REFERENCE COPY

PLEASE

DO NOT TAKE AWAY

2004

The International WHO'S WHO

2004

The International WHO'S WHO

67th Edition

Europa Publications
Taylor & Francis Group

LONDON AND NEW YORK

First published 1935

© **Europa Publications Limited 2003**
11 New Fetter Lane, London, EC4P 4EE, England
(A member of the Taylor & Francis Group)

ISBN: Book and Online 1 85743 217 7

Library of Congress Catalog Card Number 35–10257

Editor: Elizabeth Sleeman
Editor 1975–2001: Richard Fitzwilliams
Associate Editor: Alison Neale
Assistant Editor: Kate Robinson

Freelance Editorial Team: John Bailie, Julian Beecroft, Jane Carroll,
Gerard Delaney, Annabella Gabb, Peter Kirkham, David Lea, Susan Leckey,
James Merino, Eve Pickles, Elizabeth Salzman, Jenifa Sharif, Eric Smith

Editorial Co-ordinator: Mary Hill
Administrative Assistant: Haydon Lawrence

PUBLISHER'S NOTE

The International Who's Who has been published annually by
Europa Publications Limited since 1935 and provides biographical
information on the most famous and talented men and women in
the world today. We select the entries entirely on merit and our
book is recognised by librarians in every country as a standard
reference source in its field. It is compiled in our editorial offices
at 11 New Fetter Lane, London, EC4P 4EE, England. We wish to
make it clear that Europa Publications Limited has no connection
with any other business purporting to produce a publication with
the same title or a similar title to ours.

Typeset by Ignition UK Limited and printed by Unwin Brothers Limited,
The Gresham Press, Old Woking, Surrey

FOREWORD TO THE 67th EDITION

This is the 67th edition of THE INTERNATIONAL WHO'S WHO, which since its first publication in 1935 has become the standard reference work on the world's most famous and influential men and women. The present edition contains about 20,000 entries, of which over 1,000 appear for the first time.

In compiling THE INTERNATIONAL WHO'S WHO our aim is to create a reference book that answers the needs of readers seeking information on the lives of our most gifted contemporaries. We choose the entries entirely on merit and for their continuing interest and importance. Some are household names in every continent. Others are noted for their contributions in specialized fields or for their role in the political, economic, social or cultural life of their particular countries. The scope and diversity of the book is reflected in the range of activities represented, which includes architecture, art, business, cinema, diplomacy, engineering, fashion, journalism, law, literature, medicine, music, photography, politics, science, sport, technology and theatre.

Each year new entrants are sent questionnaires with a request to supply biographical details. All existing entrants are also mailed, so that they may have an opportunity to make necessary additions and amendments. Supplementary research is done by the Editor and the Europa editorial department in order to ensure that the book is as up to date as possible on publication. Valuable assistance is also given by consultants and experts in particular fields or with specialized knowledge of certain countries.

The introduction contains a list of abbreviations and international telephone codes. The names of entrants whose death has been reported over the past year are included in the Obituary. There is also a section on Reigning Royal Families.

THE INTERNATIONAL WHO'S WHO 2004 includes single-user access to the online version of the publication. This exceptional resource combines the content of the print version with a full range of sophisticated search and browse features, and with regular updates. Search types include name, nationality, place and date of birth, and occupation/profession; there is also a full-text search option. In addition, the online version includes the biographies of individuals who appeared in recent editions of the book but who have since died, and a full list of new entrants.

Not many countries have their own who's who, and not all national who's whos are published annually. THE INTERNATIONAL WHO'S WHO represents in one volume a library of information from all countries that is not found elsewhere and is unrivalled in its balance and coverage.

May 2003.

ALPHABETIZATION KEY

The list of names is alphabetical, with the entrants listed under surnames. If part of an entrant's first given name is in parentheses, this will not affect his or her alphabetical listing.

All names beginning Mc and Mac are treated as though they began Mac, e.g. McDowell before MacEachen, MacFarlane after McFadyen, Macharski before McHenry.

Names with Arabic prefixes are normally listed after the prefix except when requested by the entrant. In the case of surnames beginning De, Des, Du, van or von the entries are normally found under the prefix. Names beginning St are listed as if they began Saint, e.g. St Aubin de Teran after Sainsbury. As a general rule Chinese names are alphabetized under the first name.

In the case of an entrant whose name is spelt in a variety of ways, who is known by a pseudonym or best known by another name, a cross reference is provided, e.g.:

Kadhafi, Col Mu'ammar Muhammed al- (see Gaddafi, Col Mu'ammar Muhammed al-).

Le Carré, John (see Cornwell, David John Moore).

Lloyd, Chris(tine) Marie Evert (see Evert, Chris(tine) Marie).

ABBREVIATIONS

AAA	Agricultural Adjustment Administration
AAAS	American Association for the Advancement of Science
AAF	Army Air Force
AASA	Associate of the Australian Society of Accountants
AB	Bachelor of Arts; Aktiebolag
ABA	American Bar Association
AC	Companion of the Order of Australia
ACA	Associate of the Institute of Chartered Accountants
ACCA	Associate of the Association of Certified Accountants
Acad.	Academy; Académie
Accad.	Accademia
Accred	Accredited
ACIS	Associate of the Chartered Institute of Secretaries
ACP	American College of Physicians
ACS	American Chemical Society
ACT	Australian Capital Territory
ADC	Aide-de-camp
Adm.	Admiral
Admin(.)	Administrative; Administration; Administrator
AE	Air Efficiency Award
AERE	Atomic Energy Research Establishment
AF	Air Force
AFC	Air Force Cross
ADB	African Development Bank
affil.	affiliated
AFL	American Federation of Labor
AFM	Air Force Medal
AG	Aktiengesellschaft (Joint Stock Company)
Agric.	Agriculture
a.i.	ad interim
AIA	Associate of the Institute of Actuaries; American Institute of Architects
AIAA	American Institute of Aeronautics and Astronautics
AIB	Associate of the Institute of Bankers
AICC	All-India Congress Committee
AICE	Associate of the Institute of Civil Engineers
AIChE	American Institute of Chemical Engineers
AIDS	Acquired Immune Deficiency Syndrome
AIEE	American Institute of Electrical Engineers
AIME	American Institute of Mining Engineers; Associate of the Institution of Mining Engineers
AIMechE	Associate of the Institution of Mechanical Engineers
AIR	All-India Radio
AK	Knight of the Order of Australia
Akad.	Akademie
AL	Alabama
Ala	Alabama
ALS	Associate of the Linnaean Society
Alt.	Alternate
AM	Alpes Maritimes; Albert Medal; Master of Arts; Member of the Order of Australia
Amb.	Ambassador
AMICE	Associate Member of the Institution of Civil Engineers
AMIEE	Associate Member of the Institution of Electrical Engineers
AMIMechE	Associate Member of the Institution of Mechanical Engineers
ANU	Australian National University
AO	Officer of the Order of Australia
AP	Andhra Pradesh
Apdo	Apartado
APEC	Asia and Pacific Economic Co-operation
approx.	approximately
apptd	appointed
AR	Arkansas
ARA	Associate of the Royal Academy
ARAM	Associate of the Royal Academy of Music
ARAS	Associate of the Royal Astronomical Society
ARC	Agriculture Research Council
ARCA	Associate of the Royal College of Art
ARCM	Associate of the Royal College of Music
ARCO	Associate of the Royal College of Organists
ARCS	Associate of the Royal College of Science
ARIBA	Associate of the Royal Institute of British Architects
Ariz.	Arizona

Ark.	Arkansas
ARSA	Associate of the Royal Scottish Academy; Associate of the Royal Society of Arts
ASEAN	Association of South-East Asian Nations
ASLIB	Association of Special Libraries and Information Bureaux
ASME	American Society of Mechanical Engineers
Asoc.	Asociación
Ass.	Assembly
Asscn	Association
Assoc.	Associate
ASSR	Autonomous Soviet Socialist Republic
Asst	Assistant
ATV	Associated Television
Aug.	August
AZ	Arizona
b.	born
BA	Bachelor of Arts; British Airways
BAAS	British Association for the Advancement of Science
BAFTA	British Academy of Film and Television Arts
BAgr	Bachelor of Agriculture
BAgrSc	Bachelor of Agricultural Science
BAO	Bachelor of Obstetrics
BAOR	British Army of the Rhine
BArch	Bachelor of Architecture
Bart	Baronet
BAS	Bachelor in Agricultural Science
BASc	Bachelor of Applied Science
BBA	Bachelor of Business Administration
BBC	British Broadcasting Corporation
BC	British Columbia
BCC	British Council of Churches
BCE	Bachelor of Civil Engineering
BChir	Bachelor of Surgery
BCL	Bachelor of Civil Law; Bachelor of Canon Law
BCom(m)	Bachelor of Commerce
BCS	Bachelor of Commercial Sciences
BD	Bachelor of Divinity
Bd	Board
BDS	Bachelor of Dental Surgery
BE	Bachelor of Education; Bachelor of Engineering
BEA	British European Airways
BEcons	Bachelor of Economics
BEd	Bachelor of Education
Beds.	Bedfordshire
BEE	Bachelor of Electrical Engineering
BEM	British Empire Medal
BEng	Bachelor of Engineering
Berks.	Berkshire
BFA	Bachelor of Fine Arts
BFI	British Film Institute
BIM	British Institute of Management
biog.	biography
BIS	Bank for International Settlements
BL	Bachelor of Laws
BLA	Bachelor of Landscape Architecture
Bldg	Building
BLit(t)	Bachelor of Letters; Bachelor of Literature
BLL	Bachelor of Laws
BLS	Bachelor in Library Science
blvd	boulevard
BM	Bachelor of Medicine
BMA	British Medical Association
BMus	Bachelor of Music
Bn	Battalion
BNOC	British National Oil Corporation
BOAC	British Overseas Airways Corporation
BPA	Bachelor of Public Administration
BPharm	Bachelor of Pharmacy
BPhil	Bachelor of Philosophy
Br.	Branch
Brig.	Brigadier
BS	Bachelor of Science; Bachelor of Surgery
BSA	Bachelor of Scientific Agriculture

BSc	Bachelor of Science		CPA	Certified Public Accountant; Commonwealth Parliamentary Association
Bt	Baronet		CPhys	Chartered Physicist
Bucks.	Buckinghamshire		CPP	Convention People's Party (Ghana)
			CPPCC	Chinese People's Political Consultative Conference
c.	child(ren); circa		CPSU	Communist Party of the Soviet Union
CA	California; Chartered Accountant		cr.	created
Calif.	California		CSc	Candidate of Sciences
Camb.	Cambridgeshire		CSCE	Conference on Security and Co-operation in Europe
Cand.	Candidate; Candidature		CSI	Companion of (the Order of) the Star of India
Cantab.	of Cambridge University		CSIRO	Commonwealth Scientific and Industrial Research Organization
Capt.	Captain			
Cards.	Cardiganshire		CSSR	Czechoslovak Socialist Republic
CB	Companion of the (Order of the) Bath		CStJ	Commander of (the Order of) St John of Jerusalem
CBC	Canadian Broadcasting Corporation		CT	Connecticut
CBE	Commander of (the Order of) the British Empire		Cttee	Committee
CBI	Confederation of British Industry		CV	Commanditaire Vennootschap
CBiol	Chartered Biologist		CUNY	City University of New York
CBIM	Companion of British Institute of Management		CVO	Commander of the Royal Victorian Order
CBS	Columbia Broadcasting System			
CC	Companion of Order of Canada		d.	daughter(s)
CChem	Chartered Chemist		DArch	Doctor of Architecture
CCP	Chinese Communist Party		DB	Bachelor of Divinity
CD	Canadian Forces Decoration; Commander Order of Distinction		DBA	Doctor of Business Administration
			DBE	Dame Commander of (the Order of) the British Empire
Cdre	Commodore		DC	District of Columbia
CDU	Christlich-Demokratische Union		DCE	Doctor of Civil Engineering
CE	Civil Engineer; Chartered Engineer		DCL	Doctor of Civil Law; Doctor of Canon Law
CEAO	Communauté Economique de l'Afrique de l'Ouest		DCM	Distinguished Conduct Medal
Cen.	Central		DCMG	Dame Commander of (the Order of) St Michael and St George
CEng	Chartered Engineer			
CENTO	Central Treaty Organization		DCnL	Doctor of Canon Law
CEO	Chief Executive Officer		DComm	Doctor of Commerce
CERN	Conseil (now Organisation) Européen(ne) pour la Recherche Nucléaire		DCS	Doctor of Commercial Sciences
			DCT	Doctor of Christian Theology
CFR	Commander of the Federal Republic of Nigeria		DCVO	Dame Commander of the Royal Victorian Order
CGM	Conspicuous Gallantry Medal		DD	Doctor of Divinity
CGT	Confédération Général du Travail		DDR	Deutsche Demokratische Republik (German Democratic Republic)
CH	Companion of Honour			
Chair.	Chairman; Chairwoman; Chairperson		DDS	Doctor of Dental Surgery
CHB	Companion of Honour of Barbados		DE	Delaware
ChB	Bachelor of Surgery		Dec.	December
Chem.	Chemistry		DEcon	Doctor of Economics
ChM	Master of Surgery		Del.	Delegate; Delegation; Delaware
CI	Channel Islands		Denbighs.	Denbighshire
CIA	Central Intelligence Agency		DenD	Docteur en Droit
Cia	Compagnia (Company)		DenM	Docteur en Medicine
Cía	Compañía (Company)		DEng	Doctor of Engineering
CID	Criminal Investigation Department		Dept	Department
CIE	Companion of (the Order of) the Indian Empire		DES	Department of Education and Science
Cie	Compagnie (Company)		Desig.	Designate
CIEE	Companion of the Institution of Electrical Engineers		DèsL	Docteur ès Lettres
CIMgt	Companion Institute of Management		DèsSc	Docteur ès Sciences
C-in-C	Commander-in-Chief		Devt	Development
CIO	Congress of Industrial Organizations		DF	Distrito Federal
CIOMS	Council of International Organizations of Medical Science		DFA	Doctor of Fine Arts; Diploma of Fine Arts
			DFC	Distinguished Flying Cross
CIS	Commonwealth of Independent States		DFM	Distinguished Flying Medal
CLD	Doctor of Civil Law (USA)		DH	Doctor of Humanities
CLit	Companion of Literature		DHist	Doctor of History
CM	Canada Medal; Master in Surgery		DHL	Doctor of Hebrew Literature
CMEA	Council for Mutual Economic Assistance		DHSS	Department of Health and Social Security
CMG	Companion of (the Order of) St Michael and St George		DHumLitt	Doctor of Humane Letters
			DIC	Diploma of Imperial College
CNAA	Council for National Academic Awards		DipAD	Diploma in Art and Design
CNRS	Centre National de la Recherche Scientifique		DipAgr	Diploma in Agriculture
CO	Colorado; Commanding Officer		DipArch	Diploma in Architecture
Co.	Company; County		DipEd	Diploma in Education
COI	Central Office of Information		DipMus	Diploma in Music
Col	Colonel		DipScEconSc	Diploma of Social and Economic Science
Coll.	College		DipEng	Diploma in Engineering
Colo	Colorado		Dir	Director
COMECON	Council for Mutual Economic Assistance		Dist	District
COMESA	Common Market for Eastern and Southern Asia		DIur	Doctor of Law
Comm.	Commission		DIurUtr	Doctor of both Civil and Canon Law
Commdg	Commanding		Div.	Division; divisional
Commdr	Commander; Commandeur		DJur	Doctor of Law
Commdt	Commandant		DK	Most Esteemed Family (Malaysia)
Commr	Commissioner		DL	Deputy Lieutenant
CON	Commander of Order of Nigeria		DLit(t)	Doctor of Letters; Doctor of Literature
Conf.	Conference		DLS	Doctor of Library Science
Confed.	Confederation		DM	Doctor of Medicine (Oxford)
Conn.	Connecticut		DMD	Doctor of Dental Medicine
Contrib.	Contributor; contribution		DMilSc	Doctor of Military Science
COO	Chief Operating Officer		DMunSci	Doctor of Municipal Science
Corp.	Corporate		DMS	Director of Medical Services
Corpn	Corporation			
Corresp.	Correspondent; Corresponding			
CP	Communist Party; Caixa Postal (Post Office Box)			

ABBREVIATIONS

DMedSc	Doctor of Medical Science
DMus	Doctor of Music
DMV	Doctor of Veterinary Medicine
DO	Doctor of Ophthalmology
DPH	Diploma in Public Health
DPM	Diploma in Psychological Medicine
DPhil	Doctor of Philosophy
DrAgr	Doctor of Agriculture
DrIng	Doctor of Engineering
DrIur	Doctor of Laws
DrMed	Doctor of Medicine
DrOecPol	Doctor of Political Economy
DrOecPubl	Doctor of (Public) Economy
DrPhilNat	Doctor of Natural Philosophy
Dr rer. nat	Doctor of Natural Sciences
Dr rer. pol	Doctor of Political Science
DrSc(i)	Doctor of Sciences
DrScNat	Doctor of Natural Sciences
DS	Doctor of Science
DSC	Distinguished Service Cross
DSc(i)	Doctor of Sciences
DScS	Doctor of Social Science
DSM	Distinguished Service Medal
DSO	Companion of the Distinguished Service Order
DST	Doctor of Sacred Theology
DTech	Doctor of Technology
DTechSc(i)	Doctor of Technical Sciences
DTheol	Doctor of Theology
DTM	Diploma in Tropical Medicine
DTM&H	Diploma in Tropical Medicine (and Hygiene)
DUP	Diploma of the University of Paris
DUniv	Doctor of the University
E.	East
EBRD	European Bank for Reconstruction and Development
EC	European Commission; European Community
ECA	Economic Co-operation Administration; Economic Commission for Africa
ECAFE	Economic Commission for Asia and the Far East
ECE	Economic Commission for Europe
ECLA	Economic Commission for Latin America
ECLAC	Economic Commission for Latin America and the Caribbean
ECO	Economic Co-operation Organization
Econ.	Economic
Econs	Economics
ECOSOC	Economic and Social Council
ECSC	European Coal and Steel Community
ECWA	Economic Commission for Western Asia
ed	educated; edited
Ed.	Editor
ED	Efficiency Decoration; Doctor of Engineering (USA)
EdD	Doctor of Education
Edin.	Edinburgh
EdM	Master of Education
Edn	Edition
Educ.	Education
EEC	European Economic Community
EFTA	European Free Trade Association
eh	Ehrenhalben (Honorary)
EIB	European Investment Bank
EM	Edward Medal; Master of Engineering (USA)
Emer.	Emeritus
Eng	Engineering
EngD	Doctor of Engineering
ENO	English National Opera
EPLF	Eritrean People's Liberation Front
ESA	European Space Agency
ESCAP	Economic and Social Commission for Asia and the Pacific
est.	established
ETH	Eidgenössische Technische Hochschule (Swiss Federal Institute of Technology)
Ets	Etablissements
EU	European Union
EURATOM	European Atomic Energy Community
Exec.	Executive
Exhbn	Exhibition
Ext.	Extension
f.	founded
FAA	Fellow of the Australian Academy of Science
FAAS	Fellow of the American Association for the Advancement of Science
FAATS	Fellow of the Australian Academy of Technological Sciences
FACC	Fellow of the American College of Cardiology

FACCA	Fellow of the Association of Certified and Corporate Accountants
FACE	Fellow of the Australian College of Education
FACP	Fellow of the American College of Physicians
FACS	Fellow of the American College of Surgeons
FAHA	Fellow of the Australian Academy of the Humanities
FAIA	Fellow of the American Institute of Architects
FAIAS	Fellow of the Australian Institute of Agricultural Science
FAIM	Fellow of the Australian Institute of Management
FAO	Food and Agriculture Organization
FAS	Fellow of the Antiquarian Society
FASE	Fellow of the Antiquarian Society, Edinburgh
FASSA	Fellow of the Academy of Social Sciences of Australia
FBA	Fellow of the British Academy
FBI	Federal Bureau of Investigation
FBIM	Fellow of the British Institute of Management
FBIP	Fellow of the British Institute of Physics
FCA	Fellow of the Institute of Chartered Accountants
FCAE	Fellow of the Canadian Academy of Engineering
FCGI	Fellow of the City and Guilds of London Institute
FCIA	Fellow of the Chartered Institute of Arbitrators
FCIB	Fellow of the Chartered Institute of Bankers
FCIC	Fellow of the Chemical Institute of Canada
FCIM	Fellow of the Chartered Institute of Management
FCIS	Fellow of the Chartered Institute of Secretaries
FCMA	Fellow of the Chartered Institute of Management Accountants
FCO	Foreign and Commonwealth Office
FCSD	Fellow of the Chartered Society of Designers
FCT	Federal Capital Territory
FCWA	Fellow of the Institute of Cost and Works Accountants (now FCMA)
FDGB	Freier Deutscher Gewerkschaftsbund
FDP	Freier Demokratische Partei
Feb.	February
Fed.	Federation; Federal
FEng	Fellow(ship) of Engineering
FFCM	Fellow of the Faculty of Community Medicine
FFPHM	Fellow of the Faculty of Public Health Medicine
FGS	Fellow of the Geological Society
FGSM	Fellow of the Guildhall School of Music
FIA	Fellow of the Institute of Actuaries
FIAL	Fellow of the International Institute of Arts and Letters
FIAM	Fellow of the International Academy of Management
FIAMS	Fellow of the Indian Academy of Medical Sciences
FIAP	Fellow of the Institution of Analysts and Programmers
FIArb	Fellow of the Institute of Arbitrators
FIB	Fellow of the Institute of Bankers
FIBA	Fellow of the Institute of Banking Associations
FIBiol	Fellow of the Institute of Biologists
FICE	Fellow of the Institution of Civil Engineers
FIChemE	Fellow of the Institute of Chemical Engineers
FID	Fellow of the Institute of Directors
FIE	Fellow of the Institute of Engineers
FIEE	Fellow of the Institution of Electrical Engineers
FIEEE	Fellow of the Institute of Electrical and Electronics Engineers
FIFA	Fédération Internationale de Football Association
FIJ	Fellow of the Institute of Journalists
FilLic	Licentiate in Philosophy
FIM	Fellow of the Institute of Metallurgists
FIME	Fellow of the Institute of Mining Engineers
FIMechE	Fellow of the Institute of Mechanical Engineers
FIMI	Fellow of the Institute of the Motor Industry
FInstF	Fellow of the Institute of Fuel
FInstM	Fellow of the Institute of Marketing
FInstP	Fellow of the Institute of Physics
FInstPet	Fellow of the Institute of Petroleum
FIPM	Fellow of the Institute of Personnel Management
FIRE	Fellow of the Institution of Radio Engineers
FITD	Fellow of the Institute of Training and Development
FL	Florida
FLA	Fellow of the Library Association
Fla	Florida
FLN	Front de Libération Nationale
FLS	Fellow of the Linnaean Society
FMedSci	Fellow of Medical Science
fmr(ly)	former(ly)
FNI	Fellow of the National Institute of Sciences of India
FNZIA	Fellow of the New Zealand Institute of Architects
FRACP	Fellow of the Royal Australasian College of Physicians
FRACS	Fellow of the Royal Australasian College of Surgeons
FRAeS	Fellow of the Royal Aeronautical Society
FRAI	Fellow of the Royal Anthropological Institute
FRAIA	Fellow of the Royal Australian Institute of Architects
FRAIC	Fellow of the Royal Architectural Institute of Canada
FRAM	Fellow of the Royal Academy of Music

ABBREVIATIONS

FRAS	Fellow of the Royal Astronomical Society; Fellow of the Royal Asiatic Society
FRBS	Fellow of the Royal Society of British Sculptors
FRCA	Fellow of the Royal College of Anaesthetists
FRCM	Fellow of the Royal College of Music
FRCO	Fellow of the Royal College of Organists
FRCOG	Fellow of the Royal College of Obstetricians and Gynaecologists
FRCP	Fellow of the Royal College of Physicians
FRCPE	Fellow of the Royal College of Physicians, Edinburgh
FRCPI	Fellow of the Royal College of Physicians of Ireland
FRCPath	Fellow of the Royal College of Pathologists
FRCR	Fellow of the Royal College of Radiology
FRCS	Fellow of the Royal College of Surgeons
FRCSE	Fellow of the Royal College of Surgeons, Edinburgh
FREconS	Fellow of the Royal Economic Society
FREng	Fellow of the Royal Academy of Engineering
FRES	Fellow of the Royal Entomological Society
FRFPS	Fellow of the Royal Faculty of Physicians and Surgeons
FRG	Federal Republic of Germany
FRGS	Fellow of the Royal Geographical Society
FRHistS	Fellow of the Royal Historical Society
FRHortS	Fellow of the Royal Horticultural Society
FRIBA	Fellow of the Royal Institute of British Architects
FRIC	Fellow of the Royal Institute of Chemists
FRICS	Fellow of the Royal Institute of Chartered Surveyors
FRMetSoc	Fellow of the Royal Meteorological Society
FRNCM	Fellow of the Royal Northern College of Music
FRPS	Fellow of the Royal Photographic Society
FRS	Fellow of the Royal Society
FRSA	Fellow of the Royal Society of Arts
FRSAMD	Fellow of the Royal Scottish Academy of Music and Drama
FRSC	Fellow of the Royal Society of Canada; Fellow of the Royal Society of Chemistry
FRSE	Fellow of the Royal Society of Edinburgh
FRSL	Fellow of the Royal Society of Literature
FRSM	Fellow of the Royal Society of Medicine
FRSNZ	Fellow of the Royal Society of New Zealand
FRSS	Fellow of the Royal Statistical Society
FRSSA	Fellow of the Royal Society of South Africa
FRTS	Fellow of the Royal Television Society
FSA	Fellow of the Society of Antiquaries
FSIAD	Fellow of the Society of Industrial Artists and Designers
FTI	Fellow of the Textile Institute
FTS	Fellow of Technological Sciences
FWAAS	Fellow of the World Academy of Arts and Sciences
FZS	Fellow of the Zoological Society
GA	Georgia
Ga	Georgia
GATT	General Agreement on Tariffs and Trade
GB	Great Britain
GBE	Knight (or Dame) Grand Cross of (the Order of) the British Empire
GC	George Cross
GCB	Knight Grand Cross of (the Order of) the Bath
GCIE	Knight Grand Commander of (the Order of) the Indian Empire
GCMG	Knight (or Dame) Grand Cross of (the Order of) St Michael and St George
GCSI	Knight Grand Commander of (the Order of) the Star of India
GCVO	Knight (or Dame) Grand Cross of the Royal Victorian Order
GDR	German Democratic Republic
Gen.	General
GHQ	General Headquarters
Glam.	Glamorganshire
GLA	Greater London Authority
GLC	Greater London Council
Glos.	Gloucestershire
GM	George Medal
GmbH	Gesellschaft mit beschränkter Haftung (Limited Liability Company)
GOC	General Officer Commanding
GOC-in-C	General Officer Commanding-in-Chief
Gov.	Governor
Govt	Government
GPO	General Post Office
Grad.	Graduate
GRSM	Graduate of the Royal School of Music
GSO	General Staff Officer
Hants.	Hampshire
hc	honoris causa

HE	His Eminence; His (or Her) Excellency
Herefords.	Herefordshire
Herts.	Hertfordshire
HH	His (or Her) Highness
HI	Hawaii
HLD	Doctor of Humane Letters
HM	His (or Her) Majesty
HMS	His (or Her) Majesty's Ship
Hon.	Honourable
Hon	Honorary
Hons	Honours
Hosp.	Hospital
HQ	Headquarters
HRH	His (or Her) Royal Highness
HSP	Hungarian Socialist Party
HSWP	Hungarian Socialist Workers' Party
Hunts.	Huntingdonshire
IA	Iowa
Ia	Iowa
IAAF	International Amateur Athletic Federation
IAEA	International Atomic Energy Agency
IATA	International Air Transport Association
IBA	Independent Broadcasting Authority
IBRD	International Bank for Reconstruction and Development (World Bank)
ICAO	International Civil Aviation Organization
ICC	International Chamber of Commerce
ICE	Institution of Civil Engineers
ICEM	Intergovernmental Committee for European Migration
ICFTU	International Confederation of Free Trade Unions
ICI	Imperial Chemical Industries
ICOM	International Council of Museums
ICRC	International Committee for the Red Cross
ICS	Indian Civil Service
ICSID	International Centre for Settlement of Investment Disputes
ICSU	International Council of Scientific Unions
ID	Idaho
IDA	International Development Association
Ida.	Idaho
IDB	Inter-American Development Bank
IEA	International Energy Agency
IEE	Institution of Electrical Engineers
IEEE	Institution of Electrical and Electronic Engineers
IFAD	International Fund for Agricultural Development
IFC	International Finance Corporation
IGAD	Intergovernmental Authority on Development
IISS	International Institute for Strategic Studies
IL	Illinois
Ill.	Illinois
ILO	International Labour Organization
IMCO	Inter-Governmental Maritime Consultative Organization
IMechE	Institution of Mechanical Engineers
IMF	International Monetary Fund
IMO	International Maritime Organization
IN	Indiana
Inc.	Incorporated
Ind.	Indiana; Independent
Insp.	Inspector
Inst.	Institute; Institution
Int.	International
INTUC	Indian National Trades Union Congress
IOC	International Olympic Committee
IPU	Inter-Parliamentary Union
ISO	Companion of the Imperial Service Order
ITA	Independent Television Authority
ITU	International Telecommunications Union
ITV	Independent Television
IUPAC	International Union of Pure and Applied Chemistry
IUPAP	International Union of Pure and Applied Physics
Jan.	January
JCB	Bachelor of Canon Law
JCD	Doctor of Canon Law
JD	Doctor of Jurisprudence
JMK	Johan Mangku Negara (Malaysia)
JP	Justice of the Peace
Jr	Junior
JSD	Doctor of Juristic Science
Jt(ly)	Joint(ly)
JUD	Juris utriusque Doctor (Doctor of both Civil and Canon Law)
JuD	Doctor of Law
JUDr	Juris utriusque Doctor (Doctor of both Civil and Canon Law), Doctor of Law

ABBREVIATIONS

Kan.	Kansas
KBE	Knight Commander of (the Order of) the British Empire
KC	King's Counsel
KCB	Knight Commander of (the Order of) the Bath
KCIE	Knight Commander of (the Order of) the Indian Empire
KCMG	Knight Commander of (the Order of) St Michael and St George
KCSI	Knight Commander of (the Order of) the Star of India
KCVO	Knight Commander of the Royal Victorian Order
KG	Knight of (the Order of) the Garter
KGB	Committee of State Security (USSR)
KK	Kaien Kaisha
KLM	Koninklijke Luchtvaart Maatschappij (Royal Dutch Airlines)
KNZM	Knight of the New Zealand Order of Merit
KP	Knight of (the Order of) St Patrick
KS	Kansas
KStJ	Knight of (the Order of) St John of Jerusalem
KT	Knight of (the Order of) the Thistle
Kt	Knight
Ky	Kentucky
LA	Louisiana; Los Angeles
La	Louisiana
Lab.	Laboratory
Lancs.	Lancashire
LDP	Liberal Democratic Party
LDS	Licentiate in Dental Surgery
Legis.	Legislative
Leics.	Leicestershire
LenD	Licencié en Droit
LèsL	Licencié ès Lettres
LèsSc	Licencié ès Sciences
LG	Lady of (the Order of) the Garter
LHD	Doctor of Humane Letters
LI	Long Island
LicenDer	Licenciado en Derecho
LicenFil	Licenciado en Filosofía
LicMed	Licentiate in Medicine
Lt	Lieutenant
Lincs.	Lincolnshire
LittD	Doctor of Letters
LLB	Bachelor of Laws
LLD	Doctor of Laws
LLL	Licentiate of Laws
LLM	Master of Laws
LM	Licentiate of Medicine; Licentiate of Midwifery
LN	League of Nations
LPh	Licentiate of Philosophy
LRAM	Licentiate of the Royal Academy of Music
LRCP	Licentiate of the Royal College of Physicians
LSE	London School of Economics
Ltd	Limited
Ltda	Limitada
LTh	Licentiate in Theology
LVO	Lieutenant, Royal Victorian Order
m	metre(s)
m.	married; marriage
MA	Massachusetts; Master of Arts
MAgr	Master of Agriculture (USA)
Maj.	Major
MALD	Master of Arts in Law and Diplomacy
Man.	Management; Manager; Managing; Manitoba
MArch	Master of Architecture
Mass	Massachusetts
Math.	Mathematics; Mathematical
MB	Bachelor of Medicine
MBA	Master of Business Administration
MBE	Member of (the Order of) the British Empire
MBS	Master of Business Studies
MC	Military Cross
MCC	Marylebone Cricket Club
MCE	Master of Civil Engineering
MCh	Master of Surgery
MChD	Master of Dental Surgery
MCL	Master of Civil Law
MCom(m)	Master of Commerce
MCP	Master of City Planning
MD	Maryland; Doctor of Medicine
Md	Maryland
MDiv	Master of Divinity
MDS	Master of Dental Surgery
ME	Maine; Myalgic Encephalomyehtis
Me	Maine
mem.	member
MEconSc	Master of Economic Sciences

MEng	Master of Engineering (Dublin)
MEP	Member of European Parliament
MFA	Master of Fine Arts
Mfg	Manufacturing
Mfrs	Manufacturers
Mgr	Monseigneur; Monsignor
MI	Michigan; Marshall Islands
MIA	Master of International Affairs
MICE	Member of the Institution of Civil Engineers
MIChemE	Member of the Institution of Chemical Engineers
Mich.	Michigan
Middx	Middlesex
MIEE	Member of the Institution of Electrical Engineers
Mil.	Military
MIMarE	Member of the Institute of Marine Engineers
MIMechE	Member of the Institution of Mechanical Engineers
MIMinE	Member of the Institution of Mining Engineers
Minn.	Minnesota
MInstT	Member of the Institute of Transport
Miss.	Mississippi
MIStructE	Member of the Institution of Structural Engineers
MIT	Massachusetts Institute of Technology
MJ	Master of Jurisprudence
MLA	Member of the Legislative Assembly; Master of Landscape Architecture
MLC	Member of the Legislative Council
MM	Military Medal
MN	Minnesota
MNOC	Movement of Non-Aligned Countries
MO	Missouri
Mo.	Missouri
MOH	Medical Officer of Health
Mon.	Monmouthshire
Mont.	Montana
Movt	Movement
MP	Member of Parliament; Madhya Pradesh (India)
MPA	Master of Public Administration (Harvard)
MPh	Master of Philosophy (USA)
MPolSci	Master of Political Science
MPP	Member of Provincial Parliament (Canada)
MRAS	Member of the Royal Asiatic Society
MRC	Medical Research Council
MRCP	Member of the Royal College of Physicians
MRCPE	Member of the Royal College of Physicians, Edinburgh
MRCS	Member of the Royal College of Surgeons
MRCSE	Member of the Royal College of Surgeons, Edinburgh
MRCVS	Member of the Royal College of Veterinary Surgeons
MRI	Member of the Royal Institution
MRIA	Member of the Royal Irish Academy
MRIC	Member of the Royal Institute of Chemistry
MRP	Mouvement Républicain Populaire
MS	Mississippi; Master of Science; Master of Surgery
MSc	Master of Science
MScS	Master of Social Science
MSP	Member Scottish Parliament
MT	Montana
MTS	Master of Theological Studies
MUDr	Doctor of Medicine
MusB(ac)	Bachelor of Music
MusD(oc)	Doctor of Music
MusM	Master of Music (Cambridge)
MVD	Master of Veterinary Medicine
MVO	Member of the Royal Victorian Order
MW	Master of Wine
N.	North
NAS	National Academy of Sciences (USA)
NASA	National Aeronautics and Space Administration
Nat.	National
NATO	North Atlantic Treaty Organization
Naz.	Nazionale
NB	New Brunswick
NBC	National Broadcasting Corporation
NC	North Carolina
ND	North Dakota
NE	Nebraska
N.E.	Near East; North East
Neb.	Nebraska
NEDC	National Economic Development Council
NERC	Natural Environment Research Council
Nev.	Nevada
NH	New Hampshire
NI	Northern Ireland
NIH	National Institute of Health
NJ	New Jersey
NM	New Mexico
Northants.	Northamptonshire

ABBREVIATIONS

Notts.	Nottinghamshire	Priv Doz	Privat Dozent (recognized teacher not on the regular staff)
Nov.	November	PRO	Public Relations Officer
NPC	National People's Congress	Proc.	Proceedings
nr	near	Prof.	Professor
NRC	Nuclear Research Council	Propr	Proprietor
NS	Nova Scotia	Prov.	Province; Provincial
NSF	National Science Foundation	PRS	President of the Royal Society
NSW	New South Wales	PRSA	President of the Royal Scottish Academy
NT	Northern Territory	PSM	Panglima Setia Mahota
NV	Naamloze Vennootschap; Nevada	Pty	Proprietary
N.W.	North West	Publ.(s)	Publication(s)
NWT	North West Territories	Publr	Publisher
NY	New York	Pvt.	Private
NZ	New Zealand	PZPR	Polish United Workers' Party
NZIC	New Zealand Institute of Chemistry		
		QC	Queen's Counsel
O.	Ohio	QGM	Queen's Gallantry Medal
OAPEC	Organization of Arab Petroleum Exporting Countries	q.v.	quod vide (to which refer)
OAS	Organization of American States	QPM	Queen's Police Medal
OAU	Organization of African Unity	QSO	Queen's Service Order
OBE	Officer of (the Order of) the British Empire		
OC	Officer of the Order of Canada	RA	Royal Academy; Royal Academician; Royal Artillery
Oct.	October	RAAF	Royal Australian Air Force
OE	Order of Excellence (Guyana)	RAC	Royal Armoured Corps
OECD	Organization for Economic Co-operation and Development	RACP	Royal Australasian College of Physicians
OEEC	Organization for European Economic Co-operation	RAF	Royal Air Force
OFS	Orange Free State	RAFVR	Royal Air Force Volunteer Reserve
OH	Ohio	RAM	Royal Academy of Music
OHCHR	Office of the United Nations High Commissioner for Human Rights	RAMC	Royal Army Medical Corps
		RAOC	Royal Army Ordnance Corps
OIC	Organization of the Islamic Conference	RC	Roman Catholic
OJ	Order of Jamaica	RCA	Radio Corporation of America; Royal Canadian Academy; Royal College of Art
OK	Oklahoma		
Okla	Oklahoma	RCAF	Royal Canadian Air Force
OM	Member of the Order of Merit	RCP	Romanian Communist Party
ON	Order of Nigeria	RCPI	Royal College of Physicians of Ireland
Ont.	Ontario	Regt	Regiment
ONZ	Order of New Zealand	REME	Royal Electric and Mechanical Engineers
OP	Ordo Praedicatorum (Dominicans)	Rep.	Representative; represented
OPCW	Organization for the Prohibition of Chemical Weapons	Repub.	Republic
OPEC	Organization of the Petroleum Exporting Countries	resgnd	resigned
OPM	Office of Production Management	retd	retired
OQ	Officer National Order of Québec	Rev.	Reverend
OR	Oregon	RI	Rhode Island
Ore.	Oregon	RIBA	Royal Institute of British Architects
Org.	Organization	RMA	Royal Military Academy
OSB	Order of St Benedict	RN	Royal Navy
OSCE	Organization for Security and Co-operation in Europe	RNR	Royal Naval Reserve
Oxon.	of Oxford University; Oxfordshire	RNVR	Royal Naval Volunteer Reserve
		RNZAF	Royal New Zealand Air Force
PA	Pennsylvania	RP	Member of the Royal Society of Portrait Painters
Pa	Pennsylvania	RPR	Rassemblement pour la République
Parl.	Parliament; Parliamentary	RSA	Royal Scottish Academy; Royal Society of Arts
PC	Privy Councillor	RSC	Royal Shakespeare Company; Royal Society of Canada
PCC	Provincial Congress Committee	RSDr	Doctor of Social Sciences
PdB	Bachelor of Pedagogy	RSFSR	Russian Soviet Federative Socialist Republic
PdD	Doctor of Pedagogy	RSL	Royal Society of Literature
PdM	Master of Pedagogy	Rt Hon.	Right Honourable
PDS	Partei des Demokratischen Sozialismus	Rt Rev.	Right Reverend
PEI	Prince Edward Island	RVO	Royal Victorian Order
Pembs.	Pembrokeshire	RWS	Royal Society of Painters in Water Colours
PEN	Poets, Playwright, Essayists, Editors and Novelists (Club)		
Perm.	Permanent	s.	son(s)
PhB	Bachelor of Philosophy	S.	South
PhD(r)	Doctor of Philosophy	SA	South Africa; Société Anonyme; Sociedad Anónima
PharmD	Docteur en Pharmacie	SAARC	South Asian Association for Regional Co-operation
Phila	Philadelphia	SADC	South African Development Community
PhL	Licentiate of Philosophy	SAE	Society of Aeronautical Engineers
PLA	People's Liberation Army; Port of London Authority	Salop.	Shropshire
PLC	Public Limited Company	SALT	Strategic Arms Limitation Treaty
Pnr	Partner	Sask.	Saskatchewan
PO(B)	Post Office (Box)	SB	Bachelor of Science (USA)
POW	Prisoner of War	SC	South Carolina; Senior Counsel
PPR	Polish Workers' Party	SCAP	Supreme Command Allied Powers
PPRA	Past President of the Royal Academy	ScB	Bachelor of Science
PQ	Province of Québec	ScD	Doctor of Science
PR	Puerto Rico	SD	South Dakota
PRA	President of the Royal Academy	SDak	South Dakota
Pref.	Prefecture	SDLP	Social and Democratic Liberal Party
Prep.	Preparatory	SDP	Social Democratic Party
Pres.	President	S.E.	South East
PRI	President of the Royal Institute (of Painters in Water Colours)	SEATO	South East Asia Treaty Organization
		Sec.	Secretary
PRIBA	President of the Royal Institute of British Architects	SEC	Securities and Exchange Commission
Prin.	Principal	Secr.	Secretariat

ABBREVIATIONS

SED	Sozialistische Einheitspartei Deutschlands (Socialist Unity Party of the German Democratic Republic)
Sept.	September
S-et-O	Seine-et-Oise
SHAEF	Supreme Headquarters Allied Expeditionary Force
SHAPE	Supreme Headquarters Allied Powers in Europe
SJ	Society of Jesus (Jesuits)
SJD	Doctor of Juristic Science
SLD	Social and Liberal Democrats
SM	Master of Science
SOAS	School of Oriental and African Studies
Soc.	Society; Société
SpA	Società per Azioni
SPD	Sozialdemokratische Partei Deutschlands
Sr	Senior
SRC	Science Research Council
SSM	Seria Seta Mahkota (Malaysia)
SSR	Soviet Socialist Republic
St	Saint
Staffs.	Staffordshire
STB	Bachelor of Sacred Theology
STD	Doctor of Sacred Theology
STL	Licentiate of Sacred Theology
STM	Master of Sacred Theology
str.	strasse
Supt	Superintendent
S.W.	South West
SWAPO	South West Africa People's Organization
TA	Territorial Army
TD	Teachta Dála (mem. of the Dáil); Territorial Decoration
Tech.	Technical; Technology
Temp.	Temporary
Tenn.	Tennessee
Tex.	Texas
ThB	Bachelor of Theology
ThD	Doctor of Theology
THDr	Doctor of Theology
ThM	Master of Theology
TN	Tennessee
Trans.	Translation; Translator
Treas.	Treasurer
TU(C)	Trades Union (Congress)
TV	Television
TX	Texas
UAE	United Arab Emirates
UAR	United Arab Republic
UCLA	University of California at Los Angeles
UDEAC	L'Union Douanière et Economique de l'Afrique Centrale
UDR	Union des Démocrates pour la République
UED	University Education Diploma
UK	United Kingdom (of Great Britain and Northern Ireland)
UKAEA	United Kingdom Atomic Energy Authority
UMIST	University of Manchester Institute of Science and Technology
UMNO	United Malays National Organization
UN	United Nations
UNA	United Nations Association
UNCED	United Nations Council for Education and Development
UNCHS	United Nations Centre for Human Settlements (Habitat)
UNCTAD	United Nations Conference on Trade and Development
UNDCP	United Nations International Drug Control Programme
UNDP	United Nations Development Programme
UNDRO	United Nations Disaster Relief Office
UNEF	United Nations Emergency Force
UNEP	United Nations Environment Programme
UNESCO	United Nations Educational, Scientific and Cultural Organisation
UNHCR	United Nations High Commissioner for Refugees
UNICEF	United Nations International Children's Emergency Fund
UNIDO	United Nations Industrial Development Organization
UNIFEM	United Nations Development Fund for Women
UNITAR	United Nations Institute for Training and Research
Univ.	University
UNKRA	United Nations Korean Relief Administration
UNRRA	United Nations Relief and Rehabilitation Administration
UNRWA	United Nations Relief and Works Agency
UNU	United Nations University
UP	United Provinces; Uttar Pradesh (India)
UPU	Universal Postal Union
USA	United States of America
USAAF	United States Army Air Force
USAF	United States Air Force
USAID	United States Agency for International Development
USN	United States Navy
USNR	United States Navy Reserve
USS	United States Ship
USSR	Union of Soviet Socialist Republics
UT	Utah
UWI	University of the West Indies
VA	Virginia
Va	Virginia
VC	Victoria Cross
VI	Virgin Islands
Vic.	Victoria
Vol.(s)	Volume(s)
VSO	Voluntary Service Overseas
VT	Vermont
Vt	Vermont
W.	West
WA	Washington (State); Western Australia
Warwicks.	Warwickshire
Wash.	Washington (State)
WCC	World Council of Churches
WCT	World Championship Tennis
WEU	Western European Union
WFP	World Food Programme
WFTU	World Federation of Trade Unions
WHO	World Health Organization
WI	Wisconsin
Wilts.	Wiltshire
WIPO	World Intellectual Property Organization
Wis.	Wisconsin
WMO	World Meteorological Organization
Worcs.	Worcestershire
WRAC	Women's Royal Army Corps
WRNS	Women's Royal Naval Service
WTO	World Trade Organization
WV	West Virginia
W Va	West Virginia
WY	Wyoming
Wyo.	Wyoming
YMCA	Young Men's Christian Association
Yorks.	Yorkshire
YWCA	Young Women's Christian Association

INTERNATIONAL TELEPHONE CODES

To make international calls to telephone and fax numbers listed in *The International Who's Who*, dial the international code of the country from which you are calling, followed by the appropriate country code for the organization you wish to call (listed below), followed by the area code (if applicable) and telephone or fax number listed in the entry.

	Country code	+ or − GMT*
Afghanistan	93	+4½
Albania	355	+1
Algeria	213	+1
Andorra	376	+1
Angola	244	+1
Antigua and Barbuda	1 268	−4
Argentina	54	−3
Armenia	374	+4
Australia	61	+7 to +10
Australian External Territories:		
Christmas Island	61	+10
Cocos (Keeling) Islands	61	+10
Norfolk Island	672	+11½
Austria	43	+1
Azerbaijan	994	+5
The Bahamas	1 242	−5
Bahrain	973	+3
Bangladesh	880	+6
Barbados	1 246	−4
Belarus	375	+2
Belgium	32	+1
Belize	501	−6
Benin	229	+1
Bhutan	975	+6
Bolivia	591	−4
Bosnia and Herzegovina	387	+1
Botswana	267	+2
Brazil	55	−3 to −4
Brunei	673	+8
Bulgaria	359	+2
Burkina Faso	226	0
Burundi	257	+2
Cambodia	855	+7
Cameroon	237	+1
Canada	1	−3 to −8
Cape Verde	238	−1
The Central African Republic	236	+1
Chad	235	+1
Chile	56	−4
China, People's Republic	86	+8
Special Administrative Regions:		
Hong Kong	852	+8
Macao	853	+8
China (Taiwan)	886	+8
Colombia	57	−5
The Comoros	269	+3
Congo, Democratic Republic	243	+1
Congo, Republic	242	+1
Costa Rica	506	−6
Côte d'Ivoire	225	0
Croatia	385	+1
Cuba	53	−5
Cyprus	357	+2
'Turkish Republic of Northern Cyprus'.	90 392	+2
Czech Republic	420	+1
Denmark	45	+1
Danish External Territories:		
Faroe Islands	298	0
Greenland	299	−1 to −4

	Country code	+ or − GMT*
Djibouti	253	+3
Dominica	1 767	−4
The Dominican Republic	1 809	−4
Ecuador	593	−5
Egypt	20	+2
El Salvador	503	−6
Equatorial Guinea	240	+1
Eritrea	291	+3
Estonia	372	+2
Ethiopia	251	+3
Fiji	679	+12
Finland	358	+2
Finnish External Territory:		
Åland Islands	358	+2
France	33	+1
French Overseas Departments:		
French Guiana	594	−3
Guadeloupe	590	−4
Martinique	596	−4
Réunion	262	+4
French Overseas Collectivités Territoriales:		
Mayotte	269	+3
Saint Pierre and Miquelon	508	−3
French Overseas Territories:		
French Polynesia	689	−10
Wallis and Futuna Islands	681	+12
French Overseas Country:		
New Caledonia	687	+11
Gabon	241	+1
The Gambia	220	0
Georgia	995	+4
Germany	49	+1
Ghana	233	0
Greece	30	+2
Grenada	1 473	−4
Guatemala	502	−6
Guinea	224	0
Guinea-Bissau	245	0
Guyana	592	−4
Haiti	509	−5
Honduras	504	−6
Hungary	36	+1
Iceland	354	0
India	91	+5½
Indonesia	62	+7 to +8
Iran	98	+3½
Iraq	964	+3
Ireland	353	0
Israel	972	+2
Italy	39	+1
Jamaica	1 876	−5
Japan	81	+9
Jordan	962	+2
Kazakhstan	7	+6
Kenya	254	+3
Kiribati	686	+12
Korea, Democratic People's Republic (North Korea)	850	+9
Korea, Republic (South Korea)	82	+9
Kuwait	965	+3
Kyrgyzstan	996	+5

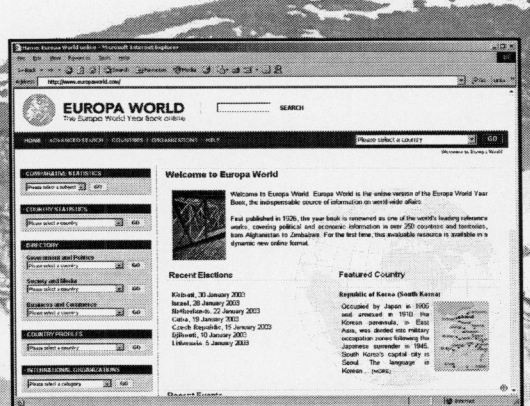
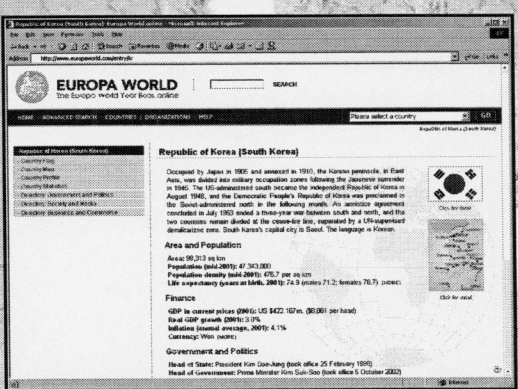

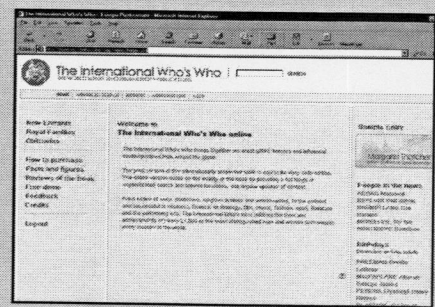
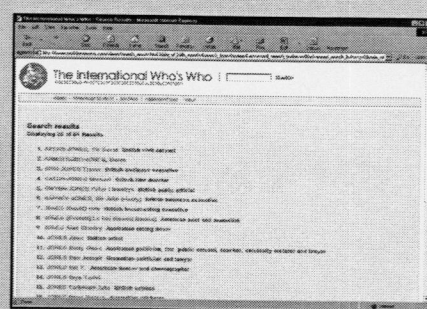

INTERNATIONAL TELEPHONE CODES

	Country code	+ or – GMT*
Laos	856	+7
Latvia	371	+2
Lebanon	961	+2
Lesotho	266	+2
Liberia	231	0
Libya	218	+1
Liechtenstein	423	+1
Lithuania	370	+2
Luxembourg	352	+1
Macedonia, former Yugoslav Republic	389	+1
Madagascar	261	+3
Malawi	265	+2
Malaysia	60	+8
Maldives	960	+5
Mali	223	0
Malta	356	+1
The Marshall Islands	692	+12
Mauritania	222	0
Mauritius	230	+4
Mexico	52	–6 to –7
Micronesia, Federated States	691	+10 to +11
Moldova	373	+2
Monaco	377	+1
Mongolia	976	+8
Morocco	212	0
Mozambique	258	+2
Myanmar	95	+6½
Namibia	264	+2
Nauru	674	+12
Nepal	977	+5¾
The Netherlands	31	+1
Netherlands Dependencies:		
Aruba	297	–4
Netherlands Antilles	599	–4
New Zealand	64	+12
New Zealand's Dependent and Associated Territories:		
Cook Islands	682	–10½
Niue	683	–11
Nicaragua	505	–6
Niger	227	+1
Nigeria	234	+1
Norway	47	+1
Norwegian External Territory:		
Svalbard	47	+1
Oman	968	+4
Pakistan	92	+5
Palau	680	+9
Panama	507	–5
Papua New Guinea	675	+10
Paraguay	595	–4
Peru	51	–5
The Philippines	63	+8
Poland	48	+1
Portugal	351	0
Qatar	974	+3
Romania	40	+2
The Russian Federation	7	+2 to +12
Rwanda	250	+2
Saint Christopher and Nevis	1 869	–4
Saint Lucia	1 758	–4
Saint Vincent and the Grenadines	1 784	–4
Samoa	685	–11
San Marino	378	+1
São Tomé and Príncipe	239	0
Saudi Arabia	966	+3
Senegal	221	0

	Country code	+ or – GMT*
Serbia and Montenegro	381	+1
Seychelles	248	+4
Sierra Leone	232	0
Singapore	65	+8
Slovakia	421	+1
Slovenia	386	+1
Solomon Islands	677	+11
Somalia	252	+3
South Africa	27	+2
Spain	34	+1
Sri Lanka	94	+5½
Sudan	249	+2
Suriname	597	–3
Swaziland	268	+2
Sweden	46	+1
Switzerland	41	+1
Syria	963	+2
Tajikistan	992	+5
Tanzania	255	+3
Thailand	66	+7
Timor-Leste	670	+8
Togo	228	0
Tonga	676	+13
Trinidad and Tobago	1 868	–4
Tunisia	216	+1
Turkey	90	+2
Turkmenistan	993	+5
Tuvalu	688	+12
Uganda	256	+3
Ukraine	380	+2
United Arab Emirates	971	+4
United Kingdom	44	0
United Kingdom Crown Dependencies	44	0
United Kingdom Overseas Territories:		
Anguilla	1 264	–4
Ascension Island	247	0
Bermuda	1 441	–4
British Virgin Islands	1 284	–4
Cayman Islands	1 345	–5
Falkland Islands	500	–4
Gibraltar	350	+1
Montserrat	1 664	–4
Saint Helena	290	0
Tristan da Cunha	2 897	0
Turks and Caicos Islands	1 649	–5
United States of America	1	–5 to –10
United States Commonwealth Territories:		
Northern Mariana Islands	1 670	+10
Puerto Rico	1 787	–4
United States External Territories:		
American Samoa	684	–11
Guam	1 671	+10
United States Virgin Islands	1 340	–4
Uruguay	598	–3
Uzbekistan	998	+5
Vanuatu	678	+11
Vatican City	39	+1
Venezuela	58	–4
Viet Nam	84	+7
Yemen	967	+3
Zambia	260	+2
Zimbabwe	263	+2

* Time difference in hours + or – Greenwich Mean Time (GMT). The times listed compare the standard (winter) times in the various countries. Some countries adopt Summer (Daylight Saving) Time—i.e. +1 hour—for part of the year.

REIGNING ROYAL FAMILIES

Biographical entries of most of the reigning monarchs and of certain other members of the reigning royal families will be found in their appropriate alphabetical order in the biographical section of this book. The name under which they can be found in the text of the book will be listed in this section in bold type.

BAHRAIN
Reigning King
SHEIKH HAMAD BIN ISA AL-**KHALIFA**; b. 28 January 1950; succeeded 6 March 1999 as Ruler of Bahrain on the death of his father, Sheikh Isa bin Sulman al-Khalifa; acceded as Amir 6 March 1999; proclaimed King 14 February 2002; married 1968, Shaikha Sabeeka bint Ebrahim al-Khalifa; three sons.

BELGIUM
Reigning King
KING **ALBERT** FELIX HUMBERT THEODORE CHRISTIAN EUGENE MARIE; b. 6 June 1934; succeeded to the throne 9 August 1993, after the death of his brother, King Baudouin I; married 2 July 1959, Donna Paola Ruffo di Calabria (b. 11 September 1937).

Children of the King
Crown Prince Philippe, Duke of Brabant, b. 15 April 1960; married 4 December 1999, Mathilde d'Udekem d'Acoz; daughter, Princess Elisabeth, b. 25 October 2001.

Prince Laurent, b. 19 October 1963; married 12 April 2003, Claire Coombs.

Princess Astrid, b. 5 June 1962; married September 1984, Archduke Lorenz; son, Prince Amedeo, b. February 1986; daughter, Princess Maria Laura, b. August 1988; son, Prince Joachim, b. December 1991; daughter, Louisa-Maria, b. October 1995.

Father of the King
King Léopold III; b. 3 November 1901, died 25 September 1983; married (1) 4 November 1926, Princess Astrid of Sweden (b. 17 November 1905, died 29 August 1935); (2) 11 September 1941, Mlle Mary Lilian Baels (died 7 June 2002) (three children).

Sister of the King
Joséphine Charlotte, Princess of Belgium; b. 11 October 1927; married 9 April 1953, Prince Jean of Luxembourg (b. 5 January 1921) (five children).

BHUTAN
Reigning King
H.M. THE DRUK GYALPO JIGME SINGYE **WANGCHUCK**; b. 11 November 1955; succeeded to the throne 24 July 1972, on the death of his father, the Druk Gyalpo Jigme Dorji Wangchuk; crowned on 2 June 1974.

Queens
H.M. Queen Ashi Dorji Wangmo Wangchuck, b. 29 December 1955.

H.M. Queen Ashi Tshering Pem Wangchuck, b. 29 December 1957.

H.M. Queen Ashi Tshering Yandon Wangchuck, b. 21 June 1959.

H.M. Queen Ashi Sangay Choden Wangchuck, b. 11 May 1963.

Children
H.R.H. Dasho Jigme Khesar Namgyal Wangchuck, Crown Prince, b. 21 February 1980.

H.R.H. Prince Jigyel Ugyen Wangchuck, b. 16 July 1984.

H.R.H. Prince Khamsum Singye Wangchuck, b. 6 October 1985.

H.R.H. Prince Jigme Dorji Wangchuck, b. 14 April 1986.

H.R.H. Princess Chimi Yangzom Wangchuck, b. 10 January 1980.

H.R.H. Princess Sonam Dechen Wangchuck, b. 5 August 1981.

H.R.H. Princess Dechen Yangzom Wangchuck, b. 2 December 1981.

H.R.H. Princess Kesang Choden Wangchuck, b. 23 January 1982.

Parents of the King
The Druk Gyalpo Jigme Dorji Wangchuck, b. 1928; married 1953, Queen Ashi Kesang Wangchuck; succeeded to the throne 28 October 1952; died 21 July 1972.

Sisters of the King
H.R.H. Ashi Sonam Choden Wangchuck, b. 26 July 1953.

H.R.H. Ashi Dechen Wangmo Wangchuck, b. 8 September 1954.

H.R.H. Ashi Pem Pem Wangchuck, b. 12 March 1959.

H.R.H. Ashi Kesang Wangmo Wangchuck, b. 11 May 1961.

BRUNEI
Reigning Sultan and Yang di-Pertuan
H.M. Sultan Haji HASSANAL **BOLKIAH**; b. 15 July 1946; succeeded his father Sultan Haji Omar Ali Saifuddien II as 29th Sultan 5 October 1967, crowned 1 August 1968; married Raja Isteri Pengiran Anak Hajjah Saleha, two sons, four daughters; also married Pengiran Isteri Hajjah Mariam 1981, two sons, two daughters.

Brothers of the Sultan
H.R.H. Prince Mohamed Bolkiah.

H.R.H. Prince Haji Sufri Bolkiah.

H.R.H. Prince Haji Jefri Bolkiah.

CAMBODIA
Reigning King
KING **NORODOM SIHANOUK**; b. 31 October 1922; elected King April 1941; abdicated March 1955; took oath of fidelity to vacant throne 1960; elected Head of State on the death of his father 1960; deposed March 1970; elected as King 24 September 1993.

Children of the King
Princess Buppha Devi; b. 8 January 1943.

Prince Yuvaneath; b. 13 October 1943.

Prince Ranariddh; b. 2 January 1944.

Prince Ravivong; b. 1944; died 1973.

Prince Chakrapong; b. 21 October 1945.

Prince Naradipo; b. 10 February 1946; died 1977.

Princess Soriya Roeungsey; b. 1947; died 1977.

Princess Kantha Bopha; b. 1948; died 14 December 1952.

Prince Khemanourak; b. 1949; died 1977.

Princess Botum Bopha; b. 1951; died 1977.

Princess Socheata; b. 1953; died 1975.

Prince Sihamoni; b. 14 May 1953.

Prince Narindrapong; b. 18 September 1954.

Princess Arun Rasmy; b. 2 October 1955.

DENMARK
Reigning Queen
QUEEN **MARGRETHE II**; b. 16 April 1940; succeeded to the throne 14 January 1972, on the death of her father, King Frederik IX; married 10 June 1967, Count Henri-Marie-Jean de Laborde de Monpezat (Prince Henrik) (b. 11 June 1934).

Children of the Queen
Prince Frederik André Henrik Christian (heir-apparent); b. 26 May 1968.

Prince Joachim Holger Waldemar Christian; b. 7 June 1969; married 18

November 1995, Alexandra Christina Manley; son, Nikolai William Alexander Frederik, b. 28 August 1999; son, Felix Henrik Valdemar Christian, b. 22 July 2002.

Parents of the Queen

King Frederik IX; b. 11 March 1899; died 14 January 1972; son of King Christian X and Queen Alexandrine; married 24 May 1935, Princess Ingrid of Sweden (b. 28 March 1910, died 7 November 2000).

Sisters of the Queen

Princess Benedikte; b. 29 April 1944; married 3 February 1968, Prince Richard zu Sayn-Wittgenstein-Berleburg; son, Prince Gustav, b. 12 January 1969; daughters, Princess Alexandra, b. 20 November 1970, Princess Nathalie, b. 2 May 1975.

Queen Anne-Marie of the Hellenes; b. 30 August 1946; married 18 September 1964, King Constantine II of the Hellenes; sons, Prince Pavlos, b. 20 May 1967, Prince Nikolaos, b. 1 October 1969, Prince Philippos, b. 26 April 1986; daughters, Princess Alexia, b. 10 July 1965, Princess Theodora, b. 9 June 1983.

JAPAN
Reigning Emperor

EMPEROR **AKIHITO**; b. 23 December 1933; succeeded his father 7th January 1989; enthroned 12 November 1990; married 10 April 1959, Michiko Shoda (b. 20 October 1934).

Children of the Emperor

Crown Prince **Naruhito** (fmrly Hiro no Miya), b. 23 February 1960, married 9 June 1993 Masako Owada; daughter, Princess Aiko (Toshi no Miya), b. 1 December 2001.

Prince Akishino (Fumihito, fmrly Aya no Miya), b. 30 November 1965; married 1990, Kiko Kawashima; two d.

Princess Sayako (Nori no Miya), b. 18 April 1969.

Parents of the Emperor

Emperor Hirohito; b. 29 April 1901; married 26 January 1924, died 7 January 1989; Princess Nagako Kuni (b. 6 March 1903, died 16 June 2000), daughter of Prince Kuni.

JORDAN
Reigning King

KING **ABDULLAH**; b. 30 January 1962; succeeded to the throne on the death of his father Hussein Ibn Talal, 7 February 1999; married 10 June 1993, Rania Yassin.

Children of the King

Prince Al Hussein; b. 28 June 1994.

Princess Iman; b. 7 September 1996.

Princess Salma, b. 26 September 2000.

Parents of the King

King Hussein Ibn Talal; b. 14 November 1935; died 7 February 1999; married 2nd Miss Antoinette Gardner, Princess Muna al-Hussein (divorced 1972).

Brothers and Sisters of the King

Crown Prince Hamzah bin Al Hussein; b. 29 March 1980.

Princess Alia; b. 13 February 1956; married 1st 11 July 1977, Nasser Wasfi Mirza (divorced 1983); son, Prince Hussein Mirza; b. 12 February 1981; married 2nd 30 July 1988, Mohammad Farid Al Saleh; son, Talal Al Saleh, b. 12 September 1989; son, Abdul Hameed Al Saleh, b. 15 November 1991.

Prince Feisal; b. 11 October 1963; married 10 August 1987, Alia al-Tabba; daughter, Princess Aya, b. 11 February 1990; son, Prince Omar, b. October 1993; daughters, Princess Aisha, b. 1996, Princess Sarah, b. 1996.

Princess Zein; b. 23 April 1968; married 3 August 1989, Majdi Farid Al Saleh; son, Jafar Al Saleh, b. 9 November 1990.

Princess Aisha; b. 23 April 1968; married 26 July 1990, Zeid Juma'a; son, Aoun Juma'a, b. 27 May 1992.

Princess Haya; b. 3 May 1974.

Prince Ali; b. 23 December 1975.

Prince Hashim; b. 10 June 1981.

Princess Iman; b. 24 April 1983.

Princess Raiyah; b. 9 February 1986.

KUWAIT
Reigning Amir

SHEIKH JABER AL-AHMAD AL-JABER AL-**SABAH**; b. 29 June 1928; succeeded his uncle, Sheikh Sabah al-Salim al-Sabah, 31 December 1977.

Crown Prince

SHEIKH SAAD AL-ABDULLAH AL-SALEM AL-**SABAH**; proclaimed Crown Prince 31 January 1978.

LESOTHO
Reigning King

KING **LETSIE III**; b. 17 July 1963; married 18 February 2000, Karabo Motsoeneng; installed as King November 1990; abdicated January 1995; reinstalled 7th February 1996.

LIECHTENSTEIN
Reigning Prince

HANS-ADAM II; b. 14 February 1945; succeeded Franz Josef II, 13 November 1989; married 30 July 1967, Countess Marie Kinsky (Princess Marie).

Children of the Prince

Hereditary Prince Alois, b. 11 June 1968; married 3 July 1993, Duchess Sophie in Bavaria; sons Prince Joseph Wenzel, b. 24 May 1995, Prince Georg, b. 20 April 1999, Prince Nikolaus, b. 6 December 2000; daughter Princess Marie Caroline, b. 17 October 1996.

Prince Maximilian, b. 16 May 1969; married 29 January 2000, Angela Gisela Brown.

Prince Constantin, b. 15 March 1972; married 17 July 1999, Countess Marie Kálnoky.

Princess Tatjana, b. 10 April 1973; married 5 June 1999, Philipp von Lattorff; son Lukas, b. 13 May 2000; daughter Elisabeth, b. 25 January 2002.

Brothers and Sisters of the Prince

Prince Philipp; b. 19 August 1946; married 11 September 1971, Mademoiselle Isabelle de l'Arbre de Malander; sons, Prince Alexander, b. 19 May 1972; Prince Wenzeslaus, b. 12 May 1974; Prince Rudolf, b. 7 September 1975.

Prince Nicolas; b. 24 October 1947; married 20 March 1982, Princess Margaretha of Luxembourg; daughters, Princess Maria-Anunciata, b. 12 May 1985, Princess Marie-Astrid, b. 26 June 1987; son Prince Josef Emanuel, b. 7 May 1989.

Princess Nora; b. 31 October 1950; married 11 June 1988, Vicente Marques de Mariño; daughter Theresa Maria, b. 21 November 1992.

Prince Wenzel; b. 19 November 1962; died 28 February 1991.

LUXEMBOURG
Reigning Monarch

GRAND DUKE **HENRI**; b. 16 April 1955; succeeded 7 October 2000 on the abdication of his father, Grand Duke Jean; married 14 February 1981, Maria-Teresa Mestre.

Children of the Grand Duke

Prince Guillaume Jean Joseph Marie; b. 11 November 1981.

Prince Félix Léopold Marie Guillaume; b. 3 June 1984.

Prince Louis Xavier Marie Guillaume; b. 3 August 1986.

Princess Alexandra Josephine Teresa Charlotte Marie Wilhelmina; b. 16 February 1991.

Prince Sebastien Henri Marie Guillaume; b. 16 April 1992.

Brothers and Sisters of the Grand Duke

Princess Marie-Astrid; b. 17 February 1954; married 6 February 1982, Charles Christian of Habsburg Lorraine, Archduke of Austria; daughter Marie-Christine Anne Astrid Zita Charlotte of Habsburg Lorraine, b. 31 July 1983, son Prince Imre, b. 8 December 1985, son Prince Christophe, b. 2 February 1988, son Prince Alexander, b. 26 September 1990, daughter Princess Gabriella, b. 26 March 1994.

Prince Jean; b. 15 May 1957; married 27 May 1987, Hélène Suzanne Vestur; daughter Marie-Gabrielle, b. 8 December 1986, son Constantin Jean Philippe, b. 22 July 1988, son Wenceslas, b. 17 November 1990, son Carl-Johann, b. 15 August 1992.

Princess Margaretha; b. 15 May 1957; married 20 March 1982, Prince Nicolas of Liechtenstein; daughter Princess Maria Annunciata, b. 12 May 1985, daughter Princess Marie-Astrid, b. 26 June 1987, son Prince Joseph-Emmanuel, b. 7 May 1989.

Prince Guillaume; b. 1 May 1963; married 24 September 1994, Sibilla Weiller; sons Paul-Louis, b. 4 March 1998, Léopold, b. 2 May 2000; daughter Charlotte, b. 2 May 2000.

REIGNING ROYAL FAMILIES

Parents of the Grand Duke

JEAN BENOÎT GUILLAUME MARIE ROBERT LOUIS ANTOINE ADOLPHE MARC D'AVIANO, FORMER GRAND DUKE; b. 5 January 1921; succeeded 12 November 1964; abdicated in favour of his son, Prince Henri, 7 October 2000; married 9 April 1953, Josephine Charlotte, Princess of Belgium (b. 11 October 1927).

MALAYSIA
Supreme Head of State (Yang di-Pertuan Agong)*

TUANKU SYED SIRAJUDDIN PUTRA JAMALULLAIL; Raja of **Perlis**; b. 17 May 1943; installed as twelfth Yang di-Pertuan Agong 25 April 2002.

* Reign ends in 2007.

MONACO

PRINCE **RAINIER III**; b. 31 May 1923; succeeded his grandfather, Prince Louis II, 9 May 1949; married 18 April 1956, Miss Grace Patricia Kelly, daughter of the late Mr. John Brendan Kelly and Mrs. Margaret Majer, of Philadelphia, USA (b. 12 November 1929, died 14 September 1982).

Children of the Prince

Princess Caroline Louise Marguerite; b. 23 January 1957; married 1st 28 June 1978, Philippe Junot (divorced 1980, marriage annulled 1992); married 2nd 29 December 1983, Stefano Casiraghi (died 3 October 1990); son, Andrea Albert Pierre, b. 8 June 1984; daughter, Charlotte Marie Pomeline, b. 3 August 1986; son, Pierre Rainier Stefano, b. 5 September 1987; married 3rd 23 January 1999, Prince Ernst August of Hanover; daughter, Princess Alexandra of Hanover, b. 20 July 1999.

Crown Prince Albert Alexandre Louis Pierre; b. 14 March 1958.

Princess Stéphanie Marie Elisabeth; b. 1 February 1965; married 1st July 1995, Daniel Ducruet (divorced 5 October 1996); son, Louis Robert Paul, b. 26 November 1992; daughter, Pauline Grace Maguy, b. 4 May 1994; daughter, Camille Marie Kelly, b. 15 July 1998.

Parents of the Prince

Princess Charlotte, Duchess of Valentinois (b. 30 September 1898; died 16 November 1977); married 19 March 1920, Comte Pierre de Polignac (b. 24 October 1895), who thus became Prince Pierre of Monaco; he died 10 November 1964.

MOROCCO
Reigning King

KING **MOHAMMED VI** (formerly Crown Prince Sidi Mohammed); b. 21 August 1963; son of late King Hassan II; succeeded to the throne 30 July 1999; married Lalla Salma Bennani 21 March 2002; son, Moulay Hassan, b. May 2003.

Brothers and Sisters of the King

Princess Lalla Myriam; b. 26 August 1962; married September 1984, Fouad Fillali (divorced 1996).

Princess Lalla Asma; b. 1965; married 7 June 1987, Khalid Bouchentouf.

Princess Lalla Hasna; b. 1967; married 13 December 1991, Khalid Benharbit.

Crown Prince Moulay Rachid; b. July 1970.

NEPAL
Reigning King

KING **GYANENDRA BIR BIKRAM SHAH DEV**; b. 7 July 1947; succeeded to the throne, 4 June 2001, on the death of his nephew King Dipendra (who had succeeded to the throne, 1 June 2001, on the death of his father King **Birendra**); married 1 May 1970, Princess Komal Rajya Laxmi Devi.

Children of the King

Crown Prince Paras Bir Bikram Shah; married 26 January 2000, Himani Rajya Laxmi Devi; son, Prince Hridayendra, b. 30 July 2002.

Princess Prearana Rajya Laxmi Devi Shah; married 22 January 2003, Raj Bahadur Singh.

NETHERLANDS
Reigning Queen

QUEEN **BEATRIX** WILHELMINA ARMGARD; b. 31 January 1938; succeeded to the throne on the abdication of her mother, 30 April 1980; married 10 March 1966, Prince Claus George Willem Otto Frederik Geert of the Netherlands, Jonkheer van Amsberg (b. 6 September 1926, died 6 October 2002).

Children of the Queen

Prince Willem-Alexander Claus George Ferdinand, Prince of Orange-Nassau; b. 27 April 1967; married 2 February 2002, Maxima Zorreguieta.

Prince Johan Friso Bernhard Christiaan David; b. 25 September 1968.

Prince Constantijn Christof Frederik Aschwin; b. 11 October 1969; married 17 May 2001, Laurentien Brinkhorst; daughter, Princess Eloise Sophie Beatrix Laurence, b. 8 June 2002.

Sisters of the Queen

Princess Irene Emma Elisabeth; b. 5 August 1939; married 29 April 1964, Prince Carlos Hugo of Bourbon Parma (divorced 1981); sons, Prince Carlos Javier Bernardo, b. 27 January 1970, Prince Jaime Bernardo, b. 13 October 1972; daughters, Princess Margarita Maria Beatriz, b. 13 October 1972, Princess Maria Carolina Christina, b. 23 June 1974.

Princess Margriet Francisca; b. 19 January 1943; married 10 January 1967, Pieter van Vollenhoven; sons, Prince Maurits Willem Pieter Hendrik van Orange-Nassau van Vollenhoven, b. 17 April 1968, Prince Bernhard Lucas Emmanuel, b. 25 December 1969, Prince Pieter-Christiaan Michiel, b. 22 March 1972, Prince Floris Frederik Martÿn, b. 10 April 1975.

Princess Maria Christina; b. 18 February 1947; married 28 June 1975, Jorge Guillermo (divorced 1996); sons, Bernardo Federico Tomás, b. 17 June 1977, Nicolas Daniel Mauricio, b. 6 July 1979; daughter, Princess Juliana Edenia Antonia, b. 8 October 1981.

Parents of the Queen

Princess **Juliana** (Louise Emma Marie Wilhelmina) of the Netherlands, Princess of Orange Nassau, Duchess of Mecklenburg; Princess of Lippe-Biesterfeld, etc.; b. 30 April 1909; succeeded to the throne on the abdication of her mother, 4 September 1948; inaugurated 6 September 1948; abdicated 30 April 1980; married 7 January 1937, Prince Bernhard Leopold Frederik Everhard Julius Coert Karel Godfried Pieter of the **Netherlands**, Prince of Lippe-Biesterfeld (b. 29 June 1911).

NORWAY
Reigning King

KING **HARALD V**; b. 21 February 1937; succeeded to the throne on the death of his father, King Olav V, 17 January 1991; married 29 August 1968, Miss Sonja Haraldsen (Queen Sonja).

Children of the King

Crown Prince **Haakon** Magnus; b. 20 July 1973; married 25 August 2001, Mette-Marit Tjessem Holby.

Princess Märtha Louise; b. 22 September 1971; married 24 May 2002, Ari Behn.

Sisters of the King

Princess Ragnhild Alexandra; b. 9 June 1930; married 15 May 1953, Erling Lorentzen; three children.

Princess Astrid Maud Ingeborg; b. 12 February 1932; married 12 January 1961, Johan Martin Ferner; five children.

OMAN
Reigning Sultan

SULTAN **QABOOS BIN SAID**; b. 18 November 1940; deposed his father, Sultan Said bin Taimur (1910–72), 23 July 1970.

QATAR
Reigning Amir

SHEIKH HAMAD BIN KHALIFA ATH-**THANI**; b. 1950; succeeded his father, 27 June 1995.

SAUDI ARABIA
Reigning King

KING **FAHD IBN ABD AL-AZIZ AS SA'UD**; b. 1921; succeeded to the throne on the death of his brother, King Khalid, 13 June 1982.

Brothers of the King include

King Saud ibn Abd al-Aziz as-Sa'ud; b. 15 January 1902; proclaimed King 12 November 1953, following the death of his father, King Abd al-Aziz as-Sa'ud; relinquished the throne 1 November 1964; died 23 February 1969.

King Faisal ibn Abd al-Aziz as-Sa'ud; b. 9 April 1906; acceded 1 November 1964; died 24 March 1975.

Amir Mohammed; b. 1912; died 1988.

King Khalid ibn Abd al-Aziz as-Sa'ud; b. 1913; acceded 25 March 1975; died 13 June 1982.

Crown Prince Abdullah ibn Abd al-Aziz as-Sa'ud; b. August 1921.

REIGNING ROYAL FAMILIES

Amir Sultan; b. 1922.

SPAIN
Reigning King

KING **JUAN CARLOS I**; b. 5 January 1938; succeeded to the throne 22 November 1975; married 14 May 1962, Princess Sofía of Greece (b. 2 November 1938), daughter of the late King Paul of the Hellenes and Queen Frederica.

Children of the King

Princess Elena; b. 20 December 1963; married Don Jaime de Marichalar y Saénz de Tejada; son, Felipe Juan Froilán de Todos los Santos, b. 17 July 1998; daughter, Victoria Federica, b. 9 October 2000.

Princess Cristina; b. 13 June 1965; m. Iñaki Urgandarin 1997; sons, Juan Valentín de Todos los Santos, b. 29 September 1999, Pablo Nicolás, b. 6 December 2000.

Prince Felipe; b. 30 January 1968.

Parents of the King

Don Juan de Borbón y Battenberg, Count of Barcelona; b. 20 June 1913; married 1935, Doña María de las Mercedes de Borbón y Orleans (died 2 January 2000); died 1 April 1993.

SWAZILAND
Reigning Monarch

KING **MSWATI III**; b. 19 April 1968; installed as Head of State 25 April 1986.

Father of the King

King Sobhuza II; b. 22 July 1899, died 21 August 1982.

SWEDEN
Reigning King

KING **CARL XVI GUSTAF**; b. 30 April 1946; succeeded to the throne 15 September 1973, on the death of his grandfather King Gustaf VI Adolf; married 19 June 1976, Silvia Renate Sommerlath (b. 23 December 1943); daughter, Victoria Ingrid Alice Désirée, b. 14 July 1977; son, Carl Philip Edmund Bertil, b. 13 May 1979; daughter, Madeleine Thérèse Amelie Josephine, b. 10 June 1982.

Parents of the King

Prince Gustaf Adolf, Duke of Västerbotten; b. 22 April 1906, died 26 January 1947; married 20 October 1932, Sibylla, Princess of Saxe-Coburg and Gotha (b. 18 January 1908, died 28 November 1972).

Sisters of the King

Princess Margaretha; b. 31 October 1934; married 30 June 1964, Mr. John Ambler; daughter, Sibylla Louise, b. 14 April 1965; sons, Charles Edward, b. 14 July 1966; James Patrick, b. 10 June 1969.

Princess Birgitta; b. 19 January 1937; married 25 May 1961, Prince of Hohenzollern Johann Georg; sons, Carl Christian, b. 5 April 1962; Hubertus, b. 9 June 1966; daughter, Desirée, b. 27 November 1963.

Princess Désirée; b. 2 June 1938; married 5 June 1964, Baron Niclas Silfverschiöld; son, Carl Otto Edmund, b. 22 March 1965; daughters, Christina Louise Madeleine, b. 29 September 1966, Hélène, b. 20 September 1968.

Princess Christina; b. 3 August 1943; married 15 June 1974, Tord Magnuson; sons, Carl Gustaf Victor, b. 8 August 1975, Tord Oscar Fredrik, b. 20 June 1977, Victor Edmund Lennart, b. 10 September 1980.

THAILAND
Reigning King

KING **BHUMIBOL ADULYADEJ**: b. 5 December 1927; succeeded to the throne on the death of his brother, King Ananda Mahidol, 9 June 1946; married 28 April 1950, Mom Rajawongse Sirikit Kitiyakara (b. 12 August 1932), daughter of H.H. Prince Chandaburi Suranath (Mom Chao Nakkhatra Mangala Kitiyakara).

Children of the King

Princess Ubol Ratana; b. 5 April 1951; married August 1972, Peter Ladd Jensen (relinquished Royal claims); daughters, Khun Ploypailin, b. 12 February 1981, Khun Sirikittiya, b. 18 March 1985; son, Khun Poomi, b. 16 August 1983.

Crown Prince Maha Vajiralongkorn; b. 28 July 1952; proclaimed Crown Prince December 1972; married 3 January 1977, Mom Luang Somsawalee Kitiyakara; daughters, Princess Bajrakitiyabha, b. 7 December 1978, Princess Siriwanwaree Mahldol, b. 8 January 1987.

Princess Maha Chakri Sirindhorn; b. 2 April 1955.

Princess Chulabhorn; b. 4 July 1957; married 7 January 1982, Squadron Leader Virayuth Didyasarin; daughter, Princess Siribhachudabhorn, b. 8 October 1982, daughter, Princess Aditayadornkitikhun, b. 5 May 1984.

Parents of the King

Prince and Princess Mahidol of Songkla.

Sister of the King

Princess Galyani Vadhana Krom Luang Naradhiwas Rajanagarindra.

TONGA
Reigning King

KING **TAUFA'AHAU TUPOU IV**; b. 4 July 1918; succeeded to the throne 15 December 1965, on the death of his mother, Queen Salote Tupou III; married 1947, Princess Halaevalu Mata'aho 'Ahome'e (b. 1926), (now Queen Halaevalu Mata'aho).

Mother of the King

Queen Salote Tupou III; b. 13 March 1900; married 1917, Prince Viliami Tungi (Prince Consort); died 15 December 1965.

Children of the King

Prince Tupouto'a (Crown Prince); b. 4 May 1948.

Princess Salote Mafile'o Pilolevu Tuku'aho Tuita; b. 17 November 1951; married 21 July 1976, Captain Ma'ulupekotofa Tuita (known as Honourable Tuita).

Prince Fatafehi Alaivahamama'o Tuku'aho (known as Honourable Maátu); b. 17 December 1954.

Prince 'Ulukalala-Lavaka-Ata (fmrly. known as 'Aho'eitu' Unuaki'otonga Tuku'aho); b. 12 July 1959; married 11 December 1982, Nanasipau'u Vaea (now Princess Nanasipau'u).

UNITED ARAB EMIRATES
Reigning Rulers

Ruler of Sharjah: Sheikh SULTAN BIN MUHAMMAD AL-**QASIMI**; succeeded to the throne 1972.

Ruler of Ras al-Khaimah: Sheikh SAQR BIN MUHAMMAD AL-**QASIMI**; succeeded to the throne 1948.

Ruler of Umm al-Qaiwain: Sheikh RASHID BIN AHMED AL-**MU'ALLA**; succeeded to the throne 1981.

Ruler of Ajman: Sheikh HUMAID BIN RASHID AN-**NUAIMI**; succeeded to the throne 1981.

Ruler of Dubai: Sheikh MAKTOUM BIN RASHID AL-**MAKTOUM**; succeeded to the throne 1990.

Ruler of Abu Dhabi: Sheikh ZAYED BIN SULTAN AN-**NAHYAN**; succeeded to the throne 1966.

Ruler of Fujairah: Sheikh HAMAD BIN MUHAMMAD ASH-**SHARQI**; succeeded to the throne 1974.

UNITED KINGDOM
Reigning Queen

QUEEN **ELIZABETH II**; b. 21 April 1926; succeeded to the throne 6 February 1952, on the death of her father, King George VI; crowned 2 June 1953; married 20 November 1947, H.R.H. The Prince Philip, DUKE OF **EDINBURGH**, K.G., K.T., O.M., G.B.E., A.C., Q.S.O. (b. 10 June 1921), son of Prince Andrew of Greece and Princess Alice of Battenberg (Mountbatten).

Children of the Queen

The Prince Charles Philip Arthur George, Prince of **Wales**, Duke of Cornwall and Rothesay, Earl of Chester and Carrick, Baron of Renfrew, Lord of the Isles and Great Steward of Scotland, K.G., K.T., G.C.B., A.K., Q.S.O., A.D.C. (heir-apparent); b. 14 November 1948; married 29 July 1981, Lady Diana Frances Spencer (divorced 1996, died 1997); sons, Prince William Arthur Philip Louis, b. 21 June 1982; Prince Henry Charles Albert David, b. 15 September 1984.

The Princess Anne Elizabeth Alice Louise, The Princess **Royal**, K.G., K.T., G.C.V.O., Q.S.O.; b. 15 August 1950; married 1st 14 November 1973, Captain Mark Phillips (divorced 1992); son, Peter Mark Andrew, b. 15 November 1977; daughter, Zara Anne Elizabeth, b. 15 May 1981; married 2nd 12 December 1992, Commodore Timothy Laurence, M.V.O., R.N.

The Prince Andrew Albert Christian Edward, Duke of **York**, Earl of Inverness, Baron Killyleagh, C.V.O., A.D.C.; b. 19 February 1960; married 23 July 1986, Miss Sarah Ferguson (divorced 1996); daughters, Princess Beatrice Elizabeth Mary, b. 8 August 1988; Princess Eugenie Victoria Helena, b. 23 March 1990.

The Prince Edward Antony Richard Louis, Earl of **Wessex**, Viscount Severn, C.V.O.; b. 10 March 1964; married 19 June 1999, Miss Sophie Rhys Jones.

REIGNING ROYAL FAMILIES

Parents of the Queen

King George VI; b. 14 December 1895; son of King George V and Queen Mary; married 26 April 1923, Lady Elizabeth Angela Marguerite Bowes-Lyon (b. 4 August 1900, died 30 March 2002); succeeded to the throne 11 December 1936; died 6 February 1952.

Sister of the Queen

The Princess Margaret Rose, Countess of Snowdon, C.I., G.C.V.O.; b. 21 August 1930; married 6 May 1960, Antony Armstrong-Jones, later the Earl of Snowdon, G.C.V.O. (divorced 1978); son, David Albert Charles, Viscount Linley, b. 3 November 1961; daughter, Lady Sarah Frances Elizabeth Chatto, b. 1 May 1964; died 9 February 2002.

The full titles of Queen Elizabeth II are as follows:

United Kingdom

"Elizabeth the Second, by the Grace of God, of the United Kingdom of Great Britain and Northern Ireland and of Her other Realms and Territories Queen, Head of the Commonwealth, Defender of the Faith."

Canada

"Elizabeth the Second, by the Grace of God, of the United Kingdom, Canada and Her other Realms and Territories Queen, Head of the Commonwealth, Defender of the Faith."

Australia

"Elizabeth the Second, by the Grace of God Queen of Australia and Her other Realms and Territories, Head of the Commonwealth."

New Zealand

"Elizabeth the Second, by the Grace of God, Queen of New Zealand and Her Other Realms and Territories, Head of the Commonwealth, Defender of the Faith."

Jamaica

"Elizabeth the Second, by the Grace of God, of Jamaica and of Her other Realms and Territories Queen, Head of the Commonwealth."

Barbados

"Elizabeth the Second, by the Grace of God, Queen of Barbados and of Her other Realms and Territories, Head of the Commonwealth."

The Bahamas

"Elizabeth the Second, by the Grace of God, Queen of the Commonwealth of The Bahamas and of Her other Realms and Territories, Head of the Commonwealth."

Grenada

"Elizabeth the Second, by the Grace of God, Queen of the United Kingdom of Great Britain and Northern Ireland and of Grenada and Her other Realms and Territories, Head of the Commonwealth."

Papua New Guinea

"Elizabeth the Second, Queen of Papua New Guinea and of Her other Realms and Territories, Head of the Commonwealth."

Solomon Islands

"Elizabeth the Second, by the Grace of God Queen of the Solomon Islands and of Her other Realms and Territories, Head of the Commonwealth."

Tuvalu

"Elizabeth the Second, by the Grace of God Queen of Tuvalu and of Her other Realms and Territories, Head of the Commonwealth."

Saint Lucia

"Elizabeth the Second, by the Grace of God, Queen of Saint Lucia and of Her other Realms and Territories, Head of the Commonwealth."

Saint Vincent and the Grenadines

"Elizabeth the Second, by the Grace of God, Queen of Saint Vincent and the Grenadines and of Her other Realms and Territories, Head of the Commonwealth."

Belize

"Elizabeth The Second, by the Grace of God, Queen of Belize and of Her Other Realms and Territories, Head of the Commonwealth."

Antigua and Barbuda

"Elizabeth the Second, by the Grace of God, Queen of Antigua and Barbuda and of Her other Realms and Territories, Head of the Commonwealth."

Saint Christopher and Nevis

"Elizabeth the Second, by the Grace of God, Queen of Saint Christopher and Nevis and of Her other Realms and Territories, Head of the Commonwealth."

The Republics of India, Ghana, Cyprus, Tanzania, Uganda, Kenya, Zambia, Malawi, Singapore, Botswana, Guyana, Nauru, The Gambia, Sierra Leone, Bangladesh, Sri Lanka, Malta, Trinidad and Tobago, Seychelles, Dominica, Kiribati, Zimbabwe, Vanuatu, Maldives, Namibia, Mauritius, South Africa, Fiji, Pakistan, Cameroon and Mozambique, together with the Federation of Malaysia, the Kingdom of Lesotho, the Kingdom of Swaziland, the Kingdom of Tonga, the Independent State of Samoa and the Sultanate of Brunei, recognize the Queen as "Head of the Commonwealth".

OBITUARY

Abdel-Rahman, Aisha	1 December 1998
Abdullojonov, Abdumalik	–
Aberconway, 3rd Baron; Charles Melville McLaren	4 February 2003
Aga Khan, Prince Sadruddin	12 May 2003
Agnelli, Giovanni	24 January 2003
Ahronovitch, Yuri (George)	31 October 2002
Aigrain, Pierre Raoul Roger	30 October 2002
Alexander, Sir Michael O'Donel Bjarne	1 June 2002
Almond, Gabriel Abraham	25 December 2002
Ambani, Dhirubhai Hirachand	6 July 2002
Ambrose, Stephen E.	13 October 2002
Amies, Sir (Edwin) Hardy	5 March 2003
Amosov, Nikolai Mikhailovich	12 December 2002
Annenberg, Walter H.	1 October 2002
Anselm, Aleksey Andreyevich	December 1999
Antrobus, Sir Charles (James)	3 June 2002
Augstein, Rudolf	7 November 2002
Baker, Wilson	3 June 2002
Balaguer Ricardo, Joaquín	14 July 2002
Baldin, Aleksandr Mikhailovich	27 April 2001
Barbieri, Fedora	4 March 2003
Beláunde Terry, Fernando	4 June 2002
Bergmann, Felix	19 February 2002
Bergson, Abram	24 April 2003
Bieler, Manfred	23 April 2002
Biesheuvel, Barend Willem	29 April 2001
Billingham, Rupert Everett	16 November 2002
Biobaku, Saburi Oladeni	8 February 2001
Birt, Lindsay Michael	28 October 2001
Black, Sir Douglas Andrew Kilgour	13 September 2002
Black, Stanley	26 November 2002
Blass, Bill (William) Ralph	12 June 2002
Boardman, Baron; Thomas Gray Boardman	10 March 2003
Boisdeffre, (Néraud le Mouton de) Pierre Jules Marie Raoul	23 May 2002
Borel, Jacques	25 September 2002
Bredsdorff, Elias	8 August 2002
Brookes, Baron; Raymond Percival Brookes	31 July 2002
Brown, Arthur Joseph	28 February 2003
Brown, Jesse	15 August 2002
Brown, Sir John Gilbert Newton	3 March 2003
Brushlinksy, Andrei Vladimirovich	30 January 2002
Buchholz, Horst	3 March 2003
Carter, HE Cardinal Gerald Emmett	6 April 2003
Cash, Sir Gerald Christopher	6 January 2003
Castiglioni, Achille	2 December 2002
Chadwick, Lynn Russell	25 April 2003
Chargaff, Erwin	20 June 2002
Chapman Nyaho, Daniel Ahmling	13 July 2001
Chillida Juantegui, Eduardo	19 August 2002
Christodoulou, Anastasios	20 May 2002
Chubb, Frederick Basil	8 May 2002
Clapham, Sir Michael John Sinclair	11 November 2002
Coburn, James	18 November 2002
Cohn, Haim Herman	10 April 2002
Corbin, Raymond Pierre Louis	1 March 2002
Cowan, William Maxwell	30 June 2002
Coxeter, Harold Scott MacDonald	31 March 2003
Cracknell, Ruth Winifred	13 May 2002
Dacre of Glanton, Baron; Hugh Redwald Trevor-Roper	26 January 2003
Daniel-Lesur, J.-Y.	2 July 2002
Degenhardt, HE Cardinal Johannes Joachim	25 July 2002
Dejmek, Kazimierz	31 December 2002
Diligensky, German Germanovich	14 June 2002
Dillon, C. Douglas	10 January 2003
Djindjić, Zoran	12 March 2003
Doinaş, Ştefan Augustin	25 May 2002
Dornbusch, Rudiger	25 July 2002
Dowiyogo, Bernard	9 March 2003
Drucker, Jean Maurice	18 April 2003
Dudinskaya, Natalya Mikhailovna	29 January 2003
Eastwick-Field, Elizabeth	8 March 2003
Eban, Abba	17 November 2002
Edelmann, Otto Karl	14 May 2003
Edwards, Sir George Robert	2 March 2003
Eicher, Lawrence D.	21 March 2003
Emslie, Baron; George Carlyle Emslie	20 November 2002
Enright, Dennis Joseph	31 December 2002
Everett, Douglas Hugh	25 June 2002
Faith, Adam	8 March 2003
Fast, Howard	12 March 2003
Fatayi-Williams, Hon. Justice Atanda	April 2002
Fauvet, Jacques	1 June 2002
Fiedler, Leslie A.	29 January 2003
Flexner, James Thomas	13 February 2003
Frankenheimer, John Michael	6 July 2002
Freeman, Orville Lothrop	20 February 2003
Frumkin, Allan	9 December 2002
Galtieri, Lt-Gen. Leopoldo Fortunato	11 January 2003
Garba, Maj.-Gen. Joseph Nanven	1 June 2002
Geens, Gaston	5 June 2002
Gélin, Daniel Yves	29 November 2002
Getty, Sir Paul	17 April 2003
Gibb, Maurice	12 January 2003
Gibson, Eleanor Jack	30 December 2002
Ginzberg, Eli	12 December 2002
Ginzburg, Aleksandr Ilyich	19 July 2002
Giroud, Françoise	19 January 2003
Gopal, Sarvepalli	20 April 2002
Gorenstein, Fridrikh Naumovich	2 March 2002
Gottlieb, Paul	5 June 2002
Grekova, Irina Nikolaevna	16 April 2002
Guest, George Howell	20 November 2002
Gröer, HE Cardinal Hans Hermann	23 March 2003
Gunther, Gerald	30 July 2002
Habakkuk, Sir Hrothgar John	3 November 2002
Hambro, Baron; Charles Eric Alexander Hambro	7 November 2002
Harris, Richard R. St Johns	25 October 2002
Hartog, Jan de	22 September 2002
Haslam, Baron; Robert Haslam	2 November 2002
Helms, Richard M.	22 October 2002
Herron, Very Rev. Andrew	27 February 2003
Hibbert, Sir Reginald Alfred	5 October 2002
Hill, George Roy	27 December 2002
Hill, (John Edward) Christopher	24 February 2003
Hiller, Dame Wendy	14 may 2003
Hnatyshyn, Rt Hon. Ramon John	18 December 2002
Holderness, Baron; Richard Frederick Wood Holderness	11 August 2002
Hoyte, Hugh Desmond	22 December 2002
Illich, Ivan	2 December 2002
Ioseliani, Dzhaba	4 March 2003
Ishii, Maki	9 April 2003
Jabłoński, Henryk	27 January 2003
Jarring, Gunnar	29 May 2002
Jenkins of Hillhead, Baron; Roy Harris Jenkins	5 January 2003
Jerie, Jan	23 September 2002
Jobert, Michel	26 May 2002
Johnson, Barry Edward	5 May 2002
Johnson, David Gale	14 April 2003
Jones, Rt Hon. Aubrey	10 April 2003
Kanakaratne, Neville	21 September 1999
Kant, Shri Krishna	27 July 2002
Kapnick, Harvey Edward, Jr	16 August 2002
Karsh, Yousuf	13 July 2002
Katz, Sir Bernard	20 April 2003
Keane, John Brendan	30 May 2002
Kendell, Robert Evan	19 December 2002
Kerr, Jean	5 January 2003
Kirk, Geoffrey Stephen	10 March 2003
Kolar, Jiri	11 August 2002

OBITUARY

Kornilov, Vladimir Nikolaevich	8 January 2002	Reinhardt, Max	19 November 2002
Koszarowski, Tadeusz Tomasz	17 August 2002	Reisz, Karel	25 November 2002
Krasucki, Henri	24 January 2003	Rheims, Maurice	6 March 2003
Kulidzhanov, Lev Aleksandrovich	18 February 2002	Ri Jong Ok	23 September 1999
		Richardson, Sir Michael (John de Rougemont)	12 May 2003
Lacant, Jacques	12 August 2002	Ringadoo, Sir Veerasamy	9 September 2000
Lagardère, Jean-Luc	14 March 2003	Ritts, Her	26 December 2002
Lanchbery, John Arthur	27 February 2003	Rivers, Larry	14 August 2002
Latsis, John	17 April 2003	Robinson, Derek Charles	2 December 2002
Lemieux, Raymond Urgel	22 July 2000	Rosenblith, Walter Alter	1 May 2002
Limerick, 6th Earl of; Patrick Edmund Pery	8 January 2003	Rostow, Eugene Victor	25 November 2002
Lippold, Richard	22 August 2002	Rostow, Walt Whitman	13 February 2003
Littlewood, Joan	20 September 2002	Ryder of Eaton Hastings, Baron; Sydney Thomas	
Logachev, Nikolay Alekseyevich	19 December 2002	Franklin (Don) Ryder	12 May 2003
Loiseau, Bernard	24 February 2003		
Lomax, Alan	19 July 2002	Sánchez Hernández, Col Fidel	28 February 2003
Long, Russell B.	9 May 2003	Sauvagnarques, Jean Victor	6 August 2002
Longford, Countess of; Elizabeth Pakenham	23 October 2002	Seefelder, Matthias	30 October 2001
Luns, Joseph Marie Antoine Hubert	17 July 2002	Seignoret, Sir Clarence (Henry Augustus)	5 May 2002
		Sellschop, Jacques Pierre Friedrich	4 August 2002
Marchandise-Franquet, Jacques	30 September 2002	Shaker, Field Marshal Sharif Zaid ibn	30 August 2002
Martin, Archer John Porter	28 July 2002	Shihata, Ibrahim F.I.	28 May 2001
Massu, Gen. Jacques	26 October 2002	Shreider, Yuly Anatolyevich	26 August 2000
Matheson, Sir (James Adam) Louis	27 March 2002	Siepmann, Mary Aline (Mary Wesley)	30 December 2002
May, Georges	28 February 2003	Siig, Arvi	23 November 1999
McCormack, Mark Hurne	16 May 2003	Siilasvuo, Gen. Ensio	10 January 2003
McKern, Leo Reginald	23 July 2002	Simone, Nina	21 April 2003
Mehdi, Mohammad T.	23 February 1998	Sisulu, Walter Max Ulyate	5 May 2003
Merton, Robert K.	23 February 2003	Smithson, Peter Denham	3 March 2003
Meyer, Jean Léon André	8 January 2003	Snowman, A. Kenneth	9 July 2002
Migulin, Vladimir Vasiliyevich	22 September 2002	Solomin, Vitaly Mefodievich	27 May 2002
Miller, Neal Elgar	23 March 2002	Solomon, Hollis	6 June 2002
Milner, Anthony Francis Dominic	22 September 2002	Souza, Francis Newton	28 March 2002
Mitchell, Sir (Edgar) William John	30 October 2002	Steiger, Rod	9 July 2002
Mitchell, James Richard	2 December 2002	Su Buqing	17 March 2003
Mokaba, Peter Ramoshoane	9 June 2002		
Monterroso, Augusto (Tito)	8 February 2003	Tchobanu, Ion	2000
Moreira Neves, HE Cardinal Lucas	8 September 2002	Thompson, J(ay) Lee	30 August 2002
Mosler, Hermann	—	Todd, Hon. Sir (Reginald Stephen) Garfield	13 October 2002
Mostafizur Rahman, A.S.M.	30 November 2001	Todea, HE Cardinal Alexandru	22 May 2002
Moynihan, Daniel Patrick	26 March 2003	Tomaszewski, Henryk	23 September 2001
Muhammadullah	—	Toscan du Plantier, Daniel	11 February 2002
		Tschudi, Hans-Peter	29 September 2002
Ne Win, U (Maung Shu Maung)	5 December 2002	Turkevich, Anthony Leonid	7 September 2002
Neumann, Bernhard Hermann	21 October 2002	Turnbull, Lyle E. J.	27 March 2003
Nguyen Van Thuan, HE Cardinal François Xavier	16 September 2002		
Noelte, Rudolf	7 November 2002	Unseld, Siegfried	26 October 2002
Norfolk, 17th Duke of; Miles Francis Stapleton			
Fitzalan-Howard	24 June 2002	Villas-Bôas, Orlando	12 December 2002
Novarina, Maurice Paul Joseph	28 September 2002		
Nozick, Robert	23 January 2002	Walker, Rev. Sir Alan Edgar	29 January 2003
		Wasserman, Lew R.	3 June 2002
Odum, Eugene P.	10 August 2002	Weinstock, Baron; Arnold Weinstock	23 July 2002
Oldenbourg, Zoé	8 November 2002	Wende, Edward	28 May 2002
Oppenheim, Sir Duncan Morris	5 January 2003	Werner, Pierre	24 June 2002
Palkhivala, Nani Ardeshir	11 December 2002	Wesley, Mary (see Siepmann, Mary Aline)	30 December 2002
Panchenko, Aleksandr Mikhailovich	28 May 2002	Whent, Sir Gerald Arthur	16 May 2002
Park Choong-Hoon	16 March 2001	Wilberforce, Baron; Richard Orme Wilberforce	15 February 2003
Pavlov, Valentin Sergeyevich	30 March 2003	Williamson, Malcolm Benjamin Graham	2 March 2003
Périer, François	29 June 2002	Wilson, Alexander	13 February 2002
Perlemuter, Vlado	4 September 2002	Wilson, Sir Robert	2 September 2002
Perry, George Edward (Ted)	9 February 2003	Wirahadikusumah, Gen. Umar	21st March 2003
Petrassi, Goffredo	2 March 2003	Wu Cheng-Chung	23 September 2002
Peugeot, Pierre	1 December 2002		
Phillips, William	13 September 2002	Yamahana, Sadao	14 July 1999
Pogorelov, Aleksey Vasiliyevich	18 December 2002	Young, Baroness; Janet Mary Young	6 September 2002
Porter of Luddenham, Baron; George Porter	31 August 2002	Younger of Leckie, 4th Viscount; Baron; George	
Powell, Sir (Arnold Joseph) Philip	5 May 2003	(Kenneth Hotson) Younger	26 January 2003
		Yushenkov, Col Sergey Nikolayevich	17 April 2003
Rawls, John	24 November 2002		
Rechter, Yacov	14 February 2001	Zahn, Joachim	8 October 2002
Reddaway, William Brian	23 July 2002	Żukrowski, Wojciech	26 August 2000

THE INTERNATIONAL WHO'S WHO

2004

A

AARNES, Asbjørn Sigurd, DPhil; Norwegian professor of European literature; b. 20 Dec. 1923, Vågbø; s. of Halvor Aarnes and Alida Olsen; m. Berit Alten 1950; one s. one d.; ed Univ. of Oslo and Ecole Normale Supérieure, Paris; Prof. of European Literature, Univ. of Oslo 1964, Dir Inst. d'Études Romanes 1966–70; Pres. Norwegian Acad. of Language and Literature 1966–84; mem. Norwegian Acad. of Science, various ed. bds and cttees; Chevalier, Ordre Nat. du Mérite; Chevalier, Légion d'honneur; Officier des Palmes académiques. *Publications:* J. S. Welhaven 1955, Gérard de Nerval 1957, Nicolas Boileau 1961, Det poetiske fenomen 1963, Litterært Leksikon 1964, Pierre Le Moyne 1965, Ved Veiskille: natur og rasjonalitet 1974, Maine de Biran 1976, René Descartes 1980, Debatten om Descartes: innvendinger og svar 1982, Fransk tanke og idéliv: Cartesianske perspektiver 1981, Henri Bergson 1989, Perspektiver og profiler i norsk poesi 1989, Cartesianische Perspektiven von Montaigne bis Paul Ricoeur 1991, (Ed.) Emmanuel Levinas, Den Annens humanisme 1996, (Ed.) Underveis mot den Annen 1998. *Leisure interest:* fishing. *Address:* Ostadalsveien 9, 0753 Oslo 7, Norway. *Telephone:* 22500789 (Home). *Fax:* 22500789 (Home).

AARON, David L., MA; American diplomatist; b. 21 Aug. 1938, Chicago; m. Chloe W. Aaron; one c.; ed Occidental Coll. Calif. and Princeton Univ.; entered Foreign Service 1962; Political and Econ. Officer, Guayaquil, Ecuador; Int. Relations Officer, Dept of State 1964–66; Political Officer, NATO, Paris 1966; Arms Control and Disarmament Agency; Sr Staff mem. Nat. Security Council 1972–74; Legis. Asst to Sen. Walter Mondale 1974–75; Task Force Leader, Senate Select Cttee on Intelligence 1975–76; mem. staff, Carter-Mondale presidential campaign; Transition Dir with Nat. Security Council and CIA 1976–77; Deputy Asst to Pres. for Nat. Security Affairs 1977–81; Vice-Pres. Oppenheimer & Co. Inc. 1981–85, Dir Oppenheimer Int. 1984; Sr Adviser, Mondale presidential campaign; writer and lecturer, Lantz-Harris Agency 1985–93; consultant, 20th Century Fund 1990–92, Sr Fellow 1992–93; U.S. Rep. to OECD 1993; U.S. Special Envoy for Cryptography 1996; Under-Sec. of Commerce for Int. Trade 1997–2001; Sr Int. Adviser, Int. Trade Practice Group, Dorsey & Whitney 2000–; Dr. hc (Occidental Coll.); Nat. Defense Medal. *Publications:* State Scarlet 1987, Agent of Influence 1989, Crossing by Night 1993; articles in newspapers and journals. *Address:* Dorsey & Whitney LLP, 1001 Pennsylvania Avenue, NW, Suite 300, Washington, DC 20004, USA (Office). *Telephone:* (202) 824-8845. *E-mail:* aaron.david@dorseylaw.com. *Website:* www.dorseylaw.com.

ABAKANOWICZ, Magdalena; Polish artist, weaver and sculptor; b. 20 June 1930, Falenty, nr Warsaw; d. of Konstanty and Helena Abakanowicz; m. Jan Kosmowski 1956; ed Acad. of Fine Arts, Warsaw; mem. of Soc. of Authors ZAIKS; work includes monumental space forms of woven fibres, cycles of figurative sculptures of burlap, wood and clay, cast metal, stone, drawings, paintings with collage and gouache; Prof. Acad. of Fine Arts, Poznań 1979–90; mem. Presidential Council for Culture 1992; Hon. mem. American Acad. of Arts and Letters 1996; Dr hc (RCA), London 1974, Rhode Island School of Design, Providence 1992, Acad. of Fine Arts, Łódź 1997, Pratt Inst., New York 2000, Massachusetts Coll. of Art, Boston 2001, School of the Art Inst. of Chicago 2002, Acad. of Fine Arts, Poznań 2002; Minister of Culture and Art Prize (1st Class) 1965; Gold Medal VIIIth Int. Biennale of Arts, São Paulo 1965; Gottfried von Herder Prize 1979; Alfred Jurzykowski Foundation Award 1982, New York Sculpture Center Award 1993, Leonardo da Vinci World Award of Arts 1997; Officier des Arts et des Lettres, Paris 1999; Commdr's Cross with Star, Order of Polonia Restituta 1998. *Works:* Sculpture for Elblag, relief woven composition for North Brabant Provincial Building, Netherlands; three-dimensional woven forms: Abakans Figurative sculptures, seated figures, Backs, Incarnations, War Games, Crowds, Hands-like Trees, Mutants, Birds; large outdoor installations: Katarsis (Italy), Negev (Israel), Space of Dragon (S Korea), Space of Nine Figures (Germany), Becalmed Beings (Hiroshima) and others; one-woman exhbns: Zachęta State Gallery, Warsaw 1965, 1975, Kunsthaus Zürich 1968, Nat. Museum Stockholm 1970, Pasadena Art Museum 1970, Düsseldorf Kunsthalle 1972, Whitechapel Art Gallery, London 1975, Art Gallery of New South Wales, Sydney, Nat. Gallery of Victoria, Melbourne 1976, Henie-Onstad Foundation, Oslo 1978, Muzeum Sztuki, Łódź 1978, Musée d'Art Moderne de la Ville de Paris 1982, Museum of Contemporary Art, Chicago 1982, Musée d'Art Moderne, Montreal 1983, Xavier Fourcade Gallery, New York 1985, Virginia Museum of Fine Art, Richmond, Muku Gallery, Hiroshima 1987, Mücsarnok Palace of Exhbns, Budapest 1988, Turske a. Turske Gallery, Zürich 1988, Städel Kunstinstitut, Frankfurt 1989, Marlborough Gallery, New York 1989, 1992, 1993, 1997, Sezon Museum of Art, Tokyo 1991, Museum of Modern Art, Shiga 1991, Art Tower, Mito 1991, Hiroshima City Art Museum 1991, Walker Art Center, Minn. 1992, Inst. of Contemporary Art, New York, BWA, Kraków, Hiroshima City Museum 1993, Muzeum Sztuki, Łódź, Marlborough Gallery, Madrid 1994, Fundació Miró, Mallorca 1994, Els Jardins de Can Altamira, Barcelona, Centre of Polish Sculpture, Orońsko, Centre for Contemporary Art, Warsaw, Yorks. Sculpture Park, Centre for Contemporary Art, Ujazdoski Castle 1995, Galerie Marwan Hoss, Paris 1996, Oriel Mostyn, England 1996, Kulturhuset, Stockholm 1996, Grounds for Sculpture, Hamilton, USA 1996, Doris Freedman Plaza, New York 1996–97, Marlborough Gallery, New York 1997–98, Metropolitan Museum of Art, New York 1999, Les Jardins du Palais Royal, Paris 1999, Marlborough Gallery, New York 2000, Three Rivers Arts Festival, Pittsburgh 2001 and others; group exhbns: Biennale: Biennale de Lausanne 1962–79, 1995; Biennale of Art, São Paulo 1965, 1979, Venice Biennale 1968, 1980, ROSC, Dublin 1980, Nat. Gallery, Berlin 1982, Museum of Ateneum, Helsinki 1983, Biennale of Sculpture, Middelheim, Antwerp 1983, Biennale of Art, Sydney 1986, Storm Kings Art Center, New York 1987, Hirshhorn Museum, Washington, DC 1988, Fuji Sankei Biennale, Japan 1993, Royal Festival Hall, London, Museum Ludwig, Cologne, Hiroshima City Museum of Contemporary Art 1995, Marwan Hoss Gallery, Paris 1997, Guggenheim Museum, New York 1997, Spoleto Festival, USA 1997, Les Jardins du Palais Royal, Paris 2000, Galerie Nationale du Jeu de Paume, Paris 2000. *Leisure interests:* swimming, walking in the countryside and forests. *Address:* ul. Bzowa 1, 02-708 Warsaw, Poland. *Telephone:* (22) 8486379 (Home). *Fax:* (22) 8486379 (Home).

ABALAKIN, Victor Kuzmich, DPhysMathSc; Russian astronomer; b. 27 Aug. 1930; m.; three c.; ed Odessa State Univ.; jr researcher, Inst. of Geophysics, USSR Acad. of Sciences 1953–55, Inst. of Theoretical Astronomy, USSR Acad. of Sciences 1955–57, Head of Div. 1965–83; researcher, Odessa Astronomy Observatory 1960–63; Docent, Odessa State Univ. 1963–65; Dir Main Astronomy Observatory, Russian Acad. of Sciences 1983–; Corresp. mem. USSR (now Russian) Acad. of Sciences 1987–; mem. Int. Acad. of Ecological Sciences, Security of Man and Nature; main research in theoretical astronomy; USSR State Prize. *Publications:* 5 books including Optical Localisation of the Moon 1981, numerous papers. *Address:* Main Astronomy Observatory, Pulkovskoye shosse 65, korp. 1, 196140 St Petersburg, Russia. *Telephone:* (812) 298 2242 (Office); (812) 277 2881 (Home).

ABALKHAIL, Sheikh Mohamed Ali, BA; Saudi Arabian government official and financial executive; b. 1935, Buraida; s. of Ali Abdullah Abalkhail and Fatima Abdulaziz Othaim; m. 1966; two s. two d.; ed Cairo Univ.; began career as Asst Dir of Office of Minister of Communications, later Dir; Dir-Gen. of Inst. of Public Admin.; Deputy Minister of Finance and Nat. Econ., then Vice-Minister, Minister of State, Minister for Finance and Nat. Econ. 1975–95; fmr Chair. Riyadh Bank, Riyadh; Chair. Centre for Econ. and Man. Studies; mem. JP Morgan Int. Council; decorations from Belgium, Egypt, France, Niger, Pakistan, Saudi Arabia, Sudan, Germany, Morocco, Spain. *Leisure interests:* reading, sports. *Address:* PO Box 287, Riyadh 11411, Saudi Arabia. *Telephone:* (1) 478-1722, (1) 476-6965. *Fax:* (1) 478-1904. *E-mail:* abakhail@kfshhub.kfshrc.edu.sa.

ABALKIN, Leonid Ivanovich; Russian economist; b. 5 May 1930, Moscow; m. Abalkina (Satarova) Anna Vartanovna 1953; one s. one d.; ed Inst. of Nat. Econ.; mem. CPSU 1956–91, mem. Cen. Cttee 1990–91; Deputy Head Acad. of Social Sciences of the Central Cttee 1976–89, Head Faculty of Political Econ. 1978–86; Dir Inst. of Econs, Acad. of Sciences 1986–; mem. USSR (now Russian) Acad. of Sciences 1987–, mem. of Presidium 1988–; Columnist, Trud; mem. bds of EKO and Voprosy ekonomiki; USSR People's Deputy 1989–91; Deputy Prime Minister, Chair. Comm. for Econ. Reforms 1989–91; adviser to Pres. Gorbachev 1991; mem. Govt's Econ. Crisis Group 1998–; Ed.-in-Chief Voprosy Ekonomiki 1992–; mem. Int. Acad. of Man., New York Acad. of Sciences, Int. Econs Acad. of Eurasia; Vice-Pres. Int. Union of Economists, Free Tcjn. Soc. of Russia;. *Publications:* Political Economy and Economic Policy 1970, Final Economic Results 1978, Direction—Acceleration 1986, New Type of Economic Thinking 1987, Perestroika—Ways and Problems 1989, Missed Chance 1991, To the Goal Through Crisis: Destiny of Economic Reform 1992, At the Crossroads 1993, The Crisis Grip 1994, To Self-Perception of Russia 1995, Zigzags of Fate: Disappointments and Hopes 1996, Postponed Changes: The Lost Year 1997, Russia: The Choice 1998 and numerous articles in Soviet press on theoretical problems of political economy under socialism. *Leisure interests:* chess, gardening. *Address:* Institute of Economics, Academy of Sciences of Russia, 117218 Moscow, Nakhimovsky Prospekt 32, Russia. *Telephone:* (095) 129-02-54 (Office); (095) 135-10-85 (Home). *Fax:* (095) 310-70-71.

ABASHIDZE, Aslan Ibragimovich; Georgian politician and economist; b. 20 July 1938, Batumi; m. Maguli Gogitidze; one s. one d.; ed Batumi State Inst., Tbilisi State Univ.; with Komsomol; Dir Tech. Colls. No. 44, No. 105; Deputy Chair. Exec. Cttee, Public Deputies Council of Batumi; Minister of Civil Service, Autonomous Repub. of Ajaria, Georgia 1984–86; Deputy Minister of Civil Service, Repub. of Georgia; mem. Georgian Parl., Deputy Chair. 1990–95; Chair. Supreme Council of Autonomous Repub. of Ajaria, Georgia 1991–2001, Head of the Repub. 2001–; est. Georgian Union of Revival Party 1991; apptd. Chief Negotiator to deal with problems created by self-proclaimed, separatist Abkhazian Repub. 2001–; Hon. Pres. Georgian Orientalist Asscn; mem. Int. Ind. Bureau's Council of European Parl.'s Humanitarian Subjects, Geneva; Hon. mem. Georgian Acad. of Political Science and Information; rank of Maj.-Gen.; Order of Friendship. *Leisure interests:* drawing, model-making. *Address:* Gogebashvili Street 4, Apt. 24, Batumi 384503, Autonomous Republic of Ajaria, Georgia. *Telephone:* (222) 700 00.

ABAZAH, Muhammad Muher, BSc; Egyptian politician and engineer; b. 12 March 1930, Sharkia; s. of Muhamed Osman Abazah; m. Ezdehar Abo El-Ela 1955; one s. one d.; ed Cairo Univ.; engineer Ministry of Public Works 1951–64; Man. Egyptian Gen. Electricity Authority 1964–66; Dir-Gen. Egyptian Electricity Authority 1966–72, Man. Dir for Studies and Projects 1973–74; Insp. Gen. Rural Electrification Authority 1972–73; First Under-Sec. of State Ministry of Electricity and Energy 1975–80, Minister 1980–99; mem. numerous comms., Inst. of Electric and Electronic Engineers, Thomas Alva Edison Foundation; Order of the Repub. (First Class, Egypt, France), Royal Order of the Polar Star (Grand Cross, Sweden), Grand Cross of the Order of Merit (Germany, Italy). *Leisure interests:* philately, photography, reading, swimming. *Address:* c/o Ministry of Electricity and Energy, Sharia Ramses, Cairo (Nasr City), Egypt.

ABBADO, Claudio; Italian conductor; b. 26 June 1933, Milan; one c.; Music Dir Teatro alla Scala, Milan 1968–86, Vienna Philharmonic Orchestra 1972–, London Symphony Orchestra 1979–88, Vienna State Opera 1986–91; f. European Community Youth Orchestra 1978; Gen. Music Dir City of Vienna 1987–; f. Gustav Mahler Jugend Orchestra 1988, Wien Modern (Modern Vienna) Contemporary Art Festival 1988, Vienna Int. Competition for Composers 1991, Encounters in Berlin (Chamber Music Festival) 1992, Lucerne Festival Orchestra 2001; Artistic Dir, Berlin Philharmonic Orchestra 1989–2002; Artistic Dir Easter Festival, Salzburg 1994; Conductor, Orchestra Giovanile Europea; Dr hc (Aberdeen) 1986, (Ferrara) 1990, (Cambridge) 1994 Grand Cross, Order of Merit (Italy) 1984, Cross of the Légion d'honneur, Bundesverdienstkreuz (Germany) 1992, Ehrenring, City of Vienna 1994; Mozart Medal (Vienna) 1973, Gold Medal, Int. Gustav Mahler Gesellschaft (Vienna) 1985, Amadeus (Ferrara) 1996, award from the Presidency of the Council of Ministers 1997, Athena-Giovani e Cultura Award (Univ. of Milan) 1999, Conductor of the Year, Opernwelt Review 2000; Oscar della Lirica 2001. *Publication:* Musica sopra Berlino (Nonino Award 1999) 1998 (revised ed. 2001), Suite Concertante from the Ballet Hawaii 2000. *Address:* c/o Askonas Holt, Lonsdale Chambers, 27 Chancery Lane, London WC2A 1PF, England (Office).

ABBAS, Mahmud (alias Abu Mazen), PhD; Palestinian politician and civil servant; b. 1935, Safad, Galilea; ed Damascus Univ., Moscow Univ.; civil servant UAE –1967; co-f. Fatah (The Palestine Nat. Liberation Movt), mem. Cen. Cttee 1967–; elected to Palestine Liberation Org. (PLO) Exec. Cttee 1980, Head Pan-Arab and Int. Affairs Dept 1984, Sec.-Gen. PLO Exec. Cttee 1996–; participated in Middle East Peace Conf. Washington and in Norwegian-mediated peace talks with Israel; Prime Minister, Palestinian Authority (PA) 2003–. *Address:* Palestinian Authority, Jericho Area, West Bank, Palestinian Autonomous Areas. *E-mail:* info@gov.ps. *Website:* www.pna.net.

ABBOTT, Anthony John (Tony), CMG, OBE; British diplomatist; b. 9 Sept. 1941, Ashton-under-Lyne, England; s. of Walter Abbott and Mary Abbott (née Delaney); m. Margaret Stuart Green 1962; three s. one d.; ed All Souls School, Salford, De La Salle Coll., Pendleton; joined British diplomatic service 1959, Vice Consul, Khorramshahr, Iran 1963–65, Helsinki, Finland 1965–68, Press Officer, FCO, London 1969–72, Passport Officer, Lusaka, Zambia 1972–75, Consul, Santiago, Chile 1976–80; with UK Presidency Secr. to EC 1981; on secondment to British Overseas Trade Bd 1981–82; Consul, Lisbon, Portugal 1983–87; First Sec., later Deputy High Commr, Calcutta, India 1987–91; EC Monitor, Croatia 1991; Chief of EC Monitoring Mission, Bosnia-Herzegovina 1991; Deputy Head, Training Dept, FCO 1992–93; Consul-Gen., Perth, Australia 1993–97; Gov. of Montserrat 1997–2001; Head Pitcairn Logistics Team, New Zealand 2001–; Officer, Order of Dom Enfante d'Enrique (Portugal) 1985, EC Monitoring Medal for Services in Former Yugoslavia 1994. *Leisure interests:* travel, driving, golf, all spectator sports, beating Australia at anything. *Address:* c/o Foreign and Commonwealth Office, Whitehall, London SW1A 2AH (Office); 5 Rye View Maisonettes, The Gardens, East Dulwich, London SE22 9QB, England (Home).

ABBOUD, A. Robert, LLB, MBA; American banker; b. 29 May 1929, Boston, Mass.; s. of Alfred Abboud and Victoria Abboud; m. Joan Grover Abboud 1955; one s. two d.; ed Harvard Coll., Harvard Law School, Harvard Business School; Asst Cashier, Int. Dept, First Nat. Bank of Chicago 1960, Asst Vice-Pres. Int. 1962, Vice-Pres. 1964, Sr Vice-Pres. 1969, Exec. Vice-Pres. 1972, Vice-Chair. 1973, Deputy Chair. of Bd 1974–75, Chair. of Bd 1975–80; Pres., COO and Dir Occidental Petroleum Corpn 1980–84; Pres. A. Robert Abboud and Co., Fox Grove, Ill., 1984–; Chair. Braeburn Capital Inc. 1984–92; Chair.

and CEO First City Bancorp of Tex. Inc., Houston 1988–91, First City Nat. Bank of Houston 1988–91; Dir AAR Corpn; fmr Dir Cities Service, ICN Biomedicals, ICN Pharmaceuticals, Inland Steel Co., AMOCO, Hartmarx Corpn, Alberto-Culver Co. *Publications:* Introduction of US Commercial Paper in Foreign Markets—Premature and Perilous? 1970, A Proposed Course for US Trade and Investment Policies 1971, A Proposal to Help Reverse the Narrowing Balance in the US Balance of Trade 1971, The Outlook for a New Monetary System 1971, Opportunities for Foreign Banks in Singapore 1971, The International Competitiveness of US Banks and the US Economy 1972, Money in the Bank: How Safe Is It? 1988. *Address:* A. Robert Abboud & Co., PO Box 33, 212 Stone Hill Center, Fox River Grove, IL 60021 (Office); 209 Braeburn Road, Barrington Hills, IL 60010, USA (Home). *Telephone:* (847) 639-0101 (Office); (847) 658-4808 (Home). *Fax:* (847) 639-0233 (Office). *E-mail:* araco@mc.net (Office).

ABD AL-HALIM ABU GHAZALA, Field Marshal Muhammad, BA, MSc(Econ), MD; Egyptian politician and army officer; b. 1 Jan. 1930, El Behaira; m. 1953; two s. three d.; ed War Coll., Egypt, US Army War Coll.; fought in Palestine War 1948, Suez War 1956, Wars of June 1967 and Oct. 1973; rank of Maj. 1958, Col 1966, Maj.-Gen. 1974, Lt-Gen. 1980, Marshal 1981; Commdr of an artillery brigade 1968, an artillery div. 1969–71; Commdr 2nd Field Army Artillery 1971 and 1973; Chief of Staff, Artillery Corps 1972 and 1973; Dir Mil. Intelligence and Reconnaissance Dept 1974–76; Defence Attaché, Embassy, USA 1976–80; Chief of Staff, Armed Forces 1980–81, C-in-C 1981–; also Minister of Defence and Mil. Production 1980–89; Deputy Prime Minister 1982–89; Asst to Pres. of Egypt 1989–; numerous awards and medals including Medal of Honour. *Publications include:* Soviet Military Strategy, History of Art of War (five vols), The Guns Opened Fire at Noon (October War), Mathematics and Warfare, After the Storm, Lessons of Modern War (two parts) and 17 books on mil. affairs. *Leisure interests:* reading, chess, tennis, basketball, soccer. *Address:* Hamouda Mahmoud Street, Elhay Eltamen, Nasr City, Cairo (Home); c/o Presidential Palace, Abdeen, Cairo, Egypt. *Telephone:* (2) 2721200 (Office); (2) 2878538 (Home). *Fax:* (2) 2748093 (Office); (2) 6708670 (Home).

ABD AL-MEGUID, Ahmed Esmat, PhD; Egyptian diplomatist; b. 22 March 1923, Alexandria; s. of Mohamed Fahmy Abd al-Meguid; m. Eglal Abou-Hamda 1950; three s.; ed Faculty of Law, Alexandria Univ. and Univ. of Paris; Attaché and Sec., Embassy, London 1950–54; Head British Desk, Ministry of Foreign Affairs 1954–56, Asst Dir Legal Dept 1961–63, Head Cultural and Tech. Assistance Dept 1967–68; Counsellor, Perm. Mission to European Office of UN, Geneva 1957–61; Minister Counsellor, Embassy, Paris 1963–67; Official Spokesman of Govt and Head Information Dept 1968–69; Amb. to France 1969–70; Minister of State for Cabinet Affairs 1970–72; Head, Perm. Del. to UN 1972–82; Minister of Foreign Affairs 1984–91; Deputy Prime Minister 1985–91; Sec.-Gen. League of Arab States 1991–2001; pvt. law practice 2001–; Chair. Cairo Preparatory Conf. for Geneva Peace Conf. 1977; Dir Cairo Int. Arbitration Centre; mem. Politbureau, Nat. Democratic Party, Int. Law Asscn, Advisory Council of the Inst. for Int. Studies, took part in UN confs on the Law of the Sea 1959, on Consular Relations 1963 and on the Law of Treaties 1969; Ordre Nat. du Mérite 1967, Grand Croix 1971, 1st Class Decoration, Arab Repub. of Egypt 1970 and numerous foreign decorations. *Publications:* several articles in Revue égyptienne de droit international. *Address:* 78 El Nile Street, Apt. 23, Giza, Cairo, Egypt (Home).

ABDEL-MALEK, Anouar I., DLit, PhD; Egyptian academic and writer; b. 23 Oct. 1924, Cairo; s. of Iskandar Abdel-Malek and Alice Zaki Ibrahim; m. Karin Konigseider 1961 (divorced 1965); one d.; ed Coll. de la Sainte Famille, British Inst., Ain Shams Univ., Cairo and Univ. de Paris-Sorbonne; leading mem. Egyptian Nat. and Progressive Movt 1941–; official, Nat. Bank of Egypt, Cairo 1941–42, Crédit Foncier Egyptien, Cairo 1943–46; Jt Ed. Actualité, Cairo 1950–59; journalist, Le Journal d'Egypte, Cairo 1950–59; contrib. to Rose el-Yusef, Al-Magallah, Al Masa, Cairo 1950–59; teacher of philosophy, Lycée Al-Hurriya, Cairo 1958–59; Research Asst, Ecole Pratique des Hautes Etudes, Paris 1959–60; Research Lecturer, later Research Reader, Research Prof., CNRS, Paris 1960–, Dir of Research 1970–90, Hon. Dir 1991–; Project Co-ordinator, The UN Univ., Tokyo 1976–86; Prof. of Sociology and Politics, Faculty of Int. Relations, Ristumeikan Univ., Kyoto 1989–92; Adviser Nat. Centre for Middle East Studies, Cairo 1990–; mem. Bd and Adviser, Centre for Asian Studies, Cairo Univ. 1994–; mem. Exec. Cttee, EEC Int. Sociological Asscn 1970–74, Vice-Pres. 1974–78; Visiting Prof., Univ. of Santiago, Chile 1969, Ain Shams 1975, Québec 1986, Cairo 1992; Visiting Fellow, Clare Coll., Cambridge 1985, Life Assoc. 1986–; Ed. Library of the Contemporary Orient 1989, Ideas of the New World 1991; Prix du Jury de l'Amitié Franco-Arabe, Paris 1970, Gold Medal, Nasser Higher Mil. Acad. 1976. *Publications include:* Egypte, société militaire 1962, Idéologie et renaissance nationale: l'Egypte moderne 1969, La pensée politique arabe contemporaine 1970, Sociologie de l'impérialisme 1970, La dialectique sociale 1972, Intellectual Creativity in Endogenous Culture 1983, The Transformation of the World 1985, The Egyptian Street and Thought 1989, Creativity and the Civilization Project 1991. *Leisure interests:* music, opera, ballet, theatre, cooking, swimming, walking, table-tennis, travelling, meditation. *Address:* 48 Nehru Street, 11351 Heliopolis, Cairo, Egypt (Home).

ABDELLAH, Faye Glenn, BS, MA, EdD; American nurse and psychologist; ed Teachers' Coll., Columbia Univ.; first woman to be apptd. Deputy Surgeon General, US Public Health Service 1981–89; Dean (a.i.) Univ. of Health Sciences 1993–96; Dean, Prof. Grad. School of Nursing, Uniformed Services

Univ. of Health Sciences 1993–; numerous academic and professional awards including 12 hon. degrees; Nat. Women's Hall of Fame. *Publications include:* Better Patient Care through Nursing Research (with E. Levine) 1986; more than 135 publs (books, monographs and articles). *Leisure interests:* piano and swimming. *Address:* 3713 Chanel Road, Annandale, VA 22003, USA. *Telephone:* (301) 443-4000.

ABDÉRÉMANE HALIDI, Ibrahim; Comoran politician; b. Anjouan Island; fmr teacher of philosophy; mem. Chuma Party; Minister of Interior 1990; leader Union des démocrates pour le développement (UDD); Prime Minister of the Comoros Jan.–May 1993; Minister of Transport, Tourism, Posts and Telecommunications 1996–97; Presidential Cand. Anjouan Island 2002. *Address:* c/o Ministry of Transport, Tourism, Posts and Telecommunications, Moroni, The Comoros.

ABDESSALAM, Belaid, BA; Algerian politician; b. July 1928, Dehemcha; m.; four s. two d.; ed Grenoble Univ.; fmr Hon. Pres. Union Générale des Etudiants Musulmans Algériens (UGEMA); Instructor Front de Libération Nationale (FLN) School, Oujda; Political Adviser in Cabinet of M. Ben Khedda 1961; in charge of Econ. Affairs, FLN Provisional Exec. 1962; Pres., Dir-Gen. Soc. Nat. pour la Recherche, la Production, le Transport, la Transformation et la Commercialisation des Hydrocarbures (SONATRACH) 1964–66; Minister of Industry and Energy 1966–77 (retaining SONATRACH post 1965–66), of Light Industry 1977–84; Prime Minister of Algeria and Minister of Economy 1992–93; Pres. of Special Econ. Comm. of Cen. Cttee of FLN 1979–81; Chair. Council OAPEC 1974. *Address:* c/o Office of the Prime Minister, Palais du Gouvernement, Algiers, Algeria.

ABDIC, Fikret 'Babo' (Papa); Bosnia and Herzegovina/Croatian politician and business executive; b. 1939; Dir Agrokomerc co. 1980s; charged with fraud in fmr Yugoslavia 1987, convicted, sentenced to two years' imprisonment, acquitted on appeal 1989; Co-Founder (with Alijah Izetbegovic, Party of Democratic Action (PDA); set up autonomous region of W Bosnia in defiance of cen. Govt in Sarajevo 1993, his forces were crushed by Pres. Izetbegovic 1995; fled to Croatia in 1995, f. pvt. food co.; f. political party Democratic People's Union (DNZ) 1996; accused of war crimes by Bosnia 2001; extradition to Bosnia repeatedly refused by Croatian Govt on account of his Croatian citizenship; sentenced by Croatian court to 20 years' imprisonment for war crimes committed during Bosnian war 1993–95 July 2002; permitted by Bosnian Election Comm. to run for Muslim post in three-man inter-ethnic presidency while still in prison Oct. 2002.

ABDIU, Fehmi, DrIur; Albanian judge; b. 5 Jan. 1944, Diber; m.; two c.; ed Faculty of Law, Tirana Univ., Teachers' Training School, Peshkopi; Judge Fieri Dist Court 1968–73, Deputy Chief 1974–77, Chief 1977–85, 1989–90; mem. Supreme Court 1985–89, Deputy Chief 1990–92; mem. Parl. 1991–98; Pres. Constitutional Court 1998–. *Publications include:* The Politic According to the Constitution and Laws, Constitution and the Constitutional Court of the Republic of Albania, The Constitution, the Law and the Justice. *Address:* President of the Constitutional Court, c/o Ministry of Justice, Ministria e Drejtësisë, Bulevard Dëshmorët e Kombit, Tirana, Albania (Office). *Telephone:* (5) 426-9174 (Office). *Fax:* (5) 422-8357 (Office). *Website:* www.gjk.gov.al (Office). *Address:* Bulevard "Zhan B'Ark" Pallati 4, Ap. 1, Kati 9, Tirana, Albania (Home). *Telephone:* (5) 422-8125 (Home).

ABDOU, Ahmed; Comoran politician; fmr special adviser to Pres. Ahmed Abdallah Abderrahman; Prime Minister of the Comoros 1996–97. *Address:* c/o Office of the Prime Minister, Moroni, The Comoros (Office).

ABDOU MADI, Mohamed; Comoran politician and tax inspector; m.; four c.; ed Algeria, Poland; tax insp. Moroni 1988; convicted of fraud, served sentence as a domestic servant; Perm. Sec. CTRAP (org. funded by UNDP to implement reforms in civil service) –1994; Sec.-Gen. Rassemblement pour la Démocratie et le Renouveau (RDR); Prime Minister of the Comoros 1994, also responsible for Public Works; Minister of Justice, Public Affairs, Employment, Professional Training, Admin. Decentralization and Institutional Reform 1998. *Address:* c/o Ministry of Justice and Islamic Affairs, Moroni, The Comoros (Office).

ABDOULAYE, Souley; Niger politician and business executive; fmr banker; Minister of Commerce, Transport and Tourism 1993–94; Prime Minister of Niger 1994–95; Minister of Transport 1996; mem. Convention démocratique et social-Rahana (CDS-Rahana). *Address:* c/o Ministry of Transport, Niamey, Niger.

ABDRASHITOV, Vadim Yusupovich; Russian film director; b. 19 Jan. 1945, Kharkov, Ukraine; s. of Yusup Sh. Abdrashitov and Galina Abdrashitov; m. Natella G. Toidze; one s. one d.; graduated VGIK, Moscow, pupil of Romm; RSFSR State Prize 1984, People's Artist of Russia. *Films include:* Witness for the Defence (USSR Riga Prize) 1977, The Turning 1978, Foxhunting 1980, The Train has Stopped 1982, The Parade of the Planets 1984, Plumbum, or a Dangerous Game 1986 (Gold Medal at Venice Festival 1987), The Servant (Alfred Bauer Prize 1989) 1988, Armavir 1991, The Play for a Passenger 1995 (Silver Bear Award, Berlin Festival 1995), Time for a Dancer 1997. *Address:* 3d. Frunzenskaya 9, Apt. 211, 119270 Moscow, Russia. *Telephone:* (095) 242-35-54.

ABDUL, Paula; American pop singer and choreographer; b. 19 June 1962, San Fernando, Calif.; d. of Harry Abdul and Lorraine Abdul; m. 1st Emilio Estevez 1992 (divorced 1994); m. 2nd Brad Beckerman 1996; ed Van Nuys

High School, California State Univ.; has choreographed work for several bands including Duran Duran, Toto, The Pointer Sisters and ZZ Top. *Choreographed works include:* Janet Jackson's videos Torture, Control, When I Think of You, Nasty, City of Crime video (from film Dragnet), Dolly Parton Christmas Special (TV), Tracey Ullman Show (TV). *Films include:* Coming to America, Bull Durham, The Doors, Mr Rock and Roll: The Alan Freed Story, The Waiting Game, Touched By Evil, Junior High School. *Television includes:* judge in American Idol competition 2002–03. *Albums include:* Straight Up, Forever Your Girl 1988, Spellbound 1991, Head Over Heels 1995, Greatest Hits 2000. *Address:* c/o Third Rail Entertainment, Tri-Star Bldg, 10202 W Washington Avenue, Suite 26, Culver City, CA 90232, USA (Office).

ABDUL-GHANI, Abdulaziz, MA; Yemeni politician and economist; b. 4 July 1939, Haifan, Taiz; s. of Abdulghani Saleh and Tohfa Moqbel; m. Aseya Hamza 1966; four s. one d.; ed Teacher's High School, Aden Coll., Colorado Coll. and Colorado Univ.; teacher, Balquis Coll., Aden 1964–67; Minister of Health, San'a 1967–68, of Economy 1968–69; Prime Minister 1975–80, 1983–90, 1994–97; mem. Presidential Council 1990–94; mem. Gen. People's Congress (GPC); mem. Command Council 1975–78; Vice-Pres. 1980–83; Dir Yemen Bank for Reconstruction and Devt 1968; Gov. Cen. Bank of Yemen 1971–75; lecturer, Univ. of San'a 1972–74; Chair. Tech. Office Bd of Planning 1969–71, Yemen Oil Co. 1971, Supreme Council for Reconstruction of Earthquake Affected Areas 1983; mem. Perm. Cttee 1983, of Presidential Advisory Council, Yemeni Econ. Soc.; Hon. PhD; Mareb Sash (First Class) 1987. *Leisure interests:* swimming, hiking. *Address:* c/o Office of the Prime Minister, San'a, Yemen.

ABDUL-JABBAR, Kareem; American basketball player; b. Ferdinand Lewis Alcindor, Jr, 16 April 1947, New York; s. of Lewis Alcindor and Cora Alcindor; ed Power Memorial High School, UCLA; graduated as the leading scorer in UCLA history (2,325 points); played for NBA (Nat. Basketball Asscn) Milwaukee Bucks 1969–75, for NBA Los Angeles Lakers 1975–89; All NBA First Team 1971–74, 1976–77, 1980–81, 1984, 1986; NBA All-Defensive First Team 1974–75, 1979–81; retd from game 1989; Asst Coach Alchesay High School (Whiteriver, AZ) 1999–2000; Asst Coach NBA LA Clippers 2000; Coach NBA Indiana Pacers 2002; Head Coach USBLs Oklahoma Storm 2002–; NBA career records include: most minutes (57,446), most points (33,387), most field goals made (15,837), most field goals attempted (28,307), most blocks (3,189); first player in NBA history to play 20 seasons; 1,560 games played; 18 NBA All-Star games played; All-City 1963–65; All-American 1963–65; Consensus All-American 1963–65; First Team All-America 1967, 1968, 1969; Nat. Player of the Year 1967, 1969; Nat. Collegiate Athletic Asscn (NCAA) Tournament Most Outstanding Player 1967, 1968, 1969; Naismith Award Winner 1969; NBA Rookie of the Year 1970; NBA Most Valuable Player—MVP 1971, 1972, 1974, 1976, 1977, 1980; NBA Finals MVP 1971, 1975; Sports Illustrated Sportsman of the Year 1985; elected to Basketball's Hall of Fame 1995. *Address:* c/o The Oklahoma Storm, P.O. Box 1873, Enid, OK 65535, USA (Office).

ABDUL LATIF, Pehin Dato' Jaya; Brunei diplomatist; b. 1939; m.; six c.; ed Manchester Univ.; Govt Deputy Agent, London 1981–82; Commr to Malaysia 1982–84, High Commr 1984–86; Amb. to the Philippines 1986–87; Perm Rep. of Brunei Darussalam to the UN 1987–93; Amb. to the USA 1993–97; apptd High Commr in the UK 1997; Pres. Brunei State Youth Council 1977–80; fmr mem. World Assembly of Youth, World Assembly of Muslim Youth and Asian Youth Council. *Address:* c/o Ministry of Foreign Affairs (Kementerian Hal Ehwal Luar Negeri), Bandar Seri Begawan, BD 2710, Brunei (Office).

ABDUL LATIF BIN HAJI IBRAHIM, Haji, PhD; Brunei university lecturer and government official; b. 8 Jan. 1944, Brunei; m. Hajah Habibah binti Abdullah 1972; four s. one d.; ed SMJA Malay School, Brunei, SOAS English School, Brunei, East West Centre, Univ. of Hawaii, British Museum Dept of Ethnography, London and Univs of N Queensland and Cambridge; Research Asst Brunei Museum 1965–70, Research Officer 1971–79, Curator of Ethnography 1980–83; Head of Research Unit, History Centre, Brunei 1983–86, Deputy Head 1986–88; Sr Lecturer, Univ. of Brunei Darussalam 1989–, Dir Acad. of Brunei Studies 1993–, later Dean, Asst Vice-Chancellor; Sec. Nat. Supreme Council, Malay Islam Monarchy, Brunei (ex officio); Pekerma Setia Brunei; Brunei Long Service Medal. *Publications:* A Short History of Brunei State Crest 1970, Bandar Seri Begawan (pictorial essay) 1976. *Address:* University of Brunei Darussalam, Tungku Link, Gadong BE 1410 (Office); 2, Simpang 254-23, Ban 3, Jan Mulaut, Sengkurong 2780, Brunei (Home). *Telephone:* (2) 249518 (Office); (2) 672068 (Home). *Fax:* (2) 249003 (Office). *E-mail:* latif@ubd.edu.bn (Office). *Website:* www.ubd.edu.bn.

ABDUL MAJID, Mimi Kamariah, PhD; Malaysian professor of law; b. 5 Dec. 1952, Kuantan; m. Abdul Hadi Zakaria 1977; three d.; ed Bukit Bintang Girls' Secondary School, Kuala Lumpur, Univ. of Malaya, Monash Univ., Australia; tutor, Faculty of Law, Univ. of Malaya 1976–79, lecturer 1979–87, Assoc. Prof. 1987–92, Prof. 1992–, Dean, Faculty of Law 1994–2000, 2002–; Head of Legal and Man. Services Unit 1996. *Publications:* Malaysian Law on Bail (co-author) 1986, Pentadbiran Keadilan Jenayah Di Malaysia (admin. of criminal justice) 1991, Undang-Undang Keluarga Di Malaysia (family law) 1992, Criminal Procedure in Malaysia 1995, Dangerous Drugs Laws 1995, Family Law in Malaysia 1999. *Address:* Faculty of Law, University of Malaya,

50603 Kuala Lumpur, Malaysia. *Telephone:* (603) 79696500 (Office). *Fax:* (603) 79573239 (Office). *E-mail:* law@um.edu.my (Office). *Website:* www.um.edu.my (Office).

ABDUL-RAHMAN, Omar, MVD, MRCVS; Malaysian professor of veterinary pathology; b. 9 Nov. 1932, Kota Bharu, Kelantan; m.; three c.; ed Sydney, Queensland and Cambridge Univs; Demonstrator in Veterinary Pathology, Queensland Univ. 1959; Veterinary Research Officer, Veterinary Research Inst., Ipoh 1960–67, Sr Research Officer 1967–70, Deputy Dir 1971–72; Foundation Prof. and Dean, Faculty of Veterinary Medicine and Animal Sciences, Univ. Pertanian Malaysia 1972–78, Prof. of Veterinary Pathology and Deputy Vice-Chancellor 1982–84; apptd Pres. Malaysian Scientific Asscn 1984, currently Adviser; fmr Pres. Asscn of Veterinary Surgeons Malaysia–Singapore; mem. Nat. Council for Scientific Research and Devt, Malaysia, Nat. Comm. for UNESCO, Nat. Devt Planning Cttee of Malaysia 1984–; Advisor to Prime Minister on Science and Tech. 1985–; Founding Fellow and Pres. Malaysian Acad. of Sciences; Fellow Islamic Acad. of Sciences; mem. ed. advisory bd Tropical Veterinarian (journal) 1983–; Dr hc (Stirling) 1986. *Publications:* over 100 publs on science and tech. *Address:* Islamic Academy of Sciences, PO Box 830036, Amman, Jordan (Office). *Telephone:* 5522104 (Office). *Fax:* 5511803 (Office). *E-mail:* secretariat@ias-worldwide.org. *Website:* www.ias-worldwide.org.

ABDULAI, Yesufu Seyyid Momoh; Nigerian economist and international organization official; b. 19 June 1940, Auchi; s. of Momoh Abdulai and Haijia Fatimah Abdulai; m. Zene Makonnen Abdulai 1982; three s. one d.; ed Mount Allison Univ. and McGill Univ.; taught econs in Canada; Tech. Asst to Exec. Dir (Africa Group I), World Bank Group, Washington 1971–73, Adviser to Exec. Dir 1973–78, Alternate Exec. Dir for Africa Group 1 1978–80, Exec. Dir 1980–82, Vice-Chair. Jt Audit Cttee Exec. Bd 1980–82; Chair. Jt Secr. African Exec. Dirs of the World Bank Group and the IMF 1975–77; Man. Dir and CEO Fed. Mortgage Bank of Nigeria 1982–83; Dir-Gen. OPEC Fund for Int. Devt 1983–. *Leisure interests:* sport, reading, photography, listening to music. *Address:* OPEC Fund for International Development, Parkring 8, PO Box 995, 1011 Vienna, Austria. *Telephone:* 515-64-0. *Fax:* 513-92-38. *E-mail:* info@opecfund.org. *Website:* www.opecfund.org.

ABDULATIPOV, Ramazan Gadzhimuradovich, D.PHIL.SC.; Russian/Dagestan politician; b. 4 Aug. 1946, Guerguta, Dagestan; m.; two s. one d.; ed Dagestan State Univ.; mem. CPSU 1973–91; CP work 1974–76; Sr teacher Dagestan Pedagogical Inst. 1975–76; Head of Murmansk Higher School of Marine Eng 1978–87; Head of Sector Div. of Int. Relations of CPSU Cen. Cttee 1988–90; RSFSR People's Deputy 1990–93, Chair. Council of Nationalities 1990–93; elected to Council of Fed. 1993, Deputy Chair. 1994–96; mem. State Duma 1995–97; Deputy Prime Minister 1997–98, Minister of Nat. Policy 1998–99; Rep. of Saratov Region in Council of Fed. 2000–; Pres. Ass. of Nations of Russia 1998–; participant of numerous peace-making missions on N Caucasus; Pres. Fed. of UNESCO Clubs in Russia; mem. Russian Acad. of Natural Sciences. *Publications:* Lenin's Policy of Internationalism in USSR, Internationalism and the Spiritual and Moral Development of the Peoples of Dagestan, What is the Essence of Your Being?, Power and Conscience, Nature and Paradoxes of National Consciousness Authority of Sense, Ethnic Question and State Structure of Russia: From Cran Tower to the Kremlin Gates, Inscriptions. *Leisure interests:* painting, aphoristic poetry. *Address:* Council of Federation, Bolshaya Dmitrovka 26, 103426, Moscow, Russia. *Telephone:* (095) 292-12-29 (Office).

ABDULLA OSMAN DAAR, Aden; Somali politician and businessman; b. 1908, Beledwin; ed Govt School, Somalia; served in Italian Admin. 1929–41; joined Somali Youth League 1944, Leader 1953, Pres. 1954–56, 1958–59; Pres. Nat. Ass. 1956–60, Constituent Ass. 1960; Acting Pres. of the Somali Repub. 1960, Pres. 1961–67; Deputy to Nat. Ass. 1967–69; detained following coup 1969, released 1973. *Address:* c/o Government Offices, Mogadishu, Somalia.

ABDULLAH, Abdullah, DMed; Afghanistan politician; b. Panjshir Valley; qualified doctor; Mujahideen activist Jamiat-i-Islami group, Sr Spokesman 1996; Deputy Minister of Foreign Affairs, Northern Alliance 1999, Minister 1999–2001; participated in Future of Afghanistan Govt Talks, Bonn Nov. 2001; Minister of Foreign Affairs Afghan Interim Authority Dec. 2001–June 2002, Afghan Transitional Authority June 2002–. *Address:* Ministry of Foreign Affairs, Shah Mahmud Ghazi Street, Shar-i-Nau, Kabul, Afghanistan (Office). *Telephone:* (93) 25441.

ABDULLAH, Datuk Ahmad Shah; Malaysian state official and civil servant; b. 9 Dec. 1946, Kampung Inanam; m. Datin Dayang Masuyah Awang Japar; three s. one d.; ed La Salle Secondary School, South Devon Coll., UK, Indiana State Univ., USA; Customs Officer, Royal Customs Dept 1968–69; Asst Dist Officer, Beaufort 1969–78, seconded to Nat. Rice and Padi Bd 1979–83; Sec. State Public Services Comm. 1983–87; Dir Missionary of the Sabah Islamic Council 1988–94; Sec. Home Affairs and Research 1994–95; Dept Dir Sabah Public Services 1995–98, Deputy State Sec. 1998–2002; Yang di-Pertua Negeri (Head) of State of Sabah Jan. 2003–; Deputy Pres. Bajau Arts and Cultural Ass. *Address:* Dewan Ungangan Negeri Sabah, Aras 4, Bangunan Dewan Undangan Negeri Sabah, Peti Surat 11247, Kota Kinabalu 88813, Malaysia (Office). *Telephone:* (88) 427533 (Office). *Fax:* (88) 427333 (Office). *E-mail:* webmaster@sabah.gov.my (Office). *Website:* www.sabah.gov.my (Office).

ABDULLAH, Farooq, MB; Indian politician; b. 21 Oct. 1937, Srinagar, Kashmir; s. of Sheikh Mohammad Abdullah and Begum Abdullah; m. Mollie Abdullah 1968; one s. three d.; Chief Minister, Jammu and Kashmir 1982–84, 1986–90, 1996–2002; Pres. State Cen. Labour Union, Jammu and Kashmir Nat. Conf.; Chair. Jammu & Kashmir Muslim Auquaf Trust, Sher-i-Kashmir Nat. Medical Inst. Trust, Sher-i-Kashmir Inst. of Medical Sciences; mem. of Parl. 1980–82, India Int. Centre; Gen. Sec. Indo-Arab Friendship Soc., Nat. Integration Council; Nat. Solidarity Award 1998, Eminent Personality of the Year, Indian Medical Asscn 1999. *Leisure interests:* golf, photography, gardening, music. *Address:* 5 Pritvi Raj Road, New Delhi 11001, India. *E-mail:* farooq.abdullah@hotmail.com (Home).

ABDULLAH, Omar Farooq, BCom; Indian politician; b. 10 March 1970; s. of Farooq Abdullah; ed Sydenham Coll., Mumbai; Pres. Youth Nat. Conf.; elected to 12th Lok Sabha, mem. Parl. for Srinagar Constituency (Nat. Conf. Party) 1998, re-elected to 13th Lok Sabha 1999; mem. Cttee of Transport and Tourism, Consultative Cttee, Ministry of Tourism 1998–99; Minister of State for Commerce and Industry 1999–2001, for External Affairs 2001–02; Pres. Jammu and Kashmir Nat. Conf. (JKNC) 2002–. *Address:* Jammu and Kashmir National Conference (JKNC), Mujahid Manzil, Srinagar 190 002, India (Office).

ABDULLAH, Yousuf bin al-Alawi bin; Omani government minister and diplomatist; b. 1942, Salalah; s. of Abdullah bin Alawi; joined Diplomatic Service 1970, Second Sec. Ministry of Foreign Affairs 1972, postings to Cairo and Beirut; Amb. to Lebanon 1973; Under-Sec. Ministry of Foreign Affairs 1974, Minister of State 1982, Minister responsible for Foreign Affairs 1997–; First Grade Sultan Qaboos Decoration, Order of Merit, Egypt, Officier, Légion d'honneur, France, Grand Decoration of Honour, Austria, Cavaliere Grande Croce, Italy and other foreign decorations. *Address:* Ministry of Foreign Affairs, P.O. Box 252, Muscat 113, Oman (Office). *Telephone:* 699500 (Office). *Fax:* 699589 (Office).

ABDULLAH IBN ABD AL-AZIZ AS-SA'UD, HRH Crown Prince; Saudi Arabian prince, army officer and politician; b. Aug. 1921; s. of the late King Abdul Aziz ibn Sa'ud; brother of HM King Fahd; Commdr Nat. Guard 1962–; Second Deputy Prime Minister 1975–82, First Deputy Prime Minister and Commdr of the Nat. Guard 1982–; became Crown Prince June 1982. *Leisure interests:* hunting, horse racing. *Address:* Council of Ministers, Murabba, Riyadh 11121, Saudi Arabia. *Telephone:* (1) 488-2444.

ABDULLAH IBN AL-HUSSEIN, HM King; King of Jordan, head of state and army officer; b. 30 Jan. 1962, Amman; s. of the late King Hussein Ibn Talal and of Princess Muna al-Hussein; m. Rania Yassin 1993 (now Queen Rania); one s. one d.; ed Islamic Educ. Coll., St Edmund's School, Surrey, Deerfield Acad., USA, Sandhurst Mil. Acad., Oxford Univ.; succeeded to the throne 7 Feb. 1999; commissioned Second Lt 1981, Reconnaissance Troop Leader 13th/18th Bn Royal Hussars (British Army), FRG and England; rank of First Lt 1984; Platoon Commdr and Co. second-in-command 40th Armoured Brigade, Jordan, Commdr Tank Co. 91st Armoured Brigade 1985–86 (rank of Capt.); Tactics Instructor Helicopter Anti-Tank Wing, 1986–87; undertook advanced studies in int. affairs School of Foreign Service, Georgetown Univ., Washington 1987–88; Commdr of a co. 17th Tank Bn, 2nd Guards Brigade then Bn second-in-command (rank of Major) 1989; attended Command and Staff Coll., Camberley, England 1990; Armour Rep. Office of the Insp. Gen. 1991, Commdr 2nd Armoured Car Regt, 40th Brigade (rank of Lt Col) 1992; promoted to rank of Col 1993; Deputy Commdr Jordanian Special Forces Jan.–June 1994; promoted to the rank of Brig. 1994 and assumed command of Royal Jordanian Special Forces; Commdr of Special Operations Command 1997–; Pres. Jordan Nat. Football Fed.; Hon. Pres. Int. Tourism Golden Rudder Soc.; Head Nat. Cttee for Tourism and Archaeological Film Production 1997–. *Leisure interests:* car racing, (fmr Jordanian Nat. Rally Racing Champion), water sports, scuba diving, collecting ancient weapons and armaments. *Address:* Royal Hashemite Court, Amman, Jordan.

ABDULOV, Aleksandr Gavrilovich; Russian actor; b. 29 May 1953, Fergana, USSR (now Uzbekistan); one d.; ed Lunacharsky State Inst. of Theatre; with Theatre of Leninsky Komsomol (now Lenkom) 1975–; debut as Lt Pluzhnikov in Missing from the Lists; numerous TV roles; Sec. Russian Union of Cinematographers 1992; People's Artist of Russia 1991. *Plays include:* The Star and Death of Joaquin Murietta, Merciless Games, Yunona and Avos', Optimistic Tragedy, Enough Simplicity for Every Wise Man, Hamlet, Mourning Pray and others. *Films include:* Golden River 1977, Never Part with the Beloved 1980, A Woman in White 1982, Carnival 1982, Recipe of Her Youthfulness 1984, To Kill the Dragon 1988, The Barbarian and the Heretic 1997, Still Waters 2000, The Yellow Dwarf 2002. *Address:* Peschanaya str. 4, Apt. 3, 125252 Moscow, Russia (Home).

ABDURIXIT, Abdulahat; Chinese politician; b. March 1942, Yining, Xinjiang; ed Xinjiang Eng Coll.; joined CCP 1960; engineer then Vice-Pres. Xinjiang Uygur Autonomous Region Construction Survey and Design Acad., Vice-Dir Xinjiang Uygur Autonomous Region Planning Comm.; Vice-Chair. Xinjiang Uygur Autonomous Region 1965–93; Chair. Xinjiang Uygur Autonomous Region 1993–2003; apptd Vice-Sec. CCP Xinjiang Uygur Autonomous Region Cttee 1993; mem. CCP 15th Cen. Cttee 1997–2002; Chair. Regional People's Congress, Xinjiang 2003–. *Address:* c/o People's Government of Xinjiang Uygur Autonomous Region, Urumqi, Xinjiang, People's Republic of China.

ABDYKARIMOV, Oralbai; Kazakhstan politician; b. 18 Dec.1944, Kievka, Karaganda region; m. Abdykarimova Jamal; three s. one d.; ed Alma-Ata Higher CPSU School, Karaganda State Univ.; leading posts in Komsomol and CP organs of Kazakhstan; Deputy Head, then Head of Admin. Office of Pres. of Kazakhstan; Chair. Mazhilis (Parl.); Chair. Higher Disciplinary Council, State Comm. for Fight with Corruption; mem. Senate (Parl.) 1999–, Chair. of Senate 1999–, mem. Security Council of Kazakhstan; Order Barys. *Address:* Houses of Parliament, Senate, Astana, Kazakhstan (Office). *Telephone:* (3172) 33-38-75 (Office).

ABEL, Edward William, CBE, PhD; British professor of chemistry; b. 3 Dec. 1931, Mid-Glamorgan; s. of Sydney J. Abel and the late Donna Maria Grabham; m. Margaret R. Edwards 1960; one s. one d.; ed Bridgend Grammar School, Glamorgan, Univ. Coll. Cardiff and Northern Polytechnic, London; Research Fellow, Imperial Coll. London 1957–59; lecturer and Reader, Univ. of Bristol 1959–71; Prof. of Inorganic Chem. Univ. of Exeter 1972–97, Deputy Vice-Chancellor 1991–94; Visiting Prof. Univ. of BC 1970, Univ. of Japan 1971, Tech. Univ. of Brunswick 1973, ANU, Canberra 1990; mem. Council, Royal Soc. of Chem. (RSC) 1978–82, 1983–2002, Chair. Scientific Affairs Bd, Univ. Grants Cttee 1986–89; Pres. RSC 1996–98, Ed.-in-Chief Tutorial Chemistry Texts (10 vols) 1999–; Hon. Fellow, Cardiff Univ. 1999; Hon. DUniv (Univ. of N London); Hon. DSc (Exeter) 2000; Tilden Medal, RSC 1981. *Publications:* Organometallic Chemistry Vols 1–25 (ed.) 1970–1995, Comprehensive Organometallic Chemistry I (ed.) nine vols 1984, II 14 vols (1995). *Leisure interest:* gardening. *Address:* Department of Chemistry, University of Exeter, Exeter, Devon, EX4 4QD (Office); 1A Rosebarn Avenue, Exeter, Devon, EX4 6DY, England (Home). *Telephone:* (1392) 263489 (Office); (1392) 270272 (Home). *Fax:* (1392) 263434. *E-mail:* ewabel@ex.ac.uk (Office); mea .rosebarn@virgin.net (Home).

ABELEV, Garry Israyelevich; Russian immunologist; b. 10 Jan. 1928, Moscow; s. of Israel Abelev and Eugenia Abelev; m. 1st Elfrida Cicart 1949 (died 1996); two s.; m. 2nd Galina Deichman 1999; ed Moscow State Univ.; sr lab. technician, researcher, Head of Lab., Head of Dept N. F. Gamaleya Inst. of Epidemiology and Microbiology 1950–77; Head of Lab. Inst. of Carcinogenesis, Cancer Research Centre 1977–; Prof. Moscow State Univ.; Corresp. mem. USSR (now Russian) Acad. of Sciences 1987–, mem. 2000–; research on immunology of tumours, immunochemistry, cell biochemistry; mem. Bd NY Inst. of Cancer; Hon. mem. American Asscn of Immunologists, European Soc. of Cancer Researchers, New York Acad. of Sciences; Gold Medal Cancer Research Inst. (USA) 1975, USSR State Prize 1978, Abbot Prize 1990, Honourable Scientist of Russia 1999. *Publications:* Virusology and Immunology of Cancer 1962, Alpha-Feto-Protein: 25 Years of Study, Tumour Biology 1989; articles in scientific journals of Russia, western Europe and USA. *Leisure interests:* music, history of science. *Address:* N. N. Blokhin Cancer Research Center, Russian Academy of Medical Sciences, 115478 Moscow, Kashirskoye Shosse 24, Russia. *Telephone:* (095) 323-59-10. *Fax:* (095) 324-12-05. *E-mail:* abelev@mx.iki.rsi.ru (Office).

ABELSON, Philip Hauge, MS, PhD; American physicist and editor; b. 27 April 1913, Tacoma, Wash.; s. of Ole Andrew Abelson and Ellen Hauge Abelson; m. Neva Martin 1936; one d.; ed Washington State Coll. and Univ. of California at Berkeley; Asst Physicist, Dept of Terrestrial Magnetism, Carnegie Inst. of Washington 1939–41, staff mem. (of Dept) 1946–53, Dir Geophysical Lab. 1953–71; Pres. Carnegie Inst. of Washington 1971–78, Trustee 1978–; Principal Physicist and Civilian-in-Charge, Naval Research Lab. Branch, Navy Yard, Philadelphia 1941–46; Co-Ed., Journal of Geophysical Research 1959–65; Ed., Science 1962–85; Resident Fellow Resources for the Future Inc. 1985–88; mem. Nat. Insts. of Health Biophysics and Biophysical Chem. Study Section 1956–59, Gen. Advisory Cttee, to Atomic Energy Comm. 1960–63, Cttee on Science and Public Policy of Nat. Acad. of Sciences 1962–63 and numerous other bodies; Consultant to NASA 1960–63; mem. NAS, AAAS (scientific adviser 1985–, Exec. Dir (acting) 1989), American Philosophical Soc. and many other learned socs; Pres. American Geophysical Union 1972–74, Int. Union of Geological Sciences 1972–76; work includes identification of uranium fission products 1939–40, co-discovery of neptunium 1940, separation of uranium isotopes 1943, biosynthesis in micro-organisms 1953, amino acids in fossils 1955, fatty acids in rocks 1956; Hon. DSc (Yale) 1964, (Southern Methodist Univ.) 1969, (Tufts Univ.) 1976; DHL (Univ. of Puget Sound) 1968; US Navy Distinguished Civilian Service Medal 1945, Physical Sciences Award, Washington Acad. of Sciences 1950, Distinguished Alumnus Award, Washington State Univ. 1962, Hillebrand Award, Chemical Soc. of Washington 1962, Modern Medicine Award 1967, Joseph Priestley Award 1973, Kalinga Prize for Popularization of Science 1973, American Medical Asscn Scientific Achievement Award 1974, Nat. Medal of Science 1989. *Publications:* author: Energy for Tomorrow 1975, Enough of Pessimism 1985; co-author: Studies in Biochemistry in *Escherichia coli* 1955; Ed.: Research in Geochemistry Vols 1 and 2 1959, 1967, Energy: Use, Conservation and Supply 1974, Food: Politics, Economics, Nutrition and Research 1975, Materials: Renewable and Nonrenewable 1976, Electronics: The Continuing Revolution 1977. *Address:* c/o AAAS, 1200 New York Avenue, NW, Suite 100, Washington, DC 20005-3941, USA.

ABERBACH, David, BA, BSc, M.LITT., DPhil; British professor; b. 17 Oct. 1953, London; s. of Prof. Moshe Aberbach and Rose Aberbach (née Firsht); m. Mimi Skelker 1980; three d.; ed Talmudical Acad. of Baltimore, Univ. Coll., London, Oxford Univ., Tavistock Clinic; lecturer Oxford and Cambridge Univs, Leo Baeck Coll. and Cornell Univ. 1982–86; Visiting Asst Prof., McGill Univ. 1986–87, Assoc. Prof. Dept of Jewish Studies 1987–; Visiting Prof. Univ. Coll. London 1992–93, 1998, 2001–02; Academic Visitor Sociology Dept LSE 1992–93, 1994–98, 2001–02. *Publications:* At the Handles of the Lock: Themes in the Fiction of S. J. Agnon 1984, Bialik 1988, Surviving Trauma: Loss, Literature and Psychoanalysis 1989, Realism, Caricature and Bias: The Fiction of Mendele Mocher Sefarim 1993, Imperialism and Biblical Prophecy 750–500 BCE 1993, Charisma in Politics, Religion and the Media: Private Trauma, Public Ideals 1996, Revolutionary Hebrew, Empire and Crisis 1998, The Roman-Jewish Wars and Hebrew Cultural Nationalism (co-author) 2000. *Leisure interests:* cinema, painting, coastal path hiking. *Address:* 32 Ravenshurst Avenue, London, NW4 4EG, England; Department of Jewish Studies, McGill University, 3438 McTavish, Montreal, Québec, H3A 1X9, Canada. *Telephone:* (514) 398-5009 (Office).

ABIRACHED, Robert, DèsSc; French writer and professor; b. 25 Aug. 1930, Beirut, Lebanon; m. Marie-France de Bailliencourt 1974; one s. one d.; ed Lycée Louis-le-Grand and Ecole Normale Supérieure, Paris; Attaché CNRS 1960–64; Drama Critic Nouvel Observateur 1964–66; Literary and Drama Critic La Nouvelle Revue Française 1956–72; Lecturer, later Prof. Univ. of Caen 1969–81, Prof. and Dir Dept of Drama, Univ. of Paris X 1988–99, Prof. Emer. 1999–; Prof. Conservatoire nat. supérieure d'art dramatique 1993–97; Dir Theatre and Exhibitions, Ministry of Culture 1981–88; Pres. Int. Festival of Francophones, Limoges, Observatory of Cultural Politics, Grenoble; Officier, Légion d'honneur, Commdr du Mérite, Commdr des Arts et Lettres, Commdr des Palmes académiques; Prix Sainte-Beuve. *Publications:* Casanova ou la dissipation (essay) 1961, l'Emerveillée (novel) 1963, Tu connais la musique? (play) 1971, La crise du personnage dans le théâtre moderne (essay) 1978, Le théâtre et le Prince 1992, La décentralisation théâtrale (ed.), four vols 1992–95. *Address:* Université Paris X (Paris-Nanterre), Bureau 224, 200 avenue de la République, 92001 Nanterre; 4 rue Robert-Turquan, 75016 Paris, France (Home). *Telephone:* 1-40-97-73-04 (Office). *Fax:* 1-40-97-73-06 (Office). *E-mail:* robert.abirached@wanadoo.fr (Office). *Website:* www .u-paris10.fr.

ABIZAID, Lt-Gen. John; American army officer; m.; three c.; ed US Mil. Acad., West Point, Harvard Univ., Univ. of Jordan, Amman; began career with 82nd Air Airborne Div., Fort Bragg, N. Carolina; fmr infantry commdr; led Ranger rifle co. during invasion of Grenada 1983; led 1st infantry div., 504th Parachute Infantry Regt; 66th Commdt US Mil. Acad.; Asst to Chair. of Jt Chiefs of Staff 1993; fmr Dir of Strategic Plans and Policy, Jt Staff, later Dir of the Jt Staff; Deputy Commdr for Combined Forces Command, US Cen. Command 2003–; US Army War Coll. Sr Fellowship, Hoover Inst., Stanford Univ. *Address:* Office of the Deputy Commander, US Central Command, 7115 South Boundary Boulevard, MacDill AFB, FL 33621-5101, USA (Office). *Telephone:* (813) 827-5894 (Office). *Fax:* (813) 827-2211 (Office). *E-mail:* pao@ centcom.mil (Office). *Website:* www.centcom.mil (Office).

ABOIMOV, Ivan Pavlovich; Russian; b. 6 Nov. 1936, Zarechnoye, Orenburg Dist; m.; two c.; ed Liepaya Pedagogical Inst. Higher Diplomatic School; mem. CPSU –1991; Komsomol work 1959–69; Sec., Deputy Head of Dept of Cen. Cttee of Latvian CP 1963–69; Ministry of Foreign Affairs 1972–; counsellor in USSR Embassy, Hungary 1972–79; First Sec. of European Dept, Ministry of Foreign Affairs 1979–83, Asst to Minister 1983–84; Minister Counsellor, Embassy, Budapest 1984–86; Chief of Personnel Admin., Ministry of Foreign Affairs 1986–88, Deputy Minister of Foreign Affairs 1988–90; Amb. to Hungary 1990–96, to Finland 1996–99, to Ukraine 1999–2001. *Address:* c/o Ministry of Foreign Affairs, Smolenskaya–Sennaya 32/34, 121200 Moscow, Russia (Office).

ABOUL-EIOUN, Mahmoud Ibrahim, BA, MSc; Egyptian central banker and economist; b. 1952; ed Univs. of Assiout and Zagazig; Econ. Adviser to Ministers of Tourism and Civil Aviation and of Econ. and Foreign Trade 1987–92; Asst to Gov. Cen. Bank 1991–92, Deputy Gov. 1999–2001, Gov. 2001–; mem. Bd Suez Canal Bank 1988–92; Econ. Adviser to Kuwait Fund for Arab Econ. Devt 1992–99. *Address:* Central Bank of Egypt, 31 Sharia Qasr en-Nil, Cairo, Egypt (Office). *Telephone:* (2) 3931514 (Office). *Fax:* (2) 3926361 (Office). *E-mail:* research@cbe.org.eg. *Website:* www.cbe.org.eg.

ABOULELA, Leila, MSc; Sudanese writer; b. 1964, Cairo, Egypt; m.; three c.; ed The Sisters' School, Khartoum, Univ. of Khartoum, LSE, UK; lived in Aberdeen, Scotland 1990–2000 (currently living in Indonesia); fmr Lecturer in Statistics and part-time Research Asst in Scotland; began writing 1992; author of short stories, a novel and co-writer of a play broadcast on BBC Radio 4; Caine Prize for African Writing (for short story The Museum) 2000. *Publications:* work included in anthologies Scottish Short Stories 1996, Ahead of Its Time 1998, Coloured Lights 2001; The Translator (novel) 1999. *Address:* c/o Africa Centre, 38 King Street, London, WC2, England (Office).

ABOVA, Tamara Yevgenyevna, DJur; Russian professor of law; b. 18 Nov. 1927; m.; one s.; ed Moscow Inst. of Law; Sr Consultant USSR Ministry of Transport 1954–64; Sr Researcher 1964–, then Head of Sector 1987, then Head of Centre of Civil Research, Inst. of State and Law; Prof. Moscow Inst. of Int. Relations 1973–; Head of Centre for Civilist Studies, Inst. of State and Law, Russian Acad. of Sciences 1993–; arbiter Commercial Arbitrary Court and Marine Arbitrary Comm., Chamber of Trade and Commerce; mem. Scientific-Consultative Council, Higher Arbitrary Court, Expert Council Cttee on Industry, Construction, Transport and Energy, Women of Russia Movt. *Publications:* over 130 scientific works. *Address:* Centre for Civilist Studies IGPRAN, Znamenka str. 10, 119841 Moscow (Office); 16 Parkova, 43-

1-82, Moscow 105523, Russia (Home). *Telephone:* (095) 291-17-09 (Office); (095) 468-53-60 (Home). *Fax:* (095) 291-85-74 (Office); (095) 468-53-60 (Home). *E-mail:* islran@rinet.ru (Office).

ABRAGAM, Anatole, DPhil; French physicist; b. 15 Dec. 1914, Griva-Semgallen, Russia; s. of Simon Abragam and Anna Maimin; m. 1st Suzanne Lequesme 1944 (died 1992); m. 2nd Nina Gordon 1996; ed Lycée Janson, Sorbonne, Oxford Univ.; Research Assoc., Centre Nat. de la Recherche Scientifique 1946; joined French Atomic Energy Comm. 1947, Physicist, later Sr Physicist 1947–55, Head of Magnetic Resonance Lab. 1955–58, Head of Solid State Physics and Nuclear Physics Dept 1959–65, Dir of Physics 1965–70, Dir of Research 1971–80; Prof. of Nuclear Magnetism, Coll. de France 1960–85, now Emer.; Pres. French Physical Soc. 1967; mem. Acad. of Sciences 1973–; Hon. Fellow, American Acad. of Arts and Sciences, Merton and Jesus Colls., Oxford 1976; Foreign mem. Royal Soc. 1983, US NAS, Russian Acad. of Sciences 1999; Hon. Fellow, Magdalen Coll., Oxford 2002; Dr. hc (Kent) 1968, (Oxford) 1976 and others; Holweck Prize, London Physical Soc. 1958, Grand Prix Cognacq-Jay, Acad. of Sciences 1970 and others, Grand Croix, Ordre nat. du Mérite, Commdr, Légion d'honneur, des Palmes académiques, Lorentz Medal 1982, Mateucci Medal 1992, Lomonosov Medal 1995. *Publications:* Discovery of Anomalous Hyperfine Structure in Solids 1950, Dynamic Polarization in Solids 1957, The Principles of Nuclear Magnetism 1961, Nuclear Anti-ferromagnetism 1969, Electron Paramagnetic Resonance of Transition Elements (with B. Bleaney) 1970, Nuclear Pseudomagnetism 1971, Nuclear Ferromagnetism 1973, Nuclear Magnetism: Order and Disorder (with M. Goldman) 1982, Reflexions of a Physicist 1985, La physique avant toute chose 1987, Time Reversal 1989. *Leisure interest:* English and Russian literature. *Address:* Collège de France, 3 rue d'Ulm, 75005 Paris (Office); 33 rue Croulebarbe, 75013 Paris, France (Home). *Telephone:* 1-47-07-62-57 (Home).

ABRAHAM, E. Spencer, JD; American politician; b. 12 June 1952, Lansing, Mich.; s. of Eddie Abraham and Juliette Sear Abraham; m. Jane Abraham; three c.; ed Michigan State Univ. E Lansing and Harvard Law School; attorney, Lansing 1980–; Prof., Thomas M. Cooley Law School 1981–; Chair. Mich. Republican Party 1983–90; Chair. Mich. Del. Republican Nat. Convention 1984; Chair. Presidential Inaugural Cttee Michigan 1985; Deputy Chief of Staff to Vice-Pres. Dan Quayle 1991–93; Co-Chair. Nat. Republican Congressional Cttee 1991–93; of counsel Canfield, Paddock and Stone 1993–94; Senator from Michigan 1995–2001; Sec. of Energy 2001–; mem Electricity Advisory Bd (also Sec.) 2001; mem. Mich., American and DC Bar Asscns. *Address:* Department of Energy, Forrestal Building, 1000 Independence Avenue, SW, Washington, DC 20585-0001, USA. *Telephone:* (202) 586-5000. *Fax:* (202) 586-4403. *Website:* www.doe.gov (Office).

ABRAHAM, F. Murray; American actor; b. 24 Oct. 1939, Pittsburgh; m. Kate Hannan 1962; two c.; ed Texas Univ.; Prof. Brooklyn Coll. 1985–; Dir No Smoking Please, Time & Space Ltd Theatre, NY; numerous Broadway plays, musicals, TV appearances and films; Obie Award (for Uncle Vanya) 1984; Golden Globe Award 1985; Los Angeles Film Critics Award 1985; Acad. Award (for Amadeus) 1985. *Films include:* Amadeus 1985, The Name of the Rose 1987, Russicum 1987, Slipstream, Hard Rain, Personal Choice, Eye of the Widow 1989, An Innocent Man 1990, Mobsters 1991, Bonfire of the Vanities 1991, By The Sword 1992, Last Action Hero 1993, Surviving the Game 1994, Nostradamus 1994, Mighty Aphrodite 1995, Children of the Revolution 1996, Mimic 1997, Star Trek IX 1998, Falcone 1999, Esther 1999, Muppets from Space 1999, Excellent Cadavers 1999, The Darkling 2000, Finding Forrester 2000, I cavalieri che fecero l'impresa 2001, 13 Ghosts 2001, Joshua 2002; narrator Herman Melville, Damned in Paradise 1985, OBS 1985. *Stage appearances:* The Wonderful Ice Cream Suit 1965, The Man in the Glass Booth 1968, 6 Rms Rivvu 1972, Bad Habits 1974, The Ritz 1976, Teibele and Her Demon 1979, Landscape of the Body 1977, The Master and Margarita 1978, King Lear 1981, Frankie and Johnny in the Clair de lune 1987, A Month in the Country 1995. *TV mini-series:* Larry McMurty's Dead Man's Walk 1996, Love of Life. *Address:* c/o Paradigm, Santa Monica Boulevard # 2500, Los Angeles, CA 90067, USA.

ABRAHAMS, Ivor, RA; British sculptor and painter; b. 10 Jan. 1935, Lancs.; s. of Harry Abrahams and Rachel Kalisky; m. 1st Victoria Taylor 1966 (divorced 1974); one s. (deceased); m. 2nd Evelyne Horvais 1974; one s.; ed Wigan Grammar School, Lancs., St Martin's School of Art and Camberwell School of Art, London; Visiting Lecturer in Sculpture and Drawing, Birmingham Coll. of Art 1960–64, Coventry Coll. of Art 1964–68; Visiting Lecturer, RCA, Slade School of Fine Art and Goldsmith's Coll. of Art 1970–80; Winston Churchill Fellow 1990, Fellow Royal Soc. of British Sculptors 1994; Visiting Lecturer RA Schools. *Exhibitions include:* many one-man and group exhbns in Europe and USA since 1962, including Environments, Sculpture, Drawings and Complete Graphics (Kölnischer Kunstverein, Germany) 1973, Ivor Abrahams Retrospective (Yorkshire Sculpture Park, Wakefield, England) 1984; works in numerous public collections including Victoria and Albert Museum and Tate Gallery, London, Wedgwood Museum, Stoke On Trent, Walker Art Gallery, Liverpool, Arnolfini Gallery, Bristol, Nat. Gallery of Australia, Canberra, Bibliothèque Nationale, Paris, Museum of Modern Art and Metropolitan Museum of Modern Art, New York, Denver Museum, Colo, Fort Lauderdale Museum, Fla Buymans Museum, Rotterdam, British Council and Arts Council of GB. *Television:* subject of several TV documentaries including Ivor Abrahams/Review BBC2 1972, Museum of Drawers/Arena produced by Alan Yentob BBC2 1979. *Publications:* Oxford Garden Sketchbook, Tales & Poems by E. A. Poe (illustrator 20 images). *Leisure interests:* books, postcards and golf. *Address:* c/o Royal Academy of Arts, Burlington House, Piccadilly, London, W1V 0DS, England.

ABRAHAMSEN, Egil, MSc, DTech; Norwegian scientist; b. 7 Feb. 1923, Hvaler; s. of Anker Christian Abrahamsen and Aagot Abrahamsen (née Kjoelberg); m. Randi B. Wiborg 1951; one s. two d.; ed Polytechnical Univ. of Norway, Univ. of Calif., Berkeley, USA, Univs of Durham, Newcastle upon Tyne, UK; surveyor Det Norske Veritas 1952–54, sr surveyor 1954–57, prin. surveyor 1957–75, Deputy Pres. 1966, Vice-Pres. 1967, Pres. 1967–85; Ed. European Shipbuilding 1955–60; Chair. and mem. numerous cttees; Chair. Bd of A/S Veda 1967–70, Bd of Dirs A.S. Computas 1967–83, Norsk Hydro 1985–92, The Abrahamsen Cttee 1984–86; Chair. Norwegian Telecom 1980–95, Royal Caribbean Cruise Line A/S (RCCL) 1985–89, OPAK 1985–, I. M. Skaugen 1990–99, Eikland 1990–99, Kosmos 1988–92, IKO Group 1988–92; Innovation 1990–; mem. Bd Den Norske Creditbank 1983–88; Kt Commdr, Order of the Lion (Finland) 1983, Kt Commdr, Order of St Olav (Norway) 1987, Légion d'honneur 1987, Kt Ordre Nat. du Mérite 1990, and numerous other decorations. *Leisure interests:* skiing, tennis. *Address:* Maaltrostveien 35, 0786 Oslo, Norway. *Telephone:* 22 46 90 05. *Fax:* 22 49 18 78. *E-mail:* egiab@online.no (Home).

ABRAHAMSON, Gen. James A.; American defence official and air force officer; b. 19 May 1933, Williston, ND; s. of Norval S. Abrahamson and Thelma B. Helle; m. Barbara Jean Northcott 1959 (died 1985); one s. one d.; ed MIT and Univ. of Oklahoma; commissioned USAF 1955, Lt-Gen. 1982, Gen. 1987; Flight Instructor Bryan AF Base, Tex. 1957–59; Spacecraft Project Officer Vela Nuclear Detection Satellite Programme, LAAF Station 1961–64; Fighter Pilot Tactical Air Command 1964; Astronaut USAF Manned Orbiting Lab. 1967–69; mem. staff Nat. Aeronautics and Space Council, White House 1969–71; Commdr 4950th Test Wing USAF 1973–74; Insp. Gen. AF Systems Command 1974–76; Dir F-16 Fighter Programme 1976–80; Deputy Chief of Staff for Systems Andrews AF Base, Md 1980–81; Assoc. Admin. for Space Transportation System, NASA HQ 1981–84; Dir Strategic Defence Initiative Org. 1984–89; Pres. Transportation Sector, Exec. Vice-Pres. for Devt Hughes Aircraft Co. 1989–92; Chair. Bd Oracle Corpn 1992–95; Lecturer of Astronautics AIAA 1993; moved to Int. Air Safety, LLC, Washington 1995; currently Chair. and CEO StratCom Int. LLC; mem. Nat. Advisory Bd Childhelp USA; numerous awards and medals. *Leisure interests:* sports, music and poetry. *Address:* StratCom International LLC, 20112 Marble Quarry Road, Keedysville, MD 21756-1508, USA. *Telephone:* (301) 432-8950. *Fax:* (301) 432-2657. *E-mail:* GenAbe@aol.com.

ABRAMOVICH, Roman Arkadyevich; Russian business executive and politician; b. 24 Oct. 1966, Saratov; s. of Arkady Nakhimovich Abramovich and Irina Vassilyevna Abramovich; m. 1st Olga Abramovich; one d.; m. 2nd Irina Malandina; one s. one d.; ed Industrial Inst., Ukhta, Komi, Moscow Gubkin Inst. of Oil and Gas; f. cos. Supertechnologia-Shishmarev, Elita, Petroltrans, GID, NPR 1992–95; Head Moscow Office Runicom SA, Switzerland 1993–96; f. (with Boris Berezovsky, Jt Stock Co. P.K. Trust 1995; f. cos. Mekong, Centurion-M, Agrofert, Multitrust, Oilimpex, Sibreal, Forneft, Servet, Branko, Vektor-A 1995–96; f. Dir-Gen. Rudicom Ltd Gibraltar 1997–99; Dir Moscow br. Sibneft 1996–97; Dir Sibneft 1996–; mem. State Duma 1998–2000; Gov. of Chukotka Autonomous Dist 2000–, Head of Govt 2001–. *Address:* Office of the Governor, Beringastr. 20, 689000 Anadyr, Chukotka Autonomous Region, Russia (Office). *Telephone:* (8427) 222-42-62 (Office). *Fax:* (8427) 222-24-66 (Office).

ABRAMS, Herbert Leroy, MD; American professor of radiology; b. 16 Aug. 1920, New York; s. of Morris Abrams and Freda Abrams (née Sugarman); m. Marilyn Spitz 1943; one s. one d.; ed Cornell Univ., State Univ. of New York; began medical practice Stanford Univ., faculty mem. School of Medicine 1951–67, Dir Div. Diagnostic Roentgenology 1961–67, Prof. of Radiology 1962–67; Philip H. Cook Prof. of Radiology, Harvard Univ. 1967–85, now Prof. Emer., Chair. Dept of Radiology 1967–80; Radiologist-in-Chief, Peter Bent Brigham Hosp., Boston 1967–80; Chair. Dept of Radiology, Brigham & Women's Hosp., Boston 1981–85; Radiologist-in-Chief, Sidney Farber Cancer Inst., Boston 1974–85; Prof. of Radiology, Stanford Univ. Medical School 1985–90, Prof. Emer. 1990–; Clinical Prof. Univ. of California Medical School 1986–; Ed.-in-Chief Postgraduate Radiology 1983–99, Cardiovascular and Interventional Radiology 1976–85; R.H. Nimmo Visiting Prof., Univ. of Adelaide 1976; numerous lectureships; mem.-in-residence Stanford Center for Int. Security and Arms Control 1985–; mem. Int. Blue Ribbon Panel on the Radiation Effects Research Foundation, Hiroshima and Nagasaki; mem. numerous medical assns; Fellow Nat. Cancer Inst.; Hon. Fellow Royal Coll. of Radiology, Royal Coll. of Surgeons (Ireland); Gold Medal (Asscn Univ. Radiologists) 1984, Gold Medal (Radiological Soc., USA) 1995. *Publications include:* Congenital Heart Disease 1965, Coronary Arteriography: A Practical Approach 1983, Ed. Abrams Angiography 1983, The President has been Shot: Confusion, Disability and the 25th Amendment in the Aftermath of the Assassination Attempt on Ronald Reagan 1992, The History of Cardiac Radiology 1996, numerous articles for professional periodicals. *Leisure interests:* English and American literature, tennis, music. *Address:* Stanford University School of Medicine, 300 Pasteure Drive, Stanford, CA 94305 (Office); 714 Alvarado, Stanford, CA 94305, USA (Home). *Telephone:* (415) 723-6258 (Office); (415) 424-8552 (Home). *Fax:* (415) 725-7296. *E-mail:* hlabrams@stanford.edu. *Website:* www-radiology.stanford.edu.

ABRAMSKY, Jennifer, CBE, BA; British radio producer and editor; b. 7 Oct. 1946; d. of Chimen Abramsky and Miriam Nirenstein; m. Alasdair Liddell 1976; one s. one d.; ed Holland Park School and Univ. of East Anglia; joined BBC Radio as Programme Operations Asst 1969, Producer The World at One 1973, Ed. PM 1978, Producer Radio Four Budget Programmes 1979–86, Ed. Today programme 1986–87, News and Current Affairs Radio 1987–93, est. Radio Four News FM 1991, Controller Radio Five Live 1993–96, Dir Continuous News (including Radio Five Live, BBC News 24, BBC World, BBC News Online, Ceefax), Dir BBC Radio 1998–2000, BBC Radio and Music 2000–; mem. Bd of Govs. BFI 2000–; mem. Econ. and Social Research Council 1992–96, Editorial Bd British Journalism Review 1993–; Hon. Prof. Thames Valley Univ. 1994; Royal Acad. Fellowship 1998; News Int. Visiting Prof. of Broadcast Media 2002; Hon. MA (Salford) 1997; Woman of Distinction, Jewish Care 1990; Sony Radio Acad. Award 1995. *Leisure interests:* theatre, music. *Address:* BBC, Room 2811, Broadcasting House, Portland Place, London, W1A 1AA, England. *Telephone:* (20) 7765-4561 (Office).

ABRASZEWSKI, Andrzej, MA, LLD; Polish diplomatist and UN official; b. 4 Jan. 1938, Paradyz; s. of Antoni Abraszewski and Maria Zaleska; m. Teresa Zagorska; one s.; ed Cen. School for Foreign Service, Warsaw and Copernicus Univ., Toruń; researcher, Polish Inst. for Int. Affairs, Warsaw 1962–71; Sec. Polish Nat. Cttee on the 25th anniversary of the UN 1970; Counsellor to the Minister for Foreign Affairs, Dept of Int. Orgs., Ministry of Foreign Affairs, Warsaw 1971–83; mem. Polish del. to Gen. Ass. of the UN 1971–90, 2001–, mem. Ad Hoc Working Group on UN's programme and budget machinery 1975, mem. Advisory Cttee on Admin. and Budgetary Questions 1977–82, 2001–, Vice-Chair. Fifth Cttee (Admin. and Budgetary) of Gen. Ass. 1979, Chair. 1982, Cttee on Contribs. 1983–88 (Vice-Chair. 1987–88); mem. Cttee for Programmes and Co-ordination (Vice-Chair. 1989, Chair. 1990); Asst to Deputy Minister for Foreign Affairs 1984–90; mem. UN Jt Inspection Unit 1991–2000, Vice-Chair. 1993, 1998, Chair. 1994; Prize of the Minister for Foreign Affairs, Prize of the Minister of Finance. *Publications:* various papers on UN affairs. *Leisure interests:* boating, skiing, swimming. *Address:* United Nations Advisory Committee on Administrative and Budgetary Questions, Room CB-60, New York, NY 10017 (Office); 300 East 33rd Street, Apt. 19E, New York, NY 10016, USA. *Telephone:* (212) 963-7456 (Office). *Fax:* (212) 963-6943 (Office). *E-mail:* abraszewski@un.org (Office). *Website:* www.un.int/poland.

ABRIKOSOV, Alexei Alexeyevich; American (b. Russian) physicist; b. 25 June 1928, Moscow; s. of Aleksei Ivanovich Abrikosov and Fanny Davidovna Vulf; m. Svetlana Yuriyevna Bun'kova 1977; two s. one d.; ed Moscow Univ.; Postgraduate Research Assoc., Scientist, Sr Scientist, Inst. of Physical Problems, USSR Acad. of Sciences 1948–65; Head of Dept, Landau Inst. of Theoretical Physics, USSR Acad. of Sciences 1965–88, Dir Inst. of High Pressure Physics 1988–91; Distinguished Scientist, Argonne Nat. Lab., Ill. 1991–; Research Assoc., Asst Prof., Prof. Moscow Univ. 1951–68, Prof. Gorky Univ. 1971–72, Prof. Moscow Physical Eng Inst. 1974–75, Head Chair. Theoretical Physics, Moscow Inst. of Steel and Alloys 1976–91; mem. USSR (now Russian) Acad. of Sciences 1964; mem. American Acad. of Arts and Sciences 1991, NAS 2000; Foreign mem. Royal Soc. 2001; Fellow American Physics Soc. 1992; Hon. ScD (Moscow) 1955; Hon. DS (Lausanne) 1975; Lenin Prize 1966, Fritz London Award 1972, USSR State Prize 1982, Landau Prize 1989, John Bardeen Prize 1991. *Publications:* Quantum Field Theory Methods in Statistical Physics 1962, Introduction to the Theory of Normal Metals 1972, Fundamentals of Metal Theory 1987 and works on plasma physics, quantum electro-dynamics, theory of superconductors, magnetism, astro-physics, quantum liquids and semimetals. *Leisure interest:* skiing. *Address:* Argonne National Laboratory, 9700 South Cass Avenue, Argonne, IL 60439, USA. *Telephone:* (630) 252-5482.

ABRIL, Victoria; Spanish actress; b. Victoria Mérida Rojas, 14 July 1959, Madrid; m.; two s. *Films include:* Obsesión 1975, Robin and Marian 1975, Robin Hood 1975, Caperucita Roja 1975, Cambio de sexo 1975, La bien plantada 1976, Doña Perfecta 1976, Esposa y Amante 1977, La muchacha de las bragas de oro 1979, Asesinato en el Comité Central 1981, La Guerrillera 1981, La Colmena 1982, La batalla del porro 1982, Le Bastard 1982, La Lune dans le Caniveau 1982, Sem Sombra de pecado 1982, J'ai Epousé un ombre 1982, Rio Abajo 1982, Bajo el signo de Piscis 1983, Le Voyage 1983, Las bicicletas son para el verano 1983, L'Addition 1983, Rouge George 1983, La noche más hermosa 1984, Padre Nuestro 1984, After Dark 1984, L'Addition 1984, La hora bruja 1985, Tiempo de Silencio 1985, Max mon Amour 1985, Vado e torno 1985, El Lute 1987, El placer de matar 1987, Barrios altos 1987, El juego más divertido 1987, Ada dans la jungle 1988, Baton Rouge 1988, Sandino 1989, Atame 1989, A solas contigo 1990, Amantes 1990, Tie Me Up! Tie Me Down! 1991, High Heels 1992, Lovers 1992 (Silver Bear for Best Actress, Berlin Film Festival), Intruso 1993, Kika 1993, Jimmy Hollywood 1994, Casque bleu 1994, Nadie hablará de nosotras cuandro hayamas muerto (Best Actress, Cannes) 1995, Gazon Maudit 1996, Freedomfighters 1996, La femme du cosmonaute 1998, Between Your Legs 1999, Mon père, ma mère, mes frères et mes soeurs 1999, 101 Reykjavik 2001, Sin noticias de Dios 2002, Don't Tempt Me 2003. *Theatre includes:* Obras de Mihura, Company Tirso de Molina 1977, Viernes, día de libertad, Company L. Prendes 1977, Nuit d'Ivresse, Paris 1986. *Address:* c/o Alsira García-Maroto, Gran Via 63–3° izda, 28013 Madrid, Spain.

ABRIL-MARTORELL HERNÁNDEZ, Fernando; Spanish telecommunications executive; began career with JP Morgan; Chief Financial Officer Telefónica SA 1997–99, CEO 2000–; Exec. Pres. TPI-Yellow Pages 1998–2000. *Address:* Telefónica, SA Beatriz de Bobadilla 3, 9°, 28040 Madrid, Spain (Office). *Telephone:* (91) 584 9107 (Office). *Fax:* (91) 534 7972 (Office). *Website:* www.telefonica.es (Office).

ABSE, Dannie, DLitt, MRCS, LRCP, FRSL; British author and physician; b. 22 Sept. 1923, Cardiff, Wales; s. of Rudolph Abse and Kate Shepherd; m. Joan Mercer 1951; one s. two d.; ed St Illtyd's Coll. Cardiff, Univ. Coll. Cardiff, King's Coll. London and Westminster Hosp., London; first book of poems published while still a medical student 1948; qualified as doctor 1950; Squadron-Leader RAF 1951–55; doctor in charge of chest clinic at Cen. Medical Establishment, Cleveland St, London 1954–89; Writer in Residence, Princeton Univ., NJ, USA 1973–74; Pres. Poetry Soc. 1979–92, Welsh Acad. 1996; Fellow Welsh Acad. 1993 (Pres. 1995), Hon. Fellow Univ. of Wales Coll. of Medicine 1999; Hon. DLitt (Univ. of Wales) 1989, (Glamorgan) 1997; Welsh Arts Council Literature Prize; Henry Foyle Award 1964; Jewish Chronicle Award; Cholmondeley Award 1983. *Publications:* Collected Poems 1948–1977, Pythagoras (a play), Ash on a Young Man's Sleeve 1954, Way Out in the Centre 1981, Ask the Bloody Horse 1986, Journals from the Ant Heap 1986, White Coat, Purple Coat 1989, The Music Lovers Literary Companion (with Joan Abse) 1989, Remembrance of Crimes Past 1990, The Hutchinson Book of Post-War British Poets (ed.) 1989, There was a Young Man of Cardiff 1991, On the Evening Road 1994, Intermittent Journals 1994, Twentieth-Century Anglo-Welsh Poetry 1997, A Welsh Retrospective 1997, Arcadia, One Mile 1998, Goodbye, Twentieth Century 2001, New and Collected Poems 2002, and many others. *Leisure interests:* chess, supporting Cardiff City Football Club. *Address:* 85 Hodford Road, London, NW11 8NH, England; Green Hollows, Craig-yr-Eos Road, Ogmore-by-Sea, Glamorgan, South Wales.

ABSHIRE, David Manker, PhD; American diplomatist and administrator; b. 11 April 1926, Chattanooga, Tenn.; s. of James Ernest Abshire and Phyllis Patten Abshire; m. Carolyn Sample Abshire 1957; one s. four d.; ed Baylor School, Chattanooga, U.S. Mil. Acad., West Point, NY, Georgetown Univ., Washington, DC; co-f. Center for Strategic and Int. Studies, Georgetown Univ. 1962, Exec. Dir 1962–70, Chair. 1973–82, Pres. 1982–83, Vice-Chair. 1999–; Asst Sec. of State for Congressional Relations 1970–73; Perm. Rep. to NATO 1983–87; Special Counsellor to Pres. Jan.–April 1987; Chancellor Center for Strategic and Int. Studies (CSIS) April–Dec. 1987, Pres. 1988–, Vice-Chair. 1999–; Co-ed. Washington Quarterly 1977–83; Chair. US Bd for Int. Broadcasting 1974–77; Dir Nat. Security Group, Transition Office of Pres.-elect Reagan 1980–81; Pres. and CEO, Center for the Study of the Presidency 1999–; Pres. Richard Lounsbery Foundation of New York 2002–; mem. Congressional Cttee on the Org. of Govt for the Conduct of Foreign Policy 1973–75; mem. Bd Procter & Gamble 1987–96, Ogden Corpn, BP American Advisory Bd; mem. Advisory Bd Pres.'s Task Force on US Govt Int. Broadcasting 1991; Order of Crown (Belgium), Commdr Ordre de Léopold (Belgium); Pres. Civilian Service Award 1989; Medal of Diplomatic Merit (Rep. of Korea) 1993; Order of the Lion of Finland (1st Class) 1994; US Mil. Acad. Castle Award 1994; Order of the Liberator (Argentina) 1999; Order of Sacred Treasure Gold and Silver Star (Japan) 2001. *Publications include:* International Broadcasting: A New Dimension of Western Diplomacy 1976, Foreign Policy Makers: President vs. Congress 1979, The Growing Power of Congress 1981, Preventing World War III: A Realistic Grand Strategy 1988, The Global Economy 1990, Putting America's House in Order: The Nation as a Family 1996, Report to the President-Elect 2000: Triumphs and Tragedies of the Modern Presidency 2000. *Leisure interest:* historical literature. *Address:* Center for Study of the Presidency, 1020 19th Street, NW, Suite 250, Washington, DC 20036 (Office); 311 South St Asaph Street, Alexandria, VA 22314, USA. *Telephone:* (202) 872-9800 (Office). *Fax:* (202) 872-9811 (Office). *E-mail:* center@thepresidency.org (Office). *Website:* www.thepresidency.org (Office).

ABU GHAZALA, Field Marshal Muhammad Abd al-Halim (see Abd al-Halim Abu Ghazala, Field Marshal Muhammad).

ABU-GHAZALEH, Talal; Palestinian/Jordanian management consultant and intellectual property expert; b. 22 April 1938, Jaffa; m. Nuha Salameh; two s. two d.; ed American Univ. of Beirut; Founder and Chair. Bd of Dirs Talal Abu-Ghazaleh Int. (TAGI) (mem. firm of Grant Thornton Int.), leading regional holding group of professional firms operating through 34 offices in Arab World and comprising, among others: Talal Abu-Ghazaleh & Co. (TAGCO), Abu-Ghazaleh Consultancy & Co. (AGCOC), Al-Dar Consulting Co. (ADCO), Talal Abu-Ghazaleh Assocs. Ltd (TAGA), Arab Int. Projects Co. (AIPC), The First Projects Man. Co. (FPMC), Talal Abu-Ghazaleh Int. Man. Inc. (TAGIMI), TMP Agents, Arab Bureau for Legal Services (ABLE), Al-Dar Gen. Trading Co. (ADTCO); Chair. Arab Knowledge Man. Soc. (fmrly Arab Man. Soc.) 1989–; Hon. DHumLitt (Canisius Coll. Buffalo, NY) 1988; Chevalier, Légion d'honneur and decorations from Tunisia, Kuwait, Bahrain and Jordan. *Publications:* Taxation in the Arab Countries, The Abu-Ghazaleh English–Arabic Dictionary of Accounting, Trade Mark Laws in the Arab Countries. *Address:* Talal Abu-Ghazaleh International, TAGI House, Queen Noor Street, Shmeisani, Amman; PO Box 921100, Amman 11192, Jordan. *Telephone:* (6) 5669603. *Fax:* (6) 5696284. *E-mail:* tagco@tagi.com. *Website:* www.tagi.com.

ABU MAZEN (see Abbas, Mahmud).

ABU-NIMAH, Hasan; Jordanian diplomatist; b. 11 Sept. 1935, Battir, Jerusalem; ed Al-Ummah Coll., Bethlehem, American Univ. of Beirut; fmr political commentator Amman Broadcasting Service and lecturer, Teacher Training Centre, Ramallah, Jordan; Third Sec. Embassy, Kuwait 1965–67, Second Sec. Embassy, Iraq 1967–70, First Sec. in USA 1970–72, with Foreign Ministry, Amman 1972–73, Counsellor Embassy, UK 1973–77, Amb. to Belgium (also accred to Netherlands and Luxembourg) 1978–90, to Italy 1990–95; Perm. Rep. to UN 1995–2000; Order of Grand Cross of Crown of Belgium, Order of Independence of Jordan, Grade I, Order of Al-Kawkab of Jordan, Medal of Pope Paul VI, Order of Grand Cross of Merit, Italy. *Address:* c/o Ministry of Foreign Affairs, PO Box 35214, Amman 11180, Jordan.

ABUBAKAR, Gen. Abdulsalami; Nigerian international official, fmr head of state and army officer; b. 13 June 1942, Minna; ed Minna, Bida, Kaduna; joined Nigerian Army 1963, with UN peacekeeping force Lebanon 1978–79, Chief of Defence Staff and Chair. Jt Chiefs of Staff of the Armed Forces 1993–98, fmrly active in Cttee of W African Chiefs of Staff; Commdr in Chief 1998; Head of Govt of Nigeria 1998–99; apptd UN Special Envoy to Democratic Repub. of the Congo 2000; Head of Commonwealth Observer Mission to Oversee Zimbabwe's Parl. Elections 2000, Mission to Monitor Pres. Elections in Zimbabwe March 2002. *Address:* c/o UN Mission in the Democratic Republic of the Congo, United Nations Plaza, New York, NY 10017, USA.

ABUBAKAR, Alhaji Atiku; Nigerian politician; b. 25 Nov. 1955, Jada, Adamawa State; ed Adamawa Prov. Secondary School, Yola, Ahmadu Bello Univ., Zaira; with Customs and Excise Dept 1969–89; joined People's Democratic Movt (PDM) 1989; fmr Gov. Adamawa State; mem. People's Democratic Party (PDP); Chair. Nat. Econ. Council; Head Fed. Exec. Council meeting 1999; Vice-Pres. of Nigeria 1999–; Turaki Adamawa 1988. *Address:* Office of the Vice-President, New Federal Secretariat Complex, Shehu Shagari Way, Central Area, Abuja, Nigeria (Office). *Website:* www.nigeria.gov.ng (Office).

ABYKAYEV, Nurtai Abykayevich; Kazakhstan politician and diplomatist; b. 15 May 1947, Dzhambul, Almaty Region; m.; three c.; ed Ural Polytech. Inst., Almaty Higher CP School; has rank of Amb.; engineer Almaty factory of heavy machine construction 1972–76; CP functionary 1976–88; Asst to Chair. Council of Ministers of Kazakh SSR 1988–89; Asst to First Sec. Cen. Cttee CP of Kazakhstan 1989–90; Head Adm. of Pres. and Prime Minister Repub. of Kazakhstan, mem. Nat. Security Council 1990–95, also served as Chair.; Amb. to UK (also accred to Denmark, Norway and Sweden) 1995–96; First Asst to Pres. of Kazakhstan 1996–99; apptd First Deputy Minister of Foreign Affairs 1999. *Address:* Ministry of Foreign Affairs, Beybitshilik str. 10, 480091 Astana, Kazakhstan.

ACCARDO, Salvatore; Italian violinist and conductor; b. 26 Sept. 1941, Turin; s. of Vincenzo Accardo and Ines Nea Accardo; m. Resy Corsi 1973; ed Conservatorio S. Pietro a Majella, Naples and Chigiana Acad., Siena; first professional recital 1954; won 1st prize Geneva Competition at age 15 and 1st prize Paganini Competition at age 17; repertoire includes concertos by Bartók, Beethoven, Berg, Brahms, Bruch, Paganini, Penderecki, Prokofiev, Saint-Saëns, Sibelius, Stravinsky and Tchaikovsky; plays with world's leading conductors and orchestras including Amsterdam Concertgebouw, Berlin Philharmonic, Boston Symphony, Chicago Symphony, Cleveland, La Scala, Milan, Santa Cecilia, Rome, BBC Symphony, London Symphony and Philharmonia; also appears as soloist/dir with the English, Scottish and Netherlands Chamber Orchestras; Artistic Dir Naples Festival; Cavaliere di Gran Croce 1982; numerous music prizes include Caecilia Prize (Brussels) and Italian Critics' Prize for recording of the Six Paganini Concertos and Diapuson d'Or for recording of the Sibelius Concerto. *Recordings include:* the Paganini Concertos and Caprices (Deutsche Grammophon), concerts by Beethoven and Brahms, complete works for violin and orchestra by Bruch, concertos by Mendelssohn, Dvořák, Sibelius and Tchaikovsky (Philips/ Phonogram). *Publications:* Edn Paganini Sixth Concerto, Paganini: Variations on "Carmagnola". *Leisure interests:* hi fi, electronics, sport and cooking. *Address:* c/o Agenzia Resia Srl Rappresentanze e Segreterie Internazionali Artistiche, Via Manzoni 31, 20121 Milan, Italy.

ACCONCI, Vito, MFA; American sculptor; b. 24 Jan. 1940, Bronx, New York; s. of Amilcar Acconci and Catherine Colombo; ed Holy Cross Coll., Worcester, Mass., Univ. of Iowa; solo exhbns. at San Francisco Museum of Modern Art, Stedelijk Museum, Amsterdam, Museum of Contemporary Art, Chicago, Kunstverein, Cologne, Padiglione d'Arte Contemporanea, Milan, Museum of Modern Art, New York, Museum für Angewandte Kunst, Vienna 1993, Museum d'Art Moderne, St-Etienne 1994; exhbns. at Le Centre Nat. d'Art Contemporain de Grenoble 1991, Centro per l'Arte Contemporanea Luigi Pecci, Prato 1992; public comms.: The Palladium, New York 1986, Coca Cola Co., Atlanta 1987, St Aubin Park, Detroit 1990, Autry Park, Houston 1990, Embarcadero Promenade, San Francisco 1992, Arvada Art Center, Arvada, Colo 1992, La Fontaine Avenue School, Bronx, New York 1992; Guggenheim Foundation Fellowship 1979; several awards from New York State Council of the Arts 1976, Nat. Endowment for the Arts; Skowhegan Award 1980. *Leisure interests:* architecture, movies, music. *Address:* Acconci Studio, 70 Washington Street #501, Brooklyn, New York, NY 11201 (Office); 39 Pearl Street, Brooklyn, New York, NY 11201, USA (Home). *Telephone:* (718) 852-6591 (Office). *Fax:* (718) 624-3178 (Office). *E-mail:* studio@acconci.com (Office). *Website:* www.acconci.com (Office).

ACHEBE, Chinua, BA, FRSL; Nigerian writer; b. 16 Nov. 1930, Ogidi, Anambra State; s. of the late Isaiah O. Achebe and Janet N. Achebe; m. Christie C. Okoli 1961; two s. two d.; ed Govt Coll., Umuahia and Univ. Coll., Ibadan; Producer, Nigerian Broadcasting Corpn, Lagos 1954–58, Regional Controller, Enugu 1958–61, Dir Voice of Nigeria, Lagos 1961–66; Sr Research Fellow, Univ. of Nigeria, Nsukka 1967–72; Rockefeller Fellowship 1960–61; UNESCO Fellowship 1963; Foundation mem. Asscn of Nigerian Authors 1982–; mem. Gov. Council, Lagos Univ. 1966, mem. E. Cen. State Library Bd 1971–72; Founding Ed., Okike 1971–; Prof. of English, Univ. of Mass. 1972–75, Univ. of Conn. 1975–76, Univ. of Nigeria, Nsukka 1976–81, Prof. Emer. 1985–; Pro-Chancellor and Chair. of Council, Anambra State Univ. of Tech., Enugu, Nigeria 1986–88; Regents Lecturer, Univ. of Calif., Los Angeles 1984; Founding Ed. African Writers' Series (Heinemann) 1962–72; Dir Heinemann Educational Books (Nigeria) Ltd, Nwamife (Publishers), Enugu; Pres. Asscn of Nigerian Authors 1981–86; mem. Tokyo Colloquium 1981; Visiting Distinguished Prof. of English, City Coll., NY 1989; Montgomery Fellow and Visiting Prof., Dartmouth Coll., Hanover 1990; Prof. of Literature, Bard Coll. 1991–; Visiting Fellow, Ashby Lecturer Clare Hall, Cambridge 1993; Hon. mem. American Acad. of Arts and Letters 1982; Hon. Fellow, Modern Language Asscn of America 1974; Neil Gunn Int. Fellow 1975; Fellow, Ghana Asscn of Writers 1975; Goodwill Amb. (UN Population Fund) 1998–; Hon. DUniv; Hon. DLitt (16 times); Hon. DHL (eight times); Hon. LLD (three times); Dr hc (Open Univ.) 1989; Margaret Wrong Memorial Prize 1959, Nigerian Nat. Trophy 1960, Jock Campbell New Statesman Award 1965, Commonwealth Poetry Prize 1972, The Lotus Prize (Afro-Asian writers) 1975, Order of the Federal Republic (Nigeria) 1979, Nigerian Nat. Merit Award 1979. *Publications:* Things Fall Apart 1958, No Longer at Ease 1960, Arrow of God 1964, A Man of the People 1966, Chike and the River 1966, Poems 1971, Girls at War 1972, Beware Soul Brother 1972, How the Leopard Got His Claws 1973, Morning Yet on Creation Day 1975, The Flute 1978, The Drum 1978, Anthills of the Savannah 1987, Hopes and Impediments—Selected Essays 1965–87 1988, Another Africa (jtly) 1998, Home and Exile 2000. *Leisure interest:* music. *Address:* Bard College, PO Box 41, Annandale-on-Hudson, NY 12504, USA.

ACHIDI ACHU, Simon; Cameroonian politician; b. 1934, Santa Mbu; ed Cameroon Protestant Coll., Bali, Yaoundé Univ., Univ. of Besançon, France, Nat. School of Magistracy, Yaoundé; worked as agricultural Asst, Cameroon Devt Corpn before entering univ.; fmr interpreter, Presidency, Yaoundé, Chief Accountant, Widikum Council, Pres. NW Provincial Co-operative Union Ltd; Minister-del. in charge of State Reforms 1971; Minister of Justice and Keeper of the Seals 1972–75; in pvt. business 1975–88; elected Cameroon People's Democratic Movt (CPDM) MP 1988; Prime Minister of Cameroon 1992–96. *Leisure interests:* farming, football. *Address:* c/o Prime Minister's Office, Yaoundé, Cameroon.

ACKEREN, Robert Van; German film maker, screenplay writer and producer; b. 22 Dec. 1946, Berlin; s. of Max Van Ackeren and Hildegard Van Ackeren; ed in film studies, Berlin; Prof. of TV and Film, Acad. of Media Arts, Cologne; German Film Prize, Ernst Lubitsch Prize, Federal Film Prize (Fed. Repub. of Germany), Max Ophüls Prize, Prix Celuloide, Premio Incontri Int., Prix Cinedecouverte, El Premio Cid, Prix L'âge d'or. *Films:* Einer weiss mehr 1964, Wham 1965, Sticky Fingers 1966, Nou Nou 1967, Ja und Nein 1968, Für immer und ewig 1969, Blondie's No. 1 1971, Küss mich, Fremder 1972, Harlis 1973, Der letzte Schrei 1975, Belcanto 1977, Das andere Lächeln 1978, Die Reinheit des Herzens 1980, Deutschland Privat 1981, Die flambierte Frau 1983, Die Tigerin 1985, Die Venusfalle 1987, Die Wahre Geschichte von Männern und Frauen 1992, Plan D. *Address:* Academy of Media Arts, Peter-Welter-Platz 2, 50676 Cologne (Office); Kurfürstendamm 132a, 10711 Berlin, Germany (Home). *Telephone:* (221) 20189-0. *Fax:* (221) 20189-124. *E-mail:* presse@khm.de. *Website:* www.khm.de.

ACKERMANN, Josef; Swiss investment banker; b. 7 Feb. 1948; mem. Bd of Dirs Deutsche Bank 1996–, Man., Global Corps and Insts., Spokesman Man. Bd and Chair. Group Exec. Cttee 2002–; mem. Bd Stora Enso; mem. Supervisory Bd Linde AG, Bayer AG. *Address:* Deutsche Bank AG, Taunusanlage 12, Tower A, 60325 Frankfurt, Germany (Office). *Telephone:* (69) 910-00 (Office). *Fax:* (69) 910-34227 (Office). *Website:* www.db.com (Office).

ACKLAND, Joss (Sidney Edmond Jocelyn), CBE; British actor; b. 29 Feb. 1928, London; s. of Norman Ackland and Ruth Izod; m. Rosemary Jean Kirkcaldy 1951; two s. (one deceased) five d.; ed Dame Alice Owens School, Cen. School of Speech Training and Dramatic Art; has worked in theatre since 1945; repertory includes Stratford-upon-Avon, Arts Theatre, Buxton, Croydon, The Embassy, Coventry, Oxford, Pitlochry; tea planter in Cen. Africa 1954–57; disc jockey in Cape Town 1955–57; mem. Old Vic Theatre Co. 1958–61; Artistic Dir Mermaid Theatre 1961–63; Dir The Plough and the Stars; mem. Drug Helpline, Amnesty Int. *Theatre roles include:* Falstaff in Henry IV, Parts I and II, Hook and Darling in Peter Pan, Clarence Darrow in Never the Sinner, Mitch in A Streetcar Named Desire, Brassbound in Captain Brassbound's Conversion, Sir in The Dresser (nat. tour), Petruchio in Taming of the Shrew (nat. tour), Gaev in The Cherry Orchard, Gus in Hotel in Amsterdam, Sam in Collaborators, Ill in The Visit, Eustace Perrin State in The Madras House, John Tarleton in Misalliance, Weller Martin in The Gin Game, Captain Shotover in Heartbreak House. *West End musical roles include:* Squeezum in Lock up Your Daughters, Romain Gary in Jean Seburg, Jorrocks in Jorrocks, Frederic in A Little Night Music, Perón in Evita, Captain Hook and Mr Darling in Peter Pan—the Musical. *Films include:*

Seven Days to Noon 1949, Crescendo 1969, Lady Jane 1984, A Zed and Two Noughts 1985, The Sicilian 1986, To Kill a Priest 1987, White Mischief 1988, Lethal Weapon II, The Hunt for Red October, To Forget Palermo, Tre Colonne in Cronaca 1989, The Object of Beauty, The Sheltering Desert, The Bridge, A Murder of Quality 1990, Voices in the Garden 1992, Georgino, Occhio Pinocchio 1993, Nowhere to Run 1993, The Bible, Miracle on 34th Street, Mad Dogs and Englishmen, A Kid at the Court of King Arthur, Citizen X 1994, Daisies in December, Till the End of Time, Surviving Picasso, Deadly Voyage 1995, Swept from the Sea 1996, Firelight 1997, Game of Mirrors, Son of Sandokan, Milk, Passion of Mind 1998, Mumbo Jumbo 2000, Painting Faces 2001, Othello 2001, K19: The Widowmaker 2001, No Good Deed 2001, The House on Turk Street 2002, I'll Be There 2003. *Radio includes:* Macbeth in Macbeth, The King in The King and I, Honoré Lachailles in Gigi, God in The Little World of Don Camillo, Victor Hugo in Les Misérables. *TV appearances include:* Kipling, The Man who lived at the Ritz, When We Are Married, The Lie, The Barretts of Wimpole Street, Shadowlands, First and Last, They Do It with Mirrors, Under the Sun. *Publication:* I Must Be in There Somewhere (autobiog.) 1989. *Leisure interests:* writing, painting, reading, 29 grandchildren, two great-grandchildren. *Address:* c/o Jonathan Altaras Associates, 2nd Floor, 13 Shorts Gardens, London, WC2H 9AT, England.

ACKNER, Baron (Life Peer), cr. 1986, of Sutton in the County of West Sussex; **Desmond James Conrad Ackner,** PC, MA; British judge and arbitrator; b. 18 Sept. 1920; s. of Conrad Ackner and Rhoda Ackner; m. Joan Evans 1946; one s. two d.; ed Highgate School, Clare Coll., Cambridge; served in RA 1941–42, Admiralty Naval Br. 1942–45; called to Bar, Middle Temple 1945; QC 1961; Recorder of Swindon 1962–71; Judge of Courts of Appeal of Jersey and Guernsey 1967–71; a Judge of the High Court of Justice, Queen's Bench Div. 1971–80; Judge of the Commercial Court 1973–80; presiding Judge, Western Circuit 1976–79; mem. Gen. Council of Bar 1957–61, 1963–70, Hon. Treas. 1964–66, Vice-Chair. 1966–68, Chair. 1968–70; Bencher, Middle Temple 1965, Deputy Treas. 1983, Treas. 1984; mem. Senate of the Four Inns of Court 1966–70, Vice-Pres. 1968–70; Pres. Senate of the Inns of Court and the Bar 1980–82; Lord Justice of Appeal 1980–86; Lord of Appeal in Ordinary 1986–92; Chair. Law Advisory Cttee, British Council 1980–90, mem. British Council 1991–, Lloyd's Arbitration Panel 1992–; Pres. Arbitration Appeal Panel, Securities and Futures Authority 1994–2002; Appeal Commr, Personal Investment Authority 1994–2002; Dir City Disputes Panel 1994–98; Hon. mem. Canadian Bar Asscn 1973–; Fellow Soc. of Advanced Legal Studies 1997; Hon. Fellow Clare Coll., Cambridge 1983. *Leisure interests:* reading, cooking, theatre. *Address:* House of Lords, Westminster, London, SW1A 0PW; 4 Pump Court, Temple, London, EC4Y 7AN; 7 Rivermill, 151 Grosvenor Road, London, SW1V 3JN, England. *Telephone:* (20) 7219-3243; (20) 7353-2656 (Temple); (20) 7821-8068 (Rivermill). *Fax:* (20) 7821-8068 (Home).

ACKROYD, Norman, RA, FRCA; British artist; b. 26 March 1938, Leeds; s. of the late Albert Ackroyd and Clara Briggs; m. 1st Sylvia Buckland 1963 (divorced 1975); two d.; m. 2nd Penelope Hughes-Stanton 1978; one s. one d.; ed Cockburn High School, Leeds, Leeds Coll. of Art, Royal Coll. of Art; Tutor in Etching, Cen. School of Art and Design 1965–93; Prof. of Etching, Univ. of Indiana 1970; exhbns at Mickelson Gallery, Wash. 1973, 1977, 1979, 1982, 1984, 1988, Anderson Oday Gallery, London 1979, 1988, Dolan Maxwell Gallery, Phila 1981, 1983, 1985, 1987, 1989 TV works include: Artists in Print (Etching) 1981, A Prospect of Rivers 1988; comms include: Haringey Cultural Centre 1985, Lloyds Bank Tech. Centre, London 1990, British Airways 1991, Freshfields, London 1992, Tetrapak, London 1993; British Int. Print Biennale Prize 1974, 1982, Royal Soc. of Etchers and Engravers 1984, 85, Bronze Medal, Frechen, Germany 1986. *Television:* . *Publications include:* Landscapes and Figures, Etchings (with William McIllvanny) 1973, The Pictish Coast (with Douglas Dunn) 1988, St Kilda: The Furthest Island 1989, Windrush 1990. *Leisure interests:* British history, archaeology, cricket. *Address:* c/o Royal Academy of Arts, Piccadilly, London, W1V 0DS, England. *Telephone:* (20) 7378-6001.

ACKROYD, Peter, CBE, MA, FRSL; British writer; b. 5 Oct. 1949, London; s. of Graham Ackroyd and Audrey Whiteside; ed St Benedict's School, Ealing, Clare Coll., Cambridge and Yale Univ.; Literary Ed. The Spectator 1973–77, Jt Man. Ed. 1978–82; Chief Book Reviewer The Times 1986–; Mellon Fellow Yale Univ.; Hon. DLitt (Exeter Univ.), (London Guildhall), (City Univ.), (Univ. Coll., London). *Play:* The Mystery of Charles Dickens 2000. *Television:* Charles Dickens (BBC 2). *Publications: novels:* The Great Fire of London 1982, The Last Testament of Oscar Wilde 1983 (Somerset Maugham Prize 1984), Hawksmoor 1985 (Whitbread Award, Guardian Fiction Prize), Chatterton 1987, First Light 1989, English Music 1992, The House of Doctor Dee 1993, Dan Leno and the Limehouse Golem 1994, Milton in America 1996, The Plato Papers 1999, The Clerkenwell Tales 2003; *non-fiction:* Notes for a New Culture 1976, Dressing Up 1979, Ezra Pound and his World 1980, T.S. Eliot 1984 (Whitbread Award, Heinemann Awards), Dickens 1990, Introduction to Dickens 1991, Blake 1995, The Life of Thomas More 1998, London: the Biography 2000, Albion: The Origins of the English Imagination 2002; *Poetry:* London Lickpenny 1973, Country Life 1978, The Diversions of Purley 1987. *Address:* Anthony Sheil Associates Ltd, 43 Doughty Street, London, WC1N 2LF, England. *Telephone:* (20) 7405-9351.

ACLAND, Sir Antony (Arthur), KG, GCMG, GCVO; British diplomatist; b. 12 March 1930, London; s. of the late Brig. P. B. E. Acland; m. 1st Clare Anne Verdon 1956 (died 1984); two s. one d.; m. 2nd Jennifer McGougan (née Dyke) 1987; ed Eton Coll., Christ Church, Oxford; joined diplomatic service 1953; at Middle East Centre for Arab Studies 1954; served in Dubai 1955, Kuwait 1956; Foreign Office 1958–62; Asst Pvt. Sec. to Sec. of State 1959–62; mem. UK Mission to UN 1962–66; Head of Chancery, UK Mission, Geneva 1966–68; FCO 1968–, Head of Arabian Dept 1970–72; Prin. Pvt. Sec. to Foreign and Commonwealth Sec. 1972–75; Amb. to Luxembourg 1975–77, to Spain 1977–79; Deputy Under-Sec. of State, FCO 1980–82, Perm. Under-Sec. of State and Head of Diplomatic Service 1982–86; Amb. to USA 1986–91; Provost of Eton 1991–2000; Chancellor Order of St Michael and St George 1994–; Dir Shell Transport and Trading 1991–2000, Booker PLC 1992–99; Chair. of the Council of the Ditchley Foundation 1991–96, Chair. Tidy Britain Group 1991–96, Pres. 1996–2002; Trustee Nat. Portrait Gallery 1991–99, Esmée Fairbairn Foundation 1991–; Hon. DCL (Exeter) 1988, (William and Mary Coll., USA) 1990, (Reading) 1991. *Address:* Staddon Farm, nr Winsford, Minehead, Somerset, TA24 7HY, England.

ACOGNY, Germaine; Senegalese dancer and choreographer; b. Benin State, Nigeria; m. Helmut Vogt; f. pvt. professional dance school, Dakar; Dir Mudra Africa Int. Dance School, Dakar –1982; worked in Brussels with Maurice Béjart; dancer, choreographer with Peter Gabriel 1984; first solo performance Sahel 1984; collaborated with drummer Arona N'Diaye to stage Ye'ou, the Awakening 1985; performance at World of Music and Dance Festival 1993; co-f. (with Helmut Vogt) Studio-Ecole-Ballet-Theatre of the Third World, Toulouse, France; f. The School of Sands (L'École des sables maison int. de danse), Toubab Dialaw, Senegal 1995; f. Jant Bi Dance Co.; Artistic Dir Dance Section, Afrique en Creations/AFAA (French Asscn for Artistic Action) 1997–2000; also Artistic Dir Contemporary African Dance Competition; London Dance and Performance Award for Ye'ou, the Awakening 1991. *Dance:* works include Le Coq est Mort (The Rooster is Dead). *Publication:* African Dance 1980. *Address:* Association Jant Bi, 22 rue de Thiong, Dakar; BP 6078, Dakar-Etoile, Senegal. *Telephone:* (221) 8210109. *Fax:* (221) 8229095.

ACZÉL, János D., PhD, FRSC; Canadian (b. Hungarian) mathematician; b. 26 Dec. 1924, Budapest; s. of Dezsö Aczél and Irén Aczél; m. Susan Kende 1946; two d.; ed D. Berzsenyi High School, Univ. of Budapest; Teaching Asst, Univ. of Budapest 1946–48; Statistician, Metal Workers' Trade Union, Budapest 1948; Asst Prof., Univ. of Szeged 1948–50; Assoc. Prof. and Dept Head, Tech. Univ., Miskolc 1950–52; Dept Head, Assoc. Prof. then Prof., L. Kossuth Univ., Debrecen 1952–65; Prof., Univ. of Waterloo, Ont., Canada 1965–, Distinguished Prof. 1969–93, Distinguished Prof. Emer. 1993–; many visiting professorships and fellowships, N America, Europe, Africa, Asia and Australia 1963–; Chair. Int. Symposia on Functional Equations 1962–96, Hon. Chair. 1997–; mem. Canadian Math. Soc., American Math. Soc., Austrian Math. Soc., New York Acad. of Science; Foreign Fellow Hungarian Acad. of Sciences 1990; Fellow Royal Soc. of Canada 1971 (Convener Math. Div. 1974–75, Chair. Acad. of Science Editorial Cttee 1977–78); donor L. Fejér-J. Aczél Scholarship, Univ. of Waterloo; Dr hc (Karlsruhe) 1990, (Graz) 1995, (Katowice) 1996, (Miskolc) 1999; M. Beke Award (J. Bolyai Math. Soc.) 1961, Award of Hungarian Acad. of Sciences 1962, Cajal Medal (Nat. Research Council of Spain) 1988. *Publications:* over 300 articles and ten books, including Lectures on Functional Equations and their Applications 1966, A Short Course on Functional Equations Based upon Recent Applications to the Social and Behavioral Sciences 1987, Functional Equations in Several Variables (with J. Dhombres) 1989; Hon. Ed.-in-Chief Aequationes Math; Ed. Theory and Decision Library, Series B and six int. mathematical journals. *Leisure interests:* reading, swimming, walking. *Address:* Department of Pure Mathematics, University of Waterloo, Waterloo, Ont., N2L 3G1 (Office); 97 McCarron Crescent, Waterloo, Ont., N2L 5M9, Canada (Home). *Telephone:* (519) 888-4567 Ext. 6846 (Office). *Fax:* (519) 725-0160. *E-mail:* jdaczel@math.uwaterloo.ca (Office).

ADA, Gordon Leslie, AO, DSc, FAA; Australian microbiologist; b. 6 Dec. 1922, Sydney; s. of W. L. Ada and Erica Flower; m. Jean MacPherson 1946; three s. one d.; ed Fort Street Boy's High School, Sydney and Univ. of Sydney; Research Scientist Nat. Inst. for Medical Research, London 1946–48, Walter and Eliza Hall Inst., Melbourne 1948–68 (Head of Unit 1962–68); apptd Fellow Australian Acad. of Science 1964, Council Mem.1972–75, Foreign Sec. 1977–81; Pres. Australian Biochemical Soc. 1966–67; Head Dept of Microbiology, John Curtin School of Medical Research, Australian Nat. Univ. 1968–88, Prof. Emer.; Pres. Australian Soc. for Immunology 1975–76; mem. and Chair. Scientific Council, Int. Agency for Research on Cancer, Lyon; mem. Scientific and Tech. Advisory Cttee WHO, UNDP and World Bank Special Programme on Tropical Diseases; mem. Global Advisory Council for Medical Research, WHO 1981–84; Chair. WHO Programme on Vaccine Devt 1984–; Consultant WHO 1988–; Assoc. Dir, then Dir, Johns Hopkins School of Hygiene and Public Health, Baltimore 1988–91, elected mem. Johns Hopkins Soc. of Scholars 2001. *Publications:* Antigens, Lymphoid Cells and the Immune Response (with G. J. V. Nossal) 1971; about 180 scientific papers on virology and immunology. *Leisure interests:* sailing, music, walking. *Address:* 71 Parkhill Street, Pearce, ACT 2605, Australia. *Telephone:* (62) 86-2044.

ADABASHYAN, Aleksander Artemovich; Russian scriptwriter, artist and actor; b. 8 March 1945, Moscow; m. Shadrina Yekaterina Igorevna; two d.; ed Moscow (Stroganov) Higher School of Art and Design; began career as art dir working with Nikita Mikhalkov. *Films include:* (art dir) At Home Among Strangers, A Stranger at Home 1975, Kinsfolk 1982, Unfinished Piece for Mechanical Piano (scriptwriter/co-scriptwriter), Five Evenings, Several

Days in the Life of Oblomov, Trans-Siberian Express, The Slave of Love (artistic designer) 1976, Mado, Poste Restante (Dir). *Address:* Novy Arbat str. 31, Apt. 36, 121099 Moscow, Russia. *Telephone:* (095) 205-00-89.

ADAM, André; Belgian diplomatist; b. Sept. 1936, Brussels; m.; four c.; ed Univ. of Brussels; fmr research Asst Dept of Applied Econs, Univ. of Brussels; joined Diplomatic Service 1962, postings in Havana, Paris, Kinshasa and London 1964–78, Chief of Staff of Minister for Foreign Affairs 1979, Head, Energy Div. Ministry for Foreign Affairs 1980–82, Consul-Gen., Los Angeles 1982–86, Amb. to Algeria 1986–90, to Zaire 1990–91, Dir-Gen. for Political Affairs 1991–94, Amb. to USA 1994–98, Perm. Rep. to UN 1998–2001. *Address:* c/o Ministry of Foreign Affairs, 15 rue des Petits Carmes, 1000 Brussels, Belgium.

ADAM, Ken, OBE; British film designer; b. 1921, Berlin, Germany; ed St Paul's School, London Univ.; studied architecture; served six years in RAF in World War II; started film career as draughtsman on set of This Was a Woman 1947; production designer of seven James Bond films. *Films include:* Artistic Dir: The Devil's Pass, Soho Incident, Around the World in Eighty Days; Production Designer: Golden Earrings 1947, Curse of the Demon 1957, Dr No 1962, Woman of Straw 1964, Goldfinger 1964, Dr. Strangelove 1964, Thunderball 1965, Funeral in Berlin 1966, Goodbye Mr Chips 1969, Diamonds Are Forever 1971, Sleuth 1972, The Last of Sheila 1973, Barry Lyndon (Acad. Award) 1975, Patriots, Chitty Chitty Bang Bang, The Spy Who Loved Me 1977, Pennies from Heaven 1981, King David 1985, Agnes of God 1985, Crimes of the Heart 1986, The Deceivers 1988, The Freshman 1990, The Doctor 1991, Company Business 1991, Undercover Blues 1993, Addams Family Values 1993, The Madness of King George (Acad. Award 1994) 1994, Boys on the Side 1995, Bogus 1996, In and Out 1997, The Out-of-Towners 1999, The White Hotel, Taking Sides; designed sets for La Fanciulla del West, Royal Opera House, London.

ADAM, Robert, RIBA; British architect; b. 10 April 1948, Hants.; s. of Robert W. Adam and Jessie M. Adam; m. Sarah J. Chalcraft 1970; one s. one d.; ed Canford School and Regent Street Polytechnic; Partner 1977–, Dir 1987–, Roberts and Partners, subsequently Winchester Design (Architects) Ltd Trustee 1989–98; Chair. Faculty of Fine Arts, British School at Rome 1993–97; Chair. Popular Housing Forum 1997–; mem. Council RIBA 1999–, Hon. Sec. 2001–; Bannister Fletcher Prize 1973; Rome Scholarship 1973–74. *Publications:* In Defence of Historicism 1981, Tin Gods 1989, Classical Architecture: A Complete Handbook 1990, Classical Design in the Late 20th Century 1990, Buildings by Design 1994; papers in Architectural Review, Architects Journal, RIBA Journal, Architectural Design, City Journal (USA), Archis (Netherlands). *Leisure interests:* medieval history, ceramics. *Address:* Robert Adam Architects, 9 Upper High Street, Winchester, Hants., SO23 8UT, England (Office). *Telephone:* (1962) 843843 (Office). *E-mail:* admin@robertadamarchitects.com (Office). *Website:* www.robertadamarchitects.com (Office).

ADAM, Theo; German concert singer; b. 1 Aug. 1926, Dresden; s. of Johannes Adam and Lisbeth Adam (née Dernstorf); m. Eleonore Matthes 1949; one s. one d.; ed Gymnasium and Conservatory; engagements with Dresden State Opera 1949, Bayreuth Festival 1952–80, Salzburg Festival 1969, 1970, 1980–89, 1992, 1995; mem. Deutsche Staatsoper, Berlin 1953–; has appeared with Vienna and Munich State Operas since 1967; Pres. of Curatorium Oper, Dresden 1985–; sang at Semper Oper House, Dresden 1985; staged Graun's Cesare e Cleopatra, Berlin State Opera 1992; performed at Royal Festival Hall, London 1994, Berlin Staatsoper 1997; numerous recordings; Österreichischer Kammersänger, Bayerischer Kammersänger; Nat. Prize (First Class) of GDR. *Publications:* Seht, hier ist Tinte, Feder, Papier 1980, Die 100 Rolle, Wie schön ist doch die Musik 1996. *Leisure interest:* swimming. *Address:* Schillerstrasse 14, 01326 Dresden, Germany. *Telephone:* (351) 2683997.

ADAMI, Franco; Italian sculptor; b. 19 Nov. 1933, Pisa; s. of Toscano Adami and Giuseppina Bertoncini; m. Jacqueline Sylvius; one s. two d.; ed Leonardo da Vinci Inst., Pisa, Scuola d'Arte, Cascina and School of Fine Arts, Florence; Sculpture Prize of Cascina 1957; Prix Fernand Dupré for sculpture (France) 1981, Prix Charles Oulmont, Fondation de France 1987. *One-man shows include:* Centroartemoderna, Pisa 1977, Galerie Matignon, Paris 1978, Galerie Mitkal, Abidjan 1979. *Other exhibitions include:* Salon des Réalités Nouvelles 1976, Crédit Lyonnais, Paris 1980, Int. Exhbn of Sculpture, Strasbourg 1981, European Biennale of Sculpture at Jouy-sur-Eure to mark anniversary of Treaty of Rome 1982, Musée Antoine Lecuyer, St Quentin 1983, Pisan Sculpture from XIVth century to Present Day, Villa Medicis de San Giuliano 1983, UNICEF, Rouen 1986, Castello Malaspina, Carrara 1986, Galerie Triade, Barbizon 1987, Theodor Zink Museum, Kaiserlauten (Germany) 1987, Gallery K, Paris 1988, Salon 'Comparaisons', Paris 1988, Galerie Reymondin, Geneva 1989, FIAC 1989 and FIAC 1990, Galerie K, Paris, Art Jonction, Galerie Capazza, Nice 1990. *Leisure interests:* antiques. *Address:* Via del Vicinato 13, Pontestrada, 55045 Piatrasanta, Italy (Studio); 250 rue du Faubourg Saint-Antoine, 75012 Paris, France. *Telephone:* (058) 471317. *Fax:* (058) 471317.

ADAMISHIN, Anatoly Leonidovich, CandHistSc; Russian diplomatist, politician (retd) and business executive; b. 11 Oct. 1934, Kiev, USSR (now Ukraine); m. Svetlana Adamishina; one d.; ed Moscow State Univ.; diplomatic service 1957–; Third, then Second Sec. Embassy, Rome 1959–65; counsellor in First European Countries Dept, Ministry of Foreign Affairs 1965–71,

counsellor in Dept of Gen. Int. Problems 1973–78, Head of First European Dept 1978–86; mem. of Collegium, Ministry of Foreign Affairs 1979; Deputy Minister of Foreign Affairs 1986–90, First Deputy Minister 1992–94; Pres. USSR Comm. for UNESCO 1987–90; USSR (now Russian) Amb. to Italy 1990–92, to UK 1994–97; Minister for Co-operation with CIS Countries 1997–98; Vice-Pres. Systema Corpn 1998–; Head of Chair., Prof. Russian Acad. of State Service 1998; mem. State Duma (Parl.) 1993–95. *Publications:* The Decline and Revival of the Great Power 1993, The White Sun of Angola 2001. *Leisure interests:* classical music, opera, tennis. *Address:* Financial Corporation Systema, Leontyevski per. 10, 103009 Moscow (Office); Apt 170, 2/1 Kutuzovski, Moscow, Russia (Home). *Telephone:* (095) 229-51-28 (Office); (095) 243-53-81 (Home). *Fax:* (095) 232-33-91 (Office); (095) 243-53-81 (Home). *E-mail:* adamishin@dialup.ptt.ru (Home).

ADAMKUS, Valdas; Lithuanian politician and fmr President; b. 3 Nov. 1926, Kaunas, Lithuania; m. Alma Adamkiene; ed Munich Univ., Univ. of Ill., Ill. Inst. of Tech.; resistance Movt World War II; left Lithuania; on staff World YMCA, Sec.-Gen. and Chair. Chief Physical Training and Sports Cttee; emigrated to USA 1949; worked in Chicago sports cars factory, draftsman Eng Co.; f. Academic Sports Club of American Lithuanians 1951; Chair. Bd of Santara Cen. of Lithuanian Students in USA 1957–58; Vice-Chair., Chair. Santara-Sviesa Fed. of Lithuanian Émigrés 1958–67; mem. of Bd Lithuanian Community in USA 1961–64; Deputy Chair. Cen. Bd, mem., Chair. American Lithuanian Community; Chair. Org. Cttee World Lithuanian Games 1983; fmr Head Scientific Research Cen. Environment Protection Agency, Admin. for Mid-W Regions Environment Protection Agency, USA, active participation in political life of Lithuania 1993–; Pres. of Lithuania 1998–2002; Dr hc (Vilnius) 1989, (Indiana St Joseph Coll.) 1991, (Northwestern Univ.) 1994, (Kaunas, American Catholic Univs) 1998, (Lithuanian Agricultural Univ., Ill. Inst. of Tech.) 1999, (Lev-Gumilev Euro-Asian Univ. Kazakhstan) 2000, (De Paul Univ.Chicago, Law Univ.of Lithuania) 2001; Gold Medal of US Environment Protection Agency, US Distinguished Service Award. *Address:* c/o Office of the President, Simono Daukanto sq. 3, 2600 Vilnius, Lithuania (Office). *Telephone:* (2) 612-811.

ADAMOV, Yevgeny Olegovich, DTechSC.; Russian politician and engineer; b. 28 April 1939, Moscow; m.; two d.; ed Moscow Aviation Inst.; engineer, Deputy Dir I. Kurchatov Inst. of Nuclear Energy (NIKIET) 1962–86; Prof. Moscow Aviation Inst. 1965–; took part in Chernobyl Nuclear Power Station recovery work May–Aug. 1986; Dir, Constructor-Gen. Research Inst. of Energy Tech. 1986–98, Scientific Dir 2001–; Minister of Nuclear Energy 1998–2001; mem. Russian Acad. of Eng, New York Acad. of Sciences. *Publications:* over 100 books, papers and articles on man., econs of energy resources, nuclear energy, informatics. *Leisure interest:* reading books. *Address:* NIKIET, Krasnoselskaya M. str. 2/8 a/y 788, 107140 Moscow, Russia. *Telephone:* (095) 264-46-10 (Office).

ADAMS, Bryan; Canadian/British rock singer and photographer; b. 5 Nov. 1959; Vancouver; signed contract with A&M Records 1979; 45 million albums sold world-wide (1995); awards: Diamond Sales Award (for Reckless), 12 Juno Awards, Recording Artist of the Decade, Canada; Order of Canada, Order of British Columbia. *Albums include:* Cuts Like a Knife 1983, Reckless 1984, Into the Fire 1987, Waking up the Neighbours 1991, So Far So Good 1992, 18 'Til I Die 1996, The Best of Me 2000. *Soundtrack:* Spirit: Stallion of Cimarron. *Photography exhibitions:* Toronto, Montréal, Saatchi Gallery London, Royal Jubilee Exhbn Windsor Castle 2002. *Publications:* Bryan Adams: The Official Biography 1995, Made in Canada, Photographs by Bryan Adams. *Address:* c/o Press Department, A&M Records, 136–144 New King's Road, London, SW6 4LZ, England. *Telephone:* (20) 7705-4343. *Fax:* (20) 7731-4606.

ADAMS, Gerard (Gerry); Northern Irish politician; b. 6 Oct. 1948, Falls Road, Belfast; s. of Gerard Adams and Annie Hannaway; m. Colette McCardle 1971; one s.; ed St Mary's Christian Bros School, Belfast; worked as a barman; founder mem. NI Civil Rights Asscn; mem. Belfast Housing Action Cttee; interned in Long Kesh under suspicion of being a terrorist March 1972; released to take part in secret London talks between Sec. of State for NI and Irish Republican Army (IRA) July 1972; rearrested 1973, attempted to escape from Maze Prison, sentenced to 18 months' imprisonment, released Feb. 1977; charged with membership of Provisional IRA Feb. 1978, freed after 7 months because of insufficient evidence for conviction; Pres. of Sinn Féin Nov. 1983– (Vice-Pres. 1978–83); MP for Belfast West 1983–92, May 1997–; mem. NI Ass. for Belfast West 1998–2000 (Ass. suspended 11 Feb. 2000); involved in peace negotiations with British Government; Thorr Award, Switzerland 1995. *Publications:* Falls Memory, Politics of Irish Freedom, Pathway to Peace 1988, Cage 11 (autobiog.) 1990, The Street and Other Stories 1992, Selected Writings 1994, Our Day Will Come (autobiog.) 1996, Before the Dawn (autobiog.) 1996, An Irish Voice 1997, An Irish Journal 2001. *Address:* Sinn Féin, 51–55 Falls Road, Belfast, BT12 4PD, Northern Ireland (Office). *Telephone:* (28) 9032-3214 (Office). *Fax:* (28) 9023-1723. *E-mail:* sinnfein@iol.ie. *Website:* www.sinnfein.ie.

ADAMS, John Coolidge; American composer and conductor; b. 15 Feb. 1947, Worcester, MA; ed Harvard Univ.; appearances as clarinettist and conductor; Head, Composition Dept, San Francisco Conservatory of Music 1971–81; Adviser on new music, San Francisco Symphony Orchestra 1978–82, Composer-in-Residence 1982–85; conducted Nixon in China at 1988 Edinburgh Festival; Creative Adviser, St Paul Chamber Orchestra, MN 1988–89; The Death of Klinghoffer premiered at Brussels, Lyon and Vienna

1991 (London premiere at Barbican Hall 2002); I Was Looking at the Ceiling performed at Berkeley, New York, Paris, Edinburgh and Hamburg 1995; Guggenheim Fellowship 1982, Grawemeyer Award for Music Composition 1995. *Compositions include:* opera: Nixon in China 1987, The Death of Klinghoffer 1991, I Was Looking at the Ceiling and Then I Saw the Sky 1995; orchestral works: Shaker Loops 1978, Common Tones in Simple Time 1979, Harmonium 1980, Grand Pianola Music 1981–82, Harmonielehre 1984–85, The Chairman Dances 1985, Short Ride in a Fast Machine 1986, Tromba Lontana 1986, Fearful Symmetries 1988, The Wound-Dresser 1989, Eros Piano 1989, El Dorado 1991, Violin Concerto 1993, Gnarly Buttons 1996; chamber and ensemble works: Christian Zeal and Activity 1973, China Gates 1977, Phrygian Gates 1977, Chamber Symphony 1992, John's Book of Alleged Dances 1994, Road Movies 1995, Naïve and Sentimental Music 1998, El Niño 2000, Guide to Strange Places 2001, On the Transmigration of Souls (Pulitzer Prize for Music 2003) 2002. *Address:* c/o Boosey & Hawkes Ltd, 295 Regent Street, London, W1R 8JH, England.

ADAMS, Norman (Edward Albert), RA, ARCA, RWS; British painter and professor of fine art; b. 9 Feb. 1927, London; s. of Albert Henry Adams and Winifred Elizabeth Rose Adams; m. Anna Teresa Butt 1947; two s.; ed Harrow School of Art, Royal Coll. of Art, London; first exhbn Young Contemporaries 1950; numerous solo exhbns. in London, N England, Scotland and USA; exhbns with British Council 1954–55; retrospective exhbn, RA 1988; fmr teacher at St Albans, Maidstone, Hammersmith Art Schools and Royal Acad. Schools; Head, School of Painting, Manchester Coll. of Art and Design 1962–70; elected Assoc. of Royal Acad. 1967; Lecturer, Leeds Univ. 1975–78; Prof. of Fine Art and Dir of King Edward VII Coll., Univ. of Newcastle-upon-Tyne 1981–86; Prof. of Painting, Royal Acad. of Arts, London 1986–99, Prof. Emer. 1999–, Keeper 1986–95, Keeper Emer. 1995–; comms: murals for St Anselm's, Kennington, London 1971–72, Stations of the Cross for Our Lady of Lourdes, Milton Keynes 1974–75, Stations of the Cross St Mary's (The Hidden Gem) Mulberry Street, Manchester (permanently installed in St Mary's) 1995; Hon. mem. Royal Soc. of British Watercolourists 1990; Korn Ferry Award (RA) 2000. *Public collections include:* Tate Gallery, London, Scottish Nat. Gallery of Modern Art, Edinburgh, Ulster Museum, Belfast, Nat. Gallery of New Zealand, Wellington, Cartwright Hall, Bradford, Leeds City Art Gallery, Wakefield City Art Gallery. *Publications:* Alibis and Convictions 1978, A Decade of Painting 1971–81 1981, Angels of Soho 1988, Island Chapters 1991, Life on Limestone 1994. *Leisure interests:* art, music, literature. *Address:* 6 Gainsborough Road, Chiswick, London, W4 1NJ (Home); Butts, Horton-in-Ribblesdale, Settle, N Yorks, BD24 0HD, England (Home). *Telephone:* (20) 8747-3073; (1729) 860284.

ADAMS, Paul Nicholas, BA; British business executive; b. 12 March 1953, Manchester; s. of Peter Charles Adams and Joan Adams; one s. two d.; ed Culford School and Ealing Coll.; Marketing Dir Beecham Int. 1983–86; Vice-Pres. of Marketing for Europe, Pepsi-Cola Int. 1986–91; joined British American Tobacco PLC 1991, Regional Dir for Asia Pacific, 1991–99, for Europe 1999–2001, Man. Dir 2002–. *Leisure interests:* theatre, golf, rugby. *Address:* British American Tobacco PLC, Globe House, 4 Temple Place, London, WC2R 2PG, England (Office). *Telephone:* (20) 7845-1936 (Office). *Fax:* (20) 7845-2184 (Office). *Website:* www.bat.com (Office).

ADAMS, Phillip Andrew, AO; Australian writer, broadcaster and film-maker; b. 12 July 1939; m. 1st (divorced); three d.; m. 2nd Patrice Newell; one d.; ed Eltham High School; columnist and critic 1956–; Chair. Film, Radio and TV Bd 1972–75; Founder-mem. Australia Council 1972–75; Vic. Govt Rep. Australian Children's TV Foundation 1981–87; Pres. Vic. Council for Arts 1982–86; Chair. Australian Film Inst. 1975–80, Australian Film Comm. 1983–90, Comm. for the Future 1985–90, Nat. Australia Day Council 1992–96; mem. Bd Ausflag 1990–; mem. Cttee for the Centenary of Fed. 1994; worked with Families in Distress 1985–, Montsalvat Artists' Soc. 1986–, CARE Australia 1995–97; mem. Bd Nat. Museum of Australia 1996–97, Festival of Ideas 1999; mem. Council, Adelaide Festival 1996; Hon. DUniv (Queensland Univ.) 1998; Sr ANZAC Fellow 1981; Raymond Longford Award 1981, Australian Arts Award 1987, Australian Humanist of the Year 1987, CSICOP Award for Responsibility in Media (New York) 1996. *Films include:* Jack and Jill: A Postcript 1970, The Naked Bunyip 1971, The Adventures of Barry McKenzie 1972, Don's Party 1975, The Getting of Wisdom 1976, Grendel Grendel Grendel 1980, We of the Never Never 1982, Lonely Hearts 1982, Fighting Back 1983. *Radio includes:* Compere, Late Night Live (ABC). *Television includes:* Death and Destiny, Short and Sweet (ABC), Adam's Australia (BBC), The Big Question, Face the Press (SBS). *Publications:* Adams With Added Enzymes 1970, The Unspeakable Adams 1977, More Unspeakable Adams 1979, The Uncensored Adams 1981, The Inflammable Adams 1983, Adams Versus God 1985, Harold Cazneaux: The Quiet Observer (with H. Ennis) 1994, Classic Columns 1994, The Penguin Book of Australian Jokes (with P. Newell) 1994, The Penguin Book of Jokes from Cyberspace (with P. Newell) 1995, The Big Questions (with P. Davies) 1996, The Penguin Book of More Australian Jokes 1996, Kookaburra 1996, Emperors of the Air 1997, Retreat from Tolerance? 1997, More Big Questions (with P. Davies) 1998, The Penguin Book of Schoolyard Jokes (with P. Newell) 1998, A Billion Voices 1999, The Penguin Book of All New Australian Jokes (with P. Newell) 2000. *Leisure interests:* archaeology, reading. *Address:* c/o Radio National, ABC, GPO Box 9994, Sydney, NSW 2001, Australia (Office).

ADAMS, Richard George, MA, FRSA, FRSL; British novelist; b. 9 May 1920, Newbury, Berks.; s. of Dr E. G. B. Adams, FRCS and Lilian Rosa (Button) Adams; m. Barbara Elizabeth Acland 1949; two d.; ed Bradfield Coll., Berks. and Worcester Coll., Oxford; army service 1940–46; Home Civil Service 1948–74; Pres. Royal Soc. for the Prevention of Cruelty to Animals 1980–82; Writer-in-Residence, Univ. of Florida, 1975, Hollins Coll., Va 1976; Carnegie Medal 1972, Guardian Award for Children's Fiction 1972, Medal of California Young Readers' Asscn 1977. *Publications:* Watership Down 1972, Shardik 1974, Nature Through the Seasons, The Tyger Voyage 1976, The Plague Dogs 1977 (filmed 1982), The Ship's Cat 1977, Nature Day and Night 1978, The Girl in a Swing 1980 (filmed 1988), The Unbroken Web (The Iron Wolf) 1980, Voyage Through the Antarctic 1982, Maia 1984, The Bureaucats 1985, A Nature Diary 1985, Occasional Poets: anthology (ed. and contributor) 1986, The Legend of Te Tuna 1986, Traveller 1988, The Day Gone By (autobiog.) 1990, Tales From Watership Down 1996, The Outlandish Knight 2000. *Leisure interests:* chess, ornithology, folk-song, country pursuits, fly-fishing, travel. *Address:* 26 Church Street, Whitchurch, Hants., RG28 7AR, England.

ADAMS, Robert McCormick, Jr., PhD; American anthropologist; b. 23 July 1926, Chicago, Ill.; s. of Robert McCormick Adams and Janet Adams (née Lawrence); m. Ruth Salzman Skinner 1953; one d.; ed Univ. of Chicago; Instructor, Univ. of Chicago 1955–57, Asst Prof. 1957–61, Assoc. Prof. 1961–62, Prof. 1962–84, Dir Oriental Inst. 1962–68, 1981–83, Prof. of Anthropology 1963, Dean of Social Sciences 1970–74, 1979–80, Univ. Provost 1982–84; Sec. Smithsonian Inst. 1984–93; Homewood Prof. Johns Hopkins Univ. 1984; Adjunct Prof. Univ. of Calif., San Diego 1993–; Chair. Ass. of Behavioral and Social Sciences, Nat. Research Council 1973–76; Visiting Prof., Harvard 1962, 1977, Univ. of Calif. (Berkeley) 1963; Annual Prof., Baghdad School, American Schools of Oriental Research 1966–67; Fellow Inst. for Advanced Study, Berlin 1995–96; field research in Iraq, Iran, Mexico, Saudi Arabia and Syria; Lewis Henry Morgan Prof. Univ. of Rochester 1965; Councillor, NAS 1981 (mem.); mem. American Acad. of Arts and Sciences, American Anthropological Asscn, AAAS, Middle East Studies Asscn, American Philosophical Soc., German Archaeological Inst.; Trustee, National Opinion Research Center 1970–94, Nat. Humanities Center 1976–83, Russell Sage Foundation 1978–91, Santa Fe Inst. 1989–; numerous hon. degrees; UCLA Medal 1989; Great Cross of Vasco Nuñez de Balboa (Panama) 1993. *Publications:* Land Behind Baghdad: A History of Settlement on the Diyala Plains 1965, The Evolution of Urban Society: Early Mesopotamia and Prehispanic Mexico 1966, (with H. J. Nissen) The Uruk Countryside 1972, Heartland of Cities 1981, (with N. J. Smelser and D. J. Treiman) Behavioral and Social Science Research: A National Resource (2 Vols) 1982, Paths of Fire 1996. *Leisure interests:* skiing, mountaineering. *Address:* 2810 31st Street, NW, Washington, DC; PO Box ZZ, Basalt, CO 81621; University of California-San Diego, 9500 Gilman Drive, La Jolla CA 92093-0532 USA (Office). *Telephone:* (202) 965-0456 (Home); (303) 927-3380 (Home). *E-mail:* rmadams@ucsd.edu (Office). *Website:* www.anthro.ucsd.edu (Office).

ADCOCK, Fleur, OBE, MA, FRSL; British writer; b. 10 Feb. 1934, New Zealand; d. of Cyril John Adcock and Irene Robinson; m. 1st Alistair Teariki Campbell 1952 (divorced 1958); two s.; m. 2nd Barry Crump 1962 (divorced 1966); Asst Lecturer Univ. of Otago 1958, Asst Librarian 1959–61; with Alexander Turnbull Library 1962; with FCO 1963–79; freelance writer 1979–; Northern Arts Fellowship in Literature Univs. of Newcastle-upon-Tyne and Durham 1979–81; Eastern Arts Fellowship Univ. of E Anglia 1984; Writer-in-Residence Univ. of Adelaide 1986; Buckland Award 1967, 1979; Jessie MacKay Award 1968, 1972; Cholmondeley Award 1976; NZ Book Award 1984. *Publications:* The Eye of the Hurricane 1964, Tigers 1967, High Tide in the Garden 1971, The Scenic Route 1974, The Inner Harbour 1979, Below Loughrigg 1979, The Oxford Book of Contemporary New Zealand Poetry 1982, Selected Poems 1983, The Virgin and the Nightingale: Medieval Latin Poems 1983, Hotspur: A Ballad for Music 1986, The Incident Book 1986, The Faber Book of 20th Century Women's Poetry 1987, Orient Express: Poems by Grete Tartler (translator) 1989, Time Zones 1991, Letters from Darkness: Poems by Daniela Crasnaru (translator) 1991, High Primas and the Archpoet (ed. and translator) 1994, The Oxford Book of Creatures (ed. with Jacqueline Simms) 1995, Looking Back 1997, Poems 1960–2000 2000. *Address:* 14 Lincoln Road, London, N2 9DL, England. *Telephone:* (20) 8444-7881.

ADDIS, Richard James, MA; British journalist; b. 23 Aug. 1956; s. of Richard Thomas Addis and Jane Addis; m. Eunice Minogue 1983 (divorced 2000); one s. two d.; ed West Downs Prep. School, Rugby, Downing Coll., Cambridge; with Evening Standard 1985–89; Deputy Ed. Sunday Telegraph 1989–91; Exec. Ed. Daily Mail 1991–95; Ed. Daily Express 1995–98, The Express on Sunday 1996–98; Consultant Ed. Mail on Sunday 1998–99; Ed. The Globe and Mail, Toronto 1999–2002; Asst Ed. and Design Ed., Financial Times 2002–; apptd Hon. Gov. York Univ., Canada 2002. *Leisure interests:* dancing, tennis, elementary music-making, mountains. *Address:* Financial Times, One Southwark Bridge, London, SE1 9HL, England (Office). *Telephone:* (20) 7873-3000. *Fax:* (20) 7873-3076. *Website:* www.ft.com.

ADDISON, Mark Eric, MA, MSc, PhD; British civil servant; b. 22 Jan. 1951; s. of Sydney Robert James Addison and Prudence Margaret Addison (née Russell); m. Lucinda Clare Booth 1987; ed Marlborough Coll., St John's Coll., Cambridge, City Univ., Imperial Coll.; with Dept of Employment 1978–95, Pvt. Sec. to Parl. Under-Sec. of State 1982, Pvt. Sec. to Prime Minister 1985–88; Regional Dir London Training Agency 1988–91, Dir Finance and Resource Man. 1991–94; Dir Safety Policy Health and Safety Exec. 1994–97; Dir Better Regulation Unit, Office of Public Service 1997–98; Chief Exec. Crown Prosecution Service 1998–2001; Dir-Gen. (Operations and Service

Delivery), Dept for Environment, Food and Rural Affairs 2001–. *Leisure interests:* British motorbikes, windsurfing, photography. *Address:* Department for Environment, Food and Rural Affairs, 1a Page Street, London, SW1P 4PQ, England. *Telephone:* (20) 7238-6951. *Fax:* (20) 7238-3329 (Office). *Website:* www.defra.gov.uk (Office).

ADEDEJI, Adebayo, the Asiwaju of Ijebu and Olotu'fore of Ijebu-Ode, BSc(Econ), MPA, PhD; Nigerian economist; b. 21 Dec 1930, Ijebu-Ode; s. of L. S. Adedeji; m. Susan Aderinola Ogun 1957; eight s. three d.; ed Ijebu-Ode Grammar School, Univ. Coll., Ibadan, Univ. Coll., Leicester and Harvard Univs; Asst Sec., Ministry of Econ. Planning, W Nigeria 1958–61, Principal Asst Sec. (Finance) 1962–63; Deputy Dir Inst. of Admin., Univ. of Ife 1963–66, Dir 1967– (on leave of absence 1971); Prof. of Public Admin., Univ. of Ife 1968– (on leave of absence 1971); Nat. Manpower Bd 1967–71; Fed. Commr for Econ. Devt and Reconstruction 1971–75; Chair. Directorate, Nigerian Youth Services Corps 1973–75; UN Under-Sec.-Gen. and Exec. Sec. UN Econ. Comm. for Africa 1975–91, Founder, Exec. Dir African Centre for Devt and Strategic Study (ACDESS) 1992–; Chair. Senate of UN Inst. for Namibia 1975; Founder and Ed., Quarterly Journal of Administration 1967–75; Fellow, Nigerian Inst. of Man., Nigerian Econ. Soc., African Acad. of Sciences, African Asscn for Public Admin. and Man.; Pres. Nigerian Econ. Soc. 1971–72; Pres. African Asscn for Public Admin. and Man. 1974–83; Vice-Chair. Asscn of Schools and Inst. of Admin. of Int. Inst. of Admin. Sciences 1970–; Head, Commonwealth Observer Group for Kenya's general elections Dec. 2002; Hon. DLitt (Ahmadu Bello Univ.); Hon. LLD (Dalhousie Univ., Univ. of Calabar, Univ. of Zambia); Hon. DSc (Obafemi Awolowo Univ.) and numerous awards and foreign decorations. *Publications:* A Survey of Highway Development in Western Nigeria 1960, Nigerian Administration and its Political Setting (Ed.) 1969, Nigerian Federal Finance: Its Development, Problems and Prospects 1969, Local Government Finance in Nigeria: Problems and Prospects (Co-ed.) 1972, Management Problems and Rapid Urbanisation in Nigeria (Co-ed.) 1973, The Tanzania Civil Service, A Decade After Independence 1974, Developing Research on African Administration: Some Methodological Issues (Co-ed.) 1974, Africa, The Third World and the Search for a New Economic Order 1977, Africa and the New International Economic Order: A Reassessment 1979, The Indigenization of the African Economy 1981, Economic Crisis in Africa: African Perspectives on Development Problems and Potentials (Co-ed.) 1985, Towards the Dawn of the Third Millennium and the Beginning of the Twenty-First Century 1986, Towards a Dynamic African Economy: Selected Speeches and Lectures 1975–1986 1989, African Within the World 1993, South Africa and Africa: Within or Apart? 1996, Nigeria: Renewal from the Roots? 1997, Comprehending and Mastering African Conflicts 1999. *Leisure interests:* photography, lawn tennis, golf, walking. *Address:* Asiwaju Court, Gra, Ijebu Ode, Nigeria. *Telephone:* 37-432208 (Office); 37-433000 (Home). *Fax:* 7-269-1746.

ADELI, (Seyed) Muhammad Hossein, PhD; Iranian banker; b. 1952, Ahwaz; m. Khadijeh Aryan; two s. one d.; Temp. Attaché in Canada 1979–80; Dir-Gen. of Econ. Affairs, Ministry of Foreign Affairs 1982–86; Amb. to Japan 1987–89; Gov. Bank Markazi Iran (Cen. Bank of Iran) 1990–95; Amb. to Canada 1995–99; Deputy Minister for Econ. Affairs, Ministry of Foreign Affairs 1999–. *Leisure interest:* reading. *Address:* Ministry of Foreign Affairs, Shahid Abd al-Hamid Mesri St, Ferdowsi Avenue, Tehran, Iran (Office). *Telephone:* (21) 3211 (Office). *Fax:* (21) 3113149 (Office). *E-mail:* matbuat@mfa.gov.ir (Office). *Website:* www.mfa.gov.ir (Office).

ADELMAN, Irma Glicman, PhD; American (b. Romanian) professor of economics; b. 14 March 1930, Romania; d. of the late Jacob Max Glicman and Raya Etingon; m. Frank Louis Adelman 1950 (divorced 1979); one s.; ed Univ. of Calif. at Berkeley; Asst Prof., Stanford Univ. 1960–62; Assoc. Prof. Johns Hopkins Univ. 1962–66; Prof. of Econs Northwestern Univ. 1967–72; Sr Economist, Devt Research Centre, IBRD 1971–72; Prof. of Econs, Univ. of Md 1972–79; Consultant US Dept of State 1963–72, IBRD 1968–, ILO, Geneva 1973–; Fellow Netherlands Inst. of Advanced Study, Cleveringa Chair Leiden Univ. 1977–78; Prof. of Econs and Agric. and Resource Econs, Univ. of Calif. at Berkeley 1979–94, Prof. Emer. 1994–; Vice-Pres. American Econ. Asscn 1979–80; Fellow American Acad. of Arts and Sciences, Econometric Soc., Royal Soc. for the Encouragement of the Arts, American Agricultural Econs Asscn; Order of the Bronze Tower (South Korea) 1971. *Publications:* Theories of Economic Growth and Development 1964, Society, Politics and Economic Development (with C.T. Morris) 1967, Economic Growth and Social Equity in Developing Countries (with C.T. Morris) 1973, Income Distribution Planning (with Sherman Robinson) 1978, Comparative Patterns of Economic Development: 1850–1914 (with C.T. Morris) 1988, Village Economies (with J. Edward Taylor) 1996, The Visible and Invisible Hand: The Case of Korea 2002. *Leisure interests:* art, theatre, music. *Address:* Agriculture and Resource Economics Department, 207 Gianninni Hall, University of California at Berkeley, Berkeley, CA 94720-3310 (Office); 10 Rosemont Avenue, Berkeley, CA 94708, USA (Home). *Telephone:* (510) 642-6417 (Office); (510) 527-5280 (Home). *Fax:* (510) 643-8911. *E-mail:* adelman@are.berkeley.edu. *Website:* are.berkeley.edu/~adelman.

ADELMAN, Kenneth Lee, PhD; American government official and university lecturer; b. 9 June 1946, Chicago, Ill.; s. of Harry Adelman and Corinne Unger; m. Carol Craigle 1971; two d.; ed Grinnell Coll., Georgetown Univ.; with USDept of Commerce 1968–70; Special Asst VISTA, Washington, DC 1970–72; Liaison Officer, AID 1975–76; Asst to Sec. of Defense 1975–77; Sr Political Scientist, Stanford Research Inst., Arlington, Va 1977–81; Amb. and Deputy Perm. Rep. to UN 1981–83; Dir Arms Control and Disarmament Agency (ACDA) 1983–88; Vice-Pres. Inst. of Contemporary Studies 1988–; Instructor in Shakespeare, Georgetown Univ. 1977–79; taught at George Washington Univ.; Co-Host Tech Cen. Station. *Publications:* The Great Universal Embrace 1989, The Defense Revolution (with N. Augustine, q.v.) 1990, Shakespeare in Charge: The Bard's Guide to Leading and Succeeding on the Business Stage (with Norman Augustine) 1999, and articles in newspapers, magazines and professional journals. *Address:* Tech Central Station, PO Box 33705, Washington, DC 20033, USA (Office). *Telephone:* (800) 619-5258. *Fax:* (202) 530-0255. *E-mail:* kadelman@techcentralstation.com. *Website:* www.techcentralstation.com.

ADELSOHN, Ulf, LLB; Swedish politician; b. 4 Oct. 1941, Stockholm; s. of Oskar Adelsohn and Margareta Adelsohn; m. Lena Liljeroth 1981; one s. one d.; legal adviser, Real Estate Co., Stockholm City 1968–70; Man.'s Asst, Swedish Confed. of Professional Asscns. 1970–73; Commr, Street and Traffic Dept, Stockholm City Admin. 1973–76; Mayor and Finance Commr 1976–79; Minister for Transport and Communications 1979–81; mem. Riksdagen (Parl.) 1982–88; Leader Moderata Samlingspartiet (Conservative Party) 1981–86; County Gov. of Stockholm 1992–2001; Chair. Luftfartsverket (Civil Aviation Authority) 1992–2002, Skansen (open air museum); Chair. Swedish Railways, Swedish Hotel and Restaurants Asscn; Sr Adviser Stockholm Chamber of Commerce, Ogilvy; King's Medal of the 12th Dimension with Ribbon of the Order of the Seraphims. *Publications:* Torsten Kreuger, Sanningen på väg (Torsten Kreuger, Truth on its Way) 1972, Kommunalmän: Hur skulle ni göra om det vore era egna pengar? (Local Politicians: What Would You Do If It Was Your Money?) 1978, Ulf Adelsohn Partiledare 1981–86 (Leader of the Party 1981–86) 1987, Priset för ett liv (The Price for a Life) 1991. *Leisure interests:* ice hockey, tennis. *Address:* Strandvägen 35, 114 56 Stockholm, Sweden. *Telephone:* (8) 212502 (Office). *E-mail:* ulf.adelsohn@setterwalls.se (Office).

ADENIJI, Oluyemi, BA; Nigerian diplomatist and international organization official; b. 22 July 1934, Ijebu-Ode; m.; ed Nigerian Coll. of Arts, Science and Technology, Ibadan, Univ. Coll., Ibadan, Univ. of London, UK; joined Foreign Service 1960; Minister in the Nigerian Perm. Mission to UN (New York) 1970–73; served in embassies in Washington DC, Freetown, Sierra Leone, and Accra, Ghana; apptd Amb. to Austria and Perm. Rep. to IAEA 1976; Amb. to Switzerland and Perm. Rep. to UN, Geneva 1977–81; with Ministry of Foreign Affairs 1981–87; Amb. to France 1987–91; Dir-Gen. Ministry of Foreign Affairs 1991–94; Special Rep. of the UN Sec.-Gen. for the Central African Republic (MINURCA); Special Rep. of the UN Sec.-Gen. for Sierra Leone and Chief of UN Mission in Sierra Leone (UNAMSIL) 1999–. *Address:* United Nations Mission in Sierra Leone (UNAMSIL), c/o Department of Peace-keeping Operations, UN, United Nations Plaza, New York, NY 10017, USA (Office). *Telephone:* (212) 963-9222 (Office). *Fax:* (212) 963-8079 (Office). *Website:* www.un.org.

ÁDER, János, DrIur; Hungarian politician; b. 1959, Csorna; s. of Terézia Szabó; m.; one s. two d.; ed Révai Miklós Grammar School, Győr, Loránd Eötvös Univ., Budapest; Council Exec. Dist VI, Budapest City Council 1983–85; researcher Sociology Research Inst., Hungarian Acad. of Sciences 1986–90; joined Fed. of Young Democrats (FIDESZ) 1988, Vice-Chair. 1993–, Exec. Vice-Chair. 1994–; MP 1990–98, MP as rep. of FIDESZ-Hungarian Civic Party coalition 1998–; Vice-Chair. of Parl. 1997–98; Speaker, Nat. Ass. 1998–2002. *Leisure interests:* angling, soccer. *Address:* c/o Magyar Polgári Párt—FIDESZ, 1062 Budapest, Lendvay u. 28, Hungary.

ADÈS, Thomas Joseph Edmund, MA, MPhil; British composer, pianist and conductor; b. 1 March 1971, London; s. of Timothy Adès and Dawn Adès; ed Univ. Coll. School, Guildhall School of Music, King's Coll., Cambridge, St John's Coll., Cambridge; Composer in Assoc., Hallé Orchestra 1993–95; lecturer Manchester Univ. 1993–94; Fellow Commoner in Creative Arts, Trinity Coll., Cambridge 1995–97; Benjamin Britten Prof. of Music, RAM 1997–99; Musical Dir Birmingham Contemporary Music Group 1998–2000; Artistic Dir Aldeburgh Festival 1999–; Royal Philharmonic Prize 1997, Elise L. Stoeger Prize 1998, Salzburg Easter Festival Prize 1999, Ernst von Siemens Prize 1999, Grawemeyer Prize 2000, Hindemith Prize 2001. *Music:* Five Eliot Landscapes, Chamber Symphony 1990, Catch 1991, Darknesse Visible 1992, Still Sorrowing, Life Story, Living Toys, ... but all shall be well, Sonata da Caccia 1993, Arcadiana (for string quartet) 1994, Powder Her Face (chamber opera) 1995, Traced Overhead, These Premises are Alarmed 1996, Asyla 1997, Concerto Conciso 1997–98, America (A Prophecy) 1999, Piano Quintet 2000, Brahms 2001. *Television includes:* Music for the 21st Century: Thomas Adès (Channel 4), Powder Her Face (Channel 4). *Address:* c/o Faber Music, 3 Queen Square, London, WC1N 3AU, England (Office). *Telephone:* (20) 7833-7911 (Office). *Fax:* (20) 7833-7939 (Office). *E-mail:* sally.cavender@fabermusic.com (Office). *Website:* www.fabermusic.com (Office).

ADESINA, Segun, DEd; Nigerian professor of education; b. 5 Jan. 1941, Abeokuta, Ogun State; s. of Samuel Adesina and Georgiette Adesina; m. 1968; five c.; ed Loyola Coll., Nigerian Coll. of Arts, Science & Tech., Univ. of Ife and N Ill. and Columbia Univs; history tutor, Loyola Coll. 1965–66; Asst Lecturer in Educ. Univ. of Lagos Coll. of Educ. 1967–69, Lecturer 1969–75; Sr Lecturer Univ. of Lagos Faculty of Educ. 1975–77, Assoc. Prof. 1977–78, Prof. of Educ. 1988–2000, now Dir Inst. of Educ.; fmr. Prof. of Educ. Ilorin Univ.; Visiting Prof. and Provost, Univ. of Ife, Adeyemi Coll. of Educ. Ondo 1984–85; Exec. Sec. Nigerian Educational Research Council 1987; Adviser on Educ. UN

Office, Geneva 1975–76; consultant, UNESCO, Senegal 1984; Fellow, Nigerian Inst. of Admin. Man.; Assoc. Inst. of Personnel Man.; mem. Nigerian Inst. of Man., Presidential Cttee on Brain Drain. *Publications:* Primary Education in Nigeria: A Book of Readings, Co-ed. Planning and Educational Development in Nigeria 1978, The Development of Modern Education in Nigeria 1988. *Address:* Nigerian Educational Research Council, 3 Jibowu Street, P.O. Box 8058, Yaba, Lagos (Office); PO Box 41, Abeokuta, Nigeria (Home). *Telephone:* (1) 822988 (Office); (39) 232226 (Home).

ADESOLA, Akin Oludele, MD, MCh, FRCS(Eng), FACS; Nigerian university professor; b. 6 Nov. 1930, Aba, Nigeria; s. of Bamgboye F. Adesola and Felicia A. Adesola; m. Oyebola Sodeinde 1959; two d.; ed Abeokuta Grammar School, Univ. of Ibadan, Queen's Univ. of Belfast, Royal Coll. of Surgeons of England, Univ. of Rochester, USA; surgical tutor Queen's Univ. Belfast 1959–61; Sr Buswell Fellow Univ. of Rochester, New York, USA 1963–64; Prof. of Surgery, Univ. of Lagos 1967–88; Pres. W Africa Soc. of Gastroenterology 1967–72, Nigerian Surgical Research Soc. 1975–79, W Africa Coll. of Surgeons 1975–77; Chair. Nat. Orthopaedic Hospitals Man. Bd 1977–78, Health Educ. Research and Man. Services 1989–, Bd of Trustees W African Coll. of Surgeons 1991–, Nat. Cttee on Medical Care and Training 1991–; Vice-Chancellor Univ. of Ilorin 1978–81, Univ. of Lagos 1981–88; Chair. Asscn of Commonwealth Univs 1984–85, Nat. Bd of Dirs, Leadership for Environment and Development (LEAD) Int. Inc. 1998–; mem. Albert Schweitzer Int. Nomination Council 1984–, Commonwealth Expert Group on Distance Educ. 1986–88; Fellow Nigerian Acad. of Science 1986–; Consultant on Higher Educ. to IBRD 1988–, to Canadian Int. Devt Agency 1988–; Ed. Nigerian Medical Journal 1970–80; mem. editorial Bd British Journal of Surgery 1968–80; mem. Expert Panel Comm. on Commonwealth Studies, Commonwealth Secr. 1995–, Rockefeller Foundation, NY 1996–; Dir Leadership for Environment and Devt (LEAD) Int. Inc. New York, Imperial Coll. London, UK 2000–; Prof. Emer. Univ. of Lagos 2001–; Hon. LLD (Queen's Univ. Belfast) 1989; Symons Medal for Distinguished Service to Commonwealth Univs 1987, Distinguished Visitor Award, Carnegie Corpn of New York 1988, Adesuyi Prize for Outstanding Contributions to Health in West Africa (West African Health Community) 1993. *Publications:* Coronary Thrombosis: The Influence of Meterological Changes 1960, Hyperparathyroidism and the Alimentary Tract 1960, Adult Intussusception in Western Nigeria 1964, Influence of Vasoactive Agents on Ascites 1965, Chronic Gastritis and Duodenal Ulcer in Nigerians 1974, Endoscopy in Upper Gastrointestinal Disease in Nigerians 1978, Technology in a Developing Economy 1983, The Nigerian University System: Meeting the Challenges of Growth in a Depressed Economy 1991, Anatomy of Service 1997, Nigerian Universities and a Nation in Crisis 1999, The State of Education in Nigeria – An Overview 2000. *Leisure interests:* golf, swimming, music. *Address:* 1 Ajani Olujare Street, Surulere, POB 51218, Falomo-Ikoyi, Lagos, Nigeria. *Telephone:* (1) 471-1123 (Office); (1) 583-4470. *Fax:* (1) 583-4470. *E-mail:* lead@lead.org.ng (Office); akinadesola@nigol.net.ng (Home). *Website:* www.lead.org.ng (Office).

ADEWOYE, Omoniyi, PhD; Nigerian university lecturer and former politician; b. 27 Oct. 1939, Inisa, Osun State; s. of late Chief James Woye and Victoria Fadunke Woye; m. Margaret Titilayo 1967; five d.; ed Kiriji Memorial Coll., Igbajo, Univ. of Ibadan, Univ. of London, Columbia Univ., New York; Lecturer in History Univ. of Ibadan 1968–75, Sr Lecturer 1975, Prof. 1984–2000, Vice-Chancellor 1996–2000, Prof. Emer. 2000–; Commr for Econ. Devt, Western State 1975–76; Commr for Finance and Econ. Devt, Oyo State 1976–77; Fed. Commr for Econ. Devt 1977–79; First Chair. Council of Ministers, Econ. Community of West African States 1977–78; Chair. Council of Ministers, Nigerian-Niger Jt Comm. 1977–78; Consultant to Econ. Comm. for Africa on Econ. Integration in W Africa 1982–83; Hon. Treas. Historical Soc. of Nigeria 1972–77; Woodrow Wilson Dissertation Scholarship (Columbia Univ.) 1967, Afgrad Fellowship (USA) 1964–68. *Publications:* The Legal Profession in Nigeria 1865–1962 1977, The Judicial System in Southern Nigeria 1854–1954 1977. *Leisure interests:* gardening, reading, writing, music. *Address:* University of Ibadan, PO Box 7321, Ibadan, Nigeria. *Telephone:* (2) 8103168 (Office); (2) 8103225 (Home).

ADEY, Christopher, ARAM, FRCM; British conductor; b. 19 Feb. 1943, London; m. Catherine Cave 1965 (divorced 1985); one s.; ed Royal Acad. of Music, London; violinist with Hallé Orchestra 1963–65, London Philharmonic Orchestra 1967–71; Assoc. Conductor, BBC Scottish Symphony Orchestra 1973–76, Ulster Orchestra 1981–83; Conductor and Prof. Royal Coll. of Music (RCM) 1979–92; Dir of Orchestral Studies, RCM Jr Dept 1973–84; now freelance conductor appearing as guest conductor with major orchestras in UK, Europe, USA and Canada including cycle of the complete Martinu symphonies for BBC 1992; Commemorative Medal of Czechoslovakian Govt 1986. *Publication:* Orchestral Performance: A Guide for Conductors and Players 1998. *Address:* c/o Richard Haigh, Performing Arts, 6 Windmill Street, London, W1P 1HF (Office); 137 Anson Road, Willesden Green, London, NW2 4AH, England.

ADIE, Kathryn (Kate), OBE, BA; British correspondent; b. 19 Sept. 1945; d. of Babe Dunnett (née Issit) and adopted d. of the late John Wilfrid Adie and of Maud Adie (née Fambely); ed Sunderland Church High School, Newcastle Univ.; technician and producer BBC Radio 1969–76; Reporter BBC TV South 1977–78, BBC TV News 1979–81, Corresp. 1982–89, Chief News Corresp. 1989–2003; freelance journalist, broadcaster and TV presenter 2003–; Visiting Fellow Univ. of Bournemouth 1998–; Hon. Prof. Sunderland Univ. 1995; Hon. Fellow, Royal Holloway, Univ. of London 1996; Hon. MA (Bath) 1987,

(Newcastle) 1990; Hon. DLitt (City) 1989, (Loughborough) 1991, (Sunderland) 1993, (Robert Gordon) 1996, (Nottingham) 1998, (Nottingham Trent) 1998; Hon. MUniv. (Open) 1996; RTS News Award 1981, 1987, Monte Carlo Int. News Award 1981, 1990, BAFTA Richard Dimbleby Award 1989; Freeman of Sunderland 1990. *Publication:* The Kindness of Strangers (auto-biog.) 2002. *Address:* c/o BBC TV, Wood Lane, London, W12 7RJ, England.

ADJANI, Isabelle; French actress; b. 27 June 1955; two s.; ed Lycée de Courbevoie; Pres. Comm. d'Avances Sur Recettes 1986–88. *Films:* Faustine et le bel été 1972, la Gifle 1974, l'Histoire d'Adèle H. 1975 (Best Actress, New York Critics 1976), le Locataire 1976, Barocco 1977, Violette et François 1977, Driver 1977, Nosferatu 1978, les Soeurs Brontë 1978, Possession 1980 (Best Actress, Cannes 1981), Clara et les chics types 1980, Quartet 1981 (Best Actress, Cannes 1982), l'Année prochaine si tout va bien 1981, Antonieta 1982, l'Eté meurtrier 1983 (Best Actress César 1984), Mortelle randonnée 1983, Subway 1985, Ishtar 1987, Camille Claudel 1988 (Best Actress César 1989, Best Actress Award, Berlin Film Festival 1989), La Reine Margot 1994 (Best Actress César 1995), Diabolique 1996. *Theatre:* la Maison de Bernarda Alba 1970, l'Avare 1972–73, l'Ecole des femmes 1973, Port-Royal 1973, Ondine 1974, Mademoiselle Julie 1983. *TV appearances include:* le Petit bougnat 1969, le Secret des flamands 1972, l'Ecole des femmes 1973, Top à Sacha Distel 1974, Princesse aux petits pois 1986. *Address:* c/o Artcomédia, 20 avenue Rapp, 75017 Paris, France.

ADJI, Boukary; Niger politician and economist; Minister of Finance 1983–87; Deputy Gov. Banque Centrale des Etats de l'Afrique de l'Ouest—BCEAO (Cen. Bank of West African States) –1996, 1997–; Prime Minister of Niger Jan.–Dec. 1996. *Address:* Banque Centrale des Etats de l'Afrique de l'Ouest, avenue Abdoulaye Fadiga, BP 3108, Dakar, Senegal. *Telephone:* 839-05-00. *Fax:* 823-93-35. *E-mail:* webmaster@bceao.int. *Website:* www.bceao.int.

ADKISSON, Perry Lee, PhD; American entomologist; b. 11 March 1929, Hickman, Arkansas; s. of Robert L. Adkisson and Imogene (née Perry) Adkisson; m. 1st Frances Rozelle 1956 (died 1995); one d.; m. 2nd Goria Ray 1998; ed Univ. of Arkansas, Kansas State Univ. and Harvard Univ.; Asst Prof. of Entomology Univ. of Missouri 1956–58; Assoc. Prof. of Entomology Texas A&M Univ. 1958–63, Prof. of Entomology 1963–67, Head, Dept of Entomology 1967–78, Distinguished Prof. of Entomology 1967–, Vice-Pres. for Agric. and Renewable Resources 1978–80, Deputy Chancellor for Agric. 1980–83, Deputy Chancellor 1983–86, Chancellor 1986–91, Regent's Prof. 1991–95; Consultant Int. AEC, Vienna 1969–74; Chair. Texas Pesticide Advisory Comm. 1972; mem. Panel on Integrated Pest Control FAO, Rome 1971–78; mem. NAS, Governing Bd Int. Crop Research Inst. for Semi-Arid Tropics 1982–88, Standing Cttee for Int. Plant Protection Congresses 1984–, Texas Science and Tech. Council 1986–88, Advisory Cttee, Export-Import Bank of the U.S. 1987; Alexander Von Humboldt Award 1980, Distinguished Service Award, American Inst. of Biological Sciences 1987, Distinguished Alumni Award (Ark. Univ.) 1990, Wolfe Prize in Agric. 1994–95, World Food Prize 1997, Medallion Alumni Award, Kansas State Univ. 1999 and numerous others. *Publications:* Controlling Cotton's Insect Pests: A New System 1982; several papers on insect diapause and other entomological topics. *Leisure interests:* gardening, fishing. *Address:* The Texas A&M University, Entomology Department, College Station, TX 77843-0001; The Reed House, 1 Reed Dr., College Station, TX 77843, USA. *Telephone:* (409) 845-2516. *Website:* insects.tamu.edu.

ADLER, Julius, PhD, FAAS; American biologist and biochemist; b. 30 April 1930, Edelfingen, Germany; s. of Adolf Adler and Irma Stern; m. Hildegard Wohl 1963; one s. one d.; ed Harvard Univ. and Univ. of Wisconsin; emigrated to USA 1938, naturalized US citizen 1943; Postdoctoral Fellow, Wash. Univ., St Louis 1957–59, Stanford Univ. 1959–60; Asst Prof., Depts of Biochemistry and Genetics, Univ. of Wis. 1960–63, Assoc. Prof. 1963–66, Prof. 1966–96, Prof. Emer. 1996–, Edwin Bret Hart Prof. 1972; Steenbock Prof. of Microbiological Sciences 1982–92; mem. American Acad. of Arts and Sciences, American Philosophical Soc., NAS, Wisc. Acad. of Sciences, Arts and Letters; Fellow American Acad. of Microbiology; Behring Lecturer, Philips Univ. of Marburg 1989, Hartman-Müller Memorial Lecturer, Univ. of Zürich 1984; Dr hc (Tübingen) 1987, (Regensburg) 1995; Selman A. Waksman Microbiology Award, NAS 1980, Otto-Warburg Medal, German Soc. of Biological Chem. 1986, Hilldale Award, Univ. of Wisconsin 1988, R. H. Wright Award, Simon Fraser Univ. 1988, Abbott-American Soc. for Microbiology Lifetime Achievement Award 1995, William C. Rose Award (American Soc. for Biochem. and Molecular Biology) 1996. *Publications:* research papers on the behaviour of simple organisms, especially bacteria. *Address:* Department of Biochemistry, University of Wisconsin-Madison, Madison, WI 53706; 1234 Wellesley Rd., Madison,WI 53705, USA. *Telephone:* (608) 262-3693. *E-mail:* adler@biochem .wisc.edu. *Website:* www.biochem.wisc.edu.

ADLERCREUTZ, (Carl) Herman (Thomas), MD, PhD; Finnish professor of clinical chemistry; b. 10 April 1932, Helsinki; s. of Erik Adlercreutz and Elisabeth Adlercreutz; m. 1st Marie-Louise Gräsbeck 1956 (divorced 1974); m. 2nd Sirkka T. Neva 1976; one s. two d.; ed Univ. of Helsinki; Research Fellow, Hormone Lab. Dept of Obstetrics and Gynaecology, Karolinska Hosp. Stockholm 1958–61; Resident in Internal Medicine, Univ. of Helsinki 1961–64, Acting Asst Prof. of Internal Medicine 1964–65, Assoc. Prof. of Clinical Chem. 1965–69, Acting Prof. of Clinical Chem. 1967–69, Prof. of Clinical Chem. 1969–97; Chief Physician, Central Lab. Helsinki Univ. Central Hosp. 1965–97; Research Prof. Acad. of Finland 1983–88; apptd Head Inst. for Preventive Medicine, Nutrition and Cancer, Folkhalson Research Centre 1997; mem. 13 foreign socs; mem. numerous bds of journals, Comm. on Health and Science Asscn of European Olympic Cttees 1985–93; Finnish White Rose Order of Knighthood, The Tenth D. R. Edwards Medal 1987 and other awards and distinctions. *Publications:* about 500 original publications mainly in the fields of steroid hormones, endocrinology, sports medicine, nutrition, phytoestrogens and cancer. *Leisure interests:* gardening, fishing, sport. *Address:* Institute of Clinical Medicine, University of Helsinki, PO Box 63, Haartmanink 8, 00014 Helsinki; Riskutie 13, 00950 Helsinki, Finland (Home). *Telephone:* (0) 320258 (Home); 47125380 (Office). *E-mail:* adlercre@ cc.helsinki.fi (Office); herman.adlercreutz@helsinki.fi (Office). *Website:* www .helsinki.fi (Office).

ADNI, Daniel; Israeli concert pianist; b. 6 Dec. 1951, Haifa; ed High Schools in Haifa and Tel Aviv, Conservatoire of Music in Paris; first Recital in Haifa 1963; professional début, London 1970; New York début 1976; has played at most musical centres in the world including UK, Germany, Israel, USA, Japan, South Africa, Switzerland, Norway, Netherlands, Romania, Australia, New Zealand, Finland, Austria; made over 20 records for EMI-His Master's Voice; First Prize, Paris Conservatoire; First Prize, Young Concert Artists' Auditions, New York. *Leisure interests:* cinema, theatre, bridge, walks, sightseeing. *Address:* c/o 64A Menelik Road, London, NW2 3RH, England. *Telephone:* (20) 7794-4076. *Fax:* (20) 7794-4076. *E-mail:* danieladni@waitrose .com (Home).

ADOBOLI, Eugène Koffi; Togolese politician; b. 1934; Prime Minister of Togo 1999–2000; fmrly with Mission to UN. *Address:* c/o Office of the Prime Minister, Lomé, Togo (Office).

ADOLFO, (Adolfo F. Sardiña); American fashion designer; b. 15 Feb. 1933, Cardenas, Matanzas, Cuba; ed St Ignacio de Loyola Jesuit School, Havana; served Cuban Army; apprentice, Cristóbal Balenciaga millinery salon, Paris 1950–52; apprentice millinery designer, Bergdorf Goodman, New York 1953–54; designer Emme (milliners), New York 1954–62; worked as unpaid apprentice, Chanel, New York summers of 1957, 1966; owner and head designer, Adolfo Inc., New York 1962–; designer, Adolfo Menswear Inc. and Adolfo Scarves Inc., New York 1978–; created perfume line for Frances Denny, New York 1979; mem. Council, Fashion Designers of America 1982.

ADOUKI, Martin, DJur; Republic of the Congo diplomatist; b. 8 April 1942, Makoua; ed Bordeaux and Paris Univs and Int. Inst. of Public Admin., Paris; Information Officer for the Group of African, Caribbean and Pacific Countries (ACP) in Brussels and attended negotiations between the ACP and the EEC; fmrly Lecturer in Law at the Marien Ngouabi Univ., Brazzaville and later Special Adviser to the Prime Minister; Perm. Rep. to the UN 1985–94, to UN Security Council 1986–87, Pres. UN Security Council 1986–87, Chair. UN African Group Sept. 1986, Rep. of Chair. of OAU to UN 1986–87, Head Congo Del. to 43rd Session of Gen. Ass. 1988; mem. of the Zone of Peace and Co-operation in the South Atlantic 1988–90, mem. Del. of UN Special Cttee on the Verification of Elections in Namibia 1989, Vice-Pres. UN Gen. Ass. (44th Session) 1989; Observer on the Gen. Elections in Nicaragua Feb. 1990, Head Del. to World Summit for Children Sept. 1990; Chair. 4th Cttee of 45th Session of Gen. Ass. 1990–91; Amb. and Diplomatic Adviser to Pres. 1998–. *Address:* c/o Ministry of Foreign Affairs and Co-operation, BP 2070, Brazzaville, Republic of the Congo.

ADRIANO, Dino B., FCCA; British business executive; b. 24 April 1943; s. of Dante Adriano and Yole Adriano; m. Susan Rivett 1996; two d.; ed Strand Grammar School and Highgate Coll.; articled clerk, George W. Spencer & Co. 1959–64; Accounting Dept trainee J. Sainsbury PLC 1964–65, Financial Accounts Dept 1965–73, Br. Financial Control Man. 1973–80, Area Dir Sainsbury's Cen. and Western Area 1986–89, Asst Man. Dir 1995–96, Deputy Chief Exec. 1996–97, Jt Group Chief Exec. 1997–98, Group Chief Exec. 1998–2000, Chair., Chief Exec. Sainsbury's Supermarkets Ltd 1997–2000; Gen. Man. Homebase 1981–86, Man. Dir 1989–95, Deputy Chief Exec. 1996–97; Dir Laura Ashley PLC 1996–98; Trustee Oxfam 1990–96, 1998–, Adviser on Retail Matters 1996–98, Vice-Chair. 2001–; Trustee Women's Royal Voluntary Service 2001–. *Leisure interests:* opera, music, soccer, cookery. *Address:* c/o J. Sainsbury PLC, 33 Holborn, London, EC1N 2HT, England.

ADVANI, Lal Krishna; Indian politician, fmr journalist and social worker; b. 8 Nov. 1927, Karachi (now in Pakistan); s. of Kishinchand Advani and Gyani Advani; m. Kamala Jagtiani 1965; one s. one d.; ed St Patrick's High School, Karachi, D.G. Nat. Coll., Hyderabad, Sind, Govt Law Coll., Bombay; joined Rashtriya Swayam Sevak Sangh (RSS, social work org.) 1942, Sec. of Karachi br. 1947; joined Bharatiya Jana Sangh (BJS) 1951; party work in Rajasthan until 1958, Sec. of Delhi State Jana Sangh 1958–63, Vice-Pres. 1965–67; mem. Cen. Exec. of BJS 1966; Jt Ed. of BJS paper Organizer 1960–67; mem. interim Metropolitan Council, Delhi 1966, Leader of Jana Sangh Gp. 1966; Chair. of Metropolitan Council 1967; mem. Rajya Sabha 1970, Head of Jana Sangh Parl. Group 1970; Pres. Bharatiya Jana Sangh 1973–77 (incorp. in Janata); detained during emergency 1975–77; Gen. Sec. Janata Party Jan.–May 1977; Minister of Information and Broadcasting 1977–79, of Home Affairs and of Kashmir Affairs 1998–99, of Home Affairs 1999–; Deputy Prime Minister of India 2002–; Gen. Sec. Bharatiya Janata Party 1980–86, Pres. 1986–90, re-apptd. June 1993; Leader of Opposition, Lok Sabha Dec. 1990–March 1991, 1991–96. *Publications:* A Prisoner's Scrap-

Book, The People Betrayed. *Leisure interests:* theatre, cinema, books. *Address:* Ministry of Home Affairs, North Block, New Delhi 110 001 (Office); C-1/6, Pandara Park, New Delhi 110 003, India (Home). *Telephone:* (11) 3011989 (Office); (11) 3782397 (Home). *Fax:* (11) 3015750 (Office); (11) 3782367 (Home). *E-mail:* mhaweb@mhant.delhi.nic.in (Office). *Website:* www .mha.nic.in (Office).

ADYRKHAYEVA, Svetlana Dzantemirovna; Russian/Ossetian ballerina; b. 12 May 1938, Khumalag, North Ossetia; d. of Taissya Gougkayeva and Dzantemir Adyrkhayev; m. Alexey Zakalinsky 1966; one d.; ed Leningrad Choreographic School, Theatre Acad. of Russia; danced with Glinka Theatre of Opera and Ballet, Chelyabinsk 1955–58; with Odessa Opera and Ballet 1958–60; dancer at Bolshoi Theatre 1960–88; USSR People's Artist 1984; Dir Svetlana Adyrkhayeva Ballet Studio, Moscow. *Principal parts include:* Odette-Odile, Princess Florine, Woman of the Bronze Mountain (Prokofiev's Stone Flower), Zarema (Asafiev's Fountain of Bakhchisaray), Mehmene Banu (Melikov's Legend of Love), Aegina (Khatchaturyan's Spartacus), Kitri (Minkus's Don Quixote). *Leisure interests:* reading, travelling. *Address:* 1st Smolensky per. 9, Apt. 74, 121099 Moscow, Russia. *Telephone:* (095) 241-13-62.

AFANASIYEV, Yuri Nikolaevich, D.HIST.SC.; Russian politician and historian; b. 5 Sept. 1934, Maina, Ulyanovsk region; m.; two c.; ed Moscow State Univ., Acad. of Social Sciences; mem. CPSU 1956–90; instructor, then sec. Comsomol org. in Krasnoyarsk Region 1957–64, mem. of Comsomol Cen. Cttee 1964–71; Deputy Head of Div. 1971, lecturer Higher Comsomol School 1971, Pro-rector 1972–83; Sr researcher Inst. of World History USSR Acad. of Sciences 1983–87; Rector Moscow Inst. of History and Archives (now Russian Humanitarian Univ.) 1987–; USSR People's Deputy 1989–91, mem. of Interregional Deputies' Group, People's Deputy of Russia 1991–92; Co-Chair. Democratic Russia Movt 1991–92. *Publications:* numerous articles and over 10 books on problems of Russian history and contemporary politics including Russia on the Crossroads (3 Vols) 2000, Dangerous Russia 2001. *Address:* Russian Humanitarian University, ul. Chayanova 15, 125267 Moscow, Russia. *Telephone:* (095) 250-63-36 (Office); (095) 921-41-69 (Home).

AFANASSIEVSKY, Nikolay Nikolayevich; Russian diplomatist; b. 1 Oct. 1940, Moscow; m.; one s.; ed Moscow Inst. of Int. Relations; mem. CPSU 1968–91; attaché, Embassy, Cameroon, 1964–66; with Ministry of Foreign Affairs 1966–76; del. to UN Gen. Ass. 1969; del. to CSCE, Geneva, Helsinki; 1973–75; counsellor, ministry counsellor, Embassy, Paris 1976–83; Deputy Chief of First European Dept, Ministry of Foreign Affairs 1983–86, Chief 1986–90; Amb. to Belgium and liaison to NATO 1990–94; Deputy Minister of Foreign Affairs 1994–98; Amb. to France 1999–2002, to Poland 2002–. *Address:* Russian Embassy, Belvederska str. 49, 00 761 Warsaw, Poland. *Telephone:* (22) 6289558.

AFEWERKI, Issaias; Eritrean politician; b. 1945, Asmara; trained as engineer; joined Eritrean Liberation Front (ELF) 1966, mil. training in China 1966, Leader fourth regional area ELF 1968, Gen. Commdr ELF 1969; founding mem. Eritrean People's Liberation Front (EPLF) (now People's Front for Democracy and Justice (PFDJ) 1977), fmr Asst Sec. Gen., Sec. Gen. 1987; Chair. State Council, Nat. Ass.; Sec. Gen. Provisional Govt of Eritrea 1991; assumed power May 1991; elected Pres. of Eritrea by Nat. Ass. June 1993–. *Address:* Office of the President, PO Box 257, Asmara, Eritrea. *Telephone:* (1) 122132. *Fax:* (1) 125123.

AFFLECK, Ben; American actor; b. 15 Aug. 1972, Berkeley, Calif. *Films include:* School Ties 1992, Buffy the Vampire Slayer, Dazed and Confused, Mallrats 1995, Glory Daze, Office Killer, Chasing Amy 1997, Going All the Way 1997, Good Will Hunting (also screenplay with Matt Damon, q.v., Acad. Award and Golden Globe for Best Original Screenplay 1997), Phantoms 1998, Armageddon 1998, Shakespeare in Love 1998, Reindeer Games 1999, Forces of Nature 1999, Dogma 1999, Daddy and Them 1999, The Boiler Room 1999, 200 Cigarettes 1999, Bounce 2000, The Third Wheel (also producer) 2000, Pearl Harbor 2001, The Sum of All Fear 2002, Changing Lanes 2002, Daredevil 2003. *Television includes:* Voyage of the Mimi, Against the Grain, Lifestories: Families in Crisis, Hands of a Stranger, Daddy. *Address:* c/o Creative Artists Agency, 9830 Wilshire Boulevard, Beverly Hills, CA 90212; c/o Endeavor Talent, 9701 Wilshire Boulevard, 10th Floor, Beverly Hills, CA 90212, USA.

AFRAH, Maj.-Gen. Hussein Kulmia; Somali politician and army officer; b. 1920, Margeh; ed Italian Secondary School, Mogadishu, Italian Officers' Acad., Rome; shopkeeper until 1943; joined Police Force 1945; criminal investigation training in Kenya 1945; then instructor and translator, Police Training School Mogadishu; at Italian Secondary School Mogadishu 1950–54, Italian Officers' Acad. 1954–55; ADC to fmr Pres. Osman 1960; mem. Supreme Revolutionary Council 1970–76, Vice-Pres. 1973–76; Chair. Econ. Cttee 1973; Sec. of State for the Interior 1970–74; Deputy Head of State 1976–80, mem. Political Bureau, Somali Revolutionary Socialist Party 1976–; Pres. Adviser on Govt Affairs 1980–84. *Address:* Somali Socialist Revolutionary Party Headquarters, Mogadishu, Somalia.

AFXENTIOU, Afxentis C., MA(Econ); Cypriot banker and government official; b. 11 Dec. 1932, Larnaca; s. of Costas Afxentiou and Terpsichore Panayi; m. 1st Stella Vanezis 1957 (deceased); one s. one d.; m. 2nd Egli Pattichis 1981; ed Pancyprian Commercial Lyceum, Larnaca, Athens School of Econs and Business and Univ. of Georgia; Hellenic Mining Co. Group 1955–62; Ministry of Finance 1962–79, Perm. Sec. 1973–79; Minister of Finance 1977–82; Gov.

Cen. Bank of Cyprus 1982–2002; Gov. IMF 1982; fmr Gov. for Cyprus, IBRD; fmr Vice-Chair. Bd Dirs Cyprus Devt Bank Ltd. *Leisure interests:* reading, walking, swimming. *Address:* 3 Idis Street, Parisinos, Strovolos, Nicosia, Cyprus (Home).

AG HAMANI, Ahmed Mohamed; Malian politician; b. 1941; diplomatic career; Rep. of Mali to EC and Head of Mission to ECSE and Euratom 2000, Amb. in Brussels 2001; Prime Minister of Mali and Minister of African Integration June 2002–. *Address:* Office of the Prime Minister, quartièr du Fleuve, BP 790, Bamako, Mali (Office). *Telephone:* 22-55-34 (Office). *Fax:* 22-85-83 (Office).

AGA KHAN IV, HH Prince Karim, Spiritual leader and Imam of Ismaili Muslims, BA; Iranian; b. 13 Dec. 1936, Creux-de-Genthod, Geneva; s. of the late Prince Aly Salomon Khan and of Princess Joan Aly Khan (late Viscountess Camrose, née Joan Barbara Yarde-Buller); m. 1st Sarah Frances Croker-Poole 1969 (divorced 1995); two s. one d.; m. 2nd Princess Gabriele zu Leiningen (Begum Inaara Aga Khan) 1998; one s.; ed Le Rosey, Switzerland, Harvard Univ., USA; became Aga Khan on the death of his grandfather Sir Sultan Mahomed Shah, Aga Khan III, GCSI, GCIE, GCVO 1957; granted title of His Highness by Queen Elizabeth II 1957, of His Royal Highness by the Shah of Iran 1959; Founder and Chair. Aga Khan Foundation 1967, Aga Khan Award for Architecture 1977–, Inst. of Ismaili Studies 1977–, Aga Khan Fund for Econ. Devt, Geneva 1984, Aga Khan Trust for Culture 1988; Founder and Chancellor Aga Khan Univ., Pakistan 1983; Founder and Chancellor, Univ. of Central Asia 2001; Hon. Fellow RIBA 1991, Founder Pres. Yacht Club Costa Smeralda, Sardinia; mem. Royal Yacht Squadron 1982–; Hon. mem. AIA (USA) 1992; Commdr Ordre du Mérite Mauritanien 1960; Grand Croix, Ordre du Prince Henry du Gouvernement Portugais 1960, Ordre Nat. de la Côte d'Ivoire 1965, de la Haute-Volta 1965, Ordre Nat. Malgache 1966; Ordre du Croissant Vert des Comores 1966; Grand Cordon Ordre du Tadj de l'Empire d'Iran 1967, Nishan-i-Imtiaz, Pakistan 1970; Cavaliere di Gran Croce dell'Ordine al Merito della Repubblica (Italy) 1977; Grand Officier de l'Ordre Nat. du Lion (Senegal) 1982, Nishan-e-Pakistan, Pakistan 1983; Grand Cordon of Ouissam-al Arch (Morocco) 1986; Cavaliere del Lavaro (Italy) 1988; Commdr, Légion d'honneur (France) 1990, Gran Cruz de la Orden del Mérito Civil, Spain 1991, Grand Croix, Order of Merit (Portugal) 1998, Order of Friendship (Tajikistan) 1998; Hon. LLD (Peshawar Univ.) 1967, (Univ. of Sind) 1970, (McGill Univ., Montreal) 1983, (McMaster Univ.) 1987, (Univ. of Wales) 1993, (Brown Univ.) 1996; Hon. DLitt (London Univ.) 1989; Thomas Jefferson Memorial Foundation Medal in Architecture, Univ. of Virginia 1984, Honor Award A.I.A. 1984, La Medalla de Oro del Consejo Superior de Colegios de Arquitectos, Spain 1987, Médaille d'Argent Académie d'Architecture, Paris 1991, Huésped de Honor de Granada, Spain 1991; Hadrian Award, World Monuments Fund (USA) 1996, Gold Medal, City of Granada (Spain) 1998; Insignia of Honour, Union. Int. des Architectes 2001. *Leisure interests:* breeding race-horses, yachting, skiing. *Address:* Aiglemont, 60270 Gouvieux, France.

AGAFANGEL, (Savvin Alexey Mikhailovich), Metropolitan of Odessa and Izmail; Ukrainian Orthodox ecclesiastic; b. 2 Sept. 1938, Burdino, Lipetsk Region; ed Lipetsk Seminary, Moscow Theological Acad.; took monastic vows 1965; ordained as archimandrite 1967; Rector Odessa Seminary 1967–75; Bishop of Vinnitsa and Bratslav 1975–81; ordained as Archbishop 1981, Archbishop of Vinnitsa and Bratslav 1981–89; ordained as Metropolitan 1989, Metropolitan of Vinnitsa and Bratslav 1989–92; Metropolitan of Odessa and Izmail 1992–; People's Deputy of Ukraine 1990–94; Rector Odessa Seminary 1993–98; rep. of Russian Orthodox Church in Ukraine; Dr. hc (Kiev) 1995. *Address:* Monastery of the Dormition, Mayatchny pereulok 6, Odessa 65038, Ukraine. *Telephone:* (48) 746-3037 (Home). *Fax:* (48) 746-3038 (Office).

AGAKHANOV, Khalnazar Amannazarovich; Turkmenistan diplomatist and politician; b. 25 Feb. 1952, Ashgabat; m.; three c.; ed Samarkand State Inst. of Co-operation; trader, Ashgabat 1969–87; First Deputy Chair. Turkmenpotrebsoyuz 1987–91; Minister of Trade 1991–94, of Trade and Resources 1994–98, of Trade and Foreign Econ. Relations 1998–99; Amb. to Kazakhstan 1999–2000, to Russia 2000–; Order of Galkynysh, For Love for Homeland and Gairat Medals. *Leisure interests:* chess, reading books, pop and folk music. *Address:* Embassy of Turkmenistan, Filippovskii per. 22, 121019 Moscow, Russia (Office). *Telephone:* (095) 291-66-36 (Office). *Fax:* (095) 291-09-35 (Office).

AGAM, Yaacov; Israeli artist; b. 1928, Rishon Le-zion; m. Clila Agam 1954; two s. one d.; ed Bezalel School of Art, Jerusalem, Atelier d'art abstrait, Paris; travelling retrospective exhbn Paris (Nat. Museum of Modern Art), Amsterdam, Düsseldorf, Tel-Aviv 1972–73. *One-man exhibitions include:* Galerie Craven, Paris 1953, Galerie Denise René, Paris 1956, 1958, Palais des Beaux-Arts, Brussels 1958, Tel-Aviv Museum 1958, Suzanne Bollag Gallery, Zürich 1959, 1962, Drian Gallery, London 1959, Marlborough Gerson Gallery, New York 1966, Galerie Denise René, New York 1971, Guggenheim Museum, New York 1980, Tokyo, Osaka, Kawasaki 1989. *Works include:* Transformes Musicales 1961, Double Metamorphosis, Shalom Liner 1964, Sculptures in the City, Reims 1970, sculpture and mural, President's mansion, Israel 1971, Water-Fire fountain, St Louis 1971, Pompidou Room, Elysée Palace 1972, environment, Elysée Palace, Paris 1972, mobile wall, School of Science, Montpellier 1972, design and realization of a square in La Défense, Paris, including water fountain and monumental sculpture 1973, Villa Regina, Miami (biggest painting in the world, at 300,000 square feet) 1984, Homage

to Mondrian (a whole building), LA 1984, Fire-Water Fountain, Tel-Aviv 1986, Visual Educ. System 1986, MS Celebration cruise ship 1987, Grand Prix Artec 1989, Nagoya, MS Fantasy cruise ship 1990; films produced include Recherches et inventions 1956, Le désert chante, 1957. *Publications:* 36 books covering his non-verbal visual learning method (visual alphabet). *Address:* 26 rue Boulard, Paris 75014, France. *Telephone:* 1-43-22-00-88.

AGANBEGYAN, Abel Gezevich; Russian/Armenian economist; b. 8 Oct. 1932, Tbilisi, Georgia; s. of Galina A. Aganbegyan; m. Zoya V. Kupriyanova 1953; one s. one d.; ed Moscow State Econ. Inst.; mem. CPSU 1956–91; Economist, Gen. Econ. Dept, State Cttee for Labour and Wages 1955–61; Head of Lab., Inst. of Econs and Industrial Eng, Siberian Branch of USSR Acad. of Sciences 1961–67, Dir Inst. of Econs and Industrial Eng 1967–85; Prof. of Econs, Novosibirsk State Univ.; Prof. Acad. of Nat. Econ.; Chair. Cttee for Study of Productive Forces and Natural Resources 1965–; Rector Acad. of Nat. Economy 1989–; mem. Presidium; Chair. All-Union Club of Managers; Corresp. mem. USSR (now Russian) Acad. of Sciences 1964, mem. 1974, Acad.-Sec. Dept of Econ. 1986–89; Foreign mem. Bulgarian and Hungarian Acads. of Sciences; Corresp. FBA; Dr. hc (Alicante and Łódź); two Orders of Lenin. *Publications:* Wages and Salaries in the USSR 1959, On the Application of Mathematics and Electronic Machinery in Planning 1961, Some Questions of Monopoly Price Theory with Reference to the USA 1961, Economical-Mathematical Analysis of Input-Output Tables in USSR 1968, System of Models of National Economy Planning 1972, Management of the Socialist Enterprises 1979, Management and Efficiency: USSR Economy in 1981–85 1981, Siberia—not by Hearsay (with Z. Ibragimova) 1981, Economic Methods in Planned Management (with D. Kazakevich) 1985, Enterprise: Managing Scientific and Technological Progress (with V. Rechin) 1986; The Challenge: Economics of Perestroika 1987, Moving the Mountain: Inside Perestroika 1989, Measures and Stages of Improving USSR Economy 1991. *Address:* Academy of National Economy, Prospect Vernadskogo 82, 117571 Moscow, Russia. *Telephone:* (095) 434-83-89 (Office).

AGARWAL, Bina, PhD; Indian academic; b. Jabalpur, India; ed Univ. of Delhi, Univ. of Cambridge, Delhi School of Econ.; Research Assoc. Council for Social Devt 1972–74; Visiting Fellow Inst. of Devt Studies, Univ. of Sussex 1978–79, Research Fellow Science Policy Research Unit 1979–80; Assoc. Prof. of Econs, Inst. of Econ. Growth, Univ. of Delhi 1981–88, Prof. 1988–, Head Population Research Center 1996–98; Fellow Bunting Inst. Radcliffe Coll. 1989–91; mem. and seminar organizer Harvard Center for Population and Devt Studies 1990–91; Visiting Prof. Harvard Univ. Cttee on Degrees in Women's Studies 1991–92, First Daniel H. H. Ingalls Visiting Prof. March–Sept. 1999; Visiting Scholar Inst. for Advanced Study, Princeton 1995; mem. of numerous nat. and int. ed. bds, advisory cttees and consultancies; K. H. Batheja Award 1995–96, Edgar Graham Book Prize 1996, Ananda Kentish Coomaraswamy Book Prize 1996. *Publications:* Mechanization in Indian Agriculture 1983, Cold Hearths and Barren Slopes: The Woodfuel Crisis in the Third World 1986, A Field of One's Own: Gender and Land Rights in South Asia 1994, Structures of Patriarchy: State, Community and Household in Modernizing Asia (Ed.) 1988, Women, Poverty and Ideology in Asia (Co-ed.) 1989, Women and Work in the World Economy 1991; numerous articles on agricultural, environmental, developmental and gender topics in learned journals. *Leisure interests:* writing poetry, reading literature and biography, walking, movies. *Address:* Institute of Economic Growth, University Enclave, University of Delhi, Delhi 110007 (Office); 111 Golf Links, New Delhi 110003, India (Home). *Telephone:* (11) 7667101 (Office); (11) 4692203 (Home). *Fax:* (11) 7667410 (Office). *E-mail:* bina@ieg.ernet.in (Office).

AGASSI, Andre; American tennis player; b. 29 April 1970, Las Vegas; s. of Mike Agassi and Elizabeth Agassi; m. 1st Brooke Shields 1997 (divorced 1999); m. 2nd Steffi Graf; one s.; coached from age 13 by Nick Bollettieri, strength coach Gil Reyes; semi-finalist, French Open 1988, US Open 1988, 1989; mem. US team which defeated Australia in Davis Cup Final 1990; defeated Stefan Edberg to win inaugural ATP World Championship, Frankfurt 1991; finalist French Open 1990, 1991, US Open 1990, 1995, 2002, Australian Open 1995, Wimbledon 1999; Men's Singles Wimbledon Champion 1992; won US Open 1994, 1999, Canadian Open 1995, Australian Open 1995, 2000, 2001, 2003, French Open 1999; winner Olympic Games tennis tournaments 1996; Asscn of Tennis Professionals World Champion 1990; one of only five players to have won all four Grand Slam titles (2001); winner of 54 singles and 9 doubles titles as at Nov. 2002; f. Andre Agassi Foundation to help at-risk youth in Las Vegas 1994. *Address:* International Management Group, 1 Erieview Plaza, Suite 1300, Cleveland, OH 44114, USA.

AGEE, William J., MBA; American business executive; b. 5 Jan. 1938, Boise, Ida; s. of Harold J. Agee and Suzanne Agee; m. 1st Diane Weaver 1957; one s. two d.; m. 2nd Mary Cunningham 1982; one d.; ed Stanford Univ., Boise Junior Coll., Univ. of Idaho, Harvard Univ.; with Boise Cascade Corpn 1963–72; Sr Vice-Pres. and Chief Financial Officer, Bendix Corpn 1972–76, Pres. and COO 1976–77, Chair. and CEO 1977–83, Pres. 1977–79; CEO Semper Enterprises, Inc., Mass. 1983–; Chair., Pres. CEO Morrison Knudsen Corpn 1988–95; Dir ASARCO, Equitable Life Assurance Soc. of US, Dow Jones & Co. Inc., Econ. Club of Detroit, Detroit Renaissance Inc., Nat. Council for US–China Trade, Gen. Foods Corpn, Detroit Econ. Growth Corpn 1978–, United Foundation, Nat. Council for US–China Trade; mem. Conf. Bd, Council on Foreign Relations, Business Roundtable, American and other insts of CPAs, Bd of Dirs, Assocs of Harvard Business School 1977–, United Negroes Coll. Fund 1977; Chair. Gov.'s Higher Educ. Capital Investment

Advisory Cttee, Pres.'s Industrial Advisory Sub-Cttee on Econ. and Trade Policy 1978–79, Advisory Council Cranbrook Educational Community 1978, Trustee 1978; Trustee Urban Inst., Cttee for Econ. Devt 1977, Citizen Research Council, Mich. 1977; numerous hon. degrees. *Leisure interests:* tennis, golf, swimming.

AGHILI, Shadmehr; Iranian musician; b. 1972; singer and writer of popular songs. *Film:* Par e Parvaz (also composed soundtrack). *Recordings include:* Mosaafer, Dehati, Bahar e Man. *Address:* c/o Radio Network 1 (Voice of the Islamic Republic of Iran), Tehran, Iran (Office).

AGIUS, Marcus Ambrose Paul, MA, MBA; British airline executive and investment banker; b. 22 July 1946, Walton-on-Thames; s. of Alfred Victor Louis Benedict Agius and Ena Eleanora Hueffer; m. Kate Juliette de Rothschild 1971; two d.; ed Univ. of Cambridge and Harvard Business School; grad. Trainee with Vickers PLC 1968–70; with Lazard Bros & Co. Ltd 1972–, Dir 1981–85, Man. Dir 1985–90, Vice-Chair. 1990–2001, Chair. 2001–; mem. Bd British Airports Authority (BAA) PLC 1995–, Deputy Chair. 1998–2002, Chair. 2002–. *Leisure interests:* gardening, shooting, tennis, skiing. *Address:* BAA PLC, 130 Wilton Road, London, SW1V 1LQ (Office); Lazard, 21 Moorfields, London, EC2P 2HT (Office); 7 South Terrace, London, SW7 2TB (Home); Marise Cottage, Exbury, Hants., SO45 1AH, England (Home). *Telephone:* (20) 7834-9449 (Office); (20) 7589-9440 (Home). *Fax:* (20) 7932-6699 (Office). *Website:* www.baa.co.uk (Office); www.lazard.com.

AGNELLI, Susanna; Italian politician; b. 24 April 1922, Turin; sister of the late Giovanni Agnelli and of Umberto Agnelli (q.v.); six c.; Mayor of Monte Argentario 1974–84; mem. Parl. 1976; mem. European Parl. 1981; Senator 1983; mem. Nat. Council, Republican Party until 1992; Jr Minister, Ministry of Foreign Affairs 1986–91; Minister of Foreign Affairs 1992–96; Adviser, John F. Kennedy School of Govt Council of Women World Leaders, Harvard Univ. 1998–; mem. Int. Comm. on Missing Persons 1998–, Bd of Dirs. of Int. Center for Missing and Exploited Children 1999–; Pres. Telethon Foundation 1992, 'Il Faro' Foundation 1997–; Hon. Pres. AMREF Italy; Hon. LLD (Mt. Holyoke Coll., MA) 1981. *Publications include:* We Always Wore Sailor Suits 1975, Ricordati Gualeguaychù 1982, Addio, addio mio ultimo amore 1985, Questo libro è tuo 1993; numerous articles in magazines and newspapers. *Leisure interest:* writing. *Address:* Comitato Telethon Fondazione ONLUS, Via G. Saliceto 5A, 00161 Rome (Office); Piazza Navona 49, 00186 Rome, Italy (Home). *Telephone:* (06) 440151 (Office). *Fax:* (06) 44202032 (Office). *E-mail:* info@telethon.it (Office). *Website:* www.telethon.it (Office).

AGNELLI, Umberto; Italian industrialist; b. 1 Nov. 1934, Lausanne, Switzerland; brother of the late Giovanni Agnelli and of Susanna Agnelli (q.v.); m. Allegra Caracciolo di Castagneto; two s. (one deceased) one d.; ed Turin Univ.; mem. Bd Istituto Finanziario Industriale SpA (IFI) 1959–80, Vice-Chair., CEO 1981–; Chair. SAI (insurance co.) 1960–76; mem. Bd FIAT SpA, Head Int. Operation Group 1964–73, Chair. FIAT France 1965–80, CEO FIAT SpA 1970–76, Vice-Pres. 1976–93, Chair. FIAT Auto 1980–90, mem. FIAT Int. Advisory Bd 1993–, Chair. 2003–; Chair. PIAGGIO SpA (motorcycles) 1965–88 (mem. Bd 1988–), IVECO (heavy vehicle sector of FIAT Group) 1975–80, Teksid (metallurgical sector of FIAT group) 1975–80, CRF (FIAT Research Centre) 1978–80, ISVOR (Inst. for Organizational Devt of FIAT Group) 1978–80, IFIL 1983–, TORO (insurance co.) 1983–93; senator 1976–79; Chair. JUVENTUS 1956–61, Hon. Chair. 1970–; Chair. Italian Football Asscn 1959–62; Vice-Pres. G. Agnelli Foundation 1966–; Chair. Cttee of Common Market Automobile Constructors (ACEA, fmrly CCMC) 1980–90, Int. Vienna Council (IVC) 1988–93 (Vice-Chair. 1993–); Pres. Italy-Japan Asscn 1982–, LUISS (Univ. of Econ. Studies) Man. School 1986– (mem. Bd LUISS 1978–); Co-Chair. Italy-Japan Business Group 1989–; mem. ALLIANZ Advisory Cttee 1980–, Steering Cttee of European Roundtable Industrialists (ERT) 1983–94, European Advisory Cttee of New York Stock Exchange 1985–96, TRILATERAL Comm. 1991–, Steering Cttee of the Bilderberg Meetings 1994–, European Advisory Bd, Schroder Salomon Smith Barney 2001–, Int. Adviser Praemium Imperiale organised by Japanese Art Asscn, Fuji TV 1996–; Grand Ufficiale al Merito 1972, Grand Officier Légion d'Honneur 1992, Trade Award (Japan) 1995, Imperial Award Grand Cordon of the Sacred Treasure (Japan) 1996. *Leisure interests:* golf, modern art, skiing. *Address:* Palazzina Fiat, Via Nizza 250, 10126 Turin, Italy (Office). *Telephone:* (011) 6861111 (Office). *Fax:* (011) 6863704 (Office). *Website:* www .fiatgroup.com (Office).

AGNELO, HE Cardinal Geraldo Majella; Brazilian ecclesiastic; b. 19 Oct. 1933, Juiz de Fora; ordained priest 1957; elected Bishop of Toledo 1978; Bishop of Londrina 1982; resgnd 1991; Archbishop of São Salvador da Bahía 1999; cr. Cardinal 2001. *Address:* Archdiocese of São Salvador da Bahia, Rua Martin Afonso de Souza 270, 40100–050 Salvador, Bahía, Brazil (Office). *Telephone:* (71) 328-6699 (Office). *Fax:* (71) 328-0068 (Office). *E-mail:* contato@arquidiocesedesalvador.org.br (Office).

AGNEW, Harold Melvin, PhD; American physicist; b. 28 March 1921, Denver, Colo; s. of Sam E. Agnew and Agusta (Jacobs) Agnew; m. Beverly Jackson 1942; one s. one d.; ed Univs. of Denver and Chicago; Los Alamos Scientific Lab. 1943–46, Alt. Div. Leader 1949–61, Leader Weapons Div. 1964–70, Dir Los Alamos Scientific Lab. 1970–79; Pres. GA Technologies Inc. 1979–85, Dir 1985–; New Mexico State Senator 1955–61; Scientific Adviser, Supreme Allied Commdr in Europe, Paris 1961–64; Chair. Army Scientific Advisory Panel 1965–70, mem. 1970–74; Chair. Gen. Advisory Cttee US Arms Control and Disarmament Agency 1972–76, mem. 1976–80; mem. Aircraft

Panel, President's Scientific Advisory Cttee 1965–73, USAF Scientific Advisory Bd 1957–69, Defense Scientific Bd 1965–70, Govt of NM Radiation Advisory Council 1959–61; Sec. NM Health and Social Services 1971–73; mem. Aerospace Safety Advisory Panel, NASA 1968–74, 1986; White House Science Council 1982–89; Adjunct Prof. Univ. of Calif., San Diego 1988–; Woodrow Wilson Nat. Fellowship Foundation 1973–80; Dir Charles Lee Powell Foundation 1993–; Fellow, American Physical Soc.; mem. NAS, Nat. Acad. of Eng; Ernest Orlando Lawrence Award 1966; Enrico Fermi Award, Dept of Energy 1978. *Leisure interests:* crafts, gardening, skiing, golf, tennis, fishing. *Address:* 322 Punta Baja Drive, Solana Beach, CA 92075, USA. *Telephone:* (858) 481-8908. *Fax:* (858) 481-8908. *E-mail:* hmabja@sdsc.edu (Office).

AGNEW, Jonathan Geoffrey William, MA; British investment banker; b. 30 July 1941, Windsor; s. of late Sir Geoffrey Agnew and Hon. Doreen Maud Jessel; m. 1st Hon. Joanna Campbell 1966 (divorced 1985); one s. two d.; m. 2nd Marie-Claire Dreesmann 1990; one s. one d.; ed Eton Coll. and Trinity Coll. Cambridge; with The Economist 1964–65, IBRD 1965–67; with Hill Samuel & Co. 1967–73, Dir 1971; Morgan Stanley & Co. 1973–82, Man. Dir 1977; with J.G.W. Agnew & Co. 1983–86; Chief Exec. ISRO 1986; with Kleinwort Benson Group PLC 1987–93, Chief Exec. 1989–93; Chair. Limit PLC 1993–2000, Henderson Geared Income and Growth Trust PLC 1995–2003, Gerrard Group PLC 1998–2000; Dir (non-exec.) Thos. Agnew & Sons Ltd 1969–; Dir (non-exec.) Nationwide Bldg Soc. 1997–, Deputy Chair. 1999–2002, Chair. 2002–; Dir (non-exec.) Beazley Group PLC 2002–; Dir Soditic Ltd 2001–; mem. Council Lloyd's 1995–98. *Address:* Flat E, 51 Eaton Square, London, SW1W 9BE, England (Home). *Telephone:* (20) 7826-2121 (Office); (20) 7235-7589 (Home). *Fax:* (20) 7826-2045 (Office). *E-mail:* jonathan.agnew@nationwide.co.uk (Office).

AGNEW, (Morland Herbert) Julian, MAFRSA; British art dealer; b. 20 Sept. 1943, London; s. of the late Sir Geoffrey William Gerald Agnew and of Hon. Doreen Maud Jessel; m. 1st Elizabeth Margaret Moncrieff Mitchell 1973 (divorced 1992); one s. two d.; m. 2nd Victoria Burn Callander 1993; one s.; ed Eton Coll. and Trinity Coll. Cambridge; joined Thomas Agnew & Sons Ltd 1965, Dir 1968, Man. Dir 1987–92, Chair. 1992–; Pres. British Antique Dealers Asscn 1979–81; Chair. Soc. of London Art Dealers 1986–90. *Leisure interests:* opera, music, books, tennis, golf. *Address:* Thomas Agnew & Sons Ltd, 43 Old Bond Street, London, W1S 4BA (Office); 76 Alderney Street, London, SW1 4EX (Home); Egmere Farm House, Egmere Nr. Walsingham, Norfolk, England. *Telephone:* (20) 7290-9250 (Office). *Fax:* (20) 7629-4359 (Office). *E-mail:* julianagnew@agnewsgallery.co.uk (Office). *Website:* www .agnewsgallery.co.uk (Office).

AGNEW, Sir Rudolph (Ion Joseph), Kt, FRSA; British business executive; b. 12 March 1934; s. of Rudolph John Agnew and Pamela Geraldine (née Campbell) Agnew; m. Whitney Warren 1980; ed Downside School; Commissioned Officer 8th King's Royal Irish Hussars 1953–57; joined Consolidated Gold Fields PLC 1957, apptd Exec. Dir 1973, Deputy Chair. 1978–82, Group Chief Exec. 1978–89, Chair. 1983–89, mem. Cttee of Man. Dirs 1986–89; Chief Exec. Amey Roadstone Corpn 1974–78, Chair. 1974–77; Chair., CEO TVS Entertainment 1990–93; Chair. Stena Int. BV (fmrly Sealink Stena Line) 1990–, Federated Aggregates PLC 1991–95, Bona Shipholding Ltd, Bermuda 1993–98, LASMO PLC 1994–2000, Redland PLC 1995–97, Star Mining Corpn 1995–98; Jt Chair. Global Stone Corpn (Canada) 1993–94; Dir (non-exec.) New London PLC 1985–96, Standard Chartered PLC 1988–97, Newmount Mining Corpn, USA 1989–98, Hanson PLC 1989–91; Vice-Pres. Nat. Asscn of Boys Clubs; mem. Council WWF (UK) 1989– (Trustee 1983–89); Fellow, Game Conservancy. *Leisure interest:* shooting. *Address:* 7 Eccleston Street, London, SW1X 9LX, England.

AGOSTINI, Giacomo (Ago); Italian motorcyclist; b. 16 June 1942, Brescia; rode for Morini 1961–64; understudy to Mike Hailwood at MV Augusta 1965, number one rider 1966–73, 1976–77; rode for Yamaha 1974–76; 311 wins; a record 122 Grand Prix wins (54 at 350cc, 68 at 500cc); 12 Isle of Man TT wins (350cc: 1966, 1967, 1968, 1969, 1970, 1972; 500cc: 1967, 1968, 1969, 1970, 1971, 1972); 18 Italian championship wins; a record 15 World Championship wins (350cc: 1968, 1969, 1970, 1971, 1972, 1973, 1974; 500cc: 1966, 1967, 1968, 1969, 1970, 1971, 1972, 1975); shares (with Mike Hailwood) record for most races won in a season (19 in 1970). *Address:* c/o Media Affairs Office, Laureus World Sports Awards, 15 Hill Street, London W1J 5QT, England (Office).

AGRAWAL, Prabhu Lal, PhD; Indian business executive and engineer; b. 22 Oct. 1926, Udaipur, Rajasthan; s. of Tilok Chand Agrawal and Narayan Devi Agrawal; m. Pushpa Devi 1948; one s. one d.; ed Banaras Hindu Univ. and Univ. of Sheffield; Asst Prof., College of Mining and Metallurgy, Banaras Hindu Univ. 1947–54, Reader 1954–56; Tech. Officer Rourkela Steel Plant, then Sr Fuel Engineer, then Asst Chief Fuel Engineer, then Supt Energy & Economy Dept 1957–65, then Chief Supt 1965–66, Asst Gen. Supt 1966–69, Gen. Man. 1971–78; Gen. Supt Alloy Steels Plant 1969–70; Gen. Supt Bokaro Steel Ltd 1970–71; Chair. Steel Authority of India 1978–80; Tech. Adviser PT Krakatan Steel, Jakarta 1980–86; Dir Secure Meters Ltd; mem. judging panel for Prime Minister's Trophy for Best Operating Integrated Steel Plant 1992–97, 2000–01; Pres. Indian Inst. of Metals 1978, Hon. mem. 1980; Trustee Sevamandir 1987–; Holkar Fellow, Banaras Hindu Univ.; Uttar Pradesh Govt Book Prize for Audyogik Indhan; Nat. Metallurgists Day Award 1966; Bundesverdienstkreuz (1st Class) 1981; FIE Foundation Award, India

1981; Tata Gold Medal, Indian Inst. of Metals 1981, Platinum Medal, Indian Inst. of Metals 1993. *Publications:* Audyogik Indhan (Hindi); several technical papers and reports. *Leisure interests:* reading, social work, walking. *Address:* Narayan Villa, 56A New Fatehpura, Sukhadia Circle, Udaipur 31300, India (Home). *Telephone:* (294) 560380 (Office). *Fax:* (294) 560380. *E-mail:* plagrawal@bppl.net.in (Office).

AGRAWALA, Surendra Kumar, MA, LLD; Indian university administrator and professor of law; b. 18 Jan. 1929, Bilgram; s. of the late Radha Krishna and Tara Devi; m. Prof. Dr Raj Kumari Agrawala 1959; one s.; ed Allahabad and Lucknow Univs and Harvard Law School; Lecturer in Law, Lucknow Univ. 1953–62; Reader in Law, Aligarh Muslim Univ. 1962–65; Prof. and Head of Dept Poona Univ. 1965–85, Prof. Emer.; Vice-Chancellor, Agra Univ. 1985–88; Sec.-Gen. Asscn of Indian Univs. 1988–93; fmr mem. Governing Council, Indian Inst. of Science, Bangalore, Acad. Council, J. Nehru Univ., Court, Aligarh Muslim Univ.; Convener, UGC Advisory Panel on Law; numerous professional appointments, cttee memberships etc.; UGC Nat. Lecturer in Law 1974, K.M. Munshi Memorial Lecturer, Indian Law Inst. 1983; Banerjee Research Prize 1962, Best Univ. Teacher Award, Maharashtra Govt. 1979. *Publications:* International Law: Indian Courts and Legislature 1965, Essays on the Law of Treaties (ed.) 1972, Legal Education in India: Problems and Perspectives (ed.) 1973, Proposed Indian Ombudsman 1971, Aircraft Hijacking and International Law 1975, New Horizons of International Law (ed.) 1983, Public Interest Litigation in India 1985; about 50 articles in anthologies and legal journals. *Leisure interests:* reading, writing, travel and sightseeing. *Address:* 3/454 Vishwas Khand, Gomtinagar, Lucknow, UP, India. *Telephone:* (522) 309515.

AGRÉ, HE Cardinal Bernard; Côte d'Ivoirian ecclesiastic; b. 2 March 1926, Monga, Abidjan; ordained priest 1953; Bishop 1968; Bishop of Yamoussoukro 1992–96; Archbishop of Abidjan 1994–; cr. Cardinal 2001. *Address:* Archevêché, av. Jean Paul II, 01 B.P. 1287, Abidjan 01, Côte d'Ivoire (Office). *Telephone:* 211246 (Office); 212299 (Home). *Fax:* 214022 (Office).

AGT, Andries A. M. van; Netherlands politician; b. 2 Feb. 1931, Geldrop; s. of Frans van Agt and Anna Frencken; m. Eugenie Krekelberg 1958; one s. two d.; ed Catholic Univ., Nijmegen; worked at Ministry of Agric. and Fisheries, then Ministry of Justice 1968; Prof. of Penal Law, Univ. of Nijmegen 1968–; Minister of Justice 1971–77; Deputy Prime Minister 1973–77; Prime Minister and Minister of Gen. Affairs 1977–82; Minister of Foreign Affairs 1982; MP 1983; Gov. Prov. of Noord-Brabant 1983–87; Amb., Head Del. of European Communities, Tokyo, later Washington –1995.

AGUADO, Victor M., MSc, MEng; Spanish international official, aviation executive and engineer; b. 9 June 1953; m. Paloma Sierra de Aguado; one s. two d.; ed Polytechnic Univ., Madrid, MIT, USA; student trainee Lufthansa 1975; Man.of Tech.Standards, Maintenance Airforce Base, Albacete 1977–78; Systems Engineer in civil and military air traffic Man., Mitre Corpn, Boston, USA 1978–83; Programme Dir Civil Aviation Authority, Madrid 1983–84; Exec. Adviser to Sec. of State for Aerospace and Telecommunications Affairs 1984–85; Chair. Inter-Govt Task Force on major aerospace programmes 1984–85; Deputy Dir-Gen. in Spanish Admin. 1985–88, Dir-Gen.1988–90; apptd CEO ISDEFE SA Systems Engineering and Consulting Co., Madrid 1990; Air Navigation Commr ICAO, Montréal, Canada, later Pres. of Air Navigation 1996–2000; Dir-Gen. Eurocontrol, Brussels 2001–. *Address:* Eurocontrol, 96 rue de la Fusée, 1130 Brussels, Belgium (Office). *Telephone:* (2) 729-90-11 (Office). *Fax:* (2) 729-90-44 (Office). *Website:* www.eurocontrol.be (Office).

ÁGÚSTSSON, Helgi; Icelandic diplomatist; b. 16 Oct. 1941, Reykjavik; s. of Ágúst H. Pétursson and Helga Jóhannesdóttir; m. Hervör Jónasdóttir 1963; three s. one d.; ed Commercial Coll. of Iceland and Univ. of Iceland; joined Ministry for Foreign Affairs 1970; First Sec. and Counsellor, London 1973–77; Dir Defence Div. Ministry for Foreign Affairs and Icelandic Chair. US–Icelandic Defence Council 1979; Minister-Counsellor, Washington, DC 1983–87; Deputy Perm. Sec., Ministry for Foreign Affairs 1987; Amb. to UK (also accred to Ireland, Netherlands and Nigeria) 1989–94; Perm. Sec. Ministry for Foreign Affairs 1995–99; Amb. to Denmark (also accred to Lithuania, Turkey, Israel and Romania) 1998–99; fmr Pres. Icelandic Basketball Fed.; Hon. GCVO; Grand Cross of Dannebrog, Kt Commdr of White Rose, Grand Cross of Mérito Civil, Kt Commdr of Pole Star, Grand Cross of the Order of the Falcon, Grand Cross Oranje-Nassau Order, Grand Cross Norwegian Service Order, Grand Cross IMR. *Leisure interest:* salmon fishing. *Address:* Embassy of Iceland, Dantes Plads 3, 1556 Copenhagen V, Denmark (Office). *Telephone:* 3318-1050 (Office). *Fax:* 3318-1059 (Office). *E-mail:* icemb.coph@utn.stjr.is (Office).

AGUTTER, Jennifer Ann; British actress and dancer; b. 20 Dec. 1952, Taunton; d. of Derek Brodie Agutter and Catherine (née Lynam); m. Johan Tham 1990; one s.; ed Elmhurst Ballet School; film debut in East of Sudan 1964; has appeared in numerous TV films, dramas and series and on stage with RSC and Nat. Theatre. *Plays include:* Tempest, Spring Awakening, Hedda Gabler, Betrayal, The Unified Field, Breaking the Code, Love's Labour's Lost, Peter Pan. *Films include:* East of Sudan 1964, Ballerina 1964, Gates of Paradise 1967, Star 1968, I Start Counting, The Railway Children 1969, Walkabout, Logan's Run 1975, The Eagle Has Landed, Equus, Man in the Iron Mask, Riddle of the Sands, Sweet William, The Survivor 1980, An American Werewolf in London 1981, Secret Places 1983, Dark Tower 1987, King of the Wind 1989, Child's Play 2 1991, Freddie as Fro 7 1993, Blue Juice 1995, English Places, English Faces 1996. *TV includes:* Amy 1980, Not a Penny More, Not a Penny Less 1990, The Good Guys, Puss in Boots 1991, Love Hurts 1994, Heartbeat 1994, September 1995, 1996, The Buccaneers 1995, And The Beat Goes On 1996, A Respectable Trade 1997, Bramwell 1998, The Railway Children 2000, Spooks 2002. *Publication:* Snap 1983. *Leisure interest:* photography. *Address:* c/o Marmont Management, Langham House, 308 Regent Street, London, W1B 3AT, England.

AHERN, Bertie; Irish politician; b. 12 Sept. 1951, Dublin; s. of Cornelius Ahern and Julia Ahern; m. Miriam P. Kelly 1975 (separated); two d.; ed Rathmines Coll. of Commerce, Dublin, Univ. Coll., Dublin; accountant; mem. Dáil 1977–; mem. Dublin City Council 1979–, Lord Mayor 1986–87; Asst Chief Whip 1980–81; Spokesman on Youth Affairs 1981; Govt Chief Whip and Minister of State, Depts of Taoiseach and of Defence March–Nov. 1982; Minister for Labour 1987–91, for Finance 1991–94; Pres. EC Council of Ministers for Social Affairs Jan.–June 1990; Leader of the Opposition 1994–97; Prime Minister of Ireland 1997–; fmr mem. Bd of Govs IMF, World Bank, European Investment Bank (Chair. 1991–92), EBRD, EU Council of Ministers for Econs and Finance (ECOFIN); Grand Cross, Order of Merit with Star and Sash (Germany). *Leisure interests:* reading, sport. *Address:* Department of the Taoiseach, Government Buildings, Upper Merrion Street, Dublin 2 (Office); St Luke's, 161 Lower Drumcondra Road, Dublin 9, Republic of Ireland (Home).

AHERN, Dermot, BCL; Irish politician; b. Feb. 1955, Drogheda, Co. Louth; s. of Jeremiah Ahern and Gertrude Alice Ahern (née McGarrity); m. Maeve Coleman; two d.; ed Marist Coll., Dundalk, Univ. Coll., Dublin, Inc. Law Soc. of Ireland; solicitor 1976–; mem. Louth Co. Council 1979–91; mem. Dáil Éireann 1987–; mem. various Parl. Cttees.; Asst Govt Whip 1988–91; Minister of State at Depts. of the Taoiseach and Defence, Govt Chief Whip 1991–92; Minister for Social, Community and Family Affairs 1997–2002, for Communications, Marine and Natural Resources 2002–; mem. British–Irish Parl. Body 1991–97 (Co-Chair. 1993–95). *Address:* Department of Communications, Marine and Natural Resources, Leeson Lane, Dublin 2, Ireland (Office). *Telephone:* (1) 6789807. *Fax:* (1) 6782029.

AHLMARK, Per, BA; Swedish politician, journalist, novelist and poet; b. 15 Jan. 1939, Stockholm; s. of Prof. Axel Ahlmark; m. 1st (divorced); one s. one d.; m. 2nd Bibi Andersson (q.v.) 1978 (divorced); m. 3rd Lilian Edström; one s.; Leader of Young Liberals 1960–62; columnist for Expressen 1961–95, for Dagens Nyheter 1997–; mem. Parl. 1967–78; Deputy Chair. Swedish-Israeli Friendship Org. 1970–97; mem. Council of Europe 1971–76; mem. Royal Comms. on Literature, Human Rights, etc. in the 1970s; Leader, Folkpartiet (Liberal Party) 1975–78; Deputy Prime Minister and Minister of Labour 1976–78; Deputy Chair. Martin Luther King Fund 1968–73; Chair. Swedish Film Inst. 1978–81; Founder and Deputy Chair. Swedish Comm. Against Antisemitism 1983–95; Adviser to Elie Wiesel Foundation for Humanity, New York 1987–; mem. UN Watch, Geneva 1993–; mem. Acad. Universelle des Cultures, Paris; Fellow Wissenschaftskolleg zu Berlin 1998–99; Hon. Fellow (Hebrew Univ., Jerusalem) 1992; Defender of Jerusalem Award 1986 (New York). *Publications:* An Open Sore, Tyranny and the Left, many political books, essays and numerous articles, three books of poetry, one novel. *Leisure interests:* books. *Address:* Folkungag 61, 11622 Stockholm, Sweden.

AHLSEN, Leopold; German author; b. 12 Jan. 1927, Munich; m. Ruth Gehwald 1964; one s. one d.; Gerhart Hauptmann Prize; Schiller-Förderungspreis; Goldener Bildschirm; Hörspielpreis der Kriegsblinden; Silver Nymph of Monte Carlo, Bundesverdienstkreuz and other awards. *Publications:* 13 plays, 23 radio plays, 68 television plays, 7 novels. *Leisure interest:* joinery. *Address:* Waldschulstrasse 58, 81827 Munich, Germany. *Telephone:* (89) 4301466. *Fax:* (89) 4301466.

AHLSTRÖM, Krister Harry, MSc; Finnish business executive; b. 29 Aug. 1940, Helsinki; s. of Harry F. Ahlström and Asta A. (née Seege) Ahlström; m. Anja I. Artto 1974; one s. four d.; ed Helsinki Univ. of Technology; Product Eng, Gen. Man. and mem. Bd of Man. Oy Wärtsilä Ab 1966–81; Dir and mem. Exec. Bd A. Ahlström Corpn 1981–82, Pres. and CEO 1982–98, Chair. 1998–99; Vice-Chair. StoraEnso, Nordea Securities; Chair. Confed. Finnish Employers 1986–92, Fed. of Finnish Metal, Eng and Electrotechnical Industries 1992–96, Orgalime (Organisme de Liaison des Industries Métalliques Européennes) Brussels 1994–96; Chair. Board of the Research Inst. of the Finnish Economy. *Leisure interests:* sailing (World winner 8mR 1975), skiing. *Address:* c/o A. Ahlström Corporation, P.O. Box 329, Eteläesplanadi 14, 00101 Helsinki (Office); Kvarnvägen 2A2 00140 Helsinki, Finland (Home). *Telephone:* (10) 8884701 (Office); 500 500788 (Home). *Fax:* (9) (10) 8884729 (Office); (9) 625560 (Home). *E-mail:* krister.ahlstrom@ahlstrom.com. *Website:* www.STORAEnso.com; www.ahlstrom.com.

AHMAD, Shamshad, MA; Pakistani diplomatist; m.; two s.; ed Univ. of Punjab; diplomatic postings to Tehran 1968–69, Dakar 1969–72, Paris 1972–74, Washington 1977–80; with Pakistan Mission to UN (Chair. Political Cttee UN Council for Namibia and mem. UN Cttee on Palestine) 1980–81, Consul Gen. 1981–85; Dir-Gen. Ministry of Foreign Affairs 1985–87; Amb. to Repub. of Korea 1987–90, to Iran 1990–92; Sec.-Gen. Econ. Cooperation Org., Tehran 1992–96; Special Sec., Ministry of Foreign Affairs 1996–97, Foreign Sec. 1997–2000; Perm. Rep. to UN 2000–02; mem. ESCAP Panel of Eminent Persons on Human Resources Devt 1994. *Address:* c/o Aizad Ahmad Chaudhury, Head Office Chancery, Perm. Mission of Pakistan in UN, UN Plaza, New York, NY 10017, USA (Office). *Telephone:* (212) 879-8600 (Office). *Fax:* (212) 744-7348 (Office). *E-mail:* pakistan@un.int (Office).

AHMED, Jameel Yusuf; Pakistani civil servant; b. 10 May 1946, Hyderabad Deccan, India; s. of Yusuf Ahmed and of Amina Yusuf; m.; one s. two d.; ed Karachi Polytechnic Inst.; industrialist in paper cone mfg co. 1969; convenor Citizen Police Liaison Cttee (CPLC) Reporting Cell (est. to restore confidence in police service) 1989, Co-Chief CPLC 1990–, mem. numerous police reform cttees; mem. Bd of Govs Karachi Public Transport and Social Educ. Soc. (KPTC) 1999–; mem. Advisory Bd Interior Div., Fed. Ministry of the Interior 2000–; Hon. Sec. Bd of Govs Al-Murtaza School Network Charitable Trust 1989–, Chair. Steering Cttee Professional Devt Centre, Al-Murtaza 2001–; mem. Man. Cttee Zainabia Housing Trust 1990–, Steering Cttee NGO Resource Centre, Aga Khan Foundation 2001–; Founder and Trustee Panah Women's Shelter 2001–; Sitara-e-Shujaat 1992, Mulla Asghar Memorial Int. Award for Excellence in Educ. 2002. *Address:* CPCL-Central Reporting Cell, Sindh Governor's Secretariat, Gate No. 4, Abdullah Haroon Road, Karachi-75580 (Office); 37-L/1, Block-6, PECHS, Karachi, Pakistan (Home). *Telephone:* (21) 568222 (Office); (21) 4546428 (Home). *Fax:* (21) 5683336 (Office). *E-mail:* clcp@gerrys.net (Office); juchief@hotmail.com (Home).

AHMED, Kazi Zafar, BA; Bangladeshi politician; b. 1 July 1940, Cheora; s. of Kazi Ahmed Ali; m.; three d.; ed Dhaka Univ.; Office Sec. East Pakistan Students Union Cen. Cttee 1957, Office Sec. 1957–62, Gen. Sec. 1962–63; imprisoned several times for political activities between 1963 and 1965; Pres. Bangla Sramik Fed. 1967; actively participated in struggle for independence 1971; Sec.-Gen. Cen. Cttee Nat. Awami Party 1972–74; f. United People's Party 1974, Sec. Gen. 1974, Chair. Cen. Cttee 1979; mem. Nationalist Front 1978 (later became part of Nat. Party); Ed. Nayajug; Minister of Educ. 1978, Deputy Prime Minister, also in charge of Ports, Shipping and River Transport 1986–87, Political Adviser to the Pres. and Minister of Information 1988–91; Prime Minister 1989–91; formed rival faction to Nat. Party with Shah Moazzen Hossein 1997; charged with corruption; living in self-exile in Australia.

AHMED, Moudud, MA; Bangladeshi politician and barrister; b. 1940, Noakhali; s. of the late Bara Moulana; m. Hasna Jasimuddin; two s.; ed Dhaka Univ.; fmr Gen. Sec. East Pakistan House, England; took an active part in struggle for independence, organising External Publicity Div. of Bangladesh Govt in exile; Ed. Bangladesh (weekly); lawyer, Bangladesh Supreme Court 1972–74; Gen. Sec. Cttee for Civil Liberties Legal Aid 1974; imprisoned during State of Emergency 1974; Head, Bangladesh delegation to 32nd Session UN Gen. Ass. 1977; Adviser to Pres. 1977; Minister of Communications 1985–86, Deputy Prime Minister in charge of Ministry of Industries 1986–88, Prime Minister and Minister of Industry 1988–89, Vice-Pres. 1989–90; under house arrest 1990–91, imprisoned Dec. 1991, later released; Minister for Law, Justice &andParliamentary Affairs 2001–; Visiting Fellow South Asian Inst. of Heidelberg Univ., Harvard Univ. Centre for Int. Affairs, Oxford Univ. *Publications:* Bangladesh Contemporary Events and Documents, Bangladesh Constitutional Quest for Autonomy 1974, Democracy and the Challenge of Development: A Study of Politics and Military Interventions in Bangladesh. *Address:* Ministry of Law, Justice and Parliamentary Affairs, Bangladesh Government Secretariat, Dhaka; Islam Chamber 9th floor 125/A, Motijheel C/A, Dhaka 1000, Bangladesh (Office). *Telephone:* (2) 8610577 (Office); (2) 9888694 (Home). *Fax:* (2) 8618557 (Office).

AHMED, Shahabuddin, MA; Bangladeshi head of state and judge; b. 1930, Pemai of Kendua, Greater Mymensingh Dist; s. of Talukder Risat A. Bhuiyan (deceased); two s. three d.; ed Dhaka Univ., Lahore Civil Service Acad., Univ. of Oxford; joined Civil Service of Pakistan 1954 as Sub-Divisional Officer, later Additional Deputy Commr; transferred to Judicial Br. 1960; fmr Additional Dist and Sessions Judge, Dhaka and Barisal; fmr Dist and Sessions Judge, Comilla and Chittagong; fmr Registrar High Court of East Pakistan; elevated to High Court Bench 1972; appointed Judge of Appellate Div., Supreme Court of Bangladesh 1980; Chief Justice 1990, 1991–95; Chair. Comm. of Enquiry into police shootings of students 1983, Nat. Pay Comm. 1984, Labour Appellate Tribunal 1973–74, Bangladesh Red Cross Soc. 1978–82; Vice-Pres. League of Red Cross and Red Crescent Soc. (Geneva); Acting Pres. of Bangladesh 1990–91, Pres. of Bangladesh Oct. 1996–2001; Hon. Master, Hon. Soc. of Gray's Inn, London. *Address:* House Dal Motia, nr Mohammadpur, Dhaka, Bangladesh.

AHMETI, Ali; Macedonian politician; b. 4 Jan. 1959, Zajas, Macedonia; ed in Pristina; fmr. political leader of rebel ethnic Albanian Nat. Liberation Army; imprisoned for taking part in demonstrations by Kosovo Albanians 1981; moved to Switzerland 1993; Co-Founder Democratic Union for Integration 1999; formed multi-ethnic coalition Govt with Prime Minister Desig. Branko Crvenkovski's Together for Macedonia coalition Oct. 2002. *Address:* Parliamentary Assembly Buildings, Stojan Andov, 1000 Skopje, 11 Oktomvri bb, Macedonia (Office).

AHMETI, Vilson; Albanian politician; b. 5 Sept. 1951; ed Univ. of Tirana; engineer Vehicles Workshop, Tirana 1973–78; mem. Foreign Trade Dept Makina-Import 1978–87; Deputy Minister of Food 1987; Minister of Industry March–June 1991, of Food June–Dec. 1991; Prime Minister of Albania 1991–92; convicted of abusing power Sept. 1993; sentenced to two years' imprisonment.

AHO, Esko Tapani, MA; Finnish politician; b. 20 May 1954, Veteli; s. of Kauko Kaleva Aho and Laura Kyllikki (née Harjupatana) Aho; m. Kirsti Hannele Söderkultalahti 1980; two s. one d.; Chair. Youth Org. of the Centre Party 1974–80, Chair. Finnish Centre Party (KESK) 1990–; Political Sec. to Minister of Foreign Affairs 1979–80; Trade Agent, Kannus 1980–; MP 1983–; Prime Minister of Finland 1991–95; Presidential Cand. 2000. *Leisure interests:* literature, tennis, theatre. *Address:* Finnish Centre Party (Suomen Keskusta), Apollonkatu 11A, 00100 Helsinki, Finland. *Telephone:* (9) 75144200. *Fax:* (9) 75144240. *Website:* www.keskusta.fi (Office).

AHOMADEGBÉ, Justin Tometin; Benin politician; b. 1917; ed William Ponty School, Dakar and School of Medicine, Dakar; medical work, Cotonou, Porto-Novo 1944–47; mem. Gen. Council, Dahomey 1947, Sec.-Gen. Bloc Populaire Africain; Sec.-Gen. Union Démocratique Dahoméenne (UDD) 1956; mem. Grand Council, A.O.F. 1957; mem. Dahomey Legis. Ass. 1959, Pres. 1959–60; medical work 1960–61; imprisoned 1961–62; Minister of Health, Public Works and Nat. Education 1963; Vice-Pres. of Dahomey, Pres. of Council of Ministers and Minister in Charge of Interior, Defence, Security and Information 1964–65, also in charge of the Plan 1965; mem. Presidential Council 1970–72; Head of State May–Oct. 1972; imprisoned 1972 released April 1981; f. Rally of Democratic Forces 1990. *Address:* c/o Ministry of Justice, Cotonou, Benin.

AHRENDS, Peter, AADipl, RIBA; British architect; b. 30 April 1933, Berlin, Germany; s. of Steffen Bruno Ahrends and Margarete Marie Sophie (née Visino) Ahrends; m. Elizabeth Robertson 1954; two d.; ed King Edward VII School, Johannesburg, Architectural Asscn, London; research into decoration in Islamic Architecture 1956; Visiting Critic and/or External Examiner Kumasi Univ., AA School of Architecture, Nova Scotia Tech. Univ., Strathclyde Univ.; with Steffen Ahrends & Partners, Johannesburg 1957–58; with Denys Lasdun & Partners 1959–60; with Julian Keable & Partners; teacher A.A. School of Architecture 1960–61; f. architectural practice Ahrends, Burton and Koralek 1961, Partner, Dir 1961–; Visiting Prof. Kingston Polytechnic 1983–84; teacher and conducted workshops A.A. School of Architecture, Canterbury Art School, Edinburgh Univ., Winter School, Edinburgh, Plymouth Polytechnic, Plymouth Art School; Prof. Bartlett School of Architecture and Planning, Univ. Coll. London 1986–89; comms. include Trinity Coll. Library, Dublin 1961 and Arts Faculty Bldg 1979, Chichester Theological Coll. residential Bldg (Grade II listed) 1965, Templeton Coll. (Grade II listed), Oxford 1969, Nebenzahl House, Jerusalem 1972, Habitat Warehouse & Showroom, Wallingford 1974, Residential Bldg, Keble Coll. (Grade II* listed), Oxford 1976, Nat. Gallery Extension 1982–85, Cummins Engines Factory, Shotts 1983, J. Sainsbury Supermarket, Canterbury 1984, W. H. Smith Retail HQ, Swindon, phase I 1985, phase 2 1995, Office Devt for Stanhope Trafalgar 1990, St Mary's Hosp., Newport, Isle of Wight 1990, John Lewis Dept Store, Kingston 1990, White Cliffs Heritage Centre, Dover 1991, Poplar Footbridge, London Docklands 1992, Docklands Light Railway, Beckton Extension Stations 1993, Techniquest Science Centre, Cardiff 1995, Whitworth Art Gallery Sculpture Court 1995, Institutes of Tech. at Tralee, Waterford and Blanchardstown 1997–, Loughborough Univ. Business School 1998, Dublin Dental Hosp. extension 1998, New British Embassy, Moscow 1999, Waterford Visitor Centre 1999, Carrickmines Croquet and Lawn Tennis Club 2000, Dublin Inner City Devt Study 2000, Co. Offices at Tullamore, Offaly and N Riding Tipperary 2000–01, Dublin Corpn NEIC Civic Centre 2000–01; exhbns. at RIBA Heinz Gallery 1980, Royal Architects Inst., Ireland 1981, Douglas Hyde Gallery, Dublin 1981, Braunschweig Tech. Univ., Hanover Tech. Univ., Finnish Architecture Museum, Helsinki 1982, Alvar Aalto Museum, Jyvaskyla 1982, Architectural Asscn, Oslo 1983; mem. Design Council, Chair. UK Architects Against Apartheid 1988–93; RIBA Good Design in Housing Award 1977, RIBA Architecture Award 1978, 1993, 1996, 1999, Structural Steel Design Award 1980, Structural Steel Design Commendation 1993; RIAI Architecture Award 1999, Gulbenkian Museum of the Year Award 1999. *Publications:* Ahrends, Burton & Koralek, Architects (monograph) 1991, numerous articles in professional journals. *Leisure interests:* architecture and architecture-related interests. *Address:* Ahrends Burton & Koralek, 7 Chalcot Road, London, NW1 8LH (Office); 16 Rochester Road, London, NW1 9JH, England (Home). *Telephone:* (20) 7586-3311 (Office). *Fax:* (20) 7722-5445 (Office). *E-mail:* abk@abklondon.com (Office). *Website:* www.abk.co.uk (Office).

AHRLAND, Karin Margareta, LLB; Swedish politician; b. 20 July 1931, Torshälla; d. of Valfrid Andersson and Greta (née Myhlén) Andersson; m. 1st Hans F. Petersson 1958 (divorced 1962); m. 2nd Nils Ahrland 1964; one s.; ed Univ. of Lund; chief lawyer, County of Malmöhus 1971–76; mem. Riksdag (Parl.) 1976–; Minister for Public Health and Medical Services 1981–82; Del. UN Comm. on Status of Women 1976–79; Chair. Nat. Cttee for Equality between Men and Women 1979–81; Chair. Nat. Arts Council 1980; Amb. 1989–90; with Consul, Montreal 1990–. *Address:* c/o Ministry for Foreign Affairs, Gustav Adolfstorg 1, P.O. Box 16121, 103 39 Stockholm, Sweden. *Telephone:* (613) 241-8553. *Fax:* (613) 241-2277.

AHRWEILER, Hélène, DenHist, DèsL; French professor; b. 28 Aug. 1926, Athens, Greece; d. of Nicolas Glykatzi and Calliroe Psaltides; m. Jacques Ahrweiler 1958; one d.; ed Univ. of Athens; Research Worker CNRS 1955–67, Head of Research 1964–67; apptd Prof. Sorbonne 1967, now Emer.; Pres. Univ. de Paris I 1976–81; Rector Acad., Chancellor Univs. of Paris 1982–89; Chair. and Pres. Terra Foundation for the Arts (Chicago); Sec.-Gen. Int. Cttee of Historical Sciences 1980–90; Vice-Pres. Conseil d'Orientation du Centre

Georges Pompidou 1975–89, Conseil Supérieur de l'Education Nationale 1983–89; Pres. Centre Georges Pompidou 1989–91; Pres. Univ. of Europe, Paris; Pres. Comité d'Ethique des Sciences (CNRS) 1994; Pres. European Cultural Center of Delphi, Nat. Theatre, Athens (Greece); mem. Greek, British, Belgian, German and Bulgarian Acads.; Dr hc (Univs of London, New York, Belgrade, Harvard (USA), Lima, New Brunswick (Canada), Athens Social Science Univ., American Univ. of Paris, Haifa); Commdr, Légion d'honneur, Officier des Palmes académiques, Commdr Ordre Nat. du Mérite, Commdr des Arts et des Lettres, numerous foreign decorations. *Publications:* Byzance et la Mer 1966, Etudes sur les structures administratives et sociales de Byzance 1971, l'Idéologie politique de l'empire byzantin 1975, Byzance: les pays et les territoires 1976, Geographica 1981, The Making of Europe 2000, Les Européens 2001, contribs to numerous books. *Leisure interests:* tennis, swimming. *Address:* Sorbonne, 47 rue des Ecoles, 75005 Paris (Office); 28 rue Guynemer, 75006 Paris, France (Home).

AHTISAARI, Martti; Finnish politician and diplomatist; b. 23 June 1937, Viipuri; s. of Oiva Ahtisaari and Tyyne Ahtisaari; m. Eeva Irmeli Hyvärinen 1968; one s.; UN Envoy, Head of operation monitoring Namibia's transition to independence 1989–90, Sr Envoy participated in peace-making efforts in fmr Yugoslavia 1992–93; Pres. of Finland 1994–2000; EU's Special Envoy on Crisis in Kosovo 1999; mem. observer group on Austrian Govt's human rights record 2000; co-inspector of IRA arms dumps 2000–01; Co-Chair. East–West Inst.; Chair. Int. Crisis Group, War-torn Societies Project Int., Balkan Children and Youth Foundation; mem. Open Soc. Inst. Int. Advisor's Group, Exec. Bd of Int. Inst. for Democracy and Electoral Assistance. *Leisure interests:* golf, music, reading. *Address:* Erottajankatu 11A, 4th Floor, 00130 Helsinki, Finland. *Telephone:* (9) 6987024. *Fax:* (9) 6127759. *E-mail:* office@ahtisaari.fi (Office). *Website:* www.ahtisaari.fi (Office).

AI ZHONGXIN; Chinese painter; b. 13 Oct. 1915, Shanghai; m. Qian Lily, 1977; ed Nanjing Central Univ. and in USSR; Prof. Cen. Inst. of Fine Arts 1954–, Deputy Dir 1980–; mem. Chinese Artists Asscn. *Works include:* Yellow River, Road to Ulumci, Seashore. *Publications:* Study of Xu Beihong, On Style of Painting, etc. *Address:* Central Institute of Fine Arts, Beijing, People's Republic of China.

AIBEL, Howard James, BA, DJur; American lawyer, arbitrator and business executive; b. 24 March 1929, New York; s. of David Aibel and Anne Aibel; m. Katherine W. Webster 1952; three s.; ed Harvard Coll., Harvard Law School; admitted New York Bar 1952, served as Vice-Pres. of Asscn of the Bar of New York City, Chair. Cttee on Fed. Legislation, Assoc. White & Case, New York 1952–57; with Gen. Electric Co. 1957–64, Anti-Trust Litigation Counsel GE 1960–64; Trade Regulation Counsel ITT Corpn, New York 1964–66, Vice-Pres., Assoc. Gen. Counsel 1966–68, Gen. Counsel 1968–92, Sr Vice-Pres. 1969–87, Exec. Vice-Pres. 1987–94, Chief Legal Officer 1992–94; Pres. Harvard Law School Asscn of New York City 1992–93; partner Le Boeuf Lamb Greene & McRae 1994–99, mem. counsel 1999–2001; fmr Trustee, Chair. Advisory Bd School of Law, Bridgeport Univ. 1989–91, Chair. Exec. Cttee Bd of Dirs American Arbitration Asscn 1992–95, Chair. Bd of Dirs 1995–98; Bd of Dirs Alliance of Resident Theaters, New York 1986–, Chair. 1989–, Chair. Emer. 2002–; Vice-Chair., Trustee The Fund for Modern Courts 1985–95, Vice-Pres. Harvard Law School Asscn 1994–2002; mem. American Law Inst., New York State, American Bar Asscns.; mem. Bd of Dirs Sheraton Corpn 1982–94, Farrel Corp. 1994–; Life Fellow American Bar Foundation; Trustee Int. Bar Asscn Foundation, Lawyers' Cttee for Civil Rights under Law 1991–95; consulting Trustee Nature Centre for Environmental Activities of Westport; Harold S. Geneen Man. Award 1994. *Leisure interests:* theatre, bird study, photography. *Address:* Le Boeuf Lamb Greene & McRae, 125 West 55th Street, New York, NY 10019 (Office); 183 Steep Hill Road, Weston, CT 06883-1924, USA (Home). *Telephone:* (212) 424-8527 (Office); (203) 227-0738 (Home). *Fax:* (212) 424-8500 (Office); (203) 454-2072 (Home). *E-mail:* haibel@llgm.com (Office); hjaibel@optonline.net (Home).

AICHINGER, Ilse; Austrian writer; b. 1 Nov. 1921, Vienna; m. Günter Eich (died 1972); ed high school and Universität Wien; formerly worked with Inge Scholl at Hochschule für Gestaltung, Ulm; later worked as a reader for S. Fischer (publishers), Frankfurt and Vienna; Förderungspreis des Österreichischen Staatspreises 1952, Preis der Gruppe 47 1952, Literaturpreis der Freien und Hansestadt Bremen 1954, Immermannpreis der Stadt Düsseldorf 1955, Literaturpreis der Bayerischen Akademie 1961, Ny-ell Sachs-Preis, Dortmund 1971, City of Vienna Literature Prize 1974, Georg Tracke Prize 1979, Petrarca Prize 1982. *Publications:* Die Grössere Hoffnung (novel) 1948, Knöpfe (radio play) 1952, Der Gefesselte (short stories) 1953, Zu keiner Stunde (dialogues) 1957, Besuch im Pfarrhaus (radio play) 1961, Wo ich wohne (stories, dialogues, poems) 1963, Eliza, Eliza (stories) 1965, Nachricht von Tag (stories) 1970.

AIDA, Takefumi, PhD; Japanese architect and university professor; b. 5 June 1937, Tokyo; s. of Takeshi Aida and Chiyo Aida; m. Kazuko Aida 1966; one s. one d.; ed School of Architecture, Waseda Univ., Tokyo; qualified architect 1967; Prof. Shibaura Inst. of Tech., Tokyo 1976–2000, Prof. and Dean Dept of Architecture and Eng 1991–94; maj. works include: Memorial at Iwo-Jima Island, Tokyo 1983, Toy Block House X, Shibuya, Tokyo 1984, Tokyo War Dead Memorial Park, Bunkyo, Tokyo 1988, Saito Memorial Hall, Shibaura Inst. of Tech., Tokyo 1990, Community Centre, Kawasato 1993, Funeral Hall, Mizuho 1998, Nenseiji Temple 2001; Japan Architects' Asscn Annual Prize for Newcomers 1982; 2nd Prize Int. Doll's Houses Competition, England 1983.

Publications: Architecture Note, Toy Block Houses 1984, Toy Block House X 1986, Takefumi Aida Buildings and Projects 1990, The Works of Takefumi Aida 1998, The Collected Edition of Takefumi Aida 1998. *Leisure interest:* Shogi. *Address:* 1-3-2 Okubo, Shinjuku-ku, Tokyo 169-0072, Japan. *Telephone:* (3) 3205-1585. *Fax:* (3) 3209-7960. *E-mail:* t-aida@kt.rim.or.jp (Office).

AIDA, Yukio; Japanese banker; b. 1 Feb. 1924, Tokyo; ed Waseda Univ.; joined Nomura Securities Co. Ltd 1947, Chief Man. Int. Dept 1961–63, Dir 1963–67, Man. Dir 1967–71, Exec. Man. Dir Int. Operation 1971–76, Exec. Vice-Pres. 1976–83, Sr Adviser 1991, Hon. Chair. 1991–92, Chair. 1992–; Pres., CEO Nomura Investment Man. Co. Ltd 1983–86, Chair. 1986–87, Sr Adviser 1987–91. *Address:* Nomura Securities Co. Ltd, 6-40-8, Shimo-Shakujii, Nerima-ku, Tokyo 103, Japan. *Telephone:* (3) 3996-0886.

AIDOO, Ama Ata; Ghanaian writer; b. Ghana; one d.; lecturer Cape Coast Univ. 1970–73; consultant at Univs. Acads. and Research Insts. in Africa, Europe and USA; Minister of Educ. 1982–83; Chair. African Regional Panel of the Commonwealth Writers' Prize 1990, 1991; currently living in Zimbabwe. *Publications include:* novels: Our Sister Killjoy or Reflections from a Black-Eyed Squint 1977, Changes: A Love Story 1991, Poetry: Someone Talking to Sometime 1985, Birds and Other Poems, Plays: The Dilemma of a Ghost 1965, Anowa 1970; short stories: No Sweetness Here 1970, The Eagle and The Chicken and Other Stories 1987; numerous contribs. to magazines and journals. *Address:* P.O. Box 4930, Harare, Zimbabwe. *Telephone:* (4) 731901.

AIELLO, Danny; American actor; b. 20 May 1933, New York; s. of Daniel Louis Aiello and Frances Pietrocova; m. Sandy Cohen 1955; three s. one d. *Theatre includes:* Lamppost Reunion 1975 (Theatre World Award), Gemini 1977 (Obie Award 1977), Hurlyburly 1985. *Films include:* Bang the Drum Slowly 1973, The Godfather II 1976, Once Upon a Time in America 1984, The Purple Rose of Cairo 1985, Moonstruck 1987, Do the Right Thing 1989 (Boston Critics Award, Chicago Critics Award, L.A. Critics Award, all for Best Supporting Actor), Harlem Nights 1989, Jacob's Ladder 1990, Once Around 1991, Hudson Hawk 1991, The Closer 1991, 29th Street 1991, Mistress 1992, Ruby 1992, The Pickle 1992, The Cemetery Club 1992, The Professional 1994, Prêt-a-Porter 1994, Léon 1994, City Hall 1995, Power of Attorney 1995, Two Days in the Valley 1996, Mojave Moon 1996, Two Much 1996, A Brooklyn State of Mind 1997, Bring Me the Head of Mavis Davis 1998, Wilbur Falls 1998, Mambo Cafe 1999, 18 Shades of Dust 1999, Prince of Central Park 2000, Dinner Rush 2000, Off Key 2001, The Russian Job 2002, Marcus Timberwolf 2002, The Last Request 2002. *TV films include:* The Preppie Murder 1989, A Family of Strangers 1993 (Emmy Award), The Last Don (mini-series) 1997, Dellaventura (series) 1997, The Last Don II (mini-series) 1998. *Address:* William Morris Agency, 151 South El Camino Drive, Beverly Hills, CA 90212, USA.

AIKEN, Linda H., PhD; American nurse sociologist; b. 29 July 1943, Roanoke; d. of William Jordan and Betty Philips (Warner) Harman; one s. one d.; ed Univ. of Florida, Gainesville, Univ. of Texas, Austin, Univ. of Wisconsin, Madison; nurse, Univ. of Fla Medical Center 1964–65; Instructor, Coll. of Nursing, Univ. of Fla 1966–67; Instructor, School of Nursing, Univ. of Mo. 1967–70, Clinical Nurse Specialist 1967–70; lecturer, School of Nursing, Univ. of Wis. 1973–74; Program Officer, Robert Wood Johnson Foundation 1974–76, Dir of Research 1976–79, Asst Vice-Pres. 1979–81, Vice-Pres. 1981–87; Prof. of Nursing and Sociology, Dir Center for Health Services and Policy Research, Univ. of Pennsylvania 1988–; mem. Pres. Clinton's Nat. Health Care Reform Task Force 1993; Commr Physician Payment Review Comm. Nat. Advisory Council, U.S. Agency for Health Care Policy and Research; Assoc. Ed. Journal of Health and Social Behaviour 1979–81; Jessie M. Scott Award, American Nurses Asscn 1984, Nurse Scientist of the Year Award 1991, Best of Image Award 1991. *Publications:* Nursing in the 1980s: Crises, Challenges, Opportunities (Ed.) 1982, Evaluation Studies Review Annual 1985 (Co-ed. with B. Kehrer) 1985, Applications of Social Science to Clinical Medicine and Health Policy (Co-ed. with D. Mechanic) 1986, Charting Nursing's Future (Co-ed. with C. Fagin) 1991, Hospital Restructuring in North America and Europe 1997, Advances in Hospital Outcomes Research 1998, Accounting for Variation in Hospital Outcomes: Cross-National Study 1999; contrib. to professional journals. *Address:* University of Pennsylvania, Center for Health Outcomes and Policy Research, 420 Guardian Drive, NEB 332R, Philadelphia, PA 19104-6096 (Office); 2209 Lombard Street, Philadelphia, PA 19146-1107, U.S.A. (Home). *Telephone:* (215) 898-9759 (Office); (215) 898-5673 (Home). *Fax:* (215) 573-2062 (Office).

AILLAGON, Jean Jacques; French politician and cultural official; b. 2 Oct. 1946, Metz; s. of Charles Aillagon and Anne-Marie Louis; two c.; ed Univs of Toulouse and Nanterre; Prof. of History and Geography, Lycée de Tulle 1973–76; Deputy Dir Ecole Nat. Supérieure des Beaux-Arts 1978–82; Admin. Musée Nat. d'Art Moderne (Centre Pompidou) 1982–85; Asst to Dir of Cultural Affairs of City of Paris 1985–88; Del.-Gen. for Cultural Programmes of City of Paris 1988–93; Dir-Gen. Vidéothèque de Paris 1992–93; Dir of Cultural Affairs of City of Paris 1993–96; Pres. Centre Georges Pompidou 1996–2002; Minister of Culture and Communication May 2002–; Pres. commission organizing year 2000 celebrations 1999–2001; Artistic Dir Commissariat for France-Egypt Year 1996–98; Chevalier, Ordre Nat. du Mérite, des Palmes académiques, Légion d'honneur. *Address:* Ministry of Culture and

Communication, 3 rue de Valois, 75001 Paris; 3 rue de Venise, 75004 Paris, France (Home). *Telephone:* 1-40-15-80-00. *Fax:* 1-42-61-35-77. *Website:* www .culture.gouv.fr.

AILLERET, François; French government official; b. 7 June 1937; s. of Pierre Ailleret and Denise Nodé-Langlois; m. Chantal Flinois 1963; four c.; served in Algeria and Côte d'Ivoire in early 1960s; various appts. at Paris Airport 1967–80; joined Electricité de France (EDF) 1980, Deputy Dir-Gen. 1987, Dir-Gen. 1994–96, Vice-Pres. 1996, Pres. EDF Int. 1996–; Pres. Int. Union of Electricity Producers and Distributors (UNIPEDE) 1997–2000; Admin. Pechiney 1996–; Officier, Légion d'honneur, Commdr Ordre Nat. du Mérite, Croix de la Valeur militaire. *Address:* EDF International, 22–30 avenue de Wagram, 75008 Paris (Office); 33 rue Desnouettes, 75015 Paris, France (Home). *Telephone:* 1-40-42-26-70 (Office). *Fax:* 1-40-42-77-78 (Office). *E-mail:* francois.ailleret@edfgdf.fr (Office).

AIMÉ, Jean-Claude C., MBA; Haitian international civil servant; b. 10 Sept. 1935, Port-au-Prince; s. of Christian F. Aimé and Carmen Amelia Gautier; m. 1st Elizabeth B. Bettison 1963 (divorced 1991); m. 2nd Lisa M. Buttenheim 1992; ed Harvard Coll., Univ. of Pennsylvania; joined UN 1962, Programme Officer Tunis 1963–64, Asst Resident Rep. UNDP Algiers 1964–67, ILO Geneva 1967–69, Deputy Perm. Rep. UNDP Amman 1969–71, UN Relief Operation Dacca 1971–72, Rep. East African Community Arusha UNDP 1972–73, Resident Rep. UNDP Amman 1973–77, Sr Adviser UNIFIL Naqoura 1978, UN Sr Adviser in the Middle East 1979–82, Dir Office of Under-Secs.-Gen. for Special Political Affairs 1982–88, Exec. Asst to Sec.-Gen. 1989–92, Asst Sec.-Gen., Chief of Staff 1992–96, Exec. Sec. UN Compensation Comm., Geneva 1997–2000. *Leisure interests:* music, reading, squash, hunting. *Address:* c/o Ministry of Foreign Affairs and Religion, blvd Harry S. Truman, Cité de l'Exposition, Port-au-Prince, Haiti. *Telephone:* 222-8482. *Fax:* 223-1668.

AIMÉE, Anouk; French actress; b. Françoise Dreyfus, 27 April 1932, Paris; d. of Henry Dreyfus and Geneviève Durand; m. 2nd Nico Papatakis 1951; one d.; m. 3rd Pierre Barouh 1966; m. 4th Albert Finney (q.v.) 1970 (divorced 1978); ed Ecole de la rue Milton, Paris, Ecole de Barbezieux, Pensionnat de Bandd, Inst. de Megève and Cours Bauer-Therond; film and TV actress 1955–; Commdr des Arts et des Lettres, Golden Globe Award 1968, Prix Féminin, Cannes. *Theatre includes:* Sud 1954, Love Letters 1990, 1994. *Films include:* Les mauvaises rencontres 1955, Tous peuvent me tuer, Pot bouille and Montparnasse 19 1957, La tête contre les murs 1958, Les drageurs 1959, La dolce vita, Le farceur, Lola, Les amours de Paris, L'imprévu 1960, Quai Notre Dame 1960, Le jugement dernier 1961, Sodome et Gomorrhe 1961, Les grands chemins 1962, Education sentimentale 1962, Huit et demi 1962, Un homme et une femme 1966, Un soir un train 1967, The Appointment 1968, Model Shop 1968, Justine 1968, Si c'était à refaire 1976, Mon premier amour 1978, Salto nel vuoto 1979, La tragédie d'un homme ridicule 1981, Qu'est-ce qui fait courir David? 1982, Le Général de l'armée morte 1983, Vive la vie and Le succès à tout prix 1984, Un homme et une femme: vingt ans déjà 1986, Docteur Norman Bethune 1992, Les Marmottes 1993, Les Cent et une Nuits 1995, Prêt-à-porter 1995. *Television:* Une page d'amour 1979, Des voix dans le jardin. *Leisure interests:* reading, life, human rights. *Address:* 9 rue Girardon, 75018 Paris (Home); Bureau Georges Beaume, 3 Quai Malaquais, 75006 Paris, France.

AINSLEY, John Mark; British tenor; b. 9 July 1963, Crewe; s. of John Alwyn Ainsley and Dorothy Sylvia Ainsley (née Anderson); ed Royal Grammar School, Worcester, Madgalen Coll. Univ. of Oxford; debut in Stravinsky's Mass, Royal Festival Hall 1984; many concert performances from 1985 with Taverner Consort, New London Consort and London Baroque; appearances in Mozart Masses at The Vienna Konzerthaus with Heinz Holliger, Handel's Saul at Götingen with John Eliot Gardiner, the Mozart Requiem under Yehudi Menuhin at Gstaad and Pulcinella at the Barbican under Jeffrey Tate; other concerts with the Ulster Orchestra and the Bournemouth Sinfonietta; debut in USA at Lincoln Center in Bach's B Minor Mass with Christopher Hogwood 1990; opera debut at the Innsbruck Festival in Scarlatti's Gli Equivoci nel Sembiante, at the ENO in the Return of Ulysses 1989; title role in Méhul's Joseph for Dutch Radio, Handel's Acis in Stuttgart and Solomon for Radio France under Leopold Hager; has sung Mozart's Tamino for Opera Northern Ireland and Ferrando for Glyndebourne Touring Opera; sang Ferrando at Glyndebourne 1992, Don Ottavio 1994, Haydn's The Seasons with the London Classical Players; BBC Proms Concerts, London 1993, Stravinsky concert under Andrew Davis at Royal Festival Hall 1997, Monteverdi's Orfeo for the Munich Festival 1999, Jupiter in Semele for ENO 1999; Grammy Award for best opera recording 1995. *Recordings include:* Handel's Nisi Dominus under Simon Preston, Purcell's Odes with Trevor Pinnock, Mozart's C Minor Mass with Christopher Hogwood, Great Baroque Aria with the King's Consort, Acis and Galatea, Saul. *Address:* c/o Askonas Holt, Lonsdale Chambers, 27 Chancery Lane, London, WC2A 1PF, England (Office).

AIPIN, Yeremey Danilovich; Russian author; b. 27 June 1948, Varyegan, Khanty-Mansisky district; s. of Danil Romanovich Aipin and Vera Savljevna Aipina; m.; two d.; ed Gorky Inst. of Literature; People's Deputy 1990–91; Pres. Asscn of Aboriginal Peoples of the North, Siberia and Far East of Russia (now Asscn of Aboriginal People of the North, Siberia and Far East of Russia) 1993; a founder of Democratic Choice of Russia party in Khanty-Mansysk Autonomous Region 1994; mem. State Duma, Deputy Chair. Cttee on Nat.

Affairs 1993–96, Deputy Chair. of Duma, Chair. Ass. of Native People's Reps; Honoured Achiever in Culture 1998, Khanty-Mansisky Governor's Prize 1999. *Publications include:* I am Listening to the Earth, Khanty or Star of Morning Dawn, In Wait for the First Snow, By the Dying Fire, and other works about peoples of N Russia. *Leisure interests:* hunting, fishing, reindeer breeding. *Address:* Mira str. 628011 Khanty-Mansisk, (Office); Lenina str. 39, apt. 27 628011 Khanty-Mansisk,Russia (Home). *Telephone:* (34671) 2-45-78 (Office); (34671) 2-25-57 (Home). *Fax:* (34671) 2-14-35 (Office). *E-mail:* aipin@ dumahmao.ru (Office).

AIREY, Dawn Elizabeth, MA, FRSA, FRTS; British television executive; b. 15 Nov. 1960, Preston, Lancs.; d. of Kelly Coll., Girton Coll. Cambridge; with Cen. TV 1985–93; ITV Network Centre 1993–94; Channel 4 1994–96; Channel 5 1996–2002, Chief Exec. 2000–02; Man. Dir Sky Networks 2002–; Vice-Pres. Royal TV Soc. 2002–; Olswang Businees Woman of the Year 2000. *Leisure interests:* cinema, tennis. *Address:* Sky Networks, British Sky Broadcasting, Grant Way, Isleworth, Middx, TW7 5QD, England (Office).

AIRLIE, 13th Earl of; David George Patrick Coke Ogilvy, KT, GCVO, PC, RVO; British business executive; b. 17 May 1926, London; s. of 12th Earl of Airlie, KT, GCVO, MC and Lady Alexandra Marie Bridget Coke; m. Virginia Fortune Ryan 1952; three s. three d.; ed Eton Coll.; Chair. Schroders PLC. 1977–84, Ashdown Investment Trust Ltd 1968–84, J. Henry Schroder Bank AG (Switzerland) 1977–84, Baring Stratton Investment Trust PLC 1986–2000; Chair. Gen. Accident Fire and Life Assurance Corpn PLC 1987–97; Dir J. Henry Schroder Wagg & Co. Ltd 1961–84, Schroder, Darling and Co. Holdings Ltd (Australia) 1977–84, Schroders Inc. (USA) 1977–84, Schroder Int. Ltd 1973–84, Scottish & Newcastle Breweries PLC 1969–83; Dir Royal Bank of Scotland Group PLC 1983–93; Lord Chamberlain of the Queen's Household 1984–97; Lord Lt of Angus 1989–2001; Chancellor Univ. of Abertay Dundee 1994–; Chair. Historic Royal Palaces 1998–2002; Pres. Nat. Trust for Scotland 1998–2002; Gov. Nuffield Hosps.; Hon. Pres. Scout Asscn in Scotland 1988–2002, JP Angus 1990; Hon. LLD (Univ. of Dundee) 1990. *Address:* Cortachy Castle, Kirriemuir, Angus, Scotland; 36 Sloane Court West, London, SW3 4TB England. *Telephone:* (1575) 540231. *Fax:* (1575) 540223 (Office); (1575) 540400.

AITCHISON, Craigie (Ronald John), CBE; British artist; b. 13 Jan. 1926, Scotland; s. of the late Rt Hon the Lord Aitchison and of Lady Aitchison; ed Slade School of Fine Art, London; British Council/Italian Govt Scholarship for Painting 1955; Edwin Austin Abbey Premier Scholarship 1970; Lorne Scholarship 1974–75; Arts Council Bursary 1976; works in public collections including Tate Gallery, Arts Council of GB, Contemporary Art Soc., London, Scottish Nat. Gallery of Modern Art, Scottish Arts Council, Walker Art Gallery, Liverpool and Newcastle Region Art Gallery, NSW, Australia, British Council Exhbn, Israel Museum, Jerusalem 1992; fmr RA, resgnd 1997, rejoined 1998; Prizewinner John Moores Liverpool Exhbn 1974–75, Johnson's Wax Award for Best Painting at Royal Academy Summer Exhibition 1982, Korn Ferry Int. Award, Royal Academy Summer Exhibition 1989, 1991, Jerwood Foundation Prize 1994, Nordstern Art Prize 2000. *One man exhibitions:* Beaux Arts Gallery, Marlborough Fine Art, Rutland Gallery, Serpentine Gallery, 12 Duke Street Gallery, Timothy Taylor Gallery, Waddington Galleries and others, London, Compass Gallery, Glasgow, Scottish Arts Council, Edinburgh, Kettle's Yard, Cambridge, Artis, Monte Carlo and others; retrospectives, Harewood House, Leeds 1954–94, Gallery of Modern Art, Glasgow 1956–96; many mixed exhbns in UK, Italy, Japan, France and India. *Address:* c/o Royal Academy of Arts, Burlington House, Piccadilly, London, W1V 0DS, England.

AITMATOV, Askar Chingizovich; Kyrghyzstan politician; b. 5 Jan. 1959, Frunze; s. of Chingiz Aitmatov; ed Moscow State Univ.; mem. staff Div. of Middle Asia, Ministry of Foreign Affairs, USSR 1982–83; Information Dept 1987–90; seconded to USSR Embassy, Turkey 1983–87; mem. Political Information Dept, Ministry of Foreign Affairs, Kyrghyzstan 1990–92, Deputy Minister of Foreign Affairs 1992–94, Minister June 2002–; Acting Perm. Rep. to UN, New York 1994–96; Adviser, Office of the Pres. 1996–98, Head Dept of Foreign Policy 1998–2002. *Address:* Ministry of Foreign Affairs, Erkindik blvd, 54, 720021 Bishkek, Kyrghyzstan (Office). *Telephone:* (312) 22-05-45 (Office).

AITMATOV, Ilgiz Torekulovich, PhD, D.TECH.SC.; Kyrgyzstan scientist; b. 8 Feb. 1931, Frunze (now Bishkek); s. of Torokul Aitmatov and Naghima (née Abdulvaliyeva) Aitmatova; m. Rosalia Jamankulovna Jenchuraeva 1961; one s. two d.; ed Moscow Inst. of Geological Survey; foreman, Eng, Head anti-avalanche surveillance service, Kyrgyz Geological Man. 1954–57; Jr researcher, Head of Lab., Deputy Dir Inst. of Physics and Mechanics of Rocks, Kyrgyz Acad. of Sciences 1960–64, Head of Lab. 1965–68, Deputy Dir 1968–70, Dir 1970–90, 1994–; mem. Kyrgyz Acad. of Sciences 1989–, Academician-Sec. Dept of Physical, Math. and Geological Sciences 1989–90; mem. Political Council People's Republican Party of Kyrgyzstan 1992–; People's Deputy XII convocation 1990–94; mem. Council 1990–91; Chair. Constant Comm. Soviet for Science, Tech., Industry, Power Industry and Communications 1984; Pres. Kyrgyz Acad. of Sciences 1990–93; People's Deputy of Kyrgyzstan 1990–94; USSR State Prize 1989, Merited Worker of Science of Kyrgyzstan; other medals and awards. *Publications:* more than 200 papers on geomechanics. *Address:* Institute of Rock Physics and Mechanics, O Mederov

Str. 98, 720035 Bishek (Office); 98 Toktoghul Str., Apartment 9, 720000 Bishkek, Kyrgyzstan (Home). *Telephone:* (312) 54-11-15 (Office); (312) 66-21-89 (Home). *Fax:* (312) 54-11-17 (Office). *E-mail:* djam@freenet.kg (Home).

AITMATOV, Tchinguiz Torekulovich; Kyrgyzstan writer and diplomatist; b. 12 Dec. 1928, Sheker Village; s. of the late Torekul Aitmatov and of Nagima Aitmatova; m. Maria Urmatova 1974; three s. one d.; ed Kyrgyz Agricultural Inst.; writer 1952–; fmrly Corresp. for Pravda; mem. CPSU 1959–91; First Sec. of Cinema Union of Kyrgyz SSR 1964–69, Chair. 1969–86; Chair. of Union of Writers of Kyrgyzstan 1986–; Cand. mem. Cen. Cttee of CP of Kyrgyz SSR 1969–71, mem. 1971–90; People's Writer of Kyrgyz SSR 1968; Vice-Chair. Cttee of Solidarity with Peoples of Asian and African Countries 1974–89; Deputy to USSR Supreme Soviet 1966–89; People's Deputy of the USSR 1989–91; mem. Presidential Council 1990–91; USSR (now Russian) Amb. to Luxembourg 1990–92; Kyrgyzstan Amb. to Benelux countries and France 1992–; mem. Kyrgyz Acad. of Science 1974, European Acad. of Arts, Science and Humanity 1983, World Acad. of Art and Science 1987; Chair. Issyk-Kul Forum 1986–; Chief Ed. Innostrannaya Literatura 1988–90; Rep. Euro–Atlantic Partnership Council, NATO; Lenin Prize for Tales of the Hills and the Steppes 1963; Austrian State Prize for European Literature 1994; Hero of Socialist Labour 1978, State Prize in Literature 1968, 1977, 1983 and other decorations and prizes from Germany, Kyrgyzstan, India, Turkey and USA. *Stories filmed include:* The First Teacher, Djamilya, My Poplar in a Red Kerchief, The White Steamship. *Publications include:* stories: Face to Face, Short Stories, Melody 1961, Tales of the Hills and the Steppes 1963; Stories 1967; Mother Earth and Other Stories 1989; novels: Djamilya 1959, My Poplar in a Red Kerchief 1960, Camel's Eye, The First Teacher, Farewell Gulsary, Mother Earth 1963, The White Steamship (English trans. 1972), The Lament of the Migrating Bird (English trans. 1972), The Ascent of Mount Fuji (with Muhamegjanov) 1973, co-author of Earth and Water 1978, Works (3 Vols) 1978, Early Storks 1979, Stories 1979, Piebald Dog, Running Along the Sea Shore, The Day Lasts More Than a Hundred Years 1980, Executioner's Block (English trans. 1987) 1986, The Place of the Skull, The White Cloud of Chingiz Khan 1991, A Conversation at the Foothill of Fudjiyama Mountain (with Daisaku Ikeda) 1992, The Brand of Cassandra (novel) 1994. *Leisure interest:* skiing. *Address:* Embassy of the Kyrgyz Republic, rue de L'Abbaye, 1050 Brussels (Office); Toktogul str. 98, Apt. 9, 720000 Bishkek, Kyrgyzstan (Home); 244, avenue Louise, 6.5, 1050 Brussels, Belgium. *Telephone:* (32) 640-18-68 (Office); (32) 672-27-22. *Fax:* (32) 640-01-31 (Office); (32) 646-37-29 (Home). *E-mail:* aitmatov@infonie.be (Office).

AIZAWA, Hideyuki, LLB; Japanese politician; b. 4 July 1919; m. Yoko Aizawa; three s.; ed Univ. of Tokyo; mem. House of Reps., Tottori Pref.; Vice-Minister of Finance; Vice-Chair. Policy Affairs Research Council Liberal Democratic Party (LDP); Dir-Gen. Research Bureau, Treasury Bureau, (LDP); Chair. Cttee on Judicial Affairs, Cttee on Foreign Affairs; Dir-Gen. Econ. Planning Agency, Minister of State 1990; Chair. Extraordinary Cttee on Revitalizing Securities and Bond Markets (LDP) 2000–, Financial Reconstruction Comm., Ministry of State 2001–. *Publications include:* A Day in My Life (autobiog.), From the Forest of Ta Taru (novel), Flower and After (photo album). *Leisure interests:* golf, photography. *Address:* 2-2-1-721, Nagata-cho, Chiyoda-ku, Tokyo 100-8981 (Office); 7-10-3, Seijo, Setaya-ku, Tokyo 167-0066 (Home); c/o Liberal Democratic Party, 1-11-23 Nagata-cho, Chiyoda-ku, Tokyo 100-8910, Japan. *Telephone:* (3) 3508-7207 (Office); (3) 3484-1234 (Home); (3) 3581-6211. *Fax:* (3) 3502-3399 (Office); (3) 3483-0017 (Home). *E-mail:* aizawahideyuki@mbg.sphere.ne.jp (Office). *Website:* www.mars .sphere.ne.jp/aizawa/ (Office).

AJAYI, Jacob Festus Ade, PhD; Nigerian professor of history; b. 26 May 1929, Ikole-Ekiti; s. of the late Chief E. Ade Ajayi and Comfort F. Bolajoko Ajayi; m. Christie Akinleye-Martins 1956; one s. four d.; ed Igbobi Coll. Lagos, Higher Coll. Yaba, Univ. Coll. Ibadan, Univ. Coll. Leicester and King's Coll. London; tutor, Ibadan Boys' High School 1948–49, 1951–52; Fellow, Inst. of Historical Research 1957–58; Lecturer, Sr Lecturer, Univ. of Ibadan 1958–63, Prof. of History 1963–89; Fellow, Center for Advanced Study in the Behavioural Sciences, Stanford 1970–71; Vice-Chancellor, Univ. of Lagos 1972–78; Pro-Chancellor, Ondo State Univ., Ado-Ekiti 1984–88; mem. UN Univ. Council 1974–80, Chair. 1976–77; Chair. Int. African Inst. 1975–87; mem. Bureau, Asscn of African Univs 1973–80, Vice-Pres. 1976–80; mem. Bureau, Int. Asscn of Univs 1980–90; Pres. Historical Soc. of Nigeria 1972–81; mem. UNESCO scientific Cttee for drafting The General History of Africa (Ed. Vol. VI) 1970–93, Council, Nat. Univ. of Lesotho 1976–82, OAU Group of Eminent Persons for Reparation 1992–, editorial Bd Encyclopaedia of Sub-Saharan Africa 1995–; mem. Bd of Dirs of SOWSCO 1994–; Corresp. Fellow Royal Historical Soc., UK; Hon. Fellow SOAS, Univ. of London 1994; Hon. LLD (Leicester) 1975; Hon. DLitt (Birmingham) 1984, (Ondo State Univ.) 1992; Bd of Trustees Nigerian Merit Award 1996–; Bobapitan of Ikole-Ekiti and Onikoyi of Ife 1983; Nigerian Order of Nat. Merit 1986; Officer of the Fed. Repub. (OFR); Univ. of Lagos Anniversary Gold Medal 1987, Distinguished Africanist Award (African Studies Asscn of USA) 1993. *Publications include:* Milestones in Nigerian History 1962, Yoruba Warfare 1964, Christian Missions in Nigeria, 1841–91: The Making of a New Elite 1965; Cementing Partnership: The Story of WAPCO 1960–90, History and the Nation and other Addresses, History of the Nigerian Society of Engineers 1995, The African Experience with Higher Education 1996, Tradition and Change: Essays of J F Ade Ajayi, A Patriot to the Core: Bishop Ajayi Crowther (with Akinseye-George), Kayode Eso: the Making of a Judge 2002; ed. or jt ed. of various vols on African history. *Leisure interests:* table tennis, dancing. *Address:* PO Box 14617, University of Ibadan, Ibadan (Office); 1, Ojobadan Avenue, Bodija, Ibadan, Nigeria (Home). *Telephone:* (2) 8100064 (Office); (2) 8101588 (Home). *Fax:* (2) 8100064 (Office). *E-mail:* jadeas@skannet.com.

AJIBOLA, Hon. Prince Bola; Nigerian judge; b. 22 March 1934, Lagos; s. of Oba A. S. Ajibola and Adikatu Ashakun Ajibola; m. Olu Ajibola 1961; three s. two d.; ed Holborn Coll. of Law, London Univ.; called to the English Bar (Lincoln's Inn) 1962; Prin. Partner, Bola Ajibola & Co., Lagos, Ikeja, Abeokuta and Kaduna, specializing in commercial law and int. arbitration; fmr Attorney-Gen. and Fed. Minister of Justice; mem. Int. Court of Justice, The Hague 1991–94; mem. Nigerian del. to UN Gen. Ass. 1986; Temporary Pres. UN Gen. Ass., 17th Special Session on Narcotic Drugs 1990; Chair. Task Force for Revision of the Laws of the Fed. 1990; initiated first African Law Ministers Conf., Abuja 1989; Chair. Gen. Council of the Bar, Disciplinary Cttee of the Bar, Advisory Cttee on the Prerogative of Mercy; Pres. African Concern 1996–; mem. Nigeria Police Council, Int. Law Comm., Perm. Court of Arbitration, The Hague, ICC Court of Arbitration, Int. Maritime Arbitration Comm., Paris, Panel of Int. Arbitrators, London Inst. of Arbitrators, Int. Advisory Cttee of World Arbitration Inst., USA; Judge and Vice-Pres. IBRD Tribunal, Washington, DC 1995–; Vice-Pres. Inst. of Int. Business Law and Practice, Paris; Nat. Chair. World Peace Through Law Centre; Ed. Nigeria's Treaties in Force 1970–1990, All Nigeria Law Reports 1961–1990; Ed.-in-Chief, Justice; Gen. Ed. Fed. Ministry of Justice Law Review Series (7 Vols); Fellow Chartered Inst. of Arbitrators, Nigerian Inst. of Advanced Legal Studies; mem. Nigerian Bar Asscn (Pres. 1984–85), African Bar Asscn, Int. Bar Asscn, Asscn of World Lawyers, ICC, Commonwealth Law Asscn, World Arbitration Inst., Soc. for the Reform of Criminal Law; Hon. LLD (Buckingham) 1996. *Publications:* Principles of Arbitration 1980, The Law and Settlement of Commercial Disputes 1984, Law Development and Administration in Nigeria 1987, Integration of the African Continent Through Law 1988, Banking Frauds and Other Financial Malpractices in Nigeria 1989, Women and Children under Nigerian Law 1990, Scheme Relating to Mutual Assistance in Criminal Matters and the Control of Criminal Activities within Africa and numerous other books on other legal topics. *Address:* c/o IBRD, 1818 H Street, NW, Washington, DC 20433, USA; 141 Igbosere Road, Lagos, Nigeria.

AJODHIA, Jules Rattankoemar; Suriname politician; Vice-Pres. and Prime Minister of Suriname 1991–96, 2000–; mem. Verenigde Hervormings Partij (VHP). *Address:* c/o Verenigde Hervormings Partij, Paramaribo, Suriname.

AKAGAWA, Jiro; Japanese author; b. 29 Feb. 1948, Fukuoka; m. Fumiko Serita 1973; one d.; ed Toho-gakuen High School; fmr proof-reader for Japan Soc. of Mechanical Engineers; mem. Japanese Mystery Writers' Asscn 1977–; All Yomimono Debut Writers' Award 1976; Kadokawa Publishing Book Award 1980. *Publications:* more than 400 works including novels: The School Festival for the Dead 1977, Ghost Train 1978, The Deduction of Tortoise-shell Holmes 1978, High School Girl with a Machine Gun 1978, The Requiem Dedicated to the Bad Wife 1980, Virgin Road 1983, Chizuko's Younger Sister 1989, The Ghost Story of the Hitokoizaka-Slope 1995. *Leisure interests:* classical music, watching movies. *Address:* 40-16-201 Ohyama-cho, Sibuya-ku, Tokyo 151-0065, Japan.

AKAKA, Daniel Kahikina; American politician; b. 11 Sept. 1924, Honolulu; s. of Kahikina Akaka and Annie Kahoa; m. Mary M. Chong 1948; four s. one d.; ed Univ. of Hawaii; schoolteacher, Hawaii 1953–60; Vice-Prin., Prin. Ewa Beach Elementary School, Honolulu 1960–64; Prin. Pohakea Elementary School 1964–65, Kaneohe Elementary School 1965–68; Dir Hawaii Office of Econ. Opportunity 1971–74; Special Asst Human Resources Office of Gov. of Hawaii 1975–76; program specialist, Hawaii Compensatory Educ. 1978–79, 1985–91; mem. 95th–101st Congresses from 2nd Dist of Hawaii 1977–90; Senator from Hawaii 1990–; Democrat. *Address:* United States Senate, 141 Hart Senate Bldg, Washington, DC 20510-0001, USA.

AKALAITIS, Joanne; American artistic director (retd); b. 29 June 1932, Chicago; d. of Clement Akalaitis and Estelle Mattis; m. Philip Glass 1965 (divorced 1974); one s. one d.; ed Univ. of Chicago and Stanford Univ. Grad. School; Artistic Dir New York Shakespeare Festival 1991–92; Rockefeller Playwright Fellow; Rosamund Gilder Fellow; Guggenheim Fellow 1978; recipient of four Obies for distinguished direction. *Works directed include:* Beckett's Cascando 1976, Dressed Like an Egg 1977, Dead End Kids 1980, A History of Nuclear Power (writer and dir of play and film), Request Concert (Drama Desk Award) 1981, The Photographer 1983, Beckett's Endgame 1984, Genet's The Balcony 1985, Green Card (writer and dir) 1986, Greg Büchner's Leon & Lena (and Lenz) 1987, Genet's The Screens 1987, Cymbeline 1989, 'Tis Pity She's a Whore 1992, Henry IV (Pts I & II) 1991, Woyzeck 1992, In the Summer House 1993. *Publication:* Green Card. *Leisure interest:* cooking. *Address:* Mabon Mines, 150 1st Avenue, New York, NY 10009, USA.

AKAMATSU, Ryoko; Japanese politician; b. 24 Aug. 1929, Osaka; d. of Rinsaku Akamatsu and Asaka Akamatsu; m. Tadashi Hanami 1953; one s.; ed Tsuda Coll. and Univ. of Tokyo; Ministry of Labour 1953, Dir Women Workers' Div. 1970–72; Dir-Gen. Yamanashi Labour Standard Bureau 1975–78; Counsellor in charge of Women's Affairs, Prime Minister's Office 1978–79; Minister, Perm. Mission to UN 1979–82; Dir-Gen. Women's Bureau, Ministry of Labour 1982–85; Amb. to Uruguay 1986–89; Pres. Japan Inst. of Workers' Evolution 1989–93; Prof. Bunkyo Women's Coll. 1992–93; Minister of Educ., Science, Culture and Sports 1993–94. *Publications:* Girls Be Ambitious (autobiog.) 1990, Beautiful Uruguay 1990. *Leisure interests:* reading, swimming, listening to classical music. *Address:* 5-11-22-309, Roppongi, Minato-ku, Tokyo 106, Japan. *Telephone:* 03-3423-3534. *Fax:* 03-3423-3534.

AKASHI, Yasushi; Japanese diplomatist; b. 19 Jan. 1931, Akita; m.; two c.; ed Univ. of Tokyo, Univ. of Virginia, Fletcher School of Law and Diplomacy and Columbia Univ.; Political Affairs Officer UN Secr. 1957–74; Chair. Univ. Seminar on Modern East Asia 1963–64; Amb. at Perm. Mission to UN, New York 1974–79; UN Under-Sec.-Gen. for Public Information 1979–87, for Disarmament Affairs 1987; UN Rep. in Cambodia 1992; Special Envoy to Fmr. Yugoslavia 1994–95; UN Under-Sec. for Humanitarian Affairs 1996–97, UN Emergency Relief Co-ordinator 1997–98; Chair. Int. Peace Co-operation Council 2002–; has represented Japan in Gen. Ass. and numerous UN confs. and orgs.; Chair. Budget and Finance Cttee Governing Council UNDP 1978; mem. Advisory Cttee on Admin. and Budgetary Questions 1974, 1977; Assoc. Columbia Univ. Seminars; Chair. Conf. of Mid-Career Asian Leaders on Devt 1967; Dir Int. Peace Acad., Better World Soc.; Sec. Founding Cttee UN Univ.; fmr Visiting Lecturer Univ. of Tokyo, Int. Christian Univ., Tokyo and Sophia Univ. *Publications:* The United Nations 1965, From the Windows of the United Nations 1984, The Lights and Shadows of the United Nations 1985 and numerous articles. *Address:* International Peace Co-operation Council, Office of the Prime Minister, 1-6-1, Nagata-cho, Chiyoda-ku, Tokyo 100-8968, Japan.

AKAYEV, Askar Akayevich, DTech; Kyrgyzstan politician; b. 10 Nov. 1944, Kyzyl-Baízak Keminsky Dist; s. of Akai Tokoyev and Aselj Tokoyeva; m. Mairam Akayeva 1970; two s. two d.; ed Leningrad Inst. of Precise Mechanics and Optics; lecturer; Prof. Frunze Politech. Inst. 1972–73, Chair. 1976–86; Prof. Inst. of Precise Mechanics and Optics 1973–76; Head of Science Dept Cen. Cttee Kyrgyz CP 1986–87; mem. CPSU 1981–91; fmr mem. Cen. Cttee Kyrgyz CP, Vice-Pres., Pres. Kirghiz SSR (now Kyrgyzstan) Acad. of Sciences 1987–90; fmr mem. CPSU Constitutional Compliance Cttee; fmr mem. USSR Supreme Soviet Cttee on Econ. Reform 1991; Exec. Pres. Kirghiz SSR 1990, Pres. of Kyrgyzstan 1991–; Hon. Academician Int. Eng Acad. and of Int. Acad. of Creation 1996. *Publications:* more than 80 articles on radiophysics and politics. *Leisure interests:* travelling with the family, mountain skiing, mountaineering. *Address:* Government House, Bishkek 720003, Kyrgyzstan. *Telephone:* (312) 21-24-66. *Fax:* (312) 21-86-27.

AKBULUT, Yildirim; Turkish politician; b. 1935, Erzincan; m.; three c.; ed Univ. of Istanbul; fmr practising lawyer; Deputy for Erzincan 1983–; Prime Minister of Turkey 1989–91; mem. Motherland Party; fmr Deputy Speaker of Parl., Speaker 1987–89; Minister of Interior 1986–87. *Address:* c/o Anavatan Partisi, 13 Cad. 3, Balgat, Ankara, Turkey.

AKCHURIN, Renat Suleimanovich, DrMed; Russian cardiosurgeon; b. 2 April 1946, Andijan, Uzbekistan; m. Natalya Pavlovna Akchurina; two s.; ed Inst. of Medicine (now Seehenov Acad. of Medicine); general practitioner polyclinics 1970–73; Ordinator, Jr, Sr Researcher Inst. of Clinical and Experimental Medicine 1973–84; in Baylor Univ., Texas, USA 1984; surgeon, Head Dept of Cardiovascular Surgery, Russian Cardiological Cen. 1984–; Corresp. mem. Russian Acad. of Medical Sciences 1997; performed first heart and lung transplantation operations in USSR; performs about 100 bypass operations a year, performed a bypass operation on Pres. Yeltsin 1996; patented several inventions of medical instruments; USSR State Prize 1982. *Publications include:* over 180 scientific papers and articles. *Leisure interests:* music, hunting, cooking. *Address:* Cardiology Scientific Centre, Cherepkovskaya str. 15a, 121552 Moscow, Russia (Office). *Telephone:* (095) 149-00-69 (Office).

AKE, Siméon; Côte d'Ivoirian lawyer, diplomatist and politician; b. 4 Jan. 1932, Bingerville; m. Anne Maud Bonful 1958; five c.; ed Univs of Dakar and Grenoble; Chef de Cabinet to Minister of Public Service, 1959–61; First Counsellor, Ivory Coast Mission to UN 1961–63; Dir of Protocol, Ministry of Foreign Affairs 1963–64; Amb. to UK, Sweden, Denmark and Norway 1964–66; Perm. Rep. of Ivory Coast to UN 1966–77; Minister of Foreign Affairs 1977–90; Amb. accred to Germany and Austria 1991; mem. Guiding Cttee, Parti Démocratique de la Côte d'Ivoire (PDCI-RDA) 1975–; Commdr Ordre Nat. de la République de la Côte d'Ivoire, de l'Ordre de St Grégoire; Grand Officer, Légion d'honneur; distinctions from Belgium, Brazil, Spain, Cameroun. *Address:* 08 Boîte Postale 2102, Abidjan, Côte d'Ivoire.

AKENSON, Donald Harman, PhD, DLitt, DHum, FRSA, FRSC, FRHistS; Canadian professor of history; b. 22 May 1941, Minneapolis, Minn.; s. of Donald Nels Akenson and Fern L. Harman Akenson; ed Yale Coll. and Harvard Univ.; Allston Burr Sr Tutor, Dunster House, Harvard Coll. 1966–67; Assoc. Prof. of History, Queen's Univ., Kingston, Ont. 1970–74; Prof. 1974–; Beamish Research Prof., Inst. of Irish Studies, Univ. of Liverpool 1998–; Guggenheim Fellow 1984–85; Molson Laureate 1996; Hon. DLitt McMaster Univ. 1995; Hon. DHumLitt Lethbridge Univ. 1995; Chalmers Prize 1985, Landon Prize 1987, Grawemeyer World Peace Prize 1993 and many other awards and distinctions. *Publications:* The Irish Education Experiment 1970, The Church of Ireland: Ecclesiastical Reform and Revolution 1800–1885 1971, Education and Enmity: The Control of Schooling in Northern Ireland 1920–50 1973, The United States and Ireland 1973, A Mirror to Kathleen's Face: Education in Independent Ireland 1922–60 1975, Local Poets and Social History: James Orr, Bard of Ballycarry 1977, Between Two Revolutions: Islandmagee, Co. Antrim 1798–1920 1979, A Protestant in Purgatory: Richard Whately: Archbishop of Dublin 1981, The Irish in Ontario: A Study of Rural History

1984, Being Had: Historians, Evidence and the Irish in North America 1985, The Life and Times of Ogle Gowan 1986, Small Differences: Irish Catholics and Irish Protestants, 1815–1921 1988, Half the World from Home: Perspectives on the Irish in New Zealand 1990, Occasional Papers on the Irish in South Africa 1991, God's Peoples: Covenant and Land in South Africa, Israel and Ulster 1992, The Irish Diaspora, A Primer 1993, Conor: A Biography of Conor Cruise O'Brien 1994, If the Irish Ran the World: Montserrat 1630–1730, Surpassing Wonder: The Invention of the Bible and the Talmuds 1998, Saint Saul: A Skeleton Key to the Historical Jesus 2000; novels: The Lazar House Notebooks 1981, Brotherhood Week in Belfast 1984, The Orangeman: The Edgerston Audit 1987, At Face Value: The Life and Times of Eliza McCormack 1990. *Address:* Department of History, Queen's University, Kingston, Ont., K7L 3N6, Canada.

AKERLOF, George Arthur, BA, PhD; American economist; b. 17 June 1940, New Haven, Conn.; m. Janet L. Yellen; one s.; ed MIT, Yale Univ.; Asst Prof. Univ. of Calif. at Berkeley 1966–70, Assoc. Prof. 1970–77, Prof. 1977–78, 1980–; Visiting Prof. Indian Statistical Inst. 1967–68; Research Assoc. Harvard Univ. 1969; Sr Staff Economist President's Council of Econ. Advisers 1973–74; Visiting Research Economist Special Studies Section, Bd of Govs. of the Fed. Reserve System 1977–78; Cassel Prof. with respect to Money and Banking, LSE 1978–80; Sr Fellow The Brookings Inst. 1994–; Vice-Pres. American Econ. Asscn; mem. Bd of Dirs Nat. Bureau for Economic Research 1997–; Assoc. Ed. several journals on Econs; Guggenheim Fellow; Fellow Inst. for Policy Reform; numerous hon. lectureships; Nobel Prize in Economics 2001 (jt recipient); numerous other awards and prizes. *Publication:* An Economic Theorist's Book of Tales 1984. *Address:* Department of Economics, 549 Evans Hall, #3880, University of California at Berkeley, CA 94720-3880, USA (Office). *Telephone:* (510) 642-5837 (Office). *E-mail:* akerlof@econ.berkeley.edu (Office).

AKERS-JONES, Sir David, KBE, CMG, JP, MA; British civil servant; b. 14 April 1927; s. of Walter George Jones and Dorothy Jones; m. Jane Spickernell 1951 (died 2002); one s. (deceased) one d.; ed Worthing High School and Brasenose Coll. Oxford; with British India Steam Navigation Co. 1945–49; Malayan Civil Service 1954–57; Hong Kong Civil Service 1957–86, Sec. for New Territories and for District Admin., Hong Kong Govt 1973–85, Chief Sec. 1985–86; Acting Gov. Hong Kong 1986–87; Hong Kong Affairs Advisor to China 1993–97; Chair. Nat. Mutual Asia Hong Kong (later AXA China Region) 1987, Hong Kong Housing Authority 1988–93, Global Asset Man. Hong Kong, AXA Life Advisory Bd 2001–; Hon. Pres. Outward Bound Trust (Hong Kong) 1986–; Vice-Pres. WWF Hong Kong 1995–; Dir Hysan Devt Co. Ltd, The Mingly Corpn Ltd, Shui On Properties Ltd; Hon. mem. RICS; Vice Pres. Hong Kong Girl Guides; Hon. DCL (Kent Univ.) 1987; Hon. LLD (Chinese Univ. of Hong Kong) 1988; Hon. DScS (City Univ., Hong Kong) 1993; Grand Bauhinia Medal (Hong Kong). *Leisure interests:* painting, gardening, walking and music. *Address:* Flat 1, Block A, 1/F, Villa Monte Rosa, 41 Stubbs Road, Hong Kong Special Administrative Region, People's Republic of China. *Telephone:* (852) 2491-9319 (Office); (852) 2491-9319 (Home). *Fax:* (852) 2491-1300 (Home). *E-mail:* akersjon@pacific.net.hk (Home).

AKHEDJAKOVA, Liya Medjidovna; Russian actress; b. 9 June 1938, Dniepropetrovsk; d. of Medjid Salekhovich Akhedjakov and Yulia Aleksandrovna Akhedjakova; m. Vladimir Nikolayevich Persyanov; ed State Inst. of Theatre Art; actress Moscow Theatre of Young Spectator 1953–71, Sovremennik Theatre 1971–; leading roles in classical and contemporary plays including Shakespeare, Tennessee Williams; in cinema 1969–; People's Artist of Russia, State Prize, Nike Prize. *Films include:* Garage, Office Romance, Blessed Heavens, Twenty Days Without War, Lost Bus. *Leisure interest:* travel. *Address:* Udaltsova str. 12, Apt. 153, 117415 Moscow, Russia (Home). *Telephone:* (095) 921-63-48 (Office); (095) 131-60-41 (Home).

AKHMADULINA, Bella (Isabella Akhatovna); Russian poet; b. 10 April 1937, Moscow; d. of Ahat and Nadya (née Lazareva) Akhmadulin; m. 1st Yevgeniy Yevtushenko 1960; m. 2nd Yuriy Nagibin; m. 3rd Boris Messerer 1974; ed Gorky Inst. of Literature; Hon. mem. American Acad. of Arts and Letters 1977; Sec. USSR (now Russian) Writers' Union 1986–91, mem. Bd Russian PEN-Centre 1989–92; State Prize USSR 1989, Pushkin Prize, Russian President's Prize 1998, Alfred Tepfer Prize. *Publications:* The String 1962, The Rain 1963, My Ancestry 1964, Summer Leaves 1968, The Lessons of Music 1969, Fever and Other New Poems (trans. into English) 1970, Tenerezza 1971, The Rain 1974, Poems 1975, The Dreams about Georgia 1977, The Candle 1978, The Snowstorm 1978, The Mystery 1983, The Garden 1987, The Seaboard 1991, Selected Works (Vols 1–3) 1996, The Ancient Style Attracts Me 1997, Beautiful Features of My Friends 1999, and translations from Georgian. *Address:* Chernyachovskogo str. 4, Apt. 37, 125319 Moscow, Russia. *Telephone:* (095) 151-22-00.

AKHMEDOV, Khan A.; Turkmenistan politician (retd); b. 16 June 1936, Pazau, Krasnovodsk Dist; m.; four c.; ed Tashkent Inst. of Railway; Transport Eng, Man. Railways of Middle Asia 1962–80; Head Dept of Transport and Communications, Turkmenistan CP Cen. Cttee 1980–85; First Sec. Ashkhabad City, CP Cttee 1985–88; First Deputy Chair. Turkmenistan SSR Council of Ministers 1988–89, Chair. 1989–90; Prime Minister of Turkmenistan 1990–91; Deputy Prime Minister 1991–92; Amb. to Turkey 1992–95; mem. Pres. Council. *Address:* Administration of the President, Karl Marx str. 24, 744017 Ashgabat, Turkmenistan (Office).

AKHTAR, Muhammad, MSc, PhD, FRS; British/Pakistani professor of biochemistry; b. 23 Feb. 1933, Punjab, India; s. of Muhammad Azeem Chaudhry; m. Monika E Schürmann 1963; two s.; ed Govt Coll. Sargodha, Govt Coll. Lahore, Univ. of Punjab and Imperial Coll., London; Research Scientist, Research Inst. for Medicine and Chem., Cambridge, Mass. 1959–63; Lecturer in Biochem. Univ. of Southampton 1963–66, Sr Lecturer 1966–68, Reader 1968–73, Prof. 1973–98, Head Dept of Biochem. 1978–93, Chair. School of Biochemical and Physiological Sciences 1983–87, Prof. Emer. of Biochemistry 1998–; Founding Fellow Third World Acad. of Sciences, Treasurer, mem. Council 1993–98, Vice-Pres. 1998–; mem. Council Royal Soc. 1983–85; Biochemical Soc.Cttee1983–86; Sitara-I-Imtiaz (Pakistan); Flintoff Medal (Royal Society of Chemistry) 1993, TWAS Medal 1996. *Publications:* numerous articles in biochemical and chemical journals. *Address:* Department of Biochemistry, University of Southampton, Southampton, SO9 3TU, England (Office). *Telephone:* (23) 8059-4338.

AKI, Keiiti, PhD; American academic; b. 3 March 1930, Yokohama, Japan; s. of Koichi Aki and Fumiko Kojima; m. Haruko Uyeda 1956; three c.; ed Univ. of Tokyo, Geophysical Inst.; Research Fellow, Calif. Inst. of Tech., USA 1958–60; Research Fellow and Assoc. Prof., Univ. of Tokyo 1960–66; Prof. of Geophysics, MIT 1966–84, R. R. Schrock Prof. of Earth and Planetary Sciences 1982–84; W. M. Keck Foundation Prof. of Geological Sciences, Univ. of Southern Calif., USA 1984–; Science Dir, Chair. Bd Dirs Southern Calif. Earthquake Centre 1991–96; Distinguished Visiting Prof., Univ. of Alaska 1981–88; mem. Nat. Council for Earthquake Prediction Evaluation 1980–, Calif. Council for Earthquake Prediction Evaluation 1984–; Fellow AAAS; mem. NAS; medal of the Seismological Society of America 1987; Hon. Foreign Fellow European Union of Geosciences 1987. *Publications:* (Co-author) Quantitative Seismology (Vols I and II) 1980, Orogeny 1983. *Leisure interests:* swimming, skiing, sailing, surfing. *Address:* Department of Geological Sciences, University of Southern California, Los Angeles, CA 90089-0740 (Office); 3 Bis Impasse Jacarandas, La Reunion, CA 90277, USA (Home). *Telephone:* (213) 743-3510.

AKIHITO, Emperor of Japan; b. 23 Dec. 1933, Tokyo; s. of the late Emperor Hirohito and of Empress Nagako; m. Michiko Shoda 1959; two s. one d.; ed Gakushuin schools and Faculty of Politics and Econs Gakushuin Univ.; official investiture as Crown Prince 1952; succeeded 7 Jan. 1989; crowned 12 Nov. 1990; has undertaken visits to some 37 countries and travelled widely throughout Japan; Hon. Pres. or Patron, Asian Games 1958, Int. Sports Games for the Disabled 1964, Eleventh Pacific Science Congress 1966, Japan World Exposition 1970, Int. Skill Contest for the Disabled 1981; mem. Ichthyological Soc. of Japan; Hon. Sec. Int. Conf. on Indo-Pacific Fish 1985; Hon. mem. Linnean Soc. (London). *Publications:* 25 papers in journal of Ichthyological Soc. of Japan. *Leisure interests:* taxonomic study of gobiid fish, natural history and conservation, history, tennis. *Address:* The Imperial Palace, 1-1 Chiyoda, Chiyoda-ku, Tokyo 100, Japan. *Telephone:* (3) 32131111.

AKILOV, Akil Gaibullayevich; Tajik politician and engineer; b. 2 Feb. 1944, Khudjand (fmrly Leninabad); m.; three c.; ed Moscow Inst. of Construction and Eng; various posts on construction orgs. Leninabad Region 1960–76; work for CP 1976–93; Minister of Construction of Tajikistan 1993–94; Deputy Prime Minister 1994–96; First Deputy Chair. Leninabad Region 1996–99; Prime Minister of Tajikistan 1999–2001. *Address:* Council of Ministers, Rudaki Prospect 80, 734021 Dushanbe, Tajikistan (Office). *Telephone:* (2) 21-18-71 (Office). *Fax:* (2) 21-51-10 (Office).

AKINKUGBE, Oladipo Olujimi, Atobase of Ife, Babalofin of Ijebu-Igbo, Adingbuwa of Ondo, Ikolaba Balogun Basegun of Ibadan, MD, DPhil, D.T.M.&H., FRCP; Nigerian professor of medicine; b. 17 July 1933, Ondo; s. of Chief Odofin David Akinkugbe and Chief (Mrs.) Grace Akinkugbe; m. Dr. Folasade Dina 1965; two s.; ed Govt Coll., Ibadan, Univ. Coll., Ibadan, Univs. of London, Liverpool and Oxford; Lecturer in Medicine, Univ. of Ibadan 1964–66, Sr Lecturer 1966–68, Prof. 1968–95, Prof. Emer. 1996–, Dean of Medicine 1970–74, Chair. of Cttee of Deans 1972–74, mem. Council 1971–74; Visiting Prof. Medicine, Harvard Univ. 1974–75; Principal, Univ. Coll., Ilorin 1975–77; Vice-Chancellor Univ. of Ilorin 1977–78, Ahmadu Bello Univ. 1978–79; Pro-Chancellor and Chair. Council, Port Harcourt Univ. 1986–90; Pres. Nigerian Asscn of Nephrology 1987–89, Nigerian Hypertension Soc. 1992–95; mem. Scientific Advisory Panel CIBA Foundation, Council of Int Soc. of Hypertension, WHO Expert Cttees. on Cardiovascular Diseases, Smoking Control, Professional and Tech. Educ. of Medical and Auxiliary Personnel, Sr Consultant 1983–84, WHO Advisory Cttee on Health Research 1990; Visiting Fellow, Balliol Coll., Oxford 1981–82; Visiting Prof. of Medicine, Oxford Univ. 1981–82; mem. Bd of Trustees, Obafemi Awolowo Foundation, Nigerian Heartcare Foundation 1994–, Chair. 2000– (also mem. Governing Council), Nigerian Educare Trust 1995, The Social Sciences and Reproductive Health Research Network 1996, Ajumogobia Science Foundation; Chair. Bd of Man., Univ. Coll. Hosp. Ibadan 2000–; Pres. African Heart Network 2001; Founding Pres. Nigerian Soc. for Information, Arts and Culture 2001–; Patron Sickle Cell Asscn of Nigeria; mem. several editorial bds.; Fellow Nigerian Acad. of Science, Hon. Fellow Univ. of Ibadan 1998; Hon. DSc (Ilorin) 1982, (Fed. Univ. Tech. Akure) 1994, (Port-Harcourt) 1997, (Ogun State Univ.) 1998; Commdr Noble Order of the Niger 1979, Officier, Ordre Nat. de la République de Côte d'Ivoire; Searle Distinguished Research Award 1989; Nigerian Nat. Order of Merit 1997. *Publications include:* High Blood Pressure in the African 1972, Priorities in National Health Planning 1974 (Ed.), Hypertension in Africa (Ed.) 1975, Cardiovascular Diseases in Africa (Ed.) 1976, Clinical Medicine in the Tropics—Cardiovascular Disease 1986, Nigeria's Health in the 90s (Co-ed.) 1996, A Compendium of Clinical Medicine (Ed.) 1999; many papers on hypertension and renal disease. *Leisure interests:* bird-watching, music, gardening. *Address:* Department of Medicine, University of Ibadan, Ibadan, Oyo State (Office); The Little Summit, Olubadan Aleshinloye Way, Iyaganku, Ibadan, Nigeria (Home). *Telephone:* (2) 2315463 (Office); (2) 2317717. *E-mail:* akin.ooihc@errands.skannet.com (Office).

AKIYA, Einosuke; Japanese religious leader; b. 15 July 1930, Tokyo; s. of late Jubei Akiya and of Yuki Akiya; m. Akiko Ishida 1957; two s.; ed Waseda Univ.; with Soka Gakkai 1951–, Young Men's Div. Chief 1956–59, Youth Div. Chief 1959–66, Dir 1961–62, Vice-Gen. Dir 1962–67, Gen. Admin. 1967–70, Vice-Pres. 1970–81, Pres. 1981–; Ed.-in-Chief Seikyo Shimbun 1968, Rep. Dir 1975–81, Pres. 1987–90, Exec. Advisor 1990–; Gen. Dir Soka Gakkai Int. 1981–92, Exec. Counsellor 1992–95, Deputy Pres. 1995–. *Leisure interests:* reading, music, theatre. *Address:* Soka Gakkai Headquarters, 32 Shinanomachi, Shinjuku-ku, Tokyo 160-8583, Japan (Office). *Telephone:* (3) 3353-7111 (Office). *E-mail:* webmaster@sokagakkai.info (Office). *Website:* www .sokagakkai.info (Office); www.sgi.org (Office).

AKRAM, Wasim (see Wasim Akram).

AKSENENKO, Nikolai Yemelyanovich; Russian politician and administrator; b. 15 March 1949, Novoaleksandrovka, Novosibirsk Region; m.; one s. one d.; ed Novosibirsk Inst. of Railway Eng, Acad. of Nat. Econs; metalworker, Novosibirsk Aviation Factory; worker on duty, Head of railway station, Head of sectors of E. Siberian and S.-E. Railways 1966–84; Deputy Dir Murmansk Div., Oktyabrskaya Railway 1984–85, Dir Leningrad–Finland Div. 1985–86, Deputy Dir, Chief Econ., First Deputy Dir 1986–92; Deputy, First Deputy Minister of Railways of Russian Fed. 1994–97, Minister 1997–2002 (resgnd); mem. Govt Comm. on Operational Problems 1997–, Chair. 1999; First Deputy Chair. of Govt 1999–2000; mem. Security Council of Russia 1999–2000. *Address:* MPS, Novobasmannaya str. 2, Moscow, Russia. *Telephone:* (095) 262-10-02 (Office). *Fax:* (095) 262-66-70.

AKSU, Abdülkadir; Turkish politician; b. 12 Oct. 1944, Diyarbakır; m.; two c.; ed Ankara Univ.; fmrly Security Dir, Malatya, Acting Gov. of Kahramanmaraş, Deputy Security Dir, Gov. and Mayor of Rize, Gov. of Gaziantep; Deputy for Motherland Party 1987; Minister of the Interior 1989–91, Nov. 2002–. *Address:* İçişleri Bakanlığı, Bakanlıklar, Ankara, Turkey. *Telephone:* (312) 4181368. *Fax:* (312) 4181795. *E-mail:* aaksu@icisleri.gov.tr. *Website:* www.icisleri.gov.tr.

AKSYONOV, Vasiliy Pavlovich; Russian writer; b. 20 Aug. 1932, Kazan; s. of Pavel V. Aksyonov and Yevgeniya Ginzburg; m. 1st Kira L. Mendeleva 1957; m. 2nd Maya A. Karmen; one s.; ed Leningrad Medical Inst.; Physician 1956–60, Moscow Tubercular Dispensary 1960–61; professional writer 1960–; emigrated to USA 1980; mem. Union of Russian Writers, Editorial Board Yunost; citizenship restored 1990; lecturer George Mason Univ., USA 1995–. *Publications:* novels: Colleagues 1960, Starry Ticket 1961, 1970, Oranges from Morocco 1963, Time, My Friend, Time 1964, The Empty Barrels 1968, Love of Electricity 1971, My Grandpa is a Monument 1972, The Box Inside Which Something Knocks (children's book) 1976, Our Golden Ironware 1980, The Burn 1980, The Island of Crimea 1981, An Aristopheana 1981, Paper Landscape 1983, The Right to the Island 1983, Say 'Cheese' 1985, In Search of a Genre 1986, In Search of Melancholy Baby 1987, Our Garden Fronburg 1989, The Moscow Saga 1993, The Negative of a Positive Hero 1996, New Sweet Style 1998; collected stories: Catapult 1964, Half-Way to the Moon 1966, Wish You Were Here 1969; screenplay for films: Colleagues, My Young Friend, When They Raise the Bridges, Travelling 1967, The Murmar House 1972; play: On Sale 1965; travel: An Unusual Journey 1963, Twenty-Four Hours Non-Stop 1976, The Steel Bird and Other Stories 1978; joint ed. Metropol 1979, Four Temperaments (comedy) 1979. *Leisure interests:* music, travelling, running. *Address:* c/o Random House Inc., 201 East 50th Street, New York, NY 10022, USA. *Telephone:* (095) 915-45-63 (Moscow).

AKSYUCHITS, Viktor Vladimirovich; Russian politician and Orthodox philosopher; b. 27 Aug. 1949, Vardantsy, Minsk region, USSR (now Belarus); m. 2nd; four c.; ed Riga Navigation School and Moscow State Univ.; mem. CPSU 1971–72; served in Navy, seasonal worker in Siberia and Far East; founder Orthodox Unity Church; edited Vybor; Chair. Duma (Bd) of Russian Christian-Democratic Movt 1990–98, Chair. of Political Council 1990–92; mem. Duma of Russian People's Congress 1992–96; People's Deputy of Russia 1990–93; adviser to Deputy Prime Minister Boris Nemtsov 1997–98; lecturer, State Acad. of Slavic Culture; Chair. Orthodox Brotherhood Resurrection. *Publications:* three books and numerous articles on problems of Orthodox ideology. *Address:* State Acad. of Slavic Culture, Geroyev-Pamfilovtsev str. 39, korp. 2, 123480 Moscow, Russia (Office). *Telephone:* (095) 948-80-89 (Office).

AKUNIN, Boris; Russian (born Georgian) writer; b. (Grigory Shalvovich Chkhartishvili), 1956; ed Moscow State Univ.; Deputy Ed.-in-Chief Inostrannaya Literatura (magazine) –2000; Ed.-in-Chief Anthology of Japanese Literature (20 vols); Chair. Exec. Bd Pushkin Library (Soros Foundation). *Publications:* Azazel, Turkish Gambit, Leviafan, Death of Achilles, Special Errands, Counsellor of State, Coronation or the Last of the Novels 1998–2000, Pelageya and the White Bulldog 2000, Lovers of Death (2 vols) 2000; Tales for Idiots (essays); The Writer and Suicide (non-fiction) 1999; numerous reviews and criticisms, numerous translations of Japanese, American and English literature. *Address:* Poema Press Publications, Zvezdny blvd 23, 129075 Moscow, Russia (Office). *Telephone:* (095) 925-42-05 (Home). *E-mail:* erikavoronova@mtu-net.ru (Office). *Website:* www.akunin.ru (Office).

AKURGAL, Ekrem, PhD; Turkish archaeologist; b. 30 March 1911, Istanbul; ed Germany; Prof. Univ. of Ankara 1941–81; has conducted excavations at Sinope, Phokaia, Daskyleion, Pitane and Erythrai 1953–, at Izmir 1967–; Visiting Prof., Princeton Univ. 1961–62, W Berlin 1971–72, Vienna 1980–81; mem. Turkish Historical Soc. (Sec.-Gen. 1951–61), Turkish High Comm. for Ancient Monuments; mem. British, Austrian, Danish, French and Swedish Acads.; Hon. mem. Soc. for Promotion of Hellenic Studies, London, German, Austrian, American Inst. of Archaeology; Dr. hc (Bordeaux) 1961, (Athens) 1989, (Lecce) 1990; Goethe Medal (Fed. Repub. of Germany) 1979; Grand Prize, Turkish Ministry of Culture 1981. *Publications:* Griechische Reliefs aus Lykien 1942, Remarques stylistiques sur les reliefs de Malatya 1946, Späthethitische Bildkunst 1949, Phrygische Kunst 1955, Die Kunst Anatoliens von Homer bis Alexander 1961, Die Kunst der Hethiter 1961, Orient und Okzident 1966, Treasures of Turkey (with Mango and Ettinghausen) 1966, Urartäische und Altiranische Kunstzentren 1968, The Art and Architecture of Turkey 1981, Alt-Smyrna 1983, Ancient Civilizations and Ruins of Turkey (5th Edn) 1983, (8th Edn 1993), Griechische und Römische Kunst in der Turkey 1987, Turquie Akurgal-Mantran-Roux 1990. *Address:* Yalı Cadı 360/7, 35530 Karşiyaka, Izmir, Turkey (Home).

ALAGIAH, George; British journalist, broadcaster and author; b. 22 Nov. 1955, Sri Lanka; m.; two s.; ed St John's Coll., Portsmouth and Univ. of Durham; family moved to Ghana 1960; worked in print journalism for South Magazine 1982–89; joined the BBC 1989, Leading Foreign Corresp. specializing in Africa and the developing world, BBC's Africa Corresp., Johannesburg 1994–98, presenter of The World News on BBC4 2002, presenter BBC Six O' Clock News 2003–; has interviewed many internationally prominent figures; has contributed to The Guardian, Daily Telegraph, The Independent and Daily Express newspapers; Patron The Presswise Trust, NAZ Project, Parenting, Educ. and Support Forum, Fairtrade Foundation; Critics' Award and Golden Nymph Award, Monte Carlo TV Festival 1992, Best Int. Report, Royal TV Soc. 1993, Best TV Journalist Award, Amnesty Int. 1994, One World Broadcasting Trust Award 1994, James Cameron Memorial Trust Award 1995, Bayeux Award for War Reporting 1996, Media Personality of the Year, Ethnic Minority Media Awards 1998, BAFTA Award (part of BBC Team) for coverage of Kosovo conflict 2000. *Publication:* A Passage to Africa 2001. *Address:* BBC, Room 1640, Television Centre, Wood Lane, London, W12 7RJ, England (Office). *Telephone:* (20) 8743-8000 (Office). *Fax:* (20) 8743-7882 (Office). *Website:* www.bbc.co.uk.

ALAGNA, Roberto; French opera singer; b. 7 June 1963, Clichy-sous-Bois; m. (wife deceased); m. 2nd Angela Gheorghiu 1996; ed Paris and Italy; debut as Alfredo in La Traviata, Glyndebourne Touring Opera; repertoire includes: Rodolfo in La Bohème, Edgard in Lucia di Lammermoor, Rigoletto, L'Elisir d'Amore, Roméo, Don Carlos, Roberto Devereux, Duke of Mantua, Don Carlos, Alfredo; Chevalier des Arts et des Lettres; winner Pavarotti Competition 1988; Personalité Musicale de l'Année 1994, Laurence Olivier Award for Outstanding Achievement in Opera 1995, Victor Award for Best Singer 1997. *Recordings include:* Duets and Arias (with Angela Gheorghiu), La Bohème 1996, Don Carlos 1996, La Rondine 1997. *Address:* c/o Lévon Sayan, 9 chemin de Plonjon, Geneva, Switzerland (Office).

ALAÏA, Azzedine; French fashion designer; b. Tunis; ed Ecole des Beaux Arts, Tunis; studied sculpture; worked with dressmakers specializing in copies of Parisian haute couture in Tunis and then began making his own designs for pvt. clients in Tunis; moved to Paris 1957; worked briefly at Christian Dior before moving to Guy Laroche workrooms for two seasons; also worked in Paris as cook and housekeeper; began made-to-order dressmaking business in 1960s; set up first atelier in Faubourg Saint Germain 1965–84; first ready-to-wear show, Bergdorf Goodman store, New York 1982; first Azzedine Alaïa boutique opened in Beverly Hills 1983; moved to Marais district of Paris 1984; retrospective exhbn Museum of Modern Art, Bordeaux 1985; named Best Designer of Year by French Ministry of Culture 1985. *Address:* 18 rue de la Verrérie, Paris, France.

ALAIN, Marie-Claire; French organist; b. 10 Aug. 1926, Saint-Germain-en-Laye; d. of Albert Alain and Magdeleine Alain (née Alberty); m. Jacques Gommier 1950; one s. one d.; ed Institut Notre Dame, Saint-Germain-en-Laye, Conservatoire Nat. Supérieur de Musique, Paris; Lecturer, Summer Acad. for organists, Haarlem, Netherlands 1956–72; organ teacher, Conservatoire de Musique de Rueil-Malmaison 1978–94; numerous concerts throughout world 1955–; lecturer at numerous univs. throughout world; expert on organology to Minister of Culture; Hon. DHumLitt (Colorado State Univ.); Hon. DMus (Southern Methodist Univ., Dallas, Boston Conservatory); Dr hc (Acad. Sibelius, Helsinki); numerous prizes for recordings and performances including Buxtehudepreis (Lübeck, Fed. Repub. of Germany); Prix Léonie Sonning, Copenhagen, Prix Franz Liszt, Budapest 1987; Commdr, Légion d'honneur, Ordre du Mérite, Arts et Lettres. *Recordings:* over 250 records, including complete works of J. Alain, C. P. E. Bach, J. S. Bach, C. Balbastre, G. Böhm, N. Bruhns, D. Buxtehude, L. N. Clérambault, F. Couperin, L. C. Daquin, C. Franck, N. de Grigny, J. A. Guilain, G. F. Handel, J.

Haydn, F. Mendelssohn, A. Vivaldi, etc. *Publication:* Notes critiques sur l'œuvre d'orgue de Jehan Alain 2001. *Address:* 4 rue Victor Hugo, 78230 Le Pecq, France. *Telephone:* 1-30-87-08-65. *Fax:* 1-30-61-43-61.

ALAINI, Mohsen Ahmed al-; Yemeni politician and diplomatist; b. 20 Oct. 1932, Bani Bahloul, N Yemen; m. Aziza Abulahom 1962; two s. two d.; ed Faculty of Law, Cairo Univ. and the Sorbonne, Paris; school-teacher, Aden 1958–60; Int. Confederation of Arab Trade Unions 1960–62; Minister of Foreign Affairs, Yemeni Repub. Sept.–Dec. 1962, 1974–80; Perm. Rep. to UN 1962–65, 1965–66, 1967–69; Minister of Foreign Affairs May–July 1965; Prime Minister Nov.–Dec. 1967, 1974–80; Amb. to USSR 1968–70; Prime Minister, Minister of Foreign Affairs Feb. 1971, 1971–72, 1974–75; Amb. to France Aug.–Sept. 1974, 1965–76, to UK 1973–74, to FRG 1982–84, to USA 1984–97; Perm. Rep. to UN 1980–82; Deputy Chair. Consultative Council 1997–. *Publications include:* Battles and Conspiracies against Yemen 1957, Fifty Years of Mounting Sands (autobiog.) 2000. *Leisure interests:* reading, exercizing. *Address:* 8 Wissa Wassif Street, Giza Cairo, Egypt (Home); P.O. Box 7922, San'a, Yemen. *Telephone:* (1) 241951 (Yemen) (Office); (2) 5702423 (Cairo). *Fax:* (2) 5701989 (Home).

ALANÍS, Joan Martí; Spanish Roman Catholic ecclesiastic; b. 29 Nov. 1928, Mila; ordained priest 1951; Bishop of Urgel and Episcopal Co-Prince of Andorra 1971–; mem. Exec. Cttee Spanish Conf. of Bishops 1978–84, Chair. Episcopal Comm. on Migration 1984–87, Comm. on Mass Media 1987–93. *Address:* Govern d'Andorra, Carrer Prat de la Creu 62-64, Andorra la Vella, Andorra (Office).

ALARCÓN DE QUESADA, Ricardo; Cuban diplomatist; b. 21 May 1937; s. of Roberto Alarcón de Quesada; m. Margarita Maza; one d.; ed Univ. de Habana; Head of Student Section, Provincial Office of 26 July Revolutionary Movement 1957–59; Pres. Univ. Students' Fed., Sec. Union of Young Communists; Dir for Regional Policies (Latin America), Ministry of Foreign Affairs 1962–66; mem. Governing Council of Inst. for Int. Politics, Ministry of Foreign Affairs, Deputy Minister of Foreign Affairs 1978, mem. Tech. Advisory Council 1980; Perm. Rep. of Cuba to the UN 1966–78; Pres. UNDP 1976–77; Alt. mem. Cen. Cttee of CP of Cuba 1980–; mem. Politburo of CP 1992–; Perm Rep. to UN 1990; Minister of Foreign Affairs 1992–94; Pres. Nat. Ass. of People's Power 1993–. *Address:* Asamblea Nacional del Poder Popular, Havana, Cuba; 42 Street No. 2308 e/23 and 25 Streets, Municipio Playa, Cuba.

ALARCÓN MANTILLA, Luis Fernando, MSc; Colombian politician and engineer; b. Aug. 1951, Bucaramanga; m.; ed Univ. of the Andes and MIT; engineer with Mejía Millan y Perry Ltd and Prof. of Civil Eng Univ. of the Andes 1980–83; Head of Public Investment Unit, Nat. Dept of Planning 1983–84; Dir-Gen. of Budget, Ministry of Finance and Public Credit 1984–86; economist at Banco Internacional de Desarrollo, Washington DC 1986; Vice-Minister at Ministry of Finance and Public Credit 1986–87, Minister 1987–91; mem. of Governing Council for Foreign Trade, Bd of Banco de la República, Nat. Council for Econ. and Social Policy 1987–. *Address:* c/o Ministry of Finance and Public Credit, 7a, No. 6-4J, Of. 308, Santa Fe de Bogotá, Colombia.

ALARCON RIVERA, Fabián Ernesto, PhD; Ecuadorean politician; b. 1947, Quito; m. Lucía Peña; two s. one d.; ed Pontifical Catholic Univ.; councillor Quito 1969; fmr Prefect of Pinchincha Prov.; fmr Deputy to Congress (three times), fmr Speaker of Congress (three times); Acting Pres. of Ecuador 6–10 Feb. 1997, Pres. of Ecuador 1997–98; arrested on charges of illegally hiring personnel March 1999; mem. Frente Radical Alfarista. *Address:* c/o Office of the President, Palacio Nacional, García Moreno 1043, Quito, Ecuador.

ALATAS, Ali; Indonesian diplomatist; b. 4 Nov. 1932, Jakarta; s. of Abdullah Alatas; m. Yunisa Alatas 1956; three d.; ed Acad. for Foreign Affairs and School of Law, Univ. of Indonesia; Financial and Econ. Ed. P.I.A. Nat. news agency, Jakarta; joined Ministry of Foreign Affairs 1954; Second Sec. (later First Sec.), Bangkok, Thailand 1956–69; Dir Information and Cultural Affairs, Jakarta 1960–65; Dir 1965–66, 1970–72; Counsellor (later Minister Counsellor), Washington, DC 1966–70; Sec. Directorate Gen. for Political Affairs, Jakarta, Chef de Cabinet to Minister of Foreign Affairs 1972–75; Minister of Foreign Affairs 1988–99; Perm. Rep. to UN 1976–78, 1982–84, 1985–87; Sec. to the Vice-Pres. of Indonesia 1978–82; Chair. First Cttee, 40th UN Gen. Ass. 1985; Indonesian Order of Merit. *Leisure interests:* golf, reading, music, swimming. *Address:* c/o Ministry of Foreign Affairs, Jalan Taman Pejambon No. 6, Jakarta 10110, Indonesia.

ALATAS, Syed Hussein, PhD; Malaysian university vice-chancellor and sociologist; b. 17 Sept. 1928, Bogor, Indonesia; m.; one s. two d.; ed Univ. of Amsterdam; Fullbright Visiting Prof. 1965; Visiting Asian Fellow, ANU Canberra 1973; corresp. Int. Social Science Journal, Paris 1973–; mem. Int. Sociological Asscn 1965–; mem. Comm. on Challenges of Devt Int. Union of Anthropological and Ethnological Studies 1979; Founder mem. Int. Asscn for Study of Peace and Prejudice, Nuremberg 1980; Research Fellow, Woodrow Wilson Int. Center for Scholars, Smithsonian Inst. Bldg Washington, DC 1982–83; mem. Nat. Consultative Council, Fed. of Malaysia 1969–71; Nat. Unity Council 1971; mem. Senate, Parl. of Malaysia 1971; formerly Prof. and Head, Dept of Malay Studies, Nat. Univ. of Singapore; Vice-Chancellor, Univ. of Malaya 1988–91; numerous professional affiliations, overseas lectureships etc. *Publications include:* The Sociology of Corruption 1968, Thomas Stamford Raffles: Reformer or Intriguer 1972, Modernization and Social Change in

Southeast Asia 1972, The Intellectuals in Developing Societies 1977, The Myth of the Lazy Native 1977, The Problem of Corruption 1986. *Leisure interests:* reading, gardening.

ALBACETE CARREIRA, Alfonso; Spanish painter; b. 14 March 1950, Málaga; s. of Alfonso Albacete Carreira and María Albacete Carreira; m. Luisa Gómez 1986; one s. one d.; studied painting, with Juan Bonafé and architecture; Asst Juan Bonafé's studio 1967–69; studied painting Valencia 1969, then in Paris; first one-man exhbn, Madrid 1972; first exhbn USA, Center for Contemporary Art, Chicago 1989; works included in numerous collections of contemporary art. *Leisure interests:* botany, architecture. *Address:* Biasco de Garay 86, 6°A, Madrid 28015, Spain. *Telephone:* 5545640.

ALBARN, Damon; British singer, musician and songwriter; b. 23 March 1968, Whitechapel, London; s. of Hazel Albarn and Keith Albarn; singer, keyboard player and songwriter with Blur (fmrly named Seymour) 1989–; has toured worldwide; gold and platinum discs in UK; co-f. Gorillaz 2000; platinum discs in New Zealand, Ireland, USA, UK, France, Mexico and Canada; gold discs in Germany, Brazil, Italy, Spain and Sweden. *Films:* acted in Face 1997; wrote original score for Ravenous 1998 (with Michael Nyman, for Ordinary Decent Criminal 1999, for 101 Reykjavik (with Einar Benediktsson) 2000. *Singles include:* (with Blur) She's So High 1990, There's No Other Way 1991, Bang 1991, Popscene 1992, For Tomorrow 1993, Chemical World 1993, Sunday Sunday 1993, Girls and Boys 1994, To The End 1994, Parklife 1994, End Of A Century 1994, Country House 1995, Universal 1995, Charmless Man 1995, Beetlebum 1997, Song 2 1997, On Your Own 1997, MOR 1997, Tender 1999, Coffee & TV 1999, No Distance Left To Run 1999, Music Is My Radar 2000; (with Gorillaz) Clint Eastwood 2000, 19-2000 2001, Rock the House 2001, Tomorrow Comes Today 2002. *Albums:* (with Blur) Leisure 1991, Modern Life is Rubbish 1993, Parklife 1994, The Great Escape 1995, Blur 1997, 13 1999, Best of 2000; (with Gorillaz) Gorillaz 2001, G-Sides 2002, Phase One Celebrity Take Down 2002; (solo) Mali Music (various contribs) 2002. *Leisure interests:* football, Tae Kwon Do. *Address:* CMO Management, Unit 32, Ransomes Dock, 35–37 Parkgate Road, London, SW11 4NP, England.

ALBEE, Edward Franklin; American playwright; b. 12 March 1928, Virginia; s. of Reed Albee and Frances Cotter; ed Lawrenceville and Choate Schools, Washington and Columbia Univ.; Comm. Chair. Brandeis Univ. Creative Arts Awards 1983, 1984; Pres. The Edward F. Albee Foundation Inc.; mem. Dramatists Guild Council, PEN America, The American Acad., Nat. Inst. of Arts and Letters; Gold Medal, American Acad. and Inst. of Arts and Letters 1980; inducted, Theater Hall of Fame 1985, Kennedy Center Award 1996, Nat. Medal of Arts 1996. *Plays include:* The Zoo Story (Vernon Rice Award 1960) 1958, The Death of Bessie Smith 1959, The Sandbox 1959, Fam and Yam 1959, The American Dream (Foreign Press Asscn Award 1961) 1960, Who's Afraid of Virginia Woolf? (Drama Critics' Circle Award for Best Play) 1961–62, stage adaptation of The Ballad of the Sad Café (Carson McCullers) 1963, Tiny Alice 1964, Malcolm (from novel by James Purdy) 1965, A Delicate Balance (Pulitzer Prize 1966) 1966, Everything in the Garden (after a play by Giles Cooper) 1967, Box 1968, Quotations from Chairman Mao Tse-tung 1968, All Over 1971, Seascape (Pulitzer Prize 1975) 1974, Listening 1975, Counting the Ways 1976, The Lady from Dubuque 1977–79, Lolita (adapted from Vladimir Nabokov) 1979, The Man Who Had Three Arms 1981, Finding the Sun 1982, Marriage Play 1986–87, Three Tall Women (Pulitzer Prize 1994) 1990–91, Fragments 1993, The Play about the Baby 1996, The Goat, or, Who is Sylvia? 2000, Occupant 2001. *Leisure interest:* collecting art. *Address:* 14 Harrison Street, New York, NY 10013; Old Montauk Highway, Montauk, NY 11954, USA.

ALBERT, Calvin; American sculptor; b. 19 Nov. 1918, Grand Rapids, Mich.; s. of Philip Albert and Ethel Albert; m. Martha Neff 1941; one d.; ed Inst. of Design, Chicago, Art Inst. of Chicago and Archipenko School of Sculpture; Teacher, New York Univ. 1949–52, Brooklyn Coll. 1947–49, Inst. of Design 1942–46; Prof. of Art, Pratt Inst. 1949–85, Prof. Emer. 1985–; sculpture and drawings in collections of Whitney Museum, Metropolitan Museum, Jewish Museum, Art Inst. of Chicago, Detroit Inst. of Arts, Univ. of Nebraska, Chrysler Museum of Art and Nelson-Atkins Museum of Art; Fulbright Advanced Research Grant to Italy 1961; Tiffany Grants 1963, 1965; Guggenheim Fellowship 1966; Nat. Inst. of Arts and Letters Award 1975. *One-man exhibitions include:* Landmark, Stable and Borgenicht Galleries, New York, Palace of Legion of Honor, San Francisco, Art. Inst. of Chicago; retrospective exhbn at Guildhall Museum, East Hampton, NY 1979; other exhbns in the USA and Galleria George Lester, Rome. *Publication:* Figure Drawing Comes to Life (with Dorothy Seckler) 1987. *Leisure interest:* boating.

ALBERT II, King of the Belgians; b. 6 June 1934, Brussels; s. of King Léopold III and Queen Astrid (née Princess of Sweden); m. Donna Paola Ruffo Di Calabria 1959; two s. one d.; fmrly Prince of Liège; succeeded to the throne 9 Aug. 1993, following death of his brother King Baudouin I; C.-in-C. of Armed Forces, rank of Gen. and Adm.; Pres. Caisse d'Epargne et de Retraite 1954–92; Pres. Belgian Red Cross 1958–93; Hon. Pres. Belgian Office of Foreign Trade 1962–93; apptd. by Council of Europe as Pres. of Conf. of European Ministers responsible for protection of cultural and architectural heritage 1969; participant in numerous int. confs. on environment including UN Conf. in Stockholm 1972; Chair. Belgian Cttee of European Year of Renaissance of the City 1981; Hon. Pres. Belgian Olympic and Interfed. Cttee. *Address:* Cabinet of the King, The Royal Palace, rue Bréderode, 1000 Brussels, Belgium. *Telephone:* (2) 551-20-20 (Office).

ALBERTI, Sir Kurt George Matthew Mayer, MA, DPhil, FRCP; British professor of medicine; b. 27 Sept. 1937, Koblenz, Germany; s. of the late William Peter Matthew Alberti and of Edith Elizabeth Alberti; m. 1st 1964; m. 2nd Stephanie Anne Amiel 1998; three s.; ed Univ. of Oxford; Research Fellow, Harvard Univ. 1966–69; Research Officer, Univ. of Oxford 1969–73; Prof. of Chemical Pathology, Univ. of Southampton 1973–78; Prof. of Clinical Biochemistry and Metabolic Medicine, Univ. of Newcastle 1978–85, Prof. of Medicine 1985–2002, Dean 1995–97; Prof. of Metabolic Medicine, Imperial Coll. London 1999–2002; Sr Research Fellow London 2002–; Nat. Dir for Emergency Access, Dept of Health 2002–; Dir Research and Devt, Northern and Yorkshire Regional Health Authority 1992–95; Pres. Royal Coll. of Physicians 1997–2002; Fellow Acad. of Medicine, Singapore, Hong Kong, Coll. of Physicians, Sri Lanka, Thailand, SA; Hon. DMed (Univ. of Aarhus), (Southampton) 2000, (Athens) 2002. *Publications:* Ed. International Textbook of Diabetes Mellitus 1997 and more than 1,000 papers, reviews and edited books. *Leisure interests:* jogging, hillwalking, crime fiction, opera. *Address:* 4 Spenser Mews, Croxted Road, West Dulwich, London SE21 8SN, England (Home). *Telephone:* (191) 222-6602 (Office). *Fax:* (191) 222-0723 (Office); (20) 8766-7132 (Home).

ALBERTSSON, Per-Åke, PhD; Swedish professor of biochemistry; b. 19 March 1930, Skurup; s. of Albert Olsson and Frideborg Olsson; m. 1st Elisabet Godberg 1955 (divorced 1978); five s. one d.; m. 2nd Charlotte Erlanson 1978; three d.; ed Swedish High School, Ystad and Univs of Lund and Uppsala; Lecturer in Biochem. Univ. of Uppsala 1960–65; Prof. of Biochem. Univ. of Umeå 1965–75, Univ. of Lund 1975–; research zoologist, Univ. of Calif. at Los Angeles 1961–62; Visiting Prof. Stanford Univ. 1971–72, Univ. of Calif. Berkeley 1984–85; mem. Swedish Acad. of Sciences, Swedish Acad. of Eng Sciences, Royal Physiographic Soc. of Lund, Röda Kapellet (symphonic band), City Council of Lund 1991–94; mem. Bd Lunds Energi AB; Gold Medal, Swedish Acad. of Eng Sciences, Gold Medal, Swedish Chem. Soc., Bror Holmberg Medal. *Publications:* Partition of Cell Particles and Macromolecules; over 140 scientific publs in journals. *Leisure interests:* playing music with flute, recorder, trombone and euphonium, tennis. *Address:* Department of Biochemistry, Box 124, S-22100 Lund, Sweden (Office). *Telephone:* (46) 222-8190 (Office). *Fax:* (46) 222-4534.

ALBERTY, Robert Arnold, PhD; American professor of chemistry; b. 21 June 1921, Winfield, Kan.; s. of Luman H. Alberty and Mattie (née Arnold) Alberty; m. Lillian Jane Wind 1944; one s. two d.; ed Lincoln High School, Lincoln, Neb., Univ. of Nebraska and Univ. of Wisconsin; Instructor, Chemistry Dept, Univ. of Wis. 1947–48, Asst Prof. 1948–50, Assoc. Prof. 1950–56, Prof. 1956–57, Assoc. Dean of Letters and Science 1962–63, Dean of Graduate School 1963–67; Prof. of Chemistry MIT 1967–91, 1996–; Prof. Emer. 1991–; Dean, School of Science 1967–82; mem. NAS 1965–, American Acad. of Arts and Sciences 1968–, Inst. of Medicine 1973–; Chair. Comm. on Human Resources, Nat. Research Council 1971–77; Fellow, AAAS 1976–; Dir Colt Industries 1978–88; Dir Inst. for Defense Analysis 1980–86; Chair. Cttee on Chemistry and Public Affairs, American Chemical Soc. 1980; Pres. Physical Chem. Div. IUPAC 1991–93; Dr. hc (Nebraska) 1967, (Lawrence) 1967; Eli Lilly Award for research in enzyme kinetics 1956. *Publications:* Experimental Physical Chemistry (with others) 1962, co-author Physical Chemistry 2001. *Leisure interest:* designing and building a summer cabin. *Address:* Massachusetts Institute of Technology, Room 6-215, 77 Massachusetts Avenue, Cambridge, MA 02139-4307 (Office); 931 Massachusetts Avenue, Cambridge, MA 02139-3171, USA (Home).

ALBERY, Tim; British theatre and opera director; b. 20 May 1952. *Plays directed include:* War Crimes 1981, Secret Gardens 1983, Venice Preserv'd 1983, Hedda Gabler 1984, The Princess of Cleves 1985, Mary Stuart 1988, As You Like It 1989, Berenice 1990, Wallenstein 1993, Macbeth 1996, Attempts on her Life 1997. *Operas directed include:* (for English Nat. Opera) Billy Budd 1988, Beatrice and Benedict 1990, Peter Grimes 1991, Lohengrin 1993, From the House of the Dead 1997, La Bohème 2000, War and Peace 2001; (for Opera North) The Midsummer Marriage 1985, The Trojans 1986, La Finta Giardiniera 1989, Don Giovanni 1991, Don Carlos 1992, Luisa Miller 1995 Così fan Tutte 1997, Katya Kabanova 1999; (for Welsh Nat. Opera) The Trojans 1987, Nabucco 1995; (for Scottish Opera) The Midsummer Marriage 1988, The Trojans 1990, Fidelio 1994, The Ring Cycle 2000– (Rheingold 2000, Die Walküre 2001); (for Australian Opera) The Marriage of Figaro 1992; (for Netherlands Opera) Benvenuto Cellini 1991, La Wally 1993, Beatrice and Benedict 2001; (for Bayerische Staatsoper) Peter Grimes 1993, Simon Boccanegra 1995, Ariadne Auf Naxos 1996; (for Batignano Festival, Italy) The Turn of the Screw 1983; (for Bregenz Festival, Austria) La Wally 1990; (for Royal Opera House) Cherubin 1994; (for Metropolitan Opera, New York) Midsummer Night's Dream 1996, The Merry Widow 2000. *Address:* c/o Harriet Cruickshank, Cruickshank Cazenove, 97 Old South Lambeth Road, London, SW8 1XU, England.

ALBERY, Wyndham John, MA, DPhil, FRS, FRSC; British professor of physical chemistry; b. 5 April 1936, London; s. of the late Michael James Albery and Mary Lawton Albery; ed Winchester Coll., Balliol Coll., Oxford; Nat. Service 1955–56; Weir Jr Research Fellow 1962, Fellow in Physical Chem., University Coll., Oxford 1964–78; Lecturer, Physical Chem., Univ. of Oxford

1964–78; Prof. of Physical Chem., Imperial Coll., London 1978–89, Visiting Prof. 1989; Master of University Coll., Oxford 1989–97; Visiting Prof., Harvard Univ. 1989; Chair. Burton-Taylor Theatre Man. Cttee 1990–93; Gov. Rugby School 1987–; Fellow, Winchester Coll. 1989–; Tilden Lecturer Royal Soc. of Chemistry 1978; Hon. DSc (Oxford) 1990; Electrochemistry Medal RSC 1989. *Publications:* Ring-Disc Electrodes 1971, Electrode Kinetics 1975; (two musicals with John Gould) Who Was That Lady? 1970, On the Boil 1972. *Leisure interests:* theatre, skiing. *Address:* 35 Falmouth House, Hyde Park Place, London W2 2NT, England. *Telephone:* (20) 7262-3909.

ALBORCH BATALLER, Maria del Carmen, LLD; Spanish politician; b. 1948, Castellón del Rugat, Valencia; ed Univ. of Valencia; Lecturer in Commercial Law, Univ. of Valencia, Dean of Law 1985–86; Dir-Gen. of Culture, Culture, Educ. and Science, Office of Autonomous Community of Valencia 1987; Dir-Gen. of Scenic Arts, Cinema and Music Inst. Valencia; Dir-Gen. of Cultural Insts. of Cultural, Educ. and Science Office, Dir, Man. Modern Art Inst. Valencia 1988–93; Minister of Culture 1993–96. *Address:* c/o Ministry of Culture, Plaza del Rey, Madrid, Spain.

ALBRECHT, Ernst Carl Julius, Dr rer. pol; German politician and economist; b. 29 June 1930, Heidelberg; s. of Carl Albrecht, MD and Dr Adda Albrecht (née Berg); m. Dr. Heidi Adele Stromeyer 1953; five s. two d.; ed Univs of Tübingen, Cornell, Basle, Bonn; Attaché to Council of Ministers, ECSC 1954; Head of Common Market section of Brussels conf. for preparation of Treaties of Rome 1956; CEO to EEC Commr Hans von der Groeben 1958; Deputy Head of Comm. del. at negotiations with Denmark, Ireland, Norway and UK for accession to EEC 1961–63; Dir-Gen. for Competition, EEC Comm. 1967–70; Financial Dir Bahlsens Keksfabrik, biscuit mfrs 1971–76; mem. Landtag (Parl.) for Lower Saxony 1970–90, Minister-Pres. of Lower Saxony 1976–90; personal consultant to Pres. and Prime Minister of Kyrgyzstan 1995–; Christlich-Demokratische Union (CDU); Grosskreuz der Bundesrepublik Deutschland. *Publication:* Der Staat—Idee und Wirklichkeit (The State—Idea and Reality) 1976–90, Erinnerungen (Memoirs) 1999. *Address:* Am Brink 2B, 31303 Burgdorf, Germany. *Telephone:* (5136) 977900 (Office); (5136) 82141. *Fax:* (5136) 977901 (Office).

ALBRECHT, Karl; German business executive; co.-f. Albrecht Discount (now Aldi) with brother Theo Albrecht (q.v.) 1948, now CEO Aldi Süd. *Address:* Aldi Einkauf GmbH, Burgstrasse 37–39, 45476, Muelheim, Germany (Office). *Telephone:* 208 99270 (Office). *Website:* www.aldi.de (Office).

ALBRECHT, Theo; German business executive; co.-f. Albrecht Discount (now Aldi) with brother Karl Albrecht (q.v.) 1948, now head of Aldi Nord; Chair. Markus Stiftung. *Address:* Aldi Einkauf GmbH, Burgstrasse 37–39, 45476, Muelheim, Germany (Office). *Telephone:* 208 99270 (Office). *Website:* www.aldi.de (Office).

ALBRIGHT, Madeleine Korbel, PhD; American politician and international affairs adviser; b. 15 May 1938, Prague, Czechoslovakia; d. of Joseph Korbel and Anna Speeglova; m. Joseph Albright 1959 (divorced 1983); three d.; ed Wellesley Coll. and Columbia Univ.; Prof. of Int. Affairs, Georgetown Univ. 1982–83; Head, Center for Nat. Policy 1985–93; fmr legis. aide to Democratic Senator Edmund Muskie; fmr mem. Nat. Security Council staff in Carter Admin.; adviser to Democrat cands Geraldine Ferraro 1984 and Michael Dukakis 1988; Perm. Rep. to UN 1993–97 (first foreign-born holder of this post); Sec. of State 1997–2001; co-f. The Albright Group 2001–; Chair. Nat. Democratic Inst., Washington, DC 2001–; mem. Council on Foreign Relations, American Political Science Asscn, American Asscn for Advancement of Slavic Studies. *Publications:* Poland: The Role of the Press in Political Change 1983 and numerous articles. *Address:* 901 15th Street, NW, Suite 1000, Washington, DC 20005, USA (Office).

ALCHOURON, Guillermo E.; Argentine farmer, lawyer and politician; b. 4 Nov. 1933; m. María Elina Albin Etchart; two s. three d.; ed Univ. of Buenos Aires; farmer specializing in breeding of Dutch, Argentine and Jersey dairy cattle and milk production at Coronel Brandsen Estate; mem. Bd of Dirs Argentine Rural Soc. 1969–96, Pres. 1984–90; Pres. Argentine Soc. of Jersey Dairy Cattle; Counsellor, Foundation for Latin American Econ. Research 1969–, Argentine Council for Int. Relations 1987–; Deputy for Acción de la República 1999–; mem. Exec. Council, Int. Fed. of Agric. Producers; Gov. World Econ. Forum for Food and Farming Production; Pres. Agric. Soc.; del. to numerous int. confs.; decorations from Spain, France, USA, Germany and Italy. *Leisure interests:* golf, tennis, cattle-raising. *Address:* La Juanita, Coronel Brandsen, Argentina.

ALDA, Alan, BS; American actor; b. 28 Jan. 1936, New York; s. of Robert Alda and Joan Browne; m. Arlene Weiss; three d.; ed Fordham Univ.; performed with Second City 1963; Trustee Museum of TV and Radio, Rockefeller Foundation; Pres. Appointee Nat. Comm. for Observance of Int. Women's Year 1976; Co-Chair. Nat. ERA Countdown Campaign 1982; five Emmy Awards (Best Actor, Best Dir and Best Writer), two Dirs' Guild Awards, Writers' Guild Award, seven People's Choice Awards, Humanitas Award for Writing, five Golden Globe Awards for M*A*S*H, elected to TV Acad. Hall of Fame 1994. *Films include:* Gone Are the Days 1963, Paper Lion 1968, The Extraordinary Seaman 1968, The Moonshine War 1970, Jenny 1970, The Mephisto Waltz 1971, To Kill a Clown 1972, California Suite 1978, Same Time Next Year 1978, The Seduction of Joe Tynan (also wrote screenplay) 1979, Crimes and Misdemeanours (D.W. Griffith Award, NY Film Critics' Award) 1989, Whispers in the Dark 1992, And the Band Played On 1993, Manhattan Murder Mystery 1993, White Mile 1994, Canadian Bacon 1995, Everybody Says I Love You 1996, Murder at 1600 1997, Mad City 1997, The Object of My Affection 1998; actor, Ddir, writer of films: The Four Seasons 1981, Sweet Liberty 1986, A New Life 1987, Betsy's Wedding 1990. *Broadway appearances include:* The Owl and the Pussycat, Purlie Victorious, Fair Game for Lovers, The Apple Tree, Our Town (London) 1991, Jake's Women 1992, etc. *TV includes:* The Glass House 1972, M*A*S*H 1972–83, Tune in America 1975, Kill Me If You Can (film) 1977; devised series We'll Get By 1975; Fair Game for Lovers (Theatre World Award); And The Band Played On 1993, White Mile 1994. *Address:* c/o Martin Bregman Productions, 641 Lexington Avenue, New York, NY 10022, USA.

ALDER, Berni Julian, PhD; American theoretical physicist (retd.); b. 9 Sept. 1925, Duisburg, Germany; s. of Ludwig Alder and Ottilie Gottschalk; m. Esther Romella Berger 1956; two s. one d.; ed Univ. of California (Berkeley) and California Inst. of Technology; Instructor, Univ. of Calif. (Berkeley) 1951–54; Theoretical Physicist, Univ. of Calif. Lawrence Livermore Nat. Lab. 1955–93; Prof. of Applied Science, Univ. of California at Davis 1987–93, Prof. Emer. 1993; Nat. Science Foundation Sr Post Doctoral Fellow, Weizman Inst. (Israel) and Univ. of Rome 1963–64; Van der Waals Prof., Univ. of Amsterdam 1971; Guggenheim Fellow, Cambridge (UK) and Leiden (Netherlands) 1954–55; Assoc. Prof., Univ. of Paris 1972; Hinshelwood Prof., Univ. of Oxford 1986; Lorentz Prof., Univ. of Leiden 1990; G. N. Lewis Lecturer 1984, Histiakowsky Lecturer 1990, Royal Soc. Lecturer 1991, Grad. Lecturer 2000; Ed. Journal of Computational Physics; mem. NAS; Fellow Japanese Promotion of Science 1989, American Physics Soc.; Hildebrand Award, American Chem. Soc. 1985; Berni J. Alder Prize est. I.U.P.P. 1999, Boltzmann Prize 2002. *Publications:* Methods of Computational Physics 1963, many chapters in books and articles in journals. *Leisure interests:* hiking, skiing. *Address:* Lawrence Livermore National Laboratory, PO Box 808, Livermore, CA 94551-0808 (Office); 1245 Contra Costa Drive, El Cerrito, CA 94530, USA (Home). *Telephone:* (925) 422-4384 (Office); (510) 231-0137 (Home). *Fax:* (925) 423-4371 (Office). *E-mail:* alder1@llnl.gov (Office).

ALDERDICE OF KNOCK, Baron (Life Peer), cr. 1996, of Knock, in the City of Belfast; **John Thomas Alderdice,** MB, BCh, BAO, FRCPsych; British politician and psychiatrist; b. 28 March 1955, Lurgan, Co. Antrim; s. of Rev. David Alderdice and Helena Alderdice (née Sheilds); m. Joan Margaret (née Hill) 1977; two s. one d.; ed Ballymena Acad., Queen's Univ. Belfast; Royal Coll. of Psychiatrists; apptd Consultant Psychotherapist, Eastern Health and Social Services Bd (EHSSB) 1988; Dir NI Inst. of Human Relations 1991–94; Exec. Medical Dir, S and E Belfast Health and Social Services Trust 1993–97; mem. Alliance Party of NI 1978–, mem. Exec. Cttee 1984–98, Chair. Policy Cttee 1985–87, Vice-Chair. 1987, Leader 1987–98; contested Belfast E 1987, 1992, NI European Parl. elections 1989; councillor, Belfast City Council 1989–97; Leader of Del. to Inter-Party and Inter-Govt Talks on the Future of NI 1991–92; Leader of Del. at Forum for Peace and Reconciliation (Dublin Castle) 1994–96; mem. NI Forum for Political Dialogue 1996–98; mem. European Liberal Democrat and Reform Party, Exec. Cttee mem. 1987–, Treas. 1995–; Vice-Pres. Liberal Int. 1992–99, Chair. Human Rights Cttee 1999; mem. House of Lords 1998–; mem. NI Ass. (Belfast E) 1998–2002, Speaker 1998–2002 (NI Ass. suspended Oct. 2002); mem. BMA, Asscn Psychoanalytic Psychotherapy, Society of Clinical Psychiatrists; Trustee Ulster Museum; Hon. Lecturer Faculty of Medicine, Queen's Univ. Belfast 1991–99, elected Fellow Royal Coll. of Psychiatrists 1997; apptd Hon. Prof. Faculty of Medicine, Univ. of San Marcos, Lima (Peru) 1999; W. Averell Harrison Award for Democracy 1998, John F. Kennedy Profiles in Courage Award 1998, Silver Medal of Congress of Peru 1999, Medal of Honour of Peru Coll. of Medicine 1999. *Publications include:* articles on eating disorders, psychotherapy, ethics and politics. *Leisure interests:* music, singing. *Address:* c/o Parliament Buildings, Stormont, Belfast, Co. Antrim, BT4 3XX, Northern Ireland (Office). *Telephone:* (28) 9052-1130 (Office). *Fax:* (28) 9052-1959 (Office). *E-mail:* alderdicej@parliament.uk (Office). *Website:* homepage.ntlworld.com/john.alderdice.

ALDERS, Hans; Netherlands politician; b. 17 Dec. 1942; ed vocational school; fmr junior man. in an employment agency; mem. Gelderland Prov. Ass. 1978, Leader Partij van de Arbeid (PvdA) Group 1979; mem. Parl. 1982–, Sec. PvdA Parl. Group 1987–89; Minister of Housing, Physical Planning and the Environment 1989–94; Commr of the Queen Prov. of Groningen Netherlands 1995–2002. *Address:* Partij van Arbeid, Nicolaas Witsenkade 30, 1017 ZT Amsterdam, Netherlands.

ALDISS, Brian Wilson, FRSL; British writer, critic and actor; b. 18 Aug. 1925, Norfolk; m. 2nd Margaret Manson 1965; two s. two d.; ed Framlingham Coll. and West Buckland School; fmrly soldier, draughtsman, bookseller and film critic; Literary Ed. Oxford Mail 1957–69; Pres. British Science Fiction Asscn 1960–65; Jt-Pres. European Science Fiction Cttees 1976–80; Chair. John W. Campbell Memorial Award 1976–77; Chair. Cttee of Man. Soc. of Authors 1977–78; mem. Literature Advisory Panel, Arts Council 1978–80; Chair. Cultural Exchanges Cttee of Authors 1978; Judge, Booker McConnell Prize 1981; Pres. World SF 1982–84; Ed. S.F. Horizons 1964–; Vice-Pres. H. G. Wells Soc., W Buckland School 1997–; Hon. DLitt; Hugo Award for Hothouse 1962, Nebula Award for The Saliva Tree 1965, Ditmar Award for World's Best Contemporary Science Fiction Writer 1969, British Science Fiction Asscn Award for The Moment of Eclipse 1972, Eurocon III Merit Award for Billion Year Spree 1976, Jules Verne Award for Non-Stop 1977, first James Blish Award for Excellence in Criticism 1977, Pilgrim Award

1978, John W. Campbell Award 1983, Kurt Lasswitz Award 1984, IAFA Distinguished Scholarship Award 1986, J. Lloyd Eaton Award 1988, Prix Utopie (France) 1999, Grand Master of Science Fiction 2000. *Plays (author):* SF Blues, Kindred Blood in Kensington Gore, Monsters of Every Day (Oxford Literary Festival) 2000, Drinks with The Spider King (Florida) 2000; acted in own productions 1985–2002. *Publications:* The Brightfount Diaries 1955, Space, Time & Nathaniel 1957, Non-Stop 1958, The Male Response 1959, Hothouse 1962, The Airs of Earth 1963, The Dark Light Years 1964, Greybeard 1964, Earthworks 1965, Best Science Fiction Stories of Brian W. Aldiss 1965, Cities and Stones: A Traveller's Jugoslavia 1966, Report on Probability A 1968, Barefoot in the Head 1969, Intangibles Inc., 1969, A Brian Aldiss Omnibus 1969, The Hand-Reared Boy 1970, The Shape of Further Things 1970, A Soldier Erect 1971, The Moment of Eclipse 1971, Brian Aldiss Omnibus 2 1971, Penguin Science Fiction Omnibus (ed.) 1973, Comic Inferno 1973, Billion Year Spree 1973, Frankenstein Unbound 1973, The Eighty-Minute Hour 1974, Hell's Cartographers (ed.) 1975, Space Odysseys, Evil Earths, Science Fiction Art 1975, The Malacia Tapestry, Galactic Empires (2 vols) 1976, Last Orders, Brothers of the Head 1977, Perilous Planets 1977, A Rude Awakening 1978, Enemies of the System 1978, This World and Nearer Ones 1979, Pile 1979, New Arrivals, Old Encounters 1979, Moreau's Other Island 1980, Life in the West 1980, An Island called Moreau 1981, Foreign Bodies 1981, Helliconia Spring 1982, Science Fiction Quiz 1983, Helliconia Summer 1983, Seasons in Flight 1984, Helliconia Winter 1985, The Pale Shadow of Science 1985, . . . And the Lurid Glare of the Comet 1986, Trillion Year Spree 1986 (Hugo Award 1987), Ruins 1987, Forgotten Life 1988, Science Fiction Blues 1988, Best SF Stories of Brian W. Aldiss 1988, Cracken at Critical 1989, A Romance of the Equator 1990, Bury My Heart at W.H. Smith's 1990, Dracula Unbound 1991, Remembrance Day 1993, A Tupolev Too Far 1993, Somewhere East of Life 1994, The Detached Retina 1995, At the Caligula Hotel (poems) 1995, The Secret of this Book 1995, Songs from the Steppes of Central Asia 1996, The Twinkling of an Eye 1998, The Squire Quartet (4 vols) 1998, When the Feast is Finished 1999, White Mars 1999, Supertoys Last All Summer Long (made into Kubrick–Spielberg film A.I. 2001) 2001, The Cretan Teat 2001, Super-State 2002, Researches and Churches in Serbia 2002, The Dark Sun Rises (poems) 2002, Affairs in Hampden Ferrers 2003. *Leisure interests:* the past, the future, obscurity. *Address:* Hambleden, 39 St Andrew's Road, Old Headington, Oxford, OX3 9DL, England. *Telephone:* (1865) 762464. *Fax:* (1865) 744435. *E-mail:* aldiss@dial.pipex.com (Office). *Website:* brianwaldiss.com (Office).

ALDOURI, Mohammed A., BL, PhD; Iraqi diplomatist and professor of law; b. 1942, Baghdad; ed Baghdad Univ. and Dijon Univ., France; Lecturer Coll. of Law and Political Science, Baghdad Univ. 1973–82, Head Dept of Law 1982–83, Prof. of Int. Law and Dean of Law Coll. 1983–98; Dir-Gen. Iraqi Cultural Relations Office, Ministry of Higher Educ. 1975–78; mem. UN Cttee for Civil and Political Rights 1980–84, also Rep. of Iraq to Comm. for Human Rights; Head of Human Rights and Legal Depts, Ministry of Foreign Affairs 1994–96, 1998; Perm. Rep. to UN, Geneva 1999–2001, New York 2001–03. *Address:* c/o Permanent Mission of Iraq to the United Nations, 14 East 79th Street, New York, NY 10021, USA (Office).

ALDRIDGE, (Harold Edward) James; British author and journalist; b. 10 July 1918; s. of William Thomas Aldridge and Edith Quayle Aldridge; m. Dina Mitchnik 1942; two s.; with Herald and Sun, Melbourne, Australia 1937–38, Daily Sketch and Sunday Dispatch, London 1939; with Australian Newspaper Service and North American Newspaper Alliance (as war correspondent), Finland, Norway, Middle East, Greece, USSR 1939–45; correspondent for Time and Life, Tehran 1944; Rhys Memorial Award 1945; Lenin Peace Prize 1972. *Plays:* 49th State 1947, One Last Glimpse 1981. *Publications:* Signed With Their Honour 1942, The Sea Eagle 1944, Of Many Men 1946, The Diplomat 1950, The Hunter 1951, Heroes of the Empty View 1954, Underwater Hunting for Inexperienced Englishmen 1955, I Wish He Would Not Die 1958, Gold and Sand (short stories) 1960, The Last Exile 1961, A Captive in the Land 1962, The Statesman's Game 1966, My Brother Tom 1966, The Flying 19 1966, Living Egypt (with Paul Strand) 1969, Cairo: Biography of a City 1970, A Sporting Proposition 1973, The Marvellous Mongolian 1974, Mockery in Arms 1974, The Untouchable Juli 1975, One Last Glimpse 1977, Goodbye Un-America 1979, The Broken Saddle 1982, The True Story of Lilli Stubek 1984 (Australian Children's Book of the Year 1985), The True Story of Spit Mac Phee 1985 (Guardian Children's Fiction Prize), The True Story of Lola MacKellar 1993. *Leisure interests:* trout and salmon fishing. *Address:* c/o Curtis Brown, 28–29 Haymarket, London, SW1Y 4SP, England.

ALDRIN, Buzz, DSc; American astronaut; b. 20 Jan. 1930, Montclair, NJ; s. of the late Col Edwin E. Aldrin and Marion Moon; m. 1st (divorced 1978); two s. one d.; m. 2nd Lois Driggs Cannon 1988; ed US Military Acad. and Massachusetts Inst. of Technology; fmr mem. US Air Force; completed pilot training 1952; flew combat missions during Korean War; later became aerial gunnery instructor, Nellis Air Force Base, Nev.; attended Squadron Officers' School at Air Univ., Maxwell Air Force Base, Ala; later Flight Commdr 36th Tactical Fighter Wing, Bitburg, Germany; completed astronautics studies at MIT 1963; selected by NASA as astronaut 1963; Gemini Target Office, Air Force Space Systems Div., LA, Calif. 1963; later assigned to Manned Spacecraft Center, Houston, Tex.; pilot of backup crew for Gemini IX mission 1966; pilot for Gemini XII 1966; backup command module pilot for Apollo VIII; lunar module pilot for Apollo XI, landed on the moon 20 July 1969; Commdt

Aerospace Research Pilot School 1971–72; Scientific Consultant, Beverly Hills Oil Co., LA; Chair. Starcraft Enterprises, Nat. Space Soc.; Fellow, American Inst. of Aeronautics and Astronautics; Hon. mem. Royal Aeronautical Soc.; retd from USAF 1972; Pres. Research & Eng Consultants Inc. 1972–; consultant to JRW, Jet Propulsion Lab.; several hon. degrees and numerous decorations and awards. *Publications:* First on the Moon: A Voyage with Neil Armstrong (with Michael Collins) 1970, Return to Earth (with Wayne Warga) 1974, Men From Earth (with Malcolm McConnell) 1989, Encounter with Tiber (with John Barnes) 1996, Encounter with Tiber—the Return 2000. *Leisure interests:* scuba diving, snow skiing, Starcraft Enterprises. *Address:* 10380 Wilshire Boulevard, Suite 703, Los Angeles, CA 90024, USA. *Telephone:* (310) 278-0384 (Office); (310) 278-0384 (Home). *Fax:* (310) 278-0388 (Office); (310) 278-0388 (Home).

ALEBUA, Rt Hon Ezekiel, PC; Solomon Islands politician; fmr Deputy Prime Minister; Prime Minister of the Solomon Is. 1986–89; mem. Solomon Is. United Party (SIUPA). *Address:* c/o Office of the Prime Minister, Honiara, Solomon Islands.

ALEGRE, Norberto José d'Alva Costa; São Tomé e Príncipe politician; fmr Minister of Econ. and Finance; Prime Minister of São Tomé e Príncipe 1992–94; mem. Partido de Convergência Democrática Grupo de Reflexão. *Address:* c/o Partido de Convergência Democrático Grupo de Reflexão, São Tomé, São Tomé e Príncipe.

ALEGRETT, Sebastián, BEcons; Venezuelan diplomatist; b. 1942, Caracas; ed Andrés Bello Catholic Univ., Caracas, Univ. of Paris, France; pvt. consultant; Pres. Export Financing Fund of Venezuela; mem. Bd of Dirs. Cen. Bank of Venezuela, CVG Siderúrgica del Orinoco CA Iron and Steel Plant, CVG Internacional, Extebandes; Integration Dir Inst. of Foreign Trade of Venezuela 1971–74, Pres. 1979–83; Prof. Andrés Bello Catholic Univ. and Central Univ. of Venezuela 1973–79; Perm. Sec. Latin American Econ. System 1983–87; Amb. to Brazil 1990–94, to Colombia 1996–97; Perm. Rep. to O.A.S. 1994–96; Rep. of Venezuela to the Andean Community of Nations and Corporación Andina de Fomento, Sec.-Gen. Andean Community of Nations Aug. 1997–. *Address:* Andean Community of Nations, Avda Paseo de la República 3895, San Isidro, Lima 27, Peru (Office). *Telephone:* (1) 2212222 (Office). *Fax:* (1) 2213329 (Office). *E-mail:* contacto@comunidadandina.org (Office). *Website:* www.comunidadandina.org (Office).

ALEKPEROV, Vagit Yusufovich; Russian-Azerbaijani businessman; b. 1 Sept. 1950, Baku; m.; one s.; ed Azerbaijan Inst. of Oil and Gas; worked as engineer for Kasporneft, Surgntneftegaz.Bashneft cos. 1975–84; Dir oil-extraction Co. Kogalymneftegas 1984–90; Deputy, then First Deputy Minister of Oil and Gas Industry of USSR 1990–91; Chair. Bd Imperial Bank, Petrocommercial Bank; founder Pres. and Chair. Oil Co. LUKoil 1992–; Deputy Chair. Oil Exporters Union of Russia; Vice-Pres. Int. Oil Consortium. *Publication:* Vertical Integrated Oil Companies in Russia. *Address:* LUKoil, Sretensky blvd 11, 101000 Moscow, Russia. *Telephone:* (095) 927-44-44.

ALEKSANDR, (Timofeyev, Nikolai Anatolyevich) Archbishop of Saratov and Volsk; Russian ecclesiastic; b. 8 Aug. 1941, Teykovo, Ivanovo region; ed Moscow Theological Acad.; mil. service 1963–66; became a monk 1971; lecturer, Moscow Theological Acad. 1973, Prof. 1981; Dean of Moscow Theological Acad. and Seminary 1982; Bishop of Dmitrov 1982–92; Archbishop 1986–, of Maykop and Armavir 1994–95, of Saratov and Volsk 1995–; Chair. of Educ. Cttee of Holy Synod 1986. *Address:* Moscow Theological Academy and Seminary, Vysoko-Petrovsky Monastery, Petrovka 28/2, 103051 Moscow, Russia. *Telephone:* (095) 209-13-10.

ALEKSANDROV, Aleksandr Pavlovich, PhD; Russian cosmonaut and pilot; b. 20 Feb. 1943, Moscow; m. Natalia Valentinovna Aleksandrova; one s. one d.; ed Baumann Tech. Inst., Moscow; mem. CPSU 1970; after service in Soviet Army started work with Space Programme 1964–; took part in elaboration of control system of space-craft, Cosmonaut since 1978, participated in Soyuz-T and Salyut programmes; successfully completed 149-day flight to Salyut-7 orbital station with V. A. Lyakhov 1983 and effected spacewalk, July 1987, with V. A. Victorenko and M. Fares; joined Yurii Romanenko in space, returned to Earth Dec. 1987; completed 160-day flight on Mir Space Station; Chief, Dept of Crew Training and Extra Vehicular Activity at Energya design and production firm; mem. Extra Vehicular Activity Cttee, IAF 1994–; Academician Int. Informatization Acad. 1997; Hero of Soviet Union 1983, 1987, Hero of Syria. *Address:* Khovanskaya str. 3, 27, 129515 Moscow, Russia. *Telephone:* (095) 513-67-88 (Office); (095) 215-56-19 (Home). *Fax:* (095) 513-61-38.

ALEKSANDROV, Kiryll Sergeyevich, DPhysMathSc; Russian physicist; b. 9 Jan. 1931; s. of Sergey Aleksandrov and Ljubov' Aleksandrov; m. Inga Chernjavskaja 1959; one d.; ed Leningrad Electrotech. Inst.; worked as researcher Inst. of Crystallography; researcher, Vice-Dir Kirensky Inst. of Physics, Siberian br. of USSR (now Russian) Acad. of Sciences, Krasnoyarsk 1958–83, Dir 1983–; Corresp. mem. USSR Acad. of Sciences 1971, mem. 1984; Chair. Scientific Council on Physics of Segnetoelectrics and Dielectrics, Dept of Gen. Physics and Astronomy, Russian Acad. of Sciences; Vice-Chair. Krasnoyarsk Scientific Centre of Russian Acad. of Sciences; USSR State Prize in Science 1989. *Publications:* works in the field of crystal physics, structural phase transitions, physics of materials. *Leisure interests:* numismatics, mushroom hunting. *Address:* L. Kirensky Institute of Physics, 600036 Akademgorodok, Krasnoyarsk, Russia. *Telephone:* (3912) 43-26-35 (Office); (3912) 44-41-75 (Home). *Fax:* (3912) 43-89-23. *E-mail:* kaleks@post.krascience.rssi.ru (Office).

ALEKSANDROV, Vassily Yegorovich; Russian pilot and aviation executive; b. 6 May 1947, Istra, Moscow region; m.; one d.; ed Tambov Higher Aviation School of Pilots, Yu. Gagarin Mil. Aviation Acad., Mil. Acad. of Gen. Staff; pilot in mil. air forces of Russian Fed., Squadron Commdr, Regt Commdr; Dir Tambov Higher Aviation School; Deputy Commdr Air Forces Siberian Mil. Command; Dir Research Inst., Ministry of Defence; Chair. Bd of Dirs Tupolev Aviation Scientific-Tech. Complex (mfrs of strategic bombers and passenger liners) 1997–98, Dir-Gen. 1998–; Corresp. mem. Russian Acad. of Aviation. *Address:* Tupolev Aviation Scientific-Technical Complex, akademik Tupolev emb. 15, 111250 Moscow, Russia (Office). *Telephone:* (095) 785-53-38 (Office). *Fax:* (095) 261-08-68 (Office).

ALEKSASHENKO, Sergey Vladimirovich; Russian banker; b. 23 Dec. 1959, Likino-Dulevo, Moscow Region; m.; two c.; ed Moscow State Univ.; mem. of staff Moscow Inst. of Econs and Math., USSR Acad. of Sciences 1986–90; leading expert USSR State Comm. on Econ. Reform; Exec. Dir Inst. of Russian Union of Industrialists and Entrepreneurs 1991–93, Dir.-Gen. 1995; Deputy Minister of Finance 1993–95; First Deputy Chair. Cen. Bank of the Russian Fed. 1995–98; Chair. Audit Comm.; Chair. Asscn of Current Stock Exchanges of Russia 1995–; First Deputy Chair. Observation Council Savings Bank 1996–99; Head Centre of Devt Analytical Group 1999–; Deputy Dir-Gen. Interros (holding co.) 2000–. *Publications:* Battle for the Rouble, Alma Mater; over 100 Publs on fiscal and econ. matters. *Leisure interests:* photography, diving. *Address:* Interros Managing Holding Company, Mashi Pozyvayevoy str. 11, 107078 Moscow, Russia (Office). *Telephone:* (095) 726-57-50 (Office). *Fax:* (095) 921-62-88 (Office). *E-mail:* webmaster@www.cbr.ru (Office).

ALEKSEEVA, Tatyana Ivanovna, PhD; Russian anthropologist and biologist; b. 7 Dec. 1928, Kazan; d. of Ivan Sharabrin and Varvara Majorova; m. Valery Alekseev (deceased); ed Moscow State Univ.; jr, sr, leading, prin. researcher Research Inst. and Museum of Anthropology 1955–; Prin. Researcher Inst. of Archaeology 1992–; Corresp. mem. USSR (now Russian) Acad. of Sciences 1991, mem. 2000; research in study of influence of geographical and social medium on aboriginal population; mem. Asscn of Human Biologists; Pres. Russian branch of European Anthropological Asscn;; Hon. mem. World Org. of Mongolian Studies; Order of Friendship 1999; Medal of Moscow. *Publications include:* Origin and Ethnic History of Russian People 1965, Ethnogenesis of East Slavs 1973, Geographical Medium and Biology of Man 1977, Adaptive Processes in Populations of Man 1986, Neolithic Population of the Eastern Europe Forest Zone 1997, Eastern Slavs: Anthropology and Ethnic History 1999, Homo Sungirensis Upper Palaeolithic Man: Ecological and Evolutionary Aspects of the Investigation 2000. *Leisure interests:* riding, pets. *Address:* Research Institute and Museum of Anthropology, Moscow State Univ., Mokhovaya str. 11, 103009 Moscow (Office); ul. Profsoyuzhaya 43-1, apt 125, 117420 Moscow, Russia (Home). *Telephone:* (095) 203-35-98 (Office); (095) 331-32-73 (Home). *Fax:* (095) 203-3554 (Office). *E-mail:* homo@antropos.msu.ru (Office).

ALEKSEYEV, Aleksander Yuryevich; Russian diplomatist; b. 20 Aug. 1946, Moscow; m.; one d.; ed Moscow Inst. of Int. Relations; diplomatic posts abroad, including India and in Ministry of Foreign Affairs of USSR and Russia; Amb. to Pakistan 1993; Deputy Dir European Co-operation Dept, Ministry of Foreign Affairs; Perm. Rep. to OSCE 2001–. *Address:* Russian Delegation to the Organization for Security and Co-operation in Europe, Erzherzog Karl Strasse 182, 1220 Vienna, Austria (Office). *Telephone:* (1) 280-27-62 (Office). *Fax:* (1) 280-31-90 (Office). *E-mail:* rfms@atnet.at (Office).

ALEKSEYEV, Sergey Sergeyevich, DJur; Russian lawyer; b. 28 July 1924; m.; two d.; ed Sverdlovsk Inst. of Law; teacher, Prof., Head of Chair Sverdlovsk (now Yekaterinburg) Inst. of Law 1949–; Dir Inst. of Philosophy and Law Ural Div. of USSR Acad. of Sciences; Corresp. mem. USSR Acad. of Sciences 1987; USSR People's Deputy 1990–91; Chair. USSR Cttee of Constitutional Inspection 1990–91; Chair. Council of Research Centre of Pvt. Law 1992–; author (with A. Sobchak) of one of projects of Constitution of Russia 1991–92; mem. Presidential Council of Russia 1993–95; USSR State Prize, Merited Worker of Science of Russia. *Publications include:* General Theory of Law (Vols 1–2, 1981–82), Theory of Law: Constitutional Concept 1991, Legal Civil Soc. 1991. *Leisure interests:* tourism, mountain skiing, reading. *Address:* Research Centre of Private Law, Yekaterinburg Branch, 620146 Yekaterinburg, Russia (Office). *Telephone:* (3432) 28-89-81 (Office).

ALEKSIY II, DCT; Russian Orthodox clergyman; b. (A. M. Ridiger), 23 Feb. 1929, Tallinn, Estonia; ed Leningrad (now St Petersburg) Theological Acad.; ordained priest 1950; Bishop of Tallinn and Estonia 1961–64; mem. Cen. Cttee of World Council of Churches 1961–68; Vice-Chair. Dept of External Church Relations, Moscow Patriarchate 1961–64; Archbishop 1961–, Admin. Manager of Moscow Patriarchy 1964–86, perm. mem. of Holy Synod 1964–, Chair. Teaching Cttee of Moscow Patriarchate 1965–86; Metropolitan of Tallinn and Estonia 1968–86; Metropolitan of Leningrad and Novgorod 1986–90; Patriarch of Moscow and All Russia 1990–; Chair. of Presidium Conf. of European Churches 1987–92; USSR People's Deputy 1989–91; Dr hc (Moscow Univ.). *Address:* Moscow Patriarchate, Chisty per. 5, Moscow 119034, Russia. *Telephone:* (095) 201-28-40. *Fax:* (095) 201-25-04.

ALEMÁN LACAYO, Arnoldo; Nicaraguan politician; b. 23 Jan. 1946, Managua; ed Nat. Autonomous Univ.; fmr leader pro-Somoza Liberal Student Youth Org. in 1960s; imprisoned for alleged counter-revolutionary activity 1980; placed under house arrest 1989; Mayor of Managua 1990; Pres. Fed. of Cen. American Municipalities 1993–95; Leader, Liberal Party Alliance 1996; Pres. of Nicaragua 1997–2001. *Address:* c/o Oficina del Presidente, Managua, Nicaragua.

ALENCAR GOMES DA SILVA, José; Brazilian politician and business executive; b. 17 Oct. 1931, Muriaé; s. of Antonio Gomes da Silva and Dolores Peres Gomes da Silva; clerk A Sedutora (textiles store), Muriaé 1946–48; salesperson Casa Bonfim, Caratinga 1948–50; est. A Queimadeira (textiles store), Caratinga 1950–53; travelling salesman Tecidos Fernandes SA 1953; co-f. Industria de Macarrão Santa Cruz (pasta factory) 1950s; inherited co. Uniãos dos Cometas from brother Geraldo Gomes da Silva 1959, renamed Geraldo Gomes da Silva Tecidos SA; f. Cia Industrial de Roupas União dos Cometas 1963, renamed Wembley Roupas SA; co-f. Companhia de Tecidos Norte de Minas—Coteminas, Montes Claros 1967; Senator for Tancredo Neves (Liberal Party); Vice-Pres. of Brazil 2003–. *Address:* Gabinete do Senador, Anexo II, 1 Andar, Gab. 57, Ala Senador Tancredo Neves, Senado Federal, 70165-900 Brasília (Office); Companhia de Tecidos Norte de Minas—Coteminas, Matrix Unit, Av. Magalhaes Pinto, No. 4000, Bairro Planalto, 39404-166 Montes Claros, MG, Brazil (Office). *Telephone:* (38) 3215-7777 (Office). *Fax:* (38) 3217-1633 (Office). *E-mail:* jose.alencar@senado.gov.br (Office).

ALENTOVA, Vera Valentinovna; Russian actress; b. 21 Feb. 1942; m. Vladimir Menshov; one d.; ed Studio School of Moscow Art Theatre; actress Moscow Pushkin Drama Theatre 1965; State Prize of Russia, Grand Prix Saint Michel, People's Artist of Russia 1992. *Theatre roles include:* Last Days, The Warsaw Melody, The Slaves, The Unattainable, Children of the Sun, Scum, Lighting But Not Heating, Chocolate Soldier; in cinema 1966–; numerous roles including Katerina in Moscow Does Not Trust Tears 1980, Time of Desires 1982, Shirli-Myrli 1995, Son for Father 1997, The Envy of the Gods 2000. *Address:* 3d Tverskaya-Yamskaya str. 52, Apt. 29, 125047 Moscow, Russia (Home). *Telephone:* (095) 250-85-43 (Home).

ALESKEROV, Murtuz Nadzhaf oglu, DJurSc; Azerbaijani politician; b. 20 Sept. 1928, Gyandzha; s. of Nadzhaf Aleskerov and Khanym Mammadova; m.; two s. one d.; ed Azerbaijan State Univ., Moscow Inst. of State and Law; Sr lecturer Azerbaijan State Univ. 1954–, Head of Chair of State Law 1965–, Prof. 1969, Rector 1993–96; after proclamation of independence of Azerbaijan took part in working out draft Constitution of new Repub.; participant in political activities since 1990; mem. Bd of People's Front 1991–92, expelled for org. of rally in support of Heydar Alijev; Deputy Chair. Party Yeni Azerbaijan (New Azerbaijan) and mem. Political Council; elected Deputy to Milli Majlis (Nat. Ass.) 1995, Chair. 1996–; mem. Int. Juridical Asscn, Bd Republican Lawyers' Union, Scientific Consulting Councils of Supreme Court, State Prosecutor's Office; Merited Lawyer of Azerbaijan, Istiglal ('Independence') Decoration. *Publications:* author of numerous monographs and textbooks and over 200 articles on problems of state and int. law. *Address:* 1 Parliamentary Avenue, Milli Majlis of the Republic of Azerbaijan, 370152 Baku, Azerbaijan. *Telephone:* (12) 98-23-63. *Fax:* (12) 98-97-22.

ALEXANDER, (Andrew) Lamar, JD; American politician; b. 3 July 1940, Knoxville, Tenn.; s. of Andrew Lamar Alexander and Genevra F. Rankin; m. Leslee K. (Honey) Buhler 1969; two s. two d.; ed Vanderbilt and New York Univs; mem. Bar of La. and Tenn.; law clerk to presiding justice, US Court of Appeals (5th circuit), New Orleans; Assoc. Fowler, Rountree, Fowler & Robertson, Knoxville 1965; Legislative Asst to Senator Howard Baker 1967–68; Exec. Asst to Bryce Harlow, White House Congressional Liaison Office 1969–70; partner, Dearborn & Ewing, Nashville 1971–78; Gov. of Tenn. 1979–87; Chair. Leadership Inst. Belmont Coll. Nashville 1987–88; Pres. Univ. of Tenn. 1988–90; mem. Pres.'s Task Force on Federalism; Chair. Nat. Govs Asscn 1985–86, President's Comm. on Americans Outdoors 1985–87; mem. Bd of Dirs Corporate Child Care Inc., Nashville, Martin Marietta Corpn Bethesda, Md; Sec. of Educ. 1990–93; Counsel Baker, Donelson, Bearman and Caldwell 1993–98; pvt. practice 1999–; Chair. Republican Neighbourhood Meeting 1993–; Senator from Tenn. 2003–; Republican; recipient of various awards and distinctions. *Publications:* Steps Along the Way 1986, Six Months Off 1988, We Know What We Do 1995. *Leisure interests:* piano. *Address:* United States Senate, SD B-40, Suite 2 , Washington, DC 20510, USA. *Telephone:* (202) 224-4944. *Fax:* (202) 228-3398. *Website:* alexander.senate.gov.

ALEXANDER, Bill; British theatre director; b. 23 Feb. 1948, Hunstanton, Norfolk; s. of Bill Paterson and Rosemary Paterson; m. Juliet Harmer 1978; two d.; ed St Lawrence Coll. Ramsgate and Keele Univ.; began career at Bristol Old Vic directing Shakespeare and the classics and contemporary drama; joined RSC 1977, Assoc. Dir 1984–91, Hon. Assoc. Artistic Dir 1991–; productions for RSC include: Tartuffe, Richard III 1984, Volpone, The Accrington Pals, Clay, Captain Swing, School of Night, A Midsummer Night's Dream, The Merry Wives of Windsor; other theatre work at Nottingham Playhouse, Royal Court Theatre, Victory Theatre, New York and Shakespeare Theatre, Washington, DC; Artistic Dir Birmingham Repertory Co. 1993–2000, productions include: Othello, The Snowman, Macbeth, Dr. Jekyll and Mr. Hyde, The Alchemist, Awake and Sing, The Way of the World, Divine Right, The Merchant of Venice, Old Times, Frozen, Hamlet, The Tempest, The

Four Alice Bakers, Jumpers, Nativity (co-author) 1999, Quarantine 2000, Twelfth Night 2000, An Enemy of the People (Theatre Clwyd) 2002, Frozen, Mappa Mundi (RNT) 2002, The Importance of Being Ernest (Northampton) 2002; Olivier Award for Dir of the Year 1986. *Films:* The Snowman 1998. *Leisure interest:* tennis. *Address:* Rose Cottage, Tunley, Glos. GL7 6LP, England.

ALEXANDER, Brooke, BA; American art dealer and publisher; b. 26 April 1937, Los Angeles; s. of Richard H. Alexander and Marion C. Alexander; m. Carolyn Rankin 1967; two d.; ed Yale Univ.; f. Brooke Alexander Inc. to publish and distribute graphic art 1968, expanded co. 1975; f. Brooke Alexander Edns., opened separate gallery for graphics 1989; partner in Madrid gallery, Galería Weber, Alexander y Cobo 1991–; mem. Governing Bd Yale Univ. Art Gallery 1988–. *Address:* 59 Wooster Street, New York, NY, USA. *Telephone:* (212) 925-4338.

ALEXANDER, Christopher, PhD; American architect, professor and consultant; b. 4 Oct. 1936, Vienna, Austria; m. Pamela Patrick 1978; two d.; ed Oundle, Trinity Coll., Cambridge, Harvard Univ.; fmrly with Center for Cognitive Studies, Harvard, with Jt Center for Urban Studies, Harvard Univ. and MIT 1959–63; Prof. of Architecture Univ. of Calif., Berkeley 1963–, Research Prof. in the Humanities 1965; Visiting Fellow Rockefeller Foundation Villa Serbelloni 1965; f., Pres., Dir Center for Environmental Structure 1967–; Trustee Prince of Wales's Inst. for Architecture 1991–97; Prof. in Grad. School, Univ. of Calif., Berkeley 1998–; Center for Environmental Structure has undertaken around 200 projects, including town and community planning worldwide; Fellow Harvard Univ. 1961–64, American Acad. of Arts and Sciences 1996; mem. Swedish Royal Acad. 1980–; Best Bldg in Japan Award 1985; Seaside Prize 1994, numerous other awards and prizes. *Major works include:* 35 bldgs. of New Eishin Univ., Tokyo, Linz Café, Linz, village school, Gujarat, low-cost housing in Mexico and Peru, Shelter for the Homeless, San José, numerous pvt. houses and public bldgs. *Publications include:* Notes on the Synthesis of Form 1964, The Oregon Experiment 1975, The Linz Café 1981, A New Theory of Urban Design 1984, The Phenomenon of Life 1998, The Process of Creating Life 1998, The Luminous Ground 1998, A Vision of the Living World 1998; over 200 articles in design journals. *Address:* 2701 Shasta Road, Berkeley, CA 94708, USA; Meadow Lodge, Binsted, near Arundel, W Sussex, BN18 0LQ, England.

ALEXANDER, Clifford L., LLD; American government official and lawyer; b. 21 Sept. 1933, Harlem, New York; s. of Clifford Alexander and Edith Alexander (née McAllister); m. Adele Logan 1959; one s. one d.; ed Harvard Univ., Yale Univ.; practised as lawyer in New York, partner in Verner, Liipfert, Bernhard, McPherson and Alexander, law firm; Foreign Affairs Officer, Nat. Security Council Staff 1963–64; Deputy Special Asst, later Deputy Special Counsel to Pres. Lyndon Johnson 1964–67; Chair. Equal Employment Opportunity Comm. 1967–69, resgnd; mem. Comm. for the Observance of Human Rights 1968; Special Amb. to Swaziland 1968; Partner in Arnold & Porter, law firm; news commentator and host, Cliff Alexander—Black on White TV programme 1971–74; Prof. of Law, Howard Univ. 1973–74; US Sec. of the Army 1977–80; Pres. Alexander & Assocs Inc. 1981–; mem. Bd of Dirs Pennsylvania Power & Light Co.; Adjunct Prof., Georgetown Univ.; Prof. Howard Univ., Washington, DC; mem. Bd of Dirs. Mexican-American Legal Defense and Educ. Fund, Dreyfus Third Century Fund Inc., MCI Corpn, Dreyfus Common Stock Fund, Dreyfus Tax Exempt Fund; mem. American and DC Bar Assens; fmr mem. Bd Overseers Harvard Univ.; Trustee, Atlanta Univ.; Hon. LLD (Univ. of Maryland, Atlanta Univ.); Frederick Douglass Award and other decorations. *Address:* Alexander & Assocs. Inc., 400 C Street, NE, Washington, DC 20002-5818; 512 A Street, SE, Washington, DC 20003-1139, USA (Home). *Telephone:* (202) 546 0111 (Office).

ALEXANDER, Jane; American actress and government official; b. 28 Oct. 1939, Boston; d. of Thomas Bartlett and Ruth Quigley (née Pearson); m. 1st Robert Alexander 1962 (divorced 1969); one s.; m. 2nd Edwin Sherin 1975; ed Sarah Lawrence Coll., Edinburgh Univ.; Chair. Nat. Endowment for Arts 1993–97; mem. Bd Dirs. Women's Action for Nuclear Disarmament 1981–88, Film Forum 1985–90, Nat. Stroke Assen 1984–91; guest artist-in-residence Oklahoma Arts Inst. 1982; mem. Bd of Trustees Wildlife Conservation Soc. 1997–, The MacDowell Colony 1997–, Arts Int. 2000–; Frances Eppes Prof. Fla State Univ. 2002–; Hon. DFA (The Juilliard School) 1994, (N.C. School of Arts) 1994, (The New School of Social Research) 1996, (Smith Coll.) 1999, (Pa State Univ.) 2000; Hon. PhD (Univ. of Pa) 1995, (Duke Univ.) 1996 and numerous other hon. degrees; Tony Award for the Great White Hope 1969, Emmy Award for Playing for Time 1980, Lifetime Achievement Award, Americans for Arts 1999, Harry S. Truman Award for Public Service 1999, Dir's Guild of America Award 2002. *Broadway appearances include:* The Great White Hope 1968–69, Find Your Way Home 1974, Hamlet 1975, The Heiress 1976, Goodbye Fidel 1980, Night of the Iguana 1988, Shadowlands 1990–91, The Visit 1992, The Sisters Rosenzweig 1993, Honour 1998. *Other stage appearances include:* Antony and Cleopatra 1981, Hedda Gabler 1981, Approaching Zanzibar 1989, The Cherry Orchard 2000, Mourning Becomes Electra 2002. *Film appearances include:* The Great White Hope 1970, All the President's Men 1976, Kramer vs. Kramer 1979, Brubaker 1980, Sweet Country 1986, Glory 1989, The Cider House Rules 1999, Sunshine State 2001. *TV appearances include:* Eleanor and Franklin 1976, Playing for Time 1980, Kennedy's Children 1981, A Marriage: Georgia O'Keeffe and Alfred Stieglitz 1991, Stay the Night 1992, The Jenifer Estess Story 2001. *Publications:* The

Bluefish Cookbook (with Greta Jacobs) 1979, (co-translator) The Master Builder (Henrik Ibsen), Command Performance: An Actress in the Theater of Politics 2000. *Address:* c/o Samuel Liff, William Morris Agency, 1325 Avenue of the Americas, New York, NY 10019, USA.

ALEXANDER, Jonathan James Graham, DPhil, FBA, FSA; British/ American professor of history of art; b. 20 Aug. 1935, London; s. of Arthur Ronald Brown and Frederica Emma Graham (who m. 2nd Boyd Alexander); m. 1st Mary Davey 1974 (divorced 1994); one s.; m. 2nd Serita Winthrop 1996 (divorced 2001); one s.; ed Magdalen Coll. Oxford; Asst, Dept of Western Manuscripts, Bodleian Library, Oxford 1963–71; Lecturer, History of Art Dept, Univ. of Manchester 1971–73, Reader 1973–87; Prof. of Fine Arts, Inst. of Fine Arts, New York Univ. 1988–; Lyell Reader in Bibliography, Oxford Univ. 1982–83; Sandars Lecturer, Cambridge Univ. 1984–85; Visiting Prof. Univ. Coll. London 1991–92; Fellow Medieval Acad. of America 1999; Hon. Fellow Pierpont Morgan Library 1995, John Simon Guggenheim Memorial Foundation Fellowship 1995–96, Distinguished Visiting Fellowship, La Trobe Univ. 1997, Visiting Fellow All Souls Coll., Oxford 1998; Prix Minda de Gunzburg 1987. *Publications:* Illuminated Manuscripts in the Bodleian Library, Oxford (with Otto Pächt) (3 vols) 1966, 1970, 1973, Italian Illuminated Manuscripts in the library of Major J. R. Abbey (with A. C. de la Mare) 1969, Norman Illumination at Mont St Michel c. 966–1100 1970, The Master of Mary of Burgundy, A Book of Hours 1970, Italian Renaissance Illuminations 1977, Insular Manuscripts 6th–9th Century 1978, The Decorated Letter 1978, Illuminated Manuscripts in Oxford College Libraries, The University Archives and the Taylor Institution (with E. Temple) 1986, Age of Chivalry (Jt Ed.), Art in Plantagenet England 1200–1400 1987, Medieval Illuminators and their Methods of Work 1993, The Painted Page: Italian Renaissance Book Illumination 1450–1550 (Ed.) 1994, The Townley Lectionary (introduction) 1997; articles in Burlington Magazine, Arte Veneta, Pantheon, Art Bulletin etc. *Leisure interest:* music. *Address:* Institute of Fine Arts, 1 East 78th Street, New York, NY 10021, USA. *Telephone:* (212) 992-5876. *Fax:* (212) 992-5807. *Website:* www.ifa.nyu.edu (Office).

ALEXANDER, (Padinjarethalakal) Cherian, DLitt; Indian government official; b. 20 March 1921, Kerala; s. of Jacob Cherian and Mariama Cherian; m. Ackama Alexander 1942; two s. two d.; ed India and UK; Indian Admin. Service, Kerala Cadre 1948; Devt Commr Small Scale Industries 1960–63; Sr Adviser, Centre for Industrial Devt, UN, New York 1963–66; Chief UN Project on Small Industries and Chief Adviser to Govt of Iran 1970–73; Devt Commr Small Scale Industries 1973–75; Sec. Foreign Trade, later Commerce Sec. 1975–78; Sr Adviser, later Exec. Dir and Asst Sec.-Gen. Int. Trade Centre, UNCTAD-GATT, Geneva 1978–81; Prin. Sec. to Prime Minister of India 1981–85; High Commr in UK 1985–88; Gov., Tamil Nadu 1988–89, Maharashtra 1993–; Hon. LLD (Pondicherry) 1994; Kanchi Parmacharya Prize for Nat. Eminence in Admin. 2000. *Publications:* The Dutch in Malabar, Buddhism in Kerala, Industrial Estates in India, My Years with Indira Gandhi, The Perils of Democracy, India in the New Millennium. *Leisure interest:* reading. *Address:* c/o Raj Bhavan, Mumbai, Maharashtra, India.

ALEXANDER, Robert McNeill, CBE, MA, PhD, DSc, FRS; British professor of zoology; b. 7 July 1934, Lisburn, Northern Ireland; s. of Robert Priestley Alexander and Janet (née McNeill) Alexander; m. Ann Elizabeth Coulton 1961; one s. one d.; ed Tonbridge School and Cambridge Univ.; lecturer Univ. Coll. of North Wales, Bangor 1958–69; Prof. of Zoology Univ. of Leeds 1969–99; Sec. Zoological Soc. of London 1992–99; Vice-Pres. Soc. for Experimental Biology 1993–95, Pres. 1995–97; Pres. Int. Soc. for Vertebrate Morphology 1997–; mem. Academia Europaea 1996; Hon. mem. American Soc. of Zoologists (now Soc. for Integrative and Comparative Biology) 1986; Foreign Hon. mem. American Acad. of Arts and Sciences 2001; Scientific Medal (Zoological Soc. of London) 1969, Linnean Medal for Zoology (Linnean Soc. of London) 1979, Muybridge Medal (Int. Soc. for Biomechanics) 1991. *Publications:* Functional Design in Fishes 1967, Animal Mechanics 1968, Size and Shape 1971, The Chordates 1975, The Invertebrates 1979, Locomotion of Animals 1982, Optima for Animals 1982, Elastic Mechanisms in Animal Movement 1988, Dynamics of Dinosaurs and Other Extinct Giants 1989, Animals 1990, Exploring Biomechanics 1992, The Human Machine 1992, Bones 1994, Energy for Animal Life 1999, Principles of Animal Locomotion 2003; and many scientific papers. *Leisure interests:* local history and history of natural history. *Address:* School of Biology, University of Leeds, Leeds, LS2 9JT (Office); 14 Moor Park Mount, Leeds, LS6 4BU, England (Home). *Telephone:* (113) 3432911 (Office); (113) 2759218 (Home). *Fax:* (113) 3432911 (Office). *E-mail:* r.m.alexander@leeds.ac.uk (Office).

ALEXANDER, Wendy, MA, MBA; British politician; b. Glasgow, Scotland; ed Park Mains High School, Erskine, Pearson Coll., Canada, Univ. of Glasgow, Univ. of Warwick and INSEAD, France; fmr int. man. consultant with Booz Allen & Hamilton (consumer products practice); joined Labour Party 1978, worked as party research officer; appt. Special Adviser to Sec. of State for Scotland 1997; Mem. Scottish Parl. (Labour) for Paisley N 1999; Minister for Communities 1999–2000, for Enterprise and Lifelong Learning 2000–01, for Enterprise, Transport and Lifelong Learning 2001–02; mem. Justice 1 Cttee, Finance Cttee (Cttee Substitute), Cross-Party Group in Scottish Parl. for Information, Knowledge and Enlightenment (SPIKE); Visiting Prof. Univ. of Strathclyde Business School 2002–; mem. Transport and Gen. Workers' Union, Royal Soc. for the Protection of Birds, Amnesty Int.; Scottish Politician of the Year (Channel 4) 2000. *Publications include:* First Ladies of Medicine 1986; contribs. to The World is Ill Divided: Women's Work in Scotland 1992,

The State and the Nations 1996, The Ethnicity Reader 1997, New Gender Agenda 2000. *Address:* The Scottish Parliament, Edinburgh, EH99 1SP (Office); Abbey Mill Business Centre, Mile End, 12 Seedhill Road, Paisley, PA1 1JS, Scotland (Office). *Telephone:* (141) 561-5800 (Office). *Fax:* (141) 561-5900 (Office). *E-mail:* Wendy.Alexander.msp@scottish.parliament.uk (Office). *Website:* www.scottish.parliament.uk/msps/biogrpahies/n-pais.htm (Office); www.scottishlabour.org.uk/WendyAlexander.html (Office).

ALEXANDER KARADJORDJEVIC, HRH Crown Prince of Yugo-slavia; b. 17 July 1945, London; s. of HM King Peter II of Yugoslavia and HRH Princess Alexandra of the Hellenes and Denmark; m. 1st HRH Princess Maria da Gloria of Orléans and Bragança 1972 (divorced 1983); m. 2nd Katherine Batis 1985; three s.; ed Le Rosey, Switzerland, Gordonstoun, Scotland, Culver Mil. Acad., USA, Royal Mil. Acad., UK; commissioned in British Army, 16th/5th The Queen's Royal Lancers, rank of Acting Capt. 1971; businessman working in Rio de Janeiro, New York, Chicago and London; in exile from birth, chose not to take the title of King on his father's death in 1970, whilst forced to live in exile; visited Belgrade for the first time Oct. 1991, returned on visits June 1992, 1995, 2000, establishing residence in Royal Palace 2001; British Army Ski Champion 1972. *Leisure interests:* skiing, scuba diving, underwater photography, family. *Address:* Royal Palace, Dedinje, Belgrade, Serbia and Montenegro (Home); 36 Dover Street, London, W1X 3RB, England. *Telephone:* (20) 7493-3715 (Office). *Fax:* (20) 7495-2889 (Office). *E-mail:* hrhcpale@royalfamily.org (Office). *Website:* www.royalfamily.org (Office).

ALEXANDER OF WEEDON, Baron (Life Peer), cr. 1988; **Robert Scott Alexander,** QC; British banker and barrister; b. 5 Sept. 1936, Newcastle; s. of the late Samuel James Alexander and of Hannah May Alexander; m. 1st; two s. two d.; m. 2nd Marie Anderson 1985; ed Brighton Coll. and King's Coll., Cambridge; called to the Bar (Middle Temple) 1961, QC 1973, Bencher, 1979; QC (NSW, Australia) 1983, Chair. of the Bar of England and Wales 1985–86; Chair. Panel of Takeovers and Mergers 1987–89; Deputy Chair. Nat. Westminster Bank PLC May–Oct. 1989, Chair. 1989–99; Trustee of Nat. Gallery 1986–93, The Economist 1990–; Gov. of Wycombe Abbey School 1986–92; Dir (non-exec.) The RTZ Corpn PLC 1991–96, The London Stock Exchange 1991–93 (Deputy Chair. Securities and Investments Bd 1994–96); Dir. Total 1993–; Chair. Deregulated Powers and Scrutiny Cttee, House of Lords 1995–; Chancellor Exeter Univ. 1998–; Gov. RSC 1995–, Chair. 2000–; Pres. MCC 2000–01; Hon. LLD (Sheffield) 1991, (Buckingham) 1992, (Keele) 1993, (Exeter) 1995. *Publications* Voice of the People: A Constitution for Tomorrow 1997. *Leisure interests:* tennis, cricket. *Address:* House of Lords, London, SW1A 0PW, England.

ALEXANDRA, HRH Princess (see Ogilvy, the Hon. Mrs. Angus).

ALEXANDROV (see Aleksandrov).

ALEXEEV (see Alekseyev).

ALEXEEV, Dmitri Konstantinovich; Russian pianist; b. 10 Aug. 1947, Moscow; s. of Konstantin Alekseyev and Gertrude Bolotina; m. Tatiana Sarkisova 1970; one d.; ed Moscow Conservatoire; studied under Dmitri Bashkirov; performs regularly in Russia, in UK and throughout Europe and USA and has toured Japan, Australia etc.; has performed with London Philharmonic Orchestra, London Symphony Orchestra, City of Birmingham Symphony Orchestra, the Royal Philharmonic Orchestra, St Petersburg Philharmonic Orchestra, Berlin Philharmonic, Chicago Symphony Orchestra, Philadelphia Orchestra, Royal Concertgebouw Orchestra of Amsterdam, Israel Philharmonic and the Munich Bavarian Radio Orchestra; worked with Ashkenazy (q.v.), Boulez (q.v.), Semyon Bychkov (q.v.), Dorati, Giulini, Jansons, Muti, Kent Nagano, Rozhdestvensky, Salonen, Klaus Tennstedt, Michael Tilson Thomas, Sian Edwards, Valery Gergiev, Andrew Litton and Yuri Temirkanov; recordings include works by Bach, Brahms, Chopin, Grieg, Liszt, Medtner, Prokofiev, Rachmaninov, Schumann, Shostakovich and Scriabin; prizewinner Int. Tchaikovsky Competition, Moscow 1974, 5th Leeds Int. Piano Competition 1975 and other int. competitions; received Edison Award, Netherlands. *Address:* c/o IMG Artists, Lovell House, 616 Chiswick High Road, London, W4 5RX, England. *Telephone:* (20) 8233-5800.

ALEXEYEV, Nikolay Gennadyevich; Russian conductor; b. 1 May 1956, Leningrad; s. of Gennady Nikolayevich Alexeyev and Tamara Andreyevna Alexeyeva; m. Nina Yefimovna Alexeyeva; two s.; ed Glinka Choir School, St Petersburg State Conservatory; Chief Conductor Ulyanovsk Philharmonic Orchestra 1983–; Prin. Guest Conductor Zagreb Philharmonic and Estonian Nat. Symphony 1994–97; Artistic Dir and mus. Conductor Estonian Nat. Symphony 2000–; performs with leading orchestras, Symphony Orchestra, Moscow, Russian Nat. Orchestra, Moscow Philharmonic, tours in Europe, USA, Japan; Assoc. Prin. Conductor St Petersburg Philharmonic 2000–; Prize Int. H. von Karajan Music Competition 1982, Int. V. Talikh Competition 1985. *Address:* St Petersburg Philharmonia, Mikhailovskaya str. 2, St Petersburg, Russia (Office). *Telephone:* (812) 931-75-88 (Office); (812) 271-04-90 (Home).

ALEXIS, Francis, LLM, PhD; Grenadian politician, author and lawyer; b. 3 Oct. 1947, Grenada; s. of John Everest Alexis and Anastasia Omega Alexis; m. Margaret de Bique 1973; three d.; ed Grenada Boys' Secondary School, Univ. of West Indies, Hugh Wooding Law School and Univ. of Cambridge; fmr clerk, Jonas Brown & Hubbards Ltd, Grenada; later civil servant, Grenada; Sr Lecturer in Law and Deputy Dean, Faculty of Law, Univ. of West Indies; Barrister-at-Law, Grenada; mem. Parl. 1984–; Minister of Labour, Co-operatives, Social Security and Local Govt 1984–87; Attorney-Gen. and Minister of Legal Affairs and Labour 1987; Opposition MP 1987–90; Founder-mem. and Deputy Leader New Nat. Party 1986, Nat. Democratic Congress 1987–95; Attorney-Gen. and Minister of Legal Affairs and Local Govt 1990–95; Acting Prime Minister on various occasions 1990–95; Leader Govt Business, House of Reps. in Parl. 1990–95, Grenada Nat. Del. to the Windward Islands Political Union Talks 1991–92, to UN Gen. Ass. 1993, to Commonwealth Parl. Asscn UK 1986, Canada 1994; Father of House of Reps. in Parl. 1995–; Founder mem., Leader Democratic Labour Party 1995–; Vice-Pres. Grenada Bar Asscn 1997–98. *Publications:* Commonwealth Caribbean Legal Essays 1981, Changing Caribbean Constitutions 1983, H. Aubrey Fraser: Eminent Caribbean Jurist 1985, The Constitution and You 1991; articles in law journals. *Leisure interests:* reading, writing, music. *Address:* Church Street, St George's (Office); St Paul's, St George's, Grenada (Home). *Telephone:* 440-6743 (Office); 440-2378 (Home). *Fax:* 440-6591.

ALEXIS, Jacques Edouard; Haitian politician; Prime Minister of Haiti, Minister of the Interior and Local Govt 1998–2000. *Address:* c/o Office of the Prime Minister, Port-au-Prince, Haiti (Office).

ALFARO, Andreu; Spanish sculptor; b. 5 Aug. 1929, Valencia; s. of Andrés Alfaro and Teresa Hernández; m. Dorothy Hofmann 1954; three c.; began work as sculptor in Valencia 1958; joined Grupo Parpalló and participated in various collective exhbns 1959–62; major one-man exhbn Sala de la Dirección Gen. de Bellas Artes de Madrid 1967; first one-man exhbn in Germany at Galerie Dreiseitel, Cologne 1974; one-man exhbn organized by Ministry of Culture, Palacio Velázquez, Parque del Retiro de Madrid 1979; other one-man shows at Universidad Complutense de Madrid 1981, Antic Mercat del Born de Barcelona 1983; exhibited in Paris and Madrid 1989; retrospective Exhbn in Instituto Valenciano de Arte Moderno 1991, then in Barcelona, Madrid and Cologne 1992–94, XLVI Venice Biennial 1995, then in Valencia, Madrid, Cologne, Munich and Rome 1996–99; exhbns on Goethe in Rome, Frankfurt, Welmar, The Hague and Scheveningen; monumental open-air sculptures in Valencia, Barcelona, Madrid, Nuremberg, Cologne, Frankfurt, Munich; Gold Medal Salón Internacional de Marzo 1964, Premi Jaume I, Barcelona 1980, Premio Nacional de Artes Plásticas 1981, Premi Creu de Sant Jordi, Barcelona 1982, Premi Alfons Roig, Valencia 1991, Premio Urbanismo, Arquitectura y Obras Públicas, Ayuntamiento de Madrid 1991, Premio Tomás Francisco de Prieto, Fundación Casa de la Moneda de Madrid 1995. *Publications:* El Arte visto por los artistas 1987, Doce artistas de vanguardia en el Museo del Prado 1991; articles in reviews. *Address:* Urbanización Sta. Bárbara 138R, 46111 Rocafort, Valencia, Spain. *Telephone:* (96) 1310956.

ALFEROV, Zhores Ivanovich, DPhysMathSc; Russian physicist; b. 15 March 1930, Vitebsk; m.; two c.; ed Leningrad Electrotech. Inst.; researcher, Head of Lab. Ioffe Inst. of Physics and Tech. USSR Acad. of Sciences 1972–87; Dir 1987–; Corresp. mem. USSR (now Russian) Acad. of Sciences 1972, mem. 1979; Vice-Pres. 1991–; Chair. Leningrad (now St Petersburg) Scientific Centre 1990–; mem. State Duma 1995–; Ed.-in-Chief Physics and Tech. of Semiconductors; mem. Acad. of Sciences of Germany, Poland, USA, European Physical Soc., and many others; Hon. Citizen of St Petersburg USSR Lenin and State Prizes, Karpinsky Prize, Nobel Prize for Physics 2000, Stuart Ballantine Gold Medal, Hewlett-Packard Europhysics Prize. *Publications:* scientific works on physics and tech. of semiconductors, quantum electronics. *Leisure interest:* history of Second World War. *Address:* St Petersburg Scientific Centre, Universitetskaya nab. 5, St Petersburg 199034 (Office); Ioffe Physico-Technical Institute, Polytechnicheskya str. 26, St Petersburg 194021 (Office); Jacques Duclos str. 8/3-82, St Petersburg 194223, Russia (Home). *Telephone:* (812) 328-23-11 (Office); (812) 552-58-55 (Home). *Fax:* (812) 328-37-87 (Office). *E-mail:* zhores.alferov@pop.ioffe.rssi.ru (Office).

ALFONSÍN FOULKES, Raúl; Argentine politician and lawyer; b. 13 March 1926, Chascomus; m. María Barreneche; three s. three d.; ed Liceo Militar General San Martín, Nat. Univ. of La Plata; journalist, Chascomus; f. El Imparcial newspaper; joined Movimiento de Intransigencia y Renovación 1944; Pres. Unión Cívica Radical 1983–91, 2001–; Municipal Councillor, Chascomus 1950; mem. Buenos Aires Prov. Legislature 1952; imprisoned 1953; mem. Chamber of Deputies 1963–66, 1973–76; f. Movimiento de Renovación y Cambio 1966; Pres. of Argentina 1983–89; Dr. hc (Univ. of New Mexico) 1985, (Santiago de Compostela) 1988; Príncipe de Asturias Prize 1985, Shared Human Rights Prize of Council of Europe 1986.

ALGABID, Hamid; Niger politician; b. 1941, Tamont; m.; five c.; ed Abidjan Univ.; fmr Minister of State for Planning, Commerce and Transportation; fmr Minister del. for Finance; Prime Minister of Niger 1983–88; Sec.-Gen. Org. of Islamic Conf. 1989–96; currently Chair. Rassemblement pour la démocratie et le progrès (RDP), Presidential cand. 1999. *Address:* c/o Organisation of the Islamic Conference, Kilo 6, P.O. Box 178, Jeddah 2411, Saudi Arabia.

ALGOSAIBI, Ghazi, PhD; Saudi Arabian diplomatist and politician; b. 2 March 1940, Al-Hasa; s. of Abdul Rahman Algosaibi and Fatma Algosaibi; m. Sigrid Presser 1968; three s. one d.; ed Univs. of Cairo, S. Calif. and London; Asst Prof. King Saud Univ. Riyadh 1965, then Prof. and Head of Political Science and Dean, Faculty of Commerce; Dir Saudi Railways 1974; Minister of Industry and Electricity 1975, of Health 1982; Amb. to Bahrain 1984, to UK (also accred. to Ireland) 1992–2002; Minister of Agric. and Water 2002–; numerous decorations. *Publications:* prose works include: Yes, (Saudi) Minister! A Life in Administration, Seven, An Apartment Called Freedom, The Dilemma of Development, The Gulf Crisis: An Attempt to Understand, Arabian Essays, Dansko; 18 collections of poems. *Leisure interests:* swimming, fishing, table tennis. *Address:* Ministry of Agriculture and Water, Airport Road, Riyadh 11195, Saudi Arabia. *Telephone:* (1) 401-6666. *Fax:* (1) 404-4592. *E-mail:* info@agrwat.gov.sa. *Website:* www.agrwat.gov.sa.

ALHAJI, Alhaji Abubakar; Nigerian politician; b. 22 Nov. 1938, Sokoto; m. Amina Abubakar 1965; three s. three d.; ed Univ. of Reading and The Hague Inst. of Social Sciences; Deputy Perm. Sec. Ministry of Trade 1974; later Dir of External Finance, Ministry of Finance; Minister of State for Budget and Planning and Special Advisor to the Pres. 1989–90; Minister of Finance and Econ. Devt 1990–92; Sardauna of Sokoto 1990–92; High Commr in UK 1992–97; Hon. KBE. *Address:* c/o Ministry of Foreign Affairs, Maputo Street, PMB 130, Abuja, Nigeria.

ALHEGELAN, Sheikh Faisal Abdul Aziz al-; Saudi Arabian diplomatist; b. 7 Oct. 1929, Jeddah; s. of Sheikh Abdul Aziz Al-Hegelan and Fatima Al-Eissa; m. Nouha Tarazi 1961; three s.; ed Faculty of Law, Fouad Univ., Cairo; Ministry of Foreign Affairs 1952–54; served Embassy in Washington, DC 1954–58; Chief of Protocol in Ministry 1958–60; Political Adviser to HM King Sa'ud 1960–61; Amb. to Spain 1961–68, to Venezuela and Argentina 1968–75, to Denmark 1975–76, to UK 1976–79, to USA 1979–83, to France 1996–; Minister of State and mem. Council of Ministers (Saudi Arabia) April–Sept. 1984, of Health 1984–96, Chair. Bd of Dirs., Saudi Red Crescent Soc. 1984–, Saudi Anti-Smoking Soc. 1985–; Chair. Bd of Trustees, Saudi Council for Health Specialties 1992–; Order of King Abdulaziz, Gran Cruz Cordon of King Abdul Aziz, Order of Isabela la Católica (Spain), Gran Cordón, Orden del Libertador (Venezuela), Grande Oficial, Orden Riobranco (Brazil), May Grand Decoration (Argentina); Hon. KBE. *Leisure interests:* bridge, golf. *Address:* Embassy of Saudi Arabia, 5 av. Hoche, 75008 Paris, France; P.O. Box 25557, Riyadh 11576, Saudi Arabia. *Telephone:* 1-56-79-40-00 (France). *Fax:* 1-56-79-40-01 (France).

ALI, Ahmad Mohamed, LLB, DPA; Saudi Arabian development banker; b. 13 April 1934, Medina; s. of Mohamed Ali and Amina Ali; m. Ghada Mahmood Masri 1968; one s. three d.; ed Cairo Univ., Univ. of Michigan, New York State Univ.; Dir Scientific and Islamic Inst., Aden 1958–59; Deputy Rector King Abdul Aziz Univ., Jeddah 1967–72; Deputy Minister of Educ. for Tech. Affairs 1972–75; Pres. Islamic Devt Bank 1975–93, 1995–; Sec.-Gen. Muslim World League 1993–95; mem. King Abdul Aziz Univ. Council, King Saud Univ., Oil and Minerals Univ., Islamic Univ., Imam Mohammed Ben Saud Univ.; mem. Admin. Bd Saudi Credit Bank, Saudi Fund for Devt. *Publications:* numerous articles and working papers on Islamic econs, banking and educ. *Leisure interests:* cycling, walking. *Address:* Islamic Development Bank, PO Box 5925, Jeddah 21432, Saudi Arabia. *Telephone:* (2) 6361400. *Fax:* (2) 6366871. *E-mail:* archives@isdb.org.sa. *Website:* www.isdb.org.

ALI, Muhammad; American boxer; b. Cassius Marcellus Clay, 17 Jan. 1942, Louisville, Ky; s. of Cassius Marcellus Clay Sr and Odessa L. Grady; m. 1st Sonji Roi (divorced 1966); m. 2nd Belinda Boyd (Khalilah Toloria) 1967 (divorced 1977); m. 3rd Veronica Porche 1977 (divorced 1986); m. 4th Yolanda Williams 1986; seven d. two s.; ed Louisville; amateur boxer 1954–60, Olympic Games Light-Heavyweight Champion 1960; turned professional 1960, won World Heavyweight title Feb. 1964, defeating Sonny Liston; adopted name Muhammad Ali 1964; stripped of title after refusing to be drafted into U.S. Army 1967, won case in U.S. Supreme Court and returned to professional boxing 1970; regained World Heavyweight title Oct. 1974, defeating George Foreman in Zaïre; lost title to Leon Spinks 1978, regained title from Spinks 1978; 56 victories in 61 fights up to Dec. 1981; lost to Larry Holmes Oct. 1980; mem. of U.S. Black Muslim movement; Special Envoy of Pres. Carter to Africa 1980 (to urge boycott of Olympic Games), of Pres. Bush to Iraq 1990 (prior to Operation Desert Storm); lit Olympic flame, Atlanta 1996; fmr mem. Peace Corps Advisory Council; named Messenger of Peace, UN 1999; Athlete of the Century, GQ Magazine; Lifetime Achievement Award, Amnesty Int.; Hon. Consul-Gen. for Bangladesh in Chicago Feb. 1978. *Film appearances include:* The Greatest 1976, Freedom Road 1980, Freedom Road (television) 1978. *Publications:* The Greatest: My Own Story (autobiog.) 1975, Healing (with Thomas Hauser) 1996, More Than a Hero (with Hana Ali) 2000. *Address:* P.O. Box 160, Berrien Springs, MI 49103, USA.

ALI, Muhammad Shamsher, PhD; Bangladeshi professor of physics; b. 9 Nov. 1940, Bheramara, Kushtia; ed Dhaka Univ. and Manchester Univ., UK; scientific officer, Atomic Energy Comm. 1961–65, Sr Scientific Officer 1965–69, Prin. Scientific Officer 1975–82; Dir Atomic Energy Centre, Dhaka 1970–78; Prof. of Physics, Univ. of Dhaka 1982–; mem. Advisory Cttee, Bangladesh Atomic Energy Comm. 1977–87; Sr Assoc. Int. Centre for Theoretical Physics, Trieste; Gen. Sec. Bangladesh Asscn of Scientists and Scientific Professions 1978–81; Fellow Bangladesh Physical Soc., Bangladesh Acad. of Sciences, Islamic Acad. of Sciences, mem. Council 1989–94; mem. New York Acad. of Sciences; Hon. Prof. of Physics (Dhaka. Univ.) 1973. *Publications:* over 70 research papers on nuclear physics. *Address:* Islamic Academy of Sciences, P.O. Box 830036, Amman, Jordan (Office). *Telephone:* 5522104 (Office). *Fax:* 5511803 (Office).

ALI, Sheikh Razzak, LLB, MA; Bangladeshi politician and diplomatist; b. 1928, Khulna; ed Univ. of Dhaka; fmr reporter and journalist with Daily Pakistan; Asst Ed. 'Enterprise' 1952; Chief Reporter and Commercial Ed. Daily Pakistan Observer 1954–58; practised law in Khulna, lawyer of High Court –1990, 1997–2001; participated in Language Movt 1952, War of Liberation 1971; joined Bangladesh Nat. Party (BNP) 1978, fmr Pres. Khulna Dist BNP, fmr Vice-Chair. BNP Cen. Cttee, fmr mem. BNP Standing Cttee;

rep. Bangladesh in UN Gen. Ass. 1980; elected Mem. Parl. 1970, 1991, 1996; State Minister for Law and Justice 1991; Deputy Speaker of Parl. April–Oct. 1991, Speaker 1991–96; High Commr to UK 2001–; Pres. and Gen. Sec. Khulna Bar Asscn 1964, 1972; Pres. Jessore Bar Asscn 1984–86; Founder-Prin. Khulna City Coll.; Founder Khulna Suburban Coll.; Founder-Pres. Khulna Shiromony Eye Hosp. *Address:* High Commission of People's Republic of Bangladesh, 28 Queens Gate, London, SW7 5JA, England (Office). *Telephone:* (20) 7584-0081 (Office). *Fax:* (20) 7225-2130 (Office). *E-mail:* bdesh .lon@dial.pipex.com (Office).

ALI, Sadiq, BA; Indian politician; b. 1910, Udaipur, Rajasthan; s. of Shri Tahir Ali; m. Shrimati Shanti Sadiq Ali 1951; ed Allahabad Univ; associated with Indian freedom movement 1930; Perm. Sec. All-India Congress Cttee 1938–47; mem. Lok Sabha 1951–52, Rajya Sabha 1958–70; Gen. Sec. Indian Nat. Congress 1958–64, 1966–69; Pres. Opposition Congress Party 1971–73; Chief Ed. AICC Econ. Review 1960–69; Chair. Gandhi Nat. Museum and Library, New Delhi 1965–, Cen. Gandhi Smarak Nidhi 1991–; Gov. of Maharashtra 1977–80, of Tamil Nadu 1980–82. *Publications:* Know Your Country, Congress Ideology and Programme, Culture of India, General Election 1957, Towards Socialist Thinking in Congress, Campaign Against Nuclear Arms. *Address:* A-23/139 Lodhi Colony, New Delhi 110003, India. *Telephone:* (11) 4697375.

ALI, Zine al Abidine Ben; Tunisian politician; b. 3 Sept. 1936, Hammam Sousse; m. Leila Ben Ali; three c.; ed as graduate in electronics, Saint-Cyr Military Acad. (France), Chalons-sur-Marne School of Artillery (France), Special School of Intelligence and Security (USA); Head of Mil. Security 1958–74; Mil. and Naval Attaché, Rabat, Morocco 1974–77; mem. of Cabinet for Minister of Nat. Defence, Dir-Gen. Nat. Security 1977–80; Amb. to Poland 1980–84; Sec. of State for Nat. Security 1984–85, Minister of the Interior 1986–87, Minister of State for the Interior May–Nov. 1987, Pres. of Tunisia Nov. 1987–; mem. politbureau of Parti Socialiste Destourien (PSD) 1986, Sec.-Gen. PSD 1986, Chair. Rassemblement Constitutionnel Démocratique (RCD); Order of Merit of Bourguiba, Order of Independence, Order of the Repub., several foreign orders. *Leisure interests:* computers, music, sports. *Address:* Présidence de la République, Palais de Carthage, Tunis, Tunisia. *Website:* www.carthage.tn (Office).

ALI SAMATER, Gen. Mohammed; Somali politician and army officer; b. 1931, Chisimaio; ed Intermediate School, Mogadishu, Mil. Acad., Rome, Mil. Acad., Moscow; Commdt Somali Police 1956, Maj.-Adjutant 1958–65; Brig.-Gen. Nat. Army 1967, Maj.-Gen. 1973; Sec. of State for Defence 1971–76, C-in-C Armed Forces 1971–78; fmr Vice-Pres. Political Bureau, Somali Socialist Revolutionary Party; Minister of Defence 1976–81, 1982–89; First Vice-Pres. Supreme Revolutionary Council (now Council of Ministers) 1982–90; Prime Minister of Somalia 1987–90; Chair. Defence and Security Cttee, Supreme Council of the Revolution 1980–82, Vice-Pres. of Council 1981–82.

ALIA, Ramiz; Albanian politician; b. 1925, Shkodër; m. Semiram Alia; active in 1939–45 war; mem. of political shock 7th brigade; political leader 2nd Div.; fought in Yugoslavia at Kosova, Metohia, Sandjak, Political Commissar of the 5th Div.; First Sec. Cen. Cttee Communist Youth –1955; Minister of Educ.; mem. of the Cen. Cttee CP since the 1st Congress; since 4th Congress mem. of the Politbureau, Sec. Cen. Cttee CP, First Sec. 1985–92; Vice-Chair. of the Gen. Council of the Democratic Front of Albania; Deputy to People's Ass. from 2nd Legislature; Pres. Presidium of People's Ass. (Head of State) 1982–92; under house arrest, imprisoned Aug. 1993; sentenced to nine years' imprisonment for abuse of power and violation of citizens' rights July 1994, released July 1995; acquitted of charges of genocide and crimes against humanity Oct. 1997.

ALIBEK, Ken, MD, PhD, ScD; American (b. Kazakh) industrial biotechnologist; b. Kauchuk, Kazakh Soviet Socialist Repub.; s. of Bayzak Alibekov and Rosa Alibekov; m. Lena Yemesheva 1976; four c.; ed Tomsk Medical Inst.; fmr mem. Communist Party; cadet intern in mil. section of Tomsk Medical Inst. 1973; Jr Lt, later Sr Lt in Soviet Army, rank of Col 1987; mem. staff E European Scientific Br., Inst. of Applied Biochem., Omutninsk, Sr Scientist Siberian Br., Berdsk 1976; Deputy Dir (later Dir) Stepnogorsk Biological Research Centre, Deputy Chief Biopreparat Biosafety Div. 1987, First Deputy Chief 1988, working for Soviet Union's offensive biological weapons programme; Dir Biomash 1990–91; visited American mil. and research sites 1991; defected to USA 1992, debriefed by US mil. on Soviet and Russian biological weapons programme, consultant to Nat. Inst. of Health and numerous US Govt agencies in fields of industrial tech., medical microbiology, biological weapons defence and biological weapons non-proliferation; currently Pres. Hadron Advanced Biosystems Inc., Corp. Vice-Pres. Hadron; Distinguished Prof. George Mason Univ.; Hon. DSc 1988. *Publications:* Biohazard (autobiog. with Stephen Handelman) 1999; more than eighty articles. *Address:* Hadron Advanced Biosystems Inc., 5904 Richmond Highway, Alexandria, VA 22303-1864 (Office); c/o Random House Publicity, 299 Park Avenue, New York, NY 10171, USA.

ALIER, Abel, LLM; Sudanese politician; b. 1933, Bor District, Upper Nile Province; s. of Kwai Alier and Anaai Alier; m. Siama Fatma Bilal 1970; one d.; ed Univs. of Khartoum and Yale; fmr advocate; District Judge in El Obeid, Wad Medani and Khartoum until 1965; participant in Round Table Conf. and mem. Twelve Man Cttee to Study the Southern Problem 1965; mem. Constitution Comms. 1966–67, 1968; fmr mem. Law Reform Comm. and Southern Front; Minister of Supply and Internal Trade 1969–70; Minister of Works

1970–71; Minister of Southern Affairs 1971–72, of Construction and Public Works 1983–85; Vice-Pres. 1971–82; Pres. Supreme Exec. Council for the South 1972–78, 1980–81; mem. Political Bureau, Sudanese Socialist Union, Bd of Dirs., Industrial Planning Corpn; mem. Nat. Scholarship Bd; Hon. LLD (Khartoum) 1978. *Leisure interests:* tennis, athletics, reading, history and literature. *Address:* c/o Ministry of Construction and Public Works, Sudan.

ALIERTA UZUEL, D. César, LLL, MBA; Spanish telecommunications executive; b. 5 May 1945, Zaragoza; m. Ana Cristina Placer; ed Univ. of Zaragoza and Columbia Univ., New York, USA; financial analyst Urquijo Bank 1970, fmr adviser to Gesfondo, Urquijo Gestión de Patrimonios, Urquijo Financial Services, later Dir Div. Area of Capital Markets 1980–85; Founder, Pres. and Delegated Adviser Capital Beta 1985; Co-Founder Creaciones Baluarte 1997; currently Chair. Telefónica; facing charges of insider trading relating to share deals while Chair. of Tabacalera in 1997 Dec. 2002. *Address:* Telefónica, SA, Beatriz de Bobadilla 3, 9°, 28040 Madrid, Spain (Office). *Telephone:* (91) 5849107 (Office). *Fax:* (91) 5347972 (Office). *Website:* www.telefonica.es (Office).

ALIMOV, Rashid; Tajikistan politician; b. 1953; m.; two c.; ed Tajik Univ.; Chair. trade union Cttee Tajik Univ. 1975–77; Head of group of lecturers Cen. Comsomol Cttee of Tajik SSR, instructor regional and city CP cttees. Dushanbe; mem. Div. of Propaganda, First Sec. Frunze Regional Cttee of Tajikistan CP 1988–89, Second Sec. Dushanbe City CP Cttee 1989; Chair. Comm. on Problems of Youth, Supreme Soviet of Tajikistan 1989–91; State Counsellor to fmr Pres. Nabiyev 1990–92; Minister of Foreign Affairs of Tajikistan 1992–94; Perm Rep. to UN 1994–. *Address:* Permanent Mission of Tajikistan to the United Nations, 136 East 67th Street, New York, NY 10021, USA; c/o Ministry of Foreign Affairs, Dushanbe, Tajikistan.

ALIMOV, Timur; Uzbekistan politician; b. 1936; ed Tashkent Inst. of Irrigation Engineering and Agric. Mechanisation; engineer on construction of channel in Afghanistan 1960–62; senior engineer, Uzgiprovodkhoz 1962–65; senior engineer, Dir of Tashkent reservoir div. 1965–67; mem. of CPSU 1967–91; Head of section of water supply and irrigation with Uzbek SSR Council of Mins. 1967–75; Man., Uzbek SSR Council of Ministers 1975–78; Pres. of Tashkent Exec. Cttee of Uzbek CP. 1978–85; First Sec. of Tashkent Exec. Cttee of Uzbek CP. 1985–91; Cand. mem. of CPSU Cen. Cttee 1986–90; Adviser to the Pres. of Uzbekistan 1991–. *Address:* Office of the President, Uzbekistansky Prosp. 43, 700163, Tashkent, Uzbekistan. *Telephone:* (712) 995746.

ALIMPIY, (Alexander Kapitonovich Gusev); Russian ecclesiastic; b. 31 July 1929, Nizhny Novgorod; worked as fireman, served in army, was housepainter, stoker; ordained as deacon of Russian Old Belief Church 1967; deacon Old Belief Church in Gorky (now Nizhny Novgorod) 1967–86; elected Archbishop of Moscow and of All Russia on Ecumenical Council of Old Belief Church 1987; elected the First Old Belief Metropolitan of All Russia 1988. *Address:* Russian Old Belief Church Society, Pokrovsky Cathedral Church, Rogozksky pos. 29, 109052 Moscow, Russia. *Telephone:* (095) 918-13-92.

ALINGTON, William Hildebrand, MArch; New Zealand architect; b. 18 Nov. 1929, Wellington; s. of Edward Hugh Alington and Beatrice McCrie Alington; m. Margaret Hilda Broadhead 1955; one s. two d.; ed Hutt Valley High School, School of Architecture, Auckland Univ. Coll., School of Architecture Univ. of Illinois; architectural cadet and architect Head Office Ministry of Works, Wellington 1950–65; architect London Office Robert Matthew & Johnson-Marshall 1956–57; partner Gabites & Beard 1965–71, Gabites Toomath Beard Wilson & Partners 1971–72, Gabites Alington & Edmondson 1972–79, Gabites Porter & Partners 1978–83; Sr Partner Alington Group Architects 1984–; Asst Ed. NZIA Journal 1964–69; Pres. Architectural Centre 1970–72; Hon. lecturer Victoria Univ. of Wellington School of Architecture 1975–85, Tutor 1986–92; Vice-Pres. and Branch Chair. N.Z.I.A. 1977–79, mem. Council 1965–79; mem. Wellington Anglican Diocesan Synod 1972–90. *Major works include:* Meteorological Office, Gisborne Courthouse, Upper Hutt Civic Centre, Massey Univ. Halls of Residence, VUW School of Music, Karori Baptist Church, St Mary's Church Extension, New Plymouth. *Publications:* numerous articles in specialist journals. *Leisure interests:* gardening, painting, church government. *Address:* 60 Homewood Crescent, Wellington, New Zealand. *Telephone:* (4) 476-8495. *Fax:* (4) 476-8495 (Home). *E-mail:* alington@xtra.co.nz (Home).

ALIYEV, Maj.-Gen. Heydar Alirza oglu; Azerbaijani politician; b. 10 May 1923, Nakhichevan; s. of Alirza Aliyev and Izzat Aliyeva; m. Zarifa Aziz gizi Aliyeva (died 1985); one s. one d.; ed Inst. of Industry, Baku, Azerbaijan State Univ.; mem. CPSU 1945–91; official of security forces and mem. Council of Ministers of Nakhichevan Autonomous Republic 1941–49; on staff of Ministry of Foreign Affairs and Cttee of State Security (KGB) of Azerbaijan SSR 1949; Deputy Chair. KGB Azerbaijan SSR 1964–67; rank of Maj.-Gen.; Cand. mem. Cen. Cttee of CP of Azerbaijan (CPA) SSR 1966–69, mem. Cen. Cttee CPA 1969, mem. Bureau 1969, First Sec. Cen. Cttee 1969–82; mem. Cen. Cttee CPSU 1971–89, mem. Politburo of Cen. Cttee CPSU 1976–87; Deputy to USSR Supreme Soviet 1974–89, Vice-Chair. Council of Union 1974–79; First Deputy Chair. U.S.S.R Council of Ministers 1982–87, retd 1987; resumed political activities 1992, Chair. New Azerbaijan Party 1992–93, elected to Supreme Medjlis of Nakhichevan Autonomous Repub. 1992; mem. and Vice Chair. Supreme Soviet of Azerbaijan Repub. 1992, Chair. Aug. 1993; Pres. of Azerbaijan Repub. Oct. 1993–; Hon. mem. Int. Acad. of Architecture of Eastern Countries 1994; Hero of Socialist Labour (twice); Dr. hc (Baku State

Univ.) 1994, (Hojjat-Tapa Univ., Ankara) 1994. *Publications:* over 300 speeches, articles and books published on social, cultural, economic and political subjects. *Leisure interests:* paintings, poetry, sport. *Address:* Office of the President of the Republic of Azerbaijan, 19 Istiglaliyyat str., 370001 Baku, Azerbaijan. *Telephone:* (12) 92-88-54. *Fax:* (12) 98-33-28; (12) 98 08 02.

ALIYEV, Ilham; Azerbaijani politician and business executive; b. 24 Dec. 1961, Baku; s. of Heydar Aliyev (q.v.), Pres. of Azerbaijan; one s. two d.; ed Moscow State Univ. of Int. Relations; teacher, Moscow State Univ. of Int. Relations 1985–90; engaged in commercial activity in Moscow and Istanbul following collapse of USSR 1991–94; First Vice-Pres. SOCAR (State Oil Co.) 1994–; Mem. Parl. 1995–; Deputy Chair. Yeni Azerbaijan (New Azerbaijan Party) 1999–2001, First Deputy Chair. 2001–; Pres. Nat. Olympic Cttee 1997–; Leader Del. to Council of Europe. *Address:* c/o Milli Majlis, Mehti Hussein Street 2, 370152 Baku, Azerbaijan (Office). *Telephone:* (12) 98-33-98 (Office). *Website:* www.ilham-aliyev.com (Office).

ALIYEV, Mukhu Gimbatovich, PhD; Russian/Dagestan politician; b. 6 Aug. 1940, Tusu; ed Dagestan State Univ.; Prin. of a secondary school; Sec. Comsomol Cttee, Dagestan State Univ. –1969; First Sec. Makhachkala City Comsomol Cttee 1969–72, Makhachkala dist. CPSU Cttee 1972–83; Deputy Head, then Head of Div., Makhachkala City CPSU Cttee 1983–90; First Deputy Chair. Dagestan Repub. CPSU Cttee 1990–91; mem. Supreme Soviet of Dagestan, Vice-Chair. 1991–95, Chair. 1995; Chair. Econs Cttee, Repub. of Dagestan 1992–94; Chair. Peoples' Ass., Repub. of Dagestan 1999–; mem. Council of Feds. of Russia 1999–, Deputy Chair. Cttee on Foreign Affairs, Fed. Ass. of Russian Fed. *Address:* House of Government, Lenina Square, 367005 Makhachkala, Dagestan, Russia (Office). *Telephone:* (8722) 67-32-48 (Office). *Fax:* (8722) 67-30-66 (Office).

ALKATIRI, Mari bin Amude; Timor-Leste politician; b. 26 Nov. 1949, Dili; m. Marina Ribeiro; three c.; fmr chartered surveyor; est. Movt for the Liberation of East Timor (Timor-Leste) 1970; Co-Founder and Sec.-Gen. Frente Revolucionário do Timor Leste Independente—Fretilin (Revolutionary Front for an Ind. Timor-Leste) 1974–; lived in political exile, teaching in Mozambique –1999; Minister for Econs in Transitional Admin; Prime Minister of Timor-Leste and Minister for Economy and Devt 2002–. *Address:* Fretilin, Rua dos Martires da Patria, Dili, Timor-Leste (Office). *Telephone:* (390) 321409 (Office). *E-mail:* opm@gov.east-timor.org. *Website:* www.gov .east-timor.org.

ALLADAYE, Lt-Col Michel; Benin army officer; b. 1940, Abomey; m.; five c.; ed Lycée Victor Ballot, Ecole Mil. de Saint-Cyr, Ecole Supérieure Technique du Génie, Versailles; Commdr 1st Eng Corps, Dahomey Armed Forces, Kandi 1963–67; promoted to rank of Capt. 1967; worked successively in Eng Unit, Army Gen. Staff Command, Services Battalion Command; Commdr 2nd Mil. Engs.; Minister of Foreign Affairs 1972–80, of Co-operation 1976–80, of Legislation and Social Affairs 1980–82, of Justice 1980–83; Vice-Pres. Parti de la Révolution Populaire du Bénin Defense and Security Comm. 1985; Chevalier, Légion d'honneur. *Address:* c/o Ministère de Justice, Cotonou, Benin.

ALLAIS, Maurice; French economist and engineer; b. 31 May 1911, Paris; s. of Maurice Allais and Louise (Caubet) Allais; m. Jacqueline Bouteloup 1960; one d.; ed Ecole Polytechnique and Ecole Nat. Supérieure des Mines de Paris; Dept of Mines and Quarries 1937–43; Dir Bureau de Documentation Minière 1943–48; econ. research 1948–70; Prof. of Economic Analysis, Ecole Nat. Supérieure des Mines de Paris 1944–88; Prof. of Econ. Theory, Inst. of Statistics, Univ. of Paris 1947–68; Dir of Research, Centre Nat. de la Recherche Scientifique 1954–80; Dir Centre for Econ. Analysis 1946–; Prof. Graduate Inst. of Int. Studies, Geneva 1967–70; Dir Séminaire Clément Juglar d'Analyse Monétaire, Univ. of Paris-X (Nanterre) 1970–85; Foreign Assoc. mem. NAS, Accad. dei Lincei, Russian Acad. of Sciences; mem. Acad. des Sciences Morales et Politiques; Dr.hc (Groningen, Mons, American Univ. of Paris, Lisbon, Hautes Etudes Commerciales, Paris); numerous hon. doctorates from European and American Univs.; Lanchester Prize, American Soc. for Operations Research, Gold Medal, Société d'Encouragement pour l'Industrie Nationale, Gold Medal, Centre National de la Recherche Scientifique 1978, Prix Laplace, Prix Rivot, Prix Robert Blanché, Grand Prix Zerilli Marimó, Académie des Sciences Morales et Politiques, Nobel Prize for Econ. Sciences 1988 and other awards; Hon. Ingénieur Général au Corps des Mines; Commdr Légion d'honneur, Officier Palmes académiques, Chevalier Ordre de l'Economie Nationale, Grand Croix, Ordre Nat. du Mérite. *Publications include:* A la Recherche d'un Discipline Economique 1943, Abondance ou misère 1946, Economie et intérêt 1947, Traité d'économie pure 1952, La gestion des houillères nationalisées et la théorie économique 1953, Les fondements comptables de la macroéconomie 1954, Le pendule paraconique 1957–59, Manifeste pour une société libre 1958, L'Europe unie, route de la prospérité 1960, Le Tiers-Monde au carrefour—Centralisation autoritaire ou planification concurrentielle 1962, L'Algérie d'Evian 1962, The Role of Capital in Economic Development 1963, Reformulation de la théorie quantitative de la monnaie 1966, L'Impôt sur le capital 1966, The Conditions of the Efficiency in the Economy 1967, Growth Without Inflation 1968, Growth and Inflation 1969, La libéralisation des relations économiques internationales 1970, Les théories de l'équilibre économique général et de l'efficacité maximale 1971, Forgetfulness and Interest 1972, The General Theory of Surplus and Pareto's Fundamental Contribution 1973, Inequality and Civilization 1973, La création de monnaie et de pouvoir d'achat par le mécanisme du crédit 1974, The Psychological Rate of Interest 1974, L'inflation française et la croissance 1974, Classes sociales et civilisations 1974, Taux d'expansion de la dépense globale et vitesse de circulation de la monnaie 1975, Inflation répartition des revenus et indexation 1976, L'impôt sur le capital et la réforme monétaire 1977, Expected Utility Hypotheses and the Allais Paradox 1979, La théorie générale des surplus 1980, Frequency, Probability and Chance 1982, The Foundations of the Theory of Utility and Risk 1984, Determination of Cardinal Utility 1985, The Concepts of Surplus and Loss and the Reformulation of the Theories of Stable General Economic Equilibrium and Maximum Efficiency 1985, The Empirical Approaches of the Hereditary and Relativistic Theory of the Demand for Money 1985, Les conditions monétaires d'une économie de marchés 1987, Pour l'indexation; Pour la réforme de la fiscalité 1990, L'Europe face à son avenir 1991, Erreurs et impasse de la construction européenne 1992, Cardinalism 1994, Combats pour l'Europe 1994, L'Anisotropie de l'espace 1997, La crise mondiale d'aujourd'hui 1999, L'Union européene, la mondialisation et le chômage 1999, La mondialisation: La destruction des emplois et de la croissance, L'évidence empirique 2000, Fondements de la dynamique monétaire 2001, La Passion de la Recherche 2001, Un Savant Méconnu 2002. *Leisure interests:* history, physics, swimming, skiing. *Address:* 60 boulevard Saint Michel, 75006 Paris (Office); 15 rue des Gâtes-Ceps, 92210 St-Cloud, France (Home). *Telephone:* 1-40-51-91-88 (Office). *E-mail:* mgendrot@club.internet.fr (Home). *Website:* allais.maurice.free.fr (Office).

ALLAN, Alexander Claud Stuart (Alex), MA, MSc; British civil servant and former diplomatist; b. 9 Feb. 1951; s. of the late Lord Allan of Kilmahew and of Maureen Catherine Flower Stuart-Clark; m. Katie Christine Clemson 1978; ed Harrow School, Clare Coll., Cambridge, Univ. Coll., London; with HM Customs and Excise 1973–76, HM Treasury 1976–92, Prin. Pvt. Sec. to Chancellor of the Exchequer 1986–89; secondments in Australia 1983–84; Under Sec. for Int. Finance 1989–90, for Public Expenditure Policy, 1990–92; Prin. Pvt. Sec. to the Prime Minister 1992–97; High Commr in Australia 1997–2000; e-Envoy Cabinet Office 1999–2000. *Leisure interests:* sailing, Grateful Dead music, cycling, computers, bridge. *Address:* 13 McCleery Street, Beaconsfield, WA 6162, Australia (Home). *Telephone:* (8) 9335-8885 (Home); (4) 3998-4442 (Home). *Fax:* (8) 9336-1360 (Home). *E-mail:* alex@whitegum.com (Home). *Website:* www.whitegum.com (Home).

ALLAN, Andrew Norman, BA, FRTS; British arts and media executive; b. 26 Sept. 1943, Newcastle-upon-Tyne; s. of Andrew Allan and Elizabeth Allan (née Davidson); m. Joanna Forrest 1978; two s. one d. and two d. from previous m.; ed Birmingham Univ.; presenter, ABC Television 1965–66; producer, Thames TV 1966–69, 1971–75; Head of News 1976–78; producer, ITN 1970; Dir of Programmes, Tyne Tees TV 1978–83, Deputy Man. Dir 1982–83, Man. Dir 1983–84; Dir of Programes, Cen. Ind. TV 1984–90, Man. Dir 1993–94; Man. Dir Cen. Broadcasting 1990–93; Chief Exec. Carlton TV 1994–95, Dir of Programmes 1996–98; Dir TV12 1999–; media consultant 1998–; Chair. Birmingham Repertory 2000–, Route 4 PLC 2001. *Leisure interests:* reading, dining. *Address:* Wardington Lodge, Wardington, Banbury, Oxon., OX17 1SE, England. *Telephone:* (1295) 750162. *Fax:* (1295) 750161.

ALLARD, A. Wayne, DMV; American politician and veterinarian; b. 12 Dec. 1943; m. Joan Malcolm 1967; two d.; ed Colo State Univ.; veterinarian, Allard Animal Hosp.; mem. Republican Party; mem. Colo State Senate 1982–91; Chair.Health, Environment and Insts Cttee; Chair. Senate Majority Caucus; mem. Congress from 4th Dist Colo 1991–96, mem. Agric. Cttee 1991–96, Small Business Cttee 1991–92, Interior and Insular Affairs Cttee 1991–92, Cttee on Cttees 1991–94, Budget Cttee 1993–96, Natural Resources Cttee 1993–96, Joint Cttee on Reorganization of Congress 1993–96; Chair. Sub-Cttee of Agric. Conservation, Forest and Water 1995–96; Senator from Colo 1997–, mem. Banking, Urban Affairs Cttee 1997–, Environment and Public Works Cttee 1997–, Intelligence Select Cttee 1997–, Senate Armed Services Cttee, and numerous other cttees; health officer Loveland, Colo; mem. Regional Advisory Council on Veterinarian Medicine, W Interstate Comm. on Higher Educ., Colo Low-Level Radioactive Waste Advisory Cttee; Chair. United Way; Founding mem. AVMA, Colo Veterinarian Medicine Asscn, Larimer Co. Veterinarian Medicine Asscn; mem. Bd Veterinarian Practitioners (charter mem.), American Animal Hosp. Asscn, Nat. Conf. State Legislatures (Vice-Chair. Human Resources Cttee 1987–); mem. Loveland Chamber of Commerce. *Address:* Office of the Senator from Colorado, US Senate, Senate Buildings, Washington, DC20510 (Office); POB 2405, Loveland, CO 80539, USA (Home).

ALLARDT, Erik Anders, MA, PhD; Finnish university chancellor and professor of sociology; b. 9 Aug. 1925, Helsinki; s. of Arvid Allardt and Marita (née Heikel) Allardt; m. Sagi Nylander 1947; one s. two d.; ed Univ. of Helsinki; Prof. of Sociology, Univ. of Helsinki 1958–85, Dean of the Faculty of Social Sciences 1969–70; Pres. Acad. of Finland 1986–91; Chancellor of the Åbo Acad. Univ. 1992–94; mem. European Science Foundation Exec. Council 1987–92, Vice-Pres. 1990–92; mem. Bd Scandinavia-Japan Sasakawa Foundation 1987–96; Founder mem. Academia Europaea 1988–; Fellow, Woodrow Int. Center for Scholars 1978–79; Visiting Prof. numerous countries and univs.; Dr. hc (Stockholm) 1978, (Åbo Akademi) 1978, (Uppsala) 1984, (Bergen) 1996, (Copenhagen) 2000. *Publications:* (with Rokkan) Mass Politics: Studies in Political Sociology 1970, Att Ha, Att Älska, Att Vara. Om Välfärd i Norden 1975, Implications of the Ethnic Revival in Modern, Industrialized Society 1979, (with Lysgaard and Sørensen) Sociologin i Sverige, vetenskap, miljö och organisation 1988, The History of the Social Sciences in Finland 1997. *Address:* Department of Sociology, PB 18, 00014 University of Helsinki (Office); Unionsgatan 45B 40, 00170 Helsinki, Finland (Home). *Telephone:* (9) 19123963 (Office); (9) 1354550 (Home). *Fax:* (9) 19123967 (Office). *E-mail:* erik.allardt@helsinki.fi (Office).

ALLCHIN, Frank Raymond, PhD, FBA, FSA; British university lecturer; b. 9 July 1923, Harrow; s. of late Frank MacDonald Allchin and Louise Maude Wright; m. Bridget Gordon 1951; one s. one d.; ed Westminster School, Regent Street Polytechnic School of Architecture, SOAS; Lecturer in Indian Archaeology, SOAS 1954–59; Lecturer in Indian Studies, Cambridge 1959–72, Reader 1972–90, Reader Emer. 1990–; Fellow of Churchill Coll., Cambridge 1963–; Jt Dir British Archaeological Mission to Pakistan 1975–92; Dir British Anuradhapura Project, Sri Lanka 1989–93; Jt Founding Trustee, Ancient India and Iran Trust 1978–, Chair. 1995–. *Publications:* Co-author: The Birth of Indian Civilization 1968, The Rise of Civilization in India and Pakistan 1982, The Archaeology of Early Historic South Asia 1995, Origins of a Civilization 1997. *Leisure interests:* walking, gardening. *Address:* 2 Shepreth Road, Barrington, Cambridge, CB2 5SB; 23 Brooklands Avenue, Cambridge, CB2 2BG, England. *Telephone:* (1223) 870494 (Shepreth Road); (1223) 356841 (Brooklands Avenue). *Fax:* (1223) 361125 (Brooklands Avenue).

ALLÈGRE, Claude Jean; French politician; b. 31 March 1937, Paris, France; s. of Prof. Roger Allègre and Lucette (née Hugoueneq) Allègre; m. Claude Blanche Simon 1967; three s. one d.; ed Lycées Saint-Maur and Saint-Louis, Faculté des Sciences, Paris; Asst Univ. de Paris 1962–68; Dir of Lab. of Geochemistry and Cosmochemistry Univ. de Paris VI and VII 1967–; Asst Physician Inst. de Physique du Globe 1968–70, Dir 1976–86; Prof. of Earth Sciences Univ. de Paris VII 1970–; Prof. of Earth Sciences Inst. of Tech., Mass. 1975–76; Special Adviser to Lionel Jospin 1988–92; MEP 1989; Minister of Nat. Educ., Research and Tech. 1997–2000; Pres. Admin Council of Bureau de Recherches Géologiques et Minières 1992–97; mem. of numerous socs.; Hon. mem. Union Européenne de Géosciences, European Biophysical Soc., Acad. of Arts and Sciences, Boston Philosophical Soc.; Foreign mem. NAS; Craaford Prize (Sweden) 1986; Officier, Légion d'honneur, Chevalier des Palmes académiques; numerous medals. *Publications include:* L'Ecume de la Terre 1983, De la Pierre à l'Etoile 1985, Les Fureurs de la Terre 1987, Economiser la Planète 1990, Introduction à une Histoire Naturelle 1992, L'Age des Savoires 1993, Ecologie des Villes, Ecologie des Champs 1993, L'Etat de la Planète 1994, La Défaite de Platon 1995, Questions de France 1996, Dieu Face à la Science 1997, Toute Vérité est Bonne à Dire 2000, Vive L'École Libre 2000. *Address:* Institut de France, 23 quai Conti, 75006 Paris, France (Office); Institut de physique du globe, 4 place Jussieu, 75005 Paris, France.

ALLÈGRE, Maurice Marie, LenD; French research co-ordinator and business executive; b. 16 Feb. 1933, Antibes; s. of Guy Allègre and Renée-Lise Bermond; m. Catherine Pierre 1962; one s. one d.; ed Ecole Polytechnique, Ecole Nat. Supérieure des Mines et Ecole Nat. Supérieure du Pétrole et des Moteurs; Engineer, Direction des Carburants, Ministry of Industry 1957–62; Dir Mines de l'Organisme Saharien 1962–64; Tech. Adviser to Ministry of Finance and Econ. Affairs 1965–67; Délégué à l'Informatique et Pres. Inst. de Recherche d'Informatique et d'Automatique 1968–74; Chief of Nickel Mission to New Caledonia 1975; Asst Dir-Gen. Inst. Français du Pétrole 1976–81; Pres. and Dir-Gen. ISIS 1976–81; Pres. FRANLAB, COFLEXIP 1976–81; Pres. Agence Nat. de Valorisation et de la Recherche (ANVAR) 1982–84; Dir Scientific and Tech. Devt, Ministry of Research and Tech. 1982–84; Dir-Gen. Bureau de Recherches Géologiques et Minières 1984–88, Pres. 1988–92; Pres. Nat. Agency for Man. of Radioactive Waste (ANDRA) 1993–98; Pres. Sicav Vauban 1998–; Pres. AGRER Asscn 1998–; consultant on energy and radioactive waste 1998–; Chevalier, Légion d'honneur, Officier Ordre Nat. du Mérite. *Leisure interests:* photography, skiing, sailing. *Address:* 85 rue de Sèvres, 75006 Paris; 50 boulevard d'Aiguillon, 06600 Antibes, France. *Telephone:* 1-45-44-94-51 (Office).

ALLEN, Charles Lamb, CBE, FRSA, FCMA; British business executive; b. 4 Jan. 1957; accountant, British Steel 1974–79; Deputy Audit Man. Gallaghers PLC 1979–82; Dir Man. Services Grandmet Int. Services Ltd 1982–85; Group Man. Dir Compass Vending, Grandmet Innovations Ltd 1986–87; Man. Dir Grandmet Int. Services Ltd 1987–88; Man. Dir Compass Group Ltd 1988–91; Chief Exec. Leisure Div., Granada Group 1991–92; Chair. Granada Leisure and Services 1993–2000, CEO LWT (following takeover by Granada) 1994–96 (Chair. 1996–), CEO Granada Group PLC 1996–2000, Chair. GMTV 1996–2000, Jt Deputy Chair. Granada Compass PLC 2000–, Exec. Chair. Granada PLC 2000–; Chair. Yorkshire Tyne Tees TV 1997–, M2002 Ltd; Dir (non-exec.) Tesco PLC 1999–; Hon. DBA (Manchester Metropolitan) 1999, (Salford) 2002. *Leisure interests:* visual and performing arts, int. travel and cultures. *Address:* Granada PLC, The London Television Centre, Upper Ground, London, SE1 9LT, England (Office); 1A Upper Phillimore Gardens, Kensington, London, W8 7HF, England (Home). *Telephone:* (20) 7620-1620 (Office); (20) 7937 7510 (Home). *Fax:* (20) 7261-3307 (Office). *Website:* www.granadamedia.com.

ALLEN, Sir Douglas Albert Vivian, GCB (see Croham, Baron).

ALLEN, Gary James, CBE, DL, BCom, FCMA, CBIM, FRSA; British business executive; b. 30 Sept. 1944, Birmingham; s. of Alfred Allen; m. Judith A. Nattrass 1966; three s.; ed King Edward VI Grammar School, Aston, Birmingham and Liverpool Univ.; Man. Dir IMI Range Ltd 1973–77; Dir IMI PLC 1978–, Man. Dir and CEO 1986–2001; Dir (non-exec.) NV Bekaert SA,

Belgium 1987–, Nat. Exhbn Centre Ltd 1989–, Marley PLC 1989–97 (Deputy Chair. 1993–97), Birmingham European Airways Ltd 1989–91, The London Stock Exchange PLC 1994–, Temple Bar Investment Trust PLC 2001; Chair. Optilon Ltd 1979–84, Eley Ltd 1981–85; mem. Nat. Council CBI 1986–99; mem. Council, Birmingham Chamber of Industry and Commerce 1983–98, Pres. 1991–92, mem. Bd 1994–96; mem. Council Univ. of Birmingham 1985–90 and Hon. Life mem. Court 1984–; mem. Bd Birmingham Royal Ballet 1993–; Pres. Midlands Club Cricket Conf. 1995–96; mem. Council Lord's Taverners 1992–2001; Pres. West Midlands Regional Cttee, Lord's Taverners 1994–; Trustee The Lord's Taverners 1995–2001; Trustee Industry in Educ. 1998–; Chair. Birmingham Children's Hosp. Appeal 1995–2000; High Sheriff W Midlands 2002; Order of Leopold II (Belgium) 2002. *Leisure interests:* sport, reading, gardening. *Address:* IMI plc, P.O. Box 216, Birmingham, B6 7BA, England (Office). *Telephone:* (121) 356-4848 (Office). *Fax:* (121) 356-7916 (Office). *Website:* www.imi.plc.uk/ (Office).

ALLEN, Sir Geoffrey, Kt, PhD, FREng, FRS, FInstP, FPRI, FIM, FRSC; British polymer scientist and administrator; b. 29 Oct. 1928, Clay Cross, Derbyshire; s. of John James Allen and Marjorie Allen; m. Valerie Frances Duckworth 1972; one d.; ed Clay Cross Tupton Hall Grammar School, Univ. of Leeds; Postdoctoral Fellow, Nat. Research Council, Canada 1952–54; Lecturer, Univ. of Manchester 1955–65, Prof. of Chemical Physics 1965–75; Prof. of Polymer Science, Imperial Coll. of Science and Tech., Univ. of London 1975–76, of Chemical Tech. 1976–81; Fellow Imperial Coll. 1986, UMIST 1994; Exec. Adviser Kobe Steel Ltd 1990–2000; Chair. Science Research Council 1977–81; Head of Research, Unilever PLC 1981–90, Dir of Unilever responsible for Research and Eng 1982–90; Dir (non-exec.) Courtaulds 1987–93; Pres. PRI, Pres. SCI 1990–92; mem. Nat. Consumer Council 1993–96; Vice-Pres. Royal Soc. 1991–93; Chancellor Univ. of E Anglia 1994–; Pres. Inst. of Materials 1994–95; Visiting Fellow, Robinson Coll., Cambridge 1980–; Hon. FIM, Hon. FIChemE; Hon. MSc (Manchester); Hon. DSc (Durham, E Anglia) 1984, (Bath, Bradford, Keele, Loughborough) 1985, (Essex, Leeds) 1986, (Cranfield) 1988, (Surrey) 1989, (N London) 1999; Dr hc (Open Univ.). *Leisure interests:* opera, walking, talking. *Address:* 18 Oxford House, 52 Parkside, London, SW19 5NE, England (Home). *Telephone:* (20) 8947-7459 (Home).

ALLEN, George; American politician and business executive; m. Susan Allen (née Brown); three c.; mem. House of Dels, Va 1982, House of Reps., Washington DC 1991; Gov. of Va 1994–98; Senator from Va 2000–; mem. Commerce, Science and Transportation Cttee, Foreign Relations Cttee, 'Small b' Business Cttee; Head of McguireWoods' Business Expansion and Relocation Team, Va; Jefferson Scholar, American Legis. Exchange Council 1998. *Address:* Office of the Senator from Virginia, US Senate, Washington, DC 20510, USA (Office). *Telephone:* (202) 224-4024 (Office).

ALLEN, Dame Ingrid Victoria, DBE, DL, MD, DSc, FMedSci, MRIA; British professor of medicine; b. 30 July 1932, Belfast; d. of Robert Allen and Doris V. Allen (née Shaw); m. 1st Alan Watson Barnes 1972 (died 1986); m. 2nd John Thompson 1990; ed Ashleigh House School, Belfast and Cheltenham Ladies Coll.; House Officer Royal Victoria Hosp. (RVH), Belfast 1957–58; Musgrave Research Fellow, Tutor in Pathology, Clavert Research Fellow, Queen's Univ. Belfast (QUB) 1958–64; Sr Registrar RVH 1964–65; Sr Lecturer and Consultant in Neuropathology, QUB/RVH 1966–78, Reader and Consultant 1978–79; Head NI Regional Neuropathology Service 1979–97; mem. MRC 1988–94; Dir for Research and Devt Health and Personal Social Services, NI 1997–2001; Visiting Prof. Univ. of Ulster 1998; Fellow Int. Soc. of Neuropathology 1993, Vice-Pres. 1988–92; Fellow Royal Soc. of Pathologists. *Publications:* Greenfield's Neuropathology 1984, McAlpine's Multiple Sclerosis (contrib.) 1990; numerous articles in learned journals on neuropathology, demyilinating diseases, neurovirology, neuro-oncology and biomedical research and devt. *Leisure interests:* reading, sailing, lying on an island off the NW coast of Ireland. *Address:* 95 Malone Road, Belfast, BT9 6SP, Northern Ireland (Home). *Telephone:* (28) 9066-6662 (Home).

ALLEN, John Robert Lawrence, DSc, FRS, FGS, FSA; British professor of sedimentology; b. 25 Oct. 1932; s. of George Eustace Allen and Alice Josephine (née Formby); m. Jean Mary Wood 1960; four s. one d.; ed St Philip's Grammar School, Birmingham, Univ. of Sheffield; mem. staff, Univ. of Reading 1959–, Prof. of Geology 1972–89, of Sedimentology 1989–93, apptd. Research Prof. Postgrad. Research Inst. for Sedimentology 1993 (now Prof. Emer.), Visiting Prof. in Archaeology; Assoc. mem. Royal Belgian Acad. of Sciences; Hon. LLD; Lyell Medal, Geological Soc. 1980, David Linton Award, British Geomorphological Research Group 1983, Twenhofel Medal, Soc. of Econ. Paleontologists and Minerologists 1987, G.K. Warren Prize, NAS, USA 1990, Sorby Medal, Int. Asscn of Sedimentologists 1994, Penrose Medal, Geological Soc. of America 1996. *Publications:* Current Ripples 1968, Physical Processes of Sedimentation 1970, Sedimentary Structures 1982, Principles of Physical Sedimentology 1985; numerous contribs. to professional journals. *Leisure interests:* cooking, music, opera, pottery, walking. *Address:* 17C Whiteknights Road, Reading, Berks., RG6 7BY, England. *Telephone:* (118) 926-4621.

ALLEN, John Walter, MA, FRSE; British physicist; b. 7 March 1928, Birmingham; s. of Walter Allen and Beryl Parsons; m. 1st Mavis Williamson 1956 (died 1972); m. 2nd Hania Szawelska 1981; one s.; ed King Edward's School, Birmingham and Sidney Sussex Coll., Cambridge; RAF Educ. Br. 1949–51; staff scientist, Ericsson Telephones, Nottingham 1951–56; Royal Naval Scientific Service, Services Electronics Research Lab. 1956–68; Vis-

iting Prof. Stanford Univ. 1964–66; Tullis Russell Fellow, Univ. of St Andrew's 1968–72, Reader in Physics, Dir of Wolfson Inst. of Luminescence 1972–81, Prof. of Solid State Physics 1981–. *Publications:* some 120 papers in scientific journals including the first account of a practical light-emitting diode. *Leisure interests:* archaeology, traditional dance. *Address:* Department of Physics and Astronomy, University of St Andrews, North Haugh, St Andrews, Fife, KY16 9SS (Office); 2 Dempster Terrace, St Andrews, Fife KY16 9QQ, Scotland (Home). *Telephone:* (1334) 463331 (Office); (1334) 474163 (Home). *Fax:* (1334) 463104 (Office). *E-mail:* jwa@st-and.ac.uk (Office).

ALLEN, Gen. Lew, Jr, MS, PhD; American air force officer; b. 30 Sept. 1925, Miami; s. of the late Lew Allen and Zella Holman; m. Barbara McKelden Frink 1949; two s. three d.; ed Gainesville Junior Coll., US Mil. Acad. West Point, Air Tactical School Tyndall, Univ. of Illinois; Pilot, Carswell Air Force Base, Tex. 1946–50; Physicist, Los Alamos Scientific Laboratory, NM 1954–57; various posts Kirkland Air Force Base, NM 1957–61; Space Tech. Office and OSD, Washington, DC 1961–65; OSAF, Los Angeles, Calif. 1965–68; OSAF Washington, DC 1968–70; OSAF, Los Angeles, Calif. 1970–71; SAMSO, Los Angeles, Calif. 1971–73; c/s, HQ AFSC, Andrews Air Force Base, Md 1973; Deputy to Dir of Cen. Intelligence for the Intelligence Community 1973; Dir NSA and Chief of Cen. Security Service, Fort Meade, Md 1973–77; Commdr, AFSC, Andrews Air Force Base 1977–78; Vice-Chief of Staff USAF April–June 1978, Chief of Staff USAF 1978–82; Dir Jet Propulsion Lab., Pasadena, Calif. 1982–90; Chair. Draper Lab., Boston 1991–95; mem. Nat. Acad. of Eng 1977–; Defense Distinguished Service Medal, Distinguished Service Medal of the Air Force, Legion of Merit with Two Oak Leaf Clusters, Joint Service Commendation and various other US awards and medals, Order of Nat. Security (Repub. of Korea). *Leisure interests:* racquet ball, scuba diving, jogging. *Address:* c/o Draper Charles Stark Laboratory Inc., 555 Technology Square, Cambridge, MA 02139, USA. *Telephone:* (818) 354-3405.

ALLEN, Mary; British arts administrator and fmr actress; b. 22 Aug. 1951, London; d. of Fergus Allen and Joan Allen; m. 1st Robin Woodhead 1980 (divorced 1990); m. 2nd Nigel Pantling 1991; ed School of St Helen and St Catherine, New Hall, Cambridge; actress, West End and repertory 1973–76; Agent, London Man. 1977–78; Arts, Sponsorship Man., Mobil Oil Co. 1978–81; Assoc. for Business Sponsorship of the Arts 1982–83; arts man. consultant 1983–90; Trustee, Public Art DevtTrust 1983–92, Chair. 1987–92; Dir Cheek by Jowl 1989–92; Dir Waterman's Arts Centre, London 1990–92; Deputy Sec.-Gen. Arts Council of GB 1992–94; Sec. Gen. Arts Council of England 1994–97; Chief Exec. Royal Opera House, London 1997–98. *Publications:* Sponsoring The Arts: New Business Strategies for the 1990s, A House Divided 1998. *Leisure interests:* gardening, cooking, theatre, collecting contemporary art.

ALLEN, Paul G.; American computer executive; ed Washington State Univ.; co-f. Microsoft Corpn 1975, Exec. Vice-Pres. 1975–83, Dir 2001–; f. Asymetrix Corpn 1985–, Starwave Corpn; Founder, Chair. Intervas Research; owner and Chair. Bd Portland Trail Blazers (Ore.) 1988–, Seattle Seahawks; Dir Egghead Discount Software, Darwin Molecular Inc.; fmrly owner, Chair., Dir Ticketmaster Holdings Group; CEO Vulcan Ventures 1987–. *Address:* The Paul Allen Group, Suite 530, 110 110th Avenue North East, Bellevue, WA 98004, USA.

ALLEN, Percival, PhD, FRS; British geologist; b. 15 March 1917, Brede, Sussex; s. of the late Norman Williams Allen and Mildred Kathleen Allen (née Hoad); m. Frances Margaret Hepworth 1941; three s. one d.; ed Rye Grammar School, Univ. of Reading; served in RAF 1941–42; Asst Lecturer Univ. of Reading 1945–46; Univ. Demonstrator, Univ. of Cambridge 1946–47, Lecturer 1947–52; Prof. of Geology, Univ. of Reading 1952–82, Prof. Emer. of Geology 1982–; Sec. Philpots Quarry Ltd; Dean of Science Faculty, Univ. of Reading 1963–66; Visiting Prof., Univ. of Kuwait 1970; a Vice-Pres. Royal Soc. 1977–79; Pres. Geological Soc. 1978–80; Adviser UNDP Nile Delta Project 1972–75; Geology Consultant, India, for UNESCO/UNDP 1976–77; Algerian Sahara Glacials Expedition 1970; Tibet Geotraverse Follow-up 1986; Chair. Int. Confs Organizing Cttees of Seventh Int. Sedimentology Congress 1967, First European Earth and Planetary Physics Colloquium 1971, First Meeting European Geological Socs. 1975; Sec.-Gen. Int. Assoc. of Sedimentologists 1967–71; Chair. Royal Soc. Expeditions Cttee 1974–; Royal Soc. Assessor to NERC 1977–80; Chair. Royal Soc., British Nat. Cttee for Geology 1982–90, British Inst. for Geological Conservation 1987–90; UK Corresp. IGCP Project 245, 1986–91; UK Del. to Int. Union of Geological Sciences, Moscow 1984; Hon. mem. of Bulgarian Geological Soc., of Geological Asscn, Soc. Econ. Palaeontologists and Mineralogists and of Int. Asscn of Sedimentologists; Council mem. Natural Environment Research Council 1971–74; Foreign Fellow, Indian Natural Sciences Acad.; Lyell Medal, Geological Soc. of London 1971. *Publications:* Papers on Purbeck-Wealden (Lower Cretaceous) and Torridonian (Proterozoic) sedimentology in various scientific journals from 1938 onwards. *Leisure interests:* chess, natural history, gardening, bicycling. *Address:* Postgraduate Research Institute for Sedimentology (PRIS), University of Reading, Reading, RG6 6AB; Orchard End, Hazeley Bottom, Hartley Wintney, Hook, Hampshire, RG27 8LU, England. *Telephone:* (118) 931-6713 (Office); (1252) 842229 (Home). *Fax:* (1734) 310279.

ALLEN, Richard V.; American international business consultant; b. 1 Jan. 1936, Collingswood, NJ; s. of C. Carroll Allen, Sr and Magdalen Buchman; m. Patricia Ann Mason 1957; three s. four d.; ed Notre Dame Univ. and Univ. of

Munich; helped found Cen. for Strategic and Int. Studies, Georgetown Univ. 1962; Consultant and fmr Prof. Hoover Inst., Stanford Univ.; with Nat. Security Council 1968–69; int. business consultant; mem. Ronald Reagan's staff, campaigns 1976, Bd Govs. Ronald Reagan Presidential Foundation 1985; Pres. Richard V. Allen Co., Washington 1982–90, Chair. 1991–; Head Nat. Security Council and Nat. Security Adviser 1981–82; Chair. Fed. Capital Bank 1987; Sr Council for Foreign Policy and Nat. Security Affairs, Repub. Nat. Cttee 1982–88; Bd Dirs. Xsirius Inc. 1991–92; Distinguished Fellow and Chair. Asian Studies Center, The Heritage Foundation 1982; Chair. German-American Tricentenial Foundation 1983; Founding mem. US Nat. Cttee for Pacific Basin 1984; Sr Fellow, Hoover Inst. 1983–; mem. Advisory Bd Catholic Campaign for America 1993–; mem. Republican Congressional Policy Advisory Bd 1998–; Hon. degrees (Hanover Coll.) 1981, (Korea Univ.) 1982; Order of Diplomatic Merit Ganghwa (Repub. of Korea) 1982, Kt Commdr.'s Cross (FRG) 1983, Order of Brilliant Star (Repub. of China) 1986, Sovereign Mil. Order of Kts. of Malta 1987. *Publications:* numerous books on political and economic affairs including Peace or Peaceful Coexistence 1966, Communism and Democracy: Theory and Action 1967. *Address:* 1615 L. Street, Suite 900, NW, Washington, DC 20036-5623, USA (Office).

ALLÉN, Sture, DPhil; Swedish professor of linguistics; b. 1928, Göteborg; s. of Bror G. Allén and Hanna Johanson; m. Solveig Janson 1954; three c.; ed Univ. of Göteborg; Asst Prof. of Scandinavian Philology, Göteborg Univ. 1965–70, Prof. of Computational Linguistics 1979–93, Pro-Rector 1980–85, Rector 1986; Assoc. Prof. of Computational Linguistics, Swedish Humanistic Research Council 1970–72, Prof. 1972–79; Perm. Sec. Swedish Acad. 1986–99; mem. Royal Soc. of Arts and Sciences of Göteborg, Royal Swedish Acad. of Letters, History and Antiquities, Academia Europaea, Royal Swedish Acad. of Eng Sciences, Norwegian Acad. of Sciences and Letters, Finnish Soc. of Science and Letters; Hon. mem. Soc. of Swedish Literature in Finland; Corresp. mem. Icelandic Soc. of Sciences; mem. Bd of Dirs, Nobel Foundation 1987–99; Dr hc (Swedish Univ. of Åbo) 1988; several awards and distinctions, including Medal of King of Sweden in the Ribbon of the Order of Seraphim for Eminent Scientific and Cultural Achievements, Gothenburg City Medal (Gold) 1994, Knight Commdr Order of the White Rose (Finland) 1994; Chester Carlson Research Prize 1988, Margit Påhlson Prize 2000, Chalmers Tech. Univ. Medal 2002. *Radio:* From a Linguistic Point of View (series). *Television:* In Plain Swedish (series). *Publications:* author and co-author of numerous textbooks, dictionaries, glossaries, etc. *Leisure interests:* music, sports. *Address:* Swedish Academy, P.O. Box 2118, SE-10313 Stockholm; c/o Språkdata Group, Department of Swedish, Göteborg University, P.O. Box 200, 40530 Göteborg, Sweden.

ALLEN, Sir Thomas, KBE, FRCM; British opera singer; b. 10 Sept. 1944, Seaham, Co. Durham; s. of Thomas Boaz and Florence Allen; m. 1st Margaret Holley 1968 (divorced 1986); one s.; m. 2nd Jeannie Gordon Lascelles 1988; one step-s. one step-d.; ed Robert Richardson Grammar School, Ryhope, Royal Coll. of Music, London; prin. baritone, Welsh Nat. Opera 1969–72, Royal Opera House, Covent Garden 1972–78, Glyndebourne Opera 1973, ENO, London Coliseum 1986, La Scala 1987, Chicago Lyric Opera 1990, Royal Albert Hall 2000; Hon. Fellow RAM, Univ. of Sunderland; Hon. MA (Newcastle) 1984, Hon. DMus (Durham) 1988; Queen's Prize 1967, Gulbenkian Fellow 1968. *Art Exhibitions:* Chelsea Festival 2001, Salisbury Playhouse 2001. *Performances include:* Die Zauberflöte 1973, Le Nozze di Figaro 1974, Così fan Tutte 1975, Don Giovanni 1977, The Cunning Little Vixen 1977 and Simon Boccanegra, Billy Budd, La Bohème, L'Elisir d'Amore, Faust, Albert Herring, Die Fledermaus, La Traviata, A Midsummer Night's Dream, Die Meistersinger von Nürnberg, etc. *Publication:* Foreign Parts: A Singer's Journal 1993. *Leisure interests:* painting, drawing, ornithology, golf, fishing. *Address:* c/o Askonas Holt Limited, Lonsdale Chambers, 27 Chancery Lane, London, WC2A 1PF, England. *Telephone:* (20) 7400-1700 (Office).

ALLEN, Tim; American actor and comedian; b. 13 June 1953, Denver; ed W Mich. Univ., Univ. of Detroit; fmr creative Dir for advertising agency; début as comedian on Showtime Comedy Club All Stars 1988; Favorite Comedy Actor, People's Choice Award 1995, 1997–99. *TV includes:* Home Improvement (series) 1991–, Tim Allen: Men Are Pigs 1990, Tim Allen Rewrites America (specials), Showtime Comedy Club All-Stars II 1988. *Films include:* Comedy's Dirtiest Dozen, The Santa Clause 1994, Toy Story (voice) 1995, Meet Wally Sparks 1997, Jungle 2 Jungle 1997, For Richer or Poorer 1997, Galaxy Quest 1999, Toy Story 2 (voice) 2000, Buzz Lightyear of Star Command: The Adventure Begins 2000, Who is Cletis Tout? 2001, Joe Somebody 2001, Big Trouble 2002, The Santa Clause 2 2002. *Publications:* Don't Stand Too Close to a Naked Man 1994, I'm Not Really Here 1996. *Address:* c/o Commercial Unlimited, 8883 Wilshire Boulevard, Suite 850, Beverly Hills, CA 90211, USA.

ALLEN, Woody (Allen Stewart Konigsberg); American actor, writer, producer and director; b. 1 Dec. 1935, Brooklyn, New York; s. of the late Martin Konigsberg and of Nettie Konigsberg (née Cherry); m. 1st Harlene Rosen (divorced); m. 2nd Louise Lasser 1966 (divorced 1969); m. 3rd Soon-Yi Previn 1997; two adopted d.; one s. by Mia Farrow (q.v.); ed City Coll. of New York and New York Univ.; made his debut as a performer in 1961 at the Duplex in Greenwich Village; has performed in a variety of nightclubs across the US; produced the play Don't Drink the Water, Morosco Theater 1966, Broadhurst Theatre 1969; made his Broadway début as Allan Felix in Play it Again, Sam, which he also wrote; during the 1950s wrote for television performers Herb Shriner 1953, Sid Caesar 1957, Art Carney 1958–59, Jack

Parr and Carol Channing, also wrote for the Tonight Show and the Gary Moore Show; D. W. Griffith Award 1996. *Films include:* What's New Pussycat? 1965, Casino Royale 1967, What's Up, Tiger Lily? 1967, Take the Money and Run 1969, Bananas 1971, Everything You Always Wanted to Know About Sex 1972, Play it Again, Sam 1972, Sleeper 1973, Love and Death 1976, The Front 1976, Annie Hall (Academy Awards for Best Director and Best Writer) 1977, Interiors 1978, Manhattan 1979, Stardust Memories 1980, A Midsummer Night's Sex Comedy 1982, Zelig 1983, Broadway Danny Rose 1984, The Purple Rose of Cairo 1985, Hannah and Her Sisters 1985, Radio Days 1987, September 1987, Another Woman 1988, Oedipus Wrecks 1989, Crimes and Misdemeanors 1989, Alice 1990, Scenes from a Mall, Shadows and Fog 1991, Husbands and Wives 1992, Manhattan Murder Mystery 1993, Bullets Over Broadway 1995, Mighty Aphrodite 1995, Everybody Says I Love You 1996, Deconstructing Harry 1997, Celebrity 1998, Antz (voice only) 1998, Wild Man Blues 1998, Stuck on You 1998, Company Men 1999, Sweet and Lowdown 1999, Small Town Crooks 2000, The Curse of the Jade Scorpion 2001, Hail Sid Caesar! 2001, Hollywood Ending 2002. *Plays written include:* Don't Drink the Water 1966, The Floating Lightbulb 1981, Death Defying Acts (one act) 1995. *Publications:* Getting Even 1971, Without Feathers 1975, Side Effects 1980, The Complete Prose 1994, has also contributed to Playboy and New Yorker. *Leisure interests:* chocolate milk shakes, poker, chess, baseball; also a noted clarinettist. *Address:* 930 Fifth Avenue, New York, NY 10021, USA.

ALLENDE, Isabel; Chilean (Peruvian-born) writer; b. 8 Aug. 1942, Lima; d. of Francisca Llona Barros and Tomás Allende; m. 1st Miguel Frias 1962; one s. one d.; m. 2nd William Gordon 1988; journalist for Paula Magazine 1967–74, Mampato Magazine 1969–74; Channel 13 World Hunger Campaign 1964; Channel 7, various humorous programmes 1970–74; Maga-Cine-Ellas 1973; Admin. Marroco School, Caracas 1978–82; freelance journalist El Nacional newspaper, Caracas 1976–83; Visiting Teacher Montclair State Coll., NJ 1985, Univ. of Virginia, Charlottesville 1988, Univ. of Calif., Berkeley 1989; Writer 1981–; Hon. mem. Acad. of Devt and Peace, Austria 2000; Prof. hc (Chile) 1991; Hon. DLitt (New York State) 1991; Novel of the Year, Panorama Literario (Chile) 1983; Point de Mire (Belgium) 1985; Author of the Year and Book of the Year (Germany) 1984; Grand Prix d'Evasion (France) 1984; Colima for Best Novel (Mexico) 1985; Author of the Year (Germany) 1986; Mulheres Best Novel (Portugal) 1987; Dorothy and Lillian Gish Prize 1998; Sara Lee Frontrunner Award 1998; GEMS Women of the Year Award 1999; Donna Dell'Anno Award (Italy) 1999; WILLA Literary Award (USA) 2000. *Plays:* Paula, Stories of Eva Luna, The House of the Spirits, Eva Luna. *Publications:* (novels) The House of the Spirits 1982, Of Love and Shadows 1984, Eva Luna 1989, Aphrodite 1998, Daughter of Fortune 1999, Portrait in Sepia 2000; (short stories) Tales of Eva Luna 1990, The Infinite Plan 1992, Paula (memoir) 1995, Aphrodite (a memoir of the senses) 1997; (children's story) La Gorda de Porcelana 1984. *Address:* 116 Caledonia Street, Sausalito, CA 94965, USA.

ALLENDE, Jorge Eduardo, PhD; Chilean biochemist and molecular biologist; b. 11 Nov. 1934, Cartago, Costa Rica; s. of Octavio Allende and Amparo Rivera; m. Catherine C. Connelly 1961; three s. one d.; ed Louisiana State and Yale Univs., USA; Research Assoc. Lab. of Prof. Fritz Lipmann at Rockefeller Univ. 1961–62; Asst Prof. Dept of Biochemistry, Univ. of Chile 1963–68, Assoc. Prof. 1968–71, Prof. of Biochemistry and Molecular Biology 1972–; Pres. Pan American Asscn of Biochemical Socs. 1976; mem. Exec. Cttee Int. Union of Biochemistry 1982–91, Int. Cell Research Org. 1976–; mem. Exec. Bd Int. Council of Scientific Unions 1986–90; Regional Co-ordinator Latin American Network of Biological Sciences 1975–; mem. UNESCO Int. Scientific Advisory Bd 1996–; Foreign Assoc. Inst. of Medicine, NAS; Fogarty Scholar-in-Residence NIH, USA; Fellow Third World Acad. of Sciences; Founder mem. Latin American Acad. of Sciences; mem. Chilean Acad. of Sciences, Pres. 1991–94; Hon. mem. Chilean Acad. of Medicine; Dr hc (Buenos Aires) 1993; Chilean Nat. Prize in Natural Sciences 1992. *Publications:* 116 research articles in learned journals. *Leisure interests:* music, reading, swimming. *Address:* Departamento de Bioquímica, Facultad de Medicina, Universidad de Chile, Casilla 70086, Santiago 7, Chile. *Telephone:* (2) 737-6320. *Fax:* (2) 737-6320.

ALLEST, Frédéric Jean Pierre d'; French engineer; b. 1 Sept. 1940, Marseilles; s. of Pierre d'Allest and Luce d'Allest; m. Anne-Marie Morel 1963; three s.; ed Ecole St Joseph and Lycée Thiers, Marseilles, Ecole Polytechnique and Ecole Nat. Supérieure d'Aéronautique; with Centre National d'Etudes Spatiales (CNES) 1966–70, Head of Ariane Project 1973–76, Dir Ariane Programme 1976–82, Dir-Gen. CNES 1982–89; with Europa III project, European Launcher Devt Org. 1970–72; Pres. Soc. Arianespace 1980–90 (Hon. Pres. 1990–), Matra Transport 1992–, Matra Hachette 1993–; Dir-Gen. Groupe Matra 1990–93, Groupe Lagardère 1996–; f. Marseille Provence 1988; Prix de l'Aéronautique, James Watt Prize (Inst. of Mechanical Engineers) 1993; Officier, Légion d'honneur, Officier Ordre Nat. du Mérite. *Leisure interests:* sport, alpinism. *Address:* Groupe Lagardère, 121 ave de Malakoff, 75216 Paris Cedex 16 (Office); 6 rue Marcel Allegot, 92190 Meudon, France (Home).

ALLEY, Kirstie; American actress; b. Wichita, Kan.; m. Parker Stevenson; one s. one d.; ed Univ. of Kan.; People's Choice Award 1998. *Films:* Star Trek II, The Wrath of Khan 1982, One More Chance, Blind Date, Champions 1983, Runaway 1984, Summer School 1987, Look Who's Talking Too 1990, Madhouse 1990, Look Who's Talking Now 1993, David's Mother (TV film) 1994,

Village of the Damned 1995, It Takes Two 1995, Sticks and Stones 1996, Nevada 1996, For Richer or Poorer 1997, Deconstructing Harry 1997, Toothless 1997, Drop Dead Gorgeous 1999, The Mao Game 1999, Back By Midnight 2002. *Stage appearances include:* Cat on a Hot Tin Roof, Answers. *Television includes:* Cheers 1987–93, Veronica's Closet 1997, Blonde 2001, Salem Witch Trials (mini series) 2002, and numerous other TV films and series. *Address:* Jason Weinberg and Associates, 122 East 25th Street, 2nd Floor, New York, NY 10010, USA.

ALLEYNE, Sir George, Kt, MD, FRCP; Barbadian physician; b. 7 Oct. 1932, Barbados; s. of Clinton Alleyne and Eileen (née Gaskin) Alleyne; m. Sylvan I. Chen 1958; two s. one d.; ed Harrison Coll., Univ. of West Indies; Sr Resident Univ. Hosp. of W Indies 1963; Research Fellow Tropical Metabolism Research Unit, Jamaica 1964–72. Prof. of Medicine W Indies Univ. 1972–81, Chair. Dept of Medicine 1976–81; Head Research Unit Pan American Health Org. 1981–83, Dir Health Programmes 1982–90, Asst Dir 1990–95, Dir 1995–; Hon. DSc (W Indies Univ.) 1988; Order of the Caribbean Community 2001. *Publications include:* The Importance of Health: A Caribbean Perspective 1989, Public Health for All 1991, Health and Tourism 1992; over 100 articles in major scientific research journals. *Leisure interests:* gardening, reading. *Address:* Pan American Health Organization, 525 23rd Street, NW, Washington, DC 20037, USA. *Telephone:* (202) 974-3408. *Fax:* (202) 974-3409.

ALLFORD, Simon, BA, DipArch, RIBA; British architect; b. 27 July 1961, London; s. of the late David Allford and of Margaret Beryl Allford (née Roebuck); ed Hampstead Comprehensive School, Sheffield Univ., The Bartlett School of Architecture, Univ. Coll. London; with Nicholas Grimshaw 1983–85, BDP 1986–89; Partner Allford Hall Monaghan Morris 1989–; lecturer, Univ. Coll. London 1987–; mem. Architectural Asscn Council 1996–, Hon. Sec. 1991–2001, Hon. Treas. 2001–; Chair. RIBA Pres.'s Medals for Architecture; external examiner, visiting lecturer several UK and int. schools; judge various int. competitions; adviser to professional bodies; contrib. to TV and radio programmes; RIBA Award for Architecture 1996, 1998, 1999, 2000, 2001, British Construction Industry Award 2000, 2001, Royal Fine Arts Comm. Award for school bldg 2000, Civic Trust Award 2000, 2001, Housing Design Award 2001. *Leisure interests:* architecture, Sheffield Wednesday Football Club. *Address:* Allford Hall Monaghan Morris, 2nd Floor, Block B, Morelands, 5–23 Old Street, London EC1V 9HL (Office); 232 Bickenhall Mansions, Bickenhall Street, London, W1V 6BW, England (Home). *Telephone:* (20) 7251-5261 (Office); (20) 7487-5391 (Home). *Fax:* (20) 7251-5123 (Office). *E-mail:* sallford@ahmm.co.uk (Office). *Website:* www.ahmm.co.uk (Office).

ALLI, Baron (Life Peer), cr. 1998, of Norbury in the London Borough of Croydon; **Waheed Alli;** British business executive; b. 16 Nov. 1964; ed Norbury Manor School; created Planet 24 Productions Ltd (fmrly 24 Hour Productions) with partner Charlie Parsons, Jt Man. Dir 1992–99; Man. Dir Carlton Productions 1998–2000; Dir Carlton TV 1998–2000; Dir (non-exec.) Chorion 2002–; mem. Teacher Training Agency 1997–98, Panel 2000, Creative Industry Taskforce; mem. Bd English Nat. Ballet 2001–; Dir Shine Entertainment Ltd, Shine M, Castaway TV, Digital Radio Group Ltd. *Address:* House of Lords, London, SW1A 0PW, England (Office).

ALLIALI, Camille Zahakro; Côte d'Ivoirian politician, lawyer and diplomatist; b. 23 Nov. 1926; m.; five c.; ed Dakar Lycée and Lycée Champollion, Grenoble; fmr Advocate, Court of Appeal, Abidjan; Press Sec. Parti Démocratique de la Côte d'Ivoire 1959, Deputy 1958–60; Vice-Pres. Nat. Ass., Ivory Coast 1957–60; Senator of French Community 1959–61; Amb. to France 1961–63; Perm. Del. UNESCO 1961–63; Minister of Foreign Affairs 1963–66; Minister of Justice 1966–83, Minister of State 1983–89; mem. Cen. Cttee of Parti Démocratique de la Côte d'Ivoire (PDCI); Commdr, Légion d'honneur and many other decorations. *Address:* c/o Parti Démocratique de la Côte d'Ivoire, Maison du Parti, Abidjan, Côte d'Ivoire.

ALLIANCE, Sir David, Kt, CBE, CBIM, FRSA; British business executive; b. June 1932; ed Iran; first acquisition, Thomas Hoghton (Oswaldtwistle) 1956; acquired Spirella 1968, then Vantona Ltd, 1975 to form Vantona Group 1975; acquired Carrington Viyella to form Vantona Viyella 1983, Nottingham Mfg 1985, Coats Patons to form Coats Viyella 1986; Group Chief Exec. Coats Viyella 1975–90, Chair. 1989–99; Chair. N. Brown Group 1968–, Tootal Group PLC 1991–99; Gov. Tel-Aviv Univ. 1989–; Hon. Fellow UMIST; Hon. FCGI 1991; Hon. LLD (Manchester) 1989, (Liverpool) 1996; Hon. DSc (Heriot-Watt) 1991. *Address:* N Brown Group, 53 Dale Street, Manchester, M60 6ES, England (Office). *Telephone:* (161) 238-2000 (Office). *Fax:* (161) 238-2020 (Office). *Website:* www.nbrown.co.uk (Office).

ALLIBONE, Thomas Edward, CBE, PhD, DSc, DEng, FRS, FREng; British scientist; b. 11 Nov. 1903, Sheffield; s. of Henry James Allibone and Eliza Allibone; m. Dorothy Margery Boulden, LRAM, ARCM 1931; two d.; ed Cen. School, Sheffield Univ. and Gonville and Caius Coll. Cambridge Univ.; High Voltage Lab. Metropolitan Vickers Co. 1930–44; Univ. of Calif. (British team, Atomic Bomb) 1944–45; Dir Research Lab., Assoc. Electrical Industries, Aldermaston 1946–63; Scientific Adviser to AEI Ltd 1963; Dir Assoc. Electrical Industries (Woolwich) Ltd 1950–63; Chief Scientist, Central Electricity Generating Bd 1963–70; External Prof. of Electrical Eng, Leeds Univ. 1967–79, Prof. Emer. 1979–; Visiting Prof. of Physics, City Univ. 1971–, Robert Kitchin (Sadlers') Research Prof. 1983–, First Frank Poynton Visiting Prof. 1984–; Vice-Pres. Inst. of Physics 1948–52; Chair. Research Cttee, Electrical Research Asscn 1955–62; Vice-Pres. Royal Inst. 1955–57, 1969–72; mem. Council, Physical Soc. 1953–57, Council of Inst. of Electrical Engineers 1937–53, Advisory Council, Royal Mil. Coll., Shrivenham; Pres. Section A British Asscn 1958, Inst. of Information Scientists 1967–69; Trustee, British Museum 1968–75; Hon. FIEE; Hon. DSc; Hon. DEng; Röntgen Medal, British Inst. of Radiology; Thornton and Cooper Hill Medals, Inst. of Electrical Engineers; Melchett Medal, Inst. of Fuel. *Publications:* High Voltage Electrical Phenomena and Thermonuclear Reactions, Release and Use of Atomic Energy, Rutherford, the Father of Nuclear Energy, The Royal Society and Its Dining Clubs; contribution to Lightning and Lightning Protection, Cockcroft and the Atom 1984, Cambridge Physics in the Thirties 1984, The Making of Physicists 1987, Philately and the Royal Society 1990, research papers for Royal Soc. *Leisure interests:* history, archaeology, gardening, handicrafts. *Address:* York Cottage, Lovel Road, Winkfield, Windsor, Berks. SL4 2ES, England. *Telephone:* (1344) 884501.

ALLIES, Bob, MA, DipArch; British architect and lecturer; b. 5 Sept. 1953, Singapore; s. of Edgar Martyn and Lily Maud; m. Jill Franklin; one s. one d.; ed Reading School, Univ. of Edin.; est. Allies and Morrison Architects Co. with Graham Morrison 1983, Partner 1983–; Lecturer Univ. of Cambridge 1984–88, George Simpson Visiting Prof. Univ. of Edin. 1995; Visiting Prof. Univ. of Bath 1996–99; mem. Faculty of Fine Arts, British School of Rome, Italy 1998–; Kea Distinguished Visiting Prof. Univ. of Maryland, USA 1999; Rome Scholar in Architecture 1981–82; Medal for Architecture, Edin. Architectural Asscn 1977. *Architectural works include:* The Clove Bldg (RIBA Award 1991); Pierhead, Liverpool (RIBA Award 1995); Sarum Hall School (RIBA Award 1996); Nunnery Square, Sheffield (RIBA Award 1996); Rosalind Franklin Bldg, Newnham Coll. Cambridge (RIBA Award 1996); British Embassy, Dublin (RIBA Award 1997); Abbey Mills Pumping Station, Stratford (RIBA Award 1997); Rutherford Information Services Bldg, Goldsmiths Coll. London (RIBA Award 1998); Blackburn House (RIBA Award 2000). *Exhibitions include:* New British Architecture (Japan) 1994; Allies and Morrison Retrospective, USA Schools of Architecture (USA) 1996–98. *Publications include:* Model Futures 1983, Allies and Morrison 1996. *Leisure interest:* contemporary music. *Address:* Allies and Morrison, 62 Newman Street, London, W1T 3EE, England (Office). *Telephone:* (20) 7612-7100 (Office). *Fax:* (20) 7612-7101 (Office). *E-mail:* boballies@alliesandmorrison.co.uk (Office). *Website:* www.alliesandmorrison.co.uk (Office).

ALLIMADI, E. Otema; Ugandan politician and diplomatist; b. 11 Feb. 1929, Kitgum; s. of the late Saulo Allimadi and of Susan Allimadi (née Layado); m. Yayina Lalela 1953; one s. three d. (one d. deceased); ed in Uganda; NCO in E African Army Medical Corps 1947–53; mem. Uganda Nat. Congress 1953, Nat. Admin. and Organizing Sec. 1956–59, Sec.-Gen. 1959, later Vice-Chair. Uganda People's Congress; Deputy Perm. Rep. to UN 1964–66; Amb. to USA 1966–71, concurrently Perm. Rep. to UN 1967–71; Minister of Foreign Affairs 1979–80; Prime Minister of Uganda 1980–85; Founder-mem. Uganda People's Congress (UPC), fmr Vice-Chair. *Address:* P.O. Box 40228, Kampala (Home); PO Box Gulu, Gulu District, Uganda. *Telephone:* (41) 285894 (Home).

ALLIOT-MARIE, Michèle Yvette Marie-Thérèse, MA, DenDroit, DenScPol; French politician; b. 10 Sept. 1946, Villeneuve-le-Roi; d. of Bernard Marie and Renée Leyko; ed Faculté de Droit et des Sciences Econ. de Paris, Faculté des Lettres de Paris-Sorbonne, Univ. de Paris I; Asst lecturer Faculté de Droit et des Sciences Econ. de Paris then at Univ. de Paris I 1970–84, Sr Lecturer in Econs and Man. 1984–; Tech. Adviser to Minister of Social Affairs 1972–73, Adviser to Minister of Overseas Territories 1973–74, to Jr Minister for Tourism March–Sept. 1974, Tech. Adviser to Jr Minister for Univs 1974–76, Chef de Cabinet to Jr Minister for Univs then to Minister for Univs 1976–78; Dir, later Prés.-Dir. Gén. UTA-Indemnité 1979–84; adviser on Admin. and Public Service Issues, Rassemblement pour la République (RPR) 1981–84, Asst Sec.-Gen. Legal Advisory Cttee 1984–, mem. Cen. Cttee 1984–, Exec. Cttee 1985–, Nat. Sec. for Educ. and Research 1985–; Deputy for Pyrénées-Atlantiques (RPR) 1986; Sec. of State in charge of schools, Ministry of Educ. 1986–88; Nat. Sec. RPR (Research and Planning) 1988–90, Asst Sec.-Gen. (Foreign Relations) 1990–92; Municipal Councillor for Ciboure 1983–89, for Biarritz 1989–91; Deputy for Pyrénées-Atlantiques 1988–; MEP (UDF-RPR) 1989; Minister for Youth and Sports 1993–95; mem. and First Vice-Pres. Regional Council of Pyrénées-Atlantiques 1995–2001; Mayor of Saint-Jean-de-Luz 1995–2002; Nat. Sec. RPR for Social Affairs 1997–, mem. Political Cttee 1998–, Nat. Sec. in charge of elections Aug. 1999–, Pres. RPR Dec. 1999–2002; Minister of Defence and Veterans 2002–; mem. Political Cttee Alliance pour la France 1998; Pres. Comm. for Defence of Rights and Freedoms 1980–, Foundation for Voluntary Orgs –2000 and many current and fmr offices in women's and children's charitable orgs; Commdr de l'Etoile équatoriale (Gabon), de l'Etoile d'Anjouan (Comoros), du Mérite de l'Educ. Nat. (Côte d'Ivoire), Ordre de la République (Egypt), Palmes Magistrales (First Class) (Peru). *Publications:* L'actionnariat des salariés 1975, La Décision politique: attention une république peut en cacher une autre 1983, La Grande peur des classes moyennes 1996, La République des irresponsables 1999. *Address:* Ministry of Defence, 14 rue St Dominique, 00450 Armées (Office); Assemblée Nationale, 75355 Paris, France (Office). *Telephone:* 1-42-19-35-20 (Office). *Fax:* 1-47-05-40-91 (Office).

ALLISON, Graham Tillett, Jr, MA, PhD; American professor of government and government official; b. 23 March 1940, Charlotte, NC; s. of Graham T. Allison, Sr and Virginia Wright; m. Elisabeth K. Smith 1968; ed Davison Coll. and Harvard and Oxford Univs.; Instr. of Govt, Harvard Univ. 1967–68, Asst Prof. of Govt 1968–70, Assoc. Prof. of Politics 1970–72, Prof. of Politics

1972–93, Assoc. Dean and Chair. Public Policy Program, John F. Kennedy School of Govt 1975–77, Dean and Don K. Price Prof. of Politics, John F. Kennedy School of Govt 1977–89, Douglas Dillon Prof. of Govt, John F. Kennedy School of Govt 1989–; Asst Sec. of Defense for Policy and Plans, Dept of Defense, Washington, DC 1993–94; Dir Belfer Center for Science and Int. Affairs 1994–; numerous professional appts. *Publications include:* Essence of Decision: Explaining the Cuban Missile Crisis 1971, Sharing International Responsibilities: A Report to the Trilateral Commission 1983; co-author: Hawks, Doves and Owls: An Agenda for Avoiding Nuclear War 1985, Fateful Visions: Avoiding Nuclear Catastrophe 1988, Windows of Opportunity: From Cold War to Peaceful Competition 1989, Window of Opportunity: The Grand Bargain for Democracy in the Soviet Union 1991, Beyond Cold War to Trilateral Cooperation in the Asia-Pacific Region (with others) 1992, Avoiding Nuclear Anarchy 1996, Realizing Human Rights: Moving from Inspiration to Impact 2000. *Leisure interests:* fishing, tennis. *Address:* Harvard University, 79 JFK Street, Cambridge, MA 02178 (Office); 69 Pinehurst Road, Belmont, MA 02478-1502, USA (Home). *Telephone:* (617) 496-6099 (Office). *Fax:* (617) 495-1905 (Office).

ALLISON, Richard Clark, BA, LLB; American judge; b. 10 July 1924, New York; s. of Albert F. and Anice (née Clark) Allison; m. Anne Elizabeth Johnston 1950; two s. one d.; ed Univ. of Virginia; called to New York Bar 1948; practised in New York City 1948–52, 1954–55, 1955–; partner law firm Reid & Priest 1961–87; mem. Iran-US Claims Tribunal, The Hague 1988–; mem. ABA (Chair. Cttee Latin American Law 1964–68, Int. Law Section 1976–77, Nat. Inst. on Doing Business in Far East 1972, Int. Legal Exchange Program 1981–85), Int. Bar Asscn (Chair. Conf. 1986, Ethics Cttee 1986–88); mem. Société Int. des Avocats, Inter-American Bar Asscn, American Foreign Law Asscn, American Arbitration Asscn (Int. Panel), Southwestern Legal Foundation, American Soc. of Int. Law, Council on Foreign Relations, American Bar Foundation, Asscn of Bar of City of New York, Inst. for Transnat. Arbitration (Advisory Bd), Raven Soc., SAR, St Andrew's Soc., New York. *Publications:* Protecting Against the Expropriation Risk in Investing Abroad 1988, revised 1998; legal articles. *Address:* Parkweg 13, 2585 JH The Hague, The Netherlands (Office); 224 Circle Drive, Manhasset, New York, NY 11030, USA (Home). *E-mail:* ra.allison@att.net (Office).

ALLISON, Robert J., Jr, BSc; American petroleum executive; m. Carolyn Allison; three c.; ed Kansas Univ.; various sr positions with Amoco Production Co. 1959–73; Vice-Pres. of Operations, Anadarko Production Co. 1973–76, mem. Bd of Dirs. 1976–, Pres. 1976–79, CEO 1979–, Chair. 1986–; mem. Bd of Dirs American Petroleum Inst., US Oil & Gas Asscn; mem. Nat. Petroleum Council, Soc. of Petroleum Engineers, Natural Gas Supply Asscn; Dir Freeport-McMoRan Copper & Gold; mem. All-American Wildcatters 1991–, Chair. 1999–2000; Assoc. mem. Univ. Cancer Foundation, Univ. of Texas M. D. Anderson Cancer Center; Trustee United Way of Texas Gulf Coast; Dir Spindletop (fmr Pres. and Chair.); mem. Bd of Dirs N. Harris Montgomery Community Coll. Dist Foundation, Sam Houston Area Council, Boy Scouts of America. *Address:* Anadarko Petroleum Corporation, 17001 Northchase Drive, Houston, TX 77060, USA (Office). *Website:* www.anadarko.com (Office).

ALLMAND, Warren, PC, QC; Canadian politician; b. 19 Sept. 1932, Montreal; s. of Harold W. Allmand and Rose Irene McMorrow; one s. two d.; ed Loyola High School, Montreal, St Francis Xavier Univ., NS, McGill Univ., Montreal, Univ. of Paris; called to Quebec Bar 1958, Ont. Bar 1976, Yukon and NWT Bars 1976; mem. Parl. for Montreal-NDG 1965–93, Minister for Indian and Northern Affairs 1976–77, for Consumer and Corp. Affairs 1977–79; Solicitor-Gen. 1972–76; mem. Exec. World Federalists of Canada 1960–65; Int. Pres. Parliamentarians for Global Action 1984–91; Pres. Int. Centre for Human Rights and Democratic Devt 1997–2002; mem. Quebec Bar Asscn, Liberal Party; Hon. LLD (St Francis Xavier Univ., NS), (St Thomas Univ., NB) 1998. *Leisure interests:* hockey, long-distance running, skiing, tennis. *Address:* 1001 De Maisonneuve East, 1100 Montréal, Québec, H2L 4P9, Canada (Office). *Telephone:* (514) 283-6073 (Office). *Fax:* (514) 283-3792 (Office).

ALLOUACHE, Merzak; Algerian film director; b. 6 Oct. 1944, Algiers; s. of Omar Allouache and Fatma Allouache; m. Lazib Anissa 1962; one d.; worked in Nat. Inst. of Cinema, Algiers, later in Inst. of Film, Paris; after return to Algeria worked as Adviser, Ministry of Culture; Silver Prize, Moscow Festival; Tanit D'Or Prize, Carthage 1979. *Films include:* Our Agrarian Revolution (documentary) 1973, Omar Gatlato, Les aventures d'un héros, L'homme qui regardait les fenêtres 1982. *Address:* Cité des Asphodèles, Bt D15, 183 Ben Aknoun, Algiers, Algeria. *Telephone:* 79 33 60.

ALMODÓVAR, Pedro; Spanish film director; b. 25 Sept. 1951, La Mancha; fronted a rock band; worked at Telefónica for ten years; started career with full-length super-8 films; made 16mm. short films, including Salome 1978–83. *Films include:* Pepe, Luci, Bom y otras montón, Laberinto de pasiones 1980, Dark Habits 1983, What Have I Done to Deserve This? 1985, Matador 1986, Law of Desire 1987, Women on the Verge of a Nervous Breakdown 1988 (Felix Award 1988), Tie Me Up, Tie Me Down 1990, Tacones Lejanos 1991, Kika 1993, The Flower of My Secret 1996, Live Flesh 1997, All About My Mother (Acad. Award for Best Foreign Language Film) 1999, Talk to Her (BAFTA Award for Best Film not in the English language 2003, Acad. Award for Best Original Screenplay 2003) 2002. *Publications:* Fuego en las entrañas 1982,

The Patty Diphusa Stories and Other Writings 1992. *Address:* c/o El Deseo SA, Ruiz Perelló 15, Madrid 28028, Spain; Miramax Films, 18 E 48th Street, New York, NY 10017, USA.

ALMOND, Lincoln Carter, LLB; American lawyer and politician; b. 1936, Central Falls, RI; ed Boston Univ.; called to RI Bar 1962; Admin. Town of Lincoln, RI 1963–67; US Attorney, RI Dept of Justice, Providence 1967–78, 1981–93; pvt. law practice 1967–69, 1978–81; Pres. Blackstone Valley Devt Foundation 1993–95; Gov. of Rhode Island 1995–2003. *Address:* c/o Office of the Governor, 222 State House, Providence, RI 02903-1196, USA.

ALMUNIA AMANN, Joaquín; Spanish politician; b. 1948, Bilbao; m.; two c.; ed Univ. of Deusto; economist, various Spanish chambers of commerce in mem. countries of EEC; econ. adviser to Exec. Cttee, Unión General de Trabajo; Sec. for trade union relations, then Head of Dept of Research and Planning, then Head of Perm. Cttee for Political Man., Partido Socialista Obrero Español 1981, Sec.-Gen. 1997–2000; Minister of Labour and Social Security 1982–86; Minister of Public Admin. 1987–91; Pres. Socialist Parl. Group 1994–2000, Budget Cttee Congreso de los Diputados 2000. *Publication:* Memorias Políticas 2001. *Address:* Carrera de San Jerónimo, s/n 28014 Madrid, Spain. *E-mail:* joaquin.almunia@diputado.congreso.esp (Office). *Website:* www.almunia.com (Office).

ALOMAR, Raphael; French business executive; b. 28 July 1941, Tourcoing; s. of Raphaël Alomar and Jeanne Alomar (née Broutin); m. Nicole Labrunie 1964; three s.; ed Sorbonne, Paris, Ecole des Hautes Etudes Commerciales and Ecole Nationale d'Admin. (ENA); Sec.-Gen. Etablissements Broutin 1966–69; Adviser to Gen. Man. Société Générale 1969–86; Prof. of Corp. Financial Man., ENA 1974–82, Pres. Alumni Assen 1984–86, mem. Bd Dirs 1987–; Assoc. Gen. Man. Cie de Navigation Mixte and of Via Banque 1986–93; Gov. Council of Europe Devt Bank 1993–; Officier, Légion d'honneur, Commdr Order of Isabella the Catholic, Commdr, Order of the Lion of Finland. *Publication:* Financing Business Development 1981. *Address:* Council of Europe Development Bank, 55 avenue Kléber, 75116 Paris, France (Office). *Website:* www.coebank.org/ (Office).

ALONEFTIS, Andreas P., MBA, FAIA; Cypriot business executive and government official; b. 24 Aug. 1945, Nicosia; s. of Polycarpos Aloneftis and Charitini Aloneftis; m. Nedi Georghiades 1967; one s. one d.; ed New York Inst. of Finance Coll. of New York Stock Exchange, Southern Methodist Univ., Dallas, Tex., Harvard Univ., Boston, Mass., USA, Henley Management Coll., UK; served Nat. Guard 1964–66; studied finance and accountancy in UK; served 16 years in Cyprus Devt Bank; Gen. Man. and Chief Exec. Officer, Cyprus Investment and Securities Corpn Ltd (CISCO) 1982–88; Minister of Defence 1988–93; Gen. Man. ALICO (Cyprus) 1993–95; Man. Dir CYPRI-ALIFE Ltd 1995–99; Gen. Man. Insurance, Cyprus Popular Bank Group 1999–; Open Fellowship, Southern Methodist Univ. 1978, Salzburg Seminar Fellow 1984. *Address:* Cyprus Popular Bank, 154 Limassol Avenue, P.O. Box 22032, 1598 Nicosia (Office); 10 Kastellorizo Street, Aglantzia, 2108 Nicosia, Cyprus (Home). *Telephone:* (2) 811560 (Office); (2) 811562 (Office); (2) 333733 (Home). *Fax:* (2) 811487 (Office); (2) 331748 (Home). *E-mail:* alonefan@ cytanet.com.cy (Office).

ALONI, Shulamit; Israeli politician and lawyer; b. 1929, Tel Aviv; three s.; participated in the defence of Jerusalem during the War of Independence; worked as a teacher; columnist for several newspapers; producer of radio programmes dealing with legislation and legal procedures; f. Israel Consumers' Council, Chair. for four years; joined Mapai 1959; mem. Knesset (Labour) 1965–69; f. Civil Rights Movt (CRM) 1973, CRM Minister without Portfolio June–Oct. 1974, CRM leader and MK 1974–, served on numerous cttees.; Minister of Educ. (representing the Meretz coalition) 1992, of Communications, Science and Tech. 1993–96; mem. Meretz (coalition party). *Publications include:* The Citizen and His/Her Country, The Rights of the Child in Israel, The Arrangement – A State of Law and Not a State of Religion, Women as People. *Leisure interests:* reading, theatre, tennis. *Address:* c/o Ministry of Communications, 23 Yaffo Street, Jerusalem 91999, Israel. *E-mail:* intmocil@ moc.gov.il (Office).

ALONSO, Alicia; Cuban ballet dancer, choreographer and ballet director; b. 21 Dec. 1920, Havana; d. of Antonio Martínez and Ernestina del Hoyo; m. 1st Fernando Alonso 1937; m. 2nd Pedro Simón 1975; one s. one d.; ed Ballet School of Sociedad Pro–Arte Musical, Havana, School of American Ballet, USA; mem. American Ballet Caravan 1938–39, American Ballet Theater 1940–41, 1943–48, 1950–55, 1958–60, Ballet Russe, Monte Carlo 1955–59; danced with Greek Theatre, LA, Calif. 1957–59, Washington Ballet 1958; Guest Artist, Teatro Colón, Buenos Aires 1958, Kirov and Bolshoi Ballets 1958, Royal Danish Ballet 1959, Paris Opera 1972, Rome Opera 1987; Founder, Prima Ballerina Assoluta, Choreographer and Gen. Dir Nat. Ballet of Cuba 1948–(99); has staged her versions of the maj. romantic and classical ballets in Paris, Rome, Milan, Naples, Vienna, Mexico, Sofia and Prague; mem. jury several int. ballet competitions, Advisory Council, Ministry of Culture and Nat. Cttee of Writers, Artists' Union of Cuba, Kennedy Center Artistic Cttee, Washington, DC; many awards including Dance Magazine Annual Award 1958, Grand Prix of Paris 1966, 1970, Anna Pavlova Award, Univ. of Dance, Paris 1966, Gold Medal of Barcelona Liceo 1971, Annual Award of Gran Teatro de La Habana 1985; several honours including Hero of Work, Cuba, Order Félix Varela, Cuba, Order Aguila Azteca, Mexico, Order Isabel la Católica, Spain, Commdr des Arts et des Lettres. *Publication:* Dialogues with the Dance 1988. *Leisure interests:* films, music, scientific discoveries. *Address:* National Ballet of Cuba, Calzada No. 510 entre D y E, C.P. 10400, El Vedado, Havana, Cuba. *Telephone:* (7) 55-2948. *Fax:* (7) 33-3317.

ALPER, Howard, OC, PhD, FRSC; Canadian professor of chemistry; b. 17 Oct. 1941, Montreal; s. of Max Alper and Frema Alper; m. Anne Fairhurst 1966; two d.; ed Sir George Williams Univ. and McGill Univ.; NATO Postdoctoral Fellow, Princeton Univ. 1967–68; Asst Prof. State Univ. of New York at Binghamton 1968–71, Assoc. Prof. 1971–74; Assoc. Prof. Univ. of Ottawa 1975–77, Prof. 1977–, Chair. Dept of Chem. 1982–85, 1988–91, 1991–94, Asst Vice-Pres. (Research) 1995–96, Vice-Pres. (Research) 1997–2002; titular mem. European Acad. of Arts, Sciences and Humanities; Guggenheim Fellowship 1985–86; Killam Research Fellow 1986–88; Pres. RSC 2001–03; Chemical Inst. of Canada Inorganic Chem. Award 1980, Catalysis Award 1984, Alfred Bader Award in Organic Chemistry 1990, Commemorative Medal (125th Anniversary of Canada) 1992, E. W. R. Steacie Award 1993, Urgel-Archambault Prize in Physical Sciences, Math. and Eng (ACFAS) 1996, Chemical Inst. of Canada Medal 1997, Bell Canada Forum Award 1998, Gerhard Herzberg Gold Medal in Science and Eng 2000, Le Sever Memorial Award 2002. *Publications:* more than 440 papers and more than 30 patents in the area of organometallic chemistry and catalysis. *Address:* Department of Chemistry, University of Ottawa, Ottawa, Ont. K1N 6N5, Canada. *Telephone:* (613) 562-5189. *Fax:* (613) 562-5871.

ALPERT, Herb; American musician; b. 31 March 1935, Los Angeles; s. of Louis Alpert and Tillie Goldberg; m. 1st Sharon Mae Lubin 1956 (divorced); two c.; m. 2nd Lani Hall; one d.; ed Univ. of Southern Calif.; Co-owner and fmr Pres. A&M Record Co., Co-Chair. 1962–94, Almo Sounds 1994–; Leader, trumpeter, arranger, music group, Tijuana Brass 1962–; concert appearances include Atlanta Symphony 1988, Philharmonic Orchestra of Florida, Miami 1988. *Recordings include:* Fandango, Magic Man, Beat of the Brass, Lonely Bull, Solid Brass, South of the Border, What Now My Love, Whipped Cream, Wild Romance, Keep Your Eye on Me, Under a Spanish Moon, Second Wind 1996, Colors 1999. *Address:* c/o Herb Alpert Foundation, 1414 Sixth Street, Santa Monica, CA 90401, USA.

ALPERT, Joseph Stephen, MD; American professor of medicine; b. 1 Feb. 1942, New Haven, Conn.; s. of Zelly C. Alpert and Beatrice A. Kopsofsky; m. Helle Mathiasen 1965; one s. one d.; ed Yale and Harvard Univs; Instructor in Medicine, Peter Bent Brigham Hosp., Harvard Univ. 1973–74; Lieut-Commdr U.S. Navy, Dir Coronary Care Unit, San Diego Naval Hospital and Asst Prof. of Medicine, Univ. of Calif., San Diego 1974–76; Dir Levine Cardiac Unit and Asst Prof. of Medicine, Peter Bent Brigham Hospital and Harvard Univ. 1976–78; Dir Div. of Cardiovascular Medicine and Prof. of Medicine, Univ. of Mass. Medical School 1978–92, Vice-Chair. Medicine Dept 1990–; Budnitz Prof. of Cardiovascular Medicine 1988–92; Prof., Chair. of Medicine Dept Ariz. Univ. 1992–; Fulbright Fellow, Copenhagen 1963–64; U.S. Public Health Service Fellow, Harvard and Copenhagen 1966–67; Nat. Inst. of Health Special Fellow, Harvard 1972–74; Fellow, American Coll. of Physicians, American Coll. of Cardiology (Trustee 1996–2001), American Heart Assen Clinical Council (Vice-Chair. 1991–92, Chair. 1993–95), American Coll. of Chest Physicians; Gold Medal of Univ. of Copenhagen and other awards. *Publications include:* The Heart Attack Handbook 1978, Physiopathology of the Cardiovascular System 1984, Modern Coronary Care 1990, Diagnostic Atlas of the Heart 1994, Valvular Heart Disease 2000; co-author of other books and author of more than 400 articles in scientific journals. *Leisure interests:* poetry, music, swimming, cycling, cooking, travel. *Address:* 1501 North Campbell Avenue, Tucson, AZ 85724-0001 (Office); 3440 E Cathedral Rock Circle, Tucson, AZ 85718, USA (Home). *Telephone:* (520) 626-6102 (Office). *Fax:* (520) 626-2919. *E-mail:* jalpert@u.arizona.edu (Office).

ALSOP, William Allen, OBE, RA, FRSA; British architect; b. 12 Dec. 1947, Northampton; s. of Francis Alsop and Brenda Hight; m. Sheila Bean 1972; two s. one d.; ed Architectural Assen; teacher of Sculpture St Martin's Coll.; worked with Cedric Price; fmrly in practice with John Lyall; designed a ferry terminal in Hamburg; undertook design work on the Cardiff barrage; conducted feasibility studies to recycle the fmr De Lorean car factory in Belfast; designed a govt bldg for Marseilles; est. own practice, collaborates with Bruce Maclean in producing architectural drawings; projects include N. Greenwich Station (with John Lyall) 2000, Peckham Library and Media Centre (Stirling Prize) 2000; commissioned to design Fourth Grace, Liverpool 2002–; Prin. Alsop & Störmer Architects 1979–2000; Prin., Dir and Chair. Alsop Architects 2001–; Chair. Architecture Foundation 2001–; Hon. LLD (Leicester) 1996; Dr hc (Nottingham Trent), (Sheffield). *Publications:* City of Objects 1992, William Alsop Buildings and Projects 1992, William Alsop Architect: Four Projects 1993, Will Alsop and Jan Störmer, Architects 1993, Le Grand Bleu-Marseille 1994, Alsop and Störmer: Selected and Current Works 1999, Will Alsop Book 1 1968–1990. *Leisure interest:* fishing. *Address:* Parkgate Studio, 41 Parkgate Road, London, SW11 4NP (Office); 72 Pembroke Road, London, W8 6NX, England (Home). *Telephone:* (20) 7978-7878 (Office); (20) 7602-4811 (Home). *Fax:* (20) 7978-7879 (Office). *E-mail:* walsop@alsoparchitects.com (Office); willalsop@hotmail.com (Home). *Website:* www.alsoparchitects.com (Office).

ALSTON, Richard Kenneth Robert, BCom, MBA, LLM; Australian politician; b. 19 Dec. 1941; m.; two c.; ed Xavier Coll., Melbourne, Melbourne and Monash Univs; Senator for Vic. 1986–; Shadow Minister for Communications 1989–90, for Social Security, Child Care and Retirement Incomes 1990–92, for

Social Security, Child Care and Superannuation 1992, for Superannuation and Child Care and Shadow Minister Assisting Leader on Social Policy 1992–93, for Communications and the Arts 1994–96; Minister for Communications and the Arts March 1996–, for Information Tech. 1998–; Deputy Leader of Opposition in Senate 1993–96, of Govt in Senate 1996–; Deputy Chair. Senate Standing Cttee on Legal and Constitutional Affairs 1986, Jt Parl. Cttee on Nat. Crime Authority 1987; mem. Senate Standing Cttee on Finance and Public Admin. 1987; State Pres. Liberal Party Vic. Div. 1979–82; mem. Amnesty Int. Parl. Group; Nat. Chair. Australian Council for Overseas Aid 1978–83; Chair. Afghan-Australia Council 1987–90; Fed. Pres. UNA of Australia 1977–79; Gov. Nat. Gallery of Australia Foundation; Fellow Inst. of Dirs 1983–88. *Leisure interests:* Aboriginal art, modern literature, Oriental rugs, jogging, reading, pumping iron. *Address:* Parliament House, Canberra, ACT 2600, Australia.

ALSTON, Robert John, BA, CMG; British diplomatist (retd); b. 10 Feb. 1938; s. of Arthur William Alston and Rita Alston; m. Patricia Claire Essex 1969; one s. one d.; ed Ardingly Coll., New Coll., Oxford; joined HM Diplomatic Service 1961, Third Sec. Kabul 1963, Eastern Dept Foreign Office 1966, Head of Computer Study Team FCO 1969, First Sec., Econ., Paris 1971, First Sec. and Head of Chancery, Tehran 1974, Asst Head, Energy, Science and Space Dept, FCO 1977, Head, Jt Nuclear Unit, FCO 1978, Political Counsellor, UK Del. to NATO 1981, Head of Defence Dept, FCO 1984; Amb. to Oman 1986–90; seconded to Home Civil Service 1990–92; Asst Under Sec. (Public Depts.), FCO 1992–94; High Commr to New Zealand, to Western Samoa (non-res.) 1994–98; Gov. of Pitcairn 1994–98; Trustee Antarctic Heritage Trust 1998–; Chair. Link Foundation for UK–NZ Relations 1999; Kent Amb. 1999; Adviser, Int. Trade and Investment Missions Ltd 1999–; Dir Romney Resource Centre 2000 1999–; Consultant on Anglican Communion affairs to Archbishop of Canterbury 1999–2003. *Leisure interests:* gardening, reading, listening to music. *Address:* 16 Carlisle Mansions, Carlisle Place, London, SW1P 1HX, England.

ALTBACH, Philip, G., PhD; American professor of education; b. 3 May 1941; s. of Milton Altbach and Josephine Huebsch; m. Edith Hoshino 1962; two s.; ed Univ. of Chicago; Lecturer on Educ., Harvard Univ. 1965–67; Asst Prof., Assoc. Prof. Dept of Educational Policy Studies, Univ. of Wisconsin-Madison 1967–75; Prof. Dept of Educational Org., Admin. and Policy, State Univ. of New York, Buffalo 1975, Chair. 1985–88, Dir Comparative Educ. Center 1978–94, Chair. Dept of Social Foundations 1978–82, Adjunct Prof. School of Information and Library Studies 1982, Adjunct Prof. Dept of Sociology 1991; Project Dir Nat. Science Foundation study of higher educ. in newly industrialising countries 1988–90; Prof. School of Educ., Boston Coll. 1994–, J. Donald Monan SJ Prof. of Higher Educ. 1996–; Dir Centre for Int. Higher Educ. 1995–; Fulbright Research Prof. Univ. of Bombay 1968; Visiting Prof. Moscow State Univ. 1982, Univ. of Malaya 1983, School of Educ. Stanford Univ. 1988–89; Visiting Fellow, Hoover Inst., Stanford Univ. 1988–89; mem. numerous professional socs; Consultant, Rockefeller Foundation; Sr Assoc. Carnegie Foundation for the Advancement of Teaching 1992–96; lecturer at many int. confs and seminars. *Publications:* N American Ed. of Higher Education 1996–, Educational Policy 1989–; author or co-author of numerous books, book chapters, articles in professional journals etc. *Address:* Boston College, 207 Campion Hall, Chestnut Hill, MA 02467, USA (Office). *E-mail:* altbach@bc.edu (Office).

ALTHER, Lisa, BA; American writer, reviewer and university professor; b. 23 July 1944, Kingsport, Tenn.; d. of John Shelton Reed and Alice Greene Reed; m. Richard Alther 1966 (divorced); one d.; ed Wellesley Coll., Radcliffe Coll.; editorial Asst Atheneum Publrs., New York 1967–68; freelance writer 1968–; lecturer, St Michael's Coll., Winooski, Vt 1980–81; Prof and Basler Chair. East Tenn. State Univ. 1999–. *Publications:* Kinflicks 1975, Original Sins 1980, Other Women 1984, Bedrock 1990, Birdman and the Dancer 1993, Five Minutes in Heaven 1995. *Address:* 1086 Silver Street, Hinesburg, VT 05461, USA. *Telephone:* (802) 482-3141. *Fax:* (802) 482-3141. *E-mail:* lalther@aol.com.

ALTMAN, Robert B.; American director, writer and producer; b. 20 Feb. 1925, Kansas City; m. 3rd Kathryn Reed; two s. (also two s. one d. from two previous marriages); ed Univ. of Missouri; mem. Dirs Guild of America; Owner Sandcastle 5 Productions; Hon. Golden Berlin Bear Award 2002. *Films include:* The Delinquents 1955, The James Dean Story 1957, Nightmare in Chicago 1964, Countdown 1968, That Cold Day in the Park 1969, M*A*S*H 1970, Brewster McCloud 1971, McCabe and Mrs. Miller 1972, Images 1972, The Long Goodbye 1973, Thieves Like Us 1973, California Split 1974, Nashville 1975, Buffalo Bill and the Indians 1976, Welcome to LA 1977, The Late Show 1977, Three Women 1977, A Wedding 1979, Remember My Name 1979, Quintet 1979, A Perfect Couple 1979, Rich Kids 1979, Popeye 1980, Health 1980, The Easter Egg Hunt 1981, Come Back to the Five and Dime, Jimmy Dean, Jimmy Dean 1982, Secret Honor 1984, Fool for Love 1986, Aria (Segment) 1987, Beyond Therapy 1987, Vincent and Theo 1990 (also TV), The Player 1991, Short Cuts 1992, Prêt à Porter 1994; producer: Mrs Parker and the Vicious Circle 1995, Kansas City, The Gingerbread Man 1998, The Cookie Fortune 1998; TV: The Laundromat 1984, The Dumb Waiter 1987, The Room 1987, The Caine Mutiny Court Martial 1987, Tanner '88 (co-Dir), Dr. T. and the Women 1999, Gosford Park (Golden Globe Award for Best Dir 2002, Best Film, Evening Standard, British Film Awards 2002, Best Dir, Best Film Silver Ribbon award 2002) 2001. *Television work includes:* Bonanza, Kraft Theatre, Bus Stop, Combat, Cannes Film Festival Grand Prize for M*A*S*H.

Achievements (miscellaneous): British Film Inst. Fellowship. *Address:* ICM, 8942 Wilshire Boulevard, Beverly Hills, CA 90211-1934 (Office); Sandcastle 5 Productions, 502 Park Avenue, Suite 15G, New York, NY 10022-1108, USA.

ALTMAN, Stuart Harold, PhD; American professor of health; b. 8 Aug. 1937, Bronx, New York; s. of Sidney Altman and Florence Altman; m. Diane Kleinberg 1959; three d.; ed City Coll. of New York and Univ. of California, Los Angeles; Labor Market Economist, Fed. Reserve Bd 1962–64; Econ. Consultant and Manpower Economist, Office of Asst Sec. of Defense, Washington, DC 1964–66; Asst Prof. of Econs, Brown Univ. 1966–68, Assoc. Prof. 1968–70; Univ. Fellow and Dir of Health Studies, Urban Inst. 1970–71; Deputy Admin., Office of Health, Cost of Living Council, Dept of Health, Educ. and Welfare 1973–74, Deputy Asst Sec. for Planning and Evaluation (Health) 1971–76; Visiting Lecturer, Graduate School of Public Policy, Univ. of Calif., Berkeley 1976–77; Sol C. Chaikin Prof. of Nat. Health Policy, Heller School, Brandeis Univ. 1977–, Dean 1977; Chair. Prospective Payment Assessment Comm., US Congress 1984–96; mem. NAS Inst. of Medicine (mem. Governing Council 1982–83), Bd Robert Wood Johnson Clinical Scholars, Bd Beth Israel Hosp., Brookline, Mass. 1979–. *Publications:* The Growing Physician Surplus: Will it Benefit or Bankrupt the U.S. Health System 1982, Ambulatory Care: Problems of Cost and Access (with others) 1983, Will the Medicare Prospective Payment System Succeed? Technical Adjustments Can Make the Difference 1986, Competition and Compassion: Conflicting Roles for Public Hospitals 1989, and other publs. *Leisure interests:* sailing, cross-country skiing, boating, tennis, golf. *Address:* Schneider Institute for Health Policy, Heller Graduate School, POB 549110, Brandeis University, Waltham, MA 02254; 11 Bakers Hill Road, Weston, MA 02493, USA (Home). *Telephone:* (617) 736-3803 (Office); (617) 988-9144 (Home). *E-mail:* altman@brandeis.edu (Office).

ALTON, Roger Martin; British journalist; b. 20 Dec. 1947, Oxford; s. of Reggie Alton and Jeanine Alton; m. (divorced); one d.; ed Clifton Coll., Exeter Coll., Oxford; grad. trainee Liverpool Post, then Gen. Reporter and Deputy Features Ed. 1969–74; Sub-Ed. News The Guardian 1974–76, Chief Sub-Ed. News 1976–81, Deputy Sports Ed. 1981–85, Arts Ed. 1985–90, Weekend Magazine Ed. 1990–93, Features Ed. 1993–96, Asst Ed. 1996–98, Ed. The Observer 1998–; Ed. of the Year, What the Papers Say Awards 2000. *Leisure interests:* mountaineering, skiing, films. *Address:* Office of the Editor, The Observer, 119 Farringdon Road, London, EC1R 3ER, England (Office). *Telephone:* (20) 7713-4744 (Office). *Fax:* (20) 7713-4250 (Office). *E-mail:* editor@observer.co.uk (Office). *Website:* www.observer.co.uk (Office).

ALVA, Dinkar Shanker, BSc, BSc(TECH.); Indian industrialist; b. 2 July 1933, Mangalore, Karnataka; s. of the late Shanker Alva and Kamala Alva; m. Shashikala Alva 1960; one s. one d.; ed Madras Univ.; Asst Weaving Master, Delhi Cloth and Gen. Mills Ltd 1954–58; Industrial Consultant IBCON Pvt. Ltd 1958–60; Sales Exec. Bombay Dyeing and Mfg Co. Ltd 1960–66, Gen. Man. (Sales) 1969–74, Sales Dir 1974–75, Dir 1976–79, Pres. 1979–88, Man. Dir 1988–98; Gen. Man. Anglo-French Textiles Ltd 1966–69; Dir V.T.C. Industries Ltd, Hindustan SPG and WUG Mills Ltd, Banswara Syntex Ltd, Sanghi Polyesters Ltd, Indian Cotton Mills Fed.; Chair. Cotton Textile Export Promotion Council; mem., Man. Cttee All India Exporters' Chamber. *Leisure interests:* music, reading, tennis. *Address:* 18-B L.D. Ruparel Marg, Mumbai 400006, India (Home). *Telephone:* (22) 3695419 (Home). *Fax:* (22) 3695420 (Home). *E-mail:* dinkaralva@hotmail.com (Home).

ALVA CASTRO, Luis; Peruvian politician and economist; b. Trujillo; ed Universidad Nacional de Trujillo; fmr Dir Corporación de Desarrollo Económico y Social de la Libertad; Deputy for Libertad; has held various posts in Partido Aprista Peruano (now Alianza Popular Revolucionaria Americana) including Sec.-Gen. of Northern Regional Org., mem. Political Comm. and Nat. Sec. for Electoral Matters; Chair. Nat Planning Comm. of Partido Aprista Peruano; Second Vice-Pres. of Repub. 1985–90, Pres. Council of Ministers (Prime Minister) and Minister of Economy and Finance 1985–87. *Publications:* La Necesidad del Cambio, Manejo Presupuestal del Perú, En Defensa del Pueblo, Endeudamiento Externo del Perú, Deuda Externa: Un reto para los Latinoamericanos and other books and essays. *Address:* c/o Alianza Popular Revolucionaria Americana, Avenida Alfonso Ugarte 1012, Lima 5, Peru.

ALVAREZ, Aida, BA; American politician; b. Aguadilla, Puerto Rico; ed Harvard Univ.; fmr news reporter, presenter Metromedia TV, NY; fmr reporter NY Post; fmr mem. NY City Charter revision Comm.; fmr Vice-Pres. NY City Health and Hospitals Corp.; investment banker First Boston Corpn NY, San Francisco 1986–93; Dir Office Fed. Housing Enterprise Oversight 1993–97; Dir Small Business Admin. 1997–2001; fmr mem. Bd Dirs. Nat. Hispanic Leadership Agenda, NY Community Trust, Nat. Civic League; fmr Chair. Bd Municipal Assistance Corp./Victim Services Agency, NY; NY State Chair. Gore Presidential Campaign 1988; Nat. Co-Chair. Women's Cttee Clinton Presidential Campaign 1992; mem. Pres. Econ. Transition Team 1992; Hon. LLD (Iona Coll.) 1985; Front Page Award 1982, Assoc. Press Award for Excellence 1982. *Address:* 75 East Wayne Avenue, Apt W404, Silver Spring, MD 20901-4263, USA (Home).

ALVAREZ, Carlos Alberto (Chacho); Argentine politician; b. 26 Dec. 1948, Balvanera; m. Liliana Chiernajowsky; one s. three d.; ed Mariano Acosta Coll.; Assessor Regional Econ. Cttee. of Nat. Senate 1983–89; elected Deputy to Nat. Ass. for Fed. Capital 1989–93; left Partido Justicialista and f. Partido Movimiento por la Democracia y la Justicia Social (MODEJUSO) 1990; f. Frente Grande; Pres. Frente Grande Bloc in Nat. Constitutional Convention

1994; Founder, Leader Frente del País Solidario—FREPASO 1994–; Vice-Pres. of Argentina 1999–2000. *Address:* c/o Frente del País Solidario—FREPASO, Edificio Anexo, Oficina 022, Planta Baja, Buenos Aires, Argentina (Office). *Telephone:* (11) 4370-7100 (Office). *E-mail:* contacto@chachoalvarez .com.ar (Office); chacho@sion.net (Office). *Website:* www.chachoalvarez.com .ar (Office).

ALVAREZ, Mario Roberto; Argentine architect; b. 14 Nov. 1913, Buenos Aires; m. Jorgelina Ortiz de Rosas 1953; one s. one d.; ed Colegio Nacional, Buenos Aires and Univ. of Buenos Aires; in pvt. practice, Buenos Aires 1937–, as Mario Roberto Alvarez and Assocs. 1947–; architect, Ministry of Public Works 1937–42; municipal architect, Avellaneda 1942–47; adviser, Secr. of Public Works, City of Buenos Aires 1958–62; Sec. to World Football Cup Stadium Comm., Buenos Aires 1972–78; Vice-Pres. Cen. Soc. of Architects 1953–55; exhibited, São Paulo Bienal 1957 and several other exhbns. of Argentine architecture in Buenos Aires and abroad; Hon. Fellow, American Inst. of Architects; Dr. hc (La Plata) 1982; Great Prize of the Nat. Fund of Arts 1976; prizewinner in numerous int. architectural competitions; Hon. mem. Inst. of City Planning, Peru 1979. *Address:* Mario Roberto Alvarez y Asociados, Solis 370, Buenos Aires, Argentina. *Website:* www .mariorobertoalvarez.com.ar (Office).

ALVAREZ ARMELLINO, Gen. Gregorio Conrado; Uruguayan politician and army officer; b. 26 Nov. 1925, Montevideo; s. of Gen. Gregorio Alvarez Lezama and Bianca Armellino de Alvarez Lezama; m. María del Rosario Flores 1978; one d.; ed José Pedro Varela High School and Uruguay Mil. Coll.; Officer, Cavalry Regt 1946–59; Head of Cavalry Operations Training, Mil. Coll. 1960–62; Chief of Republican Guard 1962–79; promoted to Gen. 1971; Joint Chief of Staff 1971–79; First Sec. Council of Nat. Security 1973–74; 4th Div. Army Commander 1974–78; C-in-C of the Army 1978–79; retd from armed forces 1979; Pres. of Uruguay 1981–84; various military decorations. *Leisure interests:* horse-riding, fishing, hunting.

ÁLVAREZ MARTÍNEZ, H.E. Cardinal Francisco; Spanish ecclesiastic; b. 14 July 1925, Santa Eulalia de Ferroñes; ordained priest 1950; Bishop of Tarazona 1973; Bishop of Calahorra and La Calzada 1976–89, of Orihuela 1989–95; Archbishop of Toledo 1995–; cr. Cardinal 2001. *Address:* Arco de Palacio 3, 45001 Toledo, Spain (Office). *Telephone:* (25) 224100 (Office); (25) 223439 (Home). *Fax:* (25) 222639 (Office); (25) 222771 (Home).

ALVAREZ RENDUELES, José Ramón, LLM, PhD; Spanish central banker and university professor; b. 17 June 1940, Gijón; s. of Ramón Alvarez Medina; m. Eugenia Villar 1964; four s. one d; State Economist 1964; rank of Full Prof. in Public Finance 1973; Head of Econ. Studies in Planning Comm. 1969; Dir Inst. of Econ. Devt 1973; Tech. Sec.-Gen. Ministry of Finance 1973–75, Under-Sec. for Econ. Affairs 1975–76; Sec. of State for Econ. Affairs 1977–78; Gov. Bank of Spain 1978–84; Chair. COFIR 1988–93, Productos Pirelli 1986–, Peugeot España 1996, Aceralia 1997–; Pres. Prince of Asturias Foundation 1996–; Vice Chair. Arcelor. *Publications:* Valoración actual de la imposición sobre consumo 1971, La Hacienda pública y el medio ambiente 1973. *Leisure interests:* golf, music, literature, lawn tennis. *Address:* Pegueriros 12-F, 28035, Madrid, Spain (Home). *Telephone:* (91) 5969527 (Office). *Fax:* (91) 5969366 (Office). *E-mail:* arendueles@aceralia.es (Office).

ALVEAR VALENZUELA, Soledad; Chilean politician and lawyer; b. 1951; m. Gutemberg Martinez; four c.; ed Univ. of Chile Law School, Latin American Inst. of Social Studies; Minister of Nat. Women's Service (SERNAM) 1991–94, of Justice 1994, of Foreign Affairs 2000–; fmr Prof. Law Faculty, Cen. Univ. of Santiago and Andres Bello Univ.; mem. Directive Congress of the Interamerican Women's Comm. (CAM) 1990–. *Address:* Ministry of Foreign Affairs, Catedral 1158, Santiago, Chile (Office). *E-mail:* mingab1@minrel.cl (Office).

ALWARD, Peter Andrew Ulrich; British record company executive; b. 20 Nov. 1950, London; s. of the late Herbert Andrew Alward and Marion Evelyne Schreiber; ed Bryanston School and Guildhall School of Music and Drama; worked for Simrock Music Publrs. 1968–70; EMI Records UK 1970–74, European Co-ordinator EMI Classical Div. (Munich) 1975–83, Exec. Producer for all EMI recordings with Herbert von Karajan 1976–89, Man. (UK) Artists and Repertoire 1983, Int. Dir A&R 1985, Vice-Pres. 1989, Sr Vice-Pres. 1997; mem. Royal Opera House Covent Garden Opera Advisory Bd 1998–99; Dir Young Concert Artists Trust 1999–; Pres. EMI Classics 2002–. *Leisure interests:* classical music, painting and sculpture, theatre, books, collecting stage and costume designs, cooking, travelling. *Address:* EMI Classics, 64 Baker Street, London, W1U 7DQ (Office); 24 Midway, Walton-on-Thames, Surrey, KT12 3HZ, England (Home). *Telephone:* (20) 7467-2203 (Office); (1932) 248985 (Home); 07785 362987 (mobile). *Fax:* (20) 7467-2245 (Office). *E-mail:* peter.alward@emic.co.uk (Office). *Website:* www.emiclassics.com (Office).

AMAD, Hani Subhi al-, MA, PhD; Jordanian librarian; b. 1938, Salt; s. of Subhi al-Amad and Suhaila al-Amad; m. Intesar Bashiti 1968; two s. two d.; ed Salt Secondary School, Cairo Univ. and in USA; Librarian, Univ. of Jordan Library 1963–73, Dir 1983; Librarian, Faculty of Arts & Human Sciences, Univ. of Moh. V, Rabat 1974–76; Dir-Gen. Culture and Arts Dept, Amman 1977–78; Asst Prof. Faculty of Arts, Univ. of Jordan 1979–, Asst Dean 1981–83; Pres. Jordan Library Assen 1984–85; Jordanian Writers' Union 1987–. *Publications:* Jordan Folk Songs 1969, Jordan Folk Proverbs 1978, Cultural Policy in Jordan 1980, Studies in Biographical Sources 1981, Jordan

Folk Elegies: Lamentation 1984, Directory of Notables in the Southern Region of Bilad Ash-Sham 1985, Literature of Writing and Authorship among Arabs: A General View 1986, Principles of Methodology in Arabic authorship extracted from Introductions 1987, Arab Character in the Biography of Princess That al-Himmah 1988. *Leisure interest:* reading and doing research. *Address:* c/o The Library, University of Jordan, Amman, Jordan.

AMADI, Elechi, BSc; Nigerian writer, fmr teacher, army officer and administrative officer; b. 12 May 1934, Aluu, Rivers State; s. of Chief Wonuchukwu Amadi and Enwere Amadi; m. 1st Dorah Nwonne Ohale 1957; m. 2nd Priye Iyalla 1991; four s. eight d.; ed Govt Coll. Umuaphia, Univ. Coll. Ibadan, Brookings Inst., USA; worked as land surveyor 1959–60, teacher 1960–63; army officer (Capt.) 1963–66, with 3rd Marine Commandos during civil war 1968–69; Prin. Asa Grammar School 1967; Perm. Sec. Rivers State Govt 1973–83, Commr of Educ. 1987–89, of Lands and Housing 1989–90; Writer-in-Residence and Lecturer Rivers State Coll. of Educ. 1984–85, Dean of Arts 1985–86, Head Dept of Literature 1991–93; Founder and Dir Elechi Amadi School of Creative Writing 1997–; Rivers State Silver Jubilee Merit Award 1992, Ikwerre Ethnic Nationality Merit Award for Literature 1995. *Publications:* (novels) The Concubine 1966, The Great Ponds 1969, The Slave 1978, Estrangement 1986; (plays) Isiburu 1973, The Road to Ibadan 1977, Dancer of Johannesburg 1978; Sunset in Biafra (war diary) 1973; Ethics in Nigerian Culture (philosophy) 1982. *Leisure interests:* reading, music, playing the piano, billiards. *Address:* 7 Mbodo Road, Aluu, P.O. Box 331, Port Harcourt, Nigeria. *Fax:* (84) 230 238.

AMADOU, Hama; Niger politician; fmr Man. Dir Niger Broadcasting Bd; fmr Pvt. Sec. to Pres. Seyni Kountche and Pres. Ali Saibou; Prime Minister of Niger 1995, Jan. 2000–; now Sec.-Gen. Mouvement national pour une société de développement—Nassara (MNSD). *Address:* Office of the Prime Minister, Niamey, Niger (Office).

AMADUZZI, Luigi, GCVO; Italian diplomatist; b. 22 March 1937, Naples; s. of Aurelio Amaduzzi; m. Giovanna Amaduzzi; one s. one d.; ed Univ. of Rome; joined diplomatic service 1963; Second Sec., London 1967; First Sec., Moscow 1969; First Sec., later Counsellor, Sec.-Gen.'s Office 1972, Head of Office 1983, 1991; Counsellor, Washington, DC 1975; Amb. to Amman 1985–88, to Romania 1988; apptd. Diplomatic Counsellor to the Pres. of the Repub. 1992; Amb. to UK 1999–. *Leisure interests:* tennis, painting. *Address:* Embassy of Italy, 14 Three Kings Yard, London, W1K 4EH, England (Office). *Telephone:* (20) 7312-2200 (Office). *Fax:* (20) 7312-2217 (Office). *E-mail:* press@embitaly .org.uk (Office). *Website:* www.embitaly.org.uk (Office).

AMAMOU, Mohamed; Tunisian diplomatist; b. 7 Oct. 1933, Kairouan; s. of Mohamed Amamou and Zohra Saadi; m. Beya Boudjaria; one s. one d.; ed Collège Sadiki and Inst. des Hautes Etudes; Chargé d'affaires, Jordan 1969–71; Amb. to Zaïre 1972–73; Gen. Consul in Paris 1973–74; Amb. to Lebanon and Jordan 1974–78; Dir of Political Affairs for the Arab World, Ministry of Foreign Affairs 1978–81; Chargé de mission, Ministry of Foreign Affairs 1981–85; Amb. to Morocco and Portugal (resident in Rabat) 1985–87, to Syria 1987–89; Sec. of State for Maghreb Affairs 1989–90; Prin. Adviser to Pres. of Tunisia 1990–91, Minister Adviser 1991; Sec.-Gen. of Arab Maghreb Union 1991–2000; Grand Officier Ordre de la République Tunisienne, Chevalier, Ordre Indépendance and several foreign decorations. *Address:* c/o Ministry of Foreign Affairs, place du Gouvernement, la Kasbah, 1006 Tunis, Tunisia. *Telephone:* (71) 660-088 (Office).

AMANN, Ronald, MSocSc, PhD, FRSA, ACSS; British academic; b. 21 Aug. 1943, North Shields; s. of George Amann and Elizabeth Towell; m. Susan Peters 1965; two s. one d.; ed Heaton Grammar School, Newcastle-upon-Tyne and Univ. of Birmingham; Consultant, OECD and Research Assoc. 1965–69; Lecturer, Sr Lecturer in Soviet Science Policy, Univ. of Birmingham 1969–83, Dir Centre for Russian and East European Studies (CREES) 1983–89, Prof. of Comparative Politics 1986–, Dean Faculty of Commerce and Social Science 1989–91, Pro-Vice-Chancellor 1991–94; Chief Exec. and Deputy Chair. Econ. and Social Science Research Council (ESRC) 1994–99; Dir Gen. Centre for Man. and Policy Studies, Cabinet Office 1999–; Chair. Centre for Research on Innovation and Competition, Univ. of Manchester; Visiting Fellow, Osteuropa Inst. Munich 1975; Specialist Adviser, House of Commons Select Cttee on Science and Tech. 1976, mem. Steering Cttee, Centre for the Analysis of Risk and Regulation, LSE; Founding Academician, Acad. of Learned Socs. for the Social Services 1999. *Publications:* co-author: Science Policy in the USSR 1969, The Technological Level of Soviet Industry 1977, Industrial Innovation in the Soviet Union 1982, Technical Progress and Soviet Economic Development 1986. *Leisure interests:* walking, modern jazz, cricket. *Address:* Department of Political Science and International Studies, University of Birmingham, Edgbaston, Birmingham, B15 2TT (Office); 26 Spring Road, Edgbaston, Birmingham, B15 2HA, England. *Telephone:* (121) 440-6186.

AMANPOUR, Christiane; British broadcasting correspondent; b. 12 Jan. 1958, London; d. of Mohammad Amanpour and Patricia Amanpour; m. James Rubin 1998; one s.; ed primary school in Tehran, Iran, Holy Cross Convent, UK, New Hall School, UK and Univ. of Rhode Island, USA; radio producer/research Asst BBC Radio, London 1980–82; radio reporter, WBRU Brown Univ. USA 1981–83; electronic graphics designer, WJAR, Providence, RI 1983; Asst CNN int. assignment desk, Atlanta, Ga 1983; news writer, CNN, Atlanta 1984–86; reporter/producer, CNN, New York 1987–90; Int. Corresp. CNN 1990, Sr Int. Corresp. 1994, Chief Int. Corresp. 1996–; assignments have included coverage of Gulf War 1990–91, break-up of USSR and subsequent war in Tbilisi 1991, extensive reports on conflict in Fmr Yugoslavia, Israel and Afghanistan and coverage of civil unrest and political crises in Haiti, Algeria, Somalia, Rwanda, Iran and Pakistan; Fellow, Soc. of Professional Journalists; Dr hc (Rhode Island); three Dupont-Columbia Awards 1986–96, two News and Documentary Emmy Awards 1999, George Foster Peabody Award 1999, George Polk Award 1999, Univ. of Missouri Honor Award for Distinguished Service to Journalism 1999. *Leisure interests:* reading, riding, tennis, swimming, sky-diving. *Address:* c/o CNN International, CNN House, 19–22 Rathbone Place, London, W1P 1DF, England. *Telephone:* (20) 7637-6800.

AMARAL, Diogo Freitas do, PhD; Portuguese politician and university professor; b. 21 July 1941, Póvoa de Varzim; s. of Duarte P. C. Freitas do Amaral and Maria Filomena Campos Trocado; m. Maria José Salgado Sarmento de Matos 1965; two s. two d.; Prof. of Admin. Law, Lisbon Univ. 1968, Head Dept of Public Law, Prof. Portuguese Catholic Univ. 1978; mem. Council of State 1974–75, Parl. 1975–82, 1992–93; Pres. Centre Democrat Party (CDS) 1974–82, 1988–91; Pres. European Union of Christian Democrats 1981–82; Deputy Prime Minister and Minister for Foreign Affairs 1980–81, Deputy Prime Minister and Minister of Defence 1981–83; Presidential cand. 1986; Pres. 50th Gen. Ass. of UN 1995–96; Founder, Chair. School of Law, New Univ. of Lisbon 1996–; Pres. Fundação Portugal Século XXI 1986–90, PETROCONTROL 1992–2000; Calouste Gulbenkian Prize (twice); Henry the Navigator Prize. *Plays:* O Magnífico Reitor 2001, Viriato 2002. *Publications:* A Utilização do Domínio Público Pelos Particulares 1965, A Execução das Sentenças dos Tribunais Administrativos 1967, Conceito e natureza do recurso hierárquico 1981, Uma Solução para Portugal 1985, Curso de Direito Administrativo I, 1986, II 2001, O Antigo Regime e a Revolução (Memórias Políticas—1941–76) 1995, História das Ideias Políticas, vol. I 1998, D. Afonso Henriques. Biografia 2000. *Leisure interests:* music, horses, reading, theatre, writing, political philosophy. *Address:* Av. Fontes Pereira de Melo 35 13A, 1050-118 Lisbon, Portugal.

AMARI, Akira; Japanese politician; worked for Sony Corpn; mem. House of Reps. of New Liberal Club for Ninami-Kanto; subsequently joined LDP, Deputy Sec.-Gen. LDP, Chief LDP Commerce and Industry Panel; Minister of Labour 1998–99. *Leisure interests:* collecting antiques. *Address:* c/o Ministry of Labour, 1-2-2, Kasumigaseki, Chiyoda-ku, Tokyo 100, Japan.

AMARJARGAL, Rinchinnyamyn, M.ECONS.; Mongolian politician; m.; one s.; ed Moscow Inst. of Econs, Univ. of Bradford, UK; officer, Cen. Council of Mongolian Trade Unions 1982–83; lecturer, Mil. Acad. and Tech. Univ. 1983–90; Dir Econs Coll., Ulan Bator 1991–96; MP 1996–99, Minister and Acting Minister of External Relations April–Dec. 1998, Prime Minister of Mongolia 1999–2000; mem. Mongolian Nat. Democratic Party (MNPP) Gen. Council; Dr. h. c. (Bradford) 2000. *Address:* c/o Office of the Prime Minister, Ulan Bator, Mongolia (Office).

AMATO, Giuliano; Italian politician; b. 13 May 1938, Turin; joined Italian Socialist Party (PSI) 1958, mem. Cen. Cttee 1978–, Leader –2000, Asst Sec.; elected Deputy for Turin-Novara-Vercelli 1983, 1987; fmr Under-Sec. of State, Presidency of Council of Ministers; Vice-Pres. Council of Ministers and Minister of the Treasury 1987–89; Prof. of Italian and Comparative Constitutional Law, Univ. of Rome; Nat. Deputy Sec. Italian Socialist Party 1988–92; Foreign debt negotiator for Albanian Govt 1991–92, Prime Minister of Italy 1992–93, 2000–01; Minister for Treasury 1999–2001; Vice-Pres. EU Special Convention on a Pan-European Constitution 2001–. *Address:* Special Convention on a European Constitution, European Union, 200 rue de la Loi, 1049 Brussels, Belgium; Socialisti Democratici, Piazza San Lorenzo in Lucina 26, Rome, Italy.

AMBANI, Mukesh D., BChemEng, MBA; Indian business executive; b. 19 April 1957, Mumbai; s. of the late Dhirubhai Hirachand Ambani and of Kokilaben Dhirubhai Ambani; m. Nita Ambani; three c.; ed Univ. of Bombay and Stanford Univ., USA; joined Reliance Industries Ltd (India's largest pvt co.) 1981, Man. Dir 1986–, Chair. 2002–, also Dir Reliance Europe Ltd; Chair. Indian Petrochemicals Corpn Ltd; mem. Prime Minister's Advisory Council on Trade and Industry, Council of Scientific and Industrial Research, Bd Govs Nat. Council of Applied Econ. Research, Advisory Council of the Indian Banks Asscn; Chair. Bd of Trustees, Indian Inst. of Software Eng; 'Global Leader for Tomorrow', World Econ. Forum, Switzerland 1994, Business India Businessman of the Year Award 1997, 'Distinguished Alumnus of the Decade', Univ. of Bombay 1999, Ernst & Young Entrepreneur of the Year Award 2000, rated one of 'India's Most Admired CEOs' in Business Barons-Taylor Nelson Sofres-Mode Survey 2002, Bombay Man. Asscn Entrepreneur of the Decade Award 2002. *Address:* Reliance Industries Ltd., Maker Chambers IV, 222, Nariman Point, Mumbai 400 021, India (Office). *Telephone:* (22) 2287 1418 (Office). *Fax:* (22) 2287 0303 (Office). *E-mail:* M_Ambani@ril.com (Office). *Website:* www.ril.com (Office).

AMBARTSUMOV, Yevgeniy Arshakovich, CandHistSc; Russian politician, social scientist, political analyst and journalist; b. 19 Aug. 1929, Moscow; s. of Arshak Ambartsumov and Alexandra Vassilevskaia; m. Nina Ignatovskaia 1978; one s.; ed Moscow Inst. of Int. Relations; with Novoye Vremya 1954–59, Problems of Peace and Socialism 1959–63; Sr Scientific Researcher, Inst. of World Econs and Int. Relations 1956–59, Head of Dept Inst. of World Int. Labour Movt 1966–69; Head of Dept, Inst. of Sociology 1969–73; Head of Dept of Politics, Inst. of Economics of World Socialist System (now Inst. of Int. Economic and Political Studies) 1973–90; Russian People's Deputy 1990–93; Chair. Foreign Affairs Cttee of Russian Supreme Soviet 1992–93; mem. State

Duma (Parl.) 1993–94; mem. Presidential Council 1993–95; Amb. to Mexico, also accred to Belize 1994–99; Prof. Universidad La Salle, Mexico 1998–. *Publications include:* How Socialism Began: Russia under Lenin 1978, NEP: A Modern View 1988, Socialism: Past and Present (Ed.). *Leisure interest:* books. *Address:* Universidad La Salle, Benjamin Franklin 47, Col Condesa, Del. Cuauhtémoc, 06140 México, DF, Mexico. *Telephone:* (095) 332-64-25 (Home).

AMBARTSUMYAN, Sergey Aleksandrovich, DTech; Armenian state official and scientist; b. 17 March 1922, Alexandropol (now Gumry); s. of Alexander G. Ambartsumyan and Anna V. Ambartsumyan; m. Seda A. Ambartsumyan 1949; one s. one d.; Rector Yerevan State Univ. 1977–92; Hon. Dir Inst. of Mechanics 1993–; Academician Armenian Acad. of Sciences 1964– (Vice-Pres. 1975–77), Armenian Eng Acad. 1992–, Armenian Philosophy Acad. 1993–; USSR People's Deputy 1989–91, mem. Supreme Soviet 1979–91; Academician Int. Acad. of Astronautics; mem. Int. Acad. of Sciences, Educ., Industry and Arts 1997–; Hon. Pres. Armenian Acad. of Eng 1997–; Hon. mem. Slovak. Acad. of Sciences, Int. Eng Acad. 1991; Hon. Prof. Peninsula Inst. of Information, Tech. and Business 1998; Dr. hc (Bratislava) 1984; many awards and prizes. *Publications:* Theory of Anisotropic Shells 1961, Theory of Anisotropic Plates 1967, General Theory of Anisotropic Shells 1974, Magnetoelasticity of Thin Shells and Plates 1977, Different Modulus Theory of Elasticity 1982, Fragments of the Theory of Anisotropic Shells 1990, Some Problems of Electro-magneto-elasticity of Plates 1991, Vibrations and Stability of Current-carrying Elastic Plates 1991, Conductive Plates and Shells in Magnetic Field 1998; over 200 articles on mechanics of solids. *Leisure interests:* painting, literature, history. *Address:* Institute of Mechanics, 24 Marshal Bagramian Avenue, 375019 Yerevan, Armenia. *Telephone:* (41) 520644, 521503 (Office); (41) 532050 (Home). *Fax:* (41) 569281. *E-mail:* samb@sd.am.

AMBRASEYS, Nicholas, PhD, FICE, FREng; British professor of engineering seismology; b. 19 Jan. 1929, Athens, Greece; s. of Neocles Ambraseys and Cleopatra Ambraseys; m. Xeni Stavrou 1955; ed Nat. Tech. Univ. of Athens and Imperial Coll. of Science and Tech., Univ. of London; Prof. of Hydro-dynamics, Nat. Tech. Univ. of Athens 1963–64; Lecturer in Soil Mechanics, Imperial Coll., London 1965–68, Reader in Eng Seismology 1968–73, Prof. 1973–94, Head of Eng Seismology Section 1969–94, Sr Research Fellow 1995–, Sr Research Investigator 1996–, currently Prof. Emer.; led UN/UNESCO earthquake reconnaissance missions to Yugoslavia, Iran, Turkey, Pakistan, Romania, Algeria, Italy, E Africa, Nicaragua and Cen. Africa 1963–81; mem. UN Advisory Bd for reconstruction of Skopje 1964–69; Chair. British Nat. Cttee for Earthquake Eng, ICE 1966–76; Vice-Pres. European Assen of Earthquake Eng 1967–75; mem. and Chair. UNESCO Advisory Cttee on Earthquake Risk 1971–81; mem. European Acad. 1996; Hon. Fellow, Int. Assen for Earthquake Eng 1992; Dr. hc (Nat. Tech. Univ. Athens) 1993; Busk Medal for Scientific Discovery (Royal Geographical Soc.) 1975. *Publications:* A History of Persian Earthquakes (with G. Melville) 1982, The Seismicity of Egypt, Arabia and the Red Sea 1994, Seismicity of Turkey 1995, Seismicity of Central America 2000, Seismicity of Iceland 2000 and over 200 papers in scientific and eng journals. *Leisure interests:* historical geography, archaeology, travel. *Address:* Department of Civil Engineering, Imperial College of Science and Technology, Imperial College, London, SW7 2BU; 19 Bede House, Manor Fields, London, SW15 3LT, England (Home). *Telephone:* (20) 7589-5111 (Office); (20) 8788-4219 (Home). *E-mail:* n.ambraseys@ic.ac.uk (Office).

AMBROZIC, HE Cardinal Aloysius; Canadian ecclesiastic; b. 27 Jan. 1930, Gabrje, Yugoslavia (now Slovenia); s. of Aloysius Ambrozic and Helen Ambrozic; ed St Augustine's Seminary, Toronto, Univ. of San Tommaso, Rome 1958, Biblicum, Rome, Univ. of Wurzburg; ordained priest 1955; curate, St Teresa's Parish, Port Colborne, Ont. 1955–56; Prof., St Augustine's Seminary, Toronto 1956–57, 1960–67, 1970–76; Prof. of New Testament Exegesis, Toronto School of Theology 1970–76; Dean of Studies, St Augustine's Seminary, Toronto 1971–76; ordained Auxiliary Bishop, Archdiocese of Toronto 1976–86, Coadjutor Archbishop 1986–90, Archbishop of Toronto 1990–; mem. Pontifical Council for Pastoral Care of Migrants 1990, Vatican Congregation for Clergy 1991–, Pontifical Council for Culture 1993; cr. Cardinal 1998; Hon. DD (Univ. of St Michael's Coll.) 1991. *Publications:* The Hidden Kingdom: A Redaction-Critical Study of the References to the Kingdom of God in Mark's Gospel 1972, Remarks on the Canadian Catechism 1974. *Address:* Catholic Pastoral Centre, 1155 Yonge Street, Toronto, Ont. M4T 1W2, Canada (Office). *Telephone:* (416) 934-0606 (Office). *Fax:* (416) 934-3452 (Office).

AMELING, Elly; Netherlands opera singer; b. (as Elisabeth Sara Ameling), 1938, Rotterdam; m. Arnold W. Beider 1964; studied singing with Jo Bolle-kamp, with Jacoba and Sam Dresden and with Bodi Rapp; studied French art song with Pierre Bernac; has given recitals in Europe, S. Africa, USA; début in USA 1968, annual tours of USA and Canada 1968–; has sung with Concertgebouw Orchestra, New Philharmonic Orchestra, BBC Symphony Orchestra, Berlin Philharmonic, Cincinnati Symphony, San Francisco Symphony, Toronto Symphony, Chicago Symphony; has appeared in Mozart Festival, Washington, DC 1974, Caramoor Festival 1974, Art Song Festival, Princeton, NJ 1974; First Prize, Concours Int. de Musique, Geneva; Grand Prix du Disque, Edison Prize, Preis der Deutschen Schallplattenkritik, Stereo Review Record of the Year Award; Knight Order of Orange-Nassau. *Recordings include:* Mozart Concert, Handel Concert, Cantatas (Bach), Mörike

Lieder (Wolf), Aimez-vous Handel?, Aimez-vous Mozart?, Christmas Oratorio (Bach), Symphony No. 2 (Mahler), Te Deum (Bruckner), Italienisches Lie-derbuch (Wolf).

AMENÁBAR, Alejandro; Spanish/Chilean film director; b. 1973, Santiago, Chile; ed Complutense Univ., Madrid. *Films:* Tésis (Thesis) 1996, Abre los Ojos (Open Your Eyes) 1997, The Others 2001. *Address:* c/o Dimension Films, 375 Greenwich Street, New York, NY 10012, USA (Office).

AMERASINGHE, Chittharanjan Felix, PhD, LLD; Sri Lankan international lawyer and judge; b. 2 March 1933, Colombo; s. of Samson Felix Amerasinghe, OBE and Mary Victorine Abeyesundere; m. Wimala Nalini Pieris 1964; one s. two d.; ed Royal Coll., Colombo, Trinity Hall, Cambridge Univ., Harvard Univ. Law School; Supervisor in Law, Trinity Hall, Cambridge Univ. 1955–57; Jr Exec., Caltex Oil Co., Colombo 1959–61; Lecturer in Law, Univ. of Ceylon 1962–65, Sr Lecturer 1965–68, Reader 1968–69, Prof. of Law 1969–71; Counsel, World Bank 1970–75, Sr Counsel 1975–81, Exec. Sec. and Dir of Secr., World Bank Admin. Tribunal 1981–96; Judge UN Tribunal, NY 1997–2000; Judge, Commonwealth Int. Arbitral Tribunal 1999–; Consultant in Int. Law, Govt of Ceylon 1963–70; mem. Ceylon Govt Comm. on Local Govt 1969; Hon. Prof. of Int. Law, Univ. of Colombo 1991–; Adjunct Prof. of Int. Law, School of Law, American Univ. 1991–93; mem. Panel of Arbitrators and Conciliators, Law of the Sea Convention, Int. Centre for Settlement of Investment Disputes, Panel of UN Compensation Comm. for Kuwait; Exec. Council mem. American Soc. of Int. Law 1980–83; Assoc. mem. Inst. de Droit Int. 1981–87, mem. 1987–; mem. Int. Law Asscn 1986–; mem. Sr Editorial Bd, Project on Governing Rules of Int. Law, American Soc. of Int. Law; mem. Advisory Bd and Hon. Cttee Int. Inst. of Human Rights 1968–, Int. Inst. of Environmental Law 1987–98, Sri Lanka Journal of Int. Law 1989–; Trinity Hall Law Studentship 1956–59, Research Fellowship, Harvard Univ. Law School 1957; Henry Arthur Thomas Classical Award, Cambridge Univ. 1953, Angus Classical Prize 1953, Clement Davies Prize for Law 1955, Major Scholar and Prizeman, Trinity Hall, Cambridge 1953–56, Yorke Prize 1964, Certificate of Merit, American Soc. of Int. Law 1988–89. *Publications:* Some Aspects of the Actio Iniuriarum in Roman-Dutch Law 1966, Defamation and Other Injuries in Roman-Dutch Law 1968, State Responsibility for Injuries to Aliens 1967, Studies in International Law 1969, The Doctrines of Sovereignty and Separation of Powers in the Law of Ceylon 1970, The Law of the International Civil Service (2 vols) 1988, Documents on International Administrative Tribunals 1989, Case Law of the World Bank Administrative Tribunal (3 vols) 1989, 1991, 1994, Local Remedies in International Law 1990, Principles of the Institutional Law of International Organizations 1996; articles in leading law and int. law journals. *Leisure interests:* classical and classical jazz music, art, artifacts, philately, photography, walking. *Address:* 6100 Robinwood Road, Bethesda, MD 20817, USA (Home). *Telephone:* (301) 229-2766 (Home). *Fax:* (301) 229-4151 (Home). *E-mail:* chameras@aol.com (Home).

AMERY, Carl (see Mayer, Christian).

AMES, Bruce Nathan, PhD, FAAS; American professor of biochemistry; b. 16 Dec. 1928, New York; s. of Dr. M. U. Ames and Dorothy Andres Ames; m. Dr. Giovanna Ferro-Luzzi 1960; one s. one d.; ed Cornell Univ. and California Inst. of Tech.; Postdoctoral Fellow, Nat. Insts. of Health 1953–54, Biochemist 1954–60; Nat. Science Foundation Fellow, Labs. of F. C. Crick, Cambridge and F. Jacob, Paris 1961; Chief Section of Microbial Genetics, Lab. of Molecular Biology, Nat. Insts. of Health 1962–67; Prof. of Biochemistry, Univ. of Calif., Berkeley 1968–, Chair. Dept of Biochemistry 1983–89; Sr Research Scientist, Children's Hospital Oakland Research Inst. 1968–; mem. Nat. Cancer Advisory Bd 1976–82, NAS, American Acad. of Arts and Sciences; Foreign mem. Royal Swedish Acad. of Sciences 1989; Eli Lilly Award, American Chem. Soc. 1964, Arthur Flemming Award 1966, Rosenstiel Award 1976, Fed. of American Socs. for Experimental Biology Award 1976, Wankel Award 1978, John Scott Medal 1979, Bolton L. Corson Medal 1980, New Brunswick Lectureship Award of American Soc. for Microbiology 1980, Gen. Motors Cancer Research Fund Charles S. Mott Prize 1983, Gairdner Foundation Award 1983, Tyler Prize for Environmental Achievement 1985, Spencer Award (American Chem. Soc.) 1986, Roger G. Williams Award in Preventive Nutrition 1989, Gold Medal American Inst. of Chemists 1991, Glenn Foundation Prize 1992, shared Japan Prize 1997, Nat. Medal of Science 1998, Linus Pauling Prize for Health Research 2001, Lifetime Achievement Award of American Soc. for Microbiology 2001. *Publications:* scientific papers in areas of operons, biochemical genetics, histidine biosynthesis, mutagenesis, detection of environmental carcinogens and mutagens, oxygen radicals as a cause of aging and degenerative diseases, anti-carcinogens, micronutrient deficiency. *Address:* Children's Hospital Oakland Research Institute, 5700 Martin Luther King Jr. Way, Oakland, CA 94609-1673 (Office); 1324 Spruce Street, Berkeley, CA 94709, USA (Home). *Telephone:* (510) 450-7625 (Office). *Fax:* (510) 597-7128 (Office). *E-mail:* bnames@uclink4.berkeley.edu (Office). *Website:* mcb.berkeley.edu./faculty/BMB/amesb.html (Office).

AMES, Michael McClean, OC, PhD, FRSC; Canadian professor of anthropology; b. 19 June 1933, Vancouver; s. of Ernest O. F. Ames and Elsie McClean; m. (separated); one s. one d.; ed Univ of British Columbia and Harvard Univ.; Asst Prof. of Sociology, McMaster Univ. 1962–64; Asst Prof. Univ. of BC 1964, now Prof. Emer. of Anthropology; Dir Museum of Anthropology, Univ. of BC 1974–; Co-ed of Manlike Monsters; consultant to various museums and projects since 1976; Guggenheim Fellowship 1970–71. *Pub-*

lications: Manlike Monsters on Trial 1980, Museums, The Public and Anthropology 1986, Cannibal Tours and Glass Boxes 1992; articles in academic and museum journals. *Leisure interests:* hiking, photography, running. *Address:* Department of Anthropology-Sociology, The University of British Columbia, 6303 NW Marine Drive, Vancouver, BC V6T 1Z1, Canada (Office). *Telephone:* (604) 822-1913 (Office). *Fax:* (604) 822-1913 (Office). *E-mail:* mames@interchange.ubc.ca (Office).

AMES, Roger; Trinidadian music company executive; b. 1949; with EMI UK 1975–79; mem. A & R (Artists and Repertoire) Dept, Phonogram, PolyGram UK 1979–83, Chair. and CEO PolyGram UK 1991–94, Group Exec. and Vice-Pres. PolyGram Int. Ltd 1996–99, Pres. PolyGram Music Group 1996–99; Gen. Man. London Records 1983, purchased back catologue of Factory Records, signed New Order, later Man. Dir.; Pres. Warner Music Int. 1999, Chair. and CEO Warner Music Group 1999–. *Address:* Warner Music Group, 75 Rockefeller Plaza, New York, NY 10019, USA (Office). *Website:* www.wmg.com (Office).

AMEY, Julian Nigel Robert, MA; British civil servant; b. 19 June 1949; s. of Robert Amey and Diana Amey (née Coles); m. Ann Victoria Brenchley 1972; three d.; ed Wellingborough School, Magdalene Coll., Cambridge; Dir Int. Sales and Marketing Longman Group Ltd 1985–89; Exec. Dir BBC English World Service 1989–94; seconded to Dept of Trade and Industry 1994–96; Dir-Gen. Canning House 1996–2001; Partner The English Place 2001–; CEO CIBSE 2001–. *Publications:* Spanish Business Directory 1979, Portuguese Business Dictionary 1981. *Leisure interests:* cricket, tennis, travel. *Address:* CIBSE, 222 Balham High Road, London, SW12 9BS, England. *Telephone:* (20) 8772-3609. *Fax:* (20) 8673-0822.

AMIN, Mudhaffar, PhD; Iraqi diplomatist; m. Zahr Amin; three c.; ed Univ. of Durham; entered Ministry of Foreign Affairs 1980s; Head of Iraqi Interests Section, Jordanian Embassy, London (Baghdad's only accred diplomat in London). *Address:* Iraqi Interests Section, 21 Queens Gate, London, SW7 5JG, England (Office). *Telephone:* (20) 7584-7141 (Office). *Fax:* (20) 7584-7716 (Office).

AMIN, Samir, DEcon; Egyptian economist; b. 4 Sept. 1931, Cairo; s. of Farid Amin and Odette Amin; m. Isabelle Eynard 1957; ed Univ. of Paris; Sr Economist, Econ. Devt Org., Cairo 1957–60; Tech. Adviser for Planning to Govt of Mali 1960–63; Prof. of Econs, Univs. of Poitiers, Paris and Dakar; Dir UN African Inst. for Econ. Devt and Planning 1970–80; Dir Third World Forum (Africa Office), Senegal 1980–. *Publications include:* Trois expériences africaines de développement, Mali, Guinée, Ghana 1965, L'économie du Maghreb (2 Vols) 1967, Le développement du capitalisme en Côte d'Ivoire 1968, Le monde des affaires sénégalais 1969, The Maghreb in the Modern World 1970, Neo-colonialism in West Africa 1973, Accumulation on a World Scale 1974, Unequal Development 1976, The Arab Nation 1978, Class and Nation 1980, The Arab Economy Today 1982, Eurocentrism 1989, Delinking: Towards a Polycentric World 1990, Maldevelopment: Anatomy of a Global Failure 1990, The Empire of Chaos 1992, Re-reading The Post War Period 1994, Capitalism in the Age of Globalisation 1996, Les défis de la mondialisation 1996, Spectres of Capitalism 1998, L'hégémonisme des Etats-Unis et l'effacement du projet européen 2000. *Leisure interest:* history. *Address:* Third World Forum, B.P. 3501, Dakar, Senegal (Office). *Telephone:* 821-11-44 (Office). *Fax:* 821-11-44 (Office). *E-mail:* ftm@refer.sn (Office). *Website:* www.refer.sn/ftm.

AMIN DADA, Field Marshal Idi; Ugandan fmr Head of State and army officer; b. 1925, Kakwa Region, West Nile; s. of the late Amin Dada; joined King's African Rifles 1946; rank of Corporal 1949, Major 1963, Col 1964; Deputy Commdr of the Army 1964; Commdr of the Army and Air Force 1966–70; rank of Brig.-Gen. 1967, Maj.-Gen. 1968, promoted Field Marshal July 1975; leader of mil. coup d'état which deposed Pres. Milton Obote Jan. 1971; Pres. and Chief of Armed Forces 1971–79 (Life Pres. 1976–79 overthrown in Tanzanian invasion, fled Uganda); Minister of Defence 1971–75; Chair. Defence Council 1972–79; Minister of Internal Affairs 1973, of Information and Broadcasting 1973, of Foreign Affairs Nov. 1974–Jan. 1975, of Health 1977–79, of Foreign Affairs 1978, of Information, Broadcasting and Tourism, Game and Wildlife 1978–79, of Internal Affairs 1978–79; Chief of Staff of the Army 1974–79; Chair. OAU Ass. of Heads of State 1975–76, presided over Kampala Summit 1975, Addis Ababa Summit 1976; Heavyweight Boxing Champion of Uganda 1951–60; resident in Libya 1979–80; in exile in Jeddah, Saudi Arabia 1980–; awarded eight highest mil. decorations of Uganda; Hon. LLD (Kampala) 1976.

AMINU, Jibril Muhammed, PhD, FRCP; Nigerian diplomatist and physician; b. 25 Aug. 1939, Song, Adamawa State; m.; eight c.; ed Ahmadu Bello Univ., Zaria, Univ. of Ibadan and London hosps.; Professor of Medicine, specializing in Cardiology and Hypertension, Univ. of Maiduguri 1979–95, Univ. Vice-Chancellor (Pres.) 1980–85; Minister of Educ. 1985–89; Minister of Petroleum and Mineral Resources, Nigeria 1989–92; mem. World Bank Preparatory Cttee on Educ. for All, Jornitien 1990; Chair. First Meeting of the Ministers of Educ. in Sub-Saharan Africa; Vice-Pres. for Africa of the Third World Acad. of Sciences Network of Scientific Orgs.; fmr Pres. African Petroleum Producers' Assocn; Pres. OPEC Conf. 1991–92; Del. to Nigerian Nat. Constitutional Conf. 1994–95; Amb. to USA 2000–; Foundation mem. Bd of Trustees, People's Democratic Party of Nigeria 1998; Fellow, Nigerian Acad. of Science (FAS) 1972, W African Coll. of Physicians (FWACP) 1980; Ordre National de la Légion d'Honneur 2001. *Publications:* Quality and Stress in

Nigerian Education 1986, Observations 1987. *Address:* Nigerian Embassy, 1333 16th Street, NW, Washington, DC 20036, USA (Office). *Telephone:* (202) 986-8400 (Office). *Fax:* (202) 986-8449 (Office). *E-mail:* jibrilaminu@nigeriaembassyusa.org (Office). *Website:* www.nigeriaembassyusa.org (Office); www.jibrilaminu.com (Home).

AMIREDJIBI, Chabua; Georgian writer, editor and politician; b. Mzechabuk I. Amiredjibi, 18 Nov. 1921, Tbilisi; s. of Irakli Amiredjibi and Maria Nakashidze; m. Tamar Djavakhishvili 1966; four s. (one deceased) two d.; ed Tbilisi State Univ., A. Pushkin Tbilisi Pedagogical Inst.; as student of Tbilisi State Univ. was arrested for political activities 1944, sentenced to 25 years' imprisonment in Gulag, released 1959; Dir Advertising-Information Bureau Goskinoprokat 1965–70; Chief Ed. Kino anthology 1970–83; Dir Mematiane documentary film studio 1983–89; MP 1992–96; Chair. Defence Fund of Georgia 1992–96; f. PEN Centre of Georgia, Pres. 1994–97, Hon. Chair. 1998–; Publr and Ed.-in-Chief Ganakhlebuli Iveria newspaper 1999–; mem. Writers' Union of Georgia 1964–; mem. editorial bds. of several journals and newspapers; USSR State Prize 1979, Sh. Rustaveli Prize 1994; Honoured Art Worker of Georgia 1987, Order of Honour 1994, Order of King Vakhtang Gorgasili (First Class) 2001. *Film screenplay:* Data Tutashkhia 1979. *Publications:* Road (short stories) 1964, Tales for Children 1966, Data Tutashkhia (novel) 1973, Gora Mborgali (novel) 1994. *Leisure interests:* sports, football, basketball. *Address:* 8/45 Tamarashvili Street, 380062 Tbilisi, Georgia. *Telephone:* (32) 99 95 27 (Office); (32) 23 06 75 (Home).

AMIS, Martin Louis, BA; British author; b. 25 Aug. 1949; s. of the late Kingsley Amis and of Hilary Bardwell; m. 1st Antonia Phillips 1984 (divorced 1996); two s.; m. 2nd Isabel Fonseca 1998; two d.; ed Exeter Coll. Oxford; Asst Ed. 1971, Fiction and Poetry Ed. Times Literary Supplement 1974; Literary Ed. New Statesman 1977–79; special writer for The Observer newspaper 1980–; Somerset Maugham Award (for The Rachel Papers) 1974. *Publications:* The Rachel Papers 1973, Dead Babies 1975, Success 1978, Other People: A Mystery Story 1981, Money 1984, The Moronic Inferno: And Other Visits to America 1986, Einstein's Monsters (five stories) 1987, London Fields 1989, Time's Arrow 1991, Visiting Mrs Nabokov And Other Excursions 1993, The Information 1994, God's Dice 1996, Night Train 1997, Heavy Water and Other Stories 1998, Experience 2000, The War Against Cliché (essays and reviews 1971–2000) 2001, Koba the Dread: Laughter and the Twenty Million 2002. *Leisure interests:* tennis, chess, snooker. *Address:* c/o Wylie Agency (UK) Ltd, 4–8 Rodney Street, London, N1 9JH, England. *Telephone:* (20) 7843-2150 (Office). *Fax:* (20) 7843-2151 (Office).

AMIT, Maj.-Gen. Meir, MBA; Israeli politician and business executive; b. Meir Slutsky, 17 March 1921, Tiberias; s. of Shimon and Haya Slutsky; m. Yona Kelman 1942; three d.; ed Columbia Univ., New York; mem. Kibbutz Alonim 1939; served in Israeli Defence Forces 1948–68, fmr Head of Mil. Intelligence and Head of Israeli Security Service; Pres. Koor Industries 1968–77; Minister of Transport and Communication 1977; mem. of Knesset 1977–81; man. consultant 1982–; Dir MA'OF 1982–85; Dir Zim Lines, Israel Corpn 1985, Yachin, DSI Teva Pharmaceutical, Lapidot Oil Drilling; Chair. Gen. Satellite Corpn, Spacecom 1982, Satellite Communications, etc.; numerous awards. *Publications:* Head On, Yes Sir. *Leisure interests:* photography, collecting dolls and educational games. *Address:* 55 Arlazorof Street, Ramat-Gan 52493, Israel (Office). *Telephone:* (3) 5477337 (Office); (3) 6729777 (Home). *Fax:* (3) 6725935 (Home). *E-mail:* amit173@netvision.net.il (Home).

AMITAL, Yehuda; Israeli politician and rabbi; b. 1925, Transylvania; m.; five c.; in Nazi labour camp 1943–44; migrated to Israel 1944; yeshiva studies in Jerusalem; ordained in Jerusalem; joined Haganah during war of independence; Head, Yeshivat Har Etzion 1968–; f. Meimad, the Movt for Religious Zionist Renewal 1993; Minister without Portfolio 1995–96; rank of capt. in army reserve. *Address:* The Knesset, Jerusalem, Israel.

AMOAKO, Kingsley Y., MSc, PhD; Ghanaian economist; b. 1947; ed Univ. of Ghana, Univ. of California, Berkeley, USA; with IBRD from the 1970s, Dir Dept of Educ. and Social Policy 1993–95; UN Under-Sec.-Gen. and Exec. Sec. Econ. Comm. for Africa (ECA) 1995–. *Address:* Economic Commission for Africa, Africa Hall, P.O.B. 3001, Addis Ababa, Ethiopia (Office). *Telephone:* (1) 510365 (Office). *Fax:* (1) 514416 (Office). *E-mail:* ecainfo@un.org (Office). *Website:* www.uneca.org (Office).

AMORIM, Celso Luiz Nunes; Brazilian diplomatist and politician; b. 3 June 1942, Santos, São Paulo; s. of Vicente Matheus Amorim and Beatriz Nunes Amorim; m. Ana Maria Amorim; three s. one d.; ed Rio Branco Inst., Diplomatic Acad. Vienna and London School of Econs; Lecturer, Dept of Political Science and Int. Relations, Univ. of Brasília 1977–; Perm. Rep. to UN, GATT and Conf. on Disarmament, Geneva 1991–93, to UN and WTO 1999–2001; Minister of Foreign Affairs 1993–94, 2003–; Perm. Rep. to UN, New York 1995–99; Amb. to UK 2001–02; Perm. mem. Dept of Int. Affairs, Inst. of Advanced Studies, Univ. of São Paulo; mem. Canberra Comm. on Elimination of Nuclear Weapons 1966, Int. Task Force on Security Council Peace Enforcement 1997; Foreign Policy Assn Medal (USA) 1999. *Publications:* several works on political theory, int. relations, cultural policies and subjects connected with science and tech. *Leisure interests:* reading, travel, art, cinema. *Address:* Ministry of Foreign Affairs, Palácio do Itamaraty, Esplanada dos Ministérios, Bloco H, 70170-900, Brasília DF, Brazil (Office). *Telephone:* (61) 411-6161 (Office). *Fax:* (61) 225-1272 (Office). *Website:* www.mre.gov.br (Office).

AMOS, Valerie Ann Amos, Baroness (Life Peer), cr. 1997, of Brondesbury in the London Borough of Brent, MA; British politician and organization official; b. 13 March 1954, Guyana; d. of E. Michael Amos and Eunice V. Amos; ed Univs of Warwick, Birmingham and East Anglia; Race Relations Adviser London Borough of Lambeth 1981–83; Women's Adviser London Borough of Camden 1983–85; Head of Training and Devt London Borough of Hackney 1985–87, Head of Man. Services 1988–89; Chief Exec. Equal Opportunities Comm. 1989–94; Dir Fraser Bernard 1994–98; Govt Whip 1998–2001; Parl. Under-Sec. of State, Foreign and Commonwealth Office 2001–03; Sec. of State for Int. Devt 2003–; Dir Hampstead Theatre 1992–98; Deputy Chair. Runnymede Trust 1990–98; mem. Advisory Cttee Centre for Educ. Devt Appraisal and Research, Univ. of Warwick 1991–98, Gen. Advisory Council BBC, King's Fund Coll. Cttee 1992–98, Council Inst. of Employment Studies 1993–98; Trustee Women's Therapy Centre 1989–; Hon. LLD (Warwick) 2000, (Staffs.) 2000, (Manchester) 2001. *Address:* Department for International Development, 1 Palace Street, London, SW1E 6QW, England (Office). *Telephone:* (20) 7023-0000 (Office). *Fax:* (20) 7023-0000 (Office). *E-mail:* general.enquiries@dfid.gov.uk (Office). *Website:* www.dfid.gov.uk (Office).

AMOUR, Salmin; Tanzanian politician; Pres. and Chair. Supreme Revolutionary Council of Zanzibar 1990–2000; Vice-Chair. C.C.M. (Revolutionary Party of Tanzania). *Address:* Chama Cha Mapinduzi (Revolutionary Party of Tanzania), Kuu St, P.O.B. 50, Dodoma, Tanzania (Office). *Telephone:* (61) 2282 (Office).

AMOUZEGAR, Jamshid, BCE, MS, PhD; Iranian politician; b. 25 June 1923; s. of Turan Amouzegar and Habibollah Amouzegar; m. Ulrike Amouzegar 1951; ed Univs. of Tehran, Cornell, Washington; UN Expert, Mission to Iran 1951; Chief, Eng Dept 1952–55; Deputy Minister of Health 1955–58; Minister of Labour 1958–59, of Agric. 1959–60; Consulting Eng 1960–64; Chair. Int. Civil Service Advisory Bd of UN 1962–67; Minister of Health 1964–65, of Finance 1965–74, of Interior and Employment 1974–76; Minister of State 1976–77; Sec.-Gen. Rastakhiz Party 1976–77, Jan.–Aug. 1978; Prime Minister of Iran 1977–78; Pres. OPEC 1974; fmr Chief Oil Negotiator to Shah; First Order of the Taj. *Leisure interests:* listening to music, reading poetry.

AMOYAL, Pierre Alain Wilfred; French violinist; b. 22 June 1949, Paris; s. of Dr. Wilfred Amoyal and Vera (Popravka) Amoyal; m. 2nd Leslie Chabot 1988; ed Cours d'Etat, Vanves, Conservatoire Nat. Supérieur de Musique, Paris, Univ. of Southern California, USA (studied with Jascha Heifetz); invited by Sir Georg Solti to perform Berg's violin concerto with Orchestre de Paris 1971; invited by Pierre Boulez to perform Schoenberg's Concerto with Orchestre de Paris 1977; Prof. of Violin, Conservatoire Nat. Supérieur de Musique, Paris 1977–88; Lausanne Conservatory 1987–; numerous performances throughout world with orchestras including Royal Philharmonic, New Philarmonia, l'Orchestre Nat. de France, Residentie-Orkest, The Hague; First Prize, Conservatoire de Versailles 1960, Conservatoire Nat. Supérieur de Musique, Paris 1962, for chamber music, Conservatoire Nat. Supérieur de Musique; Chevalier, Ordre des Arts et des Lettres; Prix Ginette Neveu; Prix Paganini; Prix Enesco 1970; Grand Prix du Disque 1974, 1977. *Numerous recordings including:* Symphonie espagnole (Lalo), Violin Concerto (Mendelssohn), Concertos Nos. 1 and 2 and 2 Sonatas (Prokofiev), Tartini's concertos, Third Concerto, Havanaise and Rondo Capriccioso (Saint-Saëns), Concerto No. 1 (Bruch), Concerto (Glazunov); Sonatas (Fauré), Horn Trio (Brahms), Concertos (Mozart), Concerto (Sibelius), Concerto (Tchaikovsky), Sonatas (Brahms), Concerto (Schoenberg). *Leisure interests:* photography, literature, sport. *Address:* c/o Jacques Thelen, 15 avenue Montaigne, 75008 Paris, France.

AMPAL, Jemar Haji, BEd, MA; Brunei diplomatist; b. 18 Feb. 1954; m.; ed Lancaster Univ., School of Advanced Int. Studies, Johns Hopkins Univ.; joined Dept of Educ. 1978, Diplomatic Officer, Foreign Ministry 1984–89, Deputy Dir Dept of Educ. 1989–93, Deputy Perm. Rep. to UN 1993–98, Perm. Rep. 1998–2000. *Address:* Ministry of Foreign Affairs, Jalan Subok, Bandar Seri Begawan BD, 2710 Brunei (Office).

AMTE, Baba, BA, LLB; Indian lawyer and social worker; b. Murlidhar Devidas Amte, 26 Dec. 1914, Hinganghat; s. of Devidas Amte and Laxmibai Amte; m. Sadhana Amte; two s.; ed Christian Coll. Nagpur, Nagpur Univ., School of Tropical Medicines, Calcutta; joined Quit India Movt, imprisoned 1942; Vice-Pres. Warora Municipality 1948; originator and developer of Maharogi Sewa Samiti leper complex near Nagpur which accommodates 1,400 lepers and includes a cottage hosp., out-patient clinic, shops, workshops, bank, schools, rehabilitation centre for the physically disabled and a technical coll.; recipient of four hon. degrees; UN Human Rights Award 1988; Templeton Prize for Progress in Religion (jtly. with L. C. Birch, 1990; Int. Gandhi Peace Prize Award 1999; numerous int. and nat. awards. *Publications:* numerous books of poems. *Address:* Maharogi Sewa Samiti, Warora, Anandwan, Dist Chandrapur 442914, India. *Telephone:* (7176) 82425 (Home); (7176) 82034. *Fax:* (7176) 82134 (Office).

AMUDUN NIYAZ; Chinese party and government official; b. 1932; joined CCP 1953; First Sec. Urumqi Municipality CCP 1977–79; Vice-Chair. Govt of Xinjiang Uygur Autonomous Region 1979–83; Chair. Standing Cttee of Xinjiang Uygur Autonomous Region People's Congress 1985; Deputy Sec., Xinjiang Uygur Autonomous Region Cttee CCP 1985; Chair. Xinjiang Uygur Autonomous Regional 8th People's Congress 1985, Standing Cttee of 7th Xinjiang PC 1989–93, of 8th Xinjiang PC 1993–. *Address:* Standing Committee of Xinjiang Uygur Autonomous Region People's Congress, Urumqi, People's Republic of China.

AMURO, Namie; Japanese pop singer; b. 20 Sept. 1977, Okinawa; m. Sam Maruyama; ed Okinawa Actor's School; mem. of group Super Monkeys 1992, leader of group 1994; Japan Records Award 1996. *Singles include:* (with Super Monkeys) Paradise Train, Try Me, Tiayo No Season, (solo) Stop the Music, Body Feels Exit, Chase the Chance, Don't Wanna Cry, You Are My Sunshine, Sweet 19 Blues, Can You Celebrate. *Albums include:* Sweet 19 Blues, Concentration 20, 181920.

AMUSÁTEGUI DE LA CIERVA, José María; Spanish banker; b. 12 March 1932, San Roque; s. of Antonio Amusategui de la Cierva and Dolores Amusategui de la Cierva; m. Amalia de León 1988 (divorced); six c.; ed Colegio de Huérfanos de la Armada and Univ. of Madrid; state lawyer, Minister of Finance, Gerona 1959–70; Deputy Chair. Instituto Nacional de Industria 1970; Deputy Chair. Prodinsa 1974; Chair. Intelsa 1975, Astilleros Españoles 1980; Deputy Chair. Instituto Nacional de Hidrocarburos 1981; Chair. Campsa 1982; Man. Dir, Deputy Chair. Banco Hispano Americano 1985, Chair. 1991–99, also Pres.; Chair. Banco Cen. Hispano 1992–99; Co.-Chair. Banco Santander Cen. Hispanoamericano (BSCH, now Banco Santander Cen. Hispano SA) 1999–2002, Hon. Chair. 2002–; Grand Cross of Civil Merit. *Leisure interests:* motorcycling, astronomy, botany. *Address:* Banco Santander Central Hispano SA, Alcalá 49, 28014 Madrid, Spain.

AN MIN, (Wang, An Min) Chinese university professor; b. 15 March 1922, Shandong; s. of Wang Jingxuan and Zhou Ailian; m. Wu Pei (Wu Guangrui) 1951; one s. one d.; ed Ming Hsien High School and Nat. Cen. Univ.; mem. Friends Ambulance Unit 1941–49; ed Faculty China Agric. Univ. 1949–, Head Dept Animal Science 1979–82, Pres. Univ. 1982–87; Vice-Chair. Scientific and Tech. Cttee Ministry of Agric. 1983–87, Consultant 1987–; Head Animal Science Section Nat. Academic Degree Cttee 1984–92; Section Head Nat. Foundation for Natural Science 1986–; Pres. Domestic Animal and Poultry Information Centre 1984–87; Dir Int. Goat Asscn 1982, China Int. Conf. Centre for Science and Tech. 1984–; Vice-Chair. Chinese Asscn of Agricultural Sciences 1983–87; Chief Ed. Chinese Journal of Animal Science 1980–84; mem. Standing Cttee China Assc'n of Animal Science and Veterinary Medicine 1986–, China Assc'n for Science and Tech. 1987–91, Nat. Awarding Cttee of Natural Science 1987–91; Deputy Chief Ed. China Agricultural Encyclopedia, Vol. Animal Science 1988–; Chief Ed. Biography of Chinese Scientists, Vol. Agricultural Animal Science 1989–; Dir Dept of Taiwan, Hong Kong and Macao Affairs, Ministry of Foreign Trade and Econ. Co-operation 1991–; Assoc. Chief Ed. China Animal Science 1993–; mem. Steering Cttee Small Ruminant Production System Network of Asia 1990–; mem. Agricultural Consultant Group, Beijing Municipality 1990–; Nat. Award for Tech. Support in Agric. Sciences 1981, 1984, Education Award for Outstanding Profs and other awards. *Publications:* Animal Reproduction and Reproductive Physiology, Reproductive Hormones, Farm Animal Reproduction and its Genetical Improvement, English-Chinese Dictionary of Animal Science and Technology. *Leisure interests:* music, theatre and travel. *Address:* 303 Building 15, China Agricultural University, Beijing 100094, People's Republic of China. *Telephone:* (10) 62892955. *Fax:* (10) 2582332.

AN QIYUAN; Chinese government official and fmr geologist; b. 1933, Lingtong Co., Shaanxi Prov.; ed Dept of Geology, Northwest China Univ.; joined CCP 1953; leader geological team of Songliao Petroleum Prospecting Bureau 1958–59; Dir of Oil Mine and Chief, Underground Operation Section of 1st HQ Oil Extracting in Daqing 1964–65; Dir Petroleum Geophysics Prospecting Bureau, Ministry of Petroleum 1973–77; Deputy Dir State Seismological Bureau 1977–80, Dir 1982–88; mem. Standing Cttee CCP Shaanxi Prov. Cttee, Sec. CCP Xian Municipal Cttee 1988; mem. Standing Cttee CCPCC Comm. for Inspecting Discipline 1992–; Sec. CCP Shaanxi Prov. Cttee 1994–. *Address:* Shaanxi Provincial Committee, Xian, Shaanxi Province, People's Republic of China.

AN ZHENDONG; Chinese government official and engineer; b. 5 Sept. 1930, Tangshan, Hebei; ed Hebei Industry Coll. 1951; engineer, Qiqihar Admin. Railroad 1952–58; engineer Heilongjiang Sillicon Rectifier Factory 1963–67; Engineer, Deputy Factory Dir Harbin Rectifier Equipment Factory 1967–81; Chief Engineer 2nd Light Industry Bureau 1981–82; Vice-Gov. Heilongjiang 1983–90; Vice-Chair. Standing Cttee Heilongjiang PPC 1990–93; Vice-Chair. 6th, 7th, 8th, 9th and 10th Cen. Cttee Jiusan Soc., 6th, 7th Deputy to the Nat. People's Congress; Vice-Pres. Chinese Package Soc.; Dir Chinese Industry Econ. Soc.; main inventions include: Signal and Radio Telephone in Railroad Cars 1958, Fire-fighting Automatic System in Cities 1963, Explosion-proof Rectifier Equipment in Coal Mines 1973, Power Factor Electricity Regulator 1976; named Model Worker of special grade of Harbin, the Model Worker of Heilongjiang Prov. *Address:* c/o People's Congress Standing Committee of Heilonjiang, Nangang District, Harbin 150001, People's Republic of China.

ANAND, Bal Krishan, MB, BS, MD; Indian physiologist; b. 19 Sept. 1917, Lahore; s. of V. D. Anand and Saraswati Anand; m. Kamla Puri 1942; one s. two d.; ed Government Coll. and K. E. Medical Coll., Lahore; Prof. of Physiology, Lady Hardinge Medical Coll., New Delhi 1949–57, All India Inst. of Medical Sciences, New Delhi 1957–74 (Dean 1964–74), Prof. Emer. 1977–; Pres. XXVI Int. Congress of Physiological Sciences, New Delhi 1974; Asst Dir WHO. (SE Asia) 1974–77; Dir Inst. of Medical Sciences, Srinagar 1982–85; Vice-Chancellor, Banaras Hindu Univ., Varanasi 1978; Pres. Indian Nat.

Acad. of Medical Sciences; Pres. Nat. Bd of Examinations 1979–82; Pres. Asscn for Advancement of Medical Educ. 1984–86; Chair. Post-graduate Cttee of Medical Council of India 1985–91; Chair. Physiology Cttee of Indian Nat. Science Acad. 1988–91, Governing Council Vallabhbhai Patel Chest Inst., Univ. of Delhi 1997–; Visiting Prof. Pa Univ. School of Medicine 1968; Commonwealth Visiting Prof., Univ. of London 1966; Hon. Mem. Fed. of Asia Oceanic Physiological Soc. 1994; Rockefeller Foundation Fellow at Yale Univ. School of Medicine 1950–51; Fellow Nat. Acad. of Medical Sciences, Nat. Science Acad., Indian Acad. of Sciences; Hon. DSc (Banaras) 1983; Indian Council of Medical Research Sr Research Award 1962, Watumull Foundation Award in Medicine 1961, Sir Shanti Swaroof Bhatnagar Memorial Award for Scientific Research in Medicine 1963, Padma Shri 1966, Medical Council of India Silver Jubilee Research Award 1969, Dr. B. C. Roy Award for Eminent Medical Man 1984. *Publications:* several specialized articles. *Leisure interests:* academic literature, photography, tennis, hiking. *Address:* B9/21, Vasant Vihar, New Delhi, India (Home). *Telephone:* 6142627.

ANAND, Dev; Indian actor and film maker; b. 1924, Gurdaspur; m. Kalpana Kartik; one s. one d.; est. Navketan Studios; Padma Bhushan 2001. *Films include:* Hum Ek Hain 1946, The Guide 1965, Des Pardes 1978, Hare Rama Hare Krishna, Bullet, Manzil, Barsaat, Jaal, Paying Guest, Censor 2001, Ishk Ishk Ishk, Taxi Driver, Tere Ghar Ke Samne, Aman ke Farishtey 2002. *Address:* 42 Pali Hill, Mumbai (Office); 2 Irish Park, Juhu, Mumbai 400 049, India (Home). *Telephone:* (22) 6497550 (Office); (22) 6202609 (Home).

ANAND, Mulk Raj, PhD; Indian writer and critic; b. 12 Dec. 1905, Peshawar; s. of Lalchand Anand and Ishwar Kaur; m. 1st Kathleen van Gelder 1939 (divorced 1948); m. 2nd Shirin Vajifdar 1950; one d.; ed Punjab and London Univs; active in Nationalist and Gandhi movements; lecturer, London County Council; BBC broadcaster, film script writer, British Ministry of Information; ed. (1956) various magazines; Leverhulme Fellow for Research in Hindustani literature; fmr Editor Marg magazine, India; mem. Indian Nat. Acad. of Letters, Indian Nat. Acad. of Arts, Indian Nat. Book Trust; fmr Tagore Prof. of Art and Literature, Punjab Univ., Chandigarh; Fellow, Nat. Acad. of Art, New Delhi; Padma Bhushan 1967; Hon. DLitt (Delhi, Benares, Andhra, Patiala, Shantiniketan); Laureate of Int. Peace Prize. *Publications:* novels: The Bubble, Morning Face, Private Life of an Indian Prince, The Big Heart, The Sword and the Sickle, Across the Black Waters, Untouchable, Coolie, The Barbers' Trade Union, Seven Summers, etc.; essays: Apology for Heroism, Seven Little Known Birds of the Inner Eye, Death of a Hero, etc. *Leisure interests:* environment, world peace. *Address:* Jassim House, 25 Cuffe Parade, Colaba, Mumbai 400005, India. *Telephone:* (22) 2181371.

ANAND, Viswanathan; Indian chess-player; b. 11 Dec. 1969; s. of K. Viswanathan and Susila Viswanathan; m. Aruna Anand; Int. Master (aged 15) 1984; first Indian Int. Grandmaster 1987; World Jr Champion 1987; beat fmr world champions Mikhail Tal and Boris Spassky at 4th Int. Games Festival 1989; captained Indian team at Chess Olympiad, Manila 1992; has participated in numerous int. chess tournaments 1987–; placed No. 2 in PCA ranking 1995; World Chess Champion 2000; FIDE World Cup Champion 2002; Arjuna Award 1985, Nat. Citizens' Award 1987, Shri Rajiv Gandhi Award 1988. *Address:* c/o FIDE, 9 Avenue de Beaumont, Lausanne 1012, Switzerland (Office); 7 (old No. 4) II Cross Street, Customs Colony, Besant Nagar, Chennai 600 090, India (Home). *Telephone:* (69) 25577236. *E-mail:* vishy@compuserve.com.

ANAND PANYARACHUN; Thai politician and business executive; ed Univ. of Cambridge; fmr Amb. to Canada, USA, UN and Fed. Repub. of Germany in 1970s; later Head, Ministry of Foreign Affairs; fmr Exec. Chair. Saha Union (industrial conglomerate); fmr Chair. Fed. of Industries; Prime Minister of Thailand 1991–92. *Address:* c/o Office of the Prime Minister, Government House, Thanon Nakhon Pathom Road, Bangkok 10300, Thailand.

ANANIASHVILI, Nina Gedevanovna; Georgian/Russian ballet dancer; b. 28 March 1963, Tbilisi, Georgia; d. of Gedevan Ananiashvili and Lia Gogolashvili; m. Gregory Vashadze 1988; ed State Choreographic Schools of Georgia and Bolshoi Theatre, Moscow; prima Bolshoi Ballet 1981–98, now freelance; has performed on tour world-wide with New York City Ballet, Royal Ballet, Royal Danish Ballet, Kirov Ballet, American Ballet Theatre, Royal Swedish Ballet, Ballet de Monte Carlo, The Munich Ballet and others; roles include: Giselle, Odette/Odile (Swan Lake) Aurora (Sleeping Beauty), Raimonda, Juliet (Romeo and Juliet), Nikya (La Bayadère); numerous awards include Grand Prix Int. Ballet Competition, Jackson 1986, People's Artist Repub. of Georgia and of Russia; State Prize of Russia 1993. *Leisure interests:* antique books, modern painting. *Address:* Frunzenskaya nab. 46, Apt. 79, 119270 Moscow, Russia. *Telephone:* (095) 242-58-64. *Fax:* (095) 476-34-70.

ANANICH, Boris Vasilyevich; Russian historian; b. 4 March 1931, Leningrad; m.; one d.; ed Leningrad State Univ.; Chief Researcher St Petersburg Br. Inst. of History, USSR Acad. of Sciences; Corresp. mem. USSR (now Russian) Acad. of Sciences 1990, mem. 1994; research in history of Russia 19th–20th centuries, econ. history, internal policy. *Publications include:* Russia and International Capital 1897–1914, Essays on History of Financial Relations 1976, Banking Houses in Russia 1860–1914, Essays on History of Private Businesses 1991, numerous articles. *Address:* Institute of History, Russian Academy of Sciences, Petrozavodskaya str. 7, 197110 St Petersburg, Russia. *Telephone:* (812) 235-41-98 (Office).

ANANYEV, Anatoliy Andreyevich; Russian writer; b. 18 July 1925, Dzhambul, Kazakhstan; m. Tatyana Kharchenko 1957; one d.; ed Kazakh State Univ.; mem. CPSU 1950–91; Deputy Ed. Znamya 1967–70; Ed.-in-Chief Oktyabr 1973–2001; Sec. USSR Writers' Union 1976–91; Chair. Council of Independent Popular Pension Funds 1993–; First Deputy Chair. Fed. of Peace and Consent; People's Deputy of USSR 1989–91; Vice-Pres. Foreign Affairs Cttee of Supreme Soviet of USSR 1989–91; mem. Russian Acad. of Natural Sciences 1995–2001; Hero of Socialist Labour 1984, Order for Merits in the Fatherland 1995. *Publications:* Tales of Vernensk 1958, Small Cover 1959, The Shadow of Jesus 1961, The Trump Cards of the Monk Grigorii 1965, Tanks are Moving in Rhombus 1964, Miles of Love 1973, Years Without War, Vols 1–4 1975–84, Tables and Bells 1989, Faces of Immortal Power 1992, The Call for Ryurikovichi, or The Millennial Mystery of Russia (Vols 1–2) 1993–98, Collection of Works: (Vols 1–8) 1995–97. *Address:* Astrakhanski per. 5, Apt. 12, 129010 Moscow, Russia. *Telephone:* (095) 280-15-20.

ANASTASIADES, Nicos; Cypriot politician and lawyer; b. 1946, Limassol; m. Andri Moustakoudes; two d.; ed Univ. of Athens, Univ. of London, UK; practising lawyer, Limassol 1972–; Dist Sec. Youth Org. of Dimokratikos Synagermos (DISY – Democratic Rally party) 1976–85 (Pres. 1987–90), Vice-Pres. DISY 1985–86, 1990–93, Parl. Leader DISY 1993–97, Deputy Pres. 1995–97, Pres. 1997–; MP 1981–, Speaker House of Reps. 1996–. *Address:* Dimokratikos Synagermos (DISY), P.O. Box 25303, 25 Pindarou Street, 1061 Nicosia, Cyprus (Office). *Telephone:* (2) 883164 (Office). *Fax:* (2) 753821 (Office). *E-mail:* disy@disy.org.cy (Office). *Website:* www.disy.org.cy (Office).

ANAYA, Rudolfo, MA; American author; b. 30 Oct. 1937, Pastura, NM; s. of Martin Anaya and Rafaela Mares; m. Patricia Lawless 1966; ed Albuquerque High School, Browning Business School, Univ. of New Mexico; teacher Albuquerque public schools 1963–70; Dir Counseling Center, Univ. of Albuquerque 1971–73; lecturer Univ. Anahuac, Mexico City 1974; Prof. Dept of Language and Literature Univ. of NM 1974–93, Prof. Emer. 1993–; Founder, Ed. Blue Mesa Review 1989–93; Martin Luther King, Jr./César Chávez, Rosa Parks Visiting Prof. Univ. of Mich., Ann Arbor 1996; now Assoc. Ed. The American Book Review, Bd Contributing Ed. The Americas Review, Advisory Ed. Great Plains Quarterly; f. PEN-NM, Teachers of English and Chicano Language Arts 1991; Founder, Pres. NM Rio Grande Writers Asscn; mem. Bd Before Columbus Foundation; mem. Nat. Asscn of Chicano Studies; Hon. D.Hum.Litt. (Albuquerque) 1981, (Marycrest Coll.) 1984, (New England) 1992, (Calif. Lutheran Univ.) 1994, (New Hampshire) 1997; Hon. Ph.D. (Santa Fe) 1991; Hon. D.Litt. (New Hampshire) 1996; recipient numerous awards. *Plays:* Billy the Kid, Who Killed Don José?, Matachines, Angie, Ay, Compadre, The Farolitos of Christmas. *Publications include:* Bless Me, Ultima 1972 (Premio Quinto Sol Award 1971), Heart of Aztlan 1976, Tortuga 1979 (American Book Award, Before Columbus Foundation 1979), Cuentos: Tales from the Hispanic Southwest (trans.) 1980, The Silence of the Llano (short stories) 1982, The Legend of La Llorona 1984, The Adventures of Juan Chicaspatas (poem) 1985, A Chicano in China 1986, Lord of the Dawn, The Legend of Quetzalcoatl 1987, Albuquerque 1992 (PEN-WEST Fiction Award 1993), The Anaya Reader (anthology) 1994, Zia Summer 1995, The Farolitos of Christmas 1995, Jalamanta, A Message from the Desert 1996, Rio Grande Fall 1996, Maya's Children 1997, Descansos: An Interrupted Journey (with Estevan Arellano and Denise Chávez) 1997, Shaman Winter 1999, Farolitos for Abuelo 1999, My Land Sings 1999, Roadrunner's Dance 2000, Elegy for Cesar Chavez 2000; short stories in literary magazines in USA and internationally; has also ed. various collections of short stories. *Leisure interests:* reading, travel, apple orchards. *Address:* Department of Language and Literature, University of New Mexico, Albuquerque, NM 87131 (Office); 5324 Cañada Vista NW, Albuquerque, NM 87120-2412, USA (Home). *Fax:* (505) 899-0014 (Home).

ANCRAM, Earl of; Michael Andrew Foster Jude Kerr, PC, QC, DL, LLB, MA; British politician; b. 7 July 1945; s. of 12th Marquess of Lothian and Antonella, Marchioness of Lothian; m. Lady Jane Fitzalan-Howard 1975; two d.; ed Ampleforth, Christ Church Coll., Oxford, Edinburgh Univ.; fmrly in business, columnist Daily Telegraph (Manchester Edn), partner in tenanted arable farm; called to Scottish Bar 1970, practised law 1970–79; MP for Berwickshire and East Lothian Feb.–Oct. 1974, Edinburgh S. 1979–87, for Devizes 1992–; mem. House of Commons Energy Select Cttee 1979–83; Parl. Under-Sec. of State Scottish Office 1983–87; Parl. Under-Sec. NI Office 1993–94, Minister of State 1994–96; Shadow Cabinet Spokesman for Constitutional Affairs 1997–98; Chair. Conservative Party 1998–2001, Deputy Leader 2001–; Shadow Sec. of State for Foreign and Commonwealth Affairs 2001–; Vice-Chair. Conservative Party in Scotland 1975–80, Chair. 1980–83; Chair. Northern Corp. Communications 1989–91; Dir CSM Parl. Consultants 1988–92; mem. Bd Scottish Homes 1988–90. *Leisure interests:* skiing, fishing, photography, folk-singing. *Address:* House of Commons, London, SW1A 0AA, England. *Telephone:* (20) 7219-4435. *Fax:* (20) 7219-2528.

ANDERS, Edward, MA, PhD; American professor of chemistry; b. 21 June 1926, Liepaja, Latvia; s. of Adolph Alperovitch and Erica Leventals; m. Joan Elizabeth Fleming 1955; one s. one d.; ed Univ. of Munich, Columbia Univ.; Instructor in Chem., Univ. of Ill. at Urbana 1954–55; Asst Prof. of Chem. Univ. of Chicago 1955–60, Assoc. Prof. 1960–62, Prof. 1960–73, Horace B. Horton Prof. of Physical Sciences 1973–91, Prof. Emer. 1991–; Visiting Prof. Calif. Inst. of Tech. 1960, Univ. of Berne 1963–64, 1970, 1978, 1980–81, 1983, 1987–88, 1989–90; Research Assoc. Field Museum of Natural History 1968–91; Fellow American Acad. of Arts and Sciences 1973–; mem. NAS

1974–; Assoc. Royal Astronomical Soc., UK 1974–; Fairchild Distinguished Scholar, Calif. Inst. of Tech. 1992–93; Hon. DChem (Latvian Acad. of Sciences) 2000; Cleveland Prize, AAAS 1959, Smith Medal, NAS 1971, Leonard Medal, Meteoritical Soc. 1974, Goldschmidt Medal, Geochemical Soc. 1990, Kuiper Prize, American Astronomical Soc. 1991, Hess Medal (American Geophysical Union) 1995. *Publications:* over 260 articles in scientific journals. *Leisure interests:* classical music, hiking, photography. *Address:* Hintere Engelhaldenstrasse 12, 3004 Berne, Switzerland. *Telephone:* (31) 302-44-56. *Fax:* (31) 302-44-56.

ANDERSEN, Bodil Nyboe, MSc; Danish central banker; b. 9 Oct. 1940; ed Univ. of Copenhagen; Asst Prin. Ministry of Econ. Affairs 1966–68; Assoc. Prof. (Money and Banking), Univ. of Copenhagen 1968–80; Man. Dir and mem. Man. Bd Andelsbanken 1981–90; Group Man. Dir Unibank and Unidanmark 1990; mem. Bd Govs. Danmarks Nationalbank 1990–, Chair. Bd of Govs. 1995–; Gov. for Denmark, IMF 1995–; mem. Bd Dirs. Danish Foreign Policy Inst. 1972–78; mem. Senate, Univ. of Copenhagen 1977–80; Dir Privatinvest 1978–80, CERD 1978–81, Great Belt Ltd 1987–91, Danish Payment Systems Ltd 1988–90, Industrial Mortgage Credit Fund 1991–92, Velux Foundation 1994–, Danish Film Inst. 2001–; mem. Council, European Monetary Inst. 1995–98, mem. Gen. Council European Cen. Bank 1998–; Businesswoman of the Year 1989. *Address:* Danmarks Nationalbank, Havnegade 5, 1093 Copenhagen K, Denmark. *Telephone:* 33-63-63-63. *Fax:* 33-63-71-06. *E-mail:* bna@nationalbanken.dk (Office). *Website:* www .nationalbanken.dk (Office).

ANDERSEN, Ib; Danish ballet dancer; b. 14 Dec. 1954, Copenhagen; s. of Ingolf Andersen and Anna Andersen; ed with Royal Danish Ballet; ballet dancer, Royal Danish Ballet 1973–80, Prin. Dancer 1975–80; Prin. Dancer, New York City Ballet 1980–94; Ballet Master Pittsburgh Ballet Theater 1994–; Nijinsky Prize. *Address:* Pittsburgh Ballet Theater, Pittsburgh, Pa, USA.

ANDERSEN, Mogens; Danish painter; b. 8 Aug. 1916, Copenhagen; s. of the late Einar F. T. Andersen and Erna Ingeborg (née Andersen); m. Inger Therkildsen 1947; one s. one d.; ed in Copenhagen under art master P. Rostrup Boyesen; art teacher Copenhagen 1952–59, Académie de la Grande Chaumière, Paris 1963; mem. Cttee Danish Art Exhbn Arrangement 1956–58; Pres. Danish State Art Foundation 1977–80; mem. Royal Acad. of Fine Arts 1956, Prof. 1970–72; mem. PEN Club; Eckersberg Medal 1949, Thorvaldsen Medal 1984, Chevalier, Légion d'honneur, Ordre des Arts et des Lettres, Kt of Dannebrog and other awards. *Exhibitions:* Copenhagen 1935–40, 1942–50, 1953–66, 1967; Paris 1950–74, 1981. *Private Exhibitions:* Copenhagen 1953, 1963, 1966, 1968, 1969, 1976 (retrospective), Alborg (Denmark) 1954, 1972, Lund (Sweden) 1959, Paris 1954, 1959, 1963, 1966, 1967, 1973, 1975, 1981, Warsaw 1973, Belgrade 1973, Zagreb, Randers 1981, Aarhus 1982, 1988, Budapest 1983, 1984, Pittsburgh 1987; group exhbns in Europe and the USA; Venice Biennale 1968, retrospective Copenhagen 1988, Aarhus Kunstmuseum 1990, Glyptoteket, Copenhagen 1991, Mikael Andersen Gallery, Copenhagen 1991, 1993, 1996, Galerie Artcurial, Paris 1995, Århus Kunstmuseum 1995; paintings hung in Modern Museum, Skopje 1965, Bridgestone Museum, Tokyo, Kunstmuseum, Malmø, Kongelige Bibliotek, Copenhagen and many other museums in Denmark, Sweden, Norway, Poland and USA. *Major works:* Composition in Niels Bohr Inst., Copenhagen 1955, Mural, Central Library, Copenhagen 1958–59, Composition in Central Library, Århus 1964, October, State Art Museum 1964, Mural, Gentofte Town Hall 1971, Restaurante Copenhagen, Paris 1973, Handelsbanken, Copenhagen 1975, Northern Feather Inst., Danmarks Tekniske Højskole 1979, Panum-instituttet, Copenhagen 1981, Kunstmuseum, Bochum 1981, Musikhuset, Aarhus 1982, Metalskolen, Holstebro, Skäfogaard, Mörke Konstmuseum, Lund, Mural in Sejs Church, Denmark 1989. *Publications:* Moderne fransk malerkunst 1948, Omkring Kilderne 1967, Nødigt, Men Dog Gerne 1976, Ungdomsrejsen 1979, Om Kunst og Samfund 1980, Huset 1986, Punktum, Punktum, Komma, Streg 1994, Efterayn 2002. *Address:* Strandagervej 28, 2900 Hellerup, Copenhagen, Denmark. *Telephone:* (39) 62-02-66.

ANDERSEN, Ronald Max, MS, PhD; American sociologist; b. 15 Feb. 1939, Omaha, Neb.; s. of Max Adolph Andersen and Evangeline Dorothy Andersen (née Wobbe); m. Diane Borella 1965; one d.; ed Univ. of Santa Clara and Purdue Univ.; Research Assoc. Purdue Farm Cardiac Project, Dept of Sociology, Purdue Univ. 1962–63; Assoc. Study Dir Nat. Opinion Research Center, Univ. of Chicago 1963–66, Research Assoc. Center for Health Admin. Studies 1963–77; Instructor Grad. School of Business, Univ of Chicago 1966–68, Asst Prof. 1968–72, Asst Prof. Dept of Sociology 1970–72, Assoc. Prof. Grad. School of Business, then Prof. 1974–90; Assoc. Dir Center for Health Admin. Studies 1977–80, Dir and Dir Grad. Program in Health Admin. 1980–90; Chair. Ed. Bd Health Admin. Press, Chicago, Ill. 1980–83, 1988–; Wasserman Prof. Health Services and Sociology Dept, Calif. Univ. at LA 1991–, Chair. Dept of Health Services 1993–96; mem. numerous cttees., advisory panels etc.; mem. American Sociological Asscn, American Statistical Asscn, American Public Health Asscn; Baxter Allegiance Prize 1999. *Publications:* author and co-author of numerous books, monographs, book chapters and articles in professional journals. *Address:* UCLA School of Public Health, Los Angeles, CA 90024 (Office); 10724 Wilshire Boulevard, Apartment 312, Los Angeles, CA 90024-4453, USA (Home).

ANDERSEN, Torkild, MSc, DPhil; Danish professor of physics; b. 19 June 1934, Randers; m. Inger Bloch-Petersen 1957; one s. one d.; ed Tech. Univ.

Copenhagen; industrial chemist 1958–59; Asst and Assoc. Prof. of Chem., Univ. of Aarhus 1958–71, Prof. of Physics (Atomic Physics) 1971–2001, Emer. Prof. 2001–; Postdoctoral Fellow, Univ. of Cambridge 1961–63; Visiting Prof. Univ. of Colo 1984–85, Flinders Univ. S. Australia 1988, 1994; Bd mem. Carlsberg Foundation 1996–; mem. Royal Danish Acad. of Science 1979–; N. Bjerrum Prize 1972. *Publications:* 200 scientific contribs to chem. or physics journals. *Address:* Institute of Physics and Astronomy, University of Aarhus, Nordre. Ringgade, 8000 Aarhus C (Office); 37 Klokkerbakken, 8210 Aarhus V, Denmark (Home). *Telephone:* 89-42-37-40 (Office). *Fax:* 86-12-07-40 (Office). *E-mail:* fystor@phys.au.dk (Office).

ANDERSON, (Angus) Gerry, MBE; British film maker; b. 14 April 1929; s. of Joseph Anderson and Deborah Anderson; m. 1st Betty Wrightman 1952; two d.; m. 2nd Sylvia Thamm 1961 (divorced); one s.; m. 3rd Mary Robins 1981; one s.; ed Willesden County Secondary School; trainee Colonial Film Unit 1943; Asst Ed. Gainsborough Pictures 1945–47; Dubbing Ed. 1949–53; Film Dir Polytechnic Films 1954–55; co-founder Pentagon Films 1955, AP Films 1956, AP Merchandising 1961; Dir of TV commercials 1961, 1988–92; Chair. Century 21 Org. 1966–75; Hon. Fellow British Kinematograph Sound and TV Soc.; Pres. Thames Valley and Chiltern Air Ambulance 2002; Silver Arrow Award. *Television series include:* Adventures of Twizzle (52 shows) 1956, Torchy the Battery Boy (26 shows) 1957, Four Feather Falls (52 shows) 1958, Supercar (39 shows) 1959, Fireball XL5 (39 shows) 1961, Stingray (39 shows) 1962–63, Thunderbirds (32 shows screened in 20 countries) 1964–66 (Royal Television Soc. Silver Medal), Captain Scarlet (32 shows) 1967, Joe 90 (30 shows) 1968, The Secret Service (13 shows) 1968, UFO (26 shows) 1969–70, The Protectors (52 shows) 1971–72, Space 1999 (48 shows) 1973–76, Terrahawks (39 shows) 1982–83, Dick Spanner (26 shows) 1987, Space Precinct 1993–95, Lavender Castle 1997, Firestorm 2002; numerous television commercials. *Films:* Thunderbirds are Go 1966, Thunderbird 6 1968, Doppelganger 1969. *Leisure interests:* walking, gardening.

ANDERSON, Campbell McCheyne, BEcons; Australian business executive; b. 17 Sept. 1941, Sydney; s. of Allen Taylor Anderson and Ethel Catherine Rundle; m. Sandra Maclean Harper 1965; two s. one d.; ed Armidale School, NSW, Univ. of Sydney; audit clerk, Priestley and Morris 1958–59; with Boral Ltd 1962–69; Gen. Man. then Man. Dir Reef Oil and Basin Oil 1969–72; with Burmah Oil Australia Ltd 1972–73, New York 1973–74, Div. Dir, then Chief Financial Officer, Burmah Oil Trading Ltd, UK 1974–75, Dir 1975–76, Exec. Dir Burmah Oil Co. Ltd 1976–82, Man. Dir Burmah Oil PLC 1982–85; Man. Dir Renison Goldfields Consolidated Ltd 1985, Man. Dir and CEO 1986–93, Dir Consolidated Gold Fields PLC 1985–89; Chair. Ampolex Ltd 1991–96, Dir 1996–97; Man. Dir North Ltd 1994–98; Chair. Energy Resources Australia Ltd 1994–98; Pres. Business Council of Australia 1999–2000; Chair. Southern Pacific Petroleum 2001–; Man. Dir and Dir of numerous cos. in UK and overseas; Pres. Australia/Japan Soc. of Vic. 1995–98; Dir CGNU Australia 1999–, IBJ Bank Australia 1999–, Reconciliation Australia 2001–; Assoc. Australian Soc. of Certified Practising Accountants. *Leisure interests:* golf, shooting, horse-racing, swimming. *Address:* 77 Drumalbyn Road, Bellevue Hill, NSW 2023, Australia. *Telephone:* (4) 1751-2187. *Fax:* (2) 9327-5035.

ANDERSON, Christopher (Chris), B. Econs; Australian journalist; b. 9 Dec. 1947; s. of C. F. Anderson and L. A. Anderson; m. Gabriella Douglas 1969; one s. one d.; ed Picton High School, NSW, Univ. of Sydney, Columbia Univ., New York; journalist and political commentator 1962–76; Deputy Ed., later Ed., The Sun-Herald 1976–79; Deputy Ed., later Ed., The Sydney Morning Herald 1980–83, Ed.-in-Chief 1983–88; Man. Dir and Group Ed. Dir John Fairfax Ltd 1987–90, Chief Exec. 1990–91; Man. Ed. Australian Broadcasting Corpn 1993–95; Chief Exec. TV New Zealand Limited 1995–97; CEO Optus Communications 1997–. *Leisure interests:* cricket, reading. *Address:* Optus Communications, 101 Miller Street, North Sydney, NSW 2060, Australia. *Telephone:* (2) 9342-7800. *Fax:* (2) 9342-7100.

ANDERSON, Don L., PhD, FAAS; American geophysicist; b. 5 March 1933, Frederick, Md; s. of Richard Andrew and Minola Andrew (née Phares); m. Nancy Lois Ruth 1956; one s. one d.; ed Rensselaer Polytechnic Inst. and California Inst. of Tech.; Geophysicist, Chevron Oil Co. 1955–56; Geophysicist, Geophysics Research Directorate, Air Force Cambridge Research Center 1956–58; Research Fellow, Calif. Inst. of Tech. 1962–63, Asst Prof. 1963–64, Assoc. Prof. 1964–68, Prof. 1968–, Dir Seismological Lab. 1967–89; Eleanor and John R. McMillan Chair. in Geophysics, Caltech. 1990–; Ed. Physics of the Earth and Planetary Interiors 1977; Assoc. Ed. Tectonophysics, Physics and Chemistry of the Earth, Journal of Geodynamics etc.; Pres. American Geophysical Union 1988–90, Past Pres. 1990–92; mem. Space Science Bd, Geophysics Research Forum (Chair. 1984–86), Bd on Earth Sciences of NAS, Arthur L. Day Award Cttee NAS (Chair. 1989–90) and several other cttees. and bds.; Fellow American Geophysical Union (Pres. 1986–88), Geological Soc. of America, NAS, Royal Astronomical Soc., American Philosophical Soc., Guggenheim Fellow 1998; mem. Seismological Soc. of America; Sloan Foundation Fellow 1964–67; H. Burr Steinbach Visiting Scholar, Woods Hole Oceanographic Inst. 1995; Distinguished Scientists Lecture Series, Trinity Univ. 1995; Cloos Memorial Scholar, Johns Hopkins Univ. 1989; Hon. Foreign Fellow, European Union of Geosciences; Hon. DSc (Rensselaer Polytechnic Inst.) 2000; J.B. Macelwane Award, American Geophysical Union 1966, Sr Fulbright-Hays Award (Australia) 1975, Newcomb Cleveland Prize (AAAS) 1976–77, NASA Distinguished Scientific Achievement Award 1977, Emil Wiechert Medal, German Geophysical Soc. 1986, Arthur L. Day Medal, Geological Soc. of America 1987, Gold Medal, Royal

Astronomical Soc. 1988, Bowie Medal, American Geophysical Union 1991, Craafoord Prize 1998, Nat. Medal of Science 1998, Guggenheim Fellowship 1998. *Address:* Seismological Laboratory 252-21, California Institute of Technology, Pasadena, CA 91125 (Office); 669 Alameda Street, Altadena, CA 91001, USA (Home). *Telephone:* (626) 395-6901 (Office); (626) 797-7426 (Home). *Fax:* (626) 564-0715.

ANDERSON, Donald Thomas, AO, DSc, FRS; Australian professor of biology; b. 29 Dec. 1931, Eton, England; s. of Thomas and Flora Anderson; m. Joanne T. Claridge 1960; one s.; ed King's Coll., London; Lecturer in Zoology, Univ. of Sydney, Australia 1958, Sr Lecturer 1963, Reader 1968, Prof. 1972, Challis Prof. of Biology 1984–91, Prof. Emer. 1992–; Visiting Prof., King's Coll., London 1970; Kowalevsky Medal 2001. *Publications:* Embryology and Phylogeny in Annelids and Arthropods 1973, Barnacles 1994, Atlas of Invertebrate Anatomy 1996, Invertebrate Zoology 1998. *Leisure interests:* photography, gardening. *Address:* 5 Angophora Close, Wamberal, NSW 2260, Australia. *Telephone:* (2) 4384-6670.

ANDERSON, Gillian, BFA; American actress; b. 9 Aug. 1968, Chicago; d. of Edward Anderson and Rosemary Anderson; m. Errol Clyde Klotz (divorced); one d.; ed DePaul Univ., Chicago, Goodman Theater School, Chicago; worked at Nat. Theatre, London; appeared in two off-Broadway productions; best known for role as Special Agent Dana Scully in TV series The X-Files (feature film 1998) 1993–; Golden Globe Awards 1995, 1997, Screen Actors Guild Awards 1996, 1997, Emmy Award 1997. *Films include:* Chicago Cab 1995, The Turning 1997, The X-Files 1998, The Mighty 1998, Playing By Heart 1998, Princess Mononoke 1999, House of Mirth 2000. *Plays include:* Absent Friends, Manhattan Theater Club (Theater World Award 1991) 1991, The Philanthropist, Along Wharf Theater 1992, What the Night is For, Comedy Theatre London 2002. *Television films include:* Home Fire Burning 1992, When Planes Go Down 1996; presenter, Future Fantastic, BBC TV. *Address:* William Morris Agency, 151 El Camino Drive, Beverly Hills, CA 90212, U.S.A. *Website:* www.gilliananderson.ws.

ANDERSON, Sir John Anthony, KBE, FCA; New Zealand banker; b. 2 Aug. 1945, Wellington; m. Carol M. Anderson 1970; two s. one d.; ed Christ's Coll. and Victoria Univ. of Wellington; Deloitte Haskins & Sells (chartered accountants), Wellington 1962–69; Guest & Bell (sharebrokers), Melbourne 1969–72; joined South Pacific Merchant Finance Ltd, Wellington 1972, Chief Exec. and Dir 1979; Deputy Chief Exec. Nat. Bank of NZ (following merger of Southpac and Nat. Bank) 1988, Chief Exec. and Dir 1990–; Chair. NZ Merchant Banks Asscn 1982–89, Petroleum Corpn of NZ Ltd 1986–88, NZ Bankers Asscn 1992, 1999, 2000; Dir NZ Steel Ltd 1986–87, Lloyds Merchant Bank (London) 1986–92, Lloyds Bank NZA (Australia) 1989–97; Chair NZ Cricket Bd 1995–, NZ Sports Foundation Inc. 1999–2002; Pres. NZ Bankers Inst. 1990–2001; Dir Exec. Bd, Int. Cricket Council 1998–; other professional and public appointments, affiliations etc.; recipient, 1990 Commemoration Medal. *Leisure interests:* rugby, cricket, golf, bridge. *Address:* The National Bank of New Zealand Ltd, 170–186 Featherston Street, P.O. Box 1791, Wellington 6000 (Office); 5 Fancourt Street, Karori, Wellington 5, New Zealand (Home). *Telephone:* (4) 802-2220 (Office). *Fax:* (4) 802-2517 (Office).

ANDERSON, John Bayard, JD, LLM; American politician; b. 15 Feb. 1922, Rockford, Ill.; s. of E. Albin Anderson and the late Mabel Ring; m. Keke Machakos 1953; one s. four d.; ed Univ. of Illinois, Harvard Law School; admitted to Ill. Bar 1946; practiced law, Rockford, Ill. 1946–48, 1950–52, 1955–56; Instructor, Northeastern Univ. Law School 1948–49; State Dept Career Diplomatic Service 1952–55; Winnebago County, Ill., State's Attorney 1956–60; Congressman, 16th Dist, Ill. 1960–80; mem. US House of Reps 1960–79; Chair. House Republican Conf. 1969–79; Ind. cand. for US Pres. 1980; Chair. Nat. Unity Party; Political Commentator WLS-TV, Chicago 1981; Visiting Prof. of Political Science Brandeis Univ. 1985, Univ. of Massachusetts 1985–, Oregon State Univ. 1986, Nova Univ. Center for Study of Law 1987–2002; Pres. and CEO World Federalist Asscn 1992–; lecturer, US State Dept 1994–; Pres. and Chair. of Bd, Center for Voting and Democracy 1993–; Lecturer in Political Science, Bryn Mawr Coll. 1985; Visiting Prof. of Law, Washington Coll. of Law of American Univ., Washington, DC 1997–; fmr Trustee, Trinity Coll., Deerfield, Ill.; Hon. LLD (Ill., Wheaton Coll., Shimer Coll., Biola Coll., Geneva Coll., North Park Coll., Houghton Coll., Trinity Coll., Rockford Coll.). *Publications:* Between Two Worlds: A Congressman's Choice 1970, Vision and Betrayal in America 1975, Congress and Conscience (Ed.) 1970, The American Economy We Need But Won't Get 1984, A Proper Institution: Guaranteeing Televised Presidential Debates 1988. *Leisure interest:* writing occasional commentary or opinion piece on political affairs, lecturing. *Address:* 418 7th Street, SE, Washington DC 2003 (Office); 4120 48th Street, NW, Washington DC 20016 (Home); 3300 36th Street, NE, Fort Lauderdale, Florida, USA. *Telephone:* (202) 546-3950 (Office); (954) 262-6183 (Office); (202) 546-3950 (Home); (954) 566-8491 (Home). *Fax:* (202) 546-3749 (Office); (202) 362-1831 (Home). *E-mail:* j.anderson@wfa.org (Office); jbafed@aol.com (Home). *Website:* wfa.org (Office).

ANDERSON, John Duncan, MA; Australian politician; b. 14 Nov. 1956; s. of D.A. Anderson; m. Julia Gillian Robertson 1987; one s. two d.; ed Kings School, Parramatta, St Paul's Coll., Univ. of Sydney; fmr farmer and grazier; MP for Gwydir, NSW; Deputy Leader Nat. Party of Australia (NPA) 1993–99, Leader 1999–; Shadow Minister for Primary Industry 1993–96; Minister for Primary Industries and Energy 1996–98, for Transport and Regional Devt 1997–; Deputy Prime Minister 1999–. *Leisure interests:* farming, shooting,

reading, photography, motoring. *Address:* Department of Transport and Regional Services, G.P.O. Box 594, Canberra, ACT 2601 (Office); 342–344 Conadilly Street, Gunnedah, NSW 2380, Australia (Home). *Telephone:* (2) 6274-7111 (Office). *Fax:* (2) 6257-2505 (Office). *E-mail:* publicaffairs@dotrs.gov.au (Office). *Website:* www.dotrs.gov.au (Office).

ANDERSON, June, BA; American opera singer (soprano) and concert and oratorio vocalist; b. 30 Dec. 1952, Boston; ed Yale Univ.; performances at Metropolitan (New York), New York City Opera, Milwaukee Florentine Opera, San Diego Opera, Seattle Opera, Royal Opera (London), La Scala (Milan). *Roles include:* Queen of the Night in The Magic Flute, New York City Opera 1978, title role in Lucia di Lammermoor, Milwaukee Florentine Opera 1982 and Chicago 1990, Gulnara in Il Corsaro, San Diego Opera Verdi Festival 1982, I Puritani, Edmonton Opera 1982–83, title role in Semiramide, Rome Opera 1982–83 and Metropolitan Opera 1990, Rosina in The Barber of Seville, Seattle Opera and Teatro Massimo 1982–83, Cunigonde in Candide 1989, Metropolitan Opera debut as Gilda in Rigoletto 1989; concert and oratorio vocalist: Chicago Pops Orchestra, Handel Festival Kennedy Center, Denver Symphony, St Louis Symphony, Cincinnati Symphony, Maracaibo (Venezuela) Symphony. *Address:* c/o Columbia Artists, 165 W 57th Street, New York, NY 10019, USA.

ANDERSON, Laurie, MFA; American performance artist; b. 1947, Wayne, Ill.; d. of Arthur T. Anderson and Mary Louise (née Rowland) Anderson; ed Columbia Univ.; Instructor in Art History, City Coll. of New York 1973–75; freelance critic Art News, Art Forum; composer and performer multi-media exhbns; several recordings; wrote, directed and performed in film Home of the Brave 1986; one-woman shows include Barnard Coll. 1970, Harold Rivkin Gallery, Washington 1973, Artists' Space, New York 1974, Holly Solomon Gallery, New York 1977, 1980–81, Museum of Modern Art 1978, Queen's Museum, New York 1984; numerous group exhbns 1972–; performance project Happiness, Barbican, London 2002; Artist-in-Residence, ZBS Media 1974; Guggenheim Fellow 1983. *Recordings include:* O Superman (single) 1981, United States (five album set) 1985, Bright Red 1994. *Publications:* The Package 1971, October 1972, Transportation, Transportation 1973, The Rose and the Stone 1974, Notebook 1976, Artifacts at The End of a Decade 1981, Typisch Frac 1981, United States 1984, Laurie Anderson's Postcard Book 1990, Empty Places: A Performance 1991, Stories from the Nerve Bible 1993.

ANDERSON, Matthew Smith, PhD; British historian and fmr university professor; b. 23 May 1922, Perth, Scotland; s. of Matthew Smith Anderson and Elizabeth Dobbie Redpath; m. Olive Ruth Gee 1954; two d.; ed Perth Acad., Edinburgh Univ.; Lecturer in Political History, LSE 1953–61, Reader in Int. History 1961–72, Prof. 1972–85, Prof. Emer. 1985–. *Publications:* Britain's Discovery of Russia 1958, Europe in the Eighteenth Century 1961, The Eastern Question, 1774–1923 1966, The Ascendancy of Europe, 1815–1914 1972, Peter the Great 1978, Historians and Eighteenth-Century Europe 1979, War and Society in Europe of the Old Regime 1618–1789 1988, The Rise of Modern Diplomacy, 1450–1919 1993, The War of the Austrian Succession, 1740–1748 1995, The Origins of the Modern European State System 1494–1618 1998. *Leisure interests:* golf, walking, photography. *Address:* 45 Cholmeley Crescent, Highgate, London, N6 5EX, England. *Telephone:* (20) 8340-0272.

ANDERSON, Michael; British film director; b. 30 Jan. 1920, London; one s.; ed in France. *Films include:* (Co-Dir) Private Angelo (with Peter Ustinov) 1949; (Dir) Waterfront 1950, Hell is Sold Out 1952, Night Was Our Friend, Dial 17, Will Any Gentleman?, The House of The Arrow 1952, The Dam Busters 1954, Around the World in Eighty Days 1956, Yangtse Incident 1957, Chase a Crooked Shadow 1957, Shake Hands with the Devil 1958, Wreck of the Mary Deare 1959–60, All the Fine Young Cannibals 1960, The Naked Edge 1961, Flight from Ashiya (in Japan) 1962, Operation Crossbow 1964, The Quiller Memorandum 1966, The Shoes of The Fisherman 1969, Pope Joan 1970–71, Doc Savage (in Hollywood) 1973, Conduct Unbecoming 1974, Logan's Run (MGM Hollywood) 1975, Orca—Killer Whale 1976, Dominique 1977, The Martian Chronicles 1978, Bells 1979–80, Millennium, Murder by Phone, Second Time Lucky, Separate Vacations, Sword of Gideon, Jeweller's Shop, Young Catherine, Millennium, Summer of the Monkeys. *Address:* c/o Film Rights Ltd, 113–117 Wardour Street, London, W1, England.

ANDERSON, Olive Ruth, BLitt, MA, FRHistS; British professor of history; b. 27 March 1926, Edinburgh; d. of Donald H. F. Gee and Ruth (Clackson) Gee; m. Matthew Smith Anderson (q.v.) 1954; two d.; ed King Edward VI Grammar School, Louth, Lincs., St Hugh's Coll., Oxford; Asst Lecturer in History, Westfield Coll., Univ. of London 1949–56, Lecturer 1958–69, Reader 1969–86, Prof. and Head of Dept 1986–89, Prof. and Deputy Head of Dept, Queen Mary & Westfield Coll. 1989–91, Prof. Emer. and Hon. Research Fellow 1991–, Fellow 1995–; James Ford Special Lecturer, Oxford Univ. 1992; mem. Acad. Council Univ. of London 1989–91 (Exec. Cttee 1990–91); Councillor Royal Historical Soc. 1986–90, Vice-Pres. 1991–95, Hon. Vice-Pres. 2001–; Trustee Theodora Bosanquet Trust 1995–98; mem. Finance Cttee British Fed. of Women Grads. Charitable Foundation 1996–99, Grants Cttee 1998–. *Publications:* A Liberal State at War 1967, Suicide in Victorian and Edwardian England 1987. *Address:* Queen Mary College, University of London, History Dept, London, E1 4NS (Office); 45 Cholmeley Crescent, Highgate, London, N6 5EX, England (Home). *Telephone:* (20) 7882-5016 (College).

ANDERSON, Paul M., BS, MBA; Australian business executive; b. 1 April 1945, USA; m. Kathy Anderson; two d.; ed Univ. of Washington, Stanford

Univ.; joined Ford Motor Co. 1969, Planning Man. 1972–74; Dir Corp. Planning Texas Eastern Corpn 1977–80, Pres. Texas Eastern Synfuels Inc. and Project Dir Tri-State Synfuels Co. 1980–82, Vice-Pres. Planning and Eng Texas Eastern Corpn 1982–85, Sr Vice-Pres. Financial and Diversified Operations 1985–90; Vice-Pres. Finance and Chief Finance Officer Inland Steel Industries Inc. 1990–91; Exec. Vice-Pres., then Pres. Panhandle Eastern Pipe Line Co. 1991–93; Pres., CEO PanEnergy Corpn 1995–97, Chair. 1997, Dir, Pres., COO Duke Energy Corpn (merger between Duke Power and PanEnergy Corpn 1997) 1997–98; Man. Dir, CEO Broken Hill Pty Co. Ltd (later BHP Ltd., now BHP-Billiton) 1998–99; Dir Kerr-McGee Corpn, Baker Hughes Inc., Temple-Inland, Inc. *Leisure interest:* motorcycling. *Address:* c/o BHP-Billton Ltd, BHP Tower, 600 Bourke Street, Melbourne, Vic. 3000, Australia (Office).

ANDERSON, Paul Thomas; American film director; b. 1 Jan. 1970, Studio City, Calif.; s. of the late Ernie Anderson; ed Montclair Coll. Prep. High School; began career as production Asst on TV films. *Films include:* The Dirk Diggler Story 1988, Cigarettes and Coffee 1993, Hard Eight 1996, Boogie Nights (Boston Soc. of Film Critics Award), Magnolia (Golden Bear Award) 1999.

ANDERSON, Reid Bryce; Canadian ballet director; b. 1 April 1949, New Westminster, BC; Prin. Dancer, Stuttgart Ballet 1969–83, Ballet Master, 1983–85; Artistic Dir Ballet BC 1987–89, Nat. Ballet of Canada 1989–; Stuttgart Ballet 1996–; Bundesverdienstkreuz; John Cranko Prize 1989, 1996. *Address:* Stuttgarter Ballett, Oberer Schlossgarten 6, D-70173 Stuttgart, Germany. *Telephone:* (711) 2032235. *Fax:* (711) 2032491.

ANDERSON, Robert Geoffrey William, MA, DPhil, FRSE, FSA, FRSC; British museum director; b. 2 May 1944, London; s. of Herbert Patrick Anderson and Kathleen Diana Burns; m. Margaret Elizabeth Callis Lea 1973; two s.; ed Woodhouse School, Finchley, St John's Coll., Oxford; Keeper Science Museum, London 1980–84; Dir Royal Scottish Museum 1984–85, Nat. Museums of Scotland 1985–92, British Museum 1992–; Curator School of Advanced Study, Univ. of London 1994–; Pres. British Soc. for the History of Science 1988–90, Scientific Instrument Comm. of the Int. Union of the History and Philosophy of Science 1982–97; mem. Bd Boerhaave Museum, Leiden 1995–99, Trustee 1994–; Hon. FSA (Scotland) 1991; Hon. Fellow St John's Coll. Oxford; Hon. DSc (Edinburgh) 1995, (Durham) 1998; Dexter Award (ACS) 1986. *Publications:* The Playfair Collection 1978, Science in India 1982, Science, Medicine and Dissent (ed.) 1987, A New Museum for Scotland (ed.) 1990, Joseph Black: A Bibliography (with G. Fyffe) 1992, Making Instruments Count (Jt) 1993, The Great Court at the British Museum 2000. *Address:* The British Museum, Great Russell Street, London, WC1B 3DG, England. *Telephone:* (20) 7636-1555 (Office). *Fax:* (20) 7323-8480 (Office). *E-mail:* randerson@thebritishmuseum.ac.uk (Office).

ANDERSON, Roy Arnold, MBA; American financial executive; b. 15 Dec. 1920, Ripon, Calif.; s. of Carl Gustav Anderson and Esther Marie Johnson; m. Betty Leona Boehme 1948; two s. two d.; ed Ripon Union High School, Humphrey's School of Business, Stanford Univ.; Man., Factory Accounting, Westinghouse Electric Corpn 1952–56; Man., Accounting and Finance, also Dir, Management Controls, Lockheed Missiles and Space Co. 1956–65; Dir of Finance, Lockheed Georgia Co. 1965–68; Asst Treas. Lockheed Aircraft Corpn (now Lockheed-Martin Corpn) 1968–69, Vice-Pres. and Controller 1969–71, Sr Vice-Pres., Finance 1971–75, Vice-Chair. of Bd, Chief Financial and Admin. Officer 1975–77, Chair. and CEO 1977–85, Dir, Chair. Exec. Cttee and Consultant 1985–88, Chair. Emer. 1991–; Chair. Weingart Foundation 1994–98. *Leisure interests:* gardening, golf, tennis. *Address:* c/o Lockheed-Martin Corporation, 606 S. Olive Street, 23rd Floor, Los Angeles, CA 90014, USA. *Telephone:* (213) 689-8701. *Fax:* (213) 688-0807 (Office).

ANDERSON, Roy Malcolm, PhD, ARCS, DIC, FRS; British professor of epidemiology; b. 12 April 1947, Herts.; s. of James Anderson and Betty Watson-Weatherborn; m. 1st Dr. Mary Joan Mitchell 1975 (divorced 1989); m. 2nd Claire Baron 1990; ed Duncombe School, Bengeo, Richard Hale School, Hertford, Imperial Coll., Univ. of London; IBM Research Fellow, Oxford Univ. 1971–73; Lecturer, King's Coll., Univ. of London 1973–77; Lecturer, Imperial Coll. 1977–80, Reader 1980–82, Prof. of Parasite Ecology 1982–93, Head of Dept of Biology 1984–93; Linacre Prof. Oxford Univ. 1993–2000, Head Dept of Zoology 1993–98, Dir The Wellcome Trust Centre for the Epidemiology of Infectious Disease 1993–2000; Head of Dept of Infectious Disease Epidemiology, Imperial Coll. Faculty of Medicine, Univ. of London 2000–; Genentech Visiting Prof., Univ. of Washington 1998; James McLaughlin Visiting Prof., Univ. of Texas 1999; Chair. Terrestrial Life Sciences Cttee, Nat. Environment Research Council; Patron Virgin Health Care Foundation; Chair. Infection and Immunity Panel for Wellcome Trust 1990–92; Council mem. Nat. Environment Research Council 1988–91, Advisory Council on Science and Tech. (ACOST) 1989–91, Royal Soc. 1989–92, Zoological Soc. 1988–90; mem. Bd of Dirs., AIDS Policy Unit 1988–89, Spongiform Encephalopathy Advisory Cttee 1997–; mem. Acad. of Medical Sciences 1998, Acad. Europaea 1998; Trustee, The Wellcome Trust 1991–92, Gov. 1992–2000; Fellow Inst. of Biology, Royal Soc. of Tropical Medicine and Hygiene, Royal Statistical Soc., Merton Coll., Oxford 1993–2000; Foreign mem. Inst. of Medicine, NAS 2000–; Joseph Smadel Lecture (Infectious Diseases Soc. of America) 1994; Hon. Fellow Linacre Coll., Oxford Univ. 1997–; Hon. FRCPath 1999–; Hon. FRSS 2002–; Hon. MRCP; Hon. ScD (East Anglia) 1997, (Stirling) 1998; Zoological Soc. Scientific Medal 1982, Huxley Memorial Medal 1983, CA Wright Memorial Medal 1986, David Starr Jordan Prize 1986, Chalmers Medal 1988, Weldon Medal 1989, John Grundy Lecture Medal 1990, Frink Medal 1993, Joseph Smadel Medal, Infectious Diseases Soc. of America 1994, Distinguished Statistical Ecologist Award 1998. *Publications:* Population Dynamics of Infectious Disease Agents: Theory and Applications (Ed.) 1982, Population Biology of Infectious Diseases (Jt Ed. with R. M. May) 1982, Infectious Diseases of Humans: Dynamics and Control (with R. M. May) 1991. *Leisure interests:* hill walking, croquet, natural history, photography. *Address:* Department of Infectious Disease Epidemiology, Imperial College Faculty of Medicine, University of London, St Mary's Campus, Norfolk Place, London, W2 1PG, England (Office). *Telephone:* (20) 7594-3398 (Office). *Fax:* (20) 7402-3927 (Office). *E-mail:* roy.anderson@ic.ac.uk (Office).

ANDERSON, Theodore Wilbur, PhD; American professor of statistics and economics; b. 5 June 1918, Minneapolis, Minn.; s. of Theodore Wilbur Anderson and Evelynn Johnson Anderson; m. Dorothy Fisher 1950; one s. two d.; ed North Park Coll., Northwestern Univ., Princeton Univ.; Research Assoc. Cowles Comm. for Research in Econs, Univ. of Chicago 1945–46; Instructor in Math. Statistics, Columbia Univ. 1946–47, Asst Prof. to Prof. 1947–67, Chair. of Dept 1956–60, 1964–65, Dir Office of Naval Research, Dept of Math. Statistics 1950–68; Prof. of Statistics and Econs, Stanford Univ. 1967–88, Prin. Investigator Nat. Science Foundation Project Dept of Econs 1969–83, Dept of Statistics 1983–92; Prin. Investigator Army Research Office Project, Dept of Statistics 1982–92; Guggenheim Fellow, Univs. of Stockholm and Cambridge 1947–48; Academic Visitor, Imperial Coll. of Science and Tech., UK, Univ. of London, Visiting Prof. of Math., Univ. of Moscow, Visiting Prof. of Statistics, Univ. of Paris 1967–68; Academic Visitor, LSE 1974–75, Univ. of Southern Calif. 1989; Research Consultant, Cowles Foundation for Research in Econs 1946–60; Consultant, Rand Corpn 1949–66; Fellow, Center for Advanced Study in the Behavioral Sciences 1957–58, Visiting Scholar 1972–73, 1980; Distinguished Scholar, Calif. Inst. of Tech. 1980; Visiting Prof. of Econs, Columbia Univ. 1983–84, New York Univ. 1983–84; Sabbaticant, IBM Systems Research Inst. 1984; Research Assoc. Naval Postgraduate School 1986–87; Visiting Distinguished Prof. of Norwegian Council for Scientific and Industrial Research, Univ. of Oslo 1989; Fellow Acad. of Arts and Sciences 1974–; mem. NAS 1976–; Pres. Inst. of Mathematical Statistics 1963, mem. Council; Vice-Pres. American Statistical Soc. 1971–73; Chair. Section U, Statistics, AAAS 1990–91; mem. Econometric Soc., Inst. of Math. Statistics (mem. Council), Royal Statistical Soc., UK, American Math. Soc., Bernoulli Soc. for Math. Statistics and Probability, Indian Statistical Inst., Int. Statistical Inst., Statistical Soc. of Canada; Foreign mem. Norwegian Acad. of Science and Letters 1994; Hon. DLit (North Park Coll.) 1988; Hon. DSc (Northwestern Univ.) 1989; Hon. PhD (Oslo) 1997; R. A. Fisher Award (Cttee of Pres. of Statistical Socs.) 1985, Distinguished Alumnus Award, North Park Coll. 1987, Samuel S. Wilks Memorial Medal, American Statistical Asscn 1988, Award of Merit, Northwestern Univ. Alumni Asscn 1989. *Publications:* An Introduction to Multivariate Statistical Analysis 1958, 1984, The Statistical Analysis of Time Series 1971, A Bibliography of Multivariate Statistical Analysis (with S.D. Gupta and G. Styan) 1972, Introductory Statistical Analysis (with S. Sclove) 1974, An Introduction to the Statistical Analysis of Data (with S. Sclove) 1978, 1986, A Guide to MINITAB for the Statistical Analysis of Data (with B. Eynon) 1986, Collected Papers of T. W. Anderson 1943–85 1990, The New Statistical Analysis of Data (with J. D. Finn) 1996 and some 165 articles in statistical journals; ed. and fmr ed. of numerous specialist journals. *Leisure interests:* tennis, swimming, travelling. *Address:* Department of Statistics, Sequoia Hall, Stanford University, Stanford, CA 94305-4065; 746 Santa Ynez Street, Stanford, CA 94305-8441, USA (Home). *Telephone:* (650) 723-4732; (650) 327-5204 (Home). *Fax:* (650) 725-8977.

ANDERSON, Sir (William) Eric (Kinloch), Kt, MA, DLitt, FRSE; British educationist; b. 27 May 1936, Edinburgh; s. of W. J. Kinloch Anderson and Margaret Harper; m. Anne Elizabeth Mason (née Poppy) 1960; one s. one d.; ed George Watson's Coll., Univ. of St Andrews and Balliol Coll. Oxford; Asst Master, Fettes Coll. Edinburgh 1960–64, 1966–70, Gordonstoun School 1964–66; Headmaster, Abingdon School 1970–75, Shrewsbury School 1975–80, Eton College 1980–94, Provost 2000–; Rector, Lincoln Coll. Oxford 1994–2000; mem. Visiting Cttee of Memorial Church, Harvard 2001–; Trustee Nat. Heritage Memorial Fund 1996–98, Chair. 1998–2001, Royal Collection Fund 2000–, Shakespeare Birthplace Trust 2001–; Chair. Cumberland Lodge 1997–. *Publications:* The Journal of Walter Scott (ed.) 1972, The Percy Letters (Vol. IX) 1988, The Sayings of Sir Walter Scott 1995; articles and reviews. *Leisure interests:* theatre, golf, fishing. *Address:* Provost's Lodge, Eton College, Windsor, Berks., SL4 6DH, England. *Telephone:* (1753) 671234.

ANDERSON, Capt. William R.; American naval officer; b. 17 June 1921, Bakerville, Tenn.; s. of David Hensley Anderson and Mary Anderson; m. 1st Yvonne Etzel 1943 (divorced 1979); two s.; m. 2nd Patricia Walters 1980; one s. one d.; ed Columbia Military Acad. and U.S. Naval Acad.; commissioned 1942; service in submarines 1942–59; Idaho Univ. Inst. of Naval Tactics 1951; Naval Reactors Branch, Atomic Energy Comm. 1956–57, 1959; Commdr Nautilus, the world's first atomic submarine 1957–59 (Nautilus achieved the first Pacific-to-Atlantic under-ice transit and was the first ship to reach the North Pole 1958); Freedoms Foundation 1962–64; mem. US House of Reps. 1964–72; Computer Corporate Exec. 1972–; Democrat; Bronze Star Combat "V", Legion of Merit 1958, Christopher Columbus Int. Medal (Italy) 1958, Patron's Medal, Royal Geographical Soc. 1959, Freedom Leadership Award

1960, Lowell Thomas Award, The Explorers Club, New York 1997, various war and campaign medals. *Publications:* Nautilus 90 North 1959, First Under the North Pole 1959, The Useful Atom 1966. *Address:* 10505 Miller Road, Oakton, VA 22124-1709, USA.

ANDERSON-IMBERT, Enrique, PhD; American (b. Argentine) university professor; b. 12 Feb. 1910, Argentina; s. of José Enrique Anderson and Honorina Imbert; m. Margot Di Clerico 1934; one s. one d.; ed Univ. Nacional de Buenos Aires; Prof., Univ. Nacional de Cuyo, Argentina 1940–41, Univ. Tucumán, Argentina 1941–46, Univ. of Michigan 1947–65; First Victor S. Thomas Prof. of Hispanic American Literature, Harvard Univ. 1965; mem. American Acad. of Arts and Sciences 1967, Academia Argentina de Letras, 1978; City of Buenos Aires Prize for novel Vigilia 1934. *Publications:* Vigilia 1934, El arte de la prosa en Juan Montalvo 1948, Historia de la literatura hispanoamericana 1954, El grimorio 1961, Vigilia-Fuga 1963, El gato de Cheshire 1965, Genio y figura de Sarmiento 1967, La originalidad de Rubén Darío 1967, La sandía y otros cuentos 1969, Una aventura de Sarmiento en Chicago 1969, La locura juega al ajedrez 1971, La flecha en el aire 1972, Los domingos del profesor 1972, Estudios sobre letras hispánicas 1974, La Botella de Klein 1975, Los primeros cuentos del mundo 1977, El realismo mágico 1978, Teoría y técnica del cuento 1979, Dos mujeres y un Julián 1982, La prosa 1984, La crítica literaria 1984, El tamaño de las brujas 1986, Nuevos estudios sobre letras hispanas 1986, Evocación de sombras en la ciudad geométrica 1989, El anillo de Mozart (included in Narraciones Completas) 1990, Mentiras y mentirosos en el mundo de las letras 1992, Y pensar que hace diez años 1994, Reloj de arena 1996, Amorios 1997, Modernidad y Postmodernidad 1997, La buena forma de un crimen 1998. *Address:* 4859 Golden Road, Pleasanton, CA 94566, USA.

ANDERSSON, Bibi; Swedish actress; b. 11 Nov. 1935; d. of Josef Andersson and Karin Andersson; m. 1st Kjell Grede 1960; one d.; m. 2nd Per Ahlmark (q.v.) 1978 (divorced); ed Terserus Drama School and Royal Dramatic Theatre School, Stockholm; Malmö Theatre 1956–59, Royal Dramatic Theatre, Stockholm 1959–62, 1968–; appearances at Uppsala Theatre 1962–. *Plays acted in include:* Erik XIV 1956, Tre systrar 1961, King John 1961, Le balcon 1961, La grotte 1962, Uncle Vanya 1962, Who's Afraid of Virginia Woolf? 1963, As You Like It 1964, After the Fall 1964–65, The Full Circle 1973, Twelfth Night 1975, The Night of the Tribades 1977, Twelfth Night 1980, Antigone 1981, A Streetcar Named Desire 1981, 1983, L'oiseau bleu 1981, Prisoners of Altona 1982, The Creditors 1984–85, Ett gästabud i Pestens tid 1986, Loner 1994. *Films acted in include:* Sjunde inseglet (The Seventh Seal) 1956, Smultronstället (Wild Strawberries) 1957, Nära livet (The Brink of Life) 1958, Sommarnöje Sökes (Summer House Wanted) 1958, Djävulens öga (Eye of the Devil) 1961, Älskarinnen (The Mistress) 1962, För att inte tala om alla dessa kvinnor (All Those Women) 1964, Juninatt (June Night) 1965, Ön (The Island) 1965, Syskonbädd (My Sister, My Love) 1966, Persona 1966, Duel at Diablo 1966, Story of a Woman 1968, The Girls 1969, The Kremlin Letter 1970, A Passion, The Touch 1971, Scenes from a Marriage 1974, I Never Promised You a Rose Garden, La rivale 1976, An Enemy of the People 1976, Babette's Feast, Quintet 1979, Svarte Fugler 1982, Berget på månens baksida 1982, Litt et Art 1989, The Hill on the Other Side of the Mountain, Manika, Fordringsagare. *Address:* c/o Royal Dramatic Theatre, Stockholm (Office); Tykövägen 27, Lidingö 18161, Sweden (Home). *Telephone:* (8) 766-46-16.

ANDERSSON, Claes, DMed; Finnish politician; b. 30 May 1937, Helsinki; s. of Oscar Andersson and Ethel Hjelt; m. Katriina Kuusi 1970; six c.; novelist and poet 1974; MP 1987–; fmrly mem. Finnish People's Democratic League 1970–90, mem. Left-Wing Alliance 1990, Chair. 1990; Chair. Finland's Swedish Union of Writers; Vice-Pres. Information Centre of Finnish Literature 1985–; Eino-Leino Prize 1985, five times recipient of State Prize of Literature. *Publications:* 14 collections of poems, three novels, 20 stage plays and several radio plays and an opera libretto. *Leisure interest:* amateur jazz piano. *Address:* Vasemmistoliitto, Siltasaarenkatu 6, 7th Floor, 00530 Helsinki, Finland. *Telephone:* (9) 774741. *Fax:* (9) 77474200.

ANDERSSON, Harriet; Swedish actress; b. 1932, Stockholm; theatre career commenced in chorus at Oscars Theatre; subsequently appeared in reviews and then started serious dramatic career at Malmö City Theatre 1953; now appears regularly at Kunigliga Dramatiska Teatern, Stockholm; German Film Critics' Grand Prize for Through a Glass Darkly, Swedish Film Asscn plaque; Best Actress Award, Venice Film Festival 1964 (for To Love). *Films include:* Summer with Monica 1953, Sawdust and Tinsel 1953, Women's Dreams 1955, Dreams of a Summer Night 1955, Through a Glass Darkly 1961, All Those Women 1964, Cries and Whispers 1973, One Sunday in September 1963, To Love 1964, Adventure Starts Here 1965, Stimulantia 1965–66, Rooftree 1966, Anna 1970, Siska 1962, Dream of Happiness 1963, Loving Couples 1964, For the Sake of Friendship 1965, Vine Bridge 1965, The Serpent 1966, The Deadly Affair 1967, The Girls 1968, The Stake. *Theatre includes:* Anne Frank in The Diary of Anne Frank, Ophelia in Hamlet, The Beggar's Opera and plays by Chekhov. *Address:* c/o Sandrew Film & Theater AB, Box 5612, 114 86 Stockholm, Sweden.

ANDERSSON, Leif Christer Leander, MD, PhD; Finnish professor of pathology; b. 24 March 1944, Esse; s. of Herman Alfons Andersson and Elvi Alina Häll; m. Nea Margareta Gustavson 1971; one s. two d.; ed Univ. of Helsinki; Visiting Investigator, Univ. of Uppsala 1975–76, Research Inst. of Scripps Clinic, La Jolla, Calif. 1989–90; Prof. of Pathology, Univ. of Helsinki 1981–; Research Prof. Finnish Acad. of Science 1987–92; Prof. of Pathology,

Karolinska Inst., Stockholm, Sweden 1996–2000, Head of Pathology, Karolinska Hosp. 1997–98; Head of Diagnostics, Div. of Pathology and Medical Genetics, Helsinki Univ. Hosp. 2002–; Anders Jahres Medical Prize, Univ. of Oslo 1981. *Publications:* about 310 original publs on cell biology, immunology, haematology, oncology and pathology. *Leisure interest:* Dixieland jazz. *Address:* University of Helsinki, Haartman Institute, Department of Pathology, P.O. Box 21 (Haartmaninkatu 3), 00014 Helsinki, Finland. *Telephone:* (9) 1911. *Fax:* (9) 19126675. *E-mail:* leif.andersson@helsinki.fi (Office).

ANDERTON, James Patrick (Jim); New Zealand politician; b. 21 Jan. 1938, Auckland; m. twice; three s. one d.; ed Seddon Memorial Tech. Coll., Auckland Teachers' Training Coll; teacher for two years; Child Welfare Officer Educ. Dept, Wanganui; Catholic Youth Movt Organiser 1960–65; Sec. Catholic Diocesan Office, Auckland 1967–69; Export Man. UEB Textiles 1969–70; Man. Dir Anderton Holdings 1971–; City Councillor Manukau 1965–69, Auckland 1974–77, Councillor Auckland Regional Authority 1977–80; joined Labour Party 1963, held posts at Electorate, Regional and Exec. levels, Pres. NZ Labour Party 1979–84, mem. Policy Council 1979–89; MP for Sydenham 1984–; resigned from Labour Party 1989 and formed the New Labour Party; re-elected MP for Sydenham (now Wigram) 1990 as N.Z.L.P. cand.; elected first leader of Alliance Party (formed 1991); Deputy Prime Minister, Minister of Econ. Devt, for Industry and Regional Devt, for Public Trust Office and Audit Dept 1999–. *Leisure interests:* chess, cricket and classical guitar. *Address:* Ministry of Economic Development, 33 Bowen Street, Wellington (Office); 286A Selwyn Avenue, Spreydon, Christchurch, New Zealand (Home). *Telephone:* (4) 472-0030 (Office); (3) 365-5459 (Home). *Fax:* (4) 473-4638 (Office). *E-mail:* info@med.govt.nz (Office). *Website:* www.med.govt.nz (Office).

ANDÒ, Salvatore; Italian politician and university lecturer in law; b. 13 Feb. 1945, Jonia, Catania; m.; two c.; Lecturer in Public Law, Univ. of Catania; Chair. Consiglio Nazionale delle Opere Universitarie; Prov. Exec. Fed. of Young Socialists 1963–69; mem. Prov. Exec. Cttee Catania Fed. of Italian Socialist Party (PSI) 1974–, mem. Exec. of Fed. 1975–, Deputy Sec. 1978–, mem. Regional Cttee PSI; Parl. Deputy 1979–; Minister of Defence 1992–93. *Address:* c/o Italian Socialist Party, Via del Corso 476, 00186 Rome, Italy.

ANDO, Tadao; Japanese architect; b. 13 Sept. 1941, Osaka; m. Yumiko Kato 1970; one c.; began as professional boxer; taught himself architecture by observing bldgs in Africa, America, Europe; Founder, Dir Tadao Ando Architect and Assocs. 1969–; Visiting Prof. Columbia, Harvard, Yale Univs; exhbn at RIBA 1993; Gold Medal of Architecture (French Acad.), Carlsberg Architecture Prize, Pritzker Prize 1995, Imperial Praemium Prize 1996, Royal Gold Medal RIBA 1997. *Works include:* school for Benetton, Northern Italy, the Church of Light, Osaka, Japan, Children's Museum, Hyogo, Japan, Water Temple, Osaka, Rokko Housing nr Osaka. *Publications include:* Tadao Ando 1981, Tadao Ando: Buildings, Project, Writings 1984. *Address:* Tadao Ando Architect and Associates, 5-23 Toyosaki, 2-chome, Kita-ku, Osaka 531, Japan.

ANDOV, Stojan; Macedonian politician and economist; b. 1935; ed Skopje Univ., Belgrade Univ.; worked as economist; political activities since late 1980s; one of founders and mem. Exec. Bd Liberal Party of Macedonia 1990; Deputy Chair. Repub. Exec. Cttee; mem. Union Veche (Parl.) of Yugoslavia; took part in negotiations between Yugoslavia and European Econ. Community; Amb. of Yugoslavia to Iraq; Del. to Nat. Ass. Repub. of Macedonia 1990–, Chair. 1990–96, Pres. Nat. Ass. 2001–; Acting Pres. of Macedonia Oct. 1995–Jan. 1996; Head faction Reform Forces of Macedonia-Liberal Party, Co-Chair. 1996. *Address:* Sobranje, 1000 Skopje, 11 Oktombri bb, Macedonia (Office). *Telephone:* (2) 112255 (Office). *Fax:* (2) 237947 (Office). *E-mail:* sgjorgi@assembly.gov.uk (Office). *Website:* www.assembly.gov.mk/sobranje.

ANDRÁSFALVY, Bertalan, PhD; Hungarian politician and ethnographer; b. 17 Nov. 1931, Sopron; s. of Károly Andrásfalvy and Judit Mezey; m. Mária Gere; three s.; ed Budapest Univ.; with Museum of Szekszárd 1955, Transdanubian Research Inst. of the Hungarian Acad. of Sciences 1960–76, Archives of Baranya County and Museum of Pécs –1985; Exec., later Dept Head Ethnographic Research Group, Hungarian Acad. of Sciences; Assoc. Prof. Univ. of Pécs 1989–93, Prof. 1993–; mem. Cttee Hungarian Democratic Forum; mem. of Parl. 1990–; Minister of Culture and Public Educ. 1990–93; Hon. mem. Finnish Literature Soc.; Eriksson Prize of the Swedish Royal Acad., István Győrffy Memorial Medal of Hungarian Ethnographic Soc.; Grand Silver Medal with Ribbon (Austria); Order of Merit Medium Cross with Star (Hungary), Grosse Verdienstkreutz (Germany), Grand Cross of Lion's Order of Knighthood (Finland). *Publications:* Contrasting Value Orientation of Peasant Communities, Die traditionelle Bewirtschaftung der Überschwemmungsgebiete in Ungarn, European Culture of the Hungarian People, Vom 'Nutzen' der Volkskunst und der Volkskunde. *Leisure interest:* gardening. *Address:* 7694 Hosszuhetény, Fő útca 26, Hungary (Home). *Telephone:* (72) 327-622-3526 (Office); (72) 490-473 (Home). *Fax:* (72) 327-622-3529 (Office).

ANDRE, Carl; American sculptor; b. 16 Sept. 1935, Quincy, Mass.; s. of George H. Andre and Margaret M. Andre (née Johnson); ed Phillips Acad., Andover, Mass., served US Army 1955–56; went to New York 1957; worked as freight brakeman and conductor of Pa Railroad 1960–64; first public exhbn 1964, numerous public collections in USA and Europe. *Address:* c/o Paula Cooper, 534 West 21st Street, New York, NY 10011-2812; Konrad Fischer,

Platanestrasse 7, 40233 Düsseldorf, Germany; Cooper Station, PO Box 1001, New York, NY 10276, USA (Home). *Telephone:* (212) 255-1105 (New York); (211) 68-59-08 (Düsseldorf).

ANDRÉ, Maurice; French trumpeter; b. 21 May 1933, Alès, Gard; s. of Marcel André and Fabienne Volpélière; m. Lilianne Arnoult 1956; four c.; ed Conservatoire nat. supérieur de musique, Paris; apprenticed as coal miner before formal music studies; won Prix d'honneur for trumpet; joined Paris Radio Orchestra; subsequently First Trumpet, Lamoureur Orchestra and other orchestras; played in jazz groups and chamber orchestras; now soloist with world's leading orchestras; specialises in baroque and contemporary music; Prof. of Trumpet, Paris Conservatoire 1967–; has made about 260 recordings, including 30 trumpet concertos; Chevalier de la Légion d'honneur; Commdr des Arts et des Lettres; First Prize, Geneva Int. Competition 1955, Munich Int. Competition 1963, Schallplattenpreis, Berlin 1970, Victoire de la musique 1987. *Leisure interests:* pen and ink drawing, gardening, swimming, sculpture in wood and stone. *Address:* Presles-en-Brie, 77220 Tournan-en-Brie, France (Home); c/o Harry Lapp Organisation, 9 avenue de la Liberté, 67000 Strasbourg.

ANDREA, Pat; Netherlands artist; b. 25 June 1942, The Hague; s. of Kees Andrea and Metty Naezer; m. 1st Cecile Hessels 1966 (divorced 1983); m. 2nd Cristina Ruiz Guiñazu 1993; three s. one d.; ed Royal Acad. of Fine Arts, The Hague; paints in figurative style, focusing on personal deformities, people in dramatic situations, sex and violence in suspense; represented in MOMA, New York, Centre Pompidou, Paris and Frissiras Museum, Athens; Prof. Ecole Nat. Supérieur des Beaux Arts, Paris 1998–; Jacob Maris Prize 1968. *Exhibitions include:* Haags Gemeentemuseum 1968, retrospective Museum of Modern Art, Arnhem 1975, Galerie Nina Dausset, Paris 1979, Paolo Baldacci Gallery, New York 1992, retrospective of works in Argentinian collections 1992, retrospectives Stedelijk Museum, Schiedam and Inst. Néerlandais, Paris 1994, retrospective in Frissiras Museum, Athens 2001. *Films:* (with Fred Compain) Du crime consideré comme un des Beaux Arts 1981, Journal de Patagonie 1985, (with Marie Binet) L'aventure Pat Andrea 2002. *Publications:* (with H. P. de Boer) Nederlands gebarenboekje 1979, (with J. Cortazar) La Puñalada 1982, Pat Andrea: conversations avec Pierre Sterckx 1993. *Address:* 18 rue Henri Regnault, 75014 Paris, France. *Telephone:* 1-45-45-44-23. *Fax:* 1-40-44-75-75. *E-mail:* andrea@noos.fr (Office); andrea@noos.fr (Home).

ANDREANI, Jacques; French diplomatist (retd.); b. 22 Nov. 1929, Paris; m. 1st Huguette de Fonclare; one s. one d.; m. 2nd Donatella Monterisi 1981; one s. one d.; ed Inst. d'Etudes Politiques, Univ. of Paris and Ecole Nat. d'Admin; Sec. French Embassy, Washington, DC 1955–60, Moscow 1961–64; Ministry of Foreign Affairs 1964–70; Deputy Rep. of France, NATO, Brussels 1970–72; Head, French Del. to CSCE, Helsinki and Geneva 1972–75; Asst Sec. for European Affairs, Ministry of Foreign Affairs 1975–79; Amb. to Egypt 1979–81; Dir of Political Affairs, Ministry of Foreign Affairs 1981–84; Amb. to Italy 1984–88; Chief of Staff, Ministry of Foreign Affairs 1988–89; Amb. to USA 1989–95; Special Asst to Minister of Foreign Affairs 1995–97; Commdr Légion d'honneur, Commdr Ordre Nat. du Mérite. *Publication:* L'Amérique et nous 2000. *Leisure interests:* arts, music, golf. *Address:* 40 rue Bonaparte, 75006 Paris, France (Home). *Telephone:* 1-43-26-14-92 (Home). *Fax:* 1-43-26-60-82 (Home). *E-mail:* jandrean@noos.fr (Home).

ANDREAS, Glenn Allen, BA, JUDr; American business executive; b. 22 June 1943, Cedar Rapids, Ia; s. of Glenn Allen Andreas and Vera Yates; m. Toni Kay Hibma 1964; one s. two d.; ed Valparaiso Univ., Ind., Valparaiso Univ. School of Law; Attorney, US Treasury Dept 1969–73; with Legal Dept, Archer Daniels Midland Co. 1973–86, Treasurer 1986–, Chief Financial Officer of European Operations 1989–94, Vice-Pres. and Counsel to Exec. Cttee 1994–96, mem. Office of CEO 1996–97, Pres., CEO 1997–99, Chair., CEO 1999–. *Leisure interest:* golf. *Address:* Archer Daniels Midland Company, 4666 Faries Parkway, P.O. Box 1470, Decatur, IL 62526-5666, USA (Office). *Telephone:* (217) 424-5426 (Office). *Fax:* (217) 424-4266 (Office).

ANDREEV, Aleksandr Fyodorovich, DrPhysSc; Russian physicist; b. 10 Dec. 1939, Leningrad; s. of Fyodor Andreev and Nina Andreeva; m. Tamara Turok 1960; one d.; ed Moscow Physico-Tech. Inst.; Jr then Sr Researcher 1964–79, Prof. 1979–; Deputy Dir USSR Acad. of Sciences, Kapitza Inst. for Physical Problems 1984–91, Dir 1991–; Lorentz Prof. Univ. of Leiden 1992; Ed.-in-Chief Priroda 1993–, JETP 1997–; Corresp. mem. USSR (now Russian) Acad. of Sciences 1981–87, mem. 1987–, Vice-Pres. 1991–; Lomonosov Prize, USSR Acad. of Sciences 1984, Lenin Prize 1986, Carus-Medaille der Deutschen Akad. der Naturforscher Leopoldina, Carus-Preis der Stadt Schweinfurt 1987, Simon Memorial Prize (UK) 1995, Kapitza Gold Medal, Russian Acad. of Sciences 1999. *Address:* Academy of Sciences, Kapitza Institute for Physical Problems, Kosygin Street 2, 117334 Moscow, Russia. *Telephone:* (095) 938-20-29. *Fax:* (095) 938-20-30. *E-mail:* andreev@kapitza.ras.ru (Home).

ANDREI, Ştefan; Romanian politician; b. 29 March 1931, Podari-Livezi, Dolj County; ed Inst. of Civil Eng, Bucharest; Asst Prof. Inst. of Civil Eng and Inst. of Oil, Gas and Geology, Bucharest 1956–63; mem. Union of Communist Youth (UCY) 1949–54; joined student movement 1951; mem. Exec. Cttee Union of Student Asscns. 1958–62; mem. Bureau Cen. Cttee UCY 1962–65; mem. Romanian Communist Party (RCP) 1954–89; alt. mem. Cen. Cttee RCP 1969–72, mem. 1972–89; First Deputy Head of Int. Section Cen. Cttee 1966–72; Sec. Cen. Cttee 1972–78; alt. mem. Exec. Political Cttee 1974–89; mem. Perm. Bureau, Exec. Political Cttee 1974–84; Minister for Foreign

Affairs 1978–85; Secr. Cen. Cttee 1985–87; Deputy Prime Minister 1987–89; mem. Grand Nat. Ass. 1975–89; mem. Nat. Council Front of Socialist Democracy and Unity 1980–89; several Romanian orders and medals.

ANDREJEVS, Georgs, DMed; Latvian politician, diplomatist and scientist; b. 30 Oct. 1932, Tukums; m. Anita Andrejeva; one s. one d.; ed Latvian Medical Inst.; on staff Stradine Repub. Clinical Hosp. 1959–62; Asst Prof., Head Dept of Surgery, Chief Anaesthesiologist and Reanimatologist of Ministry of Health 1962–92; mem. Latvian Acad. of Sciences 1995–, European Asscn of Anaesthesiologists 1997–; Deputy to Latvian Repub. Supreme Council; mem. Latvian People's Front; Sec. Comm. for Foreign Affairs of Supreme Council; Minister of Foreign Affairs 1992–93; mem. Saima (Parl.) 1993–95; Amb. to Canada 1995–98, to Council of Europe 1998–. *Address:* Latvian Mission to Council of Europe, 67075 Strasbourg, Cédex, France.

ANDREN, Anders, LèsL, MBA; Swedish business executive; b. 30 July 1939, Gothenburg; s. of Erik Andren and Birgit Flodin; m. Monika Grohmann 1967; one s.; ed Univ. of Stockholm and Institut européen de l'administration des affaires; Dir-Gen. Electrolux Canarias SA 1968–70, Electrolux Belgique 1971–74; Pres.-Dir-Gen. Electrolux SA France 1974–93, fmr Chair., Man. Dir; fmr Pres. Supervisory Bd, Arthur Martin (now Hon. Pres.); Pres.-Dir Gen. Groupe Esab SA France 1992–95, Direct Ménager France 1993–98; f. Domus France SA 1998; Hon. Pres. Swedish Chamber of Commerce in France, Chevalier, Légion d'honneur. *Address:* 13 Boucle d'en bas, 60270 Gouvieux, France (Home).

ANDREOLI, Kathleen Gainor; American university dean; b. 22 Sept. 1935, Albany, New York; d. of John Edward Gainor and Edmunda Ringelmann Gainor; m. Thomas Eugene Andreoli 1960 (divorced); one s. two d.; ed Georgetown Univ. and Vanderbilt Schools of Nursing and Univ. of Ala School of Nursing, Birmingham; Staff Nurse, Albany Hosp. Medical Center, New York 1957; Instructor, various schools of nursing 1957–70; Educational Dir, Physician Asst Program, Dept of Medicine, School of Medicine, Univ. of Ala 1970–75, subsequently Asst then Assoc. of Nursing 1970–79, Prof. of Nursing 1979; Prof. of Nursing, Special Asst to Pres. for Educational Affairs, Univ. of Texas Health Science Center, Houston 1979–82, Vice-Pres. for Educational Services, Interprofessional Educ. and Int. Programs 1983–87; Vice-Pres. Nursing Affairs and John L. and Helen Kellogg Dean of Coll. of Nursing Rush Univ., Chicago 1987–; Heart and Lung, Journal of Total Care 1971; mem. Bd of Dirs. American Asscn of Colleges of Nursing 1998–2000; mem. Nat. Advisory Nursing Council V.H.A. 1992, Advisory Bd Robert Wood Johnson Clinic Nursing School Program, Visiting Cttee Vanderbilt Univ. School of Nursing, Editorial/Advisory Bd The Nursing Spectrum 1996–, Advisory Bd Managing Major Diseases: Diabetes Mellitus and Hypertension 1999, numerous other bodies; mem. Inst. of Medicine; Fellow American Acad. of Nursing; Founders Award, NC Heart Asscn 1970; numerous other awards. *Publications:* Comprehensive Cardiac Care (jtly.) 1983; contrib. articles in professional journals. *Leisure interests:* music, art, reading, bicycling, travelling. *Address:* Rush Presbyterian—St Luke's Medical Center, 600 South Paulina Street, Suite 1080, Chicago, IL 60612-3806 (Office); 1212 South Lake Shore Drive, Chicago, IL 60605-2402, USA (Home). *Telephone:* (312) 942-7117 (Office); (312) 266-8338 (Home). *Fax:* (312) 942-3043 (Office). *E-mail:* Kathleen_G_Andreoli@rush.edu (Office). *Website:* www.rushu.rush.edu/nursing (Office).

ANDREOTTI, Giulio; Italian politician and journalist; b. 14 Jan. 1919, Rome; s. of Philip Andreotti; m. Livia Danese 1945; two s. two d.; ed Univ. of Rome; Pres., Fed. of Catholic Univs. in Italy 1942–45; Deputy to the Constituent Ass. 1945 and to Parl. 1946– (Life Senator 1992–); Under-Sec. in the Govts. of De Gasperi and Pella 1947–53; Minister for the Interior in Fanfani Govt 1954; Minister of Finance 1955–58, of Treasury 1958–59, of Defence 1959–60, 1960–66, March–Oct. 1974, of Industry and Commerce 1966–68, for the Budget and Econ. Planning and in charge of Southern Devt Fund 1974–76, Chair. Christian Democratic Parl. Party in Chamber of Deputies 1948–72; Prime Minister 1972–73, 1976–79, 1989–92; Chair. Foreign Affairs Cttee, Chamber of Deputies; Minister of Foreign Affairs 1983–89; Co-founder European Democracy 2001–; immunity lifted May 1993, charged with consorting with the Mafia March 1995 (acquitted 1999); charged with complicity in murder Nov. 1995, acquitted 1999, prosecution urged an appeals court to reconsider, sentenced to 24 years' imprisonment Nov. 2002; Hon. LLD (Beijing Univ.) 1991. *Publications:* Editor of Concretezza 1954–76, A Ogni morte di Papa 1980, Gli USA Visti da Vicino 1983, Diari 1976–79, Lives: Encounters with History Makers 1989, The USA Up Close 1992, Cosa Loro 1995, De Prima Republica 1996.

ANDRETTI, Mario Gabriele; American racing driver; b. 28 Feb. 1940, Montona, Italy; m. Dee Ann Hoch 1961; two s. one d.; began racing career at age 19 in Nazareth, Pa; Champ Car Nat. Champion 1965, 1966, 1969, 1984; winner of Daytona 500 Miles 1967; winner of 12 Hours of Sebring 1967, 1970, 1972; winner of Indianapolis 500 Miles 1969; USAC Nat. Dirt Track Champion 1974; Formula One World Champion 1978; winner of Int. Race of Champions 1979; all-time Champ Car lap leader (7,587); oldest race winner in recorded Champ Car history; Driver of the Year 1967, 1978, 1984, Driver of the Quarter Century 1992, Driver of the Century 1999–2000. *Grand Prix wins:* 1971 South African (Ferrari), 1976 Japanese (Lotus-Ford), 1977 United States (Lotus-Ford), 1977 Spanish (Lotus-Ford), 1977 French (Lotus-Ford), 1977 Italian (Lotus-Ford), 1978 Argentine (Lotus-Ford), 1978 Belgian (Lotus-Ford), 1978 Spanish (Lotus-Ford), 1978 French (Lotus-Ford), 1978 German

(Lotus-Ford), 1978 Dutch (Lotus-Ford). *Publication:* Mario Andretti: A Driving Passion (autobiog.). *Leisure interests:* golf, snowmobiling, tennis, opera. *Address:* 457 Rose Inn Avenue, Nazareth, PA 18064, USA. *Website:* www.andretti.com.

ANDREW, Christopher Robert, MBE; British rugby football player; b. 18 Feb. 1963, Richmond, Yorks.; m. Sara Andrew 1989; two d.; ed Cambridge Univ.; chartered surveyor; fly-half; fmr mem. Middlesbrough, Cambridge Univ., Nottingham, Gordon (Sydney, Australia) clubs; mem. Wasps Club 1987–91, 1992–96, Capt. until 1989–90; with Toulouse 1991–92, Barbarians, Newcastle 1996–; int. debut England versus Romania 1985; Five Nations debut England versus France 1985; Capt. England team, England versus Romania, Bucharest 1989; mem. Grand Slam winning team 1991, 1992; record-holder for drop goals in ints.; retd from int. rugby 1995, returned 1997–99; Devt Dir Newcastle Rugby Football Club 1996–. *Publication:* A Game and a Half 1995. *Leisure interests:* gardening, pushing a pram, golf. *Address:* c/o Newcastle RFC, Newcastle-upon-Tyne, NE3 2DT, England. *Telephone:* (191) 214-5588.

ANDREW, Ludmilla; Canadian soprano opera singer; b. Canada; of Russian parentage; operatic début in Vancouver as Donna Elvira; British début as Madam Butterfly with Sadler's Wells Opera; noted for Russian song repertoire; has given many broadcasts of French, German and Russian song repertoire with Geoffrey Parsons; many recital tours; now appears regularly at world's leading opera houses and at maj. int. music festivals. *Roles include:* Aida, Anna Bolena, Leonore, Norma, Senta, Sieglinde, Turandot, Der Fliegende Holländer, Die Walküre, Fidelio.

ANDREWS, Anthony; British actor; b. 1 Dec. 1948, Hampstead, London; m. Georgina Simpson; one s. two d.; ed Royal Masonic School, Herts.; started acting 1967. *TV appearances include:* Doomwatch, Woodstock 1972, A Day Out, Follyfoot, Fortunes of Nigel 1973, The Pallisers, David Copperfield 1974, Upstairs, Downstairs 1975, French Without Tears, The Country Wife, Much Ado About Nothing 1977, Danger UXB 1978, Romeo and Juliet 1979, Brideshead Revisited 1980, Ivanhoe 1982, The Scarlet Pimpernel 1983, Columbo 1988, The Strange Case of Dr. Jekyll and Mr. Hyde 1989, Hands of a Murderer 1990, Lost in Siberia 1990, The Law Lord 1991, Jewels 1992, Ruth Rendell's Heartstones, Mothertime. *Films Include:* The Scarlet Pimpernel, Under the Volcano, A War of the Children, Take Me High 1973, Operation Daybreak 1975, Les Adolescents 1976, The Holcroft Covenant 1986, Second Victory 1987, Woman He Loved 1988, The Lighthorsemen 1988, Hannah's War 1988, Lost in Siberia (also producer) 1990, Haunted (also co-producer) 1995. *Plays:* 40 Years On, A Midsummer Night's Dream, Romeo and Juliet, One of Us 1986, Coming into Land 1986, Dragon Variation, Tima and the Conways. *Address:* c/o Peters Fraser & Dunlop Ltd, Drury House, 34–43 Russell Street, London, WC2B 5HA, England. *Telephone:* (20) 7344-1010. *Fax:* (20) 7836-9539.

ANDREWS, David, SC, BCL; Irish politician; b. 15 March 1935, Dublin; s. of Christopher Andrews and Mary Coyle; m. Annette Cusack; two s. three d.; ed Mount St Joseph's Cistercian Coll., Co. Tipperary, Univ. Coll. Dublin and King's Inns, Dublin; mem. Dáil 1965–2002; Parl. Sec. to Taoiseach 1970–73; Govt Chief Whip 1970–73; Minister of State, Dept of Foreign Affairs 1977–79, Dept of Justice 1978–79; Minister for Foreign Affairs 1992–93, for Defence and the Marine 1993–94, for Defence July–Oct. 1997, for Foreign Affairs 1997–2000; Opposition Spokesman on Tourism and Trade 1995–97; mem. New Ireland Forum, Consultative Assembly of Council of Europe, British-Irish Interparl. Body 1990–92; Fianna Fáil. *Leisure interests:* cinema, sport, walking. *Address:* Dáil Éireann, Leinster House, Dublin 2 (Office); 102 Avoca Park, Blackrock, Dublin, Ireland (Home). *Telephone:* (1) 6789911 (Office); (1) 6623851 (Home).

ANDREWS, John Hamilton, AO, FTS, MArch, RIBA; Australian architect; b. 29 Oct. 1933, Sydney; s. of the late K. Andrews; m. Rosemary Randall 1958; four s.; ed N Sydney Boys' High School, Univ. of Sydney, Harvard Univ.; pvt. practice, Toronto, Canada 1962, Sydney 1970–; mem. Staff, Univ. of Toronto School of Architecture 1962–67, Chair. and Prof. of Architecture 1967–69; mem. Visual Arts Bd, Australia Council 1977–80, Bd mem. 1988–90; Chair. Architecture and Design Comm., Australia Council 1980–83, Founding Chair. Design Arts Bd, 1983–88; Architectural Juror, Australian Archives Nat. Headquarters Building 1979, Parl. House Competition 1979–80, The Peak, Hong Kong 1983, Hawaii Loa Coll. 1986, Governor Gen.'s Medals, Canada 1986; mem. Bd Australia Council 1988–; Assoc. NZ Inst. of Architects; Foundation mem. Australian Acad. of Design 1990; Fellow, Royal Architectural Inst. of Canada, Australian Acad. of Technological Science; Life Fellow, Royal Australian Inst. of Architects; Hon. Fellow, American Inst. of Architects; Hon. DArch (Sydney) 1988; Centennial Medal (Canada) 1967, Massey Medal (Canada) 1967, Arnold Brunner Award, US Acad. of Arts and Letters 1971, American Inst. of Architects Honour Award 1973, Gold Medal, Royal Australian Inst. of Architects 1980, Advance Australia Award 1982, Sulman Medal (Australia) 1983, Design Excellence 25 Year Award, Ontario Asscn of Architecture, Scarborough Coll. 1989. *Principal works:* Scarborough Coll., Toronto, Harvard Graduate School of Design, Harvard Univ., Cameron Offices, Canberra, American Express Tower, Sydney, Intelsat Headquarters Bldg, Washington, DC, Hyatt Hotel, Perth, Convention Centre Darling Harbour, Sydney, Convention Centre and Hyatt Hotel, Adelaide, World Congress Centre and Eden on the Yarra Hotel, Melbourne, The Octagon (office bldg) Parramatta, Sydney, NSW, Veterinary Conf. Centre, Univ. of

Sydney, NSW. *Publication:* Architecture: A Performing Art 1982. *Leisure interests:* fly fishing, surfing. *Address:* John Andrews International, 'Colleton', Cargo Road, Orange, NSW 2800 (Office); 'Colleton', Cargo Road, Orange, NSW 2800, Australia (Home). *Telephone:* (2) 6365-6223 (Office). *Fax:* (2) 6365-6211 (Office).

ANDREWS, Dame Julie (Elizabeth), DBE; British actress and singer; b. 1 Oct. 1935, Walton-on-Thames, Surrey; m. 1st Tony Walton 1959 (divorced 1968); one d.; m. 2nd Blake Edwards 1969; one step-s. one step-d. and two adopted d.; first stage appearance at the age of twelve as singer, London Hippodrome; played in revues and concert tours; appeared in pantomime Cinderella, London Palladium; played leading parts in The Boy Friend, New York 1954, My Fair Lady 1959–60, Camelot, New York 1960–62, Victor, Victoria 1995/96; work for UN Devt Fund for Women; Academy Award (Oscar) Best Actress 1964; three Golden Globe Awards, Emmy Award 1987, BAFTA Award 1989, Kennedy Center Honor 2001. *Films:* Mary Poppins 1963, The Americanization of Emily 1964, The Sound of Music 1964, Hawaii 1965, Torn Curtain 1966, Thoroughly Modern Millie 1966, Star! 1967, Darling Lili 1970, The Tamarind Seed 1973, 10 1979, Little Miss Marker 1980, S.O.B. 1980, Victor/Victoria 1981, The Man Who Loved Women 1983, That's Life 1986, Duet For One 1986, The Sound of Christmas (TV) 1987, Relative Values 1999, The Princess Diaries 2001. *TV appearances include:* High Tor, The Julie Andrews Hour 1972–73, Great Performances Live in Concert 1990, Our Sons 1991, The Julie Show 1992. *Publications:* (as Julie Andrews Edwards) Mandy 1972, Last of the Really Great Whangdoodles 1973. *Leisure interests:* skiing, riding. *Address:* c/o Triad Artists, 10100 Santa Monica Boulevard, 16th Floor, Los Angeles, CA 90067, USA.

ANDREYEV, Vladimir Alekseyevich; Russian actor and stage director; b. 27 Aug. 1930; m. Natalia Selezheva; one s. one d.; ed State Inst. of Theatre Arts Cinema (GITIS); actor with Yermolova Theatre Moscow 1952–70, Chief Dir 1970–85, 1990–; mem. CPSU 1962–91; Chief. Dir of Maly Theatre, Moscow 1985–88; teaches concurrently at GITIS, Prof. 1978–; mem. Int. Acad. for Life Preservation Problems 1993; USSR People's Artist 1985; Stanislavsky State Prize 1980, 1993. *Roles include:* Aleksey in V. Rozov's It's High Time!, Vasilkov in Ostrovsky's Crazy Money, Golubkov in Bulgakov's Flight, Sattarov in Valeyev's I Give You Life, Dorogin in Zorin's Lost Story, Writer in Bunin's Grammar of Love. *Productions include:* Vampilov's plays: Last Summer in Chulimsk and The Duck Hunt; Money for Mary (based on a work by V. Rasputin), The Shore (based on Yuriy Bondarev's novel), Uncle Vanya, Three Sisters (Chekhov). *Address:* Yermolova Theatre, Tverskaya 5, 103009 Moscow, Russia. *Telephone:* (095) 203-87-03.

ANDRIANARIVO, Tantely René Gabrio; Malagasy politician; Prime Minister of Madagascar, Chief of Govt, Minister of Finances and Economy 1998–2002. *Address:* c/o Office of the Prime Minister, BP 248, Mahazoarivo, 101 Antananarivo, Madagascar (Office).

ANDRIANOV, Nikolai Yefimovich; Russian gymnast; b. 14 Nov. 1953, Vladimir; m. Lyubov Burda; two s.; ed Moscow Inst. of Physical Culture; holds record for most Olympic medals won by a man; 15 Olympic medals (1972, 1976, 1980) including gold medals in free-style exercises 1972, in all-round competitions, on the rings, in jumps 1976, team championships and in jumps 1980; world champion 1974, 1978, 1979; numerous champion titles of Europe and USSR; chief coach USSR (now Russian) team, then Japan 1983–; Merited Master of Sports 1972, Int. Gymnastics Hall of Fame 2001. *Address:* Russian Federation of Gymnastics, Luzhnetskaya nab. 8, 119871 Moscow, Russia. *Telephone:* (095) 201-13-42 (Office); (9222) 23924 (Home).

ANDRIEŞ, Andrei, DPhys-MathSc; Moldovan physicist; b. 24 Oct. 1933, Chişinău (Kishinev); s. of Mihail Andrieş and Maria Andrieş; m. Lidia Vasilievna Klimanova 1959; one s.; ed Kishinev Univ., Ioffe Inst. of Physics and Tech., Leningrad; researcher Inst. of Applied Physics, Acad. of Sciences Moldavian SSR 1962–64, Learning Sec. 1964–71, Head of Lab. Inst. of Applied Physics 1971–, Gen. Learning Sec. 1984–89, Dir Centre of Optoelectronics 1993–; Corresp. mem. Acad. of Sciences Moldavian SSR (now Acad. of Sciences of Moldova) 1978, mem. 1984, Pres. 1989–; State Prize of Moldova 1983, 2001; Merited Scientific Researcher 1984; mem. Eng. Acad. of Russian Fed. 1992, New York Acad. of Sciences 1995, Int. Scientific Acad. of Life, the Universe and Nature, Toulouse 1997; State Prize 1983; Order of the Repub. of Moldova 1996; numerous other decorations and awards. *Publications:* over 300 works, including five monographs on new materials for photographic processes. *Leisure interests:* reading, travel. *Address:* Academy of Sciences of Moldova, Bd Ştefan cel Mare 1, 2001 Chişinău, Moldova. *Telephone:* (2) 27-14-78. *Fax:* (2) 27-60-14. *E-mail:* presidium@asm.md (Office). *Website:* www.asm.md (Office).

ANDRIESSEN, Franciscus H. J. J.; Netherlands politician and economist; b. 2 April 1929, Utrecht; ed Univ. of Utrecht; Dir Catholic Inst. for Housing 1954–72; mem. of Second Chamber, States-Gen. (Parl.) 1967–77, First Chamber 1980–; Minister of Finance 1977–80; Commr for Competition Policy and Relations with the European Parl., Comm. of European Communities 1981–84; for Agric. and Fisheries 1984–85, for Agric. and Forestry 1986–89, for External Relations and Trade Policy 1989–93; special adviser KPMG 1993–; Pres. Inst. of the Euro 1993–; Prof. of European Integration, Univ. of Utrecht 1990–; mem. Catholic People's Party, Christian Democratic Appeal; Kt, Order of the Lion, Grand Cross of Order of Orange-Nassau, of Order of Leopold II, Commdr du Mérite agricole. *Address:* Institut de l'Euro, 8 rue du

Président Carnot, 69002 Lyon, France; KPMG European Headquarters, avenue Louise 54, 1050 Brussels, Belgium; clôs Henri Vaes l, 1950 Kraainem, Netherlands (Home).

ANDRIKIENE, Laima Liucija, DEcon; Lithuanian politician; b. 1 Jan. 1958, Druskininkai, Lithuania; m. (husband deceased); one s.; ed Vilnius State Univ., Manchester Univ., engineer, researcher Computation Cen. Lithuanian Research Inst. of Agric. Econ. 1980–88; Asst to Deputy Chair. Council of Ministers Lithuanian SSR 1989–90; deputy Supreme Soviet 1990; signatory to Act on Re-establishment of Independent State of Lithuania 1900; mem. Independence Party 1990–92; mem. Seimas (Parl.) 1992–; mem. Homeland Union Party (Lithuanian Conservatives) 1993–; Minister of Trade and Industry 1996–98, of European Affairs 1998–2000. *Address:* R. Seimas, Gedimino pr. 53, 2002 Vilnius, Lithuania (Office).

ANDRIYASHEV, Anatoliy Petrovich; Russian zoologist; b. 19 Aug. 1910, Montpellier, France; s. of P. E Waitashevsky and N. Y. Andriasheva; m. Nina N Savelyeva 1934; two d.; ed Leningrad Univ.; Postgrad., Research Assoc., Asst Prof. Leningrad Univ. 1933–39; Sevastopol Biological Scientific Station 1939–44; Chief, Antarctic Research Div., Inst. of Zoology, USSR (now Russian) Acad. of Sciences 1944–, Prof. 1970–; Vice-Pres. European Ichthyological Union 1979–82, Hon. mem. 1982–; Arctic and Bering Sea expeditions 1932, 1936, 1937, 1946, 1951; Antarctic expeditions 1955–58, 1971–72, 1975–76; Mediterranean and N. Atlantic expedition 1979; Corresp. mem. USSR (now Russian) Acad. of Sciences 1966; Fellow Russian Acad. Natural Sciences 1994; Ed.-in-Chief Journal of Ichthyology 1977–88; Hon. Arctic explorer of the USSR (now Russia) 1947–; Hon. Foreign mem. of American Soc. of Ichthyologists and Herpetologists; Soros Hon. Prof. 1996; State prizewinner 1971; Leo S. Berg Academic Prize 1992. *Publications:* works on ichthyology, marine zoogeography and Antarctic biology, feeding habits of fishes. *Leisure interest:* skiing. *Address:* Zoological Institute, Universitetskaya Nab. 1, Academy of Sciences, 199034 St Petersburg (Office); Savushkina str. 15, Apt. 120, 197193 St Petersburg, Russia (Home). *Telephone:* (812) 430-59-69 (Home); (812) 328-06-12. *Fax:* (812) 328-29-41. *E-mail:* aap@zisp .spb.su (Office).

ANDRONIKOF, Constantin, DTheol; French interpreter, translator, author and professor; b. 16 July 1916, Petrograd, Russia; s. of Prince Yassé Andronikof and Helen von Wachter; m. 1st Nathaly de Couriss 1946 (deceased); m. 2nd Janet Wood 1989; two s. one d.; ed Ecole Gerson, Lycée Janson-de-Sailly, Paris, Sorbonne and Inst. de Théologie Orthodoxe Saint-Serge, Paris; traffic officer, British Airways, Le Bourget 1936–38; official interpreter (Russian–English), French Ministry of Foreign Affairs 1946–76, of French Presidency (Elysée) 1962; Minister-Plenipotentiary (retd); Acting Dean, Saint-Sergius Inst. until 1993, now Hon. Dean; Prof. Emer.; Dir Sophia collection, L'Age d'Homme, Lausanne, Paris; Officier, Légion d'honneur, Ordre nat. du Mérite. *Publications:* Le Sens des Fêtes I 1970, Le Cycle pascal (Sens des Fêtes II) 1985, Le Sens de la Liturgie 1988, Des Mystères Sacramentals 1995; some 20 translations from English and Russian since 1939. *Leisure interests:* family (9 grandchildren), classical music, detective stories. *Address:* 26 rue Rosenwald, 75015 Paris, France. *Telephone:* 1-45-30-00-94.

ANDROSCH, Hannes, PhD; Austrian business executive and fmr politician; b. 18 April 1938; m. Brigitte Schärf; two c.; ed Hochschule für Welthandel, Vienna; Asst Auditor Fed. Ministry of Finance 1956–66; Sec. Econ. Affairs Section, Socialist Parl. Party 1963–66, Vice-Chair. 1974–85; mem. Nationalrat (Nat. Council) 1967–85; Minister of Finance 1970–81; Vice-Chancellor 1976–81; Chair. and Gen. Man. Creditanstalt-Bankverein 1981–87; Chair. Österreichische Kontrolbank AG 1985–86; Pres. Supervisory Bd Austria Technologie & Systemtechnik AG (A.T. & S.); Chief Shareholder Salinen and Lenzing cos; Grand Gold Medal of Honour. *Address:* c/o A.T. & S., Fabriksgasse 13, 8700 Leoben, Austria (Office). *Telephone:* 3842-200-0 (Office). *E-mail:* info@ats.net (Office).

ANDROUTSOPOULOS, Adamantios, LLM, JD; Greek politician; b. 1919, Psari; ed Athens Univ., John Marshall Law School, Chicago, USA, Chicago Univ.; lawyer 1947; Prof. of Law, Chicago Industrial School; Scientific collaborator at Roosevelt Univ., Mundelein Coll., John Marshall Law School, Fengen Coll.; returned to Greece 1967; Minister of Finance 1967–71, of Interior 1971–73; Prime Minister 1973–74; mem. Athens Bar Asscn, American Judicature Soc., American Business Law Asscn. *Publications:* State Distributions and National Economy, The Problem of Causation in Maritime Law, Legal Terminology of the Greek-American Dictionary, The Spirit and Development of The American Law, The Testimony of a Prime Minister. *Address:* 63 Academias Street, 106 78 Athens, Greece.

ANDRUS, Cecil D.; American business executive, consultant and politician; b. 25 Aug. 1931, Hood River, Ore.; s. of Hal S. Andrus and Dorothy (Johnson) Andrus; m. Carol M. May 1949; three d.; ed Oregon State Univ.; served U.S. Navy 1951–55; mem. Idaho Senate 1961–66; State Gen. Man. Paul Revere Life Insurance Co. 1967–70; Gov. of Idaho 1971–77, 1987–95; Chair. Nat. Govs. Conf. 1976; Sec. of Interior 1977–81; Dir Albertson's Inc. 1985–87, 1995–; Coeur d'Alene Mines 1995–, Key Corp. 1996–; Chair. Andrus Center for Public Policy 1995–; Counsel to Gallatin Group; Dir Rentrak Corpn; Democrat; Hon. LLD (Gonzaga Univ., Spokane, Wash. 1975, Whitman Coll., Albertson Coll. of Idaho, Oregon State Univ., Univ. of Idaho, Idaho State Univ., Univ. of New Mexico); Conservationist of the Year, Nat. Wildlife Fed. 1980, Ansel Adams Award, Wilderness Soc. 1985, Audubon Medal 1985,

Torch of Liberty Award, B'nai B'rith 1991, William Penn Mott Jr Park Leadership Award, Nat. Parks Conservation Asscn 2000. *Publications:* Cecil Andrus: Politics Western Style 1998. *Leisure interests:* hunting, fishing, golf. *Address:* Andrus Center for Public Policy, Boise State University, 1910 University Drive, Boise, ID 83725-0399, USA. *Telephone:* (208) 426-4218. *Fax:* (208) 426-4208.

ANDSNES, Leif Ove; Norwegian pianist; b. 7 April 1970, Stavanger; ed Bergen Music Conservatory; debut, Oslo 1987; British debut with Oslo Philharmonic, Edinburgh Festival 1989; US debut with Cleveland Orchestra under Neeme Järvi 1990; recitals in London, Berlin, Vienna, Amsterdam, New York (Carnegie Hall); performs with Orchestre Nat. de France, Berlin Philharmonic, Chicago Symphony, BBC Symphony, London Symphony, LA Philharmonic, Japan Philharmonic, New York Philharmonic; soloist Last Night of the Proms 2002; Co-Artistic Dir Risør Music Festival; recorded works of Brahms, Chopin, Grieg, Janacek, Liszt, Schumann; First Prize, Hindemith Competition, Frankfurt am Main and prizewinner at other int. competitions, Levin Prize (Bergen) 1988, Norwegian Music Critics' Prize 1988, Grieg Prize (Bergen) 1990, Dorothy B. Chandler Performing Arts Award, Los Angeles 1992, Gilmore Prize 1997, Instrumentalist Award, Royal Philharmonic Soc. 2000, Gramophone Award (Best Concerto Recording) 2000, (Best Instrumental Recording) 2002, Commndr Royal Norwegian Order of St Olav 2002. *Address:* c/o Kathryn Enticott, IMG Artists, Lovell House, 616 Chiswick High Road, London, W4 5RX, England. *Telephone:* (20) 8233-5800. *Fax:* (20) 8233-5801. *Website:* www.andsnes.com.

ANFIMOV, Nikolai Appolonovich; Russian scientist; b. 29 March 1935, Russia; m.; one s.; ed Moscow Inst. of Physics and Tech.; Head of Group, Head of Sector, Research Inst. of Heat Processes 1958–73, Head of Div., Deputy Dir Central Research Inst. of Machine Construction 1973–; Corresp. mem. Russian Acad. of Sciences 1984, mem. 1997; State Prize of Russia. *Publications include:* Problems of Mechanics and Heat Exchange in Space Tech. 1982, Numerical Modelling in Aerohydrodynamics 1986 and numerous scientific works on heat exchange and heat protection in high-speed, high-temperature regimes, heat regimes of spaceships, radiation gas dynamics. *Leisure interest:* tennis. *Address:* Central Institute of Machine Construction, Pionerskya str. 4, 141070 Korolyev, Moscow Region, Russia (Office). *Telephone:* (095) 513-50-01 (Office); (095) 238-40-67 (Home). *Fax:* (095) 274-00-25 (Office).

ANG LEE; Taiwanese film director; b. 1954, Taipei; m. Jane Lin; ed New York Univ.; moved to USA 1978; winner of nat. script-writing contest (Taiwanese Govt) 1990. *Films:* Pushing Hands 1992, The Wedding Banquet 1993, Eat Drink Man Woman 1995, Sense and Sensibility 1996, The Ice Storm 1998, Ride with the Devil 1998, Crouching Tiger, Hidden Dragon (Acad. Award for Best Foreign Film, David Lean Award for Best Dir, BAFTA Award 2001, Golden Globe for Best Dir 2001) 1999, Chosen 2001.

ANGEL, Heather Hazel, MSc; British wildlife photographer, author and lecturer; b. 21 July 1941, Fulmer, Bucks.; d. of Stanley Paul Le Rougetel and Hazel Marie Le Rougetel (née Sherwood); m. Martin Vivian Angel 1964; one s.; ed 14 schools in UK and NZ, Bristol Univ.; Special Prof., Dept of Life Science, Nottingham Univ. 1994–; Kodak Calendar on The Thames 1987; led British Photographic Del. to China 1985; Fellow, British Inst. of Prof. Photography; Hon. Fellow Royal Photographic Soc. (RPS) (Pres. 1984–86); Hon. DSc (Bath) 1986; Hood Medal (RPS) for contrib. to advancement of nature photography through books, teaching, exhbns etc. 1975; Médaille de Salverte, Société française de photographie 1984; Louis Schmidt Laureate, Biocommunications Asscn 1998. *Exhibitions include:* The Natural History of Britain and Ireland, Science Museum, London 1981, Nature in Focus, Natural History Museum, London 1987, The Art of Wildlife Photography, Nature in Art, Gloucester 1989, Natural Visions (touring exhbn), UK 2000–03. *TV appearances in:* Me and My Camera 1981, 1983, Gardener's World 1983, Nature 1984, Nocon on Photography 1988; featured in Japanese TV documentary, filmed in UK and Sri Lanka 1983. *Publications:* Nature Photography: Its Art and Techniques 1972, Natural History of Britain and Ireland (co-author) 1982, The Family Water Naturalist 1982, The Book of Nature Photography 1982, The Book of Close-up Photography 1983, Heather Angel's Countryside 1983, A Camera in the Garden 1984, A View from a Window 1988, Nature in Focus 1988, Landscape Photography 1989, Animal Photography 1991, Kew: A World of Plants 1993, Photographing the Natural World 1994, Outdoor Photography: 101 Tips and Hints 1997, How to Photograph Flowers 1998, Pandas 1998, How to Photograph Water 1999, Natural Visions 2000. *Leisure interest:* travel and photography. *Address:* Highways, 6 Vicarage Hill, Farnham, Surrey, GU9 8HJ, England. *Telephone:* (1252) 716700. *Fax:* (1252) 727464. *E-mail:* hangel@naturalvisions.co.uk (Office). *Website:* www.naturalvisions.co.uk (Office).

ANGELINI, HE Cardinal Fiorenzo; Italian ecclesiastic; b. 1 Aug. 1916, Rome; ordained priest 1940; elected Titular Bishop of Messene 1956, consecrated 1956; Archbishop 1985; cr. Cardinal 1991; Deacon of Santo Spirito in Sassia; Pres. Papal Council on Pastoral Work among Health Workers 1989; mem. Congregation for Evangelization of the Peoples, Papal Council on the Family, Papal Comm. on Latin America. *Address:* Via Anneo Lucano 47, 00136 Rome, Italy.

ANGELL, Wayne D., PhD; American economist; b. 28 June 1930, Liberal, Kansas; s. of Charlie Francis Angell and Adele Thelma Angell (née Edwards); m.; four c.; ed Univ. of Kansas; Prof. Ottawa Univ. 1956, Dean 1969–72; mem.

Kansas House of Reps 1961–67; Dir Fed. Reserve Bank, Kansas City 1979–86; mem. of Fed. Reserve Bd 1986–94; Chief Economist, Sr Man. Dir Bear Sterns & Co. Inc. 1994–2001; with Angell Econs, Arlington Va, 2001. *Leisure interest:* tennis. *Address:* Angell Economics, 1600 North Oak Street, Suite 1915, Arlington, VA 22209, USA (Office). *E-mail:* wangell@comcast.net (Office).

ANGELOPOULOS, Theo; Greek film director; b. 27 April 1936, Athens; s. of Spyridon Angelopoulos and Katerina Krassaki; m. Phoebe Economopoulou 1980; three d.; ed Univ. of Athens and the Inst. des Hautes Etudes Commerciales, Paris; film critic for the Athens daily Allaghi 1965; Best Foreign Film at Hyères Film Festival, George Sadoul Award and five awards at the Thessaloniki Film Festival for Reconstruction; FIPRESCI Award, Berlin 1973 for Days of '36; FIPRESCI Grand Prix, Cannes, Golden Age Award, Brussels, Best Film of the Decade 1970–80, Italy, Grand Prix of the Arts and Best Film of the Year, Japan, Best Film of the Year, BFI, Interfilm Award, Berlin, Best Film, Figueira da Foz Film Festival, nine awards at the Thessaloniki Film Festival for The Travelling Players; Golden Hugo Award at the Chicago Film Festival 1978 for The Hunters; three awards at the Venice Film Festival for Megalexandros; Best Screenplay and FIPRESCI Awards at the Cannes Film Festival for Voyage to Cythera; four awards at the Venice Film Festival; two awards at the Chicago Film Festival, Best European Film of the Year 1989 for Landscape in the Mist; Palme d'Or, Cannes Film Festival for Causes for Eternity; Chevalier des Arts et des Lettres (France). *Films include:* Formix Story 1965, Broadcast 1968, Reconstruction 1970, Days of '36 1972, The Travelling Players 1974–75, The Hunters 1976–77, Megalexandros 1980, Athens 1984, Voyage to Cythera 1984, The Bee Keeper 1986, Landscape in the Mist 1988, The Hesitant Step of the Stork 1991, Ulysses Gaze 1995, Causes for Eternity. *Publications:* numerous screenplays. *Leisure interests:* cultivating tomatoes. *Address:* Solmou 18, 106 82 Athens (Office); Charitos 7, 106 75 Athens, Greece (Home). *Telephone:* 363-9120 (Office); 724-1406 (Home).

ANGELOU, Maya; American author; b. Marguerite Johnson, 4 April 1928, St Louis; d. of Bailey Johnson and Vivian Baxter; one s.; Assoc. Ed. Arab Observer 1961–62; Asst Admin., teacher School of Music and Drama, Univ. of Ghana 1963–66; feature Ed. African Review, Accra 1964–66; Reynold's Prof. of American Studies, Wake Forest Univ. 1981–; teacher of modern dance Rome Opera House, Hambina Theatre, Tel Aviv; has written several film scores; theatre appearances include: Porgy and Bess 1954–55, Calypso 1957, The Blacks 1960, Mother Courage 1964, Look Away 1973, Roots 1977, How To Make an American Quilt 1995; contrib. to numerous periodicals; Woman of Year in Communication 1976; numerous TV acting appearances; Hon. Amb. to UNICEF 1996–; Dir Down in the Delta (film) 1998; mem. Bd of Govs. Maya Angelou Inst. for the Improvement of Child and Family Educ., Winston-Salem State Univ., NC 1998–; distinguished visiting prof. at several univs.; mem. various arts orgs.; more than 50 hon. degrees, Horatio Alger Award 1992, Grammy Award Best Spoken Word or Non-Traditional Album 1994, Lifetime Achievement Award for Literature 1999, Nat. Medal of Arts, numerous other awards. *Plays:* Cabaret for Freedom 1960, The Least of These 1966, Gettin' Up Stayed On My Mind 1967, Ajax 1974, And Still I Rise 1976, Moon On a Rainbow Shawl (producer) 1988. *Theatre appearances include:* Porgy and Bess 1954–55, Calypso 19576, The Blacks 1960, Mother Courage 1964, Look Away 1973, Roots 1977, How To Make an American Quilt 1995 (feature film 1996). *Publications include:* I Know Why the Caged Bird Sings 1970, Just Give Me A Cool Drink of Water 'Fore I Die 1971, Georgia, Georgia (screenplay) 1972, Gather Together In My Name 1974, All Day Long (screenplay) 1974, Oh Pray My Wings Are Gonna Fit Me Well 1975, Singin' and Swingin' and Gettin' Merry Like Christmas 1976, And Still I Rise 1976, The Heart of a Woman 1981, Shaker, Why Don't You Sing 1983, All God's Children Need Travelling Shoes 1986, Now Sheba Sings the Song 1987, I Shall Not Be Moved 1990, Gathered Together in My Name 1991, Wouldn't Take Nothing for my Journey Now 1993, Life Doesn't Frighten Me 1993, Collected Poems 1994, My Painted House, My Friendly Chicken and Me 1994, Phenomenal Woman 1995, Kofi and His Magic 1996, Even the Stars Look Lonesome 1997, Making Magic in the World 1998. *Address:* c/o Dave La Camera, Lordly and Dame Inc., 51 Church Street, Boston, MA 02116, USA. *Telephone:* (617) 482-3593. *Fax:* (617) 426-8019.

ANGENOT, Marc, DPhil, FRSC; Canadian professor of French and comparative literature; b. 21 Dec. 1941, Brussels; s. of Marcel Angenot and Zoé-Martha DeClercq; m. 1st Joséphine Brock 1966 (divorced 1976); one s. one d.; m. 2nd Nadia Khouri 1981; one d.; ed Univ. Libre de Bruxelles; James McGill Prof. of French, McGill Univ. 1967–; Assoc. Dir Ecole des Hautes Etudes en Sciences Sociales, France 1985; Northrop Frye Prof. of Literary Theory, Univ. of Toronto 1994; Sec. Acad. des Lettres et Sciences Humaines, Royal Soc. of Canada 2001; Killam Fellowship 1987; Prix Biguet (Acad. Française) 1983, Prix des Sciences Humaines (Canada) 1996; Award for High Distinction in Research (McGill Univ.) 2001. *Publications:* Le Roman populaire 1975, Les Champions des femmes 1977, Glossaire pratique de la critique contemporaine 1979, La Parole pamphlétaire 1982, Critique de la raison sémiotique 1985, Le Cru et le faisandé 1986, Le Centenaire de la Révolution 1989, Ce que l'on dit des Juifs en 1889 1989, Mille huit cent quatre-vingt neuf 1989, L'Utopie collectiviste 1993, La Propagande socialiste 1996, Idéologies du ressentiment 1996, Colins et le socialisme rationnel 1999, La critique au service de la Révolution 2000, Religions de l'humanité et sciences de l'histoire 2000, D'où

venons-nous, où allons-nous? 2001. *Address:* 3460 McTavish Street, Montreal, Québec H3A 1X9 (Office); 4572 Harvard Avenue, Montreal, Québec, H4A 2X2, Canada. *Telephone:* (514) 488-1388. *Fax:* (514) 483-4428.

ANGERER, Paul; Austrian conductor, composer and instrumentalist; b. 16 May 1927, Vienna; s. of Otto Angerer and Elisabeth Angerer; m. Anita Rosser 1952; two s. two d.; ed Hochschule für Musik und darstellende Kunst, Vienna; viola player, Vienna Symphony 1947, leading solo viola player 1953–57; viola player, Tonhalle Zürich 1948, Suisse Romande Orchestra, Geneva 1949; Dir and Chief Conductor, Chamber Orch. of Wiener Konzerthausgesellschaft 1956–63; composer and conductor, Burgtheater, Vienna and Salzburg and Bregenz festivals 1960–; Perm. Guest Conductor, Orchestra Sinfonica di Bolzano e Trento "Haydn" 1964–90; First Conductor, Bonn City Theatre 1964–66; Music Dir Ulm Theatre 1966–68; Chief of Opera, Salzburger Landestheater 1967–72; Dir SW German Chamber Orch., Pforzheim 1971–82; Prof. Hochschule, Vienna 1983–92; Moderator ORF 1984–2001, Radio Stephansdorn 2001; Leader of Concilium Musicum; several prizes including Austrian State Prize 1956, Theodor Körner Prize 1958, Vienna Cultural Prize 1983, Cultural Prize of Lower Austria 1987; Nestroy-Ring, City of Vienna 1998. *Works include:* orchestral pieces, chamber works, viola and piano concertos, a dramatic cantata, television opera, works for organ, harp, viola, harpsichord, etc.; numerous recordings both as soloist and conductor. *Address:* Esteplatz 3/26, 1030 Vienna, Austria. *Telephone:* (1) 714 12 71. *Fax:* (1) 714 12 71. *E-mail:* PaulAngerer@concilium.at (Home).

ANGREMY, Jean-Pierre (Pierre-Jean Rémy); French diplomatist and writer; b. 21 March 1937, Angoulême; s. of Pierre Angremy and Alice Collebrans; m. 1st Odile Cail (divorced); one s. one d.; m. 2nd Sophie Schmit 1986; one s.; ed Institut d'études politiques, Paris; served Hong Kong 1963–64, Beijing 1964–66, London 1966–71, 1975–79; Cultural, Scientific and Tech. Relations, Paris 1971–72; seconded to ORTF 1972–75; seconded to Ministry of Culture and Communication 1979–84; Consul, Florence 1984–87; Dir-Gen. Cultural, Scientific and Tech. Relations 1987–90; Amb. to UNESCO 1990–94; Dir Académie de France, Rome 1994–97; Pres. Bibliothèque Nationale de France 1997–, mem. Acad. Française 1988; Officier, Légion d'honneur, Ordre nat. du. Mérite, Commdr. des Arts et des Lettres. *Publications:* Désir d'Europe 1995, Le Rose et la Blanc 1997, Callas, une Vie 1997, Retour d'Hélène 1997, Aria Di Roma 1998, La Nuit de Ferraro 1999, Demi-Siècle 2000, Etat de Grâce et Dire Perdu 2001, and numerous other pubs. *Leisure interest:* collecting books. *Address:* Bibliothèque Nationale de France, quai François Mauriac, 75706 Paris cedex 13 (Office); 134 rue de Grenelle, 75007 Paris, France (Home).

ANGUS, Sir Michael Richardson, Kt, BSc, DL, CIMgt; British company director; b. 5 May 1930, Ashford, Kent; s. of William Richardson Angus and Doris Margaret Breach; m. Eileen Isabel May Elliott 1952; two s. one d.; ed Marling School, Stroud, Bristol Univ.; served in RAF 1951–54; joined Unilever PLC 1954, Marketing Dir Thibaud Gibbs, Paris 1962–65, Man. Dir Research Bureau 1965–67, Sales Dir Lever Brothers, UK 1967–70, Dir Unilever PLC and Unilever NV 1970–92, Toilet Preparations Co-ordinator 1970–76, Chemicals Co-ordinator 1976–80, Regional Dir N America 1979–84, Chair. and CEO Unilever United States Inc., New York 1980–84, Chair. and CEO Lever Brothers Co., New York 1980–84, Vice-Chair. Unilever PLC 1984–86, Chair. 1986–92, also Vice-Chair. Unilever NV; Vice-Pres. Netherlands-British Chamber of Commerce 1990–94; Deputy Pres. CBI 1991–92, 1994–95, Pres. 1992–94; Chair. RAC Holdings Ltd 1999–; Gov. Ashridge Man. Coll. 1974–, Chair. of Govs 1991–2002; Jt Chair. Netherlands-British Chamber of Commerce 1984–89; Chair. of Govs Royal Agricultural Coll., Cirencester 1992–; Non-Exec. Dir Whitbread PLC 1986–2000 (Deputy Chair. Jan.–Aug. 1992, Chair. 1992–99), Thorn EMI PLC 1988–93, British Airways PLC 1988–2000 (Deputy Chair. 1989–2000), Halcrow Group 1999–; Dir Nat. Westminster Bank PLC 1991–2000 (Deputy Chair. 1991–94), The Boots Co. PLC 1994–2000 (Chair. 1994–98, Deputy Chair. 1998–2000); Leverhulme Trust 1984–; mem. Council, British Exec. Service Overseas 1986– (Pres. 1998); mem. Council of Man., Ditchley Foundation 1994–; Hon. DSc (Bristol) 1990, (Buckingham) 1994; Hon. LLD (Nottingham) 1996; Holland Trade Award 1990, Commdr of Order of Oranje Nassau 1992. *Leisure interests:* countryside, wine and mathematical puzzles. *Address:* Cerney House, North Cerney, Cirencester, Gloucestershire, GL7 7BX, England (Home). *Telephone:* (1285) 831300.

ANGYAL, Stephen John, OBE, PhD, DSc, FAA; Australian (b. Hungarian) professor of organic chemistry; b. 21 Nov. 1914, Budapest; s. of Charles Engel and Maria Szanto; m. Helga Ellen Steininger 1941; one s. one d.; ed Pazmany Peter Univ., Budapest; Research Chemist, Chinoin Pharmaceutical Works, Budapest 1937–40; Research Chemist, Nicholas Pty Ltd, Melbourne, Australia 1941–46; Lecturer, Univ. of Sydney 1946–52; Nuffield Dominion Travelling Fellow 1952; Assoc. Prof. of Organic Chem., Univ. of NSW 1953–60, Prof. 1960–80, Prof. Emer. 1980–, Dean of Science 1970–79; Fellow Royal Australian Chem. Inst.; Foreign mem. Hungarian Acad. of Science 1990; H. G. Smith Memorial Medal, Royal Australian Chem. Inst. 1958, Haworth Medal and Lectureship, RSC 1980, Hudson Award, ACS 1987. *Publications:* Conformational Analysis (with others) 1965; about 200 research pubs in chemical journals. *Leisure interests:* swimming, skiing, bushwalking, music. *Address:* 304 Sailors Bay Road, Northbridge, NSW 2063, Australia. *Telephone:* (2) 9958-7209. *Fax:* (2) 9385-6141. *E-mail:* s.angyal@unsw.edu.au (Office).

ANISTON, Jennifer; American actress; b. 11 Feb. 1969, Sherman Oaks, Calif.; d. of John Aniston; m. Brad Pitt 2000; ed New York High School of the Performing Arts. *Theatre includes:* For Dear Life, Dancing on Checker's Grave. *Films include:* Leprechaun 1993, She's the One 1996, Dream for an Insomniac 1996, 'Til There Was You 1996, Picture Perfect 1997, The Object of My Affection 1998, Office Space 1999, The Iron Giant 1999, Rock Star 2001, The Good Girl 2002. *TV includes:* Molloy (series) 1989, The Edge, Ferris Bueller, Herman's Head, Friends (Emmy Award for Best Actress 2002, Golden Globe for Best TV Actress in a Comedy 2003) 1994–. *Address:* c/o Patrick Whitesell, CAA, 9830 Wilshire Blvd., Beverly Hills, CA 90212, USA. *Website:* www.jenniferaniston.com.

ANJARIA, Shailendra J.; Indian international finance official; b. 17 July 1946, Bombay; s. of Jashwantrai J. Anjaria and Harvidya Anjaria; m. Nishigandha Pandit 1972; two d.; ed Univ. of Pennsylvania, Yale Univ. and London School of Econs; economist, Exchange and Trade Relations Dept, IMF 1968; IMF office, Geneva 1973; Div. Chief 1980; Asst Dir and Adviser, Exchange and Trade Relations Dept 1986; Asst Dir N African Div. of African Dept 1988; Dir External Relations Dept IMF 1991–99, Sec. IMF Aug. 1999–. *Address:* International Monetary Fund, 700 19th Street, NW, Washington, DC 20431, USA (Office). *Telephone:* (202) 623-7300 (Office). *Fax:* (202) 623-6220 (Office). *Website:* www.imf.org (Office).

ANKUM, Hans (Johan Albert), DJur; Netherlands professor of Roman Law; b. 23 July 1930, Amsterdam; s. of Leendert and Johanna (née Van Kuykhof) Ankum; m. 1st Joke Houwink 1957 (divorced 1970); m. 2nd Pelline van Es 1971; one s. three d.; ed Zaanlands Lyceum, Zaandam, Univ. of Amsterdam, Univ. of Paris; Asst Roman Law and Juridical Papyrology, Univ. of Amsterdam 1956–60; Lecturer in Roman Law and Legal History, Univ. of Leyden 1960–63, Prof. 1963–69; Prof. of Roman Law, Legal History and Juridical Papyrology, Univ. of Amsterdam 1965–95; mem. Royal Dutch Acad. of Sciences 1986–; Drz hc (Aix-Marseille, Vrije Univ., Brussels and Ruhr Universität Bochum); Winkler Prins Award. *Publications:* De geschiedenis der 'Actio Pauliana'; numerous books and articles on Roman law and legal history. *Leisure interests:* classical music, history of art, travel. *Address:* Faculty of Law, University of Amsterdam, P.O. Box 1030, 1000 BA, Amsterdam Oudermanhuispoort 4–6 (Office); Zonnebloemlaan 8, 2111 ZG Aerdenhout, The Netherlands (Home). *Telephone:* (20) 5253408 (Office); (23) 5243036 (Home). *Fax:* (20) 5253495 (Office).

ANLYAN, William George, BS, MD; American professor of surgery and medical consultant; b. 14 Oct. 1925, Alexandria, Egypt; s. of Armand Anlyan and Emmy Anlyan; two s. one d.; ed Yale Univ. and Duke Univ. Hosp.; Instructor in Surgery Duke Univ. School of Medicine 1950–51, Assoc. 1951–53, Asst Prof. of Surgery 1953–58, Assoc. Prof. 1958–61, Prof. 1961–89, Assoc. Dean 1963–64, Dean 1964–69; Assoc. Provost Duke Univ. 1969, Vice-Pres. for Health Affairs 1969–83, Chancellor for Health Affairs 1983–88, Exec. Vice-Pres. 1987–88, Chancellor 1988–90, Chancellor Emer. 1990–; numerous exec. posts Assoc of American Medical Colls. 1965–, Distinguished Service Mem. 1974–, American Medical Assoc 1971–74, American Surgical Assoc 1964–; mem. Bd of Dirs. Assoc for Acad. Health Centers 1971–, Pres. 1974–75; mem. Research Strengthening Group for Special Programme for Research and Training in Tropical Diseases, WHO 1981–85, Chair. Univ. Council's Cttee on Medical Affairs (WHO), Yale Univ. 1987–93; mem. Council Govt-Univ.-Industry Research Roundtable 1984–86; mem. several advisory and research cttees., NC 1965–; Consultant Gen. Surgery, Durham Veterans' Hosp. 1955–73; mem. U.S. dels. consulting on health and medical educ., China, Poland, Israel, Egypt, Saudi Arabia, Japan etc.; mem. Bd of Regents Nat. Library of Medicine 1968–71, Chair. 1971–72, Consultant 1972–; mem. Bd of Dirs. Wachovia Bank 1970–90, G.D. Searle and Co. 1974–90, Pearle Health Services Inc. 1983–85, NC Inst. of Medicine 1983–, Durham Chamber of Commerce 1988–; mem. Bds. of Visitors and Trustees numerous univs.; mem. numerous professional socs.; mem. Editorial Bd The Pharos 1968–93; Trustee The Duke Endowment 1990–; Hon. DS (Rush Medical Coll.) 1973; Modern Medicine Award for Distinguished Achievement 1974, Gov.'s Award for Distinguished Meritorious Service 1978, Distinguished Surgeon Alumnus, Yale Univ. School of Medicine 1979, The Abraham Flexner Award, Assoc of American Medical Colls. 1980, Civic Honor Award, Durham Chamber of Commerce 1981, Award of Merit, Duke Univ. Hosp. and Health Admin. Alumni Assoc 1987, Lifetime Achievement Award, Duke Univ. Medical Alumni 1995, Lifetime Achievement Award (for advocacy for medical research), Research America 1997, Distinguished Alumni Service Award, Yale Univ. School of Medicine 1999. *Publications:* contrib. and several books; over 100 articles in professional journals on health and surgical topics. *Leisure interests:* piano, tennis. *Address:* Duke Medical Center, P.O. Box 3626, 109 Seeley G. Mudd Building, Durham, NC 27710, USA. *Telephone:* (919) 684-3438. *Fax:* (919) 684-3518. *E-mail:* anlya001@mc.duke.edu (Office).

ANN-MARGRET; American actress, singer and dancer; b. Ann-Margret Olsson, 28 April 1941, Stockholm, Sweden; m. Roger Smith 1967; film début in Pocketful of Miracles 1961; five Golden Globe Awards, three Female Star of the Year Awards. *Films include:* State Fair, Bye Bye Birdie, Once A Thief, The Cincinnati Kid, Stagecoach, Murderer's Row, CC & Co., Carnal Knowledge, RPM, The Train Robbers, Tommy, The Twist, Joseph Andrews, Last Remake of Beau Geste, Magic, Middle Age Crazy, Return of the Soldier, I Ought to Be in Pictures, Looking to Get Out, Twice in a Lifetime, 52 Pick-Up 1987, New Life 1988, Something More, Newsies 1992, Grumpy Old Men 1993, Grumpier Old Men 1995, Any Given Sunday 1999, The Last Producer 2000,

A Woman's a Helluva Thing 2000. *TV includes:* Who Will Love My Children? 1983, A Streetcar Named Desire 1984, The Two Mrs Grenvilles 1987, Our Sons 1991, Nobody's Children, 1994, Following her Heart, Seduced by Madness: The Diane Borchardt Story 1996, Blue Rodeo 1996, Pamela Hanniman 1999, Happy Face Murders 1999, Perfect Murder, Perfect Town 2000, The Tenth Kingdom 2000. *Publication:* (with Todd Gold) Ann-Margret: My Story 1994. *Address:* William Morris Agency, 151 El Camino Drive, Beverly Hills, CA 90212, USA.

ANNADIF, Mahamet Saleh; Chadian politician; b. 25 Dec. 1956, Arada; m. twice; eight c.; with Telecommunications Dept, Office Nat. de Postes et Télécommunications (ONPT) 1981–82 (as Head of Research), 1988–89, Dir.-Gen. ONPT 1995–97; Man. Soc. des Télécommunications internationales du Tchad 1990–97; in charge of information and propaganda, Front de libération nationale du Tchad (FROLINAT)/Conseil démocratique révolutionnaire (CDR) 1982–85, Second Vice-Pres. FROLINAT/CDR 1985–88; Sec. of State for Agric. 1989–90; Minister of Foreign Affairs and Co-operation 1997–; Commdr Order nat. du Tchad. *Leisure interests:* nature, the countryside. *Address:* Ministry of Foreign Affairs, B.P. 746, N'Djamena (Office); Quartier Goudji, Rue de 40m., N'Djamena, Chad (Home). *Telephone:* 51-50-82 (Office); 51-07-51 (Home). *Fax:* 51-49-92 (Office). *E-mail:* minaffec@intnet.td (Office).

ANNAKIN, Kenneth, DL; British film director and writer; b. 10 Aug. 1914, Beverley, Yorks.; s. of Edward Annakin and Jane Annakin; m. 1959; two d. (one deceased).; ed Beverley Grammar School, Hull Univ.; has made 49 feature films and 14 documentaries. *Films include:* Across the Bridge, Swiss Family Robinson, Very Important Person, The Longest Day, The Fast Lady, The Informers, Those Magnificent Men in Their Flying Machines, Battle of the Bulge, The Long Duel, Monte Carlo or Bust, Call of the Wild, Paper Tiger, The Fifth Musketeer, The Pirate, Cheaper to Keep Her, The Pirate Movie, Pippi Longstocking, Genghis Khan. *Screenplays:* The Crystals of Lemuria, Coco Chanel 1999, Chiffon 2001, Redwing 1999, Fair Play 2001, Yours Truly, Amelia 2001, Queen Bea 2001, High Jinks at Alucard Towers 2001. *Publications:* So You Wanna Be a Director? (autobiog.) 2000. *Leisure interests:* travel, cinema, bridge. *Address:* 1643 Lindacrest Drive, Beverly Hills, CA 90210 (Home); (agent) Denise Denny, 9233 Swallow Drive, Los Angeles, CA 90069, USA. *E-mail:* flyingmachines@earthlink.net (Home).

ANNAN, Kofi A., BA(Econs), MSc; Ghanaian international civil servant; b. 8 April 1938; m. Nane Lagergren; one s. two d.; ed Univ. of Science and Tech., Kumasi, Macalester Coll., St Paul, Minn., USA, Institut des Hautes Etudes Internationales, Geneva, Switzerland, Massachusetts Inst. of Tech., USA; held posts in UN ECA, Addis Ababa, UN, New York, WHO, Geneva 1962–71, Admin. Man. Officer, UN, Geneva 1972–74; Alfred P. Sloan Fellow, MIT 1971–72; Chief Civilian Personnel Officer, UNEF, Cairo 1974; Man. Dir Ghana Tourist Devt Co. 1974–76; Deputy Chief of Staff Services, Office of Personnel Services, Office of UNHCR, Geneva 1976–80, Deputy Dir Div. of Admin. and Head Personnel Service 1980–83; Dir of Admin. Man. Service, then Dir of Budget, Office of Financial Services, UN, New York 1984–87, Asst Sec.-Gen., Office of Human Resources Man. 1987–90; Controller Office of Programme Planning, Budget and Finance 1990–92; Asst Sec.-Gen. Dept of Peace-Keeping Operations 1992–93; Under-Sec.-Gen. 1993–96; UN Special Envoy (a.i.) to fmr Yugoslavia 1995–96; Sec. Gen. of UN Jan. 1997–; hon. degrees include Hon. DCL (Oxford) 2001; Philadelphia Liberty Medal 2001; Nobel Peace Prize 2001. *Address:* United Nations, United Nations Plaza, New York, NY 10017, USA (Office). *Telephone:* (212) 963-1234 (Office). *Fax:* (212) 963-4879 (Office). *Website:* www.un.org (Office).

ANNAUD, Jean-Jacques, LèsL; French film director and screenwriter; b. 1 Oct. 1943, Juvisy/Orge; s. of Pierre Annaud and Madeleine Tripoz; m. 1st Monique Rossignol 1970 (divorced 1980); one d.; m. 2nd Laurence Duval 1982; one d.; ed Inst. des Hautes Etudes Cinématographiques, Paris and Univ. of Paris, Sorbonne; freelance commercial film Dir (500 films) 1966–75; feature film Dir 1975–; Grand Prix Nat. du Cinéma, Grand Prix de l'Acad. Française; Officier des Palmes académiques et du Mérite social, Commdr des Arts et des Lettres. *Films include:* Black and White in Colour 1976 (Acad. Award for Best Foreign Film), Hot Head 1979, Quest for Fire (César Award) 1981, The Name of the Rose (César Award) 1986, The Bear 1988 (César Award), The Lover 1992, Wings of Courage 1994, Seven Years in Tibet 1997, Enemy at the Gates 2001. *Leisure interests:* books, old cameras, world travel. *Address:* c/o ICM, 8942 Wilshire Boulevard, Beverly Hills, CA 90211, USA (Office); c/o Repérage, 10 rue Lincoln, 75008 Paris; 9 rue Guénégaud, 75006 Paris, France (Home).

ANNE, HRH The Princess (see Royal, HRH The Princess).

ANNESLEY, Sir Hugh (Norman), Kt, QPM; British police officer; b. 22 June 1939, Dublin; m. Elizabeth Ann MacPherson 1970; one s. one d.; ed St Andrew's Prep. School, Dublin and Avoca School for Boys, Blackrock; joined Metropolitan Police 1958; Asst Chief Constable of Sussex with special responsibility for personnel and training 1976; Deputy Asst Commr, Metropolitan Police 1981, Asst Commr 1985; Head Operations Dept, Scotland Yard 1987–89; Chief Constable of the Royal Ulster Constabulary 1989–96; mem. Nat. Exec. Inst., FBI 1986; Exec. Cttee Interpol (British Rep.) 1987–90, 1993–94; mem. Bd Govs Burgess Hill School for Girls 1997, Chair. 2000–. *Leisure interests:* sailing, hockey. *Address:* c/o Brooklyn, Knock Road, Belfast, BT5 6LE, Northern Ireland.

ANNINSKY, Lev Alexandrovich, PhD; Russian writer; b. (Lev Alexandrovich Ivanov Anninsky), 7 April 1934, Rostov-on-Don; s. of Alexandre

Ivanov Anninsky and Anna Alexandrova; m. Alexandra Nikolayevna Anninskaya; three d.; ed Moscow State Univ.; freelance literary critic 1956–. *Television:* TV and radio broadcaster 1992–96. *Publications include:* The Core of the Nut: Critical Reviews 1965, Married to the Idea 1971, Literary and Critical Reviews 1977; Hunting for Lev (Lev Tolstoy and Cinematography) 1980, Contacts 1982, Three Heretics: Pisemsky, Melnikov-Pechersky, Leskov 1988, Culture's Tapestry 1991, Elbows and Wings: Literature of the 1980s: Hopes, Reality, Paradoxes 1989, A Ticket to Elysium: Reflections on Theatre Porches 1989, Flying Curtain: Literary-Critical Articles on Georgia 1991, Bards 1999, Russians plus... 2001 and numerous articles on literature, theatre and cinema. *Address:* Udaltsova str. 16, Apt. 19, 117415 Moscow, Russia (Home). *Telephone:* (095) 131-62-45 (Home). *E-mail:* lanninsky@mtu-net.ru.

ANNIS, Francesca; British actress; b. 1945; d. of Anthony Annis and Mariquita Annis; one s. two d. by Patrick Wiseman; with RSC 1975–78. *Plays include:* The Tempest, The Passion Flower Hotel, Hamlet, Troilus and Cressida, Comedy of Errors, The Heretic, Mrs Klein, Rosmersholm, Lady Windermere's Fan, Hamlet, Ghosts, The Vortex. *Films include:* Cleopatra, Saturday Night Out, Murder Most Foul, The Pleasure Girls, Run With the Wind, The Sky Pirates, The Walking Stick, Penny Gold, Macbeth, Krull, Dune, Under the Cherry Moon, The Golden River (El Rio de Oro), The Debt Collector , The End of the Affair. *Television includes:* Great Expectations, Children in Uniform, Love Story, Danger Man, The Human Jungle, Lily Langtry (role of Lily), Madame Bovary, Partners in Crime, Coming Out of Ice, Why Didn't They Ask Evans?, Magnum P.I., Inside Story, Onassis—The Richest Man in the World 1990, Parnell and the Englishwoman 1991, Absolute Hell 1991, The Gravy Train 1991, Weep No More My Lady 1991, Between the Lines 1993, Reckless 1997, Deadly Summer 1997, Wives and Daughters 1999, Milk 1999, Deceit 2000. *Address:* c/o ICM, 76 Oxford Street, London, W1N 0AX, England.

ANOSOV, Dmitry Victorovich; Russian mathematician; b. 30 Nov. 1936, Moscow; m.; one d.; ed Moscow State Univ.; mem. of staff Steklov Inst. of Math., Russian Acad. of Sciences (MIAN) 1961–, Head of Dept 1997–; main research in differential equations and affiliated problems; Corresp. mem. Russian Acad. of Sciences 1990, mem. 1992–; USSR State Prize 1976, Humboldt Prize 1999. *Address:* MIAN, Vavilova str. 42, 117966 Moscow, Russia (Office). *Telephone:* (095) 135-22-91 (Office).

ANSARI, Gholamreza, BSc; Iranian diplomatist; b. 22 Nov. 1955, Shahrood; m. Shahih Shirazi; four d.; ed Allameh Tabatabaee Univ. Tehran; Gov.-Gen. Piranshahr City, Deputy Gov.-Gen. Azarbayejan Prov., Supt of Gov.-Gen. of Azarbayejan Prov., Deputy Gen. Dir of Foreign Nationals and Refugees Dept 1980–88; Chargé d'Affaires Embassy, London 1992–99, Amb. 1999–2000. *Leisure interests:* reading, jogging, swimming. *Address:* c/o Ministry of Foreign Affairs, Shahid Abd al-Hamid Mesri Street, Ferdowsi Avenue, Tehran, Iran (Office).

ANSCHUTZ, Philip F., BSc; American business executive; b. 1939, Russell, Kan.; ed Kan. of Kansas; fmr Pres. Anschutz Corpn, now Chair. and Dir 1991–; f. Quest Communication, Colorado, Chair. 1993–; Chair. Southern Pacific Rail Corpn, San Francisco 1988–96; Vice-Chair. Union Pacific, San Francisco 1996–; Dir Forest Oil Corpn 1995–; co-owner LA Kings 1995–; owner LA Galaxy 1996–. *Address:* Anschutz Corpn, 555 17th Street, Suite 2400, Denver, CO 80202-3941 (Office); Quest Communication, 1801 California Street, Inglewood, CA 80202, USA.

ANSI, Saud bin Salim al-, BA; Omani diplomatist; b. 23 Dec. 1949, Salalah; s. of Salim Ansi and Sultana Ansi; m. 1976; two s. two d.; ed Beirut Univ.; Ministry of Information and Culture and of Diwan Affairs 1974–75; Dir Dept of Research and Studies 1976–78; First Sec. Embassy, Tunis 1975–76, Consul-Gen., Karachi 1978–80, Amb. to Djibouti 1980–82, to Kuwait 1982–84; Perm. Rep. to the UN 1984–88; Under-Sec. and Dir-Gen. Council of Environment and Water Resources 1988–89; Sec.-Gen. Council of Educ. and Vocational Training 1990–92; Adviser to Ministry of Nat. Heritage and Culture 1993–94; Chief Information Dept, Ministry of Foreign Affairs 1995–. *Leisure interests:* reading, writing, sports, travelling. *Address:* P.O. Box 1128, Ruwi 112, Oman. *Telephone:* 701 207. *Fax:* 704 785.

ANSIMOV, Georgiy Pavlovich; Russian musical theatre director; b. 3 June 1922, Ladozhskaya; s. of Pavel Ansimov and Marija Sollertinskaja; m. 1st Irina Miklukho-Maklaj 1944 (died 1991); m. 2nd Lindmila Ansimova; ed Lunarcharsky State Inst. of Theatre (under B. A. Pokrovsky); Stage Dir, Bolshoi Theatre 1955–64, 1980–89; Artistic Dir and main producer, Moscow Operetta Theatre 1964–76; teaches at Lunarcharsky Inst., Prof. 1977–; Czechoslovakia State Prize 1960, USSR People's Artist 1986. *Main productions:* Story of a Real Man (Prokofiev); Carmen, The Tale of Tsar Sultan (Rimsky Korsakov), West Side Story, Orpheus in the Underworld, War and Peace (Prokofiev), Betrothal in the Monastery (Prokofiev), The Golden Cock, Eugene Onegin, The Fiery Angel, Maddalena, The Taming of the Shrew, The Magic Flute, Sunset, Love for Three Oranges, The Tsar-Carpenter. *Publications:* The Director in the Music Theatre 1980, Everything Begins Over Again Always 1983. *Leisure interest:* photography. *Address:* Karetny Ryad 5/10, Apt. 340, 103006 Moscow, Russia (Home). *Telephone:* (095) 299-39-53. *Fax:* (095) 290-05-97.

ANSTEE, Dame Margaret Joan, DCMG, BSc(Econ), MA; British/Bolivian lecturer, consultant and author; b. 25 June 1926, Writtle, Essex; d. of Edward C. Anstee and Anne A. Mills; ed Chelmsford Co. High School for Girls, Newnham Coll. Cambridge and Univ. of London; Lecturer in Spanish, Queen's Univ. Belfast 1947–48; Third Sec. Foreign Office 1948–52; UN Tech. Assistance Bd Manila 1952–54; Spanish Supervisor, Univ. of Cambridge 1955–56; UN Tech. Assistance Bd Colombia 1956–57, Uruguay 1957–59, Bolivia 1960–65; Resident Rep. UNDP Ethiopia and UNDP Liaison Officer with ECA 1965–67; Sr Econ. Adviser, Office of Prime Minister, London 1967–68; Sr Asst to Commr in charge of study of Capacity of UN Devt System 1968–69; Resident Rep. UNDP, Morocco 1969–72, Chile (also UNDP Liaison Officer with ECLAC) 1972–74; Deputy to UN Under-Sec.-Gen. in charge of UN Relief Operation to Bangladesh and Deputy Co-ordinator of UN Emergency Assistance to Zambia 1973; with UNDP, New York 1974–78; Asst Sec.-Gen. of UN (Dept of Tech. Co-operation for Devt) 1978–87; Special Rep. of Sec.-Gen. to Bolivia 1982–92, for co-ordination of earthquake relief assistance to Mexico 1985–87; Under-Sec.-Gen. UN 1987–93, Dir-Gen. of UN office at Vienna, Head of Centre for Social Devt and Humanitarian Affairs 1987–92, Special Rep. of Sec.-Gen. for Angola and Head of Angolan Verification Mission 1992–93; Adviser to UN Sec.-Gen. on peacekeeping, post-conflict peace-building and training troops for UN peacekeeping missions 1994–; Chair. Advisory Group of Lessons Learned Unit, Dept of Peacekeeping Operations, UN 1996–2002; Co-ordinator of UN Drug Control Related Activities 1987–91, of Int. Co-operation for Chernobyl 1991–92 and for countering impact of burning oil wells in Gulf War 1991–92; Sec.-Gen. 8th UN Congress on Prevention of Crime and Treatment of Offenders Aug. 1990; writer, lecturer, consultant and Adviser (ad honorem) to Bolivian Govt 1993–97 and to UN 1993–; Consultant to UN Dept of Political Affairs on post-conflict peace-building 1996–; mem. Advisory Bd UN Studies at Yale Univ. 1994–, Advisory Council Oxford Research Group 1997–, Advisory Bd UN Intellectual History Project 1999–; Trustee Helpage Int. 1994–97; Patron and Bd mem. British Angola Forum 1998–; mem. Int. Council for Conflict Resolution 2001–; Vice-Pres. UK UN Asscn 2002–; Hon. Fellow Newnham Coll. Cambridge 1991; Dr hc (Essex) 1994; Hon. LLD (Westminster) 1996; Hon. DSc (Econ.) (London) 1998; Reves Peace Prize, William and Mary Coll. (USA) 1993; Commdr Ouissam Alaouite (Morocco) 1972, Dama Gran Cruz Condor of the Andes (Bolivia) 1986, Grosse Goldene Ehrenzeichen am Bande (Austria) 1993. *Publications:* The Administration of International Development Aid 1969, Gate of the Sun: A Prospect of Bolivia 1970, Africa and the World (ed. with R. K. A. Gardiner and C. Patterson) 1970, Orphan of the Cold War: The Inside Story of the Collapse of the Angolan Peace Process 1992–93 1996. *Leisure interests:* writing, gardening, hill-walking (preferably in the Andes), bird-watching, swimming. *Address:* c/o PNUD, Casilla 9072, La Paz, Bolivia; The Walled Garden, Knill, nr Presteigne, Powys, LD8 2PR, Wales. *Telephone:* (1544) 267411 (Wales). *Fax:* (1544) 267027 (Wales); (2) 795820 (Bolivia) (Office).

ANTES, Horst; German painter and sculptor; b. 28 Oct. 1936, Heppenheim; s. of Valentin Antes and Erika Antes; m. Dorothea Grossmann 1961; one s. one d.; ed Heppenheim Coll.; worked in Florence, then Rome; Prof. at State Acad. of Fine Arts, Karlsruhe 1957–59, Berlin 1984–; mem. Acad. der Künste, Berlin, now living in Berlin, Karlsruhe and Tuscany, Italy; Villa Romana Prize, Florence 1962, Villa Massimo Prize, Rome 1963, UNESCO Prize, Venice Biennale 1966, Kulturpreis (Hesse) 1991, Bienal de Sao Paulo 1991. *One-man shows include:* Troisième Biennale de Paris, Museum Ulm, Städtische Galerie Munich, Galerie Stangl Munich, Galerie Defet, Nuremberg, Galerie Krohn, Badenweiler, Gimpel and Hanover Gallery, Zürich and London, Lefèbre Gallery, New York, 10th Biennale São Paulo, Staatliche Kunsthalle Baden-Baden, Kunsthalle Bern, Kunsthalle Bremen, Frankfurter Kunstverein, Badischer Kunstverein Karlsruhe, Galerie Gunzenhauser, Munich, Galerie Brusberg, Hanover and Berlin, Brühl, Schloss Augustenburg, Galerie Valentien, Stuttgart, Nishimura Gallery, Tokyo, Galerie Der Spiegel, Cologne, Kunsthalle, Bremen, Sprengel Museum, Hanover, Wilhelm-Hack Museum, Ludwigshafen, Guggenheim Museum, New York, Galerie Neumann, Düsseldorf, Städt. Galerie, Villingen-Schwerringen u. Kunstverein Hochrhein, Bad Säckingen, Galerie Levy, Hamburg, Freie Akad. der Künste, Hamburg, Galerie Bernd Lutze, Friedrichshafen, Palais Preysing, Munich, Haus der Kunst, Munich, Schloss Mosigkau, Dessau, Berlinische Galerie Pels-Lensden, Berlin, Galerie Organerie-Reinz, Cologne, Prinz Max Palais, Karlsruhe, Galerie Holbein, Lindau, Galerie Meyer-Ellinger, Frankfurt Maine, Galleria d'Arte Narcisco, Turin, Keramik Museum, Stanfen, Galerie Werkstatt, Reinach, Galerie Uwe Sacksofsky, Heidelberg; numerous group exhbns Europe, USA, Japan etc. *Catalogues:* Catalog of Etchings 1962–66 (G. Gerken) 1968, Catalog of Books (W. Euler) 1968, Catalog of Steel Sculptures (H. G. Sperlich) 1976, Catalog of Lithographs (B. Lutze) 1976, 25 Votive (1983/84). *Address:* Hohenbergstrasse 11, 76228 Karlsruhe (Wolfartsweier), Germany. *Telephone:* (721) 491621.

ANTHONY, Rt Hon (John) Douglas, PC, CH; Australian politician, farmer and business executive; b. 31 Dec. 1929, Murwillumbah; s. of Hubert Lawrence Anthony and Jessie Anthony (née Stirling); m. Margot Macdonald Budd 1957; two s. one d.; ed Murwillumbah High School, The King's School, Paramatta and Queensland Agricultural Coll.; mem. House of Reps 1957–84, Exec. Council 1963–72, 1975–83, Minister for the Interior 1964–67, of Primary Industry 1967–71, for Trade and Industry 1971–72, for Overseas Trade 1975–77, for Minerals and Energy Nov.–Dec. 1975, for Nat. Resources 1975–77, for Trade and Resources 1977–83; Deputy Prime Minister 1971–72, 1975–83; Deputy Leader Nat. Country Party of Australia (now Nat. Party of Australia) 1966–71, Leader 1971–84; Chair. Resource Finance Corp. Pty. Ltd

1987–; fmr Dir Poseidon Gold Ltd; Dir John Swire and Sons Pty Ltd 1988–, Clyde Agric. Ltd 1988–, Normandy Mining Ltd 1996–; Chair. JD Crawford Fund 1986–; Chair. JD Steward Foundation (Univ. of Sydney) 1986–, Commonwealth Regional Telecommunications Infrastructure Fund 1997, Governing Council of Old Parl. House, Canberra 2000; Hon. Fellow Australian Acad. of Technological Sciences and Eng 1990; Hon. LLD (Victoria Univ. of Wellington) 1983; Hon. DUniv (Sydney) 1997; Gold Medal Queensland Agric. Coll. 1985; Canberra Medal 1989; NZ Commemorative Medal 1990. *Leisure interests:* golf, tennis, swimming, fishing. *Address:* Sunnymeadows, Murwillumbah, NSW 2484, Australia.

ANTHONY, Kenny, PhD; Saint Lucia politician; b. 8 Jan.1951; leader Saint Lucia Labour Party; Prime Minister of Saint Lucia, Minister of Finance, Planning, Devt., Information and the Civil Service, May 1997–. *Address:* Office of the Prime Minister, Greaham Louisy Administrative Building, Waterfront, Castries, Saint Lucia. *Telephone:* 468-2111. *Fax:* 453-7352. *Website:* www.stlucia.gov.lc (Office).

ANTICO, Sir Tristan, Kt, AC; Australian business executive; b. 25 March 1923, Piovene, Italy; s. of Terribile Antico; m. Dorothy Bridget Shields 1950; three s. four d.; ed Sydney Boys' High School; fmr Chair. Ampol Ltd, Ampol Exploration Ltd; fmr Dir Qantas Airways Ltd; fmr Chair. St Vincent's Hosp.; fmr Pres. Italian Chamber of Commerce; Hon. Pres. Pioneer Int. Ltd (fmrly Concrete Services Ltd) 1993–; fmr mem. Export Devt Advisory Council, numerous advisory Bds.; Trustee Art Gallery NSW Foundation, Randwick Racecourse; Commdr Order of Star of Solidarity (Italy), Sovereign Mil. Hospitaller Order of St John of Jerusalem of Rhodes and Malta, Kt Commdr Order of St Gregory the Great. *Leisure interests:* horse racing, horse breeding, swimming, boating. *Address:* Tregoyd (Holdings) Pty Ltd, Suite 901, 56 Berry Street, North Sydney, NSW 2060 (Office); 161 Raglan Street, Mosman, Sydney, NSW 2088, Australia (Home). *Telephone:* 969-4070 (Home).

ANTINORI, Severino, PhD; Italian gynaecologist; b. 1945, Civitella del Tronto; m. Caterina Antinori; two d.; ed Univ. La Sapienza, Rome; Perm. Asst in obstetrics and gynaecology, Istituto Materno Regina Elena 1973–80, Prin. Asst 1980–82, Dir Reproductive Physiopathology Service 1985–87; at Ospedale Materno Regina Elena 1978–92; specialist in obstetrics and gynaecology, Univ. Cattolica di Roma 1978; Prof. Univ. degli Studi di Pisa 1993–94, Univ. degli Studi G. D'Annunzio, Chieti 1996–97, 1998–99, Univ. degli Studi di Roma 1998–99; Dir Centro RAPRUI (Ricercatori Associati per la Riproduzione Umana); Vice-Pres. APART (Int. Asscn of Pvt. Assisted Reproductive Tech. Clinics and Laboratories). *Publications:* numerous articles in medical journals. *Address:* Centro RAPRUI, Via Tacito, Quartiere Umbertino di Prati, Rome, Italy (Office). *E-mail:* antinori@raprui.org (Office). *Website:* www.raprui.org (Office).

ANTOINE, Frédéric, M.S.G.; Belgian journalist and academic; b. 27 Sept. 1955, Uccle; s. of Paul Antoine and Suzanne Degavre; m. Chantal Berque 1982; two s. one d.; ed Catholic Univ. of Louvain; journalist L'Appel 1977, La Libre Belgique 1978; Research Asst Communication Dept Catholic Univ. of Louvain 1979; News Ed. Radio 1180, Brussels 1979; Prof. Media School I.A.D., Louvain-la-Neuve 1981; Prof. Communication Dept Univ. of Louvain 1989, Dir Research Unit on Mediatic Narrative (R.E.C.I.) 1991–; Ed. L'Appel 1992–. *Publications:* On Nous a Changé la Télé 1987, La Télévision à Travers ses Programmes 1988, Télévision In: Le Guide des Médias 1989–97; ed. La Médiamorphose d'Alain Vanderbiest 1994; ed. Coupures de Presse 1996. *Address:* Ruelle de la Lanterne, Magique 14, 1348 Louvain-la-Neuve (Office); L'Appel, Rue du Hautmur 45, 4030 Liège (Office); Montagne Street, JOB 12, 1180 Brussels, Belgium (Home). *Telephone:* (1) 47-28-14 (Office); (4) 341-10-04 (Office); (2) 374-10-81 (Home). *Fax:* (1) 47-30-44 (Office); (4) 341-10-04 (Office); (2) 374-10-81 (Home).

ANTON, Ioan, DEng; Romanian professor of fluid flow machinery; b. 18 July 1924, Vintere; s. of Mihai Anton; m. Viorica Flueraş 1949; one s. one d.; ed Polytech. Inst. of Timişoara; Assoc. Prof. 1951, Prof. 1962; Dean, Faculty of Mech. Eng, Polytech. Inst. of Timişoara 1961–63, Head, Fluid Flow Machine Dept 1962–73, 1982–90, Rector 1971–81; Corresp. mem. Romanian Acad. 1963–74, mem 1974–; Dir Tech. Research Centre, Timişoara, Romanian Acad. 1969–70; Dir Research Lab. for Hydraulic Machines, Timişoara 1970–74; Vice-Pres. Nat. Council for Science and Tech. 1973–79; Vice-Pres. Romanian Acad. 1974–90; Dir of Research Centre for Hydrodynamics, Cavitation and Magnetic Fluids, Tech. Univ., Timişoara 1990–; Dir Centre for Fundamental and Advanced Tech. Research, Romanian Acad. 1997–; mem. European Acad. of Sciences and Arts, NY Acad. of Sciences 1997–; Dr. hc (Tech. Univ. of Civil Eng Bucharest) 1998, (Univ. 'Politechnica' Timişoara) 1999; State Prize 1953, Aurel Vlaicu Prize, Romanian Acad. 1958. *Publications:* Experimental Testing of Fluid Flow Machines (with A. Bărglăzan) 1952, Hydraulic Turbines 1979, Cavitation, Vol. 1 1984, Vol. 2 1985, Hydrodynamics of Bulb Type Turbines and Bulb Type Pump-Turbines (with V. Cîmpeanu and I. Carte) 1988 and over 250 papers on hydraulic machines, cavitation and boiling and magnetic fluids; Ed.-in-Chief Revue Roumaine des Sciences Techniques. *Address:* University 'Politechnica' Timişoara, Faculty of Mechanical Engineering, Department of Hydraulic Machines, 1900 Timişoara, Bd Mihai Viteazul nr 1, Romania (Office). *Telephone:* (56) 191804. *Fax:* (56) 221547.

ANTONAKAKIS, Dimitris; Greek architect; b. 22 Dec. 1933, Chania, Crete; m. Maria-Suzana Antonakakis (q.v.) (née Kolokytha) 1961; one s. one d.; ed School of Architecture, Nat. Tech. Univ. Athens; partnership with Suzana Antonakakis (q.v.), Athens 1959–; Asst Instructor in Architecture, Nat. Tech. Univ. of Athens 1959–64, Instructor 1964–78, mem. teaching staff 1978–92; Founder and Co-Prin. (with S. Antonakakis) Atelier 66 1965; mem. and Treas. Admin. Cttee, Greek Architectural Asscn 1962–63; Pres. Asscn of Assts and Instructors, Nat. Tech. Univ. 1975–77; Vice-Pres. Cen. Admin. Cttee, Asscn of Assts and Instructors of Greek Univs 1976–77; mem. Int. Design Seminar, Tech. Univ. Delft 1987, Split 1988; Visiting Prof. MIT, USA 1994–, Nat. Tech. Univ. Athens 1997–; Art Dir Centre for Mediterranean Architecture, Crete 1997–; Corresp. mem. Acad. d'Architecture, Paris; numerous awards and prizes. *Works include:* Archaeological Museum, Chios 1965–66, Hydra Beach Hotel, Hermionis 1965, vertical addition, house in Port Phaliron 1967–72, miners' housing complex, Distomo 1969, apartment bldg, Emm. Benaki 118, Athens 1973–74, Hotel Lyttos, Heraklion, Crete 1973–82, Zannas House, Philopappos Hill, Athens 1980–82, Gen. Hosp., Sitia, Crete 1982, Ionian Bank branch, Rhodes 1983, Heraklion, Crete 1987, Faculty of Humanities, Rethymnon, Crete 1982, Tech. Univ. of Crete, Chania 1982, Summer Theatre, Komotini 1989, Traditional Crafts Centre, Ioannina 1990, Museum of Acropolis, Athens 1990, Art Studio, Aegina 1990, office bldg, 342 Syngrou Ave., Athens 1990, Open-air Theatre, Thessaloniki 1995–96, Pissas House, Iraklio, Crete 1997, Rehabilitation of ancient Agora area, Athens 1997, Museum of Science and Technology, Patras 1999, Kallithea and Ano Patisia railway stations, Athens 2001–02; several pvt. houses. *Publications:* numerous architectural articles, Le Corbusier Une Petite Maison (trans.) 1998. *Address:* Atelier 66, Emm. Benaki 118, Athens 114-73, Greece. *Telephone:* (1) 3300323. *Fax:* (1) 3300322. *E-mail:* a66@otenet.gr.

ANTONAKAKIS-KOLOKYTHA, Maria-Suzana; Greek architect; b. 25 June 1935, Athens; m. Dimitris Antonakakis (q.v.) 1961; one s. one d.; ed School of Architecture, Nat. Tech. Univ., Athens; partnership with Dimitris Antonakakis (q.v.), Athens 1959–; Founder and Co-Prin. (with Dimitris Antonakakis) Atelier 66 1965; mem. Admin. Cttee Greek Architects Asscn 1971–72; Pres. Dept of Architecture, Tech. Chamber of Greece 1982–83; mem. Int. Design Seminar, Tech. Univ. Delft 1987, Split 1988; mem. Greek Secr. of UIA 1985–2002; newspaper columnist 1998–; numerous awards and prizes. *Works include:* Archaeological Museum, Chios 1965–66, Hydra Beach Hotel, Hermionis 1965, vertical additions, House in Port Phaliron 1967–72, miners' housing complex, Distomo 1969, apartment bldg, Emm. Benaki 118, Athens 1973–74, Hotel Lyttos, Heraklion, Crete 1973–82, Zannas House, Philopappos Hill, Athens 1980–82, Gen. Hosp. Sitia, Crete 1982, Ionian Bank branch, Rhodes 1983, Heraklion, Crete 1987, Summer Theatre, Komotini 1989, Art Studio, Aegina 1990, office bldg, 342 Syngrou Ave, Athens 1990, Traditional Crafts Centre, Ioannina 1990, Museum of Acropolis, Athens 1990, Open-air Theatre, Thessaloniki 1995-96, Pissas House, Iraklio, Crete 1997, rehabilitation of ancient Agora area, Athens 1997, Museum of Science and Technology, Patras 1999, Kallithea and Ano Patisia railway stations, Athens 2001–02, New Acropolis Museum, Athens 2001; several pvt. and holiday houses. *Publications:* numerous architectural articles; trans. Entretien (Le Corbusier) 1971. *Address:* Atelier 66, Emm. Benaki 118, Athens 114-73, Greece. *Telephone:* (1) 3300323. *Fax:* (1) 3300322. *E-mail:* a66@otenet.gr.

ANTONETTI, HE Cardinal Lorenzo; Italian ecclesiastic; b. 31 July 1922, Romagnano Sesia; ordained priest 1945; Archbishop, See of Roselle and Pro-Pres. of the Admin. of the Patrimony of the Apostolic See 1968–; mem. Pontifical Comm. for Vatican City State; cr. Cardinal 1998. *Address:* Administration of the Patrimony of the Holy See, Palazzo Apostolico, 00120 Città del Vaticano, Italy. *Telephone:* (06) 69884306. *Fax:* (06) 69883141.

ANTONICHEVA, Anna; Russian leading ballet dancer; b. Baku, Azerbaijan; ed Moscow Academic School of Choreography; leading ballet dancer Bolshoi Theatre; Merited Artist of Russia. *Ballets:* leading and solo parts in ballets include Shirin (Legend of Love), Swan-Princess (Swan Lake), Nikiya (Bayadera), Mirta (Giselle), Juliet (Romeo and Juliet), Frigia (Spartacus), Princess Aurora (Sleeping Beauty), Kitry, Dulcinea (Don Quixote). *Address:* Bolshoi Theatre, Teatralnaya Pl.1. Moscow, Russia (Office).

ANTONIONI, Michelangelo, L Econ and Comm; Italian film director; b. 29 Sept. 1913, Ferrara; s. of Carlo Antonioni and Elisabetta Antonioni; m. 1st Letizia Balboni 1942; m. 2nd Enrica Fico 1986; ed Univ. of Bologna; film critic Corriere Padano and L'Italia Libera 1936–40; hon. degree (Univ. of Berkeley) 1993; City of Munich Prize 1968, Hon. Acad. Award 1995, San Marco Award for Lifetime Achievement, Venice Film Festival 2002; Kt Grand Cross, Order of Merit, Commdr Ordre des Arts et des Lettres 1992, Légion d'honneur 1996. *Films include:* Gente del Po 1943–47, Amorosa Menzogna 1949, N.U. 1948, Sette Canne un Vestito, La Villa dei Mostri, Superstizione 1949 (documentaries); Cronaca di un Amore 1950, La Signora Senza Camelie 1951–52, I Vinti 1952, Amore in Città 1953, Le Amiche 1955, Il Grido 1957, L'Avventura 1959 (Critics' Award, Cannes 1960), La Notte 1961 (Silver Bear, Berlin Film Festival 1961), L'Eclisse 1962, Il Deserto Rosso 1964 (Golden Lion, XXV Venice Film Festival 1964), Blow Up 1966 (Golden Palm, Cannes Film Festival 1967; Best Dir, Annual Awards of the Nat. Soc. of Film Critics), Zabriskie Point 1970, Chung Kuo-China 1972, The Passenger 1974, Il Mistero di Oberwald 1979, Identificazione di una Donna 1982 (Grand Prix, Cannes Film Festival 1982), Kumbha Mela 1989, Roma '90 1989, Beyond the Clouds 1995. *Leisure interests:* tennis, ping-pong. *Address:* Via Flemming III, 00191, Rome (Office); Via Vincenzo Tiberio 18, 00191 Rome, Italy (Home).

ANTONOVA, Irina Aleksandrovna; Russian museum researcher; b. 20 March 1922, Moscow; ed Moscow State Univ.; worked in Pushkin Museum of Fine Arts 1945–, Sr Researcher 1945–61, Dir 1961–; organizer of numerous exhbns. and regular exchange with museums of Europe and America; f. together with Sviatoslav Richter Festival of Arts December Nights accompanied by art shows 1981–; Vice-Pres. Int. Council of Museums 1980–92, Hon. mem. 1992–; mem. Russian Acad. of Educ. 1989; Corresp. mem. San-Fernando Acad., Madrid; State Prize 1995; Commdr des Arts et des Lettres. *Publications:* more than 60 articles on problems of museum man., art of Italian Renaissance, contemporary painting. *Leisure interests:* swimming, cars, music, ballet. *Address:* A. S. Pushkin Museum of Fine Arts, Volkhonka str. 12, Moscow, Russia. *Telephone:* (095) 203-46-76 (Office).

ANTONOVICH, Ivan Ivanovich, DPhil; Belarus diplomatist; b. 1937, Brest Region; m.; two d.; ed Minsk State Inst. of Foreign Languages, Inst. of Philosophy and Law; on staff UN Secr. New York 1969–74; Perm. Rep. of Belarus in UNESCO, rep. of Belarus in UN Comm. on Human Rights 1976–77; CP service 1977–87; Pro-Rector, Prof. Acad. of Social Sciences at Cen. Cttee CPSU 1987–90; mem. Politbureau, Sec. Cen. Cttee of Russian CP; advisor to Pres. of Russian-American Univ., Dir programmes of social-political analysis 1991–92; Dir Centre of System Social-Econ. Studies, Pro-Rector (acting) Acad. of Man., Council of Ministers 1992–93; Dir Belarus Inst. of Scientific Information and Prognosis 1993–95; Deputy Minister of Foreign Affairs 1995–97, Minister 1997–98; Dir Inst. of Socio-political Studies, Pres. Admin. 1999; mem. Russian Acad. of Social-Political Sciences, Acad. of Geopolitics Belarus Repub.; Merited Worker of Science Belarus Repub. *Publications:* 15 books, numerous articles on problems of philosophy and int. relations. *Address:* c/o Ministry of Foreign Affairs, Lenina str. 19, 220050 Minsk, Belarus (Office). *Telephone:* (17) 227-29-41 (Office).

ANUSZKIEWICZ, Richard Joseph, MFA, BS; American artist; b. 23 May 1930, Erie, Pa; s. of Adam Jacob Anuszkiewicz and Victoria Jankowski; m. Sarah Feeney 1960; one s. two d.; ed Cleveland Inst. of Art, Yale Univ., Kent State Univ.; represented in numerous group exhbns including Museum of Modern Art 1960–61, 1963, 1965, Washington Gallery of Modern Art 1963, Tate Gallery, London 1964, Art Fair, Cologne 1967, etc.; represented in perm. collections at Museum of Modern Art, Whitney Museum of American Art, Albright-Knox Art Gallery, Butler Art Inst., Yale Art Gallery, Chicago Art Inst., Fogg Art Museum, Harvard Univ., etc.; Artist-in-Residence Dartmouth 1967, Univ. of Wis. 1968, Cornell Univ. 1968, Kent State Univ. 1968, Charles Foley Gallery, Columbus 1988, Newark Museum 1990, Center for Arts, Vero Beach, Florida 1993. *One-man exhbns.:* at Butler Art Inst., Youngstown, Ohio 1955, The Contemporaries, New York 1960, 1961, 1963, Sidney Janis Gallery, New York 1965–67, Dartmouth Coll. 1967, Cleveland Museum of Art 1967, Kent State Univ. 1968, Andrew Crispo Gallery, New York 1975, 1977, La Jolla Museum of Contemporary Art, Calif. 1976, Univ. Art Museum, Berkeley, Calif. 1977, Columbus Gallery of Fine Arts, Ohio 1977, Galleria Sagittaria, Pordenone, Italy 1988, Galleria Cinche D'Arte Moderna, Ferraro, Italy 1989, Mornzen Co. Ltd, Tokyo 1990, 1991, Vero Beach, Florida 1993. *Publications:* articles in learned journals. *Address:* 76 Chestnut St, Englewood, NJ 07631-3045, USA.

ANWAR, Sheikh Muhammad, MA; Pakistani television executive; b. 25 March 1943, Amritsar, India; m.; four d.; ed Fairfield Univ., Conn. and Pakistan Admin. Staff Coll.; contract producer/dir. and scriptwriter, Pakistan Television (PTV), Lahore 1964–66; programme producer 1966–72, Exec. Producer, News and Current Affairs 1972–79, Deputy Controller, Overseas Div. PTV HQ, Islamabad 1979–80, Programme Manager, PTV, Rawalpindi/Islamabad 1980–81; Communications Consultant to the Ministry of Information and Broadcasting, Islamabad 1981–83; Deputy Controller of Programmes PTV HQ, Islamabad 1983–85, Producer Group-8, PTV, Lahore 1985–86, Gen. Man. PTV, Peshawar 1986–87, Controller Programme Planning PTV HQ, Islamabad 1988, Educational TV 1988, Programmes Training Acad. 1989–90, Programmes Admin. 1990–92, Int. Relations 1990–93, Controller Programmes Admin., Sport, Archives 1994–96; Gen., Man. PTV Centre, Lahore 1992–94; Controller PTV Acad., PTV HQ, Islamabad, Exec. Producer, Local Area Transmission, PTV, Lahore 1996–97; Visiting Prof. of Communications Quaid-e-Azam Univ. of Pakistan Information Services Acad. 1983–90; Examiner Fed. Public Service Comm. (Information Group); Visiting Prof. Fine Arts Dept, Punjab Univ. 1993; mem. Int. Inst. of Communication, London 1981, Royal TV Soc., London 1983–. *Address:* 154-A, Model Town, Lahore, Pakistan (Home). *Telephone:* 851169 (Home).

ANYAOKU, Eleazar Chukwuemeka (Emeka), Ndichie Chief Adazie of Obosi, Ugwumba of Idemili, CON, BA, FRSA; Nigerian diplomatist; b. 18 Jan. 1933, Obosi; s. of the late Emmanuel Chukwuemeka Anyaoku, Ononukpo of Okpuno Ire and Cecilia Adiba (née Ogbogu); m. Ebunola Olubunmi Solanke 1962; three s. one d.; ed Merchants of Light School, Oba, Univ. of Ibadan; Commonwealth Devt Corpn, London and Lagos 1959–62; joined Nigerian Diplomatic Service 1962, mem. Nigerian Perm. Mission to UN, New York 1963–66; seconded to Commonwealth Secr., Asst Dir Int. Affairs Div. 1966–71, Dir 1971–75, Asst Sec.-Gen. of the Commonwealth 1975–77, elected Deputy Sec.-Gen. (Political) Dec. 1977, re-elected, 1984, Sec.-Gen. 1990–99; Minister of External Affairs, Nigeria Nov.–Dec. 1983; Sec. Review Cttee on Commonwealth Intergovernmental Orgs. June–Aug. 1966; Commonwealth Observer Team for Gibraltar Referendum Aug.–Sept. 1967; mem. Anguilla Comm., West Indies Jan.–Sept. 1970; Deputy Conf. Sec., meeting of Commonwealth Heads of Govt, London 1969, Singapore 1971, Conf. Sec., Ottawa 1973, Kingston, Jamaica 1975; Leader, Commonwealth Mission to Mozambique 1975; Commonwealth Observer, Zimbabwe Talks, Geneva Oct.–Dec. 1976; accompanied Commonwealth Eminent Persons Group (EPG) SA 1986;

Vice-Pres. Royal Commonwealth Soc. 1975–2000, Pres. 2000–; mem. Council of Overseas Devt Inst. 1979–90, Council of the Selly Oak Colls., Birmingham 1980–86, Council, Save the Children Fund 1984–90, Council of Int. Inst. for Strategic Studies, London 1987–93, Int. Bd of United World Colls. 1994–2000, World Comm. on Forests and Sustainable Devt 1995–; Pres. Royal Africa Soc. 2000–; Chair. Presidential Advisory Council on Int. Relations (Nigeria) 2000–; Int. Pres. WWF (WorldWide Fund for Nature) 2002–; Hon. Fellow Inst. of Educ., London 1994, Coll. of Preceptors 1998; Hon. mem. Club of Rome 1992; Hon. DLitt (Ibadan) 1990, (Buckingham) 1994, (Zimbabwe) 1999, (Rhodes) 2001; Hon. DPhil (Ahmadu Bello) 1991; Hon. LLD (Nigeria) 1991, (Aberdeen) 1992, (Reading) 1992, (Bristol) 1993, (Oxford Brookes) 1993, (Birmingham) 1993, (Leeds) 1994, (South Bank) 1994, (New Brunswick) 1995, (North London) 1995, (Liverpool) 1997, (London) 1997, (Nottingham) 1998, (Trinity Coll. Dublin) 1999, (UNIZIK) 2001; Dr hc (Bradford) 1995; Livingston Medal, Royal Scottish Geographical Soc. 1996; Commdr of the Order of the Niger (Nigeria) 1982; Freedom of City of London 1998; Trinity Cross (Trinidad and Tobago) 1999; Hon. Kt Grand Cross of the Royal Victorian Order (UK) 2000. *Publications:* The Missing Headlines (vol. of speeches) 1997, essays in various publications. *Leisure interests:* tennis, athletics, swimming, reading. *Address:* Orimili, Okpuno Ire, Obosi, Anambra State, Nigeria.

ANYIM, Anyim Pius, LLM; Nigerian lawyer and senator; b. 10 Feb. 1961, Ishiagu, Ebonyi State; s. of Chief Anyim Ivo Osita and Agnes Anyim; m. Chioma Blessing; two s. one d.; ed Imo State (now Abia State) Univ., Okigwe, Univ. of Jos, Jos; called to Nigerian Bar 1989; Legal Adviser, Directorate of Social Mobilisation (MAMSER) HQ, Abuja 1989–92; Head Protection Dept Nat. Comm. for Refugees HQ, Abuja 1992–97; fmr Registrar, Refugee Appeal Bd; Senator 1999–, Pres. of Senate 2000–; mem. Nigerian Bar Asscn; Fellow Nigerian Environmental Soc., Inst. of Purchasing and Supply Man.; Grand Patron Abuja Chapter, Soc. for Int. Devt (SID); Grand Commdr Order of Niger (GCON); Hon. DPA (Fed. Univ. of Agric., Umudike, Abia State); Hon. DD (Baptist Seminary and Theological Inst., Ogbomoso, Oyo State); Nigeria Nat. Productivity Order of Merit Award, Distinguished Service Award, Nigerian Foundation Inc., Houston, Tex., USA, and other awards. *Leisure interests:* farming, swimming, reading. *Address:* Office of the President of the Senate, National Assembly Complex, PMB 141, Garki-Abuja (Office); Legislators Quarters, Apo Mansion, Abuja, Nigeria (Home). *Telephone:* (9) 2340505 (Office); (9) 2310009 (Home). *Fax:* (9) 2341214 (Office); (9) 3143660 (Home). *E-mail:* panyim@mail.com (Office).

AOKI, Mikio; Japanese politician; b. 8 June 1934, Taisha; m. Reiko Aoki; two s. one d.; ed Waseda Univ., Tokyo; Sec. to Noboru Takeshita 1958–66; Pres. Taisha Fishery Co-operative 1966; mem. Shimane Prefectural Ass. 1967–86; mem. House of Councillors 1986–; mem. Special Cttee on Disasters, Budget Cttee, Special Cttee on Land and Environment; Vice-Chair. LDP Diet Affairs Cttee 1986; Parl. Vice-Minister of Finance 1991; Chair. House of Councillors Cttee on Agric., Forestry and Fisheries 1994; Deputy Sec.-Gen. LDP, Upper House Sec.-Gen. 1998; Chief Cabinet Sec. and Dir.-Gen. Okinawa Devt Agency 1999–2000; Chair. LDP Fed. of Shimane Pref. 1989, Shimane Fed. of Land Improvement Asscns. 1995. *Leisure interests:* golf, reading. *Address:* c/o Okinawa Development Agency, 1-6-1, Nagata-cho, Chiyoda-ku, Tokyo 100-0014, Japan (Office).

AOUN, Gen. Michel; Lebanese army officer; b. 1935, Beirut; attended Christian school, Beirut; enrolled in mil. school 1955; trained as artilleryman; training courses Châlons-sur-Marne, France 1958–59, Fort Seale, USA 1966, Ecole Supérieure de Guerre, France 1978–80; became Brigade Gen. 1984; C-in-C of Army 1984; following the abandoned presidential elections of Sept. 1988, outgoing Pres. Gemayel agreed to name him prime minister of an interim mil. admin.; following assassination of Pres. Mouawad in Nov. 1989, he refused to accept authority of successor, Pres. Elias Hrawi; evicted from Baabda Presidential Palace by Syrian forces, refuge in French Embassy 1990–91, in exile in Marseilles, France 1991.

APEL, Karl-Otto, DPhil; German professor of philosophy; b. 15 March 1922, Düsseldorf; s. of Otto Apel and Elisabeth Gerritzen; m. Judith Jahn 1953; three d.; ed Univs. of Bonn and Mainz; Prof. of Philosophy, Univ. of Kiel 1962–69, Univ. of Saarbrücken 1969–72, Univ. of Frankfurt am Main 1972–90, Prof. Emer. 1990–; many hon. degrees; Galileo Galilei Int. Prize 1988, F. Nietzsche Int. Prize 1989. *Publications include:* Idee der Sprache in der Tradition des Humanismus 1963, Transformation der Philosophie 1973, Der Denkweg von C. Peirce 1975, Die Erklären: Verstehen-Kontroverse in transzendentalpragmatischer Sicht 1979, Diskurs und Verantwortung (Vol. 1) 1988, (Vol. 2) 1999, Towards a Transcendental Semiotics (selected essays) 1994, Ethics and the Theory of Rationality (selected essays) 1996, Auseinandersetzungen 1998, From a Transcendental-Semiotic Point of View 1998, The Response of Discourse Ethics 2001. *Leisure interest:* history of art. *Address:* Am Schillertempel 6, 65527 Niedernhausen, Germany. *Telephone:* 06127-2170. *Fax:* 06127-2058. *E-mail:* karl-otto.apel@main-rheiner.de (Home).

APICELLA, Lorenzo Franco, BA, DIP.ARCH., RIBA, FCSD, FRSA; Italian architect and designer; b. 4 Feb. 1957, Ravello; s. of Belfiore Carmine Apicella and Carmina Apicella (née Nolli); ed Nottingham Univ., Canterbury Coll. of Art, Royal Coll. of Art, UK; Asst Architect Skidmore Owings & Merill, Houston, Tex., USA 1981; Project Architect CZWG Architects, London 1982; Consultant Architect, Visiting Lecturer Canterbury Coll. of Art 1983–86; Head of Architecture Interiors and Exhbn Design, Imagination, London

1986–89, f. Apicella Assocs. Architecture & Design, London 1989; Partner London Office of Pentagram Design 1998; contrib. to TV and radio programmes; Design Week Annual Awards Winner 1990, 1991, Designers Minerva Award 1993, RIBA Award 1999, Aluminium Imagination Awards 1993, 1997, IDSA Award 2001, Art Directors Club 80th Annual Awards 2001. *Address:* Pentagram, 11 Needham Road, London, W11 2RP (Office); 29 Saville Road, London, W4 5HG, England (Home). *Telephone:* (20) 7229-3477 (Office); (20) 8995-1552 (Home). *Fax:* (20) 7727-9932 (Office). *E-mail:* apicella@ pentagram.co.uk (Office). *Website:* www.pentagram.com (Office).

APONTE MARTÍNEZ, HE Cardinal Luis; American (Puerto Rican) ecclesiastic; b. 4 Aug. 1922, Lajas; s. of Santiago Evangelista Aponte and Rosa Martinez; ed St Ildefonso Seminary, San Juan and St John's Seminary, Boston, Mass., USA; ordained priest 1950; Curate, Patillas, then Pastor of Santa Isabel; Sec. to Bishop McManus, Vice-Chancellor of Diocese of Ponce 1955–57; Pastor of Aibonito 1957–60; Chaplain to Nat. Guard 1957–60; Auxiliary Bishop of Ponce and Titular Bishop of Lares 1960–63; Bishop of Ponce 1963–64; apptd. Archbishop of San Juan 1964; created Cardinal by Pope Paul VI 1973; Dir of Devt for Catholic Univ. of Puerto Rico 1960–63, fmr Chancellor; Pres. Puerto Rican Episcopal Conf. 1966; Hon. LLD (Fordham) 1966; Hon. STD (Inter-American Univ. of Puerto Rico) 1969. *Address:* c/o Arzobispado, Apartado S-1967, Calle San Jorge 201, Santurce, Puerto Rico 00902.

APPEL, Karel Christian; Netherlands painter; b. 25 April 1921, Amsterdam; ed Rijksakademie van Beeldende Kunsten, Amsterdam; began career as artist 1938; exhibitions in Europe, America and Japan 1950–; has executed murals in Amsterdam, The Hague, Rotterdam, Brussels and Paris; UNESCO Prize, Venice Biennale 1953; Lissone Prize, Italy 1958; Acquisition Prize, São Paulo Bienal 1959; Graphique Int. Prize, Ljubljana, Yugoslavia 1959; Guggenheim Nat. Prize, Netherlands 1951; Guggenheim Int. Prize 1961. *Publications:* Works on Paper 1980, Street Art 1985, Dupe of Being 1989, Complete Sculptures 1936–1990 1990, Karel Appel Sculpture: catalogue raisonné 1994. *Address:* c/o Galerie Statler, 51 rue de Seine, Paris, France (Office).

APPIAH, Kwame Anthony, PhD; American (b. British) professor of philosophy and African-American studies and writer; b. 8 May 1954, London; s. of Joe Appiah and Peggy Appiah; ed Kwame Nkrumah Univ. of Science and Tech., Ghana, Univ. of Cambridge, England; raised in Ghana; taught at Univ. of Ghana; has held position of Prof. of Philosophy and Prof. of African Studies and African-American Studies at Univ. of Cambridge, England, Yale Univ., New Haven, CT, Cornell Univ., Ithaca, NY, Duke Univ., Durham, NC and Harvard Univ., Cambridge, MA 1991–2002; Prof. of Philosophy and African-American Studies, Princeton Univ., Princeton, NJ 2002–. *Publications include:* Assertion and Conditionals 1985, For Truth in Semantics 1986, Necessary Questions: An Introduction to Philosophy 1989, Avenging Angel (novel) 1991, In My Father's House: Africa in the Philosophy of Culture (essays—Annisfield-Wolf Book Award 1993, African Studies Asscn Herskovits Award 1993) 1992, Nobody Likes Letitia (novel) 1994, Another Death in Venice (novel) 1995, Color Consciousness: The Political Morality of Race (with Amy Gutman) (North American Soc. for Social Philosophy Annual Book Award) 1996, The Dictionary of Global Culture (with Henry Louis Gates, Jr) 1996, Africana: The Encyclopedia of African and African American Experience 1999; Ed.: Early African-American Classics 1990; Co-Ed.: Critical Perspectives Past and Present (series) 1993, Identities (essays) 1995. *Address:* c/o Barker Center, Harvard University, 12 Quincy Street, Cambridge, MA 02138, USA (Office).

APPLEBY, Malcolm Arthur; British artist; b. 6 Jan. 1946, Beckenham, Kent; s. of James William Appleby and Marjory Stokes; m. Philippa Swann; one d.; ed Hansdown Co. Secondary Modern School, Beckenham School of Art, Ravensbourne Coll. of Art, Cen. School of Arts and Crafts, Sir John Cass School of Art, RCA; career artist, designer and engraver; Littledale Scholar 1969, Liveryman Worshipful Co. of Goldsmiths 1991; Hon. DLitt (Heriot-Watt) 2000. *Art Exhibition:* one-man exhbn. Aberdeen Art Gallery 1998. *Leisure interests:* garden, work, family. *Address:* Aultbeag, Grandtully, by Aberfeldy, Perthshire, PH15 2QU, Scotland. *Telephone:* (1887) 840484. *Fax:* (1887) 840785 (Home).

APRAHAMIAN, Felix; British music critic, writer and broadcaster; b. 5 June 1914, London; ed Tollington School; contributor to musical press 1931–, nat. press 1937–; broadcaster 1942–; Asst Sec. and Concert Dir London Philharmonic Orchestra 1940–46; Consultant, United Music Publishers Ltd 1946–64; Deputy Music Critic Sunday Times 1948–89; Music Ed. The Listener 1966–67; Lecturer Richmond Adult Coll. 1969–88, Stanford Univ. in UK 1969–83, City Literary Inst. 1973–88, Morley Coll. 1975–82, Surrey Univ. 1986–; Visiting Prof. Univ. of E London 1989–; Regents Lecturer, Univ. of Calif., Riverside 1991; Hon. Sec. The Organ Music Soc. 1935–70; Hon. RCO 1973, BBC Cen. Music Advisory Cttee 1958–61; Co-founder and organizer, Concerts de Musique Française 1942–64; Adviser, Delius Trust 1961–; mem. and Pres. Int. Music Juries, Geneva, Montreux and Biarritz 1963–; Hon. mem. Royal Philharmonic Soc. 1994; Hon. FRCO 1994; Hon. DMus (City Univ.) 1995; Officier, Ordre des Arts et des Lettres. *Publications:* (Ed.) Ernest Newman's Essays from the World of Music 1956; More Essays from the World of Music 1958; Essays on Music from The Listener 1967–; Co-Ed. The Heritage

of Music (Vol. 4): The Twentieth Century 1989. *Leisure interests:* horticulture, bibliophily. *Address:* 8 Methuen Park, London, N10 2JS, England. *Telephone:* (20) 8883-3783. *Fax:* (20) 8883-3783.

APTED, Michael David; British film director; b. 10 Feb. 1941, Aylesbury; m. 1st (divorced); two s.; m. 2nd Jo Apted; one s.; ed Downing Coll. Cambridge Univ.; started career as researcher, Granada TV 1963, then worked as investigative reporter for World in Action; feature film dir 1970s–. *Films include:* The Triple Echo 1972, Stardust 1975, The Squeeze 1977, Agatha 1979, The Coal Miner's Daughter 1980, Continental Divide 1981, P'TangYang Kipperbang, Gorky Park 1983, Firstborn 1984, Critical Condition, Gorillas in the Mist 1988, Class Action 1990, Incident at Oglala, Thunderheart 1992, Blink 1993, Moving the Mountain 1993, Nell 1994, Extreme Measures 1996, Inspirations 1997, Me and Isaac Newton 1999, The World Is Not Enough 1999, Enigma 2001, Enough 2002. *Television includes:* (dir) episodes of Coronation Street, comedy series The Lovers, children's series Folly Foot, Another Sunday and Sweet F.A., Kisses at Fifty, Poor Girl, Jack Point, Up documentary series including 28 Up and 35 Up, 42: Forty-two Up, Always Outnumbered. *Publications:* 7 Up 1999. *Address:* c/o PFD, Drury House, 34–43 Russell Street, London, WC2B 5HA, England.

AQUINO, (Maria) Corazon (Cory), BA; Philippine politician; b. 25 Jan. 1933, Tarlac Prov.; d. of José Cojuangco, Sr; m. Benigno S. Aquino, Jr 1954 (assassinated 1983); one s. four d.; ed Raven Hill Acad., Philadelphia, Notre Dame School, New York, Mount St Vincent Coll., New York; in exile in USA with her husband 1980–83; mem. United Nationalist Democratic Org. (UNIDO) 1985–; Pres. of the Philippines (after overthrow of régime of Ferdinand Marcos) 1986–92; William Fulbright Prize for Int. Peace 1996; Ramon Magsaysay Award for Int. Understanding 1998. *Address:* 25 Times Street., Quezon City, Philippines.

ARAD, Ron; British designer and architect; b. 24 April 1951, Tel-Aviv, Israel; ed Jerusalem Acad. of Art and Architectural Asscn; Founder One Off Ltd 1981–94, Ron Arad Assocs 1989–; Prof. of Product Design Hochschule, Vienna 1994–97; Prof. of Design Product, RCA 1997–; Oribe Art and Design Award, Japan 2001, Giò Ponti Int. Design Award, Denver, CO 2001, Barcelona Primavera Int. Award for Design 2001. *Exhibitions:* Nouvelles Tendences, Centre Georges Pompidou 1989, Ron Arad Recent Works, Tel-Aviv Museum of Art 1990, One Off and Short Runs, Centre for Contemporary Arts (Warsaw, Krakow, Prague) 1993, L'Esprit du Nomade, Cartier Foundation, Paris 1994, Sticks and Stones, Vitra Design Museum, Touring Exhbn 1990–95, Ron Arad at the Powerhouse Museum, Sydney 1997, Before and After Now, Victoria and Albert Museum 2000, Delight in Dedark, Galeria Marconi 2001, Paperwork, Galeria Marconi 2002, Centre d'Art Santa Monica, Barcelona 2003. *Leisure interests:* tennis, ping-pong. *Address:* Arad Associates, 62 Chalk Farm Road, London, NW1 8AN, England (Office). *Telephone:* (20) 7284-4963 (Office). *Fax:* (20) 7379-0499 (Office). *E-mail:* info@ronarad.com (Office). *Website:* www .ronarad.co.uk (Office).

ARAFAT, Yasser (pseudonym of Mohammed Abed Ar'ouf Arafat); Palestinian resistance leader; b. 24 Aug. 1929, Jerusalem; m. Sulia Tawil 1991; ed Cairo Univ.; joined League of Palestinian Students 1944, mem. Exec. Cttee 1950, Pres. 1952–56; formed, with others, Al Fatah Movt 1956; engineer in Egypt 1956, Kuwait 1957–65; Pres. Exec. Cttee of Palestine Nat. Liberation Movement (Al Fatah) 1968–; Chair. Exec. Cttee Palestine Liberation Org. 1968–, Pres. Cen. Cttee, Head, Political Dept 1973–; Chair., then Exec. Cttee. Palestinian Nat. Authority (PNA) known internationally as Palestinian Authority (PA) 1996–, Minister of the Interior 1994–96, (acting) 2001; Pres. Palestine Legis. Council 1996–; Gen. Commdr Palestinian Revolutionary Forces; addressed UN Gen. Assembly Nov. 1974; shared Nobel Peace Prize 1994; Joliot-Curie Gold Medal, World Peace Council Sept. 1975. *Address:* c/o Palestinian Authority, Jericho Area, West Bank, Palestinian Autonomous Areas.

ARAGALL GARRIGA, Giacomo (Jaime); Spanish opera singer (tenor); b. 6 June 1939, Barcelona; s. of Ramon Aragall and Paola Garriga; m. Luisa Aragall 1964; three s.; ed with Jaume Francisco Puig, Barcelona and Vladimiro Badiali, Milan; winner int. competition, Busseto; debut at Teatro La Fenice de Venecia, Palermo, Metropolitan, New York 1968; has sung in more than 100 opera productions at Gran Teatre del Liceu; numerous prizes include Peseta de Oro and Medalla de Plata for appearing at 1992 Olympics, Barcelona, Medalla de Oro de Bellas Artes 1992, etc. *Performances include:* El Amico Fritz, La Bohème (La Scala, Milan), Madame Butterfly, La Favorita, La Traviata, Faust, Tosca, etc. *Address:* c/o Stafford Law Associates, 6 Barham Close, Weybridge, Surrey, KT1 9PR, England.

ARAIZA ANDRADE, Francisco José; Mexican opera and concert singer and teacher; b. 4 Oct. 1950, Mexico City; s. of José Araiza and Guadalupe Andrade; m. 1st Vivian Jaffray (divorced); one s. one d.; m. 2nd Ethery Inasaridse; ed Univ. of Mexico City and Nat. School of Music, Mexico City and Munich Acads of Music; first engagement as lyric tenor in Karlsruhe, Fed. Repub. of Germany 1974; debut as Ferrando in Così fan Tutte 1975; debut at Zurich Opera House with Almaviva 1976, perm. mem. 1978–; has become one of the leading tenors world-wide, performing at all the most important opera houses, as well as recitals accompanied by piano or orchestra; Kammersänger, Vienna State Opera 1988; has participated in festivals of Salzburg (debut under von Karajan 1980), Hohenems, Bayreuth, Edinburgh, Pesaro, Verona, Aix-en-Provence, Orange, Garmisch; awarded Deutscher Schallplattenpreis, Orphée d'Or, Mozart Medal, Univ. of Mexico City, Otello d'Oro,

Goldener Merkur, Best Performer's Award, Munich 1996. *Recordings include:* The Magic Flute, Faust, Das Lied von der Erde, Die schöne Müllerin. *Address:* c/o Kunstler Management, M Kursidem, Tal 15, 80331 Munich, Germany. *Telephone:* (89) 29161661. *Fax:* (89) 29161667. *E-mail:* faraiza@aol.com. *Website:* www.francisco-araiza.ch.

ARAM I (KESHISHIAN), His Holiness, Catholicos of Cilicia, PhD; Lebanese ecclesiastic; b. 1947; ed Seminary of the Armenian Apostolic Church, Antelias, Near East School of Theology, Beirut, American Univ. of Beirut, Fordham Univ., New York, USA, WCC Graduate School of Ecumenical Studies, Bossey, Switzerland, Univ. of Oxford, UK; ordained priest 1968; named to WCC Faith and Order Comm. 1975; locum tenens of diocese of Lebanon 1978; Primate 1979; ordained Bishop 1980; elected to Cen. Cttee of WCC 1983, youngest person and first Orthodox to be elected Moderator of Cen. Cttee of WCC 1991, re-elected 1998; Catholicos of the See of Cilicia of the Armenian Apostolic Church 1995–; mem. Oriental–Eastern Orthodox and Oriental Orthodox–Roman Catholic bilateral dialogues; Hon. mem. Pro-Oriente Catholic Ecumenical Foundation, Vienna, Austria. *Publications:* 12 publs including Conciliar Fellowship: A Common Goal 1990, The Challenge to be a Church in a Changing World 1997. *Address:* World Council of Churches, 150 route de Ferney, P.O. Box 2100, 1211 Geneva 2, Switzerland (Office). *Telephone:* (22) 7916111 (Office). *Fax:* (22) 7910361 (Office).

ARAÑA OSORIO, Gen. Carlos Manuel; Guatemalan army officer and politician; b. 17 July 1918; fmr Commdr Zacapa Brigade, Guatemala Army; fmr Amb. to Nicaragua; mem. Movimiento de Liberación Nacional (MLN); Pres. of Guatemala 1970–74. *Address:* c/o Movimiento de Liberación Nacional, 5A Calle 1-20, Zona 1, Guatemala City, Guatemala.

ARANGIO-RUIZ, Gaetano; Italian professor of law; b. 10 July 1919, Milan; s. of Vincenzo Arangio-Ruiz and Ester Mauri Arangio-Ruiz; ed Univ. of Naples; Prof. Int. Law, Univ. of Padua 1955–67, Univ. of Bologna 1968–74; Prof. Int. Law, Univ. of Rome 1974–, now Prof. Emer.; mem. Iran-United States Claims Tribunal, The Hague 1989–; Visiting Prof. European Cen., Johns Hopkins School of Advanced Int. Studies 1967–75; Lecturer, Hague Acad. of Int. Law 1962, 1972, 1977, 1984; mem. UN Int. Law Comm. 1985–96; Special Rapporteur on State Responsibility 1987–96; mem. Int. Law Inst.; Dr. hc (Univ. de Paris II, France) 1997; Giuseppe Capograssi Prize 1990, Scanno Law Prize 2001. *Publications include:* Rapporti contrattuali fra Stati e organizzazione internazionale 1950, Gli enti soggetti 1951, Su la dinamica della base sociale 1954, The Normative Role of the UN General Assembly (Hague Rec.) Vol. III 1972, L'Etat dans le sens du droit des gens et la notion du droit international, 'Oesterreichische Zeitschrift für Oeffentliches Recht' 1975–76, Human Rights and Non-Intervention in the Helsinki Final Act (Hague Rec.) Vol. IV 1977, The UN Declaration on Friendly Relations 1984, Gen. Course in Int. Law (Hague Rec.) Vol. V 1990, Non-Appearance Before the International Court of Justice (report to the Int. Law Inst.) Int. Law Inst. Yearbook 1991, On the Security Council's 'Law-Making', Rivista di Diritto Internazionale 2000. *Address:* c/o Iran-United States Claims Tribunal, Parkway 13, 2585 JH The Hague, Netherlands (Office); Corso Trieste 51, 00198 Rome, Italy (Home). *Telephone:* (70) 3520064 (Office); (06) 8559720 (Home); (0564) 819200 (Italy) (Home); (70) 3551371 (Netherlands) (Home). *Fax:* (70) 3502456 (Office).

ARANZADI MARTINEZ, José Claudio, BA; Spanish politician; b. 9 Oct. 1946, Bilbao; m.; ed Bilbao Industrial Eng School and Univ. of Paris; fmr official, Banco de Vizcaya, Econ. Consultancy, Bancaya Group; worked for Study Services, Ministry of Industry, Dir Tech. Bureau; fmr Vice-Pres. Nat. Inst. of Industry and Energy, Vice-Pres. and Pres. Nat. Inst. of Industry; Minister of Industry and Energy 1989–91, of Industry, Trade and Tourism 1991–93; del. to OECD. *Address:* c/o OECD, 2 rue André Pascal, 75775 Paris, France; c/o PSOE, Ferraz 68 y 70, 28008 Madrid, Spain. *Telephone:* (91) 5820444 (Madrid). *Fax:* (91) 5820422 (Madrid).

ARARKTSYAN, Babken Gurgenovich, PhD; Armenian politician; b. 1944, Yerevan; m.; three c.; ed Yerevan State Univ., Moscow State Univ., Steklov Inst. of Math. USSR (now Russian) Acad. of Sciences; researcher Computation Cen. and Inst. of Math. Armenian Acad. of Sciences 1968–75; researcher Inst. of Scientific and Tech. Information 1975–77; concurrently Prof., Head of Dept Yerevan State Univ. 1977–; Chair. Armat Centre for Devt of Democracy and Civil Soc. 1999–; published over 30 scientific articles and textbooks; mem. Cttee Karabakh, mem. Exec. Bd of Armenian Nat. Movt 1988; mem., First Deputy Chair. Supreme Council of Armenia 1990–91, Chair. 1991–95; Chair. Armenian Parl. 1991–95; elected mem. Nat. Ass. Repub. of Armenia 1995–99, Chair. 1995–98; Chair. Armat Movt 1999–. *Leisure interests:* music, literature, tennis. *Address:* Armat Centre, 26 Buzand Street, 375010 Yerevan (Office); 3 Tamanian Street, #35, 375009 Yerevan, Armenia (Home). *Telephone:* (2) 540512 (Office); (2) 548440 (Home). *Fax:* (2) 540511 (Office); (2) 522099 (Home). *E-mail:* armat@acc.am (Office). *Website:* www.ac.am/~armat (Office).

ARASHI, Qadi Abdul Karim al-; Yemeni politician; fmr Minister for Local Govt and the Treasury; Speaker of the Constituent People's Ass. 1978; Chair. Provisional Presidential Council June–July 1978; Vice-Pres. Yemen Arab Republic 1978–90; mem. Presidential Council of Yemen 1990–. *Address:* Constituent People's Assembly, San'a, Yemen.

ARASKOG, Rand Vincent; American business executive; b. 30 Oct. 1931, Fergus Falls, Minn.; s. of Randolph Victor Araskog and Hilfred Mathilda Araskog; m. Jessie Marie Gustafson 1956; one s. two d.; ed US Mil. Acad. and Harvard Univ.; special Asst to Dir, Dept of Defense, Washington, DC 1954–59; Dir Marketing, Aeronautical Div., Honeywell Inc., Minneapolis 1960–66; Vice-Pres. ITT, Group Exec. ITT Aerospace Electronics, Components and Energy Group, Nutley, NJ 1971–76; Pres. 1979–85, CEO ITT Corpn, New York 1979–80, Chair. Bd and Exec. and Policy Comms. 1980–98, also Dir, Chair., Pres., CEO ITT Holdings Inc., New York, 1995–98, mem. Bd Dirs ITT Industries 1980–, Chair. Nat. Security Telecommunications Advisory Cttee 1983–; mem. Bd of Govs., Aerospace Industries Asscn, Exec. Council, Air Force Assocn; Officier, Légion d'honneur, Grand Officer Order of Merit (Italy). *Publications:* ITT Wars 1989, numerous articles. *Address:* ITT Industries Inc., 4 West Red Oak Lane, White Plains, NY 10604, USA.

ARASTOU, Seyed Mojtaba; Iranian diplomatist and international official; fmr Amb. and Perm. Rep. to UN, Vienna; fmr Amb. to Switzerland; fmr Dir-Gen. Protocol Dept, Ministry of Foreign Affairs; various positions with Econ. Co-operation Org. (ECO), Sec.-Gen. July 2002–. *Address:* Economic Co-operation Organization, 1 Golbon Alley, Kamranieh Street, POB 14155-6176, Tehran, Iran (Office). *Telephone:* (21) 2831733 (Office). *Fax:* (21) 2831732 (Office). *E-mail:* registry@ecosecretariat.org (Office). *Website:* www .ecosecretariat.org (Office).

ARAÚJO, HE Cardinal Serafim Fernandes de; Brazilian ecclesiastic; b. 13 Aug. 1924, Minas Novas; ordained priest 1949; Bishop 1959; Coadjutor, See of Belo Horizonte 1982, Archbishop 1986–; cr. Cardinal 1998. *Address:* Cúria Metropolitana, Av. Brasil 2079, C.P. 494, 30140-002 Belo Horizonte, MG, Brazil. *Telephone:* (31) 261-3400. *Fax:* (31) 261-5713.

ARAÚJO SALES, HE Cardinal Eugénio de; Brazilian ecclesiastic; b. 8 Nov. 1920, Acari, Rio Grande do Norte; s. of Celso Dantas and D. Josefa de Araujo Sales; ordained 1943; Bishop 1954; Apostolic Administrator, See of São Salvador da Bahia until 1968; Archbishop of São Sebastião do Rio de Janeiro 1971–; cr. Cardinal 1969. *Leisure interest:* reading. *Address:* Palácio São Joaquim, Rua da Glória 446, 20241-150 Rio de Janeiro, RJ, Brazil. *Telephone:* 292-3132; 253-8148. *Fax:* 221-8093.

ARAZOV, Rejepbay; Turkmenistan politician; b. 1947, Shakhman, Krasnovodsk region; ed Turkmen State Polytech. Inst.; joined Kumdagneft co. 1963; Minister of Petroleum, Natural Gas and Mineral Resources 1998–2000; Head of Admin. Balkan region 2000–01; Chair. Majlis (Parl.) 2001–02; Minister of Defence 2002–. *Address:* Ministry of Defence, ul. Nurberdy Pomma 15, Ashgabat, Turkmenistan. *Telephone:* (12) 29-31-80 (Office).

ARBATOV, Aleksander Arkadyevich, DrEcons; Russian geologist; b. 4 Sept. 1938, Moscow; ed Moscow Inst. of Oil; researcher, participated in geological expeditions Ministry of Geology, USSR 1960–62; researcher All-Union Research Inst. of Geological Studies 1962–76; Head of lab. All-Union Inst. of System Studies USSR (now Russian) Acad. of Sciences 1976–89; mem. staff Comm. on Natural Resources, Russian Acad. of Sciences 1989–, Chair. 1996–; mem. Russian Acad. of Natural Sciences 1993; Vice-Pres. Russian Asscn of Power Econs; mem. Int. Asscn of Power Econs; mem. editorial bd journals Natural Resources Forum, The Energy Journal. *Publications:* numerous scientific articles, Oil and Gas in the 15 Republics of the Former USSR (5 vol. treatise). *Address:* KEPS, Vavilova str. 7, 117822 Moscow, Russia (Office). *Telephone:* (095) 135-45-29 (Office).

ARBATOV, Aleksei Georgiyevich, DrHistSc; Russian politician; b. 17 Jan. 1951, Moscow; s. of Georgiy Arkadyevich Arbatov (q.v.) and Svetlana Pavlovna Goriacheva; m.; one d.; ed Moscow Inst. of Int. Relations; researcher, then Head of Div., Inst. of World Econ. and Int. Relations (IMEMO), USSR (now Russian) Acad. of Sciences 1976–, Head Centre of Geopolitical and Mil. Prognoses 1992; Dir Centre on Disarmament and Strategic Stability of Asscn of Foreign Policy; adviser in different UN bodies; mem. State Duma (Parl.) 1993–99; Deputy Chair. State Defence Cttee 1994–; mem. faction Yabloko, mem. Cen. Council Yabloko Movt (now Yabloko Party). *Publications:* numerous papers and articles on problems with Russian foreign policy, int. relations and US political system. *Address:* State Duma, Okhotny Ryad 4, 103265 Moscow, Russia (Office). *Telephone:* (095) 292-80-23 (Office). *Fax:* (095) 292-93-79 (Office).

ARBATOV, Georgiy Arkadyevich, DHistSc; Russian administrator and academician; b. 19 May 1923, Kherson; s. of Arkady Michailovich Arbatov and Anna Vasilievna Arbatova; m. Svetlana Pavlovna Goriacheva 1948; one s.; ed Moscow Inst. for Int. Relations; Soviet Army 1941–44; mem. CPSU 1943–91; ed. in publishing house for foreign literature and periodicals (Voprosy filosofii, Novoe vremya, Kommunist) 1949–60; Columnist Problems of Peace and Socialism 1960–62; Section Chief at Inst. of World Econ. and Int. Relations of USSR Acad. of Sciences 1962–64; Worked for CPSU Cen. Cttee 1964–67; Dir Inst. of US and Canadian Studies, USSR (now Russian) Acad. of Sciences 1967–95, Hon. Dir 1995–; Deputy USSR Supreme Soviet 1974–89; People's Deputy of the USSR 1989–91; personal adviser to Mikhail Gorbachev and other Soviet leaders including Brezhnev and Andropov and to Boris Yeltsin until 1993; mem. Cen. Auditing Comm. of CPSU 1971–76; Cand. mem. and mem. CPSU Cen. Cttee 1976–89; mem. Palme Comm. 1980–91; mem. USSR (now Russian) Acad. of Sciences 1974; Order of the Red Star 1943, Badge of Honour 1962, Order of the October Revolution 1971, Order of Lenin 1975, Order of the Great Patriotic War, 1st Rank 1985. *Publications:* The System (published in USA) 1993 and other books and articles on history of

Russian–American relations, disarmanent, world econs, including A Delayed Recovery 1991. *Address:* USA and Canada Institute, 2/3 Khlebny per., Moscow G-69, 121814, Russia. *Telephone:* (095) 290-58-75 (Office).

ARBEID, Murray; British fashion designer; b. 30 May 1935, London; s. of Jack Arbeid and Ida Davis; ed Quintin School, London; apprenticed to Michael Sherard 1952; opened own business 1954–; designer and design consultant, Norman Hartnell 1988–89. *Leisure interests:* music, literature, art. *Address:* 202 Ebury Street, London, SW1W 8UN, England. *Telephone:* (20) 7259-9292.

ARBER, Werner, PhD; Swiss microbiologist; b. 1929, Gränichen, Aargau; m.; two c.; ed Aargau Gymnasium, Eidgenössische Technische Hochschule, Zürich; Asst at Laboratory of Biophysics, Univ. of Geneva 1953–58, Dozent then Extraordinary Prof. of Molecular Genetics 1962–70; Research Assoc., Dept of Microbiology, Univ. of Southern Calif. 1958–59; Visiting Investigator, Dept of Molecular Biology Univ. of Calif., Berkeley 1970–71; Prof. of Microbiology, Univ. of Basel 1971–96, Rector 1986–88; Pres. Int. Council of Scientific Unions (ICSU) 1996–99; Jt Winner Nobel Prize for Physiology or Medicine 1978. *Address:* c/o Department of Microbiology, Biozentrum der Universität, Basel, 70 Klingelbergstrasse, 4056 Basel, Switzerland (Office). *Telephone:* (61) 2672130. *Fax:* (61) 2672118.

ARBHABHIRAMA, Anat, PhD; Thai scientist; b. 13 Jan. 1938, Bangkok; s. of Arun Arbhabhirama and Pathumporn Arbhabhirama; m. Mrs Benjarata 1966; three s.; ed Chulalongkorn Univ., Bangkok, Asian Inst. of Tech., Bangkok, Colorado State Univ., Vice-Pres. for Acad. Affairs and Provost, Asian Inst. of Tech. 1979–80; Deputy Minister of Agric. and Co-operatives 1980, Minister 1980–81; Head, Regional Research and Devt Center, Asian Inst. of Tech. 1981–84; Pres. Thailand Devt Research Inst. 1984–87; Chair. Intergovernmental Council of the Int. Hydrological Programme, UNESCO 1984–88; Gov. Petroleum Authority of Thailand 1987; Chair. PTT Exploration and Production Co. Ltd 1988, The Aromatics Co. Ltd (Thailand) 1990–; Outstanding Researcher of the Year 1987. *Publications:* numerous articles and papers on water resources and hydraulics. *Leisure interests:* golf, jogging, chess. *Address:* c/o The Petroleum Authority of Thailand, 555 Vibhavadirangsit Road, Bangkok 10900, Thailand.

ARBOUR, Louise, BA, LLL; Canadian judge; b. 10 Feb. 1947, Montreal; three c.; ed Univ. de Montreal; Prof. Osgoode Hall Law School, Toronto 1974–87; called to bar Ont. 1977; Judge, Supreme Court of Ont. (High Court of Justice) 1987–90; Judge, Court of Appeal for Ont. 1990–96; Chief Prosecutor, Int. Criminal Tribunals for fmr Yugoslavia and Rwanda, The Hague 1996–99; Puisne Judge, Supreme Court of Canada 1999–; mem. Bd of Trustees, Int. Crisis Group 2000–; Hon. Prof. Univ. of Warwick, England 1999–(2004); Hon. mem. American Soc. of Int. Law 2000–; Hon. Bencher Gray's Inn, London, England 2001–; 25 hon. degrees; numerous awards including Fondation Louise Weiss Prize, Paris 1999, Lord Reading Law Soc.'s Human Rights Award 2000, Franklin and Eleanor Roosevelt Four Freedoms Medal 2000. *Address:* The Supreme Court of Canada, 301 Wellington Street, Ottawa, ON K1A 0J1, Canada (Office). *Telephone:* (613) 992-5388 (Office). *Fax:* (613) 952-1967 (Office). *E-mail:* reception@scc-csc.gc.ca (Office). *Website:* www.scc-csc.gc.ca (Office).

ARBULÚ GALLIANI, Gen. Guillermo; Peruvian government official and army officer; b. 1922, Trujillo; m. Bertha Tanaka de Azcárate; one s. two d.; ed Chorillos Mil. Acad.; Sub-Lt, Eng Corps 1943, Lt 1946, Capt. 1949, Major 1955, Lt-Col.1959, Col 1964, Brig.-Gen. 1971, Div. Gen. 1975–; fmr Chief of Staff, 1st Light Div.; fmr Dir of Logistics; fmr Chief of Operations, Armed Forces Gen. Staff; fmr Dir of Mil. Eng Coll.; fmr Instructor, Higher War Coll.; fmr Adviser to Ministries of Mining and Fisheries; fmr Pres. Empresa Pública de Servicios Pesqueros (State Fishing Corpn); Pres. Joint Armed Forces Command; Prime Minister and Minister of Defence 1976–78, Amb. to Chile 1978–79, to Spain 1979–80; del. to Latin American Conf. of Ministers of Labour; rep. of Ministry of Foreign Affairs to negotiations for Andean Pact; rep. to 11th American Mil. Congress; Commdr Mil. Order of Ayacucho; Jorge Chávez Award; Grand Officer of Peruvian Crosses of Aeronautical Merit, Naval Merit; Grand Cross, Peruvian Order of Mil. Merit; Grand Officer, Mayo Cross of Mil. Merit (Argentina). *Address:* c/o Ministry of Foreign Affairs, Lima, Peru.

ARCAND, Denys; Canadian film director; b. 25 June 1941, Deschambault, Québec; ed Univ. of Montreal; worked at Office Nat. du Film, Canada 1962–65; Vice-Pres. Asscn des Réalisateurs et Réalisatrices de films du Québec. *Films directed:* Seul ou avec d'autres (co-dir) 1962, Champlain (short) 1963, Les Montrealistes (short) 1964, La Route de l'Ouest (short) 1965, Montreal, un jour d'été and Parcs atlantiques (shorts) 1966, Volleyball 1967, On est au coton 1969, Québec: Dupléssis et après 1970, La maudite galette 1971, Réjeanne Padovani 1972, Gina 1974, La lutte des travailleurs d'hôpitaux (short) 1975, Le confort et l'indifférence 1980, Empire Inc. (TV) 1982, Le crime d'Ovide Plouffe 1984, Le déclin de l'empire américain 1986, Jésus de Montréal 1989 (Cannes Jury Prize 1989), Love and Human Remains 1993, Poverty and Other Delights, Stardom 2001.

ARCAYA, Ignacio; Venezuelan diplomatist; b. 3 June 1939, Caracas; m.; two c.; ed Cen. Univ. of Venezuela; Third Sec. Perm. Mission to UN in Geneva 1966–68, Second Sec., Ministry for Foreign Affairs 1968–69, First Sec., Mission to OAS, Washington, DC 1969–72, Counsellor Inst. of Foreign Trade, Ministry of Foreign Affairs 1972–75, Minister Counsellor of Econ. Affairs,

Embassy in Paris 1975–78, Amb. to Australia (also accred to NZ, Fiji and the Philippines) 1978–84; Sec.-Gen. Asscn of Iron Ore Exporting Countries 1984–88; Amb.-at-Large, Ministry of Foreign Affairs 1988, Amb. to Chile 1989–92, to UK (also accred to Ireland) 1992–95, to Argentina 1995–98; Perm. Rep. to UN 1998. *Address:* c/o Ministry of Foreign Affairs, Torre MRE, esq. Carmelitas, Avda Urdaneta, Caracas, 1010, Venezuela. *Telephone:* (212) 862-1085 (Office). *Fax:* (212) 864-3633 (Office). *E-mail:* criptogr@mre.gov.ve (Office).

ARCHER, Mary Doreen, PhD, FRSC; British scientist; b. 22 Dec. 1944; d. of the late Harold Norman Weeden and of Doreen Weeden (née Cox); m. Jeffrey Howard Archer (now Baron Archer of Weston-super-Mare, q.v.) 1966; two s.; ed Cheltenham Ladies' Coll., St Anne's Coll. Oxford, Imperial Coll. London; Jr Research Fellow, St Hilda's Coll. Oxford 1968–71; temporary Lecturer in Chem., Somerville Coll. Oxford 1971–72; Research Fellow, Royal Inst. of GB 1972–76; Lector in Chem., Trinity Coll. Cambridge 1976–86; Fellow and Coll. Lecturer in Chem., Newnham Coll. Cambridge 1976–86; Sr Academic Fellow, De Montfort Univ. (fmrly Leicester Polytechnic) 1990–; Visiting Prof., Dept of Biochem., Imperial Coll. London 1991–2000, Visiting Prof. Centre for Energy Policy and Tech. 2001–; Visitor, Univ. of Herts. 1993–; Trustee Science Museum 1990–2000; mem. Council, Royal Inst. 1984–85, 1999–, Cheltenham Ladies' Coll. 1991–2000; Chair. Nat. Energy Foundation 1990–2000, Pres. 2000–; Dir Anglia TV Group 1987–95, Mid Anglia Radio 1988–94, Cambridge & Newmarket FM Radio (now Q103) 1988–97; Dir Addenbrookes Hosp. NHS Trust 1992–, Vice-Chair. 2000–; mem. Council of Lloyd's 1989–92; Pres. Guild of Church Musicians 1989–, Solar Energy Soc. 2001–, British Soc. of Grad. Artists and Designers 2002–; Hon. DSc (Herts.) 1994. *Publications:* Rupert Brooke and The Old Vicarage, Grantchester 1989, Clean Energy from Photovoltaics 2001–; contribs to chemical journals. *Leisure interests:* reading, writing, singing. *Address:* The Old Vicarage, Grantchester, Cambridge, CB3 9ND, England. *Telephone:* (1223) 840213.

ARCHER, Robyn, AO, BA, DipEd; Australian performer, songwriter, writer and director; b. 18 June 1948, Adelaide; d. of Clifford Charles Smith and Mary Louisa Wohling; ed Enfield High School, Adelaide Univ.; singer 1952–; recorded 10 albums including Brecht, Weill and Eisler repertoire; has toured world-wide in recital, concert and cabaret performances; has sung with Australian and Adelaide Chamber Orchestras, Adelaide, Melbourne and Tasmanian Symphony Orchestras; numerous TV appearances in Australia and UK; has written over 100 songs; writing for theatre includes Songs from Sideshow Alley, The Pack of Women (also Dir), Cut & Thrust Cabaret (also Dir), Café Fledermaus, See Ya Next Century, Ningali, A Star is Torn, Comes a Cropper; writing for TV includes The One That Got Away; also writes for radio; directing for theatre includes Accidental Death of an Anarchist; Artistic Dir Nat. Festival of Australian Theatre 1993–95, Adelaide Festival 1998, 2000 1995–2000; Creative Consultant Melbourne Museum 1995–98; Artistic Dir Melbourne Int. Festival of Arts 2002–; Chair. Community Cultural Devt Bd, Australia Council 1992–94; Patron Nat. Affiliation of Arts Educators; Hon. DUniv (Flinders); Chevalier des Arts et des Lettres 2000; Sydney Critics' Circle Award 1980, Henry Lawson Award 1980, Australian Creative Fellowship 1991–93, Australian Record Industry Award for best soundtrack for Pack of Women 1986, for Best Children's Album for Mrs Bottle 1989, Exec. Woman of the Year, Australian Women's Network 1998. *Publications:* The Robyn Archer Songbook 1980, Mrs Bottle Burps 1983, The Pack of Women 1986, A Star is Torn 1986; contrib. to books, magazines and newspapers. *Address:* c/o Rick Raftos Management, Box 445, Paddington, NSW 2021, Australia. *Telephone:* (2) 9281-9622. *Fax:* (2) 9212-7100.

ARCHER OF WESTON-SUPER-MARE, Baron (Life Peer), cr. 1992, of Mark in the County of Somerset; **Jeffrey Howard Archer,** FRSA; British author and politician; b. 15 April 1940; s. of William and Lola (née Cook) Archer; m. Mary Archer (q.v.) 1966; two s.; ed Wellington School and Brasenose Coll., Oxford; mem. GLC for Havering 1966–70; mem. Parl. for Louth (Conservative) 1969–74; Deputy Chair. Conservative Party 1985–86; sentenced to 4 years imprisonment for perjury and perverting the course of justice July 2001. *Play:* The Accused (writer and actor) 2000. *Publications:* Not a Penny More, Not a Penny Less 1975, Shall We Tell the President? 1977, Kane and Abel 1979, A Quiver Full of Arrows 1980, The Prodigal Daughter 1982, First Among Equals 1984, A Matter of Honour 1985, Beyond Reasonable Doubt (play) 1987, A Twist in the Tale (short stories) 1988, Exclusive (play) 1989, As the Crow Flies 1991, Honour Among Thieves 1993, Twelve Red Herrings (short stories) 1994, The First Miracle (with Craigie Aitchison) 1994, The Fourth Estate 1996, The Collected Short Stories 1997, The Eleventh Commandment 1998, To Cut a Long Story Short (short stories) 2000, A Prison Diary 2002, Sons of Fortune 2003. *Leisure interests:* theatre, cinema, cricket, auctioneering. *Address:* 93 Albert Embankment, London, SE1 7TY; The Old Vicarage, Grantchester, Cambridge, CB3 9ND, England.

ARCULUS, Sir Ronald, KCMG, KCVO, MA, FBIM; British diplomatist (retd); b. 11 Feb. 1923, Birmingham; s. of the late Cecil Arculus, MC and Ethel Lilian Arculus; m. Sheila Mary Faux 1953; one s. one d.; ed Solihull School, Exeter Coll., Oxford and Imperial Defence Coll.; served in Fourth Queen's Own Hussars 1942–45 (attained rank of Capt.); Foreign Office 1947; San Francisco 1948–50; La Paz 1950; Ankara 1953–56; Foreign Office 1957–60; First Sec. (Commercial), Washington 1961–65; Dir of Trade Devt, New York 1965–68; Imperial Defence Coll. 1969; Head of Science and Technology Dept, FCO 1970–73; Minister (Economic), Paris 1973–77; Amb. to Law of Sea Conference 1977–79; Amb. to Italy 1979–83; Special Adviser to Government on Channel

Tunnel trains 1987–88; Dir Glaxo PLC 1983–91, Consultant 1992–95; Chair. Kensington Soc. 1999–2001, Pres. 2001–; Dir of Appeals King's Medical Research Trust 1984–88; Trustee, Glaxo Trustees Ltd 1988–93; Freeman of the City of London; Gov. British Inst., Florence 1984–93; Consultant London and Continental Bankers Ltd 1985–90, Trusthouse Forte 1983–86; Hon. Fellow Exeter Coll., Oxford 1989. *Leisure interests:* travel, fine arts, music, antiques. *Address:* 20 Kensington Court Gardens, London, W8 5QF, England.

ARDALAN, Nader, MArch; American architect and planner; b. 9 March 1939, Tehran, Iran; s. of Abbas Gholi Ardalan and Faranguis Davar Ardalan; m. 1st Laleh Bakhtiar 1962 (divorced 1976); one s. two d.; m. 2nd Shahla Ganji 1977; one s.; ed New Rochelle High School, Carnegie-Mellon Univ. and Harvard Univ. Grad. School of Design; designer, S.O.M. 1962–64; Chief Architect, Nat. Iranian Oil Co. 1964–66; Design Partner, Aziz Farmanfarmaian & Assocs. 1966–72; Man. Dir Mandala Collaborative Tehran/Boston 1972–79; Prof. of Design, Tehran Univ. Faculty of Fine Arts 1972–77; Pres. Nader Ardalan Assocs. 1979–92; Prin. Jung/Brannen Assocs. Inc., Boston 1983–94; Man. Prin. Jung/Brannen Assocs. Inc., Abu Dhabi 1992; Senior Vice-Pres. and Dir of Design KEO Int. Consultants 1994–; Visiting Prof. Harvard Univ. Grad. School of Design 1977–78, 1981–83, Yale Univ. 1977, MIT 1980; various other professional appts.; Aga Khan Award Steering Cttee 1976–80; King Fahd Award 1987; design awards. *Publications:* Sense of Unity 1972, Habitat Bill of Rights 1976, Pardisan, Environmental Park 1976, Blessed Jerusalem 1985; articles in leading professional journals. *Leisure interests:* the study of sacred architecture, photography, swimming, hunting. *Address:* 20 Williams Street, Suite 245, Wellesley, MA 02481, USA (Home); KEO International Consultants, P.O. Box 3679, Safat 13037, Kuwait. *Telephone:* (965) 243-8011. *Fax:* (965) 244-3969. *E-mail:* nadera@keoic.com (Office).

ARDANT, Fanny; French actress; b. 22 March 1949, Monte Carlo; d. of Lieut.-Col. Jean Ardant and Jacqueline Lecoq; three c.; Grand Prix National (Ministry of Culture). *Films include:* Les Chiens 1979, Les uns et les autres, The Woman Next Door, The Ins and Outs, Life is a Novel, Confidentially Yours, Benevenuta, Desire, Swann in Love, Love Unto Death, Les Enragés, L'Eté prochain, Family Business, Affabulazione, Melo, The Family, La Paltoquet, Three Sisters, Australia, Pleure pas my love, Adventure of Catherine C., Afraid of the Dark, Rien que des mensonges, La Femme du déserteur, Amok, Colonel Chabert, Beyond the Clouds, Ridicule, Elizabeth, La Débondade, Le Fils du Français, Le Dîner et le Libertin 2000, 8 Femmes 2002. *Theatre includes:* Polyeucte, Esther, The Mayor of Santiago, Electra, Tête d'Or. *Leisure interest:* (music) piano. *Address:* Artmédia, 10 avenue George V, 75008 Paris, France (Office).

ARDEBERG, Arne Lennart, PhD; Swedish professor of astronomy; b. 10 Nov. 1940, Malmö; s. of Kurt Ardeberg and Elly Ardeberg; m. Margareta Vinberg 1969; one s. two d.; ed Lund Univ.; staff astronomer, Lund Observatory 1965–69; staff astronomer, European Southern Observatory, La Silla, Chile 1969–73; Assoc. Prof. Lund Observatory 1973–79; Astronomical Dir European Southern Observatory, La Silla 1979–81, Dir 1981–83; Dir Lund Observatory 1983–, Nordic Optical Telescope Scientific Asscn 1984–; apptd. Dean, Faculty of Science, Lund Univ. 1987–, now Prof.; mem. Royal Swedish Acad. of Sciences, Royal Physiographical Soc. (Sweden), Royal Soc. of Sciences (Sweden); Wallmark Prize (Royal Swedish Acad. of Sciences) 1977. *Publications:* 160 Publs in int. journals and books on astronomy and physics. *Leisure interests:* mountaineering, forestry. *Address:* Lund Observatory, Box 43, S-221 00 Lund, Sweden. *Telephone:* 46-10-72-90.

ARDEN, John; British playwright and novelist; b. 26 Oct. 1930, Barnsley; s. of Charles Alwyn Arden and Annie Elizabeth Layland; m. Margaretta Ruth D'Arcy (q.v.) 1957; five s. (one deceased); ed Sedbergh School, King's Coll., Cambridge and Edinburgh Coll. of Art; Fellow in Playwriting, Bristol Univ. 1959–60; Visiting Lecturer (Politics and Drama), New York Univ. 1967; Regent's Lecturer, Univ. of Calif.at Davis 1973; Writer in Residence, Univ. of New England, Australia 1975; mem. Corrandula Arts and Entertainment Club 1973, Galway Theatre Workshop 1975; PEN Short Story Prize 1992, V. S. Pritchett Short Story Prize 1999; Evening Standard Drama Award 1960, Arts Council Playwriting Award (with Margaretta D'Arcy) 1972. *Plays:* All Fall Down 1955, The Waters of Babylon 1957, Live Like Pigs 1958, Serjeant Musgrave's Dance 1959, The Happy Haven (with Margaretta D'Arcy) 1960, The Business of Good Government (with Margaretta D'Arcy) 1960, Wet Fish 1962, The Workhouse Donkey 1963, Ironhand 1963, Ars Longa Vita Brevis (with Margaretta D'Arcy) 1964, Armstrong's Last Goodnight 1964, Left Handed Liberty 1965, Friday's Hiding (with Margaretta D'Arcy) 1966, The Royal Pardon (with Margaretta D'Arcy) 1966, Muggins is a Martyr (with Margaretta D'Arcy and C.A.S.T.) 1968, The Hero Rises Up (musical with Margaretta D'Arcy) 1968, Two Autobiographical Plays 1972, The Ballygombeen Bequest (with Margaretta D'Arcy) 1972, The Island of the Mighty (with Margaretta D'Arcy) 1972, The Non-Stop Connolly Show (with Margaretta D'Arcy) 1975, Vandaleur's Folly (with Margaretta D'Arcy) 1978, The Little Gray Home in the West (with Margaretta D'Arcy) 1978, The Making of Muswell Hill (with Margaretta D'Arcy) 1979. *Radio:* The Life of Man 1956, The Bagman 1969, Keep Those People Moving (with Margaretta D'Arcy) 1972, Pearl 1977, Don Quixote (adaptation) 1980, Garland for a Hoar Head 1982, The Old Man Sleeps Alone 1982, The Manchester Enthusiasts (with Margaretta D'Arcy) 1984, Whose is the Kingdom? (with Magaretta D'Arcy) 1988, A Suburban Suicide (with Margaretta D'Arcy) 1994, Six Little Novels of Wilkie Collins (adaptation) 1997, Woe Alas, the Fatal Cashbox! 1999. *TV:* Soldier Soldier 1960, Wet Fish 1962, Profile of Sean O'Casey (documentary,

with Margaretta D'Arcy) 1973. *Publications:* essays: To Present the Pretence 1977, Awkward Corners (with Margaretta D'Arcy) 1988; novels: Silence Among the Weapons 1982, Books of Bale 1988, Cogs Tyrannic 1991, Jack Juggler and the Emperor's Whore 1995. *Leisure interests:* antiquarianism, mythology. *Address:* c/o Casarotto Ramsay Ltd., National House, 60–66 Wardour Street, London, W1V 3HP, England. *Telephone:* (20) 7287-4450. *Fax:* (20) 7287-9128.

ARDEN, Rt Hon. Dame Mary (Howarth), DBE, PC, MA, LLM; British judge; b. 23 Jan. 1947; d. of the late Lt-Col E. C. Arden and of M. M. (née Smith) Arden; m. Hon. Sir Jonathan Hugh Mance 1973; one s. two d.; ed Huyton Coll., Girton Coll., Cambridge, Harvard Law School; called to the Bar Gray's Inn 1971; admitted to Lincoln's Inn 1973, Bencher 1993; QC 1986; Dept of Trade and Industry Inspector Rotaprint PLC 1988–91; Attorney Gen. Duchy of Lancaster 1991–93; Judge of High Court of Justice, Chancery Div. 1993–2000; Chair. Law Comm. 1996–99; Lord Justice of Appeal 2000–; Bar mem. Law Soc.'s Standing Cttee on Co. Law 1976–; mem. Financial Law Panel 1993–2000, Steering Group, Co. Law Review 1998–2000; Fellow Girton Coll. Cambridge; Hon. DUniv (Essex) 1997; Hon. LLD (Liverpool) 1998, (London) 1999, (Warwick) 1999, (Royal Holloway and Bedford New College, London) 1999, (Nottingham) 2002. *Publications:* Buckley on The Companies Acts (Jt Gen. Ed.) 2000; contrib. to numerous books, articles in legal journals. *Leisure interests:* reading, swimming. *Address:* Royal Courts of Justice, Strand, London, WC2A 2LL, England.

ARDITO BARLETTA, Nicolás, PhD, MS; Panamanian politician and economist; b. 21 Aug. 1938, Aguadulce, Coclé; s. of Nicolás Ardito Barletta and Leticia de Ardito Barletta; m. María Consuelo de Ardito Barletta; two s. one d.; ed Univ. of Chicago and N. Carolina State Univ.; Cabinet mem. and Dir Planning 1968–70; Dir Econ. Affairs Org. of American States 1970–73; Minister of Planning 1973–78; Negotiator of econ. aspects of Panama Canal Treaties 1976–77; Vice-Pres. World Bank for Latin America and Caribbean 1978–84; Founder and first Pres. Latin American Export Bank 1978; Pres. Latin American Econ. System (SELA) Constituent Ass.; Pres. of Panama 1984–85; Gen. Dir of Int. Centre for Econ. Growth 1986–95; Dir Autoridad de la Región Interoceanía (ARI) 1995–2000; Chair. Asesores Estrategicos; mem. Bd of Dirs of several corpns, banks and policy insts. *Leisure interests:* tennis and music. *Address:* P.O. Box 7737, Panamá 9, Republic of Panama. *Telephone:* 269-1522. *Fax:* 264-9370.

ARDZINBA, Vladislav Grigoriyvich, D.HIS.SC.; Georgian (Abkhaz) politician and historian; b. 14 May 1945, Eshera; m. Svetlana Ardzinba; one d.; ed Sukhumi Pedagogical Inst.; mem. CPSU 1967–91; researcher Inst. of Oriental Sciences, Moscow 1969–87; Dir D. Gulia Abkhaz Inst. of Language, Literature and History, Georgian Acad. of Sciences 1987–90; USSR People's Deputy 1989–91; Chair. Supreme Soviet of Abkhazia 1990–94; leader of independence movt, self-proclaimed Repub. of Abkhazia, Pres. 1994–. *Publications:* Rituals and Myths of Ancient Anatolia 1985; numerous papers. *Address:* Supreme Soviet of Abkhazia, Sukhumi, Georgia.

AREF, Maj.-Gen. Abdul Rahman Mohammed; Iraqi politician and army officer; b. 1916; brother of late President Abdul Salam Aref; ed Baghdad Military Acad.; Head of Armoured Corps until 1962; Commdr 5th Div. Feb.–Nov. 1963; assisted in overthrow of Gen. Kassem 1963; mem. Regency Council 1965; Asst Chief of Staff Iraqi Armed Forces 1963–64; Acting Chief of Staff 1964, Chief of Staff 1964–68; Pres. of Iraq 1966–68, also Prime Minister May–July 1967.

ARENDARSKI, Andrzej, PhD; Polish politician; b. 15 Nov. 1949, Warsaw; m. Agnieszka Łypacewicz; three s. one d.; ed Warsaw Univ.; teacher, E. Dembowski Secondary School, Warsaw 1972–73, Inst. of Philosophy and Sociology of Polish Acad. of Sciences, Warsaw 1973–75; mem. Solidarity Trade Union 1980–; Ed.-in-Chief, underground journal Zeszyty Edukacji Narodowej 1981–82; co-f. Agric.-Industrial Soc., Konin 1988; mem. Soc. for Econ. and Econ. Action, Warsaw 1988–; co-f. Social Movt for Econ. Initiatives SPRING 1988; Deputy to Sejm (Parl.) 1989–93; mem. Liberal Democratic Congress (KLD) 1989–94, Deputy Chair. KLD 1989–94, mem. KLD Political Council 1991–94, now Chair.; Pres., Polish Chamber of Commerce 1990–; Minister of Foreign Econ. Co-operation 1992–93; Chair. Polish-Ukrainian Chamber of Commerce 1996–; Sec.-Gen. Polish Asscn Industry, Commerce and Finance 1997–; CEO Tel-Emergo, Telephony Service Providers. *Publications:* contribs to underground journals 1981–89; co-author: Polska lat 80-tych: Analiza stanu obecnego i perspektywy rozwoju sytuacji politycznej w Polsce 1984, Stan środowiska przyrodniczego 1984. *Leisure interests:* travel, sailing, art of cooking. *Address:* Krajowa Izba Gospodarcza, ul. Trębacka 4, 00-074 Warsaw, Poland. *Telephone:* (22) 8260221 (Office); (22) 8260143 (Office). *Fax:* (22) 8274673 (Office).

ARENS, Moshe; Israeli politician, professor and diplomatist; b. 7 Dec. 1925, Lithuania; ed Massachusetts and California Insts. of Technology, USA; Assoc. Prof. of Aeronautical Eng Technion (Israel Inst. of Tech.), Haifa; Deputy Dir Israel Aircraft Industries, Lod; Amb. to USA 1982–83; Minister of Defence 1983–84, 1999, without Portfolio –1987, of Foreign Affairs 1988–90, of Defence 1990–92; Adviser to Prime Minister 2001–; elected to Knesset, mem. Knesset Finance Cttee 1973; Israel Defence Prize 1971; Assoc. Fellow, AIAA. *Publications:* Broken Covenant 1994, several books on propulsion and flight mechanics. *Address:* c/o Office of the Prime Minister, P.O. Box 187, 3 Rehov Kaplan, Kiryat Ben-Gurion, Jerusalem 91919, Israel.

ARENY CASAL, Francesc; Andorran politician; b. 28 June 1959, Canillo; Mayor of Canillo 1988–95; Pres. Unio Pro-Turisme, Canillo 1987; mem. Partit Liberal d'Andorra; Síndic-Gen. (Speaker of the Gen. Council) 1997–. *Address:* Consell General, Andorra la Vella, Andorra (Office). *Telephone:* 821234 (Office). *Fax:* 861234 (Office). *E-mail:* consell.general@andorra.ad (Office). *Website:* www.micg.ad (Office).

ARGERICH, Martha; Argentine pianist; b. 5 June 1941, Buenos Aires; studied with V. Scaramuzzo, Friedrich Gulda, Nikita Magaloff, Madeleine Lipatti and Arturo Benedetto Michaelangeli; début Buenos Aires 1949; London début 1964; soloist with world's leading orchestras; with Chamber Orchestra of Europe, Barbican Hall, London 1991; Schumann Concerto, BBC London Proms 2000; First Prize Busoni Contest and Geneva Int. Music Competition 1957, Int. Chopin Competition, Warsaw 1965; Officier Ordre des Arts et des Lettres 1996, Accademica di Santa Cecilia di Roma 1997. *Address:* c/o Jacques Thelen Agence Artistique, 15 Avenue Montaigne, 75008 Paris, France.

ARGUETA, Manlio; Salvadorean writer and librarian; b. 24 Nov. 1935, San Miguel; lived in exile in Costa Rica for many years since 1973; apptd. Dir of Library, Univ. of El Salvador 1996; Univ. of Cen. America Prize (for One Day of Life) 1980. *Publications:* One Day of Life 1980 (trans. into English 1984), Cuscatlán (novel) 1987, Rosario de la Paz (novel) 1996, Siglo de O(g)ro 1997. *Address:* c/o Biblioteca, Universidad de El Salvador, Final 24 Avda Norte, Ciudad Universitaria, Apdo postal 2973, San Salvador, El Salvador.

ARGUETA ANTILLÓN, José Luis; Salvadorean university administrator; b. 16 July 1932, El Salvador; s. of Tomás Antillón and Andrea Argueta; m. María Luz Márquez 1969; four s. two d.; ed Univs. of El Salvador and Chile; Prof., Univ. of El Salvador 1964–67, Sec. Faculty of Econ. Sciences 1967–69, Prof. Faculty of Investigative Econs 1974–78, Asst Dir to the Dir 1973–74, Dir 1985–86, Asst to Acting Rector 1979–80, Rector 1986–; Prof. and Researcher, Cen. American Univ. 1980–85; Dr. hc (Univ. of Simón Bolívar, Colombia); Economist of the Year 1985. *Publications include:* Manual de Contabilidad Nacional 1967, La Economía Salvadoreana—Algunos Elementos de Análisis 1984, La Reedición de Reforma Universitaria de Córdoba—Una Necesidad Histórica 1989. *Leisure interest:* sport. *Address:* Universidad de El Salvador, Apdo 1703, San Salvador; Calle del Marmara no 18-A, Col Sardinas de Guadalupe, San Salvador, Ap. Post. 3210, El Salvador. *Telephone:* 25-9427. *Fax:* 25-9427.

ARGUS, (Don) Donald Robert, AO; Australian banker and business executive; b. 1 Aug. 1938, Bundaberg; s. of Dudley Francis Argus and Evelyn Argus; m. Patricia Anne Argus 1961; three d.; ed Royal Melbourne Inst. of Tech., Harvard Univ.; Chief Man. Corp. Lending, Nat. Australia Bank Ltd 1983, then Gen. Man. Credit Bureau, then Gen. Man. Group Strategic Devt, then Exec. Dir and COO, Man. Dir, CEO 1990–99; Chair. Australian Bankers' Asscn 1992–94; Dir Broken Hill Pty Co. Ltd (BHP Ltd 2000–01, BHP Billton Ltd 2001–) 1999–, Chair. 2000–; Chair. Brambles Industries Ltd 1999–; Dir Southcorp Ltd 1999–, Australian Foundation Investment Co. Ltd 1999–. *Leisure interests:* hockey, golf, reading. *Address:* Broken Hill Pty Ltd, 48th Floor, BHP Tower, 600 Bourke Street, Melbourne, Victoria 3000, Australia (Office).

ARGYRIS, John, CBE, DScEng, FREng, FRS, FAAS, FRAeS; British professor of aeronautical structures; b. 19 Aug. 1916, Volos, Greece; s. of Nicolas Argyris and Lucie Argyris (née Caratheodory); m. Inga-Lisa Johansson 1953; one s.; ed Technical Univs in Athens, Munich and Zürich; research, J. Gollnow u. Sohn, Stettin; Research and Tech. Officer, Royal Aeronautical Soc. 1943–49; Sr Lecturer, Dept of Aeronautics, Imperial Coll. London 1949, Reader in Theory of Aeronautical Structures 1950, Prof. 1955–75; Visiting Prof. 1975–78, now Prof. Emer.; Dir Inst. for Statics and Dynamics, Stuttgart 1959–84, Inst. of Computer Applications, Stuttgart 1984–; Prin. Ed. Journal of Computer Methods in Applied Mechanics and Eng 1972–; Hon. Prof., Northwestern Polytech. Univ., Xian, China, Tech. Univ. of Beijing, Qinghua Univ.; Fellow AIAA; Life mem. ASME; Foreign Assoc. US Nat. Acad. of Eng; Hon. Life mem. New York Acad. of Sciences; Hon. FCGI; Hon. FRAeS; 16 hon. degrees; Silver Medal, Royal Aeronautical Soc. (RAeS) 1971, Von Kármán Medal, American Soc. of Civil Engineers (ASCE) 1975, Copernicus Medal, Polish Acad. of Sciences 1979, Timoshenko Medal, ASME 1981, I. B. Lasko-witz Award with Gold Medal in Aerospace Eng, New York Acad. of Sciences 1982, Royal Medal, Royal Soc. 1985, Daedalus Gold Medal, Sir George Cayley Inst. 1988; Grosses Bundesverdienstkreuz (Fed. Germany) 1985, mit Stern 1990, Grand Cross of the Saviour (Greece) 1996, Golden Cross of the Order of Phoenix (Greece), Gold Medal of Volos 1996, Prince Philip Gold Medal of Royal Acad. of Eng 1997 and numerous other honours and awards. *Pub-lications:* Handbook of Aeronautics (Vol. I) 1952, Energy Theorems and Structural Analysis 1960, Modern Fuselage Analysis and the Elastic Aircraft 1963, Recent Advances in Matrix Methods of Structural Analysis 1964, Introduction into the Finite Element Method (Vols I–III) 1986–88, Dynamics of Structures 1991, An Overview of Aerolasticity 1992, The Dynamics of Chaos 1994; more than 545 articles in professional journals etc. *Leisure interests:* archaeology, nature, music, literature. *Address:* Institute of Com-puter Applications, 27 Pfaffenwaldring, 70569 Stuttgart, Germany; c/o Department of Aeronautics, Imperial College, Prince Consort Road, London, SW7, England. *Telephone:* (711) 6853594. *Fax:* (711) 6853669.

ARIARAJAH, Wesley, ThM, M.PHIL., PhD; Sri Lankan ecclesiastic; b. 2 Dec. 1941, Jaffna; s. of Ponniah David Seevaratnam and Grace Annalukshmi (née Sinnapu); m. Christine Shyamala Chinniah 1974; three d.; ed Madras Christian Coll., United Theological Coll., Bangalore, Princeton (NY) Semi-nary, Univ. of London; ordained in Methodist Church; Minister Methodist Church of Sri Lanka, Jaffna 1966–68; Lecturer Theological Coll. Lanka, Pilimatalawa 1969–71; Chair. North and East Dist, Methodist Church, Jaffna 1974–81; staff WCC programme on Dialogue with People of Living Faiths, Geneva 1981–83, Dir 1983–93, Deputy Sec.-Gen. WCC 1993–97; Prof. of Ecumenical Theology, Drew Univ., NJ; delivered Sixth Lambeth Interfaith Lecture 1987. *Publications:* Dialogue 1980, The Bible and People of Other Faiths 1986, Hindus and Christians: A Century of Protestant Ecumenical Thought, Did I Betray the Gospel?: The Letters of Paul and the Place of Women 1996, Not Without My Neighbour: Issues in Interfaith Dialogue 1998; contrib. articles to specialist journals. *Leisure interest:* reading. *Address:* Seminary Hall, School of Theology, Drew University, Madison, NJ 07940 (Office); 34B Loantaka Way, Madison, NJ 07940, USA (Home). *Telephone:* (973) 408-3979 (Office); (973) 360-9296 (Home). *Fax:* (973) 408-3808 (Office). *E-mail:* wariaraj@drew.edu (Office); ariarajah@hotmail.com (Home).

ARIAS, Inocencio F.; Spanish civil servant and diplomatist; b. 20 April 1940; m.; three c.; joined diplomatic service 1967; Dir of Diplomatic Informa-tion Office, Ministry of Foreign Affairs 1980–82, 1985–88, 1996–97; Under-Sec. Ministry of Foreign Affairs 1988–91; State Sec. for Int. Co-operation for Iberoamerican Affairs 1991–93; Gen. Dir Real Madrid 1993–95; Perm. Rep. to UN 1998–; fmr. Prof. of Int. Relations, Univ. Complutense, Univ. Carlos III, Madrid. *Publications:* numerous papers and contribs. *Address:* Permanent Mission of Spain to the United Nations, 823 United Nations Plaza, 9th Floor, New York, NY 10017, U.S.A. (Office). *Telephone:* (212) 661-1050 (Office). *Fax:* (212) 949-7247 (Office). *E-mail:* spain@un.int (Office). *Website:* www.spainun .org (Office).

ARIAS-SALGADO Y MONTALVO, Fernando; Spanish diplomatist; b. 3 May 1938, Valladolid; s. of Gabriel Arias-Salgado y Cubas and Maria Montalvo; m. María Isabel Garrigues López-Chicheri 1969; one s. one d.; ed Univ. of Madrid, Coll. of Lawyers, Madrid; entered Diplomatic School 1963; Sec. Perm. Del. of Spain to UN 1966–68; Adviser, UN Security Council 1968–69; Asst Dir-Gen. Promotion of Research, Ministry of Educ. and Science 1971, Asst Dir-Gen. of Int. Co-operation, Ministry of Educ. and Science 1972; Legal Adviser, Legal Dept (Int. Affairs), Ministry of Foreign Affairs 1973–75, Dir 1983–85; Counsellor, Spanish Del. to Int. Court of Justice 1975; Tech. Sec.-Gen. Ministry of Foreign Affairs 1976; Dir-Gen. Radiotelevisión Espa-ñola 1977–81; Amb. to UK 1981–83, to Tunisia 1993–96, to Morocco 2001–; Consul-Gen. for Spain, Zürich 1985–90; Perm. Rep. to Int. Orgs. in Vienna 1990–93. *Address:* 3 rue Madnine, B.P. 1354, 10000 Rabat, Morocco. *Tele-phone:* (3) 7707600. *Fax:* (3) 7707387. *E-mail:* infembsp@mtds.com.

ARIAS SÁNCHEZ, Oscar, PhD; Costa Rican politician and academic; b. 13 Sept. 1940; s. of Juan Rafael Arias Trejos and Líllyan Sánchez Cortes; m. Margarita Penón; one s. one d.; m.; ed Univ. of Costa Rica, Univ. of Essex, UK; Prof. School of Political Sciences Univ. of Costa Rica 1969–72; Financial Adviser to Pres. of Repub. 1970–72; Minister of Nat. Planning and Econs Policy 1972–77; Int. Sec. Liberación Nacional Party 1975, Gen. Sec. 1979–83, 1983; Congressman in Legis. Ass. 1978–82; Pres. of Costa Rica 1986–90; f. Arias Foundation for Peace and Human Progress 1988; mem. Bd Cen. Bank 1972–77, Vice-Pres. 1970–72; ad hoc Comm. mem. Heredia's Nat. Univ. 1972–75; mem. Bd Tech. Inst. 1974–77; mem. Rector's Nat. Council 1974–77; mem. Bd Int. Univ. Exchange Fund, Geneva 1976; mem. North–South Roundtable 1977; has participated in numerous int. meetings and socialist conventions; instrumental in formulating the Cen. American Peace Agree-ment 1986–87; Dr. hc (Oviedo) 1988; Nobel Peace Prize 1987; Martin Luther King Award 1987, Príncipe de Asturias Award 1988, shared Philadelphia Liberty Medal 1991. *Publications:* Pressure Groups in Costa Rica 1970 (Essay's Nat. Award 1971), Who Governs in Costa Rica? 1976, Latin American Democracy, Independence and Society 1977, Roads for Costa Rica's Develop-ment 1977, New Ways for Costa Rican Development 1980 and many articles in newspapers and in nat. and foreign magazines. *Address:* Arias Foundation for Peace and Human Progress, Apdo 8-6410-1000, San José, Costa Rica. *Telephone:* 255-2955. *Fax:* 255-2244.

ARIBAUD, Jean Roch; French diplomatist and civil servant; b. 30 Nov. 1943, Carcassonne (Aude); s. of Jean-Baptiste Aribaud and Suzanne Boyer; m. Claire Thépot 1970; three s.; ed Balwyn High School, Australia, Lycée Condorcet, Faculté des lettres, Paris, Ecole nat. d'admin.; Dir Office of Prefect, Eure-et-Loir 1971–74; Deputy Prefect Briançon 1974–77; Chef de Cabinet Sec. of State for Youth and Sport 1977, then Tech. Adviser to Sec. of State for Overseas Depts. and Territories 1978–80; Deputy Dir Social and Cultural Affairs, Sec. of State for Overseas Depts. and Territories 1980–85; Asst Dir, Local Communities Dept, Ministry of Interior 1985–89; Prefect Lozère 1989–92, Yonne 1992–93, seconded Prefect and adviser on interior affairs, Principality of Monaco 1993–97, Prefect Seine-Saint-Denis 2001–; High Commr in French Polynesia 1997–2001; Médaille d'or Jeunesse et des Sports, Chevalier Légion d'honneur, Officier Ordre Nat. du Mérite, Chevalier des Palmes académiques, Officier du Mérite agricole, Commdr. du Mérite Ordre Souverain de Malte, Officier Ordre de Saint-Charles (Monaco). *Leisure interest:* running. *Address:* c/o Ministry of the Interior, Internal Security and Local Freedoms, Place Beauvau, 75008 Paris, France.

ARIDJIS, Homero; Mexican author, poet and diplomatist; b. 1940, Con-tepec, Michoacán; m. Betty Ferber; lecturer in Mexican literature at univs in

USA; Cultural Attaché, Embassy in Netherlands 1972, later Amb. to Switzerland and the Netherlands; Man. Cultural Inst., Michoacán, organized first int. poetry festival; f. Review Correspondencias; Chief Ed. Dialogos; Visiting Prof. Univ. of Indiana and New York Univ.; Poet-in-Residence Columbia Univ. Translation Center, New York; co-f. Grupo de los Cien 1985 (100 internationally renowned artists and intellectuals active in environmental affairs); currently Pres. PEN Int.; Guggenheim Fellow 1966–67, 1979–80. *Publications include:* (trans. into English) Blue Spaces (poetry) 1974, Exaltation of Light 1981, Persephone 1986; Obra poética 1960–86 (collected poetry) 1987, ¿En quién piensas cuando haces el amor? 1996; several novels. *Address:* International PEN, 9–10 Charterhouse Buildings, Goswell Road, London, EC1M 7AT, England (Office). *Telephone:* (20) 7253-3226 (Office). *Fax:* (20) 7253-5711 (Office). *E-mail:* intpen@gn.apc.org; intpen@dircon.co.uk (Office). *Website:* www.oneworld.org (Office).

ARIDOR, Yoram, BA, M.JUR.; Israeli politician and lawyer; b. 24 Oct. 1933, Tel Aviv; m.; three c.; ed Hebrew Univ. of Jerusalem; mem. Knesset 1969–88, Chair. Cttee for Interior and Environmental Affairs 1975–77, Chair. Sub-Cttee for Constitutional Law 1975–77, mem. Cttee for Legislation and Justice 1969–81, Deputy Minister in Prime Minister's office 1977–81; Minister of Finance 1981–83, also of Communications Jan.–July 1981; Chair. Herut (Freedom) Movt in Histradrut (Gen. Fed. of Labour) 1972–77, mem. Cen. Cttee Herut Movt 1961–90, Chair. Secr. 1979–87; Amb. to UN 1990–92; fmr Gov. IMF. *Address:* 38 Haoranim Street, Ramat-Efal, Israel (Home).

ARIE, Thomas Harry David, CBE, BM, MA, DPM, FRCP, FRCPsych, FFPHM; British psychiatrist; b. 9 Aug. 1933, Prague, Czechoslovakia; s. of late Dr. O. M. Arie and H. Arie; m. Eleanor Aitken 1963; one s. two d.; ed Balliol Coll., Oxford; Sr Lecturer in Social Medicine, London Hosp. Medical Coll. 1962–74; Consultant Psychiatrist for Old People, Goodmayes Hosp. 1969–77; Foundation Prof. and Head, Dept of Health Care of the Elderly, Nottingham Univ. 1977–95, Prof. Emer. 1995–; Visiting Prof. NZ Geriatrics Soc. 1980, Univ. of the Negev 1988, Univ. of Calif., LA 1991, Keele Univ. 1997; Consultant Psychiatrist to the Nottingham Hosps. 1977–95; Vice-Pres. Royal Coll. of Psychiatrists 1984–86, Chair. Specialist Section on Old Age 1981–86; Sec., Geriatric Psychiatry Section, World Psychiatric Assen 1983–89, Chair. 1989–93; mem. Standing Medical Advisory Cttee for the Nat. Health Service 1980–84, Cttee on the Review of Medicines 1981–91, Registrar Gen.'s Medical Advisory Cttee 1990–94; Gov. Centre for Policy on Ageing 1992–98; Council mem., Vice-Chair. Royal Surgical Aid Soc. (AgeCare); Hon. Fellow Royal Coll. of Psychiatrists 2001; Dhole-Eddlestone Memorial Prize, British Geriatrics Soc. 1996; Int. Psychogeriatric Assen Award 1999. *Publications:* Ed. Health Care of the Elderly 1981, Recent Advances in Psychogeriatrics (Vol. 1) 1985, (Vol. 2) 1992; papers on the care of the aged, old age psychiatry, epidemiology and educ. *Address:* Cromwell House, West Church Street, Kenninghall, Norfolk, NR16 2EN, England. *Telephone:* (1953) 887375. *Fax:* (1953) 887375.

ARIGONI, Duilio, DrScTech; Swiss professor of organic chemistry; b. 6 Dec. 1928, Lugano; s. of Bernardino Arigoni and Emma Arigoni (née Bernasconi); m. Carla Diener 1958 (died 1998); two s. one d.; ed Swiss Fed. Inst. of Tech. (ETH), Zürich; Lecturer in Organic Chem., ETH Zürich 1961–62, Assoc. Prof. 1962–67, Full Prof. 1967–96; mem. Swiss Nat. Foundation for Scientific Research 1967–71, Bd of Govs, Weizmann Inst. of Science, Rehovot, Israel 1979–, Bd of Trustees, Sandoz Ltd 1984–96, Novartis Ltd 1996–99; mem. Deutsche Akad. der Naturforscher Leopoldina, Accademia Nazionale delle Scienze, Rome; Foreign mem. Royal Soc., London; Hon. FRSC; Foreign Assoc. Nat. Acad. of Sciences, Washington; Dr hc (Université de Paris-Sud) 1982; Davy Medal, Royal Soc. London 1983, R. A. Welch Award, Welch Foundation, USA 1985, Arthur C. Cope Award, American Chemical Soc. 1986, Wolf Prize, Israel 1989, Marcel Benoist Prize, Switzerland 1992 and other prizes and awards. *Publications:* over 180 publs in scientific journals. *Leisure interest:* music, especially Bach, Mozart. *Address:* Laboratorium für org. Chemie, ETH Hönggerberg, HCI H307, 8093 Zürich (Office); Im Glockenacker 42, 8053 Zürich, Switzerland (Home). *Telephone:* (1) 6322891 (Office); (1) 3811383 (Home). *Fax:* (1) 6321154 (Office). *E-mail:* arigoni@org.chem.ethz.ch (Office).

ARIKHA, Avigdor; French/Israeli painter and author; b. 28 April 1929, Bukovina; s. of Karl Haim and Pepi (née Korn) Dlugacz; m. Anne Atik 1961; two d.; ed Fine-Art, Bezalel, Jerusalem, Ecole des Beaux Arts, Paris and Sorbonne, Paris; after a short period of abstraction, has painted exclusively from life; painted portrait of HM Queen Elizabeth, The Queen Mother for Scottish Nat. Portrait Gallery 1983, Lord Home 1988; curator Poussin Exhbn, Louvre, Paris 1979, Ingres Exhbn, Frick Collection, New York 1986, Israel Museum, Jerusalem, Musée des Beaux-Arts, Dijon, Museum of Fine Arts, Houston, USA; fmr lecturer at univs in USA and UK; has made several films for TV; Hon. Prof. Nat. Acad. of Fine Arts, China; Hon. DPhil (Hebrew Univ., Jerusalem) 1997; Grand Prix des Arts (City of Paris) 1987, Prix des Arts, des Lettres et des Sciences, Fondation du Judaïsme Français; Gold Medal, Tenth Triennial (Milan, Italy) 1954, Chevalier, Ordre des Arts et des Lettres. *Art exhibitions:* 31 one-man public exhbns and 43 pvt. gallery exhbns 1952–2002; retrospective exhbns Israel Museum, Jerusalem and Tel Aviv Museum of Art 1998, Scottish Nat. Gallery of Modern Art, Edin. 1999, Palais des Beaux-Arts, Lille, France 1999; works in public collections including Musée du Louvre, Centre Pompidou, Paris, Tate Gallery, London, Hirshhorn Museum, Washington, DC, Uffizi Gallery, Florence, Israel Museum, Jerusalem, Los Angeles County Museum of Art, Musée des Beaux-Arts, Dijon, Metropolitan Museum of Art, New York. *Radio:* various programmes for Radio France Culture. *Television:* Avigdor Arikha on Diego Velaquez, BBC 1992, Avigdor Arikha, BBC Omnibus 1992. *Publications:* Ingres: Fifty Life Drawings 1986, Peinture et Regard 1991, On Depiction—Writings on Art 1995; scholarly catalogues for exhbns. etc.; numerous essays and articles. *Address:* c/o Marlborough Fine Art, 6 Albemarle Street, London W1X 4BY, England.

ARIMA, Akito, DSc; Japanese university professor; b. 13 Sept. 1930; s. of Johji Arima and Kazuko Arima; m. Hiroko Aota 1957; one s. one d.; ed Musashi Koto Gakko Coll., Univ. of Tokyo; Visiting Prof. Rutgers and Princeton Univs 1967–68, State Univ. of New York, Stony Brook 1968, 1971–73; Prof. of Physics, Faculty of Science, Univ. of Tokyo 1975, Dir Computer Centre 1981–87, Dean of the Faculty of Science 1985–87, Vice-Pres. Univ. of Tokyo 1987–89, Pres. 1989–93; Pres. Inst. of Physical and Chemical Research (RIKEN) 1993–98; Minister of Educ. and Dir.-Gen. of Science and Tech. Agency 1998–99; currently mem. House of Councillors; mem. Science Council of Japan 1985–94; Hon. DSc (Univ. of Glasgow); Nishina Memorial Prize 1978, Humboldt Prize 1987, John Price Wetherill Medal 1990, Bonner Prize 1993, Japan Acad. Prize 1993; Das Grosse Verdienstkreuz (Germany) 1990, Order of Orange Nassau (Netherlands) 1991. *Publication:* Interacting Boson Model 1987. *Leisure interests:* Haiku, calligraphy, reading. *Address:* RM223, Sangiin-Kaikan 2-1-1, Nagata-cho, Chiyoda-ku, Tokyo 100-8962, Japan. *Telephone:* (3) 3508-8223. *Fax:* (3) 5512-2223. *E-mail:* akito_arima@sangiin.go.jp.

ARINZE, HE Cardinal Francis A., DD, STL; Nigerian ecclesiastic; b. 1 Nov. 1932, Eziowelle, Onitsha; s. of Joseph Arinze Nwankwu and Bernadette M. Arinze; ed Bigard Memorial Seminary, Nigeria, Urban Univ., Rome and Univ. of London; ordained 1958; consecrated Bishop (Titular Church of Fissiana) 1965; Archbishop of Onitsha 1967; cr. Cardinal 1985; Pres. Pontifical Council for Inter-Religious Dialogue 1984–2002; Prefect of Divine Worship and the Discipline of the Sacraments 2002–; Hon. PhD (Univ. of Nigeria) 1986; Hon. LLD (Catholic Univ. of America) 1998; Hon. DD (Wake Foret Univ., USA) 1999; Hon. DH (Univ. of Santo Tomas, Philippines) 2001. *Publications:* Partnership in Education 1965, Sacrifice in Ibo Religion 1970, Answering God's Call 1983, Alone With God 1986, Church in Dialogue 1990, Meeting Other Believers 1997, Brücken Bauen 2000, The Holy Eucharist 2001, Religions for Peace 2002. *Leisure interests:* tennis, reading. *Address:* Congregation for Divine Worship and the Discipline of the Sacraments, Palazzo delle Congregazioni, Piazza Pio XII 10, , 00193 Rome, Italy. *Telephone:* (06) 69884316. *Fax:* (06) 69883499. *E-mail:* cultdiv@ccdds.va. *Website:* www.vatican.va/roman_curia/congregations/ccdds.

ARISMUNANDAR, Wiranto, MSc; Indonesian professor of mechanical engineering and politician; b. 19 Nov. 1933, Semarang; ed Univ. of Indonesia, Purdue and Stanford Univs; Research Assoc., Dept of Mechanical Eng, Stanford Univ. 1961–62; training in rocket propulsion, Japan 1965; Vice-Chair. Indonesian Nat. Inst. of Aeronautics and Space 1978–89; Prof. of Mechanical Eng Inst. of Tech., Bandung 1973–, Pres. 1988–97; Minister of Educ. and Culture 1998; Sr Scientist Indonesian Agency for the Assessment and Application of Tech., Technological Adviser Indonesian Aircraft Industry 1979–; Consultant Indonesian Nat. Atomic Energy Agency; mem. People's Consultative Council 1992–97, Consultative Bd Indonesian Islamic Council; mem. Nat. Energy Cttee, World Energy Conf., Nat. Telecommunication Council, Indonesian Nat. Cttee; mem. Indonesian Nat. Research Council, AIAA, Indonesian Aeronautics and Astronautics Inst., Soc. of Automotive Engineers of Indonesia (founding mem.) and many other nat. and int. eng bodies; Chief Ed. Teknology magazine; Fellow Islamic Acad. of Sciences; Satyalancana Dwidya Sistha Medal of Merit 1968, 1983, 1989, 1992, Satyalancana Karya Satya (First Class) 1990, Satyalancana Karya Satya for 30 years' service, Bindang Jasa Utama 1998. *Publications:* 13 books and over 100 papers. *Leisure interests:* sport, photography. *Address:* Institut Teknologi Bandung, Department of Mechanical Engineering, Ganesa 10, Bandung 40132 (Office); Bukit Dago Utara I/6, Bandung 40135, Indonesia (Home). *Telephone:* (22) 2504243 (Office); (22) 2503558 (Home). *Fax:* (22) 2534118 (Office); (22) 2503558 (Home).

ARISMUNANDAR, Lt-Gen. Wismoyo; Indonesian army officer; brother-in-law of fmr Pres. Suharto; fmrly special forces Commdr; fmr Army Deputy Chief, Army Chief 1993–. *Address:* c/o Ministry of Defence and Security, Jalan Merdeka Barat 13, Jakarta 10110, Indonesia.

ARISTIDE, Jean Bertrand; Haitian politician and fmr ecclesiastic; b. Salut; m. Mildred Trouillot 1996; one d.; Roman Catholic priest; expelled from Salesian Order 1988; resgnd from priesthood Nov. 1994; Pres. of Haiti Feb.–Oct. 1991, 1993–96, Feb. 2001–; in exile in Caracas, Venezuela Oct. 1991; returned Oct. 1993 after resignation of junta. *Publications:* Haiti and the New World Order 1995, Dignity 1996, Eyes of the Heart 2000. *Address:* c/o Office of the President, Palais National, Champ de Mars, Port-au-Prince, Haiti. *Telephone:* 222-3024 (Office).

ARJONA PÉREZ, Marta María; Cuban ceramic artist and sculptor; b. 3 May 1923, Havana; d. of Ernesto and Norak Arjona Pérez; ed San Alejandro Nat. School of Beaux Arts and Paris; various exhbns. in Cuba and overseas 1945–52; Dir Nuestro Tiempo Soc. Gallery 1953–59; Nat. Dir of Plastic Arts, then Museums and Monuments 1959–77, Dir of Cultural Heritage 1977–; Pres. Cuban Cttee, Int. Council of Museums; Medal, then Order of Raúl Gómez García 1975, 1982. *Works on view include:* ceramic murals at the Palacio de la Revolución (with René Portocarrero) and Escuela V. I. Lenin (with Mariano Rodríguez). *Publications:* various articles in specialist periodicals. *Address:* Quinta B, no. 8605 entre 86 y 88, Miramar, Playa, Cuba (Home); Calle A, no. 608 entre 25 y 27, Vedado, Havana (Office). *Telephone:* (7) 2-8155 (Home).

ARKHIPOVA, Irina Konstantinovna; Russian mezzo-soprano; b. 2 Jan. 1925, Moscow; d. of Vetoschkin Konstantin and Galda Evdokija; m. Piavkò Vladislav; one s.; attended vocal classes with Nadezda Malysheva at Inst. of Architecture, Moscow, from which graduated, 1948; entered Moscow Conservatoire 1959 (pupil of L. Savransky); stage début as soloist (Lubasha) of Tsar's Bride with Sverdlovsk Opera and Carmen with Bolshoi Theatre, 1956, leading soloist –1958; mem. CPSU 1963–91; mem. USSR Supreme Soviet 1962–66; People's Deputy 1989–91; Prof. at Moscow Conservatoire 1982–; Pres. Int. Union of Musicians, Irina Arkhipova Foundation; opera performances and song recitals since 1956 at Milan, Vienna, Paris, London and in USA; performs Russian, French and Italian repertoire, roles include Carmen, Amneris in Aida, Hélène in War and Peace, Eboli in Don Carlos; mem. Acad. of Creative Endeavours 1991, Int. Acad. of Sciences 1994; People's Artist of USSR 1966; Lenin Prize 1978; Hero of Socialist Labour 1984, People's Artist of Kyrgyzstan 1993, State Prize 1997. *Publications:* My Muses 1992, Music of Life 1997. *Address:* Bryusov per. 2/14, Apt. 27, 103009 Moscow, Russia. *Telephone:* (095) 229-60-29 (Office); (095) 229-43-07 (Home).

ARKIN, Alan Wolf; American actor, director and author; b. 26 March 1934; s. of David Arkin and Beatrice Arkin; m. 2nd Barbara Dana; one s.; two s. from first marriage; ed Los Angeles City Coll., Los Angeles State Coll., Bennington Coll.; made professional theatre début with the Compass Players, St Louis 1959; later joined Second City group, Chicago 1960; made New York début at Royal, in revue From the Second City 1961; played David Kolvitz in Enter Laughing 1963–64 (Tony Award 1963), appeared in revue A View Under The Bridge, 1964, Harry Berline in Luv; Theatre World Award 1964 for Enter Laughing, New York Film Critics; Best Supporting Actor Award for Hearts of the West and for The Heart is a Lonely Hunter. *Films include:* The Russians Are Coming, The Russians Are Coming (Golden Globe Award) 1966, Women Times Seven 1967, Wait Until Dark 1967, Inspector Clouseau 1968, The Heart is a Lonely Hunter 1968, Popi 1969, Catch-22 1970, Little Murders (also Dir) 1971, Last of the Red Hot Lovers 1972, Freebie and the Bean 1974, Rafferty and the Gold Dust Twins 1975, Hearts of the West 1975, The In-Laws 1979, The Magician of Lublin 1979, Simon 1980, Chu Chu and the Philly Flash 1981, Improper Channels (Canadian Acad. Award) 1981, The Last Unicorn 1982, Joshua Then and Now (also Dir, Canadian Acad. Award) 1985, Coupe de Ville 1989, Havana 1990, Edward Scissorhands 1990, The Rocketeer 1990, Glengarry Glen Ross 1992, Indian Summer 1993, So I Married an Axe Murderer 1993, Steal Big, Steal Little 1995, Mother Night 1995, Grosse Point Blank 1997, Gattaca 1998, The Slums of Beverly Hills 1998, Jakob the Liar 1999, Arigo 2000, America's Sweethearts 2001, Thirteen Conversations About One Thing 2001, Counting Sheep 2002. *TV appearances include:* The Love Song of Barney Kempinski 1966, The Other Side of Hell 1978, The Defection of Simas Kudirka 1978, Captain Kangaroo, A Deadly Business 1986, Escape from Sobibor, Necessary Parties, Cooperstown, Taking the Heat, Doomsday Gun. *Theatre includes:* (Dir) Eh? at the Circle in the Square, 1966, Hail Scrawdyke 1966, Little Murders, 1969, White House Murder Case 1970, The Sunshine Boys, Eh? 1972, Molly 1973, Joan Lorraine 1974, Power Plays (also wrote and directed), Promenade Theatre 1998, The Sorrows of Stephen, Room Service. *Publications:* Tony's Hard Work Day, The Lemming Condition, Halfway Through the Door, The Clearing 1986, Some Fine Grampha 1995, One Present from Flekmans 1998, Cassie Loves Beethoven 1999. *Address:* c/o William Morris Agency, 151 El Camino Drive, Beverly Hills, CA 90212, USA.

ARLACCHI, Pino; Italian politician and international organization official; b. 21 Feb. 1951, Gioia Tauro, Reggio Calabria; m.; two c.; Assoc. Prof. of Applied Sociology Univ. of Calabria 1982–85, Univ. of Florence 1988–94; apptd. Prof. of Sociology Univ. of Sassari 1994; elected to Chamber of Deputies 1994–95, to Senate 1995–97; Vice-Pres. Parl. Comm. on the Mafia; UN Under-Sec.-Gen. and Dir-Gen. UN Vienna Office 1997–2002; Exec. Dir UN Office for Drug Control and Crime Prevention (ODCCP) 1997–2002; Pres. Int. Asscn for the Study of Organized Crime 1989–; Hon. Pres. Giovanni Falcone Foundation 1992–; Fellow, Ford Foundation. *Publications:* numerous publs on int. organized crime. *Address:* c/o Vienna International Centre, P.O. Box 500, 1400 Vienna, Austria (Office).

ARLMAN, Paul, MA; Netherlands international civil servant and banker; b. 11 July 1946, Bussum; s. of Evert Arlman and Corrie Jacobs; m. Kieke Wijs 1971; one s. one d.; ed Hilversum Grammar School, Rotterdam Econ. Univ., Peace Research Inst., Groningen and Nice European Inst., France; served in the Treasury, The Hague 1970–74, as Treasury Rep. to the Netherlands Embassy, Washington DC 1974–78; Div. Chief Treasury, The Hague 1978–81; Dir and Deputy Asst Sec. Int. Affairs 1981–86; Exec. Dir IBRD, IDA, IFC, MIGA 1986–90; mem. Bd of Dirs, EIB 1981–86, Chair. Bd Policy Cttee 1983–84; Sec.-Gen. Amsterdam Stock Exchange 1991–96; Dir Int. Affairs Amsterdam Exchanges 1997–98; Sec.-Gen. Fed. European Securities Exchanges 1998–; mem. Bd European Capital Market Inst.; mem. Peters Cttee on Corporate Governance; Scholarships from Royal Dutch Shell, Ministry of Educ. and European Comm. *Leisure interests:* literature, tennis, skiing, outdoor sports. *Address:* Federation European Securities Exchange, Rue du Lombard 41, 1000 Brussels, Belgium (Office); Jan van Nassaustraat 33, 2596 BM The Hague, Netherlands (Home). *Telephone:* (2) 551-01-80 (Office); (70) 3244938 (Home). *Fax:* (2) 512-49-05 (Office); (70) 3240458 (Home). *E-mail:* arlman@fese.be (Office); paul@arlman.com (Home). *Website:* www.fese.org (Office).

ARMACOST, Michael Hayden, MA, PhD; American government official, politician and administrator; b. 15 April 1937, Cleveland, Ohio; s. of George H. and Verda Gay Armacost (née Hayden); brother of Samuel Henry Armacost (q.v.); m. Roberta June Bray 1959; three s.; ed Carleton Coll., Friedrich Wilhelms Univ., Columbia Univ.; Assoc. Prof. Govt, Pomona Coll., Claremont, Calif. 1962–70; Wig Distinguished Prof. 1966; Special Asst to Amb., American Embassy, Tokyo 1972–74; Amb. to Philippines 1982–84, to Japan 1989–93; mem. Policy Planning, Staff Dept, Washington, DC 1974–77; Sr Staff mem., Nat. Security Council, Washington, DC 1977–78; Dep. Asst Sec. Defence, Int. Security Affairs Defence Dept, Washington, DC 1978–79; Principal Deputy Asst Sec. E Asian and Pacific Affairs 1980–81; Undersec. Political Affairs 1984–89; Amb. to Japan 1989; mem. Council on Foreign Relations; Visiting Prof. Int. Relations, Int. Christian Univ., Tokyo 1968–69; Pres. Brookings Inst., Washington, DC 1995–2002, Trustee 2002–; White House Fellow 1969–70; Superior Honour Award, State Dept 1976; Distinguished Civilian Service Award, Defence Dept 1980; Presidential Distinguished Service Award; Sec. of State Distinguished Service Award. *Publications:* The Politics of Weapons Innovation 1969, The Foreign Relations of United States 1969, Friends or Rivals 1996. *Leisure interests:* reading, music, golf. *Address:* 9425 Tarnberry Drive, Potomac, MD 20854 (Home); c/o Brookings Institution, 1775 Massachusetts Ave., NW, Washington, DC 20036, USA.

ARMACOST, Samuel Henry; American banker; b. 1939, Newport News, Va; brother of Michael Hayden Armacost (q.v.); m. Mary Jane Armacost 1962; two d.; ed Denison Univ., Granville, Ohio, Stanford Univ.; joined Bank of America as credit trainee 1961; London branch 1969–71; State Dept Office of Monetary Affairs (executive exchange programme) 1971–72; Head Europe, Middle East and Africa Div., London 1977–79; Cashier Bank of America and Treasurer of its Holding Co. Bank-America Corpn 1979–80; Pres. and CEO Bank of America and Bank-America Corpn 1981–86, Chair. and CEO 1986 (resgnd); Investment Banker Merrill Lynch and Co. 1987; Man. Dir Merrill Lynch Capital Markets 1988–. *Address:* c/o Merrill Lynch and Co. Inc., 100 Church Street, 12th Floor, New York, NY 10080, USA.

ARMANI, Giorgio; Italian fashion designer; b. 11 July 1934, Piacenza; s. of late Ugo Armani and of Maria Raimondi; ed Univ. of Milan; window dresser, then Asst Buyer La Rinascente, Milan 1957–64; Designer and Product Developer Hitman (menswear co. of Cerruti group) 1964–70; freelance designer for several firms 1970; founded Giorgio Armani SpA with Sergio Galeotti 1975, achieved particular success with unconstructed jackets of mannish cut for women, trademarks also in babywear, underwear, accessories, perfume; appeared on cover of Time 1982; Dr. hc (Royal Coll. of Art, London) 1991; numerous awards including Cutty Sark 1980, 1981, 1984, 1986, 1987, (First Designer Laureate 1985), Ambrogino d'Oro, Milan 1982, Int. Designer Award, Council of Fashion Designers of America 1983, L'Occhio d'Oro 1984, 1986, 1987, 1988, L'Occhiolino d'Oro 1984, 1986, 1987, 1988, Time-Life Achievement Award 1987, Cristobal Balenciaga Award 1988, Woolmark Award, New York 1989, 1992, Senken Award, Japan 1989, Award from People for the Ethical Treatment of Animals, USA 1990, Fiorino d'Oro, Florence, for promoting Made in Italy image 1992, Hon. Nomination from Brera Acad., Milan 1993, Aguja de Oro Award, Spain, for Best Int. Designer 1993, Telva Triunfador Award, Madrid, for Best Designer of the Year 1993; Grand'Ufficiale dell'ordine al merito 1986, Gran Cavaliere 1987. *Leisure interests:* cinema, music, books. *Address:* Georgio Armani Corporation, 650 Fifth Avenue, New York, NY 10019 (Office); Via Borgonuovo 21, 20121 Milan, Italy; Giorgio Armani Corpn, 114 Fifth Avenue, New York, NY 10011, USA. *Telephone:* (02) 801481 (Milan). *Fax:* (02) 86461914 (Milan).

ARMATRADING, Joan; British singer and songwriter; b. 9 Dec. 1950, St Kitts, West Indies; d. of Amos Ezekiel Armatrading and Beryl Madge Benjamin; moved to Birmingham, UK 1958; began professional career in collaboration with lyric-writer Pam Nestor 1972; world tour 1995–96; Hon. Fellow John Moores Univ., Liverpool; Discs: 3 Silver, 28 Gold, 6 Platinum. *Recordings include:* Whatever's For Us 1973, Back To The Night 1975, Joan Armatrading 1976, Show Some Emotion 1977, Me Myself I 1980, Walk Under Ladders 1981, The Key 1983, Secret Secrets 1985, The Shouting Stage 1988, Hearts and Flowers 1990, The Very Best of 1991, Square the Circle 1992, What's Inside 1995, Lovers Speak 2003. *Leisure interests:* British comics, vintage cars. *Address:* c/o F. Winter & Co., Ramilies House, 2 Ramilies Street, London, W1V 1DF, England.

ARMEY, Richard Keith, PhD; American politician and economist; b. 7 July 1940, Cando, ND; s. of Glen Armey and Marion Gutschlog; m. Susan Byrd; four s. one d.; ed Jamestown Coll., ND and Univs. of N Dakota and Okla; mem. Faculty of Econs Univ. of Mon. 1964–65; Asst Prof. West Tex. State Univ. 1967–68, Austin Coll. 1968–72; Assoc. Prof. North Tex. State Univ. 1972–77, Chair. Dept of Econs 1977–83; mem. US House of Reps from 26th Tex. Dist 1985–2002; Majority Leader, House of Reps. 1995–2002; retd from Congress 2002; mem. Republican Party. *Publications:* Price Theory 1977, The Freedom Revolution 1995, The Flat Tax 1996. *Address:* Suite 3050, 9901 Valley Ranch Parkway East, Irving, TX 75063-6707, USA (Office).

ARMFIELD, Diana Maxwell, RA, RCA, RWS; British painter; b. 11 June 1920, Ringwood, Hants.; d. of Joseph Harold Armfield and Gertrude Mary Uttley; m. Bernard Dunstan 1949; three s.; ed Bedales School, Bournemouth

Art School, Slade School of Art, Cen. School of Arts & Crafts, London; teacher, Byam Shaw School of Art 1959–80; Artist in Residence, Perth, Australia 1985, Jackson, Wyoming, USA 1989; Assoc. Royal Acad. 1989–; Hon. mem. New English Art Club, Royal W of England Acad.; Hon. retd mem. Royal Cambrian Acad.; Hon. mem. Pastel Soc.; Hunting Finalist Prize 1980, 1981. *Art exhibitions:* numerous exhbns UK including Browse & Darby, London 1979–2003, Royal Cambrian Acad. 2001, also USA, Australia and Netherlands; works included in public collections: Victoria and Albert Museum (Textiles), R.W.A. Talbot Collection, Faringdon Collection, Yale Centre for British Art, Govt Picture Collection, Mercury Asset Management Collection, Royal Acad. Diploma Collection, HRH Prince of Wales Collection, Contemporary Art Soc. for Wales, R.W.S. Diploma Collection. *Publications:* Painting in Oils, Drawing. *Leisure interests:* music, gardening. *Address:* 10 High Park Road, Kew, Richmond, Surrey, TW9 4BH, England; Llwynhir, Parc, Bala, Gwynedd, LL23 7YU, Wales. *Telephone:* (20) 8876-6633. *Fax:* (20) 8876-6633.

ARMIJOS, Ana Lucia; Ecuadorean economist; b. 13 Oct. 1949, Quito; ed Pontifical Catholic Univ. of Quito, Univ. of Illinois, Univ. of Mississippi; Coordinator of Faculty of Econ., Pontifical Catholic Univ. of Quito 1976–80; analyst, Dir of Financial Planning, Cen. Bank 1976–80, Dir of Monetary Policy 1980–82, Vice-Chair. Monetary Policy 1982–87, Dir of Tech. Div. 1987–88, Dir 1992–93; Macroeconomist on West African team, World Bank 1990–92; econ. advisor to Govt of Sixto Durán Ballén; Pres. of Monetary Comm. 1993–96; Exec. Pres. of Asscn of Pvt. Banks of Ecuador 1996–97; imprisoned 1997–98; Govt Minister 1998–99, of Finance 1999; arrested in Bogotá 1999; faced five charges 1999. *Publications:* The Theoretical Considerations of External Debt 1981, Interest Rate Policy in Ecuador, 1979–1980, 1993. *Address:* Junta Monetaria Nacional (National Monetary Board), Quito, Ecuador.

ARMITT, John, CBE; British transport executive, construction manager and engineer; civil engineer John Laing Construction Co., Jt Man. Dir 1963–93; Project Man. Channel Tunnel Rail Link 1992–97; CEO Union Railways 1993–97, selected route and oversaw parl. legislation for Channel Tunnel–London St Pancras Station Rail Link; CEO Costain (eng and construction group) 1997–2001, negotiated co-operation agreement with Skanska; CEO Railtrack PLC 2001–02, Network Rail 2002–; Dir Major Projects Asscn; fmr Chair. Anglo–French venture to build Second Severn Crossing. *Address:* Network Rail, Community Relations, Railtrack House, Euston Square, London, NW1 2EE, England (Office). *Website:* www .networkrail.com (Office).

ARMSTRONG, Anne Legendre, BA; American politician, company director and diplomatist; b. 27 Dec. 1927, New Orleans, La.; d. of Armant Legendre and Olive Legendre; m. Tobin Armstrong 1950; three s. two d.; ed Foxcroft School, Middleburg, Va and Vassar Coll.; Republican Nat. Cttee woman from Texas 1968–73; Republican Nat. Comm. Co-Chair. 1971–73; Counsellor to Pres. Nixon with cabinet rank 1973–74; Counsellor to Pres. Ford with cabinet rank 1974; resigned from Govt service 1974; Amb. to UK 1976–77; Dir Halliburton, Boise Cascade, American Express Co.; Chair. English-Speaking Union of US 1977–80, Pres.'s Foreign Intelligence Advisory Bd 1981–90, Bd of Trustees Center for Strategic and Int. Studies, Washington, DC 1987–99, Chair. Exec. Cttee 1999–; Co-Chair. Reagan–Bush Campaign 1980; Chair. Texas Women's Alliance 1985–89; mem. Visiting Cttee JFK School of Govt, Harvard Univ. 1978–82, Comm. on Integrated Long-Term Strategy 1987, Gen. Motors Corpn Advisory Council, US Comm. on Nat. Security 1999–2001; mem. Bd of Regents, Smithsonian Inst., 1978–94; Trustee American Assocs of RA, of Trust 1985–, Vice-Chair. 1996; Pres. Blair House Restoration Fund 1985–91, Nat. Thanksgiving Comm. 1986–94; Regent Texas A & M Univ. 1997–; Hon. LLD (Bristol, UK) 1976, (Washington and Lee) 1976, (Williams Coll., Mass.) 1977, (St Mary's) 1978, (Tulane) 1978; Republican Woman of the Year Award 1979, Texan of the Year Award 1981, Texas Women's Hall of Fame 1986, Presidential Medal of Freedom 1987, Golden Plate Award, American Acad. of Achievement 1989. *Address:* Armstrong Ranch, Armstrong, TX 78338, USA. *Telephone:* (361) 595-5551 (Office).

ARMSTRONG, C. Michael, BS; American business executive; b. 18 Oct. 1938, Detroit, Mich.; s. of Charles H. Armstrong and Zora Jean (née Brooks) Armstrong; m. Anne Gossett 1961; three d.; ed Miami Univ., Dartmouth Inst.; joined IBM Corpn 1961, Dir Systems Man. Marketing Div. 1975–76, Vice-Pres. Market Operations East 1976–78, Pres. Data Processing Div. 1978–80, Vice-Pres. Plans and Controls, Data Processing Product Group 1980–84, Asst Group Exec. 1980–83, Group Exec. 1983–92, Sr Vice-Pres. 1984–92, fmrly Pres. IBM Corpn Europe, Pres. and Dir Gen. World Trade (Europe, Middle East, Africa) 1987–89; Chair. World Trade Corpn 1989–92; Chair., CEO Hughes Aircraft Co. 1992–93, Hughes Electronics Corpn 1993–; Chair. Pres.'s Export Council 1994–; Chair., CEO AT&T 1997–; Chair. FCC Network Reliability and Inter-Operability Council 1999–; mem. Bd of Dirs. Citigroup, Nat. Cable TV Asscn; mem. Supervisory Bd Thyssen-Bornemisza Group, Council on Foreign Relations, Nat. Security Telecommunications Advisory Cttee, Defence Policy Advisory Cttee on Trade (DPACT), numerous univ. advisory bds; mem. Bd of Trustees of Carnegie Hall; Hon. LLD (Pepperdine Univ.) 1997, (Loyola Marymount Univ.) 1998. *Address:* AT&T, 295 North Maple Avenue, Basking Ridge, NJ 07920, USA.

ARMSTRONG, David John, BA; Australian journalist; b. 25 Nov. 1947, Sydney; s. of Allan E Armstrong and Mary P. Armstrong; m. Deborah Bailey 1980; two d.; ed Marist Brothers High School Parramatta, Univ. of NSW; Ed. The Bulletin 1985–86; Deputy Ed. The Daily Telegraph 1988–89; Ed. The Australian 1989–92, Ed.-in-Chief 1996–; Ed. The Canberra Times 1992–93; Ed. South China Morning Post, Hong Kong 1993–94, Ed.-in-Chief 1994–96. *Leisure interests:* reading, golf. *Address:* News Ltd, 2 Holt Street, Surry Hills, NSW 2010, Australia (Office).

ARMSTRONG, David Malet, AO, BPhil, PhD, FBA; Australian professor of philosophy; b. 8 July 1926, Melbourne; s. of Capt. J. M. Armstrong and Philippa Suzanne Marett; m. Jennifer Mary de Bohun Clark 1982; ed Dragon School, Oxford, England, Geelong Grammar School, Sydney and Oxford Univs; Asst Lecturer in Philosophy, Birkbeck Coll., London Univ. 1954–55; Lecturer, Sr Lecturer in Philosophy, Univ. of Melbourne 1956–63; Challis Prof. of Philosophy, Univ. of Sydney 1964–91, Prof. Emer. 1992–; Fellow Australian Acad. of Humanities. *Publications:* Berkeley's Theory of Vision 1961, Perception and the Physical World 1961, Bodily Sensations 1962, A Materialist Theory of the Mind 1968, Belief, Truth and Knowledge 1973, Universals and Scientific Realism 1978, The Nature of the Mind and Other Essays 1983, What is a Law of Nature? 1983, Consciousness and Causality (with Norman Malcolm) 1984, A Combinatorial Theory of Possibility 1989, Universals, An Opinionated Instruction 1989, Dispositions: A Debate (with C. B. Martin and U. T. Place) 1996, A World of States of Affairs 1997, The Mind-Body Problem: An Opinionated Introduction 1999. *Address:* Department of Philosophy, University of Sydney, Sydney, NSW 2006; 206 Glebe Point Road, Glebe, NSW 2037, Australia. *Telephone:* (2) 9351-2466 (Office); (2) 9660-1435 (Home). *Fax:* (2) 9660-8846. *E-mail:* david.armstrong@philosophy.usyd.edu .au (Office).

ARMSTRONG, Gillian, AM; Australian film director; b. 18 Dec. 1950; m.; two d.; ed Swinburne Coll., Nat. Australian Film & TV School, Sydney; dir numerous short films and documentaries; mem. Dirs' Guild of America, Acad. of Motion Picture Arts and Sciences; Hon. Doctorate in Film (Swinburne Univ.) 1998; Hon. DLitt (Univ. of NSW) 2000; numerous awards including Women in Hollywood Icon Award 1988, Dorothy Arzner Directing Award (USA) 1993. *Feature films include:* The Singer and The Dancer 1976, My Brilliant Career (Best Film and Best Dir Australian Film Inst. Awards, Best First Feature British Film Critics Award) 1979, Starstruck 1982, Mrs Soffel 1984, High Tide (Best Film Houston Film Festival, Grand Prix Festival Int. de Creteil, France) 1987, Fires Within 1990, The Last Days of Chez Nous 1991, Little Women 1995, Oscar and Lucinda 1997, Charlotte Gray 2001. *Address:* c/o HLA Management, 87 Pitt Street, Redfern, NSW 2016, Australia (Office). *Telephone:* (2) 9310-4948 (Office). *Fax:* (2) 9310-4113 (Office). *E-mail:* hla@hlamgt.com.au (Office).

ARMSTRONG, Rt Hon. Hilary Jane, PC, BSc; British politician; b. 30 Nov. 1945, Sunderland; d. of the late Rt Hon Ernest Armstrong and Hannah P. Armstrong (née Lamb); m. Paul D. Corrigan 1992; ed Monkwearmouth Comprehensive School, Sunderland, West Ham Coll. of Tech., Univ. of Birmingham; mem. Labour Party 1960–; teacher with VSO, Murray Girls' High School, P.O. Mwatate, Kenya 1967–69; social worker Newcastle City Social Services Dept 1970–73; community worker Southwick Neighbourhood Action Project, Sunderland 1973–75; Lecturer in Community and Youth Work, Sunderland Polytech. (now Univ. of Sunderland) 1975–86; councillor, Durham City Council 1985–87; MP (Labour) for Durham NW 1987–; Frontbench Spokesperson on Educ. (under-fives, primary and special educ.) 1988–92, on Treasury Affairs 1994–95; Parl. Pvt. Sec. to Leader of the Opposition 1992–94; mem. Nat. Exec. Labour Party 1992–97; Minister of State Dept of Environment, Transport and the Regions 1997–2001; Parl. Sec. to HM Treasury and Govt Chief Whip 2001–; fmr Vice-Pres. Nat. Children's Homes; fmr mem. British Council; fmr mem. Bd VSO; fmr mem. Mfg Science Finance (MSF) Union. *Leisure interests:* reading, theatre, watching football. *Address:* House of Commons, Westminster, London, SW1A 0AA, (Office); North House, 17 North Terrace, Crook, Co. Durham, DL15 9AZ, England (Home). *Telephone:* (20) 7276-2020 (Office); (1388) 767065 (Home). *Fax:* (20) 7219-4920 (Office); (1388) 767923 (Home). *E-mail:* hilary@hilaryarmstrong .com. *Website:* www.hilaryarmstrong.com.

ARMSTRONG, Lance; American cyclist; b. 18 Sept. 1971, Plano, Texas; s. of Linda Armstrong; m. Kristin Richard 1998; three c.; U.S. Nat. Amateur Champion 1991; mem. US Olympic team 1992, 1996, 2000 (bronze medal); mem. U.S. Postal Service Pro Cycling Team 1998–; winner numerous races including Tour Du Pont 1995, 1996, Tour de Luxembourg 1998, Tour de France 1999, 2000, 2001, 2002 (first American to win four Tours); survived testicular cancer 1996; f. Lance Armstrong Foundation for Cancer 1996; Sports Illustrated Sportsman of the Year 2002. *Publications:* It's Not About the Bike, The Lance Armstrong Performance Programme. *Address:* c/o Capital Sports Ventures, 803 Presslar, Austin, TX 78703 (Office); Lance Armstrong Foundation, POB 13026, Austin, TX 78711, USA (Office). *Website:* www.lancearmstrong.com (Office).

ARMSTRONG, Neil A., FRAeS; American astronaut and professor of engineering; b. 5 Aug. 1930, Wapakoneta, Ohio; s. of Stephen Armstrong; m. Janet Shearon; two s.; ed Purdue Univ. and Univ. of Southern California; naval aviator 1949–52, flew combat missions during Korean War; joined NASA Lewis Flight Propulsion Laboratory 1955, later transferred to NASA High Speed Flight Station, Edwards, Calif., as aeronautical research pilot, was X-15 project pilot flying to over 200,000 ft. and at approx. 4,000 m.p.h.; other flight test work included X-1 rocket research plane, F-100, F-101, F-104, F5D,

B-47 and the paraglider; selected as astronaut by NASA Sept. 1962; command pilot for Gemini VIII 1966; backup pilot for Gemini V 1965, Gemini XI 1966; flew to the moon in Apollo XI July 1969, first man to set foot on the moon 20 July 1969; Chair. Peace Corps Nat. Advisory Council 1969; Deputy Assoc. Admin. for Aeronautics, NASA, Washington 1970–71; Prof. of Eng, Univ. of Cincinnati 1971–79; Chair. Cardwell Int. Ltd 1979–81; Chair. CTA Inc. 1982–92, AIL Systems Inc. 1989–2000, EDO Corpn 2000–; Dir numerous cos.; mem. Pres.'s Comm. on Space Shuttle 1986, Nat. Comm. on Space 1985–86; mem. Nat. Acad. of Eng; Fellow, Soc. of Experimental Test Pilots, American Inst. of Aeronautics and Astronautics; Hon. mem. Int. Acad. of Astronautics; Hon. Fellow, Int. Astron. Fed.; numerous decorations and awards from 17 countries including Presidential Medal of Freedom, NASA Exceptional Service Award, Royal Geographical Soc. Gold Medal and Harmon Int. Aviation Trophy 1970. *Address:* EDO Corporation, 60 East 42nd Street, Suite 5010, New York, NY 10165, USA.

ARMSTRONG, Robin Louis, BA, PhD, FRSC; Canadian professor of physics; b. 14 May 1935, Galt, Ont.; s. of Robert Dockstader Armstrong and Beatrice Jenny Armstrong (née Grill) ; m. Karen Elisabeth Hansen 1960; two s.; ed Univs of Toronto and Oxford; Asst Prof. of Physics, Univ. of Toronto 1962–68, Assoc. Prof. 1968–71, Prof. 1971–90, Adjunct Prof. 1990–99, Prof. Emer. 1999–; Assoc. Chair. Physics, Univ. of Toronto 1969–74, Chair. 1974–82, Dean Faculty of Arts and Science 1982–90, Adjunct Prof. 1990–99; Visitante Distinguido, Univ. of Córdoba, Argentina 1989; Pres. and Prof. of Physics, Univ. of New Brunswick 1990–96; Adviser to Pres., Wilfrid Laurier Univ. 1997–2000; Pres. Canadian Inst. for Neutron Scattering 1986–89, Canadian Asscn of Physicists 1990–91; Dir Canadian Inst. for Advanced Research 1981–82, Huntsman Marine Lab. 1983–87; mem. Research Council of Canadian Inst. for Advanced Research 1982–2000, Natural Science and Eng Research Council of Canada (NSERC) 1991–97 (mem. Exec. 1992–97, Vice-Pres. 1994–97); Rutherford Memorial Fellowship (Royal Soc. Canada) 1961; Herzberg Medal 1973; Medal of Achievement (Canadian Asscn of Physicists) 1990, Commemorative Medal for 125th Anniversary of Canadian Confed. 1992, Hon. DSc (Univ. of New Brunswick) 2001. *Publications:* over 180 research articles on condensed matter physics in numerous journals. *Leisure interests:* golf, gardening. *Address:* Suite 707, 95 Prince Arthur Avenue, Toronto, Ont., M5R 3P6 (Home); University of Toronto, Department of Physics, 60 St George Street, Toronto, Ont., M5S 1A7, Canada. *Telephone:* (416) 921-4293 (Home); (519) 475-6737. *E-mail:* robinl.armstrong@sympatico.ca (Home).

ARMSTRONG, Sheila Ann, FRAM; British opera and concert singer (retd); b. 13 Aug. 1942, England; d. of William R. Armstrong and Janet Armstrong; m. David E. Cooper 1980 (divorced 1999) ; ed Hirst Park Girls' School, Ashington, Northumberland and Royal Acad. of Music; has appeared in opera at Glyndebourne, Scottish National Opera, Sadlers Wells, English Nat. Opera, Opera North and Royal Opera House, Covent Garden as well as giving recitals around the world with most of the major orchestras; has made extensive recordings; Pres. Kathleen Ferrier Soc.; Trustee Kathleen Ferrier Award; Fellow Hatfield Coll., Univ. of Durham 1992; Hon. MA (Newcastle); Hon. DMus (Durham) 1991; Mozart Prize 1965, Kathleen Ferrier Memorial Award 1965. *Leisure interests:* collecting keys, interior decoration and design, flower-arranging, sewing, gardening and garden design. *Address:* Harvesters, Tilford Road, Hindhead, Surrey, GU26 6SQ, England.

ARMSTRONG-JONES, Baron (see Snowdon, Earl of).

ARMSTRONG OF ILMINSTER, Baron (Life Peer), cr. 1988, of Ashill in the County of Somerset; **Robert Temple Armstrong,** GCB, KCB, CVO, MA; British civil servant (retd); b. 30 March 1927, Oxford; s. of Sir Thomas Armstrong and of Lady Armstrong (née Draper); m. 1st Serena Mary Benedicta Chance 1953 (divorced 1985) (died 1994); two d.; m. 2nd (Mary) Patricia Carlow 1985; ed Eton Coll. and Christ Church, Oxford; Asst Prin. Treasury 1950–55, Private Sec. to Economic Sec. 1953–54; Private Sec. to Chancellor of the Exchequer (Rt Hon R. A. Butler) 1954–55; Prin. Treasury 1955–64; Asst Sec. Cabinet Office 1964–66; Asst Sec. Treasury 1966–68; Prin. Private Sec. to Chancellor of the Exchequer (Rt Hon Roy Jenkins) 1968; Under-Sec. Treasury 1968–70; Prin. Private Sec. to the Prime Minister 1970–75; Deputy Under-Sec. of State, Home Office 1975–77, Perm. Under-Sec. of State 1977–79; Sec. of the Cabinet 1979–87; Perm. Sec. Man. and Personnel Office 1981–87; Head, Home Civil Service 1981–87; Chair. Biotechnology Investments Ltd 1989–2000; Chair. Forensic Investigative Assocs PLC 1997–; Chair. Hestercombe Gardens Trust 1995–, Bd of Govs Royal Northern Coll. of Music 2000–; Sec. Radcliffe Cttee on Monetary System 1957–59; Sec. to the Dirs, Royal Opera House, Covent Garden 1968–87, Dir 1988–93; Dir Bristol and West Bldg Soc. 1988–97 (Chair. 1993–97), Bank of Ireland and other cos; Chair. Bd of Trustees, Victoria and Albert Museum 1988–98; mem. Rhodes Trust 1975–97; Fellow, Eton Coll. 1979–94; Chancellor, Univ. of Hull 1994–; Trustee Leeds Castle Foundation 1987– (Chair. 2001–); Hon. Student, Christ Church 1985; Hon. Bencher, Inner Temple 1986. *Leisure interest:* music. *Address:* House of Lords, London, SW1A 0PW, England. *Telephone:* (20) 7219-3000. *Fax:* (20) 7219-1259.

ARNAUD, Jean-Loup, L.EN.D.; French government official; b. 25 Sept. 1942, Paris; s. of Raoul Arnaud and Emilienne Lapeyre; m. Lucienne Lavallée 1966; one d.; ed Faculté de Droit, Paris and Ecole Nat. d'Admin; Auditor, Cour des Comptes 1970, Advisory Counsellor 1976; assigned to Datar 1971–72; Tech. Counsellor, Cabinet of Sec. of State, André Rossi; assigned to financial aspects

of reform of ORTF 1974–75; Advisory Counsellor, Cour des Comptes 1976; Tech. Counsellor, Cabinet of Minister of Culture and Environment 1977; Chief of Centre, Centre Nat. de la Cinématographie 1978; official in charge of relations with cinema, Soc. Nat. de Programme de France-Régions 3 (FR3) 1979–82; Admin. Soc. Française de Production Cinématographique 1983–; Head, Dept of Cinema, Ministry of Culture and Communication 1986; Dir-Gen. Soc. d'Edition de Programmes de Télévision 1987–; Admin. Fondation Européenne des métiers de l'image et du son (Femis) 1987; Dir-Gen. Télé-Hachette 1989–; Vice-Pres. Union syndicale de la production audiovisuelle 1990–; Magistrat Cour des comptes; mem. Admin. Council of France 3 1993–; Pres. Asscn pour le crédit de l'épargne des fonctionnaires de Paris et sa région 1997–; Deputy mem. Comité fiscal, douanier et des changes 2000–. *Address:* Cour des comptes, 13 rue Cambon, 75001 Paris (Office); 55 avenue du Maine, 75014 Paris, France (Home).

ARNAULT, Bernard; French business executive; b. 5 March 1949, Roubaix; s. of Jean Arnault and Marie-Jo Arnault (née Savinel) m. 1st Anne Dewavrin 1973 (divorced); two c.; m. 2nd Hélène Mercier 1991; three s.; ed Ecole Polytechnique; joined Ferret-Savinel (family construction co.) 1971, Pres. 1978–84; lived in USA 1981–84; took over Boussac Saint-Frères (parent co. of Dior) 1985; Pres. LVMH (luxury goods group which includes Louis Vuitton bags, Moët et Chandon champagne, Parfums Christian Dior, Hennessy and Hine cognac) 1989–, Chair. 1992–; Pres. Bd of Dirs Montaigne 1997–; owner Phillips auction house 1999– (merged with Bonhams & Brooks 2001); fmr Dir Diageo; through holding co. Financière Agache owns fashion houses Dior, Lacroix and Céline and dept store Bon Marché; Officier Légion d'honneur, Ordre nat. du Mérite. *Publication:* La Passion créative 2000. *Leisure interests:* music, tennis. *Address:* 11 rue François 1er, 75008 Paris; LVMH, 22 ave Montaigne, 75008 Paris, France (Office). *Telephone:* 1-44-13-22-22. *Fax:* 1-44-13-22-23.

ARNDT, Heinz Wolfgang, BLitt, MA; Australian professor of economics; b. 26 Feb. 1915, Breslau (Wrocław), Poland; s. of F. G. Arndt; m. Ruth Strohsahl 1941; two s. one d.; ed Oxford Univ., London School of Econs (Leverhulme Research Fellow), UK; Research Asst, Royal Inst. of Int. Affairs 1941–43; Asst Lecturer in Econs, Univ. of Manchester 1943–46; Sr Lecturer in Econs, Univ. of Sydney, Australia 1946–50; Prof. of Econs, School of Gen. Studies, Australian Nat. Univ. (A.N.U.) 1951–63, Dean Faculty of Econs 1959–60, Prof. of Econs, Research School of Pacific Studies 1963–80, Deputy Chair. Bd of Inst. of Advanced Studies 1976–78, 1978–80, Prof. Emer. and Visiting Fellow Nat. Centre for Devt Studies 1981–; field work, Indonesia 1964–97; Consultant, UNCTAD 1966, 1967; mem. Governing Council UN Asian Inst. for Econ. Devt and Planning, Bangkok 1969–75; Deputy Dir Country Studies Div., OECD, Paris 1972; mem. Research Cttee, Australia-Japan Research Centre, A.N.U. 1972–95; Chair. Expert Group on Structural Change and Econ. Growth, Commonwealth Secretariat, London 1980, Australian Steering Cttee, ASEAN-Australia Econ. Relations Research Project, A.N.U. 1980–86; Consultant, UNIDO 1983–85, Asian Devt Bank 1987, 1989–92; Pres. Econ. Soc. of Australia and NZ 1957–59, Australian Asscn for Cultural Freedom 1977–85; Hon. Sec. Social Science Research Council of Australia 1957–59; Distinguished Fellow Australian Econ. Soc.; Ed. Bulletin of Indonesian Economic Studies 1965–82, Asian-Pacific Economic Literature 1986–; Jt Ed. Quadrant 1981–83. *Publications:* The Economic Lessons of the Nineteen-Thirties 1944, The Australian Trading Banks 1957 and subsequent edns., The Rise and Fall of Economic Growth: A Study in Contemporary Thought 1978, The Indonesian Economy: Collected Papers 1984, A Course Through Life: Memoirs of an Australian Economist 1985, Asian Diaries 1986, Economic Development: The History of an Idea 1987, The Indonesian Economy: As Seen by a Neighbour 1991, 50 Years of Development Studies 1993, Essays in International Economics 1944–1994, 1996, The Importance of Money: Essays in Domestic Macroeconomics 1949–1999, 2000, Essays in Biography: Australian Economists 2001 and several other books; articles in learned journals. *Leisure interests:* chess, music. *Address:* Australian National University, Canberra, ACT 0200 (Office); 14 Hopetoun Circuit, Deakin, ACT 2600, Australia (Home). *Telephone:* (6) 2492637 (Office); (6) 2733625 (Home). *Fax:* (6) 2798869. *E-mail:* Heinz.Arndt@anu.edu.au (Office).

ARNELL, Richard Anthony Sayer; British composer and conductor; b. 15 Sept. 1917, London; s. of the late Richard Sayer Arnell and Hélène Marie Scherf; m. Joan Heycock 1992; three d. from previous marriages; ed Mall School, University Coll. School and Royal Coll. of Music; Music consultant, BBC North American Service 1943–46; Lecturer, Trinity Coll. of Music, London 1948–87; Lecturer, Royal Ballet School 1958–59; Ed. 'The Composer' 1961–64; Visiting Lecturer (Fulbright exchange), Bowdoin Coll., Maine, USA 1967–68; Visiting Prof., Hofstra Univ., NY 1968–70; Music Dir and mem. Bd London Int. Film School 1975–89; Chair. Composers' Guild of GB 1974–75, 1977–79 (Vice-Pres. 1992–), Young Musicians' Symphony Orch. Soc. 1975–77, 1977–79, Saxmundham Music and Arts 1993–96 (Pres. 1996–); Music Dir Ram Filming Ltd 1980–91; Dir A plus A Ltd 1984–89; Chair. London Int. Film School Trust 1981–87; Founder, Chair. Friends of London Int. Film School 1982–87, Vice-Pres. 1987–; Founder, Chair. Friends of Trinity Coll. of Music Jr Dept 1986–87, Vice-Pres. 1987–; Founder, Chair. Tadcaster Civic Soc. Music and Arts 1988–91; Hon. Fellow, Trinity Coll. of Music, London 1950–; Composer of the Year 1966 (Music Teachers' Asscn Award); Tadcaster Town Council Merit Award 1991. *Compositions include:* opera: Love in Transit 1953, Moonflowers 1958, Boudicca, Queen of East England 2002; ballet scores: Punch and the Child 1947, Harlequin in April 1951, the Great

Detective 1953, The Angels 1957, Giselle (re-orchestrated) 1965; film scores: The Land 1941, The Third Secret 1963, The Visit 1964, The Man Outside 1966, Topsail Schooner 1966, Bequest for a Village 1969, Second Best 1972, Stained Glass 1973, Wires Over the Border 1974, Black Panther 1977, Antagonist 1980, Dilemma 1981, Toulouse Lautrec 1984, Light of the World 1988; other works: Symphonic Portrait, Lord Byron, for Sir Thomas Beecham 1953, Landscapes and Figures 1956, Petrified Princess, puppet operetta for BBC 1959; Robert Flaherty, Impression for Radio Eireann 1960, Musica Pacifica for Edward Benjamin 1963, Festival Flourish, for Salvation Army 1965, Piano Concerto for Royal Philharmonic Orchestra (RPO) 1967, Overture, Food of Love, for Portland Symphony Orchestra 1968, My Ladye Greene Sleeves, for Hofstra Univ. 1968, Nocturne 1968, I Think of All Soft Limbs 1971, Astronaut One 1973, Life Boat Voluntary, for Royal Nat. Lifeboat Inst. 1974, Call, for London Philharmonic Orchestra 1980, RVW's Almanac 1984, Six Lawrence Poems 1985, Ode to Beecham, for RPO 1986, Con Amore for Cantamus Girls Choir 1988, Xanadu for Harlow Choral Soc. 1993, Symphonic Statement for Nelson Mandela 1999, "B" Queen Boudicca 2002; also six symphonies, two violin concertos, harpsichord concerto, two piano concertos, six string quartets, two quintets, organ works, music for string orchestra, wind ensembles, brass ensembles, song cycles and electronic music. *Plays:* libretti: Moonflowers 1958, The Madrigal Murders 1995. *Leisure interests:* cooking, travel. *Address:* Benhall Lodge, Benhall, Suffolk, IP17 1JD, England. *Telephone:* (1728) 602014. *Fax:* (1728) 603256 (Office).

ARNETT, Emerson James, QC, BA, LLM; Canadian business executive; b. 29 Sept. 1938, Winnipeg, Man.; s. of Emerson Lloyd Arnett and Elsie Audrey Rhind; m. Edith Alexandra Palk 1964; four c.; ed Univ. of Man., Harvard Univ.; civil litigation section, Dept of Justice, Ottawa 1964–65; Assoc. Pitblado and Hoskin (law firm), Winnipeg 1965–66; Asst to Exec. Vice-Pres. Vickers and Benson Advertising, Toronto 1966–67; Assoc./Partner Davies, Ward and Beck (law firm), Toronto 1968–73; partner Stikeman, Elliott (law firm), Toronto 1973–97, Resident partner, Washington, DC, 1993–96; Pres. and CEO Molson Inc. 1997–. *Publications:* Doing Business (co-ed.); numerous law review and newspaper articles and conf. papers. *Leisure interests:* shooting, skiing, hiking, reading. *Address:* Molson Inc., 1555 Notre Dame Street East, Montreal, Quebec, H2L 2R5 (Office); 500 Avenue Road, Suite 1203, Toronto, Ont., M4V 2J6, Canada (Home). *Telephone:* (514) 597-1786 (Office); (416) 923-7887 (Home). *Fax:* (514) 590-6352 (Office); (416) 923-5899 (Home). *E-mail:* ejarnett@molson.com (Office); ejarnett@netcom.ca (Home). *Website:* www.molson.com (Office).

ARNETT, Peter; American journalist and television reporter; b. 1934, New Zealand; m. (divorced); two c.; ed Waitaki Coll., Oamaru, New Zealand; with Associated Press (AP) 1960–; war corresp. in Viet Nam, Middle East, Nicaragua, El Salvador and Afghanistan; special writer for AP, New York; joined Cable News Network (CNN) 1981–99; served as corresp. in Moscow for two years; later nat. security reporter, Washington, DC; CNN corresp. Baghdad 1991; Chief Foreign Corresp. ForeignTV.com, New York 1998–; Pulitzer prizewinner. *Publication:* Live from the Battlefield 1994. *Leisure interests:* collector of books and oriental statuary. *Address:* ForeignTV.com Inc., 162 Fifth Avenue, Suite 105A, New York, NY 10010, USA (Office).

ARNOLD, Armin, PhD, FRSC; Swiss/Canadian professor, writer and critic; b. 1 Sept. 1931, Zug, Switzerland; s. of Franz Arnold and Ida Baumgartner; ed Univs. of Fribourg, London and Zürich; Asst Prof. of German, Univ. of Alberta 1959–61, McGill Univ. 1961–64, Assoc. Prof. 1964–68, Prof. 1968–84, Auxiliary Prof. 1984–89; Dozent, Höhere Wirtschafts- und Verwaltungsschule, Olten 1984–93, Baden 1994–. *Publications include:* D. H. Lawrence and America 1958, James Joyce 1963, Die Literatur des Expressionismus 1966, Friedrich Dürrenmatt 1969, Prosa des Expressionismus 1972, Kriminalromanführer 1978, Alfred Doeblin 1996, etc. *Address:* 9E Rang Ste-Anne de la Rochelle, Québec J0E 2B0, Canada; Rauchlenweg 332, 4712 Laupersdorf, Switzerland.

ARNOLD, Eve; photographer; b. Philadelphia, USA; m. Arnold Arnold (divorced); one s.; ed New School for Social Research; joined Magnum Photographic Agency 1954; moved to UK 1961; has worked for Sunday Times, Time, Life, etc.; worked in UK, USA, China, fmr USSR; subjects include Marilyn Monroe, Joan Crawford, John and Anjelica Huston, Francis Bacon, Yves Montand, Margot Fonteyn, Rudolph Nureyev, Malcolm X, photographs examining the status of women and numerous other topics; numerous exhbns. including Eve Arnold: In Retrospect, premièred Int. Center for Photography, NY, retrospective at Nat. Museum of Photography, Bradford 1996. *Publications include:* The Unretouched Woman, In China, In America, The Great British, Eve Arnold: In Retrospect 1996. *Address:* c/o Magnum Photographic Agency, Moreland Buildings, 2nd Floor, 5 Old Street, London, EC1V 9HL; 26 Mount Street, London, W1Y 5RB, England (Home). *Telephone:* (20) 7490-1771.

ARNOLD, Hans Redlef, PhD; German diplomatist and writer; b. 14 Aug. 1923, Munich; s. of Karl Arnold and Anne-Dora Volquardsen; m. Karin Baroness von Egloffstein 1954; three c.; ed Univ. of Munich; joined Foreign Service, FRG; served Embassy, Paris 1952–55, Foreign Office, Bonn 1955–57, Embassy, Washington, DC 1957–61, Foreign Office 1961–68, sometime head of Foreign Minister Willy Brandt's office; Amb. to Netherlands 1968–72; Head, Cultural Dept, Foreign Office 1972–77; Amb. to Italy 1977–81; Insp.-Gen. German Foreign Service 1981–82; Amb. and Perm. Rep. to UN and Int. Orgs., Geneva 1982–86; Lecturer Acad. of Political Science, Munich; several

nat. and foreign decorations. *Publications:* Cultural Export as Policy? 1976, Foreign Cultural Policy 1980, The March (co-author) 1990, Europe on the Decline? 1993, Germany's Power 1995, Europe To Be Thought Anew: Why and How Further Unification? 1999, Security for Europe (co-ed.) 2002; regular contributions to periodicals and newspapers. *Address:* 83083 Riedering-Heft, Germany. *Telephone:* (8032) 5255. *Fax:* (8032) 989755. *E-mail:* hans.r .arnold@gmx.de (Home).

ARNOLD, James R., MA, PhD; American professor of chemistry and space scientist; b. 5 May 1923, Metuchen, NJ; s. of Abraham S. Arnold and Julia J. Arnold; m. Louise C. Arnold 1952; three s.; ed Princeton Univ.; Asst Princeton 1943, Manhattan Project 1943–46; Fellow, Inst. of Nuclear Studies, Univ. of Chicago 1946; Nat. Research Fellow, Harvard 1947; Asst Prof., Univ. of Chicago 1949–55; Assoc. Prof., Princeton Univ. 1956–58; Assoc. Prof., Dept of Chem., Univ. of Calif., San Diego 1958–60, Prof. 1960–92, Harold C. Urey Prof. 1983–92; Assoc. Ed. Moon 1972–; Dir Calif. Space Inst. (S.I.O.), Univ. of Calif., San Diego 1980–89, interim Dir 1996–97; prin. investigator Calif. Space Grant Consortium 1989–; recipient of lunar samples from Apollo and Soviet missions; mem. of NAS, AAAS, ACS, American Acad. of Arts and Sciences; Nat. Council of World Federalists 1970–72; Guggenheim Fellow, India 1972–73; specialized in field of cosmic-ray produced nuclides, meteorites, lunar samples and cosmochemistry. *Publications:* over 100 articles in scientific reviews and journals. *Address:* University of California at San Diego, Department of Chemistry, Code 0524, La Jolla, CA 92093, USA. *Telephone:* (858) 534-2908. *Fax:* (619) 534-7840. *E-mail:* jarnold@ucsd.edu.

ARNOLD, Luqman; British bank executive; b. April 1950, Calcutta; m.; one s.; ed Oundle School, Univ. of London; with Mfrs Hanover Corpn, London, Hong Kong and Singapore 1976–82; with First Nat. Bank (Dallas), Singapore and London 1972–76; with Credit Suisse First Boston (CSFB), London and Tokyo 1982–92, responsible for Asia Pacific origination, Private Placements, Cen. and Eastern Europe, later Head of Investment Banking, New Business, mem. Operating Cttee; sabbatical year (research into drivers and outlook for cross-border institutional investment flows) 1992–93; Global Head of Investment Banking, Paribas Capital Markets, Banque Paribas, London 1993–95, Group Head of Business Devt, Paris 1995–96; CEO Asia Pacific UBS AG, Singapore and Tokyo 1996–98, COO, London 1998–99, Chief Financial Officer and Head of Corp. Centre, Zurich 1999–2001, Pres. and Chair., Exec. Bd, Zurich 2001; CEO Abbey National 2002–. *Address:* Abbey National Group, Abbey National House, 2 Triton Square, Regent's Place, London, NW1 3AN, England (Office). *Telephone:* (870) 607-6000. *Website:* www .abbeynational.com.

ARNOLD, Sir Malcolm Henry, Kt, CBE, FRCM, FRNCM; British composer and musician; b. 21 Oct. 1921, Northampton; s. of William Arnold and Annie Arnold; m. 1st Sheila Nicholson 1942; one s. one d.; m. 2nd Isobel Gray 1963 (died 1992); one s.; ed Royal Coll. of Music, London; Prin. Trumpet, London Philharmonic Orchestra 1942–44 and 1946–48; served army 1944–46; fulltime composer and conductor 1948–; Hon. mem. Royal Northern Coll. of Music 1997; Hon. RAM 1983; Bard of the Cornish Gorsedd 1969; Freeman City of London 1950; Hon. Freeman Borough of Northampton 1989; Hon. DMus (Exeter) 1969, (Durham) 1982, (Leicester) 1984, (Trinity Coll. London) 1991; Dr hc (Miami, Ohio) 1990; Ivor Novello Award for music for Inn of Sixth Happiness 1952, Oscar for music for film Bridge on the River Kwai 1957, Ivor Novello Award for Outstanding Services to British Music 1986, Wavendon All Music Composer of the Year 1987, BAFTA Fellowship 2001. *Works include:* Films: more than 100 film scores including St Trinians series, Hobson's Choice, Whistle down the Wind, Heroes of Telemark; symphonies: No. 1 1949, No. 2 1953, No. 3 1957, No. 4 1960, No. 5 1961, No. 6 1967, No. 7 1973, No. 8 1978, No. 9 1986, Symphony for Brass Instruments 1979; overtures: Beckus the Dandipratt 1943, Tam O'Shanter 1955, Peterloo 1967; other compositions: 18 concertos, 5 ballets, 2 one-act operas, 2 string quartets, 2 brass quintets and vocal, choral and chamber music. *Leisure interests:* reading, foreign travel. *Address:* Malcolm Arnold Society, 6 Walton Street, Barnsley, South Yorkshire (Office); Music Unites, 26 Springfields, Attleborough, Norfolk, NR17 2PA, England. *Telephone:* (1226) 284116 (Society) (Office); (1953) 455420 (Music Unites). *Fax:* (1953) 455420 (Music Unites). *E-mail:* musicunites@btopenworld.com. *Website:* www.malcolmarnold.com.

ARNOLD, Roseanne (see Roseanne).

ARNOLD, Vladimir Igorevich, DSc; Russian mathematician; b. 12 June 1937, Odessa; s. of Igor Vladimorovich Arnold and Nina Alexandrovna Isakovich; m. Voronina Elionora Aleksandrovna 1976; one s.; ed Moscow State Univ.; Asst Prof., then Prof., Moscow State Univ. 1961–86; Prof. and Chief Scientific Researcher Steklov Math. Inst., Moscow 1986–, Université Paris-Dauphine 1993–; Corresp. mem. USSR (now Russian) Acad. of Sciences 1984–90, mem. 1990–; Foreign mem. Académie des Sciences, Paris, NAS, USA, Academia Lincei, Rome, Royal Soc., London, Acad. of Arts and Sciences, Boston, USA, London Math. Soc., American Philosophical Soc., European Acad.; Dr hc (Univ. P. et M. Curie, Paris) 1979, (Warwick, UK) 1988, (Utrecht) 1991, (Bologna) 1991, (Universidad Complutense de Madrid) 1994, (Toronto) 1997; Moscow Math. Soc. Prize 1958, Lenin Prize 1965, Crafoord Prize 1982, Lobachevsky Prize 1992, Harvey Prize 1994, ADION Medal 1995, Wolf Prize 2001, American Physics Soc. Prize 2001. *Publications:* Ergodic Problems in Classical Mechanics (with A. Avez) 1968, Mathematical Methods of Classical Mechanics 1974, Catastrophe Theory 1981, Singularity Theory and its Applications (Vols 1, 2) 1982, 1984, Huygens and Barrow, Newton and Hooke

1990, Partial and Differential Equations 1995, Topological Methods in Hydrodynamics 1997, Arnold Problems 2000, and other publs. *Leisure interests:* skiing, canoeing, hiking. *Address:* Steklov Mathematical Institute, 8 Gubkina Street, GSP-1 Moscow 117966, Russia; (Jan.–June) CEREMADE, Université de Paris-Dauphine, Place du Mal de Lattre de Tassigny, Paris 75775, Cedex 16e, France. *Telephone:* (095) 135-14-90 (Moscow) (Office); 1-44-05-46-81 (Paris) (Office); (095) 132-48-02 (Moscow) (Home); 1-40-01-92-08 (Paris) (Home). *Fax:* (095) 135-05-55 (Moscow) (Office); 1-44-05-45-99 (Paris) (Office).

ARNOTT, Struther, CBE, FRSE, FRS; British university vice-chancellor and scientist; b. 25 Sept. 1934; s. of Charles McCann and Christina Struthers Arnott; m. Greta Edwards 1970; two s.; ed Hamilton Acad., Lanarkshire and Glasgow Univ.; Scientist, MRC Biophysics Research Unit, King's Coll. London 1960–70, Demonstrator in Physics 1960–67, Dir of Postgraduate Studies in Biophysics 1967–70; Prof. of Molecular Biology, Purdue Univ., West Lafayette, Ind. 1970–86, Head, Dept of Biological Sciences 1975–80, Vice-Pres. for Research and Dean, Graduate School 1980–86; Sr Visiting Research Fellow, Jesus Coll. Oxford 1980–81; Nuffield Research Fellow, Green Coll. 1985–86; Principal and Vice-Chancellor, St Andrews Univ. 1986–2000, Leverhulme Fellow 2000–02; Haddow Prof. Inst. for Cancer Research 2000–; Guggenheim Memorial Foundation Fellow 1985; Gov. Sedbergh School; Hon. ScD (St Andrews, USA) 1994; Hon. DSc (Purdue) 1998; Hon. LLD (St Andrews) 1999. *Publications:* papers in learned journals on structures of fibrous biopolymers, especially nucleic acids and polysaccharides and techniques for visualizing them. *Leisure interests:* birdwatching, botanizing. *Address:* 1 Yorkshire, South Parade, Bawtry, DN10 6JH, Scotland. *E-mail:* essaie@icr.ac.uk.

ARNOUL, Françoise (Françoise Gautsch); French actress; b. 9 June 1931, Constantine, Algeria; d. of Gen. Arnoul Gautsch and Jeanne Gradwohl; m. Georges Cravenne (divorced); ed Lycée de Rabat, Lycée Molière (Paris) and Paris Conservatoire; Chevalier Légion d'honneur, Officier des Arts et des Lettres. *Films include:* Nous irons à Paris, La maison Bonnadieu, Le désir et l'amour, La plus belle fille du monde, Les compagnons de la nuit, Les amants du Tage, French-Cancan, Des gens sans importance, Thérèse Etienne, La chatte, Asphalte, La bête à l'affût, Le bal des espions, La chatte sort ses griffes, La morte-saison des amours, Le testament d'Orphée, Les Parisiennes, Dimanche de la vie, Le Congrès s'amuse, Españolas en Paris 1970, Van der Valk 1972, Dialogue d'exiles 1975, Dernière sortie avant Roissy 1977, Ronde de Nuit 1984, Nuit Docile 1987, Voir L'Éléphant 1990; numerous TV roles; theatre debut in Les Justes (Camus), Versailles 1966. *Leisure interest:* dancing. *Address:* 53 rue Censier, 75005 Paris, France (Home).

ARNOULT, Erik (Erik Orsenna), D. ES. SC.ECON., PhD; French civil servant and writer; b. 22 March 1947, Paris; m. (divorced); one s. one d.; ed Institut d'Etudes Politiques, Paris, Univ. of Paris I; lecturer, Université de Paris I 1978–81; Adviser to Minister of Devt 1981–83, to Minister of Foreign Affairs 1990–92; Cultural Adviser to Pres. of Repub. 1983–90; Maître des Requêtes, Conseil d'Etat 1985–; mem. Acad. Française; co-screenwriter Indochine (Acad. Award for Best Foreign Film); Prix Goncourt 1988. *Publications:* L'Exposition Coloniale 1988, Deux Etés 1996, Longtemps 1998 (all novels). *Leisure interest:* yachting. *Address:* Conseil d'Etat, 1 place du Palais Royal, 75001 Paris (Office); 8 passage Sigaud, 75013 Paris, France (Home).

ARNS, HE Cardinal Paulo Evaristo; Brazilian ecclesiastic; b. 14 Sept. 1921, Forquilhinha, Criciúma, Santa Catarina; s. of Gabriel and Helena Steiner Arns; ed Univ. de Paris and Ecole des Hautes Etudes, Paris; taught theology and French, Univ. Católica de Petrópolis; pastoral work in Petrópolis; Aux. Bishop of São Paulo 1966; apptd. Archbishop of São Paulo 1970; Grand Chancellor of Pontificia Univ. Católica de São Paulo; mem. Sacred Congregation for the Sacraments (Vatican); mem. UN Int. Independent Comm. on Humanitarian Issues; cr. Cardinal by Pope Paul VI 1973; Hon. LLD (Notre Dame, Ind., USA); Nansen Prize (UN) 1985. *Publications:* numerous works and translations on religious and racial topics, including A Quem iremos, Senhor? 1968, Comunidade: União e Ação 1972, Sê Fiel 1977, Em Defesa dos Direitos Humanos 1978, Convite para Rezar 1978, Presença e Força do Cristão 1978, Discutindo o Papel da Igreja 1980, Os Ministérios na Igreja 1980, O que é Igreja 1981, Meditações para o Dia-a-Dia (Vols 1–4) 1981–83, Pensamentos 1982, Olhando o Mundo com São Francisco 1982, A Violência em nossos Dias 1983, Para Ser Jovem Hoje 1983, Santos e Heróis do Povo 1984. *Address:* Avenida Higienopolis, 890, C.P. 6778, 01064 São Paulo, S.P., Brazil. *Telephone:* (11) 826-0133. *Fax:* (11) 825-6806.

AROSEMENA MONROY, Carlos Julio, PhD; Ecuadorean politician and lawyer; b. 24 Aug. 1919, Guayaquil; s. of Carlos Julio Arosemena Tola and Laura Monroy Garaicoa; Counsellor, Ecuadorean Embassy, Washington, DC 1946–52; Chair. Chamber of Deputies 1952; Minister of Defence 1952–53; Vice-Pres. 1960–61; Pres. of Ecuador 1961–63 (deposed by coup d'état).

ARQUETTE, Patricia; American actress; b. 8 April 1968; d. of Lewis Arquette and Mardi Arquette; m. Nicolas Cage (q.v.) 1995. *Films:* Pretty Smart 1986, A Nightmare on Elm Street 3: Dream Warriors 1987, Time Out 1988, Far North 1988, The Indian Runner 1991, Prayer of the Rollerboys 1991, Ethan Frome 1993, Trouble Bound 1993, Inside Monkey Zetterland 1993, True Romance 1993, Holy Matrimony 1994, Ed Wood 1994, Beyond Rangoon 1995, Infinity 1995, Flirting with Disaster 1996, The Secret Agent 1996, Lost Highway 1997, Nightwatch 1998, In the Boom Boom Room 1999, Goodbye Lover 1999, Stigmata 1999, Bringing out the Dead 1999, Little Nicky

2000, Human Nature 2001. *Films for TV include:* Daddy 1987, Dillinger 1991, Wildflower 1991, Betrayed by Love 1994, Toby's Story 1998, The Hi-Lo Country 1998, The Badge 2002. *Address:* c/o U.T.A., 9560 Wilshire Blvd., 5th Floor, Beverly Hills, CA 90212, USA.

ARQUETTE, Rosanna; American actress; b. 10 Aug. 1959, NY; d. of Lewis Arquette and Mardi Arquette; m. 1st (divorced); m. 2nd James N. Howard (divorced); m. 3rd. John Sidel 1993; f. Flower Child Productions. *Films include:* Gorp 1980, S.O.B. 1981, Off the Wall 1983, The Aviator 1985, Desperately Seeking Susan 1985, 8 Million Ways to Die 1986, After Hours 1986, Nobody's Fool 1986, The Big Blue 1988, Life Lessons, Black Rainbow 1989; Wendy Cracked a Walnut 1989, Sweet Revenge 1990, Baby, It's You 1990, Flight of the Intruder 1990, The Linguini Incident 1992, Fathers and Sons 1992, Nowhere to Run 1993, Pulp Fiction 1994, Search and Destroy 1995, Crash 1996, Liar 1997, Gone Fishin' 1997, Buffalo '66 1997, Palmer's Pick Up 1998, I'm Losing You 1998, Homeslice 1998, Floating Away 1998, Hope Floats 1998, Fait Accompli 1998, Sugar Town 1999, Palmer's Pick Up 1999, Pigeonhood 1999, Interview with a Dead Man 1999, The Whole Nine Yards 2000, Too Much Flesh 2000, Things Behind the Sun 2001, Big Bad Love 2001, Good Advice 2001, Diary of a Sex Addict 2001. *TV films include:* Harvest Home, The Wall, The Long Way Home, The Executioner's Song, One Cooks, the Other Doesn't, The Parade, Survival Guide, A Family Tree, Promised a Miracle, Sweet Revenge, Separation, The Wrong Man, Nowhere to Hide, I Know What You Did. *Address:* c/o 8033 West Sunset Boulevard, #16, Los Angeles, CA 90046, USA (Office).

ARRABAL, Fernando; Spanish writer; b. 11 Aug. 1932, Melilla; s. of Fernando Arrabal and Carmen Terán González; m. Luce Moreau 1958; one s. one d; ed Univ. of Madrid; political prisoner in Spain 1967; founder "Panique" Movt with Topor, Jodorowsky, etc.; "Superdotado" Award 1942, Ford Foundation Award 1959, Grand Prix du Théâtre 1967, Grand Prix Humour Noir 1968, Obie Award 1976, Premio Nadal (Spain) 1983, World's Theater Prize 1984, Medalla de Oro de Bellas Artes (Spain) 1989, Prix du Théâtre (Acad. Française) 1993, Prix Int. Vladimir Nabokov 1994, Premio de Ensayo Espasa 1994, Grand Prix Soc. des Gens de Lettres 1996, Grand Prix de la Méditerranée 1996, Prix de la Francophonie 1998, Premio Mariano de Cavia 1998, Prix Alessandro Manzoni di Poesia 1999, Premio Nacional de las Letras, Premio Eninci Cine y Literatura 2000, Premio Nacional de Teatro 2001, Premio Ercilla Teatro 2001; Medal of Centre for French Civilization and Culture, New York 1997; Officier, Ordre des Arts et des Lettres 1984. *Exhibition:* Kalédescopies, Musée de Bayeux 2000. *Publications:* plays: numerous plays including Le cimetière des voitures, Guernica, Le grand cérémonial, L'architecte et l'Empereur d'Assyrie, Le jardin des délices, Et ils passèrent des menottes aux fleurs, Le ciel et la merde, Bella ciao, La Tour de Babel, L'extravagante réussite de Jésus-Christ, Karl Marx et William Shakespeare, Les délices de la chair, La traversée de l'empire, Luly, Cielito, Fando et Lis, Lettre d'amour; novels: Baal Babylone 1959, L'enterrement de la sardine 1962, Fêtes et rites de la confusion 1965, La tour prends garde, La reverdie, La vierge rouge, Bréviaire d'amour d'un haltérophile, L'extravagante croisade d'un castrat amoureux 1991, La tueuse du jardin d'hiver 1994, El Mono 1994, Le Funambule de Dieu 1998, Ceremonia por un teniente abandonado 1998, Porté disparu 2000, Levitación 2000; poetry includes: La pierre de la folie 1963, 100 sonnets 1966, Humbles paradis 1983, Liberté couleur de femme 1993, Arrabalesques 1994, Passion, Passions 1997, Le Frénétique du Spasme 1997; essays: numerous, including Le 'Panique', Le New York d'Arrabal, Lettre au Général Franco, Greco 1970, Lettre à Fidel Castro 1983, Goya-Dali 1992, La Dudosa Luz del Día 1994. *Films:* directed and written: Viva la Muerte, J'irai comme un cheval fou, L'arbre de Guernica, L'odyssée de la Pacific, Le cimetière des voitures, Adieu Babylone!, J.-L. Borges (Una Vida de Poesía) 1998. *Leisure interest:* chess. *Address:* 22 rue Jouffroy d'Abbans, Paris 75017, France. *Fax:* 1-42-67-01-26. *E-mail:* arrabal@noos.fr (Home). *Website:* www.arrabal.org (Home).

ARRIAGA, Gen. Kaúlza de; Portuguese army officer (retd); b. 18 Jan. 1915, Oporto; s. of Manuel de Arriaga Nunes and Felicidad Oliveira de Arriaga; m. Maria do Carmo Formigal 1955; three s. two d.; ed Univ. of Oporto, Portuguese Mil. Acad. and Portuguese Inst. for Higher Mil. Studies; Under-Sec. of State for Aviation, later Sec. 1955–62; High Command Course 1963–64; Brig. 1964; Prof. of Strategy and Tactics, Inst. for High Mil. Studies 1964–69; Chair. Nuclear Energy Bd 1967–69, 1973–74; Gen. 1968; C-in-C Portuguese Armed Forces in Mozambique 1970–73; mem. Overseas Council 1965–69, 1973–74; mem. Bd of Dirs and Exec. Chair. Soc. Portuguesa de Exploração de Petróleos (ANGOL Oil Corpn) 1966–69, 1973–74; Chair. Shareholders' Meeting, Finicisa Synthetic Fibres Corpn 1968–69, 1973–74; retd May 1974; arrested during coup d'état Sept. 1974, released Jan. 1976, later successfully sued Portuguese State; mem. Council, Order of Christ 1966–74; Pres. Equestrian Fed. 1968–71; Grande-Oficial Ordem Militar de Cristo, Grã Cruz, Mérito Aeronáutico, Gran Cruz (Spain), Grande Oficial Ordem do Mérito Militar (Brazil), Grand Officier, Légion d'honneur (France), Commdr Legion of Merit (USA) and other Portuguese and foreign decorations. *Publications include:* Energia Atómica 1949, Portuguese National Defence during the Last 40 Years and in the Future 1966, Guerra e Política 1987, Maastricht 1992; numerous articles. *Address:* Avenida João XXI No. 9, 6°, 1000-298 Lisbon, Portugal. *Telephone:* (21) 8482965.

ARRIGHI DE CASANOVA, Emile, DIur; French civil servant and financial executive; b. 21 Oct. 1920, Bastia, Corsica; s. of Pierre Arrighi de Casanova and Catherine Arrighi de Casanova (née Paoli); m. Geneviève Barthelemy

1946; four c.; ed Lycée Mignet, Univ. of Aix-en-Provence; Dir of Internal Trade, Ministry of Industry and Trade 1951–59; Dir of Industrial Expansion, Ministry of Industry 1959–65; Dir-Gen. Chamber of Commerce and Industry of Paris 1965–77, Hon. Dir-Gen. 1985–; Chair. Econ. and Social Cttee for Corsica 1974–83; Conseiller d'Etat en Service extraordinaire 1976–79; Chair. Soc. du Marché d'Interêt nat. de Rungis 1977–81; Hon. Pres. Assoc. Nat. des docteurs en Droit 1971–; Pres. Palais des Congrès, Paris 1977–84, Institut du Développement 1984–94; Vice-Pres. Groupement Nat. des Hypermarchés 1989–91; Pres. Egée France 1992–95 (Hon. Pres. 2000–), Institut de la Méditerranée 1994–; mem. Econ. and Social Council 1979– (Pres. 1984–94); Commdr Légion d'honneur, Ordre nat. du Mérite, Ordre nat. du Mérite artisanal, Ordre nat. du Mérite commercial. *Address:* Institut de la Méditerranée, Palais du Pharo, 58 boulevard Charles Livon, 13007 Marseille (Office); 11 boulevard du roi René, 13100 Aix-en-Provence, France (Home).

ARRILLAGA, Josu, PhD, FRS (NZ), FIEE, FIEEE; Spanish professor of electrical engineering; b. 21 Jan. 1934; s. of José María and María Mercedes Arrillaga; m. Greta Robinson 1968; two s. two d.; ed in Spain and Univ. of Manchester Inst. of Science and Tech.; Industrial Engineer, ISOLUX, Spain 1955–59; A.E.I. Engineer, Manchester 1959–61; Research student UMIST 1961–66; Lecturer Salford Univ. 1966–67; Lecturer and Sr Lecturer, UMIST 1967–75, Head Power Systems and High Voltage 1970–75; Prof. of Electrical Eng, Univ. of Canterbury, NZ 1975–, Head Dept of Electrical and Electronic Eng 1986–91, currently James Cook Sr Research Fellow; Johns Hopkins Prize, IEE 1975; Uno Lamm Medal, IEEE 1997, Int. Power Quality Award 1997, IPENZ Pres. Gold Medal 1999, Royal Soc. (NZ) Silver Medal for Tech. Innovation 1999. *Publications:* twelve books including AC-DC Power System Analysis 1998, Power System Quality Assessment 2000, 300 technical articles. *Leisure interest:* gardening. *Address:* 2/77 Hinau Street, Christchurch, New Zealand. *Telephone:* (3) 348-8492. *Fax:* (3) 364-2761 (Office). *E-mail:* arrillj@elec.canterbury.ac.uk.

ARRINDELL, Sir Clement Athelston, GCMG, GCVO, QC; St Christopher and Nevis civil servant and lawyer; b. 16 April 1932, St Kitts, West Indies; s. of George E Arrindell and Hilda I. Arrindell; m. Evelyn Eugenia O'Loughlin 1967; ed St Kitts-Nevis Grammar School (Island Scholar 1948) and Lincoln's Inn, London; practising barrister-at-law 1959–66; Dist Magistrate 1966–74; Chief Magistrate 1975–77; Puisne Judge 1978–81; Gov. of St Kitts-Nevis 1981–83; Gov.-Gen. of St Christopher and Nevis 1983–95. *Leisure interests:* gardening, piano playing, classical music. *Address:* The Lark, Bird Rock, St Christopher and Nevis, West Indies.

ARROW, Kenneth Joseph, PhD; American professor of economics; b. 23 Aug. 1921, New York; s. of Harry I. Arrow and Lillian Arrow; m. Selma Schweitzer 1947; two s.; ed The City College, Columbia Univ.; Capt. USAF 1942–46; Research Assoc. Cowles Comm. for Research in Econ., Univ. of Chicago 1947–49; Asst Assoc. and Prof. of Econs, Statistics and Operations Research, Stanford Univ., 1949–68; Prof. of Econs Harvard Univ., 1968–79; Prof. of Econs and Operations Research, Stanford Univ., 1979–91, Prof. Emer. 1991–; mem. NAS, American Acad. of Arts and Sciences, American Phil. Soc., Finnish Acad. of Sciences, British Acad., Inst. of Medicine, Pontifical Acad. of Social Sciences; Pres. Int. Soc. for Inventory Research 1983–90, Int. Econ. Asscn, Econometric Soc., American Econ. Asscn, Soc. for Social Choice and Welfare; Dir various cos; Hon. LLD (City Univ., Univ. of Chicago, Washington Univ., Univ. of Pennsylvania, Ben-Gurion Univ., Harvard Univ., Univ. of Cyprus, Univ. of Buenos Aires); Hon. Dr of Social and Econ. Sciences (Vienna); Hon. ScD (Columbia Univ.) 1973; Hon. DSocSci (Yale) 1974; Hon. LLD (Hebrew Univ. Jerusalem) 1975, Hon. DPolSci (Helsinki) 1976; Dr hc (Univ. René Descartes) 1974, (Univ. Aix-Marseille III) 1985, Univ. of Cyprus 2000); Hon. DLitt (Cambridge) 1985, (Harvard Univ.) 1999; Hon.DUniv. (Uppsala) 1995; Hon. doctorate ; Hon. PhD Tel-Aviv Univ. 2001; Nobel Memorial Prize in Econ. Science 1972; Order of the Rising Sun (Japan); John Bates Clark Medal; Von Neumann Prize; Medal of Univ. of Paris 1998. *Publications:* Social Choice and Individual Values 1951, 1963, Studies in the Mathematical Theory of Inventory and Production (with S. Karlin and H. Scarf) 1958, Studies in Linear and Nonlinear Programming (with L. Hurwicz and H. Uzawa) 1958, A Time Series Analysis of Inter-industry Demands (with M. Hoffenberg) 1959, Public Investment, The Rate of Return and Optimal Fiscal Policy (with M. Kurz) 1970, Essays in the Theory of Risk-Bearing 1971, General Competitive Analysis (with F. H. Hahn) 1971, The Limits of Organization 1973, Studies in Resource Allocation Processes (with L. Hurwicz) 1977, Collected Papers 1983–85, Social Choice and Multicriterion Decision Making (with H. Raynaud) 1985; about 200 articles in learned journals. *Leisure interests:* walking, music. *Address:* Department of Economics, Stanford Univ., Stanford, CA 94305-6072 (Office); 580 Constanzo Street, Stanford, CA 94305, USA (Home). *Telephone:* (650) 723-9165 (Office). *Fax:* (650) 725-5702 (Office). *E-mail:* arrow@leland.stanford.edu (Office).

ARSALA, Hedayat Amin; Afghanistan politician and economist; nephew of Pir Gailani; Minister of Foreign Affairs 1992–96; fmr official World Bank; Vice-Chair. and Minister of Finance Afghan Interim Authority 2001–02, Transitional Authority 2002–. *Address:* Ministry of Finance, Shar Rahi Pashtunistan, Kabul, Afghanistan (Office).

ARSENIS, Gerasimos; Greek politician and economist; b. 1931, Cephalonia; m. Louka Katseli; three s. one d.; ed Univ. of Athens and Massachusetts Inst. of Tech.; worked for UN 1960; Dir Dept of Econ. Studies, OECD Research Centre 1964–66, Sr Official, Prebisch Group, UN 1966–73; Dir UNCTAD

1973; Gov. Bank of Greece 1981–84; Minister of Nat. Economy 1982–84, of Finance and Nat. Economy 1984–85, of Merchant Marine June–July 1985, of Defence 1993–96, of Education and Religious Affairs 1996–99; expelled from PASOK 1986; f. Democratic Initiative Group 1987, Leader 1987–89; returned to PASOK 1989, mem. Exec. Bureau 1990–; MP for Athens Dist 1990–. *Address:* 15 Valaoritou Street, 106 71 Athens, Greece.

ARSENISHVILI, Georgy, DR.TECH.SC; Georgian politician and mathematician; b. 1942, Khirsa, Signakhi Region; m.; two c.; ed Tbilisi State Univ.; Jr Researcher Inst. of Applied Math., Sr Researcher, Docent, Deputy Dean Tbilisi State Univ. 1970–73; Heidelberg Univ. 1973–74; Dean, Chair of Applied Math., Methods Prof. Tbilisi Univ. 1978–; State Rep. of Pres. of Georgia to Kakhetia Dist 1995–2000; Minister of State 2000–02; mem. Int. Acad. of Communications. *Publications:* over 50 scientific works on probability theory and statistical math., application of math. methods to humanitarian and nat. science fields, econ. geography. *Address:* c/o Office of the State Minister of Republic of Georgia, Ingorka str. 7, 380034 Tbilisi, Georgia (Office).

ARTAMONOV, Sergey Pavlovich, DEcon; Russian educationalist; b. 10 Feb. 1947, Moscow; ed Higher Mil. School, Diplomatic Acad.; First Vice-Pres. Acad. of Russian Comprehensive Encyclopaedia; Exec. Sec. Acad. of Mil. Sciences; Rector Inst. of Professionalization; Dir Centre of Econ.-Legal Educ.; Dir.-Gen. Int. Inst. of Marketing, Vice-Pres. Int. Commercial Univ.; Councillor Expert Council, State Duma 1996–; mem., Sec.-Gen. Russian Acad. of Natural Sciences; Vice-Pres. Int. Acad. of Sciences; Vice-Pres. Int. Asscn of Writers; Dr hc (Dresden Acad. of Sciences); numerous awards and prizes. *Publications:* over 100 scientific works. *Leisure interest:* sport. *Address:* State Duma, Okhotny Ryad 1, 103265 Moscow, Russia (Office). *Telephone:* (095) 292-80-00 (Office); (095) 453-98-03 (Home).

ARTEH GHALIB, Omar; Somali politician; b. 1930, Hargeisa; s. of the late Arteh Ghalib and Sahra Sheikh Hassan; m. Shakri Jirdeh Hussein 1954; six s. six d.; ed St Paul's Coll., Cheltenham, UK and Univ. of Bristol; Teacher 1946–49; Headmaster, various elementary schools 1949–54; Vice-Principal, Intermediate School, Sheikh, Somalia 1954–56; Principal, Intermediate School, Gabileh 1958; Officer in charge of Adult Educ. 1959; District Commr in Public Admin. 1960–61; First Sec. Somali Embassy, Moscow 1961–62; Rapporteur, Special Cttee on South-West Africa, UN 1962–63; Counsellor, Perm. Mission of Somalia at UN 1964; Amb. to Ethiopia 1965–68; mem. Somali Nat. Assembly 1969; Sec. of State for Foreign Affairs 1969–76; Minister of Culture and Higher Education 1976–78, in the President's Office 1978–80; mem. Cttee for Social and Political Thought 1976–; Speaker, People's Ass. 1982–91; Prime Minister of Somalia 1991; attended numerous OAU Summit and Ministerial Confs.; numerous awards and decorations. *Publications include:* Back from the Lion of Judah. *Leisure interests:* reciting the Koran, writing, poetry, horse riding, social welfare activities. *Address:* c/o Office of the President, People's Palace, Mogadishu, Somalia.

ARTÉS-GÓMEZ, Mariano; Spanish professor of mechanics; b. 5 March 1947, Murcia; s. of Mariano Artés and Elisa Gómez; m. María José Caselles 1973; three s.; ed Universidad Politécnica de Madrid, Int. Centre for Theoretical Physics, Trieste; Asst Prof. of Mechanics, Universidad Politécnica de Madrid 1971–78, Assoc. Prof. 1979–80; Prof. Universidad de Oviedo 1980–81; Prof. and Head of Dept of Applied Math., Universidad Nacional de Educación a Distancia 1981–, Vice-Rector for Research 1986, Dean of Faculty of Industrial Eng 1987, Rector 1987–96; mem. Asocs Española de Informática y Automática, Asocs Española de Ingeniería Mecánica, Soc. for Research into Higher Educ. (UK); Premio Citema 1975, Premio Extraordinario de Doctorado 1977, Laurel de Murcia 1987. *Publications:* El Papel Instrumental de la Informática en el Proceso Educativo 1975, Dinámica de Sistemas 1979, Mecánica 1982, numerous articles on informatics in educ. and applied mechanics. *Leisure interests:* music, reading. *Address:* Universidad Nacional de Educación a Distancia, Ciudad Universitaria, 28040 Madrid, Spain. *Telephone:* (1) 3986420. *Fax:* (1) 3986536.

ARTHUIS, Jean Raymond Francis Marcel; French politician; b. 7 Oct. 1944, Saint-Martin du Bois, Maine-et-Loire; s. of Raymond Arthuis and Marthe Cotin; m. Brigitte Lafont 1971; one s. one d.; ed Coll. Saint-Michel, Château-Gontier, Ecole Supérieure de Commerce, Nantes and Inst. d'Etudes Politiques, Paris; chartered accountant, Paris 1971–86; Mayor of Château-Gontier 1971–; mem. Conseil, Gen., Mayenne, Château-Gontier canton 1976–, Pres. 1992–; Senator from Mayenne (Centrist Group) 1983–86, 1988–95; Sec. of State, Ministry of Social Affairs and Employment 1986–87, Ministry of Econ., Finance and Privatization 1987–88; Spokesman on Budget in Senate 1992–95; Minister of Econ. Devt and Planning May–Aug. 1995, of Econ. and Finance 1995–97; Vice-Pres. Force Démocrate (fmrly Centre des démocrates sociaux) 1995–; Vice-Pres. Nouvelle Union pour la Démocratie Française (UDF) 1998; Pres. Union centriste du Sénat 1998; Chevalier du Mérite Agricole. *Publications:* Justice sinistrée, Démocratie en danger (co-author) 1991, Les Délocalisations et l'emploi 1993, Dans les coulisses de Bercy, Le Cinquième pouvoir 1998. *Address:* Mairie, 53200 Château-Gontier (Office); Conseil général de la Mayenne, 39 rue Mazagran, BP 1429, 53014 Laval cédex (Office); 8 rue René Homo, 53200 Château-Gontier, France (Home).

ARTHUR, James Greig, PhD, FRS, FRSC; Canadian professor of mathematics; b. 18 May 1944, Hamilton; s. of John G. Arthur and Katherine (née Scott) Arthur; m. Dorothy P. Helm 1972; two s.; ed Univ. of Toronto, Yale

Univ.; Instructor Princeton Univ. 1970–72; Asst Prof. Yale Univ. 1972–76; Prof. Duke Univ. 1976–79, Univ. of Toronto 1979–; Sloan Fellow 1975–77, Stracie Memorial Fellowship 1982–84; Synge Award in Math. 1987, Henry Marshall Tory Medal 1997, Canadian Gold Medal for Science and Eng 1999. *Publications:* numerous scientific papers and articles. *Leisure interests:* tennis, squash, golf. *Address:* Department of Mathematics, University of Toronto, Toronto, M5S 3G3, Canada (Office); 23 Woodlawn Avenue West, Toronto, Ont., M4V 1G6, Canada (Home). *Telephone:* (416) 978-4254.

ARTHUR, Rt. Hon. Owen, PC; Barbadian politician and economist; b. 17 Oct. 1949; m. Beverley Jeanne Batchelor 1978; ed Harrison Coll., Univ. of W Indies, Cave Hill, Univ. of W Indies, Mona; Research Asst, Univ. of W Indies, Jamaica 1973; Asst Econ. Planner, Chief Econ. Planner Nat. Planning Agency, Jamaica 1974–79; Dir of Econs Jamaica Bauxite Inst. 1979–81; Chief Project Analyst Ministry of Finance, Barbados 1981–83; lecturer Dept of Man. Univ. of W Indies, Cave Hill 1986, Resident Fellow 1993; Senator 1983–84; Parl. Sec. Ministry of Finance 1985–86; Chair. Barbados Labour Party (BLP) July 1993–96; Prime Minister of Barbados, Minister of Defence and Security, Finance and Econ. Affairs and for the Civil Service Sept. 1994–. *Publications:* The Commercialisation of Technology in Jamaica 1979, Energy and Mineral Resource Development in the Jamaican Bauxite Industry 1981, The IMF and Economic Stabilisation Policies in Barbados 1984. *Leisure interests:* gardening, cooking. *Address:* Office of the Prime Minister, Government Headquarters, Bay Street, St Michael, Barbados. *Telephone:* 426-3179. *Fax:* 436-9280. *E-mail:* info@primeminister.gov.bb (Office).

ARTHURS, Harry William, OC, O.O., LLM, FRSC; Canadian barrister, professor of law and academic; b. 9 May 1935, Toronto; s. of Leon Arthurs and Ellen H. (Dworkin) Arthurs; m. Penelope Geraldine Ann Milnes 1974; two s.; ed Univ. of Toronto, Harvard Univ., USA; Asst, Assoc. then full Prof. of Law, Osgoode Hall Law School, York Univ., Ont. 1961–, Dean of Law School 1972–77, Pres. York Univ. 1985–92, Pres. Emer. 1992–, Univ. Prof. 1995–; Assoc. Canada Inst. of Advanced Research 1995–98; mediator and arbitrator in labour disputes 1962–85; author, lecturer 1961–; Bencher, Law Soc. of Upper Canada 1979–83; mem. Econ. Council of Canada 1978–81; Chair. Consultative Group, Research and Educ. in Law 1980–84; Chair. Council of Ont. Univs. 1987–89; Hon. LLD (Sherbrooke, McGill and Brock Univs., Law Soc. of Upper Canada); Hon. D.Litt (Lethbridge). *Publications:* Industrial Relations and Labour Law in Canada (co-author) 1984, Law and Learning (Report on Legal Research and Education in Canada) 1984, Without the Law: Administrative Justice and Legal Pluralism in Nineteenth Century England 1985. *Address:* Osgoode Law School, York University, 4700 Keele Street, North York, Ont., M3J 1P3 (Office); 11 Hillcrest Park, Toronto, Ont., M4X 1E8, Canada (Home). *Telephone:* (416) 736-5407 (Office). *Fax:* (416) 736-5736.

ARTHUS-BERTRAND, Yann Marie; French photographer; b. 13 March 1946, Paris; s. of Claude Arthus-Bertrand and Jeanne Arthus-Bertrand (née Schildge); m. 2nd Anne Thual 1984; three s.; worked on wildlife reserve, Allier River 1966–76; balloon pilot, Masai Mara Reserve, Kenya 1976–78; photographer, specializing in aerial photography 1976–; f. Altitude agency (aerial photographs) 1991. *Art exhibitions:* La terre vue du ciel, Musée du Luxembourg, Paris 2000. *Publications:* more than 60 books of photographs including La terre vue du ciel (The Earth from the Air) 1999, 365 jours pour réfléchir sur la terre 2000. *Address:* Altitude, 30 rue des Favorites, 75015 Paris, France (Office). *E-mail:* yannab@club-internet.fr (Office).

ARTSCHWAGER, Richard Ernst; American artist; b. 26 Dec. 1923, Washington, DC; m. 1st Elfriede Wejmelka 1947 (divorced 1970); one d.; m. 2nd Catherine Kord 1972 (divorced 1989); one s. one d.; m. 3rd. Molly O'Gorman (divorced 1993); one s. one d.; m. 4th Ann Sebring 1995; ed Cornell Univ.; studied with Amedee Ozenfant, New York 1949–50; baby photographer 1950–53; cabinetmaker 1953–65; has exhibited with Richard Bellamy and Leo Castelli also many group and one-man shows in USA and Europe 1963–. *Publication:* The Hydraulic Door Check 1967. *Address:* P.O. Box 12, Hudson, NY 12534-0012, USA.

ARTZT, Alice Josephine, BA; American classical guitarist, writer and teacher; b. 16 March 1943, Philadelphia, Pa; d. of Harriett Green Artzt and Maurice G. Artzt; m. Bruce B. Lawton, Jr; ed Columbia Univ. and studied composition with Darius Milhaud and guitar with Julian Bream, Ida Presti and Alexandre Lagoya; taught guitar at Mannes Coll. of Music, New York 1966–69, Trenton State Univ. 1977–80; worldwide tours as soloist 1969–; f. Alice Artzt Guitar Trio (with M. Rutscho and R. Burley) 1989; toured in duo with R. Burley; fmr mem. Bd of Dirs Guitar Foundation of America (Chair. 1986–89); several Critics' Choice awards. *Recordings include:* The Glory of the Guitar, Virtuoso Romantic Guitar, Tributes, Variations, Passacaglias and Chaconnes, American Music of the Stage and Screen, Alice Artzt Classic Guitar, Alice Artzt Plays Original Works. *Publications:* The Art of Practicing, The International GFA Guitarists' Cookbook (Ed.), Rythmic Mastery 1997; numerous articles in guitar and music periodicals. *Leisure interests:* hi-fi, travel, Chaplin movies. *Address:* 51 Hawthorne Avenue, Princeton, NJ 08540, USA. *Telephone:* (609) 921-6629. *Fax:* (609) 924-0091. *E-mail:* guitartzt@aol .com (Home).

ARTZT, Edwin Lewis, B.J.; American business executive; b. 15 April 1930, New York; s. of William Artzt and Ida Artzt; m. Ruth N. Martin 1950; one s. four d.; ed Univ. of Oregon; Account Exec. Glasser Gailey Advertising Agency, Los Angeles 1952–53; joined Proctor & Gamble Co., Cincinnati 1953, Brand Man. Advertising Dept 1956–58, Assoc. Brand Promotion Man. 1958–60, Brand Promotion Man. 1960, 1962–65, Copy Man. 1960–62, Advertisement Man. Paper Products Div. 1965–68, Man. Products Food Div. 1968–69, Vice-Pres. 1969, Vice-Pres., Acting Man. Coffee Div. 1970, Vice-Pres., Group Exec. 1970–75, Dir 1972–75, 1980–95; Group Vice-Pres. Procter & Gamble Co., Europe, Belgium 1975–80; Pres. Procter & Gamble Int. 1980–89, Chair., CEO 1995–99; Vice-Chair. Procter & Gamble Co. 1980–89, Chair. 1989–95, CEO 1995–99; Exec. Dir Barilla G.E.R. SpA 1995–; Martin Luther King, Jr Salute to Greatness Award 1995, Leadership Conf. on Civil Rights Pvt. Sector Leadership Award 1995. *Address:* 9495 Whitegate Lane, Cincinnati, OH 45243, USA (Home).

ARUTIUNIAN, Alexander Grigor; Armenian composer; b. 23 Sept. 1920, Yerevan; s. of Gregori and Eleanor Arutiunian; m. Irina Odenova Tamara 1950; one s. one d.; ed Yerevan Conservatory and Workshop at House of Armenian Culture, Moscow; mem. CPSU 1952–91; Artistic Dir Armenian Philharmonic 1954–; Prof., Yerevan Conservatory 1962–; USSR State Prize 1949, People's Artist of the USSR 1970, Armenian State Prizes 1970, 1986, Kentucky Coll. Orpheus Award 1983, Khachaturian Prize 1986. *Compositions include:* Cantata on the Motherland 1949, Trumpet concerto 1950, Concertino for piano and orchestra 1951, Symphony 1957, Legend of the Armenian People for soloists, choir and orchestra 1961, French Horn concerto 1962, Concertino for cello 1964, Sinfonietta 1966, Sayat-Nova (opera) 1969, vocal series Memorial to Mother 1970, Piano concertos 1971, 1983, Reverend Beggars (musical comedy) 1972, Theme and Variations for trumpet and orchestra, Rhapsody for piano, percussion and string orchestra 1974, Oboe concerto 1977, Symphony for choir and percussion 1982, Armenian Scenes (brass quintet) 1984, concertos for flute and string orchestra 1985, for violin and string orchestra 1988, for trombone and orchestra 1990, for tuba and orchestra 1991, Suite for clarinet, violin and piano 1992, Rhapsody for trumpet and wind orchestra 1992, Suite for oboe, clarinet and piano 1994; chamber and vocal music, music for theatre and cinema. *Leisure interest:* memoirs. *Address:* Demirchian str. 25, Apt. 19, 375002 Yerevan, Armenia. *Telephone:* (2) 524785. *Fax:* (2) 151938.

ARUTYUNYAN, Khosrov Melikovich; Armenian politician; b. 30 May 1948, Yerevan; m.; two c.; ed Yerevan Polytech. Inst.; Head of Lab., Head of Dept, Dir Ashtarak br., Byurokan Observatory 1977–82; lecturer, Yerevan Polytechnic Inst. 1978–82; Dir knitted goods factory 1983–87, Chair. Municipal Cttee Charentsavan Dist 1991; mem. Armenian Supreme Soviet 1990–92; Chair. Comm. on problems of local self-governing 1990–92; mem. Parl. 1993–; Prime Minister of Armenia 1992–93; Deputy Chair. State Legal Comm., Adviser to Prime Minster 1995–; Pres. Nat. Ass. 1998; Minister for Territorial Govt 1999–2000. *Address:* National Assembly, 19 Marshal Bughramyan Avenue, 375095 Yerevan, Armenia. *Telephone:* (2) 524614. *Fax:* (2) 529826.

ARYAL, Krishna Raj, M.ED., MA; Nepalese politician, educationist and diplomatist; b. Dec. 1928, Kathmandu; m. Shanta Laxmi 1956; one s.; ed Durbar High School, Tri-Chandra Coll., Allahabad Univ., India, Univ. of Oregon, USA Lecturer, Nat. Teachers' Training Centre 1954–56; Prof. Coll. of Educ., Dir Publs Govt Educ. Devt Project 1956–59; Ed. Education Quarterly 1956–59, Nabin Shikshya 1956–59; Founder, Admin. and Prin. Shri Ratna Rajya Laxmi Girls' Coll. 1961–71; Asst Minister for Educ. 1971–72, Minister of State 1972–73, Minister 1973–75, Minister of Foreign Affairs 1975–79; Amb. to France also accred to Spain, Italy, Portugal and Israel and Perm. Del. to UNESCO 1980–84; Chair. Asian Group and mem. Bureau Group 77, UNESCO 1982–83; Hon. mem. Raj Sabha 1985–90, Rastriya Panchayat (unicameral legis.) 1986–90; fmr Sec. Cricket Asscn of Nepal; Chair. Brahmacharya Ashram; Exec. mem. World Hindu Fed.; Gorakha Dakhinbahu (1st Class) Grand Cordon of Yugoslav Star, Order of the Rising Sun, 1st Class (Japan), Grand Officier, Order Nat. du Mérite (France), Order of Civil Merit, 1st Class (Spain) and other decorations. *Publications include:* Monarchy in the Making of Nepal (in English), Education for the Development of Nepal (in English), The Science of Education (in Nepalese). *Address:* 17/93 Gaihiri Dhara, Kathmandu, Nepal (Home).

ARYSTANBEKOVA, Akmaral K., PhD; Kazakhstan diplomatist; b. 12 May 1948, Almaty; ed Kazakh State Univ., Almaty; research work in chem., Kazakh State Univ. 1978–83; Deputy Supreme Soviet of Kazakh Soviet Socialist Repub., mem. Presidium Supreme Soviet 1985–90; Foreign Minister 1978–91; Rep. of Kazakhstan at Perm. Mission of the fmr USSR 1991–92, Perm. Rep. of Kazakhstan to UN 1992–99; Amb. to France 1999–; Deputy Chair. Kazakh Friendship Soc. 1983–84; Chair. Presidium Kazakh Soc. for Friendship and Cultural Relations with Foreign Countries 1984–89; Kurmat Order 1996. *Publication:* United Nations and Kazakhstan 2002. *Address:* Embassy of Kazakhstan, 59 rue Pierre Charron, 75008 Paris, France. *Telephone:* 1-45-61-52-00 (Office). *Fax:* 1-45-61-52-01 (Office).

ARZALLUZ ANTÍA, Xabier; Spanish politician and lawyer; b. 1932; fmr Jesuit priest; mem. Euzko Alderdi Jeltzalea/Partido Nacionalista Vasco (EAJ/PNV) (Basque Nationalist Party) 1968–, now Pres. *Address:* Ibáñez de Bilbao 16 (Sabin Etxea), 48001 Bilbao, Spain (Office). *Telephone:* (94) 40359400 (Office). *Fax:* (94) 40359412 (Office). *E-mail:* prensa@eaj-pnv.com (Office). *Website:* www.eaj-pnv.com (Office).

ARZÚ IRIGOYEN, Alvaro Enrique; Guatemalan politician; Dir. Guatemalan Tourist Inst. 1978–81; Mayor of Guatemala City 1986–91; unsuccessful presidential cand. 1990; leader Partido de Avanzada Nacional (PAN) 1991–; Minister of Foreign Relations 1991; Pres. of Guatemala 1996–2000.

Address: Partido de Avanzada Nacional (PAN), 7A Avda 10-38, Zona 9, Guatemala City, Guatemala (Office). *Telephone:* 334-1702 (Office). *Website:* www.pan.org.gt (Office).

ARZUMANYAN, Aleksander Robertovich; Armenian politician and diplomatist; b. 24 Dec. 1959, Yerevan; m.; two c.; ed Yerevan State Univ.; Eng Yerevan Research Inst. of Automatic Systems of City Man. 1985–88; Dir Information Cen. Armenian Nat. Movt 1989–90; Asst Chair. of Supreme Council of Armenia 1990–91; Rep. of Armenia to N America 1991–92; Chargé d'affaires to USA 1992–93; Perm. Rep. to UN 1992; rank of Amb. 1992; took part and headed dels. of Armenia to int. meetings; elected Deputy Chair. 49th Gen. UN Ass., concurrently mem. Gen. Cttee of UN and mem. Appellation Cttee on resolutions of Admin. Court of UN 1994; Chair. Regional Group for E Europe 1992–96; Minister of Foreign Affairs 1996–98. *Address:* c/o Mashal Bagramyan str. 10, 375019 Yerevan, Armenia.

ASADOV, Eduard Arkadevich; Russian poet; b. 7 Sept. 1923, Merv, Turkmenistan SSR; s. of Arkady Asadov and Lidya Asadova; m. 2nd Galina Asadova 1961; one s.; ed Gorky Literary Inst., Moscow; Red Army 1941, seriously wounded and lost sight 1944; started publishing 1948; mem. CPSU 1951–91. *Publications:* Again into the Line 1948, Bright Roads 1951, Snowy Evening 1956, The Soldiers Have Returned from the War 1957, Galina 1960, Lyrical Limits 1962, I Love Forever 1965, Be Happy, Dreamers 1966, Isle of Romance 1969, Goodness 1972, I Fight, I Believe, I Love 1983, The Dream of Centuries 1985, The Highest Duty 1986, Collected Works (3 Vols) 1987–88, Fates and Hearts 1989, Letter from the Battle Front 1993, Never Surrender, People 1997, Don't Dare To Beat a Man (novel) 1998, Don't Give up the Beloved 2000. *Leisure interests:* music, especially gypsy songs, books, collecting funny names of streets and people. *Address:* Astrahansky per., 5, Apt. 78, Moscow 129010, Russia. *Telephone:* (095) 280-14-58.

ASAMOAH, Obed Y., JSD; Ghanaian politician and lawyer; b. 6 Feb. 1936, Likpe Bala, Volta Region; s. of William Asamoah and Monica Asamoah; m. Yvonne Wood 1964; two s. one d.; ed Achimota Secondary School, Woolwich Polytechnic, London, King's Coll. London and Columbia Univ., New York; called to the Bar, Middle Temple, London 1960; upon return to Ghana practised as solicitor and advocate of Supreme Court of Ghana; lecturer, Faculty of Law, Univ. of Ghana, Legon 1965–69; fmr Chair. Bd of Dirs of Ghana Film Industry Corpn, Ghana Bauxite Co.; mem. Constituent Ass. which drafted Constitution for Second Repub. of Ghana 1969; elected to Parl. (Nat. Alliance of Liberals) 1969; mem. Constituent Ass. which drafted third Republican Constitution 1979; Gen. Sec. United Nat. Convention (UNC) 1979, All People's Party (APP) 1981; Sec. for Foreign Affairs 1982–93; Minister of Foreign Affairs 1993–97; Attorney-Gen. and Minister of Justice 1993–2001; mem. Ghana Bar Asscn; has served on several int. and public orgs; Order of the Star of Ghana 2001. *Publications:* The Legal Significance of the Declaration of the General Assembly of the United Nations 1967; articles in legal journals. *Leisure interests:* reading, farming. *Address:* P.O. Box 14581, Accra, Ghana. *Telephone:* (21) 668414 (Home).

ASANBAYEV, Erik Magzumovich, DEcon; Kazakhstan politician; b. 10 March 1936, Baygabul, Turgai Dist; m.; two c.; ed Kazakh Univ.; economist, Ministry of Finance 1958–59; lecturer Kazakh Univ. 1959–63; Head of Dept, Inst. of Econs 1963–67; Head of Dept, Deputy Minister of Finance 1967–75; mem. CPSU 1967–91; Sr posts in CP and Govt 1975–88; Deputy Chair. Council of Ministers 1988–89; Sec. Cen. Cttee Kazakh CP 1989–90; Chair. Kazakh SSR Supreme Soviet 1991; joined Socialist Party of Kazakhstan 1991; Vice-Pres. Kazakhstan 1991–96; Amb. to Germany 1996–2000; Rector Diplomatic Acad. 2000–. *Address:* Ministry of Foreign Affairs, Diplomatic Academy, Astana, Kazakhstan.

ASANTE, Samuel Kwadwo Boaten, LLM, JSD; Ghanaian lawyer and international official; b. 11 May 1933, Asokore; s. of Daniel Y. Asante and Mary Baafi; m. Philomena Margaret Aidoo 1961; two s. three d.; ed Achimota School, Univs of Nottingham and London and Yale Univ. Law School; State Attorney in the Ministry of Justice of Ghana 1960–61; Lecturer in Law and Acting Head of Law Dept, Univ. of Ghana 1961–65; Lecturer, Leeds Univ., UK 1965–66; Attorney World Bank, Washington, DC 1966–69; Adjunct Prof. of Law, Howard Univ. Law School, Washington, DC 1967–69; Solicitor-Gen. of Ghana 1969–74; mem. Arbitration Panel, Int. Cen. for Settlement of Investment Disputes, Washington, DC 1971–; Chair. Public Agreements Review Cttee of Ghana 1972–77; Deputy Attorney-Gen. of Ghana 1974–77; Chief Legal Adviser, UN Comm. on Transnational Corpns, New York 1977–83, Dir 1983–92; Dir UN Legal Advisory Services for Devt 1992–; Chair. Cttee of Experts on Ghana Constitution 1991; Dir Int. Third World Legal Studies Asscn, New York; mem. Bd Dirs Int. Devt Law Inst., Rome; Taylor Lecturer, Lagos Univ. 1978; Consultant, Commonwealth Secr., African Devt Bank and UNITAR; Guest Lecturer numerous univs and institutions world-wide; Guest Fellow, Berkeley Coll., Yale Univ. 1964–65; fmr Sterling, Fulbright and Aggrey Fellow; Fellow of World Acad. of Arts and Sciences 1975, Ghana Acad. of Arts and Sciences 1976; Visiting Fellow, Clare Hall, Cambridge Univ. 1978–79, Life mem.; Visiting Prof., Temple Univ. Law School, Philadelphia 1976; patron Int. Centre for Public Law, Inst. of Advanced Legal Studies, London Univ.; mem. Int. Bar Asscn; mem. Exec. Council, American Soc. of Int. Law 1979, mem. Gen. Legal Council, Ghana; mem. Advisory Bd, Foreign Investment Law Journal-ICSID Review; Ghana Book Award. *Publications:* Property Law and Social Goals in Ghana 1976, Transnational Investment Law and National Development 1979 and various articles in law journals.

Leisure interests: tennis, golf, reading biographies. *Address:* United Nations, Room DC2-1320, New York, NY 10017 (Office); 412 Pinebrook Boulevard, New Rochelle, NY 10804, USA (Home).

ÅSBRINK, Erik, BSc, BA; Swedish fmr politician and business executive; b. 1 Feb. 1947, Stockholm; m. Anne-Marie Lindgren; three c.; ed Univ. of Stockholm, Stockholm School of Econs; worked at Inst. for Soviet and E European Econ. Affairs 1972; Nat. Inst. of Econ. Research 1972–74; Ministry of Finance 1974–76; Ministry of the Budget 1976–78; Research Sec., parl. group of Social Democratic Party (SDP) 1978–82; Under-Sec. of State, Ministry of Finance 1982–90; Minister for Fiscal and Financial Affairs, Ministry of Finance 1990–91, Minister of Finance 1996–99; Man. Dir Vasakronan AB 1993–, Pres. –1996; mem. Bd First Nat. Pension Insurance Fund 1982–85; Chair. Lantbrukskredit AB 1983–85; Chair. State Housing Finance Corpn 1984–85; Chair. Governing Bd Sveriges Riksbank 1985–90; mem. Bd Fourth Nat. Pension Insurance Fund 1985–90; Vice-Chair. Systembolaget AB 1986–90; mem. Bd AB Vin & Sprit AB (Swedish Wine and Spirits Corpn) 1986–90, 1993–, AB Trav & Galopp 1989–90, Sparbanken Sverige AB 1991–93; Chair. Sparbanken Första 1992, Confortia AB 1993–, Swedish Bond Promotion 1993–; mem. Bd ABB Investment Man. 1993–, SkandiaBanken 1994–, Swedish Concert Hall Foundation 1995–, SNS, Centre for Business and Policy Studies 1995–. *Address:* c/o Ministry of Finance, Drottninggt. 21, 103 33 Stockholm, Sweden.

ASGHAR, Muhammad, LLB, DPhil; French (born Pakistani) professor of nuclear physics; b. 7 June 1936, Pakistan; s. of Muhammad Fazal and Bibi Fazal; m.; one c.; ed Univ. of Punjab, Oxford Univ.; with Pakistan Inst. of Tech., Nilore, also worked at atomic energy research stations at Harwell, UK and Saclay, France; Assoc. Prof. Univ. of Bordeaux 1968–71; physicist Inst. Laue-Langevin (ILL), Grenoble 1971–78, CCR Euratom, Ispra 1978–80, Centre d'Etudes Nucléaires, Grenoble 1980–81; Prof. of Physics Houari Boumedienne Univ., Algiers 1981–94, Inst. des Sciences Nucléaires, Grenoble 1994–; specialist in nuclear fission, has coordinated int. teams in major experiments at high flux nuclear reactor, ILL, Grenoble; Fellow Islamic Acad. of Sciences 1998. *Publications:* c. 200 research papers. *Leisure interest:* writing poetry in English, French, Persian and Urdu. *Address:* Institut des Sciences Nucléaires, 3 avenue des Martyrs, 38026 Grenoble Cedex (Office); 12 rue des Aberlles, 38240 Meylan, France (Home). *Telephone:* (4) 76-28-40-00 (Office); (4) 76-18-00-22 (Home). *Fax:* (4) 76-28-40-04 (Office).

ÁSGRÍMSSON, Halldór; Icelandic politician; b. 8 Sept. 1947, Vopnafjördur; s. of Ásgrímur Halldórsson and Guðrún Ingólfsdóttir; m. Sigurjóna Sigurðardóttir; three d.; ed Co-operative's Commercial Coll. and commerce univs. in Bergen and Copenhagen; Certified Public Accountant 1970; Lecturer in Auditing and Accounting, Univ. of Iceland 1973–75; mem. Parl. 1974–78, 1979–; mem. Bd Cen. Bank of Iceland 1976–83, Chair. 1981–83; mem. Nordic Council 1977–78, 1979–83, 1991–95, Chair. 1982–83, Chair. Icelandic Del. 1982–83, mem. Presidium 1991–94, Chair. Liberal Group 1992–94; Minister of Fisheries 1983–91, of Nordic Co-operation 1985–87, 1995, of Justice and Ecclesiastical Affairs 1988–89, of Foreign Affairs and External Trade 1995–; Vice-Chair. Progressive Party 1980–94, Chair. 1994–; Vice-Pres. Liberal Int. 1994–; Kt of Order of Falcon of Iceland. *Address:* Ministry for Foreign Affairs, Raudarárstíg 25, 150 Reykjavik (Office); c/o Progressive Party, P.O. Box 453, IS-121 Reykjavik, Iceland. *Telephone:* 5609900 (Office); 5624400. *Fax:* 5622373 (Office); 5404301. *E-mail:* external@utn.stjr.is (Office). *Website:* www.mfa.is (Office).

ASH, Sir Eric Albert, Kt, CBE, PhD, FRS, FCGI, FIEE, FIEEE, FInstP, FREng; British professor of physical electronics; b. 31 Jan. 1928, Berlin, Germany; s. of Walter Ash and Dorothea Ash (née Schwarz); m. Clare Babb 1954; five d.; ed Univ. Coll. School and Imperial Coll., London; Research Fellow, Stanford Univ. 1952–54; Research Asst, Queen Mary Coll., London 1954–55; Research Engineer, Standard Telecommunications Labs. Ltd 1955–63; Sr Lecturer, Univ. Coll, London 1963–65, Reader 1965–67, Prof. of Electrical Eng 1967–80, Pender Prof. and Head, Dept of Electronic and Electrical Eng 1980–85, Prof. of Electrical Eng 1993–97, now Prof. Emer.; Rector, Imperial Coll., London 1985–93; Dir (non-exec.) British Telecom 1987–93, Student Loans Co. PLC 1994–; Chair. BBC Science Advisory Cttee 1987–, Chair. of Council, Vice-Pres. Royal Inst. 1995– (fmr Sec., Man.); Treasurer, Royal Soc. 1997–2002; Chair. HVCo Ltd; Trustee Science Museum 1987–93, Wolfson Foundation 1988–; hon. degrees from Aston, Leicester, Edinburgh, NY Polytech., INPG Grenoble, Westminster, Sussex, Glasgow, Surrey Univs and Chinese Univ. of Hong Kong; Faraday Medal (IEE) 1980, Royal Medal (Royal Soc.) 1986; Nat. Order of Merit (France) 1990. *Publications:* papers on topics of physical electronics in various eng and physics journals. *Leisure interests:* music, skiing, writing. *Address:* c/o Royal Society, 6 Carlton House Terrace, London, SW1Y 5AG, England. *Telephone:* (20) 7451-2673 (Office); (20) 7607-4989 (Home). *Fax:* (20) 7451-2674 (Office); (20) 7700-7446 (Home). *E-mail:* eric.ash@royalsoc.ac.uk (Office); eric_ash99@yahoo.co.uk (Home).

ASH, Roy Lawrence, MBA; American industrialist; b. Roy Lawrence Ash, 20 Oct. 1918, Los Angeles, Calif.; s. of Charles K. Ash and Fay (Dickinson) Ash; m. Lila M. Hornbek 1943; three s. two d.; ed Harvard Univ.; Private to Capt., USAF 1942–46; Chief Financial Officer, Hughes Aircraft Co. 1949–53; Co-founder and Dir, Litton Industries Inc. 1953–72; Pres. 1961–72; mem. Bd of Dirs Bankamerica Corpn 1968–72, 1976–91, Bank of America NT and SA 1964–72, 1978–91, Global Marine Inc. 1965–72, 1975–81, Pacific Mutual Life Insurance Co. 1965–72, Sara Lee Corpn 1979–90; Dir Los Angeles World

Affairs Council 1968–72, (Pres. 1970–72), 1978–91; Chair. President's Advisory Council on Exec. Org. 1969–71; Asst to the Pres. of the USA for Exec. Man. 1972–75; Dir US Office of Man. and Budget 1973–75; Chair. and CEO AM Int. 1976–81; Co-Chair. Japan–Calif. Asscn 1965–72, 1980–81; Vice-Chair. Los Angeles Olympic Organizing Cttee 1979–84; mem. Bd and Chair. LA Music Center Opera 1988–93; mem. The Business Roundtable 1977–81, Bd of US Chamber of Commerce 1979–85; mem. Bd of Trustees, Calif.Inst. of Tech. 1967–72; Trustee, Cttee for Econ. Devt 1970–72, 1975–; Hon. LLD (Pepperdine) 1976; Kt of Malta; Horatio Alger Award 1966. *Address:* 1900 Avenue of the Stars, #1600, Los Angeles, CA 90067-4407 (Office); 655 Funchal Road, Los Angeles, CA 90077, USA (Home). *Telephone:* (310) 553-6244 (Office); (310) 472-6661 (Home). *Fax:* (310) 203-9530 (Office).

ASHBERY, John Lawrence, MA; American author and critic; b. 28 July 1927, Rochester, NY; s. of Chester F. Ashbery and Helen L. Ashbery; ed Deerfield Acad., Mass., Harvard Coll., Columbia and New York Univs; copywriter, Oxford Univ. Press, New York 1951–54, McGraw-Hill Book Co. 1954–55; lived in France 1955–57, 1958–65; art critic European edn New York Herald Tribune 1960–65; Paris corresp. Art News, NY 1964–65, Exec. Ed. 1965–72; art critic, Art International, Lugano 1961–64; ed. Locus Solus 1960–62, Art and Literature, Paris 1963–66; Prof. of English and co-Dir MFA Program in Creative Writing, Brooklyn Coll., NY 1974–90; Poetry Ed. Partisan Review, New York 1976–80; art critic, New York (magazine) 1978–80, Newsweek 1980–85; Chancellor American Acad. of Poets 1988–; leader, Foundation d'Art de la Napoule 1989; Charles P. Stevenson Prof. Bard Coll. 1990–; Officier, Légion d'honneur 2002; recipient of numerous awards and honours, including Pulitzer Prize 1975, MacArthur Award 1985, Gold Medal (Inst. of Arts and Letters) 1997. *Plays:* The Heroes 1952, The Compromise 1956, The Philosopher 1963, Three Plays 1978, Girls on the Run 1999, Your Name Here 2000, As Umbrellas Follow Rain 2001, Chinese Whispers 2002. *Poems include:* April Galleons 1987, Flow Chart 1992, Hotel Lautréamont 1992, And the Stars were Shining 1994, Can You Hear, Bird 1995, Wakefulness 1998. *Publications include:* non-fiction: Fairfield Porter 1983, R. B. Kitaj (with others) 1983, Reported Sightings: Art Chronicles 1957–1987 1989; novel: A Nest of Ninnies (with J. Schuyler) 1969. *Address:* c/o George Borchardt Inc., 136 East 57th Street, New York, NY 10022-2707; Bard College, Department of Languages and Literature, PO Box 5000, Annandale On Hudson, NY 12504-5000, USA.

ASHBURTON, 7th Baron, cr. 1835; John Francis Harcourt Baring, Kt, KG, KCVO, DL, FIB; British merchant banker; b. 2 Nov. 1928, London; s. of 6th Baron Ashburton and Hon. Doris Mary Therese Harcourt; m. 1st Susan Mary Renwick 1955 (divorced 1984); two s. two d.; m. 2nd Sarah Crewe 1987; ed Eton Coll. and Trinity Coll., Oxford; Chair. Barings PLC 1985–89 (Dir (non-exec.) 1989–94), Baring Bros. & Co. Ltd 1974–89 (a Man. Dir 1955–74); Dir Trafford Park Estates Ltd 1964–77; Royal Insurance Co. Ltd 1964–82, (Deputy Chair. 1975–82), Dir Outwich Investment Trust Ltd 1965–86 (Chair. 1968–86), British Petroleum Co. 1982–95 (Chair. 1992–95); Dir Dunlop Holdings 1981–84, Bank of England 1983–91, Baring Stratton Investment Trust PLC 1986–98 (Chair. 1986–98), Jaguar PLC 1989–91; mem. British Transport Docks Bd 1966–71; Vice-Pres. British Bankers Asscn 1977–81; mem. Pres.'s Cttee CBI 1976–79, Gen. Council CBI 1976–80; Chair. Accepting Houses Cttee 1977–81, NEDC Cttee on Finance for Industry 1980–87; Pres. Overseas Bankers Club 1977–78; Rhodes Trustee 1970–79, Chair. 1987–, Trustee Nat. Gallery 1981–87; Trustee and Hon. Treas. Police Foundation 1989–2000; mem. Exec. Cttee Nat. Art Collections Fund 1989–99; mem. Council Baring Foundation 1971–98, Chair. 1987–98; mem. Southampton Univ. Devt Trust 1986–96 (Chair. 1989–96); mem. Winchester Cathedral Trust 1989– (Chair. 1993–); Lord Warden of the Stannaries, Duchy of Cornwall 1990–94, Receiver-Gen. 1974–90; High Steward Winchester Cathedral 1991–; DL Hants. 1994–; Fellow, Eton Coll. 1982–97; Hon. Fellow, Hertford Coll., Oxford 1976, Trinity Coll., Oxford 1989. *Address:* 70 Bolingbroke Road, London, W14 0AH; Lake House, Northington, Alresford, Hants., SO24 9TG, England. *Telephone:* (1962) 738728 (Office).

ASHBY, Michael Farries, CBE, PhD, FRS, FREng; British professor of engineering materials; b. 20 Nov. 1935; s. of Lord Ashby and Elizabeth Helen Farries; m. Maureen Stewart 1962; two s. one d.; ed Campbell Coll., Belfast, Queens' Coll., Cambridge; Asst, Univ. of Göttingen, Fed. Repub. of Germany 1962–65; Asst Prof., Harvard Univ., USA 1965–69, Prof. of Metallurgy 1969–73; Prof. of Eng Materials, Univ. of Cambridge 1973–89, Royal Soc. Research Prof., Dept of Eng 1989–; Ed. Acta Metallurgica 1974–96, Progress in Materials Science 1995–; mem. Akad. der Wissenschaften zu Göttingen 1980; Hon. MA (Harvard) 1969. *Publications:* Deformation Mechanism Maps 1982, Engineering Materials (Vol. 1) 1989, (Vol. 2) 1996, Materials Selection in Design 1992, Cellular Solids 1997. *Leisure interests:* music, design. *Address:* 51 Maids Causeway, Cambridge, CB5 8DE, England. *Telephone:* (1223) 303015. *E-mail:* mfa2@eng.cam.ac.uk (Office).

ASHCROFT, Frances Mary, PhD, FRS, FMedSci; British professor of physiology; b. 15 Feb. 1952; d. of John Ashcroft and Kathleen Ashcroft; ed Talbot Heath School, Bournemouth; Girton Coll., Cambridge; MRC training fellow in Physiology, Leicester Univ. 1978–82; demonstrator in Physiology, Oxford Univ. 1982–85, EPA Cephalosporin Jr Research Fellow, Linacre Coll. 1983–85, Royal Soc. Univ. Research Fellow in Physiology 1985–90, Lecturer in Physiology, Christ Church 1986–87, Trinity Coll. 1988–89 (Sr Research Fellow 1992–); Tutorial Fellow in Medicine, St Hilda's Coll. 1990–91; Univ. Lecturer in Physiology 1990–96, Prof. of Physiology 1996–2001, Royal Soc. Research Prof. 2001–; G. L. Brown Prize Lecturer 1997, Peter Curran Lecturer, Yale Univ. 1999; mem. European Molecular Biology Org.; Frank Smart Prize, Cambridge Univ. 1974, Andrew Culworth Memorial Prize 1990, G. B. Morgagni Young Investigator Award 1991. *Publications:* Insulin-Molecular Biology to Pathology (jtly) 1992, Ion Channels and Disease 2000, Life at the Extremes 2000, and numerous articles in scientific journals. *Leisure interests:* reading, walking, writing, sailing. *Address:* University Laboratory of Physiology, Parks Road, Oxford, OX1 3PT, England (Office).

ASHCROFT, John David, JD; American politician; b. 9 May 1942, Chicago; m. Janet Elise; two s. one d.; ed Yale Univ. and Univ. of Chicago; admitted, Missouri State Bar, US Supreme Court Bar; Assoc. Prof. SW Missouri State Univ. Springfield; legal practice, Springfield, Mo. until 1973; State Auditor, Missouri 1973–75, Asst Attorney-Gen. 1975–77, Attorney-Gen. 1977–84; Gov. of Missouri 1985–93; Senator from Missouri 1995–2001; Attorney Gen. of USA 2001–; recordings as gospel singer; Republican. *Publications:* College Law for Business (with Janet Elise), It's the Law 1979. *Address:* Department of Justice, 950 Pennsylvania Avenue NW, Washington, DC 20530, USA. *Telephone:* (202) 514-2007 (Office). *Fax:* (202) 514-4371 (Office). *Website:* www.usdoj.gov (Office).

ASHCROFT, Baron (Life Peer), cr. 2000, of Chichester in the County of West Sussex; **Michael Ashcroft;** Belizean/British business executive and diplomatist; b. 4 March 1946; m.; three c.; ed St Catherine's Acad., Belize City, Norwich School, Mid-Essex Coll.; fmr Chair. and CEO BHI Corpn, Belize; Chair. and Chief Exec. ADT Ltd (fmrly Hawley Group Ltd and now Tyco Int. Ltd), Bermuda 1977–97; Trade and Investment Adviser to Belize High Comm. in London 1984–89; Belize's Itinerant Amb. Extraordinary and Plenipotentiary to EEC 1989; Econ. Adviser, Embassy of Belize, USA 1998–99; Perm. Rep. of Belize to UN 1998–2000; Dir Tyco 2002–; Treas. Conservative Party, UK 1998–2001; Head of Aspen Int. Devt Co.; fmr Chair. Bd of Trustees, Crimestoppers, UK, Industry in Educ., UK, Prospect Educational Trust, UK; fmr Chair. Michael A. Ashcroft Foundation, Belize and UK. *Address:* House of Lords, London, SW1A 0PW, England (Office).

ASHDOWN OF NORTON SUB-HAMDON, Baron (Life Peer), cr. 2001, of Norton Sub-Hamdon in the County of Somerset; **Sir Jeremy John Durham (Paddy) Ashdown,** KBE, PC; British politician; b. 27 Feb. 1941, Delhi, India; s. of John W. R. D. Ashdown and Lois A. Ashdown; m. Jane Courtenay 1961; one s. one d.; ed Bedford School; served Royal Marines 1959–71, Captain ; joined Diplomatic Service, First Sec. Mission to UN, Geneva 1971–76; Commercial Man.'s Dept, Westland Group 1976–78; Sr Man., Morlands Ltd 1978–81; employee Dorset Co. Council 1982–83; Parl. Spokesman for Trade and Industry 1983–86; Liberal/SDP Alliance Spokesman on Education and Science 1987; Liberal MP for Yeovil 1983–88, Liberal Democrat MP for Yeovil 1988–2001; Leader Liberal Democrats 1988–99; UN Int. High Rep. to Bosnia and Herzegovina May 2002–. *Publications:* Citizen's Britain: A Radical Agenda for the 1990s 1989, Beyond Westminster 1994, The Ashdown Diaries 1988–1997 2000, The Ashdown Diaries Vol. II 1997–1999 2001. *Leisure interests:* walking, gardening, wine making. *Address:* c/o House of Lords, London SW1A 0PW, England (Office).

ASHER, Jane; British actress, writer and businesswoman; b. 5 April 1946; d. of the late Richard A. J. Asher and of Margaret Eliot; m. Gerald Scarfe; two s. one d.; has appeared in numerous films, on TV and the London stage and has written several best-selling books; Proprietor Jane Asher Party Cakes Shop and Sugarcraft 1990–; designer, consultant for Sainsbury's cakes 1992–99; Pres. Nat. Autistic Soc.; Spokesperson and Consultant to Heinz Frozen Desserts 1999–2001; Cookware and Gift Food Designer for Debenhams 1998–; Creator of Home Baking Mixes for Victoria Foods 1999–. *Films include:* Greengage Summer, Masque of the Red Death, Alfie, Deep End, Henry the Eighth and his Six Wives, Success is the Best Revenge, Dreamchild, Paris By Night, Walter (TV), Murder Most Horrid 1991, Closing Numbers (TV) 1994, The Choir (TV) 1995. *Plays include:* Henceforward..., School for Scandal 1990, Making It Better 1992, The Shallow End 1997, Things We Do for Love 1998, House and Garden 2000, What the Butler Saw 2001. *Television includes:* Closing Numbers 1993, The Choir 1995, Good Living 1997, Crossroads 2003. *Publications include:* The Moppy Stories 1987, Keep Your Baby Safe 1988, Calendar of Cakes 1989, Eats for Treats 1990, Time to Play 1993, Jane Asher's Book of Cake Decorating Ideas 1993, The Longing (novel) 1996, The Question (novel) 1998, Losing It (novel) 2002. *Leisure interests:* reading, Times crossword. *Address:* c/o Actual Management, 7 Great Russell Street, London, WC1B 3NH; 24 Cale Street, London, SW3 3QU, England.

ASHIDA, Jun; Japanese fashion designer; b. 21 Aug. 1930, Kyoto; s. of Sadao Ashida and Ritsuko Ashida; m. Tomoko Tomita 1960; two d.; ed Tokyo High School; studied under Jun-ichi Nakahara 1948–52; consultant designer to Takashimaya Dept Store 1960; est. Jun Ashida Co. Ltd and Jun Ashida label 1963; exclusive designer to H.I.H. (now Empress) Crown Princess Michiko 1966–76, designs for several mems. Imperial family; presented first collection in Paris 1977; launched Miss Ashida and Jun Ashida for Men labels 1985–86; opened shop Paris 1989; designed uniforms for Japanese Pavilion, Expo World Fair, Seville 1992, All Nippon Airways, Fuji Xerox, Imperial Hotel, Nomura Securities, Idemitsu Kosan, Tokyo Kaijo, Japanese team at Olympic Games, Atlanta 1996; mem. Postal Service Council of Ministry of Posts and Telecommunications; FEC Award (Japan) 1971, Cavaliere, Ordine al Merito (Italy) 1989, Purple Ribbon Medal (Japan) 1991, Officier Ordre Nat. du Mérite

(France). *Publications:* Young Man (essays) 1986, Jun Ashida, 30 Years of Design 1993, Patches of Unshaven Beard 1998; articles on fashion and lifestyle in daily newspapers. *Leisure interests:* tennis, golf. *Address:* 1-3-3 Aobadai, Meguro-ku, Tokyo 153-8521, Japan. *Telephone:* (3) 3463-8631. *Fax:* (3) 3463-9638.

ASHIHARA, Yoshinobu, BA, MArch, DEng; Japanese architect; b. 7 July 1918, Tokyo; s. of Dr Nobuyuki Ashihara and Kikuko Fujita; m. Hatsuko Takahasi 1944; one s. one d.; ed Univ. of Tokyo and Harvard Univ. Graduate School; worked in architectural firms, Tokyo 1946–52; in Marcel Breuer's firm, New York 1953; visited Europe on Rockefeller Travel Grant 1954; Prin., Yoshinobu Ashihara Architect and Assocs 1956–; Lecturer in Architecture, Hosei Univ., Tokyo 1955–59, Prof. of Architecture 1959–65; Prof. of Architecture, Musashino Art Univ., Tokyo 1964–70; Visiting Prof., School of Architecture and Building, Univ. of NSW, Australia 1966, Dept of Architecture, Univ. of Hawaii 1969; Prof. of Architecture, Univ. of Tokyo 1970–79; Prof. Emer. Univ. of Tokyo, Musashino Art Univ.; Pres. Japan Inst. of Architects 1980–82; Architectural Inst. of Japan 1985–87; mem. Japan Art Acad. 1988; Hon. Fellow Architectural Inst. of Japan 1988, Royal Australian Inst. of Architects 1987; Hon. FAIA 1979; Award of Architectural Inst. of Japan for Chuo-Koron Building 1960; Special Award of Architectural Inst. of Japan for Komazawa Olympic Gymnasium 1965; Minister of Educ. Award for Japan Pavilion, Expo 1967, Montreal; NSID Golden Triangle Award (USA) 1970; Japan Art Acad. Award for Nat. Museum of Japanese History 1984; Person of Cultural Merit 1991; Commendatore, Ordine al Merito (Italy) 1970, Order of Commdr of Lion (Finland) 1985, Order of Culture 1998. *Works include:* Chuo-Koron Building 1956, Komazawa Olympic Gymnasium 1964, Sony Building 1966, Japanese Pavilion, Expo 67, Montreal, Fuji Film Bldg 1969, Nat. Museum of Japanese History 1980, Tokyo Metropolitan Art Space 1990. *Publications:* Exterior Design in Architecture 1970, The Aesthetic Townscape 1983, The Hidden Order 1989, The Aesthetics of Tokyo – Chaos and Order 1998. *Leisure interests:* sauna, travelling. *Address:* Y. Ashihara Architect and Associates, Sumitomo Seimei Building, 31-15 Sakuragaoka-cho, Shibuya-ku, Tokyo 150-0031 (Office); 47-10 Nishihara-3, Shibuya-ku, Tokyo 151-0066, Japan (Home). *Telephone:* (3) 3463-7461 (Office). *Fax:* (3) 3496-2596 (Office).

ASHKENASI, Shmuel; American violinist; b. 11 Jan. 1940, Tel-Aviv, Israel; m. Mihaela Ionescu Ashkenasi; two s.; ed Curtis Inst. of Music, Philadelphia; Concert violinist since 1962; First violinist, Vermeer String Quartet; Prof. of Music, Univ. of Northern Ill. 1969–; First Prize, Merryweather Post Contest, Washington, DC 1958; Finalist, Queen Elizabeth Competition, Brussels 1959; Second Prize, Tchaikovsky Competition, Moscow 1962. *Leisure interests:* tennis, chess. *Address:* Caecilia, 5 Place de la Fustene, 1204 Geneva, Switzerland.

ASHKENAZY, Vladimir; Icelandic concert pianist and conductor; b. 6 July 1937, Gorky, USSR; s. of David Ashkenazy and Evstolia Ashkenazy (née Plotnova); m. Thorunn Sofia Johannsdóttir 1961; two s. three d.; ed Central Music School, Moscow and Moscow Conservatoire; Second Prize, Int. Chopin Competition, Warsaw 1955; Gold Medal, Queen Elizabeth Int. Piano Competition, Brussels 1956; Joint winner (with John Ogdon) Int. Tchaikovsky Piano Competition, Moscow 1962; Prin. Guest Conductor, Philharmonia 1982–83; Music Dir Royal Philharmonic Orchestra 1987–94, Deutsches Symphonie-Orchester Berlin (fmrly Berlin Radio Symphony) 1989–99; Chief Conductor Czech Philharmonic Orchestra 1998–; Hon. RAM; concerts worldwide; many recordings; Hon. DMus (Nottingham) 1995; Icelandic Order of the Falcon. *Publication:* Beyond Frontiers (with Jasper Parrott) 1985. *Address:* Savinka, Käppelistr. 15, 6045 Meggen, Switzerland.

ASHMAWY, Muhammad Saïd al-, BA; Egyptian lawyer and writer; b. 1 Dec. 1932; Asst of Dist Attorney, Alexandria 1954; Dist Attorney 1956; Judge 1961; Chief Prosecutor, Cairo 1973; Counsellor of State for Legislation 1977; Chief Justice High Criminal Court, Cairo 1985. *Publications:* Roots of Islamic Law 1979, Political Islam 1987, Islamic Caliphate 1990, Religion for the Future 1992, Veil and Tradition in Islam 1995, The Conflict between Arabs and Israel 1997, Reason in Islam 1998, Book of Ethics 1999, Egyptian Roots of Judaism 2001, Clash of Nations 2002. *Leisure interests:* music, driving, tennis. *Address:* 9 Gezira al-Wosta Street, Zamalek, Cairo, Egypt 11211 (Home). *Telephone:* (2) 735-2060. *Fax:* (2) 735-2060. *E-mail:* ashmawy2@hotmail.com (Home).

ASHMORE, Adm. of the Fleet Sir Edward (Beckwith), GCB, DSC; British naval officer; b. 11 Dec. 1919, Queenstown, Eire; s. of Vice-Adm. L. H. Ashmore, C.B., DSO and T. V. Schutt; m. Elizabeth Mary Doveton Sturdee 1942; one s. one d.; ed Royal Naval Coll., Dartmouth; served HMS Birmingham, Jupiter, Middleton 1938–42; qualified Communications 1943; Staff, C-in-C Home Fleet 1944; Cruiser Squadron British Pacific Fleet 1945–46; mentioned in despatches 1946; Russian interpreter and Asst Naval Attaché, British Embassy, Moscow 1946–47; Squadron Communications Officer 3rd Aircraft Carrier Squadron 50; Commdr 1950; HMS Alert 1952–53; Capt. 1955; Capt. (F) 6th Frigate Squadron, Commdg Officer HMS Blackpool 1958; Dir of Plans, Admiralty and Ministry of Defence 1960–62; Commdr British Forces Caribbean Area 1963–64; Rear-Adm. 1965; Asst Chief of Defence Staff, Signals 1965–67; Flag Officer, Second-in-Command, Far East Fleet 1967–68; Vice-Adm. 1968; Vice-Chief Naval Staff 1969–71; Adm. 1970; C-in-C Western Fleet Sept.–Oct. 1971; C-in-C Fleet 1971–73; Chief of Naval Staff and First Sea Lord 1974–77; Chief of Defence Staff Feb.–Aug. 1977; First and Principal Naval ADC to Her Majesty the Queen 1974–77; Adm. of the Fleet 1977–; Dir Racal Electronics Ltd 1978–97; Gov. Sutton's Hospital in Charterhouse 1975–2000; Distinguished Service Cross 1942, Order of the Bath 1974. *Publication:* The Battle and the Breeze 1997. *Leisure interest:* travel. *Address:* c/o Naval Secretary, Victory Building, HM Naval Base, Portsmouth, Hants., England.

ASHRAWI, Hanan; Palestinian politician and academic; b. 1946; m. Emile Ashrawi; two d.; ed American Univ. of Beirut, Univ. of Virginia; joined mainstream PLO Fatah faction; Prof. of English Literature, Chair. English Dept, Dean of Arts, Birzeit Univ., West Bank 1973–90; official spokeswoman for Palestinian Del. 1991–93; mem. Advisory Cttee Palestinian Del. at Madrid Peace Conf. on Middle East; mem. Palestinian Independent Comm. for Palestinian Repub. (fmr Head); Founder, Commr Gen. Palestinian Ind. Comm. for Citizens' Rights 1993–95; mem. Palestinian Legis. Council 1996–; Minister of Higher Educ. 1996–98; currently Human Rights Commr (semiofficial ombudsman) and mem. Palestinian Council; Media Dir and Spokesperson Arab League 2001–; activist Palestinian Women's Movt 1974–; Olof Palme Prize 2002. *Publications:* A Passion for Peace 1994, This Side of Peace 1995. *Address:* Arab League, PO Box 11642, Arab League Building, Tahrir Square, Cairo, Egypt (Office); Dept of English Literature, Birzeit University, PO Box 14, Birzeit, via Israel. *Telephone:* (2) 5750511. *Fax:* (2) 5775726.

ASHTAL, Abdalla Saleh al-, MA; Yemeni diplomatist; b. 5 Oct. 1940, Addis Ababa, Ethiopia; m. Vivian Eshoo al-Ashtal; one s. one d.; ed Menelik II Secondary School, American Univ. of Beirut and New York Univ.; Asst Dir Yemeni Bank for Reconstruction and Devt, San'a 1966–67; mem. Supreme People's Council, Hadramout Province 1967–68, Gen. Command Yemeni Nat. Liberation Front 1968–70; Political Adviser, Perm. Mission to UN 1970–72, Sr Counsellor 1972–73, Perm. Rep. 1973–; Non-Resident Amb. to Canada 1974, to Mexico 1975–79, to Brazil 1985–91 (Pres. Security Council 1991). *Address:* Permanent Mission of Republic of Yemen to the United Nations, 413 East 51st Street, New York, NY 10022, USA. *Telephone:* (212) 355-1730. *Fax:* (212) 750-9613. *E-mail:* yemen@un.int (Office).

ASHWORTH, John Michael, PhD, DSc; British biologist; b. 27 Nov. 1938, Luton; s. of Jack Ashworth and Mary Ousman; m. 1st Ann Knight 1963 (died 1985); one s. three d.; m. 2nd Auriol Stevens 1988; ed Exeter Coll., Oxford, Leicester Univ., Brandeis Univ., USA, Univ. of California, San Diego; Harkness Fellow, Commonwealth Fund, New York, NY 1965–67; Lecturer, Biochemistry Dept, Univ. of Leicester 1967–71, Reader 1971–73; Prof., Biology Dept, Univ. of Essex 1973–79; Chief Scientist, Cen. Policy Review Staff, Cabinet Office 1976–81; Under-Sec. Cabinet Office 1979–81; Vice-Chancellor, Univ. of Salford 1981–89; Dir LSE and Political Science 1990–96; Chair. Bd Nat. Computer Centre 1983–91, Nat. Accreditation Council for Certification Bodies 1984–88, British Library 1996–2001; mem. Bd of Granada TV 1987–89, Dir Granada Group 1990–2002; Dir J. Sainsbury 1993–96, Strategic Health Authority NE London 2002–; mem. Council Inst. of Cancer Research 1998–; Hon. Fellow LSE 1997; Hon. DSc (Salford) 1991; Colworth Medal of Biochemical Soc. 1972. *Publications:* Ed.: Outline Studies in Biology; author: Cell Differentiation 1973, The Slime Moulds (with J. Dee) 1976, over 100 papers on biological, biochemical and educational topics in scientific journals. *Leisure interest:* sailing. *Address:* Garden House, Wivenhoe, Essex, CO7 9DB, England. *Telephone:* (1206) 822256 (Home). *E-mail:* john.ashworth@british_library.net (Home).

ASKEW, Reubin O'Donovan, LLB; American politician and lawyer; b. 11 Sept. 1928, Muskogee, Okla; s. of Leo G. Askew and Alberta N. O'Donovan; m. Donna L. Harper 1956; one s. one d.; ed Escambia County Public School System, Florida State Univ., Univ. of Florida Coll. of Law and Denver Univ.; partner in law firm, Pensacola, Florida 1958–70; Asst County Solicitor, Escambia Co., Florida 1956–58; mem. State of Florida House of Reps. 1958–62; State Senate 1962–70; Gov. of Florida 1971–79; US Trade Rep. 1979–81; dir in law firm, Miami 1981–88; Dir Akerman, Senterfitt and Eidson 1988–; Chair. Education Commission of USA 1973; Chair. Southern Govs Conf. 1974–78, Chair. Nat. Democratic Govs Conf. 1976, Nat. Govs Conf. 1976–77; Chair. Presidential Advisory Bd on Ambassadorial Appointments 1977–79, Select Comm. on Immigration and Refugee Policy 1979; Visiting Fellow, Inst. of Politics, Harvard Univ. 1979; Chubb Fellow, Yale Univ.; Distinguished Service Prof. Fla Atlantic Univ. Fort Lauderdale 1991; Democrat; Presbyterian; Dr hc (Univ. of Notre Dame, Stetson Univ., Rollins Coll., Eckerd Coll., Florida Southern Coll., Saint Leo Coll., Miami Univ., Bethune-Cookman Coll., Univ. of West Fla, Barry Univ., Univ. of Florida, Univ. of Tampa, Belmont Abbey Coll.); John F. Kennedy Award, Nat. Council of Jewish Women 1973, Hubert Harley Award (American Judicature Soc.) 1973, Nat. Wildlife Fed. Award 1972, Outstanding Conservationist of Year Award, Florida Audubon Soc. 1972, Herbert H. Lehman Ethics Award 1973, Salvation Army Gen. William Booth Award 1973, Distinguished Community Service Award, Brandeis Univ., Ethics and Govt Award, Common Cause; Order of COIF (Hon.) Coll. of Law, Univ. of Fla, Albert Einstein Distinguished Achievement Award, Yeshiva Univ. *Publications:* Trade Services and the World Econ. 1983, Opinion: Public Welfare 1984. *Address:* Akerman, Senterfitt and Edison, 255 South Orange Avenue, PO Box 321, Orlando, FL 32802; College of Urban and Public Affairs, 220 South East 2nd Avenue, Fort Lauderdale, FL 33301, USA. *Telephone:* (407) 843-7860.

ASKONAS, Brigitte Alice, PhD, FRS, FMedSci; Canadian immunologist; b. 1 April 1923; d. of the late Charles F. Askonas and Rose Askonas; ed McGill Univ., Montreal, Canada and Univ. of Cambridge, England; Research Student, School of Biochemistry, Univ. of Cambridge 1949–52; Immunology Div., Nat. Inst. for Medical Research, London 1953–88, Head 1977–88; Dept of Bacteriology and Immunology, Harvard Medical School, Boston, Mass., USA 1961–62; Basel Inst. for Immunology, Switzerland 1971–72; Visiting Prof., Dept of Medicine, St Mary's Hosp. Medical School, London 1988–95, attached to Dept of Immunology 1992–96; attached to Molecular Immunology Group, Inst. of Molecular Medicine, John Radcliffe Hosp., Oxford 1989–; Visiting Prof. Dept of Biology, Imperial Coll. London 1995–, Fellowship 2000–; Fellow Acad. of Medical Science; Hon. mem. American Soc. of Immunology, Société Française d'Immunologie, British Soc. of Immunology, German Soc. of Immunology; Hon. DSc (McGill Univ.) 1987. *Publications:* more than 200 scientific papers in biochemical and immunological journals and books. *Leisure interests:* art, travel. *Address:* Infection and Immunity Section, Department of Biology, Imperial College of Science, Technology and Medicine, Sir Alexander Fleming Building, London, SW7 2AZ; 23 Hillside Gardens, London, N6 5SU, England. *Telephone:* (20) 7594-5404/5 (Office); (20) 8348-6792 (Home). *Fax:* (20) 7584-2056. *E-mail:* b.askonas@ic.ac.uk (Office).

ASLAKHANOV, Col.-Gen. Aslanbek Akhmedovich, CandJur; Chechen politician; b. 11 March 1947, Novye Atagi; m.; two c.; ed Kharkov State Pedagogical Inst., Acad. of USSR; teacher Moscow Mining Inst. 1965–67; numerous positions in USSR Ministry of Internal Affairs 1967–, investigator, then Head of Dept, then Sr Inspector, then Deputy Head, then Head of Div., Chief Inspector Organizational Dept 1981–89; head of successful operation to end the hijacking of an aircraft in N Caucasus 1989; Pres. All-Russian Asscn of Security Veterans and Courts; mem. Soviet of Nationalities, USSR Supreme Soviet 1989–91; elected to State Duma (Parl.) 2000, representing Chechen Repub.; numerous awards. *Leisure interests:* free-style wrestling, sport. *Address:* State Duma, Okhotny Ryad 1, 103265 Moscow, Russia. *Telephone:* (095) 292-02-04.

ASMAL, Kader, LLM, MA; South African politician; b. 1934, Stanger; m. Louise Parkinson; two s.; ed Stanger High School, Univ. of SA, London School of Econs, London Univ., Trinity Coll. Dublin and Springfield Teachers' Training Coll.; law teacher Trinity Coll., Dublin for 27 years (during 30-year exile), Dean, Faculty of Arts, Trinity Coll., Dublin 1980–86; barrister Lincoln's Inn, London and King's Inn, Dublin; returned from exile 1990; Prof. of Human Rights Univ. of Western Cape 1990–94; Minister for Water Affairs and Forestry, Govt of Nat. Unity 1994–99, of Educ. 1999–; Chair. World Comm. of Dams 1997–; Pres. Irish Council for Civil Liberties 1976–90; f. Irish Anti-Apartheid Movement 1963, Chair. –1991; mem. Constitutional Comm. of ANC 1986–93, ANC Nat. Exec. Comm. 1991–, Nat. Comm. for Emancipation of Women 1992–, Nat. Ass. on ANC's Nat. List 1994–; mem. ANC negotiating team at Multi-Party Negotiating Forum 1993; Hon. Fellow LSE; Hon. LLD (Queen's Univ. Belfast) 1997, (Trinity Coll. Dublin) 1998, (Univ. of Cape Town) 1999; Hon. PhD (Rhodes Univ.) 1997; UNESCO Prize for Teaching and Devt of Human Rights 1985, Int. Stocholm Water Prize 2000; Gold Medal, WWF, SA 1996. *Publications:* Reconciliation Through Truth (jtly) 1997; over 150 articles on legal and political aspects of apartheid, labour law, Ireland and decolonization. *Address:* Ministry of Education, Private Bag X603, Pretoria 0001 (Office); Ministry of Education, Private Bag X9034, Cape Town, South Africa (Office). *Telephone:* (12) 326-0126 (Pretoria) (Office); (21) 465-7350 (Cape Town) (Office). *Fax:* (12) 323-5989 (Pretoria) (Office); (21) 461-4788 (Cape Town) (Office).

ASMODI, Herbert; German playwright; b. 30 March 1923, Heilbronn; m.1st T. Katja; m. 2nd Mascha Freifrau von Hallberg zu Broich 2002; ed Ruprecht-Karl Universität, Heidelberg; war service 1942–45; studied 1947–52; free-lance writer, Munich 1952–; wrote opera libretto Die Geschichte von dem kleinen blauen Bergsee und dem alten Adler (music by Wilfried Hiller) 1996; mem. PEN; Gerhart Hauptmann-Preis der Freien Volksbühne Berlin 1954, Tukan Prize, Munich 1971, Bayerischer Verdienstorden, Bundesverdienstkreuz. *Publications include:* plays: Jenseits vom Paradies 1954, Pardon wird nicht gegeben 1956, Die Menschenfresser 1959, Nachsaison 1970, Mohrenwäsche, Dichtung und Wahrheit 1969, Stirb und Werde 1965, Nasrin oder Die Kunst zu Träumen 1970, Marie von Brinvilliers 1971, Geld 1973; prose: Das Lächeln der Harpyjen 1987, Eine unwürdige Existenz 1988, Landleben 1991, Das Grosse Rendezvous 1993; poems: Jokers Gala 1975, Jokers Farewell 1977. *Leisure interests:* antiques, modern art. *Address:* Kufsteiner Platz 2, 81679 Munich, Germany. *Telephone:* (89) 983088. *Fax:* (89) 983088.

ASNER, Edward (Ed); American actor and film producer; b. 15 Nov. 1929, Kansas City; m. 1st Nancy Sykes 1957; three c.; m. 2nd Cindy Gilmore 1998; one s. with Carol Jean Vogelman; ed Univ. of Chicago; film and TV actor 1961–; Pres. Screen Actors Guild 1981–85; f. Quince Productions, Inc.; seven Emmy Awards, five Golden Globe Awards, Ralph Morgan Award, Screen Actors Guild 2000, Lifetime Achievement Award 2002. *Film appearances include:* Fort Apache the Bronx 1981, JFK 1991, The Golem 1995, Hard Rain 1998, The Batchelor 1999, Above Suspicion 2000, Mars and Beyond 2000, The Animal 2001, The Confidence Game (also co-producer) 2001, Academy Boyz 2001; numerous TV film appearances. *Films produced:* Payback (TV) 1997, A Vision of Murder: The Story of Donielle (TV) (exec. producer) 2000. *TV series include:* The Mary Tyler Moore Show (as Lou Grant) (five Emmy Awards) 1970–77, Lou Grant (as Lou Grant) 1977–82.

ASO, Taro; Japanese politician; m.; two c.; ed Gakushuin Univ., Stanford Univ., USA and LSE, UK; joined Aso Cement Co. Ltd 1966, Pres. 1973–79; elected Mem. House of Reps 1979; Parl. Vice-Minister, Ministry of Educ.,

Science and Sports 1988; Chair. Standing Cttee on Foreign Affairs 1991; Minister of State for Econ. Planning 1996; mem. Judge Indictment Cttee 1998; Minister of State for Econ. and Fiscal Policy 2001–; Dir Educ. Div., Liberal Democrat Party (LDP) Policy Research Council 1990, Dir Foreign Affairs Div. 1992, Deputy Sec.-Gen. LDP 1993, Deputy Chair. Policy Research Council 1999, Dir-Gen. LDP Treasury Bureau 2000, Chair. Policy Research Council 2001–; mem. Japan Olympic Shooting Team, Montréal 1976; Pres. Japan Jr Chamber of Commerce 1978. *Address:* Policy Research Council, Liberal Democratic Party—LDP (Jiyu-Minshuto), 1-11-23, Nagata-cho, Chiyoda-ku, Tokyo, 100-8910, Japan (Office). *Telephone:* (3) 3581-6211 (Office). *E-mail:* koho@ldp.jimin.or.jp (Office). *Website:* www.jimin.jp/ (Office).

ASPER, Israel Harold, OC, OM, QC, BA, LLM; Canadian business executive and lawyer; b. 11 Aug. 1932, Minnedosa, Manitoba; s. of Leon Asper and Cecilia Asper; m. Ruth M. Bernstein 1956; two s. one d.; ed Kelvin High School, Winnipeg and Univ. of Manitoba; with Drache, Meltzer, Essers, Gold & Asper 1957–59; f. Asper & Co. (now Buchwald, Asper & Co.), law firm, Winnipeg 1959, Sr Partner Asper & Co. 1959–70; Sr Partner Buchwald, Asper, Henteleff 1970–77; fmr mem. Man. Legislature 1970–75; Leader Liberal Party, Man. 1970–75; Chair. of Bd Global Television Network, CanWest Broadcasting Ltd, CanWest Communications Corpn, The CanWest Capital Group Inc., CanWest Trust Co., SaskWest TV Ltd., CPTV Inc.; Chair. and CEO CanWest Global Communications Corpn, CanWest Int. Inc., TV3 Network Holdings Ltd; Pres. The Asper Foundation Inc.; Hon. Chair. Univ. of Man. Asper Centre for Entrepreneurship; mem. Bd of Govs. Hebrew Univ. of Jerusalem; Hon. Lt-Col Canadian Militia; Hon. Fellow Hebrew Univ. of Jerusalem; Hon. LL.D. 1998; Hon. Ph.D. 1999; Univ. of Manitoba Outstanding Alumni Award; winner of several Entrepreneur of the Year awards and many other awards. *Publications:* The Benson Iceberg: A Critical Analysis of The White Paper on Tax Reform in Canada 1970; weekly newspaper column in Toronto Globe & Mail 1966–77. *Leisure interests:* music, reading, travel. *Address:* 31st Floor, 201 Portage Avenue, Winnipeg, Man. R3B 3L7 (Office); 1063 Wellington Crescent, Winnipeg, Man. R3N 0A1, Canada (Home). *Telephone:* (204) 956-2025 (Office); (204) 488-0050 (Home). *Fax:* (204) 947-9841 (Office); (204) 488-7925 (Home). *E-mail:* iasper@canwest.com (Office). *Website:* www.canwest.com (Office).

ASSAD, Lt-Gen. Bashar al-; Syrian politician, ophthalmologist and army officer; b. 11 Sept. 1965, Damascus; s. of the late Hafiz al-Assad (Pres. of Syria 1971–2000) and Anissa Makhlouf; m. Asmaa al-Akhras 2001; one s.; ed Al-Huria High School, Damascus; trained as an ophthalmologist; Capt., Medical Corps 1994, fmr Commdr armoured div., Syrian Armed Forces, apptd. Col 1999; Commdr.-in-Chief of the Armed Forces 2000–; Pres. of Syria 2000–. *Leisure interest:* surfing the net. *Address:* Office of the President, Damascus, Syria (Office). *Website:* www.assad.org (Office).

ASSENMACHER, Ivan, MD, DSc; French professor of physiology; b. 17 May 1927, Erstein; s. of Ivan Assenmacher and Mary Assenmacher (née Wetzel); m. Violette Rochedieu 1952; two s. (one s. deceased); ed Univs. of Strasbourg and Paris; Asst Faculty of Medicine Univ. of Strasbourg 1950–53; Asst Prof. Histophysiology Lab., Coll. de France, Paris 1953–57, Sub-Dir 1957–59; Assoc. Prof., Univ. of Montpellier 1959–62, Prof. Physiology 1962–95, Prof. Emer. 1995–; Head of Neuroendocrinology Lab., CNRS, Montpellier 1967–92; Exchange Prof. Physiology, Univ. of Calif., Berkeley 1976, 1982; mem. Acad. des Sciences 1982, Academia Europaea 1990; mem. Consultative Cttee for Univs., Paris 1967–80, 1986–91, Nat. Cttee for Scientific Research, Paris 1967–75, 1980–86, Gutachtergruppe für Neuroendokrinologie 1975–85 and Neuropeptide 1985–92, Deutsche Forschungsgemeinschaft, Bonn, Nat. Consultative Cttee for a Code of Ethics for Life and Health Sciences 1986–91, French Nat. Comm. for UNESCO 1997–2001, Higher Council for Scientific and Technological Research, Paris 1992–95; Officier, Légion d'honneur, Officier, Ordre Nat. du Mérite, Officier Ordre Palmes Académiques, Insigne des Réfractaires 1944–45. *Publications:* Photorégulation de la Reproduction (with J. Benoît) 1970, Environmental Endocrinology (with D. S. Farner) 1978, Endocrine Regulations as Adaptive Mechanisms to the Environment (with J. Boissin) 1987. *Leisure interest:* music. *Address:* Laboratory of Neuroendocrinology, Department of Health Sciences, University of Montpellier II, 34095 Montpellier (Office); 419 avenue d'Occitanie, 34090 Montpellier, France (Home). *Telephone:* (4) 67-52-28-25 (Office); (4) 67-63-22-20 (Home). *Fax:* (4) 67-52-28-25.

ASTAKHOV, Pavel Alekseyevich; Russian barrister; b. 8 Sept. 1966, Moscow; m. Astakhova Svetlana; two s.; ed Higher KGB School; legal adviser, pvt practice 1989–; has worked in Spain, France, USA, Greece, Czech Republic –1990; Founder, Head Advocates' Group, P. Astakhov 1990–; Rep., Int. Business Centre, Moscow 1990–; mem. Moscow City Collegiate of Advocates. *Leisure interests:* collecting lenses, hunting. *Address:* Advocates Bureau, Barshchevsky & Co., Strioteley str. 8, korp. 2, 119311 Moscow, Russian Federation (Office). *Telephone:* (095) 930-23-00 (Office). *Fax:* (095) 930-23-00 (Office). *E-mail:* astakhov@bbp.ru (Office). *Website:* advocate.org (Office).

ASTAKHOV, Yevgeny Mikhailovich, CandHist; Russian diplomatist; b. 9 March 1937, Moscow; m.; one d.; ed Tashkent Pedagogical Inst., Moscow State Inst. of Int. Relations, Diplomatic Acad.; USSR Ministry of Foreign Affairs; on staff USSR Embassy, Brazil 1963–65, attaché 1965–68, Third Sec. 1968–69; Second Sec. 1971–73, First Sec. 1973–75; Third Sec. Div. of Latin

America, USSR Ministry of Foreign Affairs 1969–71; First Sec. European Dept, USSR Ministry of Foreign Affairs 1977–78; First Sec. USSR Embassy, Spain 1979–80; counsellor 1980–85; Head of Sector IEO 1985–87, Deputy Head 1987–90; Deputy Head First European Dept, USSR Ministry of Foreign Affairs 1990; Amb. to Nicaragua 1990, to Honduras 1991, to El Salvador 1992; Russian Amb. to Uruguay 1999–2000, to Argentina 2000–; observer at Latin America Asscn of Integration. *Address:* Russian Embassy, Rodríguez Pena 1741, 1021 Buenos Aires, Argentina (Office). *Telephone:* (1) 421552 (Office). *Fax:* (1) 812 1794 (Office).

ASTLEY, Philip Sinton, CVO, BA; British diplomatist; b. 18 Aug. 1943; s. of Bernard Astley and Barbara Astley (née Sinton); m. Susanne Poulsen 1966; two d.; ed St Albans School, Magdalene Coll., Cambridge; Asst Rep., British Council, Madras 1966–70, London 1970–73; First Sec. FCO 1973–76, 1982–86, Copenhagen 1976–79; First Sec. and Head of Chancery, East Berlin 1980–82; Econ. Counsellor and Consul-Gen., Islamabad 1986–90; Deputy Head of Mission, Copenhagen 1990–94, Head of Human Rights Policy Dept, FCO 1994–96; Asst Under-Sec. of State, FCO and HM Vice-Marshal of the Diplomatic Corps 1996–99; Amb. to Denmark 1999–2003. *Address:* c/o Foreign and Commonwealth Office, London, SW1A 2AH, England (Office).

ASTRUC, Alexandre, LèsL; French film director, author and newspaperman; b. 13 July 1923, Paris; s. of Marcel Astruc and Huguette Haendel; m. Elyette Helies 1983; ed Lycée de Saint-Germain-en-Laye, Lycée Henri IV and Faculté des Lettres, Paris; journalist and film critic since 1945; TV reporter for Radio Luxembourg 1969–72; Film Critic, Paris Match 1970–72; contributor to Figaro-Dimanche 1977–; Chevalier, Légion d'honneur, Officier de l'Ordre Nat. du Mérite, Commdr des Arts et des Lettres; various film prizes and other awards. *Films directed include:* Le Rideau cramoisi 1952, Les Mauvaises rencontres 1955, Une Vie 1958, La Proie pour l'ombre 1960, Education sentimentale 1961, Evariste Galois 1965, La Longue Marche 1966, Flammes sur l'Adriatique 1968, Sartre par lui-même 1976; also TV films and series. *Publications:* Les Vacances 1945, La Tête la première, Ciel de Cendres 1975, Le Serpent jaune 1976, Quand la chouette s'envole 1978, Le Permissionnaire 1982, Le Roman de Descartes 1989, De la caméra au stylo 1992, L'Autre versant de la colline 1993, Evadiste Galois 1994, Le Montreur d'ombres 1996, La France au coeur 2000. *Leisure interests:* mathematics, literature. *Address:* 168 rue de Grenelle, 75007 Paris, France (Home). *Telephone:* 1-47-05-20-86.

ASYLMURATOVA, Altynai; Kazakhstan ballerina; b. 1962, Alma-Ata (now Almaty); m. Konstantin Zaklinsky; one d.; ed Vaganova Ballet School, Leningrad; dancer with Kirov (now Mariinsky) Ballet 1980; numerous foreign tours including Paris 1982; USA, Canada 1987. *Roles include:* Odette/Odile, in Swan Lake, Shirin, in Legend of Love, Kitzi in Don Quixote, Aurora in Sleeping Beauty, Nike in Boyaderka, Giselle. *Address:* Mariinsky Theatre, Teatralnaya pl. 1, St Petersburg, Russia. *Telephone:* (812) 116-41-64 (Office); (812) 315-57-24 (Home).

ATAEVA, Aksoltan Toreevna; Turkmenistan diplomatist, politician and medical practitioner; b. 6 Nov. 1944, Ashgabat; m. Tchary Pirmoukhamedov 1969; one s. one d.; ed Turkmenistan State Medical Inst., Ashgabat; doctor, Hosp. No. 1, Ashgabat 1968–79, Asst to Chief Dr. 1979–80; Vice-Dir Regional Health Dept, Ashgabat 1980–85; Vice Minister of Health 1985–90, Minister 1990–94; Minister of Social Security 1994–95; Amb. and Perm. Rep. to UN 1995–; mem. Democratic Party 1992–, Khalk Maslakhaty (Supreme People's Council of Turkmenistan) 1993–; Pres. Trade Unions of Turkmenistan 1994–95; Hon. Assoc. of Int. Acad. of Computer Sciences and Systems (Kiev, Ukraine) 1993; Gairat Medal 1992. *Publications:* 108 publs and 2 monographs on health and maternity care. *Leisure interests:* books, arts, sports. *Address:* Permanent Mission of Turkmenistan to UN, 866 UN Plaza, Suite 424, New York, NY 10017, USA. *Telephone:* (212) 486-8908.

ATANASOF, Alfredo; Argentine politician; b. 1949; mem. Gremios Solidarios Group; official, Gen. Confed. of Labour; fmr Minister of Labour, Employment and Social Affairs; Cabinet Chief 2002–. *Address:* General Secretariat to the Presidency, Balcarce 50, 1064 Buenos Aires, Argentina (Office). *Telephone:* (11) 4344-3662 (Office). *Fax:* (11) 4344-3789 (Office). *E-mail:* secgral@presidencia.ner.ar (Office).

ATANASOV, Georgi Ivanov; Bulgarian politician; b. 23 June 1933, Pravoslaven, Plovdiv; ed Faculty of History, Univ. of Sofia; mem. Bulgarian CP (BCP) 1956–; First Sec. Sofia Komsomol City Cttee 1953–62; mem. Komsomol Political Bureau and Sec. of Cen. Cttee 1962–65, First Sec. 1965–68; Cand. mem. BCP Cen. Cttee 1962–66, Head of Dept of Science and Educ., 1968–76, mem. BCP Cen. Cttee 1966; mem. Dept of Admin., 1976–78, Sec. 1977–86; mem. Political Bureau 1986; Deputy Chair. State Planning Cttee 1980–81; Chair. Cttee on State Control 1981–84; Pres. Council of Ministers 1986–90; charged with embezzlement Oct. 1992, convicted Nov. 1992; granted presidential pardon Aug. 1994.

ATHEL, Saleh Abdul Rahman al-, PhD; Saudi Arabian professor of mechanical engineering and university president; b. Al-Rus; m.; several c.; ed Stanford and Texas Univs.; joined teaching staff of King Saud Univ., becoming Vice-Dean, Coll. of Eng 1974–75, Dean 1975–76, Vice-Pres. for Grad. Studies and Research 1976–84; Pres. King Abdulaziz City for Science and Tech., Riyadh; mem. UN World Comm. on Environment and Devt, UN Advisory Cttee on Science and Tech. for Devt, Saudi Working Cttee for Educ. Policy and Scientific Cttee Pio Manza Int. Research Centre; fmr mem. Exec. Cttee Org. for Islamic Co-operation Ministerial Cttee of Scientific and Tech.

Co-operation; mem. American Soc. of Mechanical Engineers.; Fellow Islamic Acad. of Sciences, Vice-Pres. 1986–90. *Publications:* a book on eng. structures, trans. of three books, more than 50 articles. *Address:* Islamic Academy of Sciences, P.O. Box 830036, Amman, Jordan (Office). *Telephone:* (55) 23385 (Office). *Fax:* (55) 11803 (Office).

ATHERTON, Alfred Leroy, Jr, BSc, MA; American diplomatist; b. 22 Nov. 1921, Pittsburgh; s. of Alfred Leroy Atherton and Joan (née Reed) Atherton; m. Betty Wylie Kittredge 1946; two s. one d.; ed Harvard Univ.; joined Foreign Service 1947; Vice-Consul, Stuttgart and Bonn 1947–52; Second Sec., US Embassy, Syria 1953–56; Consul, Aleppo, Syria 1957–58, Calcutta, India 1962–65; Int. Relations Officer, Bureau of Near Eastern and S. Asian Affairs, State Dept 1959–61, Country Dir (Iraq, Jordan, Lebanon, Syria) 1966–67, (Israel and Arab-Israeli Affairs) 1967–70; Deputy Asst Sec. of State 1970–74, Asst Sec. of State 1974–78; Amb. at Large with Special Responsibility for Middle East Peace Negotiations 1978–79; Amb. to Egypt 1979–83; Dir-Gen., Foreign Service, State Dept 1983–85; Dir The Harkness Fellowships 1985–91; Visiting Prof. Hamilton Coll. 1988, 1992, 1994, Mount Holyoke Coll. 1991, Birmingham Southern Coll. 1992, 1993, 1995, 1998, 2000; Chair. New York-Cairo Sister City Cttee 1986–98; mem. Advisory Bd Hariri Foundation 1986–; mem. Nat. Council Near East Foundation 1986–; mem. Bd Dirs., US NZ Council 1987–; mem. Advisory Comm. for Initiative for Peace and Co-operation in Middle East in Search for Common Ground 1991– (Chair. 1992–2000); Trustee, the Una Chapman Cox Foundation 1985–87, Exec. Dir 1989–98; Pres. Distinguished Service Award 1983 and numerous other awards. *Leisure interests:* photography, travel. *Address:* Collington 10450, Lottsford Road 5012, Mitchellville, MD 20721-2734, USA (Home). *Telephone:* (202) 223-0887 (Office); (202) 244-1060 (Home). *E-mail:* royath@aol.com (Home).

ATHERTON, David, OBE, MA, LRAM; British conductor; b. 3 Jan. 1944, Blackpool; s. of Robert and Lavinia Atherton; m. Ann Gianetta Drake 1970 (separated 1983); one s. two d.; ed Cambridge Univ.; Répétiteur, Royal Opera House, Covent Garden 1967–68; Resident Conductor, Royal Opera House 1968–79; Artistic Dir and Conductor, London Stravinsky Festival 1979–82, Ravel/Varèse Festival 1983–84; début La Scala, Milan 1976, San Francisco Opera 1978, Metropolitan Opera, New York 1984; youngest-ever conductor at Henry Wood Promenade Concerts, London 1968; début Royal Festival Hall, London 1969; has conducted performances in Europe, Middle East, Far East, Australasia, N America 1970–; Music Dir and Prin. Conductor San Diego Symphony Orchestra 1980–87; Prin. Conductor and Artistic Adviser Royal Liverpool Philharmonic Orchestra 1980–83, Prin. Guest Conductor 1983–86; Prin. Guest Conductor BBC Symphony Orchestra 1985–89; Music Dir and Prin. Conductor Hong Kong Philharmonic Orchestra 1989–2000, Conductor Laureate 2000–; Artistic Dir Mainly Mozart Festival, S. Calif. 1989–, London Sinfonietta 1967–73, 1989–91 (Founder 1967); Prin. Guest Conductor BBC Nat. Orchestra of Wales 1994–97; Co-Founder, Pres. and Artistic Dir Global Music Network 1998–; Licentiate, Trinity Coll. of Music, Guildhall School of Music and Drama; Conductor of the Year Award, Composers' Guild of GB 1971, Edison Award 1973, Grand Prix du Disque Award 1977, Koussevitzky Award 1981, Int. Record Critics' Award 1982, Prix Caecilia 1982. *Publications:* The Complete Instrumental and Chamber Music of Arnold Schoenberg and Roberto Gerhard (Ed.) 1973, Pandora and Don Quixote Suites by Roberto Gerhard (Ed.) 1973; Contrib. to The Musical Companion 1978, The New Grove Dictionary 1981. *Leisure interests:* travel, films, theatre, computers. *Address:* c/o Askonas Holt Ltd, Lonsdale Chambers, 27 Chancery Lane, London, WC2A 1PF, England. *Telephone:* (20) 7400-1700.

ATHERTON, Michael Andrew, OBE; British cricketer; b. 23 March 1968, Manchester; s. of Alan Atherton and Wendy Atherton; ed Manchester Grammar School and Downing Coll. Cambridge; right-hand opening batsman; leg-spin bowler; played for Cambridge Univ. 1987–89 (Capt. 1988–89), Lancs. 1987–2001; England début 1989, 115 tests to 1 May 2000, 54 as Capt. (England record), scoring 7,728 runs (average 37.69) including 16 centuries (to 1 Jan. 2002); scored 18,349 first-class runs (47 centuries) to end of 2000–01 season, including 1,193 in début season; toured Australia 1990–91, 1994–95 (Capt.); 54 limited-overs internationals (43 as Capt.) to 20 Aug. 1998; toured S. Africa 1995–96, Zimbabwe and NZ 1996–97, West Indies 1998; mem. team touring Australia 1998–99, S. Africa 1999–2000, Pakistan and Sri Lanka 2000–01; retd 2001; cricket commentator for Channel 4. *Publications:* A Test of Cricket 1995, Opening Up (autobiog.) 2002. *Leisure interests:* decent novels, good movies, food, wine, travel, most sports, music. *Address:* c/o Lancashire County Cricket Club, Old Trafford, Manchester, M16 0PX, England.

ATHFIELD, Ian Charles, DipArch; New Zealand architect; b. 15 July 1940, Christchurch; s. of Charles Leonard Athfield and Ella Agnes Taylor; m. Nancy Clare Cookson 1962; two s.; ed Christchurch Boys High School, Auckland Univ. School of Architecture; a Principal of Structon Group Architects, Wellington 1965–68; own practice 1968–; Professional Teaching Fellowship, Victoria Univ. of Wellington 1987–88; Hon. DLitt (Victoria Univ. of Wellington) 2000; winner Int. Design Competition for Housing, Manila, Philippines 1976; winner of over 60 design awards including NZIA Silver Medal 1970, Bronze Medal 1975, Gold Medal 1982, AA Award 1968, 1972, NZ Tourist and Publicity Design Award 1975, Wellington Civic Centre and Public Library, jt winner Design Competition for Low Cost Housing, Fiji 1978, AAA Monier Design Award 1983, NZIA Branch Award 1984, NZIA Nat. Design Award 1984, 1985, 1986, 1987, 1988, 1989, 1993, 1997, 1998, Environmental

Design Award 1986, NZ Wool Bd Award 1987, 1991, NZ Commemoration Medal 1990, Companion NZ Order of Merit 1997. *Leisure interests:* building, gardening. *Address:* P.O. Box 3364, Wellington (Office); 105 Amritsar Street, Khandallah, Wellington, New Zealand (Home). *Telephone:* (4) 499-1727. *Fax:* (4) 499-1960. *E-mail:* ath@athfieldarchitects.co.nz.

ATIYAH, Sir Michael Francis, Kt, OM, ScD, FRS, FRSE; British mathematician; b. 22 April 1929, London; s. of Edward Selim Atiyah and Jean Atiyah (née Levens); m. Lily Brown 1955; three s.; ed Victoria Coll., Egypt, Manchester Grammar School and Trinity Coll. Cambridge; Research Fellow, Trinity Coll., Cambridge 1954–58, Hon. Fellow 1976, Master 1990–97, Fellow 1997–; Fellow, Pembroke Coll., Cambridge 1958–61 (Hon. Fellow 1983), Univ. Lecturer 1957–61; Reader, Oxford Univ. and Fellow, St Catherine's Coll., Oxford 1961–63, Hon. Fellow 1991; Savilian Prof. of Geometry, Oxford Univ. and Fellow of New Coll., Oxford 1963–69, Hon. Fellow 1999; Prof. of Mathematics, Inst. for Advanced Study, Princeton, NJ 1969–72; Royal Soc. Research Prof., Oxford Univ. 1973–90, Fellow St Catherine's Coll., Oxford 1973–90; Dir Isaac Newton Inst. of Math. Sciences, Cambridge 1990–96; Chancellor Univ. of Leicester 1995–; Hon. Fellow Darwin Coll., Cambridge 1992; Pres. London Mathematical Soc. 1974–76, Pres. Mathematical Asscn 1981; mem. Science and Eng Research Council 1984–89; Pres. Pugwash Confs 1997–2002, Council Royal Soc. 1984–85, Pres. 1990–95; Foreign mem. American Acad. of Arts and Sciences, Swedish Acad. of Sciences, Leopoldina Acad. (Germany), NAS, Acad. des Sciences (France), Royal Irish Acad., Third World Acad. of Science, Indian Nat. Science Acad., Australian Acad. of Sciences, Chinese Acad. of Sciences, American Philosophical Soc., Ukrainian Acad. of Sciences, Russian Acad. of Sciences, Georgian Acad. of Sciences, Venezuelan Acad. of Sciences, Accad. Naz. dei Lincei, Royal Spanish Acad. of Sciences, Norwegian Acad. of Science and Letters; Hon. Prof. Univ. of Edinburgh 1997–; Hon. Fellow Royal Acad. of Eng (UK) 1993, Faculty of Actuaries 1999, Univ. of Wales Swansea 1999; Hon. DSc (Bonn, Warwick, Durham, St Andrew's, Dublin, Chicago, Edinburgh, Cambridge, Essex, London, Sussex, Ghent, Reading, Helsinki, Leicester, Rutgers, Salamanca, Montreal, Waterloo, Wales, Queen's-Kingston, Keele, Birmingham, Lebanon, Open Univ., Brown Univ., Oxford, Prague, Chinese Univ., Hong Kong, Heriot-Watt); Dr hc (UMIST) 1996; Fields Medal, Int. Congress of Mathematicians, Moscow 1966, Royal Medal of Royal Soc. (UK) 1968, De Morgan Medal, London Mathematical Soc. 1980, Copley Medal of Royal Soc. (UK) 1988, Feltrinelli Prize, Accademia Nazionale dei Lincei 1981, King Faisal Int. Prize for Science 1987, Benjamin Franklin Medal (American Philosophical Soc.), Nehru Medal (Indian Nat. Science Acad.); Commdr Order of the Cedars; Order of Andreas Bello (Venezuela). *Publications:* K-Theory 1966, Commutative Algebra 1969, Geometry and Dynamics of Magnetic Monopoles 1988, Collected Works (5 vols) 1988, The Geometry and Physics of Knots 1990. *Leisure interests:* gardening, music. *Address:* University of Edinburgh, School of Mathematics, Mayfield Road, Edinburgh, EH9 3JZ (Office); 3/8 West Grange Gardens, Edinburgh, EH9 2RA, Scotland. *Telephone:* (131) 650-5086 (Office); (131) 667-0898 (Home). *E-mail:* atiyah@maths.ed.ac.uk (Home).

ATIYAT, Talal Moh'd Ismail, B.B.A., MA; Jordanian civil servant; b. 28 Dec. 1951, Amman; Chief of Div., Revenue Dept; Dir of Admin., UNESCO office; Dir of Finance, Co-operative Bank; Asst Gen. Dir, Dir of Devt Admin., Jordan Co-operative Corpn 1995–. *Leisure interest:* reading. *Address:* Jordan Co-operative Corporation, Amman (Office); P.O. Box 930008, Housing Bank Complex, Amman, Jordan. *Telephone:* 665171 (Office); 711530 (Home).

ATKINS, Dame Eileen June, DBE; British actress; b. 16 June 1934; d. of Arthur Thomas Atkins and of the late Annie Ellen Elkins; m. Bill Shepherd; ed Latymer Grammar School, Edmonton and Guildhall School of Music and Drama; BAFTA Award 1985. *Stage appearances include:* Twelfth Night, Richard III, The Tempest 1962, The Killing of Sister George (Best Actress, Evening Standard Awards) 1965, The Cocktail Party 1968, Vivat! Vivat Regina! (Variety Award) 1970, Suzanne Andler, As You Like It 1973, St Joan 1977, Passion Play 1981, Medea 1986, The Winter's Tale, Cymbeline (Olivier Award) 1988, Mountain Language 1988, A Room of One's Own 1989, Exclusive 1989, The Night of the Iguana 1992, Vita and Virginia 1993, Indiscretions 1995, John Gabriel Borkman 1996, A Delicate Balance 1997 (Evening Standard Award), The Unexpected Man (Olivier Award) 1998, 2000–01, Honour 2003. *Films include:* Equus 1974, The Dresser 1984, Let Him Have It 1990, Wolf 1994, Cold Comfort Farm 1995, Jack and Sarah 1995, The Avengers 1998, Women Talking Dirty 1999, Gosford Park 2002, The Hours 2003. *Radio work includes:* adaptation of To the Lighthouse 2000. *TV appearances include:* The Duchess of Malfi, Sons and Lovers, Smiley's People, Nelly's Version, The Burston Rebellion, Breaking Up, The Vision, Mrs Pankhurst in In My Defence (series) 1990, A Room of One's Own 1990, The Lost Language of Cranes 1993, The Maitlands 1993, Talking Heads 2 1998, Madame Bovary 2000, The Sleeper 2000, Wit 2001, Bertie and Elizabeth 2001, The Lives of Animals 2002. *Co-creator:* Upstairs Downstairs, The House of Eliott television series. *Adaptation:* Mrs Dalloway (Evening Standard Film Award) 1999. *Address:* c/o Paul Lyon Maris, ICM, Oxford House, 76 Oxford Street, London, W1D 1BS (Office); 2 The Moorings, Strand on the Green, Chiswick, London, W4 3PG, England. *Telephone:* (20) 7636-6565 (Office). *Fax:* (20) 7323-0101 (Office).

ATKINSON, Sir Anthony Barnes (Tony), Kt, MA, FBA; British professor of economics; b. 4 Sept. 1944, Caerleon; m. Judith Mary Mandeville 1965; two s. one d.; ed Cranbrook School, Kent and Churchill Coll., Cambridge; Prof. of Econs, Univ. of Essex 1970–76; Head Dept of Political Economy, Univ. Coll. London 1976–79; Prof. of Econs LSE 1980–92; Prof. of Political Economy, Cambridge Univ., Fellow Churchill Coll. 1992–94; Warden Nuffield Coll. Oxford 1994–; Ed. Journal of Public Economics 1972–97; mem. Royal Comm. on Distribution of Income and Wealth 1978–79, Retail Prices Index Advisory Cttee 1984–90, Pension Law Review Cttee 1992–93, Conseil d'Analyse Economique 1997–; Fellow, St John's Coll., Cambridge 1967–70; Fellow, Econometric Soc. 1984, Pres. 1988; Vice-Pres. British Acad. 1988–90; Pres. of the European Econ. Asscn 1989, Hon. mem. American Econ. Asscn 1985; Pres. Int. Econ. Asscn 1989–92, Royal Econ. Soc. 1995–98; Hon. Dr rer. pol (Univ. of Frankfurt); UAP Prix Scientifique 1986; Frank E. Seidman Distinguished Award in Political Economy 1995; hon. degrees from Univ. of Liège 1989, Athens Univ. of Econs 1991, Stirling Univ. 1992, Edin. Univ. 1994 and numerous others; Chevalier Légion d'honneur. *Publications:* Poverty in Britain and the Reform of Social Security 1969, Unequal Shares 1972, The Economics of Inequality 1975, Distribution of Personal Wealth in Britain (with A. Harrison) 1978, Lectures on Public Economics (with J. E. Stiglitz) 1980, Social Justice and Public Policy 1983, Parents and Children (with A. Maynard and C. Trinder), Poverty and Social Security 1989, Economic Transformation in Eastern Europe and the Distribution of Income (with J. M. Micklewright) 1992, Public Economics in Action 1995, Incomes and the Welfare State 1996, Poverty in Europe 1998, The Economic Consequences of Rolling Back the Welfare State 1999, Social Indicators (jtly) 2002. *Leisure interest:* sailing. *Address:* Nuffield College, Oxford, OX1 1NF (Office); 39 Park Town, Oxford, OX2 6SL, England (Home). *Telephone:* (1865) 278520 (Office); (1865) 556064. *E-mail:* tony.atkinson@nuf.ox.ac.uk (Office).

ATKINSON, Conrad; British artist; b. 15 June 1940, Cleator Moor, Cumbria; m. Margaret Harrison 1967; two d.; ed Whitehaven Grammar School, Carlisle and Liverpool Colls of Art and Royal Acad. Schools, London; Granada Fellow in Fine Art 1967–68; Churchill Fellow in Fine Art 1972; Fellow in Fine Art, Northern Arts 1974–76; Lecturer, Slade School of Fine Art 1976–79; Visual Art Adviser to GLC 1982–86; Power Lecturer, Univ. of Sydney 1983; Artist-in-Residence, London Borough of Lewisham 1984–86, Edin. Univ. 1986–87; Adviser Labour Party 1985–86 (Visual Arts Policy). *Exhibitions include:* Strike at Brannans, ICA 1972, Work, Wages and Prices, ICA 1974, A Shade of Green on Orange Edge, Arts Council of Northern Ireland Gallery, Belfast, Material, Ronald Feldman Fine Arts, New York, At the Heart of the Matter, ICA 1982, Ronald Feldman Fine Arts "Goldfish", New York 1985. *Leisure interest:* rock and roll music. *Address:* 172 Erlanger Road, London, SE14 5TJ, England. *Telephone:* (20) 7639-0308.

ATKINSON, Sir Frederick John, KCB, MA; British economist; b. 7 Dec. 1919, London; s. of George E. Atkinson and Elizabeth S. Cooper; m. Margaret Grace Gibson 1947; two d.; ed Jesus Coll., Oxford Univ.; Lecturer, Jesus and Trinity Colls, Oxford 1947–49; Econ. Adviser, Cabinet Office 1949–51, at Embassy, Washington 1951–54 and at Treasury 1955–69; Chief Econ. Adviser, Dept of Trade and Industry 1970–73; Asst Sec.-Gen. OECD 1973–75; Deputy Sec. Chief Econ. Adviser, Dept of Energy 1975–77; Chief Econ. Adviser, Treasury 1977–79; Hon. Fellow, Jesus Coll., Oxford 1979–. *Publication:* (jt author) Oil and the British Economy 1983. *Leisure interest:* reading. *Address:* 26 Lee Terrace, Blackheath, London, SE3 9TZ; Tickner Cottage, Church Lane, Aldington, Kent, TN25 7EG, England. *Telephone:* (20) 8852-1040; (1233) 720514.

ATKINSON, Harry Hindmarsh, PhD; British physicist; b. 5 Aug. 1929, Wellington, New Zealand; s. of late Harry Temple Atkinson and Constance Hindmarsh Atkinson (née Shields); m. Anne Judith Barrett 1958; two s. one d.; ed Canterbury Univ. Coll., NZ, Corpus Christi Coll. and Cavendish Lab., Univ. of Cambridge; Asst Lecturer in Physics, Canterbury Univ. Coll., NZ 1952–53; Research Asst, Cornell Univ., USA 1954–55; Sr Research Fellow, AERE, Harwell 1958–61; Head, General Physics Group, Rutherford Lab. 1961–69; Staff Chief Scientific Adviser to UK Govt, Cabinet Office 1969–72; Head, Astronomy, Space and Radio Div., Science Research Council 1972–78, Under Sec. and Dir, Astronomy, Space and Nuclear Physics 1983–86; Under Sec. and Dir of Science, Science and Eng Research Council 1983–88, Under Sec. and Dir (Special Responsibilities) 1988–92, Consultant 1992–; Chief Scientist (part-time) UK Loss Prevention Council 1990; Consultant North Comm. on Future of Oxford Univ. 1995–97; Chair. Anglo-Dutch Astronomy Cttee 1981–88, Steering Cttee, Inst. Laue Langevin (ILL), Grenoble 1984–88; UK Del. Council, European Space Agency 1973–87, Vice-Chair. 1981–84, Chair. 1984–87; UK Del. Intergovernmental Panel on High Energy Physics 1983–91, Council of European Synchrotron Radiation Facility 1986–88; Assessor Univ. Grants Cttee 1987–89, Consultant 1995–97; UK mem. S. African Astronomical Observatory Cttee 1979–85, Anglo-Australian Telescope Bd 1979–88; mem. Working Group on Int. Collaboration, Cabinet Office 1989, NI Cttee of Univ. Funding Council 1989–93; Co-ordinator Australia, NZ, UK Science Collaboration 1989–94; Chair. Govt Task Force on Potentially Hazardous Near Earth Objects 2000; mem. European Science Foundation Working Group on Near Earth Objects 2001–. *Address:* Atkinson Associates, Ampney Lodge, Bampton, Oxon., OX18 2JN, England. *Telephone:* (1993) 850120. *Fax:* (1993) 851529. *E-mail:* harry_atkinson@compuserve.com.

ATKINSON, Sir Robert, Kt, DSC, RD, BScEng, FREng, FIMech, FIMare; British business executive (retd); b. 7 March 1916, Tynemouth, Northumberland; s. of Nicholas and Margaret Atkinson; m. 1st Joyce Forster 1941 (died 1973); one s. one d.; m. 2nd Margaret Hazel Walker 1977; ed Christ Church School, Tynemouth Grammar School, Univ. of London, McGill Univ., Canada; served World War II (DSC and two bars; mentioned in despatches); Man. Dir William

Doxford 1957–61; Tube Investments 1961–67; Unicorn Industries 1967–72; Chair. Aurora Holdings 1972–84; Chair. and Chief Exec. British Shipbuilders 1980–84; James Clayton Gold Medal 1961. *Publications:* The Design and Operating Experience of an Ore Carrier Built Abroad 1957, Some Crankshaft Failures: Investigations into Causes and Remedies 1960, The Manufacture of Crankshafts (North East Coast of Engineers and Shipbuilders Gold Medal) 1961, British Shipbuilders' Offshore Division 1962, Productivity Improvement in Ship Design and Construction 1983, The Development and Decline of British Shipbuilding 1999. *Leisure interests:* salmon and trout fishing, walking, gardening. *Address:* Southwood House, Itchen Abbas, Winchester, Hants., SO21 1AT, England. *Telephone:* (1962) 779610.

ATKINSON, Rowan Sebastian, MSc; British actor and writer; b. 6 Jan. 1955; s. of the late Eric Atkinson and of Ella Atkinson; m. Sunetra Sastry 1990; ed Durham Cathedral Choristers' School, St Bees School and Univs of Newcastle and Oxford; stage appearances include: Beyond a Joke, Hampstead 1978, Oxford Univ. revues at Edinburgh Fringe, one-man show, London 1981, The Nerd 1985, The New Revue 1986, The Sneeze 1988. *TV appearances:* Not the Nine O'Clock News 1979–82, Blackadder 1983, Blackadder II 1985, Blackadder the Third 1987, Blackadder Goes Forth 1989, Mr Bean (13 episodes) 1990–96, Rowan Atkinson on Location in Boston 1993, Full Throttle 1994, The Thin Blue Line 1995. *Films:* Never Say Never Again, The Tall Guy 1989, The Appointments of Dennis Jennings 1989, The Witches 1990, Four Weddings and a Funeral 1994, Hot Shots—Part Deux 1994, Bean: The Ultimate Disaster Movie 1997, Blackadder—Back and Forth 2000, Maybe Baby 2000, Rat Race 2002, Scooby Doo 2002, Johnny English 2003. *Leisure interests:* motor cars, motor sport. *Address:* c/o PBJ Management Ltd, 7 Soho Street, London, W1D 3DQ, England. *Telephone:* (20) 7287-1112. *Fax:* (20) 7287-1191. *E-mail:* general@pbjmgt.co.uk (Office).

ATLANTOV, Vladimir Andreevich; Russian tenor; b. 19 Feb. 1933, Leningrad; ed Leningrad Conservatory (pupil of Natalya Bolotina); mem. CPSU 1966–88; joined Leningrad Kirov 1963; further study, La Scala, Milan 1963–65; won Tchaikovsky Competition 1966 and Int. Contest for Young Singers, Sofia 1967; soloist with Moscow Bolshoi Theatre 1968–88, with Vienna State Opera 1987–, Kammersänger 1987; major roles include German in The Queen of Spades, José in Carmen, Otello, Cavaradossi in Tosca; many tours and recordings; RSFSR People's Artist 1972, USSR People's Artist 1976. *Address:* c/o Wiener Staatsoper, Opernring 2, 1015 Vienna, Austria. *Fax:* (1) 51444-2330.

ATOPARE, Sir Sailas, GCMG; Papua New Guinea Governor-General and civil servant; b. Sailas Atopare, 1951, Kabiufa, Eastern Highlands Prov.; m.; ed Jones Missionary Coll., Rabaul, E New Britain Prov.; fmrly Agriculture Officer, Dept of Agric., Stocks and Fisheries, Asst Transport Man., Dept of Works and Supply, Man. and Sec. Assro-Watabung Rural Devt Corpn; mem. Nat. Parl. for Goroka Open, Eastern Highlands Prov. 1977; Gov.-Gen. 1997–; Sec.-Gen. Papua New Guinea Coffee Growers' Asscn; KStJ. *Leisure interests:* playing golf, going to church. *Address:* Government House, P.O. Box 79, Port Moresby 121, Papua New Guinea (Office). *Telephone:* 321-4466 (Office). *Fax:* 321-4543 (Office).

ATRASH, Muhammad al-, PhD; Syrian international official; b. 13 Nov. 1934, Tartous; s. of Hassan Sayed al-Atrash and Aziza Sayed al-Atrash; m. Felicia al-Atrash 1958; two s. one d.; ed American Univ., Beirut, Lebanon, American Univ., Washington, DC, USA, London School of Econs; joined Cen. Bank of Syria 1963, Research Dept 1963, Head of Credit Dept 1966–70; Alt. Exec. Dir IMF 1970–73; Deputy Gov. Cen. Bank of Syria 1974; Exec. Dir IBRD 1974–76, IMF 1976–78; del. to Second Cttee of UN Gen. Ass., to UNCTAD and other int. econ. confs. 1963–70; part-time lecturer, Univ. of Damascus 1963–70; mem. Deputies of IMF Interim Cttee of the Bd of Govs. on Reform of Int. Monetary System 1972–74; Assoc. mem. IMF Interim Cttee 1974–76, ex officio mem. 1976–78; Minister of Economy and Foreign Trade 1980–82; Minister of Finance 2001–. *Publications:* articles in Al-Abhath (Quarterly of the American Univ. of Beirut) 1963, 1964, 1966. *Leisure interests:* swimming, walking, reading books on history and literature. *Address:* Ministry of Finance, BP 13136, rue Jule Jammal, Damascus, Syria.

ATTALI, Bernard; French business executive; b. 1 Nov. 1943, Algiers; s. of the late Simon Attali and Fernande Abecassis; twin brother of Jacques Attali (q.v.); m. Hélène Scebat 1974; one d.; ed Lycée Gauthier, Algiers, Lycée Janson-de-Sailly, Paris, Faculté de Droit, Paris, Inst. d'Etudes Politiques, Paris and Ecole Nat. d'Admin; auditeur, Cour des Comptes 1968, adviser 1974; on secondment to Commissariat Général du Plan d'Equipement et de la Productivité 1972–74; Délégation à l'Aménagement du Térritoire et à l'Action Regionale (Datar) 1974–80, 1981–84; Finance Dir Soc. Club Meditérranée 1980–81; Pres. Regional Cttee of EEC 1981–84; Pres. Groupe des Assurances Nationales (Gan) 1984–86; Pres. Banque pour l'Industrie Française 1984–86; Adviser on European Affairs, Commercial Union Assurance 1986–88, Chair. Air France 1988–93; Pres. Supervisory Council, Sociétés Epargne de France 1986–88, Commercial Union Lard 1986–88; Pres. Euroberlin 1988, Union de Transports Aériens (UTA) 1990, Asscn des Transporteurs Aériens Européens (AEA) 1991; Vice-Pres. Supervisory Bd BIGT 1995; Admin. Aérospatiale 1989, Air Inter 1990; Chief Adviser Revenue Court 1991–93; Chair. Supervisory Bd Banque Arjil (part of Lagadère) 1993–96; Chair. Bankers Trust Co. France 1996–99; Vice-Pres. Investment Banking in Europe Div., Deutsche Bank 1999–2000; Pres. Bd Dirs Regional Devt Agency, Ile-de-France 2001–; Officier Ordre Nat. du Mérite, Chevalier, Légion d'hon-

neur. *Publication:* Les Guerres du Ciel 1994. *Address:* Deutsche Bank, 3 avenue de Friedland, 75008 Paris (Office); 12 avenue Pierre 1er de Serbie, 75016 Paris, France (Home).

ATTALI, Jacques; French international bank official and writer; b. 1 Nov. 1943, Algiers; s. of the late Simon Attali and of Fernande Attali; twin brother of Bernard Attali (q.v.); m. Elisabeth Allain 1981; one s. one d.; ed Ecole Polytechnique, Inst. d'Etudes Politiques de Paris, Ecoles des Mines de Paris, Ecole Nat. d'Admin; started career as mining engineer, then Lecturer in Econs, Ecole Polytechnique; Auditeur, Council of State; Adviser to the Pres. 1981–91; State Councillor 1989–91; Pres. European Bank for Reconstruction and Development (EBRD), London 1991–93; Pres. Attali et Associés (ACA) 1994–; mem. Council of State 1981–90, 1993–; Admin. KeeBoo 2000–; Dr hc (Univ. of Kent, Univ. of Haifa). *Publications:* Analyse économique de la vie politique 1972, Modèles politiques 1973, Anti-économique (with Marc Guillaume) 1974, La parole et l'outil 1975, Bruits, Essai sur l'économie politique de la musique 1976, La nouvelle économie française 1977, L'ordre cannibale 1979, Les trois mondes 1981, Histoires du temps 1982, La figure de Fraser 1984, Un homme d'influence 1985, Au propre et au Figuré 1988, La vie éternelle (novel) 1989, Millennium: Winners and Losers in the Coming World Order 1991, 1492 1991, Verbatim (Tome I) 1993, Europe(s) 1994, Verbatim (Tome II) 1995, Economie de l'Apocalypse 1995, Tome III 1996, Chemins de Sagesse 1996, Au delà de nulle part 1997, Dictionnaire du XXIe siècle 1998, Les portes du ciel 1999, La femme du menteur 1999, Fraternités 1999, Blaise Pascal ou le génie français 2000, Bruits 2001. *Address:* ACA, 28 rue Bayard, 75008 Paris, France.

ATTALIDES, Michalis A., PhD; Cypriot diplomatist; b. 1941; m.; two c.; ed LSE and Princeton Univ.; Lecturer in Sociology, Univ. of Leicester 1966–68; sociologist, Cyprus Town and Country Planning Project 1968–70; counterpart of UNESCO expert, Social Research Centre, Cyprus 1971, 1973–74; mil. service 1972; Guest Lecturer Otto Suhr Inst., Free Univ. of Berlin 1974–75; journalist 1975–76; worked in Int. Relations Service, House of Reps of Cyprus 1977–89, Dir 1979–89; Amb., Dir of Political Affairs Division B (Cyprus question), Ministry of Foreign Affairs 1989–91; Amb. of Cyprus to France (also accred to Morocco, Portugal and Spain) 1991–95, Amb. to Belgium (also accred to Luxembourg) and Perm. Del. of Cyprus to EU 1995–98, High Commr in UK 1998–2000; Del. of Cyprus to Convention on the Future of Europe 2001; Perm. Sec. Ministry of Foreign Affairs May 2000–; Grand Officier, Ordre Nat. du Mérite. *Publications:* Cyprus: Nationalism and International Politics 1980, Social Change and Urbanization in Cyprus: A Study of Nicosia 1971. *Address:* Ministry of Foreign Affairs, Nicosia, Cyprus. *E-mail:* mattali@spidernet.com .cy (Home).

ATTALLAH, Naim Ibrahim, FRSA; British publisher and financial adviser; b. 1 May 1931, Haifa, Palestine; s. of Ibrahim Attallah and Genevieve Attallah; m. Maria Nykolyn 1957; one s.; ed Coll. des Frères, Haifa and Battersea Polytechnic, London; Propr Quartet Books 1976–, Women's Press 1977–, Robin Clark 1980–, Pipeline Books 1978–2000, The Literary Review 1981–2001, The Wire 1984–2000, Acad. Club 1989–96, The Oldie 1991–2001; Group Chief Exec. Asprey PLC 1992–96, Deputy Chair. Asprey (Bond Street) 1992–98; Man. Dir Mappin and Webb 1990–95; Exec. Dir Garrard 1990–95; Chair. Namara Group of cos 1973–, launched Parfums Namara 1985, Avant L'Amour and Après L'Amour 1985, Naïdor 1987, L'Amour de Namara 1990; Hon. MA (Surrey) 1993; Retail Personality of the Year, UK Jewellery Awards 1993. *Films produced:* The Slipper and the Rose (with David Frost, q.v. 1975, Brimstone and Treacle (Exec. Producer) 1982 and several TV documentaries. *Theatre:* Happy End (Co-Presenter) 1975, The Beastly Beatitudes of Balthazar B. (Presenter and Producer) 1981, Trafford Tanzi (Co-Producer) 1982. *Publications:* Women 1987, Singular Encounters 1990, Of a Certain Age 1992, More of a Certain Age 1993, Speaking for the Oldie 1994, A Timeless Passion 1995, Tara and Claire (novel) 1996, Asking Questions 1996, A Woman a Week 1998, In Conversation with Naim Attalah 1998, Insights 1999, Dialogues 2001. *Leisure interests:* classical music, opera, theatre, cinema, photography and fine arts. *Address:* 25 Shepherd Market, London, W1J 7PP, England. *Telephone:* (20) 7499-2901. *Fax:* (20) 7499-2914. *E-mail:* nattallah@aol.com (Office).

ATTANASIO, Paul; American screenwriter; m. Katie Jacobs; one d.; ed Harvard Univ., Harvard Law School; began career as a journalist; fmr film critic for the Washington Post. *Films include:* Quiz Show, Disclosure, Donnie Brasco 1997, Sphere 1998. *TV includes:* Homicide (series).

ATTAR, Mohamed Saeed Al-, PhD; Yemeni politician; b. 26 Nov. 1927; m.; one s. five d.; ed Sorbonne, Paris; Research Assoc. Sorbonne and Inst. de Développement, Paris 1959–62; Gen. Man. Yemen Bank for Reconstruction and Devt 1962–65, Chair. 1965–68; mem. High Econ. Comm. 1962–68; Ministry of Econ. 1965–68; Perm. Rep. of Yemen Arab Repub. to UN 1968–71, 1973–74; Roving Amb. 1971–73; Under-Sec.-Gen. of UN and Exec. Sec. Econ. Comm. for Western Asia (ECWA) 1974–85; Deputy Prime Minister, Minister of Devt and Chair. Cen. Planning Org. 1985; Deputy Prime Minister and Minister of Industry 1990–95; Pres. Gen. Investment Authority 1993; Deputy Prime Minister and Minister of Oil and Mineral Resources 1995; mem. Supreme Council for Oil; many other public appts.; MARIB Legion decoration (Yemen); Légion d'honneur. *Publications include:* La Révolution Yemenite 1964; articles in magazines and newspapers. *Address:* c/o Ministry of Oil and Mineral Resources, P.O. Box 81, San'a, Yemen.

ATTAS, Haydar Abu Bakr al-; Yemeni politician; fmr Minister of Construction; Prime Minister of People's Democratic Repub. of Yemen 1985–86; Pres. (following overthrow of Govt of Ali Nasser Mohammed,) 1986–90; Prime Minister of Repub. of Yemen 1990–94. *Address:* c/o Office of the Prime Minister, San'a, Yemen.

ATTASSI, Lt-Gen. Louai; Syrian politician and army officer; b. 1926; ed Syrian Military Acad. and Staff Officers' Coll., Homs; took part in Palestinian War 1948; opposed Syrian break with Egypt 1961; Garrison Commdr, Aleppo April 1962; Mil. Attaché, Syrian Embassy, Washington 1962–63; C-in-C of Syrian Armed Forces and Pres. of Revolutionary Council March–July 1963.

ATTENBOROUGH, Sir David Frederick, Kt, CH, CVO, CBE, MA, FRS; British broadcaster and writer; b. 8 May 1926, London; s. of the late Frederick Attenborough and of Mary Attenborough; brother of Lord Attenborough (q.v.); m. Jane Elizabeth Ebsworth Oriel 1950 (died 1997); one s. one d.; ed Wyggeston Grammar School, Leicester and Clare Coll., Cambridge; Royal Navy 1947–49; Editorial Asst in publishing house 1949–52; with BBC Television 1952–73, Trainee Producer BBC TV 1952–54, Pproducer of zoological, archaeological, travel, political and other programmes 1954–64; Controller BBC 2 1964–68, Dir of Programmes, TV 1969–73; writer, presenter BBC series: Tribal Eye 1976, Wildlife on One, annually 1977–, Life on Earth 1979, The Living Planet 1984, The First Eden 1987, Lost World, Vanished Lives 1989, The Trials of Life 1990, Life in the Freezer 1993, The Private Life of Plants 1995, The Life of Birds 1998, State of the Planet (presenter) 2000, Ultimate Wild Paradises: The Top Ten Destinations 2001, The Blue Planet (narrator) 2001, The Life of Mammals 2002; Pres. BAAS 1990–91, Royal Soc. for Nature Conservation 1991–96; mem. Man. Bd, BBC 1969–73; freelance broadcaster and writer 1973–; mem. Nature Conservancy Council 1975–82; Fellow, Soc. of Film and Television Arts 1980; Hon. Fellow, Clare Coll., Cambridge 1980, UMIST 1980, Inst. of Biology; Int. Trustee, World Wild Life Fund 1979–86; Trustee, British Museum 1980–, Science Museum 1984–87, Royal Botanical Gardens, Kew 1986–92; Hon. DLitt (Leicester, London, Birmingham and City Univs); Hon. DSc (Liverpool, Ulster, Sussex, Bath, Durham, Keele, Heriot-Watt, Bradford, Nottingham); Hon. LLD (Bristol and Glasgow) 1977; Hon. DUniv (Open Univ.) 1980, (Essex) 1987, Antwerp 1993; Dr hc (Edin.) 1994; Special Award, Guild of TV Producers 1961, Silver Medal, Royal TV Soc. 1966, Silver Medal, Zoological Soc. of London 1966, Desmond Davis Award, Soc. of Film and TV Arts 1970, Founders Gold Medal, Royal Geographical Soc. 1985, UNESCO Kalinga Prize 1982, Medallist, Acad. of Natural Sciences, Philadelphia 1982, Encyclopedia Britannica Award 1987, Edin. Medal, Edin. Science Festival 1998. *Publications:* Zoo Quest to Guiana 1956, Zoo Quest for a Dragon 1957, Zoo Quest in Paraguay 1959, Quest in Paradise 1960, Zoo Quest to Madagascar 1961, Quest under Capricorn 1963, The Tribal Eye 1976, Life on Earth 1979, The Zoo Quest Expeditions 1982; The Living Planet 1984, The First Eden, The Mediterranean World and Man 1987, The Trials of Life 1990, The Private Life of Plants 1994, The Life of Birds 1998 (BP Natural World Book Prize), The Life of Mammals 2002, Life on Air (autobiog.) 2002. *Leisure interests:* music, tribal art, natural history. *Address:* 5 Park Road, Richmond, Surrey, TW10 6NS, England.

ATTENBOROUGH, Michael; British theatre director; b. 1951; s. of Richard Attenborough (Baron Attenborough of Richmond) (q.v.) and Sheila Sim; m. Jane Seymour 1971 (divorced); ed Sussex Univ.; Assoc. Dir Mercury Theatre, Colchester 1974; Assoc. Dir Leeds Playhouse –1979; Assoc. Dir Young Vic Theatre 1979; Dir Hampstead Theatre during the 1980s; joined RSC 1990–2001; Artistic Dir Almeida Theatre Co. July 2002–. *Productions include:* The Herbal Bed (Eileen Anderson Award), Romeo and Juliet, A Month in the Country, Othello, The Prisoner's Dilemma. *Address:* Almeida Theatre, Almeida Street, Islington, London, N1 1TA, England (Office).

ATTENBOROUGH, Philip John, CBE; British book publisher; b. 3 June 1936; s. of John Attenborough CBE and Barbara Attenborough (née Sandle); m. Rosemary Littler 1963; one s. one d.; ed Rugby School, Trinity Coll., Oxford; joined Hodder & Stoughton 1957, Dir 1963, Sales Dir 1969; Chair. Hodder & Stoughton Ltd and Hodder & Stoughton Holdings Ltd 1975–93, Deputy Chair. Hodder Headline PLC 1993–96; Chair. The Lancet Ltd 1977–91; Dir Book Tokens Ltd 1985–96; mem. Council, Publishers' Asscn 1976–92, Pres. 1983–85; UK Rep. Fédération des Editeurs Européens 1986–93; mem. Exec. Cttee, Int. Publishers' Asscn 1988–96, Vice-Pres. 1992–96; Chair., British Council Publishers' Advisory Cttee 1989–93; Adviser, UNESCO Publishing 1992–95; mem. Governing Body, SPCK 1999–. *Publication:* The Rebirth of European Publishing: An Anglo-European Perspective of '1992' (essay) 1991. *Leisure interests:* trout fishing, watching cricket. *Address:* Coldhanger, Seal Chart, Sevenoaks, Kent, TN15 0EJ, England. *Telephone:* (1732) 761516.

ATTENBOROUGH, Baron (Life Peer), cr. 1993, of Richmond-upon-Thames in the London Borough of Richmond-upon-Thames; **Richard (Samuel) Attenborough,** Kt, CBE; British actor, producer and director; b. 29 Aug. 1923; s. of late Frederick Attenborough and Mary Attenborough; brother of Sir David Attenborough (q.v.); m. Sheila Beryl Grant Sim 1945; one s. (Michael Attenborough, q.v.) two d.; ed Wyggeston Grammar School, Leicester, Royal Acad. of Dramatic Art, London; first stage appearance as Richard Miller in Ah! Wilderness, Palmers Green 1941; West End debut in Awake and Sing 1942; first film appearance In Which We Serve 1942; joined RAF 1943; seconded to RAF Film Unit for Journey Together 1944, demobilised 1946; returned to stage 1949; formed Beaver Films with Bryan Forbes (q.v.) 1959, Allied Film Makers 1960; Goodwill Amb. for UNICEF 1987–; mem. British

Actors' Equity Asscn Council 1949–73, Cinematograph Films Council 1967–73, Arts Council of GB 1970–73; Chair. Actors' Charitable Trust 1956–88 (Pres. 1988–), Combined Theatrical Charities Appeals Council 1964–88 (Pres. 1988–), BAFTA 1969–70 (Vice-Pres. 1971–94), Royal Acad. of Dramatic Arts 1970 (mem. Council 1963–), Capital Radio 1972–92 (Life Pres. 1992–), Help a London Child 1975–, UK Trustees Waterford-Kamhlaba School, Swaziland 1976– (Gov. 1987–), Duke of York's Theatre 1979–92, BFI 1981–92, Goldcrest Films and TV 1982–87, Cttee of Inquiry into the Arts and Disabled People 1983–85, Channel Four TV 1987–92 (Deputy Chair. 1980–86), British Screen Advisory Council 1987–96, European Script Fund 1988–96 (Hon. Pres. 1996); Gov. Nat. Film School 1970–81, Motability 1977–; Pres. Muscular Dystrophy Group of GB 1971– (Vice-Pres. 1962–71), The Gandhi Foundation 1983–, Brighton Festival 1984–95, British Film Year 1984–86, Arts for Health 1989–, Gardner Centre for the Arts, Sussex Univ. 1990– (Patron 1969–82); Dir Young Vic 1974–84, Chelsea Football Club 1969–82; Trustee Tate Gallery 1976–82, 1994–96, Tate Foundation 1986–, Foundation for Sport and the Arts 1991–; Patron Kingsley Hall Community Centre 1982–, RA Centre for Disability and the Arts, Leicester 1990–; Pro-Chancellor Sussex Univ. 1970–98, Chancellor 1998–; Freeman of Leicester 1990; Fellow King's Coll. London 1993, Fellow BAFTA; Hon. Fellow Nat. Film and TV School 2001; Hon. DLitt (Leicester) 1970, (Kent) 1981, (Sussex) 1987; Hon. DCL (Newcastle) 1974; Hon. LLD (Dickinson, Penn.) 1983; Evening Standard Film Award for 40 Years' Service to British Cinema 1983, Martin Luther King Jr Peace Prize 1983, Padma Bhushan, India 1983, European Film Awards Award of Merit 1988, Hon. Fellow BFI 1992, Shakespeare Prize for Oustanding Contrib. to European Culture 1992; Commdr des Arts et des Lettres, Chevalier, Légion d'honneur, Dilys Powell Award 1995. *Stage appearances include:* The Little Foxes 1942, Brighton Rock 1943, The Way Back Home (Home of the Brave) 1949, To Dorothy a Son 1965, Sweet Madness 1952, The Mousetrap 1952–54, Double Image 1956–57, The Rape of the Belt 1957–58. *Film appearances include:* School for Secrets, The Man Within, Dancing with Crime, Brighton Rock, London Belongs to Me, The Guinea Pig, The Lost People, Boys in Brown, Morning Departure, Hell is Sold Out, The Magic Box, Gift Horse, Father's Doing Fine, Eight O'Clock Walk, The Ship that Died of Shame, Private's Progress, The Baby and the Battleship, Brothers in Law, The Scamp, Dunkirk, The Man Upstairs, Sea of Sand, Danger Within, I'm All Right Jack, Jet Storm, S.O.S. Pacific, The Angry Silence (also co-prod.) 1959, The League of Gentlemen 1960, Only Two Can Play, All Night Long 1961, The Dock Brief, The Great Escape 1962, Seance on a Wet Afternoon (also prod., Best Actor, San Sebastian Film Festival and British Film Acad.), The Third Secret 1963, Guns at Batasi (Best Actor, British Film Acad.) 1964, The Flight of the Phoenix 1965, The Sand Pebbles (Hollywood Golden Globe) 1966, Dr. Doolittle (Hollywood Golden Globe), The Bliss of Mrs. Blossom 1967, Only When I Larf 1968, The Last Grenade, A Severed Head, David Copperfield, Loot 1969, 10 Rillington Place 1970, And Then There Were None, Rosebud, Brannigan, Conduct Unbecoming 1974, The Chess Players 1977, The Human Factor 1979, Jurassic Park 1992, Miracle on 34th Street 1994, The Lost World: Jurassic Park 1997, Elizabeth 1998, Puckoon 2001. *Produced:* Whistle Down the Wind 1961, The L-Shaped Room 1962. *Directed:* Young Winston (Hollywood Golden Globe) 1972, A Bridge Too Far (Evening News Best Drama Award) 1976, Magic 1978, A Chorus Line 1985, Grey Owl 2000. *Produced and directed:* Oh! What a Lovely War (16 int. Awards), Gandhi (8 Oscars, 5 BAFTA Awards, 5 Hollywood Golden Globes, Dirs' Guild of America Award for Outstanding Directorial Achievement) 1980–81, Cry Freedom (Berlinale Kamera, BFI Award for Tech. Achievement) 1987, Chaplin 1992, Shadowlands 1993 (Alexander Korda Award for Outstanding British Film of the Year, BAFTA), In Love and War 1997, Grey Owl 2000. *Publications:* In Search of Gandhi 1982, Richard Attenborough's Chorus Line (with Diana Carter) 1986, Cry Freedom, A Pictorial Record 1987. *Leisure interests:* music, collecting art, watching football. *Address:* Old Friars, Richmond Green, Richmond, Surrey, TW9 1NQ, England.

ATTERSEE; Austrian artist; b. (as Christian Ludwig), 28 Aug. 1940, Pressburg; s. of Christian Ludwig and Susanne Ludwig; ed Akademie für Angewandte Kunst, Vienna; has worked as an artist since 1963; more than 200 one-man exhbns. in Germany, France, Netherlands, Italy, Austria and Switzerland, including Venice Biennale. *Publications:* Attersee Werksquer 1962–82, Attersee, Biennale Venedig 1984. *Leisure interest:* sailing.

ATUN, Hakki, M.PHIL.; Turkish-Cypriot politician, architect and city planner; b. 1935, Ergazi; s. of Mustafa Atun and Emine Atun; m. Suna Atun 1960; one s. one d.; ed Istanbul Tech. Univ., Manchester Univ., Nottingham Univ.; with Cyprus Govt Planning and Housing Dept 1961–63, Turkish-Cypriot Admin. Planning and Housing Dept 1963–68, Dir Planning and Public Works Dept 1968–75, Under-Sec. of State for Housing 1975, Minister of Rehabilitation and Housing 1976–78, of Economy and Finance 1978–81, of Culture, Educ. and Youth 1981–83, of Housing 1983–85; mem. Turkish-Cypriot Parl. 1976–, Speaker 1985–93; Prime Minister of 'Turkish Repub. of Northern Cyprus' 1993–96; mem. Nat. Union Party (UBP) 1976–92; f. The Democratic Party, Leader 1992–96, Speaker of Legis. Ass. 1996–98. *Address:* Legislative Assembly of "Turkish Republic of Northern Cyprus", Lefkoşa (Nicosia), via Mersin 10, Turkey. *Telephone:* 2274656. *Fax:* 2282161.

ATWOOD, Margaret, CC, AM, FRSC; Canadian author; b. 18 Nov. 1939, Ottawa; m. Graeme Gibson; one d.; ed Univ. of Toronto and Harvard Univ.; taught at Univ. of British Columbia 1964–65, Sir George Williams Univ.

1967–68, Univ. of Alberta 1969–70, York Univ. 1971; Writer-in-Residence, Univ. of Toronto 1972–73, Tuscaloosa, Alabama 1985; Berg Prof. New York Univ. 1986, Maquarie Univ., Australia 1987; Guggenheim Fellowship 1981; Hon. DLitt (Trent) 1973, (Concordia) 1980, (Smith Coll.) 1982, (Univ. of Toronto) 1983, (Mount Holyoke) 1985, (Univ. of Waterloo) 1985, (Univ. of Guelph) 1985, (Oxford) 1998; Hon. LLD (Queen's Univ.) 1974; Commonwealth Literary Prize 1987; Centennial Medal (Harvard Univ.) 1990; Order of Ont. 1990; City of Toronto Book Awards, Coles Book of the Year, Canadian Booksellers Author of the Year 1989. *Publications:* poetry: The Circle Game 1966, The Animals in that Country 1969, The Journals of Susanna Moodie 1970, Procedures for Underground 1970, Power Politics 1971, You Are Happy 1974, Selected Poems 1976, Two Headed Poems 1978, True Stories 1981, Snake Poems 1983, Interlunar 1984, Selected Poems II 1986, Selected Poems 1966–1984, 1990, Margaret Atwood Poems 1965–1975, 1991, Morning in the Burned House 1995; fiction: The Edible Woman 1969, Surfacing 1972, Lady Oracle 1976, Dancing Girls 1977, Life Before Man 1979, Bodily Harm 1981, Encounters With the Element Man 1982, Murder in the Dark 1983, Bluebeard's Egg (short stories) 1983, Unearthing Suite 1983, The Handmaid's Tale 1985, Cat's Eye 1988, Wilderness Tips (short stories) 1991, The Robber Bride 1993, Bones and Murder 1995, The Labrador Fiasco 1996, Alias Grace (novel) 1996, The Blind Assassin (Booker Prize) 2000, Oryx and Crake (novel) 2003; non-fiction: Survival: A Thematic Guide to Canadian Literature 1972, Second Words: Selected Critical Prose 1982, (ed.) The New Oxford Book of Canadian Verse in English 1982, The Oxford Book of Canadian Short Stories in English (ed.) 1986, The New Oxford Book of Canadian Short Stories in English 1995, Negotiating with the Dead 2002; children's books: Up in the Tree 1978, Anna's Pet 1980, For the Birds 1990, Princess Prunella and the Purple Peanut 1995; reviews and critical articles. *Address:* c/o McClelland & Stewart, 481 University Avenue, 9th Floor, Toronto, Ont., M5G 2E9; Oxford University Press, 70 Wynford Drive, Don Mills, Ont., M3C 1J9, Canada.

ATZMON, Moshe; Israeli conductor; b. 30 July 1931, Budapest, Hungary; m. 1954; two d.; ed Tel Aviv Acad. of Music, Guildhall School of Music, London; left Hungary for Israel 1944; played the horn professionally in various orchestras for several years; has conducted in Israel, England, Australia, Germany, Sweden, Norway, Switzerland, Spain, Finland, Italy, Austria, Turkey and USA; Chief Conductor, Sydney Symphony Orchestra 1969–71; Chief Conductor, North German Symphony Orchestra 1972; Musical Dir Basel Symphony Orchestra 1972–86; Chief Conductor Tokyo Metropolitan Orchestra 1979–83, Nagoya Symphony Orchestra 1987–92; Musical Dir Dortmund Opera House and Philharmonic Orchestra 1991–; second prize Dimitri Mitropoulos Competition for Conductors, New York 1963; Leonard Bernstein Prize 1963; First Prize, Int. Conductors Competition, Liverpool, England 1964. *Leisure interests:* reading, travelling. *Address:* PMG, Top Floor, 59 Lansdowne Place, Hove, East Sussex, BN3 1FL, England (Office).

AUBERGER, Bernard, ING. CIVIL, LenD; French banker; b. 5 Dec. 1937, Gennevilliers; s. of Paul Auberger and Jeanne (née Geny) Auberger; m. Christine Baraduc 1963; three s. one d.; ed Ecole des Mines, Paris, Inst. d'Etudes Politiques, Paris, Ecole Nat. d'Admin., Paris; Investigating Officer French Ministry of Finance 1966–70; Adviser to Gen. Man. Crédit Nat., Paris 1970–72; Financial Attaché French Embassy, New York 1972–74; Dir of Cabinet for Under Sec. for Finance 1974; attached to Industrial Relations Cttee 1974–75; Dir Production and Trade, French Ministry of Agric. 1975–80; Cen. Man. Société Générale 1983–86; Insp. Gen. of Finances 1988; Advisor to Pres. of Paluel-Marmont 1990; Pres. Cortal Bank 1991–98, Banque Directe 1994–2001; Vice-Pres., Dir-Gen. Crédit du Nord 1993–94, Chair., CEO 1994–95; Pres. Asscn Opéra Comique-Salle Favart 1994–2001; Dir Compagnie Bancaire 1991–98, Banque Paribas 1994–97; mem. Econ. and Social Council 1982–; Gen. Man. Caisse Nat. de Crédit Agricole 1986–88; Adviser to Chair. Palvel-Marmont Group 1990; Officier Ordre nat. du Mérite, Chevalier du Mérite agricole, Légion d'honneur. *Address:* 13 rue du Bois-Joli, 92190 Meudon, France (Home). *Telephone:* 45-34-08-78 (Home).

AUBERT, Guy, D. ÈS SC.; French scientific director; b. 9 May 1938, Costes, Hautes-Alpes; s. of Gontran Aubert and Marguerite Vincent; m. 1962; two d.; Research Assoc. Lab. d'Electrostatique et de Physique du Metal, CNRS, Grenoble; Titular Prof. Univ. Scientifique et Médicale de Grenoble 1970, Vice-Pres. in charge of research 1981–84; Scientific Del. of CNRS for Rhône-Alpes region 1981–83; Dir Ecole Normale Supérieure de Lyon 1985–94; Dir-Gen. CNRS 1994–97; Extraordinary mem. Conseil d'Etat 1997–; mem. Universities' Higher Council, French Physics Soc.; Officier Ordre Nat. du Mérite; Chevalier Légion d'honneur, des Palmes académiques, du Mérite agricole. *Publications:* papers in scientific journals. *Leisure interests:* skiing, tennis. *Address:* Conseil d'Etat, Palais Royal, 75100 Paris RP (Office); 79 Bvd. Suchet, 75016 Paris, France.

AUBERT, Pierre; Swiss politician and lawyer; b. 3 March 1927, La Chaux-de-Fonds; s. of the late Alfred and Henriette Erni Aubert; m. Anne-Lise Borel 1953; one s. one d.; ed Univ. of Neuchatel; mem. of local Assembly, La Chaux-de-Fonds 1960–68, Pres. 1967–68; mem. Legis. Ass. of Canton of Neuchâtel 1961–75, Pres. 1969–70; Labour mem. Council of States 1971–77; mem. Fed. Council (Govt) 1978–87, Vice-Pres. Jan.–Dec. 1982; Pres. of Switzerland Jan.–Dec. 1983, Jan.–Dec. 1987; Head of Fed. Foreign Affairs Dept 1978–87. *Leisure interests:* camping, boxing, skiing, cycling, theatre, watches.

AUBOUIN, Jean Armand, D. ÈS SC.; French academic; b. 5 May 1928, Evreux; s. of Jean Aubouin and Yvonne Joubin; m. Françoise Delpouget 1953; two d.; ed Lycées Buffon and St-Louis, Ecole Normale Supérieure (St-Cloud) and Univ. of Paris; Asst Univ. of Paris 1952–62, Prof. 1962–90; mem. Acad. of Sciences Inst. of France 1981–, Vice-Pres. 1986–88, Pres. 1989–90, Pres. Inst. of France 1989; Pres. Société Géologique de France 1976, Int. Geological Congress 1980, Scientific Advisory Bds. of Bureau de Recherches Géologiques et Minières 1984–90 and Inst. Français de Recherche pour l'Exploitation de la Mer 1985–90; mem. Scientific Advisory Bds. of Inst. Français du Pétrole 1983–92, of Fondation de France 1984–89, Planning Cttee Int. Programme of Ocean Drilling 1980–84; Pres. Cttee Geological Map of the World 1984–92; mem. Scientific Advisory Bds. of various geology-related programmes; mem. Bd of Dirs. Office de Recherche Scientifique d'Outre-mer 1984–88, Bureau de Recherche Géologique et Minières 1988–93, Inst. Océanographique, Paris and Monaco 1994– (Pres. Comité Perfectionnement 1992–); mem. Conseil Supérieur Recherche et Technologie 1981–86; Pres. French Cttee of Int. Decade for the Reduction of Natural Disasters 1990–93, Parc Naturel du Verdun 1996–; Admin. Chancellery Acad. de Nice, Acad. de Paris 2000–; Foreign mem. Accademia dei Lincei, Italy 1974–, USSR (now Russia) Acad. of Sciences 1976–, Acad. of Athens, Greece 1980–, Acad. Europaea 1988–, Acad. of Zagreb, Croatia 1990–, Acad. Royale Sciences, Arts et Lettres de Belgique 1994–, Deutsche Akademie der Naturforscher Leopoldina 1995–, Acad. de la Latinité 2000–; Hon. mem. Acad. of Tech. 2001–; Hon. mem. Geological Soc. of London 1976–; Hon. Fellow Geological Soc. of America 1980–; Hon. mem. Société Physique Histoire Naturelle (Geneva) 1990–; Dr. (hc) Univ. of Athens 1992; CNRS Medal 1959, Museo de la Plata Medal 1977, Dumont Medal (Société Géologique de Belgique) 1977, Ville de Paris Medal 1980; Prize Viquesnel (Soc. Géologique de France) 1962, Prize Charles Jacob (Acad. des Sciences) 1976, Gaudry Prize (Société Géologique de France) 1990, Gold Medal Académie Royale des Sciences de Belgique 1990, Chevalier Ordre des Palmes académiques 1965, Chevalier Ordre Nat. du Mérite 1981, Chevalier Légion d'honneur 1989. *Publications:* Géologie de la Grèce septentrionale 1959, Geosynclines 1965, Manuel de Cartographie (Co-Ed.) 1970, Précis de Géologie (Co-Ed., 4 Vols) 1968–79, approx. 400 scientific articles. *Leisure interests:* reading, mountain walking and swimming at sea. *Address:* Institut de Géodynamique, avenue Albert Einstein, Sophia Antipolis, 06560 Valbonne (Office); 27 avenue des Baumettes, 06000 Nice, France (Home). *Telephone:* (4) 93-95-42-22 (Office); (4) 93-86-03-76 (Home). *Fax:* (4) 93-65-27-17 (Office); (4) 93-86-03-76 (Home).

AUBRY, Cécile (pseudonym of Anne-José Bénard); French author, scriptwriter and film director; b. 3 Aug. 1928, Paris; d. of Lucien Bénard Aubry and Marguerite Candelier; m. Prince Brahim el Glaoui 1951 (divorced); one s.; ed Lycée Victor Duruy, Paris; appeared in prin. role in Clouzot's film Manon 1948; subsequent roles in films The Black Rose 1950, Barbe Bleue 1951 and in Italian and French films 1951; author and director of numerous television scripts and series 1961–72, including Poly, Belle et Sébastien, Sébastien Parmi les Hommes, Sébastien et la Mary Morgane, Le Jeune Fabre, etc.; Officier des Arts et des Lettres. *Publications:* three novels 1974–85, several children's books. *Address:* Le Moulin Bleu, 6 chemin du Moulin Bleu, 91410 St-Cyr-sous-Dourdan, France. *Telephone:* 1-64-59-01-06.

AUBRY, Martine Louise Marie; French politician; b. 8 Aug. 1950, Paris; d. of Jacques Delors (q.v.) and Marie Lephaille; m. Xavier Aubry; one d.; ed Inst. Saint-Pierre-Fourier, Lycée Paul-Valéry, Faculté de Droit, Paris, Inst. des Sciences Sociales du Travail, Inst. d'Etudes Politiques, Paris and Ecole Nat. d'Admin; Ministry of Labour 1975–79; Instructor Ecole Nat. d'Admin. 1978; Dir of preparations for econ. competition for admin. of Univ. Paris-Dauphine 1978; civil admin. Conseil d'Etat 1980–81; Deputy Dir Pvt. Office of Minister of Labour 1981; special assignment for Minister of Social Affairs and Nat. Solidarity 1983–84; Dir of Labour Relations, Ministry of Labour 1984–87; Maître des Requêtes, Conseil d'Etat 1987; Deputy Dir-Gen. Pechiney 1989–91; Minister of Labour, Employment and Professional Training 1991–93; Pres. FACE 1993–97; First Asst Mayor of Lille 1995–2001, Mayor 2001–; Vice-Pres. Lille Urban Council 1995–; mem. Nat. Ass. for Nord region (Socialist Party) 1997–2002; Minister of Employment and Social Affairs 1997–2000; Nat. Sec. Socialist Party 2000–; Int. Press Prize, Le Trombinoscope 1999. *Publications:* Le Choix d'Agir 1994, Petit dictionnaire pour lutter contre l'extrême droite (jtly.) 1995, Il est grand temps... 1997, C'est quoi la solidarité? 2000. *Leisure interests:* tennis, skiing. *Address:* Parti Socialiste, 10 rue de Solférino, 75333 Paris Cédex 07 (Office); Mairie, B.P. 667, 59033 Lille Cédex France. *Telephone:* 1-45-56-77-00 (Office). *Fax:* 1-47-05-15-78 (Office). *E-mail:* infosp@parti-socialiste.fr (Office). *Website:* www.parti-socialiste.fr (Office).

AUCHINCLOSS, Kenneth, MA; American editor; b. 3 July 1937, New York; s. of Douglas Auchincloss and Eleanor Grant Auchincloss; m. Eleanor Johnson 1971; one s. one d.; ed Harvard Coll. and Balliol Coll. Oxford; Asst to Deputy Sec. US Dept of Commerce 1961; Exec. Asst to US Special Trade Rep. 1963; mem. staff, Inst. for Advanced Study 1965; Assoc. Ed. Newsweek 1966–68, Gen. Ed. 1968–72, Sr Ed. 1972, Exec. Ed. 1972–76, Man. Ed. 1976–95, Ed. Int. Edn 1986–95, Ed.-at-Large 1996–2002. *Leisure interest:* collecting books (fine printing). *Address:* 40 East 62nd Street, New York, NY 10021-8018, USA (Home).

AUCHINCLOSS, Louis Stanton, LLB, DLitt; American author and lawyer; b. 27 Sept. 1917; s. of Joseph Howland and Priscilla (née Stanton) Auchincloss; m. Adele Lawrence 1957; three s.; ed Groton School, Yale Univ. and Univ. of Virginia; admitted to New York Bar 1941, Assoc. Sullivan and Cromwell 1941–51, Hawkins, Delafield and Wood, New York 1954–58, partner 1958–86;

Lt U.S. Navy 1941–45; Pres. Museum of the City of New York; mem. Nat. Inst. of Arts and Letters. *Publications:* The Indifferent Children 1947, The Injustice Collectors 1950, Sybil 1952, A Law for the Lion 1953, The Romantic Egoists 1954, The Great World and Timothy Colt 1956, Venus in Sparta 1958, Pursuit of the Prodigal 1959, House of Five Talents 1960, Reflections of a Jacobite 1961, Portrait in Brownstone 1962, Powers of Attorney 1963, The Rector of Justin 1964, Pioneers and Caretakers 1965, The Embezzler 1966, Tales of Manhattan 1967, A World of Profit 1969, Motiveless Malignity 1969, Edith Wharton: A Woman in Her Time 1971, I Come as a Thief 1972, Richelieu 1972, The Partners 1974, A Winter's Capital 1974, Reading Henry James 1975, The Winthrop Covenant 1976, The Dark Lady 1977, The Country Cousin 1978, Persons of Consequence 1979, Life, Law and Letters 1979, The House of the Prophet 1980, The Cat and the King 1981, Watchfires 1982, Exit Lady Masham 1983, The Book Class 1984, Honorable Men 1985, Diary of a Yuppie 1986, Skinny Island 1987, The Golden Calves 1988, Fellow Passengers 1989, The Vanderbilt Era 1989, The Lady of Situations 1991, False Gods 1992, Three Lives 1993, Tales of Yesteryear 1994, Collected Stories 1994, The Education of Oscar Fairfax 1995, The Man Behind the Book 1996, La Gloire 1996, The Atonement 1997, Woodrow Wilson 2000. *Address:* 1111 Park Avenue, New York, NY 10028, USA (Home).

AUCOTT, George William, BS; American company executive; b. 24 Aug. 1934, Philadelphia; s. of George William Aucott and Clara Anna (Nagel) Aucott; m. Ruth Tonetta Heller 1956; one s. two d.; ed Ursinus Coll., Collegeville, Pa and Harvard Univ.; served US army 1957–60; joined Firestone Tire & Rubber Co. 1956, Pres. Firestone Industrial Products Co. 1978, Firestone Canada Inc. 1978–80, Vice-Pres. Mfg parent co., Akron, Ohio 1980; Pres. and COO Firestone Int. 1982–91, Pres., COO World Tire Group 1988–; mem. Bd of Dirs. and Exec. Vice-Pres. of Corpn 1986–; mem. Bd Dirs. Akron United Way 1968–73; Pres. and Dir Akron YMCA 1969–73; mem. Bd of Dirs Rubber Mfrs Asscn, Rubber Asscn. *Address:* 1200 Firestone Parkway, Akron, OH 44317, USA (Office).

AUDRAIN, Paul André Marie; French business executive; b. 17 May 1945, Chambéry, Savoie; s. of Jean Audrain and Margueritte Gubian; m. Danièle Pons 1967; two s.; ed Lycée d'Etat de Chambéry, Lycée du Parc Lyon, Ecole Supérieure des Sciences Economiques et Commerciales, Paris; Engineer, IBM France 1969–70; Financial and Admin. Dir Aiglon, Angers 1970–74; Financial Dir Christian Dior 1974–79, then Sec. Gen., Financial and Admin. Dir 1979–84, Chair. and CEO 1984–85, Pres. 1985–86; Int. Dir Financière Agache 1986–87; Chair. and CEO Christian Lacroix 1987–88, Pierre Balmain 1988–89; CEO Société Crillon 1990–93, Int. Consulting & Licensing; Chevalier Ordre nat. du Mérite 1985. *Address:* 27 rue du Phare, Port Navalo, 56 640 Arzon (Home); 20 Boulevard du Montparnasse, 75015 Paris, France. *Telephone:* 1-44-49-98-70 (Office); 2-97-53-85-45 (Home). *Fax:* 2-97-53-63-76. *E-mail:* polaudrain@aol.com.

AUDRAN, Stéphane (see Dacheville, Colette).

AUERBACH, Frank Helmuth; British artist; b. 29 April 1931, Berlin; s. of Max Auerbach and Charlotte Auerbach; m. Julia Wolstenholme 1958; one s.; ed St Martin's School of Art, London, Royal Coll. of Art; one-man exhbns. at Beaux-Arts Gallery, London 1956, 1959, 1961, 1962, 1963, Marlborough Fine Art, London 1965, 1967, 1971, 1974, 1983, 1987, 1990, 1997, Marlborough Gallery, New York 1969, 1982, 1994, 1998, Villiers Art Gallery, Sydney 1972, Univ. of Essex, Colchester 1973, Galleria Bergamini, Milan 1973, Municipal Art Gallery, Dublin 1975, Marlborough, Zurich 1976, Anthony d'Offay, London 1978, Retrospective Exhbn, Arts Council, Hayward Gallery, London, Fruit Market Gallery, Edinburgh 1978, Bernard Jacobson, New York 1979, Anne Berthoud, London 1983, Venice Biennale, British Pavilion 1986 (Golden Lion Award), Kunstverein, Hamburg 1986, Museum Folkwang, Essen 1987, Centro de Arte Reina Sofia, Madrid 1987, Rijksmuseum Vincent Van Gogh, Amsterdam 1989, Yale Center for British Art, New Haven 1991, Nat. Gallery, London 1995, Campbell-Thiebaud, San Francisco 1995, Rex Irwin, Sydney 1996, 2000, Charlottenborg, Copenhagen 2000, Royal Acad. of Arts, London 2001, Marlborough, Madrid 2002; numerous group exhbns including Carnegie Int. Exhbn, Pittsburg 1958, 1961, Gulbenkian Exhbn, London 1964, Peter Stuyvesant Foundation Collection, London 1967, European Painting in the Seventies, L.A. County Museum 1975, The Human Clay, Hayward Gallery, London 1976, British Painting 1952–1977, Royal Acad. of Arts, London 1977, New Spirit in Painting, RA, London 1981, Westkunst, Cologne 1981, The Hard-Won Image, Tate Gallery, London 1984, A School of London: Six Figurative Painters, Kunstnernes Hus, Oslo 1987, British Art in the Twentieth Century, RA, London 1987, The Pursuit of the Real, Manchester City Art Gallery 1990, Israel Museum, Jerusalem 1992–93, From London, Scottish Nat. Gallery of Modern Art 1995, L'Ecole de Londres, Fondation Dina Vierny—Musée Maillol, Paris 1998–99; works in public collections in UK, Australia, Brazil, USA, Mexico, Israel, S. Africa, Canada; Silver Medal for Painting, Royal Coll. of Art. *Address:* c/o Marlborough Fine Art, 6 Albemarle Street, London, W1S 4BY, England. *Telephone:* (20) 7629-5161.

AUERBACH, Stanley Irving, MS, PhD; American ecologist (retd.); b. 21 May 1921, Chicago, Ill.; s. of Abraham and Carrie Friedman Auerbach; m. Dawn Patricia Davey 1954; two s. two d.; ed Univ. of Illinois and Northwestern Univ.; Second Lt US Army 1942–44; instructor, then Asst Prof., Roosevelt Univ., Chicago 1950–54; Assoc. Scientist, then Scientist, Health Physics Div., Oak Ridge Nat. Laboratory 1954–59, Senior Scientist, Section Leader 1959–70, Dir Ecological Sciences Div. 1970–72, Environmental Sciences Div.

1972–86, Sr Research Adviser 1986–90; Visiting Research Prof. Radiation Ecology, Univ. of Georgia, Athens, Ga 1964–90; Adjunct Prof., Dept Ecology, Univ. of Tenn., Knoxville 1965–90; mem. US Cttee Int. Biological Program; Dir Eastern Deciduous Forest Biome Project 1968–76; mem. Special Comm. on Biological Water Quality of Ohio River Valley Sanitation Comm. 1971–81, Bd Environmental Consultants for Tenn.-Tombigbee Waterway, US Army Corps of Engineers 1975–82, Energy Research and Devt Admin. (ERDA) Ad Hoc Cttee on Shallow Land Burial of Transuranic Waste 1976–80, Pres.'s Cttee on Health and Ecological Effects on Increased Coal Utilization 1977–78, Research Advisory Cttee, Resources for the Future 1978–81, Environmental Advisory Bd-Chief of Engineers 1989–93; Pres. Distinguished Service Award, Ecological Soc. of America 1971–72, 1985; mem. Bd of Trustees, Inst. of Ecology 1971–74, NAS—NRC Bd on Energy Studies, Bd of Govs. American Inst. of Biological Sciences 1965–66, Ecological Soc. of America, Scientific Research Soc. of America (Pres. Oak Ridge Br. 1972–73), Cttee on Energy and the Environment, NAS Comms. on Physical Sciences, Nat. Resources (Chair. Environmental Studies Bd 1983–86), Exec. Cttee Science Advisory Bd, US Environmental Protection Agency 1986–92; mem. British Ecological Soc., Nature Conservancy, Health Physics Soc., Soc. of Systematic Zoology; Radiation Research (AAAS); Leader, Interdisciplinary Review Group, Corps of Engineers, Tennessee-Tombigbee, Waterway project 1982; Distinguished Assoc. Award, US Dept of Energy, Commdrs.' Award, US Army 1990, Award of Honour, Int. Union of Radioecologists, Distinguished Service Award, Ecological Soc. of America. *Address:* 103 Wildwood Drive, Oak Ridge, TN 37830, USA (Home). *Telephone:* (865) 483-5139 (Home). *Fax:* (865) 483-5139 (Office). *E-mail:* stanauer@juno.com (Home).

AUGUST, Bille; Danish film director; b. 9 Nov. 1948; ed Christer Stroholm School of Photography, Stockholm, Danish Film School; worked as cameraman on Homewards at Night, Manrape, The Grass is Singing, Love, before making first feature film 1978. *Television includes:* The World is So Big, So Big, May, Three Days with Magnus, Buster's World (series). *Feature films:* In My Life 1978, Zappa 1983, Twist and Shout 1986, Pelle the Conqueror 1989 (Oscar for Best Foreign Film, Palme d'Or, Cannes Film Festival, Golden Ram, Stockholm, Golden Globe, LA), The Best Intentions 1991, episode of The Young Indiana Jones, The House of the Spirits, Smilla's Feeling for Snow.

AUGUSTINE, Norman Ralph, FIEEE; American aerospace industry executive; b. 27 July 1935, Denver; s. of Ralph Harvey Augustine and Freda Irene (Immenga) Augustine; m. Margareta Engman 1962; two c.; ed Princeton Univ.; Research Asst, Princeton Univ. 1957–58; Program Man., Chief Engineer Douglas Aircraft Co. Inc., Santa Monica, Calif. 1958–65; Asst Dir of Defense Research and Eng, Office of Sec. for Defense, Washington, DC 1965–70; Vice-Pres. Advanced Systems, Missiles and Space Co., LTV Aerospace Corpn, Dallas 1970–73; Asst Sec. Army, The Pentagon, Washington 1965–70, Under-Sec. 1973–75; Vice-Pres. Operations, Martin Marietta Aerospace Corpn, Bethesda, Md 1977–82, Pres. Martin Marietta Denver Aerospace Co. 1982–85, Sr Vice-Pres. Information Systems 1985, Pres. COO 1986–87, Vice-Chair. and CEO 1987–88, Chair. and CEO 1988–95; Pres. Lockheed Martin 1995–96, Pres. CEO 1996–97, Chair. 1998–; mem. Bd of Dirs. Phillips Petroleum Co., Procter & Gamble Co., Riggs Nat. Bank Corpn; mem. NATO Group of Experts on Air Defence 1966–70, NASA Research and Tech. Advisory Council 1973–75; Chair. NASA Space Systems and Tech. Advisory Bd 1985–89; Chair. American Red Cross 1992–; Prof. Princeton Univ. 1997–; Fellow AIAA; mem. American Acad. of Arts and Sciences, Int. Acad. of Astronautics and other bodies; numerous hon. degrees; Nat. Eng Award, American Asscn of Eng Socs. 1991, Goddard Medal, AIAA 1988 and other prizes and awards. *Publications:* Augustine's Laws, The Defense Revolution (co-author) 1990, Augustine's Travels 1997, Shakespeare in Charge: The Bard's Guide to Leading and Succeeding on the Business Stage (with K. Adelman) 2001. *Address:* Amer. Red Cross National Headquarters Building, 17th & D Street NW, Washington, DC 20006 (Home); Lockheed Martin, 6801 Rockledge Drive, Bethesda, MD 20817, USA.

AUGUSZTINOVICS, Maria, DEconSci; Hungarian professor of economics; b. 12 Feb. 1930, Budapest; m. Gabor Fekecs; one s.; ed Budapest Univ. of Econs; at Ministry of Finance 1955–61; at Nat. Planning Bureau 1961–84; Sr Research Adviser, Hungarian Acad. of Sciences 1984, Prof. of Econs 1986–. *Address:* Institute of Economics, Hungarian Academy of Sciences, P.O. Box 262, 1502 Budapest, Hungary (Office). *Telephone:* (1) 309-2645 (Office); (23) 344-226 (Home). *Fax:* (1) 319-3136 (Office); (23) 344-226 (Home). *E-mail:* auguszti@econ.core.hu (Office); auguszti@axelero.hu (Home).

AUKIN, David, BA, FRSA; British theatre, film and television producer; b. 12 Feb. 1942, Harrow; s. of Charles Aukin and Regina Aukin; m. Nancy Meckler 1969; two s.; ed St Paul's School, London and St Edmund Hall, Oxford; founder of Foco Novo and Jt Stock Theatre cos. and admin. producer for various fringe theatre groups 1970–75; Admin. Dir Hampstead Theatre 1975–79, Dir 1979–84; Dir Leicester Haymarket Theatre 1984–86; Exec. Dir Royal Nat. Theatre of Great Britain 1986–90; Pres. Soc. of West End Theatres 1988–90; Head of Drama, Channel 4 TV 1990–97, Head of Film 1997–98; Jt Chief Exec. HAL Films 1998–2000; Producer and Man. Dir David Aukin Productions Ltd 2001–. *Address:* c/o Act Productions Ltd, 20–22 Stukeley Street, London WC2B 5LR, England (Office).

AULENTI, Gae; Italian architect and designer; b. 4 Dec. 1927, Palazzolo dello Stella, Udine; d. of Aldo Aulenti and Virginia Gioia; divorced; one d.; ed Faculty of Architecture, Milan Polytechnic; mem. editorial staff of review

Casabella-Continuità 1955–65; Asst, Venice Faculty of Architecture 1960–62, Milan Faculty of Architecture 1964–67; own architecture, exhbn design, interior design, industrial design, stage design practice, Milan 1956–; solo exhbn, Padiglione d'Arte Contemporanea (PAC), Milan 1979; group exhbn Museum of Modern Art, New York 1972; Hon. mem. American Soc. Interior Designers; Hon. Fellow American Inst. of Architects; Hon. DFA (RI School of Design, USA) 2001; Int. Prize for Italian Pavilion, Milan Triennale 1964, Praemium Imperiale for Architecture, Japan Art Asscn, Tokyo 1991; Chevalier, Légion d'honneur 1987, Cavaliere di Gran Croce, Rome 1995. *Major recent works:* conversion of Gare d'Orsay into museum, Paris 1980–86; new interior design of Musée Nat. d'Art Moderne, Centre Georges Pompidou, Paris 1982–85; restoration of Palazzo Grassi, Venice 1986; conversion of Palau Nacional into Museu Nacional d'Art de Catalunya, Barcelona 1987–2001; new access ramp to S. Maria Novella railway station, Florence 1990; Italian Pavilion at EXPO '92, Seville 1992; new gallery for temp. exhbns at Triennale, Milan 1994; conversion of fmr Leopolda railway station into venue for temp. exhbns, Florence 1996–; conversion of San Francisco Old Main Library into Asian Art Museum 1996–; Spazio Oberdan (new HQ of Nat. Film Hall), Milan 1999; renovation of former Papal Stables at Quirinale as temp. exhbn gallery, Rome 1999; redevt of Piazza Cadorna, Milan 2000; in progress: extension of Mt. Zion Hotel, Jerusalem, renovation of Venaria Royal Palace nr Turin, redevt. of Piazza Cavour and Piazza Dante, Naples. *Exhibition installations:* Futurism 1986, 'Renaissance, Venice and the North: Crosscurrents in the Time of Bellini, Dürer, Titian' 1999, Balthus 2001–02 and other exhbns. at Palazzo Grassi, Venice, The Italian Metamorphosis 1943–1968, Guggenheim Museum, New York and Kunstmuseum, Wolfsburg, Germany 1994–95. *Stage designs:* Elektra, La Scala, Milan 1994, King Lear, Teatro Lirico, Milan 1995, Viaggio a Reims, Rossini Opera Festival, Pesaro 1999, Viaggio a Reims, Teatro Comunale de Bologna 2001. *Industrial design:* furniture, lamps, objects for Kartell, Knoll, Fontana Arte, Louis Vuitton, Tecno, Venini, Zanotta etc. *Leisure interests:* collecting paintings and sculptures. *Address:* 4 piazza San Marco, 20121 Milan, Italy. *Telephone:* (2) 8692613. *Fax:* (2) 874125. *E-mail:* aulenti@tin.it (Office).

AUNG SAN SUU KYI; Myanmar politician; b. 19 June 1945, Rangoon; d. of the late Gen. Aung San; m. Michael Aris 1972 (died 1999); two s.; ed St Francis Convent, Methodist English High School, Lady Shri Ram Coll., Delhi Univ., St Hugh's Coll., Oxford; Asst Sec. Advisory Cttee on Admin. and Budgetary Questions UN Secr., NY 1969–71; Resident Officer, Ministry of Foreign Affairs, Bhutan 1972; Visiting Scholar Centre for SE Asian Studies, Kyoto Univ. 1985–86; Fellow Indian Inst. of Advanced Studies 1987; Co-founder, Gen. Sec. Nat. League for Democracy 1988 (expelled from party), reinstated as Gen. Sec. Oct. 1995; returned from UK 1988; under house arrest 1989–95, house arrest lifted July 1995, placed under de facto house arrest Sept. 2000, released unconditionally May 2002; numerous hon. degrees; Sakharov Prize 1990, European Parl. Human Rights Prize 1991, Nobel Peace Prize 1991, Simón Bolívar Prize 1992, Liberal Int. Prize for Freedom 1995, Jawaharlal Nehru Award for Int. Understanding 1995, Freedom Award of Int. Rescue Cttee 1995, Free Spirit Prize, Freedom Forum USA 2003. *Publications:* Aung San 1984, Burma and India: Some Aspects of Colonial Life Under Colonialism 1990, Freedom from Fear 1991, Towards a True Refuge 1993, Freedom from Fear and Other Writings 1995. *Address:* c/o National League for Democracy, 97B West Shwegondine Road, Bahan Township, Yangon, Myanmar.

AURA, Matti Ilmari, LLM; Finnish business executive and politician; b. 18 June 1943, Helsinki; s. of Teuvo Ensio Aura and Kielo Kaino Kivekäs; m. Marja H. Hiippala 1967; two s.; ed Munkkiniemi High School and Univ. of Helsinki; lawyer, Finnish Export Credit Ltd 1968–69, Confed. of Finnish Industries 1970–71; Man. Dir Cen. Bd of Finnish Wholesale and Retail Asscn 1972–85; Gen. Man. Cen. Chamber of Commerce of Finland 1986; apptd. Minister of Transport and Communications 1997. *Address:* Louhentie 1 H 25, 02130 Espoo, Finland (Home). *Telephone:* (358) 465610 (Home).

AURBACH, Gerhard, Dr rer. pol; German administrative official; b. 19 July 1936, Neuburg/Donau; m. Jennifer Thompson; two d.; ed Univ. of Munich; Asst Univ. of Munich, consultant, IFO Inst. (Econ. Research Inst.) Munich, consultant Fed. Ministry of Transport 1960–63; Admin. European Conf. of Ministers of Transport (ECMT) 1963, Prin. Admin. 1970, Head, Transport Policy Div. 1975, Deputy Sec.-Gen. 1986, apptd Sec.-Gen. ECMT 1992. *Publications:* articles on transport econs and policy. *Leisure interests:* history, classical music, skiing, tennis. *Address:* c/o European Conference of Ministers of Transport, 2 rue André Pascal, 75116 Paris Cedex 16, France.

AURE, Aud Inger, CAND.JUR.; Norwegian politician; b. 12 Nov. 1942, Avcrøy; m.; three c.; mem. Kristiansund Municipal Council 1979–83; mem. Møre og Romsdal Co. Council 1984–95; mem. Cen. Exec. Cttee Women's Org. Christian Democratic Party 1982–, Deputy Chair. 1986–88, Chair. 1988–94; Deputy mem. Storting for Møre og Romsdal Co. 1985–93, mem. 1989–90; mem. Standing Cttee on Justice; Regional Employment Officer 1992–95; Mayor of Kristiansund 1995–; mem. Cen. Exec. Cttee Christian Democratic Party 1995–; Minister of Justice 1997–99. *Address:* Kristelig Folkeparti (Christian Democratic Party), Øvre Slottzgt, 18-20, P.O. Box 478 Sentrum, 0105 Oslo, Norway (Office). *Telephone:* 23-16-28-00 (Office). *Fax:* 23-10-28-10 (Office). *E-mail:* krf@krf.no (Office). *Website:* www.krf.no (Office).

AUROUX, Jean; French politician; b. 19 Sept. 1942, Thizy, Rhône; s. of Louis and Jeanne (née Masson) Auroux; m. Lucienne Sabadie 1967; one s. one d.; ed Lycée Jean Puy, Roanne, Université Claude Bernard de Lyon; City Councillor, Roanne 1976–88, Mayor 1977–2001; mem., then Vice-Pres. Regional Assembly of Rhône-Alpes 1977–81; Pres. District de l'Agglomération Roannaise 1991–; Parti Socialiste Nat. Del. for Housing 1978; mem. Nat. Assembly 1978–81, 1986–88, mem. Finance Cttee; mem. Production and Exchange Cttee; Minister of Labour 1981–82, Minister Del. attached to Social Affairs Ministry, in charge of Labour Affairs 1982–83, Sec. of State at Ministry of Industry and Research in Charge of Energy 1983–84, at Ministry of Urban Planning, Housing and Transport 1984–85, Minister 1985–86; Pres. Socialist Group in Nat. Ass. 1990–93; Pres. Féd. des Maires des Villes Moyennes 1988–2001; mem. Conseil Nat. des Villes, Comité de Décentralisation; Chevalier Légion d'honneur, Officier Ordre nat. du Mérite. *Publication:* Géographie économique à usage scolaire, Rapport sur les nouveaux droits des travailleurs. *Address:* Parti Socialiste, 10 rue de Solférino, 75007 Paris (Office); c/o Fédération des Villes Moyennes, 42 boulevard Raspail, 75007 Paris, France. *Telephone:* 4-77-23-20-13.

AUSHEV, Lt-Gen. Ruslan Sultanovich; Russian/Ingush politician; b. 29 Oct. 1954, Volodarskoye, Kokchetav Region, USSR (now Kazakhstan); s. of Sultan Aushev and Tamara Aushev; m. Aza Ausheva 1983; two s. two d.; ed Ordzhonikidze Gen. Troops School, M. Frunze Mil. Acad.; Commdr motorized infantry co., then platoon 1975–80; Chief of HQ, then Commdr motorized Bn in Afghanistan 1980–82; Chief of Regt HQ in Afghanistan 1985–87; Commdr motorized infantry regt, then Deputy Commdr motorized infantry div. Far East Command 1987–91; at Council of Heads of Govts of CIS countries 1991–92; USSR People's Deputy 1989–91; Head of Admin in newly formed Ingush Repub. Nov.–Dec. 1992; elected Pres. of Repub. of Ingushetia 1993–2001 (resgnd); mem. Council of Fed. of Russia 1993–2000, Rep. of Ingushetia to Council of Fed. 2002–; Hero of Soviet Union (Gold Star). *Leisure interest:* football. *Address:* Council of Federation, Bolshaya Dmitrovka 26, 103426 Moscow, Russia (Office). *Telephone:* (095) 334-20-39 (Office). *Website:* www.ingushetia.ru (Office).

AUSTEN, K(arl) Frank, MD; American professor of medicine; b. 14 March 1928, Akron, Ohio; s. of Karl Arnstein and Bertle J. Arnstein; m. Jocelyn Chapman 1959; two s. two d.; ed Amherst Coll. and Harvard Medical School; Intern in Medicine, Mass. Gen. Hosp. 1954–55, Asst Resident 1955–56, Sr Resident 1958–59, Chief Resident 1961–62, Asst in Medicine 1962–63, Asst Physician 1963–66; Capt., US Army Medical Corps, Walter Reed Army Inst. of Research 1956–58; U.S.P.H.S. Postdoctoral Research Fellow, Nat. Inst. for Medical Research, Mill Hill, London, UK 1959–61; Physician-in-Chief, Robert B. Brigham Hosp. Boston 1966–80; Physician, Peter Bent Brigham Hosp. Boston 1966–80; Chair. Dept Rheumatology and Immunology, Brigham and Women's Hosp., Boston 1980–95, Dir Inflammation and Allergic Diseases Research Section, Div. of Rheumatology and Immunology 1995–; Asst in Medicine, Harvard Medical School 1961, Instr. 1962, Assoc. 1962–64, Asst Prof. 1965–66, Assoc. Prof. 1966–68, Prof. 1969–72, Theodore Bevier Bayles Prof. of Medicine 1972–; Pres. Int. Soc. of Immunopharmacology 1994; numerous cttee assignments, guest lectureships, etc.; mem. numerous professional orgs; recipient of numerous prizes and awards. *Publications:* numerous publications on immunology, etc. *Leisure interests:* skiing, jogging, gardening. *Address:* BWH Department of Rheumatology & Allergy, Smith Building, 55 Francis Street, Boston, MA 02115 (Office); Brigham and Women's Hospital, PBB-B-2, 75 Francis Street, Boston, MA 02115, USA.

AUSTER, Paul; American writer; b. 3 Feb. 1947, Newark, NJ; s. of the late Sam Auster and Queenie Auster; m. 1st Lydia Davis 1974 (divorced 1982); one s.; m. 2nd Siri Hustvedt 1982; one d.; ed Columbia High School, NJ, Columbia Coll., New York, Columbia Univ., New York; worked as census taker; oil tank utility man. on the Esso Florence; moved to Paris, France 1970, returned to USA 1974; worked as trans.; Tutor in Storywriting and Trans., Princeton Univ. 1986–90; juror, Cannes Film Festival 1997. *Publications include:* (fiction): New York Trilogy 1987, In the Country of Last Things 1988, Moon Palace 1989, The Music of Chance 1991, Leviathan 1992, Mr Vertigo 1994, Timbuktu 1999, The Book of Illusions 2002; (non-fiction): The Invention of Solitude 1988, Hand to Mouth (memoir) 1989, The Red Notebook 1995, True Tales of American Life 2001; (poetry): Selected Poems 1998; (screenplays): Smoke 1995, Blue in the Face 1996, Lulu on the Bridge 1999; (critical studies): The Art of Hunger 1997. *Address:* c/o Faber and Faber Ltd., 3 Queen Square, London, WC1N 3AU, England (Office).

AUSTIN, Colin François Lloyd, DPhil, FBA; British classical scholar; b. 26 July 1941, Melbourne, Australia; s. of late Lloyd James Austin; m. Mishtu Mazumdar 1967; one s. one d.; ed Lycée Lakanal, Paris, Manchester Grammar School, Jesus Coll. Cambridge (Scholar), Christ Church Oxford (Sr Scholar) and Freie Universität, West Berlin; Research Fellow, Trinity Hall, Cambridge Univ. 1965–69, Dir of Studies in Classics 1965–; Asst Lecturer in Classics, Cambridge Univ. 1969–73, Lecturer 1973–88, Reader in Greek Language and Literature 1988–98, Prof. of Greek 1998–; Hallam Prize 1961, Browne Medal 1961, Porson Prize 1962. *Publications:* Nova Fragmenta Euripidea 1968, Menandri Aspis et Samia 1969–70, Comicorum Graecorum Fragmenta in papyris reperta 1973, Poetae Comici Graeci (with R. Kassel): Vol. I Comoedia Dorica, Mimi, Phlyaces 2001, Vol. II Agathenor—Aristonymus 1991, Vol. III 2 Aristophanes, Testimonia et Fragmenta 1984, Vol. IV Aristophon—Crobylus 1983, Vol. V Damoxenus—Magnes 1986, Vol. VI 2 Menander, Testimonia et Fragmenta apud Scriptores Servata 1998, Vol. VII Menecrates-Xenophon 1989, Vol. VIII Adespota 1995, Posidippi Pellaei Quae Supersunt Omnia (jtly) 2002. *Leisure interests:* cycling, philately, wine tasting. *Address:* Trinity Hall, Cambridge, CB2 1TJ (Office); 7 Park Terrace, Cambridge, CB1 1JH, England (Home). *Telephone:* (1223) 332520 (Office); (1223) 362732 (Home). *Fax:* (1223) 332537.

AUSTRIAN, Robert, MD, FAAS; American physician and professor of medicine; b. 12 April 1916, Baltimore, Md; s. of Charles Robert Austrian and Florence Hochschild Austrian; m. Babette Friedmann Bernstein 1963; ed Johns Hopkins Univ.; numerous hosp. appts. at Johns Hopkins and other h osps 1941–86; Consultant in Medicine, Veterans Admin. Hosp., Pa 1968–91; Visiting Physician, Hosp. of the Univ. of Pa 1962–; teaching appts at Johns Hopkins Univ. School of Medicine, New York Univ. Coll. of Medicine, State Univ. of New York Coll. of Medicine 1942–62; John Herr Musser Prof. of Research Medicine 1962– (Chair. of Dept of Research Medicine, Univ. of Pa School of Medicine 1962–86), Prof. Emer. 1986–; Visiting Scientist, Dept of Microbial Genetics, Pasteur Inst., Paris, France 1960–61; Dir WHO Collaborating Center for Reference and Research on Pneumococci, Univ. of Pennsylvania School of Medicine 1978–; mem. WHO Expert Advisory Panel on Acute Bacterial Disease 1979–2000; mem. Editorial Bd Antimicrobial Agents and Chemotherapy, Reviews of Infectious Diseases 1979–89, Vaccine; mem. Scientific Advisory Cttee, The Wistar Inst. 1985–87; American Philosophical Soc. 1987–; Fellow American Acad. of Microbiology; Master, American Coll. of Physicians; mem. NAS; Sr mem. Inst. of Medicine 1992 and numerous socs; Hon. DSc (Hahnemann Medical Coll.) 1980, (Philadelphia Coll. of Pharmacy and Science) 1981, (Pennsylvania) 1987, (State Univ. of New York) 1996; numerous awards including Albert Lasker Clinical Medical Research Award 1978, Lifetime Science Award, Inst. for Advanced Studies in Immunology and Aging 1997. *Publications:* Life with the Pneumococcus: Notes from the Bedside, Laboratory and Library 1985; 165 scientific articles in medical journals. *Leisure interests:* ornithology, philately. *Address:* Department of Research Medicine, University of Pennsylvania, The School of Medicine, 36th Street and Hamilton Walk, Philadelphia, PA 19104-6088, USA. *Telephone:* (215) 662-3186. *Fax:* (215) 349-5111 (Office).

AUTEUIL, Daniel; French actor; b. 24 Jan. 1950, Algeria; s. of Henri Auteil and Yvonne Auteil; two d. (one by Emmanuelle Béart, q.v.); worked in musical comedies in Paris; screen debut in L'Agression 1974; stage appearances include Le Garçon d'Appartement 1980; Chevalier des Arts et des Lettres. *Films:* Attention les Yeux 1975, La Nuit Saint-Germain des Près 1976, L'Amour Violé 1976, Monsieur Papa 1977, Les Héros n'ont pas Froid aux Oreilles 1978, A Nous Deux 1979, Bête Mais Discipliné 1979, Les Sous-Doués 1980, La Banquière 1980, Clara et les Chics Types 1980, Les Hommes Préfèrent les Grosses 1981, Les Sous-Doués en Vacances 1981, T'empêches Tout le Monde de Dormir 1981, Pour Cent Briques t'as Plus Rien 1981, L'Indic 1982, Que les Gros Salaires Lèvent le Doigt 1982, P'tit Con 1983, Les Fauves 1983, Palace 1983, L'Arbalete 1984, L'Amour en Douce 1984, Jean de Florette 1985, Manon des Sources (César for Best Actor, Award for Best Actor, Cannes Film Festival) 1985, Le Paltoquet 1986, Quelques Jours Avec Moi 1988, Romuald et Juliette 1989, Lacenaire 1989, Ma Vie Est Un Enfer 1991, Un Coeur en Hiver 1992, Ma Saison Préférée 1992, Quelques Jours Avec Moi, L'Elegant Criminel, Tout Ça Pour Ça 1993, La Séparation 1994, La Reine Margot 1994, Ma Saison Préférée 1994, The Eighth Day 1996, Les Voleurs 1998, La Fille sur le Pont, The Lost Son 1999, La Veuve de Saint Pierre 2000, Sade 2000, The Escort 2000, Le Placard 2001. *Address:* c/o Artmédia, 20 avenue Rapp, 75007 Paris, France (Office).

AVDEYEV, Aleksander Alekseyevich; Russian politician and diplomatist; b. 8 Sept. 1946, Kremenchug, USSR (now Ukraine); m.; one s.; ed Moscow State Inst. of Int. Relations; diplomatic service with USSR Ministry of Foreign Affairs 1968–; Second, First Sec., USSR Embassy, France 1977–85; Counsellor; Head of Sector, First European Dept, USSR Ministry of Foreign Affairs 1985–87; USSR Amb. to Luxembourg 1987–90; First Deputy Head, First European Dept, Ministry of Foreign Affairs 1990–91; USSR Deputy Minister of Foreign Affairs 1991–92; Amb. at Large, Russian Ministry of Foreign Affairs 1992–; Amb. to Bulgaria 1992–96; Deputy Minister of Foreign Affairs 1996–98, First Deputy Minister Oct. 1998–2002, Amb. to France 2002–. *Address:* Embassy of Russia, 40–50 Boulevard Lannes, 75116 Paris, France. *Telephone:* 1-45-04-05-50 (Office). *Fax:* 1-45-04-17-65 (Office). *E-mail:* ambrus@wanadoo.fr (Office).

AVEDON, Richard; American photographer; b. 15 May 1923, New York; s. of Jack Avedon and Anna Polonsky; m. 1st Dorcas Nowell 1944; m. 2nd Evelyn Franklin 1951; one s.; ed Columbia; staff photographer Harper's Bazaar 1945–65, mem. editorial staff Theatre Arts Magazine 1952–53, Vogue magazine 1966–90; first staff photographer The New Yorker 1992–; retrospective Richard Avedon Evidence 1944–94 Whitney Museum of American Art, NY 1994; Visiting Artist Harvard Univ. 1986–87; his work is represented in collections of many maj. museums and in private collections; Fellow Timothy Dwight Coll. Yale Univ. 1975–; Pres.'s Fellow Rhode Island School of Design 1978; Dr. hc (RCA) 1989, (Kenyon Coll., OH); Highest Achievement Medal Awards, Art Dirs. Show 1950; Popular Photography World's 10 Greatest Photographers 1958; Nat. Magazine Award for Visual Excellence 1976; Citation of Dedication to Fashion Photography, Pratt Inst. 1976; Chancellor's Citation, Univ. of Calif., Berkeley 1980; Art Dirs. Club Hall of Fame 1982, American Soc. of Magazine Photographers Photographer of the Year 1985, Best Photographic Book of the Year Award, Maine Photographic Workshop 1985, Dir of the Year, Adweek magazine 1985; Lifetime Achievement Award, Council of Fashion Designers of America 1989, Harvard Univ. Certificate of Recognition, Prix Nadar 1994, Mental Health Asscn of New York City

Humanitarian Award 1996, Lifetime Achievement Award, Columbia Univ. Grad. School of Journalism 2000, Berlin Photography Prize, Deutsches Centrum for Photography 2000. *One-man exhibitions include:* Smithsonian Inst. 1962, Minneapolis Inst. of Arts 1970, Museum of Modern Art 1974, Marlborough Gallery, New York 1975, Metropolitan Museum of Art, New York 1978, Univ. Art Museum, Berkeley, Calif. 1980, Amon Carter Museum, Fort Worth, Texas 1985 and American tour. *Publications:* Observations 1959, Nothing Personal 1964, Ed. Diary of a Century (photographs by Jacques Henri Lartigue) 1970, Alice in Wonderland 1973, Portraits 1976, Rolling Stone Magazine, "The Family" 1976, Avedon: Photographs 1947–77 1978, In the American West 1985, An Autobiography 1993, Evidence 1944–1994 1994. *Address:* Richard Avedon Studio, 407 East 75th Street, New York, NY 10021-3102, USA (Office). *Telephone:* (212) 879-6325.

AVEN, Peter, CandEconSc; Russian economist; b. 16 March 1955, Moscow; s. of Oleg P. Aven; m.; two c.; ed Moscow State Univ.; researcher Research Inst. of System Studies, USSR Acad. of Sciences 1981–88; Int. Inst. of Applied System Analysis in Vienna 1989–91, First Deputy Minister of Foreign Affairs, Chair. Cttee of Foreign Econ. Relations 1991–92; Russian Minister of Foreign Econ. Relations Feb.–Dec. 1992; Pres., Deputy Chair. of Bd Alpha Bank 1994–; Chair. Bd of Dirs STS Television 1998; Chair. Bd of Dirs Golden Telecom Inc. 2001–; mem. State Duma, resgnd 1994; Trustee Bolshoi Theatre, Russian Econ. School. *Publication* The International Economy 2003. *Address:* Alfa Bank, Mashi Poryvayevoy str. 9, 107078 Moscow, Russia. *Telephone:* (095) 974-25-15. *Fax:* (095) 207-61-36. *E-mail:* odubova@alfabank.ru.

AVERCHENKO, Vladimir Alexandrovich, CandEcon; Russian politician and engineer; b. 23 July 1950, Belaya Kalitva, Rostov Region; m.; three c.; ed Novocherkassk Polytech. Inst., New York Univ.; army service 1969–71; on staff Belokalitvinsky City CPSU Cttee 1975–80; constructor maj. industrial sites Rostov Region; Head of Itominstroi, then Promstroi Rostov Region 1980–89; Deputy Chair. Novocherkassk City Exec. Cttee 1989–91; First Vice-Maj. Novocherkassk 1991–98; Deputy Gov., Minister of Econ., Int. and Foreign Relations, Rostov Region 1998–99; concurrently Head Econ. Council Asscn of Social-Econ. Devt N. Caucasus; Deputy State Duma, People's Deputies Group 1999; Head Del. of Fed. Ass. in Parl. Ass. of Black Sea Econ. Co-operation (PACHES); Deputy Chair. State Duma 2000–; State awards and Int. Award for contrib. to devt of free market relations between Russia and CIS countries 1994. *Publications:* numerous publs, 8 books on man., investment policy, ecology. *Leisure interests:* chess, basketball, collecting figurines of lions, collecting coins. *Address:* State Duma, Okhotny Ryad 1, 103265 Moscow, Russia (Office). *Telephone:* (095) 292-84-40 (Office). *Fax:* (095) 292-52-23 (Office).

AVERINTSEV, Sergey Sergeyevich, DPhil; Russian philologist; b. 10 Dec. 1937; m.; one s. one d.; ed Moscow Univ.; Researcher, Sr Researcher, Head of Div., Leading Researcher Inst. of World Literature, USSR Acad. of Sciences 1965–88, Head of Section 1982–92; Prof. Moscow Univ. 1991, Head Dept of Christian Culture 1992–; Prof. Inst. für Slavistik, Vienna Univ. 1994–; Corresp. mem. USSR (now Russian) Acad. of Sciences 1987; mem. Russian Acad. of Natural Sciences; mem. Acad. Universelle de Culture 1991, Academia Europaea 1992, Acad. dell Science Social, Rome 1994; Pres. Asscn of Culturologists of Russia; Chair. Bible Soc. of Russia; USSR People's Deputy 1989–91; USSR State Prize 1991; Leopold Lucas Prize, Tübingen Univ. 1995; Russia State Prize 1996. *Publications:* works on history and theory of literature, studies of Ancient Byzantine, Latin and Syrian Literature, on history of Russian and West European Poetry including Plato and Greek Literature 1973, Poetry of Early Byzantine Literature 1977, From the Banks of Bosphorus to the Banks of Efrat 1987, contribs to the Encyclopedia of Myths and Tales of Peoples of the World. *Address:* Moscow University, Vorob'yevy Gory, Philological Faculty, 119899 Moscow, Russia. *Telephone:* (095) 939-20-08, 939-54-38 (Moscow); (1) 4277-42830 (Vienna).

AVERY, Bryan Robert, MA, DipArch, RIBA; British architect and designer; b. 2 Jan. 1944, Aston Tirrold, Berks; one d.; ed Brockenhurst Co. High School, Leicester Coll. of Art and Essex Univ.; specialised in component devt and industrialized bldg techniques 1967–69; studied history and theory of architecture, Essex Univ. 1969–70; worked in various architect practices 1970–78; founded Avery Assocs 1978–; British Council for Offices Award 1998, RIBA Award 2001, ADAPT Trust Award 2001, National Drywall Awards 2001, USITT Architecture Award 2003, BIAT Technical Excellence in Architecture 2003, many others including Civic Trust Award, City Heritage Award, PA Award for Innovation, Westminster Soc.'s Award, Glassex Award, British Construction Industry Award, Aluminium Imagination Architectural Award, British Council for Offices Award, Millenium Products Award, Comedia Creative City Award. *Artistic achievements:* major bldgs completed include Museum of the Moving Image 1987–88, Nat. Film Theatre foyers and bookshop 1989, No. 1 Neathouse Place 1997, IMAX Cinema for the British Film Inst. 1999, RADA 2000; work in progress includes restoration and improvement of the Commonwealth Inst., the Innovation Centre at Oakham School and a West End commercial redevelopment; maj. design and research projects include Advanced Tech. Housing Project, Wilderness City Project, transformation of Oxford Street and The Mall, Ecological Beacons Project and Cellular Sedan (automobile). *Publications:* numerous articles in the UK and abroad. *Leisure interests:* film, theatre, country walking. *Address:* Avery Associates Architects, 270 Vauxhall Bridge Road, London, SW1V 1BB,

England (Office). *Telephone:* (20) 7233-6262 (Office). *Fax:* (20) 7233-5182 (Office). *E-mail:* enquiries@avery-architects.co.uk (Office). *Website:* www .avery-architects.co.uk (Office).

AVERY, Mary Ellen, AB, MD; American physician; b. 6 May 1927, New Jersey; d. of William Clarence Avery and Mary Catherine Miller; ed Wheaton Coll., Mass., Johns Hopkins School of Medicine; Eudowood Assoc. Prof. of Pediatrics, Johns Hopkins Univ. 1966–69; Prof. and Chairman, Pediatrics, Faculty of Medicine, McGill Univ., Physician-in-Chief, Montreal Children's Hosp. 1969–74; Thomas Morgan Rotch Prof. of Pediatrics, Harvard Medical School 1974–96, Dist Prof. Emer. 1997–; Physician-in-Chief, Children's Hosp., Boston 1974–85; John and Mary Markle Scholar 1961–66; Dir AAAS; mem. Council Inst. of Medicine; mem. NAS 1994–, mem. Council 1997–; Pres. American Paediatric Soc. 1990; numerous hon. degrees; Trudeau Medal, American Thoracic Soc., Nat. Medal of Science 1991, Marta Philipson Award, Karolinska Inst., Stockholm 1998, Walsh McDermott Award, Inst. of Medicine 2000. *Publications:* The Lung and its Disorders in the Newborn Infant 1981, Born Early 1983, Diseases of the Newborn 1971, Pediatric Medicine 1988. *Address:* Children's Hospital, 300 Longwood Avenue, HU432 Boston, MA 02115-5737, USA. *Telephone:* (617) 355-8330. *Fax:* (617) 732-4151.

AVERY, William Hinckley, AM, PhD; American physicist (retd); b. 25 July 1912, Fort Collins, Colo; s. of Edgar Delano Avery and Mabel A. Gordon; m. Helen W. Palmer 1938; one s. one d.; ed Pomona Coll. and Harvard Univ.; Postdoctoral Research Asst Infrared Spectroscopy, Harvard 1937–39; Research Chemist, Shell Oil Co., St Louis, Houston 1939–43; Head, Propulsion Div. Allegany Ballistics Lab. Cumberland, Md 1943–46; Consultant in Physics and Chem. Arthur D. Little Co., Cambridge, Mass. 1946–47; Professional staff mem. Applied Physics Lab. Johns Hopkins Univ. 1947–73, Asst Dir Exploratory Devt 1973–78, Dir Ocean Energy Programs 1978–89, William H. Avery Propulsion Research Lab. named in his honour 1989; mem. various govt advisory panels etc.; mem. ACS; Fellow, American Inst. of Aeronautics and Astronautics; Presidential Certificate of Merit 1948, Sir Alfred Egerton Award 1972, IR 100 Award 1979 and other awards and distinctions. *Publication:* Ocean Thermal Energy Conversion 1992, Renewable Energy from the Ocean: A Guide to OTEC 1994. *Address:* 60 Daley Terrace, Orleans, MA 02653-3318 (Office); 237 North Maine Street, #353, South Yarmouth, MA 02664, USA (Home).

AVICE, Edwige, LèsL; French politician; b. 13 April 1945, Nevers; d. of Edmond Bertrant and Hélène Guyot; m. Etienne Avice 1970; ed Cours Fénelon, Nevers, Lycée Pothier, Orléans, Univ. of Paris; worked for Nat. Cttee for Housing Improvement 1970; Int. Dept, Crédit Lyonnais 1970–73; on staff of Dir-Gen. of Paris Hospitals 1973–78; Pres. Asscn Démocratique des Français de l'Etranger 1991–93; mem. Parti Socialiste (PS) 1972, mem. Exec. Bureau 1977, Nat. Secr. 1987–94, PS Nat. Del. for Nat. Service; mem. Nat. Ass. 1978–81, 1986–88; Minister-Del. for Free Time, Youth and Sports 1981–84; Sec. of State attached to the Minister of Defence 1984–86; Minister-Del. attached to the Minister for Foreign Affairs 1988–91; Minister of Co-operation and Devt 1991–93; Conseillère de Paris 1983–88; Pres. Dir.-Gen. Financière de Brienne 1993–, Brienne Council and Finance 1996–; Pres. Econ. Defence Council 1999–. *Publication:* Terre d'élection 1993. *Leisure interests:* travelling, music, swimming, walking, fencing. *Address:* Financière de Brienne, 2 place Rio de Janeiro, 75008 Paris, France (Office).

AVILA, Rev. Fernando Bastos de; Brazilian ecclesiastic and sociologist; b. 17 March 1918, Rio de Janeiro; ed Univ. do Nova Friburgo (Brazil), Univ. de Louvain and Gregorian Univ., Rome; Prof. of Sociology, Pontificia Univ. Católica do Rio de Janeiro 1957; Social Dir Nat. Catholic Immigration Comm. 1954–; mem. Council, Nat. Fed. of Trade 1960–; Dir Inst. Brasileiro de Desenvolvimento (IBRADES). *Publications:* Economic Impacts of Immigration 1956, L'Immigration au Brésil 1957, Introdução a Sociologia 1962, Solidarismo 1965, Pequena Enciclopédia de Moral Ecivismo 1967. *Address:* 115 rua Bambina-Botatogo, Rio de Janeiro, RJ, Brazil.

AVILDSEN, John Guilbert; American film director, cinematographer and editor; b. 21 Dec. 1935, Ill.; s. of Clarence John Avildsen and Ivy (Guilbert) Avildsen; m. Tracy Brooks Swope 1987; two s. one d.; ed New York Univ.; Advertising Man. Vespa Motor Scooters 1959; served US Army 1959–61; Asst Dir Greenwich Village Story 1961; worked as asst cameraman and production man.; with Muller, Jordan & Herrick Industrial Films 1965–67; mem. Dirs' Guild of America, Motion Picture Photographers' Union, Motion Picture Eds Union, Writers' Guild of America. *Films include:* Turn On to Love 1967, Sweet Dreams 1968, Guess What We Learned in School Today 1969, Joe 1970, Cry Uncle 1971, Save the Tiger 1972, Inaugural Ball 1973, W.W. and the Dixie Dancekings 1974, Rocky 1976 (Acad. Award for Best Dir), Slow Dancing in the Big City 1978, The Formula 1980, Neighbors 1981, Traveling Hopefully 1982, A Night in Heaven 1983, The Karate Kid 1984, Happy New Year 1985, The Karate Kid II 1986, For Keeps 1987, The Karate Kid III 1989, Lean on Me 1989 (Image Award, NAACP), Rocky V 1990, The Power of One 1992, 8 Seconds 1994, Save the Everglades (documentary), A Fine and Private Place, Coyote Moon 1998. *Television:* From No House to Options House (Emmy Award). *Address:* c/o United Talent Agency Dan Aloni, 9560 Wilshire Blvd., Fl. 5, Beverly Hills, CA 90212-2401, USA.

AVINERI, Shlomo; Israeli professor of political science; b. 20 Aug. 1933, Bielsko, Poland; s. of Michael Avineri and Erna Groner; m. Dvora Nadler 1957; one d.; ed Shalva Secondary School, Tel Aviv, Hebrew Univ., Jerusalem and London School of Econs; has lived in Israel since 1939; Prof. of Political Science, Hebrew Univ. Jerusalem 1971–, Dir Eshkol Research Inst. 1971–74, Dean of Faculty of Social Sciences 1974–76; Dir-Gen. Ministry of Foreign Affairs 1976–77; Dir Inst. for European Studies, Hebrew Univ. 1997–; visiting appointments at Yale Univ. 1966–67, Wesleyan Univ., Middletown, Conn. 1971–72, Research School of Social Sciences, Australian Nat. Univ. 1972, Cornell Univ. 1973, Univ. of Calif. 1979, Queen's Coll., New York 1989, Oxford 1989; mem. Int. Inst. of Philosophy 1980–; Fellow, Woodrow Wilson Center, Washington, DC 1983–84; Carlyle Lecturer, Oxford 1989; Visiting Prof., Cardozo School of Law, NY 1996–97, 2000–01, Brookings Inst., Washington, DC 1991, Cen. European Univ., Budapest 1994, Northwestern Univ., Evanston 1997, Carnegie Endowment for Int. Peace, Washington, DC 2000–01; British Council Scholarship 1961; Fellow Collegium Budapest 2002; Rubin Prize in the Social Sciences 1968, Naphtali Prize for study of Hegel 1977, Present Tense Award for Study of Zionism 1982, Israel Prize 1996. *Publications:* The Social and Political Thought of Karl Marx 1968, Karl Marx on Colonialism and Modernization 1968, Israel and the Palestinians 1971, Marx's Socialism 1972, Hegel's Theory of the Modern State 1973, Varieties of Marxism 1977, The Making of Modern Zionism 1981, Moses Hess—Prophet of Communism and Zionism 1985, Arlosoroff—A Political Biography 1989, Communitarianism and Individualism (co-author) 1992, Herzl's Diaries 1998, Identity and Integration 1999, The Law of Religious Identity (co-author) 1999, Identities in Transformation 2002. *Address:* Faculty of Social Sciences, Hebrew University of Jerusalem, Mount Scopus, Jerusalem (Office); 10 Hagedud Ha-ivri Street, Jerusalem, Israel (Home). *Telephone:* (2) 588-3286 (Office); (2) 563-0862 (Home). *Fax:* (2) 588-1535. *E-mail:* shlomo.avineri@huji .ac.il (Office).

AVNET, Jonathan Michael, BA; American film company executive and film director; b. 17 Nov. 1949, Brooklyn, New York; m. Barbara Brody; one s. two d.; ed Sarah Lawrence Coll., Univ. of Pennsylvania, Conservatory for Advanced Film Studies; Reader United Artists, LA 1974; Dir Creative Affairs, Sequoia Pictures, LA 1975–77; Pres. Tisch/Avnet Productions, LA 1977–85; Chair. Avnet/Kerner Co., LA 1985–; Pres. Allied Communications Inc.; dir and producer (films): Fried Green Tomatoes at the Whistle Stop Cafe (3 Golden Globes), The War, Up Close and Personal, George of the Jungle; producer, writer, Ddir (TV series): Call to Glory 1984–85 (Golden Reel aAward), Between Two Women (Emmy Award); producer, exec. producer (films): Risky Business, Men Don't Leave, Less than Zero, When a Man Loves a Woman, Mighty Ducks, Deal of the Century, Miami Rhapsody, Three Musketeers; exec. producer: The Burning Bed, Silence of the Heart, Heatwave (4 Cable Ace Awards, including Best Picture), Do You Know the Muffin Man, No Other Love, Steal This Movie; Trustee LA Co. Opera; Fellow American Film Inst.; mem. Dirs' Guild of America, Writers' Guild of America, Acad. of Motion Pictures Arts and Sciences. *Leisure interests:* basketball, skiing, biking.

AVRIL, Pierre; French professor; b. 18 Nov. 1930, Pau; s. of Stanislas Avril and Geneviève Camion; m. Marie-Louise Hillion 1959; one s.; Asst Pierre Mendès France 1955–62, Ed.-in-Chief Cahiers de la Répub. 1960–62; sub.-ed. Soc. Gen. de Presse 1962–69; Prof. Faculté de Droit de Poitiers 1972–79, Univ. de Paris X 1979–88, Inst. d'études politiques 1982–97, Univ. de Paris II 1988–99; mem. Conseil supérieur de la magistrature 1998–2002; Pres. Commission de réflexion sur le statut pénal du Président de la République 2002. *Publications:* Le Régime politique de la Vᵉ République 1964, Droit parlementaire (with others) 1988; Un président pour quoi faire? 1965, Essais sur les partis politiques 1990, La Vᵉ République—histoire politique et constitutionnelle 1994, Les conventions de la Constitution 1997. *Address:* 48 rue Gay-Lussac, 75005 Paris, France (Home). *Telephone:* 1-43-26-36-43.

AVRIL, Brig.-Gen. Prosper; Haitian politician and army officer; ed Mil. Acad. Haiti and Univ. of Haiti Law School; fmr adviser to deposed Pres. Jean-Claude Duvalier; adviser to mil.-civilian junta headed by Gen. Namphy and mem. Nat. Governing Council 1986; Commdr Presidential Guard 1988; maj. participant in June 1988 coup which overthrew civilian Govt of Leslie Manigat; leader of coup which deposed regime of Gen. Namphy Sept. 1988; Pres. of Haiti 1988–90; in USA March 1990.

AWADALLAH, Babikir; Sudanese politician and jurist; b. 1917, El Citaina, Blue Nile Province; ed School of Law, Gordon Coll., Khartoum; District Judge 1947–54; resgnd to become Speaker of Sudanese House of Reps. 1954–57; Judge of the Supreme Court 1957, Chief Justice 1964–69; Prime Minister and Minister of Foreign Affairs May–Oct. 1969; Deputy Chair. Revolutionary Council, Minister of Foreign Affairs 1969–70, Minister of Justice 1969–71, Deputy Prime Minister 1970–71; First Vice-Pres. of Sudan 1971–72. *Address:* c/o Sudanese Socialist Union, Khartoum, Sudan.

AWOONOR, Kofi Nyidevu, PhD; Ghanaian writer, teacher, diplomatist and politician; b. 13 March 1935, Wheta; s. of Kosiwo Awoonor and Atsu Awoonor; m.; five s. one d.; ed Univ. of Ghana, Univ. Coll., London and State Univ. of NY, Stony Brook; Research Fellow, Inst. of African Studies; Man. Dir Film Corpn, Accra; Longmans Fellow, Univ. of London; Asst Prof. and later Chair. Comparative Literature Program, State Univ. of NY; Visiting Prof., Univ. of Texas, Austin and New School of Social Research, NY; detained in Ghana for allegedly harbouring leader of coup 1975; on trial 1976, sentenced to one year's imprisonment Oct. 1976, pardoned Oct. 1976; fmr Chair. Dept of English and Dean of Faculty of Arts, Univ. of Cape Coast; Sec.-Gen. Action Congress Party; Amb. to Brazil 1984–90 (also accred to Cuba 1988–90); Perm. Rep. to UN 1990–94; currently Minister of State; Contributing Ed., Transition and Alcheringa; Longmans and Fairfield Fellowships; Gurrey Prize for Poetry, Nat. Book Council Award for Poetry 1979, Dillons Commonwealth Prize for Poetry (Africa Div.) 1989, Order of the Volta 1977, Agbonugla of ANLO 1997, Agbaledzigla of the Wheta Traditional Area 1998. *Publications:* poetry: Rediscovery 1964, Messages 1970, Night of My Blood 1971, House by the Sea 1978, Until the Morning After (collected poems); prose: This Earth My Brother 1971, Guardians of the Sacred Word 1973, Ride Me Memory 1973, Breast of the Earth 1974 (history of African literature), Traditional African Literature (Sseries, Ed.), Alien Corn (novel) 1974, Where is the Mississippi Panorama 1974, Fire in the Valley: Folktales of the Ewes 1980, The Ghana Revolution, Ghana: A Political History 1990, Comes the Voyage at Last 1991, The Caribbean and Latin American Notebook 1992, Africa the Marginalized Continent. *Leisure interests:* jazz, walking, tennis, hunting. *Address:* c/o Secretariat for Foreign Affairs, P.O.B. M212, Accra, Ghana. *Telephone:* (21) 665415 ext. 119 (Office); (21) 503580 (Home). *Fax:* (21) 660246 (Office).

AXELROD, Julius, PhD; American biochemical pharmacologist; b. 30 May 1912, New York; s. of Isadore Axelrod and Molly Axelrod (née Leichtling); m. Sally Taub 1938; two s.; ed Coll. of the City of New York, New York Univ. and George Washington Univ. Lab.; Asst, Dept of Bacteriology, New York Univ. Medical School 1933–35; Chemist, Laboratory of Industrial Hygiene 1935–46; Research Assoc., Third New York Univ. Research Div., Goldwater Memorial Hosp. 1946–49; Assoc. Chemist, Nat. Heart Inst., Nat. Inst. of Health 1949–50, Chemist 1950–53, Sr Chemist 1953–55; Chief, Section on Pharmacology, Lab. of Chemical Science, Nat. Inst. of Mental Health, Health Services and Mental Health Admin., Dept of Health, Educ. and Welfare 1955–84; Professorial Lecturer George Washington Univ. 1959; Guest Researcher, Nat. Inst. of Mental Health 1984–; mem. Scientific Advisory Bd, Nat. Foundation, Brookhaven Nat. Lab., Center for Biomedical Educ. and many others; mem. Int. Brain Research Organization; Senior mem. Inst. of Medicine; Foreign mem. Royal Society; Fellow, American Coll. of Neuropsychopharmacology (mem. Council 1966–69); mem. ACS, American Soc. of Pharmacology and Experimental Therapeutics, American Soc. of Biological Chemists, AAAS; Fellow, American Acad. of Arts and Sciences, NAS; Corresp. mem. German Pharmacological Soc.; Foreign mem. Acad. der Naturforcher DDR; Hon. ScD (Univ. of Chicago, Medical Coll. of Wisconsin, New York Univ, Medical Coll. of Pa, Univ. of Pennsylvania); Hon. LLD (George Washington Univ.); Hon. LLD (Coll. of the City of New ; Dr hc (Univ. of Panama); Gairdner Foundation Award 1967, Distinguished Achievement Award, George Washington Univ. 1968, Dept of Health, Educ. and Welfare 1970, Modern Medicine Magazine 1970, Claude Bernard Medal, Univ. of Montreal 1969, Nobel Prize for Medicine or Physiology 1970, Albert Einstein Achievement Award, Yeshiva Univ. 1971, Torald Sollmann Award in Pharmacology 1973, Paul Hoch Award, American Psychopathological Asscn 1975, etc.; several research awards, memorial lectureships etc. *Publications:* The Pineal 1968 (with Richard J. Wurtman and Douglas E. Kelly), 450 articles in professional journals, also abstracts and press articles. *Leisure interests:* music, reading. *Address:* Department of Health Education and Welfare, National Institute of Health, 9000 Rockville Pike, Room 3A-15, Bethesda, MD 20892-0003 (Office); 10401 Grosvenor Place, Rockville, MD 20852, USA (Home). *Telephone:* (301) 493-6376. *Fax:* (301) 402-1748.

AXER, Erwin; Polish theatre producer and director; b. 1 Jan. 1917, Vienna, Austria; s. of Dr Maurycy Axer and Fryderyka Schuster; m. Bronisława Kreczmar 1945 (died 1973); two s.; ed Nat. Acad. of Theatrical Art, Warsaw; Asst Producer, Nat. Theatre, Warsaw 1938–39; Actor Polish Drama Theatre, Lvov, USSR 1939–41; Artistic Dir, Teatr Kameralny, Łódź 1946–49; Dir and Producer, Teatr Współczesny (Contemporary Theatre), Warsaw 1949–81; Dir and Chief Producer, Nat. Theatre, Warsaw 1954–57; Asst Prof. Producers' Dept, State Higher Theatrical School, Łódź 1946–49, Warsaw 1949–55, Extraordinary Prof. 1955–66, Prof. Ordinary 1966–81, Prof. Emer. 1981; mem. Presidential Council for Culture 1992–95; State Prizes for Artistic Achievement 1951, 1953, 1955, 1962, Nagroda Krytyki im. Boya-Żeleńskiego (Critics Award) 1960; Commdr's Cross, Order of Polonia Restituta, Great Cross, Order of Polonia Restituta 1996; Order of Banner of Labour (1st Class); other awards and prizes. *Productions include:* Major Barbara (Shaw) 1947, Niemcy (Kruczkowski) 1955, Kordian (Słowacki) 1956, Pierwszy dzień wolności 1959, Iphigenia in Tauris 1961, Kariera Arturo Ui (Brecht), Warsaw 1962, Leningrad 1963, Three Sisters (Chekhov) 1963, Düsseldorf 1967, Androcles and the Lion (Shaw), Warsaw 1964, Tango (Mrożek), Warsaw 1965, Düsseldorf 1966, Die Ermittlung (Weiss), Warsaw 1966, Le Piéton de l'Air (Ionesco), Warsaw 1967, Maria Stuart (Schiller), Warsaw 1969, Dwa Teatry (Szaniawski), Leningrad 1969, Matka (Witkiewicz), Warsaw 1970, Porträt eines Planeten, Düsseldorf 1970, Old Times and Macbeth, Warsaw 1972, Uncle Vanya, Munich 1972, Ein Fest für Boris, Vienna (Kainz Award) 1973, Maria Stuart (Schiller), Vienna 1974, King Lear (Bond), Warsaw, 1974, Endgame (Beckett), Vienna 1976, Kordian, Warsaw 1977, Seagull (Chekhov), Vienna 1977, Biedermann und die Brandstifter (Max Frisch), Zürich 1978, Krawiec (Tailor by Mrożek), Warsaw 1979, Wesele (Wyspiański), New York 1962, Our Town, Leningrad 1979, John Gabriel Borkman, Zürich 1979, Triptychon (Frisch), Warsaw 1980, Die Schwärmer (Musil), Vienna 1980, Triptychon (Frisch), Vienna 1981, Amphitryon (Kleist), Vienna 1982, Till Damascus (Strindberg), Munich 1983, Reigen (Schnizler), Vienna 1983, Vinzenz (Musil), Vienna 1985, Am Ziel (Bernhard), Berlin 1987, Nachtasyl (Gorky), Berlin 1987, Theatermacher (Bernhard), Warsaw 1990, When We Dead Awaken (Ibsen), Hamburg 1990, Emigranci (Mrożek), Bregenz 1990, Mein Kampf (Tabori), Hamburg 1992, The Widows, Warsaw 1992, Love in Crimea (Mrożek), Warsaw 1994, Ambassador 1995, Warsaw Semiramida (Wojtyszko) 1996, Am Ziel (Bernhard), Warsaw 1997, Androcles and the Lion (Shaw), Poznań 1999, Easter (Strindberg), Warsaw 2001. *TV:* plays by Frisch, Mrożek, Dürrenmatt and others, Warsaw 1962–, Tango (Mrożek,), Düsseldorf 1966, Die Schwärmer (Musil), Vienna 1980. *Publications include:* Listy ze sceny I (Letters from the Stage) 1955, Listy ze sceny II 1957, Sprawy teatralne (Theatrical Things) 1966, Ćwiczenia pamięci (Exercises of the Memory Series I) 1984, Exercises of the Memory Series II 1991, Exercises of the Memory Series III 1998, essays, serial, articles on theatre. *Address:* ul. Odyńca 27 m. 11, 02-606 Warsaw, Poland (Home). *Telephone:* (22) 844-01-16 (Home). *Fax:* (22) 825-52-17 (Office).

AXFORD, David Norman, MA, MSc, PhD, CEng, FIEE; British meteorologist; b. 14 June 1934, London; s. of Norman Axford and Joy A. (Williams) Axford; m. 1st Elizabeth A. Stiles 1962 (divorced 1980); one s. two d.; m. 2nd Diana R. J. Bufton 1980; three step-s. one step-d.; ed Merchant Taylors School, Plymouth Coll., St John's Coll. Cambridge and Southampton Univ.; Scientific Officer, Kew Observatory 1960–62; Sr Scientific Officer, various RAF stations 1962–68; Prin. Scientific Officer, Meteorological Research Flight, Royal Aircraft Establishment, Farnborough 1968–76; Asst Dir (SPSO) Operation Instrumentation Branch 1976–80; Asst Dir (SPSO), Telecommunications 1980–82; Deputy Dir Observational Services 1982–84; Dir of Services and Deputy to Dir-Gen. Meteorological Office 1984–89; Pres. N Atlantic Ocean Station Bd 1982–85; Chair. Cttee of Operational World Weather Watch System Evaluations—N. Atlantic (CONA) 1985–89; Deputy Sec.-Gen. World Meteorological Org., Geneva 1989–1995, Special Exec. Adviser to Sec.-Gen. Jan–May 1995; Consultant Meteorologist 1995–; Consultant to Earthwatch Europe, Oxford 1996–2000; Chair. of Trustees Stanford in the Vale Public Purposes Charity 2000–02; Hon. Sec. Royal Meteorological Soc. 1983–88, Vice-Pres. 1989–91, Chair. Accreditation Bd 1999–, Sec. Special Group on Observations and Instruments 1999–2001; Trustee Thames Valley Hospice, Windsor 1996–98; mem. Exec. Cttee British Asscn of Former UN Civil Servants (BAFUNCS) 1996–, Vice-Chair. 1998, Chair. 1999–; Chartered Meteorologist of Royal Meteorological Soc. 1994–; Vice-Pres. and Treas. European Meteorological Soc. 2002–; Groves Award 1972. *Publications:* articles in professional journals. *Leisure interests:* home and garden, food and wine, Tibetan terrier, 12 grandchildren. *Address:* Honey End, 14 Ock Meadow, Stanford-in-the-Vale, Oxon., SN7 8LN, England. *Telephone:* (1367) 718480. *E-mail:* david.axford@dial.pipex.com (Home).

AXFORD, Sir William Ian, Kt, MSc, ME, PhD, FRS; British/New Zealand scientist; b. 2 Jan. 1933, Dannevirke, NZ; s. of John Edgar Axford and May Victoria (née Thoresen) Axford; m. Catherine Joy Lowry 1955; two s. two d.; ed Canterbury Univ. Coll., NZ, Manchester Univ. and Cambridge Univ.; mem. staff Defence Research Bd, Canada 1960–62; Assoc. Prof., then Prof. of Astronomy, Cornell Univ., USA 1963–67; Prof. of Physics and Applied Physics, Univ. of Calif., San Diego, USA 1967–74; Ed. Journal of Geophysical Research 1969–73; Scientific mem. and Dir Max Planck Inst. für Aeronomie 1974–82, 1985–2002, Dir Emer. 2002–; Vice-Chancellor, Victoria Univ. of Wellington, NZ 1982–85; Pres. Cttee on Space Research 1986–94; Vice-Pres. Scientific Cttee on Solar Terrestrial Physics 1986–90; Chair. Foundation for Research, Science and Tech., NZ 1992–95; Pres. European Geophysical Soc. 1990–92; Chair. Marsden Fund, NZ 1994–98; Assoc. Royal Astronomical Soc.; Fellow American Geophysical Union; Foreign Assoc. NAS; mem. Acad. Europaea; Hon. mem. European Geophysical Soc.; Hon. FRSNZ; Hon. Prof. (Gottingen); Pei-Ling Chan Eminent Scholar in Astrophysics, Univ. of Ala 2002–; Hon. DSc (Canterbury, NZ) 1996, (Victoria, NZ) 1999; Appleton Award (Union Radio-Scientifique Int.), J. A. Fleming Award (American Geophysical Union), Space Award (AIAA), Tsiolkovski Medal, Chapman Medal (Royal Astronomical Soc.) 1994, NZ Science and Tech. Medal (Royal Soc. of NZ) 1994, Scientist of the Year and New Zealander of the Year 1995. *Publications:* c. 280 scientific articles on various aspects of astrophysics, cosmic ray physics and space physics. *Leisure interests:* reading, family history, writing on historical topics. *Address:* 2 Gladstone Road, Napier, New Zealand; Max Planck Institut für Aeronomie, Max-Planck-Str. 2, 37191 Katlenburg-Lindau, Germany. *Telephone:* (6) 8352188 (NZ); (5556) 979 439 (Germany). *Fax:* (6) 8352176 (NZ); (5556) 979 149 (Germany). *E-mail:* axford@linmpi.mpg.de (Office); axford@inhb.co.nz (Home).

AXWORTHY, Lloyd, MA, PhD; Canadian politician and academic; b. 21 Dec. 1939; s. of Norman Joseph Axworthy and Gwen Jane Axworthy; m. Denise Ommaney 1984; one s.; ed Princeton Univ.; fmr Prof. of Political Science, Univ. of Winnipeg; fmr mem. Man. Legis.; mem. House of Commons 1979–; MP for Winnipeg South-Centre 1988–; fmr Minister of Employment and Immigration, Minister responsible for Status of Women and Minister of Transport; Minister of Human Resources Devt and Minister of Western Econ. Diversification 1993–96, of Foreign Affairs 1996–2002; mem. Liberal Party. *Address:* c/o Liberal Party of Canada, 81 Metcalfe Street, Suite 400, Ottawa, Ont., K1P 6M8, Canada.

AYALA, Francisco Jose, PhD; American (naturalized) professor of genetics; b. 12 March 1934, Madrid, Spain; s. of Francisco and Soledad (née Pereda) Ayala; m. Hana Lostakova 1985; two s. (by previous m.); ed Univ. of Madrid and Columbia Univ.; Research Assoc. Rockefeller Univ., New York 1964–65, Asst Prof. 1967–71; Asst Prof. Providence Coll., RI 1965–67; Assoc. Prof., later Prof. of Genetics Univ. of Calif., Davis 1971–87, Dir Inst. of Ecology 1977–81, Assoc. Dean of Environmental Studies 1977–81; Distinguished Prof. of Biology Univ. of Calif., Irvine 1987–89, Donald Bren Prof. of Biological

Sciences 1989–; Pres. AAAS 1994–95; mem. NAS, American Acad. of Arts and Sciences, American Philosophical Soc., Pres. Cttee of Advisers on Science and Tech. 1994–2001; Dr. hc (León) 1982, (Madrid) 1986, (Barcelona) 1986, (Athens) 1991, (Vigo) 1996, (Islas Baleares) 1998, (Valencia) 1999, (Bologna) 2001. *Publications:* Studies in the Philosophy of Biology 1974, Molecular Evolution 1976, Evolution 1977, Evolving: The Theory and Processes of Organic Evolution 1979, Population and Evolutionary Genetics 1982, Modern Genetics 1984 and more than 750 scientific articles. *Leisure interests:* travel, reading, collecting fine art. *Address:* Department of Ecology and Evolutionary Biology, University of California, Irvine, CA 92697 (Office); 2 Locke Court, Irvine, CA 92612, USA (Home). *Telephone:* (949) 824-8293 (Office). *Fax:* (949) 824-2474. *E-mail:* fjayala@uci.edu (Office). *Website:* ecoevo.bio.uci.edu/faculty/ayala/ayala.html (Office).

AYALA-CASTAÑERES, Agustín, MS, D.BIOL.; Mexican professor of micropaleontology; b. 28 Aug. 1925, Mazatlán; s. of Agustín Ayala and María Luisa Castañares; m. Alma Irma López 1957; one s. two d.; ed Universidad Nacional Autónoma de México (UNAM) and Stanford Univ.; micropaleontologist, Pemex 1950–54; Prof. of Paleontology, Inst. Politécnico Nacional (IPN) 1955–60; Head, Dept of Micropaleontology and Marine Science Dept Inst. of Geology, UNAM 1956–67; Prof. of Micropaleontology, Faculty of Sciences, UNAM 1961–, Head, Dept of Biology 1965–67, Dir Inst. Biología 1967–73; full-time researcher, Centro de Ciencias del Mar y Limnología, UNAM 1970–81; Coordinator of Scientific Investigation, UNAM 1973–80; Assoc. Researcher, Scripps Inst. of Oceanography, Univ. of Calif. San Diego 1968–; Chair. Nat. Cttee Scientific Cttee on Oceanic Research (SCOR) 1971–; Dir Plan para Crear una Infraestructura en Ciencias y Tecnologías del Mar, México-UNESCO 1974–80; Pres. Acad. de la Investigación Científica (AIC) 1975–76; Chair. Intergovernmental Oceanographic Comm. UNESCO 1977–82; Exec. Dir Programa Nacional de Ciencia y Tecnología para el Aprovechamiento de los Recursos Marinos (PROMAR-CONACyT) 1974–80; Chair. Org. Cttee Jt Oceanographic Ass., Mexico 1988; mem. Bd Trustees, Int. Center for Living Aquatic Resources Man. (ICLARM) 1989–94; Gen. Coordinator, Interinst. Comms. for Evaluation of Higher Educ. 1991–; Fellow, Geological Soc. of America; mem. Int. Asscn of Plant Taxonomy and Nomenclature, American Soc. of Ecology, American Soc. of Petroleum Geologists, Soc. of Econ. Paleontologists and Mineralogists, etc.; Dr. hc (Bordeaux) 1988. *Publications:* 52 articles on fossil foraminifera, marine geology, coastal lagoons and science policy. *Address:* Apartado Postal 70-157, México 04510 DF (Office); 43 Cerro del Jabalí, México 04320 DF, Mexico (Home).

AYALA-LASSO, José; Ecuadorean diplomatist and international civil servant; b. 29 Jan. 1932, Quito; m.; four c.; ed Pontificia Universidad Católica del Ecuador, Universidad Cen. del Ecuador, Université Catholique de Louvain, Belgium; several foreign affairs posts at embassies in Japan, Repub. of Korea, China, Italy; Minister of Foreign Affairs 1977; fmr Amb. to Belgium, Luxembourg, Peru, EEC; Lecturer Int. Law Inst., Universidad Cen. del Ecuador; Deputy Legal Sec. Perm Comm. for the South Pacific; Perm. Rep. to UN 1989–94, Chair. Security Council Cttee concerning fmr Yugoslavia 1991; Chair. working group to establish post of High Commr for Human Rights 1993; UN High Commr for Human Rights 1994–97, Minister of Foreign Affairs 1997–99; Amb. to Holy See 1999–2002; Grand Cross, Nat. Order of Merit (Ecuador); numerous decorations from Japan, Belgium, Brazil, etc. *Address:* c/o Ministry of Foreign Affairs, Avda 10 de Agosto y Carrión, Quito, Ecuador.

AYARI, Chedli, LenD, DèsSc(Econ); Tunisian economist, diplomatist and politician; b. 24 Aug. 1933, Tunis; s. of Sadok and Fatouma Chedly; m. Elaine Vatteau 1959; three c.; ed Collège Sadiki and Inst. de Hautes Etudes; with Société Tunisienne de Banque 1958; Asst Faculté de Droit et des Sciences Economiques et Politiques, Tunis 1959; Econ. Counsellor, Perm. Mission of Tunis at UN 1960–64; Exec. Dir IBRD 1964–65; Dean, Faculté de Droit, Tunis 1965–67; Dir CERES 1967–69; Sec. of State in charge of Plan 1969–70; Minister of Nat. Educ., Youth and Sport 1970–71; Amb. to Belgium Feb.–March 1972; Minister of Nat. Economy 1972–74, of Planning 1974–75; Chair. of Bd and Gen. Man. Arab Bank for Econ. Devt in Africa 1975; Prof. of Economics, Agrégé de Sciences Economiques, Tunis; Assoc. Prof. Univ. of Aix-Marseilles 1989–; mem. UN Cttee of Planning for Devt; Dr hc (Aix-Marseilles) 1972; Grand Officier Légion d'honneur, Grand Cordon, Ordre de la République. *Publications:* Les Enjeux méditerranéens 1992, La Méditerranée economique 1992; books and articles on econ. and monetary problems. *Leisure interest:* music. *Address:* Rue Tanit, Gammarth, La Marsa, Tunis, Tunisia (Home). *Telephone:* 270-038.

AYATSKOV, Dmitry Fedorovich, DHistSc; Russian politician; b. 9 Nov. 1950, Stolypino, Saratov Region; s. of Fedor Kuzmich Ayatskov and Anna Petrovna Ayatskov; m.; one s. one d.; ed Saratov Inst. of Agric., Moscow Cooperation Inst.; machine-operator, electrician in kolkhoz; army service 1969–71; chief agronomist in kolkhozes, leading posts on maj. enterprises of region (Tantal, Saratovskoye) 1977–80; Vice-Mayor of Saratov 1992–96; Head of Admin. Saratov Region 1996–; Gov. 1996–; mem. Council of Fed. of Russia 1993–2000; mem. Our Home Russia 1995–99, Yedinstvo-Otechestvo 2001; Order of Honour, Order for Merits to the Homeland. *Leisure interest:* history. *Address:* Office of the Governor, Moskovskaya str. 72, 410042 Saratov, Russia (Office). *Telephone:* (8452) 72-20-86 (Office). *Fax:* (8452) 72-52-54 (Office). *E-mail:* governor@gov.saratov.ru (Office).

AYCKBOURN, Sir Alan, Kt, CBE; British playwright and theatre director; b. 12 April 1939, London; s. of Horace Ayckbourn and Irene Maud Ayckbourn (née Worley); m. 1st Christine Helen Roland 1959 (divorced 1997); two s.; m. 2nd Heather Elizabeth Stoney 1997; ed Haileybury; on leaving school went straight into the theatre as stage manager and actor with various repertory cos. in England; founder mem. Victoria Theatre Co., Stoke on Trent 1962–64; Drama Producer, BBC Radio 1964–70; Artistic Dir, Stephen Joseph Theatre, Scarborough 1971–; Prof. of Contemporary Theatre, Oxford 1992; Hon. Fellow (Bretton) 1982, (Cardiff) 1995; Hon. DLitt (Hull) 1981, (Keele, Leeds) 1987, (Bradford) 1994; Dr. hc (York) 1992, (Open Univ.) 1998; Evening Standard Award for Best New Comedy for Absurd Person Singular 1973, for Best New Play for The Norman Conquests 1974, for Best New Play for Just Between Ourselves 1977, Plays and Players Award for Best New Play for The Norman Conquests 1974, Variety Club of Great Britain Playwright of the Year 1974, Co-winner Plays and Players Award for Best New Comedy for Joking Apart 1979, London Evening Standard Award, Olivier Award and DRAMA Award for Best Comedy for A Chorus of Disapproval 1985, London Evening Standard Award for Best New Play for A Small Family Business 1987, Plays and Players Director of the Year Award for A View from the Bridge 1987, London Evening Standard Award for Best Comedy for Henceforward... 1989, for Man of the Moment 1990, Lifetime Achievement Award (Writers' Guild) 1993, Montblanc de la Culture Award for Europe 1994, Writers' Guild of GB Award for Best West End Play for Communicating Doors 1996, British Regional Theatre Awards for Best Musical for By Jeeves 1996, Lloyds Pvt. Banking Playwright of the Year Award for Things We Do For Love 1997, Sunday Times Literary Award for Excellence 2001. *Plays:* Mr Whatnot 1993, Relatively Speaking 1965, How the Other Half Loves 1969, Ernie's Incredible Illucinations 1969, Time and Time Again 1971, Absurd Person Singular 1972, The Norman Conquests 1973, Jeeves (book and lyrics for Andrew Lloyd Webber musical) 1975 (rewritten as By Jeeves 1996), Absent Friends 1974, Confusions 1974, Bedroom Farce 1975, Just Between Ourselves 1976, Ten Times Table 1977, Joking Apart 1978, Family Circles 1978, Sisterly Feelings 1979, Taking Steps 1979, Suburban Strains (musical play with music by Paul Todd) 1980, Season's Greetings 1980, Me, Myself & I (with Paul Todd) 1981, Way Upstream 1981, Intimate Exchanges 1982, It Could Be Any One Of Us 1983, A Chorus of Disapproval 1984 (film 1988), Woman in Mind 1985, A Small Family Business 1987, Henceforward... 1987, Man of the Moment 1988, Mr A's Amazing Maze Plays 1988, The Revengers' Comedies 1989, Invisible Friends 1989, Body Language 1990, This Is Where We Came In 1990, Callisto 5 1990 (rewritten as Callisto 7 1999), Wildest Dreams 1991, My Very Own Story 1991, Time of My Life 1992, Dreams from a Summer House (with music by John Pattison) 1992, Communicating Doors 1994, Haunting Julia 1994, The Musical Jigsaw Play 1994, A Word from our Sponsor (with music by John Pattison) 1995, The Champion of Paribanou 1996, Things We Do For Love 1997, Comic Potential 1998, The Boy Who Fell Into A Book 1998, House & Garden 1999, Whenever (with music by Denis King) 2000, Damsels in Distress (trilogy: GamePlan, FlatSpin, RolePlay) 2001, The Jollies 2002, Snake in the Grass 2002. *Non-fiction:* Conversations with Ayckbourn (with I. Watson) 1981, The Crafty Art of Playmaking 2002. *Leisure interests:* music, cricket. *Address:* c/o Casarotto Ramsay and Associates Ltd, National House, 60–66 Wardour Street, London W1V 4ND, England. *Telephone:* (20) 7287-4450. *Fax:* (20) 7287-9128. *Website:* www.alanayckbourn.net.

AYGI, Gennadi Nikolaevich (G. N. Lisin); Chuvash poet; b. 21 Aug. 1934, Shamurzino; m. 3rd Galina Borisovna Aygi; five s. one d.; ed Gorky Literary Inst., Moscow; started writing in Russian rather than Chuvash 1960–; worked in Mayakovsky Museum, Moscow 1961–71; trans. and writer 1971–; Prix Paul Desfeuilles 1968 (for trans. of French poetry into Chuvash), Petrarca Prize (Italy) 1993, Ordre des Arts et des Lettres 1997. *Publications include:* Poetry 1954–71, Munich 1975, A Celebrated Winter, Paris 1982, Selected Poems 1954–1988, 1991, The Field—Russia 1990, The Winter Carouses 1991, Poetry as Silence 1994, Veronica's Notebook 1997, A Bow to the Singing 2000, Continuation of Departure 2001, The Conversation at a Distance (essays) 2001. *Address:* Grishina str. 21/3, 121 354 Moscow, Russia (Home). *Telephone:* (095) 444-41-58 (Home).

AYKROYD, Daniel Edward; American actor; b. 1 July 1952, Ottawa, Canada; s. of Peter Hugh Aykroyd and Lorraine Gougeon Aykroyd; m. 1st Maureen Lewis 1974 (divorced); three s.; m. 2nd Donna Dixon 1984; two d.; ed Carleton Univ., Ottawa; started as a stand-up comedian and worked on Saturday Night Live 1975–79; created and performed as The Blues Brothers (with the late John Belushi); Emmy Award 1976–77. *Films include:* 1941 1979, Mr. Mike's Mondo Video 1979, The Blues Brothers (also screenwriter) 1980, Neighbors 1981, Doctor Detroit 1983, Trading Places 1983, Twilight Zone 1983, Ghostbusters 1984, Nothing Lasts for Ever 1984, Into the Night 1985, Spies Like Us (also screenwriter) 1985, Dragnet (co-screenwriter) 1987, Caddyshack II 1988, The Great Outdoors 1988, My Stepmother is an Alien 1988, Ghostbusters II 1989, Driving Miss Daisy 1990, My Girl, Loose Canons, Valkemania, Nothing But Trouble 1991, Coneheads 1993, My Girl II 1994, North, Casper (also co-screenwriter) 1995, Sergeant Bilko (also co-screenwriter) 1996, Grosse Point Blank (also co-screenwriter) 1997, Blues Brothers 2000 1997, The Arrow 1997, Susan's Plan 1998 (also dir and screenwriter), Antz (voice only) 1999, Diamonds (also dir and screenwriter) 1999, The House of Mirth 2000, Stardom 2000, Dying to Get Rich 2000, The Devil and Daniel Webster, Not a Girl, Pearl Harbour 2001, Evolution 2001, Crossroads 2002, Who Shot Victor Fox 2002, The Curse of the Jade Scorpion 2002. *Albums include:* Briefcase Full of Blues, Made in America, The Blues Brothers, Best of the Blues Brothers. *Address:* 9200 Sunset Boulevard, #428, Los Angeles, CA 90069 (Office); c/o CAA, 9830 Wilshire Boulevard, Beverly Hills, CA 90212, USA.

AYKUT, Imren; Turkish politician; b. 1941, Adana; s. of Şevket Şadi and Rahime Aykut; ed Istanbul Univ. and Oxford Univ.; fmr man. of trades unions; industrial relations expert in Turkish glass industries; fmr Sec.-Gen. Paper Industry Employers' Union; mem. Constitutional Ass. 1981; Deputy, Nat. Ass. 1983–; Minister of Labour and Social Security 1987–91; Govt Spokesperson 1991; Pres. Turkish Inter-Parl. Group 1991–; Motherland Party. *Publications:* over 40 articles and research papers. *Leisure interests:* hand-made carpets, antiquities. *Address:* Türkiye Büyük Millet Meclisi, Parlamentolararasi Birlik Türk Grubu, Baskanıgi, Ankara, Turkey. *Telephone:* (904) 4205431.

AYLING, Robert John; British airline executive; b. 3 Aug. 1946; m. Julia Crallan 1972; two s. one d.; ed King's Coll. School, Wimbledon; joined Elborne, Mitchell & Co. 1968; legal adviser on British accession to the EEC 1973–75, Head of Dept of Trade Aviation Law br. 1978 (responsible for parl. bill that led to privatization of British Airways), Under-Sec. for EC, int. trade, competition issues 1981; with British Shipbuilders 1975; joined British Airways (legal and govt affairs) 1985, Co. Sec. 1987, organized legal arrangements concerning BA's privatization 1987 and BA's acquisition of British Caledonian 1988, Dir Human Resources 1988, Dir Marketing and Operations 1991, Group Man. Dir 1993–95, CEO 1996–2000; Dir (non-exec.) Holidaybreak 2003, Chair. 2003–; Dir (non-exec.) Royal & SunAlliance Insurance Group PLC 1993–; Chair. New Millennium Experience Co. Ltd. 1997–2000; Gov. King's Coll. School 1996; Hon. LLD (Brunel) 1996. *Address:* Holidaybreak, Hartford Manor, Greenbank Lane, Northwich, Cheshire, CW8 1HW, England (Office). *Telephone:* (1606) 787000. *Fax:* (1606) 787001. *E-mail:* group@holidaybreak.co.uk. *Website:* www.holidaybreak.co.uk.

AYLWIN AZÓCAR, Patricio; Chilean politician, lawyer, university professor and consultant; b. 26 Nov. 1918, Viña del Mar; s. of Miguel Aylwin G. and Laura Azócar; m. Leonor Oyarzun Ivanovic 1948; five c.; ed Universidad de Chile; Senator 1965–73, Pres. of Senate 1971–72; Pres. Christian Democrat party (PDC) 1973, 1987–91, Vice-Pres. 1982–89; leader opposition coalition rejecting Gen. Augusto Pinochet in nat. plebiscite Oct. 1988; opposition coalition cand. 1989; PDC cand. for Pres. 1989; Pres. of Chile 1990–94; Pres. Corporación Justicia y Democracia; Hon. Pres. World Democratic Conf. 1997; awarded numerous hon. doctorates; North-South Prize, Council of Europe 1997, J. William Fulbright Prize for Int. Understanding 1998. *Publications:* El Juicio Arbitral 1943, La Transición Chilena: Discursos escogidos Marzo 1990–92, Crecimiento con Equidad: Discursos escogidos 1992–94, Justicia, Democracia y Desarrollo: Conferencias y discursos 1994–95. *Address:* Teresa Salas No. 786, Providencia, Santiago, Chile. *Telephone:* (562) 3411574. *Fax:* (562) 2042135.

AYNSLEY-GREEN, Albert, MA, MBBS, DPhil, MRCS, FRCP, FRCP(Edin.), FRCPCH, FMedSci; British paediatrician; b. 30 May 1943; m. Rosemary Boucher 1967; two d.; ed Glyn Grammar School, Epsom and Univs of London and Oxford; House Officer, Guy's Hosp. London, St Luke's Hosp. Guildford, Radcliffe Infirmary, Oxford and Royal Postgrad. Medical School, Hammersmith 1967–70; Wellcome Research Fellow, Radcliffe Infirmary 1970–72, Clinical Lecturer in Internal Medicine 1972–73, Sr House Officer and Registrar in Paediatrics (also John Radcliffe Hosp.) 1973–74; European Science Exchange Fellowship, Univ. Children's Hosp. Zürich 1974–75; Clinical Lecturer in Paediatrics, Univ. of Oxford 1975–78, Univ. Lecturer 1978–83; Fellow Green Coll. Oxford 1980–83, Royal Coll. of Paediatrics and Child Health; Prof. of Child Health and Head of Dept Univ. of Newcastle-upon-Tyne 1984–93; Nuffield Prof. of Child Health, Univ. of London 1993–; Dir of Clinical Research and Devt Great Ormond St Hosp. and Inst. of Child Health, London 1993–; Chair. Nat. Children's Taskforce, Dept of Health 2001–; Nat. Clinical Dir Dept of Health 2001–. *Publications:* papers on child health. *Leisure interests:* family, walking, music, photography. *Address:* Institute of Child Health, 30 Guilford Street, London, WC1N 1EH, England. *Telephone:* (20) 7813-8391. *Fax:* (20) 7813-0387. *E-mail:* a.aynsley-green@ich.ucl.ac.uk (Office).

AYONG, Most Rev. James Simon, BTheol; Papua New Guinea ecclesiastic; b. 3 Sept. 1944, Kumbun, West New Britain Prov.; s. of Julius Ayong and Margaret Ayong; m. Gawali Ayong 1967; two d. (one deceased); Local Govt Officer 1964–70, 1974–76; Prin. Newton Theological Coll. 1989–93; Archbishop of Papua New Guinea and Bishop of Diocese of Aipo Rongo 1996–; Primate of Anglican Prov. of Papua New Guinea 1996. *Leisure interest:* watching football. *Address:* Anglican Diocese of Aipo Rongo, P.O. Box 893, Mt Hagen, Western Highlands Province, Papua New Guinea (Office). *Telephone:* 542-1131 (Office). *Fax:* 542-1181 (Office). *E-mail:* achgn@global.net.pg (Office).

AYRE, Richard James, BA, JP; British journalist; b. 1 Aug. 1949, Newcastle-upon-Tyne; s. of Thomas Henry Ayre and Beth Carson; ed Univ. Coll., Durham; Pres. Univ. of Durham Students' Union 1969–70; producer and reporter BBC Northern Ireland 1973–76, Home News Ed. TV News 1979–84, Head of BBC Westminster 1989–92, Controller of Editorial Policy 1993–96, Deputy Chief Exec. BBC News 1996–2000; mem. Bd Food Standards Agency 2001–; Freedom of Information Adjudicator, Law Soc. 2001–; mem. Bd Article 19 2000–, Chair. 2002–; Benton Fellow Univ. of Chicago 1984–85. *Address:* The Old Dairy, Burgh Hall, Burgh Parva, Melton Constable, Norfolk, NR24 2PU, England. *E-mail:* richardayre@btinternet.com (Office).

AYRES, Gillian, OBE, RA; British artist; b. 3 Feb. 1930; d. of Stephen Ayres and Florence Ayres; m. Henry Mundy (divorced); two s.; ed St Paul's Girls' School and Camberwell School of Art; teacher of art 1959–81, Sr Lecturer, St Martin's School of Art and Head of Painting, Winchester School of Art 1978–81; Sr Fellow Royal Coll. of Art 1996; fmr RA, London, resgnd 1997, rejoined 2000; works in public collections at Tate Gallery, London, Museum of Modern Art, New York and Gulbenkian Foundation, Lisbon; Hon. DLitt (London); prizewinner, Tokyo Biennale 1963, Major Arts Council Bursary 1979, Charles Wolaston RA Award for best painting in the RA 1989, Gold Medal, Indian Triennale 1991. *Art exhibitions:* one-woman exhbns include: Gallery One 1956, Redfern Gallery 1958, Moulton Gallery 1960, 1962, Kasmin Gallery 1965, 1966, 1969, Knoedler Gallery 1979, 1982, 1987, Museum of Modern Art, Oxford 1981, Sackler Gallery at Royal Acad., London 1997, Alan Cristae Prints and Gimpel Fils Gallery 1999, 2001; retrospective exhbn at Serpentine Gallery 1983; works have also appeared in group exhbns in London, New York and Paris. *Address:* c/o Gimpel Fils Gallery, 30 Davies Street, London, W1Y 1LG, England.

AYUSHEYEV, Damba Badmayevich; Russian Buddhist leader; b. 1963, Russia; abbot Buddhist monastery Baldan Braybun 1995; elected Head of Buddhists of Russia (Khambo Lama) at Conf. of Buddhist Clergy, Ulan-Ude 1995–; Shiretuy Buddhist datsan Baldan-Braybun. *Address:* c/o Buddist Centre, Petrovsky blvd., 17/1, Suite 35, 103051 Moscow, Russia (Office). *Telephone:* (095) 925-16-81 (Office).

AYYOUBI, Mahmoud Ben Saleh al-; Syrian politician; b. 1932; fmr Dir-Gen. for Admin. Affairs, Euphrates Dept; Minister of Educ. 1969–71; Deputy Premier 1970–71; Vice-Pres. 1971–76; Prime Minister 1972–76; mem. Baath Party Regional Command 1971–75, 1980–. *Address:* c/o Baath Party, National Command, BP 849, Damascus, Syria.

AZA, Alberto; Spanish diplomatist; b. 22 May 1937, Tetuán, Morocco; s. of Alberto Aza and Marcela Arias; m. María Eulalia Custodio Martí 1963; two s. four d.; ed Univ. of Oviedo and Madrid; joined Diplomatic Service 1965; served Libreville, Algiers, Rome, Madrid; Dir Cabt. of Prime Minister of Spain 1977–83; Chief Dir OAS, Latin America Dept, Ministry of Foreign Affairs 1983; Minister Counsellor, Lisbon 1983–85; Amb. to OAS, Washington, DC 1985–89 (also accred to Belize); Amb. to Mexico 1990–92, to UK 1992–99; Hon. DLitt (Portsmouth) 1997; Gran Cruz del Mérito Civil 1979, Gran Cruz de la Order del Mérito Naval 1996. *Leisure interests:* golf, fishing, walking. *Address:* c/o Ministerio de Asuntos Exteriores, Plaza de la Provincia 1, 28012 Madrid, Spain (Office).

AZALI, Col. Assoumani; Comoran politician; Chief of Staff, Comoran Armed Forces –1999; seized power in coup d'état April 1999; Head of State of the Comoros and C-in-C of the Armed Forces 1999–2002, Fed. Pres. of the Union of the Comoros 2002–. *Address:* Office of the Head of State, BP 521, Moroni, The Comoros (Office). *Telephone:* (74) 4814 (Office). *Fax:* (74) 4829 (Home). *Website:* www.presidence-rfic.com (Office).

AZARNOFF, Daniel L(ester), MS, MD; American physician and business executive; b. 4 Aug. 1926, Brooklyn, New York; s. of Samuel J. Azarnoff and Kate (Asarnow) Azarnoff; m. Joanne Stokes 1951; two s. one d.; ed Rutgers Univ. and Univ. of Kansas; Instructor in Anatomy, Univ. of Kansas 1949–50, Research Fellow 1950–52, Intern 1955–56, Nat. Heart Inst. Resident Research Fellow 1956–58, Asst Prof. of Medicine 1962–64, Assoc. Prof. 1964–68, Dir Clinical Pharmacology Study Unit 1964–68, Assoc. Prof. of Pharmacology 1965–68, Prof. of Medicine and Pharmacology 1968, Dir Clinical Pharmacology-Toxicology Center 1967–68, Distinguished Prof. 1973–78, Clinical Prof. of Medicine 1982–; Asst Prof. of Medicine St Louis Univ. 1960–62; Visiting Scientist, Fulbright Scholar, Karolinska Inst., Stockholm, Sweden 1968; Clinical Prof. of Pathology and Prof. of Pharmacology, Northwestern Univ. 1978–85; Clinical Prof. of Medicine, Univ. of Kansas Coll. of Health Sciences 1984, Stanford Univ. School of Medicine 1998–; Sr Vice-Pres. Clinical Regulatory Affairs, Cellegy Pharmaceuticals 1999–; Sr Vice-Pres. Worldwide Research and Devt, G. D. Searle & Co., Chicago 1978, Pres. Searle Research and Devt, Skokie, Ill. 1979–85; Pres. D. L. Azarnoff Assocs., Inc. 1987–; mem. Bd of Dirs. De Novo Inc. 1994–, Oread Inc. 1994– (Chair. 1998–), Entropin Inc. 1999–; editorial Bd Drug Investigation 1989–; Chair. Cttee on Problems of Drug Safety, NAS 1972–76; Consultant to numerous Govt agencies; mem. Nat. Comm. on Orphan Diseases, Dept of Health and Human Services; mem. Bd of Dirs. Oread Labs. Inc. 1993; Ed. Review of Drug Interactions 1974–77, Yearbook of Drug Therapy 1977–79; Series Ed. Monographs in Clinical Pharmacology 1977–84; Fellow, American Coll. of Physicians, New York Acad. of Scientists; mem. American Soc. of Clinical Nutrition, American Nutrition Inst., American Fed. of Clinical Research, British Pharmacological Soc., Royal Soc. for the Promotion of Health, Inst. of Medicine (NAS) and others; Burroughs Wellcome Scholar 1964; Ciba Award for gerontological research 1958, Rector's Medal (Univ. of Helsinki) 1968. *Address:* 210 Robin Road, Hillsborough, CA 94010, USA. *Telephone:* (415) 340-9048. *E-mail:* dazarnoff@earthlink.com (Home).

AZAROV, Mykola Yanovych; Ukrainian politician and tax officer; fmrly Chief of State Tax Admin.; Chair. Regions of Ukraine Party –2001; First Deputy Prime Minister and Minister of Finance Nov. 2002–. *Address:*

Ministry of Finance, 01008 Kiev, vul. M. Hrushevskoho 12/2, Ukraine (Office). *Telephone:* (44) 293-74-66 (Office). *Fax:* (44) 293-21-78 (Office). *E-mail:* infomf@minfin.gov.ua (Office). *Website:* www.minfin.gov.ua (Office).

AZCONA DEL HOYO, José; Honduran politician and engineer; b. 26 Jan. 1927, La Ceiba; s. of José Simón Azcona Vélez and Carmen Hoyo Pérez de Azcona; m. Miriam Bocock Selva; two s. one d.; ed Universidad Nacional Autónoma de Honduras and Instituto Tecnológico de Estudios Superiores de Monterrey, Mexico; civil engineer, with special interest in low-cost housing, planning and urban devt; Gen. Man. Federación Hondureña de Cooperativas de Vivienda Limitada 1973–82; started political activities when a student; Liberal cand. in 1963 gen. elections (interrupted by coup d'état); apptd. Sec. for Org. and Propaganda, Movimiento Liberal Rodista 1975; mem. Cen. Exec. Council 1977, Sec. Gen. 1981; Deputy to Congreso Nacional 1982–86; Minister of Communications, Public Works and Transport 1982–83; fmr Pres. Liberal Party Cen. Exec. Council; Pres. of Honduras 1985–90. *Address:* c/o Partido Liberal, Col Miramonte Atrás del Supermercado La Colonia, No. 1 Tegucigalpa, Honduras.

AZCUNA, Adolfo, AB, LLB; Philippines lawyer; b. 16 Feb. 1939; s. of Felipe Azcuna and Carmen Sevilla; m. Maria Asuncion Aunario 1968; one s. three d.; ed Ateneo de Manila and Univ. of Salzburg; elected Del. 1971 Constitutional Convention 1971–73; mem. Constitutional Comm. 1986–87; Press Sec. 1989; Presidential Legal Counsel 1987–90, Presidential Spokesman 1989–90; Pres. Manila Hotel 1997–98; Partner, Azcuna, Yorac, Sarmiento, Arroyo & Chua Law Offices 1992–; Corazon Aquino Fellowship, Harvard Univ. 1990 (deferred). *Publications:* Doing Business in the Philippines, Foreign Judgment Enforcement in the Philippines, Asian Conflict of Law, The Philippine Writ of Amparo, The Aquino Presidency: Destiny with Valor and Grace. *Leisure interests:* reading, biking, photography. *Address:* Azcuna, Yorac, Sarmiento, Arroyo and Chua Law Offices, G/F, Cedar Mansions II, Amber Avenue, Ortigas Center, Pasig City (Office); 140 CRM Avenue, Las Pinas, Metro Manila, Philippines (Home). *Telephone:* (2) 633-5981 (Office); 801-1685 (Home). *Fax:* (2) 633-2820 (Office).

AZIM, Athar Vigar Aziz, M.A.; Pakistani television producer and director; b. 15 June 1948, Karachi; s. of Syed Vigar Azim; ed Punjab Univ., Lahore; with Pakistan Television Corpn (PTV); Best Sports TV Producer (five times), Best Current Affairs TV Producer (twice), Men's Forum Golden Jubilee Award. *Television includes:* numerous reports on current affairs; sports series including Indo-Pakistan Cricket series 1978–79, Football World Cup 1987, Hockey Champions Trophy and live coverage of Hockey, Athletics, Squash and other games. *Address:* Pakistan Television Corporation, Karachi TV Centre, Karachi (Office); Flat No. GF-3, Block B- 1, Sea View Apartment, Defence, Karachi, Pakistan. *Telephone:* (21) 9230161 (PTV) (Office); (21) 5843046. *Fax:* (21) 9231068 (PTV) (Office).

AZIM, Syed Aftab, MA; Pakistani television producer; b. 19 Dec. 1944, Lucknow, India; s. of Syed Saeem Aziz; m. Ghazala Yasmeen; ed Islamia Coll., Karachi, Univ. of Karachi; Programmes Producer Pakistan TV (PTV) 1967–83, Special Producer of Religious Programmes 1999–; Audio Visual Man., PIA 1984–99; eight PTV Awards in 1972, 1974, 2002, Gold Medal, Silver Jubilee 1989. *Television includes:* documentaries on Japan, Thailand, The Philippines, France, Germany, UK and Saudi Arabia; religious programmes: Quran-e-Hakeem 2001, Haiya Alal Falaah 2002. *Publications include:* Sou-e-Haram (official Govt Hajj book). *Leisure interest:* travel. *Address:* Karachi Television Centre, Stadium Road, Karachi (Office); 2/3 Block-E, Myanmar View, Gulshan-e-Igbal, Karachi, Pakistan. *Telephone:* (21) 9231178 (Office); (21) 4792450. *Fax:* (21) 9231043 (Office); (21) 9231068.

AZIMOV, Yakhyo Nuriddinovich; Tajikistan politician; b. 4 Dec. 1947, Khodjend (fmrly Leninabad); m.; one s. two d.; ed Tashkent Inst. of Textile Industry; worked Ura-Tubin Tricot factory 1971–75; engineer, head of rug production, Dir Kairak-Kum rug factory 1975–82; Deputy Chief Engineer, Chief Engineer, Dir-General of rug productions 1982–96; Pres. Jt Stock Co. Kolinkho, Kairakum 1996–; Chair. Council of Ministers (Prime Minister) of Tajikistan 1996–99; Minister of Econs 2000–01. *Address:* c/o Council of Ministers, Rudaki prosp. 42, 743051 Dushanbe, Tajikistan (Office). *Telephone:* (3772) 21-18-71; (3772) 23-19-47 (Office).

AZINGER, Paul William; American golfer; b. 6 Jan. 1960, Holyoke, Mass.; m. Toni Azinger; two d.; ed Florida State Univ.; started playing golf aged 5; turned professional 1981; won Phoenix Open 1987, Herz Bay Hill Classic 1988, Canon Greater Hartford Open 1989, MONY Tournament of Champions 1990, AT&T Pebble Beach Nat. Pro-Am 1991, TOUR Championship 1992, BMW Int. Open 1990, 1992, Memorial Tournament, New England Classic, PGA Championship, Inverness 1993; GWAA Ben Hogan Trophy 1995; mem. US Ryder Cup Team 1989, 1991, 1993, 2001; mem. Pres.'s Cup 1994, 2000; broadcasting debut as reporter for NBC, 1995 Ryder Cup; PGA Tour Player of the Year 1987, Ben Hogan Award 1995. *Publication:* Zinger (about his fight against cancer). *Leisure interest:* fishing. *Address:* PGA Tour, 112 Tpc Boulevard, Ponte Vedra Beach, FL 33082, USA.

AZIZ, Dato' Seri Paduka Rafidah, MEcons; Malaysian politician; b. 4 Nov. 1943, Selama Perak; m. Mohammed Basir bin Ahmad; three c.; ed Univ. of Malaya; tutor, Asst Lecturer, Lecturer and Chair. Rural Devt Div. Faculty of Econs Univ. of Malaya 1966–76; mem. Parl. 1978–; Deputy Minister of Finance 1977–80; Minister of Public Enterprise 1980–88, of Int. Trade and Industry 1988–; mem. UMNO Supreme Council 1975–; holder of many other public appts. and del. to numerous int. confs.; Ahli Mangku Negara, Datuk Paduka Mahkota Selangor. *Leisure interests:* reading, decoration, music, squash. *Address:* Ministry of International Trade and Industry, Block 10, Kompleks Rejabat Kerajaan, Jalan Duta, 50622 Kuala Lumpur, Malaysia (Office). *Telephone:* (3) 6510033 (Office). *Fax:* (3) 62031303 (Office). *E-mail:* mitiweb@miti.gov.my (Office). *Website:* www.miti.gov.my (Office).

AZIZ, Tareq; Iraqi politician; b. 1936, Mosul; ed Baghdad Univ.; mem. staff, Al-Jumhuriyah 1958; Chief Ed. Al-Jamahiir 1963; worked for Baath press in Syria until change of Govt in Feb. 1966; Chief Ed. Al-Thawra publishing house; mem. Revolutionary Command Council Gen. Affairs Bureau 1972; reserve mem. Arab Baath Socialist Party Leadership 1974–77; elected mem. Baath Regional Leadership 1977; Deputy Prime Minister 1981, 1991–2003; Minister of Foreign Affairs 1983, Acting Foreign Minister 2001.

AZIZ, Ungku Abdul, D.ECONS.; Malaysian professor and university administrator; b. 28 Jan. 1922, London, UK; m. Sharifah Azah Aziz; one d.; ed Raffles Coll. and Univ. of Malaya in Singapore, Waseda Univ., Tokyo, Johore State Civil Service; Lecturer in Econs, Univ. of Malaya in Singapore till 1952; Head, Dept of Econs, Univ. of Malaya, Kuala Lumpur 1952–61, Dean of Faculty 1961–65, Vice-Chancellor 1968–88, Royal Prof. of Econs 1978; Pres. Nat. Co-operative Movement (ANGKASA) 1971, Asscn of SE Asian Institutions of Higher Learning (ASAIHL) 1973–75; Chair. Asscn of Commonwealth Univs. 1974–75, Malaysian Nat. Council for ASAIHL, Malaysian Examinations Council 1980–; mem. UN Univ. Council; Corresp. mem. of Advisory Bd, Modern Asian Studies 1973–75; mem. Econ. Asscn of Malaysia, Int. Asscn of Agricultural Economists, Joint Advisory Cttee of FAO, UNESCO and ILO; mem. Nat. Consultative Council and Nat. Unity Advisory Council, Govt of Malaysia; mem. numerous cttees and orgs; Fellow, World Acad. of Arts and Sciences 1965–; Hon. DHumLitt (Univ. of Pittsburgh); Hon. EdD (Chulalongkorn Univ., Thailand) 1977; Hon. DJur (Waseda Univ., Japan) 1982; Hon. DLitt (Univ. of Warwick) 1982; Hon. DIur (Univ. of Strathclyde) 1986, (Utara Univ., Malaysia) 1988; Hon. DEcon (Kebangsaan Univ., Malaysia) 1986; Hon. LLD (Buckingham) 1987; Tun Abdul Razak Foundation Award 1978, Japan Foundation Award 1981; Ordre des Arts et des Lettres (France) 1965; Special Award, Muslim Pilgrim Savings Fund Bd 1988; Grand Cordon of the Order of the Sacred Treasure, Emperor of Japan 1989; ASEAN Achievement Award (Educ.) 1992, Int. Academic Prize (City of Fukoka) 1993. *Leisure interests:* jogging, reading and photography.

AZIZ M. IBRAHIM, Farouk Abdel, MD, FRCOG; Sudanese professor of obstetrics and gynaecology; b. 12 April 1941, Elgolid; s. of Abdel Aziz Mohamed and Zeinab Ahmed Hassan; m. Amal Abu Bakr Arbab 1975; two s. two d.; ed Univ. of Khartoum; Consultant and Lecturer in Obstetrics and Gynaecology, Univ. of Khartoum 1972, Head of Dept 1974, Assoc. Prof. 1980, Dir E.D.C. 1985, Man. Health Learning Materials Project 1986, Dir Staff Devt Centre 1990; Dean Ahfad School of Medicine for Girls 1993; Chief Tech. Adviser WHO 1995–. *Publications:* 5 books on obstetrics and educ., 3 books on educ., obstetrics and reproductive health and family planning, 16 scientific papers on reproductive health. *Leisure interests:* photography, reading. *Address:* P.O. Box 543, San'a, Republic of Yemen. *Telephone:* (1) 216 337. *Fax:* (1) 251 216.

AZIZAN ZAINUL ABIDIN, Tan Sri Datuk Seri; Malaysian airline executive; Chair. Kuala Lumpur City Centre (Urusharta) Berhad; Man. Dir Malaysia Airlines (MAS) 2001–; Chair. Petronas, Perbadanan Putrajaya. *Address:* P.O. Box 13214, 50802 Kuala Lumpur, Malaysia (Office). *Telephone:* (3) 3828000 (Office). *Fax:* (3) 21629200 (Office). *E-mail:* info@klcc.com.my (Office). *Website:* www.klcc.com.my (Office).

AZKOUL, Karim, PhD; Lebanese diplomatist and writer; b. 15 July 1915, Raschaya; s. of Najib Azkoul and Latifah Assaly; m. Eva Corey 1947; one s. one d.; ed Jesuit Univ. of St Joseph, Beirut and Univs of Paris, Berlin, Bonn and Munich; Prof. of History, Arab and French Literature and Philosophy in various colls in Lebanon 1939–46; Dir of an Arabic publishing house and monthly Arabic review The Arab World, Beirut 1943–45; mem. Lebanese Del. to UN, New York 1947–50, Acting Perm. Del. to UN 1950–53; Head of UN Affairs Dept, Ministry of Foreign Affairs 1953–57; Head, Perm. Del. to UN 1957–59, Rapporteur Cttee on Genocide 1948, Humanitarian, Cultural and Social Cttee of Gen. Ass. 1951, Cttee on Freedom of Information 1951; First Vice-Chair. Human Rights Comm. 1958; Chair. Negotiating Cttee for Extra Budgetary Funds 1952–54; Consul-Gen. in Australia and New Zealand 1959–61; Amb. to Ghana, Guinea and Mali 1961–64, to Iran and Afghanistan 1964–66; journalist 1966–68; Prof. of Philosophy, Beirut Coll. for Women 1968–72, Lebanese Univ. 1970–72; Chief Ed. The Joy of Knowledge, Arabic Encyclopedia (10 vols) 1978–; mem. PEN, Emergency World Council, Hague 1971–; Vice-Chair. Cttee for Defence of Human Rights in Lebanon; mem. Bd of Trustees, Bd of Man. of Theological School of Balamand, Lebanon; Order of Cedar (Lebanon), Order of Holy Sepulchre (Jerusalem), Order of St Marc (Alexandria), Order of the Brilliant Star (Repub. of China), Order of Southern Star (Brazil), Order of St Peter and Paul (Damascus). *Publications:* Reason and Faith in Islam (in German) 1938, Reason in Islam (in Arabic) 1946, Freedom (co-author) 1956, Freedom of Association (UN) 1968; trans. into Arabic: Consciencism (Nkrumah) 1964, Arab Thought in the Liberal Age (Albert Hourani) 1969. *Leisure interests:* reading and writing.

AZMI, Shabana, BSc; Indian actress and politician; b. 18 Sept. 1950, Hyderabad; d. of Shaukat Kaifi and Kaifi Azmi; m. Javed Akhtar 1984; ed St Xavier's Coll., Film Inst., Pune; mem. Rajya Sabha 1997; speaker on women's rights and communication in USA; active campaigner on social justice issues; Chair. Nivara Hakk Suraksha Samiti (campaigning org. for upgrading of slum dwellings); Chair. of Jury Montreal and Cairo Int. Film Festivals; mem. Nat. Integration Council, Advisory Council Endowment Campaign for Chair. in Indian Studies, Columbia Univ.; Soviet Land Nehru Award 1985, Padma Shri Award 1988; Rajiv Gandhi Award for Excellence in Secularism 1994, Yash Bhartiya Award for promoting women's issues, Govt of Uttar Pradesh. *Films include:* Ankur (Nat. Award Best Actress) 1974, Arth (Nat. Award) 1983, Khandhar (Nat. Award) 1984, Paar (Nat. Award) 1985, Libaas (Int. Best Actress Award, N Korea 1993), Patang (Best Actress Award, Taormina Art Festival 1994), Swami, Bhavna (Filmfare Award), Junoon, Shatranj Ke Khilan, Parinay, Amardeep, Sparsh, Massom, Doosri Dulhan, Madame Sousatzka, Bengali Night, In Custody, The Journey, Son of the Pink Panther, City of Joy, Fire (Best Actress Award, Chicago Int. Film Festival) 1996. *Leisure interests:* reading, singing. *Address:* 23 Ashoka Road, New Delhi 110001 (Office); 702 Sagar Samrat, Green Fields, Juhu, Mumbai 400049, India (Home). *Telephone:* (11) 3366874 (Office); (22) 6200066 (Home). *Fax:* (11) 3347017 (Office). *E-mail:* shabana@bom3.vsnl.net.in.

AZNAR LÓPEZ, José María; Spanish politician; b. 1953, Madrid; m. Ana Botella; two s. one d.; ed Universidad Complutense, Madrid; fmr tax inspector; fmr Chief Exec. Castile-Leon region; joined Rioja br. Alianza Popular 1978, Deputy Sec.-Gen. and mem. Cortes (Parl.) 1982; Premier Castilla y León Autonomous Region 1987; Pres. Partido Popular (PP, fmrly Alianza Popular) 1990–; Prime Minister of Spain and Pres. of the Council 1996–; Vice-Pres. European Democratic Union (EDC); Pres. Int. Democratic Centre (IDC) 2001. *Address:* Prime Minister's Chancellery, Complejo de la Moncloa, 28071 Madrid, Spain (Office). *Telephone:* (1) 3353535 (Office). *Fax:* (1) 5492739 (Office). *Website:* www.mpr.es (Office).

AZNAVOUR, Charles; French film actor and singer; b. 22 May 1924; m. 1st Micheline Rugel 1946; m. 2nd Evelyne Plessis 1955; m. 3rd Ulla Thorsel 1967; five c.; ed Ecole Centrale de T.S.F., Centre de Spectacle, Paris; with Jean Dasté Company 1941; Man. Dir French-Music 1965–; Roving UNESCO Amb. to Armenia 1995–; Hon. Pres. Belgrade Film Festival 2003; numerous song recitals in Europe and USA; film music includes: Soupe au lait, L'île du bout du monde, Ces dames préfèrent le mambo, Le cercle vicieux, De quoi tu te mêles Daniela, Douce violence, Les Parisiennes; also author and singer of numerous songs; composer of operetta Monsieur Carnaval 1965, Douchka 1973; Chevalier Légion d'honneur, Commdr des Arts et des Lettres; several prizes; Grand Prix nat. de la chanson 1986, César d'honneur 1997, Molière

amical 1999, Time Magazine Entertainer of the Century. *Films include:* La tête contre les murs 1959, Tirez sur le pianiste 1960, Un taxi pour Tobrouk, Le testament d'Orphée, Le diable et les dix commandements, Haute-infidélité 1964, La métamorphose des cloportes 1965, Paris au mois d'août 1966, Le facteur s'en va-t-en guerre 1966, Candy 1969, Les intrus 1973, Sky Riders, Intervention Delta, Folies bourgeoises, Dix petits nègres 1976, The Twist 1976, The Tin Drum 1979, Qu'est-ce qui a fait courir David? 1982, Les fantômes du chapelier 1982, La montagne magique 1983, Vive la vie 1984, Mangeclous 1988, Il Maestro 1992, Les Années Campagne 1992, Pondichéry Dernier Comptoir des Indes 1996, Les Mômes 1999, Judaicaë I 2000. *Albums include:* Jazznavour 1998, Aznavour 2000. *Leisure interests:* photography, do-it-yourself. *Address:* c/o Levon Sayan, 76–78 avenue des Champs-Elysées, bureau 322, 75008 Paris, France.

AZUELA, Arturo; Mexican writer; b. 1938; fmr mathematician and violinist in various symphony orchestras; published first novel 1973; mem. Academia Mexicana de la Lengua 1986–. *Publications:* El tamaño del infierno, La casa de las 1,000 vírgenes, Manifestación de silencios. *Address:* c/o Academia Mexicana de la Lengua, Donceles 66, Centro, Delegación Cuauhtémoc, 06010 México, DF Mexico.

AZUMA, Takamitsu, J.I.A., D.ARCH.; Japanese architect; b. 20 Sept. 1933, Osaka; s. of Yoshimatsu Azuma and Yoshiko (née Ikeda); m. Setsuko Nakaoka 1957; one d.; ed Osaka Univ.; designer Ministry of Postal Service, Osaka 1957–60; Chief Designer Junzo Sakakura Architect & Assocs., Osaka 1960–63, Tokyo 1963–67; Prin. Takamitsu Azuma Architect & Assocs., Tokyo 1968–85; Instructor Univ. of Art and Design 1976–78, Tokyo Denki Univ. 1980–82, Tokyo Univ. 1983–85; Instructor Osaka Univ. 1981–85, Prof. 1985–97, Prof. Emer. 1997–; Instructor Osaka Art Univ. 1985–87; Architect Azuma Architects and Assocs. 1985–97; Prof. Chiba Inst. of Tech. 1997–; mem. Architectural Inst. of Japan; Visiting Prof. School of Architecture, Washington Univ., St Louis, USA 1985; 1st Prize Kinki Br., Inst. of Architects Competition 1957; Architectural Inst. of Japan Architectural Design Prize 1995. *Publications:* Revaluation of the Residence 1971, On the Japanese Architectural Space 1981, Philosophy of Living in the City 1983, Device from Architecture 1986, Space Analysis of the Urban Residence 1986, White Book about Tower House 1987, On Urban Housing 1997. *Leisure interests:* travelling, reading, computing. *Address:* Azuma Architects & Assocs., 3-6-1 Minami-Aoyama Minato-ku, Tokyo 107-0016 (Office); 3-39-4 Jingumae, Shibuya-ku, Tokyo 150-0001, Japan (Home). *Telephone:* (3) 3403-5593 (Office); (3) 3404-0805 (Home).

B

BA JIN, (LI YAOTANG); Chinese writer and journalist; b. 25 Nov. 1904, Chengdu, Sichuan Prov.; m. Xiao Shan 1944 (died 1972); one s. one d.; ed Foreign Language School, Chengdu; studied in France and adopted name Ba Jin (taken from first syllable of Bakunin and the last of Kropotkin) 1926; Ed. fortnightly provincial Ban Yue 1928; writer and translator, Shanghai 1929; visited Japan 1934; Chief Ed. Shanghai Cultural Life Publishing House 1935; joined Lu Xun's China Literary Work Soc. 1936; Co-Ed. (with Mao Dun) Shouting Weekly and Bonfire Weekly 1937; Vice-Chair. Union of Chinese Writers 1953 (now Chair.); Deputy to NPC 1954; Chief. Ed. People's Literature 1957–58; Vice-Chair. China Fed. of Literary and Art Circles 1960; Chief Ed. Shanghai Literature 1961; in disgrace 1968–77; Vice-Chair. 5th Municipal CPPCC Cttee, Shanghai 1977–83; mem. Presidium 6th Nat. CPPCC Cttee 1983–88; Vice-Chair. 7th Nat. Cttee CPPCC 1988–93, 8th Nat. Cttee 1993–98, 9th Nat. Cttee 1998–; Exec. Council, China Welfare Inst. 1978–; Vice-Chair. China Fed. of Literary and Art Circles 1978–; Pres. China PEN Centre 1980–, Chinese Writers' Asscn 1981– (Chair. 2001), China Literature Foundation 1986–; Hon. Pres. Fiction Soc. 1984–; Hon. Chair. China Shakespeare Research Foundation 1984–; Hon. mem. AAAS 1985; Medal of Int. Friendship, USSR 1990. *Publications include:* Extinction 1928, The Family 1931, Trilogy of Love 1932–33, The History of the Nihilist Movement 1936, Spring 1937, Autumn 1940, Festival Day of Warsaw 1950, Living Among Heroes 1953, Three Comrades 1962, Random Thoughts (5 Vols) 1979–86, Essays by the Sickbed 1984. *Address:* c/o China PEN, Shatan Beijie 2, Beijing, People's Republic of China. *Website:* www.bajin.com (Office).

BAALI, Abdallah; Algerian diplomatist; b. 19 Oct. 1954, Guelma; m. Rafika Baali; one s. one d.; ed Ecole Nat. d'Admin., New York Univ.; Sec. of Foreign Affairs 1977–82, Head Dept. of Communication and Documentation, Foreign Affairs Ministry 1990–92; mem. Perm. Mission to UN, New York 1982–89, Algeria's Alt. Rep. to Security Council 1988–89, Perm. Rep. to UN 1996–; Amb. to Indonesia (also accred. to Australia, New Zealand and Brunei Darussalam) 1992–96. *Address:* Permanent Mission of Algeria to the United Nations, 326 East 48th Street, New York, NY 10017, USA (Office). *Telephone:* (212) 750-1960 (Office). *Fax:* (212) 759-9538 (Office). *E-mail:* algeria@un.int (Office). *Website:* www.algeria-un.org (Office).

BABADJHAN, Ramz; Uzbekistan poet and playwright; b. 2 Aug. 1921, Uzbekistan; s. of Nasriddin Babadjhan and Salomat Babadjhan; m. 1947; one s. two d.; ed Pedagogical Inst., Tashkent; Deputy Chair. Uzbek Writers' Union; mem. CPSU 1951–91; Chair. Uzbek Republican Cttee on Relations with African and Asian Writers; Pres. Soc. on Cultural Relations with Compatriots Living Abroad "Vatan" 1990–94; first works published 1935; USSR State Prize 1972. *Publications include:* Dear Friends, Thank You, My Dear, The Heart Never Sleeps, Selected Poetry, A Poet Lives Twice, Living Water, Yusuf and Zuleyha, 1001 Crane, Sides, Uncle and Nephew, You Cannot Deceive a Gipsy. *Leisure interests:* photography, travelling. *Address:* Beshchinar str. 34, 700070 Tashkent, Uzbekistan. *Telephone:* (371) 55-61-06.

BABAEV, Agadzhan Geldyevich, DrGeogSc; Turkmenistan geographer; b. 10 May 1929, Mary; s. of Geldy Babaev and Ogulbek Babaev; m. Dunyagozel Palvanova 1951; two s. six d.; ed State Pedagogical Inst., Ashkhabad (now Ashgabat), Turkmenistan State Univ.; Head Geography Dept, Turkmenistan State Univ. 1952–59; Deputy Dir Desert Research Inst., Turkmenistan Acad. of Sciences 1959–60, Dir 1960–; Chair. Scientific Council for Desert Problems 1967–; Ed.-in-Chief Problems of Desert Devt 1967–; Dir Turkmenistan Research and Training Centre on Desertification Control for ESCAP; mem. CPSU 1954–91; Deputy to USSR Supreme Soviet 1979–89; mem. Cen. Auditing Cttee CPSU 1990–91; Chair. Turkmenistan Soc. for Chinese-Soviet Friendship; mem. Turkmenistan Acad. of Sciences, Pres. 1975–86, 1989–93; Corresp. mem. USSR (now Russian) Acad. of Sciences 1976; Academician, Islamic Acad. of Sciences; mem. Turkmenistan Geographical Soc.; Vice-Pres. Turkmens of the World Humanitarian Asscn; Deputy, Turkmenistan Parl.; Sec. Democratic Party of Turkmenistan 1991–; Sign of Honour Award 1976, Heroic Labour Medal 1970, USSR State Prize 1982, Academician Vavilov Medal 1976, Academician Karpinskii Medal 1990, Jerald Piel Medal 1992. *Publications:* eight monographs, over 200 articles for professional journals. *Address:* National Institute of Deserts, Flora and Fauna, 15 Bitarap Turkmenistan Street, Ashgabat 744000 (Office); 8 Kurban Durdy Street, Ashgabat 744020, Turkmenistan (Home). *Telephone:* (1) 395427 (Office); (1) 242683 (Home).

BABANGIDA, Maj.-Gen. Ibrahim; Nigerian army officer (retd) and fmr Head of State; b. 17 Aug. 1941, Minna; m. Maryam King 1969; two s. two d.; ed Niger provincial secondary school, Bida, Kaduna Mil. Training Coll. and Indian Mil. Acad.; commissioned 1963, Lt 1966; training with RAC, UK 1966; CO during Biafran Civil War; Co Commdr and Instructor, Nigerian Defence Acad. 1970–72; rank of Maj. then Lt-Col Armoured Corps 1974; trained at U.S. Army Armoury School 1974; promoted to Maj.-Gen., Dir of Army Duties and Plans 1981; took part in overthrow of Pres. Shehu Shagari 1983; mem. Supreme Mil. Council and Chief Army Staff 1983–85; Pres. of Nigeria following coup overthrowing Maj.-Gen. Muhammadu Buhari (q.v.) 1985–93; Pres. Police Council 1989; Minister of Defence Dec. 1989–90; Hon. GCB 1989. *Publications:* Civil and Military Relationship, The Nigerian Experience 1979, Defence Policy within the Framework of National Planning 1985. *Address:* Minna, Niger State, Nigeria.

BABBAR, Raj; Indian politician, actor and film maker; b. 26 June 1952, Agra Dist, Uttar Pradesh; s. of Kaushal Kumar and Shobha Rani; m. Nadira Babbar 1975; two s. one d.; ed NSD, New Delhi; mem. Rajya Sabha 1994–99, Home Affairs Cttee, Rules Cttee, Consultative Cttee, Ministry of Civil Aviation; mem. (Socialist Party) 13th Lok Sabha 1999–, mem. Defence Cttee 1999–2000, Energy Cttee; acted in more than 150 films and 30 plays; Uttar Pradesh Govt 'Yash Bharti' Award, Punjabi Male Actor of the Millennium, Punjabi American Festival 2000. *Films include:* Shaheed Uddham Singh, LoC, Kyaa Dil Ne Kahaa, The Legend of Bhagat Singh. *Leisure interest:* charity work. *Address:* 20 Mahadev Road, New Delhi 110 001, India. *Telephone:* (11) 3710151; (11) 3557728; (11) 3352728.

BABBITT, Bruce Edward, LLB; American politician and lawyer; b. 27 July 1938; m. Hattie Coons; two c.; ed Univ. of Notre Dame, Univ. of Newcastle, UK, Harvard Univ. Law School; Attorney-Gen. Ariz 1975–78; Gov. of Arizona 1978–87; partner Steptoe & Johnson, Phoenix; Sec. of Interior 1993–2001; Sec. of Counsel, Environmental Dept, Latham & Watkins 2001–; Chair. Nat. Groundwater Policy Forum 1984–; Pres. League of Conservation Voters; Marshall Scholar 1960–62; Democrat; Thomas Jefferson Award, Nat. Wildlife Fed. 1981, Special Conservation Award 1983. *Publications:* Color and Light: The Southwest Canvases of Louis Akin 1973, Grand Canyon: An Anthology 1978. *Address:* Latham & Watkins, 555 Eleventh Street NW, Suite 1000, Washington, DC 20004, USA (Office).

BABBITT, Milton Byron, DMus, MFA; American composer; b. 10 May 1916, Philadelphia; s. of Albert E Babbitt and Sarah Potamkin; m. Sylvia Miller 1939; one d.; ed New York and Princeton Univs.; Music Faculty, Princeton Univ. 1938–, Math. Faculty 1943–45, Bicentennial Preceptor 1953–56, Prof. of Music 1966–84, Prof. Emer. 1984–; Dir Columbia-Princeton Electronic Music Center; mem. Faculty, Juilliard School 1971–; Fromm Prof., Harvard Univ. 1988; Guggenheim Fellow 1960–61; MacArthur Fellow 1986–91; mem. American Acad. of Arts and Sciences, American Acad. of Arts and Letters; Hon. D.Mus. (Glasgow); Hon. DFA (Northwestern Univ.); American Acad. of Arts and Letters Award 1959; Gold Medal, Brandeis Univ. 1970; Pulitzer Prize 1982, Schoenberg Inst. Award 1988, William Schuman Award 1992. *Works include:* Music for the Mass 1940, Composition for Four Instruments 1948, Woodwind Quartet 1953, All Set 1957, Vision and Prayer 1961, Philomel 1964, Tableaux 1972, Reflections 1975, Solo Requiem 1977, Paraphrases 1979, Ars Combinatoria 1981, Melismata 1982, The Head of the Bed 1982, Canonic Form 1983, Piano Concerto 1985, Transfigured Notes 1986, The Joy of More Sextets 1986, Whirled Series 1987, Consortini 1989, Emblems 1989, Soli e Duettini 1989–90, Play It Again Sam 1989, Envoi 1990, Preludes, Interludes and Postlude 1991. *Publication:* The Function of Set Structure in the Twelve Tone System 1946. *Leisure interest:* philosophy. *Address:* 222 Western Way, Princeton, NJ 08540-5306, USA.

BABENKO, Hector; Argentine film director; b. 7 Feb. 1946, Buenos Aires; eight years in Europe as writer, house painter, door to door salesman, film extra etc.; Best Foreign Film Award for Pixote (New York Film Critics). *Films:* Rei Da Nolte 1976, Lucio Flavio—Passageiro da Agonia 1978, Pixote 1980, Kiss of the Spider Woman 1985, Ironweed 1987, Naked Tango 1990, At Play in the Fields of the Lord 1991.

BABICH, Mikhail; Russian (Chechen) politician; sr officer in airborne troops 1990–94; worked in pvt sector 1995–99; Deputy Dir-Gen. Fed. Agency for Food Market Regulation, Ministry of Agric.; fmr Deputy Gov. Moscow Region, forced to resign following accusations of misappropriating US humanitarian aid; First Deputy Gov. Ivanovskaya Region 2001–02; Chair. of Republican Govt (Prime Minister) of Chechnya Nov. 2002–. *Address:* Office of the Chairman of the Republican Government (Prime Minister), ul. Garazhnaya 10A, Groznyi, 364000, Chechnya, Russia (Office). *Telephone:* (095) 777-92-14 (Office).

BABIKIAN, Khatchik Diran; Lebanese politician and lawyer; b. 1924, Cyprus; m. 1956; five d.; ed Collège Italien, Beirut, Faculté Française de Droit, Beirut, Faculté de Paris, Univ. of London; Barrister; Deputy for Beirut 1957, 1960, 1964, 1968, 1972, 1992; mem. Parl. Comm. on Justice; Pres. Traffic Comm., Parl. Comm. on Planning, Lebanese Management Asscn 1972, 1992, 1995; Minister for Admin. Reform 1960–61; Minister of Public Health 1968–69, of Tourism 1969–70, of Information 1972–73, of Planning 1973, 1990–95, of Justice 1980–82, 1990–92; mem. Higher Court for the trial of the Presidents and Ministers 1994–97; Pres. Armenian Nat. Ass. 1972, 1976; Pres. Exec. Council Armenian Church of Cilicia 1983–97, Asscn Libanaise contre la Drogue, Asscn Libanaise pour le Diabète, Asscn Libanaise pour l'Habitat; Vice-Pres. World Asscn of French-Speaking Parliamentarians 1982, 1997; Personal Rep. of Pres. of Repub. at Conseil Perm. de la Francophonie 1992–97; Officier Légion d'honneur; Ufficiale, Ordine del Merito (Italy). *Leisure interests:* violin, languages. *Address:* Rue Abrine, Achrafié, Beirut, Lebanon (Home). *Telephone:* 322013 (Home).

BABIUC, Victor, LLD; Romanian politician and lawyer; b. 3 April 1938, Răchiţi Commune, Botoşani Co.; s. of Victor Babiuc and Olga Babiuc; m. Lucia Babiuc 1978; one d.; ed Law School of Bucharest, Romanian Acad. for Econ. Studies, Univ. of Bucharest; juridical counsellor, judge in Braşov; Chief

Juridical Counsel Ministry of Foreign Trade, Sr Researcher at the World Economy Inst. 1977–90; mem. House of Deputies 1992–; Minister of Justice 1990–91, Minister of the Interior, 1991–92; Vice-Pres. Democratic Party; Minister of Nat. Defence 1996–98, Minister of State, Minister of Nat. Defence 1998–2000; Prof. of Int. Trade Law, Acad. of Econ. Studies of Bucharest 1992–; Chair. Cttee for Investigation into Corruption and Cases of Abuse and for Petitions of the Chamber of Deputies 1992–96; Pres. Int. Commercial Arbitration Court of Chamber of Commerce and Industry of Romania; mem. Panel of Arbitrators of American Arbitration Asscn, Moscow, Sofia, Abu Dhabi, Warsaw, New Delhi, Cairo 1991–. *Publications:* over 100 publications mainly in the field of econ. legislation and int. trade law. *Leisure interests:* theatre, walking, reading books on politics, history, memoirs. *Address:* Henri Coandă Str. No. 27, Sector 1, Bucharest (Office); Bd Libertatii No. 20, Sector 5, Bucharest, Romania (Home). *Telephone:* (21) 3151773 (Office). *Fax:* (21) 3151777 (Office). *E-mail:* office@btsa.ro (Office). *Website:* www.btsa.ro (Office).

BABURIN, Sergei Nikolaevich, LLD; Russian politician; b. 31 Jan. 1959, Semipalatinsk; s. of Nikolay Baburin and Valentina Baburina; m. Tatiana Nikolaevna Baburina; four s.; ed Omsk State Univ., Leningrad State Univ.; mem. CPSU 1981–91; mil. service in Afghanistan 1982–83; worked as lawyer; lecturer, Dean of Law Faculty, Omsk Univ. 1988–90; People's Deputy of RSFSR (now Russia); mem. Supreme Soviet 1990–93; mem. Constitutional Comm. 1991–; Co-Chair. Exec. Bd of All Russian Peoples' Union 1991; Co-Chair. Nat. Salvation Front 1992–; mem. State Duma (Parl.) 1995–99, Deputy Chair. 1996–99; Chair. All Russian People's Union 1994–2001; Deputy Chair. Parl. Ass. Union of Russia and Belarus 1996–2000; Deputy Dir for Research, Russian Acad. of Sciences (Inst. of Social and Political Researches) 2001–; Chair. Bd Inter-regional Collegium of Advocates of Businessmen and Citizens' Interactions 2001–02; Leader Party of Nat. Revival (Narodnaya Volya) 2001–. *Publications:* Russian Way: Selected Speeches and Essays 1990–95 1995, Russian Way: Losses and Acquisitions 1997, Territory of State: Law and Geopolitical Problems 1997. *Address:* Inter-regional Collegium of Lawyers, Novogireyevskaya str. 65, Moscow, Russia. *Telephone:* (095) 176-01-01.

BACA, Susana; Peruvian popular singer; b. Chortillos, Lima; m. Ricardo Pereira; formed experimental group combining poetry and song; took part in int. Agua Dulce Festival in Lima; with husband f. Instituto Negrocontinuo; first US performance in Brooklyn 1995; one US and six European tours. *Albums include:* Susana Baca 1997, Del Fuego y del Agua 1999, Eco de Sombras 2000. *Publication:* The Cultural Importance of Black Peruvians (co-author with Richard Pereira) 1992. *Address:* c/o Iris Musique, 5 Passage St-Sebastien, 75011 Paris, France.

BACALL, Lauren; American actress; b. 16 Sept. 1924, New York; m. 1st Humphrey Bogart 1945 (died 1957); 2nd Jason Robards 1961 (divorced); two s. one d.; fmr model; Commdr des Arts et des Lettres 1995. *Films include:* Two Guys from Milwaukee 1946, To Have and Have Not, The Big Sleep, Confidential Agent, Dark Passage, Key Largo, Young Man with a Horn, Bright Leaf, How to Marry a Millionaire, Woman's World, The Cobweb, Blood Alley, Written on the Wind, Designing Woman, The Gift of Love, Flame over India, Sex and the Single Girl, Harper, Shock Treatment 1964, Murder on the Orient Express 1974, The Shootist 1976, Health 1980, The Fan 1981, Appointment with Death 1988, Mr North 1988, Tree of Hands 1989, A Star For Two 1990, Misery 1990, All I Want for Christmas 1991, A Foreign Field 1993, The Portrait 1993, Prêt à Porter 1995, Le Jour et la Nuit 1996, The Mirror Has Two Faces (Golden Globe 1996, Screen Actors' Guild Award), My Fellow Americans, Day and Night, Diamonds, The Venice Project, Presence of Mind. *Plays:* Goodbye Charlie 1960, Cactus Flower 1966, Applause 1970 (Tony Award, Best Actress in a Musical 1970) (London 1972), Wonderful Town 1977, Woman of the Year 1981 (Tony Award 1981), Sweet Bird of Youth (London) 1985, The Visit (Chichester, UK), Waiting in the Wings. *Publications:* Lauren Bacall By Myself 1978, Lauren Bacall Now 1994. *Address:* c/o Johnnie Planco, William Morris Agency, 1325 Avenue of the Americas, New York, NY 10019, USA.

BACCOUCHE, Hedi; Tunisian politician; b. 1930; active mem. Tunisian Independence Movt; Pres. Fed. des Étudiants Destouriens; detained by French authorities 1952; Dir PSD Political Bureau –1987; Minister of Social Affairs April–Nov. 1987; Prime Minister 1987–89. *Address:* c/o Office of the Prime Minister, Tunis, Tunisia.

BACH NUÑEZ, Jaume; Spanish architect; b. 4 April 1943, Sabadell; s. of Miquel Bach Nuñez and Josefa Bach Nuñez; m. Carmen Triadó Tur 1978; two s.; ed Tech. Univ. of Architecture, Barcelona (ETSAB); Assoc. Dols-Millet-Páez 1971; tutor, ETSAB 1971, 1972; in partnership with Gabriel Mora Gramunt, Bach/Mora Architects 1976–; work includes grass hockey Olympic stadium, Terrassa 1989, cen. telephone exchange, Olympic Village, Barcelona 1992, apt. Bldg. agric. complex, health clinic, etc.; tutor, Int. Lab. of Architecture and Urban Design, Urbino, Italy 1978; Design tutor, ETSAB 1978–; Visiting Prof. Univ. of Dublin 1993, Univ. of Hanover 1994; Hon. DArch (Polytechnic Univ. of Barcelona) 1991; various professional awards. *Publications include:* Junge Architekten in Europa (jtly) 1983, Young Spanish Architecture (jtly) 1985. *Address:* Avenida Diagonal 335, 08037 Barcelona, Spain.

BACHA, Edmar Lisboa, PhD; Brazilian economist; b. 14 Feb. 1942; m. Maria Laura Cavalcanti; ed Fed. Univ. of Minas Gerais, Yale Univ., USA; Research Assoc., MIT, Cambridge, Mass., USA 1968–69; Prof. of Econs, Vargas Founda-

tion, Rio de Janeiro 1970–71, Univ. of Brasília 1972–78, Catholic Univ. of Rio de Janeiro 1979–93, Fed. Univ. of Rio de Janeiro 1996–; Pres. Statistical Office of Brazil, Rio de Janeiro 1985–86; Econ. Adviser to Brazilian Govt 1993; Pres. Nat. Devt Bank, Rio de Janeiro 1995; Visiting Prof. Harvard Univ. 1975, Columbia Univ. 1983, Yale Univ. 1984, Univ. of Calif. at Berkeley 1988, Univ. of Stanford 1989; mem. Exec. Cttee, Int. Econ. Asscn, Paris 1987–92, Cttee for Devt Planning, UN, New York 1987–94. *Publications:* Mitos de uma Decada 1976, Models of Growth and Distribution for Brazil 1980, El Milagro y la Crisis 1986, Social Change in Brazil 1986, Recessão ou Crescimento 1987, Requirements for Growth Resumption in Latin America 1993. *Address:* Rua Marquês de São Vicente 225, 22453 Rio de Janeiro, Brazil. *Telephone:* (21) 274-2797.

BACHCHAN, Amitabh; Indian actor; b. 11 Oct. 1942, Allahabad; s. of Harivansh Rai and Teji Bachchan; m. Jaya Bachchan; one s. one d.; ed Sherwood Coll., Delhi Univ. *Films:* over seventy films including Saat Hindustani 1969, Zanjeer 1973, Deewar 1975, Imaan Dharam 1977, Kasme Vaade 1978, Jurmana 1979, Barsaat Ki Ek Raat 1980, Manzil 1981, Shakti 1982, Pet Pyar Aur Paap 1984, Kaun A Kaun Hara 1987, Soorma Bhopali 1988, Jadugar 1989, Agneepath 1990, Ajooba 1991, Insaniyat 1994, Bade Miyan Chote Miyan 1998, Tumhare Liye 1999, Sooryavansham 1999. *Television:* presenter Kaun Banega Crorepati? (Who Wants To Be A Millionaire?). *Address:* Pratiksha, 10th Road, JVPD Scheme, Mumbai, 400 049, India (Office).

BACHELIER, Bernard; French agronomist; b. 27 July 1950, Levallois-Perret; s. of Pierre Bachelier and Claire Pardon; ed Inst. Nat. Agronomique, Paris-Grignon; worked in Africa for several years; Del. for Africa and Indian Ocean, Centre de Coopération Internationale en Recherche Agronomique pour de Développement (Cirad), Paris 1988–90; Pres. Cirad Centre, Montpellier 1993; Head of Devt Research, Ministry of Educ. and Research 1993–96; Dir-Gen. Cirad 1996–2002; Chair., Council of Admin., Centre Nat. d'Etudes Agronomiques des Régions Chaudes (CNEARC) 1998–; Chevalier, Ordre nat. du Mérite, Ordre du Mérite agricole. *Address:* 9 rue Thérèse, 75001 Paris, France (Home).

BACHELOT-NARQUIN, Roselyne, PharmD; French politician and pharmacist; b. 24 Dec. 1946, Nevers (Nièvre); d. of Jean Narquin and Yvette Narquin (née Le Dû); m. Jacques Bachelot; one c.; pharmacist, Conseillère général de Maine-et-Loire 1982–88; mem. and Vice-Pres. Regional Council, Pays de la Loire, Pres. Comm. aménagement 1998–; elected Deputy for Maine-et-Loire 1988–; mem. RPR, Sec.-Gen. 1989–92, 2001–, Del.-Gen. for the Status of Women 1992–93, for Labour and Social Exclusion 1995–97, Sec.-Gen. for Labour 1998–2001, mem. Political Bureau RPR; Reporter-Gen. Observatoire de la parité 1995–98; Pres. Nat. Consultative Council for Handicapped Persons 1996–; Minister of Ecology and Sustainable Devt 2002–. *Publications include:* Les Maires: fête ou défaite? 2001. *Address:* Ministry of Ecology and Sustainable Development, 20 avenue de Ségur, 75007 Paris, France (Office). *Telephone:* 1-42-19-20-21 (Office). *Website:* www .environnement.gouv.fr (Office).

BACHER, Aron ('Ali'), MB, B.CH.; South African cricketer and administrator; b. 24 May 1942, Johannesburg; s. of Kopel Bacher and Rose Bacher; m. Shira Ruth Teeger 1965; one s. two d.; ed King Edward VII High School and Univ. of Witwatersrand; right-hand batsman; played for Transvaal 1959–74 (Capt. 1963–74); 12 tests for S. Africa 1965–70, 4 (all won) as Capt.; scored 7,894 first-class runs (18 centuries); toured England 1965; intern, Baragwanath and Natalspruit Hosps.; pvt. practice, Rosebank, Johannesburg 1970–79; Man. Dir Delta Distributors (Pty) Ltd 1979–81; Man. Dir The Transvaal Cricket Council 1981–86; Man. Dir The South African Cricket Union 1986–91, United Cricket Bd of South Africa 1991–2000; Exec. Dir 2003 Int. Cricket Council Cricket World Cup 2001–; South African Sports Award Admin. 1991; Pres. Sports Award Admin. (Cricket) 1997; Hon. LLD (Witwatersrand, Johannesburg) 2001; African South Sports Merit Award 1972; Paul Harris Fellow Award 1989; Jack Cheetham Memorial Award 1990; Int. Jewish Sports Hall of Fame 1991. *Leisure interest:* jogging. *Address:* 2003 ICC Cricket World Cup, PO Box 782, Northlands, 2116 (Office); 17 Romajador Avenue, Sandhurst Ext. 4, Sandton, South Africa (Home). *Telephone:* (11) 446-3600 (Office); (11) 783-1263 (Home). *Fax:* (11) 883-2597 (Home).

BACHER, Robert Fox, BS, PhD; American physicist; b. 31 Aug. 1905, Loudonville, Ohio; s. of Harry Bacher and Byrl (née Fox) Bacher; m. Jean Dow 1930; one s. one d.; ed Univ. of Michigan; Nat. Research Fellow Physics, Calif. Inst. of Technology 1930–31, MIT 1931–32; Alfred Lloyd Fellow, Univ. of Michigan 1932–33; Instructor, Columbia Univ. 1934–35; Instructor to Prof., Cornell Univ. 1935–49; Radiation Laboratory, MIT 1940–45 (on leave 1943–45); Los Alamos Laboratory, Atomic Bomb Project 1943–46; Dir of Laboratory of Nuclear Studies, Cornell Univ. 1946; mem. U.S. Atomic Energy Comm. 1946–49; Prof. of Physics, Calif. Inst. of Technology 1949–76, Prof. Emer. 1976–, Chair. Div. of Physics, Mathematics and Astronomy 1949–62, Provost 1962–70; mem. President's Science Advisory Cttee 1953–55, 1957–60; Trustee, Carnegie Corpn 1959–76, Claremont Graduate School 1971–, Universities Research Assen 1965–75 (Chair. 1969–73, Pres. 1973–74), Rand Corpn 1950–60; Pres. Int. Union of Pure and Applied Physics 1969–72; mem. NAS, American Philosophical Soc., American Acad. of Arts and Sciences, American Physical Soc. (Pres. 1964), AAAS; Medal for Merit 1946. *Publications:* Atomic Energy States (with S. Goudsmit) 1932. *Address:* California Institute of Technology, Pasadena, CA 91125, USA.

BACHIRI, Mohamed, MBA; Moroccan administrator and engineer; b. 14 July 1948, Berkane; s. of Mimoun Bachiri and Aïcha Ouadi; m. Badia Khelfaoui 1972; three c.; ed Ecole Mohammedie d'Ingénieurs, Rabat, Ecole Nationale des Ponts et Chaussées, Paris, France; qualified civil engineer; responsible for public works, Berkane and Nador Provs. 1969; Asst Dir Moroccan Ports 1978; Regional Dir of Public Works, Marrakesh 1983; Dir Nat. Vocational Training 1984; Insp. Gen. Council of Public Works 1991; Founder and Dir Al Handassa Lwatania Eng journal 1981; now Chair. Bd Drapor Port Dredging Co.; Founding Pres. Public Works Foundation; Chair. CEDA–African Section (World Dredging Asscn); trophée d'Ingénieur Créateur, Royal Decoration of 'Chevalier' 1998. *Publications:* Drainage and Environment (Ed.); articles and editorials in Al Handassa Lwatania, contrib. to other prof. journals. *Leisure interest:* golf. *Address:* 5 Rue Chajarat Addor, Palmier, Casablanca (Office); 3 Avenue Ma Al Aynine, Agdal, Rabat, Morocco. *Telephone:* (2) 23-46-40 (Office); (7) 77-46-24 (Home). *Fax:* (2) 23-26-00 (Office); (7) 68-14-94 (Home). *E-mail:* bachiri@drapor.com (Office); bachiri@iam.net.ma (Home). *Website:* www.drapor.com; www.ceda-africa.com.

BACHRACH, Howard L., PhD; American biochemist; b. 21 May 1920, Faribault, Minn.; m. Shirley F. Lichterman 1943; one s. one d.; ed Univ. of Minnesota; Chemist, Jos. Seagram & Co., Lawrenceburg, Ind. 1942; Research Asst, Explosives Research Lab., Carnegie Inst. of Tech., Nat. Defense Research Cttee, OSRD 1942–45; Research Asst, Univ. of Minn. 1945–49; Biochemist, Foot-and-Mouth Disease Research Mission, US Dept of Agric., Denmark 1949–50; Research Biochemist, Biochemistry and Virus Lab., Univ. of Calif., Berkeley 1950–53; Chief Scientist and Head, Biochemical and Physical Investigations, Plum Island Animal Disease Center, US Dept of Agric. 1953–81, Research Chemist 1981–89, Consultant-Collaborator 1990–95; developed unified comparative molecular pathways of animal virus replication 1978; first purification and visualization of polio virus 1953 and of foot-and-mouth virus 1958; first immunization of livestock with protein isolated from foot-and-mouth disease virus 1975; first production through gene splicing of an effective protein vaccine against any disease of animals or humans 1981; mem. NAS; Fellow, New York Acad. of Sciences; Hon. mem. American Coll. of Veterinary Microbiologists; many awards, including U.S. Presidential Citation 1965, AAAS-Newcomb Cleveland Prize 1982, ACS Kenneth A. Spencer Medal 1983, Nat. Medal of Science 1983, Nat. Award for Agricultural Excellence 1983 and Alexander von Humboldt Award 1983, USDA Agricultural Research Service, Science Hall of Fame 1987. *Publications:* 150 Publs; patent on FMD protein vaccine. *Address:* 355 Dayton Road, P.O. Box 1054, Southold, NY 11971; 10220 Andover Coach Circle G2, Lake Worth, FL 33467, USA.

BACHYNSKI, Morrel Paul, PhD, FRSC, FIEEE; Canadian physicist; b. 19 July 1930, Bienfait, Sask.; s. of Nick Bachynski and Karolina Bachynski; m. Slava Krkovic 1959; two d.; ed Univ. of Saskatchewan and McGill Univ.; mem. Scientific Staff, RCA Ltd 1955–58, Dir Microwave Physics Laboratory 1958–65; Dir Research 1965–75, Vice-Pres. Research and Devt 1975–76; Pres. and CEO MPB Technologies Inc. 1977–; mem. Canadian Asscn of Physicists (Pres. 1968), Asscn of Scientific, Eng and Tech. Community of Canada (Pres. 1974–75), Nat. Research Council of Canada (Chair. on Fusion 1977–87), Science Council of Canada; Fellow Canadian Aeronautics and Space Inst.; American Physical Soc., Canadian Acad. of Eng; Hon. mem. Eng Inst. of Canada; Hon. LLD (Waterloo) 1993, (Concordia) 1997; Hon. DSc (McGill) 1994; Prix Scientifique du Québec 1974, Canada Enterprise Award 1977, Queen's Silver Jubilee Medal 1977, Canadian Asscn of Physicists Medal 1984, Canadian Research Man. Asscn Award 1988, Prix PME (Quebec) 1988, Canada Award for Business Excellence-Entrepreneurship 1989, 1990, Prix ADRIQ 1991, Canadian Asscn of Physicists Medal for Industrial and Applied Physics 1995, Prix du Québec – Lionel Boulet 2001. *Publications:* The Particle Kinetics of Plasmas (Co-author) 1968; more than 80 publs in scientific and eng journals. *Leisure interest:* tennis. *Address:* MPB Technologies Inc., 151 Hymus Boulevard, Pointe Claire, Québec, H9R 1E9 (Office); 78 Thurlow Road, Montreal, Québec, H3X 3G9, Canada (Home). *Telephone:* (514) 694-8751 (Office); (514) 481-2359 (Home). *Fax:* (514) 695-7492 (Office). *E-mail:* m.p.bachynski@mpbc.ca (Office). *Website:* www.mpbcommunications.com (Office).

BACKE, John David, MBA; American communications executive; b. 5 July 1932, Akron, Ohio; s. of John and Ella A. (née Enyedy) Backe; m. Katherine Elliott 1955; one s. one d.; ed Miami Univ., Ohio Xavier Univ.; various Eng, financial and marketing positions in General Electric Co. 1957–66; Vice-Pres. and Dir of Marketing, Silver Burdett Co. 1966–68, Pres. 1968–69; Exec. Vice-Pres. General Learning Corpn 1969, Pres. and CEO 1969–73; Pres. of Publishing Group, CBS Inc. 1973–76, of CBS Inc. (also CEO) 1976–80, Dir of Business Marketing, Corpn of New York 1978; Pres. CEO Tomorrow Entertainment 1981–84, Chair. 1984–; Chair. Cinema Products, Los Angeles 1992–; Chair., CEO, Backe Group Inc. 1984–; Chair. Station WRGB Schenectady, NY 1983–; Chair. Station WLNS Lansing, MI 1984; Chair. Station WKBT Lacrosse, WI 1984; Chair. Dorchester Publ Co. Inc., NY 1984; Chair. Kingswood Advertising 1988; Station WDKY-TV, Lexington 1985–93; Gulf-shore Publ Co., Naples 1986–; Gulfstream Newspapers, Pompano 1987–; Andrews Communications, Westtown, Pa 1987–; Atlantic Publs, Accomac, Va 1989–; Special Del. to UNESCO Conf. on publishing for Arabic-speaking countries 1972; mem. Nat. Advisory Cttee for Illinois Univ. Inst. for Aviation;

Hon. LLD (Miami and Xavier); Cable Ace Award 1988. *Leisure interest:* multi-engine piloting. *Address:* 399 Park Avenue, 19th Floor, New York, NY 10022, USA (Office).

BAČKIS, HE Cardinal Audrys Juozas; Lithuanian ecclesiastic; b. 1 Feb. 1937, Kaunas; ordained priest 1961; Archbishop 1988; Archbishop of Vilnius 1991–; cr. Cardinal 2001. *Address:* Šventaragio 4, 2001 Vilnius, Lithuania (Office). *Telephone:* (2) 223653 (Office); (2) 223413 (Home). *Fax:* (2) 222807 (Office).

BACKLEY, Steve, OBE; British athlete; b. 12 Feb. 1969, Sidcup, Kent; s. of John Backley and Pauline Hogg; javelin thrower; coached by John Trower; Commonwealth record-holder 1992 (91.46m); Gold Medal European Jr Championships 1987; Silver Medal World Jr Championships 1988; Gold Medal European Cup 1989, 1997, Bronze Medal 1995; Gold Medal World Student Games 1989, 1991; Gold Medal World Cup 1989, 1994, 1998; Gold Medal Commonwealth Games 1990, 1994, 2002, Silver Medal 1998; Gold Medal European Championships 1990, 1994, 1998, 2002; Bronze Medal Olympic Games 1992, Silver Medal 1996, 2000; Silver Medal World Championships 1995, 1997; Athlete of the Year, UK Athletics 2000. *Publication:* The Winning Mind.

BÄCKSTRÖM, Urban, PhD; Swedish banker; b. 25 May 1954, Sollefteå; s. of Sven-Ake Bäckström and Maj-Britt Filipsson; m. Ewa Hintze 1978; one s. one d.; ed Stockholm Univ. and Stockholm School of Econs; Research Asst Inst. for Int. Econ. Studies, Stockholm 1978–80; First Sec. Int. Dept Ministry of Foreign Affairs 1980–82; Chief Economist, Moderate Party 1982–83, 1986–89; Under-Sec. of State, Ministry of Finance 1991–93; Gov. Sveriges Riksbank (Swedish Cen. Bank) 1994–2002; Bd mem. Bank for Int. Settlements 1994–, Chair. and Pres. 1999–2002. *Address:* c/o Sveriges Riksbank, 10337 Stockholm, Sweden (Office).

BACKUS, George Edward, SM, PhD, FRSA; American theoretical geophysicist; b. 24 May 1930, Chicago, Ill.; s. of the late Milo Morlan Backus and Dora Backus (née Mendenhall); m. 1st Elizabeth E Allen 1961; two s. one d.; m. 2nd Marianne McDonald 1971; m. 3rd Varda Peller 1977; ed Thornton Township High School, Harvey, Ill. and Univ. of Chicago; Asst Examiner, Univ. of Chicago 1949–50; Junior Mathematician, Inst. for Air Weapons Research, Univ. of Chicago 1950–54; Physicist, Project Matterhorn, Princeton Univ. 1957–58; Asst Prof. of Mathematics, MIT 1958–60; Assoc. Prof. of Geophysics, Univ. of Calif. (La Jolla) 1960–62, Prof. 1962–94, Research Prof. 1994–99, Prof. Emer. 1999–; mem. Scientific Advisory Cttee to NASA on Jt NASA/CNES Magnetic Satellites; Co.-Chair. Int. Working Group on Magnetic Field Satellites 1983–92; mem. Visiting Cttee Inst. de Physique du Globe de Paris 1987; Guggenheim Fellowship 1963, 1971; Fellow American Geophysical Union, RSA, Royal Astronomical Soc.; mem. NAS; Foreign mem. Académie des Sciences de l'Institut de France; Dr hc (Inst. de Physique de Globe, Paris) 1995; Gold Medal, Royal Astronomical Soc. 1986, John Adam Fleming Medal, American Geophysical Union 1986. *Publications:* numerous scientific works 1958–. *Leisure interests:* hiking, swimming, history, reading, skiing. *Address:* Institute of Geophysics and Planetary Physics, University of California at San Diego, La Jolla, CA 92093 (Office); 9362 La Jolla Farms Road, La Jolla, CA 92037, USA (Home). *Telephone:* (619) 534-2468 (Office); (619) 455-8972 (Home). *Fax:* (619) 534-8090.

BACKUS, John, AM; American computer scientist; b. 3 Dec. 1924, Philadelphia; m. 2nd Una Stannard 1968; two d.; ed Columbia Univ.; Research Staff mem., Thomas J. Watson Research Center 1959–63; IBM Fellow, IBM Almaden Research Center, San José, Calif. 1963–91; consultant 1991–; Man. Incest Info., Bay Area 1992–; Visiting Prof., Univ. of California, Berkeley 1980; Fellow American Acad. of Arts and Sciences; mem. NAS, Nat. Acad. of Eng; Hon. DUniv (York, England) 1985; Hon. DSc (Arizona) 1988, (Indiana) 1992; Dr hc (Nancy I, France) 1989; awards include National Medal of Science 1975, A. M. Turing Award, Asscn for Computing Machinery 1977, Charles Stark Draper Prize, Nat. Acad. of Eng 1994. *Publications:* Systems Design of the IBM 704 Computer (with G. M. Amdahl) 1954, The Fortran Automatic Coding System (with others) 1957, The Syntax and Semantics of the Proposed International Algebraic Language of the Zürich ACM-GAMM Conf. 1959, Report on the Algorithmic Language ALGOL 60 (with others) 1960, Can Programming Be Liberated from the von Neumann Style? A Functional Style and Its Algebra of Programs (Communications of the Asscn for Computing Machinery) 1978, Is Computer Science Based on the Wrong Fundamental Concept of Program? An Extended Concept in Algorithmic Languages (Holland) 1981. *Leisure interests:* psychology, prevention and treatment of child abuse. *Address:* 91 St Germain Avenue, San Francisco, CA 94114, USA. *Telephone:* (415) 731-8155. *Fax:* (415) 665-6124 (Home). *E-mail:* jbackus1@pacbell.net (Home).

BACON, Edmund Norwood, BArch; American architect and planner; b. 2 May 1910, Philadelphia; s. of Ellis W Bacon and Helen Comly Bacon; m. Ruth Holmes 1938 (died 1991); two s. four d.; ed Cornell Univ. and Cranbrook Acad.; Architectural Designer, Shanghai, China 1933–34; housing projects for W Pope Barney, Architect, Philadelphia 1935; Supervisor of City Planning, Flint (Michigan) Inst. of Research and Planning 1937–39; Man. Dir Philadelphia Housing Asscn 1940–43; Co-Designer Better Philadelphia Exhibition and Senior Land Planner, Philadelphia City Planning Comm. 1946–49; Exec. Dir Philadelphia City Planning Comm. 1949–70, Devt Co-ordinator 1968–70; Adjunct Prof., Univ. of Pennsylvania 1950–87; Vice-Pres. Mondev Int. Ltd, Montreal, Canada 1971–88; Plym Distinguished Prof. Univ. of Ill. 1991–92;

mem. President's Citizens' Advisory Cttee on Environmental Quality 1969–70; numerous awards, including Sir Patrick Abercrombie Prize for Town Planning, Int. Union of Architects 1990, Planning Pioneer Award, American Inst. of Certified Planners 1993. *Films:* has produced/directed five films on architecture. *Achievements (miscellaneous):* numerous professional projects 1971– including plan for Beijing, Beijing Asscn for Cultural Exchanges with Foreign Countries. *Publication:* Design of Cities 1967 (revised 1974). *Address:* 2117 Locust Street, Philadelphia, PA 19103, USA (Home). *Telephone:* (215) 567-0693. *Fax:* (215) 567-1658.

BACON, Kevin; American actor; b. 8 July 1958, Philadelphia, Pa; m. Kyra Sedgwick; one s. one d.; ed Manning Street Actor's Theatre. *Stage appearances include:* Getting On 1978, Glad Tidyings 1979–80, Mary Barnes 1980, Album 1980, Forty-Deuce 1981, Flux 1982, Poor Little Lambs 1982, Slab Boys 1983, Men Without Dates 1985, Loot 1986, Road, Spike Heels. *Television appearances include:* The Gift 1979, Enormous Changes at the Last Minute 1982, The Demon Murder Case 1983, The Tender Age, Lemon Sky, Frasier (voice), Happy Birthday Elizabeth: A Celebration of Life 1997. *Film appearances include:* National Lampoon's Animal House 1978, Starting Over 1979, Hero at Large 1980, Friday the 13th 1980, Only When I Laugh 1981, Diner 1982, Footloose 1984, Quicksilver 1985, White Water Summer 1987, Planes, Trains and Automobiles 1987, End of the Line 1988, She's Having a Baby 1988, Criminal Law 1989, The Big Picture 1989, Tremors 1990, Flatliners 1990, Queens Logic 1991, He Said/She Said 1991, Pyrates 1991, JFK 1992, A Few Good Men 1992, The Air Up There 1994, The River Wild 1994, Murder in the First 1995, Apollo 13 1995, Sleepers 1996, Telling Lies in America 1997, Picture Perfect 1997, Digging to China 1997, Wild Things 1998, My Dog Skip 1999, The Hollow Man 1999, Stir of Echoes 1999, Novocaine 2000, We Married Margo 2000, 24 Hours 2001, Trapped 2002. *Address:* c/o Frank Frattaroli, William Morris Agency, 9830 Wilshire Boulevard, Beverly Hills, CA 90212, USA.

BACQUIER, Gabriel; French (baritone) opera singer; b. 17 May 1924, Béziers; s. of Augustin Bacquier and Fernande Severac; m. 1st Simone Teisseire 1943; one s.; m. 2nd Mauricette Bénard 1958; one s.; ed Paris Conservatoire; debut at Théâtre Royal de la Monnaie, Brussels 1953; joined Opéra de Paris 1956; debut at Carnegie Hall 1960, Metropolitan Opera, New York 1961; has appeared at the Vienna State Opera, Covent Garden, La Scala, Opéra de Paris and most leading opera houses; repertoire includes Otello, Don Giovanni, Pelléas et Mélisande, Damnation de Faust, Tosca, Falstaff; several recordings; Prix nat. du disque français 1964; Chevalier, Légion d'honneur, Officier, Ordre nat. du Mérite, Commdr des Arts et des Lettres, Médaille de Vermeil, Paris, Victoires de la Musique 1985. *Films include:* La Grande Récré, Falstaff. *Leisure interests:* painting, drawing. *Address:* c/o OIA, 16 avenue Franklin D. Roosevelt, 75008 Paris, France (Home).

BÁCS, Ludovic; Romanian conductor and composer; b. 19 Jan. 1930, Petrila; s. of Ludovic Bács and Iuliana Bács (Venczel); m. Ercse Gyöngyver, 1952; two s.; ed Dima Gh. Conservatory, Cluj-Napoca Tchaikovski Conservatory, Moscow, Cluj-Napoca Coll. of Philosophy 1948–49; began career as conductor Symphonic Orchestra of Romanian Radio, also Artistic Dir 1964–; Prof. Bucharest Conservatory 1960–66, 1990–; Conductor Romanian Radio Chamber Orchestra 1990–; f. Musica Rediviva 1966, the first group of performers to render ancient Romanian music; he conducted concerts in USSR, Poland, Czechoslovakia, Hungary, Bulgaria, the GDR, West Berlin, the FRG, Holland, Argentina, Switzerland, Spain, France; mem. Romanian Composers' Union; Cultural Merit Award, the Medal of Labour, Prize of the Theatre and Music Asscn. *Works include:* orchestration of Bach's Art of the Fugue (on record), numerous adaptations from 15th–18th centuries music: Bach, Monteverdi, Backfarg, from Codex Caioni 17th–18th c.; Suitá de Musicá Veche 17th–18th century, Variations Sinfoniques e Double Fugue sur une Thème Populaire Hongroise, Trois Madrigales pour Choeur, Variations et Fugue sur une Colinde Roumaine, Potpourri sur des Colindes. *Address:* Berthelot 63-64, Bucharest (Office); 31 D. Golescu, Sc III, Et V ap. 87, Bucharest 1, Romania (Home).

BADAL, Prakash Singh, BA; Indian politician; b. 8 Dec. 1927, Abulkhurana, Punjab; s. of Raghuraj Singh; m. Surinder Kaur; one s. one d.; mem. Akali Dal; fmr mem. Shiromani Gurdwara Prabandhak Cttee; elected to Ass. 1957, re-elected 1969; Minister for Community Devt Panchayati Raj, Animal Husbandry, Dairying and Fisheries 1969–70; Chief Minister 1970–71; imprisoned during State of Emergency 1975–77; elected to Lok Sabha 1977; Minister for Agric. 1977; Chief Minister of Punjab 1977, 1997–2002; Leader of Opposition 1980; Chair. Punjab Arts Council; mem. Nankana Sahib Educational Trust, Ludhiana. *Address:* Kothi No. 45, Sector 2, Chandigarh, India (Home). *Telephone:* (172) 740737 (Home).

BADAWI, Dato' Seri Abdullah Bin Haji Ahmad, BA; Malaysian politician; b. 26 Nov. 1939, Pulau Pinang; m. Datin Endon bint Datuk Mahmud; ed Univ. of Malaya; Asst Sec. Public Service Dept 1964; Asst Sec. MAGERAN 1969; Asst Sec. Nat. Security Council 1971; Dir (Youth), Ministry of Sport, Youth and Culture 1971–74, Deputy Sec.-Gen. 1974–78; Minister without Portfolio, Prime Minister's Dept 1982; Minister of Educ. 1984–86, of Defence 1986–87; mem. UMNO Supreme Council 1982–, Vice-Pres. 1984; Minister of Foreign Affairs 1991; Deputy Prime Minister and Minister of Home Affairs 1998–(2003), Prime Minister (desig.) of Malaysia Oct. 2003–. *Address:* Dewan Rakyat, Parliament Building, 50680 Kuala Lumpur, Malaysia.

BADAWI, Zeinab Mohammed-Khair, MA; television presenter; b. 3 Oct. 1959; d. of Mohammed-Khair El Badawi and Asia Malik; m. David Antony Crook 1991; one s. two d.; ed Hornsey School for Girls, St Hilda's Coll. Oxford and Univ. of London; presenter and journalist, current affairs and documentaries, Yorkshire TV 1982–86; current affairs reporter, BBC TV 1987–88; newscaster and journalist ITN Channel Four News 1988; now broadcaster BBC World Service, BBC Live Political Programmer; Vice-Pres. UN Int. Asscn; mem. Hansard Chair. into Scrutiny Role of Parl. Panel 2000. *Leisure interests:* languages, opera, yoga, reading. *Address:* BBC World Service, Bush House, Strand, London, WC2B 4PH, England (Office). *Telephone:* (20) 7240-3456 (Office). *Fax:* (20) 7557-1258 (Office). *E-mail:* worldservice.letters@bbc .co.uk (Office).

BADDILEY, Sir James, Kt, MA, PhD, DSc, ScD, FRS, FRSE; British professor of chemical microbiology; b. 15 May 1918, Manchester; s. of the late James Baddiley and Ivy (Logan-Cato) Baddiley; m. Hazel M. Townsend 1944; one s.; ed Manchester Grammar School and Univ. of Manchester; ICI Fellow, Univ. of Cambridge 1944–49; Fellow, Swedish Medical Research Council, Stockholm 1947–49; mem. of staff Dept of Biochemistry, Lister Inst., London 1949–54; Prof. of Organic Chem., Univ. of Durham, Kings Coll., Newcastle 1955–63; Prof. of Organic Chem., Univ. of Newcastle-upon-Tyne 1963–77, Head of the School of Chem. 1968–78, Prof. of Chem. Microbiology 1977–83, now Prof. Emer.; Science and Engineering Research Council (SERC) Sr Fellow, Univ. of Cambridge 1981–83; Dir Microbiological Chem. Research Lab., Univ. of Newcastle-upon-Tyne 1975–83; mem. Science Research Council 1979–81; mem. Council, Royal Soc. 1977–79, SERC 1979–81; editorial Bds., Biochemical Preparations 1960–70, Biochimica et Biophysica Acta 1970–77; Cambridge Studies in Biotech. 1985–; Trustee EPA Cephalosporin Fund; Vice-Pres. Alzheimer's Research Trust; Fellow (now Fellow Emer.), Pembroke Coll., Cambridge; Hon. mem. American Soc. for Biochemistry and Molecular Biology; Rockefeller Fellow, Harvard Medical School 1954; Beyer Fellow, Univ. of Manchester 1943–44; Tilden Lecturer, Chemical Soc. 1959, Karl Folkers Prof., Univ. of Illinois 1962, Leeuwenhoek Lecturer, Royal Soc. 1967, Pedler Lecturer, Chem. Soc. 1978, Bose Endowment Lecturer, Bose Inst., Calcutta 1980; Hon. DSc (Heriot-Watt) 1978, (Bath) 1986; Meldola Medal, Royal Inst. of Chem. 1947, Corday-Morgan Medal and Prize, Chem. Soc. 1952, Davy Medal, Royal Soc. 1974. *Achievements:* made first chemical synthesis of ATP (energy transfer agent in all living cells); discovered teichoic acids (major component of walls and membranes of bacteria). *Publications:* numerous publications in biochem. and microbiological chem. *Leisure interests:* gardening, music, photography, fine arts, mountaineering. *Address:* Hill Top Cottage, Hildersham, Cambridge, CB1 6DA, England. *Telephone:* (1223) 893055. *E-mail:* james@baddiley.fsnet.co.uk (Home).

BADHAM, John Macdonald, BA, MFA; American (b. British) film director; b. 25 Aug. 1939, Luton, England; s. of Henry Lee Badham and Mary Iola Hewitt; m. Julia Laughlin 1992; one d.; ed Yale Univ., Yale Drama School; joined Universal Studio as mailroom employee, then tour guide, subsequently casting Dir and assoc. producer; Pres. Great American Picture Show; Chair. Bd JMB Films Inc.; Founder and Pres. Badham Co., California 1975–; George Pal Award. *Films include:* The Bingo Long Travelling All-Stars and Motor Kings, Saturday Night Fever 1977, Dracula (Best Horror Film Award, Acad. of Science Fiction, Fantasy and Horror Films) 1979, Whose Life Is It Anyway? (San Rafael Grand Prize) 1981, War Games (Best Dir, Science Fiction/ Fantasy Acad.) 1983, Stakeout (also exec. producer) 1987, Disorganized Crime (exec. producer only), Bird on a Wire 1989, The Hard Way 1990, Point of No Return 1993, Another Stakeout (also exec. producer) 1993, Drop Zone (also exec. producer) 1994, Nick of Time (also producer) 1995, Incognito 1998, Floating Away 1998, The Jack Bull 1999, Ocean Warrior 2000. *Television includes:* The Impatient Heart (Christopher Award 1971), Isn't It Shocking? 1973, The Law, The Gun (Southern Calif. Motion Picture Council Award 1974), Reflections of Murder 1973, The Godchild 1974, The Keegans, Sorrow Floats 1998; several series episodes. *Website:* www.badhamcompany.com (Office).

BADIAN, Ernst, MA, DPhil, LittD, FBA; professor of history; b. 8 Aug. 1925, Vienna, Austria; s. of Joseph Badian and Sally Badian; m. Nathlie A. Wimsett 1950; one s. one d.; ed Christchurch Boys' High School, Canterbury Univ. Coll., Christchurch, NZ and Univ. Coll., Oxford; Asst Lecturer in Classics, Victoria Univ. Coll., Wellington 1947–48; Rome Scholar in Classics, British School at Rome 1950–52; Asst Lecturer in Classics and Ancient History, Univ. of Sheffield 1952–54; Lecturer in Classics, Univ. of Durham 1954–65; Prof. of Ancient History, Univ. of Leeds 1965–69; Prof. of Classics and History, State Univ. of NY at Buffalo 1969–71; Prof. of History, Harvard Univ. 1971–82, John Moors Cabot Prof. of History 1982–98, Prof. Emer. 1998–; Fellow, American Acad. of Arts and Sciences, American Numismatic Soc.; Corresp. mem. Austrian Acad. of Sciences, German Archaeological Inst.; Foreign mem. Finnish Acad. of Sciences; Visiting Prof. and lecturer at many univs in USA, Canada, Australia, S. Africa, Europe etc.; Hon. Fellow Univ. Coll., Oxford; Hon. mem. Soc. for Roman Studies; Hon. LittD (Macquarie), (Canterbury); Conington Prize, Oxford Univ. 1958; Cross of Honour for Science and Art (Austria) 1999. *Publications:* Foreign Clientelae (264–70 BC) 1958, Studies in Greek and Roman History 1964, Polybius 1966, Roman Imperialism in the Late Republic 1967, Publicans and Sinners 1972, From Plataea to Potidaea 1993, Zöllner und Sünder 1997; articles in classical and historical journals.

Leisure interest: parrots. *Address:* Department of History, Harvard University, Cambridge, MA 02138, USA. *Telephone:* (617) 496-5881. *Fax:* (617) 496-3425 (Office).

BADINTER, Robert, AM, LLD; French lawyer and professor of law; b. 30 March 1928, Paris; s. of Simon Badinter and Charlotte Rosenberg; m. 1st Anne Vernon 1957; m. 2nd Elisabeth Bleustein-Blanchet 1966; two s. one d.; ed Univ. of Paris, Columbia Univ., New York; Lawyer, Paris Court of Appeal 1951; Prof. of Law, Paris I (Sorbonne) 1974–81; Minister of Justice and Keeper of the Seals 1981–86; Pres. Constitutional Council 1986–95; Pres. Court of Conciliation and Arbitration of the OSCE; Senator (Hauts de Seine) 1995–. *Play:* C.3.3., Paris 1995. *Publications:* L'exécution 1973, Liberté, libertés 1976, Condorcet (with Elisabeth Badinter) 1988, Libres et égaux: L'émancipation des juifs sous la révolution française 1989, La prison républicaine 1992, C.3.3. 1995, Un antisémitisme ordinaire: Vichy et les avocats juifs 1940–44 1997, L'abolition 2000, Une Constitution européenne 2002. *Address:* Court of Conciliation and Arbitration, Organization for Security and Co-operation in Europe, 266 route de Lausanne, 1292 Chambesy, Geneva, Switzerland; 38 rue Guynemer, 75006 Paris, France (Home). *Telephone:* (22) 7580025. *Fax:* (22) 7582510. *E-mail:* info@osce.org; cca.osce@bluewin.ch. *Website:* www.osce.org.

BADRAN, Adnan, PhD; Jordanian university president and international organization official; m.; several c.; ed Oklahoma State Univ., Michigan State Univ.; Prof. of Science; Dean Faculty of Science, Univ. of Jordan 1971–76; Pres. Yarmouk Univ. 1976–86; Asst. Dir Gen. for Science, UNESCO 1990–93, Deputy Dir Gen. 1993–98; Pres. Philadelphia Univ., Jordan; fmr Minister of Agric. and Minister of Educ.; fmr Sec. Gen. Higher Council for Science and Tech.; Sec. Gen. and Fellow Third World Acad. of Sciences; mem. Arab Thought Forum 1978–, World Affairs Council 1980–, Inst. of Biological Sciences, AAAS 1993–; Fellow Islamic Acad. of Sciences, mem. Council and Treas. 1999–; Dr hc (Sung Kyuakwan Univ., Seoul); Al-Nahda Medal (Jordan), Al-Yarmouk Medal (Jordan), Istilal Medal (Jordan) 1995, Alfonso X Medal (Spain). *Publications:* author and ed. of over 18 books and 90 research papers in the fields of botany, economic devt, educ. and int. co-operation. *Address:* Islamic Academy of Sciences, P.O. Box 830036, Amman, Jordan (Office). *Telephone:* 5522104 (Office). *Fax:* 5511803 (Office). *Website:* www .ias-worldwide.org.

BADRAN, Ibrahim, PhD; Jordanian government official and foundation director; b. 19 July 1939, Nablus, Palestine; m.; four c.; ed Univs. of Cairo and London; Lecturer in Electrical Eng Univ. of Libya, Tripoli 1970–74; Chief. Eng and Head, Electricity Section, Consultancy and Architecture, Ministry of Planning, Baghdad 1974–76; Dir of Planning and Dir of Standards and Specifications, Jordan Electricity Authority 1978–80; Dir of Energy, Ministry of Trade and Industry 1980–84; Sec.-Gen. (Under-Sec.) Ministry of Industry and Trade 1984–85; Sec.-Gen. Ministry of Energy and Natural Resources 1985–90; Adviser to Prime Minister 1991–94; Co-ordinator-Gen. of Peace Process, Ministry of Foreign Affairs 1994–95; Exec. Dir Noor Al-Hussein Foundation 1995–97; Supervisor, Human Rights Unit, Prime Minister's Office; Asst Pres. Philadelphia Univ. 1999–, Dean of Faculty of Eng 2000–; Chair. Bd Dirs Jordan Glass Co. 1985–87, Commercial Centers Cooperation-Jordan 1984–85, 1990–91; fmr Dir Jordanian Petroleum Refinery, Jordanian Phosphate Co., Jordan Valley Authority, Jordan Water Authority, Jordan Electricity Authority, Jordan Natural Resources Authority, Industrial Bank of Jordan etc.; Gov. for Jordan, IAEA 1982–90; numerous other professional and academic appointments and affiliations; writes weekly column in Aldustou (daily newspaper); Order of Independence; Hussein Gold Medal for Scientific Distinctions, State Appreciation Award for Human Sciences and Arab Thoughts. *Publications:* Study on the Arab Mind, On Progress and History in the Arab World, Science and Technology in the Arab World, Culture Decline, and other books on aspects of science, tech., nuclear energy, natural resources and devt in the Arab world; two theoretical plays. *Leisure interests:* farming, reading, writing, travelling. *Address:* Philadelphia University, POB 1, Amman 19392 (Office); 29 Ali Thyabat Street, Tla'a Al Ali, Amman, Jordan (Home). *Telephone:* (2) 6374444 (Office); (2) 5347777 (Home). *Fax:* (2) 6374370 (Office); (2) 5344448 (Home). *E-mail:* philad@go.com.jo (Office); philad.pr@ lycos.com (Office). *Website:* www.philadelphia.edu.jo.

BADRAN, Mudar, BA; Jordanian politician and civil servant; b. 1934, Jerash; ed Univ. of Damascus, Syria; Lieut. and Legal Consultant, Jordanian armed forces 1957, Maj. and Legal Adviser to the Armed Forces Treasury 1962; Asst Chief, Jordanian Foreign Intelligence 1965; Deputy Chief of Gen. Intelligence 1966, Chief 1968; Retd. Maj.-Gen. 1970; Chief Chamberlain of the Royal Court 1970, Sec.-Gen.; late Nat. Security Adviser to fmr King Hussein 1970; Minister in the Royal Court 1972; Nat. Security Adviser to King Hussein 1973; Minister of Educ. 1973–74; Chief of the Royal Court 1974–76; Minister of Defence and of Foreign Affairs 1976–79; Prime Minister 1976–79, 1980–84, 1989–91; also Minister of Defence 1980–84, 1989; mem. Nat. Consultative Council 1979–; fmr mem. Exec. Council of the Arab Nat. Union; Hon. LLD (Leicester) 1991.

BADRI, Muhammad bin, PhD; Malaysian professor of chemistry and university administrator; b. May 1943; ed St Francis Xavier Univ., Dalhousie Univ., Canada; teacher 1965–72; lecturer Universiti Putra Malaysia 1972–75, Assoc. Prof. 1976–84, apptd. Dean and Prof., Faculty of Science and Environmental Studies 1984; mem. Council of Malaysia Inst. of Chem. 1980–84, Nat. Asscn of Science and Math. Educ., Malaysian Rubber Producers' Council, ACS 1984, Bd Rubber Research Inst. of Malaysia, Environ-

mental Quality Council, Ministry of Science, Malaysia; Fellow Islamic Acad. of Sciences, Acad. of Sciences, Malaysia. *Address:* Universiti Putra Malaysia, 43400 Serdang, Selangor Darul Ehsan, Malaysia (Office). *Telephone:* (3) 89486101 (Office). *Fax:* (3) 89483244 (Office).

BADURA-SKODA, Paul; Austrian pianist; b. 6 Oct. 1927; s. of Ludwig Badura and Margarete Badura (née Winter); m. Eva Badura-Skoda (née Halfar); two s. two d.; ed Realgymnasium courses in conducting and piano, Konservatorium der Stadt Wien and Edwin Fischer's Master Class in Lucerne; regular concerts since 1948; tours all over the world as soloist and with leading orchestras; conductor of chamber orchestra 1960–; yearly master classes fmrly in Edin., Salzburg and Vienna Festival 1958–63; Artist in Residence, Univ. of Wisconsin, master classes in Madison, Wis. 1966–71; recorded over 200 L.P. records and CDs including complete Beethoven and Schubert sonatas; First Prize Austrian Music Competition 1947, Austrian Cross of Honour for Science and Arts (1st Order) 1976, Bösendorfer-Ring 1978, Chevalier, Legion d'honneur 1992. *Compositions:* Mass in D, Cadenzas to Piano and Violin Concertos by Mozart and Haydn, completion of 5 unfinished Piano Sonatas by Schubert 1976 and of unfinished Larghetto and Allegro for 2 Pianos by Mozart, Elegy for Piano 1980, Sonatine Romantique for Violin and Piano 1994. *Publications:* Interpreting Mozart on the Keyboard (with Eva Badura-Skoda), Die Klaviersonaten von Beethoven (with Jörg Demus) 1970, Interpreting Bach at the Keyboard 1993; Editions of Schubert, Mozart, Chopin; numerous articles. *Leisure interest:* chess. *Address:* c/o Hochschule für Musik und darstellende Kunst, Lothringerstrasse 18, 1037 Vienna, Austria (Office); c/o 3116 Live Oak Street, Dallas, TX 75204, USA.

BAER, Olaf; German baritone; b. 19 Dec. 1957, Dresden; s. of Ernst Edwin Baer and Dora Anneliese Pfennig; m. Carola Tantz 1993; ed Music School 'Carl Maria von Weber', Dresden; mem. of Dresden Kreuzchores 1967–76; British début at Wigmore Hall 1983, American début in Bach's St Matthew Passion with Chicago Symphony Orchestra 1987; Prin. Baritone with Dresden State Opera 1983–91; recital and concert tours in all maj. cities Europe, Australia, USA and Japan; winner of inaugural Walther Gruner Lieder Competition 1983. *Leisure interests:* all aspects of music, poetry, literature, painting. *Address:* Olbersdorferstrasse 7, 01324 Dresden, Germany. *Telephone:* (351) 376952.

BAEZ, Joan Chandos; American folk singer; b. 9 Jan. 1941, Staten Island, NY; d. of Albert V. Baez and Joan (Bridge) Baez; m. David Harris 1968 (divorced 1973); one s.; ed School of Fine and Applied Arts, Boston Univ.; began career as singer in coffee houses, appeared at Ballad Room, Club 47 1958–68, Gate of Horn, Chicago 1958, Newport, RI, Folk Festival 1959–69, Town Hall and Carnegie Hall, New York 1962, 1967, 1968; gave concerts in black colls in southern USA 1963; toured Europe and USA 1960s–1990s, Democratic Repub. of Viet Nam 1972, Australia 1985; recordings with Vanguard Records 1960–72, A & M Record Co. 1972–76, Portrait Records 1977–80, Gold Castle Records 1987–89, Virgin Records 1990–93, Guardian Records 1995–, Grapevine Label Records 1995–; awarded eight gold albums, one gold single; many TV appearances; began refusing payment of war taxes 1964; detained for civil disobedience opposing conscription 1967; speaking tour of USA and Canada for draft resistance 1967–68; Founder, Vice-Pres. Inst. for Study of Non-Violence (now called Resource Center for Non-Violence) 1965–; Founder, Humanitas Int. Human Rights Comm. 1979–92; Gandhi Memorial Int. Foundation Award 1988; Chevalier, Légion d'honneur. *Albums include:* Rare, Live and Classic 1993, Gone From Danger 1997. *Publications:* Joan Baez Songbook 1964, Daybreak 1968, Coming Out (with David Harris) 1971, And Then I Wrote... (songbook) 1979, And a Voice to Sing With 1987. *Address:* Diamonds and Rust Productions, P.O. Box 1026, Menlo Park, CA 94026-1026, USA. *Telephone:* (650) 328-0266. *Website:* www.joanbaez.com.

BAFILE, HE Cardinal Corrado; Italian ecclesiastic; b. 4 July 1903; s. of Vincenzo and Maddalena Tedeschini; ed State Univ., Rome and Lateran Univ., Rome; fmr Prefect of the Sacred Congregation for the Causes of Saints; ordained priest 1936; Vatican Secretariat of State 1939–58; Privy Chamberlain to Pope John XXIII 1958–60; Papal Nuncio to Germany 1960–75; Titular Archbishop of Antiochia in Pisidia 1960–76; cr. Cardinal 1976, now Cardinal Priest. *Address:* 10 Via P. Pancrazio Pfeiffer, 00193, Rome, Italy.

BAGABANDI, Natsag, MSc; Mongolian politician; b. 22 April 1950, Zavkhan Prov.; s. of Mend Natsag and Rashjamts Dogoo; m. Oyunbileg Azadsuren 1971; one s. one d.; ed Refrigeration Jr Coll., Leningrad (now St Petersburg), USSR, Food Tech. Inst. of USSR, Odessa, Acad. of Social Science, Moscow, USSR; machine operator, mechanic and engineer, Ulan Bator City Brewery and Distillery 1972–75; Chief of Dept Mongolian People's Revolutionary Party's (MPRP) Cttee of Tuv Aimag 1980–84; Chief of Div., Div. Adviser Cen. Cttee of MPRP 1987–90; Sec., Deputy Chair. Cen. Cttee of MPRP 1990–92, Chair. Feb.–June 1997; mem. of State Great Hural, Chair. 1992–96; Pres. of Mongolia and C-in-C of the Armed Forces May 1997–; Hon. Prof. Mongolian Socio-Econ. Inst. 'Explorer XXI'; 70th Anniversary Order of the People's Revolution 1991, 'Golden Star' Olympic Order 1997, Academician Title 'Bilguun Nomch', Mongolian Nomadic Civilization Acad. and 'Ikh-Zasag' Univ. 2000, 'Peace' Order of Russian Fed. 2000, Order of Chinggis Khaan 2000; Dr hc (Nat. Food Tech. Acad. of Odessa, Ukraine) 1995, (Seng-Shui Univ., Japan) 1998, (Ankara Univ., Turkey) 1998, (Alma-Ata Univ., Kazakhstan) 1998, (Mongolian Admin Acad.) 1999, (Mongolian 'Otgontenger' Univ.) 2001, (Mongolian Defense Univ.) 2001, (Sougan Univ., S Korea) 2001, (Mongolian Science and Tech. Univ.) 2002; Sukhbaatar Fund Prize 1996,

Peter the Great Int. Prize 2001. *Publications include:* Mongolian Behaviour 1992, The President: Thought and Recommendation Before the New Century 1998, The President: Policy and Objectives Before the New Century 1998, Policy and Mind of the President 2000, Significance of Restoration and Tradition to the Development 2000, Mongolian Intelligence 2001, Policy and Diligence of the President 2001, Thought and Ideas of the President 2001, XXI Century Will Test You 2001, New Era and New Objectives of Mongolian Buddhist Religion 2001, Let Us Respect and Admire Elders 2001, Children, Youths and the President 2001, Multi-Sided National Security 2001. *Leisure interests:* reading, fishing. *Address:* State Palace, Ulan Bator 12, Mongolia. *Telephone:* (1) 323252 (Office). *Fax:* (1) 329281 (Office). *E-mail:* president@ pmis.gov.mn (Office). *Website:* www.pmis.gov.mn/president.

BAGAYEV, Sergei Nikolayevich; Russian physicist; b. 9 Sept. 1941; m.; one s.; ed Novosibirsk State Univ.; jr, sr researcher, head of lab. Inst. of Physics of Semiconductors, Siberian br. USSR Acad. of Sciences 1965–78; head of lab., head of div., Deputy Dir Inst. of Thermal Physics, Siberian br. USSR Acad. of Sciences 1978–91; Deputy Dir Inst. of Laser Physics, Siberian br. Russian Acad. of Sciences 1991–92, Dir 1992–; Corresp. mem. USSR (now Russian) Acad. of Sciences 1990, Academician 1993–; research in nonlinear laser spectroscopy of superhigh resolution, laser frequency standards, physics and their applications in precision physical experiments; State Prize of Russian Fed. 1998. *Publications include:* Laser Frequency Standards 1986 and numerous articles. *Address:* Institute of Laser Physics, Siberian Branch of Russian Academy of Sciences, Prosp. Lavrentjev 13/3, 630090 Novosibirsk, Russia. *Telephone:* (3832) 33-24-89 (Office). *Fax:* (3832) 33-20-67 (Office). *E-mail:* bagayev@laser.nsc.ru (Office).

BAGAZA, Col Jean-Baptiste; Burundian army officer and politician; b. 29 Aug. 1946, Rutovu, Bururi Prov.; m. Fausta Bagaza; four c.; ed Ecole des Cadets, Brussels and the Belgian Mil. School, Arlon; fmr Asst to Gen. Ndabemeye; Chief of Staff of the Armed Forces, rank of Lt-Col; led coup to overthrow Pres. Micombero Nov. 1976; Pres. of the Repub. of Burundi 1976–87, also Minister of Defence; Pres. Union pour le progrès national (UPRONA) 1976–87; promoted to Col 1977; in exile abroad.

BÅGE, Lennart, MBA; Swedish diplomatist; m.; two c.; ed Stockholm School of Economics; Asst Under-Sec. Ministry of Foreign Affairs; Amb. to Zimbabwe; Head Dept for Int. Co-operation, Ministry of Foreign Affairs, Deputy Dir-Gen. Ministry of Foreign Affairs –2001; Pres. and CEO IFAD April 2001–. *Address:* International Fund for Agricultural Development, Via del Serafico 107, 00142 Rome, Italy (Office). *Telephone:* (06) 54591 (Office). *Fax:* (06) 5043463 (Office). *E-mail:* ifad@ifad.org (Office). *Website:* www.ifad.org (Office).

BAGGE, Sverre Hakon, PhD; Norwegian historian; b. 7 Aug. 1942, Bergen; s. of Sverre Olsen and Gunvor Bagge; m. Guro Mette Skrove; two s. one d.; lecturer Univ. of Bergen 1973, Sr Lecturer 1974, Prof. 1991–; Prof., Head Centre for Medieval Studies 2002–; Brage Prize, Clara Lachmann's Prize. *Publications:* The Political Thought of the King's Mirror 1987, Society and Politics in Snorri Sturluson's Heimskringla 1991, From Gang Leader to the Lord's Anointed 1996, Kings, Politics, and the Right Order of the World in German Historiography c. 950–1150. *Address:* Department of History, Sydnesplass 7, N-5007 Bergen (Office); Moldbakken 13, 5035 Bergen, Norway (Home). *Telephone:* 55-58-23-25 (Office). *Fax:* 55-58-96-54 (Office).

BAGGIO, Roberto; Italian footballer; b. 18 Feb. 1967, Caldogno; s. of Fiorindo Baggio and Matilde Baggio; m. Andreina Fabbri; two d.; with Vicenza 1985, Fiorentina 1985–90, Juventus 1990–95, Milan 1995–97, Bologna 1997–98, Inter Milan 1998–2000, Brescia 2000–, 300 career goals to 15 Dec. 2002; played for Italian Nat. Team in 1990, 1994 and 1998 World Cups; Golden Ball Award (France) 1993, FIFA World Player of the Year 1993, European Footballer of the Year 1993. *Leisure interests:* hunting, music.

BAGLAY, Marat Viktorovich, DJur, DHist; Russian lawyer; b. 13 March 1931, Baku, Azerbaijan; m.; three d.; ed Rostov State Univ., Inst. of State and Law; researcher Inst. of State and Law 1957–62; Prof. Moscow Inst. of Int. Relations 1962–95; Head of Dept Inst. of Int. Workers' Movt Acad. of Sciences 1967–77; Pro-Rector, Prof. Acad. of Labour and Social Relations 1977–95; judge Constitutional Court of Russian Fed. 1996–, Chair. 1997–; Corresp. mem. Russian Acad. of Sciences 1997–; Hon. LLD (Baku Univ., Rostov-on-Don Univ., Odessa Nat. Acad. of Law); Merited Scientist of Russia. *Publications include:* Way to Freedom, Constitutional Law of Russian Federation, numerous books and articles. *Address:* Constitutional Court of Russian Federation, Ilyinka str. 21, 103132 Moscow, Russia (Office). *Telephone:* (095) 206-92-25 (Office).

BAGRATIAN, Hrant Araratovich; Armenian politician; b. 18 Oct. 1958, Yerevan; m.; one s.; ed Yerevan Inst. of Nat. Econ.; Jr researcher, Sr researcher Inst. of Econs, Armenian Acad. of Sciences 1982–90; First Deputy Chair. Council of Ministers of Armenian SSR, Chair. State Cttee on Econs 1990–; Vice-Prime Minister, Minister of Econs Repub. of Armenia 1991–93; Prime Minister of Armenia 1993–96; Leader Azatutiun (Freedom Party); in pvt. business 1996–.

BAGRI, Baron (Life Peer), cr. 1997, of Regents Park in the City of Westminster; **Raj Kumar Bagri,** CBE; British commodities executive; b. 24 Aug. 1930; m. 1954; one s. one d.; joined a metals business in Calcutta 1946; moved into int. metals trading 1949; set up UK br. office of an Indian co. 1959; f. own company in UK, Metdist Ltd, which became London Metal Exchange (LME)

ring dealing mem. 1970, currently Chair. Minmetco (UK holding co. of Metdist Group of Cos.); joined LME's Man. Cttee 1973, apptd. Dir of LME 1983, Vice-Chair. 1990, Chair. 1993–2002, Hon. Pres. 2003–; mem. Advisory Council Prince's Youth Business Trust, Governing Body SOAS; Hon. DSc (City Univ.) 1999, (Nottingham) 2000. *Leisure interest:* cricket. *Address:* Metdist Group, 80 Cannon Street, London, EC4N 6EJ, England. *Telephone:* (20) 7280-0000. *Fax:* (20) 7606-6650.

BAGSHAWE, Kenneth Dawson, CBE, MD, FRCP, FRCR, FRCOG, FRS; British physician and medical oncologist; b. 17 Aug. 1925, Marple, Cheshire; s. of Harry Bagshawe and Gladys Bagshawe; m. 1st Ann A. Kelly 1946 (divorced 1976, died 2000); m. 2nd Sylvia D. Lawler (née Corben) 1977 (died 1996); one s. one d.; m. 3rd Surinder Kanta Sharma 1998; ed Harrow Co. School, London School of Econs and St Mary's Hosp. Medical School, Univ. of London; served RN 1943–46; Research Fellow, Johns Hopkins Hosp. 1955–56; Sr Registrar, St Mary's Hosp. 1956–60; Sr Lecturer in Medicine, Charing Cross Hosp. Medical School 1961–63; Consultant Physician and Dir Dept of Medical Oncology 1961–90, Prof. Emer.; Prof. of Medical Oncology, Charing Cross Hosp. Medical School 1974–90; Chair., Zenyx Scientific Co. Ltd 1996–, Enzacta 1998–; Vice-Chair. Council Cancer Research Campaign 1988–; Pres. Asscn of Cancer Physicians 1986–93, British Asscn for Cancer Research 1990–94; mem. various cancer research cttees. etc.; Fellow. Royal Coll. of Radiologists; Hamilton Fairley Lectureship 1989; Hon. DSc (Bradford) 1990; Krug Award for Excellence in Medicine 1980; Edgar Gentilli Prize (Royal Coll. of Obstetricians and Gynaecologists) 1980, Galen Medal (London Soc. of Apothecaries) 1993. *Publications:* Choriocarcinoma 1969, Medical Oncology 1976, Germ Cell Tumours 1983, Antibody Directed Prodrug Therapy 1987 and articles in professional journals. *Leisure interests:* travel, walking, photography, music, art. *Address:* Department of Surgery, 4N, Charing Cross Hospital, London, W6 8RF (Office); 115 George Street, London, W1H T5A, England (Home). *Telephone:* (20) 8846-7517 (Office); (20) 7262-6033 (Home). *Fax:* (20) 8846-7516 (Office); (20) 7258-1365 (Home). *E-mail:* k.bagshawe@ic.ac.uk (Home).

BAHARNA, Husain Mohammad al-, PhD; Bahraini lawyer and government minister; b. 5 Dec. 1932, Manama; s. of Mohammad Makki Al-Baharna and Zahra Sayed Mahmood; m.; three s. two d.; ed Baghdad Law Coll., Iraq, London Univ. and Cambridge Univ., UK; mem. English Bar (Lincoln's Inn) and Bahraini Bar; Legal Adviser, Ministry of Foreign Affairs, Kuwait 1962–64; Legal Adviser and Analyst Arab Gulf Affairs, Arabian-American Oil Co., Saudi Arabia 1965–68; Legal Adviser, Dept of Foreign Affairs, Bahrain 1969–70; Legal Adviser to the State and mem. Council of State, Pres. Legal Cttee 1970–71; Minister of State for Legal Affairs 1971; mem. Del. of Bahrain to Sixth (Legal) Cttee UN Gen. Ass. 1986, UN Int. Law Comm., Geneva 1987, Del. of Bahrain to Summit of Heads of State of Gulf Co-operation Council 1991; fmr legal adviser and del. numerous int. confs. and summit meetings; Chair. Del. of Bahrain to UN Preparatory Comm. for Int. Sea Bed Authority and Int. Tribunal for Law of the Sea 1983; mem. Cttee of Experts on Control of Transnational and Int. Criminality and for the establishment of the Int. Criminal Court, Siracusa, Italy 1990; Council mem. Centre for Islamic and Middle East Law, SOAS, London Univ.; Editorial Bd Arab Law Quarterly; Hon. mem. Euro-Arab Forum for Arbitration and Business Law, Paris; mem. British Inst. of Int. and Comparative Law, American Soc. of Int. Law, Int. Law Asscn, Egyptian Soc. of Int. Law; Assoc. mem. Int. Comm. of Jurists; Arab Historian Medal (Union of Arab Historians) 1986. *Publications:* The Legal Status of the Arab Gulf States 1968, Legal and Constitutional Systems of the Arabian Gulf States (in Arabic) 1975, The Arabian Gulf States – Their Legal and Political Status and their International Problems 1975; articles in learned journals. *Leisure interest:* reading. *Address:* P.O. Box 790, Manama, Bahrain. *Telephone:* 255633. *Fax:* 270303.

BAHCALL, John Norris, PhD; American astrophysicist; b. 30 Dec. 1934, Shreveport, La.; m. Neta Assaf Bahcall 1966; three c.; ed Univ. of California at Berkeley, Univ. of Chicago, Harvard Univ.; Research Fellow in Physics, Ind. Univ.; joined staff Kellogg Radiation Lab., Calif. Inst. of Tech. 1962; interdisciplinary scientist, Hubble Space Working Group 1973–92; Chair. Astronomy and Astrophysics Survey Cttee, Nat. Research Council 1989–91; Prof. of Natural Sciences, Inst. for Advanced Study, Princeton 1971–; Richard Black Prof. of Natural Sciences 1997–; Visiting Prof. Princeton Univ.; Warner Prize (American Astronomical Soc.) 1970, NASA Distinguished Public Service Medal 1992, Heineman Prize (American Astronomical Soc. and American Inst. of Physics) 1994, Hans Bethe Prize (American Physical Soc.) 1998, Nat. Medal of Science 1998, Russell Prize (American Astronomical Soc.) 1999, Franklin Medal for Physics 2003. *Publications:* The Redshift Controversy (co-author) 1973, The Galaxy and the Solar System (co-ed.) 1987, Neutrino Astrophysics 1989, The Decade of Discovery in Astronomy and Astrophysics (co-author) 1991, Time for the Stars: Astronomy in the 1990s (co-author) 1994, Solar Neutrinos: The First Thirty Years (co-ed.) 1995, Unsolved Problems in Astrophysics (co-ed.) 1997. *Leisure interest:* modern novels. *Address:* School of Natural Sciences, Institute for Advanced Study, 1 Einstein Drive, Princeton, NJ 08540, USA (Office).

BAHÇELI, Devlet, DEcon; Turkish politician and academic; b. 1948, Osmaniye; ed Ankara Econ. and Commercial Sciences Acad., Gazi Univ. Social Sciences Inst.; Sec.-Gen. Turkish Nat. Students Fed. 1970–71; instructor Ankara Econ. and Commercial Sciences Acad., mem. Faculty of Econ. and Admin. Sciences, Gazi Univ. 1972–87; Sec.-Gen. Nationalist Action Party (MHP) 1987, Leader 1997–; Deputy Prime Minister and State Minister

1999–2002; Founder mem., Pres. of the Financiers and Economists Asscn. *Address:* Milliyetçi Hareket Partisi (Nationalist Action Party), Karanfil Sokak 69, 06640 Bakanlyklar, Ankara, Turkey (Office). *Telephone:* (312) 4195956 (Office). *Fax:* (312) 2311424 (Office). *E-mail:* mhp@mhp.org.tr (Office). *Website:* www.mhp.org.tr (Office).

BAHL, Kamlesh, CBE, LLB, FRSA; British solicitor and administrator; b. 28 May 1956; d. of Swinder Nath Bahl and Leela Wati Bahl; m. Nitin Lakhani 1986; ed Univ. of Birmingham; solicitor GLC 1978–81, British Steel Corpn 1981–84, Texaco Ltd 1984–87; Legal and Commercial Man. Data Logic Ltd 1987–89, Co. Sec. 1989–93, also Man. Legal Services, legal consultant 1993–; Chair. Equal Opportunities Comm. 1993–98; Chair. Law Soc. Commerce and Industry Group 1988–89, mem. Law Soc. Council 1990, Deputy Vice-Pres. 1998–99, Vice-Pres. 1999–2000; Dir (non-exec.) Parkside Health Authority 1990–93; mem. Justice Sub-Cttee on Judiciary 1991–92, Ethnic Minorities Advisory Cttee and Tribunals Cttee 1991–94, Council and Standing Cttee on Health Authorities, Nat. Asscn of Health Authorities and Trusts 1993–94, Council of Justice 1993–94; independent mem. Diplomatic Service Appeal Bd, FCO 1993–; EU Rep. EU Consultative Comm. on Racism and Xenophobia 1994–97; Patron UN Year for Tolerance 1995; Trustee Refuge 1998–; mem. Council of the Open Univ. 1999–; Hon. MA (N London) 1997; Hon. LLD (De Montfort) 1998; Dr. hc (Birmingham) 1999. *Publication:* Managing Legal Practice in Business (ed.) 1989. *Leisure interests:* travelling, swimming, theatre, fund-raising for charity. *Address:* Overseas House, Quay Street, Manchester, M3 3HN, England. *Telephone:* (161) 833-9244. *Fax:* (161) 838-8201.

BAHNASSI, Afif, MA, PhD; Syrian professor of art and architecture; b. 17 April 1928, Damascus; m. 1st Hiba Wadi 1962 (died 1966); m. 2nd Maysoun Jazairi 1971; four s. one d.; ed Univ. of Syria and Sorbonne, Paris; Dir Fine Arts Dept 1959–71; Dir Gen. of Antiquities and Museums of Syria 1972–88; mem. Arab Writers' Union 1967–; Chair. Fine Arts Asscn of Syria 1968–; Prof. of History of Art and Architecture, Damascus Univ. 1988–; co-designer of Martyr Monument 1991, October Monument 1998; Commdr des Arts and des Lettres; First Prize in Islamic Architecture 1991, ICO Award, Jeddah; numerous other awards and medals. *Publications:* General History of Arts and Architecture 1962, L'Esthétique de l'art arabe 1979, Arabic Modern Art 1979, Damascus 1981, L'Art et l'Orientalisme 1983, En Syrie 1986, The Ancient Syria 1987, The Great Mosque of Damascus 1988, Arab Architecture 1994, Dictionnaire d'architecture 1994, Dictionnaire des termes de calligraphie, The Great Mosque of San'a 1996, Aesthetics of al Tawhidi 1997, Criticism of Art 1997, Modernism and Postmodernism 1997, Islamic Tiles 1997, Arab Calligraphy 1997, Interlocution in Islamic Art 2000, Encyclopédie de l'architecture islamique 2002, Formation of Damascus 2002, Damascus – Capital of Umayyad Dynasty 2002. *Leisure interests:* painting, sculpture. *Address:* 4 Gazzi Street, Damascus, Syria. *Telephone:* 3334554 (Office); 3311827 (Home). *Fax:* 3319368 (Home).

BAHR, Egon; German government official and journalist; b. 18 March 1922, Treffurt; m. Dorothea Grob 1945; one s. one d.; journalist 1945–, contrib. Die Neue Zeitung 1948–59, Das Tagesspiegel 1950; Chief Commentator RIAS (Rundfunk im amerikanischen Sektor Berlins) 1950–60; Dir Press and Information Office of Berlin 1960–66; promoted to rank of Amb. in diplomatic service 1967; Dir of Planning Staff, Diplomatic Service 1967–68; Ministerial Dir 1968–69; State Sec., Bundeskanzleramt and Plenipotentiary of the Fed. Govt in Berlin 1969–72; mem. of Parl. (Bundestag) 1972–90; Fed. Minister without Portfolio attached to the Fed. Chancellor's Office 1972–74, for Overseas Devt Aid (Econ. Co-operation) 1974–76; Dir Institut für Friedensforschung und Sicherheitspolitik 1984–94; mem. PEN 1974–, Ind. Comm. on Disarmament and Security 1980–; Grosses Bundesverdienstkreuz; Theodor-Heuss-Preis 1976, Gustav-Heinemann-Bürgerpreis 1982. *Publications:* Was wird aus den Deutschen? 1982, Zum Europäischen Frieden 1988, Zu meiner Zeit 1996, Deutsche Interessen 1998, Nationalstaat: Überholt und unentbehrlich 1999. *Address:* Ollenhauerstrasse 1, 53113 Bonn, Germany.

BAI CHUNLI, PhD; Chinese chemist and professor of chemistry; b. 26 Sept. 1953, Liaoning; s. of Bai Fuxin and Li Fengyun; m. Li Chunfang 1981; one s.; ed Peking Univ.; Research Asst, Changchun Inst. of Applied Chem., Chinese Acad. of Sciences (CAS) 1978, Research Assoc., Inst. of Chem. 1981–85; Visiting Research Assoc., Calif. Inst. of Tech., USA 1985–87; Assoc. Prof. and Dir Study Group on Scanning Tunnelling Microscopy (STM), Inst. of Chem., CAS 1987–89, Prof. 1989–, Deputy Dir 1992–96, Chair. Div. of Fundamental Research and Vice-Chair. Acad. Cttee 1993–96, Vice-Pres. CAS 1996–; Visiting Prof. Inst. for Materials Research, Tohoku Univ., Japan 1991–92; Chair. 1st, 2nd, 3rd and 4th Nat. Confs. on STM; mem. Advisory Bd Int. Organizing Cttee of STM Conf., Co-Ed. Proc. STM '93; mem. Steering and Organizing Cttee 1st and 2nd Asian Conf. on STM 1994, 1996; Ed.-in-Chief China Basic Research, mem. editorial bds journals of nano-particle research; Pres. B-Y Research and Devt Centre for Microscopic Instruments 1988–92; Vice-Pres., China Asscn for Science and Technology;Sec.-Gen. and mem. Exec. Council Chinese Chemical Soc. 1994–98, Pres. 1999–; mem. Chinese Vacuum Soc. 1990–, Exec. Council Engineers' Asscn of CAS 1990–, Council Chinese Crystallographic Soc. 1994–, Exec. Council China Material Research Soc. 1995–99; Vice-Pres. All-China Youth Fed. 1995–2000; Pres. China Young Scientists' Asscn 1996–; mem. CPPCC 1993–98, alt. mem. 15th Cen. Cttee 1997–2002; Fellow Third World Acad. of Sciences 1997–; Academician Chinese Acad. of Sciences 1997–; Outstanding Young Scholar Hong Qiu Shi Science and Tech. Foundation 1995; numerous prizes and awards. *Pub-*

lications: 11 books and more than 300 papers in scientific journals. *Address:* Chinese Academy of Sciences, 52 San Li He Road, Beijing 100864, People's Republic of China. *Telephone:* (10) 68597606. *Fax:* (10) 68512458. *E-mail:* clbai@cashq.ac.cn (Office).

BAI DONGLU, PhD; Chinese professor of medicinal chemistry; b. Feb. 1936, Dinghai Co., Zhejiang Prov.; s. of Bai Daxi and Zhang Yunxiao; m. Ni Zhifang 1969; one d.; ed Shanghai First Medical Coll., Czechoslovak Acad. of Sciences, Prague; Prof. Shanghai Inst. of Materia Medica, Chinese Acad. of Sciences; Science and Tech. Progress Award, Nat. Natural Science Prize. *Publications:* more than 120 papers. *Leisure interest:* stamp collecting. *Address:* Shanghai Institute of Materia Medica, 294 Taiyuan Road, Shanghai 200031, People's Republic of China. *Telephone:* (21) 64311833. *Fax:* (21) 64370269. *E-mail:* dlbai@mail.shcnc.ac.cn (Office).

BAI ENPEI; Chinese politician; b. Sept. 1946, Qingjian Co., Shaanxi Prov.; ed Northwest Tech. Univ. 1965; joined CCP 1973; Vice-Sec. CCP Ya'nan Prefectural Cttee 1983; Sec. CCP Yan'an Prefectural Cttee 1985; alt. mem. 13th CCP Cen. Cttee 1987; Vice-Sec. CCP Inner Mongolia Autonomous Regional Cttee 1990; alt. mem. 14th CCP Cen. Cttee 1992; mem. 15th CCP Cen. Cttee 1997–2002; mem. 16th CCP Cen. Cttee 2002–; Vice-Sec. CCP Qinghai Prov. Cttee, Acting Gov. Qinghai Prov. 1997–2000; Chair. Qinghai Prov. People's Congress 2000–; Sec. CCP Yunnan Prov. Cttee 2001. *Address:* Chinese Communist Party Yunnan Provincial Committee, Kunming, Yunnan Province, People's Republic of China.

BAI KEMING; Chinese journalist and party official; b. Oct. 1943, Jingbian, Shanxi Prov; ed Harbin Mil. Eng Inst.; joined CCP 1975; Vice-Section Chief, Section Chief then Dir Gen. Office of the Ministry of Educ.; Head Educ. Science, Culture and Health Group, Research Office of the State Council; Sec.-Gen. Propaganda Dept of CCP Cen. Cttee, then Vice-Dir. 1993–2000; Chair. People's Daily (newspaper) 2000–01; Sec. CCP Hainan Prov. Cttee and Chair. Hainan People's Congress 2001–. *Address:* Chinese Communist Party Hainan Provincial Committee, Haikou, Hainan Province, People's Republic of China (Office). *Telephone:* (898) 5342164 (Office).

BAI LICHEN; Chinese administrator; b. 1941, Lingyuan, Liaoning; joined CCP 1971; mem. Standing Cttee CCP Prov. Cttee Liaoning 1985–87; Vice-Gov. Liaoning 1985–86; mem. 13th Cen. Cttee CCP 1987–92, 14th Cen. Cttee CCP 1992–97, 15th Cen. Cttee 1997–2002; Chair. Ningxia Hui Autonomous Regional People's Govt 1987–97; Deputy Sec. CPC Regional Cttee 1988–97; Sec. CCP Group, Nat. Office of Supply and Marketing Co-operatives 1997–2002; Vice-Chair. 9th Nat. Cttee of CPPCC 1998. *Address:* National Committee of the Chinese People's Political Consultative Conference, 23 Taiping Qiao Street, Beijing, People's Republic of China.

BAI QINGCAI; Chinese party and government official; b. 1932, Wutai Co., Shanxi Prov.; joined CCP 1955; Vice-Gov. of Shanxi Prov. 1983–93; mem. of Shanxi Standing Comm. CCP 1985–93; mem. 14th CCP Cen. Cttee 1992–97; Gov. Shaanxi Prov. 1993–94; later Vice Chair. All-China Fed. of Supply and Marketing Co-operation; Deputy Sec. CCP Shaanxi Prov. Cttee; Vice-Chair. Environment and Resource Protection Cttee of 9th NPC 1998. *Address:* c/o Standing Committee of the National People's Congress, Beijing, People's Republic of China.

BAI SHUXIAN; Chinese ballerina; b. 1939; ed Beijing Coll. of Dancing; Prin. Dancer Cen. Ballet Co. 1958–, Dir 1984–90; mem. 5th Nat. Cttee CPPCC 1978–82, 6th 1983–87, 7th 1988–92, 8th 1993–; Vice Dir Beijing Ballet 1980–; Perm. mem. Chinese Dancers' Asscn, Chair. 1992–; Vice-Chair. China Fed. of Literary and Art Circles 1996–; First Grade Dancer of the Nat. (award). *Performances include:* Swan Lake, Giselle, The Fountain of Bakhchisarai, The Emerald, Sylvia, Red Women Army, Song of Yimeng, Song of Jiaoyang. *Address:* Chinese Dancers' Association, Di An Men Dong Dajie, Beijing 100009, People's Republic of China.

BAI XUESHI; Chinese artist; b. 12 June 1915, Beijing; s. of Dong and Bai Huanzhang; m. Xie Lin; two s. three d.; studied under Liang Shunian; specializes in landscape paintings; fmr teacher Beijing Teachers' Inst. of Arts, Beijing Inst. of Arts; Prof. Cen. Acad. of Arts and Design; Pres. Beijing Research Soc. of Landscape Paintings; mem. Cttee of 7th CPPCC 1988–; exhbns. in USA, Japan, Hong Kong. *Works include:* Myriad Peaks Contending, Riverside Village, Riverboats in Springtime, Aspects of Lushan, Lijiang, Cool Waters of Lijiang, Cormorant Fishing. *Leisure interests:* Beijing opera and weiqi. *Address:* Central Academy of Arts and Design, Beijing, People's Republic of China. *Telephone:* 341308.

BAIGELDI, Omirbek, DrEconSc; Kazakhstan politician; b. 15 April 1939, Yernazar, Zhambyl Region; m.; three c.; ed Almaty Inst. of Veterinary Sciences, Acad. of Social Sciences Cen. CPSU Cttee; various posts in Dist Dept of Agric. Man. 1962–74; First Deputy Chair. Regional Dept on Agric. Man. 1974–75; First Sec. Kurdai Regional Cttee, Chair. Zhambyl Regional Exec. Cttee, First Sec. Zhambyl Regional Cttee CP of Kazakhstan, Chair. Zhambyl Soviet of People's Deputies 1975–92; Head Zhambyl Regional Admin. 1992–95; Counsellor to Pres. of Kazakhstan 1995–96; Chair. Senate (Parl.) 1996–99, mem. 1999–, Deputy Chair. 1999–; mem. Acad. of Agric. Sciences; Orders Union (Sodruzjestvo) 1991, Kurmet 1995, Otan 1999. *Address:* House of Parliament, Astana, Kazakhstan. *Telephone:* (3172) 32-78-92 (Office).

BAILEY, David, CBE, FRPS, FSIAD, FCSD; British photographer and film director; b. 2 Jan. 1938, London; s. of Herbert William Bailey and Gladys

Agnes Bailey; m. 1st Rosemary Bramble 1960; m. 2nd Catherine Deneuve 1965; m. 3rd Marie Helvin (divorced 1985); m. 4th Catherine Dyer 1986; two s. one d.; self-taught; photographer for Vogue, UK, USA, France, Italy and advertising photography 1959–; Dir Commercials 1966–, TV documentaries 1968–; photographer for Harpers and Queen 1999; directed and produced TV film Who Dealt? 1993; documentary: Models Close Up 1998; Dir feature film The Intruder 1999; Dr hc (Bradford Univ.) 2001. *Exhibitions include:* Nat. Portrait Gallery 1971, Photographers' Gallery 1973, Olympus Gallery 1980, 1982, 1983, Victoria and Albert Museum 1983, Int. Center of Photography, New York 1984, Hamilton Gallery 1990, 1992, Carla Sozzani, Milan 1997, Gallery for Fine Photography, New Orleans, Barbican 1999, Nat. Museum of Photography, Film and TV 1999. *Publications:* Box of Pinups 1964, Goodbye Baby and Amen 1969, Warhol 1974, Beady Minces 1974, Mixed Moments 1976, Trouble and Strife 1980, NW1 1982, Black and White Memories 1983, Nudes 1981–84 1984, Imagine 1985, The Naked Eye: Great Photographs of the Nude (with Martin Harrison) 1988, If We Shadows 1992, The Lady is a Tramp 1995, Rock & Roll Heroes 1997, Archive One 1999, Chasing Rainbows 2001. *Leisure interests:* photography, aviculture, travel, painting. *Address:* c/o Robert Montgomery and Partners, 3 Junction Mews, Sale Place, London, W2, England. *Telephone:* (20) 7439-1877. *E-mail:* studio@camera-eye.co.uk (Office).

BAILEY, D(avid) R(oy) Shackleton, LittD, FBA; British/American academic; b. 10 Dec. 1917, Lancaster; s. of John Henry Shackleton Bailey and Rosamund Maud Giles; m. Kristine Zvirbulis 1994; ed Gonville and Caius Coll. Cambridge; Fellow, Gonville and Caius Coll. 1944–55, Praelector 1954–55, Deputy Bursar 1964, Sr Bursar 1965–68, Univ. Lecturer in Tibetan 1948–68, Hon. Fellow 2000; Fellow, Dir of Studies in Classics, Jesus Coll. Cambridge 1955–64; Visiting Lecturer in Classics, Harvard Univ., USA 1963, Prof. of Greek and Latin 1975–82, Pope Prof. of Latin Language and Literature 1982–88, Prof. Emer. 1988–; Prof. of Latin, Univ. of Mich., Ann Arbor 1968–75, Adjunct Prof. 1989–; Andrew V. V. Raymond Visiting Prof. of Classics, State Univ. of NY at Buffalo 1973–74; Nat. Endowment for Humanities Fellow, Visiting Fellow, Peterhouse, Cambridge 1980–81; Fellow, British Acad., American Acad. of Arts and Sciences; mem. American Philosophical Soc.; Hon. mem. Soc. for the Promotion of Roman Studies 1999; Hon. DLitt (Dublin) 1984; Charles J. Goodwin Award of Merit 1978, Kenyon Medal, British Acad. 1985. *Publications:* The Satapancasatka of Matrceta 1951, Propertiana 1956, Cicero's Letters, 10 Vols 1965–81, Cicero 1971, Profile of Horace 1982, Anthologia Latina I 1982, Horatius 1985, Cicero's Philippics 1986, Lucanus 1988, Cicero's Letters (4 Vols) 1988, Quintilian 1989, Martialis 1990, Martial (3 Vols) 1993, Homeoteleuton in Latin Dactylic Poetry 1994, Selected Classical Papers 1997, Cicero's Letters to Atticus (4 Vols) 1999, Valerius Maximus (2 Vols) 2000, Cicero's Letters to Friends (3 Vols) 2000, Cicero's Letters to Quintus and Brutus etc. 2002, Statius Silvae 2003, and others; Harvard Studies in Classical Philology (ed.) 1978–85; articles on oriental and classical subjects in professional journals. *Leisure interest:* cats. *Address:* 303 North Division, Ann Arbor, MI 48104, USA. *Telephone:* (734) 665-8062.

BAILEY, Donovan; Canadian athlete and marketing consultant; b. 16 Dec. 1967, Manchester, Jamaica; s. of George Donovan and Icilda Donovan; one d. by Michelle Mullin; ed Sheridan Coll., Oakville; grew up in Jamaica and emigrated to Canada 1981; mem. Canada's winning 4×100m team, Commonwealth Games 1994, Olympic Games 1996; world indoor record-holder for 50m 1996; Canadian 100m record-holder 1995, 1996; world, Commonwealth and Olympic 100m record-holder 1996; retired from athletics 2001; partner in stockbroking, man. and construction co.; f. Donovan Bailey Foundation to assist Canadian amateur atheltes; Sprinter of the Decade, Track and Field News 1999. *Address:* c/o Flynn Sports Management, 606–1185, Eglinton Avenue East, Toronto, Ont., M3C 3C6, Canada (Office).

BAILEY, Jerry; American jockey; b. 29 Aug. 1957, Dallas; s. of James Bailey; m. Suzee; one s.; thoroughbred racing jockey 1974–, began career with win at Sunland Park, New Mexico 1974 (Fetch); moved to New York 1982; winner Gulfstream Park Handicap 1990, 1995 (Cigar), 1996, 1997, 1998; 11 Breeders' Cup titles, including Breeders' Cup Classic 1991 (Black Tie Affair), 1993 (Arcangues), 1994 (Concern), Cigar (1995); winner Belmont 1991 (Hansel); winner Preakness Stakes 1991 (Hansel), 2000 (Red Bullet); winner Hollywood Gold Cup Handicap 1992, 1995 (Cigar), 1998, 1999; winner Woodward Stakes 1992, 1995 (Cigar), 1996 (Cigar), 1998; winner Kentucky Derby 1993 (Sea Hero), 1996 (Grindstone); winner Travers Stakes 1993 (Sea Hero); winner Oaklawn Park Handicap, Pimlico Special, Jockey Club Gold Cup, Don Handicap 1995 (Cigar); winner Massachussets Handicap 1995 (Cigar), 1996 (Cigar), 1998 (Skip Away); winner Dubai World Cup 1996 (Cigar), 1997 (Singspiel); Saratoga riding title 1994, 1995, 1996, 1997, 2000; 16 straight victories on Cigar 1995–96; seven winners on one card, Florida Derby Day 1995; North America's leading money-winning rider 1995–1997 and 2001; first rider to win more than $20 million in one season (2001); fmr Nat. Pres. Jockeys' Guild; George Woolf Memorial Jockey Award 1992; Mike Venezia Award (New York Racing Assçn) 1993; Eclipse Award for Outstanding Jockey 1995, 1996, 1997, 2000, 2001; elected to racing's Hall of Fame 1995. *Address:* c/o National Museum of Racing and Hall of Fame, 191 Union Avenue, Saratoga Springs, NY 12866-3566, USA.

BAILEY, Norman Stanley, CBE, BMus; British operatic and concert singer; b. 23 March 1933, Birmingham; s. of the late Stanley Ernest and Agnes Train (Gale) Bailey; m. 1st Doreen Evelyn Simpson 1957 (divorced 1983); two s. one

d.; m. 2nd Kristine Ciesinski 1985; ed East Barnet Grammar School, England, Boksburg High School, South Africa, Prince Edward School, Rhodesia, Rhodes Univ., South Africa, Akad. für Musik und Darstellende Kunst, Vienna; engaged full time at Linz Landestheater, Austria 1960–63, Wuppertaler Bühnen 1963–64, Deutsche Oper am Rhein, Düsseldorf and Duisburg 1964–67; Prin. Baritone English Nat. Opera, Sadler's Wells 1967–71; freelance 1971–; debut at La Scala, Milan 1967, Royal Opera House, Covent Garden 1969, Bayreuth Festival 1969, Paris Opera 1973, Vienna State Opera 1976, Metropolitan Opera, New York 1976; appearances Paris Opera, Edin. Festival, Hamburg State Opera, Munich State Opera; Prof. of Voice, Royal Coll. of Music, London; Prof. Royal Coll. of Music 1990–; Hon. RAM 1981; Hon. DMus (Rhodes) 1986; Sir Charles Santley Memorial Prize 1977. *Major recordings and TV films include:* Der fliegende Holländer, Die Meistersinger von Nürnberg, King Priam, Der Ring des Nibelungen, Macbeth, La Traviata, Falstaff. *Leisure interests:* golf, chess, microcomputing, mem. Baha'i World Faith. *Address:* PO Box 655, Victor, ID 83455, USA.

BAILEY, Paul, FRSL; British writer; b. Peter Harry Bailey, 16 Feb. 1937; s. of Arthur Oswald Bailey and Helen Maud Burgess; ed Sir Walter St John's School, London; actor 1956–64, appearing in The Sport of My Mad Mother 1958 and Epitaph for George Dillon 1958; Literary Fellow at Univs. of Newcastle and Durham 1972–74; Bicentennial Fellowship 1976; Visiting Lecturer in English Literature, North Dakota State Univ. 1977–79; Somerset Maugham Award 1968; E. M. Forster Award 1978; George Orwell Memorial Prize 1978. *Publications:* At the Jerusalem 1967, Trespasses 1970, A Distant Likeness 1973, Peter Smart's Confessions 1977, Old Soldiers 1980, An English Madam 1982, Gabriel's Lament 1986, An Immaculate Mistake (autobiog.) 1990, Hearth and Home 1990, Sugar Cane 1993, The Oxford Book of London (ed.) 1995, First Love (ed.) 1997, Kitty and Virgil 1998, The Stately Homo: A Celebration of the Life of Quentin Crisp (ed.) 2000, Three Queer Lives: Fred Barnes, Naomi Jacob and Arthur Marshall 2001, Uncle Rudolf (novel) 2002; numerous newspaper articles. *Leisure interests:* visiting churches, opera, watching tennis. *Address:* 79 Davisville Road, London, W12 9SH, England. *Telephone:* (20) 8749-2279. *Fax:* (20) 8248-2127.

BAILEY, Sly; British publishing and media executive; b. Sylvia Grice, London; m. Peter Bailey; telephone sales exec. at The Guardian 1984; joined The Independent 1987; moved to IPC Magazines 1989, mem. Bd 1994–2003 (part of team that undertook man. buyout of IPC from Reed Elsevier 1998), CEO 1999–2003 (led deal to sell IPC Media to AOL Time Warner in 2001); CEO Trinity Mirror PLC Feb. 2003–. *Leisure interest:* Tottenham Hotspur Football Club. *Address:* Trinity Mirror PLC, 1 Canada Square, Canary Wharf, London, E14 5AP, England (Office). *Telephone:* (20) 7293-3000 (Office). *Fax:* (20) 7293-3280 (Office). *Website:* www.trinity.plc.uk (Office).

BAILIE, Robert Ernest (Roy), OBE; British business executive; b. 2 June 1943; s. of Robert Bailie and Rosetta Bailie; ed Harvard Business School; joined W&G Baird 1965, Man. Dir 1972, Dir 1977–, Chair. 1982–; Chair. CBI, Northern Ireland 1992–94, Northern Ireland Tourist Bd 1996–; Vice-Pres. British Printing Industries Fed. 1997–99, Pres. 1999–2001; Dir Graphic Plates Ltd 1977–, MSO Ltd 1984–, Biddles Ltd 1989–, Thanet Press Ltd 1995–; Dir (non-exec.) Blackstaff Press Ltd 1995–, UTV 1997–, Court, Bank of England 1998–, Court, Bank of Ireland 1999–, Corporate Document Services Ltd 2000–. *Leisure interests:* golf, sailing, walking. *Address:* 60 Ballymena Road, Doagh, Ballyclare, Co. Antrim, BT39 0QR, Northern Ireland. *Telephone:* (28) 9334-0383.

BAILLIE, A. Charles, Jr, BA, MBA; Canadian banker; b. 20 Dec. 1939, Orillia, Ont.; s. of Charles Baillie and Jean G. Baillie; m. Marilyn J. Michener 1965; three s. one d.; ed Trinity Coll., Univ. of Toronto, Harvard Business School, USA; joined The Toronto Dominion Bank 1964, Vice-Pres. and Gen. Man., USA Div. 1979, Sr Vice-Pres. 1981, Exec. Vice-Pres., Corp. and Investment Banking Group 1984, Vice-Chair. 1992, Pres. The Toronto Dominion Bank 1995, CEO 1997–2002, Chair. 1998–(2004); Dir The Toronto Dominion Bank, Dana Corpn; Chair. and Dir TD Waterhouse Group, Inc.; Chair. Campaign 2000, United Way of Greater Toronto; Chair. Capital Campaign, Shaw Festival; Campaign Co-Chair. Nature Conservancy; Campaign Hon. Chair. Sir Sam Steele Art Gallery; Vice-Chair. Exec. Cttee Business Council on Nat. Issues; mem. Corpn and Hon. Cabinet, Trinity Coll.; Fellow Inst. of Canadian Bankers 1967; Hon. LLD (Queen's Univ.) 2000. *Address:* The Toronto Dominion Bank, PO Box 1, Toronto Dominion Centre, Toronto, M5K 1A2, Canada.

BAILLY, Jean-Paul, MSc; French business executive and engineer; b. 29 Nov. 1946, Hénin-Beaumont (Pas-de-Calais); s. of Jean Bailly and Hélène Bailly (née Viénot); m. Michèle Moulard 1972; two s.; ed Lycées d'Oujda, Morocco, Louis-le-Grand, Paris, Ecole polytechnique, Paris and MIT, USA; engineer, Regie Autonome des Transports Parisiens (RATP) 1970, Chief Consultant SOFRETU for Mexico City Metro 1978–81, Sr Engineer 1981–88, Personnel Dir 1989, Jt Dir-Gen. 1990–94, Pres. and Dir-Gen. 1994–97; Pres. Int. Union of Public Transport (UITP) 1997–2001; Pres. La Poste 2002–; Pres. French Section, Centre européen des entreprises à participation publique (CEEP) 1998–2001; mem. Econ. and Social Council 1994–; Chevalier, Légion d'honneur, Officier, Ordre nat. du Mérite. *Address:* La Poste, 4 quai du Point du Jour, 92777 Boulogne Billancourt Cedex, France (Office). *Website:* www .laposte.fr (Office).

BAILY, Martin Neil, PhD; American economist; b. 13 Jan. 1945, Exeter, England; s. of the late Theodore Baily and Joyce Baily; m. Vickie Lyn Baily (née Hyde) 1986; two s. two d.; ed King Edward's School, Birmingham, Christ's Coll., Cambridge, MIT; teaching positions at MIT and Yale Univ. 1972–79; Sr Fellow Brookings Inst. 1979–94, 1996–99; Prof. Univ. of Maryland 1989–94; mem. Council of Econ. Advisers 1994–96, Chair. and mem. of the Cabinet 1999–2001; Prin. McKinsey and Co. 1996–99; Prizewinner in Econs, Christ's Coll., Cambridge 1967. *Publications:* Macroeconomics, Financial Markets and the International Sector 1994, Efficiency in Manufacturing (Brookings Papers) 1995, Economic Report of the President: 2000. *Leisure interests:* squash, music, travel. *Address:* c/o McKinsey Global Institute, Suite 700, 1101 Pennsylvania Avenue, NW, Washington, DC 20004, USA (Office).

BAILYN, Bernard, PhD; American historian; b. 10 Sept. 1922, Hartford, Conn.; s. of Charles Manuel Bailyn and Esther Schloss; m. Lotte Lazarsfeld 1952; two s.; ed Williams Coll. and Harvard Univ.; mem. Faculty, Harvard Univ. 1953–, Prof. of History 1961–66, Winthrop Prof. of History 1966–81, Adams Univ. Prof. 1981–93, Prof. Emer. 1993–, James Duncan Phillips Prof. in Early American History 1991–93, Prof. Emer. 1993–; Dir Charles Warren Center for Studies in American History 1983–94; Pitt Prof. of American Hist., Cambridge Univ. 1986–87; Dir Int. Seminar on History of Atlantic World 1995–; Ed.-in-Chief John Harvard Library 1962–70; Co-Ed. Perspectives in American History (journal) 1967–77, 1984–86; mem. American Historical Asscn (Pres. 1981), American Acad. of Arts and Sciences, Nat. Acad. of Educ., American Philosophical Soc.; Foreign mem. Russian Acad. of Sciences, Academia Europaea, Mexican Acad. of History and Geography; Sr Fellow, Soc. of Fellows; Hon. Fellow Christ's Coll., Cambridge Univ.; Corresp. Fellow, British Acad. 1989, Royal Historial Soc.; Trustee Inst. of Advanced Study, Princeton 1989–94; Trevelyan Lecturer, Cambridge Univ. 1971; Jefferson Lecturer, Nat. Endowment for the Humanities 1998; 15 hon. degrees; Robert H. Lord Award, Emmanuel Coll. 1967, Thomas Jefferson Medal 1993, Henry Allen Moe Prize, American Philosophical Soc. 1994, Foreign Policy Asscn Medal 1998; Catton Prize, Soc. American Historians 2000. *Publications:* The New England Merchants in the 17th Century 1955, Massachusetts Shipping 1697–1714: A Statistical Study (jtly) 1959, Education in the Forming of American Society 1960, Pamphlets of the American Revolution 1750–1776, Vol. I (ed.) (Faculty Prize, Harvard Univ. Press) 1965, The Apologia of Robert Keayne (ed.) 1965, The Ideological Origins of the American Revolution (Pulitzer and Bancroft Prizes 1968) 1967, The Origins of American Politics 1968, The Ordeal of Thomas Hutchinson (Nat. Book Award 1975) 1974, The Great Republic (co-author) 1977, The Peopling of British North America 1986, Voyagers to the West (Pulitzer Prize 1986) 1986, Faces of Revolution 1990, The Debate on the Constitution (2 Vols) (ed.) 1993, On the Teaching and Writing of History 1994; co-ed.: The Intellectual Migration 1930–1960 1969, Law in American History 1972, The Press and the American Revolution 1980, Strangers Within the Realm 1991. *Address:* History Department, Harvard University, Cambridge, MA 02138 (Office); 170 Clifton Street, Belmont, MA 02478-2604, USA (Home).

BAIN, Neville Clifford, MCom, LLD, FCA, CMA, FCIS, FRSA; British business executive and consultant; b. 14 July 1940, Dunedin, NZ; s. of Charles Alexander Bain and Gertrude Mae Bain (née Howe); m. Anne Patricia Bain (née Kemp); one s. one d. one step-d.; ed King's High School, Dunedin, Otago Univ., Dunedin, NZ; trainee insp. Inland Revenue, NZ 1957–59; Cost Accountant then Finance Dir Cadbury Schweppes, NZ 1960–75, Commercial Dir and Group Finance Dir Cadbury Schweppes, SA 1975–80, Group Strategy Dir, apptd to Main Bd Cadbury Schweppes PLC 1980–83, Man. Dir Cadbury UK 1983–86, World-wide Man. Dir Group Confectionery 1986–89, Deputy CEO and Finance Dir Cadbury Schweppes PLC 1989–90, Chief Exec. Coats Viyella PLC 1990–97; Chair. Hogg Robinson PLC 1997–, SHL 1998– (Dir 1997–), The Post Office 1998–2001; Chair. Gartmore Split Capital Opportunities Trust 1999–2001; Dir (non-exec.) Safeway PLC 1993–2000, Scottish & Newcastle PLC 1997–, Gartmore Scotland Investment Trust PLC 1991–2001; mem. Inst. of Dirs (also Chair. Audit Cttee), Council for Excellence in Man. and Leadership, Trustee Nat. Centre for Social Research 2002–. *Publications:* Successful Management 1995, Winning Ways through Corporate Governance (with D. Band) 1996, The People Advantage (with Bill Mabey) 1999. *Leisure interests:* sport, walking, music. *Address:* Hogg Robinson PLC, Global House, Victoria Street, Basingstoke, Hants., RG21 3BT, England (Office). *Telephone:* (1256) 312610 (Office). *Fax:* (1256) 346999 (Office). *E-mail:* neville.bain@hrplc.co.uk (Office). *Website:* www.hoggrobinson.com (Office).

BAINBRIDGE, Dame Beryl, DBE, FRSL; British writer and actress; b. 21 Nov. 1934, Liverpool; d. of Richard Bainbridge and Winifred (née Baines) Bainbridge; m. Austin Davies 1954 (divorced); one s. two d.; ed Merchant Taylors' School, Liverpool, Arts Educational Schools, Tring; columnist Evening Standard 1987–93; Hon. DLitt (Liverpool Univ.) 1988; Whitbread Novel Prize 1996 for Every Man For Himself, James Tait Black Fiction Prize 1996, Guardian Fiction Award for The Bottle Factory Outing, Whitbread Award for Injury Time, Author of the Year 1999, James Tait Black Memorial Prize, British Book Awards 1999, David Cohen Prize, Arts Council of England 2003. *Plays:* Tiptoe Through the Tulips 1976, The Warriors Return 1977, It's a Lovely Day Tomorrow 1977, Journal of Bridget Hitler 1981, Somewhere More Central (TV) 1981, Evensong (TV) 1986. *Publications:* A Weekend with Claude 1967, Another Part of the Wood 1968, Harriet Said... 1972, The Dressmaker 1973 (film 1989), The Bottle Factory Outing 1974, Sweet William 1975 (film 1980), A Quiet Life 1976, Injury Time 1977, Young Adolf 1978, Winter Garden 1980, English Journey (TV series) 1984, Watson's Apology

1984, Mum and Mr. Armitage 1985, Forever England 1986 (TV series 1986), Filthy Lucre 1986, An Awfully Big Adventure (staged 1992, film 1995) 1989, The Birthday Boys 1991, Something Happened Yesterday 1993, Collected Stories 1994, Northern Stories (Vol. 5.) (with David Pownall) 1996, Every Man For Himself 1996, Master Georgie 1998, According to Queeney 2001. *Leisure interests:* reading, smoking. *Address:* 42 Albert Street, London, NW1 7NU, England. *Telephone:* (20) 7387-3113 (Home).

BAIRD, Dugald Euan, MA, LLD, DSc; British oil industry executive; b. 16 Sept. 1937, Aberdeen, Scotland; s. of Dugald Baird and Matilda Deans Tennant; m. Angelica Hartz 1961; two d.; ed Univ. of Aberdeen and Trinity Coll. Cambridge; joined Schlumberger Ltd as field engineer 1960, various field assignments in Europe, Asia, Middle East, Africa until 1974, Personnel Man., Vice-Pres. (Operations) Schlumberger Technical Services, Paris 1974–79; Exec. Vice-Pres. (worldwide wireline operations) Schlumberger Ltd, New York 1979–86, Chair. Bd, Pres. and CEO 1986–; mem. Comité Nat. de la Science, France 1998–, Council of Science and Tech., UK 2000–; mem. Bd ScottishPower 2000–; mem. Bd Société Générale Group 2001–; mem. Bd Areva 2001–; Trustee Haven Man. Trust 1994–, Carnegie Inst. of Wash. 1998–; Hon. LLD (Aberdeen) 1995, (Dundee) 1998; Hon. DSc (Heriot-Watt) 1999. *Address:* Schlumberger Ltd, 153 East 53rd Street, 57th Floor, New York, NY 10022-4624, USA. *Telephone:* (212) 350-9481. *Fax:* (212) 350-9457.

BAIS, Ramesh; Indian politician; b. 2 Aug. 1948, Raipur, Madhya Pradesh; s. of late Khom Pal Bais; m.; one s. two d.; elected Councillor, Raipur Mun. Corpn 1978, mem. Madhya Pradesh Legis. Ass. 1980, Lok Sabha 1989, 1996–; Vice-Pres. Madhya Pradesh Bharatiya Janata Party (BJP) 1989–90, 1994–96, mem. BJP Nat. Exec. 1993–; Minister of State for Steel and Mines 1998-2000, for Information and Broadcasting 2000–; Chair. Seed and Agricultural Devt Corpn of Madhya Pradesh 1992–93. *Leisure interests:* woodcrafting, painting, interior decoration, gardening. *Address:* Ministry of Information and Broadcasting, Shastri Bhavan, New Delhi 110 001 (Office); 2 Safdarjung Lane, New Delhi 110 001, India (Home). *Telephone:* (11) 3014804 (Home). *Fax:* (11) 3019273 (Home).

BAJAJ, Rahul, LLB, MBA; Indian industrialist; b. 10 June 1938, Kolkata; m. Rupa Bajaj 1961; two s. one d.; ed St Stephen's Coll., Delhi, Govt Law Coll., Bombay, Harvard Univ.; Dir Bajaj Auto Ltd 1956–60, Chair. and Man. Dir 1972–; Chair. Maharashtra Scooters Ltd 1975–; Pres. Asscn of Indian Automobile Mfrs 1976–78, Mahratta Chamber of Commerce and Industries 1983–85, Confed. of Eng Industry 1979–80; Chair. Devt Council for Automobiles and Allied Industries 1975–77; mem. Exec. Cttee Confed. of Eng Industry 1978–, Governing Council, Automotive Research Asscn of India 1972–, Devt Council for Automobiles and Allied Industries 1987–, World Econ. Forum's Advisory Council 1984–; Man of the Year Award (Nat. Inst. of Quality Assurance) 1975, Business Man of the Year Award (Business India Magazine) 1985, Padma Bhushan 2001. *Address:* Mumbai-Pune Road, Akurdi, Pune 411 035, India (Office). *Telephone:* (20) 772851 (Office); (20) 82857 (Home). *Fax:* (20) 773398 (Office). *E-mail:* rahulbajaj@bajajauto.co.in (Office).

BAJAMMAL, Abd al-Qadir, BA; Yemeni politician and economist; b. 18 Feb. 1946, Seiyun-Hadhramout; m. 1976; two s. two d.; ed Cairo Univ.; First Deputy Minister of Planning and Devt People's Democratic Repub. of Yemen 1978; Lecturer in Econs Aden Univ. 1978–80; Minister of Industry, Chair. Bd Oil, Mineral and Electricity Authority 1980–85; Minister of Energy and Minerals 1985; MP Repub. of Yemen (following union of fmr People's Democratic Repub. of Yemen and fmr Yemen Arab Repub.) 1990–91; Chair. Bd Public Free Zone Authority 1991–94; Deputy Prime Minister 1994–97, 2000–01; Minister of Planning and Devt 1994–97, 1998, of Foreign Affairs 2000–01; Prime Minister of Yemen 2001–; awarded Medal of Yemeni Unity, Medal of Yemeni Revolution, Medal of Yemeni Independence. *Publications:* New Administration Accountancy 1978, The Patterns of Development in the Arab Countries (jtly) 1981, Policies and Guidelines for Privatization in the Republic of Yemen 1994. *Leisure interests:* sports, table tennis. *Address:* Office of the Prime Minister, San'a, Yemen (Office).

BAKA, András B., LLD, PhD; Hungarian judge and professor of law; b. 11 Dec. 1952, Budapest; ed St Stephen's High School, Budapest and Eötvös Loránd Univ., Budapest; Research Fellow, Comparative Law Dept Inst. for Legal and Admin. Sciences of Hungarian Acad. of Sciences 1978–82, Sr Research Fellow, Constitutional and Admin. Dept 1982–90; Prof. of Constitutional Law, Budapest School of Public Admin. 1990–; Dir-Gen. and Pres. Bd Budapest School of Public Admin. 1990–; mem. Parl. and Sec. Human Rights Comm. of Hungarian Parl. 1990–91; Judge, European Court of Human Rights 1991–; Visiting Prof. Brown Univ., Providence, RI 1986, Univ. of Virginia 1987, Univ. of Calif. at Berkeley 1987, Columbia Univ. New York 1987; Prof. Santa Clara Univ. School of Law, Inst. of Int. and Comparative Law, Santa Clara, Calif. 1991; Scientist Award, Hungarian Acad. of Sciences 1988. *Publications:* several Publs on minority rights. *Address:* School of Public Administration, 5 Ménesi Street, 1118 Budapest, Hungary. *Telephone:* (361) 186-9054. *Fax:* (361) 186-9429.

BAKATIN, Vadim Viktorovich; Russian politician (retd); b. 6 Nov. 1937, Kiselevsk, Kemerovo Dist; s. of Victor Aleksandrovich Bakatin and Nina Afanasievna Bakatina; m. Ludmila Antonovna Bakatina; two s.; ed Novosibirsk Construction Eng Inst., Acad. of Social Sciences; supervisor, chief engineer, Dir of construction works 1960–71; mem. CPSU 1964–91; chief engineer of housing construction combine, Kemerovo 1971–73; Second Sec.,

Kemerovo City Cttee 1973–75; Sec., Kemerovo Dist Cttee 1977–83; inspector, CPSU Cen. Cttee 1985; First Sec. Kirov Dist Cttee 1985–87; mem. CPSU Cen. Cttee 1986–90; First Sec. Kemerovo Dist Cttee 1987–88; USSR Minister of Internal Affairs 1988–90; mem. Presidential Council Jan.–Nov. 1990; Head KGB Aug.–Dec. 1991, Interrepublican Security Service 1991–92; Vice-Pres. and Dir Dept of Political and Int. Relations Reforma Fund 1992–98. *Publication:* The Deliverance from the KGB 1992. *Leisure interests:* painting, reading, tennis. *Address:* c/o Reforma, Kotelnicheskaya nab. 17, 103240, Moscow, Russia (Office). *Telephone:* (095) 915-96-67.

BAKER, Alan, PhD, FRS; British mathematician; b. 19 Aug. 1939, London; s. of Barnet Baker and Bessie Baker; ed Stratford Grammar School, University Coll., London and Trinity Coll., Cambridge; Fellow, Trinity Coll., Cambridge 1964–, Research Fellow 1964–68, Dir of Studies in Math. 1968–74; Prof. of Pure Math. Univ. of Cambridge 1974–; Visiting Prof. Stanford Univ. 1974 and other univs. in USA, Univ. of Hong Kong 1988, 1999; Guest Prof. ETH Zürich 1989; Hon. Fellow, Indian Nat. Science Acad. 1980; mem. European Acad. 1998; Hon. mem. Hungarian Acad. of Sciences 2001; Dr. hc (Univ. Louis Pasteur, Strasbourg) 1998; Fields Medal 1970, Adams Prize 1972. *Publications:* Transcendental Number Theory 1975, A Concise Introduction to the Theory of Numbers 1984, New Advances in Transcendence Theory (ed.) 1988; papers in scientific journals. *Leisure interests:* travel, photography, theatre. *Address:* Centre for Mathematical Sciences, Wilberforce Road, Cambridge, CB3 0WB (Office); Trinity College, Cambridge, CB2 1TQ, England. *Telephone:* (1223) 337999 (Office); (1223) 338400. *Fax:* (1223) 337920 (Office). *E-mail:* a.baker@dpmms.cam.ac.uk (Office).

BAKER, Anita; American singer; b. 26 Jan. 1958, Toledo; m. Walter Bridgeforth, Jr 1988; one s.; mem. funk band, Chapter 8, Detroit, 1978–80; worked as receptionist, Detroit 1980–82; ind. singer and songwriter 1982–; NAACP Image Award, Best Female Vocalist and Best Album of the Year. *Records:* (with Chapter 8) I Just Wanna Be Your Girl 1980; (solo albums) The Songstress 1983, Rapture 1986 (Grammy Award for Best Rhythm and Blues Vocal Performance 1987), Giving You the Best That I Got 1988 (Grammy Awards for Best Rhythm and Blues Song, Best Rhythm and Blues Performance by a Female Artist 1988, Best Album 1989), Compositions 1990 (Grammy Award for Best Rhythm and Blues Performance 1990), Rhythm of Love 1994. *Songs include:* No More Tears, Caught Up in the Rapture, Sweet Love, Been So Long. *Address:* All Baker's Music, 345 N Maple Drive, Beverly Hills, CA 90210, USA.

BAKER, Carroll; American actress; b. 28 May 1931, Johnstown, Pa; d. of William W Baker and Virginia Duffy; m. 1st Jack Garfein 1955 (divorced); one s. one d.; m. 2nd Donald Burton 1982; ed St Petersburg Jr Coll., Florida; Broadway appearances include All Summer Long 1954, Come on Strong 1962; toured Vietnam with Bob Hope 1966; mem. Acad. of Motion Picture Arts and Sciences; several acting awards. *Films include:* Giant 1956, Baby Doll 1957, The Big Country 1958, But Not for Me 1959, The Miracle 1959, Bridge to the Sun 1960, Something Wild 1961, How the West Was Won 1962, Station Six Sahara 1962, The Carpetbaggers 1963, Cheyenne Autumn 1963, Mr Moses 1964, Sylvia 1964, Harlow 1965, The Harem 1967, Honeymoon 1968, The Sweet Body of Deborah 1968, Captain Apache 1971, Bad 1977, Watcher in the Woods 1980, Red Monarch 1983, The Secret Diary of Sigmund Freud 1983, Star 80 1983, Ironweed 1987, Native Son, Red Monarch, Kindergarten Cop, Blonde Fist, Cybereden, Undercurrent, Skeletons, Just Your Luck, The Game, Nowhere to Go. *Publications:* Baby Doll (autobiog.), A Roman Tale.

BAKER, Howard Henry, Jr., LLB; American politician, government official and attorney; b. 15 Nov. 1925, Huntsville, Tenn.; s. of Howard H. Baker and Dora Ladd; m. 1st Joy Dirksen 1951 (died 1993); one s. one d.; m. 2nd Nancy Kassebaum 1996; ed The McCallie School, Chattanooga, Univ. of the South, Sewanee, Tennessee, Tulane Univ. of New Orleans and Univ. of Tennessee Coll. of Law; US Naval Reserve 1943–46; partner in Baker, Worthington, Barnett & Crossley 1949–66; Senator from Tennessee 1967–85; Minority Leader in the Senate 1977–81, Majority Leader 1981–85; partner Baker, Worthington, Crossley, Stansberry & Woolf 1985–87, 1988–95, Baker, Donelson, Bearman & Caldwell, Washington 1995–; mem. law firm Vinson and Elkins 1985–87; White House Chief of Staff 1987–88; Amb. to Japan 2001–; del. to UN 1976; mem. Council on Foreign Relations 1973–; Int. Councillor, Center for Strategic and Int. Studies 1991–; mem. Inst. of Foreign Affairs 1992–; mem. Bd The Forum for Int. Policy 1993–; Pres.'s Foreign Intelligence Advisory Bd 1985–87, 1988–90; Int. Advisory Bd Barrick Gold Corp., Bd of Regents Smithsonian Inst.; Chair. Cherokee Aviation, Newstar Inc.; mem. Bd of Dirs United Technologies Corpn, Pennzoil Co.; Republican; several hon. degrees; American Soc. of Photographers Award 1993, Presidential Medal of Freedom 1984. *Publications:* No Margin for Error 1980, Howard Baker's Washington 1982, Big South Fork Country 1993, Scott's Gulf 2000. *Leisure interests:* photography, tennis. *Address:* 1-10-15 Akasaka, Minato-ku, Tokyo 107-8420, Japan (Office); c/o Baker, Donelson, Bearman & Caldwell, 801 Pennsylvania Avenue, NW, Washington, DC 20004, USA. *Telephone:* (3) 3224-5000 (Office). *E-mail:* ustkyecn@ppp.bekkoame.or.jp (Office). *Website:* usembassy.state.gov/posts/ja1/wwwhmain.html (Office).

BAKER, James Addison, III, LLB; American government official and lawyer; b. 28 April 1930, Texas; s. of James A. Baker, Jr and Bonner Means; m. Susan Garrett 1973; eight c.; ed Princeton Univ. and Univ. of Texas Law School; served US Marine Corps 1952–54; with law firm Andrews, Kurth, Campbell and Jones, Houston, Texas 1957–75; Under-Sec. of Commerce

under Pres. Ford 1975; Nat. Chair. Ford's presidential campaign 1976; Campaign Dir for George Bush in primary campaign 1980, later joined Reagan campaign; White House Chief of Staff and on Nat. Security Council 1981–85; Trustee, Woodrow Wilson Int. Center for Scholars, Smithsonian Inst. 1977–; Sec. of the Treasury 1985–88, Sec. of State 1989–92; White House Chief of Staff and Sr Counsellor 1992–93; Gov. Rice Univ. 1993; Sr Partner Baker & Botts 1993–; UN Special Envoy to resolve W Sahara Dispute 1997–; Co-Chair. Campaign to elect Bush as Pres. *Publication:* The Politics of Diplomacy 1995. *Leisure interests:* jogging, tennis, hunting. *Address:* United Nations Mission for the Referendum in Western Sahara, Department of Peace-keeping Operations, Room S-3727-B, New York, NY 10017; Baker & Botts, 1 Shell Plaza, 910 Louisiana, Houston, TX 77002, USA. *Website:* www.un.org/Depts/dpko.

BAKER, Dame Janet (Abbott), CH, DBE, FRSA; British mezzo-soprano; b. 21 Aug. 1933, Hatfield, Yorks.; d. of Robert Abbott Baker and May Baker (née Pollard); m. James Keith Shelley 1957; ed York Coll. for Girls and Wintringham School, Grimsby; Pres. London Sinfonia 1986–; Chancellor Univ. of York 1991–; Trustee Foundation for Sport and the Arts 1991–; Hon. Fellow, St Anne's Coll., Oxford 1975, Downing Coll., Cambridge 1985; Hon. DMus (Birmingham) 1968, (Leicester) 1974, (London) 1974, (Hull) 1975, (Oxford) 1975, (Leeds) 1980, (Lancaster) 1983, (York) 1984, (Cambridge) 1984; Hon. LLD (Aberdeen) 1980; Hon. DLitt (Bradford) 1983; Daily Mail Kathleen Ferrier Memorial Prize 1956, Queen's Prize, Royal Coll. of Music 1959, Shakespeare Prize, Hamburg 1971, Grand Prix, French Nat. Acad. of Lyric Recordings 1975, Leonie Sonning Prize (Denmark) 1979; Gold Medal of Royal Philharmonic Soc. 1990; Commdr des Arts et des Lettres. *Publication:* Full Circle (autobiog.) 1982. *Leisure interest:* walking, reading. *Address:* c/o Transart (UK) Ltd, 8 Bristol Gardens, London, W9 2JG, England.

BAKER, Rt Rev John Austin, MA, MLitt, DD; British ecclesiastic; b. 11 Jan. 1928, Birmingham; s. of George Austin Baker and Grace Edna Baker; m. Gillian Mary Leach 1974; ed Marlborough Coll., Oriel Coll., Oxford and Cuddesdon Theological Coll.; ordained 1954; Official Fellow, Chaplain and Lecturer in Divinity Corpus Christi Coll., Oxford 1959–73; Lecturer in Theology Brasenose and Lincoln Colls., Oxford; Dorrance Visiting Prof. Trinity Coll., Hartford, Conn. 1967; Canon of Westminster 1973–82; Visiting Prof., King's Coll., London 1974–76; Sub-Dean of Westminster and Lector Theologiae 1978–82; Rector of St Margaret's, Westminster 1978–82; Chaplain to Speaker of House of Commons 1978–82; Bishop of Salisbury 1982–93; mem. Church of England Doctrine Comm. 1967–81, 1984–87, Chair. 1985–87; mem. Standing Comm., WCC Faith and Order Comm. 1983–87; Fellow Emer., Corpus Christi Coll., Oxford 1977–. *Publications include:* The Foolishness of God 1970, Travels in Oudamovia 1976, The Whole Family of God 1981, The Faith of a Christian 1996; numerous theological articles and trans. *Leisure interests:* music, travel. *Address:* 4 Mede Villas, Kingsgate Road, Winchester, Hants., SO23 9QQ, England. *Telephone:* (1962) 861388. *Fax:* (1962) 843089.

BAKER, John Hamilton, QC, PhD, LLD, FBA, FRHistS; British professor of English legal history; b. 10 April 1944, Sheffield; s. of Kenneth Lee Vincent Baker and Marjorie Bagshaw; m. 1st Veronica Margaret Lloyd 1968 (divorced 1997); two d.; m. 2nd Fiona Rosalind Holdsworth (née Cantlay) 2002; ed King Edward VI Grammar School, Chelmsford and Univ. Coll. London; Asst Lecturer in Law, Univ. Coll. London 1965–67, Lecturer 1967–70; Barrister Inner Temple, London 1966; Librarian, Squire Law Library, Cambridge 1971–73; Lecturer in Law, Cambridge Univ. 1973–83, Reader in English Legal History 1983–88, Prof. 1988–98, Downing Prof. of the Laws of England 1998–, Fellow of St Catharine's Coll. 1971–; Visiting Prof. New York Univ. School of Law 1988–; Corresp. Fellow American Soc. for Legal History 1992; Visiting Fellow All Souls Coll. Oxford 1995; Jt Literary Dir Selden Soc. 1981–90, Literary Dir 1991–; Fellow of Univ. Coll. London 1991; Hon. Bencher, Inner Temple, London 1988; Hon. Fellow Soc. for Advanced Legal Studies 1998; Hon. Foreign mem. American Acad. of Arts and Sciences 2001; Hon. LLD (Chicago) 1991; Yorke Prize (Cambridge) 1975; Ames Prize (Harvard Law School) 1985. *Publications:* An Introduction to English Legal History 1971, The Reports of Sir John Spelman 1977, Manual of Law French 1979, The Order of Serjeants at Law 1984, English Legal MSS in the USA (Part I) 1985, The Legal Profession and the Common Law 1986, Sources of English Legal History (with S. F. C. Milsom) 1986, The Notebook of Sir John Port 1987, Readings and Moots at the Inns of Court 1990, English Legal MSS in the USA (Part II) 1990, Cases from the Lost Notebooks of Sir James Dyer 1994, Catalogue of English Legal MSS in Cambridge University Library 1996, Spelman's Reading on Quo Warranto 1997, Monuments of Endless Labours 1998, Caryll's Reports 1999, The Common Law Tradition 2000, The Law's Two Bodies 2001, Readers and Readings 2001. *Address:* St Catharine's College, Cambridge, CB2 1RL, England. *Telephone:* (1223) 338317.

BAKER, John William, CBE; British business executive; b. 5 Dec. 1937; s. of Reginald Baker and Wilhelmina Baker; m. 1st Pauline Moore 1962; one s.; m. 2nd Gillian Bullen; ed Harrow Weald Co. Grammar School and Oriel Coll., Oxford; served army 1959–61, Ministry of Transport 1961–70, Dept of Environment 1970–74; Deputy CEO Housing Corpn 1974–78; Sec. Cen. Electricity Generating Bd 1979–80, Bd mem. 1980–89, Jt Man. Dir 1986–89; CEO Nat. Power PLC 1990–95, Chair. 1995–97; Dir (non-exec.) Royal Insurance (now Royal and Sun Alliance Insurance Group) 1995–, The Maersk Co. 1996–, Medeva PLC 1996–2000, EIC 1999–; Deputy Chair. Celltech Group 2000–; Int. Business Council mem. AP Möller; Chair. Groundwork Foundation 1995–99, World Energy Council Exec. Ass. 1995–98, ENO

1996–2001; mem. Associated Bd, Royal Schools of Music 2000–; mem. Sr Salaries Review Bd 2000–, Chair. 2002–. *Leisure interests:* tennis, bridge, music, theatre. *Address:* c/o Medeva PLC, 10 St James's Street, London, SW1A 1EF, England.

BAKER, Baron (Life Peer), cr. 1997, of Dorking in the County of Surrey; **Kenneth (Wilfred) Baker,** PC, CH; British politician; b. 3 Nov. 1934, Newport, Wales; s. of the late W. M. Baker; m. Mary Elizabeth Gray-Muir 1963; one s. two d.; ed St Paul's School and Magdalen Coll. Oxford; nat. service 1953–55; served Twickenham Borough Council 1960–62; as Conservative cand. contested Poplar 1964, Acton 1966; Conservative MP for Acton 1968–70, St Marylebone 1970–83, Mole Valley 1983–97; Parl. Sec. Civil Service Dept 1972–74, Parl. Pvt. Sec. to Leader of Opposition 1974–75; Minister of State and Minister for Information Tech., Dept of Trade and Industry 1981–84; Sec. of State for the Environment 1985–86, for Educ. and Science 1986–89; Chancellor of the Duchy of Lancaster and Chair. Conservative Party 1989–90; Sec. of State for the Home Dept 1990–92; mem. Public Accounts Cttee 1969–70; mem. Exec. 1922 Cttee 1978–81; Chair. Hansard Soc. 1978–81, MTT PLC 1996–97, Business Serve PLC, Northern Edge Ltd, Museum of British History, Belmont Press (London) Ltd, Monstermob; Pres. Royal London Soc. for the Blind; Sec. Gen. UN Conf. of Parliamentarians on World Population and Devt 1978; Dir (non-exec.) Hanson 1992–, Millennium Chemicals Inc., Collaboration Tech. Ltd, Stanley Leisure PLC; Adviser to The Blackstone Group; Chair. Information Cttee, House of Lords 2002–. *Publications:* I Have No Gun But I Can Spit 1980, London Lines (Ed.) 1982, The Faber Book of English History in Verse 1988, Unauthorized Versions (Ed.) 1990, The Faber Book of Conservatism (Ed.) 1993, The Turbulent Years 1993, The Prime Ministers, An Irreverent Political History in Cartoons 1995, The Kings and Queens: An Irreverent Cartoon History of the British Monarchy, The Faber Book of War Poetry 1996, Children's English History in Verse 2000, The Faber Book of Landscape Poetry 2000. *Leisure interests:* collecting books, political cartoons. *Address:* House of Lords, Westminster, London, SW1A 0PW, England.

BAKER, Paul Thornell, PhD; American professor of anthropology; b. 28 Feb. 1927, Burlington, Ia; s. of Palmer Ward Baker and Viola (née Thornell) Laughlin; m. Thelma M. Shoher 1949; one s. three d.; ed Univ. of New Mexico and Harvard Univ.; Research Scientist, US Army Climatic Research Lab. 1952–57; Asst Prof. of Anthropology, Penn. State Univ. 1957–61, Assoc. Prof. 1961–64, Prof. 1965–81, Head Dept of Anthropology 1980–85, Evan Pugh Prof. of Anthropology 1981–87, Evan Pugh Prof. Emer. 1987–; Vice-Pres. Int. Union of Anthropological and Ethnological Sciences 1988–93, Sr Vice-Pres. 1993–98; Pres. Int. Asscn of Human Biologists 1980–89, American Asscn of Physical Anthropologists 1969–71, Human Biology Council 1974–77; Chair. US Man and Biosphere Program 1983–85; mem. NAS; Huxley Medal (Royal Anthropological Soc., London) 1982, Gorjanovic-Krambergeri Medal (Croatian Anthropological Soc.) 1985, Order of the Golden Star with Necklace (Yugoslavia) 1988. *Publications:* The Biology of Human Adaptability (co-ed.) 1966, Man in the Andes: A Multidisciplinary Study of High Altitude Quechua 1976, The Biology of High Altitude Peoples (ed.) 1978, The Changing Samoans: Behavior and Health in Transition 1986, Human Biology (co-author) 1988. *Leisure interest:* sailing. *Address:* 337 Upton Pyne Drive, Brentwood, CA 94513-6458, USA.

BAKER, Raymond, OBE, PhD, FRS; British research scientist; b. 1 Nov. 1936; s. of Alfred Baker and May Golds; m. Marian Slater 1960; one s. two d.; ed Ilkeston Grammar School and Univ. of Leicester; Postdoctoral Fellow, Univ. of Calif. at Los Angeles 1962–64; Lecturer in Organic Chem. Univ. of Southampton 1964–72, Sr Lecturer 1972–74, Reader 1974–77, Prof. 1977–84; Dir Wolfson Unit of Chemical Entomology 1976–84; Dir of Medicinal Chem. Merck Sharpe Dohme Research Labs. 1984–89, Exec. Dir 1989–96; Chief Exec. Biotech. and Biological Sciences Research Council 1996–2001; Visiting Prof. Univ. of Edinburgh 1988–96; Visiting Prof. Univ. of Leicester 1990–93; Hon. DSc (Nottingham Trent) 1990, (Aston) 1997, (Leicester) 1998, (St Andrews) 1998, (Southampton) 1999. *Publications:* Mechanism in Organic Chemistry 1971; over 300 articles in professional journals. *Leisure interests:* golf, gardening, travel. *Address:* Angeston Court, Uley, Dursley, Glos., GL11 5AL, England (Home).

BAKER, Richard Douglas James, OBE, MA; British broadcaster and author; b. 15 June 1925; s. of Albert Baker and Jane I. Baker; m. Margaret C. Martin 1961; two s.; ed Kilburn Grammar School and Peterhouse, Cambridge; Royal Navy 1943–46; actor 1948; teacher 1949; BBC Third Programme announcer 1950–53; BBC TV newsreader 1954–82; commentator for State Occasion Outside Broadcasts 1967–70; TV introductions to Promenade concerts 1960–95; panellist, Face the Music (BBC 2) 1966–79; presenter, Omnibus (BBC TV) 1983; presenter of various shows on BBC radio including Start the Week 1970–77, These You Have Loved 1972–77, Baker's Dozen 1978–87, Mainly for Pleasure 1986–92, Comparing Notes 1987–95; presenter Classic Countdown for Classic FM radio 1995–97, Sound Stories Radio 3 1998–, Melodies for You 1999–; mem. Broadcasting Standards Council 1988–93; Hon. Fellow, London Coll. of Music; Hon. FRCM; Hon. mem. Royal Liverpool Philharmonic Soc.; Hon. LLD (Strathclyde) 1979, (Aberdeen) 1983; TV Newscaster of the Year (Radio Industries Club), 1972, 1974, 1979, BBC Radio Personality of the Year (Variety Club of GB) 1984, Sony Gold Award for Radio 1996. *Publications:* Here is the News (broadcasts) 1966, The Terror of Tobermory 1972, The Magic of Music 1975, Dry Ginger 1977, Richard Baker's Music Guide 1979, Mozart 1982, London, A Theme with Variations 1989, Richard Baker's Companion to Music 1993, Franz Schubert 1997. *Leisure interests:* gardening, music. *Address:* c/o Stephannie Williams Artists, 9 Central Chambers, Wood Street, Stratford upon Avon, CV37 6JQ, England. *Telephone:* (1789) 266272.

BAKER, Russell Wayne, DLitt; American journalist and author; b. 14 Aug. 1925, London Co., Va; s. of Benjamin R. Baker and Lucy E. Robinson; m. Miriam E. Nash 1950; two s. one d.; ed Johns Hopkins Univ.; served USNR 1943–45; with Baltimore Sun 1947–64; mem. Washington Bureau, New York Times 1954–62, author-columnist, editorial page 1962–; mem. American Acad., Inst. of Arts and Letters; Chair. Pulitzer Prize Bd 1992–; several hon. degrees; Pulitzer Prize for distinguished commentary 1979; Pulitzer Prize for Biography 1983 and other awards. *Publications:* American in Washington 1961, No Cause for Panic 1964, All Things Considered 1965, Our Next President 1968, Poor Russell's Almanac 1972, The Upside Down Man 1977, Home Again, Home Again 1979, So This is Depravity 1980, Growing Up 1982, The Rescue of Miss Yaskell and Other Pipe Dreams 1983, The Good Times (memories) 1989, There's a Country in My Cellar 1990, Russell Baker's Book of American Humor 1993. *Address:* New York Times, 229 West 43rd Street, New York, NY 10036, USA (Office).

BAKER, William Oliver, BS, PhD; American research chemist; b. 15 July 1915, Chestertown, Md; s. of Harold M. Baker and Helen (Stokes) Baker; m. Frances Burrill 1941 (died 1999); one s. one d. (deceased); ed Washington Coll., Maryland and Princeton Univ.; with AT&T Bell Labs 1939–80, in charge of polymer research and Devt 1948–51, Asst Dir of Chemical and Metallurgical Research 1951–54, Dir of Research, Physical Sciences 1954–55, Vice-Pres. Research 1955–73, Pres. 1973–79, Chair. of the Bd 1979–80; Chair. Rockefeller Univ. 1978–90, Chair. Emer. 1990–; Chair. Andrew W. Mellon Foundation 1975–90, Chair. Emer. 1990–; Dir Health Effects Inst. 1980–95; mem. NAS, Nat. Acad. of Engineering, Inst. of Medicine, American Philosophical Soc., American Acad. of Arts and Sciences, Nat. Comm. on Jobs and Small Business 1985–87, Nat. Comm. on Role and Future of State Colls and Univs 1985–87, Comm. on Science and Tech. of New Jersey 1985–, Nat. Council on Science and Tech. Educ., AAAS 1985–; numerous hon. degrees; numerous awards include Perkin Medal 1963, Priestley Medal 1966, Edgar Marburg Award 1967, ASTM Award to Executives 1967, Industrial Research Institute Medal 1970, Frederik Philips Award (IEEE) 1972, Industrial Research Man of the Year Award 1973, James Madison Medal, Princeton Univ. 1975, Gold Medal, American Inst. of Chemists 1975, Mellon Inst. Award 1975, American Chemical Soc. Parsons Award 1976, Franklin Inst. Delmer S. Fahrney Medal 1977, J. Willard Gibbs Medal, ACS 1978, Madison Marshall Award 1980, von Hippel Award, Materials Research Soc. 1978; Bush Medal, NSF 1982, Nat. Security Medal 1983, Nat. Medal of Tech. (co-recipient) 1985, Nat. Medal of Science 1988, NJ Thomas Edison Award 1988, Philip Hauge Abelson Prize, AAAS 1995. *Publications include:* Rheology, Vol. III 1960, Listen to Leaders in Engineering 1965, Perspectives in Polymer Science 1966, Science: The Achievement and the Promise 1968, 1942–1967, Twenty-five Years at RCA Laboratories: Materials Science and Engineering in the United States 1970, The Technological Catch and Society 1975, Science and Technology in America—An Assessment 1977, Resources of Organic Matter for the Future—Perspectives and Recommendations 1978; contribs to many symposia and publs, about 95 research papers in journals and holder of 13 patents. *Leisure interest:* natural history. *Address:* AT&T Bell Laboratories, 600 Mountain Avenue, Providence, NJ 07974 (Office); c/o Rockefeller University, 1230 York Avenue, New York, NY 10021, USA. *Telephone:* (908) 582-3423.

BAKEWELL, Joan Dawson, CBE, BA; British broadcaster and writer; b. 16 April 1933, Stockport; d. of John Rowlands and Rose Bland; m. 1st Michael Bakewell 1955 (divorced 1972); one s. one d.; m. 2nd Jack Emery 1975 (divorced 2001); ed Stockport High School for Girls and Newnham Coll., Cambridge; TV critic The Times 1978–81, columnist Sunday Times 1988–90; Assoc. Newnham Coll., Cambridge 1980–91, Assoc. Fellow 1984–87; Gov. BFI 1994–99, Chair. 1999–2003; Dimbleby Award, BAFTA 1995. *TV includes:* Sunday Break 1962, Home at 4.30 (writer and producer) 1964, Meeting Point, The Second Sex 1964, Late Night Line Up 1965–72, The Youthful Eye 1968, Moviemakers at the National Film Theatre 1971, Film 72, Film 73, Holiday 74, 75, 76, 77, 78 (series), Reports Action (series) 1976–78, Arts UK: OK? 1980, Heart of the Matter 1988–2000, My Generation 2000, One Foot in the Past 2000, Taboo (series) 2001. *Radio includes:* Artist of the Week 1998–99, The Brains Trust 1999–, Belief 2000. *Publications:* The New Priesthood: British Television Today (jtly) 1970, A Fine and Private Place (jtly) 1977, The Complete Traveller 1977, The Heart of the Heart of the Matter 1996; contribs to journals. *Leisure interests:* theatre, travel, cinema. *Address:* c/o Knight Ayton Management, 10 Argyll Street, London, W1V 1AB, England.

BAKHMIN, Vyacheslav Ivanovich; Russian engineer; b. 25 Sept. 1947, Kalinin (now Tver); m.; one s.; ed Moscow Inst. of Econ. Statistics; researcher Inst. of Molecular Biology 1971–, Inst. of Electronic Man. Machines 1971–73; engineer Computation Cen. Inst. of Information and Electronics 1973–79; Sr engineer Inst. of Public Hygiene and Org. of Public Health 1979–80; mem. human rights movt, arrested and imprisoned 1980–84; engineer, head of group Research Centre at Inst. of Applied Math. 1990; Head Div. of Global Problems and Humanitarian Co-operation Russian Ministry of Foreign Affairs 1991–92; Dir Dept of Int. Humanitarian and Cultural Co-operation 1992–95; Dir Inst. Open Soc. (Soros Foundation) 1995–98; Exec. Dir of Program Block, Social Contract 1998–. *Address:* Ozerkovskaya nab. 18, Moscow, Russia (Office). *Telephone:* (095) 787-88-11 (Office).

BAKHT, Sikander; Indian politician; b. 24 Aug. 1918, Delhi; s. of Hafiz Mohd Yusuf and N Yusuf; m. Raj Sharma 1952; two s.; ed Delhi Univ.; mem. of Indian Nat. Congress until 1969; mem. All-India Congress Cttee, also mem. Working Cttee 1969–77; mem. Delhi Metropolitan Council for 10 years; detained for 18 months during emergency 1975–76; mem. for Chandni Chowk, Lok Sabha 1977; Minister of Works, Housing, Supply and Rehabilitation 1977–79, of Urban Affairs, Employment and External Affairs 1996, of Industry 1998; mem. and Gen. Sec. Janata Party 1977; Gen. Sec. Bharatiya Janata Party (BJP) 1980–82, Vice-Pres. 1982–93; mem. for Madhya Pradesh, Rajya Sabha 1990–96, 1996–2002; Leader of Opposition in Rajya Sabha 1992–96, 1996–98; Chair. Parl. Standing Cttee on Commerce 1999–2002; Gov. of Kerala 2002–; Padma Vibhushan 2000. *Leisure interests:* sports, Indian classical music, Urdu poetry. *Address:* Kerala Raj Bhavan, K.G. Camp PO, Thiruvananthapuram, 695 099, India (Office). *Telephone:* (471) 2721100 (Office). *Fax:* (471) 2720266 (Office).

BAKIYEV, Kurmanbek Saliyevich; Kyrgyzstan politician; b. 1 Aug. 1949, Masadan, Jalal-Abad region; m. Bakiyeva Tatyana Vassilievna; two s.; ed Bishkek Polytech. Inst.; engineer in Moscow region –1985; Dir Kok-Zhangak factory 1985–90; elected mem. Parl. 1990; Deputy Chair. Foundation of State Property, then Head of Admin. Toguz-Toro region 1994–95; Deputy Gov., then Gov. Jalal-Abad region 1995–98; Gov. Chuyisk region 1998–2000; Prime Minister of Kyrgyzstan 2000–02; mem. Constitutional Conf. 2002–. *Address:* Constitutional Conference, House of Parliament, Bishkek, Kyrgyzstan (Office).

BAKKE, Dennis W., MBA; American business executive; m. Eileen Bakke; ed Harvard Univ.; began career with Fed. Energy Agency; later with Energy Productivity Center, Carnegie Mellon Univ.; Founder, Pres. and CEO The AES Corpn, Arlington, VA 1981–; Pres. The Mustard Seed Asscn. *Publication:* Creating Abundance – America's Least Cost Energy Strategy (Jt author). *Address:* AES Corporation, 1001 North 19th Street, Arlington, VA 22209-1722, USA (Office). *Fax:* (703) 528-4510 (Office). *Website:* www.aesc.com (Office).

BAKLANOV, Grigoriy Yakovlevich; Russian author; b. 11 Sept. 1923, Voronezh; s. of Jakov Friedman and Ida Kantor; m. Elga Sergeeva 1953; one s. one d.; ed Gorky Inst. of Literature, Moscow; served as soldier and officer 1941–45; mem. CPSU 1942–91; Ed.-in-Chief Znamya 1986–93; first works published 1950; USSR State Prize 1982, Russian State Prize 1997. *Publications include:* In Snegiri 1954, Nine Days 1958, The Foothold 1959, The Dead Are Not Ashamed 1961, July 41 1964, Karpukhin 1965, Friends 1975, Forever Nineteen 1980, The Youngest of the Brothers 1981, Our Man 1990, Time to Gather Stones 1989, Once it was the Month of May (scenario) 1990, The Moment Between the Past and the Future 1990, Come Through the Narrow Gates 1993, Short Stories 1994, Kondratiy 1995, Short Stories 1996, And Then the Marauders Come (novel) 1996, Life Granted Twice (memoirs) 1999, My General (novel) 2000. *Leisure interest:* gardening. *Address:* Lomonosovsky Prospekt 19, Apt. 82, 117311 Moscow, Russia. *Telephone:* (095) 930-12-90. *Fax:* (095) 549-57-67.

BAKLANOV, Oleg Dmitrievich, BEng; Russian politician; b. 17 March 1932, Kharkov, USSR (now Ukraine); ed All-Union Inst. of Energetics; engineer, Sr engineer, then Dir Kharkov technical appliances plant 1950–55; mem. CPSU 1953–91; gen. Dir of production unit 1975–76; Deputy Minister of Gen. Machine Construction (with special responsibility for the defence industry) in USSR 1981–83, First Deputy Minister 1981–83, Minister 1983–88; mem. CPSU Cen. Cttee 1986–91; Sec. Political Bureau 1988–91; Deputy to Supreme Soviet 1987–89; USSR People's Deputy 1989–91; arrested 22 Aug. 1991 for involvement in failed coup d'état, on trial 1993–94, released on amnesty 1994; active in Communist Movt; mem. Political Council, Russian Public Union 1996–; Chair. Soc. for Friendship and Co-operation of Russia and Ukraine 2000–; Hero of Socialist Labour 1976, Lenin Prize 1982. *Address:* ROS, Szedny Tishinski Pereulok 10, Apt. 9, 123557 Moscow, Russia (Office). *Telephone:* (095) 253-18-98.

BAKOYIANNI, Dora; Greek politician; d. of Constantine Mitsotakis, Prime Minister of Greece 1990–93; m. Pavlos Bakoyiannis (assassinated 1989); ed Univ. of Munich and Athens Law School; fled with her family to Paris to escape mil. dictatorship 1967, returned when coup collapsed 1974; Mem. Parl. (Nea Dimokratia – New Democracy) for Evritania 1989–93, for Athens 1996–2002; fmr. Under-Sec. to Prime Minister's Office; Minister of Culture 1992–93; Mayor of Athens Oct. 2002–. *Address:* New Democracy (Nea Dimokratia), Odos Rigillis 18, 106 74 Athens, Greece (Office).

BAKR, Rashid El Tahir; Sudanese politician; b. 1930, Karkoj; ed Univ. of Khartoum; fmr advocate; imprisoned for opposition to the regime of Gen. Ibrahim Abboud 1958–64; Minister of Animal Resources and Justice 1965; Amb. to Libya 1972–74; apptd mem. Political Bureau, Sudanese Socialist Union (SSU) and Sec. Farmers' Union in the SSU 1972; Asst Sec.-Gen. Sectoral Orgs, SSU 1974; Speaker, People's Nat. Ass. 1974–76, 1980–81; Second Vice-Pres. of Sudan 1976–80; Prime Minister 1976–77; Minister of Foreign Affairs 1977–80; Chair. OAU Council of Ministers 1978–79; Attorney-Gen. 1983–84; mem. group of 41 set up to revitalize policy-making organs of SSU 1982.

BAKR AL-HAKIM, Hojatoleslam Mohammed; Iraqi cleric and politician; s. of Grand Ayatollah Mohsen al-Hakim; ed theological studies in Najaf; imprisoned for political activities 1977; escaped to Syria and then to Iran 1980; built up opposition movt during Iran–Iraq War 1980–88; subsequently set up resistance group Supreme Council for Islamic Revolution in Iraq (SCIRI)/ Supreme Ass. of Islamic Revolution in Iraq (SAIRI) in 1982 consisting of 70 mems of various Islamic movts and scholars, and mil. force called Badr Corps, currently allied with other Iraqi opposition groups.

BĂLĂIȚĂ, George; Romanian writer; b. 17 April 1935, Bacău; s. of Gheorghe Bălăiță and Constantina Popa Bălăiță; m. Lucia Gavril 1959; one s.; ed Coll. of Philology; Ed. of cultural review Ateneu (Bacău) 1964–78; Dir Cartea Românească publishing house, Bucharest 1982–90, Ed.-in-Chief Arc 1991–97; Dir Literary Fund (soc. for defending authors' rights) 1997–; Vice-Pres. of the Romanian Writers' Union; Fulbright stipendiate 1980; Prize of the Romanian Writers' Union 1975; Prize of the Romanian Acad. 1978; Award of Bucharest Writers' Asscn 1994. *Publications:* novels: Lumea în două zile (The World in Two Days) 1975, Ucenicul neascultător (The Disobedient Apprentice) 1978; essays: A Provincial's Nights 1984, Gulliver in No Man's Land (essays) 1994. *Leisure interests:* music, the arts, his pet dog. *Address:* 115 Victoriei Rd., Bucharest (Office); 24–26 Bd Lascăr Catargiu, Bucharest, Romania. *Telephone:* (1) 2109964 (Office); (1) 6504859. *Fax:* (1) 2109964 (Office).

BALANANDAN, E.; Indian trade union official and politician; b. 16 June 1924, Quilon, Kerala; s. of Raman and Eswary; m.; three d. one s.; ed St Joseph's High School, Shaktikulangara, Quilon; electrician Indian Aluminium Co., Alwaye, Kerala 1942–46; various positions within trade union orgs 1944–, currently Pres. Centre of Indian Trade Unions and Pres. Electricity Employees Fed. of India; joined Communist Party of India 1944, held many positions including mem. Politbureau (Marxist) 1988–; elected to Kerala Legis. Ass. 1976–69, 1970–76; fmrly elected to Parl. (Lok Sabha); elected to Parl. (Rajya Sabha) 1988–2000. *Leisure interest:* reading. *Address:* Centre of Indian Trade Unions, BTR Bhavan, 13-A Rouse Avenue, New Delhi 110 002 (Office); Ponnamkulath, Kalamassery, Ernakulam, Kerala, India (Home). *Telephone:* (23) 2213066 (Office); 4842532415 (Home). *Fax:* (23) 221284 (Office). *E-mail:* citu@vsnl.com, eefi@eth.net (Office). *Website:* www.citu.org .in, www.eefi.ord (Office).

BALANOVSKAYA, Nadezhda Avgustovna; Russian business executive; b. 1949; ed Moscow Inst. of Textiles; textile factory worker until 1986; Chief Engineer Joint Stock Co. Trekhgornaya Manufactura 1986–88, Dir-Gen. 1988–; mem. Presidium Council on Industrial Policy at Russian Govt 1993–94, Exec. Bd Russian Union of Businessmen and Enterprise 1992–, Govt Comm. on Problems of Women 1992–. *Address:* Joint Stock co. Trekhgornaya Manufactura, Rochdelskaya str. 15, 123022, Moscow, Russia (Office). *Telephone:* (095) 252-12-91 (Office). *Fax:* (095) 255-68-83 (Office). *E-mail:* dunayev@yahoo.com (Office). *Website:* www.trekhgorka.ru (Office).

BALASSA, Sándor; Hungarian composer; b. 20 Jan. 1935, Budapest; s. of János Balassa and Eszter Bora; m. Marianna Orosz 1994; one s. one d.; ed Budapest Conservatory and Music Acad.; began career as a mechanic; entered Budapest Conservatory at age 17; studied composition under Endre Szervánszky at Budapest Music Acad., obtained diploma 1965; Music Dir Hungarian Radio 1964–80; Teacher of Instrumentation, Music. Acad. Budapest 1981; Erkel Prize 1972, Critics' Prize (Hungarian Radio) 1972, 1974, Listeners' Prize (Hungarian Radio) 1976, Distinction for Best Work of the Year, Paris Int. Tribune of Composers 1972, Merited Artist of the Hungarian People's Repub. 1978, Kossuth Prize 1983, Bartók-Pásztory Prize 1988, 1999. *Compositions include:* vocal: Eight Songs from Street Rottenbiller 1957, Two Songs to Poems by Dezső Kosztolányi 1957, Two Songs to Poems by Attila József 1958, Five Choruses (for children's choir) 1967, Legenda 1967, Antinomia 1968, Summer Night (for female choir) 1968, Requiem for Lajos Kassák 1969, Cantata Y 1970, Motetta 1973, Tresses 1979, Kyrie for female choir 1981, Madaras énekek (for children's choir) 1984, The Third Planet, opera-cantata 1986, Bánatomtól szabadulnék (for female choir) 1988, Oldott kéve for mixed choir 1992, Kelet népe for children's choir 1992, Damjanich's prayer for mixed choir 1993, Chant of Orphans 1995, Capriccio for Female Choir 1996, Spring Song, Autumn Song (for female choir) 1997, Woodcutter (for male choir) 1998, Moon-gesang and Sun-anthem (for male choir) 1998, Winter cantata (for children's chorus and string orchestra) 1999, Legend of Christmas (for female choir) 1999; opera: Az ajtón kivül (The Man Outside) 1976, Karl and Anna 1992, Földindulás 2001; instrumental: Dimensioni 1966, Quartetto per percussioni 1969, Xenia 1970, Tabulae 1972, The Last Shepherd 1978, Quintet for Brass 1979, The Flowers of Hajta 1984, Divertimento for two cimbaloms 1992, Sonatina for harp 1993, Little Garland (trio for flute, viola and harp) 1994, Five Brothers (piano) 1994, Jánosnapi muzsika (solo violin) 1994, Vonósnégyes (string quartet) 1995, Bells of Nyirbátor (for twelve brass instruments) 1996, Sonatina for Piano 1996, Preludes and Fantasia for Organ 1996, Duets (for flute and harp) 1998, Pastoral and Rondo (for violin and horn) 1998; orchestral: Violin Concerto 1965, Lupercalia 1971, Iris 1972, Chant of Glarus 1978, The Island of Everlasting Youth 1979, Calls and Cries 1980, A Daydreamer's Diary 1983, Three Phantasias 1984, Little Grape and Little Fish 1987, Tündér Ilona 1992, Prince Csaba for string orchestra 1993, Bölcske Concerto for string orchestra 1993, Dances of Mucsa 1994, Sons of the Sun 1995, Four Portraits 1996, Number 301 Parcel 1997, Pécs Concerto 1998, Hungarian Coronation Music 1998, Hun's Valley (Val d'Anniviers) 1999, Double Concerto for oboe, horn and string orchestra 2000, Eight Movements for two clarinets 2001, Secrets of Heart (cantata) 2002, Fantasy for harp and string orchestra 2002, Flowers of October for orchestra 2003. *Leisure interest:* nature. *Address:* str. 18 Sümegvár, 1118 Budapest, Hungary. *Telephone:* (1) 319-7049.

BALASURIYA, Stanislaus Tissa, BA, STL; Sri Lankan ecclesiastic; b. 29 Aug. 1924, Kahatagasdigiliya; s. of William Balasuriya and Victoria Balasuriya; ed Univ. of Ceylon, Gregorian Univ., Rome, Oxford Univ., Maris Stella Coll., Negombo, St Patrick's Coll., Jaffna and St Joseph's Coll., Colombo; helped found Aquinas Univ. with Fr. Peter Pillai 1954, Rector 1964–71; f. Centre for Soc. and Religion, Colombo 1971, Dir 1971–, Citizens Cttee for Nat. Harmony in Sri Lanka 1977–91; Visiting Prof. of Faith and Social Justice, Faculty of Theology, Univ. of Ottawa 1993–94; Ed. Logos, Quest, Voices of the Third World, Social Justice, Sadharanaya; Khan Memorial Gold Medal for Econs. *Publications:* Jesus Christ and Human Liberation, Eucharist and Human Liberation, Catastrophe July '83, Planetary Theology, Mary and Human Liberation, Liberation of the Affluent, Humanization Europe, Indicators of Social Justice, Third World Theology of Religious Life, Right Relationships: Re-rooting of Christian Theology 1991, Doing Marian Theology in Sri Lanka. *Leisure interests:* writing, organic farming. *Address:* Centre for Society and Religion, 281 Deans Road, Colombo 10, Sri Lanka. *Telephone:* 695425.

BALAYAN, Roman Gurgenovich; Armenian film director; b. 15 April 1941, Nagorno-Karabak Autonomous Region; m. Natalia Balayan; two s.; ed Kiev Theatre Inst., USSR; State Prize 1987. *Films include:* The Romashkin Effect, 1973, Kashtanka 1976, Biryuk (Morose) 1978, The Kiss 1983, Dream and Waking Flights 1983, Keep Me Safe, My Talisman 1985, Police Spy 1988, Lady Macbeth of Mtcensk 1989. *TV:* Who's Afraid of Virginia Woolf 1992, The Tale of the First Love 1995. *Address:* Leningradsky Prosp. 33, Apt. 70, 125212 Moscow, Russia. *Telephone:* (095) 159-99-74.

BALAZS, Artur Krzysztof, MEng; Polish politician, trade union leader and farmer; b. 3 Jan. 1952, Ełk; s. of Adam Balazs and Irena Balazs; m. Jolanta Balazs 1973; three d.; ed Agricultural Acad., Szczecin; worked in agric. service of Communal Office, Kołczewo 1974–76; own farm in Łuskowo 1976–; mem. Polish United Workers' Party (PZPR) 1975–81; active in Agric. Solidarity Independent Self-governing Trade Union 1980–81, participant 1st Nat. Congress of Solidarity of Pvt. Farmers Trade Union, Warsaw 1980; participant agric. strikes and co-signatory agreements in Ustrzyki, Rzeszów and Bydgoszcz 1981; mem. All-Poland Founding Cttee of Solidarity of Private Farmers Trade Union, mem. Comm. for Realization of Rzeszów-Ustrzyki Agreements; interned Dec. 1981–Dec. 1982; mem. Presidium of Solidarity Provisional Nat. Council of Farmers 1987; mem. Inter-factory Strike Cttee Szczecin 1988; mem. Civic Cttee attached to Lech Wałęsa, Chair. of Solidarity Trade Union 1988–91; participant Round Table debates, mem. group for union pluralism and team for agric. matters Feb.–April 1989; mem. Episcopate Comm. for the Pastoral Care of Farmers 1989–; Deputy to Sejm (Parl.) 1989–93, 1997–; mem. Solidarity Election Action Parl. Club 1997–; Chair. Sejm Cttee for Admin. and Internal Affairs 1992–93; Vice-Chair. Christian Peasant Party 1990–94, 1995–97, Chair. 1994–95; mem. Nat. Bd Conservative Peasant Party (SKL) 1997–, Vice-Chair. 1998–99, Chair. 2000–02, Chair. Conservative Party–New Poland Movt (SKL–RNP) 2002–; Chair. European Fund for the Devt of Polish Villages 1990–; Minister, mem. Council of Ministers 1989–90, Minister without Portfolio 1991–92; mem. Senate 1995–97; mem. Cttee for Agric.; Minister of Agric. and Rural Devt 1999–2002. *Leisure interests:* press, politics. *Address:* Biuro Krajowe SKL–Ruch Nowej Polski, pl. Dąbrowskiego 5, 00-065 Warsaw, Poland (Office). *Telephone:* (22) 8278442 (Office). *Fax:* (22) 8278441 (Office). *E-mail:* biuro@skl-rnp.pl (Office). *Website:* www.skl-rnp.pl (Office).

BALÁZS, Éva H., DrSc; Hungarian professor of modern history; b. 20 Dec. 1915, Székelyudvarhely; d. of Sándor Balázs and Judit Beczássy; m. Lajos Hunyady 1941; one s.; ed Univ. of Budapest; Asst Inst. of Political Science, Ministry of Foreign Affairs 1939–41; lecturer, Dept of Medieval History, Univ. of Budapest 1945–54; Head, Dept of History, Coll. of Pedagogy 1947; responsible for historians' affairs, Office of Prime Minister 1947–49; Fellow, Inst. of History, Hungarian Acad. of Sciences, 1949–61; lecturer, Dept of Medieval and Modern World History, Univ. of Budapest 1961–77, Prof. 1978–87, Head of Dept 1982–87; Prof. Emer. 1987–, Pres. Cttee of French and Hungarian Historians; First Prize of Renovanda Hungariae Cultura Foundation 1996; Officier des Palmes académiques, Laureate of Hungarian Acad., Officer's Cross of the Repub. of Hungary, Chevalier Légion d'honneur 1997. *Publications:* The Age of Enlightenment 1964, Gergely Berzeviczy, the Reform Politician 1967, Paysannerie française-paysannerie hongroise (ed. and contrib.) 1973, Beförderer der Aufklärung in Mittel- und Osteuropa 1979, Noblesses 1981, Intellectuels 1985, Absolutisme Eclairé 1985, Vienna and Pest-Buda 1765–1800 1988, Magyarország története 1989, Hungary and the Habsburgs 1765–1800. An Experiment in Enlightened Absolutism 1997. *Leisure interests:* music, swimming. *Address:* Eötvös Loránd Tudomány Egyetem, BTK, Múzeum krt. 6-8, Budapest, H-1088 (Office); 11 Érmelléki u. 7, Budapest, H-1026, Hungary (Home). *Telephone:* (1) 213-8986.

BALCEROWICZ, Leszek, MBA, DEconSc; Polish central banker, politician and economist; b. 19 Jan. 1947, Lipno; s. of Wacław Balcerowicz and Barbara Balcerowicz; m. 1977; two s. one d.; ed Cen. School of Planning and Statistics, Warsaw, St John's Univ., New York; staff Central School of Planning and Statistics, Warsaw 1970–, Inst. of Int. Econ. Relations 1970–80; Head, Research Team attached to Econ. Devt Inst. 1978–81, Scientific Sec. Econ.

Devt Inst. 1980–; Prof. of Comparative Int. Studies, Warsaw School of Econs 1992–; mem. Polish United Workers' Party (PZPR) 1969–81; consultant, Network of Solidarity Independent Self-governing Trade Union 1981–4; Deputy Prime Minister and Minister of Finance 1989–91, 1997–2000; Leader Freedom Union (UW) 1995–2000; Pres. Nat. Bank of Poland 2001–; Deputy to Sejm (Parl.) 1997–2000; fmr mem. Council of Econ. Advisers to Pres. Wałęsa; Head Inst. for Comparative Int. Studies, Warsaw School of Econs 1993–; Chair. Council of Centre for Social and Econ. Research, Warsaw 1992–2000; mem. Polish Econ. Soc. 1970–, Vice-Chair. Gen. Bd 1981–82; mem. Polish Sociological Soc. 1983–, European Econ. Asscn; mem. Warsaw Civic Cttee Solidarity 1989; 11 hon degrees; Awards of Minister of Science, Higher Educ. and Tech. 1978, 1980, 1981, Ludwig Erhard Prize 1992, Minister of Finance of the Year 1998, Awards of Transatlantic Leadership 1999, Central European Award 1999, Friedrich von Hayek Prize 2000, Carl Bertelsman Prize 2001, Fasel Foundation Prize for Merits for the Social Market Economy 2002. *Publications:* numerous scientific works on int. econ. relations and problems of econ. systems. *Leisure interests:* basketball, detective stories. *Address:* National Bank of Poland, Świętokrzyska 11/21, 00-919 Warsaw, Poland (Office). *Telephone:* (22) 6531000. *Fax:* (22) 6208518. *E-mail:* nbp@nbp.pl. *Website:* www.nbp.pl.

BALDACCI, John Elias, BA; American state official; b. 30 Jan. 1955, Bangor, Maine; m. Karen Weston; one s.; ed Bangor High School, Univ. of Maine; worked in family restaurant Momma Baldacci's, Bangor; mem. Bangor City Council 1978–81; mem. State Senate, Me 1982–94; mem. House of Reps 1994–2002; Gov. of Me 2003–; Nat. Energy Assistance Dirs Asscn Award 1997, Small Business Assistance Award, NASA, Big M Award, Me State Soc., Washington DC 2000. *Address:* Office of the Governor, State House, Station 1, Augusta, ME 04333, USA (Office).

BALDESCHWIELER, John Dickson, PhD; American professor of chemistry; b. 14 Nov. 1933, Elizabeth, NJ; s. of Emile L. Baldeschwieler and Isobel M. Dickson; m. Marlene Konnar 1991; two s. one d. from previous m.; ed Cornell Univ. and Univ. of Calif., Berkeley; Asst Prof. Harvard Univ. 1962–65; Assoc. Prof. Stanford Univ. 1965–67, Prof. of Chem. 1967–73; Deputy Dir Office of Science and Tech. Exec. Office of Pres. of USA 1971–73; Prof. of Chem. Calif. Inst. of Tech. 1973 (now Prof. Emer.), Chair. Div. of Chem. and Chem. Eng 1973–78; Chair. Bd of Dirs Vestar Research Inc. 1981–; mem. numerous advisory cttees and comms; Alfred P. Sloan Foundation Fellow 1962–65; ACS Award in Pure Chem. 1967, William H. Nichols Award 1990, Nat. Medal of Science 2000, ACS Award for Creative Invention 2001. *Publications:* numerous articles in professional journals. *Leisure interests:* hiking, skiing, photography, music, travel. *Address:* Division of Chemistry and Chemical Engineering, California Institute of Technology, 127-72 Pasadena, CA 91125 (Office); PO Box 50065, Pasadena, CA 91115-0065, USA (Home). *Telephone:* (626) 395-6088 (Office). *Fax:* (626) 568-0402 (Office).

BALDOCK, Brian Ford, CBE, FRSA, CIMgt, FInstM; British business executive; b. 10 June 1934; s. of Ernest A. Baldock and Florence F. Baldock; m. 1st Mary Lillian Bartolo 1956 (divorced 1966); two s.; m. 2nd Carole Anthea Mason 1968; one s.; ed Clapham Coll. London; army officer 1952–55; Procter & Gamble 1956–61; Ted Bates Inc. 1961–63; Rank Org. 1963–66; Smith & Nephew 1966–75; Revlon Inc. 1975–78; Imperial Group 1978–86; Dir Guinness PLC 1986–96, Group Man. Dir 1989–96, Deputy Chair. 1992–96; Chair. Portman Group 1989–96; Chair. Sygen Int. (fmrly Dalgety) 1992–(Dir 1992–); Dir Marks & Spencer 1996– (Chair. 1999–2000), WMC Communications 1996–99, Cornhill Insurance 1996–; Chair. Wellington Group 1998–, Mencap 1998–, First Artist Corpn PLC 2001–; Freeman, City of London 1989. *Leisure interests:* theatre, opera, sport. *Address:* Marks and Spencer PLC, Michael House, Baker Street, London, W1U 8EP, England. *Telephone:* (20) 7935-4422. *Fax:* (20) 7487-2679. *E-mail:* brian.baldock@marks-and-spencer.com. *Website:* www.marksandspencer.com.

BALDWIN, Alec (Alexander Rae Baldwin III); American actor; b. 3 April 1958, Masapequa, NY; s. of Alexander Rae Baldwin, Jr and Carol (née Martineau) Baldwin; m. Kim Basinger (q.v.) 1993; one d.; ed George Washington and New York Univs, Lee Strasberg Theater Inst.; also studied with Mira Rostova and Elaine Aiken; mem. Screen Actors' Guild, American Fed. of TV and Radio Artists, Actors Equity Asscn; Theatre World Award (for Loot) 1986. *Stage appearances include:* Loot 1986, Serious Money 1988, Prelude to a Kiss 1990, A Streetcar Named Desire 1992. *Television appearances include:* The Doctors 1980–82, Cutter to Houston 1982, Knot's Landing 1984–85, Love on the Run 1985, A Dress Gray 1986, The Alamo: 13 Days to Glory 1986, Sweet Revenge 1990, Nuremberg 2000, Path to War 2002, Second Nature 2002. *Film appearances include:* Forever Lulu 1987, She's Having a Baby 1987, Beetlejuice 1988, Married to the Mob 1988, Talk Radio 1988, Working Girl 1988, Great Balls of Fire 1989, The Hunt for Red October 1990, Miami Blues 1990, Alice 1990, The Marrying Man 1991, Prelude to a Kiss 1992, Glengarry Glen Ross 1992, Malice 1993, The Getaway 1994, The Shadow 1994, Heaven's Prisoners 1995, Looking for Richard 1996, The Juror 1996, Ghosts of Mississippi 1996, Bookworm 1997, The Edge 1997, Thick as Thieves 1998, Outside Providence 1998, Mercury Rising 1998 (also producer), The Confession 1999, Notting Hill 1999, Thomas and the Magic Railroad 2000, State and Main 2000, Pearl Harbor 2001, Cats and Dogs (voice) 2001, Final Fantasy: The Spirit's Within 2001, The Royal Tenenbaums 2001, The Devil and Daniel Webster 2001, Path to War 2002, Dr. Seuss' The Cat in the Hat 2003, The Cooler 2003.

BALDWIN, Sir Jack Edward, Kt, PhD, FRS; British professor of chemistry; b. 8 Aug. 1938, London; s. of Frederick C. Baldwin and Olive F. Headland; m. Christine L. Franchi 1977; ed Lewes County Grammar School and Imperial Coll., London; Asst Lecturer in Chem., Imperial Coll. 1963, Lecturer 1966; Asst Prof. Penn. State Univ. 1967, Assoc. Prof. 1969; Assoc. Prof. MIT 1970, Prof. 1972; Daniell Prof. of Chem. King's Coll., London 1972; Prof. of Chem. MIT 1972–78; Waynflete Prof. of Chem., Univ. of Oxford 1978–, Fellow Magdalen Coll. 1978–; Dir Oxford Centre for Molecular Sciences; Hon. DSc (Warwick) 1988, (Strathclyde); Corday Morgan Medal, Chem. Soc. 1975; Karrer Medal, Univ. of Zürich 1984; Dr P. Janssen Prize (Belgium) 1988; Davy Medal (Royal Soc.) 1993, Leverhulm Medal (Royal Soc.) 1999, Kitasako Medal 2000. *Publications:* papers in organic and biorganic chem. in Journal of American Chem. Soc., Journal of Chem. Soc. and Nature. *Address:* Dyson Perrins Laboratory, University of Oxford, South Parks Road, Oxford, OX1 3QY, England. *Telephone:* (1865) 557809.

BALDWIN, Peter, BEE, BA; Australian politician; b. 12 April 1951, Aldershot, UK; ed Univ. of Sydney, Macquarie Univ.; fmr engineer and computer programmer; mem. NSW State Parl. (Upper House) 1976–82; Australian Labor Party mem. for Sydney, House of Reps. 1983–98; Minister for Higher Educ. and Employment Services and Minister Assisting Treasurer 1990–93; Minister for Social Security 1993–96; Shadow Minister for Finance 1997–; mem. Parl. Cttee on Foreign Affairs, Defence and Trade 1987–90, House of Reps. Standing Cttee on Industry, Science and Tech. 1987–90. *Address:* Level 3, 10 Mallet Street, Camperdown, NSW 2050, Australia.

BALESTRE, Jean-Marie; French editor and press executive; b. 9 April 1921, Saint-Rémy-de-Provence (Bouches-du-Rhône); s. of Joseph Balestre and Joséphine Bayol; ed Lycée Charlemagne and Faculté de Droit, Paris; sub-, Sport et Santé 1937, L'Auto and Droit de Vivre 1938–40; Dir Int. Gen. Presse 1947; Co-founder and Assoc. L'Auto Journal 1950, Dir-Gen. 1952–71; Dir Semaine du Monde 1953; Asst Dir-Gen. Soc. Edn Diffusion Presse 1970–; Dir Presses Modernes de France, La Liberté de Seine-et-Marne, Centre-Presse, Oise-Matin, Edns. Professionnelles de France, Brunel Edns., Edns. Sport Auto, France Antilles; Dir Robert Hersant press group 1969–; Dir Agence Générale de Presse et d'Information (Hersant group) 1976–77; Treas. Office de Justification de la Diffusion de la Presse 1964–; Hon. Pres. Féd. Nat. de la Presse Hebdomadaire et Périodique; Pres. Féd. Française du Sport Automobile 1973–96, World Fed. of Automobile Clubs 1985–, Int. Fed. of Motor Sport 1978–96 (Hon. Pres. 1996–), Int. Automobile Fed. 1985–; Chevalier, Légion d'honneur, Officier, Ordre Nat. du Mérite, Médaille de la Déportation pour Faits de Résistance; Licence d'Or, Féd. Française du Sport Automobile 1976, Personnalité de l'Année 1988. *Address:* c/o Fédération Française du Sport Automobile, 17–21 avenue du Général Mangin, 75781 Paris cedex 16, France.

BALGIMBAYEV, Nurlan Utebovich; Kazakhstan politician; b. 20 Nov. 1947; ed Kazakh Polytech. Inst., Massachusetts Univ. USA; worked in petroleum industry; Minister of Petroleum and Gas Industry 1994–97; Pres. Kazakhoil Co. 1997, 2000–; Prime Minister of Kazakhstan 1997–99. *Address:* Kazakhoil Co., Astana, Kazakhstan.

BALKENENDE, Jan Pieter, DIur; Netherlands politician; b. 7 May 1956, Kapelle; ed Free Univ. Amsterdam; Legal Affairs Policy Officer, Netherlands Univs Council 1982–84; mem. Amstelveen municipal council 1982–98, leader council CDA group 1994–98; Prof. of Econs, Free Univ. of Amsterdam 1993–2002; mem. staff Policy Inst. of the Christian Democratic Alliance (CDA) 1984–98; elected mem. Parl. 1998; Leader Christian Democratic Party (CDA) 2001–; Prime Minister of the Netherlands 2002–, also Minister of Gen. Affairs 2002–. *Publications include:* numerous articles on liberal individualism and communitarianism in Dutch society. *Address:* Office of the Prime Minister, Binnenhof 20, Postbus 20001, 2500 EA The Hague, The Netherlands (Office). *Telephone:* (70) 3564100 (Office). *Fax:* (70) 3564683 (Office). *E-mail:* info@minaz.nl (Office). *Website:* www.minaz.nl (Office).

BALL, Anthony (Tony), MBA; British media executive; b. 18 Dec. 1955; ed Kingston Univ.; with Thames TV 1976–88; fmr sports broadcaster for Trans World Int.; with BSB Sport 1988–91; with Int. Man. Group 1991–93; with BSkyB 1993–95; with Fox/Liberty Network 1995–99; Exec. Dir British Sky Broadcasting (BSkyB) 1999–; Dir (non-exec.) Marks & Spencer PLC 2000–. *Address:* British Sky Broadcasting, 6 Centaurs Business Park, Grant Way, Isleworth, Middx, TW7 5QD, England (Office). *Telephone:* (20) 7705-3000 (Office). *Fax:* (20) 7705-3955 (Office). *Website:* www.sky.com.

BALL, Sir Christopher John Elinger, Kt, MA, FRSA; British academic; b. 22 April 1935, London; s. of the late Laurence Elinger Ball and Christine Florence Mary (née Howe) Ball; m. Wendy Ruth Colyer 1958; three s. three d.; ed St George's School, Harpenden, Merton Coll., Oxford; Second Lt Parachute Regt 1955–56; Lecturer in English Language, Merton Coll., Oxford 1960–61; Lecturer in Comparative Linguistics, SOAS (Univ. of London) 1961–64; Fellow and Tutor in English Language, Lincoln Coll., Oxford 1964–69, Bursar 1972–79, Warden, Keble Coll., Oxford 1980–88; Jt Founding Ed. Toronto Dictionary of Old English 1970; mem. General Bd of the Faculties 1979–82, Hebdomadal Council 1985–89, Council and Exec., Templeton Coll., Oxford 1981–92, Editorial Bd, Oxford Review of Educ. 1984–96, CNAA 1982–88; Chair. Bd of Nat. Advisory Body for Public Sector Higher Educ. in England 1982–88, Oxford Univ. English Bd 1977–79, Jt Standing Cttee for Linguistics 1979–83, Conf. of Colls. Fees Cttee 1979–85, Higher Educ. Information Services Trust 1987–90; Sec. Linguistics Assn GB 1964–67; Publications Sec. Philological Soc. 1969–75; Gov. St George's School, Harpenden 1985–89, Centre for Medieval Studies, Oxford 1987, Brathay Hall Trust 1988–91, Manchester Polytechnic 1989–91; Founding Fellow in Kellogg Forum for Continuing Education, Oxford Univ. 1988–89, RSA Fellow in Continuing Educ. 1990–92, Dir of Learning 1992–97; Founding Chair. Nat. Advisory Council for Careers and Educational Guidance (NACCEG); Pres. Nat. Campaign for Learning 1995–97, Patron 1998–; Chancellor Univ. of Derby 1995–2003; Founding Chair. The Talent Foundation 1999–; Chair. Global Univ. Alliance 2000–; Millennium Fellow, Auckland Univ. of Tech., NZ 2000; Hon. Fellow (Lincoln Coll., Oxford) 1981, (Merton College, Oxford) 1987, (Keble College, Oxford) 1989, (Manchester Polytechnic) 1988, (Polytechnic of Cen. London) 1991, (Auckland Inst. of Tech., NZ) 1992, (North East Wales Inst.) 1996; Hon. D.Litt (CNAA) 1989; Hon. DUniv (Univ. of N London) 1993, (Open Univ.) 2002; Hon. DEd (Greenwich Univ.) 1994. *Publications:* Fitness For Purpose 1985, Aim Higher 1989, Higher Education into the 1990s (Jt ed.) 1989, Sharks and Splashes!: The Future of Education and Employment 1991, Profitable Learning 1992, Start Right 1994; various contribs. to philological, linguistic and educ. journals. *Address:* 45 Richmond Road, Oxford, OX1 2JJ, England. *Telephone:* (1865) 310800. *Fax:* (1865) 310800 (Home).

BALL, James (see Ball, Sir (Robert) James).

BALL, Michael Ashley; British singer; b. 27 June 1962, Bromsgrove; s. of Anthony George Ball and Ruth Parry Ball (née Davies); pnr Cathy McGowan; ed Plymouth Coll., Farnham Sixth Form Coll., Guildford School of Acting; numerous nat. and int. concert tours; Co-Founder and Patron Research into Ovarian Cancer; Variety Club of Great Britain Most Promising Artiste Award 1989, Gold Discs for four of his albums, The Variety Club Best Recording Artiste 1998, Theatregoers Club of Great Britain Most Popular Musial Actor 1999. *Theatre appearances include:* Judas/John the Baptist in Godspell (debut), Aberystwyth 1984, Frederick in The Pirates of Penzance, Manchester Opera House 1984, Marius in Les Misérables, London 1985–86, Raoul in The Phantom of the Opera, London 1987–88, Alex in Aspects of Love, London 1989–90, New York (debut) 1990, Giorgio in Passion, London 1996, Alone Together (part of Divas Season), London 2001, Caractacus Potts in Chitty Chitty Bang Bang, London 2002–. *Film:* England My England 1995. *Television:* own TV series 'Michael Ball' 1993, 1994, Royal Variety performances, Michael Ball in Concert (video) 1997, Michael Ball at Christmas 1999; represented UK in Eurovision Song Contest 1992, hosted National Lottery Live Show 1997, Top of the Pops, An Evening with Michael Ball 1998, Lord Lloyd Webber's 50th Birthday 1998. *Recordings include:* Les Miserables (original London cast album 1986, int. cast album 1987), Rage of the Heart 1987, Aspects of Love (London cast album 1989), Michael Ball 1992, West Side Story 1993, Always 1993, One Careful Owner 1994, The Best of Michael Ball 1994, First Love 1996, Michael Ball – The Musicals 1996, Michael Ball – The Movies 1998, Christmas 1999, Live at the Royal Albert Hall 1999, This Time It's Personal 2000, Centre Stage 2001, Chitty Chitty Bang Bang (London cast album). *Leisure interests:* collecting graphic novels and single malt whiskies, country walking, music, theatre. *Address:* Michael Ball Enterprises, PO Box 173, Hampton, Middlesex, TW12 1HF (Office); Gavin Barker Associates Limited, 2D Wimpole Street, London, W1M 7AA, England (Office). *Telephone:* (20) 8979-3739 (Office); (20) 7499-4777 (agent). *Fax:* (20) 8941-4143 (Office); (20) 7499-3777 (agent). *E-mail:* mbe@michaelball.co.uk (Office).

BALL, Sir (Robert) James, Kt, PhD, CBIM, FIAM; British professor of economics; b. 15 July 1933, Saffron Walden; s. of Arnold James Hector Ball; m. 1st Patricia Mary Hart Davies 1954 (divorced 1970); one s. (deceased) three d. (one d. deceased); m. 2nd Lindsay Jackson (née Wonnacott) 1970; one step-s.; ed St Marylebone Grammar School, Queen's Coll., Oxford, Univ. of Pennsylvania; RAF 1952–54; Research Officer, Oxford Univ. Inst. of Statistics 1957–58; IBM Fellow, Univ. of Pennsylvania 1958–60; Lecturer, Univ. of Manchester 1960–63, Sr Lecturer 1963–65; Prof. of Econs, London Business School 1984–98, Prof. Emer. 1998–, Deputy Prin. 1971–72, Prin. 1972–84; Dir Barclays Bank Trust Co. Ltd 1973–86, Tube Investments 1974–84, IBM UK Holdings Ltd 1979–95, IBM UK Pensions Trust 1994–; Chair. Legal and General Group PLC. 1980–94, Royal Bank of Canada Holdings (UK) Ltd 1995–98; Dir LASMO 1988–94, Royal Bank of Canada 1990–98; Vice-Pres. Chartered Inst. of Marketing 1991–94; mem. Council British-N American Cttee 1985–98, Research Assn 1985–, Marshall Aid Commemoration Comm. 1987–94; Econ. Adviser, Touche Ross & Co. 1984–95; Trustee Foulkes Foundation 1984–, Civic Trust 1986–91, The Economist 1987–99, ReAction Trust 1991–93; mem. Advisory Bd IBM UK Ltd 1995–98; Freeman of City of London 1987; Hon. DSc (Aston) 1987, Hon. DSocSc (Manchester) 1988. *Publications:* An Economic Model of the United Kingdom 1961, Inflation and the Theory of Money 1964, Inflation (ed.) 1969, The International Linkage of National Economic Models (ed.) 1972, Money and Employment 1982, The Economics of Wealth Creation (ed.) 1992, The British Economy at the Crossroads 1998, articles in professional journals. *Leisure interests:* chess, fishing, gardening. *Address:* London Business School, Sussex Place, Regent's Park, London, NW1 4SA, England (Office). *Telephone:* (20) 7262-5050 (Office). *Fax:* (20) 7724-7875 (Office). *E-mail:* jball@london.edu (Office). *Website:* www.london.edu/economics (Office).

BALLAA, Abdelmuhsen Mohammed S. al-, MAgr; Saudi Arabian diplomatist; b. 7 Feb. 1936, Riyadh; s. of Mohammed Al-Sudeari and Lululua Al-Sudeari; m. Hissa Al-Sudeari; one s. two d.; ed Colorado State Univ. and Arizona Univ.; worked at Ministry of Agric. and Waters; Amb. to FAO 1972, Chair. NE Group; Chair. OPEC during UN Conf. on the Establishment of Int. Fund for Agric. Devt (IFAD) June 1975; Chair. World Food Programme Cttee on Food Aid Policies and Programmes 1976, Preparatory Comm. for IFAD 1976–77; Pres. IFAD 1977–84; Amb. to Sudan 1987–89, to the Netherlands 1990–; Hon. PhD (Mich. State Univ.); Gold Medal Award (Pio Manzu Centre, Italy) 1978, Int. Prize of the Italian Agricultural Press Asscn 1978; Order Francisco de Miranda (Venezuela) 1979, Chevalier, Ordre Nat. de la Légion d'honneur 1986 and numerous other awards. *Address:* Embassy of Saudi Arabia, Alexanderstraat 19, 2514 JM The Hague, Netherlands. *Telephone:* (70) 3614391. *Fax:* (70) 3630348.

BALLADUR, Edouard, LenD; French politician; b. 2 May 1929, Smyrna, Turkey; s. of Pierre Balladur and Emilie Latour; m. Marie-Josèphe Delacour 1957; four s.; ed Lycée Thiers, Marseilles, Faculté de Droit, Aix-en-Provence, Inst. d'Etudes Politiques, Paris and Ecole Nationale d'Admin; auditor, Conseil d'Etat 1957, Maître des Requêtes 1963; adviser to Dir-Gen. of ORTF 1962–63; mem. Admin. Council of ORTF 1967–68; Tech. Adviser, Office of Prime Minister Georges Pompidou 1966–68; Pres. French soc. for Bldg and Devt of road tunnel under Mont Blanc 1968–81; mem. Admin. Council, Nat. Forestry Office 1968–73; Asst Sec.-Gen. Presidency of Repub. 1969, Sec.-Gen. 1974; Pres. Dir-Gen. Générale de Service Informatique 1977–86; Pres. Compagnie Européenne d'Accumulateurs 1980–86; mem. Conseil d'Etat 1984–88, 1988–; Minister of the Econ., of Finance and Privatization 1986–88; Prime Minister of France 1993–95; Presidential Cand. 1995; Comm. on Foreign Affairs, Nat. Ass. 2002–; mem. Nat. Ass.; Chevalier, Légion d'honneur, Grand-Croix Ordre Nat. du Mérite. *Publications:* l'Arbre de mai 1979, Je crois en l'homme plus qu'en l'Etat 1987, Passion et longueur de temps (with others) 1989, Douze Lettres aux français trop tranquilles 1990, Des Modes et des convictions 1992, Dictionnaire de la réforme 1992, L'Action pour la réforme 1995, Deux ans à Matignon 1995, Caractère de la France 1997, L'Avenir de la différence 1999, Renaissance de la droite, pour une alternance décomplexée 2000. *Address:* Conseil d'Etat, 75100 Paris; Assemblée Nationale, 126 rue de l'Université, 75355 Paris, France.

BALLARD, J. G. (James Graham); British novelist and short story writer; b. 15 Nov. 1930, Shanghai, China; s. of the late James Ballard and Edna Ballard (née Johnstone); m. Helen Mary Mathews 1954 (died 1964); one s. two d.; ed Leys School, Cambridge and King's Coll. Cambridge. *Publications:* The Drowned World 1963, The 4-Dimensional Nightmare 1963, The Terminal Beach 1964, The Drought 1965, The Crystal World 1966, The Disaster Area 1967, The Atrocity Exhibition 1970, Crash 1973, Vermillion Sands 1973, Concrete Island 1974, High Rise 1975, Low-Flying Aircraft 1976, The Unlimited Dream Company 1979, Myths of the Near Future 1982, Empire of the Sun 1984, The Venus Hunters 1986, The Day of Creation 1987, Running Wild 1988, Memories of the Space Age 1988, War Fever 1990, The Kindness of Women 1991, The Terminal Beach (short stories) 1992, Rushing to Paradise 1994, A Users' Guide to the Millennium 1996, Cocaine Nights 1996, Super-Cannes 2000, The Complete Short Stories 2001. *Address:* 36 Old Charlton Road, Shepperton, Middx, TW17 8AT, England. *Telephone:* (1932) 225692.

BALLARD, Robert D., PhD; American oceanographer; b. 30 June 1942, Wichita, Kan.; Barbara Earle Ballard; two s. one d.; ed Univs of California, Southern California, Hawaii and Rhode Island; 2nd Lt, US Army Intelligence 1965–67, later transferred to USN 1967–70; served with USN during Vietnam War, Consultant, Deputy Chief of Naval Operations for Submarine Warfare 1984–90, Consultant, Nat. Research Council, Marine Bd Comm. 1984–87, Commdr USNR 1987–2001; Research Assoc. Woods Hole Oceanographic Inst., Cape Cod, Mass. 1969–74, Asst Scientist 1974–76, Assoc. Scientist 1976–83, Sr Scientist 1983–, Founder Deep Submergence Laboratory 1983–, Dir Center for Marine Exploration 1989–95, Emer. 1997–; Visiting Scholar, Stanford Univ. 1979–80, Consulting Prof. 1980–81; Founder and Chair. Jason Foundation for Educ. 1989–; Founder Inst. for Exploration, Mystic, Conn. 1995–, Pres. 1997–; Founder and Pres. Immersion Inst. 2001–; Prof. of Oceanography, URI 2002–; has led or participated in over 100 deep-sea expeditions including discoveries of German battleship Bismarck, RMS Titanic 1985, warships from lost fleet of Guadalcanal, the Lusitania, Roman ships off coast of Tunisia 1997, USS Yorktown 1998; expeditions included first manned exploration of Mid-ocean Ridge, discovery of warm water springs and their fauna in Galapagos Rift, first discovery of polymetallic sulphides; has participated in numerous educ. programmes with major TV networks in Europe, Japan and USA, hosted Nat. Geographic Explorer show 1989–91; Hon. Dir Explorers Club 1988–, Hon. Dir Sigma Pi Sigma, Physics Soc. 1996–; Dr hc Clark Univ. 1986, Univ. of Rhode Island 1986, Southeastern Massachusetts Univ. 1986, Long Island Univ. 1987, Univ. of Bath, UK 1988, Tufts Univ. 1990, Lenoir-Rhyne Coll. 1991, Skidmore Coll. 1992, Worcester Polytechnic Inst. 1992, Bridgewater State Coll. 1993, Lehigh Univ. 1993, Maine Maritime Acad. 1994, Massachusetts Maritime Acad. 1994, Univ. of Wisconsin 2000, Univ. of Hartford 2001, Univ. of Delaware 2001; Distinguished Mil. Grad., US Army 1967, Newcomb-Cleveland Award (American Asscn for the Advancement of Science) 1981, Nat.Geographic Soc. Centennial Award 1988, American Geological Inst. Award 1990, USN Robert Dexter Conrad Award 1992, The Kilby Award 1994, Explorers Medal (Explorers Club) 1995, Nat. Geographic Soc. Hubbard Medal 1996, USN Memorial Foundation Lone Sailor Award 1996, NII Award for Best Internet Site for Education 1996, American Geophysical Union 'Excellence in Geophysical Education' Award 1997, Commonwealth Award 2000, Lindbergh Award 2001, The Navy League Award Robert M. Thompson Award for Outstanding Leadership 2001; numerous other awards and prizes. *Films:* Secrets of the Titanic (Int. Film Festival Award) 1987, Search for Battleship Bismarck (Emmy Award for Best Docu-

mentary) 1990, Last Voyage of the Lusitania (Emmy Award for Best Documentary) 1994. *Publications:* Photographic Atlas of the Mid-Atlantic Ridge 1977, The Discovery of the Titanic (with Rick Archbold) (New York Times and The Times No. 1 Best Seller 1987) 1987, The Discovery of the Bismarck (New York Times and The Times No. 1 Best Seller 1990) 1990, , Bright Shark (novel) 1992, The Lost Ships of Guadalcanal (with Rick Archbold) 1993, Explorations (autobiog.) 1995, Exploring the Lusitania (with Spencer Dunmore) 1995, Lost Liners (with Rick Archbold) 1997, Return to Midway 1999, The Water's Edge 1999, Eternal Darkness: A Personal History of Deep-Sea Exploration (with Will Hively) 2000, Graveyards of the Pacific 2001, Adventures in Ocean Exploration 2001; non-fiction for children: Exploring the Titanic (Virginia State Reading Asscn Young Readers Award 1993) 1988, The Lost Wreck of the Isis 1990, Exploring the Bismarck 1991, Explorer 1992, Ghost Liners 1998; Deep Sea Explorer (CD-ROM) 1999; has also published more than 57 articles in scientific journals and numerous popular articles. *Address:* Institute for Exploration, 55 Coogan Boulevard, Mystic, CT 06355, USA. *Telephone:* (860) 572-5955 ext. 602 (Office). *E-mail:* lbradt@ife.org (Office). *Website:* ife.org (Office).

BALLE, Francis, DèsSc, PhD; French professor; b. 15 June 1939, Fourmies; s. of Marcel Balle and Madeleine (née Leprohon) Balle; m. Marie Derieux 1972; three d.; ed Inst. d'Etudes Politiques, Univ. de Paris-Sorbonne; philosophy teacher Ecole Normale d'Oran 1963–65; Asst Lecturer Faculté des Lettres, Ecole de Journalisme, Algiers 1965–67, Univ. de Paris-Sorbonne 1967–70, Univ. René Descartes, Univ. Paris VI 1970–72; Lecturer Univ. de Droit, d'Econ. et de Sciences Sociales 1972, Prof. 1978–; Pres. statistical Cttee for TV action outside France 1997–; Dir Inst. Français de Presse 1976–83, Inst. de Recherche et d'Etudes sur la Communication 1986–; Vice-Chancellor Univs. de Paris 1986–89; Visiting Prof. Univ. of Stanford, Calif. 1981–83; Dir Information and New Techs. at Ministry of Nat. Educ. 1993–95, of Scientific Information, Tech. and of Libraries 1995–; Dir French Media Inst. 1997; Prize of Acad. des Sciences Morales et Politiques for Médias et Sociétés 1995; Officier Ordre National de la Légion d'honneur, Palmes académiques. *Publications:* Médias et Sociétés 1980, The Media Revolution in America and Western Europe 1984, Les nouveaux médias (with Gerard Eymery) 1987, Et si la Presse n'existait pas 1987, La Télévision 1987, Le Mandarin et le marchand 1995, Dictionnaire des médias 1998, Les Médias 2000, Dictionnaire du Web 2002. *Leisure interests:* music, painting. *Address:* 83 bis rue Notre Dame des Champs, 75006 Paris (Office); 18 rue Greuze, 75116 Paris, France (Home). *Telephone:* 1-44-41-59-28 (Office); 1-47-27-78-31 (Home). *Fax:* 1-43-26-15-78.

BALLESTEROS SOTA, Severiano; Spanish golfer; b. 9 April 1957, Pedreña, Santander; s. of Baldomero Ballesteros Presmanes and Carmen Sota Ocejo; m. Carmen Botin Sanz 1988; two s. one d.; professional 1974–; won Spanish Young Professional title 1974; 72 int. titles; won Dutch Open and two major European tournaments and, with Manuel Pinero, World Cup 1976; won Opens of France, Switzerland and Japan, four other major tournaments in Europe, Japan and New Zealand and World Cup, with Antonio Garrido 1977; won Opens of Japan, Germany, Kenya, Scandinavia and Switzerland and tournament in USA 1978; British Open Champion (youngest this century) 1979, 1984, 1988; second European and youngest ever winner US Masters 1980; World Matchplay Title 1981, 1982, 1984, 1985; tied Gary Player's record of five victories in World Matchplay with his fifth win 1991; winner US Masters 1980, 1983, Henry Vardon Trophy 1976, 1977, 1978, 1986, Ryder Cup 1979, 1983, 1985, 1987, British/Volvo PGA Championship 1983, 1991, Mallorca Open 1988, 1990, 1991, British Masters 1991, Dubai Open 1992; acted in film Escape to Paradise 1987; mem. Laurens World Sports Acad.; resident of Monaco; Príncipe de Asturias Award 1989; Dr hc (St Andrews) 2000. *Publication:* Trouble Shooting 1996. *Leisure interests:* ping-pong, chess, fitness, shooting, reading, music. *Address:* Fairway, SA, Pasaje de Peña 2-4°, 39008 Santander, Spain; Houston Palace, 7 Avenue Princess Grace, 39009 Monte Carlo, Monaco. *Telephone:* (42) 31-45-12 (Spain). *Fax:* (42) 31-45-59 (Spain).

BALLIN, Ernst Hirsch (see Hirsch Ballin, Ernst).

BALLMER, Steve; American business executive; m. Connie Ballmer; three c.; ed Harvard Univ., Stanford Univ.; fmr accountant; Asst Product Man. Procter & Gamble, Vice-Pres. Marketing; Sr Vice-Pres. Systems Software, Microsoft Corpn, Redmond, WA 1980–, Exec. Vice-Pres. Sales and Support, Pres. 1998, CEO Jan. 2000–; Dir Accenture 2001–. *Leisure interests:* exercise, basketball. *Address:* Microsoft Corporation, 1 Microsoft Way, Redmond, WA 98052-8300, USA (Office).

BALLS, Ed(ward); British economist; b. 25 Feb. 1967; s. of Prof. Michael Balls and Carolyn J. Balls; m. Yvette Cooper 1998; one s. one d.; ed Nottingham High School, Keble Coll., Oxford, Harvard Univ.; fmr Teaching Fellow, Dept of Econs, Harvard Univ., fmr Research Asst Nat. Bureau of Econ. Research, USA; econs leader writer, Financial Times 1990–94; econs columnist, The Guardian 1994–97; Econ. Adviser to Gordon Brown (q.v.) 1994–97; Chief Econ. Adviser to HM Treasury 1999–; mem. Council Royal Econ. Soc.; Ed. European Econ. Policy 1994–97; Young Financial Journalist of the Year, Wincott Foundation 1992. *Publication:* Reforming Britain's Economic and Financial Policy (co-ed.) 2001. *Address:* HM Treasury, 1 Horse Guards Road, London, SW1A 2HQ, England (Office). *Telephone:* (20) 7270-4941 (Office). *Fax:* (20) 7270-4836 (Office). *E-mail:* ed.balls@hm-treasury.gov.uk (Office). *Website:* www.hm-treasury.gov.uk (Office).

BALOGUN, Kolawole, Chief Jagun of Otan, LLB, PhD; Nigerian politician, lawyer and diplomatist; b. 1926, Osun, Oyo State; s. of Moses and Marian Balogun; ed Govt Coll., Ibadan; on staff of Nigerian Advocate, later radio announcer, then Asst Ed. West African Pilot; legal studies in London 1948–51, called to the Bar 1951; Sec. London br. Nat. Council of Nigeria and the Cameroons (NCNC) 1951; Nat. Sec. NCNC 1951–57; mem. of Fed. Parl. 1954; Fed. Minister without Portfolio 1955, of Information 1955–58; resigned from Govt 1958; Nigerian Commr in Ghana 1959–60, High Commr 1960–61; fmr mem. of Ministry of Foreign Affairs; Chair, Nigerian Nat. Shipping Line 1962–65; Commr for Econ. Planning and Social Devt, Mil. Govt of W Nigeria 1967; Commr for Educ. 1968–70. *Publications:* Government in Old Oyo Empire 1985, Osun State: Story of Its Creation 1992, Nigeria: June 12 Election 1996. *Leisure interests:* reading and writing. *Address:* Maye Lodge, P.O. Box 50, Osogbo, Nigeria. *Telephone:* (35) 234703.

BALSAI, István, DIur; Hungarian politician; b. 5 April 1947, Miskolc; s. of József Balsai and Mária Szalontai; m. Ilona Schmidt; two s.; chemical laboratory Asst 1966; Eötvös Loránd Univ. Budapest faculty of political and legal sciences 1967–72; worked as adviser to Lawyers Asscn, Budapest; mem. Hungarian Democratic Forum 1988; mem. of Parl. 1990–; Minister of Justice 1990–94; leader of splinter group in Hungarian Democratic Forum 1998–; founding mem. Asscn of Christian Intellectuals 1989–. *Leisure interest:* folk architecture. *Address:* Széchenyi rkp. 19, 1054 Budapest, Hungary. *Telephone:* (1) 441-5139. *Fax:* (1) 441-5978 (Office). *E-mail:* istvan.balsai@mdf .parlament.hu (Office). *Website:* www.mdf.hu (Office).

BALSEMÃO, Francisco Pinto (see Pinto Balsemão).

BALTIMORE, David, PhD; American biologist; b. 7 March 1938, New York, NY; s. of Richard Baltimore and Gertrude Lipschitz; m. Alice Huang 1968; one d.; ed Swarthmore Coll. and Rockefeller Univ.; Postdoctoral Fellow, Mass. Inst. of Technology (MIT) 1963–64, Albert Einstein Coll. of Medicine, New York 1964–65; Research Assoc., Salk Inst., La Jolla, Calif. 1965–68; Assoc. Prof., MIT 1968–72, Prof. of Microbiology 1972–95; Ivan R. Cottrell Prof. of Molecular Biology and Immunology MIT 1994–97; Inst. Prof. MIT 1995–97; American Cancer Soc. Prof. of Microbiology 1973–83, 1994–97; Dir Whitehead Inst. for Biomedical Research 1982–90; Pres. Rockefeller Univ. 1990–91, Prof. 1990–94; Pres. Calif. Inst. of Tech. 1997–; mem. Nat. Insts. of Health Advisory Council on AIDS research, Chair. Vaccine Cttee 1997–2002; Eli Lilly Award in Microbiology and Immunology 1971, US Steel Foundation Award in Molecular Biology 1974, Nobel Prize 1975, Nat. Medal of Science 1999, Warren Alpert Foundation Prize 2000, American Medical Asscn Scientific Achievement Award 2002. *Address:* California Institute of Technology, MC 204-31, 1200 East California Boulevard, Pasadena, CA 91125-3100, USA (Office). *Telephone:* (626) 395-6301 (Office). *Fax:* (626) 449-9374 (Office). *E-mail:* baltimo@caltech.edu (Office).

BALTSA, Agnes; Greek opera singer; b. Lefkas; ed Acad. of Music, Athens and in Munich (Maria Callas Scholarship); opera debut as Cherubino, Frankfurt 1968; debut at Vienna State Opera (Octavian) 1970, Salzburg Festival 1970, La Scala, Milan (Dorabella) 1976, Paris Opera and Covent Garden, London (Cherubino) 1976, Metropolitan Opera, New York (Octavian) 1980; mem. Deutsche Oper Berlin 1973–; performs at all maj. opera houses in world and has given concerts in Europe, USA and Japan with Karajan, Böhm, Bernstein, Muti, etc.; Österreichische Kammersängerin 1980; has made about 30 operatic recordings; Deutscher Schallplattenpreis 1983, Prix Prestige Lyrique (French Ministry of Culture) 1984. *Leisure interests:* swimming, fashion. *Address:* c/o Management Rita Schültz, Rütistr 52, 8044 Zurich-Gockhausen, Switzerland.

BALUYEVSKY, Col.-Gen. Yuri Nikolayevich; Russian army officer; b. 9 Jan. 1947, Truskavets, Drogobych Region, Ukraine; ed Leningrad Higher Mil. Command School of Gen. Army, M. Frunze Mil. Acad., Mil. Acad. of Gen. Staff; infantry officer 1970–82; Sr officer, operator, Head of Group Chief Operation Dept of Gen. Staff; First Deputy Commdr of Group of Russian Forces in Caucasus; Deputy Head Chief Operation Dept of Gen. Staff 1982–2001, first Deputy Head of Gen. Staff 2001–; Order for Service to Motherland in Armed Forces, Order of Audacity, 9 medals. *Address:* Ministry of Defence, Znamenka str. 19, 103160 Moscow, Russia (Office). *Telephone:* (095) 293-80-20 (Office).

BAMBANG YUDHOYONO, Lt-Gen. Susilo, MA; Indonesian politician; b. 1949, East Java; m.; ed Indonesian Mil. Acad. and Webster Univ., USA; participated in Operation Seroja (invasion of Timor Leste) and commanded Dili-based Battalion 744 1970s; spent much of mil. career with Kostrad airborne units; mil. training in USA and Europe 1980s–90s; lectured at Army Staff Command Coll. (Seskoad) 1980s; worked in territorial commands in Jakarta and S. Sumatra (Pangdam II/Sriwijaya) mid 1990s; Chief Mil. Observer in Bosnia 1995–96; Chief of the Armed Forces Social and Political Affairs Staff (Kassospol Abri) (renamed Chief of Territorial Affairs (Kaster) Nov. 1998) 1997–2000; retd from active mil. service 2000; Minister of Mines 1999–2000; Co-ordinating Minister for Political Affairs, Security and Social Welfare 2000–. *Address:* Office of the Co-ordinating Minister for Political Affairs, Security and Social Welfare, Jalan Medan Merdeka Barat 15, Jakarta 10110, Indonesia (Office). *Telephone:* (21) 3849453 (Office). *Fax:* (21) 3450918 (Office).

BAMERT, Matthias; Swiss conductor; b. 5 July 1942, Ersigen; m. Susan Exline 1969; one s. one d.; Asst conductor to Leopold Stokowski 1970–71; Resident Conductor Cleveland Orchestra 1971–78; Music Dir Swiss Radio Orchestra, Basel 1977–83; Prin. Guest Conductor Scottish Nat. Orchestra 1985–90; Dir Musica Nova Festival, Glasgow 1985–90, Lucerne Festival 1992–98; Music Dir London Mozart Players 1993–2000; has appeared with Orchestre de Paris, Rotterdam Philharmonic, Cleveland Orchestra, Pittsburgh Symphony, Montreal Symphony, Royal Philharmonic Orchestra, London, London Philharmonic Orchestra, BBC Philharmonic, City of Birmingham Symphony Orchestra and at BBC Promenade Concerts, London; has toured world-wide. *Address:* c/o Scottish National Orchestra, 3 La Belle Place, Glasgow, G3 7LH, Scotland (Office).

BAMFORD, Sir Anthony (Paul), Kt; British construction executive; b. 23 Oct. 1945; s. of the late Joseph Cyril Bamford and of Marjorie Griffin; m. Carole Gray Whitt 1974; two s. one d.; ed Ampleforth Coll., Grenoble Univ.; joined JCB 1962, Chair. and Man. Dir 1975–; Dir Tarmac 1987–94; Pres. Staffs. Agricultural Soc. 1987–88, Burton-upon-Trent Conservative Asscn 1987–90; Pres.'s Cttee CBI 1986–88; mem. Design Council 1987–89; DL Staffs., High Sheriff Staffs. 1985–86; Chevalier Ordre nat. du Mérite 1989, Commendatore della Repubblica Italiana 1995; Hon. MEng (Birmingham) 1987; DUniv (Keele) 1988; Hon. DSc (Cranfield) 1994; Hon. DBA (Rober Gordon Univ., Aberdeen) 1996; Hon. DTech (Staffordshire) 1998, (Loughborough) 2002; Young Exporter of the Year (UK) 1972, Young Businessman of the Year (UK) 1979, Top Exporter of the Year (UK) 1995. *Leisure interests:* farming, gardening. *Address:* c/o J. C. Bamford Excavators Ltd, Rocester, Uttoxeter, Staffs., ST14 5JP, England.

BAN, Shigeru, BArch; Japanese architect and lecturer; b. 5 Aug. 1957, Tokyo; ed Southern Calif. Inst. of Architecture, CA, Cooper Union, NY, USA; worked for Arata Isozaki, Tokyo 1982–83; est. Shigeru Ban Architects, Tokyo 1985; Consultant UNHCR 1995; est. Voluntary Architects Network (VAN) 1995; Adjunct Prof. of Architecture Tokohama Nat. Univ. 1995–99, Nihon Univ. 1996–2000; Visiting Prof. Columbia Univ., NY, USA 2000; Prof. of Architecture Keio Univ. 2001–; 3rd Kansai Architect Grand Prize, Japan Inst. of Architecture (JIA) 1996, Best Young Architect of the Year, JIA 1997, 18th Tohoku Architecture Prize, Architectural Inst. of Japan 1998, Best Designer of the Year, Interior Magazine 2000, Best Architecture of the Year in Europe, World Architecture Awards 2001, Matsui Gengo Award 2001, Best House of the Year, World Architectural Awards 2002. *Architectural works include:* House of Double Roof 1993, MDS Gallery 1994, Curtain Wall House 1995, Furniture House 1995, Paper Church 1995, Paper Loghouse 1995, Tazawako Station 1997, Wall-less House 1997, 9 Square Grid House 1997, Hanegi Forest 1997, Paper Dome 1998, Ivy Structure House 1998, Japan Pavilion for Expo 2000 Hanover 2000, A Paper Arch, Museum of Modern Art Courtyard, NY 2000, GC Osaka Bldg 2000, Naked House 2000, Day-Care Center 2001, Gymnasium 2001, Paper Art Museum (PAM) 2002. *Publications include:* Shigeru Ban 1997, Ban Shigeru 1998, Paper Tube Architecture from Kobe to Rwanda 1998, Shigeru Ban—Projects in Progress 1999, Shigeru Ban 2001. *Address:* Shigeru Ban Architects, 5-2-4 Matsubara Ban Building, First Floor, Setagaya, Tokyo 156-0043, Japan (Office). *Telephone:* (3) 3324-6760 (Office). *Fax:* (3) 3324-6789 (Office). *E-mail:* SBA@tokyo.email.ne.jp (Office). *Website:* www.dnp.co.jp/millenium/SB/VAN.html (Office).

BANANA, Rev. Dr Canaan Sodindo, BA, MTS; Zimbabwean nationalist leader and ecclesiastic; b. 5 March 1936, Esiphezini, Essexvale Dist; s. of Aaron Banana and Zibiya Banana; m. Janet Mbuyazwe 1961; three s. one d.; ed Tegwani Training Inst., Epworth Theological Coll., Kansai Industrial Centre, Japan, Wesley Theological Seminary, USA, Univ. of SA; Chaplain, Tegwani High School 1965–66; ordained Methodist at Epworth 1966; Prin. Matjinke Boarding School 1966; Chair. Bulawayo Council of Churches 1969–70, Southern Africa Urban Industrial Mission 1970–73; founder mem. and Vice-Pres. African Nat. Council (ANC) 1971–73; ANC rep. in USA and UN 1973–75; Chaplain American Univ. 1974–75; detained 1975–76; Press Spokesman for ANC 1976; attended Geneva Conf. on Rhodesia 1976; founder mem. and publicity sec. People's Movt 1976; in detention several times and publs banned in Rhodesia; Pres. Repub. of Zimbabwe 1980–87; f. Mushandira Pamure Project 1980; f. Kushinga-Phikelela Agric. Inst. 1981; Chancellor of Univ. of Zimbabwe 1983–88; led World Council of Churches Eminent Church Persons sanctions against SA 1989; Co-Chair. UN Panel on the operations of transnat. corpns in SA 1989; Prof. of Classics, Religious Studies and Philosophy, Univ. of Zimbabwe 1989–; convicted on 11 charges of homosexual abuse 1998; sentenced to ten years' imprisonment, nine suspended conditionally, sentenced to one year's imprisonment after appeal May 2000, released 2001; Hon. LLD (American Univ., Univ. of Zimbabwe). *Publications:* The Zimbabwe Exodus, The Gospel According to the Ghetto, Theology of Promise, The Woman of My Imagination, The Ethos of Socialism 1987. *Leisure interests:* soccer, table tennis, lawn tennis. *Address:* c/o State House, Box 368, Harare, Zimbabwe. *Telephone:* (4) 26666.

BANBURY, (Frederick Harold) Frith, MBE; British theatrical director, actor and manager; b. 4 May 1912, Plymouth; s. of Rear Admiral Frederick Arthur Frith Banbury and Winifred Fink; ed Stowe School, Oxford Univ. and Royal Acad. Dramatic Art; made first stage appearance 1933 and appeared on the London stage, in plays and on television until 1947; has since concentrated on direction. *Plays directed include:* Dark Summer 1947, The Holly and the Ivy 1950, Waters of the Moon 1951, The Deep Blue Sea 1951, Morosco (New York) 1952, A Question of Fact 1953, Marching Song 1954, Love's Labours Lost, (Old Vic) 1954, The Diary of Anne Frank 1956, A Dead Secret 1957, Flowering Cherry 1957, A Touch of the Sun 1958, The Ring of Truth 1959, The Tiger and the Horse 1960, The Wings of the Dove 1963, The

Right Honourable Gentleman (New York) 1965, Howards End 1967, Dear Octopus 1967, Enter a Free Man 1968, My Darling Daisy 1970, The Winslow Boy 1970, Captain Brassbound's Conversion 1971, Reunion in Vienna 1972, The Day After the Fair 1972, In USA 1973, Glasstown 1973, Ardèle 1975, Family Matter 1976, On Approval 1977, Motherdear 1980, Dear Liar 1982, The Aspern Papers 1984, The Corn is Green 1985, The Admirable Crichton 1988, Screamers 1989, The Gin Game 1999, Savoy 1999 and others in New York, Paris, Tel Aviv, Toronto, Hong Kong, Johannesburg, Nairobi, Sydney, Melbourne. *Leisure interest:* playing the piano. *Address:* 18 Park St James, Prince Albert Road, London, NW8 7LE, England.

BANCROFT, Anne; American actress; b. 17 Sept. 1931, New York; d. of Michael Italiano and Mildred (née DiNapoli) Italiano; m. 2nd Mel Brooks (q.v.) 1964; one s.; ed Christopher Columbus High School, New York; numerous TV appearances; Academy Award for film The Miracle Worker 1962, Golden Globe Award 1968, Emmy Award for Annie, the Woman in the Life of a Man 1970, Lifetime Achievement in Comedy Award, American Comedy Awards 1996. *Theatre:* Broadway debut in Two for the Seesaw 1958, played Anne Sullivan in The Miracle Worker 1959–60; A Cry of Prayers 1968, Golda 1977, The Devils 1977, Mystery of the Rose Bouquet 1989. *Films:* The Miracle Worker, Don't Bother to Knock, Tonight We Sing, Demetrius and the Gladiators, The Pumpkin Eater, Seven Women, The Graduate 1968, Young Winston 1971, The Prisoner of Second Avenue 1974, The Hindenburg 1975, Lipstick 1976, Silent Movie 1976, The Turning Point 1977, Silent Movie, Fatso (also Dir and screenwriter), The Elephant Man 1980, To Be or Not to Be 1984, Agnes of God 1985, 84 Charing Cross Road 1986, Torch Song Trilogy 1989, Bert Rigby You're a Fool 1989, Broadway Bound 1992, How to Make An American Quilt 1995, Home for the Holidays 1995, The Homecoming 1996, Sunchasers 1997, GI Jane 1997, Critical Care 1997, Great Expectations 1998, Antz 1998 (voice only), Twain's America in 3D 1998, Up at the Villa 1999, Deep in My Heart 1999. *Address:* c/o The Culver Studios, 9336 W Washington Boulevard, Culver City, CA 90232, USA.

BANDA, Aleke Kadonaphani; Malawi politician and journalist; b. 19 Sept. 1939, Livingstone, Zambia; s. of Eliazar G. Banda and Lilian Phiri; m. Mbumba M. Kahumbe 1961; two s. one d.; ed United Missionary School, Que Que and Inyati School, Bulawayo; Sec. Nyasaland African Congress (NAC), Que Que Branch 1954; Gen. Sec. S. Rhodesia African Students Assen 1957–59; arrested and detained in Rhodesia 1959, deported to Nyasaland; Founder-mem. Malawi Congress Party (MCP), Sec.-Gen. 1959–73, mem. 1974–; Ed. Nyasaland TUC newspaper Ntendere Pa Nchito and mem. TUC Council 1959–60; Personal Political Sec. to Dr. Hastings Banda 1960–73; Sec. MCP Del. to Lancaster House Conf. resulting in self-govt for Malawi 1960; Sec. to subsequent confs. 1960, 1962; Man. Ed. Malawi News 1959–66; Dir Malawi Press Ltd 1960; Dir-Gen. Malawi Broadcasting Corpn 1964–66; Nat. Chair. League of Malawi Youth and Commdr Malawi Young Pioneers 1963–73; Dir Reserve Bank of Malawi 1965–66; Minister of Devt and Planning 1966–67, of Econ. Affairs (incorporating Natural Resources, Trade and Industry and Devt and Planning) and Minister of Works and Supplies 1967–68, of Trade and Industry (incorporating Tourism, Information and Broadcasting) 1968–69, of Finance and of Information and Tourism 1969–72, of Trade, Industry and Tourism 1972–73; dismissed from Cabinet posts and party 1973, reinstated as mem. party 1974; detained without trial 1980–92; First Vice-Pres. and Campaign Chair. United Democratic Front (UDF) Party 1993–; Minister of Finance, Econ. Planning and Devt 1994–97, of Agric. and Irrigation 1997–2000, 2001–, of Health and Population 2000–01; fmr Chair. Nat. Bank of Malawi. *Leisure interest:* tennis. *Address:* Ministry of Agriculture and Irrigation, PO Box 30134, Capital City, Lilongwe 3, Malawi (Office). *Telephone:* 788513 (Office). *Fax:* 789380 (Office).

BANDAR BIN SULTAN BIN ABDULAZIZ AL-SAUD, HRH Prince, MA; Saudi Arabian diplomatist and army officer; b. 2 March 1949, Taif; s. of HRH Prince Sultan bin Abdulaziz al-Saud; m. HRH Princess Haifa bint Faisal bin Abdulaziz al-Saud; four s. four d.; ed RAF Coll., Cranwell, USAF Advanced Program and Johns Hopkins Univ.; fighter pilot, Royal Saudi Air Force 1969–82; in charge of special Saudi Arabian liaison mission to USA for purchase of AWACS and other defence equipment 1981; Defence and Mil. Attaché, Saudi Arabian Mil. Mission to USA 1982–83; Amb. to USA 1983–. *Leisure interests:* flying, racquetball, reading. *Address:* Royal Embassy of Saudi Arabia, 601 New Hampshire Avenue, NW, Washington, DC 20037, USA (Office). *Telephone:* (202) 342-3800 (Office). *Fax:* (202) 944-5983 (Office). *E-mail:* info@saudiembassy.net (Office). *Website:* www.saudiembassy.net (Office).

BANDEEN, Robert Angus, OC, PhD, LLD, DCL, KStJ; Canadian company executive; b. 29 Oct. 1930, Rodney, Ont.; s. of John Robert and Jessie Marie (Thomson) Bandeen; m. Mona Helen Blair 1958; four s.; ed Univ. of Western Ontario and Duke Univ., USA; joined Canadian Nat. Railways 1955, Research and Devt Dept 1955–66, Dir of Corporate Planning 1966–68, Vice-Pres. Corporate Planning and Finance 1968–71, Vice-Pres. Great Lakes Region, Toronto 1971–72, Exec. Vice-Pres. Finance and Admin. 1972–74, Pres. 1974–82, CEO 1974–82; Pres. and Chair., Crown Life Insurance Co. 1982–84, Chair. and CEO 1984–85; Pres. Crownx Inc. 1984–85, Vice-Chair. 1985–86; Pres. and CEO Cluny Corpn 1986–; Dir numerous cos; fmr Chair. Counsel Life Insurance Co., Cytex Inc.; fmr Chancellor Bishop's Univ., Lennoxville, Québec; Gov. Olympic Trust of Canada; Senator Stratford Shakespearean Festival Foundation; Hon. LLD (W Ont.) 1975, (Dalhousie) 1978, (Queens) 1982; Hon. DCL (Bishops) 1978; Salzberg Medal (Syracuse

Univ.) 1982. *Leisure interests:* tennis, skiing. *Address:* Cluny Corpn, #305 1166 Bay Street, Toronto, Ont., M5S 2X8, Canada. *Telephone:* (416) 922-8238. *Fax:* (416) 928-2729.

BANDEIRA DE MELLO, Lydio Machado, DJur; Brazilian university professor emeritus; b. 19 July 1901, Abaete, Minas Gerais; s. of Dr. Lydio Alerano and Adélia Machado Bandeira de Mello; m. Amália Introcaso Bandeira de Mello 1928; two s. two d.; ed Univ. of Brazil; Prof. of Criminal Law, Univ. of Minas Gerais 1952–71, Comparative Criminal Law 1959–71, Prof. Emer. 1972–. *Publications:* O Problema do Mal 1935, A Procura de Deus 1938, Responsabilidade Penal 1941, Prova Matemática da Existência de Deus 1942, Teoria do Destino 1944, Metafísica do Número 1946, A Predestinação Para O Bem 1948, Tabu, Pecado e Crime 1949, Dezessete Aventuras no Reino de Deus 1952, O Real e o Possível 1953, Manual de Direito Penal (Vols 1-4) 1953–58, A Origem dos Sexos 1955, Filosofia do Direito 1957, Ontologia e Lógica da Contradição 1959, Metafísica do Tempo 1961, O Direito Penal Hispano-Luso Medievo (2 Vols) 1961, Tratado de Direito Penal, Crime e Exclusão de Criminalidade 1962, Da Responsabilidade Penal e Da Isenção de Pena 1962, Da Capitulação dos Crimes e da Fixação das Penas 1963, Metafísica da Gravitação 1963, Memória Espaço e Tempo (2 Vols) 1963, Cosmologia do Movimento 1965, Teologia Matemática 1965, Metafísica do Espaço 1966, A Pluralidade de Consciências 1967, Crítica Cosmológica de Física Quântica 1968, Fórmulas Gerais da Distribuição de Probabilidades 1968, Evangelho para Bacharéis 1969, O Criminoso, O Crime e a Pena 1970, Trabalhos de Algoritmia (Aritmética e Algebra) Superior 1971, A Existência e a Imortalidade da Alma 1972, As Credenciais da Razão 1973, Teoria Algébrica das Permutações Condicionadas 1972, Crítica do Principio de Razão Suficiente 1974, A Falibilidade da Indução 1974, A Conquista do Reino de Deus (2 Vols) 1975, O Possível Puro 1975, Cosmologia Científica 1976, Metafísica da Sensação 1977, A Matemática do Universo e a Matemática Dos Homens 1978, Voluntariedade da Vinda dos Homens para a Terra (A Genética Experimental 1979) 1980, Deus e cada Homem 1980, Sem Angústia Diante de Deus 1982, O Universo Físico Feito 1982, Para Receber Homens Livres 1982, Universos Abstratos em Possível Expansão Ilimitável 1983, Jesus meu Mestre 1984. *Leisure interests:* walking, cinema-going, philately. *Address:* Rua Rodrigues Caldas, 703 Belo Horizonte, Minas Gerais, Brazil. *Telephone:* (31) 3370198.

BANDERAS, Antonio; Spanish film actor; b. 1960, Málaga; m. 1st Anna Banderas; m. 2nd Melanie Griffith 1996; began acting aged 14; performed with Nat. Theatre, Madrid for six years. *Films include:* Labyrinth of Passion, El Señor Galíndez, El Caso Almería, The Stilts, 27 Hours, Law of Desire, Matador, Tie Me Up! Tie Me Down!, Women on the Verge of a Nervous Breakdown, The House of Spirits, Interview with the Vampire, Philadelphia, The Mambo Kings, Love and Shadow, Miami Rhapsody, Young Mussolini, Return of Mariaolu, Assassins, Desperado, Evita, The Mask of Zorro 1997, Never Talk to Strangers; Crazy in Alabama (Dir), The 13th Warrior, White River Kid (producer), Dancing in the Dark 2000, Malaga Burning (Dir) 2000, The Body 2000, Forever Lulu (producer) 2000, Spy Kids 2001, Femme Fatale 2002, Frida 2003. *Address:* c/o CAA, 9830 Wilshire Boulevard, Beverly Hills, CA 90212, USA; Agents Associés, 201 rue du Faubourg Saint-Honoré, 75008 Paris, France.

BANDLER, Donald K., MA, JD; American diplomatist; m. Jane Bandler; one s. two d.; ed Kenyon Coll., St John's Coll., George Washington Univ.; Dir 'Face to Face', Carnegie Endowment 1978–79; assignments in African Affairs and Congressional relations; Co-ordinator, Conf. on Security and Co-operation in Europe 1983–85; Head, Political-Mil. Affairs, Paris Embassy 1985–89; Counsellor for Political and Legal Affairs, Bonn 1989–93; Dir Israeli and Arab–Israeli Affairs, Dept of State 1994–95; Deputy Chief of Mission, then Chargé d'Affaires, Paris 1995–97; Special Asst to the Pres. and Sr Dir for European Affairs, Nat. Security Council 1997–99; Amb. to Cyprus 1999–; Légion d'honneur 1998, Superior Honor Award (four times). *Address:* American Embassy, 7 Ploutarchou, 2406 Engomi, Nicosia, Cyprus (Office). *Telephone:* (2) 776400 (Office). *Fax:* (2) 780944 (Office). *E-mail:* ambassador@spidernet.com.cy (Office). *Website:* www.americanembassy.org.cy (Office).

BANDLER, John William, PhD, DSc(Eng), FIEE, FRSC, FIEEE, FEIC; Canadian professor of electrical and computer engineering; b. 9 Nov. 1941, Jerusalem; m. 3rd Beth Budd 1990; two d.; ed Imperial Coll. London; Mullard Research Labs., Redhill, Surrey 1966; Univ. of Man. 1967–69; McMaster Univ. 1969, Prof. 1974, Prof. Emer. 2000; Chair. Dept of Electrical Eng, McMaster Univ. 1978–79, Dean of Faculty 1979–81, Dir of Research, Simulation Optimization Systems Research Lab. 1983–; Pres. Optimization Systems Assocs Inc. 1983–97, Bandler Corpn 1997–; ARFTG Automated Measurements Career Award for Automated Microwave Techniques 1994. *Publications:* more than 350 papers in journals and books and book chapters. *Address:* Department of Electrical and Computer Engineering, McMaster University, Hamilton, Ont., L8S 4K1, Canada. *Telephone:* (905) 525-9140 (Office). *Fax:* (905) 523-4407 (Office). *Website:* www.sos.mcmaster.ca (Office).

BANDLER, Vivica Aina Fanny; Finnish theatre director; b. 5 Feb. 1917, Helsingfors; d. of Erik von Frenckell and Ester Margaret Lindberg; m. Kurt Bandler; ed Univ. of Helsinki; with Helsingfors Student Theatre 1939; war service 1939–40, 1941–43; Asst film dir in France 1939, Sweden 1945–46; started as theatre Dir Swedish Theatre, Helsingfors 1948; Head, theatre section, Helsinki's 400th anniversary 1950; f. Peasants' Theatre Group, Kylänpojat 1951; Man., Prin. Dir Lilla Teatern, Helsingfors 1955–67, mem.

Bd 1983–; Man., Dir Oslo Nye Teater, Norway 1967–69; Head Stockholm City Theatre, Sweden 1969–80; theatre Dir Sweden and Finland 1980–; Artistic Dir Tampere Int. Theatre Festival, Finland 1989–95; Pres. Bd of Swedish Theatre Union/Swedish Int. Theatre Inst. (ITI) 1978–92, mem. Exec. Cttee ITI 1981–86, mem. Drama Cttee 1990–92; mem. Bd Nordic Theatre Union 1986–88; Pres. Theatre Acad. of Sweden, Stockholm 1992–2000; Patron Hangö Festival (Finland) 1996–97; Theatre Dir Eri Dance Theatre (Finland) 1989–; Hon. mem. Swedish Authors' Asscn in Finland, Union of Theatre Dirs., Finland; has written several dramatizations of novels, film scripts, musicals etc.; Golden Boot, awarded by daily newspaper Dagens Nyheter, Sweden, Medal of City of Stockholm, Medal of Swedish Parl. in Finland, August Award, Swedish Dramatists' Asscn, Letterstedt Foundation Medal for Nordic Co-operation, Thalia Award, Swedish Actors' Asscn, Finland Prize; Memory Medal of War 1939–40, Commdr of Finnish Lion, Pro Finlandis (Finland), Commdr Northern Star of Sweden. *Publications:* Adressaten okänd (Addressee Unknown) (with Carita Backström) 1992; articles about theatre, translations of plays, etc. *Leisure interests:* mice and men. *Address:* Villagatan 1 B, SF-00150 Helsinki, Finland. *Telephone:* (9) 635483 (Finland).

BANFIELD, Jillian Fiona, PhD; Australian professor of geology; b. 18 Aug. 1959, Armidale, NSW; d. of James E. Banfield and Eve Banfield; m. Perry Smith; two s. one d.; ed Australian Nat. Univ., Johns Hopkins Univ., USA; exploration geologist, Western Mining Corpn 1982–83; Asst Prof., Dept of Geology and Geophysics, Univ. of Wis., Madison 1990–95, Assoc. Prof. 1995–99, Prof. 1999–2001, Dept of Chem. 1998–2001; Prof. Dept of Earth and Planetary Science, Univ. of Calif., Berkeley 2001–; Prof. Dept of Environmental Science, Policy and Man. 2001–; Assoc. Prof. Mineralogical Inst., Univ. of Tokyo 1996–97, Prof. 1998; John D. and Catherine T. MacArthur Foundation Fellow 1999–(2004); John Simon Guggenheim Foundation Fellowship 2000; Distinguished Lecturer, Mineralogical Soc. of America 1994–95, Fellow 1997–; Gast Lecturer, Geochemical Soc. 2000; NSF Earth Science Week Lecturer (Inaugural) 2000; Geological Soc. of Australia Prize 1978, Award for Outstanding Research, Dept of Energy, USA 1995, Mineralogical Soc. of America Award 1997, D. A. Brown Medal, A.N.U. 1999 and several other prizes and awards. *Publications:* numerous scientific papers. *Address:* Department of Earth and Planetary Sciences and Department of Environmental Science, Policy and Managment, 369 McCone Hall, University of California Berkeley, Berkeley, CA 94720-4767, USA (Office). *Telephone:* (510) 642-9488 (Office); (510) 204-9147 (Home). *Fax:* (510) 643-9980 (Office). *E-mail:* jill@seismo.berkeley.edu (Office). *Website:* http://perry.geo.berkeley .edu/geology/faculty/facultyframe.htm (Office).

BANGEMANN, Martin, DJur; German telecommunications executive, fmr. politician and lawyer; b. 15 Nov. 1934, Wanzleben; s. of Martin Bangemann and Lotte Telge; m. Renate Bauer 1962; three s. two d.; ed secondary school, Emden and Univs. of Tübingen and Munich; mem. Freie Demokratische Partei (FDP) 1963–, Deputy 1969, mem. Regional Exec. Baden-Württemberg FDP 1973–78 (resgnd), mem. Nat. Exec. 1969– (resgnd as Gen. Sec. 1975), Chair. FDP 1985–88; mem. Bundestag 1972–80, 1987–88, European Parl. 1979–84; Minister of Finance 1984–88; EEC (now EU) Commr for Internal Market, Industry, relations with European Parl. 1989–92, for Industrial Affairs and Tech. 1993–95, for Industrial Affairs, Information and Telecommunications Technologies 1995–99, a Vice-Pres. 1993–95; Dir Telefonica, Madrid 1999, Sr Adviser to Chair. and CEO; Fed. Cross of Merit with Star. *Leisure interests:* philosophy, horticulture. *Address:* c/o Telefonica, Gran Via 28, 28013 Madrid, Spain (Office).

BANHAM, Sir John Michael Middlecott, Kt, MA, LL.D.; British business executive; b. 22 Aug. 1940, Torquay, Devon; s. of late Terence Middlecott Banham and of Belinda Joan Banham CBE; m. Frances Favell 1965; one s. two d.; ed Charterhouse, Queens' Coll., Cambridge; with HM Foreign Service 1962–64; Dir of Marketing, Wallcoverings Div., Reed Int. 1965–69; with McKinsey & Co. Inc. 1969, Assoc. 1969–75, Prin. 1975–80, Dir 1980–83; Controller Audit Comm. for Local Authorities in England and Wales 1983–87; Dir-Gen. CBI March 1987–92; Dir Amvescap 1999–; Chair. WestCountry TV Ltd 1992–95, John Labatt (Europe) (now Labatt Breweries of Europe) 1992–95, ECI Ventures 1992–95, Local Govt Comm. for England 1992–95, Kingfisher 1996–2000, Tarmac 2000–, Whitbread PLC 2000–, Geest 2002–, Cyclacel 2002–; Dir Nat. Westminster Bank 1992–98, Nat. Power 1992–98; Man. Trustee Nuffield Foundation 1988–97; Hon. Treas. Cancer Research Campaign 1991–2002; DL Cornwall 1999; Hon. LLD (Bath) 1987, Hon. DSc (Loughborough) 1989, (Exeter) 1993, (Strathclyde) 1995. *Publications:* Future of the British Car Industry 1975, Realising the Promise of a National Health Service 1977, The Anatomy of Change 1994 and numerous reports for Audit Comm. on educ., social services, housing, etc. 1984–87 and on the economy, skill training, infrastructure and urban regeneration for the CBI 1987–. *Leisure interests:* gardening, walking, music. *Address:* Whitbread PLC, Citypoint, One Ropemaker Street, London, EC2Y 9HX (Office); Penberth, St Buryan, nr Penzance, Cornwall, England. *Telephone:* (20) 7806-5403 (Office). *Fax:* (20) 8308-0425 (Office).

BANI, Father John; Ni-Vanuatu politician; Pres. of Vanuatu March 1999–. *Address:* Office of the President, Port-Vila, Vanuatu.

BANI-SADR, Abolhasan; Iranian politician; b. 1933, Hamadan, W Iran; s. of the Ayatollah Sayed Nasrollah Bani-Sadr; ed Sorbonne and Tehran Univs; supporter of Mossadeq (Prime Minister of Iran 1951–53); joined underground anti-Shah movement 1953; imprisoned after riots over Shah's land reforms 1963; in exile in Paris 1963–79; taught at the Sorbonne; close assoc. of the Ayatollah Ruhollah Khomeini and returned to Iran after overthrow of Shah; Minister of Econ. and Financial Affairs 1979–80; Acting Foreign Minister 1979 (dismissed); President of Iran 1980–81; mem. Revolutionary Council 1979–81 (Pres. 1980–81); fled to France 1981, subsequently formed Nat. Council of Resistance to oppose the Govt (in alliance with Massoud Rajavi, Leader of Mujaheddin Kalq and Abdel-Rahman Ghassemlov, Leader of Democratic Party of Kurdistan, Nat. Democratic Front and other resistance groups), Chair. 1981–84. *Publications:* The Economics of Divine Unity, Oil and Violence, L'espérance trahie 1982 and numerous articles and pamphlets on economics and politics.

BANJO, Ladipo Ayodeji, PhD; Nigerian university administrator and linguist; b. 2 May 1934, Ijebu-Igbo, Ogun State; s. of the late Ven. and S. A. Banjo; m. Alice Mbamali; two s. two d.; ed Nigerian Coll. of Arts, Science and Tech. Univs. of Glasgow and Leeds, Univ. of Calif. (Los Angeles), Univ. of Ibadan; Educ. Officer W Nigeria 1960–64 (Sr Educ. Officer Jan–Oct. 1966); lecturer Dept of English, Univ. of Ibadan 1966–71, Sr Lecturer 1971–73, Reader and Acting Head 1973–75, Prof. 1975–97, Head 1981, Dean Faculty of Arts 1977–79, Chair. Cttee of Deans 1978–79, Deputy Vice-Chancellor 1981–84, Vice-Chancellor 1984–91, Prof. Emer. 1997–; Dir Reading Centre 1970–72 (Co-Dir 1966–70); Chair. Int. Panel on English Language, West African Examination Council 1979–85, Advisory Cttee Nat. Language Centre 1980–85; Pres. West African Modern Languages Asscn 1981–; Vice-Pres. Int. Fed. of Languages and Literatures 1985–89, Yoruba Studies Asscn 1985–; J. P. Oyo State 1986–; Pres. and Fellow, Nigerian Acad. of Letters 2000–. *Publications:* Oral English 1971, Letter Writing 1973, Effective Use of English 1976, Developmental English 1985, New Englishes: A West African Perspective (ed. with A. Bamgbose and A. Thomas) 1995, Making a Virtue of Necessity: An Overview of the English Language in Nigeria 1996, In the Saddle: A Vice-Chancellor's Story 1997. *Leisure interests:* music, photography, reading. *Address:* University of Ibadan, P.O. Box 14341, Ibadan, Oyo State, Nigeria. *Telephone:* (2) 8104863. *Fax:* (2) 8104863. *E-mail:* banjo@ ibadan.skannet.com.ng (Home).

BANKS, Anthony Louis (Tony), BA; British politician; b. 8 April 1943; ed Archbishop Tenison's Grammar School, Kensington, York Univ. and London School of Econs; fmr trade union research worker; Head of Research Amalgamated Union of Eng Workers 1969–75; an Asst Sec. Gen. Asscn of Broadcasting and Allied Staffs 1976–83; Political Advisor to Minister for Overseas Devt 1975; joined Labour Party 1964; GLC mem. for Hammersmith 1970–77, for Tooting 1981–86; Chair. Gen. Purposes Cttee GLC 1975–77, Arts and Recreation Cttee 1981–83, GLC 1985–86; mem. Select Cttee HM Treasury 1986–87, Select Cttee on Procedure 1987–97, Select Cttee on Accommodation and Works 2000–, Jt Lords/Commons Cttee on Private Bill Procedure 1987–88; mem. Council of Europe Parl. Ass. and Western European Union 1989–97; MP for Newham North West 1983–97, West Ham 1997–; Parl. Under Sec. of State Dept of Culture, Media and Sport 1997–99; Chair. London Group of Labour MPs 1987–91; mem. Bd ENO 1981–83, London Festival Ballet 1981–83, Nat. Theatre 1981–85. *Publication:* Out of Order (jtly) 1993. *Address:* House of Commons, London, SW1A 0AA; 306 High Street, Stratford, London, E15 1AJ, England. *Telephone:* (20) 8555-0036.

BANKS, Iain; British author; b. 1954, Fife, Scotland; ed Stirling Univ.; worked as technician, British Steel 1976, IBM, Greenock 1978. *Publications:* The Wasp Factory 1984, Walking on Glass 1985, The Bridge 1986, Espedair Street 1987, Canal Dreams 1989, The Crow Road 1992 (adapted as Channel 4 TV series 1996), Complicity 1993, Whit 1995; science fiction (under name Iain M. Banks): Consider Phlebas 1987, The Player of Games 1988, Use of Weapons 1990, The State of the Art 1991, Against a Dark Background 1993, Feersum Endjinn 1994, Excession 1996, A Song of Stone 1998, Inversions 1998, The Business 1999, Look to Windward 2000, Dead Air 2002. *Address:* c/o Little, Brown, Brettenham House, Lancaster Place, London, WC2E 7EN, England. *Telephone:* (20) 7911-8000. *Fax:* (20) 7911-8100.

BANKS, Russell; American author; b. 28 March 1940, Barnstead, NH; s. of Earl Banks and Florence Banks; m. 1st Darlene Bennett (divorced 1962); one d.; m. 2nd Mary Gunst (divorced 1977); three d.; m. 3rd Kathy Walton (divorced 1988); m. 4th Chase Twichell; ed Colgate Univ. and Univ. of NC at Chapel Hill; fmr teacher of creative writing at Emerson Coll. Boston, Univ. of NH at Durham, Univ. of Ala, New England Coll.; teacher of creative writing, Princeton Univ.; Pres. Parl. Int. des Écrivains 2001–; Fels Award for Fiction 1974; John Dos Passos Award 1985; American Acad. of Arts and Letters Award 1985. *Publications include:* poetry: Waiting to Freeze 1967, 30/ 6 1969, Snow: Meditations of a Cautious Man in Winter 1974; novels: Family Life 1975, Hamilton Stark 1978, The Book of Jamaica 1980, The Relation of My Imprisonment 1984, Continental Drift 1985, Affliction 1989, The Sweet Hereafter 1991, The Angel on the Roof 2001; collected short stories: Searching for Survivors 1975, The New World 1978, Trailerpark 1981, Success Stories 1986; short stories in literary magazines. *Address:* 1000 Park Avenue, New York, NY 10028, USA.

BANKS, Victor Franklin, MA; Anguillan politician; b. 8 Nov. 1947, The Valley; m. Cerise Banks; three c.; ed ed. The Valley Secondary School, Coll. of the Virgin Islands, St Thomas and New School, New York, USA; teacher, The Valley Secondary School 1964–68; Man. Shipping Dept, SARAND, Inc., New York 1974–80; Gov. Liaison Officer, Anguilla 1980–81; elected Deputy to House of Ass. (Anguilla People's Party) for Valley N. 1981–84; Minister of

Social Services 1981–84; Leader Anguilla Democratic Party 1985–; elected Deputy (Anguilla Democratic Party) for Valley S. 1985–; Minister of Finance, Econ. Devt, Investment and Commerce (following formation of coalition govt. between Anguilla Democratic Party and Anguilla United Party) 2002–; Pres. Banx Professional Services Ltd 1981–. *Leisure interests:* community work, counselling, political educ., volleyball, squash, handball, duck shooting. *Address:* Ministry of Finance, Economic Development, Investment and Commerce, The Secretariat, The Valley, Anguilla (Office). *Telephone:* (264) 497-2545 (Office). *E-mail:* ministeroffinance@gov.ai (Office). *Website:* www.gov.ai (Office).

BANNISTER, (Richard) Matthew, LLB; British broadcasting executive; b. 16 March 1957; s. of the late Richard Neville Bannister and of Olga Margaret Bannister; m. 1st Amanda Gerrard Walker 1984 (died 1988); one d.; m. 2nd Shelagh Margaret Macleod 1989; one s.; ed King Edward VII School, Sheffield, Nottingham Univ.; Presenter, BBC Radio Nottingham 1978–81; Reporter/Presenter Capital Radio, London 1981–83, Deputy Head News and Talks 1985–87, Head 1987–88; with Newsbeat, BBC Radio 1 1983–85; Man. Ed. BBC Greater London Radio 1988–91, Project Co-ordinator, BBC Charter Renewal 1991–93, Controller BBC Radio 1 1993–96, Dir BBC Radio 1996–98; Head of Production BBC TV 1999–2000; Dir Marketing and Communications Assсn Dec. 2000; Chair. Trust the DJ 2001–; Presenter BBC Radio 5 Live 2002–; mem. Bd Chichester Festival Theatre 1999–. *Leisure interests:* rock music, collecting P. G. Wodehouse first edns. *Address:* Trust the DJ, Units 13–14, Barley Shotts Bus Park, Acklam Road, London, W10 5YG, England. *Telephone:* (20) 8962-5420. *Fax:* (20) 8962-5455. *E-mail:* contact@trustthedj.com. *Website:* www.trustthedj.com.

BANNISTER, Sir Roger G., Kt, CBE, DM, FRCP; British athlete, consultant physician, neurologist and university administrator; b. 23 March 1929, London; s. of the late Ralph Bannister and of Alice Bannister; m. Moyra Elver Jacobsson 1955; two s. two d.; ed City of Bath Boys' School, Univ. Coll. School, Exeter and Merton Colls., Oxford, St Mary's Hosp. Medical School, London; winner, Oxford and Cambridge Mile 1947–50; Pres. Oxford Univ. Athletic Club 1948; British Mile Champion 1951, 1953, 1954; world record one mile 1954, first sub-four minute mile 1954; Master Pembroke College, Oxford 1985–93; Hon. Consultant Neurologist, St Mary's Hosp. Medical School, Nat. Hosp. for Neurology and Neurosurgery, London (non-exec. Dir 1992–96), London and Oxford Dist and Region; Chair. St Mary's Hosp. Devt Trust; Chair. Govt Working Group on Sport in the Univs. 1995–97; Chair. Clinical Autonomic Research Soc. 1982–84; mem. Physiological Soc., Medical Research Soc. Assсn of British Neurologists; Fellow Imperial College; Trustee Leeds Castle Foundation 1988–, St Mary's Hosp. Medical School Devt Trust 1994–; Hon. Fellow UMIST 1974; Hon. Fellow Exeter Coll., Oxford 1980, Merton Coll., Oxford 1986; Hon. LLD (Liverpool) 1972; Hon. DSc (Sheffield) 1978, (Grinnell) 1984, (Bath) 1984, (Rochester) 1986, (Williams) 1987; Hon. MD (Pavia) 1986; Hon. DL (Univ. of Victoria, Canada) 1994, (Univ. of Wales, Cardiff) 1995, (Loughborough) 1996, (Univ. of East Anglia) 1997; Dr hc (Jyvaskylä, Finland); Hans-Heinrich Siegbert Prize 1977. *Publications:* First Four Minutes 1955 (now republished as Four Minute Mile 1989), Ed. Brain and Bannister's Clinical Neurology 1992, Autonomic Failure (co-ed.) 1993; various medical articles on physiology and neurology. *Address:* 21 Bardwell Road, Oxford, OX2 6SV, England. *Telephone:* (1865) 511413.

BANNON, John Charles, BA, LLB; Australian politician; b. 7 May 1943; s. of C. Bannon and Joyce Marion Bannon; m. 1st Robyn Layton 1968 (divorced); one d.; m. 2nd. Angela Bannon 1982; at St Peter's Coll., Univ. of Adelaide; Industrial Advocate AWU 1969–73; Adviser to Commonwealth Minister of Labour and Immigration 1973–75; Asst Dir S. Australian Dept of Labour and Industry 1975–77; mem. House Ass. 1977–93; Minister for Community Devt, Minister for Local Govt, Minister for Recreation and Sport 1978–79; Leader of the Opposition 1979–82; Premier and Treasurer of S. Australia, Minister of State Devt and Minister for the Arts 1982–85; Premier and Treasurer of S. Australia and Minister for the Arts 1985–89; Premier and Treasurer of S. Australia 1982–92; Nat. Pres. Australian Labor Party 1988–91; Dir Australian Broadcasting Corpn 1994–2000, Adelaide Symphony Orchestra Bd 1997–; mem. Council Constitutional Centenary Foundation 1995– (Chair. 1996–); Master, St Marks's Coll., Adelaide 2000–; Ed. The New Federalist (Nat. Journal of Australian Fed. History) 1998. *Publications:* The Crucial Colony 1994; articles, monographs on Fed./State relations. *Leisure interests:* running, gardening. *Address:* P.O. Box 323, Rundle Mall, Adelaide, SA 5000, Australia.

BANNY, Charles Konan; Côte d'Ivoirian central banker and economist; b. 11 Nov. 1942, Divo; ed Ecole Supérieure des Sciences Economiques et Commerciales, Paris; served as Chargé de Mission, Stabilisation and Support Fund of Agric. Product Prices; Deputy Sec.-Gen. Inter-African Coffee Org., Paris 1970, Sec.-Gen. 1971; Dir of Admin. and Social Affairs, Cen. Bank of West African States (BCEAO) 1976, later Dir of Securities, Investment, Borrowing and Lending, then Cen. Dir of Research, apptd. Nat. Dir of BCEAO for Côte d'Ivoire 1983, Gov. BCEAO 1994–. *Address:* Banque centrale des Etats de l'Afrique de l'Ouest, Avenue Abdoulaye Fadiga, B.P. 3108, Dakar, Senegal (Office). *Website:* www.bceao.int.

BANVILLE, John; Irish author; b. Wexford; m. Janet Dunham; two s.; fmrly night copy ed. on The Irish Times, Literary Ed. 1988–99, Chief Literary Critic and Assoc. Literary Ed. 1999–2002; Lannan Foundation Award 1998. *Film script:* The Last September 1998. *Plays:* The Broken Jug (after Kleist) 1994,

God's Gift (after Kleist's "Amphitryon") 2000. *Publications:* 13 novels including: Birchwood, Dr. Copernicus, Kepler, The Newton Letter, Mefisto, The Book of Evidence (Guinness Peat Aviation Prize 1989) 1989, Ghosts 1993, Athena 1995, The Untouchable 1996, Eclipse 2000, Shroud 2003. *Address:* c/o Gillon Aitken Associates Ltd, 29 Fernshaw Road, London, SW10 0TG, England.

BAO TONG; Chinese political prisoner and former official; fmr aide to CCP leader Zhao Ziyang; imprisoned following Tiananmen Square massacre 1989–96; now on probation.

BAO WENKUI; Chinese agronomist; b. 8 May 1916; ed in USA; Prof. Chinese Acad. of Agricultural Sciences; Deputy, 5th NPC 1978–83; Dir Inst. of Crop Breeding and Cultivation, Beijing 1981–; Deputy, 6th NPC 1983–88; mem. Dept of Biology, Academia Sinica 1982–. *Address:* Chinese Academy of Agricultural Sciences, Baishiqiao Road, Haidian, Beijing 100081, People's Republic of China.

BAO XUDING; Chinese politician; b. Feb. 1939, Wuxi City, Jiangsu Prov.; ed Shenyang School of Machine Bldg 1958, CCP Cen. Party School 1986; joined CCP 1961; Vice-Dir then Dir Dept of Machinery of Sichuan Prov. 1986; Dir Sichuan Provincial Planning Comm. 1988; Vice-Minister of Machine Bldg and Electronics Industries 1990; Vice-Minister of Machine Bldg Industry 1993, Minister 1996–98; Vice-Minister State Devt and Planning Comm. 1998–99; Deputy Mayor of Chongqing 1999–; mem. 15th CCP Cen. Cttee 1997–2002. *Address:* Office of the Mayor, Chongqing City, Chongqing Special Municipality, People's Republic of China.

BAQUET, Dean Paul; American journalist; b. 21 Sept. 1956, New Orleans; s. of Edward Joseph Baquet and Myrtle (née Romano) Baquet; m. Dylan Landis 1986; one s.; ed Columbia Univ., New York; investigative reporter New Orleans 1978–84; investigative reporter Chicago Tribune 1984–87, chief investigative reporter 1987–90; investigative reporter New York Times 1990–92, Projects Ed. 1992–95, Deputy Metropolitan Ed. 1995, Nat. Ed. 1995–2000; Man. Ed. Los Angeles Times 2000–; Pulitzer Prize for Investigative Reporting 1988. *Address:* Los Angeles Times, Times Mirror Co., Times Mirror Square, Los Angeles, CA 90012, USA (Office). *Telephone:* (213) 237-7811 (Office). *Fax:* (213) 237-7910 (Office). *Website:* www.latimes.com (Office).

BARABOLYA, Maj.-Gen. Petr Demidovich, CandJur; Russian lawyer and ecologist; b. 1 Jan. 1919, Poboina, Ukraine; m. (deceased); one d.; ed Berdyank Teachers' Inst., Acad. of USSR Armed Forces; history and geography teacher 1938–39; active service in army 1939; prosecutor Marine Prosecutor's Office 1950; Chief Officer for problems concerning int. law, Marine Gen. Staff 1950–54 (Chief Expert 1966–70), Operations Dept 1954–66; Head Dept of Int. Law 1970–82; Sr researcher Inst. of State and Law, USSR Acad. of Sciences 1982–86, Chair. Soviet (now Russian) Cttee for Peace, Disarmament and Ecological Security 1987–; numerous medals and decorations. *Publications:* over 100 scientific works on int. maritime law. *Address:* Mira prosp. 36, room 509, 129090 Moscow, Russia (Office). *Telephone:* (095) 280-29-45 (Office).

BARADEI, Mohamed Mostafa el-, PhD; Egyptian international organization official and diplomatist; b. 17 June 1942; m. Aida el-Kachef; one s. one d.; ed Univ. of Cairo, New York Univ., USA; with Ministry of Foreign Affairs, Dept of Int. Orgs 1964–67; mem. Perm. Mission to UN, New York 1967–71; Sr Fellow, Center for Int. Studies, New York Univ. 1973–74; Special Asst to Foreign Minister, Ministry of Foreign Affairs 1974–78; mem. Perm. Mission to UN, Geneva and Alt. Rep. Cttee on Disarmament 1978–80; Sr Fellow and Dir Int. Law and Orgs Programme, UN Inst. for Training and Research, New York 1980–84; Adjunct Prof. of Int. Law, New York Univ. 1981–87; Rep. of Dir-Gen. of IAEA to UN, New York 1984–87, Legal Adviser, then Dir Legal Div., IAEA, Vienna 1987–91, Dir of External Relations 1991–93, Asst Dir-Gen. for External Relations 1993–97, Dir-Gen. IAEA 1997–; mem. Int. Law Assсn, American Soc., of Int. Law, Nuclear Law Assсn. *Publications:* The International Law Commission: The Need for a New Direction 1981, Model Rules for Disaster Relief Operations 1982, The Role of International Atomic Energy Agency Safeguards in the Evolution of the Non-Proliferation Regime 1991, The International Law of Nuclear Energy 1993, On Compliance with Nuclear Non-Proliferation Obligations (Security Dialogue) 1996, and articles in int. law journals. *Address:* International Atomic Energy Agency, PO Box 100, Wagramerstrasse 5, 1400 Vienna, Austria (Office). *Telephone:* (1) 26000 (Office). *Fax:* (1) 26007 (Office). *E-mail:* official.mail@iaea.org (Office). *Website:* www.iaea.org (Office).

BARAK, Lt-Gen. Ehud; Israeli politician and fmr army officer; b. 2 Feb. 1942, Israel; s. of Israel Barak and Esther Barak; m. Nava Cohen; three d.; ed Hebrew Univ. Jerusalem and Stanford Univ. Calif.; enlisted in Israeli Defence Force (IDF) 1959; grad. Infantry Officers' course 1962; commando course, France 1963; Armoured Corps Co. Commdrs. course 1968; various command roles; also served in operations br. of Gen. Staff; active service in Six Day War 1967 and Yom Kippur War 1973; Commdr Tank Commdrs. course 1974; Head, Gen. Staff Planning Dept 1982–83; Dir IDF Mil. Intelligence 1983–86; Commdr Cen. Command 1986–87; Deputy Chief of Gen. Staff Israeli Defence Force 1987–91, Chief of Gen. Staff 1991–94; Minister of Interior July–Nov. 1995, of Foreign Affairs 1995–1996; Chair. Labour Party 1997–2001; Prime Minister of Israel 1999–2001; mem. Knesset (Parl.) and of

Parl. Security and Foreign Affairs Cttee 1996. *Leisure interest:* playing the piano. *Address:* Israel Labour Party, 110 Ha'yarkon Street, Tel Aviv 61032, Israel. *Telephone:* (3) 5209222. *Fax:* (3) 5271744.

BARAKAT, Nayel, PhD, FInstP; Egyptian professor of experimental physics; b. 22 Sept. 1922, Cairo; s. of M.H. Barakat Bey and N el Safty; m. Afaf Ali Nada 1956; one s. two d.; ed Univs. of Cairo and London; lecturer, Alexandria Univ. 1951–54; lecturer, Ain Shams Univ. 1954–58, Asst Prof. 1958–64, Prof. of Experimental Physics 1964–88, Prof. Emer. 1988–, Dean, Faculty of Science 1971–76; Cultural Counsellor and Dir of Educ. Mission in Fed. Repub. of Germany, Netherlands and Denmark 1976–81; Hon. DSc (London) 1992; Egyptian Nat. Award in Physics 1958, 1963; Nat. Award in Basic Science 1990. *Publications:* 85 papers in specialized journals. *Leisure interests:* Arabic and classical music, photography. *Address:* 4 Ibn Marawan Street, Appt. 504, Dokki, Cairo, Egypt. *Telephone:* 3484568.

BARAM, Uzi; Israeli politician; b. 1937, Jerusalem; co-f. Labour Party's Young Guard, Sec. 1966–70; Chair. Young Leadership Dept, World Zionist Org. 1972–75; Chair. Labour Party (Jerusalem br.) 1975–81, Sec.-Gen. 1984–88; Chair. Immigration and Absorption Cttee 1984–92; Minister of Tourism 1992–96, fmrly of Religious Affairs; mem. Knesset 1977–, Foreign Affairs and Defence Cttee. *Address:* c/o Ministry of Foreign Affairs, Hakirya, Romema, Jerusalem 91950, Israel.

BARAŃCZAK, Stanisław; Polish poet and literary critic; b. 13 Nov. 1946, Poznań; m.; one s. one d.; ed Adam Mickiewicz Univ., Poznań; Asst Adam Mickiewicz Univ. 1969–80; in the USA 1981–; Prof. Harvard Univ., Jt literary Publs 1983–, Ed. monthly The Polish Review. *Collections of poetry include:* Korekta twarzy (Face Correction) 1968, Jednym tchem (In One breath) 1970, Dziennik poranny (Morning Diary) 1972, Sztuczne oddychanie (Breathing Underwater) 1974, Ja wiem, że to niesłuszne (I know That It's Wrong) 1977, Atlantyda (Atlantis) 1986, Widokówka z tego świata (A Postcard from This World) 1988, Podróż zimowa (Winter Journey) 1994, Chirurgiczna precyzja (Surgical Precision) 1999. *Criticism includes:* Ironia i Harmonia (Irony and Harmony) 1973, Etyka i poetyka (Ethics and Poetry) 1979; Przed i po (Before and After) 1988, Tablica z Macondo (Board from Macondo) 1990, Ocalone w tłumaczeniu (Saved in Translation 1992), Fioletowa krowa (Violet Cow) 1993, Poezja i duch uogólnienia (Poetry and the Spirit of Generalization) (essay); numerous trans. of English, American and Russian poetry and of William Shakespeare. *Address:* 8 Broad Dale, Newton Wille, MA 02160, USA.

BARBA, Eugenio, MA; Danish theatre director; b. 29 Oct. 1936, Brindisi, Italy; s. of Emanuele Barba and Vera Gaeta; m. Judith Patricia Howard Jones 1965; two s.; ed Univ. of Oslo, Theatre School, Warsaw and Jerzy Grotowski's Theatre Lab. Opole; Founder and Dir Odin Teatret (Interscandinavian Theatre Lab.) 1964–; more than 20 productions 1965–; Founder and Dir Int. School of Theatre Anthropology 1979–; mem. Bd of Advisers, Int. Cttee Théâtre des Nations 1975–80; mem. Bd of Advisers, Int. Asscn of Performing Arts Semiotics 1981–85; adviser, Danish Ministry of Culture 1981–82; UNESCO adviser, Centro de Estudios Teatrales, Museo de Arte Moderno, Bogotá 1983; adviser, Centre of Theatre Exchanges, Rio de Janeiro 1987–; mem. Bd of Advisers, Int. Comparative Literature Asscn 1998; lectures regularly at univs, theatre schools, etc.; Dr hc (Århus) 1988, (Ayacucho) 1998, (Bologna) 1998, (Havana) 2002; Danish Acad. Award 1980, Mexican Theatre Critics' Prize 1984, Diego Fabbri Prize 1986, Pirandello Int. Prize 1996, Reconnaissance de Mérite Scientifique (Montreal) 1999, Sonning Prize 2000. *Publications include:* In Search of a Lost Theatre 1965, The Floating Islands 1978, Il Brecht dell' Odin 1981, La Corsa dei Contrari 1981, Beyond the Floating Islands 1985, The Dilated Body 1985, Anatomie de l'Acteur (with N Savarese) 1988, Brechts Aske, Oxyrhincus Evangeliet (two plays) 1986, The Secret Art of the Performer 1990, The Paper Canoe 1992, Theatre—Solitude, Craft, Revolt 1996, Land of Ashes and Diamonds 1999, Arar el cielo 2002; numerous articles, essays etc. *Address:* Nordisk Teaterlaboratorium, Odin Teatret, Box 1283, 7500 Holstebro, Denmark. *Telephone:* (45) 97-42-47-77. *Fax:* (45) 97-41-04-82. *E-mail:* odin@odinteatret.dk (Office). *Website:* www .odinteatret.dk (Office).

BARBENEL, Joseph Cyril, PhD, FRSE; British bioengineer; b. 2 Jan. 1937, London; s. of Tobias Barbenel and Sarah Barbenel; m. Lesley Mary Hyde Jowett 1964; two s. one d.; ed Hackney Downs Grammar School, London, London Hosp. Dental School, Univ. of London, Queen's Coll., Univ. of St Andrews, Univ. of Strathclyde, Glasgow; Dental House Surgeon, London Hosp. 1960; Royal Army Dental Corps 1960–62; gen. dental practice, London 1963; Lecturer, Dental Prosthetics, Univ. of Dundee 1967–69, Univ. of Strathclyde 1970, Sr Lecturer, Bioeng. Unit 1970–82, Reader 1982–85, Prof. 1985–, Head Dept 1992–98, Vice-Dean (Research) Faculty of Eng 1997–2001; Vice-Pres. (Int. Affairs) IPEM; Consulting Prof., Chongqing Univ., China 1986–; mem. Admin. Cttee Int. Fed. of Medical and Biological Eng; Nuffield Foundation Award 1963–66, Pres.'s Medal, Soc. of Cosmetic Scientists 1994. *Publications:* Clinical Aspects of Blood Rheology (with Lowe and Forbes) 1981, Pressure Sores (with Lowe and Forbes) 1983, Blood Flow in Artificial Organs and Cardiovascular Prostheses (with co-eds) 1988, Blood Flow in the Brain (with co-eds) 1988, numerous scientific papers. *Leisure interests:* music, theatre, reading. *Address:* University of Strathclyde, Glasgow, G4 0NW (Office); 151 Maxwell Drive, Glasgow, G41, Scotland (Home). *Telephone:* (141) 548-3221 (Office); (141) 427-0765 (Home). *Fax:* (141) 552-6098 (Office). *E-mail:* j.c.barbenel@strath.ac.uk (Office).

BARBER, Baron (Life Peer), cr. 1974, of Wentbridge in West Yorkshire; **Anthony Perrinot Lysberg Barber,** PC, TD, DL; British politician and former banker; b. 4 July 1920, Hull; s. of John Barber, CBE and Katy Lysberg; m. 1st Jean Patricia Asquith 1950 (died 1983); two d.; m. 2nd Rosemary Youens 1989; ed Retford School and Oriel Coll., Oxford; army service 1939–40, Royal Air Force 1940–45; mem. Parl. 1951–64, 1965–74; Parl. Private Sec., Air Ministry 1952–54; Govt Whip 1955–57; Lord Commissioner of the Treasury 1957–58; Parl. Private Sec. to Prime Minister 1958–59; Econ. Sec. to the Treasury 1959–62; Financial Sec. to the Treasury 1962–63; Minister of Health 1963–64; Chair. Conservative Party 1967–70; Chancellor of Duchy of Lancaster June–July 1970; Chancellor of Exchequer 1970–74; Dir British Ropes (now Bridon) 1964–70, 1974–83, several banks incl. Chartered Bank 1966–70, British Petroleum 1979–88; Chair. Redfearn Nat. Glass 1967, Standard Chartered Bank 1974–87, RAF Benevolent Fund 1991–95; Vice Chair. Charing Cross and Westminster Medical School 1984–95; mem. Cttee of Inquiry into events leading to Argentine invasion of the Falkland Islands 1982, Commonwealth Group on S. Africa 1985; Hon. Fellow, Oriel Coll., Oxford 1971. *Address:* House of Lords, London, SW1A 0PW, England.

BARBER, Brendan; British trade union official; b. Merseyside; taught in Ghana with VSO; Pres. Students' Union, City Univ., London; worked for Ceramics, Glass and Mineral Products Industrial Training Bd; joined Org. and Industrial Relations Dept, TUC 1975, Head Dept 1987–93, Head Press and Information Dept 1979–87, Deputy Gen. Sec. TUC 1993–2003, Gen. Sec. 2003–; mem. Council of Advisory, Conciliation and Arbitration Service (ACAS) 1995; mem. Bd Sport England. *Address:* TUC, Congress House, Great Russell Street, London, WC1B 3LS, England (Office). *Telephone:* (20) 7637-4030 (Office). *E-mail:* info@tuc.org.uk (Office).

BARBER, Frances Jennifer; British actress; b. 13 May 1957, Wolver-hampton; d. of S.W. Brooks and late Gladys Simpson; ed Bangor and Cardiff Univs; fmrly with Hull Truck Theatre Co., Glasgow Citizens Theatre, Tricycle Theatre, RSC. *Television appearances include:* Clem, Jackie's Story, Home Sweet Home, Flame to the Phoenix, Reilly, Ace of Spies, Those Glory Glory Days, Hard Feelings, Behaving Badly, The Nightmare Year, Real Women, Just in Time, The Ice House, Dalziel & Pascoe, Plastic Man, Love in a Cold Climate. *Film appearances include:* The Missionary 1982, A Zed and Two Noughts, White City, Castaway, Prick Up Your Ears, Sammy and Rosie Get Laid, We Think the World of You, The Grasscutter, Separate Bedrooms, Young Soul Rebels, Secret Friends, The Lake, Soft Top, Hard Shoulder, The Fish Tale, Three Steps to Heaven, Photographing Fairies, Shiner, Still Crazy, Esther Kahn, Mauvaise passe. *Stage appearances include:* Night of the Iguana, Pygmalion, Closer, Uncle Vanya. *Leisure interests* poetry, reading, swimming, walking the dog.

BARBER, John Norman Romney; British business executive; b. 22 April 1919, Leigh-on-Sea, Essex; s. of George Ernest and Gladys Eleanor Barber; m. Babette Chalu 1941; one s.; Principal, Cen. Finance Dept, Ministry of Supply 1946–55; with Ford Motor Co. Ltd 1955–65, Dir of Finance 1962–65, Founder, Chair. Ford Motor Credit Co. 1963; Dir of Finance, AEI Ltd 1966; Finance Dir Leyland Motor Corpn 1967, Dir of Finance and Planning, British Leyland Motor Corpn 1968, Deputy Man. Dir 1971, Deputy Chair. 1973–74; Deputy Chair. John E Wiltshier Gp. Ltd 1979–88; Chair. Aberhurst Ltd 1976–89, A. C. Edwards Eng Ltd 1976–81; Dir Acrow PLC 1977–85, Good Relations Group PLC 1980–87, Cox & Kings Holdings Ltd 1980–81, Spear and Jackson Int. PLC 1980–86, C & K Consulting Group 1982–86, Cox & Kings Financial Services Ltd 1980–85, C & K Exec. Search Ltd 1981–85, Economists Advisory Group Ltd 1981–98, UK Investments Ltd 1985–2001, The Communication Group Holdings PLC 1990–; Past Chair. Bd of Trade Investments Grants Advisory Cttee; fmr mem. Royal Comm. on Medical Educ.; fmr mem. Advisory Cttee on Energy Conservation to Ministry of Energy; fmr Vice-Pres., Soc. of Motor Mfrs and Traders; Companion Inst. of Management. *Leisure interests:* motor sport, photography, reading, forestry. *Address:* Woodpecker Lodge, Romsey Road, Ower, Romsey, Hants., SO51 6AE, England. *Telephone:* (23) 8081-1060. *Fax:* (23) 8081-1070.

BARBERÁ GUILLEM, Emilio, DR. MED.; Spanish university professor; b. 14 Feb. 1946, Valencia; s. of Edelmiro Barberá and Emilia Guillem; two s.; ed Univ. of Valencia; Dir Lab. of Quantitative Biol. Instituto Investigaciones Citológicas, C.A.M.P., Valencia 1969–74; Section Head, Centro Investigaciones Ciudad Sanit. 'La Fe' 1974–76; Investigator, Dept of Pathology, Faculty of Medicine, Valencia 1976–79; Asst Prof. Univ. of Valencia 1976–78, Assoc. Prof. 1978–79; Prof. Univ. of Valladolid 1979–80; Prof. of Histology and Gen. Embryology, Univ. del País Vasco 1980–; Dir Dept of Histology and Cellular Biology 1980, Rector 1986–92; other professional appts.; mem. Real Acad. de Medicina de Valencia, Real Acad. de Medicina de Vizcaya and nine int. biological socs. *Publications:* numerous scientific articles in int. reviews; book chapters. *Leisure interests:* photography, travel. *Address:* Universidad del País Vasco/Euskal Herriko Unibertsitatea, Edificio Rectorado, Apartado de Correos 1397, 48080 Bilbao, Spain. *Telephone:* (34) (4) 463-76-53.

BARBERIS, Alessandro; Italian business executive; b. 1937, Turin; m.; three c.; trained as engineer; joined Fiat SpA 1964, Dir 1972, Dir Fmb (Fiat Group in Latin America), Brazil 1976–78, Head of Metalworks 1978–1982, Dir-Gen. Magneti Marelli 1982–93, Dir of Industrial Co-ordination Fiat Auto 1993–96, COO 2002, CEO Dec. 2002–; Dir Istituto Bancario San Paulo di Torino 1996–97; Pres. Piaggio & C. SpA 1997–2002; Pres. Confindustria Toscana 1999, Unione Industriale di Pisa 1999; Chair. CDC Point SpA 2001;

Pres. ANCMA (construction asscn). *Address:* Fiat Auto SpA, Corso Agnelli 200, 10135 Turin, Italy (Office). *Telephone:* (011) 68311111 (Office). *Website:* www.fiat.com (Office).

BARBOSA, Rubens Antonio, MA; Brazilian diplomatist; b. 13 June 1938, São Paulo; m. Maria Ignez Correa da Costa 1969; one s. one d.; ed Univ. of Brazil, São Paulo and London School of Econs; Exec. Sec. Brazilian Trade Comm. with Socialist Countries of E Europe 1976–84; Chief of Staff of Minister of Foreign Affairs 1985–86; Under-Sec.-Gen. for Multilateral and Special Political Affairs 1986–87; Sec. for Int. Affairs, Ministry of Economy 1987–88; Amb. and Perm. Rep. to Latin American Integration Asscn (ALADI) 1988–91; Pres. Cttee of Reps. ALADI 1991–92; Under-Sec.-Gen. for Regional Integration, Econ. Affairs and Foreign Trade, Ministry of Foreign Affairs 1991–93; coordinator Brazilian section of Mercosul (Southern Cone Common Market) 1991–93; Amb. to UK 1994–99, to USA 1999–; fmr Pres. Asscn of Coffee Producing Countries; Grand Cross, Order of Rio Branco, Commdr Légion d'honneur, Hon. LVO, Hon. GCVO; decorations from Argentina, Mexico and Italy. *Publications:* América Latina em Perspectiva: Integração Regional da Retórica à Realidade 1991; Panorama: Visto de Londres 1998, The Mercosur Codes 2000, O Brasil dos Brasilianistas, um Guia dos Estudos sobre o Brasil nos Estados Unidos (1945–2000) 2002; essays and articles in newspapers and magazines. *Leisure interests:* classical music, tennis. *Address:* Embassy of Brazil, 3006 Massachusetts Avenue, NW, Washington, DC 20008, USA (Office). *Telephone:* (202) 238-2700 (Office). *Fax:* (202) 238-2827 (Office). *E-mail:* ambassador@brasilemb.org (Office). *Website:* www.brasilemb.org (Office).

BARBOT, Ivan, LèsL; French police commissioner; b. 5 Jan. 1937, Ploeuc; s. of Pierre Barbot and Anne (née Le Calvez) Barbot; m. Roselyne de Lestrange 1971; three c.; ed Lycée de Saint-Brieuc, Univ. of Paris; Prin. Pvt. Sec. to Chief Commr, Tarn-et-Garonne 1961; Prin. Pvt. Sec., later Dir of Staff to Chief Commr, Haute-Savoie 1962; Dir of Staff, Paris Region Pref. 1967; Deputy Chief Commr, Etampes 1969; Deputy Chief Commr without portfolio, Official Rep. to the Cabinet 1974; Tech. Adviser to Minister of the Interior 1974–77; Sec.-Gen. Seine-Saint-Denis 1977–82; Chief Commr and Supt, Dept de la Charente 1982–85, du Var 1985–87; Dir-Gén. Police Nat. 1987–89; Pres. Interpol 1988–92; Prefect Poitou-Charentes 1989, Vienne 1989–91; with Prime Minister's office, responsible for security 1991–92; Pres. Admin. Council of French concessionary co. for the construction and exploitation of the road tunnel under Mont-Blanc 1992–94; Chair., CEO OFEMA 1993–, SOFMA 1996–; Pres., Dir-Gen. SOFEMA 1997–; Officier, Légion d'honneur, du Mérite agricole, Commdr, Ordre Nat. du Mérite, Chavalier des Palmes académiques, des Arts et des Lettres. *Address:* SOFEMA, 58 ave Marceau, 75008 Paris (Office); 4 rue Marguerite, 75017 Paris, France (Home).

BARBOUR, Haley Reeves, JD; American politician; b. 22 Oct. 1947, Yazoo City, Miss.; s. of the late Jeptha F. Barbour Jr and LeFlore Johnson; m. Marsha Dickson 1971; two s.; ed Univ. of Mississippi; field rep. Miss. Republican Party 1968, Deputy Exec. Dir 1972–73, Exec. Dir 1973–76; Regional Technician, Bureau of Census 1969–70; Exec. Dir Southern Asscn of Republican State Chairmen 1973–76; Southeastern US Campaign Dir Pres. Ford Cttee 1976; Chair. 3rd Congressional Dist Cttee Miss. 1976–84; Republican nominee, US Senate 1982; Municipal Judge, Yazoo City 1980–81, City Attorney 1981–85; Chair. Republican Nat. Cttee 1993–97; Dir Deposit Guarranty Corpn; mem. Bd Deposit Guarranty Nat. Bank; mem. Bd Dirs Amtrak & Mobil Telecommunications Technologies Inc. *Publication:* Agenda for America 1996. *Address:* Republican National Committee, Dwight D. Eisenhower Republican Center, 310 First Street, SE, Washington, DC 20003, USA.

BARBOUR, Ian G., BD, PhD; American physicist and theologian; b. 5 Oct. 1923, Peking (now Beijing), (People's Republic of) China; ed Swarthmore Coll., Duke Univ., Univ. of Chicago, Yale Univ.; Prof. Emer. Dept of Religion, Carleton Coll., Northfield, Minn.; Templeton Prize 1999. *Publications:* Issues in Science and Religion 1966, Technology, Environment and Human Values 1980, Religion in an Age of Science (Gifford Lectures) 1990, Ethics in an Age of Technology 1993, Religion and Science: Historical and Contemporary Issues 1997, When Science Meets Religion 2000, Nature, Human Nature and God 2002. *Address:* Carleton College, Northfield, MN 55057, USA.

BARCHUK, Vasily Vasilievich, CEconSc; Russian politician and economist; b. 11 March 1941, Komsomolsk-on-Amur; m.; one d.; ed All-Union Inst. of Finance and Econ. USSR Acad. of Nat. Econ.; worked in tax inspection bodies in Khabarovsk Region 1958–72; staff mem. RSFSR Ministry of Finance 1972–84, USSR Ministry of Finance 1986–91, Deputy Minister of Finance April–Nov. 1991; First Deputy Minister of Finance of Russia 1991–92, Minister 1992–93; Chair. of Bd Pensions Fund of Russian Fed. 1993–99; Deputy Chair. Dept of Social Devt, Ministry of Labour and Social Devt 2001–. *Address:* Ministry of Labour and Social Development, Birzhevaya pl. 1, 103706 Moscow, Russia. *Telephone:* (095) 205-43-01.

BARD, Allen J., PhD, FAAS; American professor of chemistry; b. 18 Dec. 1933, New York; m. Frances Segal 1957; one s. one d.; ed City Coll. of New York and Harvard Univ.; Thayer Scholarship 1955–56; Nat. Science Foundation Postdoctoral Fellowship 1956–58; joined chem. staff of Univ. of Tex., Austin 1958, Prof. of Chem. 1967–, Jack S. Josey Prof. 1980–82, Norman Hackerman Prof. 1982–85, Hackerman-Welch Regents Chair. in Chem. 1985–; consultant to several labs including E.I. duPont, Texas Instruments and several govt agencies; research interests in application of electrochemical methods to study of chemical problems; Vice-Chair. Nat. Research Council; Ed.-in-Chief Journal of American Chemical Soc. 1982–2001; Chair. Nat. Acad. of Sciences Chemical Section 1996–; mem. editorial Bd of numerous journals; Gov. Weizmann Inst. 1995–; mem. ACS, Electrochemical Soc.; Dr hc (Paris) 1986; Ward Medal in Chem. 1955, Harrison Howe Award, ACS 1980, Carl Wagner Memorial Award, Electrochemical Soc. 1981, Bruno Breyer Memorial Medal, Royal Australian Chem. Inst. 1984, Fisher Award in Analytical Chem., ACS 1984, Charles N Reilley Award, Soc. of Electroanalytical Chem. 1984, New York Acad. of Sciences Award in Math. and Physical Sciences 1986, Willard Gibbs Award, ACS 1987, Olin-Palladium Award, Electrochem. Soc. 1987, Oesper Award, Univ. of Cincinnati 1989, NAS Award 1998, Linus Pauling Award 1998, Pittsburgh Analytical Chem. Award 2001, ACS Priestley Medal 2002. *Publications:* Chemical Equilibrium 1966, Electrochemical Methods (with L. R. Faulkner) 1980, Integrated Chemical Systems: A Chemical Approach to Nanotechnology 1994; approx. 700 papers and book chapters; Ed. Electroanalytical Chemistry (15 Vols) 1966–, The Encyclopedia of the Electrochemistry of the Elements, 16 Vols 1973–82. *Address:* Chemistry and Biochemistry Department, University of Texas at Austin, 1 University Station A5300, Austin, TX 78712-0165, USA (Office). *Telephone:* (512) 471-3761. *Fax:* (512) 471-0088. *E-mail:* ajbard@mail.utexas.edu (Office). *Website:* www.cm.utexas.edu/bard/.

BARDER, Sir Brian Leon, KCMG, BA; British diplomatist (retd); b. 20 June 1934, Bristol; s. of Harry Barder and Vivien Young; m. Jane M. Cornwell 1958; two d. one s.; ed Sherborne School and St Catharine's Coll., Cambridge; Colonial Office 1957–64; First Sec. UK Mission to UN, New York 1964–68; FCO 1968–70; First Sec. Moscow 1971–73; Counsellor, Canberra 1973–77; Canadian Nat. Defence Coll. 1977–78; Head of Southern Africa Dept, FCO 1978–82; Amb. to Ethiopia 1982–86, to Poland 1986–88; High Commr in Nigeria and Amb. (non-resident) to Benin 1988–91; High Commr in Australia 1991–94; Know How Fund Diplomatic Training Consultant 1996; mem. Bd of Man. Royal Hosp. for Neurodisability 1996–2003; mem. English-Speaking Union Cttee for Speech and Debate 1996–, Special Immigration Appeals Comm. 1998–. *Leisure interests:* music, the Internet, cycling, polemics. *Address:* 10 Melrose Road, London, SW18 1NE, England. *Telephone:* (20) 8874-5909. *Fax:* (20) 8871-2836 (Home). *E-mail:* brianlb@ntlworld.com (Home). *Website:* www.barder.com/brian (Home).

BARDIN, Garry Yakovlevich; Russian film director; b. 11 Sept. 1941, Orenburg; m.; ed Studio-School of Moscow Art Theatre; actor Moscow Gogol Drama Theatre; Stage Dir Moscow Puppet Theatre; debut as animation film dir in studio Sopuyzmutlfilm 1975; also scriptwriter; Founder, Pres. and Artistic Dir Animated Film Studio Stayer 1991–; Diplomas, Moscow Int. Film Festival, Bilbao Int. Film Festival, Spain, Tampere Int. Film Festival, Finland, Hon. Diploma Krakow Int. Film Festival, Poland; TV Prize, Rennes Int. Film Festival, France; Jury Prizes, Los Angeles Film Festival, USA, Hiroshima Int. Film Festival, Japan; Grand Prix Ruan Int. Film Festival, Annecy Int. Film Festival, France; Golden Dove Prize, Leipzig Int. Film Festival, Germany; Golden Palm Branch Prize, Cannes Film Festival, France; Nika Prize of Russian Acad. of Cinematic Arts (three times); State Prize of Russian Fed.; Golden Prize, New York Int. Film Festival, USA. *Films include:* The Road Tale, We Were Birds Before, The Conflict, Careless Painters, Break, Banquet, Marriage, Twists'n'Turns, Grey Wolf and Little Red Riding Hood, Choo Choo, Adagio. *Address:* Animated Film Studio Stayer, Otkrytoye shosse 28, korp.6A, 107143 Moscow (Office); Lev Tolstoy str. 3, apt. 11, 119021 Moscow, Russia (Home). *Telephone:* (095) 167-01-64 (Office); (095) 246-45-86 (Home). *Fax:* (095) 292-85-11 (Office).

BARDINI, Adolfo, DrIng; Italian industrial executive; b. 9 April 1915, Genoa; s. of the late Emilio Bardini and Eugenia Baltuzzi; m. 1st Ernestina Zampaglione 1939; two d.; m. 2nd Mirella Noli Parmeggiani 1972; ed Naples Univ.; Gen. Man. Fabbrica Macchine Industriali, Naples 1952–55; Dir and Gen. Man. Nuova San Giorgio, Genoa 1955–62; Dir and Gen. Man. Alfa Romeo SpA 1962–74; Chair. Autodelta SpA 1962–74, ANFIA (Italian Asscn of Motor Vehicle Mfrs) 1975–78, Turin Int. Motor Show 1975–78; Dir CMI SpA, Genoa 1975–82; Pres. CLCA (Comité de Liaison de la Construction Automobile pour les Pays de la Communauté Economique Européenne) 1978–80, Elettronica San Giorgio SpA ELSAG, Genoa 1979–84, Hon. Chair. 1984–94. *Address:* Corso Monforte 36, 20122 Milan, Italy (Home). *Telephone:* (02) 784320 (Home).

BARDONNET, Daniel, DJur, Dr rer. pol; French international lawyer; b. 18 May 1931, Moulins; s. of Louis Bardonnet and Marguerite Dory; m. Geneviève Paintaud-Briand 1958; two s.; ed Lycée Banville, Moulins and Faculty of Law, Univ. of Paris; Prof. Faculty of Law, Univ. of Tananarive, Madagascar 1960–66, Univ. of Rabat, Morocco 1966–72; Fellow, Woodrow Wilson Int. Center for Scholars, Washington, DC 1972–73; Prof. Faculty of Law, Univ. of Paris XII 1973–77; Prof. Inst. d'Etudes Politiques de Paris 1975–84; legal adviser, French Del. to Law of Sea Conf. 1976–82; Dir Annuaire Français de Droit Int. 1977–94; Prof. Faculty of Law, Paris Univ. of Law, Econ. and Social Sciences 1977–94, Prof. Emer. 1994–; Sec.-Gen. Hague Acad. of Int. Law 1985–99; mem. Scientific Council of Inst. du Droit Econ. de la Mer, Monaco 1985–98; mem. of the Curatorium, Hague Acad. of Int. Law 1999–; Assoc. mem. of Inst. of Int. Law 1987–; Judge, Tribunal for Nuclear Energy OECD 1990–95; arbitrator nominated by the French Govt under the UN Convention on the Law of the Sea 1998–; Prix Léon Juillot de la Morandière (Inst. de France) 1972; Chevalier Légion d'honneur, Officier des Palmes académiques, Grand Croix Ordre de José Cecilio del Valle (Honduras), Grand Croix Ordre de Mayo (Argentina), Officier Order of Orange Nassau (Pays Bas). *Publications:* Le Tribunal des conflits, juge du fond 1959, L'évolution de la structure du Parti radical 1960, La Succession d'etats à Madagascar 1970, Les Frontières terrestres et la relativité de leur tracé 1976; articles in legal journals. *Leisure interests:* sea, forest, literature, 18th-century art. *Address:* 5 rue des Eaux, 75016, Paris, France (Home). *Telephone:* 1-45-20-95-80. *Fax:* 1-40-50-19-97.

BARDOT, Brigitte; French actress; b. 28 Sept. 1934, Paris; d. of Louis and Anne-Marie (Mücel) Bardot; m. 1st Roger Vadim (died 2000); m. 2nd Jacques Charrier; one s.; m. 3rd Gunther Sachs 1966 (divorced 1969); ed Paris Conservatoire; stage and film career 1952–; Founder, Pres. Fondation Brigitte Bardot; Étoile de Cristal from Acad. of Cinema 1966; Chevalier Légion d'honneur 1985. *Films include:* Manina: la fille sans voile, Le fils de Caroline chérie, Futures vedettes, Les grandes manoeuvres, La lumière d'en face, Cette sacrée gamine, La mariée est trop belle, Et Dieu créa la femme, En effeuillant la marguerite, Une parisienne, Les bijoutiers du clair de lune, En cas de malheur, La femme et le pantin, Babette s'en va-t-en guerre, Voulez-vous danser avec moi?, La vérité, Please not now?, Le mépris, Le repos du guerrier, Une ravissante idiote, Viva Maria, A coeur joie 1967, Two weeks in September 1967, Shalako 1968, Les femmes 1969, Les novices 1970, Boulevard du rhum 1971, Les pétroleuses 1971, Don Juan 1973, L'Histoire très bonne et très joyeuse de Colinot trousse-chemise 1973. *Publication:* Initiales BB 1996 (received Prix Paul Léautaud 1996), Le Carré de Pluton 1999. *Leisure interest:* swimming. *Address:* Fondation Brigitte Bardot, 45 rue Vineuse, 75016 Paris, France. *Telephone:* 1-45-05-14-60. *Fax:* 1-45-05-14-80. *E-mail:* fbb@fondationbrigittebardot.fr (Office). *Website:* www.fondationbrigittebardot.fr (Office).

BARENBLATT, Grigory Isaakovich, MA, PhD, ScD; Russian mathematician; b. 10 July 1927, Moscow; s. of Isaak Grigorievich Barenblatt and Nadezhda Veniaminovna Kagan; m. Iraida Nikolaevna Kochina 1952; two d.; ed Moscow Univ., Univ. of Cambridge; Research Scientist, Inst. of Petroleum, USSR Acad. of Sciences, Moscow 1953–61; Prof. and Head Dept of Mechanics of Solids, Inst. of Mechanics, Moscow Univ. 1961–75; Head Theoretical Dept, Inst. of Oceanology, USSR Acad. of Sciences 1975–92; G. I. Taylor Prof. of Fluid Mechanics, Univ. of Cambridge 1992–94, Prof. Emer. 1994–; Prof. of Math., Univ. of Calif. at Berkeley 1997–; Foreign mem. American Acad. of Arts and Sciences 1975, Royal Soc. 2000; Fellow Gonville and Caius Coll., Cambridge 1994–99; Foreign Assoc. Nat. Acad. of Eng 1992, NAS 1997; mem. Academia Europaea 1993; Hon. Fellow Gonville and Caius Coll., Cambridge 1999; Hon. DTech (Royal Inst. of Tech., Stockholm) 1989; Laureate, Panetti Medal and Prize 1995, G. I. Taylor Medal, American Soc. of Eng Sciences 1999, J. C. Maxwell Prize, Int. Congress on Industrial and Applied Math. 1999, Accademia Dei Lincei Lagrange Medal 1995. *Publications:* Similarity, Self-Similarity and Intermediate Asymptotics 1979, Dimensional Analysis 1987, Theory of Fluid Flows in Porous Media (jtly) 1990, Scaling, Self-Similarity and Intermediate Asymptotics 1996; articles in scientific journals. *Leisure interest:* historical reading. *Address:* Department of Mathematics, University of California, Berkeley, CA 94720-3840 (Office); 1800 Spruce Street, apt 102, Berkeley, CA 94709-1836, USA (Home). *Telephone:* (510) 642-4162 (Office); (510) 849-0155 (Home). *Fax:* (510) 642-8204 (Office).

BARENBOIM, Daniel, FRCM; Israeli concert pianist and conductor; b. 16 Nov. 1942, Buenos Aires, Argentina; s. of Prof. Enrique and Aida (née Schuster) Barenboim; m. 1st Jacqueline du Pré 1967 (died 1987); m. 2nd Elena Bashkirova 1988; two s.; studied piano with his father and other musical subjects with Nadia Boulanger, Edwin Fischer and Igor Markevitch; début in Buenos Aires at age of seven; played Bach D Minor Concerto with orchestra at Salzburg Mozarteum at age of nine; has played in Europe regularly 1954–; yearly tours of USA 1957–; has toured Japan, Australia and S. America; has played with or conducted London Philharmonic, Philharmonia Orchestra, London Symphony Orchestra, Royal Philharmonic, Chicago Symphony Orchestra, New York Philharmonic, Philadelphia Orchestra, Israel Philharmonic, Vienna Philharmonic, Berlin Philharmonic; frequently tours with English Chamber Orchestra and with them records for EMI (projects include complete Mozart Piano Concertos and late Symphonies); other recording projects include complete Beethoven Sonatas and Beethoven Concertos (with New Philharmonia Orchestra conducted by Klemperer); has appeared in series of master-classes on BBC Television; presented Festival of Summer Music on South Bank, London 1968, 1969; leading role in Brighton Festival 1967–69; appears regularly at Edinburgh Festival; conductor, Edinburgh Festival Opera 1973; Musical Dir Orchestre de Paris 1975–89, Chicago Symphony Orchestra 1991–; Musical and Artistic Dir Deutsche Staatsoper, Berlin 1992; Hon. DMus (Manchester) 1997; Beethoven Medal 1958; Paderewski Medal 1963; Beethoven Soc. Medal 1982; Prix de la Tolérance, Protestant Acad. of Tutzing 2002. *Publication:* A Life in Music (jtly) 1991. *Address:* c/o Daniel Barenboim Secretariat, 29 rue de la Coulouvrenière, 1204 Geneva, Switzerland.

BARFIELD, Julia, MBA, RIBA; British architect; b. 15 Nov. 1952; d. of Arnold Robert Barfield and Iolanthe Mary Barfield; m. David Joseph Marks 1981; one s. one d.; ed Godophin and Latymer School, London, Architectural Asscn. School of Architecture, London; with Tetra Ltd 1978–79, Richard Rogers Partnership 1979–81, Foster Assocs. 1981–88; co-f. Marks Barfield Architects with David Marks 1989, London Eye Co. to realise London Eye project 1994; lectures include Royal Acad. of Arts 2000, 2001, RIBA 2000, The Prince's Foundation Urban Villages Forum 2000, Royal Inst. 2001, Cooper-Hewitt Nat. Design Museum, New York 2001, etc.; Civic Trust and RIBA Awards Assessor; mem. Lambeth Democracy Comm. 2000–01; RIBA Award for Architecture 2000, London First Millennium Award 2000, Royal Inst. of Chartered Surveyors Award 2000, American Inst. of Architects Design Award 2000, Design Week Special Award 2001, D Awards, Silver and Gold 2001, Blueprint Award 2001, Architectural Practice of the Year 2001. *Exhibitions include:* Architecture Foundation, Tower Power, Royal Acad. of Arts 1997, 1998, 1999, 2000, 2001, Royal Inst. of British Architects, Science Museum, Materials Gallery. *Leisure interests:* family, travel. *Address:* Marks Barfield Architects, 50 Bromells Road, London, SW4 0BG, England (Office). *Telephone:* (20) 7501-0180 (Office). *Fax:* (20) 7498-7103 (Office). *E-mail:* jbarfield@marksbarfield.com (Office). *Website:* www.marksbarfield.com (Office).

BARFOOT, Joan, BA; Canadian novelist and journalist; b. 17 May 1946, Owen Sound, Ont.; ed University of Western Ont.; reporter, Religious Windsor Star 1967–69; feature and news writer Mirror Publications, Toronto 1969–73, Toronto Sunday Sun 1973–75; with London Free Press 1976–79, 1980–94; has taught journalism and creative writing at School of Journalism, Univ. of Western Ont.; Canadian Del. First Int. Feminist Book Fair and Festival, UK 1983; Juror Books in Canada First Novel Award 1987, Gov.-Gen.'s Award for English Language Canadian Fiction 1995, Trillium Literary Award 1996, 1999; mem. Writers' Union of Canada, PEN Canada; Books in Canada First Novel Award 1978, Marian Engel Award 1992. *Publications:* Abra 1978, Dancing in the Dark 1982, Duet for Three 1985, Family News 1989, Plain Jane 1992, Charlotte and Claudia Keeping in Touch 1994, Some Things About Flying 1997, Getting Over Edgar 1999, Critical Injuries 2001. *Address:* 286 Cheapside Street, London, Ont. N6A 2A2, Canada. *E-mail:* jbarfoot@sympatico.ca (Office). *Website:* www3.sympatico.ca/jbarfoot (Office).

BARGOUTHI, Marwan Haseeb, MA; Palestinian resistance leader; b. 6 June 1959, Kobar, Ramallah; m. Fadwa Bargouthi; three s. one d.; ed Bir Zeit Univ.; joined Fatah Movt aged 15; imprisoned for involvement in an intifada (uprising) 1976; placed under admin. detention without charges for six months 1985; deported to Jordan by Israeli authorities for allegedly inciting struggle against occupation 1987; returned to W Bank, Pres. student body, Bir Zeit Univ.; served in PLO in Tunis, cen. liaison officer between PLO and Fatah; helped organize political aspects of the first Intifada 1987; mem. Revolutionary Council of Fatah 1989, Sec.-Gen. in W Bank; returned to Ramallah under Oslo Accords 1994; mem. Palestinian Legis. Council (PLC) 1996, mem. Legal Cttee, Political Cttee, Chair. Parl. Cttee with French Parl.; participated in outbreak of second Intifada in W Bank and Gaza 2000; sponsor of Tanzim (Fatah's operation dept); arrested by Israeli armed forces during incursion into Ramallah April 2002, accused of being the leader of the al-Aqsa Martyrs Brigade, indicted on terrorism charges Aug. 2002; currently detained by Israel in Maskoubieh Prison, W Jerusalem, trial commenced Sept. 2002. *E-mail:* fateh@fateh.org (Office). *Website:* www.fateh.net.

BARIANI, Didier, DèsSc; French politician; b. 16 Oct. 1943, Bellerive sur Allier; m. Chantal Maufroy (divorced); two c.; ed Inst. d'Etudes Politiques de Paris; Chargé de Mission, then Dept Head, Conseil Nat. du Patronat Français 1969–74; Dir, later Chair. Bd of Dirs., Centre de Perfectionnement et de Recherche des Relations Publiques 1974–79; Prin. Pvt. Sec. to Sec. of State for Environment, Ministry of Quality of Life June–Oct. 1974, to Sec. of State in charge of Public Admin., Prime Minister's Office 1974–76; Lecturer, Inst. d'Etudes Politiques de Paris 1975–79; Pres. Paris Fed. of Parti Radical Socialiste (PRS) 1973–78; Sec.-Gen. of party 1977–79, UDF Deputy for Paris 20th Arrondissement 1978–81, Vice-Pres. UDF Group in Nat. Ass. 1978–81, Exec. Vice-Pres. 1994–97, Nat. Vice-Pres. UDF 1979–83, 1995–97, Pres. UDF, Paris 1999–; Pres. PRS 1979–83; mem. Steering Cttee, Exec. Cttee PRS 1971; mem. UDF Nat. Council 1978–; Paris Councillor 1983, mem. Perm. Comm., Conseil de Paris; Pres. and Dir-Gen. Saemar Saint-Blaise 1983–2001; Mayor 20th Arrondissement, Paris 1983–95, Deputy Mayor of Paris 1983–2001; Sec. of State, Ministry of Foreign Affairs 1986–88; Pres. Parti Radical 1979–83; Nat. Del. of UDF (relations with int. orgs.) 1988–92; Man. Société INFORG (Information, Communication et Organisation) 1977–; Pres. Parti Radical Fédération Régionale de l'Ile de France 1988–; Exec. Vice-Pres. (in Nat. Ass.) UDF 1994–97, Chair. 1999–; Jt Sec.-Gen. responsible for UDF's relations with int. insts 1992–96; mem. Nat. Ass. 1993–97, Vice-Pres. 1995–97; mem. Comm. for Foreign Affairs 1993–97; Titular Judge High Court of Justice 1995–97; Pres. France-Israel Friendship Group 1993–97; Adviser to Mayor of Paris 1995–2001; Co-Producer UDF/RPR Project 'Gouverner ensemble' 1986, 'Projet UDF/RPR pour la France' 1993; Hon. Pres. Parti Radical, Paris Football Club; Chevalier Légion d'honneur, Officier Ordre nat. du Mérite. *Publication:* Les immigrés: pour ou contre la France? 1985, Manifeste des Radicaux (jtly) 1995, Manifestement Radical (jtly) 1996. *Leisure interests:* football, skiing, tennis. *Address:* Groupe UDF-9, Hôtel de Ville de Paris, 75196 Paris RP, France. *Telephone:* 1-42-76-51-27 (Office). *Fax:* 1-42-76-64-57 (Office).

BARING, Arnulf Martin, LLD; German academic; b. 8 May 1932, Dresden; s. of Martin Baring and Gertrud Stolze; m.; three d. one s.; ed Univs. of Hamburg, Berlin, Freiburg, Columbia Univ., NY, USA, Freie Univ. Berlin, Inst. of Admin. Science, Speyer and Fondation Nat. des Sciences Politiques, Paris; lecturer, Inst. for Public and Admin. Law, Freie Univ. Berlin 1956–58, in Political Science and Int. Relations 1966–68, Univ. Lecturer, Faculty of Econ. and Social Sciences 1968, Prof. of Political Science, Otto-Suhr-Inst. and John F. Kennedy Inst. 1969–, of Contemporary History and Int. Relations, Dept of History 1976–; Research Assoc., Center for Int. Affairs, Harvard Univ.

1968–69; Political Ed. Westdeutscher Rundfunk 1962–64; Guest Prof. Stiftung für Wissenschaft und Politik, Ebenhausen, Sr Research Assoc., Inst. for East-West Security Studies, New York, Fellow, Wilson Int. Center for Scholars, Washington, DC 1986–88; mem. Inst. for Advanced Study, Princeton, NJ 1992–93; Fellow, St Antony's Coll., Oxford 1993–94. *Publications include:* Charles de Gaulle: Grosse und Grenzen (with Christian Tautil) 1963, Aussenpolitik in Adenauers Kanzlerdemokratie 1969, Sehr verehrter Herr Bundeskanzler, Heinrich von Brentano im Briefwechsel mit Konrad Adenauer 1949–64, 1974, Zwei zaghafte Riesen? Deutschland und Japan nach 1945 (co-ed.) 1977, Machtwechsel, Die Ära Brandt-Scheel 1982, Unser neuer Grössenwahn, Deutschland zwischen Ost und West 1988, Deutschland, was nun? 1991, Scheitert Deutschland? 1997, Es lebe die Republik, es lebe Deutschland! 1999; contrib. to Frankfurter Allgemeine Zeitung, Westdeutscher und Norddeutscher Rundfunk, Sender Freies Berlin. *Leisure interests:* travel, rambling. *Address:* Freie Universität Berlin, FB Geschichtswissenschaften, Habelschwerdter Allee 45, 14195 Berlin (Office); Ahrenshooper Zeile 64, 14129 Berlin, Germany.

BARING, Hon. Sir John Francis Harcourt (see Ashburton, Baron).

BARKAUSKAS, Antanas Stase; Lithuanian government official (retd); b. 20 Jan. 1917, Paparchiai, Lithuania; s. of Stasys Barkauskas and Aleksandra Barkauskas; m. Zoya Yarashunaitė 1961; one s. one d.; ed Higher Communist Party School, Moscow and Acad. of Social Sciences; mem. of Lithuanian Young Komsomol League 1940; Soviet official in Kaunas 1940–41; served in 16th Lithuanian Div. 1942–44; mem. CPSU 1942–90, party official in Kaunas during post-war period; Sec. Vilnius (later Kaunas) Regional Cttee of Lithuanian C.P. 1950–53; Teacher, Head of Dept, Kaunas Polytechnic Inst. 1953–55; Head of Dept, Cen. Cttee of Lithuanian C.P. 1959–60, mem. Cen. Cttee 1960–90, Sec. of Cen. Cttee 1961–75, mem. Secr. 1961–91, mem. Politburo 1962–66; Deputy to Supreme Soviet of Lithuania 1959–90, Chair. Supreme Soviet of Lithuanian SSR 1959–75, Pres. of Presidium 1975–85; Deputy to Supreme Soviet of USSR 1974–89, Vice-Chair. of Presidium 1976–85; mem. Cen. Auditing Cttee of CPSU 1976–81; Cand. mem. Cen. Cttee, CPSU 1981–86 (retd); Honoured Cultural Worker of Lithuanian SSR 1967. *Publications:* Country, Culture, Rural Life 1967, Culture and Society 1975, Lithuanian Countryside: Past, Present and Future (in English, French, German, Hungarian and Arabic) 1976, Lithuania: Years and Deeds (in English) 1982. *Leisure interests:* fiction, travelling, sport. *Address:* Akmenų str. 7a, Vilnius, Lithuania. *Telephone:* (2) 62-44-45.

BARKER, David James Purslove, MD, PhD, FRS, FRCP(UK); British medical research director; b. 29 June 1938, London; s. of the late Hugh Barker and Joye Barker; m. 1st Angela Coddington 1960 (deceased); m. 2nd Janet Franklin 1983; three s. two d. and one step-s. two step-d.; ed Oundle School and Guy's Hosp. Univ. of London; Research Fellow, Dept of Medicine, Univ. of Birmingham 1963, Lecturer in Medicine 1966; Lecturer in Preventive Medicine, Makerere Univ. Uganda 1969–72; Sr Lecturer in Clinical Epidemiology and Consultant Physician, Univ. of Southampton 1972–79, Prof. of Clinical Epidemiology 1979–; Hon. Consultant Physician, Royal S. Hants. Hosp.; Dir MRC Environmental Epidemiology Unit, Univ. of Southampton 1984–; Founder FMedSci 1998; Hon. Fellow Royal Coll. of Obstetricians and Gynaecologists 1993, Royal Coll. of Paediatrics; Royal Soc. Wellcome Gold Medal 1994, Feldberg Foundation Award, Prince Mahidol Prize for Medicine. *Publications:* Practical Epidemiology 1973, Epidemiology in Medical Practice (with G. Rose) 1976, Epidemiology for the Uninitiated (with G. Rose) 1979, Fetal and Infant Origins of Adult Disease 1992, Mothers, Babies and Disease in Later Life 1998, The Best Start in Life 2003. *Leisure interests:* writing, drawing, golf, fishing, craic. *Address:* MRC Environmental Epidemiology Unit, Southampton General Hospital, Southampton, SO16 6YD (Office); Manor Farm, East Dean, nr Salisbury, Wilts., SP5 1HB, England (Home). *Telephone:* (23) 8077-7624 (Office); (1794) 340016 (Home). *Fax:* (23) 8070-4021 (Office).

BARKER, Pat, CBE, BSc(Econ); British author; b. 8 May 1943, Thornaby-on-Tees; m.; two c.; ed LSE; Hon. Fellow, LSE 1998; Hon. MLitt (Teesside) 1993; Hon. DLitt (Napier) 1996, (Durham) 1998, (Hertfordshire) 1998, (London) 2002; Dr hc (Open Univ.) 1997; Fawcett Prize 1983, Guardian Prize for Fiction 1993. *Publications:* novels: Union Street 1982, Blow Your House Down 1984, The Century's Daughter 1986 (retitled Liza's England 1996), The Man Who Wasn't There 1989; trilogy of First World War novels: Regeneration 1991, The Eye in the Door 1993, The Ghost Road (Booker Prize 1995) 1995; Another World 1998, Border Crossing 2001, Double Vision 2003. *Address:* c/o Gillon Aitken Associates, 29 Fernshaw Road, London, SW10 0TG, England. *Telephone:* (20) 7351-7561. *Fax:* (20) 7376-3594.

BARKIN, Ellen; American actress; b. 16 April 1955, New York; m. Gabriel Byrne 1988; one s.; m. 2nd Ronald Perelman 2000; ed City Univ. of New York and Hunter Coll. Ind. *Films:* Diner 1982, Daniel 1983, Tender Mercies 1983, Eddie and the Cruisers 1983, The Adventures of Buckaroo Banzai 1984, Harry and Son 1984, Enormous Changes at the Last Minute 1985, Down by Law 1986, The Big Easy 1987, Siesta 1987, Sea of Love 1989, Johnny Handsome, Switch, Man Trouble 1992, Mac 1993, This Boy's Life 1993, Into the West 1993, Bad Company 1995, Wild Bill 1995, Mad Dog Time 1996, The Fan 1996, Fear and Loathing in Las Vegas, Popcorn, Drop Dead Gorgeous, The White River Kid 1999, Crime and Punishment in Suburbia 2000, Mercy 2000, Someone Like You 2001. *Stage appearances include:* Shout Across the River 1980, Killings on the Last Line 1980, Extremities 1982, Eden Court. *TV appearances include:* Search for Tomorrow, Kent State 1981, We're Fighting Back 1981, Terrible Joe Moran 1984, Before Women Had Wings 1998 (Emmy Award). *Address:* c/o CAA, 9830 Wilshire Boulevard, Beverly Hills, CA 90212, USA (Office).

BARKWORTH, Peter Wynn; British actor and author; b. 14 Jan. 1929, Margate, Kent; s. of Walter W. Barkworth and Irene M. Barkworth; ed Stockport School and Royal Acad. of Dramatic Art; Hon. MA (Manchester); BAFTA Best Actor Award 1974, 1977; Royal Television Soc. Best Actor 1977; Writers' Guild Best Actor 1977. *Films include:* Where Eagles Dare 1968, Mr Smith, Escape from the Dark, Champions 1983, Wilde 1997. *Stage appearances in London include:* Roar Like a Dove (Phoenix) 1957–60, The School for Scandal (Haymarket and New York) 1962, Crown Matrimonial (Haymarket) 1972, Donkeys' Years (Globe) 1976, Can You Hear Me at the Back? (Piccadilly) 1979–80, A Coat of Varnish (Haymarket) 1982, Siegfried Sassoon (Apollo) 1987, Hidden Laughter (Vaudeville) 1990–91, The Winslow Boy (Globe) 1994. *Television series include:* The Power Game 1966, Manhunt 1969, Winston Churchill: The Wilderness Years 1975, Telford's Change 1978, Late Starter 1984, The Price 1984. *Publications:* About Acting 1980, First Houses 1983, More About Acting 1984, The Complete About Acting 1991, For All Occasions 1997. *Leisure interests:* walking, gardening, looking at paintings. *Address:* 47 Flask Walk, London, NW3 1HH; 26 Marlborough Court, Earls Avenue, Folkestone, Kent, CT20 2PN, England. *Telephone:* (20) 7794-4591; (1303) 245728.

BARLOW, Sir Frank, Kt, CBE; British business executive; b. 25 March 1930; s. of John Barlow and Isabella Barlow; m. Constance Patricia Ginns 1950 (died 2000), one s. two d.; ed Barrow Grammar School, Cumbria; with Nigerian Electricity Supply Corpn 1952–59; worked for Daily Times, Nigeria 1960–62; Man. Dir Ghana Graphic 1962–63, Barbados Advocate 1963, Trinidad Mirror Newspapers 1963–64, Daily Mirror 1964–67, King & Hutchings 1967–75; Dir and Gen. Man. Westminster Press 1975–83, CEO Westminster Press Group 1985–90; Dir Economist 1983–99; CEO Financial Times Group 1983–99 (Chair. 1993–96); Man. Dir Pearson PLC 1990–96; Chair. BSkyB 1991–95, Logica PLC 1995–; Pres. Les Echos, Paris 1988–90; Dir Elsevier UK 1991–94; Dir Soc. Européene des Satellites SA 2000–; Chair. Lottery Products Ltd 1997–; Dir Press Asscn 1985–93; Chair. Printers' Charitable Corpn 1995–; Dir Royal Philharmonic Orchestra 1988–93. *Leisure interests:* golf, fell walking, angling. *Address:* Logica PLC, Stephenson House, 75 Hampstead Road, London, NW1 2PL (Office); Tremarne, Marsham Way, Gerrards Cross, Buckinghamshire, SL9 8AW, England (Home). *Telephone:* (20) 7446-1786 (Office). *Website:* www.logica.com (Office).

BARLOW, Sir William, Kt, DSc, F.R.ENG., FIEE, FIMechE; British engineer; b. 8 June 1924, Oldham; s. of Albert Edward and Annice Barlow; m. Elaine Mary Atherton Adamson 1948; one s. one d.; ed Manchester Grammar School and Manchester Univ.; English Electric Co. Ltd 1947–68; Man. Dir English Electric Computers 1967–68; Chief Exec. Ransome Hoffmann Pollard Ltd 1969–77, Chair. 1971–77; Chair. Post Office Corpn 1977–80; Dir Thorn EMI PLC 1980–89, Chair. of Eng Group 1980–84; Dir BICC PLC 1980–91, Chair. 1984–91; Chair. Ericsson Ltd 1981–94, Metal Industries Ltd 1980–84, SKF (UK) Ltd 1990–92, Barking Power 1992–93, Parsons Brinckerhoff Ltd 1997–2002; Chair. Design Council 1980–86, Eng Council 1988–90; Dir Vodafone Group (fmrly Racal Telecom) 1988–98, Waste Man. Int. PLC 1992–98, Chemring Group PLC 1994–97 (Chair. 1997–98); Pres. Royal Acad. of Eng 1991–96; Vice-Pres. City and Guilds of London Inst. 1982–93; Gov. London Business School 1979–92; Pres. British Electrotechnical and Allied Mfrs Asscn (BEAMA) 1986–87; Hon. DSc (Cranfield Inst. of Tech.) 1979, (Bath) 1986, (Aston) 1988, Hon. DTech (Liverpool Polytechnic) 1988, (City Univ.) 1989, (Loughborough) 1993, Hon. DEng (UMIST) 1996. *Leisure interest:* golf, racing. *Address:* 4 Parkside, Henley-on-Thames, Oxon., RG9 1TX, England. *Telephone:* (1491) 411101. *Fax:* (1491) 410013.

BÄRLUND, Kaj-Ole Johannes, MSc(ECON.); Finnish politician and international organization official; b. 9 Nov. 1945, Porvoo; s. of Elis Bärlund and Meri Bärlund; m. Eeva-Kaisa Oksama 1972; one s. one d.; journalist, Finnish Broadcasting Co. 1967–71; Public Relations Officer, Cen. Org. of Finnish Trade Unions 1971–72; Legis. Sec. Ministry of Justice 1972–79; mem. Parl. 1979–91; Chair. Porvoo City Bd 1979–87, Nat. Cttee on Natural Resources 1979–83; Chair. Swedish Labour Union of Finland 1983–90; mem. Nordic Council, Vice-Chair. Nordic Council Social and Environment Cttee 1983–87; mem. Exec. Bd Finnish Broadcasting Co. 1982–83, Neste Oy 1983–90; Chair. Bureau of the Montreal Protocol 1989–90; Chair. UN/ECE Cttee on Environmental Policy 1991–95; Minister of the Environment 1987–91; Dir-Gen. Nat. Bd of Waters and the Environment 1990–95; Dir-Gen. Finnish Environment Agency 1995–2001; Dir Environment and Human Settlements Div. UN/ECE 1995–; Chair. Consumers' Union of Finland 1983–90, Peoples of Finland and Russia Friendship Soc. 1991–95, Union of the Pulmonary Disabled in Finland 1993–95; mem. Party Exec., Finnish Social Democratic Party 1984–91, Chair. Environmental Working Group 1981–87; State Publicity Prize (Finland) 1972. *Publications:* Miksi Ei EEC 1971, Palkat Paketissa 1972. *Leisure interests:* tennis, cross-country skiing, literature, roller skating. *Address:* Environment and Human Settlements Division, Economic Commission for Europe, Palais des Nations, 1211 Geneva 10, Switzerland. *Telephone:* (22) 917-23-70. *Fax:* (22) 907-01-07.

BARNABY, Charles Frank, PhD; British physicist; b. 27 Sept. 1927, Andover, Hants.; s. of Charles H. Barnaby and Lilian Sainsbury; m. Wendy

Elizabeth Field 1972; one s. one d.; ed Andover Grammar School and Univ. of London; Physicist, UK Atomic Energy Authority 1950–57; mem. Sr Scientific Staff, Medical Research Council, Univ. Coll. Medical School 1957–68; Exec. Sec. Pugwash Confs on Science and World Affairs 1968–70; Dir Stockholm Int. Peace Research Inst. (SIPRI) 1971–81; Prof. of Peace Studies, Free Univ., Amsterdam 1981–85; Dir World Disarmament Campaign (UK) 1982–; Chair. Just Defence 1982–; Consultant Oxford Research Group 1998–; Ed. Int. Journal of Human Rights; Hon. DSc (Frei Univ., Amsterdam) 1982, (Southampton) 1996. *Publications:* Man and the Atom 1971, Ed. Preventing the Spread of Nuclear Weapons 1971, Co-ed. Anti-ballistic Missile Systems 1971, Disarmament and Arms Control 1973, The Nuclear Age 1976, Prospects for Peace 1980, Future Warfare (ed. and co-author) 1983, Space Weapons 1984, The Automated Battlefield 1986, The Invisible Bomb 1989, The Gaia Peace Atlas 1989, The Role and Control of Weapons in the 1990s 1992, How Nuclear Weapons Spread 1993, Instruments of Terror 1997; articles in scientific journals. *Leisure interest:* natural history. *Address:* Brandreth, Chilbolton, Stockbridge, Hants., England. *Telephone:* (1264) 860423 (Home). *Fax:* (1264) 860868.

BARNALA, Surjit Singh, LLB; Indian politician and lawyer; b. 21 Oct. 1925, Ateli, Gurgaon Dist (now in Haryana); s. of Nar Singh and Jasmer Kaur; m. Surjit Kaur 1954; three s. one d.; ed Lucknow Univ.; Shiromani Akali Dal MP for Barnala 1967–77; Educ. Minister of Punjab 1969–71; MP from Sangrur 1977; Union Agric., Irrigation and Food Minister in Janata Govt 1977–80; elected Pres. Shiromani Akali Dal 1985; Chief Minister of Punjab 1985–87; Gov. Tamil Nadu 1990, Minister of Chemicals and Fertilizers –1999, of Food March 1998–2001. *Leisure interests:* painting, reading, ecology. *Address:* c/o Ministry of Food, 45 Krishi Bhavan, New Delhi 110 001 (Office); Barnala Sangrur Dist, Punjab, India.

BARNARD, Eric Albert, PhD, FRS; British biochemist; b. 2 July 1927; m. Penelope J. Hennessy 1956; two s. two d.; ed Davenant Foundation School, King's Coll., Univ. of London; Nuffield Foundation Fellow, King's Coll. 1956–59, Asst Lecturer 1959–60, Lecturer 1960–64; Assoc. Prof. of Biochemical Pharmacology, State Univ. of New York 1964–65, Prof. of Biochemistry 1965–76, Head Biochemistry Dept 1969–76; Rank Prof. of Physiological Biochemistry, Imperial Coll. of Science and Tech., London 1976–85, Chair. Div. of Life Sciences 1977–85, Head Dept of Biochemistry 1979–85; Dir MRC Molecular Neurobiology Unit, Cambridge 1985–92; Dir Molecular Neurobiology Unit, Prof. of Neurobiology, Royal Free Hosp. School of Medicine, London Univ. 1992–; Rockefeller Fellow, Univ. of Calif., Berkeley 1960–61; Guggenheim Fellow, MRC Lab. of Molecular Biology, Cambridge 1971; Visiting Prof., Univ. of Marburg, Fed. Rep. of Germany 1965, Tokyo Univ. 1993; Visiting Scientist, Inst. Pasteur, France 1973; Ed.-in-Chief Receptors and Channels 1993–; Visiting Prof. Dept of Pharmacology, Cambridge Univ. 1999–; mem. American Soc. of Biological Chemists, Int. Soc. of Neurochemistry; cttee mem. MRC; mem. editorial bd four scientific journals; Josiah Macy Faculty Scholar Award, USA 1975, Medal of Polish Acad. of Sciences 1980, Ciba Medal and Prize 1985, Eastman Kodak Award (USA) 1988, Erspamer Int. Award for Neuroscience 1991, Eli Lilly Prize for European Neuroscience 1998. *Publications:* ed. eight scientific books; numerous papers in learned journals. *Leisure interest:* the pursuit of good claret. *Address:* Department of Pharmacology, University of Cambridge, Tennis Court Road, Cambridge, CB2 1PD, England (Office). *Telephone:* (1223) 334073 (Office). *Fax:* (1223) 843090 (Office). *E-mail:* eb247@cam.ac.uk (Office). *Website:* www.phar.cam.ac.uk (Office).

BARNARD, Lukas Daniël, MA, DPhil; South African intelligence officer and university professor; b. 14 June 1949, Otjiwarongo; s. of Nicolaas Evehardus Barnard and Magdalena Catharina Beukes; m. Engela Brand 1971; three s.; ed Otjiwarongo High School, Univ. of OFS; Sr Lecturer Univ. of OFS 1976, Prof. and Head, Dept of Political Science 1978; Dir-Gen. Nat. Intelligence Service (fmrly Dept of Nat. Security) 1980–91, Head, Constitutional Devt Service 1992; mem. several cttees. and bds.; S. African Police Star for Outstanding Service 1985, Order of the Star of S. Africa (Class 1), Gold 1987, Nat. Intelligence Service Decoration for Outstanding Leadership, Gold Nat. Intelligence Service Medal for Distinguished Service, Senior Service Award, Gold (CDS) 1992. *Publications:* one book, 26 articles in popular and technical scientific journals. *Leisure interest:* tennis. *Address:* c/o Constitutional Development, Private Bag X804, Pretoria 0001, South Africa. *Telephone:* 3412400.

BARNDORFF-NIELSEN, Ole Eiler, ScD, RI; Danish professor of mathematics; b. 18 March 1935, Copenhagen; m. Bente Jensen-Storch 1956; two s. one d.; ed Univ. of Copenhagen and Aarhus Univ.; Prof. of Math. Statistics, Inst. of Math., Aarhus Univ. 1973–, Scientific Dir Math. Centre 1995–97, MaPhySto (Centre for Math. Physics and Stochastics) 1998–2003; Ed.-in-Chief Bernoulli 1994–2000; mem. Royal Danish Acad. of Sciences and Letters 1980–, Academia Europaea 1990–; Pres. Bernoulli Soc. for Math. Statistics and Probability 1993–95; Dr hc (Univ. Paul Sabatier, Toulouse) 1993, (Katholieke Univ. Leuven) 1999; Humboldt Research Award 2002. *Publications:* Information and Exponential Families in Statistical Theory 1978, Parametric Statistical Models and Likelihood 1988, Asymptotic Techniques for Use in Statistics (with D. R. Cox) 1989, Decomposition and Invariance of Measures with a View to Statistical Transformation Models (with P. Blœsild and P. S. Eriksen) 1989, Inference and Asymptotics (with D. R. Cox) 1994; numerous scientific papers. *Leisure interests:* biography, opera, tennis.

Address: Department of Mathematical Sciences, Aarhus University, 8000 Aarhus (Inst.) (Office); Dalvangen 48, 8270 Højbjerg, Denmark (Home). *Telephone:* 89423521 (Office); 86271442 (Home). *E-mail:* oebn@imf.au.dk.

BARNES, Christopher Richard, CM, BSc, PhD, FRSC, PGeol; Canadian geologist; b. 20 April 1940, Nottingham, England; m. Susan M. Miller 1961; three d.; ed Univs. of Southampton and Ottawa; NATO Research Fellow Univ. of Wales, Swansea 1964–65; Asst Prof. Univ. of Waterloo 1965–70, Assoc. Prof. 1970–76, Prof. and Chair. 1976–81, Biology Dept 1973–81; Sr Research Fellow Univ. of Southampton, UK 1971–72; Univ. of Cambridge 1980–81; Prof. and Head Memorial Univ. of Newfoundland 1981–87; Acting Dir Centre for Earth Resources Research 1984–87; Dir-Gen. Sedimentary and Marine Geosciences, Geological Survey of Canada 1987–89; Dir Centre for Earth and Ocean Research Univ. of Vic. 1989–2000, Dir School of Earth and Ocean Sciences 1991–2002; Project Dir Neptune Canada 2001–; Pres. Canadian Geoscience Council 1979, Geological Asscn of Canada 1983–84, Acad. of Sciences, Royal Soc. of Canada 1990–93; mem. Science Council of BC 1991–95, Atomic Energy Control Bd 1996–2000, Canadian Nuclear Safety Comm. 2000–; Geological Asscn of Canada Nat. Lecturer 1978; Bancroft Award 1982, Past-Pres.'s Medal 1977, Willis Ambrose Medal 1991. *Publications:* over 140 scientific works in geological journals. *Address:* School of Earth and Ocean Sciences, Univ. of Victoria, PO Box 3055, Victoria, BC, V8W 3P6, Canada. *Telephone:* (250) 721-8847. *Fax:* (250) 721-6200.

BARNES, Clive Alexander, CBE; British journalist and dance and theatre critic; b. 13 May 1927, London; s. of Arthur Lionel Barnes and Freda Marguerite Garratt; m. Patricia Winckley 1958; one s. one d.; ed King's Coll., London and Univ. of Oxford; served RAF 1946–48; Admin. Officer, Town Planning Dept, London Co. Council 1952–61; also active as freelance journalist contributing articles, reviews and criticisms on music, dance, theatre, films and television to the New Statesman, The Spectator, The Daily Express, The New York Times, etc.; Chief Dance Critic, The Times, London 1961–65; Exec. Ed., Dance and Dancers, Music and Musicians, Plays and Players 1961–65; Dance Critic The New York Times 1965–78, also Drama Critic (weekdays only) 1967–77; Assoc. Ed., Chief Drama and Dance Critic, New York Post 1977–; a New York Corresp. of The Times 1970–; Kt Order of the Dannebrog (Denmark). *Publications:* Ballet in Britain Since the War, Frederick Ashton and His Ballet, Ballet Here and Now, Dance As It Happened, Dance in the Twentieth Century, Dance Scene: USA; Ed. Nureyev 1983. *Leisure interests:* eating, drinking, walking, theatre. *Address:* c/o New York Post, 210 South Street, New York, NY 10002, USA.

BARNES, Edward Larrabee, MArch; American architect; b. 22 April 1915, Chicago Ill.; s. of Cecil Barnes and Margaret H. (Ayer) Barnes; m. Mary E Coss 1944; one s.; ed Milton Acad., Harvard Coll. and Graduate School of Design; Sheldon Travelling Fellowship 1942; architectural practice in New York 1949–; Critic of Architectural Design, Pratt Inst., Brooklyn 1954–59, Yale School of Architecture 1957–64, Eliot Noyes Critic, Harvard Graduate School of Design 1979; Jefferson Prof., Univ. of Virginia 1980; work exhibited at Museum of Modern Art (New York), Carnegie Inst. (Pittsburgh, Pa), Whitney Museum, New York and published in architectural magazines; Dir Municipal Art Soc. of New York 1960; Fellow, American Inst. of Architects; Trustee, American Acad. in Rome 1963–78, Vice-Pres. 1973, First Vice-Chair. 1975; Trustee, Museum of Modern Art, New York, 1975–93, Life Trustee 1993–; Assoc. Nat. Acad. of Design 1969, Academician 1974–; Fellow, American Acad. of Arts and Sciences 1978; mem. American Acad. of Arts and Letters 1991–; Hon. DFA (Rhode Island School of Design) 1983; Hon. DHumLitt (Amherst Coll.) 1984; Yale Award for Distinction in the Arts 1959, Arnold Brunner Prize, Nat. Inst. of Arts and Letters 1959, Silver Medal, Architectural League, (New York) 1960, AIA Medal of Hon. (New York chapter) 1971, AIA Collaborative Achievement in Architecture 1972, Hon. Award 1972, 1977, 1986, Harleston Parker Award, Boston Soc. of Architects 1972, Louis Sullivan Award 1979, Honor Award, Connecticut Soc. of Architects 1980, AIA Architectural Firm Award 1980 (25 Year Award 1994), Thomas Jefferson Award 1981 (Univ. of Virginia), Honor Award, New Mexico Soc. of Architects 1983, Excellence in Design Award, NY State Asscn of Architects 1984, Harvard Univ. 350th Anniversary Medal 1986, Interfaith Forum on Religion, Art and Architecture, Honor Award 1989, AIA 25-year Award 1994, American Craft Council Award of Distinction 1998, and other awards. *Works include:* pre-fabricated house, pvt. houses, camps, academic bldgs. and master plans, office bldgs and corporate headquarters, museums and botanical gardens including Haystack Mountain School of Arts and Crafts, Maine; master plans for State Univ. of New York at Purchase and Potsdam; office bldgs. for New England Merchants Nat. Bank, Boston, IBM headquarters in New York City and Mt. Pleasant, New York; master plan and office/retail complex, Crown Center, Kansas City; Walker Art Gallery, Minneapolis, Minn.; Sarah Scaife Gallery, Pittsburgh, Pa; Chicago Botanic Garden, Dallas Museum of Art, Minn. Sculpture Garden, etc. *Leisure interests:* music, piano, sailing, climbing. *Address:* 975 Memorial Drive, Cambridge, MA 02138, USA. *Telephone:* (617) 876-1543.

BARNES, John Arundel, DSC, MA, DPhil, FBA; British/Australian sociologist; b. 9 Sept. 1918, Reading, Berks.; s. of Thomas D. Barnes and M. Grace Barnes; m. Helen F. Bastable 1942; three s. one d.; ed Christ's Hosp., St John's Coll. Cambridge, Univ. of Cape Town and Balliol Coll. Oxford; served RN 1940–46; Research Officer, Rhodes-Livingston Inst. N Rhodesia 1946–49; Lecturer, Dept of Anthropology, Univ. Coll. London 1949–51; Fellow, St John's Coll. Cambridge 1950–53; Simon Research Fellow, Univ. of Manchester 1951–53;

Reader in Anthropology, London School of Econs 1954–56; Prof. of Anthropology, Univ. of Sydney 1956–58, Australian Nat. Univ. 1958–69; Fellow, Churchill Coll. Cambridge 1965–66, 1969–; Prof. of Sociology, Univ. of Cambridge 1969–82; Visiting Fellow, Australian Nat. Univ. 1978–79, 1984–92, Program Visitor 1993–98; Fellow, Acad. of Social Sciences, Australia; Wellcome Medal 1950, Rivers Medal 1959, Royal Anthropological Inst. *Publications:* Marriage in a Changing Society 1951, Politics in a Changing Society 1954, Three Styles in the Study of Kinship 1971, The Ethics of Inquiry in Social Science 1977, Who Should Know What? 1979, Models and Interpretations 1990, A Pack of Lies 1994. *Address:* Churchill College, Cambridge, CB3 0DS, England. *Telephone:* (1223) 365395.

BARNES, Jonathan, FBA; British professor of philosophy; b. 1942; s. of the late A. L. Barnes and K. M. Barnes; m. Jennifer Postgate 1965; two d.; ed City of London School and Balliol Coll. Oxford; Fellow, Oriel Coll. Oxford 1968–78, Balliol Coll. 1978–94; Prof. of Ancient Philosophy, Univ. of Oxford 1989–94, Univ. of Geneva 1994–2002, Univ. of Paris IV–Sorbonne 2003–; visiting posts at Inst. for Advanced Study, Princeton 1972, Univ. of Texas 1981, Wissenschaftskolleg zu Berlin 1985, Univ. of Alberta 1986, Univ. of Zurich 1987, Istituto Italiano per la Storia della Filosofia 1994, Ecole Normale Supérieure, Paris 1996, Scuola Normale di Pisa 2002; Hon. Fellow American Acad. of Arts and Sciences 1999; Condorcet Medal 1996. *Publications:* The Ontological Argument 1972, Aristotle's Posterior Analytics 1975, The Presocratic Philosophers 1979, Aristotle 1982, Early Greek Philosophy 1987, The Toils of Scepticism 1991, Companion to Aristotle 1995, Logic and the Imperial Stoa 1997. *Address:* Les Charmilles, 36200 Ceaulmont; 12 blvd Arago, 75013 Paris, France. *E-mail:* jonathanbarnes@wanadoo.fr.

BARNES, Julian (Patrick), (also writes as Dan Kavanagh); British author; b. 19 Jan. 1946, Leicester; m. Pat Kavanagh; ed City of London School, Magdalen Coll. Oxford; Lexicographer, Oxford English Dictionary Supplement 1969–72; TV Critic New Statesman 1977–81, Asst Literary Ed. 1977–79; Contributing Ed. New Review, London 1977–78; Deputy Literary Ed. Sunday Times, London 1979–81; TV Critic The Observer 1982–86; Hon. Fellow Magdalen Coll., Oxford 1996–; E. M. Forster Award, US Acad. of Arts and Letters 1986, Shakespeare Prize, Germany 1993; Officier, Ordre des Arts et des Lettres 1995. *Publications:* Metroland, Duffy (as Dan Kavanagh) 1980, Fiddle City (as Dan Kavanagh) 1981, Before She Met Me 1982, Flaubert's Parrot (Geoffrey Faber Memorial Prize, Prix Medicis 1986) 1984, Putting the Boot In (as Dan Kavanagh) 1985, Staring at the Sun 1986, Going to the Dogs (as Dan Kavanagh) 1987, A History of the World in 10½ Chapters 1989, Talking it Over (Femina Etranger Prize) 1991, The Porcupine (novel) 1992, Letters from London 1990–95 (articles) 1995, Cross Channel (short stories) 1996, England, England 1998, Love, etc (novel) 2000, Something to Declare 2002. *Address:* c/o Peters, Fraser & Dunlop, Drury House, 34–43 Russell Street, London, WC2B 5HA, England.

BARNES, Peter John, MA, DM, DSc, FRCP, FMedSci; British professor of thoracic medicine; b. 29 Oct. 1946, Birmingham; s. of the late John Barnes and Eileen Barnes; m. Olivia Harvard-Watts 1976; three s.; ed Leamington Coll., Cambridge Univ., Oxford Univ. Clinical School; medical positions Oxford, Brompton Hosp., Nat. Hosp., Univ. Coll. Hosp. 1972–78; Sr Registrar Hammersmith Hosp. 1979–82; Sr Lecturer, Consultant Physician Royal Postgrad. Medical School 1982–85 (MRC Research Fellow 1978–79); Prof. of Clinical Pharmacology Cardiothoracic Inst. 1985–87, of Thoracic Medicine, Nat. Heart and Lung Inst. 1987–; Hon. Consultant Physician Royal Brompton Hosp. 1987–; MRC Travelling Fellow Cardiovascular Research Inst., San Francisco 1981–82; numerous awards. *Publications:* Asthma: Basic Mechanics and Clinical Management, The Lung: Scientific Foundations 1991, Pharmacology of the Respiratory Tract 1993, Conquering Asthma 1994, Molecular Biology of Lung Disease 1994, Asthma (2 Vols) 1997. *Leisure interests:* ethnic art, foreign travel, gardening. *Address:* Department of Thoracic Medicine, National Heart and Lung Institute (Imperial College), Dovehouse Street, London, SW3 6LY (Office); 44 Woodsome Road, London, NW5 1RZ, England (Home). *Telephone:* (20) 7351-8174; (20) 7485-6582. *Fax:* (20) 7351-5675. *E-mail:* p.j.barnes@ic.ac.uk (Office). *Website:* www.med.ic.ac.uk.

BARNETT, Correlli Douglas, CBE, MA; British historian; b. 28 June 1927, Norbury, Surrey; s. of Douglas A. Barnett and Kathleen M. Barnett; m. Ruth Murby 1950; two d.; ed Trinity School, Croydon and Exeter Coll. Oxford; Intelligence Corps 1945–48; North Thames Gas Bd 1952–57; public relations 1957–63; Keeper of Archives, Churchill Coll. Cambridge 1977–95; Defence Lecturer, Univ. of Cambridge 1980–83; Fellow Churchill Coll., Cambridge 1977–; mem. Council, Royal United Services Inst. for Defence Studies 1973–85; mem. Cttee London Library 1977–79, 1982–84; Winston Churchill Memorial Lecturer, Switzerland 1982; Hon. DSc (Cranfield Univ.) 1993; Hon. Fellow City and Guilds of London Inst. 2003; Screenwriters' Guild Award for Best British TV Documentary (The Great War) 1964; FRSL Award for Britain and Her Army 1971; Chesney Gold Medal Royal United Services Inst. for Defence Studies 1991. *Television includes:* The Great War (BBC TV) 1964, The Lost Peace (BBC TV) 1966, The Commanders (BBC TV) 1972. *Publications:* The Hump Organisation 1957, The Channel Tunnel (with Humphrey Slater) 1958, The Desert Generals 1960, The Swordbearers 1963, Britain and Her Army 1970, The Collapse of British Power 1972, Marlborough 1974, Bonaparte 1978, The Great War 1979, The Audit of War 1986, Hitler's Generals 1989, Engage the Enemy More Closely 1991 (Yorkshire Post Book of the Year Award 1991), The Lost Victory: British Dreams, British Realities

1945–1950 1995, The Verdict of Peace: Britain Between Her Yesterday and the Future 2001. *Leisure interests:* gardening, interior decorating, eating, idling, mole-hunting. *Address:* Churchill College, Cambridge (Office); Catbridge House, East Carleton, Norwich, Norfolk, NR14 8JX, England (Home). *Telephone:* (1223) 336083 (Office); (1508) 570410 (Home).

BARNETT, Baron (Life Peer), cr. 1983, of Heywood and Royton in Greater Manchester; **Joel Barnett,** PC, JP; British politician; b. 14 Oct. 1923; s. of Louis and Ettie Barnett; m. Lilian Goldstone 1949; one d.; ed Derby Street Jewish School, Manchester Central High School; Certified Accountant 1974; Sr Partner accountancy practice, Manchester 1953–74, 1979–80; served Royal Army Service Corps and British Mil. Govt in Germany; mem. Borough Council, Prestwich, Lancs. 1956–59; Hon. Treas. Manchester Fabian Soc. 1953–65; Labour cand. for Runcorn Div. of Cheshire 1959; MP for Heywood and Royton Div. of Lancashire 1964–83, mem. House of Commons Public Accounts Cttee 1965–71, Chair. 1979–83; mem. Public Expenditure Cttee 1971–74, Select. Cttee on Tax Credits 1973–74; Vice-Chair. Parl. Labour Party Econ. and Finance Group 1966–67, Chair. 1967–70, 1972–74; Opposition Spokesman on Treas. 1970–74; Chief Sec. to the Treas. 1974–79, mem. Cabinet 1977–79; mem. Hallé Cttee 1982–93; Vice-Chair. Bd of Govs., BBC 1986–93; Chair., Dir, consultant to a number of cos.; Chair. British Screen Finance Ltd 1985–95, Hansard Soc. for Parl. Govt 1984–95; Pres. Royal Inst. of Public Admin. 1989–92, Children's Medical Charity Trust PLC; Hon. Fellow Birkbeck Coll., London Univ. 1992; Trustee Victoria and Albert Museum 1984–96, Open Univ. Foundation 1995–; Gov. Birkbeck Coll., Hon. Fellow 2002; Hon. Visiting Fellow, Univ. of Strathclyde 1980–83; Hon. LLD (Strathclyde) 1983. *Publication:* Inside the Treasury 1982. *Leisure interests:* walking, conversation, reading, good food. *Address:* 92 Millbank Court, 24 John Islip Street, London, SW1P 4LG (Home); 7 Hillingdon Road, Whitefield, Manchester, M45 7QQ, Lancs., England (Home). *Telephone:* (20) 7828-4620 (London) (Home); (1625) 505300 (Manchester). *Fax:* (1625) 505313 (Manchester).

BARNETT, Peter Leonard, AM; Australian journalist, broadcaster and administrator; b. 21 July 1930, Albany, Western Australia; s. of Leonard Stewart and Ruby Barnett; m. Siti Nuraini Jatim 1970; one s.; ed Guildford Grammar School, Western Australia, Univ. of Western Australia; Canberra Rep. and Columnist, The Western Australian 1953–57; South-East Asia Corresp., Australian Broadcasting Comm. 1961, 1963, 1964, Jakarta Rep. 1962, New York and UN Corresp. 1964–67, Washington Corresp. 1967–70; News Ed., Radio Australia, Melbourne 1971–72, Washington Corresp. 1972–80, Controller, Melbourne 1980–84, Dir 1984–89; Exec. Dir Australian Broadcasting Corpn 1984–89; Vice-Chair. Operating Cttee Council for Econ. Devt of Australia; mem. Council Australian Inst. of Int. Affairs; Australia Award 1988. *Publication:* Foreign Correspondence 2001. *Leisure interests:* swimming, gardening, literature, musical composition. *Address:* CEDA, 136 Exhibition Street, Melbourne 3000 (Office); 66/46 Lansell Road, Toorak, Vic. 3142, Australia (Home). *Telephone:* (3) 9662-3544 (Office); (3) 9827-5979 (Home).

BARNEVIK, Percy Nils, MBA; Swedish business executive; b. 13 Feb. 1941, Simrishamn; s. of Einar and Anna Barnevik; m. Aina Orvarsson 1963; two s. one d.; ed Gothenburg School of Econs, Stanford Univ., USA; Man. Corp. Devt, Group Controller, Sandvik AB 1969–74, Pres. U.S. subsidiary 1975–79, Exec. Vice-Pres. parent co. 1979–80, Chair. Sandvik AB 1983–; Pres. and Chief Exec. ASEA AB, Västerås 1980–87; Pres. and CEO ABB Ltd 1988–96, Chair. 1996–2001; Dir Du Pont Co. 1991–98; Dir Skanska 1986–92, Chair. 1992–97; Dir General Motors, USA 1996–; Chair. Investor AB 1997–2002, AstraZeneca PLC 1999–; mem. of numerous professional orgs; recipient of several hon. degrees; numerous awards. *Address:* AstraZeneca PLC, 15 Stanhope Gate, London, W1K 1LN, England (Office). *Telephone:* (20) 7304-5000 (Office). *Website:* www.astrazeneca.co.uk/ (Office).

BARNIER, Michel; French politician; b. 9 Jan. 1951; m.; three c.; ed Ecole Supérieure de Commerce, Paris; Pvt. Office of the Ministers for the Environment, Youth and Sport and for Trade and Craft Industries 1973–78; Departmental Councillor for Savoie 1973; mem. Nat. Ass. for Savoie 1978–93; Chair. Departmental Council of Savoie 1982; Co-Pres. Organizing Cttee for XVIth Olympic Games, Albertville and Savoie 1987–92; Minister of the Environment 1993–95; Minister of State for European Affairs 1995–97; Senator for Savoie 1997; Chair. French Asscn of Council of European Municipalities and Regions 1997; Pres. Senate Del. for the EU 1998–; EU Commr for Regional Policy and Institutional Reform 1999–; Chevalier, Légion d'honneur. *Publications:* Vive la politique 1985, Le défi écologique, chacun pour tous 1990, L'Atlas des risques majeurs 1992, Vers une mer inconnue 1994. *Address:* Commission of the European Communities, 200 rue de la Loi, 1049 Brussels, Belgium (Office). *Telephone:* (2) 298-15-00 (Office). *Fax:* (2) 298-15-99 (Office). *Website:* europa.eu.int/barnier (Office).

BARNSLEY, Victoria; British publisher; b. 4 March 1954; d. of the late Thomas E. Barnsley and Margaret Gwyneth Barnsley (née Llewellin); m. Nicholas Howard 1992; one d. one step-s.; ed Loughborough High School, Beech Lawn Tutorial Coll., Edinburgh Univ., Univ. Coll. London, York Univ.; with Junction Books 1980–83; Founder, Chair. and CEO Fourth Estate 1984–2000; CEO HarperCollins UK 2000–; Trustee Tate Gallery 1998–; Dir Tate Enterprises Ltd 1998–; Council Mem. Publishers Asscn 2001–. *Address:* HarperCollins, Ophelia House, 77–85 Fulham Palace Road, London, W6 8JB,

England (Office). *Telephone:* (20) 8741-7070 (Office). *Fax:* (20) 8307-4440 (Office). *E-mail:* contact@harpercollins.co.uk (Office). *Website:* www .harpercollins.co.uk (Office).

BARON, Carolyn, BA; American publishing executive, editor and author; b. 25 Jan. 1940, Detroit; d. of Gabriel Cohn and Viola Cohn; m. Richard W Baron 1975; ed Univ. of Mich.; Ed., Editorial Production Dir Holt, Rinehart & Winston, New York 1965–71; Man. Ed. E. P. Dutton Co. Inc., New York 1971–74, Exec. Ed. 1974–75; Admin. Ed. Pocket Books, Simon & Schuster, New York 1975–78, Vice-Pres., Ed.-in-Chief 1978–79; Vice-Pres., Ed.-in-Chief Crown Publs, New York 1979–81; Vice-Pres. Dell Publishing Co. New York 1981–86, Sr Pres.; Publr 1986–; Sr Vice-Pres. Bantam, Doubleday, Dell 1989–. *Publications:* The History of Labor Unions in the US 1971, Re-entry Game 1974, Board Sailboats: A Buying Guide 1977; articles in magazines. *Address:* Dell Publishing Co. Inc., 1540 Broadway, New York, NY 10036, USA.

BARON, Franklin Andrew Merrifield; Dominican business executive, politician and diplomatist; b. 19 Jan. 1923, Dominica; s. of Alexander Baron and O. M. Baron; m. Sybil Eva McIntyre 1973; ed Dominica Grammar School, St Mary's Acad.; Man. A. A. Baron & Co. 1939–45, partner 1945–78, sole owner 1987–; mem. Dominica Legis. and Exec. Councils 1954–60; rep. of Dominica to Fed. Talks 1956–60; Founder and Political Leader, Dominica United People's Party 1957–66; Minister of Trade and Production 1956–60; Chief Minister and Minister of Finance 1960–61; Man. Dir Franklyn Hotels Ltd 1970–75; Man. Sisserou Hotel 1975–76; Chair. Dominica Tourist Bd 1970–72, Dominica Electricity Services 1983–91, Nat. Commercial Bank of Dominica 1986–90, Fort Young Hotel Co. Ltd 1986–, New Chronicle Newspaper 1990–96, Paramount Printing Ltd 1992–; Propr The Chronicle 1996–; Adviser, Barclays Bank Int. 1976–84; non-resident Amb. to USA 1982–86; Perm. non-resident Rep. to UN and to OAS 1982–, Chair. OAS 1985, 1993; non-resident High Commr in UK 1986–92; mem. Industrial Devt Corpn 1984–88. *Leisure interests:* gardening, reading. *Address:* 14 Cork Street, P.O. Box 57, Roseau (Office); Syb Bar Aerie, Champs Fleurs, Eggleston, Dominica (Home). *Telephone:* 4480415 (Office); 4488151 (Home). *Fax:* 4480047 (Office). *E-mail:* thechronicle@cwdom.dm (Office); frankb@cwdom.dm (Home). *Website:* www.delphis.dm/thechronicle (Office).

BARÓN CRESPO, Enrique; Spanish politician; b. 1944, Madrid; m.; one s.; ed Calasancio de las Escuelas Pías Coll., Instituto Católico de Dirección de Empresas, Ecole Supérieure des Sciences Economiques et Commerciales, Paris; mem. Federación Universitaria Democrática Española; mem. Unión Sindical Obrero 1964; ran legal and econ. consultancy with Agapito Ramos; mem. Convergencia Socialista and Federación de Partidos Socialistas (FPS); negotiated electoral coalition of FPS with the Partido Socialista Obrero Español (PSOE); mem. Congress of Deputies 1977–, PSOE spokesman for econ. affairs, public finance and the budget 1977–82; Minister of Transport and Tourism 1982–85; mem. European Parl. 1986–, Pres. 1989–92; Chair. Parl. Group, Party of European Socialists 2000–. *Publications:* Population and Hunger in the World, Europa 92, Europe at the Dawn of the Millennium. *Leisure interests:* jazz, painting, walking, skiing. *Address:* Parlement Européen, ASP 6H 263, rue Wiertz 60, 1047 Brussels, Belgium. *Telephone:* (2) 284-5490 (Office). *Fax:* (2) 284-9490 (Office).

BARR, James, MA, DD, DTheol., FBA; British university professor; b. 20 March 1924, Glasgow, Scotland; s. of Prof. and Mrs. Allan Barr; m. Jane J. S. Hepburn 1950; two s. one d.; ed Daniel Stewart's Coll., Edinburgh, Univ. of Edinburgh; Minister, Church of Scotland, Tiberias, Israel 1951–53; Prof. of New Testament, Presbyterian Coll., Montreal, Canada 1953–55; Prof. of Old Testament, Univ. of Edinburgh 1955–61, Princeton Theological Seminary (NJ) 1961–65; Prof. of Semitic Languages and Literatures, Univ. of Manchester 1965–76; Ed. Oxford Hebrew Dictionary 1974–80; Oriel Prof. of Interpretation of Holy Scripture, Univ. of Oxford 1976–78; Regius Prof. of Hebrew, Oxford 1978–89; Prof. of Hebrew Bible, Vanderbilt Univ., USA 1989–98, Distinguished Prof. 1994–98, Prof. Emer. 1998–; mem. Governing Body SOAS 1980–85; Visiting Prof., numerous univs.; Currie Lecturer, Austin Theological Seminary, Tex. 1964; Guggenheim Memorial Fellowship for Study in Biblical Semantics 1965; Cadbury Lecturer, Univ. of Birmingham 1969; Croall Lecturer, Univ. of Edinburgh 1970; Grinfield Lecturer on the Septuagint, Univ. of Oxford 1974–78; Firth Lecturer, Univ. of Nottingham 1978; Sprunt Lecturer, Richmond, Va 1982; Schweich Lecturer, British Acad. 1986, Sarum Lecturer Univ. of Oxford 1989, Read-Tuckwell Lecturer Bristol Univ. 1990, Gifford Lecturer, Edinburgh Univ. 1991, Hensley Henson Lecturer, Oxford Univ. 1997, Robertson Lecturer, Glasgow Univ. 1999; mem. Inst. for Advanced Study, Princeton, NJ 1985; Schweich Lectures, British Acad. 1986; Fellow American Acad. of Arts and Sciences 1993; mem. American Philosophical Soc. 1993; Corresp. mem. Göttingen Acad. of Sciences, Fed. Repub. of Germany 1976, Norwegian Acad. 1977, Royal Swedish Acad. of Science, Uppsala 1991; Hon. mem. Soc. of Biblical Literature, USA 1983; Hon. Fellow, SOAS, London 1975, Oriel Coll., Oxford 1980; numerous hon. degrees. *Publications:* The Semantics of Biblical Language 1961, Biblical Words for Time 1962, Old and New in Interpretation 1966, Comparative Philology and the Text of the Old Testament 1968, The Bible in the Modern World 1973, Fundamentalism 1977, Explorations in Theology 1980; Holy Scripture: Canon, Authority, Criticism 1983, Escaping from Fundamentalism 1984, The Variable Spellings of the Hebrew Bible 1988, The Garden of Eden and the Hope of Immortality 1992, Biblical Faith and Natural Theology 1993, The

Concept of Biblical Theology 1999, History and Ideology in the Old Testament 2000. *Address:* 1432 Sitka Court, Claremont, CA 91711, USA. *Telephone:* (909) 621-4189. *E-mail:* JmsBarr@aol.com (Home).

BARR, Roseanne (see Roseanne).

BARR, William Pelham, MA, JD; American lawyer; b. 23 May 1950, New York; s. of Donald Barr and Mary Ahern; m. Christine Moynihan 1973; three d.; ed Columbia Univ., George Washington Univ.; staff officer CIA Washington 1973–77; barrister 1977–78; law clerk to US Circuit Judge 1977–78, Assoc. Shaw, Pittman, Potts & Trowbridge 1978–82, 1983–84, Partner 1985–89, 1993–; Deputy Asst Dir Domestic Staff Policy The White House, Washington 1982–83; Asst Attorney Gen. Office of Legal Counsel US Dept of Justice, Washington 1989–91; Attorney Gen. of USA 1991–93; Exec. Vice-Pres., Gen. Counsel GTE Corpn, Washington 1994–; mem. Virginia State Bar Asscn, DC Bar Asscn. *Address:* GTE Corporation, 1850 M. Street NW, Suite 1200, Washington, DC 20036, USA.

BARRAULT, Marie-Christine; French actress; b. 21 March 1944, Paris; d. of Max-Henri Barrault and Marthe Valmier; m. 1st Daniel Toscan de Plantier (divorced); one s. one d.; m. 2nd Roger Vadim 1990 (died 2000); ed Conservatoire national d'art dramatique; Officer des Arts et des Lettres, Chevalier de la Legion d'honneur. *Theatre includes:* Andorra, Othon, Un couple pour l'hiver, Travail à domicile, Conversation chez les Stein sur Monsieur de Goethe absent, Dylan, cet animal étrange, Partage du midi, L'Etrange intermède, Même heure l'année prochaine, Enfin seuls!, La Cerisaie, Le bonheur des autres qui a peur de Virginia Woolf, La mènagerie de verre, Barrage contre le pacifique. *Films include:* Ma nuit chez Maude 1966, Le Distrait 1970, Cousin, cousine 1975 (Prix Louis Delluc), Du côté des tennis 1976, L'Etat sauvage 1978, Femme entre chien et loup 1978, Ma Chérie 1979, Stardust Memories 1980, L'Amour trop fort 1981, Un Amour en Allemagne 1983, Les Mots pour le dire 1983, Un Amour de Swann 1984, Pianoforte 1985, Le Jupon rouge 1987, Adieu je t'aime 1988, Sanguines 1988, Prisonnières 1988, Un été d'orage 1989, Dames Galantes 1990, L'Amour nécessaire 1991, Bonsoir 1994, C'est la tangente que je préfère 1997, La dilettante 1999. *Musical:* L'Homme rêvé 2000. *TV includes:* Marie Curie (series; Nymphe d'argent, Monte Carlo TV Festival 1991, 7 d'Or for best comedienne 1991). *Publication:* Le Cheval dans la pierre 1999. *Address:* c/o Cine art – Marie Laure Munich, 36 rue de Ponthieu, 75008 Paris, France.

BARRE, Raymond; French politician and international civil servant; b. 12 April 1924, Saint-Denis, Réunion; s. of René Barre and Charlotte (née Déramond) Barre; m. Eve Hegedüs 1954; two s.; ed Faculté de Droit, Paris and Inst. d'Etudes Politiques, Paris; Prof. at Inst. des Hautes Etudes, Tunis 1951–54; Prof. at Faculté de Droit et de Sciences économiques, Caen 1954–63; Prof. Inst. d'Etudes politiques, Paris 1961, 1982–, Univ. de Paris I (Panthéon-Sorbonne) 1982, Faculté de Droit et Sciences économiques, Paris 1962; Dir du Cabinet to Minister of Industry 1959–62; mem. Cttee of Experts (Comité Lorain) studying financing of investments in France 1963–64; mem. Comm. of Gen. Econ. and Financing of Fifth Plan and other Govt cttees.; Vice-Pres. of Comm. of European Communities responsible for Econ. and Financial Affairs 1967–72; mem. Gen. Council, Banque de France 1973; Minister of Foreign Trade Jan.–Aug. 1976; Prime Minister 1976–78, 1978–81, also Minister of Economy and Finance 1976–78; mem. for Rhône, Nat. Ass. 1978–2002; Pres. Inst. d'études des relations int. (IERI) 1988–, Convention libérale européenne et sociale (CLES) 1988–, Inst. int. du droit d'expression française 1989–, Pres. Supervisory Council of Aspen, France 1994–; Mayor of Lyon 1995–2001; numerous decorations. *Publications:* Economie politique 1956, Une politique pour l'avenir 1982, Réflexions pour demain 1982, Au tournant du siècle 1987, Questions de confiance 1988, Un goût de liberté 2000. *Address:* Assemblée Nationale, 75355 Paris, France; 4–6 avenue Emile-Acollas, 75007 Paris (Home).

BARRÉ-SINOUSSI, Françoise Claire, D. ÈS SC.; French scientist; b. 30 July 1947, Paris; d. of Roger Sinoussi and Jeanine Fau; m. Jean-Claude Barré 1978; ed Lycée Bergson, Faculty of Science Paris VII and Paris VI; Research Asst Inst. nat. de la Santé et de la recherche médicale (Inserm) 1975–80, Researcher 1980–86, Dir of Research 1986–; Head of Lab., Biology of Retroviruses Unit, Inst. Pasteur 1988–92, Head of Unit 1993–; Prize of Fondation Körber pour la promotion de la Science européenne 1986, Prize of Acad. de médecine 1988, Faisal Prize for Medicine (Saudi Arabia) 1993; Chevalier Ordre nat. du Mérite, Chevalier Légion d'honneur. *Leisure interests:* theatre, reading. *Address:* Institut Pasteur, Unité de Biologie des Rétrovirus, 25 rue du Docteur Roux, 75724 Paris cedex 15, France.

BARRETT, Craig, PhD; American business executive; b. 29 Aug. 1939, San Francisco; m. Barbara Barrett; one s. one d.; ed Stanford Univ.; NATO Postdoctoral Fellowship, Nat. Physical Lab., England 1965; Prof. at Stanford Univ. 1964–73; Fulbright Fellowship, Tech. Univ. of Denmark 1972; joined Intel 1974, fmr Tech. Devt Man., Vice-Pres. 1984, Exec. Vice-Pres. 1987, COO 1993, Pres. 1997–, CEO 1998–; mem. Nat. Acad. of Eng; Hardy Gold Medal (American Inst. of Mining and Metallurgical Engineers). *Publications:* Principles of Engineering Materials and more than 40 tech. papers on the influence of the microstructure of materials. *Leisure interests:* hiking, skiing, horse riding, cycling, fly-fishing. *Address:* c/o Intel Corporation, 2200 Mission College Blvd., Santa Clara, CA 95052-1537, USA (Office).

BARRETT, Matthew W., O.C; Canadian banker; b. 20 Sept. 1944, Co. Kerry, Ireland; ed Harvard Business School; joined Bank of Montreal, London,

England 1962; moved to Canada 1967; Vice-Pres. Man. Services, Bank of Montreal 1978, Vice-Pres. BC Div. 1979, Sr Vice-Pres. Eastern and Northern Ont. 1980, Sr Vice-Pres. and Deputy Gen. Man. Int. Banking Group 1981, Sr Vice-Pres. and Deputy Group Exec. Treasury Group 1984, Exec. Vice-Pres. and Group Exec. Personal Banking 1985, Pres. and COO 1987, CEO 1989–99, Chair. Bd of Dirs. 1990–99; CEO Barclays Group 1999–; Trustee, First Canadian Mortgage Fund; Dir Harris Bankcorp. Inc. and subsidiaries, Nesbitt Burns Inc., Molson Cos. Ltd, Seagrams Co. Ltd; various public appts.; Hon. LLD (St Mary's Univ., Halifax, NS, York Univ., Ont., Concordia Univ., Univ. of Waterloo, Acadia Univ.); Hon. DCL (Bishop's Univ.) 1993. *Leisure interests:* fly-fishing, tennis, reading. *Address:* Barclays Group, 54 Lombard St, London, EC3P 3AH, England (Office).

BARRIE, George Napier, BA, LLD; South African professor and advocate; b. 9 Oct. 1940, Pietersburg; m. Marie Howell 1970; two s. one d.; ed Pretoria Univ., Univ. of SA and Univ. Coll. London; State advocate Supreme Court 1964–69; Sr Law Adviser Dept of Foreign Affairs 1970–80; Prof. of Int. and Constitutional Law, Rand Afrikaans Univ. 1981–, Dean Faculty of Law 2001–; Visiting Prof. Free Univ. of Brussels 1992; Leader of SA Del. to numerous int. confs.; mem. SA Del. to Int. Bar Asscn Conf. 1984, Nat. Council on Correctional Services 1996–. *Publications include:* Topical International Law 1979, Self-Determination in Modern International Law 1995 and numerous works and articles on int. and constitutional law; co-author: Nuclear Non-Proliferation: The Why and the Wherefore 1985, Constitutions of Southern Africa 1985, Law of South Africa 1986, Law of the Sea 1987, Bill of Rights Compendium 1996, Managing African Conflicts 2000. *Leisure interests:* long distance running, long distance cycling. *Address:* Faculty of Law, Rand Afrikaans University, P.O. Box 524, Auckland Park, Johannesburg 2006, South Africa. *Fax:* (11) 4892049.

BARRINGTON, Edward John, BA; Irish civil servant and diplomatist; b. 26 July 1949, Dublin; m. Clare O'Brien 1972; one s.; ed Univ. Coll. Dublin; Third Sec. Dept of Foreign Affairs, EC Div. 1971–73, First Sec. 1973–75, First Sec. EC Perm. Rep. Office, Brussels 1975–80, First Sec. Press Section, HQ Aug.–Dec. 1980, Counsellor Political Div., HQ 1980–85, Asst Sec.-Gen. Admin. Div., HQ 1985–89, Asst Sec.-Gen. EC Div., HQ 1989–91, Asst Sec.-Gen. Political Div. and Political Dir, HQ 1991–95, Deputy Sec. 1995; Amb. to UK 1995–2001. *Leisure interests:* cinema, hiking, jazz, theatre. *Address:* c/o Ministry of Foreign Affairs, 80 St Stephen's Green, Dublin, Ireland.

BARRINGTON, Sir Nicholas John, KCMG, CVO, MA, FRSA; British diplomatist; b. 23 July 1934; s. of the late Eric A. Barrington and Mildred Bill; ed Repton School and Clare Coll. Cambridge; joined HM Diplomatic Service 1957; served Kabul 1959, UK Del. to European Communities, Brussels 1963, Rawalpindi 1965, Tokyo 1972–75, Cairo 1978–81; Minister and Head, British Interests Section, Tehran 1981–83; Asst Under-Sec. of State, FCO 1984–87; Amb. to Pakistan 1987–89; High Commr 1989–94; also Amb. (Non-Resident) to Afghanistan 1994; Chair. Man. Cttee Southwold Summer Theatre 1995–2001; Co-Pres. Clare Coll. Devt Programme, Cambridge 1995–2002; Hon. Fellow Clare Coll. Cambridge 1992; Trustee Museum of British Empire and Commonwealth, Bristol 1996–; mem. numerous bodies connected with Asia; Order of the Sacred Treasure, Japan 1975. *Leisure interests:* theatre, drawing, prosopography. *Address:* 2 Banhams Close, Cambridge, CB4 1HX, England.

BARRINGTON-WARD, Rt Rev Simon, KCMG, MA, DD, DLitt; British ecclesiastic; b. 27 May 1930, London; s. of Robert McGowan Barrington-Ward and Margaret A. Radice; m. Dr Jean Caverill Taylor 1963; two d.; ed Eton Coll., Magdalene Coll. Cambridge and Westcott House, Cambridge; ordained, diocese of Ely 1956; Chaplain, Magdalene Coll. Cambridge 1956–60; Lecturer, Ibadan Univ. Nigeria 1960–63; Fellow and Dean of Chapel, Magdalene Coll. Cambridge 1963–69; Principal Church Missionary Soc. Coll. Selly Oak, Birmingham 1969–74; Gen. Sec. Church Missionary Soc. 1974–85; Canon, Derby Cathedral 1975–85; Chaplain to HM The Queen 1983–85; Bishop of Coventry 1985–97; Chair. Int. and Devt Affairs Cttee, Gen. Synod of Church of England 1986–96; Prelate to the Most Distinguished Order of St Michael and St George 1989; Asst Bishop of Ely 1997–; Hon. Fellow Magdalene Coll. Cambridge 1977–; Hon. DD (Wycliffe Coll. Toronto) 1983; Hon. DLitt (Warwick Univ.) 1988. *Publications:* Love Will Out 1988, Christianity Today 1988, The Weight of Glory 1991, Why God? 1993, The Jesus Prayer 1996, Praying the Jesus Prayer Together 2001; articles and book chapters. *Leisure interests:* hill walking, music, cycling, calligraphy. *Address:* 4 Searle Street, Cambridge, CB4 3DB, England. *Telephone:* (1223) 740460. *E-mail:* sb292@cam.ac.uk (Home).

BARRIONUEVO PEÑA, José; Spanish politician; b. 13 March 1942, Berja; m.; three c.; mem. Agrupación de Estudiantes Tradicionalistas; held posts in Sindicato Español Universitaria; became journalist; mem. Convergencia Socialista; town councillor, Madrid; Inspector de Trabajo, Madrid 1971; Asst Dir-Gen. Ministry of Labour until 1979; Socialist cand. in elections for Mayor of Madrid 1979; Minister of Interior 1982–88, of Transport, Tourism and Communications 1988–91; charged with kidnapping, misuse of public funds and assoc. with an outlaw band Jan. 1996; sentenced to ten years' imprisonment July 1998; partially pardoned and prison terms suspended Dec. 1998.

BARRIOS DE CHAMORRO, Violeta; Nicaraguan politician; b. 18 Oct. 1929, Rivas; m. Pedro Joaquín Chamorro (died 1978) 1950; two s. two d.; ed Our Lady of the Lake Catholic School, San Antonio and Blackstone Coll., USA; mem. and Dir Sociedad Interamericana de Prensa 1978–89, Prensa Freedom

Comm. 1978–89; Pres. and Dir-Gen. La Prensa (daily) 1978–89; Nat. Opposition Union cand. for Pres. 1989–90; Pres. of Nicaragua 1990–97, also Minister of Nat. Defence 1990; Grand Cross of the Order of Isabel la Católica (Spain) 1991, Grand Collar of the Order of the Aztec Eagle (Mexico) 1993, Grand Cross of the Order of Merit (Germany) 1996; six hon. degrees including Hon. LLD (American Univ., Washington, DC) 1997; Hon. DH (Catholic Univ. of Nicaragua Redemptores Mater) 1995; Dr hc (American Univ., Managua) 1998, (Univ. for Peace, Costa Rica) 1999; numerous nat. and int. awards including Louis Lyon Prize, Harvard Univ. 1986, American Soc. Gold Ensign Award 1990, Int. Rescue Cttee Freedom Award 1990, Int. Peace Asscn Woman for Peace Award 1990, Pan-American Devt Foundation Inter-american Leadership Award 1991, Lutheran Univ. of Calif. Thomas Wade Landry Award 1991, The Path to Peace Foundation Award 1997. *Publication:* Dreams of the Heart (autobiog.) 1996. *Address:* c/o Oficina del Presidente, Managua, Nicaragua.

BARRO, Robert Joseph, PhD; American professor of economics; b. 28 Sept. 1944, New York; four c.; ed Harvard Univ., California Inst. of Tech.; Prof. of Econs, Harvard Univ. 1987–; Sr Fellow Hoover Inst., Stanford Univ. 1995–; Viewpoint Columnist, Business Week 1998–; Frank Paish Lecturer, Meeting of Royal Econ. Soc., Oxford, 1985; Henry Thornton Lecturer, City Univ. Business School, London 1987; Horowitz Lecturer, Israel 1988; Lionel Robbins Lecturer, LSE 1996; Hoover Inst. Nat. Fellowship 1977–78; John Simon Guggenheim Memorial Fellowship 1982–83; Fellow Econometric Soc. 1980–; American Acad. of Arts and Sciences 1988–. *Publications:* Determinants of Economic Growth: A Cross-Country Empirical Study, Getting it Right: Markets and Choice in a Free Society, Economic Growth. *Address:* Department of Economics, Harvard University, Cambridge, MA 02138, USA (Office). *Telephone:* (617) 495-3203 (Office); (781) 894-8184 (Home). *Fax:* (617) 496-8629 (Office). *E-mail:* rbarro@harvard.edu (Office). *Website:* www.economics .harvard.edu (Office).

BARRON, Sir Donald James, Kt, DL, BCom, CA; British businessman; b. 17 March 1921, Edinburgh; s. of Albert Gibson Barron and Elizabeth Macdonald; m. Gillian Mary Saville 1956; three s. two d.; ed George Heriot's School, Edinburgh, Univ. of Edinburgh; joined Rowntree & Co. Ltd 1952, Dir 1961, Vice-Chair. 1965; Chair. Rowntree Mackintosh Ltd 1966–81; Vice-Chair. Midland Bank PLC 1981–82 (Dir 1972–87), Chair. 1982–87; mem. Bd of Banking Supervision 1987–89; Dir Canada Life Assurance Co., Toronto 1980–96; Vice-Chair. Canada Life Assurance Co. of Great Britain 1983–91, Chair. 1991–94 (Dir 1980–96); Dir Canada Life Unit Trust Mans 1980–96 (Chair. 1982), Investors in Industry Group PLC 1980–91; mem. Council of CBI 1966–81, Soc. Science Research Council 1971–72, Univ. Grants Cttee 1972–81, Council Inst. of Chartered Accountants of Scotland 1980–81, Council of British Inst. of Man. 1979–80; Trustee, Joseph Rowntree Foundation 1966–73, 1975–96, Chair. 1981–96; mem. NEDC 1983–85; Dir Clydesdale Bank 1986–87; Gov. London Business School 1982–89; Treas. Univ. of York 1966–72, a Pro-Chancellor 1982–94; Chair. York Millennium Bridge Trust 1998–2002; Dr hc (Loughborough 1982, Heriot-Watt 1983, Council for Nat. Academic Awards 1983, Edinburgh 1984, Nottingham 1985, York 1986). *Leisure interests:* golf, tennis, travelling, gardening. *Address:* Greenfield, Sim Balk Lane, Bishopthorpe, York, YO2 1QH, England (Home). *Telephone:* (1904) 705675.

BARRON, John Penrose, MA, DPhil, FSA; British professor of Greek; b. 27 April 1934, Morley, Yorks.; s. of George Barron and Leslie Barron; m. Caroline M. Hogarth 1962; two d.; ed Clifton Coll., Bristol and Balliol Coll. Oxford; Asst Lecturer, then Lecturer in Latin, Bedford Coll. London 1958–64, in Archaeology, Univ. Coll. London 1964–67, Reader in Archaeology and Numismatics 1967–71; Prof. of Greek, Univ. of London (King's Coll.) 1971–91, Dean, Faculty of Arts 1976–80, Public Orator 1978–81, 1986–88, Dir Inst. of Classical Studies 1984–91, Pro-Vice-Chancellor 1987–89; Dean, Univ. of London Insts for Advanced Study 1989–91; mem. Univs Funding Council 1989–93; Pres. Soc. for Promotion of Hellenic Studies 1990–93; Master St Peter's Coll., Oxford 1991–2003; Chair. Conf. of Colls, Oxford 1993–95; Fellow, King's Coll., London; Gov. St Paul's Schools, London 1991–, SOAS, London 1989–98 (Vice-Chair. 1992–98), Radley Coll. 1996–2003, Clifton Coll., Bristol 1996– (Pres. 1999–); Founder Trustee Prince of Wales's Inst. of Architecture; Trustee Lambeth Palace Library 1998–. *Publications:* Greek Sculpture 1965, Silver Coins of Samos 1966. *Leisure interests:* travel, gardens. *Address:* ; 9 Boundary Road, London, NW8 0HE, England (Home).

BARROT, Jacques, LenD; French politician; b. 3 Feb. 1937, Yssingeaux, Haute-Loire; s. of Noël Barrot and Marthe Pivot; m. Florence Cattani 1982; one s. two d.; ed Coll. d'Yssingeaux and Faculté de Droit, Paris and Inst. d'Etudes Politiques, Paris; Deputy to Nat. Ass. (Union Centriste) 1967–74, 1978, (Union pour la Démocratie Française) 1981–95, 1997–2002, (UMP) 2002–03, Pres. UMP Group; Sec. of State, Ministry of Equipment 1974–78; Minister of Commerce and Working Classes 1978–79, of Health and Social Security 1979–81; Pres. Conseil-Gen. Haute-Loire 1976–; Mayor of Yssingeaux 1989–2001; Minister of Labour, Social Dialogue and Participation 1995–97; Pres. Nat. Union for Environmental Improvement 1991–93; mem. Fondatems du "Dialogue et Initiations". *Publications:* Les Pierres de l'avenir 1978, Note Cordial pour l'alternance 2002. *Leisure interest:* mountain sports. *Address:* Assemblée Nationale, 75355 Paris (Office); Conseil Général de la Haute-Loire, 4 avenue du Général de Gaulle, BP 310, 43011 Le-Puy-en-Velay cedex; Rue Beuve-Méry, 43200 Yssingeaux, France (Home).

BARROW, Dean Oliver, MA, LLM; Belizean politician; b. 2 March 1951, Belize City; ed Univ. of West Indies and Center for Advanced Int. Studies, Univ. of Miami, USA; elected (United Democratic Party—UDP)) to Belize City Council 1983; elected to Nat. Ass. (UDP) for Queen Square Div. 1984–89; Deputy Leader UDP 1990, currently Leader; Minister of Foreign Affairs and Econ. Devt 1984–86; Attorney-Gen. 1986–89; apptd Deputy Prime Minister, Minister of Foreign Affairs and Econ. Devt and Attorney-Gen. 1993, also Minister of Nat. Security, Immigration and Nationality Matters 1995; Partner Barrow and Williams law firm. *Address:* United Democratic Party, South End Bel-China Bridge, POB 1898, Belize City, Belize (Office). *Telephone:* 227-2576 (Office). *Fax:* 227-6441 (Office). *E-mail:* info@udp.org.bz (Office). *Website:* www.udp.org.bz (Office).

BARROW, Dame Jocelyn (Anita), DBE, FRSA; British administrator; b. 15 April 1929, d. of Charles Newton Barrow and Olive Irene Barrow (née Pierre); m. Henderson Downer 1970; ed Univ. of London; Gen. Sec. then Vice-Chair. Campaign Against Racial Discrimination 1964–69; Vice-Chair. Int. Human Rights Year Cttee 1968; mem. Community Relations Council 1968–72, Nat. Vice-Pres. Nat. Union of Townswomen's Guilds 1978–80, 1987–; a Gov. BBC 1981–88; mem. Parole Bd 1983–87; Deputy Chair. Broadcasting Standards Council 1989–95; Chair. Ind. Cttee of Man., Optical Consumer Complaints Service 1992–; Devt Dir Focus Consultancy Ltd 1996–; Founder and Pres. Community Housing Assen, Camden; mem. EC Econ. and Social Cttee 1990–; Gov. and Patron Goldsmiths Coll.; Hon. DLitt (Univ. of East London) 1992. *Leisure interests:* cooking, music, reading, theatre. *Address:* c/o Focus Consultancy Ltd, 38 Grosvenor Gardens, London, SW1W 0EB, England (Office). *Telephone:* (20) 7730-3010 (Office). *Fax:* (20) 7730-7030 (Office). *E-mail:* jocelynbarrow@focus-consultancy.co.uk (Office).

BARROW, John David, DSc, DPhil, FRAS, FRSA, FInstP; British professor of mathematical sciences and astrophysicist; b. 29 Nov. 1952, London; s. of the late Walter Henry Barrow and Lois Miriam Barrow (née Tucker); m. Elizabeth Mary East 1975; two s. one d.; ed Van Mildert Coll., Durham Univ., Magdalen Coll., Oxford; Lindemann Fellow, Astronomy Dept Berkeley, Calif. Univ. 1977–78, Miller Fellow, Physics Dept 1980–81; research lecturer Astrophysics Dept, Oxford Univ. 1978–80; lecturer Astronomy Centre, Sussex Univ. 1981, Sr lecturer, then Prof. 1989–99, Dir Astronomy Centre 1995–99; Research Prof. of Math. Sciences, Cambridge Univ. 1999–; Dir Millennium Math. Project 1999–; Nuffield Fellow 1986–87, Leverhulme Royal Soc. Fellow 1992–93, PPARC Sr Fellow 1994–, Fellow Clare Hall Coll., Cambridge 1999–; Gifford Lecturer (Glasgow Univ.) 1988; Samuel Locker Award 1989, Scott Memorial Lecture (Leuven) 1989, Collingwood Lecture (Durham) 1990, Spinoza Lecture (Amsterdam) 1993, George Darwin Lecture (Royal Astronomical Soc.) 1993, Elizabeth Spreadbury Lecture (UCL) 1993, BBV Lectures (Spain), Robert Boyle Memorial Lecture (Oxford) 1996, RSA Lecture 1999, LMS Lectures 2000, Flamsteed Lecture (Derby) 2000, Tyndall Lecture (Bristol) 2001, Darwin Lecture (Cambridge) 2001, Whitrow Lecture (Royal Astronomical Soc.) 2002; Hon. DSc (Herts.) 1999; Templeton Award 1995, Kelvin Medal 1999. *Plays:* Infinities (dir Luca Ronconi) (Premi Ubu, Italy 2002) 2002, Ciutat de les Arts Esceniques 2002. *Publications:* The Left Hand of Creation 1983, L'Homme et le Cosmos 1984, The Anthropic Cosmological Principle 1986, The World Within the World 1988, Theories of Everything 1991, Perche il Mondo è Matematico? 1992, Pi in the Sky 1992, The Origin of the Universe 1994, The Artful Universe 1995, Impossibility 1998, Between Inner Space and Outer Space 1999, The Universe that Discovered Itself 2000, The Book of Nothing 2000, The Constants of Nature 2002. *Leisure interests:* athletics, books, theatre, writing. *Address:* Centre for Mathematical Sciences, University of Cambridge, Wilberforce Road, Cambridge, CB3 0WA, England (Office). *Telephone:* (1223) 766696 (Office). *Fax:* (1223) 765900 (Office). *E-mail:* j.d.barrow@damtp.cam.ac.uk (Office).

BARROW, Viscountess Waverley Ursula Helen, MA; Belizean diplomatist; b. 31 Oct. 1955; d. of Raymond Hugh Barrow and Rita Helen Barrow; m. Viscount Waverley; one s.; ed Newnham Coll., Cambridge Univ.; Econ. Devt Planner, Planning Unit, Govt of Belize 1978; consultant for small business affairs, urban planning and marketing, Frazier & Assocs. 1979–85; Counsellor and Deputy High Commr in London 1988–89; Perm. Rep. to UN 1989–91; Asst Dir Commonwealth Secr. 1991–93; Amb. to the EU, Belgium, France, Germany and the Holy See; awarded Belize Open Scholarship 1974, Cambridge Commonwealth Trust Scholarship 1985. *Address:* c/o Ministry of Foreign Affairs, Economic Development and Education, P.O. Box 174, Belmopan, Belize.

BARRY, Brian Michael, MA, DPhil, FBA; British professor; b. 7 Aug. 1936, London; s. of James Frederick Barry and Doris Rose Barry; m. 1st Joanna Hill 1960 (divorced 1988); one s.; m. 2nd Elizabeth Ann Parker 1991; ed Taunton's School, Southampton and Queen's Coll., Oxford; Fellow Nuffield Coll., Oxford 1966–69, 1972–75; Prof. of Govt, Univ. of Essex 1969–72; Prof. of Political Science and Philosophy, Univ. of Chicago 1977–82; Prof. of Philosophy, Calif. Inst. of Tech. 1982–86; Prof. European Univ. Inst. 1986–87; Prof. of Political Science, LSE 1987, now Emer.; Arnold A. Saltzman Prof. of Political Science, Columbia Univ., NY, USA; Fellow American Acad. of Arts and Sciences; Hon. DSc (Southampton) 1998; Johan Skytte Prize in Political Science 2001. *Publications:* Political Argument 1965, Sociologists, Economists and Democracy 1970, The Liberal Theory of Justice 1973, Theories of Justice (WJM Mackenzie Prize) 1989, Democracy, Power and Justice 1989, Democracy and Power 1991, Liberty and Justice 1991, Justice as Impartiality 1995, Culture and Equality: An Egalitarian Critique of Multiculturalism (WJM Mackenzie

Prize) 2001, Why Social Justice Matters 2003. *Leisure interests:* cooking, playing the piano, London. *Address:* Department of Political Science, Columbia University, 730 International Affairs Building, 420 West 118th Street, New York, NY 10027, USA. *Telephone:* (212) 854-7075 (Office). *Fax:* (212) 222-0598. *E-mail:* bmb21@columbia.edu. *Website:* www.columbia.edu/cu/polisci.

BARRY, Edward William, BA; American publishing executive; b. 24 Nov. 1937, Stamford, Conn.; s. of Edward Barry and Elizabeth Cosgrove; m. Barbara H. Walker 1963; one s. one d.; ed Univ. of Conn.; Pres. The Free Press, New York 1972–82, Oxford Univ. Press Inc., New York 1982–2000; Sr Vice-Pres. Macmillan Publishing Co., New York 1973–82; mem. Exec. Council Professional and Scholarly Publications 1993, Advisory Bd Pace Univ. Grad. Program in Publishing 1990–, Bd Dirs. Asscn of American Publrs. 1995; Trustee Columbia Univ. Press 2000–; Hon. LittD (Univ. of Oxford) 2000. *Address:* 266 Old Poverty Road, Southbury, CT 06488-1769, USA (Home). *Telephone:* (212) 251-0416 (Office). *E-mail:* edwardbarry@cs.com (Office).

BARRY, John, OBE; British soundtrack composer; b. John Barry Prendergast, 3 Nov. 1933, York; formed group The John Barry Seven 1957, left group 1962; stage musical, Billy 1974; first film score composed for Beat Girl. *Film scores include:* music for Monte Walsh, The Lion in Winter, Midnight Cowboy (Acad. Award), The Ipcress File, Body Heat, From Russia with Love, Goldfinger, You Only Live Twice, Octopussy, The Cotton Club, A View to a Kill, Out of Africa (Acad. Award 1985), Dances with Wolves (Acad. Award 1990), Indecent Proposal, The Specialist, Chaplin, The Scarlet Letter, Mercury Rising. *Album:* Eternal Echoes 2001.

BARRY, Marion Shepilov, Jr; American politician; b. 6 March 1936, Itta Bena, Miss.; s. of Marion S. Barry and Mattie Barry; m. 1st Effi Barry 1978; one s.; m. 2nd Cara Masters Barry 1994; ed LeMoyne Coll., Fisk Univ., Univs. of Kansas and Tennessee; Dir of Operations, Pride Inc., Washington, DC 1967; Co-Founder, Chair. and Dir Pride Econ. Enterprises, Inc., Washington, DC 1968; mem. Washington DC School Bd 1971–74; mem. Washington City Council 1974–78; Mayor of Washington, DC 1979–91; arrested and charged with possessing cocaine Jan. 1990; convicted, imprisoned for 6 months for possessing cocaine; re-elected Mayor 1995–98. *Address:* c/o Office of the Mayor, 1 Judiciary Square, 441 4th Street, N.W., Washington, DC 20001, USA.

BARRYMORE, Drew; American film actress and producer; b. 22 Feb. 1975, Los Angeles; d. of John Barrymore, Jr and Jaid Barrymore; m. 1st Jeremy Thomas 1994 (divorced); m. 2nd Tom Green 2001 (divorced 2001); appeared in dog food commercial 1976; film debut in TV movie Suddenly Love 1978; owner Flower Films production co. *Films include:* Altered States 1980, E.T.: The Extra-Terrestrial 1982, Irreconcilable Differences 1984, Firestarter 1984, Cat's Eye 1985, See You In The Morning 1988, Far From Home 1989, Motorama 1991, Guncrazy 1992, Poison Ivy 1992, Beyond Control: The Amy Fisher Story 1992, No Place to Hide 1993, Doppelganger 1993, Wayne's World 2 1993, Bad Girls 1994, Inside the Goldmine 1994, Boys On The Side 1995, Batman Forever 1995, Mad Love 1995, Scream 1996, Everyone Says I Love You 1996, All She Wanted 1997, Best Men 1997, Never Been Kissed (also producer) 1998, Home Fries 1998, The Wedding Singer 1998, Ever After 1998, Titan A.E. (voice) 2000, Charlie's Angels (also producer) 2000, Donnie Darko (also producer) 2001, Riding in Cars With Boys 2001, Confessions of a Dangerous Mind 2002, Duplex (also producer), So Love Returns (also producer), Charlie's Angels: Full Throttle (also producer) 2003. *Address:* c/o EMA, 9025 Wilshire Boulevard, Suite 450, Beverly Hills, CA 90211, USA (Office).

BARSALOU, Yves; French banking executive; b. 18 Sept. 1932, Bizanet; s. of Marcell Barsalou and Marie-Louise Salvan; m. Claire-Marie Vié 1955; two s.; ed Ecoles de Carcassonne et Narbonne; mem. Dept Centre of Young Farmers 1957–67; Pres. Caisse Locale de Crédit Agricole de Narbonne 1974–; mem. Cen. Cttee, then Vice-Pres. Caisse nat. du Crédit agricole (CNCA) 1981–88, Pres. 1988–, Chair. CNCA 1989; Vice-Pres. Fed. Nationale du Crédit Agricole (FNCA) 1992–2000; mem. Plenary Comm., Fed. nat. du Crédit agricole 1975–77, Dir 1977–81, Pres. 1982–92; Vice-Pres., Pres. Fed. Int. du Crédit Agricole (CiCa) 1993–; Vice-Pres. Bd Crédit Agricole Indosuez 1996; mem. Conseil econ. et social, numerous cttees.; Commdr, Légion d'honneur, Commdr, Mérite agricole. *Address:* CNCA, 91–93 blvd Pasteur, 75015 Paris (Office); rue Jean-Jacques Rousseau, 11200 Bizanet, France (Home).

BARSCHEVSKY, Mikhail Yuryevich; Russian lawyer; b. 29 Dec. 1955, Moscow; m. Olga Barkalova; one d.; ed All-Union Inst. of Law; legal consultant in Moscow butter factory 1973–79; sr legal consultant Dept of Trade, Reutov Town 1979–80; Founder, Head Moscow Lawyers 1991–, (Barschevsky and Partners Co. 1993–), defended Obshchaya Gazeta newspaper 1993, Oblik TV Co. 1997; TV arbiter, What? Where? When? 1997–; Prof. State Acad. of Law; Govt Rep., Constitutional Court, Supreme Court, Higher Arbitration Court 2001–; Chair. Moscow Inst. of Econ., Politics and Law; mem. Bd All Russian Co-ordination Council for Public-Political Union, Moscow Region 1999–; mem. Russian Acad. of Natural Sciences, Russian Acad. of Lawyers, Moscow Collegiate of Advocates 1980–; Advocate of Honour, Plevako Gold Medal. *Leisure interests:* theatre, chess. *Address:* Krasnopresnenskaya emb. 2, 103274 Moscow, Russian (Office). *Telephone:* (095) 205-40-51 (Office). *Fax:* (095) 205-65-25 (Office).

BARSHAI, Rudolf Borisovich; Russian/British conductor; b. 28 Sept. 1924, Labinskaya, Krasnodar Territory; s. of Boris and Maria Barshai; ed Moscow Conservatoire; performed in chamber ensembles with Shostakovich, Richter, Oistrakh, Rostropovich; Founder and Artistic Dir Moscow Chamber Orchestra 1956–77; Prin. Conductor and Artistic Adviser, Bournemouth Symphony Orchestra 1982–96; Guest Conductor Orchestre Nat. de France; numerous tours abroad; author of orchestrations and arrangements for chamber orchestra of old and contemporary music; Hon. DMus (Southampton). *Address:* Homberg Str. 6, 4433 Ramlinsburg, Switzerland. *Telephone:* (61) 931-12-84. *Fax:* (61) 931-35-64.

BARSHEFSKY, Charlene, BA, JD; American government official and lawyer; ed Univ. of Wisconsin; partner, Steptoe & Johnson (law firm), Washington, DC 1975–93; Deputy US Trade Rep. 1993–96; Acting US Trade Rep. April–Nov. 1996; US Trade Rep. 1997–2001; Sr Int. Partner Wilmer, Cutler & Pickering (law firm) 2001–; mem. Bd American Express 2001–, Estée Lauder 2001–. *Address:* Wilmer, Cutler & Pickering, 2445 M Street, NW, Washington, DC 20037, USA. *Telephone:* (202) 663-6000 (Office). *Fax:* (202) 663-6363 (Office). *Website:* www.wilmercutler.com (Office).

BARSTOW, Dame Josephine (Clare), DBE, BA; British opera singer; b. 27 Sept. 1940, Sheffield; d. of Harold Barstow and Clara Barstow; m. 1st Terry Hands 1964 (divorced 1968); m. 2nd Ande Anderson 1969 (died 1996); ed Birmingham Univ.; taught English in London area for two years; début in operatic profession with Opera for All 1964; for short time co. mem. Welsh Nat. Opera, then English Nat. Opera; now freelance singer in all nat. opera houses in GB and in Paris, Vienna, Salzburg, Zürich, Geneva, Turin, Florence, Cologne, Munich, Berlin, USSR, Chicago, San Francisco, New York, Houston and many other American opera houses; Hon. DMus (Birmingham, Kingston, Sheffield Hallam); Fidelio Medal. *Chief roles:* Violetta (Traviata), Leonora (Forza del Destino), Elisabeth (Don Carlos), Lady Macbeth, Leonore (Fidelio), Sieglinde, Arabella, Salome, Chrysothemis, Amelia, The Marschallin, Tosca, Mimi, Minnie, Manon Lescaut, Emilia Marty, Jenůfa, Katya Kabanova, Medea, Renata (The Fiery Angel), Katerina Ismailova, Kostelnicka (Jenůfa), Marie (Wozzeck), Gloriana, Lady Billows (Albert Herring); world premières of Tippett, Henze and Penderecki. *Film:* Owen Wingrave 2001. *Recordings include:* Verdi Recital Record with English National Opera Orchestra and Mark Elder, Amelia with Herbert von Karajan, Anna Maurant in Street Scene, Kate in Kiss Me Kate, Four Finales, Gloriana, Albert Herring. *Leisure interests:* farming (cattle) and breeding Arabian horses. *Address:* c/o Askonas Holt, Lonsdale Chambers, 27 Chancery Lane, London, WC2A 1PF, England. *Telephone:* (20) 7400-1700.

BART, Hon. Delano Frank, LLB; Saint Christopher and Nevis lawyer, politician and international official; b. 28 Oct. 1952; ed Basseterre Sr School, Matthew Bolton Tech. Coll., Birmingham, Queen Mary Coll. and Inns of Court School, London, UK; teacher Molineux All Age School 1970–72; Lecturer of Law (part-time) Coll. of Distributive Justice, London 1977–79; admitted to Bar of England and Wales 1977, of Anguilla 1984, of Saint Christopher and Nevis 1984, of Antigua and Barbuda 1989; in pvt. practice from Chambers, The Temple, London 1977–95, appeared in variety of criminal and civil rights cases; Asst Counsel to Comm. of Inquiry, Bahamas 1993–94; Legal Rep. of Govt 1995–; mem. Legal Affairs Cttee Org. of Eastern Caribbean States (OECS) 1995–; various positions with CARICOM 1995–, including mem. Legal Affairs Cttee, Attorney-Gen. to Caribbean Assocn of Regulators of Int. Business (CARIB), mem. Del. to Heads of Govt Meetings, Barbados, Bahamas, Canada; Head Del. to Defence Ministerial of the Americas Meetings 1995, 1996, 1998, 2000; head numerous other govt dels including Commonwealth Law Ministers Conf., Malaysia; Attorney-Gen. and Minister of Justice and Legal Affairs 2001–; mem. Lincoln's Inn, London 1976; Del. to Talks on Drafting Saint Christopher and Nevis Constitution 1982; fmr exec. mem. Soc. of Black Lawyers in England and Wales. *Leisure interests:* music, art, reading, swimming. *Address:* Ministry of the Attorney General, Justice and Legal Affairs, Government Headquarters, Church Street, POB 186, Basseterre (Office); #45 Horizon Villa, Frigate Bay, Basseterre, Saint Christopher and Nevis (Home). *Telephone:* (869) 465-2127, (869) 465-2125 Ext. 1013 (Office); (869) 465-3581 (Home). *Fax:* (869) 465-5040 (Office). *E-mail:* attnygenskn@caribsurf.com (Office).

BARTELSKI, Lesław, LLM; Polish writer; b. 8 Sept. 1920, Warsaw; s. of Zygmunt and Zofia Ulanowska; m. Maria Zembrzuska 1947; one s. one d.; ed Univ. of Warsaw; mem. of resistance movement 1939–44; mem. Sztuka i Naród (Art and Nation) 1942–44; Co-Ed. Nowiny Literackie 1947–48, Nowa Kultura 1953–63, Kultura 1963–72; mem. Presidium of Gen. Council, Union of Fighters for Freedom and Democracy 1969–79, Deputy Pres. 1979–90; mem. PEN; Chair. Warsaw Branch, Polish Writers' Asscn 1972–78, mem. Polish Writers' Asscn 1984–, Deputy Pres. 1989–2000, Hon. Pres. 2000–; mem. Bd, Janusz Korczak Int. Asscn; Visiting Prof., Univ. of Warsaw 1970–71, 1977–78; Vice-Pres. Warsaw City Council 1973–80; Lecturer on Cultural Research, Pvt. Higher School of Commerce 1993–96; State Prize (3rd class) 1951, Prize of Minister of Defence (2nd class) 1969, Pietrzak Prize 1969 and 1985, Warsaw Prize 1969, Prize of Minister of Culture and Art 1977 (1st Class), Award of Pres. of Warsaw 1990, Reymont Prize 1998; Commdr's Cross, Order of Polonia Restituta, Order of Banner of Labour (2nd Class), Order of Cyril and Methodius (1st Class) Bulgaria, Cross of Valour, Warsaw Insurgent Cross, Partisan's Cross. *Publications:* poems: Przeciw zagładzie 1948; novels include Ludzie zza rzeki 1951, Pejzaż dwukrotny 1958, Wodorosty 1964, Mickiewicz na wschodzie 1966, Dialog z cieniem 1968, Niedziela bez dzwonów

1973, Krwawe skrzydła 1975, Rajski ogród 1978; essays: Genealogia ocalonych 1963, Jeździec z Madary 1963, Cień wojny 1963, Walcząca Warszawa 1968, Z głową na karabinie 1974, Pamięć żywa 1977, Polscy pisarze współcześni 1944–74 (biographical dictionary) 1977, Kusociński 1979, Pieśń niepodległa 1988, Czas bitew 1993, Polscy pisarze współcześni 1939–91 (biographical dictionary) 1995; monograph: Powstanie Warszawskie 1965, Mokotów 1944, 1971, Pułk AK Baszta 1990, Krzyż AK 1993, Getto 1999. *Leisure interests:* history of the Second World War, sport. *Address:* ul. F. Joliot Curie 17 m. 1, 02-646 Warsaw, Poland. *Telephone:* (22) 844-31-10.

BARTH, Else M.; Norwegian/Netherlands professor of logic and analytical philosophy; b. 3 Aug. 1928, Strinda, Norway; m. Hendrik A. J. F. Misset 1953; ed Univs. of Oslo, Trondheim, Amsterdam and Leyden; Reader in Logic, Utrecht Univ. 1971–77; Prof. of Analytical Philosophy, Groningen Univ. 1977–87, of Logic and Analytical Philosophy 1987–; Pres. Evert Willem Beth Foundation 1976–; mem. Royal Netherlands Acad. of Arts and Sciences, Sciences, Norwegian Soc. of Sciences. *Publications:* The Logic of the Articles in Traditional Philosophy. A Contribution to the Study of Conceptual Structures 1974, Perspectives on Analytic Philosophy, in Mededelingen van de Koninklijke Nederlandse Akademie van Wetenschappen, afd. Letterkunde, Nieuwe Reeks 1979, From Axiom to Dialogue—A Philosophical Study of Logics and Argumentation (with E. C. W. Krabbe) 1982, Argumentation: Approaches to Theory Formation. Containing the Contributions to the Groningen Conference on the Theory of Argumentation, October 1978 (ed., with J. L. Martens) 1982, Problems, Functions and Semantic Roles—A Pragmatist's Analysis of Montague's Theory of Sentence Meaning (with R. T. P. Wiche) 1986; numerous contribs. to learned journals and published lectures. *Leisure interests:* music, cultural and political philosophy, literature, skiing. *Address:* Filosofisch Instituut, University of Groningen, Westersingel 19, 9718 CA Groningen (Office); Kamperfoelieweg 16, 9765 HK Paterswolde; Nachtegaallaan 26, 2224 JH Katwijk aan Zee, The Netherlands (Home). *Telephone:* (50) 636146 (Office); (5907) 4315 (Paterswolde); (1718) 13353 (Katwijk aan Zee).

BARTH, John Simmons, MA; American novelist and professor of English; b. 27 May 1930, Cambridge, Md; s. of John J. Barth and Georgia Simmons; m. 1st Harriette Anne Strickland 1950 (divorced 1969); two s. one d.; m. 2nd Shelly Rosenberg 1970; ed Johns Hopkins Univ.; Instructor Pennsylvania State Univ. 1953, Assoc. Prof. until 1965; Prof. of English, State Univ. of New York at Buffalo 1965–73, Johns Hopkins Univ. 1973–91, Prof. Emer. 1991–; Rockefeller Foundation Grant; Brandeis Univ. Citation in Literature; Hon. LittD (Univ. of Maryland); Hon. DHL (Pennsylvania State Univ.) 1996; Nat. Acad. of Arts and Letters Award, Nat. Book Award 1973, F. Scott Fitzgerald Award 1997, President's Medal, Johns Hopkins Univ. 1997, PEN/Malamud Award 1998, Lifetime Achievement Award, Lannan Foundation 1998, Lifetime Achievement in Letters Award, Enoch Pratt Soc. 1999. *Publications:* The Floating Opera 1956, The End of the Road 1958, The Sot-Weed Factor 1960, Giles Goat-Boy 1966; Lost in the Funhouse (stories) 1968, Chimera 1972, Letters 1979, Sabbatical 1982, The Friday Book (essays) 1984, The Tidewater Tales: A Novel 1987, The Last Voyage of Somebody the Sailor 1991, Once Upon a Time 1994, On With the Story (stories) 1996, Coming Soon!!! (novel) 2001. *Address:* Writing Seminars, Johns Hopkins University, Baltimore, MD 21218, USA.

BARTH, (Thomas) Fredrik (Weybye), MA, PhD; Norwegian social anthropologist; b. 22 Dec. 1928, Leipzig; s. of Prof. Tom Barth and Randi Barth; m. Unni Wikan 1972; one s.; ed Berg School, Oslo and Univs. of Chicago, USA and Cambridge, England; Research Fellow in Social Anthropology, Univ. of Oslo 1953–61; Prof. of Social Anthropology, Univ. of Bergen 1961–72, Univ. of Oslo 1973–86; Research Fellow, Ministry of Educ. and Science 1987–; Prof. of Anthropology, Boston Univ., USA; Visiting Prof. Columbia Univ. 1960, Univ. of Khartoum 1963–64, Yale Univ. 1972, Johns Hopkins Univ. 1977, Univ. of Calif. Berkeley 1980, City Univ. NY 1987, Emory Univ. 1989–96, Harvard Univ. 1996–97; Sir James Frazer Memorial Lecturer, Cambridge 1983; Sir Thomas Huxley Memorial Lecturer, London 1989; Hon. Life Fellow Royal Anthropological Inst. 1968; Hon. Life mem. Int. Union of Anthropological and Ethnological Sciences 1993; Dr. hc (Memorial Univ., Canada) 1988, (Univ. of Edin.) 1996; Retzius Gold Medal, Royal Swedish Soc. 1988, Lifetime Achievement Award, IUAES Comm. on Nomadic Peoples 1998. *Publications:* Political Leadership Among Swat Pathans 1959, Nomads of South Persia 1961, Models of Social Organization 1964, Ethnic Groups and Boundaries 1969, Ritual and Knowledge among the Baktaman of New Guinea 1975, Selected Essays 1981, Sohar 1983, The Last Wali of Swat 1985, Cosmologies in the Making 1987, Balinese Worlds 1993. *Leisure interests:* travel, art. *Address:* Rödkleivfaret 16, 0788 Oslo, Norway. *Telephone:* (47) 22-147483. *Fax:* (47) 22-145748.

BARTHELMEH, Hans Adolf; German business executive (retd); b. 19 Sept. 1923, Cologne; s. of Johann Barthelmeh and Gertrud (née Weiler) Barthelmeh; m. Helene Fries 1950; one s.; ed Univ. of Cologne; Internal Auditor (Taxes), Fed. Financial Admin., Cologne 1950–52; with Ford-Werke AG, Cologne 1952–73; first Head, Tax Dept, then Head Depts., Finance Div. 1955–63; Chief Controller, Operations 1963–66; mem. Bd of Man. (Finance) 1966–68, (Sales) 1968–71; Pres. and Chair. Man. Bd, Ford-Werke AG, Cologne, 1966–73; Gen. Man. Ford Motor GmbH, Salzburg, Austria 1957–59; Chair. Rank Xerox GmbH, Düsseldorf 1980–83; Chair. Bd of Dirs. Ford-Credit AG, Cologne; mem. Man. Bd, Verband der Deutschen Automobilindustrie e.V., Frankfurt; fmr mem. Bd of Dirs. American Chamber of Commerce, Fed.

Repub. of Germany; mem. Industry Cttee Chamber of Industry and Commerce, Cologne; mem. Regional Council Deutsche Bank AG, Bd of Dirs., Deutsche Automobil-Treuhand GmbH until 1973; Pres. and Chair. Man. Bd Gildemeister AG, Bielefeld 1974–78; mem. Advisory Bd, Deutsche Bank AG, Düsseldorf, Supervisory Bd, Rank Xerox Austria; fmr mem. Bd of Dirs. Gildemeister Italiana SpA, Ponte S. Pietro, Gildemeister Máquinas Operatrizes SA, Brazil. *Publications:* articles in business magazines. *Leisure interests:* swimming, walking, books on futurology, philosophy, psychology and history, playing the piano. *Address:* Herrenstrunder Strasse 2A, 51067 Cologne, Germany.

BARTHOLOMEOS I, Patriarch, DCnL; Turkish ecclesiastic; b. 29 Feb. 1940, Hagioi Theodoroi, Island of Imvros; s. of Christos Archondonis and Merope Archondonis; ed Theological School of Halki, Pontifical Oriental Inst., Rome, Ecumenical Inst. Bossey, Switzerland and Univ. of Munich; mil. service 1961–63; ordained deacon 1961, priest 1969; Asst Dean, Theological School of Halki 1968; elevated to rank of Archimandrite 1970; Admin. Pvt. Patriarchal Office of Ecumenical Patriarch Dimitrios 1972–90; Metropolitan, See of Philadelphia, Asia Minor 1973; mem. Holy and Sacred Synod 1974; Metropolitan of Chalcedon 1990–91; Archbishop of Constantinople, New Rome and Ecumenical Patriarch 1991–; mem. Exec. and Cen. Cttees, WCC 1991–; Dr hc (Athens), (Holy Cross Orthodox School of Theology, Brookline, Mass.). *Address:* Chief Secretariat of the Holy and Sacred Synod of the Ecumenical Patriarchate, Greek Orthodox Church, Rum Ortodoks Patrikhanesi, 34220 Fener-Haliç, Istanbul, Turkey (Office). *Telephone:* (212) 5319671 (Office). *Fax:* (212) 5349037 (Office). *Website:* www.patriarchate.org (Office).

BARTHOLOMEW, Reginald; American diplomatist; b. 17 Feb. 1936, Portland, Maine; m. Rose-Anne Dognin; three s. one d.; ed Dartmouth Coll., Chicago Univ.; instructor Chicago Univ. 1961–64; Wesleyan Univ., Conn. 1964–68; Deputy Dir Policy Planning Staff, Dept of State 1974; Deputy Dir Politico-Mil. Affairs Bureau 1977, Dir 1979–81; with Nat. Security Council 1977–79; Special Cyprus Co-ordinator 1981–82; Special Negotiator for U.S.-Greek defence and econ. co-operation negotiations 1982–83; Amb. to Lebanon 1983–86, to Spain 1987–89, to NATO 1992–93; Special Envoy of Pres. Clinton to Bosnia 1993; Amb. to Italy 1993–97; Vice-Chair., Man. Dir Merrill Lynch Europe Holdings Ltd 1997–; Chair. Merrill Lynch, Italy; mem. Council on Foreign Relations. *Address:* Merrill Lynch, Largo Fontanella Borghese, 00186 Rome, Italy (Office).

BARTKUS, Gintautas; Lithuanian politician and lawyer; b. 30 June 1966; m.; two c.; ed Vilnius State Univ., Helsinki Univ., Jean Moulin Univ. Lyon, France; Adviser to Dir Dept of Nat. Lithuanian Govt 1990–92; Visiting Prof. John Marshall Law School, Chicago, USA 1993–96; Founder and Partner Law Co. Lideika, Petrauskas, Valiunas and Partners 1990–2000; mem. Working Group for Drafting the Civil Code of Lithuania 1992–2000; Asst Prof. Vilnius Univ. 1989–; Minister of Justice of Lithuania 2000–01. *Address:* Vilnius University, Universiteto 3, 2734 Vilnius, Lithuania (Office). *Telephone:* (2) 62-37-79 (Office). *Fax:* (2) 22-35-63 (Office).

BARTLETT, Jennifer, MFA; American artist; b. 14 March 1941, Long Beach, Calif.; m. 1st Edward Bartlett 1964 (divorced 1972); m. 2nd Mathieu Carrière 1983; ed Mills Coll., Oakland, Calif., Yale Univ. School of Art and Architecture; taught art at Univ. of Conn., Storrs 1964–72, School of Visual Arts, New York 1972; first New York Exhbn, Alan Saret's SoHo gallery 1970; works in numerous collections, including: Museum of Modern Art, Metropolitan Museum of Art, Whitney Museum of American Art, New York; Art Gallery of S. Australia, Adelaide, Rhode Island School of Design, Yale Univ. Art Gallery and Walker Art Cente, Minneapolis; large-scale murals and other works include: Rhapsody 1976, Swimmers Atlanta (Richard B. Russel Fed. Bldg, Atlanta, Ga) 1979; 270 steel plates for Inst. for Scientific Information, Phila; murals for AT&T Bldg, New York; sculpture and other objects for Volvo Corpn.'s HQ, Göteborg, Sweden; Harris Prize, Art Inst. of Chicago 1976, Award of American Acad. and Inst. of Arts and Letters 1983. *Exhibitions include:* 1977 Documenta, Kassel, FRG and 1980 Venice Biennale. *Address:* c/o Robert Miller Gallery, 526 West 26th Street, New York, NY 10001, USA (Office). *Telephone:* (212) 366-4774 (Office). *Fax:* (212) 366-4454 (Office). *E-mail:* rmg@robertmillergallery.com (Office). *Website:* www .robertmillergallery.com (Office).

BARTLETT, John Vernon, CBE, MA, FREng, FICE; British consulting engineer; b. 18 June 1927, London; s. of the late Vernon F. Bartlett and of Olga (née Testrup) Bartlett; m. Gillian Hoffman 1951; four s.; ed Stowe School and Trinity Coll., Cambridge; Engineer, John Mowlem & Co., Ltd 1951–57; joined Mott Hay & Anderson (now Mott MacDonald Group) 1957, Partner 1966, Chair. 1973–88, Consultant 1988–95; Chair. British Tunnelling Soc, 1977–79; Pres. Inst. of Civil Engs 1982–83; mem. Governing Body Imperial Coll. London 1991–95; Master Worshipful Co. of Engineers 1992–93; Founder Bartlett Library, Nat. Maritime Museum, Falmouth, Cornwall 2002; Telford Gold Medals 1971, 1973; S. G. Brown Medal, Royal Soc. 1973. *Publications:* Tunnels: Planning, Design and Construction (with T. M. Megaw) 1981, Ships of North Cornwall 1996; various professional papers. *Leisure interests:* sailing, maritime history. *Address:* 6 Cottenham Park Road, Wimbledon, London, SW20 0RZ, England (Home). *Telephone:* (20) 8946-9576 (Home).

BARTLETT, Neil, BSc, PhD, FRS; British/American chemist; b. 15 Sept. 1932, Newcastle-upon-Tyne; s. of Norman and Ann Willins (née Vock) Bartlett; m. Christina Isabel Cross 1957; three s. one d.; ed Heaton Grammar School, Newcastle-upon-Tyne, King's Coll., Durham Univ.; Sr Chemistry Master, The

Duke's School, Alnwick, Northumberland 1957–58; Faculty mem. Dept of Chem., Univ. of BC, Canada 1958–66; Prof. of Chem. Princeton Univ., NJ, USA 1966–69; Scientist, Bell Telephone Labs., Murray Hill, NJ 1966–69; Prof. of Chem. Univ. of Calif., Berkeley 1969–94; Prof. Emer. 1994–, Prin. Investigator Lawrence Berkeley Lab. 1969–99; Brotherton Visiting Prof., Chemistry Dept, Leeds Univ. 1981; Erskine, Visiting Fellow, Univ. of Canterbury, NZ 1983; Visiting Fellow, All Souls Coll., Oxford Univ. 1984; Assoc. of Inst. Jozef Stefan, Slovenia; mem. Leopoldina Acad., Halle 1969; Corresp. mem. Göttingen Acad. 1977, American Acad. of Arts and Sciences 1977, Nat. Acad. of Sciences 1979; Associé Etranger Acad. des Sciences, France 1989, Acad. Europaea 1998; Pierre Duhem Lecturer, Bordeaux Univ. 1998; Foreign Fellow Royal Soc. of Canada 2001; Hon. FRSC 2002; Hon. DSc (Waterloo) 1968, (Colby Coll.) 1971; Dr hc (Bordeaux) 1976, (Newcastle-upon-Tyne) 1981, (Ljubljana) 1989, (Nantes) 1990, (McMaster) 1992; Hon. LLD (Simon Fraser) 1993, Hon. Dr rer. nat (Freie Univ. Berlin) 1998; Research Corpn Award 1965; Dannie Heineman Prize 1971; Robert A. Welch Award 1976, W. H. Nichols Medal, USA 1983, Moissan Fluorine Centennial Medal, Paris 1986, Prix Moissan 1988, ACS Award for Distinguished Service to Inorganic Chem. 1989, Pauling Medal (ACS) 1989, Award for Creative Work in Fluorine Chemistry (ACS) 1992, Bonner Chemiepreis 1992, Royal Soc. (London) Davy Medal 2002. *Achievements (miscellaneous):* preparation of the first compound of a noble gas ($XePtF_6$), characterization of the first salt of oxidized oxygen (O_2^+), synthesis and structural characterization of the metastable fluorides AgF_3 and NiF_3 and synthesis of new semi-conducting pseudo-graphite materials such as C_3B, C_5N and BC_2N. *Publications:* The Chemistry of the Monatomic Gases (with F. O. Sladky, A. H. Cockett and K. C. Smith) 1973, Noble-Gas Compounds (with D. T. Hawkins and W. E. Falconer) 1978, The Oxidation of Oxygen and Related Chemistry 2001; more than 160 scientific papers including reports on the first preparation of the oxidized oxygen cation O_2^+ and the first true compound of a noble gas. *Leisure interests:* watercolour painting, antique silver. *Address:* c/o Room 3307, Building 70A, Lawrence Berkeley National Laboratory, Berkeley, CA 94720 (Office); 6 Oak Drive, Orinda, CA 94563, USA (Home). *Fax:* (510) 486-6033. *E-mail:* n-bart@cchem .berkeley.edu (Office).

BARTLEY, Robert LeRoy, MS; American journalist; b. 12 Oct. 1937, Marshall, Minn.; s. of Theodore Bartley and Iva Radach; m. Edith Lillie 1960; three d.; ed Iowa State Univ. and Univ. of Wisconsin; reporter, Grinnell (Ia) Herald-Register 1959–60; staff reporter, Wall Street Journal, Chicago 1962–63, Philadelphia 1963–64; editorial writer, Wall Street Journal, New York 1964–70, Washington, DC 1970–71; Ed. editorial page, Wall Street Journal, New York 1972–78; Ed. Wall Street Journal 1979–, Vice-Pres. 1983–; mem. American Soc. of Newspaper Eds, American Political Science Asscn, Council on Foreign Relations; Hon. LLD (Macalester Coll.) 1982, (Babson Coll.) 1987; Hon. HHD (Adelphi) 1992; Pulitzer Prize for editorial writing 1980. *Publication:* The Seven Fat Years 1992. *Address:* The Wall Street Journal, 200 Liberty Street, New York, NY 10281-1003, USA. *Telephone:* (212) 416-2000.

BARTOLI, Cecilia; Italian mezzo-soprano opera singer and recitalist; b. 4 June 1966, Rome; d. of Pietro Angelo Bartoli and Silvana Bazzoni; ed Acad. of Santa Cecilia, Rome; professional career began with TV appearance aged 19; US debut in recital at Mostly Mozart Festival, New York 1990; Paris debut as Cherubino in The Marriage of Figaro, Opéra de Paris Bastille 1990–91 season; debut, La Scala, Milan in Rossini's Le Comte Ory 1990–91 season; appeared as Dorabella in Così fan tutte, Maggio Musicale, Florence 1991; debut with Montreal Symphony Orch. and Philadelphia Orch. 1990–91 season; recitals in collaboration with pianist András Schiff since 1990; appeared in Marriage of Figaro and Così fan tutte conducted by Daniel Barenboim (q.v.) in Chicago Feb. 1992; debut at Salzburg Festival 1992; appeared in recital at Rossini bicentenary celebration at Lincoln Center, New York 1992; has appeared with many leading conductors including the late Herbert von Karajan, Claudio Abbado, Riccardo Chailly, Myung-Whun Chung, William Christie, Charles Dutoit, Adam Fischer, Nikolaus Harnoncourt, Christhopher Hogwood, James Levine, Sir Neville Marriner, Zubin Mehta, Riccardo Muti, Giuseppe Sinopoli and the late Sir George Solti; particularly associated with the operas of Mozart and Rossini; highlights of the 2000–01 season included Cenerentola in Munich, Così fan tutte and Don Giovanni in Zurich, concert performances of Haydn's Orfeo with Hogwood in Birmingham, Amsterdam, Bremen and Paris, orchestral appearances with Harnoncourt and the Berlin Philharmonic in Berlin, Barenboim and the Chicago Symphony in Chicago and New York, Boulez and the London Symphony Orchestra in London and Amsterdam, Chailly and the Concertgebouw Orchestra in Amsterdam, all-Vivaldi concerts with the Giardino Armonico in Merano, Zurich, Paris, Lindau, Liechtenstein, New York, Vancouver, Los Angeles and San Francisco, baroque music concerts with the Akademie für Alte Musik in Oslo, Goteborg, Stockholm, Helsinki and Vienna; two Grammy Awards for Best Classical Vocal Album 1994, Deutsche Schallplatten Preis, La Stella d'Oro, Italy, Caecilia Award, Belgium, Diapason d'Or, France, Best Opera Recording of the Year for La Cenerentola, Japan; Chevalier des Arts et des Lettres. *Albums include:* Rossini Arias, Rossini Songs, Mozart Arias, Rossini Heroines, Chants d'amour, If You Love Me 1992, Mozart Portraits 1995, An Italian Songbook 1997, Cecilia Bartoli – Live Vivaldi Album 1999, Cecilia & Bryn, Turco in Italia, Mitridate, Rinaldo, Armida in Italy. *Address:* c/o Edgar Vincent, 481 Eighth Avenue, Suite 740, New York, NY 10001, USA (Office).

BARTON, Anne, PhD, FBA; British professor of English; b. 9 May 1933; d. of Oscar Charles Roesen and Blanche Godfrey Williams; m. 1st William Harvey Righter 1957; m. 2nd John Bernard Adie Barton 1969; ed Bryn Mawr Coll. and Cambridge Univ.; Lecturer History of Art, Ithaca Coll., NY 1958–59; Rosalind Carlisle Research Fellow, Girton Coll. Cambridge 1960–62; Official Fellow in English 1962–72; Asst Lecturer, Cambridge Univ. 1962–64, lecturer 1964–72; Hildred Carlile Prof. of English and Head Dept of English, Bedford Coll., London 1972–74; Fellow and Tutor in English, New Coll., Oxford and Common Univ. Fund Lecturer 1974–84; Prof. of English, Cambridge Univ. 1984–2000; Fellow of Trinity Coll., Cambridge 1986–; mem. Editorial Bds., Shakespeare Quarterly 1981–, Studies in English Literature 1976–, Romanticism 1995–; Hon. Fellow, Shakespeare Inst., Univ. of Birmingham, New Coll., Oxford; mem. Academia Europaea; Rose Mary Crawshay Prize, British Acad. 1990. *Publications:* Shakespeare and the Idea of the Play 1962; Ben Jonson, Dramatist 1984, The Names of Comedy 1990, Byron: Don Juan 1992, Essays, Mainly Shakespearean 1994; numerous essays in journals. *Leisure interests:* opera, travel, fine arts. *Address:* Trinity College, Cambridge, CB2 1TQ, England (Home). *Telephone:* (1223) 338466 (Office); (1223) 338466 (Home). *E-mail:* ab10004@hermes.cam.ac.uk (Home).

BARTON, Glenys, MA, RCA; British artist; b. 24 Jan. 1944, Stoke on Trent; d. of Alexander James Barton and Gertrude Elizabeth Barton (née Farmer); m. Martin Hunt; one s.; ed Royal Coll. of Art; part-time lecturer Portsmouth Polytechnic 1971–74, Camberwell School of Arts & Crafts 1971–87. *Solo exhibitions:* Museum of Decorative Art, Copenhagen 1973, Oxford Gallery, Oxford 1973, Angela Flowers Gallery, London 1974, 1981, 1983, 1986, 1994, Gallery Het Kapelhuis, Amersfoort, Netherlands 1976, Germeenttelijkmuseum, Leeuwarden, Netherlands 1976, Crafts Council Gallery, London 1977, Wedgwood New York 1978, Flowers East, London 1990, 1993, 1996, 1997, Nat. Portrait Gallery, London 1997, Manchester City Art Gallery 1997, City Museum and Art Gallery, Stoke On Trent 1998, Flowers West, Santa Monica 2000; numerous group exhbns., UK and abroad 1980–; works in numerous public collections including: Nat. Portrait Gallery, London, Royal Scottish Museum, Edin., Scottish Nat. Portrait Gallery, Edin., Victoria and Albert Museum, London, Potteries Museum, Stoke on Trent, Wedgwood Museum, Barlaston and in Birmingham, Leeds, Leicester, Manchester, Norwich, Portsmouth, Reading, Southampton, Rotterdam, Melbourne, Pennsylvania, Leeuwarden and Stockholm. *Leisure interest:* gardening. *Address:* c/o Flowers East Contemporary Gallery, 199–205 Richmond Road, London, E8 3NJ, England.

BARTON, Rev. John, MA, DPhil, DLitt; British university professor; b. 17 June 1948, London; s. of Bernard A. Barton and Gwendolyn H. Barton; m. Mary Burn 1973; one d.; ed Latymer Upper School, London and Keble Coll. Oxford; Jr Research Fellow, Merton Coll. Oxford 1973–74; Univ. Lecturer in Theology, Univ. of Oxford 1974–89, Reader in Biblical Studies 1989–91; Fellow, St Cross Coll. Oxford 1974–91; Oriel and Laing Prof. of the Interpretation of Holy Scripture and Fellow, Oriel Coll. Oxford 1991–; Canon Theologian of Winchester Cathedral 1991–; Hon. DTheol (Bonn) 1998. *Publications:* Amos's Oracles Against the Nations 1980, Reading the Old Testament 1984, Oracles of God 1986, People of the Book? 1988, Love Unknown 1990, What is the Bible? 1991, Isaiah 1–39 1995, The Spirit and the Letter 1997, Making the Christian Bible 1997, Ethics and the Old Testament 1998, The Cambridge Companion to Biblical Interpretation 1998, Oxford Bible Commentary 2001, Joel and Obadiah 2001, The Biblical World 2003. *Address:* Oriel College, Oxford, OX1 4EW, England. *Telephone:* (1865) 276537.

BARTON, John Bernard Adie, CBE, MA; British drama director and adaptor; b. 26 Nov. 1928, London; s. of Sir Harold Montagu Barton and Lady Joyce Barton (née Wale); m. Anne Righter 1968; ed Eton Coll. and King's Coll., Cambridge; Drama Lecturer, Univ. of Berkeley, Calif. 1953–54; Fellow, King's Coll. Cambridge 1954–59; Asst Dir (to Peter Hall) RSC 1959, Assoc. Dir 1964–91, Advisory Dir 1991–. *Productions for RSC include:* The Wars of the Roses (adapted, edited, co-directed) 1963, Love's Labour's Lost 1965, 1978, All's Well That Ends Well, Julius Caesar, Troilus and Cressida 1968–69, Twelfth Night, When Thou Art King 1969–70, Othello, Richard II, Henry V 1971, Richard II 1973, Dr. Faustus, King John (co-Dir), Cymbeline (co-Dir) 1974–75, Much Ado About Nothing, Troilus and Cressida, The Winter's Tale, King Lear, A Midsummer Night's Dream, Pillars of the Community 1976, The Way of the World 1978, The Merchant of Venice, Love's Labour's Lost 1978, The Greeks 1980, Hamlet 1980, Merchant of Venice, Two Gentlemen of Verona 1981, Titus Andronicus 1981, La Ronde 1982, Life's a Dream 1984, The Devils 1984, Waste 1985, Dream Play 1985, The Rover 1986, The Three Sisters 1988, Coriolanus 1989, Peer Gynt 1994, 1995, Cain 1995; also School for Scandal, London 1983, For Triumph Apollo 1983, The Vikings 1983; for Nat. Theatre, Oslo: Peer Gynt 1990, Measure for Measure, As You Like It 1991–92; The War That Still Goes On 1991, Tantalus, Denver Center Theater Co. 2000. *Television productions:* Playing Shakespeare 1982, Mallory's Morte d'Arthur 1983, The War That Never Ends (scriptwriter) 1990. *Publications:* The Hollow Crown 1962, The Wars of the Roses 1970, The Greeks 1981, Playing Shakespeare 1982. *Leisure interests:* travel, chess, work. *Address:* 14 De Walden Court, 85 New Cavendish Street, London, W1W 6XD, England. *Telephone:* (20) 7580-6196. *Fax:* (20) 7580-6196 (Office).

BARTOŠEK, Karel, DPhil; Czech historian and writer; b. 30 June 1930, Skutec; s. of Karel Bartošek and Frantiska Stepanková; m. Suzanne Bartošek (née Chastaing) 1959; one s. two d.; ed Charles Univ., Prague; research Asst, Inst. of History, Czechoslovak Acad. of Sciences 1960–68; resgnd 1969; stoker 1972–82; researcher Inst. d'Histoire du Temps Présent, CNRS 1983–99; Ed. Nouvelle Alternative 1986–. *Publications:* Les Aveux des archives 1996, Le Livre noir du communisme, crimes, terreurs, répressions (co-author) 1997, Czech Prisoner 2001. *Leisure interests:* swimming, skiing. *Address:* 6 rue du Moulin de la Pointe, 75013 Paris, France. *Telephone:* 1-45-81-44-69.

BARTOV, Omer, DPhil; professor of European history; ed Univ. of Oxford; fmrly at Rutgers Univ.; currently John P. Birkelund Distinguished Prof. of European History and Prof. of History, Brown Univ.; Visiting Fellow Davis Center, Princeton Univ., Jr Fellow Soc. of Fellows, Harvard Univ.; Fellow Nat. Endowment for the Humanities, Alexander von Humboldt Foundation, Radcliffe Inst. for Advanced Study, Harvard Univ. 2002–03; Guggenheim Fellow 2003–04. *Publications include:* The Eastern Front 1941–45: German Troops and the Barbarisation of Warfare 1985, Murder in Our Midst (Fraenkel Prize in Contemporary History) 1996, Mirrors of Destruction 2000, Germany's War and the Holocaust 2002; (Co-Ed.): The Crimes of War: Guilt and Denial in the Twentieth Century 2001; numerous book chapters, articles and reviews in several languages. *Address:* Brown University, Department of History, Peter Green House, 142 Angell Street, Box N, Providence, RI 02912, USA (Office). *Telephone:* (401) 863-2131 (Office). *Fax:* (401) 863-1040 (Office). *E-mail:* Omer_Bartov@brown.edu (Office). *Website:* www.brown.edu (Office).

BARTY-KING, Mark Baxter, MC, FRSA; British publishing executive; b. 3 March 1938; s. of George Ingram Barty-King and Barbara Baxter; m. 1st Margild Bolten 1963 (divorced 1975); two s.; m. 2nd Marilyn Scott Barrett 1976; two s.; ed Winchester Coll.; nat. service, 13th/18th Royal Hussars, Aden, Oman, Malaya 1957–61; with Abelard Schuman, NY 1962–63, John Howell Books, San Francisco 1964–65, Heinemann Group 1966–74 (Dir Peter Davies Ltd 1969, William Heinemann Ltd 1971); Editorial Dir Granada Publishing 1974–81, Man. Dir Hardback Div. 1981–83; joined Transworld Publishers Ltd 1984, Deputy Man. Dir Publishing 1992, Man. Dir, CEO 1995–2000, Chair. 2001–; f. Bantam Press 1985; Chair. Council, Publrs. Asscn 1995–99, Gen. Books Council 1999–2002, Court, Worshipful Co. of Merchant Taylors 1992–, Chair. Govs St John's School, Northwood 1997–. *Leisure interest:* the countryside. *Address:* Transworld Publishers, 61–63 Uxbridge Road, London, W5 5SA (Office); 46 Elms Road, London, SW4 9EX, England (Home). *Telephone:* (20) 8231-6620 (Office); (20) 7622-1717 (Home); (20) 7622-1544. *Fax:* (20) 8231-6813 (Office); (20) 7622-1544 (Home). *E-mail:* m.barty-king@transworld-publishers.co.uk (Office); MarkBartyKing@aol.com (Home).

BARYSHNIKOV, Mikhail (Misha); Russian/American ballet dancer; b. 28 Jan. 1948, Riga, Latvia; s. of Nikolay Baryshnikov and Aleksandra (née Kisselov) Baryshnikova; one d.; ed Riga Ballet School and Kirov Ballet School, Leningrad; mem. Kirov Ballet Co. 1969–74; guest artist with many leading ballet cos including American Ballet Theater, Nat. Ballet of Canada, Royal Ballet, Hamburg Ballet, FRG, Ballet Victoria, Australia, Stuttgart Ballet, FRG, Alvin Ailey Co., USA 1974–; joined New York City Ballet Co. 1978, resgnd 1979; Artistic Dir, American Ballet Theater 1980–89; Co-Founder (with Mark Morris) and Dir White Oak Dance Project 1990–2002; plans to open Baryshnikov Center for Dance, New York 2004; launched perfume Misha 1989; Gold Medal, Varna Competition, Bulgaria 1966, First Int. Ballet Competition, Moscow, USSR 1968; Nijinsky Prize, First Int. Ballet Competition, Paris Acad. de Danse 1968. *Ballets (world premières):* Vestris 1969, Medea 1975, Push Comes to Shove 1976, Hamlet Connotations 1976, Other Dances 1976, Pas de Duke 1976, La Dame de Pique 1978, L'Après-midi d'un Faune 1978, Santa Fe Saga 1978, Opus 19 1979, Rhapsody 1980. *Films:* The Turning Point 1977, White Nights 1985, Giselle 1987, Dancers 1987, Dinosaurs 1991. *Choreography:* Nutcracker 1976, Don Quixote 1978, Cinderella 1984. *Publication:* Baryshnikov at Work 1977. *Address:* c/o Vincent & Farrell Associates, 481 Eighth Avenue, Suite 740, New York, NY 10001, USA.

BARZEL, Amnon, MSc; Israeli art writer, critic, consultant and museum director; b. 5 July 1935, Tel Aviv; m. Shafrira Glikson 1956; one s. one d.; ed Hebrew Univ., Jerusalem, Sorbonne, Paris; Art Consultant for City of Tel Aviv 1975–76; Curator Biennale of Venice, Italy 1976–78, 1980, 'Two Environments', Forte Belvedere, Florence and Castle of Prato, Italy 1978, São Paulo Biennale, Brazil 1985; Founding Curator 'Contemporary Art Meetings', Tel Hai, Israel 1980–83, Villa Celle Art Spaces Collection, Giuliano Gori, Prato, Italy 1981–82; Founding Dir Centre of Contemporary Art Luigi Pecci, Prato, Italy 1986–; Dir School for Curators 1991–; Consultant for creation of Museum of Contemporary Art, Florence, Italy 1989; mem. Curatorial Cttee for Int. Sculpture Center (ISC), Washington, DC, USA 1990. *Publications:* Isaac Frenel 1973, Dani Karavan 1978, Art in Israel 1986, Europe Now 1988, Julian Schnabel 1989, Enzo Cucchi 1989, Contemporary Russian Artists (jt ed.) 1990. *Leisure interests:* poetry, Holy contemporary philosophy. *Address:* Centro per l'Arte Contemporanea Luigi Pecci, Viale della Repubblica 277, 50047 Prato (Office); Via Giovanni Prati, 26, 50124 Florence, Italy (Home). *Telephone:* (0574) 570620 (Office); (055) 220098 (Home).

BARZEL, Rainer, DrIur; German politician and civil servant; b. 20 June 1924, Braunsberg, East Prussia; s. of Dr. Candidus Barzel and Maria née Skibowski; m. 1st Kriemhild Schumacher 1948 (died 1980); one d. (deceased); m. 2nd Helga Henselder 1982 (died 1995); ed Gymnasium, Braunsberg (East Prussia), Berlin and Univ. of Cologne; Air Force, Second World War; Civil Service, North Rhine-Westphalia, Ministry for Fed. Affairs 1949–56, resgnd 1956; mem. Bundestag 1957–87, Pres. 1983–84; Fed. Minister for All-German Affairs 1962–63; mem. Christian Democrat Party (CDU), Deputy and Acting Chair. CDU/CSU Parl. Group in Bundestag 1963–64, Chair. 1964–73; Chair.

CDU 1971–73, Chair. Econ. Affairs Cttee of Bundestag 1977–79, resgnd 1979, Chair. Foreign Affairs Cttee 1980–82; Co-ordinator for French-German Affairs 1980, 1986–90; Fed. Minister for Inter-German Affairs 1982–83; Pres. German-French Inst., Ludwigsburg 1980–83; Grosses Bundesverdienstkreuz 1968, Grand Officier Légion d'honneur 1992 and numerous other awards. *Publications:* Die geistigen Grundlagen der politischen Parteien 1947, Souveränität und Freiheit 1950, Die deutschen Parteien 1951, Karl Arnold—Grundlegung christlich-demokratischer Politik in Deutschland 1961, Gesichtspunkte eines Deutschen 1968, Es ist noch nicht zu spät 1976, Auf dem Drahtseil 1978, Das Formular 1979, Unterwegs—Woher und Wohin? 1982, Im Streit und umstritten 1986, Geschichten aus der Politik 1987, Ermland und Masuren—zu Besuch aber nicht als ein Fremder 1988, Plädoyer für Deutschland 1989, Sternstunden des Parlaments (Ed.) 1989. *Leisure interests:* skating, mountaineering, curling, archaeology. *Address:* c/o Görrestr. 15, Bundeshaus, 53179 Bonn, Germany.

BARZUN, Jacques, PhD; American writer and university professor; b. 30 Nov. 1907, Créteil, France; s. of Henri Martin and Anna-Rose Barzun; m. 1st Mariana Lowell 1936 (died 1979); two s. one d.; m. 2nd Marguerite Lee Davenport 1980; ed Lycée Janson de Sailly and Columbia Univ.; Instructor in History, Columbia Univ. 1929, Asst Prof. 1938, Assoc. Prof. 1942, Prof. 1945, Dean of Graduate Faculties 1955–58, Dean of Faculties and Provost 1958–67, Seth Low Prof. 1960, Univ. Prof. 1967–75; Prof. Emer. 1975; Literary Adviser, Scribner's 1975–93; fmr Dir Council for Basic Educ., New York Soc. Library, Open Court Publications Inc., Peabody Inst.; mem. Advisory Council, Univ. Coll. at Buckingham, Editorial Bd Encyclopedia Britannica 1979–; mem. Acad. Delphinale (Grenoble), American Acad. and Inst. of Arts and Letters (Pres. 1972–75, 1977–78), American Historical Asscn, Royal Soc. of Arts, American Arbitration Asscn, American Philosophical Soc., Royal Soc. of Literature, American Acad. of Arts and Sciences; Extraordinary Fellow, Churchill Coll., Cambridge 1961; Chevalier Légion d'honneur. *Publications:* The French Race 1932, Race: A Study in Modern Superstition 1937, Of Human Freedom 1939, Darwin, Marx, Wagner 1941, Teacher in America 1945, Berlioz and the Romantic Century 1950, God's Country and Mine 1954, The Energies of Art 1956, Music in American Life 1956, The Modern Researcher 1957 (with H. Graff), The House of Intellect 1959, Classic, Romantic and Modern 1961, Science, the Glorious Entertainment 1964, The American University 1968, A Catalogue of Crime (with W. Taylor) 1971, On Writing, Editing and Publishing 1971, The Use and Abuse of Art 1974, Clio and the Doctors 1974, Simple and Direct 1975, Critical Questions 1982, A Stroll with William James 1983, A Word or Two Before You Go 1986, The Culture We Deserve 1989, Begin Here: On Teaching and Learning 1990, From Dawn to Decadence 2000, A Jacques Barzun Reader 2001; An Essay on French Verse for Readers of English Poetry 1991; Ed. Pleasures of Music 1951, The Selected Letters of Lord Byron 1953, New Letters of Berlioz (and trans.) 1954, The Selected Writings of John Jay Chapman 1957, Modern American Usage (with others) and numerous other books; trans.: Diderot: Rameau's Nephew 1952, Flaubert's Dictionary of Accepted Ideas 1954, Evenings with the Orchestra 1956, Courteline: A Rule is a Rule 1960, Beaumarchais: The Marriage of Figaro 1961.

BASANG; Chinese party official; b. 1937, Lang, Tibet; ed Tibetan Minorities Inst. 1956; served as a slave to the Landlord of Chika 1947–56; joined the CCP 1959; Vice-Chair. Tibet Autonomous Region Revolutionary Cttee 1968–79; Sec. Secr. CCP Cttee Tibet 1971–77; Chair. Women's Fed. of Tibet 1973; mem. 10th CCP Cen. Cttee 1973; Chair. Langxian Co. Revolutionary Cttee 1974; mem. Standing Cttee 4th NPC 1975; 5th NPC 1978; Deputy Head Leading Group for Party Consolidation CCP Cttee Tibet 1977; Sec. CCP 4th Tibet Autonomous Regional Cttee 1977; Deputy Sec. 5th Autonomous Regional Cttee 1977–; mem. CCP 11th Cen. Cttee 1977; Deputy for Tibet to 5th NPC 1978; mem. Pres. 1979; Vice-Chair. People's Govt of Tibet 1979–83; mem. 12th CCP Cen. Cttee 1982–86; mem. Cen. Discipline Inspection Comm., CCPCC; Vice-Chair. CPPCC 6th Tibet Regional Cttee 1993–. *Address:* Chinese Communist Party, Tibet Autonomous Region, Lhasa, People's Republic of China.

BASANT ROI, Rameswurlall, MA; Mauritian central bank governor; b. 17 Aug. 1946; ed Dehli School of Econs, Univ. of Delhi, India; joined Bank of Mauritius 1976, Research Officer 1984–87, Asst Dir Dept of Research 1984–87, Dir 1987–98, Gov. Dec. 1998–. *Publications include:* several papers on econs including Monetary Policy Making in Mauritius (co-author with Maxwell Fry) 1995. *Address:* Bank of Mauritius, Sir William Newton Street, POB 29, Port Louis (Office); 15 Couvent de Lorette, Vacoas, Mauritius (Office). *Telephone:* (230) 212-6127 (Office). *Fax:* (230) 208-9204 (Office). *E-mail:* bomrd@bow.intnet.mu (Office). *Website:* bom.intnet.mu (Office).

BASAYEV, Col Shamil; Russian/Chechen army officer and politician; b. 14 Jan. 1965, Vedeno; m.; one s. one d.; ed Moscow Inst. of Land Eng; served in the Soviet army as fireman; cand. in Pres. elections Chechen Repub. 1991; participant of hijacking of TU-134 from Mineralnye Vody to Turkey in protest against introduction of martial law to Chechnya Nov. 1991; returned to Chechnya as Commdr special task force of D. Dudayev, participant in armed units Confed. of Peoples of Caucasus 1991, Commdr-in-Chief 1994; participant of mil. actions in Nagorny Karabakh (with Azerbaijan), Abkhazia (with separatists); Deputy Minister of Defence, Self-Proclaimed Repub. of Abkhazia 1992; during civil war in Chechnya supported D. Dudayev 1994; after introduction of Russian troops one of leading field commdrs of resistance; Commdr of group that attacked town of Budennovsk and took hostages June 1995; after removal of Russian troops cand. for Presidency of Chechen Repub.

Ichkeriya Jan. 1997; Deputy Prime Minister 1997–; Acting Prime Minister Jan.–Sept. 1998; field commdr. of forces invading Dagestan 1999, fighting Russian troops, hiding in Chechnya mountains 1999–.

BASELITZ, Georg; German artist; b. 23 Jan. 1938, Deutschbaselitz, Saxony; m. Elke Kretzschmar 1962; two s.; ed Gymnasium, Kamenz, Kunstakad. E. Berlin and Akad. der Künste, W. Berlin; Instructor Staatliche Akad. der Bildenden Kunste, Karlsruhe 1977–78, Prof. 1978–83; Prof. Hochschule der Kunste, Berlin 1983–2003; works in public collections including Berlinisce Galerie and Staatliche Museen zu Berlin, Berlin, Kunsthalle, Hamburg, Sammlung Ludwig, Cologne, Staatsgalerie Stuttgart, Staatsgalerie Moderne Kunst, Munich, Statens Museum for Kunst, Copenhagen, Museum Moderner Kunst Stiftung Ludwig, Vienna, Stedelijk Museum, Amsterdam, Centre Pompidou, Paris, Musée d'art moderne et contemporain, Strasbourg, Ludwig Museum, Budapest, Museo Nacional Centro de Arte Reina Sofia, Madrid, Kunstmuseum, Basel, Russian State Museum, St Petersburg, Tate Gallery, London, Scottish Nat. Gallery of Modern Art, Edinburgh, Museum of Fine Arts, Boston, The Art Inst., Chicago, Metropolitan Museum of Art and Museum of Modern Art, New York, Nat. Gallery of Art, Washington, DC, Toronto Art Gallery, Ludwig Museum for Int. Art, Beijing, Nat. Museum of Modern Art Tokyo, Museum of Contemporary Art, Sydney; Commdr des Arts et des Lettres 2002; Kaiserring Prize, Goslar 1986, Rhenus Arts Prize, München-Gladbach 1999, Julio González Prize, Valencia 2001. *Art exhibitions:* exhbn with Eugen Schönebeck, Pandemomnium, W. Berlin 1961; numerous one-man shows throughout Germany, Europe, UK and USA since 1963; contrib. to numerous group shows including Documenta 5, Kassel 1972, São Paulo Bienal 1975, Venice Biennale 1980, The New Spirit in Painting, Royal Acad. London 1981, Berlinart 1961–87, Museum of Modern Art, New York 1987. *Publications:* books, pamphlets, manifestos and articles. *Address:* Schloss Derneburg, 31188 Holle, Germany.

BASESCU, Traian; Romanian politician and fmr naval officer; b. 4 Nov. 1951, Basarabi, Constanța Co.; m.; two d.; ed Inst. of Civil Marine Mircea cel Batran and Norwegian Acad.; Officer Grades III, II and I, Romanian Navy 1976–81, Capt., Merchant Navy 1981–87; Head Navrom Agency, Antwerp 1987–89; Gen. Dir State Inspectorate of Civil Navigation, Ministry of Transportation 1989–90, Under-Sec. of State and Head of Naval Transportation Dept 1990–91, Minister of Transport 1991–92, 1996–2000; mem. Democratic Party (PD), Pres. May 2001–; mem. Chamber of Deputies 1992–96, 1996–2000; Vice-Pres. Chamber of Deputies Comm. for Industry and Services 1992–96; investigated for corruption and fraud 1996; Dir electoral campaign for Petre Roman (Pres. Cand.) 1996; Gen. Mayor of Bucharest July 2000–. *Address:* Office of the General Mayor, Bucharest, Romania (Office).

BASHIR, Abu Bakar; Indonesian religious leader; b. 1938, Jombang, E. Java; joined Darul Islam (extremist Islamic movt) 1950s; ran pirate radio stations broadcasting the call to jihad (holy war), Cen. Java 1960s; Founder and Teacher Muslim boarding school, Solo 1971–; est. self-governing commune on strict Islamic lines, E. Java 1973; imprisoned for attempts to est. an Islamic militia under Suharto regime 1978–82; sought exile in Malaysia 1985–99; believed to have co-f. Jemaah Islamiah (JI—Islamic Community) network with Riduan Isamuddin with objective of establishing Pan-Asian Islamic State 1990; Founding Chair. Indonesia Mujahideen Council (MMI—fed. of extremist Islamic groups) 1999; allegedly funded numerous mil. terrorist groups fighting jihad, in particular in Maluko Islands 1999; believed to have provided logistical support to al-Qaeda operations, USA 2001; arrested on suspicion of bomb attacks on 30 Christian churches, Indonesia 2000, and bomb attacks in Bali, Oct. 2002; wanted by Malaysian Govt in connection with Operation Jabril (attempted mass terrorist attacks on US targets in Malaysia, Singapore and The Philippines 2001); charged with treason April 2003.

BASHIR, Atalla Hamad, BSc, MA, PhD; Sudanese diplomatist and international organization official; b. 23 Aug. 1946, Dongola; m.; one s. one d.; ed Khartoum Univ., Syracuse Univ., New York, USA, Acad. of Commerce, Bucharest, Romania; joined diplomatic service 1971; served in Kuwait, Bahrain, Czechoslovakia, Hungary, Malta, Italy, Romania, Ethiopia; Amb. to GDR 1989–90, to Rep. of Korea 1990–93; Amb. to Saudi Arabia and Perm. Rep. to Islamic Devt Bank and Org. of the Islamic Conf. 1995–97; Amb. to Netherlands and Resident Rep. to Int. Court of Justice 1997–2000; Dir-Gen. Bilateral and Regional Relations, Ministry of External Relations –2000; Exec. Sec. Intergovernmental Authority on Devt (IGAD) June 2000–. *Address:* Intergovernmental Authority on Development, BP 2653, Djibouti, Djibouti (Office). *Telephone:* 354050 (Office). *Fax:* 356994 (Office). *E-mail:* igad@intnet .dj (Office).

BASHIR, Munir Abdul al-Aziz; Iraqi composer and performer; b. 28 Sept. 1930, Mosul; s. of Bashir Abdul Aziz; m. Gecsy Iren 1961; two s.; ed high school and Fine Arts Inst. Baghdad; Instructor, Fine Arts Acad. 1946–60; Dir Community Arts Acad. 1950–56; Head, Music Dept Baghdad Radio and TV 1949–60; Art Adviser and Gen. Dir Music Dept Iraqi Ministry of Culture and Information 1973–93; Gen. Dir Babylon Int. Festival 1986–91; Vice-Pres. Int. Music Council (UNESCO) 1986–91; Sec.-Gen. Arab Acad. of Music 1974–; has performed solo Ud in more than 50 countries since 1954 and made many recordings; recipient of numerous honours and awards including Tchaikovsky Medal (USSR), Chopin Medal (Poland), UNESCO Int. Prize and decorations from France, Spain, Poland, Italy, Jordan, Cuba etc. *Leisure interest:* reading.

Address: Arab Academy of Music, Al-Mansour, P.O. Box 1650, Baghdad; The National Music Conservatory, P.O. Box 926687, Baghdad, Iraq. *Telephone:* 962-2-687620. *Fax:* 962-2-687621.

BASHIR, Lt-Gen. Omar Hassan Ahmad al-; Sudanese army officer; fmr Brig.; overthrew Govt of Sadiq al-Mahdi in coup 30 June 1989; Chair. Revolutionary Command Council for Nat. Salvation 1989–; Minister of Defence 1989–93; Pres. and Prime Minister of Sudan 1993–; Chair. Ass. Intergovt. Authority on Devt (I.G.A.D.) 2000–01. *Address:* Revolutionary Command Council, Khartoum, Sudan.

BASHKIROV, Dmitri Aleksandrovich; Russian pianist and professor of piano; b. 1 Nov. 1931, Tbilisi; s. of Alexandr Bashkirov and Ester Ramendik; m. Natalya Bashkirova 1988; one s.; one d. from a previous marriage; ed Moscow P. I. Tchaikovsky State Conservatory; studied in Tbilisi under A. Virsaladze, Moscow State Conservatory under A. Goldenweiser; concerts since 1955 in more than 30 countries; participated in Wiener Festwochen, Vezbier, Switzerland, Helsinki, Granada, Ruhr Piano Fest, Germany and other festivals; repertoire includes works by Mozart, Schumann, Brahms, Debussy, Prokofiev; teacher Moscow State Conservatory 1957, Prof. 1976–90; Chair. Piano Dept Queen Sofia Higher School of Music, Madrid 1991–; mem. jury numerous int. competitions; Prof. classes Acad. Mozarteum Salzburg, Sibelius Acad. Helsinki, Acad. of Music Jerusalem, Paris Conservatory and others in London, Vienna, Lisbon, Stockholm; Prof. Internat. Piano Foundation, Como-Cadenabbia, Italy 1992–; Grand Prix M. Long Int. Competition (Paris) 1955; People's Artist of Russia, Hon. R. Schumann Medal (Zwickau, Germany), Hon. Medal, Univ. Autónoma de Madrid, Hon. Prix Ruhr pianisten festivals. *Music:* numerous recordings on various labels. *Address:* Studencheskaja 31, app. 74, Moscow, Russia (Home). *Telephone:* (91) 351-1060 (Office); (095) 249-37-41 (Home). *Fax:* (095) 249-37-41 (Home).

BASHMACHNIKOV, Vladimir Fedorovich, DEcon; Russian politician; b. 27 March 1937; m.; three d.; ed Urals State Univ.; worker, deputy chair. kolkhoz, Sverdlovsk Region 1959–62; teacher, docent, Prof. Urals State Univ. 1962–65; Founder All-Russian Inst. of Labour (now All-Russian Inst. of Econ. and Man. in Agric.) 1964–72; Deputy Dir 1972–84; consultant Econ. Dept Cen. Cttee CPSU 1984–89; mem. Cttee on Land Reform Cen. Cttee CPSU 1989–91; active participant movt for privatization of land; mem. State Duma; mem. faction Our Home Russia; mem. Cttee on Agrarian Problems 1995–; Pres. Asscn of Farmers' and Agric. Co-operatives of Russia 1991–; Chair. Union of Land-Owners of Russia 1994; mem. Co-ordination Council, Round Table Business of Russia. *Publications:* over 150 books and articles on org. of labour in agric. *Address:* Association of Farmers' and Agricultural Co-operatives of Russia, Orlikov per 3, Suite 405, 107139 Moscow, Russia (Office). *Telephone:* (095) 204-40-27 (Office).

BASHMET, Yuri Abramovich; Russian viola player and conductor; b. 24 Jan. 1953, Rostov-on-Don; m. Natalia Bashmet; one d.; ed Moscow State Conservatory; concerts since 1975; gave recitals and played with maj. orchestras of Europe, America and Asia; played in chamber ensembles with Sviatoslav Richter, Vladimir Spivakov, Victor Tretyakov and others; restored chamber repertoire for viola and was first performer of music by contemporary composers, including concertos by Alfred Schnittke, Giya Kancheli, Aleksander Tchaikovsky; Founder and Artistic Dir Chamber Orchestra Soloists of Moscow 1989–; Artistic Dir and Chief Conductor Young Russian Symphony Orchestra 2002–; f. Yuri Bashmet Int. Competition for Young Viola Players 1994–; Artistic Dir Dec. Nights Festival, Moscow 1998–; Founder and Artistic Dir Elba Music Festival 1998–; f. Yu. Bashmet Viola Competition, Moscow 1999–; prize winner of int. competitions in Budapest 1975, Munich 1976; People's Artist of Russia 1986, State Prize of Russia 1993, Sonning Prize (Denmark) 1995. *Address:* c/o ICM Artists Ltd, 40 West 57th Street, New York, NY 10019, USA (Agent); Briyusov per. 7, Apt. 16, 103009 Moscow, Russia (Home). *Telephone:* (095) 561-66-96; (095) 229-73-25 (Home).

BASILASHVILI, Oleg Valeriyanovich; Russian actor; b. 26 Sept. 1934, Moscow; m. Galina Mshanskaya; two d.; ed Moscow Art Theatre; debut Leningrad Theatre of Lenin's Komsomol 1956–59; leading actor Leningrad (now St Petersburg) Bolshoi Drama Theatre of Tovstonogov 1959–; several leading roles, including Gayev (The Cherry Orchard), Voynitsky (Uncle Vanya), Khlestakov (The Government Inspector); active participant of democratic movt since end of 1980s, People's Deputy of Russia 1990–93; People's Actor of Russia 1977, USSR People's Actor 1984, State Prize of Russia 1978, Order of Friendship 1994. *Films include:* Alive Corpse 1969, Business Love Affair 1977, Autumn Marathon 1979, Railway Station for Two 1983, The Promised Heaven 1991, The Prophecy 1992, The Ticket in the Red Theatre 1994; numerous TV productions. *Address:* Borodinskaya str. 13, Apt 58, 196180 St Petersburg, Russia (Home). *Telephone:* 113-55-56 (Home).

BASIN, Yefim Vladimirovich; Russian politician and engineer; b. 3 Jan. 1940, Khislovichi, Tambov Region; m.; one s. one d.; ed Belarus Inst. of Transport Eng, Acad. of Nat. Econs; Master, Chief Engineer, Head, Yaroslavl Construction Dept 1962–69; Deputy Man., Chief Engineer, Gortransstroi, Gorky (now Nizhny Novgorod) 1969–72; Head Construction Dept, Pechorstroi 1972–78; First Deputy Head Glavbamstroi 1980–86; USSR Deputy Minister of Transport Construction; Head, Glavbamstroi and Bamtransstroi production cos. 1986–90; Deputy, State Duma of RSFSR; mem. Supreme Soviet; Chair. Cttee on Construction, Architecture and Housing 1990–92; Chair. State Cttee on Problems of Architecture and Construction 1992–94; Minister of Construction 1994–97; Chair. State Cttee on Construction Policy 1997–98;

First Deputy Head, Complex of Perspective Construction, then Head, Dept of Construction Devt, Moscow Govt May–Oct. 1998; Chair. State Cttee on Construction, Architecture and Housing Policy 1998–99; First Vice-Pres. Transstroy Corpn 1999–; Hero of Socialist Labour, Merited Constructor of Russian Fed. *Address:* Transstroy, Sadovaya-Spasskaya str. 21/1, 107217 Moscow, Russia. *Telephone:* (095) 262-3871 (Office). *Fax:* (095) 204-0546 (Home).

BASINGER, Kim; American actress; b. 8 Dec. 1953, Athens, Ga; d. of Don Basinger; m. 1st Ron Britton 1980 (divorced 1990); m. 2nd Alec Baldwin (q.v.) 1993; model 1971–76; first TV role 1976. *Films include:* Hard Country 1981, Mother Lode 1982, Never Say Never Again 1982, The Man Who Loved Women 1983, The Natural 1984, 9½ weeks 1985, Fool for Love 1985, No Mercy 1986, Batman 1989, The Marrying Man 1990, Too Hot to Handle 1991, Final Analysis 1992, Cool World 1992, The Real McCoy 1993, Getaway 1994, Wayne's World II 1994., Pret-a-Porter 1994, LA Confidential 1997 (Acad. Award and Golden Globe for Best Supporting Actress), Bless the Child 2000, I Dreamed of Africa 2000, People I Know 2002, 8 Mile 2003. *Address:* c/o Rick Nicita, CAA, 9830 Wilshire Boulevard, Beverly Hills, CA 90212; c/o Judy Hofflund, Hofflund Polone, 9465 Wilshire Boulevard, Suite 820, Beverly Hills, CA 90212, USA.

BASIR, Ismail; Malaysian banker; b. 1927, Taiping, Perak State; ed Serdang Agricultural Coll. and Durham Univ.; Lecturer, Universiti Pertanian Malaysia; Asst Agricultural Officer Serdang Agricultural Coll.; Dir Agric. Dept, Dir-Gen. Agric., later Exec. Dir Johore State Devt Corpn; Chair. Nat. Padi and Rice Authority 1981–, Food Industries Malaysia 1981–; Exec. Chair. Bank Bumiputra Malaysia Bhd. 1985; Head BMF, Kewangan Bumiputra, Bumiputra Merchant Bankers 1985; Dir Bank Negara 1981 and of several other cos.

BASOLO, Fred, PhD, FAAS; American professor of chemistry; b. 11 Feb. 1920, Coello, Ill.; s. of John Basolo and Catherine Basolo; m. Mary P. Basolo 1947; one s. three d.; ed Southern Illinois Normal Univ. and Univ. of Illinois; Research Chemist, Rohm & Haas Chemical Co. 1943–46; Instructor, subsequently Asst Prof., Assoc. Prof. and Prof. of Chem., Northwestern Univ. 1946–, Chair. of Chem. Dept 1969–72, Morrison Prof. of Chem. 1980–90, Charles E and Emma H. Morrison Prof. Emer. 1990–; NATO Distinguished Prof., Tech. Univ. of Munich 1969; NATO Sr Scientist Fellow, Italy 1981; numerous visiting lectureships USA, Australia, Europe and Asia; Ed.-in-Chief Chemtracts 1988–; Assoc. Ed. Inorganic Chemica Acta Letters 1977–; mem. Editorial Bd Inorganica Chemica Acta 1967– and other publs; Hon. Prof. Lanzhou Univ., China 1985; Chair. Chem. Section, AAAS 1979; mem. ACS (mem. Bd of Dirs 1982–84, Pres. 1983), NAS, Chemical Soc. (London); Hon. mem. Italian Chemical Soc.; Foreign mem. Accademia Naz. dei Lincei, Italy; Corresp. mem., Chemical Soc. of Peru 1983; Fellow, American Acad. of Arts and Sciences 1983, Japanese Soc. for the Promotion of Science 1979; Guggenheim Fellow, Copenhagen 1954–55; Sr Nat. Research Foundation Fellow, Rome 1962–63; Hon. DSc (Southern Ill.) 1984; ACS Award for Research in Inorganic Chem. 1964, Award for Distinguished Service in Inorganic Chem. 1975, Dwyer Medal Award 1976, Oesper Memorial Award 1983, IX Century Medal of Bologna Univ. 1988, Harry and Carol Mosher Award 1990, Padua Univ. Medal 1991, Chinese Chemical Soc. Medal 1991, Chemical Pioneer Award (American Inst. of Chemists) 1992, Humboldt Sr US Scientist Award 1992, Gold Medal Award (American Inst. of Chemists) 1993, Joseph Chatt Medal (RSC) 1996, Josiah Willard Gibbs Medal (ACS) 1996, numerous other awards and honours. *Publications:* Mechanisms of Inorganic Reactions (with R. G. Pearson), Co-ordination Chemistry (with R. C. Johnson—several edns in trans.); more than 350 scientific publs. *Address:* Department of Chemistry, Northwestern University, 2145 Sheridan Road, Evanston, IL 60208, USA.

BASS, Ronald; American songwriter; b. Los Angeles, Calif.; ed Yale Univ., Harvard Law School; began career as entertainment lawyer. *Films include:* Code Name: Emerald, Black Widow, Gardens of Stone, Rain Man (Acad. Award 1988), Sleeping with the Enemy, The Joy Luck Club, When a Man Loves a Woman 1994, Dangerous Minds 1995, Waiting to Exhale, My Best Friend's Wedding 1997, What Dreams May Come 1998, Stepmom 1998, Entrapment 1999, Snow Falling on Cedars 1999, Passion of Mind 1999. *Television includes:* Dangerous Minds (series), Moloney. *Publications:* The Perfect Thief, Lime's Crisis, The Emerald Illusion (novels). *Address:* c/o Creative Artists Agency, 9830 Wilshire Boulevard, Beverly Hills, CA 90212, USA.

BASSANI, Giuseppe Franco, DrSc; Italian professor of physics; b. 29 Oct. 1929, Milan; s. of Luigi Bassani and Claretta Riccadonna; m. Serenella Figini 1959; one s. one d.; ed Univs. of Pavia and Illinois; research physicist, Argonne Nat. Lab. 1960–65; Prof. of Physics, Univ. of Pisa 1965–70, Univ. of Rome 1970–80, Scuola Normale Superiore, Pisa 1980–; Nat. mem. Accademia dei Lincei; Dr. h.c. (Toulouse) 1979, (Lausanne) 1986, (Purdue Univ., W Lafayette, USA) 1994; Italgas Prize for Materials Science 1996. *Publications:* Electronic States and Optical Transitions in Solids (co-author) 1975, Fisica dello Stato Solido (co-author) 2000 and articles in professional journals. *Leisure interest:* history. *Address:* Lungarno Pacinotti 18, 56126 Pisa, Italy (Home); Scuola Normale Superiore, 56100 Pisa, Italy. *Telephone:* 050-509111 (Office); 050-580524 (Home).

BASSETT, Angela; American actress; b. 16 Aug. 1958, New York; ed Yale School of Drama. *Theatre includes:* Colored People's Time 1982, Antigone,

Black Girl, The Mystery Plays 1984–85, The Painful Adventures of Pericles, Prince of Tyre 1986–87, Joe Turner's Come and Gone 1986–87, Ma Rainey's Black Bottom, King Henry IV (Part I) 1987. *Films include:* F/X 1986, Kindergarten Cop 1990, Boyz 'N the Hood 1991, City of Hope 1991, Critters 4, Innocent Blood 1992, Malcolm X 1992, Passion Fish 1992, What's Love Got to Do with It 1993 (Golden Globe Award Best Actress 1994), Strange Days 1995, Panther 1995, Waiting to Exhale 1995, A Vampire in Brooklyn 1995, Contact 1997, How Stella Got Her Groove Back 1998, Music of the Heart 1999, Supernova 2000, Boesman and Lena 2000, The Score 2001, Sunshine State 2002. *TV films include:* Line of Fire: The Morris Dees Story 1991, The Jacksons: An American Dream 1992, A Century of Women 1994. *Address:* c/o Doug Chapin Management, Suite 430 9465 WilshireBoulevard, Beverly Hills, CA 90212, USA (Office).

BASSEY, Dame Shirley (Veronica), DBE; British popular singer; b. 8 Jan. 1937, Tiger Bay, Cardiff, Wales; d. of the late Henry Bassey and Eliza Bassey (née Mendi); one d.; m. 1st Kenneth Hume 1961 (divorced 1965; deceased); m. 2nd Sergio Novak 1971 (divorced 1981); one d. (deceased) one adopted s.; sang at Astor Club, London; signed up for Such is Life by impresario Jack Hylton 1955; started making records 1956; appeared in cabaret New York 1961; Artist for Peace, UNESCO 2000; Int. Amb., Variety Club 2001; many awards including 20 gold discs and 14 silver discs for sales in UK, Netherlands, France, Sweden and other countries; Best Female Singer (TV Times) 1972, 1973, (Music Week) 1974, Best Female Entertainer (American Guild of Variety Artists) 1976, Britannia Award for Best Female Singer 1977. *Films:* La Passione 1996. *Singles include:* Banana Boat Song, As I Love You, Kiss Me Honey Honey Kiss Me, As Long As He Needs Me, theme song for film Goldfinger 1964, Diamonds Are Forever 1971. *Albums include:* Born to Sing the Blues 1958, And I Love You So 1972, Magic is You 1978, Sassy Bassey 1985, I Am What I Am 1984, New York, New York 1991, Great Shirley Bassey 1999. *Address:* c/o CSS Stellar Management, Drury House, 34–43 Russell Street, London, WC2B 5HA, England (Office).

BASSIOUNI, Muhammad Abd al-Aziz; Egyptian diplomatist; b. 31 July 1937, Cairo; s. of Abdel Aziz Bassiouny; m. Nagwa Elsabouny; one s. one d.; ed Egyptian Mil. Acad.; served in Egyptian Army 1956–80; mem. teaching staff, Mil. Acad. 1959–66; Mil. Attaché to Syria 1968–76, Liaison Officer between Egyptian and Syrian Commands, War of Oct. 1973; Brig.-Gen. in Egyptian Army 1978; Mil. Attaché to Iran 1978–80; joined Foreign Service 1980; Counsellor, then Minister Plenipotentiary, Embassy, Tel Aviv 1980, Amb. to Israel 1986–2000; participated in all Egyptian-Israeli talks on normalization of relations and on Taba dispute; Dr. hc (Ben Gurion Univ., Israel) 1995; twelve mil. decorations from Egyptian Army; High Medal of Honour for Bravery with rank of Kt, Syria. *Publications:* several articles on Egyptian-Israeli relations, the peace process and the Taba talks. *Leisure interests:* sport, reading. *Address:* c/o Ministry of Foreign Affairs, Corniche en-Nil, Cairo, Egypt (Office).

BASSOLE, Bazomboué Léandre, MA; Burkinabè diplomatist; b. 21 Sept. 1946, Koudougou; s. of the late Bassole Baourla and of Kanki Eyombie; m. Louise Ouedraogo 1975; four s. one d.; ed Higher Educ. Centre, Ouagadougou, Univ. of Bordeaux and Int. Inst. for Public Admin., Paris; Counsellor State Protocol Dept, Legal Affairs and Claims Dept and Int. Co-operation Dept of Ministry of Foreign Affairs 1975–76, Dir for Admin. and Consular Affairs 1976–77; Second Counsellor, later First Counsellor, Upper Volta Embassy, Paris 1977–81; First Counsellor, Perm. Mission of Upper Volta to the UN 1981–82, Chargé d'affaires 1982–83; Perm. Rep. of Upper Volta (now Burkina Faso) to the UN 1983–86; Amb. to USA March–Aug. 1986; Minister of External Affairs and Co-operation 1986–87; Amb. to Canada 1988–91, to Côte d'Ivoire 1991–2001. *Leisure interests:* classical music, soccer, cycling, swimming, movies. *Address:* c/o Ministry of Foreign Affairs, 03 BP 7038, Ouagadougou 03, Burkina Faso (Office).

BÁSTI, Juli; Hungarian actress; b. 10 Aug. 1957, Budapest; d. of Lajos Básti and Zsuzsa Zolnay; one s.; ed Acad. of Dramatic Arts, Budapest; mem. Csiky Gergely Theatre Co., Kaposvár 1980–85, Katona József Theatre Co. 1985–; stage roles include Beatrice (The Changeling), Ophelia (Hamlet), Helena (Midsummer Night's Dream), Lady Anne (Richard III), Mother Ubu (King Ubu), Masha (Three Sisters), Anna Andrejevna (The Government Inspector), Anna Petrovna (Platonov); musicals: Velma Kelly in Chicago, Sally in Cabaret 1993; films: Wasted Lives 1980, The Red Countess 1983, The Followers 1983, Laura 1986, The Horoscope of Jesus Christ 1988, The Bride of Stalin 1990, The Holidaymaker 1990; Best Actress Award, San Remo 1982, Moscow 1985, Award for Best Acting in Theatre in Budapest 1985, Jászay Marit Prize 1985, Kossuth Prize 1993. *Leisure interest:* forests. *Address:* Krecsányi utca 6, 1025 Budapest, Hungary. *Telephone:* 2742219 (Home).

BASTIDAS CASTILLO, Adina Mercedes; Venezuelan politician and international banker; ed Central Univ. of Venezuela; Rep. of Venezuela to Inter-American Devt Bank, Washington, DC 1999–2000; fmr Vice-Pres. of Venezuela. *Address:* c/o Central Information Office of the Presidency, Torre Oeste 18, Parque Central, Caracas 1010, Venezuela (Office).

BASTOS, Márcio Thomaz de; Brazilian politician and lawyer; b. 30 Aug. 1935, Cruzeiro, São Paulo; m. Maria Leonor de Castro Bastos; one s.; ed Univ. of São Paulo; criminal lawyer 1957–, involved in over 700 cases including acting for the prosecution of Chico Mendes, Lindomar Castilho and Pimenta Neves; Minister of Justice Jan. 2003–; Co-Founder Action for the Citizenship movt. *Address:* Ministry of Justice, Esplanada dos Ministérios, Bloco T, 4° Andar, 70064-900 Brasília, DF, Brazil (Office). *Telephone:* (61) 226-4404 (Office). *Fax:* (61) 322-6817 (Office). *E-mail:* acs@mj.gov.br (Office). *Website:* www.mj.gov.br (Office).

BASU, Jyoti, BA; Indian politician and lawyer; b. 1914; ed Loreto Day School, St Xavier's School, St Xavier's Coll.; went to England to study law, called to Middle Temple Bar 1939; during stay in England actively associated with India League and Fed. of Indian Students in England, Sec. of London Majlis and came in contact with CP of Great Britain; returned to Calcutta 1940; joined undivided Communist Party CP of India; a leader of fmr Eastern Bengal Railroad Workers' Union; elected to Bengal Legis. Council 1946; after Partition remained a mem. of W Bengal Legis. Ass.; arrested for membership of CP after party was banned 1948, but released on orders of High Court; became Chair. Editorial Bd Swadhinata; mem. W. Bengal Legis. Ass. 1952–72; fmr Sec. Prov. Cttee of CP, mem. Nat. Council, Cen. Exec. Cttee and Nat. Secr. until CP split 1963; subsequently mem. Politbureau, CP of India (Marxist); imprisoned 1948, 1949, 1953, 1955, 1963, 1965; Deputy Chief Minister and Minister in charge of Finance in first United Front Govt 1967, Deputy Chief Minister in second United Front Govt; narrowly escaped assassination attempt while campaigning in Bihar 1972; MP for Satgachia 1977; subsequently Leader of Left Front Legislature Party; Chief Minister of W Bengal 1977–2000. *Address:* Chief Minister's Secretariat, Writers' Bldg, Kolkata, India.

BAT-ÜÜL, Erdeniin; Mongolian politician; b. 1 July 1957, Ulan Bator; m. B. Delgertuja 1977; two s. one d.; teacher, First Constructing Tech. Training School, Ulan Bator 1981–82, secondary school Höbsögöl Prov. 1982–85; scientist, Observatory of Acad. of Sciences 1985–89; Founder-mem. Mongolian Democratic Union, mem. Gen. Co-ordinating Council 1989–, Gen. Co-ordinator Political Consultative Centre 1990–; Deputy to Great People's Hural 1990–92, 1996–; mem. Political Consultative Centre of Mongolian Democratic Party 1992–; mem. Gen. Council and Dir Political Policy Inst. of Mongolian Nat. Democratic Party 1992–, Regional Sec. 1993–, Gen. Sec. and Presidium of Co-ordinating Council of Mongolian Democratic Union 1993–. *Address:* Mongolian National Democratic Party, Ulan Bator (Office); Suchbaatar District 1-40,000, 62-1-4 Ulan Bator, Mongolia (Home). *Telephone:* 372810 (Office); 321105 (Home). *Fax:* 372810.

BATA, Thomas John, CC; Canadian (b. Czech) shoe industry executive; b. 17 Sept. 1914, Prague; s. of the late Tomas Bata and Marie Bata; m. Sonja Ingrid Wettstein 1946; one s. three d.; ed pvt. schools England and Switzerland and Acad. of Commerce, Uherske, Hradiste; emigrated to Canada 1939; became Canadian citizen 1942; served as Capt. in Canadian Reserve Army; Chair. Bata Shoe Foundation, Expert Group on Transition Economies and Devt Issues for Cen. and Eastern Europe of the Business and Advisory Cttee to the OECD, Advisory Council Int. MBA Program at York Univ.; mem. Cttee Council for Security Co-operation in Asia Pacific, Comm. on Int. Trade and Investment Policy of ICC, Canadian Council of Chief Execs., Bd of Dirs., Jr Achievement Int.; fmr Chair. Comm. on Multinat. Enterprises, ICC; fmr Adviser UN Comm. on Transnat. Corpns.; fmr Dir Canadian Pacific Airlines, IBM World Trade Corpn; Hon. Chair. Bata Ltd; Hon. Gov. Trent Univ., Ont.; f. T. Bata Foundation, Zlín, Czech Repub.; Hon. LLD (York Univ., Toronto); Dr. hc (Tech. Univ., Brno), (Univ. of Écons, Prague); Order of T.J. Masaryk 1991, Canada 125 Year Confed. Medal 1992, Queen's Silver Jubilee Medal 1997, Order of Double White Cross, Slovakia 1999. *Publication:* Bata, Shoemaker to the World. *Leisure interests:* tennis, skiing, swimming. *Address:* 59 Wynford Drive, Toronto, Ont. M3C 1K3 (Office); 44 Park Lane Circle, Toronto, Ont. M3C 2N2, Canada (Home). *Telephone:* (416) 446-2011 (Office). *Fax:* (416) 446-2187 (Office). *E-mail:* tjbata@toronto.bata.com (Office).

BATALOV, Aleksey Vladimirovich; Russian film actor and director; b. 20 Nov. 1928, Moscow; m. Gitana Azkad'yevna Leonchenko; two d.; ed Moscow Arts Theatre Studio; actor with Cen. Theatre of Soviet Army 1950–53; with Moscow Art Academic Theatre 1953–60; film début 1954; teacher VGIK 1976–, Prof. 1979–; Order of Lenin, People's Artist of USSR 1976, Hero of Socialist Labour and other decorations. *Roles include:* Aleksei Zhurbin in A Large Family 1954, Sasha in The Rumyantsev Case 1956, Boris in The Cranes Are Flying 1957, Gusev in Nine Days in One Year 1962, Pavel Vlasov in Mother 1964, Gurov in The Lady with the Lap-dog 1965, Golubkin in The Flight 1971, Georgi Ivanovich in Moscow Does Not Believe in Tears 1980. *Films directed:* The Overcoat 1960, The Three Fat Men 1966, The Living Corpse 1969, The Flight 1971, The Gambler 1973. *Publication:* Fate and Craftsmanship 1984. *Address:* VGIK, Wilhelm Pieck str. 3, 129226 Moscow (Office); Serafimovicha 2, Apt. 91, 109072 Moscow, Russia (Home). *Telephone:* (095) 181-13-14 (Office); (095) 238-16-29 (Home).

BATALOV, Andrei Yevgenyevich; Russian ballet dancer; b. 22 Apr. 1974, Izhevsk, Udmurt Repub., Russia; ed Vaganova Acad. of Russian Ballet, St. Petersburg; Soloist St. Petersburg Mussorgsky Opera and Ballet Theatre 1992–94; with Mariinsky Theatre 1994–, soloist 1996–; prize-winner Int. Competitions in Budapest, Nagoya, Paris, Moscow. *Roles in ballets include:* James (La Sylphide), Blue Bird (Sleeping Beauty), Prince (Nutcracker), Peasants' Pas de Deux (Giselle), Clown (Legend of Love), Bozhok and Solor (La Bayadère), Basil (Don Quixote), Ali (Le Corsaire), Pas de Deux (Diana and Acteon). *Address:* c/o Mariinsky Theatre, 1 Teatralnaya Square, St. Petersburg, Russia (Office).

BATBAYAR, Bat-Erdeniin, BSc; Mongolian politician and scientist; b. 1955, Arkhangai Prov.; ed Mongolian State Univ., Imperial Coll., Univ. of London; teacher at secondary school, Hentii Prov. 1982–84; scientist, Inst. of Microbiology 1984–; Founding mem. Democratic Socialist Movt; Founding mem. Mongolian Social Democratic Party, Chair. 1990–94; mem. State Great Hural 1996–; Minister of Finance 1998–99 (resgnd). *Address:* Mongolian Social Democratic Party, P.O. Box 578, Ulan Bator 11, Mongolia. *Telephone:* 322055; 328425. *Fax:* 322055.

BATCHELOR, Paul John; Australian financial services executive; b. 22 Sept. 1950, Sydney; s. of John Eastley Batchelor and Patricia Fay Batchelor (née Smith); m. Therese Batchelor 1974; three s.; partner Touche Ross & Co. 1981–85; Financial Dir Nat. Mutual Royal Bank 1985–87; Exec. Dir of Operations Westmax 1987–89; Dir Retail Asia Man. 1993–96; Group Chief Financial Officer and Group Exec. Australasia Fiji Colonial Mutual Assurance Soc. Ltd 1995–97; Chief Financial Officer AMP Ltd 1997–99; Man. Dir and CEO 1999–2002; Dir Jardine CMG Life Holdings Ltd 1994–, Colonial Mutual Funds 1993–, Colonial Mutual Funds Man. Ltd 1993–, Colonial Investment Man. Ltd 1993–, Colonial State Bank 1995–, Jacques Martin Pty Ltd 1993–; mem. Business Council of Australia, Financial Sector Advisory Council, Investment Advisory Cttee, Australian Olympic Foundation; Fellow, Inst. of Charted Accountants. *Address:* c/o AMP, AMP Sydney Core Building, 33 Alfred Street, Sydney, NSW 2000, Australia (Office).

BATE, Jennifer Lucy, BA, FRCO, FRSA, LRAM, ARCM; British organist; b. 11 Nov. 1944, London; d. of Horace Alfred Bate and Dorothy Marjorie Bate; ed Bristol Univ.; Shaw Librarian, LSE 1966–69; full-time concert career 1969–; has performed world-wide; has organized several teaching programmes; collaboration with Olivier Messiaen 1975–92; designed portable pipe organ with N. P. Mander Ltd 1984 and a prototype computer organ 1987; gives masterclasses world-wide and lectures on a wide range of musical subjects; F. J. Read Prize (Royal Coll. of Organists), Young Musician 1972, voted Personnalité de l'Année, France 1989, one of the Women of the Year, UK 1990–97; hon. Italian citizenship for services to music 1996. *Compositions:* Toccata on a Theme of Martin Shaw, Introduction and Variations on an Old French Carol, Four Reflections, Homage to 1685, The Spinning Wheel, Lament, An English Canon, Variations on a Gregorian Theme. *Recordings:* concertos and solo works of all periods; prizes include Grand Prix du Disque (Messiaen), Diapason d'Or, Prix de Répertoire (France), Preis der deutschen Schallplattenkritik (Germany) and MRA Award for 18th century series From Stanley to Wesley. *Television:* South Bank Show on Messiaen, La Nativité du Seigneur (Channel 4). *Leisure interests:* cooking, theatre, philately, gardening. *Address:* 35 Collingwood Avenue, Muswell Hill, London, N10 3EH, England. *Telephone:* (20) 8883-3811. *Fax:* (20) 8444-3695. *E-mail:* jenniferbate@classical-artists.com (Home). *Website:* www.classical-artists.com/jbate (Home).

BATE, Jonathan, PhD, FBA; British professor of English literature; b. 26 June 1958; s. of Ronald Montagu Bate and Sylvia Helen Bate; m. 1st Hilary Gaskin 1984 (divorced 1995); m. 2nd Paula Jayne Byrne 1996; one s. one d.; ed St. Catherine's Coll., Cambridge; Harkness Fellow, Harvard Univ. 1980–81; Research Fellow, St Catherine's Coll., Cambridge 1983–85, Hon. Fellow 2000–; Fellow Trinity Hall, Cambridge, lecturer 1985–90; King Alfred Prof. of English Literature, Univ. of Liverpool 1991–; Research Reader, British Acad. 1994–96; Leverhulme Personal Research Prof. 1999–; Ed. Arden Shakespeare series. *Radio:* features for BBC Radio 3, reviews for BBC Radio 4. *Publications:* Shakespeare and the English Romantic Imagination 1986, Shakespearean Constitutions 1989, Romantic Ecology 1991, Shakespeare and Ovid 1993, The Genius of Shakespeare 1997, The Cure for Love (novel) 1998, The Song of the Earth 2000. *Leisure interests:* cricket, tennis, walking, opera. *Address:* Department of English, University of Liverpool, P.O. Box 147, Liverpool, L69 3BX, England (Office). *Telephone:* (151) 794-2704 (Office).

BATEMAN, Barry Richard James, BA; British investment executive; b. 21 June 1945; m. Christine Bateman; one s.; ed Univ. of Exeter; investment analyst Hoare Govett 1967–72, Research Dir 1972–75; Marketing Dir Datastream 1975–81; Sr Marketing Dir Fidelity Int. Man. 1981–86, Man. Dir Fidelity Investment Ltd 1986–97, Pres. Fidelity Int. Ltd 1991–; Chair. Unit Trust Assen 1991–93. *Address:* Fidelity Investment Management Ltd, Oakhill House, 130 Tonbridge Road, Hildenborough, Tonbridge, Kent, TN11 9DZ, England. *Telephone:* (1732) 361144. *Fax:* (1732) 777441.

BATEMAN, Robert McLellan, OC, BA, DFA, DLitt, DSc, LLD, RCA; Canadian artist; b. 24 May 1930, Toronto; s. of Joseph W. Bateman and Annie (née McLellan) Bateman; m. 1st Suzanne Bowerman 1960; two s. one d.; m. 2nd Birgit Freybe 1975; two s.; ed Forest Hill High School, Toronto, Univ. of Toronto, Ont. Coll. of Education; high school art teacher for 20 years; began full-time painting 1976, numerous museum exhbns. since 1959, including the Smithsonian Inst. 1987, Nat. Museum of Wildlife Art, Jackson, Wyo. 1997; Master Artist, Leigh Yawkey Woodson Museum 1982; Hon. Life mem. Fed. of Ont. Naturalists, Canadian Wildlife Fed., Audubon Soc., Sierra Club; Bd mem. Ecotrust, Jane Goodall Inst.; Hon. Dir Kenya Wildlife Fund, Sierra Legal Defense Fund; mem. Royal Acad. of Arts; nine hon. degrees; awards include: Queen Elizabeth II Jubilee Medal 1977, mem. of Honour Award, World Wildlife Fund 1985, Rachel Carson Award 1996, Golden Plate Award 1998, Rungius Medal 2001. *Publications:* with Ramsay Derry: The Art of Robert Bateman 1981, The World of Robert Bateman 1984; with Rick

Archbold: Robert Bateman: An Artist in Nature 1990, Robert Bateman: Natural Worlds 1996, Safari 1998, Thinking Like a Mountain 2000, with Kathryn Dean: Birds 2002. *Address:* POB 115, Fulford Harbour, Salt Spring Island, BC, V8K 2P2, Canada.

BATENIN, Vyacheslav Mikhailovich, DrPhys-MathSc; Russian physicist; b. 12 March 1939; m.; one s.; ed Moscow Energy Inst.; Engineer, Sr Engineer, Deputy Dir Inst. of High Temperatures USSR (now Russian) Acad. of Sciences 1962–, Dir 1987–; corresp. mem. USSR Acad. of Sciences 1987. *Publications include:* works on physics of gas explosion and low-temperature plasma, problems of applied superconductivity and magnetic hydrodynamics, unconventional energy sources. *Leisure interests:* tennis, travelling. *Address:* Institute of High Temperatures (IVTAN), Izhorskaya str. 13/19, 127112 Moscow, Russia (Office). *Telephone:* (095) 484-23-11 (Office); (095) 331-32-52 (Home).

BATES, Sir Alan, Kt, CBE; British actor; b. 17 Feb. 1934, Allestree, Derbys.; s. of Harold A. Bates and Florence M. Wheatcroft; m. Victoria Ward 1970 (died 1992); twin s. (one s. died 1990); ed Belper Grammar School and Royal Acad. of Dramatic Art (RADA); spent one year with Midland Repertory Co., Coventry; Hon. DLitt (Derby) 1997. *Stage appearances include roles in:* The Mulberry Bush, Look Back in Anger (also in Moscow and New York) 1956, The Country Wife, In Celebration, Long Day's Journey into Night (also at Edinburgh Festival), The Caretaker (also in New York), The Four Seasons, Hamlet (also in Nottingham), Butley (also in New York, Los Angeles and San Francisco), Life Class, Otherwise Engaged 1975–76, The Seagull 1976, Stage Struck; has also appeared at Canadian Shakespeare Festival, Stratford, Ont. in title role of Richard III and as Ford in The Merry Wives of Windsor; also in Poor Richard (New York), Venice Preserved (Bristol), The Taming of the Shrew (Stratford-upon-Avon), A Patriot for Me (London and Chichester) 1983, Dance of Death 1985, Yonadab 1985, Melon 1987, Ivanov 1989, Much Ado About Nothing 1989, Muse of Fire 1989, Stages (Nat. Theatre) 1992, The Showman 1993, Rat in the Skull 1995, The Master Builder 1995, Simply Disconnected 1996, Fortune's Fool 1996, Life Support 1997, Antony and Cleopatra 1999, The Unexpected Man (New York) 2001–02, Fortune's Fool (New York) 2002. *Films:* The Entertainer 1960, Whistle Down the Wind 1961, A Kind of Loving 1962, The Running Man 1962, The Caretaker 1963, Nothing but the Best 1964, Zorba the Greek 1965, Georgy Girl 1965, King of Hearts 1966, Far from the Madding Crowd 1966, The Fixer 1967, Women in Love 1968, The Three Sisters 1969, The Go-Between 1971, A Day in the Death of Joe Egg 1972, Butley 1973, The Impossible Object 1973, In Celebration 1974, Royal Flash 1974, An Unmarried Woman 1977, The Shout 1977, The Rose 1978, Nijinsky 1979, The Trespasser 1980, Quartet 1981, The Return of the Soldier 1982, The Wicked Lady 1982, Duet for One 1987, Prayer for the Dying 1987, The Lair of the White Worm 1989, Dr. M. 1989, Force Majeure, Hamlet 1990, 102 Boulevard Haussmann 1990, Mister Frost 1990, Secret Friends 1991, Shuttlecock 1991, Losing Track 1991, Silent Tongue 1992, The Grotesque 1996, Nicholas's Gift 1997, The Cherry Orchard 1999, The Mothman Prophecies 2001, The Sum of All Fears 2001, Gosford Park 2001. *Television:* Two Sundays, Plaintiff and Dependant, The Collection, The Mayor of Casterbridge, Very Like a Whale, A Voyage Round my Father 1982, An Englishman Abroad 1983, Dr. Fischer of Geneva or the Bomb Party 1984, Pack of Lies 1988, 102 Boulevard Haussmann 1991, Two Lumps of Ice 1992, Silent Tongue 1995; received Tony Award for Butley, Broadway, New York 1973, Variety Club Award for Otherwise Engaged 1975, An Englishman Abroad, Separate Tables 1983, Unnatural Pursuits 1992, Hard Times 1993, Oliver's Travels 1995, In The Beginning 2000, The Prince and the Pauper 2000, Arabian Nights 2000, St Patrick 2000, Love in a Cold Climate 2001, Bertie and Elizabeth 2002. *Radio:* Art, Man and Boy. *Leisure interests:* swimming, driving, travelling, reading. *Address:* c/o Chatto & Linnit Ltd, 123A Kings Road, London, SW3 4PL, England. *Telephone:* (20) 7352-7722. *Fax:* (20) 7352-3450.

BATES, Kathy; American actress; b. 28 June 1948, Memphis, Tenn.; d. of Langdon Doyle Bates and Bertye Kathleen (née Talbot); m. Tony Campisi 1991; ed White Station High School, Southern Methodist Univ.; singing waitress Catskill mountains, cashier Museum of Modern Art, Manhattan. *Theatre work includes:* Varieties 1976, Crimes of the Heart 1979 (won Pulitzer Prize 1981), The Art of Dining 1979, Goodbye Fidel 1980, Chocolate Cake 1980, Extremities 1980, The Fifth of July 1981, Come Back to the 5 & Dime Jimmy Dean, Jimmy Dean 1982, 'night, Mother 1983 (Outer Critics Circle Award), Days and Nights Within 1985, Rain of Terror 1985, Deadfall 1985, Curse of the Starving Class 1985, Frankie and Johnny in the Clair de Lune 1987 (Obie Award), The Road to Mecca 1988. *Films include:* Taking Off 1971, Straight Time 1978, Summer Heat 1987, Arthur 2 on the Rocks 1988, High Stakes 1989, Dick Tracy 1990, White Palace 1990, Men Don't Leave 1990, Misery 1990 (Acad. Award for Best Actress 1991, Golden Globe Award from Hollywood Foreign Press Asscn), Prelude to a Kiss 1991, At Play in the Fields of the Lord 1991, The Road to Mecca 1991, Fried Green Tomatoes at the Whistle Stop Café 1991, Used People 1992, A Home of Our Own 1993, North 1994, Curse of the Starving Class 1994, Diabolique 1996, The War at Home 1996, Primary Colors 1998, Swept from the Sea 1998, Titanic 1998, A Civil Action 1999, Dash and Lilly 1999, My Life as a Dog 1999, Bruno 2000, Rat Race 2001, American Outlaws 2001, About Schmidt 2002, Love Liza 2002, Evelyn 2003. *TV work includes guest roles in:* The Love Boat, St Elsewhere, Cagney & Lacey, LA Law, China Beach, All My Children. *TV films include:* Johnny Bull, Uncommon Knowledge, No Place like Home, One for Sorrow—Two for Joy, Signs of Life, Murder Ordained, Straight Time, Hostages, The West Side Waltz 1995, The Late Shift (Golden Globe 1997) 1996, Annie 1999, My Sister's Keeper 2002. *Address:* c/o Susan Smith and Associates, 121 N San Vicente Blvd., Beverly Hills, CA 90211-2303, USA.

BATESON, (Paul) Patrick (Gordon), PhD, FRS; British university professor; b. 31 March 1938, Chinnor Hill, Oxon.; s. of Richard Gordon Bateson and Solvi Helene Berg; m. Dusha Matthews 1963; two d.; ed Westminster School, Univ. of Cambridge; Stanford Medical Centre, Univ. of Calif.; Sr Asst in Research Sub-Dept of Animal Behaviour, Univ. of Cambridge 1965–69, Dir 1976–80, Lecturer in Zoology 1969–78, Reader in Sub-Dept of Animal Behaviour 1978–84, Prof. of Ethology 1984–; Provost of King's Coll. Cambridge 1988–(2003); Pres. Council Zoological Soc. of London 1989–92; mem. Council Museums and Galleries Comm. 1995–2000; Trustee Inst. for Public Policy Research 1988–95; Biological Sec., Royal Soc. 1998–; Scientific Medal, Zoological Soc. of London 1976, Asscn for Study of Animal Behaviour Medal 2001. *Publications:* (with others) Defended to Death 1983, Ed. Perspectives in Ethology 1973, Growing Points in Ethology 1976, Mate Choice 1983, The Domestic Cat: The Biology of its Behaviour 1988, The Development and Integration of Behaviour (ed.) 1991, Design for a Life: How Behaviour Develops (jtly.) 1999. *Address:* Sub-Department of Animal Behaviour, University of Cambridge, Madingley, Cambridge, CB3 8AA (Office); Provost's Lodge, King's College, Cambridge, CB2 1ST, England (Home). *Telephone:* (1954) 210301 (Office); (1223) 355949 (Home).

BATIZ CAMPBELL, Enrique; Mexican conductor; b. 4 May 1942, Mexico City, DF; s. of José Luis Bátiz and María Elena Campbell; m. 1st Eva María Zuk 1965 (divorced 1983); one s. one d.; m. 2nd Elena Campbell Lombardo; ed Centro Universitario México, Southern Methodist Univ., Dallas, Tex., USA, Juilliard School, New York, Warsaw Conservatoire, Poland; Founder-conductor Orquesta Sinfónica del Estado de México 1971–83, 1990–; Artistic Dir Orquesta Filarmónica de la Ciudad de México 1983–90; Prin. Guest Conductor Royal Philharmonic Orchestra, London 1984–; Guest Conductor with 130 orchestras; decorated Officer, Order of Rio Branco (Brazil) 1986. *Leisure interest:* swimming. *Address:* Cerrada Rancho de los Colorines No. 11, Col Huipulco Tabla del Llano, Código Postal 14380, Zona Postal 22, México, DF, 7, 34, Mexico. *Telephone:* (525) 671-4216 (Agent); (72) 14 46 84 (Office). *Fax:* (72) 15 62 16.

BATLINER, Gerard, DrIur; Liechtenstein lawyer; b. 9 Dec. 1928, Eschen; s. of Andreas Batliner and Karolina Batliner; m. Christina Negele 1965; two s.; ed Grammar School, Schwyz, Switzerland and Univs of Zürich, Fribourg, Paris and Freiburg im Breisgau; practice at County Court of Principality of Liechtenstein 1954–55; Lawyer, Vaduz 1956–62, 1970–; Vice-Pres. Progressive Burgher Party 1958–62; Deputy Mayor of Eschen 1960–62; Head of Govt of Principality of Liechtenstein and Minister of Justice 1962–70; Pres. Liechtenstein Parl. 1974–77, Vice-Pres. 1978–81; Head of Liechtenstein Parl. Del. to the Council of Europe 1978–81; a Vice-Pres Parl. Ass., Council of Europe, session 1981–82; mem. European Comm. on Human Rights 1983–90, European Comm. for Democracy Through Law 1991–; Arbitrator at Court of OSCE 1995–; Chair. Scientific Council of Liechtenstein-Inst. 1987–97, mem. 1998–; mem. European Comm. for Democracy Through Law (Venice Comm.) 1991–; Arbitrator at Court of OSCE 1995–; Ed.-in-Chief Liechtenstein Politische Schriften (Liechtenstein Political Publications); mem. Liecthensteinische Akademische Gesellschaft, Liechtensteinische Gesellschaft für Umweltschultz Historischer Verein, Liechtensteinische Kunstgesellschaft; Grand Cross of the Liechtenstein Order of Merit, Grand Silver Cross of Honour (Austria); Hon. DrIur (Basel) 1988; Fürstlicher Justizrat 1970. *Publications include:* Grundlagen einer liechtensteinischen Politik: Kleinstaatliche Variationen zum Thema der Integration 1972, Liechtenstein und die europäische Integration 1989, Schichten der liechtensteinischen Verfassung 1993, Aktuelle Fragen des liechtensteinischen Verfassungsrechts 1998, and other publs in field of political science. *Address:* Am Schrägen Weg 2, PO Box 185, FL-9490 Vaduz, Liechtenstein (Office). *Telephone:* 239-78-78 (Office). *Fax:* 239-78-79 (Office). *E-mail:* office@bwb-law.li.

BATLLE IBÁÑEZ, Jorge Luis, LLD; Uruguayan politician; b. 25 Oct. 1927; m. Mercedes Menafra; one s. one d.; ed Universidad de la República; journalist 1946–76; MP Partido Colorado 1959–63, 1963–67; blacklisted by mil. Govt, frequently arrested 1973–84; Senator Partido Colorado 1985–90, 1995–99; co-author constitutional reform project 1996; President of Uruguay March 2000–. *Address:* Office of the President, Casa de Gobierno, Edif. Libertad, Avda Luis Alberto de Herrera 3350, esq. Avda José Pedro Varela, Montevideo, Uruguay (Office). *Telephone:* (2) 4872110 (Office). *Fax:* (2) 4809397 (Office). *E-mail:* presidente@presidencia.gub.uy (Office).

BATT, Neil Leonard Charles, AO, BA; Australian politician; b. 14 June 1937, Hobart; s. of Clyde Wilfred Luke Batt and Miriam (née Wilkie) Batt; m. 1st Anne Cameron Teniswood 1962 (divorced 1986); three d.; m. 2nd Dr. Karen Green 1986; one s., two d.; ed Hobart High School, Univ. of Tasmania; secondary school teacher 1960–61 and 1964–66; mem., House of Ass., Tasmanian Parl. 1969–80, 1986–89; Minister of Transport and Chief Sec. 1972–74, Minister for Educ. 1974–77, Deputy Premier and Treasurer 1977–80, Minister for Forests 1978–80, Minister for Finance 1979–82; Nat. Pres. Australian Labor Party 1978–80; Dir TNT Group of Cos. for Vic. and Tasmania 1982–86, Resident Dir TNT Man. Pty Ltd 1982–86; Leader of Opposition 1987–89; fmr Exec. Dir Health Benefits Council of Vic.; Chair. Heine Man. Ltd 1995–2000; Victorian Man. Australian Health Insurance Asscn 2001–; Vice-Pres. Int. Diabetes Inst.; mem. Bd Netwealth Ltd; Ombudsman for Tasmania 1989–91; mem. Jackson Cttee; Trustee, Nat. Gallery of Vic. 1983–86, Treas. 1984–86; Commr of Commonwealth Serum Labs. 1983–86, Chair. 1984–86; mem. Bd of Australian Opera 1983–96. *Publications:* The Great Depression in Australia 1970, The Role of the University Today 1977, Information Power 1977. *Leisure interests:* swimming, yachting. *Address:* 16 Kooyong Road, North Caulfield, Vic. 3161, Australia.

BATT, Philip E.; American politician and farmer; b. 4 March 1927, Wilder, Idaho; m. Jacque Fallis 1948; one s. two d.; Chair. Idaho State Republican party; fmr mem. Idaho State Senate; fmr Lt-Gov. of Idaho; Gov. of Idaho 1995–99; first Pres. Idaho Food Producers; Dir Wilder Farm Labor Cttee. *Address:* c/o Office of the Governor, P.O. Box 83720, Boise, ID 83720, USA.

BATTEN, Alan Henry, PhD, DSc, FRSC; Canadian astronomer; b. 21 Jan. 1933, Whitstable, England; s. of George Cuthbert Batten and Gladys (Greenwood) Batten; m. Lois Eleanor Dewis 1960; one s. one d.; ed Wolverhampton Grammar School, Univs. of St Andrews and Manchester; Research Asst, Univ. of Manchester and Jr Tutor, St Anselm Hall of Residence 1958–59; Post-doctoral Fellow, Dominion Astrophysical Observatory, Victoria, BC, Canada 1959–61, staff mem. 1961–91, Sr Research Officer 1976–91, Guest Worker 1991–; Visiting Erskine Fellow, Univ. of Canterbury, NZ 1995; Vice-Pres. Astronomical Soc. of Pacific 1966–68; Pres. Canadian Astronomical Soc. 1974–76, Royal Astronomical Soc. of Canada 1976–78 (Hon. Pres. 1994–98), Comm. 30 of Int. Astronomical Union 1976–79, Comm. 42 1982–85; Vice-Pres. Int. Astronomical Union 1985–91; mem. Advisory Council, Centre for Studies in Religion and Society, Univ. of Vic. 1993–2002 (Chair. 1997–2000); mem. Editorial Bd, Journal of Astronomical History and Heritage 1998–; Sessional Lecturer in History, Univ. of Vic. 2003; Queen's Silver Jubilee Medal 1977. *Publications:* The Determination of Radial Velocities and their Applications (co-ed.) 1967, Extended Atmospheres and Circumstellar Matter in Close Binary Systems (ed.) 1973, Binary and Multiple Systems of Stars 1973, Resolute and Undertaking Characters: The Lives of Wilhelm and Otto Struve 1988, Algols (ed.) 1989, Astronomy for Developing Countries (ed.) 2001; over 160 scientific papers. *Leisure interest:* campanology. *Address:* Dominion Astrophysical Observatory, 5071 West Saanich Road, Victoria, BC, V9E 2E7 (Office); 2987 Westdowne Road, Victoria, BC, V8R 5G1, Canada (Home). *Telephone:* (250) 363-0009 (Office); (250) 592-1720 (Home). *Fax:* (250) 363-0045. *E-mail:* alan.batten@nrc.gc.ca (Office).

BATTEN, Sir John Charles, KCVO, MD, FRCP; British physician; b. 11 March 1924; s. of the late Raymond Wallis Batten and of Gladys Charles; m. Anne Margaret Oriel 1950; one s. two d. (and one d. deceased); ed Mill Hill School, St Bartholomew's Medical School; Jr appointments, St George's Hospital and Brompton Hospital 1946–58; Surgeon Capt., Royal Horse Guards 1947–49; Physician, St George's Hosp. 1958–79, Brompton Hosp. 1959–86, King Edward VII Hosp. for Officers 1968–89, King Edward VII Hosp., Midhurst 1969–89; Physician to HM Royal Household 1970–74, Physician to HM the Queen 1974–89, Head HM Medical Household 1982–89; Dorothy Temple Cross Research Fellow, Cornell Univ. Medical Coll., New York 1954–55; Deputy Chief Medical Referee, Confederation Life Insurance Co. 1958–74, Chief Medical Officer 1974–95; Examiner in Medicine, London Univ. 1968; Marc Daniels Lecturer, Royal Coll. of Physicians 1969; Croonian Lecturer, Royal Coll. of Physicians 1983; mem. Bd of Govs., Brompton Hosp. 1966–69, Medical School Council, St George's Hosp. 1969, Man. Cttee, King Edward VII Hospital Fund, Council, Royal Soc. of Medicine 1970, Chair. Medical and Survival Cttee RNLI 1992–94, Life Vice-Pres. 2000–; Censor, Royal Coll. of Physicians 1977–78, Sr Censor 1980–81, Vice-Pres. 1980–81; Hon. Physician to St George's Hospital 1980–, Royal Brompton Hosp. 1986–; Consultant to King Edward VII Convalescent Home, Isle of Wight 1975–85; Pres. Cystic Fibrosis Trust 1986–, Medical Protection Soc. 1987–95. *Publications:* articles in medical books and journals. *Address:* 7 Lion Gate Gardens, Richmond, Surrey, TW9 2DF, England. *Telephone:* (20) 8940-3282.

BATTERSBY, Sir Alan Rushton, Kt, PhD, DSc, ScD, FRS; British chemist; b. 4 March 1925, Leigh; s. of William Battersby and Hilda Battersby; m. Margaret Ruth Hart 1949 (died 1997); two s.; ed Leigh Grammar School, Manchester Univ., St Andrews Univ.; Lecturer in Chem., St Andrews Univ. 1948–53, Bristol Univ. 1954–62; Prof. of Organic Chem., Liverpool Univ. 1962–69, Cambridge Univ. 1969–92, Prof. Emer. 1992–; Baker Lectureship, Cornell Univ. 1984, Robert Robinson Lectureship 1985, Marvel Lectureship, Illinois, USA 1989, Gilman Lectureship, Iowa, USA 1989, Kurt Alder Lectureship, Univ. of Cologne, Germany 1991, Romanes Lectureship, Edin. Univ. 1993, Univ. Lectureship, Ottawa 1993, William Dauben Lectureship, Univ. of Calif., Berkeley, USA 1994, Alexander Cruickshank Lectureship, Gordon Confs., USA 1994, Linus Pauling Distinguished Lectureship, Ore. State, USA 1996, IAP Lectureship, Columbia, USA 1999; Hon. DSc (Rockefeller) 1977; Hon. LLD (St Andrew's) 1977; Hon. DSc (Sheffield) 1986, (Bristol) 1994, (Liverpool) 1996; Corday-Morgan Medal and Prize 1961, Tilden Lectureship and Medal 1963, Hugo Müller Lectureship and Medal 1972, Flintoff Medal 1975, Paul Karrer Medal 1977, Davy Medal 1977, Max Tishler Award and Lectureship (Harvard) 1978, W von Hofmann Award and Lectureship 1979, Medal for Chemistry of Natural Products 1979, Pedlar Lectureship and Medal 1980, Roger Adams Award and Medal, ACS 1983, Davy Medal, Royal Soc. 1984, Havinga Medal 1984, Longstaff Medal 1984, Royal Medal 1984, Antonio Feltrinelli Int. Prize for Chemistry, Accademia Nazionale dei Lincei, Italy 1986, Varro Tyler Award, Purdue, USA 1987, Medal of Société Royale de Chimie, Belgium 1987, Adolf Windaus Medal and Lectureship German Chem. Soc. 1987, Wolf Foundation Chemistry Prize 1989, Arun Guthikonda Award and Lectureship, Columbia Univ., USA 1991, W von Hofmann Memorial Medal 1992, Tetrahedron Prize 1995, Hans-Herloff Inhoffen Medal and Prize, Germany 1997, Robert A. Welch Award, USA 2000, Copley Medal, Royal Soc. 2000. *Publications:* original papers in the maj. chemical journals. *Leisure interests:* trout fishing, camping, hiking, gardening, classical music. *Address:* University Chemical Laboratory, Lensfield Road, Cambridge, CB2 1EW (Office); 20 Barrow Road, Cambridge, CB2 2AS, England (Home). *Telephone:* (1223) 336400 (Office); (1223) 363799 (Home). *Fax:* (1223) 336362.

BATTLE, Kathleen Deanna, M.MUS.; American opera singer; b. Portsmouth, Ohio; d. of Ollie Layne Battle and Grady Battle; ed Coll.-Conservatory of Music, Univ. of Cincinnati; professional début in Brahms Requiem, Cincinnati May Festival, then Spoleto Festival, Italy 1972; début Metropolitan Opera, New York as shepherd in Wagner's Tannhäuser 1977; regular guest with orchestras of New York, Chicago, Boston, Philadelphia, Cleveland, LA, San Francisco, Vienna, Paris and Berlin, at Salzburg, Tanglewood and other festivals and at the maj. opera houses including Metropolitan, New York, Covent Garden, London, Paris and Vienna; appearances in 1985/86 season included Sophie in Der Rosenkavalier and Susanna in Figaro, Metropolitan New York, U.S. première parts of Messiaen's St Francis of Assisi with Boston Symphony Orchestra and recitals USA and in Toronto, Paris, Vienna and Florence; appearances in 1986/87 season included Zerbinetta in Ariadne auf Naxos and Adina in L'Elisir d'amore, Metropolitan New York and recitals in Japan, London, Salzburg and Vienna; planned recordings include Fauré Requiem; Dr. hc (Cincinnati and Westminster Choir Coll., Princeton), Grammy Award 1987, 1988. *Recordings include:* Brahms Requiem and Songs, Mozart Requiem, Don Giovanni, Seraglio and concert arias, Verdi's Un Ballo in Maschera and Berg's Lulu Suite; New Year's Eve Gala, Vienna. *Leisure interests:* gardening, cooking, sewing, piano, dance. *Address:* c/o Columbia Artist Management Inc., 165 West 57th Street, New York, NY 10019, USA.

BATTLE, Lucius Durham, AB, LLB; American educationist; b. 1 June 1918, Dawson, Ga; s. of Warren L. Battle and Jewel B. Durham; m. Betty Davis 1949; two s. two d.; ed Univ. of Florida; Man. of student staff, Univ. of Florida Library 1940–42; Assoc. Admin. Analyst, War Dept 1942–43; US Naval Reserve 1943–46; Foreign Affairs Specialist, Dept of State, Washington, DC 1946–49; Special Asst to Sec. of State 1949–53, 1961–64, also Exec. Sec. Dept of State 1961–62; First Sec., Copenhagen 1953–55; Deputy Exec. Sec. NATO, Paris 1955–56; Asst Sec. of State for Educational and Cultural Affairs 1962–64; Amb. to United Arab Repub. 1964–67; Asst Sec. of State for Near Eastern and S. Asian Affairs, Washington, DC 1967–68; Vice-Pres. for Corporate Affairs, Communications Satellite Corpn, Washington, DC 1968–73; Sr Vice-Pres. for Corporate Affairs 1974–80; Pres. Middle East Inst., Washington, DC, 1973–74, 1986–90; Lucius D. Battle Assocs. 1984–85; mem. Advisory Council, Center for US–European Middle East Co-operation 1981–; Chair. UNESCO Gen. Conf., Paris 1962; Adviser, Foundation for Middle East Peace 1981, Pres. 1994–; mem. Bd of Dirs World Council of Washington, DC 1980; mem. Nat. Bd Smithsonian Assocs 1981–85; Vice-Pres. Colonial Williamsburg Inc., Williamsburg Restoration Inc. 1956–61; Pres. Bacon House Foundation; Trustee, Meridan House Int., American Univ. Cairo, The Jordan Soc. 1982; mem. Bd of Dirs Foreign Policy Asscn, School of Advanced Int. Studies, Middle East Inst., George C. Marshall Research Foundation, First American Bank, NA 1982–; mem. Bd Nat. Defense Univ. Foundation 1978–; mem. Founders' Council, Inst. for Study of Diplomacy, Georgetown Univ. 1978–87; mem. Advisory Bd Faith and Hope, WAFA WAL AMAL, Center for Contemporary Arab Studies, Georgetown Univ., Inst. for Psychiatry and Foreign Affairs; mem. American Foreign Service Asscn (Pres. 1962–63), Nat. Study Comm. on Records and Documents of Fed. Officials, Dept of State Fine Arts Cttee; Communications Exec. Dir COMSAT Gen. Corpn; Chair. Nat. Cttee to honour the 14th Centennial of Islam 1979–84; Chair. The Johns Hopkins Foreign Policy Inst., School for Advanced Int. Studies, The Johns Hopkins Univ., Washington, DC 1980–84; Order of Republic (1st class), Egypt 1978. *Address:* 4856 Rockwood Parkway, NW, Washington, DC 20016, USA (Home). *Telephone:* (202) 244-9109 (Home).

BATTS, Warren Leighton; American business executive; b. 4 Sept. 1932, Norfolk, Va; s. of John Leighton Batts and Allie Belle (née Johnson) Batts; m. Eloise Pitts 1957; one d.; ed Georgia Inst. of Tech., Harvard; with Kendall Co. 1963–64; Exec. Vice-Pres. Fashion Devt Co. 1964–66; Vice-Pres., Douglas Williams Assocs. 1966–67; Founder, Triangle Corpn 1967, Pres. and Chief Exec. Officer 1967–71; Vice-Pres., Mead Corpn 1971–73, Pres. 1973–80, CEO 1978–80; Pres. Dart Industries 1980–81, Pres. Dart & Kraft 1981–86; Chair. Premark Int. Inc. 1986–97, CEO 1986–96; Chair., CEO Tupperware Corpn 1996–97; Chair. Nat. Asscn of Corpn Dirs. 2000–; Trustee Northwestern Univ. 1989, Children's Memorial Hospital, Chicago 1984–. *Address:* c/o Premark International Inc., 1717 Deerfield Road, IL 60015, USA.

BATTY, Sir William (Bradshaw), Kt, TD; British motor executive (retd); b. 15 May 1913, Manchester; s. of Rowland Batty and Nellie Batty; m. Jean Ella Brice 1946; one s. one d. (one s. deceased); ed Hulme Grammar School, Manchester; apprentice toolmaker, Ford Motor Co. Ltd 1930, co. trainee 1933; Man. Tractor Div. 1955; Gen. Man. Tractor Group 1961; Dir of Car and Truck Group 1964; Exec. Dir Ford Motor Co. Ltd 1963, Man. Dir 1967–73, Chair. 1972–76; Dir Henry Ford and Son Ltd, Cork 1965–76; Chair. Ford Motor Credit Co. Ltd 1968–76, Automotive Finance Ltd 1970–76; Dir Ford Lusitana SARL, Portugal 1973–76; Pres. Soc. of Motor Mfrs and Traders 1975–76, Vice-

Pres. 1976–. *Leisure interests:* golf, sailing, gardening. *Address:* Glenhaven Cottage, Riverside Road West, Newton Ferrers, South Devon, PL8 1AD, England. *Telephone:* (1752) 872415.

BATU BAGEN; Chinese party and government official; b. 1924, Zhenlai Co., Jilin Prov.; s. of Chen and Ne Garibu; m. 1950; three d.; joined CCP 1946; Deputy 1st, 2nd, 4th, 5th, 6th and 7th Inner Mongolia Autonomous Regional People's Congress, Chair. 1983–95; mem. Presidium 4th, 5th, 6th and 7th Autonomous Regional People's Congress; Deputy for Inner Mongolia 4th, 5th, 6th and 7th NPC; mem. Presidium 6th, 7th NPC; Vice-Chair. Autonomous Regional Govt Inner Mongolia 1979–83; alt. mem. Cen. Cttee CCP 1982–92; mem. Standing Cttee 8th CPPCC and Vice-Chair. Ethnic Affairs Cttee CPPCC 1993–; Leader 8th Prov. Spoken and Written Mongolian Language Co-ordination Group 1983–; Vice Chair. China Sports Asscn for the Elderly 1992; Vice-Pres. China Yellow River Culture, Econs and Devt Research Inst. 1993; Pres. Inner Mongolia Yellow River Culture, Econs and Devt Research Inst. 1995. *Leisure interests:* tennis, calligraphy. *Address:* Bldg 4, Inner Yard, 1 Qingcheng Lane, Huhhot 010015, People's Republic of China.

BATURIN, Yuri Mikhailovich, DJur; Russian politician, cosmonaut, lawyer and journalist; b. 12 June 1949, Moscow; m.; one d.; ed Moscow Inst. of Physics and Tech., All-Union Inst. of Law, Moscow State Univ. School of Journalism, Military Acad. of Gen. Staff; worked in research production union Energia 1973–80; Inst. of State and Law USSR (now Russian) Acad. of Sciences 1980–91; Research Scholar, Kennan Inst. for Advanced Russian Studies, The Woodrow Wilson Center, Washington, DC, USA 1991; on staff of Pres. Mikhail Gorbachev Admin. 1991; mem. Pres.'s Council 1993–; Asst to Pres. on legal problems 1993–94, on Nat. Security Problems 1994–96; mem. Council on Personnel Policy of Pres. 1994–97; Sec. Defence Council of Russian Fed. 1996–97; Asst to Pres., Chair. Cttee for Mil. Ranks and Posts 1995–97; columnist Novaya Gazeta newspaper 1997–; cosmonaut and test pilot of the Cosmonaut Corps 1998–, Deputy Commr 2000–, participated in space flight to Mir Station Aug. 1998, second space flight to Int. Space Station 2001; Prof. of Computer Law, Moscow Inst. of Eng and Physics; Prof. Moscow Inst. of Physics and Tech.; Prof., School of Journalism, Moscow Univ., Pres. of the School, Media Law and Policy Center; Chair. Center for Anti-Corruption Research and Initiative Transparency Int. 2000–; Union of Journalists Prize 1990, Award for Outstanding Contribution to Mass-Media Law 1997, Themis Award 1998. *Exhibition:* Short Rendezvous with Earth (art photography) 1999. *Films:* documentaries: Tuch-and-go in Space 1997, Ladder to Heaven 2000. *Publications:* drafts of the laws on the freedom of the press of the USSR 1989 and of Russia 1991, Problems of Computer Law 1991. *Address:* Y. Gagarin Centre for Cosmonaut Training, Zvezdny Gorodok, 141160 Shchelkovsky Raion, Moskovskaya oblast, Russia (Office). *Telephone:* (095) 526-38-83 (Office). *E-mail:* baturin@medialaw.ru (Office); TIRussia@libfl.ru (Office).

BAUCHARD, Denis M(ichel) B(ertrand), BA; French diplomatist; b. 20 Sept. 1936, Paris; s. of Charles Bauchard and Marguerite Duhamel; m. Geneviève Lanoë 1961; two s. two d.; ed Inst. of Political Studies, Ecole nat. d'administration; Civil Admin., Ministry of Finance 1964–66, 1968–74; Financial Attaché Nr and Middle East, French Embassy Beirut 1966–68; Asst to Minister 1974–76; Financial Counsellor, French Mission to UN 1977–81; Deputy Asst Sec., Ministry of Foreign Affairs 1981–85; Asst Sec. 1986–89; Amb. to Jordan 1989–93; Asst Sec. Ministry of Foreign Affairs (N Africa and Middle East) 1993–96; Chief of Staff to Minister of Foreign Affairs 1996–97; Amb. to Canada 1998–2001; Pres. Institut du Monde Arabe 2002–; Officier, Légion d'honneur; Officier, Ordre nat. du Mérite. *Publications:* Le Jeu mondial des pétroliers 1970, Economie financière des collectivités locales 1972. *Address:* Institut du Monde Arabe, 1 rue des Fosses-Saint-Bernard, 75236 Paris Cedex 5, France; 91 rue de Rennes, 75006 Paris, France (Home). *Telephone:* 1-45-44-18-05 (Home); 1-40-51-38-13. *Fax:* 1-46-34-02-08 (Office); 1-45-44-02-08 (Home). *E-mail:* dbauchard@imarabe.org (Office); denis .bauchard@wanadoo.fr (Home). *Website:* www.imarabe.org.

BAUCUS, Max S., LLB; American senator; b. 11 Dec. 1941, Helena, Mont.; m. Wanda Minge 1983; one s.; ed Helena High School, Stanford Univ. and Stanford Law School; staff attorney, Civil Aeronautics Bd, Washington, DC 1967–69; legal staff, Securities and Exchange Comm. 1969–71; legal Asst to Chair. SEC 1970–71; private law practice, Missoula, Mont. 1971; Acting Exec. Dir and Cttee Coordinator, Mont. Constitutional Convention; elected to Montana State Legislature 1972; two terms in US House of Reps for Mont. Western Dist., mem. House Appropriations Cttee and Deputy Whip; Senator from Montana 1979–; Chair. Senate Int. Trade Sub-Cttee of Finance, Senate Environment and Public Works Cttee, Senate Agric. and Intelligence Cttee, Finance Cttee 2001; mem. several other sub-cttees; Democrat. *Address:* 511 Hart Senate Building, Washington, DC 20510-0001, USA.

BAUDO, Serge; French conductor; b. 16 July 1927, Marseille; s. of Etienne Baudo and Geneviève Tortelier; m. Madeleine Reties 1947; one s. one d.; ed Conservatoire nat. supérieur de musique, Paris; Music Dir Radio Nice 1957–59; Conductor Paris Opera Orchestra 1962–66; titular Conductor and Orchestral Dir a.i. Orchestre de Paris 1968–70; Music Dir Opéra de Lyon 1969–71, Orchestre Nat. de Lyon 1971–87; Musical Dir Orchestre Symphonique de Prague (FOK) 2001–; has conducted many of world's leading orchestras; Founder Berlioz Festival, Lyon 1979–89; Chevalier, Ordre nat. du Mérite; Officier des Arts et des Lettres, Officier, Légion d'honneur; numerous prix du disque and other awards. *Address:* Les Hauts du Ferra, Chemin

Charré, 13600 Ceyreste, France (Home); Matthias Vogt, 1714 Stockton Street, Suite 300, San Francisco, CA 94133-2930, USA. *Telephone:* (415) 788-8073. *Fax:* (530) 684-5535. *E-mail:* malthias.vogt@usa.net (Office).

BAUDOUIN, Jean-Louis, BA, BCL, PhD; Canadian lawyer and professor of law; b. 8 Aug. 1938, Boulogne, France; s. of Louis Baudouin and Marguerite Guerin; m.; four d.; ed Univ. of Paris, McGill Univ., Montreal, Canada; admitted to Bar of Québec 1959; Prof. of Law, Univ. of Montreal 1963–; Commr, Law Reform Comm. of Canada 1976–78, Vice-Chair. 1978–80, Judge, Court of Appeal, Québec 1989–; mem. RSC; Dr. h.c. (Sherbrooke) 1990, (Paris) 1994, (Namur) 1998, (Ottawa) 2001; Médaille du Burreau de Québec 1988. *Publications:* Les Obligations 1970, La Responsabilité Civile 1973, Le Secret Professionnel 1964, Produire l'Homme: de quel Droit? 1987, Ethique de la Mort, Droit à la Mort 1992. *Leisure interests:* windsurfing, fishing, wine-tasting. *Address:* Court House, #17.95, 1 Notre Dame East, Montreal, H2Y 1B6 (Office); 875 Antonine Maillet, Montreal, Québec, H2V 2Y6, Canada (Home). *Telephone:* (514) 393-4863 (Office); (514) 270-1884 (Home). *Fax:* (514) 873-0376 (Office). *E-mail:* jlbaudouin@justice.gouv.qc.ca (Office).

BAUDRIER, Jaqueline; French journalist and diplomatist; b. 16 March 1922, Beaufai; m. 1st Maurice Baudrier (divorced); m. 2nd Roger Perriard 1957; ed Univ. of Paris; political reporter, Actualités de Paris news programme and foreign news reporter and presenter on various news programmes, Radiodiffusion-Télévision Française 1950–60; Sec.-Gen. Soutien fraternel des journalistes 1955; Ed.-in-Chief of news programmes, Office de Radiodiffusion-Télévision Française (ORTF) 1963–66, in charge of main news programme 1966–68; Asst Dir of radio broadcasting, in charge of information 1968–69; Dir of Information, 2nd TV channel (A2) 1969–72; Dir 1st TV channel network (TF1) 1972–74; Chair. Radio-France (nat. radio broadcasting co.) 1975–81; mem. Bd of Dirs Télédiffusion de France (nat. TV broadcasting co.) 1975–81; Pres. Communauté radiophonique des programmes de langue française 1977–79; Vice-Chair. Programming Comm. Union européenne de radiodiffusion 1978, re-elected 1980; Perm. Rep. of France to UNESCO 1981–85; mem. Exec. Cttee, UNESCO 1984–85, Comm. nat. de la Communication et des Libertés 1986–89; columnist Quotidien de Paris 1989; Pres. Cosmo Communications 1989–95; columnist, mem. Bd L'Observatoire de la Télévision 1993–; Pres. Channel 5 TV Programming Comm. 1995; Vice-Pres. Nat. Comm. for UNESCO 1996; Prix Maurice Bourdet 1960, Prix Ondes 1969; Chevalier Légion d'honneur, Officier, Ordre nat. du Mérit, numerous other awards. *Address:* La Cinquième, 8 rue Marceau, 92136 Issy-les-Moulineaux Cedex (Office); 60 quai Louis Blériot, 75016 Paris, France (Home).

BAULIEU, Etienne-Emile, DenM, D. ÈS SC.; French biochemist; b. 12 Dec. 1926, Strasbourg; s. of Léon Blum and Thérèse Lion; m. Yolande Compagnon 1947; one s. two d.; ed Lycée Pasteur, Neuilly-sur-Seine, Faculté de Médecine and Faculté des Sciences, Paris; Intern, Paris Hosps. 1951–55; Chef de Clinique, Faculté de Médecine, Paris 1955–57, Assoc. Prof. of Biochemistry 1958; Visiting Scientist, Dept of Obstetrics, Gynaecology and Biochemistry, Columbia Univ. New York 1961–62; Dir Research Inst. 33, Hormones Lab., Inst. Nat. de la Santé et de la Recherche Médicale (INSERM) 1963–; Prof. of Biochemistry, Faculté de Médecine de Bicêtre, Univ. Paris-Sud 1970; Prof. at Collège de France 1993, a chair. 1994–; Consultant, Roussel Uclaf; mem. Editorial Bds several French and int. journals; mem. and Past Pres. INSERM, Fondation pour la Recherche Médicale Française; Pres. Société Française d'Endocrinologie 1975; Vice-Pres. Acad. of Sciences 2000–02, Pres. 2003–; mem. Organizing Cttee Karolinska Symposia on Reproductive Endocrinology, NCI-INSERM Cancer and Hormones Programme (Past French Scientific Chair.), fmr mem. Scientific Advisory Bd WHO Special Programme in Human Reproduction; inventor of RU486 abortion pill; mem. Endocrine Soc., USA 1966–, Royal Soc. of Medicine, London 1972–, Inst. de France (Acad. des Sciences) 1982–, New York Acad. of Sciences 1985–; Foreign Assoc. mem. NAS (USA) 1990–; mem. Expert Advisory Panel, Int. Fed. of Gynaecology and Obstetrics (FIGO) 1997–; Mem. Emer. Academia Europaea 1997–; Hon. mem. American Physiological Soc. 1993, Acad. Nationale de Médecine 2002; Chevalier Ordre nat. du Mérite 1967; Officier Ordre du Mérite du Gabon 1979; Commdr Légion d'honneur 1990; Dr hc (Ghent) 1991, (Tufts) 1991, (Karolinska Inst.) 1994, (Worcs. Foundation, Shrewsbury) 1994; Reichstein Award, Int. Soc. of Endocrinology 1972, Grand Prix Scientifique 1989 de la Ville de Paris 1974, First European Medallist of Soc. of Endocrinology (GB) 1985, Albert & Mary Lasker Clinical Research Award 1989, American Acad. of Achievement Golden Plate Award 1990, Premio Minerva, Rome 1990, Christopher Columbus Discovery Award in Biomedical Research (Genoa and NIH) 1992, Nat. Award, American Assn for Clinical Chem. 1992, Grand Prix Scientifique, Fondation pour la Recherche Médicale, Paris 1994, Ken Myer Medal (Australia) 2000, Int. Acad. of Humanism Laureat 2002, and numerous other prizes and awards. *Publications:* Génération pilule 1989, Hormones 1990, Contraception: Constraint or Freedom?; numerous specialist papers. *Address:* Institut de France, 23 quai de Conti, 75006 Paris (Home); INSERM, Unit 488, Building G. Pincus, 80 Rue du Général Leclerc, 94276 Le Kremlin-Bicêtre, France. *Telephone:* 1-49-59-18-82 (Office). *Fax:* 1-49-59-92-03 (Office). *E-mail:* baulieu@kb.inserm.fr (Office).

BAUM, Bernard René, PhD, FRSC; Canadian scientist; b. 14 Feb. 1937, Paris, France; s. of Kurt Baum and Marta Berl; m. Danielle Habib 1961; one d.; ed Hebrew Univ., Jerusalem; Research Scientist, Plant Research Inst., Dept of Agric., Ottawa, Canada 1966–74; Sr Research Scientist, Biosystematics Research Inst., Agric. Canada, Ottawa 1974–80, Prin. Research Scientist, Biosystematics Research Centre 1980–90, Prin. Research Scientist, Centre for Land and Biological Resources Research 1990–95, Eastern Cereal and Oilseed Research Centre 1996–; Section Chief, Cultivated Crops Section 1973–77, Section Head, Vascular Plants Section 1982–87, Acting Dir, Geostrategy Div., Devt Policy Directorate 1981–82; mem. Acad. of Sciences (RSC) 1981, Botanical Soc. of America, Societé Botanique de France, Int. Asscn for Plant Taxonomy and other socs.; Founder mem. Hennig Soc.; Fellow Linnean Soc., London; George Lawson Medal, Canadian Botanical Asscn 1979. *Publications:* Material of an International Oat Register 1973, Oats: Wild and Cultivated. A Monograph of the Genus Avena 1977, The Genus Tamarix 1978, Barley Register 1985, Triticale Register; 200 scientific publs. *Leisure interests:* swimming long distance, classical music. *Address:* Eastern Cereal and Oilseed Research Centre, Agriculture Canada, Central Experimental Farm, Ottawa, Ont., K1A 0C6 (Office); 15 Murray Street, Suite 408, Ottawa, Ont., K1N 9M5, Canada (Home). *Telephone:* (613) 759-1821 (Office); (613) 241-5871 (Home). *Fax:* (613) 759-1924 (Office). *E-mail:* baumbr@agr.gc.ca (Office); baumbd@attcanada.ca (Home). *Website:* res.agr.ca/ecorc (Office).

BAUM, Warren C., PhD; American international finance official; b. 2 Sept. 1922, New York; s. of William Baum and Elsie Baum; m. Jessie Scullen 1946; two d.; ed Columbia Coll. and Harvard Univ.; with Office of Strategic Services 1942–46; Economic Co-operation Admin. 1949–51; Mutual Security Agency 1952–53; Economist, RAND Corpn 1953–56; Chief, Office of Network Study, Fed. Communications Comm. 1956–59; Economist, European Dept World Bank 1959–62; Div. Chief, European Dept 1962–64; Asst Dir in charge of Transportation, Projects Dept 1964–68; Deputy Dir Projects Dept 1968; Assoc. Dir, Projects Nov. 1968–72; Vice-Pres. Projects Staff 1972–83, Vice-Pres. 1983–; Chair. Consultative Group on Int. Agricultural Research 1974–83, Chair. Emer. 1984–. *Publications:* The Marshall Plan and French Foreign Trade 1951, The French Economy and the State 1956, Investing in Development 1985. *Address:* 1818 H. Street, NW, Washington, DC 20433, USA.

BAUM, HE Cardinal William Wakefield, STD, STL; American ecclesiastic; b. 21 Nov. 1926, Dallas, Tex.; s. of Harold E White and Mary Leona (Hayes) White, step-father Jerome C. Baum; ed Kenrick Seminary, St Louis and Univ. of St Thomas Aquinas, Rome; ordained to priesthood 1951; Assoc. Pastor, St Aloysius, St Therese's and St Peter's parishes, Kan. City, Mo. 1951–56; Instructor and Prof., Avila Coll., Kan. City 1954–56; 1958–63; Admin. St Cyril's Parish, Sugar Creek, Mo. 1960–61; Hon. Chaplain of His Holiness the Pope 1961; Peritus (Expert Adviser), Second Vatican Council 1962–65; First Exec. Dir Bishops' Comm. for Ecumenical and Interreligious Affairs, Washington, DC 1964–67, Chair. 1972; mem. Jt Working Group of Reps of Catholic Church and World Council of Churches 1965–69; mem. Mixed Comm. of Reps of Catholic Church and Lutheran World Fed. 1965–66; Chancellor, Diocese of Kan. City, St Joseph 1967–70; Hon. Prelate of His Holiness the Pope 1968; Pastor, St James Parish, Kan. City 1968–70; Bishop, Diocese of Springfield-Cape Girardeau 1970; mem. Synod of Bishops 1971; Archbishop of Washington 1973–80; Chancellor of the Catholic Univ. 1973–80; cr. Cardinal 1976; Prefect, Sacred Congregation for Catholic Educ. 1980–91; Grand Penitentiary Cardinal 1990–; Permanent Observer-Consultant for Vatican Secr. for Promoting Christian Unity; Chair. USCC-NCCB Doctrine Cttee, Cttee for Pastoral Research and Practices; mem. Secr. for Non-Christians; Hon. DD (Muhlenberg Coll., Allentown, Pa 1967, Georgetown Univ., Wash., St John's Univ., Brooklyn, NY). *Publications:* The Teaching of HE Cardinal Cajetan on the Sacrifice of the Mass 1958, Considerations Toward the Theology on the Presbyterate 1961. *Leisure interests:* reading, music. *Address:* Via Rusticucci 13, 00193, Rome, Italy.

BAUMAN, Robert Patten, BA, MBA; American business executive; b. 27 March 1931, Cleveland; s. of John Nevan Bauman, Jr and Lucille Miller Patten; m. Patricia Hughes Jones 1961; one s. one d.; ed Ohio Wesleyan Univ., Harvard School of Business; joined Gen. Foods Corpn 1958, Corp. Vice-Pres. 1968, Group Vice-Pres. 1970, Exec. Vice-Pres. and Corp. Dir 1972–81; Dir Avco Corpn 1980, Chair. and CEO 1981–85; Vice-Chair. and Dir Textron Inc. 1985–86; Chair. and Chief Exec. Beecham Group 1986–89, CEO SmithKline Beecham 1989–94; Chair. British Aerospace PLC 1994–98, BTR PLC, London 1998–99; Dir (non-exec.) Bolero.net 2001–; Dir Cap Cities/ABC Inc., Union Pacific Corpn, Trustee, Ohio Wesleyan Univ. *Publication:* Plants as Pets 1982, From Promise to Performance 1997. *Leisure interests:* growing orchids, paddle tennis, jogging, tennis, photography, golf, sailing. *E-mail:* RPBauman@aol.com (Office).

BAUMAN, Zygmunt, PhD; British professor of sociology; b. 19 Nov. 1925, Poznań, Poland; s. of Moritz Bauman and Sophia Bauman (née Cohn); m. Janina Lewinson 1948; three d.; ed Univ. of Warsaw; held Chair. of Gen. Sociology, Univ. of Warsaw 1964–68, now Prof. Emer.; Prof. of Sociology, Univ. of Tel Aviv 1968–71, Univ. of Leeds 1971–91, now Prof. Emer.; Dr hc (Oslo) 1997, (Lapland) 1999, (Uppsala) 2000, (West of England) 2001, (London) 2002, (Sofia) 2002, (Charles Univ., Prague) 2002, (Copenhagen) 2002; Amalfi Prize for Sociology and Social Sciences 1989, Theodor W. Adorno Prize 1998. *Publications:* Culture as Praxis 1972, Hermeneutics and Social Science 1977, Memories of Class 1982, Legislators and Interpreters 1987, Modernity and the Holocaust 1989, Modernity and Ambivalence 1990, Intimations of Postmodernity 1991, Thinking Sociologically 1991, Mortality, Immortality and Other Life Strategies 1992, Postmodern Ethics 1993, Life in Fragments 1995, Postmodernity and Its Discontents 1996, Globalization: The Human Consequences 1998, Work, Consumerism and the New Poor 1998, In

Search of Politics 1999, Liquid Modernity 2000, Individualized Society 2000, Community: Seeking Safety in an Uncertain World 2001, Society Under Siege 2002, Liquid Love: On the Frailty of Human Bonds 2003. *Leisure interest:* photography. *Address:* 1 Lawnswood Gardens, Leeds, LS16 6HF, England. *Telephone:* (113) 267-8173. *Fax:* (113) 267-8173.

BAUMANIS, Aivars; Latvian diplomatist and journalist; b. 23 Dec. 1937, Riga; s. of Arturs Baumanis and Elza Finks; m. Anita Baumanis 1979; three s. one d.; ed Latvian Univ.; investigator, City Police Dept of Riga 1961–64; corresp. foreign news desk of Latvian Radio 1964–71; ed. Liesma (magazine) 1971–74; corresp. Padomfu Faunatne (newspaper) 1974–80; Exec. Sec. Furmala (newspaper) 1980–88, Ed.-in-Chief 1986–88; Dir Latvian br. Novosti News Agency 1988–90; Dir Latvian News Agency Leta 1990–91; Amb. and Perm. Rep. of Latvia to UN 1991–98; Amb. to Denmark 1998–. *Publications:* articles in various Latvian newspapers and magazines 1966–91. *Leisure interests:* jazz, movies, literature. *Address:* Latvian Embassy, Rosbaeksvej 17 2100 Copenhagen, Denmark. *Telephone:* 39-27-60-00 (Office). *Fax:* 39-27-61-73 (Office). *E-mail:* latemb@latemb.dk (Office).

BAUMANN, Herbert Karl Wilhelm; German composer and conductor; b. 31 July 1925, Berlin; s. of Wilhelm and Elfriede (née Bade) Baumann; m. Marianne Brose 1951; two s.; ed Berlin Classical High School, Schillergymnasium and Int. Music Inst.; conductor, Tchaikovsky Symphony Orch. 1947; composer and conductor, Deutsches Theater, Berlin 1947–53, Staatliche Berliner Bühnen: Schillertheater and Schlossparktheater 1953–70, Bayerisches Staatsschauspiel: Residenztheater, Munich 1971–79; freelance composer 1979–; numerous recordings; Mem. of Honour, BDZ 1990, Diploma of Honour GEMA 1998, Bundesverdienstkreuz 1998. *Works include:* stage music (ballets: Alice in Wonderland, Rumpelstilzchen), music for radio, cinema and television, orchestral, chamber and choral works, several suites for plucked instruments, music for strings, music for wind instruments, three concertos and works for organ. *Leisure interests:* travelling and wandering, reading, especially books on fine arts. *Address:* Franziskanerstrasse 16, Apt. 1419, 81669 Munich, Germany. *Telephone:* (89) 4807745. *Fax:* (89) 4807745. *Website:* www.komponisten.net/baumann (Home).

BAUMEL, Jacques; French politician; b. 6 March 1918, Marseille; m. Louise-Jacqueline Bachelot 1959; two d.; Deputy for Hauts-de-Seine (RPR); Mayor of Rueil-Malmaison; fmr Govt minister and senator; Vice-Pres. Comm. on Nat. Defence and the Armed Forces; Vice-Chair. Parl. Ass., Council of Europe; Pres. Defence Cttee WEU, Forum du Futur; Chair Ass. Nationale de Téléspectateurs français; mem. French del. to UN 1984–; Pres. Conseil nat. des collectivités territoriales pour l'audiovisuel (CNCTA) 1989–; Chevalier, Légion d'honneur, Compagnon de la Libération, Croix de Guerre, Médaille de la Résistance. *Publication:* Une Certaine Idée de la France 1985, Résister 1999, de Gaulle 2001. *Address:* Assemblée Nationale, 126 rue de l'Université, 75355 Paris (Office); 13 boulevard Foch, 92500 Rueil-Malmaison, France (Home). *Telephone:* 1-47-08-41-18 (Office). *Fax:* 1-47-08-64-16 (Office); 1-40-63-69-52. *E-mail:* jacquesbaumel@hotmail.com (Office).

BAUMOL, William Jack, PhD; American professor of economics; b. 26 Feb. 1922, New York; s. of Solomon Baumol and Lillian Baumol; m. Hilda Missel 1941; one s. one d.; ed Coll. of City of New York and Univ. of London; jr economist, US Dept of Agriculture 1942–43, 1946; Asst Lecturer, London School of Econs 1947–49; Asst Prof. Dept of Econs, Princeton Univ. 1949–52, Prof. of Econs 1952–92, Prof. Emer. and Sr Research Economist 1992–; Prof. of Econs New York Univ. 1971–, Dir C. V. Starr Center for Applied Econs 1983–2000; Pres. Eastern Econ. Asscn 1978–79, Asscn of Environmental and Resource Economists 1979, American Econ. Asscn 1981, Atlantic Econ. Soc. 1985; mem. NAS, Accademia Nazionale di Lincei, Rome 2001; Hon. Fellow, LSE; Hon. Prof. Univ. of Belgrano 1996; Hon. doctorates, Stockholm School of Econs, Univ. of Basel, Univ. of Lille, Princeton Univ. etc.; Frank E Seidman Award, Political Econ. 1987, Henry H. Villand Research Award 1997, Int. Award for Entrepreneurship and Small Business Research, Swedish Foundation for Small Business Research and Swedish Business Devt Agency 2003. *Publications:* more than 30 books including: Economic Dynamics 1951, Business Behavior, Value and Growth 1959, Economic Theory and Operations Analysis 1961, Performing Arts: The Economic Dilemma (with W. G. Bowen) 1966, Theory of Environmental Policy (with W. E. Oates) 1975, Economics, Environmental Policy and the Quality of Life (with W. E. Oates and S. A. Batey Blackman) 1979, Economics: Principles and Policy (with A. S. Blinder) 1979, Contestable Markets and the Theory of Industry Structure (with J. C. Panzar and R. D. Willig) 1982, Productivity Growth and US Competitiveness (ed. with K. McLennan) 1985, Superfairness: Applications and Theory 1986 (Best Book in Business, Man. and Econs, Asscn of American Publishers), Microtheory: Applications and Origins 1986, Productivity and American Leadership: The Long View (with S. A. Batey Blackman and E. N. Wolff) (Hon. Mention, American Publrs Asscn Annual Awards for Excellence in Publishing 1989) 1989, The Information Economy and the Implications of Unbalanced Growth (with L. Osberg and E. N. Wolff) 1989, The Economics of Mutual Fund Markets: Competition versus Regulation (jtly) 1990, Perfect Markets and Easy Value: Business Ethics and the Invisible Hand (jtly) 1991, Entrepreneurship, Management and the Structure of Payoffs 1993, Toward Competition in Local Telephony (with G. Sidak) 1994, Convergence of Productivity: Cross-National Studies and Historical Evidence (with R. R. Nelson and E. N. Wolff) 1994, Transmission Pricing and Stranded Costs in the Electric Power Industry (with J. G. Sidak) 1995, Assessing Educational Practices: The Contribution of Economics (with W. E. Becker) 1995, Baumol's

Cost Disease: The Arts and Other victims (ed. R. Towse) 1997, Global Trade and Conflicting National Interests 2000, Welfare Economics (with C. A. Wilson) 2001, The Free-Market Innovation Machine: Analyzing the Growth Miracle of Capitalism 2002, Downsizing in America: Reality, Causes, and Consequences (with A. S. Blinder and E. N. Wolff) 2003, Growth, Industrial Organization and Economic Generalities 2003, and 500 articles in professional journals. *Leisure interests:* woodcarving, painting. *Address:* Department of Economics, New York University, 269 Mercer Street, New York, NY 10003 (Office); 100 Bleecker Street, Apt 29A, New York, NY 10012, USA (Home). *Telephone:* (212) 998-8943 (New York Univ.). *Fax:* (212) 995-3932. *E-mail:* william.baumol@nyu.edu (Office). *Website:* www.econ.nyu.edu/ (Office).

BAUSCH, Pina; German dancer and choreographer; b. 27 July 1940, Solingen; one s.; ed Folkwang School, Essen, Juilliard School, New York; mem. Dance Company Paul Sanasardo and Donya Feuer, danced at Metropolitan Opera New York, New American Ballet 1960–62; became soloist, Folkwang-Ballett 1962, choreographer, 1968–73; Dir 1968–73; f. Tanztheater Wuppertal 1973; Head Dance Dept, Folkwang Hochschule Essen 1983–89; Artistic Dir Folkwang-Tanzstudio 1983–; numerous prizes and awards; Commdr Ordre des Arts et des Lettres (France), Cruz da Ordem Militar de Santiago de Espada (Portugal), Pour le Mérite Orden, Bundesverdienstkreuz mit Stern, Praemium Imperiale 1999, Hansischer Goethe-Preis 2001. *Choreographed works include:* Fritz, Iphigenie auf Tauris, Adagio – Fünf Lieder von Gustaf Mahler 1974, Orpheus und Eurydike, Frühlingsopfer 1975, Die Sieben Todsünden 1976, Blaubart, Komm Tanz mit Mir, Renate Wandert aus 1977, Café Müller, Kontakthof 1978, Arien, Keuschheitslegende 1979, Bandoneon 1980, Walzer, Nelken 1982, Auf dem Gebirge hat Man ein Geschrei gehört 1984, Two Cigarettes in the Dark 1985, Viktor 1986, Ahnen 1987, Die Klage der Kaiserin, Palermo, Palermo 1989, Tanzabend II 1991, Das Stück mit dem Schiff 1993, Ein Trauerspiel 1994, Danzón 1995, Nur Du 1996, Der Fensterputzer 1997, Masurca 1998, Lissabon-Projekt 1998, Agua 2002. *Address:* Tanztheater Wuppertal, Spinnstr. 4, 42283 Wuppertal, Germany. *Telephone:* (202) 5634253. *Fax:* (202) 5638171.

BAUTIER, Robert-Henri; French archivist and museum curator; b. 19 April 1922, Paris; s. of the late Edgar Bautier and Suzanne Voyer; m. Anne-Marie Regnier 1948; one d.; ed Ecole des Chartes, Sorbonne and Ecole des Hautes Etudes; archivist, Nat. Archives 1943; Head Archivist, Archives départementales de la Creuse 1944; mem. Ecole Française de Rome 1945; Keeper, Archives de France 1948; Prof. Ecole Nat. des Chartes 1961–90; Curator Musée Jacquemart-André, Chaalis Abbey 1990–; Pres. Comm. Int. de Diplomatique 1980 (then Hon. Pres.), Cttee Historic and Scientific Works, Ministry of Nat. Educ. 1989–; Société Française d'Héraldique et Sigillographie; mem. Inst. de France (Acad. des Inscriptions et Belles Lettres); Assoc. Fellow, British Acad.; Fellow, Medieval Acad. of America; Assoc. mem. Belgian Acad.; mem. Académie internationale d'Héraldique etc.; fellow of numerous French provincial acads. and learned socs; Officier, Légion d'honneur, Officier Ordre nat. du Mérite, Commdr des Palmes académiques, des Arts et des Lettres and other distinctions. *Publications:* numerous books and more than 300 articles in learned journals. *Address:* 13 rue de Sévigné, 75004 Paris; Les Rabuteloires, 45360 Chatillon-sur-Loire, France. *Telephone:* 1-48-87-23-38.

BAVADRA, Adi Kuini Teimumu Vuikaba, BA; Fijian politician; b. 23 Dec. 1949, Ba; d. of the late Senator Ratu Qoro Latianara and of Lanieta Vuni Latianara; m. 1st Dr. Timoci Bavadra, fmr Prime Minister of Fiji (died 1989); m. 2nd Clive Speed 1991; two s. two d. and eight step-c.; ed Suva Grammar School, Univ. of the South Pacific, Australian Nat. Univ.; rep. Fiji Public Service Asscn women at world conf. org. by Public Service Int. 1984; Pres. Fiji Labour Party (FLP) 1989–91; lived in Australia 1991–94; stood as All Nationals Congress (ANC) cand. in gen. elections 1994, Pres. ANC (now merged with Fijian Asscn-FA) 1994–; Deputy Prime Minister and Minister of Fijian Affairs 1999–2000; Head, official Fiji del. to World Conf. on UN End of Decade for Women, Nairobi 1985; past Pres. Fiji Public Servants Asscn (women's wing), Univ. of S. Pacific Alumni Asscn. *Leisure interests:* reading, Bible study, political debates, biographical documentaries of world leaders and literary figures. *Address:* General Post Office 633, Suva, Fiji. *Telephone:* 320533. *Fax:* 320533.

BAVIN, Rt Rev Dom Timothy John, MA; British monk; b. 17 Sept. 1935, Northwood, England; s. of Edward and Marjorie Bavin; ed St George School, Windsor, Brighton Coll., Worcester Coll., Oxford Univ., Cuddesdon Coll.; Asst Priest, St Alban's Cathedral, Pretoria 1961–64; Chaplain, St Alban's Coll., Pretoria 1964–69; Asst Priest, Uckfield, Sussex, England 1969–71; Vicar, Church of the Good Shepherd, Brighton 1971–73; Dean of Johannesburg 1973–74, Bishop 1974–84; Bishop of Portsmouth, England 1985–95; Monk, Order of St Benedict, Alton Abbey 1996–; mem. Oratory of the Good Shepherd 1987–95; Hon. Fellow Royal School of Church Music 1991. *Publications:* Deacons in the Ministry of the Church 1986, In Tune with Heaven (ed.) 1992. *Leisure interests:* music, walking, gardening. *Address:* Alton Abbey, Alton, Hants., GU34 4AP, England.

BAWDEN, Nina Mary, CBE, MA, JP, FRSL; English novelist; b. 19 Jan. 1925, London; d. of Charles Mabey and Ellalaine Ursula May Mabey; m. 1st H. W Bawden 1947; two s. (one deceased); m. 2nd Austen S. Kark 1954 (died 2002); one d. two step-d.; ed Ilford County High School, Somerville Coll., Oxford; Asst, Town and Country Planning Asscn 1946–47; JP, Surrey 1968; Pres. Soc.

of Women Writers and Journalists 1981–; Hon. Fellow, Somerville Coll., Oxford; Guardian Prize for Children's Literature 1975; Yorkshire Post Novel of the Year Award 1976. *Publications:* The Birds on the Trees 1970, Anna Apparent 1972, George Beneath a Paper Moon 1974, Afternoon of a Good Woman 1976, Familiar Passions 1979, Walking Naked 1981, The Ice House 1983, Circles of Deceit (also adapted for TV) 1987, Family Money (also adapted for TV) 1991, In My Own Time (autobiog.) 1994; for children: Carrie's War (Phoenix Award 1993) (also adapted for BBC TV 2003), The Peppermint Pig, The Runaway Summer, The Finding 1985, Princess Alice 1985, Keeping Henry 1988, The Outside Child, Humbug 1992, The Real Plato Jones 1993, Granny the Pag 1995, A Nice Change 1997, Devil by the Sea 1997, Off the Road 1998, Ruffian on the Stair 2001. *Leisure interests:* theatre, cinema, travel, croquet, friends. *Address:* 22 Noel Road, London, N1 8HA, England; 19 Kapodistriou, Nauplion 21100, Greece. *Telephone:* (20) 7226-2839 (Office). *Fax:* (20) 7359-7103.

BAWOYEU, Jean Alingue; Chadian politician; b. 18 Aug. 1937, N'Djamena; s. of Marc Alingue Bawoyeu and Tabita Poureng; m. Esther Azina 1960; three s. four d.; fmr Pres. of Nat. Ass.; Prime Minister of Chad 1991–92; Chair. Union pour la Démocratie et la République. *Address:* B.P. 1122, N'Djamena, Chad.

BAXANDALL, Michael David Kighley, MA, FBA; British historian; b. 18 Aug. 1933, Cardiff; s. of David K. Baxandall and Sarah I. M. Thomas; m. Katharina D. Simon 1963; one s. one d.; ed Manchester Grammar School, Downing Coll. Cambridge and Univs. of Pavia and Munich; Asst Keeper, Dept of Sculpture, Victoria & Albert Museum, London 1961–65; Lecturer in Renaissance Studies, Warburg Inst. Univ. of London 1965–72, Reader in History of the Classical Tradition 1973–80, Prof. of History of the Classical Tradition 1980–81; Slade Prof. of Fine Art, Univ. of Oxford 1974–75; A. D. White Prof.-at-Large, Cornell Univ. 1982–88; Prof. of Art History, Univ. of Calif. at Berkeley 1987–96, Prof. Emer. 1996–; Mitchell Prize for History of Art 1980; Prix Vasari de l'Essai Etranger 1986. *Publications:* Giotto and the Orators 1971, Painting and Experience in 15th Century Italy 1972, The Limewood Sculptors of Renaissance Germany 1980, Patterns of Intention 1985, Tiepolo and the Pictorial Intelligence (jtly.) 1994, Shadows and Enlightenment 1995. *Address:* 405 Doe Library, University of California, Berkeley, CA 94720, USA.

BAXENDELL, Sir Peter (Brian), Kt, CBE, BSc, ARSM, FREng; British petroleum engineer; b. 28 Feb. 1925, Runcorn; s. of Lesley Wilfred Edward Baxendell and Evelyn Mary Baxendell (née Gaskin); m. Rosemary Lacey 1949; two s. two d.; ed St Francis Xavier's Coll., Liverpool, Royal School of Mines, Imperial Coll., London; with Royal Dutch/Shell Group 1946–95; Anglo-Egyptian Oilfields 1947–50; Compañía Shell de Venezuela 1950–63; Tech. Dir Shell-BP Nigeria 1963–66, Man. Dir 1969–72; Shell Int. London, Eastern Region 1966–69; Chair. Shell UK 1973–79; Man. Dir Royal Dutch/Shell Group 1973–85; Vice-Chair. Cttee of Man. Dirs. 1979–82, Chair. 1982–85; Dir Shell Transport and Trading Co. 1973–95 (Chair. 1979–85); Dir Hawker Siddeley Group 1984–91, Chair. 1986–91; Dir Inchcape PLC 1986–93; Dir Sun Life Assurance Co. of Canada 1986–97; mem. Univ. Grants Cttee 1983–89; Fellow, Imperial Coll. Science and Tech., London 1983, mem. Governing Body 1983–99 (Deputy Chair. 1992–99); Hon. DSc (Heriot-Watt) 1982, (Queen's, Belfast) 1986, (London) 1986, (Loughborough) 1987; Commdr Order of Orange-Nassau. *Leisure interests:* fishing, tennis. *Address:* c/o Royal Dutch/Shell Group, Shell Centre, London, SE1 7NA, England (Office).

BAXTER, Glen; British artist; b. 4 March 1944, Leeds; s. of the late Charles Baxter and Florence Baxter; m. Carole Agis; one s. one d.; ed Cockburn Grammar School, Leeds and Leeds Coll. of Art; has exhibited his drawings in New York, San Francisco, Venice, Amsterdam, Lille, Munich, Tokyo and Paris and represented UK at the Sydney Biennale 1986, Adelaide Festival 1992, Hôtel Furkablick (Switzerland) 1993; major retrospectives at Musée de l'Abbaye Sainte-Croix, Les Sables d'Olonne, France 1987, 'Une Ame en Tourment', Centre nat. de l'art imprimé Chatou, Paris; illustrated Charlie Malarkey and the Belly Button Machine 1986; tapestry commissioned by French Govt. to commemorate 8th centenary of death of Richard the Lion-Heart. *Television:* The South Bank Show: Profile of Glen Baxter 1983. *Publications:* The Impending Gleam 1981, Atlas 1982 and Glen Baxter: His Life: The Years of Struggle 1983, Jodhpurs in the Quantocks 1986, Welcome to the Weird World of Glen Baxter 1989, The Billiard Table Murders, A Gladys Babbington Morton Mystery 1990, Glen Baxter Returns to Normal 1992, The Collected Blurtings of Baxter 1993, The Further Blurtings of Baxter 1994, The Wonder Book of Sex 1995, Glen Baxter's Gourmet Guide 1997, Blizzards of Tweed 1999, Podium 2000, The Unhinged World of Glen Baxter 2001, Trundling Grunts 2002. *Leisure interests:* marquetry, snood retrieval. *Address:* c/o Chris Beetles Gallery, 10 Ryder Street, St James's, London, SW1Y 6QB, England (Office). *Website:* www.glenbaxter.com (Home).

BAXTER, Rodney James, ScD, FAA, FRS; Australian professor of mathematical physics; b. 8 Feb. 1940, London, England; s. of Thomas J. Baxter and Florence Baxter; m. Elizabeth A. Phillips 1968; one s. one d.; ed Bancroft's School, Essex, Trinity Coll., Cambridge and Australian Nat. Univ.; Reservoir Engineer, Iraq Petroleum Co. 1964–65; Research Fellow, Australian Nat. Univ. 1965–68; Asst Prof. Mass. Inst. of Tech. 1968–70; Fellow, Australian Nat. Univ. 1971–81; Prof. Dept of Theoretical Physics, Research School of Physical Sciences, Australian Nat. Univ. 1981–, jtly with School of Mathematical Sciences 1989–; Royal Soc. Research Prof. Univ. of Cambridge 1992,

Sr Fellow 1992–; Pawsey Medal, Australian Acad. of Science 1975, Boltzmann Medal, Int. Union of Pure and Applied Physics 1980, Dannie Heineman Prize, American Inst. of Physics 1987, Massey Medal, Inst. of Physics 1994. *Publication:* Exactly Solved Models in Statistical Mechanics 1982, contrib. to professional journals. *Leisure interest:* theatre. *Address:* Centre for Mathematics And Its Applications, Building 27, Australian National University, Canberra, ACT 0200, Australia.

BAYE, Nathalie; French actress; b. 6 July 1948, Mainneville; d. of Claude Baye and Denise Coustet; one d. by Johnny Hallyday; ed Conservatoire nat. d'art dramatique de Paris; Femme en or–Trophée Whirlpool 2000. *Stage appearances include:* Galapages 1972, Liola 1973, les Trois Soeurs 1978, Adriana Monti 1986, les Fausses Confidences 1993, la Parisienne 1995. *Films include:* Two People 1972, La nuit américaine 1973, La gueule ouverte 1974, La Gifle 1974, Un jour la fête 1974, Le Voyage de noces 1975, Le plein de super 1976, Mado 1976, L'homme qui aimait les femmes 1977, Monsieur Papa 1977, la Communion solennelle 1977, la Chambre verte 1978, Mon premier amour 1978, La Mémoire courte 1978, Sauve qui peut 1979, Je vais craquer 1979, Une semaine de vacances 1980, Provinciale 1980, Beau-père, Une étrange affaire, L'Ombre rouge and Le Retour de Martin Guerre 1981, La Balance (César for Best Actress 1983) 1982, J'ai épousé une ombre 1982, Notre histoire 1983, Rive droite, rive gauche 1984, Détective 1984, Le neveu de Beethoven 1985, Lune de Miel 1985, De guerre lasse 1987, En toute innocence 1988, la Baule-les-Pins 1990, un Week-end sur deux 1990, The Man Inside 1990, L'Affaire Wallraff 1991, La Voix 1992, Mensonges 1993, La Machine 1994, Les Soldats de L'Espérance 1994, Enfants da salud 1996, Si je t'aime . . . prends garde à toi 1998, Food of Love 1998, Paparazzi 1998, Vénus beauté 1999, Une Liaison pornographique 1999, Ça ira mieux demain 2000, Selon Matthieu, Barnie et ses petites contrariétés 2001, Absolument fabuleux 2001. *Address:* c/o Artmédia, 20 avenue Rapp, 75007 Paris, France (Office).

BAYER, Oswald; German ecclesiastic and professor of theology; b. 30 Sept. 1939, Nagold; s. of Emil Bayer and Hermine Bayer; m. Eva Bayer 1966; ed Tübingen, Bonn and Rome; Vicar, Evangelische Landeskirche, Württemberg 1964; Asst Univ. of Tübingen 1965–68; Evangelical Stift, Tübingen 1968–71; Pastor, Tübingen 1972–74; Prof. of Systematic Theology, Univ. of Bochum 1974–79, Univ. of Tübingen 1979–, Dir Inst. of Christian Ethics 1979–95; Ed. Zeitschrift für Systematische Theologie und Religionsphilosophie. *Publications:* numerous books and essays on theological and philosophical topics. *Address:* Evangelisch-theologische Fakultät der Universität Tübingen, Liebermeisterstr. 18, 72076 Tübingen (Office); Am Unteren Herrlesberg 36, 72074 Tübingen, Germany (Home). *Telephone:* (7071) 2972882 (Office); (7071) 81897 (Home).

BAYERO, Alhaji Ado; Nigerian administrator; b. 1930, Kano; s. of Alhaji Abdullahi Bayer, Emir of Kano; m. Halimatu Sadiya; ed Kano Middle School; clerk, Bank of W Africa; MP, N House of Ass. 1955–57; Chief of Kano Native Authority Police 1957–62; Amb. to Senegal 1962–63; Emir of Kano 1963–; Chancellor, Univ. of Nigeria, Nsukka, E Nigeria 1966–75, Chancellor Univ. of Ibadan 1975–85. *Leisure interests:* photography, riding, reading. *Address:* c/o University of Ibadan, Ibadan, Nigeria.

BAYH, Evan, BS, JD; American politician; b. 26 Dec. 1955, Terre Haute, Ind.; s. of Birch Evans Bayh Jr and Marvella Hern; m.; ed Indiana Univ. and Univ. of Virginia; Sec. of State of Indiana 1987–89; Gov. of Indiana 1989–97; partner Baker & Daniel Assocs. Indianapolis 1997; Senator from Indiana 1999–; Democrat. *Address:* US Senate, 463 Russell Senate Office Building, Washington, DC 20510-0001; 10 West Market Street, Suite 1650, Indianapolis, IN 46204-2934, USA.

BAYI, Filbert, BSc; Tanzanian athlete and sports administrator; b. Habiye, 22 June 1953, Karatu, Arusha Region; s. of the late Sanka Bayi and of Magdalena Qwaray; m. Anna Lyimo 1977; two s. two d.; ed Univ. of Texas at El Paso, USA; joined Air Transport Battalion (TPDF), Dar es Salaam; beat Tanzanian Nat. Champion over 1,500 m, Dar es Salaam 1972; 1,500 m Gold Medal Nat. Championships, Dar es Salaam 1972, All African Games, Lagos, Nigeria (record time) 1973; first competed Europe June 1973; 1,500 m Gold Medal (world record), Commonwealth Games, Christchurch, New Zealand 1974; 1,500 m Gold Medal, All African Games, Algiers, Algeria 1978; 1,500 m Silver Medal Commonwealth Games, Edmonton, Canada 1978; 3,000 m Steeplechase Silver Medal, Olympic Games, Moscow, USSR 1980; has competed on all five continents; Athletic Nat. Coach; Army Chief Coach ATHL; Sec. TAAA Tech. Cttee; mem. TAAA Exec. Cttee, IAAF Tech. Cttee; IAAF Athletic Coaching Lecturer; Nat. Chief Instructor and Athletic Coach; IOC Nat. Course Dir; exec. mem. Nat. Olympic Cttee; United Republic of Tanzania Medal 1995. *Leisure interests:* reading, sports, watching TV, talking to children. *Address:* Filbert Bayi Nursery and Primary School—Kimara, Morogoro Road, PO Box 60240, Dar es Salaam, Tanzania. *Telephone:* (22) 420635 (Office); (22) 420634 (Home). *Fax:* (22) 420178. *E-mail:* fbayi@ud.co.tz (Office).

BAYKAM, Bedri; Turkish painter, writer and politician; b. 26 April 1957, Ankara; s. of Suphi and Mutahhar Baykam; m. Sibel Yağci; one s.; ed French Lycée, Istanbul, Univ. of Paris I (Panthéon-Sorbonne), France, California Coll. of Arts and Crafts, Oakland, Calif., USA; 71 solo exhbns. Paris, Brussels, Rome, New York, Istanbul, Munich, Stockholm, Helsinki, London 1963–99; mem. Cen. Bd CHP (Republican Party of the People) 1995–98; Painter of the Year, Nokta magazine 1987, 1989, 1990, 1996–97. *Publications include:* The Brain of Paint (Boyanin Beyni) 1990, Monkey's Right to Paint 1994, Mustafa Kemal's on Duty Now 1994, Secular Turkey Without Concession 1995,

Fleeting Moments, Enduring Delights 1996, His Eyes Always Rest on Us 1997, The Color of the Era 1997, The Years of 68 (Vols 1 and 2) 1998–99, I'm Nothing but I'm Everything 1999, The Last Condottiere of the Millennium, Che 2000. *Leisure interests:* tennis, football, music. *Address:* Palanga Cad 33/23, Ortaköy, Istanbul 80840, Turkey. *Telephone:* (212) 2584464. *Fax:* (212) 2273465. *E-mail:* bedbay@turk.net (Home). *Website:* www.bedribaykam.com (Office).

BAYLEY, John Oliver, MA, FBA; British professor of English literature; b. 27 March 1925; s. of F. J. Bayley; m. 1st (Jean) Iris Murdoch 1956 (died 1999); m. 2nd Audhild Villers 2000; ed Eton and New Coll. Oxford; served in army 1943–47; mem. St Antony's and Magdalen Colls. Oxford 1951–55; Fellow and Tutor in English, New Coll. Oxford 1955–74; Warton Prof. of English Literature and Fellow, St Catherine's Coll. Oxford 1974–92; Heinemann Literary Award. *Publications:* In Another Country (novel) 1954, The Romantic Survival: A Study in Poetic Evolution 1956, The Characters of Love 1961, Tolstoy and the Novel 1966, Pushkin: A Comparative Commentary 1971, The Uses of Division: Unity and Disharmony in Literature 1976, An Essay on Hardy 1978, Shakespeare and Tragedy 1981, The Order of Battle at Trafalgar 1987, The Short Story: Henry James to Elizabeth Bowen 1988, Housman's Poems 1992, Alice (novel) 1994, The Queer Captain (novel) 1995, George's Lair (novel) 1996, The Red Hat 1997, Iris and the Friends: A Year of Memories 1999, Widower's House 2001, Hand Luggage – An Anthology 2001. *Address:* c/o St Catherine's College, Oxford, England.

BAYLEY, Stephen Paul, MA; British design consultant, writer, exhibition organiser and museum administrator; b. 13 Oct. 1951, Cardiff; s. of Donald Bayley and Anne Bayley; m. Flo Fothergill 1981; one s. one d.; ed Quarry Bank School, Liverpool, Manchester Univ., Liverpool Univ. School of Architecture; Lecturer in History of Art, Open Univ. 1974–76, Univ. of Kent 1976–80; Dir Conran Foundation 1981–89; Dir Boilerhouse Project, Victoria and Albert Museum London 1982–86; Founding Dir then Chief Exec. Design Museum 1986–89; Prin. Eye-Q Ltd (design consultancy) 1991–; Creative Dir New Millennium Experience Co. 1997–98 (resgnd); lectured throughout the UK and abroad; Periodical Publrs Asscn Magazine, Columnist of the Year 1995; Chevalier des Arts et des Lettres (France). *Publications include:* In Good Shape 1979, The Albert Memorial 1981, Harley Earl and the Dream Machine 1983, Conran Directory of Design 1985, Sex, Drink and Fast Cars 1986, Commerce and Culture 1989, Taste 1991, General Knowledge 1996, Labour Camp 1998, Moving Objects (ed.) 1999, General Knowledge 2000, Sex: An Intimate History (ed.) 2001; contribs to newspapers and magazines; numerous exhbn catalogues. *Leisure interests:* travel-related services, solitary sports, books. *Address:* 176 Kennington Park Road, London, SE11 4BT, England (Office). *Telephone:* (20) 7820-8899. *Fax:* (20) 7820-9966 (Office). *E-mail:* sb@opinions.demon.co.uk (Office).

BAYM, Gordon Alan, AM, PhD, FAAS; American physicist and educator; b. 1 July 1935, New York; s. of Louis Baym and Lillian Baym; two s. two d.; ed Cornell Univ., Harvard Univ.; Fellow, Universitetets Institut for Teoretisk Fysik, Copenhagen 1960–62; Lecturer, Univ. of Calif., Berkeley 1962–63; Prof. of Physics, Univ. of Ill., Urbana 1963–; Visiting Prof., Univs of Tokyo and Kyoto 1968, Nordita, Copenhagen 1970, 1976, Niels Bohr Inst. 1976, Univ. of Nagoya 1979; Visiting Scientist, Academia Sinica, Beijing 1979; mem. Advisory Bd Inst. of Theoretical Physics, Santa Barbara, Calif. 1978–83; mem. Sub-Cttee on Theoretical Physics NSF 1980–81, Physics Advisory Cttee 1982–85; mem. Nuclear Science Advisory Cttee, Dept of Energy/NSF 1982–86; mem. Editorial Bd Procs. NAS 1986–92; Trustee Assoc. Univ. Inc. 1986–90; Fellow American Acad. of Arts and Sciences, American Physical Soc.; Research Fellow, Alfred P. Sloan Foundation 1965–68; NSF Postdoctoral Fellow 1960–62; Trustee, Assoc. Univs Inc. 1986–90; Assoc. Ed. Nuclear Physics; mem. American Astronomical Soc., Int. Astronomical Union, NAS; Sr US Scientist Award, Alexander von Humboldt Foundation 1983. *Publications:* Quantum Statistical Mechanics (jt author) 1962, Lectures on Quantum Mechanics 1969, Neutron Stars 1970, Neutron Stars and the Properties of Matter at High Density 1977, Landau Fermi-Liquid Theory (jt author) 1991. *Leisure interests:* photography and mountains. *Address:* Loomis Laboratory of Physics, University of Illinois, 1110 West Green Street, Urbana, IL 61801, USA. *Telephone:* (217) 333-4363. *Fax:* (217) 333-9819.

BAYNE, Sir Nicholas Peter, KCMG, MA, DPhil; British diplomatist (retd); b. 15 Feb. 1937, London; s. of the late Capt. Ronald Bayne, RN and of Elizabeth (née Ashcroft) Bayne; m. Diana Wilde 1961; three s. (one deceased) ed Eton Coll. and Christ Church, Oxford; joined HM Diplomatic Service 1961; served Manila 1963–66, Bonn 1969–72; seconded to HM Treasury 1974–75; Financial Counsellor, Paris 1975–79; Head of Econ. Relations Dept, FCO 1979–82; Royal Inst. of Int. Affairs 1982–83; Amb. to Zaire, also Accred to Congo, Rwanda, Burundi 1983–84; Amb. and Perm. Rep. to OECD 1985–88; Deputy Under-Sec. of State, FCO 1988–92; High Commr in Canada 1992–96; Fellow, Int. Trade Policy Unit, LSE 1997–. *Publications:* Hanging Together: the Seven-Power Summits (with R. Putnam) 1984, Hanging In There: the G7 and G8 Summit in Maturity and Renewal 2000, The Grey Wares of North-West Anatolia and their Relations to the Early Greek Settlements 2000, The New Economic Diplomacy (with S. Woolcock) 2003. *Leisure interests:* reading, sightseeing. *Address:* 2 Chetwynd House, Hampton Court, Surrey, KT8 9BS, England.

BAYROU, François; French politician; b. 25 May 1951, Bordères, Basses-Pyrénées; s. of Calixte Bayrou and Emma Sarthou; m. Elisabeth Perlant;

three s. three d.; ed Lycée de Nay-Bourdettes, Lycée Montaigne, Bordeaux and Univ. of Bordeaux III; Prof. Pau 1974–79; special attachment to Office of Minister of Agric. 1979; Ed.-in-Chief, Démocratie Moderne (weekly) 1980–; Nat. Sec. Centre des Démocrates Sociaux (now Force démocrate) 1980–86, Deputy Sec.-Gen. 1986–94, Pres. 1994–; Conseiller Gen. Pau 1982; Pres. Conseil Gen. des Pyrénées-Atlantiques 1992–; Conseiller Régional, Aquitaine 1982–86; Town Councillor, Pau 1988–92; Adviser to Pierre Pflimlin (Pres. of Ass. of EC) 1984–86; Deputy to Nat. Ass. 1986–93; Gen. Del. Union pour la Démocratie Française (UDF) 1989–91, Sec. Gen. 1991–94; Minister of Nat. Educ. 1993–95, also of Higher Educ., Research and Professional Training 1995–97; Pres. UDF 1998–, mem. European Parl. June 1999–; Presidential candidate 2002. *Publication:* 1990–2000, la Décennie des mal-appris 1990, Henri IV, le roi libre 1994, le Droit au sens 1996, Ils portaient l'écharpe blanche. L'Edit de Nantes 1998, Hors des sentiers battus 1999. *Address:* Nouvelle UDF, 133 bis rue de l'Université, 75007 Paris (Office); Parliament Européen, 97–113 rue Wiertz, 1047 Bruxelles, Belgium (Office); Conseil général des Pyrénées-Atlantiques, 2 rue du Maréchal Joffre, BP 1615, 64016 Pau cedex; 27 rue Duboué, 64000 Pau, France (Home).

BAYÜLKEN, Ümit Halük; Turkish diplomatist; b. 7 July 1921, Istanbul; s. of Staff Officer H. Hüsnü Bayülken and Melek Bayülken; m. Valihe Salci 1952; one s. one d.; ed Lycée of Haydarpasa, Istanbul and Univ. of Ankara (Political Sciences); Ministry of Foreign Affairs 1944–; Reserve Officer in Army 1945–47; Vice-Consul, Frankfurt (Main) 1947–49; First Sec., Bonn 1950–51; Ministry of Foreign Affairs 1951–53; First Sec. Turkish Perm. Mission to UN 1953–57, Counsellor 1957–59; Turkish Rep. to London Jt Cttee on Cyprus 1959–60; Dir-Gen., Policy Planning Group, Ankara 1960–63, Deputy Sec.-Gen. for Political Affairs 1963–64, Sec.-Gen. 1964–66; Amb. to UK 1966–69, concurrently Accred to Malta 1968–1969; Perm. Rep. of Turkey to UN 1969–71; Minister of Foreign Affairs 1971–74; Sec.-Gen. CENTO 1975–77; Sec.-Gen. of the Presidency 1977–80; Minister of Defence 1980–83; MP from Antalya 1983–87; Pres. Atlantic Treaty Asscn (Turkey) 1987–90; Pres. of Turkish Parl. Union 1992–; Hon. mem. Mexican Acad. Int. Law, etc.; Hon. GCVO (UK), Order of Isabel la Católica (Spain), Grosses Bundesverdienstkreuz (FRG), numerous other int. awards. *Publications:* lectures, articles, studies and essays on minorities, Cyprus, principles of foreign policy, int. relations and disputes, including the Cyprus Question in the UN 1975, Collective Security and Defence Organizations in Changing World Conditions 1976, Turkey and the Regional Security Interests 1991. *Leisure interests:* music, painting, reading. *Address:* Nergiz Sokak no. 15/20, Cankaya, Ankara, Turkey. *Telephone:* (212) 1270858.

BAZ, Farouk El-, PH.D; Egyptian/American scientist; b. 1 Jan. 1938, Zagazig; s. of late El-Sayed El-Baz and of Zahia Hammouda; m. Catherine Patricia O'Leary 1963; four d.; ed Ain Shams Univ., Cairo, Assiut Univ., Missouri School of Mines and Metallurgy, Univ. of Missouri, Massachusetts Inst. of Tech., Heidelberg Univ., Germany; demonstrator, Geology Dept, Assiut Univ. 1958–60; lecturer, Mineralogy-Petrography Inst., Univ. of Heidelberg 1964–65; exploration geologist, Pan-American UAR Oil Co., Cairo 1966; Supervisor, Lunar Science Planning and Operations, BellComm, Bell Telephone Labs., Washington, DC for Apollo Program Dir, NASA 1967–72; Research Dir, Center for Earth and Planetary Studies, Nat. Air and Space Museum, Smithsonian Inst., Washington, DC 1973–82; Science Adviser to Pres. Anwar Sadat of Egypt 1978–81; Vice-Pres. for Science and Tech. and for Int. Devt, Itek Optical Systems, Lexington, Mass. 1982–86; Dir Center for Remote Sensing, Boston Univ. 1986–; pioneering work in applications of space photography to understanding of arid terrain; Pres. Arab Soc. of Desert Research; Hon. DSc (New England Coll., NH) 1989; numerous honours and awards, including NASA Apollo Achievement Award, Exceptional Scientific Achievement Medal and Special Recognition Award, Award for Public Understanding of Science and Tech., AAAS 1992, Order of Merit (First Class), Arab Repub. of Egypt, Golden Door Award, Int. Inst. of Boston. *Publications:* Say It in Arabic 1968, Astronaut Observations from the Apollo-Soyuz Mission 1977, Egypt as Seen by Landsat 1979, Desert Landforms of Southwest Egypt 1982, Deserts and Arid Lands 1984, The Geology of Egypt 1984, Physics of Desertification 1986, The Gulf War and the Environment 1994, Atlas of Kuwait from Satellite Images 2000. *Leisure interests:* reading history, travel, swimming. *Address:* Center for Earth and Planetary Studies, National Air and Space Museum, Smithsonian Institution, Washington, DC 20560 (Office); 213 Silver Hill Road, Concord, MA 01742 (Home); Center for Remote Sensing, Boston University, Boston, MA 02215, USA. *Telephone:* (617) 353-5081. *Fax:* (617) 353-3200. *E-mail:* farouk@bu.edu (Office). *Website:* www.bu.edu/remotesensing/ (Office).

BAZÁN, Dominador Kaiser, MCE; Panamanian politician and civil engineer; b. 13 Dec. 1937, Colón prov.; m. María Isabel Kodat Duque; four c.; ed West Point Mil. Acad. and Stanford Univ., USA; civil engineer in two cos. in USA and Canada; Exec. Vice-Pres. Panavision del Istmo (Canal 5 TV channel); elected Deputy for Colón prov. in Nat. Ass. 1968; fmr Minister of Foreign Affairs, Dir of Social Security, Minister of Public Works; fmr Amb. to USA, to Canada; Second Vice-Pres. of Panama 1999–. *Address:* Oficina del Segundo Vice-Presidente, Palacio Presidencial, Valija 50, Panamá 1, Panama (Office).

BAZHANOV, Yevgeny Petrovich, CSc, DHist; Russian diplomatist, scientist and journalist; b. 6 Nov. 1946, Lvov, Ukraine; m.; ed Nanyan Univ. (Singapore), Moscow Inst. of Int. Relations, Inst. of the Far East (Moscow), Diplomatic Acad. (Moscow), Inst. of Oriental Studies (Moscow); mem. of staff

USSR Ministry of Foreign Affairs 1970–73; Vice-Consul USSR Gen. Consulate, San Francisco 1973–79; Counsellor USSR Embassy, Beijing 1981–85; consultant Int. Dept, Cen. CPSU Cttee; mem. Exec. Cttee Asscn for Dialogue and Co-operation in Asian-Pacific Region 1991; mem. Nat. Cttee on Security, 1996; Pro-Rector, Dir Inst. of Actual Int. Problems Diplomatic Acad., Ministry of Foreign Affairs, Russian Fed. 1991–; Hon. Prof. People's Univ., Beijing, China 1999; mem. Int. Ecological Acad., Acad. of Humanitarian Research, Acad. of Political Sciences, USA, Asscn of Russian Sinologists 1986–, Nat. Cttee on Trade and Econ. Co-operation with the Pacific-Asian Countries, Asscn of Russian Diplomats 1999–, Political Science Asscn, Asscn of Asian Studies, Russia's Council on Foreign Policy; Distinguished Scholar of the Russian Fed. 1997; numerous prizes for journalistic and scholarly articles. *Publications:* China and the World 1990, Studies in Contemporary International Development. Vols I–III 2002 and 14 other books and over 1,000 articles and book chapters on world affairs, foreign policies and Russia's internal and foreign policy. *Address:* Diplomatic Academy, Russian Ministry of Foreign Affairs, 4 Kozlousky Pereulok, 107078 Moscow, Russia (Office); 30 Kutuzovsky Av. #462, 12165 Moscow, Russia (Home). *Telephone:* (095) 208-94-61 (Office); (095) 249-15-60 (Home). *Fax:* (095) 208-94-66 (Office). *E-mail:* icipu@online.ru (Office).

BAZIN, Marc Louis, LenD; Haitian politician; b. 6 March 1932, Saint-Marc; s. of Louis Bazin and Simone St Vil; m. Marie Yolène Sam 1981; ed Lycée Petion, Port-au-Prince, Univ. of Paris, Solvay Inst. Brussels and American Univ. Washington, DC; Admin. Asst Ministry of Foreign Affairs 1950; Prof. of Civic Educ. Lycée Petion, Haiti 1951; Legal Adviser, Cabinet Rivière (real estate agency), Paris 1958; Lecturer in Commercial Law, Paris 1960; Tech. Adviser, Treasury Dept, Rabat, Morocco 1962, Deputy Gen. Counsel 1964; Technical Adviser, Ministry of Finance, Rabat 1965; Sr Loan Officer, IBRD, Washington, DC 1968; Deputy Chief IBRD Mission in West Africa, Ivory Coast 1970; Div. Chief, IBRD, Washington, DC 1972; Dir Riverblindness Program, WHO, Upper Volta 1976; Man. Dir Industrial Devt Fund, Port-au-Prince 1980; Minister of Finance and Econ. Affairs 1982; Special rep. of IBRD at UN 1982; Div. Chief for int. orgs IBRD 1986; Pres. Mouvement pour l'Instauration de la Démocratie en Haiti (MIDH) allied with ANDP 1986–; Prime Minister of Haiti 1992–93; Officer, Order of the Ouissam Alaouite (Morocco), Kt of Nat. Order of Merit (Burkina Faso). *Address:* 114 ave Jean Paul II, Port-au-Prince, Haiti. *Telephone:* 245-8377.

BEACH, David Hugh, PhD, FRS; British molecular biologist; b. 18 May 1954, London; s. of Gen. Sir Hugh Beach and Estelle Beach; ed Winchester Coll., Peterhouse, Cambridge, Univ. of Miami; Postdoctoral Fellow, Univ. of Sussex 1978–82; Postdoctoral Fellow, Cold Spring Harbor Lab., NY 1982–83, Jr then Sr Staff Investigator 1984–89, Tenured Scientist 1992– (Sr Staff Scientist 1989–97, Adjunct Investigator 1997–2000); Investigator, Howard Hughes Medical Inst. 1990–97; Adjunct Assoc. Prof. State Univ. of NY at Stony Brook 1990–97; f. Mitotix Inc. 1992; Founder and Pres. Genetica Inc. 1996–; Hugh and Catherine Stevenson Prof. of Cancer Biology, Univ. Coll. London 1997–; Eli Lilly Research Award 1994; Bristol-Myers Squibb Award 2000; Raymond Bourgine Award 2001. *Publications:* numerous papers in scientific journals. *Address:* Wolfson Institute for Biomedical Research, Cruciform Building, University College London, Gower Street, London, WC1E 6BT, England (Office). *Telephone:* (20) 7679-6762 (Office). *Fax:* (20) 7679-6793 (Office). *E-mail:* d.beach@ucl.ac.uk (Office). *Website:* www.ucl.ac.uk/wibr.

BEALES, Derek Edward Dawson, LittD, FBA; British professor of history; b. 12 June 1931, Felixstowe; s. of the late Edward Beales and Dorothy K. Dawson; m. Sara J. Ledbury 1964; one s. one d.; ed Bishop's Stortford Coll. and Sidney Sussex Coll. Cambridge; Research Fellow, Sidney Sussex Coll. Cambridge 1955–58, Fellow 1958–; Asst Lecturer in History, Univ. of Cambridge 1962–65, Lecturer 1965–80; Prof. of Modern History 1980–97, Prof. Emer. 1997–; Stenton Lecturer, Univ. of Reading 1992, Birkbeck Lecturer, Trinity Coll., Cambridge 1993; Recurring Visiting Prof., Cen. European Univ., Budapest 1995–; Ed. Historical Journal 1971–75; mem. Standing Cttee for Humanities, European Science Foundation 1994–99; Leverhulme Emer. 2000, Fellowship 2001–03; Prince Consort Prize, Univ. of Cambridge 1960. *Publications:* England and Italy 1859–60 1961, From Castlereagh to Gladstone 1969, The Risorgimento and the Unification of Italy 1971, History and Biography 1981, History, Society and the Churches (with G. Best) 1985, Joseph II, Vol. I: In the Shadow of Maria Theresa 1987, Mozart and the Habsburgs 1993, Sidney Sussex Quatercentenary Essays (with H. B. Nisbet) 1996, Prosperity and Plunder: European Catholic Monasteries in the Age of Revolution 2003, Enlightenment and Reform in the 18th Century 2003. *Leisure interests:* music, walking, bridge. *Address:* Sidney Sussex College, Cambridge, CB2 3HU, England (Office). *Telephone:* (1223) 338833 (Office). *E-mail:* derek@beales.ws.

BEALL, Donald Ray, BS, MBA; American business executive; b. 29 Nov. 1938, Beaumont, Calif.; s. of Ray C. Beall and Margaret (née Murray) Beall; m. Joan Frances Lange 1961; two s.; ed San Jose State Coll. and Univ. of Pittsburgh; various financial and management positions, Ford Motor Co., Newport Beach, Calif., Philadelphia and Palo Alto, Calif. 1961–68; Exec. Dir Corporate Financial Planning, Rockwell Int., El Segundo, Calif. 1968–69, Exec. Vice-Pres. Electronics Group 1969–71; Exec. Vice-Pres. Collins Radio Co., Dallas 1971–74; Pres. Collins Radio Group, Dallas Rockwell Int. 1974–76, Pres. Electronics Operations 1976–77, Exec. Vice-Pres. 1977–79; Pres. Rockwell Int. 1979–88, COO 1979–88, Chair., CEO 1988–98, CEO 1988–97, Chair. Exec. Cttee 1998–; mem. Pres.'s Export Council 1981–85;

mem. Bd Overseers Univ. of Calif. Irvine 1988–; numerous awards. *Leisure interests:* tennis and boating. *Address:* Rockwell International Corporation, 2201 Seal Beach Boulevard, Seal Beach, CA 90740, USA.

BEAN, Charles Richard, PhD; British economist; b. 16 Sept. 1953; ed Brentwood School, Emmanuel Coll., Cambridge, Mass. Inst. of Tech.; Econ. Asst, Short-Term Forecasting Div., HM Treasury 1975–79, Econ. Adviser, Monetary Policy Div. 1981–82; Lecturer in Econs, LSE 1982–86, Reader 1986–90, Prof. 1990–2000, Deputy Dir Centre for Econ. Performance 1990–94, Head of Econs Dept 1999–2000; Visiting Prof. Stanford Univ. 1990, Reserve Bank of Australia 1999; Exec. Dir, Chief Economist and mem. of Monetary Policy Cttee, Bank of England 2000–. *Address:* Bank of England, Threadneedle Street, London, EC2R 8AH, England (Office). *Telephone:* (20) 7601-4999 (Office). *Fax:* (20) 7601-4112 (Office). *Website:* www.bankofengland.co.uk (Office).

BEAN, Sean; British actor; b. 17 April 1958, Sheffield, Yorks.; ed Royal Acad. of Dramatic Art; professional debut as Tybalt in Romeo and Juliet, Watermill Theatre, Newbury. *Stage appearances include:* The Last Days of Mankind and Der Rosenkavalier at Citizens' Theatre, Glasgow, Lederer in Deathwatch, Young Vic Studio, Who Knew Mackenzie? and Gone, Theatre Upstairs, Royal Court, Starvling in Midsummer Night's Dream and Romeo in Romeo and Juliet, RSC, Stratford-upon-Avon 1986, Captain Spencer in The Fair Maid of the West, RSC, London, Macbeth in Macbeth, Albery Theatre, London 2002. *Films:* Caravaggio, Stormy Monday, The Field, Lorna Doone, Shopping, Black Beauty, Patriot Games, Goldeneye, When Saturday Comes, Anna Karenina, Airborne, Ronin, The Lord of the Rings: The Fellowship of the Ring, Don't Say a Word, Equilibrium, Tom and Thomas, The Big Empty, Windprints, Essex Boys. *Radio work:* A Kind of Loving, The True Story of Martin Guerre, Saturday Night and Sunday Morning. *TV appearances include:* The True Bride (TVS Films), Samson & Delilah (Flamingo Films), Winter Flight (Enigma), War Requiem (Anglo-International Films), My Kingdom for a Horse (BBC), Small Zones (BBC), Troubles (LWT), The Loser (Channel 4), Wedded (BBC), Tell That You Love Me (BBC), Prince (BBC), Clarissa (BBC), Inspector Morse (Central), Fool's Gold (LWT), Mellors in BBC dramatization of Lady Chatterley's Lover, Sharpe in Sharpe's Rifles series (Central), A Woman's Guide to Adultery (Carlton), Jacob (CBS), Bravo Two Zero (BBC), Extremely Dangerous (ITV). *Address:* c/o ICM Ltd, Oxford House, 76 Oxford Street, London, W1N 0AX, England. *Telephone:* (20) 7636-6565. *Fax:* (20) 7323-0101.

BEARN, Alexander Gordon, MD, FACP; American (b. British) pharmaceutical executive and professor of medicine; b. 29 March 1923, Cheam, England; s. of Edward Gordon Bearn; m. Margaret Slocum 1952; one s. one d.; ed Epsom Coll. and Guy's Hospital, Univ. of London; Postgraduate Medical School, London 1949–51; Asst to Prof., Rockefeller Univ., New York, USA 1951–64, Prof. 1964–66, Adjunct Prof., Visiting Physician 1966–; Prof. and Chair. Dept of Medicine, Cornell Univ. Medical Coll. 1966–77; Physician-in-Chief New York Hosp. 1966–77; Stanton Griffis Distinguished Medical Prof. 1976–80; Prof. of Medicine, Cornell Univ. Medical Coll. 1966–89, Prof. Emer. 1989–; Sr Vice-Pres., Medical and Scientific Affairs, Merck Sharp & Dohme Int. 1979–88; mem. Council Fogarty Centre, Nat. Insts. Health 1990–; Exec. Officer American Philosophical Soc. 1997–; mem. NAS, American Philosophical Soc.; Pres. American Soc. of Human Genetics 1971; Lowell Lecture, Harvard Univ. 1958; Hon. MD (Catholic Univ., Korea); Dr. hc (René Descartes, Paris); Alfred Benzon Prize (Denmark). *Publications:* Progress in Medical Genetics (Ed.) 1962–87, Cecil Loeb Textbook of Medicine (Assoc. Ed.) 1963, 1967, 1971, 1975, Archibald Garrodi and the Individuality of Man 1993, 1999; numerous articles in medical and scientific journals. *Leisure interest:* aristology. *Address:* American Philosophical Society, 104 S. Fifth Street, Philadelphia, PA 19106 (Office); 241 South 6th Street, #2111, Philadelphia, PA 19106, USA (Home). *Telephone:* (215) 440-3435 (Office). *Fax:* (215) 440-3436 (Office). *E-mail:* abearn@amphilsoc.org. *Website:* www.amphilsoc.org (Office).

BÉART, Emmanuelle; French actress; b. 14 Aug. 1965, Gassin; d. of Guy Béart (q.v.); one d. with Daniel Auteuil (q.v.); ed drama school; began acting career with appearance as a child in Demain les Momes 1978. *Films:* Un Amour Interdit, L'Enfant Trouvé 1983, L'Amour en Douce 1984, Manon des Sources 1985, Date with Angel 1987, A Gauche en Sortant de l'Ascenseur 1988, Les Enfants du Désordre 1989, Capitaine Fracasse 1990, La Belle Noiseuse 1991, J'embrasse Pas 1991, Un Coeur en Hiver 1991, Ruptures 1992, L'Enfer 1993, Mission Impossible 1995, Nelly and M. Arnaud 1995, Time Regained 1999, Les Destinées Sentimentales 2000, La Repetition 2001, 8 Femmes 2002.

BÉART, Guy; French singer, composer, engineer and author; b. 16 July 1930, Cairo, Egypt; s. of David Behart-Hasson and Amélia Taral; one s. one d. (Emmanuelle Béart, q.v.); ed Lycée Henri IV, Paris and Ecole Nat. des Ponts et des Chaussées; music transcriber, Prof. of Math., then Eng 1952–57; subsequently made début in cabaret in Paris; composed songs for Zizi Jeanmaire, Juliette Greco, Patachou, Maurice Chevalier, etc.; recitalist in various Paris theatres and music-halls; composer of more than 200 songs, also film music (including L'Eau vive, Pierrot la tendresse and La Gamberge); author and producer of TV series Bienvenue 1966–72; Chevalier, Légion d'honneur, Officier, Ordre Nat. du Mérite, Commdr des Arts et des Lettres, Grand Prix, Acad. du Disque 1957, Grand Prix du Disque, Acad. Charles Cros 1965, Grand Prix de la chanson Sacem 1987, Prix Balzac 1987, Grand

Médaille de la Chanson Française (Académie Française) 1994. *Publications:* Couleurs et colères du temps 1976, L'Espérance polle 1987, Il est temps 1995. *Leisure interest:* chess. *Address:* Editions Temporel, 2 rue du Marquis de Morès, 92380 Garches, France (Office).

BEASLEY, David Muldrow, JD; American politician; b. 26 Feb. 1957, Lamar, SC; s. of Richard L. Beasley and Jacqueline A. Blackwell; m. Mary Wood Payne; ed Clemson Univ. and Univ. of S. Carolina; practising attorney; Rep. for SC State, Dist 56 1979–92; Majority Leader, SC House of Reps. 1987; Gov. of S. Carolina 1995–98; Prin. Bingham Consulting Group 1999–; Fellow Inst. Politics Kennedy School of Govt, Harvard Univ. 1999–; Republican. *Address:* Institute of Politics, 79 JFK Street, Cambridge, MA 02138, USA.

BEATH, John Arnott, MA, M.PHIL.; British professor of econs; b. 15 June 1944, Thurso, Caithness, Scotland; s. of James Beath and Marion McKendrick Beath (née Spence); m. Monika Schröder 1980; ed Hillhead High School, Glasgow, Univs. of St Andrews, London, Pennsylvania and Cambridge; Thouron Scholar, Univ. of Pa. 1968–71, Fels Fellow 1971–72; Research Officer, Univ. of Cambridge 1972–79, Fellow, Downing Coll. 1978–79; Lecturer, then Sr Lecturer, Univ. of Bristol 1979–91; Prof. of Econs, Univ. of St Andrews 1991–, Head, School of Social Sciences 1997–. *Publications:* Economic Theory of Product Differentiation. *Leisure interests:* gardening, golf, walking. *Address:* Department of Economics, University of St Andrews, St Andrews, Fife, KY16 9AL, Scotland (Office). *Telephone:* (1334) 462420 (Office). *E-mail:* jab@st-and.ac.uk (Office).

BEATRIX, Queen of the Netherlands; **Beatrix Wilhelmina Armgard;** b. 31 Jan. 1938, Baarn; d. of Queen Juliana and Bernhard (q.v.), Prince of the Netherlands; succeeded to the throne on abdication of her mother 30 April 1980; m. Claus George Willem Otto Frederik Geert von Amsberg 10 March 1966 (died 2002); children: Prince Willem-Alexander Claus George Ferdinand, Prince of Orange, b. 27 April 1967; Prince Johan Friso Bernhard Christiaan David, b. 25 Sept. 1968; Prince Constantijn Christof Frederik Aschwin, b. 11 Oct. 1969; ed Baarn Grammar School, Leiden State Univ.; succeeded to the throne on abdication of her mother 30 April 1980; Hon. K.G. *Address:* c/o Government Information Service, Press and Publicity Department, Binnenhof 19, 2513 AA The Hague, Netherlands. *Telephone:* (70) 3564136.

BEATSON, Jack, QC, DCL, LLD, FBA; British judge; b. 3 Nov. 1948, Haifa, Israel; s. of the late John James Beatson and Miriam White; m. Charlotte H. Christie-Miller 1973; one s. one d.; ed Whittingehame Coll. Brighton and Brasenose Coll. Oxford; Lecturer in Law, Univ. of Bristol 1972–73; Fellow and Tutor in Law, Merton Coll. Oxford 1973–93, Hon. Fellow 1994–; Rouse Ball Prof. of Law, Univ. of Cambridge 1993–2003, Chair. Faculty of Law 2001–03; Fellow, St John's Coll. Cambridge 1994–2003; Dir Centre for Public Law, Cambridge 1997–2001; Deputy High Court Judge 2000–03, Justice of the High Court, Queen's Bench Div. 2003–; Visiting Prof. Osgoode Hall Law School, Toronto 1979, Univ. of Va Law School 1980, 1983; Sr Visiting Fellow, Nat. Univ. of Singapore 1987; Law Commr for England and Wales 1989–94; Recorder of Crown Court 1994–2003; mem. Competition Comm. 1995–2001; Hon. Bencher, Inner Temple. *Publications:* Administrative Law: Cases and Materials (with M. Matthews), The Use and Abuse of Restitution 1991; Jt Ed. Chitty on Contracts (28th Edn 1999), Good Faith and Fault in Contract Law 1995, Jt Ed. European Public Law 1998, Anson's Law of Contract (28th edn 2001), Human Rights: The 1998 Act and the European Convention (with S. Grosz and P. Duffy). *Leisure interests:* gardening, travelling. *Address:* Royal Courts of Justice, Strand, London, WC2A 2LL, England.

BEATTIE, Ann, MA; American author; b. 8 Sept. 1947, Washington; d. of James Beattie and Charlotte Crosby; m. Lincoln Perry; ed American Univ. and Univ. of Connecticut; Visiting Asst Prof. Univ. of Virginia, Charlottesville 1976–77, Visiting Writer 1980; Briggs Copeland Lecturer in English, Harvard Univ. 1977; Guggenheim Fellow 1977; mem. American Acad. and Inst. of Arts and Letters (Award in Literature 1980), PEN, Authors' Guild; Hon. LHD (American Univ.). *Publications:* Chilly Scenes of Winter 1976, Distortions 1976, Secrets and Surprises 1979, Falling in Place 1990, Jacklighting 1981, The Burning House 1982, Love Always 1985, Where You'll Find Me 1986, Alex Katz (art criticism) 1987, Picturing Will 1990, What Was Mine (story collection) 1991, My Life Starring Dara Falcon 1997, Park City: New and Selected Stories 1998, Perfect Recall 2000. *Address:* c/o Janklow & Nesbit, 445 Park Avenue, New York, NY 10022-2606, USA.

BEATTY, Hon. Perrin, BA; Canadian business executive and fmr politician; b. 1 June 1950, Toronto; s. of George Ernest Beatty and Martha (Perrin) Beatty; m. Julia Kenny 1974; two s.; ed Upper Canada Coll., Univ. of Western Ont.; Special Asst to Minister of Health, Ont.; mem. House of Commons 1972–93; Minister of State for Treasury Bd 1979; Minister of Nat. Revenue 1984–85; Solicitor-Gen. for Canada 1985–86, Acting Solicitor-Gen. 1989; Minister of Defence 1986–89, of Nat. Health and Welfare 1989–91, of Communications 1991–93, of External Affairs 1993; Pres. and CEO Canadian Broadcasting Corpn 1995–2000, Canadian Mfrs & Exporters 1999–; mem. Special Jt Cttee on Constitution 1978, Chair. Progressive Conservative Caucus Cttee on Supply and Services, Spokesperson on Communications; Co-Chair. of Standing Jt Cttee on Regulations and Other Statutory Instruments; Caucus spokesperson on Revenue Canada; Chair. of Caucus Cttee on Fed. Prov. Relations and of Progressive Conservative Task Force on Revenue Canada 1983. *Leisure interests:* music, travel, technology and reading.

Address: Canadian Manufacturers & Exporters, 1 Nicholas Street, Suite 1500, Ottawa, Ont., K1N 7B7, Canada (Office). *Website:* www.CME-MEC.ca (Office).

BEATTY, Warren; American actor; b. 30 March 1937, Richmond, Virginia; s. of Ira Beatty and Kathlyn Maclean; brother of Shirley Maclaine; m. Annette Bening (q.v.) 1992; one s. two d.; ed Stella Adler Theatre School; Fellow BAFTA 2002; Commdr Ordre des Arts et des Lettres, Irving Thalberg Special Acad. Award 2000. *Film appearances include:* Splendor in the Grass 1961, Roman Spring of Mrs. Stone 1961, All Fall Down 1962, Lilith, 1965, Mickey One 1965, Promise Her Anything 1966, Kaleidoscope 1966, Bonnie and Clyde 1967, The Only Game in Town 1969, McCabe and Mrs. Miller 1971, Dollars 1972, The Parallax View 1974, Shampoo (producer and co-screenwriter) 1975, The Fortune 1976, Heaven Can Wait (producer, co-Dir and co-screenwriter) 1978, Reds (producer, Dir, Acad. Award for Best Dir 1981) 1981, Ishtar 1987, Dick Tracy 1989, Bugsy 1991, Love Affair, Bulworth (also Dir) 1998, Town and Country 2001, Kill Bill 2002. *Theatre roles include:* A Loss of Roses 1960. *TV appearances include:* Studio One and Playhouse 90, A Salute to Dustin Hoffman 1999. *Address:* c/o Risa Gertner, CAA, 9830 Wilshire Boulevard, Beverly Hills, CA 90212, USA.

BEAUCE, Thierry M. de; French government official; b. 14 Feb. 1943, Lyon; s. of Bertrand Martin de Beauce and Simone de la Verpillere; two d.; ed Univ. of Paris and Ecole Nat. d'Admin; Civil Admin., Ministry of Cultural Affairs 1968–69; seconded to Office of Prime Minister 1969–73; Tech. Adviser, Pvt. Office of Pres. of Nat. Ass. 1974; seconded to Econ. Affairs Directorate, Ministry of Foreign Affairs 1974–76; Cultural Counsellor, Japan 1976–78; Second Counsellor, Morocco 1978–80; Vice-Pres. for Int. Affairs Société Elf Aquitaine 1981–86; Dir-Gen. of Cultural, Scientific and Tech. Relations, Ministry of Foreign Affairs 1986–87; State Sec. attached to Minister of Foreign Affairs 1988–91; Adviser to the Pres. for African Affairs 1991–94; Vice-Pres. of Conf. for Yugoslavia 1992; Amb. to Indonesia 1995–97; Special Adviser to Chair. and CEO for Int. Affairs Vivendi Universal 1997–, Sr Exec. Vice-Pres. for Int. Affairs Vivendi Environnement; Pres. MEDEF Int. for Middle East 1998–; Deputy Pres. Asscn of Democrats 1989–; Chevalier, Légion d'honneur. *Publications:* Les raisons dangereuses (essay) 1975, Un homme ordinaire (novel) 1978, L'Ile absolue (essay) 1979, Le désir de guerre 1980, La chute de Tanger (novel) 1984, Nouveau discours sur l'universalité de la langue française 1988, Le livre d'Esther 1989, La République de France 1991, La nonchalence de Dieu 1995, L'archipel des épices 1998. *Address:* Vivendi Environnement, 52 rue d'Anjou, 75008 Paris (Office); 45 rue de Richelieu, 75001 Paris, France (Home). *Telephone:* 1-71-75-01-42 (Office). *Fax:* 1-71-75-10-04 (Office). *E-mail:* thierry-de-beauce@ vivendi-environnement.net (Office).

BEAUDOIN, Hon. Gérald-A., OC, QC, MA, LLD; Canadian politician, lawyer and author; b. 15 April 1929, Montreal; s. of Armand Beaudoin and Aldéa St-Arnaud; m. Renée Desmarais 1954; four d.; ed Univs. of Montreal, Toronto, Ottawa; pvt. practice with Paul Gérin-Lajoie QC in Montreal 1955–56; mem. Advisory Counsel, Dept of Justice, Ottawa 1956–65; Asst Parl. Counsel, House of Commons 1965–69; Prof. of Constitutional Law, Univ. of Ottawa 1969–89, Visiting Prof. 1989–94, Prof. Emer. 1994–, Dean of Law 1969–79, Assoc. Dir, Human Rights Centre 1981–86, Dir 1986–88; Vice-Pres. Institut de Droit d'Expression Française 1973–; Pres. Int. Comm. of Jurists (Canadian section) 1990–92; Chair. Senate Standing Cttee on Legal and Constitutional Affairs 1993–96; mem. Canadian Senate 1988–; mem. Pepin-Roberts Royal Comm. (Task Force on Canadian Unity) 1977–79; Co-Chair. Senate and House of Commons Jt Cttee on Formula of Amendment (Beaudoin-Edwards) 1991, on the Renewal of Canada (Beaudoin-Dobbie) 1991–92; mem. Académie des Lettres du Québec, RSC; Titular mem. Int. Acad. of Comparative Law; Prix du Doyen 1953, Medal of ACFAS 1987, Ramon John Hnatyshyn Award for Law 1997, Walter Tarnopolsky Human Rights Award 2002. *Publications:* Essais sur la Constitution 1979, Le partage des pouvoirs, 3rd Edn 1983, La Constitution du Canada 1990; Ed. The Supreme Court of Canada 1986, Charter Cases 1987, Your Client and the Charter 1989, As the Charter Evolves 1990, The Charter: Ten Years Later 1992; Co-Ed. Canadian Charter of Rights and Freedoms 1982 1989, 1996, Perspectives canadiennes et européennes des droits de la personne 1986, 1989, Le fédéralisme au Canada 2000, Les droits et libertés au Canada 2000; over 100 articles on the Canadian Constitution. *Leisure interests:* reading, travels. *Address:* Senate Bldg, Centre Block, Room 474-F, Ottawa, Ont., K1A 0A4 (Office); Faculty of Law, Civil Law Section, 57 Louis Pasteur, University of Ottawa, Ottawa, Ont., K1N 6N5 (Office); 4 St-Thomas, Hull, Québec, J8Y 1L4, Canada (Home). *Telephone:* (613) 995-6128 (Office); (819) 771-4742 (Home). *Fax:* (613) 943-0685 (Office); (819) 778-1729 (Home). *E-mail:* beaudg@sen.parl.gc.ca (Office).

BEAUMONT, (John) Michael, OBE, CEng; British Seigneur of Sark and engineer (retd); b. 20 Dec. 1927, Egypt; s. of the late Lionel Beaumont and Enid Beaumont (née Ripley); m. Diana La Trobe-Bateman 1956; two s.; ed Loughborough Coll.; chief stress engineer Beagle Aircraft 1965–69, chief tech. engineer 1969–70; Sr engineer guided weapons, Filton 1970–74; inherited Fief of Sark 1974. *Leisure interests:* theatre, music, gardening. *Address:* La Seigneurie de Sark, Channel Islands, GY9 0SF. *Telephone:* (1481) 832017. *Fax:* (1481) 832628. *Website:* www.sark.gov.gg (Office).

BEAUMONT, Lady Mary Rose, BA; British art historian; b. 6 June 1932, Petersfield; d. of Charles Edward Wauchope and Elaine Margaret Armstrong-Jones; m. Lord Beaumont of Whitley, The Rev. Timothy Wentworth Beaumont 1955; one s. (one s. deceased) two d.; ed Prior's Field School, Godalming, Surrey, Courtauld Inst. of Fine Art, Univ. of London; art critic for Art Review 1978–96; Lecturer in Modern Art for Christies' Educ. 1978–2001; Exhbn curator for British Council in E Europe and Far East 1983–87; Exhbn Curator The Human Touch, Fischer Fine Art Gallery 1986, The Dark Side of the Moon, Rhodes Gallery 1990, Three Scottish Artists, Pamela Auchincloss Gallery, New York 1990; Picker Fellow Kingston Polytechnic 1986–87; Lecturer in Humanities Dept City & Guilds School of Art 1996–; mem. Exec. Cttee of Contemporary Art Soc. 1979–89, Advisory Cttee Govt Art Collection 1994–2001. *Publications include:* An American Passion: The Susan Kasen Summer and Robert D. Summer Collection of Contemporary British Painting (contrib. artists' profiles) 1995, Open Studio: Derek Healey 1997, Jean MacAlpine: Intervals in Light 1998, Carole Hodgson 1999, George Kyriacou 1999, Jock McFadyen: A Book About a Painter (contrib.) 2000, New European Artists Vol. I (contrib.) 2000. *Leisure interests:* reading novels, listening to opera. *Address:* 40 Elms Road, London, SW4 9EX, England. *Telephone:* (20) 7498-8664. *Fax:* (20) 7498-8664.

BEAZLEY, Hon. Kim Christian, MA, M.PHIL.; Australian politician; b. 14 Dec. 1948, Perth; s. of Kim Edward Beazley; m. 1st Mary Beazley 1974 (divorced 1989); two d.; m. 2nd Susie Annus 1990; one d.; ed Hollywood Sr High School, Perth, Univ. of Western Australia, Oxford Univ.; fmr Lecturer in Social and Political Theory, Murdoch Univ. Perth; MP for Swan 1980–96, for Brand 1996–; Minister for Aviation 1983–84, for Defence Dec. 1984–90, for Transport and Communications 1990–91, of Finance 1991, of Employment, Education and Training 1991–93, of Finance 1993–96; Deputy Prime Minister 1995–96; Special Minister of State 1983–84; Leader of the House 1988–96; Leader of Australian Labor Party 1996–2001. *Leisure interests:* reading, swimming, watching cricket. *Address:* c/o ALP, Centenary House, 19 National Circuit, Barton, ACT 2600, Australia.

BÉBÉAR, Claude; French businessman; b. 29 July 1935, Issac; s. of André Bebear and Simone (née Veyssière); m. Catherine Dessagne 1957; one s. two d.; ed Lycées of Périgueux and St Louis, Paris; joined Ancienne Mutuelle 1958, Dir Gen. 1975; Dir-Gen., Pres. AXA 1982–, AXA-UAP 1997–, Chair. 1996–; Chair. Advisory Bd 2000–; Dir-Gen. Finaxa; numerous directorships; Hon. Pres. Inst. des Actuaires Français 1989–; Founder and Chair. L'Institut Montaigne 2001–; Pres. Exec.-Cttee Groupement d'intérêt public (G.I.P.), Paris nomination for 2008 Olympics 2000–; Officier, Légion d'honneur, Officier, Ordre Nat. du Mérite. *Address:* AXA, 25 avenue Matignon, 75008 Paris, France. *Telephone:* 40-75-57-00.

BECERRA BARNEY, Manuel Francisco; Colombian politician and lawyer; b. 22 Nov. 1951; m.; two s. one d.; ed Instituto La Salle, Bogotá and Externado de Colombia, Bogotá; Prof. at Univ. Javeriana, Bogotá; Pres. of Colombian Del. to Ibero-American Parl., Madrid; Gov. of Valle Prov. 1986–88; Minister of Educ. 1988–90; mem. of Peace Verification Comm.; Pres. of Educative Cttee for Nat. Peace Dialogue. *Publications include:* The Exorbitant Clause in Administrative Contracts. *Address:* c/o Ministry of Education, Centro Administrativo Nacional, Of. 501, Avda Eldorado, Santa Fe de Bogotá, Colombia.

BECHERER, Hans Walter, MBA; American business executive; b. 19 April 1935, Detroit, Mich.; s. of Max Becherer and Mariele Specht; m. Michele Beigbeder 1959; one s. (deceased) one d.; ed Trinity Coll., Hartford, Conn. and Munich and Harvard Univs; Exec. Asst Office of Chair. Deere & Co., Moline, Ill. 1966–69; Gen. Man. John Deere Export, Mannheim, Germany 1969–73; Dir Export Marketing, Deere & Co., Moline, Ill. 1973–77, Vice-Pres. 1977–83, Sr Vice-Pres. 1983–86, Exec. Vice-Pres. 1986–87, Pres. 1987–90, COO 1987–89, CEO 1989–2000, Chair. 1990–2000; Dir Schering-Plough Corpn 1989–, Allied Signal Inc. 1991–, Chase Manhattan Corpn and Chase Manhattan Bank 1998–; mem. The Business Roundtable 1989–, Chase Manhattan Bank Int. Advisory Cttee 1990–98, The Business Council 1992–; Trustee Cttee for Econ. Devt 1990. *Address:* c/o Deere & Company, One John Deere Place, Moline, IL 61265-8098, USA (Office). *Telephone:* (309) 765-4448 (Office).

BECHERT, Heinz, DPhil; German professor of Indology; b. 26 June 1932, Munich; s. of the late Rudolf Bechert and of Herta Bechert; m. Marianne Würzburger 1963; ed Univs of Munich and Hamburg; Research Asst Univ. of Saarbrücken 1956–61; Univ. of Mainz 1961–64; Prof. of Indology Univ. of Göttingen 1965–; Visiting Prof. Yale Univ. 1969–70, 1974–75; Research Fellow Japan Soc. for the Promotion of Science 1990; mem. Akademie der Wissenschaften in Göttingen 1968, Académie Royale de Belgique 1973, Royal Swedish Acad. of Literature, History and Antiquities 1988, Acad. Europaea 1989. *Publications:* author and ed. of 30 books and 210 contribs in academic journals. *Address:* Hermann-Föge-Weg 1A, 37073 Göttingen, Germany. *Telephone:* (551) 485765.

BECHTEL, Marie Françoise; French jurist; b. 19 March 1946, Coarraze, Basses Pyrénées; d. of Gaston Cassiau and Marie Cassiau (née Sahores); one s. one d.; ed Univ. de Paris-Sorbonne; secondary school teacher 1972–75; student at Ecole Nat. d'Admin. 1978–80; Officer, Council of State 1980–84, Counsel 1984–85, Sr mem. 1996–; Adviser to Minister of Justice 1992–93, to Minister of the Interior 1999–2000; Dir Ecole Nat. Admin. 2000–02; Tech. Adviser to Minister of Nat. Educ. 1984–86; Sr Lecturer, Inst. d'Etudes Politiques 1983–87. *Publications:* contribs to Recueil Française d'administration publique on institutions, organization, justice, civil rights etc. 1983–99; Rapport général du Comité pour la révision de la Constitution 1993. *Leisure*

interest: modern art. *Address:* Conseil d'Etat, place du Palais Royal, 75001 Paris SP (Office); 29 bd Edgard Quinet, 75014 Paris, France (Home). *Telephone:* 1-40-20-80-00 (Office). *E-mail:* marie-francaise.bechtel@conseil-etat .fr (Office); mfbechtel@noos.fr (Home). *Website:* www.conseil-etat.fr (Office).

BECK, Béatrix Marie; Swiss writer; b. 30 July 1914; ed Lycée de St Germain-en-Laye and Université de Grenoble; fmr Sec. to André Gide; journalist; mem. Jury, Prix Fémina; Prix Goncourt for Léon Morin, prêtre; Prix Félix Fénéon; Prix Fondation Delmas 1979; Grand Prix Nat. des Lettres 1991. *Publications:* Barny, Une mort irrégulière, Léon Morin, prêtre, Des accommodements avec le ciel, Le premier mai, Abram Krol, Le muet, Cou coupé court toujours, Confidences de Gorgoulle 1999, La Petite Italie 2000. *Address:* Editions Bernard Grasset, 61 rue des Saints-Pères, 75006 Paris, France (Office).

BECK, Rev. Brian Edgar, MA, DD; British ecclesiastic; b. 27 Sept. 1933, London; s. of late A. G. Beck and C. A. Beck; m. Margaret Ludlow 1958; three d.; ed City of London School, Corpus Christi Coll., Cambridge and Wesley House, Cambridge; Asst Tutor Handsworth Coll. 1957–59; ordained Methodist Minister 1960; Circuit Minister, Suffolk 1959–62; St Paul's United Theological Coll., Limuru, Kenya 1962–68; Tutor Wesley House, Cambridge 1968–80, Prin. 1980–84; Sec. Methodist Conf. of GB 1984–98, Pres. 1993–94; Co.-Chair. Oxford Inst. of Methodist Theological Studies 1976–; Sec. E African Church Union Consultation Worship and Liturgy Cttee 1963–68; mem. World Methodist Council 1966–71, 1981–98; Visiting Prof. Wesley Theological Seminary, Washington, DC 1999. *Publications:* Reading the New Testament Today 1977, Christian Character in the Gospel of Luke 1989, Gospel Insights 1998; (contrib. to) Christian Belief, A Catholic-Methodist Statement 1970, Unity the Next Step? 1972, Suffering and Martyrdom in the New Testament 1981, Community-Unity-Communion 1998, Rethinking Wesley's Theology 1998, Managing the Church? 2000, Apostolicity and Unity 2002, and articles in theological journals. *Leisure interests:* walking and DIY. *Address:* 26 Hurrell Road, Cambridge, CB4 3RH, England. *Telephone:* (1223) 312260. *Fax:* (1223) 312260.

BECK, Sir (Edgar) Philip, Kt, MA; British business executive; b. 9 Aug. 1934; s. of the late Sir Edgar Charles Beck and of Mary Agnes Sorapure; m. 1st Thomasina Joanna Jeal 1957 (divorced); two s.; m. 2nd Bridget Alexandra Heathcoat Amory 1991; ed Jesus Coll., Cambridge; Chair. John Mowlem and Co. PLC 1979–95 (Dir 1963–95), Railtrack 1999–2001; fmr Dir numerous assoc. cos.; Chair. Fed. of Civil Eng. Contractors 1982–83; Dir (non-exec.) Invensys PLC 1991– (Interim Chair. 1998, Deputy Chair. 1998–99), Kitagawa Group Ltd, Delta PLC 1994–, Yorks. Electricity Group PLC 1995–97, Railtrack Group 1999–2001 (non-exec. Dir 1995–99). *Leisure interest:* sailing. *Address:* Pylle Manor, Pylle, Shepton Mallet, Somerset, BA4 6TD, England (Home). *Telephone:* (1749) 860292 (Home). *Fax:* (1749) 860035 (Home). *E-mail:* philipbeck98@aol.com (Home).

BECK, James (Henry); American art historian and writer; b. 14 May 1930, New York, NY; s. of Samuel Beck and Margaret Weisz; m. Darma Tercinod 1956; one s. one d.; ed New York and Columbia Univs; Asst Prof. Univ. of Ala 1958–59, Ariz. State Univ. 1959–61; joined Columbia Univ. 1961, Prof. of Art History 1972–, Chair. Dept of Art History 1984–90, Visiting Assoc. Prof. Princeton Univ. 1970; f. ArtWatch Int., Pres. 1992–; Herodotus Fellow Inst. for Advanced Study, Princeton Univ. 1967; Fellow Harvard Univ. Centre for Italian Renaissance Studies 1967–68, 1972, Visiting Scholar 1983; Guggenheim Fellow 1973–74; Commendatore of Repub. of Italy. *Publications include:* Mariano di Jacopo detto il Taccola, 'Liber Tertius' 1969, Jacopo della Quercia e San Petronio 1970, Michelangelo: A Lesson in Anatomy 1975, Raphael 1976, Masaccio: The Documents 1978, Leonardo's Rules of Painting: An Unconventional Approach to Modern Art 1979, Italian Renaissance Painting 1981, The Doors of the Florentine Baptistry 1985, The Sepulchral Monument for Ilaria del Caretto by Jacopo della Quercia 1988, Jacopo della Quercia 1991, The Tyranny of the Detail 1992, The Culture, the Business and the Scandal 1993, Raphael, the Camera della Segnatura 1993, The Three Worlds of Michelangelo 1999, Arte Violata 2002. *Address:* Columbia University, 826 Schermerhorn Hall, New York, NY 10027 (Office); 39 Claremont Avenue, New York, NY 10027, USA (Home). *Telephone:* (212) 854-4569 (Office); (212) 316-0912 (Home). *E-mail:* jhb3@columbia.edu (Office); jameshbeck@aol.com (Home).

BECK, John C., MD, FAAS; American professor of medicine; b. 4 Jan. 1924, Audubon, Ia; s. of Wilhelm Beck and Marie Beck; one s.; ed McGill Univ.; Physician-in-Chief, Royal Victoria Hospital 1964–74, Sr Physician, Dept of Medicine 1974–81; Prof. of Medicine, Univ. of Calif., San Francisco 1974–79; Visiting Prof. UCLA 1978–79, Dir Multicampus Div. of Geriatric Medicine, School of Medicine, UCLA 1979–93, Prof. of Medicine 1979–; Dir Calif. Geriatric Educ. Center 1987–93, Dir Emer. 1993–; numerous other professional appts.; Dr hc (Ben-Gurion Univ., Israel) 1981; Hon. DSc (McGill Univ., Canada) 1994; Ronald V. Christie Award, Canadian Asscn of Profs. of Medicine 1987, Duncan Graham Award, Royal Coll. of Physicians and Surgeons 1990, Distinguished Service Recognition Award, Asscn for Gerontology in Higher Educ. 2001, Donald P. Kent Award, The Gerontological Soc. of America 2001. *Publications:* over 300 articles in professional journals and book chapters. *Address:* 1562 Casale Road, Pacific Palisades, CA 90272, USA. *Telephone:* (310) 459-5927 (Office). *Fax:* (310) 454-1944 (Office). *E-mail:* egebjcb@ucla.edu (Office).

BECK, Kurt Georg; German politician; b. 5 Feb. 1949, Bad Bergzabern; m. Roswitha Beck 1968; one s.; apprenticeship as mechanic, specializing in electronics; mem. ÖTV (Public Employees' Union) 1969; mem. SPD 1972–; mem. Rhineland-Palatinate State Ass. 1979–, Whip of SPD Parl. Group 1985–91, Chair. 1991–94; Chair. Rhineland-Palatinate SPD 1993–; Minister-Pres. of Rhineland-Palatinate 1994–; Mayor of Steinfeld 1989–94; Chair. Broadcasting Comm. of Fed. States' Minister-Pres.'s 1994–; responsible for cultural matters under German-French co-operation agreement 1999–; Chair. Bd of Dirs. Zweites Deutsches Fernsehen (ZDF) 1999–. *Address:* Peter-Altmeier-Allee 1, 55116 Mainz, Germany (Office). *Telephone:* (6131) 164700 (Office). *Fax:* (6131) 164702 (Office). *E-mail:* poststelle@stk.rp.dbp.de.

BECKENBAUER, Franz; German professional football manager and administrator; b. 11 Sept. 1945, Munich; s. of the late Franz Beckenbauer Sr and of Antonia Beckenbauer; m. Brigitte Wittmann; three s.; ed Northern Coll. of Insurance Studies; played for Bayern Munich, Hanover and New York Cosmos football clubs; won West German Cup (with Bayern Munich) 1966, 1967, 1969, 1971, West German Championship 1972, 1974, European Cup Winners 1967, European Cup 1974–76, World Club Championship 1976; won European Nations Cup (with West German Nat. Team) 1972, World Cup (only man to have won the World Cup both as captain and manager) 1974; won North American Championship (with New York Cosmos) 1977, 1978–80; retd. 1984; Man. West German Nat. Team 1984–90; briefly coach for Marseilles; Pres. FC Bayern Munich 1994–; Vice-Pres. Deutscher Fusball-Bund 1998–; Pres. 2006 World Cup Organizing Cttee; f. Franz Beckenbauer Foundation 1982; Adviser Mitsubishi Mrawa Football Club 1992–; West German Footballer of the Year 1966, European Footballer of the Year 1972, 1976, Bayern Verdienstorden 1982, Order of FIFA (Int. Football Fed.) 1984, Bundesverdienstkreuz. *Publication:* Einer wie ich (Someone like Me). *Address:* DFB, Otto-Fleck-Schneise 6, 6000 Frankfurt Main 71, Germany. *Telephone:* (611) 710405.

BECKER, Boris; German tennis player; b. 22 Nov. 1967, Leimen, near Heidelberg; s. of the late Karl-Heinz and of Elvira Becker; m. Barbara Feltus (divorced 2001); one s.; started playing tennis at Blau-Weiss Club, Leimen; won West German Jr Championship 1983; subsequently runner-up US Jr Championship; coached by Ion Tiriac since 1984; quarter-finalist Australian Championship, winner Young Masters Tournament, Birmingham, England 1985, Grand Prix Tournament, Queen's 1985; won Men's Singles Championship, Wimbledon 1985 (youngest ever winner and finalist; beat Kevin Curren), also won 1986, 1989, finalist 1988, 1990, 1991, 1995; finalist Benson and Hedges Championship, Wembley, London 1985; Masters Champion 1988, finalist 1989; US Open Champion 1989; Semi-finalist French Open 1989; winner Davis Cup 1989, Australian Open Championships 1991, 1996, IBM/ATP Tour Championship 1992, 1995, Grand Slam Cup 1996; named World Champion 1991, 1995, 64 career titles (49 singles); mem. Bd Bayern Munich Football Club 2001–; Chair. Laurens Sport for Good Foundation 2002–; convicted of tax evasion, given a two-year suspended sentence Oct. 2002; Sportsman of the Year 1985, Hon. Citizen Leimen 1986. *Leisure interests:* football, basketball, chess, backgammon. *Address:* Nusslocher Strasse 51, 69181 Leimen, Baden, Germany.

BECKER, Gary Stanley, PhD; American professor of economics; b. 2 Dec. 1930, Pottsville, Pa; s. of Louis William and Anna Siskind Becker; m. 1st Doria Slote 1954 (deceased); m. 2nd Guity Nashat 1979; two s. two d.; ed Princeton Univ., Univ. of Chicago; Asst Prof., Univ. of Chicago 1954–57; Asst and Assoc. Prof. of Econs Columbia Univ. 1957–60, Prof. of Econs 1960, Arthur Lehman Prof. of Econs 1968–69; Ford Foundation Visiting Prof. of Econs, Univ. of Chicago 1969–70, Univ. Prof., Dept of Econs, 1970–83, Depts of Econs and Sociology 1983–, Chair. Dept of Econs 1984–85; Research Assoc., Econs Research Center, NORC 1980–; Univ. Prof., Grad. School of Business, Univ. of Chicago 2002–; mem. NAS, Int. Union for the Scientific Study of Population, American Philosophical Soc. and American Econ. Asscn (Pres. 1987), Mont Pelerin Soc. (Dir 1985–, Pres. 1990–92); Fellow, American Statistical Asscn, Econometric Soc., Nat. Acad. of Educ., American Acad. of Arts and Sciences; mem. Bd of Dirs UNext.com 1999–; affil. Lexecon Corpn 1990–2002; hon. degrees from Hebrew Univ. of Jerusalem 1985, Knox Coll., Galesburg, Ill. 1985, Univ. of Ill., Chicago 1988, State Univ. of New York 1990, Princeton Univ. 1991, Univs of Palermo and Buenos Aires 1993, Columbia Univ. 1993, Warsaw School of Econs 1995, Univ. of Econs, Prague 1995, Univ. of Miami 1995, Univ. of Rochester 1995, Hofstra Univ. 1997, Univ. d'Aix-Marseille 1999, Univ. of Athens 2002; W. S. Woytinsky Award (Univ. of Mich.) 1964, John Bates Clark Medal (American Econ. Assn) 1967, Frank E. Seidman Distinguished Award in Political Econ. 1985, Merit Award (Nat. Insts. of Health) 1986, John R. Commons Award, Nobel Prize for Economic Sciences 1992, Lord Foundation Award 1995, Irene Tauber Award 1997, Nat. Medal of Science 2000, Phoenix Prize, Univ. of Chicago 2000, American Acad. of Achievement 2001. *Publications:* The Economics of Discrimination 1957, Human Capital 1964, Human Capital and the Personal Distribution of Income: Analytical Approach 1967, Economic Theory 1971, Essays in the Economics of Crime and Punishment (ed. with William M. Landes) 1974, The Allocation of Time and Goods over the Life Cycle (with Gilbert Ghez) 1975, The Economic Approach to Human Behavior 1976, A Treatise on the Family 1991, Accounting for Tastes 1996, The Economics of Life 1996, Social Economics 2000; columnist Business Week 1985–, Family, Society and State (in German) 1996, L'Approccio Economico al Comportamento Umano 1998; numerous articles in professional journals. *Leisure interests:* swimming, tennis. *Address:* Department of Economics, University of Chicago, 1126 East 59th Street, Chicago, IL 60637 (Office); 1308 E 58th Street, Chicago, IL 60637,

USA (Home). *Telephone:* (312) 702-8168 (Office). *Fax:* (773) 702-8496 (Office); (312) 702-8490. *E-mail:* sw47@midway.uchicago.edu (Office). *Website:* www.src.uchicago.edu/users/gsb1 (Office).

BECKER, Gert O.; German company executive; b. 21 Aug. 1933, Kronberg; s. of Otto Becker and Henriette (née Syring); m. Margrit Bruns 1960; one s. one d.; ed Akademie für Welthandel, Frankfurt; Sales Dept, Degussa, Frankfurt 1956; with rep. office in Tehran, Iran 1960, with subsidiary in São Paulo, Brazil 1963, Div. Man., Frankfurt 1966, Dir 1971, Man. Dir Degussa, Frankfurt 1977–96, Chair. Supervisory Bd 1996–, fmr Pres. and CEO; Pres. Asscn of Chemical Industries 1994–95. *Leisure interests:* literature, book collecting, golf. *Address:* Friedrichstrasse 100, 61476 Kronberg, Germany.

BECKER, Jürgen; German writer and editor; b. 10 July 1932, Cologne; s. of Robert Becker and Else (née Schuchardt) Becker; m. 1st Mare Becker 1954 (divorced 1965); one s.; m. 2nd Rango Bohne 1965; one step-s. one step-d.; ed Univ. of Cologne; various jobs until 1959; freelance writer and contributor to W German Radio 1959–64; Reader at Rowohlt Verlag 1964–65; freelance writer; living in Cologne, Berlin, Hamburg and Rome; Dir Suhrkamp-Theaterverlag 1974; Head of Drama Dept, Deutschlandfunk Cologne; Writer in Residence, Warwick Univ. 1988; mem. Akademie der Künste Berlin, Deutsche Akademie für Sprache und Dichtung Darmstadt, PEN Club; Förderpreis des Landes Niedersachsen 1964, Stipendium Deutsche Akad. Villa Massimo, Rome 1965, 1966, Group 47 Prize 1967, Literaturpreis der Stadt Cologne 1968, Literaturpreis, Bavarian Acad. of Arts 1980, Kritikerpreis 1981, Bremer Literaturpreis 1986, Peter Huchel Prize 1994, Heinrich Böll Prize 1995, Rhein Literary Prize 1998, Uwe Johnson Prize 2001. *Publications:* Felder (short stories) 1964; Ränder (short stories) 1968, Bilder, Häuser (Radio Play) 1969, Umgebungen (short stories) 1970, Schnee (poems) 1971, Das Ende der Landschaftsmalerei (poems) 1974, Erzähl mir nichts vom Krieg (poems) 1977, In der verbleibenden Zeit (Poetry) 1979, Erzählen bis Ostende (short stories) 1981, Fenster und Stimmen (poems with Rango Bohne) 1982, Odenthals Küste (poems) 1986, Das Gedicht von der wiedervereinigten Landschaft (poem) 1988, Das Englische Fenster (poems) 1990, Frauen mit dem Rücken zum Betrachter (short stories with Rango Bohne) 1989, Foxtrott im Erfurter Stadion 1993, Korrespondenzen mit Landschaft (poems with pictures from Rango Bohne) 1996, Der fehlende Rest 1997, Aus der Geschichte der Trennungen (novel) 1999, Schnee in den Ardennen (novel) 2003; Ed. Happenings (documentary with Wolf Vostell) 1965. *Address:* Am Klausenberg 84, 51109 Cologne, Germany. *Telephone:* 841139.

BECKERS, Pierre-Olivier, BA, MBA; Belgian retail executive; ed IAG Louvain-La-Neuve, Harvard Business School; joined Delhaize Group 1983, positions include store man., buyer, dir of purchasing, mem. Exec. Cttee, later Exec. Vice-Pres. responsible for int. activities, Dir Delhaize Group 1995–, Pres. and CEO 1999–, CEO Delhaize America 2002–; Dir Food Marketing Inst.; Chair. CIES—The Food Business Forum 2002–; Man. of the Year, Trends/Tendances magazine 2000. *Address:* Office of the President, Delhaize, rue Osseghemstr. 53, Molenbeek-St-Jean, 1080 Brussels, Belgium (Office). *Telephone:* (2) 412-21-11 (Office). *Fax:* (2) 412-21-94 (Office). *Website:* 64.29.208.90/en/default.asp (Office).

BECKETT, Rt Hon Margaret (Mary), PC; British politician; b. 15 Jan. 1943, Ashton-under-Lyne, Lancs.; d. of Cyril Jackson and Winifred Jackson; m. Leo Beckett 1979; two step-s.; ed Notre Dame High School, Manchester and Norwich, Manchester Coll. of Science and Tech., John Dalton Polytechnic; Eng apprentice (metallurgy), Associated Electrical Industries, Manchester, subsequently Experimental Officer, Univ. of Manchester; researcher (Industrial Policy), Labour Party HQ 1970–74; Political Adviser to Minister of Overseas Devt Feb.–Oct. 1974; Labour MP for Lincoln 1974–79, for Derby South 1983–; Special Adviser at Overseas Devt Admin. Feb.–Oct. 1974; Parl. Pvt. Sec., Minister for Overseas Devt 1974–75; Asst Govt Whip 1975–76; Minister, Dept of Educ. 1976–79; Prin. Researcher, Granada TV 1979–83; Opposition Spokeswoman with responsibility for Social Security 1984–89; Shadow Chief Sec. 1989–92; Shadow Leader of House, Campaigns Co-ordinator, Deputy Leader of Opposition 1992–94, Leader of Opposition May–July 1994; Shadow Sec. of State for Health 1994–95; Shadow Pres. of Bd of Trade 1995–97; Pres. of Bd of Trade and Sec. of State for Trade and Industry 1997–98; Pres. of Council and Leader of the House of Commons 1998–2001; Sec. of State for Environment, Food and Rural Affairs 2001–; mem. Labour Party Nat. Exec. Cttee 1980–81, 1985–86, 1988–97, Transport & General Workers Union Parl. Labour Party Group; apptd to Privy Council 1993. *Leisure interests:* cooking, reading, caravanning. *Address:* c/o House of Commons, London, SW1A 0AA, England.

BECKETT, Sir Terence (Norman), KBE, DL, B.SC.(ECON.), F.R.ENG., FIMechE; British business executive; b. 13 Dec. 1923, Walsall, Staffs.; s. of Horace Norman and Clarice Lillian (née Allsop) Beckett; m. Sylvia Gladys Asprey 1950; one d.; ed Wolverhampton and S. Staffs. Tech. Coll., London School of Econs; Capt. Royal Electrical and Mechnical Eng, served in Britain, India and Malaya 1945–48; joined Ford Motor Co. as Man. Trainee 1950, Styling Man., Briggs Motor Bodies Ltd (Ford subsidiary) 1954, Admin. Man., Engineer, then Man. Product Staff 1955, Gen. Planning Man., Product Planning Staff 1961, Man. Marketing Staff 1963, Dir, Car Div., Ford Motor Co. Ltd 1964, Exec. Dir 1966, Dir of Sales 1968, Vice-Pres. European and Overseas Sales Operations, Ford of Europe 1969–73; Man. Dir, Chief Exec., Ford Motor Co. Ltd 1974–80, Chair. 1976–80; fmr Chair. Ford Motor Credit Co. Ltd; Dir (non-exec.) CEGB 1987–90, Deputy Chair. 1990; Pro-Chancellor Univ. of Essex 1989–98 (Chair.

1989–95); fmr Dir ICI, Ford Nederland NV, Ford Lusitana SARL, Portugal, Henry Ford & Son Ltd, Ireland, Ford Motor Co. A/S, Denmark, Ford Motor Co. AB, Sweden, Automotive Finance Ltd; fmr mem. of Council CBI, Dir-Gen. 1980–87, mem. Council and Exec. Cttee Soc. of Motor Mfrs and Traders; mem. NEDC 1980–87; mem. Court and Council Essex Univ. 1985–98, Top Salaries Review Body 1987–92; Chair. Governing Body of London Business School, London Business School Trust Co. Ltd 1979–86, Council of Motor Cycle Trades Benevolent Fund; Gov., Cranfield Inst. of Tech., Nat. Inst. of Econ. and Social Research, London School of Econs; Patron, Manpower Services Comm. Award Scheme for Disabled People; Hon. mem. REME Inst. 1990; Hon. Fellow (Sidney Sussex Coll., Cambridge) 1981–, (London Business School) 1987–, (LSE) 1995–; Hon. DSc (Cranfield Inst. of Tech.) 1977, (Heriot-Watt) 1981; Hon. DScEcon (London) 1982; Hon. DTech (Brunel) 1991, (Wolverhampton) 1995; Hon. DUniv (Essex) 1995; Hon. DLitt (Anglia) 1998; Hambro Businessman of the Year Award 1978; BIM Gold Medal 1980. *Leisure interests:* travel, music. *Address:* c/o Barclays Bank PLC, 74 High Street, Ingatestone, Essex, England.

BECKETT, Wendy (Sister Wendy), MA; British art historian and nun; b. 25 Feb. 1930, Johannesburg, South Africa; ed ed. Oxford Univ.; Carmelite nun. *Television:* several series for BBC and Public Broadcasting Service (US) including Sister Wendy's Grand Tour, Sister Wendy's Story of Painting. *Publications:* A Thousand Masterpieces, The Story of Painting, Meditations, My Favourite Things, Sister Wendy's American Collection 2000.

BECKHAM, David Robert Joseph; British footballer; b. 2 May 1975, Leytonstone; m. Victoria Adams (q.v.) 1999; two s.; player with Manchester United, trainee 1991, team debut 1992, League debut 1995, 325 appearances, 78 goals as at 14 Dec. 2002; 7 caps for England Under-21s, rep. England 1996–, Capt. 2000–, 58 caps, 9 goals Dec. 2002; five Premiership medals, two Football Asscn medals, European Cup medal, two Charity Shield winner medals; Bobby Charlton Skills Award 1987, Manchester United Player of the Year 1996–97, Young Player of the Year Professional Football Asscn 1996–97, Sky Football Personality of the Year 1997. *Publication:* David Beckham: My World 2001. *Address:* SFX Sports Group Europe Ltd., Priest House, 1624 High Street, Knowle, West Midlands, B93 0JU, England (Office). *Telephone:* (1564) 777799 (Office). *Fax:* (1564) 777766 (Office). *Website:* www.manutd.com (Office).

BECKHAM, Victoria; British singer; b. 17 April 1974; d. of Tony Adams and Jackie Adams; m. David Beckham (q.v.) 1999; two s.; ed Jason Theatre School, Laine Arts Theatre Coll.; mem. group The Spice Girls 1993–, signed to Virgin 1995; solo artist 2000–; Best Video (for Say You'll Be There), Best Single (for Wannabe) Brit Awards 1997; two Ivor Novello song writing awards 1997; Best Band Smash Hits Awards 1997; three American Music Awards 1998; Special Award for Int. Sales Brit Awards 1998. *Films:* Spiceworld: The Movie 1997. *Albums:* Spice 1996 (UK number 1), Spiceworld 1997 (UK number 1, platinum UK, double platinum USA, number 1 in numerous cos., Forever 2000; Singles from album Spice include: Wannabe 1996 (number 1 in 31 countries including UK and USA), Say You'll Be There 1996 (UK number 1), 2 Become 1 (UK number 1) 1996, Mama/Who Do You Think You Are 1997 (UK number 1, first band to go to number 1 in UK with first four singles); from album Spiceworld: Spice Up Your Life 1997 (UK number 1), Too Much 1997 (UK number 1), Stop 1998, Viva Forever 1998 (UK number 1), Goodbye 1998 (UK number 1); from album Forever: Holler/Let Love Lead The Way 2000 (UK number 1); solo album: Not Such An Innocent Girl 2001; solo singles: Out of Your Mind (jtly) 2000, Not Such an Innocent Girl 2001, A Mind of Its Own 2002. *Publication:* Learning to Fly (autobiog.) 2001. *Leisure interests:* shopping. *Address:* c/o Lee & Thompson, Green Garden House, 15–22 St. Christopher's Place, London, W1M 5HE, England (Office).

BECKINSALE, Kate; British actress; b. 26 July 1973; d. of the late Richard Beckinsale and of Judy Loe; m. Michael Sheen; one d.; ed Godolphin and Latymer School, London and New. Coll., Oxford. *Films:* Much Ado About Nothing 1993, Prince of Jutland 1994, Uncovered 1994, Haunted 1995, Marie-Louise ou La Permission 1995, Shooting Fish 1998, The Last Days of Disco 1998, Brokedown Palace 1999, The Golden Bowl 2000, Pearl Harbor 2001, Serendipity 2001. *Play:* The Seagull 1995. *Television:* One Against the Wind 1991, Rachel's Dream 1992, Cold Comfort Farm 1994, Emma 1996, Alice Through the Looking Glass 1999. *Address:* c/o International Creative Management, Oxford House, 76 Oxford Street, London W1N 0AX, England (Office). *Telephone:* (20) 7636-6565 (Office).

BECKWITH, Athelstan Laurence Johnson, DPhil, FAA, FRS; Australian professor of organic chemistry; b. 20 Feb. 1930, Perth, WA; s. of Laurence A. Beckwith and Doris G. Beckwith; m. Phyllis Kaye Marshall 1953; one s. two d.; ed Univ. of Western Australia and Balliol Coll., Oxford Univ.; Research Scientist, CSIRO, Melbourne 1957–58; Lecturer in Chem., Univ. of Adelaide 1958–62, Prof. of Organic Chem., 1965–81; Lecturer, Imperial Coll., Univ. of London 1962–63; Visiting Prof., Univ. of York 1968; Prof. of Organic Chem., ANU 1981–96, Prof. Emer. 1997–, Dean 1989–91; Pres. Royal Australian Chemical Inst. 1984–85; Vice-Pres. Australian Acad. of Science 1985–86; Chair. Ed. Bd Australian Journals of Science 1988–94; Syntex Pacific Coast Lecturer 1986, Rayson Huang Lecturer 1989, Kharasch Lecturer 1990, Centenary Lecturer 1991; Rennie Memorial Medal 1960, Centenary Medal 1991, Organic Chemistry Medal 1992, Carnegie Fellow 1968, H. G. Smith Memorial Medal 1980, Leighton Medal 1997. *Publications:* numerous scientific papers and reviews in chemistry journals, etc. *Leisure interests:* reading,

performing music, model-making, golf. *Address:* Research School of Chemistry, Australian National University, Canberra, ACT 0200 (Office); 3/9 Crisp Circuit, Bruce, ACT 2617, Australia (Home). *Telephone:* (2) 6253-0696. *Fax:* (2) 6253-0737.

BEDDALL, David; Australian politician; b. 27 Nov. 1948, Manchester, UK; s. of G. A. Beddall; m. Helen Beddall; one d.; two s. from previous marriage; mem. staff Commonwealth Banking Corpn 1967–78; Loans Officer, Australian Guarantee Corpn Ltd 1978–83; commercial finance consultant 1979–83; mem. House of Reps for Fadden, Queensland 1983, for Rankin 1984–; Minister for Small Business and Customs 1990–93, for Communications 1993, for Resources 1993–96; Chair. Jt Standing Cttee on Foreign Affairs and Defence 1984–87, House of Reps Standing Cttee on Industry, Science and Tech. 1987–93. *Address:* Inala Plaza, Corsair Avenue, Inala, Queensland 4077; House of Representatives, Canberra, ACT 2600, Australia.

BEDFORD, David, ARAM, FTCL; British composer; b. 4 Aug. 1937, London; s. of L. H. Bedford and L. F. K. Duff; m. 1st M. Parsonage 1958 (divorced); two d.; m. 2nd S. Pilgrim 1969 (divorced); two d.; m. 3rd Allison Powell 1994; one s. two d.; ed Lancing Coll. and RAM; teacher of Music, Whitefield School, Hendon, London 1966–69, Queen's Coll., Harley Street, London 1969–80; Assoc. Visiting Composer, Gordonstoun School 1980–81; Youth Music Dir English Sinfonia 1986–93, Composer in Asscn English Sinfonia 1993–; Patron Barnet Schools Music Asscn 1987; since 1980 freelance composer and arranger; Deputy Chair. Performing Right Soc. 1999, Chair. 2002; Licentiate of Trinity Coll. of Music. *Compositions:* Music for Albion Moonlight 1965, Star Clusters 1971, The Golden Wine 1974, Star's End 1974, The Rime of the Ancient Mariner 1978, The Death of Baldur 1979, Sun Paints Rainbows 1982, Symphony No. 1 1983, Symphony No. 2 1985, some music for film The Killing Fields 1984, Absolute Beginners 1985, The Mission 1986, Into Thy Wondrous House 1986, Ma non Sempere 1987, Gere Curam Mei Nobis (for Katherine) 1987, A Charm of Blessings 1996, String Quartet No. 2 1998, Oboe Concerto 1999, The Sultan's Turret 1999, The City and the Stars 2001, Like a Strand of Scarlet 2002. *Leisure interests:* squash, film, cricket, tennis. *Address:* 12 Oakwood Road, Bristol, BS9 4NR, England. *Telephone:* (117) 962-4202. *E-mail:* dvbmus@aol.com (Office). *Website:* www.jeffgower.com/bedford.html (Office).

BEDFORD, Steuart John Rudolf, BA, FRCO, FRAM; British conductor; b. 31 July 1939, London; s. of L. H. and Lesley (Duff) Bedford; m. 1st Norma Burrowes (q.v.) 1969 (divorced 1980); m. 2nd Celia Harding 1980; two d.; ed Lancing Coll., Sussex, Oxford Univ., Royal Acad. of Music; operatic training as repetiteur, Asst Conductor, Glyndebourne Festival 1965–67; English Opera Group (later English Music Theatre), Aldeburgh and London 1967–73; Co-Artistic Dir, English Musical Theatre 1976–80, Artistic Dir English Sinfonia 1981–90, Artistic Dir (also Exec. Artistic Dir) Aldeburgh Festival 1987–98; freelance conductor, numerous performances with ENO, Welsh Nat. Opera, Metropolitan Opera, New York (operas include Death in Venice, The Marriage of Figaro), Royal Danish Opera; also at Royal Opera House, Covent Garden (operas include Owen Wingrave, Death in Venice, Così fan tutte) Santa Fe Opera, Teatro Colón, Buenos Aires, Lyon etc.; conductor for Orchestre Philharmonique de Montpellier, Mahler Chamber Orchestra, Southern Sinfonia; recordings include Death in Venice, Phaedra, Beggar's Opera, Collins Britten series; Medal of the Worshipful Co. of Musicians. *Leisure interests:* golf, skiing. *Address:* 76 Cromwell Avenue, London, N6 5HQ (Home); c/o Harrison-Parrott Ltd, 12 Penzance Place, London, W11 4PA, England.

BEDFORD, Sybille, OBE, CLit; British author; b. 16 March 1911, Berlin; d. of Maximilian von Schoenebeck and Elizabeth Bernard; m. Walter Bedford 1935; ed pvt. schools in Italy, France and England; literary journalist 1930s–; Vice-Pres. English PEN 1979. *Publications:* A Visit to Don Otavio 1953, A Legacy 1956, The Best We Can Do 1958, The Faces of Justice 1961, A Favourite of the Gods 1968, A Compass Error 1968, Aldous Huxley: A Biography (Vol. I) 1973, (Vol. II) 1974, Jigsaw 1989, As It Was 1990. *Leisure interests:* wine, food, reading, travel, history, politics. *Address:* c/o Lutyens & Rubinstein, 231 Westbourne Park Road, London, W11 1EB, England. *Telephone:* (20) 7792-4855.

BEDI, Bishan Singh, BA; Indian cricketer; b. 25 Sept. 1946, Amritsar; s. of the late Gyan Singh Bedi and Rajinder Kaur Bedi; m. 1st Glenith Jill Bedi 1969; one s. one d.; m. 2nd Inderjit Bedi 1980; ed Punjab Univ.; employed by Steel Authority of India, New Delhi; slow left-arm bowler; played for Northern Punjab 1961–62 to 1966–67, Delhi 1968–69 to 1980–81, Northamptonshire 1972–77; played in 67 Tests for India (1967–68 to 1979), 22 as captain, taking 266 wickets (average 28.7); took 1,560 first-class wickets; toured England 1971, 1974, 1976 and 1975 (World Cup); Hon. Life mem. MCC 1981, nat. selector; Padma Shri Award 1969, Arjuna Award 1971. *Leisure interests:* reading, photography, swimming and letter-writing. *Address:* Ispat Bhawan, Lodhi Rd, New Delhi 3, India. *Telephone:* 43133.

BEDIE, Henri Konan, LenD; Côte d'Ivoire politician; b. 1934, Dadiekro; m. Henriette Koinzan Bomo 1958; two s. two d.; ed Univ. of Poitiers; Asst Dir Caisse de Sécurité de la Côte d'Ivoire 1959–60; Counsellor, French Embassy, Washington, DC March–Aug. 1960; mem. Perm. Mission to UN 1960; Chargé d'Affaires, Embassy of Côte d'Ivoire, Washington, DC Aug.–Dec. 1960; Amb. to USA 1960–66; Minister-Del. for Econ. and Financial Affairs 1966–68; Minister of Economy and Finance 1968–75; Special Adviser, IFC 1976–80; re-elected Deputy, Nat. Ass. 1980; Pres. Nat. Ass. 1980, re-elected 1985, 1986;

mem. Political Bureau, Parti Démocratique de la Côte d'Ivoire (PDCI); Pres. Office Africain et Malgache de la Propriété Industrielle; Pres. of Côte d'Ivoire 1993–2000.

BEDJAOUI, Mohammed; Algerian lawyer; b. 21 Sept. 1929, Sidi-Bel-Abbès; s. of Benali Bedjaoui and Fatima Oukili; m. Leila Francis 1962; two d.; ed Univ. of Grenoble and Institut d'Etudes Politiques, Grenoble; Lawyer, Court of Appeal, Grenoble 1951; research worker at CNRS, Paris 1955; Legal Counsellor of the Arab League in Geneva 1959–62; Legal Counsellor Provisional Republican Govt of Algeria in Exile 1958–61; Dir Office of the Pres. of Nat. Constituent Ass. 1962; mem. Del. to UN 1957, 1962, 1977, 1978–82; Sec.-Gen. Council of Ministers, Algiers 1962–63; Pres. Soc. Nat. des Chemins de Fer Algériens (SNCFA) 1964; Dean of the Faculty of Law, Algiers Univ. 1964; Minister of Justice and Keeper of the Seals 1964–70; mem., special reporter, Int. Law Comm. 1965–82; Amb. to France 1970–79; Perm. Rep. to UNESCO 1971–79, to UN 1979–82; Vice-Pres. UN Council on Namibia 1979–82; mem. UN Comm. of Inquiry (Iran) 1980; Pres. Group of 77 1981–82; Judge Int. Court of Justice 1982–2001 (Pres. 1994–97); fmr Pres. African Soc. of Int. and Comparative Law; Head Algerian Del. to UN Conf. on Law of the Sea 1976–80; mem. Int. Inst. of Law; Carnegie Endowment for Int. Peace 1956; Ordre du Mérite Alaouite, Morocco, Order of the Repub., Egypt, Commdr Légion d'honneur (France), Ordre de la Résistance (Algeria). *Publications:* International Civil Service 1956, Fonction publique internationale et influences nationales 1958, La révolution algérienne et le droit 1961, Succession d'états 1970, Terra nullius, droits historiques et autodétermination 1975, Non-alignment et droit international 1976, Pour un nouvel ordre économique international 1979, Droit international: bilan et perspectives 1992. *Address:* 39 rue des Pins, Hydra, Algiers, Algeria. *Telephone:* (2) 60-30-89.

BEDNARSKI, Krzysztof; Polish sculptor; b. 25 July 1953, Cracow; m.; two s.; ed Acad. of Fine Arts (ASP), Warsaw; worked for Laboratorium Theatre of Jerzy Grotowski, Wrocław 1976–82. *Works include:* installations such as Total Portrait of Karl Marx 1978 (realised in many versions up to 1999), sculptures such as Victoria-Victoria 1983, Moby Dick (Best Polish Sculpture 1987) 1987, Missing Lenin's Hand 1995; monument of Federico Fellini in Rimini under construction 1994 and Krzysztof Kieślowski's tomb in Warsaw 1997; works in numerous collections in Poland, Italy and elsewhere. *Publications:* Linda Nochlin, The Body in Pieces, The Fragment as a Metaphor of Modernity 1994, Dictionary of Contemporary Artists 2001, Achille Bonito-Oliva, Oggetti di turno. Dall'arte alla critica 1997. *Leisure interests:* beer drinking, social contacts, chess. *Address:* 00-161 Rome, Via Trapani, 17 B-C (Office); 00-186 Rome, Via Dei Banchi Vecchi 134, Italy. *Telephone:* (06) 44239722 (Office); (06) 6896068 (Home). *Fax:* (06) 6896068 (Home). *E-mail:* fbbmrn@tin.it; k.bednarksi@tiscali.it.

BEDNORZ, George, PhD; German physicist; b. 16 May 1950; ed Swiss Federal Inst. of Tech., Zürich; with IBM Research Lab., Rüschlikon, Zürich 1982–; shared Nobel Prize for Physics for discovery of new super-conducting materials 1987. *Address:* IBM Zürich Research Laboratory, Säumerstrasse 4, 8803 Rüschlikon, Zürich, Switzerland. *Telephone:* (1) 7248111.

BEDSER, Sir Alec Victor, Kt, CBE; British fmr cricketer and company director; b. 4 July 1918, Reading; s. of the late Arthur Bedser and Florence Beatrice Bedser; ed Monument Hill Secondary School, Woking; served RAF 1939–46; right-arm fast-medium bowler and right-hand lower-order batsman; played for Surrey 1939–60; played in 51 Tests for England 1946–55, taking then record 236 wickets (average 24.8) including 104 against Australia; took 1,924 first-class wickets; toured Australia 1946–47, 1950–51 and 1954–55; mem. England Cricket Selection Cttee of Test and County Cricket Bd 1962–83, Chair. 1968–81; Asst Man. (to the late Duke of Norfolk) MCC tour to Australia 1962–63, Man. MCC tour to Australia 1974–75, to Australia and India 1979–80; Pres. Surrey C.C.C. 1987–88, fmr Vice-Pres. and Cttee mem., Hon. Life Vice-Pres.; started office equipment firm in partnership with twin brother, Eric A. Bedser 1955; Freeman City of London 1968; Hon. Life mem. Surrey Cricket Club, Western Prov. Cricket Club, SA 2002, West Hill Golf Club, East India and Devonshire Club; Hon. Life Vice-Pres. MCC 1999. *Publications:* Our Cricket Story (with Eric A. Bedser) 1951, Bowling 1952, Following On (with Eric A. Bedser) 1954, May's Men in Australia 1959, Cricket Choice 1981, Twin Ambitions (autobiog. with Alex Bannister) 1986. *Leisure interests:* cricket, golf, gardening, charities. *Address:* c/o Surrey County Cricket Club, Kennington Oval, London, SE11 5SS (Office); The Coppice, Carlton Road, Woking, Surrey, GU21 4HQ, England (Home). *Telephone:* (1483) 773018 (Home).

BEEBY, Thomas Hall; American architect; b. 12 Oct. 1941, Oak Park, Ill.; m. 1st Marcia D. Greenlease 1960 (divorced 1973); one s. one d.; m. 2nd Kirsten Peltzer 1975; two s.; ed Lower Merion High School, Ardmore, Pa, Gresham's School, Holt (UK), Cornell and Yale Univs; Assoc. C.F. Murphy Assocs. Chicago 1965–71; partner, Hammond Beeby & Assocs. Chicago 1971–76; partner, Hammond Beeby & Babka (now Hammond Beeby Rupert Ainge), Chicago 1976–; Assoc. Prof. Dept of Architecture, Ill. Inst. of Tech., Chicago 1973–80; Dir School of Arch. Univ. of Ill. at Chicago 1980–85; Dean, Prof. School of Arch. Yale Univ. 1985–91, Adjunct Prof. 1992–; mem. Advisory Bd, Dept of Architecture, Illinois Inst. of Tech. 1993–, Trustee 1997–; work includes office bldgs., shopping centres, housing, libraries, museums, public bldgs. etc.; contributor to numerous exhbns. of architecture and design in USA and Europe including Venice Biennale 1980; Distinguished Building Award, American Inst. of Architects, Chicago Chapter (numerous times); Nat. Design Award 1984, 1987, 1989, 1991, 1993. *Publications:* articles in professional journals. *Address:* Hammond Beeby Rupert Ainge Inc., 440 N Wells Street, Chicago, IL 60610, USA. *Telephone:* (312) 527-3200 (Office). *Fax:* (312) 527-1256 (Office). *E-mail:* tbeeby@hbra-arch.com (Office).

BEENE, Geoffrey; American fashion designer; b. 30 Aug. 1927, Haynesville, La.; s. of Albert Beene and Lorene Waller; ed Tulane Univ., Univ. of S. Calif., Traphagen School of Fashion and Acad. Julien, Paris; designer for Samuel Winston 1949–50, Harmay 1950–57, Teal Traina 1958–62; Pres. and Designer, Geoffrey Beene Inc. New York 1962–; work represented in Costume Inst., Metropolitan Museum of Art; recipient of numerous awards including Council of Fashion Designers of America Award 1981, 1985, 1987, Achievement in Creative Arts, Philadelphia Coll. of Art 1986. *Address:* Geoffrey Beene Inc., 250 W 39th Street, 9th Floor, New York, NY 10018, USA.

BEERING, Steven Claus, MD; American fmr university president; b. 20 Aug. 1932, Berlin, Germany; s. of Steven and Alice Friedrichs Beering; m. Jane Pickering 1956; three s.; ed Univ. of Pittsburgh; Prof. of Medicine 1969–; Asst Dean, Indiana Univ. School of Medicine 1969–70, Assoc. Dean 1970–74, Dean 1974–83, Dir Indiana Univ. Medical Center 1974–83; Pres. Purdue Univ. and Purdue Univ. Research Foundation 1983–2000, Pres. Emer. and Chair. 2000–; numerous awards and prizes. *Publications:* numerous articles in professional journals. *Leisure interests:* music, photography, reading, travel. *Address:* Purdue University, Perdue Memorial Union, Room 218, West Lafayette, IN 47906-3584 (Office); 3746 Westlake Court, West Lafayette, IN 47906-8612, USA (Home). *Telephone:* (765) 496-7555 (Office); (765) 464-1122 (Home). *Fax:* (765) 496-7561 (Office). *E-mail:* scb@purdue.edu (Office).

BEERS, Charlotte Lenore; American business executive; b. 26 July 1935, Beaumont, Tex.; d. of Glen Rice and Frances Bolt; m. Donald C. Beers 1971; one d.; ed Baylor Univ. Waco, Tex.; Group Product Man. Uncle Ben's Inc. 1959–69; Sr Vice-Pres., Dir Client Services, J. Walter Thompson 1969–79; COO Tatham-Laird & Kudner, Chicago, Man. Partner, Chair. and CEO 1979–; Vice-Chair. RSCG Group Roux Seguela, Cayzac & Goudard, France; Chair. and CEO Ogilvy & Mather Worldwide, New York, Ogilvy Group Inc., New York, Chair. Emer. 1997–99; Chair. J. Walter Thompson, New York 1999–2000; Under Sec. of State for Public Diplomacy and Public Affairs 2001–. *Address:* c/o Department of State, 2201 C Street, NW, Washington, DC 20520, USA (Office).

BEEVERS, Harry, PhD; American biologist; b. 10 Jan. 1924, Shildon, England; s. of Norman Beevers and Olive Beevers; m. Jean Sykes 1949; one s.; ed Univ. of Durham; post-doctoral research, Univ. of Oxford 1946–50; Asst Prof. of Biology, Purdue Univ. 1950–53, Assoc. Prof. 1953–58, Prof. 1958–69; Prof. of Biology, Univ. of Calif., Santa Cruz 1969–90, Prof. Emer. 1990–; Pres. American Soc. of Plant Physiologists 1961; Sr U.S. Scientist, Alexander von Humboldt Foundation 1986; Fellow Crown Coll., Univ. of Calif. Santa Cruz 1969; mem. NAS; Fellow American Acad. of Arts and Sciences 1973; mem. Deutsche Botanische Gesellschaft 1982, Academia Nazionale dei Lincei 1991; Foreign mem. Academia Europaea; Hon. DSc (Purdue Univ.) 1971, (Univ. of Newcastle-upon-Tyne) 1974, (Nagoya Univ.) 1986; Sigma Xi Research Award, Purdue Univ. 1958, McCoy Research Award 1968, Stephen Hales Award, American Soc. of Plant Physiologists 1970, Barnes Award 1998. *Publications:* Respiratory Metabolism in Plants 1961; 200 articles on plant metabolism in scientific journals. *Leisure interest:* gardening. *Address:* Biology Department, University of California, Santa Cruz, CA 95064 (Office); 57 Del Mesa Carmel, Carmel, CA 93923, USA (Home). *E-mail:* hbeevers@webtv.net (Home).

BEFFA, Jean-Louis Guy Henri; French business executive; b. 11 Aug. 1941, Nice; s. of Edmond Beffa and Marguerite Feursinger; m. Marie-Madeleine Brunel-Grasset 1967; two s. one d.; ed Lycée Masséna, Nice, Ecole Nat. Supérieure des Mines and Inst. d'Etudes Politiques, Paris; Mining Engineer Clermont-Ferrand 1967; motor fuel man. 1967–74; head of refinery service 1970–73; Asst to Dir 1973–74; Chief Mining Eng 1974; Dir of Planning, Cie de Saint-Gobain-Pont-à-Mousson 1975–77; Dir-Gen. Société Pont-à-Mousson 1978, Pres. Dir-Gen. 1979–82; Deputy Dir (Pipelines) Saint-Gobain-Pont-à-Mousson 1978, Dir 1979–82; Dir-Gen. Cie de Saint-Gobain 1982–86, Pres., Dir-Gen. 1986–, Chair. Saint-Gobain Centre for Econ. Research 2000–; Pres. Inst. de L'Histoire de L'Industrie (Idni) 1992–98; Pres. Supervisory Bd Poliet 1996–; Vice-Pres. Companie Générale des Eaux 1998–; Vice-Pres. Admin. Bd BNP Paribas 2000–; mem. int. consultative Cttee Chase Manhattan Bank (fmrly Chemical Bank) 1986–, American Telephone & Telegraph 1987; mem. Admin. Council Ecole Polytechnique 1993–; Admin. Banque Nat. de Paris, Cie Gen. des Eaux, Cie de Suez et de Petrofina; Officier Légion d'honneur, Officier Ordre Nat. du Mérite, Officier des Arts es des Lettres, Commdr du Mérite (Fed. Repub. of Germany). *Leisure interests:* swimming, golf. *Address:* Les Miroirs, 92096 Paris la Défense cedex, France (Office).

BEG, Gen. Mirza Aslam, BA, MSc; Pakistani army officer; b. 2 Aug. 1931, Azamgarh, Uttar Pradesh, India; s. of Mirza Murtuza Beg; m.; one s. two d.; ed Shibli Coll., Azamgarh, Aligarh Univ., India, Command and Staff Coll., Quetta and Nat. Defence Coll., Quaid-Azam Univ., Rawalpindi; commissioned 1952; served in Baluch (Infantry) Regt; joined Special Service Group (Commandos) 1961; Brig. Maj. of an Infantry Brigade during India-Pakistan war 1965; Lt-Col 1969; in command, Infantry Bn, India-Pakistan war 1971; Brig. in command of Infantry Brigade 1974; Maj.-Gen. in command Infantry Div. 1978; Chief of Gen. Staff 1980–85; Lt-Gen. 1984; Corps Commdr 1985; Gen. and Vice-Chief of Army Staff 1987; Chief of Army Staff 1987–91; Founder, Pres. and Chair. Gen. (retd) Awami Qiyadad Party; Sitara-e-

Basalat 1981, Hilal-e-Imtiaz (Mil.) 1982, Nishan-e-Imtiaz (Mil.) 1988, Tongil (First Class) Medal (S. Korea) 1988, U.S. Legion of Merit 1989, Bintang Yudha Dharm (Indonesia) 1990, Knight Grand Cross (First Class) (Thailand) 1991. *Publications:* articles in journals and nat. and int. newspapers. *Address:* 88 Race Course Scheme Street 3, Rawalpindi Cantt, Pakistan (Office); No. 1, National Park Road, Rawalpindi, Pakistan (Home). *Telephone:* (51) 5563309 (Office); (51) 5567637 (Home). *Fax:* (51) 5564244; (51) 5521219 (Home). *E-mail:* fr786pak@isb.comsats.net.pk (Office).

BEGGS, Jean Duthie, PhD, FRS, FRSE; British molecular biologist; b. 16 April 1950; d. of William Renfrew Lancaster and Jean Crawford Lancaster (née Duthie); m. Ian Beggs 1972; two s.; ed Univ. of Glasgow; Postdoctoral Fellow, Dept of Molecular Biology, Univ. of Edin. 1974–77; Plant Breeding Inst., Cambridge 1977–79; Beit Memorial Fellow for Medical Research 1976–79; Lecturer in Biochemistry, Imperial Coll., London Univ. 1979–85; Univ. Research Fellow, Dept of Molecular Biology, Univ. of Edin. 1985–89, Professorial Research Fellow 1994–99, Prof. of Molecular Biology 1999–. *Address:* Institute of Cell and Molecular Biology, University of Edinburgh, King's Buildings, Mayfield Road, Edin., EH9 3JR, Scotland (Office). *Telephone:* (131) 650-5351 (Office). *E-mail:* j.beggs@ed.ac.uk (Home).

BÉGUIN, Bernard, LèsL; Swiss journalist; b. 14 Feb. 1923, Sion, Valais; s. of Bernard Béguin and Clemence Welten; m. Antoinette Waelbroeck 1948; two s. two d.; ed Geneva High School, Geneva Univ. and Graduate Inst. of Int. Studies; Swiss Sec. World Student Relief 1945–46; corresp. at UN European Headquarters; Journal de Geneva 1946–70, Foreign Ed. 1947, Ed.-in-Chief 1959–70; Diplomatic Commentator, Swiss Broadcasting System 1954–59, Swiss TV 1959–70; Head of Programmes, Swiss French-speaking TV 1970–73; Deputy Dir Radio and TV 1973–86; Cen. Pres. Swiss Press Assen 1958–60, Hon. mem. 1974–; Visiting Prof. in Professional Ethics, Univ. of Neuchâtel 1984–88; Pres. Swiss Press Council 1985–90; Pres. Swiss Ind. Authority on Complaints concerning Broadcasting Programmes 1991–92; consultant with UNESCO (assessment of the media environment), Belarus 1994; mem. Fed. Comm. on Cartels 1964–80; mem. Bd, Swiss Telegraphic Agency 1968–71. *Publication:* Journaliste, qui t'a fait roi? Les médias entre droit et liberté, 1988. *Leisure interests:* sailing, camping. *Address:* 41 avenue de Budé, 1202 Geneva 1, Switzerland. *Telephone:* (22) 733-75-30. *Fax:* (22) 733-75-30 (Home). *E-mail:* beguinb@worldcom.ch (Home).

BEHBEHANI, Kazem, PH.D., M.R.C.PATH.; international organization official; ed Liverpool and London Univs.; fmr Deputy Dir Gen. Kuwait Inst. for Scientific Research; Vice-Rector for Research, Kuwait Univ.; Programme Man., Special Programme for Research and Training, Tropical Diseases WHO 1991–94, Dir of Tropical Diseases 1994–99, Dir E. Mediterranean Liaison Office and in charge of Resource Mobilization for the E. Mediterranean Region 1999–; mem. British Soc. of Parasitology, American Soc. for Tropical Medicine and Hygiene, Electron Microscopy Soc. of America and European Acad. of Arts, Science and the Humanities; Fellow Islamic Acad. of Sciences; Award for Research in Medicine, Kuwait Foundation for the Advancement of Sciences. *Publications:* a book on science and tech. and more than 100 scientific papers. *Address:* World Health Organization, Ave. Appia, 1211 Geneva 27, Switzerland (Office). *Telephone:* (22) 791-21-11 (Office). *Fax:* (22) 791-31-11 (Office).

BEHMEN, Alija, PhD; Bosnia and Herzegovina politician and economist; b. 25 Dec. 1940, Split, Croatia; m.; two s.; ed Univ. of Sarajevo; worked at Inst. of Econs, Sarajevo; mem. staff Railways Enterprise ŽTO Sarajevo, Deputy Pres., Pres. Exec. Bd 1970–78; Pres. Exec. Bd INTERŠPED 1978–80; Assoc. Prof. Faculty of Transportation and Communications 1980–; fmr mem. Socialist-Democratic Party (SDP), now mem. Stranka za Bosnu i Hercegovinu – SBiH); mem. Ass. of Sarajevo Canton; Deputy Chair. Parl. of Bosnia and Herzegovina 1998–2001; Prime Minister of the Fed. of Bosnia and Herzegovina March 2001–. *Address:* Office of the Prime Minister, Alipašina 1, 71000 Sarajevo, Bosnia and Herzegovina (Office). *Telephone:* (33) 663649 (Office). *Fax:* (33) 444718 (Office). *E-mail:* ebicakcic@fbihvlada.gov.ba (Office).

BEHNISCH, Günter; German architect; b. 12 June 1922, Dresden; ed Tech. Univ., Stuttgart; Architect with Rolf Gutbrod, Stuttgart 1951–52; own practice 1952–; partner Behnisch & Partner 1979–; Prof. of Design, Industrial Bldg and Dir of Bldg Form, Inst. for Bldg Standards, Tech. Univ. Darmstadt 1967–87, Prof. Emer. 1987–; Heinrich Hertz Prof. Tech. Univ. Karlsruhe 1994; mem. Berlin Acad. of Arts 1982–, Int. Acad. of Architecture, Sofia 1994–, Bavarian Acad. of Fine Arts 1999–; Founding mem. Saxon Acad. of Fine Arts, Dresden 1996–; Hon. FRIBA; Hon. mem. Royal Incorporation of Architecture, Edin.; Dr. hc (Tech. Univ. Stuttgart) 1984; Int. Olympic Cttee Hon. Prize 1992, Gold Medal, Acad. d'Architecture, Paris 1992, Hans Molfenter Prize, Stuttgart 1993, Hon. Award, Lithuanian Architecture Assen 1994, Fritz Schumacher Prize, Alfred Toepfer Foundation 1998, Wolfgang Hirsch Award, Chamber of Architects Rheinland-Pfalz 2001; Order of Merit 1997. *Publications include:* Plenary Complex of the German Bundestag 1994, Architecture for Nature 1998, Das Bristol Projekt – The Harbourside Centre for Performing Arts 1999; over 1,200 articles in brochures and magazines. *Address:* Gorch-Fock-Strasse 30, 70619 Stuttgart, Germany (Office). *Telephone:* (711) 476560 (Office). *Fax:* (711) 4765656 (Office). *E-mail:* bp@behnisch.com (Office). *Website:* www.behnisch.com (Office).

BEHNISCH, Stefan, Dipl.Ing; German architect; b. 1 June 1957, Stuttgart; m. Petra Behnisch; two s.; with Behnisch & Partner 1987–; f. Buero Innenstadt 1989, Prin. 1990–, co. became ind. 1991, later renamed Behnisch, Behnisch & Partner; teaches at various univs.; also Visiting Prof. at several American univs and External Examiner at several European univs; frequent lecturer at architectural symposia in Germany and abroad; awards include three RIBA awards, Trophée Sommet de la terre et bâtiment, France 2002, and several German architectural prizes. *Achievements:* responsible for several well-known bldgs. in Germany and elsewhere in Europe; several maj. bldgs at planning stage or under construction in Europe, USA and Canada. *Address:* Behnisch, Behnisch & Partners, 6 Christophstrasse, 70178 Stuttgart, Germany (Office); 1517 Park Row, Venice, CA 90291, USA (Office). *Telephone:* (711) 607720 (Stuttgart) (Office); (310) 399-9003 (Los Angeles) (Office); (711) 2365652 (Stuttgart) (Home). *Fax:* (711) 6077299 (Stuttgart) (Office); (711) 2365653 (Stuttgart) (Home). *E-mail:* buero@behnisch.com (Office); stb@behnisch.com (Home); BBPLA@behnisch.com (Home). *Website:* www.behnisch.com (Office).

BEHRENS, Hildegard; German opera singer; b. 1937, Oldenburg; m. Seth Schneidmann; ed Freiburg Music Conservatory; opera debut, Freiburg 1971; resident mem. Deutsche Oper am Rhein, Düsseldorf; has appeared with Frankfurt Opera, Teatro Nacional de San Carlo, Lisbon, Vienna State Opera, Metropolitan Opera, New York; soloist, Chicago Symphony Orchestra 1984; appeared in Jenufa, Salzburg Festival 2001. *Address:* c/o Herbert H. Breslin Inc., W 57th Street, New York, NY 10019, USA.

BEHRMAN, Richard Elliot, MD, JD; American professor of pediatrics; b. 13 Dec. 1931, Philadelphia, Pa; s. of Robert Behrman and Vivian Keegan; m. Ann Nelson 1954; one s. three d.; ed Amherst Coll., Harvard Univ., Univ. of Rochester and Johns Hopkins Univ.; Oregon Regional Primate Research Center and Univ. of Oregon Medical School 1965–68; Prof. of Pediatrics and Dir Neonatal Intensive Care Unit and Nurseries, Univ. of Ill. Coll. of Medicine 1968–71; Prof. and Chair. Dept of Pediatrics and Dir Babies Hospital, Columbia Univ. Coll. of Physicians and Surgeons 1971–76; Prof. and Chair. Dept of Pediatrics and Dir Dept of Pediatrics, Rainbow Babies and Children's Hosp. Case Western Reserve Univ. School of Medicine 1976–82; Dean, School of Medicine, Case Western Reserve Univ. 1980–89, Vice-Pres. Medical Affairs 1987–89; Dir Center for Future of Children, David and Lucile Packard Foundation 1989–99; Clinical Prof. Stanford Univ. and UCSF 1989; Chair. Bd of Dirs, Lucile Packard Foundation for Children 1997–99, Sr Vice-Pres. Medical Affairs 1999–2002; Exec. Chair. Fed. of Pediatric Orgs 2002–; mem. Bd of Dirs, UCSF Stanford Health Care 1997–; mem. several bds; Fellow American Acad. of Pediatrics; mem. Inst. Medicine, NAS; Hon. DSc (Medical Coll., WI) 2000. *Publications:* The Future of Children (Ed.) 1990–, Essentials of Paediatrics (Ed.) 2002, Nelson Textbook of Paediatrics (Ed.) 2003. *Leisure interests:* running, hiking, reading. *Address:* Lucile Packard Foundation for Children's Health, Suite 350, 770 Welch Road, Palo Alto, CA 94304 (Office); 15 Crest Road, Belvedere, CA 94920, USA (Home). *Telephone:* (415) 789-0967 (Office); (415) 435-9066 (Home). *Fax:* (415) 789-0768 (Office). *E-mail:* rbehrman@fopo.org.

BEI SHIZHANG, Dr rer. nat; Chinese biologist, university professor and institute director; b. 10 Oct. 1903, Ningpo; s. of Bei Qingyang and Chen Ahua; m. Cheng Ihming 1931; two s. two d.; ed Tongji Medical and Eng School, Shanghai and Univ. of Freiburg i. Breisgau, Univ. of Munich, Univ. of Tübingen; Asst Inst. of Zoology, Univ. Tübingen 1928–29; returned home 1929; Assoc. Prof., Prof. and Chair. of Dept of Biology, Univ. of Zhejiang 1930–50, Dean of Science Faculty 1949–50; Dir Inst. of Experimental Biology, Chinese Acad. of Sciences 1950–58; Chair. Dept of Biophysics, Univ. of Science and Tech., China 1958–64; Dir Inst. of Biophysics, Chinese Acad. of Sciences 1958–83, Hon. Dir 1985–; Pres. Chinese Zoological Soc. 1978–83, Chinese Biophysical Soc. 1980–83, (Hon. Pres. 1983–86); Deputy Ed.-in-Chief Scientia Sinica 1958–83, Encyclopedia of China 1984–; Ed.-in-Chief Acta Biophysica Sinica 1985–91; mem. Div. of Biological Sciences, Chinese Acad. of Sciences; mem. 1st 1954, 2nd 1959, 3rd 1964, 4th 1975, 5th 1978 and 6th 1983 NPC. *Publications:* Cell Reformation, Series 1 (24 papers) 1988, Series 2 (18 papers) in preparation; other studies on cell reformation, chromatin, DNA and histones in yolk granules; several articles in Science Record and Scientia Sinica. *Address:* Institute of Biophysics, Chinese Academy of Sciences, Da Tun Road 15, Chao Yang District, 100101 Beijing, People's Republic of China. *Telephone:* 6202-2029; 6255-1064; 6255-4575. *Fax:* 6202-7837.

BEILIN, Yossi, PhD; Israeli politician; b. 1948; m.; two c.; ed Tel-Aviv Univ.; fmr journalist and mem. editorial Bd of Davar; Spokesman for Labour Party 1977–84; Cabinet Sec. 1984–86; Dir.-Gen. for Political Affairs of Foreign Ministry 1986–88; mem. Knesset 1988; Deputy Minister of Finance 1988–90; mem. Knesset Foreign Affairs and Defense, Immigration and Absorption and Constitution, Law and Justice Cttees 1990–92; Deputy Minister of Foreign Affairs 1992–95; Minister of Econs and Planning July–Nov. 1995; Minister without Portfolio 1995–96; mem. Knesset Foreign Affairs and Defense, Constitution, Law and Justice, Advancement of the Status of Women Cttees. 1996–99; Minister of Justice 1999–2001; Founder and Leader Social Democratic Party 2002–; Int. Activist Award, The Gleitsman Foundation 1999. *Publications:* Sons in the Shadow of their Fathers, The Price of Unity, Industry in Israel, Touching Peace, His Brother's Keeper, Israel, A Concise Political History, Touching Peace 1997, The Manual for Leaving Lebanon 1998, From Socialism to Social Liberalism 1999, His Brother's Keeper 2000, Manual for a Wounded Dove 2001. *Address:* ECF, 4 Hashalom Road, Tel-Aviv, Israel. *Telephone:* 3-6242332 (Office). *Fax:* 3-6242336 (Office). *E-mail:* beilin@ecf.org.il (Office).

BEINEIX, Jean-Jacques; French film director; b. 8 Oct. 1946, Paris; Asst Dir 1970–77; numerous prizes and awards at film festivals. *Films include:* Le Chien de Monsieur Michel 1971, Diva 1980, La Lune dans le caniveau (The Moon in the Gutter) 1983, 37.2° le matin (Betty Blue) 1985, Roselyne and the Lions 1989, IP5 1992, Mortel Transfert 2001. *Publications:* Diva 1991, L'île aux pachydermes 1992. *Address:* c/o Cargo Films, 9 rue Ambroise Thomas, 75009 Paris, France (Office). *Telephone:* 1-53-34-13-80 (Office). *Fax:* 1-53-34-13-81 (Office). *E-mail:* cargo@cargofilms.com (Office). *Website:* www.cargofilms.com.

BEIT-ARIÉ, Malachi, MA, MLS, PhD; Israeli university professor and palae-ographer; b. 20 May 1937, Petah-Tiqva; s. of Meir Beit-Arié and Esther (née Elpiner) Beit-Arié; one s. two d.; ed Hebrew Univ., Jerusalem; Dir The Hebrew Palaeography Project, Israel Acad. of Sciences and Humanities 1965–, Inst. of Microfilmed Hebrew Manuscripts 1970–78; Sr Lecturer in Codicology and Palaeography, Hebrew Univ. 1975–78, Assoc. Prof. 1979–83, Prof. 1984–; Dir Nat. and Univ. Library 1979–90; Chair. Int. Advisory Council Jewish Nat. Library 1991–; Visiting Fellow Wolfson Coll., Oxford 1984–85; Visiting Researcher IRHT (CNRS) Paris 1991; Visiting Scholar Harvard Univ. 1992; Fellow Center for Advanced Judaic Studies, Univ. of Pennsylvania 1996, 1999–2000; Anne Frank Awards for poetry 1961. *Publications:* These Streets, Those Mountains (lyrics) 1963, The Hills of Jerusalem and All the Pain (poems) 1967, Manuscrits médiévaux en caractères hébraiques (with C. Sirat), Parts I–III 1972–86, Hebrew Codicology 1977, The Only Dated Medieval MS Written in England 1985, Medieval Specimens of Hebrew Scripts 1987, The Makings of the Medieval Hebrew Book 1993, Hebrew Manuscripts of East and West: Towards Comparative Codicology 1993, Catalogue of the Hebrew MSS in the Bodleian Library (Supplement) 1994, Codices Lebraicis litteris exarati quo tempore scripti fuerint exhibentes I–II (with C. Sirat and M. Glatzer) 1997–99, Hebrew Manuscripts in the Biblioteca Palatina in Parma (with B. Richler) 2001. *Leisure interest:* classical music. *Address:* P.O. Box 34165, Jerusalem 91341 (Office); 11C Alkalai Street, Jerusalem 92223, Israel (Home). *Telephone:* 2-5619270 (Office); 2-5633940 (Home). *Fax:* 2-6511771.

BEITZ, Berthold; German industrialist; b. 26 Sept. 1913, Zemmin, West Pomerania; m. Else Hochheim 1939; three d.; ed secondary school; bank apprentice; employment in Shell, Hamburg; in charge of the Galician oilfields, Poland 1939–44; Deputy Chair. British Zonal Insurance Control Dept 1946; Dir-Gen. Iduna Germania Insurance Co. 1949–53; General-bevollmächtigter Dr. Alfried Krupp von Bohlen and Halbach 1953–67; Chair. Bd of Curators, Alfried Krupp von Bohlen und Halbach-Stiftung 1968, Chair. Supervisory Bd Friedrich Krupp GmbH 1970–89, Hon. Chair. 1989– (now ThyssenKrupp AG); Chair. Cttee of the Max-Grundig Foundation; Hon. mem. Int. Olympic Cttee; Chair. Bd, Ruhr Cultural Foundation (Kulturstiftung Ruhr); mem. 'pro Ruhrgebiet' Cttee; Direktorium der Univ. Witten-Herdecke; Hon. Chair. Supervisory Bd, Fried. Krupp AG Hoesch-Krupp, Essen, Inst. for East-West Security Studies, NY; Hon. Gov. Ernst-Moritz-Arndt Univ. (Greifswald); Hon. mem. Nat. Olympic Cttee, Univ. of Essen; Hon. Dr. Med. (Greifswald Univ.) 1983; Dr. hc (Jagiellonian Univ., Poland) 1993; DPhil hc (Ruhr-Univ., Bochum) 1999; Commandorium with Star of Order of Merit (Poland) 1974, Yad Vashem Medal (Israel), Grosses Bundesverdienstkreuz mit Stern und Schulterband 1979, Grosskreuz des Verdienstordens der Bundesrepublik Deutschland 1987, First Class Order of Madara Reiter (Bulgaria); Ring of Honour of the City of Essen; Ehrenbürger der Hanestadt Greifswald; numerous other decorations including B'nai B'rith Medal 1991, Leo Baeck Prize 2000, Leibniz Medal 2000. *Leisure interests:* yachting, hunting, jazz, modern painting. *Address:* Hügel 15, 45133 Essen, Germany. *Telephone:* (201) 1881. *Fax:* (201) 412587.

BÉJART, Maurice (Jean); French choreographer, dancer and stage director; b. 1 Jan. 1927; s. of Gaston Béjart and Germaine Berger; ed Lycée de Marseilles; début as ballet dancer with Marseilles Opera 1945; with int. Ballet 1949–50, Royal Opera, Stockholm 1951–52; co-founded Les Ballets de l'Etoile, later Ballet-Théâtre de Paris, 1954 (Dir 1954–59); Artistic Dir Béjart Ballet Lausanne (fmrly Twentieth Century Ballet Co.) 1960– (became Béjart Ballet Lausanne 1987); Dir Mudra Sch 1972; mem. Inst. (Académie des Beaux-Arts) 1994; Grand Prix Nat. de la Musique 1970, Prix Erasme de la Danse 1974, Chevalier des Arts et Lettres, Commdr Ordre de Léopold 1982, Ordre du Soleil Levant (Japan) 1986, Grand Officier Ordre de la Couronne (Belgium) 1988, Imperial Award (Japan) 1993. *Principal works include:* La Belle au Boa, Symphonie pour un homme seul 1955, Orphée 1958, le Sacre du Printemps 1959, Boléro 1961, The Tales of Hoffmann 1962, The Merry Widow, The Damnation of Faust, l'Oiseau de Feu 1964, Roméo and Juliet 1966, Messe pour le Temps Présent 1967, Firebird 1970, Song of a Wayfarer, Nijinsky: Clown de Dieu 1971, Le Marteau sans Maître, La Traviata 1973, Ce que l'amour me dit 1974, Notre Faust 1975, Heliogabale, Pli selon pli 1976, Petrouchka 1977, Gaîté Parisienne, Ce que la Mort me dit 1978, Mephisto Waltzer 1979, Casta Diva, Eros Thanatos 1980, The Magic Flute, Les Chaises, Light, Les Uns et les Autres (film) 1981, Wien Wien nur du Allein, Thalassa Mare Nostrum 1982, Salome, Messe pour le Temps Futur, Vie et mort d'une marionnette humaine 1983, Dionysos 1984, Le Concours, la Chauve Souris 1985, Arepo, Malraux ou la Métamorphose des Dieux 1986, Trois Etudes pour Alexandre, Souvenir de Léningrad, Après-midi d'un Faune, Fiche Signalé-tique, 1987, Patrice Chéreau..., Dibouk, Et Valse, Piaf, Paris-Tokyo, A force de partir... 1988, 1789 et nous, Elegie pour elle, L..., aile 1989, Ring um den Ring 1990, Nijinsky Clown de Dieu 1990, Pyramides 1990, M pour B 1990,

Mort Subite 1991, Maurice Béjart (co-choreographer) 1991, Ballade de la rue Athina, Le Mandarin merveilleux, King Lear/Prospero, Sissi, Les Chaises 1994, le Presbytère 1997, Jérusalem, cité de la paix 1997, Casse-noisette 1999, Enfant-Roi 2000, Lumière 2001. *Publications:* Mathilde, ou le temps perdu (novel) 1963, La Reine Verte (play) 1963, L'Autre chant de la danse 1974, Un instant dans la vie d'autrui 1979, La mort subite 1991, Maurice Béjart 1991 (jtly), la Vie de qui? 1997, Le Presbytère Mutation x, The Ballet for Life 2000. *Address:* Institut de France, 23 quai Conti, 75006 Paris, France (Office); Rudra Béjart Lausanne, case postale 25, 1000 Lausanne 22, Switzerland.

BEKHTEREVA, Natalya Petrovna, DrMedSc; Russian physiologist; b. 7 July 1924, Leningrad; d. of Pyotr Vladimirovich Bekhterev and Zinaida Vasilievna Bekhtereva; m. 1st Vsevolod Medvedev 1948 (divorced 1973); m. 2nd Ivan Kastelian 1973 (died 1990); one s.; ed Leningrad Medical Inst., mem. CPSU 1959–91; Jr research worker at USSR Acad. of Medical Sciences Inst. of Experimental Medicine 1950–54; on staff of Neuro-surgical Inst. of Min-istry of Health 1954–62; Head of Lab., Deputy Dir Inst. of Experimental Medicine 1962–, Dir 1970–90; Scientific Dir Inst. of the Human Brain, Russian Acad. of Science 1990–; USSR People's Deputy 1970–74, 1989–91; Corresp. mem. Austrian Acad. of Sciences; Foreign mem. Cuban Physiological Soc.; Hon. mem. Czechoslovakian Neurochirurgical Soc. J.E. Purkyne, Hun-garian Electrophysiological Soc.; mem. Finnish Acad. of Sciences, USSR (now Russian) Acad. of Sciences 1981–, USSR (now Russian) Acad. of Medical Sciences 1975, Int. Acad. of Ecology, Man and Nature Protection Sciences (IAEMNP) 1999–; Fellow Academia Medicina et Psychiatria (USA); Order of The Great Powers of Russia 1999 USSR State Prize Winner 1985, McCulloch Medal, USA Cybernetics Soc., Hans Berger Medal, GDR Electrophysiological Soc., Medal of Bulgarian Union of Research Workers, Bechterev's Gold Medal, Russian Acad. of Sciences, Century Award of the Int. Org. of Psychophysiology 1998, American Biographical Inst. Medal of Honor 2000 1998, planet N6074 discovered in 1968 named in honour of Becteræva, IAEMNP Merits in Ecology Medal 1999, I. P. Pavlov Prize, St Petersburg 2000. *Publications:* over 370 publs in Russian and English on physiology of mental activity, structural and functional org. of physiological activity of brain, including El cerebro humano sano y enfermo 1984, On the Human Brain. XX Century and its Last Decade in Human Brain Science 1997. *Leisure interests:* painting, music. *Address:* Institute of the Human Brain, Pavlova Street 9, St Petersburg 197376, Russia. *Telephone:* 234-22-21 (Office). *Fax:* 234-32-47.

BEKSIŃSKI, Zdzisław; Polish painter; b. 24 Feb. 1929, Sanok; m. (wife deceased); one s. (deceased); ed Cracow Tech. Univ.; mem. of Asscn of Polish Artists (ZPAP) 1962–83, 1989; collaborated with Piotr Dmochowski, Paris 1980–94; numerous one-man exhbns. in Poland, France, Germany and Japan. *Leisure interests:* collecting records, listening to music. *Address:* ul. Sonaty 6 m. 314, 02-744 Warsaw, Poland. *Telephone:* (22) 8470587. *E-mail:* bex@acn.waw.pl.

BELAFONTE, Harry; American singer; b. 1 March 1927, New York; s. of Harold George Belafonte Sr and Malvene Love Wright; m. 2nd Julie Robinson 1957; one s. three d.; ed George Washington High School, New York; in Jamaica 1935–39; service with US Navy 1943–45; American Negro Theater; student at Manhattan New School for Social Research Dramatic Workshop 1946–48; first engagement at the Vanguard, Greenwich Village; European tours 1958, 1976, 1981, 1983, 1988; Pres. Belafonte Enterprises Inc.; Goodwill Amb. for UNICEF 1987; Host Nelson Mandela Birthday Concert, Wembley 1988; Broadway appearances in Three For Tonight, Almanac, Belafonte At The Palace and in films Bright Road, Carmen Jones 1952, Island in the Sun 1957, The World, the Flesh and the Devil 1958, Odds Against Tomorrow 1959, The Angel Levine (also producer) 1969, Grambling's White Tiger 1981, White Man's Burden; produced with Sidney Poitier Buck and the Preacher 1971 (also acted), Uptown Saturday Night 1974; Emmy Television Award for Tonight with Belafonte 1960; Producer Strolling '20s 1965, A Time for Laughter 1967, Harry and Lena 1970, Beat Street 1984; concerts in USA, Europe 1989, Canada 1990, USA and Canada 1991, N America, Europe and Far East 1996; mem. Bd NY State Martin Luther King Jr Inst. for Non-violence 1989–; Hon. DHumLitt (Park Coll., Mo.) 1968; Hon. Dr Arts, New School of Social Research, New York 1968; Hon. DCL (Newcastle) 1997, numerous other hon. doctorates; numerous awards including Golden Acord Award, Bronx Community Coll. 1989, Mandela Courage Award 1990, Nat. Medal of the Arts 1994, NY Arts and Business Council Award 1997, Dis-tinguished American Award, John F. Kennedy Library, Boston 2002. *Leisure interests:* photography, water skiing, recording.

BÉLANGER, Gerard, MA, MSocSc; Canadian professor of economics; b. 23 Oct. 1940, St Hyacinthe; s. of Georges Bélanger and Cécile Girard; m. Michèle Potvin 1964; one d.; ed Princeton and Laval Univs; Prof. Dept of Econs Laval Univ. 1967–, Prof. of Econs 1977–; Research Co-ordinator, Howe Inst. Montreal 1977–79; mem. Task Force on Urbanization, Govt of Québec 1974–76; Sec. Acad. of Letters and Social Sciences, RSC 1985–88; Woodrow Wilson Fellow. *Publications:* The Price of Health 1972, Le financement municipal au Québec 1976, Taxes and Expenditures in Québec and Ontario 1978, Le prix du transport au Québec 1978, L'économique du secteur public 1981, Croissance du Secteur Public et Fédéralisme 1988. *Address:* Depart-ment of Economics, Université Laval, Québec, G1K 7P4, Canada. *Telephone:* (418) 656-5363 (Office); (418) 681-3075 (Home). *Fax:* (418) 656-2707. *E-mail:* gebe@ecn.ulaval.ca (Office).

BÉLAVAL, Philippe Marie; French library executive and civil servant; b. 21 Aug. 1955, Toulouse; s. of Jacques Bélaval and Marie-Thérèse (née Chazarenc) Bélaval; ed Faculté des Sciences Sociales de Toulouse, Inst. d'études politiques de Toulouse; trainee at École nationale d'admin. 1977–79, auditor 1979; technical adviser Conseil d'Etat 1983–84, counsel 1984, rep. of Sec. of State for Budget and Consumption 1984–86; Asst Dir Office of Minister of Public Affairs and Admin. Reform 1988–89, Dir 1989–90; Dir-Gen. Théâtre nationale de l'Opéra de Paris 1990–92; Dir-Gen. Bibliothèque nationale de France 1994–98; Dir-Gen. Archives de France 1998–2000; Pres. Admin. Council Groupe vocal de France 1985–90; Pres. cour administrative d'appel, Bordeaux 2001–; Council of State 1996; mem. Admin. Council of École des chartes; Sr lecturer Inst. d'études politiques de Paris; Chevalier Légion d'honneur, Chevalier Ordre nat. du Mérite, Commdr des Arts et des Lettres. *Address:* Cour administrative d'appel de Bordeux, 17 Cours de Verdun, 33074 Bordeaux Cedex (Office); Conseil d'État, place du Palais Royal, 75100 Paris, France. *Telephone:* 1-40-27-67-00 (Office). *Fax:* 1-40-27-66-06 (Office). *E-mail:* philippe.belaval@culture.gouv.fr (Office).

BELEZA, Miguel; Portuguese banker; b. 1950; ed Mass. Inst. of Tech.; Minister of Finance 1990–91; Dir (non-exec.) Siemens Portugal; fmr adviser Banco Comercial Português; fmr Asst Prof., then Assoc. Prof. Faculty of Econs, Univ. Nova de Lisboa; fmr adviser IMF; fmr adviser, then Gov. and Dir Bank of Portugal; fmr Visiting Prof. Brown Univ., Univ. dos Açores, INSEAD, Fontainebleau; now Dir Banco Expresso Atlântico Lisbon; consultant and Ed. Economia journal (Univ. Católica Portuguesa); Grand Cross, Nat. Order Cross of the South (Brazil), Grand Cross, Order of Merit. *Publications:* numerous articles in journals. *Address:* c/o Banco Expresso Atlântico, SA, Av. da Boavista 757, 4100 Porto, Lisbon, Portugal (Office). *Telephone:* (2) 6005579 (Office).

BELIGAN, Radu; Romanian actor; b. 14 Dec. 1918, Galbeni, Bacău County; m.; four c.; ed Bucharest Conservatoire; started career at Muncă și Lumină (Work and Light) Theatre in Bucharest, then played at Alhambra and Nat. Theatre; Prof. Inst. of Drama and Film Art Bucharest 1960–68; Dir Teatrul de Comedie 1960–68; Dir Nat. Theatre 1969–89; Chair. Int. Theatre Inst.; mem. Cen. Cttee Romanian CP 1969–89; mem. Exec. Bureau Nat. Council Front of Socialist Democracy and Unity 1980–89; performances in classic and modern Romanian plays and int. repertoire (Shakespeare, Gogol, Chekhov, Albee, Dürrenmatt and others); Merited Artist 1953, People's Artist 1962. *Publications:* Pretexte și subtexte (Pretexts and Understatements), essays, 1968; Luni, marți, miercuri (Monday, Tuesday, Wednesday), Memoirs 1978. *Address:* Str. Spătarului 36, 70241 Bucharest, Romania.

BELINGA-EBOUTOU, Martin; Cameroonian diplomatist; b. 17 Feb. 1940, Nkilzok; m.; six c.; ed Catholic Univ., Lavanium-Kinshasa, Univ. of Paris; joined Ministry of Foreign Affairs 1968; Chargé d'Affaires, Congo 1970–74; Chief Regional Orgs. Unit 1974–85; Head Econ. Mission of Cameroon, Paris, Rome, Tunis, Rabat 1985–89; Dir then Chief of State Protocol, Office of Pres. 1989–97, Dir Civil Cabinet 1996–97; Perm. Rep. to UN, New York 1997–; Pres. ECOSOC 2001–; Assoc. Prof. Inst. of Int. Relations 1974–76. *Address:* Permanent Mission of Cameroon to the United Nations, 22 East 73rd Street, New York, NY 10021, USA (Office). *Telephone:* (212) 794-2295 (Office). *Fax:* (212) 249-0533 (Office). *E-mail:* cameroon@un.int (Office).

BELKA, Marek, PhD; Polish politician and professor of economics; b. 28 Jan. 1952, Tczew; m.; two c.; ed Łódź Univ.; Asst Prof., then Prof. of Econs Łódź Univ. 1973–96; visiting scholar Columbia Univ. (Fulbright Foundation) 1978–79, American Council of Scholarly Socs., Univ. of Chicago 1985–86, LSE 1990; Asst Prof. Inst. of Econs, Polish Acad. of Sciences (PAN) 1986–97; consultant Cen. Planning Office, Ministry of Finance and of Privatization 1990–96; Vice-Pres. Council of Socio-Econ. Strategy, Council of Ministers 1994–96; Econ. Adviser to the Pres. of Poland 1996–97, 1997–2001; Deputy Prime Minister and Minister of Finance 1997, 2001–02. *Publications:* several books and numerous articles in Polish and foreign press on anti-inflation policy in developed countries, the Milton Friedman socio-econ. doctrine and macroecon. policy in transition periods. *Leisure interests:* travelling, basketball, music. *Address:* c/o Ministry of Finance, ul. Świętokrzyska 12, 00-916 Warsaw, Poland (Office).

BELKEZIZ, Abdelouahed, DrIur; Moroccan international organization official; b. 1939, Marrakesh; ed Univ. of Rennes, France; Dean Moroccan Univ., Rabat, Hassan II Univ. Ibn Tofail, Kenitra, Univ. Muhammad V, Rabat; Amb. to Rabat 1977; apptd. to Cabinet 1979, held portfolios of Information, Youth and Sports and Foreign Affairs; Sec.-Gen. Org. of the Islamic Conf. (OIC) Jan. 2001–. *Address:* General Secretariat, Organization of the Islamic Conference, Kilo 6, Mecca Road, P.O. Box 178, Jeddah 21411, Saudi Arabia. *Telephone:* (2) 680-0800. *Fax:* (2) 687-3568. *E-mail:* info@oic-oci.org. *Website:* www.oic-oci.org.

BELL, (Alexander) Scott, CBE; British financial executive; b. 4 Dec. 1941; s. of the late William Scott Bell and Irene Bell; m. Veronica Jane Simpson 1965; two s. one d.; ed Daniel Stewart's Coll., Edin.; Asst Actuary for Canada, Standard Life Assurance Co. 1967, Deputy Actuary 1972, South Region Man. 1974, Asst Gen. Man. (Finance) 1979, Gen. Man. (Finance) 1985–88, Group Man. Dir 1988–2001; Dir Bank of Scotland 1988–96, Hammerson PLC (fmrly Hammerson Property and Devt Corpn) 1988–98, Scottish Financial Enterprise 1989–95, Prosperity SA 1993–, Standard Life Healthcare 1994–2001, Prime Health Ltd 1994–, Standard Life Bank 1997–2001, Standard Life Investments 1998–2001; Dir Asscn of British Insurers 1999–; Chair. Assoc.

Scottish Life Offices 1994–96; Dir Univs Superannuation Scheme Ltd 1996–; Hon. Canadian Consul in Scotland 1994–; Hon. DLitt (Herriot-Watt Univ.) 1997; Fellow, Pensions Man. Inst. *Leisure interests:* golf, reading, travel.

BELL, Edward; British publisher; b. 2 Aug. 1949; s. of Eddie Bell and Jean Bell; m. Junette Bannatyne 1969; one s. two d.; ed Airdrie High School; with Hodder & Stoughton 1970–85; Man. Dir Collins Gen. Div. 1985–89; launched Harper Paperbacks in USA 1989; Deputy Chief Exec., HarperCollins UK 1990–91, Chief Exec. 1991–92, Chair. 1992–2000; Chair. HarperCollins India 1994–2000; Dir (non-exec.) Haynes Publishing 2001, Be Cogent Ltd, Management Diagnostics Ltd; Chair. (non-exec.) OAG Worldwide Ltd 2001; Chair. Those Who Can Ltd 2001; partner Bell Lomax Literary and Sport Agency 2002; Gov. St Dunstan's Coll. 1999, Kent Inst. of Art and Design 2002. *Leisure interests:* golf, supporting Arsenal, collecting old books. *Address:* The Bell Lomax Agency, James House, 1 Babmaes Street, London, SW1Y 6HF, England (Office). *Telephone:* (20) 7930-4447 (Office). *Fax:* (20) 7925-0118 (Office). *E-mail:* eddie@bell-lomax.co.uk.

BELL, (Ernest) Arthur, CB, PhD, CChem, FRSC, CBiol, FIBiol, FLS; British scientist; b. 20 June 1926, Gosforth, Northumberland; s. of Albert Bell and Rachel Enid Bell (née Williams); m. Jean Swinton Ogilvie 1952; two s. one d.; ed Dame Allan's School, Newcastle-upon-Tyne, King's Coll., Newcastle, Univ. of Durham, Trinity Coll. Dublin; Research Chemist, ICI 1946–47, Demonstrator and holder of Sarah Purser Research Award, Trinity Coll., Dublin 1947–49, Asst to Prof. of Biochemistry 1949–53; Lecturer in Biochemistry, King's Coll., London 1953–64, Reader 1964–68, Prof. of Biology and Head of Dept of Plant Sciences 1972–81, Dean of Natural Science 1980–81; Prof. of Botany, Univ. of Texas at Austin 1968–72; Dir Royal Botanic Gardens, Kew 1981–88; Consultant Dir CAB Int. Mycological Inst. 1982–86; mem. Working Party on Naturally Occurring Toxicants in Foods 1983–95; Sr Foreign Scientist Fellow of Natural Science Foundation of USA; Visiting Prof. Univ. of Kansas 1964, Univ. of Sierra Leone 1977, King's Coll., London 1982–, Univ. of Reading 1982–88; Sr Commonwealth Visiting Fellow, Australia 1980; Cecil H. and Ida Green Visiting Prof. Univ. of British Columbia 1987; Visiting Prof. Univ. of Texas at Austin 1988–90, Adjunct Prof. 1991–; Scientific Dir, Texas Botanical Garden Soc. 1988–; mem. Royal Mint Advisory Cttee 1992–98; Fellow, King's Coll., London 1982; Vice-Pres. Linnean Soc. of London 1982; Pres., Plant Biology Section, British Asscn for the Advancement of Science 1985–86; Hon. mem. Phytochemical Soc. of Europe 1985–; Visiting Fellow, Japan Soc. for the Promotion of Science 1986; Pres. King's Coll. London Asscn 1986–88; Hon. Fellow, Trinity Coll. Dublin, Ireland 1990, Leverhulme Fellow Emer. 1991–93. *Publications:* numerous publs on plant biochemistry, chemotaxonomy and chemical ecology. *Leisure interests:* walking, travel, watching rugby football. *Address:* 3 Hillview, Wimbledon, London SW20 0TA, England. *Telephone:* (20) 8946-2626.

BELL, Geoffrey Lakin, BScEcon; British international banker; b. 8 Nov. 1939, Grimsby; s. of the late Walter Lakin Bell and of Anne Bell; m. Joan Rosine Abel 1973; one d.; ed Grimsby Tech. High School and London School of Econs; HM Treasury 1961–63; Visiting Economist Federal Reserve System 1963–64; HM Treasury and Lecturer, LSE 1964–66; Adviser British Embassy, Washington, DC 1966–69; joined J. Henry Schroder Wagg and Co. Ltd 1969, Asst to Chair. 1969–72; Dir and Exec. Vice-Pres. Schroder Int. Ltd; Dir Schroder Bermuda Ltd; Exec. Sec. Group of Thirty 1978–; Pres. Geoffrey Bell and Co. Ltd 1982–; Chair. Guinness Mahon Holdings 1987–93; mem. Court of Govs LSE 1994–. *Publication:* The Euro-Dollar Market and the International Financial System 1973, contrib. The Times and numerous academic and other publs. *Address:* Apt. 15A, 455 East 57th Street, New York, NY 10022, USA; 17 Abbotsbury House, Abbotsbury Road, London, W14 8EN, England. *Telephone:* (212) 838-1193 (USA); (20) 7603-9408 (England).

BELL, John Anthony, OBE, AM; Australian theatre director and actor; b. 1 Nov. 1940, Newcastle; s. of Albert Bell and Joyce Feeney; m. Anna Volska 1965; two d.; ed Maitland Marist Bros. High School, NSW and Univ. of Sydney; actor with Old Tote Theatre Co. 1963–64, with RSC UK 1964–69; Co-Founder, Nimrod Theatre Co. 1970–85; Founder and Artistic Dir Bell Shakespeare Co. 1990–; roles include King Lear, Macbeth, Shylock, Malvolio and Richard III; Hon. D. Litt (Newcastle), (Sydney). *Leisure interests:* reading, music, painting. *Address:* The Bell Shakespeare Company, Level 1, 88 George Street, The Rocks, NSW 2000, Australia.

BELL, Joshua; American violinist; b. 9 Dec. 1967, Indiana; youngest guest soloist at a Philadelphia Orchestra Subscription concert 1982; European tour with St Louis Symphony 1985; German tour with Indianapolis Symphony 1987; European tour with Dallas Symphony 1997; European tours with Nat. Symphony Orchestra 2002, Minnesota Orchestra 2003; guest soloist with numerous orchestras in USA, Canada, Europe; has also appeared in USA and Europe as a recitalist; played premiere of violin concerto by Nicholas Maw, written for him, with Philharmonia Orchestra 1993; Visiting Prof. at RAM, London; Gramophone Award for Best Concerto Recording 1998 (for Barber Concerto), Mercury Music Award 2000, Acad. Award – Best Soundtrack for Red Violin, Grammy Award 2001. *Recordings:* Mendelssohn and Bruch concertos with the Academy of St Martin-in-the-Fields and Sir Neville Marriner, Tchaikovsky and Wieniawski concertos with the Cleveland Orchestra and Vladimir Ashkenazy, recital album of Brahms, Paganini, Sarasate and Wieniawski with Samuel Sanders, Lalo Symphonie Espagnole and Saint-Saëns Concerto with Montreal Symphony Orchestra and Charles Dutoit, Franck, Fauré and Débussy, Chausson Concerto for violin, piano and string quartet with Thibaudet and Isserlis, Poème with Royal Philharmonic Orchestra and Andrew Litton, Mozart Concertos Nos 3 and 5 with the English Chamber Orchestra and Peter Maag, Prokofiev violin concertos with Montreal Symphony Orchestra and Charles Dutoit, Barber and Walton concertos and Bloch Baal Shem with Baltimore Symphony Orchestra and David Zinman, recital disc with Olli Mustonen, Gershwin Fantasy with London Symphony Orchestra and John Williams, Short Trip Home with Edgar Meyer, The Red Violin film soundtrack with Philharmonia Orchestra, Sibelius Goldmark Concertos with Los Angeles Philharmonic Orchestra and Esa-Pekka Salonen, Maw Concerto for violin with London Philharmonic Orchestra and Roger Norrington, Bernstein Serenade and West Side Story Suite with Philharmonia Orchestra and David Zinman, Beethoven and Mendelssohn concertos with Camerata Salzburg and Sir Roger Norrington, Irish film soundtrack. *Leisure interests:* chess, computers, golf. *Address:* c/o IMG Artists, Lovell House, 616 Chiswick High Road, London, W4 5RX, England.

BELL, Marian, BA, MSc; British economist; b. 28 Oct. 1957; d. of Joseph Denis Milburn Bell and Wilhelmenia Maxwell Bell (née Miller); m.; two c.; ed Hertford Coll. Oxford, Birkbeck Coll. London; Sr Economist, Royal Bank of Scotland 1985–89, Sr Treasury Economist 1991–97, Head of Research, Treasury and Capital Markets 1997–2000; Econ. Adviser, HM Treasury 1989–91; f. Alpha Econs 2000, consultant 2000–02; External Mem. Monetary Policy Cttee, Bank of England June 2002–. *Address:* Bank of England, Threadneedle Street, London, EC2R 8AH England (Office). *Telephone:* (20) 7601-3235 (Office). *Fax:* (20) 7601-4610 (Office). *E-mail:* marian.bell@ bankofengland.co.uk (Office). *Website:* www.bankofengland.co.uk (Office).

BELL, Martin, OBE, MA; British broadcaster and politician; b. 31 Aug. 1938; s. of the late Adrian Bell and Marjorie Bell (née Gibson); m. 1st Nelly Gourdon 1971 (divorced); two d.; m. 2nd Rebecca Sobel 1985 (divorced 1993); m. 3rd Fiona Goddard 1998; ed The Leys School, Cambridge, King's Coll., Cambridge; joined BBC 1962, news Asst, Norwich 1962–64, gen. reporter, London and overseas 1964–76, Diplomatic Corresp. 1976–77, Chief N American Corresp. 1977–89, Berlin Corresp. BBC TV News 1989–93, Vienna Corresp. 1993–94, Foreign Affairs Corresp. 1994–96, Special Corresp., Nine O'Clock News 1997; has reported from over 70 countries and has covered wars in Vietnam, Middle East 1967, 1973, Angola, Rhodesia, Biafra, El Salvador, Gulf 1991, Nicaragua, Croatia, Bosnia; MP (Ind.) for Tatton 1997–2001; Humanitarian Amb. for UNICEF 2001–; Dr hc (Derby) 1996; Hon. MA (E Anglia) 1997, (Aberdeen) 1998; Royal TV Soc. Reporter of the Year 1976, 1992, TV and Radio Industries Club Newscaster of the Year 1995, Inst. of Public Relations Pres.'s Medal 1996. *Publication:* In Harm's Way 1995, An Accidental MP 2000. *Address:* 71 Denman Drive, London, W11 6RA, England (Home).

BELL, Baron (Life Peer), cr. 1998, of Belgravia in the City of Westminster; **Timothy John Leigh Bell,** Kt, FIPA; British public relations executive; b. 18 Oct. 1941; s. of Arthur Leigh Bell and Greta Mary Bell (née Findlay); m. Virginia Wallis Hornbrook 1988; one s. one d.; ed Queen Elizabeth's Grammar School, Barnet, Herts.; with ABC Television 1959–61, Colman Prentis & Varley 1961–63, Hobson Bates 1963–66, Geers Gross 1966–70; Man. Dir Saatchi & Saatchi 1970–75, Chair. and Man. Dir Saatchi & Saatchi Compton 1975–85; Group Chief Exec. Lowe Howard-Spink Campbell Ewald 1985–87, Deputy Chair. Lowe Howard-Spink & Bell PLC 1987–89; Chair. Lowe-Bell Communications 1987–89, Chime Communications 1994–; f. Lowe-Bell Govt Relations 1993–; arranged man. buy-out of Lowe-Bell Communications 1989; Special Adviser to Chair. Nat. Coal Bd 1984–86; mem. South Bank Bd 1985–86; Chair. Charity Projects 1984–93, Pres. 1993–; Dir Centre for Policy Studies; mem. Industry Cttee SCF, Public Relations Cttee Greater London Fund for the Blind 1979–86, Council Royal Opera House 1982–85, Public Affairs Cttee, Worldwide Fund for Nature 1985–88; Creative Leaders' Network Gov. British Film Inst. 1983–86. *Leisure interests:* golf, politics. *Address:* Chime Communications PLC, 14 Curzon Street, London, W1J 5HN, England (Office). *Telephone:* (20) 7495-4044. *Fax:* (20) 7491-9860 (Office).

BELL BURNELL, S. Jocelyn, CBE, PhD; British astrophysicist and university administrator; b. 15 July 1943; d. of (George) Philip Bell and (Margaret) Allison Bell (née Kennedy); m. (divorced); one s.; Lecturer Univ. of Southampton 1968–73; part-time with Mullard Space Lab., Univ. Coll. London 1974–82; part-time with Royal Observatory, Edin. 1982–91; Chair. Physics Dept Open Univ. 1991–99; Dean of Science, Univ. of Bath 2001–; Visiting Prof. for Distinguished Teaching, Princeton Univ. 1999–2000; Pres. Royal Astronomical Soc. 2002–04; discovered the first four pulsars; frequent radio and TV broadcaster on science, on being a woman in science and on science and religion; Hon. Fellow New Hall, Cambridge 1996; 14 hon. doctorates including Cambridge and London Univs; Joseph Black Medal and Cowie Book Prize, Glasgow Univ. 1962, Michelson Medal, Franklin Inst. (USA) 1973, J. Robert Oppenheimer Memorial Prize, Center for Theoretical Studies, Fla 1978, Beatrice M. Tinsley Prize, American Astronomical Soc. (first recipient) 1987, Herschel Medal, Royal Astronomical Soc., London 1989, Edinburgh Medal 1999, Magellanic Premium, American Philosophical Soc. 2000. *Publications:* two books, about 70 scientific papers and c. 35 Quaker publs. *Leisure interests:* popularizing astronomy, walking, Quaker and ecumenical activities, listening to choral music. *Address:* Faculty of Science, University of Bath, Bath, BA2 7AY, England (Office). *Telephone:* (1225) 383965 (Office). *Fax:* (1225) 383353 (Office). *E-mail:* s.j.b.burnell@bath.ac.uk (Office).

BELL LEMUS, Gustavo; Colombian politician and academic; b. 1 Feb. 1957, Barranquilla; ed Javeriana Univ. of Bogotá, Andes Univ. and Univ. of Oxford, UK; fmr Prof. Univ. del Norte e del Atlantico; fmr Man. Nat. Industrial Asscn (Andi), Barranquilla; fmr Gov. of Atlantico; Vice-Pres. of Colombia and Minister of Nat. Defence 2001–02. *Address:* c/o Ministry of National Defence, Centro Administrativo Nacional (CAN), 2°, Avda El Dorado, Santafé de Bogotá, DC, Colombia (Office).

BELLAMY, Carol, JD; American agency administrator; b. 1942, Plainfield, NJ; ed Gettysburg Coll. and New York Univ.; Peace Corps Volunteer, Guatemala; Assoc. Cravath, Swaine & Moore, New York; mem. New York State Senate; Pres. New York City Council; Prin. Morgan Stanley & Co. New York; Man. Dir Bear Stearns, New York; Dir Peace Corps, Washington, DC 1993–95; Exec. Dir UNICEF 1995–. *Address:* UNICEF, 3 United Nations Plaza, New York, NY 10017-4486, USA. *Telephone:* (212) 326-7028 (Office). *Fax:* (212) 326-7758 (Office). *E-mail:* cbellamy@unicef.org (Office). *Website:* www.unicef.org (Office).

BELLAMY, Sir Christopher (William), Kt, MA, QC; British judge; b. 25 April 1946, Waddesdon, Bucks.; s. of the late William Albert Bellamy and Vyvienne Hilda Bellamy (née Meyrick); m. Deirdre Patricia Turner 1989; one s. two d.; ed Tonbridge School, Brasenose Coll., Oxford; called to the Bar, Middle Temple 1968 (Bencher 1994), in full-time practice 1970–92, QC 1986, Asst Recorder 1989–92; Judge of Court of First Instance of the EC 1992–99; Pres. of Appeal Tribunals, Competition Comm. 1999–; Deputy High Court Judge 2000–; Judge of Employment Appeal Tribunal 2000–; mem. council, British Inst. of Int. and Comparative Law 2000–; Recorder, Crown Court 2001–; Gov. Ravensbourne Coll. of Design and Communication 1988–92. *Publication:* Common Market Law of Competition (jtly) 1973. *Leisure interests:* family life, walking, history. *Address:* Competition Commission Appeal Tribunals, New Court, 48 Carey Street, London, WC2A 2JT, England (Office). *Telephone:* (20) 7271-0400 (Office).

BELLAMY, David James, OBE, PhD, FIBiol, FLS; British botanist, writer, broadcaster and environmental organisation administrator; b. 18 Jan. 1933, London; s. of Thomas Bellamy and Winifred Green; m. Rosemary Froy 1959; two s. three d.; ed Chelsea Coll. of Science and Tech. and Bedford Coll., London Univ.; Lecturer, then Sr Lecturer, Dept of Botany, Univ. of Durham 1960–80, Hon. Prof. of Adult and Continuing Educ. 1980–82; Visiting Prof. Massey Univ., NZ 1988–89; Special Prof. of Botany Nottingham Univ. 1987–; TV and radio presenter and scriptwriter; Founder Dir Conservation Foundation; Pres. WATCH 1982; Pres. Youth Hostels Asscn 1983; Pres. Population Concern 1988–, Nat. Asscn of Environmental Educ. 1989–, Plantlife 1995–, Wildlife Trust's Partnership 1996–, British Inst. of Cleaning Science 1997–; Dir David Bellamy Assocs. (environmental consultants) 1988–97; Pres. Council Zoological Soc. of London 1991–94, BH&HPA 2000–, Camping and Caravanning Club 2002–; Hon. Fellow CIWEM; Hon. FLS; Hon. DSc; Hon. DUniv; Dr hc (CNAA) 1990; Dutch Order of the Golden Ark 1989, UNEP Global 500 Award 1990. *Television series includes:* Life in Our Sea 1970, Bellamy on Botany 1973, Bellamy's Britain 1975, Bellamy's Europe 1977, Botanic Man 1978, Up a Gum Tree 1980, Backyard Safari 1981, The Great Seasons 1982, Bellamy's New World 1983, End of the Rainbow Show 1986, S.W.A.L.L.O.W. 1986, Turning the Tide 1986, Bellamy's Bugle 1986, 1987, 1988, Bellamy on Top of the World 1987, Bellamy's Journey to the Centre of the World 1987, Bellamy's Bird's Eye View 1989, Wheat Today What Tomorrow? 1989, Moa's Ark 1990, Bellamy Rides Again 1992, Blooming Bellamy 1993, 1994, Routes of Wisdom 1993, The Peak 1994, Bellamy's Border Raids 1996, Westwatch 1997, A Welsh Herbal 1998, Salt Solutions 1999, The Challenge 1999. *Publications include:* Peatlands 1974, Life Giving Sea 1977, Half of Paradise 1979, The Great Seasons 1981, Discovering the Countryside with David Bellamy (Vols I, II) 1982, (Vols III, IV) 1983, The Mouse Book 1983, The Queen's Hidden Garden 1984, Bellamy's Ireland 1986, Bellamy's Changing Countryside (4 Vols) 1988, England's Last Wilderness 1989, Wetlands 1990, Wilderness Britain 1990, Moa's Ark 1990, How Green Are You? 1991, Tomorrow's Earth 1992, World Medicine 1992, Poo, You and the Poteroo's Loo 1997, Bellamy's Changing Countryside 1998, The Glorious Trees of Great Britain 2002, Jolly Green Giant (autobiog.) 2002, The Bellamy Herbal 2003, and books connected with TV series. *Leisure interests:* children and ballet. *Address:* Mill House, Bedburn, Bishop Auckland, Co. Durham, DL13 3NN, England. *Website:* www.wildlifebiz.com (Office).

BELLANY, John, CBE, RA; British artist; b. 18 June 1942, Port Seton, Scotland; s. of Richard Weatherhead Bellany and Agnes Maltman Bellany; m. 1st Helen Margaret Percy 1965 (remarried 1986); two s. one d.; m. 2nd Juliet Gray (née Lister) 1979 (died 1985); ed Cockenzie Public School, Preston Lodge, Prestonpans, Edinburgh Coll. of Art, Royal Coll. of Art, London; Lecturer in Fine Art, Winchester School of Art 1969–73; Head of Faculty of Painting, Croydon Coll. of Art 1973–78; Visiting Lecturer in Painting, RCA 1975–85; Lecturer in Fine Art, Goldsmiths Coll., Univ. of London 1978–84; Fellow Commoner, Trinity Hall, Cambridge 1988, Sr Fellow RCA 1999; Hon. RSA; Dr hc (Edin.) 1996; Hon. DLit (Edin.) 1998; Arts Council Award 1981, Jt 1st Prize, Athena Int. Award 1985. *One-man exhibitions include:* Arts Council Touring Show 1978, Rosa Esman Gallery, New York 1982, 1983, 1984, Ikon Gallery, Birmingham, Walker Art Gallery, Liverpool, Graves Art Gallery, Sheffield, Christine Abrahams Gallery, Melbourne, Nat. Portrait Gallery, London 1986, Galerie Kirkhaar, Amsterdam 1986, Fischer Fine Art, London 1989, Retrospective, Scottish Nat. Gallery of Modern Art, Kunsthalle, Hamburg, Serpentine Gallery, London, Ruth Siegel Gallery, New York 1990,

Raab Gallery, Berlin, Ruth Siegel Gallery, USA 1990, Fitzwilliam Museum, Cambridge, Fischer Fine Art, London 1991, Kelvingrove Museum, Glasgow, Beaux Arts Gallery 1992, Berkeley Square Gallery, London 1993, Beaux Arts Gallery, London 1997, 1998, 1999, 2000, 2001, 2002, Dintenfass Gallery, New York 1997, Elane Gallery, Boca Raton, FL 1999, Scottish Nat. Gallery of Modern Art 2002, Ricci Foundation, Barga, Italy 2002, Flowers Gallery, Los Angeles. *Radio:* regular contributor to Kaleidoscope (BBC Radio 4), Night Waves (BBC Radio 3); John Bellany 30 min. programme (BBC Radio 3) with Judith Bumphus –1995. *Television:* John Bellany (BBC TV) 1972, John Bellany – Artist with a New Liver (BBC TV) 1989. *Publications:* Scottish National Galleries 1986, National Portrait Gallery, London 1986. *Leisure interests:* opera, motoring. *Address:* The Clock House, Shortgrove Hall, Newport, Saffron Walden, Essex, CB11 3TX, England (Home); 19 Great Stuart Street, Edinburgh, EH2 7TP, Scotland (Home). *Telephone:* (1799) 541009 (England) (Home). *Fax:* (1799) 542062 (England) (Home). *E-mail:* john@bellany.com. *Website:* www.bellany.com (Office).

BELLEN, Heinz, DPhil; German professor of ancient history; b. 1 Aug. 1927, Neuss/Rhein; s. of Heinrich Bellen and Elisabeth Hussmann; m. Agnes Meuters 1958; two d.; secondary school teacher, Düsseldorf 1957–62; Asst Prof. Cologne 1962–68, Lecturer, 1968–73; Prof. of Ancient History, Univ. of Mainz 1974–93; mem. Mainz Acad. 1975–. *Publications:* Studien zur Sklavenflucht im römischen Kaiserreich 1971, Die germanische Leibwache der römischen Kaiser 1981, Metus Gallicus-Metus Punicus 1985, Grundzüge der römischen Geschichte (Vol. I) 1994, (Vol. II) 1998, Politik-Recht-Gesellschaft 1997; Ed.: Forschungen zur antiken Sklaverei 1978–. *Address:* Institüt für Alte Geschichte, Johannes Gütenberg-Universität, Saarstrasse 21, 55099 Mainz (Office); Alfred-Nobel Strasse 23, 55124 Mainz, Germany (Home). *Telephone:* (6131) 472919.

BELLENS, Didier; Belgian media executive; b. 9 June 1955; m.; two c.; ed Ecole de Commerce Solay, Univ. Libre de Bruxelles; Deputy Gen. Man. Pargesa Holding SA, Geneva –1992; Man. Dir Groupe Bruxelles Lambert SA, Brussels 1992–2000; CEO CLT-UFA, Luxembourg 2000 (merged with Pearson TV to become RTL Group 2000); apptd CEO RTL Group (owns 24 TV and 17 radio stations), Luxembourg 2000; CEO Belgacom SA, Brussels Feb. 2003–. *Leisure interests:* hikes in the Libyan desert, Morocco and Namibia. *Address:* Belgacom, 177 boulevard Emile Jacqmain, 1030 Brussels, Belgium (Office). *Telephone:* (2) 202-41-11 (Office). *Fax:* (2) 203-54-93 (Office). *E-mail:* about@belgacom.be (Office). *Website:* www.belgacom.be (Office).

BELLINGHAM, Alastair John, CBE, FRCP, FRCPE, FRCPath; British professor of haematology; b. 27 March 1938, London; m. Valerie Jill Morford 1963 (died 1997); three s.; ed Tiffin Boys' School, Univ. Coll. Hosp. Medical School, London; Sr Lecturer, Hon. Consultant Haematology Dept, Univ. Coll. Hosp. Medical School 1971; Prof. of Haematology Univ. of Liverpool 1974, King's Coll., Univ. of London 1984–97; Pres. British Soc. for Haematology 1992–93, Royal Coll. of Pathologists 1993–96; Chair. Nat. Health Service Information Authority 1999–. *Publications:* numerous publs on red cell physiology and biochemistry, inherited red cell abnormalities, sickle cell disease. *Leisure interests:* photography, wine and viticulture. *Address:* Broadstones, The Street, Teffont Magna, Salisbury, Wilts., SP3 5QP, England. *Telephone:* (1722) 716267. *E-mail:* savage@teffont.freeservcer.co.uk (Home).

BELLINI, Mario; Italian architect; fmrly designer for Olivetti office machines; commissions include: Tokyo Design Centre, Sakurada Dori Dist, Villa Erba Int. Congress and Exhbn Centre, Cernobbio on Lake Como, Exhbn bldgs. for Milan Trade Fair. *Exhibitions include:* The Renaissance from Brunelleschi to Michelangelo—The Representation of Architecture, Venice 1994, Paris 1995, Berlin 1995. *Address:* c/o Architecture Centre, 66 Portland Place, London W.1, England.

BELLOCH JULBE, Juan Alberto; Spanish politician; b. 3 Feb. 1950, Mora de Rubielos (Teruel); m.; one s.; mem. Democratic Justice; Founder, Asscn of Judges for Democracy, Asscn des Magistrats Européens pour la démocratie et les libertés; founder and Pres. Asscn for the Human Rights of the Basque Country; Judge, La Gomera, Berga Vic y Alcoy from 1975; Magistrate and Pres. Court of Justice of Biscay 1981–90; mem. Gen. Council of Judiciary 1990–93; Minister of Justice 1993–96, of the Interior 1994–96. *Address:* c/o PSOE, Ferraz 68 y 70, 28008 Madrid, Spain. *Telephone:* (91) 5820444. *Fax:* (91) 5820422.

BELLOW, Saul, BS; American writer and university professor; b. 10 June 1915, Québec, Canada; s. of Abraham Bellow and Liza (née Gordon) Bellow; m. 1st Anita Goshkin 1937 (divorced); one s.; m. 2nd Alexandra Tschacbasov 1956 (divorced); one s.; m. 3rd Susan Glassman 1961 (divorced); one s.; m. 4th Alexandra Ionesco Tuleca 1974 (divorced); m. 5th Janis Freedman 1989; one d.; ed Northwestern Univ.; Prof., Univ. of Minn. 1946–48; Prof. Princeton Univ. 1952–53; Prof. Univ. of Chicago 1964–; Prof. Boston Univ. 1993–; mem. Faculty, Boston Univ.; mem. Comm. on Social Thought 1963–; Ford Foundation Grant 1959; Fellow, American Acad. of Arts and Sciences; Nat. Book Award, Inst. of Arts and Letters 1953, Prix Int. de Littérature 1965, US Nat. Book Award for The Adventures of Augie March 1954, Herzog 1965, Mr. Sammler's Planet 1971, Pulitzer Prize for Humboldt's Gift 1976, Nobel Prize for Literature 1976; Commdr, Légion d'honneur; Malaparte Literary Award 1984, Nat. Medal of Arts 1988, Nat. Book Foundation Medal 1990, Lifetime Cultural Achievement Award, YIVO Inst. for Jewish Research 1996. *Publications:* include contribs to numerous magazines and journals; also Dangling Man 1944, The Victim 1947, The Adventures of Augie March 1953, Seize the Day 1956, Henderson the Rain King 1959, Herzog 1964, Mosby's Memoirs and Other Stories 1968, Mr. Sammler's Planet 1969, Humboldt's Gift 1975, To Jerusalem and Back: A Personal Account (non-fiction) 1976, The Dean's December 1981, Him with His Foot in His Mouth and Other Stories 1984, More Die of Heartbreak 1987, A Theft (novella) 1989, The Bellarosa Connection (novella) 1989, Something to Remember Me By 1991, Occasional Pieces 1993, It All Adds Up (essays) 1994, The Actual 1997, Ravelstein (novel) 2000, Collected Stories 2001. *Address:* University Professors, 745 Commonwealth Avenue, Boston, MA 02215, USA.

BELLUGI, Piero; Italian conductor; b. 14 July 1924, Florence; s. of Mario Bellugi and Giulia Favilli; m. Ursula Herzberger 1954 (divorced); five c.; ed Conservatorio Cherubini, Florence, Accad. Chigiana, Siena, Akad. des Mozarteums, Salzburg and Tanglewood, Mass., USA; Musical Dir Oakland (Calif.) and Portland (Ore.) Symphony Orchs. 1955–61; Perm. Conductor, Radio Symphony Orchestras, Turin 1967; Prof. courses for orchestral players and conductor, Italian Youth Orchestra 1981–; Guest Conductor, La Scala, Milan (début 1961), Vienna State Opera, Rome Opera, Aix-en-Provence Festival, Berlin Radio, Paris, Rome S. Cecilia, Chicago, San Francisco Operas, etc.; Hon. mem. Nat. Acad. Luigi Cherubini of Music, Letters and Arts. *Address:* Via della Montagnola, 50027 Strada in Chianti, Florence, Italy. *Telephone:* (55) 858556. *Fax:* (55) 858556. *E-mail:* pierobellugi@tin.it (Home).

BELMONDO, Jean-Paul; French actor; b. 9 April 1933, Neuilly-sur-Seine; s. of Paul Belmondo and Madeline Rainaud-Richard; m. 1959 (divorced 1967); one s. two d. (one deceased); ed Ecole Alsacienne, Paris, Cours Pascal and Conservatoire nat. d'art dramatique; started career on the stage; mainly film actor since 1957; Pres. French Union of Actors 1963–66; Pres. Annabel Productions 1981–; Dir Théâtre des Variétés 1991; Officier Légion d'honneur, Chevalier, Ordre nat. du Mérite, des Arts et des Lettres; Prix Citron 1972. *Plays acted in include:* L'hôtel du libre-échange, Oscar, Trésor-Party, Médée, La mégère apprivoisée, Kean 1987, Cyrano de Bergerac 1990, Tailleur pour Dames 1993, La Puce à l'oreille 1996, Frédérick ou le boulevard du crime 1998. *Films acted in include:* Sois belle et tais-toi, A pied, à cheval et en voiture, les Tricheurs, Charlotte et son Jules, Drôle de dimanche 1958, Les Copains du dimanche, Mademoiselle Ange, A double tour, Classe tous risques, Au bout de souffle, L'Amour, La Novice, La Ciociara, Moderato Cantabile, Léon Morin Prêtre, Le Doulos 1962, Dragées au poivre, L'Aîné des Ferchaux, Peau de banane, 100,000 dollars au soleil 1963, Two Women, The Man From Rio, Echappement libre 1964, Les tribulations d'un Chinois en Chine, Pierrot le Fou 1965, Paris, brûle-t-il? 1966, Le Voleur 1966, Casino Royale 1967, The Brain 1969, La Sirène du Mississippi 1969, Un Homme qui me plaît 1970, Borsalino 1970, The Burglars 1972, La Scoumoune 1972, L'Héritier 1972, Le Magnifique 1973, Stavisky 1974, Peur sur la ville 1975, L'Incorrigible 1975, L'Alpageur, Le corps de mon ennemi 1976, L'Animal 1977, Flic ou Voyou 1979, L'As de as (also produced) 1982, Le Marginal 1983, Joyeuses Pâques, Les Morfalous 1984, Hold-up 1985, Le Solitaire 1987, Itinéraire d'un enfant gâté (César for Best Actor 1988), L'Inconnu dans la Maison 1992, Les Cent et une Nuits 1995, Les Misérables 1995, Désiré 1996, Une chance sur deux 1998, Peut-être 1999, Les Acteurs 2000, Amazone 2000. *Publication:* 30 Ans et 25 Films (autobiog.) 1963. *Address:* Artmédia, 20 avenue Ropp, 75007 Paris (Office); Théâtre des Variétés, 7 blvd Montmartre, 75002 Paris, France.

BELNAP, Nuel, PhD; American professor of philosophy; b. 1 May 1930, Evanston, Ill.; s. of Nuel Dinsmore and Elizabeth (Dafter) Belnap; m. 1st Joan Gohde 1953; m. 2nd Gillian Hirth 1982; four c.; m. 3rd Birgit Herbeck 1997; ed Univ. of Illinois, Yale Univ.; instructor in Philosophy, then Asst Prof., Yale Univ. 1958–63; Assoc. Prof. of Philosophy, Univ. of Pittsburgh 1963–66, Prof. 1966–, Alan Ross Anderson Distinguished Prof. of Philosophy 1984–, Prof. of Sociology 1967–80, of History and Philosophy of Science 1971, of Intelligent Systems 1988–93; Visiting Prof. of Philosophy, Univ. of Calif. at Irvine 1973; Visiting Fellow, Australian Nat. Univ., Canberra 1976; Visiting Oscar R. Ewing Prof. of Philosophy, Indiana Univ. 1977, 1978, 1979; Visiting Leibniz-Prof., Zentrum für Höhere Studien 1996; mem. several editorial bds.; Sterling Jr Fellow 1955–56; Fulbright Fellow 1957–58; Morse Research Fellow 1962–63; Guggenheim Fellow 1975–76; Fellow Center for Advanced Studies in Behavioral Science 1982–83; Hon. DPhil (Leipzig) 2000. *Publications:* Computer Programs Bindex Tester 1976; The Logic of Questions and Answers (co-author) 1976, Entailment: The Logic of Relevance and Necessity (co-author) (Vol. I) 1975, (Vol. II) 1992, The Revision Theory of Truth (co-author) 1993, Facing the Future: Agents and Choices in Our Indeterministic World (co-author) 2001. *Address:* Department of Philosophy, University of Pittsburgh, Fifth Avenue, Pittsburgh, PA 15260 (Office); 5803 Ferree Street, Pittsburgh, PA 15217, USA (Home). *Telephone:* (412) 624-5777 (Office); (412) 521-3897 (Home). *Fax:* (412) 624-5377 (Office).

BĚLOHLÁVEK, Jiří; Czech musician and conductor; b. 24 Feb. 1946, Prague; m. Anna Fejérová 1971; two d.; ed Acad. of Performing Arts, Prague; Conductor, Orchestra Puellarum Pragensis (a chamber orchestra), Prague 1967–72; lectureship with Czech Philharmonic Orchestra 1970–71; Conductor, State Philharmonic Orchestra, Brno 1972–77; Chief Conductor, Prague Symphony Orchestra 1977–89; Conductor, Int. Philharmonic Youth Orchestra, Prague 1987–; Conductor, Czech Philharmonic 1981–90, Prin. Conductor and Music Dir 1990–92; freelance conductor 1993–; Founder and Music Dir Prague Philharmonia 1994–; Principal Guest Conductor BBC Symphony Orchestra 1995–2000, Principal Guest Conductor Nat. Theatre Prague 1998–; Prof. Acad. of Music, Prague 1995–; concert performances in many countries; many recordings for Czechoslovak Radio, TV; Supraphon

Prize 1977, Artist of Merit 1986, Supraphon Golden Disc 1986, 1987, 1994, 1999, Diapason d'Or 1992, Barclay Theatre Award 2000, Medal for Merit, Prague 2001. *Leisure interests:* gardening, hiking. *Address:* Philharmonia Prague, Krocinova 1, 110 00 Prague 1, Czech Republic. *Telephone:* (2) 24232488 (Office); 57960172. *Fax:* 57960173. *E-mail:* jiri.belohlavek@bon.cz (Home).

BELOTSERKOVSKY, Oleg Mikhailovich; Russian mathematician; b. 29 Aug. 1925, Livni, Orlov Region; m.; two c.; ed Lomonosov Moscow State Univ.; Sr Researcher, Applied Math. Div. and Computing Centre, USSR (now Russian) Acad. of Sciences 1953–76, Head of Computer Centre 1976; Rector Moscow Inst. of Physics and Tech. 1962–87; Corresp. mem. USSR (now Russian) Acad. of Sciences 1972, mem. 1979, Chair. Scientific Council on Cybernetics; Dir Inst. of Computer-Aided Design 1987–; mem. Int. Acad. of Astronautic Fed.; Order of the Red Banner of Labour 1965, 1975, 1981, Order of the October Revolution 1971, Order of Lenin 1985, Order of Merit to the Fatherland (3rd Degree) 1999N. Zhukovsky Prize and Gold Medal 1962, Lenin Prize 1966, S. Korolev Medal 1978. *Publications include:* Flow Past Blunt in Supersonic Flow—Theoretical and Experimental Results 1967, Numerical Methods in Fluid Dynamics 1976, The 'Coarse-Particle' Method in Gas Dynamics 1982, Numerical Modelling in Mechanics of Continuous Media 1984, Computational Mechanics: Contemporary Problems and Results 1991, Mathematical Modelling of Myocardial Infarction 1993, Computational Experiment in Turbulence: From Order to Chaos 1997, Turbulence and Instabilities 1999. *Leisure interests:* tennis, swimming. *Address:* Institute for Computer-Aided Design, Russian Academy of Sciences, 2 Brestskaya str. 19/18, 123056 Moscow, Russia. *Telephone:* (095) 250-02-62 (Office). *Fax:* (095) 250-95-54. *E-mail:* icad.ran@g23.relcom.ru.

BELOUS, Oleg Nikolayevich; Russian diplomatist; b. 18 Aug. 1951; ed Moscow Inst. of Int. Relations; on staff USSR (later Russian) Ministry of Foreign Affairs 1973–; Counsellor, Russian Embassy to Belgium 1991–94; Deputy Dir First European Dept 1994–96; Dir Dept of All-European Co-operation 1996–98; Perm. Rep. of Russia to OSCE, Vienna 1998–2001; Dir First European Dept, Ministry of Foreign Affairs 2001–. *Address:* Ministry of Foreign Affairs, Cadovaya-Sennaya 32/34, Moscow, Russia (Office).

BELOV, Vasiliy Ivanovich; Russian writer; b. 23 Oct. 1932, Timonikha, Vologda; m.; one d.; fmr mem. CPSU and USSR Union of Writers; worked on kolkhoz, received industrial training at a FZO school, then as a joiner and mechanic; served in Soviet Army; staff writer on regional newspaper 'Kommunar' in Gryazovets (Vologda) 1950s; secondary ed. (evening classes) 1956–59; Ed. Literary Inst. of Union of Writers 1959–64; People's Deputy of USSR 1989–91, mem. USSR Supreme Soviet 1989–91; USSR State Prize 1981. *Publications include:* My Village in the Forest 1961, Hot Summer 1963, Tisha and Grisha 1966, Carpenter Stories 1968 (English trans. 1969), An Ordinary Affair 1969, Village Tales 1971, Day after Day 1972, The Hills 1973, Looks can Kiss 1975, On the Eve 1972–87, All is Ahead 1986. *Address:* Maltseva ul. 19, Apt. 26, 160001 Vologda, Russia. *Telephone:* (81722) 2-94-65.

BELSHAW, Cyril Shirley, PhD, FRSC; Canadian anthropologist, writer and publisher; b. 3 Dec. 1921, Waddington, NZ; s. of Horace Belshaw and Marion L. S. (née McHardie) Belshaw; m. Betty J. Sweetman 1943 (deceased); one s. one d.; ed Auckland Univ. Coll. and Victoria Coll., Wellington (Univ. of New Zealand), London School of Econs; Dist Officer and Deputy Commr for Western Pacific, British Solomon Islands 1943–46; Sr Research Fellow, Australian Nat. Univ. 1950–53; Prof. Univ. of British Columbia 1953–86, Prof. Emer. 1986–; Dir Regional Training Centre for UN Fellows, Van. 1961–62; Ed. Current Anthropology 1974–84; mem. numerous UNESCO comms., working parties and consultancy groups; Pres. Int. Union of Anthropological and Ethnological Sciences 1978–83, XIth Int. Congress of Anthropological and Ethnological Sciences 1983; Exec. American Anthropological Assoc. 1969–70; Chair. Standing Cttee Social Sciences and Humanities Pacific Science Assn 1968–76; Hon. Life mem. Royal Anthropological Inst. 1978, Pacific Science Assn 1981; Ed. The Anthroglobe Journal 1998–2000; Propr Webzines of Vancouver; Man. Ed. EVE-Enjoy Vancouver Electronically 1997–, www.anthropologising.ca 2001–; Hon. Life Fellow Royal Anthropoligcal Inst., Pacific Science Assn, Assn for the Social Anthropology of Oceania. *Publications:* Island Administration in the South West Pacific 1950, Changing Melanesia 1954, In Search of Wealth 1955, The Great Village 1957, The Indians of British Columbia (with others) 1958, Under the Ivi Tree 1964, Anatomy of a University 1964, Traditional Exchange and Modern Markets (eds. in 5 languages) 1965, The Conditions of Social Performance 1970, Towers Besieged 1974, The Sorcerer's Apprentice 1976, The Complete Good Dining Guide to Restaurants in Greater Vancouver 1984, Where is Utopia – Controlling Social Evolution (online) 2000. *Leisure interests:* gardening, photography, travel, restaurants. *Address:* Suite 2901, 969 Richards Street, Vancouver, BC, V6B 1A8, Canada. *Telephone:* (604) 739-8130. *E-mail:* edit@evevancouver.ca (Office), cbelshaw@telus.net (Home). *Website:* www.evevancouver.ca; www.anthropologising.ca.

BELSTEAD, 2nd Baron (cr. 1938); **John Julian Ganzoni,** Bt, PC, JP, MA; British politician; b. 30 Sept. 1932; s. of 1st Baron Belstead and of the late Gwendolen Gertrude Turner; ed Eton Coll. and Christ Church, Oxford; Parl. Under-Sec. of State Dept of Educ. and Science 1970–73, N Ireland Office 1973–74, Home Office 1979–82, Minister of State FCO 1982–83, Ministry of Agric., Fisheries and Food 1983–87, Dept of Environment 1987–88; Lord Privy Seal and Leader of the House of Lords 1988–90; sits as Lord Ganzoni

in the House of Lords 1999–; Paymaster Gen. NI Office 1990–92; Chair. The Parole Bd 1992–97; Chair. Assen Governing Bodies of Public Schools 1974–79; JP, Borough of Ipswich 1962; DL, Suffolk 1979, Lord-Lt of Suffolk 1994–2002. *Leisure interests:* lawn tennis, sailing, skiing. *Address:* House of Lords, London, SW1A 0PW, England. *Telephone:* (20) 7219-3000.

BELTRÁN, Washington; Uruguayan newspaper executive and former politician; b. 6 April 1914, Montevideo; s. of Washington Beltrán and Elena Mullin de Beltrán; m. Esther Storace Arrosa de Beltrán 1943; three s. three d.; ed Univ. de la República; joined El País 1939, Sub-Dir 1949–61, Co-Dir 1961–; mem. House of Reps. 1946, 1955; f. Reconstrucción Blanca and Unión Blanca Democrática groups, both within Partido Nacional; elected Senator 1959, 1967, 1971; mem. Consejo Nacional de Gobierno 1962–67, Pres. of Uruguay 1965–66; proscribed by mil. Govt 1973–80; since 1980 has dedicated most of time to journalism, especially editorials (collected in a book 1985); attended UNICEF World Conf. 1982; Amb. Plenipotentiary to Vatican and companion to Pope on his visit to Uruguay 1987; mem. Bd of Dirs. Inter-American Press Assen 1998–2001; Pres. Sino-Uruguayan Foundation; Círculo de Tenis de Montevideo; numerous decorations from many countries. *Publication:* Pamperada Blanca 1990. *Address:* El País, Plaza Cagancha 1162, 11100 Montevideo, Uruguay. *Telephone:* (2) 9011929. *Fax:* (2) 9020632.

BELTRÃO, Alexandre Fontana; Brazilian coffee executive; b. 28 April 1924, Curitiba, Paraná; s. of the late Alexandre Beltrão and of Zilda Fontana Beltrão; m. Anna Emilia Beltrão 1964; two c.; ed Instituto Santa Maria, Curitiba, Univ. de São Paulo, Escola Nacional de Engenharia, Rio de Janeiro; Asst engineer 1944; army officer 1945–46; Asst engineer, Dept of Soil Mechanics, Inst. de Pesquisas Tecnológicas, São Paulo 1948; trained in regional planning at Inst. Nat. d'Aerophotogrametrie, Ministère de la Reconstruction, Paris and at Ministry of Works, London 1950–51; founder and Dir of SPL (Planning Services Ltd) 1954–; observer, Govt of State of Paraná to UN Int. Coffee Conf. 1962; special adviser to Pres. Brazilian Coffee Inst. 1964; Chief Brazilian Coffee Inst. Bureau, NY 1965–67; Pres. World Coffee Promotion Cttee of Int. Coffee Org. 1965–67; Exec. Dir Int. Coffee Org. 1968–94; Sec. of Science and Tech., Paraná 1994–; Commdr Order of Rio Branco. *Publications:* Paraná and the Coffee Economy 1963, essay on Economy of States of Paraná, Pará and Ceará (Brazil) 1958.

BELYAKOV, Rostislav Apollosovich, DTechSci; Russian mechanical scientist; b. 4 March 1919; m. Lyudmila Nikolayevna Shvernik; one s.; ed Ordzhonikidze Aviation Inst., Moscow; mem. CPSU 1944–91; leading positions as engineer and designer 1941–57; deputy gen. designer ANPK "MIG" 1957–71, gen. designer 1971–98, gen. design adviser 1998–; Corresp. mem. of USSR (now Russian) Acad. of Sciences 1974, mem. 1981–; Deputy to USSR Supreme Soviet 1974–89; A. N. Tupolev Gold Medal; Hero of Socialist Labour 1971, 1982, USSR State Prize 1952, 1989, Lenin Prize 1972. *Publications:* papers on aircraft construction. *Address:* RSK "MIG", Leningradskoye Sh. 6, 125299 Moscow, Russia. *Telephone:* (095) 155-23-10. *Fax:* (095) 943-00-27.

BELYAYEV, Spartak Timofeyevich, DrSc; Russian physicist; b. 27 Oct. 1923, Moscow; m.; two c.; ed Moscow State Univ.; Jr research worker, Head of Laboratory, I. Kurchatov Inst. of Nuclear Energy 1952–62; Inst. of Nuclear Physics, Siberian Dept, Acad. of Sciences 1962–78; Head of Dept, Kurchatov Inst. 1980–; Prof., Rector, Novosibirsk State Univ. 1965; Corresp. mem. USSR (now Russian) Acad. of Sciences 1964–68, mem. 1968–; mem. CPSU 1943–91. *Publications:* scientific works in field of theory of atomic nucleus, particle movement in cyclotron, physics of relativistic plasma, statistic physics of quantum, many body systems. *Address:* Russian Scientific Centre, Kurchatov Institute, Kurchatova str. 46, D-182 Moscow, Russia (Office). *Fax:* (095) 196-92-06 (Office).

BELZA, Svyatoslav Igorevich; Russian literary and music critic; b. 26 April 1942, Chelyabinsk; s. of Igor Belza and Zoya Gulinskaya; divorced; two s.; ed Moscow State Univ.; researcher Inst. of World Literature USSR (now Russian) Acad. of Sciences 1965–; Founder and reviewer TV programme Music on TV 1988–97; Man. and Artistic Dir TV programme Music on TV 1995–97; actively works as literary critic and TV broadcaster; mem. Russian Union of Writers; mem. Acad. of Russian Art, Acad. of Russian TV; Officer Cross of Merit (Poland) 1998, Order of St Nicholas (Ukraine) 1998, Order of Friendship (Russia) 2001; Merited Master of Arts, Golden Sign of Honour 1999, Irina Arkhipova Foundation Prize 2001. *Publications include:* Homo legens 1983, 1990 and over 300 literary works and reviews. *Leisure interests:* reading, travel. *Address:* Stroiteley str. 4, korp. 7, Apt 9, Moscow 117311, Russia (Home). *Telephone:* (095) 930-36-61 (Home). *Fax:* (095) 930-36-61 (Home).

BEM, Pavel; Czech politician; m.; two s.; ed Charles Univ., Prague and post-grad. studies in USA; specialized in psychiatry working with drug addicts; headed Govt's anti-drug comm. for three years; mem. Civic Democratic Party (ODS); fmr Mayor of Prague 6; elected Mayor of Prague Nov. 2002–. *Address:* Lord Mayor's Office of Prague, Mariánské náměstí 2, 110 00 Prague 1 – Staré Město, Czech Republic (Office). *Telephone:* (2) 24482633 (Office).

BEN ALI, Mohamed; Tunisian actor, writer and producer; b. 17 Feb. 1932, Tunis; m. 1957; one s. four d.; f. Groupe Théâtral Radio Tunisienne 1952–, Groupe Théâtre Populaire 1954–; Deputy Mayor of Ezzahra 1980–82; Municipal Councillor 1985–90; Dir Festival of Ezzahra 1987–90; mem. Assen Tunisienne Droit d'Auteur et Compositeur, Union des Acteurs Professionels;

various awards from Ministry of Culture and Asscn Audio-Visuelle. *Leisure interests:* reading, travel. *Address:* 10 rue Gabes, 2034 Ezzahra, Tunisia. *Telephone:* 451888, 388941.

BEN-AMI, Shlomo, PH.D; Israeli politician; b. 1943, Morocco; m.; three c.; ed Tel-Aviv Univ., Oxford Univ.; Head of School of History of Tel-Aviv Univ. 1982–86; Amb. to Spain 1987–91; mem. Knesset 1996–; fmr mem. Foreign Affairs and Defense Cttee; Minister of Public Security 1999–2001. *Publications:* several books in English, Spanish and Hebrew. *Address:* c/o Ministry of Public Security, P.O. Box 18182, Bldg No. 3, Kiryat Hamemshala (East), Jerusalem 91181, Israel (Office).

BEN BELLA, Mohammed; Algerian politician; b. 1916; Warrant Officer in Moroccan regiment during Second World War (decorated); Chief O.A.S. rebel military group in Algeria 1947; imprisoned 1949–52 (escaped); directed Algerian nat. movement from exile in Libya 1952–56; arrested Oct. 1956; held in France 1959–62; Vice-Premier, Algerian Nationalist Provisional Govt, Tunis 1962, Leader, Algerian Political Bureau, Algeria 1962, Premier of Algeria 1962–65, Pres. of Algeria 1963–65; detained 1965–80; restricted residence, Msila 1979–80; freed 1981; returned from exile Sept. 1990; Chair. Int. Islamic Comm. for Human Rights, London 1982–; Lenin Peace Prize 1964.

BEN-DAVID, Zadok; Israeli sculptor; b. 1949, Bayhan, Yemen; s. of Moshe and Hana Ben-David; m. Dana Pugach 1991; ed Acad. of Art and Design, Jerusalem, Reading Univ. 1974–75 and St Martin's School of Art, London 1975–76; Sculpture Teacher at St Martin's School of Art 1977–82, Ravensbourne Coll. of Art and Design, Bromley 1982–85; first one-man show at Air Gallery, London 1980; represented Israel in the Biennale di Venezia, Italy 1988. *Exhibitions include:* Antwerp, London, New York, Jerusalem, Melbourne, Munich, Glasgow, Tel Aviv 1984–. *Publications:* (catalogues) Zadok Ben-David 1987, The Israeli Pavilion—The Venice Biennale 1988. *Address:* 65 Warwick Avenue, London, W9 2PP, England (Home). *Telephone:* (20) 7266-0536 (Home). *Fax:* (20) 7266-3892.

BEN-ELIEZER, Benjamin (Fuad); Israeli politician and army officer; b. 1936, Iraq; ed Israel Nat. Defence Coll.; emigrated to Israel 1949; career officer Israel Defence Forces (IDF), Commdr Six Day War 1967, served on IDF Mil. Mission to Singapore 1970–73, Commdr Yom Kippur War 1973, First CO Southern Lebanon 1977–78, Commdr Judea and Samaria 1978–81; Govt Coordinator of Activities in the Administered Areas 1983–84; Minister of Housing and Construction 1992–96; mem. Knesset 1984–, served on Foreign Affairs Cttee 1988–92; mem. Israel Labour Party, Chair. –2002; Deputy Prime Minister and Minister of Communications 1999–2001; Minister of Defence 2001–02. *Address:* c/o Ministry of Defence, Kaplan Street, Hakirya, Tel-Aviv 67659, Israel.

BEN-NATAN, Asher; Israeli diplomatist; b. 15 Feb. 1921, Vienna; s. of Nahum Natan and Berta Natan; m. Erika (Rut) Frucht 1940; one s. one d.; ed Z. P. Hayut Hebrew Coll., Vienna and Institut des Hautes Etudes Internationales, Geneva; Co-Founder and mem. Kibbutz Mederot-Zeraim 1938–44, latterly Sec. and Treas.; Political Dept, Jewish Agency 1944–45; on mission to Europe to organize rescue of Jews and illegal immigration to Palestine: attached to office of Head of Jewish Agency 1945–47; Ministry of Foreign Affairs 1948–51; studies in Geneva 1951–53; Govt Rep. on Bd of Red Sea Inkodeh Co. 1953–56, Gen. Man. 1955–56; Rep. of Ministry of Defence in Europe 1956–58; Dir-Gen. Ministry of Defence 1959–65; Amb. to FRG 1965–70, to France 1970–75; Political Adviser to Minister of Defence 1975–78; Adviser to Prime Minister on Special Affairs 1985; Amb. on Special Mission 1993; Chair. Ben-Gurion Foundation 1983–; Pres. Israel-German Asscn 1973–; Dr. hc (Ben Gurion Univ.) 1990; Hon. DPhil (Ben Gurion Univ.) 1997; Officier Légion d'honneur; Commdr Ordre nat. (Ivory Coast); Commdr Ordre de l'Etoile équatoriale (Gabon); Louis Waiss Peace Prize 1974, Heinz Galinski Prize (Berlin) 1992; Grosses Bundesverdienstorden (Germany) 2000; Grosses Verdienstkreuz mit Mand (Germany). *Publications:* Briefe an den Botschafter 1970, Dialogue avec des Allemands 1973. *Address:* 11 Mapu Street, Tel Aviv 63377, Israel (Office); 89 Haim Levanon Street, Tel Aviv 69345, Israel. *Telephone:* (3) 527-8069 (Office); (3) 641-3398. *Fax:* (3) 527-0106 (Office).

BENACERRAF, Baruj; American (b. Venezuelan) professor emeritus of pathology; b. 29 Oct. 1920, Caracas, Venezuela; m. Annette Dreyfus 1943; one d.; ed Lycée Janson, Paris, Columbia Univ., New York, Medical Coll. of Virginia; Internship, Queens General Hosp., New York 1945–46; army service 1946–48; Research Fellow Dept of Microbiology, Coll. of Physicians and Surgeons, Columbia Univ., NY 1948–50; Chargé de Recherches, CNRS, Hôpital Broussais, Paris 1950–56; Asst Prof. of Pathology, New York Univ. School of Medicine 1956–58, Assoc. Prof. of Pathology 1958–60, Prof. of Pathology 1960–68; Chief, Lab. of Immunology, Nat. Inst. of Allergy and Infectious Diseases, Nat. Insts. of Health, Bethesda, Md 1968–70; Fabyan Prof. of Comparative Pathology and Chair. Dept of Pathology, Harvard Medical School, Boston, Mass. 1970–91; mem. Immunology "A" Study Section, Nat. Insts. of Health 1965–69; Scientific Advisor World Health Org. for Immunology; Trustee and mem. Scientific Advisory Bd, Trudeau Foundation 1970–77; mem. Scientific Advisory Bd Mass. General Hosp. 1971–74; mem. Bd of Govs. Weizmann Inst. of Science; Chair. Scientific Advisory Cttee, Centre d'Immunologie de Marseille, CNRS-INSERM; Pres. American Asscn of Immunologists 1973–74; Pres. Fed. of American Socs. for Experimental Biology 1974–75; Pres. Dana-Farber Cancer Inst., Boston, Mass. 1980–92; Pres. Int. Union of Immunological Socs.; Fellow, American Acad. of Arts and Sciences; mem. American Asscn of Immunologists, American Asscn of Pathologists and Bacteriologists, American Soc. for Experimental Pathology, Soc. for Experimental Biology and Medicine, British Asscn for Immunology, French Soc. of Biological Chemistry, Harvey Soc., New York Acad. of Sciences, American Acad. of Sciences, Inst. of Medicine; Rabbi Shai Shacknai Prize in Immunology and Cancer Research (Hebrew Univ. of Jerusalem) 1974, T. Duckett Jones Memorial Award, Helen Hay Whitney Foundation 1976, Nobel Prize for Physiology or Medicine 1980, Nat. Medal of Science 1990. *Address:* 111 Perkins Street, Boston, MA 02130, USA.

BENACHENHOU, Mourad, M.ECON., D.SOC.; Algerian economist and government minister; b. 30 July 1938, Tlemcen; s. of the late Mohammed Benachenhou and Rostane Hiba; m. Norya Berbar 1962; two s. one d.; ed Univ. D'Alger, Univ. de Bordeaux, Univ. of Maryland; Officer Nat. Liberation Army 1956–62; Adviser, Ministry of Agric. 1965–66; Dir Nat. Agronomic Inst., Algiers 1966–78; Dir Higher Ed. 1971–78; Dir Centre of Research on Agronomy 1978–82; Perm. Sec. Ministry of Finance 1982–90; int. consultant 1990–93; Minister of Econ. Affairs 1993–94, of Industrial Restructuring and Participation 1994–96, of Industry 1996; Exec. Dir World Bank 1982; Médaille de la Résistance. *Publications:* Higher Education in Algeria 1976, The Future of the University 1979, Debt and Democracy 1992, Inflation and Devaluation 1993. *Leisure interests:* tennis, chess, computers, reading, writing. *Address:* c/o Ministry of Industry, Le Colisée, Rue Roccas, Algiers, Algeria.

BENAISSA, Muhammad, BA; Moroccan politician; b. 3 Jan. 1937, Asilah; m. Laila Hajoun-Benaissa; five c.; ed Univ. of Minn., Columbia Univ., USA; Press Attaché, Perm. Mission of Morocco to UN, New York 1964–65; Information Officer, UN Dept of Information, 1965–67; Regional Information Adviser, FAO, Rome 1967–71, Head of Devt Support Communication 1971–73, Asst to Dir of Information 1973–74, Dir of Information Div. 1974–76; Asst Sec.-Gen. of UN, World Food Conf. 1975; elected to City Council of Asilah 1976–83, elected Mayor 1992; mem. Moroccan Parl. 1977–83; Co-Founder and Exec. Mem. Moroccan Social Democratic Party (Rassemblement Nat. des Independents) 1978; Consultant UNDP, IFAD, UNFPA 1978–85; Chief Ed. Al-Mithak Al-Watani and Al-Maghrab publs 1980–85; apptd Amb. to USA 1993; Minister of Foreign Affairs and Co-operation 1999–. *Publications include:* Grains de Peau 1974. *Address:* Ministry of Foreign Affairs and Co-operation, ave Franklin Roosevelt, Rabat, Morocco (Office). *Telephone:* (3) 7761583 (Office). *Fax:* (3) 7765508 (Office). *E-mail:* benaissa@maec.gov.ma (Office). *Website:* www.maec.gov.ma (Office).

BENAKIS, Anna, DJur; Greek politician and professor of criminal law; b. 12 Dec. 1934, Athens; m. Linos Benakis 1957; ed Pierce Coll. of Athens and Univs. of Athens and Bonn; Asst, Asst Prof., Univ. of Athens, Univ. of Bonn, Max-Planck Inst. for Int. Criminal Law, Freiburg 1962–78; Consultant on Higher Educ. to Ministry of Educ. 1975–77, 1980–81; mem. Legal Comms. of Ministry of Justice 1977–81; mem. foreign teaching staff, Temple Univ., Philadelphia 1981–85; now Prof. of Criminal Law, Univ. of Athens; mem. Parl. 1981–; Speaker on legal and educ. matters, Nea Democratia Party 1981–89; Alt. Minister of Educ. 1989; Alt. Minister of Culture 1991; Minister of Culture 1991; Minister of Justice 1992–93; Vice-Pres. Greek Soc. for Criminal Law 1988–. *Publications:* four books and several articles on criminal matters; political articles. *Leisure interests:* water skiing, swimming, classical music, literature. *Address:* Skoufa 75, 10680 Athens (Office); Sina 58, 10672 Athens, Greece (Home). *Telephone:* 3602634, 3602863 (Office); 3636818 (Home). *Fax:* 3602633 (Office); 3645179 (Home).

BÉNARD, André Pierre Jacques; French business executive; b. 19 Aug. 1922, Draveil, Essone; s. of Marcel Bénard and Lucie Thalmann; m. Jacqueline Preiss 1946; one s.; ed Lycée Janson-de-Sailly, Lycée Georges Clémenceau, Nantes, Lycée Thiers, Marseilles, Ecole Polytechnique, Paris; joined Royal Dutch/Shell Group 1946; with Société Anonyme des Pétroles Jupiter 1946–49; Shell Petroleum Co. Ltd, London 1949–50; Head of Bitumen Services, Société des Pétroles Shell Berre 1950–58, Head Nat. Activities Dept 1958–59; Asst Dir-Gen. Société pour l'Utilisation Rationnelle des Gaz 1960–61, Pres. Dir-Gen. 1962–64; Marketing Man. Shell Française 1964–67, Pres. Man. Dir 1967–70; Regional Co-ordinator Europe 1970; Dir Shell Petroleum N.V. 1970; Dir The Shell Petroleum Co. Ltd 1970, Barclays Bank SA, Paris 1989–; Man. Dir Royal Dutch Petroleum Co. 1971–83, mem. Supervisory Bd 1983–; Admin. Royal Dutch 1983–, INSEAD 1983–, La Radiotechnique 1983–; Hon. Pres., French Chamber of Commerce and Industry, in the Netherlands 1980–; Jt Chair. Eurotunnel 1986–90, Pres. Admin. Council 1990–94; Prix Descartes 1982, Médaille des Evadés, Médaille de la Résistance; Chevalier de l'Ordre nat. du Mérite, Commdr Légion d'honneur, Commdr Order of Orange Nassau, Chevalier du Mérite agricole; Hon. KBE. *Leisure interest:* golf.

BÉNASSY, Jean-Pascal, PhD; French economist and researcher; b. 30 Dec. 1948, Paris; s. of Jean Bénassy and Jeannine Bénassy; ed Ecole Normale Supérieure, Paris, Univ. of Berkeley, California, USA; research assoc. CEPREMAP 1973–; Dir of Research CNRS 1981–; Dir Laboratoire d'Economie Politique, Ecole Normale Supérieure 1984–88; Dept of Econs Ecole Polytechnique 1987–2002; Fellow Econometric Soc. 1981, mem. Council 1990–92; Guido Zerilli Marimo Prize, Acad. des Sciences Morales et Politiques 1990. *Publications:* The Economics of Market Disequilibrium 1982, Macroéconomie et théorie du déséquilibre 1984, Macroeconomics: An Introduction to the Non-Walrasian Approach 1986, Macroeconomics and Imperfect Competition 1995, The Macroeconomics of Imperfect Competition and Non-clearing Markets: A Dynamic General Equilibrium Approach 2002, numerous articles in specialized journals. *Address:* CEPREMAP, 142 rue du Chevaleret, 75013 Paris, France. *Telephone:* 1-40-77-84-62. *Fax:* 1-44-24-38-57. *E-mail:* jean-pascal.benassy@cepremap.cnrs.fr.

BENAUD, Richard ('Richie'), OBE; Australian cricketer and sports commentator; b. 6 Oct. 1930; s. of Louis Richard and Irene Benaud; m. Daphne Elizabeth Surfleet 1967; two s. by previous marriage; ed Parramatta High School; right-hand middle-order batsman and right-arm leg-break and googly bowler; played for New South Wales 1948–49 to 1963–64 (Capt. 1958–59 to 1963); played in 63 Tests for Australia 1951–52 to 1963–64, 28 as Capt., scoring 2,201 runs (average 24.4) including 3 hundreds, taking 248 wickets (average 27.0); first to score 2,000 runs and take 200 wickets in Tests; scored 11,719 runs (23 hundreds) and took 945 wickets in first-class cricket; toured England 1953, 1956 and 1961; int. sports consultant; TV Commentator, BBC 1960–99, Channel Nine 1977–, Channel 4 1999–; Wisden Cricketer of the Year 1962. *Publications:* Way of Cricket 1960, Tale of Two Tests 1962, Spin Me a Spinner 1963, The New Champions 1965, Willow Patterns 1972, Benaud on Reflection 1984, The Appeal of Cricket 1995, Anything But... An Autobiography 1998. *Leisure interest:* golf. *Address:* 19/178 Beach Street, Coogee, New South Wales 2034, Australia. *Telephone:* 9664-1124.

BENBITOUR, Ahmed, MBA, PhD; Algerian politician and economist; b. 20 June 1946, Ghardaia; m.; four c.; ed Univ. of Algiers, Univ. of Montreal, Canada; fmr Prof. of Business Man., Minister of Finance (three times), of Energy, Minister Del. to Treasury, Dir Ministry of Industry, Head of Mission in Office of Pres., CEO several parastatals; Prime Minister of Algeria 1999–2000. *Publications:* several publs on econ. reforms and finance. *Address:* c/o Office of the President, el-Mouradia, Algiers, Algeria (Office).

BENDA, Ernst; German politician and lawyer; b. 15 Jan. 1925, Berlin; s. of Rudolf Benda and Lilly (Krasting) Benda; m. Waltraut Vorbau 1956; one s. one d.; ed Kant-Gymnasium, Berlin-Spandau, Humboldt Univ., Freie Univ. Berlin, Univ. of Wisconsin; war service; prisoner-of-war; Humboldt Univ. 1946–48; Freie Univ., Berlin 1948–51; Univ. of Wis. 1949–55; Dist appointment, Spandau 1951–54; mem. Berlin House of Reps. 1955–57, Bundestag 1957–71; in practice as lawyer 1956–71; Chair. Berlin Christian Democratic Union Youth Dept 1952–54; mem. Fed. Govt 1966; Under-Sec. in Interior Ministry; Minister of the Interior 1968–69; Pres. Fed. Constitutional Court, Karlsruhe 1971–83; Prof. Constitutional Law Univ. of Freiburg 1983–93; Chair. Media Council Berlin-Brandenburg 1992–; Hon. Prof., Law Faculty, Trier Univ. 1977; Hon. DJur (Würzburg Univ.) 1974; Grosses Bundesverdienstkreuz. *Publications:* Notstandsverfassung und Arbeitskampf 1963, Rechtsstaat und Verjährung 1965, Industrielle Herrschaft und sozialer Staat 1966, Die Notstandsverfassung 1966, Der Rechtsstaat in der Krise 1971, Verfassungsprozessrecht 1992. *Leisure interest:* sailing. *Address:* Käthe-Kollwitz Strasse 46, 76227 Karlsruhe, Germany. *Telephone:* (721) 404661. *Fax:* (721) 496634. *E-mail:* ernst.benda@t.online.de (Home).

BENDER, Brian Geoffrey, CB, PhD; British civil servant; b. 25 Feb. 1949; s. of the late Prof. Arnold Eric Bender; m. Penelope Clark 1974; one s. one d.; ed Imperial Coll., London Univ.; joined Dept of Trade and Industry 1973; Pvt. Sec. to Sec. of State for Trade 1976–77; First Sec., Office of Perm. Rep. to EC 1977–82; Prin., Dept of Trade and Industry 1982–84; Counsellor, Office of Perm. Rep. to EC 1985–89; Under Sec. and Deputy Head of European Secr., Cabinet Office 1990–93; Head of Regulation Devt Div., Dept of Trade and Industry 1993–94; Deputy Sec. and Head of European Secr., Cabinet Office 1994–98; Head of Public Service Delivery, Cabinet Office 1998–99; Perm. Sec. Cabinet Office 1999–2000, Ministry of Agric., Fisheries and Food 2000–01, Dept for Environment, Food and Rural Affairs 2000–. *Address:* Department for Environment, Food and Rural Affairs, Nobel House, 17 Smith Square, London, SW1P 3JR, England (Office). *Telephone:* (20) 7238-5446 (Office). *Fax:* (20) 7238-6118 (Office).

BENDJEDID, Col Chadli (see Chadli, Col Bendjedid).

BENDUKIDZE, Kakha Avtandilovich; Russian business executive; b. 20 April 1956, Tbilisi, Georgia; ed Tbilisi State Univ., Moscow State Univ.; researcher, Inst. of Biochem. and Physiology of Micro-organisms, USSR (now Russian) Acad. of Sciences 1981–; Head, Lab. of Molecular Genetics, Inst. of Biotech., USSR Ministry of Medical Industry 1985–89; Founder, mem. Bd Dirs., Bioprocess 1988–90; Gen. Man. People's Oil Investment-Industrial European-Asian Corpn NIPEK 1993–; Dir-Gen. Urals machine-construction factory 1997–; Chair. Bd Promtorgbank 1998–; mem. Presidium, All-Union Movt Businessmen for New Russia 1993–94; mem. Council on Industrial Policy and Enterprise, Govt of Russian Fed. 1994–98; mem. State Cttee on Econ. Policy and Supporting Econ. Structures 1995–98; mem. Reform-Club Interaction. *Address:* Promtorgbank M. Yermolayevsky per. 27, 103379 Moscow, Russia. *Telephone:* (095) 796-90-05 (Office).

BENEDETTI, Mario; Uruguayan writer; b. 14 Sept. 1920, Paso de los Toros, Tacuarembo; s. of Brenno Benedetti and Matilde Farrugia; m. Luz López; ed Colegio Alemán; Journalist on Marcha (weekly) and Literary, Film and Theatre Critic on El Diario, Tribuna Popular and La Mañana; visited Europe 1957, 1966–67. *Publications:* fiction: Esta mañana 1949, El último viaje y otros cuentos 1951, Quién de nosotros 1953, Montevideanos 1959, La Tregua 1963, Gracias por el Fuego 1965, La muerte y otras sorpresas 1968, Con o sin nostalgia 1977, Viento del exilio 1981, El amor, las mujeres y la vida 1995;

plays: Ustedes por ejemplo 1953, El Reportaje 1958, Ida y Vuelta 1958; poetry: La víspera indeleble 1945, Sólo mientras tanto 1950, Poemas de la Oficina 1956, Poemas del Hoyporhoy 1965, Inventario 1965, Contra los puentes levadizos 1966, A ras de sueño 1967; essays: Peripecia y novela 1948, Marcel Proust y otros ensayos 1951, Literatura uruguaya siglo XX 1963, Letras del continente mestizo 1967, Sobre artes y oficios 1968. *Leisure interests:* reading, football.

BENEŠOVÁ, Libuše, DPhil, PhD; Czech politician; b. 5 July 1948, Benešov; m. Jiří Beneš; one d.; ed Charles Univ., Prague; Mayor of Lešany 1990–92; Head Dist Council, Prague-West 1993–94; Vice-Minister of Finance 1995–97; Senator 1996–2002, Pres. of Senate 1998–2001; Gen. Man. ODS 2002–; TGM Medal of Honour 2001. *Publication:* Handbook of Municipal Administration 1994. *Leisure interests:* cooking, gardening, knitting, reading, sewing. *Address:* Sněmovní č. 3, 11000 Prague 1, Czech Republic. *Telephone:* (2) 33334800 (Office). *E-mail:* info@ods.cz. *Website:* www.ods.cz.

BENEŠOVÁ, Marie; Czech lawyer; b. 17 April 1948; Supreme State Prosecutor and Attorney-Gen. of the Czech Repub. *Address:* Office of the Attorney-General, Jezuitska 4, 66055 Brno, Czech Republic (Office). *Telephone:* (5) 42512111 (Office). *Fax:* (5) 42219621 (Office).

BENETTON, Luciano; Italian business executive; s. of Rosa Benetton; m. Maria-Teresa Benetton (separated); f. Benetton 1963, now Pres. Benetton Group; mem. Italian Senate 1992–94; awarded Civiltà Veneta 1986; Premio Creatività 1992. *Address:* Benetton Group SpA, Via Minelli, 31050 Ponzano (Treviso), Italy. *Telephone:* 4224491. *Fax:* 422449586.

BENFREHA, Ahmed; Algerian politician; b. 1940, Mascara; m.; three c.; ed Inst. Abdelhamid Ben Badis, Constantine, Univ. de la Zitouna and Univ. of Algiers; research worker Agronomie-Inst. de recherches; Chargé de mission, Ministry of Agric.; Cen. Dir Ministry of Agric.; Head of Student Cell, Nat. Liberation Front, Tunis; Deputy Nat. Popular Ass.; Sec. of State for Fishing 1980–82, Fishing and Maritime Transport 1982–84; Minister of Public Works 1984–88, Hydraulics and Forests 1988–89; mem. Central Cttee Nat. Liberation Front 1979–. *Address:* le Grand Séminaire, Kouba, Algiers, Algeria. *Telephone:* (2) 58-95-00.

BENGSTON, Billy Al (Moon Doggie, Moondoggy, Moontang, Two Moons); American artist, designer and architect; b. 7 June 1934, Dodge City, Kan.; m. Wendy Al; one d.; ed Los Angeles City Coll., Calif. Coll. of Arts & Crafts, Oakland and Otis Art Inst.; instructor Chouinard Art Inst. Los Angeles 1961; lecturer, Univ. of Calif. at Los Angeles 1962–63; Guest Artist, Univ. of Okla 1967; Guest Prof. Univ. of Colo 1969; Guest Lecturer, Univ. of Calif. at Irvine 1973; Dir Pelican Club Productions Los Angeles 1981–84; Exec. Dir Westfall Arts 1995–98; numerous one-man exhbns.; works in numerous public collections including Museum of Modern Art, New York, Whitney Museum of American Art, New York, Solomon R. Guggenheim Museum, New York, San Francisco Museum of Art, The Beaubourg, Paris; Nat. Foundation for the Arts Grant 1967; Tamarind Fellow 1968, 1982, 1987; Guggenheim Fellowship 1975; numerous art exhbns; various commissions and other awards. *Publications:* contribs to Art in America, Art Forum, Paris Review. *Address:* 110 Mildred Avenue, Venice, CA 90291 (Office); 805 Hampton Drive, Venice, CA 90291, USA. *Telephone:* (310) 450-2131 (Office). *Fax:* (310) 450-3211 (Office). *E-mail:* studio@billyalbengston.com (Office). *Website:* www.billyalbengston.com (Office).

BENGU, Sibusiso Mandlenkosi Emmanuel, PhD; South African politician; b. 8 May 1934, Kranskop; s. of Rev. Jackonia Bengu and Augusta Bengu; m. Ethel Funeka 1961; one s. four d.; Prin. Dlangezwa High School 1968–76; Publicity Sec. Natal African Teachers' Asscn 1969–71; Dir Students' Advisory Services, Univ. of Zululand 1977–78; Exec. Sec. for Research and Social Action, Lutheran World Fed., Geneva 1978–91; Rector, Vice-Chancellor Univ. of Fort Hare 1991–94; Minister of Educ. Govt of Nat. Unity 1994–99; First Gen. Sec. Inkatha Freedom Party, now mem. ANC. *Publications:* African Cultural Identity and International Relations 1975, Chasing Gods Not our Own 1975, Mirror or Model. *Address:* c/o Ministry of Education, Private Bag X603, Pretoria 0001, South Africa.

BENHABIB, Seyla, MA, PhD; Turkish professor of government; b. Istanbul; ed American Coll. for Girls, Istanbul, Brandeis and Yale Univs, USA; teacher, New School for Social Research 1991–93; Prof. of Govt and Sr Research Fellow, Center for European Studies, Harvard Univ. 1993–2000; Ed.-in-Chief Constellations: An International Journal of Critical and Democratic Theory 1994–97; Visiting Sr Fellow, Institut für Wissenschaft vom Menschen, Vienna, Austria 1996; Eugene Meyer Prof. of Political Science and Prof. of Philosophy, Yale Univ. 2000–; Baruch de Spinoza Distinguished Professorship, University of Amsterdam 2000, Russell Sage Foundation Fellow 2000–01. *Publications include:* Critique, Norm and Utopia: A Study of the Foundations of Critical Theory 1986, Situating the Self: Gender, Community and Postmodernism in Contemporary Ethics 1992, The Reluctant Modernism of Hannah Arendt 1996, Feminist Contentions: A Philosophical Exchange 1996; (as Ed.): Feminism as Critique: Essays on the Politics of Gender in Late-Capitalist Societies 1987, The Communicative Ethics Controversy (co-ed with Fred Dallmayr) 1990, On Max Horkheimer (co-ed with Wolfgang Bonss and John McCole) 1993, The Philosophical Discourses of Modernity 1996, Democracy and Difference: Changes Boundaries of the Political 1996, Transformation of Citizenship—Dilemmas of the Nation-State in the Era of Globalization 2000, The Claims of Culture—Equality and Diversity in the

Global Era 2002; (trans.): Hegel's Ontology and the Theory of Historicity by Herbert Marcuse 1987; numerous articles on social and political thought, feminist theory and the history of modern political theory. *Address:* Department of Political Science, Yale University, POB 208301, 124 Prospect Street, Rm. 211, New Haven, CT 06520, USA (Office). *Telephone:* (203) 432-5246 (Office). *Fax:* (203) 432-6196. *E-mail:* seyla.benhabib@yale.edu (Office). *Website:* www.yale.edu (Office).

BENHAMOUDA, Boualem, DIur; Algerian politician and lexicographer; b. Boualem Benhamouda, 8 March 1933, Cherchell; m.; two s. one d.; ed Algiers Univ.; served with Army of Nat. Liberation 1956–62; mem. Parl. 1962–65; Minister of Ex-Combatants 1965–70, of Justice 1970–77, of Public Works 1977–80, of the Interior 1980–82, of Finance 1982–86; mem. Political Bureau of Nat. Liberation Front (FLN) 1979–, Chair. FLN Cttee on Educ. Training and Culture 1979–80, Gen. Sec. FLN 1995–2001; responsible for the Inst. of Global Studies of Strategy (political and econ. matters) 1986–90; Medal of Liberation. *Publications:* The Keys of Arabic Language 1991, The Arabic Origin of Some Spanish Words 1991, The Democratic Practice of Power (Between Theory and Reality) 1992, Spanish-Arabic Pocket Dictionary 1993, The Arabic Origin of About 1000 French Words, General French-Arabic Dictionary 1996, General Arabic-French Dictionary 2000, 2001. *Leisure interests:* reading, studying, cultural travel, philosophy, science, languages. *Address:* Siege du Parti du FLN, Rue du Stade, Hydra, Algiers (Office); 5 Rue de Frère Zennouch, El-Biar, Algiers, Algeria (Home). *Telephone:* (2) 694296 (Office).

BENIGNI, Roberto; Italian actor, director and writer; b. 27 Oct. 1952, Misericordia, Tuscany; Dr hc (Bologna) 2002. *Films include:* Belingua ti voglio bene (actor, writer) 1977, Down by Law (actor) 1986, Tutto Benigni (actor, writer) 1986, Johnny Stecchino (Dir, actor, writer), Night on Earth (actor) 1992, Son of the Pink Panther (acted) 1993, Mostro (Dir, actor, writer), Life is Beautiful (Dir, actor, writer, Acad. Award for Best Actor and Best Foreign Film) 1998, Asterisk and Obelisk (actor) 1998, Pinocchio 2002.

BENING, Annette; American actress; b. 29 May 1958, Topeka, Kan.; m. 1st Steven White (divorced); m. 2nd Warren Beatty (q.v.) 1992; three c.; ed San Francisco State Univ.; stage appearances in works by Ibsen, Chekhov and Shakespeare in San Diego and San Francisco; other stage roles in Coastal Disturbances, The Great Outdoors; European Achievement in World Cinema Award 2000. *Films:* Valmont, The Grifters, Regarding Henry, Guilty by Suspicion, Bugsy, Love Affair, The American President, Richard III, Blue Vision, Mars Attacks!, Against All Enemies, The Siege, In Dreams, American Beauty, Forever Hollywood, What Planet Are You From? *Address:* c/o Kevin Huvane, CAA, 9830 Wilshire Boulevard, Beverly Hills, CA 90212, USA.

BENIZRI, Shlomo; Israeli politician; b. 1961, Haifa; m.; seven c.; army service; ordained as a rabbi at Or Hachaim Talmudic Coll., Jerusalem; currently Head of Talmudic Coll.; mem. Knesset 1992–; mem. Finance and Anti-Drug Abuse Cttees. 1992–96; fmr Head of Shas Knesset Faction; Deputy Minister of Health 1996–99, Minister 1999–2001; Minister of Labour and Social Welfare 2001–02. *Publication:* The Sky is Talking (astrology). *Leisure interests:* sports, computers, nature. *Address:* 2 Kaplan Street, Jerusalem (Office); c/o Ministry of Labour and Social Welfare, PO Box 915, 2 Rehov Kaplan, Kiryat Ben-Gurion, Jerusalem 91008, Israel.

BENJAMIN, George William John, FRCM; British composer, conductor and pianist; b. 31 Jan. 1960, London; s. of William Benjamin and Susan Benjamin (née Bendon); ed Westminster School, Paris Conservatoire, King's Coll., Cambridge, Institut de recherche et coordination acoustique/musique, Paris; first London orchestral performance, BBC Proms 1980; Prince Consort Prof. of Composition, RCM 1984–2001; Henry Purcell Prof. of Composition, King's Coll. London 2001–; has conducted widely in GB, Europe, USA, Australia and Far East; Prin. Guest Artist, Hallé Orchestra 1993–96; operatic conducting debut Pelléas et Mélisande, La Monnaie, Brussels 1999; Carte Blanche at Opéra Bastille, Paris 1992; founding Artistic Dir Wet Ink Festival, San Francisco Symphony Orchestra 1992, Meltdown Festival, South Bank 1993; Featured Composer, 75th Salzburg Festival 1995, Tanglewood Festival 1999; Artistic Consultant BBC Sounding the Century 1996–99; Lili Boulanger Award, USA 1985, Koussevitzky Int. Record Award 1987, Grand Prix du Disque de l'Académie Charles Cros 1987, Gramophone Contemporary Award 1990, Chevalier Ordre des Arts et des Lettres 1996, Edison Award 1998, Schönberg Prize, Deutsche Sinfonie Berlin 2002. *Publications:* orchestral works: Ringed by the Flat Horizon 1980, A Mind of Winter 1981, At First Light 1982, Jubilation 1985, Antara 1987, Sudden Time 1993, Three Inventions for Chamber Orchestra 1995, Sometime Voices 1996, Palimpsest 2000; chamber music: Piano Sonata 1978, Octet 1978, Flight 1979, Sortilèges 1981, Three Studies for Piano 1985, Upon Silence 1990, Viola, Viola 1997, Shadowlines (for solo piano) 2001, Three Miniatures for violin 2001. *Address:* c/o Faber Music, 3 Queen Square, London, WC1N 3AU, England. *Telephone:* (20) 7833-7910. *Fax:* (20) 7833-7939. *E-mail:* promotion@fabermusic.com (Office). *Website:* www.fabermusic.co.uk.

BENJELLOUN, Tahar; Moroccan writer; b. 1944, Fès; m. 1986; two s. two d.; ed Lycée Regnault de Tanger, Faculté de Lettres de Rabat and Univ. of Paris; columnist Le Monde 1973–, La Repubblica (Italy) and La Vanguardia (Spain); mem. Haut Conseil de la francophonie, Conseil supérieur de la langue française; UN Goodwill Amb. for Human Rights; Chevalier des Arts et des Lettres, Légion d'honneur; Médaille du Mérite nat. (Morocco); Prix Goncourt 1987; Global Tolerance Award (UN) 1998. *Publications:* Harrouda 1973, La

Reclusion solitaire 1976, Les Amandiers sont morts de leurs blessures (poems) 1976, La plus haute des Solitudes 1977, Moha le fou, Moha le sage 1978, La Prière de l'absent 1980, L'Écrivain public 1983, L'Enfant de sable 1985, La Nuit sacrée 1987, Jour de Silence à Tanger 1990, Les Yeux baissés 1991, Giacometti 1991, L'Ange aveugle 1992, L'Homme rompu 1994, Le Premier Amour est toujours le dernier 1995, Les Raisins de la galère 1995, La Sondure fraternelle 1995, Poésie complète 1995, La Nuit de l'erreur 1997, Le Racisme expliqué à ma fille 1998, L'Auberge des Pauvres 1999, Labyrinthe des Sentiments 1999, Cette aveudlante absence de lumière 2001, L'islam expliqué aux enfants 2002, Amours sorcières 2003. *Address:* Editions du Seuil, BP 80, 27 rue Jacob, 75261 Paris cedex 06, France (Office).

BENMAKHLOUF, Alexandre; French lawyer; b. 9 Sept. 1939, Oran, Algeria; s. of Tahar Benmakhlouf and Sylviane Jan; m. Gabrielle Steinmann 1965; one s. one d.; Deputy Public Prosecutor, Meaux 1970, Versailles 1972; seconded to Chancellery 1974–84; Pres. Nanterre Magistrates' Court 1984–86; Deputy Sec.-Gen. Professional Asscn of Magistrates 1984–86; Adviser to Prime Minister Jacques Chirac 1986–89; Legal Adviser to Jacques Chirac, Mayor of Paris 1989–91; Pres. Court of Appeal, Versailles 1991–93; Dir of Civil Affairs and Dir of Cabinet of Guardian of the Seal, Ministry of Justice 1993–96; Attorney-Gen., Court of Appeal 1996–97, Solicitor-Gen. 1997–2000, First Counsel for the Prosecution 2001–; Chevalier Légion d'honneur, Ordre des Palmes académiques. *Leisure interests:* reading, travelling, cinema. *Address:* Cour de Cassation, 5 quai de l'Horloge, 75055 Paris RP, France (Office).

BENN, Rt Hon Tony, PC, MA; British politician, writer and broadcaster; b. (Anthony Neil Wedgwood Benn) 3 April 1925, London; s. of William Wedgwood Benn (1st Viscount Stansgate), PC and Margaret Eadie (née Holmes); m. Caroline de Camp 1949 (died 2000); three s. one d.; ed Westminster School and New Coll., Oxford; RAF Pilot 1943–45; Oxford Univ. 1946–49; Producer, BBC 1949–50; Labour MP for Bristol SE 1950–60, compelled to leave House of Commons on inheriting peerage 1960, re-elected and unseated 1961, renounced peerage and re-elected 1963, contested and lost Bristol East seat in 1983, re-elected as mem. for Chesterfield 1984–2001; Nat. Exec. Labour Party 1959–94; Chair. Fabian Soc. 1964; Postmaster-Gen. 1964–66; Minister of Technology 1966–70, of Power 1969–70; Shadow Minister of Trade and Industry 1970–74; Sec. of State for Industry and Minister of Posts and Telecommunications 1974–75; Sec. of State for Energy 1975–79; Vice-Chair. Labour Party 1970, Chair. 1971–72; Chair. Labour Party Home Policy Cttee 1974–82; Cand. for Leadership of Labour Party 1976, 1988, for Deputy Leadership 1971, 1981; Pres. EEC Energy Council 1977; Pres. Labour Action for Peace 1997–; Visiting Prof. of Politics, LSE 2001–; Pres. Socialist Campaign Group of Labour MPs; fmr mem. Bureau Confed. of Socialist Parties of the European Community; numerous TV and radio broadcasts; Hon. LLD (Strathclyde), (Williams Coll., USA), (Brunel), (Bristol), (Univ. of West of England), (Univ. of N London); Hon. DTech (Bradford); Hon. DSc (Aston); Dr hc (Paisley). *Television:* Speaking Up in Parliament 1993, Westminster Behind Closed Doors 1995, New Labour in Focus 1998, Tony Benn Speaks 2001. *Publications:* The Privy Council as a Second Chamber 1957, The Regeneration of Britain 1964, The New Politics 1970, Speeches by Tony Benn 1974, Arguments for Socialism 1979, Arguments for Democracy 1981, Parliament, People and Power 1982, The Sizewell Syndrome 1984, Writings on the Wall 1984, Out of the Wilderness: Diaries 1963–67, 1987, Office Without Power: Diaries 1968–72, 1988, Fighting Back 1988, Against the Tide: Diaries 1973–76, 1989, Conflicts of Interest: Diaries 1977–80, 1990, A Future for Socialism 1991, End of an Era: Diaries 1980–90 1992, Common Sense: A New Constitution for Britain (with Andrew Hood) 1993, Years of Hope—Diaries 1940–1962 1994, The Benn Diaries 1940–1990 1995; The BBC Benn Tapes (audio tapes) 1994, 1995, Writings on the Wall (with Roy Bailey) (audio tape) 1996; Free at Last: Diaries 1991–2001 2002. *Address:* 12 Holland Park Avenue, London, W11 3QU, England (Office). *Telephone:* (20) 7229-0779 (Office). *Fax:* (20) 7229-9693 (Office). *E-mail:* tony@tbenn.fsnet.co.uk.

BENNACK, Frank Anthony, Jr.; American publishing executive; b. 12 Feb. 1933, San Antonio; s. of Frank Bennack and Lula Connally; m. Luella Smith 1951; five d.; ed Univ. of Maryland and St Mary's Univ.; advertising account exec. San Antonio Light 1950–53, 1956–58, Advertising Man. 1961–65, Asst Publr 1965–67, Publr 1967–74; Gen. Man. (newspapers), Hearst Corpn New York 1974–76, Exec. Vice-Pres. and COO 1975–78, Pres. and CEO 1978–; Chair. Museum of TV and Radio, NY City 1991–; mem. Bd of Dirs. Mfrs Hanover Trust Co., New York; Pres. Tex. Daily Newspaper Asscn 1973–; Dir American Newspaper Publrs. Asscn. *Address:* Hearst Corporation, 959 8th Avenue, New York, NY 10019; The Museum of TV and Radio, 25 W 52nd Street, New York, NY 10019, USA.

BENNET, Douglas J., Jr, PhD; American public administrator; b. 23 June 1938, Orange, NJ; s. of Douglas Bennet and Phoebe Bennet; m. 1st Susanne Klejman 1959 (divorced 1995); m. 2nd Midge Bowen Ramsey 1996; two s. one d.; ed Wesleyan Univ., Middletown, Conn., Univ. of Calif. (Berkeley) and Harvard Univ.; Asst to Econ. Adviser (Dr C. E. Lindblom), Agency for Int. Devt, New Delhi 1963–64; Special Asst to Amb. Chester Bowles, US Embassy, New Delhi 1964–66; Asst to Vice-Pres. Hubert Humphrey 1967–69; Admin. Asst to Senator T. F. Eagleton 1969–73, to Senator A. Ribicoff 1973–74; Staff Dir Senate Budget Cttee 1974–77; Asst Sec. of State, Congressional Relations 1977–79; Admin. U.S. Agency for Int. Devt 1979–81; Pres. Roosevelt Center for American Policy Studies 1981–83; Pres., CEO Nat. Public Radio (NPR) 1983–93; Asst Sec. of State, Int. Organizational Affairs, Dept of State

1993–95; Pres. Wesleyan Univ. 1995–; mem. Council of Foreign Relations, North South Round Table, Soc. for Int. Devt, Carnegie Endowment Study on Organizing Int. Financial Co-operation in 1980s; Dir Overseas Educ. Fund, KTI Corpn. *Publications:* articles in newspapers and journals. *Leisure interests:* sailing, skiing. *Address:* Office of the President, Wesleyan University, 229 High Street, Middletown, CT 06457 (Office); 269 High Street, Middletown, CT 06457, USA (Home). *Telephone:* (202) 822-2010 (Office).

BENNETT, Alan; British playwright and actor; b. 9 May 1934; s. of Walter Bennett and Lilian Mary Peel; ed Leeds Modern School, Exeter Coll., Oxford; Jr Lecturer, Modern History, Magdalen Coll., Oxford 1960–62; co-author and actor Beyond the Fringe, Edin. 1960, London 1961, New York 1962; Fellow Royal Acad.; author and actor On the Margin (television series) 1966, Forty Years On (play) 1968; Hon. Fellow Exeter Coll., Oxford; Hon. DLitt (Leeds); Evening Standard Award 1961, 1969, Hawthornden Prize 1988, two Oliver Awards 1993, Evening Standard Film Award 1996, Lifetime Achievement Award, British Book Awards 2003. *Plays:* Getting On 1971, Habeas Corpus 1973, The Old Country 1977, Enjoy 1980, Kafka's Dick 1986, Single Spies 1988, The Wind in the Willows (adapted for Nat. Theatre) 1990, The Madness of George III 1991 (film 1995), The Lady in the Van 1999. *Television scripts:* A Day Out (film) 1972, Sunset Across the Bay (TV film) 1975, A Little Outing, A Visit from Miss Prothero (plays) 1977, Doris and Doreen, The Old Crowd, Me! I'm Afraid of Virginia Woolf, All Day on the Sands, Afternoon Off, One Fine Day 1978–79, Intensive Care, Our Winnie, A Woman of No Importance, Rolling Home, Marks, Say Something Happened, An Englishman Abroad 1982, The Insurance Man 1986, Talking Heads (Olivier Award) 1992, 102 Boulevard Haussmann 1991, A Question of Attribution 1991, Talking Heads 2 1998. *Films:* A Private Function 1984, Prick Up Your Ears 1987, The Madness of King George 1994. *Television Documentaries:* Dinner at Noon 1988, Poetry in Motion 1990, Portrait or Bust 1994, The Abbey 1995, Telling Tales 1999. *Publications:* Beyond the Fringe (with Peter Cook, Jonathan Miller and Dudley Moore) 1962, Forty Years On 1969, Getting On 1972, Habeas Corpus 1973, The Old Country 1978, Enjoy 1980, Office Suite 1981, Objects of Affection 1982, The Writer in Disguise 1985, Two Kafka Plays 1987, Talking Heads 1988, Single Spies 1989, The Lady in the Van 1991, The Wind in the Willows (adaptation) 1991, The Madness of George III 1992, Writing Home 1994, The Madness of King George (screenplay) 1995, The Clothes They Stood Up In 1998, Talking Heads 2 1998, The Complete Talking Heads 1998, A Box of Alan Bennett 2000, The Laying on of Hands 2001; regular contrib. to London Review of Books. *Address:* c/o Peters, Fraser & Dunlop, Drury House, 34–43 Russell Street, London WC2B 5HA, England; 23 Gloucester Crescent, London, NW1 7DS, England (Home). *Telephone:* (20) 7376-7676.

BENNETT, Bob (Robert F.), BA; American politician and businessman; b. 18 Sept. 1933, Salt Lake City, Utah; s. of Wallace Bennett; m. Joyce McKay; six c.; ed Univ. of Utah; served in USAF 1951–57; Propr Bennett Paint & Glass Co.; Congressional liaison official for Transportation Dept, Washington, DC 1968–70; became lobbyist after acquiring Robert Mullen's public relations firm 1970; CEO Franklin Quest 1984–91; Adviser to fmr US Senator Wallace Bennett 1962; Senator from Utah 1993–; Republican. *Address:* US Senate, Senate Members Office, 431 Dirksen, Washington, DC 20510-0001, USA.

BENNETT, Emmett Leslie, PhD; American classical scholar; b. 12 July 1918, Minneapolis, Minn.; s. of Emmett L. Bennett and Mary C. Buzzelle; m. Marja Adams 1942; five c.; ed Univ. of Cincinnati; Research Analyst, US War Dept 1942–45; taught in Dept of Classics, Yale Univ. 1947–58; Fulbright Research Scholar, Athens 1953–54, Cambridge 1965; mem. Inst. for Advanced Study, Guggenheim Fellow, Visiting Lecturer in Greek, Bryn Mawr Coll. 1955–56; Dept of Classical Languages, Univ. of Texas 1958–59; Univ. of Wis. Inst. for Research Humanities 1959–, Acting Dir 1968–69, 1972–75, Dept of Classics 1960–, Moses S. Slaughter Prof. of Classical Studies 1978–88, Emer. 1988–; Visiting Scholar, Univ. of Texas 1989–; Visiting Prof., Univ. of Colorado 1967, of Cincinnati 1972; Elizabeth A. Whitehead Prof., American School of Classical Studies 1986–87; Adjunct Prof., Dept of Classics, Univ. of Texas-Austin 1992–93, 1995; Corresp. mem. German Archaeological Inst.; Hon. Councillor Archaeological Soc. of Athens; mem. Comité Int. Permanent des Etudes Mycéniennes, Archaeological Inst. of America, American Philological Assscn; Gold Cross (Greece) 1991, McMicken Arts & Sciences Distinguished Alumnus Award 1997, Gold Medal, Archeological Inst. of America 2001. *Publications:* The Pylos Tablets 1951 and 1956, The Mycenae Tablets 1953 and 1958, Mycenaean Studies 1964, Re., Nestor 1957–77, etc. *Address:* 3106 Bluff Street, #2, Madison, WI 53705-3459, USA (Home); Classics Department, Van Rise, 1220 Linden Drive, University of Wisconsin–Madison, Madison, WI 53706. *Telephone:* (608) 233-2681. *Fax:* (608) 265-4173; (608) 262-8570. *E-mail:* ebennett@facstaff.wisc.edu (Home); ebennett@wiscmail .wisc.edu.

BENNETT, Hywel Thomas; British actor and director; b. 8 April 1944, Garnant, S. Wales; s. of Gorden Bennett and Sarah Gwen Lewis; m. 1st Cathy McGowan 1967 (divorced 1988); one d.; m. 2nd Sandra Layne Fulford 1998; ed Henry Thornton Grammar School, Clapham, London and Royal Acad. of Dramatic Art; London stage debut as Ophelia in Youth Theatre's Hamlet, Queen's Theatre 1959; played in repertory, Salisbury and Leatherhead 1965; Fellow Welsh Coll. of Music & Drama; Hon. Fellow Univ. of Wales, Cardiff 1997. *Stage roles include:* Puck in A Midsummer Night's Dream, Edinburgh Festival 1967; Prince Hal in Henry IV (Parts I and II), Mermaid 1970; Antony in Julius Caesar, Young Vic 1972; Stanley in The Birthday Party, Gardner Cen., Brighton 1973; Hamlet (touring S. Africa) 1974; Danny in Night Must

Fall, Sherman, Cardiff 1974 and Shaw, 1975; Jimmy Porter in Look Back in Anger, Belgrade, Coventry 1974; Konstantin in the Seagull (on tour), Birmingham Repertory Co. 1974, Otherwise Engaged, Comedy Theatre 1978, Terra Nova, Chichester 1979, The Case of the Oily Levantine, Her Majesty's 1980, She Stoops to Conquer, Nat. Theatre 1984–85; Andrey in Elijah Moshinsky's production of The Three Sisters, Albery Theatre 1987, Treasure Island 1990; has directed several plays including Rosencrantz and Guildenstern are Dead, Leatherhead 1975, A Man for All Seasons, Birmingham 1976, I Have Been Here Before, Sherman Theatre, Cardiff 1976, Otherwise Engaged, Library Theatre, Manchester 1978, What the Butler Saw, Theatre of Wales, Cardiff 1980, Fly Away Home (also producer), Hammersmith 1983. *Films include:* The Family Way 1966, Twisted Nerve 1968, The Virgin Soldiers 1969, Loot 1970, Percy 1971, Alice in Wonderland 1972, Endless Night 1972, Murder Elite, War Zone, Frankie and Johnnie 1985, The Twilight Zone, Checkpoint Chiswick, Age Unknown, Married to Malcolm 1997, Misery Harbour 1998, Nasty Neighbours, Vatel, Jesus and Mary 2000, One for the Road 2002. *Radio:* No Telegrams No Thunder, Dialogues on a Broken Sphere, Dracula, Witness for the Prosecution, Night Must Fall. *TV appearances include:* Romeo and Juliet, The Idiot, Unman, Wittering and Zigo, A Month in the Country, Malice Aforethought (serial), Shelley (two series), Tinker, Tailor, Soldier, Spy (serial) 1979, Coming Out, Pennies From Heaven, Artemis '81, The Critic, The Consultant, Absent Friends, Checkpoint Chiswick, The Secret Agent, A Mind to Kill, Casualty, Virtual Murder, Shelley, The Other Side of Paradise, Trust Me, Frontiers, Karaoke, Harpur and Isles, Hospital, Neverwhere, Dirty Work; many voice-overs and narrations; radio plays. *Leisure interests:* fishing, cooking, golf, painting, walking, swimming, reading and solitude. *Address:* c/o Gavin Barker, 2D Wimpole Street, London W1G 0EB, England.

BENNETT, Jana Eve, OBE, BA, MSc, FRTS; British broadcasting executive; b. 6 Nov. 1956, Cooperstown, USA; d. of Gordon Willard Bennett and Elizabeth Bennett (née Cushing); m. Richard Clemmow 1996; one s. one d.; ed Bognor Comprehensive School, St Anne's Coll., Oxford, LSE; News trainee BBC 1979, fmrly Asst Producer The Money Programme, Producer Newsnight, Producer/ Dir Panorama, Series Producer Antenna, Ed. Horizon, Head of BBC Science; BBC Dir of Production and Deputy Chief Exec. 1997–99, BBC Dir of TV 2002–; Exec. Vice Pres. Learning Channel, US Discovery Communications Inc. 1999–2002; Golden Nymph Award (Panorama), BAFTA, Emmy, Prix Italia (Horizon). *Publication:* (jtly) The Disappeared: Argentina's Dirty War 1986. *Leisure interests:* mountaineering, music, children, travel. *Address:* BBC TV Centre, Wood Lane, London, W12 7RJ, England (Office). *Website:* www.bbc.co .uk (Office).

BENNETT, Martin Arthur, PhD, DSc, FRS, FAA, FRSC; British/Australian professor of chemistry; b. 11 Aug. 1935, Harrow; s. of Arthur Edward Charles Bennett and Dorothy Ivy Bennett; m. Rae Elizabeth Mathews 1964; two s.; ed Haberdashers' Aske's Hampstead School, Imperial Coll. of Science and Tech., London; Postdoctoral Fellow Univ. of S. Calif. 1960–61; Turner and Newall Fellow Univ. Coll. London 1961–63, lecturer 1963–67; Fellow Research School of Chemistry, Australian Nat. Univ. 1967–70, Sr Fellow 1970–79, Professorial Fellow 1979–91, Prof. 1991–2000, Prof. Emer. 2001–; Adjunct Prof. Royal Melbourne Inst. of Tech. Univ. 2000–; various professorial and visiting fellowships in Canada, Germany, USA, New Zealand and Japan; mem. Int. Advisory Bd for Dictionary of Organometallic Compounds 1984 and Dictionary of Inorganic Compounds 1988; H. G. Smith Medal, Royal Australian Chem. Inst. 1977, RSC Award 1981, G. J. Burrows Award, Royal Australian Chem. Inst. 1987, Nyholm Medal, RSC 1991, Max Planck Soc. Research Award 1994. *Publications:* chapters on ruthenium in Comprehensive Organometallic Chemistry; over 250 papers in journals. *Leisure interests:* golf, reading, foreign languages. *Address:* Research School of Chemistry, Australian National University, Canberra, ACT 0200 (Office); 21 Black Street, Yarralumla, ACT 2600, Australia (Home). *Telephone:* (2) 6125-3639 (Office); (2) 6125-3216 (Home). *Fax:* (2) 6125-3216. *E-mail:* bennett@rsc.anu .edu.au (Office).

BENNETT, Maxwell Richard, BEng, DSc, FAA; Australian professor of physiology; b. 19 Feb. 1939, Melbourne; s. of Herman Adler Bennett (Bercovici) and Ivy G. Arthur; m. Gillian R. Bennett 1965; one s. one d.; ed Christian Brothers Coll., St Kilda, Melbourne and Univ. of Melbourne; John & Alan Gilmour Research Fellow, Univ. of Melbourne 1965; Lecturer in Physiology, Univ. of Sydney 1969, Reader 1973, Prof. of Physiology 1982–, Dir Neurobiology Research Centre 1982–90; Convener Sydney Inst. of Biomedical Research 1995; Founder Fed. Australian Scientific and Tech. Socs 1985; Co-Founder Australian Neural Networks Soc. 1990; Pres. Australian Neuroscience Soc. 1989–92; Pres. Int. Soc. for Autonomic Neuroscience 2001–03; mem. Council Int. Brain Research Org. 1995–; First Univ. Chair., Univ. of Sydney 2000; Fellow Australian Acad. of Science 1981–; Opening Plenary Lecture, World Congress of Neuroscience 1995, Goddard Research Prize Nat. Heart Foundation 1996, Ramaciotti Medal for Excellence in Biomedical Research 1996, Renenessin Research Prize Nat. Heart Foundation 1998, Almington Research Prize, Nat. Heart Foundation 1999, Burnet Medal and Lecture Australian Acad. of Science 1999, Neuroscience Distinguished Achievement 2001, Australian Neuroscience Soc. Medallion 2001; Officer Order of Australia 2001. *Publications:* Autonomic Neuromuscular Transmission 1972, Development of Neuromuscular Synapses 1983, Optimising Research and Development 1985, The Idea of Consciousness 1997, History of the Synapse 2001; 250 papers on neuroscience. *Leisure interests:* history and philosophy of science, science policy. *Address:* Department of Physiology, University of Sydney, NSW 2006, Australia. *Telephone:* (2) 9351-2034.

BENNETT, Michael Vander Laan, BS, DPhil; American professor of neuroscience; b. 7 Jan. 1931, Madison, Wis.; s. of Martin Toscan Bennett and Cornelia Vander Laan Bennett; m. 1st Ruth Berman 1963 (divorced 1993); one s. one d.; m. 2nd Ruth Suzanne Zukin 1998; ed Yale Univ. and Oxford Univ., England; research worker, Dept of Neurology, Coll. of Physicians and Surgeons, Columbia Univ. 1957–58, Research Assoc. 1958–59; Asst Prof. of Neurology, Columbia Univ. 1959–61, Assoc. Prof. 1961–66; Prof. of Anatomy, Albert Einstein Coll. of Medicine 1967–74; Co-Dir Neurobiology Course, Marine Biological Lab. 1970–74; Prof. of Neuroscience, Albert Einstein Coll. of Medicine 1974–, Dir Div. of Cellular Neurobiology 1974–, Chair. Dept of Neuroscience 1982–96, Sylvia and Robert S. Olnick Prof. 1986–; Rhodes Scholar 1952; Sr Research Fellowship, NIH 1960–62; Fellow, Nat. Neurological Research Foundation 1958–60, New York Acad. of Sciences; mem. NAS 1982–, American Asscn of Anatomists, American Physiological Soc., American Soc. for Cell Biology, American Soc. of Zoologists, Biophysical Soc., Soc. for Neuroscience, Soc. of Gen. Physiologists; mem. Editorial Bds. Brain Research 1975–, Journal of Cell Biology 1983–85, Journal of Neurobiology 1969–95 (Assoc. Ed. 1979–93), Journal of Neurocytology 1980–82, Journal of Neuroscience (Section Ed. 1981–85). *Publications:* over 290 papers in scholarly journals and books. *Leisure interests:* running, hiking, skiing and scuba. *Address:* Albert Einstein College of Medicine, Department of Neuroscience, Bronx, NY 10461, USA (Office). *Telephone:* (718) 430-2536 (Office). *Fax:* (718) 430-8944.

BENNETT, Sir Richard Rodney, Kt, CBE, FRAM; British composer; b. 29 March 1936, Broadstairs, Kent; s. of H. Rodney Bennett and Joan Esther Bennett; ed Leighton Park School, Reading, Royal Acad. of Music, London and under Pierre Boulez, Paris; commissioned to write two operas by Sadler's Wells 1962; Prof. of Composition, RAM 1963–65, Visiting Prof. 1995–; Vice-Pres. RCM 1983–; mem. Gen. Council, Performing Right Soc. 1975–; Arnold Bax Soc. Prize for Commonwealth Composers 1964; Anthony Asquith Memorial Award for Murder on the Orient Express film music, Soc. of Film and TV Awards 1974. *Compositions:* The Approaches of Sleep 1959, Journal, Calendar, Winter Music 1960, The Ledge, Suite Française, Oboe Sonata 1961, Nocturnes, London Pastoral, Fantasy 1962, Aubade, Jazz Calendar, String Quartet No. 4, Five Studies 1964, Symphony No. 1 1965, Epithalamion 1966, Symphony No. 2 1967, Wind Quintet, Piano Concerto 1968, Jazz Pastoral 1969, Oboe Concerto 1970, Guitar Concerto 1971, Viola Concerto 1973, Commedia I–IV 1972–73, Spells (choral) 1975, Serenade for Youth Orchestra 1977, Dream Songs 1986, Marimba Concerto 1988, Diversions 1989, Concerto for Stan Getz 1990, Partita 1995, Reflections on a 16th-Century Tune 1999, Seven Country Dances 2000, The Glory and the Dream 2000; opera: The Mines of Sulphur 1964, A Penny for a Song 1966, Victory 1969, All the King's Men (children's opera) 1969; Isadora (ballet) 1981; film music: Indiscreet, Devil's Disciple, Blind Date, The Mark, Only Two Can Play, Wrong Arm of the Law, Heavens Above, Billy Liar, One Way Pendulum, The Nanny, The Witches, Far from the Madding Crowd, Billion Dollar Brain, The Buttercup Chain, Secret Ceremony, Figures in a Landscape, Nicholas and Alexandra, Lady Caroline Lamb, Voices, Murder on the Orient Express, Equus, Sherlock Holmes in New York, L'Imprecateur, The Brinks Job, Yanks, Return of the Soldier, Four Weddings and a Funeral, Swann; TV music for series include: Hereward the Wake, The Christians, The Ebony Tower, Poor Little Rich Girl, Gormenghast. *Leisure interests:* cinema, modern jazz, art.

BENNETT, Roy Frederick, FCA; Canadian business executive; b. 18 March 1928, Winnipeg, Man.; s. of the late Charles William Bennett and Gladys Mabel Matthews; m. Gail Cook Bennett 1978; two s. two d.; ed Collegiate Inst., N Toronto and Inst. of Chartered Accountants; with Ford Motor Co. of Canada Ltd, Asst Controller 1960–62, Dir Vehicle Marketing 1962–63, Dir Corporate Planning 1963–64, Gen. Marketing Man. 1964–65, Vice-Pres. Finance 1965–70, Dir 1966–, Pres. and CEO 1970–81, Chair. and CEO 1981–82; Chair. Bennecon Ltd 1982–; Chair. Bd Jannock Ltd; Dir Bell Canada Inc.; Chair. Bd Midland Walwyn Inc., Talisman Energy Inc., Zalev Metals Ltd; Hon. LLD. *Leisure interests:* golf, tennis, skiing. *Address:* Suite 1416, Commercial Union Tower, P.O. Box 59, Toronto Dominion Bank Tower, Toronto, Ont. M5K 1E7, Canada. *Telephone:* (416) 365-1418. *Fax:* (416) 365-1419.

BENNETT, Tony (Anthony Dominick Benedetto), MusD; American singer and entertainer; b. 3 Aug. 1926, Astoria; s. of John Benedetto and Anna Suraci; m. 1st Patricia Beech 1952 (divorced 1971); two c.; m. 2nd Sandra Grant 1971 (divorced 1984); two d.; ed American Theatre Wing, NY and Univ. of Berkeley; frequent appearances on TV and in concert; owner and recording artist with Improv Records; paintings exhibited at Butler Inst. of American Art, Youngstown, Ohio 1994; Gold records for recordings of Because of You, I Left My Heart in San Francisco; Grammy Award for Best Traditional Pop Vocal Performer 1998. *Records include:* The Art of Excellence 1986, Bennett/Berlin 1988, Astoria: Portrait of the Artist 1990, Perfectly Frank 1992 (Grammy award for Best Traditional Vocal Performance), Steppin' Out 1993 (Grammy award for Best Traditional Pop Vocal), The Essence of Tony Bennett 1993, MTV Unplugged 1994 (Grammy award Album of the Year, Best Traditional Pop Vocal), Here's to the Ladies 1995, The Playground 1998, Cool 1999 (Grammy award), The Ultimate Tony 2000. *Publication:* The Good Life: The Autobiography of Tony Bennett. *Address:* 130 West 57th Street, Apartment 9D, New York, NY 10019, USA.

BENNEY, Adrian Gerald Sallis, CBE; British gold- and silversmith; b. 21 April 1930, Hull; s. of the late Ernest Alfred Sallis Benney and of Aileen Mary Benney; m. Janet Edwards 1957; three s. one d.; ed Brighton Grammar School, Brighton Coll. of Art, Royal Coll. of Art; est. first workshop in London 1955, Consultant Designer, Viners Ltd 1957–67; commenced designing and making Reading civic plate 1963; Prof. of Silversmithing and Jewellery, RCA 1974–83; Export Adviser and Designer, Selangor Pewter, Kuala Lumpur 1986–; Adviser to UK Atomic Energy Ceramics Centre 1979–83; Chair. Govt India Hallmarking Survey 1981; British Hallmarking Council 1983–88; created altar crosses for St Paul's and Lichfield Cathedrals and Westminster Abbey, dinner service for 240 people, Chartered Accountants in England and Wales, Gold Commonwealth Mace given to Queen Elizabeth II on the 40th Anniversary of her reign; has staged several major exhbns.; Liveryman, Worshipful Co. of Goldsmiths 1964; Freeman, City of London 1964; Freeman, Borough of Reading 1984; Royal Designer to Industry 1971; royal warrants of appt. to the Queen, the Duke of Edinburgh, Queen Elizabeth the Queen Mother and the Prince of Wales; Hon. Fellow RCA, Hon. MA (Leicester) 1963. *Publication:* Gerald Benney: Fifty Years at the Bench 1999. *Leisure interests:* landscape gardening, painting. *Address:* 73 Walton Street, London, SW3 2HT (Office); The Old Rectory, Cholderton, Nr. Salisbury, Wilts., SP4 0DW, England (Home). *Telephone:* (20) 7589-7002 (Office); (1980) 629614 (Home). *Fax:* (20) 7581-2573 (Office); (1980) 629461 (Home). *E-mail:* jbenney@benneyjfreeserve.co.uk (Home).

BENOÎT DE COIGNAC, Henri Elie Marie; French diplomatist (retd.) and international consultant; b. 3 Oct. 1935, Rodez (Aveyron); s. of Emile Benoit de Coignac and Madeleine Bonnefous; m. Nadine Vimont 1966; two s. one d.; ed Collège Saint-Joseph, Sarlat, Lycée Henry IV, Lycée Louis-le-Grand, Faculté de Droit, Univ. of Paris; Asst, Staff Dept, Ministry of Foreign Affairs, Paris 1963–65, Second Sec., Mexico 1965–67, Second Sec. then First Sec., Washington, DC 1967–71, First Sec. Tunis and Chief of Press and Information Service 1971–74, Counsellor in charge of Political Affairs 1974, Cultural Counsellor and Counsellor for Tech. and Scientific Co-operation in India 1975–77, Diplomatic Adviser to Nat. Defence Gen. Sec. and Auditeur, Nat. Defence Inst. for Higher Studies (IHEDN) 1978–79, First Counsellor, Buenos Aires 1979–82, Rep. of Pres. of France (Viguier) in Andorra 1982–84, Chief of Protocol in Paris 1984–88, Minister Plenipotentiary 1986, Amb. to Spain 1988–93, to Morocco 1993–95, to Ireland 1997–2001; Diplomatic Adviser to French Govt 1996–97; Chevalier Ordre Nat. du Mérite, Officier Légion d'honneur, Grand Coirx Ordre d'Isabelle la Catholique. *Leisure interests:* tennis, golf. *Address:* 26 rue des Boulangers, 75005 Paris (Home); Domaine de Farinières, Saint-Germain des Prés, 81700 Puylaurens, France (Home). *Telephone:* (5) 63-75-47-68 (Office); 1-46-34-21-16 (Home). *Fax:* (6) 68-42-47-97 (Office). *E-mail:* nethdecoignac@yahoo.fr (Office); hdecoignac@yahoo.es (Home).

BENSON, Andrew Alm, PhD; American biochemist and plant physiologist; b. 24 Sept. 1917, Modesto, Calif.; s. of Carl B. Benson and Emma C. Alm; m. 1st Ruth Carkeek 1942 (divorced 1969); m. 2nd Dorothy Dorgan Neri 1971; one s. (deceased) three d. (one deceased); ed Modesto High School, Univ. of Calif., Berkeley and Calif. Inst. of Tech.; Instructor, Univ. of Calif., Berkeley 1942–43; Research Assoc. Stanford Univ. 1944–45; Asst Dir Bioorganic Group, Radiation Lab., Univ. of Calif., Berkeley 1946–54; Assoc. Prof. of Agricultural Biological Chemistry Pennsylvania State Univ. 1955–60, Prof. 1960–61; Prof.-in-Residence, Physiological Chem. and Biophysics, UCLA 1961–62; Prof. Scripps Inst. of Oceanography, Univ. of Calif., San Diego 1962–88, Prof. Emer. 1988–, Assoc. Dir 1966–70, Dir Physiology Research Lab. 1970–77; Sr Queen's Fellow in Oceanography, Australia 1979; mem. advisory Bd Marine Biotech. Inst. Co. Ltd, Tokyo 1990–, NAS, AAAS, American Acad. of Arts and Sciences, Royal Norwegian Soc. of Sciences and Letters 1984–; Hon. mem. Inst. of Marine Biology, Far East Branch, Russian Acad. of Sciences 1992; Dr hc (Oslo), (Université Pierre et Marie Curie, Paris) 1986; Sugar Research Foundation Award 1950, Ernest Orlando Lawrence Memorial Award 1962, Stephen Hales Award 1972, AmOil Chemists' Soc./Supelco Research Award 1987, Riken Distinguished Scientist 1995. *Publications:* Path of Carbon in Photosynthesis 1947–55, Wax in Oceanic Food Chains 1975, Arsenic Metabolism, a Way of Life in the Sea 1984, Methanol Metabolism and Plant Growth, Paving the Path 2002; 280 articles in scientific journals, five patents. *Leisure interests:* philately, gardening, starfinder development, nutritional biochemistry. *Address:* Scripps Institution of Oceanography, La Jolla, CA 92093-0202 (Office); 6044 Folsom Drive, La Jolla, CA 92037, USA (Home). *Telephone:* (858) 534-4300 (Office). *Fax:* (858) 534-7313 (Office). *E-mail:* abenson@ucsd.edu (Office); abenson@ucsd.edu (Home).

BENSON, Sir Christopher John, Kt, FRICS; British business executive and chartered surveyor; b. 20 July 1933, Wheaton Aston; s. of Charles Woodburn Benson and Catherine Clara Bishton; m. Margaret Josephine Bundy 1960; two s.; ed Worcester Cathedral King's School, Thames Nautical Training Coll. HMS Worcester; Midshipman RNR 1949–52; Sub-Lt RDVR 1952–53; worked as chartered surveyor and agricultural auctioneer 1953–64; Dir Arndale Devts Ltd 1965–69; Chair. Dolphin Devts Ltd 1969–71, Dolphin Farms Ltd 1969–71, Dolphin Property (Man.) Ltd 1969–; Asst Man. Dir The Law Land Co. Ltd 1972–74; Dir Sun Alliance and London Insurance Group 1978–84, Chair. Sun Alliance Insurance Group PLC 1993–96 (Dir 1988, Vice-Chair. 1991, Deputy Chair. 1992), Deputy Chair. Royal and Sun Alliance Insurance Group PLC 1996–97 (Chair. 1996–97); Advisor to British Petroleum Pension Fund 1979–84; Underwriting Mem. of Lloyd's 1979–97; mem. Council CBI

1979–97; Pres. British Property Fed. 1981–83; Dir House of Fraser PLC 1982–86; Chair. London Docklands Devt Corpn 1984–88; Chair. Reedpack Ltd 1989–90; Man. Dir MEPC PLC 1976–88, Chair. 1988–93; Chair. Housing Corpn 1990–94; Chair. Boots Co. PLC 1990–94 (Dir 1989); Chair. Games for Good Causes PLC 1993–94; Chair. Costain Group PLC 1993–96; Chair. Funding Agency for Schools 1994–97; Deputy Chair. Thorn Lighting Group PLC 1994–98; Chair. Albright and Wilson PLC 1995–; Chair. Devt Bd Macmillan Cancer Relief 1995–; Chair. Partnership Bd GVA Grimley 1999–2001, Cross London Rail Links 2001–; Gov. Inns of Court School of Law 1996–2000, Prin. 2000–02; Pres. London Chamber of Commerce and Industry 2000–02; Pres. Nat. Deaf Children's Soc. 1995–; Vice-Pres. RSA 1992–97; High Sheriff of Wilts. 2002–03; mem. Advisory Bd Hawkpoint Partners Ltd 1999–2001; Chair. Air Ambulance Foundation; mem. Court of Worshipful Co. of Watermen and Lightermen of the River Thames; Liveryman of Guild of Air Pilots and Air Navigators; Lay Canon, Salisbury Cathedral; Trustee, Magna Carta Trust, Salisbury Cathedral; Patron Changing Faces; Friend, Royal Coll. of Physicians; numerous other public and charitable interests; Hon. Vice-Pres. Nat. Fed. of Housing Asscns 1994–; Hon. Fellow Wolfson Coll. Cambridge 1990, Chartered Inst. of Bldg 1992–, Royal Coll. of Pathologists 1992–; Hon. Bencher, Hon. Soc. of Middle Temple 1984–; Hon. DSc (City), (Bradford). *Leisure interests:* opera, ballet, farming in Wiltshire, flying, swimming. *Address:* Pauls Dene House, Castle Road, Salisbury, SP1 3RY (Home); Flat 2, 50 South Audley Street, London, W1K 2QE, England.

BENSON, Craig, MBA; American state official and business executive; b. 8 Oct. 1954, New York City; m. Denise Benson; two d.; ed Babson Coll., Syracuse Univ.; co-f. Cabletron Systems Inc. 1983, Pres., CEO –1999; Dir. Enterasys Networks Inc.; Gov. of New Hampshire 2003–; Adjunct Prof. of Entrepreneurship Babson Coll. 2000; Entrepreneur of the Year, Inc. Magazine 1991. *Address:* Office of the Governor, 107 North Main Street, Room 208, Concord, NH 03301, USA (Office).

BENSON, Sidney William, PhD, FAAS; American professor of chemistry; b. 26 Sept. 1918, New York; s. of Julius Benson and Dora Cohen; m. Anna Bruni 1986; one s. one d.; ed Stuyvesant High School, Columbia Coll. and Harvard Univ.; Postdoctoral Research Fellow, Harvard Univ. 1941–42; Instructor in Chem., Coll. of City of New York 1942–43, Group Leader, Manhattan Project 1943; Asst Prof., Univ. of Southern Calif. 1943–48, Assoc. Prof. 1948–51, Prof. of Chemistry 1951–64, 1976–91, Distinguished Prof. Emer. 1989; Scientific Co-Director, Loker Hydrocarbon Research Inst. 1977–90, Emer. 1991–; Chair. Dept of Kinetics and Thermochemistry, Stanford Research Inst. 1963–76; mem. Int. Editorial Bd, Elsevier Publishing Co., Amsterdam, Netherlands 1965–; Founder and Ed.-in-Chief Int. Journal of Chemical Kinetics 1967–83, Ed. Emer. 1983–; G. N. Lewis Lecturer, Univ. of Calif., Berkeley 1989; mem. Editorial Bd Journal of Physical Chem. 1981–84; Fellow American Physical Soc.; Foreign mem. Indian Acad. Science 1989; mem. ACS, NAS; Guggenheim Fellow, Chemical Kinetics and Fulbright Fellow to France 1950–51; NSF Sr Research Fellow 1957–58, in France 1971–72; Dr hc (Univ. of Nancy) 1989; ACS Award in Petroleum Chem. 1977, Tolman Medal 1978, Fellowship Award of the Japanese Soc. for Promotion of Science 1980, Irving Langmuir Award in Chemical Physics, ACS 1986, Polanyi Medal for Work in Chemical Kinetics (Royal Soc.) 1986, ACS Award, Orange Co. 1986, USC Award, Presidential Medallion 1986, Emer. Faculty Award, Univ. of SC 1990, Kapitsa Gold Medal Award, Russian Acad. of Nat. Science 1997, Citation Index for one of ten most cited papers in 25 years, Chemical Reviews Centennial Citation for two of most cited papers in Chemical Reviews. *Leisure interests:* skiing, swimming and tennis. *Address:* University of Southern California, University Park, MC-1661 Los Angeles, CA 90089-1661; 1110 North Bundy Drive, Los Angeles, CA 90049, USA (Home). *Telephone:* (213) 740-5964 (Office); (310) 471-5841 (Home). *Fax:* (213) 740-6679.

BENTHAM, Richard Walker, BA, LLB, FRSA; British professor of law; b. 26 June 1930; s. of Richard H. Bentham and Ellen W. Fisher; m. Stella W. Matthews 1957; one d.; ed Trinity Coll. Dublin and Middle Temple, London; called to Bar 1955; Lecturer in Law, Univ. of Tasmania 1955–57, Univ. of Sydney 1957–61; Legal Dept British Petroleum Co. PLC 1961–83, Deputy Legal Adviser 1979–83; Prof. of Petroleum and Mineral Law and Dir Centre for Petroleum and Mineral Law Studies, Univ. of Dundee 1983–90, Prof. Emer. 1991–; Russian Petroleum Legislation Project (Univ. of Houston, World Bank, ODA) 1991–96; mem. Council ICC Inst. of Int. Business Law and Practice 1988–95; British nominated mem. panel arbitrators IEA Dispute Settlement Centre; mem. Bd Scottish Council for Int. Arbitration 1988–98; mem. Int. Law Asscn, Int. Bar Asscn. *Publications:* publications in learned journals in the UK and overseas. *Leisure interests:* cricket, military history. *Address:* Earlham, 41 Trumlands Road, St Marychurch, Torquay, Devon, TQ1 4RN, England. *Telephone:* (1803) 314315. *Fax:* (1803) 314315.

BENTLEY, (Charles) Fred, OC, MSc, PhD, FAAS, FRSC; Canadian professor of soil science; b. 14 March 1914, Mass., USA; s. of Charles F. Bentley and Lavina A. (née MacKenzie) Bentley; m. Helen S. Petersen 1943; one s. one d.; ed Univ. of Alberta and Minnesota; Instructor in Soil Science Univ. of Minn. 1942–43; Instructor and Asst Prof. Soil Science Univ. of Sask. 1943–46; Faculty mem. Soil Science Univ. of Alberta 1946–79, Dean Faculty of Agric. 1959–68, Prof. Emer. 1979–; Special Adviser, Agric., Canadian Int. Devt Agency 1968–69; mem. Bd of Govs Int. Devt Research Centre 1970–74; Chair. of Bd Int. Crops Research Inst. for Semi-Arid Tropics, Hyderabad, India 1972–82, Int. Bd for Soil Research and Man., Bangkok, Thailand 1983–87; Consulting Agrologist, Int. Devt Volunteer 1979; Hon. DSc (Guelph) 1984, Alberta 1990; Fellow

Agric. Inst. of Canada, Canadian Soc. of Soil Science, American Soc. of Soil Science, American Soc. of Agronomy, Nat. Acad. of India; Pres. Int. Soc. of Soil Science 1975; Queen's Silver Jubilee Medal; Alberta Order of Excellence 1987, M. H. Bennett Award, Soil and Water Conservation Soc. 1989, Conf. Centre of ICRIS, India named C. Fred Bentley Conference Centre 2001; numerous other awards and distinctions. *Publications:* over 100 scientific reports and papers. *Leisure interests:* world devt, int. affairs, agriculture and human welfare, the population problem and planned parenthood. *Address:* 13103-66 Avenue NW, Edmonton, Alberta, T6H 1Y6, Canada. *Telephone:* (780) 435-6523.

BENTLEY, Gerald Eades, Jr, DPhil, DLitt, FRSC; American/Canadian scholar and professor of English; b. 23 Aug. 1930, Chicago, Ill.; s. of Gerald Eades Bentley and Esther Felt Bentley; m. Elizabeth Budd 1952; two d.; ed Princeton Univ. and Oxford Univ., UK; Instructor, Univ. of Chicago Dept of English 1956–60; Asst, later full Prof. of English, Univ. of Toronto, Canada 1960–96; Fulbright Lecturer, Univ. of Algiers 1967–68, Univ. of Poona, India 1975–76, Fudan Univ., Shanghai, People's Repub. of China 1982–83; Visiting Fellow, Univ. Coll., Swansea 1985, Univ. of Hyderabad (India) 1988, Fudan Univ. (China) 1988; Guggenheim Fellow, London 1958–59; Fellow of Canada Council and successor Social Science and Humanities Research Council of Canada 1963–64, 1970–71, 1977–78, 1984–85, 1991–94, 1995–98; Harold White Fellow, Nat. Library of Australia 1989, Connaught Fellow 1991–92; Rockefeller Research Fellow Bellaggio, Italy 1991; Prof./Visiting Research Fellow Princeton Univ. 1992, Merton Coll. Oxford 1993, Hatfield Coll., Durham 1996; Visiting Lecturer Australian Defence Force Acad. 1997; Co-Founder Conf. on Editorial Problems 1964–, Occasional Chair.; Jenkins Award for Bibliography. *Publications include:* Ed. William Blake, Vala, or The Four Zoas 1963, Ed. William Blake's Writings, 2 Vols 1978, Blake Records 1969, Blake Books 1977, Blake Records Supplement 1988, Blake Studies in Japan 1994, Blake Books Supplement 1995, The Stranger from Paradise: A Biography of William Blake 2001; The Early Engravings of Flaxman's Classical Designs 1964, A Bibliography of George Cumberland 1975, Editing Eighteenth Century Novels (Ed.) 1975, George Cumberland, the Captive of the Castle of Sennaar (Ed.) 1991. *Leisure interests:* book collecting, travel. *Address:* 246 MacPherson Avenue, Toronto, Ont., M4V 1A2, Canada; Dutch Boys Landing, Mears, MI 49436, USA (May–Sept.). *Telephone:* (416) 922-5613.

BENTON, Peter Faulkner, MA; British economic consultant; b. 6 Oct. 1934, London; s. of the late S. Faulkner Benton and Hilda Benton; m. Ruth S. Cobb 1959; two s. three d.; ed Oundle School and Queens' Coll. Cambridge; Jr man. positions in Unilever, Shell Chemicals and Berger, Jenson and Nicholson 1959–64; consultant, McKinsey & Co., London and Chicago 1964–71; Dir Gallaher Ltd 1971–77; Man. Dir Post Office Telecommunications 1978–81; Deputy Chair. British Telecom 1981–83; Special Adviser to EEC 1983–84; Chair. European Practice, Nolan, Norton & Co. 1984–87, Enfield Dist Health Authority 1986–92; Vice-Pres. European Council of Man. 1989–92; Dir Singer & Friedlander Ltd 1983–89, Tandata Holdings PLC. 1983–89, Turing Inst. 1985–95, Woodside Communications Ltd 1995–96; Dir Gen. British Inst. of Man. 1987–92; Chair. Enterprise Support Group 1993–96; Chair. Visiting Group Inst. for Systems, Eng and Informatics, Italy 1993–94, Visiting Group Inst. for Systems, Informatics and Safety, Italy 1996–99; Adviser to Arthur Andersen 1992–98; mem. Int. Advisory Bd for Science and Tech. to Govt of Portugal 1996–2002, Industrial Devt Advisory Bd (DTI) 1988–94; Adviser to Stern Stewart Inc. 1995–2001; mem. Exec. Cttee Athenaeum 1997–2002; Chair. Ditchley Conf. on Information Tech. 1980, North London Hospice 1985–89, World Bank Confs. on Catastrophe 1988, 1989, Chair. Delhi Conf. on Indian Infrastructure 1998; Adam Smith Lecturer 1991; Pres. Highgate Literary and Scientific Inst. 1981–88; Treas. Harington Scheme, London 1983–93; Gov. Molecule Theatre, London 1985–91; Ind. mem. British Library Advisory Council 1988–93; Companion Chartered Man. Inst. 1978; IEE Award 1994. *Achievements include:* led reorganization of UK gas industry 1966–71. *Publication:* Riding the Whirlwind 1990. *Leisure interests:* reading, conversation, sailing, early music. *Address:* Northgate House, Highgate Hill, London, N6 5HD (Home); Dolphins, Polruan-by-Fowey, Cornwall, PL23 1PP, England. *Telephone:* (20) 8341-1122. *Fax:* (20) 8341-1122.

BENTON II, Fletcher Chapman, BFA; American artist; b. 25 Feb. 1931, Jackson, Ohio; m. Roberta Lee 1964; one s. one d.; ed Miami Univ.; mem. Faculty, Calif. Coll. of Arts and Crafts 1959, San Francisco Art Inst. 1964–67; Prof. of Art Calif. State Univ., San José 1967–86; American Acad. of Arts and Letters Award for Distinguished Service to the Arts 1979, President's Scholar Award, Calif. State Univ. San José 1980, San Francisco Arts. Comm. Award of Honor for Outstanding Achievement in Sculpture 1982; Hon. DFA (Miami Univ.) 1993, (Columbus Univ. of Rio Grande, Rio Grande, Ohio) 1994. *Solo art exhibitions:* San Francisco Museum of Art 1965, 1970, Galeria Bonino, New York 1968, 1969, Galerie Françoise Mayer, Brussels 1969, Albright-Knox Art Gallery, Buffalo, New York 1970, Galeria Bonino, Buenos Aires 1970, Estudio Actual, Caracas, Venezuela 1970, John Berggruen Gallery, San Francisco 1971, Stanford Univ. Museum of Art, Calif. 1971, Galeria Bonino, Rio de Janeiro 1973, Art Club of Chicago 1979, American Acad. of Arts and Letters, New York 1979, Suermondt-Ludwig Museum, Aachen, FRG 1980, Klingspor Museum, Offenback, FRG 1981, Riva Yares Gallery, Scottsdale, Ariz. 1981, San Jose Museum of Art, Calif. 1982, Galerie B. Haasner, Wiesbaden, FRG 1987, Gothaer Kunstforum, Cologne 1993, Tasende Gallery, W Hollywood 1998, La Jolla, Calif. 1998, Jean Albano Gallery, Chicago 1998, Sheldon

Memorial Art Gallery and Sculpture Garden, Univ. of Neb., Lincoln 1999, Imago Galleries, Palm Desert, Calif. 2000, The Art Show, 7th Regt Armory, New York 2001; more than 30 group exhbns. throughout the world between 1966 and 2001. *Address:* 250 Dore Street, San Francisco, CA 94103, USA (Office). *Telephone:* (415) 863-7207 (Office). *Fax:* (415) 863-8052 (Office). *E-mail:* bstudio@slip.net (Office). *Website:* www.fletcherbentonStudio.com (Office).

BENYON, Margaret, MBE, PhD, BFA; British artist; b. 29 April 1940, Birmingham; m. William Rodwell 1974; one s. one d.; ed Kenya High School, Slade School of Fine Art, Univ. Coll. London, Royal Coll. of Art; Visiting Tutor Coventry Coll. of Art 1966–68, Trent Polytechnic, Nottingham 1968–71, Holography Unit, RCA 1985–89; Fellow in Fine Art, Univ. of Nottingham 1968–71; Leverhulme Sr Art Fellow, Univ. of Strathclyde 1971–73; Co-ordinator Graphic Investigation, Canberra School of Art, Australia 1977–80; Creative Arts Fellow A.N.U., Canberra 1978; Artist-in-Residence, Museum of Holography, New York 1981, Center for Holographic Arts, New York 1999; pioneered holography as an art medium; works in public collections including Australian Nat. Gallery, Nat. Gallery of Vic., Australia, MIT Museum, USA, Calouste Gulbenkian Foundation, Portugal, Victoria and Albert Museum, London; over 100 exhbns. to date, including London, Vienna, New York, Frankfurt, Lisbon, Madrid, Nagoya, Liverpool, Bradford, Berlin, Boston, Tokyo; Hon. FRPS, Audrey Mellon Prize 1964, Carnegie Trust Award 1972, Kodak Photographic Bursary 1982, Calouste Gulbenkian Holography Award 1982, Agfa 'Best of Exhibition' Award, USA 1985, Shearwater Foundation Holography Award, USA 1987, Lifetime Achievement Award, Art in Holography International Symposium, UK 1996. *Works include:* Hot Air 1970, Bird in Box 1973, Solar Markers 1979, White Rainbow 1980, Tiresias 1981, Conjugal Series 1983, Tigirl 1985, Cosmetic Series 1986–93, Cornucopia 1994–. *Publications:* articles in over 100 Publs. *Address:* Holography Studio, 40 Springdale Avenue, Broadstone, Dorset, BH18 9EU, England (Office). *Telephone:* (1202) 698067 (Office). *Fax:* (1202) 698067 (Office). *E-mail:* benyon@holography.demon.co.uk (Office). *Website:* www.holography.demon.co.uk (Office).

BENZ, Edward J., Jr, MD, MA; American professor of medicine, paediatrics and pathology, physician and hospital administrator; b. 22 May 1946, Pittsburgh; m. Margaret A. Vettese; one s. one d.; ed Allentown Cen. Catholic High School, Princeton Univ., Harvard Medical School, Yale Univ.; research fellowships Princeton and Boston Univs. 1967–71; Jr Asst Health Services Officer U.S. Public Health Service, N.J.H., NHLBI 1972–73, Sr Asst Surgeon 1973–75; intern Peter Bent Brigham Hosp., Boston 1973–74, Asst Resident Physician 1974–75; Clinical Fellow Harvard Medical School 1973–75; Fellow in Medicine (Hematology) Children's Hosp. Medical Center, Boston 1974–75; Research Assoc. Molecular Hematology Br. NHLBI, NIH, Bethesda, Md 1975–78; Fellow in Hematology Yale Univ. School of Medicine 1978–80; Assoc. Attending in Medicine Yale-New Haven Hosp. 1979–81, Attending Physician 1981–93; Asst Prof. of Medicine Hematology Section, Dept of Internal Medicine, Yale Univ. School of Medicine 1979–82, Assoc. Prof. of Medicine 1982–84, Assoc. Prof. of Human Genetics (Jt) 1983–87, Assoc. Prof. of Internal Medicine 1984–87, Prof. of Internal Medicine and Genetics 1987–93, Chief Hematology Section, Dept of Internal Medicine 1987–93, Assoc. Chair. for Academic Affairs 1988–90, Vice Chair. 1990–93; Jack D. Myers Prof. and Chair. Dept of Medicine, Univ. of Pittsburgh School of Medicine 1993–95, Prof. of Molecular Genetics and Biochem. (Jt) 1993–95; Adjunct Prof. of Biological Sciences, Carnegie Mellon Univ., Pittsburgh 1993–95; Chief Medicine Service, Univ. of Pittsburgh Medical Center 1993–95; Sir William Osler Prof. and Dir Dept of Medicine, Johns Hopkins Univ. School of Medicine 1995–2000, Prof. of Molecular Biology and Genetics 1995–2000; Physician-in-Chief Johns Hopkins Hosp. 1995–2000; Pres. and CEO Dana-Farber Cancer Inst., Harvard Univ. 2000–, CEO Dana-Farber/ Partners Cancer Care 2000–, Dir Dana-Farber/Harvard Cancer Center, mem. Governing Bd Dana-Farber/Children's Center; Richard and Susan Smith Prof. of Medicine, Prof. of Pediatrics, Prof. of Pathology, Faculty Dean for Oncology, Harvard Medical School 2000–; numerous visiting professorships and lectures in U.S., UK, Canada and France; Chair. Red Cells and Hemoglobin Sub-Cttee, American Soc. of Hematology 1983, 1989, Molecular Genetics Educ. Panel 1984–87, Hematology I Study Section, Nat. Insts. of Health Research 1993–95; Pres. American Soc. of Clinical Investigation 1992, Scientific Affairs Cttee 1992, Educ. Program 1994; mem. Exec. Cttee American Soc. of Hematology 1994–, (Vice Pres. 1998, Pres. 2000–), Scientific Advisory Bd Inst. of Molecular Medicine, Oxford Univ. 1998; mem. AAAS Asscn of American Physicians, Inst. of Medicine and many other socs. concerned with biology, medicine and genetics; mem. Editorial Bd American Journal of Hematology 1985–, Int. Journal of Hematology, Tokyo 1990–99, American Journal of Medicine 1994–; Adviser in Medicine Oxford Univ. Press 1994–; Consulting Ed. Journal of Clinical Investigation 1998–; Assoc. Ed. New England Journal of Medicine 2001–; Fellow American Asscn of Physicians 1992; Basil O'Connor Award, March of Dimes, Nat. Foundation 1980, Nat. Insts. of Health Research Career Devt Award 1982, Scientific Research Award, American Asscn of Blood Banks 1986, Inst. of Medicine Award and other awards. *Publications:* Molecular Genetics (Methods in Hematology series) (Ed.) 1989, Hematology: Principles and Practice (Jt Ed.) 1990, Oxford Textbook of Medicine (Co-Ed.) 1997 and numerous articles in professional journals. *Leisure interests:* tennis, reading, travel, hiking. *Address:* Dana-Farber Cancer Institute, Room D1628, 44 Binney Street, Boston, MA 02115 (Office); 28 Chestnut Hill Terrace, Chestnut Hill, MA 02467, USA (Home).

Telephone: (617) 632-4266 (Office); (617) 916-5345 (Home). *Fax:* (617) 632-2161 (Office); (617) 916-5681 (Home). *E-mail:* edward_benz@dfci.harvard.edu (Office); edbenz@attbi.com (Home). *Website:* www.dfci.org (Office).

BENZER, Seymour, PhD, FAAS; American biologist; b. 15 Oct. 1921, New York; s. of Mayer Benzer and Eva Naidorf; m. 1st Dorothy Vlosky 1942 (died 1978); two c.; m. 2nd Carol Miller 1980; one c.; ed Brooklyn Coll. and Purdue Univ.; Asst Prof. of Physics Purdue Univ. 1947–53, Assoc. Prof. of Biophysics 1953–58, Prof. 1958–61, Stuart Distinguished Prof. 1961–67; Biophysicist Oak Ridge Nat. Laboratory 1948–49; Research Fellow Calif. Inst. of Technology 1949–51, Visiting Assoc. 1965–67, Prof. of Biology 1967–75, Boswell Prof. of Neuroscience 1975–; Fulbright Research Scholar, Pasteur Inst., Paris 1951–52; Senior Nat. Science Foundation Research Fellow Cambridge 1957–58; mem. NAS, Harvey Soc., Biophysical Soc., American Acad. of Arts and Sciences, American Philosophical Soc., Foreign mem. Royal Soc. London; Dr. hc (Purdue) 1968, (Columbia) 1974, (Yale) 1977, (Brandeis) 1978, (City Univ. of New York) 1978, (Univ. of Paris) 1983; awards include Sigma Xi Research Award 1957, Ricketts Award, Univ. of Chicago, Lasker Award 1971, Prix Charles-Leopold Mayer, French Acad. of Sciences 1975, Harvey Prize, Technion, Israel 1977, Warren Triennial Prize, Mass. General Hosp. 1977, Dickson Prize, Carnegie-Mellon Univ. 1978, Nat. Medal of Science (USA) 1983, Rosenstiel Award, Brandeis Univ. 1986, T. H. Morgan Medal, Genetics Soc. of America 1986, Lashley Award, American Philosophical Soc. 1988, Gerard Medal, Soc. for Neuroscience 1989, Helmerich Award for Retina Research 1990, Wolf Foundation Award for Medicine 1991, Bristol-Myers Squibb Award for Neuroscience 1992, Crafoord Prize (Royal Swedish Acad. of Sciences) 1993, Feltrinelli Prize (Accademia dei Lincei) 1994, Mendel Medal (Genetical Soc. of GB) 1994, Int. Prize for Biology (Japan) 2000, Passano Award 2001, Nat. Acad. Award in Neuroscience 2001, March of Dimes Award 2002, Pasarow Award 2002. *Publications:* The Elementary Units of Heredity 1957, Induction of Specific Mutations with 5-bromouracil 1958, Topology of the Genetic Fine Structure 1959, Topography of the Genetic Fine Structure 1961, A Change from Nonsense to Sense in the Genetic Code 1962, On the Role of Soluble Ribonucleic Acid in Coding for Amino Acids 1962, A Physical Basis for Degeneracy in the Genetic Code 1962, Adventures in the rII Region 1966, Isolation of Behavioral Mutants of Drosophila by Countercurrent Distribution 1967, Genetic Dissection of the Drosophila Nervous System by Means of Mosaics 1970, Mapping of Behavior in Drosophila Mosaics 1972, Genetic Dissection of Behavior 1973, Dunce, a Mutant of Drosophila Deficient in Learning 1976, Monoclonal Antibodies Against the Drosophila Nervous System 1982, Antigenic Cross-Reaction Between Drosophila and Human Brain 1983, Neuronal Development in the Drosophila Retina, Monoclonal Antibodies as Molecular Probes 1984, From Monoclonal Antibody to Gene for a Neuron-Specific Glycoprotein in Drosophila 1985, Molecular Characterization and Expression of Sevenless, a Gene involved in Neuronal Pattern Formation in the Drosophila Eye 1987, The Fly and Eye 1990, numerous other publs on neurogenetics. *Address:* 2075 Robin Road, San Marino, CA 91108-2831, USA (Home).

BENZI, Roberto; Italian/French conductor; b. 12 Dec. 1937, Marseille; s. of Giuseppe Benzi and Maria Pastorino; m. Jane Rhodes 1966; studied conducting with Andre Cluytens; début as conductor, France 1948; tours in Europe and S. America 1949–52; opera conducting début 1954; conducted Carmen, Paris Opera 1959; guest conductor Europe, Japan, Israel, Mexico, Canada, USA, S. Africa and main music festivals; Music Dir Bordeaux-Aquitaine Orchestra 1973–87, Arnhem Philharmonic 1989–98, Dutch Nat. Youth Orchestra 1991–96; Chevalier, Légion d'honneur, Ordre National du Mérite, Ordre des Palmes Académiques, Order of Orange-Nassau. *Publications:* orchestrations of Brahms op. 23 Schumann Variations 1970, Brahms op. 24 Variations and Fugue on a theme by Handel 1973, Rossini Thème et Variations 1978, Erik Satie Je te veux, valse 1987. *Leisure interests:* wildlife, astronomy, cycling. *Address:* 12 Villa Ste.-Foy, 92200 Neuilly-sur-Seine, France. *Telephone:* 1-46-24-27-85. *Fax:* 1-46-24-55-73.

BERARDI, Antonio, BA; British fashion designer; b. 21 Dec. 1968, Grantham; ed Cen. St Martin's School of Art and Design; career launched when graduation collection was purchased by Liberty and A la Mode; first Spring/Summer own label collection also bought by Liberty and A la Mode 1995; designs featured in New Generation catwalk promotion sponsored by Marks and Spencer 1996; joined Italian Mfrs Givuesse 1996; launched Autumn/Winter label 1997; apptd design consultant Ruffo leather and suede mfrs 1997; Best New Designer, VHI Awards (USA) 1997. *Address:* St Martin's House, 59 St Martin's Lane, London, WC2N 4JS, England.

BERDENNIKOV, Grigory Vitalievich; Russian diplomatist; b. 24 Dec. 1950, Moscow; m.; one d.; ed Moscow Inst. of Int. Relations; diplomatic service 1973–, sec., atttaché Mission in UN, New York 1973–78, Sec. of Div. USSR Ministry of Foreign Affairs 1978–81, Second then First Sec. Mission to UN, Geneva 1981–86, Counsellor, Chief of Div., Deputy Chief Dept of Armament Reduction and Disarmament, USSR (now Russian) Ministry of Foreign Affairs 1986–92, Deputy Minister of Foreign Affairs of Russia 1992–94, 1999–2001, Dir Dept of Security and Disarmament 1998–99; Perm. Rep. to Disarmament Conf. Geneva 1994–98; Perm. Rep. of Russia at Int. Orgs. in Vienna 2001–; Order of Friendship 1997; 850th Anniversary of Moscow Medal 1998, Presidential Letter of Gratitude 2000. *Address:* Permanent Mission of the Russian Federation to the International Organizations in Vienna, Erzherzog Karl-Strasse 182, 1220 Vienna, Austria. *Telephone:* (1) 282-53-91; (1) 282-53-93. *Fax:* (1) 280-56-87.

BERDYEV, Batyr Atayevich; Turkmen philologist; b. 3 Oct. 1960, Ashgabat, Turkmenistan; ed Turkmen State Univ.; Corresp., Head of Div., Deputy Ed., Ed. Komsomolets Turkmenistana (newspaper) 1982–90; Consultant Int. Div. of Turkmen Presidency 1992–; Deputy Minister of Foreign Relations Turkmenistan 1992–94; Amb. to Austria (also Accred to Slovakia and Czech Repub.) 1996–2000; Minister of Foreign Relations of Turkmenistan 2000; Order of Galkynysh, Order of Bitaraplyk. *Address:* c/o Government House, Ministry of Foreign Affairs, Ashgabat, Turkmenistan (Office). *Telephone:* (2) 266211 (Office). *Fax:* (2) 253583 (Office).

BEREND, T. Ivan, PhD, DEcon; American (born Hungarian) economic historian; b. 11 Dec. 1930, Budapest; s. of Mihály Berend and Elvira Gellei; two d.; ed Univ. of Economics and Univ. of Sciences, Faculty of Philosophy, Budapest; Asst Lecturer, Karl Marx Univ. of Economics 1953, Sr Lecturer 1960, Prof. of Econ. History 1964–, Head of Dept 1967–85, Rector 1973–79; Prof. of History Univ. of Calif. at LA 1990–, Dir Center for European and Russian Studies 1993–; Gen. Sec. Hungarian Historical Soc. 1966–72, Pres. 1975–79; Corresp. mem. Hungarian Acad. of Sciences 1973–79, mem. 1979–, Pres. 1985–90; Fellowship, Ford Foundation, New York 1966–67; Visiting Fellow, St Antony's Coll., Oxford 1972–73; Visiting Prof. Univ. of Calif., Berkeley 1978; Visiting Fellow, All Souls Coll., Oxford 1980; Fellow, Woodrow Wilson Int. Center for Scholars, Washington, DC 1982–83; Co-Chair. Bd of Dirs. Inst. for East-West Security Studies 1986; mem. Exec. Cttee of Int. Econ. Soc. 1982–86, Vice-Pres. 1986–1994; First Vice-Pres. Int. Cttee of Historial Sciences 1990–95, Pres. 1995–2000; Corresp. mem. Royal Historical Soc. 1981, Academia Europe 1987, Bulgarian Acad. of Sciences 1988, British Acad. 1989, Austrian Acad. of Sciences 1989, Czechoslovak Acad. of Sciences 1988; Hon. D.Litt. (St John's Univ., New York) 1986, (Glasgow) 1990, (Janus Pannonius Univ., Pécs) 1994; Kossuth Prize 1961, State Prize 1985. *Publications:* (with György Ránki): Magyarország gyáripara 1900–1914 1955, Magyarország gyáripara a II. világháboru elött és a háboru idöszakában 1933–1944 1958, Magyarország a fasiszta Németország "életterében" 1960, Magyarország gazdasága az I. világháboru után 1919–1929 1966, Economic Development in East-Central Europe in the 19th and 20th Centuries 1974, Hungary—A Century of Economic Development, Underdevelopment and Economic Growth, The European Periphery and Industrialization 1780–1914 1982, The Hungarian Economy in the Twentieth Century 1985, The European Economy in the Nineteenth Century 1987; (as sole author): Ujjáépités és a nagytöke elleni harc Magyarországon 1945–1948 1962, Gazdaságpolitika az elsö ötéves terv meginditásakor 1948–1950 1964, Öt elöadás gazdaságról és oktatásról 1978, Napjaink a történelemben 1980, Válságos évtizedek 1982, Gazdasági utkeresés 1983, The Crisis Zone of Europe 1986, Szocializmus és reform 1986, The Hungarian Economic Reforms 1990, Central and Eastern Europe 1944–93 – Detour from the Periphery to the Periphery 1996, Decades of Crisis: Central and Eastern Europe Before World War II 1998, History Derailed: Central and Eastern Europe in the 'Long' 19th Century 2002. *Leisure interests:* walking, swimming. *Address:* Department of History, University of California, Los Angeles, 405 Hildgard Avenue, Los Angeles, CA 90096, USA. *Telephone:* (310) 825-1178. *Fax:* (310) 206-3556 (Office). *E-mail:* iberend@history.ucla.edu (Home).

BERENDT, John Lawrence; American writer; b. 5 Dec. 1939, Syracuse, NY; s. of Ralph Berendt and Carol (Deschere) Berendt; ed Nottingham High School, Syracuse, Harvard Univ.; Assoc. Ed. Esquire 1961–69, columnist 1982–94; Ed. New York magazine 1977–82; mem. PEN. *Publication:* Midnight in the Garden of Good and Evil 1994. *Address:* c/o Random House, 299 Park Avenue, New York, NY 10171, USA (Office).

BÉRENGER, Paul Raymond, BA; Mauritian politician; b. 26 March 1945, Quatre Bornes; m. Arline Perrier 1971; one s. one d.; ed Collège du Saint Esprit, Univ. of Wales and Sorbonne, Paris; Gen. Sec. Mouvement Militant Mauricien 1969–82; Minister of Finance 1982–83, of Foreign Affairs 1991, MP 1982–83; Deputy Prime Minister and Minister of Foreign Affairs and Int. and Regional Co-operation 1995; Deputy Prime Minister and Minister of Finance Sept. 2000–; Gov. IMF, African Devt Bank/African Devt Fund. *Leisure interests:* reading, swimming. *Address:* Ministry of Finance, Government Centre, Port Louis (Office); Wellington Street, Quatre Bornes, Mauritius (Home). *Telephone:* 201-2557 (Office); 54-1998 (Home). *Fax:* 208-9823 (Office). *E-mail:* mof@bow.internet.mu (Office). *Website:* ncb.intnet.mu/mof.htm (Office).

BERENGER, Tom; American actor; b. 31 May 1950, Chicago; ed Univ. of Missouri; stage appearances in regional theatre and off-Broadway including The Rose Tattoo, Electra, A Streetcar Named Desire, End as a Man. *Films:* Beyond the Door 1975, Sentinel, Looking for Mr Goodbar, In Praise of Older Women, Butch and Sundance: The Early Days, The Dogs of War, The Big Chill, Eddie and the Cruisers, Fear City, Firstborn, Rustler's Rhapsody, Platoon, Someone to Watch Over Me, Shoot to Kill, Betrayed, Last Rites, Major League, Love at Large, The Field, Shattered, Chasers, Sniper 1993, Sliver 1993, Major League 2 1994, Last of the Dogmen 1994, Gettysburg 1994, The Substitute 1996, An Occasional Hell 1996, The Gingerbread Man 1997, Takedown 2000, One Man's Hero (also producer) 1999, Diplomatic Siege 1999, A Murder of Crows 1999, The Hollywood Sign 2000, Fear of Flying 2000, Training Day 2001, Watchtower 2001, Eye See You 2001. *TV appearances include* One Life to Live (series), Johnny We Hardly Knew Ye, Flesh and Blood, If Tomorrow Comes. *Address:* c/o C.A.A., 9830 Wilshire Boulevard, Beverly Hills, CA 90212, USA.

BERENGO GARDIN, Gianni; Italian photographer; b. 10 Oct. 1930, Santa Margherita Ligure; s. of Alberto Berengo Gardin and Carmen Maffei Berengo Gardin; m. Caterina Stiffoni 1957; one s. one d.; began working as photographer 1954; has lived and worked in Switzerland, Rome, Venice; living in Milan 1965–; photographs originally published by Il Mondo magazine, now published by maj. magazines in Italy and world-wide; photographs in perm. collections of Museum of Modern Art, New York, Bibliothèque Nationale Paris, Eastman House, Rochester, NY, Musée de l'Elysée, Lausanne, Museum of Aesthetic Art, Beijing; Mois de la Photo Brassaï Award, Paris 1990; Leica Oskar Barnack Award, Arles 1995. *Exhibitions include:* Cologne Photokina, Montreal Expo, Venice Biennale, Milan, Rome, Venice, Arles, London, Lausanne, Paris, Vienna, New York. *Publications:* over 190 photographic books. *Leisure interests:* photography, farming, his little dog Olivia. *Address:* Via S. Michele del Carso 21, 20144 Milan, Italy. *Telephone:* (2) 4692877. *Fax:* (2) 4692877.

BERESFORD, Bruce; Australian film director; b. 16 Aug 1940, Sydney; s. of Leslie Beresford and Lona Beresford; m. 1st Rhoisin Beresford 1965; two s. one d.; m. 2nd Virginia Duigan 1989; one d.; ed Univ. of Sydney; worked in advertising; worked for Australian Broadcasting Comm.; went to England 1961; odd jobs including teaching; film ed. Nigeria 1964–66; Sec. to British Film Inst.'s Production Bd 1966; feature film Dir 1971–; directed many short films 1960–75. *Films directed:* The Adventures of Barry Mackenzie 1972, Barry Mackenzie Holds His Own 1974, Side by Side 1975, Don's Party 1976, The Getting of Wisdom 1977, Money Movers 1979, Breaker Morant 1980, Puberty Blues 1981, The Club 1981, Tender Mercies 1983, King David 1984, Crimes of the Heart 1986, Fringe Dwellers 1986, Aria (segment) 1987, Her Alibi 1988, Driving Miss Daisy 1989 (Acad. Award Best Film 1990), Mr. Johnson 1990, Black Robe 1990, Rich in Love 1993, A Good Man in Africa 1993, Silent Fall 1994, The Last Dance 1995, Paradise Road 1996, Double Jeopardy 1998, Rigoletto (opera) 2000, Bride of the Wind 2001, Evelyn 2002, Starring Pancho Villa as Himself 2003. *Address:* c/o Anthony A. Williams, P.O. Box 1379, Darlinghurst, NSW 2010, Australia.

BERESFORD, Meg, BA; British peace campaign organizer; b. 5 Sept. 1937, Birmingham; d. of the late John Tristram Beresford and of Anne Isobel Northcroft (née Stuart-Wortley); m. William Tanner 1959; two s.; ed Sherborne School for Girls, Dorset and Univ. of Warwick; Founder mem. and Coordinator, Campaign Atom, Oxford 1980–81; elected to Nat. Council Campaign for Nuclear Disarmament (CND) 1980; Organizing Sec. European Nuclear Disarmament 1981–83; Vice-Chair. CND 1983–85, Gen. Sec. 1985–90; Staff Co-ordinator, The Iona Community 1991–94; Asst Dir YMCA Centre, Wiston Lodge 1994–97, Man. 1997–. *Publication:* Into the Twenty First Century 1989. *Leisure interests:* walking, the environment, reading and art. *Address:* Wiston Lodge, Wiston, Biggar, ML12 6HT, Scotland. *Telephone:* (1899) 850228. *Fax:* (1899) 850693. *E-mail:* wiston@zetnet.co.uk. *Website:* www.wiston.zetnet.co.uk.

BEREZOVSKY, Boris Abramovich, DrMathSc; Russian businessman, mathematician and politician; b. 23 Jan. 1946, Moscow; m.; one s. three d.; ed Moscow Inst. of Wood Tech., Moscow State Univ.; engineer Research Inst. of Testing Machines, Equipment and Measurement Devices 1968–69; engineer Hydrometeorological Research Cen. 1969; engineer, researcher, head of div. Inst. of Problems of Man. 1969–87; author of over 100 scientific articles on applied math., theory of man.; Corresp. mem. Russian Acad. of Sciences 1991; supervisor of introduction of automatization on Togliatti Car Works (VAZ) 1973–91; one of founders and Dir-Gen. LOGOVAZ Co. 1991–96, 1997–; Dir-Gen. All-Union Automobile Alliance (AVVA) 1993–96; Deputy Chair. Bd of Dirs Public Russian TV 1995–96; Deputy Sec. Security Council of Russian Fed. 1996–97; Exec. Sec. CIS 1998–99; accused of corruption, charges dismissed 1999; again accused Dec. 2000; elected to State Duma Dec. 1999, resgnd April 2000; charged with corruption; living in self-imposed exile in London; arrested again in London March 2003 at request of Russian authorities, who seek his extradition for alleged fraud in 1994–95; f. Charity Foundation Triumph 1994.

BEREZOVSKY, Boris Vadimovich; Russian pianist; b. 4 Jan. 1969, Moscow; m. 1989; ed Moscow Conservatoire; winner, Prize of Hope competition, City of Ufa 1985; London début, Wigmore Hall 1988; Gold Medal, Int. Tchaikovsky Piano Competition, Moscow 1990; appeared with Soviet Festival Orchestra, London 1990; recitals in New York, Washington, London, Amsterdam, Salzburg, Moscow, Leningrad, Tokyo, Osaka, etc.; appearances with orchestras including Philharmonia, New York Philharmonic, Philadelphia Orchestra, NDR Hamburg and Danish Nat. Radio Symphony Orchestra. *Address:* IMG Artists, Lovell House, 616 Chiswick High Road, London, W4 5RX, England. *Telephone:* (20) 8233-5800; (095) 241-74-87 (Moscow).

BERG, Adrian, MA, ARCA; British artist; b. 12 March 1929, London; s. of Charles Berg and Sarah Berg (née Sorby); ed Charterhouse, Gonville and Caius Coll. Cambridge, Trinity Coll. Dublin, St Martin's and Chelsea Schools of Art and Royal Coll. of Art; one-man exhbns in London, Florence, Düsseldorf, Montreal, Toronto and Chicago; Arts Council Serpentine Gallery, Paintings 1977–86, Piccadilly Gallery; touring exhbn, "A Sense of Place", Barbican Centre, London, Bath, Plymouth, Gwent, Sheffield, Newcastle-upon-Tyne, Edinburgh, 1993–94; RA Elect 1992; Hon. Fellow RCA 1994; several prizes including Gold Medal, Florence Biennale 1973, Maj. Prize, Tolly Cobbold Eastern Arts Asscn Exhbn 1981 and Third Prize, John Moores Liverpool

Exhbn 1982–83, First Nat. Trust Foundation for Art Award 1987, First Prize RWS Open 2001. *Leisure interests:* music, reading, travel, walking. *Address:* c/o Royal Academy of Arts, Piccadilly, London, W1J 0BD, England. *Telephone:* (20) 7629-2875.

BERG, Christian, DPhil; Danish professor of mathematics; b. 2 June 1944, Haarslev; m. Margrete Vergmann 1967; one s. one d.; ed Univ. of Copenhagen; Assoc. Prof., Univ. of Copenhagen 1972, Prof. of Math. 1978–, Chair. Math. Dept 1996–97, Dir Inst. for Math. Sciences 1997–2002; Pres. Danish Mathematical Soc. 1994–98; mem. Danish Natural Sciences Research Council 1985–92, Royal Danish Acad. of Sciences and Letters 1982– (Vice-Pres. 1999–); Gold Medal Univ. of Copenhagen 1970. *Publications:* research monographs: Potential Theory on Locally Compact Abelian Groups (with Forst) 1975, Harmonic Analysis on Semigroups (with Christensen and Ressel) 1984, research papers on potential theory and mathematical analysis. *Address:* Department of Mathematics, Universitetsparken 5, 2100 Copenhagen Ø, Denmark. *Telephone:* 35-32-07-28. *Fax:* 35-32-07-04. *E-mail:* berg@math.ku .dk (Office).

BERG, Eivinn; Norwegian diplomatist; b. 31 July 1931, Sandefjord; s. of Morten Berg and Ester Christoffersen; m. Unni Berg 1957; one s. two d.; ed Norwegian Coll. of Econs and Business Admin., Bergen, Norway; entered Foreign Service 1957; Attaché and Vice-Consul, Chicago 1957–60; Ministry of Foreign Affairs 1960–63, 1968–70; First Sec. Norwegian Perm. Del. to EFTA/GATT, UN Office, Geneva 1963–66, Head of Dept, EFTA 1966–68; Counsellor of Embassy, Brussels and Norway's Mission to EEC 1970–73; Dir Int. Affairs Norwegian Shipowners Asscn, Oslo 1973–78; Deputy Dir-Gen. Ministry of Foreign Affairs (Dept of External Econ. Affairs) 1978–80, Dir-Gen. 1980–81, State Sec., Ministry of Foreign Affairs 1984–88; Amb. and Perm. Rep. of Norway to NATO 1984–88, to European Union 1989–96; Chief Negotiator European Economic Area 1990–92, for possible accession of Norway to EU 1993–94, for Schengen Agreement 1995–96; Sr Adviser on int. and European affairs to Statoil, Norske Skog, Statkraft; Commdr, Order of the Crown, Belgium 1974, Commdr, Henrique Infante, Portugal 1980, Caballero Gran Cruz al Mérito Civil, Spain 1982, Grand Lion Order of the Lion, Finland 1983, Grand Officier, Order Nat. du Mérite, France 1984, Commdr, Royal Order of St Olav, Norway 1987. *Leisure interests:* golf, sailing, mountain hiking. *Address:* Aasstubben 64, 0381 Oslo, Norway. *Telephone:* 22-52-50-08. *Fax:* 22-52-51-88. *E-mail:* eivinnbe@online.no (Office).

BERG, Jeffrey Spencer, BA; American theatrical agent; b. 26 May 1947, LA; ed Univ. of California, Berkeley; fmrly head literature div. Creative Man. Assocs, fmrly Vice-Pres.; Vice-Pres. Motion Picture Dept Int. Creative Man. 1975–80, Pres. 1980–85, Chair. and CEO 1985–; Dir Josephson Int. Inc., Marshall McLuhan Center of Global Communication; Pres. Letters and Science Exec. Bd Univ. of Calif., Berkeley; Co-Chair. Calif. Information Tech. Council; Trustee Univ. of Berkeley Foundation. *Address:* International Creative Management, 8942 Wilshire Boulevard, Beverly Hills, CA 90211, USA.

BERG, Knut, MA, DPhil; Norwegian art historian; b. 4 Aug. 1925, Oslo; s. of Arno Berg and Signe (née Mowinckel-Larsen) Berg; m. Marcia W Robinson 1953; two s. one d.; ed Univ. of Oslo; research scholar, Univ. of Oslo 1953–65; curator, Dept of Prints and Drawings, Nasjonalgalleriet 1965–73, Dir Nasjonalgalleriet 1973–96; mem. Norwegian Acad. of Science and the Humanities, Norwegian Cultural Council; Chair. State Cttee for Cultural Exchanges with Foreign Countries 1981, Soc. for Benefit of City of Oslo 1980; mem. numerous other bds and cttees; Hon. mem. Norwegian Soc. of Art Historians; Commdr Order of St Olav. *Publications:* Studies in Tuscan Twelfth Century Illumination 1968, King Magnus Haakonson's Laws of Norway 1983; ed. History of Norwegian Art (Vols 1–7) 1981–83, Dictionary of Norwegian Artists 1981–86. *Address:* Rosenborg gate 5, 0356, Oslo, Norway. *Telephone:* 22-60-21-07.

BERG, Paul, PhD, FAAS; American biochemist; b. 30 June 1926, New York; s. of Harry Berg and Sarah Brodsky; m. Mildred Levy 1947; one s.; ed Pennsylvania State Univ. and Western Reserve Univ.; Postdoctoral Fellow, Copenhagen Univ., Denmark 1952–53; Postdoctoral Fellow, Wash. Univ., St Louis, Mo. 1953–54, Scholar in Cancer Research 1954–57, Asst to Assoc. Prof. of Microbiology 1955–59; Prof. of Biochemistry, Stanford Univ. School of Medicine, Stanford, Calif. 1959–, Willson Prof. of Biochem. 1970–94, Chair Dept 1969–74, Dir Beckman Center for Molecular and Genetic Medicine 1985–2001, Robert W. Cahill Prof. of Cancer Research 1994–2000; Dir Nat. Foundation for Biomedical Research 1994–; Chair. Nat. Advisory Cttee Human Genome Project 1990–92; Dir several cos; Sr Post-Doctoral Fellow of NSF 1961–68; Non-resident Fellow Salk Inst. 1973–83; Foreign mem. Académie des Sciences, France 1981; mem. Inst. Medicine, NAS and several other professional bodies; Pres. American Soc. of Biological Chemists 1974–75; Eli Lilly Prize in Biochemistry 1959, Calif. Scientist of the Year 1963, V. D. Mattia Award 1972, shared Nobel Prize for Chem. 1980, Nat. Medal of Science and other awards and prizes. *Publications:* Genes and Genomes 1991, Dealing with Genes. The Language of Heredity 1992, Exploring Genetic Mechanisms 1997. *Leisure interests:* travel, art and sports. *Address:* Stanford University School of Medicine, Beckman Center, B-062, Stanford, CA 94305, USA (Office). *Telephone:* (415) 723-6170 (Office).

BERGANT, Boris; Slovenian journalist and broadcasting executive; b. 19 April 1948, Maribor; s. of Evgen Bergant and Marija Bergant; m. Verena Bergant 1969; one s.; fmrly Ed. Foreign Affairs, Ed.-in-Chief of News TV Slovenia; fmr radio journalist; former Deputy Dir-Gen. Int. Relations and Programme Cooperation RTV Slovenija, Deputy Dir.-Gen. RTV Slovenija

1992–; Pres. Slovenian Journalist Asscn 1986–90; mem. Admin. Council European Broadcasting Union 1990–92, 1996–, Vice-Chair. TV programme Cttee 1993–98, mem. radio Cttee 1993, Vice-Pres. of Union 1998–; Pres. Circom-Regional 1990–92, Sec.-Gen. 1995–2001; awarded Tomšičeva Nagrada Prize for Best Journalistic Achievement in Slovenia; awards at Monte Carlo, New York and Leipzig TV festivals. *Leisure interests:* tennis, golf. *Address:* Radio-televizija Slovenija, 1550 Ljubljana, Kolodvorska 2–4, Slovenia. *Telephone:* (61) 475-21-51 (Office). *Fax:* (61) 475-21-50 (Office). *E-mail:* boris.bergant@rtvslo.si (Office).

BERGANZA, Teresa; Spanish mezzo-soprano; b. 16 March 1935, Madrid; d. of Guillermo Berganza and Ascensión Berganza; m. 1st Felix Lavilla 1957; one s. two d.; m. 2nd José Rifa 1986; début in Aix-en-Provence 1957, in England, Glyndebourne 1958; has sung at La Scala, Milan, Opera Rome, Metropolitan, New York, Chicago Opera House, San Francisco Opera, Covent Garden, etc.; has appeared at festivals in Edinburgh, Holland, Glyndebourne; concerts in France, Belgium, Holland, Italy, Germany, Spain, Austria, Portugal, Scandinavia, Israel, Mexico, Buenos Aires, USA, Canada, etc.; appeared as Rosina in Il Barbiere di Siviglia, Covent Garden 1967; sung Carmen, at opening ceremony of Expo 92, Seville, also at opening ceremonies Barcelona Olympics 1992, mem. Real Academia de Bellas Artes de San Fernando, Spanish Royal Acad. of Arts 1994; Premio Lucrezia Arana, Premio Extraordinario del Conservatorio de Madrid, Grande Cruz, Isabel la Católica, Harriet Cohen Award, Int. Critic Award 1988; Commdr, Ordre des Arts et des Lettres, Grand Prix de Disque (six times), Grand Prix Rossini. *Film:* Don Giovanni. *Publication:* Flor de Soledad y Silencio 1984. *Leisure interests:* art, music, reading. *Address:* c/o Askonas Holt, 19A Air Street, London, W1, England (Office); La Rossiniana, Archanda 5, P.O. Box 137, 28200 San Lorenzo del Escorial, Madrid, Spain. *Telephone:* (1) 8960941 (Madrid). *Fax:* (1) 8960816 (Madrid).

BERGÉ, Pierre Vital Georges; French business executive; b. 14 Nov. 1930, l'Ile d'Oléron; s. of Pierre Bergé and Christiane (née Sicard) Bergé; ed Lycée Eugène-Fromentin, La Rochelle; Dir and Ed.-in-Chief La Patrie Mondiale 1949–61; Co-Founder and Dir-Gen. Yves Saint Laurent 1961, Pres. 1971–2002, Pres. Yves Saint Laurent of America Inc., New York 1971–2002, Pres., Dir-Gen. Yves Saint Laurent Parfums (merged with Elf-Sanofi) 1987–93, f. Fondation Yves Saint Laurent 2002; Chair. Asscn of Theatres of the Paris Opera 1988–94, Hon. Pres. 1994–; Pres. Chambre Syndicale du Prêt-à-Porter Des Couturiers et des Créateurs de Mode 1988–93; Goodwill Amb. for UNESCO 1993; Dir Lundis Musicaux de l'Athénée 1977; Admin. Cttee for the Devt and Promotion of Textile and Design, Fondation Cartier Parsons School of Design 1985–, Pres. 1991–; Pres. Inst. Français de la Mode 1985–; Pres. Asscn des Amis de l'Institut François Mitterand 1999, Gustav Mahler Library 2000; Commdr Légion d'honneur, Ordre Nat. du Mérite, Commdr des Arts et des Lettres, Officer Order of Orange-Nassau (Netherlands). *Publications:* Bernard Buffet 1957, Liberté, j'écris ton nom 1991, l'Affaire Clovis 1996, l'Inventaire Mitterand 2001, Studies on Pierre Mac-Orlan, Henry de Montherlant, Jean Anouilh, Francis Carco and Jean Giono. *Leisure interest:* modern art. *Address:* c/o Fondation Yves Saint Laurent, 5 avenue Marceau, 75116 Paris (Office); 5 rue Bonaparte, 75006 Paris, France (Home).

BERGEN, Candice Patricia; American actress and photojournalist; b. 9 May 1946, Beverly Hills; d. of Edgar Bergen and Frances (née Westerman) Bergen; m. Louis Malle 1980 (died 1995); one d.; ed Westlake School for Girls, Univ. of Pennsylvania; photojournalist work has appeared in Vogue, Cosmopolitan, Life and Esquire. *Films include:* The Group 1966, The Sand Pebbles 1966, The Day the Fish Came Out 1967, Vivre Pour Vivre 1967, The Magus 1968, Getting Straight 1970, Soldier Blue 1970, The Adventurers 1970, Carnal Knowledge 1971, The Hunting Party 1971, T. R. Baskin 1972, 11 Harrowhouse 1974, Bite the Bullet 1975, The Wind and the Lion 1976, The Domino Principle 1977, A Night Full of Rain 1977, Oliver's Story, 1978, Starting Over 1979, Rich and Famous 1981, Gandhi 1982, Stick 1985, Au Revoir les Enfants (Co-Dir) 1987, Murphy Brown (TV series Emmy Award 1989, 1990) 1989, 1990, Mary and Tim (TV movie) 1996, Miss Congeniality 2000, Sweet Home Alabama 2002. *Publications:* The Freezer (in Best Short Plays of 1968), Knock Wood (autobiog.) 1984. *Address:* c/o William Morris Agency, 151 El Camino, Beverly Hills, CA 90212, USA.

BERGER, Geneviève, MD, PhD; French university professor and medical practitioner; b. 1955, Moselle; ed Ecole normale supérieure, Cachan, Medical School, Paris; f. Parametric Imaging Lab. 1991; Pres. Treatment and Drugs: Design and Resources Section, Nat. Cttee for Scientific Research 1995–98; Dir of Tech., Ministry of Research 1998–2000; Dir.-Gen. CNRS 2000–; Chevalier, Légion d'honneur 1988, Commdr des Palmes académiques 2000; CNRS Silver Medal, Yves Rocard Prize 1997, European Grand Prix for Innovation Award 2001. *Address:* Centre National de la Recherche Scientifique, 3–5 rue Michel-Ange, 75794 Paris Cedex 16, France (Office). *Telephone:* 1-44-96-40-00 (Office). *Fax:* 1-44-96-49-13 (Office). *E-mail:* secr_dg@cnrs_dir.fr.

BERGER, Helmut; Austrian actor; b. 1942, Salzburg; ed Feldkirk Coll., Univ. of Perugia, Italy; first film role in Luchino Visconti's Le Streghe 1966. *Films include:* The Young Tigers, The Damned, Do You Know What Stalin Did To Women?, The Garden of the Finzi-Continis, The Picture of Dorian Gray, A Butterfly with Bloody Wings, The Greedy Ones, The Strange Love Affair, Ludwig, Ash Wednesday, Conversation Piece, The Romantic Englishwoman, Orders to Kill, Madame Kitty, Merry-Go-Round, Code Name: Emerald, The

Glass Heaven, Faceless, The Betrothed, The Godfather Part III, Once Arizona, Still Waters, Unter den Palmen, Die Haupter Meiner. *Publication:* Ich (autobiog.) 1998.

BERGER, John; British author and art critic; b. 5 Nov. 1926, London; s. of the late S. J. D. Berger and Miriam Berger (née Branson); ed Cen. School of Art and Chelsea School of Art, London; began career as painter and teacher of drawing; exhbns at Wildenstein, Redfern and Leicester Galleries, London; Art Critic Tribune, New Statesman; Visiting Fellow BFI 1990–; numerous TV appearances including Monitor, two series for Granada; Scenario: La Salamandre (with Alain Tanner), Le Milieu du Monde, Jonas (New York Critics Prize for Best Scenario of Year 1976); George Orwell Memorial Prize 1977. *Plays:* The Three Lives of Lucy Cabrol (with Simon McBurney) 1994, Isabelle (with Nella Bielski) 1998. *Radio:* Will It Be A Likeness? 1996. *Publications:* fiction: A Painter of Our Time 1958, The Foot of Clive 1962, Corker's Freedom 1964, G (Booker Prize, James Tait Black Memorial Prize) 1972, Pig Earth 1979, Once in Europa 1989, Lilac and Flag 1991, To The Wedding 1995, Photocopies 1996, King: A Street Story 1999; theatre: Question of Geography (with Nella Bielski) 1984 (staged in Marseille, Paris and by RSC, Stratford), Francisco Goya's Last Portrait (with Nella Bielski) 1989, I Send You This Cadmium Red (with John Christie) 2000; non-fiction: Marcel Frishman 1958, Permanent Red 1960, The Success and Failure of Picasso 1965, A Fortunate Man: The Story of a Country Doctor (with J. Mohr) 1967, Art and Revolution, Moments of Cubism and Other Essays 1969, The Look of Things, Ways of Seeing 1972, The Seventh Man 1975 (Prize for Best Reportage, Union of Journalists and Writers, Paris 1977), About Looking 1980, Another Way of Telling (with J. Mohr) 1982, And Our Faces, My Heart, Brief as Photos 1984, The White Bird 1985 (USA as The Sense of Sight 1985), Keeping a Rendezvous (essays and poems) 1992, Titian: Nymph and Shepherd (with Katya Berger) 1996, Steps Towards a Small Theory of the Visible 1996, The Shape of a Pocket 2001, John Berger Selected Essays (ed. by Geoff Dyer) 2001; poetry: Pages of the Wound: Poems, Drawings, Photographs 1956–96 1996; translations: (with A. Bostock): Poems on the Theatre by B. Brecht 1960, Return to My Native Land by Aimé Césaire 1969; Oranges for the Son of Alexander Levy by Nella Bielski (with Lisa Appignanesi) 1982. *Address:* Quincy, Mieussy, 74440 Taninges, France.

BERGER, Samuel R.; American government official; b. 28 Oct. 1945, Sharon, Conn.; ed Cornell Univ., Harvard Univ.; mem. Bar, DC 1971; Legis. Asst to Senator Harold E. Hughes 1971–72; Special Asst to Mayor John V. Lindsay, NY 1972; Deputy Dir Policy Planning Staff Dept of State 1977–80; partner Hogan & Hartson; Asst Dir Nat. Security Presidential Transitional Team 1992; Deputy Asst to Pres. for Nat. Security Affairs 1993–95, Asst 1995–97; Nat. Security Adviser 1997–2001. *Address:* c/o National Security Council, Old Executive Office Building, 17th Street and Pennsylvania Avenue, NW, Washington, DC 20504, USA (Office). *Telephone:* (202) 456-9392.

BERGER, Thomas Louis, BA; American author; b. 20 July 1924, Cincinnati, Ohio; s. of Thomas C. Berger and Mildred Berger; m. Jeanne Redpath 1950; ed Univ. of Cincinnati and Columbia Univ. Grad. School; mil. service 1943–46; Distinguished Visiting Prof. Southampton Univ. 1975–76; Visiting Lecturer, Yale Univ. 1981, 1982; Regents Lecturer, Univ. of Calif. (Davis) 1982; Dial Fellow 1962; Hon. LittD (Long Island) 1986; Rosenthal Award, Nat. Inst. of Arts and Letters 1965; Western Heritage Award 1965. *Play:* Other People 1970. *Publications:* Crazy in Berlin 1958, Reinhart in Love 1962, Little Big Man 1964, Killing Time 1967, Vital Parts 1970, Regiment of Women 1973, Sneaky People 1975, Who Is Teddy Villanova? 1977, Arthur Rex 1978, Neighbors 1980, Reinhart's Women 1981, The Feud 1983, Nowhere 1985, Being Invisible 1987, The Houseguest 1988, Changing the Past 1989, Orrie's Story 1990, Meeting Evil 1992, Robert Crews 1994, Suspects 1996, The Return of Little Big Man 1999, Best Friends 2003. *Leisure interest:* cooking. *Address:* Don Congdon Associates, 156 Fifth Avenue, Suite 625, New York, NY 10010-7002 (Office); PO Box 11, Palisades, NY 10964, USA. *Telephone:* (212) 645-1229 (Office). *Fax:* (212) 727-2688 (Office). *E-mail:* doncongdon@aol.com (Office).

BERGERON, André Louis; French trade unionist and printer; b. 1 Jan. 1922, Suarce; s. of Louis Bergeron and Marie (née Voëlin) Bergeron; m. Georgette Monnier 1954; ed Tech. Coll., Belfort; printer 1936–48; Sec.-Gen. of Typographical Union, Belfort 1946–47; Force-Ouvrière 1947–48, Perm. Sec. Belfort Area 1948; Sec.-Gen. Fédération Force Ouvrière du Livre 1948–50; Regional Del. Force Ouvrière and mem. Exec. Cttee 1950–56, mem. Bureau de la Confédération 1956–63, Sec.-Gen. Force Ouvrière 1963–89; mem. Exec. Cttee Féd. Graphique Internationale 1957, Pres. 1958–86, 1988–; Pres. Org. Commune de Consommateurs, Agriculteurs-Consommateurs 1985–; Vice-Pres. Union Nat. pour l'Emploi dans l'Industrie et le Commerce (UNEDIC) 1986, Pres. 1989–90. *Publications:* Lettre ouverte à un syndiqué 1975, Ma route et mes combats 1976, Quinze cents jours 1984, Tant qu'il y aura du grain à moudre 1988, Je revendique le bon sens 1996. *Address:* 14 rue du Stade-Buffalo, 92120 Montrouge, France (Home).

BERGGREN, Bo Erik Gunnar; Swedish company executive; b. 11 Aug. 1936, Falun; s. of Tage Berggren and Elsa Höglund; m. Gunbritt Haglund 1962; two s. two d.; ed Royal Inst. of Tech.; metallurgical research and Devt, STORA Kopparbergs Bergslags AB (now STORA), Domnarvet 1962–68, Mill Man., Söderfors 1968–74, Exec. Vice-Pres., Falun 1975–78, Pres. 1984–92, CEO 1984–94, Chair. Bd 1992–, Chair. Bd STORA Stockholm 1995–98; Pres.

Incentive AB, Stockholm 1978–84; mem. Prime Minister's Special Industry Advisory Cttee 1994–; Chair. Astra, SAS (Sweden), SAS (Sverige) AB; Vice-Chair. Investor, Fed. of Swedish Industries, Skandinaviska Enskilda Banken; mem. Bd Telefonaktiebolaget L M Ericsson, Danisco A/S, Royal Inst. of Tech.; mem. Int. Council J. P. Morgan & Co. Inc., Robert Bosch Internationale Beteiligungen Advisory Cttee, Royal Swedish Acad. of Eng Sciences, of Forestry and Agric.; Dr. hc (Royal Inst. of Tech., Stockholm) (Dalhousie Univ.) 1996; King's Medal 12th Dimension with Ribbon of Order of the Seraphim 1987. *Leisure interests:* the arts, family, music. *Address:* P.O. Box 16 100, S-103 22 Stockholm, Sweden. *Telephone:* (8) 6136600. *Fax:* (8) 106282.

BERGGREN, Thommy; Swedish actor; b. 1937; ed The Pickwick Club (private dramatic school), Atelierteatern, Stockholm and Gothenburg Theatre; Gothenburg Theatre 1959–63; Royal Dramatic Theatre, Stockholm 1963. *Plays acted in include:* Gengangaren (Ibsen) 1962, Romeo and Juliet 1962, Chembalo 1962, Who's Afraid of Virginia Woolf? 1964. *Films acted in include:* Pärlemor 1961, Barnvagnen (The Pram) 1962, Kvarteret Korpen (Ravens End) 1963, En söndag i september (A Sunday in September) 1963, Karlek 65 (Love 65) 1965, Elvira Madigan 1967, The Black Palm Trees 1969, The Ballad of Joe Hill 1971.

BERGH, Birger, DPhil; Swedish professor of Latin; b. 25 June 1935, Luleå; s. of Elsa Bergh and Ragnar Bergh; m. Gunilla Åselius 1958 (divorced 1987); two s. one d.; ed Uppsala Univ.; Asst Prof. of Latin, Uppsala Univ. 1968–75; Prof. of Latin, Lund Univ. 1975–2000, Prof. Emer. 2000–. *Publications:* Critical Editions of St Bridget's Revelations, (Book VII) 1967, (Book V) 1972, (Book VI) 1991, (Book II) 2000, 1967, 1971, 1991 of Mathias Lincopensis' Testa Nucis and Poetria 1996; works on Latin linguistics, studies in Swedish neo-Latin. *Leisure interest:* music. *Address:* Kunt den stores gata 7, 22221 Lund, Sweden. *Telephone:* (46) 15-25-06. *E-mail:* birger.bergh@e-bostad.net (Office).

BERGIN, Patrick; Irish actor; b. 1954, Dublin; m. Paula Bergin; teacher of juvenile delinquents and children with learning disabilities in London until 1980; full-time actor in repertory theatre, TV and film 1980–. *Films include:* Those Glory, Glory Days, Sleeping with The Enemy 1991, Patriot Games 1992, Map of the Human Heart 1992, Love Crimes 1992, Double Cross 1994, Soft Deceit 1994, Whitechapel 1997, The Proposition 1997, The Island on Bird Street 1997, Taxman 1999, The Lost World 1998, Eye of the Beholder 1999, Africa 1999, Treasure Island 1999, Merlin: The Return 1999, Press Run 1999, When The Sky Falls 2000, Cause of Death 2000, High Explosives 2000, Amazons and Gladiators 2001, Beneath Loch Ness 2001, Deni's Prey 2001, Gas Station Jesus 2001, The Invisible Circus 2001. *Television:* Boon, Hard Cases, The Real Charlotte (series) 1990, Robin Hood 1991, The Hummingbird Tree (BBC film) 1992, Act of Betrayal, They, Frankenstein.

BERGKAMP, Dennis; Netherlands footballer; b. 10 May 1969, Amsterdam; m. Henrita Ruizendaal; one s. one d.; striker; played for Ajax Amsterdam 1986–92, Inter Milan 1992–95, Arsenal, London, UK 1995–, for Holland 1990–2000; all-time leading scorer for Holland; Dutch Player of the Year 1992, 1993, English Player of the Year 1998, English Football Writers' Player of the Year 1998. *Leisure interests:* snooker, golf, reading, films, basketball. *Address:* c/o Arsenal F.C., Arsenal Stadium, Avenell Road, London, N5 1BU, England.

BERGLUND, Paavo Allan Engelbert; Finnish conductor; b. 14 April 1929, Helsinki; s. of Hjalmar Berglund and Siiri (Loiri) Berglund; m. Kirsti Kivekäs 1958; one s. two d.; ed Sibelius Acad. Helsinki; Violinist, Finnish Radio Symphony Orchestra 1949–56, Conductor 1956–62, Prin. Conductor 1962–71; Prin. Conductor Bournemouth Symphony Orch. 1972–79, Helsinki Philharmonic Orch. 1975–79; Prin. Conductor Royal Stockholm Philharmonic Orchestra 1987–91, Royal Danish Orchestra 1993–96, London Philharmonic 1997; State Award for Music 1972; Hon. OBE. *Recordings:* complete Sibelius symphonies including first recording of Kullervo Symphony 1971–77, Má Vlast (Smetana), Shostakovich symphonies 5, 6, 7, 10, 11, many other recordings. *Publication:* A Comparative Study of the Printed Score and the Manuscript of the Seventh Symphony of Sibelius 1970. *Address:* Munkki-niemenranta 41, 00330 Helsinki 33, Finland.

BERGMAN, Ingmar; Swedish film director and theatre producer; b. 14 July 1918, Uppsala; m. Ingrid Karlebovon Rosen 1971 (died 1995); eight c. by previous marriages; ed Stockholm Univ.; producer Royal Theatre, Stockholm 1940–42; scriptwriter and producer Svensk Filmindustri 1940–44; theatre-Dir Helsingborg 1944–46, Gothenburg 1946–49, Malmo 1954–63; leading Dir Royal Dramatic Theatre, Stockholm 1963; Dir Mme de Sade Theatre 1989; Chair. European Cinema Soc. 1989–; has written the scripts of most of his films; mem. Swedish Acad. of Letters; author of plays A Painting on Wood, The City, The Rite (TV play), The Lie (TV play), Scenes from a Marriage (TV play); Dir To Damascus 1974, The Merry Widow, Twelfth Night 1975, 1980, Tartuffe 1980, King Lear 1985, John Gabriel Borkman 1985, Miss Julie 1986, Hamlet 1986, Maria Stuart 2000; Erasmus Prize 1965, Award for Best Dir Nat. Soc. of Film Critics 1970, Order of the Yugoslav Flag 1971, Luigi Pirandello Int. Theatre Prize 1971, Goethe Award (Frankfurt) 1976, Gold Medal of Swedish Acad. 1977, European Film Award 1988, Le Prix Sonning 1989, Praemium Imperiale Prize (Japan) 1991, Dorothy and Lilian Gish Prize 1995; Dr. hc (Univ. of Rome) 1988; Commdr Légion d'honneur 1985. *Films include:* Crisis 1945, It Rains on Our Love 1946, A Ship Bound for India 1947, Music in Darkness 1947, Port of Call 1948, Prison 1948, Thirst 1949, To Joy 1949,

Summer Interlude 1950, This Can't Happen Here 1950, Waiting Women 1952, Summer with Monika 1952, Sawdust and Tinsel 1953, A Lesson in Love 1954, Journey into Autumn 1955, Smiles of a Summer Night 1955, The Seventh Seal 1956, Wild Strawberries 1957, So Close to Life 1957, The Face 1958, The Virgin Spring 1959, The Devil's Eye 1960, Through a Glass Darkly 1961, Winter Light 1962, The Silence 1962, Now About these Women 1963, Episode in Stimulantia 1965, Persona 1966, The Hour of the Wolf 1967, Shame 1968, The Rite 1970, A Passion 1970, The Touch 1971, Cries and Whispers 1972, Scenes from a Marriage 1974 (film and TV), The Magic Flute (film and TV) 1975, Face to Face (film and TV) 1975, The Serpent's Egg 1977, Sonate d'automne 1978, Aus dem Leben der Marionetten 1980, Fårö Document 1980, Fanny and Alexander 1981, After the Rehearsal 1984, Private Confessions 1998; TV: Making Noise and Acting Up 1996; scriptwriter, The Best Intentions 1991, Faithless 2000. *Publications:* Four Stories 1977, The Magic Lantern (autobiog.) 1988, Fanny and Alexander 1989, Images: My Life in Film 1993, Sunday's Child 1994, Private Confessions 1997.

BERGMAN, Stephenie Jane, DipAD; British artist; b. 18 April 1946, London; d. of Jack 'Kid' Berg and Morya Bergman; ed St Paul's Girls' School and St Martin's School of Art; has participated in group exhbns in London, France, Belgium, Australia, Zimbabwe, including 25 Years of Painting, Royal Academy, London 1976; Gulbenkian Award 1975. *One-woman exhibitions include:* Garage Art Ltd, London 1973, 1975, Nottingham 1976, Cambridge 1977, Chester 1978, Anthony Stokes, London, 1978, 1980, Riverside Studios, London 1980, Crafts Council Gallery 1984, Butler's House, Kilkenny 1984. *Leisure interest:* horse racing.

BERGMANN, Barbara Rose, MA, PhD; American professor of economics; b. 20 July 1927, New York; d. of Martin Berman and Nellie Wallenstein; m. Fred H. Bergmann 1965; one s. one d.; ed Cornell and Harvard Univs; economist, U.S. Bureau of Statistics, New York 1949–53, New York Metropolitan Regional Study 1957–61; Instr. Harvard Univ. 1958–61; Sr Research Assoc. Harvard Econ. Research Project 1960–61; Sr staff economist, Council of Econ. Advisers, Washington, DC 1961–62; Assoc. Prof. Brandeis Univ. 1962–64; mem. Sr staff, Brookings Inst. Washington, DC 1963–65; Sr econ. adviser, AID, Washington, DC 1966–67; Prof. of Econs Univ. of Md College Park 1971–88; Distinguished Prof. of Econs American Univ. Washington, DC 1988–97, Prof. Emer. 1997–; Vice-Pres. American Econ. Asscn 1976; Columnist on econ. affairs NY Times 1981–82, LA Times 1983–; Pres. American Asscn of Univ. Profs. 1990–92, Int. Asscn for Feminist Economists 1999; Hon. PhD (De Montford Univ.) 1996, (Muhlenberg Coll.) 2000. *Publications:* Projection of a Metropolis (co-author) 1961, The Impact of Highway Investment on Development (co-author), A Microsimulated Transactions Model of the U.S. Economy (co-author) 1985, The Economic Emergence of Women 1986, Saving Our Children from Poverty: What the United States Can Learn From France 1995, In Defense of Affirmative Action 1996, Is Social Security Broke? A Cartoon Guide to the Issues 1999, America's Child Care Problem: The Way Out (co-author) 2002. *Address:* c/o Department of Economics, American University, Washington, DC 20016, USA (Office). *E-mail:* bbergman@wam.umd.edu (Office).

BERGMANN, Christine, Dr rer. nat; German politician; b. 7 Sept. 1939, Dresden; m. Volker Bergmann 1963; one s. one d.; ed Leipzig Univ.; fmrly worked as apothecary; freelance work then full-time employee in pharmaceutics propagation, Berlin Pharmaceutical Inst. 1967–77, Head of Dept 1977; mem. Social Democratic Party of Germany (SPD) 1989–, State Chair. Berlin 1989, mem. Party Exec. Cttee and Presidium 1995–; Fed. Minister of Family Affairs, Sr Citizens, Women and Youth 1998–2002; Pres. Berlin Ass. of City Councillors 1990–91, Mayoress of Berlin and Senator 1991–98. *Address:* c/o Ministry of Family Affairs, Sr Citizens, Women and Youth, Taubenstrasse 42–43, 10117 Berlin, Germany.

BERGNER, Christoph, DR.AGRAR; German politician; b. 24 Nov. 1948, Zwickau; m.; three c.; ed Univs. of Jena and Halle; mem. Christian Democratic Union (CDU) without office in fmr GDR 1971; Research Asst Inst. of Biochemistry of Plants, Univ. of Halle 1974; mem. Landtag (State Parl.) of Saxony-Anhalt 1990–; Vice-Chair. Saxony-Anhalt CDU Asscn 1991–; Chair. CDU Parl. Party in Landtag 1991–93, 1994; Minister-Pres. of Saxony-Anhalt 1993–94. *Address:* Tannenweg 37, 06120 Halle, Germany.

BERGOGLIO, H.E. Cardinal Jorge Mario; Argentine ecclesiastic; b. 17 Dec. 1936, Buenos Aires; ordained priest 1969; Bishop 1992; Coadjutor 1997; Archbishop of Buenos Aires 1998–; cr. Cardinal 2001. *Address:* Arzobispado, Rivadavia 415, 1002 Buenos Aires, Argentina (Office). *Telephone:* (11) 4343-3925 (Office). *Fax:* (11) 4334-8373 (Office). *E-mail:* arzobispado@arzbaires .org.ar (Office).

BERGONZI, Carlo; Italian opera singer; b. 13 July 1924, Busseto, Parma; m. Adele; two c.; ed Parma Conservatory; début as Figaro (Il Barbiere di Siviglia) at Lecce 1948; début as tenor in title role of Andrea Chénier, Teatro Petruzzelli, Bari 1951; subsequently appeared at various Italian opera houses including La Scala, Milan; U.S. début in Il Tabarro and Cavalleria Rusticana, Lyric Opera, Chicago 1955; appeared at Metropolitan Opera, New York in Aïda (as Radames) and Il Trovatore (as Manrico) 1955–56; appeared at all the maj. opera houses in Europe and also in USA and S. America; retd 1994 with occasional appearances thereafter; currently a vocal coach. *Address:* c/o Askonas Holt Ltd, Lonsdale Chambers, 27 Chancery Lane, London, WC2A 1PF, England (Office).

BERGQUIST, Dame Patricia Rose, DBE, PhD, DSc, FRSNZ; New Zealand professor of zoology; b. 10 March 1933, Auckland; d. of William and Bertha E Smyth; m. Peter L. Bergquist 1958; one d.; ed Takapuna Grammar School and Univ. of Auckland; Lecturer in Zoology, Auckland Univ. 1958; Postdoctoral research, Yale Univ. 1961–64; subsequently career concentrated on sponge biology, chemistry, chemo-taxonomy; pioneered application of chem. and pharmacology of marine sponges to resolving maj. questions of sponge phylogeny and relationships; int. consultant in marine sponge taxonomy and marine ecology; Prof. of Zoology (Personal Chair.), Univ. of Auckland 1981–, Head of Dept 1986–, Asst Vice-Chancellor (Academic) 1989–96, Deputy Vice-Chancellor 1996, Special Asst to Vice-Chancellor 1997–98, Prof. Emer. 1999–; Hector Medal, Royal Soc. of NZ 1988. *Publications:* more than 130 articles in professional journals. *Leisure interests:* fishing, stamp collecting, classical music. *Address:* 3A Pukerangi Crescent, Ellersie, Auckland 5 (Home); Department of Anatomy, University of Auckland, Private Bag 92019, Auckland 1, New Zealand. *Telephone:* (9) 3737599 (Office); (9) 5796291 (Home). *E-mail:* pr .bergquist@auckland.ac.nz (Office).

BERGSAGEL, John Dagfinn, PhD; Danish (born Canadian) musicologist; b. 19 April 1928, Outlook, Sask.; s. of Rev. Dr. Knut Bergsagel and Alma Josephine Bergsagel née Anderson; m. 1st Sondra Rubin 1953 (divorced); 2nd Ingrid Charlotte Sørensen 1965; three s. one d.; ed Gordon Bell High School, Winnipeg, Man., Univ. of Manitoba, St Olaf Coll., Minn., USA, Cornell Univ., USA, Magdalen Coll. Oxford, UK, RAM, London, UK; Lecturer, Concordia Coll., Minn. 1954–55; Assoc. Prof., Ohio Univ. 1955–59, Exec. Ed. Early English Church Music, Oxford, UK 1961–76; Tutor in History of Music, Oxford Univ. 1962–67, Lecturer, New Coll. 1966–67; Sr Lecturer in Musicology, Manchester Univ. 1967–70; Lecturer in History and Theory of Music, Univ. of Copenhagen 1970–81, Prof. of Musicology 1981–98; Dir Monumenta Musicae Byzantinae, Exec. Bd Foundation for Publishing of Works of Niels W. Gade; Sr Arts Fellow of Canada Council 1959; Gulbenkian Foundation Grant 1961; Fellow Royal Danish Acad. of Sciences and Letters, Norwegian Acad. of Science and Letters, Academia Europaea (Chair. Musicology Section, mem. Council); Order of Dannebrog. *Publications:* The Collected Works of Nicholas Ludford 1963, Early Tudor Masses I–II 1963, 1976, Engelske Anthems fra det 16. århundrede 1973, Musikk i Norge i Middelalder og Renessanse 1982, Music in Denmark at the Time of Christian IV: Vol. 2, Music for Instrumental Ensemble 1988, Vol. 6, Anonymous Mass and Occasional Motets (with H. Glahn) 1988; numerous articles, contribs to encyclopaedias, translations of many scholarly works. *Address:* Strandvejen 63, 2100 Copenhagen Ø, Denmark. *Telephone:* 39-20-02-02. *E-mail:* jberg@hum.ku.dk (Home).

BERGSTRÖM, Lars, PhD; Swedish professor of philosophy; b. 17 July 1935, Stockholm; m. Ulla von Heland 1960; one s.; ed Stockholm Univ.; Assoc. Prof., Lecturer in Philosophy, Stockholm Univ. 1967–74; Prof. of Practical Philosophy, Uppsala Univ. 1974–87; Prof. of Practical Philosophy, Stockholm Univ. 1987–2001, Prof. Emer. 2001–; mem. Royal Swedish Acad. of Sciences 1998–. *Publications:* The Alternatives and Consequences of Actions 1966, Objektivitet 1972, Grundbok i Värdeteori 1990. *Leisure interests:* music, tennis. *Address:* Department of Philosophy, Stockholm University, 106 91 Stockholm (Office); Reimersholmsgatan 39, 117 40 Stockholm, Sweden (Home). *Telephone:* (8) 164209 (Office); (8) 6698899 (Home). *E-mail:* lars.bergstrom@ philosophy.su.se (Office). *Website:* www.philosophy.su.se/personal/bergstrom .htm (Office).

BERIO, Luciano; Italian composer; b. 24 Oct. 1925; s. of Ernesto Berio and Ada dal Fiume; m. 1st Cathy Berberian 1950 (divorced 1964, died 1983); one d.; m. 2nd Susan Oyama 1964 (divorced 1971); one s. one d.; m. 3rd Talia Pecker 1977; two s.; ed Liceo Classico and Conservatorio G. Verdi, Milan; founder of Studio di Fonologia Musicale, Italian Radio; Teacher of Composition and Lecturer at Mills Coll. (Calif.), Darmstadt and Harvard Univ.; Prof. of Composition, Juilliard School of Music, NY 1965–; Wolf Prize 1990, Praemium Imperial Prize 1996. *Compositions include:* 5 Variazioni 1951, Nones for Orchestra 1954, Alleluyah I and II 1955–57, Thema (Omaggio a Joyce) 1958, Circles 1960, Visage 1961, Epifanie 63, Passagio 1962, Laborintus II 1965, O King 1968, Sinfonia 1969, This Means That... 1970, Opera 1970, Sequenzas for solo instruments, A-Ronne for eight voices 1974–75, Coro for Chorus and Orchestra 1975–76, La Ritirata Notturna di Madrid 1975, Ritorno degli Snovidenia 1977, La Vera Storia 1978, Corale 1981, Un Re in Ascolto 1982, Requies 1983, Voci 1984, Requires 1985, Formazioni 1986, Ricorrenze 1987, Concerto II 1988, Ofanim 1988, Canticum Novissimi Testamenti 1989, Rendering (Schubert) 1990, Continuo 1991. *Address:* Il Colombaio, Radicondoli, Siena, Italy.

BERISHA, Sali, PhD; Albanian politician and cardiologist; b. 15 Oct. 1944, Tropoje; m.; two c.; ed Tirana Univ.; worked as cardiologist in Tirana Cardiology Clinic; fmr mem. Albanian Workers' Party; co-f. Democratic Party, Leader 1991–97, elected Chair. 1991; Pres. of Albania 1992–97; mem. Nat. Medical Research Cttee; mem. European Cttee on Medical Scientific Research 1986–. *Publications:* political articles in newspapers.

BERKELEY, Michael Fitzhardinge, FRAM; British composer; b. 29 May 1948, London; s. of the late Sir Lennox Berkeley and of Elizabeth Freda Berkeley (née Bernstein); m. Deborah Jane Coltman-Rogers 1979; one d.; ed Westminster Cathedral Choir School, The Oratory School, Royal Acad. of Music; writer on music and arts for the Observer, Vogue and The Listener 1970–75; presents music programmes (including Proms) for BBC TV 1975–;

BBC Radio 3 announcer 1974–79; Dir Britten-Pears Foundation 1996–; mem. Exec. Cttee Asscn of Professional Composers 1982–84, Cen. Music Advisory Cttee, BBC 1986–90; Music Panel Adviser to Arts Council 1986–90; Visiting Prof. Huddersfield Univ. (fmrly Polytechnic) 1991–94; Artistic Dir Cheltenham Festival 1995–; Co-Dir Spitalfields Festival 1994–97; Dir Royal Opera House, Covent Garden 1996–2000 (mem. 1994–98, Chair. Opera Bd 1998); Composer-in-Asscn BBC Nat. Orchestra of Wales, Welsh Coll. of Music and Drama 2002–; apart from concert works, has written music for film, TV and Radio; The Guinness Prize for Composition 1977. *Major works include:* Meditations for Strings, Oboe Concerto, Fantasia Concertante, Gregorian Variations (orchestra), For The Savage Messiah (piano quintet), Or Shall We Die? (oratorio to text by Ian McEwan), 4 String quartets, Piano Trio, Songs of Awakening Love, Entertaining Master Punch, Clarinet Concerto, Speaking Silence, Baa Baa Black Sheep (opera), Jane Eyre (opera) 2000, Viola Concerto, Catch Me If You Can (chamber), Dark Sleep (keyboard). *Publication:* The Music Pack 1994: numerous articles in newspapers and magazines. *Leisure interests:* walking, farming, reading. *Address:* c/o Oxford University Press, 70 Baker Street, London, W1U 7DN, England (Office). *Telephone:* (20) 7616-5900 (Office).

BERKOFF, Steven; British actor, writer and director; b. 3 Aug. 1937, Stepney, London; s. of Alfred Berkoff and Pauline Berkoff; m. 1st Alison Minto 1970; m. 2nd Shelley Lee 1976 (divorced). *Films include:* Octopussy, First Blood 2, Beverly Hills Cop, Absolute Beginners, War and Remembrance (TV) 1988, The Krays 1990, Decadence 1994. *Plays/Productions include:* Agamemnon (London) 1973, The House of Usher 1974, The Trial 1976, East 1978, Hamlet 1980, 2001, Greek 1980, Decadence 1981, Agamemnon (USA) 1984, Harry's Xmas 1985, Kvetch 1986, 1991, Sink the Belgrano 1987, Coriolanus 1988, Metamorphosis 1988, Salome 1989, The Trial 1991, Brighton Beach Scumbags? 1994; Dir West (London) 1983, Acapulco (LA) 1990, One Man (London) 1993, Coriolanus 1996, Mermaid 1996, Massage (LA and Edinburgh) 1997, Shakespeare's Villains 1998, Messiah 2000. *Publications:* America 1988, I am Hamlet 1989, A Prisoner in Rio 1989, The Theatre of Steven Berkoff (photographic) 1992, Coriolanus in Deutschland 1992, Overview (collected essays) 1994, Free Association (autobiog.) 1996, Graft: Tales of an Actor 1998, Shopping in the Santa Monica Mall, Ritual in Blood, Messiah, Oedipus 2000, The Secret Love Life of Ophelia 2001. *Leisure interests:* photography, travelling, table tennis. *Address:* c/o Joanna Marston, Rosica Colin Ltd, 1 Clareville Grove Mews, London, SW7 5AH, England. *Telephone:* (20) 7370-1080. *Fax:* (20) 7244-6441.

BERLUSCONI, Silvio; Italian politician and businessman; b. 1936, Milan; ed Univ. of Milan; started building and property Ddevt business aged 26; built up Fininvest, major conglomerate with interests in commercial TV, printed media, publishing, advertising, insurance and financial services, retailing and football; worked on Milan 2 Housing project 1969; Canale 5 network began broadcasting 1980; bought Italia 1 TV network 1983, Rete 4 TV network 1984; took stake in La Cinq commercial TV network 1985, Clain, Cinema 5 (largest in Italy); bought Estudios Roma 1986; Milan AC Football Club 1986; La Standa (Italy's largest Dept store chain) 1988; Chair. Arnoldo Mondadori Editore SpA Jan.–July 1990, (half-share) 1991; Founder, Pres. Forza Italia political Movt 1993–, began full-time political career 1994, declaring he had stepped down from exec. posts in Fininvest; led Forza Italia to win general elections in alliance with Lega Nord and Alleanza Nazionale parties 1994; Prime Minister of Italy April–Dec. 1994, 2001–, also Minister of Foreign Affairs 2002; has stood trial on a series of corruption charges; MEP 1999. *Address:* Office of the Prime Minister, Palazzo Chigi Piazza Colonna 370, 00187 Rome, Italy. *Telephone:* (06) 67791. *Fax:* (06) 6783998.

BERMAN, Gail, BA; American entertainment executive; m. Bill Masters; ed Univ. of Maryland Coll. of Arts and Humanities; Pres. and Partner, Regency Television Inc. –2000; Entertainment Pres., Fox Broadcasting Co. May 2000–. *Television:* Exec. Producer Buffy the Vampire Slayer, Angel. *Address:* Fox TV Entertainment Group, 10201 W. Pico Boulevard, Building 100, Room 4450, Los Angeles, CA 90035, USA (Office).

BERMAN, Harold Joseph, LLB, MA; American professor of law; b. 13 Feb. 1918, Hartford, Conn.; s. of Saul Berman and Emma Kaplan Berman; m. Ruth Harlow Berman 1941; two s. two d.; ed Dartmouth Coll., London School of Econs, Yale Univ. and Yale Law School; James Barr Ames Prof. of Law, Harvard Univ. 1948–85, Prof. Emer. 1985–; mem. Exec. Cttee of Russian Research Center, Harvard Univ. 1952–84; Robert W. Woodruff Prof. of Law, Emory Univ. 1985–; Fellow, Carter Center 1985–; Founder and Co-Dir American Law Center, Moscow 1991–97; Co-founder, Co-Chair. World Law Inst. 1997–; Dr. hc (Catholic Univ. of America) 1991, (Va Theological Seminary) 1995, (Univ. of Ghent) 1997, Russian Acad. of Sciences Law Univ. 2000; Scribes Book Award, American Bar Asscn 1984; Bronze Star Medal. *Publications:* Justice in the USSR: An Interpretation of Soviet Law 1950, The Nature and Functions of Law: An Introduction for Students of the Arts and Sciences 1958, Law and Revolution: The Formation of the Western Legal Tradition 1983, Faith and Order: The Reconciliation of Law and Religion 1993. *Leisure interests:* bridge, music. *Address:* Emory University School of Law, Gambrell Hall G534, Atlanta, GA 30322, USA. *Telephone:* (404) 727-6503. *Fax:* (404) 727-0299. *E-mail:* hberman@law.emory.edu (Office).

BERN, Howard Alan, PhD; American professor of biology and research endocrinologist; b. 30 Jan. 1920, Montreal, Canada; s. of Simeon Bern and Ethel Bern; m. Estelle Bruck 1946; one s. one d.; ed Univ. of California, Los Angeles; mil. service 1942–46; Nat. Research Council Predoctoral Fellow in Biology, U.C.L.A. 1946–48; Instructor in Zoology, Univ. of Calif., Berkeley 1948–50, Asst Prof. 1950–56, Assoc. Prof. 1956–60, Prof. of Zoology 1960–89, Prof. of Integrative Biology 1989–90, Prof. Emer. 1990–, Research Endocrinologist, Cancer Research Lab. 1960–; research interests: comparative endocrinology of prolactin, control of prolactin secretion, mammary gland biology, long-term effect of perinatal exposure to hormones; hormones and genital epithelial cell growth, developmental endocrinology and growth of fishes; neurosecretion; Fellow American Acad. of Arts and Sciences; Foreign Fellow, Indian Nat. Science Acad., Accad. Nazionale dei Lincei (Italy), Acad. of Sciences of Naples; Assoc. Nat. Museum of Natural History, Paris; mem. NAS, American Soc. of Zoologists (Pres. 1967), Int. Soc. of Neuroendocrinology, Endocrine Soc., American Physiological Soc., American Fisheries Soc.; Hon. mem. Japan Soc. of Comparative Endocrinology, Japan Soc. of Zootechnical Science; Visiting Prof. at numerous univs.; Howard A. Bern Distinguished Lectureship in Comparative Endocrinology, Soc. of Integrative and Comparative Biology 2002–; Hon. LLD (Hokkaido); Hon. PhD (Yokohama); Hon. DSc (Toho); Dr hc (Rouen); Hatai Medal 1998, Beverton Medal 2001. *Publications:* A Textbook of Comparative Endocrinology (with A. Gorbman) 1962; co-ed. of six books and author of numerous other publs. *Leisure interests:* collection of art and antiquities. *Address:* Department of Integrative Biology, University of California, Berkeley, CA 94720-3140 (Office); 1010 Shattuck Avenue, Berkeley, CA 94707, USA (Home). *Telephone:* (510) 642-2940 (Office); (510) 524-3480 (Home). *Fax:* (510) 643-6264 (Office). *E-mail:* bern@socrates.berkeley.edu (Office).

BERNABE, Franco; Italian business executive; b. 18 Sept. 1948, Vipiteno; s. of Bruno Bernabe and Clara Frigerio; m. Maria Grazia Curtetto; one s. one d.; ed Univ. of Turin; Fellow, Einaudi Foundation and Prof. of Econs Univ. of Turin 1973; Sr Economist, OECD, Paris 1976; Chief Economist, FIAT, Turin 1978; Asst to Chair. ENI SpA 1983, Dir Corp. Devt, Planning and Control 1986, Man. Dir and CEO –1998; Chair. Telecom Italia SpA –1998. *Publications include:* Financial Structure and Economic Policy in Italy 1975, Labour Market and Unemployment (with A. Boltho) 1982, Industrial Policies and Industrialization: The Case of the Automobile Industry 1982. *Address:* Telecom Italia SpA, Via Caboto 15, 20094 Corsico, Milan, Italy (Office).

BERNADOTTE, Graf (Gustaf) Lennart (Nicolaus Paul); Swedish administrator; b. 8 May 1909, Stockholm; s. of Prinz Wilhelm of Sweden and Princess Marie Pavlovna; m. 1st Karin Nissvandt 1932–72; m. 2nd Sonja Haunz 1972; four s. five d.; ed studies in forestry and land economy; owner, Insel Mainau, Lake Constance 1932–74 (now belongs to Lennart Bernadotte Foundation); Hon. Pres. Deutsche Gartenbaugesellschaft, Nobelpreisträgertagungen, Lindau; Hon. Senator, Technische Hochschule, Hannover; Hon. mem. Royal Horticultural Soc.; Hon. DrScAgr (Univ. of Hohenheim) numerous decorations and awards including Grosses Bundesverdienstkreuz mit Stern und Schulterband, Albert Schweitzer Gold Medal. *Address:* 78465 Insel Mainau, Germany. *Telephone:* (7531) 3030. *Fax:* (7531) 303-1 30. *E-mail:* info@mainau.de (Office). *Website:* www.mainau.de (Office).

BERNADOTTE, Count Sigvard Oscar Fredrik, BA; Swedish industrial designer; b. 7 June 1907; s. of the late King Gustav VI of Sweden; m. Marianne Lindberg 1961; ed Uppsala Univ., Royal Acad. of Arts, Stockholm and Munich; designed silverware, textiles, bookbindings, glass, porcelain 1930–; Partner, Bernadotte & Bjørn (Industrial Design) 1949–63, own firm Bernadotte Design AB 1964–; Pres. Int. Council of Socs. of Industrial Design (ICSID) 1961–63, Foreign mem. 1961–63, 1967–; Speaker German Advisory Service for Land Husbandry 1962–; Dr hc Univ. of Stuttgart-Hohenheim; awarded Gold Medal, Silver Medal and Diploma at the Milan Triennale. *Address:* Villagatan 10, Stockholm, Sweden.

BERNARD, Claire Marie Anne; French violinist; b. 31 March 1947, Rouen; d. of Yvan Bernard and Marie Chouquet; ed Conservatoire Régional de Musique, Rouen and Conservatoire Nat. Supérieur de Musique (CNSM), Paris; began professional career as solo violinist 1965; mem. jury, Tchaikovsky Int. Competition, Moscow 1974; Prof. of Violin at state-run conservatoires and music schools in France; Asst Conservatoire nat. supérieur de musique, Lyon 1990–; Prof. CNR, CNSM; recordings include works by Khatchaturian, Prokofiev, Barber, Milhaud, Mozart, Haydn and Sarasate; Chevalier, Ordre Nat. du Mérite; First Prize George Enesco Int. Competition 1964; other awards and prizes. *Leisure interests:* painting, gymnastics, swimming. *Address:* 53 rue Rabelais, 69003 Lyon, France (Home).

BERNARD, Daniel Louis; French diplomatist; b. 13 Sept. 1941, Lyon; s. of Célestin Bernard and Marie Corsat; m. Monique Beaumet 1964; two s. one d.; ed Lycée du Parc, Lyon, Faculté des Lettres de Lyon, Ecole nationale d'admin; Vice-Consul, Dublin 1967–71, UN Affairs Dept, Ministry of Foreign Affairs 1975–77, First Sec., Perm. Mission to EC, Brussels 1977–81, Tech. Adviser to Office of Minister of External Relations 1981–83, in charge of int. affairs, Ministry of Industry and Research 1984, Tech. Adviser to Office of Prime Minister 1984–86, Insp., Gen. Inspectorate of Foreign Affairs 1986, seconded to Comm. of EC 1987–88, Official Rep., Pres. of Nat. Ass. 1988–90, Head of Press, Information and Communication and Spokesman, Ministry of Foreign Affairs 1990–92, Minister Plenipotentiary 1991, Head, Office of Minister of State, Ministry of Foreign Affairs 1992–93; Amb. to Netherlands 1993–95, to UK 1997–2002, to Algeria 2002–; Perm. Rep. to UN in Geneva 1995–97.

Address: French Embassy, chemin Abd al-Kader Gadouche, Hydra, Algiers, Algeria (Office). *Telephone:* (21) 69-24-88 (Office). *Fax:* (21) 69-13-69 (Office). *E-mail:* daniel.bernard@diplomatie.fr (Office).

BERNAUER, David W., BPharm; American pharmaceutical executive; ed North Dakota State Univ. (NDSU); joined Walgreen Co. in 1966, Dist Man. 1979–87, Regional Vice-Pres. 1987–90, Vice-Pres. and Treas. 1990–92, Vice-Pres. of Purchasing 1992–95, Vice-Pres. 1995, Sr Vice-Pres. 1996–99, Pres. and COO 1999–2002, CEO 2002–, Chair. 2003–; mem. Bd of Dirs Nat. Asscn. of Chain Drug Stores (NACDS), Students in Free Enterprise (SIFE); Co-Chair. North Dakota State Univ. Coll. of Pharmacy Devt Fund; Hon. DPharm (NDSU); Distinguished Alumni Award, NDSU. *Address:* Office of the Chief Executive, Walgreen Co., 200 Wilmot Road, Deerfield, IL 60015, USA (Office). *Telephone:* (847) 940-2500 (Office). *Fax:* (847) 914-2804 (Office). *Website:* www.walgreens.com (Office).

BERNE, Robert Matthew, AB, MD, FAAS; American professor of physiology; b. 22 April 1918, Yonkers, New York; s. of Nelson Berne and Julia Stahl; m. Beth Goldberg 1944; two s. two d.; ed Univ. of North Carolina, Chapel Hill and Harvard Medical School; Intern, Asst Resident, Mount Sinai Hosp. of New York 1943–44; U.S. Army Medical Corps 1944–46; Resident in Medicine, Mount Sinai Hosp. 1947–48; Research Fellow in Physiology, Western Reserve Univ. 1948–49, Instructor 1949–50, Sr Instructor 1950–52, Asst Prof. 1952–55, Assoc. Prof. 1955–61, Prof. 1961–66; Chair. and Charles Slaughter Prof. of Physiology, Univ. of Va 1966–88, Alumni Prof. of Physiology 1988–94, Prof. Emer. 1995–; mem. Bd Science Counsel Nat. Heart, Lung and Blood Inst. 1986–89; mem. NAS, Inst. of Medicine, NAS 1988, American Acad. of Arts and Sciences 1995; Fellow American Coll. Cardiology; Carl J. Wiggers Award for significant contrib. towards understanding of circulation in health and diseases 1975, Research Achievement Award, American Heart Asscn 1979, Gold Heart Award, American Heart Asscn 1985, Jacobi Medallion 1987, Virginia Lifetime Science Achievement Award 1989, Daggs Award 1990, Inventor of the Year Award (Va) 1992 and numerous other awards. *Publications:* The Heart, in Handbook of Physiology 1979, Cardiovascular Physiology (with M. N. Levy) 1981, The Regulatory Function of Adenosine (with others) 1983, Physiology (Ed., with M. N. Levy) 1983, Principles of Physiology (Ed. with M. N. Levy) 1990; 243 scientific papers. *Leisure interests:* tennis and fishing. *Address:* University of Virginia School of Medicine, Dept of Molecular Physiology, Box 800736, Charlottesville, VA 22908 (Office); 1851 Wayside Place, Charlottesville VA 22903, USA (Home). *Telephone:* (804) 924-0173 (Office); (804) 295-9745 (Home). *Fax:* 804 982-1631. *E-mail:* mb9a@virginia.edu (Office).

BERNERD, Elliott; British property developer; b. 23 May 1945; s. of the late Geoffrey Bernerd and of Trudie Malawer (née Melzack); m. 1st Susan Elizabeth Lynton 1968 (divorced 1989); two d.; m. 2nd Sonia Ramsay (née Ramalho) 1992; Chair. Chelsfield PLC 1987–, London Philharmonic Trust 1987–94, Wentworth Group Holdings Ltd 1990–, South Bank Foundation 1996–, South Bank Bd Ltd 1998–2002. *Leisure interests:* tennis, skiing. *Address:* Chelsfield PLC, 67 Brook Street, London, W1K 4NJ, England. *Telephone:* (20) 7493-3977. *Fax:* (20) 7629-0971 . *E-mail:* ebernerd@chelsfield.com. *Website:* www.chelsfield.co.uk.

BERNERS-LEE, Timothy John, OBE, BA, FRS, FREng; British computer scientist; b. 8 June 1955, London; ed Emanuel School, London, Queen's Coll., Oxford; with Plessey Telecommunications Ltd 1976–78; software engineer D. G. Nash Ltd 1978; consultant software engineer CERN June–Dec. 1980, fellowship to work on distributed real-time systems for scientific data acquisition and system control 1984; with Image Computer Systems Ltd, responsible for tech. design 1981–84; began work on global hypertext project (now known as World Wide Web) 1989, launched within CERN 1990, on Internet 1991; joined Lab. for Computer Science, MIT 1994–, 3Com Founders Chair 1999–; Dir World Wide Web Consortium; Distinguished Fellow British Computer Soc., Hon. FIEE; Hon. DFA (Parsons School of Design, New York) 1996; Hon. DSc (Southampton Univ.) 1996; Hon. DUniv (Essex Univ.) 1998, (Southern Cross) 1998; Dr hc (Oxford) 2001; Young Innovator of the Year (Kilby Foundation) 1995, ACM Software Systems Award (jtly.) 1995, ACM Kobayashi Award 1996, IEEE Computer Soc. Wallace McDowell Award 1996, Computers and Communication Award (jtly) 1996, Duddell Medal, Inst. of Physics 1997, Charles Babbage Award 1998, Mountbatten Medal, Nat. Electronics Council 1998, Royal C Medal 2000, and numerous other awards. *Publication:* Weaving the Web: The Original Design and Ultimate Destiny of the World Wide Web by its Inventor 2000. *Address:* Laboratory for Computer Science, Massachusetts Institute of Technology, 545 Technology Square, Cambridge, MA 02139, USA (Office). *Telephone:* (617) 253-1000 (Office). *Fax:* (617) 253-8000 (Office).

BERNES, Thomas Anthony, BA; Canadian government official; b. 21 March 1946, Winnipeg; m. Ann Boyd 1974 (divorced 1997); one s. one d.; ed Univ. of Manitoba; Dir Gen. Trade Policy, Dept of Industry, Trade and Commerce 1981–82, Economic Policy Planning Secr. 1982–83; Head Gen. Trade Policy Div., OECD 1983–85; Dir GATT Affairs, Dept of Foreign Affairs and Int. Trade, Govt of Canada 1985–87; Dir Internal Econ. Relations, Dept of Finance 1987–88, Gen. Dir Int. Trade and Finance Br. 1988–91, Exec. Dir Coordinating Secr. on Canadian Unity, Office of the Deputy Minister 1991–92, Asst Deputy Minister, Int. Trade and Finance Br. 1992–95; G7 Finance Deputy 1995–96; Alt. Gov. for Canada, IMF, Asia Devt Bank, African Devt Bank and Inter-American Devt Bank 1996; Dir Canadian Export Devt Corpn 1996;

Exec. Dir IMF 1996–2001; Exec. Sec., Devt Cttee of Int. Bank for Reconstruction and Devt (World Bank) and IMF 2001–. *Address:* Development Committee, International Bank for Reconstruction and Development, Suite MC12-427, 1818 H Street, NW, Washington, DC 20433, USA. *Telephone:* (202) 458-9555 (Office). *Fax:* (202) 522-1618 (Office). *E-mail:* tbernes@worldbank.org.

BERNHARD, Sandra; American actress, comedienne and singer; b. 6 June 1955, Flint, Mich.; d. of Jerome Bernhard and Jeanette Bernhard; stand-up comedienne in nightclubs in Beverly Hills 1974–78. *Films include:* Cheech and Chong's Nice Dreams 1981, The King of Comedy 1983 (Nat. Soc. Film Critics Award), Sesame Street Presents: Follow That Bird 1985, Track 29 1988, Without You I'm Nothing 1990, Hudson Hawk 1991, Truth or Dare 1991, Inside Monkey Zetterland 1993, Dallas Doll 1994, Unzipped 1995, Catwalk 1995, Somewhere in the City 1997, Lover Girl 1997, The Apocalypse 1997, Exposé 1998, Wrongfully Accused 1998, Hercules: Zero to Hero (voice) 1999, Dinner Rush 2000, Playing Mona Lisa 2000, Zoolander 2001. *Stage appearances (solo):* Without You I'm Nothing 1988, Giving Till It Hurts 1992. *TV appearances:* Living in America (host) 1990, regular appearances in Roseanne (series), Ally McBeal, Superman, The Larry Sanders Shaw, Clueless. *Albums:* I'm Your Woman (co-author 8 songs) 1985, Without You I'm Nothing 1989. *Publications include:* Confessions of a Pretty Lady 1988, Love Love and Love 1993. *Address:* Noe-Man Management, 26500 West Agoura Road, Suite 575, Calabasas, CA 91302 (Office); c/o Susan DuBow, 9171 Wilshire Boulevard, Beverly Hills, CA 90210, USA.

BERNHARD LEOPOLD FREDERIK EVERHARD JULIUS COERT KAREL GODFRIED PIETER, HRH Prince (see under Netherlands).

BERNHEIM, Antoine, Des en D, LèsSc; French business executive and banker; b. 4 Sept. 1924, Paris; s. of Léonce Bernheim and Renée-Marcelle Schwob d'Héricourt; m. Francine Bernard 1947; one s. one d.; ed Lycée Janson-de-Sailly, Univs. of Paris and Grenoble; partner 1954, later Prés. Dir Gen. Soc. française gén. immobilière (fmrly Bernheim Frères et Fils) 1967–72; Man. Partner Lazard Frères et Cie 1967–, Gen. Partner and mem. Exec. Bd Lazard Partners 1984–99, Assoc. Lazard LLC 2000–; mem. Bd of Dirs. 1967, Prés. Dir Gén. La France IARD et Vie 1972; Prés. Dir Gén. La France SA 1974–; Prés. Dir Gén. Euromarché 1981–91; Vice-Prés. Dir Gén. Eurafrance 1984–, Partner 1973–, mem. Supervisory Cttee 1976, Vice-Prés. 1982–95, Prés. 1995–96; Vice-Pres. Generali France Holding 1990–95, 2001–02, Pres. Dir-Gen. 1996–99; Prés. Euralux 1973–2001; mem. Supervisory Bd then Vice-Prés. Printemps SA 1972; Dir and Vice-Pres. Mediobanca 1988–; mem. Supervisory Bd 1988–, Dir then Vice-Pres. Bd of Dirs. LVMH (Louis Vuitton Moët Hennessy) 1992–; mem. Supervisory Bd 1981, Vice-Pres. Pinault-Printemps 1992–93; Pres. Assicurazioni Generali 1995–99, Chair. 2002–; Grand Officier Légion d'honneur. *Address:* Assicurazioni Generali SpA, Piazza Duca degli Abruzzi 2, 34132 Trieste, Italy (Office); 64 avenue Henri-Martin, 75116 Paris, France (Home). *Telephone:* (04) 067-1111 (Office). *Fax:* (04) 067-1600 (Office). *Website:* www.generali.com (Office).

BERNIK, France, PhD; Slovenian academic; b. 13 May 1927, Ljubljana; s. of Franc Bernik and Cecilija Bernik (née Smole); m. Marija Kanc 1956; one d.; ed Univ. of Ljubljana; teaching Asst Slovene Literature Univ. of Ljubljana 1951–57; Ed., Sec. Slovenska Matica, Ljubljana 1961–71; affiliated with Slovenian Acad. of Sciences and Arts Research Centre 1972–99; Scientific Adviser Inst. for Slovene Literature and Literary Sciences 1977–99, Assoc. mem. 1983, mem. 1987, Pres. Slovenian Acad. of Sciences and Arts 1992–2002; lecturer, Visiting Prof. various univs; Soc. for Slovene Studies, Bloomington, USA 1992, mem., Senator Academia Scientiarum et Artium Europaea, Salzburg 1993; mem. Croatian Acad. of Sciences and Arts 1994, Int. Acad. of Energy 1997, L'Accademia del Mediterraneo 1999, numerous editorial bds; Eques commendator Ordinis sancti Gregorii Magni 1997, Golden Hon. Decoration of Freedom of Repub. of Slovenia 1997, Maréchal Ordre de Saint Fortunat 2001; Dr hc (Maribor) 2000; Int. Cultural Diploma of Honour 1996, Zois Award of Repub. of Slovenia 1999. *Publications:* The Lyrics of Simon Jenko 1962, Cankar's Early Prose 1976, Simon Jenko 1979, Problems of Slovene Literature 1980, Typology of Cankar's Prose 1983, Ivan Cankar: A Monograph 1987, Slovene War Prose 1941–80 1988, Studies on Slovene Poetry 1993, Slowenische Literatur im europäischen Kontext 1993, Ivan Cankar: Ein slowenischer Schriftsteller des europäischen Symbolismus 1997, Horizons of Slovenian Literature 1999, Ed.-in-chief Collected Works of Slovene Poets and Writers 1981–. *Address:* c/o Slovenian Academy of Sciences and Arts, Novi trg 3, 1000 Ljubljana (Office); Zidovska 1, 1000 Ljubljana, Slovenia (Home). *Telephone:* (1) 4706151 (Office); (1) 4250365 (Home). *Fax:* (1) 4253423 (Office). *E-mail:* jerka.kern@sazu.si (Office). *Website:* www.sazu.si (Office).

BERNINI, Giorgio; Italian politician, lawyer and university lecturer; b. 9 Nov. 1928, Bologna; ed Univ. of Bologna; Lecturer in Commercial Law, Univ. of Bologna; fmr adviser to EC (now EU) and Italian Govt on questions of int. commercial law, customs tariffs and tech. transfer; entered politics 1994, Forza Italia Senator 1994–; Minister for Foreign Trade 1994–95; Chair. Int. Council for Arbitration. *Publications:* articles in specialized journals and in daily newspapers. *Address:* c/o Forza Italia, Via dell'Umiltà 48, 00187, Rome, Italy.

BERNSTEIN, Baron (Life Peer), cr. 2000, of Craigweil in the County of West Sussex; **Alexander Bernstein;** British business executive; b. 15 March 1936; s. of the late Cecil Bernstein and of Myra Ella Lesser; m. 1st Vanessa Anne

Mills 1962 (divorced 1993); one s. one d.; m. 2nd Angela Mary Serota 1995; ed Stowe School, St John's Coll. Cambridge; Man. Dir Granada TV Rental Ltd 1964–68, Chair. 1977–86; Jt Man. Dir Granada TV Ltd 1971–75; Chair. Granada Group PLC 1979–96 (Dir 1964–96); acquired Forte PLC 1996; Dir Waddington Galleries 1966–; Trustee Civic Trust for the North-West 1964–86, Granada Foundation 1968–, Theatres Trust 1996–2000, Trusthouse Charitable Foundation 1996–; Chair. Royal Exchange Theatre 1983–94 (Deputy Chair. 1980–83), Old Vic Theatre Trust 1998–2002; mem. Nat. Theatre Devt Council 1996–98; mem. of Court, Univ. of Salford 1976–87, Univ. of Manchester 1983–98; Hon. DLitt (Salford) 1981; Hon. LLD (Manchester) 1996. *Leisure interests:* modern art, skiing, gardening. *Address:* c/o House of Lords, London, SW1A 0PW, England.

BERNSTEIN, Carl, LLD; American journalist and author; b. 14 Feb. 1944, Washington; s. of Alfred Bernstein and Sylvia Walker; m. Nora Ephron 1976 (divorced); two s.; ed Univ. of Maryland and Boston Univ.; copyboy, reporter, Washington Star 1960–65; reporter Elizabeth (NJ) Journal 1965–66, Washington Post 1966–77; Washington bureau chief, ABC 1979–81; corresp. ABC News, New York 1981–84; Corresp., contrib. Time Magazine 1990–91; Visiting Prof. New York Univ. 1992–93; Exec. Vice-Pres. and Exec. Dir Voter.com –2001; contributing Ed. Vanity Fair 1997–; frequent political commentator on network TV; fmr rock and music critic for the Washington Post; Drew Pearson Prize for investigative reporting of Watergate 1972, George Polk Memorial Award and other awards for journalism. *Publications:* All the President's Men (with Bob Woodward) (Pulitzer Prize 1977) 1974, The Final Days (with Bob Woodward) 1976, Loyalties: A Son's Memoir 1989, His Holiness: John Paul II and the Hidden History of Our Time (with Marco Politi) 1996; numerous articles in The New Republic, Rolling Stone, The New York Times, Newsweek and Der Spiegel. *Address:* c/o Janklow & Nesbit Assocs., 598 Madison Avenue, New York, NY 10022, USA.

BERNSTEIN, Robert Louis; American publisher; b. 5 Jan. 1923, New York City; s. of Alfred and Sylvia Bernstein; m. Helen Walter 1950; three s.; ed Harvard Univ.; U.S. Army Air Force 1943–46; with Simon & Schuster (book publrs.) 1946–57, Gen. Sales Man. 1950–57; Random House Inc. 1958–, Vice-Pres. (Sales) 1961–63, First Vice-Pres. 1963–65, Pres. and CEO 1966–89, Chair. 1975–89; Publr at Large, Adviser John Wiley & Sons Inc. 1991–98; Vice-Chair. Asscn of American Publrs. 1970–72, Chair. 1972–73; Chair. Asscn of American Publrs. Cttee on Soviet-American Publishing Relations 1973–74, on Int. Freedom to Publish 1975; Chair. U.S. Helsinki Watch Cttee, New York, 1979–92, Founding Chair. 1992; Chair. Fund for Free Expression 1975–90, Founding Chair. 1990; Founding Chair. Human Rights Watch 1975–; Co-Chair. Human Rights in China 1999–; fmr mem. Council on Foreign Relations, Nat. Advisory Cttee Amnesty Int.; mem. Americas Watch, Asia Watch, ME Watch, Africa Watch, Advisory Cttee Carter-Menil Human Rights Foundation, Advisory Bd Robert F. Kennedy Foundation Human Rights Award, Int. Liberal Education Bd Bard Coll.; Vice-Pres. Bd of Dirs. Aaron Diamond Foundation, The Century Asscn; Dr. of Laws New School for Social Research 1991; Hon. LLD (Hofstra) 1998; Human Rights Award (Lawyers' Cttee for Human Rights) 1987, Spirit of Liberty Award for the American Way 1989, Barnard Medal of Distinction, Barnard Coll. 1990, Liberty Award, Brandeis Univ. 1994, Eleanor Roosevelt Human Rights Award 1998; other awards. *Leisure interests:* skiing, tennis, swimming. *Address:* 277 Park Avenue, 49th Floor, New York, NY 10172-0003, USA (Office). *E-mail:* r.l .bernstein@att.net.

BERNSTEN, Thorbjørn; Norwegian politician and trade union official; b. 15 April 1935, Oslo; m. Adda Bernsten; ed Tech. Coll., Officers' Training School; with Nylands Shipyard 1951–66; Information Sec. Norwegian Union of Iron and Metalworkers, Leader 1965–66; Leader Akers mek. Verksted A.S. 1962–64; Chair., later Deputy Chair. Oslo Municipal Consultative Cttee for Trade and Industry 1969–83; Deputy Chair. Labour Party 1989; Minister of the Environment 1990–97; mem. Cttee of Reps. Oslo Labour Party 1962 (Chair. 1976–82), Standing Cttee on Local Govt and the Environment 1973– (Chair. 1989–90), Storting (Parl.) 1977–. *Address:* c/o Det Norske Arbeiderpartei, Youngstorget 2, P.O. Box 8743, 0028 Oslo, Norway.

BEROV, Lyuben; Bulgarian politician and economist; fmr econ. advisor to Pres. Zhelev; Prime Minister of Bulgaria 1992–94; mem. Movt for Rights and Freedoms (MRF). *Address:* c/o Movement for Rights and Freedoms, Ivan Vazov, Tzarigradsko Shosse 47/1, 1408 Sofia, Bulgaria.

BERRI, (Claude) (pseudonym of Langmann, Claude Beri); French film director; b. 1 July 1934, Paris; s. of Hirsh Langmann and Beila Bercu; m. Anne-Marie Rassam 1967; two c.; ed Lycée Turgot, Paris; theatre and film actor 1951–63; writer and dir of films 1963–; Grand Prix de l'Acad. du Cinéma 1986. *Films include:* Le Poulet 1963 (Acad. Award for best short film 1966), Le Vieil Homme et l'Enfant 1966, Mazel Tov ou le Mariage 1968, Le Pistonné 1970, Le Cinéma de Papa 1971, Sex-Shop 1972, Le Mâle du Siècle 1975, La Première Fois 1976, Un Moment d'égarement 1977, Je vous aime 1980, Le Maître d'Ecole 1981, Tchao Pantin 1983, Jean de Florette 1986, Manon des Sources 1986, Uranus 1990, My Dog Stupid 1990, Germinal 1993, La Reine Margot 1994, Lucie Albrac 1996, Astérix et Obélix contre César 1999; producer The Bear 1989. *Address:* Renn Espace d'Art Contemporain, 7 rue de Lille, 75007 Paris; Renn Production, 10 rue Lincoln, 75008 Paris, France.

BERRIDGE, Sir Michael (John), Kt, PhD, FRS; British biologist; b. 22 Oct. 1938, Gatooma, Rhodesia (now Zimbabwe); s. of George Kirton Berridge and Stella Elaine Hards; m. Susan Graham Winter 1965; one s. one d.; ed Univ.

Coll. of Rhodesia and Nyasaland, Univ. of Cambridge; Post-doctoral Fellow, Univ. of Virginia 1965–66; Post-doctoral Fellow, Case Western Reserve Univ. 1966–67, Research Assoc. 1967–69; Sr Scientific Officer, Unit of Invertebrate Chemistry and Physiology, Univ. of Cambridge 1969–72, Prin. Scientific Officer 1972–78, Sr Prin. Scientific Officer, Unit of Insect Neurophysiology and Pharmacology 1978–90, Hon. Prof. of Cell Signalling 1994–; Deputy Chief Scientific Officer, Lab. of Molecular Signalling, Babraham Inst., Cambridge 1990–, Head of Signalling Programme 1996–; mem. Soc. of Gen. Physiologists, Acad. Europaea 1989–, European Molecular Biology Org. 1991–; Acad. of Medical Sciences 1998; Hon. mem. Japanese Biochemical Soc.; Hon. Life mem. Soc. for Experimental Biology; Hon. mem. American Physiological Soc. 1992; mem. NAS 1999; Foreign Hon. mem. American Acad. of Arts and Science 1999; mem. numerous editorial bds including Biochemical Journal 1987–, Journal of Endocrinology 1989–, Molecular Biology of the Cell 1989–, Advances in Second Messenger and Phosphoprotein Research 1990–, Journal of Basic and Clinical Physiology and Pharmacology 1990–, Journal of Experimental Biology 1993–; Advisory Ed. BioEssays 1994–; Foreign Corresp., Acad. Royale de Médecine de Belgique 1994–; Fellow Trinity Coll. Cambridge 1972–; Hon. Fellow Gonville and Caius Coll. Cambridge 1998; Trustee, Isaac Newton Trust 1991–2000; has given numerous memorial lectures; Gov. Strangeways Research Lab. 1987–98; main area of research concerns the mode of action of hormones and neurotransmitters at the cellular level; Dr hc (Limburgs Universitaire Centrum, Belgium) 1993; Feldberg Prize 1984, King Faisal Int. Prize in Science 1986, Louis Jeantet Prize in Medicine 1989, William Bate Hardy Prize, Cambridge Philosophical Soc. 1987, Dr H. P. Heineken Prize for Biochemistry and Biophysics 1994, Wolf Foundation Prize in Medicine, Israel 1995, Massry Prize, USA 1996, Ernst Schering Prize 1999; numerous awards and medals including Gairdner Foundation Int. Award 1988, Baly Medal, Royal Coll. of Physicians 1989, Albert Lasker Basic Medical Research Award 1989, Royal Medal, Royal Soc. 1991. *Publications:* more than 100 scientific papers. *Leisure interests:* gardening, golf. *Address:* Laboratory of Molecular Signalling, The Babraham Institute, Babraham Hall, Babraham, Cambridge, CB2 4AT (Office). *Telephone:* (1223) 496621 (Office); (1223) 496033. *E-mail:* michael.berridge@bbsrc.ac.uk (Office). *Website:* www .babraham.ac.uk.

BERRILL, Sir Kenneth, GBE, KCB, B.SC.(ECON.), MA; British economist; b. 28 Aug. 1920, London; s. of Stanley Berrill and Lilian Blakeley; m. 1st Brenda West 1941 (divorced); one s.; m. 2nd June Phillips 1950 (divorced 1976); one s. one d.; m. 3rd Jane Marris 1977; ed London School of Econs and Trinity Coll., Cambridge; HM Treasury (Cen. Econ. Planning Staff) 1947–49; Lecturer in Econs, Cambridge Univ. 1949–69; Prof. MIT 1962; Special Adviser, HM Treasury 1967–69; Brit. Nat. Comm. for UNESCO 1967–70; Gov. Admin. Staff Coll. Henley 1969–85; mem. Council for Scientific Policy 1969–72; Chair. Univ. Grants Cttee of GB 1969–73, Moneda Chile Fund 1995–; mem. Advisory Bd for Research Councils 1972–73, 1976–78; mem. Advisory Council for Applied Research and Devt 1977–80; apptd. Head of Govt Econ. Service and Chief Econ. Adviser to HM Treasury 1973–74; Head Cen. Policy Review Staff, Cabinet Office 1974–80; Chair. Vickers Da Costa and Co. 1981–85, Securities and Investment Bd 1985–88; Deputy Chair. Universities Superannuation Scheme 1980–85; Vice-Pres. Council, Royal Econ. Soc. 1986–; Dir Nippon Credit Gartmore Investment Man. Ltd 1990–98; Chair. Commonwealth Equities Fund 1990–95; mem. Advisory Bd, Royal Coll. of Defence Studies 1974–80; mem. Stock Exchange (London) 1980–85; mem. Review Bd for Govt Contracts 1981–85; Deputy Chair. Gen. Funds Investment Trust 1981–85; Chair. Robert Horne Group 1987–90; mem. Council Lloyds of London 1983–88; Pro-Chancellor and Chair. of Council of Open Univ. 1983–96; sometime Econ. Adviser to OECD, IBRD, Guyana, Cameroon, Turkey; City Councillor, Cambridge 1964–69; Fellow Open Univ. 1997; Trustee, London Philharmonic Orchestra 1987–; Hon. Fellow (LSE, King's Coll. and St Catharine's Coll., Cambridge, King's Coll. London, Open Univ.); James S. McDonnell Fellow (WIDER) 1988, 1990; Hon. LLD (Bath, Cambridge, East Anglia, Leicester); Hon. DUniv (Open Univ.); Hon. DTech (Loughborough); Hon. ScD (Aston). *Leisure interests:* sailing, music, gardening. *Address:* Salt Hill, Bridle Way, Grantchester, Cambs., CB3 9NY, England (Home). *Telephone:* (1223) 840335. *Fax:* (1223) 845939.

BERRY, Brian Joe Lobley, BSc(ECON.), MA, PhD, FBA, FAAS; American/British geographer, political economist and policy analyst; b. 16 Feb. 1934, Sedgley, Staffs., UK; s. of Joe Berry and Gwendoline Berry (née Lobley); m. Janet E Shapley 1958; one s. two d.; ed Univ. Coll., London and Univ. of Washington; Asst Prof., then Prof. Univ. of Chicago 1958–76; Faculty mem. Brookings Inst. 1966–76; Prof. Harvard Univ. 1976–81; Prof. and Dean, School of Urban and Public Affairs, Carnegie Mellon Univ. 1981–86; Prof. Univ. of Tex. at Dallas 1986–, Lloyd Viel Berkner Regental Prof. and Prof. of Political Economy 1991–; mem. NAS (mem. Council 1999–2002), Asscn of American Geographers (Pres. 1978–79), American Inst. of Certified Planners, Regional Science Asscn Int.; Fellow, Univ. Coll. London 1983, American Acad. of Arts and Sciences, Weimar School of Land Econs, Inst. of British Geographers, Royal Geographical Soc.; Hon. AM (Harvard) 1976; Anderson Medal, Asscn of American Geographers 1987, Victoria Medal, Royal Geographical Soc. 1988, Rockefeller Prize 1991, and others. *Publications:* more than 500 books, articles and other professional publs. *Leisure interests:* family history, genealogy, travel. *Address:* School of Social Sciences GR31, University of Texas-Dallas, PO Box 83-0688, Richardson, TX 75083 (Office); 2404 Forest

Ct., McKinney, TX 75070, USA (Home). *Telephone:* (972) 883-2041 (Office); (972) 562-1058 (Home). *Fax:* (972) 883-2735 (Office); (972) 562-1058 (Home). *E-mail:* heja@utdallas.edu (Office); bjlb@attbi.com (Home).

BERRY, Chuck (Charles Edward Anderson Berry); American singer and composer; b. 18 Oct. 1926, St Louis; m. Thermetta Suggs 1948; four c.; popular artiste in rock and roll, plays guitar, saxophone, piano; concert and TV appearances 1955–; Grammy Award for Life Achievement 1984. *Albums:* After School Sessions 1958, One Dozen Berrys 1958, New Juke Box Hits 1960, Chuck Berry 1960, More Chuck Berry 1960, On Stage 1960, You Can Never Tell 1964, Greatest Hits 1964, Two Great Guitars 1964, Chuck Berry in London 1965, Fresh Berrys 1965, St Louis to Liverpool 1966, Golden Hits 1967, At the Fillmore 1967, Medley 1967, In Memphis 1967, Concerto in B Goods 1969, Home Again 1971, The London Sessions 1972, Golden Decade 1972, St Louis to Frisco to Memphis 1972, Let the Good Times Roll 1973, Golden Decade (Vol. II) 1973, (Vol. V) 1974, Bio 1973, Back in the USA 1973, I'm a Rocker 1975, Chuck Berry 75 1975, Motorvatin' 1976, Rockit 1979, Chess Masters 1983, The Chess Box 1989, Missing Berries 1990, Rarities 1990, On the Blues Side 1993, Anthology 2000. *Films:* Go, Johnny Go, Rock, Rock, Rock 1956, Jazz on a Summer's Day 1960, Let the Good Times Roll 1973, Hail! Hail! Rock 'n' Roll 1987. *Publication:* Chuck Berry: The Autobiography 1987. *Address:* Berry Park, 691 Buckner Road, Wentzville, MO 63385, USA.

BERRY, Halle; American actress and model; b. 14 Aug. 1968, Cleveland, Ohio; d. of Judith Berry (née Hawkins); m. 1st David Justice 1993 (divorced 1996); one d.; m. 2nd Eric Benet 2001; ed Cuyahoga Community Coll., Cleveland; began competing in formal beauty contests 1980s, won title Miss Ohio 1986; TV and film actress 1989–; mem. Nat. Breast Cancer Coalition; Harvard Foundation for Intercultural and Race Relations Award. *Films:* Strictly Business 1991, Jungle Fever 1991, The Last Boy Scout 1991, Boomerang 1992, Father Hood 1993, Alex Haley's Queen 1993, The Program 1993, The Flintstones 1994, Losing Isaiah 1995, The Rich Man's Wife 1996, Executive Decision 1996, Race the Sun 1996, Girl 6 1996, B.A.P.S. 1997, Why Do Fools Fall in Love 1998, The Wedding 1998, Bulworth 1998, Victims of Fashion 1999, Ringside 1999, Introducing Dorothy Dandridge (also producer) (Golden Globe for Best Actress, Screen Actors' Guild Award) 1999, X-Men 2000, Swordfish 2001, Monster's Ball (Acad. Award 2002) 2001, James Bond: Die Another Day (Nat. Asscn for the Advancement of Colored People—NAACP Award for Best Supporting Actress 2003) 2002, X-Men 2 2003. *Television:* TV debut with sitcom Living Dolls 1989, Knots Landing 1991–92. *Address:* c/o William Morris Agency, 151 South El Camino Drive, Beverly Hills, LA 90212, USA (Office).

BERRY, L(eonard) Michael; Canadian diplomatist; b. 28 Sept. 1937, Bolton, UK; s. of Leonard Berry and Margaret (née Wynne) Berry; m. 1st Linda Kathleen Randal 1963 (deceased); one s. two d.; m. 2nd Anna Sumanti 2002; ed McGill Univ.; entered Canadian Dept of External Affairs 1964, served in Berlin 1966–68 and London 1971–75; High Commr in Singapore 1979–82; Amb. to OECD 1988–91; High Commr in Australia 1991–95; Canadian Special Co-ordinator for the Reconstruction of Former Yugoslavia 1995–97; Diplomat-in-Residence Malaspina Univ., BC 1997–99; Int. Adviser Berry Assocs. 1999–; Dir Port of Nanaimo Authority; mem. Bd British Columbia Centre for Int. Educ. *Leisure interests:* skiing, golf, cricket, music, investment. *Address:* 541 St Andrew's Road, Qualicum Beach, BC V9K 1L5, Canada. *Telephone:* (250) 752-9360. *Fax:* (250) 752-9372. *E-mail:* lmichaelberry@shaw.ca (Office); michaelberry541@hotmail.com (Home).

BERRY, Mary Frances, PhD; American lawyer and historian; b. 17 Feb. 1938, Nashville; d. of George Ford and Frances Southall; ed ed. Howard Univ., Univ. of Michigan; Asst Prof. of History, Cen. Mich. Univ., Mount Pleasant 1966–68; Asst Prof. Eastern Mich. Univ., Ypsilanti 1968–69, Assoc. Prof. 1969–70; Acting Dir Afro-American Studies, Univ. of Md 1970–72, Dir 1972–74, Acting Chair. Div. of Behavioural and Social Sciences 1973–74, Provost 1973–76; Prof. of Law, Univ. of Colo 1976–80, Chancellor 1976–77; Asst Sec. for Educ. US Dept of Health, Educ. and Welfare 1977–80; Prof. of History and Law, Howard Univ., Washington 1980–; Geraldine R. Segal Prof. of American Social Thought, Univ. of Pa 1987–; mem. US Comm. on Civil Rights 1980–, now Chair.; mem. Advisory Bd Feminist Press 1980–, Inst. for Higher Educ. Law and Governance, Univ. of Houston; mem. Council UN Univ. 1986–; numerous awards and hon. degrees. *Publications:* Black Resistance/White Law 1971, Military Necessity and Civil Rights Policy 1977, Stability, Security and Continuity, Mr Justice Burton and Decision-Making in the Supreme Court 1945–58 1978, Long Memory: The Black Experience in America 1982 (jtly.), The Pig Farmer's Daughter and Other Tales of American Justice: Episodes of Racism and Sexism in the Courts from 1865 to the Present 1999. *Address:* Office of the Chairman, Commission on Civil Rights, 624 9th Street, NW, Washington, DC 30425, USA (Office).

BERRY, Nabih; Lebanese politician and lawyer; b. 1938, Sierra Leone; s. of Mustapha Berri; m. 1st; six c.; m. 2nd; ed Makassed, Ecole de la Sagesse, Beirut, Univ. Libanaise, Univ. of Paris; lawyer 1963–; led student movement, Unions of Lebanese Univs.; Pres. Shi'ite Amal Movement 1980–; fmr State Minister of Reconstruction and the South, of Justice, of Hydraulic and Electrical Resources; led Liberation Bloc 1992 parl. elections, Liberation and Devt Bloc 1996; Pres. Nat. Ass. 1992–. *Address:* Assemblée Nationale, Beirut, Lebanon.

BERRY, Richard Stephen, AM, PhD, FAAS; American professor of chemistry; b. 9 April 1931, Denver, Colo; s. of Morris Berry and Ethel (Alpert) Berry; m. Carla Lamport Friedman 1955; one s. two d.; ed Harvard Univ.; Instructor, Univ. of Mich. 1957–60; Asst Prof. Yale Univ. 1960–64; Assoc. Prof. Univ. of Chicago 1964–67, Prof. Dept of Chem., James Franck Inst. 1967–89, James Franck Distinguished Service Prof. 1989–; Gaest Prof. Univ. of Copenhagen 1967, 1979; Consultant Argonne Nat. Lab. 1976–, Los Alamos Science Lab. 1975–; Visiting Prof., Univ. de Paris-Sud 1979–80; Hinshelwood Lecturer, Oxford 1980; Chair., Numerical Data Advisory Bd, National Research Council 1978–84; Newton Abraham Prof., Oxford Univ., England 1986–87; mem. Visiting Comm. of Applied Physics, Harvard Univ. 1977–81; mem. NAS (Home Sec. 1999–2003); mem. numerous cttees. and orgs.; Foreign mem. Royal Danish Acad. of Sciences; Fellow American Acad. of Arts and Sciences (Vice-Pres. 1995–98); MacArthur Prize Fellow 1983; Alexander von Humboldt Preistraeger 1993; J. Heyrosky Medal 1997. *Publications:* (with L. Gaines and T.V. Long II) TOSCA: The Social Costs of Coal and Nuclear Power 1979, (with S. A. Rice and J. Ross) Physical Chemistry 1980, Understanding Energy: Energy, Entropy and Thermodynamics for Everyman 1991, (with others) Optimization Methods in Finite Time Thermodynamics 1999; approximately 450 scientific papers in specialist journals. *Leisure interests:* music, skiing, hiking and climbing, photography, fly fishing. *Address:* Department of Chemistry, University of Chicago, 5735 S. Ellis Avenue, Chicago, IL 60637 (Office); 5317 S. University Ave., Chicago, IL 60615, USA (Home). *Telephone:* (773) 702-7021 (Office). *Fax:* (773) 834-4049 (Office). *E-mail:* berry@uchicago.edu (Office).

BERRY, Wendell, MA; American author; b. 5 Aug. 1934, Henry County, Ky; m. Tanya Amyx 1957; one s. one d.; ed Univ. of Ky; mem. Faculty, Univ. of Ky 1964–77, 1987–, Distinguished Prof. of English 1971–72. *Publications:* novels: Nathan Coulter 1962, A Place on Earth 1967, The Memory of Old Jack 1974, Remembering 1988, The Discovery of Kentucky 1991, Fidelity 1992, A Consent 1993, Watch With Me 1994, A World Lost 1996; short stories: The Wild Birds 1986; poetry: The Broken Ground 1964, Openings 1968, Findings 1969, Farming: A Handbook 1970, The Country of Marriage 1973, Clearing 1977, A Part 1980, The Wheel 1982, Collected Poems 1985, Sabbaths 1987, Sayings and Doings and an Eastward Look 1990, Entries 1994, The Farm 1995; essays: The Long-Legged House 1969, The Hidden Wound 1970, The Unforseen Wilderness 1971, A Continuous Harmony 1972, The Unsettling of America 1977, Recollected Essays 1965–80 1981, The Gift of Good Land 1981, Standing by Words 1985, Life is a Miracle: An Essay Against Modern Superstition 2000; co-ed. Meeting the Expectations of the Land 1985, Home Economics 1987, What Are People For? 1990, Harland Hubbard: Life and Work 1990, Standing on Earth 1991, Another Turn of the Crank. *Address:* Lanes Landing Farm, Port Royal, KY 40058, USA.

BERSON, Jerome Abraham, MA, PhD; American professor of chemistry; b. 10 May 1924, Sanford, Fla; s. of Joseph and Rebecca Bernicker Berson; m. Bella Zevitovsky 1946; two s. one d.; ed City Coll. of New York, Columbia and Harvard Univs; Asst Prof., Univ. of Southern Calif. 1950–53, Assoc. Prof. 1953–58, Prof. 1958–63; Prof., Univ. of Wis. 1963–69, Yale Univ. 1969–79, Irénée duPont Prof. 1979–92, Sterling Prof. 1992–94, Sterling Prof. Emer. 1994–; Chair. Dept of Chem., Yale Univ. 1971–74; Dir Div. of Physical Sciences and Eng 1983–90; Sherman Fairchild Distinguished Scholar, Calif. Inst. of Tech. 1974–75; mem. NAS; Fellow American Acad. of Arts and Sciences; Nat. Research Council Post-doctoral Fellow; ACS (Calif. Section) Award 1963, James Flack Norris Award in Physical Organic Chemistry 1978, Sr U.S. Scientist Award, Alexander von Humboldt Foundation 1980; Townsend Harris Medal 1984; William H. Nichols Medal 1985, Roger Adams Award 1987, Nat. Insts. of Health Merit Award 1989, Arthur C. Cope Scholar Award 1992, Oesper Award 1998; Literature Prize, German Chemical Industry Asscn 2000. *Publications:* Chemical Creativity 1999; scientific papers on organic chem. published mostly in Journal of the American Chemical Society. *Leisure interests:* hiking, squash. *Address:* Department of Chemistry, Yale University, Box 208107, New Haven, CT 06520-8107, USA. *Telephone:* (203) 432-3970. *Fax:* (203) 432-6144. *E-mail:* jerome.berson@yale.edu (Office).

BERTHELOT, Yves M.; French statistician and economist; b. 15 Sept. 1937, Paris; m. Dosithée Yeatman 1961; three s. one d.; ed Ecole Polytechnique and Ecole Nationale de la Statistique et de l'Administration Economique; Dir of Studies in the Ministry of Planning, Ivory Coast 1965–68; Chief of the Study of Enterprises Div., then Chief of Service of Programmes of INSEE (Institut Nat. de la Statistique et des Etudes Economiques) 1971–75; Chief, Service des Etudes et Questions Int., French Ministry of Co-operation 1976–78; Dir of Research, Devt Centre of OECD, Paris 1978–81; Dir CEPII (Prospective Studies and Int. Information Centre) 1981–85; Deputy Sec.-Gen. of UNCTAD 1985–93; Exec. Sec. UN Econ. Comm. for Europe 1993–2000; Sr Research Fellow and Head Geneva Liaison Office, City Univ. of New York Grad. Center 2000–; Chevalier Ordre Nat. du Mérite, Officier Ordre Nat. (Côte d'Ivoire). *Publications:* numerous articles on economics. *Leisure interests:* sailing, skiing. *Address:* City University of New York, 365 Fifth Avenue, New York, NY 10021, USA. *Website:* www.gc.cuny.edu.

BERTHELSEN, Asger, DPhil; Danish geologist; b. 30 April 1928, Aarhus; s. of O.V. Berthelsen and Charlotte Berthelsen (neé Jensen); m. 1st Suoma I. Påhlman-Carlsson 1954 (died 1971); one d.; m. 2nd Mona D. Hansen (died 1979); m. 3rd Inge Halberg 1984 (died 2003); ed Copenhagen and Neuchatel Univ.; State Geologist 1959; Prof. of Geology, Aarhus Univ. 1961, Copenhagen Univ. 1966–92; mem. Royal Danish Acad. of Science, Academia Europaea; Denmark Geology Prize 1993; Order of Dannebrog (1st Class). *Publications:* On the Geology of the Rupshu District 1953, Geology of Tovqussap Nuna 1960,

Precambrian of Greenland 1965, Geological Map of Ivigtut 1975, Geologi pa Rösnäs 1975, Den lille Tektoniker 1976, The EUGENO-S Project 1988, A Continent Revealed: The European Geotraverse Project (co-author) 1992, Rejsen til den blaa Sø 1998. *Leisure interest:* oil painting. *Address:* Geological Institute, Øster Voldgade 10, 1350 Copenhagen K (Office); Fredensvej 14, I, 2920, Charlottenlund, Denmark (Home). *Telephone:* 35-32-24-58 (Office); 39-90-26-24 (Home). *E-mail:* asgerb@geo.geol.ku.dk (Office).

BERTHOIN, Georges Paul, LenD, LèsL; French civil servant; b. 17 May 1925, Nérac; s. of Jean Berthoin and Germaine Mourgnot; m. 1st Anne W Whittlesey (deceased); m. 2nd Pamela Jenkins 1965; two s. four d.; ed Univ. of Grenoble, Ecole des Sciences Politiques, Paris and Harvard and McGill Univs; Private Sec. to Minister of Finance 1948–50; Head of Staff, Prefecture of Alsace-Lorraine-Champagne 1950–52; Prin. Pvt. Sec. M. Jean Monnet, Pres. of ECSC 1952–55; Counsellor for Information, ECSC 1955–56; Deputy Chief Rep. of ECSC in UK 1956; Acting Chief Rep. of Comm. of EEC 1967–68, Deputy Chief Rep. 1968–71, Chief Rep. 1971–73; Exec. mem. Trilateral Comm. 1973–75, European Chair. 1975–92, Hon. Chair. 1993–; Int. Chair of European Movement 1978–81; Dir Int. Peace Acad., New York; Bd mem. Aspen-Berlin Inst.; mem. Int. Advisory Bd Johns Hopkins Univ., Bologna, Nine Wise Men Group on Africa; Aspen Inst. Distinguished Fellow; Hon. Chair. Jean Monnet Asscn; Chevalier, Légion d'honneur, Médaille Militaire, Croix de Guerre, Médaille de la Résistance. *Leisure interests:* art, theatre, walking, collecting objects. *Address:* 67 avenue Niel, 75017 Paris, France.

BERTI, Luciano; Italian art historian; b. 28 Jan. 1922, Florence; s. of Ferdinando Berti and Ines Berti; m. Anna Maria Tinacci 1959; ed Univ. of Florence; attached to Superintendency of Florence 1949; arranged new museums of Casa Vasari, Arezzo 1950, Palazzo Davanzati 1955, Il Museo di Arezzo 1958, Il Museo di S. Giovanni Valdarno 1959, Museum of Verna 1961, Museum of S. Croce, Florence 1962; Dir Museums of Arezzo, San Marco and Acad., Florence; Dir Museo Nazionale del Bargello; Dir Uffizi Gallery, Florence 1969–87; Dir Monuments, Pisa Gallery 1973–74; Dir of Galleries, Florence 1974–87; mem. Consiglio Superiore 1976–80; Pres. Casa Buonarroti 1990–; Gold Medal, Ministry of Cultural Heritage, Dott. Laurea in Lettere, Libera docenza in Storia dell'Arte, Accademico Emerito Arti del Disegno. *Publications:* Filippino Lippi 1957, Masaccio 1964, Pontormo 1964, Pontormo disegni 1965, Il Principe dello Studiolo 1967, Il Museo tra Thanatos ed Eros 1973–74, Catalogue to the Uffizi Gallery 1979, I Disegni di Michelangelo in Casa Buonarroti 1985, Pontormo e il suo Tempo 1993, Il Portico (novel) 1998; various articles and catalogues. *Leisure interests:* history of art, museology. *Address:* Casa Buonarroti, Via Ghibellina 70, 50122, Florence (Office); Via Giusti 6, Florence, Italy (Home). *Telephone:* 244938 (Home).

BERTINI, Catherine Ann, BA; American international public servant; b. 30 March 1950, Syracuse, New York; d. of Fulvio Bertini and Ann Vino Bertini; m. Thomas Haskell 1988; ed Cortland High School, NY, State Univ. of New York at Albany; Youth Dir, New York Republican State Cttee 1971–74, Republican Nat. Cttee 1975–76; Man., Public Policy, Container Corpn of America 1977–87; Dir Office of Family Assistance, US Dept of Health and Human Services 1987–89; Acting Asst Sec., US Dept of Health and Human Services 1989, Asst Sec. US Dept of Agriculture 1989–92; Exec. Dir World Food Programme of UN, Rome 1992–2002; UN Sec.-Gen.'s Special Envoy on Drought in the Horn of Africa 2000–02; UN Sec.-Gen.'s Personal Humanitarian Envoy to Middle East 2002–; mem. UN Sec.-Gen.'s Panel of High-Level Personalities on African Devt 1992–95; Fellow Inst. of Politics, Harvard Univ. 1986; Commr Ill. State Scholarship Comm. 1979–84, Ill. Human Rights Comm. 1985–87; Hon. DSc (McGill Univ., Montreal) 1997, (Pine Major Coll.) 2000; Hon. DHL (State Univ. of New York, Cortland) 1999, (American Univ., Rome) 2001; Leadership in Human Services Award, American Public Welfare Asscn 1990, Excellence in Public Service Award, American Acad. of Pediatrics 1991, Leadership Award, Nat. Asscn of WIC Dirs 1992, Quality of Life Award, Auburn School of Human Sciences 1996. *Address:* United Nations, New York, NY 10017, USA.

BERTMAN, Dmitry Aleksandrovich; Russian theatre director; b. 17 Oct. 1967, Moscow; ed Lunacharsky State Inst. of Theatre Arts; started career as Dir in theatres in Moscow, Tver, Odessa, Syktyvkar; Founder and Artistic Dir HELIKON Opera, Moscow 1990–; has also directed productions abroad, including in Vienna and Klagenfurt, Austria; docent Russian Acad. of Theatre Arts; Merited Worker of Arts; Golden Mask Nat. Prize 1997, 1998. *Stage productions include:* Lady Macbeth of Mtsensk, Eugene Onegin, La Traviata, Falstaff, Aida, The Rake's Progress, Lulu. *Address:* HELIKON Opera, B. Nikitskaya str. 19, 103009 Moscow, Russia (Office). *Telephone:* (095) 290-28-88 (Office); (095) 290-64-19 (Home). *Fax:* (095) 291-13-23 (Office). *E-mail:* helikon@helikon.ru (Office). *Website:* www.helikon.ru (Office).

BERTOLUCCI, Bernardo; Italian film director; b. 16 March 1941, Parma; s. of Attilio Bertolucci; m. Clare Peploe 1978; worked with Pier Paolo Pasolini on Accattone; European Film Award 1988, 9 Acad. Awards; Dr. hc (Turin) 2000. *Films directed:* La Commare Secca 1962, Prima della Rivoluzione 1964, Agonia in Aurore e Rabbia 1967, Partner 1968, La Strategia del Ragno 1970, Il Conformista 1970, Last Tango in Paris 1972, 1900 1976, La Luna 1979, Tragedy of a Ridiculous Man 1981, The Last Emperor 1987 (Acad. Awards 1988 for Best Dir and Best Screenwriter), The Sheltering Sky 1989, Little Buddha 1993, Stealing Beauty 1995, I Dance Alone 1996, Besieged (Globo D'Oro Award for Best Film 1999) 1998. *Publications:* In cerca del mistero (poems) 1962 (Viareggio Prize 1962), Paradiso e inferno (poems) 1999.

Address: c/o Recorded Picture Company, 24 Hanway Street, London, W1P 9DD, England; c/o Jeff Berg, ICM, 8942 Wilshire Boulevard, Beverly Hills, CA 90211, USA; c/o Carol Levi and Co., 2 Via Pisanelli, 00196 Rome, Italy.

BERTRAND, Françoise, BA; Canadian broadcasting executive; b. 1948, Montreal; ed Collège Ste.-Marie, Univ. of Montreal, York Univ.; Dir Soc. des Jeux du Québec 1976–78; Project Man. SORECOM Inc. 1978–80; Asst Vice-Pres. (Academic and Research) Univ. of Quebec, Montreal 1980–82; Asst Dean Research Man. 1983–84, Dean 1984–88; CEO Soc. de radio-télévision du Québec 1988–95; Sr Dir Communications Practices, KPMG Consulting 1995–96; Chair. CRTC 1996–; Chair. Bd Théâtre Populaire du Québec 1990–96; mem. Bd Asscn for Tele-Educ. in Canada (ATEC), (Chair. 1993–94), TV5 Quebec Canada 1988–95; Vice-Chair. Bd TV5 Latin America 1993–95; one of three Commrs on Fed. Water Policy Comm. 1984–85; mem. Bd of Govs. and Exec. Cttee Univ. of Quebec 1990–96; mem. various bds. and research orgs. involved in educ. and social and community orgs. *Address:* Canadian Radio-Television and Telecommunications Commission (CRTC), Ottawa, ON K1A 0N2, Canada (Office). *Telephone:* (819) 997-3430 (Office). *Fax:* (819) 994-0218 (Office). *E-mail:* info@crtc.gc.ca (Office). *Website:* www.crtc.gc.ca (Office).

BERTRANOU, Armando Victorio; Argentine professor of agricultural economics; b. 14 May 1942, Mendoza; s. of Pablo Luis Bertranou and Susana Angélica Saligari; m. Clara Alicia Jalif 1965; two s. two d.; ed Universidad Nacional de Cuyo, Univ. of California, Davis; Titular Prof., Faculty of Agricultural Sciences, Universidad Nacional de Cuyo, Rector 1988–; mem. Bd Nat. Parks Admin. *Publications:* many articles and papers on irrigation and water man. *Leisure interests:* aerobics, rugby, rowing. *Address:* Universidad Nacional de Cuyo, Centro Universitario, Parque General San Martín, 5500 Mendoza; Paso de los Andes 966, 5500 Mendoza; Casilla de Correo 589, 5500 Mendoza, Argentina. *Telephone:* 2-52152; 2-53219; 2-31352.

BERTUCCELLI, Jean-Louis Augusto; French film producer; b. 3 June 1942, Paris; s. of Louis Bertuccelli and Charlotte Feral; one d.; ed Conservatoire Régional de Musique de Nice and Faculté des Sciences, Marseille; musician, then sound engineer 1964–66; film producer 1966–; TV corresp. reporting on Japan, Thailand, Hong Kong, Bolivia, Mexico, South Africa, Senegal, USA and Spain 1968–73; Chevalier des Arts et des Lettres. *Films include:* Remparts d'argile (Prix Jean Vigo) 1970, Paulina 1980, Docteur Françoise Gailland 1975, L'Imprécateur 1977, Interdit aux moins de treize ans 1982, Aujourd'hui Peut-être 1991, Momo 1992, L'Institut 1993, Le Clandestin 1993, Le Serment d'Hypocrate 1996; also short films, TV films and series etc. *Television:* Mauvaises affaires (film) 1998, Maître Da Casta (film) 1999. *Leisure interests:* music, tennis, piano, flute. *Address:* 9 rue Bénard, 75014, Paris, France.

BĒRZIŅŠ, Andris; Latvian politician and historian; b. 4 Aug. 1951, Riga; m.; two c.; ed Latvian State Univ.; teacher and admin. in several schools 1975–82; Head Div. of Personnel Training Cttee for Vocational and Tech. Training 1982–86; Head of Div. State Cttee for Labour and Social Affairs 1986–90; Head of Div., Deputy Dir Welfare Dept Ministry of Econs 1990–92; Deputy Minister, concurrently Head of Labour Dept Ministry of Welfare 1992–93; State Minister of Labour 1993–94; Deputy Prime Minister, Minister of Welfare 1994–95; Minister of Labour 1995–97; Chair. Riga City Council 1997–2000; Prime Minister of Latvia 2000–02; Chair. Latvian Way (Latvijas ceļš). *Address:* Latvijas ceļš, Terbatas jela 4-9, 1001 Riga, Latvia (Office). *Telephone:* (2) 728-5539 (Office). *Fax:* (2) 728-1121 (Office). *E-mail:* lc@lc.lv. *Website:* www.lc.lv.

BĒRZIŅŠ, Indulis; Latvian politician; b. 4 Dec. 1957, Madona; m. Inese Berzins; one s. one d.; ed ed. Latvian State Univ.; lecturer Latvian State Univ. and Latvian Inst. of Agric. 1984–90; TV broadcaster 1988–89; Founder mem. People's Front Movt for independence 1989; Deputy, Supreme Soviet Latvian Repub., Deputy Chair. Cttee on Foreign Affairs 1990–93, later Chair.; Dir Latvias Cels Union 1993–; mem. People's Front of Latvia 1992–93, Latvia's Way Party 1993–; mem. Latvian del. to NATO 1993–95, Latvian Nat. Group to European Parl. 1995–97, 1998–99; Deputy Speaker of Saeima (Parl.) 1998–99; Minister of Foreign Affairs 1999–2002. *Address:* c/o Ministry of Foreign Affairs, Brīvības blvd 36, 1050 Rīga, Latvia (Office).

BESCH, Werner Walter, DPhil; German professor of German; b. 4 May 1928, Erdmannsweiler, Schwarzwald; s. of Matthias and Elisabeth (née Fuss) Besch; m. Katharina Müller 1957; one s. two d.; Prof. of German Language and Early German Literature, Ruhr Univ., Bochum 1965–70, Univ. of Bonn 1970–93, Prof. Emer 1993–; Rector, Univ. of Bonn 1981–83, Pro-Rector 1983–85; mem. Wiss-Rat., Inst. für Deutsche Sprache, Mannheim 1976–93; Corresp. mem. Heidelberg Akad. der Wissenschaften; mem. Nordrhein-Westfälische Akad. der Wissenschaften; Corresp. mem. Inst. of Germanic Studies, Univ. of London. *Publications:* Lautgeographie u. Lautgeschichte im obersten Neckar-u. Donaugebiet 1961, Sprachlandschaften u. Sprachausgleich im 15. Jahrhundert 1967, Dialekt/Hochsprache-Kontrastiv 1977, Handbuch Dialektologie 1983, Handbuch Sprachgeschichte 1985, Duzen, Siezen, Titulieren. Zur Anrede im Deutschen heute und gestern 1996, Zur Rolle Luthers in der deutschen Sprachgeschichte 1999, Zeitschrift für deutsche Philologie (Co-Ed.), Grundlagen der Germanistik (Co-Ed.). *Leisure interests:* joinery, walking, gardening. *Address:* Hobsweg 64, 53125 Bonn, Germany (Home).

BESSER, Gordon Michael, MB, MD, DSc, FRCP, FMedSci; British physician, professor of endocrinology and professor of medicine (retd); b. 22 Jan. 1936, London; ed Medical Coll. of St. Bartholomew's Hosp., Univ. of London; Sr Lecturer in Medicine, St Bartholomew's Hosp. Medical Coll. 1970–74, Head of Endocrinology and Hon. Consultant Physician 1970–95, Prof. of Endocrinology 1974–92, Prof. of Medicine 1992–2001; Prof. of Medicine and Head of Endocrinology, St Bartholomew's and Royal London School of Medicine and Dentistry 1995–2001, Prof. Emer. 2001–; Civilian Consultant in Endocrinology, RN 1989–97, to the Triservice Medical Service 1997–; Visiting Consultant Endocrinologist to Govt of Malta 1989–2002; Chief Exec. Barts NHS Trust 1992–94; Hon. MD (Turin); Lecturer to Royal Coll. of Physicians: Goulstonian 1974, Lumlean 1993, Simms 1999, Soc. for Endocrinology; Jubilee Medalist and Lecturer 2002; William Julius Mickle Fellowship for the Advancement of Medical Science, Univ. of London 1976; Medal of Soc. for Endocrinology 1978, Clinical Endocrinology Prize 1986; Hon. MD Univ. of Turin 1985; Medal of European Neuroendocrinology Asscn 1999. *Publications:* Clinical Endocrinology 1984, DeGroot's Endocrinology (section ed.) 1985, 26 textbooks in gen. medicine and endocrinology and over 450 articles in journals of basic and clinical endocrinology and medicine. *Leisure interests:* early Chinese ceramics, physical fitness, opera, ballet. *Address:* The London Clinic Centre for Endocrinology, 145 Harley Street, London, W1G 6BL (Office); Department of Endocrinology, St. Bartholomew's & Royal London School of Medicine, London, EC1A 7BE (Office); White Cottage, 61A Marlborough Place, London, NW8 0PT, England (Home). *Telephone:* (20) 7616-7790 (Office); (20) 7601-8342 (Office). *Fax:* (20) 7616-7791 (Office). *E-mail:* endo@thelondonclinic.co.uk (Office).

BESSMERTNOVA, Natalya Igorevna; Russian ballet dancer; b. 19 July 1941, Moscow; d. of Igor Borisovich Bessmertnov and Antonia Yakovlevna Bersmertnova; m. Yuriy N Grigorovich; ed Bolshoi Theatre Ballet School (pupil of M. Kozhukhova and S. Golovkina); soloist with Bolshoi Theatre Ballet 1961–63; prima ballerina Bolshoi Theatre Ballet 1963–95; ballet mistress/tutor 1994–95; founder, Pres. European Dance Acad. 1996–; gives masterclasses abroad; Anna Pavlova Prize 1970, People's Artist, USSR 1976, USSR State Prize 1977, Lenin Prize 1986. *Important roles include:* Mazurka and 7th Valse (Chopiniana), Pas de trois (Swan Lake), variations (Class-concert), Giselle (Giselle), The Muse (Paganini, music by Rachmaninov), Florin (Sleeping Beauty), Leila (Leila and Medjnun, by Balasanyan), Shirin (Legend of Love), Odette-Odile (Swan Lake), Girl (Le Spectre de la Rose), Maria (The Fountain of Bakhtchisaray), Phrygia (Spartacus), Juliet (Romeo and Juliet), Masha (The Nutcracker), Nikia (The Kingdom of Shades), Rita (Golden Age), Valentina (The Angara), Aurora (Sleeping Beauty), Anastasia (Ivan the Terrible), Raymonda. *Address:* Sretenskii blvd 6/1, Apt. 9, 101000 Moscow, Russia. *Telephone:* (095) 925-64-31 (Home). *Fax:* (095) 925-65-57.

BESSMERTNYKH, Aleksandr Aleksandrovich, CandJurSc; Russian diplomatist; b. 10 Nov. 1933, Biisk; s. of Aleksandr and Maria Bessmertnykh; m.; one s. one d.; ed Moscow State Inst. of Int. Relations; joined Diplomatic Service 1957, with Embassy, Washington 1970–83; fmr arms control negotiator; First Deputy Foreign Minister (with special responsibility for North America and the Middle East) 1987–90, Deputy 1986; Amb. to USA 1990–91; Minister of Foreign Affairs Jan.–Aug. 1991; mem. CP Cen. Cttee 1990–91; Head Policy Analysis Centre Soviet (now Russian) Foreign Policy Asscn 1991–92; Pres. Int. Foreign Policy Asscn March 1992–, Chair. World Council of fmr Foreign Ministers May 1993–; mem. Acad. of Social Sciences of Russian Fed.; Corresp. mem. Chilean Acad. of Social and Political Sciences; Order of Friendship of Peoples; Badge of Honour Medals. *Leisure interests:* literature, classical music, tennis. *Address:* International Foreign Policy Association, Yakovo-Apostolski per. 10, 103064 Moscow, Russia. *Telephone:* (095) 975-21-67. *Fax:* (095) 975-21-90. *E-mail:* fpa.moscow@public.mtu.ru. *Website:* www.worldmin.org.

BESSON, Luc; French film director; b. 18 March 1959, Paris; s. of Claude Besson and Danièle Plane; one d. with Anne Parillaud; worked as an Asst on films in Paris and Hollywood; first Asst for several advertising films; two features (Homme libre and Les Bidasses aux grandes manoeuvres) and four shorts; f. Les Films du Loup 1982. *Films directed:* Le Dernier Combat 1982, Subway 1984, The Big Blue 1988, Nikita 1990, Atlantis 1991, The Professional 1994, Leon 1994, The Fifth Element 1996, Joan of Arc 1999, The Messenger 1999, The Dancer 2000, Exit 2000, Yamakasi 2001, Baiser mortel du dragon 2001, Le Transporteur 2002. *Address:* Leeloo Productions, 53 rue Boissée, 91540 Mennecy (Office); c/o CBC, 11 rue de la Croix Boissée, 91540 Mennecy, France. *E-mail:* lucbesson@luc-besson.com (Office).

BEST, George; British footballer; b. 22 May 1946, Belfast; s. of Richard Best and late Anne Best (née Withers); m. 1st Angela Macdonald Janes 1978 (divorced); one s.; m. 2nd Alexandra Jane Pursey 1995; joined Manchester United 1963, 361 League appearances (137 goals), 46 Football Asscn Cup competition appearances (21 goals), 25 League Cup competition appearances (9 goals), 34 European competition appearances (11 goals); rep. N Ireland 37 times; now sports commentator Sky TV; Irish Footballer of the Year 1967, European Footballer of the Year 1968, British Footballer of the Year 1968, Sportswriters' Footballer of the Year 1968, Sportsman of the Year 1969, 1971, Sky TV Greatest Sportsman Award 1995, Total Sport Magazine Greatest Sportsman of All Time; BBC Lifetime Achievement Award 2002. *Publication:* Blessed: My Autobiography 2001. *Leisure interests:* reading, crosswords, travel, films, sports. *Address:* c/o British Sky Broadcasting Ltd, Grant Way, Middx, TW7 5QD, England.

BESTUZHEV-LADA, Igor Vassilyevich, PhD, DHist; Russian sociologist and historian; b. 12 Jan. 1927, Lada, Penza Region; m.; one s. one d.; ed Inst. of Int. Relations, Inst. of History; researcher Inst. of History USSR Acad of Sciences 1954–66; Head Dept of Social Forecasting, Inst. of Sociology USSR (now Russian) Acad. of Sciences 1967–; Prof. Moscow State Univ. 1969–2000; Academician Sec., Russian Acad. of Education 1993–; Pres. Russian Future Studies Acad. 1997–, Int. Future Research Acad. 1999–; Pres. Future Research Cttee Soviet Sociological Asscn 1967–91, Int. Sociological Asscn 1970–96; Chair. Presidium Russian Pedagogical Soc. 1989–; Hon. mem. World Future Studies Fed. 1984. *Publications:* Exploratory Social Forecasting, Normative Social Forecasting, Forecasting Grounding Social Innovations, Alternative Civilization, Anthology of Classics in Future Studies 1952–82. *Leisure interests:* classic literature, book design. *Address:* Russian Academy of Education, Pogodinskaya str. 8, 119905 Moscow (Office); Russian Future Studies Academy, Bol. Cheremushkinskaya str. 34, 117217 Moscow (Office); Shipilovsky proezd 49/1, apt. 364, 115551 Moscow, Russia (Home). *Telephone:* (095) 246-2778 (Office); (095) 343-0852 (Home). *Fax:* (095) 128-1710 (Office). *E-mail:* lada@imce.ru (Office).

BETANCUR CUARTAS, Belisario; Colombian politician and lawyer; b. 4 Feb. 1923, Amagá, Antioquia; s. of Rosendo Betancur and Ana Otilia Cuartos; m. Rosa Helena Álvarez; one s. two d.; ed Univ. Bolivariana de Medellín; mem. House of Reps., later Senator; Conservative Party Presidential Cand. 1962, 1970, 1978; Minister of Labour 1963; Amb. to Spain 1974; Pres. of Colombia 1982–86; mem. Pontifical Acad. of Social Sciences 1994; Dir Fundación Santillana para Iberoamérica. *Address:* Fundación Santillana, calle 80, No 9-75, Apartado Aéreo 3974, Santa Fe de Bogotá, Colombia (Office).

BETHE, Hans Albrecht, PhD; Alsatian-born American physicist; b. 2 July 1906; s. of Albrecht Theodore Bethe and Anna Kuhn; m. Rose Ewald 1939; one s. one d.; ed Goethe Gymnasium (Frankfurt Main) and Frankfurt Main and Munich Univs; Lecturer German Univs. 1928–33, Manchester and Bristol Univs. (England) 1933–35; Asst Prof. Cornell Univ. 1935–37, Prof. 1937–75, Prof. Emer. 1975–; Dir Theoretical Physics Div. Los Alamos Scientific Lab. 1943–46; mem., Pres.'s Science Advisory Cttee 1956–59; mem. American Philosophical Soc., NAS, American Physical Soc. (Pres. 1954), American Astronomical Soc.; Foreign mem. Royal Soc. (London); Hon. DSc (Birmingham) 1956, (Manchester) 1981; Presidential Medal of Merit 1946, Max Planck Medal 1955, Enrico Fermi Award 1961, Nobel Prize for Physics 1967, Vannevar Bush Award (NAS) 1985, Einstein Peace Prize 1993. *Publications:* Elementary Nuclear Theory 1947, Mesons and Fields 1955, Intermediate Quantum Mechanics 1964, 1968; contribs. to Handbuch der Physik 1933, 1957, Review of Modern Physics 1936–37, etc. and to scientific journals. *Address:* Newman Laboratory, Cornell University, Ithaca, NY 14853, USA.

BETTELHEIM, Charles, DenD, LèsL; French economist; b. 20 Nov. 1913, Paris; s. of Henri Bettelheim and Lucienne Jacquemin; m. Lucette Beauvallet 1937; three s. two d.; ed Paris Univ.; Dir Centre for Social Studies and Int. Relations, Ministry of Labour, Paris 1944–48; French rep. Conf. on Trade and Employment 1947; Dir at Ecole Pratique des Hautes Etudes 1948–82; Head of UN Mission for Tech. Assistance to Indian Govt 1955–56; Prof. at Ecole Nat. d'Administration; Prof. at Inst. d'Etudes du Développement Economique et Social 1958–; mem. French Sociological Inst.; Dir of the review Problèmes de Planification 1948–, Centre d'Etudes des Modes d'Industrialisation (CEMI) at Ecole des Hautes Études en Sciences Sociales 1986–; Lauréat de l'Institut. *Publications:* La Planification soviétique 1939, Les problèmes théoriques et pratiques de la planification 1946, L'économie allemande sous le Nazisme 1946, Bilan de l'économie française de 1918 à 1946 1947, Esquisse d'un tableau économique de l'Europe 1948, Initiations aux recherches sur les idéologies économiques et les réalités sociales 1948, Emploi et chômage devant la théorie économique 1949, L'économie soviétique 1950, Auxerre en 1950 1950, Théories contemporaines de l'emploi 1951, Nouveaux aspects de la théorie de l'emploi 1952, Long-Term Planning Problems 1956, Foreign Trade and Planning for Economic Development 1956, Studies in the Theory of Planning 1959, Some Basic Planning Problems 1960, Teoría de la Planificación 1961, Problemas Teóricos y Prácticos de la Planificación 1962, L'Inde indépendante 1962, Planification et croissance accélérée 1964, La construction du socialisme en Chine 1965, Los Marcos socioeconómicos y la organización de la planificación social 1966, Problèmes théoriques et pratiques de la planification 1966, La transition vers l'économie socialiste 1968, India Independent 1968, Calcul économique et formes de propriété 1970, Révolution culturelle et organisation industrielle en Chine 1973, Les luttes de classes en URSS 1917–1923 1974, Les luttes de classes en URSS 1923–1930 1977, China since Mao 1978, Les luttes de classe en URSS 1930–41, Vol. 1, Les dominés 1982, Vol. 2 Les dominants 1983, Moscou, Place du Manège 1984, Orwell ed il 1984 del Socialismo reale (jtly) 1984, Rethinking Marxism (Chapter 3) 1985, Parcours, Markets within Planning (Chapter 1) 1988, Il Socialismo Irrealizato (jtly) 1992; essays in various publs. *Address:* EHESS, Cemi, 105 boulevard Raspail, 75006 Paris, France.

BETTENCOURT, Liliane; French business executive; d. of Eugene Schueller; one d.; Chair. Man. and Remuneration Cttee, L'Oréal. *Leisure interest:* wine. *Address:* L'Oréal, Centre Eugene Schueller, 41 rue Matre, 92110 Clichy, France (Office).

BETTENCOURT SANTOS, Humberto; Cape Verde diplomatist; b. 17 Feb. 1940, Santo Antão Island; s. of Severino Santos and Inacia Santos; m.; two c.; ed Catholic Univ. of Louvain, Belgium; mem. del. in negotiations on colonial dispute with Portugal 1975; elected Deputy to Nat. Ass. 1975, re-elected 1980; Dir.-Gen. Fisheries 1975–82; Amb. to EC and to Nordic and Benelux countries 1982–87; Perm. Rep. of Cape Verde to UN 1987–91; mem. Nat. Comm. on Law of the Sea 1979–82; int. consultant; Dir of pvt. computer training centre; pvt. consultant in econ. and fisheries for FAO and UNDP 1991–. *Leisure interests:* music (guitar), tennis, golf.

BETTS, Donald Drysdale, MSc, PhD, FRSC; Canadian professor of physics; b. 16 May 1929, Montreal; s. of Wallace Havelock Betts and Mary Drysdale Betts; m. 1st Vilma Mapp 1954 (divorced 1981); m. 2nd Patricia Giles McWilliams 1986; three s. one d. two step-s.; ed Queen Elizabeth High School, Halifax, Dalhousie Univ., Halifax and McGill Univ., Montreal; Nat. Research Council Fellow Univ. of Alberta, Edmonton 1955–56, Asst Prof. of Physics 1956–61, Assoc. Prof. 1961–66, Prof. 1966–80; Dean of Arts and Science Dalhousie Univ. 1980–88, of Science 1988–90, Prof. Emer. 1994–; Adjunct Prof., St Francis Xavier Univ., Antigonish, NS 2002– Visiting Prof. of Physics King's Coll., London 1970–71, of Chemistry and Physics Cornell Univ., New York Jan.–June 1975, Univ. of NSW 1991, 1993; Gordon Godfrey Visiting Research Prof. of Theoretical Physics, Univ. of NSW 1995–2000; Dir Theoretical Physics Inst. Univ. of Alberta 1972–78; Ed. Canadian Journal of Physics 1992–; Pres. Canadian Asscn of Physicists 1969–70; Fellow Japan Soc. for Promotion of Science 1982; NATO Science Fellowship 1963–64; Nuffield Fellowship 1970; Peter Kirkby Medal for Outstanding Service to Canadian Physics (Canadian Asscn of Physicists) 1996, 2002 Queen Elizabeth Gold Medal for Outstanding Service to the Royal Soc. of Canada 2003. *Publications:* some 90 refereed articles in physics journals. *Leisure interests:* game of Go, hiking, gardening, badminton and swimming. *Address:* Department of Physics, Dalhousie University, Halifax, NS, B3H 3J5 (Office); 8 Simcoe Place, Halifax, NS, B3M 1H3 (Home); 14153 Sunrise Trail, Wallace, NS, B0K 1Y0, Canada. *Telephone:* (902) 494-5124 (Office); (902) 443-3916 (Home); (902) 257-2370. *Fax:* (902) 494-5191 (Office); (902) 494-2835. *E-mail:* dbetts@is.dal.ca (Office). *Website:* fizz.phys.dal.ca/people/dbetts.html (Office).

BEUTLER, Ernest, MD; American research scientist and professor of medicine; b. 30 Sept. 1928, Berlin, Germany; s. of Alfred David Beutler and Kaethe (Italiener) Beutler; m. Brondele Fleisher 1950; three s. one d.; ed Univ. of Chicago; Resident in Medicine, Univ. of Chicago Clinics 1951–53, Asst Prof., Univ. of Chicago 1956–59; Chair. Div. of Medicine, City of Hope Medical Centre, Duarte, Calif. 1959–78; Dept of Clinical Research, Scripps Clinic and Research Foundation, La Jolla, Calif. 1978–82, Chair. Dept of Basic and Clinical Research 1982–89, Dept Molecular and Experimental Medicine 1989–, Head, Div. of Haematology-Oncology 1982–87; Clinical Prof. of Medicine, Univ. of Southern Calif., Los Angeles 1964–79, Univ. of Calif., San Diego, La Jolla, Calif. 1979–; Spinoza Chair. Univ. of Amsterdam, Netherlands 1991; mem. NAS, American Acad. of Arts and Sciences, Asscn of American Physicians; Hon. D.Ph. (Tel Aviv Univ.) 1993; Gairdner Award 1975, Blundell Prize 1985, Mayo Soley Award (Western Soc. for Clinical Investigation) 1992, Fifth Nat. Award for Excellence in Clinical Research (NIH Gen. Clinical Research Centers Program) 1993, City of Medicine Award 1994, American Soc. of Clinical Pathologists Philip Levine Outstanding Research Award 2000, Univ. of Chicago Distinguished Alumni Award 2003. *Publications:* author of 19 books and numerous articles in medical periodicals. *Leisure interests:* music and computer programming. *Address:* Department of Molecular and Experimental Medicine, Scripps Research Institute (MEM-215), 10550 North Torrey Pines Road, La Jolla, CA 92037 (Office); 2707 Costebelle Drive, La Jolla, CA 92037, USA (Home). *Telephone:* (858) 784-8040 (Office); (858) 457-5790 (Home). *Fax:* (858) 784-2083. *E-mail:* beutler@scrlpps.edu (Office).

BEVAART, Jacob; Netherlands business executive; b. 15 Feb. 1942, Amsterdam; m. J. J. Griffioen 1965; three s.; ed Univ. of Amsterdam; Dir Concertgebouw Amsterdam 1975–82; Dir-Gen. Chamber of Commerce and Industry for Amsterdam Feb. 1984–; Chair. Buvoha Soc. (Trade Information Bureau), Judicial Comm. European Chambers of Commerce, Brussels, Consumer Arbitration Bd for Public Utilities, The Hague; mem. Bd of Man. Buma/Stemra (Co-operative Copyright Orgs.) 1982–, Amsterdam Tourists Asscn; mem. Bd Amsterdam Ports Asscn, Univ. of Amsterdam Foundation for Econ. Research; Deputy Judge Utrecht Dist Court. *Address:* Chamber of Commerce and Industry for Amsterdam, De Ruyterkade 5, 1013 AA Amsterdam, Netherlands. *Telephone:* (20) 531-4602. *Fax:* (20) 531-4699.

BEVAN, Tim; British executive producer; m. Joely Richardson; began career as a runner for John Cleese's Video Arts; f. Aldabra (music video production co.) with Sarah Radclyffe; formed Working Title (film production co.) with Eric Fellner (q.v.) 1984, now Co-Chair. *Films include:* My Beautiful Laundrette, Personal Services, Wish You Were Here, Caravaggio, Pascali's Island, The Tall Guy, The Rachel Papers, Hidden Agenda, Dakota Road, Map of the Human Heart, Bob Roberts, Posse, Romeo is Bleeding, The Hudsucker Proxy, Four Weddings and a Funeral, Dead Man Walking, Elizabeth, Notting Hill, High Fidelity, Fargo, O Brother, Where Art Thou?, Captain Corelli's Mandolin, The Big Lebowski, Plunkett & Macleane 1999. *TV includes:* Tales of the City, The Borrowers, High Fidelity. *Address:* Working Title Films, 9333 Wilshire Boulevard, Beverly Hills, CA 90210, USA (Office).

BEVAN, Sir Timothy (Hugh), Kt; British banker; b. 24 May 1927, London; s. of the late Hugh Bevan and Pleasance Bevan (née Scrutton); m. Pamela Murray (née Smith) 1952; two s. two d.; ed Eton Coll.; called to the Bar, Middle

Temple 1950; joined Barclays Bank Ltd (now Barclays Bank PLC) 1950, Dir 1966–93, Vice-Chair. 1968–73, Deputy Chair. 1973–81, Chair. 1981–87; Dir Barclays Int. Ltd 1971; Dir BET Public Ltd Co. 1987–92, Chair. 1988–91; Dir Foreign and Colonial Investment Trust PLC 1988–98 (Deputy Chair. 1993–98); fmr Dir Soc. Financière Européenne 1967, Commercial Union Assurance Co. Ltd, Union Discount Co. of London Ltd; Chair. Cttee of London Clearing Bankers 1983–85; Chair. City Communications Centre 1982–83. *Leisure interests:* sailing, gardening. *Address:* c/o Barclays Bank PLC, 54 Lombard Street, London, EC3V 9EX, England.

BEVERLOO, Cornelis Van; Netherlands painter; b. 1922; ed Amsterdam Acad. of Fine Arts; co-founder, with Appel and Constant, of the experimental "Reflex" group; co-founder of "Cobra" group 1948; rep. at numerous exhbns., including Brussels Int. Exhbn 1958, Dunn Int. Exhbn, London 1963; works under the name of "Corneille".

BEWKES, Jeff; American broadcasting executive; ed MBA Stanford Univ.; Exec. Vice-Pres. Home Box Office Inc. 1987–91, Pres., COO 1991–95, Chair., CEO 1995–2002; Chair. AOL Time Warner Inc. 2002–. *Address:* Home Box Office Inc., 1100 Avenue of the Americas, New York, NY 10036-6740, USA.

BEWLEY, Thomas Henry, MA, MD; Irish consultant psychiatrist; b. 8 July 1926, Dublin; s. of Geoffrey Bewley and Victoria Jane Wilson; m. Beulah Knox 1955; one s. four d.; ed St Columba's Coll., Dublin, Trinity Coll., Dublin Univ.; trained at St Patrick's Hosp., Dublin, Maudsley Hosp., London and Univ. of Cincinnati, USA; Consultant Psychiatrist, Tooting Bec and St Thomas' Hosps., London 1961–88; Emer. Consultant St Thomas' Hosp.; mem. Standing Advisory Cttee on Drug Dependence 1966–71, Advisory Council on Misuse of Drugs 1972–84; Consultant Adviser on Drug Dependence to Dept of Health and Social Security 1972–81; Consultant WHO 1969–78; Hon. Sr Lecturer, St George's Hosp. Medical School, Univ. of London 1974–96; Pres. Royal Coll. of Psychiatrists 1984–87 (Dean 1977–82); Jt Founder and mem. Council, Inst. for the Study of Drug Dependence 1967–96; FRCP (London and Ireland); Hon. FRCPsych; Hon. CBE. *Publications:* Handbook for Inceptors and Trainees in Psychiatry 1976; papers on drug dependence, medical manpower and side effects of drugs. *Leisure interest:* Irish Georgian Society (London Chapter). *Address:* 4 Grosvenor Gardens Mews North, London, SW1W 0JP, England. *Telephone:* (20) 7730-9592 (Home).

BEYENE, Tekie, BA; Eritrean central banker; b. 15 June 1941, Asmara; m. Maaza Haile; ed Univ. of Asmara; Gov. Cen. Bank of Eritrea. *Publications:* contribs. to magazine Hewyet (Recovery). *Leisure interest:* writing. *Address:* Bank of Eritrea, P.O. Box 849, 21 Victory Avenue, Asmara, Eritrea (Office); Tiro Alvolo St 702, No. 14-16, Asmara, Eritrea (Home). *Telephone:* (1) 123036 (Office); (1) 184351 (Home). *Fax:* (1) 122091 (Office). *E-mail:* tekieb@eol.com.er (Office).

BEYER, Frank Michael; German composer and professor of composition; b. 8 March 1928, Berlin; s. of Oskar Beyer and Margarete (née Löwenfeld) Beyer; m. Sigrid Uhle 1950; one s. one d.; ed Berliner Kirchenmusikschule, Staatliche Hochschule für Musik (HDK), piano training in Leipzig; began career in church music; Scholarship, Cité Internationale des Arts Paris 1968; Docent Berliner Kirchenmusikschule 1953–62; with Hochschule für Musik Berlin, Prof. of Composition 1968–; initiated range of 'musica nova sacra' 1970–85; promoter Inst. für Neue Musik 1990; Supervisory mem. of Gema 1973–83; Exec. mem. German Music Bds. 1978–82; mem. Akademie der Künste Berlin 1979–, Dir of Music Div. 1986–; mem. Bayerische Akademie der Schönen Künste 1981–; Kunstpreis Berlin for Young Generation 1957, Bernhard-Sprengel Prize 1962, Prix Jeunesse Musicale 1967. *Compositions:* Orchestral and chamber music, organ and solo piano works, music for TV films. *Leisure interest:* philosophy. *Address:* Akademie der Künste, Hanseatenweg 10, 10557 Berlin (Office); Söhtstrasse 6, 12203 Berlin, Germany. *Telephone:* (30) 8338051.

BEYNON, John David Emrys, PhD, FREng; British professor of electronics and college principal; b. 11 March 1939, Risca, Gwent; s. of John Emrys Beynon and Elvira Beynon; m. Hazel Janet Hurley 1964; two s. one d.; ed Univ. of Wales and Univ. of Southampton; Scientific Officer, Radio Research Station, Slough 1962–64; lecturer, Sr Lecturer, then Reader, Univ. of Southampton 1964–67; Prof. of Electronics, Univ. of Wales Inst. of Science and Tech., Cardiff 1977–79; Head, Dept of Electronic and Electrical Eng, Univ. of Surrey 1979–83, Pro Vice-Chancellor 1983–87, Sr Pro Vice-Chancellor 1987–90; Prin. King's Coll., Univ. of London 1990–92, Fellow 1990; Hon. Fellow Univ. Coll. of Swansea 1990; mem. British Library Advisory Council 1994–99, Ind. TV Comm. 1995–2000; Chair. Westminster Christian Council 1999–2000. *Publications:* Charge-coupled Devices and Their Applications (with D. R. Lamb) 1980; papers on plasma physics, semi-conductor devices and integrated circuits and Eng educ. *Leisure interests:* music, photography, travel. *Address:* Chalkdene, 13 Great Quarry, Guildford, Surrey, GU1 3XN, England. *Telephone:* (1483) 503458.

BEYNON, John Herbert, DSc, CChem, FRSC, CPhys, FInstP, FRS; British professor of chemistry; b. 29 Dec. 1923, Ystalyfera, Wales; s. of Leslie Ewart and Phyllis (née Gibbon) Beynon; m. Yvonne Lilian Fryer 1947; Scientific Officer, Tank Armament Research 1943–47; Man. and Sr Research Assoc., Physical Chemistry Research, ICI Dyestuffs Div. 1952–74; Prof. of Chemistry and Dir Mass Spectrometry Center, Purdue Univ., USA 1969–75; Assoc. Prof. of Molecular Sciences, Univ. of Warwick 1972–74; Visiting Prof. Univ. of Essex 1982–; Univ. Prof. and Royal Soc. Research Prof. Univ. of Wales,

Swansea 1974–86, Research Prof. 1987–, Prof. Emer. 1991–; Chair. Science Curriculum Devt Cttee, Cttee for Wales 1983–88; Pres. Asscn for Science Educ., Wales 1985–86; Ed. Int. Journal of Mass Spectrometry and Ion Processes 1983–85; Founder and Ed.-in-Chief Rapid Communications in Mass Spectrometry 1987–97; mem. Editorial Bd Organic Mass Spectrometry 1967–88, 1992–94, Int. Journal of Mass Spectrometry and Ion Processes 1967–97, Mass Spectrometry Reviews 1967–, Biological Mass Spectrometry 1992–94, J. Mass Spectrometry 1995–97; Chair. Swansea Sports Club 1988–92; Dir Swansea Cricket and Football Club 1991–92; Founder Pres. European Mass Spectrometry Soc. 1993–96; Assoc. Inst. Jožef Stefan, Yugoslavia; Hon. mem. mass spectrometry socs of Japan, China, Italy and Yugoslavia; Hon. Fellow Serbian Chem. Soc. 1982; Fellow Univ. of Wales Swansea 1988–; Hon. DSc (Purdue Univ., USA) 1995, (Babeş-Bolyai Univ., Romania) 1997; 3M-Boomer Award 1965, Hasler Award for Spectroscopy 1979, Jan Marc Marci Medal 1984, Gold Medal of the Int. Mass Spectrometry Soc. 1985, Frank H. Field and Joe L. Franklin Award of the American Chemical Soc. 1987, Aston Medal of British Mass Spectrometry Soc. 1990, Gold Medal, Italian Chemical Soc. 1992. *Publications:* 10 books and over 400 scientific papers. *Leisure interests:* photography, golf, rugby. *Address:* 3 Rembrandt Court, Sketty, Swansea, SA2 9FG, Wales. *Telephone:* (1792) 206377 (Home).

BEZOS, Jeffrey; American media executive; b. 1963; m.; two s.; ed Princeton Univ.; with Bankers Trust Co. 1988–90; joined D. E. Shaw & Co. 1990, Sr Vice-Pres. 1992–94; f., Chair., CEO Amazon.com Inc. 1995–. *Address:* Amazon.com Inc., 1516 2nd Avenue, Seattle, WA 98101, USA.

BHABHA, J. J. (Jamshed Jehangir), BA; Indian industrialist; b. 21 Aug. 1914, Bombay; ed Cathedral High School, Bombay, Gonville and Caius Coll., Cambridge, Lincoln's Inn, London; Chair. Tata Services Ltd, Tata McGraw-Hill Publishing Co. Ltd, Associated Bldg Co. Ltd; Dir Tata & Sons Ltd, Indian Hotels Co. Ltd, Tata Ltd, London, RDI Print and Publishing Pvt. Ltd, Titan Industries Ltd, Stewarts and Lloyds of India Ltd, Tata Press Ltd; Chair. and Trustee-in-Charge Nat. Centre for the Performing Arts; Vice-Chair. and Man. Trustee Sir Dorabji Tata Trust; Trustee Lady Tata Memorial Trust, J.H. Bhabha Memorial Trust, Prince of Wales Museum of Western India, etc.; Chair. Governing Bd Tata Inst. of Social Sciences; mem. Council Nat. Inst. Advanced Studies, Tata Memorial Centre for Cancer Research and Treatment; mem. numerous public insts.; Pres. Nat. Soc. of the Friends of Trees; Vice-Pres. Nat. Soc. for Clean Cities; Kt Commdr of the Order of Merit (Italy) 1976, Commdr.'s Cross of the Order of Merit (Fed. Repub. of Germany) 1978, Commdr.'s Cross of the Order of the Crown, Belgium 1979, Austria Award of Honour 1984. *Address:* Tata Sons Ltd, Bombay House, 24 Homi Mody Street, Mumbai 400 001 (Office); 12 Little Gibbs Road, Malabar Hill, Mumbai 400 006, India (Home). *Telephone:* 204-9131 (Office).

BHADESHIA, Harshad Kumar Dharamshi Hansraj, PhD, FRS, FREng, FInstP, FIM, CEng, CPhys; British metallurgist; b. 27 Nov. 1953, Nairobi, Kenya; s. of Dharamshi Hansraj Bhadeshia and Narmda Dharamshi Bhadeshia; m. 1978 (divorced 1992); two d.; ed City of London Polytechnic, Univ. of Cambridge; demonstrator Cambridge Univ. 1981–85, lecturer 1985–94, Reader in Physical Metallurgy 1994–99, Prof. of Physical Metallurgy 1999–; Fellow, Darwin Coll. 1993–; Royal Soc. Armourers and Braziers' Medal, Rosenhain Medal, Pfeil Medal, Larke Medal, Hume-Rothery Medal. *Publications include:* Geometry of Crystals 1987, Bainite in Steels 1992, (jtly) Steels 1995. *Leisure interest:* television, squash. *Address:* University of Cambridge, Department of Materials Science and Metallurgy, Pembroke Street, Cambridge, CB2 3QZ (Office); 57 Barrons Way, Comberton, Cambridge, CB3 7EQ, England (Home). *Telephone:* (1223) 334301 (Office). *Fax:* (1223) 334567 (Office). *E-mail:* hkdb@cus.cam.ac.uk (Office). *Website:* www .msm.cam.ac.uk/phase-trans (Office).

BHAN, Suraj, MA, LLB; Indian politician; b. 1 Oct. 1928, Mahlan Wali; s. of Garibu Ram; m. Chameli Devi; mem. All-India Working Cttee of Bharatiya Jan Sangh 1970–73; Head of Harijan Wing and Sec. of Haryana Jan Sangh 1973–76; mem. Lok Sabha 1967–70, 1977–79, 1980–84, 1996; Pres. Haryana BJP; Sec. All India BJP; Pres. All India BJP Scheduled Castes Cell; mem. Legis. Ass. from Mullana 1987–; Minister for Revenue 1987–89; Deputy Speaker Lok Sabha 1996–98; apptd. Gov. of Uttar Pradesh 1998. *Address:* Raj Bhavan, Lucknow, India (Office).

BHANDARI, Sundar Singh, LLB, MA; Indian politician and lawyer; b. 12 April 1921, Udaipur, Rajasthan; s. of Sujan Singh Bhandari and Phool Kanwar; Advocate Mewar High Court 1942–43; headmaster, Shiksha Bhawan, Udaipur 1943–46; Gen. Sec. Bharatiya Jana Sangh, Rajasthan 1951–57, All India Gen. Sec. 1967–77, All India Vice-Pres. Bharatiya Janata Party 1981–98; mem. Rajya Sabha 1966–72, 1976–82, 1992–98; Deputy Leader Janata Parl. Party 1977–80; Chair. Petition Cttee Rajya Sabha 1992–94, Parl. Standing Cttee on Transport and Civil Aviation 1996–98; Gov. of Bihar 1998–99; Gov. of Gujarat 1999–; mem. Indian del. to Inter-Parl. Union, Lisbon 1978, Seoul 1997. *Leisure interests:* reading, social service. *Address:* 7B Mograwadi, Udaipur, Rajasthan; 3/16 Kalkaji Extn., New Delhi; Raj Bhavan, Gandhinagar 382020, India. *Telephone:* 485520 (Udaipur); 641-9891 (New Delhi); 43171 (Gandhinagar).

BHANDIT RITTAKOL; Thai film director; b. 1951, Ayutthaya; ed Assumption Coll., Si Racha, Assumption Commercial Coll., Bangkok; news reporter The Nation; became film critic and screenplay writer 1975, directorial debut 1983. *Films:* Boonchu, The Seed (Thai best picture award) 1987, Classmates (best picture, best Dir, best screenplay) 1990, Miss You (best picture, best Dir best screenplay) 1993, Once Upon a Time (best Dir, best screenplay) 1995, Satang 2000, Moon Hunter 2001 (also co-writer). *Address:* c/o Five Star Production Co. Ltd, 61/1 Soi Thaweemitr 2, Rama 9 Rd., Huaykwang, Bangkok, Thailand (Office). *Telephone:* 246 9025-9 (Office). *Fax:* 246 2105 (Office). *E-mail:* info@fivestarent.com (Office). *Website:* www.fivestarent.com (Office).

BHARGAVA, Pushpa Mittra, PhD; Indian scientist; b. 22 Feb. 1928, Ajmer, Rajasthan; s. of Dr. Ram Chandra Bhargava and Gayatri Devi Bhargava; m. Edith Manorama Patrick 1958; one s. one d.; ed Lucknow Univ.; lecturer, Dept of Chemistry, Osmania Univ., Hyderabad, then mem. staff Cen. Labs. Hyderabad; Post-doctoral Fellow, Univ. of Madison 1953–56; at Nat. Inst. for Medical Research, UK 1957–58; joined Regional Research Lab. (now Indian Inst. of Chemical Tech.) 1958–77; Dir Centre for Cellular and Molecular Biology, Hyderabad 1977–90; CSIR Distinguished Fellow 1990–93; Visiting Prof. Collège de France, Paris; Scientific adviser in several industries; has worked by invitation at McArdle Lab. for Cancer Research, USA, Nat. Inst. for Medical Research, UK, Institut du Radium, France, Max-Planck Institut für Biophysikalische Chemie, Germany; has given over 250 lectures to int. meetings worldwide; Founder Guha Research Conf.; Founder-mem. Soc. for Study of Reproduction (USA); Past-Pres. Soc. of Biological Chemists; mem. numerous other Indian and int. professional socs and standing or ad hoc cttees of Int. Cell Research Org. and other int. orgs; fmr or current mem. several editorial bds of scientific journals; Fellow Indian Nat. Science Acad., Indian Acad. of Sciences, Nat. Acad. of Sciences (India), Nat. Acad. of Medical Sciences (India), World Acad. of Arts and Sciences; Corresp. mem. American Asscn for Cancer Research and other bodies; Life Fellow, Clare Hall, Cambridge, UK; Hon. DSc (Univ. of Burdwan); numerous prizes and awards, including Nat. Citizens Award 1988; Padma Bhushan conferred by Pres. of India 1986; Chevalier, Légion d'honneur 1998. *Publications:* several books, including Proteins of Seminal Plasma 1989; numerous articles. *Leisure interests:* fine arts, reading, current affairs, sports, music, films, photography. *Address:* 12-5-27 Vijayapuri, Tarnaka, Hyderabad 500 017 (Home); Anveshna Consultancy Services, Furqan Cottage, 12-13-100 Lane 1, Street No. 3, Tarnaka, Hyderabad 500 017, India. *Telephone:* (40) 7017789 (Office); (40) 7003517 (Home). *Fax:* 40-7017857 (Office). *E-mail:* pushpabhargava@usa.net (Office); chanchak@nettlinx.com (Home).

BHATTACHARYA, Basu; Indian film director, producer and writer; b. 31 Jan. 1936, Murshidabad, W Bengal; m. Rinki Bhattacharya 1963; one s. two d.; Pres. Indian Film Dirs. Asscn 1978–85; Dir Nat. Film Devt Corpn 1980–87; mem. Nat. Film Policy Working Group; mem. Jury, Moscow Int. Film Festival 1981; recipient of numerous film awards. *Films include:* Teesri Kasam 1966, Anubhav 1972, Sparsh 1981, Griha Pravesh 1982, Panchvati 1986. *Leisure interests:* poetry, painting, gardening. *Address:* Gold Mist, 36 Carter Road, Bandra, Mumbai 50, India. *Telephone:* 6424727.

BHATTACHARYYA, Birendra Kumar, BSc, MA, PhD; Indian journalist and writer; b. 16 March 1924, Suffry Sibsagar, Assam; s. of Sashidhar and Aideo Bhattacharyya; m. Binita Bhattacharyya 1958; two s. one d.; ed Jorhat Government High School, Cotton Coll., Gauhati, Calcutta Univ. and Gauhati Univ.; fmr Science Teacher, Ukrul High School, Manipur; Ed. Ramdhenu 1951–61, Sadiniya Navayung 1963–67; lecturer in Journalism, Gauhati Univ. 1974–; Exec. mem. Janata Party, Assam; Sec. Archaeological Soc. of Assam; Sahitya Akademi Award for Assamese Literature 1961, Jnanpitho Award 1979. *Publications:* novels: Iyaruingam (won Akademi Award), Rajpathe Ringiai (Call of the Main Street), Mother, Sataghai (Killer), Mrityunjay, Pratipad, Nastachandra, Ballart, Kabar Aru Phul, Ranga Megh, Daint; collections of short stories: Kolongajioboi (Still Flows the Kolong), Satsari (Necklace); Aurobindo (biog.), A Survey of Assamese Modern Culture (in Assamese), Munichunir Pohar, Kalar Humuniyah, Naga Kakar Sadhu, Chaturanga, Phul Konwarar Pathighora, Sandhya Swar. *Address:* Kharghuli Development Area, Guwahati 781004, India. *Telephone:* 25019.

BHATTARAI, Krishna Prasad; Nepalese politician; b. 24 Dec. 1924, Banaras, India; s. of the late Sankata Prasad Bhattarai and Lalita Devi; served 14 years' imprisonment for opposition to absolute monarchy in Nepal; Pres. Nepali Congress Party (banned for 29 years until 1990); Prime Minister of Nepal (presiding over interim multiparty Govt) 1990–91, 1999–2000, also Minister of Royal Palace Affairs, of Home Affairs, of Foreign Affairs, of Defence and of Women and Social Welfare. *Address:* c/o Office of the Prime Minister, Central Secretariat, Singha Durbar, Kathmandu, Nepal (Office).

BHAVSAR, Natvar, BA, AM, MFA; Indian artist; b. 7 April 1934, Gothava; s. of Prahladji Bhavsar and Babuben Bhavsar; m. Janet Brosious Bhavsar; three c.; ed Gujarat Univ., Univ. of Pennyslvania, USA; art instructor Univ. of Rhode Island, Kingston, USA; numerous solo exhbns. including ART Cologne, ACP Viviane Ehrli Gallery 1998, 1999; recent group exhibitions include: Galleria Civica d'Arte, Italy (Il Sud del Mondo. L'Altra Arte Contemporanea) 1991, Viviane Ehrli Gallery, Switzerland 1997, Dialectica, NY 2000, Sundaram Tagore Gallery 2001; work in public collections including: Australian Nat. Gallery, Boston Museum of Fine Arts, Solomon R. Guggenheim Museum, Metropolitan Museum of Art, MIT, Philadelphia Museum of Art; work in numerous pvt. collections; John D. Rockefeller III Fund Fellowship 1965–66, John Simon Guggenheim Memorial Foundation Fellowship 1975–76, Vishva Gurjari 1988. *Publication:* Monogram 1998. *Address:* 131 Greene Street, New York, NY 10012, USA. *Telephone:* (212) 674-1293.

BHOSLE, Asha; Indian vocalist and composer; b. 8 Sept. 1933, Sangli, Maharashtra; d. of Dinanath Mangeshkar; Indian film playback singer; has recorded over 12,000 songs in 18 languages; first film Chunaria 1948; first solo in Raat Ki Rani 1949; sang in styles influenced by Latin American and American Big Band Jazz; worked extensively with Kishore Kumar 1970s; numerous tours and performances world-wide; Filmfare Award 1967, 1968, 1971, 1972, 1973, 1974, 1977, 1996, Nat. Award 1981, 1986, Nightingale of Asia 1987, Lata Mangeshkar Award, Madhya Pradesh Govt 1989, Maharashtra Govt 1999, Filmfare Special Award, Rangeela Re 1996, Screen Videocon Award 1997, MTV Contrib. to Music Award 1997, five Channel V Awards, Singer of the Millennium, Dubai 2000, Kolhapuri Bhushan Award 2000, Sangli Bhushan Award 2000, Omega Excellence Lifetime Achievement Award 2000, Filmfare Lifetime Achievement Award 2001, Dada Saheb Phalke Award 2001, Dayawati Modi Award 2001, BBC Mega Mela Lifetime Achievement Award 2002. *Recordings include:* albums (soundtracks): Dus Lakh 1967, Shikhar 1968, Hare Rama Hare Krishna 1972, Naina 1973, Pran Jaye Par Vachan Na Jaye 1974, Don 1977, Umrao Jaan 1981, Ijazat 1986, Dilwale Dulhania Le Jayeng 1995, Rangeela 1996; solo: Songs of My Soul – Rare and Classic Vols. 1 and 2 2001.

BHUMIBOL ADULYADEJ, King of Thailand; b. 5 Dec. 1927, Cambridge, Mass., USA; ed Bangkok and Lausanne, Switzerland; youngest son of Their Royal Highnesses Prince and Princess Mahidol of Songkla; succeeded his brother, King Ananda Mahidol, June 1946; married Her Majesty Queen Sirikit, daughter of HH the late Prince Chandaburi Suranath, 28th April 1950; formal coronation 5th May 1950; one son, HRH Crown Prince Maha Vajiralongkorn, b. 1952; three daughters, Princess Ubol Ratana, b. 1951, HRH Princess Maha Chakri Sirindhorn, b. 1955, HRH Princess Chulabhorn, b. 1957. *Address:* Chitralada Villa, Bangkok, Thailand.

BHUTTO, Begum Nusrat; Pakistani politician; b. 1934; two s. (deceased) two d. (including Benazir Bhutto, q.v.; widow of Zulfikar Ali Bhutto (died 1979); fmr first lady of Pakistan; Co-Chair. Pakistan People's Party (PPP) –1993 and involved in the Movt for the Restoration of Democracy in Pakistan 1984–; now living in Dubai in self-imposed exile. *Address:* c/o Pakistan People's Party, 70 Clifton, Karachi 75600, Pakistan.

BHUTTO, Benazir; Pakistani politician; b. 21 June 1953; d. of the late Zulfikar Ali Bhutto (died 1979) and of Begum Nusrat Bhutto (q.v.); m. Asif Ali Zardari 1987; one s. two d.; ed Harvard Univ. and Lady Margaret Hall, Oxford; under house arrest 1977–84; leader in exile of Pakistan People's Party with her mother Nusrat and involved in the Movt for the Restoration of Democracy in Pakistan 1984–; Co-Chair. Pakistan People's Party (PPP), Chair. 1993–, re-elected Leader 2002–; returned to Pakistan 1986; Prime Minister of Pakistan 1988–90, 1993–96, also fmr Minister of Finance and Econ. Affairs; removed from position by presidential decree and charged with corruption and abuse of power Aug. 1990; dismissed by presidential decree Nov. 1996, dismissal upheld by Supreme Court Jan. 1997; charged with corruption and money laundering July 1998; charged with taking bribes Oct. 1998; Opposition Leader 1990–93; Head. Parl. Foreign Affairs Cttee 1993–96; sentenced with Asif Zardari to five years' imprisonment for corruption April 1999, disqualified from politics for five years, voluntarily went into exile in Dubai; appeal against conviction for corruption upheld April 2001; Dr. hc (Harvard) 1989, (Lady Margaret Hall, Oxford) 1989. *Publication:* Daughter of The East (autobiog.) 1988. *Address:* Bilawal House, Boat Basin Area, Clifton, Karachi, Pakistan.

BIANCHERI, Boris, BL, GCVO; Italian diplomatist; b. 3 Nov. 1930, Rome; m.; one s. one d.; ed Univ. of Rome; entered diplomatic service 1956, Office of the Sec. of State, Ministry of Foreign Affairs 1956–58; Italian Embassy, Athens 1959; Econ. Affairs Dept, Ministry of Foreign Affairs 1964–67, Counsellor 1967–71; Sec.-Gen. of Govt Comm. for 1970 Universal Osaka Exhbn 1968; Political Counsellor, Italian Embassy, London 1972–75; Head of Office of Sec.-Gen. Ministry of Foreign Affairs 1975–78, Chef de Cabinet, Sec. of State for Foreign Affairs 1978, Minister Plenipotentiary 1979; Amb. to Japan 1980–84; Dir-Gen. Personnel and Admin., Ministry of Foreign Affairs 1984, Dir-Gen. Political Affairs 1985; Amb. to UK 1987–91, to USA 1991–95, Sec.-Gen. Ministry of Foreign Affairs 1995–97; Chair. Italian News Agency (ANSA) 1997–, MARSH (Gruppo M.M.C.) 2001; Pres. Inst. for Int. Studies (ISPI), Milan 1997–; Hon. LLD (St John, NY). *Leisure interests:* gardening, boating, swimming. *Address:* ANSA, Via della Dataria 94, 00187 Rome (Office); Via dei Montecatini 5, 00186 Rome, Italy (Home).

BIANCHI, Andrés, MA, PhD; Chilean diplomatist and banking executive; b. 12 Sept. 1935, Valdivia; m. Lily Urdinola; two s. one d.; ed Univ. of Chile, Yale Univ., USA; Dir Int. Labor Office Regional Employment Program of Latin America and the Caribbean 1971–73; Visiting Research Assoc. Woodrow Wilson School of Public and Int. Affairs, Princeton Univ. 1973–75; Visiting Prof. Center for Latin American Devt Studies, Boston Univ. 1978; Dir Econ. Devt Div., UN Econ. Comm. for Latin America and the Caribbean 1981–88, Deputy Exec. Sec 1988–89; Gov. Cen. Bank of Chile 1989–91; Chair. Credit Lyonnais Chile 1992–96, Dresdner Banque Nationale de Paris, Chile 1996–2000; mem. External Advisory Group, Latin America and Caribbean Regional Office, World Bank 1994–2000; mem. Pres. of Chile's Nat. Savings Comm. 1997–98; Amb. to USA 2000–; fmr adviser to cen. banks of Bolivia, Colombia, Mexico and Venezuela. *Leisure interests:* tennis, travel, classical

music. *Address:* Embassy of Chile, 1732 Massachusetts Avenue, NW, Washington, DC 20036, USA (Office). *Telephone:* (202) 785-1746 (Office). *Fax:* (202) 887-5579 (Office). *Website:* www.chile-usa.org (Office).

BIANCHI, Tancredi; Italian professor of banking economics; ed Bocconi Univ., Milan; Prof. of Banking Econs Bocconi Univ., Milan 1979; Pres. Associazione Bancaria Italiana (ABI) 1991–2001; Pres. Centrobanca 2001–; Hon. Pres. Foundation Ente Luigi Einaudi. *Address:* Centrobanca, Corso Europa 16, 20122 Milan, Italy (Office).

BIANCINI, Angelo; Italian sculptor; b. 1911; ed Accademia di Santa Luca; Prof. and Artistic Dir Istituto d'Arte, Faenza; Regular Exhibitor Venice Biennali and Rome Quadriennali 1934–58; int. exhibitor throughout the world; Prize, Milan Triennale 1940, Venice Biennale 1958. *Major works include:* three statues, Galleria d'Arte Moderna, Rome, Canadian Temple, Rome, Mosaic Marist Fathers' Int. Coll., etc. *Address:* Istituto d'Arte di Ceramica, Faenza, Italy.

BIANCO, Jean-Louis; French civil servant; b. 12 Jan. 1943, Neuilly-sur-Seine; s. of Louis Bianco and Gabrielle (née Vandries) Bianco; m. Martine Letoublon 1971; three s.; ed Lycée Janson-de-Sailly and Inst. d'études politiques, Paris; Auditor, Conseil d'Etat 1971; Official Rep. Groupe central des villes nouvelles 1973–74; attached to Ministry of Health 1976–79; Counsel, Conseil d'Etat 1976; Official Rep. Syndicat intercommunal de Devt Durance-Bléone 1979–81; Official Rep. to the advisers of the Pres. 1981; Sec.-Gen. to the Pres. 1982–91; Minister of Social Affairs and Integration 1991–92, of Equipment, Transport and Housing 1992–93; mem. Regional Council of Provence 1992–, Pres. 1998–; Mayor of Digne-les-Bains (Alpes de Haute Provence) 1995–2001; First Deputy Mayor 2001–; Deputy from Alpes de Haute-Provence (Socialist) June 1997–; Pres. François Mitterrand Inst. 1999–; Pres. High Council for Int. Co-operation 1999–. *Address:* Conseil d'Etat, Palais Royal, 75100 Paris RP; Mairie, 1 boulevard Maître Bret, 04000 Digne-les-Bains; Conseil général des Alpes de Haute-Provence, 13 rue du Docteur Romieu, 04000 Digne-les-Bains, France.

BICHARD, Sir Michael (George), KCB, LLB, MScS, FIPD, CCMI, FRSA; British civil servant; b. 31 Jan. 1947, Southampton; s. of the late George Bichard and Nora Reeves; m. Christine Bichard; one s. two d.; ed Univ. of Manchester, Univ. of Birmingham; articled clerk, solicitor, Sr Solicitor Reading Borough Council 1969–73; Co. Liaison Officer, Berks. Co. Council 1973–77; Head of Chief Exec.'s Office, Lambeth Borough Council 1977–80; Chief Exec. Brent Borough Council 1980–86, Glos. Co. Council 1986–90, Social Security Benefits Agency 1990–95; Jt Perm. Sec. Dept for Educ. and Employment July–Dec. 1995, Perm. Sec. 1996–2002; Rector London Inst. 2001–; mem. Econ. and Social Research Council 1989–92, Prince's Trust Volunteers Nat. Bd 1992–97; mem. Bd British Council 1996–2001, Industrial Soc. 1997–2001; Chair. Rathbone Training 2001–; Trustee Windsor Leadership Trust 2001–; Hon. Fellow Inst. of Local Govt Studies (Birmingham Univ.); Hon. DUniv (Leeds Metropolitan) 1992, (Middlesex) 2001; Hon. LLD (Birmingham) 1999. *Address:* The London Institute, 65 Davies Street, London, W1K 5DA, England (Office). *Telephone:* (20) 7514-6002 (Office). *Fax:* (20) 7514-6236 (Office). *E-mail:* m.bichard@linst.ac.uk (Office). *Website:* www.linst.ac.uk.

BIČKAUSKAS, Egidijuš; Lithuanian politician and lawyer; b. 29 May 1955, Prienai; m. Jurate Bičkauskienė; ed Vilnius Univ.; investigator, special cases investigator Procurator Gen.'s Office 1978–89; joined People's Front Movt Sajudis 1988; Deputy of USSR Supreme Soviet 1989–90; elected to Parl. Restoration Seimas of Repub. of Lithuania 1990–92, signatory of the Lithuanian Repub. Independence Restoration Act 1990; Head Lithuanian diplomatic mission to Moscow 1990–96; mem. Parl. (Seimas) of Repub. of Lithuania, Deputy Chair. 1992–96, head of faction of Centre Party in Seimas of Lithuania 1996–. *Address:* L R Seimas, Gedimino p.2 53, LT-2600 Vilnius (Office); Laurų 35, LT 2046 Vilnius, Lithuania. *Telephone:* (3702) 225493 (Home).

BIDDISS, Michael Denis, PhD, FRHistS; British professor of history and author; b. 15 April 1942, Farnborough, Kent; s. of Daniel Biddiss and Eileen Biddiss (née Jones); m. Ruth Margaret Cartwright 1967; four d.; ed Queens' Coll., Cambridge, Centre des Hautes Etudes Européennes, Univ. of Strasbourg; Fellow in History, Downing Coll., Cambridge and Dir of Studies in History, Social and Political Sciences 1966–73; lecturer, then Reader in History, Univ. of Leicester 1973–79; Prof. of History, Univ. of Reading 1979–, Dean Faculty of Letters and Social Sciences 1982–85; Visiting Prof., Univ. of Victoria, Canada 1973, Univ. of Cape Town 1976, 1978, Univ. of Cairo 1985, Monash Univ., Australia 1989, Univ. of Nanjing, China 1997; Chair. History at the Univs. Defence Group 1984–87; mem. Council, The Historical Assen 1985– (Pres. 1991–94), Vice-Pres. Royal Historical Soc. 1995–99 (mem. Council 1988–92); Lister Lecturer, BAAS 1975; Hon. Fellow Faculty of the History of Medicine (Pres. 1994–98), Soc. of Apothecaries 1986–; Osler Medallist, Soc. of Apothecaries of London 1989, Locke Medallist, Soc. of Apothecaries of London 1996, Sydenham Medallist, Soc. of Apothecaries of London 2000. *Publications:* Father of Racist Ideology 1970, Gobineau: Selected Political Writings (Ed.) 1970, Disease and History (co-author) 1972, The Age of the Masses 1977, Images of Race (Ed.) 1979, Thatcherism (co-ed.) 1987, The Nuremberg Trial and the Third Reich (co-author) 1992, The Uses and Abuses of Antiquity (co-ed.) 1999, The Humanities in the New Millennium (co-ed) 2000. *Leisure interests:* cricket, music and opera, mountain walking, art, travel. *Address:* School of History, University of Reading, Whiteknights, Reading, RG6 6AA, England. *Telephone:* (118) 378 8146. *E-mail:* m.d.biddiss@reading.ac.uk (Office).

BIDDLE, Martin, OBE, MA, FBA, FSA, FRHistS; British archaeologist; b. 4 June 1937, North Harrow, Middx; s. of Reginald Samuel Biddle and Gwladys Florence Biddle (née Baker); m. Birthe Kjølbye 1966; two d. and two d. by previous m.; ed Merchant Taylors' School and Pembroke Coll. Cambridge; Asst Insp. of Ancient Monuments, Ministry of Public Building and Works 1961–63; lecturer in Medieval Archaeology, Univ. of Exeter 1963–67; Visiting Fellow, All Souls Coll. Oxford 1967–68; Dir Winchester Research Unit. 1968–; Dir Univ. Museum and Prof. of Anthropology and History of Art, Univ. of Pa 1977–81; lecturer of The House, Christ Church, Oxford 1983–86; Astor Sr Research Fellow in Medieval Archaeology, Hertford Coll. Oxford 1989–; Prof. of Medieval Archaeology, Univ. of Oxford 1997–; Dir excavations and investigations at Nonsuch Palace 1959–60, Winchester 1961–71, Repton (with wife) 1974–88, 1993, St Alban's Abbey (with wife) 1978, 1982–84, 1991, 1994–95, Holy Sepulchre, Jerusalem (with wife) 1989–90, 1992, 1993, 1998, Qasr Ibrim, Egypt (with wife) 1990, 1992, 1995, 2000; archaeological consultant to Canterbury Cathedral, St Alban's Abbey, Eurotunnel, etc.; mem. Royal Comm. on Historical Monuments for England 1984–95; Trevelyan Lecturer, Univ. of Cambridge 1991; Pres. Soc. for Medieval Archaeology 1995–98; Frend Medal, Soc. of Antiquaries (with Birthe Kjølbye-Biddle) 1986. *Publications:* The Future of London's Past (with C. Heighway) 1973, Winchester in the Early Middle Ages (with others) 1976, The History of the King's Works, Vol. IV, Pt. 2 (with others) 1982, King Arthur's Round Table 2000, Approaches in Urban Archaeology 1990, Object and Economy in Medieval Winchester 1990, Das Grab-Christi 1998, Nonsuch Palace: The Domestic Materials 1998, The Tomb of Christ 1999, King Arthur's Round Table 2000, The Church of the Holy Sepulchre 2000; papers in learned journals. *Leisure interests:* travel, especially Hellenic travel, architecture, Renaissance art. *Address:* Hertford College, Oxford, OX1 3BW (Office); 19 Hamilton Road, Oxford, OX2 7PY, England (Home). *Telephone:* (1865) 513056; (1865) 559017 (Office). *Fax:* (1865) 559017; (1865) 559017 (Office). *E-mail:* martin.biddle@hertford.ox.ac.uk (Office).

BIDE, Sir Austin (Ernest), Kt, BSc, FRSC, CBIM, CChem; British business executive; b. 11 Sept. 1915, London; s. of the late Ernest Arthur Bide and Eliza Bide (née Young); m. Irene Ward 1941; three d.; ed County School, Acton, Univ. of London; mem. of staff, Dept of Govt Chemist until 1940; Research Dept Glaxo Laboratories Ltd, Deputy Sec. 1954, Sec. 1959; Dir Glaxo Group Ltd 1963; Deputy Chair. Glaxo Holdings Ltd 1971–73, Chief Exec. 1973–80, Chair. 1973–85, Hon. Pres. 1985–95; mem. Council CBI 1974–85, Chair, Research and Tech. Cttee 1977–86, mem. Pres.'s Cttee 1983–85; mem. Council British Inst. of Man. 1976–88, Companions Cttee 1976–84, Chair. Finance Cttee 1976–79, Vice-Pres. 1992–, Dir and Chair. BIM Foundation 1977–79; Dir British Leyland (now BL Ltd) 1977–86 (non-exec. Deputy Chair. 1980–82, non-exec. Chair. 1982–86), J. Lyons and Co. 1977–78; mem. Working Party on Biotechnology, Council of the Imperial Soc. of Knights Bachelor 1980–; Chair. Visiting Cttee of the Open Univ. 1982–88; Chair. CGEA (UK) Ltd 1991–99, Onyx (UK) Ltd. 1991, Comatech (UK) Ltd. 1992–99, Tyseley Waste Disposal 1994–; mem. Advisory Cttee on Industry to Vice-Chancellors and Prins. of Univs. of UK 1984–87; mem. Review Body, Univ. Grants Cttee, mem. Council of Inst. of Manpower Studies 1985–91, Adam Smith Inst. 1985 (Chair. 1986–); Chair. Q-Ca Ltd 1985–88, Microtest Research Ltd 1987–90; Chair. United Environmental Systems Ltd 1988–90; Dir Oxford Consultancy Ltd 1988–98 (Chair. 1994–98); Trustee, British Motor Industry Heritage Trust 1983–86; mem. Court of British Shippers' Council 1984–92 (Chair. 1989–92); Chair. Salisbury Cathedral Appeal Cttee 1987–92; mem. MRC 1986, mem. Advisory Council 1985–89; Hon. Fellow, Vice-Pres. Inst. of Industrial Mans. 1983, Hon. Fellow Inst. of Chemical Engineers, Hon. Fellow, Inst. of Biotechnological Studies; Hon. DSc (Queen's, Belfast), Hon. Dr hc (CNAA) 1990; Fellow St Catharine's Coll., Cambridge. *Leisure interests:* fishing, handicrafts.

BIDEN, Joseph Robinette, Jr, JD; American politician; b. 20 Nov. 1942, Scranton, Pa; s. of Joseph R. Biden and Jean F. Biden; m. 1st Neilia Hunter (deceased); two s. one d. (deceased); m. 2nd Jill Tracy Jacobs 1977; one d.; ed Univ. of Delaware, Newark and Syracuse Univ. Coll. of Law, NY; Trial Attorney in the Public Defender's Office, Del. 1968; Founder of Biden & Walsh Law Firm, Wilmington; mem. New Castle Co., Del. and American Bar Asscns, American Trial Lawyers' Asscn; admitted to practise before the Del. Supreme Court; mem. New Castle Co. Council 1970–72; Senator from Delaware 1972–, serving as a mem. of the Cttee on Foreign Relations, Judiciary Cttee 1987– (Chair. 1987–95); named to the Democratic Steering Cttee; Democrat. *Leisure interests:* sports, history, public speaking, American architecture. *Address:* 221 Russell Building, Washington, DC 20510-0001, USA (Office). *Telephone:* (202) 224-5045 (Office).

BIDWELL, Charles Edward, PhD; American professor of education and sociology; b. 24 Jan. 1932, Chicago; s. of Charles L. Bidwell and Eugenia Campbell Bidwell; m. Helen Claxton Lewis 1959; one s.; ed Univ. of Chicago; Lecturer in Sociology, Harvard Univ. 1959–61, Assoc. Prof. 1965–70, Prof. of Educ. and Sociology 1970–85, Reavis Prof. Educ. and Sociology 1985–2001, Prof. Emer. 2001–; Chair. Dept of Educ. 1978–88; Chair. Dept of Sociology 1988–94; Dir Ogburn-Stouffer Center 1988–94; Guggenheim Fellow 1971–72; Fellow AAAS; mem. Nat. Acad. of Educ. *Publications:* The School as a Formal Organization, in Handbook of Organizations (Ed. J. March) 1965, The

Organization and its Ecosystem (with JD Kasarda) 1985, The Collegial Focus: Teaching Fields, Colleague Relationships, and Instructional Practice in American High Schools in Sociology of Education (with J. Yasumoto) 1999. *Leisure interests:* skiing and reading. *Address:* Department of Sociology, 5848 S. University Avenue, Chicago, IL 60637, USA. *Telephone:* (773) 702-0388 (Office). *Fax:* (773) 702-4617 (Office). *E-mail:* c-bidwell@uchicago.edu (Office).

BIEBER, Owen F.; American labour official; b. 28 Dec. 1929, North Dorr, Mich.; s. of Albert F. Bieber and Minnie Schwartz Bieber; m. Shirley M. Van Woerkom 1950; three s. two d.; ed High School; elected Regional Dir, United Auto Workers (UAW, now United Automobile, Aerospace and Agricultural Implement Workers of America) Region 1D 1974–80, Vice-Pres. Int. Union 1980–83, Pres. 1983–; Hon. D.Hum. (Grand Valley Coll.), Hon. Dr.Sc. (Ferris State Coll.). *Address:* United Auto Workers (UAW), 8000 E Jefferson Avenue, Detroit, MI 48214, USA (Office). *Telephone:* (313) 926 5201 (Office).

BIEDENKOPF, Kurt Hans, DJur; German politician and lawyer; b. 28 Jan. 1930, Ludwigshafen; s. of Wilhelm Biedenkopf and Agathe Biedenkopf (née Schmidt); m. Ingrid Ries 1979; Prof. of Law, Ruhr Univ., Bochum 1964–70, Rector 1967–69; Chair. Govt Comm. on Co-determination 1968–70; Gen. Sec. Christian Democratic Party (CDU) 1973–77, Vice-Pres. 1977–83; Pres. CDU Regional Asscn, North Rhine-Westphalia 1980–84; mem. Bundestag 1976–80, 1987–90; Prime Minister of Saxony 1990–2002; Chair. Kuratorium Trust of Devt and Peace; mem. Exec. Bd Henkel Corpn, Düsseldorf 1971–73; mem. Bd Inst. for Econ. and Social Policy, Bonn 1977–; mem. Bd German Nat. Trust; mem. Landtag of North Rhine-Westphalia 1980–88; mem. Senate Max Planck Gesellschaft; Dr.jur. hc (Davidson Coll.) 1974, (Georgetown) 1978, (New School for Social Research, New York) 1993, (Katholic Univ., Brussels) 1994. *Publications:* Vertragliche Wettbewerbsbeschränkung und Wirtschaftsverfassung 1958, Grenzen der Tarifautonomie 1964, Fortschritt in Freiheit 1974, Die programmierte Krise-Alternativen zur staatlichen Schuldenpolitik 1979, Die neue Sicht der Dinge 1985, Zeitsignale—Parteienlandschaft im Umbruch 1989, Einheit und Erneuerung 1994, Ordnungspolitik in einer Zeit des Umbruchs 1998, Ein deutsches Tagebuch 1989–90 2000. *Leisure interests:* skiing, sailing. *Address:* Sächsischer Landtag, Bernh.v.Lindenau-Pl. 1, 01067 Dresden, Germany. *Telephone:* (351) 4935506.

BIEGMAN, Nicolaas H., PhD; Netherlands diplomatist; b. 23 Sept. 1936, Apeldoorn; s. of Nicolaas Biegman and Aukje de Boer; m. Mirjana Cibilic; two s.; ed Univ. of Leiden; Lecturer in Turkish and Persian, Univ. of Leiden 1960–62; various posts in Netherlands foreign service 1963–84; Amb. to Egypt 1984–88; Dir-Gen. for Int. Cooperation, Ministry of Foreign Affairs 1988–92; Perm. Rep. to UN 1992–97; Perm. Rep. to NATO 1998–2001; Sr Civilian Rep. of NATO in Macedonia 2002–03; mem. Bd of Dirs. Int. Peace Acad. (IPA); Order of The Netherlands Lion, Order of Merit, UAR. *Publications:* The Turco-Ragusan Relationship 1967, Egypt-Moulids, Saints, Sufis 1990, Egypt's Sideshows 1992, An Island of Bliss 1993, Mainly Manhattan 1997. *Leisure interest:* photography. *Address:* International Peace Academy, 777 United Nations Plaza, New York, NY 10017, USA. *Website:* www.ipacademy.org/.

BIELECKI, Jan Krzysztof, MSc; Polish politician and economist; b. 3 May 1951, Bydgoszcz; s. of Anastazy Bielecki and Janina Bielecka; m. Barbara Bielecka 1976; one s. one d.; ed Gdańsk Univ.; Asst Gdańsk Univ. 1973–77; Head of Research Unit, Centre for Training Managerial Staff, Ministry of Trade and Ministry of Machine Industry 1972–82; trade union and workers' rights activist, expert for econ. affairs, Solidarity Trade Union 1980–81; continued union activity under martial law as assoc. of underground regional and nat. authorities; lorry driver 1982–85; man. Doradca consulting cooperative, Sopot 1985–91; Deputy to Sejm (Parl.) 1989–93 (mem. Civic Parl. Caucus 1989–91, leader Parl. Liberal-Democratic Congress Caucus); Prime Minister of Poland Jan.–Dec. 1991; Minister for Poland–EU Relations 1992–93; mem. Liberal-Democratic Congress (mem. Provisional Bd, the Presidium) 1989–94; currently Dir. EBRD. *Leisure interests:* horse riding, tennis, football. *Address:* European Bank for Reconstruction and Development, 1 Exchange Square, London EC2 2EA, England.

BIERRING, Ole, LLM; Danish diplomatist; b. 9 Nov. 1926, Copenhagen; s. of Knud and Ester M. (Lorck) Bierring; m. Bodil E Kisbye 1960; one s. three d.; ed Univ. of Copenhagen and Princeton Univ., USA; joined Ministry of Foreign Affairs 1951; served in Washington, DC 1956–58, Vienna 1960–63, Brussels (NATO) 1968–72; Under-Sec. for Political Affairs 1976–80, Deputy Perm. Under-Sec. 1980; Amb. to France 1980–84; Amb. and Perm. Rep. to UN 1984–88, Rep. on the Security Council 1985–86; Amb. to NATO 1988–95; Observer to WEU 1993–95; Amb.-at-Large 1995–96; Commdr Order of Dannebrog (1st class) and other decorations. *Leisure interests:* music, sailing. *Address:* Rysensteensgade 6, 5 tv, 1564 Copenhagen V, Denmark. *Telephone:* 33-91-66-36.

BIESHU, Mariya Lukyanovna; Moldovan singer (soprano); b. 3 Aug. 1935, Moldova; d. of Luca Bieshu and Tatiana Bieshu; m. Arcady Rodomsky 1965; ed Kishinev Conservatoire; soloist with Moldovan Folk Orchestra 1958–60; with Moldovan Opera and Ballet 1961–; postgrad. studies at La Scala, Milan 1965–67; Prof. Kishinev Conservatoire 1980–; Chair. Union of Musicians 1986; Vice-Pres. Int. Union of Musicians; Hon. mem. Acad. of Sciences; awards include: 1st Prize Int. Puccini Competition, Tokyo 1967, People's Artist of USSR 1970, Lenin Prize 1982. *Roles include:* Tosca 1962, Desdemona in Othello 1967, Leonora in Il Trovatore 1969, Zemphira in Aleko 1973, Mimi in La Bohème 1977, Turandot 1979, Iolanta 1979, Elizabeth of Valois in Don

Carlos 1985, Amelia in A Masked Ball 1989, Abigail in Nabucco 1991. *Leisure interests:* dogs, open country. *Address:* 24 Pushkin Str., Chişinău 2012, Moldova.

BIFFEN, Baron (Life Peer) cr. 1997, of Tanat in the County of Shropshire; **William John Biffen**, PC, BA; British politician; b. 3 Nov. 1930, Bridgwater; s. of Victor W. Biffen; m. Sarah Wood (née Drew) 1979; one step-s. one step-d.; ed Dr Morgan's School, Bridgwater, Jesus Coll., Cambridge; MP for Oswestry 1961–83, for Shropshire North 1983–97; with Tube Investments Ltd 1953–60; with Economist Intelligence Unit 1960–61; Chief Sec. to the Treasury 1979–81, Sec. of State for Trade 1981–82; Lord Privy Seal and Leader of the Commons 1983–87; Dir Glynwed Int. 1987–2000, J. Bibby and Sons 1988–97, Rockware Group 1988–91, Barlow Int. PLC 1997–2000; Trustee The London Clinic 1994–; DL Shropshire 1993. *Publication:* Inside the House of Commons 1989. *Address:* Tanat House, Llanyblodwel, Oswestry, Shropshire, SY10 8NQ, England. *Telephone:* (20) 7219-3000 (Office).

BIFFI, HE Cardinal Giacomo; Italian ecclesiastic; b. 13 June 1928, Milan; ordained 1950; consecrated Bishop (Titular Church of Fidene) 1975; Archbishop of Bologna 1984; cr. Cardinal 1985. *Address:* Arcivescovado, Via Altabella 6, 40126 Bologna, Italy. *Telephone:* (51) 238202.

BIGELEISEN, Jacob, AB, MS, PhD; American chemist; b. 2 May 1919, Paterson, NJ; s. of Harry Bigeleisen and Ida (Slomowitz) Bigeleisen; m. Grace Alice Simon 1945; three s.; ed New York Univ., Washington State Univ. and Univ. of California (Berkeley); SAM Labs, Columbia Univ. (Manhattan District) 1943–45; Ohio State Univ. 1945–46; Univ. of Chicago 1946–48; Assoc. to Senior Chemist, Brookhaven Nat. Laboratory 1948–68; Prof. of Chemistry, Univ. of Rochester 1968–78, Chair. Dept of Chemistry 1970–75, Tracy H. Harris Prof., Coll. of Arts and Sciences 1973–78, Leading Prof. of Chemistry, State Univ. of New York (Stony Brook) 1978–89, Vice-Pres. for Research 1978–80, Dean of Graduate Studies 1978–80, Distinguished Prof. and Emer. Prof. 1989–; Visiting Prof. Cornell Univ. 1953; Hon. Visiting Prof., Eidgenössische Technische Hochschule, Zürich 1962–63; Senior Postdoctoral Fellow, Nat. Science Foundation 1962–63; Gilbert N. Lewis Lecturer, Univ. of Calif. 1963; Visiting Distinguished Prof., State Univ. of New York (Buffalo) 1966; Tracy Harris Prof., Rochester 1973; Distinguished Prof. Story Book 1989; Guggenheim Fellow 1974–75; mem. NAS, American Chemical Soc.; Chair. Assembly of Math. and Physical Science 1976–80, Councilor 1982–85; Fellow, American Acad. of Arts and Sciences, American Physical Soc., AAAS; Samuel F.B. Morse Medal 1939, American Chem. Soc. Nuclear Applications to Chemistry Award 1958, E. O. Lawrence Memorial Award and Presidential Citation 1964, Distinguished Alumnus Award (Washington State Univ.) 1983. *Publications:* Calculation of Equilibrium Constants of Isotopic Exchange Reactions 1947, Relative Reaction Velocities of Isotopic Molecules 1949, The Significance of the Product and Sum Rules to Isotope Fractionation Studies 1957, Statistical Mechanics of Isotope Effects in Condensed Systems 1961, Quantum Mechanical Foundations of Isotope Chemistry 1974; and numerous publs on ionization of strong electrolytes, organic photochemistry, semiquinones, acids and bases and particularly theoretical and experimental studies on the chemistry of isotopes. *Address:* 461 Graduate Chemistry Building, State University of New York, Stony Brook, NY 11794; PO Box 217, St James, NY 11780, USA. *Telephone:* (631) 632-7905 (Office); (631) 584-5482 (Home). *Fax:* (631) 632-7960. *E-mail:* jbigeleisen@notes.cc.sunyst.edu (Office).

BIGELOW, Kathryn; American film director; b. 1952, San Carlos; m. James Cameron (q.v.) 1989 (divorced 1991); ed San Francisco Art Inst. and Columbia Univ., New York; worked with Art and Language performance group, UK; awarded scholarship to Ind. Study Program, Whitney Museum, New York. *Films include:* Set Up (short), The Loveless 1982, Near Dark 1987, Blue Steel 1990, Point Break 1991, Strange Days 1995, Weight of Water 2000, K-19: The Widowmaker 2002. *Address:* c/o Ken Stovitz, CAA, 9830 Wilshire Boulevard, Beverly Hills, CA 90210, USA (Office).

BIGGAM, Sir Robin Adair, Kt; British business executive and chartered accountant; b. 8 July 1938, Carluke; s. of Thomas Biggam and Eileen Biggam; m. Elizabeth McArthur (née McDougall) Biggam 1962; one s. two d.; ed Lanark Grammar School; CA Peat Marwick Mitchell 1960–63, ICL 1964–81; ICL Finance Dir 1981–84; Exec. Dir Dunlop 1984–85; Chair. Cadcentre Ltd 1983–86; Non Exec. Dir Chloride Group PLC 1985–87, Lloyds Abbey Life PLC (fmrly Abbey Life Group) 1985–90, Redland Group PLC 1991–97, British Aerospace PLC 1994–; Man. Dir BICC PLC 1986–87, CEO 1987–91, Deputy Chair. 1991–, Chair. 1992–96; Dir Fairey Group PLC 1995– (Chair. 1996–2001); Chair. Ind. TV Comm. 1997–; Dir (non-exec.) British Energy 1996– (Deputy Chair. 2001–); Chair. Macquarie European Infrastructure 2000–; Chancellor Univ. of Luton 2001–. *Leisure interests:* golf, gardening, swimming, watching TV, fishing. *Address:* Independent Television Commission, 33 Foley Street, London, W1P 7LB, England.

BIGGS, Barton Michael, MBA; American executive; b. 26 Nov. 1932, New York; s. of William Richardson and Georgene Biggs; m. Judith Anne Lund 1959; one s. two d.; ed Yale and New York Univs; First Lt US Marine Corps 1955–59; research analyst E. M. Hutton & Co. 1961–65, Asst to Chair. 1962–65, partner 1965; co-f. Fairfield Partners 1965, Man. Partner 1965–73; partner and Man. Dir Morgan Stanley & Co. 1973–, Man. Research Dept 1973–79, 1991–93; Chair. and CEO Morgan Stanley Asset Man. Co. 1980–, mem. Man. Cttee 1987–; mem. Exec. Cttee Bd Dirs 1991–; Chair. Morgan Stanley Funds; Dir Rand McNally & Co. *Address:* Morgan Stanley Dean

Whitter Investment Management, Room 311, 1221 Avenue of the Americas, 22nd Floor, New York, NY 10020, USA. *E-mail:* barton.biggs@msdw.com (Office).

BIGGS, Peter Martin, CBE, DSc, FRCVS, FRCPath, CBiol, FIBiol, FMedSci, FRS; British veterinary scientist; b. 13 Aug. 1926, Petersfield; s. of Ronald and Cecile (née Player) Biggs; m. Alison Janet Molteno 1950; two s. one d.; ed Bedales School, Petersfield, Cambridge School, Mass., Royal Veterinary Coll., London, Univ. of Bristol; with RAF 1944–48; with Royal Veterinary Coll., London 1948–53; Research Asst, Dept of Veterinary Anatomy, Univ. of Bristol 1953–55; Lecturer in Veterinary Clinical Pathology, Dept of Veterinary Medicine 1955–59; Prin. Scientific Officer, Houghton Poultry Research Station 1959–66, Sr Prin. Scientific Officer 1966–1971, Deputy Dir 1971–74, Dir 1974–86; Dir Inst. for Animal Health 1986–88; Chief Scientific Officer 1981–88; Visiting Prof. of Veterinary Microbiology, Royal Veterinary Coll. London 1982–; Andrew D. White Prof.-at-Large, Cornell Univ., USA 1988–94; Vice-Pres. British Veterinary Asscn 1996–98; Fellow Inst. of Biology 1973, Pres. 1990–92; Fellow Royal Coll. of Pathologists 1978, Royal Coll. of Veterinary Surgeons 1979, Royal Veterinary Coll. 1983; Hon. Fellow Royal Agricultural Soc. of England 1986; Hon. Dr of Veterinary Medicine (Ludwig-Maximilians Univ., Munich), Dr hc (Univ. of Liège) and numerous others; Wolf Foundation Prize in Agric. 1989; Dalrymple-Champneys Cup and Medal of the British Veterinary Asscn 1973, Chiron Award, British Veterinary Asscn 1999. *Publications:* more than 100 scientific papers. *Leisure interests:* music making, natural history. *Address:* 'Willows', London Road, St Ives, PE27 5ES, England. *Telephone:* (1480) 463471. *Fax:* (1480) 463471. *E-mail:* peter.biggs@bigfoot.com (Home).

BIGNONE, Maj.-Gen. Reynaldo Benito; Argentine politician and army officer; b. 21 Jan. 1928, Morón; m. Nilda Raquel Belen; three c.; ed Nat. Mil. Acad., Superior War Coll.; Capt. 1954; Commdr Cadet Corps, Nat. Mil. Acad. 1970; Sec. to Army High Command 1973; Deputy Commdr, later Commdr Nat. Mil. Insts. 1980–81; fmr Dir Nat. Mil. Acad. and Sec.-Gen. of Army; retd from active service Dec. 1981; Pres. of Argentina 1982–83; arrested Jan. 1984, released June 1984; arrested on charge of serious human rights abuses Jan. 1999, placed under perm. house arrest.

BIGOT, Charles André Marie; French aviation engineer; b. 29 July 1932, Angers; s. of Charles Bigot and Marcelle Pousset; m. Marie-Odile Lambert 1959; one s. three d.; ed Ecole Sainte-Geneviève, Versailles, Ecole Nat. Supérieure de l'Aéronautique, Ecole Polytechnique and Cranfield Coll. of Aeronautics, Centre de Perfectionnement Affaires; aeronautical Eng 1957–61; Tech. Dir of Aeronautical Services, Ministry of Aeronautics, CNRS 1961–63; Dir of launch vehicle div., Centre Nat. des Etudes Spatiales (CNES) 1963–70; Deputy Dir Centre Spatial de Brétigny 1970–71; Dir of Devt Air Inter 1971–75; Soc. d'Etudes et de Réalisations Industrielles (Seri-Renault Eng), Dir-Gen. 1975–80; Commercial Dir Soc. Nat. Industrielle Aérospatiale (Snias) 1980–82; Dir-Gen. Arianespace 1982–90, Pres.-Dir-Gen. 1990–98, Hon. Chair. 1998–; mem. Int. Acad. of Astronautics, Acad. Nat. de l'Air et de l'Espace; Chevalier, Légion d'honneur, Commdr, Ordre Nat. du Mérite, Médaille de Vermeil (CNES). *Address:* Arianespace, Bd de l'Europe, BP 117, 91006 Evry cedex; 16 rue de la Chancellerie, 78000 Versailles, France. *Telephone:* 1-39-20-01-45.

BÍLÁ, Lucie (Hana Zaňáková); Czech singer; b. 7 April 1966, Otvovice; d. of Josef Zaňák; pnr Petr Kratochvíl (separated 2000); one s.; m. Stanislav Penk 2002; co-owner Theatre Ta Fantastika, Prague; has toured throughout W Europe; has performed in charity concerts in Czech Repub.; numerous awards including Czech Grammy Prize 1992–96, Most Popular Singer (Czech Repub.) 1994–97, Czech Musical Acad. Prize 1997, Czech Nightingale Trophy 1996, 1997, 1998, 1999, 2000, 2001, 2002. *Albums:* Missariel 1993, Lucie Bílá 1994, Binoculars 1995, Stars as Stars 1998. *Theatre includes:* Les Misérables 1992, Dracula 1995, Rat-Catcher 1996, Joan of Arc (Thalia Prize) 2000. *Film:* King Ubu. *Publication:* Nyní již to vim (Now I Know it Already) 1999. *Leisure interest:* family. *Address:* Theatre Ta Fantastika, Karlova ul. 8, 110 00 Prague 1, Czech Republic. *Telephone:* (2) 24-23-25-32; (2) 24-23-27-11.

BILALI, Mohamed Gharib; Tanzanian politician; fmr Govt official; Chief Minister Supreme Revolutionary Council of Zanzibar 1995–2001; mem. C.C.M. (Party for Democracy and Progress). *Address:* c/o Office of the Chief Minister, Supreme Revolutionary Council of Zanzibar, Zanzibar, Tanzania.

BILBY, Bruce Alexander, PhD, FRS; British professor of theory of materials and consultant; b. 3 Sept. 1922, London; s. of the late George Alexander Bilby and Dorothy Jean Bilby (née Telfer); m. 1st Hazel Joyce Casken 1946 (divorced 1964); two s. one d.; m. 2nd Lorette Wendela Thomas 1966; two s.; ed Dover Grammar School, Peterhouse, Cambridge, Univ. of Birmingham; Admiralty 1943–46; Research, Birmingham 1948–51; Royal Soc. Sorby Research Fellow, Univ. of Sheffield 1951–57, J. H. Andrew Research Fellow 1957–58, Reader in Theoretical Metallurgy 1958–62, Prof. of Theoretical Metallurgy 1962–66, Prof. of the Theory of Materials 1966–84, Prof. Emer. 1984–; Rosenhain Medal 1963, Griffith Medal 1994. *Publications:* scientific papers in learned journals. *Leisure interest:* sailing. *Address:* Department of Engineering Materials, University of Sheffield, Mappin Street, Sheffield, S1 3JD (Office); 32 Devonshire Road, Totley, Sheffield, S17 3NT, England (Home). *Telephone:* (114) 222-7713 (Office); (114) 236-1086 (Home). *E-mail:* B.Bilby@sheffield.ac.uk (Office). *Website:* www.shef.ac.uk/materials (Office).

BILDT, Carl; Swedish politician; b. 15 July 1949; m. Mia Bohman 1984; one s. one d.; ed Univ. of Stockholm; Chair. Confed. of Liberal and Conservative Students 1973–74, European Democrat Students 1974–76; mem. Stockholm County Council 1974–77; Political Advisor on Policy Co-ordination Ministry of Econ. Affairs 1976–78; Under-Sec. of State for Co-ordination and Planning at the Cabinet Office 1979–81; MP 1979–2001; mem. Exec. Cttee Moderate Party 1981–, Leader 1986–99; mem. Advisory Council on Foreign Affairs 1982–99; mem. Submarine Defence Comm. 1982–83; mem. 1984 Defence Policy Comm. 1984–87; Prime Minister of Sweden 1991–94; EU Peace Envoy in fmr Yugoslavia 1995; High Rep. of the Int. Community in Bosnia and Herzegovina 1995–97; mem. Int. Inst. for Strategic Studies, London; Vice-Chair. Int. Democrat Union (IDU) 1989–92, Chair. 1992–99; Special Envoy of Sec.-Gen. of the UN to the Balkans 1999–2001; Chair. At-Large-Membership Study Cttee. Internet Corpn for Assigned Names and Numbers (ICANN) 2001–02. *Publications:* Landet som steg ut i kylan 1972, Framtid i frihet 1976, Hallanning, svensk, europe 1991, Peace Journey 1999. *E-mail:* carl@bildt.net. *Website:* www.bildt.net.

BILE, Pastor Micha Ondo, MSc; Equatorial Guinean diplomatist and mining engineer; b. 2 Dec. 1952, Nsinik-Esawong; m.; six c.; ed Inst. of Mining, Krivoi-Rog Univ.; engineer, Mines and Quarries Section, Dept of Mines and Hydrocarbons, Ministry of Mines and Energy 1982, Chief of Section 1983–84, Dir.-Gen. Dept 1984–94, Sec.-Gen. Ministry 1994–95; Perm. Rep. to UN 1995–2001; Kt (Second Class), Order of Independence. *Address:* c/o Ministry of Foreign Affairs, International Co-operation and Francophone Affairs, Malabo, Equatorial Guinea (Office).

BILLAUD, Bernard; French civil servant; b. 3 Sept. 1942, Béziers; s. of Bernaud Billaud and Raymonde Mazet; m. Claude Devitry 1967; two s. one d.; ed Inst. d'études politiques de Paris and Ecole nat. d'admin; Auditor 1968, Public Auditor Cour des Comptes 1976, Conseiller maître 1989; Adviser to French Embassy, Holy See 1974–76; Official Rep. to the Prime Minister 1976; Sr Lecturer Inst. d'études politiques de Paris 1977–92; Dir of Staff, Mayor of Paris 1979–83; mem. comm. Vieux Paris 1983–; Pres. comm. on historical works of Ville de Paris 1983–; Dir-Gen. Int. Relations, Paris 1983–84; Gen. Commr of the French Language 1987–89; Prime Minister's Rep. of Admin. Council of AFP 1993–98, France 3 1995–98; Vice-Pres. organizing Cttee for 'de la Gaule à la France' 1996; Chevalier, Légion d'honneur, Officier, Ordre nat. du Mérite, Grand Croix Ordre de Saint-Grégoire-le-Grand. *Publications:* L'Aide de l'etat à l'enseignement privé 1966, Georges Bidault – Les éditoriaux de "l'aube" (1938–1940) 2001. *Leisure interest:* history. *Address:* Cour des comptes, 13 rue Cambon, 75001, Paris (Office); 12 rue des Jardins Saint Paul, 75004 Paris, France (Home). *Telephone:* 1-42-98-99-10 (Office); 1-48-87-91-68 (Home).

BILLESKOV-JANSEN, Frederik Julius, DPhil; Danish professor; b. 30 Sept. 1907, Hvidbjerg; s. of Hans Billeskov-Jansen and Bothilde Schack-Schou; m. Vibeke Collet Henrichsen 1938; one s. two d.; ed Københavns Universitet; Asst lecturer in Danish, Univ. of Copenhagen 1935–38, Prof. 1941–77; lecturer, Univ. de Paris à la Sorbonne 1938–41; Ed. Orbis Litterarum 1943–50; mem. Emer. Royal Danish Acad. of Sciences and Letters, mem. Int. Asscn of Comparative Literature and of German Language and Literature, mem. Danish Acad., Norvediam Acad.; Pres. Søren Kierkegaard Soc., Alliance Française, Copenhagen; Commdr Order of Dannebrog, Ingenio & Arti, Officier, Légion d'honneur, Officier, Ordre des Palmes académiques. *Publications:* Danmarks Digtekunst I-III 1944–58, Holberg som Epigrammatiker og Essayist 1939, Editions of Holberg: Moralske Tanker 1943, Epistler 1954, Memoirer 1963, Vaerker i tolv Bind 1969–71, Ludvig Holberg 1974; Søren Kierkegaards Litteraere Kunst 1951, Søren Kierkegaards: Vaerker i Udvalg 1950, Poetik (Vols I and II) 1941–48, Den Danske Lyrik 1961–66, Esthétique de l'œuvre d'art littéraire 1948, L'Age d'or de la littérature danoise 1953, Anthology of Danish Literature (French Edn 1964, English Edn 1971, Italian Edn 1973, Dutch Edn 1973, Japanese Edn 1976, German Edn 1978, Portuguese Edn 1981, Spanish Edn 1984), Verdens Litteraturhistorie I-XII (Chief Ed.) 1971–74, Verdenslitteratur 1982, Humanitas Christiana; also articles in Scandinavian and int. reviews. *Address:* Frydendalsvej 20, 1809 Frederiksberg C., Denmark. *Telephone:* 31-31-63-69.

BILLINGTON, James Hadley, PhD; American historian and librarian; b. 1 June 1929, Bryn Mawr, Pa; s. of Nelson Billington and Jane Coolbaugh; m. Marjorie A. Brennan 1957; two s. two d.; ed Princeton Univ. and Univ. of Oxford; army service 1953–56; Instructor in History, Harvard Univ. 1957–58, Fellow, Russian Research Center 1958–59, Asst Prof. of History 1958–61; Assoc. Prof. of History, Princeton Univ. 1962–64, Prof. 1964–73; Dir Woodrow Wilson Int. Center for Scholars, Washington, DC 1973–87; Librarian of Congress, Library of Congress, Washington, DC 1987–; Visiting Research Prof. Inst. of History of USSR Acad. of Sciences 1966–67, Univ. of Helsinki 1960–61, Ecole des Hautes Etudes en Sciences Sociales, Paris 1985, 1988; visiting lecturer to various univs. in Europe and Asia, etc.; Guggenheim Fellow 1960–61; mem. American Acad. of Arts and Sciences, American Philosophical Soc.; Chair. Bd of Foreign Scholarships (Fulbright Program) 1971–73; writer/host The Face of Russia (TV series) 1998; 22 hon. degrees; Chevalier Ordre des Arts et des Lettres, Gwangha Medal (Repub. of Korea), Woodrow Wilson Award 1992, Kt Commdr.'s Cross of the Order of Merit (Germany) 1996, Pushkin Medal 1999, Univ. of Calif. at LA Medal 2000. *Publications:* Mikhailovsky and Russian Populism 1958, The Icon and the Axe: An Interpretive History of Russian Culture 1966, Fire in the Minds of Men: Origins of the Revolutionary Faith 1980, Russia Transformed: Breakthrough to Hope 1992, The Face of Russia 1998; contribs to books and journals. *Address:* Library of Congress, 101 Independence Avenue, Washington, DC 20540-0002, USA. *Telephone:* (202) 707-5205. *Fax:* (202) 707-1714.

BILLINGTON, Kevin, BA, DipMus; British film, theatre and television director; b. 12 June 1934; s. of Richard Billington and Margaret Billington; m. Lady Rachel Mary Pakenham 1967; two s. two d.; ed Bryanston School and Queens' Coll. Cambridge; film dir BBC programme Tonight 1960–63; documentary film dir, BBC 1963–67; freelance film, theatre and TV dir 1967–; Chair. BAFTA 1989–90, 1990–91; Screenwriters' Guild Award 1966, 1967, Guild of TV Producers and Directors Award 1966, 1967. *Feature films:* Interlude 1967, The Rise and Rise of Michael Rimmer 1969, The Light at the Edge of the World 1970, Voices 1974, Reflections 1984. *Scripts:* Looking For Love 1997, Loving Attitudes 1998, Bodily Harm 2000. *Television films:* And No One Can Save Her 1973, Once Upon a Time is Now (documentary) 1978, The Music Will Never Stop (documentary) 1979, Henry VIII 1979, The Jail Diary of Albie Sachs 1980, The Good Soldier 1981, Outside Edge 1982, The Sonnets of William Shakespeare 1984, The Deliberate Death of a Polish Priest 1986, Heartland 1989, A Time to Dance 1991. *Plays directed:* Find Your Way Home 1970, Me 1973, The Birthday Party 1974, The Caretaker 1975, Bloody Neighbours 1974, Emigrés 1976, The Homecoming 1978, Quartermaine's Terms 1982, The Deliberate Death of a Polish Priest 1985, The Philanthropist 1986, The Lover and A Slight Ache (double bill) 1987, The Breadwinner 1989, Veterans' Day 1989, Quartermaine's Terms 1993, Old Times 1994, Six Characters in Search of an Author 1999, Our Country's Good 1999, Victory 2000, Wild Honey 2002. *Leisure interests:* swimming, football (Queen's Park Rangers). *Address:* c/o Judy Daish Associates, 2 St Charles Place, London, W10 6EG, England (Home). *Telephone:* (20) 8964-8811 (Office). *Fax:* (20) 8964-8966 (Office). *E-mail:* kevin.billington@btinternet.com (Office).

BILLINGTON, Michael Keith, BA; British drama critic and author; b. 16 Nov. 1939, Leamington Spa; s. of Alfred R. Billington and Patricia Bradshaw; m. Jeanine Bradlaugh 1977; one d.; ed Warwick School and St Catherine's Coll. Oxford; Public Liaison Officer, Theatre Royal, Lincoln 1962–64; writer on theatre, film and cinema, The Times 1965–71; Drama Critic, The Guardian 1971–, Country Life 1988–; presenter of various BBC Radio arts programmes including Options, Kaleidoscope, Meridian, etc. 1971–91; writer on London arts scene for The New York Times 1984–94; writer and presenter of TV profiles of Peter Hall, Alan Ayckbourn, Peggy Ashcroft 1988–90; IPC Critic of the Year 1974, Theatre Critic of the Year 1993, 1995, 1997. *Publications:* The Modern Actor 1973, Alan Ayckbourn 1983, Tom Stoppard 1987, Peggy Ashcroft 1988, One Night Stands 1993, The Life and Work of Harold Pinter 1996, Stage and Screen Lives (Ed.) 2001. *Leisure interests:* cricket, opera, travel. *Address:* 15 Hearne Road, London, W4 3NJ, England. *Telephone:* (20) 8995-0455. *Fax:* (20) 8742-3496 (Home). *E-mail:* michael.billington@guardian.co.uk (Office).

BIN LADEN, Osama; Saudi Arabian born guerrilla leader; b. Jeddah; s. of the late Mohammad bin Laden; m. five wives including Najua Ghanem; three c.; Amal al-Sadah; one d.; (divorced from one wife); more than 20 c. including two s.; ed King Abudlaziz Univ., Jeddah; funded and joined troops fighting against Soviet Union in Afghanistan 1979; co-f. group to send aid to Afghan resistance and establish recruitment centres mid-1980s; f. org. to support Islamic opposition movements 1988; expelled from Saudi Arabia for anti-Govt activities 1991, Saudi Arabian citizenship removed for 'irresponsible activities' 1994; moved to Sudan 1991, expelled following pressure from USA and UN 1996; continued to support Islamic extremist activities from Afghanistan; as head of the al-Qaida org. believed to have masterminded attacks on World Trade Center, New York and Pentagon, Washington, on 11 Sept. 2001.

BINAISA, Godfrey Lukwongwa, LLB; Ugandan politician and lawyer; b. 30 May 1920, Kampala; ed King's Coll., Budo, Makerere Univ., King's Coll., London, Lincoln's Inn, London; in pvt. legal practice 1956–62, 1967–79; mem. of Uganda Nat. Congress, later of Uganda People's Congress; Attorney-Gen. 1962–67; Pres. Uganda Law Soc., Chair. Law Devt Centre 1968; mem. Uganda Judicial Service Comm. 1970; Chair. Organizing Cttee for Commonwealth Lawyers' Conf., 1972; went into exile; in legal practice in New York; returned to Uganda 1979 after fall of Govt of Pres. Idi Amin Dada (q.v.); Pres. of Uganda 1979–80, also Minister of Foreign Affairs June–July 1979, Minister of Defence; Chancellor, Makerere Univ. 1979–80; under house arrest 1980–81; left Uganda Jan. 1981; went to Britain.

BINCHY, Maeve; Irish writer; b. 28 May 1940, Dublin; d. of William Binchy and Maureen Blackmore; m. Gordon Snell 1977; teacher of History and French, Pembroke School, Dublin 1961–68; columnist, Irish Times 1968–2000; Hon. DLit (Nat. Univ. of Ireland) 1990, (Queen's Belfast) 1998. *Publications:* (short stories) Central Line 1978, Silver Wedding 1979, Victoria Line 1980, Dublin Four 1982, The Lilac Bus 1984; (novels) Light a Penny Candle 1982, London Transports 1983, Echoes 1985, Firefly Summer 1987, Circle of Friends 1990, Copper Beech 1992, The Glass Lake 1994, Evening Class 1996, Tara Road 1999, Scarlet Feather 2000, Quentins 2002. *Address:* Dalkey, Co. Dublin, Ireland.

BINDER, Theodor, MD; physician; b. 1919; ed Hebel-Gymnasium Lörrach, Univs. of Freiburg, Strasbourg and Basel and Swiss Tropical Inst., Basel; Clinic Chief, Swiss Tropical Inst. 1947–48; Public Health Officer, Oxapampa, Peru 1948–50; Staff, Medical School, Nacional Mayor de San Marcos de Lima 1951–56; Founder of Clinic for the Poor and constructor of Hosp. Pucallpa 1956–60, Inauguration Hosp. Amazónico Albert Schweitzer, Yarinacocha,

Pucallpa 1960, Dir 1960–; Founder and Dir Instituto Tropical Amazónico 1963–; Exec. Dir Amazonian Indian Int. Devt, Toronto and New York 1971–. *Publications:* Philosophy: Friedrich Nietzsche 1950, Goethe's Iphigenia and the Ethics 1951, A. Schweitzer as a Philosopher 1954, Heroism as an Attitude towards Life 1956, Personal Ethics in a Depersonalizing Age 1963, Tristes Tropiques or Land of Hope 1968, The Right to an Independent Development in the Third World 1970, Sense and Nonsense of the Christian Mission among Jungle Indians 1970, Problems of Intercultural Relations 1971; Medicine: Congenital Malaria 1950, Treatment of Hypertension 1952, Latin-America: Nonanalytical Psychotherapy 1958, Histoplasmosis in Eastern Peru 1964, Dermatomycosis and Deep Mycosis in Eastern Peru 1965, etc.

BINDING, Günther, DrIng, DPhil; German professor of art and architecture; b. 6 March 1936, Koblenz; s. of Kurt Binding and Margot (née Masur); m. Elisabeth Dietz 1969; one s. two d.; ed gymnasium in Arnsberg and Cologne, Technische Hochschule, Aachen and Univs. of Cologne and Bonn; Dir Lower Rhine section, Rheinisches Landesmuseum, Bonn 1964–70; Prof., Univ. of Cologne 1970–2000, Rector 1981–83, Pro-rector 1983–85; Vice-Pres. W German Rectors' Conf. 1982–84; mem. Sächsische Akademie der Wissenschaften 1999; Ruhrpreis für Kunst und Wissenschaft 1966, Josef-Humar-Preis 1986, Rheinland-Taler 1987. *Publications:* 40 books and 320 articles about European architecture and history of art. *Address:* Wingertsheide 65, 51427 Berg.-Gladbach, Germany. *Telephone:* (2204) 64956.

BINGAMAN, Jeff, JD; American politician and lawyer; b. 3 Oct. 1943, Silver City, NM; s. of Jesse Bingaman and Beth Ball; m. Ann Kovacovich 1968; one s.; ed Harvard and Stanford Univs; admitted to NM Bar 1968; partner Campbell, Bingaman & Black, Santa Fe 1972–78; Attorney-Gen., NM 1979–82; Senator from New Mexico Jan. 1983–; Chair. Energy Cttee 2001; Democrat. *Address:* US Senate, 703 Hart Senate Building, Washington, DC 20510-0001 (Office); PO Box 5775 Santa Fe, NM 87502-5775, USA (Home).

BINGHAM, John, CBE, FRS; British scientist; b. 19 June 1930; s. of Thomas Frederick Bingham and Emma Maud Lusher; m. Jadwiga Anna Siedlecka 1983; one s.; mem. staff Plant Breeding Inst. of Cambridge (subsequently Plant Breeding Int. Cambridge Ltd) 1954–86, Deputy Chief Scientific Officer 1981–91; research in plant breeding, culminating in production of improved winter wheat varieties for British agric.; Pres. Royal Norfolk Agric. Asscn 1991; Hon. Fellow Royal Agric. Soc. of England 1983; Mullard Medal of Royal Soc. 1975, Royal Agric. Soc. of England Research Medal 1975, Massey Ferguson Nat. Award for Services to UK Agric. 1984. *Leisure interests:* farming and wildlife conservation. *Address:* Hereward Barn, Church Lane, Mattishall Burgh, Dereham, Norfolk, NR20 3QZ, England. *Telephone:* (1362) 858354.

BINGHAM OF CORNHILL, Baron (Life Peer) cr. 1996, of Boughrood in the County of Powys; **Thomas (Henry) Bingham,** Kt, PC, MA; British judge; b. 13 Oct. 1933; s. of the late Dr. T. H. Bingham and Dr. C. Bingham; m. Elizabeth Loxley 1963; two s. one d.; ed Sedbergh School, Balliol Coll. Oxford; called to Bar, Gray's Inn 1959, Bencher 1979; Standing Jr Counsel to Dept of Employment 1968–72; QC 1972; Recorder of Crown Court 1975–80; Judge, High Court of Justice, Queen's Bench Div. and Judge, Commercial Court 1980–86; a Lord Justice of Appeal 1986–92; Master of the Rolls 1992–96; Lord Chief Justice of England and Wales 1996–2000; Sr Law Lord June 2000–; Leader, Investigation into supply of petroleum and petroleum products to Rhodesia 1977–78; mem. Lord Chancellor's Law Reform Cttee, Inquiry into the Supervision of BCCI 1991–92; Commr Interception of Communications 1985, 1992–94; Chair. numerous other comms.; Special Trustee St Mary's Hosp. 1985–92 (Chair. 1988–92). *Publications:* Chitty on Contracts (Asst Ed.) (22nd Edn 1961), The Business of Judging 2000. *Address:* House of Lords, Westminster, London, SW1, England.

BINMORE, Kenneth George, CBE, PhD, FBA; British professor of economics; b. 27 Sept. 1940, London; s. of Ernest Binmore and Maud Binmore (née Holland); m. Josephine Ann Lee 1972; two s. two d.; ed Imperial Coll., London Univ.; Prof. of Mathematics LSE 1974–88; Prof. of Econs, Univ. of Mich. 1988–93, Univ. Coll. London 1991–; Dir Centre for Econ. Learning and Social Evolution 1994–; Fellow Econometric Soc. *Publications include:* Mathematical Analysis 1977, Economics of Bargaining 1986, Playing Fair: Game Theory and the Social Contract I 1994, Just Playing: Game Theory and the Social Contract II 1998. *Leisure interest:* philosophy. *Address:* Department of Economics, University College London, Gower Street, London, WC1E 6BT, England (Office); Newmills, Whitebrook, Monmouth, Gwent, NP5 4TY, Wales (Home). *Telephone:* (20) 7504-5864 (Office). *Fax:* (20) 7916-2774 (Office). *E-mail:* k.binmore@ucl.ac.uk (Office); k.binmore@ucl.ac.uk (Home). *Website:* else.econ.ucl.ac.uk/people/binmore.htm (Office).

BINNIG, Gerd; German physicist; b. 20 July 1947, Frankfurt am Main; m. Lore Wagler 1969; one s. one d.; ed Univ. of Frankfurt; mem. Physics group, IBM Zürich Research Lab. Rüschlikon 1978–, Group Leader 1984–; Assignment to IBM Almaden Research Centre, San José, collaboration with Stanford Univ., Calif. 1985–86, 1987; IBM Fellow 1986; Visiting Prof. Stanford Univ. 1986–; Hon. Prof. (Univ. of Munich) 1986–; Hon. Fellow (Royal Microscopical Soc.) 1988; Foreign Assoc. mem. Acad. of Sciences, Wash. 1987; mem. IBM Acad. 1989, Bd Mercedes Automobil Holding AG 1989–93, Bd Daimler Benz Holding 1990–; shared Nobel Prize for Physics (with E Ruska and H. Rohrer) 1986, Physics prize of German Physical Soc. 1982, Otto Klung Prize 1983, shared King Faisal Int. Prize for Physics and Hewlett Packard Europhysics Prize 1984, Eliot Cresson Medal (Franklin Inst., Phila) 1987; DSM,

OM (Fed. Repub. Germany) 1987; Minnie Rosen award (Ross Univ., NY) 1988, Bayerischer Verdienstorden 1992. *Leisure interests:* music, sports. *Address:* Zurich IBM Research Laboratory, Säumer Strasse 4, CH-8803 Rüschlikon, Switzerland. *Telephone:* (1) 7248111.

BINNS, Malcolm, ARCM; British concert pianist; b. 29 Jan. 1936, Nottingham; s. of Douglas Priestley Binns and May Walker; ed Bradford Grammar School, Royal Coll. of Music; soloist with maj. British orchestras 1960–; toured with Scottish Nat. Orchestra and Limbourg Orchestra 1987–88; regular performer at the Promenade Concerts 1962–; more than 30 recordings, including Balakirev Piano Concertos 1 and 2 and Rimsky-Korsakov Piano Concerto (English Northern Philharmonia) 1992; concerts at Aldeburgh, Leeds, Three Choirs and Canterbury Festivals; performances are regularly broadcast on BBC; Chappell Medal 1956, Medal of Worshipful Co. of Musicians 1956. *Leisure interests:* gardening, collecting antique gramophone records. *Address:* 233 Court Road, Orpington, Kent, BR6 9BY, England. *Telephone:* (1689) 831056.

BINOCHE, Juliette; French actress; b. 9 March 1964, Paris; d. of Jean-Marie Binoche and Monique Stalens; one s. by André Halle; ed Nat. Conservatory of Drama and private theatrical studies. *Films include:* Les nanas, La vie de famille, Rouge Baiser, Rendez-Vous, Mon beau-frère a tué ma soeur, Mauvais Sang, Un tour de manège, Les amants du Pont-Neuf, The Unbearable Lightness of Being, Wuthering Heights 1992, Damage 1992, Trois Couleurs: Bleu 1993, Le Hussard sur le Toit 1995, The English Patient (Acad. Award for Best Supporting Actress 1996, Berlin Film Festival Award 1996, BAFTA Award 1997), Alice et Martin 1999, Les Enfants du Siècle 1999, La Veuve de Saint-Pierre 2000, Chocolat 2001, Code Unknown 2001, Décalage horaire 2002. *Play:* Naked (Almeida, London) 1998. *Address:* c/o UTA, 9560 Wilshire Boulevard, Floor 5, Beverly Hills, CA 90212, USA.

BIO, Brig.-Gen. Julius Maada; Sierra Leonean army officer; fmr Vice-Chair. Supreme Council of State; Chair. Sierra Leone Nat. Provisional Ruling Council Jan.–June 1996.

BIOKE MALABO, Capt. Cristino Seriche; Equatorial Guinean politician and army officer; Second Vice-Pres. and Minister of Health 1981–82; Prime Minister of Equatorial Guinea 1982–91; Minister of Govt Co-ordination, Planning, Economic Devt and Finance 1982–86, of Health 1986, now in Charge of Political and Admin. Co-ordination. *Address:* c/o Oficina del Primer Ministro, Malabo, Equatorial Guinea.

BIONDI, Alfredo; Italian politician and lawyer; b. 29 June 1928, Pisa; m. Giovanna Susak; two c.; fmr mem. Liberal Party (PLI), Nat. Sec. 1985–86; PLI Deputy 1968–92; Unione di Centro (Libertà) Deputy 1992–94, Forza Italia Deputy March 1994–; Minister of Justice 1994–95. *Address:* Via dell'Umiltà 36, 00187 Rome, Italy (Office). *Telephone:* (06) 67311 (Office). *Fax:* (06) 6788255 (Office). *E-mail:* lettere@forza-italia.it (Office). *Website:* www .forza-italia.it (Office).

BIONDI, Frank J., Jr., MBA; American business executive; b. 9 Jan. 1945, New York; s. of Frank Biondi and Virginia Willis; m. Carol Oughton 1974; two d.; ed Princeton and Harvard Univs.; Assoc. corporate finance, Prudential Securities, New York 1969, Shearson-Lehman Inc. New York 1970–71; Prin. Frank Biondi & Assocs. New York 1972; Dir business analysis, Teleprompter Corpn New York 1972–73; Asst Treas., Assoc. Dir Business Affairs, Children's TV Workshop, New York 1974–78; Dir Entertainment Planning, HBO, New York 1978, Vice-Pres. programming operations 1979–82, Exec. Vice-Pres. Planning and Admin. 1982–83, Pres. and CEO 1983, Chair. and CEO 1984; Exec. Vice-Pres. entertainment business sector, The Coca-Cola Co. 1985; Chair. and CEO Coca-Cola TV 1986; Pres., CEO and Dir Viacom Int. Inc. New York 1987–96; Pres., CEO and Dir Viacom Inc. 1987–96; Chair., CEO Universal Studios Inc. 1996–98; Dir Seagram 1996–; Pres. Biondi Reiss Capital Man., New York 1998–; Man. Dir Waterview Advisors. *Address:* Biondi Reiss Capital Management 1114 Avenue of the Americas, New York, NY 10036 (Office); Waterview Advisors, 2425 Olympic Boulevard, Suite 4050, West Santa Monica, CA 90404, USA.

BIONDI, Matt, MA; American swimmer; b. 8 Oct. 1965, Moraga, Calif.; m. Kirsten Biondi 1995; one s.; ed Berkeley Univ., Lewis & Clarke Coll.; mem. USA Water Polo Team, then became freestyle swimmer; career highlights: Olympic Games – 50m freestyle 1st (1988), 2nd (1992); 100m freestyle 1st (1988); 200m freestyle 3rd (1988); 100m butterfly 2nd (1988); 4x100m freestyle 1st (1984, 1988, 1992); 4x200m freestyle 1st (1988); 400m medley 1st (1988, 1992); World Championships – 100m freestyle 1st (1986, 1991); world records: 50m freestyle 22.14 (Seoul 1988), 100m freestyle 48.42 (Austin 1988), 400m medley 3:34.84 (Atlanta 1996), 4x100m freestyle 3:16.53 (Seoul 1988); spokesman Olympic Movt; mem. Int. Hall of Fame Selection Cttee; now a successful motivational speaker; Int. Swimming Hall of Fame 1997, World Swimmer of the Year 1998. *Address:* USA Swimming, 1 Olympic Plaza, Colorado Springs, CO 80909, USA (Office).

BIRCH, Sir Bill, G.N.Z.M.; New Zealand politician; b. 1934, Hastings; m.; four c.; qualified as surveyor; served six years as Deputy Mayor of Pukekohe; Nat. Party MP 1972–; apptd. Jr Opposition Whip 1974–75, Sr Govt Whip 1975; successively, Minister of Energy, of Regional Devt, of Nat. Devt and of Science and Tech. 1978–84; Opposition Leader of House 1985–90; Minister of Labour and Immigration 1990–93, also of Employment 1991–93; Minister of Health 1993–94, of Finance (including Responsibility for the Govt Superannuation

Fund) and of Revenue and Minister responsible for Ministerial Services and for the Govt Legislation Programme 1994–99, Treas. 1998–99. *Address:* 188 Kitchener Road, Pukekohe, New Zealand (Home).

BIRCH, Bryan John, PhD, FRS; British mathematician; b. 25 Sept. 1931, Burton-on-Trent; s. of Arthur Jack Birch and Mary Edith Birch; m. Gina Margaret Christ 1961; two s. one d.; ed Shrewsbury School and Trinity Coll., Cambridge; Research Fellow, Trinity Coll. 1956–60; Harkness Fellow, Princeton 1957–58; Fellow, Churchill Coll., Cambridge Univ. 1960–62; Sr Lecturer, later Reader, Univ. of Manchester 1962–65; Reader in Math., Oxford Univ. 1966–85, Prof. of Arithmetic 1985–98, Prof. Emer. 1998–, Fellow of Brasenose Coll. 1966–98, Emer. Fellow 1998–; Del. of Oxford Univ. Press 1988–98; Ed. Proc. London Math. Soc. 2001–. *Publications:* scholarly articles, particularly on number theory. *Leisure interests:* theoretical gardening, listening to music, watching marmots. *Address:* Mathematical Institute, Office S2, 24–29 St Giles, Oxford, OX1 3LB (Office); Green Cottage, Boars Hill, Oxford, OX1 5DQ, England (Home). *Telephone:* (1865) 273550 (Office); (1865) 735367 (Home). *Fax:* (1865) 273583 (Office); (1865) 730687 (Home). *E-mail:* birch@maths.ox.ac.uk (Office); bryan.birch@which.net (Home). *Website:* www.maths.ox.ac.uk (Office).

BIRCH, L. Charles, BAgrSc, DSc; Australian academic; b. 8 Feb. 1918, Melbourne; s. of Harry Milton Birch and Honoria Eleanor Hogan; ed Scotch Coll., Melbourne, Univs. of Melbourne and Adelaide; Research Fellow, Waite Agricultural Research Inst., Adelaide 1939–46; Sr Overseas Research Scholar, Zoology Dept, Univ. of Chicago, USA 1946, Oxford Univ., UK 1947; Sr Lecturer in Zoology, Univ. of Sydney 1948–54, Reader in Zoology 1954–60, Challis Prof. of Biology 1960–83, Prof. Emer. 1984–; Fulbright Research Scholar, Zoology Dept, Columbia Univ., New York 1954; Visiting Prof. Univ. of Minn. 1958; Visiting Prof. of Genetics, Univ. of Calif., Berkeley 1967; Fellow Australian Acad. of Science; mem. Club of Rome; David Syme Prize, Univ. of Melbourne 1954, Eminent Ecologist Award, Ecological Soc. America 1988, Gold Medal, Ecological Soc. Australia 1988, Templeton Prize 1990. *Publications:* Nature and God 1965, Confronting the Future 1976; (Co-author) The Distribution and Abundance of Animals 1954, Genetics and the Quality of Life 1975, The Liberation of Life 1981, The Ecological Web 1984, On Purpose 1990, Liberating Life 1990, Regaining Compassion 1993, Feelings 1995, Living with the Animals 1997, Biology and the Riddle of Life 1999. *Leisure interests:* surfing, music (organ). *Address:* 5A/73 Yarranabbe Road, Darling Point, NSW 2027, Australia. *Telephone:* (2) 9362-3788. *Fax:* (2) 9362-3551 (Home).

BIRCH, Peter Gibbs, CBE; British business executive; b. 4 Dec. 1937; m. Gillian Benge 1962; three s. one d.; ed Allhallows School, Devon; served Royal West Kent Reg. 1957–58; with Nestlé Co. 1958–65; Sales Man. Gillette 1965, Gen. Sales Man. Gillette Australia 1969, Man. Dir Gillette NZ 1971, Gen. Man. Gillette SE Asia 1973, Group Gen. Man. Gillette, Africa, Middle East, Eastern Europe 1975, Man. Dir Gillette UK 1981; Dir Abbey Nat. (fmrly Abbey Nat. Bldg Soc.) 1984–98; Chief Exec. 1984–88, Chief Exec. Abbey Nat. PLC 1988–98; Dir Hoskyns Group 1988–93, Argos 1990–98, Scottish Mutual 1992–98, Dalgety 1993–98, N. M. Rothschild and Sons 1998–, Sainsbury's Bank PLC 2002–; Sr Dir (non-exec.) Trinity Mirror PLC 1999–; Dir (non-exec) Travelex 1999–; mem. Bd Land Securities PLC 1997– (Chair. 1998–), Dah Sing Financial Holdings 1997–; Chair. Trinity PLC 1998–99, Legal Services Comm. 2000–, Kensington Group PLC 2000–, UCTX Ltd 2001; Chair. Council of Mortgage Lenders 1991–92; Pres. Middx Assocn of Boys' Clubs 1988–. *Leisure interests:* active holidays, swimming. *Address:* N. M. Rothschild and Sons, New Court, St Swithin's Lane, London, EC4P 4DU, England. *Telephone:* (20) 7280-5000.

BIRD, Adrian Peter, PhD, FRS, FRSE, FMedSci; British professor of genetics; b. 3 July 1947; s. of Kenneth George Bird and Aileen Mary Bird; m. 1st 1976; one s. one d.; m. 2nd Catherine Mary Abbott 1993; one s. one d.; ed Univ. of Sussex, Univ. of Edin.; Damon Runyon Fellow, Yale 1972–73; Postdoctoral Fellowship, Univ. of Zurich 1974–87, Medical Research Council, Edin.; mem. scientific staff Mammalian Genome Unit ; Sr Scientist Inst. for Molecular Pathology, Vienna 1988–90; Buchanan Prof. of Genetics, Edin. Univ. 1990–; Dir Wellcome Trust Centre for Cell Biology, Edin. Univ. 1999–; Gov. Wellcome Trust 2000–; Louis Jeantet Prize for Medical Research 1999; Gabor Medal, Royal Soc. 1999. *Publications:* numerous papers in scientific journals. *Address:* Wellcome Trust Centre for Cell Biology, University of Edinburgh, King's Buildings, Mayfield Road, Edinburgh, EH9 3JR, Scotland (Office). *Telephone:* (131) 650-5670 (Office). *Fax:* (131) 650-5379 (Office). *E-mail:* a.bird@ed.ac.uk (Office).

BIRD, Harold Dennis 'Dickie', MBE; British international umpire and cricketer (retd); b. 19 April 1933, Barnsley, Yorks.; s. of James Harold Bird and the late Ethel Bird (née Smith); ed Raley Secondary Modern School, Barnsley; right-hand batsman and right-arm medium-fast bowler; teams: Yorks. 1956–59, Leicestershire 1960–64; scored 3,314 runs (average 20.71) with 2 hundreds; highest first-class score 181 not out 1959; First-Class Umpire 1970–98; umpired 66 Test matches (world record 1973–96) and 69 limited-overs internationals (1973–95), including 1975, 1979, 1983 and 1987–88 World Cups (officiating in the first 3 finals) and seven Sharjah tournaments; served on Int. Umpires Panel 1994–96; Hon. Life mem. Yorks. Co. Cricket Club, Leics. Co. Cricket Club, MCC; Hon. Freeman Borough of Barnsley 2000; Dr hc (Sheffield Hallam) 1995; Hon. LLD (Leeds) 1996; voted Yorks. Personality of the Year 1977, Carlsberg-Tetley Yorkshireman of the

Year 1996, People of the Year Award 1996, Radar Abbey Nat. 1996, Special Sporting Award, Variety Club of GB 1997, Lifelong Achievement Award 1998, The Barnsley Millennium Award of Merit for outstanding services to the community and to cricket and in particular for the promotion of the image and civic pride of the borough 2000. *Radio:* Down Your Way with Brian Johnston 1975, Desert Island Discs with Sue Lawley 1996. *Television appearances include:* The Terry Wogan Show 1988, This is Your Life 1992, A Question of Sport (four times) 1999, The Clive Anderson Show 1998, Through the Keyhole, Breakfast with Frost and Songs of Praise. *Publications:* Not Out 1978, That's Out 1985, From the Pavilion End, Dickie Bird, My Autobiography 1997, White Cap and Bails (best-selling sports autobiog. in history) 1999, Dickie Bird's Britain 2002. *Leisure interest:* watching football. *Address:* White Rose Cottage, 40 Paddock Road, Staincross, Barnsley, Yorks. S75 6LE, England. *Telephone:* (1226) 384491 (Home).

BIRD, Lester Bryant, BA; Antiguan politician; b. 21 Feb. 1938; m.; one s. four d.; ed Antigua Grammar School, Univ. of Michigan and Gray's Inn, London; lawyer in pvt. practice 1969–76; Chair. Antigua Labour Party (ALP) 1971–; Senator, Upper House of Parl. and Leader of Opposition in Senate 1971–76; mem. Parl. 1976–; Deputy Premier and Minister of Econ. Devt, Tourism and Energy 1976–81; Deputy Prime Minister and Minister of Foreign Affairs, Econ. Devt, Tourism and Energy 1981–91; Minister of External Affairs, Planning and Trade 1991–94; Prime Minister of Antigua and Barbuda 1994– and Minister of External Affairs, Planning, Social Services and Information 1994, of Communications, Civil Aviation and Int. Transport 1996–98, of Foreign Affairs, Social Services, Civil Aviation and Int. Transport and Information 1998–99, of Foreign Affairs, Caribbean Community Affairs, Defence and Security and Merchant Shipping 1999–2001, of Justice and Legal Affairs 2001–; del. to numerous Caribbean and int. confs. *Address:* Office of the Prime Minister, Factory Road, St John's, Antigua, West Indies (Office). *Telephone:* 462-4956 (Office).

BIRGENEAU, Robert J., BSc, PhD, FRS, FInstP, FAAS, FRSC; Canadian professor of physics and university president; b. 25 March 1942, Toronto; m. Mary Catherine Birgeneau; ed Univ. of Toronto and Yale Univ., USA; instructor Yale Univ. 1966–67; Nat. Research Council of Canada Post-doctoral Fellow, Oxford Univ., UK 1967–68; mem. tech. staff, Bell Laboratories 1968–74, Research Head, Scattering and Low Energy Physics 1975; Prof. of Physics MIT 1975–82, Cecil and Ida Green Prof. of Physics 1982–2000, Assoc. Dir, Research Lab. of Electronics 1983–86, Head, Condensed Matter, Atomic and Plasma Physics 1987–88, Head, Dept of Physics 1988–91; Dean of Science Univ. of Toronto 1991–2000, Pres. Univ. of Toronto 2000–; Fellow American Physical Soc. (APS), American Acad. of Arts and Sciences 1987; Yale Science and Eng Alumni Achievement Award 1981, Wilbur Lucius Cross Medal, Yale Univ. 1986, Oliver E. Buckley Prize for Condensed Matter Physics, APS 1987, Bertram Eugene Warren Award, ACA 1988, DOE Materials Science Outstanding Accomplishment Award 1988, Int. Union of Pure and Applied Physics (IUPAP) Magnetism Award 1997, J.E. Lilienfeld Award, APS 2000. *Address:* Office of the President, University of Toronto, Room 206, 27 King's College Circle, Toronto, Ont. M5S 1A1 (Office); 93 Highland Avenue, Toronto, Ont. M4W 2A4, Canada (Home). *Telephone:* (416) 978-2121 (Office). *Fax:* (416) 971-1360 (Office). *E-mail:* president@utoronto.ca (Office). *Website:* www.utoronto.ca (Office).

BIRIDO, Omer Yousif, MA; Sudanese diplomatist; b. 1939; m. 1966; five c.; ed Univ. of Khartoum and Delhi Univ., India; Third Sec., Sudan Embassy, New Delhi 1963–66, Second Sec., London 1966–69; Deputy Dir, Consular Dept, Ministry of Foreign Affairs 1969–71; Counsellor Sudan Embassy, Kampala 1971–73; Minister Plenipotiary, Perm. Mission of Sudan to the UN, New York 1973–76; Dir Dept of Int. Orgs., Ministry of Foreign Affairs 1976–77, Dir Dept of African Affairs 1977–78; Perm. Rep. to UN, Geneva and Vienna, also mem. Sudan Del. and Rep. to Second Cttee at UN Gen. Ass. 1979–83; Perm. Rep. to UN 1984–86; Amb. to Saudi Arabia 1989–96. *Address:* c/o Ministry of Foreign Affairs, Nasseriya Street, Riyadh 11124, Saudi Arabia.

BIRKAVS, Valdis; Latvian politician; b. 28 July 1942, Riga; s. of Voldemars Birkavs and Veronika Birkavs (née Zihelmane); m. Aina Zileva 1967; one s.; ed Riga Industrial Polytech. School, Univ. of Latvia; expert, Sr researcher, Head of Div. Latvian Research Lab. of Forensic Medicine and Criminology 1969–86; lecturer, Univ. of Latvia 1969–86, Deputy Dean Law Faculty 1986–89; Founder and Pres. Latvian Bar Asscn 1988–; Deputy to Supreme Council of Latvian Repub. from Popular Front of Latvia 1990–93, Deputy Chair. Legis. Cttee, Deputy Chair. Supreme Council of Latvian Repub. 1992–93; Prime Minister of Latvian Repub. 1993–94; Minister of Foreign Affairs 1994–99; Minister of Justice 1999–2000. *Leisure interests:* tennis, yachting, reading, downhill skiing. *Address:* c/o Ministry of Justice, Brīvības blvd 34, Riga 1536, Latvia.

BIRKE, Adolf Mathias, PhD, FRHistS; German professor of modern and contemporary history; b. 12 Oct. 1939, Wellingholzhausen; s. of Matthias Birke and Maria Birke (née Enewoldsen); m. 1st Linde D. Birn 1968, 2nd Sabine Volk 1988; one s. two d.; ed Univ. of Berlin; Prof. of Modern History, Free Univ. of Berlin 1979; Visiting Prof. of German and European Studies, Trinity Coll., Univ. of Toronto, Canada 1980–81; Asst St Antony's Coll., Oxford; Prof. of Modern History, Univ. of Bayreuth 1982–85, Univ. of Munich 1995–2000; Dir German Historical Inst., London 1985–94; Chair. Prince Albert Soc. 1983–95; Cusanuswerk Grant 1962; Heisenberg Fellow 1979; Fed. Cross of Merit 1996. *Publications:* Bischof Ketteler und der deutsche Liberalismus 1971, Pluralismus und Gewerkschaftsautonomie 1978, Britain and Germany 1987, Nation ohne Haus. Deutschland 1945–1961 1989, Prince Albert Studies (Ed.) Vols I–XIII 1983–95, Die Herausforderung des europäischen Staatensystems 1989, Princes, Patronage and the Nobility (ed with R. Asch) 1991, The Quest for Stability (ed. with R. Ahmann and M. Howard) 1992, Control Commission for Germany (British Element) (11 Vols) Inventory (with H. Booms and O. Merker) 1993, Die Bundesrepublik Deutschland. Verfassung, Parlament und Parteien 1997, Deutschland und Grossbritannien 1999, An Anglo-German Dialogue (Jt Ed. with Magnus Brechtken and Alaric Searle) 2000; numerous articles on 19th- and 20th-century German and English history. *Leisure interests:* music, walking. *Address:* Friedenstr. 16, 06114 Halle, Germany.

BIRKERTS, Gunnar, FAIA; Latvian architect; b. 17 Jan. 1925, Riga, Latvia; s. of the late Peter Birkerts and of Merija Shop Birkerts; m. Sylvia Zvirbulis 1950; two s. one d.; ed Technische Hochschule, Stuttgart, Germany; went to USA 1949; est. own practice 1959, Pres. Gunnar Birkerts and Assocs. Inc. 1963–; Prof. of Architecture, Univ. of Mich. 1959–90; numerous guest lectureships USA, Canada, Mexico and Europe; Architect in Residence, American Acad. in Rome 1976; Fellow Latvian Architects' Asscn; mem. Latvian Acad. of Sciences; work exhibited USA, Italy, Brazil, Latvia, Estonia, Yugoslavia; Dr. h.c. (Riga Tech. Univ., Latvia) 1990; Order of Three Stars, Latvia; over 50 awards for projects. *Major projects include:* Lincoln Elementary School, Columbus, Ind., Fed. Reserve Bank of Minneapolis, Contemporary Arts Museum, Houston, Tex., IBM Corpn Computer Center, Sterling Forest, New York, Corning Museum of Glass, New York, Law Library Addition, Univ. of Mich., Ann Arbor, Coll. of Law Bldg, Univ. of Iowa, St Peter's Lutheran Church, Columbus, Ind., Domino's World HQ Bldg, Ann Arbor, Mich., Law School, Ohio State Univ., Columbus, Cen. Library Addition, Univ. of Calif. at San Diego, Kemper Museum of Contemporary Art, Kan. City, Mo., U.S. Embassy, Caracas, School of Law Addition, Duke Univ., Durham, NC; Library, Univ. of Mich.–Flint; Cathedral of Blessed Sacrament, Addition, Detroit, Mich. *In progress:* Sports Centre, Venice, Italy, Novoli Multi-Use Centre, Florence, Italy, Nat. Library, Riga, Latvia, Univ. of Turin, Italy, Performing Arts Center, Mich. Technological Univ., Houghton; Marriott Library Expansion, Univ. of Utah, Market Master Plan, Riga, Latvia, City/Univ. Library, San Jose, CA. *Leisure interests:* tennis, swimming, music. *Address:* Gunnar Birkerts Architects, Inc., 1830 E Tahquamenon Street, Bloomfield Hills, MI 48302, USA. *Telephone:* (248) 626-5661. *Fax:* (248) 626-5101. *E-mail:* gunnarbirk@aol.com (Office). *Website:* www.bunnarbirkerts.com (Office).

BIRKIN, Sir (John) Derek, Kt, TD, CBIM; British business executive; b. 30 Sept. 1929; s. of Noah Birkin and Rebecca Birkin (née Stranks); m. Sadie Smith 1952; one s. one d.; ed Hemsworth Grammar School; Man. Dir Velmar Ltd 1966–67, Nairn Williamson Ltd 1967–70; Deputy Chair. and Man. Dir Tunnel Holdings Ltd 1970–75, Chair. and Man. Dir 1975–82; Dir Rio Tinto-Zinc (then RTZ) Corpn 1982–96, Deputy Chief Exec. 1983–85, Chief Exec. and Deputy Chair. 1985–91, Chair. 1991–96; Chair. Watmoughs (Holdings) PLC 1996–98; Dir Smiths Industries Ltd 1977–84, British Gas Corpn 1982–85, George Wimpey PLC 1984–92, CRA Ltd (Australia) 1985–94, Rio Algom Ltd (Canada) 1985–92, The Merchants Trust PLC 1986–99, British Steel PLC (formerly British Steel Corpn) 1986–92, Barclays Bank PLC and Barclays PLC 1990–95, Merck & Co. Inc. (USA) 1992–2000, Carlton Communications PLC 1992–2001, Unilever PLC 1993–2000; mem. Council, Industrial Soc. 1985–97, UK Top Salaries Review Body 1986–89; Trustee Royal Opera House 1990–93, Dir 1993–97; Hon. LLD (Bath) 1998. *Leisure interests:* opera, rugby, cricket. *Address:* 21 Manchester Square, London, W1M 5AP, England.

BIRKIN, Jane, OBE; French (b. British) actress and singer; b. 14 Dec. 1946, London; d. of David Birkin and Judy Campbell; m. John Barry (divorced) (q.v.); one d.; one d. with Serge Gainsbourg one s. with Jacques Doillon; Gold Leaf Award Canada 1968, Triomphe du cinéma 1969, 1973, Victoire de la musique (for best female singer) 1992; Chevalier des Arts et des Lettres. *Theatre includes:* Carving a Statue 1964, Passion Flower Hotel 1965, La Fausse suivante 1985, L'Aide-Mémoire 1993, Créatrice et Interprète de Oh! pardon tu dormais 1999. *Films include:* The Knack 1965, Blow Up 1966, Les Chemins de Katmandou 1969, Je t'aime moi non plus 1976, Mort sur le Nil 1978, Jane B par Agnès V 1988, Noir comme le souvenir 1995, La fille d'un soldat ne pleure jamais 1999, The Last September 2000, Ceci est mon corps 2001. *Recordings of songs by Serge Gainsbourg include:* C'est la vie qui veut ça, La Baigneuse de Brighton, Je t'aime moi non plus (Le Métier trophy 1970), Di doo dah, Le Canari est sur le balcon, Baby Song, Si ça peut te consoler, Tu n'es pas le premier garçon, Lolita Go Home, Love for Sale, La Ballade, Ex-fan des sixties, Baby Alone in Babylone (Grand Prix du disque, Acad. Charles-Cros). *Address:* VMA, 20 avenue Rapp, 75007 Paris, France.

BIRRELL, Sir James Drake, Kt, FCA, FCBSI; British building society executive; b. 18 Aug. 1933; s. of James R. Birrell and Edith M. Drake; m. Margaret A. Pattison 1958; two d.; ed Belle Vue Grammar School, Bradford; articled clerk, Boyce Welch & Co. 1949–55; Pilot Officer RAF 1955–57; chartered accountant, Price Waterhouse 1957–60; accountant, ADA Halifax 1960–61; man. accountant, Empire Stores 1961–64; Dir and Co. Sec. John Gladstone & Co., 1964–68; with Halifax Bldg Soc. 1968–93, Chief Exec. 1988–93; Dir (non-exec.) Securicor 1993–2002, Wesleyan Gen. Assurance Soc. 1993–; mem. Bldg Soc.'s Comm. 1994–2001. *Leisure interests:* golf, gardening, archaeology, local history. *Address:* 4 Marlin End, Berkhamsted, Hertfordshire, HP4 3GB, England.

BIRT, Baron (Life Peer) cr. 2000, of Liverpool in the County of Merseyside; **John Birt,** Kt, MA, FRTS; British broadcasting executive; b. 10 Dec. 1944, Liverpool; s. of Leo Vincent and Ida Birt; m. Jane Frances Lake 1965; one s. one d.; ed St Mary's Coll., Liverpool, St Catherine's Coll., Oxford; Television Producer of Nice Time 1968–69, Jt Editor World in Action 1969–70, Producer of The Frost Programme 1971–72, Exec. Producer of Weekend World 1972–74, Head of Current Affairs, London Weekend Television (LWT) 1974–77, Co-Producer of The Nixon Interviews 1977, Controller of Features and Current Affairs, LWT 1977–81, Dir of Programmes 1982–87; Deputy Dir-Gen. BBC 1987–92, Dir-Gen. 1992–2000; Vice-Pres. Royal TV Soc. 1994–2000 (Fellow 1989); mem. Media Law Group 1983–94, Working Party on New Techs. 1981–83, Broadcasting Research Unit, Exec. Cttee 1983–87, Int. Museum of TV and Radio, New York 1994–2000, Opportunity 2000 Target Team, Business in the Community 1991–98; Adviser to Prime Minister on criminal justice 2000–01, Strategy Adviser 2001–; Adviser to McKinsey and Co. Inc.; Chair. Capital Ventures Fund 2000; Visiting Fellow Nuffield Coll., Oxford 1991–99; Hon. Fellow Univ. of Wales, Cardiff 1997, St Catherine's Coll., Oxford 1992; Hon. DLitt (Liverpool John Moores) 1992, (City) 1998, (Bradford) 1999; Emmy Award US Nat. Acad. of Television, Arts and Sciences. *Publication:* The Harder Path – The Autobiography. *Leisure interest:* walking. *Address:* House of Lords, London, SW1A 0PW, England.

BIRTWISTLE, Sir Harrison, Kt, CH; British composer; b. 1934, Accrington, Lancs.; m. Sheila Birtwistle 1958; three s.; ed Royal Manchester Coll. of Music and Royal Acad. of Music, London; Dir of Music, Cranborne Chase School 1962–65; Visiting Fellow Princeton Univ. (Harkness Int. Fellowship) 1966; Cornell visiting Prof. of Music, Swarthmore Coll., Pa 1973–74; Slee Visiting Prof., New York State Univ., Buffalo, NY 1975; Assoc. Dir Nat. Theatre 1975–88; Composer-in-Residence London Philharmonic Orchestra 1993–98; Henry Purcell Prof. of Composition King's Coll., London Univ. 1994–2001; Visiting Prof., Univ. of Ala at Tuscaloosa 2001–02; Hon. Fellow Royal Northern Coll. of Music 1990; Dir of Contemporary Music, RAM 1996–2001; works have been widely performed at the major festivals in Europe including the Venice Biennale, the Int. Soc. of Contemporary Music Festivals in Vienna and Copenhagen, the Warsaw Autumn Festival and at Aldeburgh, Cheltenham and Edinburgh; formed, with Sir Peter Maxwell Davies, The Pierrot Players; Chevalier des Arts et des Lettres; Siemens Prize 1995; Grawemeyer Award (Univ. of Louisville, Ky) 1987. *Works: operatic and dramatic:* The Mark of the Goat (cantata) 1965–66, The Visions of Francesco Petrarca (sonnets for baritone and orchestra) 1966, Punch and Judy (one-act opera) 1966–67. *Orchestral works:* Chorales for Orchestra 1962–63, Three Movements with Fanfares 1964, Nomos 1968, The Triumph of Time 1970. *For instrumental ensemble:* Refrains and Choruses 1957, Monody for Corpus Christi 1959, The World is Discovered 1960, Entr'actes and Sappho Fragments 1964, Ring a Dumb Carillon 1965, Tragoedia 1965, Three Lessons in a Frame 1967, Verses for Ensembles 1969, Grimethorpe Aria 1973. *Choral works: Narration:* Description of the Passing of a Year 1964, Carmen Paschale 1965. *Additional compositions:* The Mask of Orpheus (opera) 1974–81, Down By The Greenwood Side 1969, Nenia on the Death of Orpheus 1970, Melencolia I 1976, Silbury Air 1977, Meridian, For O For O the Hobby Horse is Forgot 1977, agm. 1979, On the Sheer Threshold of the Night 1980, Pulse Sampler 1980, Yan Tan Tethera 1983, Still Movement, Secret Theatre 1984, Earth Dances, Words Overheard 1985, Fanfare for Will 1987, Endless Parade 1987, Gawain (opera) 1990, Four Poems by Jaan Kaplinski 1991, The Second Mrs Kong 1992, Antiphonies 1992, Cry of Anubis 1995, Panic 1995, Pulse, Shadows 1997, Exody 1998, The Last Supper 1999, The Axe Manual 2000, The Shadow of Night 2001, Theseus Game 2002; also several pieces of instrumental music. *Theatre:* Music for The Oresteia, Nat. Theatre 1986, The Bacchae, Nat. Theatre 2002. *Address:* c/o Allied Artists Agency, 42 Montpelier Square, London, SW7 1JZ, England.

BIRULÉS, Ana Maria, PhD; Spanish politician and businesswoman; ed Univ. of Barcelona, Univ. of California, Berkeley; worked for regional Govt of Catalonia; with Banco Sabadell 1990–97, negotiated acquisition of Banco NatWest 1996; Man. Dir Retevisión 1997–2000; Minister of Science and Tech. 2000–. *Address:* Ministry of Science and Technology, Paseo de la Castellana 160, 28071 Madrid, Spain (Office). *Telephone:* (91) 3494976 (Office). *Fax:* (91) 4578066 (Office). *E-mail:* info@mcyt.es (Office). *Website:* www.mcyt.es (Office).

BISCHOFF, Manfred, D.RER.POL.; German business executive; b. 22 April 1942, Calw; ed Univs. of Tübingen and Heidelberg; Asst Prof. of Econ. Politics and Int. Trade, Alfred-Weber-Inst., Univ. of Heidelberg 1968–76; various posts, to Vice-Pres. Finance Cos. and Corp. Subsidiaries, Daimler-Benz AG (now DaimlerChrysler AG) 1976–88, mem. Bd of Man. 1995–; mem. Bd of Man. and Chief Financial Officer Mercedes do Brasil, São Paulo 1988–89; mem. Bd of Man. responsible for Finance and Controlling, Deutsche Aerospace (Dasa) AG (after merger, European Aeronautic Defence and Space Co. (EADS)) 1989–95, Chair. Bd of Man. 1995–2000, Chair. Bd 2000–; Chair. Supervisory Bd Airbus Industrie 1998–, ADtranz 1999–, TEMIC 2000–, MTU Aero Engines, Munich 2000–; Pres. European Asscn of Aerospace Industries 1995–96, Fed. of German Aerospace Industries 1996–2000. *Address:* European Aeronautic Defence and Space Company, 81663 Munich, Germany (Office). *Telephone:* (607) 0 (Office). *Fax:* (607) 8 26481 (Office).

BISCHOFF, Sir Winfried Franz Wilhelm ('Win'), Kt, BCom; British merchant banker; b. 10 May 1941, Aachen; s. of the late Paul Helmut and Hildegard (née Kühne) Bischoff; m. Rosemary Elizabeth Leathers 1972; two s.; ed Marist Bros., Johannesburg and Univ. of the Witwatersrand; Man. Dir Schroders Asia Ltd Hong Kong 1971–82; Dir J. Henry Schroder & Co. Ltd 1978– (Chair. 1983–94); Dir Schroders PLC 1983– (Group Chief Exec. 1984–95); Dir (non-exec.) Cable and Wireless PLC 1991– (Deputy Chair. 1995–); Dir (non-exec.) The McGraw Hill Cos. 1999–, Land Securities PLC 1999–; Chair. Schroders PLC 1995–2000, Citigroup Europe 2000–; Dir (non-exec.) IFIL, Finanziaria di Partecipazioni SpA, Italy, Eli Lilly and Co., Indianapolis 2000–, Siemens Holdings PLC (2001–); Johnson Hon. Fellow (St Anne's Coll., Oxford) 2001; Dr hc (City Univ.) 2000. *Leisure interests:* opera, music, golf. *Address:* Citigroup Europe, Citigroup Centre, 33 Canada Square, Canary Wharf, London, E14 5LB, England (Office). *Telephone:* (20) 7986 2600 (Office). *Fax:* (20) 7986 2599 (Office). *E-mail:* win.bischoff@citigroup.com (Office).

BISH-JONES, Trevor, BSc; British business executive; b. 23 April 1960; m. Amanda Bish-Jones 1991; two d.; ed Varndean Grammar School, Portsmouth School of Pharmacy; Research Chemist The Tosco Corpn, Colo 1980–81; Store Man. Boots PLC 1981, rising to Sr Man. position –1994; various man. positions with Dixons Group 1994–2002, including Commercial Dir PC World 1994–95, Marketing Dir Dixons PLC 1995, Man. Dir The Link, Man. Dir Dixons, Dir Currys 2000–02; CEO Woolworths PLC 2002–. *Leisure interests:* horseriding, motorbikes. *Address:* Woolworths PLC, Woolworth House, 242-246 Marylebone Road, London, NW1 6JL, England (Office). *Telephone:* (20) 7262-1222 (Office). *Fax:* (20) 7706-5416 (Office). *Website:* www.woolworths.co .uk (Office).

BISHER, Ilmar, DrScIur; Latvian politician and lawyer; b. 1 Nov. 1930, Riga, Latvia; m. 1st Benita Samuilova 1958 (divorced 1975); m. 2nd Aina Bullite 1975; two s.; ed Latvia Univ.; professor of law, Latvia Univ.; mem. Latvian Popular Front 1989–92; USSR People's Deputy (representing Latvian constituency) 1989–91; Deputy Chair. USSR Supreme Soviet Council of Nationalities 1989–90; First Vice-Chair. Council of Ministers of Latvia 1990–91; Counsellor to Prime Minister 1991–93; barrister, Chair. Bišers & Partneri 1993–; Pres. Latvian Certificate Fund 1994–95, Asscn of Securities Market Participants 1994–95; mem. Council, Democratic Party of Latvia 1992–, Parl. 1995–98. *Address:* Antonijas Iela 9, Riga, LV-1010 (Office); Sporta St 1, Apt. 3, LV-1013 Riga, Latvia. *Telephone:* 733-8882 (Office); 727-4310 (Home). *Fax:* 733-8878 (Office). *E-mail:* bisers@apollo.lv (Office).

BISHOP, James Drew, BA; British journalist; b. 18 June 1929, London; s. of late Sir Patrick Bishop and Vera Drew; m. Brenda Pearson 1959; two s.; ed Haileybury Coll., Hertford and Corpus Christi Coll., Cambridge; reporter, Northampton Chronicle 1953; editorial staff of The Times (London) 1954–70, Foreign Corresp. 1957–64, Foreign News Ed. 1964–66, Features Ed. 1966–70; Ed. The Illustrated London News 1971–87, Newsweek Int. Diary 1977–88; Dir Int. Thomson Publishing Co. 1980–85; Editorial Dir Orient Express, Connections and Natural World Magazines 1981–94; Ed.-in-Chief Illustrated London News Publs 1987–94; contrib. to The Annual Register 1960–88, mem. Advisory Bd 1970–; Chair. Editorial Bd Natural World 1981–97, Asscn of British Eds. 1987–95; Chair. Nat. Heritage 1998– (Trustee 1994–). *Publications:* A Social History of Edwardian Britain 1977, Social History of the First World War 1982, The Story of The Times (with O. Woods) 1983, Illustrated Counties of England (ed.) 1985, The Sedgwick Story 1998. *Leisure interests:* reading, walking. *Address:* 67 Parliament Hill, London NW3 2TB, England (Home). *Telephone:* (20) 7435-4403 (Home). *Fax:* (20) 7435-0778 (Home). *E-mail:* jamesbishop3@compuserve.com (Home).

BISHOP, John Michael, MD; American scientist; b. 22 Feb. 1936; m. 1959; two c.; ed Gettysburg Coll. and Harvard Univ.; intern in internal medicine Mass. Gen. Hosp., Boston 1962–63, Resident 1963–64; Research Assoc. in Virology, NIH, Washington, DC 1964–66, Sr Investigator 1966–68, Asst Prof. to Assoc. Prof. 1968–72; Prof. of Microbiology and Immunology, Univ. of Calif. Medical Center, San Francisco 1972–, Prof. of Biochemistry and Biophysics 1982–; Dir G. W. Hooper Research Foundation 1981–; Univ. Prof. Univ of Calif. Medical Center, San Francisco 1994–2000, Chancellor 1998–; Gairdner Foundation Int. Award 1984, Medal of Honor, American Cancer Soc. 1984, Nobel Prize for Physiology or Medicine 1989, and many other awards and distinctions. *Address:* University of California Hooper Research Foundation, Department of Microbiology, PO Box 552, San Francisco, CA 94143-0001, USA.

BISHOP, Sir Michael (David), Kt, CBE; British business executive; b. 10 Feb. 1942; s. of Clive Leonard Bishop; ed Mill Hill School; joined Mercury Airlines, Manchester 1963, British Midland Airways Ltd 1964–; Chair. British Midland PLC (fmrly Airlines of Britain Holdings PLC) 1978–, Manx Airlines 1982–2001, British Regional Airlines Group PLC 1982–2001, Deputy Chair. Channel 4 TV Corpn 1991–93, Chair. 1993–97; Chair. D'Oyly Carte Opera Trust Ltd 1989–; Deputy Chair. Airtours PLC 1996– (Dir 1987–2001); Dir Williams PLC 1993–2000, Kidde PLC 2000–02; Hon. DTech (Loughborough Univ. of Tech.) 1989, Hon. DLitt (Salford) 1991, Hon. LLD (Nottingham) 1993, Hon. DUniv (Cent. England) 1993, Hon. DLitt (Coventry) 1994. *Address:* Donington Hall, Castle Donington, nr Derby, DE74 2SB, England. *Telephone:* (1332) 854000.

BISHOP-KOVACEVICH, Stephen (see Kovacevich, Stephen).

BISSET, Jacqueline; British actress; b. 13 Sept. 1944, Weybridge; ed French Lycée, London; film début in The Knack 1965. *Other films include:* Two for the Road 1967, Casino Royale 1967, The Sweet Ride 1968, The Detective 1968, Bullitt 1968, The First Time 1969, Airport 1970, The Grasshopper 1970, The Mephisto Waltz 1971, Believe in Me 1971, The Life and Times of Judge Roy Bean 1972, Stand Up and Be Counted 1972, The Thief Who Came to Dinner 1973, Day for Night 1973, Murder on the Orient Express 1974, The Spiral Staircase 1974, End of the Game 1974, St Ives 1975, The Deep 1976, Le Magnifique 1977, Sunday Woman 1977, The Greek Tycoon 1978, Secrets 1978, Too Many Chefs 1978, I Love You, I Love You Not 1979, When Time Ran Out 1980, Rich and Famous 1981, Inchon 1981, Class 1982, Under the Volcano 1983, Forbidden 1986, Choices 1986, High Season 1988, Scenes from the Class Struggle in Beverly Hills 1989, Wild Orchid 1989, La Cérémonie 1995, The Maid, A Judgement in Stone, Once You Meet a Stranger 1996, The Honest Courtesan 1996, Let the Devil Wear Black 1998, Dangerous Beauty 1998, Joan of Arc 1999, In the Beginning 2000, Jesus 2000, Britannic 2000. *Address:* c/o William Morris Agency, 151 El Camino Drive, Beverly Hills, CA 90212, USA; VMA, 10 avenue George V, 75008 Paris, France.

BISSINGER, Frederick Lewis, ME, MS, JD; American chemical executive; b. 11 Jan. 1911, New York; s. of Jacob Frederick Bissinger and Rosel (Ensslin) Bissinger; m. 1st Julia E Stork 1935 (deceased); one s. one d.; m. 2nd Barbara S. Simmonds 1993; ed Stevens Inst. of Technology and Fordham Univ.; Chemistry Instructor, Stevens Inst. of Technology 1933–36; lawyer, Pennie, Davis, Marvin & Edmonds 1936–42; various exec. positions, including Pres., Industrial Rayon Corpn 1942–61; Group Vice-Pres. Midland-Ross Corpn 1961–62; Vice-Pres. and Dir Stauffer Chem. Corpn 1962–65; Vice-Pres. Allied Chemical Corpn 1965–66, Dir 1966–76, Exec. Vice-Pres. 1966–69, Pres. 1969–74, Vice-Chair. 1974–76; Counsel to Pennie & Edmonds 1976–; Chair. Bd Trustees, Stevens Inst. of Tech. 1971–83, Chair. Emer. 1983–; Trustee Fordham Univ. 1970–75, Emer. 1985–; Dir Selas Corpn; Former Dir Midatlantic Nat. Bank, Nat. Starch and Chemical Corpn, Neptune Int. Corpn, Otis Elevator Corpn, Rheingold Corpn; mem. Bar NY, Dist of Colo, Ohio, Supreme Court; Hon. DEng (Stevens Inst. of Tech.) 1973. *Address:* 9 West Irving Street, Chevy Chase, MD 20815, USA. *Telephone:* (301) 657-8373.

BISSON, Thomas Noel, PhD; American professor of medieval history; b. 30 March 1931, New York; s. of Thomas A. Bisson and Faith W Bisson; m. Margaretta C. Webb 1962; two d.; ed Port Washington (NY) High School, Haverford Coll., Univ. of Calif. (Berkeley) and Princeton Univ.; Instructor in History, Amherst Coll. 1957–60; Asst Prof. Brown Univ. 1960–65; Assoc. Prof. Swarthmore Coll. 1965–67; Assoc. Prof. Univ. of Calif. (Berkeley) 1967–69, Prof. 1969–87; Prof. Harvard Univ. 1986–, Henry Charles Lea Prof. of Medieval History 1988–, Chair. Dept of History 1991–95; mem. American Philosophical Soc.; Fellow, Medieval Acad. of America (Pres. 1994–95), Royal Historical Soc., British Acad. etc.; Guggenheim Fellow 1964–65; Creu de Sant Jordi (Generalitat of Catalonia) 2001; Dr. hc (Barcelona) 1991. *Publications:* Assemblies and Representation in Languedoc in the Thirteenth Century 1964, Medieval Representative Institutions: Their Origins and Nature 1973, Conservation of Coinage: Monetary Exploitation and its Restraint in France, Catalonia and Aragon (c. AD 1000–c. AD 1225) 1979, Fiscal Accounts of Catalonia under the Early Count-Kings 1151–1213 (2 Vols) 1985, The Medieval Crown of Aragon: a Short History 1986, Medieval France and her Pyrenean Neighbors 1989, Tormented Voices: Power, Crisis and Humanity in Rural Catalonia 1140–1200 1998; articles in journals. *Leisure interests:* classical music, English literature. *Address:* Department of History, Robinson Hall, Harvard University, Cambridge, MA 02138 (Office); 21 Hammond Street, Cambridge, MA 02138, USA (Home). *Telephone:* (617) 495-5221 (Office).

BISTA, Kirti Nidhi, MA; Nepalese politician; b. 1927; ed Tri-Chandra Coll., Kathmandu and Lucknow Univ.; Asst Minister for Education 1961–62, Minister for Educ. 1962–64, for Foreign Affairs 1964; Vice-Chair. Council of Ministers and Minister for Foreign Affairs and Educ. 1964–66; Vice-Chair. Council of Ministers and Minister for Foreign Affairs and Econ. Planning 1966–67; Deputy Prime Minister and Minister for Foreign Affairs and Educ. 1967–68, Perm. Rep. to UN 1968–69; Prime Minister 1969–70, 1971–73, 1977–79, Minister of Finance, Gen. Admin. and Palace Affairs 1969–73, of Finance, Palace Affairs and Defence 1978–79; mem. Royal Advisory Cttee 1969–70; Leader Nepalese dels. to UN Gen. Assemblies 1964, 1965, 1966 and to UNESCO Gen. Confs. 1962, 1964, 1966 and to various other confs; accompanied HM the King on many State Visits; Order of the Right Hand of Gurkhas (First Class), Fed. German Order of Merit, Légion d'honneur. *Address:* Gyaneshwor, Kathmandu, Nepal (Home).

BISWAS, Abdul Rahman; Bangladeshi politician; fmr Speaker, House of Ass.; Pres. of Bangladesh 1991–96; now retd. *Address:* Residence Dhonmondi, Dhaka, Bangladesh.

BITARAF, Habibollah, MS; Iranian government official; b. 1956, Yazd; m. Zahra Mansurie; three d.; ed Tehran Univ.; Deputy Minister for Energy 1991–95, Exec. Man. of Karon 3 and 4 (dam and energy plant) project 1995–97, Minister for Energy 1997–. *Publication:* Fluid Mechanics. *Leisure interests:* studying, mountaineering, table tennis, pilgrimage, travelling. *Address:* Ministry of Energy, North Palestine Street, Tehran, Iran. *Telephone:* (21) 890001. *Fax:* (21) 8801995 (Office). *E-mail:* webmaster@moe.or.ir (Office). *Website:* www.moe.or.ir (Office).

BITOV, Andrei Georgevich; Russian writer; b. 27 May 1937, Leningrad; m. Inga Petkevich; one d.; ed Leningrad Mining Inst.; evacuated 1939–44; worked as stevedore and lathe-operator 1958–62; researcher, Leningrad Mining Inst. 1962; started publishing 1960; mem. of 'Young Prose' group in

1960s with Vasiliy Aksyonov (q.v.) and Anatoliy Gladilin; contrib. to Metropol 1979; Pres. Russian PEN Centre 1992–; Andrey Bely Prize (Russia), Best Foreign Book Prize (Paris), Pushkin Prize (Germany), State Prize (Russia). *Publications include:* The Big Balloon 1963, Such a Long Childhood 1965, A Summer Place 1967, Apothecary Island 1968, Way of Life 1972, Seven Journeys 1976, Days of Man 1976, Pushkin House 1978, Sunday (short stories) 1980, A Man in the Landscape 1987, The Flying Monakhov 1990, We Woke Up in a Strange Country 1991, Awaiting Monkeys 1993, Empire in Four Dimensions (collected works), (Vols 1–4) 1996, Inevitability of Non-Written 1998, Life in Windy Weather 2000. *Address:* Krasnoprudnaya str. 30/34, Apt 14, 107140 Moscow, Russia. *Telephone:* (095) 209-45-89 (Office); (095) 264-12-93 (Home).

BITSCH, Hans-Ullrich; German architect and industrial designer; b. 13 June 1946, Essen; s. of Prof. Heinz W. and Lore L. (née Falldorf) Bitsch; m. Evelyn R. Koch 1981; two s.; ed High School, Saarbrücken, State Coll. of Art, Saarbrücken and Illinois Inst. of Tech.; architect, Univ. of Saarbrücken 1968; Instructor Int. Inst. of Design, Washington, DC 1969; Visiting Lecturer, Harrington Inst., Chicago, Ill. 1970–71; Prof. Dept of Architecture, Düsseldorf Univ. 1972–; Pres. German Inst. of Interior Architects 1977–82; Visiting Prof., Univ. of Texas 1981; Prof. Univ. of Naples 1997–; Pres. Professor Bitsch & Assocs (design and architectural office), Düsseldorf; work represented in Smithsonian Inst., Design Collection, Stuttgart and Stiftung Preussischer Kulturbesitz; several awards for architecture and design. *Publications:* Menschengerechte Gestaltung des Kassenarbeitsplatzes 1978, Farbe und Industrie-Design 1982, Design und Formentwicklung von Stuhlen 1988, Visuelle Wahrnehmung in Architektur und Design 1989, Projekt Hotel 1992, Architectural Visions for Europe 1994, Stilströmungen 1998, Studien aus dem Architekturbüro 1999. *Leisure interests:* skiing, sailing, photography. *Address:* Kaiser-Wilhelm-Ring 23, Rive Gauche, 40545 Düsseldorf Oberkassel, Germany. *Telephone:* (211) 95449000. *Fax:* (211) 553814 (Office).

BITTERLICH, Joachim; German diplomatist; b. 10 July 1948, Saarbrücken-Dudweiler; m. 1969; two s. one d.; ed Univ. of Saarbrücken, Ecole Nat. d'Admin.; entered Foreign Office 1976; posted to Algiers 1978–81; Perm. Rep. to EC, Brussels 1981–85; Adviser, Pvt. Office of the Minister of Foreign Affairs 1985–87; Head of European Policy Dept., Fed. Chancellor's Office 1987–93; Dir. of Foreign Policy, Econ. Co-operation and External Security Fed. Chancellor's Office and Foreign and Security Policy Adviser to Fed. Chancellor 1993–98; Amb. and Perm. Rep. to North Atlantic Council, Brussels 1998–99; Amb. to Spain 1999–; mem. Bd of Trustees, Friends of Europe, Deutsche Gesellschaft für Auswärtige Politik, Inst. Français des Relations Internationales; Assoc. mem. Int. Inst. for Strategic Studies; numerous awards and decorations including Hon. CBE 1992, two Grosses Silbernes Ehrenzeichen mit Stern (Austria) 1994, Grande Oficial do Ordem de Rio Branco (Brazil) 1995, Officier Légion d'honneur 1996, Grande Ufficiale nell Ordine al Merito (Italy) 1997, Orden do Infante Don Enrique (Portugal) 1998, Gran Cruz de la Orden del Mérito Civil (Spain) 1998. *Publications:* articles in newspapers and journals. *Address:* German Embassy, Calle de Fortuny 8, 28010 Madrid, Spain (Office). *Telephone:* (91) 5579030 (Office); (91) 5579000 (Home). *Fax:* (91) 5579059 (Office).

BIYA, Paul, LenD; Cameroonian politician; b. 13 Feb. 1933, Mvomeka'a; m. 1st Jeanne (née Atyam) Biya (deceased); one c.; m. 2nd Chantal Biya 1994; ed Ndem Mission School, Edea and Akono Seminaries, Lycée Leclerc, Yaoundé, Univ. of Paris, Inst. d'Etudes Politiques, Inst. des Hautes Etudes d'Outre-Mer, Paris; Head of Dept of Foreign Devt Aid 1962–63; Dir of Cabinet in Ministry of Nat. Educ., Youth and Culture 1964–65; on goodwill mission to Ghana and Nigeria 1965; Sec.-Gen. in Ministry of Educ., Youth and Culture 1965–67; Dir of Civil Cabinet of Head of State 1967–68; Minister of State, Sec.-Gen. to Pres. 1968–75; Prime Minister 1975–82; Pres. of Cameroon 1982–; Second Vice-Pres., Central Cttee, mem. Union Nationale Camerounaise (UNC), Pres. 1983–85; Pres. Rassemblement Démocratique du Peuple Camerounais (RDPC) 1985–; mem. Politbureau; Commdr de l'Ordre de la Valeur Camerounaise, Commdr of Nat. Order of Fed. Repub. of Germany and of Tunisia, Grand Cross of Nat. Order of Merit of Senegal, Grand Officier, Légion d'honneur. *Publication:* Communal Liberalism 1987. *Address:* Office of the President, Palais de l'Unité, Yaoundé, Cameroon (Office). *Telephone:* 23-40-25 (Office). *Website:* www.camnet.cm/celcom/homepr.htm (Office).

BIZIMUNGU, Pasteur; Rwandan politician; mem. Front patriotique rwandais (FPR); Pres. of Rwanda 1994–2000; arrested in Angola Aug. 2002. *Address:* c/o Office of the President, BP 15, Kigali, Rwanda.

BJARNASON, Gudmundur; Icelandic politician; b. 9 Oct. 1944, Húsavík; s. of Bjarni Stéfánsson and Jakobina Jónsdóttir; m. Vigdís Gunnarsdóttir; three d.; ed Húsavík Secondary School and Co-operative Coll.; with Co-operative Soc., Húsavík 1963–67; Húsavík Br. Co-operative Bank of Iceland 1967–77, Br. Dir 1977–80; elected mem. Húsavík Town Council 1970, Chair. 1974; mem. Althing 1979–99; Minister of Health and Social Security 1987–91, of Environment and Agric. 1995–99; mem. Althing Appropriation Cttee 1979–87 and 1991–95, Vice-Chair 1983–87; Chair. Cttee on Housing Affairs; mem. Jt Cttee on public projects; Man. Dir Housing Financing Fund 1999–; Bd Research Council; mem. Icelandic del. to Parl. Ass. of Council of Europe. *Address:* Housing Financing Fund, Borgartin 21, 105 R, Reykjavik (Office); Kirkjusandur 5, 105 Reykjavik, Iceland (Home). *Telephone:* 569-6900 (Office); 553-9898 (Home). *Fax:* 569-6820 (Office). *E-mail:* gudmundur@ils.is (Office). *Website:* www.ils.is (Office).

BJELKE-PETERSEN, Hon. Sir Johannes, KCMG; Australian politician; b. 13 Jan. 1911, Dannevirke, New Zealand; s. of Carl G. Bjelke-Petersen and Maren (née Poulsen) Bjelke-Petersen; m. Florence Gilmour 1952; one s. three d.; ed Taabinga Village Primary School, correspondence courses and private studies; Farmer; mem. Queensland Legislative Assembly 1947–; Minister for Works and Housing, Queensland 1963–68, later of Aboriginal and Island Affairs and Police; Leader of Country (Nat.) Party of Queensland 1968–87, (split 1987), Leader New Nat. Party of Australia (right wing of old party) 1987–88; Premier of Queensland 1968–87. *Leisure interests:* flying, reading, bush-walking. *Address:* P.O. Box 141, Kingaroy, Queensland 4610, Australia.

BJERREGAARD, Ritt; Danish politician; b. 19 May 1941, Copenhagen; d. of Rita Bjerregaard; m. Søren Mørch 1966; mem. Parl. 1971–95, 2001–; Minister of Educ. 1973, 1975–78, for Social Affairs 1979–81; Chair. Parl. Group, Social Democratic Party (SDP) 1981–92, 1987–92, Deputy Chair. 1982–87; Chair. Parl. Cttee on Public Accounts 1990–95; mem. Parl. Ass. of Council of Europe 1990–95; Pres. Danish European Movt 1992–94; Vice-Pres. Parl. Ass. of CSCE 1992–95; Vice-Pres. Socialist Int. Women 1992–94; EU Commr for Environment 1995–99; Minister of Food, Agric. and Fisheries 2000–01; mem. Trilateral Comm., Centre for European Policy Studies. *Publications:* several books on politics in general and the role of women in politics. *Leisure interests:* her apple farm, organic farming, the environment. *Address:* c/o Folketing, Christiansborg, 1240 Copenhagen K, Denmark.

BJØRNDALEN, Ole Einar; Norwegian biathlete; b. 27 Jan. 1974, Drammen; ed Norwegian Ski Gymnas; winner of six Olympic medals (two Gold Medals (Sprint, Relay) in Nagano, Japan 1998, four Gold Medals (Sprint, Pursuit, Individual, Relay) in Salt Lake City, USA 2002 (became third Olympian to win four gold medals at a single Winter Games); winner of four World Championship medals (Bronze in Pursuit, Osrblie, Slovakia 1997, Bronze in Relay, Kontiolahti, Finland 1999, Bronze in Mass, Holmenkollen, Norway 2000, Silver in Mass, Pokljuka, Slovenia 2001); winner of overall World Cup titles, Salt Lake City 2000–01. *Leisure interests:* motorbikes, climbing, off-road. *Address:* Skavelandsvei 12E, Trondheim 7022, Norway (Office). *Telephone:* 926 15691 (Office). *Website:* www.bjoerndalen.com (Office).

BJÖRCK, Anders; Swedish politician; b. 19 Sept. 1944, Nässjö; m. Py-Lotte Björck; one d.; Nat. Pres. Swedish Young Moderates 1966–71; MP 1968–; mem. Parl. Ass. Council of Europe 1976–91, Pres. (Speaker) 1989–91; Minister of Defence 1991–94; First Deputy Speaker of Swedish Parl. 1994–; mem. Bd Swedish Broadcasting Co. 1978–91, Swedish TV Co. 1979–91; mem. numerous Govt comms. dealing with constitutional matters, the mass media, environmental protection. *Publications:* various articles on defence, foreign policy and constitutional issues. *Address:* Riksdagen, 100 12 Stockholm (Office); Bashult, 555 92 Jönköping, Sweden (Home). *Telephone:* (8) 786-4031 (Office); (36) 17-40-17 (Home). *Fax:* (8) 213-525 (Office).

BJÖRK, Anita; Swedish actress; b. 25 April 1923, Tällberg Dalecarlia; m. Stig Dagerman (deceased); one s. two d.; ed Royal Dramatic Theatre School, Stockholm; has toured around USA, Canada, UK and France; O'Neill Prize; Merito Cultural (Portugal); Swedish Critics' Award 1990 and many other Swedish awards. *Films acted in include:* Himlaspelet 1942, Räkna de lyckliga stunderna blott (Count Your Blessings) 1944, Hundra dragspel och en flicka (One Hundred Concertinas and a Girl) 1946, Ingen väg tillbaka (No Return) 1947, Kvinna utan ansikte 1947, Det kom en gäst (There Came a Guest) 1947, Pa dessa skuldror (On these Shoulders) 1948, Människors rike (The Realm of Men and Women) 1949, Kvartetten som sprängdes (The Quartet that was Broken) 1950, Fröken Julie 1950–51 (First Prize, Cannes Film Festival), Han glömde henne aldrig 1952, Night People 1953, Die Hexe 1954, Giftas 1955, Der Cornet 1955, Moln över Hellesta (Dark Clouds over Hellesta) 1956, Sången om den eldröda blommen 1956, Gäst i eget hus (Guest in One's Own House) 1957, Mannekäng i rött 1958, Tärningen är kastad 1960, Goda vänner trogna grannar 1960, Vita frun 1962, Älskande par 1964, Mother and Daughter 1990. *Stage appearances at:* Royal Dramatic Theatre, Stockholm, including Miss Julie 1951, Agnes (Brand, Ibsen), Celia (The Cocktail Party, Eliot), Rosalind (As You Like It, Shakespeare), Juliet (Romeo and Juliet, Shakespeare), Eliza (Pygmalion, Shaw), Solange (Les Bonnes, Genet), the girl (Look Back in Anger, Osborne), Johanna (Les séquestrés d'Altona, Sartre), Siri von Essen (Night of The Tribades, P. O. Enquist), Madame Arkadina (The Seagull, Chekhov) 1982-83, Hanna Luise Heiberg (Life of the Rainsnakes, Enquist), Christa Wolf (Kassandra, Wolf), Mihima (The Marquise de Sade), Celestina 1998, The Image Maker 1999, Copenhagen (Michael Frayn, q.v.) 2000. *Address:* Baggensgatan 9, 111 31 Stockholm, Sweden (Office). *Telephone:* (8) 209747.

BJÖRK, (Björk Guðmundsdóttir); Icelandic singer and songwriter; b. (Björk Guðmundsdóttir), 21 Nov. 1965, Reykjavik; one c.; made first album "Bjork" 1977; formed several bands including Exodus, Tappi Tikarrass; mem. The Sugarcubes (fmrly Kukl) 1986–92; singles with The Sugarcubes include: Birthday; albums with The Sugarcubes: Life's Too Good, Here Today, Tomorrow Next Week!, Stick Around For Joy; solo artist 1992–; singles include: Human Behaviour, Venus As A Boy, Big Time Sensuality, Violently Happy, Play Dead, Army Of Me, Blow A Fuse (It's Oh So Quiet), Hyperballad, Selmasongs 2000; albums: Debut 1993, Post (platinum disc in UK), Vespertine 2001; Best Int. Female Award (MTV European Music awards). *Film Dancer in the Dark 2000. Address:* One Little Indian Records, 250 York Road, London, SW11 3SJ, England. *Telephone:* (20) 7924-1661. *Fax:* (20) 7924-4274.

BJORK, Claes; Swedish business executive; joined Skanska AB 1967, moved to USA 1971, responsible for Skanska's construction operations in USA 1983, Pres. Skanska (USA) Inc. 1987, Sr Vice-Pres. Skanska AB, Head Skanska USA Operations –1997, mem. Group Man. Skanska AB 1995–, Pres., Group Chief Exec. 1997–; Chair. Swedish-American Chamber of Commerce 1992–95; mem. Bd Banister Foundation 1990–. *Address:* Skanska AB, P.O.B. 1195, 11191 Stockholm, Sweden. *Telephone:* (8) 7538800. *Fax:* (8) 7559688.

BJORKLUND, Leni, BA; Swedish politician; b. 5 July 1944; ed Uppsala Univ.; Research Asst Dept of Pedagogical Studies, Stockholm Inst. of Educ. 1969–71; Educ. Consultant Nat. Bd of Educ. 1971–74; Expert, Dept for Cultural Affairs, Ministry of Educ. and Science 1974–76; Municipal Commr Municipality of Järfälla 1977–79; Co. Council Commr Stockholm County Council 1980–98; Man. Dir of Planning and Rationalisation, Inst. for Health and Social Services 1989–99; Sec.-Gen. Church of Sweden 1999–2002; Minister of Defence 2002–; mem. SDP, numerous positions including mem. and Vice-Chair. Exec. Cttee Stockholm Co. SDP; currently Chair. Expert Group on Public Finance (ESO); mem. Bd Nat. Heritage Bd, Mid Sweden Univ.; fmr Chair. Swedish Medical Research Council; fmr Vice-Chair. Stockholm Co. Admin Bd; fmr mem. Foundation of Strategic Research; DrMed (Karolinska Institutet). *Address:* Ministry of Defence, Jakobsgatan 8, 103 33 Stockholm, Sweden (Office). *Telephone:* (8) 405-10-0 (Office). *Fax:* (8) 723-11-89 (Office).

BJÖRKMAN, Olle Erik, PhD, DSc; American professor of plant biology; b. 29 July 1933, Jönköping, Sweden; s. of Erik Gustaf Björkman and Dagmar Kristina Björkman (Svensson); m. Monika Birgit Waldinger 1955; two s.; ed Univs. of Stockholm and Uppsala; Research Fellow, Swedish Natural Science Research Council, Univ. of Uppsala 1961–63; Postdoctoral Fellow, Carnegie Inst. Washington, Stanford, Calif. 1964–65, Faculty mem. 1966–, Prof. of Biology by courtesy, Stanford Univ. 1977–; mem. Cttee on Carbon Dioxide Effects, U.S. Dept of Energy 1977–82, Cttee on Bioscience Research in Agric. 1984–85; Scientific Adviser, Desert Research Inst., Nevada 1980–81; mem. Editorial Bd Planta 1993–96; mem. NAS; Fellow, American Acad. of Arts and Sciences, AAAS; Corresp. (Foreign) mem. Australian Acad. of Sciences, Foreign mem. Royal Swedish Acad. of Sciences; Linnaeus Prize, Royal Swedish Physiographic Soc. 1977, The Stephen Hale's Award, American Soc. of Plant Physiologists 1986, The Selby Award, Australian Acad. of Sciences 1987. *Publications:* Experimental Studies on the Nature of Species V (co-author) 1971, Physiological Processes in Plant Ecology 1980, more than 170 articles in scientific journals. *Leisure interest:* opera. *Address:* Carnegie Institution Department of Plant Biology, Stanford, CA 94305, USA (Office); 3040 Greer Road, Palo Alto, CA 94303, USA (Home). *Telephone:* (650) 325-1521 (Office); (650) 858-0880 (Home). *Fax:* (650) 325-6857.

BJØRNHOLM, Sven, DPhil; Danish physicist; b. 8 Sept. 1927, Tønder; s. of Lt-Col H. L. Bjørnholm and Inger Hillerup; m. Iran Park 1957; two s. one d.; ed Tech. Univ. of Denmark, Sorbonne, Paris and Univ. of Copenhagen; Research Asst Niels Bohr Inst. Copenhagen 1955–68; Assoc. Prof. Univ. of Copenhagen 1968–96; visiting scientist at research insts. in France, USSR, USA, Germany and Brazil 1951–97; mem. Bd Int. Fed. of Insts. of Advanced Study 1972–77, Danish Natural Science Research Council 1973–79, Danish Energy Policy Council 1976–86, Int. Union of Pure and Applied Physics (IUPAP) Comm. on Nuclear Physics 1978–84, European Community Comm. on Research and Devt 1980–82; Pres. Danish Physical Soc. 1978–80; mem. Royal Danish Acad., Danish Acad. of Tech. Sciences, Royal Physiographical Soc. of Lund, Sweden, Danish Pugwash Cttee; Ole Rømer Award 1965, Ulrich Brinch Award 1973, Officier, Ordre des Palmes Académiques. *Publications:* Energy in Denmark 1990–2005 1976; and articles on the structure and reactions of atomic nuclei and metal clusters, including fission, in professional journals. *Address:* The Niels Bohr Institute, Blegdamsvej 17, 2100 Copenhagen Ø (Office); Frederiksberg Alle 45, 1820 Frederiksberg C, Denmark (Home). *Telephone:* 35-32-52-94 (Office); 33-22-48-85 (Home).

BJØRNVIG, Thorkild Strange, DPhil; Danish poet and writer; b. 2 Feb. 1918; s. of Adda and Theodor Bjørnvig; m. 1st Grete Damgaard Pedersen 1946; m. 2nd Birgit Hornum 1970; two s. one d.; ed Cathedral School, Aarhus and Univ. of Aarhus; mem. Danish Acad. 1960; several prizes including Arisseian Prize for trans. (EU) 1996 and Rungsted Lund Prize 1998. *Publications:* poetry: Stjaernen bag Gavlen 1947, Anubis 1955, Figur og Ild 1959, Vibrationer 1966, Ravnen 1968, Udvalgte digte 1970, Morgenmørke 1977, Den dobbelte Lykke 1982, Gennem Regnbuen 1987, Siv Vand og Måne 1993; essays: Rilke og tysk Tradition 1959, Begyndelsen 1960, Kains Alter 1964, Oprør mod Neonguden 1970, Virkeligheden er til 1973, Pagten, mit Venskab med Karen Blixen 1974, Delfinen 1975, Stoffets Krystalhav 1975, Det religiøse menneskes ansigter 1975, Også for naturens skyld 1978, Barnet og dyret i industrisamfundet, Abeguder, Miljødigte 1975–80 1981, Den følende planet 1988, Epidlmeteus Miljødigte 1980–90 1991, Digtere 1991, Siv vand og måna 1993, Udsat på hjertets bjerge (trans. of poems by Rainer Maria Rilke) 1995, Samlede Digte 1947–93 1998. *Leisure interests:* walking, foreign travel. *Address:* Issehoved 41, 8305 Samsø, Denmark.

BJURSTRÖM, Per Gunnar, PhD; Swedish professor; b. 28 March 1928, Stockholm; s. of Gunnar Bjurström and Claire (née Hellgård) Bjurström; m. 1st Eva Gunnars 1957 (divorced 1983); two d.; m. 2nd Görel Cavalli-Björkman; Asst curator, National museum 1950–68, curator of prints and drawings 1968–79; Dir Nat. Swedish Art Museums 1980–89; Guest Prof., Yale Univ. 1968; Prof. Nat. Gallery of Art, Washington 1990–91; mem. Bd Gen. Art Asscn of Sweden 1964–, Prince Eugen's Waldemarsudde 1980–89; Vice-Chair. Soc. of Art History 1965–91; Chair. Int. Cttee of Museums of Fine Art 1983–88; mem. Royal Acad. of Letters, History and Antiquities and Royal Acad. of Fine Art, Ateneo Veneto, Venice. *Publications:* Giacomo Torelli and Baroque Stage Design 1961, Stage Design in Sweden 1964, Feast and Theatre in Queen Christina's Rome 1966, German Drawings in Swedish Public Collections 1972, French Drawings in Swedish Public Collections 1976, 1982, 1986, Italian Drawings in Swedish Public Collections 1979, Johan Tobias Sergel 1975, Three Decades of Swedish Graphic Art 1946–1976, Roman Baroque Scenery 1977, Philip von Schantz 1979, Claude Lorrain Sketchbook 1984, Nationalmuseum 1792–1991 1992, Karl Axel Pehrson 1992, I, Alexander Roslin 1993. *Address:* Folkungagatan 142, 116 30 Stockholm, Sweden. *Telephone:* (8) 641-7093. *Fax:* (8) 641-7093.

BLACK, Sir James (Whyte), Kt, OM, FRCP, FRS; British professor of analytical pharmacology; b. 14 June 1924; m. Rona McLeod Mackie 1994; ed Beath High School, Cowdenbeath and Univ. of St Andrews; Asst Lecturer in Physiology, Univ. of St Andrews 1946; lecturer in Physiology, Univ. of Malaya 1947–50; Sr Lecturer Univ. of Glasgow Veterinary School 1950–58; with ICI Pharmaceuticals Ltd 1958–64, Head of Biological Research and Deputy Research Dir Smith, Kline & French, Welwyn Garden City 1964–73; Prof. and Head of Dept of Pharmacology, Univ. College, London 1973–77; Prof. of Analytical Pharmacology, King's Coll. Hosp. Medical School, Univ. of London 1984–93, now Emer.; Chancellor Dundee Univ. 1992–; Dir Therapeutic Research, Wellcome Research Labs. 1978–84; mem. British Pharmacological Soc. 1961–; Mullard Award, Royal Soc. 1978, (jtly) Nobel Prize for Physiology or Medicine 1988; Hon. Fellow RSC 1989; Hon. Assoc. mem. Royal Coll. of Veterinary Surgeons 1990; Hon. MD (Edinburgh) 1989; Hon. DSc (Glasgow) 1989, (Oxford) 1996. *Address:* Analytical Pharmacology Unit, Rayne Institute, 123 Cold Harbour Lane, London, SE5 9WU (Office); James Black Foundation, 68 Half Moon Lane, London, SE24 9JE, England; University of Dundee, Dundee, DD1 4HN, Scotland. *Telephone:* (20) 7274-7437.

BLACK, Kent March; American business executive; b. 25 Oct. 1939, Carrollton, Ill.; s. of Kenneth Wilbur Black and Alta Jane (March) Black; m. Karen Anne Jones 1960; two d.; ed Univ. of Illinois; joined Rockwell Int. 1962, various posts to Exec. Vice-Pres. and COO 1989; mem. Advisory Cttee Nat. Security Telecom 1989–. *Address:* c/o Rockwell International Corporation, P.O. Box 5090, Costa Mesa, CA 92628, USA.

BLACK, Robert Lincoln, MD; American pediatrician; b. 25 Aug. 1930, Los Angeles; s. of Harold Black and Kathryn Stone; m. Jean Wilmott McGuire 1953; two s. one d.; ed Stanford Univ., Kings County Hosp., Brooklyn, Stanford Univ. Hosp., Palo Alto; Capt. US Air Force Medical Corps 1956–58; Asst Clinical Prof., Stanford Univ., Clinical Prof. 1962–, Assoc. Prof. 1968–79, Prof. of Pediatrics 1980; mem. Bd of Educ. Monterey Peninsula Unified School Dist 1965–73; mem. Bd Dirs Lyceum of Monterey Peninsula 1973–; mem. Bd Mid Coast Health System Agency 1975–81; mem. various cttees of American Acad., of Pediatrics 1962–, Alt. Chapter Chair. 1984–87; Consultant, State of Calif. Dept of Health Service 1962– and of Office of Statewide Health Planning 1975–81; mem. State Maternal, Child, Adolescent Health Care Bd 1984–93; currently Pediatrician with pvt. practice; mem. Inst. of Medicine, NAS, Calif. State Maternal, Child, Adolescent Health Bd; Martin Gershman Award for Child Advocacy, American Acad. of Pediatrics 1996. *Publications:* California Health Plan for Children, California's Use of Health Statistics in Child Health Planning. *Leisure interests:* music, hiking, travel, photography. *Address:* 920 Cass Street, Monterey, CA 93940-4507 (Office); 976 Mesa Road, Monterey, CA 93940-4612, USA (Home). *Telephone:* (831) 372-5841 (Office); (831) 372-2594 (Home). *Fax:* (831) 372-4820 (Office).

BLACK, Shirley Temple; American actress and diplomatist; b. 23 April 1928, Santa Monica, Calif.; d. of George F. Temple and Gertrude Temple; m. 1st John Agar, Jr 1945 (divorced 1949); one d.; m. 2nd Charles A. Black 1950; one s. one d.; ed privately and Westlake School for Girls; career as film actress commenced at $3^1/_2$ years; first full-length film was Stand Up and Cheer; narrator/actress in TV series Shirley Temple Storybook 1958; hostess/actress Shirley Temple Show 1960; Del. to UN, New York 1969–70; Amb. to Ghana 1974–76, to Czechoslovakia 1989–92; White House Chief of Protocol 1976–77; mem. US Comm. for UNESCO 1973–; mem. US Del. on African Refugee Problems, Geneva 1981; Dir Nat. Multiple Sclerosis Soc.; Dame, Order of Knights of Malta (Paris) 1968; American Exemplar Medal 1979, Gandhi Memorial Int. Foundation Award 1988; numerous state decorations. *Films include:* Little Miss Marker, Baby Take a Bow, Bright Eyes, Our Little Girl, The Little Colonel, Curly Top, The Littlest Rebel, Captain January, Poor Little Rich Girl, Dimples, Stowaway, Wee Willie Winkie, Heidi, Rebecca of Sunnybrook Farm, Little Miss Broadway, Just Around the Corner, The Little Princess, Susannah of the Mounties, The Blue Bird, Kathleen, Miss Annie Rooney, Since You Went Away, Kiss and Tell, That Hagen Girl, War Party, The Bachelor and the Bobby-Soxer, Honeymoon. *Publication:* Child Star (autobiog.) 1988. *Address:* c/o Academy of Motion Picture Arts & Sciences, 8949 Wilshire Blvd., Beverly Hills, CA 90211, USA.

BLACK OF CROSSHARBOUR, Baron (Life Peer), cr. 2001, of Crossharbour in the London Borough of Tower Hamlets; **Conrad M. Black,** Kt, PC, OC, LittD, LLD; British (b. Canadian) publisher and business executive; b. 25 Aug. 1944, Montreal, Québec; s. of George Montegu and Jean Elizabeth (Riley) Black; m. 1st Joanna Catherine Louise Black 1978 (divorced 1991); two s. one d.; m. 2nd Barbara Amiel 1992; ed Carleton, Laval, McGill Univs; Chair. and CEO Ravelston Corpn Ltd; acquired Daily Telegraph newspaper group

1985; Chair. The Telegraph PLC 1987; Chair. Saturday Night Magazine Inc.; Chair. and CEO Hollinger Int. Inc. 1985–, Chair. Chair.'s Exec. Cttee; Chair. Bd and Exec. Cttee Argus Corpn Ltd; Deputy Chair. American Publishing Co. (now Hollinger Int.), John Fairfax (Australia); Dir Canadian Imperial Bank of Commerce; Dir Brascan Ltd, The Spectator (1828) Ltd, UniMédia Inc., Eaton's of Canada Ltd, Financial Post Co. Ltd, Key Publishers Co. Ltd, Southam Inc. (Chair., CEO 1996–), Sotheby's 1997–; Patron The Malcolm Muggeridge Foundation; mem. Advisory Bd, The Nat. Interest, Washington, DC, Steering Cttee and Advisory Group, Bilderberg Meetings, Chair.'s Council, Americas Soc., Int. Inst. for Strategic Studies, Gulfstream Aerospace Corpn; Hon. LLD (St Francis Xavier) 1979, (McMaster) 1979, (Carleton) 1989, Hon. LittD (Windsor) 1979. *Publications:* Duplessis 1977, A Life in Progress (autobiog.) 1994. *Address:* c/o Hollinger Inc., 10 Toronto Street, Toronto, Ont. M5C 2B7, Canada; The Telegraph PLC, 1 Canada Square, Canary Wharf, London, E14 5DT, England. *Telephone:* (416) 363-8721 (Toronto). *Fax:* (416) 364-2088 (Toronto).

BLACKADDER, Elizabeth Violet, OBE, RA, RSA, MA; British artist; b. 24 Sept. 1931, Falkirk, Scotland; m. John Houston 1956; ed Falkirk High School, Edinburgh Coll. of Art and Edinburgh Univ.; teacher at art, St Thomas of Aquinas School, Edin. 1958–59; librarian, Fine Art Dept Univ. of Edin. 1959–61; teacher, Edin. Coll of Art 1962–86; Scottish Arts Council retrospective Exhbn Edin., Sheffield, Aberdeen, Liverpool, Cardiff 1981–82; participant in numerous group shows in UK, USA, Canada etc. British Painting 1952–77; Royal Acad. London 1977; HM Painter and Limner in Scotland 2000–; work includes drawings and watercolours (especially botanical), prints, lithographs, portraits, tapestries and stained glass (window commissioned by Nat. Library of Scotland 1987); Hon. Fellow Royal Soc. of Edin.; Hon. DLitt (Heriot-Watt Univ.) 1989, (Strathclyde) 1998; Dr hc (Univ. of Edin.) 1990; Hon. LLD (Aberdeen) 1997, (Glasgow) 2001; Jt winner, Watercolour Foundation Award, RA Summer Exhbn 1988. *One-woman exhibitions include:* Mercury Gallery, London 1965–; 57 Gallery, Edin. 1959, The Scottish Gallery, Edin. 1961, 1966, Vaccarino Gallery, Florence 1970, Theo Waddington Gallery, Toronto 1981–82, Lillian Heidenberg Gallery, New York 1986, Browse & Darby, London 2002. *Publication:* Favourite Flowers (with Deborah Kellaway) 1994. *Address:* 57 Fountainhall Road, Edinburgh EH9 2LH; c/o Royal Scottish Academy, The Mound, Edinburgh EH2 2EL, Scotland. *Telephone:* (131) 667-3687 (Home).

BLACKBOURN, David Gordon, PhD, FRHistS; British professor of history; b. 1 Nov. 1949, Spilsby, Lincs.; s. of Harry Blackbourn and Pamela Jean Blackbourn (née Youngman); m. Deborah Frances Langton 1985; one s. one d.; ed Leeds Modern Grammar School, Christ's Coll., Cambridge; Research Fellow, Jesus Coll., Cambridge 1973–76; lecturer in History, Queen Mary Coll., London Univ. 1976–79, Birkbeck Coll. 1979–85, Reader in Modern History 1985–89, Prof. of Modern European History 1989–92; Prof. of History Harvard Univ. 1992–97, Coolidge Prof. of History 1997–; lectures and contribs to confs in UK, Ireland, Germany, France, Italy, Yugoslavia, USA and Canada 1973–; Fellow Inst. for European History, Mainz, FRG 1974–75; Research Fellow, Alexander von Humboldt Foundation, Bonn-Bad Godesberg, FRG 1984–85, 1994–95; Visiting Kratter Prof. of German History, Stanford Univ., Calif., USA 1989–90; Fellow Guggenheim Foundation, New York 1994–95; Sec. German History Soc. 1978–81, mem. Cttee 1981–86; mem. Acad. Man. Cttee, German Historical Inst., London 1983–92; mem. Editorial Bd Past and Present 1988–; mem. European Sub-Cttee of Labour Party Nat. Exec. Cttee 1978–80, Academic Man. Cttee, Inst. for European History, Mainz, Germany 1995–, Cttee on Hon. Foreign mems, American Historical Asscn 2000–; Vice-Pres. Conf. Group on Cen. European History, American Historical Asscn 2002–03; Ed. Penguin Custom Editions: The Western World Database 2000–; consultant to SMASH/The History Channel, USA; gave Annual Lecture of German Historical Inst., London 1998; American Historical Asscn Prize 1996. *Publications:* Class, Religion and Local Politics in Wilhelmine Germany 1980, The Peculiarities of German History (with Geoff Eley) 1984, Populists and Patricians: Essays in Modern German History 1987, Volksfrömmigkeit und Fortschrittsglaube im Kulturkampf 1988, The German Bourgeoisie (ed. with Richard J. Evans) 1991, Marpingen: Apparitions of the Virgin Mary in Bismarckian Germany 1993, The Fontana History of Germany: the Long Nineteenth Century, 1780–1918 1997; scholarly articles in English, German, French, Serbo-Croat, Japanese and Italian; contribs to several magazines and the BBC. *Leisure interests:* family, reading, music, sport, politics. *Address:* Minda de Gunzburg Center for European Studies, Harvard University, 27 Kirkland Street, Cambridge, MA 02138, USA. *Telephone:* (617) 495-4303, ext. 228 (Office). *Fax:* (617) 495-8509 (Office). *E-mail:* dgblackb@fas.harvard.edu (Office).

BLACKBURN, (Jeffrey) Michael, FCIB, FRSA; British business executive; b. 16 Dec. 1941, Manchester; s. of Jeffrey Blackburn and Renee Blackburn; m. 2nd Louise Clair Jouny 1987; two s.; one s. one d. from previous m.; ed Northgate Grammar School, Ipswich; Chief Man. Business Advisory Service, Lloyds Bank 1979–83; Dir and CEO Jt Credit Card Co. Ltd (Access) 1983–87, Leeds Perm. Bldg Soc. 1987–93; CEO Halifax Bldg Soc. (now Halifax PLC) 1993–98; Dir DFS Furniture PLC 1999–, George Wimpey PLC 1999–, Town Centre Securities PLC 1999–; Pres. Chartered Inst. of Bankers 1998–99; mem. court, Leeds Univ. 1989–2000; Companion, Chartered Man. Inst.; Gov. Nat. Youth Orchestra 1999–; Trustee Duke of Edin.'s Award 1998–; DUniv

(Leeds Metropolitan) 1998, Hon. DLitt (Huddersfield) 1998. *Leisure interests:* the arts. *Address:* Town Centre Securities PLC, Town Centre House, Merrion Centre, Leeds, LS2 8LY, England (Office).

BLACKBURN, Simon W., PhD, DPhil; British professor of philosophy; b. 12 July 1944, Bristol; s. of Cuthbert Blackburn and Edna Blackburn; m. Angela Bowles 1968; one s. one d.; ed Clifton Coll. Bristol and Trinity Coll. Cambridge; Research Fellow, Churchill Coll. Cambridge 1967–69; Fellow and Tutor in Philosophy, Pembroke Coll. Oxford 1969–90; Ed. Mind 1984–90; Edna J. Koury Distinguished Prof. of Philosophy, Univ. of NC 1990–2000; Adjunct Prof. ANU 1993–; Prof. of Philosophy Cambridge Univ. 2001–; Hon. LLD (Sunderland). *Publications:* Reason and Prediction 1970, Spreading the Word 1984, Essays in Quasi-Realism 1993, Oxford Dictionary of Philosophy 1994, Ruling Passions 1998, Think 1999. *Leisure interests:* mountaineering, photography, sailing. *Address:* 141 Thornton Road, Cambridge, CB3 0NE; Faculty of Philosophy, University of Cambridge, Sidgwick Avenue, Cambridge, CB3 9DA, England. *Telephone:* (1223) 528278. *E-mail:* swb24@cam.ac.uk. *Website:* www.unc.edu/~sblackbu/.

BLACKMAN, Honor; British actress; b. 22 Aug. 1926, London; film début in Fame is the Spur 1947. *Films include:* Green Grow the Rushes 1951, Come Die My Love 1952, The Rainbow Jacket 1953, The Glass Cage 1954, Dead Man's Evidence 1955, A Matter of Who 1961, Goldfinger 1964, Life at the Top 1965, Twist of Sand 1967, The Virgin and the Gipsy 1970, To the Devil a Daughter 1975, Summer Rain 1976, The Cat and the Canary 1977, Talos—The Mummy, To Walk With Lions, Bridget Jones's Diary 2001. *Plays include:* Mademoiselle Colombe 2000. *TV appearances include:* Four Just Men 1959, Man of Honour 1960, Ghost Squad 1961, Top Secret 1962, The Avengers 1962–64, The Explorer 1968, Visit from a Stranger 1970, Out Damned Spot 1972, Wind of Change 1977, Robin's Nest 1982, Never the Twain 1982, The Secret Adversary 1983, Lace 1985, The First Modern Olympics 1986, Minder on the Orient Express 1986, Dr. Who 1986, William Tell 1986, The Upper Hand (TV series). *Address:* c/o Jean Diamond, London Management, 2–4 Noel Street, London, W1V 3RB, England.

BLACKSTAD, Theodor Wilhelm, MD; Norwegian professor of anatomy; b. 29 July 1925, Iveland; s. of Leif Blackstad and Alfhild (née Holmsen); m. Ebba Helene Dietrichson 1952; two d.; ed Univ. of Oslo; anatomy teacher, Univ. of Oslo 1953, Prof. of Medicine, Univ. of Aarhus, Denmark 1967–77, Univ. of Oslo 1977–91, Prof. Emer. 1991–; Sr Research Fellow Norwegian Research Council 1991–95; Monrad-Krohn and Nansen prizes. *Publications:* (recently) articles on computer-based analysis of brain morphology. *Address:* Department of Anatomy, Inst. of Basic Medical Sciences, Sognsvannsveien 9, P.O. Box 1105 Blindern, 0317 Oslo (Office); Jernbaneveien 83, 1369 Stabekk, Norway (Home). *Telephone:* 22851271 (Office); 67532885 (Home). *Fax:* 22851278 (Office); 22851278. *E-mail:* t.w.blackstad@basalmed.uio.no (Office); t.w.blackstad@basalmed.uio.no (Home).

BLACKSTONE, Baroness (Life Peer), cr. 1987, of Stoke Newington in Greater London; **Rt. Hon. Tessa Ann Vosper Blackstone,** PC, PhD; British politician and fmr college principal; b. 27 Sept. 1942, London; d. of the late Geoffrey Vaughan Blackstone, CBE, GM and of Joanna Blackstone; m. Tom Evans 1963 (divorced, died 1985); one s. one d.; ed Ware Grammar School, LSE, Univ. of London; Assoc. Lecturer, Enfield Coll. 1965–66; Asst Lecturer, then Lecturer, Dept of Social Admin., LSE 1966–75; Fellow, Centre for Studies in Social Policy 1972–74; Adviser, Cen. Policy Review Staff, Cabinet Office 1975–78; Prof. of Educational Admin., Univ. of London Inst. of Educ. 1978–83; Deputy Educ. Officer (Resources), then Clerk and Dir of Educ., Inner London Educ. Authority 1983–87; Master, Birkbeck Coll., Univ. of London 1987–97; Minister of State in Dept of Educ. and Employment 1997–2001; Minister of State for the Arts, Dept for Culture, Media and Sport 2001–; Opposition Spokesperson on Educ. and Science, House of Lords 1990–92, on Foreign Affairs 1992–97; Dir Royal Opera House 1987–97; Chair. General Advisory Council BBC 1987–91; Chair. Bd of Trustees, Inst. for Public Policy Research 1988–97; Trustee British Museum (Natural History) 1992–97; Dir Thames TV 1991–92; Fellow Birkbeck Coll., Univ. of London 1998; Hon. Fellow LSE 1995; Hon. DLit (Bristol Polytechnic) 1991, (Bradford); Hon. DUniv (Middx); Hon. LLD (Aberdeen) 1994, (St Andrews) 1995; Dr. hc (Strathclyde) 1996; Hon. Dauphine (Sorbonne, Paris) 1998. *Publications:* A Fair Start 1971, Education and Day Care for Young Children in Need 1973, Social Policy and Administration in Britain 1975; co-author: Students in Conflict 1970, The Academic Labour Market 1974, Disadvantage and Education 1982, Education Policy and Educational Inequality 1982, Response to Adversity 1983, Testing Children 1983, Inside the Think Tank: Advising the Cabinet 1971–83, 1988, Prisons and Penal Reform 1990, Race Relations in Britain 1997. *Leisure interests:* tennis, walking, ballet, opera. *Address:* Department for Culture, Media and Sport, 2–4 Cockspur Street, London, SW1Y 5DH, England. *Telephone:* (20) 7211-62003. *E-mail:* tessa.blackstone@culture.gov.uk (Office). *Website:* www.culture.gov.uk.

BLACKWELL, Julian (Toby); British bookseller; b. 10 Jan. 1929; s. of the late Sir Basil Henry Blackwell and Marion Christine Soans; m. Jennifer Jocelyn Darley Wykeham 1953; two s. one d.; ed Winchester Coll. and Trinity Coll., Oxford; served 5th Royal Tank Regt 1947–49; 21st SAS (TA) 1950–59; Dir and Chair. various Blackwell cos 1956–; Pres. Blackwell Ltd 1995–, Chair. 1996–99; Chair. Council, ASLIB 1966–68; Pres. Booksellers' Asscn 1980–82; Chair. Thames Business Advice Centre 1986–97, Heart of England TEC 1989–94, Fox FM 1989–98, Cottontail

Ltd 1990–; Chair. Son White Memorial Trust 1991–; DL (Oxfordshire) 1988; Hon. DLitt (Robert Gordon) 1997, DUniv (Sheffield Hallam) 1998. *Leisure interests:* sawing firewood, sailing. *Address:* c/o Blackwell, 50 Broad Street, Oxford, OX1 3BQ, England. *Telephone:* (1865) 792111. *Website:* www .blackwell.com.

BLACKWELL, Baron (Life Peer) cr. 1997, of Woodcote in the County of Surrey; **Norman Roy Blackwell,** PhD, MBA; British business executive and fmr civil servant; b. 29 July 1952, London; s. of Albert Edward Blackwell and Frances Evelyn Blackwell (née Lutman); m. Brenda Clucas 1974; three s. two d.; ed Latymer Upper School, Trinity Coll., Cambridge, Wharton Business School, Univ. of Pa (Thouron Scholar); Jr Exhibitioner RAM 1963–69; Chair. Cambridge Univ. Conservative Asscn 1973; with Strategic Planning Unit, Plessey Co. 1976–78, McKinsey & Co. 1978–86, 1988–95 (partner 1984), Prime Minister's Policy Unit 1986–88, Head 1995–97; Dir of Group Devt NatWest Group 1997–2000; Dir Dixons Group 2000–; Special Adviser KPMG Corp. Finance 2000–, Corp. Services Group 2000–, Slough Estates 2001–; Chair. Centre for Policy Studies 2000–, Smartstream Technologies Group 2001–; mem. Bd Office of Fair Trading 2003–; Deputy Chair. British Urban Regeneration Asscn 1991–92. *Leisure interests:* classical music, walking. *Address:* c/o House of Lords, London, SW1A 0PW, England. *Telephone:* (20) 7311-4997.

BLAGOJEVICH, Rod R., BA, JD; American state official; b. 10 Dec.1956, Chicago; s. of Rade Blagojevich and Millie Blagojevich (née Govedarica); m. Patricia Blagojevich; one d.; ed Northwestern Univ., Pepperdine Univ.; est. pvt. law practice, Chicago 1983; Asst State Attorney, Cook Co. 1983–92; mem. House of Reps. for Ill. 1992–96; mem. Congress 1997–2003; Gov. of Ill. 2003–; Democrat; Library Man of the Year, American Library Asscn, Friends of Libraries USA, Whitehouse Conf. on Libraries. *Address:* Office of the Governor, 207 State House, Springfield, IL 62706, USA (Office).

BLAHNIK, Manolo; Spanish couturier; b. 28 Nov. 1943, Santa Cruz, The Canary Islands; ed Univ. of Geneva; f. and Dir Manolo Blahnik Int. Ltd; opened shop in Chelsea, London 1973, USA 1981; biannual collections in London and New York; Fashion Council of America Award 1988, 1991, 1997, American Leather New York Award 1991, British Fashion Award 1992, Nieman Marcus Award 1993. *Publications:* various int. publs on fashion. *Leisure interests:* painting, reading. *Address:* 15 West 55th Street, New York, NY 10019, USA; 49–51 Old Church Street, London, SW3, England. *Telephone:* (20) 7352-8622.

BLAINEY, Geoffrey Norman, AO; Australian historian and author; b. 11 March 1930, Melbourne; s. of Rev. Samuel C. Blainey and Hilda Blainey; m. Ann Heriot 1957; one d.; ed Ballarat High School, Wesley Coll., Univ. of Melbourne; freelance historian 1951–61; Reader in Econ. History, Univ. of Melbourne 1963–68, Prof. 1968–76, Ernest Scott Prof. 1977–88, Dean of Faculty of Arts 1982–87; Prof. of Australian Studies, Harvard Univ. 1982–83; columnist in daily newspapers 1974–; Chair. Australia Council 1977–81, Fed. Govt.'s Australia-China Council 1979–84, Commonwealth Literary Fund 1971–73; Pres. Council, Queen's Coll., Univ. of Melbourne 1971–89; Chair. Australian Selection Cttee Commonwealth Fund (Harkness) Fellowships 1983–90; Chancellor Univ. of Ballarat 1994–98; Dir Royal Humane Soc. 1996–; Gov. Ian Potter Foundation 1991–; Councillor Australian War Memorial 1997–; Del. to Australian Constitutional Convention 1998; Councillor Nat. Council for the Centenary of Fed. 1997–2002 (Chair. 2001–02); Gold Medal, Australian Literature Soc. 1963, Capt. Cook Bicentenary Literary Award 1970, Britannica Award for dissemination of learning, NY 1988. *Publications include:* The Peaks of Lyell 1954, Centenary History of the University of Melbourne 1957, Gold and Paper: a History of the National Bank 1958, Mines in the Spinifex 1960, The Rush That Never Ended 1963, The Tyranny of Distance 1966, Across a Red World 1968, The Rise of Broken Hill 1968, The Steel Master 1971, The Causes of War 1973, Triumph of the Nomads: A History of Ancient Australia 1975, A Land Half Won 1980, Our Side of the Country 1984, All for Australia 1984, The Great Seesaw 1988, A Game of Our Own 1990, Eye on Australia 1991, Odd Fellows 1992, The Golden Mile 1993, Jumping over the Wheel 1993, A Shorter History of Australia 1994, White Gold 1997, A History of AMP 1999, In Our Time 1999, A Short History of the World 2000, This Land is all Horizons 2001. *Leisure interests:* travel, wood-chopping, Australian football. *Address:* P.O. Box 257, East Melbourne, Vic. 3002, Australia. *Telephone:* (3) 9417-7782. *Fax:* (3) 9417-7920 (Home).

BLAIR, Rt Hon Anthony Charles Lynton (Tony), PC; British politician; b. 6 May 1953, Edinburgh; s. of Leo Blair and the late Hazel Blair; m. Cherie Booth (q.v.) 1980; three s. one d.; ed Fettes Coll., Edinburgh, St John's Coll., Oxford; barrister, specializing in trade union and employment law; MP for Sedgefield 1983–; Shadow Treasury Spokesman 1984–87, Trade and Industry Spokesman 1987–88, Energy Spokesman 1988–89, Employment Spokesman 1989–92, Home Affairs Spokesman 1992–94; Leader of the Labour Party July 1994–, Prime Minister, First Lord of the Treasury and Minister for the Civil Service May 1997–; Hon. Bencher Lincoln's Inn 1994; Hon. LLD (Northumbria) 1995; Charlemagne Prize 1999. *Publications:* New Britain: My Vision of a Young Country 1996, The Third Way 1998. *Address:* 10 Downing Street, London SW1A 2AA; Myrobella, Trimdon Station, County Durham, TS29 6DU, England. *Telephone:* (20) 7270-3000. *Website:* www.pm.gov.uk.

BLAIR, Cherie (see Booth, Cherie).

BLAIR, Dennis Cutler, BA; American naval officer; m. Diane Blair; one s. one d.; commissioned as ensign in US Navy; rank of Vice-Adm.; Commdr. USS Cochrane 1984–86, Naval Staff Pearl Harbor 1988–89, Kittyhawk Battlegroup 1993–95; Assoc. Dir. Cen. Intelligence Mil. Support 1995–96; Dir Jt. Staff 1996–99; C.-in-C. US Pacific Command, Hawaii 1999–; Rhodes Scholar, Oxford Univ.; White House Fellow, Naval Operations Fellow; Legion of Merit with three gold stars, Service Medal with two oak leaf clusters. *Address:* Commander in Chief US Pacific Command, Box 64028, Camp HM Smith Hawaii 96861, USA (Office).

BLAIR, Gordon Purves, CBE, PhD, DSc, FR.ENG., FIMechE; British professor of mechanical engineering; b. 29 April 1937, Larne, Northern Ireland; s. of Gordon Blair and Mary H.J. Blair; m. Norma Margaret Millar 1964; two d.; ed Larne Grammar School and The Queen's Univ. of Belfast; Asst Prof., Mechanical Eng, New Mexico State Univ. 1962–64; Lecturer in Mechanical Eng, Queen's Univ. Belfast 1964–71, Sr Lecturer 1971–73, Reader 1973–76, Prof. 1976–96, Prof. Emer. 1996–, Prof. and Head of Dept of Mechanical and Industrial Eng 1982–88, Dean of Faculty 1985–88, Pro-Vice-Chancellor 1989–94; consultant to many industries world-wide on engine design; Fellow SAE; Colwell Technical Merit Award (SAE),Crompton Lanchester Medal (IMechE), Trident TV Award (IBA). *Publications:* The Basic Design of Two-Stroke Engines 1990, The Design and Simulation of Two-Stroke Engines 1996, The Design and Simulation of Four Stroke Engines 1999; more than 100 tech. papers in int. journals. *Leisure interests:* golf, fishing, motorcycling. *Address:* 9 Ben Madigan Park South, Newtonabbey, Co. Antrim, BT36 7PX (Home); Ashby Building, The Queen's University of Belfast, Belfast, BT9 5AH, Northern Ireland. *Telephone:* (1232) 370368. *Fax:* (1232) 370372. *E-mail:* gpb@profblairandassociates.com (Office); g.p.blair@qub.ac.uk (Home). *Website:* www.profblairandassociates.com.

BLAIS, Marie-Claire, CC; Canadian writer; b. 5 Oct. 1939, Québec City; d. of Fernando Blais and Veronique Nolin; ed Québec, Paris and United States; Guggenheim Foundation Fellowship, New York 1963, 1964; Hon. Prof. Calgary Univ. 1978; mem. Royal Soc. of Canada, Acad. Royale de Belgique; Hon. mem. Boivin Center of French Language and Culture, Univ. of Massachusetts, USA; Chevalier de la Légion d'honneur; Dr hc (York Univ., Toronto) 1975; Prix de la langue française 1961, Prix France-Québec 1964, Prix Médicis 1966, Prix de l'Acad. Française 1983, Prix Athanase-David (Québec) 1983, Prix Nessim Habif (Acad. Royale de Belgique) 1991 and others. *Publications:* La belle bête 1959, Tête blanche 1960, Le jour est noir 1962, Existences (poems), Une saison dans la vie d'Emmanuel 1965, L'insoumise 1966, David Sterne 1967, Manuscrits de Pauline Archange 1968, Vivre, vivre 1969, Les voyageurs sacrés 1966, Les apparences 1970, Le loup 1972, Un Joualonais sa Joualonie 1973, Une liaison parisienne 1976, Les nuits de l'underground 1978, Le sourd dans la ville 1980, Visions d'Anna 1982, Pierre 1984, Dans la foudre et la lumière 2002 (novels), Pays voilés (poems) 1964; L'océan 1967, L'exécution 1968, Fièvre 1974, La nef des sorcières 1976, Sommeil d'hiver 1985, Fière 1985, L'île 1988 (plays), L'ange de la solitude (novel) 1989, Un jardin dans la tempête (play) 1990, Parcours d'un Ecrivain: Notes Americaines (essay) 1993, L'Exile (short stories) 1993, Soifs (novel) 1995, Dans la foudre et la lumière (novel), Théatre (Ed.). *Leisure interests:* painting and drawing, biking, handwriting analysis. *Address:* 4411 Rue St Denis, Apt 401, Montreal, H2J 2LN, Québec, Canada. *Telephone:* (514) 842-8026.

BLAIS, Pierre, BA, LLL; Canadian politician; b. 30 Dec. 1948, Berthier-sur-Mer, Québec; m. Chantal Fournier; two s. two d.; ed Laval Univ.; partner, Montmagny law practice 1976–84; Prof. Univ. du Québec à Rimouski 1982; Prof. Laval Univ. 1982–84; Parl. Sec. to Minister of Agric. 1984–86, to Deputy Prime Minister 1987–87; Minister of State (Agric.) 1987–93, Minister of Consumer and Corp. Affairs 1990–93; Minister of Justice and Attorney-Gen. 1993; Privy Council Pres. 1993; Solicitor-Gen. of Canada 1989–90; Progressive Conservative. *Leisure interests:* skiing, reading, swimming. *Address:* Langlois, Gaudreau s.e.n.c., 801 chemin St-Louis, bur. 160, Québec, G1S 1C1, Canada. *Telephone:* (418) 682-1212. *Fax:* (418) 682-2272.

BLAKE, John Clemens, MA, RCA; American artist; b. 11 Jan. 1945, Providence, RI; s. of John Holland Blake and Elizabeth Clemens (now Romāno); ed Carnegie Inst. of Tech. (now Carnegie-Mellon Univ.), Yale Univ., Royal Coll. of Art, London; freelance visual artist in various media including drawing, installations, photographic constructions, audio constructions, film, etc.; approx. 40 solo exhbns in Europe and USA 1972–, including Victoria and Albert Museum, London, Museum of Modern Art, Oxford, Project Studios One (PS1), New York, ICA, London, Krzysztofory, Kraków, Poland, Corps de Garde, Groningen, de Vleeshal, Middelburg and Bonnefantenmuseum, Maastricht, Netherlands, Orchard Gallery, Londonderry, Northern Ireland; teaching has included Hull Polytechnic 1975–76; London Coll. of Printing 1978–82; S. Glamorgan Inst. of Higher Educ., S. Wales 1983–84; Fulbright Fellow 1967–69; Nat. Endowment (USA) 1977; Arts Council Award (UK) 1979, Hokkaido Foundation Award (Japan) 1984. *Publications:* John Blake 1980, de Vleeshal 1983, Their Eyes 1983, Drawings and Constructions 1986. *Address:* Oz. Voorburgwal 131, 1012-ER Amsterdam, Netherlands. *Telephone:* (20) 277-740.

BLAKE, Peter Jost, BArch, FAIA; American architect; b. 20 Sept. 1920, Berlin, Germany; one s. one d; ed Grünewald Gymnasium, Berlin, Bootham School, York, Univ. of London, Regent Street Polytechnic, London, Univ. of Pennsylvania and Pratt Inst. School of Architecture, New York City; apprentice architect, London 1938–39, Philadelphia 1940–42; Curator, Dept of

Architecture and Industrial Design, Museum of Modern Art, New York 1948–50; Assoc. Ed., later Ed.-in-Chief, The Architectural Forum, New York 1950–72; registered architect 1956–; architectural practice, New York, Boston, Washington, DC and Berlin 1956–; Ed.-in-Chief, Architecture Plus, New York 1972–75; Chair. School of Architecture, Boston Architectural Center 1975–79; Chair. Dept of Architecture and Planning, Catholic Univ. of America, Washington, DC 1979–86, Prof. of Architecture 1979–91, Prof. Emer. 1991–; Visiting Prof. Washington Univ. St Louis 1991–93; bldgs and projects include: apt bldg, Berlin; various experimental theatres in New York, Nashville, Tenn. and elsewhere; institutional and industrial bldgs in USA and Europe; housing projects and several exhbns; Architecture Critic's Medal, American Inst. of Architects 1975. *Publications:* The Master Builders 1960, God's Own Junkyard 1964, Form Follows Fiasco–Why Modern Architecture Hasn't Worked 1977, No Place Like Utopia 1993, Philip Johnson 1996; contribs to books and articles in newspapers, magazines and journals. *Leisure interest:* photography. *Address:* 474 West 238th Street, Apartment 3A, Bronx NY 10463-2027, USA (Office). *Telephone:* (718) 884-4967 (Office). *Fax:* (718) 884-4967 (Office).

BLAKE, Peter (Thomas), CBE, RA, ARCA; British artist; b. 25 June 1932; s. of Kenneth William Blake; m. 1st Jann Haworth 1963 (divorced 1982); two d.; m. 2nd Chrissy Wilson 1987; one d.; ed Gravesend Tech. Coll., Gravesend School of Art, Royal Coll. of Art; third assoc. artist of Nat. Gallery, London 1994–96; works exhibited in Inst. of Contemporary Art 1958, 1960, Guggenheim Competition 1958, Cambridge 1959, Royal Acad. 1960, Musée d'Art Moderne, Paris 1963; works in perm. collections, Trinity Coll., Cambridge, Carlisle City Gallery, Tate Gallery, Arts Council of GB, Museum of Modern Art, New York, Victoria and Albert Museum and other maj. galleries; Dr hc (RCA). *Retrospective exhibitions include:* City Art Gallery, Bristol 1969, Tate Gallery, London 1983, Nat. Gallery, London 1996. *Publications:* illustrations for Oxford Illustrated Old Testament 1968, several Arden Shakespeares and in various periodicals and magazines. *Leisure interests:* sculpture, wining and dining, going to rock and roll concerts. *Address:* c/o Waddington Galleries Ltd, 11 Cork Street, London, W1X 2LT, England.

BLAKE, Quentin Saxby, OBE, RDI, MA, FCSD; British artist, illustrator and teacher; b. 16 Dec. 1932, Sidcup, Kent; s. of William Blake and Evelyn Blake; ed Downing Coll., Cambridge, London Inst. of Educ., Chelsea School of Art; freelance illustrator since 1957; Tutor, Royal Coll. of Art 1965–86, Head of Illustration Dept 1978–86, Visiting Prof. 1989–; Senior Fellow Royal Coll. of Art 1988; Hon. Fellow Brighton Univ. 1996, Downing Coll. Cambridge 2000; Hon. RA; Chevalier des Arts et des Lettres 2002; Dr hc (London Inst.) 2000, (Northumbria) 2001, RCA 2001; Children's Laureate 1999. *Publications:* illustrations for over 250 works for children and adults, including collaborations with Roald Dahl, Russell Hoban, Joan Aiken, Michael Rosen, John Yeoman; non-fiction: La Vie de la Page 1995, Quentin Blake Words and Pictures 2000, Tell Me a Picture 2001, Laureate's Progress 2002. *Address:* Flat 8, 30 Bramham Gardens, London, SW5 0HF, England. *Telephone:* (20) 7373-7464.

BLAKE, Baron (Life Peer), cr. 1971, of Braydeston, Norfolk; **Robert Norman William Blake,** DLitt, MA, FBA, JP; British academic; b. 23 Dec. 1916, Blofield, Norfolk; s. of William J. Blake and Norah L. Daynes; m. Patricia M. Waters 1953 (died 1995); three d.; ed King Edward VI School, Norwich and Magdalen Coll., Oxford; mil. service during World War II (RA), POW in Italy 1942–44, escaped 1944; MI6 1944–46; Lecturer in Politics, Christ Church, Oxford 1946–47, Student and Tutor in Politics 1947–68, Hon. Student 1977; Censor 1950–55; Sr Proctor 1959–60; Ford's Lecturer in English History 1967–68; mem. Hebdomadal Council 1959–81; Provost, The Queen's Coll., Oxford 1968–87; Pro-Vice-Chancellor, Univ. of Oxford 1971–87; Jt Ed. Dictionary of Nat. Biog. 1980–90; Pres. Electoral Reform Soc. 1986–93; mem. Royal Comm. on Historical Manuscripts (Chair. 1982–89), Bd of Trustees of British Museum 1978–88; Rhodes Trustee 1971–87, Chair. 1983–87; mem. Bd of Channel 4 TV 1983–87; Hon. DLitt (Glasgow) 1972, (East Anglia) 1983, (Buckingham) 1988. *Publications:* The Private Papers of Douglas Haig (ed.) 1952, The Unknown Prime Minister (Life of Andrew Bonar Law) 1955, Disraeli 1966, The Conservative Party from Peel to Churchill 1970, The Office of Prime Minister 1975, A History of Rhodesia 1977, Disraeli's Grand Tour 1982, The English World (ed.) 1982, The Conservative Party from Peel to Thatcher 1985, The Decline of Power 1985, Salisbury: the man and his policies (co-ed.) 1987, World History: From 1800 to the Present Day (ed.) 1988, Churchill (co-ed.) 1993, The Conservative Party from Peel to Major 1997, Churchill, a Pocket Biography 1998, Jardine Matheson, Traders of the Far East 1999. *Leisure interests:* reading and writing. *Address:* Riverview House, Brundall, Norfolk, NR13 5LA, England. *Telephone:* (1603) 712133.

BLAKEMORE, Colin (Brian), PhD, ScD, DSc, FIBiol, CBiol, FMedSci, FRS; British neurophysiologist and professor of physiology; b. 1 June 1944, Stratford-on-Avon; s. of Cedric Norman and Beryl Ann Blakemore; m. Andrée Elizabeth Washbourne 1965; three d.; ed King Henry VIII School, Coventry, Corpus Christi Coll., Cambridge, Univ. of Calif. Berkeley; Harkness Fellowship, Univ. of Calif. 1965–67; Univ. Demonstrator, Physiological Laboratory, Cambridge 1968–72; Lecturer in Physiology, Cambridge 1972–79; Fellow and Dir of Medical Studies, Downing Coll. 1971–79; Visiting Prof. New York Univ. 1970, MIT 1971; Locke Research Fellow, Royal Soc. 1976–79; Waynflete Prof. of Physiology, Oxford 1979–; Professorial Fellow of Magdalen Coll. Oxford 1979–; Chief Exec. European Dana Alliance for the Brain 1996–; Pres. British Asscn for the Advancement of Science 1997–98 (Chair. 2001–), British

Neuroscience Asscn 1997–2000, Physiological Soc. 2001–; Vice-Pres. BAAS 1990–; Visiting Scientist, The Salk Inst., San Diego 1982–83; Dir McDonnell-Pew Centre for Cognitive Neuroscience, Oxford 1990–, MRC Interdisciplinary Research Centre for Cognitive Neuroscience, Oxford 1996–; Assoc. Dir MRC Research Centre in Brain and Behaviour, Oxford 1990–; Visiting Prof. McMaster Univ. 1992; mem. Editorial Bd Perception 1971, Behavioral and Brain Sciences 1977, Journal of Developmental Physiology 1978–86, Experimental Brain Research 1979–89, Language and Communication 1979, Reviews in the Neurosciences 1984–, News in Physiological Sciences 1985, Clinical Vision Sciences 1986, Chinese Journal of Physiological Sciences 1988, Advances in Neuroscience 1989–, Vision Research 1993–; Assoc. Ed. Neuro-Report 1989–; Ed.-in-Chief IBRO News 1986–; Leverhulme Fellowship 1974–75; BBC Reith Lecturer 1976; Lethaby Prof., RCA, London 1978; Storer Lecturer, Univ. of Calif. at Davis 1980, Regents' Prof. 1995–96; Macallum Lecturer, Univ. of Toronto 1984; Fellow World Econ. Forum 1994–98, Hon. Fellow Corpus Christi Coll., Cambridge 1994–, Founder Fellow Acad. of Medical Sciences 1998–; Foreign mem. Royal Netherlands Acad. of Arts and Sciences 1993; mem. Worshipful Co. of Spectacle Makers and Freeman of the City of London 1997, mem. Livery 1998; Patron and mem. Professional Advisory Panel Headway (Nat. Head Injuries Asscn) 1997–; Patron Asscn for Art, Science, Eng and Tech. (ASCENT) 1997–; Hon. Fellow Cardiff, Univ. of Wales 1998, Downing Coll., Cambridge 1999–; Hon. mem. Physiological Soc. 1998–, Maverick Club 1999–, British Asscn for the Advancement of Science 2001–; Hon. Assoc. Rationalist Press Asscn 1986–, Rationalist Int. 2000–; Hon. DSc (Aston) 1992, (Salford) 1994; Robert Bing Prize, Swiss Acad. of Medical Sciences 1975, Man of the Year (Royal Soc. for Disability and Rehabilitation) 1978; Christmas Lectures for Young People, Royal Inst. 1982; John Locke Medal, Worshipful Soc. of Apothecaries 1983, Netter Prize of Acad. Nat. de Médecine, Paris 1984, Bertram Louis Abrahams Lecture, Royal Coll. of Physicians 1986, Cairns Memorial Lecture and Medal, Soc. of British Neurological Surgeons 1986, Norman McAllister Gregg Lecture and Medal, Royal Australian Coll. of Ophthalmologists 1988, Royal Soc. Michael Faraday Medal 1989, Robert Doyne Medal, Oxford Ophthalmology Congress 1989, John P. McGovern Science and Society Lecture and Medal 1990, Montgomery Medal 1991, Sir Douglas Robb Lectures, Univ. of Auckland 1991, Osler Medal (Royal Coll. of Physicians) 1993, Ellison-Cliffe Medal (Royal Soc. of Medicine) 1993, Charles F. Prentice Award (American Acad. of Optometry) 1994, Annual Review Prize Lecture (Physiological Soc.) 1995, Centenary Lecture, Univ. of Salford 1996, Alcon Prize 1996, Newton Lecture 1997, Cockcroft Lecture, UMIST 1997, Memorial Medal (Charles Univ., Prague) 1998, Alfred Meyer Award (British Neuropathological Soc. 2001, Inst. of Biology Charter Award and Medal 2001, Baly Medal, Royal Coll. of Physicians (Dyster Trust) 2001, British Neuroscience Asscn Outstanding Contribution to Neuroscience 2001. *Television:* presenter The Next Big Thing (series, BBC2) 2000, 2002. *Publications:* Ed. Handbook of Psychobiology 1975, Mechanics of the Mind 1977, Ed. Mindwaves 1987, The Mind Machine 1988, Ed. Images and Understanding 1990, Vision: Coding and Efficiency 1990, Sex and Society 1999, Oxford Companion to the Body 2001; contribs to Constraints on Learning 1973, Illusion in Art and Nature 1973, The Neurosciences Third Study Program 1974 and to professional journals. *Leisure interests:* running and the arts. *Address:* University Laboratory of Physiology, Parks Road, Oxford OX1 3PT, England (Office). *Telephone:* (1865) 272471 (Office). *Fax:* (1865) 272488 (Office). *E-mail:* blakemore@physiol.ox.ac.uk (Office).

BLAKEMORE, Michael Howell, OBE; Australian theatre and film director; b. 18 June 1928, Sydney; s. of Conrad Blakemore and Una Mary (née Litchfield) Blakemore; m. 1st Shirley Bush 1960; one s.; m. 2nd Tanya McCallin 1986; two d.; ed The King's School, NSW, Sydney Univ., Royal Acad. of Dramatic Art, UK; actor with Birmingham Repertory Theatre, Shakespeare Memorial Theatre etc. 1952–66; Co-Dir Glasgow Citizens' Theatre 1966–68 (first production The Investigation); Assoc. Artistic Dir Nat. Theatre, London 1971–76; Dir Players, New York, USA 1978; Resident Dir Lyric Theatre, Hammersmith, London 1980; Best Dir, London Critics 1972, Drama Desk Award 1982, Outer Critics' Circle Awards 1982, 1989, Hollywood Dramalogue Award 1983, Drama League Award 1997, Standard Film Award 1982, Film Critics' Award 1994, two Tony Awards 2000, two Drama Desk Awards 2000. *Films include:* A Personal History of the Australian Surf (writer and Dir) 1981, Privates on Parade (Dir) 1983, Country Life (writer and Dir) 1994. *Productions include:* A Day in the Death of Joe Egg 1967, Arturo Ui 1969, The National Health 1969, Long Day's Journey into Night 1971, The Front Page, Macbeth 1972, The Cherry Orchard 1973, Design for Living 1973, Separate Tables 1976, Plunder 1976, Privates on Parade 1977, Candida 1977, Make and Break 1980, Travelling North 1980, The Wild Duck 1980, All My Sons 1981, Noises Off 1982 (Drama Desk Award, New York 1983–84), Benefactors 1984, Lettice and Lovage 1987, Uncle Vanya 1988, City of Angels 1989, Lettice and Lovage 1990, After the Fall 1990, The Ride Down Mount Morgan 1991, Tosca (Welsh Nat. Opera) 1992, The Sisters Rosensweig 1994, Death Defying Acts 1995, Now You Know 1995, Sylvia 1996, The Life 1997, Copenhagen 1998, Kiss Me Kate 1999. *Television productions include:* Long Day's Journey into Night 1972, Hay Fever (Denmark) 1978, Tales from the Hollywood Hills (USA) 1988. *Publications:* Next Season (novel) 1969, Australia Fair? (anthology) 1985. *Leisure interest:* surfing. *Address:* 18 Upper Park Road, London, NW3 2UP, England. *Telephone:* (20) 7483-2575. *Fax:* (20) 7483-2476.

BLAKENEY, Allan Emrys, PC, OC, QC, LLB, MA, FRSC; Canadian politician (retd); b. 7 Sept. 1925, Bridgewater, Nova Scotia; s. of John Cline Blakeney and Bertha May Davies; m. 1st Mary Elizabeth Schwartz 1950 (died 1957); one s. one d.; m. 2nd Anne Louise Gorham 1959; one s. one d.; ed Dalhousie and Oxford Univs.; Sec. and legal adviser to Crown Corpn, Govt of Sask. 1950–55; Chair. Sask. Securities Comm. 1955–58; partner law firm of Davidson, Davidson & Blakeney 1958–60; mem. Legis. Ass. 1960–88 (retd); Govt of Sask. Minister of Educ. 1960–61, Provincial Treas. 1961–62, Minister of Health 1962–64, Leader of the Opposition 1970–71, Premier 1971–82, Leader of the Opposition 1982–87; mem. Senate, Univ. of Sask. 1960–62; Chair. of Wascana Centre Authority 1962–64; partner Griffin, Blakeney, Beke (law firm) 1964–70; Pres. New Democratic Party of Canada 1969–71; Laskin Prof. of Constitutional Law, Osgoode Hall Law School, York Univ. 1988–90; Law Foundation Prof. of Public Law, Univ. of Sask. 1990–91, Visiting Scholar 1991–; Dr. hc (Mount Allison Univ.) 1980, (Dalhousie) 1980, (York) 1991, (Univ. of W Ont.) 1991, (Univ. of Regina) 1993, (Univ. of Sask.) 1995. *Publications:* Political Management in Canada (with S. Borins) 1992; articles on public affairs. *Address:* Room 107, College of Law, 15 Campus Drive, University of Saskatchewan, Saskatoon, Saskatchewan, S7N 5A6 (Office); 1752 Prince of Wales Avenue, Saskatoon, Saskatchewan, S7K 3E5, Canada (Home). *Telephone:* (306) 966-5881 (Office); (306) 934-0626 (Home). *Fax:* (306) 966-5900 (Office); (306) 665-2581 (Home). *E-mail:* blakeney@duke.usask.ca.

BLAKENHAM, 2nd Viscount (cr. 1963), of Little Blakenham; **Michael John Hare,** PC, OBE, DL; British business executive; b. 25 Jan. 1938, London; s. of the late 1st Viscount Blakenham and Hon. Beryl Nancy Pearson; m. Marcia P. Hare 1965; one s. two d.; ed Eton Coll. and Harvard Univ.; nat. service 1956–57; with English Electric Co. 1958; Lazard Brothers 1961–63; Standard Industrial Group 1963–71; Royal Doulton 1972–77; Chief Exec. Pearson PLC 1978–90, Chair. 1983–97; Chair. Financial Times 1983–93; Partner Lazard Partners 1984–97 (Dir Lazard Bros. 1975–97); Dir Sotheby's Holdings Inc. 1987–, MEPC PLC 1990–98 (Chair. 1993–98); mem. Int. Advisory Bd Lafarge 1979–97 (Dir 1997–); mem. Int. Advisory Group Toshiba 1997–; Dir UK–Japan 2000 Group 1990–; Chair. Royal Soc. for Protection of Birds 1981–86; Pres. Sussex Wildlife Trust 1983–, Bristol Trust for Ornithology 2001–; mem. House of Lords Select Cttee on Science and Tech. 1984–88, Nature Conservancy Council 1986–90; Trustee The Royal Botanic Gardens, Kew 1991– (Chair. 1997–); Conservative. *Address:* House of Lords, London, SW1A 0PW; 1 St Leonard's Studio, London, SW3 4EN, England (Home).

BLANC, Christian; French business executive; b. 17 May 1942, Talence, Gironde; s. of Marcel Blanc and Emcarma Miranda; m. Asa Hagglund 1973; two d.; ed Ecole Montgolfier, Bordeaux, Lycée Montesquieu, Bordeaux and Inst. d'Etudes Politiques, Bordeaux; Asst Dir Sopexa-Scandinavie 1969; Société centrale d'équipement du territoire 1970–74; Chef du bureau, State Secr. for Youth and Sport 1974–76; Asst Del.-Gen. Agence technique interministérielle pour les loisirs et le plein air 1976–80; Dir du Cabinet to Edgard Pisani, mem. of Comm. of EC, Brussels 1981–83; Prefect, Commr, République des Hautes-Pyrénées 1983–84; special Govt assignment, New Caledonia 1985; Prefect for Seine-et-Marne 1985–89; Special Prefect 1989; Chair. and CEO RATP 1989–93; Chair. and CEO Air France (Admin. Council) 1993–97; Dir Middle E Airlines 1998–99, Marceau Investissements 1999–; Chair. Merrill Lynch France SA 2000–02; Presidential Cand. 2002; Dir Action contre la Faim 1998–; Pres. Karaval 2001–; f. L'Ami Public; Chevalier, Légion d'honneur, Officier Ordre Nat. du Mérite. *Publication:* Le Lièvre et La Tortue (jtly) 1994.

BLANC, Georges; French chef, author and business executive; b. 2 Jan. 1943, Bourg-en-Bresse; s. of Jean Blanc and Paule Blanc (née Tisserand); m. Jacqueline Masson 1966; two s.; ed Ecole Hôtelière de Thonon-les-Bains; worked at Réserve de Beaulieu and Grand Hôtel de Divonne; mil. service as chef to Adm. Vedel on the Foch and the Clémenceau; returned to work in family business 1965, became head of firm 1968; Man. Dir Georges Blanc SA; Maître Cuisinier de France 1975; finalist in Meilleur Ouvrier de France competition 1976; has organized numerous events abroad to promote French cuisine; Founder mem., Second Vice-Pres. Chambre Syndicale de la Haute Cuisine Française 1986; Muncipal Councillor, Vonnas 1989; Officier, Ordre nat. du Mérite, Commdr du Mérite agricole, Officier des Arts et des Lettres, Chevalier, Légion d'honneur. *Publications:* Mes recettes 1981, La cuisine de Bourgogne (Co-author), la nature dans l'assiette 1987, Le livre blanc des quatre saisons 1988, Les Blanc (jtly.) 1989, Le Grand Livre de la Volaille (jtly.) 1991, De la vigne à l'assiette 1995, la Cuisine de nos mères 2000, Cuisine de la vigne à la Carte 2000. *Leisure interests:* skiing, tennis. *Address:* Le Mère Blanc, 01540 Vonnas (Ain), France. *Telephone:* (4) 74-50-90-90.

BLANC, Pierre-Louis, MenD, MèsL; French diplomatist; b. 18 Jan. 1926; s. of Lucien Blanc and Renée Blanc; m. 1st (wife deceased); one s. two d.; m. 2nd Jutta Freifrau von Cramm 1988; ed Univ. of Paris, Paris Inst. of Political Studies and Ecole Nat. d'Admin; served French embassies in Rabat 1956, Tokyo 1962, Madrid 1965; served Office of Pres. of Repub. 1967–69; pvt. staff of Gen. de Gaulle 1969–70; Acting Deputy Dir for Asia/Oceania, Govt of France 1969–71; Cultural Counsellor, London 1971–75; Deputy Dir for Personnel and Gen. Admin. Ministry of Foreign Affairs 1975; Dir École Nat. d'Admin. 1975–82; Amb. to Sweden 1982–85, to Greece 1985–87; Perm. Rep. to UN 1987–91; Pres. Council of Francophone Affairs 1992–; Vice-Pres. Soc. des Amis des Archives de France 1994–2000; Commdr Légion d'honneur 1992. *Publication:* De Gaulle au soir de sa vie. *Leisure interest:* writing. *Address:* Quartier de Gergouven, 84560 Ménerbes, France. *Telephone:* 4-90-72-26-52 (Home). *Fax:* 4-90-72-26-45 (Home).

BLANC, Raymond René Alfred; French chef; b. 19 Nov. 1949, Besançon; s. of Maurice Blanc and Anne-Marie Blanc; two s.; ed Besançon Tech. Coll.; various positions 1968–76, Mil. Service 1970–71; Man. and Chef de cuisine, Bleu, Blanc, Rouge, Oxford 1976–77; opening of Les Quat'Saisons, Oxford as Chef Proprietor 1977; opening of Maison Blanc, patisserie and boulangerie 1978, Dir and Chair. 1978–88; opening of Le Manoir aux Quat'Saisons 1984; opening of Le Petit Blanc in Oxford 1996, in Cheltenham 1998, in Birmingham 1999 in Manchester 2000; weekly recipe column in the Observer 1988–90; mem. Acad. Culinaire de France, British Gastronomic Acad.; mem. Restaurateurs Asscn of GB; rep. GB at Grand Final of Wedgwood World Master of Culinary Arts, Paris 2002; Hon. DBA (Oxford Brookes Univ.) 1999;European Chef of the Year 1989; Personalité de l'Année 1990, Craft Guild of Chefs Special Award 2002; many awards for both the restaurant and hotel. *Television:* Blanc Mange (series) 1994, Passion for Perfection (series, Carlton TV) 2002. *Publications:* Recipes from Le Manoir aux Quat'Saisons 1989, Cooking for Friends 1991, Blanc Mange 1994, Best A Blanc Christmas 1996; contrib.: Take Six Cooks 1986, Taste of Health 1987, Masterchefs of Europe 1998, Blanc Vite 1998; Restaurants of Great Britain 1989, Gourmet Garden 1990, European Chefs 1990, Foolproof French Cooking 2002. *Leisure interests:* classical music, opera, swimming, tennis, sailing. *Address:* Le Manoir aux Quat'Saisons, Church Road, Great Milton, Oxford, OX44 7PD, England. *Telephone:* (1844) 278881 (Office). *Fax:* (1844) 279433 (Office); (1844) 278847. *E-mail:* raymond@blanc.co.uk (Home). *Website:* www.manoir.com (Home).

BLANCHARD, Francis, LLB; French international civil servant; b. 21 July 1916, Paris; s. of Antoine and Marie (née Séris) Blanchard; m. Marie Claire Boué 1940 (deceased); two s. (one deceased); ed Univ. of Paris; French Ministry of the Interior 1942–47; Int. Org. for Refugees, Geneva 1947–51; Int. Labour Office, Geneva 1951; Asst Dir-Gen. 1956–68, Deputy Dir-Gen. 1968–74, Dir-Gen. 1974–89; Préfet 1956, Hon. Préfet 1977; mem. French Econ. and Social Council 1989–94; mem. council Centre d'étude des revenus et des coûts 1989–, de la population et de la famille 1990–, Econ. and Social Council 1989; Dr. hc (Brussels, Manila, Seoul and Cairo Univs.); Commdr Légion d'honneur. *Leisure interests:* skiing, tennis. *Address:* Prébailly, 01170 Gex (Ain), France (Home). *Telephone:* 4-50-41-51-70 (Home).

BLANCHARD, James J., MBA, JD; American politician; b. 8 Aug. 1942, Detroit, Mich.; m. Paula Parker (divorced); m. 2nd Janet Eifert; one s.; ed Michigan State Univ. and Univ. of Minnesota; admitted to Mich. Bar 1968; Legal Aid, elections bureau, Office of the Sec. of State, Mich. 1968–69; Asst Attorney-Gen., Mich. 1969–74, Admin. Asst to Attorney-Gen. 1970–71, Asst Deputy Attorney-Gen. 1971–72; mem. House of Reps 1975–83; Gov. of Mich. 1983–91; Partner Verner, Liipfert, Bernhard, McPherson and Hand 1991–93, 1996–; Amb. to Canada 1993–96; admitted to DC Bar 2000; fmr mem. Pres.'s Comm. on Holocaust; Democrat; numerous awards including Foreign Affairs Award for Public Service 1996. *Address:* 1901 15th Street, NW, 700 Washington, DC 20005, USA.

BLANCHARD, Olivier Jean, PhD; French professor of economics; b. 27 Dec. 1948, Amiens; m. Noelle Golinelli 1973; three d.; ed Univ. of Paris and Massachusetts Inst. of Tech.; Asst Prof. Harvard Univ. 1977–81, Assoc. Prof. 1981–83; Assoc. Prof. MIT 1983–85, Prof. of Econs 1985–, Class of 1941 Prof. 1994–, Chair. Econs Dept 1998–; Vice-Pres. American Econ. Asscn 1995–96; Fellow Econometric Soc.; mem. American Acad. of Arts and Sciences. *Publications:* Lectures on Macroeconomics (with S. Fischer) 1989, Reform in Eastern Europe 1991, Pour l'Emploi et Cohésion Sociale 1994, Spanish Unemployment: Is There a Solution? 1994, The Economics of Transition 1996, Macroeconomics 1997. *Leisure interest:* tennis. *Address:* Department of Economics, E52-373, Massachusetts Institute of Technology, Cambridge, MA 02139, USA. *Telephone:* (617) 253-8891 (Office). *Fax:* (617) 258-8112.

BLANCHEMAISON, Claude Marie; French diplomatist; b. 6 March 1944, Loches, Indre et Loire; s. of Roger Blanchemaison and Louise Blanchemaison (née Lacour); ed Faculté de Droit et de Sciences Economiques, Paris; First Sec., then Counsellor to perm. rep. at EC 1978–82; Asst Gen. Sec. to the Interministerial Cttee for Questions of European Econ. Cooperation 1982–85; Chargé d'Affaires, S.A. 1985–86; Deputy Dir, Cen. Admin., Ministry of Foreign Affairs 1986–89; Amb. to Vietnam 1989–92, to India 1996–2000, to Russia 2000–; Minister Plenipotentiary 1991; Dir for Europe Ministry of Foreign Affairs 1992–93, for Asia and Oceania 1993–96; Chevalier Legion d'honneur, Ordre nat. du Mérite agricole. *Address:* French Embassy, 117049 Moscow, ul. B. Yakimanka 45, Russia (Office). *Telephone:* (095) 937-15-00 (Office). *Fax:* (095) 937-14-00 (Office).

BLANCHETT, Cate; Australian actress; b. 1969; m. Andrew Upton 1997; ed Melbourne Univ., Nat. Inst. of Dramatic Art; BAFTA Award for Best Actress 1999, Best Actress, Nat. Bd of Review 2001, Golden Camera Award 2001. *Plays include:* Top Girls, Kafka Dances (1993 Newcomer Award), Oleanna (Rosemont Best Actress Award), Hamlet, Sweet Phoebe, The Tempest, The Blind Giant is Dancing, Plenty. *Films include:* Parkland, Paradise Road 1997, Thank God He Met Lizzie 1997, Oscar and Lucinda 1997, Elizabeth 1998 (Golden Globe Award), Dreamtime Alice (also co-producer), The Talented Mr Ripley, An Ideal Husband, Pushing Tin 1999, Bandit 2000, The Man Who Cried 2000, The Gift 2000, Bandits 2000, Heaven 2001, The Lord of the Rings: The Fellowship of the Ring 2001, Charlotte Gray 2001, The Shipping News 2002. *TV includes:* Heartland 1994, G.P., Police Rescue. *Address:* c/o Robyn Gardiner, PO Box 128, Surry Hill, 2010 NSW, Australia.

BLANCO, Salvador Jorge; Dominican Republic politician; b. 1926; Attorney-Gen. 1965; mem. comm. negotiating withdrawal of US troops from Dominican Repub. 1965; mem. Senate; presidential cand. Partido Revolucionario Dominicano (PRD) 1982; Pres. Dominican Repub. 1982–86; sentenced to 20 years' imprisonment for misappropriation of public funds Aug. 1991.

BLANCO, Serge; French rugby football player; b. 31 Aug. 1958, Caracas, Venezuela; m. Lilianne Blanco; two s.; fmr fitter, Dassault aeronautical factory; played for Biarritz Olympique; first B cap, France v. Wales 1978, first full cap, France v. S Africa 1980; retd from int. rugby with 93 caps (233 Test points); now Chair. Nat. Rugby Union League (LNR); business interests include the Serge Blanco Hotel and Health Spa on the Basque coast of France.

BLANCO-CERVANTES, Raúl; Costa Rican politician and chest specialist; b. 1903, San José, s. of Macedonio Blanco Alvarez and Dolores Cervantes Castro; m. Dora Martín Chavarría 1939; one s. four d.; ed Liceo de Costa Rica and Ludwig-Maximilians-Univ. Munich; Medical Dir, Sanatorio Carlos Durán 1933–67; Dir of Anti-Tuberculosis Dept, Ministry of Public Health 1937–67; Minister of Public Health 1948–49; Pres. Coll. of Physicians and Surgeons of Costa Rica 1946, 1947; Dir-Gen. of Assistance, Ministry of Public Health 1950, 1951; First Vice-Pres. of Costa Rica 1953–58, 1962–66; Acting Pres. of Costa Rica 1955; Dir Hospital Nacional para Tuberculosis 1958–; Pres. Colegio de Médicos y Cirujanos de Costa Rica 1946–47; mem. of WHO Expert Advisory Panel on tuberculosis 1954–71; Gov. American Thoracic Soc., American Coll. of Chest Physicians until 1966; First Pres. and Founder Sociedad Centroamericana de Tisiología; Hon. mem. Sociedad Mexicana de Tisiología; several decorations. *Leisure interests:* reading, gardening. *Address:* Apdo. 918, San José, Costa Rica. *Telephone:* 21-20-82.

BLAND, Sir (Francis) Christopher (Buchan), Kt; British business executive; b. 29 May 1938, Japan; s. of James Franklin MacMahon Bland and Jess Buchan Bland (née Brodie); m. Jennifer Mary, Viscountess Enfield 1981; one s. and two step-s. two step-d.; ed Sedbergh and Queen's Coll. Oxford; 2nd Lt 5th Royal Inniskilling Dragoon Guards 1956–58; Lt N Irish Horse (TA) 1958–69; Dir N Ireland Finance Corpn 1972–76; Deputy Chair. IBA 1972–80; Chair. Sir Joseph Causton & Sons 1977–85, LWT (Holdings) 1984–94, Century Hutchinson Group 1984–89, Life Sciences Int. (fmrly Philicom) PLC 1987–97, NFC 1994–2000; Chair. British Telecommunications PLC 2001–; Dir Nat. Provident Inst. 1977–88, Storehouse PLC 1988–93; mem. for Lewisham, GLC 1967–70; mem. Burnham Cttee 1970; Chair. Bow Group 1969–70; Ed. Crossbow 1971–72; mem. Prime Minister's Advisory Panel on Citizen's Charter 1991–94; Chair. NHS Review Group on Nat. Training Council and Nat. Staff Cttees. 1982, Hammersmith and Queen Charlotte's Hosps. (fmrly Hammersmith) SHA 1982–94, Hammersmith Hosps. NHS Trust 1994–96, BBC Bd of Govs. 1996–2001; Hon. LLD (South Bank) 1994. *Leisure interests:* fishing, skiing. *Address:* BT Centre, 81 Newgate Street, London EC1A 7AJ (Office); 10 Catherine Place, London, SW1E 6HF; Blissamore Hall, Clanville, Andover, Hants., SP11 9HL, England. *Telephone:* (20) 7356-5000 (Office); (20) 7834-0021; (1264) 772274 (Andover). *Fax:* (20) 7356-5520 (Office). *Website:* www.bt.com (Office).

BLANDY, John Peter, CBE, MA, DM, MCh, FRCS, FACS; British professor of urology and consultant surgeon; b. 11 Sept. 1927, Calcutta, India; s. of Sir E. Nicolas Blandy and Dorothy Kathleen Blandy, (née Marshall); m. Anne Mathias 1953; four d.; ed Clifton Coll., Balliol Coll., Oxford, London Hosp. Medical Coll.; House Physician and House Surgeon, London Hosp. 1952, Surgical Registrar and Lecturer in Surgery 1956–60, Sr Lecturer 1961, Consultant Surgeon 1964–92, now Consulting Surgeon; served RAMC 1953–55; Exchange Fellow, Presbyterian St Luke's Hosp., Chicago, USA 1960–61; Resident Surgical Officer, St Paul's Hosp. 1963–64; Consultant Surgeon, St Peter's Hosp. for the Stone 1969–92, now Consulting Surgeon; Prof. of Urology, Univ. of London 1969–92, Prof. Emer. 1992–; mem. BMA, Royal Soc. of Medicine (Hon. Fellow 1995), Council, Royal Coll. of Surgeons 1982–94 (Vice-Pres. 1992–94), Int. Soc. of Pediatric Urology Surgeons, Int. Soc. of Urological Surgeons, British Asscn of Urological Surgeons (Pres. 1984–86), European Asscn of Urology (Pres. 1986–88); Pres. European Bd of Urology 1991–92; Fellow Asscn of Surgeons; Hon. Fellow Balliol Coll. Oxford, Royal Coll. of Surgeons, Ireland 1992, Urological Soc. of Australasia, Mexican Coll. of Urology, American, Dutch, Canadian, Romanian and Danish Urological Asscns etc.; Hon. Freeman Worshipful Soc. of Barbers 2000; St Peter's Medal, Freyer Medal, Diaz Medal 1988, Grégoir Medal 2001. *Publications:* Tumours of the Testicle (with A.D. Dayan and H.F. Hope-Stone) 1970, Transurethral Resection 1971, Urology (Ed.) 1976, Lecture Notes on Urology 1976, Operative Urology 1978, The Prostate (Ed. with B. Lytton) 1986, Urology for Nurses (with J. Moors) 1989, Urological and Genital Cancer (ed. with R. T. D. Oliver and H. F. Hope-Stone) 1989, Urology (with C. G. Fowler) 1995, The Royal College of Surgeons of England (ed. with J.P.S. Lumley) 2000; papers in scientific journals. *Leisure interests:* painting and sculpture. *Address:* 362 Shakespeare Tower, Barbican, London, EC2Y 8NJ, England. *Telephone:* (20) 7638-4095. *Fax:* (20) 7382-9387. *E-mail:* john@blandy.net (Home).

BLANK, Sir (Maurice) Victor, Kt, MA; British business executive; b. 9 Nov. 1942; s. of Joseph Blank and Ruth Blank (née Levey); m. Sylvia Helen Richford 1977; two s. one d.; ed Stockport Grammar School, St Catherine's Coll., Oxford; solicitor Supreme Court; joined Clifford-Turner as articled clerk 1964, solicitor 1966, partner 1969; Dir and Head Corp. Finance Charterhouse Bank 1981, Chief Exec. 1985–96, Chair. 1985–97, Chief Exec. Charterhouse PLC 1985–96, Chair. 1991–97, Dir Charterhouse Europe Holding 1993–, Chair. 1993–97; Chair. Wellbeing 1989–; Deputy Chair. Great Universal Stores (now GUS PLC) 1996–2000, Chair. 2000– (Dir 1993–); Chair. Trinity Mirror 1999–; Dir (non-exec.) Coats Ltd (formerly Coats Viyella PLC), Chubb PLC (formerly Williams PLC); Chair. Industrial Devt Advisory Bd; mem. Council, Oxford Univ. 2000–. *Publication:* Weinberg and Blank on Take-overs and Mergers (jtly) 1971. *Leisure interests:* cricket, family, tennis, theatre. *Address:* GUS PLC, 1 Stanhope Gate, London, W1K 1AF, England (Office). *Telephone:* (20) 7318-6209 (Office). *Fax:* (20) 7318-6233 (Office). *Website:* www.gusplc.com.

BLANNING, Timothy Charles William, LittD, FBA; British professor of history; b. 21 April 1942, Wells, Somerset; s. of Thomas Walter Blanning and Gwendolen Marchant-Jones; m. Nicky Susan Jones 1988; one s.; ed King's School, Bruton, Somerset, Sidney Sussex Coll., Cambridge; Research Fellow, Sidney Sussex Coll. 1965–68, Fellow 1968–, Asst Lecturer in History, Cambridge Univ. 1972–76, lecturer 1976–87, Reader in Modern European History 1987–92, Prof. of Modern European History 1992–. *Publications:* Joseph II and Enlightened Despotism 1970, Reform and Revolution in Mainz 1743–1803 1974, The French Revolution in Germany 1983, The Origins of the French Revolutionary Wars 1986, The French Revolution: Aristocrats versus Bourgeois? 1987, Joseph II 1994, The French Revolutionary Wars 1787–1802 1996, The French Revolution: Class War or Culture Clash? 1998, The Culture of Power and the Power of Culture 2002; Ed.: The Oxford Illustrated History of Modern Europe 1996, The Rise and Fall of the French Revolution 1996, History and Biography: Essays in Honour of Derek Beales (with Peter Wende), Reform in Great Britain and Germany 1750–1850 1999, The Short Oxford History of Europe: The Eighteenth Century 2000, The Short Oxford History of Europe: The Nineteenth Century 2000. *Leisure interests:* music, gardening, dog-walking. *Address:* Sidney Sussex College, Cambridge, CB2 3HU, England. *Telephone:* (1223) 335308. *Fax:* (1223) 335968 (Office). *E-mail:* tcb1000@cam.ac.uk (Office).

BLASHFORD-SNELL, Col John Nicholas, OBE, FRSGS; British explorer, author and broadcaster; b. 22 Oct. 1936, Hereford; s. of Rev. Prebendary Leland John Blashford Snell and Gwendolen Ives Sadler; m. Judith Frances Sherman 1960; two d.; ed Victoria Coll., Jersey, RMA, Sandhurst; commissioned Royal Engineers 1957; Commdr Operation Aphrodite (Expedition), Cyprus 1959–61; Instructor Jr Leaders Regt Royal Engineers 1962–63; Instructor, RMA, Sandhurst 1963–66; Adjt. 3rd Div. Engineers 1966–67; Commdr The Great Abbai Expedition (Blue Nile) 1968; attended Staff Coll., Camberley 1969; Chair. Scientific Exploration Soc. 1969–; Commdr Dahlak Quest Expedition 1969–70, British Trans-Americas Expedition (Darien Gap) 1971–72; Officer Commdg 48th Field Squadron Royal Engineers 1972–74; Commdr Zaire River Expedition 1974–75; CO Jr Leaders Regt Royal Engineers 1976–78; Dir of Operations Operation Drake 1978–81; Staff Officer Ministry of Defence 1978–91, Consultant 1992–; Commdr Fort George Volunteers 1982; Operations Dir Operation Raleigh 1982–88, Dir-Gen. 1989–91; Dir SES Tibet Expedition 1987; Leader Kalahari Quest Expedition 1990, Karnali Quest Expedition 1991, Karnali Gorges Expedition 1992, numerous exploration projects thereafter; Trustee, Operation New World 1995–; Chair. Just a Drop Charity 2002–; Hon. DSc (Durham); Hon. DEng (Bournemouth) 1997; The Livingstone Medal, The Darien Medal (Colombia), The Segrave Trophy, Freeman of the City of Hereford, Paul Harris Fellow (Rotary Int.), Royal Geographical Soc. Patrons' Medal 1993, Gold Medal (Inst. of Royal Engineers) 1994, La Paz Medal (Bolivia) 2000. *Publications:* Weapons and Tactics (with T. Wintringham) 1972, Where the Trails Run Out 1974, In the Steps of Stanley 1975, Expeditions the Experts' Way (with A. Ballantine) 1977, A Taste for Adventure 1978, Operation Drake (with M. Cable) 1981, Mysteries, Encounters with the Unexplained 1983, Operation Raleigh, The Start of an Adventure 1987, Operation Raleigh, Adventure Challenge (with Ann Tweedy) 1988, Operation Raleigh, Adventure Unlimited (with Ann Tweedy) 1990, Something Lost Behind the Ranges 1994, Mammoth Hunt (with Rula Lenska) 1996, Kota Mama (with Richard Snailham) 2000, East to the Amazon (with Richard Snailham) 2002. *Leisure interests:* shooting, photography, food and wine. *Address:* c/o Scientific Exploration Society, Expedition Base, Motcombe, nr Shaftesbury, Dorset, SP7 9PB, England. *Telephone:* (1747) 854456 (Office). *Fax:* (1747) 851351 (Office). *E-mail:* jbs@ses-explore.org (Office). *Website:* www.ses-explore.org (Office).

BLATHERWICK, Sir David (Elliott Spiby), KCMG, OBE, MA; British diplomatist (retd); b. 13 July 1941, Lincoln; s. of Edward S. Blatherwick; m. (Margaret) Clare Crompton 1964; one s. one d.; ed Lincoln School and Wadham Coll. Oxford; Foreign Office 1964; Second Sec. Kuwait 1968–70; First Sec. Dublin 1970–73; FCO 1973–77; Head of Chancery, Cairo 1977–80; Northern Ireland Office, Belfast 1981–83; FCO 1983–85; sabbatical, Stanford Univ. 1985–86; Head of Chancery, Perm. Mission to UN, New York 1986–89; Prin. Finance Officer and Chief Insp. FCO 1989–91; Amb. to Ireland 1991–95, to Egypt 1995–99; Chair. Egyptian–British Chamber of Commerce 1999–. *Publication:* The Politics of International Telecommunications 1987. *Leisure interests:* walking, sailing, music. *Address:* Egyptian–British Chamber of Commerce, PO Box 4EG, 299 Oxford Street, London, W1A 4EG England (Office). *Telephone:* (20) 7499-3100 (Office). *Fax:* (20) 7499-1070 (Office). *E-mail:* info@theebcc.com (Office). *Website:* www.theebcc.com (Office).

BLATTER, Joseph Sepp; Swiss international organization official and sports administrator; b. 10 March 1936, Viège; ed Sion and St Maurice Colls

Univ. de Lausanne; fmr Sec. Tourist Office, Valais; Sec.-Gen. Swiss Fed. of Ice-Hockey 1964; fmr journalist; fmr Dir of sports timing and public relations Longines SA; Tech. Dir of Devt Programmes, FIFA 1975–81, Gen. Sec. 1981–98, Pres. 1998–; mem. Swiss Asscn of Sports Journalists, Panathlon Club. *Address:* FIFA , Hitzigweg 11, PO Box 85, 8030 Zurich, Switzerland (Office). *Telephone:* (1) 3849595 (Office). *Fax:* (1) 3849696 (Office). *Website:* www.fifa.com.

BLATTY, William Peter, MA, DHumLitt; American author; b. 7 Jan. 1928, New York; s. of Peter Blatty and Mary (née Mouakad) Blatty; m. Julie Alicia Witbrodt 1983; three s. three d.; ed Georgetown Univ., George Washington Univ. and Seattle Univ.; served in USAF 1951–54; ed. with U.S. Information Agency 1955–57, Publicity Dir Univ. Southern Calif. 1957–58, Public Relations Dir Loyola Univ., Los Angeles 1959–60; Academy Award of Acad. Motion Picture, Arts and Sciences 1973. *Author of screenplays:* The Man from the Diner's Club 1961, Promise Her Anything 1962, A Shot in the Dark 1964, The Great Bank Robbery 1967, What Did You Do in the War, Daddy? 1965, Gunn 1967, Darling Lili 1968, The Exorcist 1973, The Exorcist III 1990. *Film directed:* The Ninth Configuration 1981; awards include: Golden Globe award for best movie screenplay (Twinkle, Twinkle, 'Killer' Kane, The Exorcist) 1981. *Publications:* Which Way to Mecca, Jack? 1959, John Goldfarb, Please Come Home 1963, I, Billy Shakespeare 1965, Twinkle, Twinkle, 'Killer' Kane 1966, The Exorcist 1970, I'll Tell Them I Remember You 1973, The Exorcist: From Novel to Film 1974, The Ninth Configuration 1978, Legion 1983.

BLAU, Peter Michael, PhD; American professor of sociology; b. 7 Feb. 1918, Vienna, Austria; s. of Theodore Blau and Bertha Selka; m. 1st Zena Smith 1948; m. 2nd Judith Fritz 1968; two d.; ed Elmhurst Coll., Ill., Columbia Univ.; Instructor, Wayne State Univ. 1949–51, Cornell Univ. 1951–53; Asst Prof., Univ. of Chicago 1953–58, Assoc. Prof. 1958–63, Prof. 1963–70; Pitt Prof. of American History and Insts, Univ. of Cambridge 1966–67; Prof. Columbia Univ. 1970–88, Quetelet Prof. 1977–88, Chair Sociology Dept 1982–85; Visiting Prof., State Univ. of New York at Albany 1978–79, Distinguished Prof. 1979–82; Robert Broughton Distinguished Research Prof., Univ. of NC Chapel Hill 1988–; Hon. DLitt (Elmhurst Coll.) 1974; ASA Sorokin Award 1968, ASA Distinguished Scholarship Award 1980. *Publications:* The Dynamics of Bureaucracy 1955, Bureaucracy in Modern Society 1956, Formal Organizations: A Comparative Approach (with W. Richard Scott) 1962, Exchange and Power in Social Life 1964, The American Occupational Structure (with Otis Dudley Duncan) 1967, The Structure of Organizations (with Richard A. Schoenherr) 1971, The Organization of Academic Work 1973, On the Nature of Organizations 1974, Approaches to the Study of Social Structure (Ed.) 1975, Inequality and Heterogeneity 1977, Crosscutting Social Circles (with Joseph E. Schwartz) 1984, Continuities in Structural Inquiry (ed. with R. K. Merton) 1984, Structural Contexts of Opportunities 1994. *Leisure interests:* theatre, reading, travel. *Address:* Department of Sociology, University of North Carolina, Chapel Hill, NC 27514 (Office); 12 Cobb Terrace, Chapel Hill, NC 27514, USA (Home). *Telephone:* (919) 929-7885. *Fax:* (919) 962-7568.

BLAUDIN De Thé, Guy (see de Thé, Guy Blaudin).

BLEANEY, Brebis, CBE, FRS, DPhil; British physicist and university professor; b. 6 June 1915, London; s. of Frederick Bleaney and Eva Johanne Petersen; m. Betty Isabelle Plumpton 1949; one s. one d.; ed St John's Coll., Oxford; lecturer in Physics, Oxford 1945–57; Fellow of St John's Coll., Oxford 1947–57, Hon. Fellow 1968–; Dr. Lee's Prof. of Experimental Philosophy, Oxford 1957–77; Fellow of Wadham Coll. 1957–; Royal Soc. Warren Research Fellow 1977–80, Leverhulme Emer. Fellow 1980–82; many visiting Professorships; Corresp. mem. Acad. des Sciences de l'Institut de France 1974–78, Associé Etranger 1978–; Abigail and John Van Vleck lecturer, Minneapolis 1985; Foreign Hon. mem. American Acad. of Arts and Sciences 1978–; DSc hc (Porto) 1987; Hughes Medal, Royal Soc. 1962; C. V. Boys Prize, Physical Soc. of London 1952, ISMAR Prize 1983, Holweck Prize, British and French Physical Socs. 1984, Zavoisky Award (Kazan) 1992, Hon. Prof., Kazan Univ. 1994, Gold Medal, Int. EPR(ESR) Soc. 1999. *Publications:* Electricity and Magnetism (with B. I. Bleaney) 1957, Electron Paramagnetic Resonance (with A. Abragam) 1970. *Leisure interests:* music, travel. *Address:* Clarendon Laboratory, Parks Road, Oxford, OX1 3PU; Garford House, Garford Road, Oxford, England (Home). *Telephone:* (1865) 272324 (Laboratory); (1865) 559589 (Home).

BLEASDALE, Alan; British playwright and novelist; b. 23 March 1946; s. of George Bleasdale and Margaret Bleasdale; m. Julia Moses 1970; two s. one d.; ed Wade Deacon Grammar School, Widnes, Padgate Teachers Training Coll.; schoolteacher 1967–75; Hon. DLitt (Liverpool Polytechnic) 1991; BAFTA Writers Award 1982, Royal TV Soc. Writer of the Year 1982; Best Writer Monte Carlo Int. TV Festival 1996 (for Jake's Progress). *Publications:* Scully 1975, Who's Been Sleeping in My Bed? 1977, No More Sitting on the Old School Bench 1979, Boys from the Blackstuff 1982, Are You Lonesome Tonight? (Best Musical, Evening Standard Drama Awards 1985) 1985, No Surrender (film script) 1986, Having a Ball 1986, It's a Madhouse 1986, The Monocled Mutineer (televised 1986) 1986, GBH (TV series) 1991, On the Ledge 1993, Jake's Progress (TV) 1995, Oliver Twist 1999 (Best Drama Series, TV and Radio Industries Club 2000). *Leisure interest:* rowing. *Address:* c/o The Agency, 24 Pottery Lane, Holland Park, London, W11 4LZ, England. *Telephone:* (20) 7727-1346. *E-mail:* info@theagency.co.uk.

BLECHA, Karl; Austrian politician; b. 16 April 1933, Vienna; s. of Karl Matthias Blecha and Rosa Blecha; m. 1st Ilse Steinhauser 1965; m. 2nd Burgunde Teuber 1982; two d.; m. 3rd Rosi Bahmüller 1999; one d.; ed Univ. of Vienna; became vocational adviser in Vienna Employment Exchange and later worked as reader in publishing firm; Founder, Dir Inst. for Empiric Social Research 1963–75; mem. Lower Austrian SPÖ (Austrian Socialist Party) Exec. 1964–90; Gen. Sec. SPÖ H.Q. 1976–81, Vice-Chair. SPÖ 1981–89; Federal Minister of the Interior 1983–89; Dir Mitropa Inst. for Econ. and Social Research, Vienna 1989–; fmr Chair. Socialist Student Movt, Socialist Young Generation, Austrian Asscn for Cultural Affairs; Pres. Austrian Soc. for Promotion of Research 1994–; Pres. Austrian Union of Pensioners 1999–; Pres. Council of Srs. in Austria 1999–. *Address:* Mitropa Institute, Reinergasse 38, A-1050 Vienna, Austria.

BLEEHEN, Norman Montague, CBE, MA, FRCP, FRCR; British professor of clinical oncology; b. 24 Feb. 1930, Manchester; s. of Solomon Bleehen and Lena Bleehen; m. Tirza Loeb 1959; ed Haberdashers' Aske's Hampstead School and Univ. of Oxford; Registrar and Sr Registrar, The Middx Hosp. London and Mt. Vernon Hosp. Northwood 1961–67; Research Fellow, Dept of Radiology, Stanford, Calif. 1966–67; Locum Consultant Radiotherapist, The Middx Hosp. 1967–69; Prof. of Radiotherapy and Head, Academic Dept of Radiotherapy, Middx Hosp. Medical School 1969–75, Hon. Consultant Radiotherapist 1975; Cancer Research Campaign Prof. and Head of Dept of Clinical Oncology and Radiotherapeutics, Univ. of Cambridge 1975–95; Hon. Consultant, Dir MRC Unit, Clinical Oncology and Radiotherapeutics 1975–95; Dir Radiotherapeutic Centre, Addenbrooke's Hosp. Cambridge 1984–92; Fellow St John's Coll., Cambridge 1976–; Hon. FACR; Dr hc (Bologna); Roentgen Prize, British Inst. of Radiology 1986. *Publications:* contribs. to numerous books and scientific journals. *Leisure interests:* reading, music, television. *Address:* 21 Bentley Road, Cambridge, CB2 2AW, England (Home). *Telephone:* (1223) 354320 (Home).

BLEGEN, Judith; American opera and concert singer; b. Lexington, Ky; d. of Dr. Halward Martin Blegen and Dorothy Mae (Anderson) Blegen; m. 1st Peter Singher 1967 (divorced 1975); one s.; m. 2nd Raymond Gniewek 1977; ed Curtis Inst. of Music, Philadelphia, Pa, Music Acad. of the West, Santa Barbara, Calif.; leading soprano, Nuremberg Opera, Fed. Republic of Germany 1965–68, Staatsoper, Vienna, Austria 1968–70, Metropolitan Opera, New York 1970–; Vienna roles include Zerbinetta (Ariadne auf Naxos), Rosina (The Barber of Seville), Aennchen (Der Freischütz), Norina (Don Pasquale); numerous performances at Metropolitan include Marzelline (Fidelio), Sophie (Werther), Mélisande (Pelléas et Mélisande), Sophie (Der Rosenkavalier), Adina (L'Elisir d'amore), Juliette (Roméo et Juliette), Susanna (The Marriage of Figaro); other appearances include Susanna (The Marriage of Figaro), San Francisco, title-role in Manon, Tulsa Opera, Gilda (Rigoletto), Chicago, Despina (Così fan tutte), Covent Garden, Blondchen (The Abduction from the Seraglio), Salzburg Festival, Mélisande (Pelléas et Mélisande), Spoleto Festival, Susanna (The Marriage of Figaro), Edinburgh Festival, Sophie, Paris Opera; Fulbright Scholarship; Grammy Awards. *Recordings include:* La Bohème (Puccini), Carmina Burana (Orff), Symphony No. 4 (Mahler), Harmonienmesse (Haydn), The Marriage of Figaro (Mozart), A Midsummer Night's Dream (Mendelssohn), Lord Nelson Mass (Haydn), Gloria (Poulenc), Peer Gynt Suite (Grieg), Lieder recital (Richard Strauss and Hugo Wolf), baroque music recital. *Address:* c/o Thea Dispeker, 59 East 54th Street, New York, NY 10022, USA.

BLEGVAD, Mogens, DPhil; Danish professor of philosophy; b. 25 June 1917, Copenhagen; s. of Dr. Olaf Blegvad Overlaege and Gudrun Schrøder; m. 1st Marianne Holm; m. 2nd Victoria Britt-Mari Persson 1961; two s. one d.; ed Univ. of Copenhagen; Psychologist, Copenhagen Municipal Inst. of Vocational Psychology 1943–48; Librarian, Royal Library, Copenhagen 1949–58; Lecturer, Danish Library School 1960–64; Prof. of Philosophy, Univ. of Copenhagen 1964–87, Prof. Emer. 1987–; Chair. Danish Soc. for Legal and Social Philosophy 1989–96; Fellow, Royal Danish Acad. of Sciences and Letters. *Publications:* The Naturalistic Fallacy 1959, Morals and Conscience 1963, Social Thought through One Hundred Years—Themes and Figures 1984, On Morals and Ethics 1986, The Royal Danish Academy of Sciences and Letters 1942–92 1992. *Leisure interests:* music, theatre, films. *Address:* Soldalen 7, 2100 Copenhagen Ø, Denmark. *Telephone:* 39-29-37-78.

BLEICKEN, Jochen, DPhil; German professor of history; b. 3 Sept. 1926, Westerland-Sylt; s. of Max Bleicken and Marie (née Jensen) Bleicken; ed Univs. of Kiel and Frankfurt a. M; Asst Althistorische Seminar, Göttingen 1955–62, Teacher in Early History 1961; Prof. in Ancient History, Hamburg 1962–67, Frankfurt a. M. 1967–77, Göttingen 1977–91; Prof. Emer. 1991–; mem. Wissenschaftliche Geschichte, Johann Wolfgang Goethe Univ., Frankfurt 1967–, Deutsches Archäologisches Institut (DAI) 1976–, Akad. der Wissenschaften in Göttingen 1978. *Publications:* Das Volkstribunat der klassische Republik 1955, Staatliche Ordnung und Freiheit in der Römische Republik 1972, Lex Publica: Studien zu Gesetz und Recht in der Römische Republik 1975, Verfassung und Sozialgeschichte der Römische Kaiserzeit 1981, Geschichte der Römische Republik 1982, Die Athenische Demokratie 1985, Die Verfassung der Römische Republik 1985, Augustus: Eine Biographie 1998. *Leisure interest:* numismatics. *Address:* Obernjesaer Strasse 8, 37133 Friedland, Germany. *Telephone:* (5504) 381.

BLENDON, Robert J., ScD, MPH, MBA; American professor of health policy and political analysis; b. 19 Dec. 1942, Philadelphia, Pa; s. of Edward G.

Blendon and Theresa M. Blendon; m. Marie C. McCormick 1977; ed Marietta Coll., Univ. of Chicago and Johns Hopkins Univ.; Instructor Johns Hopkins Univ. School of Hygiene and Public Health, Baltimore 1969, Asst to Assoc. Dean (Health Care Programs) 1969–70, Asst Prof. 1970–71, Asst Dir for Planning and Devt, Office of Health Care Programs 1970–71; Special Asst for Health Affairs to Deputy Under-Sec. for Policy Co-ordination, Dept of Health Educ. and Welfare 1971–72, Special Asst for Policy Devt to Asst Sec. for Health and Scientific Affairs 1971–72; Visiting Lecturer, Princeton Univ. 1972–80, Co-ordinator, Medicine in Modern America Course 1980–; Sr Vice-Pres. The Robert Wood Johnson Foundation 1980–87; Prof. Dept of Health Policy and Political Analysis, Harvard Univ. School of Public Health 1987–, Chair. 1987–96; Prof. Kennedy School of Govt 1987– and numerous other professional appts.; Distinguished Investigator Award, AHSR 2000. *Publications:* articles in professional journals. *Address:* Harvard University School of Public Health, 677 Huntington Avenue, Boston, MA 02115 (Office); 478 Quinobequin Road, Newton, MA 02468, USA. *Telephone:* (617) 432-4502.

BLESSED, Brian; British actor; b. 9 Oct. 1936, Mexborough, South Yorkshire; s. of William Blessed and Hilda Wall; m. Hildegard Zimmermann 1978; one d.; ed Bolton-on-Dearne Secondary Modern School; studied at Bristol Old Vic; subsequently worked in repertory cos., mainly Nottingham and later Birmingham Repertory Co.; appeared with RSC as Claudius in Hamlet, Hastings in Richard III, Exeter in Henry V; appearance with Nat. Theatre include State of Revolution; also appeared in Metropolis, Cats, The Lion in Winter, Hard Times; one-man show An Evening with Brian Blessed. *Films:* Flash Gordon, Return to Treasure Island, Trojan Women, Man of La Mancha, Henry V, War and Remembrance, Robin Hood Prince of Thieves, Prisoners of Honour, Much Ado About Nothing, Hamlet, King Lear, Tarzan, Star Wars–The Phantom Menace, Mumbo Jumbo. *Theatre:* Chitty Chitty Bang Bang, London Palladium 2002–03. *Television appearances include:* role of Fancy Smith in Z Cars and roles in BBC serializations of The Three Musketeers, I, Claudius, My Family and Other Animals, Black Adder and Tom Jones. *Publications:* The Turquoise Mountain, The Dynamite Kid, Nothing's Impossible, Blessed Everest, Quest to the Lost World. *Leisure interests:* mountaineering, judo (black belt), Koi Carp and animal welfare. *Address:* c/o Derek Webster, A.I.M., Nederlander House, 7 Great Russell Street, London WC1B 3NH, England. *Telephone:* (20) 7637-1700 (Office); (20) 7637-8666. *E-mail:* info@aim.demon.co.uk (Office). *Website:* www.a-i-m.net (Office).

BLETHYN, Brenda Anne, OBE; British actress; b. 20 Feb. 1946, Ramsgate, Kent; d. of William Charles Bottle and Louisa Kathleen Bottle; partner Michael Mayhew 1977; ed St Augustine's RC School, Ramsgate, Thanet Tech. Coll., Guildford School of Acting; with Nat. Theatre (now Royal Nat. Theatre) 1975–90; mem. Poetry Soc. 1976–; Hon.DLitt (Kent) 1999; numerous awards including Boston Film Critics' Award 1997, LA Film Critics Award 1997, Golden Globe 1997, London Film Critics Award 1997, BAFTA 1997. *Theatre appearances include:* for Royal Nat. Theatre: A Midsummer Night's Dream, Troilus and Cressida, Bedroom Farce, Tales From the Vienna Woods, The Guardsman, Fruits of Enlightenment, Madras House, The Provoked Wife, Strife, Force of Habit, Tamburlaine, Plunder (also Old Vic), Camilla Ringbinder Show, Bloody Neighbours (at ICA), The Mysteries 1979, The Double Dealer 1982, Dalliance 1987, The Beaux Stratagem 1989; for Comedy Theatre, London: Steaming (Theatre Critics' Best Supporting Actress Award) 1981; for Vaudeville Theatre, London: Benefactors 1984; for Royal Exchange Theatre, Manchester: A Doll's House 1987, Born Yesterday 1988, An Ideal Husband 1992; for RSC: Wildest Dreams 1993; for Bush Theatre, London: Crimes of the Heart; for Almeida Theatre, London: The Bed Before Yesterday 1994; for Donmar Theatre, London, Habeas Corpus 1996; for Nuffield Theatre, Southampton: The Dramatic Attitudes of Miss Fanny Kemble; for Manhattan Theater Club, New York: Absent Friends (Theatre World Award for Outstanding New Talent 1996) 1996; Mrs Warren's Profession (West End, London) 2002–03. *Films:* Witches, A River Runs Through It 1992, Secrets and Lies (Golden Globe Best Actress 1996, Best Actress Award, Cannes Film Festival 1996, London Film Critics' Circle Best Actress of the Year Award 1996, Boston Critics' Circle Best Actress Award 1996, LA Critics' Circle Best Actress Award 1996, British Acad. Award: Best Actress 1997, Premier Magazine Best Actress Award 1997) 1996, Remember Me 1996, Music From Another Room 1997, Girls' Night 1997, Little Voice (Dallas Fort Worth Critics' Asscn Best Supporting Actress 1999) 1999, Saving Grace (Sundance Film Festival Audience Award 2000, Variety Club of Great Britain Best Screen Actress Award 2001) 1999, On the Nose, In the Winter Dark, Night Train 1999, Daddy and Them 1999, RKO 281 1999, The Sleeping Dictionary 2000, Yellow Bird, Pumpkin 2000, Anne Frank – The Whole Story 2001, Lovely and Amazing 2001, Plots with a View 2002, Sonny 2002, Blizzard 2002. *Television includes:* Mona, All Good Things, Grown Ups, The Imitation Game, That Uncertain Feeling, Floating Off, Claws, Sheppey, Yes Minister, Alas Smith and Jones, King Lear, The Shawl, Rumpole, Maigret, Bedroom Farce, The Double Dealer, Death of an Expert Witness, The Storyteller, The Richest Woman in the World, The RNT Mysteries, Henry VI (Part I) 1981, King Lear 1983, Chance in a Million 1983–85, The Labours of Erica 1987, The Bullion Boys 1993, The Buddha of Suburbia 1993, Sleeping with Mickey 1993, Outside Edge (Television's Best Comedy Actress Award) 1994–96, First Signs of Madness 1996. *Leisure interests:* reading, swimming, cryptic crosswords, running. *Address:* c/o ICM, 76 Oxford Street, London, W1N 0AX, England. *Telephone:* (20) 7636-6565.

BLEWETT, Neal, AC, MA, DPhil, FRHistS, FASSA; Australian politician; b. 24 Oct. 1933, Sydney; s. of James Blewett and Phyllis Blewett (née Kerrison); m. Jill Myford 1962 (died 1988); one s. one d.; ed Launceston High School, Tasmania, Univ. of Tasmania, Oxford Univ.; Lecturer, Oxford Univ. 1959–64; Prof., Dept of Political Theory and Insts, Flinders Univ. 1974–77; MP for Bonython, S. Australia 1977–94; Minister for Health 1983–87, for Community Services and Health 1987–90, for Trade and Overseas Devt 1990–91, Minister for Social Security 1991–93; High Commr in UK 1994–98; Pres. Australian Inst. of Int. Affairs 1998–; Pres. Alcohol and Other Drugs Council of Australia 2002–; mem. Exec. Bd WHO 1995–98; Visiting Prof., Faculty of Medicine Sydney Univ. 1999–; Hon. Fellow, Jesus Coll. (Oxford); Hon. DLit (Hull), Hon. LLD (Tasmania). *Publications:* Playford to Dunstan: The Politics of Transition (with Dean Jaensch) 1971, The Peers, the Parties and the People 1972, A Cabinet Diary 1999. *Leisure interests:* reading, bush walking, cinema. *Address:* 32 Fitzroy Street, Leura, New South Wales 2780, Australia. *Telephone:* (2) 4784-3478 (Home). *Fax:* (2) 4784-3478 (Home). *E-mail:* nealb@med.usyd.edu.au (Home).

BLEY, Carla Borg; American jazz composer; b. 11 May 1938, Oakland, Calif.; d. of Emil Carl Borg and Arlene Anderson; m. 1st Paul Bley 1959 (divorced 1967); m. 2nd Michael Mantler 1967 (divorced 1992); one d.; freelance composer 1956–; pianist, Jazz Composers Orchestra, New York 1964–; European concert tours with Jazz Realities 1965–66; founder, WATT 1973–; toured Europe with Jack Bruce Band 1975; leader, Carla Bley Band, touring USA and Europe 1977–; Cultural Council Foundation grantee 1971, 1979; Guggenheim Fellow 1972; Nat. Endowment for Arts grantee 1973; Winner, int. jazz critics' poll, Down Beat magazine seven times (1966, 1971, 1972, 1978, 1979, 1980, 1983), Best Composer of Year, Down Beat readers' poll 1984 and Composer/Arranger of Year 1985–92, Best in Field Jazz Times critics' poll 1990, Prix Jazz Moderne for The Very Big Carla Bley Band (Acad. du Jazz) 1992, Best Arranger Down Beat critics' poll 1993, 1994. *Music:* composed and recorded: A Genuine Tong Funeral 1967, Escalator Over the Hill (opera) 1970–71 (Oscar du Disque de Jazz 1973), Tropic Appetites 1973; composed chamber orchestra 3/4 1974–75, Mortelle Rautonnée (film score) 1983; recordings include: Dinner Music 1976, The Carla Bley Band–European Tour 1977, Music Mecanique 1979, Fictitious Sports 1980, Social Studies 1980, Carla Bley Live! 1981, Heavy Heart 1984, I Hate to Sing 1984, Night Glo 1985, Sextet 1987, Live 1987, Duets 1988, Fleur Carnivore 1989, The Very Big Carla Bley Band 1991, Go Together 1993, Big Band Theory 1993, Songs with Legs 1995, Goes to Church 1996, Fancy Chamber Music 1998, Are We There Yet? 1999, 4×4 2000, Looking for America 2003. *Leisure interests:* gardening, cooking. *Address:* c/o Watt Works, P.O. Box 67, Willow, NY 12495, USA.

BLIER, Bertrand; French film director; b. 14 March 1939, Paris; s. of the late Bernard Blier and of Gisèl e Brunet; m. Catherine Florin 1973; one d.; also one s. by Anouk Grinberg; ed Lycée Claude Bernard, Paris; worked as Asst to several film directors; Grand Prix Nat. du Cinema 1989. *Films include:* Hitler, connais pas 1963, Si j'étais un espion (Breakdown) 1967, Les valseuses (Making It) 1974, Calmos 1975, Préparez vos mouchoirs (Oscar for Best Foreign Film) 1977, Buffet froid (three Césars) 1979, Beau-père 1981, La femme de mon pote (My Best Friend's Girl) 1983, Notre histoire (Separate Rooms) 1984, Tenue de soirée 1986, Trop belle pour toi (Cannes Special Jury Prize 1989) 1988, Merci la Vie 1991, Tango 1992, Un Deux Trois—Soleil 1993, Mon Homme 1996. *Publications:* several novels and film scripts. *Address:* c/o Artmédia, 10 avenue Georges V, 75008 Paris (Office); 11 rue Margueritte, 75017 Paris, France (Home).

BLIGE, Mary J.; American singer and songwriter; b. 11 Jan. 1971, New York; solo recording artiste; support to Jodeci, British tour 1995; has collaborated with numerous musicians including George Michael, Lauryn Hill. *Recordings include:* Albums: What's The 411 1992, My Life 1994, Mary Jane 1995, Share My World 1997, The Tour 1998, Mary 1999, No More Drama 2001, Ballads 2001; Singles: What's The 411 1992, Sweet Thing 1993, My Love 1994, You Bring Me Joy 1995, All Night Long 1995, Not Gon' Cry 1996, Love Is All We Need 1997, Everything 1997, Seven Days 1999, All That I Can Say 1999, As (with George Michael) 1999; also appears on Father's Day 1990, Changes 1992, Close To You 1992, Panther 1995, Show 1995, MTV Party To Go 1995, Waiting To Exhale 1995, Nutty Professor 1996, Case 1996, Ironman 1996, Love and Consequences 1998, Miseducation of Lauryn Hill 1998, Nu Nation Project 1998. *Address:* c/o Steve Lucas Associates, 156 West 56th Street, New York, NY 10019, USA (Office).

BLIKLE, Andrzej, Prof.Math.; Polish mathematician and confectioner; b. 24 Sept. 1939, Warsaw; s. of Jerzy Blikle and Aniela Blikle; m.; one s.; ed Warsaw Univ.; Prof. 1976; master of confectioner's trade 1975; scientific worker Inst. of Math. Polish Acad. of Sciences 1963–71; Computational Centre Polish Acad. of Sciences 1971–77; Inst. of Computer Science Polish Acad. of Sciences 1977–; Pres. A. Blikle Ltd 1991–; mem. Polish Math. Soc. 1962–, Polish Information Processing Soc. 1981– (Pres. 1987), Asscn for Theoretical Computer Science 1982–, Academia Europaea 1993. *Leisure interests:* skiing, windsurfing, films, history. *Address:* ul. Nowy Świat 35, 00-029 Warsaw (Office); ul. Czarnieckiego 82, 01-541 Warsaw, Poland (Home). *Telephone:* (22) 8430621 (Office); (22) 8396365 (Home). *Fax:* (22) 8430601 (Office). *E-mail:* blikle@medianet.com.pl (Office).

BLIN-STOYLE, Roger John, DPhil, FRS; British academic; b. 24 Dec. 1924, Leicester; s. of Cuthbert Basil St John Blin-Stoyle and Ada Mary Blin-Stoyle (née Nash); m. Audrey Elizabeth Balmford 1949; one s. one d.; ed Alderman Newton's Boys' School, Leicester, Wadham Coll., Oxford; Lecturer in Mathematical Physics Birmingham Univ. 1953–54; Sr Research Officer in Theoretical Physics Oxford 1952–62, Fellow and Lecturer in Physics Wadham Coll. 1956–62, Hon. Fellow 1987; Visiting Assoc. Prof. of Physics MIT 1959–60; Dean, School of Mathematical and Physical Sciences Sussex Univ. 1962–68, Prof. of Theoretical Physics 1962–90, Emer. Prof. 1990–, Pro-Vice-Chancellor 1965–67, Deputy Vice-Chancellor 1970–72, Pro-Vice-Chancellor (Science) 1977–79; Chair. School Curriculum Devt Cttee 1983–88; Pres. Inst. of Physics 1990–92, Asscn for Science Educ. 1993–94; Hon. DSc (Sussex) 1990; Rutherford Medal and Prize, Inst. of Physics 1976, Silver Jubilee Medal 1977. *Publications:* Theories of Nuclear Moments 1957, Fundamental Interactions and the Nucleus 1973, Nuclear and Particle Physics 1991, Eureka! Physics of Particles, Matter and the Universe 1997; Ed. Students Physics Series and various articles in scientific and educational journals. *Leisure interest:* making music. *Address:* School of Chemistry, Physics and Environmental Sciences, Arundel 233, University of Sussex, Brighton, Sussex, BN1 9QJ (Office); 14 Hill Road, Lewes, Sussex, BN7 1DB, England (Home). *Telephone:* (1273) 678069 (Office); (1273) 872940 (Office); (1273) 473640 (Home). *E-mail:* blin-stoyle@mistral.co.uk (Home). *Website:* www.cpes.sussex.ac.uk.

BLINDER, Alan Stuart, AB, MSc, PhD; American professor of economics; b. 14 Oct. 1945, Brooklyn, New York; s. of Morris Blinder and Shirley Blinder; m. Madeline Schwartz 1967; two s.; ed Princeton Univ., London School of Econs, Mass. Inst. of Tech.; Deputy Asst Dir Congressional Budget Office 1975; Gordon S. Rentschler Memorial Prof. of Econs, Princeton Univ., NJ 1982–, Dir Center for Econ. Policy Studies 1989–93, Co.-Dir 1996–; mem. Council of Econ. Advisers to Pres. Clinton 1993–94; Vice-Chair. Bd of Govs. of Fed. Reserve System 1994–96; Vice-Chair. G7 Group 1997–; Fellow American Acad. of Arts and Sciences 1991–; mem. American Philosophical Soc. 1996–; partner Promotory Financial Group 2000–. *Publications include:* Growing Together: An Alternative Economic Strategy for the 1990s 1991, Central Banking in Theory and Practice 1998, Asking About Prices: A New Approach to Understanding Price Stickiness (jtly) 1998, Economics, Principles and Policy (jtly) 2000, The Fabulous Decade: Macroeconomic Lessons from the 1990s (jtly) 2001. *Leisure interests:* tennis, skiing. *Address:* Department of Economics, Princeton University, 105 Fisher Hall, Princeton, NJ 08544, USA. *Telephone:* (609) 258-3358. *Fax:* (609) 258-5398.

BLISS, John William Michael, CM, PhD, FRSC; Canadian historian and writer; b. 18 Jan. 1941, Kingsville, Ont.; s. of Quartus Bliss and Anne L. Crow; m. Elizabeth J. Haslam 1963; one s. two d.; ed Kingsville Dist High School and Univ. of Toronto; Teaching Asst Harvard Univ. 1967–68; Dept of History, Univ. of Toronto 1968–72, Prof. 1975–99, Univ. Prof. 1999–; Hon. DLitt (McGill) 2001; numerous awards including Tyrrell Medal, Royal Soc. of Canada 1988. *Publications:* A Living Profit 1974, A Canadian Millionaire: The Life of Sir Joseph Flavelle 1978, The Discovery of Insulin 1982, Banting: A Biography 1984, Northern Enterprise: Five Centuries of Canadian Business 1987, Plague: A Story of Smallpox in Montreal 1991, Right Honourable Men: The Descent of Canadian Politics from Macdonald to Mulroney 1994, William Osler: A Life in Medicine 1999. *Address:* Department of History/History of Medicine, University of Toronto, 88 College Street, Toronto, M5G 1L4, Canada. *Telephone:* (416) 978-8480 (Office). *Fax:* (416) 971-2160. *E-mail:* m .bliss@sympatico.ca (Office).

BLISS, Timothy Vivian Pelham, PhD, FRS, FMedSci; British neuroscientist; b. 27 July 1940, Weymouth; s. of Pelham Marryat Bliss and Elizabeth Bliss (née Sproule); m. 1st Virginia Catherine Morton-Evans 1975; one step-s. two step-d.; m. 2nd Isabel Frances Vasseur; two step-s.; one d. by Katherine Clough; ed McGill Univ., Montreal; mem. of scientific staff MRC at Nat. Inst. for Medical Research 1967–, Head Div. of Neurophysiology 1988–, Head Neurosciences Group 1996–; Visiting Prof. Dept of Physiology, Univ. Coll. London 1993–; Bristol Myers Squibb Prize for Neuroscience 1991, Feldberg Prize 1994. *Publications:* over 80 papers in scientific journals relating to the neural basis of learning and memory. *Leisure interests:* architecture, food, wine, naval history, travelling. *Address:* National Institute for Medical Research, Mill Hill, London, NW7 1AA, England. *Telephone:* (20) 8816-2382 (Office); (20) 8341-1215 (Home). *Fax:* (20) 8906-4477 (Office). *E-mail:* tbliss@ nimr.mrc.ac.uk (Office).

BLIX, Hans Martin, LLD, PhD; Swedish international official and lawyer (retd); b. 28 June 1928, Uppsala; s. of Gunnar Blix and Hertha (née Wiberg) Blix; m. Eva Kettis 1962; two s.; ed Uppsala Univ., Univ. of Cambridge, Columbia Univ., New York, Univ. of Stockholm; Asst Prof. of Int. Law, Univ. of Stockholm 1960–63; Legal Consultant on Int. Law, Foreign Ministry 1963–76; Under-Sec. of State for Int. Devt Co-operation, Foreign Ministry 1976–78, 1979–81; Minister for Foreign Affairs 1978–79; Dir-Gen. Int. Atomic Energy Agency (IAEA), Vienna 1981–97; mem. Swedish del. to UN Gen. Ass. 1961–81; mem. del. to Conf. on Disarmament, Geneva 1962–78; Exec. Chair. UN Monitoring, Verification and Inspection Comm. for Iraq Jan. 2000–; Hon. Chair. World Nuclear Asscn; Dr. hc (Moscow State Univ.) 1987; Henry de Wolf Smyth Award 1988, Gold Medal, Uranium Inst. (now World Nuclear Asscn) 1997. *Publications:* Treaty-Making Power (dissertation), Statsmyndigheternas Internationella Förbindelser (monograph) 1964, Sovereignty, Aggression and Neutrality 1970, The Treaty-Maker's Handbook 1973; and articles in scientific journals. *Leisure interests:* Oriental rugs, hiking, art. *Address:* c/o United Nations, United Nations Plaza, New York, NY 10017, USA.

BLOBEL, Günter, MD, PhD; American (b. German) professor of cell biology; b. 21 May 1936, Waltersdorf, Silesia (now Poland); m. Laura Maioglio-Blobel; ed Tübingen and Wisconsin Univs; emigrated to USA 1960 (now naturalized citizen); internship in various German hosps 1960–62; joined cell biology lab. of George Palade, Rockefeller Univ., New York, Asst Prof. 1969–73, Assoc. Prof. 1973–76, Prof. 1976–; continued and developed Palade's work, now Head Cell Biology Lab.; Investigator Howard Hughes Medical Inst., Rockefeller Univ. 1986–; Nobel Prize in Physiology or Medicine for work on signal and transport mechanisms of proteins 1999, Ellis Island Medal of Hon. 2000. *Leisure interests:* architecture, classical music, landscapes. *Address:* Rockefeller University Cell Biology Laboratory, 66th and York Avenue, New York, NY 10021 (Office); The Howard Hughes Medical Institute, The Rockefeller University, 1230 York Avenue, New York, NY 10021 (Office); 1100 Park Avenue, Apt 10D, New York, NY 10128, USA (Home). *Telephone:* (212) 327-8096 (Office); (212) 369-3552 (Home). *Fax:* (212) 327-7880 (Office); (212) 534-5556 (Home). *E-mail:* blobel@rockvax.rockefeller.edu (Office). *Website:* www .rockefeller.edu/labheads/blobel/blobel-lab.html (Office); www.rockefeller .edu (Home).

BLOCHER, Christoph; Swiss politician and business executive; b. 11 Oct. 1940; m. Sylvia Blocher; one s. three d.; joined legal dept EMS Chemie 1969, took over the co. in 1983; mem. Meilen Dist Council 1974–78; mem. Zurich Canton Council 1975–80; Pres. Swiss People's Party, Zurich Canton 1977–; mem. Nat. Ass. 1979–; Pres. Aktion für eine unabhängige und neutrale Schweiz (AUNS) 1986–. *Address:* Schweizerische Volkspartei, Brückfelderstr. 18, 3000 Bern, Switzerland (Office). *Telephone:* (31) 3025858 (Office). *Fax:* (31) 3017585 (Office). *Website:* www.svp.ch (Office).

BLOCK, Ned Joel, PhD; American professor of philosophy; b. 22 Aug. 1942, Chicago; s. of Eli Block and Blanche Rabinowitz; m. Susan Carey 1970; one d.; ed Mass. Inst. of Tech., St John's Coll. Oxford and Harvard Univ.; Asst Prof. MIT 1971–77, Assoc. Prof. 1977–83, Prof. of Philosophy, Dept of Linguistics and Philosophy 1983–96, Chair. of Philosophy 1989–95; Prof. of Philosophy New York Univ. 1996–; Visiting Prof. Harvard Univ. 2002–03; Pres. Soc. for Philosophy and Psychology 1978–79; Chair. MIT Press Cognitive Science Bd 1992–95; NSF Fellow 1985–86, 1988–89; Fellow, American Council of Learned Socs, Center for Study of Language and Information; Guggenheim Fellow; Sloan Foundation Fellow. *Publications:* The IQ Controversy (with G. Dworkin) 1976, Readings in Philosophy of Psychology (Vol. 1) 1980, (Vol. 2) 1981, Imagery 1981, The Nature of Consciousness (with O. Flanagan and G. Güzeldere). *Address:* Department of Philosophy, New York University, Main Bldg, 100 Washington Square E, New York, NY 10003 (Office); 37 Washington Square West, New York, NY 10011, USA (Home). *Telephone:* (212) 998-8322. *Fax:* (212) 995-4179.

BLOEMBERGEN, Nicolaas, DPhil; American (naturalized 1958) professor of applied physics; b. 11 March 1920, Dordrecht, Netherlands; s. of Auke Bloembergen and Sophia M. Quint; m. Huberta D. Brink 1950; one s. two d.; ed Univs of Utrecht and Leiden; Research Fellow, Leiden Univ. 1947–49; Soc. of Fellows, Harvard Univ. 1949–51, Gordon McKay Assoc. Prof. 1951–57, apptd Prof. of Applied Physics 1957, Rumford Prof. of Physics 1974–80, Gerhard Gade Univ. Prof. 1980–90, Prof. Emer. 1990–; Prof. of Optics, Univ. of Arizona 2001–; Guggenheim Fellow 1957; Lorentz Guest Prof., Leiden 1973; Raman Visiting Prof., Bangalore Univ. 1979; Visiting Prof., Coll. de France 1980; mem. NAS (USA); Corresp. mem. Royal Dutch Acad. of Sciences; Foreign mem. Indian Acad. of Sciences, Akad. Leopoldina (GDR), Royal Norwegian Inst. of Science; Foreign Assoc. mem. Acad. des Sciences, Inst. de France 1981–; Commdr, Order of Orange 1988; Hon. DSc (Laval Univ., Québec, Univ. of Conn., Hartford Univ., Univ. of Mass., Univ. of Cen. Fla); Hon. DSc (Moscow State Univ.) 1997, (N Carolina State Univ.) 1998, (Harvard Univ.) 2000; Buckley Prize, American Physical Soc., Liebmann Prize, Inst. of Radio Engineers, Ballantine Medal, Franklin Inst., Royal Dutch Acad. of Arts and Sciences, Half Moon Trophy, Netherland Club of New York, Nat. Medal of Science 1974, Lorentz Medal, Royal Dutch Acad. of Sciences 1978, Frederick Ives Medal, Optical Soc. of America 1979, Alexander von Humboldt Sr US Scientist Award, Munich 1980, shared Nobel Prize in Physics 1981 for contrib. to development of laser spectroscopy, Medal of Honor, Inst. of Electrical and Electronics Engineers 1983, Byvoet Medal, Univ. of Utrecht 2001. *Publications:* Nuclear Magnetic Relaxation 1961, Nonlinear Optics 1965, Encounters in Magnetic Resonance 1996, Encounters in Nonlinear Optics 1996; over 300 papers in professional journals. *Leisure interests:* travel, skiing, tennis. *Address:* Optical Sciences Center, University of Arizona, 1630 East University Boulevard, Tucson, AZ 85747, USA (Office). *Telephone:* (520) 626-3479 (Office); (520) 647-3772 (Home). *Fax:* (520) 621-5300 (Office). *E-mail:* nbloembergen@optics.arizona.edu (Office).

BLOKHIN, Alexander Victorovich; Russian politician and engineer; b. 12 Jan. 1951, Ivanovo, Russia; m.; one d.; ed Ivanovo Inst. of Energy; Sr engineer, deputy head of workshop, deputy chief energy expert factory Fizpribor, Leningrad 1974–77; with USSR Ministry of Defence in Mongolia 1977–78; chief mechanic, garment factory Ivanovo 1978–80; chief energy expert, State Schelkovo Biological Co., Moscow Region 1983–90; Chair. subcttee, Sec. Cttee of Supreme Soviet on Devt of self-govt, Moscow 1990–92; Counsellor of Minister of Foreign Affairs, Russian Fed. 1992–93; Dir Dept Ministry of Foreign Affairs, Russian Fed. 1993–95; Amb. for special missions 1995; Amb. to Azerbaijan 1995–2000; Minister for Nationalities and Regional Policy 2000–02; Amb. to Belarus 2002–. *Address:* Embassy of the Russian Federation, Starovilencka str. 48, 220002 Minsk, Belarus (Office). *Telephone:* (72) 50-36666 (Office). *Fax:* (72) 50-3664 (Office). *E-mail:* karp@rusamb.belpak .minsk.by (Office).

BLOKHIN, Oleg Vladimirovich; Ukrainian footballer and politician; b. 5 November 1952, Kiev; s. of Volodimir Ivanovich Blokhin and Katerina Zakharivna Adamenko (fmr sprint hurdler); m. Irina Ivomovna Deryugina; one d.; ed Kiev Physical Culture Inst. and Kiev Univ.; played for Dinamo Kiev 1969–88; played 432 matches in USSR Championships, 109 matches in USSR team (record), scoring over 200 goals; played for Austrian club Vorwärts Steyr 1998; fmr coach Greek clubs Olympiaos, PAOK Saloniki (twice), AEK and Ionikos (twice); Chair. Oleg Blokhin Int. Fund 1994–; Ukraine People's Deputy 1998, mem. Cttee on Problems of Youth Policy and Sport; mem. Batkishchina faction 1999–, CP faction 2002–; Golden Boot Award 1975; European footballer of the Year 1975, Best Footballer of USSR 1973–75, seven times Champion USSR, five times winner USSR Cup, eight times winner European Cup, one Supercup 1975. *Address:* c/o Ministry of Youth and Sport, Espladra 42, 252023 Kiev, Ukraine. *Telephone:* 220-02-00.

BLOM-COOPER, Sir Louis Jacques, Kt, QC, FRSA; British lawyer and author; b. 27 March 1926; s. of Alfred Blom-Cooper and Ella Flesseman; m. 1st 1952 (dissolved 1970); two s. one d.; m. 2nd Jane E Smither 1970; one s. two d.; ed Seaford Coll., King's Coll., London, Municipal Univ. of Amsterdam and Fitzwilliam Coll., Cambridge; army service 1944–47; called to Bar, Middle Temple 1952, Bencher 1978; mem. Home Sec.'s Advisory Council on the Penal System 1966–78; Chair. Howard League for Penal Reform 1973–84, Vice-Pres. 1984–; Chair. Panel of Inquiry into death of Jasmine Beckford 1985; on several comms. of inquiry 1986–87; Judge Court of Appeal, Jersey and Guernsey 1989–96; Ind. Commr for the Holding Centres, Northern Ireland 1993–2000; Chair. Mental Health Act Comm. 1987–94, Press Council 1989–90, Nat. Asscn for Victim Support Schemes (NASS) 1994–97; Dr hc (Ulster) 1995; Hon. LittD (E Anglia) 1997; Hon. LLD (Loughborough), Hon. LLD (Ulster), Hon. LLD (Univ. of East Anglia). *Publications:* Bankruptcy in Private International Law 1954, The Law as Literature 1962, The A6 Murder (A Semblance of Truth) 1963, A Calendar of Murder (with T. P. Morris) 1964, Language of the Law 1965, Separated Spouses (with O. R. McGregor and C. Gibson) 1970, Final Appeal: A Study of the House of Lords in its Judicial Capacity (with G. Drewry) 1972; ed. Progress in Penal Reform 1975, Law and Morality (with G. Drewry) 1976, The Falling Shadow (jtly) 1995, The Birmingham Six and Other Cases 1997. *Leisure interests:* watching and reporting on Association football, reading, music, writing, broadcasting. *Address:* 1 Southgate Road, London, N1 3JP, England (Home); Glebe House, Montgomery, Powys, SY15 6QA, Wales (Home). *Telephone:* (20) 7704-1514 (London) (Home); (1686) 668458 (Montgomery). *Fax:* (20) 7226-5457 (London) (Home). *E-mail:* blomcooper@aol.com (Home).

BLOMSTEDT, Herbert Thorson; Swedish music director and conductor; b. 7 Nov. 1927, Springfield, Mass., USA; s. of Adolphe Blomstedt and Alida Armintha Thorson; m. Waltraud Regina Peterson 1955; four d.; ed Royal Acad. of Music, Stockholm and Uppsala Univ.; Music Dir, Norrköping Symphony Orchestra 1954–61; Prof. of Conducting, Swedish Royal Acad. of Music 1961–70; Perm. Conductor, Oslo Philharmonic 1962–68; Music Dir of Danish Radio Symphony Orchestra 1967–77, of Dresden Staatskapelle Orchestra 1975–85, of Swedish Radio Symphony Orchestra 1977–82; Music Dir and Conductor, San Francisco Symphony Orchestra 1985–95; Hon. Conductor NHK Symphony, Tokyo 1985; Music Dir Leipzig Gewandhaus Orchestra 1998–; Hon. DMus (Andrews); Jenny Lind Scholarship, Swedish Royal Acad. of Music; Kt Royal Order of the North Star (Sweden), Kt Royal Order of Dannebrog (Denmark); Litteris et Artibus, Gold Medal (Sweden). *Leisure interests:* hiking, reading, art. *Address:* c/o Kuenstlep Sekretariat am Gasteig, Rosenheimer Strasse 52, 81669 Munich, Germany (Office); Inter-artists, Frans van Mierisstraat 43, 1071 RK, Amsterdam, Netherlands.

BLÖNDAL, Halldór; Icelandic politician; b. 1938, Reykjavík; m. Kristrún Eymundsdóttir; ed Akureyri High School; teacher and journalist, Morgun-bladid 1959–80; mem. staff Authorised Public Accountant office, Akureyri 1976–78; Chief Surveyor of the State Account 1976–87; mem. Bd Dirs. Regional Devt Inst. 1983–91, Agric. Bank of Iceland 1985–91; mem. Inde-pendence Party, Vice-Chair. Parl. Group 1983–91; MP for Northeastern Dist 1979–; Rep. to UN Gen. Ass. 1983; mem. Icelandic Del. to Council of Europe 1984–86, Minister of Communications and Agric. 1991–95; Speaker of the Althingi (Parl.) 1999–. *Address:* Althingi, v/Austurvöll, 150 Reykjavík, Ice-land (Office). *Telephone:* 5630500 (Office). *Fax:* 5630910 (Office). *E-mail:* parlsecalthingi.is (Office). *Website:* www.althingi.is (Office).

BLOOM, Claire; British actress; b. 15 Feb. 1931, London; d. of Edward Bloom and Elizabeth Grew; m. 1st Rod Steiger 1959 (divorced 1969); m. 2nd Philip Roth 1990 (divorced 1995); ed London, Bristol and New York; Oxford Repertory Theatre 1946, Stratford-on-Avon 1948; first major stage appear-ances in The Lady's Not For Burning 1949, Ring Around the Moon 1950; at Old Vic 1951–53; Fellow Guildhall School of Music and Drama 1975. *Other stage performances include:* Duel of Angels 1956, Andromache in The Trojan Women 1964, Sascha in Ivanov, London 1966, Nora in A Doll's House, New York 1971, London 1973, Hedda Gabler in Hedda Gabler, New York 1971, Mary Queen of Scots in Vivat, Vivat Regina!, New York 1972, A Streetcar Named Desire, London (Evening Standard Drama Award for Best Actress) 1974, The Innocents, USA 1976, Rosmersholm, London 1977, The Cherry Orchard, Chichester Festival 1981, When We Dead Awaken 1990, The Cherry

Orchard, USA 1994, Long Day's Journey into Night, USA 1996, Electra, New York 1998, Conversations after a Burial, London 2000, A Little Night Music 2003. *Films include:* Limelight, Man Between, Richard III, Alexander the Great, Brothers Karamazov, Buccaneer, Look Back in Anger, Three Steps to Freedom 1960, The Brothers Grimm, The Chapman Report 1962, The Haunting 1963, 80,000 Suspects 1963, Alta Infedeltà 1963, Il Maestro di Vigevano 1963, The Outrage 1964, Spy Who Came in from the Cold 1965, Charly 1966, Three into Two Won't Go 1967, Illustrated Man 1968, Red Sky at Morning 1970, A Doll's House 1973, Islands in the Stream 1975, The Clash of the Titans 1979, Always 1984, Sammy and Rosie Get Laid 1987, Brothers 1988, Crimes and Misdemeanours 1989, Mighty Aphrodite 1994, Daylight 1995, Shakespeare's Women and Claire Bloom, The Book of Eve 2001, Imagining Argentina 2002. *Television appearances:* A Legacy 1975, The Oresteia 1978, Henry VIII 1979, Brideshead Revisited 1979, Hamlet 1980, Cymbeline 1981, Separate Tables 1982, The Ghost Writer 1982, King John 1983, Time and the Conways 1984, Shadowlands (BAFTA Award for Best Actress) 1985, Promises to Keep 1985, Oedipus the King 1985, Lightning Always Strikes Twice 1985; miniseries in USA: Ellis Island 1984, Florence Nightingale 1984, Liberty 1985, Anastasia 1986, Queenie 1986, The Belle of Amherst 1986, Intimate Contact 1987, A Shadow on the Sun 1988, The Camomile Lawn 1991, The Mirror Crack'd from Side to Side 1992, Remember 1993, A Village Affair 1994, Family Money 1996, The Lady in Question, Love and Murder, Yesterday's Children; also performs her one-woman shows Enter the Actress and These are Women, A Portrait of Shakespeare's Heroines, throughout the USA. *Publications:* Limelight and After 1982, Leaving a Doll's House 1996. *Leisure interests:* walking, music. *Address:* c/o Jeremy Conway, 18–21 Jermyn Street, London SW1Y 6HB, England. *Telephone:* (20) 7287-0077. *Fax:* (20) 7287-1940.

BLOOM, Floyd Elliott, AB, DSc, MD, FAAS; American research scientist; b. 8 Oct. 1936, Minneapolis; m. 1st D'Nell Bingham 1956 (died May 1973); two c.; m. 2nd Jody Patricia Corey 1980; ed S. Methodist Univ., Washington Univ., Hahnemann Univ., Univ. of Rochester, Mount Sinai Univ. Medical School, Thomas Jefferson Univ.; intern Barnes Hosp., St Louis 1960–61, resident internal medicine 1961–62; research assoc. Nat. Inst. of Mental Health (NIMH), Washington 1962–64; Fellow Depts. of Pharmacology, Psychiatry and Anatomy, Yale School of Medicine 1964–66, Asst Prof. 1966–67, Assoc. Prof. 1968; Chief Lab. of Neuropharmacology, NIMH 1968–75, Acting Dir Div. of Special Mental Health 1973–75; Commissioned Officer Public Health Service 1974–75; Prof. Salk Inst., La Jolla, Calif. 1975–83; Dir Div. of Preclinical Neuroscience and Endocrinology, Scripps Research Inst., La Jolla 1983–89, Chair. Dept of Neuropharmacology 1989–; Ed.-in-Chief Science Magazine 1995–2000; CEO Neurome, Inc. 2000–02, Chair. of Bd 2002–; mem. Nat. Advisory Mental Health Council 1976–80, Comm. on Alcoholism 1980–81; mem. Scientific Advisory Bd Neurocrine Inc. 1993–2000, Neuro-biological Tech. Inc. 1994–98, Healthcare Ventures Inc. 1998–2000; Trustee Wash. Univ., St Louis 1998–; Chair. Nat. Medical Council 2000–; currently Chair. AAAS; mem. NAS, Inst. of Medicine, American Philosophical Soc., Acad. of Arts and Sciences, Swedish Acad. of Sciences; A. Cressy Morrison Award, NY Acad. of Sciences 1971, Mathilde Solowey Award 1973, McAlpin Research Achievement Award, Mental Health Asscn 1980, Steven Beering Medal 1985, Janssen Award, World Psychiatry Asscn 1989, Herman von Helmholtz Award 1991, Meritorious Achievement Award, Council of Biology Eds. 1999, Distinguished Service Award, American Psychiatric Asscn 2000. *Publications include:* Biochemical Basis of Neuropharmacology (with J.R. Cooper and R.H. Roth) 1971, Brain, Mind and Behavior (with Lazerson and Hofstadter) 1984, Brain Browser (with W. Young and Y. Kim) 1989; ed. Peptides: Integrators of Cell and Tissue Function 1980, Neuro-Psycho-pharmacology: The Fourth Generation of Progress 1994, Handbook of Chem-ical Neuroanatomy 1997, The Primate Nervous System 1997, Funding Health Sciences Research (with M. Randolph) 1990. *Address:* Scripps Research Institute, 10550 North Torrey Pines Road, La Jolla, CA 92037-1000 (Office); 628 Pacific View Drive, San Diego, CA 92109, USA (Home). *E-mail:* fbloom@ scripps.edu (Office).

BLOOM, Harold, PhD; American professor of humanities; b. 11 July 1930, New York; s. of William Bloom and Paula Lev; m. Jeanne Gould 1958; two s.; ed Cornell and Yale Univs; mem. Faculty, Yale Univ. 1955–, Prof. of English 1965–77, DeVane Prof. of Humanities 1974–77, Prof. of Humanities 1977–, Sterling Prof. of Humanities 1983–; Visiting Prof. Hebrew Univ. Jerusalem 1959, Breadloaf Summer School 1965–66, Soc. for Humanities, Cornell Univ. 1968–69; Visiting Univ. Prof. New School of Social Research, New York 1982–84; Charles Eliot Norton Prof. of Poetry, Harvard Univ. 1987–88; Berg Visiting Prof. of English, New York Univ. 1988–; mem. American Acad. and Inst. of Arts and Letters, American Philosophical Soc.; Guggenheim Fellow 1962; Fulbright Fellow 1955; Hon. Dr St Michael's Coll., Univ. of Rome, Univ. of Bologna, Univ. of Coimbra, Boston Coll., Yeshiva Univ., Univ. of Mass. at Dartmouth, Univ. of Córdoba; Newton Arvin Award 1967; Melville Cane Award, Poetry Soc. of America 1970; Zabel Prize, American Inst. of Arts and Letters 1982; MacArthur Prize Fellowship 1985; Gold Medal for Criticism, American Acad. of Arts and Letters 1999, Int. Prize of Catalonia 2002. *Publications:* Shelley's Mythmaking 1959, The Visionary Company 1961, Blake's Apocalypse 1963, Commentary to Blake 1965, Yeats 1970, The Ringers in the Tower 1971, The Anxiety of Influence 1973, Wallace Stevens: The Poems of Our Climate 1977, A Map of Misreading 1975, Kabbalah and Criticism 1975, Poetry and Repression 1976, Figures of Capable Imagination 1976, The Flight to Lucifer: A Gnostic Fantasy 1979, Agon: Towards a Theory of Revisionism 1981, The Breaking of the Vessels 1981, The Strong Light of the Canonical 1987, Freud: Transference and Authority 1988, Poetics of Influence: New and Selected Criticism 1988, Ruin the Sacred Truths 1989, The Book of J 1990, The American Religion 1991, The Western Canon 1994, Omens of Millennium 1996, Shakespeare: The Invention of the Human 1998, How to Read and Why 2000, Stories and Poems for Extremely Intelligent Children of All Ages 2000, Genius: A Mosaic of One Hundred Exemplary Creative Minds 2002, Hamlet: Poem Unlimited 2003. *Leisure interest:* reading. *Address:* 179 Linden Street, New Haven, CT 06511, USA.

BLOOM, Myer, PhD, FRSC, F.A.P.S.; Canadian professor of physics; b. 7 Dec. 1928, Montreal; s. of Israel Bloom and Leah Ram; m. Margaret P. Holmes 1954; one s. one d.; ed Baron Byng High School, McGill Univ. and Univ. of Illinois at Urbana; NRC Travelling Postdoctoral Fellow, Univ. of Leiden, Netherlands 1954–56; Research Assoc. Univ. of BC 1956–57, Asst Prof. 1957–60, Assoc. Prof. 1960–63, Prof. of Physics 1963–94; Emer. Prof. 1995–; Visiting Prof. Harvard 1964–65, Kyoto Univ. 1965, Univ. de Paris Sud 1971–72, 1978–79, Univ. of Rome 1986, Danish Tech. Univ. 1986; mem. Canadian Asscn of Physicists; Alfred P. Sloan Fellow 1961–65; Fellow Canadian Inst. for Advanced Research 1991–2000; Hon. DTech (Tech. Univ. of Denmark) 1994; Hon. DIur (Concordia Univ., Montreal) 1995; Hon. DSc (British Columbia) 2000; Steacie Prize 1967, Biely Prize 1969; Canadian Asscn of Physicists Gold Medal 1973; Science Council of BC Chair.'s Award for Career Achievements 1992, Izaak Walton Killam Memorial Prize for Natural Sciences 1995. *Publications:* numerous research and review articles. *Leisure interests:* hiking, skiing, squash, wine-making. *Address:* Department of Physics and Astronomy, University of British Columbia, 6224 Agricultural Road, Vancouver, BC, V6T 1Z1 (Office); 5669 Kings Road, Vancouver, BC, V6T 1K9, Canada (Home). *Telephone:* (604) 822-2136 (Office). *Fax:* (604) 822-5324. *E-mail:* bloom@physics.ubc.ca (Office).

BLOOM, Stephen Robert, MA, MD, DSc, FRCP, FRCPath, FMedSci; British physician, educator and biomedical researcher; b. 24 Oct. 1942, Maidstone, Kent; s. of Arnold Bloom and Edith Nancy Bloom (née Fox); m. Margaret Janet Sturrock 1965; two s. two d.; ed Univ. of Cambridge; Medical Unit Registrar, Middx Hosp., London 1970–72; MRC Clinical Research Fellow 1972–74; Sr Lecturer, Royal Postgrad. Medical School, Hammersmith Hosp. 1974–78, Reader in Medicine 1978–82, Prof. of Endocrinology 1982–, Head Dept of Endocrinology and Metabolic Medicine; Prof. of Medicine, Imperial Coll. School of Medicine (fmrly Royal Postgrad. Medical School) 1982–, Dir of Metabolic Medicine and Chief of Service for Chemical Pathology 1994–; Chair. Div. of Investigative Science, ICSM 1997–; Vice-Pres. (Sr. Censor) Royal Coll. of Physicians 1999–2001; Sec. Soc. for Endocrinology 1999–2001, Chair. 2001–. *Publications:* Gut Hormones (ed.) 1978, Endocrine Tumours 1985, Surgical Endocrinology 1992. *Leisure interests:* jogging, classical music, computing. *Address:* Department of Metabolic Medicine, Division of Investigative Science, Imperial College London at Hammersmith Hospital, 6th Floor, Commonwealth Building, Du Cane Road, London, W12 0NN, England (Office). *Telephone:* (20) 8383-3242 (Office). *Fax:* (20) 8383-3142 (Office). *E-mail:* s.bloom@imperial.ac.uk (Office).

BLOOMBERG, Michael Rubens; American business executive; b. 14 Feb. 1942, Boston; m. (divorced); two c.; ed Johns Hopkins Univ., Harvard Univ.; with Salomon Brothers (investment bank) 1966–81; founder, Chief Exec., Chair. Bloomberg Financial Markets 1981–; founder, Pres. Bloomberg L.P. 1982–; publr Bloomberg Business News, Bloomberg Magazine, Bloomberg Personal Magazine; gen. man. Bloomberg Television, Bloomberg Radio WBBR-AM 1130; Mayor of New York 2001–; Chair. Bd Trustees Johns Hopkins Univ.; Trustee Big Apple Circus, Lincoln Center for Performing Arts, Jewish Museum, NY, Police and Fire Widow's and Children's Fund, Metropolitan Museum of Art and numerous other bodies. *Publication:* Bloomberg by Bloomberg (autobiog.) 1998. *Address:* Office of the Mayor, City Hall, New York, NY 10007 (Office); Bloomberg LP, 499 Park Avenue, FL. 15, New York, NY 10022, USA.

BLOOMER, Jonathan, BSc, ARCS, FCA, CIMgt; British insurance executive; b. 23 March 1954; m. Judy Bloomer (née May); one s. two d.; ed Imperial Coll., London; joined Arthur Andersen 1974, Man. Partner of European Insurance Practice –1994; Group Finance Dir Prudential PLC 1995–2000, Group CEO 2000–. *Leisure interests:* rugby, boats. *Address:* Prudential PLC, Laurence Pountney Hill, London, EC4R 0HH, England (Office). *Telephone:* (20) 7548-3100. *Fax:* (20) 7548-3930. *E-mail:* jonathan.bloomer@prudential.co.uk (Office). *Website:* www.prudential.co.uk (Office).

BLOOMFIELD, Sir Kenneth Percy, KCB, MA; British civil servant; b. 15 April 1931, Belfast; s. of late Harry Percy Bloomfield and Doris Bloomfield; m. Mary E Ramsey 1960; one s. one d.; ed Royal Belfast Academical Inst. and St Peter's Coll., Oxford; joined N Ireland Civil Service 1952; Private Sec. to Ministers of Finance 1956–60; Deputy Dir British Industrial Devt Office, New York 1960–63; Asst later Deputy Sec. to Cabinet, N Ireland 1963–72; Under-Sec. N Ireland Office 1972–74; Perm. Sec. Office of Exec. N Ireland 1974–75; Perm. Sec. Dept of Environment, N Ireland 1975–81, Dept of Econ. Devt 1981–84; Head, N Ireland Civil Service and Second Perm. Under-Sec. of State, N Ireland Office 1984–91; Nat. Gov., Chair. Broadcasting Council for N Ireland, BBC 1991–99; Chair. Children in Need Trust 1992–98, N Ireland Higher Educ. Council 1993–2001, N Ireland Victims Commr 1997–98, Bangor and Holywood Town Centre Man. Ltd 2001, BBC Audit Cttee, N Ireland Chief Execs Forum, Higher Educ. Council for N Ireland; Pres. Ulster People's Coll.

1996–; mem. N Ireland Advisory Bd Bank of Ireland 1991–2001, Green Park Trust 1996–2001; Hon. Fellow St Peter's Coll. Oxford; numerous other appointments; Hon. LLD (Belfast); Hon. DUniv (Open Univ.) 2000; Hon. DLitt (Univ. of Ulster) 2002; Northern Ireland Chamber of Commerce Award for Personal or Corporate Excellence 1990. *Publication:* Stormont in Crisis (a memoir) 1994. *Leisure interests:* reading history and biographies, writing, swimming. *Address:* 16 Larch Hill, Holywood, Co. Down, BT18 0JN, Northern Ireland (Home). *Telephone:* (28) 9042-8340 (Home). *Fax:* (28) 9042-8340 (Home). *E-mail:* kenneth@bloomfield1810.freeserve.co.uk (Home).

BLOUT, Elkan R(ogers), AB, PhD; American biochemist; b. 2 July 1919, New York; s. of Eugene Blout and Lillian Blout; m. 1st Joan Dreyfus Blout 1939; two s. one d.; m. 2nd Gail Ferris Blout 1985; one d.; ed Phillips Exeter Acad. and Princeton and Columbia Univs; Assoc. Dir of Research, Polaroid Corpn 1948–58, Vice-Pres. and Gen. Man. of Research 1958–62; Lecturer on Biophysics, Harvard Medical School 1960–62, Prof. of Biological Chem. 1962–89, Edward S. Harkness Prof. of Biological Chem. 1964–90, Emer. Prof. 1990–, Chair. Dept of Biological Chem. 1965–69, Dean Academic Affairs, Harvard School of Public Health 1978–89, Chair. Dept of Environmental Science and Physiology 1986–88, Dir Div. of Biological Sciences 1987–91; Dir Center for Blood Research 1972–92, CHON Corpn 1974–83; Scientific adviser, Affymax Research Inst. 1988–95; Gov. Weizmann Inst. of Science, Rehovot, Israel 1977–90, Gov. Emer. 1990–; mem. Finance Cttee, NAS 1976–, Inst. of Medicine 1979–, Advisory Cttee on the USSR and Eastern Europe 1979–84; mem. Boston Biomedical Research Inst. 1972– (Vice-Pres. 1990–94, trustee 1990–), Finance Cttee American Soc. of Biological Chemists 1973–82, Corpn of the Museum of Science, Boston 1974–, Advisory Council of the Dept of Biochemical Sciences, Princeton Univ. 1974–83 and of Programme in Molecular Biology 1983–95, Finance Cttee American Acad. Arts and Sciences 1976–84, Conseil de Surveillance, Compagnie Financière du Scribe 1975–81, Editorial Bd International Journal of Peptide and Protein Research 1978–89, Editorial Bd Journal of the American Chemical Society 1978–82, Assembly of Math. and Physical Sciences, Nat. Research Council 1979–82, Scientific Advisory Council, American Cttee for the Weizmann Inst. of Science 1979–, Governing Bd, Nat. Research Council 1980–92, Council, NAS 1980–92, Exec. Cttee of Governing Bd, Nat. Research Council 1980–92, Investments Advisory Cttee, Fed. of American Socs. for Experimental Biology 1981–85, Council, Int. Org. for Chemical Sciences in Devt 1981– (Vice-Pres. and Treas. 1985–); Comm. on Physical Sciences, Maths and Resources, Nat. Research Council 1982–87; Treas. Nat. Acad. of Sciences 1980–92, Advisory Council of the Program in Molecular Biology, Princeton Univ. 1983–95; mem. Bd of Dirs, ESA Inc. 1985–91, Auburn Investment Man. Corpn (also Investment Manager) 1985–; mem. Bd of Dirs, Nat. Health Research Foundation 1985–92, Organization for Chemical Sciences in Devt 1985– and Sec.-Treas., Nat. Acads Corpn 1986–92; Chair., Research Advisory Cttee, Children's Hosp. Medical Center 1986–90; Prof. and Dir Emer. Harvard School of Public Health 1991–; Sr Advisor for Science, Food and Drug Admin. 1991–99; Gen. Partner, Gosnold Investment Fund Ltd Partnership; Chair. Budget Comm., American Acad. of Arts and Sciences, Treas. 1992–98; Pres. Inst. for Int. Vaccine Devt 1996–; mem. Sr Advisory Bd The Encyclopedia of Molecular Biology 1991, Council of Visitors Marine Biological Lab. 1992–, Kuratorium of the German–American Academic Council 1995–; Foreign mem. Russian Acad. of Sciences 1976; Nat. Research Fellow, Harvard Univ.; Fellow, American Acad. of Arts and Sciences, AAAS, Optical Soc. of America, New York Acad. of Sciences; Trustee, Bay Biochemical Research 1973–82, Boston Biomedical Research Inst. 1972– (Vice-Pres. 1990–94); Hon. AM (Harvard Univ.) 1962, Hon. DSc (Loyola Univ.) 1976; Class of 1939 Achievement Award, Princeton Univ. 1970, Nat. Medal of Science Award 1990, Ralph F. Hirschmann Award in Peptide Chemistry, American Chem. Soc. 1991, John Phillips Award, Phillips Exetar Acad. 1998. *Publications:* various articles in specialized journals, including Journal of American Chemical Soc., etc. *Leisure interests:* boating, deep-sea fishing. *Address:* Dept of Biological Chemistry and Molecular Pharmacology, Harvard Medical School, 240 Longwood Avenue, Boston, MA 02115 (Office); 1010 Memorial Drive, Apt 12A, Cambridge, MA 02138-4859, USA (Home).

BLOW, David Mervyn, PhD, FRS; British professor of biophysics; b. 27 June 1931; s. of Rev. Edward Mervyn Blow and Dorothy Laura Blow; m. Mavis Sears 1955; one s. one d.; ed Kingswood School, Corpus Christi Coll., Cambridge; Fulbright Scholar, Nat. Inst. of Health, Bethesda, Md and MIT, USA 1957–59; MRC Unit for Study of Molecular Biological Systems, Cambridge 1959–62; MRC Lab. of Molecular Biology, Cambridge 1962–77; Coll. Lecturer and Fellow, Trinity Coll., Cambridge 1968–77; Prof. of Biophysics, Imperial Coll., Univ. of London 1977–94, Head, Dept of Physics 1991–94, Prof. Emer., Sr Research Fellow 1994–; Dean of Royal Coll. of Science 1981–84; Pres. British Crystallographic Asscn 1984–87; foreign assoc. mem. Acad. des Sciences, Paris 1992; Biochemistry Soc. CIBA Medal 1967, Charles Léopold Meyer Prize 1979, Wolf Foundation Prize for Chem. 1987. *Publications:* Outline of Crystallography for Biologists 2002; papers and reviews in scientific journals. *Leisure interests:* walking, sailing. *Address:* Department of Biological Sciences, Biophysics Division, Imperial College London, London, SW7 2AZ, England (Office). *Telephone:* (20) 7594-7683 (Office). *E-mail:* d .blow@ic.ac.uk (Office).

BLOW, Isabella; English stylist and fashion consultant; b. Nantwich, Cheshire; d. of Sir Evelyn Delves Broughton and Helen Mary Shore; m. Detmar Blow 1989; ed Heathfield School, Ascot and Columbia Univ., New

York; various jobs including domestic cleaner, shop Asst, waitress, etc.; worked on American Vogue, The Tatler, British Vogue magazines; Fashion Dir The Sunday Times 1997–; contrib. to The Face and French Vogue. *Leisure interests:* art, Gloucester Cathedral, rare breeds of agricultural animals and birds, reading, my husband. *Address:* c/o The Sunday Times Style, 1 Pennington Street, London, E1 9XW, England. *Telephone:* (20) 7782-5437 (Office). *Fax:* (20) 7782-5120 (Office).

BLOW, Sandra, RA, FRCA; British artist; b. 14 Sept. 1925; d. of Jack Blow and Lily Blow; ed St Martin's School of Art, Royal Acad. Schools, Accademia di Belle Arti, Rome; tutor, Painting School, RCA 1960–75; works in collections of Peter Stuyvesant Foundation, Nuffield Foundation, Arts Council of GB, Arts Council of Northern Ireland, Walker Art Gallery, Liverpool, Allbright Knox Art Gallery, Buffalo, New York, Museum of Modern Art, New York, Tate Gallery, Gulbenkian Foundation, Ministry of Public Bldg and Works, Contemporary Art Soc., Royal Acad. of Arts; silk screen prints in Victoria and Albert Museum, Fitzwilliam Museum, Cambridge, City of Leeds Art Gallery, Graves Art Gallery, Sheffield; painting purchased for liner Queen Elizabeth II; won British Section of Int. Guggenheim Award 1960; Second Prize, John Moore's Liverpool Exhbn 1961; Arts Council Purchase Award 1965–66; Korn/Ferry Picture of the Year Award 1998. *One-person exhibitions include:* Gimpel Fils 1952, 1954, 1960, 1962, Saidenbury Gallery, New York 1957, New Art Centre, London 1966, 1968, 1971, 1973, Francis Graham-Dixon Gallery 1991, Sackler Galleries, London 1994, Tate St Ives 2001. *Group exhibitions include:* UK, USA, Italy, Denmark and France, Barbican, London 2002. *Publications:* illustrations for book Waves on Porthmeor Beach (by Alaric Summer) 1995, 2000. *Address:* c/o Royal Academy of Arts, Piccadilly, London, W1V 0DS; Bullans Court, Bullans Lane, St Ives, Cornwall, TR26 1RB, England (Home). *Telephone:* (20) 7300-5670; (1736) 797279 (Home).

BLÜM, Norbert, DPhil; German politician; b. 21 July 1935, Rüsselsheim; s. of Christian Blüm and Margarete (née Beck) Blüm; m. Marita Binger 1964; one s. two d.; ed Volksschule; apprentice, Opel AG, Rüsselsheim, 1949–53, toolmaker 1953–57; worked in building trade and as lorry driver while studying evenings 1957–61; univ. student in Cologne and Bonn 1961–67; Ed. Soziale Ordnung 1966–68; Chief Man. Social Comm. of Christian Democrat employees' Asscn 1968–75, Regional Chair. Rhineland-Palatinate 1974–77, Fed. Chair. 1977–87; mem. Fed. Exec. C.D.U. 1969–; mem. Bundestag 1969–; Deputy Chair. CDU 1981–2000; Senator for Fed. Affairs for Berlin 1981; Minister of Labour and Social Affairs 1982–98; Regional Chair. CDU North Rhine-Westphalia 1987–98; mem. IG Metall; Karl-Valentin-Orden 1987, Heinrich-Brauns Preis 1990 and numerous other awards and prizes. *Publications:* Reform oder Reaktion—Wohin geht die CDU 1972, Gewerkschaften zwischen Allmacht und Ohnmacht 1979, Werkstücke 1980, Die Arbeit geht weiter—zur Krise der Erwerbsgesellschaft 1983, 40 Jahre Socialstaat Bundesrepublik Deutschland 1989, Politikals Balanceakt 1993, Dann Willichs mal probieren-Geschichten vom Lachen und Weinen 1994, Sommerfrische-Regentage inclusive 1995, Die Glücksmargerite-Geschichten zum Vorlesen 1997, Diesseits und Jenseits die Politik 1998. *Leisure interests:* reading, walking. *Address:* Platz der Republik, 11011 Berlin, Germany.

BLUM, Yehuda Z., M.JUR., PhD; Israeli diplomatist and lawyer; b. 2 Oct. 1931, Bratislava; m. Moriah Rabinovitz-Teomim; two s. one d.; ed Hebrew Univ., Jerusalem, Univ. of London; detained in Nazi concentration camp of Bergen-Belsen 1944; Asst to Judge Advocate-Gen. of Israel Defence Forces 1956–59; Sr Asst to Legal Adviser, Ministry for Foreign Affairs 1962–65; UNESCO Fellow, Univ. of Sydney July–Aug. 1968; Office of UN Legal Counsel Sept.–Dec. 1968; Sr Research Scholar, Univ. of Michigan Law School 1969; Visiting Prof., School of Law, Univ. of Texas, Austin 1971, New York Univ. 1975–76, Univ. of Mich. Law School 1985, Cardozo School of Law, New York 1991, 2000, Univ. of Southern Calif., Los Angeles 1991–92, Tulane Univ., New Orleans 1994, 2003, Univ. of Miami 1999, Univ. of Calif. at Berkeley 2002; Hersch Lauterpacht Prof. of Int. Law, Hebrew Univ., Jerusalem 1991–; mem. Israeli del., Third UN Conference on Law of the Sea 1973, 31st Session of UN Gen. Ass. 1976; Perm. Rep. to UN 1978–84; Law Ed. Encyclopedia Hebraica 1973–; DJur hc (Yeshiva Univ.) 1981; Jabotinsky Prize 1984. *Publications:* Historic Titles in International Law 1965, Secure Boundaries and Middle East Peace 1971, For Zion's Sake 1987, Eroding the UN Charter 1993. *Address:* Faculty of Law, Hebrew University, Mount Scopus, Jerusalem, Israel. *Telephone:* 2-5882562. *E-mail:* msblumy@mscc.huji.ac.il.

BLUMBERG, Baruch Samuel, MD, PhD, FRCP; American research physician; b. 28 July 1925, New York; s. of late Meyer Blumberg and of Ida (Simonoff) Blumberg; m. Jean Liebesman 1954; two s. two d.; ed Union Coll., Schenectady, Columbia Univ. Coll. of Physicians and Surgeons, Balliol Coll., Oxford; served US Navy 1943–46; Intern and resident, First (Columbia) Div., Bellevue Hosp., New York 1951–57; Ship's Surgeon 1952; Fellow in medicine, Presbyterian Hosp., New York 1953–55; Dept of Biochem., Oxford Univ., UK 1955–57; Chief of Geographic Medicine and Genetics Section, Nat. Insts of Health, Bethesda, Md 1957–64; Assoc. Dir for Clinical Research, Inst. for Cancer Research, Philadelphia 1964–86, Vice-Pres. for Population Oncology, Fox Chase Cancer Center 1986–89; Univ. Prof. of Medicine and Anthropology, Univ. of Pennsylvania 1977–; George Eastman Visiting Prof., Univ. of Oxford 1983–84, Raman Visiting Prof., Indian Acad. of Sciences, Bangalore, India, Jan.–April 1986; Ashland Visiting Prof., Univ. of Ky 1986–87; Master Balliol Coll., Oxford 1989–94; Dir NASA Astrobiology Inst., Ames Research Center, Moffett Field, Calif. 1999–; attending physician, Pa Hosp., Hosp. of Univ. of Pennsylvania; Fox Chase Distinguished Scientist and Sr Adviser to Pres., Fox Chase Cancer Center 1989–; admin. NASA HQ, Washington 2000–; mem. Asscn of American Physicians, various other medical socs; Fellow NAS; Hon. Fellow Balliol Coll., Oxford 1976; numerous hon. degrees; Bernstein Award, Medical Soc. of New York, 1969, Passano Award 1974, Modern Medicine Distinguished Achievement Award 1975, Karl Landsteiner Award 1975, Showa Emperor Memorial Award, Japan, 1994, shared Nobel Prize in Physiology or Medicine for discoveries concerning new mechanisms for origin and dissemination of infectious diseases 1976, and numerous other awards. *Publications:* Australia Antigen and the Biology of Hepatitis B 1977; numerous papers to scientific journals. *Leisure interests:* canoeing, mountain walking, cycling. *Address:* Fox Chase Cancer Center, 7701 Burholme Avenue, Fox Chase, Philadelphia, PA 19111, USA (Office). *Telephone:* (215) 728-3164 (Office).

BLUMENTHAL, W(erner) Michael, PhD; American business executive; b. 3 Jan. 1926, Germany; s. of Ewald Blumenthal and Rose Valerie (Markt) Blumenthal; ed Univ. of California at Berkeley and Princeton Univ.; went to U.S. 1947, naturalized 1952; Research Assoc., Princeton Univ. 1954–57; Vice-Pres., Dir Crown Cork Int. Corpn 1957–61; Deputy Asst Sec. of State for Econ. Affairs, Dept of State 1961–63; also served as USA Rep. to UN Comm. on Int. Commodity Trade; President's Deputy Special Rep. for Trade Negotiations (with rank of Amb.) 1963–67; Chair. U.S. Del. to Kennedy Round tariff talks in Geneva; Pres. Bendix Int. 1967–70; Dir Bendix Corpn 1967–77, Vice-Chair. June–Dec. 1970, Pres. and Chief Operating Officer 1971–72, Chair. and CEO 1972–77; Sec. of the Treasury 1977–79; Dir Burroughs Corpn (now Unisys) 1979–90, Vice-Chair. 1980, CEO 1981–90, Chair. 1990; Sr Advisor Lazard Frères & Co 1990–96; mem. Bd of Dirs. Daimler-Benz InterServices, Int. Advisory Bd Chemical Bank, Tenneco Co., The Business Council, Charter Trustee Emer., Princeton Univ. *Leisure interests:* tennis, skiing. *Address:* 227 Ridgeview Road, Princeton, NJ 08540, USA.

BLUMGART, Leslie Harold, BDS, MD, FACS, FRCS, FRCSE, FRCPS; British professor of surgery; b. 7 Dec. 1931, South Africa; s. of Harold Herman Blumgart and Hilda Blumgart; m. 1st Pearl Navias 1955 (deceased); m. 2nd Sarah Raybould Bowen 1968; two s. two d.; ed Jeppe High School, Johannesburg, Univ. of Witwatersrand, Johannesburg, Univ. of Sheffield, England; Sr Lecturer and Deputy Dir, Dept of Surgery, Welsh Nat. School of Medicine, Cardiff 1970–72; St Mungo Prof. of Surgery, Univ. of Glasgow, Hon. Consultant Surgeon, Glasgow Royal Infirmary 1972–79; Prof. of Surgery and Dir Dept of Surgery, Royal Postgraduate Medical School, Univ. of London and Hon. Consultant, Hammersmith Hosp., London 1979–86; Prof. of Visceral and Transplantion Surgery, Univ. of Bern and Inselspital Bern, Switzerland 1986–91; Enid A. Haupt Prof. of Surgery, Memorial Sloan-Kettering Cancer Center 1991–, Chief of Section of Hepato-Biliary Surgery 1995–, Dir Hepato-Biliary Program; Prof. of Surgery, Cornell Univ. Medical Coll. 1993, American Surgery Soc.; Moynihan Fellowship, Asscn of Surgeons of GB and Ireland 1972; Hon. mem. Soc. for Surgery of the Alimentary Tract, USA, Danish Surgical Soc. 1988, Asscn Française Chirurgie; mem. Hong Kong Surgical Soc., Hellenic Surgical Soc., LA Surgical Soc.; Pres. Int. Biliary Asscn 1986; Hon. mem. Yugoslav Soc. of Surgery; Hon. DSc (Sheffield) 1998; Order of Prasidda Prabala Gorkha-Dakshin Bahu (Nepal) 1984. *Publications include:* Essentials of Medicine and Surgery for Dental Students (with A. C. Kennedy), 4th Edn 1982, The Biliary Tract, in Clinical Surgery Int., Vol. 5 1982, Liver Surgery, in Clinical Surgery Int., Vol. 12 (with S. Bengmark) 1986, Surgery of the Liver and Biliary Tract, Vols 1 and 2 1988, Difficult Problems in General Surgery 1989; numerous publs concerned with medical educ., gastrointestinal surgery and aspects of oncology with particular interest in surgery of the liver, pancreas and biliary tract. *Leisure interests:* watercolour painting, wood carving. *Address:* Memorial Sloan-Kettering Cancer Center, 1275 York Avenue, New York, NY 10021 (Office); 447 East 57th Street, 3E, New York, NY 10022, USA (Home). *Telephone:* (212) 639-5526 (Office); (212) 755-0836 (Home). *Fax:* (212) 794-5852 (Office).

BLUNDELL, Pamela; British fashion designer; b. 23 Feb. 1969; ed Southampton Univ., Epsom School of Art & Design; fmrly worked on samples, design and marketing with late John Flett; numerous freelance clients including English Nat. Opera, Liberty of London; fmr lecturer St Martin's School of Art, London; formed Copperwheat Blundell with Lee Copperwheat (q.v.) 1993; Visiting Lecturer Cen. St Martin's School of Art, Univ. of Nottingham, Brighton Polytechnic 1991–95; winner Courtaulds knitwear competition; Smirnoff Fashion Award for Best Young Designer 1987; Young Designer of the Year 1994 (with Lee Copperwheat). *Address:* Copperwheat Blundell, 14 Cheshire Street, London, E2 6EH, England. *Telephone:* (20) 7613-0651. *Fax:* (20) 7729-8600.

BLUNDELL, Sir Tom Leon, Kt, DPhil, FRS; British professor of biochemistry; b. 7 July 1942, Brighton; s. of Horace Leon Blundell and Marjorie Blundell; m. Bancinyane Lynn Sibanda 1987; one s. two d.; ed Steyning Grammar School and Brasenose Coll., Oxford; Jr research fellow in molecular physics, Linacre Coll. 1968–70; lecturer, Hertford Coll., Oxford 1970–72; lecturer in Biological Sciences, Sussex Univ. 1973–76; Prof. of Crystallography, Birkbeck Coll., London Univ. 1976–90; Dir-Gen. Agricultural and Food Research Council 1991–94; Chief Exec. Biotechnology and Biological Sciences Research Council 1994–96; Sir William Dunn Prof. of Biochemistry, Univ. of Cambridge 1995–, Fellow Sidney Sussex Coll. 1995–, Head Dept of Biochem., 1996–; Dir Int. School of Crystallography 1982–; Chair. Scientific Advisory Bd Bioprocessing Ltd 1996–99; Dir (non-exec.) Celltech 1997– (Chair. Scientific

Advisory Bd 1998–); Scientific Adviser Oxford Molecular Ltd 1996–99; mem. R&D Bd SmithKline Beecham 1997–99, Bd Babraham Inst., Cambridge 1996–2003; Hon. Dir of Imperial Cancer Research Fund Unit of Structural Molecular Biology 1989–96; Chair. Biological Sciences, Science and Eng Research Council (SERC) Council 1983–87, SERC Council 1989–90, AFRC Council and Food Cttee 1985–90, Advisory Council on Science and Tech. 1988–90, Royal Comm. on Environmental Pollution 1998–, Science Advisory Bd 2000–; Dir (non-exec.) Astex Tech. 1999–; Consultant, Pfizer 1983–90; mem. Academia Europaea 1993, Council, Royal Soc. 1997–99; Fellow, EMBO 1985–; Fellow Birkbeck Coll., Univ. of London 1997; mem. Acad. of Med. Sciences 1999–; Foreign Fellow, Indian Nat. Science Acad. 1994; Trustee Daphne Jackson Trust 1996–, Lawes Trust 1996; mem. Bd Parl. Office of Science and Tech. 1998–; Hon. Fellow Royal Agricultural Soc. of England 1993; Hon. Fellow, Brasenose Coll., Oxford 1999–, Linacre Coll., Oxford 1991–Dr hc (Stirling) 2000, (Sussex) 2001, (Pavia) 2002 and numerous other hon. degrees; Gold Medal, Inst. of Biotechnologies 1987, Sir Harry Krebs Medal 1987, CIBA Medal 1988, Feldberg Prize 1988, Medal of Soc. for Chemical Industry 1995, Nat. Equal Opportunities Award 1996, Pfizer European Prize for Innovation 1998. *Publications include:* Protein Crystallography 1976, Progress in Biophysics and Molecular Biology (Ed.) 1980–; various publs in Nature, Journal of Molecular Biology. *Leisure interests:* opera, playing jazz, foreign travel, walking. *Address:* Department of Biochemistry, 80 Tennis Court Road, University of Cambridge, Cambridge, CB2 1GA, England. *Telephone:* (1223) 333628. *Fax:* (1223) 766082. *E-mail:* tom@cryst.bioc.cam.ac.uk (Home).

BLUNDEN, Sir George, Kt, MA; British central banker; b. 31 Dec. 1922, Sutton, Surrey; s. of George Blunden and Florence Holder; m. Anne Bulford 1949; two s. one d.; ed City of London School, Univ. Coll., Oxford; war service, Royal Sussex Regt 1941–45; Bank of England 1947–55; Economist, Balance of Payments Div., Int. Monetary Fund 1955–58; various posts, Bank of England 1958–65, Deputy Principal, Discount Office 1965–67, seconded to Monopolies Comm. 1968, Deputy Chief Cashier 1968–73, Chief of Man. Services 1973–74, responsible for banking supervision with rank of Head of Dept 1974–76, Exec. Dir 1976–84, Non-Exec. Dir 1984–85, Deputy Gov. 1986–90; Chair. Group of Ten Cttees. on banking supervision 1975–77 and on payments systems 1981–83; Chair. London Pensions Fund Authority 1990–92; Jt Deputy Chair. Leopold Joseph Holdings 1984–85, 1990–94; Pres. Inst. of Business Ethics 1994–96; Chair. Centre for Study of Financial Innovation 1995–98; Adviser Union Bank of Switzerland (London br.) 1990–94. *Address:* Ashdale, Gunthorpe, Melton Constable, Norfolk, NR24 2NS, England. *Telephone:* (1263) 860359.

BLUNKETT, Rt. Hon. David, PC, BA; British politician; b. 6 June 1947; m. (divorced); three s.; ed Sheffield Univ.; worked for E Midlands Gas Bd before entering univ.; subsequently taught industrial relations and politics at Barnsley Coll. of Tech.; joined Labour Party 1963; mem. Sheffield City Council 1970–87, Leader 1980–87; mem. S. Yorks. Co. Council 1973–77; MP for Sheffield Brightside 1987–; elected to Nat. Exec. Cttee (NEC) of Labour Party 1983, Chair. NEC Local Govt Cttee 1984; Local Govt Front Bench Spokesman in Opposition's Environment Team 1988–92; Shadow Sec. of State for Health 1992–94, for Educ. 1994–95, for Educ. and Employment 1995–97; Sec. of State for Educ. and Employment 1997–2001, for the Home Dept 2001–; Vice-Chair. Labour Party 1992–93, Chair. 1993–94. *Publications:* On a Clear Day (autobiog.) 1995; co-author: Local Enterprise and Workers' Plans 1981, Building from the Bottom: the Sheffield Experience 1983, Democracy in Crisis: the Town Halls Respond 1987, Politics and Progress 2001. *Leisure interests:* walking, sailing, poetry. *Address:* Home Office, 50 Queen Anne's Gate, London, SW1H 9AT (Office); House of Commons, London, SW1A 0AA, England. *Telephone:* (20) 7273-4000 (Office); (20) 7219-4043. *Fax:* (20) 7273-2065 (Office); (20) 7219-5903. *E-mail:* public .enquiries@homeoffice.gsi.gov.uk (Office). *Website:* www.homeoffice.gsi.gov .uk (Office).

BLUNT, Charles William, BEcons, CPA; Australian politician and businessman; b. 19 Jan. 1951; s. of late R. S. G. Blunt; m. Gail Blunt; two s.; mem. House of Reps. (for Richmond, NSW) 1984–90; Shadow Minister for Sport, Recreation and Tourism 1984, for Social Security 1985, for Community Service 1987; Exec. Dir Nat. Party 1980–84, Leader 1989–90; CEO American Chamber of Commerce in Australia 1990–. *Leisure interests:* tennis, squash, golf. *Address:* Suite 4, Gloucester Walk, 88 Cumberland Street, Sydney, NSW 2000, Australia.

BLY, Robert, MA; American writer and poet; b. 23 Dec. 1926, Madison, Minn.; s. of Jacob Thomas Bly and Alice (Aws) Bly; m. 1st Carolyn McLean 1955 (divorced 1979); m. 2nd Ruth Counsell 1980; five c.; ed Harvard Univ. and Univ. of Iowa; served US Navy 1944–46; f. and Ed. The Fifties 1958–, later The Sixties and Seventies Press; f. American Writers Against the Vietnam War 1966; Fulbright Award 1956–57; Amy Lowell Fellow 1964–65; Guggenheim Fellow 1965–66; Rockefeller Foundation Fellow 1967; Nat. Book Award in Poetry 1968. *Publications include:* (poems) Silence in the Snowy Fields 1962, The Light Around the Body 1967, This Tree Will Be Here for a Thousand Years 1979, Sleepers Joining Hands 1973, Jumping out of Bed 1973, Old Man Rubbing his Eyes 1975, The Man in the Black Coat 1982, Loving a Woman in Two Worlds 1985, Selected Poems (Ed.) 1986, Meditations on the Insatiable Soul 1994, Morning Poems 1997, Eating the Honey of Words: New and Selected Poems 1999, The Best American Poetry (Ed.) 1999, The Night Abraham Called to the Stars 2001; (prose poems) The Morning Glory 1973,

This Body is Made of Eating the Honey of Words: New and Selected Poems 1999, The Best American Poetry (Ed.) 1999, Camphor and Gopherwood 1977; (criticism) Leaping Poetry 1975; Forty Poems Touching on Recent American History (Ed.) 1967, A Poetry Reading Against the Vietnam War 1966, The Sea and the Honeycomb 1966, The Soul is Here for its Own Joy 1995; trans. of vols of poetry from Swedish, Norwegian, German, Spanish and Hindi. *Address:* 1904 Girard Avenue South, Minneapolis, MN 55403, USA.

BLYTH OF ROWINGTON, Baron (Life Peer), cr. 1995, of Rowington in the County of Warwickshire; **James Blyth,** Kt, FRSA, MA; British business executive; b. 8 May 1940; s. of Daniel Blyth and Jane Power Carlton; m. Pamela Anne Campbell Dixon 1967; one d. (one s. deceased); ed Spiers School, Glasgow Univ.; with Mobil Oil Co. 1963–69, Gen. Foods Ltd 1969–71, Mars Ltd 1971–74; Dir and Gen. Man. Lucas Batteries Ltd 1974–77, Lucas Aerospace Ltd 1977–81; Dir Joseph Lucas Ltd 1977–81; Head of Defence Sales, Ministry of Defence 1981–85; Man. Dir Plessey Electronic Systems 1985–86; CEO Plessey Co. PLC 1986–87; CEO Boots Co. PLC 1987–98, Deputy Chair. 1994–98, Chair. 1998–2000; Non-Exec. Dir Imperial Group PLC 1984–86, Cadbury-Schweppes PLC 1986–90, British Aerospace 1990–94, Anixter Int. Inc. 1995–, NatWest Group 1998–2000; Dir Diageo PLC 1998– (Chair. 2000–); Sr Adviser Greenhill & Co. 2000–; mem. Council, Soc. of British Aerospace Cos. 1977–81; Gov. London Business School 1987–96 (Hon. Fellow 1997); Pres. ME Asscn 1988–93; Chair. Advisory Panel on Citizen's Charter 1991–97; Patron Combined Services Winter Sports Asscn 1997–2002; Liveryman, Coachmakers' and Coach Harness Makers' Co.; Hon. LLD (Nottingham) 1992. *Leisure interests:* skiing, tennis, paintings, theatre. *Address:* Diageo PLC, 8 Henrietta Place, London, W1G 0NB, England (Office). *Telephone:* (20) 7927-5993 (Office). *Website:* www.diageo.com.

BO, Jørgen; Danish architect; b. 8 April 1919, Copenhagen; s. of Alf Bo and Anne Marie Bo; m. Gerda Bennike 1941 (divorced 1966); two s. two d.; ed Royal Danish Acad. of Fine Arts; own firm since 1943; tech. consultant for Soc. for Preservation of Natural Amenities of Denmark 1944–52; mem. Danish Nature Conservancy Bd 1952–61; mem. Charlottenborg Adjudicating Bd 1958–61; mem. Slotsholm Cttee 1961–63; mem. San Cataldo Council, Italy 1966; Fellow, Royal Danish Acad. in Rome 1968–70; consultant planner for Danish Nat. Museum; mem. of various int. juries; Fellow, Royal Danish Acad. of Fine Arts, Prof. 1960–89; Kt of the Dannebrog. *Works include:* domestic housing 1945–58, the Louisiana Museum 1956–58, Educ. Centre, Monastir, Tunisia 1960, Museum of Music History 1965, IBM HQ in Denmark 1968–73, Danish Embassy in Brasília 1968–73, IBM Int. Educ. Centre, Belgium 1969–75, Ny Carlsberg Glyptotek 1971–78, restoration work for Carlsberg Foundation and Royal Danish Acad. 1973–76, Extension of Louisiana Museum, Art Museum, Bochum and offices and housing in Baghdad 1978–83, Lübcke Museum, Hamm, Fed. Repub. of Germany 1984–, Weisbord Pavilion, Israel Museum, Jerusalem 1987–88, 20th Century Art Pavilion, Israel Museum 1988. *Address:* Lindevangsvej 22, 3460 Birkerød, Denmark.

BO XILAI; Chinese politician; b. July 1949, Dingxiang, Shanxi Prov.; s. of Bo Yibo (q.v.); ed Grad. School, Chinese Acad. of Social Sciences; joined CCP 1980; fmrly cadre Research Dept of Secr. of CCP Cen. Cttee and Gen. Office of CCP Cen. Cttee; Vice-Sec. then Sec. CCP Cttee of Dalian Econ. and Technological Devt Zone; Sec. CCP Jinzhou Dist Cttee; Vice-Mayor then Mayor of Dalian; Vice-Sec. then Sec. CCP Dalian City Cttee; Acting Gov., then Gov. Liaoning Prov. 2001–. *Address:* Office of the Governor, Shenyang, Liaoning Province, People's Republic of China (Office).

BO YIBO; Chinese government official (retd); b. 1908, Dinxian Co.; m. Hu Ming (died 1966); five s. two d.; ed Taiyuan Elementary School and Beijing Univ.; joined Chinese CP 1925; arrested for subversive activities 1932; organized Sacrifice for Nat. Salvation League in Taiyuan 1937; during Sino-Japanese War was Chair. SE Admin. Office of Shanxi Govt, Commdr Taiyuan Mil. Area and Special Commissar in 3rd Admin. Commissar's Office 1937–45; mem. Cen. Cttee of CP 1945–67; Chair. Shanxi-Hebei-Shandong-Henan Border Region Govt 1945–47, also reportedly Vice-Chair. Revolutionary Mil. and Political Acad. for Korean Cadres, Yenan; Deputy Political Commissar Cen. China PLA, Commdr 8th Column 1947–48; Political Commissar N China Mil. Area, First Vice-Pres. N China People's Govt, Chair. NE Finance and Econ. Cttee and mem. CPN China Bureau 1948; mem. Preparatory Cttee for CPPCC 1949; mem. Govt Admin. Council, Vice-Chair. Cttee of Finance and Econs and Minister of Finance 1949–53; Political Commissar Suiyuan Mil. Area 1949; mem. Bd All-China Fed. of Co-operatives 1950; Chair. Govt Econ. Investigation Cttee (led anti-corruption drive) 1951; mem. State Planning Comm. 1952–67, Deputy Chair. 1962–67; mem. Constitution Drafting Cttee 1953; mem. NPC 1954–67, May 1979–; Chair. State Construction Comm. 1954–56; Head of Third Office, State Council 1955–59; Vice-Chair. Planning Comm. for Scientific Devt 1956–67; Chair. State Econ. Comm. 1958–67; Alt. Mem. Politburo of CP 1958–69; Vice-Premier 1958–67; Deputy Dir State Office of Industry and Communications 1959–61, Dir 1961–67; criticized during Cultural Revolution 1966; arrested 1967; rehabilitated 1979; Vice-Premier, State Council 1979–82; Minister in Charge of State Machine Building Comm. 1979–82; mem. 11th Cen. Cttee CCP 1979–82; Vice-Chair. Cen. Advisory Comm., CCP 1982–92; State Councillor, State Council 1982–83; Vice-Minister, State Comm. for Restructuring Econ. System 1982–83; mem. Party Cttee of Special Orgs. 1983–92; Vice-Chair. Cen. Party Consolidation Comm. 1983–; mem. Presidium 14th CCP Nat. Congress 1992; Hon. Pres., Finance Soc., Acad. of Social Sciences 1980–; Hon. Chair. China Council for Promotion of Int. Trade 1984–; Hon. Chair. Bd of Dirs. China Nat.

Tech. Import Corpn 1984–; Hon. Pres. Beijing Garment Asscn 1984–; Hon. Chair. All-China Fed. of Handicraft Cooperatives 1986–, China Council for Promotion of Int. Trade (China Chamber of Int. Commerce); Hon. Pres. Industrial Economy Soc. May 1988–, Township Enterprises Asscn Jan. 1990–, Nat. Self-Employed Workers Asscn, Political Restructuring Research Soc., numerous other appointments. *Address:* c/o The State Council, Beijing, People's Republic of China.

BOARDMAN, Christopher (Chris) Miles, MBE, MSc; British cyclist; b. 26 Aug. 1968; s. of Keith Boardman and Carole Boardman; m. Sally-Anne Edwards 1988; three s. one d.; ed Hilbre Secondary School and Withens Coll.; has competed in nine world championships; holder of various nat. records and 20 nat. titles; bronze medal, Commonwealth Games, Edinburgh 1986; two bronze medals, Commonwealth Games, Auckland 1990; gold medal, 4,000m individual pursuit, Olympic Games, Barcelona 1992; Double World Champion (pursuit and time trial) 1994; winner Tour de France Prologue and holder Yellow Jersey 1994, 1997, 1998; World Record for distance cycled in one hour 1993 and 1996; won World 4,000m cycling championships, broke his own world record Sept. 1996; retd Oct. 2001; Co. Dir; mem. English Sports Council 1996–; Hon. DSc (Brighton) 1997, Hon. MSc (Liverpool); Man of Year Award, Cheshire Life magazine 1997. *Publication:* Chris Boardman's Complete Book of Cycling. *Leisure interests:* carpentry, swimming, family. *Address:* c/o Beyond Level Four Ltd, Lindfield House, Station Approach, Meols, Wirral, L47 8XA, England. *Telephone:* (151) 632-3383 (Office).

BOARDMAN, Sir John, Kt, MA, FSA, FBA; British archaeologist; b. 20 Aug. 1927; s. of late Frederick Boardman and Clare Wells; m. Sheila Stanford 1952; one s. one d.; ed Chigwell School and Magdalene Coll. Cambridge; Asst Dir British School, Athens 1952–55; Asst Keeper, Ashmolean Museum, Oxford 1955–59; Reader in Classical Archaeology, Univ. of Oxford 1959–78, Lincoln Prof. of Classical Archaeology and Art 1978–94, Hon. Fellow 1995; Fellow, Merton Coll. Oxford 1973–78, Hon. Fellow 1978–, Sub-warden 1975–78; Prof. of Ancient History, Royal Acad. of Arts 1989–; conducted excavations on Chios 1953–55, Crete 1964–65, in Tocra, Libya 1964–65; Visiting Prof. Columbia Univ. 1965; Geddes-Harrower Prof. Univ. of Aberdeen 1974; Fellow, Inst. of Etruscan Studies, Florence 1983, Austrian and German Archaeological Insts.; Foreign mem. Royal Danish Acad.; Assoc. mem. Acad. des Inscriptions et des Belles Lettres, Inst. de France; corresp. mem. Bavarian Acad. of Sciences; foreign mem. American Philosophical Soc., Accademia dei Lincei, Rome; Hon. MRIA; Hon. RA; Dr. hc (Athens) 1991, (Sorbonne) 1994; Kenyon Medal (British Acad.) 1995. *Publications include:* Cretan Collection in Oxford 1961, Island Gems 1963, Archaic Greek Gems 1968, Athenian Black Figure Vases 1974, Escarabeos de Piedra de Ibiza 1984, The Oxford History of the Classical World (with others) 1986, Athenian Red Figure Vases: Classical period 1989, Oxford History of Classical Art 1993, The Diffusion of Classical Art in Antiquity 1994, Greek Sculpture, Later Classical 1995, Runciman Prioxe 1995, Early Greek Vase Painting 1997, Persia and the West 2000, The History of Greek Vases 2001, Greek Gems and Finger Rings 2001, The Archaeology of Nostalgia 2002; articles in learned journals. *Address:* 11 Park Street, Woodstock, Oxford, OX20 1SJ, England. *Telephone:* (1993) 811259. *Fax:* (1865) 278082.

BOARDMAN, Norman Keith, AO, PhD, ScD, FAA, FRS; Australian biochemist; b. 16 Aug. 1926, Geelong, Vic.; s. of William R. and Margaret Boardman; m. Mary C. Shepherd 1952; two s. five d.; ed Melbourne Univ. and St John's Coll., Cambridge; Research Officer, Wool Research Section, CSIRO 1949–51; Sr Research Scientist, Div. of Plant Industry, CSIRO 1956–61, Prin. Research Scientist 1961–64; Fulbright Scholar, Univ. of Calif., Los Angeles 1964–65; Sr Prin. Research Scientist, Div. of Plant Industry, CSIRO 1966–68, Chief Research Scientist 1968–77, mem. of Exec., CSIRO 1977–85, Chair. and Chief Exec. 1985–86, CEO 1986–90, post-retirement Fellow 1990–97; Pres. Australian Biochem. Soc. 1976–78; Chair. Nat. Science and Industry Forum 1998–; Treas. Australian Acad. of Science 1978–81; Dir Sirotech Ltd 1986–90, Landcare Australia Ltd 1990–98; Sec. for Science Policy, Australian Acad. of Science 1993–97; mem. Australian Research Grants Cttee 1971–75, Australian Nat. Univ. Council 1979–89, 1990–91, Australian Centre for Int. Agric. Research (ACIAR) 1982–88, CRA Scientific Advisory Bd 1983–98, Prime Minister's Scientific Council 1989–90; Fellow Australian Acad. of Tech. Sciences and Eng; David Syme Research Prize, Melbourne Univ. 1967; Lemberg Medal, Australian Biochem. Soc. 1969. *Publications:* scientific papers on plant biochemistry, particularly photosynthesis and structure, function and biogenesis of chloroplasts. *Leisure interests:* listening to music, fishing, reading, tennis. *Address:* 6 Somers Crescent, Forrest, ACT 2603, Australia. *Telephone:* (2) 6295-1746 (Home). *Fax:* (2) 6295-1158. *E-mail:* boardman@u030.aone.net.au (Home).

BOASE, Martin, MA; British advertising and marketing executive; b. 14 July 1932, Sheffield; s. of Alan Boase and Elizabeth Grizelle Boase (née Forster); m. 1st Terry Ann Moir 1960 (divorced 1971); one s. one d.; m. 2nd Pauline Valerie Brownrigg 1974; one s. one d.; ed Rendcomb Coll., New Coll., Oxford; with Pritchard Wood and Partners 1961–68; Partner, The Boase Massimi Pollitt Partnership (subsequently Boase Massimi Pollitt PLC, now part of Omnicom UK PLC), Chair. 1977–89; Chair. Omnicom UK PLC 1989–95, Predator Three PLC 1990–97; Chair. Advertising Asscn 1987–92, Kiss 100 FM 1993–2000, Maiden Outdoor 1993–, British TV Advertising Awards Ltd 1993–2000, Herald Investment Trust 1994–, Investment Trust of Investment Trusts 1995–, Heal's 1997–, Jupiter Dividend and Growth Investment Trust 1999–, Global Professional Media PLC 1999–, Newstar Investment Trust 2000–, New Media Industries PLC 2001–; Dir Omnicom Group Inc. 1989–93, EMAP PLC 1991–2000, Taunton Cider PLC 1993–97, Matthew Clark PLC 1995–98. *Leisure interest:* the Turf. *Address:* c/o Omnicom UK PLC, 12 Bishops Bridge Road, London, W2 6AA, England. *Telephone:* (20) 7258-3979. *Fax:* (20) 7706-3854.

BOATENG, Ozwald; British fashion designer; has designed for Pierce Brosnan (q.v.), Mick Jagger, Will Smith, Stephen Baldwin, Laurence Fishburne (q.v.), Billy Zane and others; signed exclusive licensing deal with Marchpole Holdings to produce new formal and casual wear ranges 2002–; British Menswear Designer of the Year Award 2001. *Showings include:* New York 2001. *Address:* 9 Vigo Street, London, W1X 1AL, England (Office). *Telephone:* (20) 7734-6868 (Office).

BOATENG, Rt. Hon. Paul (Yaw), PC, LLB; British politician, lawyer and broadcaster; b. 14 June 1951, Hackney; s. of Kwaku Boateng and Eleanor Boateng; m. Janet Alleyne 1980; two s. three d.; ed Ghana Int. School, Accra Acad., Apsley Grammar School and Univ. of Bristol; solicitor Paddington Law Centre 1976–79; solicitor and partner B. M. Birnberg & Co. 1979–87; called to the Bar, Gray's Inn 1989; Legal Adviser, Scrap Sus Campaign 1977–81; Mem. GLC (Labour) for Walthamstow 1981–86, Chair. Police Cttee 1981–86, Vice-Chair. Ethnic Minorities Cttee 1981–86; MP (Labour) for Brent S. 1987–; Home Office mem., House of Commons Environment Cttee 1987–89; Opposition Frontbench Spokesman on Treasury and Econ. Affairs 1989–92, on Legal Affairs, Lord Chancellor's Dept 1992–97; Parl. Under-Sec. of State, Dept of Health 1997–98; Minister of State 1998–2001, Deputy Home Sec. 1999–2001; Minister for Young People 2000–01; Financial Sec. to HM Treasury 2001–02, Chief Sec. 2002–; Chair. Afro-Caribbean Educ. Resource Project 1976–86, Westminster CRC 1979–81; Gov. Police Staff Coll., Bramshill 1981–84; mem. Home Sec.'s Advisory Council on Race Relations 1981–86, WCC Comm. on Programme to Combat Racism 1984–91, Police Training Council 1981–85; Exec. Nat. Council for Civil Liberties 1980–86; mem. Court of Univ. of Bristol 1994–; mem. Bd ENO 1984–97. *Publications include:* Reclaiming the Ground (contrib.) 1993. *Address:* House of Commons, Westminster, London, SW1A 0AA, England (Office). *Telephone:* (20) 7219-6816 (Sec.) (Office); (20) 7219-0335 (Personal Asst) (Office). *Fax:* (20) 7219-4970 (Office).

BOBBITT, Philip Chase, JD, PhD; American academic and government official; b. 22 July 1948, Temple, Texas; ed Princeton Univ., Yale Univ., Oxford Univ., UK; Asst Prof. of Law, Univ. of Texas School of Law 1976–79, Prof. 1979–, A. W. Walker Centennial Chair 1996–; Jr Research Fellow, Nuffield Coll., Univ. of Oxford 1982–84, Research Fellow 1984–85, Anderson Sr Research Fellow 1985–91, mem. Modern History Faculty 1984–91; Sr Research Fellow, War Studies Dept, Kings Coll. London, UK 1994–97; Assoc. Counsel to Pres. of USA for Intelligence and Int. Security 1980–81; Legal Counsel to U.S. Senate Intra-Contra Cttee 1987–88; Counsellor on Int. Law, U.S. State Dept 1990–93; Dir for Intelligence, Nat. Security Council 1997–98, Sr Dir of Critical Infrastructure 1998–99, Sr Dir for Strategic Planning 1999; mem. American Law Inst., Council on Foreign Relations, Pacific Council on Int. Policy, Int. Inst. for Strategic Studies; fmr Trustee Princeton Univ. *Publications include:* Tragic Choices (co-author) 1978, Constitutional Fate 1982, Democracy and Deterrence 1987, U.S. Nuclear Strategy (co-author) 1989, Constitutional Interpretation 1991, The Shield of Achilles: War, Peace and the Course of History 2002. *Address:* The University of Texas School of Law, TNH4.107, D1800, 727 East Dean Keeton Street, Austin, TX 78712, USA (Office). *Telephone:* (512) 232-1376 (Office); (512) 474-6460 (Home). *Fax:* (512) 471-6988 (Office). *E-mail:* pbobbitt@mail.law.utexas.edu (Office). *Website:* www.utexas.edu (Office).

BOBROW, Martin, CBE, D.SC.MED., FRCP, FRCPath, FMedSci; British professor of genetics; b. 6 Feb. 1938, Johannesburg, South Africa; s. of Joe Bobrow and Bessie Bobrow; m. Lynda Strauss; three d.; ed Univ. of Witwatersrand; Prof. and Head Dept of Medical Genetics, Cambridge Univ. 1995–; Prof. of Human Genetics, Univ. of Amsterdam 1981–82; Prince Philip Prof. of Paediatric Research, United Medical and Dental Schools of Guy's and St Thomas' Hosps., London, 1982–95; mem. Black Advisory Group on possible increased incidence of cancer in W Cumbria 1983–84, Cttee to examine ethical implications of gene therapy 1989–93, NHS Cen. R&D Cttee, Dept of Health 1991–97, Gene Therapy Advisory Cttee 1993–94, Lewisham NHS Trust Bd 1994–95, Nuffield Council on Bioethics 1996–, Human Genetics Advisory Comm. 1997–99; Gov. Wellcome Trust 1996–; Founder FMedSci 1998. *Publications:* papers in science books and journals 1967–. *Address:* Department of Medical Genetics, Cambridge Institute for Medical Research, Wellcome/MRC Building, Addenbrooke's Hospital, Cambridge, CB2 2XY (Office); The Old School, High Street, Balsham, Cambridge, CB1 6DJ, England (Home). *Telephone:* (1223) 331154 (Office). *Fax:* (1223) 331206 (Office); (1223) 894453 (Home). *E-mail:* mb238@cam.ac.uk (Office). *Website:* www.cimr.cam.ac.uk/medgen/ (Office).

BOBUȚAC, Valeriu; Moldovan politician; b. 13 March 1945, Khankaun; m.; two c.; ed Lvov Trade-Econ. Inst., Ukraine, Higher CP School, Kiev, Ukraine; worked in Comsomol, First-Sec. Cen. Cttee then Sec. Cen. Cttee Moldovan CP; Deputy Minister of Econs and Reforms; Amb. to Russia 1997–99, 2001, resigned from diplomatic service 2001; Prime Minister of Moldova 1999–2000. *Address:* Kuznetsky Most str. 18/7, Moscow, Russia (Office). *Telephone:* (095) 924-63-42 (Office).

BOCELLI, Andrea; Italian tenor; b. 22 Sept. 1958, Lajatico, Tuscany; m. Enrica Bocelli; two c.; fmr. lawyer. *Singles include:* Miserere 1996, Con Te Partirò, Canto della terra 1999, O mare e tu 1999, Ave Maria 1999. *Albums include:* Romanza 1996, Bocelli 1997, Viaggio Italiano 1997, Il mare calmo della sera 1997, The Opera album: Aria 1998, Sogno 1999, Sacred Arias 1999.

BOCHEŃSKI, Jacek; Polish writer; b. 29 July 1926, Lvov; m.; one d.; ed State College of Theatrical Arts, Warsaw; literary samizdat Zapis 1977–81; Pres. Polish PEN Club 1996–99. *Radio:* Caprices of an Old Gentleman (weekly five-minute slot). *Television and stage plays:* Taboo, After the Collapse. *Publications include:* novels: Farewell to Miss Syngilu 1960, Divine Julius 1961, Taboo 1965, Naso Poet 1969, After the Collapse 1987; stories: Bloody Italian Rarities 1982, Retro 1990; several essays and contribs. to magazine. *Address:* ul. Sonaty 6 m. 801, 02-744 Warsaw, Poland (Home). *Telephone:* (22) 8435853 (Home). *E-mail:* jacek.bochenski@poczta.gazeta.pl (Home).

BOCHNIARZ, Henryka, PhD; Polish business executive; b. 29 Oct. 1947, Świebodzin; m. Zbigniew Bochniarz; one s. one d.; ed Main School of Planning and Statistics, Warsaw; Asst, Deputy Head Agric. Div., Foreign Trade Research Inst., Warsaw 1976–80, Asst Prof., Lecturer 1980–84, Dir Agric. Div. and Negotiator 1984–90; Sr Fulbright Scholar and Visiting Prof. Dept of Agric. and Applied Econs, Univ. of Minn., USA 1985–87; Pres. NICOM Consulting Ltd, Warsaw 1990–, Asscn of Econs Consultants in Poland 1991; Minister of Industry and Trade 1991–92; Pres. Polish Business Roundtable 1996–99; Co-Chair. (with Leszek Balcerowicz, q.v.) Cttee on Deregulation of the Polish Economy 1998–; mem. Bd Dirs TVN SA, Computerland SA, ITI SA; Pres. Polish Confed. of Pvt. Employers 1999–. *Leisure interests:* skiing, volleyball, theatre. *Website:* www.nicom.pl (Office).

BOCK, Hans, PhD, D.HABIL.; German professor of inorganic chemistry; b. 5 Oct. 1928, Hamburg; s. of Paul Bock and Hedwig (née Lis) Bock; m. Dr. Luise (née Eisenreich) Bock 1954; two s. three d.; ed Ludwigs Maximilians Univ., Munich; Visiting Scientist, Fed. Inst. of Tech., Zürich 1965–68; Prof. and Dir Johann Wolfgang Goethe Univ., Frankfurt 1969–; Adjunct Prof. Univ. of Michigan, Ann Arbor, USA 1983–84; External Scientific mem. Max Planck Soc. 1977–; mem. Acad. of Science, Mainz 1984–; Corresp. mem. Acad. of Science, Göttingen 1986, Acad. of Natural Scientists Leopoldina, Halle 1991, Bavarian Acad. of Sciences 1994; Dr hc (Hamburg) 1988, (Montpellier) 1993; Chemistry Award, Acad. of Science, Göttingen 1969, Frederic Stanley Kipping Award, ACS 1974, Wilhelm Klemm Award of the German Chemical Soc. 1987, Hieber Award 1993; Heyrovsky Medal, Prague Acad. of Science 1996. *Publications:* 500 scientific Ppubls in int. journals, The HMO Model and its Application, (3 Vols, with Edgar Heilbronner) 1965–68. *Leisure interests:* Norman art, philately. *Address:* c/o Institut für Anorganische Chemie der J. W Goethe-Universität, Marie-Curie-Str. 11, 60439 Frankfurt am Main (Office); Rombergweg 1A, 61462 Königstein, Germany (Home). *Telephone:* (69) 79829180 (Office); (6174) 931016 (Home). *Fax:* (69) 79829188 (Office). (6174) 931017 (Home).

BOCK, Jerry (Jerrold Lewis); American composer; b. 23 Nov. 1928, New Haven; s. of George Bock and Rebecca (Alpert) Bock; m. Patricia Faggen 1950; one s. one d.; ed Univ. of Wisconsin; wrote scores for high school and coll. musicals; author of sketches for television 1951–54; mem. NY Bd Educiradio broadcasts 1961–; composed songs for film Wonders of Manhattan 1956; composed music for show Mr. Wonderful 1956 and with Sheldon Harnick The Body Beautiful 1958, Fiorello 1959 (Pulitzer Prize, Antoinette Perry (Tony) Awards), Tenderloin 1960, She Loves Me 1963, Fiddler on the Roof 1964, The Apple Tree 1966, The Rothschilds 1970, Jerome Robbins Broadway 1989, A Stranger Among Us 1992; mem. Wilderness Soc., Horticultural Soc., New York, Broadcast Music Inc., American Civil Liberties Union; Johnny Mercer Award, Songwriters Hall of Fame 1990, Theatre Hall of Fame 1990, Olivier Award for Best Musical Revival (She Loves Me) 1994.

BOCUSE, Paul; French restaurateur; b. 11 Feb. 1926, Collonges-au-Mont-d'Or (Rhône); s. of Georges Bocuse and Irma Roulier; m. Raymonde Duvert 1946; one s. one d.; ed Ecole primaire, Collonges-au-Mont-d'Or and Pensionnat Saint-Louis, Lyons; restaurateur (in business passing from father to son since 1765), Collonges-Mont-d'Or; restaurateur, French Pavilion, Disneyworld, Orlando, Fla, USA; Pres. Assn Eurotoques 1989–, L'Ecole des Arts Culinaires et de l'Hôtellerie Ecully 1991–95; Pres. Meilleur Ouvrier de France—Section Cuisine-Restauration 1991–; mem. Assn des maître-cuisiniers de France; Officier, Légion d'honneur, Ordre nat. du Mérite, Chevalier des palmes académiques, Officier du Mérite agricole. *Publications:* La Cuisine du marché 1976, Bocuse dans votre cuisine 1982, La cuisine du gibier (in collaboration) 1984, Bon Appétit 1989, Cuisine de France 1990, La bonne chère 1995. *Leisure interest:* underwater fishing. *Address:* Restaurant Paul Bocuse, 40 rue de la Plage, 69660 Collonges-au-Mont d'Or, France. *Telephone:* (4) 72-42-90-90. *Fax:* (4) 72-27-85-87. *E-mail:* paul.bocuse@bocuse.fr (Office). *Website:* www.bocuse.fr (Office).

BOD, Péter Ákos, PhD; Hungarian economist and politician; b. 28 July 1951, Szigetvár; s. of Andor Bod and Rózsa Nagy; m. Katalin Monostori; one d.; ed high school, Miskolc, Univ. of Econ., Budapest; worked as researcher, later Dept head, Inst. for Econ. Planning; UNDP adviser in Ghana; mem. of Parl. (Hungarian Democratic Forum) 1990–91; Minister of Industry and Trade 1990–91; Pres. Nat. Bank of Hungary 1991–94; mem. Bd EBRD, London 1995–97; Prof. and Dept Chair., Budapest Univ. of Econ. Sciences and Public Admin. 2001–; Personal Econ. Adviser to Pres. of the Repub. 2001–. *Publications:* The Entrepreneurial State in the Contemporary Market Economy

1987, Foundations of Economic Theory and Policy 1999, The World of Money—The Money of the World 2001, Economic Policy 2002. *Leisure interests:* tennis, soccer, music, history. *Address:* Fövam tér 9, Budapest University of Economic Sciences and Public Administration, 1093 Budapest (Office); Office of the President of the Republic, 1051 Budapest, Kossuth tér. 4, Hungary. *Telephone:* (1) 2174271 (Office). *Fax:* (1) 441-3527. *E-mail:* petera .bod@bkae.hu (Office); dsuni@axelero.hu (Home).

BODE, Thilo, PhD; German business executive and consultant; b. 1947, nr Munich; ed Munich and Regensburg Univs; int. consultant Lahmeyer Int., Frankfurt; Project Man. German Bank for Reconstruction and Devt 1978–81; ind. consultant for int. orgs, govts and businesses 1981; Special Asst to Chief Exec. of int. pvt. corpn 1986; Exec. Dir Greenpeace Germany 1989–95, Greenpeace Int. 1995–2001. *Address:* c/o Greenpeace International, Keizergracht 176, Amsterdam 1016 DW, Netherlands. *E-mail:* thilobode@hotmail .com.

BODELÓN, Rogelio, DrIng; Spanish business executive; b. 21 Sept. 1936, Ponferrada; s. of Carlos Bodelón and Adela López; ed Escuela Técnica Superior Ingenieros Industriales, Madrid; mem. Bd of Dirs. Sefanitro 1973–77; Commercial Dir HIDRONITRU 1977–83; Gen. Dir ENSIDESA 1983–88; Asst Dir Instituto Nacional de Industria (INI) Aug. 1988–; Pres. AGCISA Jan. 1989–; Vice-Pres. TARNOS, SA 1991–; mem. Bd of Dirs. Ferroatlántica 1993–, Fertiberia 1995–, SEFANITRO 1997–. *Publications:* numerous articles in newspapers. *Leisure interests:* golf, dominoes. *Address:* Paseo Habana 26-6-12, 28036 Madrid, Spain. *Telephone:* 5614586. *Fax:* 5636840.

BODEN, Margaret Ann, OBE, ScD, PhD, FBA; British professor of philosophy and psychology; b. 26 Nov. 1936, London; d. of Leonard F. Boden and Violet Dorothy (Dawson) Boden; m. John R. Spiers 1967 (divorced 1981); one s. one d.; ed Newnham Coll., Cambridge (Major Scholar) and Harvard Grad. School (Harkness Fellow); lecturer in Philosophy, Univ. of Birmingham 1959–65; lecturer, then Reader in Philosophy and Psychology, Univ. of Sussex 1965–80, Prof. 1980–, Founding Dean School of Cognitive and Computing Sciences 1987, Research Prof. of Cognitive Science 2002–; Curator Univ. of London Inst. for Advanced Study 1995–; co-founder, Harvester Press Ltd 1970, Dir 1970–85; Vice-Pres. British Acad. 1989–91, Royal Inst. of GB 1993–95, Chair. of Council, Royal Inst. of GB 1993–95; mem. Advisory Bd for the Research Councils 1989–90, Council, Royal Inst. of Great Britain 1992–95, Academia Europaea 1993–, Animal Procedures Cttee 1995–99; Fellow American Assn for Artificial Intelligence 1993–; Fellow European Coordinating Cttee for Artificial Intelligence 1999–. *Publications:* Purposive Explanation in Psychology 1972, Artificial Intelligence and Natural Man 1977, Piaget 1979, Minds and Mechanisms 1981, Computer Models of Mind 1988, Artificial Intelligence in Psychology 1989, The Philosophy of Artificial Intelligence (ed.) 1990, The Creative Mind 1990, Dimensions of Creativity (ed.) 1994, Artificial Intelligence and the Mind (co-ed.) 1994, The Philosophy of Artificial Life (ed.) 1996, Artificial Intelligence (ed.) 1996. *Leisure interests:* dressmaking, travelling, passion for India. *Address:* c/o School of Cognitive and Computing Sciences, Room 5C3, University of Sussex, Falmer, Brighton, BN1 9QH, England. *Telephone:* (1273) 678386. *Fax:* (1273) 671320. *E-mail:* maggieb@ cogs.susx.ac.uk. *Website:* www.cogs.susx.ac.uk.

BODEWIG, Kurt; German politician; b. 26 April 1955, Rheinberg; m.; one s.; ed commercial coll.; joined SPD 1973; held various party posts 1982–98; member of Bundestag 1998–; Minister of Transport, Building and Housing 2000–02. *Address:* Bundestag, Platz der Republik 1, 11011 Berlin, Germany (Office). *Telephone:* (30) 22775313 (Office). *Fax:* (30) 22776313 (Office). *E-mail:* kurt.bodewig@bundestag.de (Office). *Website:* www.kurt-bodewig.de.

BODEWITZ, Hendrik Wilhelm, PhD; Netherlands professor of Sanskrit; b. 13 Oct. 1939, Gramsbergen; s. of Johan Adriaan Bodewitz and Jennigjen Lenters; m. Janneke van Uchelen 1964; one s. one d.; ed Lyceum Coevorden, Univ. of Utrecht; lecturer in Sanskrit, Utrecht Univ. 1966–68, Prof. 1976–92, Dean of Faculty 1980–82 and 1984–86; Sr Lecturer, Leiden Univ. 1969–76, Prof. 1992–2002; mem. Netherlands Royal Acad.; founding mem. Academia Europaea; Ed. Indo-Iranian Journal, Gonda Indological Studies; Co-Ed. Groningen Oriental Studies; Sec. Gonda Foundation. *Publications:* Jaiminīya Brāhmaṇa I, 1-65, with a study of the Agnihotra and the Prāṇāgnihotra 1973, The daily evening and morning offering according to the Brāhmaṇas 1976, The Jyotiṣṭoma Ritual: Jaiminīya Brāhmaṇa I, 66-364 1990, Kauṣṭtaki Upaniṣad 2002. *Address:* KERN Institute, POB 9515, 2300 RA, Leiden, Netherlands (Office); Stolberglaan 29, 3583 XL Utrecht, Netherlands. *Telephone:* (71) 5272909 (Office); (30) 2510047.

BODIN, Manfred; German banker; b. 14 Nov. 1939, Münster; m.; Stadtsparkasse, Münster 1960–64; Stadtsparkasse, Witten 1964–70; mem. Man. Bd Kreissparkasse Recklinghausen 1970–75, Chair. Man. Bd 1976–83; Chair. Man. Bd Sparkasse Essen 1984–91; Chair. Man. Bd NORD/LB 1991–; Dr. hc (Tech. Univ. Braunschweig). *Address:* Norddeutsche Landesbank Girozentrale, Georgsplatz 1, 30159 Hannover, Germany. *Telephone:* (511) 361-0. *Fax:* (511) 361-5242. *Website:* www.nordlb.de (Office).

BODMAN, Samuel Wright, III; ScD; American business executive; b. 26 Nov. 1938, Chicago, Ill.; s. of Samuel W Bodman Jr and Lina B. Bodman; m. 1st Lynda Schubert 1984; three c.; m. 2nd Diane Barber 1997; ed Cornell Univ. and Massachusetts Inst. of Tech.; Instructor, MIT 1964, Asst Prof. 1964–68, Assoc. Prof. 1968–70, Dir School of Chemical Eng Practice, American Cyanamid Co. 1965–67; Tech. Dir American Research and Devt Corpn 1964–70; Founding Partner Fidelity Ventures Ltd 1970–86, Vice-Pres. Commercial Devt 1971–75, Pres. Fidelity Man. and Research Co. 1976–86, Pres. and COO FMR Corpn (parent holding co. of Fidelity Investments) 1982–86, Exec. Vice-Pres. and Dir Fidelity Group of Mutual Funds 1980–86; Pres. and COO Cabot Corpn 1987–88, Chair., CEO 1988–; Dir Cabot Corpn, Bank of Boston Corpn, Westvaco Inc., Continental Cablevision Inc., Index Tech. Corpn, John Hancock Financial Services, Thermo Electron Corpn, Security Capital Group Inc.; Trustee Mitre Corpn, Babson Coll., Isabella Stewart Gardner Museum, New England Aquarium; mem. Corpn, MIT, Chair. Chemical Eng Visiting Cttee; mem. American Acad. of Arts and Sciences. *Address:* Cabot Corpn, 2 Seaport Lane, Suite 1300, Boston, MA 02210-2019, USA.

BODMER, Sir Walter Fred, Kt, PhD, FRCPath, FRS, FMedSci; British research scientist; b. 10 Jan. 1936, Frankfurt am Main, Germany; s. of the late Ernest Julius Bodmer and Sylvia Emily Bodmer; m. Julia Gwynaeth Pilkington 1956 (died 2001); two s. one d.; ed Manchester Grammar School and Clare Coll., Univ. of Cambridge; Research Fellow, Clare Coll., Cambridge 1958–60, Fellow 1961, Hon. Fellow 1989; Demonstrator, Dept of Genetics, Univ. of Cambridge 1960–61; Fellow, Visiting Asst Prof., Dept of Genetics, Stanford Univ. 1961–62, Asst Prof. 1962–66, Assoc. Prof. 1966–68, Prof. 1968–70; Prof. of Genetics, Univ. of Oxford 1970–79; Vice-Pres. Royal Inst. 1981–82; Pres. Royal Statistical Soc. 1984–85; Pres. British Asscn for Advancement of Science 1987–88, Chair. of Council 1996–; mem. Advisory Bd for the Research Councils 1983–88; Chair. BBC Science Consultative Group 1981–87; mem. BBC Gen. Advisory Council; Chair. Bd of Trustees, British Museum (Natural History) 1989–93; Pres. Human Genome Org. 1990–92; Dir-Gen. Imperial Cancer Research Fund 1991–96 (Dir of Research 1979–91); Chancellor of Salford Univ. 1995–; Prin. Hertford Coll., Oxford 1995–; Chair. Cttee on the Public Understanding of Science (COPUS) 1990–94; Pres. Int. Fed. of Asscns. for the Advancement of Science and Tech. 1992–94; Hon. Vice-Pres. Research Defence Soc. 1990–; Dir non-exec. Fisons PLC 1990–96; British Assoc. for Cancer Research 1998–; Foreign Hon. mem. American Acad. of Arts and Sciences, American Asscn of Immunologists; Foreign Assoc. NAS; Hon. Fellow, Green Coll., Oxford, Keble Coll., Oxford, Clare Coll., Cambridge, Royal Soc. of Medicine; Hon. FRCP; Hon. FRCS, Hon. FRSE; Hon. MD (Bologna, Birmingham); Hon. DSc (Bath), (Oxford), (Hull), (Edin.) 1990, (Aberdeen) 1994, (Lancaster) 1994, (London), (Plymouth), (Salford) 1996, (UMIST) 1997; Hon. DUniv (Surrey) 1990; William Allan Memorial Award (American Soc. of Human Genetics) 1980, Conway Evans Prize (Royal Coll. of Physicians/Royal Soc.) 1982, Rabbi Shai Shacknai Memorial Prize Lectureship in Immunology and Cancer Research 1983, John Alexander Memorial Prize and Lectureship (Univ. of Pa Medical School) 1984, Rose Payne Distinguished Scientist Lectureship 1985, Ellison Cliffe Lecture and Medal 1987, Neil Hamilton-Fairley Medal, Royal Coll. of Physicians 1990, Faraday Award, Royal Soc. 1994, Dalton Medal, Manchester Literary and Philosophical Soc. 2002. *Publications:* co-author: The Genetics of Human Populations 1971, Our Future Inheritance—Choice or Chance? 1974, Genetics, Evolution and Man 1976, The Book of Man 1994; papers in scientific and medical journals. *Leisure interests:* playing piano, riding, swimming, scuba diving. *Address:* Hertford College, Catte Street, Oxford, OX1 3BW, England. *Telephone:* (1865) 279407. *E-mail:* walter.bodmer@hertford.ox.ac.uk. *Website:* www.hertford.ox.ac.uk.

BODROV, Sergey Vladimirovich; Russian scriptwriter and film director; b. 28 July 1948, Khabarovsk; m. (divorced); ed All-Union Inst. of Cinematography. *Films include:* (scriptwriter) Trouble-Maker, Don't Get Married, Girlies, Sailors Have No Questions, (Dir) Sweet Juice Inside 1985 (Silver Prize, Moscow Film Festival 1985, Int. Film Festival Prize, Portugal 1986), Laymen (Special Prize, Int. Film Festival, Tbilisi, Int. Film Festival, Turin), SIR (Grand Prix, American Int. Film Festival, Montreal 1989, Special Prize, Int. Film Festival, Sorrento), Prisoner of Caucasus (Grand Prix, Kinotaurus 1996, Best Script, Int. Film Festival Berlin 1996), Let's Make it Fast 2001. *Address:* Leninsky prosp. 129, korp. 3, Apt. 20, 117513 Moscow, Russia. *Telephone:* (095) 438-38-04.

BOEHM, Gottfried Karl, DPhil; German art historian; b. 19 Sept. 1942, Braunau, Bohemia; s. of Karl Boehm and Olga Boehm; m. Margaret Hunold 1980; one d.; ed Univs. of Cologne, Vienna and Heidelberg; lecturer, History of Art, Ruhr Univ. Bochum 1975–79, Prof. 1977; Prof. of History of Art, Justus Liebig Univ., Giessen 1979–86, Univ. of Basel 1986–; Perm. Fellow Inst. für die Wissenschaften vom Menschen, Vienna 1981–; Fellow Wissenschaftsholleg, Berlin 2001–02; Ehrenkreuz für Wissenschaft und Kunst (First Class), Repub. of Austria. *Publications:* Studien zur Perspektivität, Philosophie und Kunst in der frühen Neuzeit 1969, Zur Dialektik der ästhetischen Grenze 1973, Philosophische Hermeneutik 1976, Die Hermeneutik und die Wissenschaften 1978, Bildnis und Individuum, Über den Ursprung der Porträtmalerei in der italienischen Renaissance 1985, Paul Cézanne, Montagne Sainte-Victoire 1988, Konrad Fiedler, Schriften zur Kunst 1991, Was ist ein Bild? 1994, Beschreibungskunst-Kunstbeschreibung. Ekphrasis von der Antike bis zur Gegenwart 1995, Canto d'amore. Klassizistische Moderne in Musik und bildender Kunst 1996, Paul Cézanne und die Moderne 1999, Der Maler Max Weiler. Das Geistige in der Natur 2001, Homo Pictor 2001, Zwischen-Räume. Malerei, Relief und Skulptur im Werk von Ellsworth Kelly 2002. *Address:* Kunstgeschichtliches Seminar, St Alban-Graben-8, 4051 Basel (Office); Sevogelplatz 1, 4051 Basel, Switzerland (Home). *Telephone:*

(61) 2066292/3 (Office); (61) 3116241 (Home). *Fax:* (61) 2066297 (Office). *E-mail:* gottfried.boehm@unibas.ch (Office). *Website:* www.unibas.ch/kunsthist (Office).

BOEKELHEIDE, Virgil Carl, PhD; American professor of chemistry; b. 28 July 1919, S. Dakota; s. of Charles F. Boekelheide and Eleanor Toennies; m. Caroline A. Barrett 1945; two s. one d.; ed Univ. of Minnesota; Instructor, Univ of Illinois 1943–46; Asst Prof. Univ. of Rochester 1946–60; Prof. of Chem., Univ. of Oregon 1960–; mem. NAS 1962–; Guggenheim Fellow 1953–54; Swiss American Foundation Fellow 1960; Roche Anniversary Fellow 1963–64; Welch Lecturer 1968; Fulbright Distinguished Prof., Yugoslavia 1972; Distinguished Scholar Exchange Program, People's Repub. of China 1981; mem. Bd of Eds. Organic Reactions 1956–, Organic Syntheses 1956–64, Journal of American Chemical Society 1964–74; mem. Council for Int. Exchange of Scholars (Sr Fulbright-Hayes Awards); Centenary Lecturer, Royal Soc. of GB 1983–; Alexander v. Humboldt Prize (Fed. Repub. of Germany) 1974–75; Coover Award 1981. *Publications:* over 200 original research papers. *Leisure interests:* tennis and music. *Address:* 2017 Elk Avenue, Eugene, OR 97403, USA.

BOENISCH, Peter H.; German journalist; b. 4 May 1927, Berlin; s. of Konstantin Boenisch and Eva Boenisch (née Premysler); m. 1st Victoria von Schack 1959 (divorced); m. 2nd Susanne Fischer (divorced); m. 3rd Julia Schramm 1998; one d.; ed Dr. Hugo Eckner Coll., Berlin Univ.; Political Ed. Die Neue Zeitung 1945–49; Ed. Tagespost 1949–52; Special Asst to Pres. Nordwest-Deutsche-Rundfunk 1952–55; Ed. Kindler Publishing Co. 1955–59, Springer Publishing Corpn (Berliner Illustrierte, Bild-Zeitung, Bild am Sonntag) 1959–81; Chair. Ed. Bd Die Welt 1978–81; fmr Vice-Chair. Axel Springer Group, responsible for planning and Devt; Chief Govt Spokesman and Leader, Fed. Press and Information Office 1983–85; Man. Dir of Burda Magazines 1986–92; mem. Bd of Dirs. Axel Springer Verlag 1999; Bundesverdienstkreuz, Bayerischer Verdienstorden 1976, Order of Leopold II (Belgium) 1985. *Leisure interests:* golf, antiques. *Address:* Kaltenbrunnerstr. 14, 83703 Gmund, Germany.

BOESAK, Rev. Allan; South African clergyman; b. 23 Feb. 1946, Kakamas; s. of Andreas Boesak and Sarah Helena Boesak; m. 1st Dorothy Rose Martin 1969; one s. three d.; m. 2nd Elna Botha 1991; two d.; ed Univ. of Western Cape, Theological Univ., Kampen, Netherlands, Union Theological Seminary; prominent anti-apartheid campaigner; elected Pres. World Alliance of Reformed Churches, Ottawa 1982; Pres. Asscn of Christian Students in SA 1984–90; Vice-Pres. SA Council of Churches 1984–87; fmr mem. Dutch Reformed Mission Church; Leader ANC in Western Cape 1991; Dir Foundation for Peace and Justice 1991; faced 32 theft and corruption charges 1997; on trial for fraud Aug. 1998; sentenced to six years' imprisonment March 1999, sentence halved on appeal May 2000; conviction for misuse of aid money set aside, conviction for theft upheld 2000; released on parole June 2001; co-f. United Democratic Front 1983; Hon. DD (Victoria) 1983, (Yale) 1984, (Interdenominational Theological Center Atlanta) 1985; Hon. DIur (Warwick) 1989; Third World Prize 1989, numerous other awards and hon. degrees. *Publications:* Farewell to Innocence 1976, Black and Reformed 1984, Walking on Thorns 1984, A Call for an End to Unjust Rule 1986, If This is Treason, I am Guilty (Speeches) 1988, Comfort and Protest 1988, Shadows of the Light 1996, Tot Sterwens Toe (poems) 2001. *Leisure interests:* reading, walking, sports, music. *Address:* 16 Villa Bellini, Constantia Street, Strand 7140, South Africa (Home). *Telephone:* (21) 854-4937 (Home). *E-mail:* boesak@mweb.co.za (Home).

BOETSCH, Wolfgang, DJur; German politician; b. 8 Sept. 1938, Bad Kreuznach; m.; two c.; ed Univ. of Würzburg and Verwaltungshochschule, Speyer; municipal lawyer, Kitzingen 1968–74; legal adviser to Govt of Lower Franconia 1974; mem. Christian Social Union (CSU) 1960–; mem. Würzburg City Council 1972–76; mem. Bavarian Parl. 1974–76; Chair. of CSU, Würzburg 1973–91, also mem. Presidium of CSU; mem. Bundestag 1976–; Minister for Posts and Telecommunications 1993–97. *Address:* Waltherstrasse 5a, 97074 Würzburg, Germany. *Telephone:* (931) 83080. *Fax:* (931) 14-8872.

BOFF, Leonardo Genezio Darci, DPhil, DTheol; Brazilian professor of theology, writer and editor; b. 14 Dec. 1938, Concórdia, SC; s. of Mansueto Boff and Regina Fontana Boff; ed Inst. Teológico Franciscano, Petrópolis and Nat. Univ. of Rio de Janeiro; Prof. of Systematic Theology and of Franciscan Spirituality, Inst. Teológico Franciscano, Petrópolis, Rio de Janeiro 1971–92, also Prof. of Theology of Liberation; Adviser to Latin American Conf. of Religions (CLAR) 1971–80, to Nat. Conf. of Brazilian Bishops (CNBB) 1971–80; mem. Editorial Bd of Revista Eclesiástica Brasileira 1971–92; mem. Bd of Dirs. Vozes publishing house 1971–92; Pres. Bd of Eds., Theology and Liberation collection 1985–; mem. Editorial Bd Concilium; ordered by Roman Curia to begin unspecified period of "obedient silence" 1985; Dr. hc (Turin, Lund); Paz y Justicia Award, Barcelona, Menschenrechte in der Kirche Award, Herbert Haag Foundation, Fed. Repub. of Germany and Switzerland. *Publications:* Jesus Christ Liberator 1971, Die Kirche als Sakrament im Horizont der Welterfahrung 1972, Theology of Captivity and Liberation 1972, Ecclesiogenesis 1977, The Maternal Face of God 1979, Church: Charisma and Power 1980, Theology Listening to People 1981, St Francis: A Model for Human Liberation 1984, Trinity and Society 1988, The Gospel of the Cosmic Christ 1989, The New Evangelization: The Perspective of the Oppressed 1990, Ecology and Spirituality 1991, Mística e Espiritualidade 1994, Nova Era: a Consciência Planetária 1994. *Leisure interests:* gardening, social work at the "favelas", child minding. *Address:* Pr. Martins Leão 12/204, Alto Vale Encantado, 20531-350 Rio de Janeiro, Brazil. *Telephone:* (21) 326-5293. *Fax:* (21) 326-5293.

BOFILL, Ricardo; Spanish architect; b. 5 Dec. 1939, Barcelona; s. of Emilio Bofill and Maria Levi; two s.; ed Ecole Française, Barcelona, architectural studies in Geneva; founder mem. and leader Taller de Arquitectura (design team), Paris, Barcelona. *Works include:* Les Espaces d'Abraxas, Marne-la-Vallée, Les Echelles du Baroque, Paris, Antigone, Montpellier, Le Lac and Le Viaduc, Versailles, airports (Barcelona), theatres (Metz and Barcelona), offices, wine cellars Congress Palace, Madrid, Christian Dior Corpn HQ, Paris, Shepherd School of Music, Houston, Tex., USA, 77 W. Wacker office tower, Chicago, Ill., USA, Harajuku United Arrows shopping centre, Tokyo. *Exhibitions include:* Architectural Asscn, London Jan. 1981, Museum of Modern Art, New York June–Sept. 1985. *Address:* Taller de Arquitectura, 14 Avenue Industria, 08960 Saint Just Desvern, Barcelona, Spain. *Telephone:* (3) 4999900. *E-mail:* rbofill@bofill.com (Office). *Website:* www.bofill.com (Office).

BOFINGER, Helge; German architect and university professor; b. 30 March 1940, Stettin/Pommern; s. of Christa Bofinger and Hans Ullrich Bofinger; m. Margret Schreib Schmitz-Mathies 1965; ed Ratsgymnasium Goslar, Tech. Univ. of Brunswick; Scientific Asst T.U. Brunswick 1968–69; est. own office Bofinger and partner with Margret Bofinger, Brunswick 1969–81, Berlin 1974–, Wiesbaden 1978–; Asst Prof., Univ. of Dortmund 1979–81, Prof. of Design and Bldg Theory, Faculty of Architecture 1986–; Hon. Prof., Univ. of Buenos Aires, Argentina 1985; Visiting Prof. and Lecturer, Venice, Amsterdam, Rotterdam, Buenos Aires, São Paulo, Brasília, Curitiba, Shanghai 1984–91; rep. in numerous exhbns. Germany, USA, Canada, Israel, Italy, Argentina, UK, France, USSR 1979–90; Prof. hc (Tbilisi) 1995; Deubau Special Prize 1979, German Architectural Prize 1983, Hon. Prize, Transcaucasian Biennale, Tbilisi 1988. *Works include:* Castle Park, Brunswick 1972–74, Unitéhabitation, Göttingen 1972–74, Piazza Ledenhof, Osnabrück 1976–77, school, Friedland 1977–79, Villa S. Kronberg 1980–82, German Cinema Museum 1979–84, Frankfurt Fair Tower 1984, IBA Berlin, Wilhemstr., Stresemannstr. 1981, 1988–89, Telecommunications Bldg, German Post/Telecom 1987–90, Commerzbank, Frankfurt 1991, Willy-Brandt-Haus (SPD HQ), Berlin 1992, town hall extension, Saarbrücken 1992. *Exhibitions:* (with Margret Bofinger): Architekturzeichnungen 1479–1979, Berlin 1979, Bauen für Frankfurt, New Building in a Historic Context, Frankfurt 1984, USA and Canada 1985–87, Italy 1985, Israel 1986, Bauen Heute, Frankfurt 1986, New German Architecture, RIBA-Heinz Gallery, London 1986, Biennale Buenos Aires 1987, IBA, Berlin 1987, Denkmal oder Denkmodell Berlin, Paris 1988, Tanskaukasische Biennale Tbilisi/USSR 1988, Paris – Architecture et Utopie, Paris, 1989, Künstlerhauser, eine Architekturgeschichte des Privaten, Frankfurt 1989, Architects for Snoopy, Musée des Beaux-Arts de Montréal 1992, Martin-Gropius-Bau, Berlin 1996, Ausstellung Willy-Brandt-Haus, Vienna 1999. *Publications:* Architecture in Germany 1979, Young Architects in Europe 1983; Helmut Jacoby – Master of Architectural Drawing (Ed.); numerous contribs. to German and int. architectural magazines. *Leisure interest:* architecture. *Address:* Biebricher Allee 49, 65187 Wiesbaden, Germany. *Telephone:* (611) 87094. *Fax:* (611) 87095. *E-mail:* bofinger@bofinger-partner.de (Office). *Website:* www.bofinger-partner.de (Office).

BOGAERS, Petrus Clemens Wilhelmus Maria, DrsEcon; Netherlands politician and trade unionist; b. 2 July 1924, Cuyk a/d Maas; s. of Petrus P. M. J. Bogaers and Henrica Maria Hermans; m. 1st Femmigje Visscher 1950 (divorced 1980); m. 2nd Yvonne M. H. L. Bogaers 1981 (divorced 1986); m. 3rd Ida Heyne 1994; four s. three d.; ed Episcopal Coll. Grammar School, Roermond and Tilburg School of Economics; official Red Cross Army 1945; Asst to Prof. v.d. Brink 1947; Econ. Adviser to Roman Catholic Workers' Union 1948, Head Scientific Advisory Section 1957–63; mem. Socio-Economic Council 1954; mem. EEC Econ. and Social Cttee 1958; mem. Second Chamber, Netherlands Parl. 1959; Minister of Housing and Building 1963–65; Minister of Housing and Physical Planning 1965–66; Pres. Gooiland Region 1968–74, Netherlands Asthma Foundation 1976–89 (Hon. mem. 1989); mem. Supervisory Bds. various Dutch cos 1976–95; Sec. Employee Participation Foundation BERGEYK 1986–96; mem. Supervisory Bd Dutch Employee Participation Inst. 1994–96; Dutch Efficiency Prize 1963; Officer Order of Orange-Nassau 1963, Queens House Medal of Orange-Nassau 1965, Commdr Order of Orange-Nassau 1966. *Leisure interests:* reading, tennis, open-air life. *Address:* Volta Street 53, Amersfoort, Netherlands. *Telephone:* (33) 4615093.

BOGDANOR, Vernon, CBE, MA, FRSA, FBA; British professor of government; b. 16 July 1943, London; s. of Harry Bogdanor and Rosa Weinger; m. Judith Beckett 1972 (divorced 2000); two s.; ed Queen's Coll. and Nuffield Coll. Oxford; Fellow, Brasenose Coll. Oxford 1966–, Sr Tutor 1979–85, 1996–97; mem. Council of Hansard Soc. for Parl. Govt 1981–97; Special Adviser, House of Lords Select Cttee on European Communities 1982–83; adviser to Govts. of Czech Repub., Slovakia, Hungary and Israel on constitutional and electoral matters 1988–; Reader in Govt Univ. of Oxford 1989–96, Prof. of Govt 1996–; Special Adviser, House of Commons Public Service Cttee 1996; mem. UK del. to CSCE Conf. Oslo 1991; Mishcon Lecturer 1994; Hon. Fellow Soc. for Advanced Legal Studies 1997. *Publications:* Devolution 1979, The People and the Party System 1981, Multi-party Politics and the Constitution 1983, What is Proportional Representation? 1984, The Blackwell Encyclopaedia of Political Institutions (ed.) 1987, Comparing Constitutions (co-author) 1995, The

Monarchy and the Constitution 1995, Politics and the Constitution 1996, Power and the People 1997, Devolution in the United Kingdom 1999, The British Constitution in the Twentieth Century (Ed.) 2003. *Leisure interests:* music, walking, talking, journalism. *Address:* Brasenose College, Oxford, OX1 4AJ, England. *Telephone:* (1865) 277830. *Fax:* (1865) 277822.

BOGDANOV, Aleksey Alekseyevich; Russian biochemist; b. 11 Oct. 1935; s. of Aleksey Bogdanov and Irina Bogdanova; m. Suzanna Bogdanova; two s.; ed Moscow State Univ.; Jr, Sr researcher, docent Moscow State Univ. 1958–69, Prof. 1973–; head of Dept 1969–; corresp. mem. USSR (now Russian) Acad. of Sciences 1984, mem. 1994; research in bioorganic chem. and molecular biology; USSR State Prize. *Publications include:* Chemistry of Nucleic Acids and their Components 1978, Advanced Organic Chemistry of Nucleic Acids (VCH) 1994; numerous articles in scientific journals. *Leisure interest:* classical music. *Address:* Moscow State University, Vorobyevy gory, 119899 Moscow, Russia. *Telephone:* (095) 939-31-43 (Office).

BOGDANOV, Michael, MA; British theatre, film and television director and writer; b. 15 Dec. 1938, London; s. of Francis Bogdin and Rhoda Rees; m. 1st Patricia Ann Warwick 1966; two s. two d.; m. 2nd Ulrike Engelbrecht 2000; one d. one s.; ed Trinity Coll., Dublin, Munich Univ., Sorbonne; Producer/Dir. Radio Telefis Eireann 1966–68; Asst Dir RSC 1969–71; Assoc. Dir Tyneside Theatre Co. 1971–73; Dir Phoenix Theatre, Leicester 1973–77; Dir Young Vic Theatre 1978–80; Assoc. Dir Nat. Theatre 1980–88, also Co. Dir; f. (with Michael Pennington) English Shakespeare Co. 1986, Artistic Dir 1986–98; Intendant Deutsches Schauspielhaus, Hamburg 1989–92; Sr Fellow De Montfort Univ. 1992; Assoc. Dir Peter Brook (q.v.) 's production of A Midsummer Night's Dream, RSC 1971; Hon. Prof. Univ. of Wales 1993; Hon. Fellow Welsh Coll. of Music and Drama 1994; Hon. Fellow in Drama, Trinity Coll., Univ. of Dublin 1997; Hon. Fellow Univ. of Sunderland 1997; Dir of Year, Soc. of West End Theatres, for the Taming of the Shrew 1979. *Plays include:* Two Gentlemen of Verona, Teatro Escobar, São Paulo, Brazil, Rabelais (Jean-Louis Barrault) 1971, Gawain and the Green Knight, Hunchback of Notre Dame, Nat. Theatre 1977, The Taming of the Shrew, RSC, Hamlet, Stuttgart and Düsseldorf 1978–79, Shadow of a Gunman, Knight of the Burning Pestle, RSC, The Seagull, Tokyo 1980, The Romans in Britain, Mayor of Zalamea, The Hypochondriac, A Spanish Tragedy, Uncle Vanya, all for Nat. Theatre; Hiawatha (Nat. Theatre Christmas production) 1980, 1981, 1982; Lorenzaccio, You Can't Take it With You, National Theatre 1983; Hamlet, Dublin Abbey Theatre 1983, Romeo and Juliet, Tokyo Imperial Theatre 1983; The Story of a Horse, Ancient Mariner, both for Nat. Theatre 1984; The Mayor of Zalamea, Washington 1984, Measure for Measure, Stratford, Ont. 1985, Mutiny, London 1985, Donnerstag aus Licht, Covent Garden 1985, Romeo and Juliet, Royal Shakespeare Co. 1986, Julius Caesar, Hamburg 1986, Henry IV (parts I and II), Henry V, UK, Europe, Canada, USA 1986–87, Reineke Fuchs, Hamburg 1987, The Wars of the Roses (7-play history cycle) 1987–89 (Dir of the Year, Laurence Olivier award 1989); Montag aus Licht, (Stockhausen) La Scala 1988; Coriolanus, The Winter's Tale, Macbeth, The Tempest, The Venetian Twins, RSC 1993, 1998, 1999, Hair, Old Vic 1993, Peer Gynt 1995, 1999, Faust 1996, Macbeth 1997, Timon of Athens 1997, Troilus and Cressida 2000, The Merry Wives of Windsor 2001. *Television includes:* Channel 4 series Shakespeare Lives, also for Channel 4, Hiawatha, Macbeth (Channel 4), The Tempest in Bute Town (BBC Wales) 1996, A Light in the Valley (BBC), A Light on the Hill (BBC), A Light in the City (BBC), Killing Time (BBC). *Film:* Shakespeare on the Estate 1995 (BAFTA Award), A Light in the Valley (RST Award), The Tempest in Britain (BBC), Macbeth (Granada/Channel 4), The Welsh in Shakespeare (BBC Wales). *Publications:* Hiawatha 1981, The Magic Drum 1983, Ancient Mariner, Reineke Fuchs 1988, The English Shakespeare Company (jtly) 1992. *Leisure interests:* cricket, reading, music, wine. *Address:* Dogo Cymru Ltd, 21 Dogo Street, Pontcanna, Cardiff, CF11 9JJ (Office); 21 Dogo Street, Cardiff, CF11 9JJ, Wales (Home). *Telephone:* (29) 2064-0069 (Office); (29) 2022-1502 (Home). *Fax:* (29) 2064-0069 (Office). *E-mail:* dogocymru@info.com (Office); michael@bogdanov.freeserve.co.uk (Home). *Website:* www.dogocymru.com (Office).

BOGDANOV, Vsevolod Leonidovich; Russian journalist; b. 6 Feb. 1944, Arkhangelsk Region; m.; two d.; ed Leningrad State Univ.; corresp.; ed in newspapers, radio and TV Magadan 1961–76; Head Chief Dept of Periodicals State Cttee of Publs 1976–89; Dir-Gen. TV programmes State Radio and TV Cttee 1989–92; Chair. Russian Union of Journalists 1992–; Pres. Nat. Journalist Trade Union 1999–; Pres. Int. Confed. of Journalists' Unions 1999–. *Leisure interests:* book rarities, fishing, hunting, Russian cuisine, music. *Address:* Union of Journalists, Zubovsky blvd 4, 119021 Moscow, Russia (Office). *Telephone:* (095) 201-51-01 (Office).

BOGDANOVICH, Peter; American film director, writer, producer and actor; b. 30 July 1939, Kingston, NY; s. of Borislav Bogdanovich and Herma (Robinson) Bogdanovich; m. 1st Polly Platt 1962 (divorced 1970); two d.; m. 2nd L. B. Straten 1988; Actor, American Shakespeare Festival, Stratford, Conn. 1956, NY Shakespeare Festival 1958; Dir, Producer off-Broadway plays, The Big Knife 1959, Camino Real, Ten Little Indians, Rocket to the Moon 1961, Once in a Lifetime 1964; film feature-writer for Esquire, New York Times, Village Voice, Cahiers du Cinéma, Los Angeles Times, New York Magazine, Vogue, Variety etc. 1961–; owner The Holly Moon Co. Inc. 1992–; mem. Dirs. Guild of America, Writers' Guild of America, Acad. of Motion Picture Arts and Sciences; NY Film Critics' Award (1971) and BAFTA Award for Best Screenplay (The Last Picture Show) 1971, Writers' Guild of America

Award for Best Screenplay (What's Up, Doc?) 1972, Pasinetti Award, Critics' Prize, Venice Festival (Saint Jack) 1979 and other awards and prizes. *Films include:* The Wild Angels (2nd Unit Dir, co-wrote, acted in) 1966, Targets (Dir, co-wrote, produced, acted in) 1968, The Last Picture Show (Dir, co-wrote) 1971, Directed by John Ford (Dir, wrote) 1971, What's Up Doc? (Dir, co-wrote, prod.) 1972, Paper Moon (Dir, prod.) 1973, Daisy Miller (Dir, prod.) 1974, At Long Last Love (Dir, wrote, prod.) 1975, Nickelodeon (Dir, co-wrote) 1976, Saint Jack (Dir, co-wrote, acted in) 1979, They All Laughed (Dir, wrote) 1981, Mask (Dir) 1985, Illegally Yours (Dir, prod.) 1988, Texasville (Dir, prod., wrote) 1990, Noises Off (Dir, exec. producer) 1992, The Thing Called Love (Dir) 1993, Who The Devil Made It (Dir) 1997, Mr Jealousy (actor) 1997, Highball (actor) 1997, Coming Soon (actor) 1999, Rated X (actor) 2000, The Independent (actor) 2000. *Television:* The Great Professional: Howard Hawks (co-Dir, wrote), BBC 1967; regular commentator for CBS This Morning 1987–89, actor in Northern Exposure, CBS 1993, Fallen Angels 1995, Painted Word 1995, To Sir With Love II 1996, Naked City: A Killer Christmas 1998, The Saintly Switch 1999, The Sopranos 1999. *Publications:* The Cinema of Orson Welles 1961, The Cinema of Howard Hawks 1962, The Cinema of Alfred Hitchcock 1963, John Ford 1968, Fritz Lang in America 1969, Allan Dwan, the Last Pioneer 1971, Pieces of Time, Peter Bogdanovich on the Movies 1961–85, The Killing of the Unicorn: Dorothy Stratten (1960–80) 1984, A Year and a Day Calendar (ed.) 1991, This is Orson Welles (with Orson Welles) 1992, Who the Devil Made It 1997. *Address:* c/o William Pfeiffer, 30 Lane of Acres, Haddonfield, NJ 08033; c/o CAA, 9830 Wilshire Boulevard, Beverly Hills, CA 90212-1804, USA (Office).

BOGIANCKINO, Massimo, PhD; Italian opera director; b. 10 Nov. 1922, Rome; s. of Edoardo T. Bogianckino and Fiorangela Liberi; m. Judith Matthias 1950; ed Conservatory of Music and Acad. Santa Cecilia, Rome and Univ. of Rome; fmr musicologist and concert pianist; Dir Enciclopedia dello Spettacolo 1957–62; Dir Accademia Filarmonica, Rome 1960–63; Dir Teatro dell' Opera, Rome 1963–68; Artistic Dir Festival of Two Worlds, Spoleto 1968–71; Dir of Concert Programs, Accad. Santa Cecilia, Rome 1970–71; Artistic Dir La Scala, Milan 1971–74; Gen. Man. Teatro Comunale, Florence 1974–82; Admin. Gen. Paris Opera 1982–85; apptd. Mayor of Florence 1985; Grosses Bundesverdienstkreuz (Fed. Repub. of Germany). *Publications:* L'arte clavicembalistica di D. Scarlatti 1956 (English version 1968), Aspetti del teatro musicale in Italia e in Francia nell' età Barocca 1968, Le canzonette e i madrigali di V. Cossa 1981. *Address:* c/o Palazzo Vecchio, 50122 Florence, Italy (Office).

BOGLE, Ellen Gray; Jamaican diplomatist and government official; b. 9 Oct. 1941, St Andrew; d. of Victor Gray Williams and Eileen Averil (née Rampie); one s. one d.; ed St Andrew High School, Univ. of the West Indies; Dir Foreign Trade Div., Ministry of Foreign Affairs, with responsibility for formulation of Jamaica's Foreign Trade policy 1978–81; Dir Jamaica Nat. Export Corpn; High Commr in Trinidad & Tobago 1981–89; High Commr in UK 1989–94; Amb., Ministry of Foreign Affairs and Foreign Trade 1996–; Amb. and Special Envoy to the Asscn of Caribbean States (A.C.S.) and C.A.R.I.C.O.M. 1997–; Under-Sec. Bilateral and Regional Affairs, Ministry of Foreign Affairs and Foreign Trade 2001–; has represented Jamaica at numerous int. confs.; Order of Distinction (Commdr) 1987. *Leisure interests:* gardening, reading, cooking, table tennis. *Address:* Ministry of Foreign Affairs and Foreign Trade, 21 Dominica Drive, Kingston 5, Jamaica. *Telephone:* 926-4220 (Office). *Fax:* 754-4862 (Office). *E-mail:* acs_caricomfa@ cwjamaica.com (Home).

BOGNER, Willy; German business executive, film director and producer; b. 23 Jan. 1942, Munich; s. of late Willy Bogner and Maria Bogner; m. Sonia Ribeiro 1973; ed Altes Realgymnasium, Munich and business and technical studies in Munich and Hohenstein; Man. Willy Bogner GmbH & Co. KG (sportswear co.), Willy Bogner Film GmbH, Munich; mem. German Nat. Olympic Cttee; Dir of documentary, advertising, sports (especially skiing) films, etc. and special cameraman for James Bond films 1960–; several times German ski champion and participated in Winter Olympics 1960, Squaw Valley 1960, Innsbruck 1964 and World Ski Championships, Chamonix 1962, Portillo (Chile) 1966. *Films include:* Skivision 1974, 1975, 1979, Skifaszina-tion, Ski Fantasie 1981, Crystal Dreams 1982, Feuer und Eis 1986, Feuer, Eis und Dynamit 1990, White Magic 1994. *Leisure interests:* sport (tennis, skiing, golf), sailing, flying, filming and photography. *Address:* Firma Willy Bogner GmbH & Co. KG, Sankt-Veit-Strasse 4, 81673 Munich, Germany. *Telephone:* (89) 41491.

BOGOLEPOV, Nikolai Nikolayevich, DrMed; Russian physiologist; b. 30 Nov. 1933, Moscow; m. Lidia Nikolayevna Rybina; two d.; ed Moscow Inst. of Medicine; corresp. mem. Russian Acad. of Medical Sciences 1988–; researcher, head of lab., Dir Research Inst. of the Brain, Russian Acad. of Medical Sciences 1957–; mem. Scientific Soc. of Anatomy, Histology; mem. Int. Brain Research Org.; main research in morphology and structure of brain. *Publications include:* 8 books and over 200 scientific papers and articles. *Address:* Institute of the Brain, Russian Academy of Natural Sciences, Obukha str. 5, 107120 Moscow, Russia (Office). *Telephone:* (095) 917-80-07 (Office).

BOGOLYUBOV, Mikhail Nikolayevich, DPhilSci; Russian philologist; b. 24 Jan. 1918, Kiev; m.; two s.; ed Leningrad Univ.; service in the army 1941–45; lecturer and researcher Leningrad Univ. 1944–60, Prof. of Iranian Studies 1959–, Dean Oriental Dept 1960–95, Hon. Dean 1995–; Corresp. mem. USSR

(now Russian) Acad. of Sciences 1966–, mem. 1990; researcher into oriental philology and Iranian languages; ed. Russian trans. of Mahabharata 1987. *Publications:* over 150 books and articles on oriental philology and history. *Address:* St Petersburg State Univ., Oriental Faculty, 11 Universitetskaya Naberezhnaya, St Petersburg, Russia. *Telephone:* (812) 328-77-32 (Office); (812) 448-51-46 (Home). *E-mail:* mb@mb1018.spb.edu (Home).

BOGOMOLOV, Oleg Timofeyevich; Russian economist; b. 20 Aug. 1927, Moscow; s. of T. I. Bogomolov and K. P. Zhelybaeva; m. 1st Larisa Sokolova, one s. (died 1962); m. 2nd Inna Yermakova 1966 (divorced 1977); m. 3rd Tatyana Yarikova 1978; ed Moscow Inst. of Foreign Trade; Ministry of Foreign Trade 1949–50; with CMEA 1954–56; Scientific Inst. for Economical Researches of State Cttee for Planning 1956–62; mem. CPSU 1950–90, Head of Advisors Group (Cen. Cttee) 1962–69; Section Chief, Econ. Research Inst., State Planning Cttee 1958–62; lecturer, then Prof. Moscow Univ. 1967–; Dir Inst. of Econs of the World Socialist System of Acad. of Sciences (now Inst. of Int. Econ. and Political Studies) 1969–97, Hon. Dir 1997–; Pres. Int. Econ. Asscn 1992–, Council of Ministers Cttee for Mutual Cooperation with Socialist Countries 1970–86; People's Deputy of USSR 1989–91; Deputy, State Duma (Parl.) 1993–95; adviser to Pres. 1998–; mem. USSR (now Russian) Acad. of Sciences 1981, Exec. Cttee of Int. Social Science Council, UNESCO 1996–; decorations include Order of October Revolution, Order of Red Banner (twice). *Publications:* Socialism between Past and Future 1990, Russia and the Commonwealth of Independent States, Trends and Risks of Post-Soviet Development; Europe in Global Change 1993, Market Transformation in Russia: Prospects Still Uncertain, Economics in a Changing World of the Tenth Congress of the IEA 1994, Reformy glazami amerikanskikh i rossiy-skikh ucheynykh 1996. *Leisure interests:* photography, music, tennis. *Address:* Institute of International Economic and Political Studies, 117418, Novo-Cheremushkinskaya 46, Moscow, Russia. *Telephone:* (095) 120-82-00 (Office). *Fax:* (095) 310-70-61.

BOGORAD, Lawrence, PhD; American biologist; b. 29 Aug. 1921, Tashkent, USSR; s. of Boris Bogorad and Florence (Bernard) Bogorad; m. Rosalyn G. Sagen 1943; one s. one d.; ed Univ. of Chicago; Instructor, Dept of Botany, Univ. of Chicago 1948–51, Asst Prof. 1953–57, Assoc. Prof. 1957–61, Prof. 1961–67; Visiting Investigator, Rockefeller Inst. 1951–53; Prof. Dept of Biology, Harvard Univ. 1967–92, Maria Moors Cabot Prof. of Biology 1980–92, Prof. Emer. 1992–; Chair. Dept of Biology 1974–76; Dir Maria Moors Cabot Foundation, Harvard Univ. 1976–87; mem. NAS, NAS Council 1989–92, Chair. Botany Section 1974–77, Ed. and Chair. Editorial Bd Proceedings of the NAS 1991–95; mem. American Philosophical Soc., Space Studies Bd 1995–98; Foreign mem. Royal Danish Acad. of Sciences and Letters; Fellow, American Acad. of Arts and Sciences; Pres. American Soc. of Plant Physiologists 1968; Pres. Soc. of Developmental Biology 1983–84; mem. Bd of Dirs AAAS 1982–86, Pres. 1986–87, Chair. Bd of Dirs 1987–88; Fulbright Fellowship 1960; Stephen Hales Award 1982 and other academic awards. *Publications:* various papers in scientific journals. *Address:* Harvard University, Department of Molecular and Cellular Biology, 16 Divinity Avenue, Cambridge, MA 02138, USA. *E-mail:* bogorad@mcb.harvard.edu (Office).

BOGOSIAN, Eric, BA; American actor; b. 24 April 1953, Boston; s. of Henry Bogosian and Edwina Bogosian; m. Jo Anne Bonney 1990; ed Univ. of Chicago and Oberlin Coll.; author, star, Off-Broadway productions, Men Inside, New York Shakespeare Festival 1982, Funhouse, New York Shakespeare Festival 1983, Actor's Playhouse, New York 1983, Drinking in America, American Place, New York 1986, Talk Radio, New York Shakespeare Festival 1987, Sex, Drugs, Rock & Roll, Orpheum Show Theatre, New York 1990, Pounding Nails in the Floor with my Forehead 1994, Suburbia 1994, Office Killer 1997, Deconstructing Harry 1997, Griller 1998, Gossip 2000, In the Weeds, Wake Up and Smell the Coffee, Ararat; appearances in several TV shows and films including Caine Mutiny Court Martial, Drinking in America, Talk Radio 1988, Sex, Drugs, Rock & Roll 1991, Under Siege 2 1995, The Substance of Fire 1996, Deconstructing Harry 1997, Office Killer 1997, Gossip 1999; Obie Award 1986, 1990, 1994; Drama Critics' Circle Award; Berlin Film Festival Silver Bear Award 1988.

BOGSCH, Arpad, LLD; American international official and lawyer; b. 24 Feb. 1919, Budapest, Hungary; s. of Arpad Bogsch and Emilia Taborsky; one s. one d.; m. Adèle Fankhauser 1994; ed Univs of Budapest and Paris and George Washington Univ., Washington, DC; attorney-at-law, Budapest 1942–48; legal officer, UNESCO, Paris 1948–54; legal counsellor, US Copyright Office, Washington, DC 1954–63; Deputy Dir-Gen. World Intellectual Property Org. Geneva 1963–73, Dir-Gen. 1973–97; Hon. Prof. of Law, Beijing Univ. 1991; Dr hc (Jabalpur) 1978, (George Washington Univ.) 1985, (Colombo) 1987, (Kyung Hee Univ., Repub. of Korea) 1991, (Eötvös Lóránd Univ. Budapest) 1991, (Bucharest) 1991, (Delhi) 1992, (Prague) 1994, (Kiev) 1995, (Mathias Bel, Slovakia) 1996, (Tbilisi) 1996, (Riga) 1997; numerous awards and decorations. *Publications:* books and articles in the field of patents, trademarks and copyright. *Leisure interest:* music. *Address:* 12, chemin du Vieux-Bois, 1292 Chambesy, Switzerland (Home). *Telephone:* (22) 7582267 (Home). *Fax:* (22) 7582267 (Home). *E-mail:* abogsch@infomaniak.ch (Home).

BOGUSLAVSKY, Mark Moiseyevich, DJur; Russian professor of law; b. 8 June 1924, Moscow; m. 1st Iren Gorodetskaya 1960; m. 2nd Valentina Mazourova 1993; ed Inst. of Foreign Trade; prof. and Sr researcher, USSR (now Russian) Academy of Sciences Inst. of State and Law; Head of Int. Pvt.

Law Sector 1985–; Dir Inst. für Osteuropäisches Recht, Kiel 1998, Lecturer 1998–, Arbiter Int. Commercial Court of Arbitration at Moscow; specialist in pvt. and econ. int. law, intellectual property and foreign investment legislation; mem. Bd Russian Asscn of Int. Law. *Publications:* over 400 publications on pvt. international law. *Address:* Institute of State and Law, Russian Academy of Sciences, Znamenka str. 10, 119841 Moscow, Russia. *Telephone:* (095) 291-86-03 (Office); (095) 118-85-71 (Home). *Fax:* (095) 291-85-74.

BOHAN, Marc; French couturier; b. 22 Aug. 1926, Paris; s. of Alfred Bohan and Geneviève Baudoux; m. Huguette Rinjonneau (deceased); one d.; ed Lycée Lakanal, Sceaux; Asst with Piguet 1945, later with Molyneux and Patou; Dior org.; London 1958, later Paris; Artistic Dir Soc. Christian Dior 1960–89; Artistic Dir Hartnell, London 1990–92; designed costumes for numerous films 1961–89, for Athens Opera 1992–96; Chevalier, Légion d'honneur, Ordre de Saint-Charles (Monaco). *Exhibitions:* Theatre Costumes 1987, Paris, French Embassy, Vienna 1988. *Leisure interests:* classical music, theatre, reading, antiques. *Address:* 35 rue du Bourg à Mont, 21400 Châtillon-sur-Seine, France (Home). *Telephone:* 3-80-91-39-75 (Office); 3-80-91-28-35 (Home).

BOHIGAS GUARDIOLA, Oriol, DArch; Spanish architect; b. 10 Dec. 1925, Barcelona; s. of Pere Bohigas and María Guardiola; m. Isabel Arnau 1957; five c.; ed Escuela Técnica Superior de Arquitectura, Barcelona; Founder-mem. of Grupo R; partnership with Josep Martorell 1951– and with David Mackay 1962–, forming MBM Arquitectes; Chair. of Composition, Escuela Técnica Superior de Arquitectura, Barcelona (ETSAB) 1971–, Head of ETSAB 1977–80; Head of Urban Planning Dept, Barcelona City Council 1980–84; Councillor of Culture 1991–94; mem. Colegio de Arquitectas de Venezuela 1976, Foundation Européenne des Sciences, des Arts et de la Culture 1983; Academician Accad. Nazionale di San Luca 1981; Foreign mem. Royal Swedish Acad. of Eng Sciences (IVA) 1991; Corresp. mem. Acad. d'Architecture de Paris 1991; Hon. Prof. Universidad Politécnica de Barcelona) 1995; Hon. mem. Sociedad Colombiana de Arquitectos 1982, Asscn of Architects of Bulgaria 1987, Die Bund Deutscher Architecten 1990; Hon. Fellow AIA 1993, FRIBA 1996; Dr hc (Darmstadt) 1992, (Menéndez y Pelayo) 1995; Gold Medal for Artistic Merits, City of Barcelona 1986, Sikkens Award, Rotterdam 1989, Gold Medal for Architecture, Consejo Superior de Arquitectas de España, Madrid 1990, Volker Stevin Innovatieprijs Award, Rotterdam 1992, RIBA Royal Gold Medal to City of Barcelona (with others) 1999; firm awarded First Prize in many architectural competitions including Foment de les Arts Decoratives for best bldg in Barcelona 1959, 1962, 1966, 1976, 1979, 1984, 1991, Delta de Plata (industrial design) 1966, First Prize, Internationale Bauhausstellung Berlin 1981, 'Un Progetto per Siena', Italy 1990, 'Operations Sextius Mirabeau', Aix-en-Provence, France 1990, 'Cardiff Bay', Wales 1993, Eric Lyons Housing Award for bldg in Olympic Village, Barcelona 1994, 'Mission Perrache-Confluent', Lyon, France 1997, 'London's Arc of Opportunity', UK 1999, 'Programma di riqualificazione urbana dell'area De-Cecco', Pescara, Italy 2000, Prize of Barcelona City for the bldg of Pompeu Fabra Univ. 2001, Int. Competition for Arts and Crafts, Barcelona 2001, Canfranch railway station transformation, Huesca, Spain 2001, Urban Design, Dublin, Ireland 2001. *Major works include:* urban design for the Olympic Village and Port, Barcelona 1986–92, hotel in Puerto Vallarto, Mexico 1990, urban projects in Aix-en-Provence 1990, new city plan for Salerno, Italy 1991, Pavilion of the Future, Expo '92, Seville 1992, housing in Berlin 1993, urban design of waterfront, Rio de Janeiro, Brazil 1997, urban design in Newham, London, UK 1998, school in the Olympic Village, Barcelona 1999, apartments and student housing in Aix-en-Provence 1999, housing in Kleine Circus, Maastricht, the Netherlands 1999, refurbishment of Roger de Llúria Barracks, Barcelona 2001, Gymnasium Sartre, Berlin 2001. *Publications include:* Barcelona entre el plà Cerdà i el barraquisme 1963, Arquitectura modernista 1968, Contra una arquitectura adjetivada 1969, La arquitectura española de la Segunda República 1970, Polemica d'arquitectura catalana 1970, Reseña y catálogo de la arquitectura modernista 1972, Proceso y erótica del diseño 1972, Once arquitectos 1976, Reconstrucció de Barcelona 1985, Combat d'incerteses. Dietari de records 1989, Dit o fet. Dietari de records II 1992, Gràcies i desgràcies de Barcelona 1993, el Present des del Futur. Epistolari Públic 1994–1995 1996, Del dubte a la Revolució. Epistolari públic 1995–1997 1998, Modernidad en la arquitectura de la España Republicana 1998. *Address:* MBM Arquitectes, Plaça Reial 18, E-08002 Barcelona 21 (Office); MBM Arquitectes, Plaça Reial 18, 08002 Barcelona (Office); Plaça Reial 8, 08002 Barcelona, Spain (Home). *Telephone:* (93) 3170061 (Office); (93) 4124771 (Home). *Fax:* (93) 3177266 (Office). *E-mail:* mbm@mbmarquitectes .com (Office). *Website:* www.mbmarquitectes.com (Office).

BOHL, Heinrich Friedrich; German politician and lawyer; b. 5 March 1945, Rosdorf, Göttingen; s. of Heinrich Bohl and Gerda Heyden; m. Elisabeth Bocking; two s. two d.; ed Univ. of Marburg; lawyer 1972–, notary 1976–; mem. CDU and Jungen Union (JU) 1963–; local Chair. JU Marburg-Biedenkopf 1964–70; Dist Chair. JU Mittelhessen 1969–73; mem. Provincial Parl. Hessen 1970–80, Chair. Legal Cttee 1974–78; Acting Chair. CDU Landtagsfraktion 1978–80; Chair. CDU Kreistagsfraktion Marburg-Biedenkopf 1974–90; mem. Fed. German Parl. 1980–, Parl. Man. CDU/CSU Bundestagsfraktion 1984–91; Fed. Minister for Special Tasks and Head of Fed. Chancellery 1991–98; Head of Press and Information, Fed. Govt 1998; now Gen. Rep. Deutscher Vermögensberatung AG; Bundesverdienstkreuz (1st Class) 1987.

Address: Deutscher Vermögensberatung AG, Querstr. 1, 60322 Frankfurt am Main (Office); Bundestag, 5300 Bonn (Office); Finkenstrasse 11, 35043 Marburg Cappel, Germany (Home). *Telephone:* 41333 (Home).

BÖHME, Helmut, DPhil; German university president; b. 30 April 1936, Tübingen; s. of Helmut B. Böhme and Elisabeth Müller; m. Bertheide Mittinger 1982; one s. three d.; ed Univs. of Tübingen and Hamburg; Prof. 1969; Pres. Darmstadt Univ. 1971–; Hon. PhD. *Publications include:* Deutschlands Weg zur Grossmacht 1966, Prolegomena 1968; essays and other publs on history of banking. *Leisure interest:* painting. *Address:* Jacques-Offenbach-Gesellschaft e.V, Römerstrasse 1, 56130 Bad Elms, Germany (Office). *Telephone:* (2603) 506030 (Office). *Fax:* (2603) 506031 (Office). *E-mail:* j.offenbach@t-online.de. *Website:* www.offenbach-festival.de (Office).

BOHR, Aage Niels, DPhil, DSc; Danish physicist; b. 19 June 1922, Copenhagen; s. of Prof. Niels Bohr and Margrethe Nørlund; m. 1st Marietta Bettina (née Soffer) (died 1978); two s. one d. m. 2nd Bente Scharff (née Meyer) 1981; ed Univ. of Copenhagen; Assoc. D.S.I.R., London 1943–45; Research Asst, Inst. of Theoretical Physics, Copenhagen 1946; Prof. of Physics, Univ. of Copenhagen 1956; Dir Niels Bohr Inst. 1963–70, Nordita 1975–81; mem. Danish, Norwegian, Pontifical, Swedish, Polish, Finnish, Yugoslav Acads. of Science, Nat. Acad. of Sciences, USA, American Acad. of Arts and Sciences, American Philosophical Soc., Royal Physiograph Soc., Lund, Sweden, Acad. of Tech. Sciences, Copenhagen, Deutsche Acad. der Naturforscher Leopoldina, Kungl. Vetenskaps-Societeten, Uppsala, Sweden; Hon. PhD (Oslo, Heidelberg, Trondheim, Manchester, Uppsala); Dannie Heineman Prize 1960, Pius XI Medal 1963, Atoms for Peace Award 1969, Ørsted Medal 1970, Rutherford Medal 1972, John Price Wetherill Medal 1974, Nobel Prize for Physics 1975, Ole Rømer Medal 1976. *Publications:* Rotational States of Atomic Nuclei 1954, Nuclear Structure Vol. I 1969, Vol. II 1975 (with Ben R. Mottelson), Genuine Fortuitousness – Where Did That Click Come From? (with Ole Ulfbeck) 2001. *Address:* c/o Niels Bohr Institute, Blegdamsvej 15–17, 2100 Copenhagen, Denmark.

BOHRER, Karl Heinz, PhD; German academic; b. 26 Sept. 1932, Cologne; m. Undine Gruenter 1991; one s. one d.; Prof. of History of Modern Literature, Univ. of Bielefeld 1982–; Ed. Merkur; J.H. Merck Prize 1978, Lessing Prize 2000. *Publications:* Die gefährdete Phantasie oder Surrealismus und Terror 1970, Der Lauf des Freitag—Die lädierte Utopie und der Dichter 1973, Die Ästhetik des Schreckens 1978, Plötzlichkeit. Der Augenblick des ästhetischen Scheins 1981, Mythos und Moderne 1983, Der romantische Brief, Die Entstehung aesthetischer Subjektivität 1987, Nach der Natur, Über Politik und Ästhetik 1988, Die Kritik der Romantik 1989, Das absolute Präsens. Die Semantik ästhetischer Zeit 1994, Der Abschied. Theorie der Trauer 1996, Die Grenzen des Aesthetischen 1998. *Address:* Universtät Bielefeld, Fakultät für Linguistik und Literaturwissenschaft, 33501 Bielefeld (Office); 11 rue Robert Planquette, 75018 Paris, France; Franziskastr. 9, Cologne, Germany.

BOIDEVAIX, Serge Marie-Germain, LèsL, LenD; French diplomatist; b. 15 Aug. 1928, Aurillac, Cantal; s. of Jean Boidevaix and Hélène Orcibal; m. Francine Savard 1966; two d.; ed Lycée d'Aurillac, Lycée Louis-le-Grand, Faculté de Droit and Faculté des Lettres, Paris and Ecole Nat. d'Admin; joined Ministry of Foreign Affairs 1954; served Vienna, Washington, DC and Bonn; Adviser, Pvt. Office of Minister of Defence 1969–73; Dir Office of Minister of Foreign Affairs 1973–74; Adviser on int. affairs and cooperation, Office of Prime Minister 1974–76; Amb. to Poland 1977–80, to India 1982–85, to Germany 1986–92; Deputy Sec.-Gen. Ministry of Foreign Affairs 1985–86; Sec. Gen. 1992–93; Sr mem. Council of State 1993–97; Chair. SB Consultant 1997–, Franco-Arab Chamber of Commerce 2002–; Commdr, Légion d'honneur, Ordre Nat. du Mérite. *Address:* 8 rue des Eaux, 75016 Paris, France. *Telephone:* 1-40-50-30-10 (Office). *Fax:* 1- 40-50-14-91 (Office). *E-mail:* stesb@ cybercable.fr (Office).

BOISSET, Yves; French author and film director; b. 14 March 1939, Paris; s. of Raymond Boisset and Germaine Bonnet; m. Micheline Paintault 1964; two s.; ed Lycée Louis-le-Grand, Faculté des Lettres, Paris and Inst. des Hautes Etudes Cinématographiques; journalist on Cinéma, Paris-Jour etc. 1958–63; Asst Dir to Yves Ciampi 1959, to Jean-Pierre Melville 1962, Claude Sautet and Antoine Bourseiller 1964, Vittorio de Sica and René Clément 1965, Ricardo Freda 1966; television and film Dir 1967–; Chevalier des Arts et des Lettres. *Films include:* Coplan sauve sa peau 1968, Cran d'arrêt 1969, Un condé 1970, Le Saut de l'ange 1971, L'Attentat 1972, R.A.S. 1973, Dupont Lajoie 1974, Folle à tuer 1975, Le Juge Fayard dit le Sheriff 1976 (Prix Louis Delluc 1977), Un taxi mauve 1977, La Clé sur la porte 1978, La Femme flic 1979, Allons z'enfants 1981, Espion lève-toi 1982, Le Prix du danger 1983, Canicule 1984, Bleu comme l'Enfer 1986, La Travestie 1988, Radio Corbeau 1989, La Tribu 1991. *Publication:* 20 ans de cinéma américain 1962. *Leisure interests:* athletics, basketball, tennis. *Address:* 61 boulevard Inkerman, 92200 Neuilly-sur-Seine, France.

BOISSIER, Patrick Marie René; French business executive; b. 18 Feb. 1950, Versailles; s. of Pierre Boissier and Françoise Boissier (née Hennebicque); m. Isabelle July 1972; two s. one d.; ed Ecole Polytechnique, Harvard Business School, USA; engineer Cegedur Rhenalu 1973–75, Forges de Crans 1976–79, Asst Factory Man. Cegedur 1980–83, Man. pipes div. 1984–87, Gen. Man. 1987–90; Deputy Chair. and CEO Tréfimétaux 1990–93; Dept Head Péchiney 1994; Gen. Man. heating and air-conditioning div. Elfi 1994–97; Chair. and CEO Technibel 1994–97; Gen. Man., then Chair. and CEO Chantiers d'Atlantique 1997–; CEO GEC Alsthom Leroux Naval (later

Alstom Leroux Naval) 1997–; Chair. Alstom marine 1998–; Chevalier, Ordre nat. du Mérite. *Leisure interest:* sailing. *Address:* Chantiers de l'Atlantique, 38 avenue Kléber, 75116 Paris (Office); 24 rue de l'Ermitage, 78000 Versailles, France (Home). *E-mail:* patrick.boissier@marine.alstom.com (Office).

BOISSIEU DEAN DE LUIGNÉ, Gen. Alain Henri Paul Marie-Joseph de; French army officer; b. 5 July 1914, Chartres; s. of Henri de Boissieu Dean de Luigné and Marguérite Froger de Mauny; m. Elisabeth de Gaulle, d. of Gen. Charles de Gaulle, 1946; one d.; ed Saint-Cyr Mil. Acad.; Cavalry Second Lt 1938, First Lieut, 1940; prisoner of war, escaped, later detained in USSR; joined Free French Forces 1941; Capt. 1942; Staff, High Commr in Indian Ocean 1944–45; Maj. 1945, Lt-Col 1953; Commdg Officer 4th Regiment of Chasseurs, Algeria 1956–58; Col 1958; Chief Mil. Staff, High Commr in Algeria 1958; Chief of Staff Armoured Directorate 1959; Commdg Officer 2nd Armoured Brigade 1962; Brig.-Gen. 1964; Commdg Gen. Saint-Cyr Mil. Acad. and Ecole Mil. Inter-Armes de Coëtquidan 1964–67; Commdg Gen. 7th Div. 1967; Maj.-Gen. 1968; Inspector of Armour 1969; Lt-Gen. 1970; mem. Army Council 1971; Gen., Chief of Staff of French Army 1971–75; fmr Grand Chancellor, Légion d'honneur, fmr Chancellor, Ordre national du Mérite 1975–81; Grand-Croix Légion d'honneur, Compagnon de la libération, Grand-Croix de l'Ordre national du Mérite, Croix de guerre, Croix de la Valeur militaire, Knight of Malta; Hon. KBE and other decorations. *Leisure interests:* riding, hunting. *Address:* 233 rue de Vaugirard, 75015 Paris, France.

BOISSON, Jacques-Louis, PhD, LLD; Monegasque diplomatist; b. 8 Jan. 1940, Monaco; m. Carmen Gómez Parejo; one s.; ed Institut d'Etudes Politiques, Institut de Droit Int., Paris, Faculté de Droit et de Sciences Economiques, Aix-en-Provence; int. civil servant (responsible for training, research and protection of human rights) UNESCO 1968–83; Amb. to France 1984–93; Perm. Rep. to UN 1993–; Commdr Ordre de Grimaldi; Officier Ordre de St Charles. *Publications:* Le Particularisme Institutionnel de la Principalité de Monaco 1966, Le Droit de la Nationalité Monégasque 1968, La Protection Internationale des Minorités, Vers un Enseignement Universel des Droits de l'Homme, L'Autorité internationale des Fouds Marin 2001; numerous articles on the protection and promotion of int. human rights 1971–99. *Leisure interests:* baroque music, opera, philosophy, poetry. *Address:* Permanent Mission of Monaco to United Nations, 866 United Nations Plaza, Suite 520, New York, NY 10017 (Office); 100 United Nations Plaza, Apt. 36A, New York, NY 10017 (Home); 48 blvd du Jardin Exotique, 98000 Monaco. *Telephone:* (212) 832-0721 (USA) (Office); (212) 753-7049 (USA) (Home); 93-25-59-64 (Monaco). *Fax:* (212) 832-5358 (USA) (Office). *E-mail:* monaco@un.int (Office).

BØJER, Jørgen R. H.; Danish diplomatist; b. 5 March 1940, Hjørring; s. of Svend Rud Hansen Bøjer and Ingeborg Bøjer (née Frederiksen); m. Lone Heilskov 1964; two d.; ed Univ. of Aarhus, Institut d'Etudes Politiques, Paris; Foreign Service Officer 1967; Sec. of Embassy, Prague 1971; Head of Section Ministry of Foreign Affairs, Copenhagen 1973, Dir 1982, Deputy Undersec. 1992; Visiting Fellow Stanford Univ. 1978; Counsellor, Embassy, Washington, DC 1979; Amb. to Egypt (also accred to Sudan and Somalia), then to Austria, Slovenia, Bosnia and Herzegovina; Perm. Rep. to Int. Orgs in Vienna 1993; Perm. Rep. to UN 1997–2001, Co-Chair. UN Int. Conf. on Financing for Devt 2001; Amb. to the Czech Republic 2001–. *Address:* Royal Danish Embassy, Maltezké Námĕsti 5, 11801 Prague 1, Czech Republic.

BOJINOV, Bojidar; Bulgarian lawyer; b. 30 Jan. 1939, Pleven City; s. of Boris Bojinov and Nikolinka Bojinova (née Makaveeva); m. Fani Vladimorova; one s. two d.; ed Charles Univ., Prague; lawyer, Pleven 1967–72; Legal Adviser to Bulgarian Chamber of Commerce and Industry (BCCI), Sofia 1972–77, Dir Patent and Trade Marks Div. 1977–85, Vice-Pres. BCCI 1985–93, Pres. 1993–; Arbitrator at BCCI Court of Arbitration 1975–2003; mem. Advisory Council to Pres. of Repub. on Foreign Investments, Nat. Council for Tripartite Cooperation, Council of Econ. Growth 2002–; fmr Pres. Asscn of Black Sea Zone Chambers of Commerce and Industry, Asscn Balkan Chambers, Bulgarian Nat. Group of AIPP. *Leisure interests:* music, art, skiing, tennis. *Address:* Office of the President, Bulgarian Chamber of Commerce and Industry, 42 Parchevich Street, 1000 Sofia (Office); Patents and Trademarks Bureau, Bojinov & Bojinov Ltd., 38 Alabin Street, P.O. Box 728, 1000 Sofia (Office); 38 Alabin Street, P.O. Box 728, 1000 Sofia, Bulgaria (Home). *Telephone:* (2) 9872528 (Office); (2) 9862974 (Home). *Fax:* (2) 9873209 (Office); (2) 9863508 (Home). *E-mail:* bojinov@bcci.bg (Office). *Website:* www .bcci.bg (Office).

BOK, Derek, MA, JD; American university administrator; b. 22 March 1930, Bryn Mawr, Pa; s. of late Curtis Bok and Margaret Plummer (now Mrs. W. S. Kiskadden); m. Sissela Ann Myrdal (d. of Karl Gunnar and Alva Myrdal) 1955; one s. two d.; ed Univs of Stanford, Harvard, George Washington and Inst. of Political Science, Paris Univ.; served US Army 1956–58; Asst Prof. of Law, Harvard Univ. 1958–61, Prof. 1961–, Dean 1968–71; Dean, 300th Anniversary Univ. Prof. 1991–; Harvard Law School 1968–71; Pres. Harvard Univ. 1971–91; Dir, Nat. Chair. Common Cause 1999–; Chair. Spencer Foundation 2002–; Facility Chair. Haupen Center for Non-Profit Orgs 2002–. *Publications include:* The First Three Years of the Schuman Plan, Cases and Materials on Labor Law (with Archibald Cox), Labor and the American Community (with John Dunlop), The Federal Government and the University, Beyond the Ivory Tower: Social Responsibilities of the Modern University 1982, Higher Learning 1986, Universities and the Future of America 1990, The Cost of Talent 1993, The State of the Nation 1997, The

Shape of the River (jtly.) 1998. *Leisure interests:* gardening, tennis, swimming. *Address:* Harvard University, J.F.K. School of Government, Cambridge, MA 02138, USA. *Telephone:* (617) 495-1502.

BOKERIA, Leonid (Leo) Antonovich, DrMedSci; Russian cardiologist; b. 21 Dec. 1939; m.; two c.; ed I. M. Sechenov Medical Inst., Moscow; with A. Bakulev Scientific Centre of Cardio-Vascular Surgery (SCCVS) 1968–, Dir 1991–; Dir, Prof. Burakovsky Research Inst. of Cardiosurgery at SCCVS; mem. Russian Acad. of Medicine; main research in cardio-vascular surgery, hyperbaric oxygenation, treatment of cardiopulse violation problems; Lenin Prize 1975, USSR State Prize 1986. *Publications:* articles on cardiosurgery. *Leisure interests:* painting, collecting of encyclopaedias and dictionaries. *Address:* A. Bakulev Scientific Centre, Leninsky prosp. 8 korp. 7, 117931 Moscow, Russia. *Telephone:* (095) 414-75-71 (Office).

BOKROS, Lajos, PhD; Hungarian banker; b. 26 June 1954, Budapest; s. of Lajos Bokros and Irén Szarka; m. Maria Gyetuai; one s. one d.; ed Univ. of Econs Budapest, Univ. of Panama; researcher Financial Research Inst., Budapest 1980–85, Chief Public Finance Div. 1986–87; Deputy Head Econ. Dept Nat. Bank of Hungary 1988–89, Dir Capital Market Dept 1989–91; Chair. Budapest Stock Exchange 1990–95; Chair., CEO Budapest Bank 1991–95; Minister of Finance 1995–96; mem. Bd of dirs. State Property Agency 1990–91, mem. Council of Dirs. World Bank 1996–. *Publications:* Development Commodity Production, Market Economy 1984, Market and Money in the Modern Economy 1985. *Address:* c/o World Bank, 1818 H Street, NW, Washington, DC 20433, USA. *Telephone:* (202) 458-7290 (Office). *Fax:* (202) 522-2758 (Office). *E-mail:* lbokros@worldbank.org (Office). *Website:* www.worldbank.org (Office).

BOKSENBERG, Alexander, CBE, PhD, FRS, FRAS; British astronomer; b. 18 March 1936; s. of Julius Boksenberg and Ernestina Steinberg; m. Adella Coren 1960; one s. one d.; ed Stationers' Co.'s School, Univ. of London; SRC Research Asst, Dept of Physics and Astronomy, Univ. Coll. London 1960–65, Lecturer in Physics 1965–75, Head of Optical and Ultraviolet Astronomy Research Group 1969–81, Reader in Physics 1975–78, SRC Sr Fellow 1976–81, Prof. of Physics and Astronomy 1978–81; Sherman Fairchild Distinguished Scholar Calif. Inst. of Tech. 1981–82; Dir Royal Greenwich Observatory 1981–93, Royal Observatories (Royal Greenwich Observatory, Royal Observatory, Edin., Isaac Newton Group of Optical Telescopes, Canary Islands, Jt Astronomy Centre, Hawaii) 1993–96; Research Prof. Univ. of Cambridge and PPARC Sr Research Fellow Univs. of Cambridge and London 1996–; Extraordinary Fellow Churchill Coll., Cambridge 1996–; Visiting Prof., Dept of Physics and Astronomy, Univ. Coll. London 1981–, Astronomy Centre, Univ. of Sussex 1981–89; Hon. Prof. of Experimental Astronomy, Univ. of Cambridge 1991–; Exec. Ed. Experimental Astronomy 1995–; Hon. Pres. Astronomical Soc. of Glasgow; Chair. New Industrial Concepts Ltd 1969–81; Pres. West London Astronomical Soc. 1978–; Chair. SRC Astronomy Cttee 1980–81 and numerous other cttees. on astronomy 1980–; mem. ESA Hubble Space Telescope Instrument Definition Team 1973–, SA Astronomical Observatory Advisory Cttee 1978–85, British Council Science Advisory Cttee 1987–91, Fachbeirat of Max Planck Institut für Astronomie 1991–95, past mem. of over 30 other councils, bds., cttees. etc. 1970–; Fellow Royal Soc. 1978–, Univ. Coll. London 1991–; Liveryman 1989; mem. of court 1994; Asteroid (3205) named Boksenberg 1988; Dr hc (l'Observatoire de Paris) 1982, Hon. DSc (Sussex) 1991; Freeman Clockmakers Co. 1984; Hannah Jackson Medal 1998. *Publications:* Modern Technology and its Influence on Astronomy 1990 (ed.); 220 contribs to learned journals. *Leisure interest:* skiing. *Address:* University of Cambridge, Institute of Astronomy, The Observatories, Madingley Road, Cambridge, CB3 0HA, England. *Telephone:* (1223) 339909. *Fax:* (1223) 339910.

BOLAÑOS GEYER, Enrique; Nicaraguan politician and business executive; b. 13 May 1928, Masaya, nr Managua; s. of Nicolás Bolaños Cortés and Amanda Geyer; m. Lila T. Abaunza; four s. (one deceased) one d.; ed Colegio Centro-América, Granada, St Louis Univ., USA, Instituto Centroamericano de Administración de Empresas, Managua; farmer 1952–59; Gen. Man. Fábrica de Calzados Lorena SA, Masaya 1956–59; Spanish teacher Berlitz School of Languages, St Louis, Mo., USA 1960–62; Gen. Man. Cía. Leonesa de Productos Lácteos SA, León 1962–64; Chair. Bd Impresora Serigráfica SA, Managua 1967–73; Founder and Chair. numerous cos. in Grupo Bolaños-SAIMSA; Head COSEP pvt. business Asscn 1979–90; Vice-Pres. of Nicaragua 1997–2000; Pres. of Nicaragua Jan. 2002–; mem. Constitutionalist Liberal Party (PLC). *Address:* Oficina del Presidente, Managua, Nicaragua (Office).

BOLDON, Ato; Trinidadian athlete; b. 30 Dec. 1973, Port of Spain; ed Univ. of Calif. at LA; resident in USA since 1988; coached by John Smith; Cen. American and Caribbean record-holder at 60m indoors (6.49 seconds), 100m (9.86 seconds) and 200m (19.77 seconds); gold medal World Jr Championships 100m and 200m 1992; fourth Commonwealth Games 100m 1994; bronze medal World Championships 100m 1995; gold medal NCAA Championships 100 m 1996; bronze medals Olympic Games 100m and 200m 1996; 100m World Champion 1997, 1999; gold medal World Championships 200m 1997; gold medal Goodwill Games, New York 200m 1998; gold medal Commonwealth Games 100m 1998; silver medal Olympic Games 100m 2000, bronze medal 200m; youngest sprinter ever to run under 10 seconds in the 100m and under 20 seconds in the 200m (at end of 2001). *Website:* www.atoboldon.com (Office).

BOLDYREV, Yuri Yuryevich; Russian politician; b. 29 May 1960, Leningrad; m. 1990; one s.; ed Leningrad Electrotech. Inst., Leningrad Inst. of Finance and Econs; worked as engineer Cen. Research Inst. of Vessel Electronics and Tech. 1983–89; mem. CPSU 1987–90; USSR People's Deputy 1989–91; del. of 28 CPSU Congress; left CPSU 1990; mem. Council of Reps., then of Co-ordination Council of Democratic Russia Movt 1990–91; mem. Higher Advisory Council to Chair. of Russian Supreme Soviet (later to Pres. of Russian Fed.) 1990–92; consultant Russian Govt Feb.–March 1992; Chief State Inspector of Russian Fed., Chief Control Man. of Admin. of Presidency 1992–93; mem. Centre of Econ. and Political Research (Epicentre) 1993–94; mem. Duma (Parl.) 1993–95; Founder-mem. and Deputy Chair. Yabloko Movt 1993–95, left Party Sept. 1995; Deputy Chair. Accountant Chamber of Russian Fed. 1995–2001. *Address:* c/o Accountant Chamber, Zubovskaya pl. 2, 31, Suite 1, 129090 Moscow, Russia (Office). *Telephone:* (095) 247-59-06 (Office).

BOLGER, Dermot; Irish author; b. 1959, Finglas, Dublin; s. of Roger Bolger and the late Bridie Flanagan; m. Bernadette Clifton 1988; two s.; ed St Canice's BNS, Finglas and Benevin Coll. Finglas; worked as factory hand, library Asst and professional author; Founder and Ed. Raven Arts Press 1979–82; Founder and Exec. Ed. New Island Books, Dublin 1992–; mem. Arts Council of Ireland 1989–93; elected mem. Aosdána 1991–; Playwright in Association, The Abbey (Nat.) Theatre 1997; recipient of various awards. *Publications include:* novels: Night Shift 1985, The Woman's Daughter 1987, The Journey Home 1990, Emily's Shoes 1992, A Second Life 1994, Father's Music 1997, Finbar's Hotel (co-author) 1997, Ladies Night at Finbar's Hotel (co-author) 1999, Temptation 2000, The Valparaiso Voyage 2001; plays: The Lament for Arthur Cleary 1989, Blinded by the Light 1990, In High Germany 1990, The Holy Ground 1990, One Last White Horse 1991, A Dublin Bloom 1994, April Bright 1995, The Passion of Jerome 1999, Consenting Adults 2000; TV film: Edward No Hands 1996; poetry: The Habit of Flesh 1979, Finglas Lilies 1980, No Waiting America 1981, Internal Exile 1986, Leinster Street Ghosts 1989, Taking My Letters Back, New and Selected Poems 1998; Picador Book of Contemporary Irish Fiction (ed.) 1994 (revised Edn 2000). *Leisure interests:* soccer, golf. *Address:* c/o A.P. Watt, 20 John Street, London, WC1N 2DR, England. *Telephone:* (20) 7405-6774. *Fax:* (20) 7831-2154.

BOLGER, James Brendan, PC, ONZ; New Zealand politician, diplomatist and business executive; b. 31 May 1935, Taranaki; s. of Daniel Bolger and Cecilia (née Doyle) Bolger; m. Joan Maureen Riddell 1963; six s. three d.; ed Opunake High School; farmer of sheep and beef cattle, Te Kuiti 1965–72; mem. Parl. 1972–98; Parl. Undersec. to Minister of Agric. and Fisheries, Minister of Maori Affairs, Minister in Charge of Rural Banking and Finance Corpn 1975–77; Minister of Fisheries and Assoc. Minister of Agric. 1977–78; Minister of Labour 1978–84, of Immigration 1978–81; Prime Minister of New Zealand and Minister in Charge of Security Intelligence Service 1990–97; Leader Nat. Party 1986–98; Leader Opposition 1986–90; Amb. to USA 1998–2002; Chair. Kiwibank 2001–, New Zealand Post 2002–; Pres. ILO 1983; Hon. DSc (Khon Kaen Univ., Thailand) 1994; Queen's Silver Jubilee Medal 1977, NZ Commemoration Medal 1990, NZ Suffrage Centennial Medal 1993. *Publication:* A View from the Top (political autobiog.). *Leisure interests:* hiking, reading, politics. *Address:* Kiwibank Ltd, Level II, 155 The Terrace, Private Bag 39888, Wellington (Office); PO Box 406, Te Kuiti, New Zealand (Home). *Telephone:* (4) 462-7936 (Office); (7) 8786-213 (Home). *Fax:* (7) 8786-215 (Home).

BOLING, Edward J., MS, EdD; American academic; b. 19 Feb. 1922, Sevier County, Tenn.; s. of Sam R. and Nerissa (Clark) Boling; m. Carolyn Pierce 1950; three s.; ed Univ. of Tennessee and George Peabody Coll.; with Union Carbide Corpn of Oak Ridge, Tenn. 1951–54; State Budget Dir 1954–58; Commr of Finance and Admin. 1958–61; Vice-Pres. for Devt and Admin., Univ. of Tenn. 1961–70, Pres. Univ. of Tenn. 1970–88, Pres. Emer. 1988–; Univ. Prof. 1988–92; mem. Educ. Comm. of States 1970–92, mem. Southern Regional Educ. Bd 1957–61, 1970–81, 1983–90, 1992–96; Chair. Tenn. Resource Valley 1991–92, fmr Corpn Bd mem. Magnavox, The Signal Co., Philips Electronics, Allied Signal, Home Fed. Bank and numerous others. *Publications:* Forecasting University Enrolment (with D. A. Gardiner) 1952, Methods of Objectifying the Allocation of Tax Funds to Tennessee State Colleges 1961. *Leisure interests:* boating, tennis, skiing, travel. *Address:* Suite 731, Andy Holt Tower, University of Tennessee, Knoxville, TN 37996 (Office); 4911 Westover Terrace, Knoxville, TN 37914, USA (Home). *Telephone:* (865) 974-3500 (Office); (865) 523-6882 (Home). *E-mail:* ejb@utk.edu (Home).

BOLKESTEIN, Frederik (Frits), MPh, LLM; Dutch politician; b. 1933; m.; three c.; ed Oregon State Coll., Gemeentelijke Univ. Amsterdam, Univ. of London, Univ. of Leiden; with Shell Group 1960–76; Dir Shell Chimie, Paris 1973–76; Mem. of Parl. for VVD (Liberals) 1978–82, 1986–88, 1989–99; Minister for Foreign Trade 1982–86; Chair. Atlantic Comm., Netherlands 1986–88; Minister of Defence 1988–89; Chair. VVD Parl. Group 1990–98; Pres. Liberal Internationale 1996–99; EU Commr for Internal Market, Financial Services, Customs and Taxation 1999–; mem. Royal Inst. of Int. Affairs. *Play:* Floris Count of Holland. *Leisure interest:* tennis. *Address:* Commission of the European Communities, 200 rue de la Loi, 1049 Brussels, Belgium (Office). *Fax:* (2) 298-07-99 (Office).

BOLKHOVITINOV, Nikolai Nikolaevich, DHist; Russian historian; b. 26 Oct. 1930, Moscow; s. of Nikolai Feodosievich Bolkhovitinov and Lidiia Bolkhovitinova (née Komarova); m. Ludmila Bolkhovitinova (née Povel'nenko)1965; ed Moscow Inst. of Int. Relations; on staff Dept of History of Diplomacy USSR Ministry of Foreign Affairs 1957–58; Jr, Sr researcher Inst. of History 1958–68; Sr Leading Researcher, Head Dept of History of USA and Canada, Dir Centre for North American Studies, Inst. of World History USSR (now Russian) Acad. of Sciences 1968–; Corresp. mem. USSR (now Russian) Acad. of Sciences 1987, full mem. 1992; research in history of USA and history of int. relations in 18th–19th centuries, Russian-American relations and foreign policy of Russia, geographic discoveries on N Pacific and in N America; mem. Russian Geographical Soc., New York Acad. of Sciences, Vargas Historical Centre, Venezuela; Koontz Memorial Award (American Historical Assen); State Prize of Russian Fed. 1997. *Publications include:* Monroe's Doctrine 1959, USA: Problems of History and Contemporary Historiography 1980, History of Russian America 1732–1867 (3 Vols) 1997–99; series of monographs on history of Russian–American relations 1966–96, and numerous articles, including Beginnings of Russian–American Relations 1775–1815 1966, Russia and the American Revolution 1976, Russia and the United States 1986, Russian–American Relations and the Sale of Alaska 1834–1867 1990. *Leisure interest:* tennis. *Address:* Institute of World History, Russian Academy of Sciences, Leninskii pr. 32A, 117334 Moscow (Office); Timiriazevskaya str. 33/11, 125422 Moscow, Russia (Home). *Telephone:* (095) 938-00-97 (Office); (095) 210-27-41 (Home). *Fax:* (095) 938-22-86. *E-mail:* amercenter@pochtamt.ru (Office); ighac@g23.relcom.ru (Home); bolkhovitinovn@mail.ru (Home).

BOLKIAH, HRH Prince Jefri; Brunei politician; fmrly Minister of Culture, Youth and Sports, Deputy Minister of Finance; Minister of Finance 1988–97; fmr Chair. Royal Brunei Airlines, Brunei Investment Agency; fmr Propr Asprey & Garrad. *Address:* c/o Ministry of Finance, Bandar Seri Begawan, Brunei. *Telephone:* (2) 242405.

BOLKIAH, HRH Prince Mohamed; Brunei politician; b. 27 Aug. 1947; ed Royal Mil. Acad., Sandhurst, UK; Minister of Foreign Affairs 1984–. *Address:* Ministry of Foreign Affairs, Jalan Subok, Bandar Seri Begawan (Office); Hijau Baiduri, Bukit Kayangan, Jalan Tutong, Bandar Seri Begawan BD 2710, Brunei (Home). *Telephone:* (2) 261177 (Office); (2) 244101 (Office). *Fax:* (2) 261709 (Office); (2) 244659 (Office).

BOLKIAH MU'IZUDDIN WADDAULAH, HM Sultan Sir Muda Hassanal, Sultan of Brunei, DK, PSPNB, PSNB, PSLJ, SPBM, PANB; b. 15 July 1946; s. of former Sultan Sir Muda Omar Ali Saifuddin, KCMG; m. 1st Rajah Isteri Anak Saleha 1965; one s. three d.; m. 2nd Pengiran Isteri Hajjah Mariam 1981 (divorced 2003); two s. two d.; ed privately and Victoria Inst., Kuala Lumpur, Malaysia and Royal Mil. Acad., Sandhurst; Appointed Crown Prince and Heir Apparent 1961; Ruler of State of Brunei Oct. 1967–; Prime Minister of Brunei Jan. 1984–, Minister of Finance and Home Affairs 1984–86, of Defence Oct. 1986–, also of Finance and of Law; Hon. Capt. Coldstream Guards 1968, Hon. Marshal RAF 1992; Sovereign and Chief of Royal Orders instituted by Sultans of Brunei. *Address:* Istana Darul Hana, Bandar Seri Begawan, BA 1000, Brunei (Office); The Aviary, Osterley, Middx, England. *Telephone:* (2) 229988 (Office). *Fax:* (2) 241717 (Office). *E-mail:* pro@jpm.gov.bn (Office).

BOLLING, Claude; French jazz pianist, composer and band leader; b. 10 April 1930, Cannes; s. of Henri Bolling and Geneviève Brannens; m. Irène Dervize-Sadyker 1959; two s.; studied with pvt. music teachers including Bob Colin, Earl Hines, Maurice Duruflé, Willie 'The Lion' Smith, André Hodeir; US and Canada Gold Records, Médaille d'or Maurice Ravel, Officier Arts et Lettres, Chevalier Ordre Nat. du Mérite, Chevalier Légion d'honneur, Hon. Citizen of LA. *Music:* compositions and recordings: piano solos, duos, trios and all instrumental combinations including jazz, big band and symphony orchestra; collaborated with Roy Eldridge, Lionel Hampton, Duke Ellington's men and many other jazz musicians and vocalists; written and recorded with Jean-Pierre Rampal (Suite for Flute), Alexandre Lagoya (Guitar Concerto), Maurice André (Toot Suite), Pinchas Zukerman (Suite for Violin), Yo-Yo Ma (Suite for Cello); composed more than 100 film soundtrack scores including, The Awakening, Le Jour et l'Heure, Borsalino, Lucky Luke, Le Magnifique, Willie and Phil, California Suite, La Mandarine, L'Homme en Colère, Flic Story, Le Mur de l'Atlantique, On ne meurt que deux fois, Netchaiev est de retour. *Television:* compositions: Jazz Memories, Les Brigades du Tigre, Chantecler; many jazz and variety shows. *Leisure interests:* ecology, model railroading. *Address:* 20 avenue de Lorraine, 92380 Garches, France (Office). *Telephone:* 1-47-41-41-84. *Fax:* 1-47-01-03-63. *E-mail:* claude@claude-bolling.com (Home). *Website:* www.claude-bolling.com (Home).

BOLLINGER, Lee C.; American university president; b. 1946, Santa Rosa, CA; m. Jean Magnano Bollinger; one s. one d.; ed Univ. of Oregon, Columbia Law School; began career as law clerk, US Court of Appeal 1971–72, US Supreme Court 1972–73; Faculty mem. Univ. of Mich. Law School 1973–94, Dean 1987–94; Provost and Prof. of Govt Dartmouth Coll. 1994–96; Pres. Univ. of Mich. 1996–2002; Pres. Columbia Univ. 2002–; Fellow, American Acad. of Arts and Sciences; mem. Bd Gerald R. Ford Foundation, RSC. *Publications:* The Tolerant Society: Freedom of Speech and Extremist Speech in America 1986, Images of a Free Press 1991, Eternally Vigilant: Free Speech in the Modern Era 2002; numerous books, articles and essays in scholarly journals. *Address:* Office of the President, Columbia University, 2960 Broadway, New York, NY 10027-6902, USA (Office). *Telephone:* (212) 854-5573 (Office). *Website:* www.columbia.edu (Office).

BOLLORÉ, Vincent Marie; French financial investor; b. 1 April 1952, Boulogne-sur-Seine; s. of Michel Bolloré and Monique Bolloré (née Follot); m.

Sophie Fossorier 1977; three s. one d.; ed Lycée Janson-de-Sailly, Faculté de droit de Paris; with EIB 1970–75; Deputy Man. Cie financière Rothschild 1976–81; Chair. and CEO Bolloré Group and Bolloré Papermills 1981–. Bolloré, Inc., USA 1981–, Banque Rivaud 1996–; mem. Bd of Dirs. Banque de France 1988–; mem. Exec. Cttee Conseil nat. du patronat français (CNPF) 1987–96; Chair. Cen. Cttee Armateurs de France 1993–95, Fondation de la deuxième chance 1998; Entrepreneur de l'année 1986, Man. de l'année 1987; Chevalier, Légion d'honneur, Grand Officier, Ordre du Lion (Senegal), Légion d'honneur (Côte d'Ivoire). *Address:* Groupe Bolloré, Tour Bolloré, 31–32 quai Dion Bouton, 92811 Puteaux Cedex, France (Office).

BOLLOYEV, Taimuraz Kazbekovich; Russian/Ossetian business executive; b. 23 Feb. 1953, N Ossetia; m.; ed Moscow Inst. of Food Industry; mechanic, then head of beer production Stepan Razin factory, Leningrad, chief technologist 1987–91; Dir Industrial Union, Vsevolzhsk, Leningrad Region 1984–87; Dir.-Gen. Baltika (beer mfr.) 1991–; Order of Honour. *Leisure interests:* classical music, football, Russian baths, wrestling. *Address:* Baltica Co. Promzona Parnas, 6th Verkhniy proyezd, block 9, 194292 St Petersburg, Russia (Office). *Telephone:* (812) 329-91-01 (Office). *Fax:* (812) 329-99-148 (Office).

BOLSHAKOV, Aleksey Alekseyevich; Russian politician and radio engineer; b. 17 Dec. 1939, Dno, Pskov Dist; m.; two s.; ed M. Bonch-Bruyevich Electromechanical Inst. of Telecommunications, Leningrad; worked as engineer in factories of Leningrad; Dir-Gen. production union Dalnaya Svyaz; First Deputy Chair. Leningrad City Exec. Cttee, Chair. Planning Comm. 1988–91; Dir-Gen. Jt-Stock Co. Vysokoskorostnye Linii 1991–94; one of initiators of construction of high-speed St Petersburg–Moscow highway; Chair. Intergovernmental Cttee of CIS 1994–; Deputy Chair. Russian Council of Ministers 1994–96, First Deputy Chair. 1996–97; Chair. Bd of Dirs Polimetal 1998–; Chair. Bd of Trustees Fund for Devt of North and North-West Territories 1998–; mem. Bd of Trustees Fund for Devt of St Petersburg and North West Region of Russia 1999–, Chair. 2000–. *Address:* Fund for Development of St Petersburg and North-West Region of Russia, Smolny, 193060 St Petersburg (Office); Polimetal, Narodnogo opolcheniya Prosp. 2, 198216 St Petersburg, Russia (Office). *Telephone:* (812) 377-38-21 (Office). *Fax:* (812) 376-65-20. *E-mail:* info@polymetal.ru (Office).

BOLSHOV, Leonid Aleksandrovich; Russian power engineering scientist; b. 23 July 1946, Moscow; m.; two c.; ed Moscow State Univ.; engineer, Jr then Sr researcher, later Head of Lab. Moscow Kurchatov Inst. of Nuclear Energy 1970–78, Head of Lab. Troitsk br. 1978–91; Dir Inst. of Problems of Safe Devt of Nuclear Power, Russian Acad. of Sciences 1991–, concurrently Dir Inst. of Problems of Nuclear Power Safety 1991–; participated in inquiry into Chernobyl nuclear accident 1986; mem. Scientific Council Ministry of Emergency Affairs; mem. Ed. Bd journal Atomnaya Energetika; corresp. mem. Russian Acad. of Sciences 1997; USSR State Prize 1988; Order of Courage 1997. *Publications:* over 300 scientific Ppubls and monographs on physics of solid surfaces, non-linear optics, physics of laser thermonuclear synthesis and problems of nuclear power safety. *Address:* Institute of Problems of Safe Development of Nuclear Power, Russian Academy of Sciences, B. Tulskaya str. 52, Moscow, Russia (Office). *Telephone:* (095) 952-24-21 (Office). *Fax:* (095) 958-00-40 (Office).

BOLTANSKI, Christian; French artist; b. 6 Sept. 1944, Paris; s. of Etienne Boltanski and Marie-Elise Ilari-Guérin; participant in numerous group exhbns in Europe, USA, Canada and Australia; Prof. Ecole Nationale Supérieure des Beaux Arts 1986; Grand Prix nat. de la Sculpture 1990. *One-man exhibitions include:* Museum of Contemporary Art, Chicago, Museum of Contemporary Art, Los Angeles, New Museum of Contemporary Art, New York, Galerie Pablo and Pandora van Dijk, Rotterdam, Ydessa Hendeles Art Foundation, Toronto, El Caso, Centro de Arte Reina Sofia, Madrid, Maria Goodman Gallery, New York 1988, Galerie Ghislaine Hussenot, Paris, Vancouver Art Gallery, Museum of Contemporary Art, Basel, Jean Bernier Gallery, Athens, Marika Malacorda Gallery, Geneva, Univ. Art Museum, Berkeley, Calif., Israel Museum, Jerusalem, Foksal Museum, Warsaw 1989, Galerie des Beaux Arts, Brussels, Kaufmann Gallery, Basel, Whitechapel Gallery, London, Musée de Grenoble, Inst. of Contemporary Arts, Nagoya, Marion Goodman Gallery, New York 1990, Kunsthalle, Hamburg, Lisson Gallery, London 1991, Lost: New York Project 1995, Musée d'art moderne (Arc) 1998. *Publications:* L'Album de la Famille B. 1971, Les Compositions Photographiques 1976, Murales 1977. *Address:* 146 boulevard Carmélina, 92240 Malakoff, France.

BOLTON, John Robert, BA, JD; American lawyer and government official; b. 20 Nov. 1948, Baltimore, MD; s. of Edward Jackson Bolton and Virginia Bolton (née Godfrey); m. Gretchen Brainerd 1986; one d.; ed Yale Univ.; Assoc. Covington & Burling, Washington DC 1974–81, Partner 1983–85; legal consultant to The White House 1981; 1983–84; Asst Attorney-Gen. Legis. Affairs, Dept of Justice 1985–88, Asst Attorney-Gen. Civil Div. 1988–89; Asst. Sec. Int. Org. Affairs Bureau, Dept of State 1989–93; Partner Lerner, Reed, Bolton & McManus (and predecessor firms), Washington DC 1993–99; Partner of counsel Kutak Rock 1999–2001; Sr Vice-Pres. American Enterprise Inst., Washington DC 1997–2001; Under-Sec. of State for Arms Control and Int. Security, Dept of State 2001–; Sr Fellow Manhattan Inst. 1993; Adjunct Prof. George Mason Univ. Law School 1994–2001; Pres. Nat. Policy Forum

1995–96; mem. Republican Party. *Address:* Department of State, 21st and C Streets, NW, Washington, DC 20520, USA (Office). *E-mail:* j.bolton@state.gov (Office). *Website:* www.state.gov (Office).

BON, Michel; French business executive; b. 5 July 1943; s. of Emmanuel Bon and Mathilde Bon (née Aussedat); m. Catherine Brunet de Sairigné; four c.; ed Ecole Supérieure Sciences Economiques et Commerciales, Paris Inst. of Political Studies, Ecole Nationale d'Admin., Stanford Business School; auditor Ministry of Finance 1971–75; banker Crédit Nat. 1975–78; joined Crédit Agricole 1978, Head of Commitments, Chair. and Deputy CEO Unicrédit –1985; Chair. then CEO Carrefour 1985–92; Head Nat. Job Placement Agency 1993–95; Chair. France Télécom 1995–2002, Hon. Chair. 2002–; Chair. (non-exec.) Orange (after merger with France Télécom) 2001–02; Chair. Editions du Cerf 1997–; fmr mem. Advisory Bd Banque de France; Chair. Supervisory Council Ecole Supérieure Sciences Economiques et Commerciales; Vice-Pres. Inst. Pasteur; Chair. Institut de l'Entreprise; Officier Légion d'honneur, Chevalier du Mérite agricole, Officier Ordre nat. du Mérite; Man. of the Year 1991, 1992, 1998. *Address:* France Télécom, 10 rue de Bassano, 75116, Paris (Office); 4 avenue de Camoëns, 75116 Paris, France (Home). *Telephone:* 1-44-44-01-00 (Office). *E-mail:* michel.bon@ francetelecom.com (Office).

BON JOVI, Jon; American musician, singer, songwriter and actor; b. 2 March 1962, Perth Amboy, NJ; m. Dorothea Bon Jovi; two c.; f. rock band Bon Jovi, singer, songwriter 1984–; world tour 1995; has performed over 2,000 concerts in 47 countries; band won Best Int. Group Brit Award 1995. *Singles include:* Runaway. *Albums include:* 7800° Fahrenheit, Slippery When Wet, New Jersey, Keep The Faith, Cross Road 1994 (12m copies sold worldwide), These Days 1996, Destination Anywhere (solo) 1997, Bon Jovi 1999, Crush (MY VH-1 Award for My Favorite Video for 'It's My Life' 2000) 1999, One Wild Night Live, Blaze of Glory: Young Guns II soundtrack (solo) (Golden Globe Award for Best Original Song from a Motion Picture). *Films include:* Moonlight and Valentino (Motion Picture Club's Premier Performance Award), The Leading Man, Long Time, Nothing New 1997, Little City 1997, Homegrown 1997, No Looking Back, Row Your Boat 1998, U-571 2000, Pay It Forward 2001. *Television includes:* The Late Show 1992, Unsolved Mysteries 1988, Sex and the City 1998, Ally McBeal (special guest star). *Address:* c/o Mercury Records, PO Box 237040, New York, NY 10023, USA (Office); PO Box 1425, 136–140 New Kings Road, London, SW6 4 FX, England. *Telephone:* (212) 336-9413 (New York) (Office); (20) 7705-4200 (London) (Office). *Fax:* (212) 336-5385 (New York) (Office); (20) 7705-4201 (London) (Office). *Website:* www .bonjovi.com.

BOND, Alan, AO; Australian business executive; b. 22 April 1938, London, England; s. of Frank Bond and Kathleen Bond; m. 1st Eileen Hughes 1956 (divorced); two s. two d.; m. 2nd Diana Bliss 1995; ed Perivale School, London and Fremantle Boys' School, WA; f. and Exec. Chair. Bond Corpn Holdings Ltd 1969–90, now consultant; interests in brewing, property, oil and gas, electronic media, minerals, airships; declared bankrupt April 1992; sentenced to 2$\frac{1}{2}$ years' imprisonment for dishonesty but found not guilty after retrial Nov. 1992; sentenced to three years' imprisonment for fraud 1996; sentenced to four years' imprisonment for fraud Feb. 1997; sentence extended to seven years Aug. 1997; released March 2000; Syndicate Head Americas Cup Challenge 1983 Ltd; with Money Centre 2000–; Australia Winners of 1983 Americas Cup Challenge; named Australian of the Year 1977. *Leisure interest:* yachting.

BOND, Alan Maxwell, PhD, DSc, FAA, FRACI, FRSC; Australian professor of chemistry; b. 17 Aug. 1946, Cobden, Vic.; s. of late Ian T. Bond and Joyce M. Bond; m. Tunde-Maria Bond 1969; two s.; ed Univ. of Melbourne; Sr Demonstrator, Dept of Inorganic Chem. Univ. of Melbourne 1970–73, Research Fellow 1973–78; Foundation Prof. of Chem. Deakin Univ. 1978–90; Prof. of Chem. La Trobe Univ. 1990–95, Deputy Head Dept of Chem. 1996, 1997, 1999; Prof. of Chem., Monash Univ. 1995–, Deputy Head Dept of Chem. 1996–97, 1999, Head School of Chem. 2000–02; 150th anniversary Royal Soc. of Chem. Robert Boyle Fellow in Analytical Chem. Univ. of Oxford 1991; Hinshelwood Lecturer Univ. of Oxford 1998; mem. Chem. Panel, Australian Research Council 1993–95, Council Australian Acad. of Science 1993–96, Vice-Pres. 1995–96, ACS, USA Electrochemical Soc.; Fulbright Fellow 1972; Fellow, Japan Soc. for Promotion of Science 1990, IUPAC, Royal Australian Chemical Inst.; Erskine Fellowship 1993; Christensen Fellowship, St Catherine's Coll., Oxford 1998; Fed. of Asian Chemical Socs Foundation Lectureship 1993; mem. numerous editorial bds including Reviews in Analytical Chem. 1971–, Bulletin of Electrochemistry 1987–, Inorganica Chimica Acta 1988–, Journal of Electroanalytical Chem. 1997–, Green Chemistry 1999, Encyclopedia of Analytical Science (2nd edn) 2001–; Rennie Medal 1975, David Syme Prize 1978, Australian Analytical Chem. Medal 1989, Stokes Medal 1992, Liversidge Award, Australian and NZ AAS 1992, Australian Research Council Special Investigator Award 1997–99, Royal Soc. of Chem. (London) Electrochemistry Group Medal 1997, Royal Australian Chemical Inst. H.G. Smith Medal 1998, Royal Soc. of Vic. Medal 1999, Burrows Medal 2000, Faraday Medal, Royal Soc. of Chem. 2000. *Publications:* Modern Polarographic Methods in Analytical Chemistry 1981, Broadening Electrochemical Horizons 2002; more than 500 publs on different aspects of electrochemistry. *Leisure interest:* cricket. *Address:* School of Chemistry, PO Box 23, Monash University, Clayton, Vic. 3800 (Office); 7 Canterbury Road, Toorak, Vic. 3142,

Australia (Home). *Telephone:* (3) 9905-1338 (Office); (3) 9827-8466 (Home). *Fax:* (3) 9905-4597 (Office). *E-mail:* alan.bond@sci.monash.edu.au. *Website:* www.monash.edu.au.

BOND, Christopher Samuel, BA, LLB; American politician and lawyer; b. 6 March 1939, St Louis; s. of Arthur Doerr and Elizabeth Green Bond; m. Carolyn Reid 1967; one s.; ed Deerfield Acad., Mass., Woodrow Wilson School of Public and Int. Affairs, Princeton Univ., Univ. of Virginia; Clerk, Fifth Circuit, U.S. Court of Appeals 1963–64; with law firm, Covington and Burling, Washington, DC 1964–67; private practice 1968; Asst Attorney-Gen., Chief Counsel of Consumer Protection Div. 1969–70; State Auditor, Missouri 1970–72; Gov. of Missouri 1973–77, 1981–84; Chair. Republican Govs.' Asscn 1974–75, Midwestern Govs.' Conf. 1976; Exec. Cttee Nat. Govs.' Conf. 1974–75; Chair. NGA Cttee on Econ. Devt 1981-82; Pres. Great Plains Legal Foundation, Kansas City, Mo. 1977–81; partner, law firm Gage and Tucker, Kansas City and St Louis 1981–87; Senator from Missouri Jan. 1987–; Republican; Hon. LLD (Westminster and William Jewell Colls., Mo.) 1973, Hon. DLitt (Drury Coll., Springfield, Mo.) 1976. *Address:* US Senate, 274 Russell Senate Building, Room 293, Washington, DC 20510 (Office); 14 S. Jefferson Road, Mexico, MO 65265, USA (Home).

BOND, Edward; British playwright and director; b. 18 July 1934, London; m. Elisabeth Pablé 1971; Northern Arts Literary Fellowship 1977–79; Resident Theatre Writer, Univ. of Essex 1982–83; Hon. DLitt (Yale) 1977; winner, George Devine Award, John Whiting Award 1968. *Publications:* plays: The Pope's Wedding 1962, Saved 1965, Narrow Road to the Deep North 1968, Early Morning 1968, Passion 1971, Black Mass 1971, Lear 1972, The Sea 1973, Bingo 1974, The Fool 1976, A-A-America! (Grandma Faust and The Swing) 1976, Stone 1976, The Bundle 1978, The Woman 1979, The Worlds 1980, Restoration 1981, Summer: A Play for Europe 1982, Derek 1983, Human Cannon 1985, The War Plays (Red Black and Ignorant, The Tin Can People, Great Peace) 1985, Jackets 1989, In the Company of Men 1990, September 1990, Olly's Prison 1993, Tuesday 1993, Coffee: A Tragedy 1994, At the Inland Sea (A Play for Young People) 1996, Eleven Vests (A Play for Young People) 1997, The Crime of the Twenty-first Century 1999, The Children (A Play for Two Adults and Sixteen Children) 2000, Chair 2000, Have I None 2000, Existence 2002; librettos: We Come to the River 1977, The English Cat 1983; translations: Chekhov's The Three Sisters 1967, Wedekind's Spring Awakening 1974, Wedekind's Lulu: A Monster Tragedy (with Elisabeth Bond-Pablé) 1992; others: Theatre Poems and Songs 1978, Collected Poems 1978–1985 1987, Notes on Post-Modernism 1990, Letters (5 Vols) 1994–2000, Notes on Imagination 1995, Selected Notebooks (Vol. 1) 2000, (Vol. 2) 2001, The Hidden Plot: Notes on Theatre and the State 2000. *Address:* c/o Casarotto Ramsay, National House, 60–66 Wardour Street, London, W1V 3HP, England. *Telephone:* (20) 7287-4450. *Fax:* (20) 7287-9128.

BOND, Sir John (Reginald Hartnell), Kt; British banker; b. 24 July 1941, Oxford; s. of the late Capt. R. H. A. Bond and of E. C. A. Bond; m. Elizabeth Caroline Parker 1968; one s. two d.; ed Tonbridge School, Kent, Cate School, California, USA; joined The Hongkong and Shanghai Banking Corpn 1961; worked in Hong Kong, Thailand, Singapore, Indonesia and USA; Chief Exec. Wardley (merchant banking subsidiary) 1983; Gen. Man. and CEO Hongkong and Shanghai Banking Corpn Americas 1988–89, Chair 1997–; Chair. Hongkong Bank of Canada 1987–97; Dir (Exec. Dir Americas) Hongkong and Shanghai Banking Corpn 1988–, Exec. Dir Banking 1990; Dir (non-exec.) London Stock Exchange 1994–99, British Steel 1994–98; Pres. and CEO Marine Midland Banks, Inc., USA (subsidiary of HSBC Holdings PLC) 1991–93, now Chair.; Chair. HSBC Bank Middle East 1998–; Group CEO HSBC Holdings PLC 1993–98, Group Chair. 1998– (Dir 1990–), Chair. HSBC Bank (fmrly Midland Bank) 1998–; Dir (non-exec.) Visa Int. 1995–97, Orange PLC 1996–99, Ford Motor Co. 2000–; Gov. The English-Speaking Union 1997–; Hon. DEcon (Richmond) 1998; Hon. DLit (Loughborough) 2000. *Leisure interests:* golf, skiing. *Address:* HSBC Holdings PLC, 10th Floor, 10 Lower Thames Street, London, EC3R 6AE, England. *Telephone:* (20) 7260-9158. *Fax:* (20) 7260-6686 (Office). *Website:* www.hsbc.com.

BOND, Julian; American civil rights leader and university professor; b. 14 Jan. 1940; s. of Horace Mann Bond and Julia Agnes (née Washington); m. 1st Alice Louise Clopton 1961 (divorced 1989); three s. two d.; m. 2nd Pamela Sue Horowitz 1990; ed Morehouse Coll.; Co-founder, Cttee on Appeal for Human Rights, Atlanta Univ. 1960; Co-founder Student Non-violent Co-ordinating Cttee 1960, Communications Dir 1961–66; reporter, feature writer Atlanta Inquirer 1960–61, Man. Ed. 1963; mem. Ga House of Reps. 1966–75, excluded 1966 by House for criticizing U.S. involvement in Viet Nam, exclusion overruled in Supreme Court; mem. Ga Senate 1975–87; Prof. Drexel Univ. 1988–89; Pappas Fellow, Univ. of Pennsylvania 1989; Visiting Prof. Harvard Univ. 1989, 1991, Univ. of Va 1990; Distinguished Prof. American Univ. 1990–; Prof., Univ. of Va 1993–; Chair. Bd, Southern Elections Fund, Nat. Asscn for the Advancement of Colored People 1998–; Pres. Emer. Southern Poverty Law Center; Pres. Inst. of Southern Studies; mem. Bd of Dirs. Delta Ministry Project of Nat. Council of Churches, Robert F. Kennedy Memorial Fund, Martin Luther King Jr Center for Social Change, Center for Community Change, Southern Regional Council, New Democratic Coalition and other bodies; mem. Nat. Advisory Council of American Civil Liberties Union, Southern Correspondents Reporting Racial Equality Wars; hon. degrees from 20 colls. and univs. *Publications:* A Time to Speak, A Time to Act, Gonna Sit

at the Welcome Table; poems and articles in books and periodicals. *Address:* 5435 41st Place, NW, Washington, DC 20015, USA. *Telephone:* (202) 244-1213.

BONDARENKO, Vitaly Mikhailovich; Russian architect; b. 22 June 1925; m.; ed Kharkov Inst. of Eng and Construction; fmr master constructor Zaporozhstal Factory; chief engineer Div. of Mining Construction and Towns, Donbass 1952–62; Head, then Pro-Rector Kharkov Inst. of Eng and Construction 1962–72; Dir All-Union Research Inst. Giproniiselkhoz, Moscow 1972–76; Head of Dept, Prof. Moscow Inst. of Communal Econs and Construction (now Communal Industry) 1976–94, 1999–; Vice-Pres. Russian Acad. of Architecture and Construction Sciences 1994–; mem. Nat. Bd of Dirs. Chamber of Cultural and Historical Heritage of Russia, Russian Acad. of Eng, Int. Acad. of Eng, Int. Acad. of Ecological Reconstruction, British Inst. of Civil Eng; Foreign mem. Ukraine Acad. of Construction; numerous awards and prizes. *Publications:* ten books and over 200 tech. Ppubls. *Leisure interest:* 20th-century Russian history. *Address:* Moscow Institute of Communal Industry, Srednaya Kalitnikovskaya str. 30, 109807 Moscow, Russia (Office). *Telephone:* (095) 157-75-07 (Office); (095) 202-48-66 (Home).

BONDAREV, Yuriy Vasiliyevich; Russian writer; b. 15 March 1924, Orsk; s. of Vasili Vasilevich Bondarev and Claudia Iosifovna Bondareva; m. Valentina Nikitichna Mosina 1950; two d.; ed Gor'kiy Inst., Moscow 1951; writer 1949–; mem. CPSU 1944–91; First Deputy Chair. of RSFSR Writers' Union, Chair. of Bd 1990–93; Pres. Yedineniye (Unity) Asscn 1995–; served Soviet Army 1941–45; Deputy to Supreme Soviet 1975–80 and Deputy Chair.; Co-Chair. Int. Community of Writers' Unions; Hero of Socialist Labour 1984, two State prizes, Lenin Prize, RSFSR Prize, Tolstoy Prize 1993, Sholokhov Prize 1994. *Publications include:* novels: On the Big River 1953, Young Commanders 1956, Fire for the Battalions 1957, Last Salute 1959, Silence 1962, Relatives 1965, Hot Snow 1969, The Shore 1975, A Choice 1980, The Game 1984, Temptation 1991, Instants (essays) 1981–87 and 1987–94, Collected Works (8 Vols) 1993–94, Non-Resistance to Evil 1994. *Leisure interest:* collecting painting albums. *Address:* Lomonosovsky Prospekt N19, Apt. 148, 117311 Moscow, Russia. *Telephone:* (095) 334-59-92.

BONDEVIK, Kjell Magne; Norwegian politician; b. 3 Sept. 1947, Molde; s. of Margit Bondevik and Johs Bondevik; m. Björg Bondevik 1970; two s. one d.; ed Free Faculty of Theology, Univ. of Oslo; ordained minister 1979; Deputy Chair. Christian Democratic youth Asscn 1968–70, Chair. 1970–73; Deputy mem. Storting 1969–73, mem. 1973–; Political Vice-Chair. Christian Democratic Party 1975–83, Chair. 1983–95; Minister of Church and Educ. 1983–86, of Foreign Affairs 1989–90, Deputy Prime Minister 1985–86; Prime Minister of Norway 1997–2000, 2002–; Chair. Christian Democratic Party's Parl. Group 1981–83, 1986–89, 1993–97; Hon. DTech (Brunel) 1997; Dr. h.c. (Suffolk) 2000, (Wonkurang) 2000; Wittenberg Award, Luther Inst. 2000. *Address:* Office of the Prime Minister, Akersgt. 42, P.O. Box 8001 Dep., 0030 Oslo, Norway. *Telephone:* (47) 22-24-90-90 (Office). *Fax:* (47) 22-24-95-00 (Office).

BONDI, Sir Hermann, KCB, MA FRS; British mathematician; b. 1 Nov. 1919, Vienna, Austria; s. of the late Samuel and Helene Bondi; m. Christine M. Stockman 1947; two s. three d.; ed Real Gymnasium, Vienna and Trinity Coll., Cambridge; Fellow, Trinity Coll., Cambridge 1943–49, 1952–54; Lecturer in Math., Cambridge Univ. 1948–54; Research Assoc. Cornell Univ. 1951, Harvard Coll. Observatory 1953; Visiting Prof. Cornell Univ. 1960; Prof. of Math. King's Coll., Univ. of London 1954–71, Titular Prof. 1971–84, Prof. Emer. 1985–; Dir-Gen. European Space Research Org. (ESRO), Paris 1967–71; Chief Scientific Adviser to Ministry of Defence 1971–77; Chief Scientist Dept of Energy 1977–80; Chair. Offshore Energy Bd, Dept of Energy 1977–80, Advisory Council on Research and Devt for Fuel and Power 1977–80, Severn Barrage Cttee 1978–81; Chair. and Chief Exec. Natural Environment Research Council 1980–84; Fellow, Royal Soc. 1959, Royal Astronomical Soc. (Sec. 1956–64), Cambridge Philosophical Soc.; Chair. Nat. Cttee for Astronomy 1964–67; Pres. Inst. of Math. and its Applications 1974–75, Asscn of British Science Writers 1981–83, British Humanist Asscn 1982–99, Pres. Hydrographical Soc. 1985–87; Master, Churchill Coll., Cambridge 1983–90, Fellow 1990–; Hon. Fellow Regent's Coll. 1988, Inst. of Physics 1992, Inst. of Math. and its Applications 1993, Indian Acad. of Sciences 1996; Hon DSc (Sussex, Bath, Surrey) 1974, (York) 1980, (Southampton) 1981, (Salford) 1982, (Birmingham) 1984, (St Andrews) 1985, (Vienna) 1993, (Plymouth) 1995; Gold Medal (Inst. of Math. and its Applications) 1988, G. D. Birla Int. Award for Humanism 1990, Planetary Award (Asscn of Space Explorers) 1993, Pres.'s Decoration for Science and Arts (Austria) 1997, Gold Medal, Royal Astronomical Soc. 2001. *Publications:* Cosmology 1952, The Universe at Large 1961, Relativity and Common Sense 1964, Assumption and Myth in Physical Theory 1967, Science, Churchill and Me (autobiog.) 1990; numerous papers. *Address:* Churchill College, Cambridge, CB3 0DS, England.

BONDS, Barry Lamar; American baseball player; b. 24 July 1964, Riverside, Calif.; s. of Bobby Bonds (fmr San Francisco Giants player); m.; three c.; ed Arizona State Univ.; with Pittsburgh Pirates baseball team 1985–92, San Francisco Giants 1992–; led Nat. League in int. walks 1992–94; scored 73 home runs 2001 (single-season home run record); MVP Baseball Writers' Asscn of America 1990, 1992, 1993, 2001, Maj. League Player of Year, Sporting News 1990, Nat. League Player of Year, Sporting News 1990, 1991, Gold Glove Award 1990–94, 1996, Silver Slugger Award 1990–96 and other awards. *Address:* San Francisco Giants, Pacific Bell Park, 24 Willie Mays Plaza, San Francisco, CA 94107, USA (Office). *Telephone:* (415) 972-2000 (Office). *E-mail:* baseball@giants.mlb.com (Office).

BONDURANT, Amy L., JuD; American diplomatist and lawyer; b. Union City, Tenn.; d. of Judge John C. Bondurant; m. David E. Dunn III; one s.; ed Univ. of Kentucky, American Univ., Washington DC; legis. aide to Senator Wendell Ford 1975; Counsel, then Sr Counsel, Senate Cttee on Commerce, Science and Transportation; pvt. practice with law firm 1987–; Chair. Commercial Space Transportation Advisory Cttee 1993; Perm. Rep. to OECD 1997–2001; Sec.-Treas. and mem. Bd Vice-Pres.'s Residence Foundation 1993–97; mem. American, Dist of Columbia and Kentucky Bar Asscns.; mem. Founding Cttee of Forum 21 Conf. on Trans-Atlantic Dialogue 2001. *Publication:* Physician Heal Thyself: Can International Organisations Reform? 2001. *Address:* Department of State, 2201 C Street, NW Washington, DC 20520 U.S.A. (Office). *E-mail:* albond@attglobal.net (Office). *Website:* www .state.gov (Office).

BONDURANT, Stuart, BS, MD; American professor and university administrator; b. 9 Sept. 1929, Winston-Salem, NC; m. 1st Margaret Fortescue 1954 (divorced); one s. two d.; m. 2nd Susan Haughton Ehringhaus 1991; ed Univ. of North Carolina at Chapel Hill, Duke Univ. School of Medicine, Durham, NC; Assoc. Dir Indiana Univ. Cardiovascular Research Center, Indiana Univ. Medical Center, Indianapolis, Ind. 1961–67; Chief, Medical Br. Artificial Heart-Myocardial Infarction Program, Nat. Health Inst., Nat. Insts. of Health 1966–67; Prof. and Chair., Dept of Medicine, Albany Medical Coll., Physician-in-Chief, Albany Medical Center Hosp., New York 1967–74, Pres. and Dean 1974–79; Prof. of Medicine, Univ. of NC 1979–, Dean, Univ. of NC School of Medicine 1979–94; Dir Center for Urban Epidemiology Studies, NY Acad of Medicine 1994–96; Hon. FRCP (E); Hon. DSc (Indiana 1980); Thomas Jefferson Award, Univ. of NC 1998. *Address:* University of North Carolina School of Medicine, Dept of Medicine CB. 7005, Chapel Hill, NC 27599-7000 (Office); 205 University Drive, Chapel Hill, NC 27516, USA . *Telephone:* (919) 966-4161 (Office).

BONELL, Carlos Antonio; British musician, teacher, guitarist and composer; b. 23 July 1949, London; s. of Carlos Bonell and Ana Bravo; m. Pinuccia Rossetti 1975; two s.; ed William Ellis School, Highgate and Royal Coll. of Music, under John Williams; solo début as solo guitarist, Wigmore Hall, London 1971; concerto début with Royal Philharmonic Orchestra 1975; American début, Avery Fisher Hall, New York 1978; concert appearances with all the prin. British orchestras; appearances with John Williams, Teresa Berganza (q.v.), Pinchas Zukerman 1975–; formed Carlos Bonell Ensemble 1983; Prof. Royal Coll. of Music 1972–, London Coll. of Music 1983–; Hon. ARCM. *Recordings include:* Guitar Music of Spain 1975, Guitar Music of the Baroque 1976, Showpieces 1981, Rodrigo Concerto 1981, Paganini Trios and Quartets 1983, Twentieth Century Music for Guitar 1987, Once Upon a Time, with Xer-Wai (violin) 1992, Walton Bagatelles and Anon in Love 1993, Britten Folksongs (with Philip Langridge) 1994, The Sea in Spring 1997, The Private Collection 1994, Kinkachoo I Love You (Millennium Guitar, The First 1000 Years) 2000. *Publications:* 20 First Pieces 1982, Tarrega: Fantasia on "La Traviata", 3 Spanish Folk Songs, Purcell: Music from the Fairy Queen, Fantasy for 3 Guitars 1995, Technique Builder 1997, Millennium Guitar, The First 1000 Years 2000. *Leisure interests:* reading, walking, snooker, films. *Address:* Bravo Music International, PO Box 19060, London, N7 0ZD; 5A Dalmeny Mansions, 77 Anson Road, London, N70AX, England (Home). *Fax:* (20) 7689-9964. *E-mail:* carlos@carlosbonell.com (Home). *Website:* www .carlosbonell.com (Home).

BONELLO DU PUIS, George, LLD, K.O.M.; Maltese politician and notary; b. 24 Jan. 1928; m. Iris Gauci Maistre; two s. one d.; ed St Catherine's High School, Sliema, the Lyceum and Univ. of Malta; practising notary 1952; MP 1971–96; mem. Nationalist Party, Spokesman on Finance, State Industry, Tourism, Trade and Industry; Minister of Finance 1987–92, for Economic Services 1992–95; fmr Chair. Parl. Standing Cttee on Foreign Affairs, EU Malta Jt Parl. Cttee; High Commr in UK 1999–; Companion of the Nat.Order of Merit. *Address:* Malta High Commission, 36–38 Piccadilly, London, W1V 0PQ, England; The Park, Antonio Nani Street, Ta'Xbiex, Malta. *Telephone:* (20) 7937-5535. *Fax:* (20) 7734-1831.

BONET, Pep; Spanish architect and designer; b. 19 Nov. 1941, Barcelona; m. Marta Monné 1964; three s.; ed High School of Architecture, Barcelona; f. Studio Per architectural practice, with Cristian Cirici, Lluis Clotet and Oscar Tusquets 1965; began producing furniture and Bldg components, co-f. BD Ediciones de Diseño 1972; taught at School of Architecture, Barcelona 1975–78, Washington School of Architecture, St Louis, Mo., USA 1981; Deltas ADI-FAD award 1967, 1976, 1986, 1990, 1991, Azulejo de Oro award 1970, Nat. Restoration award 1980, FAD award for architecture 1965, 1970, 1972, 1987, Architecture and Town Planning award 1987 for Triángulo de Oro Sports Centre, Madrid. *Major works include:* (Feria de Barcelona) Plaza Universo 1983–85, Rius i Taulet pavilion 1987, Iberia pavilion 1987, Lleida-Parallel pavilion 1989; Triángulo de Oro Sports Centre 1985, Canillejas civic centre 1985 (Madrid); Granollers Olympic sports centre, COOB-92. *Leisure interest:* playing jazz (tenor saxophone). *Address:* C/Pujades 63, 08005 Barcelona, Spain. *Telephone:* (93) 4855494. *Fax:* (93) 3091472.

BONETTI, Mattia; Swiss designer, decorator and artist; b. 2 May 1952, Lugano; s. of Giorgio Bonetti and Stella Frossard; m. Isabelle Forestier 1990; two d.; ed Centro Scolastico Industrie Artistiche, Lugano; decorated Bernard

Picasso's Boisgeloup Castle 1987, Christian Lacroix Showroom and Graphics 1987–88; designs for cafeteria, Schloss Regensburg Thurn und Taxis Museum, Germany 1990, Banque Bruxelles-Lambert, Geneva 1991, packaging for Nina Ricci Cosmetics 1992, 1994, Water Carafe design for Ricard 1995, designed tramway for city of Montpellier 1998; Hon. Citizen City of Villeurbanne; "Créateurs de l'Année 1991" (France), Chevalier, Ordre des Arts et des Lettres 1995. *Exhibitions include:* Musée des Arts Décoratifs, Bordeaux 1985, Galerie Neotu, Paris 1985–87, 1993, 1994, Furniture of the 20th Century, New York 1985, 1987, 1988, Mairie de Villeurbanne 1986, Vic. and Albert Museum, London 1988, 1994, Seibu, Tokyo, Japan, 1989, Galerie Wunderhaus, Munich 1990, Galerie Néotú, New York 1990, 1993, Galleria Ex-Ante, Rome 1990, Galleria Iannone, Milan 1992, Galerie Wohn Tendenz, Innsbruck 1993, Musée de Riom, France 1993, Galerie Naila de Monbrison, Paris 1993, Liberty, London 1993, Kulturring, Sundern 1994, Galerie Raab, Berlin 1994, Design Museum, Frankfurt 1994, La Monnaie de Paris 1995, 'Premises' group show, Guggenheim Museum, New York 1998, David Gill Gallery, London 1999; one-man show Centre Georges Pompidou, Paris 1997; 'Le Grand Hornu', retrospective one-man show Mons 2001–02. *Publications:* Mattia Bonetti and Elizabeth Garouste 1990, Garouste and Bonnetti 1996, 1998, Elizabeth Garouste and Mattia Bonetti 1981–2001. *Leisure interests:* swimming, photography. *Address:* 10 rue Rochebrune, 75011 Paris (Office); 1 rue Oberkampf, 75011 Paris, France (Home). *Telephone:* 1-48-05-61-21 (Office); 1-48-05-86-51 (Home). *Fax:* 1-48-05-61-29 (Office); 1-48-05-86-51 (Home). *E-mail:* bonettiforestier@aol.com (Home).

BONFIELD, Sir Peter (Leahy), Kt, CBE, FIEE, FRSA, FREng; British business executive; b. 3 June 1944; s. of George Bonfield and Patricia Bonfield; m. Josephine Houghton 1968; ed Hitchin Boys' Grammar School and Univ. of Loughborough; Div. Dir Texas Instruments Inc. Dallas, TX, USA 1966–81; Group Exec. Dir Worldwide Operations, ICL 1981–84, Man. Dir 1984, Chair. and CEO ICL PLC 1987–97, Deputy Chair. 1997–2000; Deputy Chief Exec. STC PLC 1987–90; Chair. and CEO British Telecommunications PLC 1996–2002; Dir BICC PLC 1992–96, AstraZeneca 1995– (Sr Dir 2002–), MCI Inc. 1996–98, Ericsson 2002–, Mentor Graphics Corpn 2002–; Vice-Pres. British Quality Foundation 1993–; mem. CS Coll. Advisory Council 1993–97, Salomon Smith Barney Int. Advisory Bd, European Round Table 1996–2002, EU–Japan Business Dialogue Round Table 1999–2002; Amb. for British Business; Liveryman, Information Technologists' Co. 1992; Fellow British Computer Soc. 1990, Chartered Inst. of Marketing 1990; Freeman, City of London 1990, Hon. Citizen, Dallas, TX; Commdr, Order of the Lion (Finland) 1995; Nat. Electronics Council Mountbatten Medal 1995, Inst. of Man. Gold Medal 1996; Dr hc (Open Univ.) 1997; Hon. DTech (Loughborough) 1988, (Brunel) 1997, (Nottingham) 1998, (Northumbria) 1999. *Leisure interests:* music, sailing, skiing. *Address:* PO Box 129, Shepperton, Middlesex, TW17 9WL, England.

BONGARD-LEVIN, Grigory Maximovich; Russian historian; b. 26 Aug. 1933, Moscow; s. of Maxim Bongard-Levin and Lussy Bongard-Levin; m. Irina Bongard-Levin (deceased) 1956; one s.; ed Moscow State Univ.; Jr, Sr researcher. head of div. Inst. of Oriental Studies USSR Acad. of Sciences 1956–87, chief researcher 1987–; Corresp. mem. USSR (now Russian) Acad. of Sciences 1987, mem. 1990; Ed.-in-Chief Vestnik Drevnei Istorii; mem. Nat. Cttee of History of Russia; head Comm. on Sanskrit Studies at Asscn of Oriental Studies; Hon. Fellow Royal Asiatic Soc., London 1997; Dr. hc Sarnath Tibetan Inst. 1991; Nehru Prize 1975, Gold Medal, Asiatic Soc. of Bengal 1979; USSR State Prize 1988, Int. Prize of St Mark, Venice 1990. *Publications:* works on culture and ethnogenesis of peoples of Asia, of old civilizations of Orient and W, including books Ancient India 1969, India of the Epoch of Mauryas 1974, Ancient Indian Civilization 1980, From India to Scythia 1983, India in Ancient Times, Indian Texts from Central Asia (2 Vols) 1985–90, Scythian Novel 1997. *Leisure interests:* paintings, literature, antique furniture. *Address:* Institute of Oriental Studies, Rozhdestvenka 12, 103777 Moscow (Office); 117334, Leninsky Prospekt 2, R. 1503, VDI, Moscow, Russia (Home). *Telephone:* (095) 938-52-28 (Office); (095) 245-46-96 (Home). *Fax:* (095) 938-19-12 (Office).

BONGO, Martin; Gabonese politician; b. 4 July 1940, Lekei; ed Ecole Normale de Mitzic; fmrly school Dir in Franceville, then Insp. for Primary Instruction for Upper-Ogooué Region; fmr Dir of Cabinet to the Vice-Pres.; Deputy Dir of Cabinet to the Pres. 1968–69; Commr-Gen. for Information April–Dec. 1969; Sec. of State to the Presidency, for Penitentiary Services 1969–70, for Nat. Educ. in charge of Special Missions 1970–72, Head of State's Personal Rep. 1972–73; Minister of Educ. and Scientific Research 1973–75, of Nat. Educ. 1975–76, of Foreign Affairs and Co-operation 1976–81, of State for Foreign Affairs and Co-operation 1981–89; Commdr Order of the Equatorial Star, Grand Officer, Nat. Order of Merit (Mauritania), Grand Officer, Order of Merit (Italy), Commdr Ordre nat. du Mérite. *Address:* c/o Ministère des Affaires Etrangères et de la Coopération, Libreville, Gabon.

BONGO, El Hadj Omar (Albert-Bernard); Gabonese politician; b. 30 Dec. 1935, Lewai, Franceville; m.; three c.; ed primary school at Bacongo (Congo–Brazzaville) and technical coll., Brazzaville; Civil Servant; served Air Force 1958–60; entered Ministry of Foreign Affairs 1960; Dir of Private Office of Pres. Léon Mba 1962, in charge of Information 1963–64, Nat. Defence 1964–65; Minister-Del. to Presidency in charge of Nat. Defence and Co-ordination, Information and Tourism 1965–66; Vice-Pres. of Govt, in charge of Co-ordination, Nat. Defence Planning, Information and Tourism 1966–67; Vice-Pres. of Gabon March–Nov. 1967, Pres. 1967–, Minister of Defence

1967–81, of Information 1967–80, of Planning 1967–77, Prime Minister 1967–75, Minister of the Interior 1967–70, of Devt 1970–77, of Women's Affairs 1976–77 and numerous other portfolios; Pres. UDEAC 1981; Founder and Sec.-Gen. Parti Démocratique Gabonais 1968; High Chancellor, Ordre Nat. de l'Etoile Equatoriale; decorations from the Ivory Coast, Niger, Chad, Cameroon, Central African Republic, Mauritius, Togo, Taiwan, Zaire, France, UK and Guinea. *Address:* Présidence de la République, Boîte Postale 546, Libreville, Gabon.

BONHAM CARTER, Helena; British actress; b. 26 May 1966; d. of Hon. Raymond Bonham Carter and Elena Bonham Carter; (great granddaughter of British Prime Minister Lord Asquith). *Films include:* Lady Jane, A Room with a View, Maurice, Francesco, The Mask, Getting it Right, Hamlet, Where Angels Fear to Tread, Howard's End 1991, A Dark Adapted Eye (TV) 1994, Mary Shelley's Frankenstein 1994, The Glace Bay Miners' Museum 1994, A Little Loving 1995, Mighty Aphrodite 1995, Twelfth Night 1996, Margaret's Museum 1996, Parti Chinois 1996, The Theory of Flight 1997, Keep the Aspidistra Flying 1997, The Wings of the Dove 1998, The Revengers' Comedies 1998, Women Talking Dirty 1999, Fight Club 1999, Until Human Voices Wake Us 2000, Planet of the Apes 2001, The Heart of Me 2002, Novocaine 2002, The Heart of Me 2003, Till Human Voices Wake Us 2003. *Plays include:* The Barber of Seville 1992, Trelawny of the "Wells" 1992. *Television appearances include:* A Pattern of Roses, Miami Vice, A Hazard of Hearts, The Vision, Arms and the Man, Beatrix Potter. *Address:* c/o Conway van Gelder Limited, 18/21 Jermyn Street, London, SW1Y 6HP, England. *Telephone:* (20) 7287-0077.

BONIN, Bernard, D. EN SC.(ECON.), FRSC; Canadian economist; b. 29 Sept. 1936, Joliette; s. of Georges Bonin and Thérèse Racette; m. Andrée Gregoire 1960; one s. one d.; ed Ecole des Hautes Etudes Commerciales, Montreal and Univ. of Paris; Prof. of Econs Ecole des Hautes Etudes Commerciales, Montreal 1962–74; Asst Deputy Minister for Immigration, Govt of Québec 1974–77, for Intergovernmental Affairs 1977–81; Prof. of Econs, Ecole Nat. d'Admin. Publique, Montreal 1979–88; Deputy Gov. Bank of Canada 1988–94, Sr Deputy Gov. 1994–99; currently Pres. Asscn des Économistes Québécois, Université de Montréal. *Publications:* L'investissement étranger à long terme au Canada 1967, A propos de l'association économique Canada-Québec 1980, L'entreprise multinationale et l'état 1984, Innovation industrielle et analyse économique 1988. *Leisure interests:* music, reading, sport. *Address:* Association des Économistes Québécois, C.P. 6128, succursale Centre-Ville, Montréal, Quebec, H3C 3J7, Canada (Office). *Telephone:* (514) 342–7537. *Fax:* (514) 342–3967. *E-mail:* national@asdeq.org. *Website:* www.asdeq.org.

BONINGTON, Sir Christian John Storey, CBE; British mountaineer, writer and photographer; b. 6 Aug. 1934; s. of the late Charles Bonington and Helen Anne (née Storey) Bonington; m. Muriel Wendy Marchant 1962; three s. (one s. deceased); ed Univ. Coll. School and RMA; Royal Tank Regt 1956–59; Instructor Army Outward Bound School 1959–61; Man. Trainee Unilever 1961–62; writer and photographer 1962–; Vice-Pres. Army Mountaineering Asscn 1980–; Pres. LEPRA 1985–, British Orienteering Fed. 1986–, British Mountaineering Council 1988–91 (Vice-Pres. 1976–79, 1985–88), Council for Nat. Parks 1992–2000, The Alpine Club 1995–99, Chair. (non-exec.) Berghaus 1998–; numerous climbs include Annapurna South Face Expedition 1970, British Everest Expedition 1972, Brammah, Himalayas 1973, Changabang, Himalayas 1974, British Everest Expedition (first ascent, SW Face) 1975, Mount Vinson, Antarctica 1983, Panch chuli II, Himalayas (first ascent, W Ridge) 1992, Maslin, Greenland (first ascent) 1993, Rangrik Rang, India (first ascent) 1994, Drangnag-Ri, Nepal (first ascent) 1995, Danga II 2000; reached Everest summit 1985; motivational/after-dinner speaker; Hon. Fellow UMIST, Lancs. Polytechnic; Hon. MA (Salford); Hon. DSc (Sheffield) 1976, (Lancaster) 1983; Hon. DCL (Northumbria) 1996; Hon. DUniv (Sheffield Hallam) 1998; Hon. DLitt (Bradford) 2002; Founders Medal (Royal Geographical Soc.) 1971, Lawrence of Arabia Medal 1986, Livingstone Medal 1991; David Livingstone Medal Royal Scottish Geographical Soc. 1991. *Publications include:* I Chose to Climb (autobiog.) 1966, The Next Horizon (autobiog.) 1973, Quest for Adventure 1981, The Everest Years 1986, Mountaineer 1989, The Climbers 1992, Sea, Ice and Rock (jtly) 1992, Tibet's Secret Mountain (jtly) 1999, Chris Bonington's Everest 2002. *Leisure interests:* mountaineering, orienteering. *Address:* Badger Hill, Hesket Newmarket, Wigton, Cumbria, CA7 8LA, England. *Telephone:* (16974) 78286. *Fax:* (16974) 78238. *E-mail:* chris@bonington.com (Home). *Website:* www.bonington.com (Office).

BONINO, Emma, PH.D; Italian politician; b. 9 March 1948, Bra, Turin; ed Univ. of Milan; mem. Chamber of Deputies 1976–1983, re-elected 1986, 1992, 1994; Pres. Parl. Group, Radical Party 1981; mem. European Parl. 1979–; Founder, Centro Informazione Sterilizzazione e Aborto 1975; Pres. Transnat. Radical Party 1991–93, Sec. 1993–94; EC Commr for Consumer Policy, EC Humanitarian Office and Fisheries 1995–99; Cand. in Presidential elections 1999; presented own list in general elections 2001; Gran Cruz de la Orden de Mayo (Argentina) 1996, Premio Principe de Asturias (Spain) 1998. *Leisure interests:* sailing, diving. *Address:* European Parliament, 60 rue Wiertz, 1047 Brussels, Belgium (Office). *Telephone:* (332) 284-52-88 (Office). *Fax:* (332) 284-92-88 (Office). *E-mail:* ebonino@visto.com (Office). *Website:* www .radicalparty.org (Office).

BONNAIRE, Sandrine; French film actress; b. 31 May 1967, Gannat, Auvergne; one d.; Film debut in La Boum 1980; Venice Film Festival award

1995, Grand prix nat. du cinéma, Ministry of Culture 1987. *Films include:* A Nos Amours 1983, Vagabond 1985, Monsieur Hire 1989, Joan of Arc 1992, La Cérémonie 1995, Judgment in Stone, Circle of Passion 1996, Secret Défense 1998, The Colour of Lies 1999, East–West 2000, Mademoiselle 2001. *Address:* c/o Intertalent, 4 rue Clément Marot, 75008 Paris, France (Office).

BONNEFOY, Yves Jean, LÈsL; French writer; b. 24 June 1923, Tours; s. of Elie Bonnefoy and Hélène Maury; m. Lucille Vines 1968; one d.; ed Lycée Descartes, Tours, Faculté des Sciences, Poitiers and Faculté des Lettres, Paris; Prof. Collège de France 1981; contrib. to Mercure de France, Critique, Encounter, L'Ephémère, La Nouvelle Revue Française etc.; has travelled in Europe, Asia and N America; lectures or seminars at Brandeis, Johns Hopkins, Princeton, Williams Coll., Calif., Geneva, Nice, Yale and other univs.; Commdr des Arts et des Lettres; Hon. DHumLitt (American Coll., Paris, Univ. of Chicago, Univ. of Neuchâtel, Trinity Coll., Dublin, Rome, Edin.); Prix Montaigne 1980, Grand Prix de poésie (Acad. Française) 1981, Prix Florence Gould 1987, Grand Prix national 1993, Prix de la Fondation Cino-del-Duca 1995, Prix Balzan 1995, Prix Prince Louis de Polignac 1998, American Acad. of Arts and Letters Award, and numerous other prizes. *Publications:* poems: Du mouvement et de l'immobilité de Douve 1953 (English 1968), Hier régnant désert 1958, Pierre écrite 1964 (English 1976), Selected Poems 1968, Dans le leurre du seuil 1975, Poèmes (1947–1975) 1978, Ce qui fut sans lumière 1987, Entretiens sur la Poesie 1990, Début et fin de la neige 1991, Les planches courbes 2001; essays: L'Improbable 1959, Arthur Rimbaud 1961 (English trans. 1973), Un rêve fait à Mantoue 1967, Le nuage rouge 1977, Rue traversière 1977; on art: Peintures murales de la France Gothique 1954, Miró 1963, Rome 1630 1969, L'Arrière-Pays 1972, Entretiens sur la poésie 1981, La Présence et l'Image 1983, Récits en rêve 1987, La Vérité de Parole 1988, Alberto Giacometti 1991, La vie errante 1993, Remarques sur le dessin 1993, Dessin, couleur et lumière 1995, Théâtre et poésie: Shakespeare et Yeats, l'Encore aveugle 1998, Zao-Wou-ki (jtly) 1998, Lieux et destins de l'image 1999, La Communauté des traducteurs 2000, Baudelaire: Le Tentation de l'oubli 2000, Keats et Léopardi 2000, Sous l'Horizon du Langage 2001, Remarques sur le regard 2001, Breton à l'avant de soi 2001, Poésie et architecture 2001, L'Enseignement de Léopardi 2001; Co-Ed. L'Ephémère, trans. of Shakespeare, W. B. Yeats, Keats, Léopardi. *Address:* Collège de France, 11 place Marcelin Berthelot, 75005 Paris, France.

BONNEMAIN, François; French broadcasting executive and fmr journalist; b. 9 Oct 1942; s. of Georges Bonnemain and Renée Charpentier; ed Centre de formation des journalistes de Paris; with Associated Press (AP), Agence France-Presse (AFP), then France-Soir; joined TF 1 TV channel, in charge of political news 1972; Ed. in Chief TF 1 1977; apptd Ed. FR 3 TV channel 1981; Dir News and Current Affairs, France-Inter 1982; Political Ed. Hebdo (weekly magazine); Tech. Adviser to Prime Minister (Jacques Chirac, q.v.) on Audiovisual Information 1986–88, to Mayor of Paris (Chirac) 1988–94; Man. Dir Radio-Télévision française d'outre-mer (RFO) 1994–95; mem. Conseil Supérieur de l'audiovisuel (CSA) 1996–99; Dir Chaîne Parl.-Sénat 2000–; Dir Human Resources, France Télévision 2000–. *Leisure interest:* fine cuisine. *Address:* France Télévision, 7 esplanade Henri de France, 75907 Paris Cedex 15 (Office); Chaîne Parlementaire-Sénat, 15 rue de Vaugirard, 75291 Paris Cedex 06 (Home).

BONNER, Elena Georgievna; Russian human rights activist and writer; b. 25 Feb. 1923, Moscow; m. Andrei Sakharov 1970 (deceased); one s. one d; ed 1st Leningrad Medical Inst.; active as nurse 1941–45; partially blinded; Lt 1945; doctor 1953–83; founder of Moscow group to monitor observation of 1975 Helsinki accords; regular visitor to Sakharov during latter's exile in Gorky 1980–84; sentenced to five years' exile 1984, released 1986; political activist after husband's death; Chair. Comm. for perpetuation of Andrei Sakharov's memory. *Publications:* Alone Together 1986 (memoirs), P.S. (post scriptum) 1991. *Address:* A. D. Sakharova Museum, Zemlyanoy val 57, Bldg 6, 107120 Moscow, Russia. *Telephone:* (095) 923-41-15.

BONNER, Gerald, MA, FSA; British university teacher (retd); b. 18 June 1926, London; s. of Frederick J. Bonner and Constance E. Hatch; m. Priscilla J. Hodgson 1967; one s. one d.; ed The Stationers' Co.'s School, London and Wadham Coll. Oxford; mil. service 1944–48; Asst Keeper, Dept of Manuscripts, British Museum 1953–64; Lecturer in Theology, Univ. of Durham 1964, promoted to personal Readership 1969, Reader Emer. 1989–; Convener and Sec. Bedan Conf. Durham 1973; Distinguished Prof. of Early Christian Studies, Catholic Univ. of America 1991–94; delivered Cathedral Lecture, Durham 1970, Augustine Lecture, Villanova Univ. Pa, 1970, Otts Lectures, Davidson Coll. NC 1992; Visiting Prof. in Augustinian Studies, Villanova Univ. Pa 1999; Johannes Quasten Medal 1994. *Publications:* The Warfare of Christ 1962, St Augustine of Hippo: Life and Controversies 1963, Famulus Christi: Essays in Commemoration of the Thirteenth Centenary of the Venerable Bede (ed.) 1976, God's Decree and Man's Destiny 1987, St Cuthbert, His Cult and His Community (ed. with D. Rollason and C. Stancliffe) 1989, Church and Faith in the Patristic Tradition: Augustine, Pelagianism and Early Christian Northumbria 1996; articles in the Augustinus-Lexikon (Basle) and other learned journals. *Leisure interests:* reading, antiquarianism, (moderate) wine-drinking and any sort of history. *Address:* 7 Victoria Terrace, Durham, DH1 4RW, England. *Telephone:* (191) 386-3407.

BONNER, John Tyler, PhD, DSc; American biologist; b. 12 May 1920, New York; s. of Paul Hyde Bonner and Lilly Marguerite Stehli; m. Ruth Ann Graham 1942; three s. one d.; ed Harvard Univ.; U.S. Air Corps 1942–46; Asst

Prof., then Prof., Princeton Univ., NJ 1947–58, George M. Moffett Prof. 1966–90, Chair. Dept of Biology 1965–77, 1983–84, 1987–88, Prof. Emer. June 1990–; Bernard Visiting Prof., Williams Coll. 1989; Raman Visiting Prof., Indian Acad. of Sciences 1990; Sheldon Travelling Fellow, Panama, Cuba 1941; Rockefeller Travelling Fellow, Paris 1953; Guggenheim Fellow, Edin. 1958, 1971–72; Nat. Science Foundation Sr Postdoctoral Fellow, Cambridge, England 1963; Commonwealth Foundation Book Fund Fellow, Edin. 1971 and 1984–85; Josiah Macy Jr Foundation Book Fund Fellow, Edin. 1978; Fellow American Acad. of Arts and Sciences, AAAS; mem. American Philosophical Soc., NAS; mem. Oxford Surveys in Evolutionary Biology 1982–93; fmr mem. Editorial Bd American Naturalist, American Scientist and other Publs; Hon. Fellow Indian Acad. of Sciences. *Television:* Professor Bonner and the Slime Moulds (BBC Horizon programme) 1984. *Publications:* Morphogenesis: An Essay on Development 1952, Cells and Societies 1955, The Evolution of Development 1958, The Cellular Slime Molds 1959, The Ideas of Biology 1962 (several edns. in trans.), Size and Cycle 1965, The Scale of Nature 1969, On Development: The Biology of Form 1974, The Evolution of Culture in Animals 1980 (several edns. in trans.), On Size and Life 1983, The Evolution of Complexity 1988, Life Cycles 1993, Sixty Years of Biology: Essays on Evolution and Development 1996, First Signals: The Evolution of Multicellular Development 2000, Lives of a Biologist 2002. Ed. abridged Edn of Growth and Form (D'Arcy Thompson) 1961. *Leisure interests:* fishing, walking. *Address:* Department of Ecology and Evolutionary Biology, Guyot Hall, Princeton University, Princeton, NJ 08544 (Office); 52A Patton Avenue, Princeton, NJ 08540, USA (Home). *Telephone:* (609) 258-3841 (Office); (609) 924-1255 (Home).

BONNER, Paul Max, OBE; British television executive; b. 30 Nov. 1934, Banstead, Surrey; s. of Frank and Jill Bonner; m. Jenifer Hubbard 1956; two s. one d.; ed Felsted School; with Longmans Green & Co., Publrs. 1952; trainee reporter, Southend Standard 1953; Nat. Service 1953–55; Asst Press Officer, E.K. Cole Ltd 1955; freelance work for Evening Standard 1955; Trainee Studio Asst, BBC, Bristol 1955–56, Studio Man. 1956–58, Acting Asst Producer, Talks Dept, West Region 1958–59, Production Asst, Talks Dept, TV 1961–65, Sr Producer, Travel and Features Programmes 1965–74, Ed. BBC Community Programmes 1974–77, Special Asst to Controller BBC2 1977, Chair. Small Integrated Multi-Role Production Unit Study Group 1977, Head of Science and Features Dept, TV 1978–81; Channel Controller, Channel Four TV Co. Ltd 1981–83, Controller of Programmes and Exec. Dir 1983–87; Dir of Programme Planning Secr. ITV Asscn 1987–92, Dir ITV Network Centre Secr. 1993–94; Dir House of Commons Broadcasting Unit Ltd 1989–94; Chair. Edin. TV Festival 1979; a Man., Royal Inst. 1982–85; Gov. of Nat. Film and TV School 1981–88; Bd mem., Broadcasting Support Services 1981–93; Chair. Media Group, Cttee on Public Understanding of Science 1981–93; Fellow Royal TV Soc. *Television documentaries include:* Climb up to Hell 1967, The Search for the Real Che Guevara 1971, Who Sank the Lusitania? 1972. *Publications:* The Third Age of Broadcasting 1983, Ind. TV in Britain (Vol. 5: ITV and IBA 1981–92) 1998, (Vol. 6: C4, TV-am, Cable & Satellite 1981–92) 2002. *Leisure interests:* photography, sailing, walking. *Address:* 5 North View, Wimbledon Common, London, SW19 4UJ, England. *Telephone:* (20) 8947-6635. *Fax:* (20) 8947-6635.

BONNET, Christian, DenD; French politician and industrialist; b. 14 June 1921, Paris; s. of Pierre Bonnet and Suzanne Delebecque; m. Christiane Mertian 1943 (died 1999); five c. (one s. deceased); ed Univ. of Paris and Ecole des sciences politiques; Pres. Les Grandes Marques de la conserve 1952–61, Del. Conseil supérieur de la conserve; MRP Deputy for Morbihan 1956–58; Deputy for the second constituency of Morbihan 1956–83; Gen. Councillor, Belle-Ile 1958, 1964, 1970, 1976, 1982; Mayor of Carnac 1964–; fmr Sec.-Gen. Républicains Indépendants; Chair. Cttee on the Merchant Marine budget; Pres. Supervisory Council, Caisse des dépots et consignations; Sec. of State for Supply, Housing and Territorial Devt 1972–74; Minister of Agric. 1974–77, of the Interior 1977–81; Senator for Morbihan 1983. *Address:* Palais du Luxembourg, 75291 Paris Cedex 06 (Office); 56340 Carnac, France (Home).

BONNEY, Barbara; American soprano opera singer; b. 14 April 1956, Montclair, NJ; d. of Alfred Bonney III and Janet Gates; m. 1st Håkan Hagegård 1989; m. 2nd Maurice Whittaker; ed Univ. of New Hampshire and Mozarteum, Salzburg; maj. appearances include: Der Rosenkavalier, Covent Garden 1984, Metropolitan Opera, New York 1990, Die Zauberflöte, La Scala 1985, Falstaff, Metropolitan Opera 1990, The Marriage of Figaro, Covent Garden 1995, Zurich Opera, Metropolitan Opera 1998, 1999, Les Boréades, Salzburg Festival 1999, Idomeneo, San Francisco 1999; noted especially for Mozart and Strauss interpretations; appears regularly as recitalist accompanied by Geoffrey Parsons. *Recordings include:* works by Schönberg, Haydn, R. Strauss, Donizetti, Mozart, Mendelssohn, Wolf etc. *Leisure interests:* textiles, interior decorating, calligraphy. *Address:* c/o IMG, 3 Burlington Lane, Chiswick, London, W4 2TH, England. *Telephone:* (20) 8233-5800. *Fax:* (20) 8233-5801.

BONNICI, Carmelo Mifsud (see Mifsud Bonnici, Carmelo).

BONNICI, Josef, MA, PH.D(ECON.); Maltese economist and politician; b. 15 April 1953; m. Rita Oliva; two c.; ed Univ. of Malta and Simon Fraser Univ., Canada; Sr Lecturer in Econs, Deakin Univ., Australia; Prof. of Econ., Univ. of Malta 1988; Econ. Adviser to Prime Minister 1988–92; appointed adviser to Council of Europe in Co-ordinated Social Research Programme 1992; mem. Parl. 1992–; Parl. Sec. Ministry of Finance 1993–95; Minister of Econ.

Services 1995–96; Shadow Minister and Opposition Spokesman for Econ. Devt 1996–98; Minister for Econ. Services 1998–; mem. Del. to Org. for Security and Co-operation in Europe, to Council of Europe, Jt Malta EU Parl. Cttee; Nationalist Party; Dr. hc (Rikkyo) 1996. *Publications:* books and articles on Econs in Malta and in professional econ. journals. *Address:* Ministry for Economic Services, Auberge d'Aragon, Valletta CMR 02, Malta. *Telephone:* 249198. *Fax:* 250955.

BONNICI, Ugo Mifsud (see Mifsud Bonnici, Ugo).

BONO, (Paul Hewson); Irish rock singer; b. (Paul Hewson), 10 May 1960; s. of Bobby Hewson and Iris Hewson; m. Alison Stewart 1982; two d.; ed Mount Temple School; formed band with friends, Dublin 1976, named U2 1978; numerous nat. and int. tours including Drop The Debt World Tour 2001; numerous prizes and awards for recordings and videos including Best Int. Group and Award for Outstanding Contrib. to the Music Industry, Brit Awards 2001. *Recordings include:* Boy 1980, October 1981, War 1983, Under a Blood Red Sky 1983, The Unforgettable Fire, The Joshua Tree 1987, Desire 1988, Rattle and Hum 1988, When Love Comes to Town 1989, Achtung Baby 1991, The Fly 1991, Stay 1993, Zooropa 1993, Pop 1997, All That You Can't Leave Behind 2000; film Rattle and Hum 1988. *Address:* c/o Regine Moylett Publicity, 9 Ivebury Court, 325 Latimer Road, London, W10 6RA, England. *Telephone:* (20) 8969-2600. *Fax:* (20) 7221-8532.

BONYNGE, Richard, AO, CBE; Australian conductor; b. 29 Sept. 1930, Sydney; s. of C. A. Bonynge; m. Dame Joan Sutherland 1954; one s.; ed NSW Conservatorium of Music, Royal Coll. of Music; trained as a pianist; début as conductor with Santa Cecilia Orchestra, Rome 1962; conducted first opera Faust, Vancouver 1963; Musical Dir Sutherland/Williamson Grand Opera Co., Australia 1965; Artistic Dir Vancouver Opera 1974–77; Musical Dir Australian Opera 1976–86; has conducted La Sonnambula, La Traviata, Faust, Eugene Onegin, L'Elisir d'amore, Orfeo, Semiramide, Giulio Cesare, Lucia di Lammermoor, Norma, Orfeo and The Tales of Hoffmann; has revived many operas not in the repertoire including Les Huguenots, La Fille du Régiment, Maria Stuarda, Lucrezia Borgia and Thérèse; Commdr des Arts et Lettres 1989. *Videos include:* Les Huguenots, La Fille du Régiment, The Merry Widow, Norma, Die Fledermans and The Magic Flute. *Major recordings include:* Alcina, La Sonnambula, Norma, Beatrice di Tenda, I Puritani, Faust, Semiramide, Lakmé, La Fille du Régiment, Messiah, Don Giovanni, Les Huguenots, L'Elisir d'amore, Lucia di Lammermoor, Rigoletto, The Tales of Hoffmann, Thérèse, Le Toréador, The Land of Smiles and Giuditta, numerous orchestral works, ballet including Giselle, Coppélia, Sylvia, The Nutcracker, Sleeping Beauty, Swan Lake. *Publication:* The Joan Sutherland Album (with Dame Joan Sutherland) 1986. *Address:* c/o Ingpen and Williams, 26 Wadham Road, London, SW15 2LR, England.

BOOLELL, Sir Satcam, Kt, QC, LLB; Mauritian politician; b. 11 Sept. 1920, New Grove; s. of Sahadewoo Boolell and Cossilah Choony; m. 1st Premila K. Inderjeet (died 1986); two s. one d.; m. 2nd Myrtha Poblete; ed LSE, UK; called to Bar (Lincoln's Inn) 1952; mem. Legis. Council of Moks-Flacq (Ind.) 1953; joined Labour Party 1955; Minister of Agric. and Natural Resources 1959–67, 1968–82, of Educ. 1967–68, of Econ. Planning and Devt 1984; Pres. Mauritius Labour Party 1993–92; Deputy Prime Minister, Attorney-Gen., Minister of Justice and of External Affairs and Emigration 1986–87, 1987–90; High Commr in UK 1996–2000 (also Accred to Sweden, Norway, Denmark, Finland and Holy See); now retd; Commdr Légion d'honneur 1990, Grand Officer Order of the Star and Key of the Indian Ocean 1999, Cavalier Grand Cross of the Order of Saint Gregory the Great 1999; Hon. DCL (Univ. of Mauritius) 1985; Hon. LLD (South Bank) 2001. *Publications:* Untold Stories 1996, Reminiscences of Travels Abroad 1998, Mauritius through the Looking Glass (short stories) 2000. *Leisure interests:* reading travel literature, walking in the countryside, numismatics. *Address:* 4 Bis, Bancilhon Street, Port Louis, Mauritius (Home). *Telephone:* (20) 7581-0294 (Office). *Fax:* (20) 7823-8437 (Office).

BOON, David Clarence, MBE; Australian cricketer; b. 29 Dec. 1960, Launceston; s. of Clarence Leonard Boon and Lesley Mary Boon; m. Philippa Louise Wright 1983; one s. two d.; ed Launceston Church Grammar School; right-hand batsman; teams: Tasmania 1978–79 to 1998–99 (Capt. 1992–93 to 1998–99), Durham, England (Capt.) 1997–99, for Australia played 107 Test matches 1984–96, scoring 7,422 runs (average 43.6) including 21 hundreds and holding 99 catches; toured England 1985, 1989 and 1993; scored more than 23,000 first-class runs (68 hundreds); 181 limited-overs internationals; Marketing Man. Trust Bank Australia 1991–; Marketing and Special Events Co-ordinator 1999; Australian selector 2000–; Patron Road Trauma Support Group, World Vision; Int. Cricketer of the Year 1987–88, Wisden Cricketer of the Year 1994. *Publications:* In the Firing Line (with A. Mark Thomas), Under the Southern Cross (autobiog.) 1996. *Leisure interests:* gardening, golf, music. *Address:* Tasmanian Cricket Association, Bellerive Oval, Bellerive, Tasmania 7018; c/o Australian Cricket Board, 90 Jollimont Street, Vic. 3002, Australia; c/o Durham County Cricket Club, County Ground, Riverside, Chester-le-Street, Co. Durham, DH3 3QR, England.

BOONSITHI CHOKWATANA; Thai business executive; Chair. Saha Group (consumer goods conglomerate). *Address:* Saha Group, 2156 New Petchburi Road, Bangkapi, Huay Kwang, Bangkok 10320, Thailand (Office). *Website:* www.sahagroup.thailand.com (Office).

BOORMAN, John, CBE; British film director, producer and screenwriter; b. 18 Jan. 1933; s. of George Boorman and Ivy (Chapman) Boorman; m. 1st Christel Kruse 1956; one s. three d.; m. 2nd Isabella Weibrecht 1994; one s. two d.; ed Salesian Coll., Chertsey; Broadcaster and critic, BBC Radio, also contributor to Manchester Guardian and magazines 1950–54; army service 1951–53; Film Editor, ITN London 1955–58; Dir and Producer Southern TV 1958–60; Head of Documentaries, Bristol, BBC TV; left BBC to work as film director; Chair. Nat. Film Studios of Ireland 1975–85; Gov. British Film Inst. 1983–94, co-f. Merlin Films Group 1989; Best Director Prize, Cannes Festival 1970, 1998, many film awards; Chevalier de l'Ordre des Arts et Lettres 1985. *Television:* founded magazine Day by Day, Dir Citizen 1963, The Newcomers 1960–64. *Films:* Catch us if you Can 1965, Point Blank 1967, Hell in the Pacific 1968, Leo the Last 1969, Deliverance 1970, Zardoz 1973, The Heretic 1976, Excalibur 1981, The Emerald Forest 1985, Hope and Glory 1987 (Golden Globe Award 1988), Where the Heart Is 1989, I Dreamt I Woke Up 1991, Beyond Rangoon 1994, Two Nudes Bathing 1995, The General 1998, The Tailor of Panama 2001. *Publications:* The Legend of Zardoz 1973 (novel), Money into Light 1985, Hope and Glory 1987, Projections 1 1992, Projections 2 1993, Projections 3 1994, Projections $4^{1}/_{2}$ (Co.-ed.) 1995, Projections 5 1996, Projections 6 1997, Projections 7 1997, Projections 8 1998; co-ed. A Year in Film 1993. *Leisure interests:* hacking the Wicklow Hills, losing gracefully at tennis, planting trees. *Address:* Merlin Films Group, 16 Upper Pembroke Street, Dublin 2, Ireland. *Telephone:* (1) 6764373. *Fax:* (1) 6764368. *E-mail:* info@merlinfilms.com. *Website:* www.merlinfilms.com.

BOORSTIN, Daniel J., MA, LLD; American historian, author and administrator; b. 1 Oct. 1914, Atlanta, Ga; s. of late Samuel Boorstin and Dora Olsan; m. Ruth Carolyn Frankel 1941; three s.; ed Harvard Coll., Balliol Coll., Oxford, Cambridge and Yale Univs.; Harvard Coll. and Harvard Law School 1938–42; Office of Lend-Lease Admin., Washington 1942; Asst Prof., Swarthmore Coll. 1942–44; Prof. of American History and Preston and Sterling Morton Distinguished Service Prof. of History, Univ. of Chicago 1944–69; Prof. American History, Univ. of Paris 1961–62; Pitt Prof. American History and Institutions and Fellow, Trinity Coll. Cambridge 1964–65; Dir Nat. Museum of History and Tech. 1969–73; mem. Comm. on Critical Choices for Americans 1973–; Shelby and Kathryn Cullom Davis Lecturer, Graduate Inst. of Int. Studies, Geneva 1973–74; Senior Historian Smithsonian Inst., Washington, DC 1973–75; The Librarian of Congress 1975–87, Librarian Emer. 1987–; mem. Bd Trustees Colonial Williamsburg, Bd Dirs. Thomas Gilcrease Museum, Comm. on Critical Choices for Americans, Bd Eds. Encyclopedia Britannica; mem. task force on exploration NASA 1989–91, Cafritz Foundation Bd of Dirs. 1991; numerous hon. degrees; Pulitzer Prize for History 1974 and several other prizes; Chevalier Légion d'honneur 1984, Grand Officer of the Order of Prince Henry the Navigator (Portugal) 1985, Japanese Order of the Sacred Treasure, (First Class) 1986, Watson-Davis Prize of the History of Science (Soc. for Discoverers) 1986, Charles Frankel Prize of the Nat. Endowment for the Humanities 1989, Nat. Book Award Medal for Distinguished Contribution to American Letters 1989. *Publications include:* The Mysterious Science of the Law 1941, Delaware Cases 1792–1830 (3 Vols) 1943, The Lost World of Thomas Jefferson 1948, The Genius of American Politics 1953, The Americans: The Colonial Experience 1958, America and the Image of Europe 1960, The Image or What Happened to the American Dream 1962, The Americans: The National Experience 1965, The Landmark History of the American People (2 Vols) 1968, 1970, The Decline of Radicalism 1969, The Sociology of the Absurd 1970, The Americans: The Democratic Experience 1973, Democracy and its Discontents 1974, The Exploring Spirit 1976, The Republic of Technology 1978, A History of the United States (with Brooks Kelley) 1980, The Discoverers 1983, Hidden History 1987, The Creators 1992, Cleopatra's Nose 1994, The Daniel J. Boorstin Reader 1995; Ed.: An American Primer 1966, American Civilization 1972, The Seekers 1998. *Leisure interests:* gardening, bird watching, hiking. *Address:* Library of Congress, Washington, DC 20540 (Office); 3541 Ordway Street, NW, Washington, DC 20016, USA (Home). *Telephone:* (202) 707-1500 (Office); (202) 966-1853 (Home).

BOOS, Georgy Valentinovich, CandTechSc; Russian politician; b. 22 Jan. 1963, Moscow; m.; one d.; ed Moscow Energy Inst.; Sr engineer, All-Union Research Inst. of Light Tech., also teacher of math., secondary school 1986–91; Founder, Dir-Gen., then Pres., Svetoservis Co. 1991–96; mem. State Duma 1996–98; Head, State Taxation Service of Russian Fed. Sept.–Dec. 1998; Minister of Revenue Dec. 1998–May 1999; Head, pre-election staff "Otechestvo-Vsya Rossiya" Movt; mem. State Duma 1999–, Deputy Chair. 2000; joined Yedinstvo and Otechestvo Union 2000–; Pres., Nat. Soc. of Light Tech.; designer of architectural illumination of Moscow 1996; State Prize 1996. *Address:* State Duma, Okhotny Ryad 1, 103265, Moscow, Russia. *Telephone:* (095) 292-62-40 (Office). *Fax:* (095) 292-80-07 (Office).

BOOTH, Cherie, QC, LLD, FRSA; British barrister; b. 23 Sept. 1954, Bury, Lancs.; d. of Anthony Booth and Gale Booth (née Smith); m. Anthony Charles Lynton Blair (Tony Blair, q.v.); three s. one d.; ed Seafield Grammar School, Crosby, Liverpool, LSE; called to Bar (Lincoln's Inn) 1976, Bencher 1999; pupillage with Alexander Irvine (now Lord Irvine of Lairg) 1976–77; Tenant New Court Chambers 1977–91, 4/5 Gray's Inn Square, London 1991–2000, Matrix Chambers 2000–; appointed QC April 1995; Asst Recorder 1996–99, Recorder 1999–; Bencher Lincoln's Inn 1999; Hon. Bencher King's Inn, Dublin 2002; Gov. London School of Econs 1998–; Fellow John Moores Univ., Liverpool (Chancellor 1998–); Patron Sargent Cancer Care for Children 1998–, Breast Cancer Care 1997–, SHADO (Liverpool) 1998–, Islington Music Centre 1999–; Hon. DUniv (Open) 1999, Hon. LLD (Westminster). *Leisure interests:* reading, working out, the arts. *Address:* Matrix Chambers, Griffin Building, Gray's Inn, London, WC1R 5LN (Office); 10 Downing Street, London, SW1A 2AA England. *Telephone:* (20) 7404-3447 (Office); (20) 7980-4433 (Home). *Fax:* (20) 7404-3448 (Office). *E-mail:* cheriebooth@matrixlaw.co .uk (Office). *Website:* www.matrixlaw.co.uk (Office).

BOOTH, Chris; New Zealand sculptor; b. 30 Dec. 1948, Kerikeri, Bay of Islands; m.; one s. one d.; ed Ilam School of Fine Arts, Univ. of Canterbury, Christchurch; undertook specialist sculpture studies with Barbara Hepworth, Denis Mitchell, John Milne and Quinto Ghermandi 1968–70; numerous solo and collective exhbns; represented in public and pvt. collections including Int. Land Art Collection; Frances Hodgkins Fellowship, Univ. of Otago 1982; int. mem. Royal Soc. of British Sculptors 1990–; Christchurch/Seattle Sister City Comm. Award 1996, Winner Greenham Common Trust Prize 1998; winner 10th Millfield Int. Sculpture Comm., Somerset, England 1998, Artists in Industry Project, Victoria, Australia 1998–99, Hanover 2000 Expo, Steinbergen, Germany 2000, winner Kinetic Art Org. int. competition, USA 2002, selected for the Art in Motion Biennale, Bos van Ypeij, Netherlands 2003. *Major commissions:* Gateway, Albert Park, Auckland 1990, Rainbow Warrior Memorial, Matauri Bay 1990, Cave, Takahanga Marne, Kaikoura 1996, Wairan Strata, Seresin Estate, Marlborough 2000, Bukker Tillabul, Swinburne Univ., Lilydale, Melbourne 2001. *Television documentaries include:* When a Warrior Dies 1991, documentary on bombing of Greenpeace ship Rainbow Warrior and the creation of the memorial of the ship and its crew 1995, Sculpture in the Park 1996. *Publications include:* Chris Booth Sculpture 1993, Balanced Stone 1998, Chris Booth: Sculpture in Europe, Australia and New Zealand 2001. *Address:* PO Box 816, Kerikeri, 0470, New Zealand. *Telephone:* (9) 407-1331. *E-mail:* chris@chrisbooth.co.nz (Office). *Website:* www.chrisbooth.co.nz (Office).

BOOTHROYD, Baroness (Life Peer), cr. 2000, of Sandwell in the County of West Midlands; **Rt Hon Betty Boothroyd,** PC; British politician; b. 8 Oct. 1929, Dewsbury, Yorks.; d. of Archibald Boothroyd and Mary Boothroyd; ed Dewsbury Coll. of Commerce and Art; sec. Labour Party HQ 1955–60; legis. Asst to US congressman, Washington, DC 1960–62; sec. and personal asst to various sr Labour politicians 1962–73; mem. Hammersmith Borough Council 1965–68; contested various elections and by-elections 1957–70; mem. Parl. for W Bromwich 1973, for W Bromwich West 1974–92; Asst Govt Whip 1974–76; mem. Labour Party Nat. Exec. 1981–87; Deputy Speaker 1987–92; Speaker of the House of Commons 1992–2000; Chancellor Open Univ. 1994–; several hon. degrees from British univs including Hon. LLD (Cambridge) 1994 and Hon. DCL (Oxford) 1995. *Publication:* Betty Boothroyd—The Autobiography 2001. *Address:* House of Lords, Westminster, London, SW1A 0PW, England.

BOR, Naci; Turkish professor of physiology; b. 1928, Bor; s. of Cemal Bor and Zekiye Bor; m. Sema Bor; two d.; ed Istanbul Univ.; researcher in cardiac physiology, Emory Univ., Atlanta 1958–61; est. research in foetal physiology, Philadelphia Presbyterian Hosp.; lecturer Univ. of Pa.; Founding Dir of Physiology, Ankara Medical School 1963, f. Medical and Surgical Research Centre 1976, Chair. 1976–; Prof. of Physiology, Hacettepe Univ. Medical Faculty, Prof. Emer. 1995–; Prof. of Physiology, East Mediterranean Univ. Medical Faculty; Chair. Anadolu Health and Research Foundation, fmr. Chair. Research Centre, Hacettepe Univ.; mem. Science Council, Turkish Scientific and Tech. Nat. Research Council; f. and Ed. Doga (scientific journal), Turkish Journal for Medical Sciences; Founding Fellow Islamic Acad. of Sciences (IAS), mem. Council 1994–, Founding Ed. IAS Journal 1988, Medical Journal of IAS; numerous TV and radio broadcasts on health and health research; A. H. Asscn Research Award 1958, Science Council Prize for Lifetime Medical Research 1992. *Leisure interest:* essentials of Sofism. *Address:* Mithatpasa Cad. 66/5 06420 Kizilay, Ankara (Office); Yukari Ayranci Ömür Sok. No. 4/16, Cankaya, Ankara, Turkey (Home). *Telephone:* (312) 4250319 (Office); (312) 4273027 (Home). *Fax:* (312) 4259487 (Office). *E-mail:* nacibor@bir.net.tr (Office). *Website:* www.medicaljournal-ias.org (Office).

BORCHERDS, Richard Ewen, PhD, FRS; British mathematician; b. 29 Nov. 1959, South Africa; s. of Dr. Peter Howard Borcherds and Margaret Elizabeth Borcherds (née Greenfield); m. Ursula Gritsch; ed Trinity Coll., Cambridge; Research Fellow, Trinity Coll. 1983–87; Morrey Asst Prof., Univ. of Calif. at Berkeley 1987–88, Prof. of Math. 1993–96, 1999–; Royal Soc. Univ. Residential Fellow, Univ. of Cambridge 1988–92, lecturer 1992–93, Royal Soc. Prof., Dept of Math. 1996–99; Jr Whitehead Prize 1992, Prize of the City of Paris 1992, Fields Medal 1998. *Publications:* numerous papers in mathematical journals. *Leisure interest:* films. *Address:* Department of Pure Mathematics and Mathematical Statistics, 16 Mill Lane, Cambridge, CB2 1SB, England (Office). *Telephone:* (1223) 337999 (Office).

BORCHERS, Elisabeth; German editor; b. 27 Feb. 1926, Homberg; d. of Rudolf Sarbin and Claire (née Beck) Sarbin; m. (divorced); two s.; Ed. Luchterhand 1960–71, Suhrkamp Verlag and Insel Verlag 1971–98; mem. PEN, Acad. of Sciences and Literature, Mainz, Acad. of Language and Poetry, Darmstadt; Erzahlerpreis Suddeutscher Rundfunk, German Industry Culture Prize, Roswitha-Gedenk-Medaille 1976, Friedrich-Hölderlin-Preis 1986. *Publications:* poetry, prose, translations, children's books. *Address:* Arndtstrasse 17, 60325 Frankfurt, Germany. *Telephone:* (69) 746391.

BORCHERT, Jochen; German politician; b. 25 April 1940, Nahrstedt, Kreis Stendal; m.; two c.; ed studies in agric. and Econs; mem. Christian Democratic

Union (CDU) 1965–; mem. Bochum City Council 1976–80; mem. Bundestag 1980–, Vice-Pres. Farmers' Asscn, Westfalen-Lippe; Chair. Absatzforderungsfonds der Deutschen Land- und Ernährungswirtschaft 1989–93; CDU/CSU Spokesman on Budgetary Policy in Bundestag; Minister of Agric. Food and Forestry 1993–98; Fed. Chair. Protestant Working Group CDU/CSU, mem. Fed. Bd CDU. *Address:* c/o Bundesministerium für Ernährung, Landwirtschaft und Forsten, Rochusstrasse 1, 53123 Bonn, Germany.

BORD, André; French politician; b. 30 Nov. 1922, Strasbourg; s. of Alphonse Bord and Marie-Anne Sigrist; m. 1st Germaine Fend (deceased); two s.; m. 2nd Francine Heisserer 1981; ed St-Etienne Coll., Strasbourg; mem. of Nat. Assembly 1958–81; mem. Municipal Council, Strasbourg 1959–71, 1977–89, Deputy Mayor 1959–65; mem. Conseil Général, Strasbourg-Est and Hun Neudorf 1961–79; Pres. Conseil-Général du Bas-Rhin 1967–79; Pres. Groupe de l'Union démocratique européenne, European Parl. 1961–66, mem. European Parl. 1982–84; Sec. of State for Interior 1966–72, for Ex-Servicemen and War Victims 1972–76, for Relations with Parl. 1976–78; Sec.-Gen. UDR 1975–76; Founder, Pres. Asscn for Industrial Devt, Alsace 1967; Pres. Regional Council of Alsace 1973–77, Comm. Interministérielle de Coopération France–République Fédérale d'Allemagne 1986–; Médaille militaire, Médaille de la France libre, Médaille de la Résistance; Croix de guerre avec palme; Grand Officer, Order of Orange-Nassau (Netherlands), Order of Polonia Restituta (Poland), Commdr Légion d'honneur and others. *Address:* Ministry of Foreign Affairs, 23 rue Lapérouse, 75775 Paris, cedex 16 (Office); 27 route de Wolfisheim, 67810 Holtzheim, France (Home). *Telephone:* 1-43-17-63-93 (Office); 3-88-23-44-50 (Home). *Fax:* 1-43-17-65-75 (Office); 3-88-22-48-14 (Home).

BORDABERRY AROCENA, Juan María; Uruguayan politician; b. 17 June 1928, Montevideo; s. of Domingo Bordaberry and Elisa Arocena de Bordaberry; m. Josefina Herrán Puig; seven s. one d.; ed Univ. Montevideo; Chair., Nat. Meat Bd 1959; mem. Hon. Comm. for Agric. Devt Plan 1960; mem. Nat. Wool Bd 1960–62; Chair. Comm. Against Foot and Mouth Disease 1962; mem. Senate 1962–64; Chair. Liga Federal de Acción Ruralista 1964; Minister of Agric. 1969–72; Pres. of Uruguay 1972–76 (deposed). *Address:* Joaquín Suárez 2868, Montevideo, Uruguay. *Telephone:* 20-14-12.

BORDER, Allan Robert, AO; Australian cricketer; b. 27 July 1955, Cremorne, Sydney; s. of John Border and Sheila Border; m. Jane Hiscox 1980; two c.; ed Mosman Primary School, N Sydney Tech. School, N Sydney Boys' High School; fmr clerk; work in motor trade; left-hand middle-order batsman, left-arm slow bowler; teams: NSW 1976–80, Glos., England 1977 (1 match), Queensland 1980–96 (Capt. 1983–89), Essex, England 1986–88; Capt. Australian Nat. Team 1984–94; 156 (record) Tests for Australia 1978–94, including record unbroken sequence of 153 matches, record 93 (unbroken sequence 1984–94) as Capt., scoring 11,174 runs (average 50.5) including 27 hundreds and then holding record 156 catches; scored 27,131 first-class runs (70 hundreds); toured England 1979 (World Cup), 1980, 1981, 1983 (World Cup), 1985, 1989, 1993 (last three as Capt.); then record 273 limited-overs internationals, record 178 as Capt.; with Ronald McConnell Holdings 1980–84; with Castlemaine Perkins 1984–; mem. Nat. Cricket Selection Panel 1998–, Queensland Cricket Bd 2001–; Int. Cricket Council (ICC) Amb. to developing regions, mem. ICC Cttee; Wisden Cricketer of the Year 1982. *Publication:* A Peep at the Poms 1986. *Leisure interests:* golf, tennis, reading. *Address:* c/o Australian Cricket Board, 90 Jolimont Street, Jolimont, Vic. 3002, Australia.

BORDIER, Roger; French writer; b. 5 March 1923, Blois; s. of Robert Bordier and Valentine Jeufraux; m. Jacqueline Bouchaud; ed secondary school; journalist in the provinces, later in Paris; contrib. to Nouvelles Littéraires and Aujourd'hui; radio and TV writer; Prix Renaudot 1961, Officier Ordre des Artes et des Lettres. *Publications:* poems: Les épicentres 1951; novels: La cinquième saison 1959, Les blés 1961, Le mime 1963, L'Entracte 1965, Un âge d'or 1967, Le tour de ville 1969, Les éventails 1971, L'océan 1974, Meeting 1976, Demain l'été 1977; plays: Les somnambules 1963, Les visiteurs 1972; essays: L'objet contre l'art 1972, Le progrès: Pour qui? 1973, L'art moderne et l'objet 1978; novels: La grande vie 1981, Les temps heureux 1983, La longue file 1984, 36 La fête 1985, La belle de mai 1986, Les saltimbanques de la Révolution 1989, Vel d'hib 1989, Les fusils du 1er Mai 1991, Chroniques de la Cité Joyeuse 1995, L'Interrogatoire, dialogue 1998. *Address:* Editions Albin Michel, 22 rue Huyghens, 75014 Paris, (Office); 8 rue Geoffroy St Hilaire, 75005 Paris, France.

BORDYUZHA, Gen. Nikolai Nikolayevich; Russian politician; b. 22 Oct. 1949, Orel; m.; one s.; service in army and state security forces 1972–91; First Deputy Head, Personnel Dept, Fed. Agency of Govt Communications and Information of Russian Presidency 1991–92; Deputy Commdr, Frontier Forces 1992–95; Deputy Dir, Fed. Frontier Service, C-in-C, Frontier Forces 1995–98; mem. Russian Security Council 1998–99, Sec. March 1999, Head Office of the Pres. 1998–99; Amb. to Denmark 2000–. *Address:* Embassy of Russian Federation, Kristianagade 5, 2100 Copenhagen, Denmark. *Telephone:* 31-42-55-85. *Fax:* 31-42-37-41.

BOREL, Jacques Paul; French restaurant and hotel executive; b. 9 April 1927, Courbevoie; s. of William Borel and Marie (née Le Monnier) Borel; m. Christiane Roubit 1949; two s. one d.; ed Lycées Condorcet and Carnot, Paris, Ecole des Hautes Etudes Commerciales; mem. Sales Force IBM France 1950–57, Man. Saigon (Viet Nam) Br. Office IBM; Founder Restaurant Chain Jacques Borel 1957, became Compagnie des Restaurants Jacques Borel

(CRJB) 1960, then Jacques Borel Int. (J.B. Int.) 1970, Pres., Dir-Gen. –1977; Pres. J.B. Enterprises Soc. 1977; Dir Sofitel Jacques Borel, Jacques Borel Belgie NV-Belgique SA, Jacques Borel Do Brasil, Jacques Borel Deutschland, Jacques Borel Italia, Jacques Borel Nederland, Jacques Borel Iran, Jacques Borel Misr (Egypt), Jacques Borel Venezuela, Hoteles Jacques Borel (Barcelona), Farah Maghreb (Casablanca); Founder Syndicat Nat. des Restaurants Economiques 1966; became Syndicat Nat. des Chaînes d'Hôtels et de Restaurants de Tourisme et d'Entreprise 1970; Pres. until 1972, then Founder-Pres.; Pres. Groupement HEC Tourisme-Hôtellerie. *Leisure interests:* music, painting, sailing. *Address:* 100 avenue du Président Kennedy, 75016 Paris, France.

BOREN, David Lyle, MA, JD; American politician and lawyer; b. 21 April 1941, Washington, DC; s. of Lyle H. Boren and Christine (McKown) Boren; m. 1st; one s. one d.; m. 2nd Molly W Shi 1977; ed Yale, Oxford and Oklahoma Univs., Rhodes Scholar 1965; mem. Okla House of Reps. 1966–74; Chair. Govt Dept, Okla Baptist Univ. 1969–74; Gov. of Okla 1975–79; Senator from Okla 1979–94; Pres. Univ. of Okla 1994–. *Leisure interests:* family, reading, rowing, tennis. *Address:* University of Oklahoma, 660 Parrington Oval, Norman, OK 73019; 750 West Boyd, Norman, OK 73019, USA (Home).

BORG, Alan Charles Nelson, CBE, PhD, FSA; British museum director; b. 21 Jan. 1942; s. of late Charles J. N Borg and Frances M. O Hughes; m. 1st Anne Blackmore 1964 (divorced); one s. one d.; m. 2nd Lady Caroline Hill 1976; two d.; ed Westminster School, Brasenose Coll. Oxford and Courtauld Inst. of Art; lecteur d'anglais, Univ. d'Aix-Marseille 1964–65; lecturer History of Art, Ind. Univ. 1967–69; Asst Prof. of History of Art, Princeton Univ. 1969–70; Asst Keeper of the Armouries, HM Tower of London 1970–78; Keeper, Sainsbury Centre for Visual Arts, Univ. of E Anglia 1978–82; Dir-Gen. Imperial War Museum 1982–95; Chair. Nat. Inventory of War Memorials 1988–95, Advisory Cttee on Public Records 1993; Dir Vic. and Albert Museum 1995–2000; Pres. Elizabethan Club 1994–2000; Hon. Fellow RIBA 2001; Dr. hc (Sheffield Hallam) 2000. *Publications include:* Architectural Sculpture in Romanesque Provence 1972, European Swords and Daggers in the Tower of London 1974, Torture and Punishment 1975, Heads and Horses 1976, Arms and Armour in Britain 1979, The Vanishing Past 1981, War Memorials 1991; articles in learned journals. *Leisure interests:* fencing, music, travel. *Address:* Telegraph House, 36 West Square, London, SE11 4SP, England.

BORG, Björn Rune; Swedish tennis player and business executive; b. 6 June 1956, Stockholm; s. of Rune Borg; m. 1st Mariana Simionescu 1980 (divorced 1984); one s. by Jannike Bjorling; m. 2nd Loredana Berte 1989 (divorced 1992); ed Blombacka School; professional player since 1972; Italian Champion 1974, 1978; French Champion 1974, 1975, 1978, 1979, 1980, 1981; Wimbledon Champion 1976, 1977, 1978, 1979, 1980 (runner-up 1981); WCT Champion 1976; four times runner-up in U.S. Open; Grand Prix Masters Champion 1980, 1981; World Champion 1979, 1980; played Davis Cup for Sweden 1972, 1973, 1974, 1975, 1976, 1977, 1978, 1979, 1980; Winner Stockholm Open 1980; announced retirement from tennis Jan. 1983, two brief comebacks 1984, 1992; later played in srs tour; f. Björn Borg Enterprises Ltd; Sweden's Sportsperson of the Century, voted second-best tennis player ever by Sports Illustrated and l'Equipe newspaper. *Publication:* Bjorn Borg – My Life and Game (with Eugene Scott) 1980. *Leisure interest:* fishing. *Address:* c/o International Management Group, The Pier House, Strand on the Green, Chiswick, London W4 3NN, England.

BORG, Joseph, LLD; Maltese politician and lawyer; b. 19 March 1952; m. Isabelle Agius; one s. one d.; ed Lyceum and Univ. of Malta; practising lawyer 1976–; legal adviser to cos. and corpns. in Malta and abroad; lecturer, Univ. of Malta 1979–88, Sr Lecturer 1988; adviser on EU matters to Minister of Foreign Affairs 1989–95; mem. Bd Govs. Malta Int. Business Authority 1989–92, Bd Dirs. of Cen. Bank 1992–95; MP 1995–; Shadow Minister for Industry and EU Impact on Malta; mem. Foreign Affairs Parl. Cttee, EU-Malta Jt Cttee 1996–98; Parl. Sec. Ministry of Foreign Affairs 1998–99; Minister of Foreign Affairs 1999–; Int. Sec. Nationalist Party 1997–; Hon. LLM (Wales). *Address:* Palazzo Parisio, Merchants Street, Valletta, CMR 02, Malta (Home). *Telephone:* (356) 242853 (Home). *Fax:* (356) 237822 (Home).

BORG, Per O.; Swedish businessman and civil servant; b. 27 Sept. 1943; m. Kerstin Borg Wallin; two c.; ed Univ. of Gothenburg; served Ministry of Finance 1969–71, Ministry of Commerce 1971–78, of Defence 1978–81; Man. Dir IMPOD 1981–82; Under-Sec. of Defence 1982–88; Dir Gen. FMV 1988–. *Leisure interests:* opera, sailing, skiing. *Address:* FMV, 115 88 Stockholm, Sweden. *Telephone:* (8) 782-63-50.

BORG, Tonio, LLD; Maltese politician and lawyer; b. 12 May 1957; s. of Carmelo Borg and Maria Gemma Zarb; m. Adele Galea 1982; one s. two d.; ed St Aloysius Coll. and Univ. of Malta; Lecturer in Public Law, Univ. of Malta; exec. mem. of European Union Young Christian Democrats 1983–85; Dir Mid-Med Bank 1987–92; Pres. of Nationalist Party Gen. Council 1988–95; mem. of European Cttee for Prevention of Torture and Inhuman or Degrading Punishment or Treatment 1990–95; MP 1992–; mem. Planning Authority 1992–95; mem. of Council of Europe Ass. 1992–95; mem. Jt Parl. Cttee of the European Parl. and Maltese House of Reps. 1992–95, 1996–98; Minister for Home Affairs 1995–96, 1998–, Nationalist Party. *Leisure interests:* reading, cycling. *Address:* Ministry for Home Affairs and the Environment, Casa Leoni, 476 St Joseph High Road, St Venera, HMR 18, Malta (Office). *Telephone:* 485100. *Fax:* 493744.

BORGE MARTÍNEZ, Tomás; Nicaraguan politician, writer and journalist; b. 13 Aug. 1930, Matagalpa; s. of Tomás Borge Delgado and Ana Martínez Rivera; m. 1st Yelba Mayorga (assassinated by Nat. Guard 1979); m. 2nd Josefina Cerda; eight d.; ed Nat. Univ. León and Granada; first took part in activities against Somoza 1943, sentenced to eight years in prison 1956, escaped 1958, founder Frente Sandinista de Liberación Nacional (FSLN) 1961, guerrilla leader in Río Coco-Bocay, Pancasán and in clandestine struggle in the cities, captured by Somoza's agents 1976 and sentenced to 180 years of imprisonment, suffered torture and thirty months isolation, liberated in 1978 after attack on Nat. Palace; mem. Nat. Directorate FSLN 1978–; Minister of the Interior 1979–90, Adjoint Commdr Armed Forces, First Vice-Pres. Perm. Conference of Political Parties in Latin America (COPPPAL); founder Espartaco (magazine) 1946 and El Universitario (newspaper) 1950; jury mem. Festival of New Latin American Film 1990, House of Americas Award 1991; Dr. hc Autonomous Univ. of Puebla, Mexico 1981. *Publications:* Carlos, el Amanecer ya no es una Tentación 1979, Los Primeros Pasos 1981, Estamos Creando una Nueva Sociedad 1981, La Mujer en la Revolución 1983, La Revolución Combate Contra la Teología de la Muerte 1983, El Axioma de la Esperanza 1984, Nicaragua: Justicia y Revolución 1986, Cristianismo y Revolución 1987, Una Relación Mágica 1989, La Paciente Impaciencia (House of America Award) 1989, La Ceremonia Esperada 1990. *Leisure interest:* film. *Address:* Apartado 1229, Managua, Nicaragua. *Telephone:* 43853-52.

BORGEAUD, Pierre, DIPL.ENG; Swiss business executive; b. 31 March 1934; m.; three c.; ed Swiss Fed. Inst. of Tech.; Research Dept of Sulzer Bros. Ltd 1959–73, Man. of Sulzer Eng Works and of Swiss Locomotive and Machine Works, Winterthur 1973–75, Gen. Man., Sulzer Bros. Ltd (now Sulzer Man. Ltd) 1975–81, Pres., CEO 1981–88 (Chair. 1988–2000, Del. 1999), mem. Bd Dirs.; Chair. Presidential Bd of Swiss Fed. of Commerce and Industry 1987–93; mem. Bd of Dirs. Winterthur Insurance Co., Swiss Bank Corpn, Bühler Ltd, Pirelli Int. Ltd. *Address:* c/o Sulzer Ltd, Zuercherstr. 12, CH-8401 Winterthur, Switzerland.

BORGES, Jacobo; Venezuelan painter; b. 28 Nov. 1931; ed Escuela de Artes Plásticas Cristóbal Rojas, Caracas and Ecole des Beaux Arts, Paris; mem. of Young Painters' Group and illustrator of magazines and record covers while in Paris 1951–56, also exhibited in French Nat. Exhbns.; Prof. of Scenography and Plastic Analysis, Escuela de Artes Plásticas Cristóbal Rojas, Caracas 1958–65; Prof. of Scenography, Theatre School of Valencia and Dir Experimental Art Centre, Univ. Cent. de Venezuela 1966–; Int. Exhbns. at Guggenheim Museum, New York 1964, 1965; Artist in residence, Mexico City 1993; Museo Jacobo Borges created to house his work 1995; Nat. Painting Prize 1963, Armando Reverón Bienal Prize 1965. *Major works:* La Lámpara y la Silla 1951, La Pesca 1957, Sala de Espera 1960, Todos a la Fiesta 1962, Ha Comenzado el Espectáculo 1964, Altas Finanzas 1965; series of Las Jugadoras and Las Comedoras de Helados 1965–66. *One-man exhibitions include:* Caracas at Galería Lauro 1956, Museo de Bellas Artes 1956, Galería G 1963 and Galería Techo 1965, Staatische Kunsthalle, Berlin 1987, Galería Avril, Mexico 1988, Galería der Bruecke, Buenos Aires 1990, Casa de la América, Granada, Spain 1993. *Group exhibitions include:* São Paulo Bienal 1957, 1963, 1965, Venice Biennale 1958, Brussels World Fair 1958. *Address:* c/o Museo Jacobo Borges, Catia, Caracas, Venezuela.

BORGNINE, Ernest; American actor; b. 24 Jan. 1917, Hamden, Conn.; s. of Charles B. Borgnine and Anna (née Baselli) Borgnine; m. Tova Newman 1972; ed New Haven public schools, Randall School of Dramatic Arts, Hartford; Acad. Award for Best Performance in Marty 1956. *Films include:* From Here to Eternity, Bad Day at Black Rock, Marty, Violent Saturday, Square Jungle, Three Brave Men, Hell Below, The Rabbit Trap, Man on String, Barabbas, Flight of the Phoenix 1966, The Oscar 1966, The Split, Ice Station Zebra, The Dirty Dozen 1968, Willard 1971, The Poseidon Adventure 1972, Emperor of the North 1972, Sunday in the Country 1974, Law and Disorder 1975, Convoy 1978, Goin' South 1979, The Black Hole 1980, All Quiet on the Western Front 1980, Last Days of Pompeii 1984, Dirty Dozen: The Next Mission 1985, Any Man's Death 1990, Mistress 1992, All Dogs go to Heaven 2 1996, McHale's Navy 1997, Gattaca 1997. *Television includes:* Little House on the Prairie, Love Boat, Murder She Wrote. *Leisure interest:* golf.

BORGOMEO, Rev. Pasquale, SJ, DLit; Italian ecclesiastic; b. 20 March 1933, Naples; s. of Vincenzo Borgomeo and Letizia De Meo; ed Pontano Coll.; entered Soc. of Jesus 1948; ordained Priest 1963; Ed.-in-Chief Vatican Radio 1970–78, Programme Dir 1983–85, Asst Dir Gen. 1985–; mem. Bureau Univ. Radiophonique et Télévisuelle Int., Paris 1976–98, Bd of Dirs Centro Televisivo Vaticano 1983–97; Pres. Int. Broadcasting Working Party of European Broadcasting Union 1983–93; Consultant to Pontifical Council for Social Communications 1989–, Unione Cattolica Stampa Italiana 1997–; Chevalier Légion d'honneur 1994. *Publication:* L'Eglise de ce temps dans la prédication de Saint Augustin 1972. *Address:* Vatican Radio, Palazzo Pio, Piazza Pia 3, 00193 Rome (Office); Via dei Penitenzieri, 20, 00193 Rome, Italy (Home). *Telephone:* (6) 698-83945 (Office); (6) 689-77240 (Home). *E-mail:* borgomeo@vatiradio.va (Office).

BORISEVICH, Nikolai Aleksandrovich; Belarus physicist; b. 21 Sept. 1923, Luchnoy Most, Beresinsky District; m. Irina Pavlovna Borisevich 1949; two s.; ed Byelorussian State Univ., Minsk; served in Soviet Army 1941–45; Deputy Dir Inst. of Physics, Byelorussian Acad. of Sciences 1955–69 (Head of Lab. 1957–); Head of Lab. Lebedev Inst. of Physics, USSR (now Russian) Acad. of Sciences 1987–; Deputy to USSR Supreme Soviet 1969–89; mem. Byelo-

russian (Belarus) Acad. of Sciences 1969 (Pres. 1969–87, Hon. Pres. 1992–); Corresp. mem. USSR (now Russian) Acad. of Sciences 1972–81, mem. 1981; Foreign mem. Czechoslovakian Acad. 1977, Slovenian Acad. of Sciences and Arts 1981; titular mem. European Acad. of Arts, Sciences and Humanities 1991; Order of Red Star 1944, 1945, Order of Patriotic War (First Degree) 1945, (Second Degree) 1995, Order of Red Banner of Labour 1967, Order of Lenin 1971, 1975, 1978, 1983, Order of October Revolution 1973, Order of Friendship 2000, Hon. PhD (Jena) 1985; USSR State Prize 1973; Hero of Socialist Labour 1978; Lenin Prize 1980, Gold Medal Czechoslovak Acad. 1983, Slovenian Acad.1983, Belarus State Prize 1998. *Publications:* Exited States of Complex Molecules in Gas Phase 1967, Infrared Filters 1977; over 250 scientific articles. *Address:* P. N. Lebedev Institute of Physics, B-333, Leninski Prospekt 53, 117924 Moscow, Russia; 66 Skariny Avenue, Minsk, 220072 (Office); 7, Apt. 20, Y. Kupala str. Minsk, 220030, Belarus (Home). *Telephone:* (095) 135-75-98 (Moscow) (Office); (17) 232-1401 (Minsk) (Office); (17) 227-4559 (Minsk) (Home). *Fax:* (17) 284-0030 f(Minsk) (Office). *E-mail:* lirp@imaph.bas-net.by (Office).

BORITH, Ouch; Cambodian diplomatist; b. 2 Nov. 1951, Phnom-Penh; m.; five c.; ed Medical Faculty, Phnom-Penh, Inst. of Sociology, Moscow; French translator, Ministry of Foreign Affairs 1979–80, Dir Dept UN Humanitarian Org., Ministry of Foreign Affairs 1980–83, Dir Dept of Asia and Pacific Affairs 1987–90; Counsellor in charge of Political Affairs, Embassy, Moscow 1983–87; Amb. to Viet Nam 1990–92; Chargé d'Affaires, Perm. Mission to UN 1992–93, Deputy Perm. Rep. 1993–97, Perm. Rep. 1998–. *Address:* Permanent Mission of Cambodia to the United Nations, 866 United Nations Plaza, Room 420, New York, NY 10017, USA (Office). *Telephone:* (212) 223-0676 (Office). *Fax:* (212) 223-0425 (Office). *E-mail:* cambodia@un.int (Office). *Website:* www.un.int/cambodia (Office).

BORJA CEVALLOS, Rodrigo, DJur; Ecuadorean politician and academic; b. 19 June 1935, Quito; s. of Luis Felipe Borja de Alcázar and Aurelia Cevallos; m. Carmen Calisto de Borja; one s. three d.; ed Cen. Univ. of Ecuador; Deputy in Nat. Congress 1962–82; Founder and Leader Partido Izquierda Democrática; Prof. of Political Sciences, Cen. Univ. of Ecuador 1963–88; Pres. of Ecuador 1988–92; Pres. Law School Assn, Cen. Univ. of Ecuador 1958; mem. Special Comm. of Lawyers on Ecuador's Political Constitution 1966. *Publications:* Political Constitutional Law (2 Vols) 1964, 1971, Democratic Socialism 1983, Diplomatic Asylum in the Americas, Democracy in Latin America, A Political Dictionary; numerous essays.

BORK, Robert Heron, JD; American judge, lawyer and educationalist; b. 1 March 1927, Pittsburgh; s. of Harry Philip Bork and Elizabeth Kunkle; m. 1st Claire Davidson 1952 (died 1980); two s. one d.; m. 2nd Mary Ellen Pohl 1982; ed Univ. of Chicago; admitted to Illinois Bar 1953; Assoc., mem. Kirkland, Ellis, Hodson, Chaffetz & Masters 1955–62; Assoc. Prof. Yale Law School 1962–65, Prof. of Law 1965–73, Chancellor Kent Prof. of Law 1977–79, Alexander M. Bickel Prof. of Public Law 1979–81; Solicitor-Gen. 1973–77; Acting Attorney-Gen. 1973–74; mem. Kirkland & Ellis, Washington 1981–82; Circuit Judge for Dist of Columbia Circuit 1982–88; nominated as Justice of US Supreme Court and rejected by Senate 1987; John M. Olin Scholar in Legal Studies, American Enterprise Inst. 1988–99, Sr Fellow 2000–; Prof. of Law, Ave Maria School of Law 2000–; Resident Scholar, American Enterprise Inst., Washington, DC 1977, adjunct scholar 1977–82; Co-Chair. Bd of Trustees Federalist Soc.; mem. perm. Cttee Oliver Wendell Holmes Devise 1989; Fellow, American Acad. of Arts and Sciences; Hon. LLD (Creighton Univ.) 1975, (Notre-Dame) 1982; Hon. DHumLitt (Wilkes-Barre Coll.) 1976, Juris Dr hc (Brooklyn Law School) 1984; Francis Boyer Award, American Enterprise Inst. 1984, Shelby Cullom Davis Award 1989. *Publication:* The Antitrust Paradox: A Policy at War with Itself 1978, The Tempting of America: The Political Seduction of the Law 1990, Slouching Towards Gomorrah 1996, Coercing Virtue: The Worldwide Rule of Judges 2002. *Address:* 5171 Palisade Lane, NW, Washington, DC 20016, USA (Home). *Telephone:* (202) 862-5851 (Office). *E-mail:* rbork@aei.org (Office).

BORKH, Inge; Swiss soprano opera singer; b. 26 May 1921; ed Drama School, Vienna and Vienna Acad.; theatre performances (dancing, piano) in Vienna and Milan, then in Switzerland in German version of The Consul (Menotti); Int. career 1951–, Bayreuth, Paris, Vienna, Edin. Festival; first visit to USA 1953; World Première of Irische Legende (Egk) 1955; appeared as Salome and Elektra, Carnegie Hall, New York 1958; Metropolitan Opera, NY 1958; Bavarian Court Singer 1963; appeared at opening of Nationaltheater, Munich, in Die Frau ohne Schatten 1963; Grand Prix du Disque for Elektra, Antigone (Orff) and Schönberg's Gurrelieder; Reinhard Ring Award 1973. *Publication:* Ich komm vom Theater nicht los (autobiog.). *Address:* Florentinerstrasse 20, Apt. 2018, 100 Stuttgart 75, Germany. *Telephone:* 47022018. *Fax:* 47022018 (Home).

BORKO, Yuri Antonovich, DEcon; Russian economist; b. 6 Feb. 1929, Rostov-on-Don; m. Yelena Borisovna Borko; two s.; ed Moscow State Univ.; researcher, Inst. of World Econ. and Int. Relations USSR Acad. of Sciences 1962–63; Ed. and mem. of Bd journal World Econ. and Int. Relations 1963–69; Head of Div. Inst. of Information on Social Sciences, USSR Acad. of Sciences 1970–90; Head of Div., Deputy Dir, Head Research Centre of European Integration, Prof. Inst. of Europe, Russian Acad. of Sciences 1990–, Jean Monnet Chairholder 2001–; Pres. Asscn of European Studies 1992–. *Publications include:* works on problems of European integration, European Community policy and int. relations between Russia and European Community. *Leisure interests:* skiing, books, music. *Address:* Institute of Europe, Mokhovaya str. 8, stroenye 3B, 103873 Moscow (Office); Sovetskoy Armii str. 13–43, 127018 Moscow, Russia (Home). *Telephone:* (095) 201-67-75 (Office); (095) 201-67-04 (Office); (095) 289-21-66 (Home). *Fax:* (095) 200-42-98 (Office). *E-mail:* aes@aes.org.ru (Office); aes@centro.ru (Office); yborko@aes .org.ru (Home). *Website:* isn.rsuh.ru/iu (Office); www.aes.org.ru (Office).

BORLAUG, Norman Ernest, PhD; American agricultural scientist; b. 25 March 1914, Cresco, Ia; s. of Henry OBorlaug and Clara (Vaala) Borlaug; m. Margaret G. Gibson 1937; one s. one d.; ed Univ. of Minnesota; with US Forest Service 1935–38; Instructor, Univ. of Minn. 1941; Microbiologist, E. I. DuPont de Nemours Foundation 1942–44; Research Scientist, Wheat Rockefeller Foundation, Mexico 1944–60, Centro Internacional de Mejoramiento de Maíz y Trigo (Int. Maize and Wheat Improvement Center), Mexico 1964–79; Leonard L. Klinck Lecturer, Agric. Inst. of Canada 1966; mem. Citizens' Comm. on Science, Law and Food Supply 1973, Comm. on Critical Choices for America 1973, Council of Agric. Science and Tech. 1973–; Assoc. Dir Rockefeller Found. 1960–63, Life Fellow 1983–, Consultant 1983; A. D. White Distinguished Prof. at Large, Cornell Univ. 1983–85; Distinguished Prof. of Int. Agriculture, Texas A&M Univ. 1984–; Sr Consultant (Agriculture), Carter Center, Atlanta; mem. NAS; Foreign mem. Royal Swedish Acad. of Agric. and Forestry 1971, Indian Nat. Science Acad. 1973; Pres. Sasakawa Africa Asscn (SAA); Hon. Foreign mem. Acad. Nacional de Agronomía y Veterinaria de Argentina, N I. Vavilovi Acad. (USSR); Hon. Fellow Indian Soc. of Genetics and Plant Breeding 1968; Life Fellow Rockefeller Foundation 1983–; Hon. DSc (Punjab Agric. Univ.) 1969, (Royal Norwegian Agric. Coll.) 1970, (Mich. State Univ.) 1971, (Univ. of Florida) 1973, (Columbia) 1980, (Tulsa) 1991, (De Montfort) 1997 and many others; Nobel Peace Prize 1970; Medal of Freedom 1977, and numerous Mexican and other awards. *Leisure interests:* hunting, fishing, baseball, wrestling, football, golf. *Address:* Texas A&M University System, Department of Soil and Crop Sciences, College Station, TX 77843-2474, USA (Office); CIMMYT, Apartado Postal 6-641, 06600 Mexico, DF, Mexico (Home). *Telephone:* (979) 845-8247 (Texas) (Office); 5804-7508 (Mexico) (Office). *Fax:* (979) 845-0456 (Texas) (Office); 5804-7558/ 59 (Mexico) (Office). *Website:* coals.tamu.edu.

BORMAN, Frank; American astronaut and business executive; b. 14 March 1928, Gary, Ind.; s. of Edwin Borman and late Marjorie Borman; m. Susan Bugbee 1950; two s.; ed U.S. Military Acad., Calif. Inst. of Tech.; pilot training, Williams Air Force Base, Arizona; assigned to various fighter squadrons in U.S. and Philippines; Instructor in Thermodynamics and Fluid Mechanics, U.S. Mil. Acad. 1957; Master's degree from Calif. Inst. of Tech. 1957; graduated from U.S. Air Force Aerospace Research Pilots School 1960; Instructor 1960–62; selected by NASA as astronaut Sept. 1962; Command Pilot Gemini VII 1965; Commdr Apollo VIII spacecraft which made flight round the moon Dec. 1968; Deputy Dir for Flight Operations, NASA, until May 1969; Field Dir of a NASA Space Station Task Group 1969–70; Vice-Pres. Eastern Airlines Inc. 1970–74, Vice-Pres. for Eastern Operations 1974–75, Pres. 1975–85, CEO 1975–86, Chair. of Bd 1976–86; Vice-Chair., mem. Bd of Dirs. Texas Air Corp. 1986–92; now Chair. Bd Autofinance Group Inc., Chair., CEO, Dir Patlex Corp. 1992–; Dir Continental Airlines Holdings, Inc. 1992–; NASA Exceptional Service Medal, Harmon Int. Aviation Trophy 1966, Gold Space Medal, Int. Aeronautics 1969, Encyclopedia Britannica Achievement in Life Award 1980. *Leisure interests:* restoring aeroplanes, building model aeroplanes. *Address:* Patlex Corporation, 745 Leonard Bryran Alley, Las Cruces, NM 88005 (Office); Autofinance Group Inc., Suite 350, Oakmont Circle 1, 601 Oakmont Lane, Westmont, IL 60559 (Office); 4530 Blue Lake Drive, Boca Raton, FL 33431, USA (Home). *Telephone:* (505) 523-8081 (Las Cruces). *Fax:* (505) 524-4050 (Las Cruces).

BORN, Adolf; Czech artist; b. 12 June 1930, České Velenice; m. Emilie Košáková; one d.; ed Acad. of Graphic and Plastic Arts; illustration, animated cartoons, film co-operation with Jiří Brdečka 1955–; illustrated 250 children's books including Robinson Crusoe 1971, The Isle of Penguins, La Fontaine's Fables; Gold Medal for Brecht's Mother Courage, Leipzig 1965, Premio preferri di Imperie, Italy 1965, Dattero d'Oro 1966, Albatross Prize for Lifelong Work, Prague 2000. *Art exhibitions:* numerous exhbns in Prague, Montreal, Istanbul, Oslo, Nantes, Lucerne, Czech Centre, Paris 2000, Jihlava 2001. *Films:* co-dir. (with Macourek and Doubrava) of films The Life of Birds, The Life of Children. *Television:* serial Mach and Šebestová. *Leisure interests:* travel, animals. *Address:* Dvorecká 18, Prague 4, 14700, Czech Republic (Office).

BORN, Gustav Victor Rudolf, DPhil, MB, ChB, FRS, FRCP; British professor of pharmacology; b. 29 July 1921; s. of the late Prof. Max Born, Jt winner of the 1954 Nobel Prize for Physics; m. 1st Wilfrida Ann Plowden-Wardlaw 1950 (divorced 1961); two s. one d.; m. 2nd Dr. Faith Elizabeth Maurice-Williams 1962; one s. one d.; ed Oberrealschule, Göttingen, Germany, Perse School, Cambridge, Edinburgh Acad. and Univs. of Edinburgh and Oxford; Medical Officer, RAMC 1943–47; Research Asst, Graham Research Lab., Univ. Coll. Hosp. Medical School, London 1947–49; Studentship, training in research methods of MRC 1949–52; mem. scientific staff, Toxicology Research Unit, MRC 1952–53; Sr Research Officer Nuffield Inst. for Medical Research and Medical Lecturer St Peter's Coll., Oxford 1953–60; Vandervell Prof. of Pharmacology, Royal Coll. of Surgeons and London Univ. 1960–73; Sheild Prof. of Pharmacology, Cambridge Univ. and Fellow, Gonville and Caius Coll. Cambridge 1973–78; Prof of Pharmacology, King's Coll., London Univ. 1978–86, Prof. Emer. 1986–, Research Prof., William Harvey Research Inst.,

St Bartholomew's Hospital Medical Coll. 1988–; fmr mem. Council of the Int. Soc. of Thrombosis and Haemostasis (Pres. 1977–79), Cttee of British Pharmacological Soc., Working Party on Antihaemophilic Globulin of MRC, Official Cttee of Enquiry into Relationship of Pharmaceutical Industry with Nat. Health Service, Medical Advisory Bd, British Council and numerous other cttees. and bds.; mem. Akademie Leopoldina; Hon. Fellow St Peter's Coll., Oxford; Hon. FRCS; Hon. Life mem. New York Acad. of Sciences, and other hon. memberships; Chevalier Ordre nat. du Mérite; Hon. DSc (Bordeaux, Paris, Brown Univ.); Hon. MD (Münster, Leuven, Edinburgh, Munich, Loyola Univ., Chicago, Düsseldorf); Royal Soc. Royal Medal, Paul Morawitz Prize, Robert Pfleger Prize, Alexander von Humboldt Award 1995, Gold Medal for Medicine, Jung Foundation. *Publications:* more than 300 scientific publs. *Leisure interests:* music, history. *Address:* The William Harvey Research Institute, St Bartholomew's and the Royal London School of Medicine and Dentistry, Charterhouse Square, London, EC1M 6BQ; 5 Walden Lodge, 48 Wood Lane, London, N6 5UU, England. *Telephone:* (20) 7882-6070 (College). *Fax:* (20) 7882-6071.

BORNER, Silvio, DrOec; Swiss professor of economics; b. 24 April 1941; s. of Walter Borner and Meta Borner; m. Verena Barth 1966; two d.; ed St Gall Grad. School and Yale Univ.; Prof. of Econs Univ. of St Gallen 1974–78, of Political Econs Univ. of Basel 1978–. *Publications:* Die 'sechste Schweiz'—überleben auf dem Weltmarkt, New Forms of Internationalization: An Assessment, Einführung in die Volkswirtschaftslehre, International Finance and Trade in a Polycentric World. *Leisure interests:* sports (active) and culture. *Address:* Institut für Volkswirtschaft, WWZ Universität Basel, Petersplatz 1, CH-4003 Basle, Switzerland. *Telephone:* (61) 29-31-11.

BORODIN, Pavel Pavlovich; Russian economist; b. 25 Oct. 1946, Shakhudya, Nizhnii-Novgorod region; m. Valentina Borodina; one d. three adopted s.; ed Higher CPSU School, Moscow Inst. of Chemical Machine Construction, Ulyanovsk Inst. of Agric.; joined Yakutskgeologiya co. as economist 1978, Deputy Dir-Gen. until 1990; Mayor of Yakutsk 1993; Russian Soviet Federated Socialist Repub. People's Deputy, mem. Cttee on Problems of Women, Family Protection and Childhood 1990–93; moved to Moscow 1993; mem., then Man., then Chair. of Presidential Admin. 1993–2000; State Sec. Union of Russia and Belarus Jan. 2000–; detained in USA on request of Swiss Govt Prosecutor, extradited to Switzerland, found guilty of money laundering 2002; State Prize of Russian Fed.; Order for Service to Motherland. *Leisure interests:* football, pets. *Address:* Executive Committee of Russia and Belarus, Union. Kirova str. 17, 220000 Minsk, Belarus (Office). *Telephone:* (17) 229-34-34 (Office).

BORODIN, Stanislav Vladimirovich; Russian jurist; b. 18 Sept. 1924; m.; two s.; ed Moscow Juridical Inst.; mem. Supreme Court RSFSR 1952–61; Head of Higher School, Ministry of Internal Affairs 1961–65, Deputy Head, then Head All-Union Research Inst. 1965–79, Rector of Acad., Ministry of Internal Affairs 1979–83; Sr researcher, then leading researcher, then chief researcher Inst. of State and Law 1983–; mem. Higher Attestation Comm., Scientific Council, Supreme Court of Russian Fed. *Address:* Institute of State and Law, Znamenka str. 10, 119841 Moscow, Russia (Office). *Telephone:* (095) 291-87-92 (Office).

BORODINA, Olga Vladimirovna; Russian mezzo-soprano; b. 29 July 1963, Leningrad; d. of Vladimir Nikolaevich and Galina Fedorovna Borodin; one s.; ed Leningrad Conservatory (student of Irina Bogacheva); soloist of Kirov (now Mariinsky) Theatre of Opera and Ballet 1987–; debut as Siebel (Faust); winner of First Prizes: All-Union Glinka Competition 1987, Int. Rosa Poncell Competition (New York) 1987, Int. Francisco Vignas Competition (Barcelona) 1989; leading parts in operas Eugene Onegin (Olga), Khovanshchina (Marfa), Prince Igor (Konchakovna), Queen of Spades (Poline), Sadko (Lubava), Boris Godunov (Marina Mnichek), La Cenerentola (Cinderella), Carmen (Carmen), Amneris (Aida), Eboli (Don Carlos), Delilah (Samson and Delilah); regular performances in all maj. opera houses as well as recitals and concerts around the world. *Leisure interest:* fishing. *Address:* c/o Askonas Holt, Lonsdale Chambers, 27 Chancery Lane, London, WC2A 1PF, England. *Telephone:* (20) 7400-1780 (Home). *Fax:* (20) 7400-1799 (Office). *E-mail:* nicola-fee.bahl@ askonasholt.co.uk (Office).

BOROSS, Péter, PhD; Hungarian politician; b. 27 Aug. 1928, Nagybajom; m.; two c.; ed Eötvös Loránd Univ. of Budapest; with Budapest Metropolitan Council 1951–56; dismissed for membership of revolutionary Cttee and revolutionary council 1956; kept under police surveillance until 1959; employed as unskilled worker 1964; organized catering and tourist coll. training; catering chain Dir 1971; mem. Council Coll. of Trade and Catering; mem. Hungarian League of Human Rights, Hungarian Chamber of Economy; Founder Nation Bldg Foundation 1988; Minister of State for the Office of Information and the Office of Nat. Security 1990–94; Minister of the Interior 1990–93; Prime Minister of Hungary 1993–94; mem. Parl. 1994–98; Chair. Nat. Security Cttee of Parl. 1994–96; Sr Counsellor and Adviser to Prime Minister 1998–; mem. Hungarian Democratic Forum Nat. Presidium 1993–. *Address:* 1055 Budapest, Kossuth Lajos tér 1–3, Hungary. *Telephone:* (1) 441-3000. *Fax:* (1) 441-4888.

BOROVKOV, Aleksandr Alekseyevich; Russian mathematician; b. 6 March 1931, Moscow; s. of Aleksey and Klaudia Borovkov; m. Svetlana Borovkov 1975; two s.; ed Moscow Univ.; Postgraduate, Research Assoc. Moscow Univ. 1954–60; Head of Dept Inst. of Math., Siberian Branch USSR (now Russian) Acad. of Sciences 1960–, Deputy Dir 1981–91; Prof., Novosibirsk Univ. 1965–; Corresp. mem. USSR (now Russian) Acad. of Sciences 1966–90, full mem. 1990–; mem. Int. Statistical Inst. and Bernulli Soc.; State Prize 1979. *Publications:* Stochastic Processes in Queuing Theory 1976, Wahrscheinlichkeitstheorie 1976, Asymptotic Methods in Queuing Theory 1980, Statistique Mathématique 1987, Ergodicity and Stability of Stochastic Processes, 1998, Probability Theory 1998, Mathematical Statistics 1998; works on contiguous problems of theory probabilities and mathematical statistics. *Address:* Sobolev Institute of Mathematics, Koptyng prospekt 4, Novosibirsk, 630090, Russia. *Telephone:* (3832) 33-34-98 (Office); (3832) 30-23-53 (Home). *Fax:* (3832) 33-25-98. *E-mail:* borovkov@math.nsc.ru (Office).

BOROVOI, Konstantin Natanovich, CTechSc; Russian politician and businessman; b. 30 June 1948, Moscow; m.; two d.; ed Moscow Inst. of Railway Eng, Moscow State Univ.; worked in field of applied math., taught in Moscow State Univ. and Inst. of Land Utilization 1975–87, business activities since 1987–; publishes journal We and Computer 1988–90; co-founder and Pres. Russian Stock and Raw Materials Exchange 1990–92; Pres. Agency of Econ. News 1990; Chair. Bd of All-Russian Nat. Commercial Bank 1990–; Pres. Russian Investment Co. Rinako 1991–; mem. Council of Businessmen of Pres. of Russia 1991–; Co-chair. Foundation of External Policy of Russia 1992–; founder Commercial TV Co. 1992–; founder and Co-Chair. Party of Econ. Freedom 1992–; mem. State Duma 1995–99; Pres. Borovoi Trust Co. 1995–; Chair. Export Council, Russian Stock Exchange 1998–. *Publications:* The Price of Freedom; numerous articles. *Leisure interests:* tennis, computer graphics. *Address:* Economic Freedom Party, Novoslobolskaya, str. 9, Korp. 3, 103030 Moscow, Russia. *Telephone:* (095) 973-12-18 (Office); (095) 250 95 02 (Home).

BOROWSKI, Marek Stefan; Polish politician; b. 4 Jan. 1946, Warsaw; m.; one s.; ed Main School of Planning and Statistics (now Warsaw School of Econs), Warsaw; Sr Economist Centrum Dept stores, Warsaw 1968–82; Ministry of Nat. Economy 1982–91, Deputy Minister 1989; deputy to Sejm (Parl.) 1991–2001; Deputy Prime Minister, Minister of Finance and Head Econ. Cttee of Council of Ministers 1993–94; Minister/Head Council of Ministers Office 1995–96; Vice-Marshal of Sejm 1996–2001, Marshal 2001–; mem. Polish United Workers' Party (PZPR) 1967–68, 1975–90; mem. Social Democracy of Polish Repub. 1990–99, Democratic Left Alliance 1999– (Vice-Chair.). *Leisure interests:* literature, films, theatre, classical music. *Address:* Sejm RP, ul. Wiejska 4/6/8, 00-902 Warsaw, Poland. *Telephone:* (22) 6942155.

BORRELL FONTELLES, José, D.ECON.SCI.; Spanish politician; b. 24 April 1947, Pobla Segur, Lérida; m.; two c.; ed Polytechnic Univ. and Complutense Univ. Madrid, Stanford Univ., USA; mem. Socialist Workers' Party (PSOE) Madrid 1975–; fmr Dir Dept of Systems CESPA (Compañía Española de Petróleos); Deputy, Treasury and Economic Planning for Provincial Del. Madrid 1979; Under-Sec. Budget and Public Spending 1982–84, Sec. of State for the Treasury 1984–86, Deputy for Barcelona in the Legis. Ass. 1986–91; Minister of Public Works and Transport 1991–96, of the Environment 1993–96. *Address:* c/o Ministerio de Obras Públicas y Transportes, Nuevos Ministerios, 28071 Madrid, Spain.

BORRELLI, Mario, MSc; Italian sociologist; b. 19 Sept. 1922, Naples; s. of Gennaro Borrelli and Lucia Morvillo; m. Jilyan West 1971; one d.; ed Posillipo Theological Univ., School of States Archives, Naples, London School of Econs; Founder of "Casa dello Scugnizzo", Naples 1950 (Pres. 1993–); Founder-Dir Lo Scugnizzo (monthly magazine) 1950–; Founder Materdei Community Centre, Naples 1970. *Publications:* La Concezione Copernico Galileiana e la Filosofia di Tomaso D'Aquino 1961, La Relazione tra il Conservatorio dei Poveri di Gesù Cristo e l'Oratorio di Napoli 1961, Il Largo dei Girolamini 1962, A Streetlamp and the Stars 1963, Memorie Baroniane dell'Oratorio di Napoli 1963, Opere e Documenti sul Baronio Presso The British Museum Library 1964, I Documenti dell'Oratorio Napoletano 1964, Le Testimonianze Baroniane dell'Oratorio di Napoli, Documenti sul Baronio Presso The Bodleian Library, L'Epistolario del Giusto Calvino nei suoi Rapporti col Baronio 1965, L'Architetto Nencioni Dionisio Di Bartolomeo 1967, Le Costituzioni dell' Oratorio Napoletano 1968, Diario delle Baracche 1969, Unearthing the Roots of the Sub-Culture of the South Italian Sub-Proletariat 1969, Socio-political Analysis of the Sub-Proletarian Reality of Naples and Lines of Intervention for the Workers of the Centre 1973, Basic Concepts for Community Action in the Urban Sub-Proletariat 1974, Practical Directions for Intervention in a Community Action in Favour of the Urban Sub-Proletariat 1974, Hypothesis of the Existence of a "Peripheral" Europe with consequent different types of Social Policy Intervention 1975, Exclusion from the Productive Process, Social Deviance and Mental Illness 1975, Alimentation and Directions of Social Intervention among the Neapolitan Sub-Proletariat 1975, Communication and Consciousness-Raising 1975, Socio-political Analysis of the Neapolitan Reality and Programme of Intervention for the Social Operators of the Centre 1976, Integration between Peace Research, Peace Education and Peace Action 1977, New Trends in the International Division of Labour and their Effects on the Conditions of Workers in Industrialized and "Third World" Countries 1977, Tourism as an Expression of Economic Subordination: Relationships between Emigration and Tourism 1977, Italian Compulsory School and Mental Retardation 1978, Human Needs, Human Rights and Peace Education (An Analysis by Means of the Practical Experience of the Materdei Community Centre of Naples), Exploration of the Preliminary Conditions for a Defensive and Economic Strategy for Central Europe leading to its Balance Insertion in the Mediterranean and African Areas 1981, Human Rights and a Methodology for Peace 1983, The Development of the Concept of Peace

Education in the IPRA Archipelago 1983, An Approach to the Political Dimension of Disarmament Education 1984, The Periphery of Europe and the Community Integration of 1992 (an Analysis from the Southern Italian Scene) 1990, 4 contributions to Council of Europe research on street children. *Address:* Via Vecchia, S. Gennaro, 100/A-Pozzuoli, Naples, Italy. *Telephone:* (81) 526-57-01 (Home).

BORRIE, Baron (Life Peer) cr. 1995, of Abbots Morton in the County of Hereford and Worcester; **Gordon Johnson,** Kt, QC, FRSA; British lawyer; b. 13 March 1931; s. of Stanley Borrie; m. Dorene Toland 1960; ed John Bright Grammar School, Llandudno and Univ. of Manchester; called to Bar, Middle Temple 1952; Bencher 1980; Barrister, London 1954–57; Lecturer, later Sr Lecturer in Law, Coll. of Law 1957–64, Univ. of Birmingham 1965–68, Prof. of English Law and Dir Inst. of Judicial Admin. 1969–76, Dean Faculty of Law 1974–76; Dir-Gen. Office of Fair Trading 1976–92; Dir Woolwich Bldg Soc. 1992–2000; Dir (non-exec.) Three Valleys Water Services 1992–, Mirror Group Newspapers 1993–99, Telewest Communications 1994–2001, General Utilities 1998–; Chair. Accountancy Foundation 2000–, Advertising Standards Authority 2001–; mem. Parole Bd for England and Wales 1971–74, Consumer Protection Advisory Cttee 1973–76, Equal Opportunities Comm. 1975–76; Pres. Inst. of Trading Standards Admin. 1992–97; Chair. Comm. on Social Justice 1992–94, Money Advice Trust 1993–95; mem. Council of Ombudsman for Corp. Estate Agents 1992–98; Labour cand. Croydon 1955, Ilford 1959; Gov. Birmingham Coll. of Commerce 1966–70; Hon. LLD (City of London Polytechnic) 1989, (Manchester Univ.) 1990, (Hull Univ.) 1991, (Dundee Univ.) 1993, (Nottingham Trent Univ.) 1996, (Univ. of the West of England) 1997. *Publications:* Commercial Law 1962, The Consumer, Society and the Law (with Prof. A. L. Diamond) 1963, Law of Contempt (with N V. Lowe) 1973, The Development of Consumer Law and Policy 1984. *Leisure interests:* gastronomy, piano playing, travel. *Address:* Manor Farm, Abbots Morton, Worcestershire, WR7 4NA; 4 Brick Court, Temple, London EC4Y 9AD, England; Advertising Standards Authority, 2 Torrington Place, London, WC1E 7HW (Office). *Telephone:* (1386) 792330; (20) 7580-5555 (Office); (20) 7353-4434. *Fax:* (20) 7583-6148 (Home).

BORRIE, Wilfred David, CBE, MA; Australian demographer; b. 2 Sept. 1913, Waimate, New Zealand; s. of Peter Borrie and Isobella Borrie; m. Alice H. Miller 1941; one d.; ed Waitaki Boys High School, Oamaru, New Zealand, Univ. of Otago, NZ and Cambridge Univ; Lecturer, Social History and Econs, Sydney Univ. 1944–46, Senior Lecturer 1946–48; Research Fellow, Research School of Social Sciences, Australian Nat. Univ. 1949–52, Reader 1952–57, Prof. and Head of Dept of Demography 1957–68, Dir Research School of Social Sciences 1968–73, Prof. of Demography 1973–78, Emer. Prof. 1979–; Visiting Prof., Office of Population Research, Princeton Univ. 1959–60; Vice-Pres. Int. Union for Scientific Study of Population 1961–63; Pres. Social Science Research Council of Australia 1962–64, Australian Council of Social Services 1963–64, Australian and New Zealand Asscn for the Advancement of Science (ANZAAS) 1975; Chair. UN Population Comm. 1965–69; Chair. and Dir Nat. Population Inquiry 1970–78; Dir Acad. of Social Sciences in Australia 1979–85; mem. Immigration Planning Council of Australia 1965–74, Australian Population and Immigration Council 1972–81; Patron Australian Population Asscn 1980–; Laureate Int. Union for the Scientific Study of Population 1996; Hon.D.Litt (Tasmania) 1975, Hon. DSc (Sydney) 1979; Hon. LLD (Australian Nat. Univ.) 1982, Laureate IUSSP 1996. *Publications:* Immigration 1948, Population Trends and Policies 1949, Italians and Germans in Australia 1954, The Cultural Integration of Immigrants (Part I and General Ed.) 1959, Australia's Population Structure and Growth (with G. Spencer) 1965, The Growth and Control of World Population 1970, Population Environment and Society 1973, Population and Australia (First Report of the Nat. Population Inquiry, 2 Vols) 1975, Supplementary Report (Recent Trends and their Implications) 1978, Implications of Australian Population Trends (Ed.) 1981, Immigration to New Zealand 1854–1938, The European Peopling of Australasia: A Demographic History, 1788–1988 1994. *Leisure interests:* reading, walking, gardening. *Address:* 49 The Grange, 67 MacGregor Street, Deakin, ACT 2600, Australia.

BORSIK, János, DJur; Hungarian trade union officer; b. 22 June 1946; m.; two s.; ed Janus Pannonius Univ. of Sciences, Pécs; locomotive fitter 1964–88; locomotive driver 1968–86; trade union officer 1986–; consultant on labour law; Pres. Autonomous Trade Union Confed. (ATUC) 2000–. *Leisure interests:* literature, theatre, sports. *Address:* ATUC, Benczúr utca 45, 1068 Budapest (Office); Oktogon 3, 1066 Budapest, Hungary (Home). *Telephone:* (1) 220-3822 (Office). *Fax:* (1) 220-3822 (Office). *E-mail:* autonom@euroweb.hu (Office).

BORST, Piet, MD, PhD; Netherlands biochemist; b. 5 July 1934, Amsterdam; s. of Prof. J. Borst and A. Borst-de Geus; m. Jinke C. S. Houwing 1957; two s. one d.; ed Gymnasium, Amsterdam, Univ. of Amsterdam; research Asst Lab. of Biochemistry, Univ. of Amsterdam 1958–61; post-doctoral research Fellow Dept of Biochemistry, New York Univ. 1963–64; Prof. of Biochemistry and Molecular Biology, Univ. of Amsterdam 1965–83, Head of Section for Medical Enzymology, Lab. of Biochemistry 1966–83, Dir Inst. of Animal Physiology 1972–80, Extraordinary Prof. of Clinical Biochemistry 1983–; Dir of Research Netherlands Cancer Inst., Amsterdam 1983–99, staff mem. 1999–; mem. European Molecular Biology Org. 1974, Royal Netherlands Acad. of Arts and Sciences 1978, Hollandsche Maatschappij der Wetenschappen 1983, Academia Europaea 1989; Foreign mem. Royal Soc. 1986, Foreign Assoc. NAS 1991; Foreign Hon. mem. American Acad. of Arts and Sciences 1995; Commdr Order of the Dutch Lion 1999; Dr hc (Leiden) 2003;

Royal Dutch/Shell Prize for the Life Sciences 1981, Federatie van Medisch Wetenschappelijke Verenigingen Prize 1984, Paul-Ehrlich and Ludwig-Darmstaedter Prize (jtly) 1984, Ricketts Award of Univ. of Chicago 1989, Dr G. Wander Award of the Wander Foundation, Berne 1990, Gold Medal of the Genootschap voor Natuur-, Genees- en Heelkunde, Amsterdam 1990, Dr H. P. Heineken Prize for Biochem. and Biophysics, Amsterdam 1992, Gold Medal of the Koch Foundation, Bonn 1992. *Publications:* over 300 scientific articles in biochemistry, molecular biology and cell biology. *Leisure interests:* tennis, windsurfing, skiing, cello, bridge. *Address:* Netherlands Cancer Institute, Plesmanlaan 121, 1066 CX Amsterdam (Office); Meentweg 87, 1406 KE Bussum, Netherlands (Home). *Telephone:* (20) 5122881 (Office); (35) 6914453 (Home). *Fax:* (20) 6691383 (Office). *E-mail:* pborst@nki.nl (Office).

BORTEN, Per; Norwegian politician and agronomist; b. 3 April 1913, Fl·a Gauldal; s. of Lars Borten and Karen Borten; m. Magnhild Rathe 1948; three c.; ed Norwegian Agricultural Univ; Asst Head, Tech. Section, Provincial Agric. Admin., Sör-Tröndelag 1946–65; Chair. Fl·a Municipal Council 1945, Provincial Council, Sör-Tröndelag 1948; fmr Head of Youth Movement of Agrarian Movement, Sör-Tröndelag; mem. Storting 1950–77, Pres. Odelsting 1961–65, 1973–77; Chair. Senterpartiet 1955–67, Chief Spokesman 1958–65; Prime Minister 1965–71. *Address:* c/o Storting, Oslo, Norway.

BORUBAYEV, Altai; Kyrgyzstan mathematician and politician; b. 1950, Kara-oy, Kyrgyzia; ed Kyrgyz State Univ.; teacher Frunze Polytech. Inst. 1975–76; teacher, Sr teacher, Head of Chair., Dean, Pro-rector Kyrgyz State Univ. 1976–92, Rector 1998–2000; Rector Kyrgyz State Pedagogical Inst. 1994–98; First Deputy Minister of Educ. 1992–94; Chair. (Speaker) Ass. of People's Reps. Chamber of Zhogorku Kenesh (Parl.) April 2000–; mem. Nat. Acad. of Sciences 2000, Russian Acad. of Social and Pedagogical Sciences. *Publications:* three monographs, over 100 articles. *Address:* Zhogorku Kenesh, Assembly of People's Representatives, 720003 Bishkek, Kyrgyzstan (Office). *Telephone:* (312) 27-17-19 (Office).

BORZOV, Valeriy Filippovich; Ukrainian athlete, sports administrator and politician; b. 20 Oct. 1949, Sambor, Lvov Region, Ukraine; s. of Philipp Petrovich Borzov and Valentina Georgiyevna Borzova; m. Lyudmila Turish-cheva 1978 (divorced); one d.; ed Kiev State Inst. of Physical Culture; competed Olympic Games Munich 1972, winning gold medals at 100m and 200m; bronze medal at 100m, Montreal 1976; European Junior Champion 100m and 200m 1968; European Champion 100m 1969; 100m and 200m 1971, 100m 1974; European Indoor Champion 60m 1970, 1971, 1972, 50m 1974, 1975, 1976; held European record at 100m and 200m and world record at 60m; Minister of Sport and Youth Ukrainian Repub. 1990–; Chair. State Cttee for Physical Culture and Sport 1996–97; Chair. Nat. Olympic Cttee of Ukraine 1990–; mem. Int. Olympic Cttee, Jt Asscn of Summer Olympic Sports 1994–; f. Nat. Olympic Acad. of Ukraine; Merited Master of Sport. *Leisure interests:* fishing, hunting. *Address:* c/o National Olympic Committee of Ukraine, Esplanadna Street 42, 252023 Kiev, Ukraine. *Telephone:* (44) 220-05-50. *Fax:* (44) 220-05-09.

BOS, Caroline Elisabeth, BA; Netherlands architect; b. 17 June 1959, Rotterdam; d. of Peter Bos and Ellen Guibal; ed Birkbeck Coll., Univ. of London; freelance journalist 1982–88; co-founder and Dir Van Berkel & Bos Architectur Bureau 1988–99; co-founder and Dir UN Studio 1999–; Eileen Gray Award 1983, British Council Fellowship 1986, Charlotte Köhler Prize 1991; winning entry for Police HQ, Berlin 1995, Museum Het Valkof 1995, Music Theatre, Graz 1998. *Projects include:* switching substation, Amersfoort 1989–93, Erasmus Bridge, Rotterdam 1990–96, Villa Wilbrink, Amersfoort 1992–94, Möbius House, 't Gooi 1993–98, Rijksmuseum Twente, conversion and extension, Enschede 1992–96, Museum Het Valkhof, Nijmegen 1995–99, Masterplan of station area, Arnhem 1996–(2005), Willemstunnel, Arnhem 1996–99, City Hall and Theatre, Ijsselstein 1996–2000, Lab. for NMR facilities, Utrecht 1996–2000, Switching station, Innsbruck 1998–2001, Music Faculty, Graz 1998–2002; *Group Exhibitions include:* Architecture et Utopie, Paris and Berlin 1989–90, Architectural Biennale of Venice 1991–93, 1996, 2000, Crossing Points, Berlin and Zürich 1993, Das Schloss, Berlin, Vienna and Stuttgart 1993–94, Light Construction, Museum of Modern Art, New York 1995, Mobile Forces, UCLA, LA and New York 1997, The Un-Private House, Museum of Modern Art, New York 1999, UCLA, LA 2000–01. *Address:* UN Studio Van Berkel & Bos, Stadhouderskade 113, 1073 AX Amsterdam, The Netherlands (Office). *Telephone:* (20) 5702040 (Office). *Fax:* (20) 5702041 (Office). *E-mail:* info@unstudio.com (Office). *Website:* www.unstudio.com (Office).

BOS, Wouter; Dutch politician; b. 14 July 1963, Vlaardingen; ed Grammar School, Zeist and Free Univ. of Amsterdam; Man. Consultant Shell Nether-lands Refinery BV 1988–90, Policy Adviser, Rotterdam 1990–92, Gen. Affairs Man. Shell Romania Exploration BV, Bucharest 1992–93, Staff Planning and Devt. Man., Shell Cos in China, Hong Kong 1993–96, Consultant New Markets, Shell Int. Oil Products, London 1996–98; mem. Parl. (Partij van de Arbeid) 1998–; Sec. of State for Finance (Taxes) 2002–02; Leader Partij van de Arbeid (PvdA) 2002–. *Address:* Partij van de Arbeid, Herengracht 54, POB 1310, 1000 BH Amsterdam, Netherlands (Office). *Telephone:* (20) 5512155 (Office). *Fax:* (20) 5512330 (Office). *E-mail:* pvda@pvda.nl (Office). *Website:* www.pvda.nl (Office).

BOSHOFF, Carel Willem Hendrik, MA, DD; South African theologian; b. 9 Nov. 1927, Nylstroom; s. of W. S. Boshoff and A. M. Boshoff; m. Anna Verwoerd, d. of late Hendrik Verwoerd (Prime Minister of SA 1958–66) 1954;

five s. two d.; ed Nylstroom High School, Pretoria Univ.; Missionary Dutch Reformed Church 1953–63, Sec. of Missions 1963–66; Prof. and Head of Dept of Theology, Missiology and Science of Religion, Univ. of Pretoria 1967–88, Dean, Theology Faculty 1978–80; Chair. SA Bureau of Racial Affairs (SABRA) 1972–99; Chair. N. G. Kerkboekhandel 1976–88; Chair. Afrikaner Volkswag Cultural Org. 1984–99, Council of Inst. for Missiological Research 1978–88; Exec. Chair. Afrikaner Vryheidstigting 1988–; Chair., Dir Orania Bes-tuurdienste Ltd 1990–; Leader, Die Voortrekkers 1981–89; mem. numerous theological and scholarly cttees; Pres. Burger Council Afrikaner Vryheid-stigting 1994–; Provincial Leader, Freedom Front of Northern Cape 1994–; mem. legislature, Prov. of Northern Cape 1994–; mem. SA Akad. vir Weken-skap en Kuns. *Publications:* Die Begin van die Evangelie van Jesus Christus 1963, Uit God Gebore 1968, Die Nuwe Sendingsituasie 1978, Swart Teologie van Amerika Tot in Suid-Afrika 1980; numerous articles in various journals. *Leisure interests:* small farming, breeding Nooitgedacht ponies, hiking. *Address:* PO Box 199, Orania 8752, South Africa. *Telephone:* (53) 207-0061 (Office); (53) 207-0008 (Home). *Fax:* (53) 207-0091.

BOSKIN, Michael Jay, PhD; American economist, government official, university educator and consultant; b. 23 Sept. 1945, NY; s. of Irving Boskin and Jean Boskin; m. Chris Dornin 1981; ed Univ. of California, Berkeley; Asst Prof., Stanford Univ., Calif. 1970–75, Assoc. Prof. 1976–78, Prof. 1978–; Dir Centre for Econ. Policy Research 1986–89; Wohlford Prof. Econs 1987–89; Chair. of the Pres.'s Council of Econ. Advisers 1989–93; Chair. Congressional Comm. on the Consumer Price Index; Friedman Prof. of Econs and Hoover Inst. Sr Fellow, Stanford Univ., Calif. 1993–; Pres. Boskin & Co., Calif. 1993–; Research Assoc. Nat. Bureau of Econ. Research 1976–; Visiting Prof. Harvard Univ., Mass. 1977–78; Faculty Research Fellow Mellon Foundation 1973; Distinguished Faculty Fellow Yale Univ. 1993; Scholar American Enterprise Inst.; mem. Bd of Dirs Exxon Corpn, Oracle Corpn, Vodaphone Group PLC, First Health Corpn; several prizes and awards. *Publications:* Too Many Promises: The Uncertain Future of Social Security 1986, Reagan and the Economy: Successes, Failures, Unfinished Agenda 1987, Frontiers of Tax Reform 1996, Capital Technology and Growth 1996, Toward a More Accurate Measure of the Cost of Living 1996; contrib. articles in various professional journals. *Leisure interests:* tennis, skiing, reading, theatre. *Address:* Stanford University, 213 HHMB, Stanford, CA 94305, USA. *Telephone:* (650) 723-6482. *Fax:* (650) 723-6494 (Office). *E-mail:* boskin@hoover.stanford.edu (Office).

BOSNICH, Brice, PhD; Australian chemist; b. 1936, Queensland; ed Univ. of Sydney, Australian Nat. Univ.; Dept. of Industrial and Scientific Research Postdoctoral Fellow, Univ. Coll., London 1962–63; ICI Fellow, 1963–66; lecturer, Univ. of Toronto 1966–69, Assoc. Prof. 1970–75, Prof. 1975–87; Prof. Univ. of Chicago 1987–; Noranda Award, Royal Soc. of Chemistry Award, Organic Chem. Award (American Chemical Soc.), Organometallic Medal, Nyholm Medal. *Address:* University of Chicago, 5801 S Ellis Avenue, Chicago, IL 60637, USA (Office). *Telephone:* (773) 702-1234 (Office). *E-mail:* bos5@midway.uchicago.edu (Office).

BOSSANO, Hon. Joseph J., B.SC.(ECON.), BA; Gibraltarian politician; b. 10 June 1939; m. 1st Judith Baker 1967 (divorced 1988); three s. one d.; m. 2nd Rose Torilla 1988; ed Gibraltar Grammar School, Birmingham Univ., Univ. of London; factory worker 1958–60; merchant seaman 1960–64; Sec. Inte-gration with Britain Movt 1964; mem. Man. Cttee Tottenham Constituency Labour Party 1965–68; fmr mem. IWBP Exec. Cttee; Leader Gibraltar Socialist Labour Party 1977–; Leader of the Opposition 1984–88, 1996–; Sec. Gibraltar Br. Commonwealth Parl. Asscn 1980–88; Br. Officer TGWU (Gibraltar) 1974–88; Chief Minister of Gibraltar, with responsibility for Information 1988–96. *Leisure interests:* carpentry, fishing, thinking and linguistics. *Address:* 2 Gowland's Ramp, Gibraltar (Home); Gibraltar Socialist Labour Party, Suite 16, Watergardens 3, Gibraltar (Office). *Telephone:* 50700 (Office). *Fax:* 78983 (Office). *E-mail:* gslp@gibnet.gi (Home).

BOSSARD, André, DIur; French international police official (retd); b. 18 June 1926, St Ouen; s. of Charles and Aline (Sirugue) Bossard; m. Francine Agen 1956; two d.; ed Lycée Louis le Grand, Paris Univ.; called to Bar 1949; joined police service with rank of Commissaire 1950, Commissaire Principal 1958, Commissaire Divisionnaire 1968; Tech. Adviser at Police Judiciaire HQ 1970; Head of a Div. Int. Criminal Police Org. (INTERPOL) 1971–77; Contrôleur Gén. de la Police Nat. 1977; Sec.-Gen. INTERPOL 1978–85; Visiting Adjunct Prof., Univ. of Illinois 1988–91, 1998; Hon. Research Fellow, Univ. of Exeter 1991; Chevalier Légion d'honneur. *Publications:* Transna-tional Crime and Criminal Law 1987, Law Enforcement in Europe 1993, Carrefours de la grande truanderie 1998. *Leisure interest:* painting. *Address:* 228 rue de la Convention, 75015 Paris, France. *Telephone:* 1-48-28-21-45.

BOSSI, Umberto; Italian politician; b. 1941, Cassano Magnago, Varese; m. (separated); two c. by Manuela Marrone; ed Pavia Univ.; f. Lombard Autonomy League 1982; Leader, Lombard League 1984–; Senator 1987; Sec. Fed. of Northern League Movts. 1989–; sentenced to five months' imprison-ment for libel and eight months for illegal financing of his party Nov. 1995; Minister without Portfolio, responsible for Reforms and Devolution 2001–. *Address:* Lega Nord, via C. Bellerio 41, 20161 Milan, Italy (Office). *Telephone:* (02) 662341 (Office). *Fax:* (02) 66234266 (Office). *E-mail:* webmaster@leganord.org (Office). *Website:* www.leganord.org (Office).

BOSSIDY, Lawrence Arthur, BA; American business executive; b. 5 March 1935, Pittsfield, Mass.; m. Nancy Bossidy 1956; three s. six d.; ed Colgate Univ.; joined Gen. Electric Co. 1957, Vice-Chair. 1984–91; Chair., CEO Allied

Signal Inc. 1991–2000; Chair. Honeywell Inc. (after merger of Allied Signal and Honeywell 1999) 2001–02; sometime Chair. and Dir Gen. Electric Credit Corpn New York; Dir numerous cos. *Publication:* Execution: The Discipline of Getting Things Done 2002. *Address:* Honeywell Inc., 101 Columbia Road, Morristown, NJ 07960, USA. *Telephone:* (973) 455-2000. *Fax:* (973) 455-4807. *Website:* www.honeywell.com (Office).

BOSSON, Bernard; French politician; b. 25 Feb. 1948, Annecy; s. of Charles Bosson and Claire Bosson; m. Danielle Blaise 1976; one d.; ed Coll. Saint-Michel and Faculté de Droit de Lyon; barrister, Annecy 1976–; Mayor of Annecy 1983–; Deputy to Nat. Ass. 1986–93, 1995–; Sec. of State, Ministry of the Interior 1986, Del. Minister, Ministry of Foreign Affairs 1986–88; Minister of Public Transport and Tourism 1993–95; Deputy Vice-Pres. Del. for EC 1988; Vice-Pres. Mouvement européen 1990–97; Sec.-Gen. Centre des Démocrates sociaux 1991; mem. Union pour la démocratie française, Vice. Pres 1998–. *Address:* Assemblée nationale, 75355 Paris; Mairie, place de l'Hôtel de Ville, BP 2305, 74001 Annecy cedex, France. *E-mail:* bbosson@assemblee-nationale.fr (Office).

BØSTERUD, Helen; Norwegian politician; b. 15 Feb. 1940, Oslo; mem. Akershus Co. Council 1975–79; mem. Storting 1977; State Sec. Ministry of Health and Social Affairs 1980–81; Chair. Storting's Standing Cttee on Justice 1981–86, on Defence 1989–94; Minister of Justice 1986–89; Dir-Gen. Directorate for Civil Defence and Emergency Planning 1993–. *Address:* Directorate for Civil Defence and Emergency Planning, Sandakervn 12, P.O. Box 8136, Dep. 0033, Oslo, Norway.

BOSTRIDGE, Ian Charles; British opera singer (tenor); b. 25 Dec. 1965; s. of the late Leslie John Bostridge and of Lilian Winifred (née Clark); m. Lucasta Miller 1992; one s.; ed Westminster School, Univs of Oxford and Cambridge; debut recital performance in Wigmore Hall, London 1993; operatic debut in Edin. Festival 1994; has since performed in numerous inst. concert halls, including tour of USA Oct. 2000, European recital tour 2001; awards include Gramophone Solo Vocal Awards 1996, 1998, Time Out Classical Music Award 1999, Edison Award 1999, 2002, Grammy Award (opera) 1999, Critics' Choice Classical Brit Award (for The English Songbook) 2000, Preis der Deutschen Schallplattenkritik 2001, Acad. Charles Cros, Grand Prix di Disque 2001. *Television:* Winterreise 1997. *Opera:* A Midsummer Night's Dream, Edin. Festival 1994, The Magic Flute, English Nat. Opera (ENO) 1996, The Turn of the Screw, Royal Opera House 1997, 2002, The Bartered Bride, Sadler's Wells 1998, L'incoronazione di Poppea, Munich Festival 1998, The Diary of One who Vanished, Munich and NY 1999. *Publication:* Witchcraft and its Transformations 1650–1750 1997. *Leisure interests:* reading, cooking. *Address:* c/o Askonas Holt Ltd, Lonsdale Chambers, 27 Chancery Lane, London, WC2A 1PF, England.

BOSTRÖM, Rolf Gustav, PhD; Swedish professor of space physics; b. 15 April 1936, Kalmar; s. of Gustav Boström and Greta Boström (née Bergström); m. Barbro Backlund 1962; one s.; ed Royal Inst. of Tech.; Research Assoc., Dept of Plasma Physics, Royal Inst. of Tech. 1961–71, Sr Physicist 1971–75, Assoc. Prof. 1975–76; Prof. Uppsala Div. of Swedish Inst. of Space Physics (fmrly Uppsala Ionospheric Observatory) 1976–; Head Dept of Space Physics, Uppsala Univ. 1988–96; mem. Royal Swedish Acad. of Sciences. *Publications:* scientific papers on space plasma physics. *Leisure interests:* hiking, angling. *Address:* Swedish Institute of Space Physics, Uppsala Division, 75591 Uppsala (Office); Klippvägen 23, 75652 Uppsala, Sweden (Home). *Telephone:* (18) 303-61-0 (Office); (18) 320-26-1 (Home).

BOSWORTH, Stephen Warren; American diplomatist; b. 4 Dec. 1939; s. of Warren Charles Bosworth and Mina Phillips; m. Christine Holmes; two s. two d.; ed Dartmouth Coll. and George Washington Univ.; joined Foreign Service 1962, assignments in Paris, Madrid and Panama City, later Amb. to Tunisia 1979–81, the Philippines 1984–87, Repub. of Korea 1997–2001; various positions with Dept of State including Deputy Asst Sec. for Econ. Affairs and for Inter-American Affairs, Dir of Policy Planning and Head Office of Fuels and Energy; Pres. US-Japan Foundation 1988–96; Exec. Dir Korean Peninsula Energy Devt Corpn 1995–97; Dean Fletcher School of Law and Diplomacy, Tufts Univ. 2001–; Adjunct Prof. School of Int. and Public Affairs, Columbia Univ. 1990–94; Diplomat of the Year Award, American Acad. of Diplomacy 1987. *Address:* Fletcher School of Law and Diplomacy, 160 Packard Avenue, Tufts University, Medford, MA 02155, USA (Office). *Telephone:* (617) 627-3700 (Office). *E-mail:* stephen.bosworth@tufts.edu. *Website:* www.fletcher.tufts.edu.

BOT, Bernard Rudolf, DJur; Netherlands diplomatist; b. 21 Nov. 1937, Djakarta, Indonesia; s. of Th. H. Bot and E.W. van Hal; m. Christine Bot-Pathy 1962; three c.; ed St Aloysius Coll. The Hague, Univ. of Leiden, Acad. of Int. Law, The Hague and Harvard Law School; Deputy Perm. Rep. of Netherlands to North Atlantic Council, Brussels 1982–86; Amb. to Turkey 1986–89; Sec.-Gen. Ministry of Foreign Affairs 1989–92; Perm. Rep. to EU 1992–; Kt, Order of Netherlands Lion and other decorations. *Publication:* Non-recognition and Treaty Relations 1968. *Leisure interests:* cycling, painting, skiing. *Address:* Permanent Representation of the Netherlands to the European Union, avenue Hermann Debroux 48, 1160 Brussels, Belgium. *Telephone:* 679-15-02 (Office). *Fax:* 679-17-95 (Office).

BOTCHARNIKOV, Mikhail Nikolayevich; Russian diplomatist; b. 6 March 1948, Moscow; one d.; ed Moscow Inst. of Int. Relations; mem. staff Ministry of Foreign Affairs until 1992; Amb. to Zambia 1992–96; Dir Dept of

African Countries, Ministry of Foreign Affairs 1996–99; Amb. to Greece 1999–. *Address:* Embassy of Russian Federation, Odos Nikiforou Litra 28, Palaio-Psychico, Athens, Greece. *Telephone:* (1) 6714594 (Office). *Fax:* (1) 6479703 (Office).

BOTELHO, João; Portuguese film director; b. 11 May 1949, Lamego; ed Nat. Conservator Film School, Lisbon; involved in film socs. in Coimbra and Oporto; film critic for newspapers; f. film magazine M. *Films include:* Alexandre e Rosa (short, co-Dir) 1978, Conversa acabada (The Other One) 1980, Um adeus português (A Portuguese Goodbye) 1985, Tempos difíceis (Hard Times) 1987. *Address:* c/o Associação Portuguesa de Realizadores, Rua de Palmeira 7, r/c, 1200 Lisbon, Portugal.

BOTELHO, Maurício; Brazilian business executive; Pres. and C.E.O. Empresa Brasiliera de Aeronautica S.A.; BACCF Excellence Award 1999. *Address:* EMBRAER, Av. Brig. Faria Lima 2170, Putim 12227-901, S. Jose dos Campos, Sao Paulo, Brazil (Office). *Telephone:* (12) 345-1000 (Office). *Fax:* (12) 321-8238 (Office).

BOTERO, Fernando; Colombian artist; b. 19 April 1932, Medellín; s. of David Botero and Flora Botero; m. Cecilia Botero 1964; four c.; first group Exhbn, Medellín 1948; first one-man exhbn, Galería Leo Matiz, Bogotá 1951; studied at Acad. San Fernando and El Prado Museum, Madrid 1952; visited Paris and Italy and studied art history with Roberto Longhi, Univ. of Florence 1953–54; lived in Mexico 1956; one-man exhbn Pan American Union, Washington, DC 1957, Colombia 1958–59; lived in New York 1960–; first one-man exhbn in Europe, Baden-Baden and Munich 1966; visited Italy and Germany 1967, studied work of Dürer; travelling retrospective exhbn of 80 paintings in five German museums 1970; one-man exhbn Hannover Gallery, London 1970; moved to Paris 1973; concentrated on Sculpture 1976–77, first one-man exhbn of sculpture, Foire Int. d'Art Contemporain, Paris 1977; retrospective exhbn, Hirshorn Museum and Sculpture Garden, Washington, DC 1979; first one-man exhbn in Japan, Tokyo, Osaka 1981; outdoor sculpture exhbn, Chicago 1994; paintings in public collections in Belgium, Finland, Germany, Israel, Italy, S. America, Spain and USA; Guggenheim Nat. Prize for Colombia 1960.

BOTERO RESTREPO, Oscar; Colombian politician and army officer; b. 11 May 1933, Armenia, Caldas; s. of Jaime Botero and Felisa Restrepo; m. Lucía Restrepo Mejía 1963 (deceased); three s.; ed Univ. of Gran Colombia and José María Cordova Mil. School; Commdr Intelligence Bn 1967–70; Commdr Charry Solano Bn 1971–72; Chief of Mil. Household of the Palacio Nacional 1973–74; Mil. Attaché, Colombian Embassy, Madrid 1974–76; Chief of Dept of E-1 Commando 1976; Commdr 8th Brigade 1977–78; Chief of Dept of D-2 of Jt Staff 1979–81; Commdr 5th Brigade 1981–82; Chief of Mil. Household of the Presidency 1982–83; Commdr 5th Div. 1983–84; Army Inspector 1984–85; Second-in-Command and Army Chief of Staff 1985–86; Commdr of Army 1986–88; Gen. Commdr of Mil. Forces 1988–89; Minister of Nat. Defence 1989; rank of Gen. 1987; Commdr of Order of the Liberator, Star of Carabobo; Cross of the Land Forces of Venezuela. *Address:* c/o Ministry of National Defence, Avda Eldorado, Bogotá, Colombia.

BOTHA, Pieter Willem, DMS, MP; South African politician; b. 12 Jan. 1916, Paul Roux district, OFS; m. 1st Anna Elizabeth Rossouw 1943 (died 1997); two s. three d.; m. 2nd Barbara Robertson 1998; ed Univ. of Orange Free State; mem. Parl. for George 1948–84; Chief Sec. Cape Nat. Party 1948–58, Deputy Minister of the Interior 1958–61; Minister of Community Devt, Public Works and Coloured Affairs 1961–66, of Defence 1966–80, of Nat. Security 1978–84; Prime Minister 1978–84; State Pres. of South Africa 1984–89; C-in-C of the Armed Forces 1984–89; Leader Nat. Party 1978–89; Leader Nat. Party in Cape Prov. 1966–86; Chancellor Univ. of Stellenbosch 1984–88; acquitted of charges brought by Truth and Reconciliation Comm. 1998; Dr. hc (Univs. of OFS, Pretoria and Stellenbosch); Decoration for Meritorious Service (SA) 1976, Order of the Star of SA and various foreign awards and decorations. *Publications:* Voice from the Wilderness (biog.), Fighter and Reformer, P.W. (biog.). *Leisure interests:* horse riding, hunting game, reading, walking. *Address:* Die Anker, Wilderness 6560, South Africa.

BOTHA, Roelof Frederik (Pik), BA, LLB; South African politician; b. 27 April 1932, Rustenburg; m. 1st Helena Bosman 1953; two s. two d.; m. 2nd Ina Joubert 1998; ed Volkskool, Potchefstroom, Univ. of Pretoria; joined Dept of Foreign Affairs 1953; served with diplomatic missions in Europe 1956–66; mem. S. African legal team in SW Africa case, Int. Court of Justice, The Hague 1963–66, 1970–71; Agent of S. African Govt, Int. Court of Justice 1965–66; Legal Adviser Dept of Foreign Affairs 1966–68, Under-Sec. and Head SW Africa and UN sections 1968–70; mem. Parl. for Wonderboom 1970–74, for Westdene 1977–94, re-elected 1994–96, served on various select Parl. cttees. 1970–74; Sec. Foreign Affairs Study Group of Nat. Party's mems. of Parl. 1974; Amb. and Perm. Rep. to UN 1974–77; Amb. to USA 1975–77; Minister of Foreign Affairs 1977–94, of Mineral and Energy Affairs 1994–96, for Information 1980–86; mem. S. African Del. to UN Gen. Assembly 1967–69, 1971, 1973–74; Leader Nat. Party in Transvaal 1992–96; Grand Cross, Order of Good Hope, Decoration for Meritorious Service (SA), Grand Cordon, Order of the Brilliant Star (Taiwan). *Leisure interests:* hunting and fishing. *Address:* P.O. Box 16176, Pretoria North 0116, South Africa.

BOTHAM, Ian Terence, OBE; British cricketer; b. 24 Nov. 1955; s. of Leslie Botham and Marie Botham; m. Kathryn Waller 1976; one s. two d.; ed Buckler's Mead Secondary School, Yeovil; right-hand batsman, right-hand, fast-medium bowler; teams: Somerset 1974–86 (Capt. 1984–85), Worcs.

1987–91, Queensland 1987–88, Durham 1992–93; 102 Tests for England 1977–92, 12 as Capt., scoring 5,200 runs (average 33.5) including 14 hundreds, taking 383 wickets (average 28.4) and holding 120 catches; scored 1,673 runs and took 148 wickets v. Australia; became first player to score a century and take 8 wickets in an innings in a Test match, v. Pakistan (Lord's) 1978; took 100th wicket in Test cricket in record time of 2 years 9 days 1979; achieved double of 1,000 runs and 100 wickets in Tests to create world record of fewest Tests (21) and English records of shortest time (2 years 33 days) and at youngest age (23 years 279 days) 1979; became first player to have scored 3,000 runs and taken 250 wickets in Tests (55) Nov. 1982; first player to score a century and take 10 wickets in a Test match, v. India; scored 19,399 runs (38 hundreds) and took 1,172 wickets in first-class cricket; toured Australia 1978–79, 1979–80, 1982–83 and 1986–87; has also played soccer for Scunthorpe United and Yeovil; mem. Sky cricket commentary team 1995–; Tech. Dir of bowling, England Cricket Team 1996–; Chair. Mission Logistics Ltd. 2000–, mem. MCC Cricket Cttee 1995, Sports Council 1995–, Laurens World Sports Acad.; Hon. MSc (UMIST); Wisden Cricketer of the Year 1978. *Publications include:* It Sort of Clicks 1986, Cricket My Way 1989, Botham: My Autobiography 1994, The Botham Report (with Peter Hayter) 1997. *Leisure interests:* shooting, golf, flying, fishing. *Address:* Mission Sports Management, Kirmington Vale, Barnetby, North Lincs., DN38 6AF, England (Office). *Telephone:* (1652) 688900 (Office). *Fax:* (1652) 688899 (Office). *E-mail:* adam@missionsportsmanagement.com (Office). *Website:* www.missionsportsmanagement.com (Office).

BOTHWELL, Thomas Hamilton, DSc, MD, FRCP, FRSSA; South African physician and professor of medicine; b. 27 Feb. 1926; s. of Robert Cooper Bothwell and Jessie Isobel (née Hamilton) Bothwell; m. Alexandrine Moorman Butterworth 1957; one s. two d.; ed St John's Coll., Johannesburg, Univ. of Witwatersrand and Univs. of Oxford and Washington; physician, later Sr Physician Dept of Medicine, Univ. of the Witwatersrand 1956–67, Prof. of Medicine and Head Dept of Medicine 1967–91; Chief Physician Johannesburg Hosp. 1967–91; Dir MRC Iron and Red Cell Metabolism Research Unit, Univ. of the Witwatersrand 1969–91, Dean of Medicine 1992–93, Hon. Professorial Research Fellow 1993–; Hon. FACP; Dr hc (Univs of Cape Town, Natal, Witwatersrand); Gold Medal, SA Medical Research Council; Medal of the SA Asscn for the Advancement of Science 1980, Biennial Award of the Nutrition Soc. of Southern Africa 1988, John F.W. Medal of the the Royal Soc. of South Africa (1993). *Publications:* 250 articles in the field of iron metabolism, 50 chapters, 7 monographs and two books: Iron Metabolism 1962, Iron Metabolism in Man 1979. *Leisure interests:* reading, walking, dogs. *Address:* Faculty of Medicine, University of the Witwatersrand, Medical School, 7 York Road, Parktown 2193, Johannesburg, South Africa.

BOTÍN, Emilio; Spanish banker; b. 1934, Santander; m. Paloma O'Shea; six c.; ed Univ. of Duesto, Bilbao; inherited Banco de Santander 1986, Pres. 1986–99 (introduced high-interest accounts and low-interest mortgages, absorbed Banesto 1993); Co-Pres. Banco Santander Cen. Hispano (following merger of Banco de Santander with Banco Hispano Americano and Banco Central 1999) 1999–2002, Exec. Chair. Feb. 2002–. *Leisure interests:* hunting, fishing, golf, the arts. *Address:* Santander Central Hispano, Paseo de la Castellana 75, Edificio Azca - Planta 12, 28046 Madrid, Spain (Office). *Telephone:* (91) 3423175 (Office). *Fax:* (91) 3423177 (Office). *Website:* www.bsch.es (Office).

BOTNARU, Ion, PhD; Moldovan diplomatist; b. 19 Aug. 1954, Chişinău; s. of Toma Botnaru and Tatiana Sheremet; m. 1979; one s. one d.; ed Inst. of Oriental Studies, Moscow, Moscow State Univ.; fmr translator and interpreter of Turkish and English; Sr Researcher, Inst. of History Studies, Nat. Acad. of Science, Chişinău 1983–84; Prof. of Contemporary History of Asia and Africa, Chişinău State Univ. 1987–89; Deputy Dir.-Gen. Dept of Protocol, Ministry of Foreign Affairs 1989–90, Dir.-Gen. Dept of Political Affairs 1990–92, Deputy Minister 1992–93, Minister 1993–94; Amb. to Turkey (also Accred to Kuwait and Egypt) 1994–98; Perm. Rep. to UN, New York 1998–2002; mem. Moldovan del. to UN Gen. Ass. 1992; Head Moldovan del. to UN World Conf. on Human Rights 1993; mem. Asscn of Orientalists 1985–. *Publications:* The Army and Politics in Turkey 1986, Islam and Political Parties in Turkey 1989, The Process of Democratisation in Moldova—Political Aspects 1993; numerous papers and articles. *Address:* c/o Ministry of Foreign Affairs, Chişinău, Moldova (Office).

BOTT, Martin Harold Phillips, MA, PhD, FRS; British professor of geophysics; b. 12 July 1926, Stoke-on-Trent; s. of Harold Bott and Dorothy Bott (née Phillips); m. Joyce Cynthia Hughes 1961; two s. one d.; ed Clayesmore School, Dorset, Keble Coll. Oxford (army short course) and Magdalene Coll. Cambridge; Nat. Service in army (Royal Signals) 1945–48, rank of Lt; Turner & Newall Research Fellow, Univ. of Durham 1954–56, Lecturer in Geophysics 1956–63, Reader 1963–66, Prof. 1966–88, Research Prof. in Geophysics 1988–91, Prof. Emer. 1991–; Head of Dept of Geological Sciences 1970–73, 1976–82; Chair. British Nat. Cttee for Geodesy and Geophysics 1985–89; Murchison Medal, Geological Soc. of London 1977, Clough Medal, Geological Soc. of Edinburgh 1979, Sorby Medal, Yorks. Geological Soc. 1981, Wollaston Medal, Geological Soc. of London 1992. *Achievements:* completed climbing the Scottish Munros at age of 76 Sept. 2002. *Publications:* The Interior of the Earth 1971, Structure and Development of the Greenland–Scotland Ridge: new methods and concepts (Co-Ed.) 1983, Sedimentary Basins of Continental Margins and Cratons (Ed.) 1976 and many scientific papers in journals.

Leisure interests: Reader (Anglican Church), mountain walking, garden slavery, etc. *Address:* 11 St Mary's Close, Shincliffe, Durham, DH1 2ND, England.

BOTT, Raoul, DSc; American (naturalized) mathematician; b. 24 Sept. 1923, Budapest, Hungary; s. of Rudolph Bott and Margit (Kovacs) Bott; m. Phyllis H. Aikman 1947; one s. three d.; ed McGill Univ. and Carnegie Inst. of Tech.; mem. Inst. for Advanced Study, Princeton 1949–51, 1955–57; Instructor in Math., Univ. of Mich. 1951–52, Asst Prof. 1952–55, Prof. 1957–59; Prof. of Math., Harvard Univ. 1959–, Higgins Prof. of Math. 1967–79, Graustein Prof. of Math. 1969–99, William Casper Graustein Research Prof. 2000–; Ed. Topology, Annals of Mathematics 1958–59, American Journal of Mathematics 1969; mem. Nat. Acad. of Sciences, American Math. Soc., American Acad. of Arts and Sciences, French Acad. of Sciences; Master Dunster House 1978–84; Hon. Fellow London Math. Soc. 1983, St Catherine's Coll., Oxford 1984; several hon. degrees and awards; Nat. Medal of Science 1987, Stole Prize 1990, shared Wolf Prize in Math. 2000. *Leisure interests:* music, swimming, skiing. *Address:* Mathematics Department, Harvard University, Science Center, 1 Oxford Street, Cambridge, MA 02138 (Office); 1 Richdale Avenue No. 9, Cambridge, MA 02140, USA (Home). *Telephone:* (616) 864-2482 (Home).

BOTTOMLEY, Rt Hon Virginia (Hilda Brunette Maxwell), PC, BA, MSc, JP; British politician; b. 12 March 1948; d. of the late W. John Garnett and of Barbara Garnett (née Rutherford-Smith); m. Peter Bottomley, MP; one s. two d.; ed Putney High School, Univ. of Essex, LSE; researcher for Child Poverty Action Group and lecturer in a further educ. coll. 1971–73, Psychiatric Social Worker Brixton and Camberwell Child Guidance Units 1973–84; Vice-Chair. Nat. Council of Carers and their Elderly Dependants 1982–88; Dir Mid Southern Water Co. 1987–88; mem. MRC 1987–88; MP Surrey South-West May 1984–; Parl. Pvt. Sec. to Minister of State for Educ. and Science 1985–86, to Minister for Overseas Devt 1986–87, to Sec. of State for Foreign and Commonwealth Affairs 1987–88; Parl. Under-Sec. of State Dept of Educ. and Science 1988–89; Sec. Conservative Backbench Employment Cttee 1985; Fellow Industry Parl. Trust 1987; Minister of State (Minister for Health) –1992; Sec. of State for Health 1992–95, with responsibility for Family Policy 1994–95; Sec. of State for Nat. Heritage 1995–97; Partner, Odgers Ray Berndtson Int. 2000–; mem. Supervisory Bd Akzo Nobel 2000–; Co-Chair. Women's Nat. Comm. 1991–92; mem. Court of Govs LSE 1985–, British Council 1997–, House of Commons Select Cttee on Foreign Affairs 1997–99; JP Inner London 1975 (Chair. Lambeth Juvenile Court 1981–84); Hon. LLD (Portsmouth) 1992. *Leisure interest:* family. *Address:* House of Commons, London, SW1A 0AA, England. *Telephone:* (20) 7219-6499.

BOUBAKER, Sidi Mohamed Ould; Mauritanian politician; b. 19 May 1954; ed Nat. School of Admin., Univ. of Nancy; fmr civil servant; Sec.-Gen. Democratic and Social Republican Party (DSRP); fmr Minister of Finance; Prime Minister of Mauritania 1992–96. *Address:* c/o Office of the Prime Minister, Nouackchott, Mauritania.

BOUBLIL, Alain Albert; French author and dramatist; b. 5 March 1941, Tunis; four s.; wrote libretto and lyrics for: La Révolution Française 1973, Les Misérables 1980, Abbacadabra 1984, Miss Saigon 1989, Martin Guerre 1996; Le Journal d'Adam et Eve (play) 1994; two Tony Awards, Two Grammy Awards, two Victoire de la Musique Awards, Molière Award (all for Les Misérables), Evening Standard Drama Award (for Miss Saigon), Laurence Olivier Award (for Martin Guerre). *Leisure interests:* theatre, opera, cinema, tennis. *Address:* c/o Cameron Mackintosh Limited, 1 Bedford Square, London, WC1B 3RA, England. *Telephone:* (20) 7637-8866. *Fax:* (20) 7436-2683.

BOUCHARD, Benoît, BA; Canadian politician; b. 16 April 1940, Roberval, Québec; m. Jeannine Lavoie; three c.; ed Laval Univ.; teacher Coll. Classique, Coll. Notre-Dame, then Prin. Coll. Notre-Dame and Villa étudiante, Roberval; Dir-Gen. St Félicien CEGEP 1979–; alderman, Roberval 1973–80; Minister of State (Transport) 1984–85, Minister of Communications 1985–86, of Employment and Immigration 1986–88, of Transport 1988–90, of Industry, Science and Tech. 1990–91, of Nat. Health and Welfare 1991–93; Amb. to France 1993–96; apptd. Chair. Transportation Bd of Canada 1996. *Address:* c/o Transport Safety Board of Canada, 200 promenade du Portage, Hull, QC K1A 1K8, Canada (Office).

BOUCHARD, Lucien, BA, BSc; Canadian politician; b. 22 Dec. 1938, Saint-Coeur-de-Marie, Lac Saint-Jean, Québec; s. of Philippe Bouchard and Alice Simard; m. Audrey Best; two s.; ed Laval Univ.; admitted Québec Bar 1964; pvt. law practice in Chicoutimi until 1985; mem. numerous comms. and orgs. connected with labour relations, both in public and pvt. sectors; Pres. Saguenay Bar 1978; Amb. to France 1985–88; Sec. of State of Canada 1988; MP 1988–2001; Minister of the Environment 1989–90; resgnd from Conservative Party 1990 to lead Bloc Québécois; Chair. and Leader, Bloc Québécois 1991–96; Leader Parti Québécois 1996–2001; Leader of Opposition, House of Commons 1993–95; Prime Minister of Québec 1996–2001. *Publications:* À visage découvert 1992; articles in legal and labour relations journals. *Address:* Parti Québécois, 1200 avenue Papineau, Bureau 150, Montreal, QC H2K 4R5, Canada (Office).

BOUCHARDEAU, Huguette; French politician; b. 1 June 1935, St-Etienne; d. of Marius Briaut and Rose (née Noël) Briaut; m. Marc Bouchardeau 1955; one s. two d.; teacher of philosophy, Lycée Honoré d'Urfé 1961–70; lecturer in educ. sciences, Univ. of Lyon 1970; Sec.-Gen. Parti Socialiste unifié 1979–83;

unsuccessful presidential cand. 1981; Sec. of State for Environment and Quality of Life 1983–84; Minister for the Environment 1984–86; f., Ed. H.B. Editions 1995–; Mayor Aigues-Vives 1995–; Chevalier Légion d'honneur. *Publications:* Pas d'histoire, les femmes 1977, Hélène Brion: La voie feministe 1978, Un coin dans leur monde 1980, Le ministère du possible 1986, Choses dites de profil 1988, George Sand, La lune et les sabots 1990, Rose Noël 1990, La grande verrière 1991, Carnets de Prague 1992, Le Déjeuner 1993, La Famille Renoir 1994, Simone Weil 1995, Les Roches rouges 1996, Faute de regard 1997, Agatha Christie 1999, Voyage autour de ma bibliothèque 2000, Elsa Triolet 2001, Mes Nuits avec Descartes 2002. *Address:* H.B. Editions, 8 rue Ménard, Nîmes 30000, France (Office). *E-mail:* bouchardeau-hb-editions@wanadoo.fr (Office).

BOUCHÈNE, Abderrahmane; Algerian publisher; b. 1941, Algiers; m.; four c.; ed Algeria and Lausanne Univs.; worked in family clothing shop; admin. posts at Société nat. d'édition et de diffusion, Entreprise nat. du livre and Ministry of Culture; f. Editions Bouchène publishing house, Kouba, in late 1980s; by 1990 owner of two bookshops in Algiers, one in Riad-El-Feth; forced to flee Algeria and close business 1994; exile in Tunisia 1994–96; moved to Paris and set up new co. specializing in Algerian historical texts and historical anthropology of Maghreb socs. *Address:* Editions Bouchène, 113–115 rue Danielle-Casanova, 93200 Saint-Denis, Paris, France (Office). *Telephone:* 1-48-20-93-75 (Office). *E-mail:* edbouchene@aol.com (Office).

BOUCHER, Carlston B., BSc, MA; Barbadian diplomatist and international civil servant; b. 18 May 1933; m.; ed Univs. of London and Sussex; Govt appointments 1957–72; Research Economist, Econ. Programmes Dept, World Bank 1972–74, Country Economist for SA, Botswana, Lesotho and Swaziland, Africa Regional Dept 1974–78, Deputy Special Rep. of World Bank to UN 1978–83, Sr Economist, Strategic Planning and Review Dept 1983–87, Adviser, External Relations Dept 1987–90, Prin. Econ. Affairs Officer, Operations Policy Dept, Int. Econs Div. 1990–93, Special Rep. to UN, New York and Geneva 1993–95; Perm. Rep. to UN 1995–2001. *Address:* c/o Ministry of Foreign Affairs and Foreign Trade, 1 Culloden Road, St Michael, Barbados (Office).

BOUCHIER, Ian Arthur Dennis, CBE, MB, CH.B., MD, FRCP, FRCPE, FRSA, FRSE, FFPHM, FIBiol, FMedSci; British professor of medicine; b. 7 Sept. 1932, Cape Town, S. Africa; s. of E. A. Bouchier and May Bouchier; m. Patricia N. Henshilwood 1959; two s.; ed Rondebosch Boys' High School and Univ. of Cape Town; junior staff positions, Groote Schuur Hosp. Cape Town 1955–60; Registrar, Lecturer, Royal Free Hosp. London 1961–63; Research Fellow, Instr. Boston Univ. 1963–65; Sr Lecturer, Univ. of London 1965–70, Reader in Medicine 1970–73; Prof. of Medicine, Univ. of Dundee 1973–86, Univ. of Edin. 1986–97; Sec.-Gen. World Org. of Gastroenterology 1982–90, Pres. 1990–98; Chief Scientist for Scotland 1992–97; mem. Chief Scientist Cttee; Visiting Prof. Univ. of Michigan 1979, Madras Medical Coll. 1981, McGill Univ. 1983, Royal Postgrad. Medical School 1984, Univ. of Hong Kong 1988, China Medical Univ. 1988, Univ. of Dunedin 1989, Keio Univ. 1991; mem. Council British Soc. of Gastroenterology 1987–90 (Pres. 1994–95); mem. Council, Royal Soc. of Edin. 1986–89; mem. Council British Soc. of Gastroenterology 1992–; Fellow, Inst. of Biology; Hon. mem. South African Soc. of Gastroenterology, Japanese Soc. of Gastroenterology; Corresp. mem. Italian Soc. of Gastroenterology, Royal Catalonian Acad. of Medicine; mem. numerous editorial bds; Hon. FCP (South Africa); Hon. MD (Iasi). *Publications:* 28 textbooks and 600 articles mainly on gastroenterological topics. *Leisure interests:* music of Berlioz, history of whaling, cooking. *Address:* 8A Merchiston Park, Edinburgh, EH10 4PN, Scotland.

BOUDART, Michel, MA, PhD; American professor of chemical engineering; b. 18 June 1924, Brussels, Belgium; s. of François Boudart and Marguerite Swolfs; m. Marina M. D'Haese 1948; three s. one d.; ed Princeton Univ., Univ. of Louvain; Asst then Assoc. Prof. Princeton Univ. 1954–61; Prof. Univ. of Calif. (Berkeley) 1961–64; adjunct Prof. of Chemical Eng 1994–; Prof. of Chemical Eng and Chemistry Stanford Univ. 1964–80, William M. Keck Prof. 1980–94, Prof. Emer. 1994–; mem. tech. advisory Bd British Petroleum 1992–98, Nova 1997–, numerous editorial bds.; co-founder and Dir Catalytica Inc. 1973; mem. NAS, Nat. Acad. of Eng, American Acad. of Arts and Sciences, Calif. Acad. of Sciences, Royal Belgian Acad. of Sciences, Acad. Nat. de Pharmacie. *Publications include:* Kinetics of Chemical Processes 1968, Kinetics of Heterogeneous Catalytic Reactions 1984 (with G. Djéga-Mariadassou), Jt (with J. R. Anderson) Catalysis: Science and Technology, 11 Vols 1981–96, (with Marina Boudart and René Bryssinck) Modern Belgium 1990. *Leisure interest:* travel. *Address:* Department of Chemical Engineering, Stanford University, Stanford, CA 94305 (Office); 228 Oak Grove Avenue, Atherton, CA 94027, USA (Home). *Telephone:* (650) 723-4748 (Office). *Fax:* (650) 723-9780 (Office). *E-mail:* lindi@chemeng.stanford.edu (Office).

BOUDRIA, Don, PC, BA; Canadian politician; b. 30 Aug. 1949, Hull, Québec; m. Mary Ann Morris 1971; one s. one d.; ed Eastview High School, Univ. of Waterloo; entered Fed. Govt 1966, held various positions including Chief Purchasing Agent –1981; Councillor, Cumberland Township 1976–80, fmr mem. Cumberland Township Housing Corpn; mem. Ontario Legis. (mem. Prov. Parl. for Prescott-Russell) 1981–84, Opposition Critic of Govt Services 1981–82, of Community and Social Services 1982–83, of Consumer and Commercial Relations 1983–84; mem. Parl. for Glengarry-Prescott-Russell 1984–; Opposition Critic on Fed. Supply and Services; mem. Standing Cttee on Agriculture 1984; mem. Ont. Liberal Caucus 1984, Chair. 1985–87;

Opposition Critic on Public Works 1985, Govt Operations 1987, Canada Post and Govt Operations 1988; Deputy Opposition Whip 1989; Asst House Leader for the Official Opposition and Govt Operations Critic 1990–93; Deputy Govt Whip 1994; Minister of Int. Co-operation and Francophonie 1996–97; Minister of State and Leader of Govt in House of Commons 1997–2002; Minister of Public Works and Govt Services Jan.–May 2002; Minister of State and Leader of the Govt in House of Commons 2002–; Founding Pres. Ont. Section, Int. Asscn of French-speaking Parliamentarians; Founding mem. Sarsfield Knights of Columbus. *Leisure interests:* history, music, downhill skiing. *Address:* 215-S Centre Block, House of Commons, Ottawa, Ont., K1A 0A6 (Office); 3455 Dessaint Crescent, Sarsfield, Ont., K0A 3E0, Canada (Home).

BOUGIE, Jacques, OC; Canadian business executive; b. 1947, Montreal; ed Univ. de Montréal; joined Alcan 1979, Man. Beauharnois Works, then various positions in Winnipeg, Toronto and Montreal in maj. project Devt, planning and gen. man., responsible for fabricating operations in N America, Pres., COO Alcan Aluminium Ltd 1989–93, Pres., CEO 1993–; Vice-Chair. Business Council on Nat. Issues; mem. Bd Dirs. Asia Pacific Foundation of Canada. *Address:* Office of the President, Alcan Aluminium Limited, 1188 Sherbrooke Street W, Montreal, Québec, H3A 3G2, Canada. *E-mail:* jacques.bougie@ alcan.com (Office). *Website:* www.alcan.com (Office).

BOUHAFS, Abdelhak; Algerian government official; b. 15 Aug. 1945; m.; one c.; ed Algiers and Grenoble Univs.; with Sonatrach 1974, Asst to Vice-Pres. and responsible for Devt and for valorization of hydrocarbons 1974–80, Co-ordinator of Energy Studies 1980–83; joined Ministry of Energy and Petrochemical Industries 1983; Dir-Gen. of Energy Coordination and of Commercialization 1984–86; responsible for Studies and Synthesis in sphere of Int. Relations 1986–88; Chef de Cabinet to Minister of Energy and Petrochemical Industries 1988–89; Dir-Gen. Sonatrach 1989. *Address:* c/o Sonatrach, 10 rue du Sahara, Hydra, Algiers, Algeria.

BOULANGER, Daniel; French writer; b. 24 Jan. 1922, Compiègne, Oise; s. of Michel Boulanger and Hélène Bayart; m. 2nd Clémence Dufour; four s. three d.; ed Petit Séminaire Saint-Charles, Chauny; sub-editor, Affaires économiques 1946–48; writer 1948–; wrote scripts or screenplays for over 100 films, including Cartouche 1962, L'Homme de Rio 1963, Les Tribulations d'un Chinois en Chine 1965, La Vie de Château 1966, Le Voleur 1967, Le Diable par la Queue 1968, Le Roi de Coeur (Prix Louis-Delluc) 1969, Les Maries de l'An II 1971, L'Affaire Dominici 1973, Prieu Puthon 1975, Une femme fidèle 1976, La Menace 1976, Cheval d'Orgueil 1980, Chouans 1988, La Révolution Française 1989; numerous plays; mem. Acad. Goncourt 1983; Prix Pierre de Monaco for his complete body of work 1979, Prix Kléber Haedens 1983; Officier Légion d'honneur, Officier Ordre nat. du Mérite, Commdr des Arts et des Lettres. *Publications include:* (novels, novellas and short stories) Les Noces du Merle 1963 (Prix de la Nouvelle 1963), Retouches 1969 (Prix Max Jacob 1970), Vessies et Lanternes 1971 (Prix de l'Académie française 1971), Fouette Cocher 1974 (Prix Goncourt de la Nouvelle 1974), La Confession d'Omer 1991, Un Eté à la diable 1992, Ursacq 1993, A la courte paille 1993, Le Retable Wasserfall et Etiquettes 1994, Caporal Supérieur 1994, Le Miroitier 1995, Taciturnes 1995, Tombeau d'Héraldine 1997, Talbard 1998, Le Ciel de Bargetal 1999, Clémence et Auguste 2000; several collections of poetry including L'été des femmes 1964, Le chemin des Caruoles, Fête Ste. Beuve 1966, Memoire de la Ville 1970. *Address:* 22 rue du Heaume, 60300 Senlis, France.

BOULARÈS, Mohamed Habib; Tunisian politician, writer and journalist; b. 29 July 1933, Tunis; s. of Sadok Ben Mohamed and Zoubeida Bent Abdelkader Aziz; m. Line Poinsignon 1966; one d.; ed Collège Sadiki, Tunis; mem. staff exec. office, Parti Destourien 1955; Deputy Ed. daily Essabah 1956; in charge of publications, Ministry of Information 1957; Ed. Nat. Radio news service 1958; Ed. Al Amal (Parti Destourien daily newspaper) 1960; first Man. Dir Tunis Afrique Presse news agency 1961; Dir Radio Télévision Tunisienne, Dir of Information, Ministry of Cultural Affairs and Information 1962; mem. Econ. and Social Council 1964–70; Minister of Cultural Affairs and Information 1970; Dir Ecole Internationale de Bordeaux, France 1972–73; teacher, Institut de Langues Orientales, Paris for four years; mem. Parl. 1981–86, 1989–94, 1994–; Amb. to Egypt 1988; Minister of Culture 1988–89, of Culture and Information 1989–90, of Foreign Affairs 1990–91, of Nat. Defence Feb.–Oct. 1991; Special Adviser to Pres. of Repub. March 1990; Pres. Nat. Ass. 1991–94; (Mediterranean Africa prize of Asscn des Ecrivains en langue française ADELF) 1984; Grand Officier Ordre de l'Indépendance, Grand Cordon Ordre de la République, Commdr Ordre du 7 Novembre, numerous foreign decorations. *Publications:* L'Islam, la peur et l'espérance (trans. in English); several other non-fiction works and plays. *Address:* c/o Assemblée Nationale, 2000 Le Bardo, Tunis, Tunisia. *Telephone:* (1) 510-200. *Fax:* (1) 514-608.

BOULEZ, Pierre; French composer and conductor; b. 26 March 1925, Montbrison; s. of Léon Boulez and Marcelle Calabre; ed Paris Conservatoire; studied with Messiaen, Vaurabourg-Honegger and Leibowitz; Dir of Music to Jean-Louis Barrault theatre co. 1948; aided by Barrault and Madeleine Renaud Barrault he founded the Concert Marigny which later became the Domaine Musical, Paris; Prin. Guest Conductor Cleveland Symphony Orchestra 1968; Prin. Conductor BBC Symphony Orchestra 1971–75; Musical Dir New York Philharmonic 1971–77; Dir Inst. de Recherches et de Coordination Acoustique/Musique (IRCAM) 1975–91, Hon. Dir 1992–; Founder and Pres. Ensemble Intercontinental 1977–98; Prof. Collège de

France 1976–95; Prin. Guest Conductor Chicago Symphony Orchestra 1995–; conducted the centenary production of Wagner's Ring, Bayreuth 1976–80; Hon. CBE; Dr hc (Cambridge) 1980, (Bâle) 1980, (Los Angeles) 1984, (Oxford) 1987, (Brussels) 1988; Prize of the Siemens Foundation 1979, Praemium Imperiale, Japan Art Asscn 1989, Polar Music Prize Sweden 1996, Grawemeyer Award 2001. *Works:* First Piano Sonata 1946, Sonatina for Flute and Piano 1946, Le Visage nuptial (5 poems of René Char for 2 solo voices, female choir and orch.) 1946–50, Second Piano Sonata 1948, Le Soleil des eaux (2 poems of René Char for voice and orch.) 1948, Livre pour Quatuor (string quartet) 1949, Le Marteau sans maître (cantata for voice and instruments to texts by René Char, also ballet 1965) 1955, Structures (2 pianos) 1964, Third Piano Sonata 1957–58, Improvisations sur Mallarmé (soprano and chamber ensemble) 1958, Doubles (orch.) 1958, Poésie pour pouvoir (orch.) 1958, Tombeau (soprano and orch.) 1959, Pli selon Pli 1958–62, Figures–Doubles-Prismes 1964/74, Eclat and Eclat/Multiples 1965, Domaines 1968–69, cummings ist der dichter 1970, explosante-fixe for 8 solo instruments 1973, Rituel 1974, Messagesquisse 1977, Notations 1979, Répons 1981–86, Dérive 1984, Dialogue de l'ombre double 1984, Mémoriale 1985, le Visage nuptial 1989, . . . explosante-fixe . . . for Midi-flute, 2 solo flutes, ensemble and electronics 1993, Anthèmes 2 1997, sur Incises 1998, Notations VII 1999, Dérive 2 2001. *Publications:* Penser la musique aujourd'hui 1966, Relevés d'apprenti (essays) 1967, Par volonté et par hasard 1975, Points de repère 1981, Le pays fertile: Paul Klee 1989, Orientations: Collected Writings 1986. *Address:* IRCAM, 1 place Igor Stravinsky, 75004 Paris, France; Postfach 100022, 76481 Baden-Baden, Germany.

BOUMA, Johannes, PhD; Netherlands soil scientist; b. 29 Oct. 1940, 't Bildt; s. of S. Bouma and J. Bouma (née Werff); m. Marianne Wiebols 1969; one s. one d.; ed Agricultural Univ., Wageningen, Univ. of Wisconsin, Madison; Asst Prof. Soils Dept, Univ. of Wis., Madison 1969–73, Assoc. Prof. 1973–75; Head of Soil Physics Dept, Netherlands Soil Survey Inst., Wageningen 1975–82, Deputy Dir in charge of research 1982–86; Prof. of Soil Science, Agricultural Univ. of Wageningen 1986–2002, Scientific Dir Environmental Sciences Group Research Centre 2002–04; mem. Netherlands Scientific Council for Govt Policy 1998–2003; mem. Royal Dutch Acad. of Sciences 1989; Corresp. mem. German Soil Science Asscn 1982; Fellow Soil Science Soc. of America 1985; Officer of the Order of Orange-Nassau 2001. *Publications:* several books and various articles in tech. journals. *Leisure interests:* jogging, cycling. *Address:* Alterra, PO Box 47, 6700 AA Wageningen (Office); Spoorbaanweg 35, 3911 CA Rhenen, Netherlands (Home). *Telephone:* (317) 613469 (Home). *E-mail:* johan.bouma@wur.nl (Office); johan.bouma@planet.nl (Home).

BOUQUET, Carole; French actress; b. 1953, Neuilly-sur-Seine; two s.; Face of Chanel No. 5 1986–. *Films include:* Cet Obscur Objet du Désir 1977, Buffet Froid 1979, Le Manteau d'Astrakan 1979, For Your Eyes Only 1981, Le Jour des Idiots 1981, Bingo Bango 1982, Dream One 1983, Mystère 1983, Dagobert 1984, Rive droite, Rive gauche 1984, Double Messieurs 1985, Special Police 1985, Le Mal d'Aimer 1986, Jenatsch 1986, On se dépêche d'en rire 1987, Bunker Palace Hotel 1988, Trop Belle pour toi (César for Best Actress) 1990, Grosse Fatigue 1994, A Business Affair 1994, Lucie Aubrac 1997, In All Innocence, The Bridge, Tango 1993, En plein cœur 1998, Un pont entre deux rives 1999, Le Pique-nique de Lulu Kreutz 2000, Embrassez qui vous voudrez 2002. *Plays include:* Phèdre, Théâtre Dejazet, Paris 2002. *Address:* c/o Intertalent, 5 rue Clément-Marot, 75008 Paris, France (Office).

BOURDEAU, Philippe François, PhD; Belgian fmr European Community official and university professor; b. 25 Nov. 1926, Rabat, Morocco; s. of Michel Bourdeau and Lucienne Imbrecht; m. Flora Gorirossi 1954; three d.; ed Gembloux, Belgium and Duke Univ. USA; Asst Prof. State Univ. of NC 1954–56, Yale Univ. 1956–58, 1960–62; Prof. Univ. of Belgian Congo 1958–60; Head, Radiobiology Dept EURATOM, Jt Research Centre, Ispra, Italy 1962–71; Head of Div. then Dir research programmes in environment and in non-nuclear energy, Comm. of EC, Brussels 1971–91; Prof. Univ. Libre de Bruxelles 1972–; Head, European Environment Agency Task Force 1991; Chair. Scientific Cttee, European Environmental Agency (EEA); Fellow, AAAS. *Publications:* scientific papers in the fields of environment policy, ecophysiology, ecotoxicology. *Leisure interests:* reading, sport. *Address:* U.L.B., CP 130/02, 50 ave F. D. Roosevelt, 1050 Brussels, Belgium (Office).

BOURGES, Hervé; French administrator and journalist; b. 2 May 1933, Rennes, Ile-et-Vilaine; s. of Joseph Bourges and Marie-Magdeleine Desjeux; m. Marie-Thérèse Lapouille 1966; ed Lycée de Biarritz, Coll. Saint-Joseph, Reims, École supérieure de journalisme; Ed. then Ed.-in-Chief Témoignage Chrétien 1956–62; attached to the Keeper of the Seals 1959–62, Dir Algerian Ministry of Youth and Popular Education, attached to Ministry of Information; Asst Lecturer Univ. de Paris II 1967–; Founder and Dir École supérieure de journalisme de Yaoundé, Cameroun 1970–76; Dir then Pres. Admin. Council École nat. supérieure de journalisme de Lille 1976–80; Dir Information Service and Dir-Gen.'s Messenger UNESCO 1980–81, Amb. to UNESCO 1994–95; Dir then Dir-Gen. Radio France Int. 1981–83; Chair. Dir-Gen. TV Française 1 (TF1) 1983–87, Hon. Pres. 1987–93; Hon. Pres. Admin. Council, Ecole Supérieure de Journalisme de Lille 1992–; Dir-Gen. Radio Monte Carlo (RMC) 1988; Pres., Dir-Gen. Société financière de radiodiffusion (Sofirad) 1989–91; Pres. Canal Horizon 1990–91, Conseil Supérieur de L'Audio-Visuel (CSA) 1995–2001; Pres. L'Union internationale des journalistes et de la presse de langue française (UIJPLF); Docteur d'état en sciences politiques; Chevalier, Légion d'honneur; Croix de la Valeur Militaire. *Publications:* L'Algérie à l'épreuve du pouvoir 1967, La Révolte étudiante 1968, Décoloniser l'information 1978, Les cinquante Afriques (jtly) 1979, Le village planétaire (jtly) 1986, Une Chaîne sur les bras 1987, Un amour de télévision (jtly) 1989, La Télévision du Public 1993, De mémoire d'éléphant (autobiog.) 2000. *Address:* UIJPLF, 3 cité Bergère, 74009 Paris (Office); 12 rue Magellan, 75008 Paris, France. *Telephone:* 1-45-68-10-00. *Fax:* 1-45-67-16-90.

BOURGES, Yvon, LenD; French politician and overseas administrator; b. 29 June 1921, Pau; s. of Jacques Bourges and Nancy Dardenne; m. Odile Fontaine 1943; two s. three d.; ed Univ. de Rennes; Chef de Cabinet to Prefect of the Somme 1944–45, of Bas-Rhin 1945–47; Sub-Prefect of Erstein 1947–48; with Ministry of Overseas Territories 1948, Dir de Cabinet, High Comm. in French Equatorial Africa 1948–51, in French West Africa 1951–56; Gov. Upper Volta 1956–58; High Commr (French) Equatorial Africa 1958–61; Chef de Cabinet, Ministry of Interior 1961–62; Deputy for Ille-et-Vilaine 1962–80; Mayor of Dinard 1962–67, 1971–89; Sec. of State for Scientific Research 1965–66, for Information 1966–67, for Co-operation 1967–72; Minister of Commerce 1972–73, of Defence 1975–80; Chair. Regional Council of Brittany 1986–98; mem. Senate 1980–98, EU Cttee of the Regions; Chair. French Cttee for a Pan-European Union 1993–2001; Officier Légion d'honneur and numerous foreign decorations. *Address:* Palais du Luxembourg, 75291 Paris Cedex 06; 24 place du Général Catroux, 75017 Paris, France (Home).

BOURGUIBA, Habib, Jr, LèsD; Tunisian diplomatist (retd); b. 9 April 1927, Paris, France; s. of the late Pres. Habib Bourguiba; m. Neila Zouiten 1954; two s. one d.; ed Collège Sadiki, Law School, France; collaborated in nat. liberation movt, especially 1951–54; Counsellor, Tunisian Embassy, Washington 1956–57; Amb. to Italy 1957–58, to France 1958–61, to USA 1961–63, to Canada 1961–62, to Mexico 1962–63; Perm. Rep. to UN 1961–62; Sec.-Gen., Govt of Repub. 1963–64; in charge of Dept of Youth and Sports, Dept of Tourism, Nat. office of Artisanship and Information Dept 1963–64; elected mem. Nat. Assembly Nov. 1964; Sec. of State for Foreign Affairs 1964–70; Special Adviser to the Pres. 1977–86; Pres., Gen. Man. Banque de Développement de l'Economie de la Tunisie 1971–88; consultant 1988–; many Tunisian and foreign decorations. *Leisure interests:* staying home with family, computers, golf. *Address:* Dar Essalam, 14 rue Chedli Zouiten, La Marsa 2070, Tunisia (Home). *Telephone:* 71-74-85-09 (Home). *Fax:* 71-74-26-66 (Home). *E-mail:* hb.jr@planet.tu (Home).

BOURGUIGNON, Philippe Etienne, M.SC.ECON., MBA; French business executive; b. 11 Jan. 1948, Salins les Bains; s. of Jacques Bourguignon and Paule Clément; m. Martine Lemardeley 1977; one s. one d.; ed Univ. of Aix; analyst, Synthèse Documentaire, Paris 1971–72; Project Man. Systembau, Munich 1973; Vice-Pres. Devt Accor, Novotel Asia, Middle East 1974–79; Exec. Vice-Pres. Accor North America, New York 1979–84; Pres. and CEO Accor Asia Pacific, Los Angeles 1984–88; Sr Vice-Pres. Real Estate Devt Euro Disney, Paris 1989–92; Pres. Euro Disney SA, Paris 1992, Chair. and CEO 1993–97; Exec. Vice-Pres. for Europe Walt Disney Co. 1996–97; Chair. Bd of Dirs. Club Méditerranée 1997–; Pres. Exec. Comm. for Paris' bid for Olympic Games 2008 1998; Pres. Young Pres. Org. 1990; mem. Bd of Dirs. American Chamber of Commerce in France; mem. Econ. Council Confed. of French Industries and Services; Chair. YPO French Chapter 1990; Chevalier Légion d'honneur, Officier Ordre nat. du Mérite. *Leisure interests:* sailing, reading, tennis, skiing. *Address:* Club Méditerranée, 11 rue Cambrai, 75957 Paris Cedex 19, France (Office). *E-mail:* philippe.bourguignon@clubmed.com (Office).

BOURHANE, Ali; Comoran international civil servant; b. 2 April 1946, Comoros; m. Beatrice Bourhane; one s. one d.; ed Univ. of Bordeaux and Ecole Nationale d'Administration, Paris; Research Fellow, Univ. of Toulouse 1971; Prof. of Math. Comoros 1972–75; civil servant 1980–85; Sr Economist, IMF, Washington, DC 1985–90; Alt. Exec. Dir IBRD 1990–94, Exec. Dir 1994–99; currently Sr Adviser African Devt Bank. *Leisure interests:* reading (religion, African history and anthropology, Devt Econs), tennis, running. *Address:* African Development Bank, Rue Joseph Anoma, 01 B.P. 1387, Abidjan, Côte d'Ivoire; 3 Greenlance Court, Potomac, MD 20854, USA (Home). *Telephone:* (301) 299-1933 (Home).

BOURHANE, Nourdine; Comoran politician; Prime Minister of Comoros 1997–98. *Address:* B.P. 551, Moroni, Comoros. *Telephone:* 73-07-83.

BOURJAILY, Vance, BA, DLit; American novelist; b. 17 Sept. 1922, Cleveland, Ohio; s. of Monte Ferris Bourjaily and Barbara Webb Bourjaily; m. 1st Bettina Yensen 1946; one s. two d.; m. 2nd Yasmin Mogul 1985; one s.; ed Handley High School, Va and Bowdoin Coll., Maine; American Field Service 1942–44; US Army 1944–46; Publisher, Record, New Castle, Va 1947–48; Staff Writer, San Francisco Chronicle 1949–50; Ed. Discovery 1951–53; Instructor, Mexico City Coll. 1953; Dramatic Critic, The Village Voice 1955–56; freelance TV writer 1956–57; Visiting lecturer, Univ. of Iowa 1957–59, Prof. 1961; Specialist, U.S. State Dept 1960; Boyd Prof. of English, La. State Univ. 1985–; Acad. Award in Literature, American Acad. of Arts and Letters 1993. *Publications:* novels: The End of My Life 1947, The Hound of Earth 1953, The Violated 1957, Confessions of a Spent Youth 1960, The Man Who Knew Kennedy 1967, Brill Among the Ruins 1970, Now Playing at Canterbury 1976, The Great Fake Book 1986, Old Soldier 1990, Fishing by Mail: The Outdoor Life of a Father and Son 1993; non-fiction: The Unnatural Enemy 1963, Country Matters 1973; plays: Time is a Dancer 1950, The Quick Years 1956, Confessions 1971. *Leisure interests:* politics, mycology, conservation. *Address:* Carlisle & Co., 24 East 64th Street, New York, NY 10021 (Office). *Telephone:* (504) 766-6231 (Home).

BOURJINI, Salah Amara, M.A.(Econs), PhD; Tunisian United Nations official; b. 17 Jan. 1938, Lekef; m. 1967; one s. two d.; Eng in planning and statistics, Tunis 1963–67; Lecturer in Econs, Univ. of Kansas 1969–72; Prof., Univ. of Tunis 1972–80; Adviser to Minister of Economy 1972–76; Deputy Dir-Gen. Ministry of Foreign Affairs 1976–80; Deputy UN Resident Rep. and UN Co-ordinator, Algeria 1980–82; Chief, Div. for Regional Programme, Arab States, UNDP, New York 1982–87; UN Resident Rep. and UN Co-ordinator, Iraq 1987–92; UN Resident Rep. and UN Co-ordinator, Libya 1992–; Chevalier de la République; various UN service awards. *Publications:* Human Capital Investment and Economic Growth 1974, New International Economic Order 1978; articles on Devt, educ. and trade. *Leisure interests:* tennis, swimming, music. *Address:* United Nations Development Programme, P.O. Box 358, Tripoli, Libya. *Telephone:* (21) 3330855. *Fax:* (21) 3330856.

BOURNE, Larry Stuart, PhD, DèsS, FRSC, MCIP, RPP; Canadian professor of geography and planning; b. 24 Dec. 1939, London, Ont.; s. of Stuart H. Bourne and Florence (Adams) Bourne; m. Paula T. O'Neill 1967; one s. one d.; ed Univs of Western Ontario, Alberta and Chicago; Asst Prof. of Geography, Univ. of Toronto 1967–69, Assoc. Prof. and Assoc. Dir, Centre for Urban and Community Studies (CUCS) 1969–82, Prof. and Dir 1973–78, 1979–84, Prof. of Geography and Planning, Co-ordinator of Grad. Studies 1985–89, 1991–94; Dir Grad. Planning Program 1996–98, 1999–2002; Visiting Scholar, Univ. of Monash, Australia and LSE, UK 1972–73, Centre for Environmental Studies, London, UK 1978–79; Visiting Prof., Univ. of Alberta, Univ. of Tex., USA 1984, Marburg (W Germany) 1985, Melbourne 1988, Meiji Univ., Tokyo 1991, Univ. of Tokyo 1996, Ben Gurion Univ. 1998, Seoul Nat. Univ. 1999; Chair. Comm. on Urban Systems and Devt, Int. Geographical Union 1988–92; consultant to local, nat. and int. agencies; Pres. Canadian Asscn of Geographers 1993–94, North American Regional Science Council 1994–95; Dr hc (Waterloo) 1999; Award for Scholarly Distinction, Canadian Asscn of Geographers 1985, Honors Award, Asscn of American Geographers 1985, Award for Service to Geography (Ont. Div. Canadian Asscn of Geographers) 1990, Teaching Award, Univ. of Toronto 1999. *Publications:* 18 books, including Urban Systems: Strategies for Regulation 1975, The Geography of Housing 1981, Internal Structure of the City 1982, Urbanization and Settlement Systems 1984, Urban Systems in Transition 1986, The Changing Geography of Urban Systems 1989, Urbanization and Urban Growth 1991, Changing Social Geography of Canadian Cities 1993; over 210 articles in journals and professional reports. *Address:* Department of Geography, University of Toronto, 100 St George Street, Toronto, Ont., M5S 3G3 (Office); 26 Anderson Avenue, Toronto, Ont., M5P 1H4, Canada (Home). *Telephone:* (416) 978-3375 (Office); (416) 486-7819 (Home). *Fax:* (416) 946-3886 (Office); (416) 978-6729. *E-mail:* bourne@geog.utoronto.ca (Office); larry.bourne@utoronto.ca (Home).

BOURNE, Matthew Christopher, OBE, BA; British dancer and choreographer; b. 13 Jan. 1960, London; s. of Harold Jeffrey (Jim) Bourne and June Lillian Bourne (née Handley); ed Laban Centre for Movt and Dance, London; f. Adventures in Motion Pictures 1987; Dir Spitfire Trust 1996–; Founding Dir New Adventures 2002–; mem. Hon. Cttee Dance Cares 1995–; Hon. Fellow of the Laban Centre 1997 (mem. Bd 1999–); Tony Award 1999, Astaire Award 1999, numerous other dance awards and prizes. *Dance:* Overlap Lovers 1987, Town and Country 1991, Nutcracker 1992, 2002, Highland Fling 1994, Swan Lake 1995, Cinderella 1997, The Car Man 2000–01 (also televised Channel 4), My Fair Lady (Olivier Award for Best Theatre Choreographer 2002) 2001, South Pacific 2002, Play Without Words (Olivier Awards for Best Entertainment and Best Theatre Choreographer 2003) 2002. *Publication:* Matthew Bourne & His Adventures in Motion Pictures 1999. *Leisure interests:* theatre, cinema, music. *Address:* c/o Duncan Heath, ICM, Oxford House, 76 Oxford Street, London, W1N 0AX (Office); 21 Stamford Road, London, N1 4JP, England (Home). *Telephone:* (20) 7636-6565 (Office). *Fax:* (20) 7323-0701 (Office). *E-mail:* matthewatamp@hotmail.com (Office).

BOURSEILLER, Antoine; French theatre director and producer; b. 8 July 1930, Paris; s. of Marcel Edouard Bourseiller and Denise Fisteberg; m. Chantal Darget 1966 (deceased); one s. one d.; Dir of Theatre, Studio des Champs-Elysées 1960–63, Poche 1964–66, Centre Dramatique National de Marseille 1966–75, Recamier 1975–78, Orléans 1980–82; Dir-Gen. Opéra-Théâtre de Nancy et de Lorraine 1982–96; Artistic Adviser, Théâtre de Tarascon 2003; Chevalier, Légion d'honneur; Commdr des Arts et Lettres. *Operas directed:* La Clémence de Titus (Aix-en-Provence Festival) 1973, Le Barbier de Seville (Théâtre Lyrique du Sud) 1979, Mireille (Geneva) 1981, (London) 1983, Carmen (Nancy) 1981, Woyzeck (Angers) 1982; Boulevard Solitude 1984, Cantate d'Octobre, Erwartung 1986, Donna Abbandonata 1987, King Priam 1988 (all at Nancy); Lulu (Nantes), Lady Macbeth de Mtsensk (Nancy) 1989; La Noche Triste 1989, Lohengrin L'Homme de Mancha (Brussels-Liège) 1994, 1998, Voyage à Reims (Liège) 2000. *Films:* Cleo de 5 à 7, 2 places pour le 26, Masculin Feminin, La Guerre est finie. *Plays directed:* Va donc chez Torpe 1961, Axel 1963, L'Amérique 1964, Metro Fantôme 1965, Striptease 1965, Silence, l'arbre. . . 1967, Les Brigands 1972, Jean Harlow 1972, Leuco 1974, Kennedy's Children 1975, La Tour 1976, S.T. 1979. *Address:* 20 Villa Seurat, 75014 Paris, France. *Telephone:* 1-43-35-26-17.

BOUTALEB, Abdelhadi, BA; Moroccan politician and educationist; b. 28 Dec. 1923, Fez; m. Touria Chraïbi 1946; two s. one d.; ed Al Qarawiyin Univ.; Prof. of Arabic History and Literature and Tutor to Prince Moulay Hassan and Prince Moulay Abdallah; Founder-mem. Democratic Party of Independence 1944–51, Shura and Istiqlal Party 1948, mem. Politburo –1959; campaigned, through the Party, for Moroccan independence and for this purpose attended UN Session, Paris 1951 and Negotiating Conf. at Aix-les-Bains 1955; Minister of Labour and Social Affairs 1956; Chief Ed. of journal Al-Rai-Alaam 1956–61; Amb. to Syria 1962; Sec. of State, Ministry of Information Nov. 1962, Ministry of Information, Youth and Sports Jan. 1963; Interim Minister in Charge of Mauritania and Sahara Nov. 1963; Minister of Justice 1964–67, of Nat. Educ. and Fine Arts 1967; Minister of State 1968; Minister of Foreign Affairs 1969–70; Pres. Chamber of Reps. 1970–71; lecturer in Constitutional Law and Political Insts., Rabat Law Univ. 1974, in Constitutional Law and Political Insts. 1979–; Amb. to USA, 1974–76, to Mexico 1976; Adviser to HM Hassan II 1977–78, 1992–96, Tutor to Crown Prince Sidi Mohamed 1978; Minister of State in Charge of Information 1978; Dir-Gen. Islamic Educ., Scientific and Cultural Org., Rabat May 1982; Vice-Pres. Int. Comm. for the Presentation of Int. Cultural Heritage 1983–; mem. Royal Acad. for Islamic Civilization Research, Royal Acad. of Morocco 1982, Hon. Cttee of Pascual de Gayancos Arab-Spanish Foundation 1985, Consulting Council of Human Rights 1994–; Commdr of the Throne of Morocco, Grand Cordon of the Repub. of UAR and other decorations. *Publications:* many cultural and literary works. *Leisure interests:* sports, music, reading. *Address:* 100 rue des Oudayas, 20300 Casablanca, Morocco. *Telephone:* (2) 61-82-85. *Fax:* (2) 62-11-95.

BOUTEFLIKA, Abdul Aziz; Algerian politician; b. 2 March 1937, Oujda; ed Morocco; Maj., Nat. Liberation Army and Sec. of Gen. Staff; mem. Parl. for Tlemcen 1962; Minister of Youth, Sports and Tourism 1962–63, of Foreign Affairs 1963–79; Counsellor to the Pres. March 1979–80; Pres. of Algeria 1999–; mem. F.L.N. Political Bureau 1964–81, mem. Cen. Cttee 1989; mem. Revolutionary Council 1965–79; led negotiations with France 1963, 1966, for nationalization of hydrocarbons 1971; leader of dels. to many confs. of Arab League, OAU 1968, Group of 1977 1967, Non-aligned countries 1973, Pres. 7th Special Session of UN Gen. Ass. 1975, Int. Conf. on Econ. Co-operation, Paris 1975–76; Pres. 29th UN Gen. Ass. 1974; mem. Nat. Council Moujahidin (Nat. Liberation Army) 1990–. *Address:* Office of the President, el-Mouradia, Algiers (Office); 138 Chemin Bachir Brahimi, El Biar, Algiers, Algeria. *Telephone:* 69 15 15 (Office); 60 34 59 (Home). *Fax:* 69 15 95 (Office).

BOUTIN, Bernard Louis, PhB; American management consultant; b. 2 July 1923, Belmont, NH; s. of Joseph L. Boutin and Annie E (Laflam) Boutin; m. Alice M. Boucher 1945; six s. five d.; ed St Michael's Coll., Winooski, Vt and Catholic Univ. of America, Washington, DC; Pres. and Treas., Boutin Insurance Agency Inc., Laconia, NH 1948–63; Proprietor, Boutin Real Estate Co., Laconia 1955–63; Mayor of Laconia 1955–59; Deputy Admin. Gen. Services Admin. (GSA), Washington DC Feb.–Nov. 1961; Admin. GSA 1961–64; Exec. Vice-Pres. Nat. Asscn Home Builders 1964–65; Admin. of Small Business Admin. 1966–67; Deputy Dir Office of Econ. Opportunity 1965–66; Exec. Sanders Assoc. Inc. 1967–69; Chair. NH State Bd of Educ. 1968–69; mem. Nat. Highway Safety Comm. 1969–70; Democratic Candidate for Gov. of NH 1958, 1960; Pres. St Michael's Coll. 1969–75; Exec. Vice-Pres. Burlington Savings Bank (Vt) 1975–76, Pres., Treas., Trustee 1976–80; Treas. and Trustee Medical Center Hospital of Vermont 1978–80; Dir New England College Fund 1979–80; Dir First Deposit Nat. Bank 1991–94; numerous awards including Kt of the Equestrian Order of the Holy Sepulchre of Jerusalem; Hon. LLD (St Michael's Coll.); Hon. LHD (Plymouth Coll. of the Univ. of New Hampshire), Hon. HHD (Franklyn Pierce Coll.). *Publication:* Echoes of Me 1991. *Leisure interests:* reading, use of my computer. *Address:* 631 Benton Drive, Laconia, NH 03241, USA (Home). *Telephone:* (603) 528-1014. *E-mail:* bboutin@cyberpostal.net (Home).

BOUTON, Daniel; French business executive; b. 1950; ed Ecole nat. d'Admin.; Insp. of Finance, Ministry of Finance 1973–76, Budget Dept, Ministry of Finance 1977–86, Chief of Staff to Alain Juppé, Deputy Minister in charge of the Budget 1986–88; Exec. Vice-Pres. Société Générale 1991, CEO 1993, Chair. 1997–; Dir Schneider, TotalFina, Vivendi Environment; Chevalier, Légion d'honneur, Ordre nat. du Mérite. *Address:* Office of the Chief Executive, 29 Blvd. Haussman,Paris,75009,France (Office). *Telephone:* (1) 42142000 (Office). *Website:* www.socgen.comb (Office).

BOUTROS, Fouad; Lebanese politician and lawyer; b. 1918, Beirut; m. Tania Shehade 1953; one s. two d.; ed Coll. des Frères, Beirut; Judge, Civil and Mixed Commercial Court, Beirut 1944–47; Judge Mil. Tribunal and Court Lawyer 1947–50; Govt Lawyer 1951–57; Minister of Nat. Educ. and of the Plan 1959–60; mem. Chamber of Deputies 1960–; Deputy Speaker, Chamber of Deputies 1960–61; Minister of Justice 1961–64; Vice-Pres. of the Council, Minister of Educ. and Defence 1966; Vice-Pres., Council of Ministers, Minister of Foreign Affairs and of Tourism Feb.–Oct. 1968; Deputy Prime Minister and Minister of Foreign Affairs 1976–82, of Defence 1976–80; numerous decorations including the Grand Cross of the Order of Gregory the Great 1997. *Publications:* Ecrits politiques 1997; numerous lectures and political articles in the press, in Arabic and French. *Leisure interests:* reading, walking. *Address:* Hazmieh, Gardenia Street, Ghaleb Center, Beirut POB 45-224 (Office); Sursock Street, Fouad Boutros Building, Beirut, Lebanon (Home). *Telephone:* (5) 459411 (Office); (1) 201500 (Home). *Fax:* (5) 457992 (Office); (5) 458933 (Office); (1) 217216 (Home). *E-mail:* tboutros@dm.net.lb (Home).

BOUTROS GHALI, Boutros, LLB, PhD; Egyptian international civil servant and politician; b. 14 Nov. 1922, Cairo; m. Leia Nadler; ed Cairo Univ. and Paris Univ.; fmr Prof. of Int. Law and Int. Relations and Head Dept of Political Sciences, Cairo Univ. 1949–77; fmr mem. Cen. Cttee Arab Socialist Union;

Pres. Cen. of Political and Strategic Studies; f. Al Ahram Al Iktisadi, Ed. 1960–75, f. Al-Siyassa Ad-Dawlya, Ed.; Minister of State for Foreign Affairs 1977–91, Deputy Prime Minister for Foreign Affairs 1991–92; Sec. Gen. of UN 1992–96; Sec.-Gen. Org. Int. de la Francophonie 1997–; Vice-Pres. Egyptian Soc. of Int. Law 1965–; mem. Cttee on Application of Conventions and Recommendations of Int. Labour Org. 1971–79; Pres. Centre of Political and Strategic Studies (Al-Ahram) 1975–; mem. Int. Comm. of Jurists, Geneva and Council and Exec. Cttee of Int. Inst. of Human Rights, Strasbourg; mem. UN Comm. of Int. Law 1979–92, Secretariat Nat. Democratic Party 1980–92, Parl. 1987–92; Onassis Foundation Prize 1995, recipient of honorary titles and awards from 24 countries. *Publications include:* Contribution à l'étude des ententes régionales 1949, Cours de diplomatie et de droit diplomatique et consulaire 1951, Le principe d'égalité des états et les organisations internationales 1961, Foreign Policies in World Change 1963, L'Organisation de l'unité africaine 1969, La ligue des états arabes 1972, Les Conflits aux frontières en Afrique 1973; also numerous books in Arabic and contribs. to periodicals. *Leisure interests:* the works of Matisse, collecting old pens from the Ottoman Empire. *Address:* 2 avenue Epnipgiza, Cairo, Egypt (Home).

BOUYGUES, Corinne Suzanne Marie Edmée; French broadcasting executive; b. 24 Aug. 1947, Laval; d. of Francis Bouygues and Monique Tèze; m. Sergio Gobbi 1995; two s. one d.; Head of Public Relations Compagnie Européene de Publication (CEP) 1979–81; Press Attaché Bouygues Group 1981, Asst Dir Communication 1987–89, Dir-Gen. Communication 1989–; Dir of Communication TF1 1989, Asst Dir Gen. TF1 Publicity 1990–91, Dir Gen. 1991, Admin. 1992, Admin. TF1 1993, Chair., Dir-Gen. TF1 Enterprises 1995, of Une Musique 1994–97, of Téléshopping SA 1994–97. *Address:* Villa Montmorency, 21 Avenue des Tilleuls, 75016 Paris, France (Home).

BOVÉ, José; French trade union leader and political activist; b. 1953, Bordeaux; partner Ghislaine Ricez; ed Univ. of Bordeaux; anti-globalization activist; arrested during protests opposing extension of local army base, Larzac 1975, sentenced to three weeks' imprisonment; Co-Founder and Spokesperson Confédération Paysanne 1987–; helped organize 'Ploughing the Champs Elysées' protest against EC set-aside policies, Paris 1988; led hunger strikes for more Govt subsidies for sheep farmers 1990; joined Greenpeace activists on Rainbow Warrior II to protest against French nuclear trials 1995; involved in destruction of Novartis seed production facility 1997; sentenced to three months' imprisonment for damaging McDonald's restaurant in Millau, S. France, as protest against American import tariffs on French farm products Aug. 1999, went on partial hunger strike for four weeks; co-led 1,300 farmers in the damaging of genetically modified maize and soybean fields manufactured by Monsanto, Brazil 2001; sentenced to one month suspended prison term and two years' probation in Montpellier for destroying genetically modified rice plants inside a research lab. March 2001, appealed unsuccessfully, re-sentenced to six months' jail term Dec. 2001, has appealed against sentence; arrested in Ramallah, W Bank for protesting on behalf of Palestinian farmers June 2001; arrested by Israeli Defence Forces outside compound of Yasser Arafat and deported to Paris April 2002. *Publications include:* The World is Not For Sale 2001. *Address:* Confédération Paysanne, 81 avenue de la République, 93170 Bagnolet, France (Office). *Telephone:* 1-43-62-04-04 (Office). *Fax:* 1-43-62-80-03 (Office). *E-mail:* contact@confederationpaysanne.fr (Office).

BOVIN, Aleksandr Yevgeniyevich, JUDr; Russian journalist and diplomatist; b. 9 Aug. 1930, Leningrad; s. of Yevgeni Bovin and Agnessa Bovin; m. Lena Bovin 1962; one d.; ed Rostov Univ.; mem. CPSU 1952–91; party and man. work in Krasnodar Dist 1954–56; served on editorial staff of Kommunist 1959–63; adviser, Chief of advisers group, Cen. Cttee CPSU 1963–72; political observer for Izvestiya 1972–91, 1997–; mem. Cen. Auditing Comm., CPSU 1981–86; Amb. to Israel 1991–97. *Publications:* numerous articles and papers. *Leisure interest:* business. *Address:* Tverskaya str. 18, 103791 Moscow (Office); B. Pirogovskaya str. 5, Apt. 79, 119021 Moscow, Russia (Home). *Telephone:* (095) 299-61-36 (Office); (095) 245-19-94 (Home).

BOVONE, HE Cardinal Alberto; Italian ecclesiastic; b. 11 June 1922, Frugarolo; ordained priest 1945; Archbishop, See of Cesarea in Numidia and Pro-Prefect Congregation for the Causes of Saints 1984; cr. HE Cardinal Feb. 1998. *Address:* Congregation for the Causes of Saints, Piazza Pio XII 10, 00193 Rome, Italy. *Telephone:* (06) 69884247. *Fax:* (06) 69881935.

BOWE, Riddick Lamont; American professional boxer (retd); b. 1967, Brooklyn; s. of Dorothy Bowe; m. Judy Bowe 1986; one s. two d.; amateur boxer 1982–89, professional boxer 1989–, won World Boxing Assn, World Boxing Confed., Int. Boxing Fed. titles 1992, World Boxing Assn, Int. Boxing Fed. titles 1993, World Boxing Org. title 1995, defeating two challengers in that year to retain title; Silver Medal Super Heavyweight Div., Olympic Games, Seoul, 1988; ranked Undisputed Heavyweight Champion 1992–93, 1995; retd from boxing 1996; briefly with U.S. Marine Corps; pleaded guilty to fed. charge of abduction June 1998.

BOWEN, Lionel Frost, AC, LLB; Australian politician; b. 28 Dec. 1922, Sydney; m. Claire Bowen 1953; five s. three d.; ed Univ. of Sydney; fmrly in practice as solicitor; mem. NSW Parl. 1962–69; mem. House of Reps. (Fed. Parl.) 1969–90; Postmaster-Gen., Special Minister of State and Minister for Mfg Industry 1974–75; Deputy Leader of Opposition 1977–83; Deputy Prime Minister, Minister for Trade and Minister assisting Prime Minister in Commonwealth-State Affairs 1983–84, Deputy Prime Minister, Attorney-Gen. 1984–90; Minister assisting the Prime Minister 1984–88, Vice-Pres. of

Exec. Council 1984–87; Deputy Chair. Advertising Standards Cttee 1990; Chair. Nat. Gallery, Canberra 1991–94, Verus Investments Ltd, The Benwood Property Trust 1997–; Australian Labor Party. *Leisure interests:* golf, tennis, riding. *Address:* 24 Mooramie Avenue, Kensington, NSW 2033, Australia.

BOWEN, Most Rev. Michael George, STL, PhL; British ecclesiastic; b. 23 April 1930, Gibraltar; s. of the late Maj. C. L. J. Bowen and Mary J. Pedley; ed Downside Abbey School, Trinity Coll., Cambridge and Gregorian Univ., Rome; wine trade 1951–52; Venerable English Coll., Rome 1952–59; ordained RC priest 1958; curate, Earlsfield and Walworth, Diocese of Southwark 1959–63; teacher of Theology, Pontifical Beda Coll., Rome 1963–66; Chancellor, Diocese of Arundel and Brighton 1966–70, Coadjutor Bishop 1970–71, Bishop of Arundel and Brighton 1971–77; Archbishop and Metropolitan, Diocese of Southwark 1977–; Vice-Pres. Catholic Bishops' Conf. England and Wales 1996–99; Pres. 1999–2000; Freeman City of London 1984. *Leisure interests:* golf, tennis. *Address:* Archbishop's House, 150 St George's Road, London, SE1 6HX, England. *Telephone:* (20) 7928-2495. *Fax:* (20) 7928-7833.

BOWEN, Ray M., PhD; American university administrator; b. 30 March 1936, Fort Worth, TX; s. of Winfred Herbert Bowen and Elizabeth Williams Bowen; m. Sara Elizabeth Gibbons Bowen 1958; one s. one d.; ed Texas A&M Univ., California Inst. Tech.; Assoc. Prof. Mechanical Eng, Louisiana State Univ. 1965–67; Prof. Mechanical Eng, Rice Univ. 1967–83, Chair. Dept Mechanical Eng 1972–77; Div. Dir Nat. Science Foundation 1982–83, Acting Asst Dir Eng to Dep. Asst Dir 1990–91; Prof. and Dean of Eng Univ. of Kentucky 1983–89; Vice-Pres. Academic Affairs, Okla State Univ. 1991–93, Interim Pres. 1993–94; Pres. Texas A&M Univ. 1994–2000; Soc. of Scholars, Johns Hopkins Univ.; A.S.E.E. Fellows. *Publications:* Introduction to Continuum Mechanics for Engineers; Introduction to Vectors and Tensors (co-author); Rational Thermodynamics (contrib.); contrib. numerous articles in professional journals. *Leisure interests:* travelling, opera. *Address:* Office of the President, Texas A&M University, Room 805, Rudder Tower, College Station, TX 77843 (Office); One College Drive, College Station, TX 77840, USA (Home). *Telephone:* (979) 845-2217 (Office); (979) 845-4323 (Home). *Fax:* (979) 845-5027 (Office); 409-845-5027. *E-mail:* r-bowen@tamu.edu (Office). *Website:* www.tamu.edu/president (Office).

BOWEN, William Gordon, PhD; American academic; b. 6 Oct. 1933, Cincinnati, Ohio; s. of Albert A. Bowen and Bernice Pomert; m. Mary Ellen Maxwell 1956; one s. one d.; ed Denison and Princeton Univs; Asst Prof. of Econs, Princeton Univ. 1958–61, Assoc. Prof. 1961–65, Prof. 1965–87; Dir of Graduate Studies, Woodrow Wilson School of Public and Int. Affairs, Princeton Univ. 1964–66; Provost, Princeton Univ. 1967–72, Pres. 1972–88; lecturer Oxford Univ. 2000; Pres. Andrew W. Mellon Foundation, New York 1988–; Dir NCR Corpn 1975–91; Regent Smithsonian Inst. 1980, now Regent Emer.; Trustee, Denison Univ. 1966–75, 1992–2000, Center for Advanced Study in the Behavioral Sciences 1973–84, 1986–92, Reader's Digest 1985–97, American Express 1988–, ISTOR 1995–, Merck and Co. 1986–, Ithaka Harbors, Inc., Univ. Corpn for Advanced Internet Devt 1998–; mem. Bd of Overseers Teachers Insurance and Annuity Asscn and Coll. Retirement Equities Fund 1995–; Dr hc. (Oxford) 2001; Joseph Henry Medal, Smithsonian Inst. 1996, Grawemeyer Award in Educ., Univ. of Louisville 2001. *Publications:* The Wage-Price Issue: A Theoretical Analysis 1960, Performing Arts: The Economic Dilemma (with W. J. Baumol) 1966, The Economics of Labor Force Participation (with T. A. Finegan) 1969, Ever the Teacher 1987, Prospects for Faculty in the Arts and Sciences 1989 (with J. A. Sosa), In Pursuit of the PhD 1992 (with Neil L. Rudenstine), Inside the Boardroom: Governance by Directors and Trustees 1994, (with S. Nygren, S. Turner and E. Duffy) The Charitable Nonprofts 1994, Universities and Their Leaderships (ed. Harold Shapiro) 1998, The Shape of the River: Long-Term Consequences of Considering Race in College and University Admissions (with Derek Bok) 1998, The Game of Life: College Sports and Educational Values 2001, At a Slight Angle to the Universe (also Romanes Lecture, Univ. of Oxford) 2001, Reclaiming the Game: College Sports and Educational Values (with Sarah A. Levin) 2003. *Address:* Andrew W. Mellon Foundation, 140 East 62nd Street, New York, NY 10021, USA (Office).

BOWER, Gordon H., MS, PhD; American professor of psychology; b. 30 Dec. 1932, Scio, Ohio; s. of Clyde W. Bower and Mabelle Bosart Bower; m. Sharon Anthony 1957; one s. two d.; ed Western Reserve (now Case Western Reserve) and Yale Univs; Asst Prof. Stanford Univ. 1959, Assoc. Prof. 1963, Prof. 1965, A. R. Lang Chair Prof. 1975–, Chair. Dept of Psychology 1978–82, Assoc. Dean, Stanford Univ. 1983–86; Ed. The Psychology of Learning and Motivation 1964–92; mem. NAS, American Acad. of Arts and Sciences, Soc. of Experimental Psychologists; Hon. degrees from Univ. of Chicago, Indiana State Univ.; Distinguished Scientist Contrib. Award, American Psychology Asscn 1979, Warren Medal, Wilbur Cross Medal, Yale Univ. *Publications:* co-author of five books and over 250 scientific papers. *Leisure interests:* reading, sport. *Address:* Department of Psychology, Stanford University, Stanford, CA 94305, USA.

BOWERING, George Henry, OC, MA; Canadian writer and lecturer; b. 1 Dec. 1936, Penticton, BC; s. of Ewart Bowering and Pearl Bowering (née Brinson); m. Angela Luoma 1962; one d.; ed Univ. of British Columbia; served Royal Canadian Air Force 1955–58; lecturer Univ. of Calgary 1963–66; Writer-in-Residence Sir George Williams Univ., Montreal 1967–71; lecturer Simon Fraser Univ., Burnaby, BC 1972–2001; Parl. Poet Laureate of Canada

2002–04; Hon. DLit (British Columbia) 1997; Gov.-Gen.'s Award (poetry) 1967, (fiction) 1980. *Publications:* Mirror on the Floor 1967, A Short Sad Book 1977, Burning Water 1980, Caprice 1987, Harry's Fragments 1990, Shoot! 1994, Parents from Space 1994, The Rain Barrel 1994, Piccolo Mondo 1998, Diamondback Dog 1998, Bowering's BC, Egotists and Autocrats – the Prime Ministers of Canada 1999, A Magpie Life 2001, Stone Country 2003. *Leisure interests:* baseball, fastball. *Address:* 2499 W 37 Avenue, Vancouver, BC V6M 1P4, Canada (Home). *Telephone:* (604) 261-2954 (Home). *Fax:* (604) 266-9000. *E-mail:* bowering@sfu.ca (Home).

BOWERS-BROADBENT, Christopher Joseph, FRAM; British organist and composer; b. 13 Jan. 1945, Hemel Hempstead; s. of Henry W. Bowers-Broadbent and Doris E Mizen; m. Deirdre Cape 1970; one s. one d.; ed King's Coll. Cambridge, Berkhamsted School and Royal Acad. of Music; Organist and Choirmaster of St Pancras Parish Church 1965–88; Organist of West London Synagogue 1973–; Organist and Choirmaster of Gray's Inn 1983–; debut organ recital, Camden Festival 1966; Prof. of Organ, Royal Acad. of Music 1976–92; Recordings include: Trivium, O Domina Nostra, Meditations Sur, Mattins Music, Duets and Canons; Three Choirs Festival Composers' Competition Prize 1978. *Operas include:* The Pied Piper 1972, The Seacock Bane 1979, The Last Man 1983–2000. *Leisure interests:* sketching, silence. *Address:* 94 Colney Hatch Lane, Muswell Hill, London, N10 1EA, England. *Telephone:* (20) 8883-1933. *Fax:* (20) 8883-8434; (20) 8888-8434 (Home). *E-mail:* chris@christopherbowers-broadbent.com (Home). *Website:* christopherbowers-broadbent.com (Home).

BOWIE, David (David Robert Jones); British musician and actor; b. 8 Jan. 1947, Brixton, London; s. of Hayward Stenton Jones and of the late Margaret Mary Jones (née Burns); m. 1st Angela Barnett 1970 (divorced 1980); one s.; m. 2nd Iman Abdul Majid 1992; one d.; singer/songwriter 1967–; first hit single Space Oddity 1969, numerous tours and TV appearances; appeared in TV play Baal (Brecht) 1982; exec. producer and wrote musical score for The Delinquents 1989; Commdr Ordre des Arts et des Lettres, Grammy Award 1984, inducted into Rock and Roll Hall of Fame 1996, Star of the Walk of Fame 1997. *Recordings include:* The Man Who Sold The World, Hunky Dory 1971, The Rise and Fall of Ziggy Stardust and the Spiders From Mars 1972, Aladdin Sane, Pin Ups 1973, David Live, Diamond Dogs 1974, Young Americans 1975, Station to Station 1976, Low, Heroes 1977, Lodger (with Brian Eno) 1979, Scary Monsters and Super Creeps 1980, Let's Dance 1983, Never Let Me Down 1987, Tin Machine (with group) 1989, Earthling 1997, David Bowie 1998, Heathen 2002. *Films include:* The Man Who Fell to Earth 1976, Just a Gigolo 1981, The Hunger 1983, Merry Christmas Mr Lawrence 1983, Ziggy Stardust and the Spiders from Mars 1983, Absolute Beginners 1986, Labyrinth 1986, The Last Temptation of Christ 1988, The Linguini Incident 1990, Basquiat 1996, Trainspotting 1996, Il Mio West 1998, Everybody Loves Sunshine 1999, Mr Rice's Secret 2000; appeared in play The Elephant Man, New York 1980. *Television:* The Hunger (series) 1999–. *Leisure interests:* boxing, martial arts instruction, listening to Polish and Chinese Communist music. *Address:* c/o Isolar, Suite 220, 641 5th Avenue, New York, NY 10022, USA.

BOWIE, Stanley Hay Umphray, DSc, FRS, FREng, FRSE, FMSA, FSA(Scot); British economic geologist; b. 24 March 1917, Bixter; s. of James Cameron Bowie and Mary Nicolson; m. Helen Elizabeth Pocock 1948; two s.; ed Aberdeen Grammar School, Univ. of Aberdeen; with Meteorological Office 1942; commissioned RAF 1943–46; Geologist, Sr Geologist, Prin. Geologist, Geological Survey of Great Britain (GSGB) 1946–55, Chief Geologist, Atomic Energy Div. 1955–68; Chief Geochemist, Asst Dir Inst. of Geological Sciences 1968–77; Chief Consultant Geologist to UKAEA 1955–77; Visiting Prof. of Applied Geology, Univ. of Strathclyde 1968–85; Prin. Investigator Apollo 11 and 12 Lunar samples 1969–71; Geological Consultant 1977–97; Dir Liquid Crystals Ltd 1977–2001; Visiting Prof., Royal School of Mines, Imperial Coll. 1985–92; Chair. Comm. on Ore Microscopy, Int. Mineralogical Asscn 1970–78; Chair. Steering Cttee, Mineral Deposits of Europe 1970–89; Chair. DOE Research Advisory Group, Radioactive Waste Man. 1984–85; Chair. Shetland Sheep Breeders' Group 1989–91, Vice-Pres. 1992–; Hon. Fellow Inst. Materials, Minerals and Mining; Silver Medal RSA, Sr Kilgour Research Scholarship, Mitchell Prize for Geology (Univ. of Aberdeen), Team mem. Queen's Award for Tech. Achievement 1990. *Achievements (miscellaneous):* new rhodium, iridium sulphide mineral named Bowieite in recognition of research in opaque mineral identification 1984. *Publications:* contrib. to Nuclear Geology 1954, Physical Methods in Determinative Mineralogy 1967, Applied Environmental Geochemistry 1963, The Bowie Simpson System for the Microscopic Determination of Ore Minerals (with P. R. Simpson) 1980 and others, Ed. (jt) Uranium Prospecting Handbook 1972, Mineral Deposits of Europe 1978, Environmental Geochemistry and Health 1985, Radon and Health – The Facts (with C. Bowie) 1991, Shetland Sheep 1994, Shetland Wool 1994, Shetland Cattle 1995; numerous articles on rare breeds of domesticated animals. *Leisure interests:* photography, gardening, survival of endangered breeds of domesticated animals. *Address:* Tanyard Farm, Clapton, Crewkerne, Somerset, TA18 8PS, England.

BOWLES, Erskine; American government official; b. 1945; s. of Hargrove "Skipper" Bowles; m. Crandall Bowles; three c.; with Morgan Stanley & Co. New York; Bowles Hollowell Conner & Co. Charlotte, NC 1975–93; Admin. Small Business Admin. Washington, DC 1993–94; Deputy Chief of Staff, The White House, Washington, DC 1994–97, Chief of Staff to Pres. 1997–99;

partner Forstmann Little & Co. 1999–; Pres. Juvenile Diabetes Foundation. *Address:* Forstmann Little and Co., 767 Fifth Avenue, Suite 4402, New York, NY 10153-4499, USA (Office).

BOWN, Jane Hope, CBE; British photographer; b. 13 March 1925, Ledbury; d. of Charles Wentworth Bell and Daisy Bown; m. Martin Grenville Moss 1954; two s. one d.; ed William Gibbs School for Girls, Faversham, Kent; photographer for the Observer 1950–; Hon. DLitt (Bradford). *Publications:* The Gentle Eye 1980, Women of Consequence 1985, Men of Consequence 1986, The Singular Cat 1988, Pillars of the Church 1991, Jane Bown Observer 1996, Faces 2000. *Leisure interests:* animals, the country, antiques. *Address:* Old Mill House, 50 Broad Street, Alresford, Hants., SO24 9AN, England. *Telephone:* (1962) 732419.

BOWNESS, Sir Alan, Kt, CBE; British art historian; b. 11 Jan. 1928; s. of George Bowness and Kathleen Bowness (née Benton); m. Sarah Hepworth-Nicholson 1957; one s. one d.; ed Univ. Coll. School, Downing Coll., Cambridge, Courtauld Inst. of Art, Univ. of London; with Friends' Ambulance Unit and Friends' Service Council 1946–50; Regional Art Officer, Arts Council of GB 1955–57; Courtauld Inst. 1957–79, Deputy Dir 1978–79; Reader, Univ. of London 1967–78, Prof. of History of Art 1978–79; Visiting Prof. Humanities Seminar, Johns Hopkins Univ., Baltimore 1969; Dir Tate Gallery 1980–88, Henry Moore Foundation 1988–94 (Trustee 1984–88, 1994–); mem. Arts Council 1973–75, 1978–80, Art Panel 1960–80 (Vice-Chair. 1973–75, Chair. 1978–80), Arts Film Cttee 1968–77 (Chair. 1972–75); mem. Fine Arts Cttee, British Council 1960–69, 1970–93 (Chair. 1981–93); mem. Exec. Cttee, Contemporary Art Soc. 1961–69, 1970–86, Cultural Advisory Cttee, UK Nat. Comm. for UNESCO 1973–82; Gov. Chelsea School of Art and London Inst. 1965–88; Hon. Sec. Asscn of Art Historians 1973–76; Dir Barbara Hepworth Museum, St Ives, Cornwall 1976–88; mem. Council Royal Coll. of Art 1978–99; Trustee Yorkshire Sculpture Park 1979–, Handel House Museum 1994–2001 (Chair. 1997–2001); mem. int. juries for Premio Di Tella, Buenos Aires 1965, São Paulo Bienal 1967, Lehmbruck Prize, Duisburg 1970, Rembrandt Prize 1982, Venice Biennale 1986, Heiliger Prize 1998; Hon. Fellow, Downing Coll., Cambridge 1980, UWE Bristol Polytechnic 1980, RCA 1982 (mem. Council 1978–99); Hon. DLitt (Liverpool) 1988, (Leeds) 1995, (Exeter) 1996; Chevalier Ordre des Arts et des Lettres 1973. *Publications:* William Scott Paintings 1964, Impressionists and Post Impressionists 1965, Henry Moore: Complete Sculpture 1955–64 1965, Modern Sculpture 1965, Barbara Hepworth Drawings 1966, Alan Davie 1967, Recent British Painting 1968, Gauguin 1971, Barbara Hepworth: complete sculpture 1960–69 1971, Modern European Art 1972, Ivon Hitchens 1973, Picasso 1881–1973 (contrib.) 1973, The Genius of British Painting (contrib.) 1975, Henry Moore: Complete Sculpture 1964–73 1977, Henry Moore: Complete Sculpture 1974–80 1983, Henry Moore: Complete Sculpture 1981–86 1988, The Conditions of Success 1989, British Contemporary Art 1910–1990 (contrib.) 1991, Bernard Meadows 1995. *Leisure interests:* going to concerts, opera, theatre. *Address:* 91 Castelnau, London, SW13 9EL; 16 Piazza, St Ives, Cornwall, TR26 1NQ, England. *Telephone:* (20) 8846-8520 (London); (1736) 795444 (St Ives).

BOWRING, Peter, CBE, FID, FRSA, FZS; British company director; b. 22 April 1923, Bromborough; s. of Frederick Clive and Agnes Walker (née Cairns) Bowring; m. Barbara Ekaterina Brewis 1946 (divorced); one s. one d.; m. 2nd Carol Gillian Hutchings 1979 (divorced); m. 3rd Carole Mary Dear 1986; ed Shrewsbury School; commissioned, Rifle Brigade 1942, served in Egypt, North Africa, Italy and Austria (mentioned in despatches); Dir C. T. Bowring & Co. Ltd 1956; Chair. C. T. Bowring Trading (Holdings) Ltd 1967; Deputy Chair. C. T. Bowring and Co. Ltd 1973; Chair. Bowmaker (Plant) Ltd 1972–83, Bowmaker Ltd 1978–82, C. T. Bowring & Co. Ltd 1978–82; Dir Marsh and McLennan Companies Inc. 1980–85, Vice-Chair. 1982–84; Dir Aldeburgh Foundation 1975–90, Chair. 1982–89, Vice-Pres. 1991–; Chair. Help the Aged Ltd 1977–87, Pres. 1987–2000; Chair. Inter-Action Social Enterprise Trust Ltd 1989–91; Chair. Wakefield (Tower Hill, Trinity Square) Trust 2002–; Master Worshipful Co. of World Traders 1989–90; Trustee Zoological Soc. Devt Trust 1987–90, Ironbridge Gorge Museum Devt Trust 1987–93 (Companion 1993), Upper Severn Navigation Trust (now Spry Trust Ltd) 1987–; mem. Lloyds 1968–98, Worshipful Company of Insurers, Company of Watermen and Lightermen; Freeman of City of London; Bd of Govs. St Dunstan's Educational Foundation 1974–94, Chair. 1977–90 (Companion 1998); Bd of Govs. Shrewsbury School 1969–97; Dir Independent Primary and Secondary Educ. Trust 1986–, Centre for Policy Studies 1983–88, City Arts Trust 1984–94 (Chair. 1987–94), Int. Human Assistance Programs Inc. 1985–89, Rhein Chemie Holding GmbH 1968–. *Publication:* The Last Minute 2000. *Leisure interests:* photography, sailing, motoring, music, walking, cooking. *Address:* Flat 79, New Concordia Wharf, Mill Street, London, SE1 2BB, England. *Telephone:* (20) 7237-0818.

BOWYER, William, RA, RP, RWS; British artist; b. 25 May 1926, Leek, Staffs.; s. of Arthur Bowyer and Emma Bowyer; m. Vera Mary Small 1951; two s. one d.; ed Burslem School of Art, Royal Coll. of Art; Head of Fine Art, Maidstone Coll. of Art 1971–82; Hon. Sec. New English Art Club 1968–98; mem. Royal Soc. of British Artists. *Leisure interests:* cricket, snooker. *Address:* 12 Cleveland Avenue, Chiswick, London, W4 1SN, England. *Telephone:* (20) 8994-0346.

BOX, John Allan Hyatt, OBE, ARIBA, FRSA; British set designer; b. 27 Jan. 1920; s. of the late Allan Cyril Box and of Bertha Box (née Storey); m. 1st Barbara Courtenay Linton 1944 (divorced 1951); m. 2nd Doris Lee 1953 (deceased); two d.; ed Ceylon, Highgate School, School of Architecture, London Polytechnic; served RAC, Royal Tank Regt 1940–46 (despatches); has worked in films 1948–; BAFTA Award for special contrib. to films 1991, Royal Designer for Industry RSA 1992; Critics' Circle Award for Lifetime Achievements in Films 1998. *Films include:* The Million Pound Note 1954, The Inn of the Sixth Happiness 1958, Our Man in Havana 1959, The World of Suzie Wong 1960, Lawrence of Arabia 1962 (Acad. Award), Doctor Zhivago 1965 (Acad. Award), A Man For All Seasons 1967 (BAFTA Award), Oliver! 1968 (Acad. Award), Nicholas and Alexandra 1971 (Acad. Award), Travels With My Aunt 1972, The Great Gatsby 1974 (BAFTA Award), Rollerball 1975 (BAFTA Award), A Passage to India 1984, Black Beauty 1994, First Knight 1995, producer The Looking Glass War 1969. *Leisure interests:* painting, art, cricket, rugby. *Address:* 5 Elm Bank Mansions, The Terrace, Barnes, London, SW13 0NS, England. *Telephone:* (20) 8876-9125.

BOXER, Barbara, BA; American politician; b. 11 Nov. 1940, Brooklyn, New York; d. of Ira Boxer and Sophie (Silvershein) Levy; m. Stewart Boxer 1962; one s. one d.; ed Brooklyn Coll.; stockbroker, New York 1962–65; journalist, Assoc. Ed. Pacific Sun 1972–74; Congressional Aide to Rep. 5th Congressional Dist San Francisco 1974–76; mem. Marin Co. Bd of Supervisors, San Rafael, Calif. 1976–82, Pres. 1980–81; Democrat mem. 98th–102nd Congresses from 6th Calif. Dist, Senator from California 1993–; mem. Bd of Dirs. Golden Gate Bridge Highway and Transport Dist, San Francisco 1978–82; Pres. Democratic New Mems Caucus 1983–; numerous awards. *Address:* US Senate, 112 Hart Senate Office Building, Washington, DC 20510-0001, USA.

BOXSHALL, Geoffrey Allan, PhD, F.R.S.; British/Canadian zoologist; b. 13 June 1950, Oyen, Alberta; s. of Sybil Irene Baker and John Edward Boxshall; m. Roberta Gabriel Smith 1972; one s. three d.; ed Churcher's Coll., Leeds Univ.; joined Natural History Museum 1974, Deputy Chief Scientific Officer 1997–. *Publications:* (co-author) Dictionary of Ecology, Evolution and Systematics, Illustrated Dictionary of Natural History, Copepod Evolution. *Leisure interests:* travel, tennis, lexicography. *Address:* Natural History Museum, Cromwell Road, London, SW7 5BD, England (Office). *Telephone:* (20) 7942-5749 (Office); (20) 8248-4577 (Home). *Fax:* (20) 7942-5433 (Office). *E-mail:* g.boxshall@nhm.ac.uk (Office). *Website:* www.nhm.ac.uk/science/ (Office).

BOYARCHIKOV, Nikolai Nikolayevich; Russian choreographer; b. 27 Sept. 1935, Leningrad; s. of Maria Boyarchikova; m. Larissa Klimova; ed Leningrad Vaganova School of Choreography, Leningrad State Conservatory; soloist Mussorgsky Academic Opera and Ballet Theatre 1954–71, chief choreographer 1977–; chief choreographer Perm Opera and Ballet Theatre 1971–77; Glinka Prize 1977, People's Artist of Russia 1985, State Prize of Russian Fed. *Theatre productions include:* Romeo and Juliet 1972, Tsar Boris 1975, Robber 1982, Quiet Don 1988. *Address:* Iskusstvo pl. 1, Mussorgsky Theatre, St Petersburg, Russia. *Telephone:* (812) 219-19-78.

BOYARCHUK, Aleksander Alekseyevich; Russian astrophysicist; b. 21 June 1931, Grozny; s. of Aleksei Boyarchuk and Maria Boyarchuk; m. Margarita Yevgenyevna Boyarchuk (née Kropotova) 1955; one s.; ed Leningrad State Univ.; researcher, Deputy Dir Crimea Astrophysical Observatory USSR Acad. of Sciences 1953–87; Dir Inst. of Astronomy 1987–; mem. USSR (now Russian) Acad. of Sciences 1987; Acad.-Sec. Dept of Gen. Physics and Astronomy 1996–; published over 200 works on astrospectroscopy, physics of star atmospheres, construction of astronomic equipment, cosmic studies, Ed.-in-Chief Astronomical journal, Pres. Int. Astronomical Union 1994–; mem. Int. Astronomical Acad., Royal Astronomical Soc. of UK, American Astronomical Soc., American Physical Soc.; USSR State Prize. *Address:* Institute of Astronomy, Pyatnitskaya str. 48, 109017 Moscow, Russia. *Telephone:* (095) 951-54-61 (Institute) (Office); (095) 938-16-95 (Academy) (Office). *Fax:* (095) 230-20-81 (Office).

BOYARSKY, Mikhail Sergeyevich; Russian actor; b. 26 Dec. 1949, Leningrad; m.; one s. one d.; ed Leningrad Inst. of Theatre, Music and Cinematography, fmrly with Lensovet Theatre, appeared in musicals Interview in Buenos Aires, Troubadour and His Friends; cinema debut 1974, more than 60 roles; artistic Dir Benefice Theatre; People's Actor of Russian Fed., People's Artist of Russia 1995. *Films include:* D'Artagnan and The Three Musketeers, Elder Son, Tartuffe, Mother, Extra Ticket, Queen Margot. *Address:* Naberezhnaya Moiki 31, Apt. 2, 191186 St Petersburg, Russia. *Telephone:* (812) 311-37-97.

BOYCE, Adm. Sir Michael (Cecil), GCB, KStJ, OBE; British naval officer; b. 2 April 1943, Cape Town, SA; s. of Commdr Hugh Boyce and of the late Madeline Boyce (née Manley); m. Harriette Gail Fletcher 1971 (separated 1994); one s. one d.; ed Hurstpierpoint Coll., Royal Naval Coll., Dartmouth; joined RN 1961; qualified submariner 1965, TAS 1970, served in HM submarines Anchorite, Valiant and Conqueror 1965–72, commanded HM submarines Oberon 1973–74, Opossum 1974–75, Superb 1979–81, frigate HMS Brilliant 1983–84, Capt. (SM) Submarine Sea Training 1984–86; Royal Coll. Defence Staff 1988; Sr Naval Officer ME 1989; Dir Naval Staff Duties 1989–91; Flag Officer, Sea Training 1991–92; Surface Flotilla 1992–95; Commdr Anti-Submarine Warfare Striking Force 1992–94; Second Sea Lord and C-in-C Naval Home Command 1995–97; Flag ADC to the Queen 1995–97; C-in-C Fleet, C-in-C Eastern Atlantic Area and Commdr Naval Forces NW Europe 1997–98; First Sea Lord 1998–2001; Chief of Defence Staff 2001–03; First and Prin. Naval ADC to the Queen 1998–2001, ADC 2001–03; Gov. Alleyn's School 1995–; Freeman City of London 1999; Younger Brother

Trinity House 1999; Commdr Legion of Merit (U.S.) 1999. *Leisure interests:* squash, tennis, photography, windsurfing, opera, ballet. *Address:* c/o Naval Secretary, Victory Building, HM Naval Base, Portsmouth, PO1 3LS, England.

BOYCE, Ralph L. ('Skip'), BA, MPA; American diplomatist; b. 1 Feb. 1952, Washington, DC; m. Kathryn Sligh; two c.; ed George Washington Univ., Princeton Univ.; joined Foreign Service 1976; Staff Asst to Amb., Tehran 1977–79; Commercial Attaché, Tunis 1979–81; Financial Economist, Islamabad 1981–84; Special Asst, then Adviser to Deputy Sec. of State, State Dept 1984–88; Political Counsellor, Bangkok 1988–92; Deputy Chief of Mission, Singapore 1992–93; Chargé d'Affaires 1993–94; Deputy Chief of Mission, Bangkok 1994–98; Deputy Asst Sec. for E Asia and Pacific Affairs 1998–2001; Amb. to Indonesia 2001–. *Address:* Embassy of the USA, Jalan Merdeka Selatan 4-5, Jakarta 10110, Indonesia (Office). *Telephone:* (21) 3442211 (Office). *Fax:* (21) 3802259 (Office). *Website:* www.usembassyjakarta.com (Office).

BOYCOTT, Geoffrey, OBE; British cricketer and sports commentator; b. 21 Oct. 1940, Fitzwilliam, Yorks.; s. of the late Thomas Wilfred Boycott and Jane Boycott; m. Rachael Swinglehurst 2003; one d.; ed Kinsley Modern School and Hemsworth Grammar School; fmrly in civil service; right-hand opening batsman; teams: Yorkshire 1962–86 (Capt. 1971–78), Northern Transvaal 1971–72; 108 Tests for England 1964–82, 4 as Capt., scoring then record 8,114 runs (average 47.7) including 22 hundreds; scored 48,426 first-class runs (151 hundreds); completed 100 hundreds for Yorkshire 1985, 7th batsman to achieve this for a county; toured Australia 1965–66, 1970–71, 1978–79 and 1979–80; only Englishman to achieve average of 100 in English County season 1971; repeated this achievement in 1979; scored 100th hundred, England v. Australia, Headingly, Leeds Aug. 1977; became 18th batsman in history of game to score 100 hundreds and the first to achieve this in a Test match; mem. Gen. Cttee; served as coach for Pakistan's Nat. Acad. 2001; cricket commentator; Wisden Cricketer of the Year 1965. *Publications:* Geoff Boycott's Book for Young Cricketers 1976, Put to the Test: Ashes Series in Australia 1978/79 1979, Geoff Boycott's Cricket Quiz 1979, Boycott on Batting 1980, Opening Up 1980, In the Fast Lane 1981, Master Class 1982, Boycott—The Autobiography 1987, Boycott on Cricket 1990, Geoffrey Boycott on Cricket 1999. *Leisure interests:* golf, tennis. *Address:* c/o Yorkshire County Cricket Club, Headingley Cricket Ground, Leeds, Yorks., LS6 3BY, England.

BOYCOTT, Rosie; British journalist and author; b. 13 May 1951; d. of Charles Boycott and Betty Boycott; m. 1st David Leitch (divorced); one d.; m. 2nd Charles Howard 1999; ed Cheltenham Ladies Coll., Kent Univ.; f. Spare Rib 1972; est. Virago Books 1973; worked on Village Voice (magazine), New York; subsequently edited Arabic women's magazine in Kuwait; Features Ed. Honey; Deputy Ed. Daily Mail's Male and Femail pages; Ed. Discount Traveller; Commissioning Ed. The Sunday Telegraph; Deputy Ed. Harpers & Queen 1989; Deputy Ed. and Features Ed. (British) Esquire 1991, Ed. 1992–96, of Ind. on Sunday 1996–98, of the Ind. 1998, of the Express 1998–2001, of the Express on Sunday 1998–2001; Chair., Panel of Judges, Orange Prize for Fiction 2001. *Publications:* A Nice Girl Like Me (autobiog.) 1983, All For Love 1985. *Address:* c/o Express Newspapers PLC, Ludgate House, 245 Blackfriars Road, London, SE1 9UX, England.

BOYD, Rt. Hon. Colin, PC, QC, BA(Econ), LLB, FRSA; British lawyer; b. 7 June 1953, Falkirk; s. of David Hugh Aird Boyd and Betty Meldrum Boyd; two s. one d.; ed Wick High School, George Watson's Coll., Edinburgh, Univ. of Manchester and Univ. of Edinburgh; qualified as solicitor 1978; called to Bar 1983; Legal Assoc. Royal Town Planning Inst. 1990; Advocate Depute (prosecutor) 1993–95; Queen's Counsel 1995; MSP 1997–; Solicitor-Gen. for Scotland, UK Govt 1997; Solicitor-Gen., Scottish Exec. 1999–2000; Lord Advocate of Scotland 2000–; chief prosecutor at Lockerbie trial; Hon. Fellow, Inst. of Advanced Legal Studies 2001. *Leisure interests:* reading, walking. *Address:* Office of the Lord Advocate, Crown Office, 25 Chambers Street, Edinburgh, EH1 1LA, Scotland (Office). *Telephone:* (131) 226-2626 (Office). *Fax:* (131) 226-6910 (Office).

BOYD, Sir John Dixon Iklé, KCMG, MA; British diplomatist (retd) and university administrator; b. 17 Jan. 1936, Cambridge; s. of the late Prof. James Dixon Boyd and of Amélie Lowenthal; m. 1st Gunilla Kristina Ingregerd Rönngren 1968 (divorced 1977); one s. one d.; m. 2nd Julia Daphne Raynsford 1977; three d.; ed Westminster School, Clare Coll., Cambridge, Yale Univ., USA; joined HM Foreign Service 1962; in Hong Kong 1962–64, Beijing (Third Sec.) 1965–67; at FCO 1967–69, Asst Under-Sec. of State 1984, Deputy Under-Sec. of State 1987–89, Chief Clerk 1989–92; with Embassy, Washington 1969–73; First Sec. Embassy, Beijing 1973–75; on secondment to Treasury 1976; Econ. Counsellor Embassy, Bonn 1977–81; Counsellor (Econ. and Social Affairs) Perm. Mission to UN 1981–84; Political Adviser, Hong Kong 1985–87; Amb. to Japan 1992–96; Master Churchill Coll., Cambridge 1996–; Chair. Bd of Govs Bedales School 1966–2001, David Davies Memorial Inst. 1997–2001; Co-Chair. Nuffield Languages Inquiry 1998–2000; Vice-Chair. Yehudi Menuhin Int. Violin Trust Ltd 1996–; Dir (non-exec.) British Nuclear Fuels PLC 1997–2000; Adviser and mem. Bd, East Asia Inst., Univ. of Cambridge 1998–; mem. ASEM "Vision Group" 1998–2000, Trustee British Museum 1996– (Chair. 2001–), Sir Winston Churchill Archive Trust 1996–, Cambridge Union (also Chair.) 1997–, Margaret Thatcher Archive Trust 1997–, Cambridge Foundation 1997–, The Wordsworth Trust 1997–2000, Great Britain-Sasakawa Foundation 2001–, Council of Senate Cambridge Univ. 2001–, Hsuang Hsing Foundation 2001–, RAND (Europe) UK 2001;

Syndic Fitzwilliam Museum 1997–; Gov. RSC 1996–; Hon. Fellow Clare Coll. Cambridge 1994–. *Leisure interests:* music, fly-fishing. *Address:* Master's Lodge, Churchill College, Cambridge, CB3 0DS, England. *Telephone:* (1223) 336142 (Office); (1223) 336226 (Office). *Fax:* (1223) 336177 (Office).

BOYD, Joseph Aubrey, MS, PhD; American business executive; b. 25 March 1921, Oscar, Ky; s. of Joseph R. Boyd and Relda J. Myatt; m. Edith A. Atkins 1942; two s.; ed Univs. of Kentucky and Michigan; Instr., Asst Prof. of Electrical Eng Univ. of Ky 1947–49; mem. Faculty, Univ. of Mich. 1949–62, Prof. of Electrical Eng 1958–62, Dir Willow Run Labs. 1958–62, Dir Inst. of Science and Tech. 1960–62; Exec. Vice-Pres. Radiation Inc., Melbourne, Fla 1962–63, Pres. 1963–72; Exec. Vice-Pres. Electronics, Harris Corpn Cleveland (now in Melbourne, Fla) 1967–71, Exec. Vice-Pres. Operations 1971–72, Dir 1972–87, Chair. Exec. Cttee 1987–, Pres. 1972–85; Chair., CEO Fairchild Space and Defense Corpn 1992–94, Fairchild Controls 1994–; consultant, Inst. for Defense Analyses 1956–, Nat. Security Agency 1957–62; special consultant to Army Combat Surveillance Agency 1958–62; Chair. Advisory Group, Electronic Warfare, Office of Dir of Defense Research, Dept of Defense 1959–61, consultant 1959–; Fellow, AAAS, IEEE. *Publications:* articles in professional journals. *Address:* Fairchild Controls, 540 Highland Street, Frederick, MD 21701 (Office); 4650 Hamilton Terrace, Vero Beach, FL 32967, USA (Home).

BOYD, Joseph Walker, BA; American music industry executive and film producer; b. 5 Aug. 1942, Boston; s. of Joseph M. Boyd and Elizabeth Walker Boyd; ed Harvard Coll.; Gen. Man. Elektra Records UK 1965–66; Man. Dir Witchseason Productions Ltd 1966–71; Dir Music Services, Warner Bros. Films 1971–73; Man. Dir Osiris Films 1976–79; Vice-Pres. Broadway Pictures, New York 1979–80; Man. Dir Hannibal Records Ltd 1980–91; Vice-Pres. A & R Rykodisc Inc. 1991–98; A & R Dir Hannibal/Ryko Latino Labels 1999–; Grammy Award 1974. *Leisure interests:* history, tennis. *Address:* Fifth Floor, 4 Columbus Circle, New York, NY 10019, U.S.A. *Telephone:* (212) 506-5865. *Fax:* (212) 506-5809.

BOYD, Michael, MA; British theatre director; b. 6 July 1955, Belfast; s. of John Truesdale Boyd and Sheila Boyd; partner Caroline Hall; one d.; one s. one d. by previous partner; ed Latymer Upper School, London, Daniel Stewart's Coll., Edin. and Univ. of Edin.; Trainee Dir Malaya Bronnaya Theatre, Moscow; Trainee Asst Dir Belgrade Theatre, Coventry, Asst Dir 1980–82; Assoc. Dir Crucible Theatre, Sheffield 1982–84; Founding Artistic Dir Tron Theatre, Glasgow 1985–89; Assoc. Dir RSC 1996–2003, Artistic Dir March 2003–; Drama Dir New Beginnings Festival of Soviet Arts, Glasgow 1999. *Productions include:* for Tron Theatre: The Trick is to Keep Breathing, Macbeth, Good, The Real World, Crow, Century's End, Salvation, The Baby, Clyde Nouveau, The Guid Sisters; for the RSC: The Broken Heart 1994–95, Measure for Measure 1996–97, The Spanish Tragedy, Much Ado About Nothing 1997–98, Troilus and Cressida 1998–99, A Midsummer Night's Dream 1999–2000, Romeo and Juliet 2000–01, Henry VI, Parts I, II and III and Richard III (Olivier Award for Best Dir) 2000–01, The Tempest 2002; other theatre productions include: Miss Julie (Haymarket Theatre, West End) 1999, Commedia (Lyric Hammersmith) 1983, Othello 1984, Hard to Get (Traverse Theatre, Edin.), Hedda Gabler (Leicester Haymarket), The Alchemist (Cambridge Theatre Co.). *Leisure interests:* walking, reading, music. *Address:* Royal Shakespeare Company, Royal Shakespeare Theatre, Waterside, Stratford-upon-Avon, Warwickshire, CV37 6BB, England (Office). *Telephone:* (1789) 403404 (Office). *Fax:* (1789) 412658 (Office). *E-mail:* info@rsc.org.uk (Office). *Website:* www.rsc.org.uk (Office).

BOYD, Robert, MA, MB, BChir, FRCP, FFPHM, FRCPCH, FMedSci; British paediatrician; b. 14 May 1938, Cambridge; s. of James Dixon Boyd and Amélie Boyd; m. Meriel Cornelia Talbot 1966; one s. one d.; ed Ley's School, Clare Coll. Cambridge, Univ. Coll. Hosp. London; jr posts Hosp. for Sick Children, Gt. Ormond St, Brompton Hosp., Univ. Coll. Hosp. (UCH), London 1962–65; Sir Stuart Halley Research Fellow and Sr Registrar, UCH 1966–71; Goldsmiths MRC Travelling Fellow, Univ. of Colo Medical Center, USA 1971–72; Sr Lecturer and Hon. Consultant UCH Medical School 1972–80; Sec. Academic Bd, British Paediatric Asscn 1976–79, Chair. 1987–90; Asst Registrar Royal Coll. of Physicians 1980–81; Prof. of Paediatrics, Univ. of Manchester 1981–86, Dean 1989–93; Prin. St. George's Hosp. Medical School and Prof. of Paediatrics 1996–, Pro-Vice-Chancellor for Medicine, Univ. of London 2000–, Deputy Vice-Chancellor 2002–; Hon. Consultant St Mary's Hosp., Manchester and Booth Hall Children's Hosp., Manchester 1981–96, St George's Healthcare NHS Trust, London 1996–; Chair. Manchester Health Authority 1994–96, Nat. Primary Care R&D Centre, Manchester, Salford and York Univs. 1994–96, Council of Heads of UK Medical Schools 2001–; Ed. Placenta 1989–95; mem. Health Cttee Universities UK 1997–, Asscn of Medical Research Charities Scientific Advisory Cttee 1996–, Task Force 'Supporting Research & Devt in the NHS' 1994; mem. Council, Royal Veterinary Coll. 1999–; Gov. Kingston Univ. 1998–. *Publications:* Paediatric Problems in General Practice (jtly) 1982; contribs. to Placental and Fetal Physiology and Paediatrics. *Leisure interests:* cooking, reading, holidays. *Address:* St George's Hospital Medical School, Cranmer Terrace, London, SW17 0RE (Office); The Stone House, Adlington, Macclesfield, Cheshire, SK10 4NU, England (Home). *Telephone:* (20) 8725-5008 (Office); (1625) 872400 (Home). *Fax:* (20) 8672-6940 (Office). *E-mail:* rboyd@sghms.ac.uk (Office). *Website:* www.sghms.ac.uk (Office).

BOYD, Sir Robert Lewis Fullarton, Kt, CBE, PhD, ACGI, FRS; British emeritus professor of physics and chartered engineer; b. 19 Oct 1922, Saltcoats, Ayrshire; s. of the late Dr W J. Boyd; m. 1st Mary Higgins 1949 (died 1996); two s. one d.; m. 2nd Betty Robinson 1998; ed Whitgift School, Croydon, Imperial and Univ. Colls., London; experimental officer, Admiralty Mining Establishment 1943–46; Research Asst, Dept of Math., Univ. Coll., London 1946–49, ICI Research Fellow 1949–50, ICI Research Fellow, Dept of Physics 1950–52, Lecturer in Physics 1952–58, Reader 1959–62, Prof. 1962–83, now Emer., Hon. Research Fellow 1983–88; Dir Mullard Space Science Lab., Univ. Coll., London 1965–83; Prof. of Astronomy (part-time), Royal Inst. 1961–67; Fellow, Inst. of Physics, IEE, Royal Astron. Soc.; Fellow, Univ. Coll. London 1988; Hon. DSc (Heriot-Watt) 1979; Royal Soc. Bakerian Prize Lecture 1978. *Publications:* over 100 scientific books and papers. *Leisure interests:* elderly Rolls-Royce motor cars and 'live steam' model making. *Address:* Bethaven, 9 Cherwell Gardens, Chandlers Ford, Eastleigh, Hants., SO53 2NH, England. *Telephone:* (23) 8027-3717. *E-mail:* sirrobertboyd@bethaven.freeserve.co.uk (Home).

BOYD, William Andrew Murray, MA, FRSL; British author; b. 7 March 1952; s. of Dr. Alexander Murray Boyd and Evelyn Boyd; m. Susan Anne (née Wilson) Boyd 1975; ed Gordonstoun School, Glasgow Univ., Jesus Coll., Oxford; lecturer in English, St Hilda's Coll., Oxford 1980–83; TV critic, New Statesman 1981–83; Hon. DLitt (St Andrews), (Glasgow), (Stirling); Chevalier des Arts et des Lettres. *Publications include:* A Good Man in Africa (Whitbread Prize 1981, Somerset Maugham Award 1982) 1981, (screenplay 1994), On the Yankee Station 1981, An Ice-Cream War (John Llewellyn Rhys Prize) 1982, Stars and Bars 1984 (screenplay 1988), School Ties 1985, The New Confessions 1987, Scoop (screenplay) 1987, Brazzaville Beach (McVities Prize and James Tait Black Memorial Prize) 1990, Aunt Julia and the Scriptwriter (screenplay) 1990, Mr. Johnson (screenplay) 1990, Chaplin (screenplay) 1992, The Blue Afternoon (novel) 1993, The Destiny of Nathalie "X" 1995, Armadillo 1998, Nat Tate: An American Artist 1998, The Trench (screenplay, also dir) 1999, Sword of Honour (screenplay) 2001, Armadillo (screenplay) 2001, Any Human Heart 2002. *Leisure interests:* tennis, strolling. *Address:* c/o The Agency, 24 Pottery Lane, Holland Park, London, W11 4LZ, England.

BOYD DE LA GUARDIA, Aquilino Edgardo; Panamanian diplomatist and lawyer; b. 30 March 1921; m. Dora Brind; five s.; ed La Salle, Panama City, Holy Cross Coll., USA, Univs. de la Habana and Panamá; First Sec. Cuba 1946–47, Washington 1947–48; mem. Panama Nat. Assembly 1948–64; Pres. Nat. Assembly 1949; Minister Foreign Affairs 1956–58, 1976–77; Perm. Rep. to UN 1962–67, 1968–76, 1983–86; Amb. to USA 1983–86, to UK 1994–97. *Address:* c/o Ministry of Foreign Affairs Panamá 4, Panama.

BOYD OF MERTON, 2nd Viscount (cr. 1960) of Merton-in-Penninghame, Co. Wigtown; **Simon Donald Rupert Neville Lennox-Boyd,** MA; British business executive; b. 7 Dec. 1939, London; s. of the late Alan Lennox-Boyd (1st Viscount Boyd of Merton) and of Lady Patricia Guinness; m. Alice Mary Clive 1962; two s. two d.; ed Eton, Christ Church, Oxford; Deputy Chair. Arthur Guinness & Sons 1981–86; Vice-Chair. Save the Children Fund 1979–82, Chair. 1987–93; Chair. Stonham Housing Asscn 1992–98, Trustee, Guinness Trust 1974–; Dir The Iveagh Trustees Ltd. *Leisure interest:* forestry. *Address:* The Iveagh Trustees Ltd, Iveagh House, 41 Harrington Gardens, London, SW7 4JU (Office); 9 Warwick Square, London, SW1V 2AA; Ince Castle, Saltash, Cornwall, PL12 4QZ, England. *Telephone:* (20) 7373-7261 (Iveagh House); (20) 7821-1618 (Warwick Square); (1752) 842672 (Saltash). *Fax:* (20) 7244-8281 (Iveagh House); (1752) 847134 (Saltash) (Home). *E-mail:* boydince@aol.com (Home).

BOYE, Madior; Senegalese politician and lawyer; ed Faculty of Legal and Econ. Sciences, Dakar, Centre Nat. d'Etudes Judiciaires, Paris; fmr Deputy Procurator of Repub.; Judge, First Vice-Pres. First Class Regional Court, Dakar; fmr Pres. Dakar Court of Appeal; Minister of Justice and Keeper of the Seals 2000–01; Prime Minister of Senegal 2001–02; mem. Parti Démocratique Sénégalais (PDS). *Address:* c/o Office of the Prime Minister, Building Administratif, Avenue Léopold Sédar Senghor, Dakar, Senegal (Office).

BOYER, Paul Delos, PhD; American professor of biochemistry; b. 31 July 1918, Provo, Utah; s. of Dell Delos Boyer and Grace Guymon; m. Lynda Wicker 1939; one s. two d.; ed Brigham Young Univ. and Univ. of Wisconsin; Research Asst, Univ. of Wis. 1939–43; Instructor, Stanford Univ. 1943–45; Assoc. Prof., Univ. of Minn. 1947–53, Prof. 1953–56, Hill Prof. of Biochem. 1956–63; Prof. of Biochemistry, Univ. of Calif. at Los Angeles 1963–89, Dir Molecular Biology Inst. 1965–83, Biotechnology Program 1985–89, Prof. Emer. 1989–; mem. Nat. Acad. of Sciences; Fellow, American Acad. of Arts and Sciences, Vice-Pres. Biological Sciences 1985–87; Pres. American Soc. of Biol. Chemists 1969–70; Guggenheim Fellowship 1955; American Chem. Soc. Award 1955; Tolman Medal 1981; Rose Award (American Soc. of Biochemistry and Molecular Biology) 1989; shared Nobel Prize for Chem. 1997; Dr hc, (Stockholm) 1974, (Minn.) 1996, (Wis.) 1998. *Publications:* Author or co-author of over 200 scientific papers in biochem. and molecular biology; Ed. Annual Biochemistry Review 1964–89, Ed. Biochemical and Biophysical Research Communications 1968–80, The Enzymes 1970–. *Leisure interest:* tennis. *Address:* Department of Chemistry and Biochemistry, University of California at Los Angeles, 639A MBT Building, 607 Charles B. Young Drive East, Los Angeles, CA 90095-0001 (Office); 1033 Somera Road, Los Angeles, CA 90077-2625, USA (Home). *E-mail:* pdboyer@ucla.edu (Office).

BOYER, Yves, PhD; French defence research director; b. 9 Oct. 1950, Blois; m. Isabelle Kraft 1978; one s. one d.; ed Inst. d'Etudes Politiques, Paris and Paris-Panthéon Univ.; Deputy Gen. Sec. SOFRESA, Paris 1978–80; Bureau des Etudes Stratégiques et des Négociations Internationales, Secr. Gén. de la Défense Nationale 1980–82; Defence Consultant and Research Assoc. Int. Inst. for Strategic Studies, London 1982–83; Sr Researcher, Inst. Français des Relations Internationales 1983–88; Research Fellow, Woodrow Wilson Center 1986; fmr Deputy Dir CREST, Ecole Polytechnique; Prof. Army Acad. 1986–, Staff Coll. 1992–; currently Deputy Dir Fondation pour la Recherche Stratégique; Chair. French Soc. for Mil. Studies (SFEM), Working Groups for the French Ministry of Defence's Scientific Advisers; mem. Bd Centre d'Analyse de la Sécurité Européenne (CASE); Ed. Les Cahiers du CREST. *Address:* Fondation pour la Recherche Stratégique, 27 rue Damesme, 75013 Paris (Office); 2 rue de Haut Bourg, 41000 Blois, France (Home). *E-mail:* y.boyer@frstrategie.org (Office).

BOYER SALVADOR, Miguel; Spanish politician; b. 5 Feb. 1939, San Juan de Luz, France; m. 1st Elena Arnedo; two s.; m. 2nd Isabel Preysler 1988; joined Spanish Socialist Workers' Party 1960, imprisoned for 6 months for political activities; fmr economist, Studies Group of Banco de España; Dir Studies, Nat. Industrial Inst., Strategic Planning Group, Explosivos Río Tinto SA, Strategic Planning, Nat. Hydrocarbons Inst.; Minister of Economy, Finance and Commerce 1982–85; Chair. Banco Exterior de España 1985–88, Cartera Central, Grueyersa 1989–93; Vice-Chair. FCC Construcción 1993–; Gov. IBRD; Rep. to IDB 1983–85. *Address:* Capitán Haya nr 41, 28020 Madrid, Spain. *Telephone:* (1) 556-70-00. *Fax:* (1) 556-90-07.

BOYLE, Danny; British film director; b. 20 Oct. 1956, Bury, Lancs.; Artistic Dir Royal Court Theatre 1982–87; produced Elephant (TV Film) 1989; Dir The Greater Good (TV series) 1991, Mr. Wroe's Virgins (TV) 1993, Not Even God is Wise Enough (TV) 1993; Golden Ephebe Award 1997. *Films:* Shallow Grave 1994, Trainspotting 1996, A Life Less Ordinary 1996, The Beach 1999, Alien Love Triangle 1999, 28 Days Later 2002; exec. producer Twin Town 1996. *Address:* c/o D6A, 7920 West Sunset Boulevard, Los Angeles, CA 90046 (Office); c/o ICM, 6th Floor, 76 Oxford Street, London, W1N 0AX, England.

BOYNTON, Robert Merrill, PhD; American professor of psychology; b. 28 Oct. 1924, Evanston, Ill.; s. of Merrill Holmes Boynton and Eleanor Matthews Boynton; m. 1st Alice Neiley 1947 (died 1996); three s. one d.; m. 2nd Sheleah Maloney 1998; ed Amherst Coll. and Brown Univ.; Asst Prof., Univ. of Rochester 1952–57, Assoc. Prof. 1957–61, Prof. 1961–74, Dir and Founder, Center for Visual Science 1963–71, Chair. Dept of Psychology 1971–74; Prof., Dept of Psychology, Univ. of Calif. at San Diego 1974–91, Emer. Prof. 1991–; Assoc. Dean, Graduate Studies and Research 1987–91; Chair. Visual Sciences B Study Section, Nat. Inst. of Health 1972–75; Chair. Bd of Eds. Vision Research 1982–85; mem. NAS; Fellow AAAS; Godlove Award, Inter-society Color Council 1982, Tillyer Medal, Optical Soc. of America 1972, Ives Medal and Quinn Prize, Optical Soc. of America 1995, Prentice Award, American Acad. of Optometry 1997, Distinguished Achievement Award (Brown Univ.) 1986; Snaker Heights High School Hall of Fame 1996. *Publications:* Human Color Vision 1979; 150 scientific articles and 12 articles on baseball. *Leisure interest:* baseball research. *Address:* 376 Bellaire Street, Del Mar, CA 92014, USA (Home). *Telephone:* (858) 481-0263 (Home). *E-mail:* rboynton@ucsd.edu (Office).

BOYSE, Edward Arthur, MD, FRS; British/American research physician; b. 11 Aug. 1923, Worthing, Sussex; s. of Arthur Boyse and Dorothy V. (née Mellersh) Boyse; m. 1st Jeanette Grimwood 1951; two s. one d.; m. 2nd Judith Bard 1987; ed St Bartholomew's Hosp. Medical School, Univ. of London; RAF pilot 1941–46; various hospital appts 1952–57; Research Fellow in Pathology, Guy's Hosp., London 1957–60; Assoc. mem. Sloan-Kettering Inst., New York 1964–67, mem. 1967–89; Prof. of Biology, Cornell Univ. Grad. School of Medical Sciences 1969–89; Adjunct Prof. of Pathology New York Univ. School of Medicine 1964; Distinguished Prof. of Microbiology and Immunology, Univ. of Ariz. 1989–94, Prof. Emer. 1994–; Harvey Lecturer 1975; Fellow American Acad. of Arts and Sciences 1977, NAS 1979; Cancer Research Inst. Award in Tumour Immunology 1975; Isaac Adler Award of Rockefeller and Harvard Univs. 1976; C. Chester Stock Award, Sloan-Kettering Inst. 1995. *Publications:* papers relating to genetics and immunology to devt and cancer. *Address:* Department of Microbiology and Immunology, University of Arizona, Health Sciences Center, P.O. Box 24-5049, 1501 N Campbell Ave, Tucson, AZ 85724, USA.

BOZANGA, Simon-Narcisse; Central African Republic politician; b. 26 Dec. 1942, Bangassou; Dir of Legal Studies, Ministry of Foreign Affairs 1972–74, Sec.-Gen. 1974–78; Amb. to Gabon 1978–79; Sec.-Gen. to Govt 1979–80; Minister of Justice 1980–81; Prime Minister and Head of Govt April–Sept. 1981 (deposed by mil. coup); Dir-Gen. Société Centrafricaine des Hydrocarbures (CentraHydro) 1982.

BOZER, Ali Husrev; Turkish jurist; b. 28 July 1925, Ankara; s. of Mustafa Fevzi Bozer and Zehra Bozer; m.; three s.; ed Ankara and Neuchâtel Univs. and Harvard Law School; Asst judge, Ankara 1951; Asst, Faculty of Law, Ankara Univ. 1952–60, Agrégé 1955–60, Head of Dept 1961, apptd. Prof. of Commercial Law 1965; lawyer at bar, Ankara 1952–; Dir Inst. de Recherche sur le Droit commercial et bancaire 1960–; Judge, European Court of Human Rights 1974–76; mem. Admin. Council, Turkish Radio-TV Corpn 1968–71, Vice-Pres. 1971–73; Minister of Customs and Monopolies 1981–83, of State for Relations with EEC 1986–90; Deputy Prime Minister and Minister of State

1989–90; Minister of Foreign Affairs Feb.–Oct. 1990. *Publications:* Les droits d'administration et de jouissance de père et mère sur les biens de l'enfant, Nantissement commercial, Aperçu général sur le droit des assurances sociales en droit turc, Droit commercial pour les employés de banques, Papiers valeurs pour les employés de banques; monographs and articles in several reviews in Turkish and French. *Leisure interest:* tennis. *Address:* Ahmet Rasim sok. 35/5, Cankaya, Ankara, Turkey. *Telephone:* 271845, 191322.

BOZIZE, Gen. François; Central African Republic army officer and politician; opposition leader 1981–93, led unsuccessful coup 1983; spent many years in exile in Togo; Presidential Cand. 1993; supported Pres. Ange-Felix Patasse in suppressing coups 1996–97; sacked as Army Chief; participated in unsuccessful coup against Pres. 2001, took control of N. Bangui before escaping to Chad with 300 supporters; launched several rebel attacks from base in Chad 2001–02; led successful coup March 2003, suspended constitution and dissolved parl.; self-proclaimed Pres. of Cen. African Repub. March 2003–. *Address:* c/o Ministry of National Defence, Bangui, Central African Republic (Office).

BOŽOVIĆ, Radoman, PhD; Serbia and Montenegro (Serbian) politician and economist; b. 1953, Serbia; m.; two c.; ed Belgrade Univ.; academic 1976–89; fmr deputy to Vojvodina Ass., later head of provincial Govt; mem. Socialist Party of Serbia (SPS) (fmrly League of Communists of Yugoslavia (LCY)); Deputy Serbian Ass. 1990–, Head SPS parl. group.; Prime Minister of Serbia 1991–92; Chair. Council of Citizens, Fed. Ass. 1992–97; f. Bancor Group Sept. 1997; Prof., Univ. Subotica. *Publications:* numerous books and articles including Political Economy (2 vols), Accumulation and Economic Development, Types of Prosperity in Socialism, Problems of Economic System Reform in Yugoslavia.

BRABECK-LETMATHE, Peter; business executive; fmrly with Findus Austria; joined Nestlé Group as new products specialist 1968, Nat. Sales Man., later Head Marketing, Savory (Chile) 1970, frozen food and ice-cream specialist, Nestlé HQ 1975, Marketing and Sales Div. Man., Chiprodal, Chile 1976, Asst to Regional Man. for S. America, Nestlé HQ 1980, Man. Dir Nestlé Ecuador 1981, Nestlé Venezuela 1983, Sr Vice-Pres. and Head Culinary Products Div., Nestlé S.A., Vevey 1987, Exec. Vice-Pres. and Head Strategic Business Group 2 1992, Group CEO (desig.) Nestlé S.A., Vevey 1995–97, Group CEO 1997–. *Address:* Nestlé, Ave. Nestlé, 1800 Vevey, Switzerland (Office).

BRABHAM, Sir Jack (John Arthur), Kt, OBE; Australian professional racing driver (retd); b. 2 April 1926, Sydney, Australia; s. of C.T. Brabham; m. 1st Betty Evelyn (divorced); three s.; m. 2nd Margaret Brabham; ed Hurstville Tech. Coll., Sydney; served in RAAF 1944–46; started own engineering business 1946; Midget Speedway racing 1946–53; numerous wins driving a Cooper-Bristol, Australia 1953–54; went to Europe 1955; Australian Grand Prix 1955, 1963; World Champion, Formula II 1958; Formula II Champion of France 1964; World Champion Driver 1959–60, 1960–61, 1966; came first in Monaco and UK Grandes Epreuves 1959; won Grand Prix of Netherlands, Belgium, France, UK, Portugal, Denmark 1960, Belgium 1961, France 1966, 1967, UK 1966; began building own cars 1961; Chair. Jack Brabham (Ewell) Ltd; Dir Engine Devts. Ltd; winner Formula I Mfrs Championship 1966, 1967; Ferodo Trophy 1964, 1966; BRDC Gold Star 1966, BARC Gold Medal 1959, 1966, 1967. *Publications:* Jack Brabham's Book of Motor Racing 1960, When the Flag Drops 1971. *Leisure interests:* flying, scuba diving, water skiing. *Address:* Suite 404, Bag No. 1, Robina Town Centre, Queensland, 4230, Australia.

BRABOURNE, 7th Baron, cr. 1880; John Ullick Knatchbull, 16th Bt, cr. 1641, CBE; British film and television producer; b. 9 Nov. 1924, London; s. of 5th Baron Brabourne and Lady Doreen Geraldine Browne; m. Lady Patricia Edwina Victoria Mountbatten (Countess Mountbatten of Burma) 1946; four s. (and one s. deceased) two d.; ed Eton Coll. and Univ. of Oxford; Dir. Copyright Promotions Group 1974– (Vice-Chair. 1995); Dir Thames TV 1975–93 (Chair. 1991–93); Dir Thorn EMI 1981–86; Gov. BFI 1979–94 (Fellow 1979); Gov. Nat. Film and TV School 1981–95; mem. British Screen Advisory Council 1985–97; Trustee, BAFTA Science Museum, Nat. Museum of Photography, Film and TV; Gov. United World Colls 1965–96; Pro-Chancellor, Univ. of Kent 1993–98; Vice-Pres. Royal Soc. for Nature Conservation 1988–98; other public appts; Hon. DCL (Kent). *Films produced:* Harry Black 1958, Sink the Bismarck! 1959, HMS Defiant 1961, Othello 1965, The Mikado 1966, Romeo and Juliet 1968, Up the Junction 1967, Dance of Death 1968, Tales of Beatrix Potter 1971, Murder on the Orient Express 1974, Death on the Nile 1978, Stories from a Flying Trunk 1979, The Mirror Crack'd 1980, Evil Under the Sun 1982, A Passage to India 1984, Little Dorritt 1987. *Television productions include:* National Gallery 1974, A Much-Maligned Monarch 1976, Leontyne 1987. *Address:* Mersham Productions Ltd, Newhouse, Mersham, Ashford, Kent, TN25 6NQ (Office); Newhouse, Mersham, Ashford, Kent, TN25 6NQ, England (Home). *Telephone:* (1233) 503636. *Fax:* (1233) 502244. *E-mail:* b@knatchbull.com (Home).

BRACHER, Karl Dietrich, DPhil; German historian and political scientist; b. 13 March 1922, Stuttgart; s. of Theodor Bracher and Gertrud Zimmermann; m. Dorothee Schleicher (niece of Dietrich Bonhoeffer) 1951; one s. one d.; ed Gymnasium, Stuttgart, Univ. of Tübingen and Harvard Univ.; Research Asst and Head of Dept, Inst. of Political Science, Berlin 1950–58; lecturer, German Hochschule für Politik, Berlin; Privatdozent and Prof. Free Univ., Berlin 1955–58; Prof. of Political Science and Contemporary History, Univ. of Bonn

www.worldwhoswho.com

1959–; Pres. Comm. for History of Parl. and Political Parties, Bonn 1962–68; Fellow Center for Advanced Study in the Behavioral Sciences, Stanford, USA 1963–64; Chair. German Asscn of Political Science 1965–67; mem. Inst. for Advanced Study, Princeton, USA 1967–68, 1974–75; mem. Wilson Center, Wash. 1980–81; Chair. Bd, Inst. für Zeitgeschichte, Munich 1980–88, German Asscn of Foreign Policy, German PEN Centre; Visiting Prof. Sweden 1962, Oxford Univ. 1971, Tel-Aviv Univ. 1974, Japan 1975, European Univ. Inst. (Florence) 1975–76, Seattle 1984; Hon. mem. American Acad. of Arts and Sciences; Corresp. Fellow, British Acad., American Philosophical Soc., Austrian Akad. der Wissenschaften; mem. Deutsche Akad. für Sprache und Dichtung, Rhenish-Westfalian Acad. of Sciences; Ed. Vierteljahrshefte für Zeitgeschichte; mem. Editorial Bd, Politische Vierteljahresschrift until 1970, Neue Politische Literatur, Bonner Historische Forschungen, Journal of Contemporary History, Government and Opposition, Societas, Zeitschrift für Politik, Tempo Presente, Risorgimento, European Journal of Int. Affairs, History of the Twentieth Century, Bonner Schriften zur Politik und Zeitgeschichte, Quellen zur Geschichte des Parliamentarismus, Dokumente zur Deutschlandpolitik; Ordre of Merit for Sciences and Arts 1992–Hon. DHumLitt (Fla.), DJur (Graz), Dr rer. pol (Berlin); Dr hc (Paris); Premio Storia Acqui 1973, Bentinck-Preis 1981, Curtius-Preis 1994. *Publications:* Conscience in Revolt (with others) 1954, Die Auflösung der Weimarer Republik 1955, Staat und Politik (with E. Fraenkel) 1957, Die Nationalsozialistische Machtergreifung (with others) 1960, Propyläen Weltgeschichte (Vol. 9) (Dutch trans.) 1960, The Foreign Policy of the Federal Republic of Germany 1963, Problems of Parliamentary Democracy in Europe 1964, Adolf Hitler 1964, Deutschland zwischen Demokratie und Diktatur 1964, Theodor Heuss 1965, Modern Constitutionalism and Democracy (Jt Ed., 2 Vols) 1966, Internationale Beziehungen (with E. Fraenkel) 1969, The German Dictatorship (English, Italian, Spanish, French, Japanese, Hebrew trans.) 1970, Nach 25 Jahren (Ed.) 1970, Das deutsche Dilemma 1971 (English trans. 1974), Western Europe (in Times History of Our Times) 1971, Democracy (in Europe Tomorrow) 1972, Zeitgeschichtliche Kontroversen 1976, Die Krise Europas seit 1917 1976 and 1992 (Italian trans.), Schlüsselwörter in der Geschichte 1978, Geschichte und Gewalt 1981, Bibliographie zur Politik (Jt Ed.) 1970, 1976, 1982, Zeit der Ideologien 1982 (English, Spanish and Italian trans. 1985), Nationalsozialistische Diktatur 1983, Das Gewissen steht auf 1984, Die totalitäre Erfahrung 1987, Geschichte der BR Deutschland 1981–87, Verfall und Fortschritt im Denken der frühen römischen Kaiserzeit 1987, Die Weimarer Republik 1998, Deutschland zwischen Krieg und Frieden 1991, Staat und Parteien (Co-Ed.) 1992, Wendezeiten der Geschichte 1992, Deutschland 1933–1945 1993, Hitler et la dictature allemande 1995, Turning Points in Modern Times 1995, Geschichte als Erfahrung 2001. *Leisure interest:* playing piano and chamber music, mountain walking. *Address:* Stationsweg 17, 53127 Bonn, Germany. *Telephone:* 284358.

BRACHES, Dr Ernst; Netherlands professor (retd); b. 8 Oct. 1930, Padang, Indonesia; s. of Godfried Daniel Ernst Braches and Zeni Jansz; m. Maartje van Hoorn 1961; three s. and one foster s.; ed Univ. of Amsterdam; Asst Univ. of Amsterdam 1957–65; Keeper, Western Printed Books, Univ. Library, Leiden 1965–73; Asst Dir Rijksmuseum Meermanno-Westreenianum, The Hague 1973–77; Librarian, Univ. of Amsterdam 1977–88; Prof. History of the Printed Book, Univ. of Amsterdam; hon. mem. Soc. de la Reliure Originale, Paris. *Publications:* Het Boek als Nieuwe Kunst 1973, Engel en Afgrond 1983, Borneo in World War II; publications on Goethe, Henry James, Thomas Mann, typography. *Address:* Vrijburglaan 53, 2051 LB Overveen, Netherlands (Home). *Telephone:* (23) 5253246 (Home). *Fax:* (23) 5253246 (Home).

BRACKS, Hon. Stephen Philip (Steve); Australian politician; b. 15 Oct. 1954, Ballarat; m.; two s. one d.; ed Ballarat Univ.; secondary commerce teacher 1976–81; employment project worker and municipal recreation officer 1981–85; Exec. Dir Ballarat Educ. Centre 1985–89; Statewide Man. Vic.'s Employment Programmes 1989–1993; Adviser to Premier of Vic. 1990; Prin. Adviser to Fed. Parl. Sec. for Transport and Communications 1993; Exec. Dir Victorian Printing Industry Training Bd 1993–94; mem. Parl. (Labor) 1994–; Deputy Chair. Public Accounts and Estimates Cttee 1996–99; Shadow Minister for Employment, Industrial Relations and Tourism 1994–96; Shadow Treas., Shadow Minister for Finance and Industrial Relations 1996–99; Premier of Vic., Minister for Multicultural Affairs 1999–, Treas. of Vic. 1999–2000. *Leisure interests:* camping, distance swimming, tennis. *Address:* Office of the Premier, 1 Treasury Place, Melbourne, Vic. 3000, Australia (Office). *Telephone:* 9651-5000 (Office). *Fax:* 9651-5054 (Office). *E-mail:* steve.bracks@parliament.vic.gov.au (Office). *Website:* www.premier.vic.gov.au (Office).

BRADBEER, Sir (John) Derek (Richardson), Kt, MA, OBE, TD; British lawyer; b. 29 Oct. 1931; s. of the late William Bertram Bradbeer and Winifred Bradbeer (née Richardson); m. Margaret Elizabeth Chantler 1962; one s. one d.; ed Canford School, Sidney Sussex Coll. Cambridge; admitted Solicitor 1959; partner Wilkinson Maughan (fmrly Wilkinson Marshall Clayton & Gibson) 1961–97; mem. Criminal Injuries Compensation Bd 1988–2000, Criminal Injuries Compensation Appeals Panel 1996–; mem. Disciplinary Cttee, Inst. of Actuaries 1989–96, Insurance Brokers Registration Council 1992–96; mem. Council, Law Soc. 1973–94, Vice-Pres. 1986–87, Pres. 1987–88; Pres. Newcastle-upon-Tyne Inc. Law Soc. 1982–83; Gov. Coll. of Law 1983–2002 (Chair. 1990–99); Dir Newcastle and Gateshead Water PLC 1978–90, Sunderland and South Shields Water PLC 1990–2002; Chair. North East Water 1992–2002; Deputy Chair. Northumbrian Water Group 1996–2002; UK Vice-Pres. Union Int. des Avocats 1988–92; Vice-Chair. N of England Territorial Auxiliary and Volunteer Reserve Asscn 1988–90, Chair. 1990–96; DL Tyne and Wear 1988; DUniv Open 2000. *Leisure interests:* reading, gardening, sport. *Address:* Forge Cottage, Shilvington, Newcastle-upon-Tyne, NE20 0AP, England (Home). *Telephone:* (1670) 775214 (Home).

BRADBURY, Ray (Douglas); American author; b. Aug. 1920, Ill.; s. of Leonard Bradbury and Esther Bradbury; m. Marguerite McClure 1947; four d.; Pres. Science-Fantasy Writers of America 1951–53; mem. Bd of Dirs Screen Workers Guild of America 1957–61; numerous awards including Lifetime Medal, Nat. Book Foundation. *Publications include:* Dark Carnival 1947, The Meadow (play) 1948, The Martian Chronicles 1950, The Illustrated Man 1951, It Came from Outer Space (screenplay) 1952, Fahrenheit 451 1953, The Golden Apples of the Sun 1953, Moby Dick (screenplay) 1954, The October Country 1955, Switch on the Night 1955, Dandelion Wine 1957, A Medicine for Melancholy (play as The Day it Rained Forever) 1966, Icarus Montgolfier Wright (screenplay) 1961, R is for Rocket 1962, Something Wicked This Way Comes 1962, The Anthem Sprinters and Other Antics (play) 1963, The World of Ray Bradbury (play) 1964, The Machineries of Joy (short stories) 1964, The Vintage Bradbury 1965, The Wonderful Ice-Cream Suit (play) 1965, The Autumn People 1965, Tomorrow Midnight 1966, The Pedestrian (play) 1966, S is for Space 1966, The Picasso Summer (screenplay) 1968, I Sing the Body Electric! 1969, Christus Apollo (play) 1969, Old Ahab's Friend and Friend to Nosh, Speaks His Piece: A Celebration 1971, The Halloween Tree 1972, The Wonderful Ice Cream Suit and Other Plays: For Today, Tomorrow and Beyond Tomorrow 1972, When Elephants Last in the Dooryard Bloomed (poetry) 1972, The Small Assassin 1973, Zen and the Art of Writing 1973, Mars and the Mind of Man 1973, The Son of Richard III 1974, Long After Midnight (stories) 1976, Pillar of Fire and Other Plays 1976, Where Robot Mice and Robot Men Run Round in Robot Towns, New Poems Both Light and Dark 1977, Beyond 1984 1979, The Stories of Ray Bradbury 1980, The Ghosts of Forever 1981, The Haunted Computer and the Android Pope 1981, The Last Circus 1981, The Complete Poems of Ray Bradbury 1982, The Love Affair 1983, The Dinosaur Tales 1983, A Memory for Murder 1984, Forever and the Earth 1984, Death is a Lonely Business (novel) 1985, The Toynbee Convector 1989, A Graveyard for Lunatics (novel) 1990, Yestermorrow, Obvious Answers to Impossible Futures, Green Shadows, White Whale 1992, Journey to Far Metaphor: Further Essays on Creativity, Writing, Literature and the Arts 1994, The First Book of Dichotomy, The Second Book of Symbiosis 1995, Driving Blind 1998. *Leisure interests:* oil painting, ceramics, collecting native masks. *Address:* Bantam Doubleday Dell, 1540 Broadway, New York, NY 10036 (Office); c/o Avon Books, 1350 Avenue of the Americas, New York, NY 10019 (Office); 10265 Cheviot Drive, Los Angeles, CA 90064, USA.

BRADEMAS, John, DPhil; American politician and former university president; b. 2 March 1927, Mishawaka, Ind.; s. of Stephen J. Brademas and Beatrice Goble; m. Mary Ellen Briggs 1977; ed Harvard Univ. and Univ. of Oxford; Legis. Asst to Senator Pat McNamara; Admin. Asst to Rep. Thomas L. Ashley 1955; Exec. Asst to presidential nominee Stevenson 1955–56; Asst Prof. of Political Science, St Mary's Coll. Notre Dame, Ind. 1957–58; mem. 86th–96th Congresses from 3rd Ind. Dist; Chief Deputy Majority Whip 93rd–94th Congresses; Majority Whip 95th–96th Congresses; Pres. New York Univ. 1981–92, Pres. Emer. 1992–; Chair. Pres.'s Comm. on the Arts and Humanities 1994, American Ditchley Foundation; fmr Chair. Fed. Reserve Bank of New York, Nat. Endowment for Democracy 1993–2001; Dir RCA/NBC, Scholastic Inc., New York Stock Exchange, Rockefeller Foundation; fmr mem. Cen. Comm. WCC, Trilateral Comm.; many other public appts; Fellow, American Acad. of Arts and Sciences; Hon. Fellow Brasenose Coll., Oxford; numerous hon. degrees; many other awards and distinctions. *Publications:* Anarcosindicalismo y revolución en España, 1930–37 1974, Washington, DC to Washington Square 1986, The Politics of Education: Conflict and Consensus on Capitol Hill 1987. *Leisure interests:* reading, travel. *Address:* c/o Office of the President Emeritus, New York University, 53 Washington Square South, New York, NY 10012, USA. *Telephone:* (22) 998-3636 (Office). *Fax:* (212) 995-4810 (Office).

BRADFORD, Barbara Taylor; British author and journalist; b. 10 May 1933, Leeds, England; d. of Winston Taylor and Freda Walker; m. Robert Bradford 1963; reporter, Yorkshire Evening Post 1949–51, Women's Ed. 1951–53; Fashion Ed. Woman's Own 1953–54; columnist, London Evening News 1955–57; Exec. Ed. London American 1959–62; Ed. Nat. Design Center Magazine 1965–69; syndicated columnist, Newsday Specials, Long Island 1968–70; nat. syndicated columnist, Chicago Tribune-New York (News Syndicate), New York 1970–75, Los Angeles Times Syndicate 1975–81; Dir Library of Congress, DL; mem. Bd American Heritage Dictionary, Police Athletic League, Author's Guild Foundation 1989–; Girls Inc.; Hon. DLit (Leeds) 1990, (Bradford) 1995, Hon. DHumLit (Teikyo Post Univ.) 1996; numerous awards and prizes. *Television:* ten novels adapted into TV mini-series. *Publications:* Complete Encyclopaedia of Homemaking Ideas 1968, A Garland of Children's Verse 1968, How to be the Perfect Wife 1969, Easy Steps to Successful Decorating 1971, How to Solve your Decorating Problems 1976, Decorating Ideas for Casual Living 1977, Making Space Grow 1979, A Woman of Substance (novel) 1979, Luxury Designs for Apartment Living 1981, Voice of the Heart 1983, Hold the Dream 1985, Act of Will (novel) 1986, To Be The Best 1988, The Women in his Life (novel) 1990, Remember (novel) 1991, Angel (novel) 1993, Everything to Gain (novel) 1994, Dangerous to Know (novel) 1995, Love in Another Town (novel) 1995, Her Own Rules 1996, A Secret

Affair 1996, Power of a Woman 1997, A Sudden Change of Heart 1998, Where You Belong 2000, The Triumph of Katie Byrne 2001, Three Weeks in Paris 2002. *Leisure interests:* boating, travelling, art collecting. *Address:* Bradford Enterprises, 450 Park Avenue, New York, NY 10022, USA. *Telephone:* (212) 308-7390. *Fax:* (212) 935-1636.

BRADFORD, Max, MCom; New Zealand politician and economist; b. 1942, Christchurch; s. of Robert Bradford and Ella Bradford; m. 1st Janet Grieve (divorced); m. 2nd Rosemary Bradford; two step-d.; ed Univ. of Canterbury, NZ; fmr mem. staff of Treasury and of IMF, Washington, DC, Chief Exec. NZ Bankers' Asscn; econ. and financial consultant; Nat. Party MP for Tarawera (now for Rotorua) 1990–; Minister of Labour, Energy, Immigration and Business Devt 1996–98, of Labour, Energy, Defence, Enterprise and Commerce 1998–99, of Tertiary Educ. 1999; fmr Chief Exec. Nat. Party. *Leisure interests:* fishing, music, reading, sailing. *Address:* Parliament Buildings, Wellington, New Zealand (Office). *Telephone:* (4) 471-9577 (Office); (4) 971-1011 (Office). *Fax:* (4) 472-4169 (Office). *E-mail:* max.bradford@parliament .govt.nz (Office). *Website:* www.maxbradford.co.nz (Home).

BRADFORD, William E.; Canadian insurance executive; b. 14 Oct. 1933, Montreal; s. of the late Elwood Joseph Bradford and Jessie (née Murray) Bradford; m. Dolores MacDonnell 1954; three s. four d.; ed Concordia Univ., Montreal; with Northern Electric Co. Ltd 1950–59, Canada Iron Foundries Ltd 1959–62; Asst Controller, Reynolds Extrusion Co. Ltd 1962–66; Vice-Pres. and Controller, Churchill Falls (Labrador) Corpn Ltd 1967–70; Vice-Pres. and Sr Financial Officer, Brinco 1970–74; Exec. Vice-Pres. for Finance, Bank of Montreal 1975, for Finance and Admin. 1976, Exec. Vice-Pres. and Deputy Gen. Man. Domestic Banking 1978, also Gen. Man. 1979, Exec. Vice-Pres., Chief Gen. Man. Bank of Montreal 1980, Pres. 1981–83, Deputy Chair. 1983–87; Pres. and CEO N American Life Assurance Co. (now Manulife Financial) 1987–93, Deputy Chair. and CEO 1993–94; Fellow, Certified Gen. Accountants' Asscn of Ont., Financial Execs. Inst. *Leisure interests:* tennis, squash, golf, skiing, hunting, fishing. *Address:* Manulife Financial, 5650 Yonge Street, North York, Ont., M2M 4G4; 1333 Watersedge Road, Mississauga, Ont., L5J 1A3, Canada (Home). *Telephone:* (416) 229-3010 (Office).

BRADLEE, Benjamin Crowninshield, AB; American newspaper editor; b. 26 Aug. 1921, Boston; s. of Frederick Bradlee and Josephine de Gersdorff; m. 1st Jean Saltonstall 1942; one s.; m. 2nd Antoinette Pinchot 1956; one s. one d.; m. 3rd Sally Quinn 1978, one s.; ed Harvard Univ.; reporter, NH Sunday News, Manchester 1946–48, Washington Post 1948–51; Press Attaché, US Embassy, Paris 1951–53; European corresp. Newsweek, Paris 1953–57; reporter, Washington Bureau, Newsweek 1957–61, Sr Ed. and Chief of Bureau 1961–65; Man. Ed. Washington Post 1965–68, Vice-Pres. and Exec. Ed. 1968–91, Vice-Pres. at Large 1991–; Chair. History of St Mary's City Comm. 1992–; Burton Benjamin Award 1995. *Publications:* That Special Grace 1964, Conversations with Kennedy 1975, A Good Life: Newspapering and Other Adventures (autobiog.) 1995. *Address:* c/o Washington Post, 1150 15th Street, NW, Washington, DC 20071-0001 (Office); 3014 N Street, NW, Washington, DC 20007-3404, USA (Home).

BRADLEY, Bill, MA; American politician; b. 28 July 1943, Crystal City, Mo.; s. of Warren W Bradley and Susan Crowe; m. Ernestine Schlant 1974; one d.; ed Princeton and Oxford Univs.; player, New York Knickerbockers Professional Basketball Team 1967–77; Senator from New Jersey 1979–96; Payne Dist Prof., Inst. for Int. Studies, Stanford Univ., Calif. 1997–98; Democrat. *Publications:* Life on the Run 1976, The Fair Tax 1984, Time Present, Time Past 1996, Values of the Game 1998. *Address:* 1661 Page Mill Road, Palo Alto, CA 94304, USA (Home).

BRADLEY, Clive, CBE, MA; British publishing and media executive; b. 25 July 1934, London; s. of late Alfred Bradley and Annie K. Bradley; ed Felsted School, Essex, Clare Coll. Cambridge and Yale Univ.; barrister; BBC 1961–63; Broadcasting Officer, Labour Party 1963–65; Political Ed., The Statist 1965–67; Group Labour Adviser, Int. Publishing Corpn and Deputy Gen. Man. Mirror Group Newspapers 1967–73; Dir The Observer 1973–75; Chief Exec. The Publishers Asscn 1976–97; Dir Confed. of Information Communication Industries 1984–; Deputy Chair. Central London Valuation Tribunal; Chair. Age Concern, Richmond 2001–; Gov. Felsted School. *Publications:* many articles and broadcasts on politics, econs, industrial relations, industry media and current affairs. *Leisure interests:* politics, reading, walking. *Address:* 8 Northumberland Place, Richmond-upon-Thames, Surrey, TW10 6TS, England (Home). *Telephone:* (20) 8940-7172 (Home). *Fax:* (20) 8940-7603 (Home). *E-mail:* bradley_clive@btopenworld.com (Office).

BRADLEY, Daniel Joseph, PhD, FRS, FIEEE, FInstP; Irish professor of optical electronics; b. 18 Jan. 1928; s. of late John Bradley and Margaret Bradley; m. Winefride M. T. O'Connor 1958; four s. one d.; ed St Columb's Coll., Derry, St Mary's Training Coll., Belfast, Birkbeck and Royal Holloway Colls., London; primary school teacher, Londonderry 1947–53, secondary school teacher, London area 1953–57; Asst Lecturer, Royal Holloway Coll. 1957–60; lecturer, Imperial Coll. of Science and Tech. 1960–64; Reader, Royal Holloway Coll. 1964–66; Prof. and Head of Dept of Pure and Applied Physics, Queen's Univ., Belfast 1966–73; Prof. of Optics, Imperial Coll. 1973–80, Head, Dept of Physics 1976–80, Emer. Prof. London Univ. 1980–; Prof. of Optical Electronics, Trinity Coll., Dublin 1980–; Visiting Scientist MIT 1965; Consultant, Harvard Observatory 1966; Chair. Laser Facility Cttee SRC 1976–79, British Nat. Cttee for Physics 1979–80, Quantum Electronics Comm. IUPAP 1982; mem. Rutherford Lab. Establishment Cttee SRC 1977–79, Science Bd, SRC

1977–80; mem. Council, Royal Soc. 1979–80; Fellow, Optical Soc. of America; Fellow Trinity Coll., Dublin; mem. Royal Irish Acad.; DSc hc (New Univ., Ulster) 1983, (Belfast) 1986; Thomas Young Medal, Inst. of Physics 1975; Royal Medal, Royal Soc. 1983, Charles Hard Townes Award of Optical Soc. of America 1989. *Publications:* papers on optics, lasers, spectroscopy, chronoscopy and astronomy in learned journals. *Leisure interests:* television, walking. *Address:* Trinity College, Dublin 2, Ireland. *Telephone:* (1) 6772941.

BRADLEY, David John, MA, DM, FRCP, FRCPath, FFPHM, FIBiol, FMedSci; British professor of tropical hygiene; b. 12 Jan. 1937; s. of the late Harold Robert Bradley and Mona Bradley; m. Lorne Marie Farquhar 1961 (divorced 1989); two s. two d.; ed Wyggeston Grammar School, Leicester, Selwyn Coll. Cambridge and Univ. Coll. Hosp. Medical School, London; Univ. Coll. Hosp. 1960–61; Medical Research Officer, Ross Inst. Bilharzia Research Unit, Mwanza, Tanzania 1961–64; lecturer, Makerere Medical School, Univ. of E Africa 1964–66, Sr lecturer in Preventive Medicine 1966–69; Royal Soc. Tropical Research Fellow 1969–73; Sr Research Fellow, Staines Medical Fellow, Exeter Coll. Oxford 1971–74; Clinical Reader in Pathology, Univ. of Oxford Clinical Medical School 1973–74; Prof. of Tropical Hygiene, Univ. of London, Dir and Head of Dept Ross Inst. of Tropical Hygiene, London School of Hygiene and Tropical Medicine 1974–2000, Ross Prof. Emer. 2000–, Chair. Div. of Communicable and Tropical Diseases 1982–88; Visiting Prof. Univ. of Wales Coll. of Medicine 1995–; numerous professional appointments, consultancies to int. orgs etc.; corresp. mem. German Tropenmedizingesellschaft; foreign corresp. mem. Royal Belgian Acad. of Medicine; numerous awards and distinctions. *Publications:* five books and more than 150 papers on tropical medicine and related topics. *Leisure interests:* natural history, landscape gardens, travel. *Address:* Ross Institute, London School of Hygiene and Tropical Medicine, Keppel Street, London, WC1E 7HT (Office); Flat 3, 1 Taviton Street, London, WC1H 0BT, England (Home). *Telephone:* (20) 7927-2216 (Office); (20) 7383-0228 (Home). *Fax:* (20) 7580-9075 (Office). *E-mail:* David.Bradley@lshtm.ac.uk. *Website:* www.lshtm.ac.uk.

BRADLEY, Donald Charlton, PhD, DSc, FRSC, FRSA, FRS; British inorganic chemist; b. 7 Nov. 1924, London; m. 1st Constance Joy Hazeldean 1948 (died 1985); one s.; m. 2nd Ann Levy (née MacDonald) 1990; ed Hove Co. School for Boys, Birkbeck Coll., Univ. of London; Research Asst, British Electrical and Allied Industries Research Asscn 1941–47; Asst Lecturer in Chem., Birkbeck Coll. 1949–52, Lecturer 1952–59; Prof. of Chem., Univ. of Western Ont. 1959–64; Prof. of Inorganic Chem., Queen Mary Coll., Univ. of London 1965–87, Emer. Prof. 1988–, Head of Chem. Dept 1978–82, Fellow 1988; Chair. Bd of Studies in Chem. and Chemical Industries, Univ. of London 1977–79; mem. Senate, London Univ. 1981–87; Pres. Dalton Div. Royal Soc. Chem.; MRI (mem. Council 1987–93, Hon. Sec. 1988–93); Exec. Ed. Polyhedron 1982–97; Fellow Royal Soc. 1980; Freeman City of London 1996; Ludwig Mond Medal and Lectureship, Royal Soc. Chem. 1987, Royal (Queen's) Medal, Royal Soc. 1998. *Publications:* Metal Alkoxides (jt author) 1978, Alkoxo and Aryloxo Derivatives of Metals (jt author) 2001; over 260 scientific papers. *Leisure interests:* travelling, gardening, music, archaeology. *Address:* Department of Chemistry, Queen Mary College, University of London, Mile End Road, London, E1 4NS (Office); 171 Shakespeare Tower, Barbican, London, EC2Y 8DR, England (Home). *Telephone:* (20) 7882-5025 (Office); (20) 7638-2054 (Home). *E-mail:* d.c.bradley@qmul.ac.uk (Office); don@bradleyhome.net (Home).

BRADLEY, Michael Carl, MBE; British trade union official; b. 17 Feb. 1951, Birmingham; s. of Ronald William Bradley and Doris Florence Bradley (née Hill); m. Janice Bradley (née Holmes) 1973; ed Aldridge Grammar School, Brooklyn Coll., Birmingham; Exec. Officer Inland Revenue 1971–74; Payroll Admin. Smedley H. P. Foods 1974–80; Researcher Transport and Gen. Workers Union (TGWU) 1980–82; Staff Section Organizer Nat. Union of Lock and Metal Workers 1982–97, Gen. Sec. 1988–92; Gen. Sec. Fed. of Trade Unions 1993–; mem. Unity Trust Advisory Cttee 1986–, Social Security Appeals Tribunal 1986–98, Governing Council, Ruskin Coll. Oxford 1994–, Trade Union Labour Party Liaison Cttee 1996–; Gov. The Northern Coll., Barnsley 2000–; Trustee Trade Union Unit Charitable Trust 2000–. *Leisure interests:* sport, reading, music. *Address:* General Federation of Trade Unions, Central House, Upper Woburn Place, London, WC1H 0HY (Office); 7 Park Lane, Gayton, Northamptonshire, NN7 3HB, England (Home). *Telephone:* (20) 7388-0852 (Office). *Fax:* (20) 383-0820 (Home). *E-mail:* gftuhq@gftu .uk (Office). *Website:* www.gftu.org.uk (Office).

BRADMAN, Godfrey Michael, FCA; British business executive; b. 9 Sept. 1936; s. of William I. Bradman and Anne Bradman (née Goldsweig); m. Susan Bennett 1975; two s. three d.; Sr Partner, Godfrey Bradman & Co. (chartered accountants) 1961; Chair. London Mercantile Corpn 1969; Chair. Rosehaugh PLC 1979–91; Chair. European Land and Property Corpn PLC 1992–; European Land and Property Investments Co. 1993–, Ashpest Finance Ltd 1993–, Jt Chair. Vic. Quay 1993–, Pondbridge Europe Ltd 1994–; founder, mem. CLEAR (Campaign for Lead-Free Air) 1981–91; Jt founder and Pres. Campaign for Freedom of Information 1983–, Founder, Chair. Citizen Action, European Citizen Action 1983–91; Chair. Friends of the Earth Trust 1983–91; Dir AIDS Policy Unit 1987–90; Pres. Soc. for the Protection of Unborn Children Educational Research Trust 1987–; mem. Council UN Int. Year of Shelter for the Homeless 1987; mem. governing body London School of Hygiene and Tropical Medicine 1988–91; founder and Jt Chair. Parents Against Tobacco Campaign; Founder Opren Victims Campaign; Hon. Fellow

King's Coll. London; Hon. DSc (Salford). *Leisure interests:* family, reading, horseriding. *Address:* 15 Hanover Terrace, London, NW1 4RJ, England. *Telephone:* (20) 7706-0189. *Fax:* (20) 7723-5341.

BRADSHAW, Anthony David, MA, PhD, FIEEM, FLS, FRS; British ecologist; b. 17 Jan. 1926; m. Betty Margaret Bradshaw; three d.; ed St Paul's School, London, Jesus Coll., Cambridge; Lecturer Univ. Coll. N Wales, Bangor 1952–63, Sr Lecturer 1963–64, Reader in Agricultural Botany 1964–68; Holbrook Gaskell Prof. of Botany, Univ. of Liverpool 1968–88, Prof. Emer. 1988–; mem. Nature Conservancy Council 1969–78, Natural Environment Research Council 1969–74; Bd of Man. Sports Turf Research Inst. 1976, Vice-Pres. 1986–; Pres. British Ecological Soc. 1981–83, Inst. of Ecology and Environmental Man. 1991–94; Pres. Merseyside Environment Trust; mem. Bd of Man. Groundwork Trust, St Helens, Knowsley, Sefton 1982–, Nat. Urban Forestry Unit 1998–; Hon. Corresp. Mem., American Soc. of Botany 1988, Foreign Fellow Indian Nat. Acad. of Sciences 1990, Croonian Lecturer, Royal Soc. 1991; Hon. DSc (Lancaster) 1998, (Hong Kong Baptist Univ.) 2000. *Publications:* (jt) Teaching Genetics 1963, (with M. J. Chadwick) The Restoration of Land 1980, (with others) Quarry Reclamation 1982, (with others) Mine Wastes Reclamation 1982, (with R. A. Dutton) Land Reclamation in Cities 1982, (jt) Ecology and Design in Landscape 1985, Transforming our Waste Land (with A. Burt) 1986, (jt) The Treatment and Handling of Wastes 1991, Trees in the Urban Landscape (with B. Hunt and T. J. Walmsley) 1995; numerous learned papers. *Leisure interests:* sailing, gardening, landscape appreciation. *Address:* 58 Knowsley Road, Liverpool, L19 0PG, England. *Telephone:* (151) 280-2292. *Fax:* (151) 291-4987. *E-mail:* tonybradshaw@ blueyonder.co.uk (Home).

BRADSHAW, Peter, BA, FRS; American (b. British) professor of aerodynamics; b. 26 Dec. 1935, Torquay; s. of J. W. N. Bradshaw and F. W. G. Bradshaw (née Finch); m. Sheila Dorothy Brown 1968; ed Torquay Grammar School, St John's Coll., Cambridge; Scientific Officer, Aerodynamics Div., Nat. Physical Lab., Teddington 1957–69; Sr Lecturer, Dept of Aeronautics, Imperial Coll., Univ. of London 1969–71, Reader 1971–78, Prof. of Experimental Aerodynamics 1978–88; Thomas V. Jones Prof. of Eng, Dept of Mechanical Eng, Stanford Univ. 1988–95, Prof. Emer. 1996–; Hon. DSc (Exeter) 1990; Royal Aeronautical Soc. Bronze Medal 1971, Royal Aeronautical Soc. Busk Prize 1972, AIAA Fluid Dynamics Award 1994. *Publications:* Experimental Fluid Mechanics 1964, An Introduction to Turbulence 1971, Momentum Transfer in Boundary Layers (with T. Cebeci) 1977, Engineering Calculation Methods for Turbulent Flow (with T. Cebeci and J. H. Whitelaw) 1981, Convective Heat Transfer (with T. Cebeci) 1984. *Leisure interests:* ancient history, walking. *Address:* Thermosciences Division, Department of Mechanical Engineering, Stanford Univ., Stanford, CA 94305-3030, USA (Office). *Telephone:* (650) 725-0704 (Office). *Fax:* (650) 723-4548 (Office). *E-mail:* bradshaw@stanford.edu (Office). *Website:* vonkarman.stanford.edu/tsd/resp_b.html (Office).

BRADY, Conor, MA; Irish journalist; b. 24 April 1949, Dublin; s. of Conor Brady and Amy MacCarthy; m. Ann Byron 1971; two s.; ed Mount St Joseph Cistercian Abbey, Univ. Coll. Dublin; Asst Ed. The Irish Times 1978–81, Deputy Ed. 1984–86, Ed. 1986–, Dir Ltd 1986–; Ed. The Sunday Tribune 1981–82; Chair. Bd of Counsellors European Journalism Centre, Maastricht 1994–98; Pres. World Ed.'s Forum, Paris 1995–98; Award for Outstanding Work in Irish Journalism 1979. *Publication:* Guardian of the Peace 1974. *Leisure interests:* travel, reading, swimming. *Address:* c/o The Irish Times, 10–16 d'Olier Street, Dublin 2, Ireland. *Telephone:* (1) 6792022. *Fax:* (1) 6793910. *E-mail:* itemail@irish-times.com (Office). *Website:* www.ireland.com (Office).

BRADY, James S., BS, JD; American government official and lawyer; b. 17 Sept. 1944, Grand Rapids, Mich.; s. of George Joseph Brady and Emily Mae (Sherman) Brady; m. Catherine Ann Yared 1966; two s., one d.; ed Univs. of Western Michigan and Notre Dame; admitted to Mich. bar 1969; assoc. Roach, Twohey, Maggini and Brady law firm 1969–77, partner 1972–77; Adjunct Prof. Cooley Law School, Lansing, Mich. 1975–76; U.S. Attorney Western Dist, Mich. Grand Rapids 1977–81; mem. Miller, Johnson, Snell and Cummiskey 1981–, Chair. Litigation Section 1992–99; Press Sec. to Pres. Reagan 1981; mem. American, Fed., Mich. and Grand Rapids bar asscns., State Bar, Mich., American Trial Lawyers' Asscn; Presidential Medal of Freedom 1996. *Address:* 800 Calder Plaza Building, Grand Rapids, MI 49503 (Office); 1700 Fisk SE, Grand Rapids, MI 49506, USA (Home).

BRADY, Nicholas F.; American politician and financier; b. 11 April 1930, New York; s. of James C. Brady and Eliot Brady; m. Katherine Douglas 1952; three s. one d.; ed Yale and Harvard Univs.; with Dillon, Read and Co. Ltd 1954–82, fmr Chair., CEO 1982–88; U.S. Treasury Sec. 1988–93; appointee to U.S. Senate from NJ 1982; Chair. Templeton Latin American Investment Trust 1994–, Darby Overseas Investments 1994–; Dir Amerada Hess Corpn, C2 Inc., H. J. Heinz Co.; Dir/Trustee U.S. Templeton Funds; Chair. Presidential Task Force on Market Mechanisms; mem. Scowcroft Comm. on Strategic Forces, Kissinger Comm. on Cen. America, Packard Comm. on Defense Man.; fmr Chair. Jockey Club, New York. *Address:* c/o Darby Overseas Investments Ltd 1133 Connecticut Avenue, NW Suite 200, Washington, DC 20036, USA.

BRADY, Roscoe Owen, MD; American medical research scientist; b. 11 Oct. 1923, Philadelphia, Pa; s. of Roscoe O. Brady and Martha Roberts Brady; m. Bennett Carden Manning 1972; two s.; ed Pennsylvania State Univ., Harvard Medical School and Univ. of Pennsylvania; Thyroid Clinic Assoc., Massachusetts Gen. Hosp., Boston; Nat. Research Council Special Fellow, Dept of Biochemistry, Univ. of Pa School of Medicine 1948–50; Officer-in-Charge, Dept of Chemistry, US Naval Medical School 1952–54; Section Chief. Nat. Inst. of Neurological Diseases and Blindness (now Nat. Inst. of Neurological Disorders and Stroke) 1954–67, Acting Chief, Laboratory of Neurochemistry 1967–68, Asst Chief 1969–71, Chief, Developmental and Metabolic Neurology Branch 1972–; Professorial Lecturer, Dept of Biochemistry, George Washington Univ. School of Medicine 1963–73; Adjunct Prof. of Biochemistry, Dept of Biochemistry, Georgetown Univ. School of Medicine 1965–; mem. of medical staff Children's Hosp. Wash. 1992–; mem. NAS, Inst. of Medicine (NAS); Gairdner Foundation Int. Award, Passano Foundation Award, Lasker Foundation Award, Cotzias Award, American Acad. of Neurology, Kovalonko Medal, NAS, Alpert Foundation Prize, Harvard Medical School and other awards and prizes. *Publications:* Neurochemistry of Nucleotides and Amino Acids (ed. with D. B. Tower) 1960, The Basic Neurosciences (ed.) 1975, The Molecular Basis of Lysosomal Storage Disorders (ed. with J. A. Barranger) 1984; and more than 400 scientific pubs. *Leisure interests:* piano, tennis, bridge. *Address:* Building 10, Room 3D04, National Institutes of Health, 9000 Rockville Pike, Bethesda, MD 20892-1260 (Office); 6026 Valerian Lane, Rockville, MD 20852, USA (Home). *Telephone:* (301) 496-3285 (Office); (301) 881-3474 (Home). *Fax:* (301) 496-9480 (Office). *E-mail:* bradyr@ninds.nih.gov (Office). *Website:* neuroscience.nih.gov/MyLab.asp?Org_ID=61.

BRADY, Most Rev. Sean, DCnL; Irish ecclesiastic; b. 16 Aug. 1939, Laragh, Co. Cavan; s. of the late Andrew Brady and Teresa Smith; ed Caulfield Nat. School, St Patrick's Coll., Cavan, St Patrick's Coll., Maynooth, Irish Coll., Rome and Lateran Univ.; ordained priest 1964; language teacher, St Patrick's Coll. Cavan 1967–80; Diocesan Sec., Kilmore 1973–80; Vice-Rector, Irish Coll., Rome 1980, Rector 1987–94; Parish Priest, Ballyhaise 1994; Coadjutor Archbishop of Armagh 1995–96, Archbishop of Armagh and Primate of All Ireland 1996–. *Leisure interest:* Gaelic football. *Address:* Ara Coeli, Armagh, BT61 7QY, Northern Ireland. *Telephone:* (28) 37522045. *Fax:* (28) 37526182. *E-mail:* admin@aracoeli.com. *Website:* www.armagharchdiocese.org.

BRAGG, Baron (Life Peer), cr. 1998, of Wigton in the County of Cumbria; **Melvyn Bragg,** MA, FRSL, FRTS; British author and television presenter; b. 6 Oct. 1939; s. of Stanley Bragg and Mary E Park; m. 1st Marie-Elisabeth Roche 1961 (deceased); one d.; m. 2nd Catherine M. Haste 1973; one s. one d.; ed Nelson-Thomlinson Grammar School, Wigton and Wadham Coll. Oxford; BBC Radio and TV Producer 1961–67; TV Presenter and Ed. The South Bank Show for ITV 1978–; Head of Arts, London Weekend TV 1982–90, Controller of Arts and Features 1990–; Deputy Chair. Border TV 1985–90, Chair. 1990–96; novelist 1965–; writer and broadcaster 1967–, writer and presenter of BBC Radio Four's Start the Week 1988–98, In Our Time 1998–, Routes of English 1999–, The Adventure of English 2001; mem. Arts Council and Chair. Literature Panel of Arts Council 1977–80; Pres. Cumbrians for Peace 1982–, Northern Arts 1983–87, Nat. Campaign for the Arts 1986–; Gov. LSE 1997–; Chancellor Leeds Univ. 1999–; mem. Bd Really Useful Co. 1989–90; Pres. Nat. Acad. of Writing; Pres. MIND; Appeal Chair. Royal Nat. Inst. for the Blind Talking Books Appeal; Hon. Fellow Lancashire Polytechnic 1987, The Library Asscn 1994, Wadham Coll. Oxford 1995, Univ. of Wales, Cardiff 1996; Domus Fellow St Catherine's Coll. Oxford 1990; Hon. DLitt (Liverpool) 1986, (Council for Nat. Academic Awards) 1990, (Lancaster) 1990, (South Bank) 1997, (Leeds) 2000, (Bradford) 2000; Hon. DUniv (Open Univ.) 1988; Hon. DCL (Northumbria) 1994; Hon. DSc (UMIST) 1998, (Brunel) 2000; Dr hc (St. Andrews) 1993, (Sunderland) 2001. *Plays:* Mardi Gras 1976, Orion 1977, The Hired Man 1985, King Lear in New York 1992. *Screenplays:* Isadora, The Music Lovers, Jesus Christ Superstar, A Time to Dance. *Novels:* For Want of a Nail 1965, The Second Inheritance 1966, Without a City Wall 1968, The Hired Man 1969, A Place in England 1970, The Nerve 1971, The Hunt 1972, Josh Lawton 1972, The Silken Net 1974, A Christmas Child 1976, Autumn Manoeuvres 1978, Kingdom Come 1980, Love and Glory 1983, The Cumbrian Trilogy 1984, The Maid of Buttermere 1987, A Time to Dance (televised 1992) 1990, Crystal Rooms 1992, Credo 1996, The Sword and the Miracle 1997, The Soldier's Return 1999, A Son of War 2001. *Other publications:* Speak for England 1976, Land of the Lakes 1983, Laurence Olivier 1984, Rich, The Life of Richard Burton 1988, The Seventh Seal: a study on Ingmar Bergman 1993, On Giants' Shoulders 1998. *Leisure interests:* walking, watching football. *Address:* 12 Hampstead Hill Gardens, London, NW3 2PL, England.

BRAGHIȘ, Dumitru; Moldovan politician and business executive; b. 28 Dec. 1957, Grătieşti; ed Institutul Politehnic din Chişinău; First Sec. Komsomol, Moldovan SSR 1989–91; Dir.-Gen. Dept Foreign Econ. Relations, Ministry of the Economy and Reform 1995; First Deputy Minister of Economy and Reform 1997–99; Prime Minister of Moldova Dec. 1999–2001; mem. Parl. 2000–; Leader Chair. Social-Democratic Alliance 2001–. *Address:* c/o Office of the Council of Ministers, Piaţa Marii Adunări Naţionale 1, 2033 Chişinău, Moldova (Office).

BRAHAM, Allan John Witney, PhD; British fmr gallery curator and author; b. 19 Aug. 1937, Croydon; s. of Dudley Braham and Florence Mears; m. Helen Clare Butterworth 1963; two d.; ed Dulwich Coll., London Univ. and the Courtauld Inst.; Asst Keeper Nat. Gallery 1962, Deputy Keeper 1973, Keeper and Deputy Dir 1978–88; Hitchcock Medal, Bannister Fletcher Prize for writings. *Publications include:* François Mansart (with Peter Smith) 1973, Carlo Fontana: The Drawings at Windsor (with Hellmut Hager) 1977, The

Architecture of the French Enlightenment 1980, El Greco to Goya 1981, Italian Paintings of the Sixteenth Century 1985. *Leisure interest:* history of architecture. *Address:* 1/55 Buckley Road, London, NW6 7LX, England.

BRAHIMI, Abdelhamid, DEcon; Algerian politician; b. 2 April 1936, Constantine; m.; one c.; officer, Nat. Liberation Army 1956–62; Wali of Annaba (Govt rep. in province of Annaba) 1963–65; Dir O.C.I. (Algerian-French Bd for promotion of industrial co-operation) 1968–70; Prof. of Econs, Univ. of Algiers 1970–75; Chair. SONATRACH Inc., USA 1976–78; Minister of Planning and Regional Devt 1979–83; Prime Minister of Algeria 1984–88.

BRAHIMI, Lakhdar; Algerian United Nations official, diplomatist and politician; b. 1 Jan. 1934; m.; three c.; ed in Algeria and France; FLN Rep. in SE Asia 1956–61; Perm. Rep. to Arab League, Cairo 1963–70; Amb. to UK 1971–79, to Egypt and Sudan; Diplomatic Adviser to Pres. of Algeria 1982–84; Under-Sec.-Gen., League of Arab States 1984–91, Special Envoy Arab League Tripartite Cttee to Lebanon 1989–91; Minister of Foreign Affairs 1991–93; Rapporteur, UN Conf. on Environment and Devt (Earth Summit) 1992; Special Rep. of UN Sec.-Gen. in South Africa –1994, in Haiti 1994–96; Under Sec.-Gen. for Special Assignments in Support of Preventive and Peacemaking Efforts of the Sec.-Gen. 1997; Special Envoy of UN Sec.-Gen. in Afghanistan, UN Special Mission to Afghanistan (UNSMA) 1997–99, Special Rep. Oct. 2001–; Special Envoy of UN Sec.-Gen. in Angola 1998; Chair. UN panel for evaluation of peace keeping operations March-Aug. 2000; other special missions to Zaïre (now Democratic Repub. of the Congo) Yemen and Liberia. *Address:* Dept of Peace Keeping Operations, Room S-3727B, United Nations, New York, NY 10017, USA (Office). *Telephone:* (212) 963-9222 (Office). *Fax:* (212) 963-8079 (Office).

BRAIBANT, Guy; French public servant; b. 5 Sept. 1927, Paris; s. of Charles Braibant and Evelyne Curiel; m. Françoise Fabiani 1989; one s. one d. by previous marriage; ed Ecole Nat. d'Admin, Inst. d'Etudes Politiques de Paris; Auditeur, Conseil d'Etat 1953–60, Counsel 1960–78, Conseiller d'Etat 1978–85, Chair. Reports and Studies Section 1985–92, Vice-Pres. Comm. Supérieure de Codification 1989–, responsible for section dealing with legal questions posed by Internet 1997–; Dir-Gen. Int. Inst. of Admin. Sciences 1979–81, Pres. 1992–95; Head of Mission, Minister of Transport 1981–84; Prof., Inst. d'Etudes Politiques de Paris 1971–92; Grand Officier, Légion d'honneur, Commdr, Ordre Nat. du Mérite. *Publications:* Les grands arrêts de la jurisprudence administrative 1956, Le contrôle de l'administration et la protection des citoyens 1973, Le droit administratif français 1985, Les archives en France 1996, Données personelles et société de l'information 1998, Charte des droits fondamentaux de l'Union Européenne 2000–2002. *Address:* Commission Supérieure de Codification, 35 rue Saint-Dominique, 75007 Paris (Office); 208 rue de Rivoli, 75001 Paris, France (Home). *Telephone:* 1-42-75-58-40 (Office); 1-42-96-17-96 (Home). *Fax:* 1-42-75-72-06 (Office). *E-mail:* guy.braibant@sgg.pm.gouv.fr (Office).

BRAININ, Norbert, OBE; British (b. Austrian) violinist; b. 12 March 1923, Vienna; s. of Adolph Brainin and Sophie Brainin; m. Kathe Kottow 1948; one d.; ed Vienna High School, started studies Vienna; emigrated to UK 1938; studied with Carl Flesch and Max Rostal; won Carl Flesch prize for solo violinists, Guildhall School of Music, London 1946; fmrly leader of Amadeus String Quartet, f. 1947; Founder, Leader of Ensemble Amadeus 1988–; Prof. of Chamber Music, Hochschule für Musik, Cologne 1976–92; Prof. for Chamber Music RAM 1986–93, Prof. annual Amadeus Quartet course; Prof. of Violin Scuola di Musica di Fiesole 1974, Accad. Europea del Quartetto, Summer Acad., Reichenau, Austria, Hochschule für Musik 'Franz Liszt', Weimar 1995, Summer Festival, Val Gardena, Italy; mem. Royal Soc. of Musicians 1980; Hon. mem. RAM 1977; Hon. DUniv (York) 1968; Dr hc (London, Caracas); Grand Cross of Merit, First Class (FRG) 1972; Cross of Honour for Arts and Science (Austria) 1972; Goldener Verdienst Kreuz Stadt Wien 1999. *Music:* ten famous quartets and quintets of Mozart, most of Haydn quartets, all the Beethoven quartets, all the Brahms quartets and quintets, most of Schubert quartets and quintets. *Address:* 19 Prowse Avenue, Bushey, Herts., WD23 1JS, England. *Telephone:* (20) 8950-7218. *Fax:* (20) 8209-1907.

BRAITHWAITE, Sir Rodric (Quentin), GCMG; British fmr diplomatist; b. 17 May 1932, London; s. of Henry Warwick Braithwaite and Lorna Constance Davies; m. Gillian Mary Robinson 1961; four s. (one deceased) one d.; ed Bedales School, Christ's Coll., Cambridge; Mil. Service 1950–52; joined Foreign Service 1955; Third Sec. Jakarta 1957–58; Second Sec. Warsaw 1959–61; Foreign Office 1961–63; First Sec. (Commercial) Moscow 1963–66; First Sec. Rome 1966–69; FCO 1969–72, Head of European Integration Dept (External) 1973–75, Head of Planning Staff 1979–80, Asst Under-Sec. of State 1981, Deputy Under-Sec. of State 1984–88; Head of Chancery, Office of Perm. Rep. to EEC, Brussels 1975–78; Minister, Commercial, Washington 1982–84; Amb. to Soviet Union 1988–92; Foreign Policy Adviser to Prime Minister 1992–93; Chair. Jt Intelligence Cttee 1992–93; Man. Dir. and Sr Adviser Deutsche Bank 1994–2002; Chair. Britain Russia Centre 1994–2000, Moscow School of Political Studies 1998–; mem. European Strategy Bd ICL 1994–2000, Supervisory Bd Deutsche Bank Moscow 1998–99, Bd UralMash Zavody (Moscow and Ekaterinburg) 1998–99; mem. Advisory Bd. Sirocco Aerospace 2000–; mem. Royal Acad. of Music 1993–2002 (Chair. of Govs 1998–2002); Hon. Fellow Christ's Coll. Cambridge, Royal Acad. of Music; Visiting Fellow All Souls Coll. Oxford 1972–73; Dr hc (Birmingham) 1998;

Hon. Prof. (Birmingham) 2000. *Publications:* Engaging Russia (with Blackwill and Tanaka) 1995, Russia in Europe 1999, Across the Moscow River 2002. *Leisure interests:* chamber music (viola), sailing, Russia.

BRAKS, Gerrit J. M., MAgr; Netherlands politician; b. 23 May 1933, Odiliapeel; s. of Theodorus H. Braks and Helena Johanna Kroef; m. Frens Bardoel 1965 (died 2000); two s. three d.; ed Agricultural Univ., Wageningen; worked on parents' farm –1955; Asst Govt Agricultural Advisory Service, Eindhoven 1955–58; Directorate for Int. Econ. Co-operation, Ministry of Agric. and Fisheries 1965–66; Deputy Agricultural Attaché, Perm. Mission of Netherlands to EEC, Brussels 1966–67; Sec. North Brabant Christian Farmers' Union (NCB), Tilburg 1967–69; Agricultural Counsellor, Perm. Mission of Netherlands to EEC 1969–77; mem. Second Chamber of Parl. 1977–80, 1981–82; Chair. Standing Cttee on Agric., Second Chamber 1979–80 parl. year; Minister of Agric. and Fisheries 1980–81, 1982–90; mem. First Chamber of Parl. 1991–; Pres. Catholic Broadcasting Org. 1991–96; Chair. and Pres. Céhavé Farmers Cooperative 1995–; mem. Interparl. Benelux Council 1996–2001; Pres. of Senate 2001–; Commdr Order of Netherlands Lion. *Leisure interests:* gardening and golf. *Address:* Ruwenbergstraat 4, 5271 AG Sint-Michielsgestel, Netherlands. *Telephone:* (73) 5514759. *Fax:* (73) 5517353. *E-mail:* g.braks@planet.nl (Home).

BRAMALL, Baron (Life Peer), cr. 1987, of Bushfield in the County of Hampshire; **Field Marshal The Lord Edwin Noel Westby Bramall,** KG, GCB, OBE, MC; British army officer (retd); b. 18 Dec. 1923, Tunbridge Wells, England; s. of the late Maj. Edmund Haselden Bramall and Katherine Bridget Bramall (née Westby); m. Dorothy Avril Wentworth Vernon 1949; one s. one d.; ed Eton Coll.; commissioned in King's Royal Rifle Corps 1943, served in North-west Europe 1944–45, occupation of Japan 1946–47; Instructor, School of Infantry 1949–51; served Middle East 1953–58; Instructor, Army Staff Coll. 1958–61; on staff of Lord Mountbatten with special responsibility for reorg. of Ministry of Defence 1963–64; CO 2nd Green Jackets (King's Royal Rifle Corps) 1965–66; Commdr 5th Airportable Brigade 1967–69; GOC 1st Div. BAOR 1972–73; rank of Lt-Gen. 1973; Commdr British Forces Hong Kong 1973–76; Col Commdt 3rd Royal Green Jackets 1973–84; Col 2nd Gurkhas 1976–86; rank of Gen. 1976; C-in-C UK Land Forces 1976–78; Vice-Chief of Defence Staff (Personnel and Logistics) 1978–79; Chief of Gen. Staff and ADC Gen. to HM The Queen 1979–82; rank of Field Marshal 1982; Chief of Defence Staff 1982–85; Lord Lt of Greater London 1986–98; Pres. of MCC 1988–89; Trustee Imperial War Museum 1983–, Chair. 1989–98; JP London 1986; KStJ 1986; Golden Medallion for Service to Christian-Jewish Dialogue 2001. *Publication:* The Chiefs: The Story of the United Kingdom Chiefs of Staff (co-author) 1993. *Leisure interests:* cricket, painting, travel, tennis. *Address:* House of Lords, London, SW1A 0PW, England.

BRANAGH, Kenneth; British actor and director; b. 10 Dec. 1960, Belfast; s. of William Branagh and Frances Branagh; m. Emma Thompson 1989 (divorced 1998); ed Meadway Comprehensive School, Reading, Royal Acad. of Dramatic Art (RADA); f. Renaissance Theatre Co. 1987 (resgnd 1994), Renaissance Films PLC 1988 (resgnd 1994), Shakespeare Film Co. 1999; mem. Bd BFI 1993–97; Officer des Arts et des Lettres; Hon. DLitt (Queen's Univ., Belfast) 1990, (Univ. of Birmingham) 2001; Bancroft Gold Medal RADA 1982; BAFTA Award (best dir) 1990. *Theatre:* Another Country 1982 (Soc. of W End Theatres Award for Most Promising Newcomer), The Madness 1983, Francis, Henry V, Hamlet, Love's Labour's Lost, Golden Girls, Tell Me Honestly (writer and dir) 1986, Romeo and Juliet (producer and dir) 1986, Public Enemy (writer, actor) 1986, Napoleon (dir) 1987, Twelfth Night (dir) 1987, Much Ado About Nothing, As You Like It, Hamlet, Look Back in Anger 1989, Napoleon: The American Story (dir) 1989, King Lear (actor, dir) 1989, Midsummer Night's Dream (actor, dir) 1989, Uncle Vanya (co-dir) 1991, Coriolanus (actor), Hamlet (actor, RSC) 1992, The Play What I Wrote (dir) 2001–02, Richard III (actor) 2002. *Television:* The Boy in the Bush, Billy (Trilogy), To the Lighthouse, Maybury, Derek, Coming Through, Ghosts, Fortunes of War, Strange Interlude, The Lady's Not for Burning, Shadow of a Gunman, Conspiracy (Emmy Award for Best Actor 2001), Shackleton 2002. *Radio:* Hamlet (actor, dir) 1992, Romeo and Juliet (actor, dir) 1993, King Lear (actor) 1994. *Films:* High Season, A Month in the Country, Henry V (actor, dir, writer) (Evening Standard Best Film, NY Film Critics' Circle Best Dir Award) 1989, Dead Again (actor, dir) 1991, Peter's Friends (actor, dir, producer) 1992, Swing Kids (actor) 1992, Swan Song (dir) 1992, Much Ado about Nothing (actor, dir, producer) 1993, Mary Shelley's Frankenstein (actor, dir), Othello (actor) 1995, In the Bleak Midwinter (dir, writer) 1995, Hamlet (actor, dir, producer) 1996, The Theory of Flight 1997, The Proposition 1997, The Gingerbread Man 1997, Celebrity 1998, Wild, Wild West 1998, Love's Labour's Lost (actor, dir, producer) 2000, How to Kill Your Neighbor's Dog 2002, Rabbit Proof Fence 2002, Harry Potter and the Chamber of Secrets (actor) 2002. *Publications:* Public Enemy (play) 1988, Beginning (memoirs) 1989; The Making of Mary Shelley's Frankenstein 1994, In the Bleak Midwinter 1995, screenplays for Henry V, Much Ado About Nothing, Hamlet. *Address:* Shepperton Studios, Studio Road, Shepperton, Middx, TW17 0QD, England.

BRANCA, Vittore (Felice Giovanni), DLitt; Italian educationist; b. 9 July 1913, Savona; s. of Antonio Branca and Lucia Branca; m. Olga Montagner 1938; one s. three d.; ed Univ. of Pisa; Prof. Accad. della Crusca, Florence 1937–48; Prof. of Italian Literature, Maria Assunta Univ., Rome 1948–50; Prof. of Italian Literature, Univ. of Catania 1950–53, Univ. of Padua 1953–; Rector Univ. of Bergamo 1968–72; Head, Div. of Arts and Letters, UNESCO

1950–53; Hon. Pres. Int. Asscn for Study of Italian Language and Literature; Gen. Sec. and Pres. Fondazione Giorgio Cini 1953–96; mem. Cttee Int. Fed. of Modern Languages and Literatures; literary adviser to publishing houses; Ed. Lettere Italiane and Studi sul Boccaccio (magazines) and of numerous series of classical texts and essays; Pres. Istituto Veneto Scienze Lettere e Arti 1979–85; mem. Accad. dei Lincei, Accad. Arcadia, Accad. Polacca della Scienze, Acad. du Monde Latin (Inst. de France), Medieval Acad. of America; Hon. mem. Modern Language Asscn of America, American Acad. of Arts and Sciences, Union of Writers, Moscow, British Acad.; Dr hc (Univs of Budapest, New York, Bergamo, Paris Sorbonne, McGill, Montreal, Cologne); Gold Medal of Italian Ministry of Educ. and of Polish Ministry of Culture; Kt Grand Cross Italian Repub., Chevalier Legion d'honneur, Commdr Polonia Liberta, Commdr Order of Malta. *Publications:* editions and critical studies of St Francis, Petrarch, Boccaccio, Poliziano, Alfieri, Manzoni, other classical authors and Romanticism; methodological works including Boccaccio Medievale 1958, Filologia e critica 1977, Poliziano e l'umanesimo della parola 1983, Dizionario critico della letteratura italiana 1986, Mercanti scrittori 1987, Ponte Santa Trinità 1988, Esopo Toscano 1989, Tradizione delle opere di Giovanni Boccaccio 1991, Esopo Veneto 1992, Con Amore Volere 1996, La Sapienza civile 1998, Merchant Writers of the Italian Renaissance 1999; Boccaccio visualizzato 1999, Il capolavoro del Boccaccio e due diverse redazioni 2002. *Leisure interests:* swimming, climbing. *Address:* San Marco 2885, Venice, Italy. *Telephone:* 5289819.

BRAND, Stewart, BS; American editor, writer and publisher; b. 14 Dec. 1938, Rockford, Ill.; m. 1st Lois Jennings 1966 (divorced 1972); m. 2nd Ryan Phelan 1983; one s. from a previous relationship; ed Phillips Exeter Acad., Stanford Univ.; served U.S. Army 1960–62; fmrly with Merry Pranksters; consultant to Gov. of Calif. 1976–78; research scientist Media Lab., MIT 1986; Visiting Scholar Royal Dutch/Shell 1986; f. America Needs Indians, The Well (Internet bulletin Bd) 1984–; co-f. Global Business Network consultancy 1988–, The Long Now Foundation 1996– (also Pres.), All Species project 2000–; Trustee Santa Fe Inst. 1989–. *Television:* How Buildings Learn (writer and presenter) 1997. *Publications:* writer: Two Cybernetic Frontiers 1974, The Media Lab 1987, How Buildings Learn 1994, The Clock of the Long Now 1999; ed., Publr: The Last Whole Earth Catalog 1968–71 (Nat. Book Award), Whole Earth Epilog 1974, The Co-Evolution Quarterly 1974–85, The Next Whole Earth Catalog 1980–81, Whole Earth Software Catalog (Ed.-in-Chief) 1983–85. *Address:* 3E Gate 5 Road, Sausalito, CA 94965-1401, USA (Office).

BRANDAUER, Klaus Maria; Austrian actor; b. 6 Feb. 1944, Bad Aussee; m. Karin Brandauer 1965; ed Acad. of Music and Dramatic Arts, Stuttgart; mem. Burgtheater, Vienna; extensive stage repertoire; Cannes Film Festival Prize for film Mephisto 1981; appeared as Jedermann at Salzburg Festival 1983, as Speer, Almeida Theatre, London 1999; Acad. Award (Oscar) for title role in film Mephisto 1982. *Films include:* Mephisto 1980, Colonel Redl 1985, Out of Africa 1985, Burning Secret 1988, Hannussen 1988, Russia House, Angel in Hell 1989, Streets of Gold 1989, The French Revolution 1989, The Artisan (also Dir), Becoming Colette 1991, White Fang 1991, The Resurrected, Seven Minutes (also Dir), Felidae (voice), Marco and the Magician (also Dir), Die Wand (Dir), Rembrandt, Introducing Dorothy Dandridge 1999, Druids 2001. *Television includes:* Quo Vadis? *Address:* Bartensteingasse 8/9, A-1010 Vienna, Austria.

BRANDO, Marlon; American actor; b. 3 April 1924, Omaha; s. of Marlon and Dorothy Penebaker (née Myers) Brando; m. 1st Anna Kashfi 1957 (divorced 1959); one s.; m. 2nd Movita Brando (divorced); one c.; ed Shattuck Military Acad.; Acad. Award for the best actor of the year 1954, Golden Globe Award for the most popular actor 1972; refused Oscar for The Godfather 1973. *Stage appearances include:* I Remember Mama, Candida, A Flag is Born, The Eagle has Two Heads, A Streetcar Named Desire, etc. *Film appearances include:* The Men 1950, A Streetcar Named Desire 1951, Viva Zapata 1952, Julius Caesar 1953, The Wild Ones 1953, Desirée 1954, On the Waterfront 1954, Guys and Dolls 1955, Teahouse of the August Moon 1956, Sayonara 1957, The Young Lions 1958, The Fugitive Kind 1960, The One-Eyed Jacks (also Dir) 1960, Mutiny on the Bounty 1962, The Ugly American 1963, Bedtime Story 1964, The Saboteur 1965, The Chase 1966, Appaloosa 1966, A Countess from Hong Kong 1967, Southwest to Sonora 1966, Reflections in a Golden Eye 1967, Candy 1968, The Night of the Following Day 1969, Queimada 1970, The Nightcomers 1971, The Godfather 1972, Last Tango in Paris 1972, The Missouri Breaks 1975, Apocalypse Now 1977, Superman 1978, The Formula 1980, Dry White Season 1989, Jericho (wrote and acted in) 1989, The Freshman 1989, Christopher Columbus 1992, Don Juan DeMarco 1994, The Island of Dr. Moreau 1996, The Brave 1997, Free Money 1998, The Score 2001, Apocalypse Now Redux 2001, Autumn of the Patriarch 2002. *TV appearance:* Roots: The Next Generations 1979. *Publication:* Brando: Songs My Mother Taught Me 1994. *Address:* Tetiarou Island, South Pacific.

BRANDT, Elmar, DPhil; German cultural institute director; b. 18 Nov. 1936, Berlin; s. of Arthur Brandt and Anna Maria Brandt (née Monscheuer); m. Holle Behncke 1983; one d. one step-s.; ed Univs of Frankfurt Main, Berlin and Munich; Dir Goethe-Institut, Yaoundé, Cameroon 1965–68, Deputy Dir Goethe-Institut, Tokyo 1968–70, Dir Goethe-Institut Osaka, Japan 1970–77, Head, Media Dept, Goethe-Institut Head Office, Munich 1977–83, Dir Goethe-Institut, São Paulo, Brazil 1983–89, London 1989–95, Rome 1995–. *Publications include:* Fundamentals of a Theory of Meaning 1963–64, Cur-

rent Problems of Consumer Protection 1978, The Woman in the Twentieth Century 1988, New Strategies of Urban Planning 1992. *Leisure interests:* gardening, photography, painting.

BRANSCOMB, Lewis McAdory, MS, PhD; American physicist; b. 17 Aug. 1926, Asheville, NC; s. of Bennett Harvie Branscomb and Margaret Vaughn Branscomb; m. Anne Wells 1951; one s. one d.; ed Duke and Harvard Univs; Instructor in Physics, Harvard Univ. 1950; Lecturer in Physics, Univ. of Maryland 1950–51; Chief, Atomic Physics Section, Nat. Bureau of Standards, Washington, DC 1954–60, Chief Atomic Physics Div. 1960–62; Chair. Jt Inst. for Laboratory Astrophysics 1962–65, 1968–70; Chief, Lab. Astrophysics Div., Nat. Bureau of Standards, Boulder, Colo 1962–69; Dir Nat. Bureau of Standards 1969–72; Chief Scientist, Vice-Pres. IBM Corpn 1972–86; Prof., Dir Public Policy Program Kennedy School of Govt, Harvard Univ. 1986–96, AETNA Prof. in Public Policy and Corp. Man. 1988–96, Prof. Emer. 1996–; Visiting Prof. Vanderbilt Univ. 1999–2000; mem. tech. assessment advisory council, Office of Tech. Assessment, US Congress 1990–95; mem. Bd, Mobil Corpn, MITRE Corpn; mem. Nat. Acad. of Sciences (mem. Council 1972–75, 1998–), Inst. of Medicine, Nat. Acad. of Eng; Fellow, American Acad. of Arts and Sciences, American Philosophical Soc.; mem. Nat. Acad. of Public Admin, Harvard Univ. Bd of Overseers, Comm. on Global Information/Infrastructure 1995–; Trustee, Carnegie Inst. of Washington 1973–90, Vanderbilt Univ., Nat. Geographic Soc., Woods Hole Oceanographic Inst., LASPAU 1999–; several awards and hon. degrees. *Publications:* Empowering Technology 1993, Confessions of a Technophile 1994, Korea at the Turning Point 1996, Investing in Innovation 1998, Taking Technical Risks 2000; numerous articles in professional journals. *Leisure interests:* skiing, sailing. *Address:* Kennedy School of Government, Harvard University, 79 J. F. Kennedy Street, Cambridge, MA 02138-5801, USA. *E-mail:* branscomb@harvard.edu (Office).

BRANSON, Richard (Charles Nicholas), Kt; British business executive; b. 18 July 1950; s. of Edward James Branson; m. 1st Kristen Tomassi 1969 (divorced); m. 2nd Joan Templeman 1989; one s. one d.; ed Stowe School; set up Student Advisory Centre (now Help) 1970; founded Virgin mail-order co. 1969, first Virgin record shop 1971, recording co. 1973, nightclub (The Venue) 1976, Virgin Atlantic Airlines 1984; f. and Chair. Virgin Retail Group, Virgin Communications, Virgin Travel Group, Voyager Group; took Virgin Music Group public 1986, bought back shares 1988 (rotating chairmanship 1991, Chair. 1991–92, now Life Pres. after sale of shares); Group also includes publishing, broadcasting, construction, heating systems, holidays; Chair. UK 2000 1986–88, Pres. 1988–; Dir Intourist Moscow Ltd 1988–90; f. The Healthcare Foundation 1987, Virgin Radio 1993, Virgin Rail Group Ltd 1996; launched Virgin Cola (drink) 1994, Babylon (restaurant) 2001; crossed Pacific in hot air balloon with Per Lindstrand 1991; Blue Riband Title for Fastest Atlantic Crossing 1986, Segrave Trophy 1987. *Publication:* Losing My Virginity (autobiog.) 1998. *Leisure interest:* sailing. *Address:* c/o Virgin Group PLC, 120 Campden Hill Road, London, W8 7AR, England. *Telephone:* (20) 7229-1282.

BRANSTAD, Terry Edward, BA, JD; American state governor; b. 17 Nov. 1946, Leland, Iowa; s. of Edward Arnold Branstad and Rita Garland; m. Christine Ann Johnson 1972; two s. one d.; ed Univ. of Iowa and Drake Univ.; admitted to Iowa Bar; sold interest in Branstad/Schwarm, Lake Mills, Iowa; farmer, Lake Mills; mem. Iowa House of Reps. 1972–78; Lt-Gov. of Iowa 1979–82, Gov. of Iowa 1983–99; Republican. *Address:* Regency West 5, Suite 201, 4500 Westown Parkway West, Des Moines, IN 50266, USA.

BRASH, Donald Thomas, MA, PhD; New Zealand banker and politician; b. 24 Sept. 1940, Wanganui; s. of Rev. Dr. Alan A. Brash and Mrs. Brash; m. 1st Erica Beatty 1964, 2nd Je Lan Lee 1989; two s. one d.; ed Christchurch Boys' High School, Canterbury Univ. and Australian Nat. Univ.; Gen. Man. Broadbank Corpn Ltd 1971–81; Gen. Man. Finance and Computer Sector, Fletcher Challenge Ltd 1981–82; Man. Dir NZ Kiwifruit Authority 1982–86; Man. Dir Trust Bank Group 1986–88; Gov. Reserve Bank of New Zealand 1988–2002; mem. NZ Monetary and Econ. Council 1974–78, NZ Planning Council 1977–80; mem. Nat. Party; mem. Parl. (Nat. Party) 2002–; Nat. Spokesperson (Opposition) on Finance 2002–; also mem. Finance and Expenditure Select Cttee; Dr hc (Canterbury) 1999; NZIER-QANTAS Econs Award 1999. *Publications:* New Zealand's Debt Servicing Capacity 1964, American Investment in Australian Industry 1966. *Leisure interest:* kiwifruit growing. *Address:* Parliament Buildings, Wellington, New Zealand. *Telephone:* (4) 471-9509. *Fax:* (4) 472-4208. *Website:* www.parl.govt.nz.

BRASSEUR, Claude; French actor; b. 15 June 1936, Paris (as Claude Espinasse); s. of late Pierre Espinasse (known as Pierre Brasseur) and of Odette Joyeux; m. 2nd Michèle Cambon 1970; one s.; ed René Girard and René Simon drama schools, Paris; Beatrix Dussane trophy 1974, César awards for Best Supporting Actor in Un éléphant ça trompe énormément 1976, Best Actor in La guerre des polices 1980; Chevalier, Ordre Nat. du Mérite. *Plays include:* Un ange passe, L'enfant du dimanche, Match 1964, La calèche 1966, Britannicus 1966, Du côté de chez l'autre 1971, Les jeux de la nuit 1974, George Dandin 1987, Le Souper 1989, Dîner de cons 1993, La Dernière salve 1995, À torts et à raisons 1999. *Films include:* Rue des prairies, Les yeux sans visage 1959, Le noeud de vipères, La verte moisson, Pierrot la tendresse 1960, Le caporal épinglé, La bride sur le cou 1961, Germinal 1962, Dragées au poivre, Peau de banane 1963, Bande à part, Lucky Joe 1964, L'enfer (unfinished), Le chien fou, Du rififi à Paname 1966, Un homme de trop, Caroline chérie 1967, La chasse royale, Catherine ou il suffit d'un amour 1968, Le viager, Le portrait de Marianne, Un cave 1971, Une belle fille comme moi 1972, Bel ordure 1973, Les seins de glace 1974, Il faut vivre dangereusement, L'agression 1975, Attention les yeux 1976, Barocco, Le grand Escogriffe, Un éléphant ça trompe énormément 1976, Monsieur papa, Nous irons au paradis, L'état sauvage 1977, L'argent des autres, Une histoire simple 1978, La guerre des polices 1979, La boume 1980, Une langouste au petit déjeuner, Une robe noire pour un tueur, L'ombre rouge, Une affaire d'hommes 1981, Josepha, Guy de Maupassant 1982, Légitime violence 1982, T'es heureuse? Moi toujours 1983, la Crime 1983, Signes extérieurs de richesse 1983, Souvenir, Le Léopard 1984, Palace 1985, Les loups entre eux 1985, La gitane 1986, Taxi Boy 1986, Descente aux enfers 1986, George Dandin 1988, Radio Corbeau 1989, l'Union sacrée 1989, l'Orchestre Rouge 1989, Dancing Machine 1990, Sale comme un Ange 1991, Le Bal des Casse-Pieds 1992, Le Souper 1992, le Fil de L'Horizon 1993, Le plus beau pays du monde et fait d'hiver 1999, Fait d'hiver 1999, La Taule 2000, Toreros et les Acteurs 2000. *Television appearances include:* Le paysan parvenu, La misère et la gloire, Don Juan, Le mystère de la chambre jaune (as Rouletabille), Les eaux mêlées, Vidocq, Les nouvelles aventures de Vidocq, l'Équipe, l'Argent, Véga 1999. *Leisure interests:* boxing, swimming, football, bobsleighing, skiing. *Address:* c/o Artmédia, 20 avenue Rapp, 75007 Paris, France.

BRATHWAITE, Rt Hon Sir Nicholas, Kt, OBE, PC, BEd; Grenadian educationalist, administrator and politician (retd); b. 8 July 1925, Carriacou; s. of Charles Brathwaite and Sophia Brathwaite; m.; three s. one d.; ed Univ. of West Indies; fmr teacher, Sr Tutor, Prin. Teachers' Coll.; fmrly Chief Educ. Officer; fmr Minister of Social Affairs; fmr Commonwealth official; Chair. Interim Council set up after US invasion of Grenada and deposition of fmr mil. Govt 1983–84; leader Nat. Democratic Congress (NDC) 1989–94; Prime Minister 1990–95, also fmr Minister of Home Affairs, Nat. Security, Foreign Affairs, Finance, Personnel and Man. and Carriacou and Petit Martinique Affairs. *Address:* Villa 'A', St George's, Grenada (Home).

BRAUER, Arik; Austrian artist; b. 4 Jan. 1929, Vienna; s. of Simon Moses Brauer and Hermine Brauer; m. Naomi Dahabani 1957; three d.; ed Wiener Kunstakademie; underground, Vienna 1942–45; after studies in Vienna travelled in Africa, France, Spain, Austria, Greece and Israel 1950–58, USA, E Africa, Ethiopia, Japan 1965–74; Prof. Acad. of Fine Arts Vienna 1986; one-man exhbns 1956–, in Austria, Germany, Switzerland, France, Denmark, Liechtenstein, Italy, Canada, Sweden, Yugoslavia, Bulgaria, Norway, Japan, Israel and USA; world travelling exhbn 1979–; group exhbns, including travelling exhbns with Wiener Schule des Phantastischen Realismus 1962–, in W Europe, USA, S. America, Poland, Yugoslavia, Israel, Iran, Turkey, Japan; Scenery for The Seven Mortal Sins (Vienna 1972), Bomarzo (Zürich 1970); scenery and costumes for Medea (Vienna 1972), The Magic Flute (Paris 1977); book, design and costumes for Sieben auf einen Streich (Vienna 1978); mural design for Univ. of Haifa, Israel 1982–; designer Brauerhaus, Vienna 1983–95; Guest Lecturer, Int. Summer Acad. for Fine Arts, Salzburg 1982, 83; two gold records for Erich Brauer LP (poetry, music and songs) 1971. *Publications:* Zigeunerziege 1976, Runde Fliegt 1983. *Leisure interests:* alpinism, skiing, windsurfing. *Address:* c/o Academy of Fine Arts, Schillerplatz 3, Vienna 1010, Austria.

BRAUER, Stephen Franklin, BEcons; American diplomatist; b. 3 Sept. 1945, St Louis, MO; m. Camilla Thompson Bauer 1971; three c.; ed Westminster Coll.; First Lieut., US Army Corps of Engineers 1967–70, tour of duty in Viet Nam; joined Hunter Engineering Co. 1971, Exec. Vice-Pres. and COO 1978–81, Pres. and CEO 1981–2001; Amb. to Belgium 2001–; Hon. Consul of Belgium in Missouri state 1987–2001; partner and part-owner of St Louis Cardinals baseball team; Trustee St Louis Art Museum, Missouri Botanical Garden (Pres. Bd Trustees), Smithsonian Inst., Washington, DC, Washington Univ. *Leisure interest:* baseball. *Address:* Embassy of the USA, Executive Office, 27 boulevard du Régent, 1000 Brussels, Belgium (Office). *Telephone:* (2) 508-24-44 (Office). *Fax:* (2) 508-21-60 (Office). *E-mail:* SniderPW@state .gov (Office). *Website:* www.usinfo.be (Office).

BRAUMAN, John I., PhD; American professor of chemistry; b. 7 Sept. 1937, Pittsburgh, Pa; s. of Milton Brauman and Freda S. Brauman; m. Sharon Lea Kruse 1964; one d.; ed MIT and Univ. of California (Berkeley and Los Angeles); Asst Prof., Stanford Univ. 1963–69, Assoc. Prof. 1969–72, Prof. 1972–80, J. G. Jackson-C. J. Wood Prof. 1980–, Chair. 1979–83, 1995–96; Deputy Ed. Science 1985–2000, Chair. Sr Editorial Bd 2000–; mem. editorial bds several journals including Nouveau Journal de Chimie 1977–85, Chemical Physics Letters 1982–85, Chemical and Engineering News 1982–84, Journal of Physical Chemistry 1985–87; mem. Nat. Research Council Bd on Chemical Sciences and Tech., advisory panels of NASA, Nat. Science Found., Atomic Energy Comm.; mem. NAS and AAAS; Award in Pure Chemistry and Harrison-Howe Award, American Chemical Soc., James Flack Norris Award in Physical Organic Chemistry, Arthur C. Cope Scholar Award, NAS Award in Chemical Sciences 2001. *Publications:* over 270 publs in scientific journals. *Address:* Department of Chemistry, Stanford University, Stanford, CA 94305 (Office); 849 Tolman Drive, Palo Alto, CA 94305, USA (Home). *Telephone:* (415) 723-3023 (Office); (415) 493-1378 (Home).

BRAUN, Carol Moseley (see Moseley-Braun, Carol).

BRAUN, Ewa; Polish interior decorator and art director; b. 2 Aug. 1944, Cracow; ed Warsaw Univ.; costume designer Documentary Film Producers 1967–72; interior decorator, art Dir Film Production Agency 1972–99; mem. of Polish Film makers 1994–; lecturer at Polish Film, Television and Theatre School, Łódź 1999–. *Films:* interior decorations and designs in over 60 films including: Illumination 1972, Jealousy and Medicine 1973, Hotel Pacific 1975, Camouflage 1976, Career of Nikodem Dyzma 1979, Queen Bona 1980, C.K. Dezerterzy 1985, Young Magician (Gdańsk Bronze Lions 1987) 1986, Europe, Europe 1990, Schindler's List (Acad. Award 1994) 1993, Les Milles 1995, Holy Week 1995, Bandit 1996, Palais de la Santé 1997, Brother of Our God 1997, Jacob the Liar 1997, Gold Deserts 1998. *Leisure interests:* movies, travels, music, literature. *Address:* Polish National Film, Television and Theatre School, ul. Targowa 61/ 63, 90-323 Łódź, Poland. *Telephone:* (42) 6749494 (Office); (22) 6428153 (Home). *Fax:* (42) 6748153 (Office). *E-mail:* braunewa@ hotmail.com (Home); ebraun@parta.onet.pl (Home).

BRAUN, Pinkas; Swiss actor and director; b. 7 Jan. 1923, Zürich; s. of Chaja and Nathan Braun; m. (divorced); one s. two d.; partner Ingrid Resch; ed drama school, Zürich; mem. of co. of Schauspielhaus Zürich 1945–50, 1952–56; own co. 1950–51; freelance 1957–; has undertaken theatre work as actor and dir in Germany, Austria and Israel and TV and cinema work in Germany, Austria, France, Italy and UK. *Roles include:* Woyzeck, Baron (in Nachtasyl), Pelegrin (in Santa Cruz), Salieri (in Amadeus), Shylock (in The Merchant of Venice), Iago (in Othello), Otto Frank (in The Diary of Anne Frank), George Bernard Shaw (in The Best of Friends). *Publications:* trans. into German of most of Edward Albee's plays. *Address:* Dorfstrasse 32, CH 8261 Hemishofen, Switzerland (Home). *Telephone:* (52) 7413370. *Fax:* (52) 7413370 (Home). *E-mail:* ip.resch-brown@bluewin.ch.

BRAUN, Volker; German poet and playwright; b. 7 May 1939, Dresden; ed Univ. of Leipzig; Asst Dir Deutsches Theater, Berlin 1972–77, Berlin Ensemble 1979–90; mem. Akademie der Künste, Berlin; Heinrich Mann Prize 1980, Bremen Literature Prize 1986, Nat. Prize, 1st Class 1986, Berlin Prize 1989, Schiller Commemorative Prize 1992, Büchner Prize 2000. *Plays:* Grosser Frieden 1979, Dmitri 1982, Die Ubergangsgesellschaft 1987, Lenins Tod 1988, Transit Europa: Der Ausflug der Toten 1988, Böhmen am Meer 1992. *Publications:* poetry: Gegen die symmetrische Welt 1974, Training des aufrechten Gangs 1979, Langsamer knirschender Morgen 1987, Der Stoff zum Leben 1990, Lustgarten Preussen 1996; prose: Unvollendete Geschichte 1977, Hinze-Kunze-Roman 1985, Bodenloser Satz 1990, Der Wendehals: Eine Enterhaltung 1995; essays: Verheerende Folgen magnelnden Anscheins innerbetrieblicher Demokratie 1988. *Address:* Wolfshagenerstrasse 68, 13187 Berlin, Germany (Home).

BRAUNFELS, Michael; German composer, pianist and teacher; b. 3 April 1917, Munich; s. of Walter Braunfels and Bertele (von Hildebrand) Braunfels; m. Mechthild Russel 1954; two s. three d.; studied piano in Basle under Paul Baumgartner and composition with Frank Martin; concert pianist in all West European music centres, Near East, Asia and Africa 1949–; Prof. of Piano, Cologne Music Coll. 1954–. *Compositions include:* 2 piano concertos, Cembaloconcerto 1956, Oboe concerto 1960, Symphony for 12 celli 1975, Concerto for cello and piano with orchestra 1976, Concerto for string trio and string orch. 1978, Das Parlament (variations for orchestra) 1982, Sinfonietta serena seria 1984, The King's Messenger (musical for children), chamber music, lieder and piano music. *Leisure interest:* history. *Address:* Dransdorferstrasse 40, 50968 Cologne, Germany. *Telephone:* (221) 383660 (Home). *Fax:* (221) 383660 (Home).

BRAUNWALD, Eugene, MD; American professor of medicine; b. 15 Aug. 1929, Vienna, Austria; m. 1st Nina Starr 1952 (deceased); three d.; m. 2nd Elaine Smith 1994; ed New York Univ.; successively Chief of Section of Cardiology, Clinic of Surgery, Cardiology Br. and Clinical Dir Nat. Heart, Lung & Blood Inst. 1958–68; Prof. and Chair. Dept of Medicine, Univ. of Calif. San Diego School of Medicine 1968–72; Hersey Prof. of Theory and Practice of Medicine, Harvard Medical School 1972–96, Distinguished Hersey Prof. of Theory and Practice of Medicine 1996–, Faculty Dean for Academic Programs 1996–; Sr Consultant in Medicine Mass. Gen. Hosp. 1994–; Vice-Pres. Academic Programs Partners Healthcare System 1996–; Herrmann Blumgart Prof. of Medicine 1980–89; Chair. Dept of Medicine, Peter Bent Brigham Hosp. (now Brigham & Women's Hosp.) 1972–96; eight hon. degrees; J. Allyn Taylor Int. Prize in Medicine 1993, and many other awards. *Publications:* over 100 articles, reviews and book chapters. *Address:* Partners Healthcare, 800 Boylston Street, Boston, MA 02199, USA.

BRÄUTIGAM, Hans Otto, DJur, LLM; German diplomatist and politician; b. 6 Feb. 1931, Völklingen, Saar; s. of Maximilian Bräutigam and Margarethe Sauerwald; m. Dr Hildegard Becker 1961; two s. one d.; ed Bonn Univ. and Harvard Law School; research Asst in int. law, Heidelberg 1958–62; served in foreign service of FRG 1962–74; Deputy Head, Perm. Representation of FRG to GDR 1974–77, Dir Fed. Chancellor's Office, Bonn 1977–80; Foreign Office, Bonn 1980–82, Perm. Rep. to GDR 1982–89; Perm. Rep. of FRG to UN 1989–90; Brandenburg Minister of Justice 1990–99; mem. Bd Dirs Foundation for Remembrance, Responsibility and Future Berlin 2000–02; Grosses Verdienstkreuz mit Stern der Bundesrepublik Deutschland. *Leisure interests:* arts, literature, mountain climbing. *Address:* Eichenallee 37, 14050 Berlin, Germany. *Fax:* (30) 3048037.

BRAWNE, Michael, MArch, MA, A.A.DIP., FRIBA; British architect; b. 5 May 1925, Vienna; m. 1st Rhoda Dupler 1954; m. 2nd Charlotte Baden-Powell 1983; two s. one d.; ed Univ. of Edinburgh, Architectural Asscn, London and Mass. Inst. of Tech.; Prin. Michael Brawne & Assocs. 1964–; lecturer, Univ. of Cambridge 1964–78; Prof. of Architecture, Univ. of Bath 1978–90; Aga Khan Prof. M.I.T. 1992; designer of numerous exhbns. including Henry

Moore, Tate Gallery, London 1968, Ceramic Art of China, Victoria & Albert Museum, London 1971, The Age of Neo-Classicism, Royal Acad. London 1972, Arts of Islam, Hayward Gallery, London 1976, The Architecture of Information, British Pavilion, Venice Biennale 1996; museums in Dorchester, Bath, Rochdale and Barnsley; also museums and library in Germany and projects for museums in Jordan and Oman; multi-screen audio-visual shows for museums in London, Paris and Berlin; UNESCO consultant on library design in Sri Lanka, Pakistan, Yemen, Mozambique, China and Yugoslavia; architect, Nat. Library of Sri Lanka, Research and Teaching Labs. and Students' Union, Univ. of London. *Publications:* The New Museum 1965, University Planning and Design (ed.) 1967, Libraries, Architecture and Equipment 1970, Arup Associates 1983, The Museum Interior 1983, Museum für Kunsthandwerk 1992, From Idea to Building 1992, Kimbell Art Museum 1992, The University of Virginia: The Lawn 1994, The Getty Center 1998. *Leisure interests:* architecture, travel, gardening. *Address:* 28 College Road, Bath, BA1 5RR, England. *Telephone:* (1225) 319242. *Fax:* (1225) 442857. *E-mail:* michael.brawne@virginnet.co.uk (Office).

BRAYBROOKE, David, PhD, FRSC; Canadian/American philosopher, university professor and author; b. 18 Oct. 1924, Hackettstown, NJ; s. of Walter Leonard Braybrooke and Netta Rose Braybrooke (née Foyle); m. 1st Alice Boyd Noble 1948 (divorced 1982); two s. one d.; m. 2nd Margaret Eva Odell 1984 (divorced 1994); m. 3rd Gomyo Michiko 1994; ed Hobart Coll., New School for Social Research, Downing Coll., Cambridge, UK, Harvard and Cornell Univs, USA, New Coll., Oxford, UK; Instructor, History and Literature, Hobart and William Smith Colls 1948–50; Teaching Fellow, Econ., Cornell Univ. 1950–52; Instructor, Philosophy, Univ. of Mich., USA 1953–54; Bowdoin Coll. 1954–56; Asst Prof. of Philosophy, Yale Univ., USA 1956–63; Assoc. Prof. of Philosophy and Politics, Dalhousie Univ., Halifax 1963–65, Prof. 1965–88, McCulloch Prof. of Philosophy and Politics 1988–90, Prof. Emer. 1990–; Prof. of Govt, Prof. of Philosophy and Centennial Comm. Chair in the Liberal Arts Univ. of Texas at Austin 1990–; Fellowship American Council of Learned Socs. 1952–53; Rockefeller Foundation Grant 1959–60; Guggenheim Fellow 1962–63; Visiting Fellow, Wolfson Coll., Cambridge, UK 1985–86. *Publications:* A Strategy of Decision: Policy Evaluation as a Social Process (with C. E. Lindblom) 1963, Philosophical Problems of the Social Sciences 1965, Three Tests for Democracy 1968, Traffic Congestion Goes through the Issue-Machine 1974, Ethics in the World of Business 1983, Philosophy of Social Science 1987, Meeting Needs 1987, Logic on the Track of Social Change (with B. Bryson and P. K. Schotch) 1995, Social Rules 1996, Moral Objectives, Rules and the Forms of Social Change 1998, Natural Law Modernized 2001. *Leisure interests:* reading (poetry, fiction, history), listening to music, walking, swimming. *Address:* Department of Philosophy, Dalhousie University, Halifax, NS, B3H 3J5, Canada (Office); 1 Prince Street 510, Dartmouth, NS, B2Y 4L3, Canada (Home); Department of Government, University of Texas at Austin, Austin, TX 78712 (Office); 1500 Scenic Drive, 300, Austin, TX 78703, USA (Home). *Telephone:* (902) 494-3810 (Canada) (Office); (902) 466-3660 (Canada) (Home); (512) 471-5121 (USA) (Office); (512) 479-8963 (USA) (Home).

BRAYFIELD, Celia Frances; British author and journalist; b. 21 Aug. 1945, Wembley Park; d. of the late Felix Brayfield and Ellen (née Jakeman) Brayfield; one d.; ed St. Paul's Girls' School; feature writer Daily Mail 1969–71; TV critic Evening Standard 1974–82, The Times 1983–88; columnist Sunday Telegraph 1989–90, The Times 1998–; contrib. to numerous other media; Dir Nat. Acad. of Writing, 1999–; mem. Cttee of Man. Nat. Council for One Parent Families 1990–. *Publications:* Glitter: The Truth About Fame 1985, Pearls 1987, The Prince 1990, White Ice 1993, Harvest 1995, Bestseller 1996, Getting Home 1998, Sunset 1999, Heartswap 2000, Mr Fabulous and Friends 2003. *Leisure interests:* family life, the arts. *Address:* c/o Curtis Brown Ltd, Haymarket House, 28/29 Haymarket, London, SW1Y 4SP, England. *Telephone:* (20) 7396-6600. *Fax:* (20) 7396-0110. *Website:* www.celiabrayfield.com.

BRAZAUSKAS, Algirdas Mikolas, DEcon; Lithuanian politician; b. 22 Sept. 1932, Rokishkis; s. of Zofija Brazauskienė and Kazimieras Brazauskas; m. Julija Styraitė-Brazauskienė 1958; two d.; ed Kaunas Polytechnic Inst.; Sr Engineer Kaunas Hydroelectric Power Station 1956–57; Chair. Energy Bldg Trust Bd 1958–65; Minister for the Construction Materials Industry of Lithuanian SSR 1965–67; Deputy, Supreme Council of Lithuania 1967–90; First Deputy Chair. of State Planning Cttee, Lithuanian SSR 1967–77; cand. mem. Cen. Cttee of Lithuanian CP 1966–76, mem. 1976–92, Sec. Cen. Cttee of Lithuanian CP 1977–88, First Sec. 1988–90; Chair. Democratic Labour Party 1990–93; Chair. Presidium Lithuanian SSR 1990; Deputy Chair. USSR Supreme Soviet 1990; Deputy Premier of Lithuania 1990–91; Acting Pres. of Lithuania 1992; Pres. of Lithuania 1993–97; Chair. Social-Democratic Party 2000–; Prime Minister of Lithuania 2000–. *Publications:* Lithuanian Divorce 1998; numerous articles. *Leisure interest:* yachting. *Address:* Turniškiu 30, 2016 Vilnius, Lithuania (Home); Gedimino Prosp. 11, 2039 Vilnius (Office). *E-mail:* kasp@lrvk.lt (Office). *Website:* www.lrvk.lt (Office).

BREAM, Julian, CBE, FRCM; British guitarist and lutenist; b. 15 July 1933, London; s. of Henry G. Bream; m. 1st Margaret Williamson; one adopted s.; m. 2nd Isobel Sanchez 1980 (divorced); ed Royal Coll. of Music; began professional career Cheltenham 1947, London début, Wigmore Hall 1950; has made many transcriptions for guitar of Romantic and Baroque works; commissioned new works from Britten, Walton, Henze and Arnold; tours throughout the world, giving recitals as soloist and with the Julian Bream Consort (f. 1960); many recitals with Sir Peter Pears and Robert Tear, and as guitar duo with John Williams; 60th Birthday Concert, Wigmore Hall, London 1993; Fellow Royal Northern Coll. of Music 1983; Hon. DUniv (Surrey) 1968, Hon. DMus (Leeds) 1984; Villa-Lobos Gold Medal 1976; numerous recording awards. *Leisure interests:* playing the guitar, cricket, table tennis, gardening, backgammon. *Address:* c/o Hazard Chase, Norman House, Cambridge Place, Cambridge, CB2 1NS, England.

BREARLEY, John Michael (Mike), OBE; British cricketer and psychoanalyst; b. 28 April 1942, Harrow, Middlesex; s. of Horace Brearley and of the late Midge Brearley; pnr Mana Sarabhai; two c.; ed City of London School and St John's Coll., Cambridge; right-hand opening batsman, occasional wicketkeeper; played for Cambridge Univ. 1961–64, captained Cambridge Univ. 1963, 1964; awarded county cap (Middlesex) 1964; Capt. of Middlesex (winning County Championships four times and Gillette Cup twice) 1971–82; Test debut 1976; Capt. of England 1977–80, 1981 (39 Tests in all); went on tours of South Africa 1964–65, Pakistan 1967, India, Sri Lanka and Australia 1976–77, Pakistan 1977–78, Australia 1978–79, Australia and India 1979–80; holds record for most runs scored at Cambridge Univ. (4,310 at an average of 38.48) 1964; scored 312 not out for MCC under-25 v. North Zone, Peshawar 1966–67; Lecturer in Philosophy, University of Newcastle-upon-Tyne 1968–71; Assoc. mem. British Psycho-Analytical Soc. 1985, Full mem. 1990; occasional cricket journalism and after-dinner speaking; Hon. DCL (Lancaster) 1999; Wisden Cricketer of the Year 1977. *Publications:* (with Dudley Doust) The Return of the Ashes 1978, The Ashes Retained (with Dudley Doust) 1979, Phoenix: the Series that Rose from the Ashes 1982, The Art of Captaincy 1985, Arlott in Conversation with Mike Brearley (with John Arlott) 1986. *Address:* c/o Middlesex County Cricket Club, Lord's Cricket Ground, St John's Wood Road, London, NW8 8QN, England. *Telephone:* (20) 7289-1300.

BREAUX, John B., JD; American politician; b. 1 March 1944, Crowley, La.; s. of Ezra Breaux and Katie Breaux; m. Lois Gail Daigle 1964; two s. two d.; ed Southwestern Univ. and State Univ. of Louisiana; called to La. Bar 1967; Partner Brown, McKernan, Ingram and Breaux 1967–68; Legislative Asst to US Congressman 1968–69; Dist Asst 1969–72; mem. 92nd–99th Congresses from 7th Dist., La. 1971–87; Senator from Louisiana 1987–; mem. House of Democrats Policy and Steering Cttee, Finance Cttee 1990–, Chief Deputy Whip 1993–; mem. Senate Cttee on Commerce, Science and Transportation, on Environment and Public Works, Special Cttee on Aging, Democratic Leadership Council; Chair. Nuclear Regulation Subcttee., Democratic Senatorial Campaign Cttee, Nat. Water Alliance 1987–88; fmr Chair House Subcttee. on Fisheries and Wildlife and the Environment; Co-chair. Nat. Bipartisan Comm. on Future of Medicare 1998–99; American Legion Award, Neptune Award, American Oceanic Org. 1980. *Address:* 503 Hart Senate Office Building, US Senate, Washington, DC 20510-0001, USA. *Telephone:* (202) 224-4623.

BRECHER, Michael, PhD, FRSC; Canadian professor of political science; b. 14 March 1925, Montreal; s. of Nathan Brecher and Gisela Hopmeyer; m. Eva Danon 1950; three d.; ed McGill and Yale Univs; mem. Faculty, McGill Univ. 1952–, R. B. Angus Prof. of Political Science 1993–; Pres. Int. Studies Asscn 1999–2000; Visiting Prof. Univ. of Chicago 1963, Hebrew Univ. Jerusalem 1970–75, Univ. of Calif. Berkeley 1979, Stanford Univ. 1980; Nuffield Fellow 1955–56; Rockefeller Fellow 1964–65; Guggenheim Fellow 1965–66; f. Shashtri Indo-Canadian Inst. 1968; Watumull Prize (American Hist. Asscn) 1960; Killam Awards (Canada Council) 1970–74, 1976–79; Woodrow Wilson Award (American Political Science Asscn) 1973, Fieldhouse Award for Distinguished Teaching (McGill Univ.) 1986, Distinguished Scholar Award (Int. Studies Asscn) 1995, Léon-Gérin Quebec Prize 2000, Award for High Distinction in Research, McGill Univ. 2000; many other awards and distinctions. *Publications:* The Struggle for Kashmir 1953, Nehru: A Political Biography 1959, The New States of Asia 1963, Succession in India 1966, India and World Politics 1968, Political Leadership in India 1969, The Foreign Policy System of Israel 1972, Israel, the Korean War and China 1974, Decisions in Israel's Foreign Policy 1975, Studies in Crisis Behavior 1979, Decisions in Crisis 1980, Crisis and Change in World Politics 1986, Crises in the 20th Century (Vols I, II) 1988, Crisis, Conflict and Instability 1989, Crises in World Politics 1993, A Study of Crisis 1997, 2000, Millennial Reflections on International Studies (Vols 1–5) 2002; over 85 articles in journals. *Address:* Department of Political Science, McGill University, 855 Sherbrooke Street West, Montreal, PQ, H3A 2T7, Canada; 5 Dubnov Street, P.O. Box 4438, Jerusalem 91043, Israel (Home). *Telephone:* (514) 398-4816 (Office). *Fax:* (514) 398-1770. *E-mail:* michael.brecher@mcgill.ca.

BRÉCHIGNAC, Catherine, DSc; French physicist; b. 12 June 1946; d. of Jean Teillac and Andrée Teillac (née Kerleguer); m. Philippe Bréchignac 1969; two s. one d.; ed Ecole Normale Supérieure, Fontenay-aux-Roses; research asst CNRS 1971–78, supervisor 1978–85, Dir of Research 1985–91, Del. to the Scientific Dir, Dept of Physical and Math. Sciences 1985–89, Dir of Aimé Cotton Lab. 1989–95, Scientific Dir, Dept of Physical and Math. Sciences 1995–97, Dir-Gen., CNRS 1997–2000; corresp. mem. Acad. des Sciences 1997–; mem. American Acad. of Arts and Sciences; Chevalier, Légion d'honneur, Ordre Nat. du Mérite, Acad. des Sciences Prize 1991, CNRS Gold Medal 1994. *Leisure interests:* opera, painting, literature. *Address:* Centre National de la Recherche Scientifique, 3 rue Michel Ange, 75794 Paris cedex 16, France (Office). *Telephone:* 1-44-96-40-00 (Office). *Fax:* 1-44-96-50-00 (Office).

BRÉCHOT, Christian, PhD; French medical researcher and professor of cell biology; b. 23 July 1952, Paris; s. of Claude Bréchot and Marie-Louise Bréchot (née Tisne); m. 1st (divorced); one s. two d.; m. 2nd Patrizia Paterlini; two s.; ed Lycée Montaigne, Paris, Lycée Louis le Grand, Paris, Univ. of Paris VII, Inst. Pasteur; Prof. of Cell Biology, Necker-Enfants Malades Faculty of Medicine, Univ. of Paris V 1989–; Head Hybridotest Lab., Inst. Pasteur 1990–98; Head Institut nat. de la santé et de la recherche médicale (INSERM) Research Unit U.370, Necker Hosp., Paris 1993–, Head Liver Unit, Necker Hosp. 1997–, Head Nat. Reference Centre on the molecular epidemiology of viral hepatitis, Inst. Pasteur and INSERM U.370 1998–; Dir-Gen. INSERM 2001–; WHO study co-ordinator for standardization of PCR in diagnosis of HIV infections 1988–91; mem. Scientific Cttee, Asscn pour la Recherche sur le Cancer 1988–2001, Agence Française du Sang 1993–96; mem. Inst. Universitaire de France 1992–, European Asscn for Virological Diagnosis, American Asscn for the Study of Liver Diseases, French Asscn for the Study of the Liver, European Asscn for the Study of the Liver (Sec. 1993–97); Biotrol Award 1982, Fondation pour la Recherche Médicale Award 1982, Abott Award for research on viral hepatitis 1983, Ligue Française contre le cancer Paris Award for research on liver cancer and hepatitis B virus 1985, APMS Award for research on prevention of transmissible diseases 1987, French Medical Soc., René Fauvert Award 1987, French Acad. of Medicine Award 1996, Fondation de France Jean Valade Award 2000. *Leisure interests:* paintings, tennis, rugby. *Address:* Institut National de la Santé de la Recherche Médicale (INSERM), 101 rue de Tolbiac, 75654 Paris Cédex 13, France (Office). *Telephone:* 1-44-23-60-60 (Office). *Fax:* 1-44-23-60-65 (Office). *E-mail:* brechot@tolbiac.inserm.fr (Office). *Website:* www.inserm.fr (Office).

BRECKENRIDGE, Alasdair Muir, CBE, MD, MSc, FRCP, FRCPE, FRSE; British professor of clinical pharmacology; b. 7 May 1937, Arbroath, Scotland; s. of Thomas Breckenridge and Jane Breckenridge; m. Jean M. Boyle 1967; two s.; ed Bell-Baxter School, Cupar, Fife and Univ. of St Andrews; House Physician and Surgeon, Dundee Royal Infirmary 1961–62; House Physician, Registrar, Lecturer, Sr Lecturer, Hammersmith Hosp. and Royal Postgrad. Medical School 1963–74; Prof. of Clinical Pharmacology, Univ. of Liverpool 1974–2002, Prof. Emer. 2002–; mem. Cttee on Safety of Medicines 1981–, Chair. 1999–; Councillor Int. Union of Pharmacology 1981–87; Foreign Sec. British Pharmacological Soc. 1983–91, Dir Research and Devt, Mersey Region 1992–96; Vice-Chair. Advisory Cttee. on Drugs 1985–98; mem. Council Royal Coll. of Physicians 1983–86, Panel of Tropical Diseases, Wellcome Trust 1984–88, WHO Steering Cttee on Chemotherapy of Malaria 1987–91, MRC Physiological Systems and Disorders Bd 1987–91, Council MRC 1992–96, Cen. Research and Devt Cttee Nat. Health Service 1991–95; Chair. NW Regional Office of the Nat. Health Service 1996–99; Chair. Jt. Medical Advisory Cttee. of Higher Educ. Funding Councils of the UK 1998–2002; Goulstonian Lecturer, Royal Coll. of Physicians 1975; Paul Martini Prize for Clinical Pharmacology 1974; Poulson Medal (Norwegian Pharmacological Soc.) 1988; Lilly Prize (British Pharmacological Soc.) 1993. *Publications:* articles in scientific and medical journals. *Leisure interests:* stock market, golf. *Address:* Department of Pharmacology and Therapeutics, University of Liverpool, Liverpool, L69 3BX (Office); Cree Cottage, Feather Lane, Wirral, L69 3BX, England (Home). *Telephone:* (151) 794-5542 (Office); (151) 342-1096 (Home).

BREDESEN, Philip Norman, AB; American state official; b. 21 Nov. 1943, Oceanport, NJ; s. of Phillip Norman Bredesen, Sr and Norma Bredesen (née Walborn); m. 1st Susan Cleaves 1968 (divorced 1974); m. 2nd Andrea Conte 1974; one s.; ed Red Jacket Cen. School, NY, Harvard Univ.; computer programmer Itek Corpn, Mass. 1967–70; Dir of Systems Devt G.D. Seale & Co. 1971–73, Div. Man. 1973–75; Dir of Special Projects Hosp. Affiliates Int. 1976–80; f. Healthplans Corpn (later HealthAmerica Corpn) 1980, Chair., CEO 1980–86; co-f. Coventry Corpn 1986, Chair. 1986–90; co-f. Clinical Pharmaceuticals 1986, Chair. 1986–93; Mayor of Nashville 1991–99; Pres. Bredex Corpn 2000–02; Gov. of Tenn. 2003–; f. Nashville's Table 1989, mem. Bd Dirs 1989–91; f. Land Trust for Tenn. 1999, Chair. 1999–2001; mem. Bd Dirs. Tenn. State Univ. Foundation, Nashville Publrs' Library Foundation 1997–; mem. Bd Trustees Frist Center for Visual Arts 1998–. *Leisure interests:* oil painting, flying glider planes, jogging, hunting, fishing, skiing, hiking. *Address:* Office of the Governor, State Capitol Building, Nashville, TN 37243 (Office); 1724 Chickering Road, Nashville, TN 37215-4908, USA (Home). *Telephone:* (615) 741-2001 (Office). *Fax:* (615) 741-1416 (Office).

BREDIN, Frédérique Marie Denise Colette; French politician; b. 2 Nov. 1956, Paris; d. of Jean-Denis Bredin (q.v.) and Danièle Hervier; m. Jean-Pascal Beaufret 1985; two c.; ed Inst. d'Etudes Politiques, Paris and Ecole Nat. d'Admin; Insp. Gen. of Finance 1980–84; special assignment to Minister of Culture 1984–86, to Pres. of Repub. 1986–88; Socialist Deputy to Nat. Ass. 1988–91, 1995–, to European Parl. 1994–96; Mayor of Fécamp 1989–95; Minister of Youth and Sport 1991–93; Nat. Sec. Socialist Party, with responsibility for Culture and Media 1996–2000; Dir of Strategies and Devt, Lagardère Médias Group 2000–. *Address:* Lagardère Médias, 4 rue de Presbourg, 75116 Paris, France (Office).

BREDIN, Jean-Denis, LèsL; French lawyer; b. 17 May 1929, Paris; m. Danièle Hervier; two c. (including Frédérique Bredin, q.v.); ed Lycée Charlemagne and Facultés de Droit et des Lettres, Paris; advocate, Court of Appeal, Paris 1950–; Prof. Faculté de Droit, Rennes 1958, Lille 1967; Adviser to Council for Higher Educ. 1968–69; Prof. of Pvt. Law, Univ. of Paris-Dauphine 1969; Prof. Univ. of Paris I 1971–93, Prof. Emer. 1993–; Vice-Pres. Mouve-ment des radicaux de gauche 1976–80; Pres. Man. Bd Bibliothèque Nationale 1983–88; Vice-Pres. Comm. Moinot 1981; Pres. Comm. for Reform of Cinema 1982; Adviser on Audiovisual Matters to Prime Minister 1985; mem. Acad. Française; Prix Gobert 1984. *Publications include:* Traité de droit commercial international 1967, La République de Monsieur Pompidou 1974, Les Français au pouvoir 1977, Eclats 1976, Joseph Cailleux 1980, L'Affaire 1983, Un coupable 1985, L'Absence 1986, La Tâche 1988, Weisbuch 1989, Un enfant sage 1990, Battements de coeur 1991, Bernard Lazare 1992, Comédie des Apparences 1994, Encore un peu de temps 1996, Convaincre, dialogues sur l'éloquence 1997, L'Affaire 1998, Une singulière famille 1999, Rien ne va plus 2000, Lettre à Dieu le fils 2001, Un tribunal au garde-à-vous 2002. *Address:* 130 rue du Faubourg Saint-Honoré, 75008 Paris; Institut de France, 23 quai de Conti, 75006 Paris, France. *Telephone:* 1-44-35-35-35 (Office).

BREGGIN, Peter R., BA, MD; American psychiatrist; b. 11 May 1936, New York; m. 3rd Ginger Ross 1984; one c. (and three c. from two previous marriages); ed Harvard Coll., Case Western Reserve School of Medicine, State Univ. of New York, Upstate Medical Center, Massachusetts Mental Health Centre; consultant Nat. Inst. of Mental Health 1966–68; psychiatrist in pvt. practice 1968–; Founder and Dir Int. Center for Study of Psychiatry and Psychology 1972–2002, Dir Emer. 2002–; Adjunct Prof. of Conflict Resolution George Mason Univ. 1990–96; Faculty Assoc. Dept of Counselling Johns Hopkins Univ. 1996–99; Ed. numerous journals, including Journal of Mind and Behaviour, Int. Journal of Risk and Society in Medicine, The Humanistic Psychologist, Review of Existential Psychology and Psychiatry; Founding Ed. Ethical Human Sciences and Services 1999–; Ludwig von Mises Award of Merit 1987, Minn. Mental Health Asscn Advocacy Award 1990, honours from Harvard Coll. *Publications:* Toxic Psychiatry 1991, Talking Back to Prozac (with Ginger Breggin) 1994, Brain-Disabling Treatments in Psychiatry 1997, The Heart of Being Helpful 1997, The War Against Children of Color (with Ginger Breggin) 1998, Talking Back to Ritalin 1998, Your Drug May Be Your Problem (with David Cohen) 1999, Reclaiming Our Children 2000, The Ritalin Fact Book 2001, The Antidepressant Fact Book 2002. *Address:* 101 East State Street, PMB 112, Ithaca, NY 14850, USA. *Telephone:* (607) 272-5328. *Fax:* (607) 272-5329. *Website:* www.breggin.com (Office).

BREGVADZE, Nani Georgievna; Georgian singer; b. 21 July 1938; ed Tbilisi Conservatoire (pianoforte class under Machutadze); soloist with Georgian State Philharmonia 1959–, with Georgian popular orchestra 'Rero' 1959–64, with 'Orera' 1964–80; specializes in Georgian music and Russian romances; has toured abroad on numerous occasions; People's Artist of USSR 1983; Hon. Citizen of Tbilisi 1995; Order of Honour 1995; People's Artist of Georgia 1996; State Prize of Georgia 1997. *Address:* Irakly Abashidze str. 18A, Apt. 10, 380079 Tbilisi, Georgia. *Telephone:* (32) 22-37-22.

BREIEN, Anja; Norwegian film director; ed Inst. des hautes études cinématiques, France; Dir of short films and feature films 1967–. *Short films include:* 17. Mai – en film om ritualer 1969, Ansikter 1971, Murer rundt fengslet 1972, Herbergister 1973, Mine Søsken, goddag 1974, Gamle 1975, Solvorn 1997, Å se en båt med seil (UIP/EFA Prize, Berlin Film Festival, Best Short Feature, Toronto) 2001. *Feature films include:* Vokse opp (Part 1 of Dager fra 100 år) 1967, Voldtekt (Rape) 1971, Hustruer (Wives) 1975, Den Allvarsamme Leken (Games of Love and Loneliness) 1977 (Silver Hugo Award, Chicago 1977), Arven (Next of Kin/The Inheritance) 1979, Forfølgelsen (Witch Hunt) 1981, Papirfuglen (Paper Bird) 1984 (Silver Hugo Award, Chicago 1984), Hustruer—ti år etter (Wives—Ten Years After) (Norwegian Film Prize Amanda) 1985, Smykketyven (Twice upon a Time) 1990, Hustruer III (Wives III) 1996; has also written script for film Trollsyn (Second Sight), Dir Ola Solum 1994. *Publications:* Forfølgelsen (script) 1981, Trollsyn (script) 1995. *Leisure interest:* skiing. *Address:* c/o Norsk Film, Filmparken-Wedel Jarlsbergs vei 36, 1342 Jar; Mellbyedalen 8, 0287 Oslo, Norway. *Telephone:* 67-52-53-00 (Jar). *Fax:* 67-12-51-08 (Jar).

BREILLAT, Catherine; French film director, screenwriter and novelist; b. 1948, Bressuire; Prof. of Auteur Cinema, European Grad. School, Switzerland. *Films roles include:* Last Tango in Paris 1972, Dracula Père et Fils 1977. *Films directed include:* Une vraie jeune fille (A Real Young Girl) 1975 (released 2000), Tapage nocturne (Nocturnal Uproar) 1979, 36 Fillette (Virgin) 1988, Sale comme un ange (Dirty Like an Angel) 1990, Parfait Amour (Perfect Love, jtly) 1996, Romance 1999, À ma soeur! (Fat Girl) 2001, Brève traversée (TV) 2001, Scènes intimes 2002, Sex is Comedy. *Publications include:* L'homme facile (novel), Tapage nocturne 1979, Romance 1999, Le livre du plaisir 1999, Une vraie jeune fille 2000, À ma soeur! 2001, Pornocratie 2001, Ein Mädchen 2001. *Screenplays include:* Catherine et Cie. (Catherine & Co., jtly) 1975, Bilitis 1977, La peau (The Skin) 1981, Et la nave va (And the Ship Sails On) 1983, L'araignée de satin (The Satin Spider) 1984, Police 1985, Milan noir (Black Milan, jtly) 1987, Zanzibar (jtly) 1988, La nuit de l'océan (The Night of the Ocean, jtly) 1988, Aventure de Catherine C. (The Adventure of Catherine C., jtly) 1990, Le diable au corps 1990, La Thune (Money, jtly) 1991, Couples et amants (Couples and Lovers, jtly) 1994, Viens jouer dans la cour des grands (TV) 1997, Selon Matthieu 2000. *Address:* c/o European Graduate School, Ringacker, 3953 Leuk-Stadt, Switzerland (Office). *Telephone:* (27) 474 9917 (Office). *Fax:* (27) 474 9969 (Office).

BREITENSTEIN, (Fredrik) Wilhelm, LLM; Finnish diplomatist (retd.); b. 17 May 1933, Tampere; s. of B. Rafael Breitenstein and Ebba Huikarinen; m. 1st Dorrit I. Martin (divorced 1977); one s. three d.; m. 2nd Satu Marjatta Lefkowitz (née Nuorvala) 1978; one d.; ed Univ. of Helsinki; intern, UN Secr.

New York 1957–58; Ministry of Foreign Affairs 1960–62, 1966–68, 1978–83; Attaché and Sec. of Embassy, Perm. Mission to UN, New York 1962–66; Deputy Perm. Rep. to EFTA and Int. Orgs. Geneva 1968–72, Perm. Mission to UN, New York 1972–78; Gov. Asian Devt Bank 1978–83, African Devt Bank 1978–83; Alt. Gov. Inter-American Devt Bank 1978–83; Perm. Rep. to OECD and UNESCO 1983–91, Vice-Pres. UNESCO Gen. Conf. 1986, Chair. Head Comm. UNESCO 1986–88, Chair. Advisory Bd for Devt Centre, OECD 1989–90; Perm. Rep. to UN 1991–98; Pres. Gov. Council UNPD 1993, Co-Chair. Open-ended Work Group of Gen. Ass. for Reform of UN Security Council 1994–98; Vice-Pres. Preparatory Comm. for 50th Anniversary of UN; mem. Exec. Bd. Int. Asscn of Perm. Reps. to UN; del. to numerous UN and other int. confs. *Leisure interests:* art and antiques. *Address:* c/o Ministry of Foreign Affairs, Merikasarmi, P.O. Box 176, 00161 Helsinki, Finland (Office).

BREJON DE LAVERGNÉE, Arnauld, DenL; French museum curator; b. 25 May 1945, Rennes; s. of Jacques Brejon de Lavergnèe and Monique Perquis; m. Barbara Mercillon 1977; four c.; ed Univ. of Sorbonne, Paris; trainee curator Louvre Museum, Museums of Cluny and Dijon 1969–70; Visiting Fellow Acad. of France in Rome 1971–72; Curator Museum of Cluny 1973–76; Curator Dept of Painting, Louvre Museum 1976–87; Gen. Curator of Heritage 1987; Curator Museum of Fine Arts, Lille 1987–, (oversaw 220 million french franc restoration project 1992–97); Corresp. mem. Acad. of Fine Arts, Acad. of Bologne; Chevalier, Légion d'honneur, Ordre nat. du Mérite, Ordre Nat. des Arts et des Lettres; Prix Nat. de Muséographie 1987. *Publications include:* L'art italien dans les collections françaises, La collection du Bailli de Breteuil, Une monographie sur Simon Vouet. *Address:* Musée des beaux-arts de Lille, 18 bis rue de Valmy, 59000 Lille (Office); 13 rue de Fleurus, 59000 Lille, France (Home).

BREKHOVSKIKH, Leonid Maksimovich, DSc; Russian physicist; b. 6 May 1917, Strunkino Village, Arkhangelsk Region; s. of Maxim Vasilievich and Nadezda Alexandrovna Brekhovskikh; m. Lidia Andreevna Popova 1940 (died 1998); one s. two d.; ed Perm. State Univ.; jr research worker, sr research worker, Deputy Head of Dept, Inst. of Physics, USSR Acad. of Sciences 1939–54; Prof. Moscow Univ.1953–75, Moscow Physics Tech. Inst. 1975–97; Dir Inst. of Acoustics 1954–64, Head of Laboratory 1964–80; Head Ocean Acoustics Dept Shirsov Inst. of Oceanology 1980–; discovered (with others) super-distant propagation of sound in the sea and existence of mesoscale eddies in the sea; Head of Dept of Oceanography, Physics of Atmosphere and Geography, USSR (now Russian) Acad. of Sciences 1969–91; Counsellor Presidium of Russian Acad. of Sciences 1992–; mem. CPSU 1959–91; Corresp. mem. USSR (now Russian) Acad. of Sciences 1953–68, mem. 1968–; mem. Polish Acad. of Sciences 1971–, NAS 1991–; Hon. Fellow Acoustical Soc. of USA 1999; State Prize 1950, 1976, Lenin Prize 1970, Rayleigh Gold Medal, British Inst. of Acoustics, Karpinsky Prize 1986, FVS Foundation, Hamburg, Hero of Socialist Labour 1987; Munk Medal of Oceanographic Soc. 1996. *Publications:* numerous scientific works in fields of ocean acoustics, radiophysics and theoretical physics. *Leisure interest:* yoga exercises. *Address:* P. P. Shirshov Oceanology Institute, Russian Academy of Sciences, Nakhimovsky pr. 36, B-218 Moscow, Russia. *Telephone:* (095) 146-96-17 (Home); (095) 124-85-38 (Home); (095) 938-14-63 (Home). *Fax:* (095) 124-59-83. *E-mail:* abrekh@mail.ru.

BREMAN, Jan; Netherlands professor of comparative sociology; b. 24 July 1936, Amsterdam; Dir Centre of Asian Studies, Univ. of Amsterdam; Prof. Inst. of Social Studies, The Hague; extensive anthropological research in India and Indonesia 1962–; Devt consultant on social policies in Asia; mem. Nat. Advisory Council on Devt Cooperation in the Netherlands; mem. Royal Netherlands Acad. of Sciences. *Publications:* Of Patronage and Exploitation 1974, Landless Labour in Colonial Java 1984, Of Peasants, Migrants and Workers 1985, Taming the Coolie Beast 1989, Beyond Patronage and Exploitation 1993, Wage Hunters and Gatherers 1994, Footloose Labour: Working India's Informal Economy (Edgar Graham Prize 1998) 1996. *Address:* Oude Hoogstraat 24, 1012 CE Amsterdam, Netherlands. *Telephone:* (20) 5252745. *Fax:* (20) 525 2446.

BREMI, Ulrich; Swiss business executive and politician; b. 6 Nov. 1929, Zürich; s. of Heinrich Bremi-Sennhauser and Johanna Bremi-Sennhauser; m. Anja Bremi-Forrer; two d.; ed School of Mechanical Eng, Winterthur and Swiss Fed. Inst. of Tech., Zürich; CEO Kaba Holding Ltd Zürich 1962–90; Chair. Bd Neue Zürcher Zeitung 1988–99, Georg Fischer AG 1989–98, Swiss Reinsurance Co. 1992–2000, Flughafen-Immobilien-Gesellschaft 1992–2000; mem. Swiss Nat. Parl. 1975–91, Chair. 1990–91; Hon. Senator St Gallen Univ. 2000. *Address:* Swiss Reinsurance Company, Mythenquai 50/60, P.O. Box 8022, Zürich, Switzerland. *Telephone:* (1) 2853553. *Fax:* (1) 2854180 (Office). *E-mail:* ulrich_Bremi@swissre.com (Office).

BRENCIU, Marius; Romanian singer (tenor); b. 1974, Brasov; s. of Radu Brenciu and Maria-Elena Brenciu; m.; ed Andrei Saguna High School, Univ. of Music, Bucharest; began singing in choir of local Orthodox church, aged 12; teaching Asst Univ. of Music, Bucharest 1997–2000; permanent leading singer Romanian Nat. Opera, Bucharest; 1st Prize Young Artists Int. Auditions, New York; winner Cardiff Singer of the World (also Song Prize) 2001. *Music: Operatic roles include:* Lenski (Eugene Onegin), Steva (Jenufa), Alfredo (La Traviata), Idomeneo (Idomeneo). *Other repertoire includes:* Requiem (Verdi), Mass in C Minor (Mozart), Messa di Gloria (Puccini), Messe Solennelle (Gounod), A Child of our Time (Tippett). *Address:* c/o Young Concert Artists, Inc., 250 West 57th Street, Suite 1222, New York, NY 10107, USA (Office). *Telephone:* (212) 307-6655 (Office). *Fax:* (212) 581-8894 (Office). *E-mail:* yca@yca.org (Office). *Website:* www.yca.org (Office).

BRENDEL, Alfred; Austrian pianist and writer; b. 5 Jan. 1931, Wiesenberg; s. of Ing. Albert and Ida (née Wieltschnig) Brendel; m. 1st Iris Heymann-Gonzala 1960 (divorced 1972); one d.; m. 2nd Irene Semler 1975; one s. two d.; studied piano under Sofija Deželi (Zagreb), Ludovika v. Kaan (Graz), Edwin Fischer (Lucerne), Paul Baumgartner (Basel), Edward Steuermann (Salzburg); studied composition under A. Michl (Graz) and harmony under Franjo Dugan (Zagreb); first piano recital 1948; concert tours through Europe, Latin America, North America 1963–; Australia 1963, 1966, 1969, 1976; has appeared at many music festivals, including Salzburg 1960–, Vienna, Edinburgh, Aldeburgh, Athens, Granada, Puerto Rico and has performed with most of the major orchestras of Europe and USA, etc.; numerous recordings, including complete piano works of Beethoven, Schubert's piano works 1822–28; mem. Acad. of Arts and Sciences (USA); Hon. RAM; Hon. RCM; Hon. Fellow, Exeter Coll. Oxford 1987; Commdr des Arts et des Lettres 1985, Hon. KBE 1989, Ordre pour le Mérite (Germany) 1991; Hon. DMus (London) 1978, (Oxford) 1983, (Exeter) 1998, (Southampton) 2002; Hon. DLitt (Sussex) 1981; Dr hc (Warwick) 1991, (Yale) 1992, (Cologne) 1995; Premio Città de Bolzano, Concorso Busoni 1949, Grand Prix du Disque 1965, Edison Prize (five times 1973–87), Grand Prix des Disquaires de France 1975, Deutscher Schallplattenpreis (four times 1976–84, 1992), Wiener Flötenuhr (six times 1976–87), Gramophone Award (six times 1977–83), Japanese Record Acad. Award (five times 1977–84, with Scottish Symphony Orchestra/Sir Charles Mackerras 2002), Japanese Grand Prix 1978, Franz Liszt Prize (four times 1979–83), Frankfurt Music Prize 1984, Diapason D'Or Award 1992, Heidsieck Award for Writing on Music 1990. *Publications:* essays on music and musicians in Phono, Fono Forum, Österreichische Musikzeitschrift, Music and Musicians, Hi-Fi Stereophonie, New York Review of Books, Die Zeit, Frankfurter Allgemeine Zeitung, Musical Thoughts and Afterthoughts 1976, Music Sounded Out (essays) 1990, Fingerzeig 1996, Störendes Lachen während des Jaworts 1997, One Finger Too Many 1998, Kleine Teufel 1999, Collected Essays on Music 2000, Augerechnet Ich 2001 (English edn The Veil of Order: In Conversation with Martin Meyer 2002). *Leisure interests:* books, theatre, the visual arts, films, baroque and romanesque architecture, unintentional humour, kitsch. *Address:* c/o Ingpen and Williams, 26 Wadham Road, London, SW15 2LR, England. *Telephone:* (20) 8874-3222. *Fax:* (20) 8877-3113.

BRENDISH, Clayton (Clay), CBE; British business executive; co-f. Admiral PLC 1979, Exec. Chair. 1979–2000; Exec. Deputy Chair. CMG PLC (following CMG's merger with Admiral) 2000; fmr Chair. Exec. Bd Inst. of Man. (IM), Pres. IM 2001–, Chair. Information Tech. Task Group, mem. Remuneration Cttee; fmr Adviser to Chancellor of Duchy of Lancaster and Parl. Sec., Office of Public Services; Dir (non-exec.) Ordnance Survey 1993–96; Chair. (non-exec.) Beacon Investment Fund 1995–; external mem. Defence Meteorological Bd 1995–; mem. Ind. TV Comm. 2000–, Council City Univ., London 2000–; Trustee, Economist Newspapers Ltd. *Address:* Institute of Management, 2 Savoy Court, Strand, London, WC2R 0EZ, England (Office). *Telephone:* (20) 7497-0580 (Office). *Fax:* (20) 7592-0463 (Office). *Website:* www.inst-mgt.org.uk (Office).

BRENNAN, Edward A.; American business executive; b. 16 Jan. 1934, Chicago; s. of Edward Brennan and Margaret Bourget; m. Lois Lyon 1955; three s. three d.; ed Marquette Univ.; joined Sears, Roebuck and Co., Madison, Wis. as salesman 1956, held several positions in co.'s nat. HQ and elsewhere, Exec. Vice-Pres. South 1977, Pres. of Sears 1980, Chair. and CEO Sears Merchandise Group 1981, Pres. and COO Sears, Roebuck and Co. 1984–86, Chair., Pres. and CEO 1986–95; Exec. Adviser Seiyu Ltd 1995–; mem. Bd of Trustees Atlanta, DePaul and Marquette Univs. and Chicago Museum of Science and Industry; mem. Bd of Govs. United Way of America; mem. Chicago Urban League 1980–. *Address:* c/o Sears, Roebuck and Co., 3333 Beverly Road, Hoffman Estates, IL 60179, USA.

BRENNAN, Hon. Sir (Francis) Gerard, AC, KBE, LLB; Australian judge (retd); b. 22 May 1928, Rockhampton, Queensland; s. of Hon. Mr. Justice Frank T. Brennan and Gertrude Brennan; m. Dr Patricia O'Hara 1953; three s. four d.; ed Christian Brothers' Coll., Rockhampton, Downlands Coll., Toowoomba and Univ. of Queensland, Brisbane; admitted to Bar 1951, QC 1965; Pres. Bar Asscn of Queensland 1974–76, Australian Bar Asscn 1975–76, Admin. Review Council 1976–79, Admin. Appeals Tribunal 1976–79; mem. Exec. Law Council of Australia 1975–76, Australian Law Reform Comm. 1975–77; Additional Judge, Supreme Court of ACT 1976–81; Judge, Australian Industrial Court 1976–81, Fed. Court of Australia 1977–81; Justice, High Court of Australia 1981–95; Chief Justice of Australia 1995–98; External Judge, Supreme Court of Fiji 1999–2000; Non-permanent Judge, Court of Final Appeal of Hong Kong 2000–; Foundation Scientia Prof. of Law, Univ. of NSW 1998; Chancellor, Univ. of Tech., Sydney 1998–; Hon. LLD (Univ. of Dublin Trinity Coll.) 1988, (Univ. of Queensland) 1996, (ANU) 1996, (Melbourne Univ., Univ. of Tech., Sydney) 1998; Hon. DLitt (Central Queensland Univ.) 1996; Hon. DUniv (Griffiths Univ.) 1996. *Address:* c/o Suite 2604, Piccadilly Tower, 133 Castlereagh Street, Sydney, NSW 2000, Australia. *Telephone:* (2) 9261-8704 (Office). *Fax:* (2) 9261-8113 (Office).

BRENNAN, Séamus, BA, MComm; Irish politician; b. 16 Feb. 1948, Salthill, Galway; s. of the late James Brennan and of Teresa Brennan; m. Ann O'Shaughnessy 1972; two s. four d.; ed St Joseph's Secondary School, Galway,

Univ. Coll., Galway, Univ. Coll., Dublin; has worked as an accountant and man. consultant; Gen. Sec. Fianna Fáil Party 1973–80; Govt Deputy Whip, Seanad Éireann 1977–81; Senator 1977–81; Dáil Deputy for Dublin South 1981–; Minister of State, Dept of Industry and Commerce with responsibility for Trade and Marketing 1987–89; Minister for Tourism and Transport 1989–92, for Educ. 1992–93, for Commerce and Technology 1993–94; Front Bench Spokesperson on Transport, Energy and Communications 1994–97; Minister of State to the Taoiseach, Govt Chief Whip and Minister of State at the Dept of Defence 1997–2002; Minister for Transport 2002–; mem. Oireachtas Cttee on Procedure and Privileges 1977–81; Vice-Chair. Oireachtas Cttee on State Sponsored Bodies 1981; mem. Jt Cttee on Commercial State Sponsored Bodies and Small Business 1994–97; mem. Oireachtas Jt Cttee on the Secondary Legislation in the EEC 1982; mem. Dublin Co. Council 1985–87. *Leisure interests:* boating, golf, reading, tennis. *Address:* Transport House, 44 Kildare Street, Dublin 2 (Office); 9 Braemor Road, Churchtown, Dublin 14, Ireland (Home). *Telephone:* (1) 6707444 (Office). *Fax:* (1) 6041183 (Office). *E-mail:* minister@transport.ie (Office). *Website:* www.transport.ie (Office).

BRENNER, Sydney, CH, MB, DPhil, FRS, FRCP; British scientist; b. 13 Jan. 1927, Germiston, South Africa; s. of Morris Brenner and Lena Brenner (née Blacher); m. May Woolf Balkind; two s. (one step-s.) two d.; ed Univ. of the Witwatersrand, Johannesburg and Oxford Univ.; Lecturer in Physiology, Univ. of Witwatersrand 1955–57; mem. Scientific Staff, MRC 1957–92, Dir MRC Lab. of Molecular Biology, Cambridge 1979–86, Dir Molecular Genetics Unit, Cambridge 1986–92; mem. Scripps Inst., La Jolla, Calif. 1992–94; Dir Molecular Sciences Inst., Berkeley, Calif. 1996–2001; Distinguished Research Prof. Salk Inst., La Jolla, Calif., USA 2001–; mem. Medical Research Council 1978–82, 1986–90; Fellow of King's Coll., Cambridge 1959–; Hon. Prof. of Genetic Medicine, Univ. of Cambridge Clinical School 1981–87; Foreign Assoc. NAS 1977; Foreign mem. of American Philosophical Soc. 1979; Foreign Assoc. Royal Soc. of S. Africa 1983, Hon. Fellow, Exeter Coll. 1985; Foreign mem. of Real Academia de Ciencias 1985; External Scientific mem. Max Planck Soc. 1988; mem. Academia Europaea 1989; Corresp. Scientifique Emérite de l'INSERM, Associé Etranger Académie des Sciences, France, Fellow American Acad. of Microbiology; Foreign Hon. mem. American Acad. of Arts and Sciences 1965, Hon. mem. Deutsche Akademie der Natursforscher Leopoldina 1975, Soc. for Biological Chemists 1975; Hon. FRSE; Hon. Fellow Indian Acad. of Sciences 1989; Hon. mem. Chinese Soc. of Genetics 1989; Hon. Fellow Royal Coll. of Pathologists 1990; Hon. Fellow Acad. Medical Sciences 1999; Hon. mem. Assoc. of Physicians of GB and Ireland 1991; Hon. DSc (Dublin, Witwatersrand, Chicago, London, Leicester, Oxford, La Trobe); Hon. LLD (Glasgow) 1981, (Cambridge) 2001; Hon. DLitt (Singapore); Hon. Dr rer. nat (Jena); Warren Triennial Prize 1968, William Bate Hardy Prize, Cambridge Philosophical Soc. 1969, Gregor Mendel Medal of German Acad. of Science Leopoldina 1970, Albert Lasker Medical Research Award 1971, Gairdner Foundation Annual Award (Canada) 1978; Royal Medal of Royal Soc. 1974, Prix Charles Leopold Mayer, French Acad. 1975, Krebs Medal, Fed. of European Biochemical Socs 1980, Ciba Medal, Biochemical Soc. 1981, Feldberg Foundation Prize 1983, Neil Hamilton Fairley Medal, Royal Coll. of Physicians 1985, Croonian Lecturer Royal Soc. of London 1986, Rosenstiel Award, Brandeis Univ. 1986, Prix Louis Jeantet de Médecine (Switzerland) 1987, Genetics Soc. of America Medal 1987, Harvey Prize, Israel Inst. of Tech. 1987, Hughlings Jackson Medal, Royal Soc. of Medicine 1987, Waterford Bio-Medical Science Award (The Research Inst. of Scripps Clinic) 1988, Kyoto Prize (Inamori Foundation) 1990, Gairdner Foundation Award (Canada) 1991, Copley Medal (Royal Soc.) 1991, King Faisal Int. Prize for Science (King Faisal Foundation) 1992, Bristol-Myers Squibb Award for Distinguished Achievement in Neuroscience Research 1992, Albert Lasker Award for Special Achievement 2000, Nobel Prize for Physiology or Medicine 2002. *Leisure interest:* rumination. *Address:* Kings College, Cambridge, CB2 1ST (Office); 22 Black Hill, Ely, Cambs. CB7 2BZ, England (Home).

BRENT, Richard Peirce, PhD, DSc, FAA, FIEEE; Australian professor of computing science; b. 20 April 1946, Melbourne; s. of Oscar Brent and Nancy Brent; m. Erin O'Connor 1969; two s.; ed Melbourne Grammar School, Monash Univ., Stanford Univ., USA; Research Scientist, IBM T. J. Watson Research Center, Yorktown Heights, New York, USA 1971–72; Research Fellow etc., ANU, Canberra 1972–78, Prof. of Computer Sciences 1978–98, now Adjunct Prof.; Prof. of Computing Science, Oxford Univ. 1998–; Fellow Asscn for Computing Machinery, USA; Forsythe Memorial Lecturer 1990; Australian Math. Soc. Medal 1984. *Publications:* Algorithms for Minimization without Derivatives 1973, Topics in Computational Complexity and the Analysis of Algorithms 1980. *Leisure interests:* music, chess, astronomy. *Address:* Oxford University Computing Laboratory, Wolfson Building, Parks Road, Oxford, OX1 3QD, England. *Telephone:* (1865) 283505.

BRENTON, Howard, BA; British playwright; b. 13 Dec. 1942, Portsmouth; s. of Donald Henry Brenton and Rose Lilian Brenton (née Lewis); m. Jane Fry 1970; two s.; ed Chichester High School for Boys and St Catharine's Coll., Cambridge; resident writer, Royal Court Theatre, London 1972–73; writer-in-residence, Warwick Univ. 1978–79; Granada Artist in Residence, Univ. of Calif. at Davis 1997; Arts and Humanities Research Bd Fellowship, Birmingham Univ. 2000; Hon. Dr of Arts (Univ. of N London) 1996; John Whiting Award 1970, Standard Best Play of the Year Award 1976, Standard Best Play of the Year (jtly with David Hare) 1985. *Publications:* Revenge 1969, Christie in Love 1969, Hitler Dances 1972, Magnificence 1973, Brassneck (with David Hare) 1973, The Churchill Play 1974, Government Property 1975, The Saliva Milkshake 1975, Weapons of Happiness 1976, Sore Throats 1979, Plays for the Poor Theatre 1980, The Romans in Britain 1980, Thirteenth Night 1981, The Genius 1983, Sleeping Policemen (with Tunde Ikoli) 1983, Bloody Poetry 1984, Pravda (with David Hare) 1985, Dead Head 1986, Greenland 1988, Diving for Pearls (novel) 1989, Iranian Nights (with Tariq Ali) 1989, Hess is Dead 1990, Moscow Gold (with Tariq Ali) 1990, Berlin Bertie 1992, Hot Irons (Essays and Diaries) 1995, Playing Away (opera) 1994, Goethe's Faust, Parts I and II 1995, Plays I 1996, Plays II 1996, in Extremis 1997, Ugly Rumours (with Tariq Ali) 1998, Collateral Damage (with Tariq Ali and Andy de la Tour), Nasser's Eden (play for radio) 1999, Snogging Ken (with Tariq Ali and Andy de la Tour) 2000, Kit's Play 2000, Bacchae/Backup 2001, Spooks (TV series) 2002. *Leisure interest:* painting. *Address:* c/o Cassarotto Ramsay Ltd, 60/66 National House, Wardour Street, London, WC1V 3HP, England. *Telephone:* (20) 7287-4450. *Fax:* (20) 7287-9128.

BRESLOW, Lester, BA, MD, MPH; American professor of public health; b. 17 March 1915, Bismarck, ND; s. of Joseph Breslow and Mayme Danziger; m. Devra Miller 1967; three s.; ed Univ. of Minnesota; Dist Health Officer, Minn. 1941–43; US Army 1943–46; Chief, Bureau of Chronic Diseases, Calif. Dept of Public Health 1946–60, Div. of Preventative Medicine 1960–65; Dir Calif. Dept of Public Health 1965–68; Prof. School of Public Health, Univ. of Calif. (Los Angeles) 1968–, Dean 1972–80, Dir for Cancer Control Research, Jonsson Comprehensive Cancer Center 1982–86, Dir Health Promotion Center 1986–91; Pres. Int. Epidemiological Asscn 1967–68; Pres. American Public Health Asscn 1968–69; Pres. Asscn of Schools of Public Health 1973–75; mem. Inst. of Medicine 1975–; Founding Ed. Annual Review of Public Health 1980–90 consultant Nat. Cancer Inst. 1981–; Lasker Award 1960, Sedwick Medal 1977, American Public Health Asscn, Dana Award 1988, Healthtrac Prize 1995, Lienhard Award, Inst. of Medicine 1997, The Porter Prize 1998. *Publication:* Health and Ways of Living: The Alameda County Study 1983. *Leisure interest:* gardening. *Address:* School of Public Health, UCLA, 650 South Young Drive, Los Angeles, CA 90095 (Office); 10926 Verano Road, Los Angeles, CA 90077, USA (Home). *Telephone:* (310) 825-1388 (Office); (310) 472-6906 (Home). *Fax:* (310) 825-3317 (Office). *E-mail:* breslow@ph.ucla.edu (Office).

BRESLOW, Ronald Charles, PhD; American professor of chemistry; b. 14 March 1931, Rahway, NJ; s. of Alexander Breslow and Gladys Fellows; m. Esther Greenberg 1956; two d.; ed Harvard Univ.; Instructor, Columbia Univ. 1956–59, Assoc. Prof. 1959–62, Prof. 1962–67, Mitchill Prof. of Chem. 1966–, Univ. Prof. 1992–; Ed. Benjamin Inc. 1962–; Sloan Fellowship 1961–63; Fellow AAAS 1986; mem. Nat. Acad. of Sciences, American Acad. of Arts and Sciences, American Philosophical Soc., Exec. Cttee of Organic Div. of American Chemical Soc.; mem. Ed. Bd Organic Syntheses 1965–, Bd of Eds Journal of Organic Chem. 1968, Tetrahedron, Tetrahedron Letters 1977, Chemical Eng News 1980–83; Hon. mem. Korean Chemical Soc. 1996, Royal Soc. of Chem. (UK) 1996; Procurator, NAS 1984; Trustee, American-Swiss Foundation for Scientific Exchange Inc. 1969–71; Chair. Div. of Organic Chem., American Chemical Soc. 1970–71, Pres. of Soc. 1996; Chair. Div. of Chem., NAS 1974; Chair. Dept of Chem., Columbia Univ. 1976–; mem. Advisory Bd, Chemical and Engineering News 1980; Foreign mem. Royal Soc.; Chair. Bd of Scientific Advisers, Sloan Foundation 1981–; mem. Bd of Scientific Advisers, Gen. Motors 1982–; Centenary Lecturer, London Chemical Soc. 1972; Trustee, Rockefeller Univ. 1981–; A. R. Todd Visiting Prof., Univ. of Cambridge 1982; Foreign Fellow Indian Acad. of Science 1992; Annual Ciba Foundation Lecturer, London 1982; Hon. mem. Japan Chemical Soc. 2002; Foreign Hon. mem. Royal Soc. 2000; ACS Award in Pure Chem. 1966, Fresinius Award 1966, Mark van Doren Award 1969, Baekeland Medal 1969, Harrison Howe Award 1974, Remsen Medal 1977, Roussel Prize 1978, American Chemical Soc. James Flack Norris Award in Physical Organic Chemistry 1980, Richards Medal in Chemistry 1984, Arthur Cope Award 1987, George Kenner Award 1988, Nichols Medal 1989, Nat. Acad. of Sciences Chemistry Medal 1989, Paracelsus Medal, Swiss Chemical Soc. 1990, US Nat. Medal of Science 1991, Priestley Medal, American Chemical Soc. 1999, New York City Mayor's Award in Science 2002, ACS Bader Award in Bioorganic Chem. 2002, Esselen Award for Chem. in the Public Interest 2002. *Publications:* Organic Reaction Mechanisms 1965, Chemistry Today and Tomorrow 1996; over 400 scientific papers. *Leisure interest:* piano performance. *Address:* 566 Chandler Laboratories, Department of Chemistry, Columbia University, New York, NY 10027 (Office); 275 Broad Avenue, Englewood, NJ 07631, USA (Home). *Telephone:* (212) 854-2170. *E-mail:* rb33@columbia.edu (Office).

BRESSANI, Ricardo, PhD; Guatemalan biochemist; b. 28 Sept. 1926, Guatemala; s. of César Bressani and Primina Castignoli de Bressani; m. Alicia Herman 1949; five s. two d.; ed Univ. of Dayton, Iowa State Univ. and Purdue Univ.; Visiting Prof. MIT, Rutgers Univ.; Ed.-in-Chief, Archivos Latino-americanos de Nutrición; Head and Research Dir, Div. of Agric. and Food Sciences, Inst. of Nutrition of Cen. America and Panama (INCAP) 1988–; Head Food Science and Tech. Center, Research Inst. Univ. de Valle; mem. Directive Cttee Agroindustrial Rural Devt (PRODAR) Costa Rica 1991–; Corresp. Academic mem., Acad. of Medical, Physical and Natural Sciences of Guatemala 1990–; Foreign mem. NAS (USA); mem. American Inst. of Food Technologists, Acad. of Science of the Int. Union for Food Science and Tech.; Orden del Quetzal en el Grado de Gran Cruz 1999; Dr hc (Purdue), (Universidad del Valle de Guatemala); Babcock Hart Award 1970, McCollum

Award 1976, World Science Award 'Albert Einstein' 1984, Abraham Horowitz Award 1990, Ibero-American Prize in Science and Technology, Mexico 2001. *Publications:* over 500 scientific publications in related professional fields including books, monographs and articles in scientific journals. *Leisure interests:* swimming, horseback riding, agricultural conservation. *Address:* Institute of Nutrition of Central America and Panama, Calzada Roosevelt zona 11, 01011 Guatemala City (Office); Centro de Ciencia y Tecnología de Alimentos, Instituto de Investigaciones, Universidad del Valle de Guatemala, 18 avenida 11-95 zona 15, 01015, Vista Hermosa III, Guatemala City (Office); 6a calle 'A' 7-74 zona 9, Guatemala City, 01009 Guatemala (Home). *Telephone:* (502) 332-6125 (Home); (502) 472-3762 (Inst. of Nutrition); (502) 364-0336 (University). *Fax:* (502) 473-6529 (Inst. of Nutrition) (Office); (502) 364-0212 (University) (Office). *E-mail:* bressani@incap.org.gt (Office); bressani@ incap.ops-oms.org (Office); bressani@uvg.edu.gt (Office). *Website:* www.incap .org.gt (Inst. of Nutrition) (Office); www.uvg.edu.gt (University) (Office).

BRETH, Andrea; German theatre director; b. 31 Oct. 1952, Rieden, Allgau; d. of Prof. Herbert Breth and Maria Breth (née Noether); ed Darmstadt, Heidelberg; Dir Bremen, Hamburg, Berlin 1976, Zürich, Bochum 1980, Freiburg (Bernarda Albas Haus, Lorca) 1984, Schauspielhaus Bochum (Le Sud, Green; The Last, Gorki) 1986–90, Burgtheater, Vienna (Zerbrochener Krug, Kleist) 1990, Schaubühne Berlin (Einsamer Weg, Schnitzler) 1991 and (Nachtasyl, Gorki) 1992, Burgtheater Vienna (End of the Beginning, O'Casey) 1991, Tschulimsk, Wampilow (Letzten Sommer) 1992, Kaiser (Von morgens bis mitternachts) 1993, (Hedda Gabler) 1993, (Orestes) 1995 (Die Möwe) 1995; mem. Berlin Acad. of Arts; Deutscher Kritiker Preis, Nordrhein-Westfalen Literaturpreis, Kortner Preis. *Leisure interests:* literature, music, paintings, theatre. *Address:* c/o Schaubühne am Lehniner Platz, Kurfürstendamm 153, 10709 Berlin, Germany.

BRETON, Thierry; French business executive; b. 15 Jan. 1955; m.; three c.; ed Lycée Louis Le Grand, Supelec Electrical Eng. School, Paris and French Inst. for Nat. Defence Studies (IHEDN); nat. service as teacher of information tech. and math., French Lycée, New York 1979–81; Chair. and CEO Forma Systèmes 1981–86; Chief Adviser of Minister for Information and New Technologies, Ministry of Educ. and Research 1986–88; CEO Futurescope de Poitiers (science and tech. theme park) and CEO Futurescope Telecommunications Platform 1986–90; CEO CGI Group 1990–93; CEO and Vice-Chair. Bd Dirs Bull Group 1993–97; Chair. and CEO Thomson SA and Thomson Multimedia 1997–2002; Dir France Telecom 2002–, Chair. and CEO Oct. 2002–; mem. Bd Schneider Electric, Dexia, La Poste; mem. Supervisory Bd AXA; Chevalier, Légion d'honneur, Officier, Ordre nat. du Mérite. *Address:* France Telecom, 6 place d'Alleray, 75505 Paris Cédex 15, France (Office). *Telephone:* 1-44-44-89-34 (Office). *Fax:* 1-44-44-03-59 (Office). *Website:* www .francetelecom.fr (Office).

BRETSCHER, Mark Steven, MA, PhD, FRS; British/Swiss research scientist; b. 8 Jan. 1940, Cambridge; s. of Hanni Bretscher (née Greminger) and Egon Bretscher; m. Barbara M. F. Pearse 1978; one s. one d.; ed Abingdon School, Gonville and Caius Coll., Cambridge; Research student, Gonville and Caius Coll., Cambridge 1961–64; Scientific Staff mem. MRC, Lab. of Molecular Biology, Cambridge 1965–, Head, Div. of Cell Biology 1984–95; Visiting Prof. Harvard Coll., USA 1974–75, Stanford Univ., USA 1984–85; Friedrich-Miescher Prize 1979. *Publications:* scientific papers in professional journals. *Leisure interest:* silviculture. *Address:* Medical Research Council, Laboratory of Molecular Biology, Hills Road, Cambridge, CB2 2QH (Office); Ram Cottage, Commercial End, Swaffham Bulbeck, Cambridgeshire, CB5 0ND, England (Home). *Telephone:* (1223) 248011 (Office); (1223) 811276 (Home). *Fax:* (1223) 412142. *E-mail:* msb@mrc-lmb.cam.ac.uk (Office). *Website:* www2.mrc-lmb .cam.ac.uk/personal/bretscher/msb_home.html (Office).

BREUEL, Birgit; German business executive and politician; b. 1937, Hamburg; d. of late Alwin Münchmeyer and Gertrud Nolte; m. Ernst Breuel 1959; three s.; ed Univs. of Hamburg, Oxford and Geneva; mem. Hamburg State Parl. 1970; Minister of Econs Lower Saxony 1978, of Finance 1986–90; mem. CDU Bundesvorstand, Bonn 1986; Chief Exec. Treuhandanstalt, Berlin (formed to manage and/or sell all fmrly state-owned cos. in East Germany) 1990, Pres. 1991–95; Gen. Sec. Expo 2000, Hannover 1995–; mem. Bd Volkswagen AG, Norddeutsche Landesbank AG, Deutsche Bundesbahn AG, Salzgitter AG, PREAG; Chair. Bd Deutsche Messe AG, Hannover; adviser, Hamburg-Mannheimer Versicherung AG, Zweites Deutsches Fernsehen; coordinator and chief del. for EXPO 2000, Hannover 1995–2000; Senator, Max Planck Gesellschaft, Munich; Dr. hc (Cologne) 1994, Bernhard-Harms Medal 1994, Ludwig-Erhard Medal 1994. *Publications:* Es gibt kein Butterbrot umsonst 1976, Der Amtsschimmel absatteln 1979, Der Mensch lebt nicht nur von Umsatzzahlen 1987. *Address:* EXPO 2000 Hannover GmbH, EXPO Plaza11-Gelände, 30521 Hannover, Germany (Office).

BREUER, Rolf E., DJur; German banker; deputy mem. of Bd of Managing Dirs. Deutsche Bank AG, Frankfurt, CEO 1997–2000; Chair. Supervisory Bd Deutsche Grundbesitz Anlagegesellschaft mbH, Cologne, Deutsche Börse AG, Frankfurt, Deutsche Vermögensbildungsgesellschaft mbH, Frankfurt, Lombardkasse AG, Frankfurt; Vice-Chair. Supervisory Bd Deutscher Auslandskassenverein AG, Frankfurt, Frankfurter Kassenverein AG, Frankfurt; mem. of Bd Asia Fund Management Co. SA, Luxembourg; Chair. Deutsche Bank Capital Markets (Asia), Euro-Clear Clearance System Ltd, London; Vice-Chair. Deutsche Bank Capital Corp., Frankfurt, Deutsche Bank Capital

Markets Ltd, London and numerous other commercial appointments. *Address:* c/o Deutsche Bank, Taunusanlage 12, 60325, Frankfurt am Main, Germany (Office).

BREWER, Derek Stanley, LittD, PhD; British professor of English; b. 13 July 1923, Cardiff; s. of Stanley Leonard Brewer and Winifred Helen Forbes; m. Lucie Elisabeth Hoole 1951; three s. two d.; ed Crypt Grammar School, Gloucester, Magdalen Coll., Oxford; war service in infantry 1942–45; Asst Lecturer then lecturer, Univ. of Birmingham 1949–56, Sr Lecturer 1958–64; Prof. Int. Christian Univ., Tokyo 1956–58; lecturer, Univ. of Cambridge 1965–76, Reader 1976–83, Prof. 1983–90, Prof. Emer. 1990–; f. D. S. Brewer Ltd (now part of Boydell and Brewer), publrs of academic books; Fellow, Emmanuel Coll., Cambridge 1965–77, Master 1977–90, Life Fellow 1990–; Corresp. Fellow Medieval Soc. of America 1987; Franqui Prof. des Sciences Humaines (Belgium) 1998; Hon. Fellow English Asscn 2001; Hon. mem. Japan Acad. 1981; hon. degrees from Univs of Keio (Tokyo), Harvard, York, Birmingham, Paris IV (Sorbonne), Liège, Williams Coll., USA; Seatonian Prize for Poetry (ten times); Medal, Japan Acad. 1997; Medal des Sciences Humaines (Belgium) 1998. *Publications include:* Chaucer 1953, Proteus 1958, Chaucer's Parlement of Foulys (ed.) 1960, Malory's Morte d'Arthur Parts 7 and 8 (ed.) 1968, Chaucer and his World 1978, Symbolic Stories 1980, English Gothic Literature 1983, Introduction to Chaucer 1984, Medieval Comic Tales (ed.) 1996, A Critical Companion to the Gawain-poet (ed.) 1996, A New Introduction to Chaucer 1998, Seatonian Exercises and other verses 2000, The World of Chaucer 2000. *Leisure interests:* reading, walking. *Address:* Emmanuel College, Cambridge, CB2 3AP (Office); 240 Hills Road, Cambridge, CB2 2QE, England. *Telephone:* (1223) 210782 (Home); (1223) 334200. *Fax:* (1223) 241104. *E-mail:* dsb27@cam.ac.uk (Office); dsb27@cam .ac.uk (Home).

BREWER, Leo, PhD; American professor of chemistry; b. 13 June 1919, St Louis, Mo.; s. of Abraham Brewer and Hannah (Resnik) Brewer; m. Rose Strugo 1945; one s. two d.; ed Calif. Inst. of Tech. and Univ. of California (Berkeley); Research Assoc. Manhattan Dist Project, Univ. of Calif. (Berkeley); Research Assoc. Lawrence Berkeley Lab. (Univ. of Calif.) 1943–61, Head Inorganic Materials Div. 1961–75, Prin. Investigator 1961–94; Assoc. Dir Lawrence Berkeley Lab. 1975–; Asst Prof. Coll. of Chem., Univ. of Calif. 1946–50, Assoc. Prof. 1950–55, Prof. 1955–89, Prof. Emer. 1989–; mem. NAS 1959–, American Acad. of Arts and Sciences 1979–; Great Western Dow Fellow 1942, Guggenheim Fellow 1950, Berkeley Fellow 1992; several hon. lectureships 1963–67, 1970–72, 1974, 1979, 1981, 1983, 1986, 1989; Leo H. Baekland Award 1953, E. O. Lawrence Award 1961, Palladium Medal and Award of Electrochemical Soc. 1971, Distinguished Alumni Award (Calif. Inst. of Tech.) 1974, William Hume-Rothery Award 1983, Henry B. Linford Award 1988, Berkeley Citation 1989, Extractive Metallurgy Science Award 1991. *Publications:* Thermodynamics (co-author) 1961; and numerous articles in professional journals. *Leisure interest:* gardening. *Address:* Department of Chemistry MC 1460, University of California, Berkeley, CA 94720 (Office); 15 Vista del Orinda Road, Orinda, CA 94563, USA (Home). *Telephone:* (510) 643-5555. *Fax:* (510) 642-4136.

BREWER, Richard George, PhD; American atomic physicist; b. 8 Dec. 1928, Los Angeles; s. of Louis Ludwig and Elise Brewer; m. Lillian Magidow 1954; one s. two d.; ed California Inst. of Technology and Univ. of California, Berkeley; Instructor, Harvard Univ. 1958–60; Asst Prof., Univ. of Calif., Los Angeles 1960–63; IBM Research Staff mem., San José, Calif. 1963–73, 1973–94, Fellow Emer. 1994–; Consulting Prof., Applied Physics, Stanford Univ. 1977–; IBM Fellow; mem. NAS 1980; Fellow American Physical Soc. and Optical Soc. of America; Albert A. Michelson Gold Medal, Franklin Inst. 1979; Distinguished Alumni Award, CIT 1994, Charles H. Townes Silver Medal, Optical Soc. of America 2000. *Publications:* more than 145 papers in scientific journals. *Leisure interests:* growing magnolias, classical music, reading Italian literature. *E-mail:* rgbrewer@worldnet.att.net (Home).

BREYER, Stephen, BA, LLB; American judge; b. 15 Aug. 1938, San Francisco, Calif.; s. of Irving Breyer and Anne Breyer; m. Joanna Hare 1967; one s. two d.; ed Stanford Univ., Magdalen Coll. Oxford and Harvard Law School; law clerk to Mr Justice Goldberg, US Supreme Court 1964–65; Special Asst to Asst Attorney-Gen. Antitrust Div. US Dept of Justice 1965–67; Asst Prof. of Law, Harvard Univ. 1967–70; Prof. of Law, Harvard Law School 1970–80; Prof. Kennedy School of Govt Harvard Univ. 1977–80; lecturer, Harvard Law School 1981–; Asst Special Prosecutor, Watergate Special Prosecution Force 1973; Special Counsel, Admin. Practices Subcttee US Senate Judiciary Cttee 1974–75; Chief Counsel, Senate Judiciary Cttee 1979–80; Circuit Judge, US Court of Appeals for the First Circuit 1980–94, Chief Judge 1990–94; mem. US Sentencing Comm. 1985–89; Assoc. Justice, Supreme Court of USA 1994–; Visiting lecturer, Coll. of Law, Sydney 1975; Visiting Prof. Univ. of Rome 1993; Fellow, American Acad. of Arts and Sciences. *Publications:* The Federal Power Commission and the Regulation of Energy (with P. MacAvoy) 1974, Administrative Law and Regulatory Policy (with R. Stewart) 1979, Regulation and Its Reform 1982, Breaking the Vicious Circle: Towards Effective Risk Regulation 1993; numerous articles and book chapters. *Address:* Supreme Court of the United States, 1 First Street, NE, Washington, DC 20543, USA (Office). *Telephone:* (202) 479-3000 (Office).

BREZIGAR, Barbara; Slovenian politician and lawyer; b. 1 Dec. 1953, Ljubljana; ed Univ. of Ljubljana; Dist State Prosecutor, Ljubljana Public Prosecutor's Office 1980, Vice-Pres. 1994, Head of Office 1995, apptd. head of special team of prosecutors dealing with organized crime 1996–99; Supreme Court Prosecutor 1998–; affiliated with SDS party; Minister of Justice in caretaker Govt of Andrej Bajuk 2000; Presidential cand. 2001. *Address:* Supreme Court, Tavčarjeva 9, 1000 Ljubljana, Slovenia (Office).

BREZIS, Haim; French professor of mathematics; b. 1 June 1944, Riom-ès-Montagnes; s. of Jacob Brezis and Rebecca Brezis; m. Michal Govrin 1982; two d.; ed Univ. of Paris; Prof. Pierre et Marie Curie Univ. 1974–, Inst. Universitare de France 1997–; Visiting Prof. New York Univ., Univ. of Chicago, Princeton Univ., MIT, Hebrew Univ.; Visiting Distinguished Prof. Rutgers Univ.; mem. Acad. des Sciences, Academia Europaea; Foreign Hon. Mem. American Acad. of Arts and Sciences; Hon. mem. Romanian Acad., Hon. mem. Real Academia Madrid, Royal Acad. of Belgium; numerous hon. degrees; Prix. Ampère 1985. *Publications:* Analyse Fonctionnelle 1983, Ginzburg-Landau vortices 1994, Un mathématicien juif 1999. *Leisure interest:* Hebraic studies. *Address:* Analyse Numérique, Université Pierre et Marie Curie, 4 place Jussieu, 75252 Paris Cedex 05 (Office); 18 rue de la Glacière, 75013 Paris Cedex 13, France (Home). *Telephone:* 1-44-27-42-98 (Office); 1-43-36-15-10 (Home). *Fax:* 1-44-27-72-00. *E-mail:* brezis@ccr.jussieu.fr (Office).

BRIALY, Jean-Claude; French actor and director; b. 30 March 1933, Aumale, Algeria; s. of Roger Brialy and Suzanne Abraham; ed Coll. St-Etienne and Conservatoire d'art dramatique, Strasbourg; Dir Théâtre Hébertot 1977, Théâtre des Bouffes Parisiens 1986–, Anjou Festival 1985–; numerous stage, TV and film appearances; Officier Légion d'honneur, Commdr Ordre nat. du Mérite, Commdr des Arts et des Lettres; recipient of César awards for roles in films Julie pot de colle 1976 and Les Innocents 1988. *Films directed include:* Eglantine 1971 (Prix Jean Le Duc, Acad. Française), Les Volets clos 1973, L'Oiseau rare 1973, Un amour de pluie 1974, Quelques hommes de bonne volonté, Un Bon petit diable 1983, L'Homme de vie (also actor) 1999, Les Acteurs (also actor) 2000, In Extremes (also actor) 2000. *Other films include:* La nuit de Varennes 1982, La Fille de Trieste, Sarah, Cap canaille, Mortelle randonnée, Le Démon dans l'île, Edith et Marcel, Stella, Le Crime 1983, Pinot simple flic 1984, Le Mariage du siècle 1985, Inspecteur Lavardin, Suivez mon regard, Le Débutant 1986, Grand guignol, Lévy et Goliath, Le Moustachu, Maladie d'amour 1987, Comédie d'Eté, Au bonheur des chiens 1990, S'en Fout la Mort 1990, Août 1992, Les Cents et Une Nuits 1995, L'Homme de ma vie 1999, Les Acteurs 2000, In Extremis 2000. *Television appearances include:* Quelques Hommes de Bonne Volonté 1983, Mariage Mortel 1991. *Theatre appearances include:* Le Nègre 1986, La Jalousie 1992, Mon père avait raison 1999. *Publication:* Les Volets clos 1973, Le Ruisseau des singes 2000. *Leisure interests:* collecting old watches and books, swimming and riding. *Address:* Théâtre des Bouffes Parisiens, 4 rue Monsigny, 75002 Paris (Office); 25 Quai Bourbon, 75004 Paris (Home); Château de Monthyon, 77122 Monthyon, France (Home).

BRIANÇON, Pierre, LLM; French journalist; b. 3 Aug. 1954, Tunis, Tunisia; s. of Claude Briançon and Geneviève Pochard; three c.; ed Université Paris II, Institut d'Etudes Politiques, Paris; journalist, Forum International 1979; Econs and Business Ed. Libération 1981–88, Moscow Corresp. 1988–91, USA Bureau Chief, Washington 1992–95, Ed.-in-Chief 1996–98; contrib. France Inter radio 1982–86; Asst. Editorial Dir. L'expansion 1998–2000; Dir. Startup Avenue (econ. information site) 2000–; Pres., Dir.-Gen. B to B Avenue.com. *Publications:* A Droite en sortant de la gauche? 1986, Héritiers du désastre 1992. *Address:* B to B Avenue, 12 rue Charlot, 75003 Paris, France (Office).

BRICEÑO, Hon. John, BBA; Belizean politician; b. 17 July 1960, Orange Walk Town; m. Rossana Briceño; two s.; ed Muffles High School, St. John's Coll., Belize City, Univ. of Texas at Austin, USA; MP for Orange Walk Cen. Div. (People's United Party) 1993–; Deputy Prime Minister 1998–, also Minister of Natural Resources and the Environment 1998–, of Commerce Trade and Industry 1999–. *Leisure interests:* reading, music, cinema. *Address:* Office of the Deputy Prime Minister, Ministry of Natural Resources, the Environment, Commerce, Trade and Industry, Belmopan, Belize (Office). *Telephone:* 822-630 (Office). *Fax:* 822-2333 (Office). *E-mail:* lincenbze@btl.net (Office). *Website:* www.belize.gov.bz.

BRIDGEMAN, John Stuart, CBE, TD, DL, BSc, CIMgt, FRSA, FRGS, FID; British business executive; b. 5 Oct. 1944; s. of the late James Alfred George Bridgeman and Edith Celia Bridgeman (née Watkins); m. Lindy Jane Fillmore 1967; three d.; ed Whitchurch School, Cardiff, Univ. Coll., Swansea, McGill Univ., Montreal; with Alcan Industries 1966–69, Aluminium Co. of Canada 1969–70, Alcan Australia 1970, Commercial Dir Alcan UK 1977–80, Vice-Pres. (Europe) Alcan Basic Raw Materials 1978–82, Man. Dir Extrusion Div. British Alcan Aluminium PLC 1983–87, British Alcan Enterprises 1987–91, Dir Corp. Planning Alcan Aluminium Ltd, Montreal 1992–93, Man. Dir British Alcan Aluminium PLC 1993–95, Monopolies and Mergers Comm. 1990–95; Dir.-Gen. of Fair Trading 1995–2000; Dir Regulatory Impact Unit, Cardew & Co. Corp. Financial Advisers 2000–; Chair. Dir Marketing Authority 2000–; Oxford Psychologists Press; Consultant with law firm Norton Rose; Chair. Standards Cttee Worcs. Co. Council; Visiting Prof. of Man. Keele Univ. 1992–, Imperial Coll. London 2001–; Chair. N Oxon. Business Group 1984–92, Enterprise Cherwell Ltd 1985–91, N Oxon Coll. 1989; Vice-Pres. Aluminium Fed. 1995, UK-Canada Chamber of Commerce 1995–96 (Pres. 1997–98); Gov. N Oxon Coll. 1985–98; Deputy Chair. Heart of England Trading and Enterprise Council 1989–, Chair. 2000–; Chair. Oxfordshire Econ. Partnership 2000–; Commissioned TA and Reserve Forces 1978, Queen's Own Yeomanry 1981–84, Maj. REME (V) 1985–94, Staff Coll. 1986,

mem. Territorial Auxiliary and Volunteer Reserve Asscn Oxon. and E Wessex 1985–2000; mem. British Airways NE Consumer Council 1978–81, Defence Science Advisory Council 1991–94, Nat. Employer Liaison Cttee for Reserve Forces 1992– (Chair. 1997–), UK–Canada Colloquium 1993–2000; numerous trusteeships; High Sheriff, Oxon. 1995–96; DL (Oxon.) 1989; US Aluminum Asscn Prize 1988; FRGS; Dr hc (Sheffield Hallam) 1996; Fellow, Univ. of Wales, Swansea 1997. *Leisure interests:* education, gardening, public affairs, shooting, skiing. *Address:* Regulatory Impact Unit, Cardew & Co., 12 Suffolk Street, London, SW1Y 4HQ (Office); The Reform Club, 104 Piccadilly, London, SW1Y 5EW, England. *Telephone:* (20) 7930-0777 (Office). *Fax:* (20) 7925-0646 (Office). *E-mail:* john@cardew.co.uk (Office). *Website:* www.cardew.co.uk (Office).

BRIDGEMAN, Viscountess Victoria Harriet Lucy, MA, FRSA; British fine arts specialist, library executive and editor; b. 30 March 1942, Co. Durham; d. of Ralph Meredyth Turton and Mary Blanche Turton (née Chetwynd Stapylton); m. Viscount Bridgeman 1966; four s. (one deceased); ed St Mary's School, Wantage, Trinity Coll., Dublin; Exec. Ed. The Masters 1965–69; Ed. Discovering Antiques 1970–72; est. own co. producing books and articles on fine and decorative arts; f., Man. Dir The Bridgeman Art Library; European Woman of the Year (Arts Section) Award 1997. *Publications:* Encyclopaedia of Victoriana, Needlework: An Illustrated History, The British Eccentric 1975, Society Scandals 1977, Beside the Seaside 1977, Guide to the Gardens of Europe 1980, The Last Word 1982 (all jtly. with Elizabeth Drury), eight titles in Connoisseur's Library series. *Leisure interests:* reading, family, travel. *Address:* The Bridgeman Art Library, 17–19 Garway Road, London, W2 4PH (Office); The Bridgeman Art Library International, 65 East 93rd Street, New York 10128, USA (Office); The Bridgeman Art Library, 36 rue des Bourdonnais, 75001 Paris, France (Office); 19 Chepstow Road, London, W2 5BP; Watley House, Sparsholt, Nr. Winchester, Hants., SO21 2LU, England. *Telephone:* (20) 7727-4065 (Office); (20) 7727-5400 (London); (1962) 776297 (Hants.). *Fax:* (20) 7792-8509 (Office); (20) 7792-9178 (Home); (1962) 776297 (Hants.). *E-mail:* harriet@bridgeman.co.uk (Office). *Website:* www .bridgeman.co.uk (Office).

BRIDGES, Alan; British film director; b. 28 Sept. 1927, Liverpool; m. Eileen Middleton 1954; one s. one d.; Dir of numerous films and dramas for TV including The Intrigue, The Ballad of Peckham Rye, Alarm Call: Z Cars, The Brothers Karamazov, The Idiot, Days to Come, Great Expectations, Les Miserables, Dear Brutus, Army Captain (376285); Palme d'Or, Cannes Film Festival, Golden Globe, Emmy Award, Moscow Film Festival Award. *Films include:* Act of Murder, Invasion, The Lie, The Wild Duck, Shelley, The Hireling (Palme d'Or, Best Film, Cannes Festival 1973), Brief Encounter, Out of Season, Summer Rain, The Girl in Blue Velvet, Very Like a Whale, Rain on the Roof, The Return of the Soldier, The Shooting Party, Displaced Persons, Apt Pupil, Secret Places of the Heart, Fire Princess, Pig Robinson. *Leisure interests:* reading, music, sport, theatre. *Address:* 29 Nursery Gardens, Sunbury-on-Thames, Middx, TW16 6LQ, England.

BRIDGES, Jeff; American actor; b. 4 Dec. 1949, Los Angeles; s. of the late Lloyd Bridges and of Dorothy Bridges; m. Susan Bridges; three d.; acting début at the age of 8. *Films include:* Halls of Anger 1970, The Last Picture Show 1971, Fat City 1971, Bad Company 1972, The Last American Hero 1973, The Iceman Cometh 1973, Thunderbolt and Lightfoot 1974, Hearts of the West 1975, Rancho Deluxe 1975, King Kong 1976, Stay Hungry 1976, Somebody Killed her Husband 1978, Winter Kills 1979, The American Success Company 1980, Heaven's Gate 1980, Cutter's Way 1981, Tron 1982, Kiss Me Goodbye 1982, The Last Unicorn 1982, Starman 1984, Against All Odds 1984, Jagged Edge 1985, 8 Million Ways to Die 1986, The Morning After 1986, Nadine 1987, Tucker, the Man and his Dream 1988, See You in the Morning 1990, Texasville 1990, The Fabulous Baker Boys 1990, The Fisher King 1991, American Heart, The Vanishing, Blown Away 1994, Fearless 1994, Wild Bill, White Squall 1995, The Mirror Has Two Faces 1996, The Big Lebowski 1997, Arlington Road 1998, Simpatico 1999, The Muse 1999, The Contender 2000, Raising the Hammoth (TV, voice) 2000, K-Pax 2002, Lost in La Mancha (voice) 2002. *Address:* c/o Rick Nicita, Creative Artists Agency, 9830 Wilshire Boulevard, Beverly Hills, CA 90212, USA.

BRIDGES, 2nd Baron; Thomas Edward Bridges, GCMG, MA; British diplomatist (retd); b. 27 Nov. 1927, London; s. of Edward, 1st Baron Bridges, KG, and Hon. Katharine D. Farrer; m. Rachel M. Bunbury 1953; two s. one d.; ed Eton and New Coll., Oxford; joined diplomatic service 1951; served Bonn, Berlin, Rio de Janeiro, Athens and Moscow; Asst Private Sec. to Foreign Sec. 1963–66; Private Sec. (Overseas Affairs) to Prime Minister 1972–74; Commercial Minister, Washington, DC 1976–79; Deputy Sec. (for int. econ. affairs), FCO 1979–83; Amb. to Italy 1983–87; Dir Consolidated Gold Fields PLC 1988–89; mem. Select Cttee on the European Communities, House of Lords 1988–92, 1994–98; Chair. UK Nat. Cttee of UNICEF 1989–97; Ind. Bd mem. Securities and Futures Authority Ltd 1989–97, Pres. Dolmetsch Foundation; Trustee Rayne Foundation. *Address:* 56 Church Street, Orford, Woodbridge, Suffolk, IP12 2NT, England.

BRIERLEY, Sir Ronald Alfred; New Zealand business executive; b. 2 Aug. 1937, Wellington; s. of J. R. Brierley; ed Wellington Coll.; Chair. Brierley Investments Ltd 1961–89 (Founder 1961, Founder Pres. 1990–); Deputy Chair. Bank of NZ 1987–89; Chair. Industrial Equity Pacific Ltd 1966–90, Guinness Peat Gp. PLC 1990–, Tozer Kemsley & Millbourn Holdings PLC 1986, The Citizens & Graziers Life Assurance Co. Ltd 1990–91; Dir Ariadne

Australia Ltd 1989–91, The Australian Gas Light Co. 1987–, Australian Oil & Gas Corpn Ltd, Mid-East Minerals Ltd 1992–, Metals Exploration Ltd 1992–, Tyndall Australia Ltd 1992–, Advance Bank Australia 1990–; mem. NZ Cricket Council, NZ Cricket Foundation; Dir Sydney Cricket & Sports Ground Trust. *Leisure interests:* cricket, ballet, stamp collecting, chess. *Address:* Guinness Peat Group PLC, 2nd Floor, 21–26 Garlick Hill, London, EC4V 2AU, England.

BRIERS, Richard David, OBE; British actor; b. 14 Jan. 1934, Merton; s. of Joseph Briers and Morna Richardson; m. Ann Davies 1957; two d.; ed Rokeby Prep. School, Wimbledon, Ridgeway School, Wimbledon and Royal Acad. of Dramatic Art; Hon. DLit (South Bank Univ.); Royal TV Soc. Hall of Fame 1996, Comic Heritage Lifetime Achievement Award 2000. *Films:* Henry V 1988, Much Ado About Nothing 1992, Swan Song 1993, Mary Shelley's Frankenstein 1995, In the Bleak Midwinter 1995, Hamlet 1996, Love's Labours Lost 1999, Unconditional Love 2000. *Stage roles include:* Gilt and Gingerbread 1956, Arsenic and Old Lace 1965, Relatively Speaking 1966, The Real Inspector Hound 1968, Cat Among the Pigeons 1969, The Two of Us 1970, Butley 1972, Absurd Person Singular 1973, Absent Friends 1975, Middle Age Spread 1979, The Wild Duck 1980, Arms and the Man 1981, Run for Your Wife 1983, Why Me? 1985, The Relapse 1986, Twelfth Night 1987, King Lear 1990, Midsummer Night's Dream 1990, Coriolanus 1991, Uncle Vanya 1991, Home 1994, A Christmas Carol 1996, The Chairs 1997, Spike 1999, Bedroom Farce 2002. *Television series include:* Brothers-in-Law, Marriage Lines, The Good Life, OneUpManShip, the Other One, Norman Conquests, Ever-Decreasing Circles, All in Good Faith, Monarch of the Glen. *Publications:* Natter Natter 1981, Coward and Company 1987, A Little Light Weeding 1993, A Taste of the Good Life 1995. *Leisure interests:* gardening, reading. *Address:* Hamilton Asper Management, Ground Floor, 24 Hanway Street, London, W1P 9DD, England. *Telephone:* (20) 7636-1221.

BRIGGS, Baron (Life Peer), cr. 1976, of Lewes in the County of Sussex; **Asa Briggs,** BSc, MA, FBA; British historian; b. 7 May 1921, Keighley, Yorks.; s. of William Walker Briggs and Jane Briggs; m. Susan Anne Banwell 1955; two s. two d.; ed Keighley Grammar School and Sidney Sussex Coll., Cambridge; Fellow, Worcester Coll., Oxford 1945–55, Reader in Recent Social and Econ. History, Univ. of Oxford 1950–55; Prof. of Modern History, Leeds Univ. 1955–61; Prof. of History, Univ. of Sussex 1961–76, Dean of Social Studies 1961–65, Pro-Vice-Chancellor 1961–67, Vice-Chancellor 1967–76; Provost Worcester Coll., Oxford 1976–91; Chancellor, Open Univ. 1979–94; Pres. Workers Educational Asscn 1958–67; Chair. Appts Comm. Press Council 1972–88; mem. Univ. Grants Cttee 1959–67; Trustee, Int. Broadcast Inst. 1968–86, Hon. Trustee 1990–; Gov. British Film Inst. 1970–76, Chair. European Inst. of Educ. 1974–84; mem. Council of UN Univ. 1974–80; Chair. Cttee on Nursing 1970–72, Heritage Educ. Group 1976–86, Commonwealth of Learning 1988–93; Pres. Social History Soc. 1976–, Ephemera Soc. 1984–, Victorian Soc. 1983–; Vice-Pres. Historical Asscn 1986–; Vice-Chair. of Council, UN Univ. 1974–80; Hon. mem. American Acad. of Arts and Sciences 1970–; Hon. LLD, Hon. DLitt, Hon. DSc; Marconi Medal for Services to Study of Broadcasting 1975, Medal of French Acad. for Architecture 1982, Wolfson History Prize 2001. *Publications:* Patterns of Peacemaking (with D. Thomson and E. Meyer) 1945, History of Birmingham, 1865–1938 1952, Victorian People 1954, Friends of the People 1956, The Age of Improvement 1959 (revised Edn 2000), Ed. Chartist Studies 1959, History of Broadcasting, Vol. I 1961, Vol. II 1965, Vol. III 1970, Vol. IV 1979, Vol. V 1995, Victorian Cities 1963, The Nineteenth Century (ed.) 1970, Cap and Bell (with Susan Briggs) 1972, Essays in the History of Publishing (ed.) 1974, Essays in Labour History 1918–1939 1977, Governing the BBC 1979, From Coalbrookdale to the Crystal Palace 1980, The Power of Steam 1982, Marx in London 1982, A Social History of England 1983 (Haut-Brion: An Illustrious Lineage 1994), The BBC—The First Fifty Years 1985, The Collected Essays of Asa Briggs, (Vol. 1, 2, 3), The Franchise Affair (with Joanna Spicer) 1986, Victorian Things 1988, The Longman Encyclopedia (ed.) 1989, The Channel Islands: Occupation and Liberation 1940–45 1995, Fins de Siècle (co-ed.) 1996; co-author Modern Europe 1789–1989 1996, The History of Bethlem 1997, Chartism 1998, Go to It! War: Working for Victory on the Home Front, 1939–45, Michael Young: Social Entrepreneur 2000, A Social History of the Media (with Peter Burke) 2002. *Leisure interest:* travel. *Address:* 26 Oakmede Way, Ringmer, East Sussex, BN8 5JL (Office); The Caprons, Keere Street, Lewes, Sussex, England (Home). *Telephone:* (1273) 814472 (Office); (1273) 474704 (Home). *Fax:* (1273) 814462 (Office); (1273) 474704 (Home). *E-mail:* veronicahumphrey@tinyworld.co.uk.

BRIGGS, Raymond Redvers, N.D.D., DFA; British writer, illustrator and cartoonist; b. 18 Jan. 1934, Wimbledon; s. of Ernest R. Briggs and Ethel Bowyer; m. Jean T. Clark 1963 (died 1973); ed Rutlish School, Merton, Wimbledon School of Art and Slade School of Fine Art, London; freelance illustrator 1957–; children's author 1961–; awards include Kate Greenaway Medal 1966, 1973, BAFTA Award, Francis Williams Illustration Award (Victoria & Albert Museum) 1982, Broadcasting Press Guild Radio Award 1983, Children's Author of the Year Award 1992, Kurt Maschler Award 1992, Illustrated Book of the Year Award 1998, Smarties Silver Award 2001. *Publications:* The Strange House 1961, Midnight Adventure 1961, Sledges to the Rescue 1963, Ring-a-Ring o' Roses 1962, The White Land 1963, Fee Fi Fo Fum 1964, The Mother Goose Treasury 1966, Jim and the Beanstalk 1970, The Fairy Tale Treasury 1972, Father Christmas 1973 (also film version), Father Christmas Goes on Holiday 1975, Fungus the Bogeyman 1977, The

Snowman 1978 (also film version), Gentleman Jim 1980 (also stage version), When the Wind Blows 1982 (stage and radio version 1983, animated film version 1987), The Tinpot Foreign General and the Old Iron Woman 1984, The Snowman Pop-Up 1986, Unlucky Wally 1987, Unlucky Wally Twenty Years On 1989, The Man 1992, The Bear 1994 (also film version), Ethel and Ernest 1998, UG 2001. *Leisure interests:* second-hand books, walking, gardening, fishing. *Address:* Weston, Underhill Lane, nr Hassocks, Sussex, England.

BRIGGS, Winslow Russell, MA, PhD; American biologist; b. 29 April 1928, St Paul, Minn.; s. of John Briggs and Marjorie (Winslow) Briggs; m. Ann Morrill 1955; three d.; ed Harvard Univ.; Instructor in Biological Sciences, Stanford Univ. 1955–57, Asst Prof. 1957–62, Assoc. Prof. 1962–66, Prof. 1966–67, 1973–93; Dir Dept of Plant Biology, Carnegie Inst. of Washington, Stanford 1973–93; Prof. of Biology, Harvard Univ. 1967–73; Guggenheim Fellow 1973–74; mem. Nat. Acad. of Sciences; Stephen Hales Award American Society of Plant Physiologists 1994, Sterling Hendricks Award, American Chem. Soc. and US Dept of Agric. 1995; Philip C. Hamm Award (Minn.) 1999; Anton Lang Memorial Lecturer, Mich. State Univ. 1999, Finsen Medal, Asscn Int. de Photobiologie. *Publications:* Life on Earth (with others) 1973; over 200 articles in professional journals. *Leisure interests:* hiking, Chinese cooking, park volunteer. *Address:* Department of Plant Biology, Carnegie Institution of Washington, 260 Panama St, Palo Alto, CA 94305 (Office); 480 Hale Street, Palo Alto, CA 94301-2207, USA (Home). *Telephone:* (650) 325-1521 (Office); (650) 324-1455 (Home). *Fax:* (650) 325-6857 (Office). *E-mail:* briggs@andrew2 .stanford.edu (Office).

BRIGHTMAN, Baron (Life Peer), cr. 1982, of Ibthorpe in the County of Hampshire; **John Anson Brightman,** Kt, PC; British lawyer; b. 20 June 1911, St Albans, Herts.; s. of William Henry Brightman and Minnie Boston Brightman (née Way); m. Roxane Ambatielo 1945; one s.; ed Marlborough Coll., St John's Coll., Cambridge; called to the bar, Lincoln's Inn 1932; Able Seaman 1939–40; Lt-Commdr RDVR 1940–46; Asst Naval Attaché Ankara 1944; QC 1961; Bencher 1966; Attorney-Gen., Duchy of Lancaster 1969–70; Judge, High Court 1970–79; a Lord Justice of Appeal 1979–82; a Lord of Appeal in Ordinary 1982–86; Judge, Nat. Industrial Relations Court 1971–74; mem. Gen. Council of the Bar 1956–60, 1966–70, Cttee on Parl. Procedures for Tax Simplification 1996, Ecclesiastical Cttee 1997–, Advisory Cttee, Inst. of Advanced Legal Studies 2000–, Jt Cttee on Tax Simplification Bills 2001; Hon. Fellow, St John's Coll., Cambridge 1982; Hon. FRGS 2000. *Leisure interests:* arctic travel, sailing, skiing, mountain walking. *Address:* House of Lords, London, SW1A 0PW, England. *Telephone:* (20) 7219-2034. *Fax:* (20) 7219-5979 (Office).

BRIGHTMAN, Sarah; British actress and singer; d. of Grenville Brightman and Pauline Brightman (née Hall); m. Andrew Lloyd Webber 1984 (divorced 1990); partner Frank Peterson; fmr mem. Pan's People and Hot Gossip groups; concerts world-wide. *Performances include:* Cats, Requiem, The Phantom of the Opera, Aspects of Love (music all by Andrew Lloyd Webber), I and Albert, The Nightingale, The Merry Widow, Trelawney of the Wells, Relative Values, Dangerous Obsession, The Innocents. *Albums include:* Eden 1999. *Address:* c/o Sunhand Limited, 63 Grosvenor Street, London, W1X 9DA, England. *Telephone:* (20) 7493-7831.

BRIGHTY, (Anthony) David, CMG, CVO; British diplomatist (retd); b. 7 Feb. 1939; m. 1st Diana Porteous 1963 (divorced 1979, died 1993); two s. two d.; m. 2nd Jane Docherty 1982 (divorced 1996); m. 3rd Susan Olivier 1997; ed Clare Coll. Cambridge; entered FCO 1961; Third Sec. Brussels 1962–64; Third Sec. Havana 1964–66, Second Sec. 1966–67; FCO 1967–69; Asst Man. S.G. Warburg & Co. 1969–71; FCO 1971–73; Head of Chancery, Saigon 1973–75; First Sec. UK Mission, New York 1975–78; Royal Coll. of Defence Studies 1979; FCO 1979–83; Counsellor, Lisbon 1983–86; Dir of Cabinet of Sec.-Gen. to NATO, FCO 1986–87; Amb. to Cuba 1989–91; Amb. to Czech Repub. and Slovakia (non-resident) 1991–94; Amb. to Spain and Andorra (non-resident) 1994–98; Dir (non-exec.) EFG Pvt. Bank 1999–; Chair. Co-ordinating Cttee on Remuneration (NATO, OECD, etc.) 1999–; Dir (non-exec.) Henderson European Microcap Trust 2000–; Chair. Anglo-Spanish Soc. 2001–; Robin Humphries Fellow, ILAS, Univ. of London 2003. *Address:* 15 Provost Road, London, NW3 4ST, England.

BRILLINGER, David Ross, PhD, FRSC; Canadian professor of statistics; b. 27 Oct. 1937, Toronto; s. of Austin C. Brillinger and Winnifred E Simpson; m. Lorie Silber 1961; two s.; ed Univ. of Toronto and Princeton Univ.; lecturer in Math. Princeton Univ., concurrently mem. tech. staff, Bell Telephone Labs. 1962–64; lecturer, then Reader, LSE 1964–69; Prof. of Statistics, Univ. of Calif. Berkeley 1969–; International Statistical Review 1987–9; Guggenheim Fellow 1975–76, 1982–83; Fellow American Acad. of Arts and Sciences 1993; Wald Lecturer 1983; R. A. Fisher Award 1991, Gold Medal, Statistical Soc. of Canada 1992. *Publications:* Time Series: Data Analysis and Theory 1975, Directions in Time Series 1980. *Address:* Department of Statistics, University of California, Berkeley, CA 94720, USA. *Telephone:* (510) 642-0611.

BRIM, Orville Gilbert, Jr., PhD; American foundation administrator and author; b. 7 April 1923, Elmira, New York; s. of Orville Gilbert and Helen Whittier Brim; m. Kathleen J. Vigneron 1944; two s. two d.; ed Yale Univ.; Instructor in Sociology, Univ. of Wis. 1952–53, Asst Prof., Sociology 1953–55; Sociologist, Russell Sage Foundation, New York 1955–60, Asst Sec. 1960–64, Pres. 1964–72; author and consultant 1972–74; Pres. Foundation for Child Devt 1974–85; Chair. Bd of Dirs., Automation Eng Lab. 1959–67, Special Comm. on the Social Sciences, Nat. Science Foundation 1968–69; mem. Drug

Research Bd, NAS 1964–65; Vice-Chair., Bd of Trustees, American Insts. for Research 1971–88, Chair. 1988–90; MacArthur Foundation Research Program on Successful Aging 1986–89; Dir McArthur Foundation Research Network on Successful Midlife Devt 1989–2002; Pres. Life Trends Inc. 1991–2002; Interim Pres. Social Science Research Council 1998–99; Kurt Lewin Memorial Award 1979, Soc. Research in Child Devt Award for Distinguished Scientific Contribs. to Child Devt Research 1985, American Psychological Asscn Presidential Citation 2003. *Publications:* Sociology and the Field of Education 1958, Education for Child Rearing 1959, Personality and Decision Processes 1962, Intelligence: Perspectives 1965, Socialization after Childhood: Two Essays 1966, American Beliefs and Attitudes Toward Intelligence 1969, The Dying Patient 1970; Ed.: Lifespan Development and Behavior, Vols II–VI 1979–84, Constancy and Change in Human Development 1980, Ambition: How we manage success and failure throughout our lives 1992, How Healthy Are We?: A National Study of Well-being at Midlife 2003. *Leisure interests:* sports and world ocean beaches. *Address:* 2029 Club Drive, Vero Beach, FL 32963, USA (Home). *Telephone:* (772) 231-3329 (Home).

BRINDLE, Ian, FCA, BA; British business executive; b. 17 Aug. 1943; s. of John Brindle and Mabel Brindle (née Walsh); m. Frances Elisabeth Moseby 1967; two s. one d.; ed Blundells School, Manchester Univ.; articled Price Waterhouse London 1965, Toronto 1975, partner 1976–2001, mem. Supervisory Cttee 1988–98, Dir Auditing and Business Advisory Services 1990–91, Sr Partner 1991–98; Chair. PricewaterhouseCoopers UK (following merger with Coopers and Lybrand) 1998–2001, Sr Partner UK 1991–98; mem. Auditing Practices Cttee Consultancy Cttee of Accounting Bodies 1986–90, Chair. 1990; mem. Accounting Standards Bd 1993–2001; mem. Council Inst. of Chartered Accountants in England and Wales 1994–97; mem. Financial Reporting Council 1995–; Deputy Chair. Financial Reporting Review Panel 2001–. *Leisure interests:* tennis, golf, classical music. *Address:* c/o Financial Reporting Review Panel, Holborn Hall, 100 Gray's Inn Road, London, WC1X 8AL (Office); Milestones, Packhorse Road, Bessels Green, Sevenoaks, Kent, TN13 2QP, England (Home). *Website:* www.frrp.org.uk/committee.

BRINDLEY, Giles Skey, MA, MD, FRCP, FRS; British physiologist; b. Giles Skey, 30 April 1926, Woking, Surrey; s. of the late Arthur James Benet Skey and Dr Margaret Beatrice Marion Skey (née Dewhurst), later Brindley; m. 1st Lucy Dunk Bennell 1959 (divorced); m. 2nd Dr Hilary Richards 1964; one s. one d.; ed Leyton Co. High School, Downing Coll., Cambridge, London Hosp. Medical School; clinical and research posts 1950–54; Russian Language Abstractor, British Abstracts of Medical Sciences 1953–56; Demonstrator, then Lecturer and Reader in Physiology, Univ. of Cambridge 1954–68; Prof. of Physiology, Univ. of London Inst. of Psychiatry 1968–91, Prof. Emer. 1991–; Hon. Dir MRC Neurological Prostheses Unit 1968–92; partner Brindley Surgical Implants 1991–2001; Hon. Consultant Physician Maudsley Hosp. 1971–92; Hon. FRCS 1988, Hon. FRCSE 2000; Fellow King's Coll., Cambridge 1959–62, Trinity Coll., Cambridge 1963–68; Chair. Editorial Bd Journal of Physiology 1964–66; Visiting Prof. Univ. of Calif., Berkeley 1968; Liebrecht-Franceschetti Prize, German Ophthalmological Soc. 1971, Feldberg Prize, Feldberg Foundation 1974, St Peter's Medal, British Asscn of Urological Surgeons 1987. *Publications:* Physiology of the Retina and Visual Pathway 1960, numerous scientific papers. *Leisure interests:* designing and playing musical instruments, composing chamber music. *Address:* 102 Ferndene Road, London, SE24 0AA, England (Home). *Telephone:* (20) 7274-2598. *E-mail:* gsbrindley@rcsed.ac.uk (Home).

BRINDLEY, Lynne Janie, MA, FLA, FRSA; British librarian; b. 2 July 1950, London; d. of Ivan Blowers and Janie Blowers (née Williams); adopted d. of Ronald Williams and Elaine Williams (née Chapman); m. Timothy Stuart Brindley 1972; ed Truro High School, Univ. of Reading, Univ. Coll. London; Head of Marketing and of Chief Exec.'s Office, British Library 1979–85, Chief Exec. British Library 2000–; Dir of Library and Information Services, also Pro-Vice Chancellor, Aston Univ. 1985–90; Prin. Consultant, KPMG 1990–92; Librarian and Dir of Information Services, LSE 1992–97; Librarian and Pro-Vice Chancellor, Univ. of Leeds 1997–2000, Visiting Prof. of Knowledge Man., 2000–; Visiting Prof. of Information Man., Leeds Metropolitan Univ. 2000–; mem., Int. Cttee on Social Science Information, UNESCO 1992–97, Lord Chancellor's Advisory Cttee on Public Records 1992–98, Stanford Univ. Advisory Council for Libraries and Information Resources 1999; Trustee, Thackray Medical Museum, Leeds 1999–; mem. Resource Bd 2002–, EPSRC User Panel 2002–; Hon. DLitt (Nottingham Univ.) 2001, (Oxford) 2002, (Leicester) 2002, Hon. DPhil (London Guildhall) 2002; Fellow, Univ. Coll. London 2002; Freeman, City of London 1989; Liveryman, Goldsmiths' Co. 1993. *Publications:* numerous articles on electronic libraries and information man. *Leisure interests:* classical music, theatre, modern art, hill walking. *Address:* The British Library, 96 Euston Road, London, NW1 2DB (Office); 85 New River Head, 173 Rosebery Avenue, London, EC1R 4UP, England (Home). *Telephone:* (20) 7412-7273 (Office). *Fax:* (20) 7412-7268 (Office). *E-mail:* chief-executive@bl.uk (Office). *Website:* www.bl.uk (Office).

BRINK, André Philippus; South African writer; b. 29 May 1935, Vrede; s. of Daniel and Aletta (née Wolmarans) Brink; m.; three s. one d.; ed Potchefstroom Univ., Sorbonne, Paris; began writing at an early age; first novel (Afrikaans) published 1958; on return from Paris became mem. and spokesman of young Afrikaans writers' group Sestigers; returned to Paris 1968; went back to South Africa to resist apartheid through writing; novel Kennis van die Aand banned 1973 (first Afrikaans novel to be banned); began

to write in English as well; Dir several plays, but abandoned theatre owing to censorship; resumed playwriting 1996; Founder-mem. Afrikaans Writers' Guild; Prof. of Afrikaans and Dutch Literature, Rhodes Univ. (previously lecturer) 1980–89; Prof. of English, Univ. of Cape Town 1991–2000; Chevalier Légion d'honneur 1983; Commdr Ordre des Arts et des Lettres 1992; Hon. DLitt (Witwatersrand) 1985, (Univ. of Free State) 1997, (Montpellier) 1998, (Rhodes) 2001, (Pretoria) 2003; CNA Award for Literature, South Africa 1965, 1978 and 1982, Martin Luther King Memorial Prize 1979, Prix Médicis Etranger, France 1979, Biannual Freedom of Speech Prize by Monismanien Foundation, Univ. of Uppsala 1991, Premio Mondello (Italy) 1997. *Publications include:* novels: Looking on Darkness 1974, An Instant in the Wind 1976, Rumours of Rain 1978, A Dry White Season 1979, A Chain of Voices 1982, Mapmakers (essays) 1983, The Wall of the Plague 1984, The Ambassador 1985, States of Emergency 1988, An Act of Terror 1991, The First Life of Adamastor 1993, On the Contrary 1993, Imaginings of Sand 1996, Reinventing a Continent (essays) 1996, Devil's Valley 1998, The Rights of Desire 2000, The Other Side of Silence 2002; several plays 1965–75, The Jogger 1997. *Address:* Department of English, University of Cape Town, Rondebosch 7701, South Africa. *Fax:* (21) 685-3945.

BRINK, Andries Jacob, MD, DSc, FRCP, FACC; South African professor of medicine; b. 29 Aug. 1923, Potchefstroom; s. of Andries J. Brink and Petronella J. Havenga; m. Maria Ruskovich 1949; two s. two d.; ed Jeppe High School, Univs of Witwatersrand, Pretoria and Stellenbosch, Johns Hopkins Univ., Baltimore, USA, Postgrad. Medical School, London, UK; Post-Graduate Medical School, Hammersmith Hosp., London 1951; Fellow in Paediatrics, Johns Hopkins Hosp., USA 1952; Internist, Sr Lecturer, Univ. of Pretoria 1953–56; Founder Prof. Dept of Medicine, Univ. of Stellenbosch 1956, Chief Cardiologist and Founder, Dept of Cardiology 1956–78, Dean, Faculty of Medicine 1971–83; Dir Molecular and Cellular Cardiac Research Unit, MRC 1956–69; Pres. (part-time) SA Medical Research Council 1969–84, Fulltime Pres. 1984–89; Man. Dir Clinics Cardive Publishing Co. 1990–, Tygerberg Clinical Trial Centre 1991–; Nat. Dir MC Research Pty Ltd 1998–2000; mem. Bd Scientific Advisory Council 1972–83, 1990–94, SA Medical and Dental Council 1971–83, World Asscn of Medical Eds 2002–; Founder Heart Foundation of SA; Founder-Ed. Cardiovascular Journal of SA; Hon. DSc (Natal) 1976, (Potchefstroom) 1985; Hon. MD (Stellenbosch) 1989; nearly 80 major awards and prizes, including Recht Malan Award, (for Dictionary of Afrikaans Medical Terms), Merit Awards (Gold), SA Medical Research Council 1986; Decoration for Meritorious Service (Gold) 1981. *Publications:* 120 scientific and general medical pubs, including 6 books and a medical dictionary. *Leisure interests:* reading, music, cycling, painting, oenology, viticulture. *Address:* PO Box 62, Durbanville, 7551 (Office); 4 King Street, Durbanville 7550, South Africa (Home). *Telephone:* (21) 976-8129 (Office); (21) 976-1786 (Home). *Fax:* (21) 976-8984 (Office); (21) 976-1786 (Home). *E-mail:* andries.medcon@cvjsa.co.za (Home); andries.medcon@absamail.co.za. *Website:* www.cvjsa.co.za (Office).

BRINKHUES, Josef; German ecclesiastic; b. 21 June 1913, Aachen; s. of Heinrich Brinkhues and Cläre (neé Führen); m. Dr. Ilse Volckmar 1946; one s. one d.; ed Frankfurt and Bonn; ordained priest 1937; consecrated bishop 1966; mem. Int. Old Catholics Bishops' Conf. of Utrecht Union 1966–1986; Bishop Emer. of Old-Catholic Church in Germany. *Leisure interest:* music. *Address:* Oberdorf 18, 53347 Impekoven Alfter, Germany. *Telephone:* (228) 643301.

BRINKLEY, David; American broadcaster (retd); b. 10 July 1920, Wilmington, NC; s. of William G. Brinkley and Mary West; m. 1st Ann Fischer 1946; three s.; m. 2nd Susan Adolph 1972; one c.; reporter, Wilmington, NC Star-News 1938–41; reporter, bureau man. various cities, United Press Asscn 1941–43; news writer, broadcaster, radio and TV, NBC, Washington 1943–, Washington Corresp. 1951–81; anchorman, This Week (ABC) 1981–97; retd. 1997; duPont Award, Peabody Award and other awards for journalism; Presidential Medal of Freedom 1992. *Publications:* David Brinkley (autobiog.) 1996, David Brinkley's Homilies 1996, Everybody is Entitled to my Opinion 1996. *Address:* c/o ABC News, 1717 DeSales Street, NW, Washington, DC 20036, USA.

BRINKLEY, Robert, MA; British diplomatist; b. 21 Jan. 1954; m. Mary Brinkley; three s.; ed Stonyhurst Coll., Lancs., Corpus Christi Coll. Oxford; joined FCO, London 1977, mem. staff 1982–88, 1992–96; mem. UK Del. to Comprehensive Test Ban Negotiations, Geneva 1978; assigned to Embassy in Moscow 1979–82, 1996–99, to Embassy in Bonn 1988–92; with FCO/Home Office Jt Entry Clearance Unit 2000–02; Amb. to Ukraine 2002–. *Leisure interests:* reading, walking, music (violin). *Address:* British Embassy, vul. Desyatinna 9, 01025 Kiev, Ukraine (Office). *Telephone:* (44) 462-00-11 (Office). *Fax:* (44) 462-00-13 (Office). *Website:* www.britems-ukraine.net (Office).

BRINKMAN, Leonard Cornelis (Eelco), Dr rer. pol; Netherlands politician; b. 5 Feb. 1948, Dirksland; m. J. Salentijn; three c.; ed Gymnasium, Dordrecht, Free Univ., Amsterdam; research post in the Public Admin. Dept, Free Univ. 1969–74; mem. Co-ordination Office for North of West Holland conurbation 1974–75; Head of Office of Sec.-Gen., Ministry of Home Affairs 1976–79, Dir-Gen. 1980–82; Minister for Welfare, Health and Cultural Affairs 1982–89; Pres. Netherlands Red Cross 2001–; Christian Democratic Alliance. *Publications:* articles on public admin. in specialist journals.

BRISVILLE, Jean-Claude Gabriel; French author; b. 28 May 1922, Bois-Colombes/Hauts-de-Seine; s. of Maurice Brisville and Geneviève Gineste; m. 2nd Irène Kalaschnikowa 1963; one s. one d. by first m.; ed Lycée Jacques Decour, Paris; literary journalist 1946–; Reader, Hachette 1951–58; Sec. to Albert Camus 1957–59; Deputy Literary Dir Juillard 1959–64, Literary Dir 1964–70; Head of Drama Video Section, ORTF 1971–75; Literary Dir Livre de poche 1976–81; Chevalier Légion d'honneur, Chevalier des Arts et des Lettres; Prix du Théâtre de la Société des Auteurs et Compositeurs Dramatiques (SACD). *Publications:* narrative works: Prologue 1948, D'un amour (Prix Sainte-Beuve) 1954, La Fuite au Danemark 1962, La Zone d'ombre 1976; plays: Le Fauteuil à bascule (Prix Ibsen, Prix de la meilleure création dramatique) 1982, Le Bonheur à Romorantin, L'entretien de M. Descartes avec M. Pascal le jeune, La Villa bleue, Les Liaisons dangereuses (adaptation), Le Souper (Prix du Théâtre, Acad. Française) 1990, L'Officier de la Garde 1990, L'Antichambre 1991, Contre-jour 1993, Dernière Salve 1995; essays; stories for children. *Address:* SACD, 12 rue Ballu, 75009 Paris, France.

BRITTAN OF SPENNITHORNE, Baron (Life Peer), cr. 2000, of Spennithorne in the County of North Yorkshire; **Rt Hon. Leon Brittan,** Kt, PC, QC, DL; British politician, barrister and investment banker; b. 25 Sept. 1939, London; s. of the late Dr Joseph Brittan and of Rebecca Brittan; brother of Sir Samuel Brittan (q.v.); m. Diana Peterson 1980; two step-d.; ed Haberdashers' Aske's School, Trinity Coll., Cambridge, Yale Univ.; Chair. Cambridge Univ. Conservative Asscn 1960; Pres. Cambridge Union 1960, debating tour of USA 1961; called to Bar, Inner Temple 1962 (Bencher 1983); Chair. Bow Group 1964–65; contested N Kensington seat 1966, 1970; Ed. Crossbow 1966–68; mem. Political Cttee Carlton Club, Cttee of the British Atlantic Group of Young Politicians 1970–78; Vice-Chair. of Govs of Isaac Newton School 1968–71; MP for Cleveland and Whitby 1974–83, for Richmond (N Yorks.) 1983–88; Queen's Counsel 1978; Vice-Chair. Parl. Conservative Party Employment Cttee 1974–76; Opposition Spokesman on Devolution and House of Commons Affairs 1976–78, on Devolution and Employment 1978–79; Minister of State, Home Office 1979–81; Chief Sec. to the Treasury 1981–83, Home Sec. 1983–85; Sec. of State for Trade and Industry 1985–86; Commr with responsibility for Competition Policy and Financial Insts, Comm. of the European Communities (now European Comm.) 1989–92, for Econ. Relations 1993–94, for External Trade and Relations with N America and parts of Asia 1995–99, a Vice-Pres. 1989–99; Consultant Herbert Smith 2000–; Vice-Chair. UBS Warburg 2000–; Advisory Dir Unilever 2000–; Chair. Lotis group of Int. Financial Services London (IFSL) 2001–; Distinguished Visiting Fellow Inst. of Policy Studies 1988; Hersch Lauterpacht Memorial Lecturer, Univ. of Cambridge 1990; Chair. Soc. of Conservative Lawyers 1986–89; Vice-Chair. Nat. Asscn of School Govs and Mans 1970–78; Chancellor Univ. of Teesside 1993–; Deputy Lt, Co. of N Yorkshire 2001–; Hon. DCL (Newcastle) 1990, (Durham) 1992; Hon. LLD (Hull) 1990, (Bath) 1995; Hon. DL (Bradford) 1992; Hon. DEcon (Korea Univ.); Dr hc (Edin.) 1991. *Publications:* The Conservative Opportunity (contrib.), Millstones for the Sixties (jt author), Rough Justice, Infancy and the Law, How to Save your Schools, A New Deal for Health Care 1988, Defence and Arms Control in a Changing Era 1988, Discussions on Policy 1989, Monetary Union: the Issues and the Impact 1989, Europe: Our Sort of Community (Granada Guildhall Lecture) 1989, Hersch Lauterpacht Memorial Lectures (Cambridge Univ.) 1990, European Competition Policy 1992, Europe: The Europe We Need 1994, A Diet of Brussels 2000. *Leisure interests:* walking, cricket, opera. *Address:* 1 Finsbury Avenue, London, EC2M 2PP (Office); House of Lords, London, SW1A 0PW, England. *Telephone:* (20) 7568-6305 (Office). *Fax:* (20) 7568-6520 (Office). *E-mail:* leon.brittan@ubsw.com (Office).

BRITTAN, Sir Samuel, Kt, MA; British economist and journalist; b. 29 Dec. 1933, London; brother of Lord Brittan; ed Kilburn Grammar School, Jesus Coll., Cambridge; journalist on The Financial Times 1955–61, prin. economic commentator 1966–, Asst Ed. 1978–95; Econs Ed. The Observer 1961–64; Adviser, Dept of Econ. Affairs 1965; Research Fellow, Nuffield Coll., Oxford 1973–74, Visiting Fellow 1974–82; Visiting Prof., Chicago Law School, USA 1978; mem. Peacock Cttee on Finance of the BBC 1985–86; Hon. Prof. of Politics Univ. of Warwick 1987–92; Hon. Fellow Jesus Coll., Cambridge 1988; Chevalier, Légion d'honneur 1993; Hon. DLitt (Heriot-Watt) 1985; Hon. DUniv (Essex) 1995; first winner Sr Harold Wincott Award for financial journalists 1971, George Orwell Prize for political journalism 1980, Ludwig Erhard Prize 1987. *Publications:* Steering the Economy (3rd edn 1978), Left or Right: The Bogus Dilemma 1968, The Price of Economic Freedom: A Guide to Flexible Rates 1970, Is There an Economic Consensus? 1973, Capitalism and the Permissive Society 1973 (new edn A Restatement of Economic Liberalism 1988), The Delusion of Incomes Policy (with Peter Lilley) 1977, The Economic Consequences of Democracy 1977, How to End the 'Monetarist' Controversy 1981, Role and Limits of Government: Essays in Political Economy 1983, There Is No Such Thing As Society 1993, Capitalism with a Human Face 1995, Essays, Moral, Political and Economic 1998. *Address:* The Financial Times, Number 1 Southwark Bridge, London, SE1 9HL, England (Office). *Telephone:* (20) 7873-3000 (Office).

BRITTEN, Roy John, PhD; American biophysicist and molecular biologist; b. 1 Oct. 1919, Washington, DC; s. of Rollo H. Britten and Marion (Hale) Britten; m. (divorced); two s.; m. 2nd Jacqueline Aymar Reid 1986 (died 2001); ed Univ. of Virginia, Johns Hopkins and Princeton Univs.; staff mem. Biophysics Group, Dept of Terrestrial Magnetism, Carnegie Inst. of Washington 1951–71; inventor, quadrupole focusing of energetic beams; discoverer, repeated DNA sequences in genomes of higher organisms; Visiting Assoc. Calif. Inst. of Tech. and staff mem. Dept of Terrestrial Magnetism, Carnegie Inst. of Washington 1971–73; Sr Research Assoc. Calif. Inst. of Tech. and staff mem. Carnegie Inst. of Washington 1973–81; Distinguished Carnegie Sr Research Assoc. in Biology, Calif. Inst. of Tech. and staff mem. Carnegie Inst. of Washington 1981–89; Distinguished Carnegie Sr Research Assoc. in Biology, Calif. Inst. of Tech. 1989–99; Distinguished Carnegie Sr Research Assoc. in Biol., Emer., Calif. Inst. of Tech. 1999–; Adjunct Prof. Univ. of Calif., Irvine 1991–; mem. NAS, Acad. Arts and Sciences. *Publications:* articles in professional journals. *Leisure interests:* inventing, sailing, music, painting. *Address:* Kerckhoff Marine Laboratory, California Institute of Technology, 101 Dahlia Avenue, Corona del Mar, CA 92625-2814, USA (Office). *Telephone:* (949) 675-2159.

BRITZ, Robert, BSc; American financial executive; b. 1951; ed Manhattan Coll., Harvard Business School; joined New York Stock Exchange (NYSE) 1972, various man. posts in corp. marketing, then Man. Dir Corp. Business Devt, Vice-Pres. New Listings and Client Service, Sr Vice-Pres., Exec. Vice-Pres., Group Exec. Vice-Pres. overseeing operation of NYSE market, tech. and information products, mem. Office of Chair. 1995–2001, apptd. Co-COO, Pres. and Exec. Vice-Pres. 2001–; mem. Bd of Dirs. Securities Industry Automation Corpn (SIAC), Sector Inc. *Address:* New York Stock Exchange, 11 Wall Street, 6th Floor, New York, NY 10005, USA (Office). *Website:* www.nyse.com (Office).

BRIXNER, Ulrich, Dr rer. pol; German banker; b. 1941, Munich; ed Univ. of Mannheim; fmrly CEO GZ Bank; Chair. and CEO DZ BANK (formed by merger of GZ Bank and DG Bank Deutsche Genossenschaftsbank) 2001–. *Address:* DZ BANK Deutsche Zentral-Genossenschaftsbank AG, Am Platz der Republik, D-60325 Frankfurt am Main, Germany (Office). *Telephone:* (69) 74472382 (Home). *Fax:* (69) 74476784 (Office). *Website:* www.dgbank.de (Office).

BRIZOLA, Leonel; Brazilian politician; b. 1922, Carazinho, Rio Grande do Sul; s. of the late José Brizola; m. Neusa Goulart 1950; ed Tech. School, Porto Alegre; shoeshine boy; warehouse labourer; joined Brazilian Labour Party (PTB) 1945; State Deputy, Constituent Ass., Rio Grande do Sul; State Sec. for Public Works; elected Fed. Deputy 1954; Mayor of Porto Alegre 1955; Gov. Rio Grande do Sul 1958; Fed. Deputy, State of Guanabara, Rio de Janeiro 1962; exiled for attempt to organize armed resistance to mil. regime 1964; lived in Uruguay until 1977; expelled from Uruguay under pressure from Brazilian military 1977; lived in Lisbon 1977–79; returned to Brazil 1979; Pres. Democratic Labour Party (PDT); Vice-Pres. Socialist Int. 1979; Gov. Rio de Janeiro 1982–86. *Address:* Partido Democrático Trabalhista, Rua Marechal Câmara 160, 4°, 20050 Rio de Janeiro, R.J., Brazil. *Fax:* (21) 262-8834. *E-mail:* pdtnac@domain.com.br (Office). *Website:* www.pdt.org.br (Office).

BROAD, Eli, BA, CPA; American philanthropist; b. 6 June 1933, New York; s. of Leon Broad and Rebecca Broad (née Jacobson); m. Edythe Lois Lawson 1954; two s.; ed Michigan State Univ.; Asst Prof. Detroit Inst. of Tech. 1956; Co-Founder, Chair., Pres. and CEO AIG SunAmerica Life Insurance Co. (fmrly Kaufman & Broad, Inc.), LA 1957–2001, Chair. 2001–; Chair. of numerous cos including CalAmerica Life Insurance Co., KB Home (fmrly Kaufman & Broad Home Corpn) 1989–93, Stanford Ranch Co.; mem. Exec. Cttee Nat. Mortgage Asscn 1972–73; mem. Calif. Business Roundtable 1986–2000; co-owner Sacramento Kings and Arco Arena 1992–99; Dir LA World Affairs Council 1988– (Chair. 1994–99), DARE America 1989–95 (Hon. Dir 1995–); Chair. Mayor's Housing Policy Comm. 1974–75; mem. Advisory Council, Town Hall of Calif. 1985–87; mem. Contemporary Art Comm., Harvard Univ. Art Museum 1992–; mem. Bd of Overseers, Univ. of Southern Calif. Keck School of Medicine 1999–, Bd of Dirs EdVoice 2001–; Fellow American Acad. of Arts and Sciences 2001–; Trustee Pitzer Coll., Claremont, CA 1970–82 (Chair. Bd of Trustees 1973–79, Life Trustee 1982–), Haifa Univ., Israel 1972–80, Windward School, Santa Monica, CA 1972–77, Calif. State Univ. 1978–82 (Vice Chair. Bd of Trustees 1979–80, Trustee Emer. 1982–), Museum of Contemporary Art, LA 1980–93, Univ. of Calif. at LA (UCLA) Foundation 1986–, Caltech 1993–, Trustee Comm. for Econ. Devt 1993–95; Founder and Trustee The Broad Foundation 1999–; numerous philanthropic donations including funds to build the Frank Gehry-designed Walt Disney Concert Hall 2003; Chevalier, Légion d'honneur; Golden Plate Award, American Acad. of Achievement 1971, Humanitarian Award, NCCJ 1977, Public Affairs Award, Coro Foundation 1987, KCET-Los Angeles Visionary Award 1999, Julius Award, Univ. of Southern Calif. 2001, Teach for America Educational Leadership Award 2001, United Way Alexis de Tocqueville Award 2002, Exemplary Leadership in Man. Award, Anderson School, Univ. of Calif., Los Angeles 2002. *Exhibitions:* Jasper Johns to Jeff Koons: Four Decades of Art from the Broad Collections, Los Angeles Co. Museum of Art 2001, Museum of Fine Arts, Boston 2001, Corcoran Gallery of Art 2002, Guggenheim Museum, Bilbao, Spain 2003. *Address:* AIG SunAmerica Inc., 10900 Wilshire Boulevard, 12th Floor, Los Angeles, CA 90024, USA (Office).

BROADBENT, Jim; British actor and writer; b. 24 May 1949; s. of the late Roy Broadbent and Dee Broadbent; m. Anastasia Lewis 1987; two step-s.; ed Leighton Park School, Reading, Hammersmith Coll. of Art, London Acad. of Music and Dramatic Arts (LAMDA); actor Nat. Theatre and RSC; wrote and appeared in short film A Sense of History (Clermont-Ferrand Int. Film Festival Award). *Theatre:* The Recruiting Officer, A Winter's Tale,

The Government Inspector, A Flea in Her Ear, Goose Pimples, Our Friends in the North, Habeas Corpus. *Films include:* The Shout, Breaking Glass, The Dogs of War, The Good Father, Superman IV, Life is Sweet, Enchanted April, The Crying Game, Widow's Peak, Princess Caraboo, Richard III, The Borrowers, Little Voice, The Avengers, Topsy Turvy 1999, Moulin Rouge (Acad. Award for Best Supporting Actor 2002, BAFTA Award for Best Supporting Actor 2002) 2001, Bridget Jones's Diary 2001, Iris (Golden Globe for Best Supporting Actor) 2001, Gangs of New York 2002. *Television includes:* Not the Nine O'Clock News, Sense of History (also writer), Murder Most Horrid, Only Fools and Horses, The Victoria Wood Show, Silas Marner, Blackadder, Birth of a Nation, Gone to the Dogs, Gone to Seed, The Peter Principle, The Gathering Storm. *Address:* c/o Harriet Robinson, ICM, 76 Oxford Street, London W1D 1BS, England. *Telephone:* (20) 7636-6565.

BROADBENT, Hon. John Edward, OC, PhD; Canadian politician and professor; b. 21 March 1936, Oshawa, Ont.; s. of Percy E. Broadbent and Mary A. Welsh; m. Lucille Munroe 1971; one s. one d.; ed High School in Oshawa, Univ. of Toronto, London School of Econs and Political Science; Prof. of Political Science, York Univ., Ont. 1965–68; mem. House of Commons 1968–89; Co-Chair. Policy Review Cttee for New Democratic Party Fed. Convention 1969; Chair. Fed. Caucus 1972–74, Parl. Leader of Fed. Caucus 1974–75; Nat. Leader of New Democratic Party 1975–89; Vice-Pres. Socialist Int. 1978–90, Hon. Pres. 1991–; Pres. Int. Centre for Human Rights and Democratic Devt 1990–96; J. S. Woodsworth Chair. Inst. for the Humanities, Simon Fraser Univ. 1997–; LLD hc (Dalhousie Univ.) 1990, (York Univ.) 1991, DLitt (Trinity Coll., Oxford) 1990, (Toronto Univ.) 1990. *Publication:* The Liberal Rip-Off 1970. *Leisure interests:* reading contemporary fiction, listening to music, skiing.

BROCKES, Jeremy Patrick, PhD, FRS; British biologist; b. 29 Feb. 1948, Haslemere; s. of Bernard Brockes and Edna Heaney; ed St John's Coll., Cambridge, Edinburgh Univ.; Asst, then Assoc. Prof. of Biology Caltech 1978–83; mem. MRC Biophysics Unit, King's Coll., London 1983–88; mem. Ludwig Inst. for Cancer Research 1988–97; Prof. of Cell Biology Univ. Coll. London 1992–97, MRC Research Prof. Dept of Biochemistry 1997–. *Publication:* Amphibian Limb Regeneration: Rebuilding a Complex Structure, Neuroimmunology. *Leisure interest:* soprano saxophone. *Address:* Department of Biochemistry and Molecular Biology, University College London, Gower Street, London, WC1E 6BT, England.

BROCKHOUSE, Bertram Neville, CC, PhD, FRS; Canadian physicist; b. 15 July 1918, Lethbridge, Alberta; s. of Israel Bertram Brockhouse and Mable Emily Neville Brockhouse; m. Doris Isobel Mary Miller 1948; four s. two d.; ed Univ. of British Columbia, Univ. of Toronto; served with Royal Canadian Navy 1939–45; lecturer Univ. of Toronto 1949–50; Research Officer Atomic Energy of Canada Ltd 1950–59, Head Neutron Physics Br. 1959–62; Prof. of Physics, McMaster Univ. 1962–84, Prof. Emer. 1984–; Foreign mem. Royal Swedish Acad. of Sciences, American Acad. of Arts and Sciences; Hon. DSc (Waterloo) 1969, (McMaster) 1984, (Toronto) 1995, (Univ. of BC) 1996; Dr. hc (Dalhousie) 1996, (Lethbridge) 1997; shared Nobel Prize for Physics 1994 for pioneering neutron scattering techniques and elaboration on theory of phonons. *Publications:* numerous articles. *Leisure interests:* natural philosophy, social bridge. *Address:* P.O. Box 7338, Ancaster, Ont., L9G 3N6, Canada. *Telephone:* (905) 648-6329. *Fax:* (905) 648-7246.

BROCKINGTON, Ian Fraser, M.PHIL., MD, FRCP, F.R.C.PSYCH.; British professor of psychiatry; b. 12 Dec. 1935, Chillington, Devon; s. of Fraser Brockington and Joyce Brockington; m. Diana Hilary Pink 1969; two s. two d.; ed Winchester Coll., Univ. of Cambridge, Univ. of Manchester Medical School; Wellcome Research Fellow, Royal Postgraduate Medical School and Univ. of Ibadan, Nigeria 1966–69; Visiting Prof. Univ. of Chicago, USA 1980–81, Washington Univ., St Louis, USA 1981; Prof. of Psychiatry, Univ. of Birmingham 1983–; Pres. the Marcé Society 1982–84; founder and first Pres. Women's Mental Health section, World Psychiatric Asscn; Cottman Fellow, Monash Univ. 1988. *Publications:* papers on African heart diseases 1966–80, on schizoaffective psychosis, methods of clinical psychiatric research, pregnancy-related psychiatric disorders; Motherhood and Mental Health 1996. *Leisure interests:* family activities, choral singing, French, Italian and German literature, bookbinding, distance running. *Address:* Faculty of Medicine and Dentistry, University of Birmingham, Edgbaston, Birmingham, B15 2TT; Lower Brockington Farm, Bredenbury, Bromyard, Herefordshire, England (Home). *Telephone:* (121) 678-2453 (Office).

BRÖDER, Ernst-Günther, DEcon; German banker and economist; b. 6 Jan. 1927, Cologne; ed Univs. of Cologne, Mainz, Freiburg and Paris; mem. Corpn staff, Bayer AG, Leverkusen 1956–61; Projects Dept World Bank (IBRD) 1961–64; joined Kreditanstalt für Wiederaufbau 1964, Deputy Man. 1968–69, Man. 1969–75, mem. Man. Bd 1975–84, Man. Bd Spokesman 1980–84; Dir European Investment Bank (EIB) 1980–84, Pres. and Chair. Bd of Dirs 1984–93, Hon. Pres. 1993–; Chair. Inspection Panel, IBRD 1994–96, 1998–99, mem. 1997–98; mem. Supervisory Bd DEG Deutsche Finanzierungsgesellschaft für Beteiligungen in Entwicklungsländern GmbH 1980–84; mem. Panel of Conciliators, Int. Centre for Settlement of Investment Disputes 1976–, Special Advisory Group, Asian Devt Bank 1981–82; high decorations in Germany, Belgium, Italy and Luxembourg. *Address:* 15 Op den Aessen, 6231 Bech, Luxembourg (Home). *Telephone:* (352) 79-98-62 (Home). *Fax:* (352) 79-98-63 (Home). *E-mail:* erdobro@pt.lu.

BRODER, Samuel, MD; American physician; b. 24 Feb. 1945, Łódź, Poland; m. Gail Broder; two d.; moved to USA 1949; ed Univ. of Michigan Ann Arbor and Stanford Univ.; clinical assoc. Nat. Cancer Inst. (NCI), Bethesda, Md 1972, investigator, medicine br. 1975, Sr investigator, metabolism br. 1976, in charge of lab. overseeing new drug trials 1981–89; Dir NCI 1989–; has played prominent role in HIV research. *Publications:* AIDS: Modern Concepts and Therapeutic Challenges (ed.) 1987; more than 250 articles. *Leisure interests:* long walks, playing cards, cinema, dinner with friends. *Address:* Office of the Director, National Cancer Institute, National Institutes of Health, 9000 Rockville Pike, Building 31, Bethesda, MD 20892, USA.

BRODERICK, Matthew; American actor; b. 21 March 1962, New York; s. of James Broderick and Patricia Broderick; m. Sarah Jessica Parker 1997; one s. *Theatre includes:* Valentine's Day (workshop production), Torch Song Trilogy, Brighton Beach Memoirs (Tony Award), Biloxi Blues, The Widow Claire, How to Succeed in Business Without Really Trying (Tony Award), The Producers. *Films include:* War Games, Ladyhawke, 1918, On Valentine's Day, Ferris Bueller's Day Off, Project X, Biloxi Blues, Torch Song Trilogy, Glory, Family Business, The Freshman, Lay This Laurel, Glory, Out on a Limb, The Night We Never Met, The Lion King (voice), Road to Welville, Mrs Parker and the Vicious Circle, Infinity (also dir), The Cable Guy, Addicted to Love, The Lion King II: Simba's Pride (voice), Godzilla, Election, Inspector Gadget 1999, Walking to the Waterline 1999, You Can Count on Me 2000, Suspicious Minds 2001. *Television includes:* Master Harold . . . and the Boys, Cinderella, Jazz 2001, The Music Man 2003. *Address:* c/o CAA, 9830 Wilshire Boulevard, Beverly Hills, CA 90212, USA.

BRODIE, Harlow Keith Hammond, MD, FRSM; American academic; b. 24 Aug. 1939, Stamford; s. of Lawrence Sheldon and Elizabeth Hammond Brodie; m. Brenda Ann Barrowclough 1967; three s. one d.; ed Princeton Univ. and Columbia Univ. College of Physicians and Surgeons; Internship, Ochsner Foundation Hosp., New Orleans 1965–66; Asst Resident in Psychiatry, Columbia-Presbyterian Medical Center, New York 1966–68; Clinical Asscn, Sec. on Psychiatry, Lab. of Clinical Science, Nat. Inst. of Mental Health 1968–70; Asst Prof., Dept of Psychiatry, Stanford Univ. School of Medicine 1970–74; Program Dir, Gen. Clinical Research Center, Stanford Univ. School of Medicine 1973–74; Prof. and Chair., Dept of Psychiatry, Duke Univ. School of Medicine 1974–82; Chief, Psychiatry Service, Duke Univ. Hosp. 1974–82; Chancellor Duke Univ. 1982–85, Acting Provost 1982–83, Pres. 1985–93, Pres. Emer. 1993–, James B. Duke Prof. of Psychiatry and Behavioral Sciences 1981–, Prof. Dept of Psychology, Prof. Law 1980–; Chair. Cttee on Substance Abuse and Mental Health Issues in AIDS Research 1992–95; mem. Coll. of Physicians and Surgeons of Columbia Univ. Asscn of Alumni Gold Medal 1985, Carnegie Council on Adolescent Devt 1986–97, Nat. Review and Advisory Panel for Improving Campus Race Relations, Ford Foundation 1990–94; Hon. LLD (Richmond) 1987; Strecker Award, Inst. of Pennsylvania Hosp. 1980, Distinguished Alumnus Award, Ochsner Foundation Hosp. 1984, Distinguished Medical Alumni Award, Columbia Univ. 1985, NC Award for Science 1990, William C. Menninger Memorial Award 1994. *Publications:* The Importance of Mental Health Services to General Health Care 1979, co-author Modern Clinical Psychiatry 1982, co-ed. American Handbook of Psychiatry (Vol. 6 1975, Vol. 7 1981, Vol. 8 1986), co-Critical Problems in Psychiatry 1982, Signs and Symptoms in Psychiatry 1983, Aids and Behavior: An Integrated Approach 1994, Keeping an Open Door: Passages in a University Presidency 1996; also numerous articles. *Leisure interests:* tennis, reading, hiking. *Address:* 205 East Duke Building, Duke Univ., Durham, NC 27708 (Office); 63 Beverly Drive, Durham, NC 27707, USA (Home). *Telephone:* (919) 493-2447 (Home).

BRODIE, James William, OBE, MSc, FRSNZ; New Zealand scientist; b. 7 Oct. 1920, Bebington, Cheshire, UK; s. of James Thomas Fielding Brodie and Isabella Garner; m. Audrey Jacobsen 1945; two s.; ed Napier Boys' High School, Victoria Coll., Univ. of New Zealand; with NZ Lands and Survey Dept 1937–45; staff of Head Office, NZ Dept of Scientific and Industrial Research 1945–49, Geophysics Div. 1949–54, Dir NZ Oceanographic Inst. 1954–1977; Dir Fisheries Research Div., NZ Marine Dept 1964–67; Consultant on Marine Sciences, UNESCO; SE Asia, Paris, Indonesia 1965–79, Marine Science Adviser for SE Asia, Jakarta, Indonesia 1978–79, Chair. West Pacific Oceanographic Workshop, Tokyo 1979; Chair. Tech. Advisory Group, S. Pacific Offshore Prospecting, ESCAP 1975, 1976, 1978, Chair. Marine Geoscience Symposium, Suva, Fiji 1976; Pres. Geological Soc. of NZ 1960–61, NZ Marine Sciences Soc. 1966–67; Hon. Librarian Royal Soc. of NZ 1965–78, Home Sec. 1983–87, Vice-Pres. 1986–87; Ed. NZ Stamp Collector 1980–85; mem. Bd of Trustees, Nat. Art Gallery and Museum 1982–92, Project Devt Bd, Museum of NZ 1988–92; Marsden Medal, NZ Asscn of Scientists 1978; NZ Marine Sciences Soc. Award 1985, Fellow Royal Philatelic Soc. of NZ 1978, Rhodes Medal 1988. *Publications:* Bathymetry of the NZ Region 1964, Terawhiti and the Goldfields 1986, The First Seven Thousand: A Jubilee History of Scots College 1991; Ed. (with Audrey Brodie) Haddenham Quaker History 1988, NZ Journeys of Lucy Violet Hodgkin 1989, Seeking a New Land: Quakers in New Zealand 1993, Go Anywhere, Do Anything: New Zealanders in the Friends' Ambulance Unit in China 1945–1951 1996, Keeping Touch: the Quaker Population in Nineteenth Century New Zealand 1999, Remembrance of Friends Past: Lives of New Zealand Quakers 1843–1998 1999, A View of the Bay: From the Journals of Lucy Violet Holdsworth 1922–24 2000, John Holdsworth and the House Called Swarthmoor 2001; contribs to Dictionary of New Zealand Biography 1993–2000; papers on geological, marine science and local history topics; philatelic monographs. *Leisure interests:* archaeology, historical research. *Address:* 1 Fettes Crescent, Wellington 3, New Zealand. *Telephone:* (4) 388-6894.

BRODY, Adrien; American actor; b. 14 April 1973, New York; s. of Sylvia Plachy; ed American Acad. of Dramatic Arts, High School for the Performing Arts; first worked in off-Broadway productions; television debut in PBS movie Home at Last 1988; other TV appearances include Home at Last 1988, Annie McGuire (series) 1988. *Films include:* New York Stories 1989, King of the Hill 1993, Jailbreakers 1994, Angels in the Outfield 1994, Solo 1996, Bullet 1996, The Undertaker's Wedding 1997, The Last Time I Committed Suicide 1997, The Thin Red Line 1998, Sweet Jersey 1998, Ten Benny 1998, Summer of Sam 1999, Six Ways to Sunday 1999, Oxygen 1999, Liberty Heights 1999, Restaurant 2000, Harrison's Flowers 2000, Bread and Roses 2001, Love the Hard Way 2001, The Affair of the Necklace 2001, Dummy 2002, The Pianist (Acad. Award for Best Actor 2003) 2002, Harrison's Flowers 2002, The Singing Detective 2003.

BRODY, Alexander, BA; American advertising executive; b. 28 Jan. 1933, Budapest, Hungary; s. of John Brody and Lilly Pollatschek; ed Princeton Univ.; with Young & Rubicam Inc. 1953–83; Vice-Pres., Man. Young & Rubicam Inc., Frankfurt, Germany 1965–70; Sr Vice-Pres., Head, European Operations, Young & Rubicam Inc. 1967–70; Int. Pres. Young & Rubicam Inc., Brussels and New York 1970–82; Pres. and CEO DYR Worldwide, New York 1984–87; Pres. Int. Ogilvy & Mather Worldwide 1987–93, consultant 1993–, now Pres. and CEO Int. Operations. *Address:* Ogilvy & Mather Worldwide, Worldwide Plaza, 309 W 49th Street, New York, NY 10019, USA.

BRODY, Jane Ellen, MS; American journalist; b. 19 May 1941, Brooklyn; d. of Sidney Brody and Lillian Kellner; m. Richard Engquist 1966; twin s.; ed New York State Coll. of Agric., Cornell Univ. and Univ. of Wis.; reporter, Minn. Tribune 1963–65; science writer, personal health columnist, New York Times 1965–; mem. Advisory Council, New York State Coll. of Agric. 1971–77; numerous awards including Howard Blakeslee Award, American Heart Asscn 1971, Science Writers' Award, ADA 1978, J.C. Penney–Univ. of Mo. Journalism Award 1978, Lifeline Award, American Health Foundation 1978. *Publications:* Secrets of Good Health (with R. Engquist) 1970, You Can Fight Cancer and Win (with A. Holleb) 1977, Jane Brody's Nutrition Book 1981, Jane Brody's New York Times Guide to Personal Health 1982, Jane Brody's Good Food Book 1985, Jane Brody's Good Food Gourmet 1990, Jane Brody's Good Seafood Book (with Richard Flaste) 1994, Jane Brody's Cold and Flu Fighter 1995, Jane Brody's Allergy Fighter 1997, The New York Times Book of Health 1997, The New York Times Book of Women's Health 2000, The New York Times Book of Alternative Medicine 2001. *Address:* c/o New York Times, 229 W 43rd Street, New York, NY 10036-3913, USA.

BROERS, Sir Alec Nigel, Kt, ScD, FREng, FRS; British professor of electrical engineering; b. 17 Sept. 1938, Calcutta; s. of late Alec W. Broers and Constance A. (Cox) Broers; m. Mary T. Phelan 1964; two s.; ed Geelong Grammar School, Melbourne Univ. and Gonville & Caius Coll. Cambridge; mem. research staff and man. of photon and electron optics groups, IBM Thomas Watson Research Center 1965–80; Man. Semiconductor Lithography and Process Devt and Advanced Devt IBM East Fishkill Lab. 1981–84; mem. Corp. Tech. Cttee IBM Corp. HQ 1984; Prof. of Electrical Eng., Univ. of Cambridge 1984–96, Emer. 1996–; Head Electrical Div. 1984–92, of Dept of Eng 1992–96; Dir (non-exec.) Vodafone Group 1998–2000, Vodafone Airtouch PLC 2000–, Lucas Industries Group 1995–96; Fellow Trinity Coll., Cambridge 1984–90; Master, Churchill Coll., Cambridge 1990–96, Fellow 1996–; Vice-Chancellor Univ. of Cambridge 1996–2003; Pres. Royal Acad. of Eng 2001–; Foreign Assoc. Nat. Acad. of Eng (USA); IBM Fellow 1977; Hon. Fellow (Gonville and Caius Coll., Cambridge) 1996–, (Trinity Coll., Cambridge) 1999–, (Univ. of Wales, Cardiff) 2001–; Hon. DEng (Glasgow) 1996; Hon. DSc (Warwick) 1997; Hon. LLD (Melbourne) 2000; Hon. DUniv (Anglia Polytechnic) 2000; Dr hc (Greenwich) 2000, (UMIST) 2002, (Peking) 2002; Prize for Industrial Applications of Physics, American Inst. of Physics 1982; Cledo Brunetti Award, Inst. of Electrical and Electronic Engineers 1985. *Publications:* patents, papers and book chapters on electron microscopy, electron beam lithography and integrated circuit fabrication. *Leisure interests:* music, small-boat sailing, skiing, tennis. *Address:* The Old Schools, Trinity Lane, Cambridge CB2 1TN, England. *Telephone:* (1223) 332291. *E-mail:* v-c@admin . cam.ac.uk (Office).

BROKAW, Thomas John, BA; American journalist; b. 6 Feb. 1940, Webster, S. Dakota; s. of Anthony O. Brokaw and Eugenia Conley; m. Meredith Lynn Auld 1962; three d.; ed Univ. of South Dakota; morning news KMTV, Omaha 1962–65; news ed., anchorman, WSB-TV, Atlanta 1965–66; reporter, corresp., anchorman KNBC-TV, Los Angeles 1966–73; White House corresp. NBC, Washington, DC 1973–76; anchorman, Saturday Night News, New York 1973–76; host, Today Show, New York 1976–82; anchorman, NBC Nightly News 1982–, Corresp. Exposé NBC 1991–; mem. advisory cttee Reporters Cttee for Freedom of Press, Gannett Journalism Center, Columbia Univ.; Trustee, Norton Simon Museum of Art, Pasadena, Calif.; Dr hc (Washington Univ., St Louis and Syracuse and Hofstra Univs). *Publication:* The Greatest Generation 1999. *Address:* NBC News, 30 Rockefeller Plaza, 3rd Floor, New York, NY 10112-0002, USA.

BROMLEY, David Allan, PhD, FRSA; American professor of physics; b. 4 May 1926, Westmeath, Ont., Canada; s. of Milton E and Susan (Anderson) Bromley; m. Patricia J. Brassor 1949 (died 1990); one s. one d.; ed Queen's

Univ., Kingston, Ont. and Univ. of Rochester, NY; operating engineer, Hydro Electric Power Comm., Ont. 1947–48; research officer, Nat. Research Council of Canada 1948; Instructor, then Asst Prof. of Physics, Univ. of Rochester 1952–55; Sr Resident Officer, Atomic Energy Canada Ltd 1955–60; Assoc. Prof. of Physics, Yale Univ. 1960–61, Prof. 1961–89, Chair. Dept of Physics 1970–77, Henry Ford II Prof. of Physics 1972–93, Sterling Prof. of Sciences 1993–, Dean of Eng, Yale Univ. 1994–2000; mem. White House Science Council 1981–89; Science and Tech. Asst to the Pres., Washington 1989–93, Chair. Pres.'s Council Advisers on Science and Tech. 1989–93, Fed. Coordinating Council, Science, Eng and Tech. 1989–93, Dir Office of Science and Tech. Policy 1989–93; Co-Founder and Principal, Washington Advisory Group LLC 1994–; discovered first nuclear molecules, created first completely integrated computer-based nuclear data acquisition system; Dir and consultant of several cos and mem. various scientific advisory bodies; Pres. AAAS 1981–85; Pres. Int. Union of Pure and Applied Physics 1984–87; Assoc. Ed. of several learned journals; Fellow AAAS, American Physical Soc., Brazilian Acad. of Sciences 1987–, Royal Soc. of SA 1988–; Benjamin Franklin Fellow Royal Soc. of Arts. 1979; mem. NAS 1990–; 33 hon. doctorates; Gov. Gen. of Canada Medal 1948, Guggenheim Fellowship 1977–78, Nat. Medal of Science 1988, Distinguished Public Service Medal 1991, Louis Pasteur Medal, Univ. of Strasbourg 1991, Commdr's Cross, Order of Merit, FRG 1993, Abelson Prize, AAAS 1977, Carey Medal, AAAS, 1993, Tenth Anniversary Medal, Human Frontier Science Program, Strasbourg 1999, Nicholson Medal, American Physical Soc. 2001. *Publications:* Large Electrostatic Accelerators 1976, Detectors in Nuclear Science 1978, Nuclear Science in China 1980, Heavy Ion Science, 8 Vols 1984, A Century of Physics 2001, A Life of Physics, Engineering and Public Policy 2003, A Golden Age of Canadian Science 2003; numerous scientific and tech. publs. *Leisure interests:* photography, golf, electronic systems, audio systems, travel. *Address:* Yale University, A. W. Wright Nuclear Laboratory, 272 Whitney, Box 208124, New Haven, CT 06520-8124; 35 Tokeneke Drive, North Haven, CT 06473, USA (Home). *Telephone:* (203) 432-3082 (Office). *Fax:* (203) 432-3522 (Office). *E-mail:* d .allan.bromley@yale.edu.

BRON, Eleanor, BA; British actress and author; b. 14 March 1938, Stanmore; d. of Sydney Bron and Fagah Bron; ed North London Collegiate School and Newnham Coll. Cambridge; started at Establishment Night Club, toured USA 1961; TV satire, Not So Much a Programme, More a Way of Life; co-wrote and appeared in TV series Where was Spring?, After That This, Beyond A Joke; Dir Actors' Centre 1982–93, Soho Theatre Co. 1993–2000. *Stage appearances include:* Private Lives, Hedda Gabler, Antony and Cleopatra, Madwoman of Chaillot, Hamlet; appeared at Royal Exchange in Uncle Vanya, Heartbreak House, Oedipus, The Prime of Miss Jean Brodie, Present Laughter; appeared at Nat. Theatre in The Duchess of Malfi, The Cherry Orchard, The Real Inspector Hound, The Miser, The White Devil and recently in Desdemona — If You Had Only Spoken! (one-woman show), Dona Rosita The Spinster, A Delicate Balance, Be My Baby, Making Noise Quietly. *Television:* appearances in Rumpole, Dr Who, French & Saunders, Absolutely Fabulous, Vanity Fair; BBC TV Play for Today: Nina, A Month in the Country, The Hour of the Lynx, The Blue Boy, Ted and Alice, Fat Friends. *Films:* Help!, Alfie, Two for the Road, Bedazzled, Women in Love, The National Health, Turtle Diary, Little Dorritt, The Attic, Deadly Advice 1994, Black Beauty 1993, A Little Princess 1994, The House of Mirth 2000, Iris 2001, The Heart of Me 2002, Love's Brother 2003. *Concert appearances (as narrator) include:* Façade, Carnival des Animaux, Peter and the Wolf, Bernstein's Symphony No. 3 with BBC Symphony Orchestra. *Publications include:* Song Cycle (with John Dankworth) 1973; verses for Saint-Saëns Carnival of the Animals 1975; Is Your Marriage Really Necessary? (with John Fortune) 1972, Life and Other Punctures 1978, The Pillow Book of Eleanor Bron 1985, Desdemona—If You Had Only Spoken! (translation of original by Christine Brückner) 1992, Double Take (novel) 1996. *Address:* c/o Rebecca Blond, 69A King's Road, London, SW3 4NX, England. *Telephone:* (20) 7351-4100. *Fax:* (20) 7351-4600.

BRON, Zakhar; violinist and teacher; b. 1947, Uralsk; ed Stoliarski School of Music, Odessa, Gnessin Conservatoire, Moscow, Tchaikovsky Conservatoire; studied with Boris Goldstein and Igor Oistrakh; has taught at Musikhochschule, Lübeck, Glinka Conservatoire, Novosibirsk, Royal Acad. of Music, London, Rotterdam Conservatoire, Reina Sofia School, Madrid, Musikhochschule, Cologne; lectures and gives masterclasses in many countries; has performed with many maj. int. orchestras; prizewinner Wieniawski Int. Violin Competition, Poznan, Queen Elizabeth Competition, Brussels; Verdienstkreutz am Bande (Germany). *E-mail:* mail@zakharbron.com (Home). *Website:* www.zakharbron.com (Home).

BRONEVOY, Leonid Sergeyevich; Russian actor; b. 17 Dec. 1928, Kiev, Ukraine; m.; one d.; ed Tashkent Inst. of Theatre Art, Studio School, Moscow Art Theatre; with Malaya Bronnaya Theatre 1961–88, with Moscow Lenkom Theatre 1998–; USSR People's Artist, State Prize of Russian Fed. *Films include:* Pokrovsky Gates. *Theatre includes:* Capulet in Romeo and Juliet, Don Louis in Don Juan, Shpigelsky in A Month in the Country, Krutitsky in Wizard, Dr. Dorn in The Seagull. *TV includes:* Seventeen Moments of Spring (series). *Address:* Tverskoy blvd 3, Apt. 22, 103104 Moscow, Russia. *Telephone:* (095) 291-73-46.

BRONFMAN, Charles Rosner, PC, CC; Canadian philanthropist; b. 27 June 1931, Montreal, Québec; s. of the late Samuel Bronfman and Saidye (Rosner) Bronfman; m. 2nd Andrea Morrison 1982; one s. one d. from previous m.; ed Selwyn House School, Montreal, PQ, Trinity Coll., Port Hope, Ont., McGill

Univ., Montreal; joined The Seagram Co. Ltd 1951, Co.-Chair. 1986–2000; Chair., prin. owner Montreal Expos 1968–90; Chair. Koor Industries Ltd; Chair. The Jerusalem Report, Andrea and Charles Bronfman Philanthropies, The CRB Foundation, United Jewish Communities; mem. Int. Advisory Corpn of Canada; Bd, Power Hon. Pres. United Israel Appeal of Canada; mem. of Bd Washington Inst. for Near E Policy, The Kravis Center for Performing Arts, Fla; Co-Chair. Birthright Israel; Chair. (non-exec.) The Nat. Jewish Center for Learning and Leadership; DPhil hc (Hebrew Univ. of Jerusalem), DL hc (McGill Univ., Montreal), (Concordia Univ., Montreal), (Univ. of Waterloo), (Univ. of Toronto), DHumLitt hc (Branders). *Leisure interests:* tennis, golf. *Address:* The Andrea and Charles Bronfman Philanthropies, c/o 375 Avenue, New York, NY 10152, USA. *Telephone:* (212) 572-7715 (Office); (514) 987-5200.

BRONFMAN, Edgar M., Jr; American business executive; b. 1955; m.; with J. Seagram Corpn 1976–, Asst to Pres. 1982, Man. Dir Seagram Europe 1982–84, Pres. House of Seagram 1984–88, Exec. Vice-Pres. US Operations 1988–89; Pres. and COO J.E. Seagram Corpn New York 1989–; now Pres. and CEO Seagram Co. Ltd (now Vivendi Universal); Acting Pres. MCA Inc. 1995–; mem. Bd of Dirs French & Associates 2001–. *Address:* Vivendi Universal, 42 avenue de Friedland, 75380 Paris, Cedex 08, France (Office). *Telephone:* 1-71-71-10-00 (Office). *Fax:* 1-71-71-10-01 (Office). *Website:* www.vivendiuniversal.com (Office).

BRONFMAN, Edgar Miles, BA; American business executive; b. 20 June 1929, Montreal, Québec; s. of the late Samuel Bronfman and Saidye (Rosner) Bronfman; m. Jan Aronson; four s. three d.; ed Trinity Coll. School, Port Hope, Ont., Williams Coll., Williamstown, Mass. and McGill Univ., Montreal; joined Distillers Corpn-Seagrams Ltd (renamed The Seagram Co. Ltd 1975) 1951, Pres. 1971–75, Chair. 1975–2000, CEO 1975–94 (Seagram Co. Ltd merged with Vivendi and CANAL+ to form Vivendi Universal Dec. 2000), Dir Vivendi Universal 2000–; Dir Int. Exec. Service Corps, American Technion Soc.; Chair. Clevepak Corpn, Pres. World Jewish Congress; Dir E.I. duPont de Nemours & Co., United Negro Coll. Fund, Weizmann Inst. of Science, American Cttee; Trustee Salk Inst. for Biological Studies, Mt Sinai Hosp. and School of Medicine; mem. Bd of Dirs Inter-racial Council for Business Opportunity; mem. Foreign Policy Asscn, Center for Inter-American Relations Inc., Cttee for Econ. Devt, Dir US–USSR Trade and Econ. Council, Inc.; Chevalier Légion d'honneur; Hon. DHumLitt (Pace) 1982, (Rochester) 1999; Hon. LLD (Williams Coll.) 1986, (Tulane Univ. Freeman Business School) 1995; Hon. DCS (New York) 1997; Hon. PhD (Hebrew Univ. of Jerusalem) 1997; Brandeis Award, Zionist Org. of America 1986. *Publications:* The Making of a Jew 1996, Good Spirits: The Making of a Businessman 1998. *Address:* Vivendi Universal, 375 Park Avenue, New York, NY 10152-0192, USA (Office). *Telephone:* (212) 572-7000 (Office). *Website:* www.vivendiuniversal.com (Office).

BRONIAREK, Zygmunt; Polish journalist and broadcaster (retd); b. 27 Aug. 1925, Warsaw; s. of Wacław Broniarek and Marianna Broniarek; m. Elzbieta Sarcewicz 1972; ed Main School of Planning and Statistics, Warsaw; Radio-telegraphic operator and stenographer, Czytelnik publishers, Warsaw 1945–48; Corresp. Trybuna Ludu 1950–90, Perm. Corresp. in USA 1985; in USA 1955, 1958, 1974, Latin America 1956, Paris 1959–60, 1969–73, Washington 1960–67, East Africa 1975, West Africa 1976, Nordic Countries 1977–82; mem. Polish United Workers' Party (PZPR) 1956–90; Corresp., Polish Radio and TV, for Finland and Sweden; Chair. Polish Asscn of Int. Journalists and Writers 1974–77; mem. Bd of Foreign Press Asscn, Stockholm 1979–81; mem. Presidium of Journalists' Asscn Polish People's Repub. 1983–85; Vice-Pres. Polish Club of Int. Journalism 1984–85, Vice-Pres. 1991–; Corresp. Trybuna Ludu, LA Olympic Games 1984; Special Corresp. in Australia 1984; Corresp. Trybuna Ludu, USA 1985–90; Presenter The Guests of Mr. Broniarek (TV), The Inner History of the Great Policy (TV) 1983, Behind the Scenes of Int. Politics (TV) 1983–85, retd 1990; columnist Trybuna 1996–; with Rynki Zagraniczne 1998–; Gold Cross of Merit, Order of Banner of Labour (Second Class) 1984, Commdr's Cross with Star of Infante Dom Henrique the Navigator (Portugal), Commdr's Cross with Star of Polonia Restituta 2002; Int. Journalists Club of Polish Journalistic Asscn Prize 1978, Golden Screen Award of Weekly Ekran 1984, Victor Prize (TV) 1985, Polish Club of Int. Journalism (1st Prize) 1990, Bolesław Prus Award, First Class (SD PRL) 1984, Hon. Silver Ace of Polish Promotion Corpn 1995, City of Warsaw Award of Merit 2000, Gold Medal, Polish Acad. of Success 2000. *Publications:* Od Hustonu do Mississipi 1956, Gorące dni Manhattanu 1960, Walka o Pałac Elizejski 1974, Kto się boi rewolucji (co-author) 1975, Angola zrodzona w walce 1977, Od Kissingera do Brzezińskiego 1980, Szaleństwo zbrojeń (co-author) 1982, Źródła spirali zbrojeń (co-author) 1985, Szczeble do Białego Domu 1986, Tajemnice Nagrody Nobla 1987, Ronald Reagan w Białym Domu 1989, Jak nauczyłem się ośmiu języków 1991, Biały Dom i Jego Prezydenci 1992, Wesoła spowiedź 1993, Książę Karol w Polsce 1994, Sekrety korespondenta zagranicznego 1995, Okiem światowca 1999, Kronika towarzyska Warszawy 2002, 365 dni z angielskim 2002. *Leisure interests:* good company, good food. *Address:* ul. Gałczyńskiego 12 m. 9, 00-362 Warsaw, Poland. *Telephone:* (22) 8263304.

BRONSON, Charles (Charles Buchinsky); American actor; b. 3 Nov 1922, Ehrenfield, Pa; m. 1st Harriet Tendler (divorced); two c.; m. 2nd Jill Ireland 1969 (deceased); one d. two step-c.; played small parts in Hollywood films in the 1950s before coming into prominence in The Magnificent Seven 1960. *Films include:* A Thunder of Drums, 1961, Lonely Are the Brave 1962, The Great Escape 1963, The Sandpiper 1965, Battle of the Bulge 1965, This Property is Condemned 1966, The Dirty Dozen 1967, Guns for San Sebastian 1969, Rider in the Rain 1969, Twinky 1969, You Can't Win Them All 1970, Cold Sweat 1971, The Family 1971, Chato's Land 1972, The Mechanic 1972, The Valachi Papers 1972, Wild Horses 1973, The Stone Killer 1973, Mr. Majestyck 1974, Death Wish 1974, Breakout 1975, Hard Times 1975, Breakheart Pass 1976, From Noon till Three 1976, St Ives 1976, The White Buffalo 1976, Telefon 1977, Love and Bullets 1979, Cabo Blanco, Death Wish II 1981, Murphy's Law 1986, Assassination 1987, Messenger of Death 1988, Kinjite 1989, The Indian Runner 1991, Death Wish V 1993, Dead to Rights 1995. *Television includes:* Raid on Entebbe 1976, The Legend of Jesse James, Act of Vengeance 1986, A Family of Cops I, II and III; also appeared on many American series during 1950s and 1960s. *Address:* c/o William Morris Agency, 1515 S. El Camino Drive, Beverly Hills, CA 90212, USA. *Website:* www.charles-bronson.com (Home).

BRONSTEIN, Alexander Semenovich, DrMed; Russian surgeon; b. 19 Sept. 1938, Khmelnitsky, Ukraine; s. of Semen Bronstein and Rebecca Yangaber; m. Irina Vladimirovna Kunina 1939; two d.; ed Moscow Sechenov Inst. of Med.; gen. practitioner of polyclinic, therapist Moscow hosp.; intern, Jr, then Sr researcher Inst. of Proctology 1964–76; Head Div. of Gastroenterology Moscow clinic 1976–90; Pres., Dir-Gen. Cen. of Endosurgery and Lithotripsy 1993–; Prof. Moscow Sechenov Acad. of Med.; mem. editorial Bd Int. Med. Journal; mem. Int. Acad. of Informatization 1978; corresp. mem. Russian Acad. of Nat. Sciences; Order of St Constantine the Great, Merited Dr of Russian Fed. *Publications:* Clinical Medicine (two vols.) and over 90 scientific works. *Leisure interests:* classical music, tennis, singing. *Address:* Centre for Endosurgery and Lythotripsy, Entusiastov shosse 62, 111125 Moscow, Russia (Office). *Telephone:* (095) 305-11-72 (Office).

BROOK, Adrian G., PhD; Canadian professor of chemistry; b. 21 May 1924, Toronto; s. of Frank A. Brook and Beatrice M. Wellington; m. Margaret E Dunn 1954; two s. one d.; ed Lawrence Park Collegiate and Univ. of Toronto; Lecturer in Chem. Univ. of Toronto 1953–56, Asst Prof. 1956–60, Assoc. Prof. 1960–62, Prof. 1962–89, Acting Chair. Dept of Chem. 1969–71, Chair. 1971–74, Chair. Univ. of Toronto Research Bd 1976–81, Univ. Prof. 1987, Univ. Prof. Emer. 1989–; Nuffield Fellow 1950–51; Stanley Kipping Award (American Chem. Soc.) 1973; CIC Medal (Chem. Inst. of Canada) 1986, Killam Prize (Canada Council) 1994. *Publications:* over 140 papers on aspects of organic chemistry. *Leisure interests:* windsurfing, computer hacking. *Address:* Department of Chemistry, University of Toronto, 80 Saint George Street, Toronto, M5S 3H6 (Office); 7 Thornwood Road, Apt. 202, Toronto, M4W 2R8, Canada (Home). *Telephone:* (416) 978-3573 (Office); (416) 920-8383 (Home). *Fax:* (416) 978-8775. *E-mail:* abrook@alchemy.chem.utoronto.ca (Office).

BROOK, Peter Stephen Paul, CH, CBE, MA; British theatre director, film director and writer; b. 21 March 1925; s. of Simon Brook; m. Natasha Parry 1951; one s. one d.; ed Westminster and Gresham's Schools and Magdalen Coll., Oxford; joined Royal Shakespeare Co. 1962; Producer, Co-Dir Royal Shakespeare Theatre; f. Centre for Theatre Research, Paris 1970, opened Théâtre des Bouffes du Nord, Paris 1974; Dir Int. Centre for Theatre Creations; Hon. DLitt (Birmingham), (Strathclyde) 1990; Freiherr von Stein Foundation, Shakespeare Award 1973, Wexner Prize (Ohio State Univ.) 1991, Onassis Int. Award 1993, Times Award 1994; Officier des Arts et des Lettres, Officier Légion d'honneur, Praemium Imperiale. *Films include:* The Beggar's Opera 1952, Moderato Cantabile 1959, Lord of the Flies 1963, Marat/Sade 1967, Tell Me Lies 1967, King Lear 1969, Meetings With Remarkable Men 1976–77, La Tragédie de Carmen 1983, The Mahabharata 1989, The Tragedy of Hamlet 2002. *Productions include:* Dr. Faustus 1943, Pygmalion, King John, Lady from the Sea 1945, Romeo and Juliet (at Stratford) 1947, Dir of Productions at Covent Garden Opera 1949–50, Faust (at Metropolitan Opera, NY) 1953, The Dark is Light Enough (London) 1954, House of Flowers (NY) 1954, Cat on a Hot Tin Roof (Paris) 1956, Eugene Onegin (NY) 1958, View from the Bridge (Paris) 1958, The Fighting Cock (NY) 1959, Irma la Douce 1960, King Lear 1963, The Physicists (NY) 1964, The Marat/Sade (NY) 1965, Oedipus (Seneca) 1968, A Midsummer Night's Dream 1970, The Conference of the Birds 1973, Timon of Athens (Paris) 1974, The Ik (Paris) 1975, (London) 1976, (USA) 1976, Ubu (Paris) 1977, Meetings with Remarkable Men (film, also Dir screenplay) 1977, Antony and Cleopatra (Stratford and London) 1978, Measure for Measure (Paris) 1978, Conference of the Birds, L'os (Festival Avignon and Paris) 1979, (New York) 1980, The Cherry Orchard (Paris) 1981, (New York) 1988, (Moscow) 1989, La Tragédie de Carmen (opera) (Paris) 1981, (film) 1983, Le Mahabharata (Avignon and Paris) 1985, (World tour) 1988, Woza Albert! (Paris) 1989, The Mahabharata (film) 1989, La Tempête (Paris) 1990, Impressions de Pelléas (opera) 1992, L'Homme Qui (Paris) 1993, 1997, The Man Who 1994, Oh! Les Beaux Jours (Lausanne) 1995, (Paris) 1996, Don Giovanni (opera) 1998, Je suis un phénomène (Paris) 1998, Le Costume (Paris) 1999, The Tragedy of Hamlet (Paris) 2000, Far Away (Paris) 2002, La Tragédie d'Hamlet (Paris) 2002. *Publications:* The Empty Space 1968, The Shifting Point: Forty years of theatrical exploration 1946–87, 1987, There Are No Secrets 1993 (appeared in USA as The Open Door: Thoughts on Acting and the Theatre), Threads of Time (autobiog.) 1998, Evoking Shakespeare 1999. *Leisure interests:* painting, playing the piano, air travel. *Address:* c/o CICT, 37 bis blvd de La Chapelle, 75010 Paris, France.

BROOK, Robert H., MD, ScD, FACP; American professor of medicine; b. 3 July 1943, New York; s. of Benjamin N. Brook and Elizabeth Berg; m. 1st Susan

Weiss 1966; m. 2nd Jacqueline Kosecoff 1981; one s. three d.; ed Univ. of Arizona, Johns Hopkins Medical School, Johns Hopkins School of Hygiene and Public Health; mil. service, US Public Health Services 1972–74; Dir Health Sciences Program, Rand Corpn 1990–, Vice-Pres. 1998–; Prof. of Medicine and Public Health, Univ. of Calif. Center for Health Sciences 1974–; Dir Robert Wood Johnson Clinical Scholars Program 1974–; mem. Inst. of Medicine, Nat. Acad. of Sciences, American Soc. of Clinical Investigation, American Asscn of Physicians; Commendation Medal; Richard and Hinda Rosenthal Foundation Award; Baxter Health Services Research Prize 1988; Sonneborn Distinguished Lecturer, Univ. of Pa, Distinguished Health Services Researcher, Asscn of Health Services Research; Robert J. Glaser Award of Soc. of Gen. Internal Medicine, Johns Hopkins Soc. of Scholars; Hollister Univ. Lecturer, Northwestern Univ.; Nat. Cttee for Quality Assurance Health Quality Award 2001, Research America 2000 Advocacy Award for Sustained Leadership 2001. *Publications:* over 300 articles on quality of medical care. *Leisure interests:* tennis, swimming, golf. *Address:* The Rand Corporation, PO Box 2138, 1700 Main Street, Santa Monica, CA 90401-3297 (Office); 1474 Bienvenida Avenue, Pacific Palisades, CA 90272-2346, USA (Home). *Telephone:* (310) 393-0411 (Office); (310) 454-0766 (Home). *Fax:* (310) 451-6917 (Office); (310) 454-2797 (Home). *E-mail:* brook@rand.org. *Website:* www.rand.org (Office).

BROOKE, Christopher Nugent Lawrence, CBE, MA, LittD, FBA, FRHistS, FSA; British historian; b. 23 June 1927, Cambridge; s. of Zachary Nugent Brooke and Rosa Grace (Stanton) Brooke; m. Rosalind Beckford Clark 1951; three s. (one deceased); ed Gonville and Caius Coll. Cambridge; Asst Lecturer, Univ. of Cambridge 1953–54, Lecturer 1954–56; Prof. of Medieval History, Univ. of Liverpool 1956–67; Prof. of History, Westfield Coll., Univ. of London 1967–77; Dixie Prof. of Ecclesiastical History, Univ. of Cambridge 1977–94; Pres. Soc. of Antiquaries 1981–84; Fellow Gonville and Caius Coll. Cambridge 1949–56, 1977–; Corresp. Fellow Medieval Acad. of America; Corresp. mem. Monumenta Germaniae Historica; Fellow Società Internazionale di Studi Francescani; mem. Royal Comm. on Historical Monuments 1977–83, Reviewing Comm. on Export of Works of Art 1979–82; corresp. mem. Bavarian Acad. of Sciences; Hon. DUniv (York) 1984. *Publications:* The Dullness of the Past 1957, From Alfred to Henry III 1961, The Saxon and Norman Kings 1963, Europe in the Central Middle Ages 1964, Time the Archsatirist 1968, The Twelfth Century Renaissance 1969, Structure of Medieval Society 1971, Medieval Church and Society (selected papers) 1971, Marriage in Christian History 1977, A History of Gonville and Caius College 1985, The Church and the Welsh Border in the Central Middle Ages 1986, The Medieval Idea of Marriage 1989, A History of the University of Cambridge IV, 1870–1970 1993, Jane Austen: Illusion and Reality 1999, Churches and Churchmen in Medieval Europe 1999; co-author of numerous works, including Gilbert Foliot and his Letters (with A. Morey) 1965, London 800–1216 (with G. Keir) 1975, Popular Religion in the Middle Ages, 1000–1300 (with Rosalind Brooke) 1984, Oxford and Cambridge (with Roger Highfield and Wim Swaan) 1988, David Knowles Remembered (with R. Lovatt, D. Luscombe and A. Sillem) 1991, A History of Emmanuel College, Cambridge (with S. Bendall and P. Collinson) 1999; ed. of numerous works, including Oxford (fmrly Nelson's) Medieval Texts, Nelson's History of England (Gen. Ed.); articles and reviews in professional journals. *Address:* Gonville and Caius College, Cambridge, CB2 1TA, England.

BROOKE, Edward William, LLD; American politician and lawyer; b. 26 Oct. 1919, Washington, DC; s. of Edward Brooke and Helen Brooke; m. 2nd Anne Fleming 1979; ed Howard Univ. and Boston Univ; admitted to Mass. Bar 1948; Chair. Finance Comm., Boston 1961–62; Attorney-Gen. of Mass. 1963–67; U.S. Senator from Mass. 1967–79; Chair. Boston Opera Co.; fmr Partner, O'Connor and Hannan, Washington, DC; Chair. Nat. Low-Income Housing Coalition 1979–; Counsel Csaplar and Bok, Boston 1979–; Ltd Partner, Bear and Stearns, NY 1979; Fellow, American Bar Asscn, American Acad. of Arts and Sciences; Republican; numerous hon. degrees. *Address:* Hanied Brooke, Suite 301-S, 6437 Blantyre Road, Warrenton, VA 20187, USA (Office).

BROOKE OF SUTTON MANDEVILLE, Baron (Life Peer), cr. 2001, of Sutton Mandeville in the County of Wiltshire; **Peter Leonard Brooke,** PC, CH, MA, MBA, FSA; British politician; b. 3 March 1934, London; s. of Lord Brooke of Cumnor, CH, PC and Baroness Brooke of Ystradfellte, DBE; m. 1st Joan Smith 1964 (died 1985); four s. (one deceased); m. 2nd Lindsay Allinson 1991; ed Marlborough Coll., Balliol Coll., Oxford, Harvard Business School, USA; Research Asst, Inst. pour l'Etude des Méthodes de Direction de l'Entreprise (IMEDE), Lausanne and Swiss Corresp. of Financial Times 1960–61; Spencer Stuart Man. Consultants 1961–79, Chair. of parent co. 1974–79; MP for City of London and Westminster S. 1977–97, for Cities of London and Westminster 1997–2001; Govt Whips' Office 1979–83; Dept of Educ. and Science Parl. Under-Sec. 1983–85; Minister of State, HM Treasury 1985–87, Paymaster Gen. 1987–89; Chair. Conservative Party 1987–89; Sec. of State for Northern Ireland 1989–92, for Nat. Heritage 1992–94; Chair. Commons Select Cttee on Northern Ireland 1997–2001; mem. House of Lords 2001–; Trustee, Wordsworth Trust 1974–2001, Cusichaca Project 1978–98; Lay Adviser, St Paul's Cathedral 1980–99; Chair. Churches Conservation Trust 1995–98; lay mem. Univ. of London Council 1994–, Deputy Chair. 2001–02, Chair. and Pro-Chancellor 2002–; Sr Fellow, RCA 1987; Presentation Fellow, King's Coll. London 1989; Hon. Fellow Queen Mary and Westfield Coll. 1996; Hon. DLitt (Westminster) 1999, (London Guildhall

Univ.) 2001. *Leisure interests:* churches, conservation, cricket, visual arts. *Address:* House of Lords, London, SW1A 0PW, England (Office). *Telephone:* (20) 7219-2150 (Office).

BROOKE-LITTLE, John Philip Brooke, CVO, KStJ, MA, FSA; British heraldic official (retd); b. 6 April 1927; s. of the late Raymond Brooke-Little; m. Mary Lee Pierce 1960; three s. one d.; ed Clayesmore School, New Coll., Oxford; mem. Earl Marshal's Staff 1952–53; Gold Staff Officer at Coronation of Queen Elizabeth II 1953; Bluemantle Pursuivant of Arms 1956–67; Richmond Herald 1967–80; Registrar Coll. of Arms 1974–82, Librarian 1974–94, Treas. 1978–95; Norroy and Ulster King of Arms, King of Arms, Registrar and Kt Attendant on the Most Illustrious Order of St Patrick 1980–95; Clarenceux King of Arms 1995–97; f., Chair. Heraldry Soc. 1947–97, Pres. 1997–; f. Coat of Arms Magazine 1950, Hon. Ed. 1950–; Chair. Bd of Govs Clayesmore School 1971–83; Chair. Harleian Soc. 1984–; Pres. English Language Literary Trust 1985–93; Dir Heralds' Museum 1991–93; Fellow Soc. of Antiquaries 1961, Soc. of Genealogists 1969; Adviser on heraldry to Nat. Trust, Shrievalty Assocn 1983–; Hon. Fellow Inst. of Heraldic and Genealogical Studies 1979; Kt of Malta 1955, numerous decorations. *Publications:* Royal London 1953, Pictorial History of Oxford 1954, Boutell's Heraldry (several edns 1963–83), Knights of the Middle Ages 1966, Prince of Wales 1969, Fox-Davies Complete Guide to Heraldry 1969, Kings and Queens of Great Britain 1970 (jtly), An Heraldic Alphabet 1973, Beasts in Heraldry 1974 (jtly), The British Monarchy in Colour 1976, Royal Arms, Beasts and Badges 1977, Royal Ceremonies of State 1979; articles on genealogy and heraldry. *Address:* Heyford House, Lower Heyford, Bicester, Oxon., OX25 5NZ, England. *Telephone:* (1869) 340337.

BROOKNER, Anita, CBE; British teacher and author; b. 16 July 1928; d. of Newson and Maude Brookner; ed James Allen's Girls' School, King's Coll., London, Courtauld Inst. and Paris; Visiting Lecturer, Univ. of Reading 1959–64; Slade Prof., Univ. of Cambridge 1967–68; lecturer, Courtauld Inst. of Art 1964, Reader 1977–87; Fellow, New Hall Cambridge, King's Coll. London; Hon. DLitt (Loughborough Univ. of Tech.) 1990, Dr hc (Smith Coll., USA); Booker Prize for Fiction for Hôtel du Lac 1984. *Publications:* Watteau 1968, The Genius of the Future 1971, Greuze: The Rise and Fall of an Eighteenth Century Phenomenon 1972, Jacques-Louis David 1980, The Stories of Edith Wharton (ed.) 1988; novels: A Start in Life 1981, Providence 1982, Look at Me 1983, Hôtel du Lac 1984, Family and Friends 1985, A Misalliance 1986, A Friend from England 1987, Latecomers 1988, Lewis Percy 1989, Brief Lives 1990, A Closed Eye 1991, Fraud 1992, A Family Romance 1993, A Private View 1994, Incidents in the rue Laugier 1995, Altered States 1996, Visitors 1997, Soundings 1997, Falling Slowly 1998, Undue Influence 1999, The Bay of Angels 2000; articles in Burlington Magazine etc. *Address:* 68 Elm Park Gardens, London, SW10 9PB, England. *Telephone:* (20) 7352-6894.

BROOKS, Albert (pseudonym of Albert Einstein); American actor, writer and director; b. 22 July 1947, LA; s. of Harry Brooks and Thelma (Leeds) Einstein. *Films include:* (actor) Taxi Driver 1976, Private Benjamin 1980, Twilight Zone: The Movie 1983, Unfaithfully Yours 1983, Terms of Endearment 1983, Broadcast News 1987, I'll Do Anything 1994, The Scout 1994, Critical Care 1997, Out of Sight 1998, Dr Dolittle (voice only) 1998, The Muse 1999; (dir, writer and actor) Real Life 1979, Modern Romance 1982, Lost in America 1985, Defending Your Life 1991, Mother 1996 (NY Soc. of Film Critics' Award, Nat. Soc. of Film Critics' Award for Best Screenplay), My First Mister 2000. *Television includes:* The Tonight Show, Merv Griffin Show, Steven Allen Show, Gold Diggers, The Simpsons (voice only) 1993; dir, writer short films Saturday Night Live 1975–76. *Recordings include:* Comedy Minus One, A Star is Bought.

BROOKS, Diana B.; American business executive; b. 1950; m. Michael C. Brooks; two c.; ed Yale Univ.; lending officer Nat. Banking Group, Citibank 1973–79; fmrly Sr Vice Pres., then Pres., CEO Sotheby's N. America; Pres., CEO Sotheby's N. and S. America 1990–2000; Pres., CEO Sotheby's Holdings Inc. 1994–2000; sentenced to three years' probation for price-fixing April 2002; Pres. Council of Assocs Frick Art Reference Library; Dir New York City Partnership; Trustee Yale Univ., Deerfield Acad., Allen-Stevenson School. *Address:* c/o Sotheby's, 1334 York Avenue, New York, NY 10021, USA.

BROOKS, Garth (Troyal Garth Brooks), BS; American country music singer; b. 7 Feb. 1962, Tulsa, Okla; s. of Troyal Raymond and Colleen Carroll Brooks; m. Sandy Mahl 1986; two c.; ed Oklahoma State Univ.; Acad. Country Music Entertainer of the Year Award 1991, 1992, 1993, 1994, Male Vocalist of the Year Award 1991, Horizon Award, Country Music Assocn Entertainer of the Year award 1991, 1992, Grammy Award for Best Male Country Vocalist 1992, Best Male Country Music Performer 1992, 1993, Best Male Musical Performer, People's Choice Awards 1992–95, Artist of Decade, Country Music Awards 1999 Favourite, Country Artist and Album, American Music Awards 2000; inducted into Grand Ole Opry. *Albums include:* Garth Brooks, No Fences (Acad. Country Music Album of the Year 1991), Ropin' The Wind 1991, Beyond the Season 1992, The Chase 1992, In Pieces 1993, The Hits 1994, Fresh Horses 1995, Sevens 1997, The Limited Series 1998, Double Live 1998, In the Life of Chris Gaines 1999, The Colors of Christmas 1999, Scarecrow 2001. *Songs include:* The Dance (Acad. Country Music Song of Year 1991), Friends in Low Places (Acad. Country Music Single Record of Year 1991), If Tomorrow Never Comes (American Music Country Song of Year 1991), The Thunder Rolls, We Shall Be Free, Somewhere Other Than The Night,

Learning to Live Again. *Television specials:* This is Garth Brooks 1992, This is Garth Brooks Too 1994, Garth Brooks: The Hits 1995, Garth Brooks Live in Cen. Park 1997. *Address:* 1111 17th Avenue S, Nashville, TN 37212, USA.

BROOKS, James L.; American screenwriter, director and producer; b. 9 May 1940, Brooklyn, NY; s. of Edward M. Brooks and Dorothy Helen Sheinheit; m. 1st Marianne Catherine Morrissey 1964 (divorced); one d.; m. 2nd Holly Beth Holmbert 1978; one s. one d.; ed New York Univ.; writer CBS News, New York 1964–66; writer-producer documentaries Wolper Productions, LA 1966–67; founder and owner Gracie Films 1984; mem. Guild of America, Writers' Guild of America, TV Acad. of Arts and Sciences, Acad. of Motion Picture Arts and Sciences. *TV series include:* creator Room 222 1968–69 (Emmy Award for Outstanding New Series); co-creator, producer Mary Tyler Moore Show 1970–77 (Emmy Awards for Comedy Writing, Outstanding Comedy Series, Peabody Award, Writers' Guild of America Award, Humanitas Award and others); writer, producer Paul Sand in Friends and Lovers 1974; co-creator, co-exec. producer series Rhoda Show 1974–75 (Emmy and Humanitas Awards); co-creator, exec. producer Taxi 1978–80 (Emmy, Film Critics' Circle, Golden Globe and Humanitas Awards); co-exec. producer, co-writer Cindy 1978; co-creator, exec. producer The Associates 1979; exec. producer, co-exec. producer, co-creator The Tracey Ullman Show 1986–90 (3 Emmy Awards for Outstanding Variety or Comedy Series, 2 Emmy Awards Outstanding Writing Variety or Music Show), The Simpsons 1990– (3 Emmy Awards). *Films include:* producer, writer, dir Terms of Endearment 1983 (Golden Globe Best Screenplay and Best Picture Awards, Acad. Awards for Best Film, Best Dir, Best Screenplay, Dirs' Guild of America Award for Best Dir); writer, dir, producer Broadcast News 1987 (New York Film Critics' Awards for Best Picture, Best Dir, Best Screenplay); exec. producer Big 1988, The War of the Roses 1989; producer Jerry Maguire 1996, As Good As It Gets 1997, Riding in Cars With Boys. *Address:* Gracie Films/Columbia Pictures, Poitier Building, 10202 Washington Boulevard, Culver City, CA 90232, USA (Office).

BROOKS, Mel (Melvin Kaminsky); American actor, writer, producer and director; b. 1926, New York; m. 1st Florence Baum; two s. one d.; m. 2nd Anne Bancroft (q.v.) 1964; one s.; script writer for TV series Your Show of Shows 1950–54, Caesar's Hour 1954–57, Get Smart 1965; set up feature film production co. Brooksfilms; Academy awards for The Critic 1964, The Producers (Best Screenplay) 1968. *Television:* Mad About You (Emmy Award for Outstanding Guest Actor in a Comedy Series 1997, 1998, 1999). *Films include:* The Critic (cartoon) 1964, The Producers 1968, The Twelve Chairs 1970, Blazing Saddles 1974, Young Frankenstein 1974, Silent Movie 1976, High Anxiety 1977, The Elephant Man 1980, History of the World Part I 1981, My Favourite Year 1982, To Be or Not to Be 1983, Fly I 1986, Spaceballs 1987, 84 Charing Cross Road 1987, Fly II 1989, Life Stinks 1991, Robin Hood: Men in Tights 1993, Dracula: Dead and Loving It 1995. *Musical:* The Producers: The New Mel Brooks Musical (producer, co-writer, composer) (Tony Awards for Best Book, Best Score, Best Musical) 2001. *Address:* c/o The Culver Studios, 9336 W Washington Boulevard, Culver City, CA 90232, USA.

BROOME, David McPherson, CBE; British professional show jumper and farmer; b. 1 March 1940, Cardiff; s. of Fred Broome and Amelia Broome; brother of veteran show jumper Liz Edgar; m. Elizabeth Fletcher 1976; three s.; ed Monmouth Grammar School for Boys; European show jumping champion, riding Sunsalve, Aachen 1961, riding Mr. Softee, Rotterdam 1967 and Hickstead 1969; world champion, riding Beethoven, La Baule (France) 1970; professional world champion, riding Sportsman and Philco, Cardiff 1974; mem. of six British Olympic teams (including Barcelona 1992); Master of Foxhounds. *Publications:* Jump-Off 1970, Horsemanship (with S. Hadley) 1983. *Leisure interests:* hunting, shooting, golf. *Address:* Mount Ballan Manor, Crick, Caldicot, Monmouthshire, NP26 5XP, Wales. *Telephone:* (1291) 420778.

BROPHY, Theodore F., BA, LLB; American business executive; b. 4 April 1923, New York; s. of Frederick H. Brophy and Muriel W. (née Osborne) Brophy; m. Sallie M. Showalter; one s. one d.; ed Yale Univ. and Harvard Univ. Law School; Assoc. law firm of Root, Ballantine, Harlan, Bushby & Palmer 1950–55; Gen. Counsel, The Lummus Co. 1955–58; GTE Corpn, Counsel 1958–59, Vice-Pres. and Gen. Counsel 1959–68, Exec. Vice-Pres. 1968–69, Dir 1969, Pres. 1972–76, 1992–95, Chair. and CEO 1976–88; Chair. US Del., World Admin. Conf. on Space Services –1988; Dir Procter and Gamble Co., Readers' Digest Asscn; Trustee Dewitt and Lilla Wallace Readers' Digest Funds, Smith Coll., Kent School; mem. American Bar Asscn and Past Chair. Public Utility Law Section; mem. Fed. Communications Bar Asscn; Public mem. Admin. Conf. of the US 1970–72. *Address:* 60 Arch Street, Greenwich, CT 06830, USA (Office).

BROSNAN, Pierce; Irish actor; b. 16 May 1953, Navan, Co. Meath; s. of Tom Brosnan and May Smith; m. Cassandra Harris (died 1991); one s.; m. Keely Shaye Smith 2001; two s.; ed Drama Center; London stage appearances include Wait Until Dark, The Red Devil Battery Sign (cast in role of McCabe in British premiere by Tennessee Williams), Filumenia. *Films include:* The Mirror Crack'd 1980, The Long Good Friday, Nomads, The Fourth Protocol, Taffin, The Deceivers, Mister Johnson, The Lawnmower Man, Mrs Doubtfire 1993, Love Affair 1994, Robinson Crusoe 1995, Mars Attacks! 1996, The Mirror Has Two Faces 1996, Dante's Peak 1997, The Nephew 1998, The Thomas Crown Affair 1999, Grey Owl 2000; role of James Bond in Goldeneye 1994, Tomorrow Never Dies 1997, The World is Not Enough 1999, The Tailor

of Panama 2001, Die Another Day 2002, Evelyn 2003. *TV appearances include:* role of detective in Remington Steele (series), Noble House (NBC mini-series), Nancy Astor, Around the World in Eighty Days, The Heist, Murder 101, Victim of Love, Live Wire, Death Train, Robinson Crusoe 1994, The James Bond Story 1999. *Address:* c/o Guttman Associates, 118 South Beverly Drive, Suite 201, Beverly Hills, CA 90212, USA (Office).

BROTODININGRAT, Soemadi Djoko Moerdjono; Indonesian diplomatist; b. 13 June 1941, Solo, Central Javan Province; m.; one s. one d.; with Dept of Foreign Affairs 1965–, Head of Section (and later of Staff), Directorate of Information 1965–71; Second, then Third Sec., Embassy in Brussels 1971–75; Deputy Dir of Social and Cultural Relations, Dept of Foreign Affairs 1975–78; First Sec., Counsellor, Perm. Mission to UN, New York 1978–82, Minister Counsellor 1984–88; Deputy Dir, Directorate of Multilateral Econ. Co-operation, Dept of Foreign Affairs 1982–84, Dir 1988–91; Dir-Gen. for Foreign Econ. Relations, Dept of Foreign Affairs 1995–98; Amb. to Japan and Federated States of Micronesia 1998–2002, to USA 2002–. *Address:* Embassy of Indonesia, 2020 Massachusetts Avenue, NW, Washington, DC 20036, USA (Office). *Telephone:* (202) 775-5200 (Office). *Fax:* (202) 775-5365 (Office). *E-mail:* indonesia@dgs.dgsys.com (Office). *Website:* www.embassyofindonesia.org (Office).

BROUGHTON, Martin Faulkner, FCA; British business executive; b. 15 April 1947, London; s. of Edward Broughton and Laura Faulkner; m. Jocelyn Mary Rodgers 1974; one s. one d.; ed Westminster City Grammar School; chartered accountant Peat Marwick Mitchell; joined British-American Tobacco Co. (BAT) 1971; with group's Brazilian subsidiary Souza Cruz 1980–85; Finance Dir BAT Industries 1988–93; Group Chief Exec. and Deputy Chair. 1993–98, Chair. BAT PLC (following demerger) 1998–; Finance Dir Eagle Star 1985–88, Chair. 1992–93, Chair. Wiggins Teape Group 1989–90; Dir (non-exec.) Whitbread 1993–2000, British Airways 2000–; Ind. Dir British Horseracing Bd 1999–; mem. Financial Reporting Council 1998–. *Leisure interests:* horseracing, golf, theatre. *Address:* British American Tobacco PLC, Globe House, 4 Temple Place, London, WC2R 2PG, England (Office). *Telephone:* (20) 7845-1000 (Office); (20) 7845-1901. *Fax:* (20) 7845-2191. *Website:* www.bat.com (Office).

BROWALDH, Tore, BA, LLM, DEng, DEcon; Swedish banker; b. 23 Aug. 1917, Västerås; s. of Ernfrid Browaldh and Ingrid (née Gezelius) Browaldh; m. Gunnel Ericson 1942; three s. one d.; Financial Attaché Swedish Legation, Washington, DC 1943; Asst Sec. Swedish Royal Cttee of Post-War Econ. Planning 1944–45: Admin. Sec. Swedish Industrial Inst. for Econ. and Social Research 1944–45; Sec. Bd of Man., Svenska Handelsbanken 1946–49, Chief Gen. Man. 1955–66, Chair. 1966–78, Vice-Chair. 1978–88, Hon. Chair. 1988–; Dir Econ., Social, Cultural and Refugee Dept, Sec.-Gen. Council of Europe 1949–51; Exec. Vice-Pres. Confed. of Swedish Employers 1951–54; mem. Bd Swedish Bankers Asscn, Chair. 1959–61; Chair. AB Industrivärden 1966–88, Svenska Cellulosa AB 1960–88, Swedish IBM 1960–88, Swedish Unilever AB 1968–; Deputy Chair. Nobel Foundation 1966–88, AB Volvo; mem. Bd IBM World Trade Corpn 1976–88; mem. Advisory Bd Unilever, Rotterdam 1976–88; mem. Bd Dag Hammarskjöld Foundation 1961–63, Swedish Govt Research Advisory Bd 1966–70, Swedish Govt Industrial Policy Comm. 1968–70, Swedish Govt Econ. Planning Comm. 1962–80; Special Adviser to Int. Fed. of Insts. for Advanced Studies; mem. UN Group to Study Multinational Corpns.; mem. Swedish Royal Acad. of Sciences 1980, Swedish Acad. of Eng Sciences 1961–, Royal Acad. of Arts and Sciences, Uppsala; St Erik Medal, Commdr Order of Vasa, Commdr Grand Cross Order of the Northern Star. *Publications:* Management and Society 1961, The Pilgrimage of a Journeyman 1976, The Road Ahead 1980, Ascent and Tailwind 1984. *Leisure interests:* playing jazz on piano, golf, computer technology. *Address:* Svenska Handelsbanken, Kungsträdgårdsgatan 2, S-106 70 Stockholm (Office); 14 Sturegatan, 114 36 Stockholm, Sweden (Home). *Telephone:* (8) 661-96-43 (Home).

BROWDER, Felix Earl, MA, PhD; American professor of mathematics and university administrator; b. 31 July 1927, Moscow, Russia; s. of Earl Browder and Raissa Berkmann; m. Eva Tislowitz 1949; two s.; ed Yonkers High School and Princeton Univ.; CLE Moore Instructor in Math. MIT 1948–51; Instructor in Math. Boston Univ. 1951–53; US Army 1953–55; Asst Prof. of Math. Brandeis Univ. 1955–56; Asst Prof. then Prof. Yale Univ. 1956–63; Prof. of Math. Univ. of Chicago 1963–72, Louis Block Prof. of Math. 1972–82, Max Mason Distinguished Service Prof. 1982–87, Chair. Math. Dept 1971–76, 1979–85; Visiting Prof. MIT 1961–62, 1977–78; Vice-Pres. for Research Rutgers Univ. 1986–91, Univ. Prof. 1986–; Pres. American Mathematical Soc. 1999–2001; ed. numerous journals; mem. NAS (mem. Council 1992–95, Governing Bd Nat. Research Council 1994–95); Fellow, American Acad. of Arts and Sciences; Dr. hc (Paris) 1990; Nat. Medal of Science 1999. *Publications:* Problèmes non-linéaires 1966, Functional Analysis and Related Fields 1970, Nonlinear Functional Analysis (2 Vols) 1970, 1976, Mathematical Heritage of Henri Poincaré 1984, Nonlinear functional analysis and its applications (2 Vols) 1985; numerous papers in mathematical journals. *Leisure interests:* reading, especially in philosophy, history and classics. *Address:* Rutgers University, P.O. Box 201, New Brunswick, NJ 08903, USA. *Telephone:* (732) 445-2393 (Office); (732) 297-6040 (Home). *E-mail:* browder@math.rutgers.edu.

BROWN, Alexander Claude, PhD, DSc, FRSSA; South African professor of zoology and marine biology; b. 19 Aug. 1931, Cape Town; s. of Alexander John

Brown and Doris Hilda (née Todd) Brown; m. Rosalind Jane Roberts 1957; three s.; ed Rhodes Univ. and Univ. of Cape Town; lecturer in Zoology, Rhodes Univ. 1954; Research Officer Council for Scientific and Industrial Research 1954–57; lecturer and Sr Lecturer Univ. of Cape Town 1957–74, Prof. and Head Dept of Zoology 1975–96, Prof. Emer. 1997–; Dir Univ. Centre for Marine Studies 1997–2000; Deputy Dean, Faculty of Music 1970–80; worked at the Univs. of London, Manchester, Cambridge and Plymouth Marine Lab.; expeditions to Chile and Antarctica; mem. Ed. Bd Journal of Experimental Marine Biology and Ecology; Past Pres. Royal Soc. of South Africa; Life Fellow Univ. of Cape Town; Gold Medal, Zoological Soc. of Southern Africa, Gilchrist Medal for Outstanding Marine Research. *Publications:* Ed. A History of Scientific Endeavour in South Africa (Royal Soc. of South Africa), several textbooks; Ed. Transactions of the Royal Soc. of South Africa 1968–82; Ecology of Sandy Shores (with A. McLachlan) 1990; about 200 research papers on the ecophysiology of sandy beach animals and marine pollution. *Leisure interests:* music, musicological research. *Address:* Department of Zoology, University of Cape Town, Rondebosch 7701 (Office); 10 Monroe Road, Rondebosch 7708, South Africa (Home). *Telephone:* (21) 6503628 (Office); (21) 6713504 (Home). *Fax:* (21) 6503301 (Office). *E-mail:* acbrown@botzoo.uct.ac.za (Office).

BROWN, Cedric Harold, FREng, FICE; British business executive; b. 7 March 1935; s. of the late William Herbert Brown and Constance Dorothy Brown (née Frances); m. Joan Hendry 1956; one s. three d.; ed Sheffield, Rotherham and Derby Colls of Tech.; East Midlands Gas Bd 1953–59; Eng Asst Tunbridge Wells Borough Council 1959–60; Eng posts, East Midlands Gas Bd 1960–75; Dir of Eng East Midlands Gas 1975–78; joined British Gas Corpn (now British Gas PLC) 1978; Dir Morecambe Bay Project 1980–87; Regional Chair. British Gas West Midlands 1987–89; Dir and Man. Dir Exploration and Production 1989; Man. Regional Services 1989–91; Sr Man. Dir 1991; Chief Exec. British Gas PLC 1992–96; Chair. CB Consultants 1996–, Intellihome PLC 1997–, Atlantic Caspian Resources PLC 1999–, Business Champions-East Midlands Devt Agency 2001–, Lachesis Investment Advisory Cttee 2002–; Pres. Institution of Gas Engineers 1996–97, Fellow; Dir Bow Valley Industries 1988–92, Orb Estates 2000–; mem. Advisory Council on Business and the Environment 1993–95. *Publications:* tech. papers. *Leisure interests:* sport, countryside, places of historic interest. *Address:* CB Consultants Limited, 1 Great Cumberland Place, London, W1H 7AL, England.

BROWN, David Arthur, PhD, DSc, MRIA; British emeritus professor of inorganic chemistry; b. 5 June 1929, High Wycombe; s. of Arthur Percy Brown and Fanny Catherine (née Withell) Brown; m. Rita Brown; two s. four d.; ed Watford Grammar School, Queen Mary Coll., King's Coll., Cambridge; lecturer, Univ. Coll. Dublin 1959; Prof. of Inorganic Chem. 1964, Head of Dept 1974–77, 1983–86, 1989–, Dean of Faculty of Science 1984–87, mem. of Governing Body 1979–81, 1985–87; Pres. Inst. of Chem. of Ireland 1976–77; Wheeler Lecturer 1999; Boyle-Higgins Medal 1996. *Publications:* over 180 publs on organo-metallic chem., bioinorganic chem. and theoretical chem. *Leisure interests:* walking, travelling, reading, music. *Address:* Department of Chemistry, University College, Belfield, Dublin 4, Ireland. *Telephone:* Dublin 7162297.

BROWN, Donald David, MS, MD; American biologist; b. 30 Dec. 1931, Cincinnati, Ohio; s. of Albert L. Brown and Louise R. Brown; m. Linda Weil 1957; one s. two d.; ed Walnut Hills High School, Cinn., Dartmouth Coll and Univ. of Chicago; Intern, Charity Hosp., New Orleans 1956–57, Sr Asst Surgeon, US Public Health Service, Bethesda 1957–59; Postdoctoral Fellow, Pasteur Inst. 1959–60, Chief Asst; Dept of Embryology, Carnegie Inst. of Washington, Baltimore 1960–62, staff mem. 1963–, Dir 1976–94; Prof., Dept of Biology, Johns Hopkins Univ. 1968–; Pres. Life Sciences Research Foundation 1981–; Pres. American Soc. of Cell Biology 1992; US Steel Award in Molecular Biology 1973, V. D. Mattia Award 1976, Boris Pregel Award, New York Acad. of Science 1977, Rose Harrison-ISDB Award 1981, Ernst W. Bertner Award, Texas Univ. Cancer Center 1982, Louisa Gross Horwitz Award, Columbia Univ. 1985, Rosenstiel Award 1985, Feodor Lynen Medal, Miami Winter Symposium 1987, E. Wilson Award 1996. *Address:* Carnegie Institution Washington, 115 W University Parkway, Baltimore, MD 21210 (Office); 5721 Oakshire Road, Baltimore, MD 21209, USA (Home). *Telephone:* (410) 554-1252 (Office); (410) 466-0902 (Home). *Fax:* (410) 243-6311 (Office). *E-mail:* brown@ciwemb.edu (Office).

BROWN, Edmund Gerald, Jr, AB, JD; American politician and lawyer; b. 7 April 1938, San Francisco; s. of Edmund G. Brown and Bernice Layne; ed Univ. of California at Berkeley, Yale Law School; Research Attorney, Calif. Supreme Court 1964–65, Attorney, Los Angeles 1966–69; Sec. of State, Calif. 1971–74; Gov. of Calif. 1975–83; Chair. Calif. State Democratic Party 1989–90; unsuccessful Democratic Presidential Cand. 1992; Mayor of Oakland, Calif. 1999–; partner Reavis and McGarth; Trustee, Los Angeles Community Colls. 1969. *Publication:* Dialogues 1988. *Address:* 1 Frank Ogawa Plaza, 1 City Hall Plaza, 3rd Floor, Oakland, CA 94612-1997, USA (Office).

BROWN, Fred, OBE, PhD, FRS; British chemist; b. 31 Jan. 1925, Clayton, Lancs.; s. of Fred Brown and Jane E Fielding; m. Audrey Alice Doherty 1948; two s.; ed Burnley Grammar School, Victoria Univ. of Manchester; Head, Biochem. Dept, Animal Virus Research Inst., Pirbright, Surrey 1955–83, Deputy Dir 1980–83; Head, Virology Dept, Wellcome Biotechnology Ltd 1983–90; Adjunct Prof. of Epidemiology, Yale Univ. 1990–95; Professorial

Fellow Queen's Univ., Belfast 1986–; Scientific Sec. Int. Asscn of Biological Standardisation; Visiting Scientist, US Dept of Agric., Plum Island Animal Disease Center, New York 1995–; Hon. DSc (Queen's Univ., Belfast) 1992. *Publications:* numerous papers on virology. *Leisure interests:* fell walking, reading scientific biographies, watching cricket and association football. *Address:* Plum Island Animal Disease Center, Greenport, P.O. Box 848, NY 11944-0848, USA (Office); Syndal, Glaziers Lane, Normandy, Surrey GU3 2DF, England (Home); 14 Cromwell Place, Old Saybrook, CT 06475, USA (Home). *Telephone:* (631) 323-3338 (USA) (Office); (1483) 811107 (England) (Home); (860) 388-1527 (USA) (Home). *Fax:* (631) 323-3044 (USA) (Office). *E-mail:* aciupryk@piadc.ars.usda.gov.

BROWN, Gavin, MA, PhD; Australian mathematician and academic; b. 27 Feb. 1942, Fife, Scotland; s. of Frank Brown and Alexandria Duncanson; m. Barbara Routh (died 2001); one s. one d.; ed Madras Coll., St Andrews, Univ. of St Andrews, Univ. of Newcastle upon Tyne; Asst Lecturer, Lecturer, Sr Lecturer Univ. of Liverpool 1966–75; Visiting Prof., Univ. of Paris 1975, Univ. of York 1979, Univ. of Cambridge 1986; Prof. of Pure Math., Univ. of NSW 1976–92, Dean Faculty of Science 1989–92; Deputy Vice-Chancellor Univ. of Adelaide 1992–93, Vice-Chancellor 1994–96; Vice-Chancellor and Principal Univ. of Sydney 1996–; Fellow Australian Acad. of Science 1981, Australian Math. Soc. Medal 1982, Hon. LLD (St Andrews Univ.) 1998. *Publications:* numerous publs in math. journals. *Leisure interest:* racing. *Address:* University of Sydney, Sydney, NSW 2006, Australia (Office). *Telephone:* (2) 9351-5051 (Office). *Fax:* (2) 9351-4596 (Office). *E-mail:* vice-chancellor@vcc.usyd.edu.au (Office).

BROWN, Gordon (see Brown, James Gordon).

BROWN, Hank, JD, LLM, CPA; American university president, lawyer and fmr politician; b. 12 Feb. 1940, Denver, Colo; s. of Harry W. Brown and Anna M. Hanks; m. Nana Morrison 1967; one s. two d.; ed Univ. of Colo and George Washington Univ.; Lt US Navy 1962–66; tax accountant, Arthur Andersen 1967–78; admitted Colo Bar 1969; Asst to Pres. Monfort of Colo Inc., Greeley 1969–70, Corp. Counsel 1970–71, Vice-Pres. Monfort Food Distributing 1971–72, Vice-Pres. Corp. Devt 1973–75, Int. Operations 1975–78, Lamb Div. 1978–80; mem. US House of Reps (97th–101st) Congresses from Colo 4th Dist; mem. Colo State Senate 1972–76, Asst Majority Leader 1974–76; US Senator from Colorado (102nd Congress) 1991–97; mem. Senate Judiciary, Budget and Foreign Affairs Cttees 1991–97; Pres. Univ. of N Colo 1998–; Republican; Hungarian Presidential Gold Medal, Air Medal, Viet Nam Service Medal Order of Merit, Poland, Grand Cordon of the Order of the Brilliant Star, Repub. of China, Nishan-I-Quaid-I-Azam, Pakistan. *Leisure interest:* skiing. *Address:* University of Northern Colorado, Campus Box 59, Greeley, CO 80639-0001, USA (Home). *Telephone:* (970) 351-2222 (Office). *Fax:* (970) 351-1110.

BROWN, Harold, PhD; American fmr government official and physicist; b. 19 Sept. 1927, New York City; s. of A. H. Brown and Gertrude Cohen; m. Colene McDowell 1953; two d.; ed New York City public schools and Columbia Univ.; Lecturer in Physics, Columbia Univ. 1947–48, Stevens Inst. of Tech. 1949–50; Univ. of Calif. Radiation Laboratory, Berkeley 1950–52; Livermore Radiation Laboratory, 1952–61, Dir 1960–61; mem. Polaris Steering Cttee, Dept of Defense 1956–58; Consultant to Air Force Scientific Advisory Bd 1956–57; mem. Scientific Advisory Cttee on Ballistic Missiles to Sec. of Defense 1958–61; mem. President's Science Advisory Cttee 1961; Sec. of Air Force 1965–69; Pres. Calif. Inst. of Tech. 1969–77; US Sec. of Defense 1977–81; Distinguished Visiting Prof. of Nat. Security Affairs, School of Advanced Int. Studies, Johns Hopkins Univ. 1981–84, Chair. Johns Hopkins Univ. Foreign Policy Inst. 1984–92; business consultant 1981–; Dir Philip Morris, Evergreen Holdings Inc., Mattel; Pnr Warburg, Pincus and Co. 1990–; Counsellor Center for Strategic and Int. Studies 1992–; mem. Del. to Strategic Arms Limitation Talks 1969; mem. NAS; Hon. DEng (Stevens Inst. of Tech.); Hon. LLD (Long Island Univ., Gettysburg Coll., Occidental Coll., Univ. of Calif., Univ. of S Carolina, Franklin and Marshall Coll., Univ. of the Pacific, Brown Univ.); Hon. DSc (Univ. of Rochester); Presidential Medal of Freedom 1981, Fermi Award 1993. *Publications:* Thinking About National Security 1983, The Strategic Defense Initiative: Shield or Snare? (ed.) 1987. *Leisure interests:* tennis, swimming, reading. *Address:* Center for Strategic and International Studies, 1800 K Street, Suite 400, NW, Washington, DC 20006, USA.

BROWN, Helen Gurley (see Gurley Brown, Helen).

BROWN, James; American singer and broadcasting executive; b. 3 May 1928; m. Adrienne Brown (died 1996); leader, Famous Flames (musical group) 1956–; now solo performer and recording artist with King, Smash Records; more than 75 albums recorded including I'm Real 1988, Universal James 1992; Pres. J.B. Broadcasting, Ltd 1968–, James Brown Network 1968–; arrested Dec. 1988 for attempted assault, received six-year sentence (served two years); Grammy award 1965; 44 Gold Record awards. *Films include:* Come to the Table 1974, The Blues Brothers 1980. *Recordings include:* Original Disco Man, Please, Please, Please, Hot on the One, Poppa's Got a Brand New Bag, Gravity, The Big Payback, Living in America, Sex Machine. *Address:* c/o Brothers Management Associates, 141 Dunbar Avenue, Fords, NJ 08863, USA.

BROWN, Rt Hon (James) Gordon, PC, MA, PhD; British politician; b. 20 Feb. 1951, Glasgow; s. of the late Rev. Dr J. Brown and of J. Elizabeth Brown; m.

Sarah Macaulay 2000; ed Kirkcaldy High School and Edinburgh Univ.; Rector, Edinburgh Univ. 1972–75, Temporary Lecturer 1976; Lecturer, Glasgow Coll. of Tech. 1976–80; Journalist and Current Affairs Ed., Scottish TV 1980–83; MP (Labour) Dunfermline East 1983–; Chair. Labour Party Scottish Council 1983–84; Opposition Chief Sec. to the Treasury 1987–89; Shadow Sec. of State for Trade and Industry 1989–92; Shadow Chancellor of the Exchequer 1992–97; Chancellor of the Exchequer May 1997–; Mem. Chair. Interim Cttee IMF 1999–; mem. Transport and Gen. Workers' Union. *Publications:* The Red Paper on Scotland (ed.) 1975, The Politics of Nationalism and Devolution (with H. M. Drucker) 1980, Scotland: The Real Divide (ed.) 1983, Maxton 1986, Where There is Greed 1989, John Smith: Life and Soul of the Party (with J. Naughtie) 1994, Values, Visions and Voices (with T. Wright) 1995. *Leisure interests:* reading, writing, football and tennis. *Address:* HM Treasury, 1 Horse Guards Road, London, SW1A 2HQ, England (Office). *Telephone:* (20) 7270-5000 (Office). *Website:* www.hm-treasury.gov .uk (Office).

BROWN, James Nathaniel (Jim); American football player (retd) and actor; b. 17 Feb. 1936, St. Simons Island, Ga; m. Sue Jones; two s. one d.; ed Manhasset High School Long Island, Syracuse Univ.; All-American running back and lacrosse player at Syracuse Univ.; fullback for Cleveland Browns 1957–65; played in nine straight NFL (Nat. Football League) Pro Bowls; NFL's leading rusher in eight of his nine seasons; NFL Most Valuable Player—MVP 1958, 1963, 1965; All-NFL 1957–61, 1963–65; career totals include: 118 games played, 12,312 rushing yards, 262 receptions, 15,459 combined net yards, 756 points scored, 126 touchdowns, 106 rushing touchdowns, average 104 yards per game, 5.2 yards per carry; retd from football to pursue acting career 1966; co-f. Negro Industrial Economic Union—NIEU 1966; works with Coor Golden Door, Barriers and Vital Issues inmates and ex-convicts training programmes 1980–; Founder and Pres. Amer-I-Can Programme Inc.1988–, Chair. Amer-I-Can Foundation for Social Change 1993–; mem. Bd Rebuild LA Project 1992–; served 4 months of a 6-month jail sentence in 2002 for vandalizing his wife's car during a domestic dispute; Syracuse All-America 1956, NFL Rookie of the Year 1957, Joe Thorpe Trophy 1965; elected to Pro Football Hall of Fame 1971 (second youngest ever, at 35), to Lacrosse Hall of Fame 1984, to Coll. Football Hall of Fame 1995; Walter Camp All-Century Team. *Films include:* The Dirty Dozen 1967, El Condor 1970, Slaughter and Black Gunn 1972, Original Gangstas 1996, Mars Attacks 1996, Ice Station Zebra, The Running Man, Any Given Sunday, He Got Game. *Address:* 269 South Beverly Drive 1048, Los Angeles, CA 90212, USA. *Telephone:* (310) 652-7884. *Fax:* (310) 652-9353. *E-mail:* info@amer-i-can.org. *Website:* www.amer-i-can.org.

BROWN, John Joseph, AO; Australian politician; b. 19 Dec. 1931, Sydney; s. of Norman Leslie Brown and Eva May Spencer; m. Jan Murray 1963; four s. one d.; ed St Patrick's Coll., Strathfield and Sydney Univ.; worked as distributor and co. dir in wholesale meat business; Alderman, Parramatta City Council 1977–70; MP for Parramatta, NSW 1977–90; Minister for Sport, Recreation and Tourism 1983–87 (also Minister assisting the Minister for Defence), for Admin. Services 1983–84; Chair. NSW Wholesale Meat Traders' Asscn 1974–76, Tourism Task Force Ltd 1989–, Environmental Choice 1992–94, London/Sydney Air Race; Dir Tourism Assets Ltd 1992–98, Sea World Man. Ltd 1993–98, Duty Free Operators Accreditation Bd 1998–, Sport Industry Australia, Macquarie Tourism and Leisure, Canterbury Bankstown Leagues Club; mem. Australasian Meat Industry Employees' Union, Sport and Tourism, Advisory Council of the Australian Opera, Advertising Standards Council; Labor Party; Patron Les Clefs d'Or; Olympic Silver Order of Merit 1986; "Australian of the Year" 1986, Gold Award, Australian Inst. of Marketing, Distinguished Service Award, US Sports Acad., Australian Sport Medal 2000. *Leisure interests:* golf, jogging, horse racing, theatre, opera, gardening. *Address:* Tourism Task Force, Level 10, Westfield Towers, 100 William Street, Sydney, NSW 2011, Australia (Office). *Telephone:* (2) 9368-1500. *Fax:* (2) 9368-0933. *E-mail:* jbrown@ttf.org.au.

BROWN, Lawrence Michael, MA, DSc,PhD; FRS; Anglo-Canadian physicist; b. 18 March 1936, Windsor, Ont.; s. of B. W. and Edith Brown; m. Susan Drucker 1965; one s. two d.; ed Univ. of Toronto, Univ. of Birmingham, England; work in Cambridge 1960–, Fellow, Gonville and Caius Coll. 1963–77, Univ. Demonstrator in Physics 1966, Reader in Structure and Properties of Materials, Dept of Physics 1983–89, Prof. of Physics 1989–2001, Prof. Emer. 2001–; Fellow Robinson Coll. 1977–; Rosenhain Medal, Inst. of Metals 1980; Robert Franklin Mehl Award, TMS 1991; Van Horn Distinguished Lecturer, Case Western Reserve Univ. 1994; Guthrie Medal and Prize, Inst. of Physics 2000. *Publications:* many papers in Philosophical Magazine and Acta Metallurgica (now Acta Materialia). *Leisure interests:* reading, gardening. *Address:* Cavendish Laboratory, Madingley Road, Cambridge, CB3 0HE; 74 Alpha Road, Cambridge, CB4 3DG, England (Home). *Telephone:* (1223) 337291 (Office); (1223) 362987 (Home). *Fax:* (1223) 337333 (Office). *E-mail:* lmb12@cam.ac.uk (Office).

BROWN, Michael Stuart, BA, MD; American professor of genetics; b. 13 April 1941, New York; s. of Harvey Brown and Evelyn Katz; m. Alice Lapin 1964; two d.; ed Univ. of Pennsylvania; Intern, then Resident, Mass. Gen. Hosp. Boston 1966–68; served with US Public Health Service 1968–70; Clinical Assoc. Nat. Inst. of Health 1968–71; Asst Prof. Univ. of Texas Southwestern Medical School, Dallas 1971–74, Paul J. Thomas, Prof. of Genetics and Dir Center for Genetic Diseases 1977–; mem. NAS and other scientific socs.; Pfizer Award (American Chemical Soc.) 1976; numerous hon.

degrees; Lounsbery Award (NAS) 1979, Lita Annenberg Hazen Award 1982, Albert Lasker Medical Research Award 1985, Nobel Prize in Medicine or Physiology 1985, Nat. Medal of Science USA 1988. *Address:* University of Texas Health Science Center, Department of Molecular Genetics, 5323 Harry Hines Boulevard, Dallas, TX 75390-9046, USA. *E-mail:* mike.brown@ ut-southwestern.edu (Office).

BROWN, Rt Hon Nicholas (Hugh), PC, BA; British politician; b. 13 June 1950; s. of the late R. C. Brown and G. K. Brown (née Tester); ed Swatenden Secondary Modern School, Tunbridge Wells Tech. High School, Univ. of Manchester; trade union officer Gen. and Municipal Workers' Union, Northern Region 1978–83; mem. Newcastle-upon-Tyne City Council 1980–83; MP (Labour) for Newcastle-upon-Tyne E 1983–97, for Newcastle-upon-Tyne E and Wallsend 1997–; Labour spokesman on Legal Affairs 1987–92, on Treasury Affairs 1988–94, on Health 1994–95; Deputy Chief Opposition Whip 1995–97; Chief Whip and Parl. Sec. to the Treasury 1997–98, Sec. of State for Agric., Fisheries and Food 1998–2001; Minister of State for Work, Dept for Work and Pensions 2001–. *Address:* c/o House of Commons, London, SW1A 0AA, England.

BROWN, Ronald Drayton, PhD, FAA; Australian professor of chemistry; b. 14 Oct. 1927, Melbourne; s. of William Harrison Brown and Linda Grace Drayton; m. Florence Catherine Mary Stringer 1950; two s. one d.; ed Wesley Coll., Melbourne, Univs. of Melbourne and London; lecturer, Univ. Coll., London, UK, Melbourne Univ.; Prof. of Chem., Monash Univ. 1960–93, Head Chem. Dept 1959–92, Prof. Emer. 1993–; current research interests cover theoretical chem., spectroscopy, galactochemistry and life in space; past Pres. Comm. 51 (Bioastronomy) of Int. Astronomical Union; fmr mem. of Exec. Cttee and Bureau, Int. Union of Pure and Applied Chem.; Fellow Australian Acad. of Science (fmr mem. Council, Vice-Pres. and Sec. of Physical Sciences); Matthew Flinders Lecturer 1988; Masson Medal, Royal Chemical Inst. 1948, Rennie Medal 1951, Smith Medal 1959, David Syme Prize for Research, Univ. of Melbourne 1959, Edgeworth-David Medal, Royal Soc. of NSW 1961, Royal Soc. Medal of Victoria 1977. *Publications:* Manual of Elementary Practical Chemistry (co-author), Atomic Structure and the Theory of Valency, The ABZ of Valency, Valency; more than 300 research papers in int. journals. *Leisure interests:* golf, skiing, tennis. *Address:* Department of Chemistry, Monash University, Wellington Road, Clayton, Victoria, 3168 (Office); 3 Moonya Rd, Glen Iris, 3146 Victoria, Australia (Home). *Telephone:* (3) 9905-4550 (Office); (3) 9885-4069 (Home).

BROWN, Tina (Christina Hambley Brown), MA, CBE; British writer and magazine editor; b. 21 Nov. 1953, Maidenhead; d. of the late George Hambley Brown and Bettina Iris Mary Brown (née Kohr); m. Harold Matthew Evans 1981; one s. one d.; ed Univ. of Oxford; columnist, Punch magazine 1978; Ed.-in-Chief Tatler Magazine 1979–83, of Vanity Fair Magazine, New York 1984–92, London 1991–92; Ed. The New Yorker 1992–98, Talk magazine 1999–2002; Partner and Chair. Talk Media 1998–, Talk Miramax Books 1998–; Most Promising Female Journalist, Katherine Pakenham Prize Sunday Times 1973, Young Journalist of the Year 1978, USC Distinguished Achievement in Journalism Award 1994. *Publications:* Under the Bamboo Tree (play) 1973 (Sunday Times Drama Award), Happy Yellow (play) 1977, Loose Talk 1979, Life as A Party 1983. *Address:* c/o Miramax, 375 Greenwich Street, New York, NY 10013, USA. *Fax:* (212) 830-5838.

BROWN, Trisha, BA; American choreographer; b. 25 Nov. 1936, Aberdeen, Wash.; ed Mills Coll., Calif.; with Judson Dance Theater 1960s; f. The Trisha Brown Dance Co. 1970; mem. Nat. Council on the Arts 1994–97; Hon. mem. American Acad. of Arts and Letters; numerous hon. doctorates; Nat. Endowment for the Arts Fellowship in Choreography (five times), John Simon Guggenheim Memorial Foundation Fellowship in Choreography (twice), MacArthur Foundation Fellowship Award 1991, Samuel H. Scripps American Dance Festival Award 1994, Prix de la Danse de la Soc. des Auteurs et Compositeurs Dramatiques 1996, NY State Gov.'s Arts Award 1999; Officier des Arts et des Lettres 2000. *Dance:* has choreographed numerous dances for alternative spaces including rooftops and walls 1961–; Opal Loop/Cloud Installation 1980, Son of Gone Fishin' 1981, Set and Reset 1982, Lateral Pass 1985, Carmen (opera) 1986, Newark 1987, Astral Convertible 1989, Foray Forêt 1990, Astral Converted (50") 1991, For M.G.: The Movie 1991, One Story as in Falling 1992, Another Story as in Falling 1993, Yet Another Story 1994, Long and Dream 1994, If You Couldn't See Me 1994, You Can See Us 1995, M.O. 1995, Twelve Ton Rose 1996, Canto/Pianto 1997, L'Orfeo (opera) 1998, Five Part Weather Invention 1999, Rapture to Leon James 2000. *Address:* Trisha Brown Dance Company, 211 West 61st Street, Floor 4, New York, NY 10023, USA (Office).

BROWN, William Charles Langdon, CBE; British banker (retd); b. 9 Sept. 1931, London; s. of Charles Leonard Brown and Kathleen May Tizzard; m. Nachiko Sagawa 1959; one s. two d.; ed John Ruskin School, Croydon, Ashbourne Grammar School, Derbyshire; with Chartered Bank of India, Australia and China, serving throughout Far East 1954–75, Area Gen. Man., Hong Kong 1975–87, Sr Gen. Man. (London) for Asia Pacific Region 1987; Exec. Dir Standard Chartered Bank PLC (SCB) 1987, Man. Dir 1988, Deputy Group Chief Exec. 1988, Group Deputy Chair. 1989–91, non-exec. Dir 1991–94; Dir and Treasurer Royal Commonwealth Soc. 1991–95, Commonwealth Trust 1991–95; Dir HongKong Investment Trust PLC 1991–97; Dir (non-exec.) Kexim Bank UK Ltd 1992–, Arbuthnot Latham & Co. Ltd 1993–99; Chair. (non-exec.) Atlantis Japan Growth Fund Ltd 1996–2002;

Unofficial mem. Legis. Council of Hong Kong 1980–85; Hon. DScS (Chinese Univ., Hong Kong) 1987. *Leisure interests:* mountain walking, yoga, skiing, philately, photography, classical music. *Address:* Penthouse B, 15 Portman Square, London, W1H 6LJ; Appleshaw, 11 Central Avenue, Findon Valley, Worthing, Sussex, BN14 0DS, England. *Telephone:* (20) 7487-5741; (1903) 873175. *Fax:* (20) 7486-3005; (1903) 873175. *E-mail:* wclbrown@yahoo.co.uk.

BROWNBACK, Sam, BS, JD; American politician; b. Parker, Kan.; m. Mary Brownback; three c.; ed Kansas State Univ. and Univ. of Kansas; partner, law firm in New York; Instructor in Law, Kansas State Univ.; City Attorney, Ogden and Leonardville, Kan.; mem. 104th Congress 1994–97; Senator from Kansas 1996–; Republican. *Address:* United States Senate, 303 Hart Senate Office Building, Washington, DC 20510-0001, USA.

BROWNE OF MADINGLEY, Baron (Life Peer), cr. 2001, of Madingley in the County of Cambridgeshire; **(Edmund) John (Philip) Browne,** BSc, MS, FInstP, FInstPet, CIMgt; British oil company executive; b. 20 Feb. 1948, Hamburg, Germany; ed Cambridge Univ., Stanford Univ., Calif., USA; joined BP 1966; various exploration and production posts Anchorage, New York, San Francisco, London and Canada 1969–83; Group Treas. and Chief Exec. BP Finance Int. 1984–86; Exec. Vice-Pres. and Chief Financial Officer The Standard Oil Co., Cleveland, Ohio 1986–87, BP America and CEO Standard Oil Production Co. (following BP/Standard merger) 1987–89; Man. Dir and CEO BP Exploration, London 1989–91; Man. Dir The British Petroleum Co. PLC 1991–95, Group Chief Exec. 1995–98, Group Chief Exec. BP Amoco (now BP PLC) 1998–; Dir Conservation Int.; Dir (non-exec.) Intel Corpn, Goldman Sachs, SmithKline Beecham 1996–99; mem. Supervisory Bd, Daimler Chrysler AG 1998–2001, Chair.'s Council 2001–; Chair. Emer. Advisory Bd, Stanford Grad. School of Business; Vice-Pres. Prince of Wales Business Leaders Forum; mem. Int. Advisory Bd of the Financial Times, British-American Chamber of Commerce (also fmr Chair.), Cambridge Consultative Cttee and Chem. Appeal (also fmr Chair.), Guild of Cambridge Benefactors, Int. Council of the Field Museum, Advisory Bd Reutgers/Carnegie Endowment for Int. Peace, Advisory Bd of Freshfields, Bruckhaus Deringer, Council of the Foundation for Science and Tech., Bd of Catalyst, Asia-Pacific Council of the Nature Conservancy, School of Econs and Man., Tsinghua Univ.; Trustee British Museum; mem. Bd of Trustees Conference Bd, Inc.; Fellow Royal Acad. of Eng; Fellow Inst. of Mining and Metallurgy; Sr Mem. St Anthony's Coll. Oxford; Hon. Fellow St John's Coll. Cambridge; Hon. FIChemE; Hon. FGS; Hon. FIMechE; Hon. FRSC; Hon. Trustee Chicago Symphony Orchestra; Hon. DEng (Heriot Watt); Hon. DTech (Robert Gordon); Hon. LLD (Dundee, Thunderbird, Notre Dame); Hon. DUniv (Sheffield Hallam); Hon. DSc (Cranfield, Hull, Leuven, Warwick); Prince Philip Medal, Royal Acad. of Eng 1999, Henry Shaw Medal, Missouri Botanical Gardens, Gold Medal, Inst. of Man., Ernest C. Arbuckle Award, Stanford Business School Alumni Asscn 2001, Soc. of Petroleum Engineers Public Service Award 2002. *Address:* BP PLC, 1 St James's Square, London, SW1Y 4PD (Office); BP PLC, Britannic House, 1 Finsbury Circus, London, EC2M 7BA, England (Office). *Telephone:* (20) 7496-4000 (Office). *Fax:* (20) 7496-4630 (Office). *Website:* www.bp.com (Office).

BROWNE-WILKINSON, Baron (Life Peer) cr. 1991, of Camden, in the London Borough of Camden; **Nicolas Christopher Henry Browne-Wilkinson,** PC, QC, BA; British judge; b. 30 March 1930, London; s. of the late Canon A. R. Browne-Wilkinson and Molly Browne-Wilkinson; m. 1st Ursula de Lacy Bacon 1955 (died 1987); three s. two d.; m. 2nd Hilary Tuckwell 1990; ed Lancing Coll., Magdalen Coll., Oxford; called to Bar, Lincoln's Inn 1953, Bencher 1977; QC 1972; Jr Counsel to Registrar of Restrictive Trading Agreements 1964–66, to Attorney-Gen. in Charity Matters 1966–72, in bankruptcy, to Dept of Trade and Industry 1966–72; a Judge of the Courts of Appeal of Jersey and Guernsey 1976–77; Judge of the High Court, Chancery Div. 1977–83; a Lord Justice of Appeal 1983–85; Vice-Chancellor of the Supreme Court 1985–91; Lord of Appeal in Ordinary 1991–2000, Sr Law Lord 1998–2000; Pres. Employment Appeal Tribunal 1981–83, Senate of the Inns of Court and the Bar 1984–86; Fellow St Edmund Hall (Oxford) 1986, Magdalen Coll. 1993, American Coll. of Trial Lawyers, American Law Inst. *Leisure interests:* gardening, music. *Address:* House of Lords, London, SW1A 0PW, England. *Telephone:* (20) 7219-3202.

BROWNER, Carol, JD; American politician and lawyer; b. 1956; m. Michael Podhorzer; one s.; ed Univ. of Florida; gen. counsel of a Cttee of Fla Legis. 1979–83; Assoc. Dir Citizen Action, Washington, DC 1983–86; mem. staff Senator Lawton Chiles 1986–89; mem. staff Senate Cttee on Energy and Natural Resources 1989; Legis. Dir on staff of Senator Al Gore 1989–90; Head Dept of Environmental Regulation, State of Fla 1990–93; Admin. Environmental Protection Agency (EPA) 1993–2001, co-f. The Albright Group 2001–. *Address:* The Albright Group, Washington, DC, USA. *Telephone:* (202) 842-7222. *Fax:* (202) 354-3888. *Website:* www.thealbrightgroupplc.com.

BROWNING, Most Rev. Edmond L., DD; American ecclesiastic; b. 11 March 1929, Texas; s. of Edmond L. Browning and Cora M. Lee; m. Patricia Sparks 1953; four s. one d.; ed Univ. of the South, Sewanee, Tenn., School of Theology, Sewanee and Japanese Language School, Okinawa; First missionary Bishop of Okinawa 1968–71; Bishop-in-Charge, Convocation of American Churches in Europe 1971–74; Exec. for Nat. and World Mission, Episcopal Church Center 1974–76; Bishop of Hawaii 1976–85; Presiding

Bishop, Episcopal Church, USA 1986–98; Hon. Canon St. Michael's Cathedral (Kobe, Japan), St. George's Cathedral (Jerusalem). *Address:* 5164 Imai Road, Hood River, OR 97031, USA.

BROWNING, Keith Anthony, PhD, ARCS, DIC, FRS; British meteorologist; b. 31 July 1938, Sunderland; s. of the late James Anthony Browning and of Amy Hilda Greenwood; m. Ann Baish 1962; one s. two d.; ed Imperial Coll. of Science and Tech., Univ. of London; Research Atmospheric Physicist, Air Force Cambridge Research Labs., Mass., USA 1962–66; Prin. then Chief Meteorological Officer, Meteorological Office Radar Research Lab., Royal Signals and Radar Establishment, Malvern, Worcs. 1966–74, 1975–85; Chief Scientist, Nat. Hail Research Experiment, Nat. Center for Atmospheric Research, Boulder, Colo, USA 1974–75; Deputy Dir (Physical Research), Meteorological Office, Bracknell, Berks. 1985–89; Dir of Research 1989–91; Visiting Scientist, Joint Centre for Mesoscale Meteorology, Univ. of Reading 1991–92, Dir 1992–2003; Prof. in Dept of Meteorology, Univ. of Reading 1995–2003; Dir Univs. Weather Research Network 2000–03; Dir Univs. Facility for Atmospheric Measurements 2001–03; Chair. Meteorology & Atmospheric Physics Sub-Cttee of British Cttee for Geodesy and Geophysics 1985–89; mem. Natural Environment Research Council 1984–87; Visiting Prof., Dept of Meteorology, Univ. of Reading 1988–94; Pres. Royal Meteorological Soc. 1988–90; Jt Scientific Cttee, World Climate Research Programme 1990–94; mem. Scientific Steering Cttee, World Weather Research Programme 1996–; mem. Academia Europaea 1989–; Foreign Assoc., Nat. Acad. of Eng (USA) 1992–; Fellow American Meteorological Soc. 1975–; Chartered Meteorologist, Royal Meteorological Soc.; awards from Royal Meteorological Soc., American Meteorological Soc. and Inst. of Physics. *Publications:* numerous articles on meteorology. *Leisure interests:* home and garden. *Address:* Department of Meteorology, University of Reading, PO Box 243, Reading, RG6 6BB, England. *Telephone:* (1189) 316521. *Fax:* (1189) 318791.

BROWNLIE, Ian, CBE, QC, DCL, FBA; British international law practitioner and barrister; b. 19 Sept. 1932, Liverpool; s. of Amy Isabella Atherton and John Nason Brownlie; m. 1st Jocelyn Gale 1957; one s. two d.; m. 2nd Christine Apperley, 1978; ed Alsop High School, Liverpool, Hertford Coll. Oxford and King's Coll. Cambridge; called to Bar (Gray's Inn) 1958; in practice 1967–; QC 1979; mem. Blackstone Chambers; Bencher of Gray's Inn 1988; Fellow Wadham Coll. Oxford 1963–76; Prof. of Int. Law, London Univ. (attached to LSE) 1976–80; Chichele Prof. of Public Int. Law, Oxford and Fellow of All Souls 1980–99; Dir of Studies, Int. Law Asscn 1982–91; lecturer, Hague Acad. of Int. Law 1995; Judge, European Nuclear Energy Tribunal 1995–2000, Pres. 1996–2000; mem. Inst. of Int. Law 1983, mem. Int. Law Comm. of UN 1997–; Commdr, Order of Merit of the Norwegian Crown. *Publications:* International Law and the Use of Force by States 1963, Principles of Public International Law 1966, Encyclopaedia of African Boundaries 1979, State Responsibility, Part I 1983, Liber Amicorum for Lord Wilberforce 1987; British Year Book of International Law (Jt Ed.) 1974–99. *Leisure interests:* travel, book collecting, maps. *Address:* Blackstone Chambers, Temple, London, EC4Y 9BW, England (Office). *Telephone:* (20) 7583-1770 (Office). *Fax:* (20) 7822-7350 (Office).

BROWNLOW, Kevin; British film historian and television director; b. 2 June 1938, Crowborough, Sussex; s. of Robert Thomas Brownlow and Niña Fortnum; m. Virginia Keane 1969; one d.; ed University College School, Hampstead; joined World Wide Pictures 1955; became film Ed., then Jt Dir 1964; with Thames TV 1975–90. *Films include:* It Happened Here 1964, Winstanley 1975 (both with Andrew Mollo). *Television includes:* 13-part series Hollywood 1980, three-part Unknown Chaplin 1983, three-part British Cinema 1986, three-part Buster Keaton – A Hard Act to Follow 1987, two-part Harold Lloyd 1988, three-part D. W. Griffith 1993, six-part Cinema Europe: the other Hollywood 1995 (all with David Gill), Universal Horror 1998, Lon Chaney – A Thousand Faces 2000, The Tramp and the Dictator (with Michael Kloft) 2002. *Publications:* Parade's Gone By . . . 1968, The War, the West and the Wilderness 1978, Napoleon (Abel Gance's Classic Film) 1983, Behind the Mask of Innocence 1990, David Lean: A Biography 1996, Mary Pickford Rediscovered 1999. *Address:* c/o Photoplay Productions, 21 Princess Road, London, NW1, England (Office). *Telephone:* (20) 7722-2500.

BROWSE, Sir Norman Leslie, Kt, MD, FRCP, FRCS; British state official and surgeon (retd); b. 1 Dec. 1931, London; s. of Reginald Browse and Margaret Browse; m. Jeanne Menage 1957; one s. one d.; ed St Bartholomew's Hosp. Medical Coll. and Univ. of Bristol; Capt. RAMC 1957–59; Sr House Officer and Registrar, Bristol 1959–62; Lecturer in Surgery, Westminster Hosp. 1962–65; Harkness Fellow, Research Assoc. Mayo Clinic, Rochester, Minn. 1964–65; Reader in Surgery and Consultant Surgeon, St Thomas' Hosp. 1965–72, Prof. of Vascular Surgery 1972–81, Prof. of Surgery 1981–96, Consulting Surgeon 1996–; Hon. Consultant to Army and RAF 1980–96; Prof. of Surgery, United Medical and Dental Schools 1981–96; Prof. Emer. Univ. of London 1996–; Pres. States of Alderney, CI 2002–04; Pres. Royal Coll. of Surgeons of England 1992–95; Chair., Jt Consultants Cttee 1994–98, Lord Brock Memorial Trust 1994–2001; Vice-Chair. British Vascular Foundation 1997–; Visiting Prof. and Lecturer, Cape Town, Johannesburg, Perth, Sydney, Melbourne, Brisbane, Boston, Ann Arbor, San Diego, Los Angeles, Vancouver, Seattle, Singapore, Hong Kong, Madras, Sri Lanka, Delhi, Kuwait, Paris, Marseille, Barcelona, Amsterdam, Copenhagen, Stockholm, Helsinki; mem. Council Marlborough Coll. 1990–2001; Gov. American Coll. of Surgeons 1997–2003; Hon. Fellow Royal Coll. of Physicians and Surgeons (Glasgow) 1993; Hon. FRACS 1994; Hon. Fellow in Dental Surgery 1994; Hon. Fellow Royal Coll.

of Surgeons in Ireland 1995; Hon. FACS 1995; Hon. Fellow Faculty of Accident and Emergency Medicine 1995; Hon. FRCSE 1996; Hon. Fellow Coll. of Medicine of S Africa 1996; Distinguished Alumnus, Mayo Clinic 1993; Hon. Freeman Worshipful Co. of Barbers 1997; Arris and Gale Medal 1968, Abraham Colles Medal 1990, Kinmouth Medal 1991, Vicary Medal 2000. *Publications:* Physiology and Pathology of Bed Rest 1964, Symptoms and Signs of Surgical Disease 1978, Reducing Operation for Lymphoedema 1986, Diseases of the Veins 1989, Diseases of the Lymphatics 2003. *Leisure interests:* marine art, medieval history, sailing. *Address:* Corbet House, Butes Lane, Alderney, GY9 3UW, Channel Islands. *E-mail:* norman.browse@virgin .net.

BROYLES, William Dodson, Jr, MA; American journalist; b. 8 Oct. 1944, Houston; s. of William Dodson and Elizabeth (née Bills) Broyles; m. Sybil Ann Newman 1973; one s. one d.; ed Rice Univ., Houston, Oxford Univ.; US Marine Corps Reserve 1969–71; teacher Philosophy US Naval Acad. 1970–71; Asst Supt Houston Public Schools 1971–72; Ed.-in-Chief Texas Monthly 1972–82; Ed.-in-Chief California Magazine 1980–82; Ed.-in-Chief Newsweek Magazine 1982–84; Columnist, US News and World Report 1986; Co-producer, exec. consultant China Beach (TV programme) 1988–; screenwriter Apollo 13 1995; Bronze Star.

BRUBAKER, Charles William, BArch; American architect; b. 28 Sept. 1926, South Bend, Ind.; s. of Ralph Brubaker and Mary Brubaker; m. Elizabeth Rogers 1955; two s. one d.; ed Univ. of Tex. at Austin; architect Perkins & Will, architects, Chicago 1950–58, partner 1958–70, Vice-Pres. 1980–85, Pres. 1985–86, Vice-Chair. 1986–; architect for numerous school, coll. and univ. bldgs. and responsible for campus planning both in USA and worldwide; mem. Bd of Dirs. Chicago Architecture Foundation 1976–; Fellow, American Inst. of Architects, Chancellor 1988–89. *Publication:* Planning Flexible Learning Places 1977. *Leisure interests:* sketching, history of architecture, music, sailing. *Address:* Perkins and Will Inc., 330 N Wabash Avenue, Chicago, IL 60611 (Office); 82 Essex Road, Winnetka, IL 60093, USA (Home). *Telephone:* (708) 446-2624 (Home).

BRUBECK, David Warren, BA; American musician; b. 6 Dec. 1920, Concord, Calif.; s. of Howard P. Brubeck and Elizabeth Ivey; m. Iola Whitlock 1942; five s. one d.; ed Pacific and Mills Colls; Leader Dave Brubeck Octet, Trio and Quartet 1946–; formed Dave Brubeck Quartet 1951; numerous tours and recordings; Duke Ellington Fellow, Yale Univ.; composer of 250 jazz pieces and songs, mem. American Jazz Hall of Fame 1995; Hon. PhD (Univ. of Pacific, Fairfield Univ., Univ. of Bridgeport, Mills Coll., Niagara Univ., Kalamazoo Coll.); many awards from trade magazines, Metronome, Downbeat, Billboard, Melodymaker; Jazz Pioneer Award, BMI 1985; Compostela Humanitarian Award 1986; Connecticut Arts Award 1987; American Eagle Award, Nat. Music Council 1988; Gerard Manley Hopkins Award 1991; Nat. Medal of the Arts 1994; Lifetime Achievement Award Nat. Acad. of Recording Arts and Sciences 1996. *Extended works:* ballets: Points on Jazz 1962, Glances 1976; orchestral: Elementals 1963, They All Sang Yankee Doodle 1976; flute and guitar: Tritonis 1979; piano: Reminiscences of the Cattle Country 1946, Four by Four 1946; Oratorios: The Light in the Wilderness 1968, Beloved Son 1978, Voice of the Holy Spirit 1985; cantatas: Gates of Justice 1969, Truth is Fallen 1971, La Fiesta de la Posada 1975, In Praise of Mary 1989; chorus and orchestra: Pange Lingua Variations 1983, Upon this Rock Chorale and Fugue 1987, Lenten Triptych 1988, Joy in the Morning 1991; Mass: To Hope! A Celebration 1980; SATB Chorus: I See, Satie 1987, Four New England Pieces 1988; Earth is our Mother 1992. *Address:* Derry Music Company, 1299 4th Street, Suite 409, San Rafael, CA 94901; c/o Sutton Artists Corporation, 20 West Park Avenue, Suite 305, Long Beach, NY 11561; Box 216, Wilton, CT 06897, USA.

BRUCE, Christopher, CBE; British artistic director and choreographer; b. 3 Oct. 1945, Leicester; s. of Alexander Bruce and Ethel Parker; m. Marian Meadowcroft 1967; two s. one d.; ed Rambert School, London; dancer, Ballet Rambert, London 1963–80; Assoc. Dir Ballet Rambert 1975–79, Assoc. Choreographer 1979–87; Assoc. Choreographer, English Nat. Ballet (fmrly London Festival Ballet), London 1986–91; Resident Choreographer, Houston Ballet 1989–; Artistic Dir Rambert Dance Co. 1994–2003; choreographer for Kent Opera, Nederlands Dans Theater, Ballet du Grand Théâtre de Genève, etc; Dr hc (De Montfort) 2000; Hon. DLitt (Exeter) 2001; Evening Standard Inaugural Dance Award 1974; Int. Theatre Inst. Award 1993; Evening Standard Ballet Award 1996. *Ballets include:* George Frideric 1969, For Those Who Die as Cattle 1971, There Was a Time 1972, Weekend 1974, Ancient Voices of Children 1975, Black Angels 1976, Cruel Garden 1977, Night with Waning Moon 1979, Dancing Day 1981, Ghost Dances 1981, Berlin Requiem 1982, Concertino 1983, Intimate Pages 1984, Ceremonies 1986, Swansong 1987, Symphony in Three Movements 1989, Waiting 1993, Crossing 1994, Meeting Point 1995 (for 'United We Dance' Int. Festival celebrating 50 years of UN), Quicksilver (tribute to Marie Rambert to celebrate Rambert Dance Co.'s 70th anniversary) 1996, Stream 1996, Four Scenes 1998, God's Plenty 1999, Hurricane 2000, Grinning in Your Face 2001. *Address:* c/o Rambert Dance Company, 94 Chiswick High Road, London, W4 1SH, England.

BRUCKHEIMER, Jerry, BA; American film producer; b. 1945, Detroit; m. Linda Bruckheimer; ed Univ. of Arizona; fmr producer of TV commercials; formed Don Simpson/Jerry Bruckheimer Productions with the late Don Simpson 1983; formed Jerry Bruckheimer Films 1997; ShoWest Producer of the Year 1999, David O. Selznick Lifetime Achievement Award 2000. *Films*

include: (assoc. producer) Culpepper Cattle Company 1972, Rafferty and the Gold Dust Twins 1975, (producer) Farewell My Lovely 1975, March or Die 1977, Defiance 1980, American Gigolo 1980, Thief 1981, Cat People 1982, Young Doctors in Love 1982, Flashdance 1983, Beverly Hills Cop 1984, Thief of Hearts 1984, Top Gun 1986, Beverly Hills Cop II 1987, Days of Thunder 1990, The Ref (exec. producer) 1994, Dangerous Minds 1995, Bad Boys 1995, Crimson Tide 1995, The Rock 1996, Con Air 1997, Enemy of the State 1998, Armageddon 1998, Gone in 60 Seconds 2000, Coyote Ugly 2000, Remember the Titans 2000, Pearl Harbor 2001, Black Hawk Down 2002, Bad Company 2002, Kangaroo Jack 2003. *Television:* exec. producer CSI: Crime Scene Investigations, The Amazing Race, CSI: Miami, Without a Trace. *Leisure interest:* hockey. *Address:* c/o Jerry Bruckheimer Films Inc., 1631 10th Street, Santa Monica, CA 90404, USA (Office). *Telephone:* (310) 664-6260 (Office). *Fax:* (310) 664-6261 (Office). *Website:* www.jbfilms.com (Office).

BRUCKMANN, Gerhart, PhD, MP; Austrian politician and statistician; b. 9 Jan. 1932, Vienna; s. of Friedrich Bruckmann and Anny (née Pötzl) Bruckmann; m. Hilde Bartl 1961; two s.; ed Univ. of Graz, Vienna and Rome, Antioch Coll., USA; with Austrian Fed. Chamber of Commerce 1957–67; Prof. of Statistics, Univ. of Linz 1967–68, Univ. of Vienna 1968–92; Dir Inst. for Advanced Studies 1968–73; Consultant Int. Inst. for Applied Systems Analysis 1973–83, Council mem. 1983–86; MP 1986–94, 1999–2002; Bd mem. Austrian Sr Citizens' Union 1998–; Exec. Officer European Sr Citizens' Union 1998–2001; mem. Austrian Acad. of Sciences, Club of Rome; Hon. PhD (Linz) 1998. *Publications:* Auswege in die Zukunft 1974, Sonnenkraft statt Atomenergie 1978, Groping in the Dark (with D. Meadows and J. Richardson) 1982, Megatrends für Österreich 1988, Österreicher wer bist du? 1989. *Leisure interest:* collecting anchor building blocks. *Address:* Österr. Seniorenbund, Lichtenfelsgasse 7, A-1010 Vienna (Office); Zehenthofgasse 11, 1190 Vienna, Austria (Home). *Telephone:* (431) 40126-151 (Office). *Fax:* (431) 4066-266 (Office).

BRUCKNER, Pascal, DèsSc, PhD; French writer and lecturer; b. 15 Dec. 1948, Paris; s. of René Bruckner and Monique Bruckner; m. Violaine Barret 1970 (divorced 1973); one s.; also one d. by Caroline Thompson; ed Lycée Henri IV, Univs de Paris I (Sorbonne), Paris VII (Jussieu); annual travels in Asia 1977–90; lecturer Inst. d'Etudes Politiques, Paris 1990–; Visiting Prof. Univs of San Diego and New York 1986–95; Chevalier des Arts et des Lettres, Légion d'honneur 2002; Prix Médicis de l'Essai 1995, Prix Renaudot 1997. *Theatre:* many of his books have been played on stage throughout Europe and in India. *Publications:* Le Nouveau Désordre Amoureux 1977, Lune de Fiel 1982 (adapted for screen by Roman Polanski under the title Bitter Moon 1992), Le sanglot de l'homme blanc 1983, Le Divin Enfant 1992, La Tentation de l'Innocence 1995, Les Voleurs de Beauté 1997, Les ogres anonymes 1998, L' Euphorie perpétuelle, essai sur Le devóir de bonheur 2000, Misère de la prospérité. La religion marchande et ses ennemis (Sénat Prix du Livre d'économie) 2002; translations in 25 countries. *Leisure interests:* piano, sports, fantasy films. *Address:* 8 rue Marie Stuart, 75002 Paris, France. *Telephone:* 1-40-26-68-79. *Fax:* 1-40-56-34-37. *E-mail:* bruckner@wanadoo.fr (Home).

BRUECKNER, Keith Allan, MA, PhD; American professor of physics (retd); b. 19 March 1924, Minneapolis, Minn.; s. of Leo John and Agnes Holland Brueckner; m. Bonnie Brueckner; two s. one d.; ed Univs of Minnesota and California (Berkeley), Inst. for Advanced Study, Princeton; Asst Prof. Indiana Univ. 1951–54, Assoc. Prof. 1954–55; Physicist, Brookhaven Nat. Lab. (NY) 1955–56; Prof. of Physics, Univ. of Pa 1956–59; Prof. of Physics, Univ. of Calif. (San Diego) 1959–; Vice-Pres. and Dir of Research, Inst. for Defense Analyses, Wash., DC 1961–62; Tech. Dir KMS Tech. Center, San Diego 1968–71; Exec. Vice-Pres. and Tech. Dir KMS Fusion Inc., Ann Arbor 1971–74; Consulting Ed., Pure and Applied Physics Series, Academic Press 1964–; mem. NAS; Hon. DSc (Indiana) 1976; Dannie Heinemann Prize for Mathematical Physics 1963. *Publications:* numerous articles in scientific journals. *Leisure interests:* mountain climbing, skiing, sailing, surfing. *Address:* Department of Physics, University of California at San Diego, La Jolla, CA 92093 (Office); 3120 Almahurst Row, La Jolla, CA 92037, USA. *Telephone:* (619) 452-2892 (Office).

BRUEL, Jean-Marc André; French business executive; b. 18 Feb. 1936, Akbou, Algeria; s. of René Bruel and Jeanine Poirson; m. Anne-Mary Barthod 1962; two s. two d.; ed Ecole Centrale des Árts et Manufactures; Head of tech. services, Rhodiaceta, Brazil 1964; Dir nylon polyester factory, Rhône-Poulenc, Brazil 1968; Deputy Dir-Gen. of textile production Rhône-Poulenc, Brazil 1971; Deputy Dir-Gen. Div. of plant hygiene, Groupe Rhône-Poulenc 1975, Dir-Gen. 1976; Asst to Pres. and mem. Exec. Cttee Rhône-Poulenc 1979–80, Deputy Dir-Gen. 1980, Dir-Gen. 1982–84; mem. Exec. Cttee Sandoz, Basle 1985–87; Dir-Gen. Rhône Poulenc 1987–92, Vice-Pres. 1992–; mem. Rhône Poulenc Chimie 1987–92; Vice-Pres. European Council of Fed. of Chemical Industry (Cefic) 1988; Pres. Soc. of Chemical Industry 1993–94, Villette Enterprises 1995–, Institut Curie 1998–; Chevalier Légion d'honneur, Officier Ordre nat. du Mérite. *Leisure interests:* tennis, sailing. *Address:* Rhône Poulenc, 25 quai Paul Doumer, 92408 Courbevoie Cedex (Office); Aventis, 46 quai de la Rupée, 75601 Paris Cedex 12 (Office); 105 bis rue de Longchamp, 92200 Neuilly-sur-Seine, France (Home).

BRUGUERA, Sergi; Spanish tennis player; b. 16 Jan. 1971, Barcelona; s. of Luis Bruguera; coached by his father; Nat. Jr Champion 1987; turned professional 1988; winner French Open 1993, 1994, finalist 1997; Olympic silver medal, Atlanta, USA 1996; winner of 17 titles (3 doubles) at end Dec. 2002.

BRUIJN, Inge de; Netherlands swimmer; b. 24 Aug. 1973, Barendrecht; 6th 50m free (26.79), 7th 100m free (58.88), 8th 100m butterfly (1:04.93), 2nd 4x100m medley relay, 3rd 4x100m free relay LC Junior European Championships 1987; 3rd 50m free (26.56), 3rd 100m butterfly (1:03.41) LC Junior European Championships 1988; 8th 100m butterfly (1:01.35), 10th 100m free (56.58), 3rd 4x100m free, 4th 4x100m medley relay LC World Championships 1991; 2nd 100m butterfly (1:01.64), 3rd 50m free (25.84), 1st 4x100m free, 3rd 4x100m medley relay LC European Championships 1991; 8th 50m free (25.84), 9th 100m butterfly (1:01.02), 8th 4x100m medley relay Olympic Games 1992; 3rd 50m free (25.86), 4th 100m butterfly (1:01.22), 12th 100m free (57.40) LC European Championships 1993; 7th 100m butterfly (1:01.14) LC World Championships 1994; 4th 50m free (25.95), 4th 100m butterfly (1:01.26), 6th 4x100m free relay LC European Championships 1995; retd from swimming 1995; returned to the sport under the tutelage of US coach Paul Bergen 1998; 7th 100m butterfly (1:00.09), 8th 100m free (56.49), 5th 4x100m free relay, 6th 4x100m medley relay LC World Championships 1998; 1st 50m free (24.41), 1st 50m butterfly (26.09), 3rd 100m butterfly (58.39), 2nd 4x50m free, 3rd 4x50m medley relay SC European Championships 1998; 1st 50m free (24.99), 1st 100m butterfly (58.49), 2nd 100m free (55.24), 4th 4x100m free, 4th 4x100m medley relay LC European Championships 1999; 1st 50m free (24.35), 3rd 50m butterfly (26.41), 5th 100m free (54.07), 2nd 4x100m free, 4th 4x100m medley relay SC World Championships 1999; 1st 50m free (24.32), 1st 100m free (53.83), 1st 100m butterfly (56.61, WR), 2nd 4x100m free relay (3:39.83) Olympic Games 2000; 1st 50m free (24.47), 1st 100m free (54.18), 1st 50m butterfly (25.90), LC World Championships 2001; 1st 50m free (23.89), 1st 100m free (52.65), 2nd 4x50m free relay (1:39.02), 3rd 4x50m medley relay (1:50.00) SC European Championships 2001; world records 50m 24.13 (Sydney, Australia 22 Sept. 2000), 100m free 53.77 (Sydney 20 Sept. 2000), 50m butterfly 25.64 (Sheffield, UK 26 May 2000), 100m butterfly 56.61 (Sydney 17 Sept. 2000); European Female Swimmer of the Year 1999; Best Female Swimmer at the World Championships 2001. *E-mail:* cyang2001@yahoo.com (Office).

BRUMMELL, Paul, BA; British diplomatist; b. 28 Aug. 1965, Harpenden; s. of Robert George Brummell and June Brummell (née Rawlins); ed St Albans School, St Catharine's Coll. Cambridge; joined HM Diplomatic Service 1987; Third Sec., later Second Sec., Islamabad 1989–92; with FCO, London 1993–94; First Sec., Rome 1995–2000; Deputy Head Eastern Dept, FCO 2000–01; Amb. to Turkmenistan 2002–. *Address:* c/o Foreign and Commonwealth Office (Ashgabat), King Charles Street, London, SW1A 2AH, England (Office). *Telephone:* (12) 36-34-62 (Office). *Fax:* (12) 36-34-65 (Office). *E-mail:* beasb@online.tm (Office). *Website:* www.britishembassytm.org.uk (Office).

BRUNDIN, Clark Lannerdahl, BS, PhD; American/British university administrator and engineer; b. 21 March 1931, Los Angeles, Calif.; s. of the late Ernest Brundin and of Elinor (née Clark) Brundin; m. Judith Anne Maloney 1959; two s. two d.; ed Whittier High School, Calif. Inst. of Tech. and Univ. of Calif., Berkeley; electronics petty officer, US Navy 1951–55; Assoc. in Mech. Eng, Univ. of Calif., Berkeley 1956–57, Research Engineer, Inst. of Eng Research 1959–63; Demonstrator Dept of Eng Science, Univ. of Oxford 1957–58, lecturer 1963–85; Vice-Chair. Gen. Bd of Faculties, Univ. of Oxford 1984–85; Fellow and Tutor in Eng, Jesus Coll., Oxford 1964–85, Sr Tutor 1974–77, Estates Bursar 1978–84, Hon. Fellow 1985–; Gov. Oxford Polytechnic 1978–83, Cokethorpe School 1983–96, Magdalen Coll. School 1987–99, Coventry School Foundation; Vice-Chancellor Univ. of Warwick 1985–92; Visiting Prof. Univ. of Calif., Santa Barbara 1978; Visiting Scholar Center for Study of Higher Educ., Univ. of Calif. Berkeley 1997–; Chair. Anchor Housing Asscn 1985–91; Dir Blackwell Science Ltd 1990–98; Dir Heritage Projects (Oxford) 1986–97, Oxford Univ. School of Man. Studies 1992–96, Finsbury Growth Trust PLC 1995–2000, Charities Aid Foundation America 1997–2000 (Pres. 1998–2000); Pres. Templeton Coll., Oxford 1992–96; mem. Eng Bd, CNAA 1976–82. *Publications:* articles on rarefied gas dynamics and education. *Leisure interests:* sailing, mending old machinery, all types of music. *Address:* Jesus College, Oxford, OX1 3DW, England (Office).

BRUNDTLAND, Gro Harlem, MD, MPH; Norwegian politician and physician; b. 20 April 1939, Oslo; d. of Gudmund Harlem and Inga Harlem; m. Arne Olav Brundtland 1960; three s. (one deceased) one d.; ed Oslo and Harvard Univs.; Consultant, Ministry of Health and Social Affairs 1965–67; Medical Officer, Oslo City Health Dept 1968–69; Deputy Dir School Health Services, Oslo 1969; Minister of Environment 1974–79; Deputy Leader Labour Party 1975–81, Leader Labour Parl. Group 1981–92; Prime Minister of Norway Feb.–Oct. 1981, 1986–89, 1990–96; mem. Parl. Standing Cttee on Foreign Affairs, fmr mem. Parl. Standing Cttee on Finance; mem. of Storting (Parl.) 1977–97; Dir-Gen. WHO 1998–2003; Chair. UN World Comm. on Environment and Devt; fmr Vice-Chair. Sr Secondary Schools' Socialist Asscn, Students' Asscn of Labour Party; Dr h.c. (Oxford) 2001; Third World Prize for Work on Environmental Issues 1989, Indira Gandhi Prize 1990, Onassis Foundation Award 1992. *Publications:* articles on preventive medicine, school health and growth studies. *Leisure interest:* cross-country skiing. *Address:* c/o World Health Organization, Avenue Appia, 1211 Geneva 27, Switzerland (Office).

BRUNEI, Sultan of (see Bolkiah Mu'izuddin Waddaulah, HM Sultan Sir Muda Hassanal).

BRUNER, Jerome Seymour, PhD; American professor of psychology and professor of law; b. 1 Oct. 1915, New York; s. of Herman Bruner and Rose Bruner; m. 1st Katherine Frost 1940 (divorced 1956); one s. one d.; m. 2nd Blanche Marshall McLane 1960 (divorced 1984); m. 3rd Carol Fleisher Feldman; ed Duke and Harvard Univs; US Intelligence 1941–42; Assoc. Dir Office of Public Opinion Research, Princeton 1942–44; Political Intelligence, France 1943; Research, Harvard Univ. 1945–72, Prof. of Psychology 1952–72, Dir Center for Cognitive Studies 1961–72; Ed. Public Opinion Quarterly 1943–44; Lecturer, Salzburg Seminar 1952; Bacon Prof., Univ. of Aix-en-Provence 1965; Watts Prof. of Psychology, Oxford Univ. 1972–80; Univ. Prof., New School for Social Research, New York 1981–88; Research Prof. of Psychology, New York Univ. 1988–96, Sr Researcher Fellow, Law School 1991–96, Univ. Prof. 1996–; Fellow, New York Inst. for the Humanities; mem. American Acad. of Arts and Sciences; Hon. DSc (Northwestern) 1965, (Sheffield) 1970, (Bristol) 1965, (Columbia) 1991; Hon. MA (Oxford) 1972; Hon. LLD (Temple) 1965, (Cincinnati) 1966, (New Brunswick) 1969, (Yale) 1978; Hon. DLitt (N Mich.) 1969, (Duke) 1969, (York Univ.) 1993; Dr hc (Sorbonne) 1974, (Leuven) 1976, (Ghent) 1977, (Madrid) 1986, (Free Univ. of Berlin) 1988, (Rome) 1992, (Harvard) 1996, (Bologna) 2001, (Crete) 2002; Int. Balzan Foundation Prize 1987. *Publications:* Mandate from the People 1944, The Process of Education 1960, On Knowing: Essays for the Left Hand 1962, Toward a Theory of Instruction 1966, Processes of Cognitive Growth: Infancy, (Vol. III) 1968, The Relevance of Education 1971, Under Five in Britain 1980, Communication as a Language 1982, In Search of Mind 1983, Child's Talk 1983, Actual Minds, Possible Worlds 1986, Acts of Meaning 1990, The Culture of Education 1996, Minding the Law 2000, Making Stories 2002; also co-author of several books. *Leisure interests:* sailing, drama. *Address:* 200 Mercer Street, New York, NY 10012, USA. *Telephone:* (212) 674-7816. *Fax:* (212) 673-6118.

BRUNETTA, Renato; Italian professor of labour economics; b. 26 May 1950, Venice; ed Marco Foscarini Liceo Classico, Venice and Univs. of Padua, Cambridge and Rotterdam; researcher in political sciences, Univ. of Padua 1975–77, Prof. of Labour Econs 1978–82; Gen. Sec. Fondazione G. Brodolini, Rome 1980–; Ed. Economia & Lavoro (quarterly review), Rome 1980–; chief consultant, econ. adviser to Italian Ministry of Labour 1983–88; Sec. Italian Asscn of Labour Economists 1985–87; Vice-Pres., OECD Manpower and Social Affairs Cttee 1986–88; Founder and Ed. Labour (4-monthly journal) 1987–; Pres. Comm. on Information for CNEL (Nat. Council of Economy and Labour) 1989–94, European Asscn of Labour Economists 1989–93, Scientific Cttee on European Integration of Ministry of Foreign Affairs 1990–92; Prof. of Labour Econs Rome Univ. II 'Tor Vergata' 1990–; mem. ASPEN-Italy 1989–, Taskforce for Programming and Econ. Policy, Ministry of the Budget 1990–; Councillor, CNEL 1995–; mem. European Parl. 1999–, Vice-Pres. Cttee on Industry, External Trade, Research and Energy; Premio St Vincent (for Econs) 1988, Premio Tarantelli (for Econs) 1993. *Publications:* Economia del Lavoro 1981, Multilocalizzazione produttiva come strategia d'impresa 1983, Squilibri, conflitto, piena occupazione 1983, Spesa pubblica e conflitto 1987, Microeconomia del lavoro: Teorie e analisi empiriche 1987, Labour Relations and Economic Performance (ed.) 1990, Il Modello Italia 1991, Economics for the New Europe 1991, Il conflitto e le relazioni di lavoro negli anni '90 1992, Disoccupazione, Isteresi, Irreversibilità 1992, Retribuzione, costo del lavoro. Regolazione e deregolazione; il capital umano; la destrutturazione del mercato (Ed.) 1992, La fine della società dei salariati 1994, Sud: Alcune idee perché il Mezzogiorno non resti com'è 1995; articles and essays on labour econs and industrial relations. *Leisure interests:* photography, history of Venice, gastronomy. *Address:* European Parliament, Centre Européen, Plateau du Kirchberg, B.P. 1601, 2929 Luxembourg.

BRUNI-SAKRAISCHIK, Claudio Alberico; American (b. Italian) art consultant and critic; b. 5 May 1926, Udine, Italy; s. of Bruno Bruni and Caterina Ellero; ed Univs of Bologna and Rome; Pres. La Medusa Gallery Inc., New York; Art Expert by appt of Tribunal of Rome; Curator Gen. Catalogue of Works of Giorgio de Chirico; Vice-Pres. Giorgio and Isa de Chirico Foundation, Rome; Hon. Pres. Italian Art Dealers' Asscn; lectures on de Chirico. *Publications:* General Catalogue of the Works of Giorgio de Chirico (Vols 1–9), several books and articles on the artist. *Address:* Via Margutta 60, 00187 Rome, Italy. *Telephone:* (212) 744-5593 (New York); (06) 3207749 (Rome).

BRUNO, Franklin Roy (Frank), MBE; British boxer; b. 16 Nov. 1961, London; s. of the late Robert Bruno and of Lynette Bruno (née Campbell); m. Laura Frances Mooney 1990 (divorced 2001); one s. two d.; ed Oak Hall School, Sussex; began boxing with Wandsworth Boys' Club, London 1970; mem. Sir Philip Game Amateur Boxing Club 1977–80; won 20 out of 21 contests as amateur; professional career 1982–96; won 38 out of 42 contests as professional 1982–89; European heavyweight champion 1985–86 (relinquished title), world heavyweight title challenges against Tim Witherspoon 1986, Mike Tyson 1989; staged comeback, won first contest 1991; lost 4th world title challenge against Lennox Lewis Oct. 1993; WBC heavyweight champion 1995–96, lost title to Mike Tyson 1996; announced retirement Aug. 1996; appearances in pantomimes 1990, 1991, 1996, 1997, 1999; fmr presenter, BBC TV; SOS Sports Personality of the Year 1990; TV Times Sports Personality of the Year 1990, Lifetime Achievement Award, BBC Sports Personality of the Year Awards 1996. *Publication:* Personality: From Zero to Hero (with Norman Giller) 1996. *Leisure interests:* music, training, swimming. *Address:* c/o PO Box 2266, Brentwood, Essex, CM15 0AQ, England. *Fax:* (1277) 822209.

BRUNTON, Sir Gordon Charles, Kt; British business executive; b. 27 Dec. 1921, London; s. of Charles A. Brunton and Hylda Pritchard; m. 1st Nadine Sohr 1946 (divorced 1965); one s. (one s. deceased) two d.; m. 2nd Gillian A. Kirk 1966; one s. one d.; ed Cranleigh School and London School of Econs; war service 1942–46; joined Tothill Press 1947, Exec. Dir 1956; Man. Dir Tower Press Group 1958; Exec. Dir Odhams Press 1961; joined Thomson Org. 1961, Dir 1963, Man. Dir and CEO Int. Thomson Org. PLC (fmrly Thomson British Holdings) and Thomson Org. Ltd 1968–84; Man. Dir Thomson Publications 1961; Chair. Thomson Travel 1965–68; Pres. Int. Thomson Org. Ltd 1978–84; Dir Times Newspapers Ltd 1967–81, Bemrose Corpn 1974 (Chair. 1978–91), Sotheby Parke Bernet Group PLC 1978–85, Cable and Wireless PLC 1981–91, Yattendon Investment Trust PLC 1985–2001; fmr non-exec. Dir Cable and Wireless PLC, South Bank Bd (Arts Council); Pres. Periodical Publishers' Asscn 1972–74, 1981–82, Nat. Advertising Benevolent Soc. 1973–75; Chair. Econ. Devt Council for Civil Eng 1978–84, Appeals Cttee, Independent Adoption Soc., Communications and Gen. Consultants Ltd 1985–, Mercury Communications Ltd 1986–90, Cavendish Shops 1985–93, Community Industry Ltd 1985–92, The Racing Post PLC 1985–97, Ingersoll Publications 1988–91, Verity Group PLC (fmrly Wharfedale PLC) 1991–97, Green Field Leisure Group Ltd 1992–, PhoneLink PLC (now Telme.com PLC) 1993–2001, Euram Consulting Ltd, Focus Investments Ltd, Cavendish Retail, Racing Int. Ltd and other limited cos; Gov. and Fellow LSE, Henley Man. Coll. 1983–86; Pres. The History of Advertising Trust 1981–84; mem. Council, Templeton Coll. (fmrly Oxford Cen. for Man. Studies); mem. South Bank Bd, Arts Council 1985–92. *Leisure interests:* books, breeding horses. *Address:* North Munstead Stud Farm, North Munstead Lane, Godalming, Surrey, GU8 4AX, England. *Telephone:* (1483) 424181 (Office); (1483) 416313 (Home). *Fax:* (1483) 426043 (Office).

BRUSKIN, Grisha (Brouskine Grigori); Russian artist; b. 21 Oct. 1945, Moscow; s. of David Brouskin and Bassia Strunina; m. 1st Ludmila Dmitrieva 1975 (divorced 1978); m. 2nd Alexandra Makarova 1982; one d. one adopted s.; ed Art High School, Moscow, Moscow Textile Inst.; became mem. Soviet Artists' Union 1968; work includes paintings, gouaches, drawings, sculptures, performances; work included in first Sotheby's auction in Moscow, designed poster for Chicago Art Exhbn 1988; now lives and works in New York, USA; solo exhbns in Moscow 1976, 1984, Vilnius, Lithuania 1983, Marlborough Gallery, New York 1990; numerous group exhbns including The Painter and Modernism, Moscow 1987, 100 Years of Russian Art, Barbican, London and in Chicago, Berne, Seoul, Cologne, Chicago, New York, Barcelona, Paris, Munich, Düsseldorf, Lisbon, Brussels, Berlin, Copenhagen 1988–; works in Art Inst. of Chicago, Jewish Museum, New York, Museum of Modern Art, New York, Nat. Museum of Israel, Jerusalem etc. *Leisure interests:* literature, music.

BRUSTEIN, Robert Sanford, MA, PhD; American drama critic, actor and producer; b. 21 April 1927, New York, NY; m. 1st Norma Cates 1962 (deceased 1979); one s. one step-s; m. 2nd Doreen Beinart 1996; two step-c.; ed Amherst Coll. Yale Univ. Drama School, Columbia Univ.; played about 70 roles in theatre groups and TV plays 1950–; Instructor, Cornell Univ. 1955–56, Vassar Coll. 1956–57; lecturer, Columbia Univ. 1957–58, Asst Prof. 1958–63, Assoc. Prof. 1963–65, Prof. 1965–66; Prof. of English, Yale Univ., Dean of Yale Drama School, Artistic Dir and Founder, Yale Repertory Theatre 1966–79; Artistic Dir and Founder American Repertory Theatre Ensemble, Loeb Drama Center, Cambridge, Mass. 1979–; Prof. of English, Harvard Univ. 1979–; Drama Critic, The New Republic 1959–67, 1978–, Contributing Ed. 1959–79; host and writer, The Opposition Theatre (Net TV) 1966–; regular contributor to New York Times 1972–; Founder, Artistic Dir Yale Repertory Theatre 1966–79; Advisory Ed., Theatre Quarterly 1967–; Guest Critic, The Observer, UK 1972–73, 1978–, Contributing Ed. 1959–; Trustee, Sarah Lawrence Coll. 1973–77; Panel mem. Nat. Endowment for the Arts 1970–72, 1981–84; mem. Nat. Acad. Arts and Sciences; Fulbright Fellow 1953–55, Guggenheim Fellow 1961–62, Ford Fellow 1964–65; LittD (Lawrence Univ.) 1968, (Amherst Coll.) 1972, LHD (Beloit Coll.) 1975; Hon. Dr of Arts (Bard Coll.) 1981; George G. Nathan Prize in Criticism 1962, George Polk Memorial Award in Criticism 1964, Jersey City Journal Award in Theatre Criticism 1967, Eliot Norton Award for Theatre, New England Theatre Conf. Award for Excellence in Theme, Award, Outstanding Achievement in American Theater, New England Theater Council 1985, Tiffany Award for Excellence in Theater, Soc. for Performing Arts Administrators 1987, American Acad. of Arts and Letters Distinguished Services to Arts Award 1995, ATHE Award for Lifetime Achievement in the Theater 2000. *Publications:* Introduction to The Plays of Chekhov 1964; Ed. The Plays of Strindberg 1964; author: The Theatre of Revolt 1964, Seasons of Discontent 1965, The Third Theatre 1969, Revolution as Theatre 1971, The Culture Watch 1975, The Plays and Prose of Strindberg (editor), Critical Moments 1980, Making Scenes 1981, Who Needs Theatre 1987, Reimagining American Theatre 1991, Dumbocracy in America 1994, Demons 1995 (play), Nobody Dies on Friday 1996 (play), Culturak Calisthenics 1998, Poker Face 1999, The Face Lift 1999, Chekhov on Ice 2000, Three Farces and a Funeral 2000, Divestiture 2001, The Siege of the Arts 2001. *Address:* Loeb Drama Center, Harvard University, Cambridge, MA 02138, USA.

BRUTON, John Gerard, BA, BL; Irish politician and farmer; b. 18 May 1947, Dublin; s. of Matthew Joseph Bruton and Doris Mary Delany; m. Finola Gill 1981; one s. three d.; ed Clongowes Wood Coll., Univ. Coll., Dublin, King's Inn, Dublin; mem. Dáil Éireann (House of Reps) 1969–; Fine Gael Spokesman on Agric. 1972–73; Parl. Sec. to Minister for Educ. 1973–77, to Minister for Industry and Commerce 1975–77; Fine Gael Spokesman on Agric. 1977–81, on Finance Jan.–June 1981; Minister of Finance 1981–82, of Industry, Trade, Commerce and Tourism 1982–86, of Finance 1986–87; Deputy Leader of Fine Gael 1987–90, Leader 1990–2001, Fine Gael Spokesman on Industry and Commerce 1987–89, on Educ. 1989–90; mem. Parl. Ass., Council of Europe 1989–91, British-Irish Parl. Body 1993–94, Parl. Ass., WEU 1997–; Prime Minister of Ireland 1994–97; Leader of Opposition 1997–2001; barrister; Hon. Citizen, Sioux City, Iowa, USA. *Publications:* Reform of the Dail 1980, A Better Way to Plan the Nation's Finances 1981. *Leisure interests:* history, folk music, tennis. *Address:* Dáil Éireann, Leinster House, Dublin 2; Cornelstown, Dunboyne, County Meath, Ireland (Home). *Telephone:* (1) 6183000 (Home).

BRUTUS, Dennis, BA; South African educationist and poet; b. 28 Nov. 1924, Salisbury, S Rhodesia (now Harare, Zimbabwe); s. of Francis Henry Brutus and Margaret Winifred Brutus (née Bloemetjie); m. May Jaggers 1950; four s. four d.; ed Paterson High School, Port Elizabeth, Fort Hare and Witwatersrand Univs; language teacher, Paterson High School, Cen. Indian High School; office boy and law student, Witwatersrand Univ.; imprisoned for opposition to apartheid 1964–65, exiled 1966, political asylum in USA 1983; Dir World Campaign for Release of S African Political Prisoners; worked for Int. Defence and Aid Fund, fmrly UN Rep.; Visiting Prof. Denver Univ.; Prof. of English, Northwestern Univ., Evanston, Ill.; Visiting Prof., English Dept, African and Afro-American Studies and Research Center, Univ. Tex., Austin, 1974–75; Visiting Prof., Dept of English, Amherst Coll., Mass. 1982–83, Dartmouth Coll., NH 1983; Adjunct Prof. Northeastern Univ., Boston, Mass. 1984; Pres. S African Non-Racial Olympic Cttee (SAN-ROC); Chair. Int. Campaign Against Racism in Sport (ICARIS), Africa Network 1984–; Dir Program on African and African-American Writing in Africa and the Diaspora 1989–; Interport lecturer Univ. of Pittsburgh; Founding Chair., Exec. mem. African Literature Asscn, fmr Chair. ARENA (Inst. for Study of Sport and Social Issues); mem. of Bd, Black Arts Celebration, Vice-Pres. Union of Writers of the African People; mem. Bd of Dirs UN Asscn of Chicago and Ill., Editorial Bd Africa Today; Dir Troubadour Press; Fellow, Int. Poetry Soc.; mem. Modern Language Asscn 1972, Int. Platform Asscn 1979–, Int. Jury Books Abroad Award 1976; Hon. HLD (Worcester State Coll.) 1982; Mbari Prize for Poetry in Africa, Chancellor's Prize for Bilingualism (Univ. of S. Africa); Freedom Writers' Award, Kenneth David Kaunda Humanism Award, Academic Excellence Award, Nat. Council for Black Studies 1982, UN Human Rights Day Award 1983. *Publications:* Sirens, Knuckles, Boots 1963, Letters to Martha 1968, Poems from Algiers 1970, Thoughts Abroad (John Bruin) 1971, A Simple Lust 1973, China Poems 1975, Strains 1975, Stubborn Hope 1978, 1979, 1983, Salutes and Censures 1980. *Leisure interests:* sport, music, chess.

BRYAN, Sir Arthur, Kt; British company director; b. 4 March 1923, Stoke-on-Trent; s. of William Woodall Bryan and Isobel Alan (née Tweedie); m. Betty Ratford 1947; one s. one d.; ed Longton High School; served with RAFVR 1941–45; joined Wedgwood Ltd 1947, sales rep. 1949, Asst London Man. 1950–53, London Man. and Gen. Man. of Wedgwood Rooms 1953–59, Gen. Sales Man. 1959–60; Dir and Pres. Josiah Wedgwood & Sons Inc. of America 1960–62; Man. Dir Wedgwood PLC 1963–85, Chair. 1968–86; Pres. Waterford Wedgwood Holdings PLC 1986–88; Dir Waterford Glass Group PLC 1986–88; Dir Friends' Provident Life Asscn 1985–92, UK Fund Inc. 1987–2001, Dartington Crystal Group 1995–2001; Pres. British Ceramic Mfrs Fed. 1970–71; mem. Court, Univ. of Keele; Chair. Consumer Market Advisory Cttee, Dept of Trade and Industry 1988–; Companion, British Inst. of Man. 1968; Fellow, Inst. of Marketing, Royal Soc. of Arts 1964; Companion, Inst. Ceramics; KStJ 1972; Lord Lt of Staffordshire 1968–93. *Leisure interests:* walking, reading. *Address:* Wedgwood Museum Trust, Barlaston, Stoke-on-Trent, Staffs., ST12 9HQ (Office); Parkfields Cottage, Tittensor, Stoke-on-Trent, Staffs., ST12 9HQ, England (Home).

BRYAN, John Henry, BA; American business executive; b. 5 Oct. 1936, West Point, Miss.; s. of John H. Bryan, Sr; m. Neville Frierson Bryan 1958; two s. two d.; ed Southwestern Univ. (now Rhodes Coll.), Memphis; joined Bryan Packing Co. 1960, Pres., CEO 1968–74; Exec. Vice-Pres., Dir Sara Lee Corpn March–Oct. 1974, Pres. 1974–75, CEO 1975–, Chair. 1976–; Dir (non-exec.) Gen. Motors 1993–; mem. Bd of Dirs Amoco Corpn, First Chicago Corpn, The First Nat. Bank of Chicago; fmr Chair. and mem. Bd of Dirs of Grocery Mfrs of America, Inc.; mem. Business Roundtable, Bds Catalyst, Nat. Women's Econ. Alliance, Art Inst. of Chicago; Dir Business Cttee for Arts; Prin. of Chicago United; Trustee Rush-Presbyterian-St Luke's Medical Center, Univ. of Chicago; Trustee Cttee for Econ. Devt; Légion d'honneur, Order of Orange Nassau (Netherlands), Order of Lincoln Medallion and numerous other awards. *Address:* Sara Lee Corpn, 3 First National Plaza, Chicago, IL 60602-4260, USA (Office). *Telephone:* (312) 726-2600 (Office).

BRYAN, Richard H., LLB; American politician; b. 16 July 1937, Washington; m. Bonnie Fairchild; three c.; ed Univ. of Nevada and Hastings Coll. of Law, Univ. of California; admitted to Nev. Bar 1963, US Supreme Court Bar 1967; Deputy Dist Attorney, Clark Co., Nev. 1964–66; Public Defender, Clark Co. 1966–68; Counsel Clark Co. Juvenile Court 1968–69; mem. Nev. Assembly 1969–71; Nev. Senate 1973–77; Attorney-Gen., Nev. 1979–82; Gov. of Nevada 1983–89; Senator from Nevada 1989–2001; Partner and mem. Exec. Cttee Lionel, Sawyer & Collins 2001–; adjunct Prof. of Political Science Univ. of

Nev., Las Vegas 2001–; mem. Bd Trustees Nev. Devt Authority 2001–; Democrat. *Address:* Lionel Sawyer & Collins, 1700 Bank America Plaza, 300 South Fourth Street, Las Vegas, NV 89101, USA (Office).

BRYANT, John Martin, MA, CEng, FIM, FREng; British business executive; b. 28 Sept. 1943, Cardiff; s. of William George Bryant and Doris Bryant; m. Andrea Irene Emmons 1965; two s. one d.; ed W Monmouth School, Pontypool, St Catharine's Coll., Cambridge; grad. trainee Steel Co. of Wales 1965–68; various tech., production, personnel positions British Steel 1968–78, Works Man. Hot Rolled Products 1978–87, Dir Coated Products 1987–90, Dir Tinplate 1990–92, Man. Dir Strip Products 1992–96, Exec. Dir 1996–98, Chief Exec. 1999; Chief Exec. Corus PLC; Dir ASW PLC 1993–95, Bank of Wales PLC 1996–2001, Welsh Water PLC 2001–, Glas Cymru Ltd 2001–, Costain Group PLC 2002–; Hon. DSc (Wales) 2000. *Leisure interests:* all sports, particularly squash and rugby, family. *Address:* Park House, Merryhole Lane, Old Down, Tockington, Bristol, BS32 4PT, England (Home).

BRYANT, Thomas Edward, MD, JD; American physician and attorney; b. 17 Jan. 1936, Ala; s. of Howard Edward Bryant and Alibel Nettles Bryant; m. Lucie Elizabeth Thrasher 1961 (divorced); one s. one d.; ed Emory Univ., Atlanta; Dir of Health Affairs, US Office of Econ. Opportunity 1969–70; Pres. Nat. Drug Abuse Council 1970–78; Chair. Pres. Comm. on Mental Health 1977–78; Dir Children of Alcoholics Foundation 1983–; mem. Inst. of Medicine, NAS 1972; Chair. The Public Cttee on Mental Health 1977–79, Council for Understanding Mental Illnesses 1983–87, Aspirin Foundation of America 1987–, Non-Profit Man. Assocs Inc. 1989–; Exec. Dir Co. Behavioral Health Inst. 1997–; Practising Attorney specializing in Health Law with Webster and Sheffield 1980–84; Chair. The Rosalynn Carter Inst. 1986–; Pres. The Friends of the Nat. Library of Medicine 1985–; Emory Outstanding Alumnus Medal 1986. *Address:* Non Profit Management Associates Inc., 1555 Connecticut Ave., NW, Suite 200, Washington, DC 20036, USA.

BRYANTSEV, Dmitri Aleksandrovich; Russian choreographer; b. 18 Feb. 1947, Leningrad; ed Leningrad Higher School of Choreography, Moscow State Inst. of Theatre; soloist Moscow Choreographic Ensemble Classical Ballet 1966–77; ballet master and choreographer since 1975; chief ballet master K. Stanislavsky and V. Nemirovich-Danchenko Musical Theatre 1985–; staged numerous productions, incl. Choreographic Miniatures (Kirov Theatre), Hussars' Ballad by T. Khrennikov (Kirov and Bolshoi Theatres 1979, 1980), Othello, Corsair, Optimistic Tragedy, Hunchback Horse; author of TV ballet productions Galatea, Old Tango; staged dances in opera productions including Dead Souls by R. Shchedrin (Bolshoi Theatre) and drama productions (Turandot, Taganka Theatre); People's Artist of Russia 1989. *Address:* Musical Theatre, Bolshaya Dmitrovka 17, 103009 Moscow, Russia. *Telephone:* (095) 229-28-35 (Office).

BRYARS, Gavin, BA; British composer and professor of music; b. 16 Jan. 1943, Goole, Yorks.; s. of Walter Joseph Bryars and Miriam Eleanor Bryars; m.1st Angela Margaret Bigley 1971 (divorced 1993); two d.; m. 2nd Anna Tchernakova 1999; one s. one step d.; ed Goole Grammar School, Sheffield Univ. and pvt. composition study with George Linstead; freelance double bassist 1963–66; freelance composer/performer 1968–70; Lecturer in Dept of Fine Art, Portsmouth Polytechnic 1969–70; Sr Lecturer, School of Fine Art, Leicester Polytechnic 1970–78, Sr Lecturer and Head of Music, School of Performing Arts 1978–85, Prof. of Music 1985–96; mem. Collège de Pataphysique, France 1974–; Ed. Experimental Music Catalogue 1972–81; British Rep. Int. Soc. for Contemporary Music Festival 1977; Visiting Prof. Univ. of Herts.; Arts Council Comms 1970, 1980, 1982, Bursary 1982. *Radio:* I Send You This Cadmium Rec (BBC Radio 3, with John Berger and John Christie) 2002. *Television:* Last Summer (CBC TV, Dir Anna Tchernakova) 2000. *Works include:* The Sinking of the Titanic 1969, Jesus' Blood Never Failed Me Yet 1971, Out of Zaleski's Gazebo 1977, The Vespertine Park 1980, Medea (opera with Robert Wilson) 1982, My First Homage 1978–82, Effarene 1984, String Quartet No. 1 1985, Pico's Flight 1986, By the Vaar 1987, The Invention of Tradition 1988, Glorious Hill 1988, Cadman Requiem 1989, String Quartet No. 2 1990, The White Lodge 1991, Three Elegies for Nine Clarinets 1994, After Handel's Vesper 1995, Cello Concerto 1995, The Adnan Songbook 1996, Doctor Ox's Experiment 1997 (opera), String Quartet No. 3 1998, The Porazzi Fragment 1999, Biped (ballet) 1999, First Book of Madrigals 2000, Violin Concerto 2000, G (opera) 2001, Second Book of Madrigals 2002, Double Bass Concerto 2002; recordings on Point Music, Decca, ECM (Munich), GB Records, CBC Records. *Leisure interests:* cricket (mem. Yorks. County Cricket Club), football, Dalmatians. *Address:* c/o Schott and Co. Ltd, 48 Great Marlborough Street, London, W1V 2BN, England. *Telephone:* (20) 7494-1487. *Fax:* (20) 7287-1529. *E-mail:* questions@gavinbryars.com (Office). *Website:* www .gavinbryars.com (Office).

BRYDEN, Alan; British/French international organization executive; b. 1945; m. Laurence Bryden; three c.; ed ed. Ecole Polytechnique, Paris, Ecole des Mines, Paris and Univ. d' Orsay, France; began career in metrology with Nat. Bureau of Standards (now Nat. Inst. of Standards and Tech.), USA; Dir-Gen. Laboratoire Nat. d'Essais 1981–99; f. Eurolab (European Fed. of Measurement, Testing and Analytical Labs), Pres. 1990–96; Dir-Gen. AFNOR (French nat. standardization inst.) 1999–2003; mem. Council Int. Org. for Standardization (ISO) 1999–2003, Sec.-Gen. March 2003–; European Cttee. for Standardization; fmr Vice-Pres. Cttee on Tech. Barriers to Trade in GATT (now WTO); fmr Chair. Labs Cttee of Int. Lab. Accreditation Co-operation; Chevalier, Légion d'honneur, Ordre nat. du Mérite. *Leisure interests:* riding, sailing. *Address:* International Organization for Standardization, Case Postale 56, 1211 Geneva 20, Switzerland (Office). *Telephone:* (22) 7490111 (Office). *Website:* www.iso.ch (Office).

BRYDON, Donald Hood, OBE; British investment executive; b. 25 May 1945; s. of James Hood Brydon and Mary Duncanson Brydon (née Young); m. 1st Joan Victoria Brydon 1971 (divorced 1995), one s. one d.; m. 2nd Corinne Susan Jane Green 1996; ed George Watson's Coll., Edinburgh, Univ. of Edinburgh; with Econs Dept Univ. of Edinburgh 1967–70; with British Airways Pensions Fund 1970–77; Barclays Investment Man.'s Office 1977–81, Deputy Man. Dir Barclays Investment Man. Ltd 1981–86; Dir BZW Investment Man. 1986–88, Man. Dir 1988–91, Chair., CEO BZW Asset Man. Ltd 1991–94, Chair. (non-exec.) 1994–95, Deputy Chief Exec. Barclays de Zoete Wedd 1994–96, Acting CEO 1996; Chair., CEO AXA. Asset Man. Europe 1997–; Pres. European Asset Man. Assn 1999–2001; Dir Stock Exchange 1991–98; Dir Edinburgh Inca Investment Trust 1996–, Allied Domecq 1997–, AXA UK (fmrly Sun Life and Provincial Holdings) 1997–; Chair. European Children's Trust 1999–2001, Fund Man. Assn 1999–, Financial Services Practitioner Forum 2001–. *Publications:* Economics of Technical Information Services (jtly) 1972. *Address:* AXA Investment Managers Ltd, 7 Newgate Street, London, EC1A 7NX, England (Office). *Telephone:* (20) 7003-1500.

BRYMER, Charles; American business executive; fmrly with BBDO Inc. Houston and New York; joined Interbrand Group (int. consultancy specializing in brands and branding) 1985, later CEO. *Address:* Interbrand Schechter Inc., 437 Madison Avenue, New York, NY 100022, USA. *Telephone:* (212) 752-4400. *Fax:* (212) 752-4503.

BRYMER, Jack, OBE, FGSM; British clarinettist; b. 27 Jan. 1915, South Shields, Co. Durham; s. of John Brymer and Mary Dixon; m. Joan Richardson 1939; one s.; ed Goldsmith's Coll., London Univ.; Prin. Clarinet, Royal Philharmonic Orchestra 1947–63, BBC Symphony Orchestra 1963–72, London Symphony Orchestra 1972–87; Prof., Royal Acad. of Music 1950–56; Prof. of Clarinet, Royal Mil. School of Music, Kneller Hall 1970–73; Prof. of Clarinet, Guildhall School of Music and Drama 1981–89; Dir Shell London Symphony Orchestra Scholarship 1982–; mem. Wigmore Ensemble, Prometheus Ensemble, London Baroque Ensemble, Delme Ensemble, Robles Ensemble and Founding Dir London Wind Soloists; world-wide soloist recitals and numerous recordings; lecturer on musical topics on radio and TV; two demonstration films on history, devt and use of the clarinet as a solo and orchestral instrument; Fellow Northern Coll. of Music; Fellow Goldsmith's Coll., London Univ. 1991; Hon. FRAM; Hon. MA (Newcastle) 1973; Hon. DMus (Kingston) 1992, (De Montfort, Leicester) 1995; Cobbett Medal of Worshipful Co. of Musicians 1989. *Publications:* The Clarinet 1976, From Where I Sit (autobiog.) 1978, In the Orchestra 1987, Learn the Clarinet (video) 1990. *Leisure interests:* golf, tennis, swimming, gardening, carpentry, photography. *Address:* 31 Sycamore Court, Hoskins Road, Oxted, Surrey, RH8 9JQ, England (Home). *Telephone:* (1883) 712843 (Home).

BRYNGDAHL, Olof; Swedish university professor; b. 26 Sept. 1933, Stockholm; s. of Carl Olof Bryngdahl and Ingeborg M. Pihlgren; m. Margaretha Schraut 1959; ed Royal Inst. of Tech. Stockholm; Research Assoc. Inst. for Optical Research, Stockholm 1956–64; staff mem. Xerox Research Lab. Rochester, NY 1964–65; Man. IBM Research Lab. San José, Calif. 1966–69; Sr scientist, IBM Research Lab. Yorktown Heights NY 1970; Prin. scientist, Xerox Research Lab. Palo Alto, Calif. 1970–77; Prof. Inst. d'Optique, Univ. of Paris 1975–76; Prof. Univ. of Essen 1977–; Fellow, Optical Soc. of America. *Publications:* more than 200 scientific articles; 14 patents in optics. *Address:* University of Essen, 45117 Essen, Universitätsstrasse 2, Germany. *Telephone:* (201) 1832562. *E-mail:* olof.bryngdahl@uni-essen.de (Office).

BRYNTSALOV, Vladimir Alekseyevich; Russian businessman; b. 23 Nov. 1946, Cherkessk; m. 1st; one d.; m. 2nd Natalya Bryntsalova; one s. one d.; ed Inst. of Construction and Eng; engineer, then Head Construction Dept in Stavropol 1970–80; expelled from CPSU for construction of a house of his own; pvt. enterprise activities started late 1980s; f. co-operative Pchelka (Bee) 1987, set up candle factory 1988; in Moscow from 1989; bought stock shares of pharmaceutical factories, f. Co. Ferein 1992– (produces over one third of all medicaments in Russia); mem. State Duma (Parl.) 1995–, joined Our Home–Russia faction 1997; f. Russian Socialist Party 1998; re-elected as ind. cand. 1999–; Deputy Chair. Yedinstvo faction; Cand. for Presidency of Russia 1996. *Address:* Ferein, Nagatinskaya str. 1, 113105 Moscow, Russia. *Telephone:* (095) 111-00-79 (Office).

BRYSON, Bill; American author; b. 1951, Des Moines, IA; m.; four c.; ed Drake Univ.; author of travel books and books on linguistics; travelled to England and worked as orderly in mental hosp. 1973; worked as journalist for The Times and the Independent; returned with his family to USA 1993; apptd to selection panel, Book of the Month Club 2001. *Publications include:* (linguistics): Penguin Dictionary of Troublesome Words 1985, The Mother Tongue: English and How It Got That Way, Made in America 1994; (travel): The Lost Continent 1987, Neither Here Nor There, Notes From a Small Island 1995, A Walk in the Woods, I'm a Stranger Here Myself (essays) 1999, In a Sunburned Country 2000, The Best American Travel Writing (Ed.). *Address:* c/o Random House, 1540 Broadway, New York, NY 10036, USA (Office).

BRYSON, Adm. Sir Lindsay Sutherland, KCB, FRSE, FRAeS; British naval officer (retd) and engineer; b. 22 Jan. 1925, Glasgow; s. of James McAuslan Bryson and Margaret Whyte; m. Averil Curtis-Willson 1951; one s. two d.; ed

Allan Glen's School, Glasgow; entered Royal Navy as Electrical Mechanic 1945, rank of Lt 1948, Commdr 1960, Capt. 1967; Commdg Officer, RN Air Station, Lee-on-Solent 1970–71; Dir Naval Guided Weapons 1973–75; Dir Surface Weapon Projects as Commodore 1975–76; rank of Rear-Adm. 1977; Dir Gen. Weapons (Navy) 1977–80; rank of Vice-Adm. 1979; Chief Naval Engineer Officer 1979–80; Controller of the Navy 1981–84; rank of Admiral 1983; retd from Navy 1985; Pres. IEE 1985–86; Dir (non-exec.) ERA Tech. Ltd 1985 (Chair. 1990–97), Molins PLC 1998–99; Chair. Marine Technology Directorate Ltd 1986–92; Lord Lt of E Sussex 1989–2000; Pres. Soc. of Underwater Tech. 1989–91; Chair. of Council, Sussex Univ. 1989–95; Chair. New Sussex Opera 1990–99, Brighton Festival Trust 1990–2000, Brighton Coll. Council 1990–98; Pres. Asscn of Project Mans 1991–95; Chair. Brighton West Pier Trust 1995–; Chair. Old Market Trust 1996–2001; Trustee Hanover Band 1997–2001; Hon. Fellow, Paisley Coll. of Tech. 1986; Hon. FIEE 1991; Hon. FIMechE 1991; Hon. Fellow Asscn of Project Mans 1996; Hon. DSc (Strathclyde) 1987; Hon. DEng (Bristol) 1988; Hon. LLD (Sussex) 1995. *Leisure interests:* opera, sailing. *Address:* 74 Dyke Road Avenue, Brighton, Sussex, BN1 5LE, England. *Telephone:* (1273) 553638. *Fax:* (1273) 562478.

BRZEZINSKI, Zbigniew K., PhD; American (naturalized 1958) professor of government; b. 28 March 1928, Warsaw, Poland; s. of Tadeusz Brzezinski and Leonia Roman; m. Emilie Anna (Muska) Benes 1955; two s. one d.; ed McGill and Harvard Univs; settled in N America 1938; Instructor in Govt and Research Fellow, Russian Research Center, Harvard Univ. 1953–56; Asst Prof. of Govt, Research Assoc. of Russian Research Center and of Center for Int. Affairs, Harvard Univ. 1956–60; Assoc. Prof. of Public Law and Govt, Columbia Univ. 1960–62, Prof. 1962–89 (on leave 1966–68, 1977–81) and Dir Research Inst. on Communist Affairs 1961–77 (on leave 1966–68); mem. Policy Planning Council, Dept of State 1966–68; mem. Hon. Steering Cttee, Young Citizens for Johnson 1964; Dir Foreign Policy Task Force for Vice-Pres. Humphrey 1968; Asst to the Pres. for Nat. Security Affairs 1977–81; mem. Nat. Security Council 1977–81; Counsellor, Center for Strategic and Int. Studies, Washington, DC 1981–; Robert Osgood Prof. of American Foreign Policy, Paul Nitze School of Advanced Int. Studies, Johns Hopkins Univ. 1989–; Fellow, American Acad. of Arts and Sciences 1969–; mem. Council on Foreign Relations, New York, Bd of Trustees, Freedom House; Guggenheim Fellowship 1960, Ford Fellowship 1970; Hon. Dr (Alliance Coll.) 1966, (Coll. of the Holy Cross) 1971, (Fordham Univ.) 1979, (Williams Coll.) 1986, (Georgetown Univ.) 1987, (Catholic Univ. of Lublin) 1990, (Warsaw Univ.) 1991; Presidential Medal of Freedom 1981, Order of White Eagle (Poland) 1995, Order of Merit (Ukraine) 1996, Masaryk Order 1998, Gedymim Order 1998. *Publications include:* Political Controls in the Soviet Army 1954, The Permanent Purge–Politics in Soviet Totalitarianism 1956, Totalitarian Dictatorship and Autocracy (co-author) 1957, The Soviet Bloc–Unity and Conflict 1960, Ideology and Power in Soviet Politics 1962, Africa and the Communist World (Ed. and contrib.) 1963, Political Power: USA/USSR (co-author) 1964, Alternative to Partition: For a Broader Conception of America's Role in Europe 1965, Dilemmas of Change in Soviet Politics (Ed. and contrib.) 1969, Between Two Ages: America's Role in the Technetronic Era 1970, The Fragile Blossom: Crisis and Change in Japan 1972, Power and Principle 1983, Game Plan 1986, The Grand Failure: The Birth and Death of Communism in the 20th Century, 1989, Out of Control 1993, The Grand Chessboard: American Primacy and its Geostrategic Imperatives 1997. *Address:* Centre for Strategic and International Studies, Suite 400, 1800 K Street, NW, Washington, DC 20006, USA (Office). *Telephone:* (202) 833-2408 (Office). *Fax:* (202) 833-2409 (Office). *E-mail:* zb@csis.org (Office). *Website:* www.csis.org (Office).

BU HE, (YUN SHUGUANG); Chinese party and government official; b. 24 March 1926, Inner Mongolia; s. of late Ulanfu and Yun Ting; m. Zhulanqiqige 1947; one s. two d.; ed Yan'an Inst. for Nationalities and Nationalities Coll. of Yan'an Univ.; joined CCP 1942; Lecturer and Deputy Dir Political Dept of Nei Mongol Autonomous Coll. in Chifeng 1946; CCP Br. Sec. and Dir of Nei Mongol Art Troupe 1947–53; Leading Party Group Sec. and Deputy Dir Nei Mongol Cultural Bureau 1954–64; Acting mem. Standing Cttee of CCP Cttee, Nei Mongol and Sec. and Dir of CCP Cttee of Cultural and Educ. Comm., Nei Mongol 1966; Sec. Municipal Party Cttee of Baotou 1974–77; Dir Propaganda Dept of CCP Cttee, Nei Mongol 1978; Deputy Dir State Nationalities Affairs Comm. 1978–81; Sec. CCP Cttee and Mayor of Huhhot City 1978–81; Deputy Sec. CCP Cttee, Nei Mongol 1981–82; mem. of 12th CCP Central Cttee 1982–87; Deputy Sec. CCP Cttee and Chair. Provincial Govt, Nei Mongol 1983; mem. 13th CCP Cen. Cttee 1987–92; Vice-Chair. 8th NPC Standing Cttee 1993–98, 9th NPC 1998–; Chair. Regional Fed. of Literary and Art Circles 1954–65; mem. 2nd, 3rd, 4th Council of Chinese Fed. of Literary and Art Circles. *Publications:* The Basic Knowledge of Autonomy in the Nationalities Region, the Nationalities Theory of Marxism and the Party's Nationalities Policies, The Animal Husbandry in Inner Mongolia Today, In the Sea of Poems (poetry collection), Bu He's Collection of Theses in Literature and Art. *Leisure interests:* calligraphy, literature and art-writing. *Address:* Office of the Regional Governor, Hohhot, Nei Mongol, People's Republic of China.

BUALLAY, Yassim Muhammad, B.B.A.; Bahraini diplomatist; b. 15 March 1942, Muharraq; s. of Muhammad Buallay and Balkees Buallay; m. Satia Buallay 1969; two s. two d.; ed American Univ. of Beirut; supervisor, Bursaries Section, Ministry of Educ. 1963–69; int. civil servant, UNESCO, Paris 1970–74; Amb. to France 1974–79, to Tunisia 1987–94; Dir of Econ. Affairs, Ministry of Foreign Affairs, Bahrain 1979–87; Perm. Rep. to UN, 1994–; Ordre nat. du Mérite, France, decorations of Morocco (Alawite) and Tunisia. *Leisure interests:* reading, theatre, music, tennis, gastronomy. *Address:* Permanent Mission of Bahrain to the United Nations, 866 Second Avenue, 14th/15th Floor, New York, NY 10017, USA (Office). *Telephone:* (212) 223-6300 (Office). *Fax:* (212) 319-0689 (Office). *E-mail:* bahrain@un.int (Office).

BUBKA, Sergey Nazarovich; Ukrainian politician, athlete and sports official; b. 4 Dec. 1963, Voroshilovgrad (now Lugansk); s. of Nazar Bubka and Valentina Bubka; m. Lilya Tioutiounik 1983; two s.; former pole vaulter; set 17 world records outdoors and 10 indoors; cleared 6m or better in more than 44 competitions; first man to clear 20 feet both indoors and out 1991; holder of indoors and outdoors world records (Dec. 2002); 6-time world champion 1983, 1987, 1991, 1993, 1995, 1997; winner Olympic gold medal, Seoul, South Korea 1988; mem. IOC Exec. Bd, IOC Evaluation Comm. for 2008, IOC Athletes' Comm., IAAF Council 2001–, Nat. Olympic Cttee Bd; Chair. EOC Athletes' Comm.; Pres. S. Bubka Sports Club; elected to Parl. (United Union faction) 2002–; L'Equipe Sportsman of the Year 1997, Track and Field Best Pole Vaulter of the Last Half-Century. *Address:* c/o State Committee of Physical Culture and Sport, 42 Esplanadnaya, 252023 Kiev, Ukraine. *Telephone:* (44) 220-02-43. *Fax:* (44) 220-02-94.

BUCARAM ORTIZ, Abdala Jaime, MA, LLM, EdM; Ecuadorean politician; b. 20 Feb. 1952, Guayaquil; s. of Jacobo Bucaram Elmalhin and Rina Ortiz Caicedo de Bucaram; m. María Rosa Pulley Vergara; three s. one d.; ed Colegio Salesiano 'Cristóbal Colón', Univ. Estatal de Guayaquil; rep. Ecuador Olympic Games, Munich 1972; holder of nat. Jr 100m record (10.5 seconds); a founder of Ecuador's Naval Sports Foundation, has been responsible for codes of conduct for sporting orgs; taught at Colegio San José La Salle, training colls for marines, navy; Gov.-Gen. of Police, Guayas 1979–80, Advisor to nat. Superintendency; Prov. Councillor for Guayas 1980; f. Partido Roldosista Ecuatoriano 1982, Chief Exec. 1983–85, 1991–93; Mayor of Guayaquil 1984; Presidential cand. (Partido Roldosista) 1988, 1992; Pres. of Ecuador 1996–97; granted political asylum in Panama 1997; sentenced in absentia to two years' imprisonment on charges of slandering two political rivals; indicted on corruption charges May 2001; Dir various agricultural, commercial and media cos; Pres. Fondo de Desarrollo Urbano de Guayaquil (FODUR) 1984–85, Club Barcelona (football club), Guayaquil 1997–; numerous sporting awards at nat. and regional level including Vicecampeón Sudamericano de Atletismo. *Publications:* Ideario Político del Partido Roldosista Ecuatoriano con sus antecedentes históricos: Principios y Estatutos, Principios de Liberación Nacional, Principios de Justicia Social, Principios de Democracia, Principios de Política Humanística, Principios de Libertad, Desarrollo Económico, Principios de Política Internacional, Las verdades de Abdalá, Roldos y Abdalá: Epopeya del pensamiento ecuatoriano. *Leisure interests:* football, athletics and basketball.

BUCCLEUCH, 9th Duke of, cr. 1663, **AND QUEENSBERRY,** 11th Duke of, cr. 1684; Baron Scott of Buccleuch, Earl of Buccleuch, Baron Scott of Whitchester and Eskdaill, Earl of Doncaster and Baron Tynedale (England), Earl of Dalkeith, Marquis of Dumfriesshire, Earl of Drumlanrig and Sanquhar, Viscount of Nith, Torthorwold and Ross, Baron Douglas; **Walter Francis John Montagu Douglas Scott,** KT, VRD, JP; b. 28 Sept. 1923, London; s. of 8th Duke of Buccleuch, KT, PC, GCVO and Vreda Esther Mary Lascelles; m. Jane McNeill 1953; three s. one d.; ed Eton, Christ Church, Oxford; served RDVR World War II: MP (C) Edin. North 1960–73; Parl. Pvt. Sec. to Sec. of State for Scotland 1962–64; Pres. Royal Asscn for Disability and Rehabilitation, Buccleuch Heritage Trust 1985–, Living Landscape Trust 1986–; Pres. Royal Highland and Agric. Soc. of Scotland 1969, Malcolm Sargent Cancer Fund for Children, Scotland 1974–97, St Andrew's Ambulance Asscn, Royal Scottish Agric. Benevolent Inst., Scottish Nat. Inst. for War Blinded, Royal Blind Asylum and School, Galloway Cattle Soc., E of England Agric. Soc. 1976, Commonwealth Forestry Asscn 1979–99, Royal Scottish Forestry Soc. 1994–96; Chair. Asscn of Lord Lts 1990–98; Vice-Pres. Children First; Hon. Pres. Moredun Foundation for Animal Welfare, Scottish Agric. Org. Soc.; DL Selkirk 1955, Midlothian 1960, Roxburgh 1962, Dumfries 1974; JP Roxburgh 1975; Chancellor of the Order of the Thistle 1992; Hon. Capt. RNR; Lord-Lt of Roxburgh 1974–98, of Ettrick and Lauderdale 1975–98; Fellow Royal Agric. Soc. 1995; Countryside Award, Countryside Comm. and Country Landowners Asscn 1983, Bledisloe Agric. Award 1992. *Leisure interests:* works of art, historic buildings, country sports, painting, classical music, travel. *Address:* Bowhill, Selkirk, TD7 5ET, Scotland. *Telephone:* (1750) 20732.

BUCHACHENKO, Anatoly Leonidovich, DrChemSc; Russian chemical physicist; b. 7 Sept. 1935, Arkhangelsk region; s. of L. P. Buchachenko and A. S. Buchachenko; m. M. S. Buchachenko 1960; one s. one d.; ed Gorky Univ.; postgrad., Jr then Sr scientific Asst 1958–68; Head of Lab. of USSR (now Russian) Acad. of Sciences Inst. of Chemical Physics 1970–, Vice-Dir 1989–94, Dir 1994–96; Head of Dept 1996; Head of Dept of Chemical Kinetics, Moscow State Univ. 1988–; Prof. 1975–; mem. USSR (now Russian) Acad. of Sciences 1987; State Prize 1977, Lenin Prize 1986. *Publications:* works on the physical chemistry of free radicals, chemical reactions, spin chemistry, molecular ferromagnets. *Leisure interests:* wood architecture modelling. *Address:* N. N. Semenov Institute of Chemical Physics of the Russian Academy of Sciences, Kosygin Street 4, 117977 Moscow, Russia (Office). *Telephone:* (095) 137-32-32 (Office); (095) 331-31-70 (Home). *Fax:* (095) 938-2484.

BUCHANAN, Isobel Wilson; British soprano; b. 15 March 1954, Glasgow; d. of Stewart Buchanan and Mary Buchanan; m. Jonathan Stephen Geoffrey King (actor Jonathan Hyde) 1980; two d.; ed Cumbernauld Comprehensive High School and Royal Scottish Acad. of Music and Drama; professional début in Sydney, Australia with Richard Bonynge and Joan Sutherland 1976–78; British début, Glyndebourne 1978; US and German débuts 1979; Vienna Staatsoper début 1979; ENO début 1985, Paris Opera début 1986; now freelance artist working with all major opera cos and orchestras. *Recordings:* Beethoven's Ninth Symphony, Werther, Mozart Arias and Duets. *Leisure interests:* cooking, reading, gardening, yoga, knitting. *Address:* c/o Marks Management Ltd, 14 New Burlington Street, London, W1X 1FF, England (Office).

BUCHANAN, J. Robert, MD; American professor of medicine; b. 8 March 1928, Newark, NJ; m. Susan Carver; one s. one d.; ed Amherst Coll. and Cornell Univ. Medical School; Intern, then Asst Resident Physician, New York Hosp. 1954–58, Research Fellow in Medicine 1956–57; Research Fellow in Endocrinology, Cornell Univ. Medical Coll., New York 1960–61; WHO Travelling Fellow 1963; Instructor in Medicine, Cornell Univ. Medical Coll. 1961–63, Asst Prof. 1963–67, Asst to Chair. Dept of Medicine 1964–65, Assoc. Dean 1965–69, Clinical Assoc. Prof. 1967–69, Assoc. Prof. 1969–71, Prof. 1971–76, Acting Dean, then Dean 1969–76; Prof. of Medicine, Univ. of Chicago, Ill. 1977–82; Assoc. Dean, Pritzker School of Medicine, Chicago 1978–82; Prof. of Medicine, Harvard Medical School, Boston, Mass. 1982; Gen. Dir, Mass. Gen. Hosp. 1982–94; Gen. Dir Emer. 1994–; physician at hosps in New York, Chicago and Boston 1956–; mem. Admin. Bd, Council of Teaching Hosps 1984–89, mem. Exec. Council 1985–; Dir Mass. Div., American Cancer Soc. 1984–; Bd of Dirs Bank of New England 1986–91, AMI Holdings 1991–, Exec. Cttee Mass. Hosp. Asscn 1987– (Chair. 1990–91), Charles River Labs; Chair. Council of Teaching Hosps., Assocn of American Medical Colls 1988–89; mem. NAS Cttee to review Inst. of Medicine, American Cancer Soc., Mass. Div., Soc. of Medical Admins; Chair. Educ. Comm. for Foreign Medical Grads 1994–; Fellow American Coll. of Physicians. *Publications:* numerous papers and articles in journals. *Address:* RSTAR/ATI, One Cambridge Center, Cambridge, MA 02142 (Office); 19 Shipway Place, Charlestown, MA 02129, USA (Home).

BUCHANAN, James McGill, MA, PhD; American academic; b. 3 Oct. 1919, Murfreesboro, Tenn.; s. of James Buchanan and Lila Scott; m. Anne Bakke 1945; ed Middle Tenn. State Coll. and Univs of Tenn. and Chicago; Prof. of Econs Univ. of Tenn. 1950–51, Fla State Univ. 1951–56, Univ. of Va 1956–62; Paul. G. McIntyre Prof. of Econs Univ. of Va 1962–68; Prof. of Econs Univ. of Calif. Los Angeles 1968–69; Univ. Distinguished Prof. of Econs Va Polytechnic Inst. 1969–83, Dir Center for Study of Public Choice 1969–88, Advisory Gen. Dir 1988–, Prof. Emer. 2000–; Univ. Distinguished Prof. of Econs George Mason Univ. 1983–99, Prof. Emer. 1999–; Fulbright Research Scholar, Italy 1955–56; Ford Faculty Research Fellow 1959–60; Fulbright Visiting Prof. Univ. of Cambridge 1961–62; Assoc. Prof. Francesco Marroquin Univ., Guatemala 2001–; Fellow, American Acad. of Arts and Sciences; Distinguished Fellow, American Econ. Assocn; Dr hc (Giessen) 1982, (Zürich) 1984, (Valencia) 1987, (Lisbon) 1987, (Fairfax) 1987, (London) 1988, (Rome) 1993, (Bucharest) 1994, (Catania) 1994, (Valladolid) 1996; Nobel Prize for Econs 1986; Seidman Award 1984. *Publications:* author and co-author of numerous books on financial policy and other econ. matters; articles in professional journals. *Address:* Center for the Study of Public Choice, George Mason University, Buchanan House Mail Stop 1 E6, Fairfax, VA 22030-4443 (Office); PO Box G, Blacksburg, VA 24063-1021, USA (Home).

BUCHANAN, John Machlin, DSc, PhD; American professor of biochemistry; b. 29 Sept. 1917, Winamac Ind.; s. of Harry J. Buchanan and Eunice B. (Miller) Buchanan; m. Elsa Nilsby 1948; two s. two d.; ed De Pauw Univ., Univ. of Michigan and Harvard Univ.; Instructor, Dept of Physiological Chem., School of Medicine, Univ. of Pa 1943–46, Asst Prof. 1946–49, Assoc. Prof. 1949–50, Prof. 1950–53; Nat. Research Council Fellow in Medicine, Nobel Inst., Stockholm 1946–48; Prof., Head, Div. of Biochem., Dept of Biology, MIT 1953–67, Wilson Prof. of Biochem. 1967–88, Prof. Emer. 1988–; mem. Medical Fellowship Bd 1954–; Fellow, Guggenheim Memorial Foundation; mem. NAS, American Soc. of Biological Chemists, American Chem. Soc., Int. Union of Biochemists, American Acad. of Arts and Sciences; Hon. DSc (De Pauw) 1975, (Michigan) 1961; Eli Lilly Award in Biological Chem., ACS 1951. *Leisure interests:* golf, reading. *Address:* Room 68-333B, Department of Biology, Massachusetts Institute of Technology, Cambridge, MA 02139 (Office); 56 Meriam St, Lexington, MA 02420-3622, USA (Home). *Telephone:* (617) 253-3702 (Office); (781) 862-1066 (Home). *Fax:* (617) 253-8699 (Office).

BUCHANAN, Patrick Joseph, MS; American government official and journalist; b. 2 Nov. 1938, Washington; s. of William Buchanan and Catherine Crum; m. Shelley A. Scarney 1971; ed Georgetown and Columbia Univs.; editorial writer, St Louis Globe Democrat 1962–64, Asst editorial writer 1964–66; Exec. Asst to Richard Nixon 1966–69; Special Asst to Pres. Nixon 1969–73; consultant to Pres. Nixon and Ford 1973–74; Asst to Pres., Dir of Communications, White House, Washington, DC 1985–87; syndicated columnist, political commentator, New York Times special features 1975–78; Chicago Tribune-New York News Syndicate 1978–85, Tribune Media Services 1987–91, 1993–95; commentator, NBC Radio Network 1978–82; co-host Crossfire (TV Show) Cable News Network 1982–85, 1987–91, 1993–95, 1997–; appeared as host and panellist in TV shows 1978–; Ed.-in-Chief PJB—From the Right (newsletter) 1990–91; moderator Capital Gang TV show CNN 1988–92; Chair. The American Cause 1993–95, 1997–, Pat Buchanan & Co., Mutual Broadcasting System 1993–95; Cand. for Republican Presidential nomination 1992, 1996; Republican. *Publications:* The New Majority 1973, Conservative Votes, Liberal Victories 1975, Right from the Beginning 1988; Barry Goldwater, The Conscience of A Conservative 1990, The Great Betrayal 1998, A Republic, not an Empire 2000. *Address:* 1017 Savile Lane, McLean, VA 22101, USA.

BUCHHEIM, Lothar-Günther; German author and publisher; b. 6 Feb. 1918, Weimar, Thüringen; m. Diethild Wickboldt 1955; one s. one d.; ed Dresden Acad., Art Acad., Munich; served in German navy; f. Kunstbuchverlag, Feldafing and started collection, "the most important private collection", of the work of German Expressionists; owner and Publr Buchheim Verlag, Feldafing; Dr hc (Duisburg) 1985; Ernst-Hoferichter Prize, Munich 1993; Bundesverdienstkreuz, Grosses Verdienstkreuz des Verdienstordens, Bayerischen Verdienstorden, Ehrenbürger von Chemnitz, Grosses Verdienstkreuz mit Stern des Verdienstordens, Bayerischen Maximiliansorden 1998; Max-Pechstein-Ehrenpreis der Stadt Zwickau 1999, Ehrenpreis des Landkreises Weilheim-Schongau 2002. *Publications:* Tage und Nächte steigen aus dem Strom 1941, Die Künstlergemeinschaft "Brücke" 1956, Der Blaue Reiter und die Neue Künstlervereinigung Munich 1958, Graphik des deutschen Expressionismus 1959, Max Beckmann 1959, Otto Mueller 1963, Das Boot 1973, U-Boot-Krieg 1976, Staatsgala 1977, Mein Paris 1977, Die Tropen von Feldafing 1978, Staatszirkus 1978, Der Luxusliner 1980, U 96 1981, Der Film-Das Boot 1981, Das Segelschiff 1982, Die U-Boot-Fahrer 1985, Das Museum in den Wolken 1986, Zu Tode gesiegt–Der Untergang der U-Boote 1988, Malerbuch 1988, Die Festung 1995, Jäger im Weltmeer 1996, Der Abschied 2000. *Address:* Biersackstr. 23, 82340 Feldafing, Germany. *Telephone:* (8157) 1221. *Fax:* (8157) 3143. *Website:* buchheimmuseum.de.

BUCHTHAL, Fritz, MD, PhD; Danish neurophysiologist (retd); b. 19 Aug. 1907, Witten, Germany; s. of Sally Buchthal and Hedvig Weyl; m. Margaret A. Lennox, MD; ed Albert-Ludwig-Universität, Freiburg im Breisgau, Germany, Stanford Univ., Calif., USA and Humboldt-Universität zu Berlin; Asst in Physiology, Univ. of Berlin 1930–32; Inst. for Theory of Gymnastics, Copenhagen Univ. 1933–43; Physiological Inst., Lund Univ. 1943–45; Dir Inst. of Neurophysiology, Copenhagen Univ. 1946–77, Prof. of Neurophysiology 1955–77; Chief, Dept of Neurophysiology, Univ. Hospital 1945–77; Consultant, Nat. Inst. of Health, USA 1959; Visiting Scientist, Nat. Inst. of Neurological and Communicative Disorders and Stroke, Nat. Inst. of Health, Bethesda 1982–84, Consultant 1984–; Consultant Dept of Neurology, San Francisco Calif., Calif.-Pacific Medical Centre 1985–; Visiting Prof. Univ. of California 1962, Academia Sinica 1964, NY Univ. 1965; mem. Royal Danish Acad. Sciences 1946, Danish Acad. of Technical Sciences, Royal Swedish Acad. of Sciences 1968, Royal Soc. of Sciences (Sweden) 1972, Polish Acad. of Sciences 1988; Hon. Fellow Royal Soc. Medicine 1991; Hon. mem. French Neurological Soc., British Assocn of Neurologists, Polish Neurological Soc., Danish Neurological Soc., American Neurological Assocn, American Acad. of Neurophysiology, San Francisco Neurological Soc., German EEG Soc., English EEG Soc., Italian and Danish EEG and Clinical Neurophysiological Soc., American Soc. for Electrodiagnosis and Electromyography, Polish Soc. for EEG and Clinical Neurophysiology; Corresp. mem. German Physiological and Neurological Socs, Italian Neurological Soc., Acad. de Ciencias Médicas, Córdoba; Hon. MD (Münster, Zürich, Lund, Munich); Hon. DSc (Medical Coll., Wisconsin); numerous awards. *Publications:* Mechanical Properties of Muscle Fibre 1942, Rheology of Muscle 1951, An Introduction to Electromyography 1957, Electrophysiological Aspects of Myopathy 1963, Evoked Action Potential and Conduction Velocity in Human Sensory Nerve 1966, Electrical and Mechanical Responses of Normal and Myasthenic Muscle 1968, Human Nerve Potentials Evoked by Tactile Stimuli 1982. *Leisure interest:* gardening. *Address:* 289 El Cielito Road, Santa Barbara, CA 93105, USA. *Telephone:* (805) 966-5304.

BUCHWALD, Art; American journalist, author and playwright; b. 20 Oct. 1925, New York; s. of Helen Kleinberger and Joseph Buchwald; m. Ann McGarry 1952; one s. two d.; ed Univ. of Southern Calif., Los Angeles; columnist, Herald Tribune, Paris 1948–62, Wash. 1962–; syndicated columnist to 550 newspapers throughout the world 1952–; mem. American Acad. and Inst. of Arts and Letters 1986; Prix de la Bonne Humeur; Pulitzer Prize for Outstanding Commentary 1982; Horatio Alger Award 1989. *Publications:* Paris After Dark, Art Buchwald's Paris, I Chose Caviar, More Caviar, A Gift from the Boys, Don't Forget to Write, How Much Is That in Dollars? 1961, Is It Safe to Drink the Water? 1962, I Chose Capitol Punishment 1963, And Then I Told the President 1965, Son of the Great Society 1967, Have I Ever Lied to You? 1968, Oh, to Be a Swinger 1970, Getting High in Government Circles 1971, I Never Danced at the White House 1973, I Am Not a Crook 1974, Washington Is Leaking 1976, Down the Seine and Up the Potomac 1977, The Buchwald Stops Here 1978, Laid Back in Washington with Art Buchwald 1981, While Reagan Slept 1983, You *Can* Fool All of the People All of the Time 1985, I Think I Don't Remember 1987, Whose Rose Garden Is It Anyway? 1989, Lighten Up, George 1991, Leaving Home: A Memoir 1994, I'll Always Have Paris (memoir) 1996. *Address:* Suite 3804, 540 Park Avenue, New York, NY 10021, USA; 200 Pennsylvania Avenue NW, Washington DC 20006 (Office). *Telephone:* (212) 393-6680.

BUCHWALD, Christoph; German publishing executive; fmrly Ed. Hanser, Munich; fmrly Publr Luchterhand Literaturverlag; now with Suhrkamp

Verlag KG, Frankfurt 1998–. *Address:* Suhrkamp Verlag KG, Frankfurt a.M., Postfach 101945, Germany (Office). *Telephone:* (69) 756010 (Office). *Fax:* (69) 75601522 (Office). *Website:* www.suhrkamp.de (Office).

BUCKINGHAM, Amyand David, CBE, FRS, FRSC, FInstP; Australian professor of chemistry; b. 28 Jan. 1930, Sydney; s. of the late Reginald Joslin Buckingham and Florence Grace Buckingham; m. Jillian Bowles 1965; one. s. two d.; ed Barker Coll., Hornsby, NSW, Univ. of Sydney, Corpus Christi Coll., Cambridge; Lecturer, then Student and Tutor, Christ Church, Univ. of Oxford 1955–65, Univ. Lecturer in Inorganic Chem. 1958–65; Prof. of Theoretical Chem., Univ. of Bristol 1965–69; Prof. of Chem., Univ. of Cambridge 1969–97, Fellow, Pembroke Coll., Cambridge 1970–97, Prof. Emer. 1997–; Pres. Faraday Div. of Royal Soc. of Chem. 1987–89, Cambridge Univ. Cricket Club 1990–; Foreign mem. American Acad. of Arts and Sciences; Foreign Assoc. (US) NAS; Foreign mem. Royal Swedish Acad. of Sciences; Fellow Royal Australian Chemical Inst., American Physical Soc., Optical Soc. of America; mem. ACS, mem. Council Royal Soc. 1999–2001; Harrie Massey Medal, Inst. of Physics 1995, Hughes Medal, Royal Soc. 1996, Faraday Medal, RSC 1998, Townes Medal, Optical Soc. of America 2001. *Publications:* over 320 papers in scientific journals, The Laws and Applications of Thermodynamics 1964, Organic Liquids: Structure, Dynamics and Chemical Properties 1978, The Principles of Molecular Recognition 1993. *Leisure interests:* cricket, tennis, woodwork, travel, walking. *Address:* Crossways, 23 The Avenue, Newmarket, CB8 9AA, England (Home). *Telephone:* (1638) 663799 (Home). *Fax:* (1638) 661772. *E-mail:* adb1000@cam.ac.uk (Office).

BUCKLAND, David John; British artist and theatre director; b. 15 June 1949, London; s. of Denis Buckland and Valarie Buckland; partner, Siobhan Davies 1978; one s. one d.; ed Dorchester Secondary Modern School, Dorset, Hardye's Grammar School, Dorchester, Deep River High School, Ottawa and London Coll. of Printing; has participated in group exhbns and work appears in public collections in London, New York, Chicago, Los Angeles, Paris etc; Artistic Dir Siobhan Davies Dance Co.; lecturer, Royal Coll. of Art, London Coll. of Printing, Chicago Art Inst.; 21 set and costume designs for dance including Rambert Dance Co., Siobhan Davies Dance Co., English Nat. Ballet and work for TV; Northern Arts Fellow 1972–73; Kodak Bursary 1978; Minn. First Bank Award 1988–90. *One-man exhibitions include:* Photographers Gallery London, 1977, 1987, Air Gallery, London 1978, Sander Gallery New York 1979, 1984, Moria Kelly Gallery, London 1981, Pompidou Centre, Paris 1982, Tom Peek Gallery, Amsterdam 1985, Espace Photo, Paris 1988, Nat. Portrait Gallery 1999. *Leisure interests:* multi-hull sailor, arts, theatre, travel, hill walking. *Address:* 239 Royal College Street, London, NW1 9LT, England. *Telephone:* (20) 7485-3228. *Fax:* (20) 7485-3228.

BUCKLAND, Sir Ross, Kt, FCIS; Australian business executive; b. 19 Dec. 1942, Sydney; s. of William Buckland and Elizabeth Buckland; m. Patricia Bubb 1966; two s.; ed Sydney Boys' High School; various positions in banking, Eng and food industries 1958–66; Dir Finance and Admin. Elizabeth Arden Pty Ltd 1966–73; Kellogg (Australia) Pty Ltd 1973–77, 1978; Man. Dir Kellogg Salada Canada Inc., Pres. and Chief Exec. 1979–80; Chair. Kellogg Co. of GB Ltd, Dir European Operations and Vice-Pres. Kellogg Co. USA 1981–90; Chief Exec. Unigate PLC 1990–; Dir Allied Domecq 1998–; Pres. Nat. Australia Bank Europe 1999; Fellow Inst. of Grocery Distribution, Chartered Inst. of Secs and Admins, Australian Soc. of Certified Practising Accountants; mem. MRC 1998–. *Leisure interest:* walking. *Address:* Unigate PLC, Unigate House, Wood Lane, London W12 7RP, England. *Telephone:* (20) 8576-6002. *Fax:* (20) 8576-6003.

BUCKLEY, James Lane, LLB; American judge; b. 9 March 1923, New York, NY; s. of William F. Buckley and Aloise Steiner Buckley; m. Ann F. Cooley 1953; five s. one d.; ed Yale Univ.; served US Navy 1943–46; Senator from New York 1971–77; Under-Sec. of State for Security Assistance 1981–82; Pres. Radio Free Europe–Radio Liberty 1982–85; Circuit Judge, US Court of Appeals, DC Circuit 1985–2001, Sr Judge, retd 2001; Co-Chair. US Del. to UN Conf. on Environment, Nairobi 1982; Chair. US Del. to UN Conf. on Population, Mexico City 1984; Republican. *Publication:* If Men Were Angels 1975. *Leisure interests:* natural history, American History. *Address:* PO Box 597, Sharon, CT, 06069 (Office); c/o United States Court of Appeals, 333 Constitution Avenue, NW, Washington, DC 20001, USA.

BUCKLEY, Michael; Irish banker; b. Cork; m. Anne Buckley; fmr stockbroker and civil servant in Ireland and EU; joined Allied Irish Bank PLC (AIB) 1991, Exec. Dir 1995–2001, Man. Dir Capital Markets Div. 1994–99, Head Polish Div. 1999–2001, Group Chief Exec. 2001–. *Address:* AIB Bankcentre, PO Box 452, Ballsbridge, Dublin 4, Ireland (Office). *Telephone:* (1) 6600311 (Office). *Website:* www.aibgroup.com (Office).

BUCKLEY, Stephen, MFA; British artist and university professor; b. 5 April 1944, Leicester; s. of Nancy Throsby and Leslie Buckley; m. Stephanie James 1973; one s. one d.; ed Univs of Newcastle-upon-Tyne and Reading; taught at Canterbury Coll. of Art 1969, Leeds Coll. of Art 1970, Chelsea School of Art 1971–80; Artist in Residence, King's Coll., Cambridge 1972–74; Prof., Head Dept of Fine Art, Univ. of Reading 1994–; one-man exhbn throughout world including Museum of Modern Art, Oxford 1985, Yale Center for British Art, New Haven, Conn., USA 1986; worked with Rambert Dance Co., London 1987–88; works in public collections in Chile, Sweden, UK, Venezuela, USA, NZ, Australia; comms include Neal St Restaurant 1972, mural painting for Penguin Books 1972, Leith's Restaurant 1973; prizewinner, John Moores Exhbn 1974, 1985, Chichester National Art Exhbn 1975, Tolly-Cobbold

Exhbn 1977. *Address:* Department of Fine Art, University of Reading, 1 Earley Gate, Whiteknights Road, Reading, RG6 6AT, England. *Telephone:* (118) 931-8050. *Fax:* (118) 926-2667. *E-mail:* fineart@reading.ac.uk (Office).

BUCKLEY, William Frank, Jr; American editor and author; b. 24 Nov. 1925, New York; s. of William Frank Buckley and Aloise (Steiner) Buckley; m. Patricia Taylor 1950; one s.; ed Univ. of Mexico and Yale Univ.; fmrly on staff American Mercury; Ed. National Review 1955–88, Ed.-in-Chief 1988–90, Ed.-at-Large 1991–; syndicated columnist 1962–; host of weekly TV series Firing Line 1966–99; lecturer New School for Social Research 1967; mem. USIA Advisory Comm. 1969–72; mem. US del. to UN 1973; contrib. to Harper's, Esquire, Foreign Affairs, Atlantic, etc.; numerous hon. degrees; Presidential Medal of Freedom 1991. *Publications:* God and Man at Yale 1951, Up from Liberalism 1959, Rumbles Left and Right 1963, The Unmaking of a Mayor 1966, The Jeweler's Eye 1968, The Governor Listeth 1970, Cruising Speed 1971, Inveighing We Will Go 1972, Four Reforms 1973, United Nations Journal 1974, Execution Eve 1975, Saving the Queen 1976, Airborne, Stained Glass 1978, A Hymnal 1978, Who's on First 1980, Marco Polo, If You Can 1982, Atlantic High 1982, Overdrive 1983, The Story of Henri Tod 1984, See You Later, Alligator 1985, Right Reason (articles and essays) 1985, The Temptation of Wilfred Malachey 1986, High Jinx 1986, Racing through Paradise 1987, Mongoose RIP 1988, On the Firing Line 1989, Gratitude 1990, Tucker's Last Stand 1990, Wind Fall: The End of the Affair 1992, Happy Days Were Here Again 1993, A Very Private Plot 1994, Buckley! The Right Word 1996, Nearer My God–An Autobiography of Faith 1998, The Lexicon 1998, A Redhunter: A Novel Based on the Life of Senator Joe McCarthy 1999, Spytime 2000; co-author McCarthy and His Enemies 1954; Ed. The Committee and Its Critics 1962, Odyssey of a Friend 1970, Did You Ever See a Dream Walking 1970. *Leisure interests:* skiing, sailing, music. *Address:* National Review, 215 Lexington Avenue, New York, NY 10016-6023, USA. *Telephone:* (212) 679-7330.

BUCKOVSKI, Vlado, PhD; Macedonian politician; b. 2 Dec. 1962, Skopje; ed Univ. of Skopje; expert legal collaborator for Parl. 1987–88; Jr Teaching Asst of Roman Law, Univ. of Skopje 1988–91, Sr Teaching Asst 1992–99, Docent 1999–; mem. State Election Comm. 1998–2000; Party Spokesman Socijaldemokratski Sojuz na Makedonije—SDSM (Social Democratic Alliance of Macedonia—SDSM) 1999–2001, Vice-Pres. SDSM 1999–; Chair. Council of Skopje 2000–01; Minister of Defence May–Nov. 2001, Oct. 2002–. *Publications include:* academic papers on public law. *Address:* Ministry of Defence, bb Orce Nikolar, Skopje, 1000 Macedonia (Office). *Telephone:* (2) 230928 (Office). *Fax:* (2) 230928 (Office). *E-mail:* info@morm.gov.mk (Office). *Website:* www.morm .gov.mk (Office).

BUCKSTEIN, Mark Aaron, JD, BS; American lawyer; b. 1 July 1939, New York; s. of Henry Buckstein and Minnie Buckstein; m. Rochelle J. Buchman 1960; one s. one d.; ed New York Univ. Law School and City Coll. of New York; Sr Partner, Baer, Marks & Upham (law firm), New York 1968–86; Special Prof. of Law, Hofstra Univ. School of Law 1981–93; Adjunct Prof. of Law, Rutgers Univ. Law School 1993–96; Sr Vice-Pres. and Gen. Counsel, Trans World Airlines Inc. 1986; Exec. Vice-Pres., Gen. Counsel GAF and Int. Speciality Products, NJ 1993–96; Dir Bayswater Realty and Capital Corpn, Travel Channel Inc., TWA; Counsel, Greenberg, Traurig, Fort Lauderdale, Fla 1996–99, Professional Dispute Resolution Inc., Boca Raton 1999–; mem. nat. arbitration and mediation cttee NASD 1998–2001. *Leisure interests:* tennis, puzzles, reading, music. *Address:* Professional Dispute Resolution, 1200 North Federal Highway, Boca Raton, FL 33432–2803 (Office); 5832 Waterford, Boca Raton, FL 33496, USA (Home). *Telephone:* (561) 447-8215 (Office); (561) 994-6067 (Home). *Fax:* mabresolve@aol.com (Office).

BUDD, Sir Alan Peter, Kt, PhD; British economist; b. 16 Nov. 1937, Kent; s. of Ernest Budd and Elsie Budd; m. Susan Millott 1964; three s.; ed Oundle School, London School of Economics, Cambridge Univ.; Lecturer in Econs, Southampton Univ. 1966–69; Ford Foundation Visiting Prof., Carnegie-Mellon Univ., USA 1969–70; Sr Econ. Adviser, HM Treasury 1970–74; Sr Research Fellow, London Business School 1974–81, Prof. of Econs 1981–88, Fellow 1997; Econ. Adviser, Barclays Bank 1988–91; Chief Econ. Adviser to HM Treasury 1991–97; Provost, The Queen's Coll. Oxford 1999–; mem. Bank of England Monetary Policy Cttee 1997–99; Visiting Prof., Univ. of NSW, Australia 1983; Grocers' Co. Scholarship; Leverhulme Undergraduate Scholarship; Chair. Gambling Review Body 2000–01; Gov. Nat. Inst. of Econ. and Social Research 1998–; Chair. (non-exec.) Oxford Biosensors Ltd 2001–02. *Publication:* Politics of Economic Planning 1978. *Leisure interests:* music, gardening, reading. *Address:* The Queen's College, Oxford, OX1 4AW, England. *Telephone:* (1865) 279123 (Office).

BUDDEN, Kenneth George, MA, PhD, FRS; British physicist; b. 23 June 1915, Portsmouth; s. of the late George Easthope Budden and Gertrude Homer Rea; m. Nicolette Ann Lydia de Longesdon Longsdon 1947; ed Portsmouth Grammar School and St John's Coll. Cambridge; Telecommunications Research Establishment 1939–41; British Air Comm. Washington, DC 1941–44; Air Command, SE Asia 1945; Fellow, St John's Coll. Cambridge 1947–; Reader in Physics, Univ. of Cambridge 1965–82, Emer. 1982–. *Publications:* Radio Waves in the Ionosphere 1961, The Wave-Guide Mode Theory of Wave Propogation 1961, Lectures on Magnetoionic Theory 1964, The Propogation of Radio Waves 1985. *Leisure interest:* gardening. *Address:* 15 Adams Road, Cambridge, CB3 9AD, England. *Telephone:* (1223) 354752.

BUDIŠA, Dražen; Croatian politician; b. 25 July 1948, Drniš; m. Nada Budiša; three s.; ed Zagreb Univ.; Pres. of Students' League of Zagreb 1971; Pres. Croatian Social-Liberal Party 1990–; Minister in Croatian Govt 1991–92; mem. House of Reps (Parl.) of Croatia 1992, 1995–. *Publications:* Beginning of Printing in Europe 1984, Heritage of Croatian Reformers in Custody of the National and University Library 1985, Humanism in Croatia 1988, Croatian Books Published in Venice from 15th to 18th Centuries 1990. *Leisure interest:* gardening. *Address:* c/o Croatian Social-Liberal Party, 10000 Zagreb, trg N. S. Zrinskog 17 (Office); Galovicéva 8, 41000 Zagreb, Croatia. *Telephone:* (41) 215704.

BUDOWSKI, Gerardo, PhD; Venezuelan agronomist and forester; b. Gert Budowski, 10 June 1925, Berlin, Germany; s. of Dr Issar Budowski and Marguerite Wolfgang; m. Thelma T. Palma 1958; two d.; ed Univ. Central de Venezuela, Inter-American Inst. of Agricultural Sciences, Turrialba, Costa Rica and Yale Univ. School of Forestry; Div. of Research, Ministry of Agriculture Forestry Service 1947–49, Head 1949–52; Forester, Inter-American Inst. of Agricultural Sciences, Havana 1953–55, Turrialba 1956–58, Head, Forestry Dept 1958–67; Visiting Prof. of Geography and Forestry, Univ. of Calif., Berkeley 1967; Programme Specialist for Ecology and Conservation, UNESCO, Paris 1967–70; Dir-Gen. Int. Union for Conservation of Nature and Nat. Resources 1970–76; Head, Renewable Natural Resources Dept, Tropical Agricultural Research and Training Centre (CATIE), Costa Rica 1976–86, Prof. Emer. 1996–; Dir Natural Resources, Univ. for Peace, Costa Rica, Vice-Rector 1999–2000; Int. Co-ordinator for Agroforestry, UN Univ. (Tokyo) 1978–; Special Adviser to Worldwide Fund for Nature (WWF) 1995–; Pres. The Ecotourism Soc. 1993–97, Life mem. 2000–; mem. Tech. Advisory Cttee, Consultative Group on Int. Agricultural Research 1989–93, Earth Council Advisory Cttee 1992–, Deputy Dir 1997–99; Hon. mem. Int. Union for Conservation of Nature and Natural Resources, Int. World Wide Fund for Nature, Soc. of American Foresters; Order of the Golden Ark (Netherlands) 1976, Order Henry Pittier, 1st Class (Venezuela) 1979, IUCN Fred Packard Award 1991, Order Semper Virens (Nicaragua) 1994. *Publications:* La Conservación como instrumento para el desarrollo 1985 and more than 250 articles. *Leisure interest:* chess (several times champion of Venezuela and mem. of Olympic team). *Address:* PO Box 198, 2300 Curridabat, San José, Costa Rica (Home). *Telephone:* (506) 205-9000 (Office); (506) 2253008 (Home). *Fax:* (506) 249-1929 (Office); (506) 253-4227 (Home). *E-mail:* upaznego@sol .racsa.co.cr (Office); smiles@sol.racsa.co.cr (Home). *Website:* www.upaz.org.

BUENAVENTURA, Enrique; Colombian playwright; b. 23 Aug. 1924, Cali; s. of Cornelio Buenaventura and Julia Emma Alder; m. Jacqueline Vidal 1961; one s.; sailor 1950–52; fmrly painter, magazine illustrator, journalist; Dir Teatro Experimental de Cali (TEC—Experimental Theatre of Cali) 1955–; has written 60 plays most of which have been staged; Hon. DLitt and Philosophy (Valle Univ.); various nat. and int. awards. *Publications include:* Teatro 1963, A la Diestra de Dios Padre (included in Teatro Hispanoamericano Contemporáneo) 1964, La Orgía and La Maestra (included in Modern One-Act Plays from Latin America) 1974, Los papeles del infierno, Seis horas en la vida de Frank Kulak. *Address:* Calle 7, No. 8-63, PO Box 2055, Cali (Office); Carrera 9, No. 7-40, Piso 3, Cali (Home); Teatro Experimental de Cali, Calle 7, Numero 8-63, Apdo Aéreo 2050, Cali, Colombia. *Telephone:* (2) 884-3820 (Office); (2) 885-3861. *Fax:* (2) 883-2632 (Office).

BUERGENTHAL, Thomas, DJur, LLM, JSD; American (born Czechoslovakian) judge and professor of international law; b. 11 May 1934, Lubochna, Czechoslovakia; s.of Mundek Buergenthal and Gerda Buergenthal; m. 2nd Marjorie Julia Buergenthal (née Bell); three s. from previous marriage; ed Bethany Coll., W Va, New York Univ. Law School (Root Tilden Scholar), Harvard Law School; became US citizen 1957; mem. (Judge, then Pres.) Inter-American Court on Human Rights 1979–91; mem. (Judge, then Pres.) Admin. Tribunal, Inter-American Devt Bank 1989–94; mem. UN Human Rights Comm. 1995–99; mem. Claims Resolution Tribunal for Dormant Accounts, Switzerland 1998–99, Vice-Chair. 1999; Judge, Int. Court of Justice March 2000–; Lobingier Prof. Emer. of Int. and Comparative Law, George Washington Univ. Law School, Washington, DC; Hon. LLD (Bethany Coll.) 1981, (Heidelberg Univ.) 1986, (Free Univ. of Brussels) 1994, (State Univ. of New York) 2000, (American Univ., Washington, DC) 2002; Manley O. Hudson Medal, American Soc. of Int. Law 2002, and numerous other awards. *Publications include:* Law-Making in the International Civil Aviation Organization 1969, International Protection of Human Rights (with L. B. Sohn) 1973, Protecting Human Rights in the Americas (with D. Shelton, 4th edn) 1995, International Human Rights (with D. Shelton and D. Stewart, 3rd edn) 2002, Public International Law (with S. Murphy, 3rd edn) 2002. *Address:* Peace Palace, Carnegieplein 2, 2517 KJ The Hague, Netherlands (Office). *Telephone:* (70) 3022323 (Office). *Fax:* (70) 3649928 (Office). *E-mail:* information@icj-cij.org (Office).

BUFE, Uwe-Ernst, PhD; German business executive and chemist; b. 22 May 1944, Teschen; m.; two c.; ed Technische Universität, Munich; with Spang and Co. 1971–74; Product Man. Degussa Frankfurt 1974, Corp. Devt and Inorganic Chemicals 1981, mem. Bd Degussa AG 1987, Corp. Devt Degussa Corpn 1977, Exec. Vice-Pres. Chemical Group 1985, Chair. Bd, CEO 1996–99, Chair. Degussa-Hüls AG 1999–. *Address:* Degussa-Hüls AG, 60287 Frankfurt am Main, Germany. *Telephone:* (69) 21801. *Fax:* (69) 2183218.

BUFFET, Marie-George; French politician; b. 7 May 1949, Sceaux (Hauts-de-Seine); d. of Paul Kossellek and Raymonde Rayer; m. Jean-Pierre Buffet 1972; two c.; joined Parti Communiste Français (PCF) 1969, elected to PCF Cen. Cttee 1987, mem. Nat. Bureau 1994, Head Nat. Women's Cttee 1996, elected to Nat. Secr. 1997, Nat. Sec. April 2001–; municipal councillor, then Deputy Mayor Châtenay-Malabry (Hautes-de-Seine) 1977–83; Nat. Ass. Deputy for Seine-Saint-Denis 1997–; Minister for Youth and Sport 1997–2002. *Address:* c/o Parti Communiste Français, 2 place du Colonel Fabien, 75940 Paris, France.

BUFFETT, Warren Edward; American investment banker; b. 30 Aug. 1930, Omaha; s. of Howard Homan Buffett and Leila Stahl; m. Susan Thompson 1952; two s. one d.; ed Columbia Univ. Business School; Chair. Berkshire Hathaway (investment co.), Omaha , Neb. 1970–, Nat. Indemnity Co., Buffalo Evening News; mem. Bd of Dirs Salomon Brothers 1987–, CEO Aug. 1991; f. Buffet Foundation. *Address:* Berkshire Hathaway Inc., 1440 Kiewit Plaza, Omaha, NE 68131, USA.

BUFI, Ylli; Albanian politician; b. 25 May 1948, Tiranë; m. Zana Bufi 1978; two d.; Minister of Foodstuff Industry 1990–91, of Food and Light Industry Feb.–May 1991, of Nutrition May–June 1991; Prime Minister of Albania June–Dec. 1991; fmr Minister of the Public Econ. and Privatization; mem. Leading Cttee of Socialist Party; mem. Parl.; Chair. Cttee on Industry, Energetics, Transport and Telecommunications. *Address:* c/o Ministry of the Public Economy and Privatization, c/o Këshilli i Ministrave, Tirana, Albania.

BUGAYEV, Sergey Petrovich; Russian scientist; b. 3 Aug. 1933; m.; one s. one d.; ed Tomsk Polytech. Inst.; fmr Head of Lab., Inst. of High-Current Electronics, Russian Acad. of Sciences, Siberia, Deputy Dir then Dir; Corresp. mem. Russian Acad. of Sciences 1987, mem. 2000; USSR State Prize, Prize of Lenin's Comsomol. *Publications:* more than 200 scientific papers in learned journals. *Leisure interests:* fiction, gardening. *Address:* Institute of High-Current Electronics, Akademicheskiy prosp. 4, 634055 Tomsk, Russia (Office). *Telephone:* (3822) 25-85-44 (Office); (3822) 25-88-84 (Home).

BUHARI, Maj.-Gen. Muhammadu; Nigerian government official and army officer; b. 17 Dec. 1942, Daura, Katsina Province of Kaduna; m. Safinatu Yusuf 1971; two d.; ed Katsina Provincial Secondary School, Nigerian Mil. Training Coll., Mons Officers' Cadet School, Aldershot, England; joined Army 1962; commissioned 1963; served 2nd Bn in Congo (now Zaire) 1963–64; Army Service Corps 1964–66; staff and command appointments in 1st and 3rd Infantry Divs; Defence Service Staff Coll., Wellington, India 1972–73; Acting Dir of Supply and Transport, Nigerian Army 1974–75; Mil. Gov. of North Eastern State (divided into three States Feb. 1976) 1975–76, of Borno State Feb.–March 1976; Fed. Commr for Petroleum 1976–78; Chair. Nigerian Nat. Petroleum Corpn 1976–80; Mil. Sec. Nigerian Army 1978; mem. Supreme Mil. Council 1976–77; overthrew Govt of Shehu Shagari; Head of State, Chair. Supreme Mil. Council and C-in-C of Armed Forces 1983–85; detained 1985–88, released 1988; mem. All Nigeria's People's Party (ANPP); Presidential Cand. 2003; Chair. Special Trust Fund 1994–. *Leisure interests:* tennis, squash, golf. *Address:* GRA, Daura, Katsina State, Nigeria.

BUICAN, Denis, D.ÈS SC.NAT., D.ÈS L.ET SC.HUM.; Romanian/French professor of history of science; b. 21 Dec. 1934, Bucharest; s. of Dumitru Peligrad and Elena Buican; ed Bucharest Univ., Faculté des Sciences de Paris, Univ. de Paris I-Sorbonne; teaching Asst, Bucharest Univ. 1956–57, Prin. Scientific Researcher 1957–60, Course Leader Gen. Biology and Genetics with History of Science course 1960–69, Invited Prof. 1990–; Invited Prof. First Class, History of Sciences, Faculté des Sciences, Univ. de Paris 1969–70, Univ. de Paris-Sorbonne 1970–74, Assoc. Prof. History and Philosophy of Science 1970–74; Assoc. History and Philosophy of Science, Univ. of Dijon 1974–80; Assoc. History of Sciences, Univ. de Paris I Panthéon-Sorbonne 1980–83; Assoc. Prof. First Class, History of Sciences, Univ. de Paris X 1983–86; Invited Prof. Collège de France 1984, 1993; Prof. First Class Univ. de Paris X Nanterre 1986–; Grand Prix, Acad. Française 1989. *Publications include:* Histoire de la génétique et de l'évolutionnisme en France 1984, La Génétique et l'évolution 1986, Génétique et pensée évolutionniste 1987, Darwin et le darwinisme 1987, Lyssenko et le lyssenkisme 1988, L'Evolution et les évolutionnismes 1989, La Révolution de l'évolution 1989, L'Explosion biologique, du néant au Sur-être 1991, Dracula et ses avatars de Vlad l'Empaleur à Staline et Ceausescu 1991, Charles Darwin 1992, Mendel et la génétique d'hier et d'aujourd'hui 1993, Les Métamorphoses de Dracula 1993, Biognoséologie: Evolution et révolution de la connaissance 1993, Jean Rostand 1994, Histoire de la Biologie 1994, Evolution de la pensée biologique 1995, L'Evolution aujourd'hui 1995, L'Evolution: la grande aventure de la vie 1995, Ethologie comparée 1996, Dictionnaire de la Biologie 1997, L'Evolution et les théories évolutionnistes 1997; poetry books: Arbre seul 1974, Lumière aveugle 1976, Mamura 1993. *Leisure interests:* literature and the arts. *Address:* Université de Paris X Nanterre, 92001 Nanterre (Office); 15 rue Poliveau, 75005 Paris, France (Home). *Telephone:* 1-40-97-72-00 (Office); 1-43-36-33-97 (Home). *Fax:* 1-40-97-70-86 (Office).

BUIJNSTERS, Piet J.; Netherlands professor of Dutch literature; b. 18 Oct. 1933, Breda; s. of Adriaan Buijnsters and Johanna Wirken; m. Leontine Smets 1961; two s. two d.; ed Univs of Nijmegen and Tübingen; f. Werkgroep 18e Eeuw (with CM Geerars) 1968; Prof. of Dutch Literature, Univ. of Nijmegen 1971–; mem. Royal Netherlands Acad. of Arts and Sciences; Anne Frank Foundation Prize 1964, Jan Campbert Stiching Prize 1974, Menno Hertzberg Prize 1981. *Publications:* Tussen twee werelden: Rhijnvis Feith als dichter van 'Het Graf' 1963, Hieronymus van Alphen 1746–1803 1973, Nederlandse literatuur van de acht-tiende eeuw 1984, Wolff en Deken, een biografie 1984, Briefwisseling van Betje Wolff en Aagje Deken 1987, Het verzamelen van boeken 1985. *Leisure interest:* book collecting. *Address:* University of Nijmegen, Department of Language and Literature, Erasmusplein 1, 6525 GG Nijmegen (Office); Witsenburgselaan 35, 6524 TE Nijmegen, Netherlands (Home). *Telephone:* (80) 512888 (Office); (80) 225466 (Home).

BUIRA, Ariel, MA; Mexican economist; b. 20 Sept. 1940, Chihuahua; s. of Antonio Buira and Enriqueta Seira de Buira; m. Janet Clark 1965; two s.; ed Univ. of Manchester, England; Lecturer, Centre for Econ. and Demographic Studies, El Colegio de México 1966–68; Prof. of Econs, Graduate School of Business, Instituto Tecnológico de Monterrey 1968–70; Economist, IMF 1970–74; Econ. Adviser to Gov., Man. for Int. Research, Banco de México, SA 1975–78, Deputy Dir then Dir for Int. Orgs and Agreements 1982–94, then Deputy Gov. and mem. Bd of Govs; Del. to Conf. on Int. Econ. Co-operation (CIEC) (Financial Affairs Comm.) 1976–77; Alt. Exec. Dir, IMF 1978–80, Exec. Dir for Mexico, Spain, Venezuela, Cen. America 1980–82; Special Envoy of the Pres. of Mexico and Chair. of the Panel, UN Int. Conf. on Financing for Devt 2002; First Prize, Course on Econ. Integration, Coll. Européen des Sciences Sociales et Economiques 1963. *Publications:* 50 Años de Banca Central (jtly) 1976, LDC External Debt and the World Economy 1978, Directions for Reform – The Future of the International Monetary System (jtly) 1984, México: Crisis Financiera y Programa de Ajuste in América Latina: Deuda, Crisis y Perspectivas 1984; Is There a Need for Reform? 1984; contrib.: Politics and Economics of External Debt Crisis – The Latin American Experience 1985, Incomes Policy (ed. V. L. Urquidi) 1987, Money and Finance Vol. I (R. Tandon) 1987, Adjustment with Growth and the Role of the IMF 1987, La Economía Mundial: Evolución y Perspectivas 1989, Una Evalución de la Estrategia de la Deuda 1989, Los Determinantes del Ahorro en México 1990, Evolución de la Estrategia de la Deuda 1990, International Liquidity and the Needs of the World Economy (Vol. IV) 1994, Reflections on the International Monetary System 1995, Can Currency Crises be Prevented or Better Managed? (ed. Jan Joost Teunissen) 1996, The Potential of the SDR for Improving the International Monetary System 1996, Reflections on the Mexican Crisis of 1994 1996; and numerous articles. *Leisure interests:* music, literature. *Address:* Sierra Tezonco No. 174, Lomas de Chapultepec, Delegación Miguel Hidalgo, 11000-México, DF, Mexico. *Telephone:* 520-46-17; 540-02-37.

BUITER, Willem Hendrik, CBE, PhD, FBA; American/British professor of economics; b. 26 Sept. 1949, The Hague, Netherlands; s. of Hendrien Buiter van Schooten and Harm Geert Buiter; m. 1st Jean Archer 1988; two c.; m. 2nd Anne C. Sibert 1998; ed Cambridge Univ., Yale Univ.; Asst Prof. of Econs and Int. Affairs, Woodrow Wilson School, Princeton Univ. 1975–79; Prof. of Econs Bristol Univ. 1980–82; Cassel Prof. of Econs with Special Reference to Money and Banking, LSE 1982–85; Prof. of Econs Yale Univ. 1985–94, Juan T. Trippe Prof. of Int. Econs 1990–94; Prof. of Int. Macroecons Univ. of Cambridge 1994–; mem. Monetary Policy Cttee, Bank of England 1997–2000; Chief Economist and Special Counsellor to the Pres., EBRD 2000–; Consultant IMF, IBRD, IDB 1979–; Adviser House of Commons Treasury Select Cttee, UK 1980–82, Netherlands Ministry of Educ. 1985–86, EC, DGII 1982–85; Corresp. mem. Royal Netherlands Acad. of Sciences 1995–, Research Assoc. Nat. Bureau of Econ. Research, Research Fellow Centre for Econ. Policy Research; N. G. Pierson Medal (Netherlands) 2000. *Publications:* Temporary and Long-run Equilibrium 1979, Budgetary Policy, International and Intertemporal Trade in the Global Economy 1989, Macroeconomic Theory and Stabilization Policy 1989, Principles of Budgetary and Financial Policy 1990, International Macroeconomics 1990, Financial Markets and European Monetary Cooperation: The Lessons of the 92–93 ERM crisis (with Giancarlo Corsetti and Paolo Pesenti) 1997. *Leisure interests:* tennis, theatre, westerns, science fiction and fantasy novels, poetry. *Address:* European Bank for Reconstruction and Development, One Exchange Square, London EC2A 2JN (Office); 2 St David's Square, London, E14 3WA, England (Home). *Telephone:* (20) 7338-6805 (Office); (20) 7517-9289 (Home); (20) 7338-6037. *Fax:* (20) 7338-6110 (Office). *E-mail:* buiterw@ebrd.com (Office); willembuiter@ whsmithnet.co.uk (Home). *Website:* ebrdnet.ebrd.com; www.nber.org/ wbuiter (Home).

BUJAK, Zbigniew; Polish politician and union leader; b. 29 Nov. 1954, Łopuszno; ed Warsaw Univ.; worked in Polfa Pharmaceutical plant, Grodzisk Mazowiecki, then Ursus Mechanical Works 1973–81; nat. service in airborne commando div. 1974–76; organizer of strike in Ursus Works in July 1980; assoc. Workers' Cttee for solidarity with striking coastal workers Aug. 1980; Chair. Founding Cttee Solidarity Trade Union, Mazowsze Region 1980; mem. Nat. Consultative Comm. of Solidarity, took part in negotiations with Govt 1981; under martial law in hiding, continued union activity 1981–86; Chair. Bd Mazowsze Region in Provisional Exec. Comm. of Solidarity 1982–86; arrested May 1986, pardoned Sept. 1986; mem. Nat. Exec. Comm. of Solidarity 1987–90; Chair. Citizens' Cttee of Solidarity 1988–90; took part in Round Table debates in Groups for Political Reform and for Economy and Social Policy Feb.–April 1989; Chair. Council of Warsaw Agreement of Citizens' Cttees 1990–91; one of founders and leaders Citizens' Movt.–Democratic Action (ROAD) 1990–91; Deputy to Sejm (Parl.) 1991–97, Chair. Sejm Comm. of Admin. and Internal Affairs 1993–97; Chair. Cen. Bd of Customs 1999–2001; Chair. of Democratic-Social Movt 1991; Co-Founder and Vice-Chair. Union of Labour (UP) 1992–98; mem. Freedom Union (UW) 1998–; fmr mem. Socialist Rural Youth Union; Robert F. Kennedy Human Rights Award 1988. *Publication:* Przepraszam za Solidarnośćć 1991. *Address:* Główny

Urząd Ceł, ul. Świętokrzyska 12, 00-916 Warsaw, Poland. *Telephone:* (22) 6944946 (Office). *E-mail:* gabinet_prezesa_guc@guc.gov.pl (Office). *Website:* www.guc.gov.pl (Office).

BUJOLD, Genevieve; Canadian actress; b. 1 July 1942, Montreal; m. Paul Almond 1967 (divorced); one s.; ed Montreal Conservatory of Drama; fmr cinema usherette in Montreal. *Films include:* La guerre est finie, La fleur de l'age, Entre la mer et l'eau douce, King of Hearts, The Thief of Paris, Isabel, Anne of the Thousand Days, The Act of the Heart, The Trojan Women, The Journey, Earthquake, Alex and the Gypsy, Kamouraska, Obsession, Swashbuckler, Another Man Another Chance, Coma, Murder by Decree, Final Assignment, The Last Flight of Noah's Ark, Monsignor, Tightrope, Choose Me, Trouble in Mind, The Moderns, Dead Ringers, False Identity, Secret Places of the Heart, A Paper Wedding, Star Trek: Generations, An Ambush of Ghosts, Mon Ami Max, Dead Innocent 1996, The House of Yes 1997, Last Night 1998, Eye of the Beholder 1999. *Stage appearances include:* The Barber of Seville, A Midsummer Night's Dream, A House . . . A Day. *TV appearances include:* St Joan, Antony and Cleopatra, Mistress of Paradise, Red Earth, White Earth, Star Trek. *Address:* c/o William Morris Agency, 151 South EL Camino Drive, Beverly Hills, CA 90212, USA (Office).

BUJON DE L'ESTANG, François; French diplomatist and business executive; b. 1940, Neuilly sur Seine; m. Anne de Margerie; four c.; ed Institut Politique de Paris, Ecole Nat. d'Admin; Office of Perm. Sec., Ministry of Foreign Affairs 1966; Special Adviser on staff of Pres. of Repub. 1966, Deputy to Pres.'s Diplomatic Adviser –1969; Second, then First Sec. Embassy in Washington, DC 1969–73; First Sec. and Second Counsellor in London 1973–75; Adviser on Int. Affairs to Del. Gen. for Energy, Ministry of Industry 1975–77; Dir for Int. Relations, Atomic Energy Commissariat 1978–79, Chief of Staff 1980–81; French Rep. on Bd of Govs IAEA 1979; f. COGEMA Inc., Washington, DC 1982, Pres. and CEO 1982–86; apptd Amb. to Mexico 1986 (did not take up post); Sr Adviser to Pres. Chirac for Diplomatic Affairs, Defence and Co-operation 1986–88; Amb. to Canada 1989–91, to USA 1995–2002; mem. Bd Dirs Sofratome, Technicatome and Eurodif 1979–, Copperweld Corpn (Imetal Group) 1982–86; Sr Vice-Pres. Compagnie de Navigation Mixte and Via Banque 1991–92; Chair. and CEO SFIM 1991–92, mem. Bd Dirs 1991–93; f. FBE Int. Consultants 1992; mem. Bd Dirs Banque INDOSUEZ, Int. Advisory Bd of TOTAL, Institut Français des Relations Internationales –1995, Chair. Citigroup France 2003–; mem. Ed. Bd Revue des Deux Mondes –1995; Pres. Harvard Business School Club of France –1995; Chevalier, Legion d'Honneur, Officier, Ordre nat. du Mérite. *Address:* Citigroup, 19 Le Parvis, La Defense 7, 7th Floor, 92073 Paris, France (Office). *Telephone:* 1-49-06-14-15. *Fax:* 1-49-06-14-17. *Website:* www.citibank.fr (Office).

BUJONES, Fernando; American ballet dancer; b. 9 March 1955, Miami, Fla; s. of Fernando and Maria (Calleiro) Bujones; m. Marcia Kibitschek 1980; ed School of American Ballet; joined American Ballet Theater 1972, Soloist 1973, Prin. Dancer 1974–85, Guest Prin. 1976; Guest Artist, Boston Ballet 1987–; artistic Dir Miss. Ballet, Jackson –1994, Bay Ballet Theater, Tampa, Fla 1994–; has danced with Nat. Ballet of Canada, Berlin Opera, Vienna State Opera, Scottish Ballet, Rome Opera and Stuttgart Ballet; appeared in film The Turning Point; has produced own dance Corpn Bujones Ltd; choreographed Grand Pas Romantique 1985; Varna Gold Medal 1974, Dance Magazine Award 1982, Florida Prize 1986, Elliott Norton Award, Boston Theater 1992. *Ballets:* Coppelia 1974, Swan Lake 1975, Sleeping Beauty 1976, Giselle 1977.

BUKAYEV, Gennadii Ivanovich; Russian politician and engineer; b. 15 Sept. 1947, Stepnoye, Orenburg Region; m.; one s.; ed Ufa Inst. Oil., Sverdlovsk Higher CPSU School; Sr Engineer 1972–75; Head of Div. Ufa Inst. of Oil 1975–77; Deputy Chair. Ufa Regional Exec. Cttee 1977–78; Instructor Bashkiria Regional Exec. CPSU Cttee 1980–85; Chair. Belebelyevo City CP Exec. Cttee. 1985–90; Head Div. of Trade Council of Ministers Bashkiria Autonomous Repub. 1990–92; Head State Taxation Inspection Repub. of Bashkortostan 1992–99; mem. Exec. Bd Ministry of Taxes and Levies of Russian Fed. 1999–2000, Minister 2000–. *Address:* Ministry of Taxes and Levies, Neglinnaya str. 23, 103381 Moscow, Russia (Office). *Telephone:* (095) 200-06-01 (Office). *Website:* www.nalog.ru (Office).

BUKOVAC, Martin J., PhD; American professor of horticulture; b. 12 Nov. 1929, Johnston City, Ill.; s. of John Bukovac and Sadie Fak; m. Judith A. Kelley 1956; one d.; ed Michigan State Univ.; Asst Prof., Dept of Horticulture, Mich. State Univ. 1957–61, Assoc. Prof. 1961–63, Prof. 1963–92, Univ. Distinguished Prof. 1992; Biological Science Collaborator, USDA/ Agricultural Research Service 1982–; Postdoctoral Fellow, Univs of Oxford and Bristol, England 1965–66; Dir Mich. State Univ. Press 1983–91; Adviser, Eli Lilly Co. 1971–88; Pres. Martin J. Bukovac Inc. 1996–; Fellow AAAS, American Soc. of Horticultural Science; mem. NAS, Editorial Advisory Bd Horticultural Abstracts 1990–, Editorial Bd Encyclopedia of Agricultural Science 1991–96, Int. Editorial Bd, Horticultural Science, Kertészete Tudomány, Budapest 1994–; mem. Int. Advisory Bd, Life Sciences Div., Center for Nuclear Sciences, Grenoble 1993–2000; Hon. DrAgr (Bonn) 1995; Alexander von Humboldt Award for Sr Scientist 1995 and numerous awards. *Publications:* over 350 research articles. *Leisure interests:* photography, sports. *Address:* Department of Horticulture, Michigan State University, East

Lansing, MI 48824-1112; 4428 Seneca Drive, Okemos, MI 48864-2946, USA (Home). *Telephone:* (517) 355-5207 (Office); (517) 349-1952 (Home). *Fax:* (517) 353-0890. *E-mail:* bukovacm@msu.edu.

BUKOVSKY, Vladimir Konstantinovich, MA; Russian writer and scientist; b. 30 Dec. 1942, Belebey; s. of Konstantin and Nina Bukovsky; ed Moscow State Univ., Cambridge Univ.; worked at Moscow Centre of Cybernetics; arrested for possessing banned literature 1963, confined to Leningrad Psychiatric Prison Hospital for 15 months; arrested for demonstration on behalf of Soviet writers 1965, confined for 8 months in psychiatric institutions; arrested for civil rights work 1967, on trial Sept. 1967 and sentenced to 3 years' corrective labour; arrested for delivering information on psychiatric abuse to the West 1971, on trial 1972 and sentenced to 2 years in prison, 5 in a labour camp and 5 in exile; after world-wide campaign for his release, was exchanged for Chilean Communist Party leader Luis Corvalán in Zürich Dec. 1976; citizenship restored 1992; research work, Stanford Univ., Calif. 1982–90; f. Centre for Democracy in Support of New Russia, New York; Hon. mem. several human rights orgs, several PEN clubs; lives in England; Konrad Adenauer Freedom and Literature Prize 1984. *Publications:* short stories in Russia's Other Writers 1970 and in Grani, Opposition–Eine neue Geisteskrankheit in der USSR (German edition) 1972, A Manual on Psychiatry for Dissenters (with Semyon Gluzman) 1974, To Build a Castle: My Life as a Dissenter (in English; trans. in Swedish, Italian, Spanish, French and German) 1978, Cette lancinante douleur de la liberté 1981, The Peace Movement and the Soviet Union 1982. *Leisure interests:* the arts, architecture.

BULAI, Igor Borisovich, CandHist; Russian diplomatist; b. 17 May 1947, Moscow; m.; two c.; ed Moscow State Inst. of Int. Relations, Inst. of USA and Canada Acad. of Sciences; Jr researcher Inst. of USA and Canada 1973–79; instructor Div. of Information Cen. Cttee CPSU 1979–85; counsellor USSR Embassy to USA 1985–91; with Dept of Information USSR Ministry of Foreign Affairs 1991–92; Head Dept of Information and Press, Ministry of Foreign Affairs of Russia 1992–98; Consul-Gen. in Edin. 1998–2001; mem. staff Dept for Information and Press and Head Press Centre, Ministry of Foreign Affairs 2001–. *Address:* Ministry of Foreign Affairs, Sadoraya-Sennaya 32/34, Moscow, Russia.

BULATOVIĆ, Momir, CEconSc; Serbia and Montenegro (Montenegrin) politician; b. 1956, Montenegro; ed Titograd Univ.; fmr mem. League of Communists of Montenegro, then leader Republican League of Communists; Chair. Democratic Party of Socialists (DPS) 1990–98; Chair. Socialist People's Party of Montenegro (SNP) 1998–; elected Pres. of Montenegro 1990–97; Prime Minister of Yugoslavia 1998–2001. *Address:* Socialist People's Party of Montenegro, Podgorica, Serbia and Montenegro (Office).

BULDAKOV, Aleksey Ivanovich; Russian actor; b. 26 March 1951, Makarovka, Altai Territory; m.; ed Pavlodar Drama Theatre Studio; worked in theatres in Pavlodar, Ryazan, Karaganda, Moscow. *Films include:* Through Fire 1982, Semen Dezhnev, Two Steps From Elysium, Sign of Trouble, Burn, Peculiarities of Russian Hunting, Quiet Investigation, Moonzund, Hey, Fools. *Address:* Kastanayevskaya str. 23, korp. 4, Apt 27, 121096 Moscow, Russia. *Telephone:* (095) 144-02-73.

BULGAK, Vladimir Borisovich, CandTechSc, DEconSc; Russian politician and business executive; b. 9 May 1941, Moscow; m.; one d.; ed Moscow Electrotech. Inst. of Communications, Inst. of Man. of Nat. Econ., USSR State Cttee on Science and Tech.; instructor, then sec. Moscow City Komsomol Cttee 1963–68; for 15 years worked in Moscow radio trans. network; head of depts USSR Ministry of Telecommunications 1983–90; Minister 1990–91; Minister of Telecommunications Russian Fed. 1991–97; Deputy Chair. Govt of Russian Fed. 1997–98, 1998–99; Minister of Science and Tech. April–Sept. 1998; Chair. Bd of Dirs TV-Holding Svyazinvest 1999–2001, Insurance Group Nasta; mem. Int. Acad. of Informatization, Russian Acad. of Tech. Sciences, Russian Acad. of Natural Sciences; USSR State Prize. *Publications:* over 100 articles and papers; several textbooks on communication techniques. *Address:* Nasta Group, Lva Tolstogo str. 5/1, 119021 Moscow, Russia (Office). *Telephone:* (095) 967-17-81 (Office).

BULIN, Gen. René Henri; French aeronautical engineer; b. 8 Aug. 1920, Langres; s. of Louis Bulin and Louise (née Walter) Bulin; m. 1st Claudine Prostot 1955 (deceased); m. 2nd Catherine Tambuscio 1982; ed Ecole Polytechnique Paris, Ecole Nationale Supérieure de l'Aéronautique; engineer responsible for setting up Centre d'Essais des Propulseurs (Fort de Villeras) 1946–53; Head Operations Dept and Instructor, Ecole Nationale de l'Aviation Civile 1953–56; Deputy Dir, then Dir Air Navigation Secrétariat Général de l'Aviation Civile, France 1956–61; first Dir-Gen. European Org. for the Safety of Air Navigation (EUROCONTROL) 1961–78, responsible for having set up the Air Traffic Services Agency, Brussels and the EUROCONTROL Experimental Centre, Brétigny-sur-Orge and for establishing the Upper Area Control Centres, Maastricht, Netherlands, Karlsruhe, Germany, Shannon, Ireland, the EUROCONTROL Inst. of Air Navigation Services, Luxembourg and the Users Charge Service, Brussels; Adviser Thomson-CSF 1978–83; Special Adviser to European Community Aeronautical Comm.; Commdr Légion d'honneur, Grand Croix du Mérite (Germany), Grand Croix du Mérite Aeronautique (Spain). *Address:* Altirama, 23 avenue Frédéric Mistral, 06130, Grasse, France (Home). *Telephone:* 4-93-70-50-58 (Home). *E-mail:* renebulin1@libertysurf.fr (Home).

BULL, Deborah Clare, CBE; British ballerina, writer, broadcaster and artistic director; b. 22 March 1963, Derby; d. of Rev. Michael John Bull and Doreen Audrey Franklin Bull (née Plumb); ed Royal Ballet School; joined Royal Ballet 1981, prin. dancer 1992–2001; teacher of Nutrition, Royal Ballet School 1996–99; Dir Clore Studio Upstairs, Royal Opera House 1999–2001, Artistic Dir Royal Opera House 2002–; mem. Dance Panel, Arts Council 1996–98, Arts Council 1998–; Gov. S Bank Centre 1997–; columnist The Telegraph 1999–2002; Patron Nat. Osteoporosis Soc., Foundation for Community Dance; Dr hc (Derby) 1998, (Sheffield) 2001; Prix de Lausanne 1980; Dancer of the Year, Sunday Express and The Ind. on Sunday 1996, Overall Prize Dancescreen Monaco 2002. *Dance:* appearances with Royal Ballet include leading roles in La Bayadère (Gamzatti), Swan Lake (Odette/Odile), The Sleeping Beauty (Aurora), Don Quixote (Kitri), Steptext (cr. for her by William Forsythe) 1995; appeared in Harrogate Int. Festival 1993, 1995, An Evening of British Ballet, Sintra Festival, Portugal 1994, 1995, Diamonds of World Ballet Gala, Kremlin Palace, Moscow 1996, Rite of Spring, Teatro dell'Opera, Rome 2001–02. *Radio:* regular contrib. to BBC Radio 4 including Breaking the Law 2001, Law in Order 2002, A Dance Through Time 2002. *Television:* Dance Ballerina Dance (writer, presenter) 1998, Travels with my Tutu (writer, presenter) 2000, Coppélia, Royal Ballet (live broadcast), Rambert Dance Co., Sadlers Wells (live broadcast), The Dancer's Boy 2002. *Publications:* The Vitality Plan 1998, Dancing Away 1998; numerous articles and reviews in newspapers and dance magazines. *Leisure interests:* mountain pursuits, food and wine, reading, writing, cycling, kayaking, walking. *Address:* Royal Opera House, Covent Garden, London, WC2E 9DD, England (Office). *Telephone:* (20) 7240-1200 (Office). *Website:* deborahbull.com (Office).

BULL, Sir George, Kt; British business executive; b. 16 July 1936, London; s. of Michael Bull and Hon. Noreen Hennessy; m. Jane Freeland 1960; four s. one d.; ed Ampleforth Coll.; Coldstream Guards 1954–57; joined Twiss Browning & Hallowes 1958; Gilbey Vintners Ltd 1970; Dir Int. Distillers and Vintners (IDV) 1973; Man. Dir IDV Europe 1977; Deputy Man. Dir IDV Ltd 1982; Dir Grand Metropolitan Ltd 1985; Chief Exec. IDV Ltd 1987; Chair. and CEO IDV Ltd (Drinks Sector of Grand Metropolitan PLC) 1988; Chair. and CEO Grand Met Food Sector 1992; Group Chief Exec. Grand Metropolitan PLC 1993, Chair. Grand Metropolitan PLC 1996–97; Co.-Chair. Diageo (after merger with Guinness PLC) 1997–98; Chair. J. Sainsbury PLC 1998–; Dir (non-exec.) BNP Paribas UK Holdings 2000–, The Maersk Co. Ltd 2001–; mem. Advisory Bd Marakon Assocs 2002–; Chevalier, Légion d'honneur 1994. *Leisure interests:* golf, photography. *Address:* J. Sainsbury PLC, Stamford House, Stamford Street, London, SE1 9LL (Office); The Old Vicarage, Arkesden, Saffron Walden, Essex, CB11 4HB, England (Home). *Telephone:* (20) 7695-6000 (Office); (1799) 550445 (Home). *Fax:* (20) 7695-0320 (Office).

BULL, William V. S., MA; Liberian diplomatist; b. 1946, Monrovia; ed Univ. of Liberia, Univ. of Pittsburgh, USA; joined Bureau of African and Asian Affairs, Ministry of Foreign Affairs 1972; Counsellor and Deputy Chief of Mission, Washington, DC 1976, Chargé d'affaires 1980; Asst Minister for American Affairs, Monrovia 1981, for African and Asian Affairs 1982–86, Prin. Deputy to Minister of Foreign Affairs 1987–90; Amb. and Perm. Rep. to UN, New York 1990–98; Amb. to UK 1998–2000, to USA 2000–. *Address:* Embassy of Liberia, 5201 16th Street, NW, Washington, DC 20011, USA (Office). *Telephone:* (202) 723-0437 (Office). *Fax:* (202) 723-0436 (Office). *E-mail:* info@liberiaemb.org (Office). *Website:* www.liberiaemb.org (Office).

BULLARD, Sir Julian (Leonard), GCMG; British diplomatist (retd); b. 8 March 1928, Athens; s. of the late Sir Reader Bullard and Miriam Smith; m. Margaret Stephens 1954; two s. two d.; ed Rugby School, Magdalen Coll., Oxford; nat. service Army 1950–52; joined HM Diplomatic Service 1953, served at Foreign Office 1953–54, Vienna 1954–56, Amman 1956–59, Foreign Office 1960–63, Bonn 1963–66, Moscow 1966–68, Dubai 1968–70, FCO (Head of E European and Soviet Dept) 1971–75; Minister, Bonn 1975–79; Deputy Under-Sec. of State 1979–84; Deputy to Perm. Under-Sec. of State and Political Dir 1982–84; Amb. to Fed. Repub. of Germany 1984–88; Pro-Chancellor, Univ. of Birmingham 1989–94, mem. Council 1988–96; Fellow All Souls Coll., Oxford 1950–67, 1988–; Hon. Fellow St. Anthony's Coll., Oxford; Hon. LLD (Birmingham) 1994. *Publications:* (ed. with Margaret Bullard) Inside Stalin's Russia, The Diaries of Reader Bullard 1930–34 2000. *Address:* 18 Northmoor Road, Oxford, OX2 6UR, England. *Telephone:* (1865) 512981. *Fax:* (1865) 510718. *E-mail:* julian.bullard@all-souls.ox.ac.uk (Office).

BULLER, Arthur John, BS, ERDFRCP, FIBiol, FRSA; British physiologist; b. 16 Oct. 1923; s. of Thomas Alfred Buller and Edith May Buller (née Wager); m. Helena Joan Pearson 1946; one s. two d. (one deceased); ed Duke of York's Royal Mil. School, Dover, St Thomas's Hospital Medical School; Kitchener Scholar 1941–45; Lecturer in Physiology St Thomas's Hosp. 1946–49; Maj. RAMC, Specialist in Physiology, Jr Sec. Mil. Personnel Research Cttee 1949–53; Lecturer in Medicine St Thomas's Hosp. 1953–57; Reader in Physiology King's Coll., London 1961–65; Gresham Prof. of Physic 1963–65; Prof. of Physiology Univ. of Bristol 1965–82 (Prof. Emer. 1982–), Dean Faculty of Medicine 1976–78; Chief Scientist (on secondment) Dept of Health and Social Security 1978–81; Visiting Prof. Monash Univ., Australia 1972; Long Fox Memorial Lecturer, Bristol 1978; Hon. Consultant in Clinical Physiology, Bristol Dist Hospital 1970–85; Royal Soc. Commonwealth Fellow, Canberra, Australia 1958–59; mem. Bd of Govs Bristol Royal Infirmary 1968–74, Avon Health Authority 1974–78, MRC 1975–81; Chair. Neurosciences and Mental Health Bd, MRC 1975–77; External Scientific Adviser, Rayne Inst. St Thomas's Hosp. 1979–85; Research Devt Dir, Muscular Dystrophy Group of

GB and NI 1982–90; mem. BBC, IBA Cen. Appeals Advice Cttee 1983–88; Milroy Lecturer, Royal Coll. of Physicians 1983. *Publications:* articles in books and journals on normal and abnormal physiology. *Leisure interests:* clarets and conversation. *Address:* Lockhall Cottage, Cow Lane, Steeple Aston, Bicester, Oxon., OX25 4SG, England. *Telephone:* (1869) 347502.

BULLOCK, Baron (Life Peer), cr. 1976, of Leafield in the County of Oxfordshire; **Alan Louis Charles Bullock,** Kt, FBA, MA, DLitt; British historian and university administrator; b. 13 Dec. 1914, Trowbridge; s. of Rev. Frank A. Bullock; m. Hilda Yates Handy 1940; three s. two d. (one deceased); ed Bradford Grammar School, Wadham and Merton Colls, Oxford; BBC European Service diplomatic and political corresp. 1940–45; Fellow, Dean and Tutor of New Coll., Oxford 1945–52; Founding Master of St Catherine's Coll., Oxford 1960–80, Hon. Fellow 1980–; Trustee, The Observer 1957–69, Dir 1977–81; mem. Arts Council 1961–64, British Library Organizing Cttee 1972–73, Cttee of Vice-Chancellors and Prins 1969–73; Vice-Chancellor, Univ. of Oxford 1969–73; Chair. Inquiry into Teaching of Reading and Other Uses of Language 1972–74; Chair. Trustees of Tate Gallery 1973–79; Chair. Cttee on Industrial Democracy 1975–76; Trustee, Wolfson Foundation 1974–87; Aspen Inst., Berlin; Chair. Research Cttee and mem. Council, Royal Inst. of Int. Affairs (Chatham House) 1954–78; fmr Chair. Nat. Advisory Council on Training and Supply of Teachers; mem. Advisory Council on Public Records to 1976; fmr Chair. The Schools Council, Bd of Int. Asscn for Cultural Freedom; Joint Ed. Oxford History of Modern Europe, Int. Comm. of Historians for publication of documents on German Foreign Policy 1918–45; mem. Acad. Europaea; Foreign Mem. American Acad. of Arts and Sciences; Hon. Fellow Merton Coll., New Coll., Wadham Coll., Wolfson Coll., Linacre Coll. and St Antony's Coll., Oxford; Hon. FRIBA; Chevalier Légion d'honneur 1970, Grosses Dienstkreuz, Germany; Dr hc (Aix-Marseilles, Bradford, Newfoundland, Reading, Open Univ., Leicester, Sussex, Warwick, Essex, Leeds Univs). *Publications:* Hitler, a Study in Tyranny 1952, 1962, The Liberal Tradition 1956, Schellenberg Memoirs 1956, The Life and Times of Ernest Bevin, Vol. I 1960, Vol. II 1967, Vol. III 1983, The Twentieth Century (ed.) 1971, The Fontana Dictionary of Modern Thought (co-ed. with Oliver Stallybrass) 1977, Faces of Europe 1979, Fontana Dictionary of Modern Thinkers (co-ed. with R. B. Woodings) 1983, The Humanist Tradition in the West 1985, Hitler and Stalin: Parallel Lives 1991, Building Jerusalem 2000, Ernest Bevin 2002. *Address:* St Catherine's College, Oxford, OX1 3UJ; Gable End, 30 Godstow Road, Oxford, OX2 8AJ, England. *Telephone:* (1865) 271700; (1865) 513380 (Home).

BULLOCK, Peter, BA, MSc, PhD; British soil scientist; b. 6 July 1937, Bridgnorth; s. of Cecil Bullock and Alice Bullock; m. Patricia Standidge 1963; one s. (deceased) one d.; ed Birmingham, Leeds and Cornell Univs; Scientific Officer, Soil Survey of England and Wales 1958, Sr Scientific Officer 1970, Prin. Scientific Officer 1975, Dir 1985; Dir Soil Survey and Land Research Centre 1987–97; Visiting Prof. Inst. of Water and Environment, Cranfield Univ.; Vice-Pres./Pres. British Soc. of Soil Science; mem. Govt and Research Council Cttees on Soil Science, Climate Change, Environmental Protection, Impacts of Environmental Change; mem. Governing Body of Inst. of Grassland and Environmental Research, Advisory Cttee of European Soil Bureau (Chair. 1998–2002); mem. Cttee of Land Degradation and Desertification Working Group of IUSS 1998–; mem. Biotech. and Biological Sciences Research Council Sr Man. Review Cttee 2002–; Fulbright Scholar 1964–66; Fellow Inst. of Professional Soil Scientists. *Publications:* eight books on soil science; over 85 scientific papers. *Leisure interests:* sport including: football, cricket, most ball games; theatre, art, walking. *Address:* Cranfield University at Silsoe, Silsoe, Beds., MK45 4DT (Office); 11 Wood End Hill, Harpenden, Herts., AL5 3EZ, England (Home). *Telephone:* (1525) 863251. *Fax:* (1525) 863344 (Office). *E-mail:* p.bullock@cranfield.ac.uk (Office); peterubullock@aol.com (Home).

BULLOCK, Sandra; American actress; b. July 1964, Washington; d. of John Bullock and Helga Bullock; ed East Carolina Univ.; grew up in Germany and Washington, DC; frequent appearances on European stage with opera-singer mother; appeared in off-Broadway productions including No Time Flat (WPA Theatre); numerous awards. *Films include:* Love Potion # 9 1992, When the Party's Over 1992, The Vanishing 1993, The Thing Called Love 1993, Fire on the Amazon 1993, Demolition Man 1993, Wrestling Ernest Hemingway 1993, Speed 1994, While You Were Sleeping 1995, The Net 1995, Two If By Sea 1996, Moll Flanders, A Time to Kill 1996, In Love and War 1996, Practical Magic 1998, Forces of Nature 1999, Gun Shy 1999, Making Sandwiches 1996 (also writer), Speed 2 1997, Hope Floats (also exec. producer) 1998, Prince of Egypt (voice only) 1998, 28 Days 2000, Famous 2000, Miss Congeniality 2000, Murder by Numbers 2001, Exactly 3:30 2001, Divine Secrets of the Ya-Ya Sisterhood 2002, Two Weeks' Notice 2002. *Television includes:* The Preppy Murder (film), Lucky Chances (miniseries), Working Girl (NBC series). *Address:* CAA, 9830 Wilshire Boulevard, Beverly Hills, CA 90212, USA.

BULLOCK, Theodore Holmes, PhD; American professor of neurosciences; b. 16 May 1915, Nanking, China; s. of A. Archibald Bullock and Ruth Beckwith Bullock; m. Martha Runquist 1937; one s. one d.; ed Univ. of California, Berkeley; Sterling Fellow, Yale Univ. 1940–41; Rockefeller Fellow 1941–42; Instructor in Neuroanatomy, Yale Univ. 1942–44; Asst Prof. of Anatomy, Univ. of Missouri 1944–46; Instructor and sometime Head, Invertebrate Zoology, Marine Biol. Lab., Woods Hole, Mass.; Asst Prof., Assoc. Prof., Prof. of Zoology, Univ. of Calif., Los Angeles 1946–66; Prof. of Neurosciences, Univ. of Calif. San Diego School of Medicine 1966–82, Prof. Emer.

1982–; Head of Neurobiology Unit, Scripps Inst. of Oceanography; mem. American Acad. Arts and Sciences, NAS, American Phil. Soc., Int. Soc. for Neuroethology; fmr Pres. American Soc. of Zoology, Soc. for Neuroscience; Dr hc (Frankfurt) 1988; Hon. DSc (Loyola Univ., Chicago) 2001; Lashley Prize, American Philosophical Soc. 1968, Gerard Prize, Soc. for Neuroscience 1984. *Publications:* Structure and Function in the Nervous Systems of Invertebrates (with G. A. Horridge) 1965, Introduction to Nervous Systems (with R. Orkand and A. D. Grinnell) 1977, Electroreception (with W. Heiligenberg) 1986, Brain Dynamics (with E. Basar) 1989, Induced Rhythms in the Brain (with E. Basar) 1992, How Do Brains Work? 1993. *Address:* Department of Neurosciences, University of California, San Diego, La Jolla, CA 92093, USA. *Telephone:* (858) 534-3636. *Fax:* (858) 534-3919 (Office). *E-mail:* tbullock@ucsd.edu (Office). *Website:* cogprints.soton.ac.uk (Office).

BULMAHN, Edelgard, BA; German politician; b. 4 March 1951, Minden; m.; ed Petershagen Aufbaugymnasium and Hanover Univ.; secondary school teacher for seven years; joined SPD party 1969; mem. Bundestag (SPD) 1987–, mem. Exec. Cttee SPD Parl. Group 1991–98, Exec. Cttee SPD 1993–; Deputy Spokesman on Research and Tech. SPD Parl. Group 1990–94; Chair. Cttee on Educ., Science, Research, Tech. and Tech. Assessment 1995–96; spokesman on Educ. and Research SPD Parl. Group 1996–98; Fed. Minister of Educ. and Research 1998–; Chair. European Space Agency (ESA) at ministerial level 2001–. *Address:* Ministry of Education and Research, Heinemannstr. 2, 53175 Bonn; Ministry of Education and Research, Hannoverschestr. 28-30, 10115 Berlin, Germany. *Telephone:* (228) 570. *Fax:* (228) 573601. *E-mail:* edelgard.bulmahn@bmbf.de (Office). *Website:* www.bmbf.de (Office).

BULMER-THOMAS, Victor Gerald, OBE, MA, DPhil; British professor of economics and international consultant; b. 23 March 1948, London; s. of the late Ivor Bulmer-Thomas and of Joan Bulmer; m. Barbara Swasey 1970; two s. one d.; ed Westminster School, New Coll. and St Antony's Coll. Oxford; Research Fellow, Fraser of Allander Inst. 1975–78; Lecturer in Econs Queen Mary Coll. London 1978–87, Reader 1987–92, Prof. of Econs 1990–98; Dir Inst. of Latin American Studies, Univ. of London 1992–98; Sr Research Fellow 1998–2001; Prof. Emer. of Econs Univ. of London 1998–; Dir Royal Inst. of Int. Affairs 2001–; Dir Schroders Emerging Countries Fund 1996–; Order of San Carlos (Colombia) 1998, Nat. Order of the Southern Cross (Brazil) 1998. *Publications:* Input-Output Analysis for Developing Countries 1982, The Political Economy of Central America since 1920 1987, Studies in the Economics of Central America 1988, Britain and Latin America: A Changing Relationship (Ed.) 1989, The Economic History of Latin America since Independence 1994, The New Economic Model in Latin America and Its Impact on Income Distribution and Poverty (Ed.) 1996, Thirty Years of Latin American Studies in the UK 1997, United States and Latin America: The New Agenda (Ed.) 1999, Regional Integration in Latin America and the Caribbean: The Political Economy of Open Regionalism (Ed.) 2001. *Leisure interests:* music (viola), tennis, walking, canoeing, underwater photography. *Address:* Royal Institute of International Affairs, Chatham House, 10 St James's Square, London, SW1Y 4LE, England (Office). *Telephone:* (20) 7957-5702 (Office). *Fax:* (20) 7314-3626 (Office). *E-mail:* director@riia.org (Office). *Website:* www.riia.org (Office).

BUMBRY, Grace; American opera singer; b. 4 Jan. 1937, St Louis, Mo.; d. of Benjamin Bumbry and Melzia Bumbry; ed Boston and Northwestern Univs, Music Acad. of the West; début, Paris Opera as Amneris in Aida March 1960; Basel Opera 1960–63; Carmen with Paris Opera and toured Japan; Royal Opera, Brussels; Die Schwarze Venus, Tannhäuser, Bayreuth Festival 1961 and 1962; Vienna State Opera 1963; Covent Garden 1963, 1968, 1969, 1976, 1978; Salzburg Festival 1964; Metropolitan Opera 1965–79; La Scala 1964–79, Chicago Lyric 1962–78; Porgy and Bess, NY Metropolitan Opera 1985; Hon. Citizen of Baltimore, LA, Philadelphia, St Louis; Hon. DH (Univ. of St Louis), (Rust Coll.); Hon. DMus (Rockhurst Coll.); Richard Wagner Medal 1963; Grammy Award 1979, Royal Opera House Medal 1988, Puccini Award 1990; Commdr des Arts et des Lettres 1996. *Leisure interests:* interior decorating, designing clothes. *Address:* J.F. Mastroianni Associates, 161 West 61st Street, New York, NY10032, USA.

BUMPERS, Dale Leon, LLD; American politician; b. 12 Aug. 1925, Charleston, Ark.; s. of William Rufus Bumpers and Lattie (née Jones) Bumpers; m. Betty Flanagan 1949; two s. one d.; ed Univ. of Arkansas and Northwestern Law School; Propr Charleston Hardware and Furniture Co. 1951–66, Angus Breeding Farm 1966–70; Attorney, Charleston, Ark. 1951–70; Gov. of Arkansas 1971–74; Senator from Arkansas 1975–99; Attorney Arent Fox Kintner Plotkin & Kahn, Washington 2000–02; Democrat. *Leisure interests:* reading, tennis, hunting. *Address:* Arent Fox Kintner Plotkin & Kohn, 1050 Connecticut Avenue, NW, Washington, DC 20036-5339, USA.

BUND, Karlheinz, DrIng, Dr rer. pol; German business executive; b. 18 March 1925, Saarlouis; m. Anni Kronenberger; ed Technische Hochschule, Darmstadt; Chair. Bd of Ruhrkohle AG 1973–85; Chair. EVG and Chair. Advisory Bd INNOTEC 1985, ENRO Energie und Rohstoff GmbH; mem. Supervisory Bd ASEA Brown, Boveri, Deutsche Babcock Anlagen AG; Pres. World Coal Inst. (WCI); Chair. ENRO GmbH; Grosses Bundesverdienstkreuz 1975. *Address:* Huyssenallee 86-88, 45128 Essen, Germany. *Telephone:* (201) 245 360. *Fax:* (201) 245 3639.

BUNDU, Abass, PhD; Sierra Leonean diplomatist and lawyer; b. 3 June 1948; s. of Isatu Kallay Bundu and Pa Santigie; m. Khadija Allie 1976; two s. three d.; ed Australian Nat. Univ., Canberra, Cambridge Univ., England; Asst Dir, Commonwealth Secr., London 1975–82; MP for Port Loko NE 1982–90; Minister of Agric., Natural Resources and Forestry 1982–85; Exec. Sec., Econ. Community of W African States (ECOWAS) 1989–93; Sec. of State for Foreign Affairs and Int. Co-operation 1993–95; Presidential Cand. People's Progressive Party 1996, currently Leader; Yorke Award, Univ. of Cambridge. *Leisure interests:* tennis, swimming. *Address:* c/o Department of Foreign Affairs, Gloucester Street, Freetown, Sierra Leone.

BUNE, Poseci Wagalevu; Fijian diplomatist; ed Queen Victoria School, Royal Coll. of Public Admin., London; joined Public Service Dept 1966, apptd Sr Admin. Officer 1972, attached to Australian Embassy, Bangkok 1973, joined Perm. Mission to UN, New York 1973, apptd First Sec. 1973, Counsellor, Mission to EEC 1976–80; Western Divisional Commr, Ministry of Rural Devt 1981–85; Amb. to EEC (also Accred to Belgium, Luxembourg, Netherlands, France and Italy) 1985–87; Perm. Sec. for Public Service 1987–95, Perm. Sec. to Govt and for Public Service 1990–95; Perm. Rep. to UN 1995–2000; mem. Parl. for Macuata 2001–. *Address:* House of Representatives, Suva, Fiji.

BUNGEY, Michael, BSc (Econs); British advertising executive; b. 18 Jan. 1940; s. of William Frederick George Bungey and Irene Edith Bungey; m. Darleen Penelope Cecilia Brooks 1976; one s. two d.; ed St Clement Danes Grammar School and London School of Econs; marketing with Nestlé 1961–65; Assoc. Dir Crawfords Advertising 1965–68; Account Dir S. H. Benson Advertising 1968–71; Chair. Michael Bungey DFS Ltd 1972–84; Chair., CEO DFS Dorland 1987, Bates Dorland 1988, Bates Europe 1989; Deputy Chair. Dorland Advertising (now Bates Dorland Advertising Ltd) 1984, Chair. 1987–96, CEO 1987; Chair., CEO Bates Worldwide (fmrly BSB Worldwide) 1994–; Chair. Backer Spielvogel Bates Europe 1988–, Pres., COO Backer Spielvogel Bates Worldwide 1993–94, CEO 1994–; Chair., CEO Bates Worldwide 1994–; CEO Cordiant Communications Group PLC 1997–; Dir Cordiant PLC (fmrly Saatchi & Saatchi)1995. *Address:* c/o Bates UK, 121–141 Westbourne Terrace, London, W2 6JR, England. *Website:* www.batesww.com.

BUNIN, Igor Mikhailovich; Russian political administrator; b. 25 Feb. 1946, Moscow; m; one d.; ed ed. Moscow State Univ.; Sr Researcher Inst. of World Econ. and Int. Relations, USSR Acad. of Sciences 1973–82; Chief Researcher Inst. of Int. Workers' Movt 1982–92; Chief Scientific Expert Int. Foundation of Socio-Econ. and Political Studies (Gorbachev Foundation) 1992–93; Dir Centre of Business Initiatives, Ekspertiza 1992–93; Dir-Gen. Centre of Political Technologies 1993–; Dir-Gen. Ind. Information Site of Political Comments, www.politcom.ru 2001–. *Publications include:* Socialists and Political Struggle in France in the 1980s 1989, New Russian Businessmen and Myths of Post-Communist Mentality 1993, Businessmen of Russia: 40 Stories of Success 1994, Experience of Formation 1994, Financial and Industrial Groups and Conglomerates in Economics and Politics of Russia 1997, Political Processes in the Regions of Russia 1998. *Address:* Centre of Political Technologies, Bolshoi Zlatoustovsky per. 8/7 office 73–95, 101000 Moscow, Russian Federation (Office). *Telephone:* (095) 206-80-30 (Office). *Fax:* (095) 20682-58 (Office). *E-mail:* info@cpt.ru (Office). *Website:* www.cpt.ru (Office).

BUNKIN, Fedor Vasilyevich, DrPhysMathSc; Russian physicist; b. 17 Jan. 1929; m.; two c.; ed Moscow State Univ.; Jr, Sr researcher, head of sector, head of lab. Physical Inst. USSR Acad. of Sciences 1955–82; Deputy Dir Inst. of Gen. Physics USSR Acad. of Sciences 1982–; corresp. mem. USSR (now Russian) Acad. of Sciences 1976, mem. 1992–; main research in quantum physics, electronics, nonlinear optics, acoustics; mem. Co-ordination Council on problem Coherent and Nonlinear Optics Russian Acad. of Sciences; USSR State Prize. *Publications include:* 6 books; numerous articles in scientific journals. *Address:* Physical Institute, Vavilova str. 38, 117942 Moscow, Russia (Office). *Telephone:* (095) 135-82-34 (Office); (095) 331-32-62 (Home).

BUNNAG, Marut; Thai politician; b. 21 Aug. 1925, Bangkok; s. of Phra Sutthikarnvinijchai and Mrs Phongsri; m. Phantipha Bunnag; two c.; ed Thammasat Univ.; with Ministry of Justice until 1952; law practice 1952–; Minister of Justice 1979; MP (Democratic Party) 1983–; Minister of Public Health 1983–86, Sept.–Dec. 1990; Minister of Education 1988; Deputy Leader, Democrat Party, Sr Adviser. *Address:* Marut Bunnag International Law Office, Forum Tower, 22nd Floor, 184/130–136 Patchadaphisek Road, Huaykwang, Bangkok, 10320 (Office); 45/1 Pradipat Road, Kwaeng Samsane-nai, Khet Phyathai, Bangkok, 10400, Thailand (Home); c/o House of Representatives, Bangkok. *Telephone:* (2) 645-2556 (Office); (2) 271-1081 (Home). *Fax:* (2) 645-2568 (Office). *E-mail:* marut@loxinfo.co.uk. *Website:* www.marut.th.com (Office).

BUNNING, Jim, BS; American politician and fmr baseball player; b. 23 Oct. 1931, Southgate, Ky; m. Mary Bunning; nine c.; ed Xavier Univ.; professional baseball player 1955–71; with Detroit Tigers 1955–63, Phila Phillies 1964–67, 1970–71, Pittsburgh Pirates 1968–69, LA Dodgers 1969; retd 1971; congressman Ky State Senate 1979–83; mem. 100th–104th Congresses from 4th Ky Dist 1987–99; Senator from Kentucky 1998–; mem. Senate Finance Cttee Dec. 2002–; Republican; Nat. Baseball Hall of Fame 1996. *Address:* US Senate, 316 Hart Senate Office Building, Washington, DC 20510, USA.

BURBIDGE, (Eleanor) Margaret Peachey, PhD, FRS; American (born British) astronomer; b. 12 Aug. 1919, Davenport, England; d. of Stanley John and Marjorie (née Stott) Peachey; m. Geoffrey Burbidge (q.v.) 1948; one d.; ed Frances Holland School, London and Univ. Coll., London; Second Asst, Asst Dir and acting Dir Univ. of London Observatory 1946–51; Research Fellow, Yerkes Observatory, Harvard Coll. Observatory 1951–53, Calif. Inst. of Technology 1955–57; Research Fellow and Assoc. Prof. Univ. of Chicago 1957–62; Assoc. Research Physicist, Univ. of Calif., San Diego 1962–64, Prof. 1964–, Univ. Prof. 1984–91, Emer. 1991–, Research Prof., Dept of Physics 1990–; Dir Royal Greenwich Observatory 1971–73; Dir Center for Astrophysics and Space Sciences, Univ. of Calif., San Diego 1979–88; Ed. Observatory 1948–51; mem. Editorial Bd Astronomy and Astrophysics 1969–85; Lindsay Memorial Lecture NASA 1985; mem. Royal Astronomical Soc., American Astronomical Soc. (Pres. 1978), American Acad. of Arts and Science, NAS, AAAS (Fellow 1981, Pres. 1982), American Philosophical Soc., Soc. Royale des Sciences de Liège, Astronomical Soc. of the Pacific, New York Acad. of Sciences; Fellow, Univ. Coll., London, Lucy Cavendish Coll., Cambridge, Girton Coll., Cambridge; Hon. DSc (Smith Coll., Mass., Rensselaer Political Inst. and Univ. of Sussex, Leicester, Bristol, Chicago, Mich., Mass., City Univ., London, Notre Dame, London and Williams Coll.); numerous prizes and awards including Helen B. Warner Prize (jtly with Geoffrey Burbidge) 1959; Bruce Gold Medal, Astronomical Soc. of the Pacific 1982, Nat. Medal of Science, USA 1983, Einstein Medal 1988. *Publications:* Quasi-Stellar Objects (with Geoffrey Burbidge) 1967; numerous articles in scientific journals. *Address:* Center for Astrophysics and Space Sciences, University of California at San Diego, Mail Code #0424, La Jolla, CA 92093, USA. *Telephone:* (858) 534-4477. *Fax:* (858) 554-7051 (Office). *E-mail:* mburbidge@ucsd.edu (Office).

BURBIDGE, Geoffrey, PhD, FRS; British physicist; b. 24 Sept. 1925, Chipping Norton, England; s. of Leslie and Eveline Burbidge; m. Margaret Peachey (q.v. 1948 Eleanor Margaret Peachey Burbidge); one d.; ed Bristol Univ. and Univ. Coll., London; Asst Lecturer, Univ. Coll. London 1950–51; Agassiz Fellow, Harvard Univ. 1951–52; Research Fellow, Cavendish Lab., Cambridge 1953–55; Carnegie Fellow, Mount Wilson and Palomar Observatories 1955–57; Asst Prof. Dept of Astronomy, Univ. of Chicago 1957–58; Assoc. Prof. 1958–62; Assoc. Prof. Univ. of Calif. (San Diego) 1962–63, Prof. 1963–84, Prof. Emer. 1984–88, Prof. 1988–; Dir Kitt Peak Nat. Observatory 1978–84; Phillips Visiting Prof., Harvard Univ. 1968; Pres. Astronomical Soc. of the Pacific 1974–76; Dir Associated Univs for Research in Astronomy 1971–74; Fellow, Univ. Coll., London; Ed. Annual Review of Astronomy and Astrophysics 1973–, Scientific Ed. Astrophysical Journal 1996–2002; Trustee, Associated Univs Inc. 1973–82; Helen B. Warner Prize (jtly with Margaret Burbidge) 1959, Bruce Gold Medal, Astronomical Soc. of the Pacific 1999. *Publications:* Quasi-Stellar Objects, (with Margaret Burbidge) 1967, A Different Approach to Cosmology (with F. Hoyle and J. V. Narlikar) 2000; more than 400 astrophysics papers in scientific journals. *Address:* Department of Physics, Center for Astrophysics and Space Sciences, 0424, University of California, San Diego, La Jolla, CA 92093, USA. *Telephone:* (858) 534-6626.

BURBULIS, Gennady Eduardovich; Russian politician; b. 4 Aug. 1945, Pervouralsk, Sverdlovsk (now Ekaterinburg); s. of Eduard Kazimirovich Burbulis and Valentina Ivanovna Belonogova; m. Natalia Kirsanova; one s.; ed Ural State Univ.; Lecturer Ural Polytechni Inst. 1974–83; Head of Chair., Deputy Dir Inst. of Non-Ferrous Metals 1983–89; USSR People's Deputy 1989–90; formed Discussion Tribune, Sverdlovsk 1988; elected to Congress of People's Deputies 1989; mem. Inter-Regional Group; Chief of Staff to Boris Yeltsin 1991; State Sec. RSFSR (now Russian Fed.) 1991–92, State Council Sec. 1991–92; First Deputy Chair. Russian Govt 1991–92, Sec. of State May–Nov. 1992, Head of Advisors' Team Nov.–Dec. 1992; Founder and Pres. Int. Humanitarian and Political Cen. Strategy 1993–; mem. State Duma (Parl.) 1993–99, mem. Cttee for Geopolitics; Deputy Gov. Novgorod Region 1999–2001; Chair. Observational Bd Novotrubny factory, Pervouralsk 1997–98; Rep. of Novgorod Region to Council of Fed. 2002–; Chair. Fed. Council Comm. on Methodology of Exercising the Fed. Council's Constitutional Powers 2002–. *Publication:* Profession – Politician 1999. *Leisure interests:* poetry, playing soccer and tennis. *Address:* Council of Federation, B. Dmitrovca 26, 103426, Moscow, Russia (Office). *Telephone:* (095) 292-61-23 (Office). *Fax:* (095) 926-69-50 (Office). *E-mail:* GEBurbulis@council.gov.ru (Office).

BURCHAM, William Ernest, CBE, PhD, FRS, FInstP; British emeritus professor of physics; b. 1 Aug. 1913, Norfolk; s. of Ernest Barnard Burcham and Edith Pitcher; m. 1st Isabella Mary Todd 1942 (died 1981); two d. (one deceased); m. 2nd Patricia Newton Marson 1985; ed City of Norwich School, Trinity Hall and Pembroke Coll., Cambridge; Scientific Officer, Ministry of Supply 1939–44; with UK Atomic Energy 1944–45; Lecturer, Fellow, Selwyn Coll., Univ. of Cambridge 1945–51; Demonstrator, Lecturer, Univ. of Cambridge 1945–51; Oliver Lodge Prof. of Physics, Univ. of Birmingham 1951–80, Emer. Prof. of Physics 1981–; Hon. Life Fellow, Coventry Polytechnic 1984. *Publications:* Nuclear Physics: An Introduction 1963, Elements of Nuclear Physics 1979, Nuclear and Particle Physics (with M. Jobes) 1995. *Address:* 95 Witherford Way, Birmingham, B29 4AN, England. *Telephone:* (121) 472-1226.

BURCHFIELD, Robert William, CBE, MA; New Zealand author and lecturer in English language (retd); b. 27 Jan. 1923, Wanganui, New Zealand; s. of Frederick Burchfield and Mary Blair; m. 1st Ethel May Yates 1949 (divorced 1976); one s. two d.; m. 2nd Elizabeth Austen Knight 1976; ed Wanganui Tech. Coll., Victoria Univ. Coll., Wellington and Magdalen Coll., Oxford; war service with Royal NZ Artillery 1941–46; NZ Rhodes Scholar

1949; Jr Lecturer in English Language, Magdalen Coll., Oxford 1952–53; Lecturer in English Language, Christ Church, Oxford 1953–57; Lecturer, St Peter's Coll., Oxford 1955–63, Tutorial Fellow 1963–79, Sr Research Fellow 1979–90, Emer. Fellow 1990–; Ed., Notes and Queries 1959–62, A Supplement to the Oxford English Dictionary 1957–86; Chief Ed., The Oxford English Dictionaries 1971–84; Pres. English Asscn 1978–79; Hon. Sec. Early English Text Soc. 1955–68, mem. Council 1968–80; Hon. Foreign mem. American Acad. of Arts and Sciences 1977–; Hon. DLitt (Liverpool) 1978, Hon. Lit.D. (Victoria Univ. of Wellington) 1983; Shakespeare Prize (FVS Foundation, Hamburg) 1994; Freedom of City of Wanganui 1986. *Publications:* The Oxford Dictionary of English Etymology (with C. T. Onions and G. W. S. Friedrichsen) 1966, A Supplement of Australian and New Zealand Words (in the Pocket Oxford Dictionary) 1969, A Supplement to the Oxford English Dictionary (Vol. I) 1972, (Vol. II) 1976, (Vol. III) 1982, (Vol. IV) 1986, The Quality of Spoken English on BBC Radio (with D. Donoghue and A. Timothy) 1979, The Spoken Language as an Art Form 1981, The Spoken Word 1981, The English Language 1985, The New Zealand Pocket Oxford Dictionary 1986, Studies in Lexicography 1987, Unlocking the English Language 1989, Points of View 1992, The Cambridge History of The English Language, Vol. V: English in Britain and Overseas 1994, The New Fowler's Modern English Usage 1996. *Leisure interests:* travelling, English grammar, country life. *Address:* 14 The Green, Sutton Courtenay, Oxon., OX14 4AE, England; St. Peter's College, Oxford, OX1 2DL (Office). *Telephone:* (1235) 848645.

BURDA, Hubert, DPhil; German publisher and author; b. 9 Feb. 1940, Heidelberg; s. of Dr Franz Burda and Aenne Lemminger; ed Univ. of Munich; Man. Bild & Funk 1966–74; partner, Burda GmbH 1974, now Chair. Burda Group; Co-Publr Elle-Verlag GmbH, Munich; co-f. Europe Online SA, Luxembourg; Publr Anna, Bunte, Burda Moden, Das Haus, Elle, Elle Bistro, Elle Deco, Elle TopModel, Focus, Focus Online, Focus TV, Freundin, Freizeit Revue, Futurekids, Glücks Revue, Haus + Garten, Lisa, Lisa Kochen & Backen, Lisa Wohnen & Dekorieren, Mein schöner Garten, Meine Familie & ich, Norddeutsche Neueste Nachrichten, Schweriner Volkszeitung, Starwatch Navigation, Super Illu, Super TV, TraXXX, Verena; mem. Bd German School of Journalism, Munich; f. Petrarca Prize (for poetry), Bambi (Media-Prize), Corp. Art Prize 1997. *Address:* Arabellastrasse 23, 81925 Munich, Germany.

BURDETT-COUTTS, William Walter, MA; British artistic director and film and television producer; b. 17 Feb. 1955, Harare, Zimbabwe; s. of William A. F. Burdett-Coutts and Nancy C. Burdett-Coutts (née Gervers); one s., two d.; ed Radley Coll., Oxford, Rhodes Univ., South Africa, Univ. of Essex; Artistic Dir Ass. Rooms Edinburgh 1981–; Festival Dir Mayfest, Glasgow 1987–90; Head of Arts Granada TV 1990–93; Dir Riverside Studios 1993–; Exec. Producer Ass. Film and TV 1994–; Chair. Kiss 102 1993–97, Kiss 105 1996–97, Riverside TV Studios Ltd 2002–; Festival Dir Brighton Comedy Festival 2002–. *Address:* Riverside Studios, Crisp Road, London, W6 9RL, England. *Telephone:* (20) 8237-1075 (Office). *Fax:* (20) 8237-1071 (Office). *E-mail:* wbc@riversidestudios.co.uk (Office). *Website:* www.riversidestudios .co.uk (Office).

BUREAU, Jérôme, DHist; French journalist; b. 19 April 1956, Paris; m. Fabienne Pauly 1999; two c. (and two from a previous marriage); journalist with Libération 1978–81; Sr Reporter L'Équipe Magazine 1981–87, Ed.-in-Chief 1989–93; Ed.-in-Chief Le Sport 1987–88; Editorial Dir L'Équipe, L'Équipe-TV 1997–, L'Équipe Magazine, Vélo, XL, Tennis de France 1993–, lequipe.fr 1999–. *Publications:* L'Amour-Foot 1986, Les Géants du football 1996. *Leisure interests:* cookery, bullfighting. *Address:* 4 rue Rouget de l'Isle, 92793 Issy-les-Moulineaux, Cedex 09; 102 avenue Denfert-Rochereau, 75014 Paris, France (Home).

BURELLI RIVAS, Miguel Angel, LLB, DR.POL.SC.; Venezuelan diplomatist and lawyer; b. 8 July 1922; ed Univ. de Los Andes, Bogotá, Univ. Central de Venezuela y de Ecuador, Univ. Nacional de Bogotá, Univ. de Madrid and Univ. di Firenze; pre-seminary Prof. of Political Sociology and Chief Prof. of Mining and Agrarian Legislation, Faculty of Law, Univ. de Los Andes, Bogotá, Chief Prof. of Humanities I and II, Faculty of Civil Eng, Dir of Univ. Culture, Founder of School of Humanities, Founder-Dir of Univ. reviews, Bibliotheca and Universitas Emeritensis; Political Dir Ministry of the Interior; Dir-Gen. Ministry of Foreign Affairs (nine times Acting Minister); Interim Minister of Foreign Affairs; returned to legal profession 1961; mem. Venezuelan Supreme Electoral Council 1961; Minister of Justice 1964–65; Amb. to Colombia 1965–67, to UK 1967–69; Presidential Candidate 1968, 1973; Amb. to USA 1974–76; Minister of Foreign Affairs 1994–99; numerous decorations. *Address:* c/o Ministry of Foreign Affairs, Casa Amarilla Biblioteca Central, esq. Principal, Caracas 1010, Venezuela.

BURENGA, Kenneth L.; American publishing executive; b. 30 May 1944, Somerville, NJ; s. of Nicholas Burenga and Louanna Chamberlin; m. Jean Case 1964; one s. one d.; ed Rider Coll.; budget accountant, Dow Jones & Co., S Brunswick, NJ 1966–67, Asst Man. data processing control 1968–69, staff asst for systems devt 1970–71, Man. systems devt and control 1972–76, circulation marketing Man. 1977–78, circulation sales dir 1979–80, Vice-Pres. circulation and circulation dir 1980–86; Chief Financial Officer and Admin. Officer, Dow Jones & Co., New York 1986–88, Exec. Vice-Pres., Gen. Man. 1989–91, Pres. COO Dow Jones & Co. Inc. 1991–; Gen. Man. Wall Street

Journal 1989–; mem. Bd of Dirs Dow Jones Courier. *Leisure interest:* cattle farming. *Address:* Dow Jones & Co. Inc., 200 Liberty St, New York, NY 10281, USA.

BURG, Avraham, BA; Israeli politician; b. 1955; m.; six c.; ed Hebrew Univ., Jerusalem; army service; mem. Knesset 1988–; mem. Finance and State Control Cttees 1988–92; Chair. Educ. Cttee 1992–95; mem. Cttee for the Advancement of the Status of Women 1992–95; Chair. Jewish Agency for Israel 1995–99; fmr Chair. Zionist Movt; Speaker of Knesset 1999–. *Address:* The Knesset, Kiryat Ben-Gurion, Hakirya, Jerusalem 91950, Israel (Office).

BURGELIN, Jean-François, LenD; French civil servant; b. 17 Dec. 1936, Metz (Moselle); s. of Pierre Burgelin and Berthe du Mesnil du Buisson 1960; three s.; Deputy Public Prosecutor Nancy 1965; Premier Judge Pontoise 1973; Sec.-Gen. First Presidency Court of Appeal, Paris 1975, Solicitor-Gen. 1994–96; Prin. Pvt. Sec. (Sec. of State responsible for immigrant workers) 1976, to Minister of Work 1976; Sec. Higher Magistrate's Council 1977; Dir Ecole Nationale de la Magistrature 1978; Vice-Pres. Tribunal, Paris 1981; Pres. Court of Appeal, Paris 1982; Dir Office of Minister of Justice 1986; Councillor Court of Cassation 1986–94; Chief Public Prosecutor, Court of Appeal, Paris 1994; Solicitor-Gen., Court of Cassation 1996–; Commdr Légion d'honneur. *Address:* Cour de Cassation, 5 quai de l'Horloge, 75001 Paris, France. *Telephone:* 1-44-32-64-14. *Fax:* 1-44-32-77-10.

BURGEN, Sir Arnold (Stanley Vincent), Kt, MD, FRS; British scientist; b. 20 March 1922, London; s. of the late Peter and Elizabeth Burgen (née Wolfers); m. 1st Judith Browne 1946 (died 1993); two s. one d.; m. 2nd Olga Kennard 1993; ed Christ's Coll., Finchley, London, Middlesex Hospital Medical School; Demonstrator, later Asst Lecturer, Middlesex Hospital Medical School 1945–49; Prof. of Physiology, McGill Univ., Montreal 1949–62; Deputy Dir McGill Univ. Clinic, Montreal Gen. Hospital 1957–62; Sheild Prof. of Pharmacology, Univ. of Cambridge 1962–71; Dir Nat. Inst. of Medical Research, London 1971–82; Master Darwin Coll., Cambridge 1982–89; Deputy Vice-Chancellor, Cambridge Univ. 1983–89; mem. Medical Research Council (MRC) 1969–71, 1973–77, Hon. Dir MRC Molecular Pharmacology Unit 1967–72; Pres. Int. Union of Pharmacology 1972–75; Vice-Pres. Royal Soc. 1970–76, Foreign Sec. 1981–86; Fellow Downing Coll., Cambridge 1962–71, Hon. Fellow 1972; mem. Deutsche Akad. der Naturforscher Leopoldina 1984; mem. Bureau, European Science and Tech. Ass. 1994–; Ed. European Review 1993–; Corresp. mem. Royal Acad. of Spain 1984; Foreign Assoc. Nat. Acad. of Sciences, USA; Pres. Acad. Europaea 1988–94; Academician of Finland; Hon. FRCP, Canada; Hon. DSc (McGill, Leeds, Liverpool); Hon. MD (Zürich) 1983, (Utrecht); Hon. DUniv (Surrey) 1983; Wellcome Gold Medal 1999. *Publications:* papers in journals of pharmacology and physiology. *Leisure interests:* sculpture, music. *Address:* 8A Hills Avenue, Cambridge, CB1 7XA, England. *Telephone:* (1223) 415381. *Fax:* (1223) 334040. *E-mail:* asvb@cam.ac.uk (Office).

BURGER, Alewyn Petrus, FRSSA, MSc, DSc (Tech); South African scientist; b. 31 Jan. 1927, Middelburg, Transvaal; s. of the late D. J. Burger and M. M. Burger; m. Erica L. van der Merwe 1952; one s. four d.; ed Univ. of Pretoria and Tech. Univ., Delft; Research Meteorologist SA Weather Bureau, Pretoria 1950–57; Head Dept of Applied Math., Nat. Physics Research Lab., Council for Scientific and Industrial Research (CSIR) 1957–61; Dir Nat. Research Inst. for Math. Sciences, CSIR 1961–73, Vice-Pres. CSIR 1973–76; Chair. Scientific Advisory Council, Scientific Adviser to Prime Minister and Head of Science Planning 1977–81; Consultant in Atmospheric Sciences 1982–; Man. Impetus Magazine 1985–89; Dir Inst. of World Concerns 1990–; Chair. SA Math. Soc. 1961–63, 1973–75; Pres. Jt Council of Scientific Socs 1972–73; Pres. SA Soc. of Atmospheric Sciences 1989–91, 1995–97; Founder mem. Acad. of Science of SA 1996–; mem. SA Council for Natural Scientists 1988–91; Fellow SA Acad. for Sciences and Arts 1968–; accred professional trans., SA Trans. Inst. 2001; Hon. Prof. of Applied Math., Univ. of Stellenbosch 1979–80; Hon. mem. SA Soc. for Atmospheric Sciences 2001; Havenga Prize for Math. Sciences 1973. *Publications:* numerous scientific articles in int. journals. *Leisure interests:* Christian work, piano, athletics, tennis. *Address:* PO Box 17071, Groenkloof 0027, South Africa.

BURGESS, Ian Glencross, AO, BSc; Australian business executive; b. 26 Nov. 1931, Sydney; m. Barbara J. Hastie 1957; ed The King's School, Parramatta and Univ. of NSW; Man. Dir CSR Ltd 1987–93, Chair. 1997–; Chair. AMP Ltd 1994– (Dir 1989–); Dir Western Mining Co., Deputy Chair. 1997–, Chair. 1999–. *Leisure interests:* reading, golf. *Address:* AMP Ltd, Corner Phillip and Alfred Streets, Circular Quay, NSW 2000, Australia. *Telephone:* (2) 9257-7764 (Office).

BURGESS, Robert George, PhD, BA; British university vice-chancellor; b. 23 April 1947; s. of George Burgess and Olive Burgess (née Andrews); m. Hilary Margaret Mary Joyce 1974; ed Univ. of Durham, Univ. of Warwick; lecturer, Univ. of Warwick 1974–84, Sr lecturer 1984–88, Dept Chair. 1985–88, Dir Centre for Educational Devt Appraisal and Research 1987–99, Chair. Faculty of Social Sciences 1988–91, Prof. of Sociology 1988–99, Founder Chair. Grad. School 1991–95, Pro-Vice-Chancellor 1995–99; Vice-Chancellor, Univ. of Leicester 1999–; mem. Research Resources Bd, Econ. and Social Research Council 1991–96, mem. Council 1996–2000, Chair. Postgrad. Training Bd 1997–2000 (mem. 1989–93, Vice-Chair. 1996–97); Founder Chair. UK Council for Grad. Educ. 1993–99; Chair. East Midlands Univs Asscn 2001–; mem. Higher Educ. Funding Council for England Review of Postgrad. Educ. 1995–96, Bd UCAS 2001–, Jt Equality Steering Group 2001–;

Academician, Acad. of Learned Socs in the Social Sciences. *Publications* Experiencing Comprehensive Education 1983, In the Field 1984, Education, Schools and Schooling 1985, Sociology, Education and Schools 1986, Implementing In-Service Education (jtly) 1993, Research Methods 1993 and Ed. of 20 books on methodology and educ. *Leisure interests:* gardening, music, walking. *Address:* Vice-Chancellor's Office, University of Leicester, Leicester, LE1 7RH, England (Office). *Telephone:* (116) 252-2322 (Office). *Fax:* (116) 255-8691 (Office). *E-mail:* vc@admin.le.ac.uk (Office). *Website:* www.le.ac.uk.

BURGH, Sir John Charles, KCMG, CB, BSc (Econ), MA, FRCM; British administrator; b. 9 Dec. 1925, Vienna, Austria; m. Ann Sturge 1957; two d.; ed Friends' School, Sibford, London School of Economics; Leverhulme post-intermediate Scholarship, LSE, Pres. of Union 1949; mem. UK Del. to UN Conf. on Trade Devt 1964; Asst Sec., Dept of Econ. Affairs 1964; Prin. Pvt. Sec. to successive First Secs of State and Secs of State for Econ. Affairs 1965–68; Under-Sec., Dept of Employment 1968–71; Deputy Chair. Community Relations Comm. 1971–72; Deputy Sec. Cabinet Office (Cen. Policy Review Staff) 1972–74, Dept of Prices and Consumer Protection 1974–79, Dept of Trade 1979–80; Dir-Gen. British Council 1980–87; Pres. Trinity Coll., Oxford 1987–96; Dir English Shakespeare Co. 1988–94; Gov. LSE 1980–, Chair. 1985–87; mem. Exec., Political and Econ. Planning 1972–78, Council, Policy Studies Inst. 1978–85, Council Voluntary Service Overseas 1980–87, Wilton Park 1984–87; Chair. Assoc. Bd Royal Coll. of Music 1987–94, Nat. Opera Coordinating Cttee 1991– (Sec. 1972–91), Oxford Educational Trust for Devt of the Arts 1991–96; Vice-Chair. Int. Student House 1985–86, Chair. 1987–92; Vice-Chair., The Yehudi Menuhin School 1995–; Chair. New Berlioz Edn 1993–; Hon. Fellow LSE 1983, Trinity Coll. 1997; Hon. LLD (Bath); Hon. mem. Royal Northern Coll. of Music. *Leisure interests:* friends, music, the arts generally. *Address:* 2 Oak Hill Lodge, Oak Hill Park, London, NW3 7LN, England.

BURGHARDT, Walter J., MA, PhL, STL, STD; American theologian; b. 10 July 1914, New York; s. of John A. Burghardt and Mary Krupp; ed Woodstock Coll., The Catholic University of America; Prof. Patristic (Historical) Theology, Woodstock Coll. 1946–74; Lecturer Union Theological Seminary, New York City 1971–74; Prof. Patristic Theology, The Catholic Univ. of America 1974–78, Prof. Emer. 1978–; Visiting Lecturer in Theology, Princeton Theological Seminary 1972–73; Ed. Theological Studies 1967–90, Man. Ed. 1946–67; Co-ed. Ancient Christian Writers 1958–; mem. Bd of Patrons, Ecumenical Inst. for Advanced Theological Studies in Jerusalem (Tantur) 1981–; Chair. Cttee on Theology and Ethics, The Catholic Health Asscn of the US 1985–89; Dir Preaching the Just Word 1990–; mem. Corpn Jesuit Int. Volunteers Inc. 1986–90; mem. American Theological Soc., Asscn Int. d'Etudes Patristiques, Catholic Comm. on Intellectual and Cultural Affairs, Catholic Theological Soc. of America, Mariological Soc. of America, North American Acad. of Ecumenists, North American Patristic Soc.; Sr Fellow Woodstock Theological Center, Washington, DC 1990–; Mariological Award 1958, HE Cardinal Spellman Award 1962; 22 hon. degrees. *Publications include:* The Image of God in Man According to Cyril of Alexandria 1957, All Lost in Wonder: Sermons on Theology and Life 1960, Saints and Sanctity 1965, Seasons That Laugh or Weep: Musings on the Human Journey 1983, Preaching: The Art and the Craft 1987, Lovely in Eyes Not His: Homilies for an Imaging of Christ 1988, To Christ I Look: Homilies at Twilight 1989, Dare to be Christ 1990, When Christ meets Christ 1993, Speak the Word with Boldness 1994, Love is a Flame of the Lord 1995, Preaching the Just Word 1996, Let Justice Roll Down Like Waters 1998, Christ in Ten Thousand Places 1999, Long Have I Loved You: A Theologian Reflects on His Church 2000, Hear the Just Word and Live It 2000, To Be Just Is To Love: Homilies for a Renewing Church 2001; also author and ed. of many booklets, radio and TV programmes, lectures. *Leisure interests:* reading mysteries, theatre. *Address:* 19 Eye Street, NW, Washington, DC 20001, USA. *Telephone:* (202) 336-7187 (Office); (202) 336-7185 (Home). *Fax:* (202) 336-7217. *E-mail:* burgharw@georgetown.edu (Office). *Website:* www.georgetown.edu/centers/woodstock/pjw.htm (Office).

BURGIN, Victor, ARCA, MFA; British artist, author and lecturer; b. 24 July 1941, Sheffield; s. of Samuel Burgin and Gwendolyne A. Crowder; m. 1st Hazel P. Rowbotham 1964 (divorced 1975); m. 2nd Francette Pacteau 1988; two s.; ed Firth Park Grammar School, Sheffield, Sheffield Coll. of Art, Royal Coll. of Art, London and Yale Univ., USA; Sr Lecturer, Trent Polytechnic, Nottingham 1967–73; Prof. of History and Theory of Visual Arts, Faculty of Communication, Polytechnic of Cen. London 1973–; Prof. of Art History, Univ. of Calif., Santa Cruz 1988–95, Prof. of History of Consciousness 1995–2001, Prof. Emer. of History of Consciousness 2001–; Millard Chair. of Fine Art Goldsmiths Coll., London 2001–; Deutscher Akademischer Austauschdienst Fellowship 1978–79; Picker Professorship, Colgate Univ., Hamilton, New York 1980; mem. Arts Advisory Panel, Arts Council of GB 1971–76, 1980–81; numerous mixed and one-man exhbns at galleries around the world since 1965. *Publications:* Work and Commentary 1973, Thinking Photography 1982, The End of Art Theory 1986, Between 1986, Passages 1991, In/Different Spaces 1996, Some Cities 1996, Venice 1997, Shadowed 2000 and exhbn catalogues. *Address:* c/o Goldsmiths College, New Cross, London, SE14 6NW, England (Office); 1223 Diamond Street, San Francisco, CA 94131, USA. *Telephone:* (415) 821-4384.

BURGO, Carlos Duarte de; Cape Verde politician; b. 5 March 1958, Nova Sintra, Ilha da Brava; Prof. of Econs and Dir Instituto Amílcar Cabral; Pres. Municipal Ass. of Brava; Deputy for Nação; Pres. Special Perm. Comm. for Finance; currently Minister of Finance, Planning and Regional Devt; consultant for nat. and int. insts; mem. Nat. Council and Political Comm. of PAICV. *Address:* Ministry of Finance, Planning and Regional Development, 107 Avda Amílcar Cabral, CP 30, Praia, Santiago, Cape Verde (Office). *Telephone:* 61-43-50 (Office).

BURGON, Geoffrey; British composer and conductor; b. 15 July 1941, Hambledon; s. of Alan Wybert Burgon and Ada Vera Isom; m. 1st Janice Garwood 1963 (divorced); one s. one d.; m. 2nd Jacqueline Krofchak 1992; one s.; ed Pewley School, Guildford, Guildhall School of Music; freelance trumpeter/composer 1964–71; conductor 1964–; full-time composer 1971–; recipient of Ivor Novello Awards 1980, 1981, Gold Disc 1986, BAFTA Award 2001. *Compositions include (dramatic works):* Epitaph for Sir Walter Raleigh 1968, Joan of Arc 1970, The Fall of Lucifer 1977, Orpheus 1982, Hard Times (opera) 1990; (*orchestral and solo music*): Concerto for String Orchestra 1963, Gending 1968, Alleluia Nativitas 1970, Paradise Dances (Brass Band) 1994, City Adventures 1997, Singapore Vtns 1997, Fantasia on REX 1997, A Different Dawn 1999; (*with voices*): Acquainted with Night 1965, Think on Dredful Domesday 1969, Canciones del Alma 1975, Requiem 1976, Magnificat and Nunc dimittis 1979, The World Again 1983, Revelations 1984, Title Divine 1986, A Vision 1990, Trumpet concerto 1992, First Was the World 1993, Music's Empire 1993, Merciless Beauty 1997; (*ballet music*): The Golden Fish 1964, The Calm 1974, Running Figures/Goldberg's Dream 1975, Songs, Lamentations and Praises 1979, Mass 1984, Prometheus 1988; (*chamber music*): Four Guitars 1977, Six Studies 1980, Waiting (for solo pianoforte) 1993, Almost Peace 1995, The Wanderer 1998, Recitativo 1998, Dancers in a Landscape 1999; (*with voices*): Hymn to Venus 1966, Five Sonnets of John Donne 1967, Worldës Blissë 1971, Two Love Songs, Lunar Beauty 1986, Nearing the Upper Air 1988, Heavenly Things 2000; (*choral music*): Three Elegies 1964, Short Mass 1965, Golden Eternity 1970, The Fire of Heaven 1973, Dos Coros 1975, A God and Yet a Man 1984, Prayer to St Richard 1989, Songs of the Creation 1989, The Song of the Creatures 1989, Five Love Songs, The First World 1991, Christ's Love 2000, Magic Words 2000; (*music for children*): Divertimento 1964, Five Studies 1965, Now Welcome Summer 1966, Beginnings 1969; (*film music*): Life of Brian 1979, Dogs of War 1980, Turtle Diary 1985, Robin Hood 1991, When Trumpets Fade 1998; (*TV music*): Dr Who 1975, Tinker Tailor Soldier Spy 1979, Brideshead Revisited 1981, Testament of Youth 1979, How Many Miles to Babylon 1981, Bewitched 1983, The Death of the Heart 1985, Happy Valley 1987, The Old Wives Tale 1988, Sophia and Constance 1988, The Chronicles of Narnia 1988–90, Children of the North 1990, A Foreign Field 1992, Martin Chuzzlewit 1994, Silent Witness 1995, Turning World 1996, Cider with Rosie 1998, Longitude 2000, Labyrinth 2001, The Forsyte Saga 2002. *Leisure interests:* cricket, jazz, wasting money on old Bristols. *Address:* Chester Music, 8–9 Frith Street, London W1V 5TZ, England. *Telephone:* (20) 7434-0066. *Fax:* (20) 7287-6329.

BURGOS, Norma, B.A., M.P.A.; Puerto Rican politician and city planner; two s.; ed Univ. of Puerto Rico, Georgia Inst. of Tech.; various admin. posts with San Juan municipality 1976–; Pres. and Exec. Dir Corpn for Redevt of Old San Juan (CODEVISA) 1986–90; in charge of special project Puerto Rico 2005; Assoc. mem. and Chair Puerto Rico Planning Cttee; Sec. of State 1995–99; Exec. Dir Gov.'s Council for Econ. Productivity; Senator 1999–; Hon. Dr rer. pol (Caribbean Univ.), Eagle Award, Distinguished Citizen of Puerto Rico 1966. *Publications:* Transnacionalización en la Década del 80 (co-author) 1984, Administración Pública en Puerto Rico ante el Nuevo Siglo (co-author) 1996. *Address:* Partido Nuevo Progresista, POB 1992, Fernández Zuncos Station, San Juan 00910, Puerto Rico.

BURJANADZE, Nino, PhD; Georgian politician; b. 16 July 1964; m. Bitsadze Badri; two s.; ed Tbilisi State Univ., Moscow State Univ.; Prof. Tbilisi State Univ. 1991–; expert Georgian Ministry of Environmental Protection 1992–94; consultant Foreign Relations Cttee 1992–95; mem. Georgian Del. to OSCE Parl. Ass. 1995–, Vice-Pres. OSCE Parl. Ass. 2000–; mem. Parl. 1995–; Deputy Chair. Cttee on Constitutional, Legal Affairs and Rule of Law 1995–98, Chair. 1998–99; Chair. Perm. Parl. Del. to UK 1995–98; rapporteur Gen. Cttee on Democracy, Human Rights and Humanitarian Issues 1998–2000; Chair. Cttee on Foreign Relations 2000–01, Perm. Parl. Del. to European Parl. 2000–; Chair. Parl. of Georgia 2001–; Political Sec. Citizen's Union of Georgia 1997–2000. *Publications:* numerous articles and papers in Russian and Georgian on int. law and int. relations. *Address:* Parliament of Georgia, Tbilisi, Georgia (Office). *Telephone:* (32) 99-90-60 (Office).

BURKE, Bernard Flood, PhD; American physicist and astrophysicist; b. 7 June 1928, Boston, Mass.; s. of Vincent Paul Burke and Clare Aloyse Brine; m. 1st Jane Chapin Pann 1953 (died 1993); three s. one d.; m. 2nd Elizabeth King Platt 1998; ed Mass. Inst. of Technology; mem. of staff, Carnegie Inst. of Washington 1953–65; Chair. Radio Astronomy Section, Carnegie Inst. of Washington, Dept of Terrestrial Magnetism 1962–65; Prof. of Physics, MIT 1965–2000, William Burden Prof. of Astrophysics 1981–2000; Visiting Prof., Leiden Univ. 1971–72, Manchester Univ. 1992–93; Pres. American Astronomical Soc. 1986–88; Ed. Comments on Astrophysics 1984–87; Trustee Associated Univ. Inc. 1972–90; Trustee and Vice-Chair. NE Radio Observatory Corpn 1973–82, Chair. 1982–95; Oort lecturer Leiden Univ. 1993, Karl Jansky Lecturer, Nat. Radio Astronomy Observatory 1998; mem. Nat. Science Bd 1990–96; mem. Nat. Science Bd American Acad. of Arts and Sciences, NAS; Sr Fellow Carnegie Inst. of Washington 1997; Fellow, AAAS; Sherman Fairchild Scholar, Calif. Inst. of Tech. 1984–85; Smithsonian Regents Fellow

1985; Helen B. Warner Prize, American Astron. Soc. 1963, Rumford Prize, American Acad. of Arts and Sciences 1971, NASA Achievement Award 1989. *Publications:* Microwave Spectroscopy 1953–54, Radio Noise from Jupiter 1955–61, Galactic Structure 1959–, Very Long Baseline Interferometry 1968–, Interstellar Masers 1968–, Gravitational Lenses 1980–, Interferometry in Space 1984–; miscellaneous publs in radio astronomy 1955–. *Leisure interests:* skiing, sailing, hiking, chamber music. *Address:* c/o Massachusetts Institute of Technology, Department of Physics, Cambridge, MA 02139 (Office); 10 Bloomfield Street, Lexington, MA, USA (Home). *Telephone:* (617) 862-8939 (Home).

BURKE, Kathy; British actress; b. London; ed Anna Scher's Theatre School, London. *TV includes:* Harry Enfield and Chums, Absolutely Fabulous, Common as Muck, Mr Wroe's Virgins (Royal TV Soc. Award), Tom Jones, Gimme Gimme Gimme. *Films:* Scrubbers, Nil by Mouth (Best Actress, Cannes Film Festival 1997, Best Actress, British Ind. Film Awards 1998), Elizabeth 1998, This Year's Love 1999, Love, Honour and Obey 2000, The Martins 2001. *Theatre includes:* Mr Thomas, London, Boom Bang-a-Bang, London (Dir).

BURKE, Philip George, CBE, PhD, FInstP, FAPS, MRIA, FRS; British professor of mathematical physics; b. 18 Oct. 1932, London; s. of Henry Burke and Frances Mary Burke (née Sprague); m. Valerie Mona Martin 1959; four d.; ed Univ. Coll. of SW of England, Exeter, Univ. Coll., Univ. of London; Research Fellow Univ. Coll., Univ. of London 1956–57, Lecturer Computer Unit 1957–59; Research Physicist, Alvarez Bubble Chamber Group, Theory Group, Lawrence Radiation Lab., Berkeley, Calif. 1959–62; Prin. Scientific Officer, then Sr Prin. Scientific Officer, Atomic Energy Research Establishment, Harwell 1962–67; Prof. of Math. Physics Queen's Univ., Belfast 1967–98, Emer. Prof. 1998–, Head Dept of Applied Math. and Theoretical Physics 1974–77, Dir School of Math. and Physics 1988–90; Chair. Inter-Council High Performance Computing Man. Cttee 1996–98; Head Div. Theory and Computational Science, Science and Eng Research Council, Daresbury Lab., Cheshire 1977–82 (Jt appointment with Queen's Univ.); mem. UK Science and Eng Research Council 1989–94, Chair. Supercomputing Man. Cttee 1991–94; mem. Council Royal Soc. 1990–92; Fellow Univ. Coll., London 1986; Hon. DSc (Exeter) 1981, (Queens Univ., Belfast) 1999; Inst. of Physics' Guthrie Medal and Prize 1994, Sir David Bates Prize 2001. *Publications:* over 350 articles in many specialist journals; author or co-author of seven books. *Leisure interests:* walking, books, music. *Address:* Department of Applied Mathematics and Theoretical Physics, Queen's University, Belfast, BT7 1NN, Northern Ireland (Office); Brook House, Norley Lane, Crowton, Northwich, Cheshire, CW8 2RR, England (Home). *Telephone:* (2890) 335047 (Office); (1928) 788301 (Home). *Fax:* (2890) 239182 (Office). *E-mail:* p.burke@qub.ac.uk (Office).

BURKE, Ray; Irish politician; b. 30 Sept. 1943, Dublin; m. Anne Fassbender; two d.; ed O'Connell's Co. Boys' School, Dublin; mem. Dublin County Council 1967–78, Chair. 1985–87; mem. Dail 1973–; Minister of State, Dept of Industry and Commerce and Energy 1978–80, Minister for Environment 1980–81, 1982, for Energy and Communications 1987–88, for Industry, Commerce and Communications 1988–89, for Justice and for Communications 1989–92, for Foreign Affairs July–Oct. 1997; Fianna Fáil. *Address:* Dáil Éireann, Dublin 2; Briargate, Malahide Road, Swords, Co. Dublin, Ireland (Home).

BURKE, Sir Thomas Kerry, Kt, BA; New Zealand politician; b. 24 March 1942, Christchurch; m. 1st Jennifer Shiel (divorced 1984); two s.; m. 2nd Helen Paske 1984 (died 1989); one s.; ed Univ. of Canterbury, Christchurch Teachers' Coll.; general labourer in Auckland 1965–66, Factory del., Auckland Labourers' Union; teacher, Rangiora High School 1967, Chair. Rangiora Post-Primary Teachers' Asscn 1969–71; MP for Rangiora 1972–75, for West Coast 1978–90; teacher Greymouth High School 1975–78; Minister of Regional Devt and of Employment and Immigration 1984–87; Speaker, New Zealand Parl. 1987–91; Labour. *Leisure interests:* skiing, swimming.

BURKE, Tom, CBE, BA, FRSA; British environmental policy adviser; b. 5 Jan. 1947, Cork, Ireland; s. of J. V. Burke and Mary Bradley; ed St Boniface's, Plymouth, Liverpool Univ.; Great George's Community Arts Project 1969–70; lecturer, W Cheshire Coll. 1970–71, Old Swan Tech. Coll. 1971–73; Local Groups Co-ordinator, Friends of the Earth 1973–75, Exec. Dir 1975–79, Dir of Special Projects 1979–80, Vice-Chair. 1980–81; Press Officer European Environment Bureau 1979–87, mem. Exec. Cttee 1987–91; Dir The Green Alliance 1982–92; Sec. Ecological Studies Inst. 1987–92; Special Adviser to Sec. of State for Environment 1991–97; Adviser to Rio Tinto PLC 1996–, to BP PLC 1997–2001; Adviser, Cen. Policy Group, Office of the Deputy Prime Minister 2002–; mem. Bd of Dirs Earth Resources Research 1975–87, Waste Man. Advisory Council 1976–81, Packaging Council 1978–82, Exec. Cttee Nat. Council for Voluntary Orgs 1984–89, UK Nat. Cttee European Year of the Environment 1986–88, Council, Royal Soc. for Nature Conservation 1993–97, mem. Council Royal Soc. of Arts 1990–92, Overseas Cttee, Save the Children Fund 1992–97; mem. High Level Advisory Group on the Environment, OECD 1996–97; stood as Social Democrat Party cand. Gen. Elections 1983, 1987; Visiting Prof. Imperial Coll. London Univ. 1997–; Visiting Fellow, Cranfield 1991–94; mem. Council English Nature 1999–, American Chem. Council Leadership Dialogue 2002–; Hon. Visiting Fellow Manchester Business School 1984; Royal Humane Soc. Testimonials on Vellum 1966, on Parchment 1968; UNEP Global 500 Laureate 1993. *Publications:* Europe:

Environment 1981, Pressure Groups in the Global System (jtly) 1982, Ecology 2000 (jtly) 1984, The Green Capitalists (jtly) 1987, Green Pages (jtly) 1988. *Leisure interests:* photography, birdwatching. *Address:* Studio 2, Clink Wharf Studios, Clink Street, London, SE1 9DG, England. *Telephone:* (20) 7357-9146.

BURKE, (Ulick) Peter, MA, FRHistS, FBA; British historian; b. 16 Aug. 1937, Stanmore; s. of John Burke and Jenny Burke (née Colin); m. 1st Susan Patricia Dell 1972 (divorced 1983); m. 2nd Maria Lucía García Pallares 1989; ed St Ignatius' Coll., Stamford Hill, St John's Coll., Oxford, St Antony's Coll., Oxford; Asst Lecturer, then Lecturer, then Reader in History (later Intellectual History) School of European Studies, Univ. of Sussex 1962–78; Lecturer in History Univ. of Cambridge 1979–88, Reader in Cultural History 1988–96, Prof. of Cultural History 1996–; Fellow Emmanuel Coll. Cambridge 1979–; Visiting Prof. Univ. of São Paulo, Brazil 1986, 1987, Nijmegen Univ. 1992–93, Groningen Univ. 1998–99; Fellow Wissenschaftskolleg, Berlin 1989–90; Erasmus Prize, Academia Europaea 1999. *Publications:* Culture and Society in Renaissance Italy 1972, Venice and Amsterdam 1974, Popular Culture in Early Modern Europe 1978, Historical Anthropology of Early Modern Italy 1987, The Fabrication of Louis XIV 1992, The Fortunes of the Courtier 1995, The European Renaissance 1998, A Social History of Knowledge 2000, Eyewitnessing 2001, (jtly) A Social History of the Media 2002. *Leisure interest:* travel. *Address:* Emmanuel College, Cambridge, CB2 3AP (Office); 14 Warkworth Street, Cambridge, CB1 1EG, England (Home). *Telephone:* (1223) 334272.

BURLAND, John Boscawen, PhD, FRS, FREng, FICE, FIStructE; British professor of engineering and civil engineer; b. 4 March 1936, Little Chalfont; s. of John Whitmore Burland and Margaret Irene Burland (née Boscawen); m. Gillian Margaret Burland (née Miller) 1963; two s. one d.; ed Parktown Boys' High School, Univ. of the Witwatersrand, Johannesburg, Cambridge Univ.; engineer Ove Arup and Partners, London 1961–63; SSO then PSO, Bldg Research Station (BRS), Watford 1966–72, Head Geotechnics Div. 1972–79, Asst Dir BRS 1979–80; Prof. of Soil Mechanics, Imperial Coll. of Science, Tech. and Medicine, London Univ. 1980–; Kelvin Medal, Baker Medal, Kevin Nash Gold Medal, Gold Medal, Inst. of Structural Engineers, Gold Medal, Inst. of Civil Engineers, Kt Commdr of the Royal Order of Francis I, Italy. *Publications:* numerous papers on soil mechanics and civil eng. *Leisure interests:* golf, painting, sailing. *Address:* Department of Civil Engineering, Imperial College Road, London, SW7 2BU, England (Office). *Telephone:* (20) 7594-6079 (Office). *Fax:* (20) 7225-2716 (Office). *E-mail:* j.burland@ic.ac.uk (Office).

BURLATSKY, Fedor Mikhailovich, DPhil; Russian journalist, writer and politician; b. 4 Jan. 1927, Kiev; s. of Mikhail Burlatsky and Sofia Burlatsky; m. 1st Seraphyma Burlatsky 1952 (divorced 1974); two s.; m. 2nd Kyra Burlatsky 1974; one d.; ed Tashkent Law Inst.; journalist Tashkent 1948–50; postgrad. at Inst. of State Law, USSR Acad. of Sciences 1950–53; journalist with Kommunist 1953–59; head of section in Cen. Cttee Dept for Liaison with Communist and Workers' Parties of Socialist Countries 1959–65; political observer with Pravda 1965–67; Deputy Dir of USSR Inst. of Sociological studies 1968–72; head of section, USSR Inst. of State and Law (later Chief Scientific Researcher 1990–) and Head of Philosophy Dept, Inst. of Social Science, Cen. Cttee of CPSU 1975–88; Vice-Pres. Soviet Assoc. of Political Science 1976; USSR People's Deputy 1989–91; Chair. Subcttee on Humanitarian, Scientific and Cultural Co-operation, Cttee on Foreign Affairs 1989–91; political observer Literaturnaya Gazeta 1983–90, Ed.-in-Chief 1990–91; Chair. of Public Comm. for Int. Co-operation on Humanitarian Problems and Human Rights 1987–90; Dir Public Consultative Council to Chair. of State Duma 1993–96; Chief Scientific Researcher Inst. of State and Law 1992–; Visiting Prof. Heidelberg Univ. 1988, Harvard Univ. 1992, Oxford Univ. 1993; Pres. Euro-Asian Fund for Humanitarian Co-operation 1996–, Int. League for Defence of Culture; Chair., Scientific Council on Politology, Pres. Russian Acad. of Sciences 1995–; mem. Acad. of National Sciences 1993, Acad. of Socio-Political Sciences 1996; Italian Senate Prize 1988. *Publications include:* Mao Zedong (biography) 1976, The Modern State and Politics 1978, The Legend of Machiavelli 1987, New Thinking 1988, Leaders and Advisers 1990, Khrushchev and the First Russian Spring 1992, The End of the Red Empire 1993, Russian Sovereigns–Age of the Reformation 1996. *Leisure interest:* tennis. *Address:* Institute of State and Law, Znamenka str. 10, 119841 Moscow, Russia (Office); Novovagankovsky per. 22, Apt 90, 123022 Moscow, Russia (Home). *Telephone:* (095) 291-88-16 (Office); (095) 291-85-06 (Home). *Fax:* (095) 291-87-56 (Office). *E-mail:* isl-ran@rinet.ru (Office).

BURLEIGH, A. Peter; American diplomatist and government official; b. 7 March 1942, Los Angeles; ed Colgate Univ.; teaching fellow Wharton School, Univ. of Pa; Deputy Asst Sec. of State, Bureau of Near Eastern and South Asian Affairs 1987–89, Prin. Deputy Asst Sec. of State for Intelligence and Research 1989–91; Co-ordinator Office of Counter-Terrorism 1991–92; Prin. Deputy Asst Sec. of State for Personnel 1992–95; Amb. to Sri Lanka (also Accred to the Maldives) 1995–97; Deputy Rep. to UN 1997–99, Chargé de Mission 1998–99; Amb. to Repub. of Philippines (also Accred to Palau) 1999–2000; Fulbright Scholar; mem. Asia Soc., American Foreign Service Asscn; numerous Dept of State Superior Honor Awards, Sr Foreign Service Presidential Award, Meritorious Service Award. *Address:* c/o Department of State, 2201 C Street, Washington, DC 20520 (Office); 2300 Riverlane Terrace, Fort Lauderdale, FL 33312-4762, USA (Home). *E-mail:* apburl@bellsouth.net (Home).

BURNET, Alastair (see Burnet, Sir J. W A).

BURNET, Sir James William Alexander (Alastair), Kt; British journalist; b. 12 July 1928, Sheffield, Yorks.; s. of the late Alexander Burnet and Schonaid Burnet; m. Maureen Campbell Sinclair 1958; ed The Leys School, Cambridge and Worcester Coll., Oxford; Sub-Ed. and Leader Writer, Glasgow Herald 1951–58, Leader Writer The Economist 1958–62; Political Ed., Independent Television News 1963–64, with ITN 1976–91, Dir 1982–90, Assoc. Ed. ITN 1981–91; Ed. The Economist 1965–74; Ed. Daily Express 1974–76; Contributor to TV current affairs programmes, This Week, Panorama, News at Ten, etc.; Ind. Dir Times Newspapers Holdings Ltd 1982–; mem. Council of the Banking Ombudsman 1985–96; Dir United Racecourses Ltd 1985–94; Hon. Vice-Pres. Inst. of Journalists 1990; Richard Dimbleby Award, BAFTA 1966, 1970, 1979, Royal Television Society Judges' Award 1981, Hall of Fame 1999. *Address:* 43 Hornton Court, Campden Hill Road, London, W8 7NT, England. *Telephone:* (20) 7937-7563.

BURNEY, Mohammad Ilyas, MBBS, MCPath, FCPS, FRCPath; Pakistani professor of virology; b. 1 Jan. 1922; est. first Dept of virology at Armed Forces Inst. of Pathology, Pakistan 1959, later first Measles and HDC Rabies Vaccine Production Labs in the developing world; isolated Congo virus 1976 and Chlamydia trachomatis and EV-70 and Coxsackie-21 viruses in the course of his career; new species of Phlebotomus named after him in recognition of pioneering work on viruses; Emer. Prof. Army Medical Coll.; Fellow Islamic Acad. of Sciences, Pakistan Acad. of Sciences Nat. Acad. of Medical Sciences, Pakistan; Hilal-i-Imtiaz Prize 1982, Shousha Award, WHO 1984. *Publications:* 7 books/monographs and over 80 research papers. *Address:* Islamic Academy of Sciences, PO Box 830036, Amman, Jordan (Office). *Telephone:* 5522104 (Office). *Fax:* 5511803 (Office).

BURNEY, Sayed Muzaffir Hussain, MA; Indian politician; b. 14 Aug. 1923, Bulandshahr, Uttar Pradesh; s. of Ejaz Hussain Burney and Imtiazi Burney; m. Sabeeha Burney; three s. two d.; entered Indian Admin. Service; various posts, including Jt Sec., Ministry of Agric. 1965–72, Additional Sec. in Ministry of Petroleum and Chemicals 1973–75, Sec., Ministry of Information and Broadcasting 1975–77, Sec., Ministry of Home Affairs 1980–81; served Orissa Govt as Divisional Commr and Chief Sec. 1979–80; Gov. of Nagaland, Manipur and Tripura, then Haryana 1981–88; Chair. Minorities Comm. 1988–92 and Chancellor Jamia Millia Islamia. *Publications:* Iqbal Poet – Patriot of India, Collected Letters of Iqbal (in Urdu), Collected Speeches. *Address:* F-3/17, Vasant Vihar, New Delhi 110057, India.

BURNHAM, James B., PhD; American banker; b. 22 Oct 1939, New York; s. of James Burnham and Marcia Lightner; m. Anne Mullin 1964; two s. two d.; ed Milton Acad., Princeton Univ., Washington Univ., St Louis; Economist and special Asst, Federal Reserve Bd, Washington, DC 1969–71; Sr Economist, Mellon Bank, Pittsburgh, Pa 1971–74, Vice-Pres. 1974–81, Sr Vice-Pres. 1985–, Office of Govt Affairs 1979–81, Chair. Country Review Cttee 1977–81; Staff Dir and Special Asst to Chair., Pres.'s Council of Economic Advisers, Washington, DC 1981–82; US Exec. Dir IBRD, Washington, DC 1982–85; Fulbright Scholar, Univ. of São Paulo, Brazil 1962. *Publications:* articles on contemporary economic subjects. *Leisure interests:* canoeing, bridge. *Address:* Mellon Bank, 1 Mellon Bank Center, Suite 0400, Pittsburgh, PA 15258, USA.

BURNS, Conrad Ray; American politician; b. 25 Jan. 1935, Gallatin, Mo.; s. of Russell Burns and Mary Frances Burns (née Knight); m. Phyllis Jean Kuhlmann; one s. one d.; ed Univ. of Missouri; Field Rep. Polled Hereford World magazine, Kansas City 1963–69; Public Relations Officer Billings Livestock Cttee, Montana 1969–73; Founding Pres. Ag-Network 1975–86; Farm Dir KULR TV 1974; Commr Yellowstone Co. 1987–89; mem. Republican Party; Senator from Montana 1989–, Chair. Appropriations Sub-cttee of Mil. Construction, Cttee on Science and Transportation, Sub-cttee of Cttees, Energy and Natural Resources Cttee; mem. Ageing Cttee, Small Business Cttee; mem. Nat. Asscn of Farm Broadcasters. *Leisure interest:* football officiating. *Address:* Office of the Senator from Montana, US Senate, Senate Buildings, Washington, DC 20510, USA (Office).

BURNS, Duncan Thorburn, PhD, DSc, CChem, FRSC, MRIA, FRSEdin.; British professor emeritus of analytical chemistry; b. 30 May 1934, Wolverhampton; s. of James Thorburn Burns and Olive Mary Constance Burns (née Waugh); m. 1st Valerie Mary Vinton 1961 (divorced 1994); one s. two d.; m. 2nd Celia Mary Thorburn-Burns 1994; ed Whitcliffe Mount School and Leeds Univ.; Asst Lecturer in Physical Chem., Medway Coll. of Tech. 1958–59, 1959–63; Sr Lecturer in Analytical Chem., Woolwich Polytechnic 1963–66, Loughborough Univ. 1966–71, Reader 1971–75; Prof. of Analytical Chem., Queen's Univ., Belfast 1975–99, Prof. Emer. 1999–; Redwood Lecturer, Royal Soc. of Chem. 1982, Pres. Analytical Div. 1988–90; Fellow Inst. of Chemistry in Ireland, European Chemist; Hon. mem. Pharmaceutical Soc. of NI 2001; Reagents and Reactions Royal Soc. of Chemistry Medal and Award 1982, Boyle/Higgens Gold Medal, Inst. of Chem. of Ireland 1990, Ehren Nadel in Gold, Analytical Inst. Technische Univ. Wien 1990, AnalaR Gold Medal, Royal Soc. of Chem. 1990, SAC Gold Medal, Royal Soc. of Chem. 1993, Fritz Pregl Medal, Austrian Chemical Soc. 1993, Tertiary Chemical Educ. Medal and Award, Royal Soc. of Chem. 1995, Sigillum Magnum, Univ. of Bologna 1996. *Publications:* seven books and over 350 papers. *Leisure interest:* history of chemistry. *Address:* 318 Stranmillis Road, Belfast, BT9 5EB, Northern Ireland (Home). *Telephone:* (2890) 668567. *Fax:* (2890) 668567. *E-mail:* profburns@chemistry.fsbusiness.co.uk (Office).

BURNS, John Fisher; British journalist; b. 4 Oct. 1944, Nottingham, England; s. of Air Cdre R. J. B. Burns and Dorothy Burns (née Fisher); m. 1st Jane Pequegnat 1972 (divorced); m. 2nd Jane Scott-Long 1991; two s. one d.; ed Stowe School, McGill Univ., Canada and Harvard Univ., USA; Foreign Corresp. New York Times 1975–80, Soviet Union 1981–84, China 1984–86, Canada 1987–88, Afghanistan 1989–90, Persian Gulf 1990, Balkans 1991–94, India 1994–98, currently Special Corresp. for Islamic Affairs 1999–; Pulitzer Prize for Int. Reporting 1993 (co-winner for reporting from Bosnia), 1997 (for coverage of the Taliban regime in Afghanistan); George Polk Prize for Foreign Correspondence 1978, 1997. *Leisure interests:* golf, music, motor racing. *Address:* New York Times, 229 W 43rd Street, New York, NY 10036, USA.

BURNS, John Joseph, PhD; American pharmacologist; b. 8 Oct. 1920, Flushing, NY; s. of Thomas F. Burns and Katherine Kane; ed Queens Coll. and Columbia Univ.; Deputy Chief, Lab. of Chemical Pharmacology, Nat. Heart Inst. 1958–60; Dir of Research, Pharmacodynamics Div. The Wellcome Research Labs 1960–66; Vice-Pres. for Research and Devt Hoffman-La Roche 1966–84; Adjunct Prof. Rockefeller Univ. 1984–94; Adjunct mem. Roche Inst. of Molecular Biology 1984–96; Visiting Prof. of Pharmacology, Cornell Univ. Medical Coll. 1996–; mem. NAS; mem. NAS Inst. of Medicine; Fellow American Inst. Chemists. *Leisure interests:* equestrian sports. *Address:* 331 Lansdowne, Westport, CT 06880-5651, USA. *Telephone:* (203) 255-6374. *Fax:* (203) 255-5508.

BURNS, R. Nicholas, MA; American diplomatist; b. 28 Jan. 1956, Buffalo, NY; m. Elizabeth Baylies; three d.; ed Univ. of Paris, Boston Coll., Johns Hopkins School of Advanced Int. Studies; before entering Foreign Service worked in US Embassy in Mauritania and as programme officer for AT Int.; Vice-Consul and Staff Asst to Amb., Cairo 1983–85; political officer, Consulate-Gen., Jerusalem 1985–87; staff officer, Operations Center and Secr., Dept of State 1987–88, Special Asst to Counsellor 1989–90; Adviser to Pres. George Bush on Greece, Turkey and Cyprus and Dir for Soviet (later Russian) Affairs; Special Asst to Pres. Clinton and Sr Dir for Russia, Ukraine and Eurasia Affairs; Spokesman, Dept of State and Acting Asst Sec. for Public Affairs 1995–97; Amb. to Greece 1997–2001; Perm. Rep. to NATO, Brussels 2002–; mem. Council on Foreign Relations, Int. Inst. for Strategic Studies; Dr hc (Worcester Polytechnic Inst.) 1997, Superior Honor Award (three times), Order of the Terra Mariana (Estonia) and other awards; OStJ. *Address:* North Atlantic Treaty Organization, boulevard Léopold III, 1110 Brussels, Belgium (Office). *Telephone:* (2) 707-41-11 (Office). *Fax:* (2) 707-45-79 (Office). *E-mail:* natodoc@hq.nato.int. *Website:* www.nato.int.

BURNS, Sir Robert Andrew, KCMG, MA; British diplomatist; b. 21 July 1943, London; s. of the late Robert Burns CB, CMG and Mary Burns (née Goodland); m. Sarah Cadogan 1973; two s. one d.; ed Highgate School, Trinity Coll. Cambridge, School of Oriental and African Studies, London Univ.; joined Diplomatic Service 1965, served in New Delhi 1967–71, FCO, London and UK Del. to CSCE 1971–75, First Sec. and Head of Chancery, Bucharest 1976–78, Pvt. Sec. to Perm. Under-Sec. and Head of Diplomatic Service, FCO 1979–82, Counsellor (Information) and Head of British Information Services, Washington, DC and New York 1983–86, Head S Asian Dept, FCO 1986–88, Head News Dept 1988–90, Asst Under-Sec. of State (Asia), FCO 1990–92; Amb. to Israel 1992–95; Deputy Under-Sec. of State (non-Europe, Trade and Investment Promotion) 1995–97; British Consul-Gen., Hong Kong Special Admin. Region and Macau 1997–2000; High Commr in Canada 2000–. *Publication:* Diplomacy, War and Parliamentary Democracy 1989. *Leisure interests:* music, theatre, country pursuits. *Address:* British High Commission, 80 Elgin Street, Ottawa, Ont. K1P 5K7, Canada (Office). *Telephone:* (613) 237-1530 (Office). *Fax:* (613) 237-7980 (Office).

BURNS, Baron (Life Peer), cr. 1998, of Pitshanger in the London Borough of Ealing; **Terence Burns,** GCB, BAEcon; British economist; b. 13 March 1944, Durham; s. of the late Patrick Owen Burns and Doris Burns; m. Anne Elizabeth Powell 1969; one s. two d.; ed Houghton-le-Spring Grammar School and Victoria Univ. of Manchester; held various research positions at the London Business School 1965–70, Lecturer in Econs 1970–74, Sr Lecturer in Econs 1974–79, Dir Centre for Econ. Forecasting 1976–79, Prof. of Econs 1979; Chief Econ. Adviser to the Treasury and Head Govt Econ. Service 1980–91; Perm. Sec. to Treasury 1991–98; Chair. Inquiry into Hunting 1999; Chair. Financial Services and Markets Jt Cttee 1999–, Nat. Lottery Comm. 2000–01, Abbey National PLC 2002–; Dir Pearson 1999–; Dir (non-exec.) Legal and General Group PLC 1999–; Vice-Pres. Soc. of Business Economists 1985–99, Pres. 1999–; Fellow, London Business School 1989–; mem. Council Royal Econ. Soc. 1986–91, Vice-Pres. 1992–; Visiting Prof. Durham Univ. 1995–; Gov. Royal Acad. of Music 1998–; Hon. DScS (Manchester) 1992. *Leisure interests:* Dir Queen's Park Rangers Football team 1996–2001, music and golf. *Address:* Abbey National PLC, Abbey House, 2 Triton Square, Regent's Place, London, NW1 3AN (Office); House of Lords, London, SW1A 0PW, England. *Telephone:* (20) 7219-0312 (Office). *E-mail:* burnst@parliament.uk (Office).

BURNS, William Joseph, PhD; American diplomatist; m. Lisa Carty; ed LaSalle Univ., Oxford Univ.; entered Foreign Service 1982; political officer, US Embassy, Amman; mem. staff Bureau of Near E Affairs, Office of Deputy Sec. of State; Special Asst to the Pres., Sr Dir for Near E and S Asian Affairs, Nat. Security Council; Acting Dir and Prin. Deputy Dir State Dept's Policy Planning; Minister-Counsellor for Political Affairs, Moscow; Exec. Sec., State Dept and Special Asst to Sec. of State; Amb. to Jordan 1998–2000; Asst Sec.

of State for Nr Eastern Affairs 2001–; Distinguished Honor Award, James Clement Dunn Award, five Superior Honor Awards. *Publication:* Economic Aid and American Policy toward Egypt, 1955–1981. *Address:* c/o Department of State, 2201 C Street, NW, Washington, DC 20520-6243, USA (Office).

BURNSTOCK, Geoffrey, PhD, DSc, FAA, FMedSci, FRS; Australian/British university professor; b. 10 May 1929, London, England; s. of James Burnstock and Nancy Green; m. Nomi Hirschfeld 1957; three d.; ed London and Melbourne Univs; Nat. Inst. for Medical Research, London 1956–57; Dept of Pharmacology, Oxford Univ. 1957–59; Dept of Physiology, Illinois Univ. 1959; Sr Lecturer, Dept of Zoology, Melbourne Univ. 1959–62, Reader 1962–64, Prof. and Chair. 1964–75, Assoc. Dean (Biological Sciences) 1969–72, Prof. Emer. 1993–; Visiting Prof., Dept of Pharmacology, Univ. of Calif. 1970; Vice-Dean, Faculty of Medical Sciences, Univ. Coll., London 1980–83, Prof. of Anatomy 1975–, Head of Dept of Anatomy and Developmental Biology 1975–97, Convenor, Centre for Neuroscience 1979–, Fellow 1996, Dir Autonomic Neuroscience Inst., Royal Free and Univ. Coll. Medical School UCL 1997–; Contract Prof., Univ. of Siena 1985–87, Univ. of Milan 1993–94; Visiting Prof., Royal Soc. of Medicine Foundation, New York 1988; Chair. Scientific Advisory Bd, Eisai London Ltd 1990–96; Chair. Bd of Clinical Studies, Royal Nat. Orthopaedic Hosp. Trust 1996; Pres. Int. Soc. for Autonomic Neuroscience 1995–2000, Int. Neurovegetative Soc. 1995–, British Asscn (Medical); Founder FMedSci 1998; mem. Academia Europaea 1992; mem. Russian Soc. of Neuropathology 1993; Ed.-in-Chief, Journal of the Autonomic Nervous System 1992–; mem. Bd of over 30 journals; Hon. FRCS; Hon. FRCP; Hon. MRCP 1987; Dr hc (Antwerp) 2002; Royal Soc. of Vic. Silver Medal 1970, Special Award, NIH Conf., Bethesda 1989, Royal Medal, Royal Soc. 2000, Janssen Award for Lifetime Achievement 2000. *Publications include:* Adrenergic Neurons: Their Organisation, Function and Development in the Peripheral Nervous System 1975, An Atlas of the Fine Structure of Muscle and its Innervation 1976; Ed. Purinergic Receptors 1981, Somatic and Autonomic Nerve-Muscle Interactions 1983, Nonadrenergic Innervation of Blood Vessels 1988, Peptides: A Target for New Drug Development 1991, Nitric Oxide in Health and Disease 1997, Cardiovascular Biology of Purines 1998; series Ed. The Autonomic Nervous System (Vols 1–14) 1992–97, Neural-Endothelial Interactions in the Control of Local Vascular Tone 1993, Nitric Oxide in Health and Disease 1997, Cardiovascular Biology of Purines 1998; also author of over 1,000 publs in scientific and medical journals and books. *Leisure interests:* wood sculpture, tennis. *Address:* Autonomic Neuroscience Institute, Royal Free and University College Medical School, Royal Free Campus, Rowland Hill Street, London, NW3 2PF, England (Office). *Telephone:* (20) 7830-2948 (Office). *Fax:* (20) 7830-2949 (Office). *E-mail:* g.burnstock@ucl.ac.uk (Office). *Website:* www.ucl.ac.uk/ani (Office).

BURNYEAT, Myles Fredric, FBA; British professor of philosophy; b. 1 Jan. 1939; s. of Peter James Anthony Burnyeat and Cynthia Cherry Warburg; m. 1st Jane Elizabeth Buckley 1971 (divorced 1982); one s. one d.; m. 2nd Ruth Sophia Padel 1984 (divorced 2000); one d.; ed Bryanston School and King's Coll., Cambridge; Asst Lecturer in Philosophy, Univ. Coll., London 1964, Lecturer 1965; Lecturer in Classics, Cambridge Univ. 1978, Lecturer in Philosophy, Robinson Coll. 1978, Fellow 1978–96; Laurence Prof. of Ancient Philosophy, Cambridge 1984–96, Sr Research Fellow in Philosophy, All Souls Coll., Oxford 1996–; Foreign Hon. mem. American Acad. of Arts and Sciences 1992–. *Publications:* Co-Ed. Philosophy As It Is 1979, Doubt and Dogmatism 1980, Science and Speculation 1982; The Sceptical Tradition 1983 (Ed.), The Theaetetus of Plato 1990, The Original Sceptics 1997 (Co-Ed.), A Map of Metaphysics Zeta 2001. *Leisure interest:* travel. *Address:* All Souls College, Oxford, OX1 4AL, England.

BURRELL, Leroy; American athlete; b. 21 Feb. 1967, Lansdowne, Philadelphia; m. Michelle Finn (fmr Olympic sprinter); two s.; ed Pen Wood High School, Lansdowne and Univ. of Houston, TX; fmr world-class sprinter and long jumper; set world record, running 100m in 9.9 seconds at US Championships, New York June 1991; set another world record 100m July 1994; Olympic gold medal 4×100m relay, Barcelona 1992; Head Track and Field Coach, Univ. of Houston 1998–. *Address:* c/o USA Track and Field Press Information Department, 1 RCA Dome, Suite 140, Indianapolis, IN 46225, USA.

BURRINGTON, Ernest; British newspaper executive; b. 13 Dec. 1926; s. of the late Harold Burrington and of Laura Burrington; m. Nancy Crossley 1950; one s. one d.; reporter, Oldham Chronicle 1941–44, reporter and sub-ed. 1947–49; mil. service 1945–47; sub-ed. Bristol Evening World 1950; sub-ed. Daily Herald, Manchester 1950, night ed. 1955, London night 1957; night ed. IPC Sun 1964, Asst ed. 1965; Asst ed. and night News Int. Sun 1969; deputy night ed. Daily Mirror 1970; Deputy Ed. Sunday People 1971, Assoc. Ed. 1972; Ed. The People 1985–88, 1989–90; Dir Mirror Group Newspapers 1985–92, Deputy Chair. and Asst Publr 1988–91, Man. Dir 1989–91, Chair. 1991–92; Chair. Syndication Int. 1989–92; Deputy Chair. Mirror Publishing Co. 1989–91; Dir Mirror Group Magazine and Newsday Ltd 1989–92, Legionstyle Ltd 1991–92, Mirror Colour Print Ltd 1991–92; Dir (non-exec.) Sunday Correspondent 1990, The European 1990–91, IQ Newsgraphics 1990–92, Sygma Picture Agency, Paris 1990–91; Deputy Publr Globe Communications, Montreal, Canada 1993–95, Exec. Vice-Pres. and Assoc. Publr 1995–96; Pres. Atlantic Media 1996–98; Consultant Head of Marketing Harveys PLC, UK 1998–2000; mem. Council Nat. Press Asscn 1988–92, Int. Press Inst. British Exec. 1988–92, Foreign Press Asscn; Trustee Int. Centre for Child Studies 1986–90; Life mem. NUJ 1960–; Hon. Life mem. NUJ 1996; Hon. Red Devil (Manchester United FC) 1985. *Leisure interests:* travel, bridge, Manchester United FC, East India Club. *Address:* 17499 Tiffany Trace Drive, Boca Raton, FL 33487, USA; South Hall, Dene Park, Shipbourne Road, Tonbridge, TN11 9NS, England. *Telephone:* (561) 995-9897 (USA); (1732) 368517 (England). *Fax:* (561) 995-9897 (USA); (1732) 368517 (England). *E-mail:* ernestburrington@aol.com (Home); burringtone@aol.com (Home).

BURRIS, Robert Harza, PhD, DSc; American professor of biochemistry; b. 13 April 1914, Brookings, S Dak.; s. of Edward Thomas Burris and Mable Harza Burris; m. Katherine Irene Brusse 1945; one s. two d.; ed S Dakota State Coll. and Univ. of Wisconsin; Research Asst, Univ. of Wis. 1936–40; Nat. Research Council Postdoctoral Fellow, Columbia Univ. 1940–41; Instructor in Bacteriology, Univ. of Wis. 1941–44, Asst Prof. of Biochemistry 1944–46, Assoc. Prof. 1946–51, Prof. 1951–, Chair. Dept of Biochemistry 1958–70; mem. NAS, American Acad. of Arts and Sciences, American Philosophical Soc., Foreign Fellow of the Indian Nat. Science Acad. 1985; Guggenheim Fellow 1954; Pres. American Soc. of Plant Physiologists 1960; Hon. DSc (S Dakota State Univ.) 1966; Merit Award of Botanical Soc. of America 1966; American Soc. of Plant Physiologists Stephen Hales Award 1968, Charles Reid Barnes Award 1977, Soc. for Industrial Microbiology Charles Thom Award 1977, American Soc. of Agronomy Edward W Browning Award 1978, Nat. Medal of Science 1980, NAS Carty Award 1984, Wolf Award 1985, ACS Spencer Award 1990. *Publications:* Manometric Techniques 1945, Biological Nitrogen Fixation 1992; 350 scientific papers 1936–2001. *Leisure interests:* photography, lapidary, vitreous enamelling. *Address:* 1015 University Bay Drive, Madison, WI 53705 (Home); Department of Biochemistry, University of Wisconsin, 433 Babcock Drive, Madison, WI 53706, USA. *Telephone:* (608) 262-3042. *Fax:* (608) 262-3453. *E-mail:* burris@biochem.wisc.edu (Office).

BURROW, John Wyon, MA, PhD, FBA; British professor of history; b. 4 June 1935, Southsea; s. of Charles Burrow and Alice (Vosper) Burrow; m. Diane Dunnington 1958; one s. one d.; ed Exeter School and Christ's Coll. Cambridge; Research Fellow, Christ's Coll. Cambridge 1959–62; Fellow and Dir of Studies in History, Downing Coll. Cambridge 1962–65; Reader, School of European Studies, Univ. of E Anglia 1965–69; Reader in History, Univ. of Sussex 1969–82, Prof. of Intellectual History 1982–95; Visiting Fellow All Souls Coll. Oxford Univ. 1994–95, Prof. of European Thought and Fellow of Balliol Coll. 1995–2000, Emer. Fellow 2001–; Research Prof. of History, Univ. of Sussex 2000–; Visiting Prof. Univ. of Calif. Berkeley 1981; Visiting Fellow, History of Ideas Unit, Australian Nat. Univ. 1983; Carlyle Lecturer, Oxford Univ. 1985; Ed. History of European Ideas 1996–; delivered Gauss Seminars, Princeton Univ. 1988; Hon. Dr Political Sciences (Bologna) 1988; Distinguished Visiting Prof. Ben Gurion Univ. of the Negev 1988; Wolfson Prize for History 1981. *Publications:* Evolution and Society 1966, A Liberal Descent 1981, That Noble Science of Politics 1983, Gibbon 1985, Whigs and Liberals 1988, The Crisis of Reason 2000. *Leisure interest:* cooking. *Address:* Arts Building, University of Sussex, Falmer, Brighton, East Sussex, BN1 9QN; 22 Bridge Street, Witney, Oxon. OX18 2HY, England (Home). *Telephone:* (1993) 700306.

BURROW, Sharan; Australian trade unionist; b. 1954, Warren, NSW; ed Univ. of New South Wales; fmr Pres. Bathurst TLC; fmr Sr Vice-Pres. NSW Teachers' Fed.; fmr mem. Bd Curriculum Corpn; Vice-Pres. Educ. Int. 1995; Pres. Australian Educ. Union 1993–2000; Pres. Australian Council of Trade Unions (ACTU) May 2000–. *Address:* Australian Council of Trade Unions (ACTU), 2nd Floor, 393 Swanston Street, Melbourne, Vic. 3000, Australia (Office). *Website:* www.actu.asn.au.

BURROWES, Norma Elizabeth, BA, FRAM; British opera and concert singer; b. Bangor, Co. Down; d. of Henry Burrowes and Caroline Burrowes; m. 1st Steuart Bedford (q.v.) 1969 (divorced 1980); m. 2nd Emile Belcourt 1987; one s. one d.; ed Queen's Univ., Belfast, Royal Acad. of Music; début with Glyndebourne Touring Opera singing Zerlina in Don Giovanni 1969, début with Royal Opera House, Fiakermili in Arabella 1976; sings regularly with Glyndebourne Opera, Scottish Opera, Aldeburgh Festival, English Nat. Opera, Welsh Nat. Opera and others; abroad: Salzburg, Paris, Munich, Aix-en-Provence, Avignon, Ottawa, Montreal, New York, Vienna, Chicago, Buenos Aires; has sung with all the prin. London orchestras and on BBC radio and TV; numerous recordings; Hon. DMus (Queen's Univ., Belfast) 1979; Order of Worshipful Co. of Musicians. *Roles include:* Blöndchen in The Abduction from the Seraglio, Oscar (Ballo in Maschera), Despina (Così Fan Tutte), Woodbird (Siegfried), Sophie (Der Rosenkavalier), Cunning Little Vixen, Manon (Massenet), Titania (Midsummer Night's Dream), Nanetta (Falstaff), Gilda (Rigoletto), Marie (Daughter of the Regiment), Juliet (Romeo and Juliet), Adina (Elisir d'Amore), Susanna (Nozze di Figaro), Lauretta (Gianni Schicchi). *Leisure interests:* gardening, embroidery. *Address:* c/o Royal Academy of Music, Marylebone Road, London, NW1, England.

BURROWS, Gen. Eva, AC, BA, MEd; Australian Salvation Army leader (retd); b. 15 Sept. 1929, Newcastle, Australia; d. of Robert J. Burrows and Ella M. Watson; ed Brisbane State High School and Queensland, London and Sydney Univs; Missionary educator, Howard Inst., Zimbabwe 1952–67; Prin. Usher Inst., Zimbabwe 1967–69; Vice-Prin. Int. Coll. for Officers, London 1970–73, Prin. 1974–75; Leader, Women's Social Services in GB and Ireland 1975–77; Territorial Commdr Sri Lanka 1977–79, Scotland 1979–82, Australia 1982–86; Gen. of the Salvation Army 1986–93; Dr hc (Ewha Woman's Univ., Seoul) 1988, (Melbourne Coll. of Divinity) 2000; Hon. LLD (Asbury Coll., USA) 1988, (Univ. of NSW) 1996; Hon. DD (Olivet Univ., USA) Hon. PhD (Queensland Univ.) 1993; Hon. DUniv (Griffith Univ.) 1994. *Leisure interests:* classical music, reading, travel. *Address:* 102 Domain Park, 193 Domain Road, South Yarra, Vic. 3141, Australia. *Telephone:* (3) 9820-9701. *Fax:* (3) 9866-5240.

BURROWS, (James) Stuart; British opera singer; b. 7 Feb. 1933, Cilfynydd, S. Wales; s. of Albert Burrows and Irene (Powell) Burrows; m. Enid Lewis 1957; one s. one d.; ed Trinity Coll., Carmarthen; school teacher until début Royal Opera House, Covent Garden 1967; a leading lyric tenor and has sung in world's major opera houses including San Francisco, Vienna, Paris, Buenos Aires (Théâtre Cologne) and Brussels (Théâtre de la Monnaie) as well as Covent Garden and Metropolitan Opera, New York; toured Far East with Royal Opera 1979 and sang with co. at Olympic Festival, Los Angeles 1984; four US tours with Metropolitan Opera; concert appearances throughout Europe and N America, under Solti, Barenboim, Mehta, Ozawa, Bernstein and Ormandy, including two recitals in Brahmssaal, Vienna; BBC TV series Stuart Burrows Sings 1978–85 also radio broadcasts; many recordings, including Die Zauberflöte, Don Giovanni, Die Entführung aus dem Serail, La Clemenza di Tito, La Damnation de Faust, Les Contes d'Hoffmann, Maria Stuarda, Anna Bolena, Eugene Onegin, The Midsummer Marriage, Messiah, Grande Messe des Morts (Berlioz), Les Nuits d'Eté, Das Klagende Lied, Beethoven's 9th (Choral) Symphony and single discs of Mozart arias, Operetta Favourites, German and French songs, popular ballads and Welsh songs; Pres. Save the Children, Cancer Research; Hon. DMus (Wales) 1981; Dr hc (Univ. Coll. of Wales, Aberystwyth). *Leisure interests:* breeding koi carp, gardening, snooker, listening to music. *Address:* 29 Blackwater Grove, Alderholt, Dorset, SP6 3AD, England (Office). *E-mail:* stuartburrows@nicholls.f9.co.uk (Office). *Website:* www.stuartburrows.f9.co.uk (Office).

BURSON, Harold, BA; American public relations consultant; b. 15 Feb. 1921, Memphis; s. of Maurice Burson and Esther Burson; m. Bette Foster 1947; two s.; ed Univ. of Mississippi; Acting Dir Ole Miss News Bureau 1938–40; Reporter Memphis Commercial Appeal 1940; Asst to Pres. and Public Relations Dir, H. K. Ferguson Co. 1941–43; operated own Public Relations firm for six years; Chair. Burson-Marsteller 1953–, CEO 1953–88; Public Relations Adviser to Pres. Reagan 1989–94; Dir World Environmental Center 1998–; Exec. Vice-Pres. of Young and Rubicam Inc., mem. Exec. Cttee 1979–85; Garrett Lecturer on Social Responsibility, Columbia Univ., Grad. School of Business 1973; Hon. Prof. Fudan Univ., Shanghai 1999; Exec.-in-residence, Univ. Kentucky Coll. Comm. 2000; Visiting Prof. Leeds Univ. 2001; Vice-Pres. and Mem. Exec. Cttee Nat. Safety Council 1964–77; Int. Trustee World Wildlife Fund 1977–81; Trustee and mem. Exec. Cttee Foundation for Public Relations Research and Educ. 1978–84; Founder and Sec. Corporate Fund, John F. Kennedy Centre for the Performing Arts 1977; Dir Kennedy Cen. Productions Inc. 1974–89; presidential appointee to Fine Arts Comm. 1981–85; White House appointee to Exec. Cttee Young Astronauts Co. 1984–88; mem. Advisory Cttee, Medill School of Journalism, Northwestern Univ. 1985, Grad. School of Business, Emory Univ. 1986; Trustee Ray Simon Inst. of Public Relations, Syracuse Univ. 1985; mem. Public Relations Soc. of America, Int. Public Relations Asscn of Business Communicators, Overseas Press Club, NY Soc. of Security Analysts, Exec. Cttee, Catalyst Inc. 1977–88, Public Relations Advisory Cttee, US Information Agency 1981; Assoc. mem. NY Acad. of Medicine; Counsellor Nat. Press Foundation; Trustee The Economic Club of NY; Chair. Jt Council on Econ. Educ., Public Relations Seminar 1983; Hon. DHumLitt (Boston Univ.) 1988, Hon. Prof. (Shanghai) 1999; Public Relations Professional of the Year Award (Public Relations News) 1977, Gold Anvil Award (Public Relations Soc. of America) 1980, Univ. of Mississippi Alumni Hall of Fame 1980, Silver Em Award (Mississippi Press Asscn) 1982, Arthur Page Award, Univ. of Texas 1986, Horatio Alger Award 1986, Nat. Public Relations Achievement Award, (Ball State Univ.), Inside PR Life Achievement Award 1993. *Leisure interests:* stamp collection, West Highland White terriers. *Address:* Burson-Marsteller, 230 Park Avenue South, New York, NY 10003-1513, USA. *Telephone:* (212) 614-4444 (Office). *Fax:* (212) 598-5679 (Office). *E-mail:* harold_burson@nyc.bm.com (Office).

BURSTYN, Ellen; American actress; b. 7 Dec. 1932, Detroit, Mich.; d. of John Austin and Coriene Marie (née Hamel) Gillooly; m. 1st William C. Alexander; m. 2nd Paul Roberts; m. 3rd Neil Burstyn; one s.; ed Cass Tech. High School, Detroit, Mich.; Co-Artistic Dir The Actor's Studio, New York 1982–88; Pres. Actors' Equity Asscn 1982–88; Dir Judgement (off Broadway) 1981, Into Thin Air 1985; Best Supporting Actress, The Last Picture Show (New York Film Critics' Award, Nat. Soc. of Film Critics' Award); Best Actress, Alice Doesn't Live Here Anymore (Acad. Award, British Acad. Award); Best Actress, Same Time Next Year (Tony Award, Drama Desk Award, Outer Critics' Circle Award). *Stage Productions include:* Fair Game 1957, Same Time Next Year 1975, 84 Charing Cross Road, Shirley Valentine 1989–90. *Films include:* Goodbye Charlie 1964, For Those Who Think Young 1965, Tropic of Cancer 1969, Alex in Wonderland 1970, The Last Picture Show 1971, The King of Marvin Gardens 1972, Thursday's Game (TV), 1973, The Exorcist 1973, Harry and Tonto 1974, Alice Doesn't Live Here Anymore 1975, Providence 1976, Dream of Passion 1978, Same Time Next Year 1978, Resurrection, Silence of the North 1980, Alamo Bay 1985, Twice in a Lifetime 1985, Hannah's War 1987, When You Remember Me (TV Film), The Colour of Evening 1990, Dying Young 1990, The Cemetery Club 1993, When a Man Loves A Woman 1994, Roommates 1994, How to Make an American Quilt 1995, The Babysitters Club 1995, Deceiver 1997, You Can Thank Me Later 1998, Playing By Heart 1998, Walking Across Egypt 1999, Requiem for a Dream 1999, The Yards 1999, Divine Secrets of the Ya-Ya Sisterhood 2002. *Television films:* Into Thin Air 1985, Getting Out 1994, The Matchmaker 1996, A Will of Their Own 1998, Deceiver 1998, Night Ride Home 1999, Mermaid 2000, Dodson's Journey 2001, Within These Walls 2001. *Address:* c/o CAA, 9830 Wilshire Blvd, Beverly Hills, CA 90212, USA.

BURT, Sir Peter Alexander, Kt, MA, MBA, FCIBS, FIB (Scot.); British banker; b. 6 March 1944; s. of Robert W. Burt and May H. Rodger; m. Alison Mackintosh Turner 1971; three s.; ed Merchiston Castle School, Edin., Univs of St Andrews and Pennsylvania; joined Hewlett Packard, Calif. 1968–70; worked for CSL, Edin. 1970–74, then Edward Bates & Sons Ltd 1974; moved to Bank of Scotland 1975, Int. Div. 1975–88 (Head 1985), Asst Gen. Man. 1979–84, Divisional Gen. Man. 1984–85, Jt Gen. Man. 1985–88, Treas. and Chief Gen. Man. 1988–96, mem. Bd of Dirs 1995–03, Chief Exec. 1996–2001, Gov. 2001–03; Exec. Deputy Chair. HBOS (formed after merger of Halifax PLC with Bank of Scotland) 2001–03; mem. High Constables and Guard of Honour Holyrood House, Edin. *Leisure interests:* golf, skiing, gardening, reading. *Address:* c/o Bank of Scotland, The Mound, Edinburgh, EH1 1YZ, Scotland (Office).

BURT, Robert Amsterdam, MA, JD; American professor of law; b. 3 Feb. 1939, Philadelphia, Pa; s. of Samuel Mathew Burt and Esther Amsterdam Burt; m. Linda Gordon Rose 1964; two d.; ed Princeton, Oxford and Yale Univs; Law Clerk, US Court of Appeals, Dist of Columbia Circuit 1964–65; Asst Gen. Counsel, Exec. Office of the Pres. of USA 1965–66; Legis. Asst, US Senate 1966–68; Assoc. Prof. of Law, Chicago Univ. 1968–70; Assoc. Prof. of Law, Michigan Univ. 1970–72, Prof. of Law 1972–73, Prof. of Law and Prof. of Law in Psychiatry 1973–76; Prof. of Law, Yale Univ. 1976–, Southmayd Prof. of Law 1982–93, Alexander M. Bickel Prof. 1993–; Special Master US Dist Court, Conn. 1987–92; Rockefeller Fellowship in Humanities 1976; mem. Bd of Dirs, Benhaven School for Autistic Persons 1977–, Chair. 1983–96, Mental Health Law Project 1985–, Chair. 1990–2000; Dir Yale Hillel Foundation 1996–; mem. Inst. of Medicine and NAS 1976, Advisory Bd Open Soc. Inst. Project on Death in America; John Simon Guggenheim Fellowship 1997. *Publications:* Taking Care of Strangers: The Rule of Law in Doctor-Patient Relations 1979, Two Jewish Justices: Outcasts in the Promised Land 1987, The Constitution in Conflict 1992, Death is That Man Taking Names 2002. *Leisure interests:* cello, swimming, bicycling. *Address:* Yale Law School, PO Box 208215, 127 Wall Street, New Haven, CT 06520 (Office); 66 Dogwood Circle, Woodbridge, CT 06525, USA (Home). *Telephone:* (203) 432-4960 (Office); (203) 393-3881 (Home). *Fax:* (203) 432-4982 (Office); (203) 393-1292 (Home). *E-mail:* robert.burt@yale.edu (Office).

BURTON, Ian, MA, PhD, FRSC; Canadian/British environmental scientist, geographer, scholar and consultant; b. 24 June 1935, Derby, England; s. of Frank Burton and Elsie Victoria Barnes; m. 1st Lydia Demodoff 1962 (divorced 1977); one s. one d.; m. 2nd Anne V. T. Whyte 1977 (divorced 1995); one s. two d.; ed Derby School, Univ. of Birmingham, Univ. of Chicago and Oberlin Coll., Ohio; Lecturer Univ. of Ind. 1960–61; Queen's Univ., Kingston, Ont. 1961; Consultant Ford Foundation, India 1964–66; Prof. Univ. of Toronto 1968–90, Adjunct Prof. 1990–, Dir Inst. for Environmental Studies 1979–84; Prof. of Environmental Science Univ. of E Anglia 1972–73; Sr Adviser Int. Devt Research Centre, Ottawa 1972–75; Sr Connaught Fellow, École des Hautes Études en Sciences Sociales, Paris 1984–86; Dir Int. Fed. of Insts for Advanced Study 1986–92; Dir Environmental Adaptation Research, Atmospheric Environmental Service 1990–96, Scientist Emer. 1996–; mem. Bd of Dirs Foundation for Int. Training 1994–; mem. Ind. World Comm. on the Oceans 1995–98; mem. Int. Soc. of Biometeorology, Vice-Pres. 1996–2002, Pres. 2002–; numerous Cttee and consultant assignments with UNESCO, WHO, UNEP, Rockefeller Foundation, UNDP, World Bank Global Environment Facility, World Resources Inst., Intergovernmental Panel on Climate Change, European Comm., Ford Foundation, projects in Sudan and Nigeria etc.; Fellow World Acad. of Art and Sciences; mem. Jury, St Francis Environment Prize; Order of Zvonkova (USSR) 1968. *Publications:* co-wrote: The Human Ecology of Coastal Flood Hazard in Megalopolis 1968, The Hazardousness of a Place: A Regional Ecology of Damaging Events 1971, The Environment as Hazard 1978; co-ed.: Readings in Resource Management and Conservation 1986, Environmental Risk Assessment 1980, Living with Risk 1982, Geography, Resources and Environment 1986. *Leisure interests:* swimming, sailing, hiking, cricket. *Address:* Atmospheric Environment Service, 4905 Dufferin Street, Downsview, Ont., M3H 5T4 (Office); 72 Coolmine Road, Toronto, Ont., M6J 3E9, Canada (Home). *Telephone:* (416) 538-2034. *Fax:* (416) 739-4297.

BURTON, Richard St John Vladimir, CBE, RIBA; British architect; b. 3 Nov. 1933, London; s. of Percy Basil Harmsworth Burton and Vera (née Poliakoff Russell); m. Mireille Dernbach-Mayen 1956; three s. one d.; ed Bryanston, Architectural Asscn School of Architecture; Dir Ahrends Burton and Koralek 1961–; founder and Trustee, Makepeace School for Craftsmen in Wood 1977–83; Chair. of numerous cttees including Arts Council of England Architecture Advisory Group, Nat. Steering Cttee Per Cent for Art 1990–92, RIBA Steering Group on Architectural Educ. 1991–93, Health Bldgs for the 21st Century; NHS Estates 1991–93, Patient Care Study 1993, Building a 2020 Vision: Future Heathcare Environments; Chair. NHS Design Brief Working Group 2001–02; mem. ACE Visual Arts Panel 1994–98; Patron, Arts for Health, Axis, Healing Arts, Isle of Wight. *Design projects include:* Chichester Theological Coll. 1964, Trinity Coll. Dublin Library 1967, Templeton Coll., Oxford 1965–96, Hooke Park Coll., Dorset 1983–90, St Mary's Hosp., Isle of Wight 1991, Lawson Practice Primary Care Centre, London

1997, Housing Estates, Basildon, Essex 1974–80, New British Embassy, Moscow 1988–2000. *Publications:* Ahrends Burton and Koralek 1991, (jtly) The Architecture of ABK 2002. *Leisure interests:* building and writing. *Address:* Ahrends Burton and Koralek, Unit 1, 7 Chalcot Road, London, NW1 8LH (Office); 1B Lady Margaret Road, London, NW5 2NE, England (Home). *Telephone:* (20) 7586-3311 (Office); (20) 7267-1198 (Home). *Fax:* (20) 7722-5445 (Office). *E-mail:* abk@abklondon.com (Office); r.burton@abklondon.com (Home). *Website:* www.abk.co.uk (Office).

BURTON, Tim; American film director; b. 25 Aug. 1958, Burbank, Calif.; ed Calif. Arts Inst.; began career as animator, Walt Disney Studios (projects included The Fox and the Hound and The Black Cauldron); animator and Dir Vincent; short-length film awards include two from Chicago Film Festival. *Films directed:* Frankenweenie (short, for Disney) 1984, Pee-Wee's Big Adventure 1985, Beetlejuice 1988, Batman 1989, Edward Scissorhands 1991, Batman Returns 1992, Ed Wood 1994, Mars Attacks! 1996, Sleepy Hollow 1999, Planet of the Apes 2001, The Heart of Me 2002; producer The Nightmare Before Christmas 1993, Cabin Boy 1994, Batman Forever 1996, James and the Giant Peach 1996, Lost in Oz (TV) 2000. *Publications:* My Art and Films 1993, The Melancholy Death of Oyster Boy and Other Stories 1997. *Address:* Chapman, Bird & Grey, 1990 South Bundy Drive, Suite 200, Los Angeles, CA 90025, USA.

BURWITZ, Nils, BA; German artist, sculptor and university professor; b. 16 Oct. 1940, Swinemünde; s. of Ulrich Burwitz and Johanna Lohse; m. Marina Schwezoff 1964; two s. one d.; ed Univ. of Witwatersrand and postgrad. studies in London, Fribourg and Salzburg; emigrated to S Africa 1958; settled in Balearic islands 1976; 102 one-man exhbns including 36 Exposures 1971 and restrospective exhbn in Sollerich Palace, Palma, Majorca 1985, Pretoria Art Museum, Pretoria 1991, Nat. Gallery 1992, Kunsthalle Munich-Germering 1995; visual concept for stage works Iconostasis 1967–68, 8 Birds 1969, 8 Beasts 1970, Gentlemen (with R. Kirby) 1972, Mobile (with V. Rodzianko), London 1972, Retalls de l'Ignorancia (with R. Esteras) 1978, Llagrimes del Vienès (with A. Ballester 1995; stained glass windows in churches of St Philip and St James and Sta Eulalia, Palma de Mallorca, Monastery of Lluch and La Ermita de la Santísima Trinidad, Valldemossa, Majorca; founder, Libra Press 1984; opened Funda Art Centre, Soweto, SA 1986; works in 84 public collections including: Albertina, Vienna, Ludwig Museum, Cologne, Nat. Portrait Gallery, Wash., Museum of Modern Art, Tokyo, Vic. and Albert Museum, London; has made three video documentaries in SA and Namibia; corresp. mem. European Acad., Rome; portfolios: Locust Variations 1967, It's About Time 1973, Tidal Zone 1974, Heads or Tails? 1981, 9 Terraces 1986, The Journey to Dresden 1989, The Invisible Miró 1995, Marinas Terraces 1995; numerous honours and awards including Gold Medal (Design), Johannesburg 1963, African Arts Centre Award, Durban 1971, Art Critics' Award, XI Graphic Biennale, Ljubljana 1975, Prix de la Ville de Monaco 1981, Primer Premio 'Ciutat de Palma' 1982, Merit Award, II Biennale of Painting, Barcelona 1987. *Publication:* On the Razor's Edge 1995. *Leisure interests:* swimming, diving. *Address:* Calle Rosa 22, Valldemossa, E-07170 Majorca, Spain. *Telephone:* (971) 612838. *Fax:* (971) 612839.

BURY, Pol; Belgian sculptor; b. 26 April 1922, Haine-St Pierre; s. of Jules Bury and Augusta Modave; m. Velma Horne 1971; one d.; ed Ecole St Joseph, Haine-St Paul, Athénée Provinciale, La Louvière and Acad. des Beaux Arts, Mons; painter 1938–; sculptor 1953–; Prof. Univ. of Calif. Berkeley 1970, Minneapolis Coll. of Art 1972, Ecole Nat. Supérieure des Beaux Arts, Paris 1983–87; one-man exhbns in USA, Germany, Netherlands, Belgium, Mexico; fountains at Univ. of Iowa 1964, Palais Royal, Paris 1985, Univ. of Yamagata 1994, etc.; mirrors at Newark Airport 1987; Dr hc (Minneapolis Coll. of Art); Grand Prix Nat. de Sculpture, Paris 1985; Médaille de la Résistance; Chevalier, Légion d'honneur, Officier Ordre de la Couronne (Belgium). *Exhibitions include:* Fontaines Hydrauliques, San Francisco 1990, Monotypes Numeriques, Gallerie Caré, Paris 2002. *Publications:* L'Art à Bicyclette et la Révolution 1972, Les Gaîtes de l'Esthétique 1984, Le Monochrome Bariolé 1991. *Leisure interest:* reading. *Address:* 12 Vallée de la Taupe, 78200 Perdreauville; 236 boulevard Raspail, 75014 Paris, France. *Telephone:* 1-34-78-33-31; 1-43-21-52-11. *Fax:* 1-34-78-04-77.

BUSEK, Erhard, DJur; Austrian politician; b. 25 March 1941, Vienna; m. Helga Busek; ed Univ. of Vienna; Second Sec. Parl. Austrian People's Party (ÖVP); joined Fed. Exec. Cttee of Austrian Econ. Fed. 1968, Deputy Sec.-Gen. 1969, Sec.-Gen. 1972–76; Gen. Sec. ÖVP 1975–76; mem. Parl. 1975–78; City Councillor, Vienna City Senate 1976–78, 1987–89; Deputy Mayor of Vienna 1978–87; Deputy Fed. Chair. ÖVP 1983–91, Chair. 1991–95; Pres. Austrian Research Community; Fed. Minister of Science and Research 1989–94, of Educ. and Culture 1994–95, Vice-Chancellor 1992–95; with Instituts für den Donauraum und Mitteleuropa (IDM) 1995–; Co-ordinator for Southeastern European Co-operative Initiative 1996–; Pres. European Forum Alpbach 2000–; Special Co-ordinator Stability Pact for SE Europe 2002–; Guest Prof., Duke Univ., USA 1995–; Perm. Sr Fellow Centre for Research into European Integration, Bonn; Pres. Gustav Mahler Youth Orchestra, Österreichischen Volksliedwerkes, Stipendienwerkes 'pro scientia'; Jt-Pres. Technologieforums Sloweniens; Dr hc (Univs of Kraków, Bratislava, Czernowitz and Ruse). *Publications:* Projekt Mitteleuropa 1986, Aufbruch nach Mitteleuropa (with G. Wilflinger) 1986, Wissenschaft, Ethik und Politik (with M. Peterlik) 1987, Wissenschaft und Freiheit – Ideen zu Universität und Universalität (with W. Mantl and M. Perterlik) 1989, Heimat – Politik mit sitz im Leben 1994, Mensch im Wort 1994, Mitteleuropa: Eine Spurensicherung 1997, Politik am

Gängelband der Medien 1998, Österreich und der Balkan – Vom Umgang mit dem Pulverfass Europas 1999, Eine Reise ins Innere Europas – Protokoll eines Österreichers 2001. *Address:* Special Co-ordinator, Stability Pact for South Eastern Europe, rue Wiertz 50, 1050 Brussels, Belgium (Office). *Telephone:* (2) 401-87-01 (Office). *Fax:* (20) 401-87-12 (Office). *E-mail:* e .busek@idm.at. *Website:* www.stabilitypact.org (Office).

BUSER, Walter Emil, DrIur; Swiss government official; b. 14 April 1926, Lausen; s. of Emil Buser and Martha Buser; m. Renée Vuille 1947; ed Humanistic Gymnasium, Basel, Univs of Basel and Berne; Ed. Sozialdemokratische Bundeshauskorrespondenz 1950–61; Legal Consultant 1962–64; Head, legal and information service, Fed. Dept of Interior 1965–67; Vice-Chancellor of the Swiss Confed. 1968–81, Chancellor 1981–92; Hon. Dozent (Basel). *Publications:* Das Bundesgesetz über die Ordnung des Arbeitsverhältnisses vom 27.6.19, Die Rolle der Verwaltung und der Interessengruppen im Entscheidungsprozess der Schweiz, Betrachtungen zum schweizerischen Petitionsrecht, Die Organisation der Rechtsetzung, in Hundert Jahre Bundesverfassung 1874–1974, Das Institut der Volksinitiative in rechtlicher und rechtspolitischer Sicht. *Address:* c/o Federal Chancellery, Swiss Confederation, 3003 Berne, Switzerland.

BUSH, Barbara Pierce; fmr First Lady; b. b. 8 June 1925, Rye, NY; d. of Marvin Pierce and Pauline (née Robinson) Pierce; m. George Herbert Walker Bush (q.v.) 1945; four s. one d.; ed Smith Coll.; mem. Bd of Dirs, Reading is Fundamental (also Hon. Chair. Advisory Bd), Business Council for Effective Literacy; mem. advisory council, Soc. of Memorial Sloan-Kettering Cancer Center; Hon. Chair. advisory council, Literacy Volunteers of America; Pres. Ladies of the Senate 1981–88; mem. staff Office of George Bush 1992–; numerous other appointments; numerous hon. degrees; Outstanding Mother of the Year Award 1984, Distinguished Leadership Award, United Negro Coll. Fund 1986, Distinguished American Woman Award, Coll. Mt St Joseph 1987, Free Spirit Award, Freedom Forum 1985. *Publication:* Barbara Bush: A Memoir 1994. *Address:* 490 E L'Enfant Plaza, SW, Room 6125, Washington, DC 20594, USA.

BUSH, George Herbert Walker, BA(ECONS); American politician; b. 12 June 1924, Milton, Mass.; s. of the late Prescott Sheldon Bush and of Dorothy Walker; m. Barbara (Pierce) Bush (q.v.) 1945; four s. one d.; ed Phillips Acad., Andover, Mass. and Yale Univ.; naval carrier pilot 1942–45 (DFC, three Air Medals); Co-Founder, Bush-Overbey Oil Devt Co. 1951; Co-Founder, Dir Zapata Petroleum Corpn 1953–59; Founder, Pres. Zapata Offshore Co. 1956–64, Chair. 1964–66; mem. House of Reps for 7th Dist of Texas 1967–71; Perm. Rep. to UN 1971–72; Chair. Republican Nat. Cttee 1973–74; Head US Liaison Office, Peking (now Beijing) 1974–75; Dir CIA 1976–77; Vice-Pres. of USA 1981–89, Pres. of USA 1989–93; Republican; numerous hon. degrees; Churchill Award 1991; Hon. GCB 1993. *Publications:* Looking Forward: An Autobiography (with Victor Gold) 1988, A World Transformed (with Brent Scowcroft) 1998, All the Best, George Bush 1999. *Leisure interests:* tennis, jogging, boating, fishing, golf. *Address:* Suite 900, 10000 Memorial Drive, Houston, TX 77024-3422, USA (Office). *Telephone:* (713) 686-1188 (Office).

BUSH, George W(alker), MBA; American politician and business executive; b. 6 July 1946; s. of George Herbert Bush (q.v.) (fmr Pres. of USA) and Barbara Bush (née Pierce) (q.v.); m. Laura Bush; twin d.; ed Yale and Harvard Univs; Chair. and CEO Spectrum 7 Energy Corpn (merged with Harken Energy Corpn 1986), Midland, Tex.; Dir Harken Energy Corpn; professional baseball team exec. Tex. Rangers; Gov. of Texas 1995–2000; Pres. of USA Jan. 2001–; Republican. *Publication:* A Charge To Keep (with Karen Hughes) 2000. *Address:* The White House, 1600 Pennsylvania Avenue NW, Washington, DC 20500, USA.

BUSH, John Ellis ('Jeb'), BA; American politician and business executive; b. 11 Feb. 1953, Midland, Tex.; s. of George Herbert Bush (q.v.), fmr Pres. of USA and Barbara Bush (q.v.); brother of George W. Bush (q.v.), Pres. of USA ; m. Columba Bush; two s. one d.; ed Univ. of Texas at Austin; co-f. Codina Group (real estate devt co.), Miami, Fla 1981–, Pres. COO; Sec. of Commerce, State of Fla 1987–88; Gov. of Florida 1998–; Founder, Chair. Foundation for Fla's Future 1995; Co-founder Liberty City Charter School; Republican. *Address:* Office of the Governor, The Capitol, Tallahassee, FL 32399-0001, USA (Office). *E-mail:* fl_governor@eog.state.fl.us (Office).

BUSH, Kate (Katherine); British singer and performer; b. 30 July 1958, Welling; contributed to soundtracks of Castaway (Be Kind to My Mistakes) and She's Having a Baby (This Woman's Work); Dir Novercia Ltd; BPI Award for Best Vocalist 1979, 1987. *Singles include:* Wuthering Heights, The Man with the Child in His Eyes, Wow, Symphony in Blue, Babooshka, Army Dreamers, Breathing, Sat in Your Lap, The Dreaming, Running Up That Hill, Don't Give Up (with P. Gabriel), The Sensual World, This Woman's Work. *Albums include:* The Kick Inside, Lionheart, Never Forever, The Dreaming, The Single File, Hounds of Love, The Sensual World, The Whole Story, The Red Shoes. *Film:* The Line, The Cross and The Curve 1993. *Address:* PO Box 120, Welling, Kent, DA16 3DA, England (Home); c/o EMI Records (UK), EMI House, 43 Brook Green, London, W6 7EF.

BUSQUIN, Philippe; Belgian politician; b. 6 Jan. 1941; m.; ed Université Libre de Bruxelles; fmr Prof. of Biology and Physics; Deputy for Hainaut 1977–78, for Charleroi 1981–; Minister of Nat. Educ. 1980–81, of the Interior and Nat. Educ. Feb.–Dec. 1981, for the Budget and Energy (French region) 1982–85, of the Economy and Employment (French region) Feb.–May 1988, of Social Affairs 1988–92; Chair. Parti Socialiste (PS) 1992–99; Vice-Pres. Socialist Int. 1992–, PES 1995–; EU Commr for Science, Research and Devt 1999–. *Address:* European Commission, 200 rue de la Loi, 1049 Brussels, Belgium (Office). *Telephone:* (2) 299-11-11 (Office). *Fax:* (2) 295-01-38 (Office). *Website:* europa.eu.int (Office).

BUSSELL, Darcey Andrea, OBE; British ballet dancer; b. 27 April 1969, London; d. of Philip M. Bussell and Andrea Williams; m. Angus Forbes 1997; one d.; ed Arts Educational School and Royal Ballet School; joined Sadlers Wells Royal Ballet (now Birmingham Royal Ballet) 1987; debut with leading role in The Prince of The Pagodas (Kenneth MacMillan) 1988; soloist, Royal Ballet 1988, first soloist 1989, prin. ballerina 1989–; appearances with Royal Ballet include leading roles in The Spirit of Fugue (created for her by David Bintley), first Royal Ballet performances of Balanchine's Rubies and Stravinsky Violin Concerto and leading roles in Agon, Symphony in C, Tchaikovsky pas de deux, Apollo (Terpsichore), Prodigal Son (Siren), Duo Concertante, Ballet Imperial and Serenade, Kenneth Macmillan's The Prince of the Pagodas (role of Princess Rose created for her), Winter Dreams (role of Masha created for her), Manon (title role), Song of the Earth, Elite Syncopations, Raymonda, Romeo and Juliet, Requiem, Mayerling and Anastasia, Frederick Ashton's Cinderella (title role), Monotones II, Les Illuminations (Sacred Love), Birthday Offering , Les Rendezvous, William Forsyth's In the middle, somewhat elevated and Herman Scherman (pas de deux), Glen Tetley's La Ronde (Prostitute), Ninette de Valois' Checkmate (Black Queen), Ashley Page's Bloodlines (creator of leading role) and ...now langourous, now wild..., Twyla Tharp's Push Comes to Shove (co. premiere), Jerome Robbins' The Concert (Ballerina), Antony Tudor's Lilac Garden (Caroline); classical repertory includes leading roles in Swan Lake (Odette/Odile), The Sleeping Beauty (Princess Aurora), The Nutcracker (Sugar Plum Fairy), La Bayadère (Nikiya and Gamzatti), Cinderella (title role), Giselle (title role), Raymonda Act III (title role); numerous appearances on TV and abroad and as guest with other ballet cos in Paris, St Petersburg and New York; Prix de Lausanne 1989, Dance and Dancers Magazine Dancer of the Year 1990, Variety Club of GB Sir James Garreras Award 1991, Evening Standard Ballet Award 1991, jt winner Cosmopolitan Achievement in the Performing Arts Award 1991, Olivier Award 1992. *Publications:* My Life in Dance 1998, Favourite Ballet Stories, The Young Dancer. *Leisure interests:* sketching/painting, arts. *Address:* The Royal Opera House, Covent Garden, London, WC2E 9DD. *Telephone:* (20) 7240-1200.

BUTCHER, Hon. David John, BA (HONS.); New Zealand economic consultant; b. 1948, England; s. of Frank George Butcher and Dorothy May Butcher; m. Mary Georgina Hall 1980; two d.; ed Victoria Univ. of Wellington; fmr union field officer and research officer for Dept of Labour, Wages Tribunal and Industrial Comm.; mem. Parl. 1978–90; fmr Parl. Under-Sec. to Ministers of Agric., Lands and Forests; Minister of Energy, of Regional Devt and Assoc. Minister of Finance 1987–88, of Regional Devt 1987–90, of Commerce 1988–90, of Energy 1989–90; Man. Dir David Butcher and Assocs 1992–; mem. Labour Party; Commemorative Medal 1990. *Publications:* Agriculture in a More Market Economy 1985, Lessons for the Future from the Free Market Economy, A Politician's View 1987, Forum Island Countries and the Single European Market 1992 1993; and numerous speeches and articles. *Leisure interests:* tramping, reading, classical music, family history, photography. *Address:* H6 109 Featherston Street, Wellington (Office); PO Box 5279, Wellington, New Zealand. *Telephone:* (4) 476-9001 (Office); (4) 476-9001 (Home). *Fax:* (4) 476-9001. *E-mail:* 100251.611@compuserve.com (Office). 100251.611@compuserve.com (Home).

BUTCHER, John Charles, PhD, DSc, FRSNZ; New Zealand professor of mathematics; b. 31 March 1933, Auckland; s. of Charles Hastings Butcher and Alice Lilac Cornwall (née Richards) Butcher; m. 1st Patricia Frances Nicolas 1957 (divorced 1989); two s. one d.; m. 2nd Jennifer Ann Wright (née Bowman) 1990; ed Dargaville, Taumarunui and Hamilton High Schools, Univ. of New Zealand and Sydney; Lecturer in Applied Math., Univ. of Sydney 1959–61; Sr Lecturer in Math., Univ. of Canterbury 1961–64; computer scientist, Stanford Linear Accelerator Center 1965–66; Prof. of Math., Univ. of Auckland 1966–79 (Head Math. Dept 1967–73), of Computer Science 1980–88 (f. Dept of Computer Science 1980), Head, Applied and Computational Math. Unit 1989–94, 1997–98, Prof. of Math. 1989–98, Hon. Research Prof. and Prof. Emer. 1999–; various visiting lectureships and professorships USA, UK, Sweden, Austria, Germany, USSR, Netherlands 1965–; Fellow Inst. of Math. and its Applications (UK) 1972; Fellow and Past Pres. NZ Math. Soc.; mem. American Math. Soc. 1966; mem. Soc. for Industrial and Applied Math. (Pa, USA), Australian and NZ Industrial and Applied Mathematics; mem. Bd of various journals; Award for Math. Research (NZ Math. Soc.) 1991, Hector Medal (Royal Soc. of NZ) 1996. *Publications:* The Numerical Analysis of Ordinary Differential Equations: Runge-Kutta and General Linear Methods 1987, papers on numerical analysis and other topics. *Leisure interests:* classical music, bridge. *Address:* Department of Mathematics, University of Auckland, Private Bag 92019, Auckland (Office); 16 Wallace Street, Herne Bay, Auckland, New Zealand (Home). *Telephone:* (9) 3737999 (Office); (9) 3762743 (Home). *Fax:* (9) 3737457 (Office). *E-mail:* butcher@mat .auckland.ac.nz (Office).

BUTHELEZI, Rt. Rev. Bishop Manas, STM, PhD; South African ecclesiastic; b. 10 Feb. 1935, Mahlabathini; s. of Absalom Buthelezi and Keslinah Mkhabase; m. Grace Mhlungu 1963; two s. two d.; ed St Francis Coll. and Yale and Drew Univs, USA; high school teacher 1957; Visiting Prof., Heidelberg

Univ., Fed. Repub. of Germany 1972, Wesley Seminary 1975; Bishop, Central Diocese, Evangelical Lutheran Church 1977–; fmr Pres. SA Council of Churches 1984–91; mem. Comm. on Studies, Lutheran World Fed. 1970–77, Comm. on World Mission and Evangelism, WCC 1975–83; mem. Standing Cttee Faith and Order Comm., Pvt. Sector Council on Urbanization, Int. Comm. on Lutheran/Catholic Dialogue, Iliff School of Theology; several hon. degrees. *Leisure interests:* music and photography. *Address:* PO Box 1210, Roodepoort 1725, South Africa.

BUTHELEZI, Chief Mangosuthu Gatsha, BA; South African politician and Zulu leader; b. 27 Aug. 1928, Mahlabatini; s. of the late Chief Mathole Buthelezi and Princess Magogo; m. Irene Audrey Thandekile Mzila 1952; three s. four d.; ed Adams Coll., Fort-Hare Univ.; installed as Chief of Buthelezi Tribe 1953; assisted King Cyprian in admin. of Zulu people 1953–68; elected leader of Zululand territorial authority 1970; Chief Minister of KwaZulu 1976–94; Minister of Home Affairs (in Gov. of Nat. Unity) 1994–; Pres. Inkatha Freedom Party; Hon. LLD (Zululand and Cape Town); George Meany Human Rights Award 1982; Kt Commdr Star of Africa (Liberia), Commdr Ordre Nat. du Mérite 1981 and numerous other awards. *Publication:* South Africa: My Vision of the Future 1990. *Address:* Ministry of Home Affairs, Private Bag X741, Pretoria 0001 (Office); Inkatha Freedom Party, Albany House North, 4th Floor, Albany Grove, PO Box 443, Durban 4000, South Africa. *Telephone:* (12) 3268081 (Office); (31) 3074962. *Fax:* (12) 3216491 (Office); (12) 3074964. *Website:* www.fp.org.za.

BUTLER, Alan, BSc; British public relations and management consultant; b. 6 Dec. 1940, Wallingford; s. of Albert Frederick Butler and Lilian Elizabeth Butler; m. Gail Butler 1981; two s.; ed Raine's Foundation Grammar School, London and Univ. Coll., London; Dir of Public Affairs, Honeywell 1970–75; Dir Carl Byoir and Assocs Ltd 1970–85, Man. Dir 1975–85; Man. Dir Countrywide Communications (London) Ltd 1987–89, Int. Dir 1989–93, Deputy Chair. 1989–93, Chair. Countrywide Political Communications 1988–91; Man. Partner, Kudos Communications 1993–; Chair. Wentworth Gate Man. Co. 1999–; Partner Speakers Bureau Int. 2000–; Dir YTJ Communications, Singapore 1994–; mem. British Computer Soc., Marketing Soc., Int. Public Relations Assch, Int. Assch of Business Communicators; Liveryman Worshipful Co. of Marketers; Fellow, Inst. of Dirs, Inst. of Public Relations; mem. British Universities Soccer Team 1962. *Leisure interests:* sport, travel. *Address:* Kudos Communications, 36 St David's Drive, Egham, Surrey, TW20 0BA, England. *Telephone:* (1784) 430461. *Fax:* (1784) 473204. *E-mail:* abutler@kudoscomms.com (Office).

BUTLER, Basil Richard Ryland, CBE, MA, FREng; British business executive; b. 1 March 1930, Hexham; s. of Hugh Montagu Butler and Annie Isabel Butler (née Wiltshire); m. Lilian Joyce Haswell 1954; one s. two d.; ed Denstone Coll., Staffs., St John's Coll., Cambridge; Operations Man. Sinclair and BP Colombian Inc. 1968–70, Operations Man. BP Alaska Inc. 1970–72, Gen. Man. BP Petroleum Devt Ltd 1978–81, Chief Exec. BP Exploration Co. Ltd 1981–86, Dir 1986–89, Man. Dir BP Co. PLC 1986–91; Dir BP Solar Int. 1991–98, Chair. 1991–95; Chair. European Council of Applied Sciences and Eng 1993–98; Dir Brown and Root Ltd 1991–97, Chair. 1993–97; Dir Murphy Oil Corpn 1991–; Gen. Man. of Kuwait Oil Co. Ltd 1972–75, of Sullom Voe Devt 1975–78; Chair. KS Biomedix Holdings PLC 1995–2001; Pres. Inst. of Petroleum 1990–92; mem. Council Royal Acad. of Eng 1993–, Hon. Sec. Int. Activities 1995–98, Sr Vice-Pres. 1996–99; Liveryman Shipwrights' Co. 1988. *Leisure interests:* sailing, music. *Address:* c/o Royal Academy of Engineering, London, SW1P 3LW, England.

BUTLER, David Edgeworth, CBE, MA, DPhil, FBA; British psephologist; b. 1924; s. of late Prof. Harold E Butler and Margaret Pollard; m. Marilyn S. Evans (Marilyn Butler, q.v., 1962; three s.; ed St Paul's School, Princeton Univ., USA and New Coll. Oxford; J.E. Procter Visiting Fellow, Princeton Univ. 1947–48; student, Nuffield Coll. Oxford 1949–51, Research Fellow 1951–54, Fellow 1954–, Dean and Sr Tutor 1956–64; Personal Asst to British Amb. in Washington 1955–56; co-ed Electoral Studies 1982–92; Hon. DUniv (Paris) 1978, (Essex) 1993; Hon. DSc (Queen's Univ. Belfast) 1985, (Teesside) 1998; Hon. LLD (Plymouth) 1997. *Publications include:* The Study of Political Behaviour 1958, Elections Abroad (ed.) 1959, British Political Facts 1900–1960 (with J. Freeman), Political Change in Britain 1969, The Canberra Model 1973, Coalitions in British Politics (ed.) 1978, Policy and Politics (ed. with A.H. Halsey), Referendums (with A. Ranney) 1978, British Political Facts 1900–79 (with A. Sloman), European Elections and British Politics (with D. Marquand) 1981, Democracy at the Polls (with A. Ranney) 1981, Democracy and Elections (with V. Bogdanor) 1983, Governing without a Majority 1983, A Compendium of Indian Elections 1984, Party Strategies in Britain (with P. Jowett) 1985, British Political Facts 1900–2000 (with G. Butler) 2000, Sovereigns and Surrogates (with A. Low) 1991, Failure in British Government (with others) 1994, India Decides (with P. Roy) 1995, Referendums Around the World (ed. jtly) 1995, British Politics and European Elections (with Martin Westlake) 2000, The British General Election of 2001 2001; also numerous books on the British electoral system and British elections since 1945. *Address:* Nuffield College, Oxford, OX1 1NF, England. *Telephone:* (1865) 278500.

BUTLER, James Walter, RA, RWA, FRBS; British sculptor; b. 25 July 1931, London; s. of the late Rosina Kingman and Walter Arthur Butler; m. Angela Elizabeth Berry 1975; five d.; ed Maidstone Grammar School, Maidstone School of Art, St Martin's School of Art, City & Guilds of London Art School,

Royal Coll. of Art; worked as stone carver; taught sculpture and drawing, City & Guilds Art School; professional sculptor working on public and pvt. comms. and exhbns.; work in various galleries. *Major works:* statues of Jomo Kenyatta, Field Marshal Alexander, John Wilkes, Thomas Cook, James Brindley; memorials to Green Howards, D-Day, Richard III, Royal Electrical & Mechanical Engineers, Fleet Air Arm; portrait busts of Sir Frank Whittle, Robert Beldam, Jack Walker, R. J. Mitchell; Royal Seal of the Realm. *Leisure interests:* golf, astronomy. *Address:* Valley Farm Studios, Radway, Warwick, CV35 0UJ, England (Office). *Telephone:* (1926) 641938 (Office). *Fax:* (1926) 640624 (Office).

BUTLER, Sir James (Jim), Kt, K.B., CBE, FCA; British chartered accountant; b. 15 March 1929, Batheaston; m. Margaret Butler; one s. two d.; ed Marlborough Coll., Clare Coll. Cambridge; articled clerk, Peat Marwick (chartered accountants) 1952; negotiated Peat Marwick's merger with Klynveld Main Goerdeler to form KPMG 1986–87; Sr Partner, Peat Marwick (UK arm of KPMG) 1987–93; Chair. KPMG Int. 1991–93; Dir Camelot PLC 1994– (Deputy Chair. 1995–), Royal Opera House 1994–99, Wadworth and Co. Ltd 1994–, Nicholson, Graham & Jones 1994–. *Leisure interests:* shooting, bridge. *Address:* 110 Cannon Street, London, EC4N 6AR (Office); Littleton House, Crawley, Winchester, Hants., SO21 2QF, England. *Telephone:* (20) 7648-9000 (Office); (1962) 880206 (Home). *Fax:* (20) 7648-9001 (Office); (1962) 886177 (Home).

BUTLER, Marilyn Speers, DPhil, FRSL, FRSA; British academic; b. 11 Feb. 1937, Kingston-upon-Thames, Surrey; d. of Trevor Evans and Margaret Evans (née Gribbin); m. David Edgeworth Butler (q.v.) 1962; three s.; ed Wimbledon High School, St Hilda's Coll. Oxford; BBC trainee and producer 1960–62; Jr Research Fellow, St Hilda's Coll. Oxford 1970–73; Fellow and Tutor, St Hugh's Coll. Oxford 1973–86; King Edward VII Prof. of English Literature, Cambridge Univ. 1986–93; Fellow King's Coll. Cambridge 1987–93; Rector Exeter Coll., Oxford 1993–; Titular Prof. of English Language and Literature, Univ. of Oxford 1998–; British Acad. Reader 1982–85; Foreign mem. US Acad. of Arts and Sciences 1999; Hon. Fellow St Hilda's Coll. Oxford, St Hugh's Coll. Oxford, King's Coll. Cambridge; Hon. LittD (Leicester) 1992, (Birmingham) 1993, (Oxford Brookes) 1994, (Williams Coll., Mass.) 1995, (Lancaster, Warwick, Surrey) 1997, (Kingston) 1998. *Publications:* Maria Edgeworth: A Literary Biography 1972, Jane Austen and the War of Ideas 1975, Peacock Displayed 1979, Romantics, Rebels and Reactionaries 1981, Burke, Paine, Godwin and the Revolution Controversy (ed.) 1984, Collected Works of Wollstonecraft (Ed. with J. Todd) 1989, Edgeworth's Castle Rackrent and Ennui (ed.) 1992, Mary Shelley's Frankenstein (ed.) 1993, Jane Austen's Northanger Abbey (ed.) 1995, Collected Works of Edgeworth (ed. with M. Myers) 1999. *Address:* The Rector's Lodgings, Exeter College, Oxford, OX1 3DP, England. *Telephone:* (1865) 279647 (College); (1865) 279644 (Home). *Fax:* (1865) 279674. *E-mail:* rector@exeter.ox.ac.uk (Office).

BUTLER, Sir Michael Dacres, GCMG; British diplomatist (retd); b. 27 Feb. 1927, Nairobi, Kenya; s. of Thomas D. and Beryl M. (née Lambert) Butler; m. Ann Clyde 1951; two s. two d.; ed Winchester Coll. and Trinity Coll., Oxford; joined Foreign Office 1950; served UK Mission to UN 1952–56, Baghdad 1956–58, Paris 1961–65, UK Mission to UN at Geneva 1968–70; sabbatical year at Harvard 1970–71; served at Washington, DC 1971–72; Head of European Integration Dept, FCO 1972–74, Under-Sec. for European Community Affairs 1974–76, Deputy Under-Sec. for Econ. Affairs 1976–79; Perm. Rep. to EC 1979–85; Labour Party's Special Envoy on Enlargement 1996–97; Adviser to Robin Cook on Europe 1997–98; mem. Council Britain in Europe 1999–, Bd 2001–; mem. Advisory Council Foreign Policy Centre 1998–; Adviser to Pres. Honda Motor Europe 1993–; Chair. Guide Phone Ltd 1998–2002; Deputy Chair. Bd of Trustees, Victoria and Albert Museum 1985–97; Chair. Council, Royal Coll. of Art 1991–96, Sr Fellow 1997; Dir The Wellcome Foundation, PLC 1985–94; Exec. Dir Hambros Bank 1986–97, Hambros PLC 1986–97, Eurosynergies (France) 1990–98, Incofina (Portugal) 1990–93; Chair. Oriental Art Magazine 1987–94, European Strategy Bd I.C.L. 1988–2001, European Cttee of British Invisibles 1988–93, Editorial Advisory Panel of Treasury Man. Int. 1992–, Business Link Dorset 1994–2001, Halo Ltd 1994–96, Rudolfinia Ltd 1994–, Pathway Group Ltd 1995–2000; Hon. DBA (Bournemouth) 1998; Adolphe-Bentinck Prize 1987; Kt Grand Cross of Portuguese Order of Merit 1998. *Publications:* Chinese Porcelain at the End of the Ming (O.C.S. Transactions, Vol. 48) and at the Beginning of the Qing (O.C.S. Transactions, Vol. 49), Europe – More than a Continent 1986, Seventeenth-Century Porcelain from the Butler Family Collection 1990, Shunzhi Porcelain – Treasures of an Unknown Reign 2002. *Leisure interests:* collecting Chinese porcelain, skiing. *Address:* 54c Lennox Gardens, London, SW1X 0DJ, England (Home).

BUTLER, Richard Edmund, AM, AASA, CPA; Australian international telecommunications policy adviser; b. 25 March 1926, Melbourne; s. of late Claude Colombia Butler and Florence Margaret Butler; m. Patricia Carmel Kelly 1951; three s. two d.; held various positions in Postmaster-General's Dept including Chief Industrial Officer, Man. Industrial Relations Arbitration and Employment Conditions 1955–60, Exec. Officer, Deputy Asst Dir-Gen. (Ministerial and External Relations) 1960–68; apptd in absentia Sec. of Australian Telecommunications Comm. 1975, later Dir Corporate Planning Directorate; Deputy Sec.-Gen. ITU 1968–83, Sec.-Gen. 1983–89; mem. Admin. Cttee of Co-ordination for UN and Heads of Specialized Agencies; fmr mem. Australian Del. Int. Telecommunication Satellite Consortium, Plenipotentiary Conf. 1965; mem. Admin. Council and Planning Cttees 1962–68;

Chair. ITU Staff Pension Cttee 1968–83; UN System Co-ordinator World Communications Year 1983; Gov. Int. Computer Communications Conf. 1975–85; ITU Rep. and Adviser, Ind. Comm. of Latin American and Caribbean Broadcasting Union (ULCRA) 1990–; mem. Advisory Bd Man. Centre for Information Tech. Research Wollongong Univ., NSW 1990–, Minister's Advisory Cttee Implementation of Australian Telecommunications Reform, Minister of Transport and Communications 1990–92; Pres. Asia-Pacific Div., IC&C World Leaders Council 1993; Chair. ASIASPACE Ltd, Australia 1995–; mem. Advisory Bd Sky Station Int. Inc. 1996; mem. Bd Volunteers in Tech. Assistance Inc. (USA) 1993–; Fellow Royal Inst. of Public Admin., Inst. of Electronic and Telecommunication Engineers; Hon. Fellow, Inst. of Electronics and Telecommunications, India, Inaugural Fellow, Telecommunications Soc. of Australia 1995; mem. Bd of Advisors Pacific Telecommunications Council, Hawaii 1993, mem. Man. Bd Centre for Int. Research on Communication and Information Technologies, (CIRCIT), Melbourne 1993, mem. Advisory Bd, Telematics, India 1994; mem. MCC (Melbourne), CTA, Sydney, Royal Commonwealth Soc., Royal Overseas League; Hon. mem. Greek Soc. of Air and Space Law 1984; Grand Insignia of Order of Merit for Telecommunications (Spain) 1983, Philipp Reis Medal 1987; several other awards and decorations. *Leisure interests:* golf and reading. *Address:* 40 Barrington Avenue, Kew, 3101 Victoria, Australia. *Telephone:* (3) 9817-4231. *Fax:* (3) 9817-4231.

BUTLER, Richard William, AO, DUniv; Australian diplomatist; b. 13 May 1942; s. of H. H. Butler; m. Barbara Evans 1974; three s. one d.; ed Randwick Boys High School, Univ. of Sydney, Australian Nat. Univ.; Second Sec. Embassy and Perm. Mission to UN, Deputy Perm. Rep. IAEA, Vienna 1966–69; First Sec. Mission to UN, New York 1970–73; Deputy High Commr, Singapore, 1975–76; Prin. Pvt. Sec. to Leader of Opposition 1976–77; Counsellor, Bonn Embassy 1978–81; Minister-Del. to OECD, Paris, Amb. and Perm. Rep. to UN (Disarmament Matters), Geneva 1983–88; Amb. to Thailand 1989–92; Amb. and Perm. Rep. to Supreme Nat. Council of Cambodia 1991–92; Amb. and Perm. Rep. to UN, New York 1992–97; Exec. Chair. UN Special Comm. on Iraqi Disarmament 1997–99; Diplomat-in-Residence, Council on Foreign Relations, New York 1999–. *Publications:* The Greatest Threat 2000, Saddam Defiant 2000. *Leisure interests:* art, music, rugby. *Address:* c/o Council on Foreign Relations, 58 East 68th Street, New York, NY 10021, USA.

BUTLER, William Elliott, JD, MA, PhD, LLD, FRSA, FSA; American/British professor of law; b. 20 Oct. 1939, Minneapolis, Minn.; s. of the late William E Butler and of Maxine Swan Elmberg; m. 1st Darlene Johnson (died 1989); two s.; m. 2nd Maryann Gashi 1991; ed Hibbing Jr Coll., The American Univ., Harvard Law School, Russian Acad. of Sciences and Johns Hopkins School of Advanced Int. Studies; Research Asst Washington Center for Foreign Policy Research, Johns Hopkins Univ. 1966–68; Research Assoc. in Law and Assoc. Russian Research Center, Harvard Univ. 1968–70; Reader in Comparative Law, Univ. of London 1970–76, Prof. of Comparative Law 1976–, Dean, Faculty of Laws 1988–90; mem. Council, School of Slavonic and E European Studies 1973–93; Dean, Faculty of Laws, Univ. Coll. London 1977–79, Vice-Dean 1979–81; Dir Vinogradoff Inst. Univ. Coll. London 1982–; Dean Faculty of Law, Speranskii Prof. of Int. and Comparative Law, Moscow Higher School of Social and Econ. Sciences 1995–; partner, White & Case 1994–96; partner, Price Waterhouse Coopers (law firm) 1997–2001; Sr Partner Phoenix Law Assocs. Moscow 2002–; Special Counsel, Comm. on Econ. Reform, USSR Council of Ministers 1989–91; consultant, IBRD; adviser and consultant, Russian Fed., Belarus, Ukraine, Kirgiz Repub., Repub. of Kazakhstan, Republic of Tajikistan, Republic of Uzbekistan; Visiting scholar, Moscow State Univ. 1972, 1980, Mongolian State Univ. 1979, Inst. of State and Law, USSR Acad. of Sciences 1976, 1981, 1983, 1984, 1988, Harvard Law School 1982; Visiting Prof. New York Univ. Law School 1978, Ritsumeikan Univ. 1985, Harvard Law School 1986–87; mem. Russian Court of Int. Commercial Arbitration 1995–; Academician, Russian Acad. of Natural Sciences, Nat. Acad. of Sciences of Ukraine, Int. Acad. of the Book and Art of the Book, Russian Acad. of Legal Sciences; numerous professional appts., affiliations etc. *Publications:* more than 900 books, articles, reviews and translations including Soviet Law 1983, The Non-Use of Force in International Law 1989, Perestroika and International Law 1990, The History of International Law in Russia 1647–1917 1990, Foreign Investment Legislation in the Republics of the Former Soviet Union 1993, Russian Law of Treaties 1997, Russian Legal Texts 1998, Russian Law 1999, 2003, Constitutional Foundations of the CIS Countries 2000, American Bookplates 2000, Russian Company Law 2000, Russian-English Legal Dictionary 2001, Foreign Investment Laws in the Commonwealth of Independent States 2002, The Law of Treaties in Russia and the Commonwealth of Independent States 2002, Civil Code of the Russian Federation 2003, Russian Company and Commercial Law 2003. *Leisure interests:* book collecting and bookplate collecting. *Address:* The Vinogradoff Institute, University College London, 4–8 Endsleigh Gardens, London, WC1H 0EG (Office); Stratton Audley Park, Bicester, Oxon., OX27 9AB, England (Home). *Telephone:* (20) 7679-1469 (Office); (1869) 278960 (Home). *Fax:* (1869) 277820 (Home). *E-mail:* webakademik@aol.com (Home).

BUTLER, William Joseph; American lawyer; b. 22 March 1924, Brighton, Mass.; s. of Patrick L. Butler and Delia Conley; m. Jane Hays 1945; one s. one d.; ed Harvard Univ. and New York Univ. School of Law; mem. New York Bar 1950; Assoc. Hays, St John, Abramson & Schulman, New York 1949–53; partner Butler, Jablow & Geller, New York 1953–; special counsel American

Civil Liberties Union; Attorney for petitioner in Engel v. Vitale (school prayer case, landmark case in history of US constitutional law), US Supreme Court 1962; Lecturer, Practising Law Inst. 1966; Sec., Dir, Cen. Counsel, Walco Nat. Corpn, FAO Schwarz, New York; mem. Comm. on Urban Affairs, American Jewish Congress 1965–70; mem. Bd of Dirs. New York Civil Liberties Union, Int. League for Rights of Man; mem. Exec. Cttee League to Abolish Capital Punishment; mem. Standing Cttee on Human Rights, World Peace Through Law Center, Geneva; Chair. Advisory Cttee Morgan Inst. for Human Rights; mem. Int. Comm. of Jurists (Pres. American Asscn for the Int. Comm. of Jurists), American Bar Asscn, Council on Foreign Relations, Int. Law Asscn, American Soc. of Int. Law, etc.; int. legal observer, Int. Human Rights Org. at trials in Greece, Burundi, Iran, Nicaragua, S. Korea, Philippines, Uruguay, Israel, at Int. Criminal Tribunal for fmr Yugoslavia, The Hague 1996–; Special Regional Adviser for N America on Human Rights to the UN High Comm. for Human Rights 1998; originator of Princeton Project on Universal Jurisdiction; Hon. DHumLitt (Cincinnati) 1988. *Publications include:* Human Rights and the Legal System in Iran 1976, The Decline of Democracy in the Philippines 1977, Human Rights in United States and United Kingdom Foreign Policy 1977, Guatemala, a New Beginning 1987, Palau: A Challenge to the Rule of Law in Micronesia 1988, The New South Africa – The Dawn of Democracy 1994; contribs to professional journals. *Address:* 280 Madison Avenue, New York, NY 10016 (Office); 24 E 10th Street, New York, NY 10003, USA. *E-mail:* wjb@iopener.net (Office). *Website:* www.law.uc.edu/archives/index.html (Office).

BUTLER OF BROCKWELL, Baron (Life Peer), cr. 1998, of Herne Hill in the London Borough of Lambeth; **Frederick Edward Robin Butler,** GCB, CVO; British public servant; b. 3 Jan. 1938, Poole, Dorset; s. of the late Bernard Butler and Nora Butler (née Jones); m. Gillian Lois Galley 1962; one s. two d.; ed Harrow School, University Coll., Oxford; with HM Treasury 1961–69, Private Sec. to the Financial Sec. 1964–65, Sec. Budget Cttee 1965–69; seconded to Cabinet Office as mem. Central Policy Review Staff 1971–72; Private Sec. to Prime Minister 1972–74, 1974–75, 1982–85; Head of General Expenditure Policy Group 1977–80; Principal Establishment Officer, HM Treasury 1980–82; Second Perm. Sec., Public Services 1985–87; Sec. to Cabinet and Head of Home Civil Service 1988–98; Master Univ. Coll., Oxford 1998–; Chair. of Govs Dulwich Coll. 1997–; Gov. Harrow School 1975–91 (Chair. of Govs 1985–91); mem. Royal Comm. for Lords' Reform 1999–; Hon. Fellow, Univ. Coll. Oxford 1989; Hon. DSc (Cranfield) 1994, Hon. LLD (Exeter) 1998, Hon. DCL (London) 1999. *Leisure interests:* competitive games, opera. *Address:* University College, Oxford, OX1 4BH, England. *Website:* www.univ.ox.ac.uk.

BUTLER-SLOSS, Rt Hon. Lady Justice, Dame (Ann) Elizabeth (Oldfield), DBE, PC, FRSM; British judge; b. 10 Aug. 1933; d. of the late Sir Cecil Havers and Enid Snelling; m. Joseph William Alexander Butler-Sloss 1958; two s. one d.; ed Wycombe Abbey School; called to Bar, Inner Temple 1955, Bencher 1979; contested Lambeth, Vauxhall as Conservative Cand. 1959; practising barrister 1955–70; Registrar, Prin. Registry of Probate, later Family Div. 1970–79; Judge, High Court of Justice, Family Div. 1979–87; Lord Justice of Appeal 1988–99; Pres. of Family Div. 1999–; Chair. Crown Appointments Comm. 2002–; a Vice-Pres. Medico-Legal Soc.; Chair. Cleveland Child Abuse Inquiry 1987–88, Advisory Council, St Paul's Cathedral; Pres. Honiton Agricultural Show 1985–86; Treas. Inner Temple 1998; mem. Judicial Studies Bd 1985–89; Hon. Fellow St Hilda's Coll., Oxford 1988; Fellow Kings Coll., London 1991, mem. Council 1992–98; Chancellor Univ. of W of England 1993–; Hon. LLD (Hull) 1989, (Bristol) 1991, (Keele) 1991, (Brunel Univ.) 1992, (Exeter) 1992, (Manchester) 1995, (Cambridge) 2000, (Greenwich) 2000, (East Anglia) 2001, (Liverpool) 2001; Hon. DLit (Loughborough Univ. of Tech.) 1993, Hon. DUniv (Univ. of Central England) 1994; Hon. mem. British Pediatric Asscn, Hon. FRCP, FRCPsych, FRCPaed. *Publications:* Jt Ed. Phipson on Evidence (10th Edn), Corpe on Road Haulage (2nd Edn), fmr Ed. Supreme Court Practice 1976, 1976. *Address:* c/o Royal Courts of Justice, Strand, London, WC2A 2LL, England.

BUTLER-WHEELHOUSE, Keith Oliver, BComm; British business executive; b. 29 March 1946, Walsall; s. of the late Kenneth Butler-Wheelhouse and May Butler-Wheelhouse; m. Pamela Anne Bosworth Smith 1973; two s.; ed Technicon, Port Elizabeth, Univ. of Witwatersrand and Univ. of Cape Town Grad. School of Business; Ford Motor Co. S. Africa 1965–85; Dir of Tech. Operations, Gen. Motors S. Africa 1985–86; Chair. and CEO Delta Motor Corpn 1987–92; Pres. and CEO Saab Automobile 1992–96; Chief Exec. Smiths Group (fmrly Smiths Industries) PLC 1996–; Non-Exec. Dir J. Sainsbury PLC 1999–. *Leisure interests:* golf, tennis, shooting, skiing, keeping fit. *Address:* Smiths Group PLC, 765 Finchley Road, London, NW11 8DS, England (Office). *Telephone:* (20) 8458-3232 (Office). *Fax:* (20) 8458-4380 (Office). *E-mail:* plc@smiths-group.com (Office). *Website:* www.smiths-group.com/plc (Office).

BUTLIN, Martin Richard Fletcher, CBE, MA, DLit, FBA; British museum curator and art historian; b. 7 June 1929, Birmingham; s. of K. R. Butlin and Helen M. Butlin (née Fletcher); m. Frances C. Chodzko 1969; ed Trinity Coll., Cambridge and Courtauld Inst. of Art., Univ. of London; Asst Keeper, Tate Gallery, London 1955–67, Keeper of the Historic British Collection 1967–89; consultant to Christie's 1989–; Mitchell Prize (jtly) 1978. *Publications:* works on J. M. W. Turner, William Blake, Samuel Palmer, catalogues, articles, reviews etc. *Leisure interests:* music, travel. *Address:* 74C Eccleston Square, London, SW1V 1PJ, England.

BUTOR, Michel; French writer and lecturer; b. 14 Sept. 1926, Mons-en-Baroeul, Nord; s. of Emile Butor and Anne Brajeux; m. Marie-Josephe Mas 1958; four d.; ed Univ. of Paris; teacher at Sens (France) 1950, Minieh (Egypt) 1950–51, Manchester (England) 1951–53, Salonica (Greece) 1954–55, Geneva (Switzerland) 1956–57; Visiting Prof. Bryn Mawr and Middlebury, USA 1960, Buffalo, USA 1962, Evanston, USA 1965, Albuquerque, USA 1969–70, 1973–74, Nice and Geneva 1974–75; Assoc. Prof. Vincennes 1969, Nice 1970–73; Prof. of Modern French Literature, Geneva 1975–91; Reader Éditions Gallimard 1958–; Hon. DSc (Univ. of Thessaloniki) 2001; Chevalier, Ordre nat. du Mérite, Ordre des Arts et des Lettres; Prix Felix Féneon 1957, Prix Renaudot 1957, Grand prix de la critique littéraire 1960. *Publications:* Novels: Passage de Milan 1954, L'emploi du temps 1956, La modification 1957, Degrés 1960, Intervalle 1973; Essays: Le Génie du lieu 1958, Répertoire 1960, Histoire extraordinaire 1961, Mobile 1962, Réseau aérien 1963, Description de San Marco 1963, Les oeuvres d'art imaginaires chez Proust 1964, Répertoire II 1964, Portrait de l'artiste en jeune singe 1967, Répertoire III 1968, Essais sur les essais 1968, Les mots dans la peinture 1969, La rose des vents 1970, Le génie du lieu II 1971, Dialogue avec 33 variations de L. Van Beethoven 1971, Répertoire IV 1974, Matière de rêves 1975, Second sous-sol 1976, Troisième dessous 1977, Boomerang 1978, Quadruple Fond 1981, Répertoire V 1982; Poetry: Illustrations 1964, 6,801.000 litres d'eau par second 1965, Illustrations II 1969, Travaux d'approche 1972, Illustrations III 1973, Illustrations IV 1976, Envois 1980, Brassée d'Avril 1982, Exprès 1983, Herbier Lunaire 1984, Mille et un plis 1985, Le Retour du Boomerang 1988, Improvisations sur Flaubert 1991, Patience, Collation 1991, Transit A, Transit B 1993, Improvisations sur Michael Butor 1994, L'Utilité Poétique 1995, Le Japon depuis la France, un rêve à l'ancre 1995, Curriculum Vitae 1996 (jtly.), Gyroscope 1996, Ici et là 1997, Improvisations sur Balzac 1998, Entretiens 1999. *Leisure interest:* teaching. *Address:* à l'Ecart, 216 Place de l'Eglise, 74380 Lucinges, France.

BUTROS, Albert Jamil, PhD; Jordanian diplomatist and professor of English; b. 25 March 1934, Jerusalem; s. of Jamil Issa Butros and Virginie Antoine (Albina) Butros; m. Ida Maria Albina 1962; four d.; ed London Univ. and Univ. of Exeter, UK, Columbia Univ., USA; taught English and Math. in two pvt. schools, Amman 1950–55; instructor, Teachers' Coll., Amman 1958–60; lecturer in English, Hunter Coll., City Univ. of New York 1961; Instructor, Miami Univ., Oxford, Ohio 1962–63; Asst Prof. of English, Univ. of Jordan 1963–65, Assoc. Prof. 1965–67, Prof. 1967–79, Acting Chair. Dept of English 1964–67, Chair. 1967–73, 1974–76, Dean Research and Graduate Studies 1973–76, Prof. of English 1985–; Visiting Prof. of English, Ohio Wesleyan Univ., Delaware, Ohio 1971–72, Jordan Univ. for Women, Amman 1995–96; Dir-Gen. and Pres. Royal Scientific Soc., Amman 1976–84; Sr Research Fellow, Int. Devt Research Centre, Ottawa, Canada 1983–84, Gov. 1986–98; Special Adviser to HRH Crown Prince Hassan of Jordan 1984–85; Amb. to UK 1987–91, (also Accred to Ireland 1988–91, to Iceland 1990–91); mem. Bd of Trustees, Philadelphia Univ., Amman, 1995–; Fellow World Acad. of Art and Sciences 1986–; Rapporteur Cttee on the Jordan Incentive State Prize in Trans. 2001, Cttee on Selection for the Shoman Foundation Prize for Young Arab scholars in the Humanities and Social Sciences 2002; Istiqlal Order, First Class 1987, Order of Merit (Grande Ufficiale), Italy 1983, KStJ 1991. *Publications:* Leaders of Arab Thought 1969; several articles in learned journals; several translations including parts of Chaucer into Arabic. *Leisure interests:* reading, writing, translation, art, world affairs. *Address:* Department of English, University of Jordan, Amman (Office); P.O. Box 309, Amman 11941, Jordan (Home). *Telephone:* (6) 535 5000 (Office); (6) 515 7870 (Home). *Fax:* (6) 535511 (Office). *E-mail:* butros@nol.com.jo (Home).

BUTT, Michael Acton, MA, MBA; British business executive; b. 25 May 1942, Thruxton; s. of Leslie Acton Kingsford Butt and Mina Gascoigne Butt; m. 1st Diana Lorraine Brook 1964; two s.; m. 2nd Zoe Benson 1986; ed Rugby School, Magdalen Coll., Oxford and Inst. Européen d'Administration des Affaires (INSEAD), France; joined Bland Welch Group 1964; Dir Bland Payne Holdings 1970; Chair. Sedgwick Ltd 1983–87; Deputy Chair. Sedgwick Group PLC 1985–87; Chair. and CEO Eagle Star Holdings PLC 1987–91; Chair. and CEO Eagle Star Insurance Co. 1987–91; Dir BAT Industries PLC 1987–91, Marceau Investissements SA (France) 1987–94; Dir Phoenix Int. (Bermuda) 1992–97, Bank of N. T. Butterfield & Son Ltd (Bermuda) 1996–2002; Pres. and CEO Mid Ocean Ltd 1993–98, Chair. and CEO Mid Ocean Reinsurance Co. Ltd 1993–98; Dir Exel Capital Ltd 1998–99, XL Capital Ltd1998–; Dir Istituto Nazionale delle Assicurazioni (INA) 1994–97; Bd mem. Int. Advisory Council, INSEAD 1982–. *Leisure interests:* travel, tennis, opera, reading, family, the European movt. *Address:* XL Capital Ltd, PO Box HM 1066, Hamilton, HM EX (Office); Leamington House, 50 Harrington Sound Road, Hamilton Parish, CR O4, Bermuda (Home). *Telephone:* (441) 292-1358 (Office); (441) 293-1378 (Home). *Fax:* (441) 292-5226 (Office); (441) 293-8511 (Home).

BUTT, Noor Mohammed, PhD; Pakistani nuclear physicist (retd); ed Punjab Univ., Birmingham Univ.; fmrly Chief Scientist Pakistan Inst. of Nuclear Science and Tech.; fmr Vice-Pres. Crystallography Soc. of Pakistan; Pres. Pakistan Nuclear Soc. 1995–97; Treas. Pakistan Acad. of Sciences 1994–98; fmr Dir-Gen. Pakistan Inst. of Nuclear Science and Tech.; Visiting Scientist AERE, Harwell, UK, Oxford Univ., ICTP, Trieste and Reactor Inst., Stockholm; IAEA nuclear energy consultant; Fellow Islamic Acad. of Sciences; Open Gold Medal in Physical Sciences, Pakistan Acad. of Sciences 1990, Sitara-I-Imtiaz 1991, 8th Kharazmi Prize (jtly) (Iran) 1995, Scientist Emer.

(Pakistan). *Publications:* more than 100 research papers on nuclear solid state physics. *Address:* H. No. 155, St No. 15, Sector E-7, Islamabad, Pakistan (Office).

BUTTERWORTH, David, BSc(Eng), FREng., FIChemE, FRSA; British chemical engineer; b. 24 Oct. 1943; m. Pauline Morgan 1966; one s.; ed Univ. Coll. London; Visiting Engineer, MIT, USA 1976–77; Group Leader, UKAEA 1977–89; Man. Dir Heat Transfer and Fluid Flow Service 1989–95, Sr consultant in heat transfer 1995–; Visiting Prof. Bristol Univ. 1993–, Cranfield Univ. 1995–2002, Aston Univ., Birmingham 1996–2001; Pres. UK Heat Transfer Soc. 1988–89; Gen. Sec. Aluminium Plate-Fin Heat Exchanger Mfrs Asscn 1995–; American Inst. of Chemical Engineers Kern Award 1986. *Publications:* Introduction to Heat Transfer 1977, Two-Phase Flow and Heat Transfer 1977 (Russian trans. 1980), Design and Operation of Heat Exchangers (Jt Ed.) 1992, New Developments in Heat Exchangers (Jt Ed.). *Leisure interests:* landscape painting, cooking. *Address:* 29 Clevelands, Abingdon, Oxon., OX14 2EQ, England. *Telephone:* (1235) 525955. *Fax:* (1235) 200906. *E-mail:* davebutterworth@alpema.org (Office); davebutterworth@aol .com (Home). *Website:* www.alpema.org (Office); members.aol.com/davebutterworth (Home).

BUTTERWORTH, Ian, CBE, FRS; British professor of physics; b. 3 Dec. 1930, Tottington; s. of Harry Butterworth and Beatrice Butterworth; m. Mary Therese Gough, 1964; one d.; ed Bolton County Grammar School, Univ. of Manchester; Scientific Officer, then Sr Scientific Officer UKAEA, Harwell AERE 1954–58; Lecturer in Physics Imperial Coll., Univ. of London 1958–64, Sr Lecturer 1965–68, Head High Energy Nuclear Physics Group, Univ. Prof. of Physics 1971–91, Head of Physics Dept 1980–83, Prof. Emer. 1991–; Visiting Physicist Lawrence Berkeley Lab., Univ. of Calif. 1964–65; Sr Prin. Scientific Officer Rutherford Lab. 1968–71; Research Dir CERN (on leave of absence from Imperial Coll.) 1983–86; Prin. Queen Mary and Westfield Coll. 1989–91 (of Queen Mary Coll. 1986–89); Pro Vice-Chancellor for European Affairs, Univ. of London 1989–91; Chair. IOP Publs Ltd 1993–97; Vice-Pres. Inst. of Physics 1993–97; Vice-Pres. Academia Europaea 1997– (mem. 1989); Sr Research Fellow Imperial Coll. 1991–; Fellow Imperial Coll. 1988; Dr hc (Soka Univ.) 1989. *Publications:* numerous papers on particle physics in scientific journals. *Leisure interest:* history of art. *Address:* Blackett Laboratory, Imperial College, Prince Consort Road, London, SW7 2BZ (Office); 48 Burntwood Grange Road, London, SW18 3JX, England (Home). *Telephone:* (20) 7594-7525. *Fax:* (20) 7823-8830. *E-mail:* i.butterworth@imperial.ac.uk (Office). *Website:* www.hep.ph.ic.ac.uk (Office).

BUTTON, John Norman, BA, LLB; Australian politician; b. 30 June 1932, Ballarat, Vic.; m. 1st Marjorie Batten 1960; two s.; m. 2nd Dorothy O'Neill 1985; ed Univ. of Melbourne; former Sr partner in Melbourne law firm specializing in industrial law; mem. Senate 1974–93; Professorial Fellow, Syme Faculty of Business and Econs, Monash Univ., Vic. 1993–; Opposition Spokesman 1976–83; Deputy Leader of Opposition in Senate 1978–80, Leader 1980–83; Leader of Govt in Senate, Minister for Industry and Commerce 1983–93, for Tech. 1984–93; Special Trade Rep. 1993–96; Labor Party; numerous hon. degrees. *Publications:* Flying the Kite 1994, On the Loose 1996, As it Happened 1998. *Leisure interests:* skiing, languages, films, literature, theatre and the arts. *Address:* 85 Rowena Parade, Richmond, Vic. 3121, Australia. *Telephone:* (3) 9428-9302 (Office). *Fax:* (3) 9428-9302 (Office).

BUXTON, Andrew Robert Fowell, FIB; British banker; b. 5 April 1939, London; m. Jane Margery Grant 1965; two d.; ed Winchester Coll. and Pembroke Coll. Oxford; joined Barclays Bank Ltd 1963; Gen. Man. Barclays Bank PLC 1980, CEO 1992–93, Chair. 1993–99; Deputy Chair. (non-exec.) Xansa PLC 1999–; Pres. British Bankers' Asscn 1997–2002; mem. Court, Bank of England 1997–2001, Guild of Int. Bankers 2001, Panel on Takeovers and Mergers 2001; Gov. Imperial Coll. of Science; Hon. DSc (City). *Address:* c/o Xansa PLC, Atlantic House, Imperial Way, Worton Grange, Reading, Berks., RG2 0TD, England. *Telephone:* (8702) 416181. *E-mail:* information@xansa.com. *Website:* www.xansa.com.

BUYOYA, Maj. Pierre; Burundian politician; b. 1949; ed Royal Mil. Acad., Brussels; mem. Cen. Cttee UPRONA party 1982–87; fmr COO Ministry of Nat. Defence; led mil. coup against fmr Pres. Bagaza Sept. 1987; Pres. of Third Repub. and Minister of Nat. Defence 1987–93; Chair. Mil. Cttee for Nat. Salvation 1987–93; Pres. of Burundi 1996–2003. *Address:* Office of the President, Bujumbura, Burundi (Office). *Telephone:* 226063 (Office).

BUYSSE, Baron Paul; Belgian business executive; b. 17 March 1945, Antwerp; m.; five c.; with Ford Motor Co. 1966–76; Gen. Man. Car Sales & Marketing, Deputy Man. Dir British Leyland Belgium NV 1976–79, Man. Dir Tenneco Belgium 1979–81, J.I. Case Benelux 1979–81, Gen. Man. Europe N, J.I. Case 1986–88; Man. Dir Hansen Transmissions Int. 1988–89; Group Chief Exec. BTR Automotive & Eng Group 1989–91, BTR Eng and Dunlop Overseas 1991–94, Exec. Dir BTR PLC 1994–98; CEO Vickers PLC 1998–; Dir (non-exec.) Bd of Generale Bank, Censor Nat. Bank of Belgium; Chair., mem. Exec. Cttee and Dir King Baudouin Foundation; Chair. Prince Filip Foundation; Hon. Pres. Antwerp Chamber of Commerce & Industry; Hon. Dean of Labour; Officier Order nat. du mérite, Officer Order of Orange-Nassau, Kt Order of Leopold, Hon. CBE. *Address:* Vickers PLC, Vickers House, 2 Bessborough Gardens, London, SW1V 2JE, England (Office). *Telephone:* (20) 7828-7777 (Office). *Fax:* (20) 7331-4735 (Office).

BUZATU, Gheorghe, DHist; Romanian historian and research institute director; b. 6 June 1939, Sihlea, Vrancea Co.; s. of Ilie Buzatu and Maria Buzatu; m. Constanța Huiban 1970; one s.; ed Iași Univ.; Prof. Univ. of Craiova; scientific researcher and Dir European History and Civilization Centre of Romanian Acad./Filiala, Iași; Vice-Pres. of the Senate; mem. Parl. Ass. of the Council of Europe 2003–; mem. editorial bds Romanian Civilization, Europa XXI, Neamul Românesc, Dosarele Istoriei; Prize of the Romanian Acad. 1981, Prize of Flacăra magazine 1992, Prize of Revista de Istorie Militară 1993, 1995, 1996. *Publications include:* (in Romanian): Files of the World War 1939–45 1979, Romania and the International Oil Trusts up to 1929 1981, From the Secret History of World War II Vols I and II 1988, 1995, Romania and World War II: A Bibliography (with others) 1981, Titulescu and the Strategy of Peace (Ed.) 1982, The Romanians in World History Vols 1–100 (Ed.) 1986–99, Marshal Antonescu versus History, Vols I–V (with others) 1990–2002, Forbidden History 1990, Romania with and without Antonescu 1991, The Romanians in the American Archives (Ed.) 1992, The Trial of Corneliu Zelea Codreanu (with others) 1994, Geopolitics (Vol. I) (Ed.) 1994, N Iorga, The Man and the Word (Vols I–III) 1971–99, Romania and the World War of 1939–1945 1995, The Romanians in the Kremlin's Archives 1995, How the Holocaust against the Romanians Began 1995, The Romanian Right (Ed.) 1996, The Secret Archives, Vols I–II (with others) 1998, A History of Romanian Oil 1998, History of the Romanians 1918–1948 (with others) 1999, Stalin (with others) 1999, Romania and the Second World War (with others) 2002, Diplomacy and Romanian Diplomats (Vols 1–2) (with others) 2001–02, Marshal Antonescu at the Judgement of Historians 2002; (in English): Anglo-Romanian Relations after 1821 (Ed.) 1983, N Titulescu and Transylvania 1984, Romania's Options in June 1940 1995; (in Spanish): Breve Historia de Rumania (with others) 1982. *Address:* European History and Civilization Centre, Strada Cuza Vodă, nr 41, etaj I, Iași 6600 (Office); Splai Bahlui nr 20 A, Bloc I/1, apt. 5, Iași 6600, Romania (Home). *Telephone:* (32) 212441 (Office); (32) 130331 (Home); (723) 633764. *Fax:* (21) 3126226 (Office). *E-mail:* ghbuzatu@senat.ro (Office).

BUZEK, Jerzy Karol; Polish politician and chemical engineer; b. 3 July 1940, Śmiłowice; m. Ludgarda Buzek; one d.; ed Silesian Tech. Univ., Gliwice; scientific researcher and prof. Chemical Eng Inst. Polish Acad. of Sciences, Gliwice 1963–97; mem. Solidarity Trade Union 1980–; organizer of Solidarity underground structures in Silesia; activist of union's regional and nat. leadership; Chair. 1st, 4th, 5th and 6th Nat. Congresses of Dels.; expert and co-author economic program of the Solidarity Election Action (AWS); Deputy to Sejm (Parl.) 1997–2001; Prime Minister of Poland 1997–2001; Chair. Nat. Bd of Social Movt of Solidarity Election Action 1999–2001; Researcher and Pro-Rector Polonia Univ., Częstochowa 2002–. *Publications include:* several dozen articles and monographs on mathematical modelling, desulphurization of exhaust gases and optimization of processes. *Leisure interests:* poetry, theatre, horse riding, tennis, yachting. *Address:* Polonia University in Częstochowa, ul. Kazimierza Putaskiego 4/6, 42-200 Częstochowa, Poland (Office). *Telephone:* (34) 3680921 (Office). *E-mail:* jbuzek@ap.edu.pl (Office). *Website:* www.ap.edu.pl (Office).

BUZOIANU, Cătălina; Romanian stage director; b. 13 April 1938, Brăila; d. of Roman Buzoianu and Elena Buzoianu; m. Papil Panduru 1963; one s. one d.; ed Bucharest Theatrical and Cinematographic Art Inst.; started career at the Nat. Theatre Iași with Le Malade Imaginaire (Molière) 1970; at Teatrul Tineretului (Youth Theatre) in Piatra Neamț, Prin. Dir at Teatrul Mic, Bucharest 1978–85; has directed plays by Chekhov, Strindberg, Bulgakov, Anski, Pirandello, Shepard, Kleist and Goldoni; tours abroad and participation in int. festivals; Prof. Theatre and Cinema Institute; Dean of Theatre Dept, Theatre and Film Acad. 1990–; numerous awards including Salvo Randoni Award for whole career and especially for Pirandello performances, Italy 1995, Prix théâtre vivant, Radio France Int. 1994, Prize for Excellence, Int. Asscn of Critics, Romanian Section. *Publications:* Novele teatrale (essays), Meridiane (Ed.) 1987; articles and essays in various periodicals. *Address:* Bulandra Theatre, 1 Bd Schitu Măgureanu, 70626 Bucharest (Office); C. A. Rosetti Str., Et.7, Ap.19, Sect. 1, Bucharest, Romania (Home). *Telephone:* (1) 211-00-88 (Home). *Fax:* (1) 312-28-97 (Office).

BYAM SHAW, Nicholas Glencairn; British publisher; b. 28 March 1934, London; s. of the late Lt-Commdr David Byam Shaw and Clarita Pamela Clarke; m. 1st Joan Elliott 1956 (divorced 1973); two s. one d.; m. 2nd Suzanne Filer (née Rastello) 1974; m. 3rd Constance Mary Wilson (née Clarke) 1987; ed Royal Naval Coll., Dartmouth; served RN, retiring with rank of Lt 1951–56; on staff of Collins (printers and publrs), Sales Man. 1956–64; joined Macmillan Publrs Ltd as Sales Man. 1964, Deputy Man. Dir 1968, Man. Dir 1970–90, Chair. 1990–97, Deputy Chair. 1998–99; Dir St Martin's Press 1980–99 (Deputy Chair. 1997–99), Pan Books Ltd 1983–99 (Chair. 1986–99), Gruppe Georg von Hotzbrinck, Stuttgart, Germany 1996–99; mem. British Council Publrs' Advisory Cttee, Byam Shaw School Council. *Leisure interests:* travel, gardening, reading, music. *Address:* 9 Kensington Park Gardens, London, W11 3HB, England. *Telephone:* (20) 7221-4547.

BYAMBASÜREN, Dashiyn; Mongolian politician; b. 20 June 1942, Binder somon Dist, Hentii Prov.; s. of Lombyn Dash and Tsevegeen Perenlee; m. Sanjeen Dulamlkhand 1968; three s. three d.; ed Inst. of Economics and Statistics, Moscow, USSR; apptd. Dept Chief, State Statistics Bd; Deputy Chair., then Chair. State Cttee for Prices and Standardization 1970–76; apptd. Chair. Construction and Repair Work Trust for Auto Transport 1984, Chief Research Officer, Research Inst. of Project Drafts for Automated Man.

Systems 1985, Dir Manager Training Inst., Council of Ministers 1986; Deputy Chair. Council of Ministers 1989–90, First Deputy Chair. March–Sept. 1990, Prime Minister 1990–92; Pres. Mongolian Devt Foundation, World Mongolian Fed. 1993; fmr mem. Parl; Chair. Mongolian Democratic Renewal Party 1994–; Rector Inst. of Admin. and Man. 1998–2000; Rector Acad. of Man.; Dir Centre for Devt Strategy and System Research 2001–; Prof. and Academician, Nat. Acad. of Science. *Publications:* Orchlongiin hurd, Sergen mandakh ireedui, Uuriin javar. *Address:* CDSSR, Apt. 4, Building 35, Khudaldaanii gudamj-13, Ulan Bator, Mongolia (Office). *Telephone:* 317098 (Office). *Fax:* 317098 (Office); 318828. *E-mail:* byambasuren@cdssr.mn (Office). *Website:* www.cdssr.mn.

BYATT, Dame Antonia Susan, DBE, BA, FRSL; British author; b. 24 Aug. 1936; d. of His Honour John F. Drabble, QC and the late Kathleen M. Bloor; sister of Margaret Drabble; m. 1st Ian C. R. Byatt (q.v.) 1959 (dissolved 1969); one s. (deceased) one d.; m. 2nd Peter J. Duffy 1969; two d.; ed Sheffield High School, The Mount School, York, Newnham Coll., Cambridge, Bryn Mawr Coll., Pa, USA and Somerville Coll., Oxford; Extra-Mural Lecturer, Univ. of London 1962–71; Lecturer in Literature, Cen. School of Art and Design 1965–69; Lecturer in English, Univ. Coll., London 1972–81, Sr Lecturer 1981–83; Assoc. Newnham Coll., Cambridge 1977–82; mem. BBC Social Effects of TV Advisory Group 1974–77; mem. Bd of Creative and Performing Arts 1985–87, Bd of British Council 1993–98; Kingman Cttee on English Language 1987–88; Man. Cttee Soc. of Authors 1984–88 (Chair. 1986–88); mem. Literature Advisory Panel of the British Council 1990–98; Hon. Fellow Newnham Coll. Cambridge, London Inst.; broadcaster, reviewer and judge of literary prizes; Hon. DLitt (Bradford) 1987, (Durham, York) 1991, (Nottingham) 1992, (Liverpool) 1993, (Portsmouth) 1994, (London) 1995 (Cambridge) 1999, (Sheffield) 2000; Premio Malaparte Award, Capri 1995, Toepfer Foundation Shakespeare Prize, Hamburg 2002. *Radio:* dramatisation of quartet of novels (BBC Radio) 2002. *Television:* profile on Scribbling (series, BBC2) 2002. *Publications:* Shadow of the Sun 1964, Degrees of Freedom: The Novels of Iris Murdoch 1965, The Game 1967, Wordsworth and Coleridge in their Time 1970, Iris Murdoch 1976, The Virgin in the Garden 1978, George Eliot: The Mill on the Floss (ed. and introduction) 1979, Still Life (PEN-Macmillan Silver Pen 1986) 1985, Sugar and Other Stories 1987, Possession (Irish Times–Aer Lingus Int. Fiction Prize 1990, Eurasian Regional Award of the Commonwealth Writers' Prize 1991, Booker Prize for Fiction 1990) 1990 (film 2002), George Eliot: Selected Essays, Poems and Other Writings (ed. and introduction) 1990, Robert Browning: Dramatic Monologues (ed. and introduction) 1990, Passions of the Mind (selected essays) 1991, Angels and Insects (novellas) 1992, The Matisse Stories (short stories) 1993, The Djinn in the Nightingale's Eye (Mythopoeic Award (Fantasy) Award 1998) 1994, Imagining Characters (with Ignês Sodré) 1995, Babel Tower 1996, New Writing 4 (co-ed.) 1995, New Writing 6 (co-ed.) 1997, Elementals: Stories of Fire and Ice (short stories) 1998, The Oxford Book of English Short Stories (ed. and introduction) 1998, The Biographer's Tale 2000, On Histories and Stories (essays) 2000, Portraits in Fiction 2001, Bird Hand Book (with V. Schrager) 2001, A Whistling Woman 2002. *Leisure interests:* none. *Address:* 37 Rusholme Road, London, SW15, England. *Website:* asbyatt.com (Office).

BYATT, Sir Ian Charles Rayner, Kt, BA, DPhil; British economist and government official; b. 11 March 1932, Preston; s. of Charles Rayner Byatt and Enid Marjorie Annie (née Howat) Byatt; m. 1st Antonia Susan Drabble (q.v. Antonia Susan Byatt) 1959 (dissolved 1969); one s. (deceased) one d.; m. 2nd Prof. Deirdre Kelly 1997; two step-s.; ed Kirkham Grammar School, St Edmund Hall and Nuffield Coll., Oxford, Harvard Univ.; Lecturer in Econs, Durham Coll., Univ. of Durham 1958–62, LSE 1964–67; Econ. Consultant, HM Treasury 1962–64; Sr Econ. Adviser, Dept of Educ. and Science 1967–69; Dir of Econs, Ministry of Housing and Local Govt (and subsequently Dept of Environment) 1969–72; Under-Sec., HM Treasury 1972–78, Deputy Chief Econ. Adviser 1978–89, Dir-Gen. of Water Services 1989–2000; Sr Assoc. Frontier Economics 2001–; Pres. Econs and Business Educ. Asscn 1998–2001; mem. Econ. Policy Cttee of EC 1978–89 (Chair. 1982–85), Bd of Man., Int. Inst. of Public Finance 1987–90, Council, Royal Econ. Soc. 1983–90, Council of Man., Nat. Inst. of Econ. and Social Research 1996–2002, Governing Body of Birkbeck Coll. 1997–, Bd of Advisers, St Edmund Hall 1998–, Bd Acad. of Youth, Birmingham 2001–, Int. Inst. of Public Finance 2001–; Vice-Pres. Strategic Planning Soc. 1993–; Chair. Friends of Birmingham Cathedral 1999–; Hon. DUniv (Brunel) 1994, (Univ. of Cen. England) 2000. *Publications:* The British Electrical Industry 1875–1914 1979; articles and book chapters on nationalized industries and public utilities; contribs to govt reports on micro-econ. policy. *Leisure interest:* painting. *Address:* Frontier Economics, 150 Holborn, London, EC2N 2NJ (Office); 34 Frederick Road, Birmingham, B15 1JN, England (Home). *Telephone:* (20) 7611-9496 (Office); (121) 689-7946 (Home). *Fax:* (20) 7611-9495 (Office); (121) 454 6438 (Home). *E-mail:* ian .byatt@frontier-economics.com (Office); ianbyatt@blueyonder.co.uk (Home).

BYATT, Ronald (Robin) Archer Campbell, CMG; British diplomatist (retd); b. 14 Nov. 1930; s. of the late Sir Horace Byatt and Lady Byatt (née Olga Campbell); m. Ann Brereton Sharpe 1954; one s. one d.; ed Gordonstoun, New Coll., Oxford; joined Diplomatic Service 1959; Foreign Office 1959, 1963; served in Havana 1961, Kampala 1970; with UK Mission to UN, New York 1966, Counsellor and Head of Chancery 1977–79; Head of Rhodesia Dept, FCO 1972–75; Asst Under-Sec. of State for Africa 1979–80; High Commr in Zimbabwe 1980–83; Amb. to Morocco 1985–87, High Commr in NZ (also Accred to Western Samoa and Gov. of Pitcairn Island) 1987–90; Visiting

Fellow, Glasgow Univ. 1975–76; Civilian Dir Royal Coll. of Defence Studies, London 1983–84; Panel Chair. Civil Service Selection Bd 1992–95; mem. Forestry Comm. Home-Grown Timber Advisory Cttee (Chair. Environment Sub-Cttee) 1993–98; Trustee Beit Trust 1987–, UK Antarctic Heritage Trust 1993–2001; Wissem Alaouite (First Class) (Morocco) 1987. *Leisure interests:* birdwatching, sailing, gardening. *Address:* Drim-na-Vullin, Lochgilphead, Argyll, Scotland (Home).

BYCHKOV, Aleksey Mikhailovich, DCT; Russian evangelist; b. 15 July 1928; s. of Michael Bychkov and Evdokia Bychkova; m. Zoia Bychkova 1950; one s. two d.; ed as engineer; active from early age in helping to prepare theological training material; Vice-Pres. All-Union Council of Evangelical Christian-Baptists 1969–71, 1990–, Gen. Sec. 1971–92; clergyman in Golgotha church; Vice-Pres. Russian Bible Soc. 1990–; Pres. Moscow Evangelical Christian Seminary 1995–; expanded Bible correspondence course, responsible for printing and distributing Bibles in USSR. *Leisure interest:* photography. *Address:* Muzanovskaya str. 8, 136260, Moscow 127549, Russia. *Telephone:* (095) 407-75-03 (Home).

BYCHKOV, Semyon; Russian-born conductor; b. 1952, Leningrad; ed Leningrad Conservatory (pupil of Musin); invited to conduct Leningrad Philharmonic Orchestra; left. USSR 1975; debut with Concertgebouw, Amsterdam and Berlin Philharmonic 1984–85; toured Germany with Berlin Philharmonic 1985; Music Dir Buffalo Philharmonic Orchestra 1986–87, Orchestre de Paris 1989–98; conducted Czech Philharmonic 1989–90; Prin. Guest Conductor Maggio Musicale Fiorentino 1992–; Franco Abbiati Prize 1996. *Address:* c/o IMG Artists (UK) Inc., Media House, 3 Burlington Lane, Chiswick, London, W4 2TH, England.

BYCZEWSKI, Iwo; Polish diplomatist and lawyer; b. 29 Feb. 1948, Poznań; m.; two d.; ed Adam Mickiewicz Univ., Poznań; Collège d'Europe, Bruges; mem. staff Ministry of Justice 1977–82; researcher Inst. of Econ. Sciences, Polish Acad. of Sciences (PAN) 1982–89; Prin. Expert, Sec. Comm. in Senate Chancellery; Ministerial Adviser, Vice-Dir Council of Minister's Office 1989–90; Dir Personnel Dept Ministry of Foreign Affairs 1990–91, Under-Sec. of State 1991–95; Perm. Rep. to EU 2001–; Chair. Supervisory Bd Alcatel Polska SA 1995–; consultant Hogan and Hartson (American law firm) 1996–; Chair. Centre of Int. Affairs Foundation 1997–.

BYERS, Rt Hon. Stephen (John), PC, LLB, FRSA; British politician; b. 13 April 1953, Wolverhampton; s. of the late Robert Byers; ed Chester City Grammar School, Chester Coll., Liverpool Polytech.; Sr Lecturer of Law Newcastle Polytech. 1977–82; Labour Party MP for Wallsend 1992–97, for Tyneside N 1997–; Opposition Whip 1994–95, frontbench spokesman on educ. and employment 1995–97; Minister of State Dept for Educ. and Employment 1997–98; Chief Sec. to the Treasury 1998–99; Sec. of State for Trade and Industry 1999–2001, for Transport, Local Govt and the Regions 2001–02. *Address:* House of Commons, London, SW1A 0AA, England (Office).

BYFORD, Mark, LLB; British broadcasting executive; b. 13 June 1958, Castleford; s. of Sir Lawrence Byford and Lady Muriel Byford (née Massey); m. Hilary Bleiker 1980; two s. three d.; ed Christ's Hospital School, Lincoln, Univ. of Leeds; joined BBC as Holiday Relief Assistant 1979, Controller Regional Broadcasting 1991–94, Deputy Man. Dir 1994–96, Dir 1996–98; Dir BBC World Service and Global News 1998–; Fellow Radio Acad. 2000; Royal TV Soc. Journalism Awards 1980, 1982, 1988, Webby Award (World Service) 2001, Sony Radio Special Award (World Service) 2002, One World Special Award (World Service) 2002. *Leisure interests:* family life, soccer, cricket, rock music, being surrounded by children. *Address:* BBC World Service, Bush House, PO Box 76, Strand, London, WC2B 4PH (Office); Bolberry House, 1 Clifton Hill, Winchester, Hants., SO22 5BL, England (Home). *Telephone:* (20) 7557-2057 (Office); (1962) 860197 (Home). *Fax:* (20) 7557-1900 (Office); (1962) 860944 (Home). *E-mail:* mark.byford@bbc.co.uk (Office); markbyford@beeb .net (Home). *Website:* bbc.co.uk/worldservice (Office).

BYKOV, Oleg Nikolayevich, DrHist; Russian political scientist; b. 15 Oct. 1926, Tula; m.; one d.; ed Moscow State Inst. of Int. Relations; mem. staff Soviet Cttee of Peace 1952–55, Deputy Exec. Sec. 1959–64; mem. staff World Peace Council, Vienna 1953–59; Sr Researcher, Head of Int. Relations Dept, Deputy Dir Inst. of World Econs and Int. Relations, Russian Acad. of Sciences 1964–98, Counsellor Russian Acad. of Sciences 1998–; mem. UN Consultative Bd on Studies of Disarmament Problems; Govt expert UN Research Group on Measures of Confidence; Ed.-in-Chief Year of the Planet (yearly journal) 1992–; Corresp. Mem. USSR (now Russian) Acad. of Sciences 1987; Soviet Orders of Labour Red Banner (1981, 1986), Russian Fed. Order of Merit 1999; USSR State Prize; four medals. *Publications:* over 600 scientific pubs on contemporary int. relations, Russian foreign policy, mil. and political problems; monographs: Russia in the System of International Relations of the Coming 10 Years 1995, Russian and International Stability 1995, National Security of Russia 1997, International Relations: The Global Structure Transformed (two vols) 2003. *Address:* Institute of World Economics and International Relations, Russian Academy of Sciences, Profsoyuznaya str. 23, Moscow, Russia (Office). *Telephone:* (095) 120-23-40 (Office).

BYKOV, Vasily (Bykaŭ, Vasil'), Belarus writer; b. 19 June 1924, Chernovshchina, Vitebsk district; m. 1980; two s.; ed Vitebsk School of Art; writer 1951–; USSR People's Deputy 1989–91; mem. Belarus Democratic Movt, in opposition to Pres. Lukashenko; lived in Finland 1998–99, Germany 1999–2000; emigrated to Czech Repub. Dec. 2002; Kolas Literature Prize

1964, Lenin Prize 1986, Order of the Red Star, Hero of Socialist Labour. *Publications include:* The Cry of the Cranes 1960, Frontline Pages 1960, The Third Rocket 1962, Alpine Ballad 1963, The Dead Feel No Pain 1966, Cursed Height 1968, Kruglyansky Bridge 1969, Sotnikov 1972, Obelisk. Stories 1973, When You Want to Live (play) 1974, The Wolf-Pack 1975, The Mark of Doom 1982, The Sandpit 1986, In the Mist 1987, The Round-up 1988, Collected Works (6 Vols) 1992–94. *Address:* c/o Tankova str. Apt. 10-132, 194292 Minsk, Belarus.

BYRD, Harry Flood, Jr; American newspaperman and politician; b. 20 Dec. 1914; s. of late Harry Flood Byrd; m. Gretchen B. Thomson 1941 (died 1989); two s. one d.; ed John Marshall High School, Richmond, Virginia Military Inst. and Univ. of Virginia; ed. and writer Winchester Evening Star 1935, Ed. and Publr 1935–81, Ed. and Publr Harrisonburg Daily News-Record 1937–2000; also active in firm of H. F. Byrd, Inc., apple growers; mem. Virginia State Senate 1947–65; mem. Democratic State Cen. Cttee 1940–70; served USNR 1941–46; Dir Associated Press 1950–66; US Senator from Virginia (succeeding his father, Harry Flood Byrd) 1965–83; Independent. *Address:* Rockingham Publishing Co. Inc., 2 North Kent Street, Winchester, Virginia, VA 22601 (Office); 411 Tennyson Avenue, Winchester, Virginia, VA 22601, USA (Home). *Telephone:* (540) 662-7745 (Office). *Fax:* (540) 667-6729 (Office).

BYRD, Robert C., JP; American politician; b. 20 Nov. 1917, North Wilkesboro, NC; s. of Cornelius Sale and Ada Byrd; m. Erma O James 1936; two d.; ed George Washington Univ. Law School and Washington Coll. of Law (American Univ.); mem.W Va House of Delegates 1946–50, W Va Senate 1950–52; mem. US House of Reps rep. 6th Dist of W Va 1952–58; Senator from West Virginia 1959–; Asst Democratic Leader in Senate 1971–77, Majority Leader 1977–81, Minority Leader 1981–87, Majority Leader 1987–88; Chair. Appropriations Cttee 2001–; mem. Senate Appropriations, Armed Services and Rules and Admin. Cttees; Democrat. *Publications:* The Senate 1789–1989 (four vols) 1989–94, The Senate of the Roman Republic: Addresses on the History of Roman Constitutionalism 1995. *Address:* 311 Hart Senate Office Building, Washington, DC 20510-0001, USA.

BYRNE, David; American musician, composer and director; b. 14 May 1952, Dumbarton, Scotland; s. of Thomas Byrne and Emily Anderson (née Brown) Byrne; m. Adele Lutz 1987; one c.; ed Rhode Island School of Design; performer with Talking Heads group 1974–92; musician, composer, producer 1980–; producer Index Video 1983–; Dir videotapes 1981–; designer stage sets, lighting, LP covers and posters 1977–; f. Luaka Bop label 1988. *Group albums:* Fear of Music 1979, Remain in Light 1980, My Life in the Bush of Ghosts 1981, Speaking in Tongues 1983, Stop Making Sense 1984, Little Creatures 1985, Naked 1988, Popular Favourites 1976–1991 1992. *Solo albums include:* The Knee Plays 1985, Rei Momo 1989, The Forest 1991, Uh Oh 1992, David Byrne 1994, Feelings 1997, Look Into The Eyeball. *Film scores include:* The Last Emperor 1987 (Acad. Award winner); film appearances in Stop Making Sense 1984, True Stories (also Dir and Co-screenwriter) 1986, Checking Out 1988. *Publications:* Stay Up Late 1987, What the Songs Look Like 1987, Strange Ritual 1995.

BYRNE, David, BA, BL, SC, FRCPI; Irish European Union official, politician and barrister; b. 26 April 1947; m.; three c.; ed Dominican Coll., Newbridge, Univ. Coll. Dublin, King's Inns, Dublin; called to the Bar 1970; mem. Bar Council 1974–87; mem. Exec. Cttee, Irish Maritime Law Asscn 1974–92; Hon. Treasurer, Bar Council 1982–83; called to Inner Bar 1985; mem. Nat. Cttee ICC 1988–97; mem. Govt Review Body on Social Welfare Law 1989; mem. ICC Int. Court of Arbitration, Paris 1990–97; mem. Constitution Review Group 1995–96; External Examiner for Arbitration and Competition Law, King's Inns 1995–97; Attorney-Gen. 1997–99; mem. Council of State, Cabinet Sub-Cttees on Social Inclusion, European Affairs, Child Abuse; EU Commr for Health and Consumer Protection (with particular responsibility for Food Safety, Public Health and Consumer Protection) 1999–; mem. Barristers' Professional Practices and Ethics Cttee 1995–97; participated in negotiation of Good Friday Agreement April 1998; Fellow Chartered Inst. of Arbitrators of England and Ireland 1998–; f. Free Legal Advice Centre, Dublin. *Publications:* numerous papers on legal affairs. *Address:* European Commission, B232, 8/120, 1049 Brussels, Belgium (Office). *Telephone:* (2) 298-14-00 (Office). *Fax:* (2) 298-14-99 (Office). *Website:* europa.eu.int (Office).

BYRNE, Gabriel; Irish actor; b. 1950, Dublin; m. Ellen Barkin (q.v.) 1988 (separated); two c.; ed Univ. Coll. Dublin; archaeologist, then teacher, began acting in amateur productions; joined an experimental repertory co. 1980; first TV appearance in series The Riordans 1982; first cinema role in Excalibur; several roles Nat. Theatre, London; moved to New York 1987. *Films include:* Hanna K, Gothic, Julia and Julia, Siesta, Miller's Crossing, Hakon Hakenson, Dark Obsession, Cool World, A Dangerous Woman, Little Women, Usual Suspects, Frankie Starlight, Dead Man, Last of the High Kings, Mad Dog Time, Somebody is Waiting, The End of Violence (Dir), Toby's Story, Polish Wedding, This is the Sea, The Man in the Iron Mask, Quest for Camelot, An Ideal Husband, Enemy of the State, Stigmata, End of Days, Spider, Ghost Ship; co-producer In the Name of the Father. *Address:* c/o ICM, 8942 Wilshire Boulevard, Beverly Hills, CA 96211, USA (Office).

BYRNE, John V., MA, PhD, FAAS; American academic; b. 9 May 1928, Hempstead, NY; m. Shirley O'Connor 1954; one s. three d.; ed Hamilton Coll., Clinton, NY, Columbia Univ. and Univ. of S. Calif., Los Angeles; research geologist, Humble Oil & Refining, Houston, Tex. 1957–60; Assoc. Prof. Oregon State Univ., Corvallis, Ore. 1960–66, Prof. of Oceanography 1966–, Chair, Oceanography 1968–72, Dean, Oceanography 1972–76, Dean, Research 1976–80, Vice-Pres. Research and Grad. Studies 1980–81, Pres. 1984–95; Program Dir Oceanography, Nat. Science Foundation 1966–67; US Commr to Int. Whaling Comm. 1982–85; Exec. Dir Kellogg Comm. on Future of State and Land Grant Univs 1996–2000; Admin. Nat. Oceanic & Atmospheric Admin., Washington, DC 1981–84; Hon. Assoc. of Arts (Lynn-Benton Community Coll., OR); Hon. JD (Hamilton Coll.) 1994; Distinguished Service Award (Oregon State Univ.) 1996. *Leisure interests:* fishing, skiing, music. *Address:* 811 SW Jefferson Avenue, Corvallis, OR 97333, USA (Office). *Telephone:* (541) 737-3542. *Fax:* (541) 737-4380. *E-mail:* john.byrne@orst.edu (Office).

BYSTRITSKAYA, Elina Avraamovna; Russian actress; b. 4 April 1928; ed Kiev Inst. of Theatre Art; began career in Vilnius Drama Theatre 1953–58; leading actress, Moscow Maly Theatre 1958–; over 50 roles in theatre and films; Prof. Moscow Lunacharsky State Inst. of Theatre Art. *Films include:* Peaceful Days 1951, Quiet Don. *Leisure interests:* billiards, fishing. *Address:* Stanislavskogo str. 14, Apt. 13, 103009 Moscow, Russia.

BYUL-BYUL OGLU, Polad, PhD; Azerbaijani composer, singer and film actor; b. 4 Feb. 1945, Baku; s. of Bul-Bul; ed Azerbaijan State Conservatory; head of pop-music ensembles 1975–87; Head Azerbaijan State Philharmonic 1987–88; Minister of Culture 1988–; mem. Milli-Medjlis 1995–; Dir.-Gen. int. org. TURKSOI 1994; Hon. Prof. Azerbaijan Univ. of Culture and Arts; Prof. Int. Humanitarian Acad.; People's Artist of Azerbaijan. *Music:* symphonic works, chamber and instrumental music, musical, vocal cycles, incidental music, pop-songs. *Address:* Ministry of Culture, Azadlyg sq. 1, 370016 Baku (Office); Fioletova str. 6/8, Apt. 53, Baku, Azerbaijan (Home). *Telephone:* (12) 934398 (Office); (12) 932177 (Home). *Fax:* (12) 935605 (Office).

BYZANTINE, Julian Sarkis, ARCM; British classical guitarist; b. 11 June 1945, London; s. of Carl Byzantine and Mavis Harris; ed Royal Coll. of Music, London and Accademia Chigiana, Siena, Italy; studied with John Williams at RCM, subsequently with Julian Bream and with Andrés Segovia and Alirio Diaz in Siena; taught at RAM 1966–68; Sr Lecturer in Guitar, Queensland Conservatorium, Griffith Univ., Australia; London début Wigmore Hall 1969, New York début Carnegie Hall 1980; has performed in 75 countries and has toured widely for the British Council; has performed concerts with leading British orchestras including Royal Philharmonic, City of Birmingham Symphony, Scottish Chamber, BBC Symphony; numerous radio and TV appearances; recordings: 4 solo albums for Classics for Pleasure, solo album for Meridian Records, recording with flautist Gerhard Mallon for Walsingham Classics (Australia); awarded first ARCM for guitar 1966; Scholarships to study with Segovia from Vaughan Williams and Gilbert Foyle Trusts. *Publications:* Schotts Arrangements of Six Albéniz Piano Works for Guitar 1984, Guitar Technique Rationalised. *Leisure interests:* collecting oriental art, archaeology, tennis. *Address:* Flat 1, 42 Ennismore Gardens, London, SW7 1AQ, England. *Telephone:* (20) 7584-7486.

C

CAAN, James; American actor and director; b. 26 March 1940, Bronx, New York; s. of Arthur and Sophie Caan; m. 1st DeeJay Mathis 1961 (divorced 1966); one d.; m. 2nd Sheila Ryan 1976 (divorced 1977); one s.; m. 3rd Linda O'Gara 1995; two c.; ed Hofstra Coll.; made theatre debut in the off-Broadway production of La Ronde 1960; Broadway debut in Blood Sweat and Stanley Poole, 1961; Outstanding Achievement in Acting, Hollywood Film Festival 1999. *Films include:* Irma La Douce 1963, Lady in a Cage 1964, The Glory Guys 1965, Countdown 1967, Games 1967, Eldorado 1967, Journey to Shiloh 1968, Submarine XI 1968, Man Without Mercy 1969, The Rain People 1969, Rabbit Run 1970, T. R. Baskin 1971, The Godfather 1972, Slither 1973, Cinderella Liberty 1975, Freebie and the Bean 1975, The Gambler 1975, Funny Lady 1975, Rollerball 1975, The Killer Elite 1975, Harry and Walter Go to New York 1976, Silent Movie 1976, A Bridge Too Far 1977, Another Man, Another Chance 1977, Comes a Horseman 1978, Chapter Two 1980, Thief 1982, Kiss Me Goodbye 1983, Bolero 1983, Gardens of Stone 1988, Alien Nation 1989, Dad 1989, Dick Tracy 1990, Misery 1991, For the Boys 1991, Dark Backward 1991, Honeymoon in Vegas 1992, Flesh and Bone 1993, The Program 1994, North Star 1995, Boy Called Hate 1995, Eraser 1996, Bullet-proof 1996, Bottle Rocket 1996, This Is My Father 1997, Poodle Springs 1997, Blue Eyes 1998, The Yards 1999, The Way of the Gun 1999, In the Boom Boom Room 2000, Luckytown 2000, Viva Las Nowhere 2000, In the Shadows 2001, Night at the Golden Eagle 2002, City of Ghosts 2002, dir and actor Hide in Plain Sight 1980, dir Violent Streets 1981; starred in television movie, Brian's Song, 1971, The Warden 2000. *Television includes:* numerous TV appearances. *Address:* c/o Fred Specktor, Endeavor, 9701 Wilshire Boulevard, 10th Floor, Beverly Hills, CA 90212, USA (Office). *Telephone:* (818) 905-9500 (Home).

CABALLÉ, Montserrat; Spanish (soprano) opera singer; b. Barcelona; m. Bernabé Marti (tenor) 1964; one s. one d.; ed Conservatorio del Liceo; studied under Eugenia Kemeny, Conchita Badia and Maestro Annovazi; début as Mimi (La Bohème), State Opera of Basel; N American début in Manon, Mexico City 1964; U.S. début in Lucrezia Borgia, Carnegie Hall 1965; appeared at Glyndebourne Festival as the Marschallin in Der Rosenkavalier and as the Countess in The Marriage of Figaro then; début at Metropolitan Opera as Marguerite (Faust) Dec. 1965; now appears frequently at the Metropolitan Opera and numerous other opera houses throughout the USA; has performed in most of the leading opera houses of Europe including Gran Teatro del Liceo, Barcelona, La Scala, Milan, Vienna State Opera, Paris and Rome Operas, Bayerische Staatsoper (Munich), etc. and also at Teatro Colón, Buenos Aires; repertoire of over forty roles; Most Excellent and Illustrious Doña and Cross of Isabella the Catholic, numerous hon. degrees, awards and medals, including Commdr des Arts et des Lettres 1986. *Recordings include:* Lucrezia Borgia, La Traviata, Salomé, Aida.

CABALLERO, Gladys Aida; Honduran politician; Vice-Minister of Justice 1996; Vice-Pres. of Honduras 1998–2001. *Address:* c/o Office of the Vice-President, Palacio José Cecilio del Valle, Boulevard Juan Pablo II, Tegucigalpa, Honduras (Office).

CABIBBO, Nicola; Italian professor of elementary particle physics; b. 30 April 1935, Rome; Prof. of Theoretical Physics 1965–, of Elementary Particle Physics, Univ. of Rome; Pres. Istituto Nazionale di Fisica Nucleare 1983–93, ENEA (Nat. agency for new tech. energy and the environment) 1993–, Pontifical Acad. of Sciences 1993–. *Address:* c/o ENEA, Viale Regina Margherita 125, 00198 Rome, Italy; c/o Pontificia Academia Scientiarum, Casina Pio IV, 00120 Vatican City (Office). *Telephone:* (06) 85282214; (06) 69883451 (Office). *Fax:* (06) 69885218 (Office); (06) 85282313. *E-mail:* academy .sciences@acdscience.va (Office).

CABRAL, Alfredo Lopes, BSc; Guinea-Bissau diplomatist; b. 1946, Dakar, Senegal; m.; joined Mouvement de Libération Nationale de la Guinée-Bissau 1964; Chef de Cabinet, Foreign Ministry 1973–75, Dir Afro-Asian Div. 1975–79, First Counsellor, Perm. Mission to UN 1979–83, Perm. Rep. 1996–2000; Amb. to Algeria 1983–86, to USA 1990–96; Sec.-Gen.'s Rep. and Head of UN Civilian Police Mission in Haiti 1999–2000. *Address:* c/o Ministry of Foreign Affairs, Rua General Omar Torrijo, Bissau, Guinea-Bissau (Office).

CABRAL, Luís de Almeida; Guinea-Bissau politician; b. 1931, Bissau; brother of late Amílcar Cabral; f. Partido Africano da Independência da Guiné e Cabo Verde (PAIGC) with Amílcar Cabral 1956; mem. Political Bureau and Cen. Cttee, PAIGC 1956–70; fled to Senegal; Sec.-Gen. Nat. Union of Workers of Guinea-Bissau 1961; mem. PAIGC Council of War 1965–80, Perm. Comm. of Exec. Cttee, in charge of Nat. Reconstruction of the liberated areas 1970–72, Asst Sec.-Gen. 1972–80; Pres. State Council (Head of State) of the self-proclaimed independent state of Guinea-Bissau 1973–74, Pres. of State Council of Guinea-Bissau 1974–80 (deposed in coup); under arrest 1980; released 1 Jan. 1982; went to Cuba.

CABRERA INFANTE, Guillermo; British writer; b. 22 April 1929, Gibara, Cuba; s. of Guillermo Cabrera and Zoila Infante; m. 1st Marta Calvo 1953 (divorced 1961); m. 2nd Míriam Gómez 1961; two d.; ed School of Journalism, Havana; wrote first short story 1947; film critic Carteles Magazine 1954–60, Man. Ed. 1957–60; f. Cinemateca de Cuba 1950; Ed. Lunes 1959–61; diplomatist in Belgium 1962–65; film writer 1966–; scripts include Wonderwall 1967, Vanishing Point 1970, Under the Volcano (not produced) 1972, The Lost City 1990; feature writer for English, Spanish and S. American magazines

and newspapers; Lecturer in USA, Spain and England 1978–; Guest Dir Telluride Film Festival 1992, Miami Film Festival 1993; mem. jury Cannes Film Festival 1994; Dr. hc (Fla Int. Univ.) 1993; Biblioteca Breve Prize, Barcelona 1964, Guggenheim Fellowship Award 1970, Prix du Meilleur Livre Etranger, Paris 1971, Writer of the Year at Puterbaugh Conf., Univ. of Okla 1987, Sancho IV Medal (Universidad Complutense, Madrid) 1993, Premio Letterario Illa (Italy) 1994, Premio Cervantes (Spain) 1997. *Publications:* Así en la paz como en la guerra (short stories) 1960, Un oficio del siglo XX (film criticism) 1963, Tres tristres tigres 1967 (novel), Vista del amanecer en el trópico, O, Exorcismos de estilo 1976–77, Arcadia todas las noches 1978, La Habana para un infante difunto (novel) 1979, Holy Smoke: Smoking and the Cinema 1985, A Twentieth Century Job 1991, Mea Cuba 1992, Writes of Passage 1993, Delito por bailar el chachachá (short stories) 1995, Ella cantaba boleros (novellas) 1995, Cine o sardina (essays) 1997, Vidas para leerlas (biogs.) 1998, Todo está hecho con espejos (complete short stories) 1999, Libro de las ciudades (travel) 1999, Infantería (anthology) 2000. *Leisure interest:* watching old and new movies and taping them. *Address:* 53 Gloucester Road, London, S.W.7, England. *Telephone:* (20) 7589-4254. *Fax:* (20) 7584-7370.

CACCIAVILLAN, HE Cardinal Agostino, DCnL, DCL; Italian ecclesiastic; b. 14 Aug. 1926, Novale; ordained Priest of Vicenza 1949; joined Holy See diplomatic service 1959, served in Philippines, Spain, Portugal; Head Documentation and Information Office, Secr. of State, Vatican City 1969–76; Apostolic Pro-Nuncio to Kenya, Apostolic Del. to Seychelles 1976–81; Apostolic Pro-Nuncio to India 1981–90, to Nepal 1985–90, to USA 1990–98; Pres. Admin. Patrimony of the Apostolic See 1998–2002, now Pres. Emer.; mem. Pontifical Comm. for Vatican City State; Perm. Observer to OAS 1990–98; cr. Cardinal 2001; Knight Grand Cross of the Order of the Holy Sepulchre. *Address:* c/o Patrimony of the Apostolic See, Palazzo Apostolico, 00120 Vatican City, Italy.

CACHAREL, Jean (pseudonym of Jean Léon Henri Bousquet); French politician and couturier; b. 29 March 1932, Nîmes; s. of Célestin Bousquet and Rosa Pyronnet; m. Dominique Sarrut 1965; one s. one d.; ed Ecole Tech. de Nîmes; dress cutter, Jean Jourdan, Paris 1955–57; f. and Pres.-Dir-Gen. Soc. Jean Cacharel 1964–, of subsidiaries abroad 1972–; Mayor of Nîmes 1983–95; Deputy from Gard (UDF), Assemblée Nat. 1986–97; mem. Radical Party 1993–96; Oscar for export achievement 1969, Man of the Year, Jeune Chambre économique française 1985. *Leisure interests:* travel, football, golf, skiing. *Address:* Cacharel, 36 rue Tronchet, 75009 Paris, France.

CACOYANNIS, Michael; Greek film and stage director and actor; b. 11 June 1922, Limassol, Cyprus; s. of the late Sir Panayotis Cacoyannis and Lady Cacoyannis; brother of Stella Soulioti; ed Greek Gymnasium and London at Gray's Inn, Cen. School of Dramatic Art and Old Vic School; called to the Bar 1943; Producer for Overseas Service of BBC 1941–50; screen and stage producer-director 1950–; Hon. Doctorate (Columbia Coll., Chicago) 1981, (Athens Univ.) 2002; Order of the Phoenix (Greece) 1965, Commdr des Arts et des Lettres 1987; Hon. Citizen Limassol 1965, Dallas 1982; Special Jury Prize for Electra, Cannes 1962, 3 Acad. Awards for Zorba the Greek 1964, Prix Femina for Iphigenia 1977, Grand Prix Special des Amériques, Montreal 1999, Life Achievement Award, Jerusalem Film Festival 2000, Lifetime Achievement Award, Cairo Film Festival 2002. *Stage appearances include:* Wilde's Salomé as Herod 1947, in Camus's Caligula 1949, in Two Dozen Red Roses 1949, etc. *Directed films:* Windfall in Athens 1953, Stella 1955, A Girl in Black 1957, A Matter of Dignity 1958, Our Last Spring 1959, The Wastrel 1960, Electra 1961, Zorba the Greek 1964, The Day the Fish Came Out 1967, The Trojan Women 1971, The Story of Jacob and Joseph 1974, Attila 74 1975, Iphigenia 1977, Sweet Country 1986, Up, Down and Sideways 1992, The Cherry Orchard 1999; also a number of stage productions in Athens, New York, etc., including The Trojan Women, Paris 1965, 1995, The Devils, New York 1966, Mourning Becomes Electra, Metropolitan Opera, New York 1967, Romeo and Juliet, Paris 1968, Iphigenia in Aulis, New York 1968, La Bohème, New York 1972, King Oedipus, Dublin 1973, The Bacchae, Comédie Française, Paris 1977, Antony and Cleopatra, Athens 1979, The Bacchae, New York 1980, Zorba (musical), USA 1983, Sophocles' Electra, Epidaurus Festival 1983, Gluck's Iphigenia in Aulis and Iphigenia in Taulis, Frankfurt State Opera 1987, La Clemenza di Tito, Aix-en-Provence Music Festival 1988, Athens 1994, Cherubini's Medea, Athens 1995, The Trojan Women, Epidaurus 1997, Master Class, Athens 1998, Euripdes' Medea, Spain 2001–02. *Publications:* translations into Greek of Shakespeare: Antony and Cleopatra 1980, Hamlet 1985, Coriolanus 1990, The Trojan Women 1995, Othello 2001; into English: The Bacchae 1982, Collected Writings 1991, Stella (screenplay) 1991. *Address:* 15 Mouson Street, Athens 117-41, Greece. *Telephone:* 922-2054. *Fax:* 921-6483. *E-mail:* micaco@otenet.gr.

CADBURY, Sir (Nicholas) Dominic, Kt, MBA; British business executive; b. 12 May 1940; s. of the late Laurence John Cadbury and Joyce Cadbury (née Mathews); m. Cecilia Sarah Symes 1972; three d.; ed Eton Coll., Trinity Coll. Cambridge, Stanford Univ. (USA); Chief Exec. Cadbury Schweppes PLC 1984–93, Chair. 1993–2000; Dir Economist Group 1990–, Chair. 1994–; Jt Deputy Chair. Guinness (now Diageo PLC) 1994–97, Deputy Chair. 1996 (Dir

1991–); Jt Deputy Chair EMI Group PLC 1999–; Chair. Wellcome Trust 2000–, Transense Techs 2000–; Pres. Food and Drink Fed. 1999; Dir (non-exec.) Misys PLC 2000–; mem. Royal Mint Advisory Cttee 1986–94, Pres.'s Cttee CBI 1989–94, Food Asscn 1989–2000, Stanford Advisory Council 1989–95. *Leisure interests:* tennis, golf, shooting. *Address:* The Wellcome Trust, 183 Euston Road, London, NW1, England (Office). *Telephone:* (20) 7611-8888 (Office).

CADBURY-BROWN, Henry Thomas, OBE, TD, RA, FRIBA; British architect; b. 20 May 1913; s. of Henry William Cadbury Brown and Marion Ethel Sewell; m. Elizabeth Romeyn Elwyn 1953 (died 2002); ed Westminster School, Architectural Asscn School of Architecture; pvt. practice since winning competition for British Railway Branch Offices 1937; taught at Architectural Asscn School 1946–49; Tutor, Royal Coll. of Art. 1952–61; architect in partnership with John Metcalfe 1962–84; Visiting Critic, School of Architecture, Harvard Univ. 1956; Prof. of Architecture, Royal Acad. 1975–88; mem. group partnership with Eric Lyons, Cunningham partnership for W Chelsea redevt. for Royal Borough of Kensington and Chelsea; mem. RIBA Council 1951–53, British Cttee of Int. Union of Architects 1951–54, Modern Architectural Research group (MARS); Pres. Architectural Asscn 1959–60; Hon. Fellow, RCA, Kent Inst. of Art and Design 1992. *Work includes:* pavilions for 'The Origins of the People', main concourse and fountain display, Festival of Britain; schools, housing, display and interiors; new civic centre, Gravesend; halls of residence, Birmingham Univ.; new premises for Royal Coll. of Art (with Sir Hugh Casson and Prof. Robert Goodden); lecture halls, Univ. of Essex. *Address:* 3 Church Walk, Aldeburgh, Suffolk, IP15 5DU, England. *Telephone:* (1728) 452591.

CADOGAN, Sir John Ivan George, Kt, CBE, PhD, FRS, FRSE, CChem, FRSC; British chemist; b. 8 Oct. 1930, Pembrey, Carmarthenshire; s. of the late Alfred Cadogan and of Dilys Cadogan; m. 1st Margaret Jeanne Evans 1955 (deceased 1992); one s. one d.; m. 2nd Elizabeth Purnell 1997; ed Grammar School, Swansea and King's Coll., London; research at King's Coll., London 1951–54; Civil Service Research Fellow 1954–56; Lecturer in Chem., King's Coll., London 1956–63; Purdie Prof. of Chem. and Head of Dept, St Salvator's Coll., Univ. of St Andrews 1963–69; Forbes Prof. of Organic Chem., Univ. of Edin. 1969–79; Chief Scientist, BP Research Centre 1979–81; Dir of Research, British Petroleum 1981–92, CEO BP Ventures 1988–92; Dir Gen. Research Council 1994–99; Chair. DNA Research Innovations Ltd 1999–; Science Policy Adviser, Science Foundation Ireland 2000–; Dir BP Chemicals Int. Ltd, BP Venezuela Ltd; Visiting Prof., Imperial Coll., London 1979–; Professorial Fellow, Univ. Coll. of Swansea, Univ. of Wales 1979–; mem. Council, Royal Inst. 1984–87, Royal Comm. on Criminal Justice 1991–93; Past Pres. Royal Soc. of Chemistry 1982–84; Gov. Jt Research Centre, EC 1994–; Science Policy Adviser, Science Foundation, Ireland, 1999; Chair. DNA Research Innovations Ltd, 1999; mem. numerous scientific cttees; Hon. Fellow Royal Acad. of Eng 1992; recipient of several prizes and 19 hon. degrees and fellowships. *Publications:* about 300 papers in professional journals. *Leisure interests:* supporting rugby football, being in France, gardening. *Address:* Department of Chemistry, Imperial College of Science, Technology and Medicine, Prince Consort Road, South Kensington, London, SW7 2AY (Office). *Telephone:* (20) 7594-5864 (Imperial Coll.) (Office). *Fax:* (20) 7271-2018 (Office). *E-mail:* d.pappoe@ic.ac.uk (Office).

CAFU, Marcos Evangelista; Brazilian footballer; b. 19 June 1970, São Paulo; defender (right back) São Paulo 1988–93, Zaragoza 1994–95, Palmeiras 1995–97, Roma 1997–; mem. nat. team 1994–; 112 int. caps (end 2002); only player to have played in three World Cup finals; Brazilian record of 16 World Cup appearances. *Address:* Fundação Cafu, Rua Edward Joseph, 122, cj. 85/86 Morumbi, São Paulo, SP 05709-020, Brazil. *Telephone:* (11) 3772-6630. *E-mail:* cafu@fundacaocafu.org.br (Office). *Website:* www.fundacaocafu.org.br.

CAGATAY, Mustafa; Cypriot politician; b. 20 April 1937, Limassol; s. of Ali Hasan and Fehime Ali; m. Tuncay Çağatay 1965; two s. one d.; ed Nicosia Turkish Lycée; started Law Practice in Limassol 1963; elected dep. for Limassol, Turkish Communal Chamber 1970; elected mem. for Kyrenia, Legis. Assembly, Turkish Federated State of Cyprus 1976; Minister of Finance 1976, of Labour, Social Security and Health May–Dec. 1978; Prime Minister 1978–83; mem. Turkish Cypriot Cttee, Turkish and Greek Cypriot Talks on Humanitarian Issues 1974; mem. Nat. Unity Party. *Leisure interests:* reading, swimming, walking. *Address:* 6 D Kolordu Street, Kyrenia (Office); 60 Cumhuriyet Caddesi, Kyrenia, Cyprus (Home).

CAGE, Nicolas (pseudonym of Nicolas Coppola); American actor; b. 7 Jan. 1964, Long Beach, Calif.; nephew of Francis Ford Coppola (q.v.); m. 1st Patricia Arquette (q.v.) 1995 (divorced 2000); m. 2nd Lisa Marie Presley 2002 (divorced 2002); one s. with Christina Fulton; Dr. hc (Calif. State, Fullerton); numerous awards including Acad. Award for Best Actor 1996, Golden Globe Award for Best Actor 1996, Lifetime Achievement Award 1996, P. J. Owens Award 1998, Charles A. Crain Desert Palm Award 2001. *Films include:* Valley Girl 1983, Rumble Fish, Racing with the Moon, The Cotton Club, Birdy, The Boy in Blue, Raising Arizona, Peggy Sue Got Married, Moonstruck, Vampire's Kiss, Killing Time, The Short Cut, Queens Logic, Wild at Heart, Wings of the Apache, Zandalee, Red Rock West, Guarding Tess, Honeymoon in Vegas, It Could Happen to You, Kiss of Death, Leaving Las Vegas 1996 (Golden Globe Award for Best Actor 1996, Acad. Award for Best Actor 1996), The Rock 1996, The Funeral 1996, Con Air 1997, Face Off 1997, 8MM 1999, Bringing Out the Dead 1999, Gone in 60 Seconds 2000, The Family Man 2001, Captain Corelli's Mandolin 2001, Christmas Carol: The Movie (voice) 2001, Windtalkers 2002, Sonny 2002, Adaptation 2003. *Address:* Saturn Films, 9000 West Sunset Boulevard, Suite 911, West Hollywood, CA 90069 (Office); c/o Creative Artists Agency, 9830 Wilshire Boulevard, Beverly Hills, CA 90212, USA (Office).

CAGIATI, Andrea, LLB; Italian diplomatist; b. 11 July 1922, Rome; s. of Filiffo Cagiati and Germaine Dewies; m. Sigrid von Morgen 1968; one s. one d.; ed Univ. of Siena; entered Foreign Service 1948; Sec., Paris 1950–51; Prin. Pvt. Sec. to Minister of State for Foreign Affairs 1951–53; Vice-Consul-Gen., New York 1953–55; Prin. Pvt. Sec. to Minister of State for Foreign Affairs, then with Dept of Political Affairs 1955–57; Counsellor, Athens 1957–60, Mexico 1960–62; Del. Disarmament Cttee, Geneva March–Dec. 1962; mem. Italian del. to UN June 1962; Head NATO Dept 1962–66; Minister-Counsellor, Madrid 1966–68; Amb. to Colombia 1968–71; Inst. for Diplomatic Studies 1971–72; Diplomatic Adviser to Prime Minister 1972–73; Amb. to Austria 1973–80, to UK 1980–86, to the Vatican 1986–88; Vice-Chair. Alitalia 1989–94 (Dir 1987–94); Hon. Pres. Circolo Studi Diplomatici, Eurodéfence Italia; Vice-Pres. Fondazione De Gasperi, Amb. to Malta; Hon. GCVO 1980; Grand Cross of Merit, Italy, Austria, Holy See, Malta. *Publications:* La Diplomazia 1945, Verso quale avvenire? 1957, I sentieri della vita 1990, Scritti di politica estera (4 Vols) 1991–2000; and numerous articles on foreign policy and int. affairs. *Leisure interests:* sculpture, golf, shooting. *Address:* Largo Olgiata, 15 (49D), 00123 Rome, Italy. *Telephone:* (06) 30888135. *Fax:* (06) 30888135.

CAĞLAR, Cavit; Turkish business executive and fmr. government minister; b. 1946, Greece; moved to Turkey as a child; founder and owner Yeşim clothing and home furnishings industry; acquired commercial bank Interbank 1996, 50% stake in Etibank 1998; after collapse of both banks, arrested in connection with alleged financial mismanagement 2001. *Address:* Yeşim Tekstil San. Ve Tic. A.S., Ankara Yolu 10.km Gursu Kavsagi, Bursa, Turkey (Office). *Telephone:* (224) 3725000 (Office). *Fax:* (224) 3721882 (Office).

CAHILL, Teresa Mary, LRAM, AGSM; British opera and concert singer; b. 30 July 1944, Maidenhead, Berks.; d. of Henry D. Cahill and Florence Cahill (née Dallimore); m. John Anthony Kiernander 1971 (divorced 1978); partner Dr Robert Saxton; ed Notre Dame High School, Southwark, Guildhall School of Music and Drama and London Opera Centre; debut at Glyndebourne 1969, Covent Garden 1970, La Scala, Milan 1976, Philadelphia Opera 1981; Prof. Royal Northern Coll. of Music and Trinity Coll. of Music, London; Vocal Consultant Univ. of York; specializes in works of Mozart, Strauss, Mahler, Elgar and Tippett; has given concerts with all the London orchestras, Boston Symphony Orchestra, Chicago Symphony Orchestra, Berlin, Vienna and Bath Festivals and throughout Europe, USA and the Far East; masterclasses, Dartington Festival 1984, 1986, Oxford Univ. 1995–96, Peabody Inst. Baltimore 1999; Artistic Adviser Nat. Mozart Competition 1997–; Adjudicator Live Music Now 1988– (Musical Adviser 2000–); Gov. Royal Soc. of Music 2000–; mem. Guildhall School of Music and Drama; masterclasses, Royal Acad. of Music, 2002, 's-Hertogenbosch 1988, 2000; Worshipful Company of Musicians Silver Medal 1966, John Christie Award 1970. *Recordings include:* works by Elgar, Strauss, Mahler, Mozart & contemporary music. *Publications:* contrib. to 'Divas in their Own Words', compiled by Andrew Palmer. *Leisure interests:* cinema, theatre, travel, photography, reading and going to sales, from car boots to Sothebys. *Address:* 65 Leyland Road, London, SE12 8DW, England.

CAI RUO-HONG; Chinese painter; b. 29 Jan. 1910, Jio Jang City; s. of Cai Yi-ting and Zhang Zhen-mai; m. Xia Lei 1939; three d.; ed Art Coll. of Shanghai; caricaturist 1932–38; Prof. Lu Xun Art Inst., Yan-an 1939–45; Vice-Dir of Art, Bureau of Ministry of Culture 1949–54; Deputy to 3rd NPC 1964–68, Deputy to 5th and 6th NPC 1978–88; Vice-Chair. Chinese Artists' Asscn 1960–; Vice-Chair. Acad. of Chinese Painting 1981–83; mem. Standing Cttee of China Fed. of Literary and Art Circles 1949–88. *Publications:* What Caused the Miserable Life? (album of paintings) 1954, Ruo-hong's Poems and Paintings (albums of poems) 1985, Collection of Art Theory of Cai Ruo-hong 1988, Collection of Poems of Cai Ruo-hong (Vol. II, Songs of Soul) 1997, The Ideal is More Perfect than Reality (theory of art) 1998, The Social Customs in the Small Attic in Shanghai (memoir) 1999, Being Barefoot in Paradise (memoir) 2000. *Leisure interests:* reading, writing. *Address:* 9-2-2 Nan Sha Go, San Li He Street, Beijing, People's Republic of China. *Telephone:* 68523346.

CAI ZHENHUA; Chinese table tennis coach; b. 1961, Wuxi, Jiangsu Prov.; Chief Coach of Chinese Men's Table Tennis Team 1991–95; Head Coach of Chinese Table Tennis Team 1995–, former chief coach for Italian table tennis team. *Address:* c/o State General Bureau for Physical Culture and Sports, 9 Tiyuguan Road, Chongwen District, Beijing, People's Republic of China.

CAI ZIMIN; Chinese politician; b. 1926, Zhanghua City, Taiwan Prov.; ed in Japan; Chair. Taiwan Democratic Self-Govt League 1988–97, Hon. Chair. 1997–; Adviser Asscn for Relations across the Taiwan Straits (ARATS) 1991–; mem. 8th Standing Cttee NPC 1993–98; Vice-Chair. Cttee for Hong Kong, Macao, Taiwan and Overseas Chinese Affairs, 9th Nat. Cttee of CPPCC 1998–. *Address:* c/o National Committee of Chinese People's Political Consultative Conference, 23 Taipingqiao Street, Beijing, People's Republic of China.

CAIN, John, LLB; Australian politician; b. 26 April 1931; s. of late John Cain; m. Nancye Williams 1955; two s. one d.; ed Northcote High School, Scotch Coll. and Melbourne Univ.; mem. Council Law Inst. of Vic. 1967–76, Exec. Law

Council of Australia 1973–76; Vice-Chair. Vic. Br. Australian Labor Party 1973–75; Pres. Law Inst., Vic. 1972–73, Chair. Council 1971–72; mem. Legis. Ass. for Bundoora, Vic. 1976–92; Leader of Opposition 1981–82; Premier of Vic. 1982–90; Professorial Assoc., Melbourne Univ. 1991–; Attorney-Gen. 1982–83; Minister for Fed. Affairs 1982, Minister for Women's Affairs 1982–90, for Ethnic Affairs 1990; Treas. Law Inst., Vic. 1969–70; part-time mem. Law Reform Comm. of Australia 1975–77; mem. Commonwealth Observer Group, South African elections 1994; Trustee, Melbourne Cricket Club 1982–98, 1999–; Trustee Nat. Tennis Centre 1990–94. *Publications:* John Cain's Years: Power, Parties and Politics 1994, On With the Show 1998. *Leisure interests:* tennis, swimming, jogging. *Address:* 9 Magnolia Road, Ivanhoe, Victoria 3079, Australia.

CAINE, Sir Michael, Kt, CBE; British actor; b. Maurice Joseph Micklewhite, 14 March 1933, London; s. of late Maurice Joseph Micklewhite and of Ellen Frances Marie Micklewhite; m. 1st Patricia Haines 1954 (divorced); one d.; m. 2nd Shakira Khatoon Baksh 1973; one d.; ed Wilson's Grammar School, Peckham; army service, Berlin and Korea 1951–53; worked at repertory theatres, Horsham and Lowestoft 1953–55; Theatre Workshop, London 1955; mem. IBA 1984–; Hon. Fellow (Univ. of London) 1994; BAFTA 2000; Acad. Award for Best Supporting Actor (Hannah and Her Sisters) 1986, Golden Globe Award (Jack the Ripper TV mini-series) 1988, Acad. Award for Best Supporting Actor (The Cider House Rules) 2000. *Films include:* A Hill in Korea 1956, How to Murder a Rich Uncle 1958, Zulu 1964, The Ipcress File 1965, Alfie 1966, The Wrong Box 1966, Gambit 1966, Funeral in Berlin 1966, Billion Dollar Brain 1967, Woman Times Seven 1967, Deadfall 1967, The Magus 1968, Battle of Britain 1968, Play Dirty 1968, The Italian Job 1969, Too Late the Hero 1970, The Last Valley 1970, Kidnapped 1971, Pulp 1971, Get Carter 1971, Zee and Co. 1972, Sleuth 1973, The Black Windmill, The Marseilles Contract, Peeper, The Wilby Conspiracy 1974, Fat Chance, The Romantic Englishwoman, Harry and Walter Go to New York, The Eagle has Landed, The Man Who Would be King 1975, A Bridge Too Far, The Silver Bears 1976, The Swarm, California Suite 1977, Ashanti 1978, Beyond the Poseidon Adventure 1979, The Island 1979, Dressed to Kill 1979, Escape to Victory 1979, Deathtrap 1981, The Hand 1981, Educating Rita 1982, Jigsaw Man 1982, The Honorary Consul 1982, Blame it on Rio 1983, Water 1984, The Holcroft Covenant 1984, Sweet Liberty 1985, Mona Lisa 1985, The Whistle Blower 1985, Half Moon Street 1986, The Fourth Protocol 1986, Hannah and Her Sisters 1986, Surrender 1987, Without a Clue 1988, Dirty Rotten Scoundrels 1988, A Shock to the System 1989, Mr. Destiny 1989, Bullseye 1989, Noises Off 1991, Blue Ice 1992, The Muppet Christmas Carol 1992, On Deadly Ground 1993, Bullet to Beijing 1994, Blood and Wine 1995, 20,000 Leagues under the Sea 1996, Mandela and De Klerk 1996, Curtain Call, Shadowrun, Little Voice 1997, The Debtors 1998, The Cider House Rules 1998, Quills 1999, Shiner 2000, Last Orders 2000, Quick Sand 2000, The Quiet American 2001, Austin Powers: Gold Member 2002, The Actors 2002, The Quiet American 2002, The Secondhand Lion. *TV includes:* over 100 TV plays 1957–63, World War 2 – When Lions Roared (NBC TV) 1993, Jack the Ripper (mini-series) 1988. *Plays include:* Next Time I'll Sing to You 1963. *Publications:* Michael Caine's File of Facts 1987, Not Many People Know This 1988, What's It All About? 1992, Acting in Film 1993. *Leisure interests:* gardening, reading. *Address:* c/o Duncan Heath, International Creative Management, Oxford House, 76 Oxford Street, London, W1R 0AX, England.

CAINE, Uri; American jazz pianist and classical composer; b. Philadelphia; ed Univ. of Penn.; began studying piano with Bernard Pfeiffer; played in bands led by Philly Joe Jones, Johnny Coles, Odean Pope, Hank Mobley, Grover Washington, Mikey Roker and Jymmie Merritt during high school; studied music composition with George Crumb and George Rochenberg at univ. and performed with Joe Henderson, Donald Byrd, J.J. Johnson, Stanley Turrentine, Lester Bowie and Freddie Hubbard; recently performed in groups led by Don Byron, Dave Douglas, Terry Gibbs and Buddy DeFranco, Clark Terry, Rashid Ali, Arto Lindsay, Sam Rivers and Barry Altschul, Bobby Watson, Craig Handy, Annie Ross, Arto Lindsay, The Enja Band, Global Theory, The Woody Herman Band, The Master Musicians of Jajouka; performed at What is Jazz? Festival (NY), North Sea Jazz Festival (The Hague), Montréal Jazz Festival, Jazz Across the Borders (Berlin), Texaco Jazz Festival (NY), Umbria Jazz Festival, Gustav Mahler Festival (Toblach, Italy), Vittoria Jazz Festival, San Sebastian Jazz Festival, Newport Jazz Festival, Salzburg Festival, Munich Opera, Holland Festival, Israel Festival, ICRAM and others; Toblacher Komponierhäuschen Award for Best Mahler CD 1997. *Albums include:* Sphere Music 1993, Toys 1995, Urlicht/Primal Light 1996, Wagner e Veneza 1997, Blue Wail 1998, Sidewalks of New York 1999, Love Fugue 2000, The Goldberg Variations 2000 (performed by Penn. Ballet 2001), Solitaire 2001, Rio 2001, Bedrock3 2001. *Compositions include:* ballet composed for Vienna Volksoper 2000, version of Diabelli Variations for Concerto Köln 2001, Mahler Reimagined, London 2002. *E-mail:* ucaine@worldnet.att.net (Office). *Website:* www.uricaine.com (Office).

CAIO, Francesco; Italian business executive; founder and fmr CEO Omnitel Pronto Italia; CEO Olivetti and C. SpA, July–Sept. 1996; fmr CEO Merloni; f. Netscalibur, CEO –2003; mem. Bd Dirs Motorola; CEO Cable & Wireless 2003–. *Address:* Cable & Wireless, 124 Theobalds Road, London, WC1X 8RX, England (Office). *Telephone:* (20) 7315-4000 (Office). *Fax:* (20) 7315-5000 (Office). *Website:* www.cwplc.com.

CAIRD, Most Rev. Donald Arthur Richard, MA, BD, DipEd; Irish ecclesiastic; b. 11 Dec. 1925, Dublin; s. of George R. Caird and Emily F. Dreaper; m. Nancy B. Sharpe 1963; one s. two d.; ed Wesley Coll., Dublin Trinity Coll., Dublin and Univ. of Dublin; Curate-Asst St Mark's, Dundela, Belfast 1950–53, Asst Master and Chaplain The Royal School, Portora 1953–57; Lecturer in Philosophy, Univ. of Wales 1957–60; Rector Rathmichael Parish, Co. Dublin 1960–69; Asst Lecturer in Philosophy, Trinity Coll. Dublin 1962–63; Dean of Ossary, Kilkenny 1969–1970; Bishop of Limerick, Ardfert and Aghadoe 1970–76; of Meath and Kildare 1976–1985; Archbishop of Dublin, Primate of Ireland and Bishop of Glendalough 1985–96; Chair. Council Alexandra Coll. (Dublin); Chair. Church of Ireland Coll. of Educ.; mem. Bórd na Gaelge (Govt Bd for Irish Language); Patron Nat. Youth Council of Ireland; Fellow of St Columba's Coll. (Dublin); Visiting Prof. of Anglican Studies, Gen. Theological Seminary, New York 1997; Sr Exhibitioner, Foundation Scholar and Sr Moderator, Univ. of Dublin; Life mem. Royal Dublin Soc. 1995–; Hon. DD (Trinity Coll., Dublin) 1988; Hon. LLD (Nat. Univ. of Ireland) 1995; Hon. PhD (Pontifical Univ., Maynooth, Co. Kildare) 2002; Nat. Council for Educational Awards 1993, . *Publication:* The Predicament of Natural Theology since the Criticism of Kant, in Directions 1970. *Leisure interests:* walking and swimming. *Address:* 3 Crofton Avenue, Dun Laoghaire, Co. Dublin, Ireland. *Telephone:* (1) 2807869. *Fax:* (1) 2301053.

CAIRNS, Christopher Lance; New Zealand cricketer; b. 13 June 1970, Picton, Marlborough; s. of Lance Cairns; right-hand batsman, right-arm fast-medium bowler; teams: Northern Districts, Nottinghamshire, Canterbury, New Zealand; in 55 Tests scored 2,853 runs (average 32.79), 197 wickets (average 28.8) to Nov. 2002; in 151 One Day Ints. scored 3,615 runs (average 29.15), 154 wickets (average 31.9) to Feb. 2002; 9,231 first-class runs (average 35.4), 594 wickets (average 27.5) in 189 matches to Nov. 2002; out of action from March to Nov. 2002 through injury; with father Lance Cairns (former Test Player), the only father and son to have captured 10 wickets in single Test matches; Wisden Cricketer of the Year 2000, PricewaterhouseCoopers No 1 All-rounder in the World 2000, New Zealand Nat. Bank Player of the Year 2001, Redpath Cup for Batting, Winsor Cup for Bowling.

CAIRNS, David Adam, CBE, MA; British journalist and musicologist; b. 8 June 1926, Loughton; s. of Sir Hugh William Bell Cairns and Barbara Cairns (née Smith); m. Rosemary Goodwin 1959; three s.; ed Winchester Coll., Univ. of Oxford, Princeton Univ.; Library Clerk, House of Commons 1951–53; critic, Record News 1954–56; mem. Editorial Staff, Times Educational Supplement 1955–58; music Critic, Spectator 1958–63, Evening Standard 1958–63; Asst Music Critic, Financial Times 1963–67; Music Critic, New Statesman 1967–70; mem. staff, Philips Records, London 1968–70, Classic Programme Co-ordinator 1970–73; Asst Music Critic, Sunday Times 1975–84, Music Critic 1985–92; Visiting Prof. of Music, Univ. of Calif., Davis 1985; Leverhulme Research Fellow 1972–74; Officier, Ordre des Arts et des Lettres. *Publications:* The Memoirs of Hector Berlioz 1969 (Ed. and Trans.), Responses: Musical Essays and Reviews 1973, (jtly) ENO Opera Guides (The Magic Flute 1981) (Falstaff 1982), Berlioz: The Making of an Artist 1803–1832 1989, Berlioz: Servitude and Greatness 1832–1869 1999. *Leisure interests:* conducting, reading, walking, cinema, theatre, cricket. *Address:* 49 Amerland Road, London, SW18 1QA, England. *Telephone:* (20) 8870-4931.

CAIRNS, 6th Earl; **Simon Dallas Cairns,** CVO, CBE; British businessman; b. 27 May 1939; s. of 5th Earl Cairns and Barbara Jeanne Harrisson; m. Amanda Mary Heathcoat Amory 1964; three s.; ed Eton, Trinity Coll., Cambridge; Chair. Voluntary Service Overseas 1981–92 (Treas. 1974–81); mem. City Capital Markets Cttee 1989–95; Dir S.G. Warburg Group PLC (fmrly Mercury Int. Group) 1985–95, Vice-Chair. 1987–91; Jt Chair. S. G. Warburg and Co. 1987–95, CEO, Deputy Chair. 1991–95; Chair. Commonwealth Devt Corpn (CDC Group PLC) 1995–, BAT Industries 1996–98 (Deputy Chair. June–Dec. 1995); Chair. Allied Zurich 1998–2000, Vice-Chair. Zurich Allied 1998–2000, Zurich Financial Services 1998–2000; Chair. Commonwealth Business Council 1997–2003, Overseas Devt Inst. 1994–2002; Receiver Gen. Duchy of Cornwall 1990–2000. *Address:* Bolehyde Manor, Allington, Nr Chippenham, Wilts., SN14 6LW; c/o 1 Bessborough Gardens, London, SW1V 2JQ, England (Office).

CALABRESI, Guido, MA, BS, LLB; American judge and professor of law; b. 18 Oct. 1932, Milan, Italy; s. of Massimo Calabresi and Bianca Maria Finzi-Contini Calabresi; m. Anne Gordon Audubon Tyler 1961; one s. two d.; ed Yale Coll., Magdalen Coll., Oxford and Yale Law School; Asst Instr. Dept of Econs Yale Coll. 1955–56; Thacher & Bartlett (law firm), New York 1957; mem. Conn. Bar 1958; law clerk to Mr Justice Hugo Black, US Supreme Court 1958–59; Asst Prof. of Law, Yale Univ. School of Law 1959–61; Assoc. Prof. Yale Law School 1961–62, Prof. of Law 1962–70; John Thomas Smith Prof. of Law, Yale Univ. 1970–78, Sterling Prof. of Law 1978–95, Sterling Prof. of Law Emer. 1995–, Dean Yale Univ. Law School 1985–94; Judge, US Court of Appeals (Second Circuit) 1994–; Visiting Prof. at Univs in USA and abroad; mem. various comms, cttees etc.; Corresp. Mem. British Acad.; mem. Royal Acad. of Sweden, Accademia delle Scienze di Torino, Accademia Nazionale dei Lincei, American Acad. of Arts and Sciences, American Philosophical Soc.; numerous hon. degrees and awards including Laetare Medal, Univ. of Notre Dame 1985, Thomas Jefferson Medal in Law 2000. *Publications:* The Costs of Accidents: A Legal and Economic Analysis 1970, Tragic Choices (with P. Bobbit) 1978, A Common Law for the Age of Statutes 1982, Ideals, Beliefs, Attitudes and the Law: Private Law Perspectives on a Public Law Problem 1985. *Leisure interests:* walking, reading (especially history), gardening, travel, bridge. *Address:* United States Court of Appeals for the Second Circuit, 157 Church Street, New Haven, CT 06510-2100 (Office); 639 Amity Road,

Woodbridge, CT 06525-1206, USA (Home). *Telephone:* (203) 773-2291 (Office); (203) 393-0008 (Home). *Fax:* (203) 773-2401 (Office); (203) 393-1575 (Home). *E-mail:* guido.calabresi@yale.edu (Office).

CALATRAVA VALLS, Santiago, PhD; Spanish architect, artist and civil engineer; b. 28 July 1953, Benimamet, nr Valencia; m. Robertina Caltrava Valls; three s. one d.; ed Escuela Tecnica Superior de Arquitectura, Fed. Inst. of Tech. (ETH), Zürich, Switzerland; asst Fed. Inst. of Tech. (ETH), Zürich 1979; undertook small eng comms 1980s; est. firm Santiago Calatrava SA, Zürich, 1983, second office Paris 1989, third office Valencia 1991; won competitions to design and construct Stadelhofen Station, Zürich 1983, Bach de Roda Bridge (commissioned by Olympic Games), Barcelona 1984, Cathedral of St John the Divine, New York 1991; sculptural works include Shadow Machine (large-scale sculpture with undulating concrete fingers) 1993; recently selected to design Christ the Light Cathedral, Oakland, Calif., the expansion of Museo dell'Opera del Duomo, Florence and Symphony Center for the Atlanta Symphony Orchestra, Georgia; mem. Acad. des Arts et Lettres, Paris; Creu Sant Jordi, Barcelona (Spain), Gold Medal for Merit in the Fine Arts, Ministry of Culture (Granada); twelve hon. doctorates; Gold Medal, Inst. of Structural Engineers (UK), City of Toronto Urban Design Award (Canada), Global Leader for Tomorrow, World Econ. Forum, Davos (Switzerland), Algur H. Meadows Award for Excellence in the Arts, Meadows School of the Arts, Gold Medal, Circolo de Bellas Artes, Valencia, Sir Misha Black Medal, Royal Coll. of Art (UK), Leonardo da Vinci Medal, Société pour les Formations des Ingénieurs (France); Principe de Asturias Art Prize. *Architectural works include:* Alamillo Bridge Viaduct, Seville 1987–92, BCE Place Mall, Toronto 1987–92, Campo Volantin Footbridge, Bilbao 1990–97, Alameda Bridge and Underground Station, Valencia 1991–95, Lyon Airport Station, France 1989–94, City of Arts and Sciences, Valencia 1991–, Oriente Railway Station, Lisbon, Portugal 1993–98, Sondica Airport, Bilbao 2000, The Bridge of Europe, Orléans, France 2000, Bodegas Ysios Winery, Laguardia 2001, Milwaukee Art Museum, USA (Time Magazine 'Best of 2001' designation) 2001; Works in progress: Blackhall Place, Dublin, Ireland (2003), Tenerife Auditorium, Santa Cruz, Canary Islands (2003), Petach Tikvah Bridge, Tel Aviv, Israel 2003, Quatro Ponte sul Canal Grande, Venice, Italy (2003–04), Turtle Bay Bridge, Redding, Calif., USA (2004), Athens Olympic Sports Complex, Greece (2004), Valencia Opera House (2004). *Exhibitions include:* Jamileh Weber Gallery, Zürich, Switzerland 1985, Royal Inst. of Architects, London, UK 1992, 'Structure and Expression', Museum of Modern Art, New York City, USA 1993, 'Santiago Calatrava: Artist, Architect, Engineer', Palazzo Strozzi, Florence, Italy 2000–01, Meadows Museum, Dallas TX, USA 2001, Alexandro Soutzos Museum, Nat. Gallery, Athens, Greece. *Address:* Santiago Calatrava SA, Parkring 11, 8002 Zürich, Switzerland (Office). *Telephone:* (1) 2045000 (Office). *Fax:* (1) 2045001 (Office). *E-mail:* zurich@scsa-mail.com (Office). *Website:* www.calatrava.com (Office).

CALCUTT, Sir David Charles, Kt, QC, MA, LLB, BMus, FRCM; British barrister; b. 2 Nov. 1930; s. of the late Henry Calcutt; m. Barbara Walker 1969; ed Christ Church Oxford (chorister), Cranleigh School (music scholar), King's Coll. Cambridge (choral scholar, Stewart of Rannoch Scholar 1952); called to Bar, Middle Temple 1955 (Bencher 1981, Treasurer 1998); Harmsworth Law Scholar 1956; Deputy Chair. Somerset Quarter Sessions 1970–71; a Recorder 1972–89; Fellow Commoner, Magdalene Coll. Cambridge 1980–85, Master 1986–94, Hon. Fellow 1994–; a Judge of the Courts of Appeal of Jersey and Guernsey 1978–2000; Chair. Civil Service Arbitration Tribunal 1979–94; Deputy Pres., Lloyd's of London Appeal Tribunal 1983–87, Pres. 1987–97; Chair. Inst. of Actuaries' Appeal Bd 1985–94; conducted Falkland Islands Comm. of Inquiry 1984, Cyprus Servicemen Inquiry 1985–86, Review of Press Self-Regulation 1992–93; Chair. City Panel on Takeovers and Mergers 1989–2000; Chair. Council of the Banking Ombudsman 1994–2001 mem. Criminal Injuries Compensation Bd 1977–97, Council on Tribunals 1980–86; mem. Gen. Council of the Bar 1968–72, Senate of the Inns of Court and the Bar 1979–85, Chair. of the Senate 1984–85, Chair. of the Bar 1984–85; mem. UK Del., Consultative Cttee, Bars and Law Socs., EEC 1979–83, Interception of Communications Tribunal 1986–2001 (Vice-Pres. 1996–2001), Investigatory Powers Tribunal 2000–; Chancellor of Dioceses of Exeter and Bristol 1971–, and in Europe 1983–; Arbitrator Int. Centre for Settlement of Investment Disputes, Washington DC 1986–; Ind. mem. Diplomatic Service Appeal Bd 1986–92; Home Office Assessor of Compensation for Miscarriages of Justice 1989–2001, for Ministry of Defence 1994–; Deputy Chair. RCM 1988–90; Chair. Cttee on Privacy and Related Matters 1989–90; Fellow Winchester Coll. 1992–; Hon. mem. American Bar Asscn 1985–, Canadian Bar Asscn 1985–; Hon. LLD (Exeter) 1996, (Staffs.) 1997, (Southampton) 1998, (Univ. of W of England) 1998. *Leisure interest:* living on Exmoor. *Address:* 35 Essex Street, Temple, London, WC2R 3AR, England. *Telephone:* (20) 7353-6381.

CALDER, Elisabeth Nicole, BA; British publisher; b. 20 Jan. 1938, New Zealand; d. of Ivor George Baber and Florence Mary Baber; m. Richard Henry Calder 1958 (divorced 1972); one s. one d.; ed Palmerston North Girls' High School, NZ and Univ. of Canterbury, NZ; reader Metro-Goldwyn-Mayer Story Dept 1969–70; Publicity Man. Victor Gollancz 1971–74, Editorial Dir 1975–78; Editorial Dir Jonathan Cape 1979–86; Publishing Dir Bloomsbury Publishing 1986–; Chair. Royal Court Theatre 2001–. *Leisure interests:* junking, thinking about gardening, reading. *Address:* Bloomsbury Publishing, 38 Soho Square, London, W1V 5DF, England. *Telephone:* (20) 7494-2111.

CALDER, John Mackenzie; British publisher, critic and playwright; b. 25 Jan. 1927; m. 1st Mary A. Simmonds 1949; one d.; m. 2nd Bettina Jonic 1960 (dissolved 1975); one d.; ed Gilling Castle, Yorks., Bishops Coll. School, Canada, McGill Univ., Montreal, Sir George Williams Coll. and Univ. of Zürich, Switzerland; f. and Man. Dir John Calder (Publishers) Ltd 1950–91, Calder Publs Ltd 1991–, Calder and Boyars Ltd 1964–75, f. Calder Bookshop; expanded to Edin. 1971; organized literature confs., Edin. Festival 1962, 1963, Harrogate Festival 1969; f. Ledlanet Nights (music and opera festival) Kinross-shire 1963–74; Pres. Riverrun Press Inc., New York 1978–; Prof. of Literature and Philosophy, Ecole Active Bilingue, Paris 1994–96; lecturer in History, Univ. of Paris-Nanterre 1995; acquired book-selling business of Better Books, London 1969; Chair. North American Book Clubs 1982–89, Fed. of Scottish Theatres 1972–74; Co-founder, Defence of Literature and the Arts Soc.; Dir of other cos assoc. with opera, publishing etc.; f. Samuel Beckett Theatre, Waterloo, London; Chevalier des Arts et des Lettres, Officier et Chevalier Ordre nat. du Mérite. *Plays include:* Lorca, The Voice, The Trust. *Publications:* A Samuel Beckett Reader, The Burroughs Reader 1981, New Beckett Reader 1983, Henry Miller Reader 1985, Nouveau Roman Reader 1986, The Defence of Literature 1991, The Garden of Eros 1992, The Philosophy of Samuel Beckett 1998, What's Wrong, What's Right (poetry) 1999, Pursuit (autobiog.) 2001. *Leisure interests:* writing, reading, music, theatre, opera, chess, conversation, travelling, promoting good causes, good food and wine. *Address:* Calder Publications Ltd, 51 The Cut, London, SE1 8LF, England (Office); Riverrun Press Inc., 100 Newfield Avenue, Edison, NJ 08837, USA (Office); 9 rue de Ramainville, 93100 Montreuil, France. *Telephone:* (20) 7633-0599 (UK) (Home); (212) 889-6850 (USA) (Office); 1-49-88-75-12 (France). *Fax:* 1-48-59-66-68 (France). *E-mail:* info@calderpublications.com (Office). *Website:* www.calderpublications.com (Office).

CALDERA, Louis Edward, BS, MBA, JD; American federal official; b. 1 April 1956, El Paso; s. of Benjamin Luis Caldera and Soledad Siqueiros; m. Eva Orlebeke Caldera; ed U.S. Mil. Acad., Harvard Univ.; called to Bar, Calif. 1987; Commdr 2nd Lt U.S. Army 1978, advanced through ranks to Capt. 1982, resigned comm. 1983; Assoc. O'Melveny & Myers, LA 1987–89, Buchalter, Nemer, Fields & Younger, LA 1990–91; Deputy Co. Counsel, Co. of LA 1991–92; mem. Calif. State Ass., 46th Dist, LA 1992–97, Chair. Banking and Finance Cttee; Man. Dir, COO Corpn for Nat. Service, Washington 1997–98; Sec. of U.S. Army 1998–2001; Vice-Chancellor for Univ. Advancement, Calif. State Univ. System 2002–; Democrat. *Address:* California State University, 401 Golden Shore, Long Beach, CA 90802, USA.

CALDERA CARDINAL, Norman José, DPhil; Nicaraguan politician, economist and consultant; b. 21 Oct. 1946, Managua; m. Nora Maria Mayorga Arg Üello; one s. two d.; ed Wentworth Mil. Acad., Lexington, Missouri, Univ. of Texas at Austin, Columbia Univ., New York, USA; fmr Marketing Supervisor, then Product Man. Kimberley Clark Co.; Finance Gen. Empresas Universales SA 1972, Exports Man. 1975, Gen. Man. 1976; consultant to Agricultural Devt of Latin America (ADELA) Investment Co. 1979, to OAS 1979, to UNCTAD/GATT 1980–96, to GUATEXPRO 1980–84 (apptd Chief Adviser 1984); Adjunct Sec.-Gen. SIECA and COMIECO (Cabinet of Integration and Commerce of Cen. America) 1992–95; consultant to Inter-American Devt Bank 1995–96, UNCTAD 1996; Econ. Adviser to Pres. of Nicaragua 1996–97; Exec. Sec. Cttee to Reform the Public Admin (CERAP) 1997; Minister of Trade, Industry and Commerce 1999–2001, of Foreign Affairs Jan. 2002–. *Address:* Ministry of Foreign Affairs, detrás de restaurante Los Ranchos, Managua, Nicaragua (Office). *Telephone:* (2) 66-1159 (Office). *E-mail:* norman.caldera@cancilleria.gob.ni (Office). *Website:* www.cancilleria.gob.ni (Office).

CALDERA RODRÍGUEZ, Rafael; Venezuelan politician and lawyer; b. 24 Jan. 1916, San Felipe, Yaracuy; s. of Dr. Rafael and Rosa Sofia R. Caldera; m. Alicia P. Caldera 1941; three s. three d.; Sec., Cen. Council of Soc. of Venezuelan Catholic Youth 1932–34; founded U.N.E. (Nat. Union of Students) 1936; graduated as lawyer 1939; founded Acción Nacional 1942; mem. Chamber of Deputies 1942; unsuccessful Pres. Candidate for Partido Social-Cristiano (COPEI) 1947; Fellow of Acad. of Political and Social Sciences 1952, 1983; unsuccessful COPEI Pres. Candidate 1958; Pres. of Chamber of Deputies 1959–61; unsuccessful COPEI Pres. Candidate 1963, 1986; Pres. of Dem. Christian Org. of America (ODCA) 1964–69; Pres. of Venezuela 1969–74, 1994–99; Senator-for-life 1974; Pres. of Inter-Parliamentary Council 1980–83; Prof. Emer. of Sociology and Labour Jurisprudence, Univ. Cen. de Venezuela; Fellow of Venezuelan Acad. of Languages; mem. many Venezuelan and Latin American Insts. of Political Science, Spanish Language and Sociology; Dr. hc from more than 20 American and European univs.; numerous decorations. *Publications:* essays on legal matters, sociology and politics. *Address:* c/o Central Information Office of the Presidency, Palacio de Miraflores, Avenida Urdaneta, Caracas 1010, Venezuela. *Telephone:* (2) 81-0811.

CALDERÓN, Sila María, MPA; Puerto Rican politician; b. 23 Sept. 1942, San Juan; three c.; ed Convent of the Sacred Heart, San Juan, Manhattanville Coll., New York, Univ. of Puerto Rico; Special Asst to the Gov. of Puerto Rico, Pres. of Commonwealth Investment Co., Product Man. for Business Devt, Citibank, 1973–84; Chief of Staff, Sec. of State for Gov. of Puerto Rico, 1985–90; Mayor of San Juan 1996–2000; Gov. of Puerto Rico Jan. 2001–; Pres. and Leader Partido Popular Democrático (PPD); Orden Isabel la Católica 1987; Honorary doctorates (Manhattanville Coll., Boston Univ., New School Univ.). *Address:* Office of the Governor, La Fortaleza, Puerto Rico, PR 00901,

USA (Office). *Telephone:* (787) 721-7000 (Office). *Fax:* (787) 721-7483 (Office). *E-mail:* webmaster@govpr.org (Office). *Website:* www.fortaleza.gobierno.pr (Office).

CALDERON FOURNIER, Rafael Angel; Costa Rican politician; b. 14 March 1949, Diriamba, Nicaragua; s. of fmr Pres. Rafael Calderón Guardia; m. Gloria Bejarano; lawyer; Minister of Foreign Affairs 1978–82; cand. for Pres., Social Christian Unity Party 1982, 1986, 1989; Pres. of Costa Rica 1990–94. *Address:* c/o Partido Unidad Social Cristiana, San José, Costa Rica.

CALDERÓN SOL, Armando; Salvadorean politician; b. 24 June 1948, San Salvador; m. Elisabeth Aguirre; three c.; ed Univ. of El Salvador; f. Alianza Republicana Nacionalista (ARENA) 1981, elected leader 1988; deputy 1985–88; Mayor of San Salvador 1988–94; Pres. of El Salvador 1994–99. *Address:* c/o Ministry for the Presidency, Avda. Cuba, Calle Darió González 806, Barrio San Jacinto, San Salvador, El Salvador.

CALDICOTT, Dame Fiona, DBE, MA, BM, BChir, FRCP, FRCPsych, FRCPI; British psychiatrist; b. 12 Jan. 1941; d. of Joseph Maurice Soesan and Elizabeth Jane Soesan (née Ransley); m. Robert Gordon Woodruff Caldicott 1965; one d. (one s. deceased); ed City of London School for Girls, St Hilda's Coll., Oxford Univ.; House Surgeon and Physician, Coventry Hosps 1966–67; GP, Family Planning and Child Welfare 1968–70; training in psychiatry 1970–76; Sr Registrar in Psychiatry, W Midlands Regional Training Scheme 1977–79; Consultant Psychiatrist, Univ. of Warwick 1979–85; consultant Psychotherapist Uffculme Clinic, Birmingham 1979–96; Sr Clinical Lecturer in Psychotherapy, Univ. of Birmingham 1982–96; Unit Gen. Man., Mental Health, Central Birmingham 1989–91; Clinical Dir Adult Psychiatric and Psychotherapy Service, Mental Health Unit, S Birmingham 1991–94; Medical Dir S Birmingham Mental Health National Health Service (NHS) Trust 1994–96; mem. Sec. of State's Standing Advisory Cttee on Medical Manpower (now Workforce) Planning 1991–2001, on Postgrad. Medical Ed. 1993–99, Council Univ. of Oxford 1998–; Chair. Monospecialist Cttee for Psychiatry 1995– (Sec. 1991–95); Sec. European Bd of Psychiatry 1992–96; Sub-Dean Royal Coll. of Psychiatrists 1987–90, Dean 1990–93, Pres. 1993–96; Chair. Conf. of Medical Royal Colls. 1995–96; Prin. Somerville Coll., Oxford Univ. 1996–; Pro-Vice-Chancellor Oxford Univ. 2001–02; mem. Union of European Medical Specialists, Broadcasting Standards Council 1996–, Czech Psychiatric Soc. 1994; Fellow Acad. of Medicine, Singapore 1994; Hon. DSc (Warwick) 1997, Hon. MD (Birmingham) 1997; Chevalier du Tastevin 1991. *Publications:* contrib. to Discussing Doctors' Careers (ed. Isobel Allen) 1988; papers in learned journals on psychiatry. *Leisure interests:* family, friends, reading, theatre, wine. *Address:* Somerville College, Oxford, OX2 6HD (Office); The Old Rectory, Manor Farm Lane, Balscote, Banbury, OX15 6JJ, England (Home). *Telephone:* (1865) 270630 (Office); (1295) 730293 (Home). *Fax:* (1295) 730549 (Home); (1865) 280623 (Office). *E-mail:* fiona.caldicott@somerville.ox.ac.uk (Office).

CALDWELL, John Bernard, OBE, PhD, DSc, FREng, FRINA; British professor of naval architecture; b. 26 Sept. 1926, Northampton; s. of John R. Caldwell and Doris (Bolland) Caldwell; m. Jean M. F. Duddridge 1955; two s.; ed Bootham School, York and Univs. of Liverpool and Bristol; Prin. Scientific Officer, RN Scientific Service 1957–60; Asst Prof. RN Coll., Greenwich 1960–66; Visiting Prof. MIT 1962–63; Prof. of Naval Architecture, Univ. of Newcastle-upon-Tyne 1966–91, Emer. Prof. 1991–, Head, Dept of Naval Architecture 1966–83, Head, School of Marine Tech. 1975–80, 1986–88, Dean, Faculty of Eng 1983–86; Pres. Royal Inst. of Naval Architects 1984–87; Dir Nat. Maritime Inst. Ltd 1983–85, Marine Design Consultants Ltd 1985–89, Marine Tech. Directorate 1986–90; mem. Eng Council 1988–94; Gold Medal of NECIS 1973, Froude Medal of RINA 1984, David Taylor Medal of SNAME (USA) 1987, Pres.'s Award of Eng Council 1995. *Publications:* over 70 papers in various eng and scientific publs. *Leisure interests:* music, walking, reading. *Address:* Barkbooth, Winster, Windermere, Cumbria, LA23 3NZ, England. *Telephone:* (15395) 68222.

CALDWELL, Philip, MBA; American motor manufacturing executive; b. 27 Jan. 1920, Bourneville, Ohio; s. of Robert Clyde Caldwell and Wilhelmina (née Hemphill) Caldwell; m. Betsey Chinn Clark 1945; one s. two d.; ed Muskingum Coll. and Harvard Univ.; served US Navy, later Lt 1942–46; Navy Dept 1946–53, Deputy Dir of Procurement Policy Div. 1948–53; joined Ford Motor Co. 1953, Vice-Pres. 1968–73, Dir 1973–90; Gen. Man. Truck Operations 1968–70; Pres. and Dir Philco-Ford Corpn 1970–71; Vice-Pres. of Mfg Group 1971–72; Chair., CEO and Dir Ford Europe Inc. 1972–73; Exec. Vice-Pres. with responsiblity for int. automotive operations 1973–77, Vice-Chair. and Deputy CEO 1978–79, Pres. of Ford Motor Co. 1978–80, CEO 1979–85, Chair. 1980–85; also Dir of Ford Latin America 1973–85, Ford Asia-Pacific Inc. 1973–85, Ford of Europe 1972–85, Ford Motor Credit Co. 1977–85, Ford of Canada 1977–85, Ford Mid-East and Africa Inc. 1973–85, Chase Manhatten Corpn, Chase Manhattan Bank N.A. 1982–85, Digital Equipment Corpn, Kellogg Co., Federated Dept Stores Inc. 1984–88, Zurich Holding Co. America, Russell Reynold Assocs. Inc.; Sr Man. Dir Shearson Lehman Bros. Inc. 1985–93; mem. Int. Advisory Cttee, Chase Manhattan Bank 1979–85, Business-Higher Educ. Forum, numerous cttees., bds. and forums; Trustee, Cttee for Econ. Devt, Muskingum Coll. Policy Comm. Business Roundtable 1980–85; Dir Harvard Business School Assocs. 1977–93, INSEAD Int. Council 1978–81; Sec. Motor Vehicle Mfrs.' Asscn; Dir Detroit Symphony Orchestra 1979–85; Hon. DH (Muskingum Coll.) 1974; Hon. DBA (Upper Iowa) 1978; Hon. LLD (Boston Univ. 1979, Eastern Mich. Univ. 1979, Miami Univ. 1980, Davidson Coll. 1982, Lawrence Inst. of Tech. 1984, Ohio Univ. 1984); Meritorious civilian service award, US Navy 1953, 1st William A. Jump memorial award 1950, Golden Plate Award, American Acad. of Achievement 1984 and several other awards. *Address:* c/o Ford Motor Co., West Building, 225 High Ridge Road, Suite 180, Stamford, CT 06905-3000, USA (Office).

ČALFA, Marián, DrIur; Czech politician and lawyer; b. 1946, Trebišov, Slovakia; m. Jiřina Čalfová; two d.; studied law in Prague, subsequently worked in legal and admin. depts. of official press agency CTK; Minister without portfolio 1988–89; resgnd from CP of Czechoslovakia; Prime Minister of Czechoslovakia 1989–92; Chair. State Defence Council 1990–92; Deputy to House of Nations of Fed. Ass. CSFR 1990–92; official, Fed. Govt of CSFR July–Oct. 1992; Deputy Chair. Civic Democratic Union—Public Against Violence 1991–92; Co-founder CTL Consulting, Prague 1992–95, Čalfa, Bartošík a partneři, Prague 1995–; Chair. Supervisory Bd I. Silas, Deputy Chair. Alia Chem. 1995–; Ed.-in-Chief Legal Adviser 1993–95, Chair. Editorial Bd 1995–99; mem. M. R. Štefánik Foundation 2000–; Grand Cross of the Order of the Crown, Belgium 1990. *Address:* Čalfa, Bartošík a Partneři, právní kancelář Přemyslovská 28, 130 00 Prague 3, Czech Republic.

CALIFANO, Joseph Anthony, Jr., AB, LLB; American lawyer, government official and writer; b. 15 May 1931, Brooklyn, New York; s. of Joseph A. Califano and Katherine Gill Califano; m. 2nd Hilary Paley Byers 1983; two s. one d. from previous marriage; one step-s. one step-d.; ed Holy Cross Coll. and Harvard Univ.; admitted to New York Bar 1955; USNR 1955–58; with firm Dewey Ballantine, Bushby, Palmer Wood, New York 1958–61; Special Asst to Gen. Counsel, Dept of Defense 1961–62; Special Asst to Sec. of Army 1962–63; Gen. Counsel, Dept of Army 1963–64; Special Asst to Sec. and Deputy Sec. of Defense 1964–65; Special Asst to Pres. 1965–69; Sec. of Health, Educ. and Welfare 1977–79; Special Counsel to House of Reps. Cttee on Standards of Official Conduct 1982–83; admitted to U.S. District Court; U.S. Court of Appeals for 2nd Circuit; U.S. Supreme Court Bar 1966; mem. Fed. Bar Asscn, American Bar Asscn, American Judicature Soc.; mem. firm Arnold & Porter 1969–71, Williams, Connolly & Califano 1971–77, Califano, Ross & Heineman 1980–82, Dewey, Ballantine, Bushby, Palmer & Wood 1983–92; General Counsel, Democratic Nat. Cttee 1971–72; Prof. of Public Health Policy, Schools of Medicine and Public Health, Columbia Univ. 1992–; Chair. Nat. Center on Addiction and Substance Abuse, Columbia Univ. 1992–; mem. Democratic Party's Nat. Charter Comm. 1972–74; Chair. Inst. for Social Policy in the Middle East, Kennedy School of Govt, Harvard Univ.; mem. Bd of Dirs., Primerica Corpn, Automatic Data Processing Inc., KMart Corpn, True North Communications, Inc., Warnaco; Trustee, Urban Inst.; Distinguished Civilian Service Medal, Dept of Army 1964, Dept of Defense 1968; Man of Year Award, Justinian Soc. Lawyers 1966; hon. degrees from Coll. of Holy Cross, Coll. of New Rochelle, Univ. of Michigan, Davis and Elkins Coll., Howard Univ., Univ. of Notre Dame, City Coll., New York. *Publications:* The Student Revolution, A Global Confrontation 1969, A Presidential Nation 1975, The Media and the Law (with Howard Simons) 1976, The Media and Business (with Howard Simons) 1978, Governing America: An Insider's Report from the White House and the Cabinet 1981, Report on Drug Abuse and Alcoholism 1982, America's Health Care Revolution: Who Lives? Who Dies? Who Pays? 1985; numerous articles for various newspapers and other publications. *Leisure interest:* jogging. *Address:* c/o School of Public Health, University of Columbia, Morningside Heights, New York, NY 10027, USA.

CALISHER, Hortense, AB; American author; b. 20 Dec. 1911, New York; d. of Joseph H. Calisher and Hedwig (Lichtstern) Calisher; m. 1st Heaton Bennet Heffelfiner 1935; one s. one d.; m. 2nd Curtis Harnack 1959; ed Barnard Coll., New York; Adjunct Prof. of English, Barnard Coll. 1956–57; Visiting Lecturer, State Univ. of Iowa 1957, 1959–60, Stanford Univ. 1958, Sarah Lawrence Coll. Bronxville, New York 1962, 1967; Adjunct Prof. Columbia Univ., New York 1968–70, City Coll. of New York 1969; Visiting Prof. of Literature, Brandeis Univ. 1963–64, Univ. of Pa 1965, State Univ. of New York, Purchase 1971–72; Regent's Prof. Univ. of Calif. 1976; Visiting Prof. Bennington Coll. 1978, Washington Univ., St Louis 1979, Brown Univ. 1986; Guggenheim Fellow 1952, 1955; mem. American Acad. and Inst. Arts and Letters (Pres. 1987–90); American PEN (Pres. 1986–87); Hon. LittD (Skidmore Coll.) 1980, Hon. LLD (Grinnell) 1986; Acad. of Arts and Letters Award 1967; Nat. Council Arts Award 1967, Kafka Prize for The Bobby Soxer, Nat. Endowment for the Arts Award For Lifetime Achievement 1989. *Publications:* In the Absence of Angels (short stories) 1951, False Entry (novel) 1961, Tale for the Mirror (short stories) 1962, Textures of Life (novel) 1963, Extreme Magic (short stories) 1964, Journal from Ellipsia (novel) 1965, The Railway Police and The Last Trolley Ride (two novellas) 1966, The New Yorkers (novel) 1966, Queenie (novel) 1971, Standard Dreaming (novel) 1972, Herself (autobiog.) 1972, Eagle Eye (novel) 1973, On Keeping Women (novel) 1977, Mysteries of Motion (novel) 1983, Saratoga, Hot 1985 (short fiction), The Bobby Soxer (novel) 1986, Age (novel) 1987, Kissing Cousins 1988 (memoir), The Small Bang (novel) (under pseudonym Jack Fenno) 1992, In the Palace of the Movie King (novel) 1993, In the Slammer with Carol Smith 1996; several novellas and volumes of short stories, articles and reviews etc. *Leisure interests:* the other arts. *Address:* c/o Marion Boyars Publishers, 237 East 39th Street, New York, NY 10016-2110, USA.

CALLADINE, Christopher Reuben, ScD, FRS, FREng; British professor of structural mechanics; b. 19 Jan. 1935, Derby; s. of Reuben Calladine and Mabel Calladine (née Boam); m. Mary Ruth Howard Webb 1964; two s. one d.; ed Nottingham High School, Peterhouse, Cambridge, Massachusetts Inst.

of Tech., USA; lecturer, Dept of Eng, Cambridge Univ. 1963–79, Reader 1979–86, Prof. of Structural Mechanics 1986–2002, Fellow Peterhouse 1960–92, Sr Fellow 1992–2002, Emer. Fellow 2002–; mem. Gen. Bd Univ. of Cambridge 1984–88; mem. Council The Royal Soc. 2000–02; Ludwig Mond Prize, Inst. of Mechanical Engineers 1966; James Alfred Ewing Medal, Inst. of Civil Engineers 1998; Hon. DEng (Malaysian Univ.of Tech.) 2002. *Publications:* Engineering Plasticity 1969, Theory of Shell Structures 1983, Understanding DNA (with H. R. Drew) 1992; many articles in eng and biological journals. *Leisure interests:* make do and mend. *Address:* Department of Engineering, University of Cambridge, Cambridge, CB2 1PZ; 25 Almoners Avenue, Cambridge, CB1 8NZ, England. *Telephone:* (1223) 766206. *Fax:* (1223) 332662. *E-mail:* crc@eng.cam.ac.uk (Office).

CALLAGHAN OF CARDIFF, Baron (Life Peer), cr. 1987, of the City of Cardiff in the County of South Glamorgan; **(Leonard) James Callaghan,** KG, PC; British politician; b. 27 March 1912, Portsmouth; m. Audrey Elizabeth Moulton 1938; one s. two d.; ed Portsmouth Northern Secondary School; Tax Officer 1929; Asst Sec. Inland Revenue Staff Fed. 1936–47; service in Royal Navy 1942–45; MP 1945–87; Parl. Sec. Ministry of Transport 1947–50; Parl. and Financial Sec., Admiralty 1950–51; Chancellor of the Exchequer 1964–67; Home Sec. 1967–70; Sec. of State for Foreign and Commonwealth Affairs 1974–76; Leader of Parl. Labour Party 1976–80; Prime Minister 1976–79; Leader of the Opposition 1979–80; mem. Consultative Assembly, Council of Europe 1948–50, 1954; Chair. Advisory Cttee on Protection of the Sea 1953–2000; Consultant to Police Fed. 1955–64; mem. Nat. Exec. Cttee Labour Party 1957–80; Treas. Labour Party 1967–76, Chair. 1973–74; Hon. Life Fellow, Nuffield Coll., Oxford 1967; Hon. Fellow (Univ. Coll. Cardiff – now Univ. of Wales, Cardiff) 1978, (Portsmouth Polytechnic – now Portsmouth Univ.) 1981, (Univ. Coll. Swansea – now Univ. of Wales, Swansea) 1992; Pres. UK Pilots' Asscn 1963–76, Univ. Coll. Swansea 1986–95; Hon. Pres. Int. Maritime Pilots' Asscn 1971–76; Hon. LLD (Univ. of Wales) 1976, Hon. LLD (Sardar Patel Univ., India) 1978, Hon. LLD (Univ. of Birmingham) 1981, Hon. LLD (Univ. of Sussex) 1988, (Univ. of Westminster) 1993, (Open Univ.) 1996, (Liverpool) 1996; Freedom of City of Cardiff 1975, City of Sheffield 1978, City of Portsmouth 1991, City of Swansea 1993; Hon. Master of the Bench of the Inner Temple 1976; Hubert Humphrey Int. Award 1978; Grand Cross (1st Class) of the Order of Merit (Fed. Repub. of Germany) 1979. *Publications:* A House Divided 1973, Time and Chance (autobiog.) 1987. *Address:* House of Lords, London, SW1A 0PW, England.

CALLAWAY, Howard Hollis; American public official; b. 2 April 1927, LaGrange, Ga; s. of Cason J. Callaway and Virginia Hand Callaway; m. Elizabeth Walton 1949; three s. two d.; ed U.S. Military Acad.; served in Infantry, participating in Korean War in Far Eastern Command, later becoming Instructor, Infantry School, Fort Benning, Ga 1949–52; mem. 89th Congress, rep. third district of Georgia 1965–66; Republican cand. for Gov. of Georgia 1966; Civilian Aide for Third Army Area 1970–73; Sec. of the Army 1973–75; fmr Campaign Man. for President Ford, 1976 Pres. Election; fmr Chair. Interfinancial Inc. of Atlanta; Chair. Crested Butte Mountain Resort Inc., GOPAC; Chair. Colo Republican Party; Dir United Bank of Denver; mem. Regents Univ. System of GaNat. 4-H Service Cttee 1953–54, 1966–70, 1993–; mem. Bd of Trustees, Nat. Recreation Assc; Chair., Ida Cason Callaway Foundation; Chair. tourism cttee Ga Dept of Industry, Trade and Tourism 2001–; Dept of Defence Medal 1975. *Leisure interests:* skiing, sailing, tennis, trout fishing. *Address:* Callaway Gardens, Pine Mountain, GA 31822, USA. *Telephone:* (706) 663-5075 (Office); (706) 628-4994 (Home). *Fax:* (706) 663-5081 (Office). *E-mail:* bocallaway@callawaygardens.com (Office). *Website:* www.callawaygardens.com (Office).

CALLEJAS, Rafael Leonardo; Honduran politician and agronomist; b. 1 Nov. 1943, Tegucigalpa; s. of Rafael Callejas Valentine and Emma Rumero; m. 1st Nan López (divorced); m. 2nd Norma Regina Taborit; ed Univ. of Mississippi; fmr Pres. Cen. Cttee, Partido Nacional; Undersec. for Natural Resources 1972–75; Minister for Agric. and Natural Resources 1978–81; cand. for Pres. 1985, 1989; Pres. of Honduras 1990–93. *Address:* c/o Partido Nacional, Tegucigalpa, Honduras.

CALLEY, John; American business executive and producer; b. 1930, NJ; m. 1st Olinka Schoberova 1972 (divorced); m. 2nd Meg Tilly 1995; four step-c.; Dir of Night-time Programming and Dir Programming Sales NBC 1951–57; production exec. and TV producer Henry Jaffe Enterprises 1957; Vice-Pres. Radio and TV Ted Bates Advertising Agency 1958; Exec. Vice-Pres. and film producer Filmways Inc. 1960–69; with Warner Bros. Inc., Burbank, Calif. 1969–87, Exec. Vice-Pres. Worldwide Production 1969–75, Pres. 1975–80, Vice-Chair. Bd 1977–80, consultant 1980–87; film producer 1987–; Pres., COO United Artists Pictures 1993–96; Pres., COO Sony Pictures Entertainment Inc., Culver City, Calif. 1996–98, Pres., CEO 1998, Chair., CEO 1998–; mem. Bd American Film Inst. (AFI). *Address:* c/o Sony Pictures Entertainment Inc., 10202 Washington Boulevard, Culver City, CA 90232, USA (Office).

CALLIL, Carmen Thérèse, F.R.S.A, BA; Australian publisher; b. 15 July 1938, Melbourne; d. of Lorraine Claire Allen and Frederick Alfred Louis Callil; ed Star of the Sea Convent, Loreto Convent, Melbourne and Melbourne Univ.; settled in England 1963; Buyer's Asst, Marks and Spencer 1963–65; Editorial Asst, Hutchinson Publishing Co. 1965–66, B. T. Batsford 1966–67, Publicity Man., Granada Publishing 1967–70, André Deutsch 1971–72; f. Carmen Callil Ltd, Book Publicity Co. and Virago Press 1972; Chairwoman

and Man. Dir Virago Press 1972–82, Chairwoman 1982–95, Man. Dir Chatto and Windus, The Hogarth Press 1983–93; Publr-at-Large Random House, UK 1993–94; Ed.-at-Large Knopf, NY 1993–94; mem. Bd Channel 4 1985–91, Random Century Bd 1989–94; Gov. Museum of London 1992–; Chair. Booker Prize for Fiction 1996; Hon. DLitt (Sheffield) 1994, (Oxford Brookes Univ.) 1995; Hon. DUniv (York) 1995, (Open) 1997; Distinguished Service Award (Int. Women's Writing Guild). *Publication:* The Modern Library: the 200 best novels in England since 1950 (jtly.) 1999. *Leisure interests:* friends, reading, animals, films, gardening, politics. *Address:* 30 Bedford Square, London, WC1B 3EG, England.

CALLOW, Simon Philip Hugh, CBE; British actor, director and writer; b. 15 June 1949; s. of Neil Callow and Yvonne Mary Callow; ed London Oratory Grammar School, Queen's Univ., Belfast, Drama Centre; debut Edin. Festival 1973; repertory seasons, Lincoln and Traverse Theatre, Edin.; work at the fringe theatre, the Bush, London; joined Joint Stock Theatre Group 1977, Nat. Theatre 1979; Hon. DLitt (Queen's Univ., Belfast) 1999, (Birmingham) 2000; Evening Standard Patricia Rothermere Award 1999. *Stage appearances include:* Passing By 1975, Plumbers Progress 1975, Arturo Ui 1978, Titus Andronicus 1978, Mary Barnes 1978, As You Like It 1979, Amadeus 1979, Sisterly Feeling 1979, Total Eclipse 1982, Restoration 1982, The Beastly Beatitudes of Balthazar B 1982, The Relapse 1983, On The Spot 1984, Melancholy Jacques 1984, Kiss of the Spider Woman 1985, Faust 1988, Single Spies 1988, 1989, The Destiny of Me 1993, The Alchemist 1996, The Importance of Being Oscar 1997, Chimes at Midnight 1997, The Mystery of Charles Dickens 2000–01. *Films include:* Amadeus 1983, A Room With A View 1984, The Good Father 1985, Maurice 1986, Manifesto 1987, Mr and Mrs Bridge 1991, Postcards from the Edge 1991, Soft Top Hard Shoulder 1992, Four Weddings and A Funeral 1994, Jefferson in Paris 1994, Victory 1994, Le Passager Clandestin 1995, England, My England 1995, Ace Ventura: When Nature Calls 1995, James and the Giant Peach (voice) 1996, The Scarlet Tunic 1996, Woman In White 1997, Bedrooms and Hallways 1997, Shakespeare in Love 1997, No Man's Land 2000, Thunder pants 2001, A Christmas Carol 2001, George and the Dragon 2002. *TV appearances:* Wings of Song 1977, Instant Enlightenment inc. VAT 1979, La Ronde 1980, Man of Destiny 1982, Chance in a Million 1982–84, Deadhead 1984, Handel 1985, David Copperfield 1986, Cariani and the Courtesan 1987, Old Flames 1989, Patriot Witness 1989, Trial of Oz 1991, Bye Bye Columbus 1992, Femme Fatale 1993, Little Napoleons 1994, An Audience with Charles Dickens 1996, A Christmas Dickens 1997, The Woman in White 1998, Trial-Retribution 1999 2000, Galileo's Daughter, The Mystery of Charles Dickens 2002. *Directed:* Loving Reno 1983, Passport 1985, Nicolson Fights Croydon 1986, Amadeus 1986, The Infernal Machine 1986, Così Fan Tutte 1987, Jacques and His Master 1987, Shirley Valentine (theatre production) 1988/89, Die Fledermaus 1989/90, Facades 1988, Single Spies 1988/89, Stevie Wants to Play the Blues 1990, The Ballad of the Sad Café (film) 1991, Carmen Jones 1991, My Fair Lady 1992, Shades 1992, The Destiny of Me 1993, Carmen Jones 1994, Il Trittico 1995, Les Enfants du Paradis (RSC) 1996, Stephen Oliver Trilogy 1996, La Calisto 1996, Il Turco in Italia 1997, HRH 1997, The Pajama Game 1999, The Consul 1999, Tomorrow Week (play for radio) 1999. *Publications:* Being An Actor 1984, A Difficult Actor: Charles Laughton 1987, Shooting the Actor, or the Choreography of Confusion (with Dusan Makevejev) 1990, Acting in Restoration Comedy 1991, Orson Welles: The Road to Xanadu 1995, Les Enfants du Paradis 1996, Snowdon – On Stage 1996, The National 1997, Love is Where it Falls 1999, Shakespeare on Love 2000, Charles Laughton's the Night of the Hunter 2000, Oscar Wilde and His Circle 2000, The Nights of the Hunter 2001, Dicken's Christmas 2002; Henry IV Part One 2002; translations of works of Cocteau, Kundera, Prévert; weekly column in Sunday Express, Independent, Country Life; contrib. to The Times, The Sunday Times, The Observer, Evening Standard, etc. *Leisure interest:* 'dreaming' the future of the British theatre. *Address:* c/o BAT, 180 Wardour Street, London, W1V 3AA, England.

CALLWOOD, June, CC; Canadian journalist; b. 2 June 1924, Chatham; d. of Harold Callwood and Gladys Lavoie; m. Trent Frayne 1944; two s. (one deceased) two d.; Columnist Toronto Globe and Mail 1983–89; Guest Lecturer on Human Rights, Univ. of Ottawa 1984; Margaret Laurence Lecture 1993; Writer-in-Residence NY Public Library 1995–96; founding mem. and Vice-Pres. Canadian Civil Liberties Assc 1965–88 (Hon. Dir for Life 1988); Pres. and founder Nellie's Hostel for Women 1974-78, Dir 1985–89, 1990–92; Pres. and founder Jessie's Centre for Teenagers 1982–83, 1987–89; Pres. and founding mem. Learnx Foundation 1977–79, Justice for Children 1979–80; Pres. and founder Casey House Hospice (for AIDS) 1988–89, Hon. Dir 1989–; Pres. Casey House Foundation 1992–93 (Hon. Dir 1993–), Maggie's Prostitute Community Service Org. 1990–94; Chair. The Writers' Union of Canada 1979–80 (Life mem. 1994–); mem. Council, Amnesty International (Canada) 1978–85; Dir Canadian Inst. for Admin. of Justice 1983–84, The Electronic Rights Licensing Agency 1997–99; Vice-Pres. PEN (Canada) 1987–88, Dir 1988–89, Pres. 1989–90; Vice-Pres. Ward's Retreat 1990–91, Book and Periodical Council 1994–95 (Chair. 1995–96), Bd of Govs. Etobicoko Gen. Hosp. 1994–98; Dir Frosst Health Care Foundation 1999–2002; Judge, Gov.-Gen.'s Literary Awards 1983–86; involved in many other public and humanitarian activities; Bencher Law Soc. of Upper Canada 1987–91, Duthie Lecture (Simon Fraser Univ.) 1990, Sechelt, B.C. Margaret Laurence Lecture 1993; Harmony Movement Patron 1994–; Writer-in-Residence, North York Public Library 1995–96; Co-Chair. Campaign Against Child Poverty 1997–; Bruce Hutchison Lecture 1998, Carmelita Lawlor Lecture (Univ. of Toronto)

2000; mem. Advisory Cttee Law Comm. of Canada 2000–03; First Lecturer Dalton Camp Lectures, St Thomas W. 2002; Order of Ontario 1988; Hon. DUniv (Ottawa) 1987; Hon. Dr. of Sacred Letters (Trinity Coll.) 1988; Hon. LLD (Memorial Univ., Newfoundland, Univ. of Toronto, York Univ.) 1988, (Univ. of Western Ont.) 1993, (McMaster) 1994, (Law Soc. of Upper Canada, Univ. of Calgary) 1997; Hon. LittD (Carleton Univ., Univ. of Alberta) 1988, (Guelph Univ.) 1989, (Univ. of New Brunswick) 1990; Hon. DCL (Acadia Univ.) 1993; Hon. DHumLitt (Mount St Vincent Univ.) 1993; Canadian Newspaper Hall of Fame 1984, Toronto Arts Foundation Lifetime Achievement Award 1990, and other awards. *Radio includes:* Court of Opinions 1959–67, Human Sexuality 1966. *Television includes:* (Host) Generations 1966, In touch 1975–78, Callwood's National Treasures 1991–98, Caregivers 1998. *Publications:* Love, Hate, Fear and Anger 1964, The Law is Not for Women 1973, Portrait of Canada 1981, Emma 1984, Emotions 1986, Twelve Weeks in Spring 1986, Jim: A Life with AIDS 1988, The Sleepwalker 1990, June Callwood's National Treasurers 1994, Trial Without End 1995, The Man Who Lost Himself 2000 and 16 other books. *Leisure interests:* swimming, books, gliding. *Address:* 21 Hillcroft Drive, Toronto, Ont., M9B 4X4, Canada. *Telephone:* (416) 231-1923. *Fax:* (416) 231-1923. *E-mail:* callwood@interlog .com (Home).

CALMAN, Sir Kenneth (Charles), DL, MD, PhD, KCB, FRCP, FRCPE, FRCS, FFPHM, FRSE; British chief medical officer; b. 25 Dec. 1941; s. of Arthur McIntosh Calman and Grace Douglas Don; m. Ann Wilkie 1967; one s. two d.; ed Allan Glen's School, Glasgow, Univ. of Glasgow; Hall Fellow in Surgery, Western Infirmary, Glasgow 1968; Lecturer in Surgery, Univ. of Glasgow 1969, Prof. of Clinical Oncology 1974, Dean of Postgrad. Medicine and Prof. of Postgraduate Medical Educ. 1984–88; MRC Clinical Research Fellow Inst. of Cancer Research, London 1972; Chief Medical Officer, Scottish Office Home and Health Dept 1989–91, (at Dept of Health and Social Security) Dept of Educ. and Science (later Dept for Employment, then Dept for Educ. and Employment) 1991–98; Vice-Chancellor and Warden, Univ. of Durham 1998–; Founder FMedSci 1998; mem. Statistics Comm. 2000–; Fellow Royal Coll. of Surgeons (Glasgow) 1971; Fellow Royal Coll. of Gen. Practitioners 1989; Hon. Fellow Inst. of Cancer Research; Hon. MD (Nottingham) 1994, (Newcastle) 1995, (Birmingham) 1996; Hon. DSc (Strathclyde) 1993, (Westminster) 1995, (Glasgow Caledonian) 1995, (Glasgow) 1996, (Birmingham) 1996, (Brighton) 2000; Hon. DUniv (Stirling) 1992, (Open Univ.) 1996, (Paisley) 1997; Medals include: Sir Thomas and Lady Dixon, Belfast 1994, Francis Bissett Hawkins, RCP 1995, Crookshanks, RCR 1995, Alexander Hutchinson, Royal Soc. of Medicine (RCS) 1995, Gold, Macmillan Cancer Relief 1996, Heberden (also Orator), British Soc. of Rheumatology 1996, Silver, Royal Coll. of Surgeons in Ireland 1997, Allwyn Smith, Faculty of Public Health Medicine 1998, Bradlaw, RCS Dental Faculty 1999, Thomas Graham, Royal Philosophical Soc., Glasgow 1999, D.L. Durham 2000. *Publications:* Basic Skills for Clinical Housemen 1971, Basic Principles of Cancer Chemotherapy 1982, Invasion 1984, Healthy Respect 1987, The Potential for Health 1998, Storytelling, Humour & Learning in Medicine 2000. *Leisure interests:* gardening, golf, collecting cartoons, Scottish literature, sundials. *Address:* Old Shire Hall, Durham, DH1 3HP, England.

CALMON DE SÁ, Angelo (see Sá, Angelo Calmon de).

CALMY-REY, Micheline; Swiss politician; b. 8 July 1945, Sion, Valais canton; m. André Calmy; two c.; ed Ecole de commerce, St. Maurice, Valais, Grad. Inst. of Int. Studies, Geneva; ran family books business 1977–97; joined Social Democratic Party 1979, Pres. 1986–90; elected Deputy Geneva Grand Council 1981–97, fmr Pres. Finance Comm., fmr Pres. Grand Council; elected to Geneva Conseil d'Etat (Head Dept of Finances) 1997–, Vice-Pres. 2000–01, Pres. 2001–02; elected to Fed. Council Dec. 2002–; Minister of Foreign Affairs Dec. 2002–; mem. Conseil d'admin. de la Caisse d'épargne, Geneva 1986–93, Conseil d'admin., Geneva Int. Airport 1994–97; Vice-Pres., later Pres. Caisse de la pension des employées de la fonction publique 1998–2002; mem. Conseil d'admin. du Fonds d'équipement communal 1998–2002, Conseil d'admin. de la Banque Nat. Suisse 2002–. *Address:* Department of Finances, Rue du Stand 26, Case postale 3937, 1211 Geneva 3, Switzerland (Office). *Telephone:* (22) 3275500 (Office). *Fax:* (22) 3275033 (Office). *E-mail:* micheline.calmy-rey@ etat.ge.ch (Office). *Website:* www.calmy-rey.net (Office).

CALNE, Sir Roy Yorke, Kt, MA, MS, FRCP, FRCS, FRS; British professor of surgery; b. 30 Dec. 1930; s. of Joseph R. Calne and Eileen Calne; m. Patricia D. Whelan 1956; two s. four d.; ed Lancing Coll. and Guy's Hosp. Medical School, London; RAMC 1954–56; Departmental Anatomy Demonstrator, Univ. of Oxford 1957–58; Sr House Officer, Nuffield Orthopaedic Centre, Oxford 1958; Surgical Registrar, Royal Free Hosp. 1958–60; Harkness Fellow in Surgery, Peter Bent Brigham Hosp. Harvard Medical School 1960–61; Lecturer in Surgery, St Mary's Hosp. London 1961–62; Sr Lecturer and Consulting Surgeon, Westminster Hosp. 1962–65; Prof. of Surgery, Univ. of Cambridge 1965–98, Emer. Prof. 1998; Ghim Seng Prof. of Surgery, Nat. Univ. of Singapore 1998–; Fellow, Trinity Hall Cambridge 1965–98, Emer. 1998–; Hon. Consulting Surgeon, Addenbrooke's Hosp. Cambridge 1965–98; Hon. FRCS (Edinburgh) 1992; Hon. MD (Oslo) 1986, (Athens) 1990, (Hanover) 1991, (Thailand) 1993, (Belfast) 1994, (Edin.) 2001; Royal Coll. of Surgeons: Hallet Prize, Jacksonian Prize, Hunterian Prof. 1962, Cecil Joll Prize 1966; numerous other honours and awards including Lister Medal 1984, Hunterian Oration 1989, Cameron Prize 1990, Ellison-Cliffe Medal 1990, Ernst-Jung Prize, Gold Medal of Catalan Transplantation Soc. 1996, Grand Officer of the Repub. of Italy 2000, King Faisal Int. Prize for Medicine 2001, Prince Mahidol Prize for Medicine 2002. *Publications:* Too Many People 1994, Art, Surgery and Transplantation 1996, The Ultimate Gift 1998; books and scientific papers on renal and liver transplantation and gen. surgery. *Leisure interests:* painting, tennis, squash, sculpture. *Address:* Department of Surgery, Douglas House Annexe, 18 Trumpington Road, Cambridge, CB2 2AH (Office); 22 Barrow Road, Cambridge, England. *Telephone:* (1223) 361467 (Office); (1223) 359831. *Fax:* (1223) 301601 (Office). *E-mail:* cpr1000@cam.ac.uk (Office).

CALOW, Peter, OBE, PhD, FIBiol, FRSA; British professor of zoology; b. 23 May 1947; two c.; ed Univ. of Leeds; lecturer, Reader, Univ. of Glasgow 1972–84, Warden Wolfson Hall 1975–84; Prof. of Zoology, Univ. of Sheffield 1984–, Dir Inst. of Environmental Sciences and Tech. 1991–96; Dir Environmental Businesses Network 1998–2000; founding ed. Functional Ecology 1986–1999; Pres. SETAC (Europe) 1990–91; Chair. UK Govt Advisory Cttee on Hazardous Substances 1991–2000; Trustee Health and Environmental Sciences Inst. 1996–2002, Int. Life Sciences Inst. 1999–2001; mem. Council Freshwater Biology Asscn 1995–99, Univ. of Buckingham 1997–2002. *Publications:* author, jt author of 20 books; more than 220 articles in tech. journals. *Leisure interests:* tennis, reading, writing. *Address:* Department of Animal and Plant Sciences, University of Sheffield, Sheffield, S10 2TN, England. *Telephone:* (114) 222-4692. *Fax:* (114) 278-0694. *E-mail:* p.calow@sheffield.ac.uk (Office).

CALVET, Jacques; French business executive and banker; b. 19 Sept. 1931, Boulogne-sur-Seine; s. of Prof. Louis Calvet and Yvonne Olmières; m. Françoise Rondot 1956; two s. one d.; ed Paris Univ. and Nat. School of Admin.; at Cour des Comptes 1957–63; Chargé de mission to office of Valéry Giscard d'Estaing (Sec. of State for Finance) 1959–62, Dir 1962–66; Dir Financial Affairs, Paris Dist 1966–68; Prin. Pvt. Sec. to Minister of Finance 1968–74; Deputy Gen. Man., Banque Nat. de Paris (BNP) 1974–75, Gen. Man. 1975–79, Chair. 1979–82, Hon. Chair. 1997–; Vice-Chair. Peugeot SA 1982–84, Pres. 1984–97; Chair. Automobiles Peugeot 1982–84, Bd Pres. 1984–, Vice-Pres., Dir-Gen. 1984–89, Pres. 1990–97; Pres. Citroën 1983–97; Pres. Conseil d'Admin. de la Publicité Française 1991–97; Dir Petrofina; Chair. European Automobiles Mfrs Asscn 1996; Pres. Supervisory Bd Bazar de l'Hôtel de Ville (BHV) 2000–; Commdr, Légion d'honneur; Officier Ordre nat. du Mérite, du Mérite agricole; Chevalier des Palmes académiques. *Publication:* La Grande faillite: Comment l'éviter 1988. *Leisure interest:* tennis. *Address:* Bazar de l'Hôtel de Ville, 14 rue du Temple, 75189 Paris Cedex 04 (Office); 31 avenue Victor Hugo, 75116 Paris, France (Home).

CALVO-SOTELO Y BUSTELO, Leopoldo, D.C.ENG.; Spanish politician and engineer; b. 14 April 1926, Madrid; s. of Leopoldo Calvo-Sotelo Bustelo and Mercedes Calvo-Sotelo Bustelo; m. Pilar Ibáñez Martín Mellado 1954; seven s. one d.; ed Escuela de Ingenieros de Caminos, Canales y Puertos, Madrid; Pres. Spanish Railways 1967–68; Dir-Gen. Unión Explosivos Rio Tinto 1963–67, 1968–75; Procurador 1971; Minister of Commerce 1975–76, of Public Works 1976–77; Minister for Relations with European Communities 1978–80; Second Deputy Prime Minister, Econ. Affairs 1980–81, Prime Minister of Spain 1981–82; mem. of European Parl. 1986; Pres. Union of the Democratic Centre (UCD) 1981–82. *Publications:* Memoria Viva de la Transición 1990, Papeles de un Cesante 1999. *Address:* Alcala, 93–, Madrid 28009, Spain (Office); Buho 1, Somosaguas, Madrid, Spain. *Telephone:* (91) 431-79-68 (Office). *Fax:* (91) 575-74-69 (Office).

CALVOCORESSI, Peter (John Ambrose); British writer, book publisher and university lecturer; b. 17 Nov. 1912, Karachi, Pakistan; s. of Pandia J. Calvocoressi and Irene (Ralli) Calvocoressi; m. Barbara Dorothy Eden 1938; two s.; ed Eton Coll. and Balliol Coll., Oxford; called to Bar 1935; RAF Intelligence 1940–45; assisted Trial of Major War Criminals, Nuremberg 1945–46; on staff, Royal Inst. of Int. Affairs 1949–54; partner Chatto & Windus, publishers 1955–65; Reader in Int. Relations, Sussex Univ. 1965–71; Ed. Dir Penguin Books 1972, Publr and Chief Exec. 1973–76; Chair. Open Univ. Educational Enterprises Ltd 1979–88; mem. UN sub-comm. on the Prevention of Discrimination 1961–71; Chair. The London Library 1970–73; Hon. DUniv (Open Univ.) 1989. *Publications:* Nuremberg: The Facts, the Law and the Consequences 1947, Survey of International Affairs: Vols for 1947–48, 1949–50, 1951, 1952 and 1953, Middle East Crisis (with Guy Wint) 1957, South Africa and World Opinion 1961, World Order and New States 1962, Total War (with Guy Wint) 1972, The British Experience: 1945–75, Top Secret Ultra 1980, A Time for Peace 1987, Who's Who in the Bible 1987, Resilient Europe 1991, Threading My Way 1994, Fall Out: World War II and the Shaping of Postwar Europe 1997, World Politics 1945–2000 2001. *Leisure interest:* music. *Address:* 1 Queens Parade, Bath, BA1 2NJ, England. *Telephone:* (1225) 333903.

CAMACHO, Felix; American politician; m. Joann Camacho; three c.; ed Father Duenas Memorial School and Marquette Univ., WI, USA; fmr Account Admin. IBM Corpn; fmr Insurance Man. Pacific Financial Corpn; served in 22nd, 23rd and 24th Guam Legislatures; fmr Senator and Chair. 26th Guam Legislature's Cttee on Tourism, Transportation and Econ. Devt; Gov. of Guam 2002–; fmr mem. and Exec. Dir Civil Service Comm. *Address:* Office of the Governor, POB 2950, Adelup, Hagåtña, GU 96932, Guam (Office). *E-mail:* governor@mail.gov.gu (Office). *Website:* www.mail.gov.gu (Office).

CAMAÑO, Eduardo Oscar; Argentine politician; Pres. Partido Justicialista de Quilmes; Pres. of Bloc in Consejal 1983–85; Provincial Deputy 1985–87; Municipal Council, Quilmes 1987–91; Deputy to Nat. Ass. 1991–, Vice-Pres. Bloc Justicialista 1994–98, Second Vice-Pres. Chamber of Deputies

1999–2001, Pres. 2001–. *Address:* Cámara de Diputados, Rivadavia 1864, CP.AAV 1033, Buenos Aires, Argentina (Office). *Telephone:* (11) 6310-7100 (Office). *E-mail:* ecamano@diputados.gov.ar (Office).

CAMARA, Assan Musa; Gambian politician; b. 1923, Mansajang; ed St Mary Anglican Mission School, Bathurst (now Banjul) and Anglican Mission School, Kristu Kunda; Teacher in Govt and mission schools 1948–60; mem. House of Assembly (Independent) 1960–; Minister without Portfolio 1960, of Health and Labour 1960–62, of Educ. and Social Welfare 1962–65, of Works and Communications 1965–66, of Educ., Labour and Social Welfare 1966–68, of External Affairs 1968–74, of Local Govt and Lands 1974–77, of Educ., Youth and Sports 1977, 1981–82, of Finance and Trade 1977–79; Vice-Pres. of The Gambia 1973–77, 1978–82; Order of the Cedar of Lebanon, Commdr Nat. Order of Senegal, Grand Band, Order of Star of Africa, Grand Cross, Brilliant Star of China. *Address:* c/o Office of the Vice-President, Banjul, The Gambia.

CAMARENA BADÍA, Vicente, PhD; Spanish professor of mathematics; b. 26 Aug. 1941, Xátiva, Valencia; s. of Vicente Camarena and Victoria Badía; m. Carmen Grau; one s. four d.; ed Universidad de Zaragoza; Asst Prof. of Math. Universidad de Zaragoza 1966–81, Prof. 1981–84, Rector 1984–92, Prof. of Applied Math. Dept 1992–; mem. Spanish Asscn of Math., Spanish Soc. of Gen. Systems, American Math. Soc., Soc. for Industries and Applied Math., Int. Astronomical Union. *Publications:* Curso de Mecánica 1977–78, Optimización de Trayectorias y efecto de Trampolín Lunar 1972, Formulación Sistemática de la Teoría de Perturbaciones en el Movimiento Orbital 1976, Determinación del Vector Primer de Lawden en Forma Universal y su Aplicación a Problemas de Optimización 1979–83, Elementos Orbitales y Osculadores en Teoría de Perturbaciones, Uniformización de Métodos Canónicos de Perturbaciones 1984, Números y Cálculo con Números: Del 1 al 0, hasta el ∞ 1999. *Leisure interests:* cycling and swimming. *Address:* Universidad de Zaragoza, Centro Politécnico Superior, Mª Luna 3, Zaragoza 50015 (Office); Latassa 17, Zaragoza, Spain (Home). *E-mail:* camarena@posta.unizar.es (Office). *Website:* www.cps.unizar.es (Office).

CAMARGO, Sérgio de; Brazilian sculptor; b. 1930; ed Academia Altamira, Buenos Aires and Univ. de Paris à la Sorbonne; in France 1948–50, 1951–54, 1961–; visited China 1954; specializes in wood reliefs; Int. Sculpture Prize, Paris Biennale 1963; works are in permanent collections of Nat. Museum of Art, Rio de Janeiro, Museum of Art, São Paulo, Musée d'Art Moderne de la Ville de Paris, Tate Gallery, London, Galleria d'Arte Moderna, Rome and in numerous private collections; represented in exhbns. in Paris and Brussels 1963, Mannheim, Arras, London and Paris 1964, 1974, New York 1965 and Latin-American exhbns. 1954–.

CAMBA, Erme Reamon, DTheol; Philippine ecclesiastic; b. 27 Nov. 1937, Camalig, Albay; s. of Mequias Camba and Erlina Reamon-Camba; m. Eugenia D'Lunsod 1964; two d.; ed Silliman Univ. Dumaguete City and Southeast Asia Grad. School of Theology; Church Minister, Guinobatan Evangelical Church, Guinobatan, Albay 1961–62, 1963–64, Albay Evangelical Church, Legazpi City 1964–69; Instr. in Applied Theology, Divinity School, Silliman Univ. 1970–71; Assoc. Prof. in Pastoral Theology and Social Ethics, Union Theological Seminary, Dasmariñas, Cavite (Manila) 1971–82; Jurisdictional Bishop, United Church of Christ in the Philippines (UCCP) 1982–86; Gen. Sec. UCCP 1986–94; Assoc. Prof. in Pastoral Theology, Divinity School, Silliman Univ. 1994–; co-founder and Chair. of several ecumenical orgs. in the Philippines; Chair. Nat. Council of Churches in the Philippines 1983–85; Pres. Christian Conf. of Asia 1985–90; now Co-Moderator, Unit II Comm. WCC. *Publications:* articles in church magazines. *Leisure interest:* reading. *Address:* Divinity School, Silliman University, Dumaguete City 6200, Philippines. *Telephone:* (35) 225-7541 (Office); (912) 515-0368 (Home). *Fax:* (35) 225-7541.

CAMBRELING, Sylvain; French conductor; b. 2 July 1948, Amiens; conducting debut with Orchestre de Lyon 1975; Prin. Guest Conductor, Ensemble Intercontemporain, Paris 1976; subsequent appearances in Paris with Orchestre de Paris, Nat. Orchestra of France and Ensemble Intercontemporain; has worked regularly at Paris Opéra since conducting Chéreau's production of Les Contes d'Hoffmann; Glyndebourne Opera debut (The Barber of Seville) 1981; Music. Dir Nat. Opera, Théâtre Royal de la Monnaie, Brussels 1981–; debut at La Scala (Lucio Silla) 1984, Metropolitan Opera, New York (Romeo et Juliette) 1986; has also appeared at Salzburg, Aix-en-Provence and Bregenz festivals; has worked in UK with Halle and Royal Liverpool Philharmonic orchestras, in Germany with Berlin Philharmonic, Berlin Radio Symphony and other orchestras and in USA. *Address:* c/o Frankfurt Opera, Staedtische Buehnen, 60275 Frankfurt am Main, Germany.

CAMDESSUS, Michel Jean; French international civil servant; b. 1 May 1933, Bayonne; s. of Alfred Camdessus and Madeleine Cassembon; m. Brigitte d'Arcy 1957; two s. four d.; ed Notre Dame Coll., Betharram, Inst. of Political Studies, Paris, Nat. School of Admin.; civil servant, Treasury, Ministry of Finance 1960–66; Chief, Bureau of Industrial Affairs, Treasury, Ministry of Econ. and Finance 1969–70; Chair. 'Investissements' Sub-Cttee of Treasury 1971; Deputy Dir of Treasury 1974–82, Dir 1982–84; Financial Attaché, Perm. Representation, EEC, Brussels 1966–69; mem. Monetary Cttee, EEC 1978, Pres. 1982; Sec. Conseil de Direction du Fonds de Développement Economique et Social 1971; Asst Dir 'Épargne et Crédit' Sub-Cttee 1972; Deputy Gov. Banque de France 1984, Gov. 1984–87, Hon. Gov. 1987–; Man.

Dir IMF 1987–2000; Pres. Centre d'études prospectives et d'informations internationales (CEPII) 2000–; UN Sec.-Gen. Special Envoy to the Monterrey Conf. 2002; Dir Banque Européenne d'Investissements, Banque Cen. des États de l'Afrique de l'Ouest, Air France, Soc. Nat. des Chemins de fer Français, Crédit Lyonnais (all 1978); Pres. Club de Paris 1978–84, Semaines Sociales de France 2001, Centre d'études prospectives et d'informations internationales 2001; Pres. Semaines Sociales de France 2001–; Personal Rep. to Africa for French Govt and G8 Heads of State 2002; Officier, Légion d'honneur, Chevalier, Ordre nat. du Mérite, Croix de la Valeur militaire. *Publications:* Notre foi dans ce siècle (M. Camdessus, M. Albert, J. Boissonnat). *Address:* Banque de France, 4 Place de Victoires, 75001 Paris; 27 rue de Valois, 75001 Paris, France (Home). *Telephone:* 1-42-97-73-38 (Office). *Fax:* 1-42-97-76-42. *E-mail:* lyliane.huot@banque-france.fr.

CAMERON, Averil Millicent, CBE, FBA, FSA, MA, PhD; British historian of late antiquity and Byzantine studies; b. 8 Feb. 1940, Leek, Staffs.; d. of Tom Roy Sutton and Millicent Drew; m. Alan Douglas Edward Cameron 1962 (divorced 1980); one s. one d.; ed Somerville Coll., Oxford, Univ. Coll., London; Asst Lecturer Classics, King's Coll., London 1965, Lecturer 1968, Reader in Ancient History 1970, Prof. 1978–88, Prof. Late Antique and Byzantine Studies 1988–94, Dir Centre for Hellenic Studies 1989–94, Fellow 1987–; Warden of Keble Coll., Oxford 1994–; Prof. of Late Antique and Byzantine History, Oxford Univ. 1997–; Pro-Vice-Chancellor Univ. of Oxford 2001–; Visiting Prof., Columbia Univ., New York 1967–68; Visiting mem., Inst. for Advanced Study, Princeton 1977–78, Distinguished Visitor 1992; Summer Fellow, Dumbarton Oaks 1980; Sather Prof. of Classical Literature, Univ. of Calif. 1985–86; Visiting Prof. Coll. de France 1987, Lansdowne Lecturer, Victoria, BC 1992; Hon. Fellow Somerville Coll., Oxford; Ed. Journal of Roman Studies 1985–90; Pres. Soc. for the Promotion of Roman Studies 1995–98; Chair. Cathedrals Fabric Comm. for England 1999–, Review Group on the Royal Peculiars 1999–2000; Hon. DLitt (Warwick, St Andrews, Queen's, Belfast, Aberdeen), Hon. DTheol (Lund). *Publications:* Procopius 1967, Agathias 1970, Corippus, In laudem Iustini minoris 1976, Images of Women in Antiquity (ed.) 1983, Continuity and Change in Sixth-Century Byzantium 1981, Constantinople in the Eighth Century (ed.) 1984, Procopius and the Sixth Century 1985, 1996, History as Text (ed.) 1989, The Greek Renaissance in the Roman Empire (ed.) 1990, Christianity and the Rhetoric of Empire 1991, The Byzantine and Early Islamic Near East I (ed.) 1992, II () 1994, III (ed.) 1995, The Later Roman Empire 1993, The Mediterranean World in Late Antiquity A.D. 395–600 1993, Changing Cultures in Early Byzantium (ed.) 1996, Cambridge Ancient History vol. XIII. The Late Empire () 1998, Eusebius, Life of Constantine (ed. and trans.) 1999, Cambridge Ancient History vol. XIV. Late Antiquity: Empire and Successors (ed.) 2000, Fifty Years of Prosopography (ed.) 2003. *Address:* Keble College, Oxford, OX1 3PG, England. *Telephone:* (1865) 272700 (Office). *Fax:* (1865) 272785 (Office). *E-mail:* averil.cameron@keb.ox.ac.uk (Home).

CAMERON, Ian Rennell, CBE, MA, DM, FRCP, FMedSci; British professor of medicine; b. 20 May 1936, London; s. of James Cameron and Frances Cameron; m. 1st Jayne Bustard 1964 (divorced); one s. one d.; m. 2nd Jennifer Payne 1980; ed Westminster School, Corpus Christi Coll. Oxford and St Thomas's Hosp. Medical School; Jr appts. St Thomas's Hosp. 1961–64; lecturer, St Thomas's Hosp. Medical School 1967, Sr Lecturer 1969, Reader 1975, Prof. of Medicine 1979–94, Dean 1986–89; Research Asst Dept of Physiology, Univ. Coll. London 1966–68; NIH Postdoctoral Fellowship, Cedars-Sinai Medical Center, Los Angeles and Asst Prof. Dept of Physiology, Univ. of Calif. at Los Angeles 1968–69; Prin. United Medical and Dental Schools of Guys and St Thomas's Hosps. 1989–92; Dir Research and Devt South-East Thames Health Authority 1993–94; Bro Taf Health Authority (non-exec.) 1996–; Provost and Vice-Chancellor, Univ. of Wales Coll. of Medicine 1994–2001; mem. and Treas. GMC 1995–2001; mem. Comm. for Health Improvement 1999–; Hon. Fellow King's Coll. London 1998, Corpus Christi Coll. Oxford 2000; Hon. LLD (Univ. of Wales) 2001; Hon. DSc Univ. of Glamorgan) 2001; Hon. PhD (Tokyo Women's Medical Univ., Kobe Gakuin Univ. Japan) 2001. *Publications:* Respiratory Disorders (with N. T. Bateman) 1983; papers in medical and physiological journals. *Leisure interests:* collecting paintings, books and china. *Address:* The Old Vicarage, Llanblethian, Vale of Glamorgan, CF71 7JF, Wales. *Telephone:* (1446) 77 4128. *E-mail:* i.r.cameron@btinternet.com.

CAMERON, James; film director and screenwriter; b. 16 Aug. 1954, Kapuskasing, Ont.; m. Linda Hamilton 1996; one d.; ed Fullerton Jr Coll.; formed Lightstorm Entertainment 1990, Head 1992–; CEO Digital Domain 1993–. *Films include:* Piranha II—The Spawning (Dir), The Terminator (Dir and screenplay) 1984, Rambo: First Blood Part II (co-screenwriter), Aliens (Dir and screenplay), The Abyss (Dir and screenplay), Terminator 2: Judgment Day (co-screenwriter, Dir and producer) 1994, Point Break (exec. producer) 1994, True Lies, Strange Days (writer), Titanic (Acad. Award for Best Dir, film won 11 Acad. Awards equalling record) 1996, Solaris 2002. *Publications:* Strange Days 1995. *Address:* Lightstorm Entertainment, 919 Santa Monica Boulevard, Santa Monica, CA 90401, USA.

CAMERON, Peter Duncanson, LLB, PhD; British professor of international energy law; b. 21 June 1952, Glasgow; s. of Stewart Cameron and Margaret Cameron; ed Bishop Vesey Grammar School, High School of Stirling and Univ. of Edinburgh; Lecturer in Law, Univ. of Dundee 1977–86; Visiting Research Assoc., Oxford Univ. Centre for Socio-Legal Studies 1980, Visiting Scholar, Stanford Law School 1985; Adviser UN Centre on Transnat. Corpns.

1985–86; Dir Int. Inst. of Energy Law, Univ. of Leiden 1986–97; Prof. of Int. Energy Law, Univ. of Dundee 1997–; Chair. Academic Advisory Group and mem. Council, Int. Bar Asscn Section on Energy and Natural Resources Law 1996–2001; Jean Monnet Fellow European Univ. Inst., Florence, Italy 2001–02, Prof. 2002–; Adviser UN ESCAP 1988–89; Consultant World Bank 1990–; Visiting Prof. Univ. Autónoma de Madrid 1997–2000; Ed. Bd Oil and Gas Law and Taxation Review 1989–97; Assoc. Ed. Journal of Energy and Natural Resources Law 1990–97, Jt Ed. 1997–. *Publications:* Property Rights and Sovereign Rights: the Case of North Sea Oil 1983, Petroleum Licensing 1984, The Oil Supplies Industry: a Comparative Study of Legislative Restrictions and their Impact 1986, Nuclear Energy Law after Chernobyl (ed.) 1988, The Regulation of Gas in Europe 1995, Gas Regulation in Western and Central Europe 1998, Kyoto: From Principles to Practice (ed.) 2001, Competition in Energy Markets 2002. *Leisure interests:* long-distance running, travel, cinema. *Address:* Centre for Energy, Petroleum and Mineral Law and Policy, University of Dundee, Park Place, Dundee, DD1 4HN (Office); 12 Vernonholme, Riverside Drive, Dundee, Fife, DD2 1QJ, Scotland (Home). *Telephone:* (1382) 344388 (Office); (1382) 630227 (Home). *Fax:* (1382) 322578 (Office); (1382) 630341 (Home). *E-mail:* p.d.cameron@dundee.ac.uk (Office); cameron1pd@aol.com (Home). *Website:* www.cepmlp.org (Office).

CAMERON OF LOCHBROOM, Baron (Life Peer), cr. 1984, of Lochbroom in the District of Ross and Cromarty; **Kenneth John Cameron,** MA, LLB, QC, FRSE; British lawyer; b. 11 June 1931, Edin.; s. of the late Lord Cameron and Eileen Dorothea Burrell; m. Jean Pamela Murray 1964; two d.; ed The Edinburgh Acad., Corpus Christi Coll. Oxford and Univ. of Edinburgh; called to Bar 1958; QC 1972; Chair. Industrial Tribunals (Scotland) 1966–81; Pres. Pensions Appeal Tribunal (Scotland) 1976–84; Chair. Cttee for Investigation in Scotland of Agricultural Marketing Schemes 1980–84; Advocate Depute 1981–84; Lord Advocate 1984–89; Senator of Coll. of Justice in Scotland 1989–2003; Chair. Royal Fine Art Comm. for Scotland; Pres. Scottish Council for Voluntary Orgs. 1989–2001; Chancellor's Assessor, Univ. of Edin. 1997–; Hon. Bencher, Lincoln's Inn, London; Hon. Fellow, Corpus Christi Coll. Oxford, Royal Incorporation of Architects in Scotland. *Leisure interests:* fishing, sailing. *Address:* Stoneyhill House, Musselburgh, Edinburgh, EH21 6RP, Scotland. *Telephone:* (131) 665-1081.

CAMERON WATT, Prof. Donald, MA, DLitt, FBA, FRHistS; British historian; b. 17 May 1928, Rugby; s. of Robert Cameron Watt and Barbara Bidwell; m. 1st Marianne R. Grau 1951 (died 1962); m. 2nd Felicia Cobb Stanley 1962 (died 1997); one s., one step-d.; ed Rugby School and Oriel Coll. Oxford; Asst ed. (Foreign Office Research Dept), Documents on German foreign policy 1918–1945, 1951–54, 1951–59; Asst Lecturer in Political History, London School of Econs 1954–56, Lecturer in Int. History 1957–63, Sr Lecturer 1964–65; Reader in Int. History, Univ. of London 1966–72, Prof. in Int. History 1972–82, Stevenson Prof. in Int. History 1982–93, Emer. Prof. of Int. History 1993–; Ed. Survey of International Affairs, Royal Inst. of Int. Affairs 1962–71; Historian, Cabinet Office Historical Section 1977–94; Rockefeller Fellow in Social Sciences 1960–61; Fellow Polish Acad. of Arts and Sciences, Cracow; fmr FRSA; Hon. Fellow Oriel Coll., Oxford 1998; Wolfson Prize for History 1990. *Publications:* Oxford Poetry 1950 (ed.) 1951, Britain and the Suez Canal 1956, Personalities and Policies 1965, Hitler's Mein Kampf (ed.) 1969, 1992, Too Serious a Business 1975, 1992, Succeeding John Bull 1984, How War Came 1989. *Leisure interests:* exploring London, science fiction, cats. *Address:* c/o Department of International History, London School of Economics, Aldwych, London, WC2A 2AE, England. *Telephone:* (20) 7955-7924. *Fax:* (20) 7955-6800.

CAMI, Foto; Albanian party official (retd) and academician; b. 4 Oct. 1925, Labove, Gjirokastër Dist; s. of Premito Cami and Olimbi Cami; m. Zhaneta Cami 1960; two d.; ed Moscow Univ.; partisan in Second World War; mem. Albanian CP 1944; propaganda dept of Albanian Workers' Party (AWP) Cen. Cttee apparatus 1953–66; cand. mem. AWP Cen. Cttee 1967–71, mem. 1971–; mem. and mem. Presidium Albanian Acad. of Sciences 1972–; deputy to People's Ass. (Tirana Dist) 1970–76, 1982–; cand. mem. Politburo 1981–86, mem. 1986; First Sec. of AWP Krujë and Shkodër Dist Cttees. 1975–79, Tirana Dist Cttee 1982–85; Propaganda Sec. of AWP Cen. Cttee 1985–; Chair. Comm. for Foreign Affairs of Albanian People's Ass. 1987–91; various orders. *Leisure interests:* politics and philosophy, fishing.

CAMILIÓN, Oscar Héctor, PhD; Argentine politician; b. 6 Jan. 1930, Buenos Aires; s. of Oscar Juan Camilión and Lucía Fernández; m. Susana María Lascano 1956; two s. two d.; ed Colegio San Salvador, Univ. Nacional de Buenos Aires; Asst, then Head of Research, Inst. of Constitutional Law, Univ. Nacional de Buenos Aires, Sec.-Gen. 1955, Prof. of Constitutional Law, concurrently at Univ. Católica de La Plata 1957; Prof. of Int. Law, Argentine Inst. of Hispanic Culture; Prof. of Int. Politics, Argentine Nat. Coll. of Defence; entered Ministry of Foreign Affairs 1958, held posts of Minister, Chief of Cabinet, Dir of Personnel, Minister-Counsellor, Argentine Embassy, Brazil 1959–61, Under-Sec. 1961–62; mem. dels. to UN Gen. Assembly, Confs. of OAS and other regional orgs., to Conf. of Guaranteeing Countries of Peru-Ecuador Peace Protocol 1960, 1981; Chief Ed. Clarín newspaper, Buenos Aires 1965–72; Amb. to Brazil 1976–81; Minister of Foreign Affairs and Worship March–Dec. 1981, of Defence 1993–96; f. Argentine Council of Int. Relations; mem. Interamerican Dialogue, Atlantic Confs.; decorations from Brazil, Peru, Bolivia, Venezuela, Colombia, Honduras, El Salvador. *Pub-*

lications: several papers on historical, political and diplomatic subjects. *Leisure interests:* golf, classical music, history. *Address:* Montevideo 1597-4°, Buenos Aires 42-9557, Argentina.

CAMILLERI, Charles, MUS.BAC.; British/Maltese composer; b. 7 Sept. 1931, Malta; s. of Carmel Camilleri and Josephine Quinton; m. Doris Vella 1957; one s. one d.; ed Lyceum High School and Toronto Univ., Canada; composer, teacher, lecturer, conductor in Malta up to 1949, Australia 1949–53, UK 1954–57, Toronto, conductor with CBC, Toronto 1958–63, London 1964–; apptd. Dir Inst. of Mediterranean Music Foundation of Int. Studies, UNESCO 1987; Prof. of Music, Univ. of Malta 1990; comm. by UNESCO Songs of Infant Species for soprano and piano 1987; commissioned by Aga Khan Foundation: Mimar for piano, vibraphone and gongs 1987; visits to many cos. in Far East, Europe and N America 1949–; many Arts Council Awards. *Publications:* over 80, including Missa Mundi 1968, 2nd Piano Concerto 1969, Piano Trio 1970, String Quartet 1973, Cosmic Visions 1974, Five Books on Improvisation 1983, 3rd Piano Concerto 1985, Interchangeable Galaxies, Diaphanion 1987, The Elements (ballet), Music of the Mediterranean 1987, Compostella (opera in two Acts) 1988, City of Brass 1989, Cello Concerto 1989, Ombras 1990. *Leisure interest:* research in primitive and folk music. *Address:* 24 Orchard Avenue, Finchley, London, N3 3NL, England. *Telephone:* (20) 8349 1728.

CAMILLERI, Louis C., BA; American (b. Egyptian) business executive; b. 1955, Alexandria, Egypt; m. (divorced); three c.; ed Univ. of Lausanne, Switzerland; joined Philip Morris Europe, Lausanne as an analyst 1978, Sr Vice-Pres. of Corp. Planning, Philip Morris Cos. Inc., New York 1995–96, Sr Vice-Pres. and Chief Financial Officer 1996–2002, Pres. and CEO April–Aug. 2002, Chair. and CEO Aug. 2002–; Pres. and CEO Kraft Foods Int. 1995, currently Chair. Bd Dirs; Dir (non-exec.) SABMiller 2002–. *Leisure interests:* motorsports, scuba diving. *Address:* Philip Morris, 120 Park Avenue, New York, NY 10017, USA (Office). *Website:* www.philipmorris.com (Office).

CAMILLERI, Victor; Maltese diplomatist; b. 1942, St Venera; m. Elizabeth B. Heaney 1967; two s.; ed Lyceum, Malta, Univ. of Birmingham, UK, Columbia Univ., USA; fmr teacher, Educ. Dept; joined External Affairs Service, Ministry of Commonwealth and Foreign Affairs 1968; First Sec., Perm. Mission to UN, New York 1974–81; Perm. Rep. to UNIDO and UNESCO 1981–84; apptd. Head Multilateral Section, Ministry of Foreign Affairs, Valletta 1984, Acting Sec. 1985–87; Amb. and Head Malta's del. to Stockholm Conf., Conf. on Security and Co-operation in Europe on Confidence and Security Bldg Measures 1984–85; Deputy High Commr in London 1987–90, High Commr (also Accred to Sweden) 1991; Chef de Cabinet, Office of Pres. of 45th Session of UN Gen. Ass. 1990; Perm. Rep. to UN 1991–93; Amb. to Belgium 1997–. *Address:* Maltese Embassy, 65–67 rue Belliard, 1040 Brussels, Belgium (Office). *Telephone:* (2) 343-01-95 (Office). *Fax:* (2) 343-01-06 (Office). *E-mail:* victor.camilleri@magnet.mt.

CAMILO, Michel; Dominican Republic pianist and composer; b. Santo Domingo; ed Nat. Conservatory, Santo Domingo, Mannes and Juilliard School of Music, New York; mem. Nat. Symphony Orchestra, Santo Domingo, conductor 1987; moved to New York 1979; debut at Carnegie Hall with trio 1985; Musical Dir Heineken Jazz Festival, Dominican Rep. 1987–92; guest soloist with numerous orchestras 1994–; Co-Artistic Dir Latin-Caribbean Music Festival, Washington, DC 1998; has performed in N America, the Caribbean, Japan, Europe, S. America and Israel; Prof. Emer., Univ. Autónoma de Santo Domingo, 1992; Dr hc (Univ. Tecnológica de Santiago) 1994, (Berklee Coll.of Music) 2000; Int. Jazz Award, Clearwater Jazz Holiday 1993; Kt Heraldic Order of Christopher Columbus; Silver Cross of the Order of Duarte, Sanchez y Mella (Award of the Govt of the Dominican Republic) 2001. *Film:* Michel Camilo trio featured in "Calle 54" (documentary on Latin Jazz). *Albums include:* Why Not!, Suntan/Michel Camilo in Trio, Michel Camilo 1988, On Fire, On the Other Hand, Rendezvous 1993, One More Once 1994, Thru My Eyes 1997, Spain 2000; *Compositions include:* Why Not! (Grammy award) 1983, The Goodwill Games Theme (Grammy award), Rhapsody for Two Pianos 1992, Piano Concerto 1998, Triangulo 2002, Concerto for Piano and Orchestra 2002; *Compositions of music for films include:* Amo Tu Cama Rica (also performed and recorded) 1991, Los Peores Años de Nuestra Vida (also recorded) 1994, Two Much 1995. *Address:* c/o Sandra Camilo, PO Box 216, Katonah, NY 10536, USA (Office). *Telephone:* (914) 232-2683 (Office). *Fax:* (914) 232-0316 (Office). *E-mail:* Mijazz@ix .netcom.com (Office). *Website:* www.michelcamilo.com.

CAMOYS, 7th Baron (cr. 1264, called out of abeyance 1839); **(Ralph) Thomas Campion George Sherman Stonor,** GCVO, PC; British banker; b. 16 April 1940; s. of 6th Baron Camoys and Mary Jeanne Stourton; m. Elisabeth Mary Hyde Parker 1966; one s. three d.; ed Eton Coll., Balliol Coll., Oxford; Man. Dir Rothschild Intercontinental Bank Ltd 1969–75; with Amex Bank Ltd 1975–78; Man. Dir Barclays Merchant Bank 1978–84, Exec. Vice-Chair. 1984–86; Dir Barclays Bank PLC 1984–94; Chief Exec. Barclays de Zoete Wedd Holdings Ltd 1986–87, Deputy Chair. 1987–98; Deputy Chair. Sotheby's Holdings Inc. 1994–97; Dir 3i Group 1991–2002, Perpetual PLC 1994–2000, British Grolux Ltd 1994–; Lord Chamberlain of HM Household 1998–2000; Perm. Lord in Waiting to the Queen 2000–; mem. Court of Assistants, Fishmongers' Co. 1980–; Consultor Extraordinary Section of Admin. of the Patrimony of the Holy See 1991–; Hon. DLitt (Sheffield) 2001; Lord-in-Waiting to HM the Queen 1992–; DL Oxfordshire 1994–; Order of

Gorkha Dakshina Bahu, 1st Class (Nepal). *Leisure interests:* the arts, shooting. *Address:* Stonor Park, Henley-on-Thames, Oxon., RG9 6HF, England. *Telephone:* (1491) 638644.

CAMP, Jeffery Bruce, RA; British artist; b. 1923, Oulton Broad, Suffolk; s. of George Camp and Caroline Denny; m. Laetitia Yhap 1963; ed Lowestoft and Ipswich Art Schools and Edin. Coll. of Art (under William Gillies); Andrew Grant Scholarship for travelling and study 1944, 1945, David Murray Bursary for landscape painting 1946; painted altarpiece for St Alban's Church, Norwich 1955; lecturer Slade School of Fine Art, London 1963–88; mem. London Group 1961; in numerous mixed exhbns 1958–; works in numerous public collections in UK; Athena Art Award 1987. *One-man exhibitions include:* Edin. Festival 1950, Galerie de Seine, London 1958, 1959, Beaux Arts Gallery, London 1961, 1963, New Art Centre, London 1968, Fermoy Art Gallery, King's Lynn 1970, S. London Art Gallery 1973, Royal Shakespeare Theatre, Stratford 1974, Serpentine Gallery, London (Arts Council) 1978, Bradford City Art Gallery 1979, Browse and Darby 1984, 1993, 1997, The 29th Aldeburgh Festival 1986, Nigel Greenwood Gallery, London 1986, 1990, 1993, Royal Acad. Retrospective 1988. *Publications:* Draw 1981, Paint 1996. *Address:* c/o Browse & Darby, 19 Cork Street, London, W1X 2LP; 27 Stirling Road, London, SW9 9EF, England. *Telephone:* (20) 7734-7984.

CAMPBELL, Alastair John, MA; British civil servant and journalist; b. 25 May 1957; s. of Donald Campbell and Elizabeth (née Caldwell) Campbell; partner Fiona Millar; two s. one d.; ed City of Leicester Boys School, Gonville and Caius Coll., Cambridge; trainee reporter Tavistock Times and Sunday Independent 1980–82; freelance reporter 1982–83; reporter Daily Mirror 1982–86, Political Ed. 1989–93; News Ed. Sunday Today 1985–86; Political Corresp. Sunday Mirror 1986–87, Political Ed. 1987–89, columnist 1989–91; Asst Ed. and columnist Today 1993–95; Press Sec. to Leader of the Opposition 1994–97; Press Sec. to Prime Minister 1997–2001, Dir of Communications 2001–; Pres. Keighley Br., Burnley Football Supporters' Club. *Leisure interests:* bagpipes, Burnley Football Club. *Address:* Prime Minister's Office, 10 Downing Street, London, SW1A 2AA, England.

CAMPBELL, Hon. Alexander Bradshaw, PC, QC, LLB, LLD; Canadian politician and lawyer; b. 1 Dec. 1933, Summerside, PEI; s. of late Thane A. Campbell and Cecilia Bradshaw; m. Marilyn Gilmour 1961; two s. one d.; practised law in Summerside, PEI 1959–66; mem. PEI Legislature 1965–78, Leader of Liberal Party for PEI Dec. 1965–78; Premier of PEI 1966–78; Minister of Devt 1969–72, of Agriculture and Forestry 1972–74, Pres. Exec. Council, Minister of Justice, Attorney and Advocate-Gen. 1974–78; Justice, Supreme Court of PEI 1978–94; mem. Privy Council for Canada 1967; mem. and fmr Sec. Summerside Bd of Trade; Past Pres. of Y's Men's Club; fmr Vice-Pres. and Exec. mem. PEI Young Liberal Asscn; Pres. Summerside YMCA 1981–91; Elder, United Church, Summerside; Founding Pres. Summerside Area Historical Soc. 1983–88; Founding Chair. Duke of Edinburgh's Awards Cttee (PEI) 1984; Trustee Wyatt Foundation 1990; mem. Heedless Hoarsemen Men's Chorus, Largo, FL; co-founder PEI Day, Florida; Hon. LLD (McGill, PEI). *Leisure interests:* golf, swimming, gardening. *Address:* Stanley Bridge, Kensington, R.R. # 6, Prince Edward Island, C0B 1M0, Canada; 7100 Ulmerton Road, Lot 314, Largo, FL 33771, USA (Winter). *Telephone:* (902) 886-2081 (Summer); (727) 530-9499 (Winter). *E-mail:* alexbcampbell@auracom.com (Home).

CAMPBELL, Allan McCulloch, MS, PhD; American professor of biology; b. 27 April 1929, Berkeley, Calif.; s. of Lindsay and Virginia Campbell; m. Alice Del Campillo 1958; one s. one d.; ed Univ. of Calif. (Berkeley) and Univ. of Ill.; Instructor in Bacteriology, Univ. of Mich. Medical School, Ann Arbor 1953–57; Research Assoc., Carnegie Inst. of Washington, Dept of Genetics 1957–58; Asst Prof. to Prof. of Biology, Univ. of Rochester, 1958–68; Prof. of Biological Sciences, Stanford Univ. 1968–, Barbara Kimball Browning Prof. of Humanities and Sciences 1992–; Fellow, American Acad. of Arts and Sciences; mem. Nat. Acad. of Sciences; Hon. DSc (Univ. of Chicago) 1978, (Univ. of Rochester) 1981. *Publications:* Episomes 1969, General Virology 1978. *Address:* Department of Biological Sciences, Stanford University, Stanford, CA 94305 (Office); 947 Mears Court, Stanford, CA 94305-1041, USA (Home). *Telephone:* 723-1170 (Office); 493-6155 (Home). *Fax:* 725-1848. *E-mail:* AMC@stanford.edu (Office).

CAMPBELL, Ben Nighthorse, BA; American politician; b. 13 April 1933, Auburn, Calif; m. Linda Price; two c.; ed Univ. of California, San José; educator Sacramento Law Enforcement Agency; Democrat mem. Colo Gen. Ass. 1983–86, U.S. House of Reps. 1987–93, Senator from Colorado 1993–; fmr Democrat, now Republican; rancher, jewellery designer; Chief Northern Cheyenne Tribe; mem. American Quarter Horse Asscn, American Indian Educ. Asscn, Aircraft Owners and Pilots Asscn. *Address:* U.S. Senate, 380 Russell Senate Office Building, Washington, DC 20510, USA.

CAMPBELL, Bonnie Jean, BA, JD; American lawyer; b. 9 April 1948, Norwich, NY; d. of Thomas Pierce and Helen Slater; m. Edward Campbell 1974; called to Bar, Iowa 1985, U.S. Dist (N and S. Dist) Iowa 1985, U.S. Court of Appeals (8th circuit) 1989, U.S. Supreme Court 1989; Clerk, U.S. Dept of Housing and Urban Devt Washington, DC 1965–67, U.S. Senate Subcttee. on Intergovernmental Relations 1967–69; case-worker, Harold E Hughes, Washington, DC 1969–74; Field rep. Senator John C. Culver, Des Moines 1974–80; Assoc. Wimer, Hudson, Flynn & Neugent, PC, Des Moines 1984–89; of counsel, Belin, Harris, Helmick, Des Moines 1989–91; Attorney-Gen. State of

Iowa 1991–95; Head, Agency for Combating Violence Against Women, U.S. Dept of Justice 1995–. *Address:* Department of Justice, 10th Street and Constitution Avenue, Washington 20530, DC, USA.

CAMPBELL, Carroll Ashmore, DHumLitt; American politician; b. 24 July 1940, Greenville, SC; s. of Carroll Ashmore Campbell Sr and Anne Williams; m. Iris Rhodes 1959; two s.; ed American Univ. and Sherman Coll.; Pres. Handy Park Co. 1960–78; mem. SC House of Reps. 1970–74, SC Senate 1976; Exec. Asst to Gov. of SC 1975; Asst Regional Whip to various State dels. at Repub. Convention 1976, 1980, 1984; mem. 96th–99th Congresses from SC 4th Dist; Gov. of South Carolina 1987–95; mem. Advisory Council, White House Conf. on Handicapped Individuals; numerous awards including Guardian of Small Businesses Award, Watchdog of Treasury Award, Humanitarian Award, Rutledge Coll. and Leadership Award, American Security Council; Republican. *Address:* c/o Office of Governor, P.O. Box 11369, Columbia, SC, USA.

CAMPBELL, Colin Kydd, FRSC, FRSA, LFIEEE, FEIC; Canadian/British professor of electrical and computer engineering; b. 3 May 1927, St Andrew's, Scotland; s. of David Walker Campbell and Jean Bell Campbell; m. Vivian G. Norval 1954; two s. one d.; ed Madras Coll. St Andrew's, Univ. of St Andrew's and Mass. Inst. of Technology; mil. service 1944–46; communications engineer, Diplomatic Wireless Service and Foreign Office, London, Washington and New York 1946–48; electronics engineer, Atomic Instrument Co., Cambridge, Mass. 1954–57; research scholar, Royal Naval Scientific Service, St Andrew's Univ. 1957–60; Asst Prof. Electrical Eng McMaster Univ. 1960–63, Assoc. Prof. 1963–67, Prof. of Electrical and Computer Eng 1967–89, Emer. Prof. 1989–; Visiting Research Fellow Rand Afrikaans Univ., Johannesburg, S. Africa 1995; Invitation Fellow Japan Soc. for the Promotion of Science 1995; Visiting Research Scholar Virginia Polytechnic Inst. and State Univ. 2000, 2002; Hon. BSc (Eng), Hon. SM, Hon. PhD, Hon. DSc, Eadie Medal (Royal Soc. of Canada) 1983. *Publications:* Surface Acoustic Wave Devices and their Signal Processing Applications 1989, Surface Acoustic Wave Devices for Mobile and Wireless Communications 1998; numerous scientific and eng publs in professional and tech. journals with specialization in surface acoustic wave devices. *Leisure interests:* fishing, travelling. *Address:* 160 Parkview Drive, Ancaster, Ont., L9G 1Z5, Canada (Home). *E-mail:* colin.kydd .campbell@sympatico.ca (Home). *Website:* www3.sympatico.ca/colin.kydd .campbell (Home).

CAMPBELL, Sir Colin Murray, Kt, LLB; British academic; b. 26 Dec. 1944, Aberdeen; s. of late Donald Campbell and of Isobel Campbell; m. 1st Elaine Carlisle 1974 (divorced 1999); one s. one d.; m. 2nd Maria Dale 2002; ed Robert Gordon's Coll. Aberdeen and Univ. of Aberdeen; lecturer, Faculty of Law, Univ. of Dundee 1967–69, Univ. of Edin. 1969–73; Prof. of Jurisprudence, Queen's Univ. Belfast 1974–88, Prof. Emer.; Vice-Chancellor, Univ. of Nottingham 1988–; mem. Council, Soc. for Computers and Law 1973–88, Standing Advisory Comm. on Human Rights 1977–80, Legal Aid Advisory Cttee, Northern Ireland 1978–82, Mental Health Legislation Review Cttee, Northern Ireland 1978–82, Nottingham Devt Enterprise 1988–91, Inquiry into Police Responsibilities and Rewards 1992–93; Chair. Ind. Advisory Group on Consumers' Protection in Northern Ireland 1984, Northern Ireland Econ. Council 1987–94 (mem. 1985–94), Lace Market Devt Co. 1989–97, Human Fertilisation and Embryology Authority 1990–94, Medical Workforce Standing Advisory Cttee 1991–2001, Food Advisory Cttee 1994–2001, Human Genetics Advisory Comm. 1996–99; Chair. QUBIS Ltd 1983–88, Zeton Ltd 1990; Dir (non-exec.) Swiss Re GB 1999–; Her Majesty's First Commr for Judicial Appointments 2001–; Hon. LLD (Aberdeen) 2001. *Publications:* Law and Society 1979 (jtly.), Do We Need a Bill of Rights? (ed.) 1980, Data Processing and the Law (ed.) 1984; numerous articles in books and journals. *Leisure interests:* walking, sport, music, reading. *Address:* University of Nottingham, University Park, Nottingham, NG7 2RD, England. *Telephone:* (115) 951-3001. *Fax:* (115) 951-3005. *E-mail:* colin.campbell@nottingham.ac .uk (Office).

CAMPBELL, Finley Alexander, PhD, FRSC; Canadian geologist; b. 5 Jan. 1927, Kenora, Ont.; s. of Finley McLeod Campbell and Vivian Delve; m. Barbara E Cromarty 1953; two s. one d.; ed Kenora High School, Portland Univ., Brandon Coll., Univ. of Manitoba, Queen's Univ. Kingston, Ont. and Princeton Univ.; exploration and mine geologist 1950–58; Asst, Assoc. Prof. Univ. of Alberta 1958–65; Prof. and Head Dept of Geology, Univ. of Calgary 1965–69; Vice-Pres. Capital Resources, Univ. of Calgary 1969–71, Vice-Pres. (Academic) 1971–76, Prof. of Geology 1976–84, Vice-Pres. Priorities and Planning 1984–88, Prof. Emer. Dept of Geology and Geophysics 1988–; Vice-Chair. Bd of Dirs. Canadian Energy Research Inst.; Pres. Emer. Asscn, Univ. of Calgary; Queen's Jubilee Medal, Commemorative Medal for 125th Anniversary of Canada, Distinguished Service Award (Brandon Univ.) 1993 and other awards and distinctions. *Publications:* over 50 publs on geological topics. *Leisure interests:* sailing, golf, music, skiing, ballet. *Address:* Department of Geology and Geophysics, University of Calgary, 2500 University Drive NW, Calgary, T2N 1N4 (Office); 3408 Benton Drive NW, Calgary Alta, T2L 1W8, Canada (Home).

CAMPBELL, Gordon Arden, MA, FIChemE, FREng; British chemical engineer; b. 16 Oct. 1946; s. of late Hugh Eric Campbell and Jessie Campbell; m. Jennifer Vaughan 1970; two d.; ed Oldershaw Grammar School, Churchill Coll., Cambridge; joined Courtaulds Research 1968; Man. Dir British Celanese Ltd 1980–85, Saiccor (Pty) Ltd, S. Africa 1985–87; Dir Courtaulds PLC

1987–, Chief Exec. 1996–98; Chair. Acordis Group 1999–2000; Chair. and CEO Babcock Int. Group PLC 2000–; Pres. Inst. of Chemical Engineers 1998; Pres. Comité Int. de Rayonne et Fibres Synthétiques 1995–98; mem. (non-exec.) UKAEA 1993–96; Dir (non-exec.) A.E.A. Tech. 1996–97, Argos PLC 1997–98, British Nuclear Fuel PLC 2000–; Chair. Wade-Allied Holdings 1999–, Jupiter Split Trust PLC 2001; Vice-Pres. Acad. of Engineers 2001–. *Leisure interests:* golf, skiing, rugby. *Address:* Babcock International, 2 Cavendish Square, London, W1G 0PX, England (Office).

CAMPBELL, Iain Donald, MA, PhD, FRS; British biochemist; b. 24 April 1941, Perth, Scotland; s. of Daniel Campbell and Catherine Campbell (née Lauder); m. Karin C. Wehle 1967; one s. two d.; ed Univs. of St Andrews and Oxford; with Dept of Physics, Univ. of Bradford 1966–67; with Physical Chemistry Lab., Univ. of Oxford 1967–70, Dept of Biochemistry 1970–, tutor in Biochemistry and Fellow St John's Coll. 1987–, Prof. of Structural Biology 1992–, Assoc. Head of Dept of Biochemistry 1998–; del. to Oxford Univ. Press 1996–; mem. Wellcome Trust MC Panel 1997–2002; BHD Medal (Biochemical Soc.) 1990; Hon. DSc (Portsmouth) 2000; Hon. DTech (Lund) 2000; Novartis Medal (Biochemical Soc.) 2003. *Publications:* papers and reviews in scientific journals. *Address:* Department of Biochemistry, University of Oxford, South Parks Road, Oxford, OX1 3QU, England. *Telephone:* (1865) 275346. *Fax:* (1865) 275253.

CAMPBELL, John, MA; Irish diplomatist; b. 23 June 1936, Dublin; s. of Ernest Campbell and Bertha Campbell (née Willan); m. Nicole Lafon 1964; two s.; ed Trinity Coll. Dublin, Yale Univ.; Amb. to People's Repub. of China 1980–83, to F.R.G.1983–86, to EC 1986–91, to France 1991–95; Perm. Rep. to UN, New York 1995–98; Amb. to Portugal (also Accred to Brazil and Morocco) 1999–. *Address:* Irish Embassy, rua da Imprensa à Estrela 1–4°, 1200–684 Lisbon, Portugal (Office). *Telephone:* (21) 3929440 (Office). *Fax:* (21) 3977363 (Office).

CAMPBELL, Juliet Jeanne d'Auvergne, CMG, MA; British fmr diplomatist and university college head (retd.); b. 23 May 1935, London; d. of Wilfred d'Auvergne Collings and Harriet Nancy Draper Bishop; m. Alexander Elmslie Campbell 1983 (died 2002); ed schools in S. Africa, Palestine, Lebanon and UK, Lady Margaret Hall, Oxford; joined Foreign Office, London 1957, Del. to Conf. negotiating Britain's proposed entry to EC 1961–63, Second Sec., Bangkok 1964–67, First Sec. Paris (NATO) 1966, First Sec., FCO News Dept 1967–70, Head of Chancery, The Hague 1970–74, First Sec. then Counsellor FCO 1974–77, Counsellor, Paris 1977–80, Royal Coll. Defence Studies 1981, Counsellor, Jakarta 1982–83, Head, Training Dept 1983–87; Amb. to Luxembourg 1987–91; mem. Wilton Park Acad. Council 1992–2000; Mistress Girton Coll., Cambridge 1992–98; Deputy Vice-Chancellor, Cambridge Univ. 1993–98; Hon. Fellow Lady Margaret Hall Coll. (Oxford Univ.) 1992; Trustee Cambridge European Trust 1994–98, Kurt Hahn Trust 1995–98; mem. Council Queen's Coll., Harley St 1992–2002; Gov. Marlborough Coll. 1999–; Trustee Changing Faces (Charity). *Address:* 3 Belbroughton Road, Oxford, OX2 6UZ, England. *Telephone:* (1865) 558685 (Home). *Fax:* (1865) 302912. *E-mail:* jencampbell@aol.com (Home).

CAMPBELL, Kim (Avril Phaedra), PC; Canadian politician and lawyer; b. 10 March 1947; ed Univ. of British Columbia; lecturer in Science and History, Vancouver Community Coll., in Political Science, Univ. of BC; mem. BC Legis.; elected Progressive Conservative House of Commons 1988; Minister of State Affairs and Northern Devt 1989–90, Minister of Justice and Attorney-Gen. of Canada 1990–93; Minister of Defence 1993; Prime Minister of Canada June–Nov. 1993; mem. Advisory Bd Youth Option Program, Visiting Cttee Center for Int. Affairs, Harvard Univ. 1995–; Hon. Dir Volunteer Grandparents Asscn; Progressive Conservative leader June–Nov. 1993; Hon. Fellow LSE 1994. *Publication:* Time and Chance: A Political Memoir of Canada's First Woman Prime Minister 1996.

CAMPBELL, Naomi; British fashion model; b. 1970, London; d. of Valerie Morris; ed Barbara Speake Stage School, Italia Conti; fashion model 1985–; recording artist with Sony Epic. *Film appearances include:* Ready To Wear 1994, Miami Rhapsody 1995, Catwalk 1995, Invasion of Privacy 1996, Beautopia 1996, Prisoner of Love 1999, Destinazione Verna 2000. *Albums:* Baby Woman 1994, Love and Tears 1994. *Publication:* Swan (novel) 1994. *Address:* Women Model Agency, 2nd Floor, 107 Greene Street, New York, 10012, USA. *Telephone:* (20) 7333-0891 (Office). *Fax:* (20) 7323-1221 (Office).

CAMPBELL, Neve Adrienne; Canadian actress; b. 3 Oct. 1973, Guelph, Ont.; m. Jeff Colt 1995 (divorced 1997); ed Nat. Ballet School, Canada; Saturn Award for Best Actress 1996 (for Scream); MTV Movie Award for Best Female Performance 1996 (for Scream), 1997 (for Scream 2); Blockbuster Entertainment Award for Favourite Actress – Horror 1997 (for Scream 2). *Dance:* The Phantom of the Opera, The Nutcracker, Sleeping Beauty. *Films include:* Paint Cans 1994, The Dark 1994, Love Child 1995, The Craft 1996, Scream 1996, A Time to Kill 1996, Simba's Pride 1997, Scream 2 1997, Wild Things 1998, Hairshirt 1998, 54 1998, Three to Tango 1999, Scream 3 2000. *Television includes:* Catwalk 1992–93, Web of Deceit 1993, Baree 1994, The Forget-Me-Not Murders 1994, Party of Five 1994–98, The Canterville Ghost 1996. *Address:* Creative Artists Agency, 9830 Wilshire Boulevard, Beverly Hills, CA 90212, U.S.A. (Office).

CAMPBELL, Philip Henry Montgomery, PhD, FInstP, FRAS; British journalist and academic; b. 19 April 1951; s. of Hugh Campbell and Mary Montgomery Campbell; m. Judie Yelton 1980 (died 1992); two s.; ed Shrews-bury School, Bristol Univ., Queen Mary Coll., Univ. of London, Leicester Univ.; researcher Leicester Univ. 1977–79; Asst Ed. Nature magazine 1979–82, Physical Sciences Ed. 1982–88; f. Physics World (magazine), Ed. 1988–95; Dir Nature Publ Group 1997–; Hon. DSc (Leicester) 1999. *Radio:* broadcasts on BBC World Service. *Publications:* numerous papers and articles in journals, magazines and newspapers. *Leisure interest:* music. *Address:* Nature, 4 Crinan Street, London, N1 9XW, England (Office). *Telephone:* (20) 7833-4000 (Office).

CAMPBELL, Roderick Samuel Fisher, AM, PhD, DSc, MRCVS, FRSE; Australian professor of tropical veterinary science; b. 5 June 1924, Glasgow, Scotland; s. of Robert Campbell and Harriet Hodson; m. Barbara M. Morris 1956; three s.; ed Allan Glens School, Glasgow, McLaren High School, Callander and Glasgow Veterinary Coll.; Lecturer in Veterinary Pathology, Univ. of Glasgow 1948, Sr Lecturer 1956–69; Prof. and Head, Grad. School of Tropical Veterinary Science, James Cook Univ. Townsville 1969–87, Emer. Prof. 1987–, Chair. Convocation 1992–94, Dir Anton Breinl Centre for Tropical Health and Medicine, Townsville 1990–91; Visiting Prof. Khartoum Univ. 1964–65, Purdue Univ., USA 1967–68; Deputy Chair. Australian Veterinary Schools Accreditation Cttee 1988–92; Project Man. Balitvet Inst. Project, Bogor, Indonesia 1981–; Consultant, FAO, World Bank, Australian Centre for Int. Agric. Research, Int. Devt Program of Australian Univs., Australian Devt Asst Bureau, Ove Arup; Trustee, Indonesia Int. Animal Science Research and Devt Foundation 1990–93; Fellow Australian Coll. of Veterinary Science, Australian Coll. of Tropical Medicine, Royal Coll. of Pathology; Hon. DSc (James Cook), Hon. Dr Veterinary Medicine and Surgery (Glasgow) 2000; Kesteven Medal for Contrib. to Int. Veterinary Science, Pegasus Medal. *Publications:* numerous scientific papers on infectious diseases, veterinary educ., devt assistance etc. *Leisure interests:* history, music, golf. *Address:* Australian Institute of Tropical Veterinary and Animal Sciences, James Cook University, Townsville, Queensland 4811 (Office); 4/49 Quinn Street, Townsville, Queensland 4812, Australia (Home). *Telephone:* 4781-4278 (Office); 4728-8192 (Home). *Fax:* 4779-1526 (Office). *E-mail:* roderick.campbell@jcu.edu.au; rs8c@ozemail.com.au.

CAMPBELL, Steven MacMillan, BA; British artist; b. 19 March 1953, Glasgow; s. of George Campbell and Martha (née MacMillan) Dallas; m. Carol Ann Thompson 1975; one s. two d.; ed Rutherglen Acad., Glasgow School of Art, Pratt Inst., NY; Major works for Hirshhorn Museum, Tate Gallery, British Council, Wadsworth Atheneum, Metropolitan Museum; Glenfiddich Gold Medal Winner 1998, Creative Scotland Award 2000, Bram Stoker Gold Medal 1982, Fulbright Scholarship 1982, Leverhulme 1992. *One-man exhibitions include:* Barbara Toll Fine Art 1985, Marlborough Fine Art, NY 1988, 1994, Tokyo 1990, The Third Eye Centre, Glasgow 1990, Southampton City Art Gallery 1991, Talbot Rice Gallery, Edin. 1993, Marlborough Fine Art, London 1993, Pier Art Centre, Orkney 1997, Talbot Ric Gallery, Edin. 2002. *Television:* Artworks Scotland (documentary) 2002. *Leisure interests:* angling, reading mathematics, detective novels, opera. *Address:* Marlborough Fine Art (UK) Ltd, 6 Albemarle Street, London, W1X 4BY, England; Rennies Loan, The Cross, Kippen, Stirlingshire, FK8 3DX, Scotland. *Telephone:* (20) 7629-5161 (London); (1786) 870370 (Stirling). *Fax:* (20) 7629-6338 (London).

CAMPBELL OF CROY, Baron (Life Peer), cr. 1974, of Croy in the County of Nairn; **Rt. Hon. Gordon Thomas Calthrop Campbell,** PC, MC; British politician; b. 8 June 1921, Quetta, Pakistan; s. of Maj.-Gen. and Mrs J. A. Campbell; m. Nicola Madan 1949; two s. one d.; ed Wellington Coll.; served in regular army 1939–46 (Maj. 1942), wounded and disabled 1945; diplomatic service 1946–57, mem. UK mission to UN 1949–52, Cabinet Office 1954–56; MP (Conservative) for Moray and Nairn 1959–74; Lord Commr of the Treasury 1962; Parl. Under-Sec. of State for Scotland 1963–64; Shadow Cabinet 1969–70; Sec. of State for Scotland 1970–74; Opposition Spokesman in House of Lords 1975–79; Oil Industry Consultant 1975–; Partner in Holme Rose Farms and Estate 1969–; Dir and Chair. Scottish Bd of Alliance and Leicester Building Soc. 1985–; Chair. Advisory Cttee on Pollution of the Sea 1987–89; Chair. Scottish Council of Independent Schools; Chair. Stoic Insurance Services 1979–96; Chair. Scottish Cttee, Int. Year of Disabled 1981; Vice Lord Lt of Nairnshire 1988–99; Trustee, Thomson Foundation 1977–2002; Pres. Anglo-Austrian Soc. 1991–2001; Austrian Grand Cross and Star. *Publication:* Disablement: Prospects and Problems in the UK 1981. *Leisure interests:* music, birds. *Address:* 907 Howard House, Dolphin Square, London, SW1V 3PQ, England. *Telephone:* (20) 7219-5353; (20) 7798-5571.

CAMPBELL-WHITE, Martin Andrew, FRSA; British business executive; b. 11 July 1943; s. of late John Vernon Campbell-White and Hilda Doris Ash; m. Margaret Mary Miles 1969; three s.; ed Dean Close School, Cheltenham, St John's Coll., Oxford, Univ. of Strasbourg; with Thomas Skinner & Co. Ltd (Publrs) 1964–66, Ibbs & Tillett Ltd (Concert Agents) 1966–72, Dir 1969–72, Harold Holt Ltd (Concert Agents), subsequently Askonas Holt Ltd 1972–, Dir 1973–, Deputy Chair. 1989–92, Chief Exec. 1992– (Jt Chief 1998–); Chair. British Asscn of Concert Agents 1978–81; Council mem. London Sinfonietta 1973–86; Dir Chamber Orchestra of Europe 1983–93; Asst Dir Festival of German Arts 1987; Founding Dir Japan Festival 1991; mem. Bd Première Ensemble 1991–, Riverside Studios 1998–; Trustee Abbado Trust for Young Musicians 1987–, Salzburg Festival Trust 1996–; Sebetia Ter prize for Culture, Naples, Italy 1999. *Leisure interests:* golf, watching cricket, classical music, travel. *Address:* c/o Askonas Holt Ltd., Lonsdale Chambers, 27

Chancery Lane, London, WC2A 1PF, England (Office). *Telephone:* (20) 7400-1700 (Office). *Fax:* (20) 7400-1799. *E-mail:* martin.campbell-white@askonasholt.co.uk.

CAMPESE, David Ian; Australian rugby football player; b. 21 Oct. 1962, Queanbeyan, NSW; s. of Tony Campese and Joan Campese; m. Lara Berkenstein 2003; partner Campo's Sports Store; int. debut Australia versus NZ 1982; Capt. Australia team; winner World Cup 1991; world's leading try scorer with 64; scored 310 points; Australia's most capped player (represented Australia 101 times); Dir David Campese Man. Group 1997–; Australian Writers Player of the Year 1991, English Rugby Writers Player of the Year 1991, Int. Rugby Hall of Fame 2001, Order of Australia Medal (for services to rugby union) 2002. *Publication:* On a Wing and a Prayer (biog.). *Leisure interests:* golf, cooking, music, reading. *Address:* David Campese Management Group, Suite 4, 870 Pacific Highway, Gordon, NSW 2072, Australia.

CAMPION, Jane, BA; New Zealand film director and writer; b. 30 April 1954, Wellington; d. of Richard Campion and Edith Campion; ed Victoria Univ., Chelsea School of Arts, London, Australian Film, TV and Radio School, Sydney Coll. of the Arts; Adjunct Prof. Sydney Coll. of the Arts, Univ. of Sydney 2000; Hon. DLitt (Victoria Univ. of Wellington) 1999; numerous awards and prizes. *Films directed:* Peel 1981–82 (Palme d'Or, Cannes Film Festival 1986), Girls Own Story 1984 (won awards at Sydney and Melbourne Film Festivals, Australian Film Inst. Awards, Cinestud Amsterdam Film Festival), Mishaps of Seduction and Conquest 1984–85, Passionless Moments 1984–85, After Hours 1984, Dancing Daze 1985, Two Friends 1986, Sweetie (co-writer also) 1988, An Angel at my Table 1990 (voted Best Woman Dir, Best Film at Venice Film Festival 1990), The Piano (Palme d'Or, Cannes Film Festival) 1993, The Portrait of a Lady (Best Film, Venice Film Festival 1996) 1996, Holy Smoke 1999, In the Cut 2003. *Address:* HLA Management Pty Ltd, 87 Pitt Street, Redfern, NSW 2016 (Office); PO Box 1536, Strawberry Hills, NSW 2012 (Office); HLA Management Pty Ltd, 87 Pitt Street, Redfern, NSW 2016, Australia. *Telephone:* (612) 9310-4948 (Office). *Fax:* (612) 9310-4113 (Office). *E-mail:* hla@hlamgt.com.au (Office).

CÁMPORA, Mario, PhD; Argentine diplomatist; b. 3 Aug. 1930, Mendoza; s. of Pedro Cámpora and Ana Miralles; m. Magdalena Díaz Gavier 1972; one s. two d.; ed Nat. Univ. of Rosario; joined Foreign Service 1955; served Geneva, Washington, DC, The Hague, New Delhi; active in politics as mem. Justicialist Party 1971–73; resgnd from diplomatic service 1975; following 1976 coup was active in opposition seeking restoration of civil liberties, law and order 1976–83; Amb. Argentine Special Mission for Disarmament, Geneva 1985; Asst to presidential cand., Dr Carlos Menem 1988; Sec. of State, Ministry of Foreign Affairs 1989; Amb. to UK 1990–94, to Belgium (also Accred to Luxembourg) 1996–99. *Address:* c/o Ministry of Foreign Affairs, International Trade and Worship, Esmeralda 1212, 1007 Buenos Aires, Argentina (Office).

CAMUS, Philippe; French business executive; b. 28 June 1948, Paris; ed Ecole Normale Supérieure, Paris, Inst. d'Etudes Politiques de Paris; Special Project Man. Caisse des Dépôts et Consignations 1972–82; Dir, Sr Man. Lagardère Groupe, Co-Pres. Chair. Financial Cttee 1993–98, Co-CEO Lagardère SCA 1998–; Chair. Financial Cttee Matra Group 1982–92; Chair. and CEO ARCO (gen. partner Lagardère Group) 1992–; CEO, Chair. Man. Bd Aérospatiale Matra 1999–; Co-CEO European Aeronautic Defence and Space Co. (EADS) 2000–; Chair. Supervisory Bd Banque Arjil 1987–93; Dir Crédit Lyonnais, Chair. Risk and Accounts Cttee 1997–; Dir CERUS 1997–; mem. Conseil des Marchés Financiers 1996–; Aviation Week Aerospace Laureate 1989; Chevalier Légion d'honneur 2001; Prix de la meilleure opération financière 2000. *Address:* E.A.D.S., 37 boulevard de Montmorency, 75781 Paris, Cedex 16, France (Office). *Telephone:* (607) 3 42 83 (Office). *Fax:* (607) 3 42 85 (Office).

CANALES CLARIOND, Fernando, MBA; Mexican politician; b. Monterrey, Nuevo León; m. Angela Stelzer; two s. two d.; ed Escuela Libre de Derecho, Inst. of Tech. and Higher Studies, Monterrey, Univ. of the Sorbonne, Paris, France; fmr Gen. Dir for Vice-Pres. of Admin. Council, IMSA group; dir of activities with Admin. Business Council of USA, Colombia, Venezuela, Brazil, Argentina and Chile; mem. Partido Accion Nacional 1978; mem. Congress (First Dist. of Nuevo León) 1979–81; Gov. of Nuevo León 1997–2002; Minister for the Economy 2003–; Pres. Fed. Chamber of Commerce of Nuevo León and Pres. Monterrey Chamber of Commerce; mem. Alternative Cabinet of Manuel Clouthier in Secr. of Patrimony and Industrial Devt. *Address:* Secretariat of State for the Economy, México, DF, Mexico (Office). *Telephone:* (1) 56-29-95-00 (Office). *E-mail:* gsanchez@economia.gob.mx (Office). *Website:* www.economia.gob.mx (Office).

CÂNDEA, Virgil; Romanian historian; b. 29 April 1927, Focşani; s. of Lucian Cândea and of Elena Cândea; m. Alexandrina M. Anastasiu 1957; two s. one d.; ed Bucharest Univ.; head documentation Dept of the Romanian Acad. Library 1950–61; Dir Int. Asscn of South-East European Studies, Bucharest 1963–68, Sec.-Gen. 1988–94; Sr Fellow Inst. of South-East European Studies, Bucharest 1968–72; Prof. Institut Universitaire de Hautes Etudes Internationales, Geneva 1967–71; Gen. Sec. of Romania Asscn 1972–90; Prof. Bucharest Univ.; Vice-Pres. Centro italo-rumeno di Studi Storici, Milan 1978–92; mem. Romanian Writers' Union 1971, Hellenic Soc. of Archaeology, Athens 1989–, Romanian Acad. 1992– (Pres. 1998–), European Acad. of Arts, Sciences and Humanities, Paris 1996–; Corresp. mem. Sudosteuropa Gesellschaft, Munich 1990–; Fellow Wilson Center, Smithsonian Inst. 1984; Ordre

du Cèdre Award (Lebanon); Prize of Romanian Acad. *Publications:* Pagini din istoria diplomaţiei româneşti (Pages from the History of Romanian Diplomacy) 1966, co-author: Stolnicul între contemporani (The High Steward Among Contemporaries) 1971, An Outline of Romanian History 1971, Raţiunea dominantă (The Prevailing Reason) 1979, co-author: Witnesses to the Romanian presence in Mount Athos 1979, Romanian Culture Abroad 1982, Présences culturelles roumaines 1985, Mărturii româneşti peste hotare, Mică enciclopedie, I (Romanian Testimonies Abroad) 1991, Icônes grecques, mel-kites, russes 1993; critical edns. of works by N. Bălcescu, Al. Odobescu and D. Cantemir; Romanian trans. from Nikitin, Bacon, Dante and others. *Leisure interests:* history of culture, spirituality. *Address:* 125, Calea Victoriei, 71102 Bucharest (Office); 8 Intr. Procopie Dumitrescu, s. 2, 70262 Bucharest, Romania (Home). *Telephone:* (1) 3125342 (Office); (1) 6192063 (Home).

CANE, Louis Paul Joseph; French artist; b. 13 Dec. 1943, Beaulieu-sur-Mer; s. of Albert Cane and Andrée (née Pasquier) Cane; m. Nicole Rondinella 1970; two d.; ed Collège des Frères Dominicains de Sorèze, Lycée Gassendi de Digne, Ecole Nationale des Arts Décoratifs, Nice, Ecole Nationale Supérieure des Arts Décoratifs, Paris; first exhbn 1970; exhbns Galerie Yvon, Lambert, Paris 1972, Galerie Templon, Paris, Milan 1973–75, Castelli Gallery, New York 1982, Galerie Beaubourg, Paris (sculptures) 1985–90, Musée de l'Orangerie des Tuileries 1994; regular exhbns in Germany, Sweden, Spain, Belgium, Italy, Australia, Japan, fmr USSR, UK; Officier des Arts et des Lettres. *Publications:* Louis Cane, artiste-peintre 1967, Toiles découpées 1971, Toiles sol/mur 1972, Annonciations 1982, Déluges 1983, Accouchements 1983, Déjeuners sur l'herbe 1985, Trois graces 1987, 1988, Fleurs et tampons 1989, Nymphéas 1992. *Leisure interests:* 18th-century France, studying 18th-century French bronzes. *Address:* 184 rue Saint Maur, 75010 Paris (Office); 37 rue d'Enghien, 75010 Paris, France (Home). *Telephone:* 1-42-03-73-31. *Fax:* 1-42-03-01-19.

CANELLA, Guido; Italian architect and university professor; b. 19 Jan. 1931, Bucharest, Romania; m. Laura Testori 1960; two s. two d.; ed Polytechnic of Milan; Founding partner Canella & Achilli architetti 1959–; Prof. of Architectural Composition, Polytechnic of Milan 1970–, Dir Inst. of Architectural Composition 1970–79, Dir Dept of Architectural Design 1979–81; Dir Architecture Section, Triennale of Milan 1978–82; Ed.-in-Chief Hinterland 1977–85, Zodiac 1989–; S. Luca Nat. Acad.; mem. Scientific Cttee Nat. Group of Architecture of Nat. Research Council; Inst. of Architects Prize 1968, Int. Cttee of Architecture Critics Prize 1991. *Major Works:* Segrate Town Hall, Milan 1963, social services and Piazza, Villaggio Incis, Milan 1968; civic centres in Pieve Emanuele, Milan 1971 and Pioltello, Milan 1976; school centres in Opera, Milan 1974, Cesano Boscone, Milan 1975 and Parma 1985; residential complexes in Bollate, Milan 1974, Peschiera Borromeo, Milan 1983, Milan 2002; Law Courts redevelopment in Ancona 1975; town offices and law courts in Legnano, Milan 1982; social services, housing and Piazza in Monte d'Ago, Ancona 1984; theatre projects in Taranto 1988, Aosta 1989, Varese 1990; Church projects at Casamassima, Bari 1991, Modena 2001; auditorium, church and health complex in Peschiera Borromeo, Milan 1983–91; Italian Embassies' projects in Washington and Berlin 1992; Pescara Airport 1992; city planning projects for Milan 1991, Berlin 1992, Como 1993, Beirut 1994, Bucharest 1996, Pordenone 2001; Cinema multiplex, Milan 1997; Motel Inter-Continental, Asmara, Eritrea 1999; museum, Meina, Novara 1997; New City Hall, offices and car park building, Bari 1998; opera house and theatre, Taranto 1998; City Hall extension, Gorgonzola, Milan 2001; New Theatre of Porta Romana and residential complex, Milan 2002; private residence, Woodland, Houston, Texas 2003; restaurant and bookstore complex, Milan 2003. *Publications:* Il sistema teatrale a Milano 1966, Università: ragione, contesto, tipo 1975; articles in various specialist journals. *Address:* Via Revere 7, 20123 Milan, Italy. *Telephone:* (02) 4695222-333. *Fax:* (02) 4813704 (Office). *E-mail:* info@canella-achilli.com (Office). *Website:* www.canella-achilli.com (Office).

CANESTRI, HE Cardinal Giovanni; Italian ecclesiastic; b. 30 Sept. 1918, Alessandria; ordained 1941, elected to the titular Church of Tenedo 1961, consecrated Bishop 1961; transferred to Tortona 1971; prefect at the titular Church of Monterano 1975 with title of Archbishop; transferred to Cagliari 1984, Genoa 1987; cr. HE Cardinal 1987.

CANETE, Alfredo; Paraguayan diplomatist; b. 14 March 1942, Asunción; m.; one s.; Sec. in Paraguayan Mission to UN 1961–62, Perm. Rep. to UN 1983–91; Deputy Dir Econ. Dept, Ministry of Foreign Affairs, then Dir Dept of Foreign Trade; Alt. Rep. to Latin-American Trade Asscn 1973–78; Consul-Gen. and Chargé d'Affaires in UK 1978; Minister in Embassy, USA 1980–81; Amb. to Belgium, Netherlands and Luxembourg 1981–83, to Belgium 1992–96; Head of Mission to EEC (now EU) 1982–83, 1992–96; Exec. Dir Paraguayan Centre for Int. Studies 1997–; Dir Diplomatic Acad., Ministry of Foreign Affairs 1999–; Kt.'s Cross, Order of Civil Merit (Spain), Great Cross, Cóndor de Los Andes (Bolivia). *Address:* c/o Ministry of Foreign Affairs, Juan E. O'Leary y Presidente Franco, Asunción, Paraguay.

CANGEMI, Joseph P., MS, EdD; American professor of psychology and consultant; b. 26 June 1936, Syracuse, NY; s. of Samuel Cangemi and Marion Cangemi; m. Amelia Elena Santalo' 1962; two d.; ed State Univ. of New York, Oswego, Syracuse and Indiana Univs; taught at Syracuse public schools and in Dominican Repub. 1960–64; Chair. and lecturer in psychology, State Univ. of NY 1962–65; Supervisor of Educ. and of Training and Devt, US Steel Corpn, Venezuela 1965–68; Teaching Assoc., Ind. Univ., Bloomington, Ind. 1972,

1973; Asst Prof. to Assoc. Prof., Western Ky Univ., Bowling Green, Kentucky 1968–79, Prof. of Psychology and Full mem. Graduate Faculty 1979–; consultant to Firestone, General Motors and numerous cos; Ed. Journal of Human Behavior and Learning 1983–90, Psychology—A Journal of Human Behavior 1977–, Organization Development Journal 1983–88; mem. Editorial Bd Educ. and several other publs; mem. American Psychological Asscn, Inter-American Soc. of Psychology, Int. Registry of Org. Devt Professionals, Psychologists in Man.; mem. Bd of Trustees, William Woods Univ. 1988–; numerous awards including Distinguished Alumnus Award, State Univ. of NY 1983, Distinguished Public Service Award, Western Ky Univ. 1983, Diplomate in Professional Counselling, Int. Acad. of Behavioural Medicine, Counselling and Psychotherapy 1994; Hon. LLD (William Woods Univ.) 1996; Dr hc (State Univ. of Humanities, Moscow) 2001, Diplomate American Coll. of Counsellors, American Coll. of Forensic Examiners 1996, Excellence in Productive Teaching Award, Coll. of Educ. and Behavioral Sciences, Western Ky Univ. 1977, 1991, 1999, Excellence in Research/Creativity Award, Western Ky Univ. Coll. of Ed. and Behavioral Sciences 1987. *Publications:* author, ed. or co-ed. of 16 books and monographs in Spanish, Portuguese, Russian and Chinese and over 300 papers and articles published in over 80 periodicals, including 31 foreign journals. *Leisure interests:* Latin American music, foreign travel, international exchanges. *Address:* Western Kentucky University, Department of Psychology, Bowling Green, KY 42101 (Office); 1409 Mt. Ayr Circle, Bowling Green, KY 42103-4708, USA. *Telephone:* (270) 745-2695 (Office); (270) 842-3436 (Home). *Fax:* (270) 842-0432 (Office). *E-mail:* joseph.cangemi@wku.edu.

CANI, Shkëlqim, DEcon; Albanian central banker, economist and politician; b. 6 May 1956, Tirana; m.; ed Univ. of Tirana; Credit Officer State Bank of Albania (SBA), Tirana br. 1979–81, Export-Import Officer, SBA Head Office 1981–83, Chief Economist, Research Div. 1984–85, Dir Overseas Dept, mem. Bd of Dirs. Cen. Bank 1985–90; Exec. Gen. Man. Commercial Bank of Albania (CBA) 1990–91, Deputy Gen. Man. 1991–92; ind. financial adviser 1996–97; Gov. Bank of Albania 1997–; Chair. Tirana Stock Exchange 1997–; Gov. IMF for Albania 1997–; mem. People's Ass. 1991–96, July–Aug. 1997, Deputy Prime Minister of Albania 1991; mem. Econ. Policies Comm. *Address:* Bank of Albania, Sheshi Skenderbeu 1, Tirana, Albania (Office). *Telephone:* 4228421 (Office). *Fax:* 4227821 (Office). *E-mail:* ehaxhi@bankofalbania.org (Office). *Website:* www.bankofalbania.org (Office).

CANIVET, Guy, JD; French judge; b. 23 Sept. 1943, Lons-le-Saunier, Jura; s. of Pierre Canivet and Henriette Barthélémy; m. Françoise Beuzit 1981; two s. two d.; ed Univ. of Dijon; judge, Trial Court of Chartres 1972–75; Public Prosecutor, Paris 1975–77; Sec.-Gen., Trial Court of Paris 1977–83, judge 1983–86; Justice, Court of Appeal, Paris 1986–94, Chief Justice 1996–99; Justice, Cour de Cassation 1994–96, Chief Justice 1999–; Hon. Bencher Gray's Inn, London; Officier Légion d'honneur, Officier Ordre nat. du Mérite, Officier des Palmes académiques. *Publication:* Droit français de la concurrence 1995. *Leisure interests:* music, outdoor recreational activities. *Address:* Cour de Cassation, Palais de Justice, 5 quai de l'Horloge, 75001 Paris (Office); 8 rue Nicolas Charlet, 75015 Paris, France (Home). *Telephone:* 1-44-32-73-70 (Office). *Fax:* 1-44-32-78-28 (Office). *E-mail:* pp.courdecassation@justice.fr (Office). *Website:* www.courdecassation.fr (Office).

CANNADINE, David Nicholas, DPhil, LittD, FRHistS, FBA, FRSA, FRSL; British professor of history; b. 7 Sept. 1950; s. of Sydney Douglas Cannadine and Dorothy Mary Hughes; m. Linda Jane Colley (q.v.) 1982; one d. (deceased); ed King Edward's Five Ways School, Birmingham, Cambridge, Oxford and Princeton Univs.; Resident Fellow, St John's Coll. Cambridge 1975–77, Asst Lecturer in History 1976–80, lecturer 1980–88; Fellow, Christ's Coll. Cambridge 1977–88, Dir of Studies in History 1977–83, Tutor 1979–81; Prof. of History, Columbia Univ. 1988–92, Moore Collegiate Prof. 1992–98; Dir Inst. of Historical Research 1998–; Prof. Univ. of London 1998–; Visiting Mem., Inst. for Advanced Study, Princeton Univ. 1980–81; Visiting Prof., Birkbeck Coll., London Univ. 1995–97; Visiting Fellow, Whitney Humanities Center, Yale Univ. 1995–96; Visiting Scholar, Pembroke Coll., Cambridge 1997; Pres. Worcs. Historical Soc. 1999–; Vice-Pres. British Records Soc. 1998–, Royal Historical Soc. 1998–; Chair. IHR Trust 1999; mem. Advisory Bd. Centre for Study of Soc. and Politics, Kingston Univ. 1998–, ICBH 1998–, Advisory Council Warburg Inst. 1998–, Inst. of US Studies 1999–, Public Record Office 1999–, Inst. of English Studies 2000–, Inst. of Latin American Studies 2000–, Kennedy Memorial Trust 2000–, Nat. Trust Eastern Regional Cttee 2000–; Gov. Ipswich School 1982–88; Fellow Berkeley Coll., Yale Univ. 1985, J. P. Morgan Library, New York 1992–98; American Council of Learned Societies Fellowship 1990–91; regular radio and TV broadcaster; Ed.-in-Chief, Journal of Maritime History 1999–; Gen. Ed. Studies in Modern History 1979–, Penguin History of Britain 1989–, Penguin History of Europe 1991–, Historical Research 1998–; Trustee Kennedy Memorial Scholarship Fund 1999–, Nat. Portrait Gallery 2000–; Hon. DLitt (East Anglia) 2001, (South Bank) 2001, (Birmingham) 2002; T. S. Ashton Prize (Econ. History Soc.) 1977, Silver Jubilee Prize (Agric. History Soc.) 1977, Lionel Trilling Prize 1991, Governors' Award 1991, Dean's Distinguished Award in the Humanities, Columbia Univ. 1996. *Publications:* Lords and Landlords: the aristocracy and the towns 1774–1967 1980, (ed. and contrib.) Patricians, Power and Politics in Nineteenth-Century Towns 1982, (jt and contrib.) H. J. Dyos, Exploring the Urban Past 1982, (jt and contrib.) Rituals of Royalty: power and ceremonial in traditional societies 1987, The Pleasures of the Past 1989, (ed. and contrib.) Winston Churchill's Famous Speeches 1989, (jt and contrib.) The First Modern Society: essays in English history in honour of Lawrence Stone 1989, The Decline and Fall of the British Aristocracy (Lionel Trilling Prize) 1990, G. M. Trevelyan: A Life in History 1992, Aspects of Aristocracy: Grandeur and Decline in Modern Britain 1994, (jt and contrib.) History and Biography: essays in honour of Derek Beales 1996, Class in Britain 1998, History in Our Time 1998, Making History Now 1999, Ornamentalism: How the British Saw Their Empire 2001, What is History Now? (ed.) 2001, In Churchill's Shadow: Confronting the Past in Modern Britain 2002, numerous contribs to other books and learned journals. *Leisure interests:* life, laughter. *Address:* Institute of Historical Research, Senate House, Malet Street, London, WC1E 7HU, England. *Telephone:* (20) 7862-8740.

CANNELL, Melvin Gilbert Richard, PhD, DSc, FRSE; British research scientist; b. 12 Aug. 1944, Bungay; s. of Charles Cannell and Joyce Cannell; m. Maria Rietdijk 1966; two d.; ed Bungay Grammar School and Univ. of Reading; research officer, coffee research station, Kenya 1966–71; Nat. Environment Research Council (NERC), Inst. of Tree Biology 1971–74; NERC Inst. of Terrestrial Ecology 1974–87; Dir (Edin.) NERC Centre for Ecology and Hydrology 1987–. *Publications:* Jt Tree Physiology and Yield Improvement 1976, Trees as Crop Plants 1985; over 100 other scientific Publs. *Address:* Centre for Ecology and Hydrology (Edinburgh), Bush Estate, Penicuik, Midlothian, EH26 0QB (Office); Easter Greyfield, Eddleston Road, Peebles, Tweeddale, EH45 9JB, Scotland (Home). *Telephone:* (131) 445 4343 (Office); (1721) 720144 (Home). *Fax:* (131) 445 3943 (Office). *E-mail:* mgrc@ceh.ac.uk (Office).

CANNY, Nicholas Patrick, PhD, FRHistS, MRIA; Irish professor of history; b. 4 Jan. 1944; s. of Cecil Canny and Helen Joyce; m. Morwena Denis 1974; one s. one d.; ed St Flannan's Coll., Ennis, Univ. Coll., Galway, Univ. of Pennsylvania, London, Harvard and Yale Univs.; Lecturer in History, Univ. Coll., Galway 1972–79, Prof. of History 1980–; mem. Inst. for Advanced Study, Princeton 1979–80; Fellow Nat. Humanities Center, NC 1985–86; mem. Irish Manuscripts Comm. 1980–, Nat. Archives Advisory Council 1986–96; Chair. Irish Comm. Historical Sciences 1991–97; Distinguished Visiting Prof., New York Univ. 1995; mem. Academia Europaea 1995–; Acad. Dir Centre for the Study of Human Settlement and Historical Change 2000; Fellow-in-Residence, Netherlands Inst. for Advanced Study 2000–01; Irish Historical Research Prize 1976. *Publications include:* The Elizabethan Conquest of Ireland 1976, The Upstart Earl: the social and mental world of Richard Boyle 1982, From Reformation to Restoration: Ireland 1534–1660 1987, Colonial Identity in the Atlantic World 1500–1800 1987, Kingdom and Colony: Ireland in the Atlantic World 1560–1800 1988, Europeans on the Move: Studies on European Migration 1500–1800 1994, The Oxford History of the British Empire (Vol. I): The Origins of Empire 1998; Making Ireland British 1580–1650 2000. *Leisure interests:* reading, walking, music. *Address:* Department of History, National University of Ireland, Galway (Office); Furramelia West, Barna, Co. Galway, Ireland (Home). *Telephone:* (91) 512264 (Office); (91) 592351 (Home). *Fax:* (91) 750556 (Office). *E-mail:* nicholas.canny@nuigalway.ie (Office).

CANOGAR, Rafael, BA; Spanish painter; b. 17 May 1935, Toledo; s. of Genaro Rafael Canogar and Alfonsa Canogar; m. 1st Ann Jane McKenzie 1960; m. 2nd Purificación Chaves 1992; six c.; studied under Daniel Vázquez Díaz 1949–54; founder mem. El Paso group 1957–60; Visiting Prof. Milles Coll., Oakland, Calif. 1965–66; artist-in-residence D.A.A.D., Berlin 1972, 1974; mem. Exec. Cttee Círculo de Bellas Artes, Madrid 1983–86, Advisory Bd Dept of Fine Arts, Ministry of Culture 1981–82, 1983–84, Bd of Trustees, Museo Nac. de Arte Contemporáneo, Madrid 1983, Admin. Bd Nat. Art Collections 1984–90, Exec. Cttee Fundación de Gremios, Madrid 1984–87; more than 120 one-man shows and numerous group exhbns; works in many public art collections world-wide; mem. Real Acad. de Bellas Artes de San Fernando 1998; Golden Palette Award, Int. Painting Festival, Cagnes-sur-Mer 1969, Grand Prize, São Paulo Biennale 1971, Special Award, Int. Painting Triennale, Sofia 1982, Premio Nacional de Artes Plásticas, Madrid 1982, Chevalier, Ordre des Arts et des Lettres 1985, Special Commendation, Orden de Isabel la Católica 1991; Dr hc (Universidad nacional de educación a distancia (UNED), Madrid) 2001; nominated "Hijo predilecto" of City of Toledo 2001. *Retrospective exhibitions include:* Museo Nac. de Arte Contemporáneo, Madrid, Musée d'Art Moderne de la Ville de Paris, Sonia Heine Foundation, Oslo, Lund Konsthalle, Sweden, Biblioteca Nacional, Madrid, Paris Art Centre, Bochum Art Museum, Instituto di Storia dell'Arte, Parma, Museo de Bellas Artes, Bilbao; 50 Years of Painting, Museo Nac. Reina Sofía, Madrid 2001. *Address:* Calle de la Bolsa 14, 28012 Madrid (Office); Avenida Menéndez Pelayo 11-bis, 28009 Madrid, Spain (Home). *Telephone:* (91) 5328171. *Fax:* (91) 5217096. *E-mail:* rcanogar@ctv.es (Home).

CANTACUZÈNE, Jean Michel, DS; French director of research (retd); b. 15 Dec. 1933, Bucharest, Romania; s. of Dr. Alexandre Cantacuzène and Marianne (née Labeyrie) Cantacuzène; m. 1st Anne-Marie Szekely 1956 (divorced); one s. one d.; m. 2nd Danièle Ricard 1971; one s.; ed Ecole Supérieure Chem. Industry, Lyon, Ecole Normale Supérieure, Paris; Asst Prof., Ecole Normale Supérieure, Paris 1960–62, Deputy Dir, Lab. Chimie 1964–67; Scientific attaché, French Embassy, Moscow 1962–64, Counsellor for Science and Tech., Washington, DC 1977–80; Prof. Organic Chem., Univ. of Paris 1967–73, Titular Prof. 1972–; Dir Chem. Scientific Dept, CNRS Paris 1973–77, Sr Counsellor for Industrial Affairs 1988; Scientific Dir Total Co. Française des Pétroles, Paris 1980–90; Counsellor for Scientific Affairs, Ministry of Foreign Affairs, Paris 1971–77; Chair. Bd SOLEMS 1983–86,

AVRIST 1982; mem. Conseil pour l'innovation industrielle 1989–91, Applications cttee and cttee to evaluate relations, Acad. of Science (Cadas) 1989–2000, exec. cttee groupe Climents français 1990–92; mem. Advisory Comm. for Science and Tech. 1971–75, Chair. Industrial R and D Advisory Cttee, EEC, Brussels 1983–86; mem. council Nuclear Safety Cttee, 1981–90; Pres. Adit 1992–95; mem. Académie des Technologies (Paris) 2001–; Le Bel Award of the Chem. Soc. of France 1968; Officier Ordre Nat. Légion d'honneur, Officier Ordre nat. du Mérite, Grand Cross of the Romanian Merit Nat. Order 2000. *Publications:* Chimie Organique 3 Vols (co-author) 1971–75, America, Science and Technology in the 80s, 2 Vols 1981, Mille Ans dans les Balkans, Chronique des Cantacuzène dans la Tourmente des Siècles 1992; over 100 papers in scientific journals. *Leisure interests:* book collecting, history. *Address:* Académie des Technologies, 16 rue Mazarine, 75006 Paris, France (Office); 52 bis route de Damiette, 91190 Gif-sur-Yvette, France (Home). *E-mail:* canta@magic.fr (Office); jcantacuzene@9online.fr (Home).

CANTALUPO, Jim; American business executive; b. 1943; m.; two c.; with Arthur Young & Co 1966–74; joined McDonalds Corpn 1974, Controller 1974–75, Vice-Pres. 1975–81, Sr Vice-Pres. 1981, Dist Man. Chicago Region, Zone Man. responsible for North-East USA 1985–87, Pres. McDonalds Int. 1987–1991, Pres. and CEO 1991, Vice-Chair. McDonalds Corpn, Pres. and Vice-Chair. –2002, retd 2002, reapptd Chair. and CEO Jan. 2003–; mem. Bd Dirs Sears, Robuck & Co, Rohm & Haas Co, Ill. Tool Works Inc., World Business Chicago, Chicago Council of Foreign Relations; mem. Bd Trustees Ronald McDonald House Charities; fmr Pres. Int. Fed. of Multiple Sclerosis Socs; fmr. Chair. Nat. Multiple Sclerosis Soc. (Chicago Chapter); fmr Dir Northern Trust Bank/DuPage; fmr mem. Bd Dirs Int. Flavors and Fragrances Inc.; Hon. mem. Bd Trustees Nat. Multiple Sclerosis Soc. (Chicago Chapter). *Address:* McDonalds Corporation Head Office, Kroc Drive, Oak Brook, IL 60523, USA (Office). *Website:* www.mcdonalds.com (Office).

CANTARELLA, Paolo; Italian business executive; b. 4 Dec. 1944, Varallo Sesia/Vercelli; m. Clara Cantarella; ed Turin Polytechnic; began working in car components 1977; Commercial Dir Ages (Fiat Group) 1978; Intersectoral Coordinator and Asst to Man. Dir, Fiat Group 1980; Man. Dir Comau (machine tools) 1985; Man. of Supplies and Distribution, Fiat Auto SpA 1989; Vice-Chair., Maserati SpA (luxury sports cars), Modena 1989, Chair. 1993–96; Man. Dir and Gen. Man. Fiat Auto SpA 1990–96, Chair. 1996–2002; Pres. CEO Fiat SpA 1996–2002; Pres. European Automobile Mfrs Asscn (ACEA) 2000–02; Co-Chair. EU–Russia Industrialists' Round Table (IRT) 2001; Chair IVECO NV, Business Solutions (Fiat Group) 2001–02; mem. Bd, CNH Global and HDP; Knight, Order of Labour Merit 1997. *Address:* c/o Fiat SpA, 250 via Nizza, 10126 Turin, Italy.

CANTENOT, Jean; French business executive and engineer; b. 19 Sept. 1919, Paris; s. of Joseph Cantenot and Marcelle (née Tournay) Cantenot; m. Nicole Berrier 1948; two d. (one deceased); ed Ecole Polytechnique and Ecole des Mines de Paris; Dept of iron-smelting, Ministry of Industry 1948–50; Chief Engineer, ARBED factory, Burbach-Saar 1950–57; Chief Engineer Schneider SA 1957, Asst Dir 1963–68; Man. Dir, then Chair. Droitaumont-Bruville Mining Co. 1957–69; Chair. and Man. Dir Aciéries de Pompey 1968–82; Pres. Asscn pour la gestion du régime d'assurance des créances des salariés (AGS) 1974–; Chair. and Man. Dir SACILOR (Steel Co.) 1980–83; Pres. Union des industries métallurgiques et minières 1973–85, Hon. Pres. 1985, Lormines 1979–85; Pres. Centre d'Entraide des Ingénieurs (Cedi) 1988, Hon. Pres. 1994; Officier, Légion d'honneur, Officier Ordre nat. du Mérite; Croix de guerre. *Address:* 1 rue Perronet, 92200 Neuilly-sur-Seine, France (Home); AGS, 3 rue Paul Cézanne, 75008 Paris (Office).

CANTERBURY, Archbishop of (see Williams, Most Rev. and Rt Hon. Rowan Douglas).

CANTONA, Eric; French football player and actor; b. 24 May 1966, Paris; s. of Albert Cantona and Léonor Raurich; m. Isabelle Ferrer 1987; one c.; player, Auxerre 1980–88, Bordeaux, Marseille 1988–89, Montpellier 1989–90, Nîmes 1992; player, Leeds United (League Champions 1992) 1992–93, Manchester United (League Champions 1993, 1994, 1995–96) 1993–97, Capt. 1996–97 (scoring 80 goals in 182 appearances); announced retirement May 1997; Player of the Year (Professional Footballers' Asscn) 1994, Footballer of the Year (Football Writers' Asscn) 1996. *Films include:* Le Bonheur est dans le Pré 1995, Elizabeth 1998, Les Enfants du marais 1999. *Leisure interest:* painting. *Address:* c/o Mikado, 105 avenue Raymond Poincaré, 75016 Paris, France (Office).

CANTONI, Giulio Leonardo, MD; American laboratory chief; b. 29 Sept. 1915, Milan, Italy; s. of Umberto L. Cantoni and Nella Pesaro Cantoni; m. Gabriella S. Cantoni 1965; two d.; ed Univ. of Milan, Italy; Instructor, New York Univ. 1943–45; Asst Prof., Long Island Coll. of Medicine, New York 1945–48; Sr Fellow, American Cancer Soc., New York 1948–50; Assoc. Prof., Western Reserve Univ., Cleveland, Ohio 1950–54; Chief, Lab. of Gen. and Comparative Biochemistry, Nat. Inst. of Mental Health 1956–96, Prof. Emer. 1996–; mem. NAS; Distinguished Service Award, Dept of Health and Human Services. *Publications:* Onium compounds, in Handbook of Comparative Biochemistry (Eds. Florkin and Mason) 1960; papers in scientific journals. *Leisure interest:* chamber music. *Address:* National Institute of Mental Health, Building 36, Room 3D-06, 9000 Rockville Pike, Bethesda, MD 20892, USA; 6938 Blaisdell Road, Bethesda, MD 20817 (Home). *Telephone:* (301) 496-3241.

CANTOR, Charles Robert, PhD, FAAS; American molecular biologist; b. 26 Aug. 1942, New York; s. of Ida Diane Banks and Louis Cantor; ed Columbia Coll. and Univ. of Calif., Berkeley; Asst Prof. of Chemistry, Columbia Univ. 1966, Assoc. Prof. 1969, Prof. 1972, Chair. and Prof. of Genetics and Devt 1981, Higgins Prof. 1988; Dir Human Genome Center, Lawrence Berkeley Lab. 1989–90, Prin. Scientist, Department of Environment Human Genome Project 1990–92; Prof. of Molecular and Cell Biology, Univ. of Calif., Berkeley 1989–92; Prof. of Biomedical Eng Boston Univ. 1991–92, Chair. 1995–98, Dir Center for Advanced Biotech. 1995–; Prof. of Pharmacology 1995–; Chief Scientific Officer Sequenon Inc. 1998–, mem. Bd of Dirs 2000–; Pres. in the Americas Human Genome Org. 1991–98; Consultant Samsung Advanced Inst. Tech. 2000–, numerous professional appointments; mem. NAS, American Acad. of Arts and Sciences; mem. Bd of Dirs and Scientific Advisory Cttee Odyssey Inc. 2002–; Analytica Prize 1988, Emily Gray Prize 2000. *Publications:* Biophysical Chemistry (3 vols, with Paul Schimmel), Genomics: The Science and Technology behind the Human Genome Project. *Leisure interests:* gastronomy, running, skiing. *Address:* Sequenom Inc., 3595 John Hopkins Court, San Diego, CA 92121 (Office); 526 Stratford Court, Apt E, Del Mar, CA 92014-2767, USA (Home). *Telephone:* (858) 202-9012 (Office). *Fax:* (858) 858-9020 (Office). *E-mail:* ccantor@sequenom.com (Office). *Website:* www.sequenom.com (Office).

CANTWELL, Maria, BA; American politician; b. 1958, Indianapolis; d. of Paul Cantwell and Rose Cantwell; ed Univs of Miami and Ohio; f. coalition to build a library in Mountlake Terrace; joined start-up software co. 1995; elected mem. Congress from Seattle 1992; Senator from Washington 2000–. *Address:* Office of the Senator from Washington, US Senate, Senate Buildings, Washington, DC 20510, USA (Office).

CAO BOCHUN; Chinese politician; b. Nov. 1941, Zhuzhou City, Hunan Prov.; ed Zhuzhou Aeronautical Industrial Training School; joined CCP 1966; Vice-Sec. CCP Zhuzhou City Cttee 1983, Sec. 1984; Sec. CCP Xiangtan City Cttee 1990; Vice-Gov. Hunan Prov. 1991; Vice-Sec. CCP Liaoning Prov. Cttee, Sec. Dalian City Cttee 1992; alt. mem. 14th CCP Cen. Cttee 1992; Sec. CCP Guangxi Zhuang Autonomous Regional Cttee 1997–; mem. 15th CCP Cen. Cttee 1997–. *Address:* Chinese Communist Party Guangxi Zhuang Autonomous Regional Committee, Naning City, Guangxi Zhuang Autonomous Region, People's Republic of China.

CAO GANGCHUAN, Gen.; Chinese army officer; b. Dec. 1935, Wuyang Co., Henan Prov.; ed Third Artillery Tech. School, Zhengzhou City, PLA Russian Tech. School, Dalian, Artillery Mil. Eng Acad. Moscow and PLA Univ. of Nat. Defence; joined PLA 1954; mem. CCP 1956–; Deputy Commdr artillery troops during Sino-Vietnamese border conflict 1979; Deputy Dir Equipment Dept Gen. Staff H.Q. 1985; Dir Mil. Affairs Dept Gen. Staff H.Q. and Dir Mil. Products Trade Office of Mil. Cttee of Cen. Cttee of CCP 1990; Deputy Dir Leading Group for Placement of Demobilized Army Officers; Deputy Sec. Comm. for Disciplinary Inspection; Deputy Chief of Gen. Staff, PLA 1992–96; Minister State Comm. of Science, Tech. and Industry for Nat. Defence 1996–98; mem. Cen. Mil. Comm. 1998–; Dir PLA Gen. Equipment Dept 1998–; rank of Gen. 1996; mem. 15th Cen. Cttee CCP 1997–98; Minister of Nat. Defence 2003–. *Address:* c/o Ministry of National Defence, 20 Jing-shanqian Jie, Beijing 100009, People's Republic of China. *Telephone:* (10) 66730000. *Fax:* (10) 65962146.

CAO QINGZE; Chinese government and party official; b. 1932, Lixian Co., Hunan Prov.; joined CCP 1952; Sec. Comm. for Discipline Inspection of CCP Sichuan Provincial Cttee 1986–93; Minister of Supervision 1993–98; Deputy Sec. CCP Cen. Comm. for Inspecting Discipline 1997–; Hon. Pres. Soc. of Supervision. *Address:* c/o Ministry of Supervision, 35 Huayuanbei Lu, Haidan Qu, Beijing 100083, People's Republic of China.

CAO SHUANGMING, Lt-Gen.; Chinese army officer and party official; b. 1929, Linxian Co., Henan Prov.; joined CCP 1946; Deputy Commdr PLA Shengyang Mil. Area Command 1987–92, Commdr 1992–; rank of Lt-Gen. 1988; mem. 14th CCP Cen. Cttee 1992–. *Address:* Shengyang Military Area Command, People's Liberation Army, Shengyang City, Liaoning Province, People's Republic of China.

CAO ZHI; Chinese politician; b. 1928, Shangzhi Co., Heilongjiang Prov.; joined CCP 1947; Deputy Sec.-Gen. 7th Standing Cttee NPC 1988–92; Sec.-Gen. 8th Standing Cttee NPC 1993–98; Vice-Chair. Standing Cttee 9th NPC 1998–; a Vice-Chair. Cen. Cttee for Comprehensive Man. of Social Security 1993–. *Address:* Standing Committee, National People's Congress, Tian'anmen Square, Beijing, People's Republic of China.

CAPA, Cornell; American photographer; b. (Friedman), 10 April 1918, Budapest, Hungary; ed Imre Madách Gymnasium, Budapest; moved to New York 1937; began work in darkroom of Life magazine 1938; first photo story published in Picture Post, UK 1939; worked in USAF Photo-Intelligence Unit and for USAF public relations 1941–46; staff photographer Life magazine 1946–54, resident photographer in England 1950–52; returned to USA 1952, covered maj. political events for Life until 1967; mem. Magnum Photos. Inc. 1954–; extensive travel in S. America 1961–64; organizer Exhbn The Concerned Photographer shown throughout USA and in Europe and Israel 1964; covered Six-Day War in Israel 1967; photographic work in El Salvador and Honduras 1970–73, Papua New Guinea 1973; founder, Int. Center of Photography, New York 1974, Dir 1974–. *Publications include:* Retarded Children Can Be Helped 1957, Margin of Life 1974; numerous photo-essays for Life 1946–72. *Address:* 275 5th Avenue, New York, NY 10016, USA.

CAPECCHI, Mario Renato, PhD; American (born Italian) geneticist and university professor; b. 6 Oct. 1937, Verona; m. 1963; ed Antioch Coll., Harvard Univ.; Jr Fellow in Biophysics, Harvard Univ. 1966–69, Asst Prof. to Assoc. Prof. of Biochem., Medical School 1969–73; Prof. of Biology, Univ. of Utah 1973–88, Prof. of Human Genetics, School of Medicine 1989–, Distinguished Prof. 1993–, Investigator Howard Hughes Inst., Univ. of Utah 1988–; mem. Bd Scientific Counsellors, Nat. Cancer Inst.; mem. NAS, American Biochem. Soc., American Soc. of Microbiology, New York Acad. of Science, Int. Genome Soc., Genetics Soc. of America; Biochem. Award, American Chem. Soc. 1969, Gairdner Foundation Int. 1993, Gen. Motors Corpn Alfred P. Sloan Jr Prize 1994, Kyoto Prize in Basic Sciences 1996, Franklin Medal 1997, Lasker Award 2001. *Address:* Howard Hughes Medical Institute, University of Utah, 15 N 2030 E, Rm 5100, Salt Lake City, UT 84112-5331, USA (Office).

CAPELING-ALAKIJA, Sharon, BEd; Canadian international organization official; b. 6 May 1944, Moose Jaw, Sask.; m. 1985 (deceased); three s.; ed Univ. of Sask.; teacher, Sask. 1966–67; Volunteer Dept Head and teacher in Tanzania and Barbados, Canadian Univ. Service Overseas 1967–72, Co-ordinator Local Cttee, London, Ont. 1972–74, Co-ordinator Orientation Dept, Ottawa 1974–77, Dir Public Affairs and Programme Funding 1977–82, Dir Human Resources Div. 1978–79, Dir West Africa Region, Lomé, Togo 1982–89; Dir UN Devt Fund for Women, New York 1989–94; Dir Office of Evaluation and Strategic Planning, UNDP, New York 1994–97; Exec. Co-ordinator UN Volunteers 1998–; Patron Global Co-operation Council, Nord-Süd Forum e.V. Feb. 1998; Hon. PhD (Univ. of Sask.) 1998. *Address:* United Nations Volunteers, Martin-Luther-King-Str. 8, PO Box 260111, 53153 Bonn, Germany (Office). *E-mail:* hq@unvolunteers.org (Office).

CAPELLAS, Michael; American business executive; m. Marie Capellas; two c.; systems analyst and mfr. with Republic Steel Corpn 1976–81; joined Schlumberger Ltd 1981, holding successive posts as First Corp. Dir for Information Systems, Controller and Treas. of Asia Pacific Operations, Chief Financial Officer Dowell Schlumberger, Operations Man. Schlumberger's Fairchild Semiconductor unit 1981–96; Founder and Man. Partner Bench-marking Partners, Cambridge, MA 1996; Dir of Supply-Chain Man., SAP America 1996–97; Sr Vice-Pres. and Gen. Man. Global Energy Business, Oracle Corpn 1997–98; Chief Information Officer Compaq 1998, Pres. and CEO Compaq/HP (following acquisition of Compaq by Hewlett-Packard) 2001–02; CEO WorldCom 2002–. *Leisure interests:* community leadership and charity work, golf. *Address:* WorldCom, 500 Clinton Center Drive, Clinton, MS 39056, USA (Office). *Website:* www.worldcom.com (Office).

CAPELLINO, Ally, BA; British fashion designer; b. 1956; ed Middlesex Univ.; worked in Courtaulds Cen. Design Studio 1978–79; est. Ally Capellino Little Hat, initially selling hats and accessories 1979; developed clothing line with accessories for Moscow Olympics collection 1979–80; began selling Ally Capellino label to int. markets 1980; launched menswear collection 1986; first London fashion show 1986; opened shop in Soho, London 1988; launched Hearts of Oak sportswear collection 1990, Mini Capellino children's wear 1991; signed promotional and licensing agreement with Coats Viyella PLC 1992; launched 'ao' collection 1996; opened Ally Capellino shop, London 1997; opened flagship store Tokyo, Japan 1998. *Address:* N1R, Metropolitan Wharf, Wapping Wall, London, E1 9SS, England. *Telephone:* (20) 7488-9777. *Fax:* (20) 7488-9852.

CAPELLO, Fabio; Italian professional football manager; b. 18 June 1946, Pieris; fmr football player with Spal, A.S. Roma, Juventus, AC Milan and the Italian national team 1962–79; Man. AC Milan (Serie A) 1991–96, 1997–2000, winner four championships and European Cup 1994; Man. Real Madrid 1996–97, winner La Liga; currently Man. A.S. Roma, winner Serie A 2000–01. *Address:* c/o A.S. Roma SPA, Via di Trigoria Km 3600, 00128 Rome, Italy (Office). *Website:* www.asromacalcio.it (Office).

CAPITANICH, Jorge Milton; Argentine politician and accountant; b. 28 Nov. 1964, Roque Saenz Peña; Head, Under-Secr. of Social Planning, Ministry of Social Devt 1998; Senator for Chaco Dec. 2001–; Acting Minister of Trade 2001; Cabinet Chief of Argentina Jan. 2002–. *Publications:* Investigación Sobre El Orígen de las Crisis Provinciales, Federalismo Fiscal y Copartici-pación, La Sumergida. Chaco, Propuestas para la Integración. *Address:* General Secretariat to the Presidency, Balcarce 50, 1064 Buenos Aires, Argentina. *Telephone:* (11) 446-9841 (Office).

CAPLIN, Mortimer Maxwell, BS, LLB, JSD; American government official, lawyer and educator; b. 11 July 1916, New York; s. of Daniel Caplin and Lillian Epstein; m. Ruth Sacks 1942; three s. one d.; ed Univ. of Virginia and New York Univ. Law School; law Clerk to US Circuit Judge 1940–41; legal practice with Paul, Weiss, Rifkind, Wharton & Garrison, New York 1941–50; USNR, Beachmaster in Normandy landings 1942–45; Prof. of Law, Univ. of Virginia 1950–61, lecturer and Visiting Prof. 1965–87, Prof. Emer. 1988–; Counsel to Perkins, Battle & Minor 1952–61; US Commr of Internal Revenue 1961–64; Sr Partner, Caplin & Drysdale, Washington, DC 1964–; Chair. Nat. Civil Service League 1965–80, American Council on Int. Sports 1975–80, Nat. Citizens' Advisory Cttee 1975–80, Asscn of American Medical Colls., Univ. of

Virginia Council of the Arts; Dir Fairchild Corpn, Presidential Reality Corpn, Danaher Corpn; mem. Public Review Bd, Arthur Andersen & Co. 1980–88; mem. House of Dels 1980–92, DC and Fed. Bar Asscns., Va and NY State Bars, American Law Inst.; Ed.-in-Chief Virginia Law Review 1939–40; mem. Bd of Trustees, George Washington Univ. 1964, Bd of Visitors, Univ. of Va Law School Foundation 1982–; Emer. Trustee Shakespeare Theatre, Wolf Trap Foundation and Arena Stage; Hon. LLD (St Michael Coll.) 1964; Order of the Coif, Raven Award, Alexander Hamilton Award, Univ. of Virgina/Thomas Jefferson Memorial Foundation Medal in Law 2001 and other awards. *Publications:* Doing Business in Other States, Proxies, Annual Meetings and Corporate Democracy; numerous articles on tax and corporate matters. *Leisure interests:* swimming, horseback riding, gardening. *Address:* One Thomas Circle, NW, Washington, DC 20005-5802 (Office); Apartment 18E, 5610 Wisconsin Avenue, Chevy Chase, MD 20815-4415, USA (Home). *Telephone:* (202) 862-5050 (Office). *E-mail:* mmc@capdale.com.

CAPPE, Mel, MA, LLD; Canadian diplomatist and economist; b. 3 Dec. 1948, Toronto; m. Marline Cappe (née Marni); two c.; ed Univs of Toronto and Western Ontario; joined Canadian public service as a policy analyst 1975; with Treasury Bd 1975–78, Deputy Sec. 1990–94; with Dept of Finance 1978–82; Deputy Dir Investigation and Research, Dept of Consumer and Corp. Affairs 1982–90; Deputy Asst Sec. Dept of Finance 1990, Deputy Sec. Program Br. 1990; fmr Asst Deputy Minister Competition Policy; fmr Asst Deputy Minister Policy Co-ordination; fmr Asst Deputy Minister Corp. Affairs and Legis. Policy; Deputy Minister of the Environment 1994–96; Deputy Minister of Human Resources Devt 1996–99; Chair. Employment Insurance Comm. 1996–99; Deputy Minister of Labour 1996–99; Clerk of the Privy Council, Sec. to Cabinet and Head of the Public Service 1999–2002; Special Adviser to Prime Minister 2002–; High Commr to UK 2002–; Nat. Vice-Chair. Govt for Gov.-Gen.'s Canadian Study Conf. 2000; Hon. PhD Univ. of Western Ontario. *Address:* Canadian High Commission, Macdonald House, 1 Gros-venor Square, London, W1K 4AB, England (Office). *Telephone:* (20) 7258-6301 (Office). *Fax:* (20) 7258-6303 (Office). *E-mail:* mel.cappe@dfait-maeci.gc.ca (Office). *Website:* www.dfait-maeci.gc.ca/london (Office).

CAPPELLO, Carmelo; Italian sculptor; b. 21 May 1912; m. Selene Varale Cappello; one s. one d.; ed Istituto Superiore d'Arte di Monza; sculptor 1937–; regular exhibitor at Venice Biennali, Milan Triennali and Rome Quadriennali since 1947; represented in maj. collections and int. exhbns. throughout the world; mem. Nat. Cttee of UNESCO Div. of Plastic Arts; mem. Accad. Nazionale di San Luca; numerous awards. *Major works:* Freddoloso 1938, Uomo nello spazio 1955, Tempestà 1956, Cristo e i due ladroni 1955, Volo Stratosferico 1958, Il Folle 1948, Il Filosofo 1949, Tuffatori 1958, Gli Acrobati 1955, Eclisse 1959, Fughe ritmiche 1961, Involuzione del cerchio 1962, Fontana per curve d'acqua 1958, Ala 1960, Ritmi Chiusi 1963, Superficie-Spazio: Itinerario Circolare 1964, Traiettoria Dal Piano Dello Spazio 1965, Occhio di Cielo 1966, Cerchi in Movimento, Milan. *Address:* Bastioni Porta Nuova 11, 20121 Milan, Italy. *Telephone:* 6552431.

CAPPUCCILLI, Piero; Italian baritone opera singer; b. 9 Nov. 1929, Trieste; m. Graziella Bossi; ed architectural studies in Rome; studied singing with Maestro Luciano Donaggio at Teatro Giuseppe Verdi, Trieste; debut as Tonio (I Pagliacci), Teatro Nuovo, Milan 1957; debut at La Scala Milan in Lucia di Lammermoor 1964; Covent Garden debut in La Traviata 1967; U.S. debut in I Due Foscari at Lyric Opera of Chicago 1969; appears at all leading Italian opera houses and maj. opera houses throughout the world. *Recordings include:* Lucia di Lammermoor (with Callas), La Gioconda, Aida, La Forza del Destino, Un Ballo in Maschera, Macbeth, Rigoletto, Don Carlos, Nabucco. *Address:* c/o SA Gorlinsky Ltd., 33 Dover Street, London, W1X 4NJ, England.

CAPRA, Carlo; Italian professor of history; b. 14 Nov. 1938, Quartu S. Elena, Cagliari; s. of Agostino Capra and Maria Maxia; m. Maria Grazia Bosi 1964; one s.; ed Univ. of Milan; teacher of English in state secondary schools until 1970; Asst lecturer in History, Milan State Univ. 1970–72, Reader 1972–81, Assoc. Prof. 1981–86, Prof. 1986–, Head, Dept of History 1989–92; mem. Scientific Council, Società Italiana di Studi sul XVIII Secolo. *Publications:* Giovanni Ristori da illuminista a funzionario (1755–1830) 1968, Il giorna-lismo nell'età rivoluzionaria e napoleonica 1976, La Lombardia austriaca nell'età delle riforme 1984, 1987; Ed.: Cesare Beccaria, Carlegio Vols IV–V of Edizione Nazionale delle Opere 1995. *Leisure interests:* music, cinema. *Address:* Istituto di Storia medievale e moderna, Via Chiaravalle 7, Milan 20122 (Office); Corso Garibaldi 71, Milan 20121, Italy (Home). *Telephone:* (02) 58308008 (Office); (02) 86461509 (Home).

CAPRIATI, Jennifer Maria; American tennis player; b. 29 March 1976, New York; d. of Stefano Capriati and Denise Capriati; ed Pasco High School, Fla; coached by her father; winner, French Open Jr 1989, US Open Jr 1989, Wimbledon and US Open Jr Doubles 1989; youngest player in Whiteman Cup 1989; competitor on pro tour 1990–Nov. 1993, 1994, 1996–; gold medal (Olympic Games of 1992); Wimbledon debut 1990; semi-finalist French Open 1990, US Open 1991, 2001, Wimbledon 1991 (youngest Grand Slam Finalist in tennis history), Boca Raton 1991, German Open 1991; won Australian Open 2001, 2002, French Open 2001, Int. Tennis Fed. World Champion 2001; finished 2002 season as world number 3. *Leisure interests:* dancing, golf, music, reading, writing. *Address:* International Management Group, c/o Barbara Perry, 22 E 71 Street, New York, NY 10021, USA.

CAPRIO, HE Cardinal Giuseppe, JCD, STL; Italian ecclesiastic; b. 15 Nov. 1914, Lapio, Avellino; ed Diocesan and Regional Seminaries, Benevento,

Pontifical Gregorian Univ., Rome, Pontifical Ecclesiastical Acad., Rome; ordained Roman Catholic Priest 1938; Attaché, Secretariat of State, Vatican City 1943–47; Sec., Apostolic Nunciature, Nanking, China 1947–51; Auditor, Apostolic Nunciature, Brussels, Belgium 1952–56; Apostolic Visitor to Repub. of Viet Nam and later Regent of Apostolic Del. in Saigon 1956–59; Apostolic Nuncio to China, serving in Taiwan 1959–67; Titular Archbishop of Apollonia 1961; Apostolic Pro-Nuncio to India 1967–69; Sec. of Admin. of Patrimony of the Holy See 1969–77; Substitute of the Secretariat of State 1977–79; Pres. of Admin. of the Patrimony of the Holy See 1979–81; mem. Sacred Congregation for the Evangelization of Peoples, Pontifical Comm. for the Revision of Canon Law; created HE Cardinal 1979. *Address:* Piazza del S. Uffizio 11, 00193 Rome, Italy. *Telephone:* (06) 69883572 (Office).

CAPRON, Alexander Morgan, LLB; American professor of law; b. 16 Aug. 1944, Hartford, Conn.; s. of William M. and Margaret (Morgan) Capron; m. 1st Barbara A. Brown 1969 (divorced 1985); m. 2nd Kathleen M. West 1989; four c.; ed Palo Alto High School, Swarthmore Coll. and Yale Law School; law clerk, US Court of Appeals, DC Circuit 1969–70; Lecturer and Research Assoc. Yale Law School 1970–72; Asst Prof. to Prof. of Law and Prof. of Human Genetics, Univ. of Pa 1972–82; Exec. Dir President's Comm. for Study of Ethical Problems in Medicine and Biomedical and Behavioural Research 1979–83; Prof. of Law, Ethics and Public Policy, Georgetown Univ. 1983–84; Topping Prof. of Law, Medicine and Public Policy, Univ. of Southern Calif. 1985–89, Univ. Prof. of Law and Medicine 1989–, Co-Dir Pacific Center for Health Policy and Ethics 1990–; Henry W. Bruce Prof. of Law 1991–; Pres. American Soc. of Law and Medicine 1988–89; Chair. Bio-medical Ethics Advisory Cttee, US Congress 1988–91; mem. Nat. Bioethics Advisory Comm. 1996–2001; several honours and awards. *Publications:* books including Catastrophic Diseases: Who Decides What? (with J. Katz) 1975, Law, Science and Medicine (with others) 1984, Treatise on Health Care Law (with others) 1991 and 200 articles in journals and books. *Leisure interests:* gardening, films, travel. *Address:* The Law School, University of Southern California, University Park, MC 0071, Los Angeles, CA 90089-0071, USA. *Telephone:* (213) 740-2557. *Fax:* (213) 740-5502. *E-mail:* acapron@law.usc.edu (Office).

CAPUTO, Dante; Argentine politician, diplomatist and professor; b. 25 Nov. 1943, Buenos Aires; m. Anne Morel; three s.; ed Salvador Univ. of Buenos Aires, Univ. of Paris, Tufts Univ. and Harvard, Boston; Adjunct Prof. of Political Sociology, Salvador Univ., Buenos Aires; Adjunct Prof. of Public Services and State Enterprises, Univ. of Buenos Aires; Dir Center for Social Investigations on State and Admin. 1976; Adjunct investigator Nat. Center for Scientific Investigation, France; Minister of Foreign Affairs and of Worship 1983–88; Pres. UN Gen. Ass. 1988–89; fmr Sec. of State for Tech., Science and Useful Innovations; fmr Special Rep. of UN Sec.-Gen. in Haiti. *Address:* c/o Ministerio de Relaciones Exteriores y Culto, Reconquista 1088 C.P. 1003, Buenos Aires, Argentina.

CARAM, A. R.; Aruban (b. Suriname) central banker; majority of banking career in the Netherlands, fmrly with Nederlandsche Bank; joined Cen. Bank of Aruba 1992, later Exec. Dir, Gov. 2002–. *Address:* Centrale Bank van Aruba, Havenstraat #2, Oranjestad, Aruba (Office). *Telephone:* 822509 (Office). *E-mail:* cbaua@setarnet.aw (Office). *Website:* www.cbaruba.org (Office).

CARAMITRU, Ion; Romanian actor, theatre director and politician; b. 9 March 1942, Bucharest; s. of Aristide Caramitru and Maria Caramitru; m. Michaela Caracas 1975; three s.; ed Theatre and Cinema Art Inst., Bucharest; mem. Exec. Bureau, Council of Nat. Salvation Front Dec. 1989–, Pres. of Cultural Cttee 1990; Vice-Pres. of Prov. Council for Nat. Unity (responsibility for cultural and youth problems) 1990–; Pres. ITI Romanian Centre, Romanian Theatre Union (UNITER) 1990–, Artistic Dir Bulandra Bucharest 1990–92; Minister of Culture 1996–2000; numerous awards. *Principal roles include:* Romeo, Hamlet, Julius Caesar, Feste, Brutus, Leonce (Büchner), Eugene Marchbanks (Bernard Shaw), Cotrone (Pirandello), Perdican (Musset), Riccardo Fontana (Rolf Hochhuth) etc. *Directed:* Remembrances (Aleksei Arbuzov), Insignificance (Terry Johnson), Dialogues (author's performance), The Third Stake (Marin Sorescu), The Shape of the Table (David Edgar), Home (David Storey); musical theatre: Eminescu (Paul Urmuzescu), My Fair Lady; opera: The Little Sweep (Benjamin Britten), Carmen (Bizet) for Belfast Opera 1993, Eugene Onegin (Tchaikovsky) for Belfast Opera 1994, Bastien and Bastienne (Mozart) for Țăndărică puppet theatre, Bucharest. *Films include:* The Treasure from Old River Bed, The City Blue Gates, Luchian, Oak – Extreme Urgency, The Purse with Dragonflies, High-School Pupils, Civic Education Test-Write, Darkness, Citizen X, Mission Impossible. *Television appearances:* Jude City (BBC serial) 1992, An Exchange of Fire 1993, A Question of Guilt 1993, Two Deaths (BBC TV) 1994. *Leisure interests:* collecting icons, tennis, writing, painted popular eggs. *Address:* UNITER, 2–4, George Enescu Str., Bucharest (Office); 16, Caderea Bastiliei, Sector i, Bucharest, Romania (Home). *Telephone:* (1) 311 32 14 (Office); (1) 210 63 37 (Home). *Fax:* (1) 312 09 13 (Office); (1) 210 57 83 (Home).

CARAZO ODIO, Rodrigo; Costa Rican politician; b. 27 Dec. 1926, Cartago; s. of Mario Carazo Paredes and Julieta Odio Cooper; active mem. of Partido de Liberación Nacional (PLN) until resignation 1969, occupying posts as Dir Nat. Inst. of Housing and Urbanization 1954–59, Adviser on Housing and Finance, Banco Obrero de Venezuela 1959–63, Dir Banco Central de Costa Rica 1963–65; Deputy to Legislative Ass. of Costa Rica 1966, then Pres., Dir Recope (state enterprise controlling distribution of petroleum products);

founded Renovación Democrática, taking fourth place in presidential elections 1974; Leader of coalition party Unidad (Renovación Democrática, Republicano Calderonista, Unión Popular, Demócrata Cristiano) 1976–82; Pres. of Costa Rica 1978–82; Prof. of Econs, Admin., Econ. Devt and History, visiting lecturer to USA and S. America; agricultural, commercial and industrial activities. *Address:* University for Peace, Apdo 199, San José, Costa Rica.

CARCIERI, Donald L.; American state official; b. E Greenwich; s. of Nicola Carcieri and Marguerite Carcieri; m. Suzanne Owren; four c.; ed E Greenwich High School, Brown Univ.; fmr math. teacher; with Old Stone Bank –1981, rising to Exec. Vice-Pres.; headed Catholic Relief Service's W. I. operation, Kingston, Jamaica 1981–83; joined Cookson America 1983, CEO Cookson America, Jt Man. Dir Cookson Group Worldwide; Gov. of R. I. 2003–; co-f. Acad. Children's Science Center; Dir Providence Center; mem. Catholic Relief Services Leadership Council. *Address:* Office of the Governor, 222 State House, Providence, RI 02903, USA (Office).

CARD, Andrew, BS; American public servant and business executive; b. 1949, Brockton, Mass.; m.; three c.; ed Univ. of South Carolina; mem. Mass. House of Reps. 1975–83; mem. staff White House, Dir of Intergovernmental Affairs 1983–87, New Hampshire Campaign Man. 1987–88, Deputy Chief of Staff 1989–92, Chief of Staff 2001–; Sec. of Transportation 1992–93; Pres. and CEO American Automobile Mfrs Asscn 1993–98; Vice-Pres. Governmental Relations, Gen. Motors. *Address:* The White House Office, 1600 Pennsylvania Avenue, NW, Washington DC 20500, USA (Office).

CARDEN, Joan Maralyn, AO, OBE; Australian opera singer; b. b. 9 Oct. 1937, Melbourne; d. of late Frank Carden and of Margaret Carden (née Cooke); m. William Coyne 1962 (divorced 1980); two d.; ed schools in Melbourne, language studies in London, Trinity Coll. of Music, London and London Opera Centre; voice studies with Thea Phillips and Henry Portnoj, Melbourne and Vida Harford, London; first opera engagement, world premiere of Williamson's Our Man in Havana, Sadler's Wells; joined The Australian Opera 1971; Covent Garden debut as Gilda (Rigoletto) 1974; Glyndebourne debut as Anna (Don Giovanni) 1977; U.S. debut at Houston as Amenaide (Tancredi) 1977; Metropolitan Opera Tour as Anna (Don Giovanni) 1978; perf. regularly in concert repertoire of Sydney Symphony Orchestra and Australian Broadcasting Corpn; Dame Joan Hammond Award for Outstanding Service to Opera in Australia 1987, Australia Creative Fellowship 1993. *Leisure interests:* gardening, theatre, reading. *Address:* c/o The Australian Opera, P.O. Box 291, Strawberry Hill, NSW 2012, Australia; c/o Avere Artists Management, 26 Oxley Drive, Bowral, N.S.W. 2576 (Office).

CARDENAS CONDE, Victor Hugo, BA; Bolivian politician and academic; b. 4 June 1951, Achica Abajo Aymara Indian community, Omasuyos Prov., Dept of La Paz; m. Lidia Katari 1980; one s. two d.; ed Ayacucho High School, Universidad Mayor de San Andrés (UMSA); univ. lecturer, then Prof. in Educ. Sciences, Linguistics and Languages, Faculty of Humanities and Educ., UMSA State Univ. 1975–92; Chair. First Nat. Congress for Peasant Unity 1979; consultant on educational issues UNESCO and UNICEF 1990, various other orgs. 1992; Prof. Latin American Coll. of Social Sciences 1992–93; Nat. Rep. Tupac Katari Revolutionary Liberation Movt party (MRTKL), Exec. Sec. (Nat. Exec. Cttee) 1993, currently Leader; Pres. Nat. Congress 1993–94, Andean Parl. 1993–94, Science and Tech. Nat. Council 1993–94; Vice-Pres. of Bolivia 1993–97; mem. Culture and Educ. Comm., Bolivian Workers Union 1979, Educ. and Culture Comm., House of Reps. 1985–86, political forum of Latin American Inst. for Social Research 1992–93, Exec. Council UNESCO 1995–2000; Fray Bartolomé de las Casas Award (Spain) 1994. *Publications:* articles on culture, educ. and history in local and foreign books, journals and newspapers. *Address:* Avda Baptista 939, Casilla 9133, La Paz, Bolivia.

CÁRDENAS SOLÓRZANO, Cuauhtémoc; Mexican politician; b. 1 May 1934, Mexico City; s. of Lázaro Cárdenas and Amalia Solórzano; m. Celeste Batel; two s. one d.; ed Escuela Nacional de Ingenieros, Universidad Nacional Autónoma de México; Senator of Michoacán 1976–82; Under-Sec. for Forestry and Wildlife 1976–80; Gov. of Michoacán 1980–86; Cand. for Presidency (Frente Democrático Nacional) 1988, (Partido de la Revolución Democrática—PRD) 1994, (Allianza por México) 2000; Pres. PRD 1988–93; Pres. Fundación para la democracia—alternativa y debate 1995–; Mayor of Mexico City 1997–99; Grand officier, Ordre nat. du Mérite (France) 1999; Cardenal Cisneros Medal, Universidad Complutense, Madrid (Spain) 1991. *Publications include:* Nuestra lucha a penas comienza 1988, Nace—una esperanza 1990, El proyecto nacional de la Revolució mexicana, un camino a retomar 1990, La esperanza en marcha. Ideario político 1998, Palambras de Cárdenas 1999. *Leisure interests:* reading, travel. *Address:* Fundación para la democracia, Guadalajara No. 88, 06700 México, DF (Office); Edgar Allan Poe No. 28–1102, 11560 México, DF, Mexico (Home). *Telephone:* (55) 5286-1114 (Office). *Fax:* (55) 5286-1114 (Office). *E-mail:* c_cardenas@mexico.com (Office).

CARDIFF, Jack, OBE; British film director and cameraman; b. 18 Sept. 1914; s. of John Joseph Cardiff and Florence Cardiff; m. Julia Lily Mickleboro 1940; three s.; ed various schools, including Medburn School, Herts.; began career as child actor 1918; switched to cameras 1928; Asst to many Hollywood cameramen 1936; world travelogues 1937–39; photographer for Ministry of Information Film Unit on War Dept films, including Western Approaches 1942; films as cameraman include: Caesar and Cleopatra 1945, A Matter of Life and Death 1946, Black Narcissus 1946 (Golden Globe Award 1947), The

Red Shoes 1948, Scott of the Antarctic, Under Capricorn, Black Rose, Pandora and the Flying Dutchman 1951, Magic Box, African Queen, War and Peace 1956, The Vikings 1958; began to direct films 1958; Hon. mem. BAFTA 1995; Hon. Dr of Art (Rome) 1953, (RCA) 2000, Hon. DLitt (Bradford) 1996, Hon. PhD (APU) 2001; Hon. mem. Asscn Française de Cameramen 1971; Film Achievement Award, Look Magazine, BSC Award for War and Peace, New York Critics Award for best film direction, Golden Globe Award for outstanding Dir for Sons and Lovers, Acad. Award for Black Narcissus; Hollywood Int. Life Achievement Award 1995, British Acad. of Cinematographers Contrib. to Art of Photography Award 1996, Special Acad. Award 2001. *Films include:* directed Intent to Kill 1958, Beyond This Place 1959, Scent of Mystery 1960, Sons and Lovers 1960, My Geisha 1962, The Lion 1963, The Long Ships 1964, Young Cassidy 1965, The Liquidator 1967, The Mercenaries 1968, Girl on a Motor Cycle (also producer) 1969, The Mutation, Penny Gold 1974, Ride a Wild Pony 1976; Dir of photography: The Prince and the Pauper, Beyond the Iron Mask, Death on the Nile, Avalanche Express, The Awakening, The Dogs of War, Ghost Story, Last Days of Pompeii, The Wicked Lady, Conan the Destroyer, Catseyes, First Blood II, Blue Velvet, Tai-Pan, Million Dollar Mystery, Journey into Space, Magic Balloon 1990, Vivaldi's Four Seasons 1991, Dance of Shiva 1998. *TV includes:* The Far Pavilions, Coup de Soir (France) 1951. *Publication:* Autobiography 1975, Magic Hour (autobiog.) 1996. *Leisure interests:* cricket, tennis, painting. *Address:* 32 Woodland Rise, London, N10, England.

CARDIN, Pierre; French couturier; b. 2 July 1922, San Biagio di Callatla, Italy; fmrly worked with Christian Dior; founded own fashion house 1949; founded Espace Pierre Cardin (theatre group); Dir Ambassadeurs-Pierre Cardin Theatre (now Espace Pierre Cardin Theatre) 1970–; Man. Société Pierre Cardin 1973; Chair. Maxims 1982–; Hon. UNESCO Amb. 1991; Exhbn at Victoria and Albert Museum 1990; mem. Acad. des Beaux-Arts; Fashion Oscar 1985; Officier, Légion d'honneur 1997; Grand Officer, Order of Merit (Italy) 1988, Order of the Sacred Treasure (Gold and Silver Star) 1991. *Publications:* Fernand Léger, Sa vie, Son oeuvre, Son rêve 1971, Le Conte du Ver à Soie 1992 (Prix Saint-Exupéry valeurs-jeunesse 1992). *Address:* 27 avenue Marigny, 75008 Paris, France (Office); Institut de France, 23 quai Conti, 75006 Paris; Pierre Cardin, 7 rue Royale, 75008 Paris (Office).

CARDINAL, Douglas Joseph, OC, BArch, FRAIC, RCA; Canadian architect; b. 7 March 1934, Calgary, Alberta; s. of Joseph Treffle Cardinal and Frances Margarete Rach; m. 1st Marilyn Zahar 1973; three s. three d.; m. 2nd Idoia Arana-Beobide 1996; ed Univ. of Texas; design architect, Bissell & Halman, Red Deer 1963–64; Prin. Douglas Cardinal Architect, Red Deer 1964–67, Edmonton 1967–76, Douglas J. Cardinal Architect Ltd, Edmonton 1976–, Douglas Cardinal Architect, Washington, DC 1995–. *Major works include:* St Mary's Church, Red Deer, Alberta, Grande Prairie Regional Coll., Grande Prairie, Alberta, Ponoka Provincial Bldg, Ponoka, Alberta, St Albert Place, St Albert, Alberta, Canadian Museum of Civilization, Hull, Québec, Nat. Museum of the American Indian, Washington, DC; awards include Honour Award, Alberta Asscn of Architects, for St Mary's Church 1969 and Award of Excellence, Canadian Architect Magazine, for Grande Prairie Regional Coll. 1972. *Publications:* contribs. to Of the Spirit 1977 and Human Values: A Primary Motive in Planning 1981. *Address:* Suite 4200, 490 E L'Enfant Plaza, SW, Washington DC 20024, USA.

CARDINALE, Claudia; Italian film actress; b. 15 April 1939, Tunis; d. of Franco and Yolanda Cardinale; m. Franco Cristaldi 1966; one s.; ed Lycée Carnot and Collège Paul Cambon, Tunis; made first film 1958; awards include Nastro d'Argento, David di Donatello, Grolla d'Oro; UNESCO Goodwill Amb. *Films include:* 8½, The Pink Panther, The Leopard, The Professionals, Once Upon a Time in the West, Fury, The Magnificent Showman, La Scoumoune, Fitzcarraldo 1982, Le Ruffian 1982, History (TV), A Man in Love 1988, The French Revolution 1989, Hiver '54, L'abbé Pierre, Mother, 588 Rue Paradis, Son of the Pink Panther 1993, Women Only Have One Thing On Their Minds, My Best Friend 1999. *Address:* c/o Carole Levi, Via Pisanelli 2, 00196 Rome, Italy.

CARDONA, Manuel, PhD; Spanish/American professor of physics; b. 7 Sept. 1934, Barcelona, Spain; s. of Juan Cardona and Angela Castro; m. Inge Hecht 1959; two s. one d.; ed Univs. of Barcelona and Madrid and Harvard Univ.; Research Asst Harvard Univ. 1956–59; mem. tech. staff, RCA Labs. Ltd, Zürich 1959–61; Princeton, NJ 1961–64; Assoc. Prof. of Physics, Brown Univ., Providence, RI 1964–66, Prof. 1966–71; Scientific mem. and Dir Max Planck Inst. for Solid State Research, Stuttgart 1971–, now Emer. Dir, Business Man. Dir 1973–74; mem. various advisory bds., professional bodies, etc.; mem. NAS (USA), Acad. Europaea; mem. Comité Nat. d'Evaluation de Recherche (France) 1999–2002; Fellow American Physical Soc.; A.D. Sloan Fellowship 1965–68; Guggenheim Fellowship 1969–70; lecturer Air NZ 2001; Dr. hc (Madrid) 1985, (Barcelona) 1985, Sherbrook Univ. (Canada) 1993, (Regensburg) 1994, (Rome) 1995, (Toulouse) 1998, (Thessaloniki) 2001, (Brno) 2002; Prince of Asturias Prize 1988, Italgas Prize 1993, J. Wheatley Prize, American Physical Soc. 1997; Grand Cross of Alfonso X el Sabio, E. Mach Medal (Czech Repub.) 1999, Mott Medal and Award (UK) 2001; numerous other awards and distinctions. *Publications:* Modulation Spectroscopy 1969, Light Scattering in Solids, Vols I–IV 1975–91, Photoemission in Solids, Vols I–II 1978–81, Fundamentals of Semiconductors 1996. *Address:* Max-Planck-Institut für Festkörperforschung, Heisenbergstrasse 1, 70569 Stuttgart, Germany. *Telephone:* (711) 6891710 (Office). *Fax:* (711) 6891712 (Office). *E-mail:* cardona@fkf.mpg.de (Office).

CARDOSO, Fernando Henrique, DSc; Brazilian sociologist and politician; b. 18 June 1931, Rio de Janeiro; m.; three c.; ed Univs. of São Paulo and Paris; Prof. Latin American Inst. for Econ. and Social Planning (ILPES/CEPAL), Santiago 1964–67; Prof. of Sociological Theory, Univ. of Paris-Nanterre 1967–68; Prof. of Political Science, Univ. of São Paulo 1968–69; Visiting Prof. Stanford Univ. 1972, Inst. for Econ. and Social Devt Univ. of Paris 1977, Univ. of Calif. 1981; Simon Bolivar Prof. Univ. of Cambridge 1976; Assoc. Dir of Studies, Inst. for Higher Studies in Social Sciences, Univ. of Paris 1980–81; many other professional appts.; Fed. Senator for State of São Paulo 1983–94; fmr Leader, Brazilian Social Democratic Party (PSDB) in Fed. Senate; Govt Leader in Congress 1985–86; Minister of Foreign Affairs 1992–93; Minister of Economy and Finance 1993–94; Pres. of Brazil 1995–2002; Prof. Coll. de France 1981; Foreign Hon. mem. American Acad. of Arts and Sciences; Dr. hc (Rutgers), (Notre Dame, Ill.) 1991, (Santiago) 1993, (Central of Caracas), (Porto and Coimbra), (Sofia, Japan), (Free Univ. of Berlin), (Lumière Lyon 2), (Bologna), (Cambridge, UK), (London, UK); Grand Cross, Order of Rio Branco, Chevalier, Légion d'honneur, Grand Cross, Order of Merit of Portugal. *Publications:* (jtly) São Paulo Growth and Poverty 1978, Dependency and Development in Latin America 1979, The New Global Economy in the Information Age 1993, Charting a New Course (co-ed.) 2001. *Address:* c/o Gabinete do Presidente, Palácio do Planalto, Praça dos Três Poderes, 70150-900 Brasília, Brazil (Office).

CARDOSO E CUNHA, António José; Portuguese politician and agriculturist; b. 28 Jan. 1933; m.; four c.; ed Inst. Superior Technico; worked in petrochem. industries, foreign trade and agric.; in Angola 1966–76; Sec. of State for Foreign Trade, Third Constitutional Govt; Minister for Industries, Fourth Constitutional Govt; mem. Ass. of the Repub., Social Democratic Party (PSD) 1979; Minister of Agric. and Fisheries 1980–81; EC Commr for Fisheries 1986–88, for Personnel and Admin., Energy, Tourism, Small and Medium-Sized Business 1989–92; Commr Gen. EXPO '98 1993–.

CAREY OF CLIFTON, Baron (Life Peer), cr. 2002, of Clifton in the City and County of Bristol; **Rt Rev and Rt Hon George Leonard Carey,** PC, BD, MTh, PhD; British clergyman; b. 13 Nov. 1935, London; s. of George Thomas Carey and Ruby Catherine Carey; m. Eileen Harmsworth Hood 1960; two s. two d.; ed Bifrons Secondary Modern School, Barking, Essex, King's Coll., London Univ.; Nat. Service, RAF 1954–56; univ. studies and theological training 1957–62; Curate St Mary's, Islington 1962–66; lecturer, Oak Hill Theological Coll. 1966–70, St John's Coll., Nottingham 1970–75; Vicar St Nicholas' Church, Durham 1975–82; Prin. Trinity Theological Coll., Bristol 1982–87; Bishop of Bath and Wells 1987–91; Archbishop of Canterbury 1991–2002; Patron or Pres. of 300 orgs; Fellow King's Coll., London; Hon. Bencher Inner Temple; Freeman Cities of London and of Wells 1990; Hon. DLitt (Polytechnic of E London) 1991, Hon. DD (Kent) 1991, (Nottingham) 1992; Hon. LLD (Bath) 1992; hon. degrees from American univs.; Greek, Hebrew and theological prizes. *Publications:* I Believe in Man 1978, The Great Acquittal 1981, The Church in the Market Place 1983, The Meeting of the Waters 1985, The Gate of Glory 1986, The Great God Robbery 1988, I Believe 1991, Spiritual Journey 1994, My Journey Your Journey 1996, Canterbury – Letters to the Future 1998, Jesus 2000 1999. *Leisure interests:* walking, football, poetry, music. *Address:* House of Lords, London, SW1A 0PW, England.

CAREY, John, MA, DPhil, FRSL, FBA; British literary critic and university professor; b. 5 April 1934; s. of Charles William and Winifred Ethel (née Cook) Carey; m. Gillian Mary Florence Booth 1960; two s.; ed Richmond and East Sheen County Grammar School, St John's Coll., Oxford; served East Surrey Regt 1953–54; Harmsworth Sr Scholar, Merton Coll., Oxford 1957–58; lecturer, Christ Church, Oxford 1958–59; Andrew Bradley Jr Research Fellow, Balliol Coll., Oxford 1959–60; Tutorial Fellow, Keble Coll., Oxford 1960–64, St John's Coll. 1964–75; Merton Prof. of English Literature, Oxford Univ. 1976–2001; T. S. Eliot Memorial Lecturer, Univ. of Kent 1989; Chair. Booker Prize Judges 1982, 2003, Judge, W.H. Smith Prize 1989–; Hon. Fellow St John's Coll. Oxford 1991, Balliol Coll. Oxford 1992. *Publications:* The Poems of John Milton (Ed. with Alastair Fowler) 1968, Milton 1969, The Violent Effigy: a Study of Dickens' Imagination 1973, Thackeray: Prodigal Genius 1977, John Donne: Life, Mind and Art 1981, The Private Memoirs and Confessions of a Justified Sinner, by James Hogg (Ed.), William Golding: The Man and His Books (Ed.) 1986, Original Copy: Selected Reviews and Journalism 1987, The Faber Book of Reportage (Ed.) 1987, John Donne (Oxford Authors) (Ed.) 1990, The Intellectuals and the Masses 1992, The Faber Book of Science (Ed.) 1995, The Faber Book of Utopias (Ed.) 1999, Pure Pleasure 2000; articles in Review of English Studies, Modern Language Review, etc. *Address:* Brasenose Cottage, Lyneham, Oxon., OX7 6QL; 57 Stapleton Road, Headington, Oxford, England. *Telephone:* (1865) 764304.

CAREY, Mariah; American singer and songwriter; b. 1969, Long Island, NY; signed contract with Columbia Records 1989; f. Crave record label 1997; over 80 million albums sold worldwide; f. Camp Mariah holiday project for inner-city children; awards include two Grammy awards (Best New Artist, Best New Pop Vocal, Female) 1990, three Soul Train Music Awards (Best New Artist, Best Album, Female, Best Single, Female) 1990, four American Music Awards 1992–96, eight World Music Awards 1991–95, seven Billboard Awards 1991–96. *Albums include:* Mariah Carey 1990, Emotions 1992, MTV Unplugged 1992, Music Box 1993, Merry Christmas 1994, Daydream 1995, Butterfly 1997, Rainbow 1999, Glitter 2001, Greatest Hits 2001, Charm-bracelet 2002. *Film:* Glitter (also soundtrack) 2001. *Address:* c/o LD Publicity Ltd, Fenton House, 55–57 Great Marlborough Street, London, W1V 1DD, England.

CAREY, Peter, FRSL; Australian author; b. 7 May 1943, Bacchus March, Vic.; m. 2nd Alison Summers 1985; two s.; ed Geelong Grammar School and Monash Univ.; fmr partner, McSpedden Carey Advertising Consultants, Sydney; now teacher Columbia Univ. and Princeton Univ.; Hon. LittD (Queensland). *Screenplays* (jtly): Bliss, Until the End of the World, Oscar and Lucinda 1998. *Publications:* The Fat Man in History (short stories) 1974 (in UK as Exotic Pleasures 1981), War Crimes (short stories) 1979 (NSW Premier's Award), Bliss (novel) 1981 (Miles Franklin Award, Nat. Book Council Award, NSW Premier's Award), Illywhacker (novel) 1985 (Age Book of the Year Award, Nat. Book Council Award, Victorian Premier's Award), Oscar and Lucinda 1988 (Booker Prize for Fiction 1988, Miles Franklin Award, Nat. Book Council Award, Adelaide Festival Award, Foundation for Australian Literary Studies Award), The Tax Inspector (novel) 1991, The Unusual Life of Tristan Smith (novel) 1994 (Age Book of the Year Award), Collected Stories 1995, The Big Bazoohley (children's novel) 1995, Jack Maggs 1997, The True History of the Kelly Gang (Booker Prize 2001) 2000, 30 Days in Sydney: A Wildly Distorted Account 2001. *Address:* c/o Amanda Urban, ICM, 40 West 57th Street, New York, NY 10019, USA.

CARIDIS, Miltiades; Greek/Austrian conductor; b. 9 May 1923, Danzig; s. of Xenophon Caridis and Barbara Fuchs-Caridis; m. Sonja Caridis 1945; one d.; ed Kreuzschule, Dresden, Dörpfeldt Gymnasium, Athens and Musikhochschule, Vienna; Opernhaus, Graz 1948–59; Opernhaus, Cologne 1959–62; Philharmonia Hungarica 1960–67; Staatsoper, Vienna 1962–69; Radio Symphony Orchestra, Copenhagen 1962–70; Oslo Philharmonic Soc. 1969–75; Duisburger Sinfoniker, Duisburg 1975–81; Tonkünstler-Orchester, Vienna 1979–85; Artistic and Music Dir Athens Radio Symphony Orchestra 1995–. *Address:* Himmelhofgasse 10, A-1130 Vienna, Austria. *Telephone:* 8779233. *Fax:* 8779233.

CARL XVI GUSTAF, King Carl Gustaf Folke Hubertus; b. 30 April 1946; s. of Prince Gustaf Adolf and Sibylla, Princess of Saxe-Coburg-Gotha; m. Silvia Sommerlath 1976; one s., Prince Carl Philip Edmund Bertil, b. 13 May 1979; two d., Crown Princess Victoria Ingrid Alice Désirée, b. 14 July 1977 and Princess Madeleine Thérèse Amelie Josephine, b. 10 June 1982; ed in Sigtuna and Univs of Uppsala and Stockholm; created Duke of Jämtland; became Crown Prince 1950; succeeded to the throne on death of his grandfather, King Gustaf VI Adolf 15 Sept. 1973; Chair. Swedish Branch, World Wide Fund for Nature; Hon. Pres. World Scout Foundation; Dr hc (Swedish Univ. of Agricultural Sciences, Stockholm Inst. of Tech., Åbo Acad., Finland); US Environmental Protection Agency Award. *Leisure interests:* hunting, sailing and water sports, motor sport, cross-country and down-hill skiing, art, music and food. *Address:* The Royal Palace, 111 30 Stockholm, Sweden. *Telephone:* (8) 402-60-00. *Fax:* (8) 402-60-05. *Website:* www.royalcourt.se (Office).

CARLIN, John William; American fmr state governor; b. 3 Aug. 1940, Smolan, Kan.; s. of Jack W and Hazel L. (Johnson) Carlin; m. Ramona Hawkinson 1962 (divorced 1980); one s. one d.; ed Lindsborg High School, Kansas Univ.; farmer, dairyman, Smolan, Kan. 1962–; mem. Kan. House of Reps. for 93rd Dist 1970–73, 73rd Dist 1973–79, Minority Leader of House 1975–77, Speaker 1977-79; Gov. of Kansas 1979–87; Visiting Prof. of Public Admin. and Int. Trade Wichita State Univ. 1987–88; Visiting Fellow Kansas Univ. 1987–88; Archivist of the United States Nat. Archives and Records Admin. 1995–; Pres. Econ. Devt Asscn 1987–92, Vice-Chair. Midwest Superconductivity Inc. 1990–94; fmr Chair. Nat. Govs Asscn; mem. Nat. Govs Asscn (NGA) Exec. Cttee; fmr Chair. Midwestern Govs Conf.; Democrat; Hon. DIur (Kansas). *Leisure interests:* golf, swimming. *Address:* National Archives and Records Administration, 7th and Pennsylvania Avenue, Washington, DC 20408-0001 (Office); 8601 Adelphi Road, Room 4200, College Park, MD 20740-6002, USA. *E-mail:* john.carlin@nara.gov (Office).

CARLING, William David Charles, OBE; British rugby football player and sports commentator; b. 12 Dec. 1965, Bradford-on-Avon, Wilts.; m. 1st Julia Carling 1994 (divorced 1996); m. 2nd Lisa Cooke 1999; one s. one step-s. one step-d.; ed Durham Univ.; owner Inspirational Horizons Co., Insights Ltd; centre; fmr mem. Durham Univ. Club; mem. Harlequins club; int. debut England versus France 1988; Capt. England team 1988–96; announced retirement from int. rugby 1997 (brief return to the game with Harlequins 1999); played 72 times for England, Capt. 59 times (world record); rugby football commentator 1997–. *Publications:* Captain's Diary 1991, Will Carling (autobiog.) 1994, The Way to Win (with Robert Heller) 1995, My Autobiography 1998. *Leisure interests:* painting and sketching. *Address:* c/o Mike Burton Management, Bastian House, Brunswick House, Brunswick Road, Gloucester, GL1 1JJ, England (Office). *Telephone:* (1542) 419666 (Office). *Fax:* (1306) 713605 (Office). *E-mail:* will@willcarling.com (Office).

CARLISLE, Sir James (Beethoven), Kt, GCMG, BDS; Antiguan Governor-General; b. 5 Aug. 1937; s. of the late James Carlisle and of Jestina Jones; m. 1st Umilta Mercer 1963 (divorced 1973); one s. one d.; m. 2nd Anne Jenkins 1973 (divorced 1984); one d.; m. 3rd Nalda Amelia Meade 1984; one s. one d.; ed Univ. of Dundee; dentist 1972–92; Gov.-Gen. Antigua and Barbuda 1993–; Chair. Nat. Parks Authority 1986–90; Chief Scout Antigua and Barbuda 1986–90; mem. British Dental Asscn, American Acad. of Laser Dentistry, Int. Asscn of Laser Dentistry; Hon. Fellow Dental Surgery Royal Coll. of Surgeons

of Edin.; Hon. LLD (Andrews Univ., USA) 1995; Kt Grand Cross, Order of Queen of Sheba (Ethiopia) 1995. *Address:* Governor-General's Office, St John's, Antigua, West Indies (Office). *Telephone:* (809) 462-0003 (Office).

CARLOS MOCO, Marcolino José, PhD; Angolan politician; Prime Minister of Angola 1992–96; mem. Movimento Popular de Libertação de Angola – Partido do Trabalho (MPLA – PT). *Address:* c/o Movimento Popular de Libertação de Angola, Luanda, Angola.

CARLOT KORMAN, Maxime; Ni-Vanuatu politician; fmr Minister of Foreign Affairs, of Public Service, Planning and Statistics, of Media and Language Services; Prime Minister of Vanuatu 1991–95, Feb.–Sept. 1996; fmr Leader, Union of Moderate Parties; currently Leader Vanuatu Republikan Pati (VRP). *Address:* Vanuatu Republikan Pati (VRP), P.O. Box 698, Port Vilan, Vanuatu.

CARLSON, Arne Helge, BA; American politician; b. 24 Sept. 1934, New York; s. of Helge William and Kerstin (Magnusson) Carlson; m. Susan Shepard 1985; one d. and one s. one d. by previous m.; ed Williams Coll., Univ. of Minnesota; with Control Data, Bloomington, Minn. 1962–64; Councilman Minneapolis City Council 1965–67; in pvt. business, Minneapolis 1968–69; Legislator, Minn. House of Reps., St Paul 1970–78; State Auditor, State of Minn. 1978–90, Gov. 1991–98; Chair. Bd IDS Mutual Fund Group, Minneapolis 1999, American Express Funds 1999–; mem. Bd of Dirs. Minn. Land Exchange Bd, Exec. Council St Paul; Trustee Minn. State Bd Investment; Sec. Minn. Housing Finance Agency 1979–91; Republican; several awards including Small Business Guardian Award, Nat. Fed. of Ind. Businesses 1994. *Leisure interests:* reading, squash, Univ. of Minn. basketball and football games. *Address:* American Express Funds, 901 Marquette Avenue, Suite 2810, Minneapolis, MN 55402 (Office); 22005 Iden Avenue N, Forest Lake, MN 55025, USA (Home).

CARLSSON, Arvid, MD, PhD; Swedish pharmacologist; b. 25 Jan. 1923, Uppsala; physician, Univ. of Lund 1951, Asst Prof. 1951–56, Assoc. Prof. 1956–59; Prof. of Pharmacology, Univ. of Göteborg 1959–89, Prof. Emer. 1989–; mem. Scientific Advisory Bd, ACADIA Pharmaceuticals 1999–; mem. Swedish Acad. of Sciences; Foreign mem. N.A.S.; numerous awards and prizes include: Magnus Blix Prize, Univ. of Lund 1947, Wolf Prize in Medicine, Jerusalem (Jt recipient) 1979, Paul Hoch Prize, American Psychopathological Asscn 1990, Japan Prize in Psychology and Psychiatry 1994, Gold Medal and Hon. Diploma, Swedish Parkinson Asscn 1996, Gold Medal, Soc. of Biological Psychiatry, Toronto 1998, Antonio Feltrinelli Int. Award, Accad. Dei Lincei, Rome 1999, Nobel Prize for Medicine (Jt recipient) 2000. *Publications:* several hundred specialist articles in journals. *Address:* Department of Pharmacology, University of Göteborg, Medicinaregatan 7, Box 431, SE-405 30 Göteborg, Sweden (Office). *Telephone:* (31) 773-34-35 (Office). *Fax:* (31) 82-17-95 (Office). *E-mail:* arvid.carlsson@pharm.gu.se (Office).

CARLSSON, Ingvar Gösta, MA; Swedish politician; b. 9 Nov. 1934, Borås; m. Ingrid Melander 1957; two d.; ed Lund Univ. and Northwestern Univ. USA; Sec. in Statsradsberedningen (Prime Minister's Office) 1958–60; Pres. Social Democratic Youth League 1961–67; Mem. Parl. 1964–; Under Sec. of State, Statsradsberedningen 1967–69; Minister of Educ. 1969–73, of Housing and Physical Planning 1973–76, Deputy Prime Minister 1982–86, Minister of the Environment 1985–86, Prime Minister 1986–91, 1994–96; Co-Chair. Comm. on Global Governance 1995–; mem. Exec. Cttee Social Democratic Party, Chair. 1972–96. *Address:* c/o Parliament Buildings, 10012 Stockholm, Sweden.

CARLUCCI, Frank Charles; American fmr politician and business executive; b. 18 Oct. 1930, Scranton, Pa; s. of Frank and Roxann Carlucci; m. 1st Jean Anthony 1954 (divorced 1974); one s. one d.; m. 2nd Marcia Myers Carlucci 1976; one d.; ed Princeton Univ. and Harvard Graduate School of Business Admin.; with Jantzen Co., Portland, Ore. 1955–56; Foreign Service Officer, Dept of State 1956; Vice-Consul, Econ. Officer, Johannesburg 1957–59; Second Sec. Political Officer, Kinshasa 1960–62; Officer in charge of Congolese Political Affairs, Zanzibar 1962–64, Consul-Gen. 1964–65; Counsellor for Political Affairs, Rio de Janeiro 1965–69; Asst Dir for Operations, Office of Econ. Opportunity 1969–70, Dir OEO 1970; Assoc. Dir Office of Management and Budget 1971–72; Deputy Dir 1972; Under-Sec. Dept of Health, Educ. and Welfare 1972–74; Amb. to Portugal 1974–77; Deputy Dir CIA 1977–81, Deputy Sec. of Defense 1981–82, Sec. 1987–89; Pres. COO Sears World Trade Inc. 1983–84, Chair. and CEO 1984–86; Nat. Security Adviser to Pres. of USA 1986–87; Vice-Chair. Carlyle Group, Washington 1989–93, Chair. 1993–; Hon. DHumLitt; Superior Service Award and Superior Honour Award, Dept of State, Presidential Citizens Award, Distinguished Intelligence Medal and other awards. *Leisure interests:* tennis, swimming. *Address:* Carlyle Group, 1001 Pennsylvania Avenue, NW, Washington, DC 20004, USA.

CARLYLE, Joan Hildred; British soprano opera singer and teacher; b. 6 April 1931; d. of late Edgar J. Carlyle and Margaret M. Carlyle; m.; two d.; ed Howell's School, Denbigh, N Wales; prin. Lyric Soprano, Covent Garden 1955; teaches privately (and also in London 2003), gives masterclasses, promotes young singers and judges prestigious competitions. *Major roles sung in UK include:* Oscar, Un Ballo in Maschera 1957–58, Sophie, Der Rosenkavalier 1958–59, Nedda, Pagliacci (Zeffirelli production) 1959, Mimi, La Bohème 1960, Titania, Midsummer Night's Dream, Britten (Gielgud production) 1960, Pamina, Magic Flute 1962, 1966, Countess, Marriage of Figaro

1963, Zdenka, Arabella (Hartman Production) 1964, Suor Angelica 1965, Desdemona, Othello 1965, Arabella 1967, Marschallin, Der Rosenkavalier 1968, Jenifer, Midsummer Marriage 1969, Donna Anna, Don Giovanni 1970, Reiza, Oberon 1970, Adrianna Lecouvreur 1970, Russalka, Elisabetta, Don Carlos 1975. *Major roles sung abroad include:* Oscar, Nedda, Mimi, Pamina, Zdenka, Micaela, Donna Anna, Arabella, Elisabetta and Desdemona; has sung at La Scala Milan, Staatsoper Vienna, Munich, Berlin, Teatro Colón Buenos Aires, San Carlo Naples, Monet Monte Carlo, Nico Milan, Cape Town, Brussels, Geneva, Zurich, Amsterdam, Boston, New York; several recordings including Von Karajan's production of Pagliacci as Nedda, Midsummer Marriage as Jenifer, Medea, Pagliacci from Buenos Aires, Mavra, Purcell Anthology. *Recordings include:* Voice from the Old House (1/11) 2002, (12/29), (30/42) 2003, Complete versions of Otello, Arabella, Suor Angelica, Highlights from La Bohème 2003. *Leisure interests:* gardening, travel, preservation of the countryside, interior design, cooking. *Address:* Laundry Cottage, Hanmer, SY13 3DQ, Wales. *Telephone:* (1948) 830265. *E-mail:* joan@joancarlyle.co.uk (Home). *Website:* www.joancarlyle.co.uk (Home).

CARLYLE, Robert, OBE; British actor; b. 14 April 1961, Glasgow; s. of Joseph Carlyle and Elizabeth Carlyle; m. Anastasia Shirley 1997; ed N Kelvinside Secondary School, Royal Scottish Acad. of Music and Drama; f. Rain Dog Theatre Co. 1990, productions include: Wasted, One Flew Over the Cuckoo's Nest (Paper Boat Award), Conquest of the South Pole, Macbeth (Paper Boat Award 1992); Scottish BAFTA Award 1995, Royal TV Award 1996, Salerno Film Festival Award 1997, Evening Standard Outstanding British Actor Award 1998, Film Critics' Circle Award for Best Actor 1998, Variety Club Actor of the Year 1998, Bowmore Whisky/Scottish Screen Award for Best Actor 2001, Michael Elliot Award for Best Actor 2001, David Puttnam Patrons Award. *Stage appearances include:* Twelfth Night, Dead Dad Dog, Nae Problem, City, No Mean City, Cuttin' a Rug, Othello. *Television includes:* The Part of Valour 1981, Hamish Macbeth 1995, Cracker 1993, 1997, 1999, Safe 1993, The Advocates, Arena, Byrne on Byrne, Taggart, The Bill, Looking After Jo Jo 1998. *Films include:* Marooned, Riff Raff 1990, Silent Scream 1990, Safe 1993, Being Human 1993, Priest 1994, Go Now 1995, Trainspotting 1996, Carla's Song 1996, Face 1997, The Full Monty (BAFTA Award for Best Actor 1998) 1997, Ravenous 1999, Apprentices, Plunkett and Macleane 1999, The World is Not Enough 1999, Angela's Ashes 2000, The Beach 2000, There's Only One Jimmy Grimble 2000, To End All Wars 2000, 51st State 2001, Once Upon a Time in the Midlands 2002. *Address:* c/o ICM, Oxford House, 76 Oxford Street, London, W1D 1BS, England (Office).

CARMACK, John; American computer software executive; worked for Softdisk Publishing; co-f. id Software 1991; created computer games Wolfenstein 3-D, Doom and Quake notable for enhanced graphic detail and three-dimensional illusion, also Quake II and Quake III; numerous awards from gaming Publs. *Address:* id Software, Town East Tower, Suite 615, 18601 LBJ Freeway, Mesquite, TX 75150, U.S.A. (Office).

CARMONA ESTANGA, Pedro; Venezuelan politician, economist and oil executive; b. 6 June 1941, Barquisimeto; ed Universidad Católica Andrés Bello, Université Libre de Bruxelles, Belgium; with Aditivos Orinoco 1889–93, Química Venoco 1989–2000, Industrias Venoco 1990–2000, Promotora Venoco 2001; First Vice-Pres. Fedecamaras 1999–2001, Pres. 2001–02; Pres. Andean Enterprise Consultative Council 2000–01; also worked for Venezuelan Confed. of Industry—Conindustria, Venezuelan Asscn of the Chemical and Petrochemical Industries, Venezuelan Asscn of Exporters—AVEX, Chamber of Commerce, Venezuelan–Columbian Integration—CAVECOL; fmr mem. Directive Council Inst. de Estudios Superiores de la Administración de Empresas—IESA; fmr mem. Junta del Acuerdo de Cartagena, fmr Pres. Venezuelan Del. to Comisión del Acuerdo de Cartagena; fmr mem. Corporación Andina de Fomento—CAF; fmr Dir Inst. de Comercio Exterior—ICE, Sistema Económico Latinoamericano—SELA; fmr adviser to Directorate of Econ. Policy, Ministry of Foreign Affairs; installed by mil. officers as interim Pres. of Venezuela 12 April 2002 following violent anti-govt protests against Pres. Chavez; placed under house arrest 14 April 2002, accused of rebellion and usurping the presidency, later granted asylum by Colombian govt; Order of the Sun (Peru), Nat. Order of Merit (Colombia), Bernardo O'Higgins Order (Chile).

CARNEGIE, Sir Roderick Howard, Kt, BSc, MA, MBA, FTS; Australian mining executive; b. 27 Nov. 1932, Melbourne; s. of D. H. Carnegie and Margaret F. Carnegie; m. Carmen Clarke 1959; three s.; ed Trinity Coll. Melbourne Univ., New Coll., Oxford, Harvard Business School; Assoc. McKinsey and Co., Melbourne and New York 1959–64, Prin. Assoc. 1964–68, Dir 1968–70; Dir Conzinc Riotinto of Aust. Ltd (now CRA Ltd) 1970, Joint Man. Dir 1971–72, Man. Dir and Chief Exec. 1972–74, Chair. and Man. Dir 1974–83, Chair. and Chief Exec. 1983–86; Dir Comalco Ltd, CRA Ltd, Rio Tinto-Zinc Corpn Ltd; Chair. Consultative Cttee on Relations with Japan 1984–87; Pres. German-Australian Chamber of Industry and Commerce 1985; Pres. Business Council of Australia 1987–88; Chair. Hudson Conway Ltd 1987–2000; Vice-Pres. Australian Mining Industry Council; Chair. Salvation Army Council 1992–, G10 Australia Holdings Ltd 1992–94, Valiant Consolidated Ltd 1993–98, GPT Ltd 1994–, Newcrest Mining Ltd 1994–; Dir John Fairfax Holdings Pty Ltd 1991–, Lexmark Holdings Inc. (USA) 1994–, Adacel Techs Ltd 1998–; mem. Int. Council Morgan Guaranty Trust, The Asia Soc., The Brookings Inst.; mem. IBM World Trade Asia/Pacific Group Bd; Hon. DSc (Newcastle) 1985. *Address:* Adacel Technologies Ltd., 250 Bray Street, Brighton, Vic. 3186, Australia (Office).

CARNEY, Rt. Hon. Patricia, PC, MA; Canadian politician and economist; b. 26 May 1935, Shanghai, China; d. of James Carney and Dora Sanders; m. 2nd Paul S. White 1998; one s. one d. from previous marriage; ed Univ. of British Columbia; Adjunct Prof. Univ. of BC; fmrly econ. journalist; f. Gemini North Ltd (consulting firm for socio-econ. impact studies) 1970; first elected MP 1980; Minister of State for Finance, Minister of Finance, Energy, Mines and Resources; Minister of Energy, Mines and Resources 1984–86, of Int. Trade 1986–88; Pres. Treasury Bd April–Oct. 1988; Chair. Cabinet Cttee on Trade; mem. Senate 1990–; fmr Chair. Standing Senate Cttee on Energy, the Environment and Natural Resources; mem. Standing Senate Cttee on Foreign Affairs; mem. Canadian Inst. of Planners, Asscn of Professional Economists of BC; fmr mem. Econ. Council of Canada; Hon. Fellow Royal Architectural Inst. of Canada 1989; Hon. LLD (Univ. of BC) 1990, (BC Open Univ.) 1991. *Address:* The Senate, Ottawa, Ont., K1A 0A4, Canada.

CARNLEY, Most Rev. Peter Frederick, AO, DD, PhD; Australian archbishop and theologian; b. 17 Oct. 1937, New Lambton, NSW; s. of F. Carnley; m. Carol Ann Dunstan, 1966; one s. one d.; ed St John's Theological Coll., NSW, Trinity Coll., Melbourne Univ., St John's Coll., Univ. of Cambridge; Deacon 1962; Priest 1964; Chaplain Mitchell Coll. of Advanced Educ., NSW 1970–72; Research Fellow St John's Coll., Cambridge 1971–72; Warden St John's Coll., Univ. of Queensland 1973–81; Anglican Archbishop of Perth and Metropolitan of the Province of Western Australia 1981–, Primate of the Anglican Church of Australia –2000; mem. Archbishop of Canterbury's Comm. on Communion and Women in the Episcopate 1988, Int. Anglican Theological and Doctrinal Comm. 1994; Visiting Prof. of Anglican Studies, Gen. Theological Seminary, New York 1993, 1996, 1999; Hon. Fellow Trinity Coll., Univ. of Melbourne 2000, Fellow St John's Coll., Cambridge 2000; Dr hc (Newcastle) 2000, (Western Australia) 2000, (Charles Sturt) 2001, (Queensland) . *Publications:* The Poverty of Historical Scepticism in Christ, Faith and History 1972, The Structure of Resurrection Belief 1987, The Yellow Wallpaper and Other Sermons 2001, Faithfulness in Fellowship: Reflections on Homosexuality and the Church 2001. *Leisure interests:* gardening, music. *Address:* G.P.O. Box W2067, Perth, WA 6846, Australia. *Telephone:* (8) 9325-7455. *Fax:* (8) 9325-6741. *E-mail:* abcsuite@perth .anglican.org (Office). *Website:* www.perth.anglican.org (Office).

ČARNOGURSKÝ, Ján, LLD, DJur; Slovak politician and lawyer; b. 1 Jan. 1944, Bratislava; s. of Pavol Čarnogurský and Kristína Fašungová; m. Marta Stachová 1970; two s. two d.; ed Charles Univ., Prague 1966–69; lawyer, Bratislava 1970–81; mem. of Slovak Lawyers' Cen. Office and Czech Lawyers' Cen. Office; banned from legal profession after defence in a political trial 1981; driver, lawyer for a co. Bratislava 1982–86; unemployed, after expulsion from legal profession, continued giving legal advice to members of the political opposition and religious activists 1987–89; held in custody, released and pardoned, Aug.–Nov. 1989; First Deputy Premier, Govt of Czechoslovakia 1989–90, Deputy Premier June 1990; Chair. Legis. Council Feb.–Aug. 1990; Chair. Christian Democratic Movt 1990–2000; First Deputy Premier, Govt of Slovak Repub. 1990–91, Prime Minister of Slovak Govt 1991–92; mem. State Defence Council 1991–92; Deputy to Slovak Nat. Council (Slovak Parl.) for KDH (Christian Democratic Movt) 1992–98; Deputy Chair. Parl. Ass. of CSCE 1993–95; Minister of Justice 1998–2002; advocate in pvt sector 2002–; Trustee Order of the German Kts 1994–; Slovak Literary Fund Prize (Journalists' Section) 1992. *Publications:* The Bratislava Letters (samizdat), Suffered for the Faith 1987, Seen from Danube 1997. *Leisure interests:* history, jogging. *Address:* Law Office, Dostojevského rad 1, 81109 Bratislava (Office); Karola Adlera 10, 84102 Bratislava; KDH, Žabotova 2, 811 04 Bratislava, Slovakia. *Telephone:* (2) 5263-6954 (Office). *Fax:* (2) 5263-6955 (Office); (7) 391 647 (KDH). *E-mail:* jancarnogursky@slovanet.sk (Home); carnogursky@ba.psg .sk. *Website:* www.justice.gov.sk (Office).

CARO, Sir Anthony, Kt, OM, CBE, MA; British sculptor; b. 8 March 1924, London; s. of Alfred and Mary Caro; m. Sheila Girling 1949; two s.; ed Charterhouse School, Christ's Coll., Cambridge, Regent St Polytechnic and Royal Acad. Schools, London; served Fleet Air Arm RN; Asst to Henry Moore 1951–53; Part-time Lecturer St Martin's School of Art, London 1953–79; taught at Bennington Coll. Vermont 1963–65; works in over 150 public collections throughout the world; initiated Triangle Summer Workshop, Pine Plains, New York 1982; undertook comm. for new East Building, Nat. Gallery of Art, Washington, DC, 1977; mem. Council RCA 1981–83, Slade School of Art 1982–92; Hon. Fellow, Christ's Coll. Cambridge 1981, RCA, London 1986, Wolfson Coll., Oxford 1992, RIBA; Foreign Hon. mem., American Acad. of Arts and Sciences, 1988, Acad. di Belle Arte di Brera; Trustee, Tate Gallery 1982–89, Fitzwilliam Museum, Cambridge 1984; Hon. DLitt (E Anglia, York Univ., Toronto, Cambridge), Hon. DUniv (Surrey) 1987, Hon. DFA (Yale) 1989, Dr hc (RCA) 1994 and others; Sculpture Prize, Paris Biennale 1959, David E Bright Award, Venice Biennale 1967, Prize for Sculpture, São Paulo Biennale 1969, presented with Key of City of New York 1974; Henry Moore Grand Prize 1991, Praemium Imperiale 1992, Int. Sculpture Centre Lifetime Achievement Award 1997. *Exhibitions include:* one-man Exhbn in Milan 1956, others subsequently in UK, USA, France, Netherlands, Greece, Italy, Germany, Finland, Spain, Switzerland, Canada, Japan, NZ and Australia; retrospective Exhbn Arts Council (Hayward Gallery, London) 1969, Museum of Modern Art, New York, Walker Art Center, Minneapolis, Houston Museum of Fine Art, Boston Museum of Fine Art 1975–76, Trajan Markets, Rome 1992, Annely Juda Fine Art 1994; Museum of Contemporary Art, Tokyo 1995; exhibited André Emmerich Gallery, New York 1964–94 (17 shows), Kasmin

Knoedler Gallery, London 1978–91 (7 shows), Annely Juda Fine Art 1989– (4 shows), Marlborough Gallery, USA 1997–2001 (4 shows); over 180 group shows in Europe, USA, Canada, Australia and the Far East including Venice Biennale six times 1958–99. *Leisure interest:* listening to music. *Address:* c/o Barford Sculptures, 38c Georgiana Street, London, NW1 0EB, England (Office). *Website:* www.barford.org (Office).

CARO, David Edmund, AO, OBE, MSc, PhD, FInstP, FAIP, FACE; Australian university chancellor; b. 29 June 1922, Melbourne; s. of George and Alice Caro; m. Fiona Macleod 1954; one s. one d.; ed Geelong Grammar School, Univs. of Melbourne and Birmingham; war service, RAAF 1941–46; Demonstrator in Physics, Univ. of Melbourne 1947–49, Lecturer 1952, Sr Lecturer 1954, Reader 1958, Prof. of Experimental Physics and Head of Dept of Physics 1961–72, Deputy Vice-Chancellor 1972–77, Vice-Chancellor and Prin. 1982–87; Vice-Chancellor, Univ. of Tasmania 1978–82; Chair. Antarctic Research Policy Advisory Cttee 1979–84, Australian Vice-Chancellors Cttee 1982–83, Melbourne Theatre Co. 1982–87, UniSuper Ltd 1984–94, Sarou Pty Ltd 1991–; mem. Council Asscn Commonwealth Univs. 1982–84, Royal Melbourne Hosp. Cttee of Man. 1982–92; Interim Vice-Chancellor, N Territory Univ. 1988–89; mem. Council Victorian Coll. of the Arts 1989–2001, Pres. 1989–92; mem. Council Univ. of S. Australia 1991–94; Chancellor Univ. of Ballarat 1998– (mem. Council 1994–); Exhbn of 1851 Overseas Research Scholar 1949–51; Hon. LLD (Melbourne) 1978, (Tasmania) 1982; Hon. DSc (Melbourne) 1987. *Publication:* Modern Physics (co-author) 1961. *Leisure interests:* skiing, gardening, theatre. *Address:* 17 Fairbairn Road, Toorak, Vic. 3142, Australia. *Telephone:* 9827-2004.

CAROLUS, Cheryl, BA; South African organization executive and diplomatist; m. Graeme Bloch 1989; ed Univ. of the Western Cape; Gen. Sec. of Nat. Exec. Cttee, United Democratic Front (UDF) 1983–87, Fed. of S. African Women (FedSAW) 1987, UDF Western Cape Region 1983; UDF Del. Int. Centre for Swedish Labour Movt 1986; mem. Interim Leadership Group S. African Communist Party 1990; mem. Interim Leadership Cttee African Nat. Congress (ANC) 1990, ANC Rep. at talks with Govt at Groote Schnurr, Cape Town 1990, Deputy Sec.-Gen. ANC 1994; High Commr to UK 1998–2001; CEO South African Tourism Board—SATOUR 2001–; mem. Congress of S. African Trade Unions, Nat. Educ. Crisis Cttee 1989, Org. of African Unity, Harare; detained under emergency regulations 1986, 1989. *Address:* South African Tourism Board, 442 Rigel Ave South, Erasmusrand 0181, Private Bag X164, Pretoria 0001, South Africa (Office). *Telephone:* (12) 4826200. *Fax:* (12) 3478753. *E-mail:* jhb@satour.com. *Website:* www.za.satour.com (Office).

CARON, Leslie Claire Margaret; French actress and ballet dancer; b. 1 July 1931, Boulogne-Billancourt; m. 1st George Hormel; m. 2nd Peter Reginald Frederick Hall 1956 (dissolved 1965); one s. one d.; m. 3rd Michael Laughlin 1969 (dissolved); ed Convent of the Assumption, Paris and Conservatoire de Danse; with Ballet des Champs Elysées 1947–50, Ballet de Paris 1954; Chevalier Légion d'honneur, Officier Ordre nat. du Mérite. *Films include:* An American in Paris, Man with a Cloak, Glory Alley, Story of Three Loves, Lili, Glass Slipper, Daddy Long Legs, Gaby, Gigi, The Doctor's Dilemma, The Man Who Understood Women, The Subterranean, Fanny, Guns of Darkness, The L-Shaped Room, Father Goose, A Very Special Favor, Promise Her Anything, Is Paris Burning?, Head of the Family, Madron, The Contract, The Unapproachable 1982, Deathly Moves 1983, Génie du Faux 1984, The Train 1987, Guerriers et Captives 1988, Courage Mountain 1988, Damage 1992, Funny Bones 1995, Let It Be Me 1995, The Reef 1996, The Last of the Blonde Bombshells 1999, Chocolat 2000, Murder on the Orient Express 2001. *Plays include:* Orvet (Jean Renoir), La Sauvage (Anouilh), Gigi (Anita Loos), 13 rue de l'Amour (Feydan), Ondine (Giraudoux), Carola (Renoir), La Répétition (Anouilh), On Your Toes (Rogers and Hart), Apprends-moi Céline (Maria Pacôme) (played in English in USA as One for the Tango 1985), Grand Hotel (Vicky Baum), George Sand (Bruno Villien), Le Martyre de Saint Sébastien (Debussy), Nocturne for Lovers (Villien), Babar the Elephant (Poulenc); toured France in Apprends-moi Céline 1998–99; stage appearances in Paris, London, USA, Germany and Australia; readings of Colette, USA and Australia. *Publication:* Vengeance 1983. *Address:* Fraser and Dunlop, Drury House, 34–43 Russell Street, London, WC2B 5HA, England; Merritt Blake Agency, 1327 Ocean Avenue, Santa Monica, CA 90401, USA. *Fax:* (310) 899-3858 (Office).

CARP, Daniel A., MS, MBA; American business executive; b. Wytheville, VA; ed Ohio Univ., Rochester Inst. of Tech., Sloan School of Man., MIT; with Kodak 1970–, Asst Gen. Man. Latin American Region 1986–88, Vice-Pres. Gen. Man. 1988–90, Gen. Man. European Marketing Cos. 1991, Gen. Man. European, African and Middle Eastern Region 1991, Exec.-Vice-Pres., Asst COO Eastman Kodak Co. 1995–97, Dir, Pres., COO 1997–2000, Chair., Pres., CEO 2000–01, Chair., CEO 2001–; Dir Texas Instruments Inc. *Address:* Eastman Kodak, 343 State Street, Rochester, NY 14650-0001, USA (Office).

CARPENTER, John Howard; American film director and screenwriter; b. 16 Jan. 1948, Carthage, NY; s. of Howard Ralph Carpenter and Milton Jean (née Carter) Carpenter; m. 1st Adrienne Barbeau 1979; m. 2nd Sandy King 1990; ed Univ. of Southern California; mem. American Soc. of Composers, Authors and Publrs., Acad. of Motion Picture Arts and Sciences, Dirs. Guild of America, West, Writers Guild of America. *Films directed:* The Resurrection of Bronco Billy 1970, Dark Star 1974, Assault on Precinct 13 1976, Someone's Watching Me, Halloween, Elvis 1978, The Fog 1979, Escape from New York 1980, The Thing 1982, Christine 1983, Starman 1984, Big Trouble in Little

China 1986, Prince of Darkness 1987, They Live 1987, Memoirs of an Invisible Man 1992, Body Bags (TV) 1993, In the Mouth of Madness 1995, Village of the Damned 1995, Escape from LA 1996, Vampires 1998, Halloween H20 1998, Ghosts of Mars 2001. *Leisure interests:* music, helicopter piloting. *Address:* c/o International Creative Management, 8942 Wilshire Boulevard, Beverly Hills, CA 90211, USA.

CARPENTER, Leslie Arthur; British business executive; b. 26 June 1927; s. of William Carpenter and Rose Carpenter; m. 1st 1952; one d.; m. 2nd Louise Botting 1989; ed Hackney Tech. Coll.; Dir Country Life 1965, George Newnes 1966; Man. Dir Odhams Press Ltd 1968; Dir Int. Publishing Corpn 1972, IPC (America) Inc. 1975; Chair. Reed Holdings Inc. 1977, Reed Publishing Holdings Ltd 1981; Chair. and Chief Exec. IPC Ltd 1974; Dir Reed Int. PLC 1974, CEO 1982–86, Chair. 1985–87; Dir Watmoughs (Holdings) PLC 1988–98. *Leisure interests:* racing, gardening. *Address:* Gable House, High Street, Broadway, Worcs., WR12 7DP, England.

CARPENTIER, Jean Claude Gabriel; French aeronautical engineer; b. 13 April 1926, Haspres; m. Micheline Robinet 1950; ed Ecole Polytechnique, Ecole Nationale Supérieure Aéronautique et Espace; Service technique de l'aéronautique 1950; Direction des recherches et moyens d'essais 1961; Dir Direction des recherches, études et techniques, Ministry of Defence 1977; Pres. Office Nat. d'études et de recherches aérospatiales (ONERA) 1984–91, Sr Consultant 1991–; Scientific Adviser; Pres. Man. Cttee Nat. Meteorological Bureau; Pres. Comité Avion-Ozone 1992; Ed. Aerospace Research 1994–; Co-Ed.-in-Chief Aerospace Science and Tech. 1997–, Revue Scientifique et Technique de la Défense; mem. Acad. Nat. de l'Air et de l'Espace; Commdr Légion d'honneur, Ordre Nat. du Mérite; Médaille de l'Aéronautique. *Publications:* Flight Mechanics 1952, Autopilots 1953, Inertial Navigation 1962, Recherche Aéronautique et Progrès de l'Aviation 1999. *Address:* Office National d'études et de recherches aérospatiales, 29 avenue de la Division Leclerc, P.O. Box 72, 92322 Chatillon Cedex, France. *Telephone:* 1-46-73-40-01 (Office). *Fax:* 1-46-73-41-65 (Office).

CARPENTIER, Michel André Georges, LenD, L. EN SC.(ECON.); French European Union official; b. 23 Oct. 1930, Billy Montigny, Pas de Calais; m. Annick Puget 1956; four s.; ed Ecole des Hautes Etudes Commerciales, Ecole des Science Politiques and Univ. of Paris; Commissariat à l'Energie Atomique (CEA) 1958; EURATOM 1959; Head of Dept Industrial, Technological and Scientific Affairs, EC Comm. 1967, Dir-Gen. Environment 1977, Dir-Gen. Energy 1981; Dir-Gen. Task Force for Information Technologies and Telecommunications, EC Comm. 1984; Dir-Gen. Information Technologies and Telecommunications, EC Comm. 1986; Dir-Gen. DG XIII, Telecommunications, Information Markets and Exploitation of Research, EC Comm. 1993–95; Hon. Dir-Gen. and Special Adviser EU Comm.; Industrial Adviser; mem. Econ. and Social Cttee, EC Comm., Paris 1995–96; Pres. Centre Informatique Documentaire (CID), Paris, Scientific Cttee AEC, Bordeaux; Hon. mem. Inst. of Electrical and Electronic Engineers (USA), Royal Swedish Acad. of Eng Science; Dr. hc (Loughborough, Madrid); Chevalier, Légion d'honneur, Ehrenkreuz für Wissenschaft und Forschung (Austria), Commdr Mérite (Luxembourg), Order of the Rising Sun, Japan. *Publications:* Telecommunications in Transition (with others) 1992, The French Space Policy 1998. *Leisure interests:* fishing, classical music, opera, reading. *Address:* Domaine de Lespinassat, 24230 Montcaret, France (Home). *Telephone:* (5) 53-58-66-05. *Fax:* (5) 53-58-66-05. *E-mail:* mcarpent@club.internet.fr (Home).

CARPER, Thomas Richard, BA, MBA; American politician; b. 23 Jan. 1947, Beckley, W Va; s. of Wallace Richard Carper and Mary Jean (Patton) Carper; m. Martha Stacy 1986; two s.; ed Ohio State Univ., Univ. of Delaware; Commdr USN 1968–73, Capt., Reserve 1973–91; industrial devt specialist, then State Treasurer, State of Del., Dover 1976–83; Democrat mem. 98th–102nd Congresses from Del. 1983–93; Gov. of Delaware 1993–2001; Senator from Delaware 2001–; mem. Nat. Govs. Asscn (Vice-Chair. 1997–98, Chair. 1998–99); Hon. Chair. Delaware Special Olympics 1987–. *Leisure interests:* physical fitness, running, weightlifting, tennis, reading, raising two sons. *Address:* 600 West Matson Run Parkway, Wilmington, DE 19802 (Home); 513 Hart building, US Senate, Washington, DC 20510, USA (Office). *Telephone:* (202) 224-2441. *E-mail:* carper@senate.gov.

CARR, Sir (Albert) Raymond (Maillard), Kt, MA, DLitt, FRSL, FRHistS, FBA; British historian; b. 11 April 1919, Bath; s. of Reginald Henry Maillard Carr and Ethel Gertrude Marion Carr; m. Sara Ann Mary Strickland 1950; three s. one d.; ed Brockenhurst School and Christ Church Oxford; Gladstone Research Exhibitioner, Christ Church 1941; Fellow All Souls Coll. Oxford 1946–53, New Coll. 1953–64, St Antony's Coll. 1964–; Dir Latin American Centre 1964–68, Chair. Soc. for Latin American Studies 1966–68; Prof. of History of Latin America, Oxford Univ. 1967–68, Warden St Antony's Coll. 1968–87; mem. Nat. Theatre Bd 1980; Corresp. mem. Royal Acad. of History, Madrid 1968; Hon. Fellow Christ Church Coll., St Antony's Coll., Oxford; Exeter Univ.; DLitt (Madrid); Grand Cross of the Order of Alfonso El Sabio (for services to Spanish history) 1983; Prince of Asturias Award in Social Sciences 1999. *Publications:* Spain 1808–1939 1966, Latin American Affairs 1969 (ed.), The Spanish Civil War 1971, English Fox Hunting 1976, The Spanish Tragedy: the Civil War in Perspective 1977, Spain: Dictatorship to Democracy 1979, Modern Spain 1980, Fox-Hunting 1982, Puerto Rico: A Colonial Experiment 1984; The Spanish Civil War (ed.) 1986, Visiones de fin

278

de siglo 1999, Spain – A History (ed.) 2001. *Leisure interest:* foxhunting. *Address:* Burch, North Molton, South Molton, EX36 3JU, England. *Telephone:* (1769) 550267.

CARR, Jack, DPhil, FRSE; British mathematician; b. 29 Aug. 1948, Newcastle-upon-Tyne; s. of John George Carr and Elizabeth Eleanor Carr; m. Teresa Nancy Thorpe 1976; one s. two d.; ed Walbottle Secondary School, Univ. of Bath, St Catherine's Coll., Oxford; Lecturer, Heriot-Watt Univ., Edin. 1974–83, Reader in Math. 1983–; Visiting Prof., Brown Univ., USA 1978–79, Mich. State Univ., USA 1982, Ecole Polytechnique, Lausanne, Switzerland 1983. *Publication:* Applications of Centre Manifolds 1981. *Leisure interests:* spreading urban myths, playing cricket for the W.C.C. *Address:* 42 Balgreen Avenue, Edinburgh, EH12 5SU, Scotland.

CARR, R. M., LLB, BCom, MA, MBA, PhD; New Zealand banker; b. 26 Nov. 1958; ed Wharton Business School, Univ. of Penn., Columbia Univ., NY, USA, Otago Univ.; fmr Head of Global Payments Nat. Australian Bank; currently Deputy Chief Exec. and Deputy Gov. Reserve Bank of NZ. *Publication:* Productivity and Efficiency in the US Life Insurance Industry. *Leisure interests:* running, swimming, hiking. *Address:* Reserve Bank of New Zealand, 2 The Terrace, POB 2498, Wellington, New Zealand (Office). *Telephone:* (4) 471-3675 (Office). *E-mail:* rod@carr.co.nz (Office).

CARR, Willard Zeller Jr, BS, JD; American attorney; b. 18 Dec. 1927, Richmond, Ind.; s. of Willard Z. Carr and Susan E Brownell Carr; m. Margaret Paterson Carr 1952; two s.; ed Purdue Univ., Indiana Univ. School of Law; Capt. Judge Advocate Gen.'s Dept USAF 1951–52; partner Gibson, Dunn & Crutcher, Attorneys 1952–; admitted to US Supreme Court 1963; mem. Los Angeles County Bar Asscn, Calif. State Bar Asscn, American Bar Asscn, Int. Bar Asscn (Chair. Labour Law Cttee 1973–83); mem. Bd of Visitors Southwestern Univ. Law School, Indiana Univ. School of Law; mem. Advisory Council Int. and Comparative Law Center, Southwestern Legal Foundation, Nat. Panel of Arbitrators, American Arbitration Asscn, World Affairs Council, Republican State Cen. Cttee for Calif.; Chair. Calif. Chamber of Commerce; Jurisprudence Award (Anti-Defamation League) 1987. *Publications:* International Handbook on Contracts of Employment 1976, Symposium on Private Investments Abroad – Problems and Solutions in International Business 1982; numerous specialist articles. *Leisure interests:* tennis, travel. *Address:* Gibson, Dunn & Crutcher, 333 South Grand Avenue, 49th floor, Los Angeles, CA 90071-3197 (Office); 2185 Century Hill, Los Angeles, CA 90067-3516, USA (Home). *Telephone:* (213) 229-7238. *E-mail:* wcarr@gibsondunn.com.

CARR OF HADLEY, Baron (Life Peer), cr. 1975, of Monken Hadley in Greater London; **(Leonard) Robert Carr,** PC, MA; British politician and business executive; b. 11 Nov. 1916, London; s. of the late Ralph Edward and of Katie Elizabeth Carr; m. Joan Kathleen Twining 1943; one s. (deceased) two d.; ed Westminster School and Gonville and Caius Coll., Cambridge; MP 1950–75, Parl. Pvt. Sec. to Sec. of State for Foreign Affairs 1951–55, to Prime Minister April–Dec. 1955, Parl. Sec. Ministry of Labour and Nat. Service 1955–58, Sec. for Tech. Co-operation May 1963–Oct. 1964; Sec. of State for Employment 1970–72; Lord Pres. of Council and Leader of House of Commons April–Nov. 1972; Sec. of State Home Dept 1972–74; joined John Dale Ltd 1938, Chief Metallurgist 1945–48, Dir of Research and Development 1948–55, Chair. 1959–63 and 1965–70; Dir Carr, Day & Martin Ltd 1947–55, Isotope Developments Ltd 1950–55; Deputy Chair. and Joint Man. Dir Metal Closures Group Ltd 1960–63, Dir 1965–70; Dir Scottish Union and Nat. Insurance Co. (London) 1958–63; Dir S. Hoffnung and Co. 1963, 1965–70, 1974–80, Securicor Ltd 1965–70, 1974–85; Dir Norwich Union Insurance Group (London) 1965–70, 1974–76; Dir S.G.B. Group Ltd 1974–86; Dir Prudential Assurance Co. 1976–85, Deputy Chair. 1979–80, Co-Chair. 1980–85; Dir Prudential Corpn Ltd 1978–89, Deputy Chair. 1979–80, Chair. 1980–85; Dir Cadbury Schweppes Ltd 1979–87; Chair. Strategy Ventures 1988–2001; mem. Political Honours Scrutiny Cttee 1977–87; Fellow, Imperial Coll., London 1985; Conservative. *Publications:* (Co-author) One Nation 1950, Change is our Ally 1954, The Responsible Society 1958, One Europe 1965. *Leisure interests:* lawn tennis, gardening, music. *Address:* House of Lords, Westminster, London, SW1 (Office); 14 North Court, Great Peter Street, London, SW1P 3LL, England (Home).

CARRARD, François Denis Etienne, LLD; Swiss lawyer and international organization official; b. 19 Jan. 1938, Lausanne; ed Lausanne, John Muir High School, Pasadena, Calif., USA, Univ. of Lausanne; with audit co., Lausanne 1962; with attorney's practice, Stockholm, Sweden 1963–64; Attorney, Lausanne 1965–, admitted to bar of Vaud (Swiss bar) 1967, Sr Partner Etude Carrard, Paschoud, Heim et Associés; Dir and Chair. of Bds. of several cos.; Dir-Gen. Int. Olympic Cttee Sept. 1989–; Chair. Montreux Jazz Festival Foundation, Gabriella Giorgi-Cavaglieri Foundation; Pres. Automobile-Club de Suisse; fmr Vice-Pres. Bd of Vintage Brands of Vaud; fmr mem. Swiss Fed. Comm. of Foreign Indemnities; mem. Ordre des Avocats Vaudois, Fédération Suisse des Avocats, Int. Bar Asscn, Assoc Suisse de l'Arbitrage, Union Internationale des Avocats; Commdr Orden del Mérito Civil (Spain) 1992; Officier Ordre de Saint-Charles (Monaco) 1993. *Address:* International Olympic Committee, Château de Vidy, 1007 Lausanne, Switzerland (Office). *Telephone:* (21) 6216111 (Office). *Fax:* (21) 6216351 (Office).

CARRARO, Franco; Italian sports administrator and politician; b. 6 Dec. 1939, Padua; graduated in econ. and commercial sciences; Chair. football team Milan Calcio 1967–71; fmr Chair. Comm. for Amateur and Professional Football, Chair. Sub-comm. for Professional Football, UEFA; Vice-Pres.

Italian Nat. Olympic Cttee 1976–78, Pres. 1978–; mem. Int. Olympic Cttee; Pres. Italian Football Fed. (Federazione Italiana Gioco Calcio) 1976–78, 2001–, Extraordinary Commr 1986–; Chair. Asscn of European Olympic Cttees 1980–; Chair. Organizing Cttee World Cup Football Championship 1990; fmr champion water skier; Minister of Tourism and Performing Arts 1989–90; Mayor of Rome 1989–93.

CARRELL, Robin Wayne, MA, PhD, DSc, FRCP, FRSNZ, FRS; New Zealand professor of haematology; b. 5 April 1936, Christchurch; s. of Ruane George Carrell and Constance Gwendoline (née Rowe) Carrell; m. Susan Wyatt Rogers 1962; two s. two d.; ed Christchurch Boys' High School, Univs. of Otago, Canterbury and Cambridge; mem. MRC Haemoglobin Unit, Cambridge 1965–68; Dir Clinical Biochemistry Christchurch Hosp., NZ 1968–75; lecturer Clinical Biochemistry Univ. of Cambridge 1976–78, Prof. of Haematology 1986–; Prof. of Clinical Biochemistry and Dir Molecular Research Lab. Christchurch Clinical School of Medicine, Otago Univ. 1978–86; Commonwealth Fellow St John's Coll., Cambridge and Visiting Scientist MRC Lab. of Molecular Biology 1985; Fellow Trinity Coll., Cambridge 1987–; Gov. Imperial Coll. London 1997–98, mem. Court 1999-; Pres. British Soc. of Thrombosis and Haemostasis 1999; Hector Medal (Royal Soc. of NZ) 1986. *Publications:* articles in scientific journals on genetic abnormalities of human proteins and new protein family, serpins. *Leisure interests:* gardening, walking. *Address:* 19 Madingley Road, Cambridge, CB3 0EG; Haematology Department, University of Cambridge, Cambridge Institute for Medical Research, Hills Road, Cambridge, CB2 2XY, England (Office). *Telephone:* (1223) 312 970; (1223) 336828 (Office). *Fax:* (1223) 336827. *E-mail:* rwc1000@cam.ac.uk (Office).

CARRERAS, José; Spanish tenor; b. 5 Dec. 1947, Barcelona; s. of José Carreras and Antonia Carreras; m. Ana Elisa Carreras; one s. one d.; opera début as Gennaro in Lucrezia Borgia, Liceo Opera House, Barcelona 1970–71 season; appeared in La Bohème, Un Ballo in Maschera and I Lombardi alla Prima Crociata at Teatro Regio, Parma, Italy 1972; U.S. début as Pinkerton in Madame Butterfly with New York City Opera 1972; début Metropolitan Opera as Cavaradossi 1974; début La Scala as Riccardo in Un Ballo in Maschera 1975; has appeared at maj. opera houses and festivals including Teatro Colón, Buenos Aires, Covent Garden, London, Vienna Staatsoper, Easter Festival and Summer Festival, Salzburg, Lyric Opera of Chicago; recordings include Un Ballo in Maschera, La Battaglia di Legnano, Il Corsaro, Un Giorno di Regno, I Due Foscari, Simone Boccanegra, Macbeth, Don Carlos, Tosca, Thais, Aida, Cavalleria Rusticana, Pagliacci, Lucia di Lammermoor, Turandot, Elisabetta, regina d'Inghilterra, Otello (Rossini); Pres. José Carreras Int. Leukaemia Foundation 1988–; Hon. mem. Royal Acad. of Music 1990; Grammy Award 1991, Sir Lawrence Olivier Award 1993, Gold Medal of City of Barcelona, Albert Schweizer Music Award 1996; Commdr des Arts et des Lettres, Chevalier Légion d'honneur and numerous other awards and prizes. *Films include:* La Bohème, I Lombardi, Andrea Chenier, Turandot, Carmen, Don Carlos, La Forza del Destino, Fedora, Jerusalem, My Life. *Publication:* Singing from the Soul 1991. *Address:* c/o José Carreras International Leukaemia Foundation, Muntaner, Barcelona (Office); c/o Opera Caballé, via Augusta 59, Barcelona (Office); c/o FIJC, Muntaner 383, 2°, 08021 Barcelona, Spain. *Telephone:* (93) 4145566 (Office). *Fax:* (93) 2010588 (Office). *E-mail:* fundacio@fcarreras.es. *Website:* www.fcarreras.es (Office).

CARRÈRE D'ENCAUSSE, Hélène, DèsSc; French professor specializing in Soviet affairs; b. 6 July 1929, Paris; d. of Georges Zourabichvili and Nathalie von Pelken; m. Louis Carrère 1952; one s. two d.; ed Sorbonne, Paris; fmr Prof. Univ. of Paris (Sorbonne); now Prof. Inst. d'Etudes Politiques, Paris and Dir of Research, Fondation Nationale des Sciences Politiques; fmr mem. Bd of Dirs. East-West Inst. for Security Studies; Visiting Prof. at numerous univs. in USA; mem. Acad. Française, Sec. for Life 2000–; Assoc. mem. Acad. Royale de Belgique; mem. European Parl. 1994–99; Dr hc (Montréal); Officier, Légion d'honneur; Prix Aujourd'hui 1978; Prix de la Fondation Louis-Weiss 1986. *Publications include:* Le marxisme et l'Asie 1965, Réforme et révolution chez les musulmans de l'Empire russe 1966, L'URSS et la Chine devant les révolutions dans les sociétés pré-industrielles 1970, L'Empire éclaté 1978, Lénine: la révolution et le pouvoir 1979, Staline: l'ordre par la terreur 1979, Le pouvoir confisqué 1982, Le Grand Frère 1983, La déstalinisation commence 1984, Ni paix ni guerre 1986, Le Grand Défi: bolcheviks et nations 1917–30 1987, Le Malheur russe 1988, La Gloire des nations ou la fin de l'Empire soviétique 1991, Victorieuse Russie 1992, Nicholas II: la transition interrompue 1996, Lénine 1998, La Russie inachevée 2000, Catherine II 2002. *Address:* Académie Française, 23 quai Conti, 75006 Paris, France (Office). *Telephone:* 1-44-41-43-00 (Office). *Fax:* 1-43-29-47-45 (Office).

CARREY, Jim; Canadian film actor; b. 17 Jan. 1962, Newmarket, Ont.; s. of Percy Carrey and Kathleen Carrey; m. 1st Melissa Worner 1986 (divorced); one d.; m. 2nd Lauren Holly 2001; began performing in comedy clubs in Toronto aged 17 before moving to Hollywood; Star on Hollywood Walk of Fame 2000. *Films include:* Peggy Sue Got Married 1986, The Dead Pool 1988, Earth Girls Are Easy 1989, Ace Ventura! Pet Detective, The Mask, Dumb and Dumber, Liar Liar (Blockbuster Entertainment Award) 1996, Batman Forever, The Cable Guy (MTV Movie Award) 1996, The Truman Show (Golden Globe for Best Performance) 1997, Man on the Moon, How the Grinch Stole Christmas 2000, Me, Myself and Irene 2000. *TV appearances include:* In Living Colour (sit-com). *Address:* UTA, 9560 Wilshire Boulevard, 5th Floor, Beverly Hills, CA 90212, USA.

CARRICK, Hon. Sir John Leslie, KCMG, BEcons; Australian politician (retd) and educationalist; b. 4 Sept. 1918, Sydney; s. of Arthur James and Emily Ellen (Terry) Carrick; m. Diana Margaret (Angela) Hunter 1951; three d.; ed Sydney Technical High School, Univ. of Sydney; commissioned Univ. of Sydney Regt 1939, served in Australian Imperial Force, Sparrow Force; POW 1942–45; mem. Citizen Mil. Force 1948–51; Gen. Sec. NSW Div. of Liberal Party of Australia 1948–71; mem. Senate 1971–87; mem. Library Cttee 1971–73, Senate Standing Cttee on Educ., Science and the Arts 1971–75, Senate Standing Cttee on Foreign Affairs and Defence 1971–74, Jt Cttee on Foreign Affairs 1971–72, on Foreign Affairs and Defence 1973–75, Senate Standing Cttee on Standing Orders 1978–83, Senate Select Cttee on Human Embryo Experimentation Bill 1985 1985–, Standing Cttee on Regulations and Ordinances 1983–86, Jt Select Cttee on Electoral Reform 1983–87; Opposition Spokesman for Federalism and Intergovernment Relations 1975; Minister for Housing and Construction, for Urban and Regional Devt Nov.–Dec. 1975; Minister for Educ. 1975–79, Minister assisting the Prime Minister in Fed. Affairs 1975–78; Leader of Govt in the Senate 1978–83, Vice-Pres. of Exec. Council 1978–82; Minister for Nat. Devt and Energy 1979–83; Chair. NSW State Govt Cttee Review of Schools 1988–89, Advisory Cttee GERRIC, Univ. of NSW 1997–; Pres. Univ. of Sydney Dermatology Research Foundation 1989–2003; Chair. Gas Council of NSW 1990–95; mem. NSW Exec. Cttee, Foundation for Aged Care 1989–2000, Ministerial Advisory Council on Teacher Educ. and Quality of Teaching 1992–95, Advisory Bd Inst. of Early Childhood Foundation, Macquarie Univ. 1992–2000, Chair. Macquarie Univ. IEC Foundation 2001–; Commonwealth Gov. Roundtable on Indigenous Capacity 2000; Hon. Fellow Australian Coll. of Educ. 1994; Hon. DLitt (Sydney) 1982, (Macquarie) 2000. *Leisure interests:* swimming, running, reading. *Address:* Apt. 21, 162E Burwood Road, Concord, NSW 2137, Australia (Home). *Telephone:* (2) 747-8320 (Home). *Fax:* (2) 747-8340 (Home).

CARRICK, Sir Roger John, KCMG, LVO; British diplomatist and international consultant; b. 13 Oct. 1937, Middx; s. of John Carrick and Florence Carrick; m. Hilary E. Blinman 1962; two s.; ed Isleworth Grammar School, Jt Services School for Linguists and School of Slavonic and E European Studies, Univ. of London; RN 1956–58; joined HM Diplomatic Service 1956; served Sofia 1962, FCO 1965, Paris 1967, Singapore 1971, FCO 1973–77; Visiting Fellow, Inst. of Int. Affairs, Univ. of Calif. Berkeley 1977–78; Counsellor, Washington, DC 1978; Head, Overseas Estate Dept FCO 1982; Consul-Gen. Chicago 1985–88; Asst Under-Sec. of State (Econ.) FCO 1988–90; Amb. to Indonesia 1990–94; High Commr in Australia 1994–97; Deputy Chair. Britain-Australia Soc. 1998–99, Chair. 1999–2002; Dir (non-exec.) cmb technologies 2000–02; Chair. (non-exec.) Charteris Mackie & Baillie Ltd 2001–; Deputy Chair. The D Group 2001–; Dir Strategy International Ltd 2001–; Trustee Chevening Estate 1998–, Britain-Australia Bicentennial Trust; Churchill Fellow, Westminster Coll., Miss. 1986. *Publications:* East-West Technology Transfer in Perspective 1978, RolleroundOz 1998. *Leisure interests:* sailing, reading, music, theatre, public speaking, avoiding gardening. *Address:* Windhover, Wootton Courtenay, Somerset, TA24 8RD, England. *Telephone:* (20) 7480-5652; (1643) 841162. *Fax:* (20) 7488-9643; (1643) 841670. *E-mail:* rjc@dgroup.co.uk (Office); roger.carrick@talk21.com (Home).

CARRIER, George Francis, PhD; American professor of applied mathematics; b. 4 May 1918, Millinocket, Maine; s. of Charles Mosher Carrier and Mary Marcoux Carrier; m. Mary Casey Carrier 1946; three s.; ed Cornell Univ.; Research Engineer, Harvard Univ. 1944–46; Asst Prof. Brown Univ. 1946–47, Assoc. Prof. 1947–48, Prof. 1948–52; Gordon McKay Prof. of Mech. Eng, Harvard Univ. 1952–72; T. Jefferson Coolidge Prof. of Applied Math. 1972–88, Emeritus 1988–; Emer. mem. Council for Eng Coll. Cornell Univ.; mem. NAS, American Philosophical Soc., Int. Soc. for Interaction of Mechanics and Math.; Fellow, American Acad. of Arts and Sciences, Nat. Acad. of Eng; Assoc. Ed., Quarterly of Applied Math.; Hon. mem. ASME; Hon. Fellow, Inst. for Maths. and its Applications; Pi Tau Sigma Richards Memorial Award, ASME 1963, Von Karman Medal, American Soc. of Civil Engineers 1977, Timoshenko Medal, ASME 1978, Von Karman Prize, SIAM 1979, NAS Award in Applied Math. and Numerical Analysis 1980, ASME Silver Centennial Medal 1980, Fluid Dynamics Prize, American Physical Soc. 1984, Dryden Medal, AIAA 1989, Pres.'s Nat. Medal of Science 1990. *Publications:* Functions of a Complex Variable: Theory and Technique (with M. Krook and C. E. Pearson) 1966, Ordinary Differential Equations (with C. E. Pearson) 1968, Partial Differential Equations (with C. E. Pearson) 1976; numerous articles. *Address:* Harvard University, Division of Engineering and Applied Sciences, Pierce 311, Cambridge, MA 02138, USA.

CARRIER, Hervé; Canadian sociologist and Jesuit; b. 26 Aug. 1921, Grand-Mère, Québec; s. of Fortunat Carrier and Cora Gélinas; ed Univ. de Montreal, Jesuit Faculty, Montreal, Catholic Univ. of America, Washington and Sorbonne, Paris; Prof. of Sociology, Gregorian Univ. Rome 1959–, Rector 1966–78; Pres. Int. Fed. of Catholic Univs. 1970–80, Dir Centre for Coordination of Research 1978–82; Sec. Pontifical Council for Culture, Vatican City 1982–93; mem. Acad. des Lettres et des Sciences Humaines of Royal Soc. of Canada, European Acad. of Sciences and Arts; Dr. hc (Sogang Univ., Seoul and Fu Jen Univ., Taipei); Officier, Légion d'honneur. *Publications:* Psychosociology of Religious Belonging 1965, Higher Education facing New Cultures 1982, Cultures: notre avenir 1985, Evangile et cultures 1987, Psico-sociologia dell'appartenenza religiosa 1988, Gospel Message and Human Cultures 1989, The Social Doctrine of the Church Revisited 1990, Evangélisation et Développement des Cultures 1990, Lexique de la Culture 1992, Evangelizing the Culture of Modernity 1993, Diccionario de la Cultura 1994, Guide pour l'inculturation de l'Evangile 1997, Dizionario della cultura 1997. *Address:* 25 Jarry Street, W Montreal, Québec, H2P 1S6, Canada. *Telephone:* (514) 387-2541. *Fax:* (514) 387-4244. *E-mail:* hcarrier@qc.aira.com (Office).

CARRIERE, Berthold, M.MUS.; Canadian composer and musical director; b. 27 Feb. 1940, Ottawa; s. of Rolland and Berthe (Paradis) Carriere; m. Nancy Carpenter 1969; ed Univs. of Montreal and Western Ontario; Musical Dir Banff School of Fine Arts 1968–72; Resident Musical Dir, Theatre London 1972–74, Dir of Music 1976–77, Assoc. Dir 1976; Dir of Music, Stratford Shakespearean Festival 1976–83, 1985–; Musical Dir, Talk of Toronto 1980–82; Conductor/Arranger, Dominion Day Celebrations 1967; Man of the Year, City of Ottawa 1967, Guthrie Award, Stratford Shakespearean Festival 1976, Dora Mavor Moore Musical Dir Award 1981, 1982, 1987. *Address:* Stratford Festival, Box 520, Stratford, Ont., N5A 6V2 (Office); Box 1273, St Mary's, Ont., N0M 2V0, Canada (Home).

CARRIÈRE, Jean Paul Jacques; French author; b. 6 Aug. 1928, Nîmes; s. of Edmond Carrière and Andrée Paoli; m. 1st Michèle Bollé; two s.; m. 2nd Françoise Battistini 1978; one s.; ed Coll. Saint Stanislas, Coll. de l'Assomption and Lycée Alphonse Daudet, Nîmes; disc-jockey, Manosque 1958–63; producer, Radio Languedoc-Roussillon 1965–74; television producer, ORTF 1969–; mem. PEN Club; Prix de l'Acad. Française 1968, Prix Goncourt 1972, Prix des Journalistes de la Presse Parisienne 1999, Prix du Roman de l'Été 1999, Screen Laurel Award, Writer's Guild of America 2000, Prix du Sud 2000. *Publications:* Les forêts du nouveau monde 1956, Lettre à un père sur une vocation incertaine 1956, Retour à Uzes 1968, L'Epervier de Maheux 1972, Jean Giono 1973, L'univers de Jean Carrière 1975, Noémie, Célestin, Joseph et autres paysans d'Ardèche 1976, La Caverne des Pestiférés (two vols) 1978, 1979, Le nez dans l'herbe 1980, Les années sauvages (novel) 1986, Julien Gracq 1986, Le Prix du Goncourt (novel) 1986, Le Dernier Été d'Occident 1987, Voyage d'hiver en Provence 1987, Cévennes 1988, Jean Fusaro, ou La chorégraphie de l'instant 1988, Un grain de beauté sur la lune (novel) 1990, Sigourney Weaver ou Portrait et itinéraire d'une femme accomplie 1989, Droits, Devoirs et Crocodile: essai politique (co-author) 1992, L'Indifférence des Etoiles (novel) 1994, Achigan (novel) 1995, L'Etoffe des rêves (novel) 1996, L'Empire des songes (novel) 1996, Un jardin pour l'éternel (novel) 1997, Le fer dans la plaie (novel) 1999, L'outsider 2002. *Leisure interests:* bicycling, walking, piano, cinema, swimming. *Address:* Les Broussanes, Domessargues, 30350 Ledignan; Le Devois, Super Camprieu, 30750 Trèves, France. *Telephone:* 66-83-30-76; 67-82-61-12. *Fax:* 66-83-33-84.

CARRILLO, Santiago; Spanish politician and journalist; b. 18 Jan. 1915, Gijón; s. of Wenceslao Carrillo and Rosalía (Solares) Carrillo; m. Carmen Menéndez; three s.; Sec.-Gen. de la Juventud Socialista Unificada 1936; Councillor of Public Order, Junta de Defensa de Madrid 1936; Sec.-Gen. Partido Comunista de España 1960–82, expelled from CP 1985; mem. Congress of Deputies 1977–, Deputy for Madrid 1982–; Dir Ahora June 1984–; Pres. de Unidad Comunista 1985. *Publications:* Después de Franco, ¿Qué?, Nuevos enfoques a problemas de hoy, Mañana España, Eurocomunismo y Estado, El año de la Constitución, Memoria de la transición 1983, Le communisme malgré tout 1983.

CARRINGTON, Alan, CBE, MA, PhD, FRS; British professor of chemistry; b. 6 Jan. 1934, Greenwich; s. of Albert Carrington and Constance (Nelson) Carrington; m. Noreen H. Taylor 1959; one s. two d.; ed Colfe's Grammar School and Univs. of Southampton, Oxford and Cambridge; Asst in Research, Univ. of Cambridge 1960, Asst Dir of Research 1963; Fellow, Downing Coll. Cambridge 1960, Hon. Fellow 1999; Prof. of Chem. Univ. of Southampton 1967, Royal Soc. Research Prof. 1979–84, 1987–; Royal Soc. Research Prof. and Fellow, Jesus Coll. Oxford 1984–87; Pres. Faraday Div., Royal Soc. of Chemistry 1997–99; Foreign Hon. mem. American Acad. of Arts and Sciences; Foreign Assoc. NAS; Hon. DSc; numerous medals and awards. *Publications:* Introduction to Magnetic Resonance (with A. D. McLachlan) 1967, Microwave Spectroscopy of Free Radicals 1974, Rational Spectroscopy of Diatomic Molecules 2003; papers in learned journals. *Leisure interests:* family, music, fishing. *Address:* 46 Lakewood Road, Chandler's Ford, Hants., SO53 1EX, England. *Telephone:* (23) 8026-5092 (Home). *E-mail:* ac@soton.ac.uk (Home).

CARRINGTON, Edwin Wilberforce, MSc; Trinidad and Tobago economist and international organization official; b. 23 June 1938; m.; two s. one d.; ed Univ. of the W Indies, McGill Univ., Montreal, Canada; Admin. Cadet, Cen. Planning Unit, Prime Minister's Office 1964; Chief of Econs and Statistics, Caribbean Community and Common Market (CARICOM) 1973–76, Dir Trade and Integration Div. 1973–76, Sec.-Gen. CARICOM 1992–; Deputy Sec.-Gen. African, Caribbean and Pacific (ACP) states 1976–85, Sec.-Gen. 1985; High Commr to Guyana 1991; Sec.-Gen. Caribbean Forum ACP states. *Publications:* Industrialization by Invitation: The Case of Trinidad and Tobago 1968, The Solution of Economic Problems through Regional Groupings (jtly.), Tourism as a Vehicle for Economic Development 1975. *Address:* Caribbean Community and Common Market, Bank of Guyana Building, P.O. Box 10827, Georgetown, Guyana. *Telephone:* (2) 69281 (Office). *Fax:* (2) 67816 (Office). *E-mail:* carisec3@caricom.org (Office).

CARRINGTON, 6th Baron; Peter Alexander Rupert Carington, KG, GCMG, CH, MC, PC; British politician and international administrator; b. 6 June 1919, London; s. of 5th Baron Carrington and the Hon. Sybil Marion Colville; m. Iona McClean 1942; one s. two d.; ed Eton Coll. and Royal Mil.

Coll., Sandhurst; Grenadier Guards 1939, served NW Europe; Parl. Sec. Ministry of Agriculture 1951–54, Ministry of Defence 1954–56; High Commr in Australia 1956–59; First Lord of the Admiralty 1959–63; Minister without Portfolio (at the Foreign Office), Leader of the House of Lords 1963–64; Leader of the Opposition in the House of Lords 1964–70, 1974–79; Sec. of State for Defence 1970–74, also Minister of Aviation Supply 1971–74; Chair. Conservative Party 1972–74; Sec. of State for Energy Jan.–March 1974, for Foreign and Commonwealth Affairs 1979–82, Minister of Overseas Devt 1979–82; Chair. GEC 1983–84; Sec.-Gen. NATO 1984–88; Chair. Christie's Int. PLC 1988–93 (Dir 1988–); sits in the House of Lords as Lord Carrington of Upton 1999–; Dir The Daily Telegraph 1990–; EC Negotiating Cttee on Yugoslavia 1991 (resgnd Aug. 1992); Chancellor Univ. of Reading 1992–; Sec. for Foreign Correspondence and Hon. mem. RA of Arts 1982–; Chancellor, Order of the Garter 1994–; Chair. Bd of Trustees, Victoria and Albert Museum 1983–88; Pres. The Pilgrims 1983–, Voluntary Service Overseas 1993–; mem. Kissinger Asscn 1982–84, 1988–; Pres. Chiltern Open Air Museum 1983–; Dir Int. Bd Fiat 1995–; Hon. Bencher of the Middle Temple 1983; Hon. Fellow, St Antony's Coll., Oxford 1982–; Hon. LLD (Cambridge) 1981, (Leeds) 1981, (Univ. of Philippines) 1982, (Univ. of Aberdeen) 1985, (Sussex) 1989; Hon. DUniv (Essex) 1983; Hon. Dr. Laws (Univ. of SC) 1983, (Harvard Univ.) 1986; Dr. hc (Buckingham) 1989; Hon. DLit (Reading) 1989; Hon. DSc (Cranfield) 1983; Hon. LLD (Nottingham) 1993, (Birmingham) 1993; Chancellor, Order of St Michael and St George 1984–94; Order of the Garter 1994–; Grand Officier, Légion d'honneur; Presidential Medal of Freedom 1988, Four Freedoms Award 1992, Freedom from Fear Award (Franklin Delano Inst.) 1992. *Publication:* Reflect on Things Past: The Memoirs of Lord Carrington 1988. *Address:* House of Lords, London, SW1; 32A Ovington Square, London, SW3 1LR; Manor House, Bledlow, Princes Risborough, Bucks., HP27 9PB, England. *Telephone:* (20) 7584-1476 (London); (1844) 343499 (Bucks.). *Fax:* (20) 7823-9051 (London).

CARRIO, Elisa Maria Avelina ('Lilita'); Argentine politician; b. 1956; four c.; ed Universidad Nacional del Nordeste; fmr Prof. of Law, Chaco; mem. Constitutional Convention 1994; mem. Chamber of Deputies for Prov. of Chaco 1995–; Founder and Pres. Alternative for a Republic of Equals (ARI) party; mem. Comm. of Asuntos Constitutionales, Pres. 2000–01; mem. Comm. of Juicio Político; mem. Women's Leadership Conf. of the Americas (WLCA), Soc. for Int. Devt Emerging Leaders of the Western Hemisphere Conf., Argentinian Asscn of Constitutional Law, Argentinian Soc. of Philosophy, Argentine Soc. of Political Science; Corresp. mem. Inst. of Parl. Law; Premio Parlamentario 1996, 1997, 1998; Dipl. Al mérito 'Konex' 1998, 'Actitud de Vida' Award, Constitutional Convention Gold Medal; Día Internacional de la Mujer Award, NEXO Award 1998. *Publications include:* Interpretando la Constitución, Acerca de la praxis interpretativa Constitucional, Recurso de Inconstitucionalidad Local (jtly); more than 50 articles on law, sociology and political science. *Address:* c/o Alternativa por una República de Iguales (ARI), Buenos Aires, Argentina (Office). *Telephone:* 6310-7100 (Office). *E-mail:* ecarrio@diputados.gov.ar (Office).

CARRON, René Joseph; French banking executive; b. 13 June 1942, Yenne, Savoie; s. of Albert Carron and Claudine Philippe Carron (née Genoud); m. Françoise Dupasquier 1963; three s. one d.; fmr dairy farmer in Yenne; Pres. Yenne br. Crédit Agricole 1981–, Pres. regional br. in Savoie 1992, all Savoie 1994, mem. Bureau 1995–, Pres. Fédération nationale du crédit agricole (FNCA) 2000–, Dir. 1999–, Vice-Pres. Caisse nationale de crédit agricole (CNCA, renamed Crédit agricole S.A. 2000) 2000–, mem. Supervisory Council, Crédit agricole indosuez 2000–, Chair. CNCA Dec. 2002–; Chair. SAS La Boétie 2001–; Pres. Savoie Chamber of Agric. 1983–92, Savoie 92 (asscn to promote Winter Olympics in Albertville 1992) 1988–92, Mission prospective du département de la Savoie 1988–98, Groupe d'étude et de mobilisation Espaces ruraux 1991, Steering Cttee for Savoie Strategic Plan Year 2000 1991–98; Counsellor Banque de France de la Savoie 1991– (mem. 1992–, mem. Perm. Comm. 1992–); Vice-Pres. Conseil géneral of Savoie 1995–98; Mayor of Yenne 1995–; mem. Econ. and Social Council 2000–, Man. Bd. Groupement Européen des Banques Coopératives; Dir. Société de banque de financement pour le commerce (Sofinco); Chevalier, Légion d'honneur, Chevalier, Ordre nat. du Mérite, Officier du Mérite agricole. *Address:* Crédit Agricole (CNCA), SA, 91–93 blvd Pasteur, 75015 Paris, France (Office). *Telephone:* 1-43-23-52-02 (Office). *Fax:* 1-43-23-20-28 (Office). *Website:* www.credit-agricole.fr (Office).

CARSBERG, Sir Bryan (Victor), Kt, MSc, MA; British public servant and university professor; b. 3 Jan. 1939, London; s. of Alfred Victor and Maryllia Ciceley Carsberg (née Collins); m. Margaret Linda Graham 1960; two d.; ed London School of Econs; sole practice CA 1962–64; Lecturer in Accounting, LSE 1964–68, Arthur Andersen Prof. of Accounting 1981–87, Visiting Prof. 1987–89; Visiting Lecturer, Grad. School of Business, Univ. of Chicago 1968–69; Prof. of Accounting, Univ. of Manchester 1969–78; Visiting Prof. of Business Admin. Univ. of Calif., Berkeley 1974; Asst Dir Research and Tech. Activities, US Financial Accounting Standards Bd 1978–81; Dir of Research, Inst. of W. B. Peat Medal and Prize (Inst. of Chartered Accountants, England in England and Wales 1981–87; Dir-Gen. of Telecommunications, Oftel 1984–92; mem. Accounting Standards Bd 1990–94 (Vice-Chair. 1990–92); Dir-Gen. of Fair Trading 1992–95; Sec. Gen. Int. Accounting Standards Cttee (IASC) 1995–2001; Dir Nynex Cable Comms. 1996–97, Cable & Wireless Communications 1997–2000; Chair. MLL Telecoms Ltd 1999–; Chair. Pensions Compensation Bd 2001–; mem. Bd Radio Communications Agency 1990–92; mem. Council Univ. of Surrey 1990–92, Loughborough Univ. 1999– (Chair. 2001–); Hon. Fellow, LSE; Hon. DSc (East Anglia) 1992; Hon. DLitt (Loughborough) 1994; Hon. DUniv. (Essex) 1995; Hon. LLD (Bath) 1990; Inst. Medal, W. B. Peat Medal and Prize (Inst. of Chartered Accountants, England); Chartered Accountants Founding Socs Centenary Award 1988, Blaew Prize for Telecommunications 1992. *Publications:* An Introduction to Mathematical Programming for Accountants 1969, Analysis for Investment Decisions 1974, Economics of Business Decisions 1975 and others. *Leisure interests:* running, theatre, music, opera. *Address:* c/o International Accounting Standards Committee, 166 Fleet Street, London EC4A 2DY, England.

CARSON, Anne, MA, PhD; Canadian professor of classics, poet and writer; b. 21 June 1950, Toronto; ed Univ. of Toronto; Prof. of Classics, Univ. of Calgary 1979–80, Princeton Univ. 1980–87, Emory Univ. 1987–88; John MacNaughton Prof. of Classics, McGill Univ. 1988–, Dir of Grad. Studies, Classics; Guggenheim Fellowship 1999; John D. and Catherine T. MacArthur Foundation Fellowship 2001; Lannan Literary Award 1996, Pushcart Prize for Poetry 1997. *Publications include:* Eros the Bittersweet: An Essay 1986, Short Talks 1992, Plainwater 1995, Glass, Irony and God 1995, Autobiography of Red 1998, Economy of the Unlost 1999, Men in the Off Hours (Griffin Poetry Prize 2001) 2000, The Beauty of the Husband (Poetry Book Soc. T. S. Eliot Prize 2001—first female winner) 2001, Sophocles Electra 2001; contribs. to anthologies and journals. *Address:* Department of Classics, Room 823, Stephen Leacock Building, 855 Sherbrooke Street West, Montréal, QC H3A 2T7 (Office); 5900 Esplanade Avenue, Montréal, QC H2T 3A3, Canada (Home). *E-mail:* decreation@hotmail.com (Office).

CARSON, Hampton L(awrence), AB, PhD; American professor of genetics; b. 5 Nov. 1914, Philadelphia, Pa; s. of Joseph and Edith Bruen Carson; m. Meredith Shelton 1937; two s.; Instructor in Zoology, Pa 1938–42, Washington (St Louis) 1943–46, Asst Prof. 1946–49, Assoc. Prof. 1949–55, Prof. 1956–71; Prof. of Genetics, Univ. of Hawaii 1971–85, Prof. Emer. 1985–, Geneticist, Dept of Entomology 1967–68; Visiting Prof. of Biology, Univ. of São Paulo 1951, 1977; Fulbright Research Scholar Dept of Zoology, Univ. of Melbourne 1961; mem. American Acad. of Arts and Sciences, American Soc. of Naturalists (Pres. 1973), Genetics Soc. of America (Pres. 1982), Hawaiian Acad. of Sciences (Pres. 1975), NAS, Soc. for the Study of Evolution (Pres. 1971); Hon. Assoc. in Entomology and Trustee B. P. Bishop Museum 1982–88; Medal for Excellence in Research, Univ. of Hawaii 1979, Leidy Medal, Acad. of Natural Sciences, Philadelphia 1985, Charles Reed Bishop Medal, Bishop Museum, Honolulu, Hawaii 1992, George Gaylord Simpson Award (Soc. for Study of Evolution) 1996. *Publications:* Heredity and Human Life and over 290 scientific articles. *Leisure interest:* bonsai training. *Address:* Department of Cell and Molecular Biology, John A. Burns School of Medicine, 1960 East-West Road, University of Hawaii, Honolulu, HI 96822 (Office); 1314 Kalakaua Ave., Apt. 1111 Honolulu, HI 96826, USA (Home). *Telephone:* (808) 956-7662 (Office); (808) 983-4522 (Home). *Fax:* (808) 956-5506 (Office); (808) 983-4495 (Home). *E-mail:* hampton@hawaii.edu .

CARSON, Johnny; American television personality; b. 23 Oct. 1925, Corning, Ia; s. of Homer Carson and Ruth (née Hook) Carson; m. 1st Jody Wolcott 1948 (divorced 1963); three c.; m. 2nd Joanne Copeland 1963 (divorced); m. 3rd Joanna Holland 1972 (divorced 1983); m. 4th Alexis Maas 1987; ed Univ. of Nebraska; announcer, radio station KFAB, Lincoln, Neb. 1948, then radio WOW and WOW-TV, Omaha, Neb., station KNXT, Los Angeles, Calif. 1950; TV show Carson's Cellar 1951; writer for comedian Red Skelton; introduced TV quiz show Earn Your Vacation 1954; The Johnny Carson Show, CBS 1955; introduced TV quiz show Who Do You Trust?, ABC-TV 1958–63; host Tonight programme, NBC-TV 1962–92; numerous other TV appearances; performer Las Vegas 1954–; Presidential Medal of Freedom 1992; Entertainer of Year Award, American Guild of Variety Artists, Kennedy Center Honor for Lifetime Achievement 1993. *Publication:* Happiness is a Dry Martini 1965. *Address:* c/o NBC, 6962 Wildlife Road, Malibu, CA 90265-4309, USA.

CARSON, William Hunter, OBE; British jockey and thoroughbred-horse breeder; b. 16 Nov. 1942, Stirling, Scotland; s. of Thomas Whelan and Mary Hay (Hunter) Carson; m. 1st Carole Jane Sutton 1962 (dissolved 1979); three s.; m. 2nd Elaine Williams 1982; ed Riverside School, Stirling, Scotland; apprentice with Capt. Gerald Armstrong 1957–62; rode first winner Pinker's Pond at Catterick 1962; first jockey to Lord Derby 1968, to Bernard van Cutsem 1971–75, to Maj. Dick Hern 1977–89, to HM The Queen 1977; champion jockey 1972, 1973, 1978, 1980, 1983; rode the winners of 18 English Classics, 8 Irish Classics and 68 English Group One races; rode 6 winners at one meeting July 1990; best horses ridden Nashwan and Dayjur; bred and rode St Leger winner Minster Son 1988; 3,828 career winners in U.K. (1997); retd 1997 as 4th-most successful ever UK jockey; racing pundit BBC 1997–; racing man. for Thoroughbred Corpn 1997–; owner Minster Stud; Dir Swindon Town Football Club 1997–98, Head of Public Relations 1997–, Chair. 2001–; Dr. hc (Stirling). *Publication:* Willie Carson Up Front: A Racing Autobiography 1993. *Leisure interests:* golf, football. *Address:* Minster House, Barnsley, Cirencester, Glos., GL7 5DZ, England. *Telephone:* (1285) 658919. *Fax:* (1285) 885355. *Website:* williecarson.com.

CARSWELL, Rt. Hon. Sir Robert Douglas, Kt, PC; British judge; b. 28 June 1934, Belfast; s. of Alan E Carswell and Nance E Carswell; m. Romayne Winifred Ferris 1961; two d.; ed Royal Belfast Academical Inst., Pembroke Coll. Oxford, Univ. of Chicago Law School; called to the Bar, Northern Ireland

1957, to English Bar, Gray's Inn 1972; Counsel to Attorney-Gen. for Northern Ireland 1970–71; QC 1971; Sr Crown Counsel for Northern Ireland 1979–84; Judge High Court of Justice in Northern Ireland 1984–93; Lord Justice of Appeal, Supreme Court of Judicature 1993–97; Lord Chief Justice of Northern Ireland 1997–; Chancellor, Dioceses of Armagh and of Down and Dromore 1990–97; Chair. Council of Law Reporting for Northern Ireland 1987–97, Law Reform Advisory Cttee for Northern Ireland 1989–97, Distinction and Meritorious Service Awards Cttee, DHSS 1995–97; Pres. Northern Ireland Scout Council 1993–; Pro-Chancellor, Chair. Council, Univ. of Ulster 1984–94; Hon. D. Litt. (Ulster) 1994. *Publications:* Trustee Acts (Northern Ireland) 1964; articles in legal periodicals. *Leisure interests:* golf, hillwalking, music, architecture, antiques and conservation, wildlife. *Address:* Royal Courts of Justice, Belfast BT1 3JF, Northern Ireland (Office). *Telephone:* (28) 9072-4603. *Fax:* (28) 9023 6838.

CARTAN, Henri Paul, D. ÈS SC.; French mathematician; b. 8 July 1904, Nancy; s. of Elie Cartan; m. Nicole Weiss 1935; two s. three d.; ed Lycée Buffon, Lycée Hoche (Versailles) and Ecole Normale Supérieure; teacher, Lycée, Caen 1928; Lecturer, Faculty of Science, Lille Univ. 1929–31; Prof. Faculty of Science, Strasbourg Univ. 1931–40, Univ. of Paris 1940–69, Univ. de Paris-Sud (Orsay) 1969–75; Pres. French Section, European Asscn of Teachers 1957–75; Pres. Int. Mathematical Union 1967–70; Pres. Mouvement Fédéraliste Européen (France) 1974–85; mem. Royal Acad., Denmark 1962; Corresp. Acad. des Sciences 1965, mem. 1974–; Foreign mem. Royal Soc. 1971; Foreign Hon. mem. American Acad. 1950, Foreign Assoc. Nat. Acad. of Sciences, Washington 1972, Acad. Royale Belgique 1978; Corresp. Akad. der Wissenschaften Göttingen 1971, Royal Acad. of Sciences, Madrid 1971, Bayerische Akad. der Wissenschaften 1974; hon. mem. Japan Acad. 1979; fmr mem. Acad. Finland 1979; Foreign mem. Royal Swedish Acad. of Sciences 1981, Polish Acad. 1985, Russian Acad. 1999; Hon. DSc (ETH, Zurich) 1955, (Münster) 1952, (Oslo) 1961, (Sussex) 1969, (Cambridge) 1969, (Stockholm) 1978, (Oxford) 1980, (Zaragoza) 1985, (Athens) 1992; Wolf Prize in Math. 1980; Commdr Légion d'honneur 1989. *Address:* 95 boulevard Jourdan, 75014 Paris, France; Institute de France, 23 quai de Conti, 75006 Paris (Office). *Telephone:* 1-45-40-51-78.

CARTELLIERI, Ulrich; German banker; b. 21 Sept. 1937; mem. Bd Deutsche Bank AG, Frankfurt; Chair. Deutsche Bank (Asia Credit) Ltd, Singapore, DB Finance (Hong Kong) Ltd, Hong Kong; Chair. Supervisory Bd European Asian Bank AG, Hamburg, Karstadt AG 1990–98; mem. Supervisory Bd Deutsche Solvay-Werke GmbH, Solingen, Deutsche Telephonwerke und Kabelindustrie AG, Berlin, Euro-Pacific Finance Corpn Ltd, Melbourne, Girmes-Werke AG, Grefrath-Oedt, Th. Goldschmidt AG, Essen, Wilhelm Karmann GmbH, Osnabrück, Thyssen Edelstahlwerke AG, Düsseldorf, G. M. Pfaff AG, Kaiserslautern. *Address:* Taunusanlage 12, 60325 Frankfurt am Main, Germany.

CARTER, Brandon, DSc, FRS; British theoretical physicist; b. 26 May 1942, Sydney, Australia; s. of Harold B. Carter and Mary Brandon-Jones; m. Lucette Defrise 1969; three d.; ed George Watson's Coll., Edinburgh, Univ. of St Andrews, Univ. of Cambridge (Pembroke Coll.); Research Fellow, Pembroke Coll., Univ. of Cambridge 1967–72; staff mem., Inst. of Astronomy, Cambridge 1968–72; Asst Lecturer, Dept of Applied Math. and Theoretical Physics, Univ. of Cambridge 1973; lecturer 1974; Maître de Recherche, Centre Nat. de la Recherche Scientifique, Paris 1975–85, Directeur-Adjoint, Group d'Astrophysique Relativiste, Observatoire de Paris-Meudon 1975–82, Directeur 1983–86; apptd. Dir of Research Centre Nat. de la Recherche Scientifique 1986. *Publications:* Global Structure of the Kerr Family of Gravitational Fields 1968, Black Hole Equilibrium States 1973, Large Number Coincidences and the Anthropic Principle in Cosmology 1974, The General Theory of the Mechanical Electromagnetic and Thermodynamic Properties of Black Holes 1979, The Anthropic Principle and its Implications for Biological Evolution 1983, Covariant Mechanics of Simple and Conducting Strings and Membranes 1990. *Address:* L.U.T.H., Observatoire de Paris-Meudon, 92190 Meudon (Office); 19 rue de la Borne au Diable, 92310 Sèvres, France (Home). *Website:* www.luth.obspm.fr (Office).

CARTER, (Edward) Graydon; American magazine editor; b. 14 July 1949; s. of E P. Carter and Margaret Ellen Carter; m. Cynthia Williamson 1982; three s. one d.; ed Carleton Univ., Univ. of Ottawa; Ed. The Canadian Review 1973–77; writer Time 1978–83, Life 1983–86; founder, Ed. Spy 1986–91; Ed. New York Observer 1991–92; Ed.-in-Chief Vanity Fair 1992–; Hon. Ed. Harvard Lampoon 1989. *Leisure interest:* fly fishing. *Address:* Vanity Fair, Condé Nast Building, 4 Times Square, New York, NY 10036-6522, USA.

CARTER, Elliott, Jr., AB, AM; American composer; b. 11 Dec. 1908, New York; s. of Elliott and Florence (née Chambers) Carter; m. Helen Frost-Jones 1939; one s.; ed Harvard Univ., Ecole Normale de Musique, Paris; Musical Dir Ballet Caravan 1937–39; critic Modern Music 1937–42; tutor St John's Coll., Annapolis 1939–41; teacher of composition Peabody Conservatory 1946–48, Columbia Univ. 1948–50, Queen's Coll. (NY) 1955–56; Prof. of Music, Yale Univ. 1960–61; Prof. Dept of Composition, Juilliard School, New York 1966–82; Andrew White Prof.-at-Large, Cornell Univ. 1967; mem. Bd of Trustees, American Acad., Rome; mem. Int. Soc. for Contemporary Music, Dir 1946–52, Pres. American Section 1952, Nat. Inst. of Arts and Letters; mem. American Acad. of Arts and Sciences; Hon. degrees Swarthmore Coll. and Princeton Univ. 1969, Univs. of Harvard, Yale and Boston 1970, Univ. of Cambridge 1983; American Composers' Alliance Prize (for Quartet for Four

Saxophones) 1943, First Prize Liège Int. Music Competition 1953, Prix de Rome 1953, Pulitzer Prize (for Second String Quartet), Sibelius Medal (Harriet Cohen Foundation) 1960, New York Critics Circle Award (for Double Concerto) 1961, Pulitzer Prize (for Third String Quartet) 1973; Ernst Von Siemens Prize, Munich 1981; Gold Medal, Nat. Inst. of Arts and Letters 1971, Handel Medallion of New York 1978, awarded Nat. Medal of Art by Pres. Reagan 1985, Commdr des Arts et des Lettres, Gold Medal, Royal Philharmonic Soc. 1996. *Works include:* Orchestral: Symphony No. 1 1942, Variations for Orchestra 1955, Double Concerto 1961, Piano Concerto 1965, Concerto for Orchestra 1969, Symphony of Three Orchestras 1977, Oboe Concerto 1987, 3 Occasions for Orchestra 1989, Violin Concerto 1990, Clarinet Concerto 1996, Symphonia 1998, Asko Concerto 2000, Cello Concerto 2001, Boston Concerto 2002; Chamber: Elegy 1943, Sonata for Cello and Piano, Woodwind Quintet 1948, Sonata for Flute, Oboe, Cello and Harpsichord 1952, Brass Quintet 1974, five String Quartets 1951–93, Triple Duo 1982, Penthode 1985, Oboe Quartet for Heinz Holliger 2001; Vocal: A Mirror on Which to Dwell 1975, In Sleep In Thunder 1983, Of Rewaking 2002; Choral: The Defense of Corinth 1949; Instrumental: Piano Sonata 1946, Night fantasies (piano) 1980, A Six-letter Letter (for English Horn); Stage Works: Pocahontas 1939, The Minotaur 1947, What Next? (opera) 1999 and numerous others. *Leisure interests:* literature, art. *Address:* Boosey & Hawkes Inc., 35 East 21st Street, New York, NY 10010, USA.

CARTER, Jimmy (James Earl, Jr.), BSc; American politician and farmer; b. 1 Oct. 1924, Plains, Ga; s. of the late James Earl Carter Sr and Lillian Gordy; m. Eleanor Rosalynn Smith 1946; three s. one d.; ed Plains High School, Georgia Southwestern Coll., Georgia Inst. of Tech., US Naval Acad., Annapolis, Md, Union Coll., New York State; served U.S. Navy 1946–53, attained rank of Lt (submarine service); peanut farmer, warehouseman 1953–77, businesses Carter Farms, Carter Warehouses, Ga; State Senator, Ga 1962–66; Gov. of Georgia 1971–74; Pres. of USA 1977–81; Distinguished Prof., Emory Univ., Atlanta 1982–; leader int. observer teams Panama 1989, Nicaragua 1990, Dominican Repub. 1990, Haiti 1990; host peace negotiations Ethiopia 1989; visit to Democratic People's Repub. of Korea (in pvt. capacity) June 1994; negotiator in Haitian crisis Sept. 1994; visit to Bosnia Dec. 1994; f. Carter Presidential Center 1982; Chair. Bd of Trustees, Carter Center Inc. 1986–, Carter-Menil Human Rights Foundation 1986–, Global 2000 Inc. 1986–, Council of Freely Elected Heads of Govt 1986–, Council of Int. Negotiation Network 1991–; mem. Sumter County, Ga, School Bd 1955–62 (Chair. 1960–62), Americus and Sumter County Hospital Authority 1956–70, Sumter County Library Bd 1961; Pres. Plains Devt Corpn 1963; Georgia Planning Asscn 1968; Dir Ga Crop Improvement Asscn 1957–63 (Pres. 1961); Chair. West Cen. Ga Area Planning and Devt Comm. 1964; State Chair. March of Dimes 1968–70; District Gov. Lions Club 1968–69; Chair. Congressional Campaign Cttee, Democratic Nat. Cttee 1974; Democrat; several hon. degrees; Ansel Adams Conservation Award, Wilderness Society 1982, World Methodist Peace Award 1984, Albert Schweitzer Prize for Humanitarianism 1987, Onassis Foundation Award 1991, Notre Dame Univ. Award 1992, Matsunaga Medal of Peace 1993, J. William Fulbright Prize for Int. Understanding 1994, shared Houphouët Boigny Peace Prize, UNESCO 1995, UNICEF Int. Child Survival Award (jtly with Rosalynn Carter) 1999, Presidential Medal of Freedom 1999, Eisenhower Medallion 2000, Nobel Peace Prize 2002. *Publications:* Why Not the Best? 1975, A Government as Good as Its People 1977, Keeping Faith: Memoirs of a President 1982, The Blood of Abraham: Insights into the Middle East 1985, Everything to Gain: Making the Most of the Rest of Your Life 1987, An Outdoor Journal 1988, Turning Point: A Candidate, a State and a Nation Come of Age 1992, Always a Reckoning (poems) 1995, Sources of Strength 1997, The Virtues of Ageing 1998, An Hour Before Daylight 2001. *Leisure interests:* reading, tennis. *Address:* The Carter Center, 453 Freedom Parkway, 1 Copenhill Avenue, NE Atlanta, GA 30307, USA. *Telephone:* (404) 331-3900 (Office).

CARTER-RUCK, Peter Frederick; British solicitor and commissioner for oaths; b. 26 Feb. 1914, Hove, Sussex; s. of Frederick Henry Carter-Ruck and Nell Mabel Carter-Ruck (née Allen); m. Pamela Ann Maxwell 1940; one s. (deceased) one d.; ed St Edward's School, Oxford; qualified as solicitor of the Supreme Court of Judicature (England) 1937; served with RA 1939–44; Sr Partner Oswald Hickson Collier & Co. 1945–81, Peter Carter-Ruck and Partners 1981–98, Media and Trust Consultant 2000–; Specialist mem. Council of Law Soc. 1971–84, Chair. Law Society Law Reform Cttee 1980–83, mem. Intellectual Property Cttee; Pres. City of Westminister Law Soc. 1976; Chair. Media Cttee, Int. Bar Asscn 1983–85; mem. Council of Justice 1968–, Council of NSPCC; Hon. Consulting Solicitor and Life Mem. Chartered Inst. of Journalists; mem. and Past Pres. Council, Media Soc.; Gov. St Edward's School, Oxford 1950–78; Past Chair. and Founder Gov. Shiplake Coll., Henley; Fellow Soc. for Advanced Legal Studies; mem. Livery, City of London Solicitors' Co. 1949–; media and trust consultant Pellys 1999–. *Publications:* Libel and Slander 1953, 1997, The Cyclist and the Law (with Ian Mackrill) 1953, Copyright: Modern Law and Practice (with Edmund Skone James) 1965, Memoirs of a Libel Lawyer (autobiog.) 1990. *Leisure interests:* writing, cinematography, wood-turning, ocean racing and cruising. *Address:* 8 Carlton Mansions, York Buildings, London, WC2N 6LS (Office); Latchmore, Great Hallingbury, Bishop's Stortford, Herts., CM22 7PE, England (Home); Eilagadale, N Ardnamurchan, Argyll, PH36 4LG, Scotland (Home); 8 Carlton Mansions, York Buildings, London, WC2N 6LS, England (Home). *Telephone:* (20) 7839-7515 (Office); (1279) 654357 (Bishop's Stortford) (Home); (1972)

510267 (N Ardnamurchan) (Home). *Fax:* (1279) 504921 (Home); (1279) 504921 (Bishop's Stortford). *E-mail:* peter-carter-ruck@dial.pipex.com (Office); peter-carter-ruck@dial.pipex.com (Home).

CARTIER, Jean-Albert; French theatre director; b. 15 May 1930, Marseille; s. of Albert Cartier and Myriem Bordes; m. Solange Ottavy 1959; two d.; ed Lycée Perrier, Marseilles and Ecole du Louvre; art critic, Combat and numerous reviews; artistic collaborator, France-Inter; arranged several exhbns for Marseille Museum; participated Paris Biennale 1959, 1961, 1963, 1965; founder and Dir Asscn technique pour l'action culturelle 1966–72; creator, Ballet-Théâtre contemporain, Centre choréographique nat. 1968–72; Dir Centre choréographique et lyrique nat. 1972; Dir Angers Mun. Theatre 1972–78; founder and Dir Anjou Arts Festival 1975–77; creator and Dir Ballet-Théâtre français de Nancy 1978–87; Dir-Gen. Grand Théâtre de Nancy 1979–81; Dir Théâtre Musical, Paris-Châtelet 1980–88; Dir Festival of Paris 1988, 1989, 1991; Dir Théâtre Nat. de l'Opéra de Paris 1988, Gen. Man. 1989–91; Dir of Music, Radio France 1991–94; Dir-Gen. L'Opéra de Nice 1994–97; Creator and Dir Europa Danse 1999–2003; Chevalier des Arts et des Lettres, Officier Ordre nat. du Mérite, Chevalier Légion d'honneur. *Publication:* L'oeuvre du peintre POUGNY (2 vols). *Address:* 8 rue Vernier, 06000 Nice; 18 rue de l'Hotel de Ville, 75004 Paris; 24 rue Saint-Pave, 75004 Paris, France. *Telephone:* 1-42-77-31-34; 1-44-54-06-48. *Fax:* 1-42-77-32-34.

CARTIER-BRESSON, Henri; French photographer; b. 22 Aug. 1908, Chanteloup; s. of André and Marthe Cartier-Bresson (née Leverdier); m. 2nd Martine Franck 1970; ed Ecole Fénelon and Lycée Condorcet, Paris; studied painting in André Lhote's studio; took up photography 1931; Asst Dir to Jean Renoir 1936, 1939; prisoner of war 1940–43, escaped; f. Magnum-Photos with Capa, Chim and Rodger 1947; exhbns Madrid, New York 1933, New York Museum of Modern Art 1947, 1968, The Louvre (Pavillon de Marsan), Paris 1954, Phillips Collection, Washington 1964, Tokyo 1965, Victoria and Albert Museum, London 1969, Grand Palais, Paris 1970, Palais de Tokyo, Paris 1985, Maison Européenne de la Photographie, Paris 1998, Nat. Portrait Gallery, London 1998, Tokyo 1999; drawing exhbns. New York, Zürich 1975, Musée d'art moderne, Paris, Museo de arte moderno, Mexico 1982; drawings, photographs and paintings exhbns. French Inst., Stockholm, Padiglione d'Arte Contemporanea, Milan, Univ. of Rome 1983, Museum of Modern Art, Oxford 1984, Palais Liechtenstein, Vienna, Salzburg 1986, Kunstverein Mannheim 1986, Museum of Modern Art, New York 1988, Printemps, Tokyo 1991, Museum of Modern Art, Taipei 1991, Parma 1992, Saragossa 1993, Minneapolis Art Inst. 1996, European Museum of Photography 1997, Musée d'art moderne, Montreal 1997, Royal Coll. of Art, London 1998, Kunsthaus, Zurich; collection of 390 photographs at Menil Foundation, Houston, USA, Victoria and Albert Museum, London, Univ. of Fine Arts, Osaka, Japan and Bibliothèque Nationale, Paris, exhibited Edin. Festival, Hayward Gallery, London 1978; made various documentary films; CD recording Le Bon Plaisir d'HCB (interviews by Vera Feyder) 1991; mem. American Acad. of Arts and Science 1974; DLit hc, Oxford Univ. 1975, Grand Prix national 1981; Hasselbladt Award 1983; Overseas Press Club awards, Prize Novocento Palermo 1986; Commdr des Arts et des Lettres. *Publications:* Images à la sauvette (U.S. edition The Decisive Moment), The Europeans, From One China to the Other, The People of Moscow, Danses à Bali, The World of Henri Cartier-Bresson 1968, L'homme et la machine 1968, Vive la France 1970, Cartier-Bresson's France 1971, Faces of Asia 1972, About Russia 1974, Henri Cartier-Bresson, Photographer 1979, Photoportraits 1983, America in Passing 1991, Carnets mexicains (preface by Carlos Fuentes) 1996, L'Imaginaire d'après nature, Des européens (preface by Jean Clair) 1997, Tête-à-tête (preface by E H. Gombrich 1998, Landscape (preface by Gerard Mace and Erik Orsenna) 1999, Vers un autre futur, un regard libertaire 2000, Paysages 2001. *Address:* c/o Magnum-Photos, 19 rue Hégésippe Moreau, 75018 Paris, France (Home).

CARTLEDGE, Sir Bryan George, KCMG; British retd diplomatist and college principal; b. 10 June 1931; s. of Eric Cartledge and Phyllis Shaw; m. 1st Ruth Hylton Gass 1960 (dissolved), one s. one d.; m. 2nd Freda Gladys Newcombe 1994 (died 2001); ed Hurstpierpoint and St John's Coll., Cambridge; served Queen's Royal Regt 1950–51; Commonwealth Fund Fellow, Stanford Univ., Calif. 1956–57; Research Fellow, St Antony's Coll., Oxford 1958–59; joined Foreign Service 1960, served Foreign Office 1960–61, British Embassy, Stockholm 1961–63, Moscow 1963–66, Diplomatic Service Admin. Office 1966–68, Tehran 1968–70, Harvard Univ. 1971–72, Counsellor, Moscow 1972–75, Head of E European and Soviet Dept, FCO 1975–77, Pvt. Sec. (Overseas Affairs) to Prime Minister 1977–79, Amb. to Hungary 1980–83, Asst Under Sec. of State, FCO 1983–84, Deputy Sec. of the Cabinet 1984–85, Amb. to USSR 1985–88; Prin. Linacre Coll., Oxford 1988–96; Hon. Fellow, St John's Coll., Cambridge 1985, St Antony's Coll., Oxford 1987, Linacre Coll., Oxford 1996. *Publications:* Monitoring the Environment (Ed.) 1992, Energy and the Environment (Ed.) 1993, Health and the Environment (Ed.) 1994, Population and the Environment (Ed.) 1995, Transport and the Environment (Ed.) 1996, Mind, Brain and Environment (Ed.) 1997. *Address:* 52 Middle Way, Oxford, OX2 7LG, England.

CARTWRIGHT, Nancy Delaney, PhD, FBA; American professor of philosophy; b. 24 June 1944, Pennsylvania; d. of Claudis Delaney and Eva Delaney; m. 1st Bliss Cartwright 1966 (divorced); m. 2nd Ian Hacking 1974 (divorced); m. 3rd Sir Stuart Hampshire 1985; two d.; ed Univs of Pittsburgh and Illinois; Prof. of Philosophy, Stanford Univ. 1983–91; Prof. of Philosophy, Logic and Scientific Method, LSE 1991–; Dir Centre for the Philosophy of the Natural and Social Sciences 1993–; Prof. of Philosophy, Univ. of California at San

Diego 1997–; Macarthur Foundation Award 1993, Leopoldina 1999. *Publications:* How the Laws of Physics Lie 1983, Nature's Capacities and Their Measurement 1989, Otto Neurath: Between Science and Politics (with others) 1994, The Dappled World: A Study of the Boundaries of Science. *Address:* Centre for the Philosophy of Natural and Social Science, London School of Economics, Houghton Street, London, WC2A 2AE, England (Office). *Telephone:* (20) 7955-7573 (Office). *Fax:* (20) 7242-0392 (Office).

CARTWRIGHT, Dame Silvia Rose, DBE, PCNZM; New Zealand Governor-General and judge; b. 7 Nov. 1943; d. of Monteith Poulter and Eileen Jane Poulter; m. Peter John Cartwright 1969; ed Univ. of Otago; partner Harkness Henry & Co. barristers and solicitors, Hamilton 1971–81; Dist Court and Family Court Judge 1981–89, Chief Dist Court Judge 1989–93; Judge High Court of NZ 1993–2001; Gov.-Gen. of NZ 2001–; mem. Comm. for the Future 1975–80, Cttee UN Human Rights Convention to eliminate discrimination against women 1992–2000; Hon. LLD (Otago) 1993, (Waikato) 1994, (Canterbury) 2002. *Address:* Government House, Wellington, New Zealand (Office).

CARTY, Donald J.; Canadian airline executive; m. Ana Carty; ed Queen's Univ., Kingston, Ont., Harvard Grad. School of Business Admin., USA; various man. positions Celanese Canada Ltd, Air Canada, Canadian Pacific Railway, American Airlines Inc., Pres. and CEO CP Air 1985–87; Sr Vice-Pres. (Airline Planning) AMR Corpn 1987–89, Exec. Vice-Pres. (Finance and Planning) AMR Corpn and American Airlines Inc. 1989–95, Pres. AMR Airline Group and American Airlines Inc. 1995–98, Chair., Pres. and CEO AMR Corpn and American Airlines Inc. 1998–2003 (resgnd); mem. Bd Dirs Dell Computer Corpn, Brinker Int., Canada-US Foundation for Educational Exchange; Assoc. mem. Dallas Citizens Council. *Address:* c/o AMR Corporation, Maoi Drop 5624, 4200 Almon Carter Boulevard, Fort Worth, TX 76155, USA.

CARUANA, Peter R., QC; Gibraltarian politician and lawyer; b. 15 Oct. 1956; m.; six c.; ed Christian Brothers School, Grace Dieu Manor, Leicester, Ratcliffe Coll. Leicester, Queen Mary Coll., Univ. of London, Council of Legal Educ., London; joined law firm Triay & Triay, Gibraltar 1979, partner (specializing in commercial and shipping law) 1990–95; joined Gibraltar Social Democrats 1990, Leader Feb. 1991–; elected in Gibraltar's first-ever by-election to House of Ass. May 1991; Leader of Opposition 1992–96; Queen's Counsel for Gibraltar 1998; Chief Minister of Gibraltar 1996–, re-elected 2000; Hon. Fellow Queen Mary Coll., Univ. of London. *Leisure interests:* golf, political and current affairs. *Address:* 6 Convent Place (Office); 10/3 Irish Town, Gibraltar (Home).

CARUANA LACORTE, Jaime; Spanish central bank governor; b. 14 March 1952, Valencia; ed Univ. Complutense Madrid; fmr telecommunications engineer; various posts with Ministry of Trade 1979–84; Commercial attaché to the Spanish Commercial Office, New York 1984–87; Man. Dir and CEO Renta 4, SA, SVB 1987–91, Pres. 1991–96; Gen. Dir of the Treasury and Financial Policy 1996–99; mem. Bd SEPP (State Holding Co.) 1996–99; mem. EU Monetary Cttee 1996–99; Pres. SETE (Euro State Co.) 1997–99; Gen. Dir for Supervision, Banco de España 1999–2000, Gov. 2000–; mem. Governing Council, European Cen. Bank 2000–. *Publications:* numerous articles on the Spanish financial system, the financing of public admins. and the man. of public debt. *Address:* Banco de España, Alcalá 50, 28014 Madrid, Spain (Office). *Telephone:* (91) 3385000 (Office). *Fax:* (91) 5310059 (Office). *Website:* www.bde.es (Office).

CARVALHO, Evaristo de; São Tomé e Príncipe politician; mem. Acção Democrática Independente (ADI); Prime Minister of São Tomé e Príncipe 2001–02. *Address:* Office of the Prime Minister, Rua Município, CP 302, São Tomé, São Tomé e Príncipe (Office). *Telephone:* (12) 23913 (Office). *Fax:* (12) 21670 (Office).

CARVALHO, Mário Costa Martins de; Portuguese writer, lawyer and professor; b. 25 Sept. 1944, Lisbon; s. of Domingos Martins Carvalho and Maria Luísa Costa Carvalho; m. Maria Helena Taborda Duarte 1969; two d.; ed Univ. of Lisbon Law School; involved in student resistance to dictatorship; received conviction for political activities; served with Army; in exile in Paris and Lund, Sweden 1973–74; returned to Portugal after revolution of 1974; involved in politics 1974–77; f. law practice 1981; Prof. of Scriptwriting, Cinema School; mem. Bd Portuguese Asscn of Writers; Prof. of Playwriting Univ. of Lisbon; City of Lisbon Prize, Theatre Prize 1999, several other awards and prizes. *Plays include:* 'Se perguntarem Por Mim, Não Estou', a Rapariga de Varsóvia. *Film:* F.F. Preto e Branco. *Publications:* Contos da Sétima Esfera 1981, O Livro Grande de Terras, Navio e Mariana 1982, A Paixão do Conde de Fróis 1986, Os Alferes 1989, Um Deus Passeando Pela Brisa da Tarde 1995, Era Bom que Trocassemos umas Ideias sobre o Assunto 1995. *Address:* Av. Eng Arantes e Oliveira 6-8° C, 1900 Lisbon; R. António Pereira Carrilho 27 R/C, 1000-046 Lisbon, Portugal. *Telephone:* (21) 8491042 (Av. Eng Arantes e Oliveira); (21) 8460576 (R. António Pereira Carrilho). *Fax:* (21) 8464227 (R. António Pereira Carrilho).

CARVER, John Henry, AM, PhD, FAA, FTS, FAIP; Australian physicist; b. 5 Sept. 1926, Sydney; s. of the late J. F. Carver; m. Mary Fielding 1955; two s. two d.; ed Fort St Boys' High School, Sydney, Univs. of Sydney and Cambridge, UK; Cavendish Lab., Cambridge, UK 1949–53; Research School of Physical Sciences, Australian Nat. Univ. 1953–61; Atomic Energy Research Establishment, Harwell, UK 1958–59; Elder Prof. of Physics, Univ. of Adelaide 1961–78, Emer. Prof. 1979–; Naval Research Lab., Washington, DC, USA

1968–69; Dir and Prof. of Physics, Research School of Physical Sciences and Eng, Australian Nat. Univ. 1978–92, Emer. Prof. 1993–, Deputy Vice-Chancellor and Dir Inst. of Advanced Studies 1993–94; Visiting Fellow Research School of Physical Sciences and Eng Australian Nat. Univ. 1994–; mem. Radio Research Bd of Australia 1964–82, Australian Science and Tech. Council 1979–86, Anglo-Australian Telescope Bd 1978–89, Australian Space Bd 1986–92; Chair. UN Scientific and Tech. Sub-Cttee on the Peaceful Uses of Outer Space 1970–95; mem. Int. Acad. of Astronautics. *Publications:* numerous articles on nuclear, atomic, molecular, atmospheric and space physics in scientific journals. *Address:* Research School of Physical Sciences and Engineering, Australian National University, Canberra, ACT 0200 (Office); 8 Holmes Crescent, Campbell, ACT 2612, Australia (Home). *Telephone:* (2) 6249-3567 (Office); (2) 6249-8732 (Home). *Fax:* (2) 6249-0390. *E-mail:* jhc121@rsphy1.anu.edu.au (Office).

CARVILLE, James; American political strategist and author; b. 25 Oct. 1944, Fort Benning, Georgia; s. of Lucille Carville; m. Mary Matalin 1993; ed Louisiana State Univ.; litigator Baton Rouge 1973–79; managed first campaign for Senate 1982; managed campaign for Gov. of Texas 1983; co.-f. Carville and Begala (political consulting co.) 1989; co-managed Clinton Presidential Campaign 1992, later Sr political adviser to Pres.; numerous int. political clients 1993–; Campaign Man. of the Year 1993. *Publications:* All's Fair: Love, War and Running for President (with Mary Matalin), We're Right, They're Wrong (with Mary Matalin), And The Horse He Rode In On – The People v. Ken Starr (with Mary Matalin), Stickin': The Case for Loyalty. *Website:* www.jamescarvillesoffice.com.

CASA-DEBELJEVIC, Lisa Della (Della Casa); Swiss singer; b. 2 Feb. 1919; ed Berne Conservatoire; début at Zürich Opera House 1943; mem. Vienna State Opera Co. 1947–, New York Metropolitan Opera Co. 1953–; has appeared at Festivals at Salzburg 1947, 1948, 1950, 1953–58, Glyndebourne 1951, Bayreuth, Edin. 1952, Zürich, Lucerne, Munich 1951–58; has also appeared in London, Berlin, Paris, Milan, San Francisco and in South America, etc.; apptd. Austrian State Kammersängerin. *Address:* Schloss Gottlieben, Thurgau, Switzerland.

CASADESUS, Jean Claude (pseudonym of Probst); French conductor; b. 7 Dec. 1935, Paris; s. of Lucien Probst and Gisèle Casadesus; m. Anne Sevestre; two s. one d.; ed Paris Nat. Conservatoire and Ecole Normale, Paris; solo timpanist, Concert Colonne 1959–68; percussion soloist, Domaine Musical (with Boulez); Conductor, Paris Opéra 1969–71; Co-Dir Orchestre Pays de Loire 1971–76; Founder and Dir Lille Nat. Orchestra 1976–; appears as guest conductor with leading orchestras in UK, USA, France, Germany, Norway, Russia, Czech Repub., int. music festivals etc.; Gen. Sec. Conseil Supérieur de la Musique; Pres. Musique Nouvelle en Liberté; Grand Prix de la SACEM and several other prizes and awards for recordings; Commdr Légion d'honneur, Commdr Ordre nat. du Mérite, Commdr des Arts et des Lettres, Chevalier Ordre des Palmes académiques, Commdr Order of Orange Nassau (Netherlands), Officer Order of Crown (Belgium). *Recordings include:* works by Dutilleux (1st Symphony), Berlioz, Mahler, Bizet, Stravinsky, Mozart, Beethoven, Ravel, Debussy, Poulenc, Groupe des Six, Prokofiev, Dukas, Massenet, Milhaud, Honneger, Mussorgsky, Franck. *Publications:* Le plus court chemin d'un coeur à un autre 1998, Stock (ed.). *Leisure interests:* yachting, sailing, skiing, tennis. *Address:* Orchestre National de Lille, 30 place Mendès France, B.P. 119, 59027 Lille Cedex (Office); 23 blvd de la Liberté, 59800 Lille, France (Home). *Telephone:* 3-20-12-82-40 (Office). *Fax:* 3-20-40-22-89 (Home); 3-20-78-29-10 (Office). *E-mail:* casajc@wanadoo.fr (Home).

CASANOVA, Jean-Claude, DEcon; French economist; b. 11 June 1934, Ajaccio, Corsica; s. of Jean Casanova and Marie-Antoinette Luciani; m. Marie-Thérèse Demargne 1962; two s.; ed Lycée Carnot, Inst. des hautes études, Tunis, Univ. of Paris, Harvard Univ.; Asst Fondation nat. des sciences politiques 1958; Chief of Staff to Minister of Industry 1958–61; Asst in Law Faculty, Univ. of Dijon 1963; Sr Lecturer then Prof. Faculty of Law and Econ. Sciences, Univ. of Nancy 1964–68; with Univ. of Paris-Nanterre 1968; with Inst. d'études politiques, Paris 1969–; Dir of Studies and Research Fondation nat. des sciences politiques 1965–90; Tech. Adviser to Minister of Educ. 1972–74; Adviser to Prime Minister Raymond Barre 1976–81; Ed. Commentaire 1978–; leader writer L'Express 1985–95; regular contrib. to Le Figaro 1996–; mem. Econ. and Social Council 1994–, Acad. des sciences morales et politiques 1996–. *Address:* Fondation nationale des sciences politiques, 27 rue Saint-Guillaume, 75007 Paris (Office); Commentaire, 116 rue du Bac, 75007 Paris (Office); 87 boulevard Saint-Michel, 75005 Paris, France (Home).

CASAS-GONZALEZ, Antonio; Venezuelan banker; b. 24 July 1933, Mérida; m. Carmen Elena Granadino de Casas; five s. one d.; ed George Washington Univ., Georgetown Univ.; fmrly Prof. of Econs at various insts.; Adviser Venezuelan Petrochemical Inst. and Asst to Minister of Mines and Hydrocarbons 1957–59; Petroleum and Econ. Counsellor Washington Embassy 1959–61; with Interamerican Devt Bank 1961–69; Vice-Minister of Devt 1969; Minister for National Planning Office (CORDIPLAN) 1972; Man. Dir Petróleos de Venezuela (UK) SA 1990–94; Gov. Banco Cen. de Venezuela 1994–99; Vice.-Pres. Intergovernmental Group of Twenty-Four on Int. Monetary Affairs 1996–; mem. Bd Dirs. Venezolana de Aviación (VIASA) 1970–73, Corp. Andina de Fomento 1970–73, Banco Cen. de Venezuela 1972–75, Corp. Venezolana de Guyana 1979–82, Petróleos de Venezuela SA 1979–90; currently Sr Adviser, Tecnoconsult, mem. Int. Bd Elliot School of Int. Affairs,

George Washington Univ.; sixteen decorations from nine countries. *Publications:* co-author América Latina y los problemas de Desarrollo 1974, Venezuela y el CIAP (jtly) 1974, La planificación en América Latina (jtly) 1975, World Development (jtly) 1977; articles for various publs. *Leisure interest:* golf. *Address:* c/o Banco Central de Venezuela, Av. Urdaneta, Esq. Las Carmelitas, Caracas 1010, Venezuela.

CASDIN-SILVER, Harriet, AB; American artist; b. 10 Feb. 1925, Worcester, Mass.; d. of Samuel Casdin-Cohen and Rose Fanya Ostroff; m. Simon Silver 1952; two d.; ed Univ. of Vermont, Vt, Columbia Univ., NY, New School for Social Research, NY, Cambridge Goddard Grad. School, Mass.; artist in residence American Optical Research Labs., Framingham, Mass. 1968–73, Ukrainian Inst. of Physics, Kiev 1989; Asst Prof. of Physics Brown Univ., RI 1974–78; Fellow Center for Advanced Visual Studies, MIT 1976–85; consultant Rockefeller Foundation Arts Program 1980–81; Visiting Lecturer RCA, London 1992, also Univ. of Ghent; Prof. of Art Mass. Coll. of Art and Design, Boston 1999–; Presenter SKYART Conf., Delphi & Ikaria, Greece 2002; also independent artist; Rockefeller Foundation Awards: 1978–79, 1980–82, Lifetime Achievement Award for Art in Holography (Univ. of Nottingham, England) 1996; Visible Repub. Award for Public Art 2001; Shearwater Foundation Award for Excellence in Holography 2001. *Exhibitions:* Documenta 6, Germany 1977, Vienna Bienale, Austria 1979, São Paulo Bienal, Brazil 1985, The Art of Holography (retrospective), Decordova Museum, USA 1998–99, Celebration of Aging (audio-holographic installation), Boston 2000, Univ. of Rhode Island 2001, Is Freedom Visible?, Massachusetts State House 2002, Museum of Afro-American History 2003, We Are Here, South Station Concourse, Boston 2002. *Publications include:* My First 10 Years as Artist/Holographer 1989, Holographic Installations: Sculpting with Light 1991. *Leisure interests:* reading, walking, ocean watching. *Address:* 99 Pond Avenue, D403, Brookline, MA 02445 (Home); 51 Melcher Street, 5th Floor, Boston, MA 02210, USA (Studio). *Telephone:* (617) 739-6869 (Home); (617) 423-4717 (Studio). *Fax:* (617) 739-6869 (Home). *E-mail:* casdinsilver@hotmail.com.

CASE, Stephen M., MA; American business executive; b. 21 Aug. 1958, Honolulu; m. Joanne Case (divorced); three d.; ed Williams Coll.; marketing dept Procter & Gamble 1980–82; man. new pizza devt, Pizza Hut Div. PepsiCo 1982–83; with Control Video 1983–85; with Quantum Computer Services 1985–92; CEO America Online 1992–2000, Chair. 1995–2000; Chair. AOL Time Warner (created after merger of Time Warner and America Online) 2001–03, Dir with jt responsibility for Corp. Strategy 2003–; Entrepreneur of the Year, Incorporated Magazine 1994. *Leisure interests:* reading political science and history. *Address:* AOL Time Warner, 75 Rockefeller Plaza, New York, NY 10019-9302, USA (Office).

CASEY, Gavin; British business executive; b. 18 Oct. 1946; trained as chartered accountant; joined County NatWest 1972, latterly Deputy Chief Exec.; Finance Dir Smith New Court (brokers) 1989, COO 1994; Chief Admin. Officer for Int. Equities, Merrill Lynch (following takeover of Smith New Court) 1994–96; Chief Exec. The Stock Exchange 1996–2000; Dir Kinetic Info System Service Ltd 2001–, Lawrence PLC 2002–; Chair. Tragus Holdings Ltd 2002–; Deputy Chair. Corp. Finance Advisory Bd PricewaterhouseCoopers 2003–. *Leisure interests:* shooting, racing, theatre. *Address:* 44 Eaton Terrace, London, SW1Y 8TY, England (Home). *Telephone:* (20) 7730–2483 (Office). *Fax:* (20) 7730–9070 (Office). *E-mail:* gavincasey@btinternet.com (Home).

CASH, J. R. (Johnny); American entertainer; b. 26 Feb. 1932, Kingsland, Ark.; s. of the late Ray Cash and Carrie Cash (née Rivers); m. 1st Vivian Liberto 1950; four d.; m. 2nd June Carter 1968; one s.; ed Gardner-Webb Coll., Nat. Univ. San Diego; served with USAF; acted in films A Gunfight, North and South 1985, Stagecoach 1986; wrote, produced and narrated film The Gospel Road 1993; compositions include: I Walk the Line, Folsom Prison Blues, At Folsom Prison, Man In Black, Don't Take Your Guns to Town; composer movie sound tracks: I Walk the Line, Little Fauss and Big Halsy; over 53 million albums sold.; Pres. House of Cash Inc., Song of Cash Inc.; Vice-Pres. Family of Man Music Inc.; mem. Country Music Asscn, Country Music Hall of Fame 1980; mem. Songwriters' Hall of Fame 1992, Rock and Roll Hall of Fame 1992; Hon. DHumLitt (San Diego) 1976; Grammy Living Legend Award 1993, Kennedy Center Honor 1996, Grammy Lifetime Achievement Award 1999, President's Nat. Medal of Arts 2002–; 11 Grammy awards. *Albums include:* Folsom and San Quentin, John R. Cash, Last Gunfighter, The Baron, Believer Sings the Truth, The Holy Land, The True West, Water from the Wells of Home, The Sun Years, Boom Chicka Boom, Mystery of Life 1991, Unchained (Grammy Award) 1998, Solitary Man 1999 (Grammy Award), The Man Comes Around 2002. *TV appearances include:* The Johnny Cash Show 1969–71, Muscular Dystrophy Telethon 1972, Johnny Cash at San Quentin; documentary films: Trail of Tears, Johnny Cash, The Man, His World, His Music, United Way of America 1972. *Publications:* Man in Black (autobiog.) 1975, Man in White (religious novel) 1986, CASH (autobiog.) 1997. *Leisure interest:* theological studies. *Address:* House of Cash, Inc., 700 Johnny Cash Parkway, Hendersonville, TN 37077, USA. *Telephone:* (615) 824-5110. *Fax:* (615) 822-7332. *Website:* www.johnnycash.com.

CASH, Pat; Australian tennis player; b. 27 May 1965, Melbourne; s. of Patrick Cussen and Dorothy Hart Cash; m. Emily Cash; one s. one d.; ed Whitefriars Coll.; winner US Open Jr 1982; winning Australian Davis Cup team 1983; mem. quarter-finals Wimbledon 1985; finalist Australian Open 1987, 1988; Wimbledon Champion 1987; retd 1997; co-est. a tennis training and coaching centre in Queensland; sports commentator; Australian Tennis Hall of Fame 2003. *Leisure interests:* music, football. *Address:* c/o Pat Cash and Associates, PO Box 2238, Footscray, Vic. 3011, Australia (Office).

CASHMORE, Roger John, BA, DPhil, FRS, FInstP; British physicist; b. 22 Aug. 1944, Birmingham; s. of C. J. C. Cashmore and E. M. Cashmore; m. Elizabeth Ann Lindsay 1971; one s.; ed Dudley Grammar School, St John's Coll., Cambridge, Balliol Coll., Oxford; Weir Jr Research Fellow Univ. Coll., Oxford 1967–69; 1851 Research Fellow 1968; Research Assoc. Stanford Linear Accelerator, Calif. 1969–74; Research Officer Oxford Univ. 1974–79, lecturer 1979–90, Reader in Experimental Physics 1990–91, Prof. 1991–98; Research Dir CERN 1999–, Deputy Dir CERN 2003–; Boys Prize, Inst. of Physics 1983; Humboldt Research Award 1995. *Publications:* contribs to Physics Review. *Leisure interests:* sports, wine. *Address:* CERN, 1211 Geneva 23, Switzerland. *Telephone:* (22) 7673838 (Office). *Fax:* (22) 7679590 (Office). *E-mail:* roger .cashmore@cern.ch (Office).

CASIDA, John Edward, MS, PhD, FRS; American entomologist; b. 22 Dec. 1929, Phoenix, Ariz.; s. of Lester Earl Casida and Ruth Casida (née Barnes); m. Katherine Faustine Monson 1956; two s.; ed Univ. of Wisconsin; served with USAF 1953; research Asst Univ. of Wisconsin 1951–53, Asst. Prof. and Assoc. Prof. 1954–63, Prof. of Entomology 1959–63; Prof. of Entomology Univ. of Calif. at Berkeley 1964–, William Muriece Hoskins Chair in Chemical and Molecular Entomology 1996–, faculty research lecturer 1998; Dir Environmental Chemistry and Toxicology Lab. 1964–; scholar in residence Bellagio Study and Conf. Centre, Rockefeller Foundation, Lake Como, Italy 1978; Messenger Lecturer Cornell Univ. 1985; Sterling B. Hendicks lecturer USDA and ACS 1992–; lecturer in Science Third World Acad. of Sciences, Univ. of Buenos Aires 1997; mem. NAS, ACS, Entomological Soc. of America, Soc. of Environmental Toxicology and Chemistry; Haight Travelling Fellow 1958–59; Guggenheim Fellow 1970–71; Fellow of Entomological Soc. of America 1989; Hon. mem. Soc. of Toxicology; Hon. DUniv (Buenos Aires) 1997; Int. Award for Research in Pesticide Chemistry, ACS 1970, Spencer Award in Agric. and Food Chemistry, ACS 1978, Bussart Memorial Award, Entomological Soc. of America 1989, Wolf Prize in Agric. 1993, Founder's Award Soc. of Environmental Toxicology and Chemistry 1994, Kôrô-sho Prize Pesticide Science Soc. (Japan) 1995. *Address:* University of California, Department of Environmental Science Policy Management, 115 Wellman Hall, Berkeley, CA 94720 (Office); 1570 La Vereda Road, Berkeley, CA 94708, USA (Home).

ČÁSLAVSKÁ, Věra; Czech gymnast; b. 3 May 1942, Prague; d. of Václav Čáslavský and Anna Čáslavská; m. Josef Odložil 1968 (divorced 1988); one s. one d.; ed Faculty of Physical Training and Sport, Charles Univ., Prague; overall, vault and beam gold medals, Olympic Games, Tokyo 1964; overall, floor, asymmetric bars and vault gold medals, beam silver medal, Olympic Games, Mexico City 1968; won more individual Olympic gold medals (seven) than anyone in history, as at 2000; overall and vault first place, beam and floor second place and mem. winning team World Championships, Dortmund 1966; five first places, European Championships, Sofia 1965 and Amsterdam 1967; signed The Two Thousand Words 1968, a declaration of the principles of anticommunist rule; coach, Sports Centre, Sparta Prague 1970–79; coach, Mexico 1979; Adviser to Pres. of CSFR on Social Policy and mem. Pres. Havel's Advisory Bd 1990–92; Pres. Czechoslovak Olympic Cttee 1990–92, Czech Olympic Cttee 1992–96; mem. Int. Olympic Cttee 1995–2001; Meritorious Master of Sports 1962, Christopher Columbus Prize 1964, Order of the Republic 1968, Pierre de Coubertin Fair Play Prize 1989, Silver Olympic Order 1992, Sievert Prize 1993, Medal for Merit, Czech Repub. 1995, Hiranuma Prize 1996, Int. Gymnastics Hall of Fame 1998, Gymnast of the Century (Czech Repub.) 2000, Emil Zatopek Prize, Sports Legend (Czech Repub.) 2001; only current member of Czech Olympians' Club. *Publication:* Věra Čáslavská Narrates 1965. *Address:* c/o Czech Olympic Committee, Benesovska 6, 101 00, Prague 10, Czech Republic.

CASORATI, Francesco; Italian artist; b. 2 July 1934, Turin; s. of Felice Casorati and Daphne Maugham; m. Paola Zanetti 1959; three s.; ed Liceo Artistico dell'Accademia al Torino; first one-man show, Milan 1954; has since exhibited at numerous int. exhbns. including Pittori Italiani, Moscow, Budapest, Prague, Sofia 1957–58, Expo, Brussels 1958, Venice Biennale, etc.; numerous one-man and group shows in various European cities; taught at Liceo Artistico di Torino 1959–75, Accad. Albertina di Torino 1970–75; holder, Chair. of Decorative Art, Accad. Albertina di Torino 1975–84. *Address:* Via Mazzini 52, Turin (Studio); C.so Kossuth 19, Turin, Italy (Home). *Telephone:* (011) 831491 (Studio); (011) 894950 (Home).

CASPER, William Earl (Billy); American golfer; b. 24 June 1931, San Diego, Calif.; m. Shirley Casper; six c., five adopted c.; ed Univ. of Notre Dame; fmr fruit farmer; professional golfer since 1954; winner, U.S. Open 1959, 1966; winner, Vardon Trophy for lowest scoring average 1960, 1963, 1965, 1966, 1968; winner, the Masters 1970; played eight times in Ryder Cup 1961–75; winner of 51 tournaments on pro circuit and several more on seniors tour; won Brazilian Open twice, the Lancôme 1974, Italian Open 1975, Mexican Open 1977; U.S. PGA Player of the Year 1966, 1970, PGA Hall of Fame 1982.

CASPERSEN, Sven Lars, M.ECON.; Danish professor of statistics and university rector; b. 30 June 1935, Aabenraa; s. of Jes P. Caspersen and Carla Caspersen; m. Eva Caspersen 1962; three s.; Asst Sec. Danish Cen. Bureau of Statistics 1962–64; Deputy Chief, Cen. Statistical Centre of Danish Insurance Cos at Danish Insurance Asscn 1964–68; Assoc. Prof. of Statistics, Copenhagen School of Econs and Business Admin. 1968–73, Head, Dept of Statistics 1970–73; Prof. of Statistics, Aalborg Univ. 1973–76, Rector 1976–; Chair. Bd Copenhagen Stock Exchange 1989–96; Chair. Liaison Cttee of Rectors' Conferences of mem. states of the EC 1992–94; Chair. Govt Advisory Council on EU Matters 1993–; Chair. European Capital Markets Inst. 1993–95; Vice-Pres. Fed. of Stock Exchanges of the EC 1993–95, Pres. 1995–96; Pres. Int. Asscn of Univ. Pres.'s 1999–2002; Chair. Bd Aalborg Theatre 1986–; Dr hc (Vilnius Tech. Univ.) 1993; recipient, Tribute of Appreciation, US Dept of State 1981. *Leisure interests:* chess, bridge, tennis. *Address:* Aalborg University, Postboks 159, 9100 Aalborg (Office); Duebrødrevej 6, 9000 Aalborg, Denmark (Home). *Telephone:* 96-35-95-01 (Office). *Fax:* 98-15-15-22. *E-mail:* sc@aua.auc.dk (Office).

CASS, Sir Geoffrey (Arthur), Kt, MA, CIMgt, CBIM, FRSA; British publishing executive and arts and lawn tennis administrator; b. 11 Aug. 1932, Bishop Auckland; s. of the late Arthur Cass and Jessie Cass (née Simpson); m. Olwen Mary Richards 1957; four d.; ed Queen Elizabeth Grammar School, Darlington and Jesus Coll., Oxford; Nuffield Coll., Oxford 1957–58; RAF 1958–60; ed. Automation 1960–61; Consultant, PA Man. Consultants Ltd 1960–65; Pvt. Man. Consultant, British Communications Corpn and Controls and Communications Ltd 1965; Dir Controls and Communications Ltd 1966–69; Dir George Allen & Unwin 1965–67, Man. Dir 1967–71; Dir Weidenfeld Publrs. 1972–74, Univ. of Chicago Press, UK 1971–86; Chief Exec. Cambridge Univ. Press 1972–92, Consultant 1992–; Sec. Press Syndicate, Univ. of Cambridge 1974–92; Univ. Printer 1982–83, 1991–92; Fellow, Clare Hall, Cambridge 1979–; Hon. Fellow, Jesus Coll., Oxford 1998; Trustee Shakespeare Birthplace Trust 1982–94 (Life Trustee 1994–); Chair. Royal Shakespeare Co. 1985–2000 (Deputy Pres. 2000–), Royal Shakespeare Theatre Trust 1983–, British Int. Tennis and Nat. Training 1985–90, Nat. Ranking Cttee; mem. Bd of Man., Lawn Tennis Asscn of GB 1985–90, 1993–2000, Deputy Pres. 1994–96, Pres. 1997–99; mem. Cttee of Man., Wimbledon Championships 1990–2002; Pres., Chair. or mem. numerous other trusts, bds, cttees, charitable appeals and advisory bodies particularly in connection with theatre, sport and medicine; Oxford tennis Blue and badminton; played in Wimbledon Tennis Championships 1954, 1955, 1956, 1959; British Veterans Singles Champion, Wimbledon 1978; Chevalier, Ordre des Arts et des Lettres. *Publications:* articles in professional journals. *Leisure interests:* tennis, theatre. *Address:* Middlefield, Huntingdon Road, Cambridge, CB3 0LH, England.

CASSAB, Judy, AO, CBE; Australian painter; b. (Judith Kaszab), 15 Aug. 1920, Vienna, Austria; d. of Imre Kaszab and Ilona Kont; m. John Kampfner 1939; two s.; ed Budapest and Prague; mem. Council for the Honours of Australia 1975–79; Trustee, Art Gallery of NSW 1981–88; has held 65 individual exhbns. in galleries throughout Australia, in London and Paris since 1953 and works are in all maj. Australian galleries including Nat. Gallery, Canberra, galleries in UK including Nat. Portrait Gallery, London, in USA and at Nat. Gallery of Budapest; Dr hc (Sydney) 1995; several prizes including Sir Charles Lloyd Jones Memorial Prize (four times), The Trustees Watercolour Prize 1994, Foundation for Australian Literary Studies Prize 1996, Nita Kibble Literary Award (for Judy Cassab Diaries) 1996, two Archibald Prizes. *Publications:* Ten Australian Portraits (lithographs) 1984, Judy Cassab, Places, Faces and Fantasies 1985, Artists and Friends 1988, Judy Cassab Diaries 1995, Judy Cassab, Portraits of Artists and Friend 1998. *Leisure interest:* writing my diary. *Address:* 16A Ocean Avenue, Double Bay, Sydney, NSW, Australia 2028. *Telephone:* (9) 326-1348. *E-mail:* judycassab@ hotmail.com.au.

CASSAR, Joseph, BA, LLD, MP; Maltese politician; b. 22 Jan. 1918, Qrendi; s. of the late Giuseppe Cassar and Giovanna Cassar (née Magri); m. Janie Pace 1948 (died 1989); ed Bishop's Seminary, Gozo, the Lyceum, Malta, Univ. of Malta; with Home Guard Voluntary Force 1940–44; Barrister 1943–; mem. Council of Govt 1945–46, Speaker, Legis. Ass. 1947–48; Minister of Justice 1949–50, 1951–53, 1955–58; Minister of Labour, Employment and Welfare 1971–74, Minister of Educ. and Culture 1974–76, Minister of Justice, Lands, Housing and Parl. Affairs 1976, Deputy Prime Minister 1976 and Deputy Leader for Govt Affairs 1976, 1981; Minister of Finance, Customs and People's Financial Investments 1979–81, Sr Deputy Prime Minister and Minister of Justice and Parl. Affairs 1981–87; Perm. Rep. to UN 1993–97; mem. House of Reps. 1987–92; Maltese Labour Party; Companion Nat. Order of Merit (K.O.M.) 1993. *Leisure interests:* reading, swimming, travel. *Address:* Dar-is-Sliem, Tal-Ibragg Road, St Andrew's, Malta. *Telephone:* 370045.

CASSEL-CROCHON, Jean-Pierre; French actor; b. 27 Oct. 1932, Paris; m. 2nd Anne Célérier 1981; two s. one d.; film debut in 1959; frequent TV appearances, regular theatre activity, music hall. *Theatre includes:* Roméo et Juliette, Chorus Line, Little Black Book, Who's Afraid of Virginia Woolf?, The Collection, Elvire, Festen. *Films include:* Les Jeux de l'Amour, Le Caporal Epinglé, Paris brûle-t-il? Those Magnificent Men in Their Flying Machines, Oh What A Lovely War!, Baxter, The Discreet Charm of the Bourgeoisie, The Three Musketeers, Le Mouton Enragé, Murder on the Orient Express, That Lucky Touch, The Twist, Someone is Killing—The Great Chefs of Europe, Les Rendezvous d'Anna, From Hell to Victory, The Return of the Musketeers, Mangeclous, La Truite, Chouans, Mr. Frost, Phantom of the Opera, Theo and Vincent, The Favour, The Watch and the Very Big Fish, Amour et Petit Doigt de Pied, Pétain, Thé Noir au Citron, Casque Bleu, Prêt à Porter 1994, La Cérémonie 1995, Sade, La Patinoire, Les Rivières Pourpres 2000, Michel

Vaillant 2002. *TV includes:* Love in a Cold Climate, Shillingbury Tales, Liberty, Casanova, Secret of Sahara, Matter of Convenience, Warburg, The Maid, The French Kill, Notorious, Dust and Blood, Young Indy, La 13e Voiture, Printemps de Chien, Le Fils de Paul, Le Président et la Garde Barrière 1996, Un printemps de chien, Les Tiers mondains 1996, Le Coeur et l'epée, Les Montagnes bleues 1998, Le Coup du Lapin, Histoire d'Amour (Crimes en Série) 1999, Rastignac 2000, Pique-Nique chez Osiris 2000, L'Amour toujours 2001, La faux 2002. *Music:* album: Et maintenant 2000. *Address:* Art-Ciné, 36 rue de Ponthieu, 75008 Paris, France. *Telephone:* 1-42-56-04-20 (Office). *Fax:* 1-42-56-04-19 (Home). *E-mail:* cecilpro@noos.fr (Home).

CASSELLS, Peter; Irish civil servant and trade union official; b. 20 Oct. 1949, Co. Meath; legislation officer, Irish Congress of Trade Unions 1973–80, econ. and social affairs officer 1980–85, Asst Gen. Sec. 1985–87, Gen. Sec. 1987–2000, Exec. Chair. Nat. Centre for Partnership and Performance 2003–; Dr hc (Nat. Univ. of Ireland) 2002. *Address:* National Centre for Partnership and Performance, 16 Parnell Square, Dublin 1, Ireland (Office). *Telephone:* 35318146300 (Office). *Fax:* 35318146301 (Office). *E-mail:* info@ncpp.ie. *Website:* www.ncpp.ie.

CASSELS, John William Scott, MA, PhD, FRS, FRSE; British mathematician; b. 11 July 1922, Durham City; s. of the late John William Cassels and Muriel Speakman Cassels (née Lobjoit); m. Constance Mabel Merritt (née Senior) 1949 (died 2000); one s. one d.; ed Neville's Cross Council School, Durham, George Heriot's School, Edinburgh and Edinburgh and Cambridge Univs; lecturer, Manchester Univ. 1949–50, Cambridge Univ. 1950–65; Reader in Arithmetic, Cambridge Univ. 1965–67; Sadleirian Prof. of Pure Mathematics, Cambridge Univ. 1967–84; Fellow of Trinity Coll., Cambridge 1949–. *Publications:* An Introduction to Diophantine Approximations 1957, An Introduction to the Geometry of Numbers 1959, Rational Quadratic Forms 1979, Economics for Mathematicians 1981, Local Fields 1986, Lectures on Elliptic Curves 1991, Prolegomena to a middlebrow arithmetic of curves of genus 2 (with E. V. Flynn) 1996. *Leisure interests:* The Higher Arithmetic, gardening. *Address:* c/o Department of Pure Mathematics and Mathematical Statistics, Centre for Mathematical Sciences, Wilberforce Road, Cambridge, CB3 0WB (Office); 3 Luard Close, Cambridge, CB2 2PL, England (Home). *Telephone:* (1223) 246108 (Home).

CASSELTON, Lorna Ann, PhD, DSc, FRS; British professor of genetics; b. 18 July 1938; d. of William Charles Henry Smith and Cecille Smith (née Bowman); m. 1st Peter John Casselton 1961 (divorced 1978); m. 2nd William Joseph Dennis Tollett 1981; ed Southend High School for Girls, Univ. Coll., London; Asst lecturer Royal Holloway Coll. 1966–67, lecturer 1967–76; reader Queen Mary Coll. (now Queen Mary and Westfield Coll.) 1976–89, Prof. of Genetics 1989–91, Visiting Prof. of Genetics 1997–; Agricultural and Food Research Council (now Biotech. and Biological Sciences Research Council) Postdoctoral Fellow, Univ. of Oxford 1991–95, Sr Research Fellow 1995–2001, Prof. of Fungal Genetics 1997–2003; Fellow St Cross Coll., Oxford 1993–2003; Hon. Fellow St Hilda's Coll. Oxford 2000. *Publications:* numerous articles in scientific journals. *Leisure activities:* classical music, dancing, reading, walking. *Address:* 83 St Bernards Road, Oxford, OX2 6EJ, England (Home). *Telephone:* (1865) 559997 (Home). *E-mail:* lorna.casselton@plants.ox.ac.uk (Office).

CASSESE, Sabino; Italian professor of law; b. 20 Oct. 1935, Atripalda; Prof. Faculté Int. de droit comparé, Luxembourg 1966; Prof. of Public Admin. and Prof. of Govt, Dept of Econs Univs. of Ancona and Naples, Political Science Dept, Univ. of Rome, School for Higher Civil Servants, Rome; Dir Inst. of Public Law, Law Dept, Univ. of Rome 1991–93, Prof. of Admin. Law 1993–; Fellow European Inst. of Public Admin., Maastricht 1985–86; Prof. Univ. de Paris I 1986, 1994; Assoc. Prof. Univ. of Nantes 1987; Visiting Prof., Inst. d'Etudes Politiques, Paris 1991; Visiting Scholar, Law School, Univ. of Calif., Berkeley 1965, LSE 1969, Law School, Stanford Univ., USA 1970, 1975, 1981, 1986; Guest Scholar, W. Wilson Int. Center for Scholars, Washington, DC 1983; Visiting Scholar and Jemolo Fellow, Nuffield Coll., Oxford 1987–89, 1995; mem. editorial bds. many journals including Rivista di Diritto Pubblico, Int. Review of Admin. Sciences, Revue européenne de droit administratif, W European Politics, Revue française d'admin. publique; mem. Prime Minister's policy unit 1988–89; fmr consultant to many Govt ministries and Bank of Italy; Minister for the Public Service 1993–94; Campano d'Oro, Associazione Laureati Ateneo Pisano 1994, Premio Tarantelli 1993, Prix Alexis de Tocqueville, Inst. européen d'admin. publique 1997 and other prizes; Grande Ufficiale della Repubblica Italiana, Cavaliere di Gran Croce, Ordino al Merito della Repubblica Italiana. *Publications:* Lo Stato introvabile 1998, Maggioranza e Minoranza. Il problema della democrazia in Italia 1995, La nuova Costituzione economica 2000, Le basi del diritto amministrativo 2000 and many other books. *Address:* Department of Law, University of Rome, Via Orazio Raimondo 00173 Rome, Italy (Office). *Telephone:* (06) 72591 (Office). *Fax:* (06) 7234368 (Office).

CASSIDY, Charles Michael Ardagh, MA, BD, HLD; South African evangelist and author; b. 24 Sept. 1936, Johannesburg; s. of Charles Stewart Cassidy and Mary Craufurd Cassidy; m. Carol Bam 1969; one s. two d.; ed Parktown School, Johannesburg, Michaelhouse, Natal, Cambridge Univ., UK, Fuller Theological Seminary, Calif., USA; Founder and Int. Team Leader, interdenominational evangelistic mission team African Enterprise 1962–2002; conducted missions in cities including Cape Town, Johannesburg, Nairobi,

Cairo, Lusaka, Gaborone, Monrovia (Liberia), Mbabane (Swaziland); initiated SA Congress on Mission and Evangelism 1973, Pan African Christian Leadership Ass. 1976, SA Christian Leadership Ass. 1979, Nat. Initiative for Reconciliation 1985; speaker at events including Lausanne II conf., Manila, Philippines 1989, Missionsfest 1990, N American Renewal Conf. 1990, UN 50th Anniversary, Dublin Castle, Repub. of Ireland 1995; admitted to the Anglican Order of Simon of Cyrene 1983; Hon. HLD (Azusa Pacific Univ., USA) 1993; Paul Harris Fellow Rotary Award 1997, Michaelhouse St Michael's Award 1997. *Radio:* Daywatch (weekly South African radio programme). *Publications:* Decade of Decisions 1970, Where Are You Taking the World Anyway? 1971, Prisoners of Hope 1974, Relationship Tangle 1974, Bursting the Wineskins 1983, Chasing the Wind 1985, The Passing Summer 1989, The Politics of Love 1991, A Witness For Ever 1995, Window on the Word 1997. *Leisure interests:* music, photography, scrapbooks, sport. *Address:* African Enterprise, P.O. Box 13140, Cascades 3202, South Africa (Office). *Telephone:* (33) 347-1911 (Office). *Fax:* (33) 347-1915 (Office). *E-mail:* aesa@africanenterprise.org.za (Office). *Website:* www.africanenterprise.org.za (Office).

CASSIDY, Denis Patrick; British business executive; b. 2 Feb. 1933, Tyneside; various posts with British Home Stores, rising to Chair. 1969–87; Chair. Ferguson Int. Holdings 1988–2000, Kingsbury Group 1988–94, Boddington Group 1989–95, The Oliver Group 1992–, Liberty PLC 1995–97; Dir (non-exec.) BAA 1986–92, Seeboard PLC 1994–96, Compass Group PLC 1994–, Newcastle United Football Club PLC 1997–98. *Leisure interests:* cricket, football. *Address:* Granada Compass PLC, Stornoway House, 13 Cleveland Row, London, SW1A 1GG, England (Office). *Telephone:* (20) 7451-3000 (Office). *Fax:* (20) 7451-3002 (Office).

CASSIDY, HE Cardinal Edward Idris, DCnL; Australian ecclesiastic (retd); b. 5 July 1924, Sydney; s. of Harold Cassidy and Dorothy Philipps; ed Parramatta High School, Sydney, St Columba's Seminary, Springwood, St Patrick's Coll. Manly, Lateran Univ. Rome and Pontifical Ecclesiastical Acad. Rome; ordained priest 1949; Asst Priest, Yenda, NSW 1950–52; diplomatic service in India 1955–62, Ireland 1962–67, El Salvador 1967–69, Argentina 1969–70; consecrated Archbishop 1970; Titular Archbishop of Amantia 1970; Apostolic Pro-Nuncio in Taiwan 1970–79 (also Accred to Bangladesh and Burma 1973–79); Apostolic Del. to Southern Africa and Apostolic Pro-Nuncio to Lesotho 1979–84; Apostolic Pro-Nuncio to the Netherlands 1984–88; Substitute of the Secr. of State 1988–89; Pres. Pontifical Council for Promoting Christian Unity and Comm. for Religious Relations with the Jews 1989–2001; cr. Cardinal 1991; Cavaliere, Gran Croce dell'Ordine al Merito della Repubblica Italiana; decorations from El Salvador, Taiwan, Netherlands, Australia, France, Sweden and Germany. *Leisure interests:* tennis, golf, music. *Address:* 16 Coachwood Drive, Warabrook, NSW 2304, Australia (Home). *Telephone:* (2) 4968-9025 (Home). *Fax:* (2) 4968-9064 (Home). *E-mail:* iecassidy@bigpond.com (Home).

CASSIDY, Sheila Anne, BM, BCh, MA; British medical practitioner; b. 18 Aug. 1937, Lincs.; d. of the late Air Vice-Marshal John Reginald Cassidy and of Barbara Margaret Cassidy (née Drew); ed Our Lady of Mercy Coll., Parramatta, NSW, Univ. of Sydney and Oxford Univ.; resident posts, Radcliffe Infirmary, Oxford 1963–68, Leicester Royal Infirmary 1968–70; Medical Asst 1970–71; Asst Surgeon, Asistencia Pública, Santiago, Chile 1971–75; tortured and imprisoned for treating wounded guerrilla Nov.–Dec. 1975; human rights lecturing 1976–77; studied monastic life, Ampleforth Abbey, York 1977–79; novice in Bernardine Cistercian Convent 1979–80; resident in radiotherapy, Plymouth Gen. Hosp. 1980–82, Research Registrar, Dept Radiotherapy 1982; Medical Dir, St Luke's Hospice, Plymouth 1982–93; Palliative Care Physician, Plymouth Gen. Hosp. 1993, Specialist in Psychosocial Oncology, Plymouth Oncology Centre 1996–2002; Hon. DSc (Exeter) 1991, Hon. DLitt (Council for Nat. Academic Awards) 1992; Valiant for Truth media award. *Publications:* Audacity to Believe (autobiog.) 1977, Prayer for Pilgrims 1979, Sharing the Darkness 1988, Good Friday People 1991, Light from the Dark Valley 1994, The Loneliest Journey 1995, Creation Story 1996. *Leisure interests:* writing, broadcasting, drawing, walking, swimming. *Address:* c/o St Luke's Hospice, Plymouth, PL9 9XA, England.

CASSIRER, Henry R., PhD; American radio and television administrator; b. 2 Sept. 1911, Berlin; s. of Kurt and Eva (née Solmitz) Cassirer; m. 1st Marta Reyto (divorced); one d.; m. 2nd Arlette Freund (divorced); one s. one d.; ed Odenwaldschule, Univs. of Frankfurt, Paris, Cologne, London School of Econs and London Univ.; Announcer/translator, BBC European Service 1938–40; Foreign News Ed., Columbia Broadcasting System (CBS), New York 1940–44; Television News Ed., CBS 1944–49; freelance producer of TV documentary programmes 1949–52; teacher of TV Production and Public Affairs Programming, New School for Social Research, New York Univ. School of Radio Techniques; with UNESCO 1952–71, Dir Use of Mass Media in Out-of-School Educ.; Adviser on Educational Radio/TV to Govt of India 1957, Pakistan 1960–, Israel 1961–, Senegal 1963–, Brazil 1967–, Mali 1968–, Algeria 1969–, Singapore, United States (Alaska) 1970, Morocco 1974–, Ghana 1975, Fed. Repub. of Germany and Ford Foundation for West Africa projects 1976, Portugal for World Bank 1976; Int. Consultant communication and educ. 1971–, parent educ. 1979 (Int. Year of the Child); Visiting Prof. Ontario Inst. for Studies in Educ. 1974; Hon. Devt Consultant Univ. of London Dept of Extra-Mural Studies 1979–88; Communication and Educ. Consultant on Disability, UNESCO 1981–, Educ. Section Consultant 1995–; Consultant to European Space Agency 1986–88; Consultant to Govt. for European Year of the Disabled 2003; Hon. Pres. Groupement français des personnes handicapées (GFPH) 1993–; Vice-Pres. Collectif handicap de la région Annecienne; mem. French organising cttee, European Year of the Disabled 2003; Chevalier Ordre Nat. du Mérite 1990. *Publications:* Television, a World Survey 1954, Television Teaching Today 1960, Bildung und Kommunikation 1974; films: Man of our Age – The Sculpture of Jo Davidson, Buma-African Sculpture Speaks 1952, Television Comes to the Land 1958, Adult Education and the Media 1984, Co-operation between the Media and Adult Education Bodies, UNESCO 1985, Seeds in the Winds of Change through Education and Communication 1989, Und alles kam anders . . . 1992, Un siècle de combat pour un monde humaniste 2000. *Leisure interests:* stereo photography, organic gardening. *Address:* Les Jardins d'Arcadie, 2 rue de Venetie, 74940 Annecy-le-Vieux, France. *Telephone:* 4-50-27-98-26. *Fax:* 4-50-27-98-26. *E-mail:* cassirer@ifrance.com (Home). *Website:* cassirer.ifrance.com (Home).

CASSON, Mark Christopher, BA, FRSA; British professor of economics; b. 17 Dec. 1945, Grappenhall, Cheshire; s. of Stanley Christopher Casson and Dorothy Nowell Barlow; m. Janet Penelope Close 1975; one d.; ed Manchester Grammar School, Univ. of Bristol, Churchill Coll., Cambridge; lecturer in Econs, Univ. of Reading 1969–77, Reader 1977–81, Prof. 1981–, Head Dept of Econs 1987–94; Fellow Acad. of Int. Business, Univ. of Leeds 1993, Visiting Prof. of Int. Business 1995–; mem. Council Royal Econ. Soc. 1985–90; Chair. Business Enterprise Heritage Trust 2000–;. *Publications:* The Future of the Multinational Enterprise 1976, The Entrepreneur: An Economic Theory 1982, Economics of Unemployment: An Historical Perspective 1983, The Firm and the Market: Studies in Multinational Enterprise and the Scope of the Firm 1987, The Economics of Business Culture: Game Theory, Transaction Costs and Economic Welfare 1981, Entrepreneurship and Business Culture 1995, Information and Organization: A New Perspective on the Theory of the Firm 1997, Economics of International Business 2000, Enterprise and Leadership 2000. *Leisure interests:* railway history, Church of England activities, book collecting. *Address:* Department of Economics, University of Reading, PO Box 218, Reading, Berks., RG6 6AA (Office); 6 Wayside Green, Woodcote, Reading, RG8 0QJ, England (Home). *Telephone:* (118) 931-8227 (Office); (1491) 681483 (Home). *Fax:* (118) 975-0236 (Office); (1491) 681483 (Home). *E-mail:* m.c.casson@reading.ac.uk (Office); mark@casson14.freeserve.co.uk (Home).

CASTA, Laetitia; French model and actress; b. 11 May 1978, Pont-Audemer; d. of Dominique Casta and Line Casta; one d. (with partner Stephane Sednaoui); launched by Yves Saint Laurent; first maj. advertising campaign for Guess jeans 1993; model, Victoria's Secret 1996–; appeared in Sports Illustrated 1997, 1998, 1999, on covers of Vogue, Elle, Cosmopolitan, Rolling Stone; contracts with L'Oréal, Galeries Lafayette; chosen to represent Marianne (nat. emblem of France) 2000. *Films include:* Astérix et Obélix contre César 1999, La Bicyclette bleue, Les Ames fortes 2001. *Address:* c/o Artmedia, 10 ave Georges V, 75008 Paris, France (Office).

CASTAÑEDA-CORNEJO, Ricardo Guillermo; Salvadorean public servant; b. 11 March 1938; m.; two c.; ed Nat. Univ. of El Salvador, Princeton Univ. and Univ. of Michigan, USA; Deputy Minister for Foreign Affairs 1970–72; Head El Salvador's del. to UN Ass. 1972–76; External Dir Banco Cuscatlan SA 1980–81; Pres. Nat. Cttee and Dir for El Salvador, Cen. American Inst. of Business Man. 1981–88; Perm. Rep. to UN 1989–2000. *Address:* c/o Ministry of Foreign Affairs, 5500 Alameda Dr Manuel Enrique Araújo, Km 6, Carretera a Santa Tecla, San Salvador, El Salvador.

CASTEEN, John Thomas. III, LLD, PhD; American university administrator; b. 11 Dec. 1943, Portsmouth, Va; s. of John T. Casteen, Jr and Naomi Irene Casteen; two s. one d.; ed Univ. of Va; Asst Prof. of English, Univ. of Calif., Berkeley 1970–75; Assoc. Prof. and Dean Univ. of Va 1975–81; Prof. Va Commonwealth Univ. 1982–85; Sec. of Educ., Commonwealth of Va 1982–85; Pres. and Prof., Univ. of Conn. 1985–90; Pres. Univ. of Va 1990–; George M. Kaufman Presidential Prof., Prof. of English 1990–; Hon. LLD (Shenandoah Coll.), (Bentley Coll.) 1992, (Piedmont Community Coll.) 1992, (Bridgewater Coll.) 1993, Transylvania Univ.) 1999, Dr hc (Athens) 1996; Raven Award, Univ. of Va, Gold Medal, Nat. Inst. of Social Sciences 1998. *Publications:* 16 stories 1982; numerous essays and articles 1970–. *Leisure interest:* sailing. *Address:* Office of the President, University of Virginia, Madison Hall, PO Box 9011, Charlottesville, VA 22906, USA. *Fax:* (804) 924-3792. *E-mail:* jtc@virginia.edu (Office).

CASTELLANOS ESCALONA, Diego Luis, PhD; Venezuelan banker; b. 1 September 1930, Caracas; ed Cen. Univ. of Venezuela; Prof. Cen. Univ. of Venezuela 1959–; Dir Advisory Council to SELA (Foundation for the Coordination of Latin American Economies) 1980–82; Sec. of Nat. Econ. Council 1991–98; financial consultant Industrial Investment Fund (FONCREI) 1984–86; Exec. Sec. Venezuelan Council of Industry 1982–83; Exec. Dir Fundafuturo 1999. *Publications:* Export: Market Studies Manual 1951, Markets and Commercialization 1963, Principles and Objectives 1972. *Address:* c/o Banco Central de Venezuela, Av. Urdaneta, Esq. Las Carmelitas, Caracas 1010, Venezuela (Office).

CASTELLI, Roberto; Italian politician and engineer; b. 12 July 1946, Lecco, Lombardy; ed Politecnico di Milano; researcher developing a technological system of electronic noise reduction; adviser to EC on environmental affairs; joined Lega Nord 1986, elected Deputy for Lecco 1992, fmr Vice-Pres. of Lega Nord in Chamber of Deputies; elected Senator for Lecco e Bergamo 1996–, Pres. Lega Nord Parl. Group 1999–; Minister of Justice 2001–; fmr mem.

Comm. for Regional Affairs, Comm. on Terrorism. *Address:* Ministry of Justice, Via Arenula 71, 00186 Rome, Italy (Office). *Telephone:* (06) 6875419 (Office). *Fax:* (06) 6875419 (Office). *Website:* www.giustizia.it (Office).

CASTELLINA, Luciana, LLB; Italian journalist and politician; b. 9 Aug. 1929, Rome; m. (divorced); one s. one d.; ed Univ. of Rome; Ed. Nuova Generazione (weekly) 1958–62, Il Manifesto (daily) 1972–78, Pace e Guerra (weekly) then Liberazione (weekly) 1992–94; elected mem. Parl. 1976, 1979, 1983; MEP 1979, 1984, 1989, 1994; Chair. Culture and Media Cttee European Parl. 1994–96, later Chair. External Econ. Relations Cttee; fmr mem. Presidence Italian Women's Union, directorate Italian Communist Party; Adviser Italia Cinema Srl (fmr Pres.); mem. Lega Ambiente; Kt Commdr of the Argentine Repub. *Publications:* Che c'è in America (reports from America) 1972, Family and Society in Marxist Analysis 1974. *Leisure interest:* films. *Address:* c/o Italia Cinema Srl, Via Aureliana 63, 00187 Rome (Office); Via di San Valentino 32, 00197 Rome, Italy (Home).

CASTILLO, Michel Xavier Janicot del, LèsL, L. EN P.; French writer; b. 2 Aug. 1933, Madrid, Spain; s. of Michel Janicot and Isabelle del Castillo; ed Coll. des jésuites d'Ubeba, Spain, Lycée Janson-de-Sailly, Paris; mem. Soc. des gens de lettres, PEN; Prix des Neufs 1957, Prix des Magots 1973, Grand Prix des libraires 1973, Prix Chateaubriand 1975, Prix Renaudot 1981, Prix Maurice Genevoix 1994; Chevalier Légion d'honneur, Commdr des Arts et des Lettres. *Publications:* Tanguy 1957, La Guitare 1958, Le Colleur d'affiches 1959, Le Manège espagnol 1960, Tara 1962, Gerardo Laïn 1969, Le Vent de la nuit 1973, Le Silence des pierres 1975, Le Sortilège espagnol 1977, Les Cyprès meurent en Italie 1979, Les Louves de l'Escurial 1980, La nuit du décret 1981, La Gloire de Dina 1984, Nos Andalousies 1985, Le Démon de l'oubli 1987, Mort d'un poète 1989, Une Femme en Soi 1991, Le Crime des Pères 1993, Rue des Archives 1994, Mon frère l'idiot 1995, La Tunique d'infamie 1997, De père français 1998, Colette, une certaine France (Prix Femina 1999), L'Adieu au siècle 2000, Droit d'auteur 2000. *Address:* Editions Stock, 27 rue Cassette, 75006 Paris (Office); Le Colombier, 7 avenue Camille Martin, 30190 La Calmette, France (Home).

CASTILLO LARA, HE Cardinal Rosalio José, S.B.D.; Venezuelan ecclesiastic; b. 4 Sept. 1922, San Casimiro, Maracay; s. of Rosalio Castillo and Guillermina Lara; ordained 1949; consecrated Bishop (Titular See of Praecausa) 1973, Archbishop 1982; cr. HE Cardinal 1985; Pres. Admin. Patrimony of the Holy See 1989; Pres. Pontifical Comm. for Vatican City State 1990–, Pres. Emer. *Address:* Palazzo del Governatorato, 00120 Città del Vaticano, Rome, Italy.

CASTLE, Michael N., JD; American politician and lawyer; b. 2 July 1939, Wilmington, Del.; s. of J. Manderson and Louisa B. Castle; ed Hamilton Coll. and Georgetown Univ.; admitted Del. Bar 1964, DC Bar 1964; Assoc. Connolly, Bove and Lodge, Wilmington 1964–73, partner, 1973–75; Deputy Attorney-Gen. State of Del. 1965–66; Partner, Schnee & Castle 1975–80; Lt-Gov. State of Del. 1981–85; Prin. Michael N. Castle 1981–; Gov. of Delaware 1985–93; mem. Del. House of Reps. 1966–67, 1993–, Del. Senate 1968–76, House of Reps. from Delaware 1993–; Republican. *Address:* House of Representatives, 1233 Longworth Building, Washington, DC 20515-0801, USA. *Telephone:* (202) 225-4165 (Office).

CASTLEMAN, Christopher Norman Anthony, MA; British banker; b. 23 June 1941, Beaconsfield, Bucks.; s. of the late S. Phillips and J. D. S-R-Pyper; m. 1st Sarah Victoria Stockdale 1965 (died 1979); one s. one d.; m. 2nd Caroline Clare Westcott 1980; two d.; m. 3rd Susan Mary Twycross 1990; one s. one d.; ed Harrow School and Clare Coll., Cambridge; joined M. Samuel and Co. Ltd 1963; Gen. Man. Hill Samuel Australia 1970–72; Officer of Hill Samuel Inc., New York 1972–73; Dir Hill Samuel and Co. Ltd, 1970–87; Man. Dir Hill Samuel Int. Ltd 1975–77, Hill Samuel Group (SA) Ltd and Hill Samuel South Africa Ltd 1978–80; Chief. Exec. Hill Samuel Group PLC 1980–87, Manpower PLC 1987–88, LIT Holdings PLC 1989–90, Chair. 1991–95; Financial Adviser, Christopher Castleman and Co. 1988–89; Exec. Dir Standard Chartered Bank 1991–2001, Advisory Dir 2001–; Sr Adviser UBS Warburg 2001–. *Leisure interests:* sport, travel. *Address:* Standard Chartered Bank, 2 Billiter St, London, EC3M 2RY (Office); UBS Warburg, 2 Finsbury Avenue, London, EC2M 2PG (Office); Tofte Manor, Souldrop Road, Sharnbrook, Beds., MK44 1HH, England (Home). *Telephone:* (1234) 781425 (Home); (20) 7280-7008 (Office). *Fax:* (1234) 781877 (Home); (1234) 781918 (Office). *E-mail:* christopher.castleman@un.standard_chartered.com/ christopher.castleman@ubsw.com (Office); castleman@toftemanor.com (Home).

CASTON, Geoffrey Kemp, CBE, MA, MPA; British university administrator; b. 17 May 1926, Beckenham, Kent; s. of Reginald Caston and Lilian Caston; m. 1st Sonya Chassell 1956; two s. one d.; m. 2nd Judy Roizen 1983; ed St Dunstan's Coll., Peterhouse, Cambridge, Harvard Univ.; Sub-Lt RDVR 1945–47; Colonial Office 1951–58; First-Sec. UK Mission to UN 1958–61; Dept of Tech. Co-operation 1961–64; Asst Sec. Dept of Educ. and Science 1964–66; Sec. Schools Council 1966–70; Under-Sec. Univ. Grants Cttee 1970–72; Registrar of Univ. and Fellow of Merton Coll., Oxford 1972–79; Sec. Gen. Cttee of Vice-Chancellors 1979–83; Vice-Chancellor, Univ. of South Pacific, Fiji 1983–92; Visiting Assoc. Center for Studies in Higher Educ., Calif. Univ. at Berkeley 1978–; Distinguished Lecturer in Pacific Studies, Univ. of Hawaii 1992; GAP Project Man. S. Pacific 1994–; Chair. Commonwealth Scholarship Comm. in the UK 1996–; mem. or chair. numerous dels. and cttees., nat. and int., including UN Tech. Assistance Cttee 1962–64, Visiting

Mission to Trust Territory of Pacific Islands 1961, OECD Workshops on Educational Innovation 1969, 1970, 1971, Nat. Inst. for Careers Educ. and Counselling 1975–83, Exec. Cttee Inter-Univ. Council for Higher Educ. Overseas 1977–83, Library Advisory Council (UK) 1973–78, Council, Univ. of Papua New Guinea; Hon. LLD (Dundee) 1982, Hon. DLitt (Deakin) 1991; George Long Prize for Jurisprudence 1950. *Publication:* The Management of International Cooperation in Universities 1996. *Address:* 3 Pennsylvania Park, Exeter, EX4 6HB, England. *Telephone:* (1392) 272986. *Fax:* (1392) 421360.

CASTRILLÓN HOYOS, HE Cardinal Dario; Colombian ecclesiastic; b. 4 July 1929, Medellín; ed Pontifical Gregorian Univ., Univ. of Louvain; ordained priest 1952; Bishop 1971; Archbishop of Bucaramanga 1992–99; Pro-Prefect Congregation for the Clergy 1996–98; Pres. Congregation for the Clergy 1998, Pontifical Comm. "Ecclesia Dei" 2000–; cr. Cardinal 1998. *Address:* c/o Arzobispado, Calle 33, N 21-18, Bucaramanga, Santander, Colombia.

CASTRO, Fidel (see Castro Ruz, Fidel).

CASTRO, Gen. Raúl (see Castro Ruz, Gen. Raúl).

CASTRO CALDAS, Júlio de Lemos de; Portuguese politician and lawyer; b. 19 Nov. 1943, Lisbon; s. of Eugénio Queiroz de Castro Caldas and Maria Lusitana Mascarenhas de Lemos de Castro Caldas; m. Ana Cristina Ribeiro Sobral Cid; one s. two d.; Leader Students' Asscn, Classical Univ. of Lisbon 1963; f. Associação para o Desenvolvimento Económico e Social (SEDES) 1970, Partido Popular Democrático 1974; Democratic Alliance mem. Parl. for Viana do Castelo 1979; Leader Parl. Group of Democratic Alliance 1979–82; Minister of Defence, Socialist Party 1999–2001; mem. Supreme Council of Public Prosecutor Dept 1980–92; Treas. Nat. Bars Asscn 1988–91, Dean 1993–98; Pres. European Bars Fed. 1997–99; Chair. Bilbao Vizcaya Bank (Portugal) 1995–99; fmr chair. several cos.; Dir (non-exec.) Companhia le Seguros Global S.A., Carrefour S.A. *Address:* c/o Ministry of Defence, Av. Ilha da Madeira, 1449-004 Lisbon, Portugal (Office).

CASTRO JIJÓN, Rear-Adm. Ramón; Ecuadorean politician and naval officer; b. 1915; studied naval eng in USA; fmr Naval Attaché, London; C-in-C of Navy, Ecuador; Pres. Mil. Junta 1963–66; in exile 1966–.

CASTRO RUZ, Fidel, DIur; Cuban politician; b. 13 Aug. 1926; brother of Raúl Castro Ruz (q.v.); m. Mirta Diaz-Bilart 1948 (divorced 1955); one s.; ed Jesuit schools in Santiago and Havana, Univ. de la Habana; law practice in Havana; began active opposition to Batista regime by attack on Moncada barracks at Santiago 26th July 1953; sentenced to 15 years' imprisonment 1953; amnestied 1956; went into exile in Mexico and began to organize armed rebellion; landed in Oriente Province with small force Dec. 1956; carried on armed struggle against Batista regime until flight of Batista Jan. 1959; Prime Minister of Cuba 1959–76; Head of State and Pres. of Council of State 1976–, Pres. of Council of Ministers 1976–; Chair. Agrarian Reform Inst. 1965–; First Sec. Partido Unido de la Revolución Socialista (PURS) 1963–65, Partido Comunista 1965– (mem. Political Bureau 1976–), Head Nat. Defence Council 1992–; Lenin Peace Prize 1961, Muammar Gaddafi Human Rights Prize 1998; Dimitrov Prize (Bulgaria) 1980; Hero of the Soviet Union 1963; Order of Lenin 1972, 1986, Order of the October Revolution 1976, Somali Order (1st Class) 1977, Order of Jamaica 1977, Gold Star (Vietnam) 1982. *Publications:* Ten Years of Revolution 1964, History Will Absolve Me 1968, Fidel (with Frei Betto) 1987, How Far We Slaves Have Come: South Africa and Cuba in Today's World (with Nelson Mandela) 1991. *Address:* Palacio del Gobierno, Havana, Cuba. *Website:* www2.cuba.cu/politica/webpcc (Office).

CASTRO RUZ, Gen. Raúl; Cuban politician; b. 3 June 1931; ed Jesuit schools; younger brother of Fidel Castro Ruz (q.v.); sentenced to 15 years' imprisonment for insurrection 1953; amnestied 1954; assisted his brother's movement in Mexico and in Cuba after Dec. 1956; Chief of the Armed Forces 1960; First Deputy Prime Minister 1972–76; First Vice-Pres. Council of State 1976–, First Vice-Pres. Council of Ministers 1976–; Medal for Strengthening of Brotherhood in Arms 1977; Order of Lenin 1979, Order of the October Revolution 1981. *Address:* Oficina del Primer Vice-Presidente, Havana, Cuba. *Website:* www2.cuba.cu/politica/webpcc (Office).

CASULE, Slobodan; Macedonian politician and journalist; b. 27 Sept. 1945, Skopje; ed Pontifical Catholic Univ., Lima, Peru; journalist and interpreter, Skopje TV 1965–67, Ed., Foreign Corresp. 1967–74; Latin America Corresp. TANJUNG News Agency 1974–80, Chief Ed. 1980–90; Dir, Chief Ed. Macedonian Radio 1990–94, Ed., Commentator 1994–99; Dir.-Gen. Nova Makedonija, 1999; Govt Adviser 2000–; Minister of Foreign Affairs 2001–02; Founder and mem. Human Rights Forum of Macedonia, Int. Relations Forum; mem. European Inst. of Media, Inst. of East–West Dialogue, Int. Fund for Media, US Democratic Inst., Helsinki Watch, Peace in the Country–Peace in the World Org., Journalists' Asscn of Macedonia, Int. Journalists' Asscn. *Address:* c/o Ministry of Foreign Affairs, Dame Gruev 6, Skopje 1000, Macedonia (Office).

CATARINO, Pedro Manuel; Portuguese diplomatist; b. 12 May 1941, Lisbon; m. Cheryl A. Steyn 1969; one s. one d.; ed Univ. of Lisbon; served Embassy, Pretoria 1967–69; Defence Counsellor, Del. to NATO, Brussels 1974–79; Consul-Gen. Hong Kong 1979–82; mem. int. staff, NATO, Brussels 1983–89; Head, del. to negotiations for a new defence and cooperation agreement with USA 1989–92; Pres. Inter-ministerial Comm. of Macau and

Head, Portuguese del. to Joint Luso-Chinese Liaison Group; Perm. Rep. to UN 1992–97; currently Amb. to China; Silver Medal for Distinguished Services. *Leisure interest:* tennis. *Address:* 8 Sarv Li Tun Dong Wu Jie, Beijing 100600, People's Republic of China (Office). *Telephone:* (10) 6532 3497 (Office). *Fax:* (10) 6532 4637 (Office).

CATER, Sir Jack, KBE; British colonial administrator; b. 21 Feb. 1922, London; s. of Alfred Francis Cater and Pamela Elizabeth Cater (née Dukes); m. Peggy Gwenda Richards 1950; one s. two d.; ed Sir George Monoux Grammar School, Walthamstow; war service 1939–45, Squadron Leader, RAFVR; British Mil. Admin., Hong Kong 1945; joined Colonial Admin. Service, Hong Kong 1946; attended 2nd Devonshire Course, Queen's Coll., Oxford 1949–50; various posts incl. Registrar of Co-operative Socs. and Dir of Marketing, Dir of Agric. and Fisheries, Deputy Econ. Sec.; Imperial Defence Coll. (now Royal Coll. of Defence Studies) 1966; Defence Sec., Special Asst to Gov. and Deputy Colonial Sec. (Special Duties) 1967; Exec. Dir Hong Kong Trade Devt Council 1968–70; Dir Commerce and Industry, Hong Kong 1970–72; Sec. for Information 1972, for Home Affairs and Information 1973; Founding Commr Ind. Comm. Against Corruption 1974–78; Chief Sec., Hong Kong 1978–81 (Acting Gov. and Deputy Gov. on several occasions); Hong Kong Commr, London 1981–84; Man. Dir Hong Kong Nuclear Investment Co. 1987–89, Consultant 1990–; Dir Guangdong Nuclear Power Jt Venture Co. Ltd 1986–89 (First Deputy Gen. Man. 1985–86); Dir TV Broadcasts Ltd, TVE (Holdings) Ltd 1992–96; Adviser to Consultative Cttee for the Basic Law, Hong Kong 1986–90; Pres. Agency for Volunteer Service 1982–99; Chair. Project Evaluation Cttee, Hong Kong Inst. of Biotech., Chinese Univ. of Hong Kong 1990–95, Oriental Devt Co. Ltd 1992–2001 (Dir 1991), H.G. (Asia) Ltd 1992–95; Consultant Philips China and Hong Kong 1990–92, Int. Bechtel Ind. 1990–97, DAO Heng Bank Ltd 1996–; Dir HKIB Syntex Ltd 1991–95, Springfield Bank and Trust Ltd, Gibraltar 1994–99; mem. Court, Univ. of Hong Kong 1982–2000, Hoare Govett (Asia) Ltd 1990–92, Hong Kong Cable Communications Ltd 1990–91; mem. Bd of Govs., Hong Kong Baptist Univ. 1990–95, Int. Bd of United World Coll. 1981–92; Dir Li Po Chun United World Coll. Ltd 1991–2001; Hon. DScS (Hong Kong Univ.) 1982. *Leisure interests:* walking, bridge, reading. *Address:* c/o Hong Kong Nuclear Investment Co. Ltd, 147 Argyle Street, Kowloon, Hong Kong Special Administrative Region (Office); Bryanston, Clos du Petit Bois, Rue Cauchez, St Martins, Guernsey GY4 6NX, Channel Islands (Home).

CATHALA, Thierry Gerard, DenD; French judge; b. 23 Feb. 1925, Bordeaux; s. of Jean Cathala and Juliette Monsion; m. Marie F. Mérimée 1954; two s. one d.; ed Saint-Genes Coll., Lycée Montaigne, Faculté de droit de Bordeaux and Paris; trainee barrister Bordeaux Bar 1946–48; Deputy Judge, Bordeaux 1948–51, Examining Magistrate 1951–65; Prin. Admin. EEC Comm., Brussels 1965–73; Judge Nanterre and Paris Courts 1974–81; Chief Justice French Polynesia Court of Appeal 1981–85; Counsellor Supreme Court of Cassation 1985–94; French Rep. South Pacific Judicial Conf. 1982–84; mem. Supreme Judiciary Council 1987–91; Chair. Ninth South Pacific Judicial Conf., Tahiti 1991; mem. Comm. Informatique et Libertés 1994–99; Chair. Judicial Court, Monaco 1999–; Pres. Asscn of Friends of French Polynesia 1994–; Officier Légion d'honneur, Ordre Nat. du Mérite. *Publications:* Le Contrôle de la légalité administrative par les tribunaux judiciaires 1966; numerous articles on law. *Leisure interests:* geography, travelling, religious questions. *Address:* CNIL, 21 rue Saint-Guillaume, 75340 Paris; 8 rue Ploix, 78000 Versailles, France (Home); Aybrams, Crampagna, 09120 Varilhes, France. *Telephone:* 39-50-31-98 (Home).

CATHCART, Kevin James, MA, PhD, MRIA; Irish professor of Near Eastern Languages; b. 9 Oct. 1939, Derrylin, Co. Fermanagh, N Ireland; s. of Andrew Cathcart and Elizabeth (née Flannery) Cathcart; m. Ann McDermott 1968; two s.; ed Salesian Coll., Cheshire, England, Mellifont Abbey, Co. Louth, Trinity Coll., Dublin, Ireland and Pontifical Biblical Inst., Rome, Italy; Lecturer in Hebrew Pontifical Biblical Inst., Rome 1968, in Near Eastern Studies, Univ. of Ottawa, Canada 1968–71, Asst Prof. 1971–73, Assoc. Prof. 1973–74; Sr Lecturer in Semitic Languages and Dept Head, Univ. Coll. Dublin 1974–79; Prof. of Near Eastern Languages and Dept Head 1979–2001, Emeritus Prof. of Near Eastern Languages 2001–; Visiting Fellow St Edmund's Coll., Cambridge 1987–88, 1993–94; Visiting Academic St Benet's Hall, Oxford 1994; Visiting Prof. Heidelberg 1981, 1986, 1992, Ottawa 1983, Aarhus 1986, Toronto 1989, Mainz 1992; Bd of Electors (Regius Professorship of Hebrew) Univ. of Cambridge 1989–; editorial consultant Journal of Semitic Studies 1991–; Trustee, Chester Beatty Library, Dublin 1974–89, Chair. Bd of Trustees 1984–86; mem. Royal Irish Acad., Royal Danish Acad. *Publications include:* Nahum in the Light of Northwest Semitic 1973, Back to the Sources: Biblical and Near Eastern Studies (with J.F. Healey) 1989, The Targum of the Minor Prophets (with RP Gordon) 1989, The Aramaic Bible (20 Vols, co-Ed.), The Edward Hincks Bicentenary Lectures 1994, Targumic and Cognate Studies (with M. Maher) 1996, The Letters of Peter le Page Renouf (1822–97) (2 Vols) 2002. *Leisure interests:* birdwatching, medieval architecture. *Address:* 8 Friarsland Road, Clonskeagh, Dublin 14, Ireland (Home). *Telephone:* (1) 2981589 (Home). *E-mail:* kevincathcart@yahoo.co.uk (Office).

CATHCART, (William) Alun; British business executive; b. 1943; Chair. (non-exec.) Selfridges 1998–, Avis Europe PLC Dir (non-exec.) Avis Rent A Car Inc.1980–98; Deputy Chair. (non-exec.) Nat. Express Group PLC 1992–; Deputy Chair. Belron Int. *Address:* Selfridges, Oxford Street, London, W.1

(Office); Avis Rent A Car Ltd., Trident House, Station Road, Hayes, UB3 4DJ, England. *Telephone:* (20) 7629-1234 (Office); (20) 8848-8765. *Fax:* (20) 8569-1436.

CATHERWOOD, Sir (Henry) Frederick (Ross), Kt; British public official and industrialist; b. 30 Jan. 1925, Castledawson, N Ireland; s. of the late Stuart Catherwood and of Jean Catherwood; m. Elizabeth Lloyd-Jones 1954; two s. one d.; ed Shrewsbury School and Clare Coll., Cambridge; Chartered Accountant 1951; Sec. Laws Stores Ltd, Gateshead 1952–54; Sec. and Controller, Richard Costain Ltd 1954–55, Chief Exec. 1955–60; Asst Man. Dir British Aluminium Co. Ltd 1960–62, Man. Dir 1962–64; Chief Industrial Adviser, Dept of Econ. Affairs 1964–66; mem. Nat. Econ. Devt Council (NEDC) 1964–71, Dir Gen. 1966–71; mem. British Nat. Export Council 1965–70; Vice-Chair. British Inst. of Man. 1972–74, Chair. 1974–76, Vice-Pres. 1976–; Chair. British Overseas Trade Bd 1975–79; Chair. Mallinson-Denny Ltd 1976–79 (Dir 1974); Dir John Laing Ltd (Group Man. Dir and Chief Exec. 1972–74) 1971–80, Goodyear Tyre and Rubber Co. (GB) Ltd 1975–89; Pres. Fellowship of Ind. Evangelical Churches 1977–78; mem. European Parl. for Cambridgeshire and Wellingborough, 1979–84, for Cambridgeshire and N Bedfordshire 1984–94, Vice-Pres. European Parl. 1989–92 (mem. Del. to U.S. Congress 1983–89, to Hungary 1989, to Canada 1991–94), Chair. Cttee for External Econ. Relations 1979–84, Vice-Pres. European Democratic Group 1983–87, Chair. Land Use and Food Policy Inter-group 1987–92, Vice-Chair. Foreign Affairs Comm. 1992–94); mem. Council Royal Inst. of Int. Affairs 1964–77; Treas. Int. Fellowship Evangelical Students 1979–93, Vice-Pres. 1995–2003; Pres. Evangelical Alliance 1992–2001; Hon. Fellow Clare Coll. Cambridge 1992; Hon. DSc (Aston) 1972, Hon. DScEcon (Queen's Univ., Belfast) 1973, Hon. DUniv (Surrey) 1979. *Publications:* The Christian in Industrial Society 1964, Britain with the Brakes off 1966, The Christian Citizen 1969, A Better Way 1975, First Things First 1979, God's Time God's Money 1987, Pro-Europe? 1991, David: Poet, Warrior, King 1993, At the Cutting Edge (memoirs) 1995, Jobs and Justice, Homes and Hope 1997, It Can be Done 2000, Work and Wealth 2002. *Leisure interests:* reading, writing, walking. *Address:* Sutton Hall, Balsham, Cambs., England. *Telephone:* (1223) 894017. *Fax:* (1223) 894032.

CATLOW, (Charles) Richard (Arthur), MA, DPhil, FRSC, FInstP; British professor of natural philosophy; b. 24 April 1947, Simonstone, Lancs.; s. of Rolf M. Catlow and Constance Catlow (née Aldred); m. 1st Carey Anne Chapman 1978; one s.; m. 2nd Nora de Leeuw 2000; ed Clitheroe Royal Grammar School and St John's Coll. Oxford; grad. scholar, Jesus Coll. Oxford 1970–73; Research Fellow, St John's Coll. Oxford 1970–76; lecturer, Univ. Coll. London 1976–85, Head Dept of Chemistry 2002–; Prof. of Chemistry, Univ. of Keele 1985–89; Wolfson Prof. of Natural Philosophy, Royal Inst. of GB 1989–, Dir Davy Faraday Research Lab. 1998–; Royal Soc. of Chem. Medal (Solid State Chemistry) 1992, Royal Soc. of Chem. Award (Interdisciplinary Science) 1992, 1998. *Publications:* jtly: Computer Simulation of Solids 1982, Mass Transport in Solids 1983, Computer Simulation of Fluids, Polymers and Solids 1989, Applications of Synchrotron Radiation 1990; over 600 research papers and several monographs, New Frontiers in Materials Chemistry (jtly) 1997, Microscopic Properties or Processes in Minerals (jtly) 1999. *Leisure interests:* reading, walking, music. *Address:* Royal Institution of Great Britain, 21 Albemarle Street, London W1X 4BS; Department of Chemistry, University College London, Christopher Ingold Laboratories, 20 Gordon Street, London, WC1H 0AJ, England. *Telephone:* (20) 7670-2901 (RI); (20) 7679-7482 (UCL). *Fax:* (20) 7670-2920 (RI); (20) 7679-7463 (UCL). *E-mail:* richard@ri.ac.uk; c.r.a.catlow@ucl.ac.uk. *Website:* www.ri.ac.uk; www.chem.ucl.ac.uk.

CATON-JONES, Michael; British film director; b. 15 Oct. 1957, Broxburn, nr Edinburgh, Scotland; ed Nat. Film School; worked as stagehand in London West End theatres, wrote and directed first film The Sanatorium and several other short films before being accepted by Nat. Film School; films made while a student include: Liebe Mutter (first prize European film school competition), The Making of Absolute Beginners (for Palace Productions), The Riveter; left School to make serial Brond for Channel 4 TV, then Lucky Sunil (BBC TV). *Films:* Scandal 1989, Memphis Belle 1990, Doc Hollywood 1991, This Boy's Life 1993, Rob Roy 1994, The Jackal 1997, City By The Sea 2002.

CATTANACH, Bruce MacIntosh, PhD, DSc, FRS; British geneticist (retd); b. Bruce MacIntosh Cattanach, 5 Nov. 1932, Glasgow; s. of James Cattanach and Margaretta May (née Fyfe) Cattanach; m. 1st Margaret Bouchier Crewe 1966 (died 1996); two d.; m. 2nd Josephine Peters 1999; ed Heaton Grammar School, Newcastle-upon-Tyne, King's Coll., Univ. of Durham and Univ. of Edinburgh; Scientific Staff MRC Induced Mutagenesis Unit, Edinburgh 1959–62, 1964–66; NIH Post-Doctoral Research Fellow Biology Div., Oak Ridge, Tenn., USA 1962–64; Sr Scientist City of Hope Medical Centre, Duarte, Calif. 1966–69; Sr Scientist 1997–98; MRC Radiobiology Unit, Chilton, Oxon. 1969–86, Head of Genetics Div. 1987–96; Acting Dir MRC Mammalian Genetics Unit, Harwell, Oxfordshire 1996–97; retd worker 1998–. *Publications:* numerous papers in scientific journals. *Leisure interests:* control of inherited disease in pedigree dogs; Boxer dog breeding, exhibiting and judging. *Address:* Downs Edge, Reading Road, Harwell, Oxon., OX11 0JJ, England (Home). *Telephone:* (1235) 834393 (Office); (1235) 835410 (Home). *Fax:* (1235) 835691 (Office); (1235) 820584 (Home). *E-mail:* b.cattanach@har.mrc.ac.uk (Office); bcattanach@steynmere.freeserve.co.uk (Home).

CATTAUI, Maria Livanos, BA; Swiss international organization official; b. 25 June 1941, New York, USA; m. Stéphane Cattaui (deceased); two s.; ed Harvard Univ., USA; staff writer and researcher Encyclopedia Britannica 1965–67; Ed. Time Life Books 1967–69; Consultant European Man. Symposium 1977–79, Dir 1979–82; Man. Dir World Econ. Forum 1982–96; Sec.-Gen. ICC 1996–. *Address:* Office of the Secretary-General, International Chamber of Commerce, 38 Cours Albert 1er, 75008 Paris, France (Office). *Telephone:* 1-49-53-28-18 (Office). *Fax:* 1-49-53-28-35 (Office). *E-mail:* sg@iccwbo.org (Office).

CATTO, Sir Graeme Robertson Dawson, Kt, DSc, MD, FRCP, FRSA, FRSE, FRCPE, FRCPGlas, FMedSci, FRSA; British professor of medicine; b. 24 April 1945, Aberdeen, Scotland; s. of William D. Catto and Dora E Catto (née Spiby); m. Joan Sievewright 1967; one s. one d.; ed Robert Gordon's Coll., Univ. of Aberdeen; house officer Aberdeen Royal Infirmary 1969–70, Hon. Consultant Physician/Nephrologist 1977–2000; Research Fellow, then Lecturer Univ. of Aberdeen 1970–75, Sr Lecturer then Reader in Medicine 1977–78, Prof. of Medicine and Therapeutics 1988–2000, Dean, Faculty of Medicine and Medical Sciences 1992–98, Vice-Prin. 1995–2000; Vice-Prin., King's Coll. London 2000–; Dean Guy's, King's and St Thomas' Medical and Dental School, King's Coll. London 2000–; Chief Scientist, Scottish Office 1997–2000; Vice-Chair. Aberdeen Royal Hosp. NHS Trust 1992–99; mem. Gen. Medical Council 1994–, Chair. GMC Educ. Centre 1999–2002, Pres. GMC 2002–; Treas. Acad. of Medical Sciences 1998–; Chair. of Govs. Robert Gordon's Coll., Aberdeen 1995–; mem. Scottish Higher Educ. Funding Council 1996–2002, mem. Specialist Training Authority 1999–; mem. Lambeth, Southwark and Lewisham HA 2000–02; Founder FMedSci 1998 (Treas. 1998–2001); Chair. Robert Gordon's Coll. Aberdeen 1995–; Harkness Fellow Commonwealth Fund of NY, Harvard Univ., Peter Bent Brigham Hosp., Mass. 1975–77; Hon. Fellow Royal Coll. of Gen. Practitioners 2001; Hon. LLD, Hon. FRSCEd (Aberdeen) 2002. *Leisure interests:* curling, fresh air, France. *Address:* Vice Principal's Office, King's College, James Clerk Maxwell Building, Waterloo Road, London, SE1 8WA, England (Office); 4 Woodend Avenue, Aberdeen, AB15 6YL, Scotland (Home). *Telephone:* (20) 7848-3428 (Office); (1224) 310509 (Home). *Fax:* (20) 7848-3439 (Office); (1224) 699884. *E-mail:* graeme.catto@kcl.ac.uk (Office). *Website:* www.kcl.ac.uk (Office).

CATTO, Henry Edward; American diplomatist and business executive; b. 6 Dec. 1930, Dallas; s. of Henry Edward Catto and Maureen (née Halsell) Catto; m. Jessica Oveta Hobby 1958; two s. two d.; ed Williams Coll.; partner Catto & Catto, San Antonio 1955–; Dep. Rep. Org. of American States 1969–71; Amb. to El Salvador 1971–73; Chief of Protocol, The White House 1974–76; Amb. to the UN Office, Geneva 1976–77; Asst Sec. of Defense, Pentagon, Washington 1981–83; Dir Cullen-Frost Bankers, San Antonio, Nat. Public Radio, Wash.; Amb. to the UK 1989–91; Dir US Information Agency 1991–93; Adjunct Prof. of Political Science Univ. of Texas, San Antonio 1993–; mem. Council on Foreign Relations 1979; Vice Chair. Aspen Inst. 1993–, H and C Communications 1983–89; Chair. Atlantic Council 1999–; columnist San Antonio Light 1985–89; Hon. LLD (Aberdeen) 1990. *Publication:* Ambassador at Sea 1999. *Leisure interest:* skiing. *Address:* 200 Navarro, San Antonio, TX 78205, USA (Office). *Telephone:* (210) 222-2161 (Office). *Fax:* (210) 228-0332 (Office).

CAUCHON, Hon. Martin, DCL, LLM; Canadian politician and lawyer; b. 1962, La Malbaie, Québec; m.; ed Univ. of Ottawa, Bar School of Québec, Univ. of Exeter, UK; practised as civil and commercial lawyer 1985–93; MP for Outremont 1993, 1997–; Vice-Chair. Public Accounts Cttee 1994; apptd. Sec. of State responsible for the Econ. Devt Agency of Canada for the Regions of Quebec 1996, Minister of Nat. Revenue 1999–2001, Minister of Justice, Attorney-Gen. and Minister responsible for Québec 2002–; Pres. Canada-France Inter-parl. Asscn 1994–95; Pres. Liberal Party of Canada (Quebec) 1993–95; Vice-Chair. Standing Cttee on Public Accounts 1994; mem. Standing Cttee on Human Resources Devt 1994–96. *Publications:* articles in Revue du Barreau and Bulletin de la Société de droit int. économique. *Address:* Department of Justice Canada, East Memorial Building, 284 Wellington Street, Ottawa, Ont., K1A 0H8, Canada (Office). *Telephone:* (613) 957-4222 (Office). *Fax:* (613) 954-0811 (Office). *E-mail:* cauchm@parl.gc.ca (Office); www.canada.justice.gc.ca (Office).

CAULFIELD, Patrick Joseph, CBE, RA; British artist; b. 29 Jan. 1936, London; s. of Patrick Caulfield and Annie Caulfield; m. 1st Pauline Jacobs 1968 (divorced); three s.; m. 2nd Janet Nathan 1999; ed Acton Cen. Secondary Modern School, Chelsea School of Art and RCA; taught at Chelsea Coll. of Art 1963–71; first exhibited, FBA Galleries 1961; design for ballet Party Game, Covent Garden 1984, The Ballet Rhapsody, Covent Garden 1995; work in public collections include Tate Gallery, Vic. & Albert Museum, Manchester City Art Gallery and other museums and galleries in UK, USA, Australia, Germany and Japan; Sr Fellowship, RCA 1993; Hon. Fellow London Inst. 1996. *Exhibitions include:* Robert Fraser Gallery, London 1965, 1967, Robert Elkon Gallery, New York 1966, 1968, Waddington Galleries 1969, 1971, 1973, 1975, 1979, 1981, 1985, 1997, 1998, 2002, also in France, Belgium, Italy, Australia, USA and Japan; retrospective exhbn Tate Gallery, London 1981, Serpentine Gallery, London 1992, Hayward Gallery, London 1999; has participated in numerous group exhbns in UK, Europe and New York. *Address:* 19 Belsize Square, London, NW3 4HT; c/o Waddington Galleries, 2 Cork Street, London, W1X 1PA, England.

CAUSLEY, Charles Stanley, CBE, FRSL, CLit; British poet; b. 24 Aug. 1917, Launceston, Cornwall; s. of Charles Causley and Laura Causley (née Bartlett); ed Horwell Grammar School, Launceston Coll., Peterborough Training

Coll.; served in RN 1940–46; worked as a teacher for many years until 1976; Hon. DLitt (Exeter) 1977, Hon. MA (Open Univ.) 1982; Queen's Gold Medal for Poetry 1967, Cholmondeley Award 1971, shared Ingersoll Prize 1990, Heywood Hill Literary Prize 2000. *Publications:* Union Street 1957, Johnny Alleluia 1961, Underneath the Water 1968, Figgie Hobbin 1971, Puffin Book of Magic Verse (Ed.) 1974, St Martha and the Dragon (libretti, music by Phyllis Tate) 1977, Puffin Book of Salt-Sea Verse (ed.) 1978, The Ballad of Aucassin and Nicolette 1981, The Sun, Dancing (ed.) 1982, Secret Destinations 1984, Kings' Children (trans. German ballads) 1986, 21 Poems 1986, Early in the Morning (poems) 1986, Jack the Treacle Eater 1987, A Field of Vision 1988, Jonah (libretto, music by William Mathias) 1990, The Young Man of Cury 1991, Bring in the Holly 1991, All Day Saturday 1994, Going to the Fair (Selected Poems for Children) 1994, Collected Poems for Children 1996, Collected Poems 1951–97 1997, Selected Poems for Children 1997, Collected Poems 1951–2000 2000. *Leisure interests:* theatre, cinema, foreign travel. *Address:* 2 Cyprus Well, Launceston, Cornwall, PL15 8BT, England. *Telephone:* (1566) 772731.

CAUTE, (John) David, MA, DPhil, JP, FRSL; British writer; b. 16 Dec. 1936; m. 1st Catherine Shuckburgh 1961 (divorced 1970); two s.; m. 2nd Martha Bates 1973; two d.; ed Edinburgh Acad., Wellington, Wadham Coll., Oxford; St Antony's Coll. 1959; army service Gold Coast 1955–56; Henry Fellow, Harvard Univ. 1960–61; Fellow, All Souls Coll., Oxford 1959–65; Visiting Prof. New York Univ. and Columbia Univ.; 1966–67; Reader in Social and Political Theory, Brunel Univ. 1967–70; Regents' Lecturer, Univ. of Calif. 1974, Visiting Prof. Univ. of Bristol 1985; Literary Ed. New Statesman 1979–80; Co-Chair. Writers' Guild 1982; Authors' Club Award & John Llewelyn Rhys Award for novel At Fever Pitch both 1960. *Plays:* Songs for an Autumn Rifle 1961, The Demonstration 1969, The Fourth World 1973, Brecht and Company (BBC TV) 1979. *Radio plays:* Fallout 1972, The Zimbabwe Tapes (BBC Radio) 1983, Henry and the Dogs (BBC Radio) 1986, Sanctions (BBC Radio) 1988, Animal Fun Park (BBC Radio) 1995. *Publications:* At Fever Pitch (novel) 1959, Comrade Jacob (novel) 1961, Communism and the French Intellectuals 1914–1960 1964, The Left in Europe Since 1789 1966, The Decline of the West (novel) 1966, Essential Writings of Karl Marx (Ed.) 1967, Fanon 1970, The Confrontation: a trilogy, The Demonstration (play), The Occupation (novel), The Illusion 1971, The Fellow-Travellers 1973, Collisions 1974, Cuba, Yes? 1974, The Great Fear 1978, Under the Skin: the Death of White Rhodesia 1983, The Baby-Sitters 1978, Moscow Gold 1980 (novels, both as John Salisbury), The K-Factor (novel) 1983, The Espionage of the Saints 1986, News from Nowhere (novel) 1986, Sixty Eight: the Year of the Barricades 1988, Veronica or the Two Nations (novel) 1989, The Women's Hour (novel) 1991, Joseph Losey: A Revenge on Life 1994, Dr Orwell and Mr Blair (novel) 1994, Fatima's Scarf (novel) 1998. *Address:* 41 Westcroft Square, London, W6 0TA, England.

CAUTHEN, Stephen Mark "Steve"; American jockey (retd); b. 1 May 1960, Walton, Kentucky; s. of Ronald Cauthen and Myra Cauthen; m. Amy Rothfuss 1992; two d.; rode first race 1976, first winner 1976, top jockey USA with 487 winners 1977; at 18, youngest person to win US racing's Triple Crown; moved to UK 1979; champion jockey 1984, 1985, 1987; won Derby on Slip Anchor 1985, on Reference Point 1987; rode 1,704 winners including 10 classics 1979–93 (retd); only jockey to have won Ky, Epsom, Irish, French and Italian Derbys; now works on family farm, Ky and as racing commentator on TV; Vice-Pres. Turfway Racing Assn, Ky; Seagram Prize 1977, Eclipse Award 1977; youngest person to be elected to Racing Hall of Fame.

CAUVIN, Patrick, LèsL; French writer; b. (as Claude Klotz), 6 Oct. 1932, Marseille; s. of Joseph Klotz and Victoria Cauvin; m. Evelyne Berrot 1959; two s. one d.; served in Algeria 1958–60; became a full-time writer 1968–. *Publications:* L'Amour aveugle, E=MC² mon amour, Monsieur Papa, Laura Brams, Ville Vanille, Pythagore, je t'adore, Pov chéri 1987, Belles galères 1991, Menteur 1993, Villa vanille 1995, Torrentera 2000, La Reine du Monde 2001. *Leisure interest:* football. *Address:* 59 rue Caulaincourt, 75018 Paris, France.

CAVACO SILVA, Anibal, PhD; Portuguese politician and university professor; b. 15 July 1939, Loulé; s. of Teodoro Silva and Maria do Nascimento Cavaco; m. Maria Cavaco Silva 1963; one s. one d.; ed Univ.of York, UK and Inst. of Econ. and Financial Studies; taught Public Econs and Political Economy, Inst. of Econ. and Financial Studies 1965–67, then at Catholic Univ. 1975– and New Univ. of Lisbon 1977–; Research Fellow, Calouste Gulbenkian Foundation 1967–77; Dir of Research and Statistical Dept, Bank of Portugal 1977–85; Minister of Finance and Planning 1980–81; Pres. Council for Nat. Planning 1981–84; Leader, PSD 1985–95; Prime Minister of Portugal 1985–95; mem. Real Academia de Ciencias Morales y Políticas, Spain; Econ. Adviser to Cen. Bank; Social Democrat (PSD) mem. Exec. Cttee Club of Madrid in Democratic Transition and Consolidation; Dr hc (Univ. of York, UK, Universidade da Coruña, Spain); Joseph Bech Prize 1991, Max Schmidleinz Foundation Prize. *Publications:* Budgetary Policy and Economic Stabilization 1976, Economic Effects of Public Debt 1977, The Economic Policy of Sá Carneiro's Government 1982, Public Finance and Macroeconomic Policy 1992, A Decade of Reforms 1995, Portugal and the Single Currency 1997, European Monetary Union 1999, Political Autobiography 2002; over 20 articles on financial markets, public economics and Portuguese economic policy. *Leisure interests:* golf, gardening. *Address:* c/o Bank of Portugal, Av. Almirante Reis 71, 1150–012 Lisbon, Portugal. *Fax:* (21) 314-4580 (Office).

CAVALCANTI, Giacomo, Marchese di Verbicaro; Italian artist; b. 17 March 1952; s. of Bruno Cavalcanti and Angela Valente; m. Antonella De Rosa 1987; one d.; studied graphic art and photography; active in ecology, anti-drug activity and anti-vivisection movts.; writes for magazine Eco. *Publications:* La rondine da terra non sa volare 1986, Maribo 1988, Incarico Colombiano 1990, L'Aquilone innamorato, La Cicogna non porta i fratellini, L'Ippopotamo e la Farfalla 1992, Serigrafie 1993. *Leisure interests:* sport, photography, travel, horses.

CAVALIER-SMITH, Thomas, PhD, FRS, FRSC, FLS, FIBiol; British/Canadian biologist; b. 21 Oct. 1942, London; s. of Alan Hailes Spencer Cavalier-Smith and Mary Maude Cavalier-Smith (née Bratt); m. 1st Gillian Glaysher 1967 (divorced); one s. one d.; m. 2nd Ema E-Yung Chao 1991; one d.; ed Norwich School, Gonville and Caius Coll. Cambridge, King's Coll. London; guest investigator and Damon Runyon Memorial Fellow, Rockefeller Univ., New York 1967–69; lecturer in Biophysics, King's Coll., Univ. of London 1969–82; Reader 1982–89; Prof. of Botany, Univ. of BC 1989–99; NERC Research Prof., Dept of Zoology, Univ. of Oxford 1999–, Prof. of Evolutionary Biology 2000–; Fellow Canadian Inst. for Advanced Research (CIAR) Evolutionary Biology Programme 1988–. *Publications:* Biology, Society and Choice (Ed.) 1982, The Evolution of Genome Size (Ed.) 1985; over 140 scientific papers. *Leisure interests:* reading, natural history. *Address:* Department of Zoology, University of Oxford, Oxford, OX1 3PS (Office); 2 Wharf Close, Abingdon, Oxon, OX14 5HS, England (Home). *Telephone:* (1865) 281065 (Office); (1235) 200931 (Home). *Fax:* (1865) 281310 (Office). *E-mail:* tom.cavalier-smith@zoo.ox.ac.uk (Office).

CAVALLI-SFORZA, Luigi Luca, M.D., M.A.; Italian/American geneticist; b. 25 Jan. 1922, Genoa; ed Univs. of Pavia and Cambridge, UK; Dir of Research in Microbiology, Istituto Sieroterapico Milanese, Milan 1950–57; Prof. of Genetics Univ. of Parma 1960–62; Prof. of Genetics Univ. of Pavia 1962–70, Dir Inst. of Genetics 1962–70; Prof. of Genetics Stanford Univ. 1970–92, Chair. Dept of Genetics 1986–90, Prof. Emer. School of Medicine 1992–; numerous awards. *Publications:* The History and Geography of Human Genes, Genes, Peoples and Languages 2000. *Address:* Department of Genetics, School of Medicine, Stanford University, Stanford, CA 94305, U.S.A. (Office). *Telephone:* (415) 723-2300 (Office). *Website:* www.stanford.edu/genetics (Office).

CAVALLO, Domingo Felipe, DEcon, PhD; Argentine politician; b. 21 July 1946, San Francisco, Córdoba; m. Sonia Abrazián; three s.; ed Nat. Univ. of Córdoba and Harvard Univ.; Under-Sec. for Devt Govt of Prov. of Córdoba 1969–70; Vice-Pres. Bd of Dirs. Banco de la Provincia de Córdoba 1971–72; Titular lecturer, Nat. and Catholic Univs. 1970–83; founding Dir Inst. for Econ. Studies of Mediterranean Found. 1977–87; fmr Pres., then Gov. Argentine Cen. Bank; mem. Advisory Cttee Inst. for Econ. Devt of World Bank (IBRD) 1988, Nat. Deputy for Córdoba 1987–91; Minister of Foreign Affairs and Worship 1989–91, of the Economy 1991–92, of the Economy and Public Works 1992–96, 2001; Visiting Prof., Stern School of Business, New York Univ. 1996–97; elected Nat. Deputy for Buenos Aires 1997; f. Acción por la República Party 1997; arrested for alleged involvement in arms smuggling April 2002, released June 2002. *Publications:* Volver a Crecer 1986, El Desafío Federal 1986, Economía en Tiempos de Crisis 1989, La Argentina que pudo ser 1989, El Peso de la Verdad 1997; numerous tech. publs and articles in Argentine and foreign newspapers. *Address:* Acción por la República, Buenos Aires (Office); Hipólito Yrigoyen 250, 1310 Buenos Aires, Argentina. *Telephone:* (11) 4349-5000. *E-mail:* edinfpub@mecon.gov.ar (Office). *Website:* www.mecon.gov.ar (Office).

CAWLEY, Charles M.; American financial services executive; ed Georgetown Univ.; began career in financial services 1963; sr mem. man. team that est. MBNA America 1982, currently Chair., Pres. and CEO MBNA Corpn; mem. Bd of Dirs MasterCard Int.; mem. Bd Grand Opera House, Wilmington, Delaware, St Benedict's Preparatory School, George Bush Presidential Library Foundation, Metropolitan Wilmington Urban League; mem. Bd of Regents Georgetown Univ., American Architectural Foundation. *Address:* MBNA Corporation, Wilmington, DE 19884 USA (Office). *Website:* www.mbna.com (Office).

CAWLEY, Evonne Fay Goolagong, AO, MBE; Australian tennis player; b. 31 July 1951, Griffith, NSW; d. of the late Kenneth Goolagong and Linda Hamilton; m. Roger Anson Cawley 1975; one s. one d.; ed Willoughby High School, Sydney; professional player 1970–83; Wimbledon Champion 1971, 1980 (singles), 1974 (doubles); Australian Champion 1974, 1975, 1976, 1977; French Champion 1971; Italian Champion 1973; SA Champion 1972; Virginia Slims Circuit Champion 1975, 1976; played Federation Cup for Australia 1971, 1972, 1973, 1974, 1975, 1976; Capt. Australian Fed. Cup Team 2001–; consultant to Indigenous Sports Programme; Sports Amb. to Aboriginal and Torres Strait Island Communities 1997–; Amb. and Exec. Dir Evonne Goolagong Sports Trust; f. Evonne Goolagong Getting Started Programme for young girls; Hon. DUniv (Charles Sturt) 2000; Australian of the Year 1982, Int. Tennis Hall of Fame 1988. *Publications:* Evonne Goolagong (with Bud Collins) 1975, Home: The Evonne Goolagong Story (with Phil Jarratt) 1993. *Leisure interests:* fishing, reading, researching Aboriginal heritage, movies, soccer. *Address:* c/o IMG, 281 Clarence Street, Sydney, NSW 2000; PO Box 1347, Noosa Heads, Queensland 4567, Australia. *Telephone:* (7) 5474-0112. *Fax:* (7) 5474-0113.

CAYETANO, Benjamin Jerome, BA, JD; American politician and lawyer; b. 14 Nov. 1939, Honolulu; m. 1st Lorraine Gueco 1958; m. 2nd Vicky Tiu 1997; two s. three d.; ed Farrington High School, Honolulu, Univ. of Calif. Los Angeles and Loyola Law School, Los Angeles; practising lawyer 1971–86; partner, Schutter Cayetano Playdon (law firm) 1983–86; mem. Hawaii State Legis. 1975–78, 1979–86; Lt-Gov. of Hawaii 1986–94, Gov. 1994–2002; Chair. W Gov.'s Asscn 1999; Democrat; Hon. LLD (Univ. of the Philippines) 1995, Hon. Dr. of Public Service (Loyola Marymount Univ.) 1998; numerous awards for public service including Medal of Univ. of Calif. at LA 1995, The Aloha Council Boy Scouts of America Harvard Foundation Leadership Award 1996, Distinguished Citizens Award 1997, Edward A. Dickson Alumnus of the Year Award, Univ. of Calif. at LA 1998, Distinguished Alumnus of the Year, Loyola Law School 2002. *Address:* c/o Office of the Governor, State Capitol, 415 South Beretania Street, Floor 5, Honolulu, HI 96813-2407, USA (Office).

CAYGILL, Hon. David Francis, LLB, MP; New Zealand politician and lawyer; b. 15 Nov. 1948, Christchurch; s. of Bruce Allott Caygill and Gwyneth Mary Caygill; m. Eileen E Boyd 1974; one s. three d.; ed Univ. of Canterbury; practised law in Christchurch legal firm 1974–78; mem. Christchurch City Council 1971–80; mem. House of Reps. 1978–90; Minister of Trade and Industry, Minister of Nat. Devt, Assoc. Minister of Finance 1984–87, of Health, Trade and Industry 1987–88, Deputy Minister of Finance 1988, Minister of Finance 1988–90, of Revenue 1988–89, Deputy Leader of the Opposition 1994–96; partner Buddle Findlay, Barristers and Solicitors 1996–; Chair. Accident Compensation Corpn 1998–; Chair. Ministerial Inquiry into the Electricity Ind. 2000; mem. Canterbury Regional Planning Authority 1977–80; Labour Party. *Leisure interests:* collecting classical music records, science fiction, following American politics. *Address:* c/o Buddle Findlay, P.O. Box 322, Christchurch, New Zealand. *E-mail:* david.caygill@buddlefindlay.com (Office).

CAYROL, Jean, LenD; French author; b. 6 June 1910, Bordeaux; s. of Antoine Cayrol and Marie A. Berrogain; m. Jeanne Durand 1971; started literary review, Abeilles et Pensées 1926; later launched Les Cahiers du Fleuve; Librarian, Chamber of Commerce of Bordeaux 1937; served in navy and secret service 1939–42; prisoner-of-war 1942–45; literary adviser to Editions du Seuil 1949; collaborated with Alain Resnais in film Nuit et brouillard 1956 and wrote screenplay for Resnais' Muriel 1963; with Claude Durand produced four short films and Le coup de grâce 1964; mem. Acad. Goncourt; Prix Renaudot for Je vivrai l'amour des autres 1947; Grand Prix littéraire Prince-Pierre-de-Monaco 1968, Prix international du Souvenir 1969, Grand Prix nat. des Lettres 1984; Commdr des Arts et des Lettres; Officier, Légion d'honneur; Croix de Guerre. *Publications:* poetic works: Ce n'est pas la mer 1935, Les Poèmes du pasteur Grimm 1936, Le Hollandais volant 1936, Les phénomènes célestes 1939, L'Age d'or 1939, Miroir de la Rédemption 1944, Poèmes de la nuit et du brouillard 1946, Passe-temps de l'homme et des oiseaux 1947, La vie répond 1948, Le charnier natal 1950, Les mots sont aussi des demeures 1952, Pour tous les temps 1955, Poésie-Journal I 1969, II 1977, III 1980, Poèmes clefs 1985, De jour en jour 1988; novels: Je vivrai l'amour des autres, La Noire 1949, Le feu qui prend 1950, Le vent de la mémoire 1952, L'espace d'une nuit 1954, Le déménagement 1956, Les corps étrangers 1959, Le froid du soleil 1963, Midi-minuit 1966, Je l'entends encore 1968, Histoire d'une prairie 1970, N'oubliez pas que nous nous aimons 1971, Histoire d'un désert 1972, Histoire de la mer 1973, Kakemono Hôtel 1974, Histoire de la fôret 1975, Histoire d'une maison 1976, L'homme dans le rétroviseur 1981, Un mot d'auteur 1983, Des Nuits Plus Blanches que Nature 1986, A Voix Haute 1990, De Vive Voix 1991, A Pleine Voix 1992, D'une voix celeste 1994, Alerte aux ombres 1997, Nuit et brouillard 1997; essays, narratives and short stories. *Address:* c/o Editions du Seuil, 27 rue Jacob, 75006 Paris, France.

CAYROL, Roland; French researcher, author and producer; b. 11 Aug. 1941, Rabat, Morocco; m. Annabelle Gomez 1989; two s. two d.; Prof. and Researcher Nat. Foundation of Political Sciences 1968, Research Dir 1978–; Scientific Adviser Louis Harris France 1977–86; Dir CSA 1986–98, Assoc. Dir CSA–TMO 1998–; with Radio-France 1971–, France 3 1981–, Radio Méditerranée internationale 1999–; Dir Calmann-Levy collection 1995–; Chevalier du Mérite agricole. *Television productions include:* Portrait d'un Président: François Mitterrand (with A. Gaillard) 1985. *Publications:* François Mitterrand 1967, Le Député Français (with J. L. Parodi and C. Ysmal) 1970, La Presse écrite et audiovisuelle 1973, La télévision fait-elle l'élection? (with G. Blumler and G. Thoveron) 1974, La nouvelle communication politique 1986, Les médias 1991, Le grand malentendu, Les Français et la politique 1994, Médias et démocratie: la dérive 1997, Sondages mode d'emploi 2000. *Address:* Fondation Nationale des Sciences Politiques, 10 rue de la Chaise, 75007 Paris (Office); 6 rue de Cerisoles, 75008 Paris, France (Office). *Telephone:* 1-41-86-22-00 (Office). *Fax:* 1-41-86-22-07. *E-mail:* cayrol@imaginet.fr (Home).

CAZALET, Sir Peter (Grenville), Kt, MA; British business executive; b. 26 Feb. 1929, Weymouth; s. of Vice-Adm. Sir Peter Cazalet, KBE, CB, DSO, DSC and Lady (Elise) Cazalet (née Winterbotham); m. Jane Jennifer Rew 1957; three s.; ed Uppingham School and Univ. of Cambridge; Gen. Man. BP Tanker Co. Ltd 1968–70, Regional Co-ordinator, Australasia and Far East, BP Trading Ltd 1970–72, Pres. BP North America Inc. 1972–75, Dir BP Trading Ltd 1975–81, Chair. BP Oil Int. Ltd 1981–89, Man. Dir BP 1981–89, Deputy Chair. 1986–89; Chair. APV PLC 1989–96; Chair. Armed Forces Pay Review Body 1989–93; mem. Top Salaries Review Body 1989–94; mem. Lloyds Register of Shipping Bd 1981–86 and Gen. Cttee 1981–99; Deputy Chair. (non-exec.) GKN PLC 1989–96; Dir Standard Oil Co., Cleveland, Ohio 1973–76, Peninsular & Oriental Steam Navigation Co. Ltd 1980–99, De La Rue Co. PLC 1983–95, Energy Capital Investment Co. 1995–98, Seascope Shipping Holdings PLC 1997–2002 (Chair. 2000–02); Chair. Hakluyt & Co. 1998–99, Breamar Seascope Group PLC 2000–02; Vice-Pres. ME Asscn 1982–, China–Britain Trade Group 1993–96 (Pres. 1996–98); Trustee Wellcome Trust 1989–92, Uppingham School 1976–95; Gov. Wellcome Trust Ltd 1992–96; Hon. Sec. King George's Fund for Sailors 1999–2000; mem. Liveryman, Tallow Chandlers' Co. (Master 1991–92), Shipwrights' Co. *Leisure interests:* golf, theatre, fishing. *Address:* c/o 22 Hill Street, London, W1X 7FU, England. *Telephone:* (20) 7496-4423. *Fax:* (20) 7496-4436 (Office).

CAZENEUVE, Jean, DèsSc; French academic; b. 17 May 1915, Ussel; s. of Charles Cazeneuve and Yvonne Renoul; m. Germaine Aladane de Paraize 1963; one s. two d.; ed Ecole normale supérieure and Harvard Univ.; Prof. of Sociology, Paris-Sorbonne 1966–84, Prof. Emer. 1984–; Pres. and Dir-Gen. TF1 1974–78, Hon. Pres. 1978–; Amb. to the Council of Europe 1978–80; Vice-Pres. Haut Comité de la langue française 1980–81; mem. Acad. des Sciences morales et politiques 1973–; mem. Prix Mondial Cino del Duca Jury 1988–; Chair. Prix Educ. et Liberté 1989–; Dr. hc (Univ. of Brussels); Commdr Légion d'honneur, Commdr Ordre de Léopold. *Publications include:* Les Dieux dansent à Cibola 1957, Bonheur et civilisation 1966, Les pouvoirs de la télévision 1970, Sociologie du rite 1971, Dix grandes notions de la sociologie 1976, La raison d'être 1981, Le mot pour rire 1989, Les hasards d'une vie 1990, Et si plus rien n'était sacré 1991, La télévision en 7 procès 1992, Du calembour au mot d'esprit 1996, Les roses de la vie 1999. *Leisure interest:* tennis. *Address:* 3 rue Marcel Loyau, 92100 Boulogne; Centre d'études politiques et de la communication, 54 avenue Marceau, 75008 Paris (Office); 43 Avenue Maréchal Joffre, 14390 Cabourg, France. *Telephone:* 40-72-64-28.

CAZENOVE, Christopher de Lerisson; British actor; b. 17 Dec. 1943, Winchester; s. of Brig. Arnold Cazenove and Elizabeth L. Cazenove (née Gurney); m. Angharad M. Rees 1974 (divorced 1993); two s.; ed Dragon School, Oxford and Eton Coll.; trained as actor at Bristol Old Vic Theatre School. *Films:* Zulu Dawn, East of Elephant Rock, Eye of the Needle, Heat and Dust, Until September, Mata Hari, The Fantasist, Souvenir, Hold My Hand I'm Dying, Three Men and a Little Lady, Aces: Iron Eagle III, The Proprietor, Shadow Run, A Knight's Tale, Trance, Beginner's Luck. *Stage roles include:* The Lionel Touch, My Darling Daisy, The Winslow Boy, Joking Apart, In Praise of Rattigan, The Life and Poetry of T. S. Eliot, The Sound of Music, An Ideal Husband, Goodbye Fidel, Brief Encounter, London Suite. *Television appearances include:* The Regiment (two series), The Duchess of Duke Street (two series), Jennie: Lady Randolph Churchill, The Riverman, Jenny's War, Dynasty, Hammer's House of Mystery, Lace, Windmills of the Gods, Shades of Love, Souvenir, The Lady and the Highwayman, Tears in the Rain, Ticket to Ride (A Fine Romance), To be the Best, Judge John Deed, Johnson County War, La Femme Musketeer. *Address:* c/o Peters, Fraser & Dunlop, Drury House, 34-43 Russell Street, London, WC2B 5HA, England. *Telephone:* (20) 7344-1010.

CEBRIÁN ECHARRI, Juan Luis; Spanish writer and journalist; b. 30 Oct. 1944, Madrid; s. of Vicente Cebrián and Carmen Echarri; m. 1st María Gema Torallas 1966 (divorced); two s. two d.; m. 2nd Teresa Aranda 1988; one s. one d.; ed Univ. of Madrid; founder-mem. of magazine Cuadernos para el Diálogo, Madrid 1963; Sr Ed. newspapers Pueblo, Madrid 1962–67, Informaciones, Madrid 1967–69; Deputy Ed.-in-Chief, Informaciones 1969–74, 1974–76; Dir News Programming, Spanish TV 1974; Ed.-in-Chief newspaper El País, Madrid 1976–88; CEO PRISA 1988–, Canal Plus 1989–, Estructura 1989–; Publr, CEO El País 1988–; Vice-Pres. SER 1990–; mem. Int. Press Inst. (Vice-Pres. 1982–86, Chair. 1986–88); Dr. hc (Iberoamericana Univ., Santo Domingo) 1988; Control Prize for Outstanding Newspaper Ed. 1976, 1977, 1978, 1979; Víctor de la Serna Prize for Journalism, Press Asscn Fed. 1977; Outstanding Ed. of the Year (World Press Review, New York) 1980, Spanish Nat. Journalism Prize 1983; Freedom of Expression Medal, F. D. Roosevelt Four Freedoms Foundation 1986; Medal of Honor, Univ. of Miss. 1986; Trento Int. Prize for Journalism and Communication 1987; Gold Medal, Spanish Inst. New York 1988. *Publications:* La Prensa y la Calle 1980, La España que bosteza 1980, ¿Qué pasa en el mundo? 1981, Crónicas de mi país 1985, El Tamaño del elefante 1987, Red Doll 1987, La isla del viento 1990, El siglo de las sombras 1994. *Leisure interests:* music, literature. *Address:* Gran Vía 32-6a, 28013 Madrid, Spain.

CEBUC, Alexandru, PhD; Romanian art historian and critic; b. 5 April 1932, Păuşeşti-Măglabi; s. of Ion and Ana Cebuc; m. Florica Turcu 1958; one d.; ed Univ. of Bucharest; Head of Dept, Museum of History of City of Bucharest 1957–69; Vice-Pres. Culture Cttee of City of Bucharest 1969–77; Dir Art Museum of Romania 1977–90; Gen. Man. Publishing and Printing House ARC 2000 1990–; Order of Cultural Merit, Knight of Italian Repub. *Publications:* The History of the City of Bucharest 1966, The History of Passenger Transportation 1967, Historical and Art Monuments of the City of Bucharest 1968, The Nat. Gallery 1983, Ion Irimescu (monograph) 1983, Etienne Hadju (monograph) 1984, Nicolae Grigorescu (monograph) 1985, H. H. Catargi (monograph) 1987, I. Iancheleviei (monograph) 1989, I. Irimescu – Album Drawings 1994, Encyclopaedia of Plastic Artists in Romania (Vol. I) 1994, Encyclopaedia of Plastic Artists in Romania, (Vol. II) 1999, (Vol. III) 2000. *Leisure interests:* art, music, travelling. *Address:* B. Dul. Carol I, HR 23, AP. 10, Bucharest (Office); Str. Spatarului No. 36, ET. II AP. 5, Bucharest, Romania. *Telephone:* (1) 3124018 (Office). *Fax:* (1) 3124018 (Office); (1) 2118617 (Home).

CECCATO, Aldo; Italian director of music and conductor; b. 18 Feb. 1934, Milan; m. Eliana de Sabata; two s.; ed Milan Conservatory, Hochschule für Musik Berlin; Musical Dir Detroit Symphony 1973–77, Hamburg Philharmonic 1974–82; Chief Conductor Hannover Radio Orchestra 1985–, Bergen Symphony 1985–; guest conductor to all maj. symphony orchestras and opera houses in four continents; Hon. D. Mus. (Eastern Michigan Univ.). *Music:* numerous recordings. *Leisure interests:* tennis, stamps, books. *Address:* c/o Rundfunkorchester Hannover, Rudolf von Bennigsen Ulfer 22, 3000 Hannover, Germany (Office); Chaunt da Crusch, 7524 Zuoz, Switzerland.

CECH, Thomas Robert, PhD; American professor of chemistry and biochemistry; b. 8 Dec. 1947, Chicago; s. of Robert Franklin Cech and Annette Marie (née Cerveny) Cech; m. Carol Lynn Martinson 1970; two d.; ed Grinnell Coll., Univ. of Calif., Berkeley; Postdoctoral Fellow, Dept of Biology, MIT, Cambridge, Mass. 1975–77; Asst Prof., then Assoc. Prof. of Chem., Univ. of Colo, Boulder 1978–83, Prof. of Chem. and Biochem. and of Molecular, Cellular and Devt Biology 1983–, Distinguished Prof. 1990–; Research Prof., American Cancer Soc. 1987–; investigator Howard Hughes Medical Inst. 1988–99, Pres. 2000–; Deputy Ed. Science; mem. Editorial Bd Genes and Devt; Nat. Science Foundation Fellow 1970–75; Public Health Service Research Fellow, Nat. Cancer Inst. 1975–77; Guggenheim Fellow 1985–86; mem. American Acad. of Arts and Sciences, NAS; Hon. DSc (Grinnell Coll.) 1987, (Univ. of Chicago) 1991, (Drury Coll.) 1994, (Colorado Coll.) 1999, (Univ. of Maryland) 2000, (Williams Coll.) 2000, (Charles Univ., Prague) 2002; Medal of American Inst. of Chemists 1970, Research Career Devt Award, Nat. Cancer Inst. 1980–85, Young Scientist Award, Passano Foundation 1984, Harrison Howe Award 1984, Pfizer Award 1985, U.S. Steel Award 1987, V.D. Mattia Award 1987, Heineken Prize 1988, Gairdner Foundation Award 1988, Lasker Award 1988, Warren Triennial Prize 1989, Nobel Prize for Chem. 1989, Rosenstiel Award 1989, Nat. Medal of Science 1995, Gregor Mendel Medal 2002. *Leisure interest:* skiing. *Address:* Howard Hughes Medical Institute, 4000 Jones Bridge Road, Chevy Chase, MD 20815, USA (Office). *Telephone:* (301) 215-8550 (Office). *Fax:* (301) 215-8558. *E-mail:* president@hhmi.org (Office). *Website:* www.hhmi.org (Office).

CECIL, Henry Richard Amherst; British racehorse trainer; b. 11 Jan. 1943; s. of late Horace Henry Kerr Auchmury Cecil and of Elizabeth Rohays Mary Burnett; m. 1st Julie Murless 1966 (divorced 1990); one s. one d.; m. 2nd Natalie Payne 1992 (divorced 2002); one s.; ed Canford School; Asst to Sir Cecil Boyd-Rochfort; started training under flat race rules 1969; 1st trainer to win more than £1 million in a season (1985); leading trainer 1976, 1978, 1979, 1982, 1984, 1985, 1987, 1988, 1990, 1993: won 23 classics (to end of 2002 flat season). *Publication:* On the Level (autobiog.) 1983. *Leisure interest:* gardening. *Address:* Warren Place, Newmarket, Suffolk, CB8 8QQ, England (Home). *Telephone:* (1638) 662387 (Office). *Fax:* (1638) 669005 (Office). *E-mail:* henry.cecil@dial.pipex.com.

CEDAIN ZHOIMA; Chinese singer; b. 1 Aug. 1937, Xigaze, Xizang; ed Shanghai Music Coll.; joined CCP 1961; performed in USSR 1963; in political disgrace during Proletarian Cultural Revolution 1966–76; rehabilitated 1977; mem. Standing Cttee 5th NPC 1978–83; Vice-Chair. 6th CPPCC Tibet Regional Cttee 1987–; Vice-Chair. Chinese Musicians Asscn 1979–; mem. Standing Cttee 6th NPC 1983–88, 7th CPPCC 1988–; Exec. Vice-Chair. China Fed. of Literary and Art Circles 1988–. *Address:* Chinese Musician's Association, Beijing, People's Republic of China.

CEJAS, Paul L., BBA, CPA; American diplomatist and business executive; b. 4 Jan. 1943, Havana, Cuba; ed Univ. of Miami; Chair. and CEO PLC Investments, Inc.; Founder, Chair. and CEO CareFlorida Health Systems Inc.; Amb. to Belgium 1998–2001; Chair. Dade Co. School Bd; mem. Bd of Regents, Fla Univ. System 1994; Post-Summit Cttee, Hemispheric Summit of the Americas 1994; Fla Partnership of the Americas 1994–97; Rep., US Del. to Gen. Ass., OAS 1996; Hon. PhD (Florida Int. Univ.) 1988. *Address:* c/o Department of State, 2201 C Street, NW, Washington, DC 20520, USA.

CELESTE, Richard F., PhB; American state governor; b. 11 Nov. 1937, Cleveland, Ohio; s. of Frank Celeste; m. Dagmar Braun 1962; three s. three d.; ed Yale Univ. and Oxford Univ.; Staff Liaison Officer, Peace Corps 1963; Special Asst to U.S. Amb. to India 1963–67, 1997–2001; mem. Ohio House of Reps. 1970–74, Majority Whip 1972–74; Lt-Gov. of Ohio 1975–79, Gov. 1983–91; Chair. Midwestern Govs.' Conf. 1987–88; Great Lakes Govs.' Assn 1987–89; Pres. Colorado Coll. 2002–. *Address:* Colorado College, 14 E. Cache La Poudre, Colorado Springs, CO 80903, U.S.A. *Website:* www.cc.colorado.edu.

CELIŃSKI, Andrzej, MA; Polish politician; b. 26 Feb. 1950, Warsaw; m.; three s.; ed Warsaw Univ.; co-f. Underground Soc. for Scholarly Courses; mem. Workers' Defence Cttee (KOR) and Solidarity Ind. Self-governing Trade Union; mem. Civic Cttee attached to Solidarity leader Lech Wałęsa 1988–90; participant Round Table plenary debates 1989; Senator 1989–93 (mem. Civic Parl. Caucus, then Democratic Union Caucus); Deputy to Sejm (Parl.) 1993–; Vice-Chair. Democratic Union (UD) 1993–94; mem. Freedom Union (UW) 1994–99; Chair. Programme Comm., then Vice-Chair. Democratic Left Alliance (SLD) 1999–; Minister of Culture and Nat. Heritage 2001–02. *Address:* c/o Ministry of Culture and National Heritage, ul. Krakowskie Przedmieście 15/17, 00-071 Warsaw, Poland (Office).

CELLUCCI, Argeo Paul, JD; American politician, lawyer and diplomatist; b. 24 April 1948, Marlboro, Mass.; s. of Argeo R. Cellucci and Priscilla Rose Cellucci; m. Janet Garnett 1971; two d.; ed Boston Coll.; attorney, Kittredge, Cellucci and Moreira, Hudson, Mass. 1973–90; mem. Charter Comm. Hudson 1970–71, Selectman 1971–77; State Rep. Third Middx Dist, Mass. 1977–84; State Senator Middx and Worcs. Dists., Mass. 1985–90; Lt-Gov. of Massachusetts 1991–97, Gov. 1997–2000; Amb. to Canada 2001–; Capt., USAR; mem. American Bar Asscn, Mass. Bar Asscn; Republican. *Address:* Embassy of the United States of America, 490 Sussex Drive, PO Box 866, Station B, Ottawa, Ont. K1N 1G8, Canada (Office). *Telephone:* (613) 238-5335 (Office). *E-mail:* reference@usembassycanada.gov (Office).

CEM, İsmail; Turkish politician; fmrly journalist; fmrly Dir Turkish TV network; fmr. mem. Democratic Left Party; mem. Parl. 1995–; Minister of Foreign Affairs 1997–2002; Founder and Leader New Turkey Party (Yeni Turkiye Partisi—YTP) July 2002–. *Leisure interest:* photography. *Address:* Yeni Turkiye Partisi (YTP), Hoşdere Cad. 144, 06550 Ayrancı, Ankara, Turkey (Office). *Telephone:* (312) 4420033 (Office). *Fax:* (312) 4429740 (Office). *Website:* www.ytp.org.tr (Office).

CENAC, Winston Francis, LLB, QC; Saint Lucia politician and lawyer; b. 14 Sept. 1925, St Lucia; s. of Frank and Leanese (née King) Cenac; m. Flora Marie Cenac 1952; ed St Mary's Coll. and Univ. of London; worked as Chief Clerk in District Court, then as Deputy Registrar, Supreme Court; called to the Bar Lincoln's Inn, London 1957; Registrar, Supreme Court, St Lucia 1957; Acting Magistrate, Southern District, St Lucia 1958; Chief Registrar of Supreme Court of Windward and Leeward Islands 1959; Attorney-Gen. of St Lucia 1962, of St Vincent 1964, of Grenada 1966; del. Constitutional Conf., Little Eight Constitution, London 1962; Dir of Public Prosecutions, Grenada 1967; pvt. practice in St Lucia 1969; Puisne Judge of St Vincent 1971, of Antigua 1971, of St Kitts, Nevis and Virgin Islands 1972; returned to pvt. practice, St Lucia 1973; Senator of St Lucia Legis. 1978; mem. House of Ass. for Soufrière 1979–; Attorney-Gen. of Saint Lucia 1979–80, Prime Minister 1981–82; Pres. St Lucia Bar Asscn 1989; Chair. Org. of Eastern Caribbean States, Bar Asscn 1989, Bd of Appeal of Income Tax Commrs. 1989; Life mem. Commonwealth Parl. Asscn. *Publication:* Coutume de Paris to 1988: The Evolution of Land Law in Saint Lucia. *Leisure interests:* reading, gardening, music. *Address:* 7 High Street, Box 629, Castries, Saint Lucia. *Telephone:* 27919; 23891. *Fax:* 27919.

CENTERMAN, Jörgen, MSc; business executive; b. 1952; ed Univ. of Tech. of Lund; joined ABB 1976, worked in Singapore, Sweden, Germany, USA, Switzerland, fmr Head, Automation Segment, Pres. and CEO 2001–. *Address:* ABB, Haselstrasse, 5400 Baden, Switzerland (Office). *Telephone:* (56) 2052012 (Office). *Fax:* (56) 2057045 (Office).

ČEPANIS, Alfreds; Latvian politician; b. 3 Aug. 1943, Kalsnava, Madona Region; m. Ilma Čepane; one d.; ed Jaungolbene School of Agric., Higher CP School in Moscow by correspondence; Comsomol functionary 1968–74; Deputy Chair., Chair. Ventspils District Exec. Cttee 1975–79; Sec. Preili Regional Cttee Latvian CP 1979–84; First Sec. Liepaja regional CP Cttee 1983–88; Deputy Chair. Council of Ministers 1989–90; mem. Supreme Soviet of Latvia 1990–93; mem. Saeima (Parl.), Deputy Speaker 1993–95; mem. faction Demikratiska Partija Samnieks 1995, Speaker 1996–98; now business executive. *Leisure interests:* hunting, literature, theatre. *Address:* Saeima, Jēkaba iela 11, 226811 Riga, Latvia. *Telephone:* 708-71-11.

CEREZO ARÉVALO, Mario Vinicio; Guatemalan politician; b. 26 Dec. 1942; s. of Marco Vinicio Cerezo; m. Raquel Blandón 1965; four c.; ed Univ. of San Carlos; mem. Christian Democratic Party; Pres. of Guatemala 1986–91. *Address:* c/o Partido Democracia Cristiana Guatemalteca, Avda Elena 20-66, Zona 3, Guatemala City, Guatemala.

ČERNÁK, Ľudovít, DipTech; Slovak politician and industrialist; b. 12 Oct. 1951, Hliník nad Hronom; m.; three c.; ed Univ. of Tech., Bratislava; man. training in UK 1990; worked for SNP Works, Žiar nad Hronom 1975–92; Minister of Economy –1993, 1998–2000; Vice-Chair. Nat. Council 1993–94; now mem. Parl. of Slovakia; Vice-Chair. Democratic Union; Chair. pvt. Investment Co.; mem. Int. Cttee for Econ. Reform and Co-operation; in pvt business (investment and finance) 2000–. *Leisure interests:* family, detective novels. *Address:* Sitno Holdings a.s., Medena 12, Bratislava; Liscie údolie 29, Bratislava, Slovakia (Home). *Telephone:* (7) 5292-1775 (Office). *Fax:* (7) 5292-6700 (Office). *E-mail:* info@sitno.sk (Office). *Website:* www.sitno.sk (Office).

CEROVSKÝ, Lt.-Gen. Milan, DipEng; Slovak army general; b. 10 Oct. 1949, Kalinov; m.; two c.; ed Mil. Acad., Vyškov; Mil. Acad., Brno, Royal Coll. of Defence, London, UK; Platoon Commdr.; Co. Commdr; Deputy Chief of Staff 60th Tank Regt, 14th Tank Div., E Mil. Dist, Commdr Tank Battalion; Chief of Staff 63rd Mechanized Regt, 14th Tank Div., Commdr; Chief of Staff 13th Tank Div., Deputy Commdr of Operations, Commdr 1993–94; Commdr 1st Army Corps 1994–97; Chief of Integration and Standardization Admin. of Army Gen. Staff. 1998, Head of Gen. Staff 1998–; rank of Lt-Gen. 1999–. *Leisure interest:* sport. *Address:* Ministry of Defence, Kutuzovova 8, 83247 Bratislava, Slovakia (Office). *Telephone:* (2) 44455054. *Fax:* (2) 44258878. *E-mail:* www.admin@army.sk. *Website:* www.army.sk.

CÉSAIRE, Aimé Fernand, LèsL; French politician, poet and dramatist; b. 25 June 1913, Basse-Pointe, Martinique; s. of Fernand and Marie (Hermine) Césaire; m. Suzanne Roussi 1937; four s. two d.; ed Fort-de-France (Martinique) and Lycée Louis-le-Grand (Paris), Ecole Normale Supérieure and the

Sorbonne; teaching career 1940–45; mem. Constituent Assemblies 1945 and 1946; Deputy for Martinique 1946–93; Pres. Parti Progressiste Martiniquais; Mayor of Fort-de-France 1945–2001; Pres. Conseil régional, Martinique 1983–86; Pres. Soc. of African Culture, Paris; Grand Prize for Verse 1982. *Publications:* Verse: Cahier d'un retour au pays natal, Les armes miraculeuses, Et les chiens se taisaient, Soleil cou coupé, Corps perdu, Cadastre, Ferrements, Moi, laminaire 1982, Poetry: Oeuvres complètes et inédites 1994; Essays: Discours sur le colonialisme; Plays: La tragédie du roi Christophe, Une saison au Congo, Une tempête. *Address:* c/o La Mairie, boulevard de général de Gaulle, 97200 Fort-de-France, Martinique, West Indies.

ÇETÎN, Hikmet; Turkish politician; b. 1937, Diyarbakir; m.; two c.; ed Ankara Univ. Political Sciences Faculty, Williams Coll., USA; Sec.-Gen. Social Democratic Populist Party (SHP) (merged to form Republican People's Party), Chair. 1995; deputy from Gaziantep; Minister of Foreign Affairs 1991–95; Deputy Prime Minister and Minister of State 1995–96. *Address:* c/o Deputy Prime Minister's Office, Bakanlıkar, Ankara, Turkey.

CHAABANE, Sadok; Tunisian politician and professor of law; b. Sadok Chaabane, 23 Feb. 1950, Syphax; s. of Jilani Chaabane; m. Dalenda Nouri 1974; one s. two d.; Prof. of Law, Univ. of Tunis 1973–; Dir of Studies, Research and Publ Centre 1975–82; Perm. Sec. of R.C.C. 1988; Sec. of State for Higher Educ. and Scientific Research 1989; Adviser to the President on Political Affairs 1990; Sec. of State for Scientific Research 1991; Prin. Adviser to the Pres. on Human Rights 1991; Minister of Justice 1992–97, of Higher Educ. Nov. 1999–; Founder mem. Int. Acad. of Constitutional Law, Int. Law Asscn; Commdr Order of Nov. 7, Great Cordon of Order of the Repub. *Publications:* The Law of International Institutions 1985, Ben Ali and The Way to Pluralism in Tunisia 1997, The Challenges of Ben Ali 1999. *Address:* Ministry of Higher Education, Avenue Ouled Haffouz, 1030 Tunis (Office); 30 Rue Mannoubia Ben Nasr, Manar 3, 2092, Tunis, Tunisia (Home). *Telephone:* (71) 784-170 (Office); (71) 889-690 (Home); (98) 315-050. *Fax:* (71) 786-711 (Office). *E-mail:* sadok.chaabane@mes.rnu.tn (Office).

CHABON, Michael, MFA; American writer; b. 1964, Columbia, Md; m.; one s. one d.; ed Univ. of Pittsburgh, Univ. Coll. Irvine. *Publications:* The Mysteries of Pittsburgh 1988, A Model World (short stories), Wonder Boys (film 2000), Werewolves in Their Youth (short stories), The Amazing Adventures of Kavalier & Clay (Pulitzer Prize for fiction) 2001; short stories published in several magazines. *Address:* c/o Random House Inc., 201 East 50th Street, New York, NY 10022, USA (Office).

CHABROL, Claude; French film director and producer; b. 24 June 1930, Paris; s. of Yves Chabrol and Madeleine Delarbre; m. 1st Agnès Goute; two s.; m. 2nd Colette Dacheville (Stéphane Audran, q.v.); one s.; m. 3rd Aurore Pajot 1983; ed Paris Univ., Ecole Libre des Sciences Politiques; fmrly film critic and Public Relations Officer in Paris for 20th-Century Fox; dir and producer 1958–; Locarno Festival Grand Prix 1958, Berlin Festival Golden Bear 1959. *Films directed include:* Le beau Serge 1957, Les cousins 1958, A double tour 1959, Les bonnes femmes 1959, Les godelureaux 1960, Ophélia 1962, L'oeil du malin 1961, Landru 1962, Les plus belles escroqueries du monde 1963, Le tigre aime la chair fraîche 1964, Le tigre se parfume à la dynamite 1965, Marie-Chantal contre le Docteur Kha 1965, Le scandale 1967, Les biches 1968, La femme infidèle 1968, Que la bête meure 1969, Le boucher 1970, La rupture 1970, Juste avant la nuit 1971, Doctor Popaul 1972, La décade prodigieuse 1972, Les noces rouges 1973, Nada 1973, Une partie de plaisir 1975, Les innocents aux mains sales 1976, Alice ou la dernière fugue 1977, Les liens de sang 1977, Violette Nozière 1978, The Twist, Blood Relations 1979, Le Cheval d'Orgueil 1980, Les fantômes du chapelier 1982, Cop au vin 1985, Inspecteur Lavardin 1986, Masques 1987, Une Affaire des Femmes 1988, Story of Women 1989, Dr. M 1989, Quiet Days in Clichy 1989, Madame Bovary 1991, Betty 1991, L'Enfer 1993, La Cérémonie, Through the Eyes of Vichy, A Judgement in Stone, Rien ne va plus 1997, Merci pour le chocolat 2000, La fleur du mal 2003. *Publications:* Alfred Hitchcock (with E. Rohmer), Les Noces rouges, Et pourtant je tourne. *Address:* c/o Artmedia, 10 avenue Georges V, 75008 Paris; 15 Quai Conti, 75006 Paris, France.

CHADERTON MATOS, Roy; Venezuelan politician and diplomatist; b. 17 Aug. 1942; ed Cen. Univ. of Venezuela, Instituto de Altos Estudios de Defensa Nacional; Second Sec. Embassy in Poland 1969–72; First Sec. Embassy in FRG 1973, Embassy in Canada 1975, in Ministry of Foreign Affairs 1973–75, Counsellor 1979, Minister Counsellor 1979–82, Amb. 1983–85, Gen. Dir of Int. Political Affairs 1990–93, Gen. Dir (Vice-Pres.) 1994–95; Counsellor Embassy in Belgium 1977–78; Counsellor Perm. Mission to UN, New York 1978–79, Deputy Perm. Rep. 1982–83; Amb. to Gabon 1985–87, to Norway and Iceland 1987–90, to Canada 1993–94, to UK and Ireland 1996–2000, to Colombia 2000–02, to USA 2002–; Minister of Foreign Affairs 2002–; mem. Social Christian Party of Venezuela (COPEI) 1958–, Official Rep. 1994; Caballero de Madara Order (Bulgaria), Francisco de Miranda Order, First Class (Venezuela), Bernardo O'Higgins Order (Chile), Great Cross, May Order (Argentina), Great Cross, San Olav Order (Norway), Great Cross, Cruceiro do Sul National Order (Brazil), Great Cord Libertador Order (Venezuela). *Address:* Ministry of Foreign Affairs, Torre MRE, Avda Urdaneta, al lado del Correo de Carmelitas, Caracas 1010, Venezuela (Office). *Telephone:* (212) 860-0209 (Office). *Fax:* (212) 861-0894 (Office). *E-mail:* ministro@mre.gov.ve. *Website:* www.mre.gov.ve (Office).

CHADIRJI, Rifat Kamil, DipArch, FRIBA; Iraqi architect; b. 6 Dec. 1926, Baghdad; s. of Kamil Chadirji; m. Balkis Sharara 1954; ed Hammersmith School of Arts and Crafts, London; f. and Sr Partner and Dir Iraq Consult 1952–; Section Head, Baghdad Bldg Dept Waqaf Org. 1954–57; Dir-Gen. Housing, Ministry of Planning, Baghdad 1958–59, Head Planning Cttee Ministry of Housing 1959–63; returned to full-time private practice with Iraq Consult 1963–78; apptd Counsellor to Mayoralty of Baghdad 1980–82; mem. Iraqi Tourist Bd 1970–75; Loeb Fellow, Harvard Univ. 1983; many awards and prizes including First Prize for Council of Ministers Bldg, Baghdad 1975, First Prize New Theatre, Abu Dhabi, UAE 1977, First Prize, Council of Ministers, Abu Dhabi, UAE 1978. *Exhibitions include:* Gulbenkian Hall, Baghdad 1966, Univ. of Khartoum, Sudan 1966, Ministry of Art and Culture, Accra, Ghana 1966, Kwame Nkrumah Univ. of Science and Tech., Ghana 1966, Middle East Tech. Univ., Ankara, Turkey 1966, Athens Insts., Greece 1966, American Univ. of Beirut, Lebanon 1966, Arab Engineers Conf., Jordan 1966, Amman, Jordan 1966, Hammersmith Coll. of Art 1966, Ain Shamis Univ., Cairo, Egypt 1967, Arab Engineers Conf., Kuwait 1975, Kuwait Engineers Union 1975, Iraqi Cultural Cen., London 1978, Middle East Construction Exhbn, Dubai, UAE 1978, Vienna Tech. Univ., Austria 1978. *Works include:* Council of Ministers Bldg, Baghdad 1975, Cabinet Ministers' Bldg, UAE 1976, Nat. Theatre, Abu Dhabi, UAE 1977, Al-Ain Public Library, UAE 1978. *Leisure interests:* photography, travel. *Address:* 28 Troy Court, Kensington High Street, London, W8, England. *Telephone:* (20) 7937 3715.

CHADLI, Col Bendjedid; Algerian politician and army officer; b. 14 April 1929, Sebaa; six c.; joined Maquisards (guerrilla forces) in fight for independence against French 1955; mem. General Staff of Col Boumédienne's army 1961; Commdr Constantine Mil. Region, East Algeria 1962, of Second Mil. Region (Oran) 1963–79; mem. Revolutionary Council 1965; Acting Chief of Staff 1978–79; Sec.-Gen. Nat. Liberation Front 1979; Pres. of Algeria, C-in-C of the Armed Forces 1979–91; Medal of the Resistance 1984.

CHADLINGTON, Baron (Life Peer), cr. 1996, of Dean in the County of Oxfordshire; **Peter Selwyn Gummer,** MA, FRSA; British business executive; b. 24 Aug. 1942, Bexley; s. of the late Rev. Canon Selwyn Gummer and Sybille Gummer (née Mason); brother of John Selwyn Gummer; m. Lucy Rachel Dudley-Hill 1982; one s. three d.; ed King's School, Rochester, Selwyn Coll., Cambridge; with Portsmouth & Sunderland Newspaper Group 1964–65, Viyella Int. 1965–66, Hodgkinson & Partners 1966–67, Industrial & Commercial Finance Corpn (3i Group) 1967–74; Founder, Chair. and Chief Exec. Shandwick PLC 1974–94, Chair. 1994–2000; Dir (non-exec.) CIA Group PLC 1990–94, Halifax Bldg Soc. London Bd 1990–94, Halifax PLC 1994–2001, Black Box Music Ltd 1999–, Oxford Resources 1999–, hotcourses.com 2000–; Dir Huntsworth PLC 2000–; mem. EU Select Sub-Cttee B (Energy, Ind. and Transport), House of Lords 2000–; Chair. Action on Addiction 2000–; mem. Nat. Health Service Policy Bd 1991–95, mem. Arts Council of Great Britain 1991–94, Arts Council of England 1994–96; Chair. Royal Opera House 1996–97; Chair. Understanding Industry Trust 1991–96, Marketing Group of GB 1993–95, Nat. Lottery Advisory Bd for the Arts and Film 1994–96, guideforlife.com 1999–2002; Dir Walbrook Club 1999–2001; mem. Council, Cheltenham Ladies Coll. 1998–, Bd of Trustees, American Univ. 1999–2001; Hon. Fellow Bournemouth Univ. 1999–; Trustee Atlantic Partnership 1999–; Inst. of Public Relations Pres.'s Medal 1988. *Publications:* articles and booklets on public relations and marketing. *Leisure interests:* opera, rugby, cricket. *Address:* Huntsworth PLC, 15–17 Huntsworth Mews, London, NW1 6DD (Office); c/o House of Lords, London, SW1A 0PW; Chapel Road, Chadlington, Oxon., OX7 3LZ, England (Home). *Telephone:* (20) 7408-2232 (Office); (1608) 676437 (Home); (20) 7219-3000. *Fax:* (20) 7493-3048 (Office). *E-mail:* lordchadlington@huntsworth.com (Office). *Website:* www .huntsworth.co.uk.

CHADWICK, Sir Henry, KBE, FBA, DD, MusB; British professor of divinity; b. 23 June 1920, Bromley, Kent; s. of John Chadwick and Edith M. Chadwick; m. Margaret E Brownrigg 1945; three d.; ed Eton Coll. and Magdalene Coll. Cambridge; Fellow, Queens' Coll. Cambridge 1946–58, Hon. Fellow 1958–; Regius Prof. of Divinity, Univ. of Oxford 1959–69, Dean of Christ Church 1969–79; Regius Prof. of Divinity, Univ. of Cambridge 1979–83, Prof. Emer. 1983–, Fellow, Magdalene Coll. 1979–86; Master Peterhouse, Cambridge 1987–93, Hon. Fellow 1993; Del. Oxford Univ. Press 1960–79; hon. degrees from Glasgow, Leeds, Manchester, Surrey, Uppsala, Yale, Harvard, Jena and Chicago; German Order pour le mérite 1993, Humboldt Prize 1983, Lucas Prize (Tübingen) 1991. *Publications:* Origen Contra Celsum 1953, Early Christian Thought and the Classical Tradition 1966, The Early Church 1967, Priscillian of Avila 1976, Boethius 1981, History and Thought of the Early Church 1982, Augustine 1986, Heresy and Orthodoxy in the Early Church 1991, Augustine's Confessions 1991, Tradition and Exploration 1994, The Church in Ancient Society from Galilee to Gregory the Great 2001, East and West: The Making of a Rift in the Church 2003. *Leisure interest:* music. *Address:* 46 St John Street, Oxford, OX1 2LH, England. *Telephone:* (1865) 512814.

CHADWICK, Michael J., MA, PhD; British environmental scientist; b. 13 Sept. 1934, Leicester; s. of John Chadwick and Hilda Corman; m. Josephine Worrall 1958; one s. two d.; ed Godalming Co. Grammar School and Univ. Coll. of N Wales, Bangor; lecturer, Dept of Botany, Univ. of Khartoum 1959–62; univ. demonstrator, School of Agric., Univ. of Cambridge 1962–66; lecturer, Prof. Dept of Biology, Univ. of York 1966–91; Dir Stockholm Environment Inst., Stockholm 1991–96; Dir LEAD-Europe, Geneva 1996–; fmr Sec. British

Ecological Soc. *Publications:* Restoration of Land (with A. D. Bradshaw) 1980, The Relative Sensitivity of Ecosystems in Europe to Acidic Depositions (with J. C. I. Kuylenstierna) 1990. *Leisure interests:* music, gardening, travel.

CHADWICK, Owen, OM, KBE, FBA; British historian; b. 20 May 1916, Bromley, Kent; s. of John Chadwick and Edith Chadwick (née Horrocks); m. Ruth Hallward 1949; two s. two d.; ed St John's Coll., Cambridge; Fellow, Trinity Hall, Cambridge 1947–56; Master of Selwyn Coll., Cambridge 1956–83, Fellow 1983–; Dixie Prof. of Ecclesiastical History, Cambridge Univ. 1958–68, Regius Prof. of Modern History 1968–83; Vice-Chancellor of Cambridge Univ. 1969–71; Pres. British Acad. 1981–85; Chancellor Univ. of E Anglia 1985–94; Chair. of Trustees, Nat. Portrait Gallery 1988–94; Hon. mem. American Acad. of Arts and Sciences; Hon. DD (St Andrew's) 1960, (Oxford) 1973, (Wales) 1993, Hon. DLitt (Kent) 1970, (Columbia Univ.) 1977, (East Anglia) 1977, (Bristol) 1977, (London) 1983, (Leeds) 1986, (Cambridge) 1987, Hon. LLD (Aberdeen) 1986; Wolfson Literary Award 1981. *Publications:* From Bossuet to Newman 1957, The Victorian Church (2 Vols) 1966–70, John Cassian (2nd Edn) 1968, The Reformation (20th Edn) 1986, The Secularization of the European Mind 1976, The Popes and European Revolution 1981, Britain and the Vatican during the Second World War 1987, Michael Ramsey: A life 1990, The Christian Church in the Cold War 1992, A History of Christianity 1995, A History of the Popes 1830–1914 1998, The Early Reformation on the Continent 2001; numerous articles and reviews in learned journals. *Leisure interests:* music and gardening. *Address:* 67 Grantchester Street, Cambridge, CB3 9HZ, England. *Telephone:* (1223) 314000 (Home).

CHADWICK, Peter, PhD, ScD, FRS; British mathematician; b. 23 March 1931, Huddersfield; s. of Jack Chadwick and Marjorie (Castle) Chadwick; m. Sheila G. Salter 1956; two d.; ed Huddersfield Coll., Univ. of Manchester and Pembroke Coll. Cambridge; Scientific Officer, then Sr Scientific Officer, Atomic Weapons Research Establishment, Aldermaston 1955–59; Lecturer, then Sr Lecturer in Applied Math. Univ. of Sheffield 1959–65; Prof. of Math. Univ. of E Anglia 1965–91, Emer. Prof. 1991–, Dean, School of Math. and Physics 1979–82; Visiting Prof. Univ. of Queensland 1972; Leverhulme Emer. Fellow 1991–93;; Hon. DSc (Glasgow) 1991. *Publications:* Continuum Mechanics: Concise Theory and Problems 1976, 1999; articles in books and learned journals. *Leisure interests:* walking, music. *Address:* 8 Stratford Crescent, Cringleford, Norwich, NR4 7SF, England. *Telephone:* (1603) 451655 (Home).

CHAFEE, Lincoln Davenport, BA; American politician; b. 26 March 1953, Warwick, Providence; m. Stephanie Chafee; one s. two d.; ed Brown Univ., Montana State Univ. Horseshoeing School, Bozeman; blacksmith 1977–83; planner Gen. Dynamics, Quonset Point 1983; Exec. Dir Northeast Corridor Initiative 1980s; began political career as del. to RI Constitutional Convention 1985–86; with Warwick City Council 1986–92, Mayor of Warwick 1992–; Gov. of RI 1999; Senator from RI 2000–, mem. Cttee on the Environment and Public Works, Cttee on Foreign Relations, Jt Econ. Cttee, Chair. Sub-Cttee on Superfund, Waste Control and Risk Assessment, Sub-Cttee on Western Hemisphere, Peace Corps, Narcotics and Terrorism; mem. Republican Party; Francis M. Driscoll Award for Leadership, Scholarship and Athletics, Brown Univ. *Leisure interests:* skiing, horseback trail riding. *Address:* Office of the Senator from Rhode Island, US Senate, Senate Buildings, Washington, DC 20510, USA (Office).

CHAGULA, Wilbert K., MB, CH.B., MA; Tanzanian public servant and administrator; b. 3 Feb. 1926, Shinyanga, Tanganyika; s. of Kiyenze Chagula; ed Tabora Govt School, Makerere Univ. Coll., Uganda, King's Coll., Cambridge Univ., Univ. of W Indies, Jamaica, Yale Univ., USA; Asst Medical Officer, Tanganyika 1952; Asst in Dept of Anatomy, Asst Lecturer, Lecturer in Anatomy, Makerere Univ. Coll. 1953–61; Rockefeller Foundation Fellow in Histochemistry, Jamaica and Yale Univs. 1961–63; Registrar and Vice-Prin., Univ. Coll., Dar es Salaam 1963–65, Prin. 1965–70; Minister for Water Devt and Power 1970–72, for Econ. Affairs and Devt Planning 1972–75, of Water Energy and Minerals 1975–77; Minister for Finance and Admin. (East African Community) 1977–78; Amb. to the UN, Geneva, 1978–86, to the UN, New York, 1986–91; Chair. Tanzania Nat. Scientific Research Council 1972; mem. UN Advisory Cttee for the Application of Science and Tech. to Devt 1971– (Chair. sessions 1973–78), WHO Advisory Cttee on Medical Research and WHO Expert Advisory Panel on Public Health Admin. 1976–77, UN Univ. Council 1977, Bd of Trustees Int. Fed. of Science 1975, Editorial Bd of Mazingira 1977–, E African Acad. (Pres. 1963–, Fellow 1971), Medical Asscn of Tanzania, Econ. Soc. of Tanzania, The Third World Forum, Tanganyika African Nat. Union Nat. Exec. Cttee 1969–75, Tanganyika Soc. of African Culture, Tanzania Soc.; Adviser Int. Fed. of Insts. of Advanced Studies. *Publications:* books and articles on education and health. *Leisure interests:* reading, writing. *Address:* c/o Ministry of Foreign Affairs, P.O. Box 9000, Dar es Salaam, Tanzania.

CHAHINE, Youssef; Egyptian film director; b. 25 Jan. 1926, Alexandria; 50th Anniversary Prize, Cannes Film Festival 1997. *Films include:* Papa Amine 1950, Cairo Station 1953, Struggle in the Valley 1953, Saladin 1963, The Land 1969, The Choice 1970, The Sparrow 1973, Return of the Prodigal Son 1976, Alexandria . . . Why? 1978, An Egyptian Story 1982, Adieu Bonaparte 1984, Alexandria Again and Always 1990.

CHAI SONGYUE; Chinese politician; b. Nov. 1941, Putuo Co., Zhejiang Prov.; joined CCP 1961; Vice-Gov., mem. CCP Zhejiang Provincial Cttee, Dir Zhejiang Provincial Planning Comm. 1988; alt. mem. 14th CCP Cen. Cttee 1992; Vice-Gov. Zhejiang Prov. 1993, Gov. 1997–; mem. 15th CCP Cen. Cttee 1997–. *Address:* Office of the Governor, Zhejiang Provincial Government, Hangzhou City, Zhejiang Province, People's Republic of China.

CHAIGNEAU, Pascal Gérard Joël, DèsSc, DenScPol, DenScEcon, DenD; French academic; b. 8 Feb. 1956, Paris; s. of André Chaigneau and Hélène Alexandre; m. Marie-Claude Ratsarazaka-Ratsimandresy 1983; three s.; ed Coll. St Michel de Picpus and Facultés de Droit et des Lettres, Paris; practical work 1974–75; Asst 1976–78, Prof. Ecole des Hautes Etudes Internationales et Ecole Supérieure de Journalisme 1978–; Research, Fondation pour les Etudes de Défense Nationale 1980–82; in charge of course, Univ. de Paris II 1982–90; Maître de conférences, Univ. de Paris V 1990–2000, Professeur des universités 2000–; Dir of Studies, Ecole des Hautes Etudes Internationales 1984–85, Dir-Gen. 1985–90; Admin.-Gen. Ecole des Hautes Etudes Internationales, Ecole des Hautes Etudes Politiques et Sociales, Ecole Supérieure de Journalisme 1990–; Sec.-Gen. Centre de Recherches Droit et Défense, Univ. de Paris V 1985–; Founder and Dir Centre d'Etudes Diplomatiques et Stratégiques 1986–; Advocate, Court of Appeal, Paris 1990–; Prof. Centre des Hautes Etudes sur l'Afrique et l'Asie Modernes; lecturer, Inst. des Hautes Etudes de Défense Nationale; in charge of course, Ecole des Hautes Etudes Commerciales 1990–92, Prof. 1992–; Prof. Collège Interarmes de Défense 1994–; with Bolivian Consulate in France 1994–97; Foreign Trade Counsellor 1995–; many other public appointments; mem. Acad. des Sciences d'Outremer, Soc. d'Economie Politique; Dr hc (Nat. Univ. of Bolivia); Hon. LLD (Richmond, USA); Grand Prix de l'Asscn. des Ecrivains de Langue Française 1987, Prix de l'Acad. des Sciences Morales et Politiques 1993 and other prizes, awards and distinctions; Chevalier, Légion d'honneur, Officier, Ordre nat. du mérite, Commdr, Ordre des Palmes Académiques, Commdr des Arts et des Lettres; decorations from Bolivia, Burkina Faso, Belgium, Honduras, Chad, Madagascar, Niger, etc. *Publications:* La Stratégie soviétique 1978, La Politique militaire de la France en Afrique 1984, Rivalités politiques et socialisme à Madagascar 1985, Les Pays de l'Est et l'Afrique 1985, Franceocéan indien-mer rouge (with others) 1986, Pour une analyse du commerce international 1987, La Guerre du Golfe 1991, Europe: la nouvelle donne stratégique 1993, Les grands Enjeux du monde contemporain 1997, Dictionnaire des Relations Internationales 1998, Gestion des Risques internationaux 2001. *Address:* CEPC, 54 avenue Marceau, 75008 Paris (Office); 68 avenue de Gravelle, 94220 Charenton-le-Pont, France (Home).

CHAIKA, Yurii Yakovlevich; Russian jurist; b. 1951, Moscow; fmr investigator in prosecution offices; Head of E Siberian Transport Prosecutor's Office; Prosecutor Irkutsk Region 1976–95; First Deputy Prosecutor-Gen., Russian Fed. 1995–99, Acting Prosecutor-Gen. 1999–2000; Minister of Justice 2000–. *Address:* Ministry of Justice, Vorontsovo pole 4, 109830 Moscow GSP 28, Russia (Office). *Telephone:* (095) 206-05-54 (Office). *Fax:* (095) 916-29-03 (Office). *Website:* www.scli.ru (Office).

CHAILLY, Riccardo; Italian conductor; b. 20 Feb. 1953, Milan; s. of the late Luciano Chailly and of Anna Marie Motta; m. Gabriella Terragni 1987; two s.; ed Giuseppe Verdi and Perugia Conservatories and with Franco Caracciolo and Franco Ferrara; Asst to Claudio Abbado, La Scala, Milan 1972–74; début as Conductor with Chicago Opera 1974; début, La Scala 1978, Covent Garden (operatic début) 1979; concert début with London Symphony Orchestra and Edin. Festival 1979; American concert début 1980; played with major orchestras 1980; début, Metropolitan Opera 1982; Prin. guest Conductor, London Philharmonic Orchestra 1982–85; début, Vienna State Opera 1983; appearances Salzburg Festival 1984, 1985, 1986; Japan début, with Royal Philharmonic Orchestra 1984; début, New York Philharmonic Orchestra 1984; Chief Conductor of Radio Symphony Orchestra Berlin 1982–89; Music Dir Bologna Orchestra 1986–93; Prin. Conductor Royal Concertgebouw Orchestra, Amsterdam 1988–, Giuseppe Verdi, Milan 1999–; Hon. mem. Royal Acad. of Music, London; Gramophone Award Artist of the Year 1998, Diapason d'Or Artist of the Year 1999; Grand' Ufficiale della Repubblica Italiana, Knight of Order of Netherlands Lion, Cavaliere di Gran Croce (Italy), Abrogino d'Oro, Comune Milano (Italy). *Leisure interests:* music, paintings, the arts in general. *Address:* Royal Concertgebouw Orchestra, Jacob Obrechtstraat 51, 1071 Amsterdam, Netherlands. *Telephone:* (20) 5730573 (Office). *Fax:* (20) 6763331 (Office). *Website:* www .concertgebouworkest.nl (Office).

CHAISANG, Chaturon, MA; Thai politician; b. 1 Jan. 1956, Chachoengsao; ed State Univ. of New York at Buffalo, American Univ., Washington DC; Asst Sec. to Minister of Finance 1986–87; Sec. Econ. Cttee, House of Reps. 1986–88; mem. Parl. Chachoengsao 1986–92, 1995–; Sec. Cttee on Finance, Banking and Financial Insts., House of Reps. 1988–91 (mem. 1992); Sec. to Minister of Commerce and adviser to Minister of Agric. 1991; adviser Minister of Science, Tech. and Environment 1992, Ministry of Labour and Social Welfare 1995; Spokesman for New Aspiration Party 1992–95, now Sec.-Gen.; Deputy Minister of Finance 1996–2001, Minister attached to Prime Minister's Office 2001, Minister of Justice 2002–; Chair. Cttee of Science and Tech., House of Reps.; Kt. Grand Cross (First Class) of Crown of Thailand. *Address:* Ministry of Justice, Thanon Ratchadaphisek, Chatuchak, Bangkok 10900 (Office); 441/ 12 Supakij Road, Maung, Chachoengsao 24000, Thailand. *Telephone:* (2) 502-8051 (Office). *Telex:* (2) 502-8059 (Office). *Website:* www.moj.go.th (Office).

CHAKAIPA, Archbishop Patrick Fani; Zimbabwean ecclesiastic; b. 25 June 1932, Mhondoro; ed St Michael's Mission, Mhondoro, Kutama Training

Coll.; ordained Roman Catholic priest 1965; Titular Bishop of Rucuma and Auxiliary Bishop of Salisbury (now Harare) 1972–76; Archbishop of Salisbury (now Harare) 1976–; first Nat. Dir Pontifical Mission Aid Societies for Zimbabwe 1974–78; Pres. Zimbabwe Catholic Bishops' Conf. 1977–1982; Pres. IMBISA (Inter-regional Meeting of Bishops of Southern Africa) 1992–95; Chancellor Catholic Univ. in Zimbabwe 1998–; Hon. DD (Gregorian Univ.) 1973. *Publications:* Karikoga Gumiremiseve 1958, Pfumo Reropa 1961, Rudo Ibofu 1961, Garandichauya 1963, Dzasukwa Mwana Asina Hembe 1967. *Leisure interest:* chess. *Address:* Archbishop's House, 66 Fifth Street, Harare, Zimbabwe (Home); Archdiocese of Harare, P.O. Box CY330, Causeway, Harare (Office). *Telephone:* (4) 792125 (Home); (4) 727386 (Office). *Fax:* (4) 721598 (Office). *E-mail:* hrearch@zol.co.zw (Office).

CHALABI, Ahmad, PhD; Iraqi politician and business executive; b. 1945, Baghdad; m.; four c.; ed in UK, MIT and Univ. of Chicago, USA; family moved to England following coup d'état and assassination of King of Iraq 1958; fmr Prof. of Math., American Univ. of Beirut; f. Bank of Petra, Jordan 1980, taken over by mil. decree 1989, charged with embezzlement, fraud and misuse of depositor funds by Jordanian court 1991, sentenced in absentia to 22 years' imprisonment 1992; organized conf. of 400 opposition leaders in Northern Iraq 1991; Chair. Exec. Council, Iraqi Nat. Congress (INC) 1992–; survived failed coup 1995; lived in exile in London 1996–2003; returned to Iraq to help establish an interim govt following the overthrow of Saddam Hussein's regime April 2003. *Address:* c/o Iraqi National Congress, 17 Cavendish Square, London, W1M 9AA (Office); c/o Iraqi National Congress, 9 Pall Mall Deposit, 124–128 Barlby Road, London, W10 6BL, England (Office). *Telephone:* (20) 7665-1812 (Office). *Fax:* (20) 7665-1201 (Office). *E-mail:* pressoffice@inc.org.uk (Office). *Website:* www.inc.org.uk (Office); www.afsc .org/iraq/chalabi.htm (Office).

CHALANDON, Albin Paul Henri, LèsL; French politician and businessman; b. 11 June 1920, Reyrieux, Ain; s. of Pierre Chalandon and Claire Cambon; m. Princess Salomé Murat 1951; two s. one d.; ed Lycée Condorcet, Paris; Inspecteur des Finances; Dir Banque Nationale pour le Commerce et l'Industrie (Afrique) 1950–51; Admin. and Dir-Gen. Banque Commerciale de Paris 1952–64, Président-Directeur Général 1964–68; MP 1967–76; Minister of Industry May 1968, of Public Works, Housing and Urban Devt 1968–72, of Justice 1986–88; Special Asst, Ministry of Foreign Affairs Feb.–Aug. 1974; Treas. Cen. Cttee Union pour la Nouvelle République (now Union des Démocrates pour la République) 1958–59, Sec.-Gen. 1959, Deputy Sec.-Gen. UDR 1974–75; Pres., Dir-Gen. Soc. Nat. ELF Aquitaine (SNEA) 1976–83; Pres., Dir-Gen. Texmaille 1989–; mem. Social and Econ. Council 1963–67; Grand Officier Légion d'honneur, Croix de guerre. *Publications:* Le système monétaire international 1966, Les joueurs de flûte, Le rêve économique de la Gauche 1977, Quitte ou Double 1986. *Address:* 12 rue de Lota, 75016 Paris, France (Home). *Telephone:* 1-47-04-51-71.

CHALAYAN, Hussein, BA; fashion designer; ed Cyprus and Cen. St Martin's School of Art, London; student final year collection featured in Brown's window; set up own label; exhbn of first solo collection, West Soho Galleries, London 1994; second collection shown during London Fashion Week and in Kobe and Tokyo; fourth collection received Absolut Vodka's Absolut Creation Sponsorship Award (first recipient) 1996; solo exhbn (key pieces from past collections), The Window Gallery, Prague 1996; exhibited Buried and Path dresses, Jam (style, music and media) exhbn, Barbican Art Gallery 1996; designs selected for Cutting Edge exhbn, Victoria and Albert Museum 1997; invited to exhibit in Challenge of Materials exhbn, Science Museum 1997; talk at Tate Gallery (with Zaha Hadid, Michael Bracewell and Georgina Starr) on parallels between fashion, art and architecture 1997; Designer of the Year, London Fashion Awards 1998, 2000. *Address:* 71 Endell Road, London, WC2 9AJ, England.

CHALFONT, Baron (Life Peer), cr. 1964; **(Arthur) Alun Gwynne Jones,** PC, OBE, MC, FRSA; British politician; b. 5 Dec. 1919, Lantarnam, Wales; s. of Arthur Gwynne Jones and Eliza Alice Hardman; m. Dr. Mona Mitchell 1948; one d. (deceased); ed West Monmouth School; commissioned into S. Wales Borderers (24th Foot) 1940; served in Burma 1941–44, Malaya 1955–57, Cyprus 1958–59; resgnd comm. 1961; Defence Corresp. The Times, London 1961–64; Consultant on foreign affairs to BBC TV, London 1961–64; Minister of State for Foreign Affairs 1964–70, Minister for Disarmament 1964–67, 1969–70, in charge of day-to-day negotiations for Britain's entry into Common Market 1967–69; Perm. Rep. to Western European Union 1969–70; Foreign Ed. New Statesman 1970–71; Chair. All-Party Defence Group House of Lords 1980–96, Pres. 1996–; Chair. Industrial Cleaning Papers 1979–86, Peter Hamilton Security Consultants Ltd 1984–86, UK Cttee for Free World 1981–89, European Atlantic Group 1983–, VSEL Consortium PLC 1987–93, Marlborough Stirling Group 1994–99; Deputy Chair. IBA 1989–90; Chair. Radio Authority 1991–94; Pres. Hispanic and Luso Brazilian Council 1975–80, Royal Nat. Inst. for Deaf 1980–87, Llangollen Int. Music Festival 1979–90; Chair. Abington Corpn (Consultants) Ltd 1981–, Nottingham Building Soc. 1983–90, Southern Mining Corpn 1997–99; Dir W S. Atkins Int. 1979–83, IBM UK Ltd 1973–90 (mem. IBM Europe Advisory Council 1973–90), Lazard Brothers and Co. Ltd 1983–90, Shandwick PLC 1985–95, Triangle Holdings 1986–90, TV Corpn PLC 1996–2001; Pres. Freedom in Sport Int.; mem. Int. Inst. of Strategic Studies, Royal Inst.; Hon. Fellow Univ. Coll. Wales, Aberystwyth 1974. *Publications:* The Sword and the Spirit 1963, The Great Commanders 1973, Montgomery of Alamein 1976, (Ed.) Waterloo: Battle of Three Armies 1979, Star Wars: Suicide or Survival 1985, Defence of

the Realm 1987, By God's Will: A Portrait of the Sultan of Brunei 1989, The Shadow of My Hand 2000; contribs to The Times and nat. and professional journals. *Leisure interests:* music, theatre. *Address:* House of Lords, London, SW1A 0PW, England.

CHALIAND, Gérard; French professor of international relations and writer; f. magazine Partisans during Algerian war; fmr Dir Centre européen d'étude des conflits; Prof. Ecole nat. d'administration (ENA), Collège interarmes de défense; Visiting Prof. Harvard Univ., Univ. of Calif. at Berkeley. *Publications:* Mythes révolutionnaires du tiers-monde, Atlas stratégique (with J.-P. Rageau), Anthologie mondiale de la stratégie, Voyage dans le demi-siècle (with Jean Lacouture). *Address:* c/o Département des relations internationales, Ecole Nationale d'Administration, 13 rue de l'Université, 75007 Paris, France (Office).

CHALIDZE, Valeriy Nikolayevich; Russian writer, physicist and publisher; b. 1938, Moscow; m.; ed Moscow Univ., then Faculty of Physics, Tbilisi Univ. 1965; head of research unit in Plastics Research Inst., Moscow 1965–70; removed from post 1970; mem. of USSR Human Rights Cttee; dissident activity 1969–, when started samizdat journal Obshchestvennyye problemy (Problems of Society), trip to USA to lecture on human rights in USSR, subsequently deprived of Soviet citizenship 1972; currently living in New York. *Publications include:* numerous samizdat articles and books and Ugolovnaya Rossiya (Capital Punishment in Russia) 1977, USSR – The Workers' Movement 1978. A Foreigner in the Soviet Union. A Juridical Memoir 1980, Communism Vanquished (Stalin) 1981, The Responsibility of a Generation 1982, National Problems and Perestroika 1988, The Dawn of the Legal Reform 1990, Responsibility of the Generation 1991, A Hierarchical Man 1991.

CHALKER OF WALLASEY, Baroness (Life Peer), cr. 1992, of Leigh-on-Sea in the County of Essex; **Lynda Chalker,** PC; British politician; b. 29 April 1942, Hitchin, Herts.; d. of the late Sidney Henry James Bates and Marjorie Kathleen Randell; m. 1st Eric Robert Chalker 1967 (divorced 1973); m. 2nd Clive Landa 1981; ed Heidelberg Univ., Germany, London Univ., Cen. London Polytechnic; statistician with Research Bureau Ltd (Unilever) 1963–69; Deputy Market Research Man., Shell Mex & BP Ltd 1969–72; Chief Exec. Int. Div. of Louis Harris Int. 1972–74; MP for Wallasey 1974–92; Parl. Under-Sec. of State, Dept of Health and Social Security 1979–82, Dept of Transport 1982–83; Minister of State, Dept of Transport 1983–86, FCO 1986–97, Minister for Overseas Devt 1989–97; ind. consultant on Africa and Devt 1997–; Chair. Africa Matters Ltd 1998–; Advisory Dir Unilever PLC and N.V. 1998–; Dir (non-exec.) Capital Shopping Centres 1997–2000, Landell Mills Ltd 1999–2001, Ashanti Goldfields Co. 2000–, Group Five Ltd, Devt Consultants Int. 2001–; Chair. Greater London Young Conservatives (GLYC) 1969–70; Nat. Vice-Chair. Young Conservatives 1970–71; Chair. London School of Hygiene and Tropical Medicine 1998–; mem. BBC Gen. Advisory Cttee 1975–79; Hon. Fellow Queen Mary and Westfield Coll.; Dr. hc (Bradford) 1995, (Liverpool), (John Moores), (Cranfield), (Warwick), (Westminster), (East London). *Publications:* We Are Richer Than We Think 1978 (co-author), Africa: Turning the Tide 1989. *Leisure interests:* music, cooking, theatre, driving. *Address:* 51 Causton Street, London, SW1P 4AT (Office); House of Lords, London, SW1A 0PW, England. *Telephone:* (20) 7976-6850 (Office). *Fax:* (20) 7976-4999 (Office); (20) 7834-5880 (Office). *E-mail:* lchalker@ africamatters.com (Office).

CHALMERS, Sir Neil Robert, Kt, PhD; British natural history museum director; b. 19 June 1942, Surrey; s. of William King and Irene Margaret Chalmers (née Pemberton); m. Monica Elizabeth Byanjeru Rusoke 1970; two d.; ed King's Coll. School, Wimbledon, Magdalen Coll., Oxford, St John's Coll., Cambridge; lecturer in Zoology, Makerere Univ. Coll., Kampala, Uganda 1966–69; Scientific Dir Natural Primate Research Centre, Nairobi, Kenya 1969–70; lecturer, subsequently Sr Lecturer then Reader in Biology, The Open Univ. 1970–85, Dean of Science 1985–88; Dir The Natural History Museum, London 1988–(2004); Warden (desig.) Wadham Coll., Oxford (Oct. 2004–). *Publications:* Social Behaviour in Primates 1979, and other books on animal behaviour; numerous papers in Animal Behaviour and other learned journals. *Leisure interests:* music, tennis, swimming. *Address:* The Natural History Museum, Cromwell Road, London, SW7 5BD, England. *Telephone:* (20) 7942-5471. *Fax:* (20) 7942-5095. *Website:* www.nhm.ac.uk.

CHALONER, William Gilbert, PhD, FRS; British professor of botany; b. 22 Nov. 1928; s. of the late Ernest J. Chaloner and L. Chaloner; m. Judith Carroll 1955; one s. two d.; ed Kingston Grammar School and Univ. of Reading; Lecturer and Reader, Univ. Coll. London 1956–72, Visiting Prof. 1995–; Visiting Prof. Pa State Univ. 1961–62; Prof. Univ. of Nigeria 1965–66; Prof. of Botany, Birkbeck Coll. London 1972–79; Hildred Carlile Prof. of Botany and Head School of Life Sciences, Royal Holloway and Bedford New Coll. 1985–94 (Bedford Coll. 1979–85), Prof. Emer., Geology Dept, Royal Holloway, Univ. of London 1994–; Wilmer D. Barrett (Visiting) Prof. of Botany, Univ. of Mass., USA 1987–91; mem. Bd of Trustees, Royal Botanic Gdns. Kew 1983–96; Pres. Linnean Soc. 1985–88; fmr mem. Senate London Univ.; fmr mem. National Environment Research Council; corresp. mem. Botanical Soc. of America 1987–, Associé Etranger de l'Acad. des Sciences; Hon. Fellow Royal Holloway 2002. *Publications:* papers in scientific journals. *Leisure interests:* swimming, tennis, visiting USA. *Address:* 20 Parke Road, London, SW13 9NG, England. *Telephone:* (20) 8748-3863. *E-mail:* w.chaloner@rhul.ac.uk (Office).

CHAMBAS, Mohamed Ibn, JD, PhD; Ghanaian lawyer, diplomatist and political scientist; b. 7 Dec. 1950; m.; ed Univ. of Ghana, Legon, Cornell Univ., New York, Case Western Reserve Univ., Cleveland, USA; teacher Oberlin Coll., Ohio; practised law with Forbes, Forbes and Teamor Legal Practice, Ohio; Deputy Foreign Minister 1987; mem. Parl. for Bimbilla 1993–96, 2000–; First Deputy Speaker of Parl. 1993–94; Deputy Foreign Minister 1994–, Chair. Foreign Affairs Cttee 1993–94; Deputy Minister of Educ. 1997–2000; Exec. Sec. Econ. Community of W. African States (ECOWAS) 2002–; fmr Del. to UN Gen. Ass., OAU, Non-aligned Movt, Commonwealth; mem. Nat. Democratic Congress. *Address:* Economic Community of West African States, ECOWAS Secretariat and Conference Centre, 60 Yakubu Gowon Crescent, Asokoro District PMB 401, Abuja, Nigeria (Office). *Telephone:* (9) 3147647 (Office). *Fax:* (9) 3147646 (Office). *E-mail:* info@ecowasmail.net (Office). *Website:* www.ecowas.int (Office).

CHAMBERLAIN, (George) Richard; American actor; b. 31 March 1935, Los Angeles; s. of Charles Chamberlain and Elsa Chamberlain; ed Los Angeles Conservatory of Music and drama studies with Jeff Corey. *Films include:* Secret of Purple Reef 1960, Thunder of Drums 1961, Twilight of Honor 1963, Joy in the Morning 1965, Petulia 1968, The Madwoman of Chaillot 1969, The Music Lovers 1971, Julius Caesar 1971, Lady Caroline Lamb 1971, The Three Musketeers 1974, Towering Inferno 1974, The Four Musketeers 1975, The Slipper and the Rose 1977, The Swarm 1978, Murder by Phone 1982, King Solomon's Mines 1985, Alan Quartermain and The Lost City of Gold 1987, The Return of the Musketeers 1989, Bird of Prey 1996, River To Drown In 1997, All the Winters That Have Been 1997, The Pavilion 1999. *Stage appearances include:* King Lear, Hamlet, Richard II, The Lady's Not for Burning, Night of the Iguana, Cyrano de Bergerac, My Fair Lady; numerous TV appearances include Dr. Kildare 1961–65, Portrait of a Lady 1968, The Woman I Love 1973, The Count of Monte Cristo 1975, The Man in the Iron Mask 1978, Shogun 1980 (Golden Globe Award), The Thorn Birds 1983, Wallenberg: A Hero's Story 1985, Dream West 1986, The Bourne Identity 1988, Ordeal in the Arctic 1993, The Thorn Birds, The Missing Year.

CHAMBERLAIN, Owen, PhD; American physicist; b. 10 July 1920, San Francisco; s. of Edward Chamberlain and Genevieve Lucinda (Owen) Chamberlin; m. 1st 1943 (divorced 1978); one s. three d.; m. 2nd June Steingart Chamberlain 1980 (deceased); m. 3rd Senta Pugh Chamberlain 1998; ed Germantown Friends School, Dartmouth Coll. and Univ. of Chicago; Research physicist Manhattan Project, Berkeley 1942–43, Los Alamos 1943–46; graduate student (under Enrico Fermi) Univ. of Chicago 1946–48; Instructor in Physics, Univ. of Calif., Berkeley 1948–50, Asst Prof. 1950–54, Assoc. Prof. 1954–58, Prof. 1958–89, Prof. Emer. 1989–; on leave at Univ. of Rome as Guggenheim Fellow 1957–58; Loeb Lecturer, Harvard Univ. 1959; mem. NAS; Fellow, American Acad. of Arts and Sciences, American Physics Soc.; has specialized in research in spontaneous fission, proton scattering, discovery of antiproton, properties of antinucleons, etc.; shared Nobel Prize for Physics with Emilio Segrè 1959; Berkeley citation, Univ. of Calif. 1989. *Leisure interests:* nuclear security and disarmament issues, global population issues. *Address:* Department of Physics, 367 Le Conte Hall, University of California, Berkeley, CA 94720, USA.

CHAMBERLIN, Wendy J.; American diplomatist; b. 12 Oct. 1948, Bethesda, Md; ed Northwestern, Boston and Harvard Univs.; joined Foreign Service, Dept of State, Washington, DC 1975; Consular and Econ. Officer, Vientiane 1976–78; Staff Aide E Asia Bureau, Washington, DC 1978–79; Special Asst to Deputy Sec. of State 1979; Political Officer, Kinshasa 1980–82; Pearson Fellow, U.S. Senate, Washington, DC 1982–83; Political-Mil. Officer, Office of Israel Affairs, Dept of State 1983–85; Dir (acting) Office of Regional Affairs, Bureau of Nr E–S Asian Affairs 1985–87; Asst Gen. Service Officer, Rabat 1988–89; Special Asst to Under-Sec. for Political Affairs, Dept of State 1989–90; Dir of Counter-Terrorism, Nat. Security Council, Washington, DC 1990–91; Dir Office of Press–Public Affairs, Bureau of Nr E–S Asian Affairs 1991–93; Deputy Chief of Mission, Kuala Lumpur 1993–96; Amb. to Laos 1996–99; Prin. Deputy Asst Bureau of Int. Narcotics and Law Enforcement Programs, Washington, DC 1999–2001; Amb. to Pakistan 2001–02; Asst Admin. for Asia and Near East, Agency for Int. Devt 2002–; Nat. Security Fellow 1984. *Address:* c/o Department of State, 2201 C Street, NW, Washington, DC 20520, U.S.A.

CHAMBERS, John T., BA, BSc; American computer executive; m. Elaine Chambers; two c.; ed West Virginia Univ., Indiana Univ.; fmrly worked for Wang Laboratories and IBM; Sr Vice-Pres. for world-wide operations Cisco Systems Inc., San Jose, Calif. 1991–94, Exec. Vice-Pres. 1994–95, Pres., CEO 1995–; Chair. NetAid 1999–; Dir Clarify Inc., Arbor Software. *Address:* Cisco Systems Inc., Building 10, 170 West Tasman Drive, San Jose, CA 95134-1706, USA (Office). *E-mail:* jochambe@cisco.com (Office).

CHAMBERS, Richard Dickinson, PhD, DSc, FRS; British professor of chemistry; b. 16 March 1935, West Stanley, Co. Durham; s. of Alfred Chambers and Elizabeth Chambers (née Allsop); m. Anne Boyd 1959; one s. one d.; ed Stanley Grammar School, Univ. of Durham; postdoctoral research at Univ. of British Columbia, Vancouver 1959–60; lecturer Univ. of Durham 1960–69, Reader 1969–76, Prof. of Chemistry 1976–, Chair. and Head of Dept of Chemistry 1983–86; Sir Derman Christopherson Research Fellow 1988–89, Research Prof. 2000–; Tarrant Visiting Prof., Univ. of Fla, Gainesville 1999; Fulbright Scholar Case Western Reserve Univ., Ohio 1966–67; Dir (non-exec.) BNFL Fluorochemicals Ltd 1995–2000; ACS Award for Creative Work in

Fluorine Chemistry 1991. *Publications:* Fluorine in Organic Chemistry 1973; also numerous articles in scientific journals. *Leisure interests:* opera, golf, watching soccer. *Address:* University of Durham, Department of Chemistry, Science Laboratories, South Road, Durham, DH1 3LE, England. *Telephone:* (191) 374-3120. *Fax:* (191) 384-4737. *E-mail:* r.d.chambers@durham.ac.uk (Office).

CHAMBLISS, Saxby, BA, JD; American politician and lawyer; b. 10 Nov. 1943, Warrenton, NC; m. Julianne Chambliss (née Frohbert); ed Univ. of Georgia, Univ. of Tenn.; fmr small businessman and attorney, Moultrie; mem. Republican Party; mem. Congress from 8th Dist Georgia 1988–2003; apptd to House of Reps Perm. Select Cttee on Intelligence 2001, Chair. Intelligence Sub-Cttee on Terrorism and Homeland Security, Chair. Agric. Gen. Farm Commodities and Risk-Man. Cttee 2001, mem. Armed Services Cttee (f. Congressional Air Power Cttee); fmr Chair. Congressional Sportsmen's Caucus; Senator from Georgia 2003–; Friend of the Farmer Award, Georgia Farm Bureau 1995, Distinguished Service Award, Georgia Peanut Comm. 1997, W. Stuart Symington Award, Air Force Assen.; named Fed. Legislator of the Year, Safari Club Int. 1999. *Leisure interests:* Little League baseball volunteer, YMCA basketball coach. *Address:* Office of the Senator from Georgia, US Senate, Senate Buildings, Washington, DC 20510, USA (Office).

CHAMBON, Pierre, MD, L. ÈS. SC.; French professor of biochemistry; b. 7 Feb. 1931, Mulhouse; s. of Henri Chambon and Yvonne Weill; m. Brigitte Andersson 1957; two s. one d.; ed Univ. of Strasbourg; Research Asst Strasbourg Medical School, Assoc. Prof. 1962–66; Dept of Biochem. Stanford Univ. Medical School 1966–67; Prof. of Biochem. Inst. de Chimie Biologique, Faculté de Médecine, Strasbourg 1967–91; Prof. Louis Pasteur Univ., Strasbourg 1974–93; Prof. Inst. Universitaire de France, Faculté de Médecine, Strasbourg 1991–; Dir Lab. de Génétique Moléculaire des Eucaryotes (LGME), CNRS 1977–; Dir Unité 184 de Biologie Moléculaire et de Génie Génétique, Inst. Nat. de la Santé et de la Recherche Médicale (INSERM) 1978–; Prof. Collège de France 1993–; mem. numerous scientific and editorial bds. etc.; mem. Acad. des Sciences; Foreign mem. NAS, Royal Swedish Acad.; corresp. mem. Liège Acad.; hon. mem. Chinese Soc. of Genetics; Prix Rosen 1976; CNRS Gold Medal 1979; Freeman Foundation Prize of NY Acad. 1981; Lounsbery Prize (NAS and Acad. des Sciences) 1982, Oberling Prize 1986, Prix Griffuel 1987, King Faisal Int. Prize 1988, Krebs Medal 1990, Prix Roussel 1990, Prix Louis Jeantet 1991, Grand Prix, Fondation for Medical Research 1996, Prix Welch 1998, Prix AFRT 1999; other honours and awards; Foreign hon. mem. American Acad. of Arts and Science, Acad. Royale de Médecine, Belgium. *Publications:* 400 articles in scientific reviews. *Address:* Institut de France, 23 quai Conti, 75006 Paris (Office); IGBMC, 1 rue Laurent Fries, B.P. 163, 67404 Illkirch cedex, C.U. Strasbourg, France. *E-mail:* chambon@igbmc.u-strasbg.fr (Office).

CHAMLING, Pawan Kumar; Indian politician; b. 22 Sept. 1950, Yangang Busty, South Sikkim; m. Tika Maya Chamling; four s. four d.; began career as ind. farmer; Pres. of Yangang Gram Panchayat 1982; mem. Sikkim Legis. Ass. 1985–; Minister for Industries, Printing and Information and Public Relations 1989–91; formed Sikkim Democratic Front Party 1993, Leader 1993–; Chief Minister of Sikkim 1994–; Chair. Sikkim Distilleries Ltd 1985–; Pres. Sikkim Handicapped Persons Welfare Mission; numerous awards including Chinton Puraskar 1987, Bharat Shiromani 1996, Man of the Year 1998, The Greenest Chief Minister of India 1998, Man of Dedication 1999, Secular India Harmony Award 1998, Manav Sewa Puraskar 1999, Pride of India Gold Award 1999, Best Citizen of India 1999. *Publications:* numerous works including: Antahin Sapana Meroh Bipana 1985; Perennial Dreams and My Reality, Prarambhek Kabitaharu 1991, Pratiwad 1992, Damthang Heejah ra Aajah 1992, Sikkim ra Narikoh Maryadha 1994, Crucified Prashna Aur Anya Kabitaye 1996, Sikkim ra Prajatantra 1996, Democracy Redeemed 1997, Prajatantra koh Mirmireymah 1997, Mah koh hun. *Leisure interests:* reading, writing. *Address:* CM Secretariat, Tashiling, Gangtok, Sikkim (Office); Ghurbisay, Namchi, Pin. 63748/63399, Sikkim 737126, India (Home). *Telephone:* 22575 (Office); 22536 (Home). *Fax:* 22245 (Office); 24710 (Home). *E-mail:* cm-skm@hub.nic.in. *Website:* www.sikkiminfo.com/sdf (Office).

CHAMORRO, Violeta Barrios de (see Barrios de Chamorro, Violeta).

CHAN, Florinda da Rosa Silva, M.B.A.; Macao civil servant; b. June 1954; ed Int. Open Univ. of Asia (Macao), Univ. of Languages and Culture, Beijing, Nat. Inst. of Public Admin., Beijing; joined Macao Govt 1974, Dir Macao Economy Services 1998, Sec. for Admin. and Justice, Macao Special Admin. Region 1999–; Medal of Professional Merit 1987, Medal of Dedication 1988. *Address:* Office of the Secretary of Administration and Justice, Rua de S. Lourenço 28, Edif. dos Secretários, Macao SAR, People's Republic of China (Office). *Telephone:* 9895179 (Office). *Fax:* 726880 (Office). *E-mail:* florindachan.saj@raem.gov.mo (Office). *Website:* www.macau.gov.mo (Office).

CHAN, Heng Chee, MA, PhD; Singaporean diplomatist and academic; b. 19 April 1942, Singapore; ed Cornell Univ. and Nat. Univ. of Singapore; Asst Lecturer, Nat. Univ. of Singapore 1967–70, lecturer 1970–75, Sr Lecturer 1976–80, Assoc. Prof. of Political Science 1981–, Head Dept of Political Science 1985–88, Prof. 1990–; Dir Inst. of Policy Studies, Singapore Jan.–Dec. 1988; Perm Rep. to UN 1989–91; Amb. to Mexico 1989–91; High Commr in Canada 1989–91; Exec. Dir Singapore Int. Foundation 1991–; Dir Inst. of SE Asian Studies 1993; mem. Int. Council of Asia Soc. 1991–, Singapore Nat. Cttee of Council for Security Co-operation in the Asia-Pacific 1993–, Int. Inst. for

Strategic Studies Council, Hong Kong, 1995–; Int. Advisory Bd of Council on Foreign Relations, New York 1995–; Amb. to U.S.A. 1996–; Hon. DLit (Newcastle, Australia) 1994; Nat. Book Award (non-fiction) 1978, 1986, Woman of the Year (Singapore) 1991. *Publications:* The Dynamics of One Party Dominance: The PAP at the Grassroots 1976, A Sensation of Independence 1984, Government and Politics of Singapore (co-ed.), The Prophetic and the Political 1987. *Address:* Embassy of Singapore, 3501 International Place, N.W., Washington, DC 20008, U.S.A. (Office); Singapore International Foundation, 111 Somerset Road, 11-07 Devonshire Wing, Singapore 238164. *Telephone:* (202) 537-3100 (Office). *Fax:* (202) 537-0876 (Office). *E-mail:* singemb@bellatlantic.net (Office). *Website:* www.mfa.gov.sg/washington (Office).

CHAN, Jackie; Chinese actor and stuntman; b. Chan Kong-Sang, 7 April 1954, Hong Kong; s. of Charles Chan and Lee-Lee Chan; ed Chinese Opera Research Inst.; worked in Australia; returned to Hong Kong, roles as stuntman or extra, Shaw Brothers Studios; signed with Golden Harvest 1980; Best Picture Award, Hong Kong Film 1989, MTV Lifetime Achievement Award 1995, Best Action Choreography, Hong Kong Film 1996, 1999, Maverick Tribute Award Cinequest San Jose Film Festival 1998. *Films:* Little Tiger from Canton 1971, Enter the Dragon 1973, Snake in the Eagle's Shadow 1978, Half a Loaf of Kung Fu 1980, The Young Master (Dir and actor) 1980, Battle Creek Brawl 1980, The Cannonball Run 1981, Dragon Lord (Dir and actor) 1982, Project A (Dir) 1983, Wheels on Meals 1984, Police Story 1985 (Hong Kong Best Film Award), Armour of God 1986, Rumble in the Bronx 1995, Police Story IV: First Strike 1996, Rush Hour 1998, Shanghai Noon 2000, Accidental Spy 2001, Rush Hour II 2001, The Tuxedo 2002. *Website:* www.jackiechan.com.hk (Home).

CHAN, Rt. Hon. Sir Julius, GCMG, KBE, PC; Papua New Guinea politician; b. 29 Aug. 1939, Tanga, New Ireland; s. of Chin Pak and Tingoris Chan; m. Stella Ahmat 1966; one d. three s.; ed Marist Brothers Coll., Ashgrove, Queensland and Univ. of Queensland, Australia; Co-operative Officer, Papua New Guinea Admin. 1960–62; Man. Dir Coastal Shipping Co. Pty Ltd; mem. House of Ass. 1968–75, 1982–97, Deputy Speaker, Vice-Chair. Public Accounts Cttee 1968–72; Parl. Leader, People's Progress Party 1970–97; Minister of Finance and Parl. Leader of Govt Business 1972–77; Deputy Prime Minister and Minister for Primary Industry 1977–78, Prime Minister 1980–82, Deputy Prime Minister 1986–88, Minister of Trade and Industry 1986–88, Deputy Prime Minister 1992–94, Minister for Finance and Planning 1992–94, for Foreign Affairs and Trade 1994–96; Prime Minister 1994–97; Gov. for Papua New Guinea and Vice-Chair. Asian Devt Bank 1975–77; Fellowship mem. Int. Bankers' Asscn Inc., USA 1976; fmr Gov. IBRD/IMF; Hon. Dr. (Econ.), Dankook Univ., Seoul 1978; Hon. DTech (Univ. of Tech., Papua New Guinea) 1983. *Leisure interests:* boating, swimming, walking. *Address:* P.O. Box 6030, Boroko, Papua New Guinea.

CHAN FANG ON SANG, Anson; Chinese government official; b. Shanghai, China; ed in Hong Kong; fmr appts. include Dir Social Welfare Dept 1984; Sec. for Econ. Services 1987; Head (Sec.), Hong Kong Civil Service until 1993; Chief Sec. of Hong Kong 1993–2001; retd April 2001. *Address:* c/o Office of the Chief Secretary, Central Government Offices, Lower Albert Road, Hong Kong Special Administrative Region, People's Republic of China.

CHANCE, Britton, MS, PhD, DSc; American biophysicist; b. 24 July 1913, Wilkes-Barre, Pa; s. of Edwin M. and Eleanor (Kent) Chance; m. 1st Jane Earle 1938 (divorced); m. 2nd Lilian Streeter Lucas 1955 (divorced); four s. four d., two step s. two step d.; ed Univ. of Pennsylvania and Cambridge Univ.; Acting Dir Johnson Foundation, Univ. of Pa 1940–41, Dir 1949–83, Asst Prof. of Biophysics and Physical Biochem. 1941–49, Prof. 1949–77, Chair. of Dept of Biophysics and Physical Biochem. 1949–75, Eldridge Reeves Johnson Prof. of Biophysics 1964–75, Prof. of Biochem. and Biophysics 1975–83, Prof. Emer. 1983–; Investigator Office of Scientific Research and Devt 1941; staff mem. Radiation Lab., MIT 1941–46; Dir Inst. for Functional and Structural Studies, Pa 1982–90, Inst. for Biophysical and Biomedical Research 1990–99; Pres. Medical Diagnostic Research Foundation, Phila 1998–; Guggenheim Fellow, Nobel and Molteno Inst. 1946–48; scientific consultant, research attaché, U.S. Navy, London 1948; consultant, Nat. Science Foundation 1951–56; President's Scientific Advisory Cttee 1959–60; mem. Council, Nat. Inst. on Alcohol Abuse and Alcoholism 1971–75, Nat. Cancer Inst. Working Group on Molecular Control 1973–; Vice-Pres. Int. Union Pure and Applied Biophysics 1972–75, Pres. 1975–79; mem. NAS, American Acad. of Arts and Sciences, American Philosophical Soc., Royal Acad. of Arts and Sciences, Biophysical Soc., Royal Soc. of Arts, Acad. Leopoldina, etc.; Foreign mem. Max-Planck-Gesellschaft zur Förderung der Wissenschaften, Munich 1974, Royal Soc. of London 1981; Fellow, Pa Coll. of Physicians 1974; Philip Morris Lecturer 1978; 10 hon. degrees; numerous awards and honours including Presidential Certificate of Merit 1950, Paul Lewis Award in Enzyme Chemistry, American Chemical Soc. 1950, William J. Morlock Award in biochemical electronics, IEEE 1961, Netherlands Biochemical Soc. Award 1965, Harrison Howe Award, American Chemical Soc. 1966, Franklin Medal 1966, Heineken Medal, Netherlands 1970, Gairdner Award 1972, Festschrift Symposium, Stockholm 1973, Semmelweis Medal 1974, Nat. Medal of Science 1974, DaCosta Oratusi 1976, Gold Medal for Distinguished Service to Medicine, Coll. of Physicians 1987, Benjamin Franklin Medal for Distinguished Achievement in the Sciences, American Philosophical Soc. 1990, Lifetime Achievement Award in Biomedical Optics 2001. *Publications:* Waveforms (with Williams, Hughes, McNichol, Sayre) 1949, Electronic Time Measure-

ments (with Hulsizer, McNichol, Williams) 1949, Enzyme-Substrate Compounds 1951, Enzymes in Action in Living Cells 1955, The Respiratory Chain and Oxidative Phosphorylation 1956, Techniques for Assay of Respiratory Enzymes 1957, Energy-Linked Functions of Mitochondria 1963, Rapid Mixing and Sampling Techniques in Biochemistry 1964, Control of Energy Metabolism 1965, Hemes and Hemoproteins 1966, Probes of Structure and Function of Macromolecules and Enzymes 1972, Alcohol and Aldehyde (3 Vols), Tunneling in Biological Systems 1979. *Leisure interests:* yacht sailing and cruising, amateur radio. *Address:* Department of Biochemistry and Biophysics, University of Pennsylvania, 250 Anatomy Chemistry Building, Philadelphia, PA 19104-6059 (Office); 4014 Pine Street, Philadelphia, PA 19104, USA (Home). *Telephone:* (215) 898-4342 (Office). *Fax:* (215) 898-1806 (Office). *E-mail:* chance@mail.med.upenn.edu (Office).

CHANCELLOR, Alexander Surtees, BA; British journalist; b. 4 Jan. 1940, Ware, Herts.; s. of Sir Christopher Chancellor, CMG and Sylvia Mary Chancellor (née Paget); m. Susanna Elizabeth Debenham 1964; two d.; ed Eton Coll., Trinity Hall, Cambridge; Reuters News Agency 1964–74, Chief Corresp., Italy 1968–73; ITV News 1974–75; Ed. The Spectator 1975–84; Ed. Time and Tide 1984–86; Deputy Ed. Sunday Telegraph 1986; Washington Ed. The Independent 1986–88; Ed. The Independent Magazine 1988–92; The New Yorker (Ed. The Talk of the Town) 1992–93; Columnist The Times 1992–93, The Guardian 1996–, Slate 1997, The Daily Telegraph 1998–; Assoc. Ed. Sunday Telegraph 1994–95, The Guardian 1996–. *Publication:* Some Times in America 1999. *Address:* 1 Souldern Road, London, W14 0JE, England. *Telephone:* (20) 7602-8686. *E-mail:* chancellor@dial.pipex.com.

CHAND, Lokendra Bahadur, BA, LLB; Nepalese politician; b. 15 Feb. 1940, Kurkuriya Village, Bashulinga Village Devt Cttee, Baitadi; s. of Mahavir Chand and Laxmi Chand; m.; seven c.; ed Pithauragarh, India, Tri-Chandra Coll., Kathmandu, DSB Degree Coll., Nainital, India and DAV Post-Grad. Coll., Dehradun, India; Founding mem. Shree Basudev High School, Liskita, served voluntarily as teacher 1961–64; practising advocate 1964–68; Vice-Chair. Lisakita Village Panchayat, Baitadi Dist 1968, later Chair. Baitadi Dist Panchayat 1970, later Pres. Mahakali Zonal Panchayat 1973, later Vice-Chair. and Chair. Rastriya Panchayat (Nat. Ass.) 1974; Founder Rastriya Prajatantra Party (RPP), Chair. 1991, Leader and Pres. Parl. Bd after unification of Thapa and Chand Group 1994; elected mem. Parl. (RPP) for both constituencies of Baitadi Dist 1995; Prime Minister of Nepal 1983–85, 1990, 1997, Oct. 2002–; Founding Chair. Mahakali Sewa Samaj 1967; mem. Nepal Red Cross Soc. Cen. Exec. Cttee 1970. *Publications include:* Bahraun Kheladi (Twelfth Player), Visarjan (short stories) (Madan Puruskar Prize), Hiunko Tanna, Indra Dhanush, Aparichit Netako Saathi; also satirical essays, humorous plays and collections of short stories. *Leisure interest:* reading books on contemporary literature. *Address:* Prime Minister's Office, Singha Durbar, Kathmandu, Nepal (Office). *E-mail:* info@pmo.gov.np (Office). *Website:* www.pmo.gov.np (Office).

CHANDLER, Sir Colin (Michael), Kt, FCMA; British business executive; b. 7 Oct. 1939; s. of Henry John Chandler and Mary Martha Chandler (née Bowles); m. Jennifer Mary Crawford 1964; one s. one d.; ed St Joseph's Acad., Hatfield Polytechnic; commercial apprentice, De Havilland Aircraft Co. 1956–61; Contracts Officer, Hawker Siddeley Aviation 1962–66, Commercial Man. 1967–72, Exec. Dir (Commercial) 1973–76, Exec. Dir and Gen. Man. 1977; Div. Man. Dir British Aerospace 1978–82, Group Marketing Dir 1983–85; Head of Defence Export Services, Ministry of Defence 1985–89; Man. Dir Vickers PLC 1990–92, Chief Exec. 1991–96, Deputy Chair. and Chief Exec. 1996, Chair. 1997–99, Chair. Vickers Defence Systems (subsidiary of Rolls-Royce) 2000–; Chair. (non-exec.) easyJet 2002–; Dir (non-exec.) Siemens Plessey Electronic Systems 1990–95, TI Group (subsequently Smiths Group) 1992–, Guardian Royal Exchange 1995–99, Racal Electronics PLC 1999–2000 (Chair. 2000–), Thaler PLC 2000–, Hoggett Bowers 2000–; mem. Cttee, Dept Trade and Industry Priority Japan Campaign 1992–2001; mem. Nat. Defence Industries Council 1992–2002; Chair. Overseas Project Bd Healthcare Sector Group; Pro-Chancellor Cranfield Univ. 2001–; Dr hc (Herts) 1999; Commdr Order of Lion of Finland 1982. *Leisure interests:* jogging, playing tennis, reading, listening to music. *Address:* c/o easyJet Airline Company Ltd, easyLand, London Luton Airport, Beds., LU2 9LS, England.

CHANDLER, Kenneth A.; British journalist; b. 2 Aug. 1947, Westcliff-on-Sea, Essex; s. of Leonard Gordon Chandler and Beatrix Marie (née McKenzie) Chandler; m. Linda Kathleen Chandler 1975; one s. two d.; Man. Ed. The New York Post 1978–86, 1993–99, Ed.-in-Chief, then Publr 1999–2002; Ed. Boston Herald 1986–93; Exec. Producer Fox TV's A Current Affair 1993; CEO Natural Energy Solutions Corpn 2002–. *Address:* c/o New York Post, Suite 1910, 1211 Avenue of the Americas, Floor 10, New York, NY 10036, USA (Office).

CHANDRA, Avinash; Indian artist; b. 28 Aug. 1931, Simla; s. of Kundan Lal and Ram Parai; m. Prem Lata; one c.; ed Delhi Polytechnic, Delhi; on staff of Delhi Polytechnic, Delhi 1953–56; in London 1956, then New York 1966; executed glass mural for Pilkington Brothers' Head Office, St Helens, Lancs. and fibreglass mural for Indian Tea Centre, London 1964; John D. Rockefeller Third Fund Fellowship 1965. Works in following collections: Nat. Gallery of Modern Art, New Delhi, Tate Gallery, London, Victoria and Albert Museum, London, Arts Council of Great Britain, London, Ashmolean Museum, Oxford, Ulster Museum, Belfast, City Art Gallery, Birmingham, Gulbenkian

Museum, Durham, Musée Nat. d'Art Moderne, Paris, Whitworth Art Gallery, Manchester, Museum of Modern Art, Haifa, Punjab Museum, Chandigarh, etc.; Gold Medal, Prix Européen, Ostend 1962. *One-man exhibitions include:* Srinagar, New Delhi, Belfast, London, Oxford, Paris, Bristol, Arnhem, Amsterdam, Zürich, Copenhagen, Stockholm, Chicago, Toronto, Geneva, etc.

CHANDRA, Subhash; Indian media executive; fmr rice packer in Hissar, Haryana; now Chair. Zee Telefilms Ltd (satellite TV network), Patco, Siti-Cable; launched TV channel in Marathi language 1999; fmr jt owner (with Rupert Murdoch, of Zee Cinema, Zee TV and Zee India TV/Zee News. *Address:* Zee Telefilms Ltd, 135 Continental Building, Dr. A B Road (Worli), Mumbai 400 018, India (Office). *Telephone:* (22) 4965506 (Office). *Fax:* (22) 4964334 (Office). *Website:* www.zeetelevision.com (Office).

CHANDRA MUNGRA, Subhas, MA; Suriname diplomatist and economist; b. 2 Sept. 1945, Paramaribo; m.; three c.; ed Municipal Univ. of Amsterdam; Lecturer in Finance and Banking, Monetary Theory, Anton de Kom Univ. of Suriname 1976–86; Chair. Nat. Cardboard Industry 1985–86; Dir Nat. Devt Bank 1983; Minister of Foreign Affairs 1991–96, of Finance 1986–90; Chair. Jt Governing Bd of Centre for the Devt of Industry on behalf of the African, Caribbean and Pacific Group in Brussels 1988–90; fmr Perm. Rep. to UN; Vice-Chair. Third UN Conf. on Least Developed Countries 2000; Pres. (acting) UN Gen. Ass. Jan. 2001. *Publications:* numerous articles on econ. issues. *Address:* c/o Permanent Mission of Suriname to the United Nations, 866 United Nations Plaza, Suite 320, New York, NY 10017, U.S.A. (Office).

CHANDRASEKHAR, Bhagwat Subramanya, BSc; Indian cricketer and bank executive; b. 17 May 1945, Mysore; m. Sandhya Rajarao 1975; one s.; ed Nat. Educ. Soc., Bangalore; right-arm leg-spin, googly bowler; bowling arm withered by attack of polio at age of 6; played for Mysore/Karnataka 1963–64 to 1979–80; played in 58 Tests for India 1963–64 to 1979, taking 242 wickets (average 29.7); toured England 1967, 1971, 1974 and 1979; Hon. Life mem. MCC 1981–; Arjuna Award; Padma Shri Award 1972; Wisden Cricketer of the Year 1972. *Leisure interests:* badminton, Indian classical music. *Address:* 571 31st Cross, 4th Block, Jayanagar, Bangalore 560011, India.

CHANDRASEKHAR, Sivaramakrishna, PhD, DSc, ScD, FRS; Indian physicist; b. 6 Aug. 1930, Calcutta; s. of the late S. Sivaramakrishnan and Sitalaxmi Sivaramakrishnan; m. Ila Pingle 1954; one s. one d.; ed Univs. of Nagpur and Cambridge; Research Scholar, Raman Research Inst., Bangalore 1950–54; 1851 Exhbn Scholar, The Cavendish Lab., Cambridge 1954–57; DSIR Fellow, Dept of Crystallography, Univ. Coll., London 1957–59; Research Fellow, Royal Inst., London 1959–61; Prof. and Head, Dept of Physics, Univ. of Mysore 1961–71; Prof. Raman Research Inst. 1971–90; Nehru Visiting Prof. and Fellow of Pembroke Coll., Cambridge 1986–87; Bhatnagar Fellow 1990–95; Dir Centre for Liquid Crystal Research 1991–; Fellow Indian Nat. Science Acad. etc.; Royal Medal of the Royal Soc. 1994, Niels Bohr–UNESCO Gold Medal 1998, Chevalier, Ordre des Palmes Académiques, Freedericksz Medal, Russian Liquid Crystal Society 2000; several Indian and int. honours for outstanding contribs to science. *Publications:* Liquid Crystals 1992; numerous scientific articles on crystal physics and liquid crystals. *Leisure interest:* painting. *Address:* Centre for Liquid Crystal Research, PO Box 1329, Bangalore 560013, India. *Telephone:* (80) 8382924 (Office); (80) 8386582 (Home). *Fax:* (80) 8382044 (Office). *E-mail:* uclcr@glasbg01.vsnl.net.in (Office).

CHANDRASEKHARAN, Komaravolu, MA, MSc, PhD; Indian mathematician and professor of mathematics; b. 21 Nov. 1920, Masulipatam, India; m. A. Sarada 1944; two s.; ed Presidency Coll., Madras and Inst. for Advanced Study, Princeton; Head, School of Math., Tata Inst. of Fundamental Research, Bombay 1949–65; Prof. Eidgenössische Technische Hochschule (Swiss Fed. Inst. of Tech.), Zürich 1965–; Sec. Int. Mathematical Union 1961–66, Pres. 1971–74; Vice-Pres. Int. Council of Scientific Unions 1963–66, Sec.-Gen. 1966–70; mem. Scientific Advisory Cttee to Cabinet, Govt of India 1961–66; Fellow Nat. Inst. of Sciences of India, Indian Acad. of Sciences; Foreign mem. Finnish Acad. of Science and Letters 1975; Hon. mem. Austrian Acad. of Sciences 1996, American Math. Soc. 1998; Hon. Fellow Tata Inst. 1970; lectured at more than 50 univs in the USA, USSR, Europe and Asia; Padma Shri 1959, Shanti Swarup Bhatnagar Memorial Award for Scientific Research 1959, Ramanujan Medal 1966. *Publications:* Fourier Transforms (with S. Bochner) 1949, Typical Means (with S. Minakshisundaram) 1952, Lectures on the Riemann Zeta-function 1953, Analytic Number Theory 1968, Arithmetical Functions 1970, Elliptic Functions 1985, Classical Fourier Transforms 1989, Siegel's Lectures on the Geometry of Numbers (ed.) 1989, Lectures on Topological Groups 1996, Integration Theory 1996; over 70 research papers. *Leisure interests:* painting, English literature, music. *Address:* Eidgenössische Technische Hochschule, 8092 Zürich, Rämistrasse 101 (Office); Hedwigstrasse 29, 8032 Zürich, Switzerland (Home). *Telephone:* (1) 6324199 (Office); (1) 3819686 (Home).

CHANEY, Frederick Michael, AO, LLB; Australian politician and lawyer; b. 28 Oct. 1941, Perth; s. of the late Frederick Charles Chaney and of Mavis Mary Bond; m. Angela Margaret Clifton 1964; three s.; ed Univ. of Western Australia; public service, Papua New Guinea 1964–66; pvt. law practice 1966–74; Senator from Western Australia 1974–90; Senate Opposition Whip 1975, Govt Whip 1976–78; Minister for Admin. Services 1978, Assisting the Minister for Educ. 1978–79, for Aboriginal Affairs 1978–80, Assisting the Minister for Nat. Devt and Energy 1979–80, for Social Security 1980–83; Leader of Opposition in Senate 1983–90; Shadow Minister for Industrial

Relations 1987–88, 1989–90, for the Environment 1990–92; Deputy Leader of the Opposition 1989–90; Chair. Fightback! (Co-ordination and Marketing Group) 1992–93; Researcher, lecturer Grad. School of Man., Univ. of Western Australia 1993–95; Chancellor Murdoch Univ., Western Australia 1995–; mem. House of Reps. for Pearce 1990–93; mem. Nat. Native Title Tribunal 1995–2000, Deputy Pres. 2000–; Liberal. *Leisure interests:* swimming, reading. *Address:* 23B Brown Street, Claremont, WA 6010, Australia.

CHANG, John H., BA, MS; Taiwanese politician; b. 2 May 1941, Kiangsi; m. Helen Chang Huang; three c.; ed Soochow Univ., Georgetown Univ.; Third then Second Sec., Washington Embassy 1974–78; Section Chief Dept of N American Affairs, Ministry of Foreign Affairs 1978, Deputy Dir 1980–81; Sec.-Gen. Coordination Council of N American Affairs (now TECO/TECRO) 1981–82, Dir of Dept 1982–86; Admin. Vice-Minister of Foreign Affairs 1986–90; Dir-Gen. Dept of Overseas Affairs Kuomintang Cen. Cttee 1990; Political Vice-Minister of Foreign Affairs 1990–93; Minister Overseas Chinese Affairs Comm. and Minister of State 1993–96; Minister of Foreign Affairs 1996–97, Deputy Prime Minister 1997; mem. Kuomintang Cen. Cttee and Cen. Standing Cttee 1993–. *Publication:* Damansky Island Incident. *Address:* Executive Yuan, 1 Chung Hsiao E Road, Taipei, Taiwan.

CHANG, Jung, PhD; British author; b. 25 March 1952, Yibin, China; d. of Shou-Yu Chang and De-Hong Xia; m. Jon Halliday 1991; ed Univ. of York; came to UK to study linguistics 1978; now full-time writer; Dr hc (Buckingham Univ.) 1996, (Warwick, York) 1997, (Open Univ., UK) 1998; NCR Book Award (UK) 1992, UK Writers' Guild Best Non-Fiction Book 1992, Fawcett Soc. Book Award (UK) 1992, Book of the Year (UK) 1993, Golden Bookmark Award (Belgium) 1993, 1994, Best Book of 1993, Humo (Belgium), Bjørnsonordenen, Den Norske Orden for Literature (Norway) 1995. *Publication:* Wild Swans: Three Daughters of China 1991. *Address:* c/o Toby Eady Associates, 9 Orme Court, London, W2 4RL, England. *Telephone:* (20) 7792-0092. *Fax:* (20) 7792-0879.

CHANG, Kwang-chih, PhD; American professor of anthropology; b. 15 April 1931, Peiping (now Beijing), China; s. of Chang Wo-chün and Lo Hsin-hsiang; m. Li Hwei 1957; one s. one d.; ed Nat. Taiwan Univ., Harvard Univ.; Lecturer on Anthropology, Harvard Univ. 1960–61, Prof. 1977–96, Chair. Dept of Anthropology 1981–84, John E. Hudson Prof. of Archaeology 1984–96, Curator of E Asian Archaeology, Peabody Museum of Archaeology and Ethnology; Instructor in Anthropology, Yale Univ. 1961–63, Asst Prof. 1963–66, Prof. 1969–77, Chair. Dept of Anthropology 1970–73, Prof. Emer. 1995–; mem. Acad. Sinica (Taipei) 1974 (Vice-Pres. 1994–96), NAS (Washington, DC) 1979–; Hon. MA. *Publications:* The Archaeology of Ancient China 1963, Rethinking Archaeology 1967, Prehistory of Taiwan 1969, Early Chinese Civilization 1972, Shang Civilization 1980, Art, Myth and Ritual: The Path to Political Authority in Ancient China 1983, Chinese Bronze Age (Vol. I) 1983, (Vol. II) 1990. *Address:* Department of Anthropology, 57 C–D, Peabody Museum, Harvard University, Cambridge, MA 02138, USA. *Telephone:* (617) 495-4389.

CHANG, Michael; American tennis player; b. 22 Feb. 1972, Hoboken, NJ; s. of Joe Chang and Betty Chang; coached by his brother Carl and others; aged 15 was youngest player since 1918 to compete in men's singles at US Open 1987; turned professional 1988; first played at Wimbledon 1988; winner, French Open 1989, becoming youngest player of a Grand Slam tournament; Davis Cup debut 1989; winner Canadian Open 1990; semi-finalist, US Open 1992, finalist 1996; finalist French Open 1995, semi-finalist Australian Open 1995, finalist 1996; by end of 2002 winner of 34 singles titles; highest singles ranking: 2nd (1996). *Address:* Advantage International, 1751 Pinnacle Drive, Suite 1500, McLean, VA 22102, USA.

CHANG CHIN-CHEN, PhD, FIEE; Taiwanese computer scientist and university professor; b. 12 Nov. 1954, Taiwan; m. Ling-Hui Hwang 1981; one s. two d.; ed Nat. Tsing Hua Univ., Hsinchu and Nat. Chiao Tung Univ., Hsinchu; Assoc. Prof., Dept of Computer Eng, Nat. Chiao Tung Univ. 1982–83; Assoc. Prof., Dept of Applied Math., Nat. Chung Hsin Univ. 1983–85; Prof. 1985–89; Prof. and Chair. Dept of Computer Eng, Nat. Chung Cheng Univ. 1989–92, Prof. and Dean Coll. of Eng 1992–95, Prof. and Dean of Academic Affairs 1995–, Acting Pres. 1996–99; Ed. Journal of Information Science and Eng 1988–93, Journal of Chinese Inst. of Engineers 1990–93, Information Science Applications 1994–; Ed.-in-Chief Information and Education 1987–; reviewer, numerous int. journals of information science; Outstanding Talent in Information Science Award of Repub. 1989, several Distinguished Research Awards of Nat. Science Council 1986–. *Publications:* more than 300 tech. papers on database design and information security in leading scientific journals and conf. proceedings; 12 books in Chinese on database design, data structures, computer viruses, information security, cryptography etc.; Ed. Advanced Database Research and Development Series (Vols 1, 2, 3) 1992. *Address:* Department of Computer Science and Information Engineering, National Chung Cheng University, Chiayi, Taiwan. *Telephone:* (5) 272-0411 (Office); (4) 325-9100 (Home); (5) 272-0405. *Fax:* (5) 272-0839; (4) 327-7423 (Home); (5) 272-0404. *E-mail:* ccc@cs.ccu.edu.tw (Office). *Website:* www.cs.ccu.edu.tw/-ccc (Office).

CHANG CHUN-HSIUNG, LLB; Chinese politician; b. 23 March 1938; m.; three s. one d.; ed Nat. Taiwan Univ.; defence lawyer in mil. trial following Kaohsiung Incident 1980; mem. Legis. Yuan 1983–, a Founder mem. Democratic Progressive Party (DPP) 1986–, mem. Cen. Standing Cttee and Cen. Exec. Cttee DPP 1986–2000, Exec. Dir DPP Caucus in Legis. Yuan 1987–88,

Gen. Convenor 1990, 1998–99, Sec.-Gen. Office of Pres. 2000; Vice-Premier 2000; Premier 2000–02. *Address:* c/o Office of the Premier, Taipei, Taiwan (Office).

CHANG DAE-WHAN, MA, PhD; South Korean politician and business executive; b. 21 March 1952; m.; two c.; ed Univ. of Rochester, USA, Coll. of Europe, Belgium, George Washington Univ., New York Univ., USA; Instructor (Capt.), Korea Air Force Acad. 1977–83; mem. Acad. of Int. Business, USA 1984; Dir Planning Office, Maeil Business Newspaper 1986, mem. Bd of Dirs. and Dir of Business Devt HQ 1986, Man. Dir 1987, Exec. Dir 1988, Pres. and Publr 1988–2002, Pres. Maeil Business News TV Co. 1993–2002; Acting Prime Minister of Repub. of Korea 9–28 Aug. 2002; Lecturer in Int. Business Man., Grad. School of Seoul Nat. Univ. 1988–97; Auditor IPI Korean Nat. Cttee 1988–2002, PFA Korean Nat. Cttee 1991–2002; Dir Korea Newspapers Asscn 1986–2002, Auditor 1996–2002; Founder Vision Korea Campaign 1997–2002, World Knowledge Forum 1998–2002; Chair. Press Foundation of Asia March–Aug. 2002; mem. Advisory Bd Sungkyunkwan Univ. Grad. School of Business, World Asscn of Newspapers 1986–2002; Order of Civil Merit 1992, Dong-bag Medal 1992. *Publications include:* (in Korean): International Business Negotiation 1989, New Product Millennium (jtly.) 1997. *Address:* Maeil Business Newspaper Building, 51-9, 1-ga, Bil-dong, Jung-gu, Seoul 100-728 (Office); c/o National Assembly, 1 Yeouido-dong, Yeong-deungpo-gu, Seoul, Republic of Korea (Office). *Telephone:* (2) 2000-2114 (Office). *E-mail:* mkmaster@mk.co.kr (Office). *Website:* www.mk.co.kr (Office).

CHANG-HIM, Rt Rev French Kitchener, LTh; Seychelles ecclesiastic; b. 10 May 1938, Seychelles; s. of Francis Chang-Him and Amelia Zoé; m. Susan Talma 1975 (died 1996); twin d.; ed Seychelles Coll., Lichfield Theological Coll., St Augustine's Coll. Canterbury and Univ. of Trinity Coll. Toronto; primary school teacher 1958; man. of schools 1973–77; Chair. Teacher Training Coll. Bd of Govs. 1976–77; Vicar-Gen. Diocese of Seychelles 1973–79; Archdeacon of Seychelles 1973–79; Bishop of Seychelles 1979–; Dean, Prov. of Indian Ocean 1983–84, Archbishop 1984–95; Hon. DD (Univ. of Trinity Coll., Toronto) 1991. *Publication:* The Seychellois: In Search of an Identity 1975. *Leisure interests:* international affairs, cooking, gardening, reading. *Address:* Bishop's House, PO Box 44, Victoria, Seychelles. *Telephone:* 224242. *Fax:* 224296. *E-mail:* angdio@seychelles-net (Office).

CHANG KING-YUH, LLM, PhD; Taiwanese government official; b. 27 April 1937, Hsiangtan County, Hunan; s. of Shao Chu Chang and Hsi-chen Huang; m. Grace Yu 1964; two s.; ed Nat. Taiwan Univ., Nat. Chengchi Univ. and Columbia Univ.; lecturer, Hofstra Univ., USA 1968–69; Asst Prof. Western Ill. Univ. 1972; Assoc. Prof. Nat. Chengchi Univ. 1972–75, Chair. Dept of Diplomacy 1974–77, Dir Grad. School of Int. Law and Diplomacy 1975–77, Prof. 1975–, Deputy Dir Inst. of Int. Relations 1977–81, Dir 1981–84, Pres. Nat. Chengchi Univ. 1989–94; Visiting Fellow, Johns Hopkins Univ. 1976–77; Distinguished Visiting Scholar, Inst. of E Asian Studies, Univ. of Calif., Berkeley 1983; Dir-Gen. Govt Information Office 1984–87; Dir Inst. of Int. Relations 1987–90; Minister of State. Exec. Yuan 1994–96. *Leisure interests:* reading, mountain climbing and sports. *Address:* 1 Chung Hsiao East Road, Sec. 1, Taipei, Taiwan. *Telephone:* (2) 3561703. *Fax:* (2) 3513038.

CHANG SANG, BSc, MDiv, DPhil; South Korean politician and professor of theology; b. 9 Oct. 1939; ed Ewha Women's Univ., Yonsei Univ., Yale Univ. and Princeton Theological Seminary, USA; Prof. of New Testament Theology, Dept of Christian Studies, Ewha Women's Univ. (EWU) 1977–2002, Dir of Academic Affairs, Grad. School 1980, Chair. Dept of Christian Studies 1988, Dir Korea Cultural Research Inst., EWU 1989, Dean Student Affairs 1990, Dean Coll. of Liberal Arts 1993, Dean Grad. School of Information Science 1995, Vice-Pres. EWU 1996, Pres. 1996–2002; ordained to the Ministry of the Word 1988; mem. Exec. Cttee YWCA Korea 1979–97 (Vice-Pres. 1983–97), Exec. Cttee World Alliance of Reformed Churches (WARC) 1982–89 (Moderator Dept of Co-operation and Witness 1989–97), Exec. Cttee World YWCA 1987–91; mem. Public Official Ethics Cttee, Ministry of Admin. and Home Affairs 1997–99, Women's Policies Cttee 1997–2002; mem. Advisory Council on Korean Unification 1998–2002; Vice-Pres. Advisory Council on Democratic and Peaceful Unification 1998–2002; mem. Presidential Comm. for the New Millennium 1999–2002, Admin. Negotiating Cttee 2000–02; nominated Prime Minister of S. Korea July 2002, appointment vetoed by Parl.; Chair. Press Asscn of Pvt. Univs. 1999–2002; Vice-Pres. Korean Council for Univ. Educ. 1999–2002; Chair. Korean Council for Pres. of Pvt. Univs 1999–2002; Trustee United Bd for Christian Higher Educ. in Asia 1995–2002, Int. Women's Univ., Hanover, Germany 2000–02, Bd Korea Research Foundation 2000–02, Korea Inst. of Science and Tech. Evaluation and Planning 2001–02; Order of Civil Merit 1999, Moran Medal 1999. *Publications include:* On Interpretation of Paul's Thoughts, Women's Status and Role in First Christian Movement, Paul's Somatic Understanding of Human Beings, The Origin and Development of Feminist Theology, Christianity and World Korean Theology in Transition, Korean Women's Studies, Paul's Understanding of History and Gospel. *Address:* c/o National Assembly, 1 Yeouido-dong, Yeong-deungpo-gu, Seoul (Office); 1901, Samdok Ever Villa, 105-1, Namgajwa-dong, Seodaemun-gu, Seoul, Republic of Korea (Home).

CHANG SHANA; Chinese artist; b. 26 March 1931, Lyon, France; one s.; ed Dunhuang, Boston Museum of Fine Art School and New York; returned to China 1950; Asst to architect Liang Sicheng, Qinghua Univ. 1951–56; Prof. Cen. Acad. of Arts and Design 1957–85; del. 12th Conf. CCP 1982; Pres. Cen.

Acad. of Arts and Design 1985–; mem. New York Students League 1953, Cen. Acad. of Arts and Design; mem. Educ., Science, Culture and Public Health Cttee 8th NPC. *Address:* Central Academy of Arts and Design, 34 North Dong Huan Road, Beijing 100020, People's Republic of China (Office). *Telephone:* 65026391 (Office).

CHANG XIANGYU; Chinese actress and opera singer; b. 15 Sept. 1923, Gongxian Co., Henan Prov.; d. of Zhang Fuxian and Wei Cairong; m. Chen Xianzhang 1944; three d. two s.; ed Drama Training, Ministry of Culture; opera debut 1936; est. Xiangyu Henan Opera School 1948, Xiangyu Henan Opera Troupe 1949; Pres. Henan Opera Acad. 1956; Prin. Traditional Opera School 1978; Hon. Prof. Henan Univ., 1983, Shenyang Conservatory of Music 1985; mem. 1st NPC 1954–58, 5th NPC 1978–83; Vice-Pres. Dramatists' Asscn 1980–; mem. Presidium 5th NPC 1980–83, 6th NPC 1983–87, 7th NPC 1988; Pres. Henan School of Traditional Operas 1982; mem. 5th Nat. Cttee, Fed. Literary and Art Circles 1988; Certificate of Merit, Ministry of Culture 1980, First Chinese Art Festival Honour Prize 1987, First Golden Gramophone Record Prize 1989. *Leisure interests:* painting, calligraphy. *Address:* 113-16 Chengdong Road, 450004 Zhengzhou City, Henan Province (Home); The Dramatists' Association, Beijing, People's Republic of China. *Telephone:* (371) 229006 (Home).

CHANGEUX, Jean-Pierre, DR. ÈS SC.; French research professor; b. 6 April 1936, Domont; s. of Marcel Changeux and Jeanne Benoît; m. Annie Dupont 1962; one s.; ed Lycées Montaigne, Louis le Grand and St Louis, Paris and Ecole Normale Supérieure, Ulm; research asst 1958–60; Asst lecturer, Science Faculty, Univ. of Paris 1960–66; post-doctoral Fellow, Univ. of Calif. 1966, Columbia Univ., New York 1967; Vice-Dir Coll. de France (Chair. of Molecular Biology) 1967; Prof. Institut Pasteur 1974–; Prof. Coll. de France 1975–; Pres. Interministerial Comm. for Preservation of Nat. Artistic Heritage 1989–, Consultative Cttee on Ethics for Life and Medical Sciences 1992–98 (Hon. Pres. 1999–); corresp. mem. numerous comms., Turin Acad. of Medicine, Académie des Sciences, Akademia Leopoldina, Halle, NAS, Swedish and Belgian acads.; Alexandre Joannidès prize (Académie des Sciences), Gairdner Foundation Award 1978, Lounsbery Prize (NAS, USA) 1982, Co-recipient Wolf Foundation Prize 1982, Céline Prize 1985, F.O. Schmitt Prize (Neurosciences Research Inst., New York) 1985, Fidia Neuroscience Award 1989, Bristol-Myers-Squibb Award in Neuroscience 1990; Carl-Gustav Bernhard Medal (Swedish Acad. of Sciences) 1991, Médaille d'Or (CNRS) 1992, Prix Jeantet (Geneva) 1993, Goodman and Gilman Award 1994, Camillo Golgi medal (Accad. Nazionale dei Lincei, Rome) 1994, Sir Hans Krebs medal (Helsinki) 1994, Grand Prix (Fondation de la Recherche Médicale) 1997, Eli Lilly Award 1999, Langley Award, Washington 2000; Commdr, Légion d'honneur, Grand Croix, Ordre nat. du mérite, Commdr, Ordre des arts et des lettres. *Publications:* L'homme neuronal 1983, Matière à pensée 1989 (with Alain Connes), Raison et Plaisir 1994, Conversations on Mind, Matter and Mathematics (with Alain Connes) 1995, La Nature et la Règle (with Paul Ricoeur) 1998; author and co-author of several research papers on allosteric proteins, on the acetylcholine receptor and on the Devt of the nervous system. *Leisure interests:* baroque paintings, organ music. *Address:* Laboratoire de Neurobiologie Moléculaire, Institut Pasteur, 25 rue du Docteur Roux, 75015 Paris (Office); 47 rue du Four, 75006 Paris, France (Home). *Telephone:* 1-45-68-88-05 (Office); 1-45-48-44-64 (Home). *Fax:* 1-45-68-88-36 (Office). *E-mail:* changeux@pasteur.fr (Office).

CHANNING, Carol; American actress; b. 31 Jan. 1923; d. of George Channing and Carol Glaser; m. 3rd Charles Lowe 1956; one s.; m. 4th Harry Kullijian 2003; Critics' Circle Award for Lend an Ear; Tony Award for Hello Dolly 1963, Golden Globe Award for Best Supporting Actress, Thoroughly Modern Millie 1967, Tony Award 1968, Lifetime Achievement Tony Award 1995. *Plays include:* No for an Answer, Let's Face It, So Proudly We Hail, Lend an Ear, Gentlemen Prefer Blondes, Wonderful Town, The Vamp, Hello Dolly, Lorelei. *Films include:* The First Traveling Saleslady 1956, Thoroughly Modern Millie 1967, Skidoo 1968, Sgt. Pepper's Lonely Hearts Club Band 1978, Hans Christian Andersen's Thumbelina 1994 (voice), The Line King: Al Hirschfield 1996, Homo Heights 1998. *Address:* c/o William Morris Agency, 151 S. El Camino Boulevard, Beverly Hills, CA 90212, USA.

CHANNING, Stockard, BA; American actress; b. (Susan Stockard), 13 Feb. 1944, New York; m. four times; ed Harvard Univ.; performed in experimental drama with Theatre Co. of Boston 1967. *Films include:* Comforts of the Home 1970, The Fortune 1975, Sweet Revenge 1975, The Big Bus 1976, Grease 1978, The Cheap Detective 1978, Boys Life 1978, Without A Trace 1983, Heartburn 1986, Men's Club 1986, Staying Together 1987, Meet the Applegates 1987, Married to It 1993, Six Degrees of Separation 1993, Bitter Moon 1994, Smoke 1995, Up Close and Personal 1996, Moll Flanders, Edie and Pen, The First Wives Club 1996, Practical Magic 1998, Twilight 1998, Lulu on the Bridge (voice) 1998, The Red Door 1999, Other Voices 1999, Isn't She Great 1999, The Venice Project 1999, Where the Heart Is 2000, The Business of Strangers 2001, Life or Something Like It 2002. *Stage appearances include:* Two Gentlemen of Verona, New York, San Francisco, LA 1972–73, No Hard Feelings, New York 1973, Vanities, LA 1976, As You Like It 1978, They're Playing Our Song, Lady and the Clarinet 1983, The Golden Age 1983, A Day in the Death of Joe Egg 1985 (Tony Award for Best Actress), House of Blue Leaves 1986, Woman in Mind 1988, Love Letters 1989, Six Degrees of Separation, New York 1990 (also London stage début, Royal Court Theatre 1992), Four Baboons Adoring the Sun 1992. *Television appearances include:* The Stockard Channing Show 1979–80, The West Wing 1999–, Batman

Beyond 1999 and various television movies including The Truth About Jane 2000, The Piano Man's Daughter 2000, Confessions of an Ugly Stepsister 2002. *Address:* ICM, c/o Andrea Eastman, 40 W 57th Street, New York, NY 10019, USA.

CHANNON, Rt Hon (Henry) Paul Guinness (see Kelvedon of Ongar, Baron).

CHANTURIA, Lado; Georgian lawyer and professor of civil and economic law; b. 14 Apr. 1963, Jvari; ed Iv. Javakhishvili Tbilisi State Univ., Moscow Legislation Inst., Göttingen Univ., Germany; Asst Prof., Assoc. Prof., then Prof. Faculty of Law, Tbilisi State Univ. 1985–2002; co-ordinator Civil and Econ. Law Reform Project 1993–96; mem. Council of Justice 1997; Minister of Justice 1998–99; Chief Justice of the Supreme Court of Georgia 1999–. *Publications:* over 50 published works. *Leisure interests:* soccer, travel. *Address:* Supreme Court of Georgia, Zubalashvili St 32, 380010 Tbilisi (Office); Phanaskerteli st. 9/97, 380001, Tbilisi, Georgia (Home). *Telephone:* (32) 99-65-46 (Office); (32) 25-26-90 (Home). *Fax:* (32) 99-01-64 (Office). *E-mail:* lado_chanturia@supremecourt.ge (Office). *Website:* www.supremecourt.ge (Office).

CHANTURYA, Valentin Alekseyevich; Russian metallurgist; b. 15 Oct. 1938; m. 2nd Yelena Leonidovna Chanturya; two s. two d.; ed Moscow Inst. of Steel and Alloys; Jr, Sr researcher, head of lab. Moscow Inst. of Earth Sciences 1969–74; Sr researcher, head of lab. Inst. for Problems of Complex Devt of Depth 1974–, deputy Dir 1993–; corresp. mem. Russian (fmrly USSR) Acad. of Sciences 1990, mem. 1994; research in physical and chemical aspects of processing mineral raw materials; Prize of USSR Council of Ministers, Govt Prize, Russian Fed. 1983, 1990, 1998. *Publications include:* Chemistry of Surfacial Phenomena at Flotation 1983, Electrochemistry of Sulphides 1993, Mining Sciences 1997. *Leisure interest:* fishing. *Address:* Institute for Problems of Complex Development of Depth, Kryukovsky tupir 4, 111020 Moscow, Russia. *Telephone:* (095) 360-06-06 (Office); (095) 348-93-94 (Home).

CHAO, Elaine L., BEcons, MBA; politician; m. Mitch McConnell 1993; three d.; ed Mount Holyoke Coll., Harvard Business School, Mass. Inst. of Tech., Dartmouth Coll., Columbia Univ.; banker Citicorp 1979–83; White House Fellow 1983–84; Vice-Pres. Syndications BankAmerica Capital Markets Group, San Francisco 1984–86; Deputy Admin. Maritime Admin. 1986–88, Chair. Fed. Maritime Comm. 1988–89; Deputy Sec. Dept of Transportation; Dir Peace Corps, est. first Peace Corps in Baltic nations and newly ind. states of fmr USSR; Pres. and CEO United Way America 1992–96; Sec. of Labor 2001–; Fellow Heritage Foundation, Washington, DC 1996–, Chair. Asian Studies Center Advisory Council 1998–; Sr Ed. Policy Review: The Journal of American Citizenship; mem. Bd Dirs Dole Food Co., Vencor, Protective Life Corpn; Hon. doctorates Villanova Univ., Sacred Heart Univ., St John's Univ., Drexel Univ., Niagara Univ., Thomas More Coll., Bellarmine Coll., Univ. of Toledo, Univ. of Louisville; Goucher Outstanding Young Achiever Award, Nat. Council of Women 1986; Harvard Univ. Grad. School of Business Alumni Achievement Award 1994. *Address:* Department of Labor, 200 Constitution Avenue, NW, Washington, DC 20210, USA (Office). *Telephone:* (202) 219-5000 (Office). *Fax:* (202) 219-7312 (Office). *Website:* www.dol.gov (Office).

CHAO SHAO-K'ANG; Taiwanese politician; fmr mem. Kuomintang (KMT); f. New Party Aug. 1993. *Address:* New Party, 4th Floor, 65 Guang Fuh South Road, Taipei, Taiwan. *Telephone:* (2) 2756-2222.

CHAPIN, Schuyler Garrison; American musical impresario; b. 13 Feb. 1923, New York; s. of L. H. Paul Chapin and Leila H. Burden; m. 1st Elizabeth Steinway 1947 (died 1993); four s.; m. 2nd Catia Zoullas Mortimer 1995; ed Longy School of Music; Spot Sales, NBC Television, New York 1947–50; Gen. Man. Tex and Jinx McCrary Enterprises, New York 1950–53; Booking Dir Judson O'Neill and Judd Div., Columbia Artists Man. 1953–59; CBS Dir Masterworks, Columbia Records Div. 1959–62, Vice-Pres. Creative Services 1962–63; Vice-Pres. Programming, Lincoln Center for the Performing Arts Inc. 1964–69; Exec. Producer, Amberson Productions 1969–72; Gen. Man. Metropolitan Opera Asscn Inc. 1972–75; Dean of Faculty of Arts, Columbia Univ., New York 1976–87, Dean Emer. 1987–; Vice-Pres. Worldwide Concert & Artists Activities, Steinway & Sons 1990–92; Commr of Cultural Affairs for City of New York 1994–2002; Special Consultant, Carnegie Hall Corpn 1976–79, trustee and mem. artistic cttee; Trustee, Naumburg Foundation 1962–; Bagby Music Lovers Foundation 1959–2002, mem. Bd of Dirs, Amberson Group Inc. 1972–; mem. The Century Asscn, The Knickerbocker Club; Chair. Exec. Cttee Franklin and Eleanor Roosevelt Inst. 1983–; Curtis Inst. of Music 1986–, Lincoln Center Theatre 1985; Hon. LHD (New York Univ. and Hobart-William Smith Colls.) 1974, (Hofstra Coll.) 1999; Hon. LittD (Emerson Coll.) 1976, Hon. DMus (Mannes Coll., New York) 1990, (Curtis Inst. of Music) 2000; Air Medal 1945; NY State Conspicuous Service Cross 1951; Christopher Award 1972, Emmy Awards 1972, 1976, 1980; Chevalier, Légion d'honneur 2002. *Publications:* Musical Chairs, A Life in the Arts 1977, Leonard Bernstein: Notes from a Friend 1992, Sopranos, Mezzos, Tenors, Basses and Other Friends 1995. *Leisure interests:* bridge, reading, swimming. *Address:* 655 Park Avenue, New York, NY 10021, USA (Home). *Telephone:* (212) 734-5553 (Home). *Fax:* (212) 628-8631 (Home).

CHAPLIN, Geraldine; American actress; b. 3 July 1944, Santa Monica, Calif.; d. of Charles Chaplin and Oona (O'Neill) Chaplin; one s.; ed pvt. schools, Royal Ballet School, London, UK. *Films include:* Doctor Zhivago 1965, Stranger in the House 1967, I Killed Rasputin 1968, The Hawaiians 1970, Innocent Bystanders 1973, Buffalo Bill and the Indians or Sitting Bull's History Lesson, The Three Musketeers 1974, The Four Musketeers, Nashville 1975, Welcome to LA Cria, Roseland 1977, Remember My Name, A Wedding 1978, The Mirror Crack'd 1980, Voyage en Douce 1981, Bolero 1982, Corsican Brothers, The Word, L'Amour Par Terre, White Mischief 1988, The Moderns 1988, The Return of the Musketeers, I Want To Go Home, The Children, Chaplin 1992, Jane Eyre, In the Name of God's Poor 1997, Cousin Bette 1998, In the Beginning 2000, Las Caras de la Luna 2001, En la Ciudad sin Límites 2002, Hable con Ella 2002. *Television appearances include:* My Cousin Rachel, A Foreign Field 1994, To Walk With Lions 1999, Dinotopia (series) 2002. *Address:* c/o Ames Cushing, William Morris Agency, 151 S. El Camino Drive, Beverly Hills, CA 90212, USA.

CHAPMAN, Dinos, MA; British artist; b. 1962, London; brother of Jake Chapman (q.v.); two d.; ed Ravensbourne Coll. of Art, RCA; studied painting at RCA; teacher of textiles in boys' school; worked as asst to artists Gilbert and George; now works jtly with brother Jake; co-owner Chapman Fine Arts Gallery, E London. *Solo exhibitions:* We Are Artists, Hales Gallery, London 1992, The Disasters of War (sculpture), Victoria Miro Gallery, London 1993, Great Deeds Against the Dead, Victoria Miro Gallery, London 1994, Mummy and Daddy, Galleria Franco Toselli, Milan 1994, Gavin Brown's Enterprise, New York 1995, Zygotic Acceleration, Biogenetic, De-sublimated Libidinal Model (Enlarged × 1000), Victoria Miro Gallery, London 1995, Five Easy Pissers, Andréhn-Schiptjenko Gallery, Stockholm 1995, P-House, Tokyo 1996, Zero Principle, Giò Marconi, Milan 1996, Chapmanworld, ICA, London 1996, Six Feet Under, Gagosian Gallery, New York 1997, Chapmanworld, Grazer Kunstverein, Graz 1997, Galerie Daniel Templon, Paris 1998, Disasters of War (etchings), Jay Jopling/White Cube Gallery, London 1999, The Rape of Creativity, Modern Art Oxford 2003. *Group exhibitions include:* General Release: Young British Artists, Venice Biennale 1995, Future, Present, Past, Venice Biennale 1997, Sensation: Young British Artists from the Saatchi Collection, RA, London 1997; works in collections of Deste Foundation, Athens, Rubell Family Collection, Fla, Saatchi Collection, London, Walker Art Center, Minneapolis. *Address:* Chapman Fine Arts, 39 Fashion Street, London, E1 6PX, England. *Fax:* (20) 7247-6914.

CHAPMAN, (F.) Ian, CBE, FRSA, CBIM, FFCS; British publisher; b. 26 Oct. 1925, St Fergus, Aberdeenshire, Scotland; s. of late Rev. Peter Chapman and Frances Burdett; m. Marjory Stewart Swinton 1953; one s. one d.; ed Shawlands Acad., Ommer School of Music, Glasgow; served RAF 1943–44; miner (nat. service) 1945–47; with William Collins Sons & Co. Ltd (fmrly W.M. Collins Holdings PLC, now Harper Collins) 1947, Man. Trainee New York br. 1950–51, Sales Man. London br. 1955; mem. main operating Bd, Group Sales Dir 1959, Jt Man. Dir 1967–76, Deputy Chair. 1976–81, Chair. CEO 1981–89; Deputy Chair. Orion Publishing Group 1993–94, Dir William Collins overseas cos. 1968–89: Canada 1968–89, USA 1974–89, S. Africa 1978–89, NZ 1978–89, William Collins Int. Ltd 1975–89; Chair. Scottish Radio Holdings PLC (fmrly Radio Clyde) 1972–96 (Hon. Pres. 1996–2000), Harvill Press 1976–89, Hatchards Ltd 1976–89, William Collins Publrs Ltd 1979–81, The Listener Publs PLC 1988–93, RadioTrust PLC 1997–2001, Guinness Publrs Ltd 1991–98; Dir Pan Books Ltd 1962–84 (Chair. 1973–76), Book Tokens Ltd 1981–94, Ind. Radio News 1984–85, Stanley Botes Ltd 1986–89, Guinness PLC (non-exec.) 1986–91; Pres.-Dir Gen. Guinness Media SAS, Paris 1996–99; f. Chapmans Publrs. Chair. and Man. Dir 1989–94; Trustee Book Trade Benevolent Soc. 1982–2003; Trustee The Publrs Asscn 1989–97; mem. Gov. Council SCOTBIC; mem. Council Publishers Asscn 1962–77, Vice-Pres. 1978, Pres. 1979–81; Chair. Nat. Acad. of Writing 2000; mem. Bd Book Devt Council 1987, Ancient House Bookshop 1972–89, Scottish Opera, Theatre Royal Ltd 1974–79, IRN Ltd 1983–85; Chair. Advisory Bd Strathclyde Univ. Business School 1985–88; Hon. DLitt (Strathclyde Univ.) 1990; Scottish Free Enterprise Award 1985. *Leisure interests:* grandchildren, music, golf, reading. *Address:* Kenmore, 46 The Avenue, Cheam, Surrey, SM2 7QE, England (Home). *Telephone:* (20) 8642-1820 (Home). *Fax:* (20) 8770-0225. *E-mail:* fic@onetel.net.uk.

CHAPMAN, Jake, MA; British artist; b. 1966, Cheltenham; brother of Dinos Chapman (q.v.); ed North East London Polytechnic, RCA; studied sculpture at RCA; now works jtly with brother Dinos; co-owner Chapman Fine Arts Gallery, E London. *Solo exhibitions:* We Are Artists, Hales Gallery, London 1992, The Disasters of War (sculpture), Victoria Miro Gallery, London 1993, Great Deeds Against the Dead, Victoria Miro Gallery, London 1994, Mummy and Daddy, Galleria Franco Toselli, Milan 1994, Gavin Brown's Enterprise, New York 1995, Zygotic Acceleration, Biogenetic, De-sublimated Libindral Model (Enlarged × 1000), Victoria Miro Gallery, London 1995, Five Easy Pissers, Andréhn-Schiptjenko Gallery, Stockholm 1995, P-House, Tokyo 1996, Zero Principle, Giò Marconi, Milan 1996, Chapmanworld, ICA, London 1996, Six Feet Under, Gagosian Gallery, New York 1997, Chapmanworld, Grazer Kunstverein, Graz 1997, Galerie Daniel Templon, Paris 1998, Disasters of War (etchings), Jay Jopling/White Cube Gallery, London 1999, The Rape of Creativity, Modern Art Oxford 2003. *Group exhibitions include:* General Release: Young British Artists, Venice Biennale 1995, Future, Present, Past, Venice Biennale 1997, Sensation: Young British Artists from the Saatchi Collection, RA, London 1997; works in collections of Deste Foundation, Athens, Rubell Family Collection, Fla, Saatchi Collection, London, Walker Art Center, Minneapolis. *Publications:* articles in Frieze art magazine. *Address:* Chapman Fine Arts, 39 Fashion Street, London, E1 6PX, England (Office). *Fax:* (20) 7375-3592.

CHAPMAN, Orville Lamar, PhD; American professor of chemistry; b. 26 June 1932, New London, Conn.; m. 2nd Susan Parker Chapman 1981; two s. (from previous m.); ed Virginia Polytechnic Inst. and Cornell Univ.; Prof. of Chem., Iowa State Univ. 1957–74, Univ. of Calif., Los Angeles 1974–2000; Arthur C. Cope Award (American Chem. Soc.), Texas Instrument Foundation Founders Prize, American Chem. Soc. Award in Pure Chem., Computerworld-Smithsonian Inst. Award in Educ. 1995. *Publications:* over 130 research articles. *Address:* 1213 Roscomare Road, Los Angeles, CA 90077-2202, USA (Home). *Telephone:* (310) 825-4883. *E-mail:* chapman@chem.ucla.edu.

CHAPPELL, Gregory (Greg) Stephen, MBE; Australian cricketer and business executive; b. 7 Aug. 1948, Adelaide; s. of Arthur Martin Chappell and Jeanne Ellen (Richardson) Chappell; grandson of V.Y. Richardson (Australian Cricket Capt. 1935–36); brother of I.M. Chappell (Australian Cricket Capt. 1971–75); m. Judith Elizabeth Donaldson 1971; two s. one d.; ed St Leonards Primary School and Plympton High School, Adelaide and Prince Alfred Coll., Adelaide; teams: S. Australia 1966–73, Somerset 1968–69, Queensland 1973–84 (Capt. 1973–77, 1979–80); 87 Tests for Australia 1970–84, 48 as Capt., scoring 7,110 runs (average 53.8) including 24 hundreds and holding 122 catches; scored 108 on Test debut v. England, Perth 1970; only capt. to have scored a century in each innings of 1st Test as capt. (versus West Indies, Brisbane 1975); holds record for most catches in a Test match (7, versus England, Perth 1975); scored 24,535 first-class runs (74 hundreds); toured England 1972, 1975, 1977 and 1980; Man. Dir AD Sports Technologies (fmrly Fundamental Golf and Leisure Ltd) 1993–95 (Dir 1992–), Greg Chappell Sports Marketing 1995–98; mem. Australian Cricket Bd 1984–88; State Man. of Cricket, S. Australian Cricket Asscn 1998–; coach, S. Australian 'Redbacks' cricket team 2002; Patron Leukaemia Foundation of SA 1998–, Happi Foundation 2001–; Hon. MBE 1979; Wisden Cricketer of the Year 1973; Australian Sportsman of the Year 1976; Hon. Life mem. MCC 1985; Chosen for Australian Team of the Century 2000; Australian Cricket Hall of Fame 2001. *Publications:* Greg Chappell's Health and Fitness Repair Manual 1998, Greg Chappell's Family Health and Fitness Manual 1999. *Leisure interests:* golf, tennis, reading, listening to music. *Address:* c/o South Australian Cricket Association, Adelaide Oval, North Adelaide, SA 5006, Australia.

CHAPPLE, Field Marshal Sir John (Lyon), GCB, CBE, MA, FZS, FLS, FRGS; British army officer; b. 27 May 1931; s. of C. H. Chapple; m. Annabel Hill 1959; one s. three d.; ed Haileybury and Trinity Coll., Cambridge; joined 2nd King Edward's Own Gurkhas 1954, served Malaya, Hong Kong, Borneo; Staff Coll. 1962, Jt Services Staff Coll. 1969; Commdr 1st Bn 2nd Gurkhas 1970–72; Directing Staff, Staff Coll. 1972–73; Commdr 48 Gurkha Infantry Brigade 1976; Gurkha Field Force 1977; Prin. Staff Officer to Chief of Defence Staff 1978–79; Commdr British Forces, Hong Kong and Maj.-Gen. Brigade of Gurkhas 1980–82; Dir of Mil. Operations 1982–84; Deputy Chief of Defence Staff (Programmes and Personnel) 1985–87; Col 2nd Gurkhas 1986–94; C-in-C UK Land Forces 1987–88; Aide-de-Camp Gen. to the Queen 1987–92; Chief of Gen. Staff 1988–92; Gov. and C-in-C Gibraltar 1993–95; Pres. Zoological Soc. of London 1991–94; Vice-Lord Lt of Greater London 1997–; Services Fellow Fitzwilliam Coll., Cambridge 1973; mem. Council Nat. Army Museum 1980–93; Pres. Combined Services Polo Asscn 1991–, Indian Mil. History Soc. 1991–, Mil. History Soc. 1992–, Soc. for Army Historical Research 1993–, Trekforce 1998–, Sir Oswald Stoll Foundation 1998–, British Schools Exploring Soc. Expeditions 1999–; Trustee World Wide Fund for Nature (UK) 1985–93, King Mahendra Trust for Conservation, Nepal 1993–.

CHARALAMBOPOULOS, Yannis; Greek politician; b. 1919, Psari, Messinia Pref.; m. Aga Stafila; one s. one d.; ed Mil. Acad., Woolwich Inst., London; co. Commdr fighting invading Italians in Albania 1939; served in Greek units attached to allied armies in Middle East during World War II; teacher at Mil. Acad. 1953; Tech. Adviser, Ministry of Finance 1954–58; resigned from army 1961 and joined Centre Union Party; Deputy to Parl. 1963, 1964–67, 1974–; political prisoner 1967–72; leader, illegal Panhellenic Liberation Movt 1972; arrested and imprisoned 1973–74; founding mem. Pasok, mem. of Cen. Cttee and Exec. Cttee 1977; Pasok Parl. Rep. to European Parl. 1981; Minister of Foreign Affairs 1981–85, Deputy Prime Minister 1985–88, Minister of Defence 1986–90. *Address:* 17 Pringipos Petrou Street, 166 74 Glyfada, Greece. *Telephone:* (1) 8932 333.

CHARASSE, Michel Joseph; French politician; b. 8 July 1941, Chamalières; s. of Martial Henri Charasse and Lucie Castellani; m. Danièle Bas 1978; ed Lycée Blaise Pascal, Clermont-Ferrand, Institut d'Etudes Politiques and Faculté de Droit de Paris; mem. staff Ministry of Finance 1965–92; Asst Sec.-Gen. Socialist group in Nat. Ass. 1962–67, 1968–81 and FGDS group 1967–68; Mayor Puy-Guillaume, Puy-de-Dôme 1977–; Regional Councillor, Auvergne 1979–87; Adviser to Pres. of the Repub. 1981–95; Senator from Puy-de-Dôme 1981–88, 1992–; Sec. of Senate 1995–98; Minister-Del. for Budget 1988–92, Minister for Budget April–Oct. 1992; Treas. Assch of Mayors of France; mem. High Council for Co-operation 2000–. *Publications:* 55 Faubourg St Honoré 1996, Pensées, Répliques et Anecdotes de François Mitterrand 1998. *Leisure interests:* hunting, fishing, reading. *Address:* Mairie, place Jean Jaurès, 63290 Puy-Guillaume; Sénat, Palais du Luxembourg, Paris 6ème, France. *Telephone:* 4-73-94-70-49 (Puy-Guillaume); 1-42-34-20-00 (Sénat).

CHARBONNEAU, Hubert, MA, PhD; Canadian demographer; b. 2 Sept. 1936, Montreal; s. of Léonel Charbonneau and Jeanne Durand; m. Marie-Christiane Hellot 1961; one d.; ed Univs. of Montreal and Paris; Sr Lecturer, Univ. of Montreal 1962–68, Asst Prof. 1968–70, Assoc. Prof. 1970–76, Prof. 1976–97, Prof. Emer. 1997–; Visiting Prof. Univ. do Paraná, Brazil 1978, 1980, 1983, Univ. de Buenos Aires 1994, 1997; Killam Sr Research Scholarship 1974, 1975, 1976; J. B. Tyrrell Historical Medal of the Royal Soc. of Canada 1990. *Publications:* author and co-author of several books on demographic topics. *Leisure interests:* genealogy, billiards, cross-country skiing. *Address:* Département de démographie, Université de Montréal, CP 6128, succ. "Centre-Ville", Montréal, PQ, H3C 3J7 (Office); 19 avenue Robert, Outremont, PQ, H3S 2P1, Canada (Home). *Telephone:* (514) 343-7229 (Office); (514) 731-5503 (Home). *Fax:* (514) 343-2309. *E-mail:* hubert.charbonneau@umontreal.ca (Office); hubert.charbonneau@videotron.ca (Home).

CHAREST, Jean J., PC, LLB; Canadian politician; b. 24 June 1958, Sherbrooke, Québec; m. Michèle Dionne 1980; one s. two d.; ed Université de Sherbrooke; mem. Sherbrooke Legal Aid Office 1981; Assoc. Beauchemin, Dussault et Charest 1981–84; Progressive Conservative MP for Sherbrooke 1984–; Asst Deputy Speaker, House of Commons 1984; Minister of State (Youth) 1986–90, (Fitness and Amateur Sport) 1988–90; Deputy Govt Leader in House of Commons 1989–90; Minister for the Environment 1991–93; Deputy Prime Minister of Canada and Minister of Industry; Leader Progressive Conservative Party 1993–98; Leader Liberal Party in Québec 1998–, Leader of the Opposition 1998–2002; Premier of Québec 2003–; mem. numerous Cabinet Cttees.; mem. Québec Bar Assch, Canadian Bar Assch. *Leisure interests:* skiing, sailing. *Address:* Office of the Premier, 885 Grande-Allée est, Edif. J, 3e étage, Québec, QC G1A 1A2, Canada (Office). *Telephone:* (418) 643-5321 (Office). *Fax:* (418) 643-3924 (Office). *E-mail:* premier.ministre@mcegouv.qc.ca (Office). *Website:* www.premier.gouv.qc.ca.

CHARETTE DE LA CONTRIE, Hervé Marie Joseph de; French politician; b. 30 July 1938, Paris; s. of Hélion de Charette de la Contrie and Jeanne de Nolhac; m. 2nd Michèle Delor; one c. and three c. by previous m.; ed Ecole des Hautes Etudes Commerciales, Inst. d'Etudes Politiques, Paris and Ecole Nat. d'Admin.; Deputy Sec.-Gen. Council of State 1969–72, Maître des requêtes 1973; Ministry of Labour 1973–78; Pres. Admin. Council, Nat. Immigration Office 1977; Dir Office of Minister of Educ. 1978; Pres. Sonacotra 1980–81; Deputy Sec.-Gen. Parti Républicain 1979; returned to Council of State 1981; Deputy to Nat. Ass. 1986, 1988–93, 1997–; Asst Minister, Office of Prime Minister 1986–88; Mayor of St-Florent-Le-Vieil 1989–; Vice-Pres. Union pour la Démocratie Française (UDF) 1991; Vice-Pres. Conseil Régional, Pays de la Loire 1992–; Minister of Housing 1993–95, of Foreign Affairs 1995–97; Pres. Parti populaire pour la démocratie française 1995. *Publications:* Ouragon sur la République 1995, Lyautey 1997. *Address:* Mairie, 49410 St-Florent-le-Vieil, France; Assemblée Nationale, 75355, Paris.

CHARKIN, Richard Denis Paul, MA; British publishing executive; b. 17 June 1949, London; s. of Frank Charkin and Mabel Doreen Charkin (née Rosen); m. Susan Mary Poole 1972; one s. two d.; ed Haileybury, Imperial Service Coll., Cambridge Univ.and Harvard Business School; Science Ed. Harrap & Co. 1972; Sr Publishing Man. Pergamon Press 1973; Medical Ed. Oxford Univ. Press 1974, Head of Science and Medicine 1976, Head of Reference 1980; Man. Dir Academic and Gen. 1984; joined Octopus Publishing Group (Reed Int. Books) 1988; Chief Exec. Reed Consumer Books 1993–94, Exec. Dir Reed Books Int. 1988–96, Chief Exec. 1994–96; CEO Current Science Group 1996–97; Chief Exec. Macmillan Ltd 1998–; Visiting Fellow Green Coll. Oxford 1987; Chair. Common Purpose 1998–; Dir (non-exec.) Scoot.com PLC 2000–, X-Refer Ltd 2000–; mem. Man. Cttee John Wisden. *Leisure interests:* music, cricket. *Address:* Macmillan Ltd, The Macmillan Building, 4 Crinan Street, London, N1 9XW (Office); 3 Redcliffe Place, London, SW10 9DB, England (Home). *Telephone:* (20) 7843-3600 (Office). *Fax:* (20) 7843-3648 (Office). *Website:* www.macmillan.co.uk.

CHARKVIANI, Gela; Georgian politician; b. 1 March 1939, T'bilisi, Georgia; s. of Candide Charkviani and Tamar Djaoshvili; m. Nana Toidze-Charkviani; one s. one d.; ed Tbilisi Inst. of Foreign Languages, Univ. of Michigan; teacher Tbilisi Inst. of Foreign Languages; author and narrator TV monthly programme Globe, Georgian TV 1976–94; Vice-Pres. Georgian Soc. for Cultural Relations with Foreign Countries 1984–92; Chief Adviser to Pres. Shevardnadze on Foreign Affairs, Head of Int. Relations Georgian State Chancellery 1992–; Chair. Presidential Comm. on Peaceful Caucasus; Order of Honour 1998. *Publications include:* trans. of King Lear; Georgia, Transcaucasus and Beyond 1996; articles in numerous journals. *Leisure interests:* piano music, exotic cuisines. *Address:* State Chancellery of Georgia, Ingorokva str. 7, Tbilisi (Office); Gamsakhurdia str. 14, Tbilisi, Georgia (Home). *Telephone:* (32) 934739 (Office); (32) 989679 (Home). *Fax:* (32) 997096 (Office). *E-mail:* gelacharkviani@hotmail.com (Office).

CHARLES, Caroline, OBE; British fashion designer; b. 18 May 1942, Cairo, Egypt; d. of Noel St John Fairhurst and Helen T. Williams; m. Malcolm Valentine 1966; one s. one d.; ed Sacred Heart Convent, Woldingham, Surrey, Swindon Art School; f. Caroline Charles 1963; established retail outlet in London selling Caroline Charles Collection 1979; launched first Caroline Charles House of Design, London 1989; wholesale business suppliers to leading British shops and stores and exports to USA, Japan, Australia and Europe; Evening Standard Design Award 1983 and other design awards. *Publication:* Weekend Wardrobe. *Leisure interests:* travel, theatre, gardening, tennis. *Address:* 56–57 Beauchamp Place, London, SW3 1NY, England. *Telephone:* (20) 7225-3197. *Website:* www.carolinecharles.co.uk.

CHARLES, Dame (Mary) Eugenia, DBE, BA; Dominican politician; b. 15 May 1919, Pointe Michel; d. of John B. and Josephine (née Delauney) Charles; ed Univ. Coll., Univ. of Toronto, London School of Econs; mem. Inner Temple, London 1947; legal practice, Barbados, Windward and Leeward Islands; political career began 1968; co-f. and first leader Dominica Freedom Party; MP 1970–95; Leader of the Opposition 1975–79; Prime Minister, Minister of Finance and Devt 1980–95; Minister of Foreign Affairs 1980–90; mem. Council Women World Leaders, John F. Kennedy School of Govt, Harvard Univ.; fmr Minister of Tourism and Trade; Pres. Int. Fed. of Women Lawyers 1990–; fmr Dir Dominica Co-operative Bank; fmr mem. Bd Dominica Infirmary. *Leisure interests:* reading, travel. *Address:* P.O. Box 121, 1 Cross Lane, Roseau, Dominica. *Telephone:* 4482855.

CHARLES, Pierre; Dominican politician and business executive; b. 30 June 1954; m.; ed teacher training coll.; Senator interim Govt 1979–80; Operations Man., Farm to Market 1979–88; mem. Dominican Labour Party 1986–2000; Minister for Communications and Works Jan.–Oct. 2000; Prime Minister Oct. 2000–, also Minister for Foreign Affairs and Caribbean Affairs, then Minister for Finance; Pres. Nat. Youth Council 1977–79; Councillor Grand Bay Village Council 1984–99; mem. Dominica Br., Commonwealth Parl. Asscn, 1985–95, Bd of Dirs Grand Bay Credit Union 1998–2000; Man. Midnight Groovers Band 1995–98. *Leisure interests:* basketball, Creole music, hiking, law. *Address:* Office of the Prime Minister, Government HQ, Kennedy Avenue, Roseau, Dominica (Office). *Telephone:* (767) 448-2401 (Office); (767) 446-3845 (Home). *Fax:* (767) 448-8960 (Office); (767) 448-5200. *E-mail:* pmoffice@cwdom.dm.

CHARLES, Ray; American jazz musician; b. (Ray Charles Robinson), 23 Sept. 1930, Albany, Ga; s. of late Bailey and Aretha Robinson; m. (divorced); nine c.; ed St Augustine's School, Orlando, Fla; taught himself to play and write for every bass and wind instrument in the orchestra, specializing in piano, organ and saxophone; composes and arranges; played at Rockin' Chair Club, Seattle Elks Club, Seattle; joined Lowell Fulsom's Blues Band, toured for a year; played at Apollo, Harlem; formed group to accompany singer Ruth Brown; Leader of Maxim Trio; with Atlantic Records 1954–59, ABC Records 1959–62, formed own cos, Tangerine 1962–73, Crossover Records Co. 1973–, Columbia Records 1982–; tours with Ray Charles Revue; Songwriters Hall of Fame, Rock and Roll Hall of Fame 1986; Commdr des Arts et des Lettres 1986; Nat. Medal of Arts 1993; Kennedy Center Honor 1986; Polar Munc Prize 1998. *Albums include:* Ray Charles' Greatest Hits, Modern Sounds in Country and Western Music (Vols 1 and 2), Message from the People, Volcanic Action of my Soul, Through the Eyes of Love, Would You Believe, My World, Blue and Jazz. *Address:* c/o Ray Charles Entertainment, 2107 West Washington Boulevard, Los Angeles, CA 90018, USA.

CHARLES-ROUX, Edmonde; French writer; b. 17 April 1920, Neuilly-sur-Seine; d. of François Charles-Roux and Sabine Gounelle; m. Gaston Defferre 1973 (deceased); ed Italy; served as nurse, then in Resistance Movement, during Second World War, in which she was twice wounded; Reporter, magazine Elle 1947–49; Features Ed., French Edn of Vogue 1949–54, Ed.-in-Chief 1954–66; mem. Acad. Goncourt 1983–, Pres. 2002; Croix de guerre 1940–45; Prix Goncourt 1966, Grand Prix Littéraire de Provence 1977; Officier, Légion d'honneur 2003. *Publications:* Oublier Palerme 1966, Elle Adrienne 1971, L'irrégulière ou mon itinéraire Chanel 1974, Le temps Chanel 1979, Stèle pour un bâtard, Don Juan d'Autriche: 1980, Une enfance sicilienne 1981, Un désir d'Orient: La jeunesse d'Isabelle Eberhardt 1988, Nomade j'étais: Les années africaines d'Isabelle Eberhardt 1995, L'homme de Marseille 2001. *Leisure interests:* music, sea and sailing. *Address:* Editions Grasset, 61 rue des Saints-Pères, Paris 75006, France (Office).

CHARLTON, Jack (John), OBE, DL; British footballer and manager; b. 8 May 1935, Ashington, Northumberland; s. of late Robert Charlton and of Elizabeth Charlton; brother of Sir Robert Charlton; m. Patricia Charlton 1958; two s. one d.; ed Hirst Park School, Ashington; player Leeds United 1952–73; 35 full England caps 1965–70; played with winning teams League Championship 1969, Football Asscn Cup 1972, League Cup 1968, Fairs Cup 1968, 1971, World Cup (England v. Germany) 1966; Man. Middlesbrough (Div. 2 Champions 1974) 1973–77, Sheffield Wednesday 1977–83, Newcastle United 1984–85, Repub. of Ireland (qualified for European Championships W Germany 1988, World Cup Italy 1990) 1986–95; Football Writers' Asscn Footballer of the Year 1967. *Publications:* Jack Charlton's American World Cup Diary 1994, Jack Charlton: The Autobiography 1996. *Leisure interests:* shooting, fishing. *Address:* Cairn Lodge, Dalton, Ponteland, Northumbria, England.

CHARLTON, Sir Robert (Bobby), Kt, CBE; British footballer, professional football manager and sports official; b. 11 Oct. 1937, Ashington, Northumberland; s. of late Robert Charlton and of Elizabeth Charlton; brother of Jack Charlton (q.v.) ; m. Norma Charlton 1961; two d.; ed Bedlington Grammar School, Northumberland; professional footballer with Manchester United 1954–73, played 751 games, scored 245 goals; F.A. Cup winners' medal 1963; First Div. championship medals 1956–57, 1964–65, 1966–67; World Cup winners' medal (with England) 1966; European Cup winners' medal 1968; 106 appearances for England 1957–73, scored record 49 goals; Man. Preston North End 1973–75; Chair. NW Council for Sport and Recreation 1982–; Dir Manchester United Football Club 1984–; Hon. Fellow Manchester Polytechnic 1979; Hon. MA (Manchester Univ.); mem. Laurens World Sports Acad. *Publications:* My Soccer Life 1965, Forward for England 1967, This

Game of Soccer 1967, Book of European Football, Books 1–4 1969–72. *Leisure interest:* golf. *Address:* Garthollerton, Chelford Road, Ollerton, nr Knutsford, Cheshire, WA16 8RY, England.

CHARMOT, Guy, MD; French physician; b. 1914, Toulon; s. of Ulysse Charmot and Claire Esmieu; m. Edith Dubuisson 1948; one d.; Medical Officer in forces 1938; war service in Free French Forces 1940–45; fmr Prof. Service de Santé des Armées: served various hospitals in French-speaking Africa: Chad, Senegal, Congo, Madagascar 1945–66; later worked at Hôpital Bichat (infectious and tropical diseases), Paris–1994 (now retd); fmr Pres. Société de Pathologie exotique; mem. Acad. des Sciences d'Outre-Mer; Commdr Légion d'honneur, Companion de la Libération, Croix de guerre. *Publications:* numerous papers concerned chiefly with diseases of the liver and spleen, human immunodeficiency virus (HIV), hereditary anaemia, malaria and amoeba-caused diseases. *Leisure interest:* mountaineering. *Address:* 72 boulevard de Reuilly, 75012 Paris, France. *Telephone:* 1-46-28-97-73.

CHARPAK, Georges, PhD; French physicist; b. 1 Aug. 1924, Dabrovica, Poland; s. of Anna Szapiro and Maurice Charpak; m. Dominique Vidal 1953; two s. one. d.; ed Ecole des Mines de Paris, Collège de France; prisoner in Dachau 1943–45; physicist CNRS 1948–59, CERN 1959–94; Dir Fimalac 1997–; f. Soc. for Biospace Measurement 1997; mem. Higher Council of Integration 1994–; mem. French Acad. of Sciences 1985; Foreign Assoc. NAS 1986; Hon. mem. Austrian Acad. of Sciences 1993; Foreign mem. Russian Acad. of Sciences 1994; Nat. Corresp. mem. French Acad. of Medicine 2002; hon. degrees from univs of Geneva 1977, Thessalonica 1993, Brussels, Coimbra 1994, Ottawa 1995, Rio de Janeiro 1996; Prize of European Physics Soc.; Nobel Prize for Physics 1992 and others; Mil. Cross 1939–45, Chevalier, Légion d'honneur 1993, Officier, Ordre Nat. du Mérite 1997. *Publications:* La Vie à fil tendu 1993 (jtly), Feu follet et champignon nucléaire (jtly) 1997, Enfants, chercheurs et citoyens 1998, Megawatts and Megatons (jtly) 2001, Devenez sorcier, devenez savant 2002; numerous papers in learned journals. *Leisure interests:* skiing, music, trekking. *Address:* CERN, 1211 Geneva 23, Switzerland (Office); 2 rue de Poissy, 75005, Paris, France (Home). *Telephone:* (22) 7672144 (Office). *Fax:* (22) 7677555 (Office).

CHARTIER, Roger; French university professor; b. 9 Dec. 1945, Lyons; s. of Georges Chartier and Laurence Fonvielle; m. Anne-Marie Trépier 1967; one s. one d.; ed Ecole Normale Supérieure, St Cloud; Prof. Lycée Louis-Le-Grand, Paris 1969–70; Asst Prof. Univ. Paris I, Panthéon-Sorbonne 1970–75; Assoc. Prof. Ecole des Hautes Etudes en Sciences Sociales 1975–83, Dir of Studies 1984–; Visiting Prof. Univ. of Calif. (Berkeley) 1987, Cornell Univ. 1988, Johns Hopkins Univ. 1992; Annual Award, American Printing History Asscn 1990; Grand Prix d'Histoire, Acad. Française 1992. *Publications:* The Cultural Uses of Print in Early Modern France 1987, The Culture of Print (ed.) 1987, Cultural History: Between Practices and Representations 1988, The Cultural Origins of the French Revolution 1991. *Address:* Ecole des Hautes Etudes en Sciences Sociales, 54 boulevard Raspail, 75006 Paris, France.

CHARTRES, Rt Rev and Rt Hon Richard John Carew, PC, DD, DLitt, FSA; British ecclesiastic; b. 11 July 1947; s. of Richard Chartres and Charlotte Chartres; m. Caroline Mary McLintock 1982; two s. two d.; ed Hertford Grammar School, Trinity Coll. Cambridge, Cuddesdon Theological Coll. Oxford and Lincoln Theological Coll.; ordained deacon 1973, priest 1974; Asst Curate, St Andrew's Bedford 1973–75; Domestic Chaplain to Bishop of St Albans 1975–80; Chaplain to Archbishop of Canterbury 1980–84; Vicar, St Stephen with St John, Westminster 1984–92; Dir of Ordinands for London Area 1985–92; Gresham Prof. of Divinity 1986–92; Bishop of Stepney 1992–95, of London 1995–; Dean of the Chapels Royal 1995–; rep. of London Church Leaders on London Pride Partnership; Ecclesiastical Patron Prayer Book Soc.; Prelate of Imperial Soc. of Kt.'s Bachelor; Liveryman Merchant Taylors' Co.; Hon. Freeman Weavers' Co. 1998, Leathersellers' Co. 1999, Woolmen's Co. 2000, Vintners' Co. 2001; Prelate of OBE 1995–; Chair. Churches Main Cttee 1998–2001, Church of England Heritage Forum 1998–; Hon. Bencher, Middle Temple; Hon. DLitt (London Guildhall) 1998, Hon. DD (London) 1999, (City) 1999, (Brunel) 1999. *Publication:* The History of Gresham College 1597–1997 1998. *Address:* The Old Deanery, Dean's Court, London, EC4V 5AA, England. *Telephone:* (20) 7248-6233 (Office). *Fax:* (20) 7248-9721 (Office). *E-mail:* bishop@londin.clara.co.uk (Office).

CHARUSATHIRA, Gen. Prapas; Thai politician and army officer; b. 25 Nov. 1912, Udorn Prov.; m. Khunying Sawai; one s. four d.; ed Chulachomklao Royal Mil. Acad. and Nat. Defence Coll; Army service 1933, rose through infantry to Gen. 1960; Minister of Interior 1957–71; Deputy Prime Minister 1963–71; Army Deputy Commdr and Deputy Supreme Commdr 1963–64; Supreme Commdr 1964; mem. Nat. Exec. Council and Dir of Security Council (Defence and Interior) 1971–72; Deputy Prime Minister, Minister of Interior 1972–73; Vice-Pres. and Rector, Chulalongkorn Univ. 1961–69; in exile 1973–77, returned to Thailand Jan. 1977; numerous decorations. *Publications:* The Role of the Ministry of Interior in the Development of National Security, The Role of the Ministry of Interior in Maintenance of National Peace and Order. *Leisure interests:* sport: boxing, soccer, golf, hunting, amateur ranching, arms collecting. *Address:* 132–5 Suan Puttan Residence, Bangkok, Thailand.

CHASE, Chevy (Cornelius Crane), MA; American comedian, actor and writer; b. 8 Oct. 1943, New York; s. of Edward Tinsley Chase and Cathalene Crane (née Widdoes) Chase; m. 1st Jacqueline Carlin 1976 (divorced 1980); m. 2nd Jayni Chase; three d.; ed Bard Coll., Inst. of Audio Research, MIT;

writer and actor, Channel One (satirical revue), The Great American Dream Machine, co-writer and actor, Lemmings (Nat. Lampoon satirical musical), writer and performer Nat. Lampoon Radio Hour, Saturday Night Live (TV series); writer Mad magazine 1969; mem. American Fed. of Musicians, Stage Actors Guild, Actors Equity, American Fed. of TV and Radio Artists; 3 Emmy Awards, Writers Guild of America Award, Man of the Year, Harvard Univ. Theatrical Group 1992. *Films include:* Tunnelvision 1976, Foul Play 1978, Oh Heavenly Dog 1980, Caddyshack 1980, Seems Like Old Times, Under the Rainbow 1981, Modern Problems 1981, Vacation 1983, Deal of the Century 1983, European Vacation 1984, Fletch 1985, Spies Like Us 1985, Follow that Bird 1985, The Three Amigos 1986, Caddyshack II 1988, Funny Farm 1988, Christmas Vacation 1989, Fletch Lives 1989, Memoirs of an Invisible Man 1992, Hero 1992, Last Action Hero 1993, Cops and Robbersons 1994, Man of the House 1995, National Lampoon's Vegas Vacation 1997, Snow Day 1999. *Television appearances include:* The Great American Machine, Smothers Brothers Show, Saturday Night Live. *Address:* Cornelius Productions, Box 257, Bedford, NY 10506, USA.

CHASE, Rodney Frank, CBE; business executive; b. 12 May 1943; s. of Norman Maxwell Chase and Barbara Chase; m. Diana Lyle 1968; one s. one d.; with British Petroleum PLC London, joined depts. of shipping, refining and marketing, distribution, oil trading, gas; CEO BP Finance, Group Treas.; Chief Financial Officer, fmr Exec. Vice-Pres. BP America Inc., CEO, Chair. 1992–94; CEO BP Exploration Inc. (Western Hemisphere), Man. Dir The British Petroleum Co. PLC (now BP Amoco PLC) 1992–98, Deputy Group Chief Exec. 1998–; Dir (non-exec.) BOC Group PLC 1995–; mem. UK Advisory Cttee on Business and the Environment (ACBE), UK Roundtable on Sustainable Devt; Bd mem. World Conservation Monitoring Centre; Fellow Asscn of Corp. Treas. *Leisure interests:* downhill skiing, golf. *Address:* BP Amoco PLC, Britannic House, 1 Finsbury Circus, London, EC2M 7BA, England. *Telephone:* (20) 7496 4000. *Fax:* (20) 7496 4574.

CHASKALSON, Arthur, SC, LLB; South African judge; b. 24 Nov. 1931, Johannesburg; s. of Harry Bernard Chaskalson and Mary Dorothea (née Oshry) Chaskalson; m. Lorraine Diane Ginsberg 1961; two s.; ed Univ. of Witwatersrand; admitted to bar 1956, SC 1971; Chair. Johannesburg Bar Council 1976, 1982 (mem. 1967–71, 1973–84); Vice-Chair. Gen. Council of SA Bar 1982–87, Int. Legal Aid Div., Int. Bar Asscn 1983–93; Nat. Dir Legal Resources Centre 1979–93; Hon. Prof. of Law Univ. of Witwatersrand 1981–95; Visiting Prof. Col Univ., NY 1987–88; Chair. Rhodes Scholarship Selection Cttee for SA 1988–93; consultant to Namibian Constituent Ass. (in relation to the drafting of the Namibian Constitution) 1989–90, to African Nat. Congress (ANC) on drafting the S. African Constitution 1990–94; mem. Tech. Cttee on Constitutional Issues during the Multi-Party Negotiating Process May–Dec. 1993; Pres. Constitutional Court 1994–; Commr Int. Comm. of Jurists 1995–; Hon. mem. Bar Asscn of NY City 1985; mem. Nat. Council of Lawyers for Human Rights 1980–91, numerous other memberships; four hon. degrees; Human Rights Award (Foundation for Freedom and Human Rights, Switzerland) 1990, numerous other awards. *Address:* Constitutional Court, Private Bag X32, Braamfontein 2017, South Africa. *Telephone:* (11) 403-8032.

CHATAWAY, Rt. Hon. Sir Christopher John, Kt, PC; British business executive, fmr politician and fmr athlete; b. 31 Jan. 1931; m. 1st Anna Lett 1959 (divorced 1975); two s. one d.; m. 2nd Carola Walker 1976; two s.; ed Sherborne School and Magdalen Coll., Oxford; rep. UK at Olympic Games 1952, 1956; holder of world 5,000 metres record 1954; Jr Exec., Arthur Guinness, Son and Co. 1953–55; Staff Reporter, Ind. Television News 1955–56; Current Affairs Commentator, BBC Television 1956–59; mem. London County Council 1958–61; MP for Lewisham North 1959–66, for Chichester 1969–74; Parl. Private Sec. to Minister of Power 1961–62; Joint Parl. Under-Sec. of State, Dept of Educ. and Science 1962–64; Alderman, Greater London Council 1967–70; Minister of Posts and Telecommunications 1970–72, for Industrial Devt 1972–74; Man. Dir Orion Royal Bank 1974–88; Chair. Civil Aviation Authority 1991–96; Chair. Bletchley Park Trust 2000–; Dir BET PLC 1974–96; Chair. UK Athletics 1999–2000; Pres. Commonwealth Games Council for England 2002; Pres. Advisory Council, ActionAid; Trustee Foundation for Sport and the Arts 1991–; Hon. DLitt (Loughborough) 1980, (Macquarie Univ., Australia) 2000; Hon. DSc (Cranfield) 1955. *Address:* 80 Maida Vale, London W9 1PR, England. *E-mail:* cjchataway@hotmail.com.

CHATER, Keith Frederick, PhD, FRS; British geneticist; b. 23 April 1944, Croydon, Surrey; s. of Frederick Ernest Chater and Marjorie Inez Chater (née Palmer); m. Jean Wallbridge 1966; three s. one d.; ed Trinity School of John Whitgift, Croydon, Univ. of Birmingham; scientist, John Innes Centre 1969–, Deputy Head Dept of Genetics 1989–98, Head 1998–2001; Head Dept of Molecular Microbiology 2001–; Hon. Prof. Univ. of East Anglia 1988–, Chinese Acad. of Sciences Inst. of Microbiology, Beijing 1998–, Huazhong Agricultural Univ., Wuhan 2000; Fred Griffith Review Lecturer, Soc. for Gen. Microbiology 1997. *Publications:* (jtly) Genetic Manipulation of Streptomyces 1985, (ed jtly) Genetics of Bacterial Diversity 1989, (jtly) Practical Streptomyces Genetics 2000. *Leisure interests:* art, birdwatching, gardening, cooking. *Address:* Department of Molecular Microbiology, John Innes Centre, Norwich Research Park, Colney, Norwich, NR4 7UH (Office); 6 Coach House Court, Norwich, NR4 7QR, England (Home). *Telephone:* (1603) 450297 (Office); (1603) 506145 (Home). *Fax:* (1603) 450045 (Office). *E-mail:* keith.chater@bbsrc.ac.uk (Office). *Website:* www.jic.bbsrc.ac.uk/staff/keith-chater.

CHAUDHRY, Amir Husain; Pakistani politician; b. 1942, Jammu, India; elected mem. Nat. Ass., 1985–, Speaker 2002–; mem. Council, Azad Jammu and Kashmir Council 1985–90; Vice-Pres. Muslim Conf., Azad Jammu 1985–90. *Address:* Pakistan National Assembly, Constitution Avenue, Islamabad, Pakistan (Office).

CHAUDHRY, Mahendra; Fijian politician; b. Mahendra Pal Chaudhry, 02 Sept. 1942, Ba, Fiji; s. of Raan Gopal Chaudhry and Devi Chaudhry (née Nair) (both deceased); two s. one d.; Sr Auditor, Office of the Auditor Gen. 1960–75; Gen. Sec. Nat. Farmers' Union 1978–; Gen. Sec. Fiji Public Service Asscn 1970–99; Nat. Sec. Fiji Trades Union Congress 1988–92; Minister of Finance April–May 1987, ousted in May 1987 coup; Founding mem. Fiji Labour Party 1985, Parliamentary Leader 1992, Sec.-Gen. 1994–; Prime Minister and Minister for Finance, Public Enterprise, Sugar Industry and Information 1999–2000; ousted in coup by George Speight May 2000; reassumed post of Prime Minister 1 March 2001, dismissed 14 March 2001 by Pres. of Fiji. *Leisure interests:* reading, music, gardening. *Address:* Fiji Labour Party, P.O. Box 2162, Suva, Fiji; 74 Augustus Street, Suva (Office); 3 Hutson Street, Suva, Fiji (Home). *Telephone:* (679) 3305811 ext. 405 (Office); (679) 3001865 (Home). *Fax:* (679) 3307829 (Office). *E-mail:* mahendrachaudhry42@hotmail.com.

CHAUDHURI, Naranarain (Sankho), BA; Indian sculptor; b. 25 Feb. 1916, Santhal Parganas, Bihar; s. of Narendra Narain and Kiron Moyee; m. Ira Chaudhuri; two s. one d.; ed Armanitoba High School, Dhaka and Bishwa Bharti Santiniketan, West Bengal; freelance artist 1947–; Reader and Head Dept of Sculpture, Univ. of Baroda 1949–50, Prof. of Sculpture 1957, Dean, Faculty of Fine Arts 1966–68; Prof. of Fine Arts, Univ. of Dar-es-Salaam 1980; mem. Lalit Kala Akademi 1956– (Sec. 1974, Chair. 1984–); Pres. Indian Sculptors' Asscn 1964–65; mem. Indian Cttee Int. Asscn of Plastic Arts, All India Handicrafts Bd, Int. Jury 5th Triennale-India, Lalit Kala Acad. 1956 (Sec. 1974, Fellow 1982); exhibited São Paulo Bienal 1961; numerous Indian awards; Padma Shri 1971. *One-man exhibitions include:* Mumbai, New Delhi and Kolkata. *Major works:* Sculptures, All India Radio, Delhi 1955, Statue of Mahatma Gandhi, Rio de Janeiro 1964, sculpture for Jyoti Ltd, Baroda 1968, brass sculpture for World Bank commissioned by Govt of India 1976, Mahatma Gandhi, Copenhagen 1985 and works in collections in India, UK and USA. *Address:* c/o Lalit Kala Academy, Copernicus Marg, New Delhi 110001, India.

CHAUNU, Pierre, DèsSc; French professor of history; b. 17 Aug. 1923, Belleville, Meuse; m. Huguette Catella 1947; five s. (one deceased) one d.; School of Advanced Hispanic Studies, Madrid 1948–51; CNRS 1956–59, now mem. Directorate; Univ. de Caen 1959; Prof. of Modern History, Univ. de Paris à la Sorbonne 1970–; Assoc. Prof., Faculté de Théologie Réformée, Aix-en-Provence 1974; mem. of Section, Conseil Econ. et Social 1976–77; Pres. Conseil Supérieur des Corps Universitaires 1977; Columnist Le Figaro 1982–; mem. Social and Econ. Council 1976–; mem. Scientific Cttee (history section), CNRS 1980–, numerous other cttees; Pres. Fed. Nat. des syndicats autonomes de l'enseignement supérieur 1988–90; mem. Acad. des Sciences morales et politiques 1982– (Pres. 1993), High Council for Integration 1994–; Commdr., Légion d'honneur. *Publications:* forty books including: Seville et l'Atlantique (1504–1650) (12 Vols), Le Pacifique des Ibériques, Civilisation de l'Europe classique, Civilisation de l'Europe des lumières, Temps des Réformes, L'Espagne de Charles Quint, La Mort à Paris, Histoire et Prospective, La Mémoire et le sacré, Le refus de la vie, La violence de Dieu, Un futur sans avenir, La mémoire de l'éternité, Le sursis 1979, Histoire et foi, Histoire et imagination 1980, Réforme et contre-réforme, Eglise, Culture et Société, Histoire et Décadence 1981, La France 1982, Ce que je crois 1982, Le chemin des mages 1983, Combats pour l'histoire 1983, L'historien dans tous ses états 1984, L'historien en cet instant 1985, Rétrohistoire, Au coeur religieux de l'histoire, L'aventure de la réforme 1986, Une autre voie (jtly) 1986, Du Big Bang à l'enfant 1987, L'obscure mémoire de la France 1988, Apologie pour l'histoire 1988, Le grand déclassement 1989, Journal de Jean Héroard 1989, Trois millions d'années, Quatre-vingts millards de destins 1990, Reflets et miroir de l'histoire 1990, Colère contre Colère 1991, Dieu, Apologie 1991, L'Aventure de la Réforme, Le monde de Jean Calvin 1992, Brève histoire de Dieu 1992, l'Axe du temps 1994, l'Instant éclaté 1994, Les Enjeux de la Paix 1995, L'Héritage 1995, Baptême de Clovis, Baptême de la France 1996, Danse avec l'histoire 1998, Le Basculement religieux de Paris 1998, Charles Quint 2000, La Femme et Dieu 2001; 120 articles. *Address:* Université Paris-Sorbonne, 1 rue Victor-Cousin, 75230 Paris Cedex 05 (Office); 12 rue des Cordeliers, 14300 Caen, France (Home). *Telephone:* (31) 81-61-51 (Caen) (Home).

CHAUVIRÉ, Yvette; French ballerina; b. 22 April 1917, Paris; d. of Henri Chauviré and Berthe Pinchard; ed Paris Opera Ballet School; joined Paris Opera Ballet 1930, Danseuse Etoile 1942; with Monte Carlo Opera Ballet 1946–47; Artistic and Technical Adviser to Admin. of Paris Opera 1963–68; Dir Acad. int. de danse, Paris 1970; Pres. Europa Danse 1999–; Commdr Légion d'honneur; Commdr des Arts et des Lettres; Grand Officier Ordre nat. du Mérite. *Ballets include:* Istar, Les deux pigeons, Sleeping Beauty, David triomphant, Giselle, Les créatures de Prométhée, Roméo et Juliette, L'écuyère, Les suites romantiques, Lac des cygnes, L'oiseau de feu, Petrouchka, Sylvia, La belle Hélène, Casse-Noisette, Les mirages, Le cygne, La dame aux camélias. *Films include:* Carrousel Napolitain 1953, Le cygne 1984, Une étoile pour l'exemple. *Publications:* Je suis ballerine, Autobiographie 1997. *Leisure interests:* drawings, watercolours, collecting swans. *Address:* 21 Place du Commerce, 75015 Paris, France.

CHAVALIT, Gen. Yongchaiyudh; Thai politician; b. 15 May 1932; m. Khunying Phankrua Yongchaiyudh; ed Chulachomklao Royal Mil. Acad., Army Command and Gen. Staff Coll., Fort Leavenworth, USA; Dir of Operations 1981, Chief of Staff 1985, C.-in-C. 1986–90, Acting Supreme Commdr 1987–90; Deputy Prime Minister and Minister of Defence March–June 1990, 1995–1996, 2001–; Minister of the Interior 1992–94, of Labour and Social Welfare 1993–94; Leader New Aspiration Party. *Address:* New Aspiration Party, Ban Mittraphap, Thanon Rama IV, Bangkok, Thailand. *Telephone:* (2) 243-5000.

CHAVAN, Shankarrao Bhaorao, BA, LLB; Indian politician; b. 14 July 1920, Paithan, Aurangabad Dist; s. of Bhaorao and Laxmibi Chavan; m. Kusumati Chavan; one s.; ed Univs. of Madras and Osmania; entered politics 1945; Pres. Nanded Town Municipality 1952–56; mem. Mumbai Legis. Council 1956, Ass. 1957; Deputy Minister for Revenue, Mumbai Govt 1956–60; Minister for Irrigation and Power, Maharashtra Govt 1960–75; Deputy Leader Congress Legis. Party 1967–75, apptd. Leader 1975–; Chief Minister, Maharashtra Govt 1975–77, 1986–88; mem. (Congress (I)) Lok Sabha 1980–; Minister of Educ. 1980–81, of Planning 1981–84, of Defence 1984–85, of Home Affairs 1985–86, 1991–96, of Finance 1988–89; Vice-Presidential cand. 1984; Vice-Pres. Nanded Co-operative Bank; Dir Hyderabad State Co-operative Bank; mem. Rajya Sabha (Congress), Exec. of Cen. Co-operative Union, Hyderabad; Exec. Cttee of Maharashtra Pradesh Congress Cttee, A.I.C.C. *Address:* 4 Krishna Menon Marg, New Delhi 110 011 (Office); Dhanegaon, Shivajinagar, Dist Nanded 431602, India (Home). *Telephone:* (11) 3014809 (Office); (2462) 34081 (Home); (22) 3633190 (Mumbai). *Fax:* (11) 3010780 (Office).

CHAVES DE MENDONÇA, Antônio Aureliano; Brazilian politician and teacher; b. 13 Jan. 1929, Três Pontas, Minas Gerais; s. of Jose Vieira and Luzia Chaves de Mendonça; m. Vivi Sanches de Mendonça; one s. two d.; ed Itajuba Fed. School of Eng, Fluminense Faculty of Eng, War Coll.; teaching posts at Itajuba Fed. School of Eng and Polytech. Inst. of Catholic Univ. of Minas Gerais; Tech. Dir ELETROBRAS 1961; Majority Leader in State Congress of Minas Gerais 1963–67; State Sec. for Educ. 1964, for Transport and Public Works 1965; Fed. Deputy 1967–75, Chair. Comm. for Mines and Energy 1971, later of Comm. for Science and Tech., also posts in various other comms.; Vice-Pres. of Brazil 1979–85, Acting Pres. Sept.–Nov. 1981; Minister of Mines and Energy 1988; mem. Brazilian Geographical Soc., Brazilian Comm. for Large Dams, Brazilian Centre for Physical Research; Arena party; various Brazilian medals. *Publications:* several text books.

CHÁVEZ FRÍAS, Hugo Rafael, MA; Venezuelan politician; b. 28 July 1954, Sabaneta, Barinas State; s. of Hugo de los Reyes Chávez and Elena de Chávez; m. 1 (divorced); three d.; m. 2nd María Isabel Rodríguez; one s.; ed Liceo O'Leary, Barinas State, Mil. Acad., Univ. Simón Bolívar, Caracas; f. Movimiento Bolivariano Revolucionario 1982; Lt-Col Venezuelan Paratroops 1990; led failed mil. coup against Pres. Carlos Pérez 1992; f. Movimiento Revolucionario V República 1998; represents Patriotic Pole coalition; Pres. of Venezuela 1999–12 April 2002, 14 April 2002–; Estrella de Carabobo Cruz de las Fuerzas Terrestres, Orden Militar Francisco de Miranda, Orden Militar Rafael Urdaneta, Orden Militar Libertador V Clase. *Publication:* Cómo salir del Laberinto? (co-author) 1992. *Address:* Central Information Office of the Presidency, Torre Oeste 18°, Parque Central, Caracas 1010, Venezuela. *Telephone:* (2) 572-7110. *Fax:* (2) 572-2675.

CHAVUNDUKA, Gordon Lloyd, MA, PhD; Zimbabwean university professor and politician; b. 16 Aug. 1931, Umtali (now Mutare); s. of Solomon and Lillian Chavunduka; m. Rachel Chavunduka 1959; two s. four d.; ed Univ. of California at Los Angeles, Univs. of Manchester and London; lecturer in Sociology, Univ. of Rhodesia, Salisbury 1966–78, Acting Head, Dept of Sociology 1974–75, Head 1978–86; mem. Univ. Senate 1972–96; Dean, Faculty of Social Studies 1978–88, 1991–; Pro-Vice-Chancellor, Univ. of Zimbabwe 1991–92, Vice-Chancellor 1992–96; Prof. Emer. 1997–; Zimbabwe Govt Commr for Public Enterprises 1988–90; Sec.-Gen. African Nat. Council 1973–76; Pres. Asscn of Univ. Teachers of Rhodesia 1974–, Zimbabwe Nat. Traditional Healers Asscn 1980–; Chair. Traditional Medical Practitioners Council 1983–. *Publications:* Traditional Healers and the Shona Patient, Professionalisation of African Medicine, Traditional Medicine in Modern Zimbabwe; also papers in the field of sociology and contribs. to INCIDI, The Society of Malawi Journal, etc. *Leisure interests:* gardening, boxing (spectator), football. *Address:* 40 The Chase, Mount Pleasant, Harare, Zimbabwe (Home). *Telephone:* 332958.

CHAZOT, Georges-Christian; French business executive; b. 19 March 1939, Algiers; s. of Raymond Chazot and Suzanne Monnet; m. Marie-Dominique Tremois 1962; one s. two d.; ed Lycée Bugeaud, Algiers, Ecole Polytechnique, Harvard Int. Marketing Inst. and MSEE Univ. of Florida; electronic engineer EMR Sarasota, Florida 1962; Man., Space Electronics, Schlumberger 1965–68, Tech. Dir for Industrial Control 1968–70, Commercial Dir for Instruments and Systems 1970–74, Audio-professional Dir-Gen. 1974–76; Dir-Gen. for Alkaline Accumulators, SAFT 1976–80, Dir-Gen. 1981–83, Pres., Dir-Gen. 1983–88, Hon. Pres. and Admin. 1989; Pres., Dir-Gen. Centre d'Etudes et de Services pour le Développement Industriel (CEI) 1983–86; Vice-Pres., Dir-Gen. Télic Alcatel and Opus Alcatel 1989–90; Pres., Dir-Gen. Alcatel Business Systems 1990–91; Pres. Business Systems Group, Vice-Pres. Alcatel NV 1990–92; Pres., Dir-Gen. Adia France 1992–94; Group Man. Dir Eurotunnel 1994–, Chair. eurotunnel Developments Ltd 2002–;

Chair. GCC Consultants; Vice-Pres. French Chamber of Commerce in GB –2000; Chair. Paris Notre-Dame magazine 2001–; Vice-Chair. Radio Notre Dame 2001; Dir Giat Industries 2002–; Fellow Chartered Inst. of Transport; Chevalier Légion d'honneur 1990, Officier Ordre nat. du Mérite 1996. *Leisure interests:* opera, sailing, skiing. *Address:* 24 rue de Réservoirs, 78000 Versailles, France. *Telephone:* 1-30-21-83-14 (Office). *Fax:* 1-30-21-83-14-(Office). *E-mail:* chazotg@compuserve.com (Office). *Website:* www.eurotunnel.com (Office).

CHAZOV, Yevgeny Ivanovich, MD, PhD; Russian politician and cardiologist; b. 10 June 1929, Gorky; ed Kiev Medical Inst.; mem. CPSU 1962–91, mem. Cen. Cttee 1982–90; Sr Scientific Worker, Inst. of Therapy 1959; Deputy Dir Inst. of Therapy, USSR Acad. of Medical Science 1963–65, Dir Inst. of Cardiology 1965–67; Deputy Minister of Public Health 1967–87, Minister 1987–91; mem. Supreme Soviet 1974–89; Dir Cardiology Research Centre, Acad. of Medical Science 1975–; personal physician to Brezhnev, Andropov, Chernenko and Gorbachev; mem. Cen. Cttee CSPU 1982–90; mem. USSR (now Russian) Acad. of Medical Sciences 1971, USSR (now Russian) Acad. of Sciences 1979; Pres. USSR (now Russian) Soc. of Cardiology 1975; Co-Pres. Int. Physicians for Prevention of Nuclear War (IPPNW) 1980–87, IPPNW awarded Nobel Prize for Peace 1985; mem. Acads. of USA, Germany, Hungary; State Prize 1969, 1976; Hero of Socialist Labour 1978; Lenin Prize 1982, UNESCO Peace Prize 1984. *Publications:* Myocardial Infarction (with others) 1971, Cardiac Rhythm Disorders 1972, Anti-coagulants and Fibrinolytics 1977, Health and Power (memoirs) and other monographs; over 300 articles on cardiology. *Leisure interests:* hunting, photography. *Address:* Cardiology Scientific Centre, Rublerskoye shosse 135, 121552 Moscow, Russia. *Telephone:* (095) 415-00-25.

CHECA CREMADES, Fernando, DenFil y Letras, LicEnD; Spanish professor of art history and arts administrator; b. 14 May 1952, Madrid; s. of Francisco Checa and Concepción Cremades; lecturer in art history, Univ. Complutense de Madrid 1976–, Prof. of Art History –1996, 2002–; specialist in Renaissance and Baroque periods; Dir Prado Museum 1996–2002; Summer Visiting Prof. Inst. of Advanced Studies, Princeton Univ. 1988; Paul Mellon Sr Fellow Center of Advanced Studies in Visual Arts, Nat. Gallery of Art, Washington 1989; Fae Norton Prof. Okla State Univ. 1995; fmr mem. Ministerial Comm. for Classification of State Collections; organizer of 4 major exhbns; Premio Extraordinario de Doctorado 1981, Nat. Prize for History 1993. *Publications include:* Pintura y escultura del Renacimiento en España 1983, La imagen impresa en el Renacimiento y el Manierismo 1987, Carlos V y la imagen del héroe en el Renacimiento 1987, Felipe II: mecenas de las artes 1992 (Nat. History Prize, Spain), Tiziano y la Monarquía Hispánica 1994, El coleccionismo en España (jtly) 1984, Las casas del Rey: Casas reales, cazaderos, jardines. Siglos XVI y XVII (jtly) 1986, Carlos V. La imagen del poder en el Renacimiento 1999. *Address:* Department of Art History, Universidad Complutense de Madrid, Ciudad Universitaria, Avda. Seneca 2, 28040 Madrid, Spain (Office). *Website:* www.ucm.es (Office).

CHECHELASHVILI, Valeri, PhD; Georgian diplomatist and international organization official; b. 17 March 1961, Tbilisi; s. of Karlo Chechelashvili and Tina Chechelashvili; m. Marine Neparidze; two s. one d.; ed Kyiv State Univ., Ukraine; mem. staff Foreign Econ. Relations Dept, Ministry of Light Industry 1987–88; Deputy Head of Foreign Econ. Relations section, Jt Stock Co. Gruzkurort 1988–89; First Sec. Dept of Int. Econ. Relations, Ministry of Foreign Affairs 1989–90, Deputy Dir 1990–91, First Deputy Dir 1991–92, Dir 1992–94, Deputy Minister of Foreign Affairs 1998–2000; Amb. to Ukraine 1994–98; Sec.-Gen. Black Sea Econ. Co-operation (BSEC) 2000–; Second Degree Order for Service, Ukraine 1998. *Publications:* several articles in learned journals on econ. co-operation. *Leisure interests:* classical music, fiction, tennis. *Address:* Office of the Secretary-General, BSEC, Istinye Cad. Musir Fuad Pasa Yalisi Eski Tersane, 80860 Istinye-Istanbul, Turkey (Office). *Telephone:* 2296330 (Office); 2824133 (Home). *Fax:* 2296336 (Office). *E-mail:* bsec@turk.net (Office); valeri_bsec@superonline.com (Home). *Website:* www.bsec-organization.org. (Office).

CHECKLAND, Sir Michael, Kt, BA, FCMA; British broadcasting executive; b. 13 March 1936, Birmingham; s. of Leslie and Ivy Florence Checkland; m. 1st Shirley Checkland 1960 (divorced 1983) (deceased); two s. one d.; m. 2nd Sue Zetter 1987; ed King Edward's Grammar School, Five Ways, Birmingham and Wadham Coll., Oxford; Accountant, Parkinson Cowan Ltd 1959–62, Thorn Electronics Ltd 1962–64; Sr Cost Accountant, BBC 1964–67, Head, Cen. Finance Unit 1967, Chief Accountant, Cen. Finance Services 1969, Chief Accountant, BBC TV 1971, Controller, Finance 1976, Controller, Planning and Resource Man., BBC TV 1977, Dir of Resources, BBC TV 1982, Deputy Dir-Gen. BBC 1985–87, Dir-Gen. 1987–92, Dir BBC Enterprises 1979–92 (Chair. 1986–87); Dir Visnews 1980–85; Vice-Pres. RTS 1985–94, Fellow 1987–; Trustee Reuters 1994–; Pres. Commonwealth Broadcasting Asscn 1987–88; Vice-Pres. EBU 1991–92; Chair. NCH (fmrly Nat. Children's Home) 1991–2001; Gov. Westminster Coll. Oxford 1992–97, Birkbeck Coll. London 1993–97, Brighton Univ. 1996–97, 2001–; Dir Nat. Youth Music Theatre 1991–2002, Nynex Cablecomms 1995–97, Wales Millennium Centre 2003–; Chair. City of Birmingham Symphony Orchestra 1993–2001, Brighton Int. Festival 1993–2002, Higher Educ. Funding Council for England 1997–2001, Brighton Univ. 2002–; Vice-Pres. Methodist Conf. 1997; Hon. Fellow Wadham Coll. Oxford 1989; mem. Ind. TV Comm. 1997–; numerous other appointments; Dr hc (Birmingham Univ.) 1999, (Open Univ.) 1999. *Leisure interests:* sport, music, travel. *Address:* Orchard Cottage, Park Lane, Maplehurst, West Sussex, RH13 6LL, England (Home).

CHEDID, Andrée, BA; French writer; b. 20 March 1920, Cairo; d. of Selim Saab and Alice K. Haddad; m. Louis A. Chedid 1942; one s. one d.; ed French schools, Cairo and Paris, American Univ. in Cairo; has lived in Paris since 1946; Prix Louise Labé 1966, L'aigle d'or de la poésie 1972, Grand Prix des Lettres Françaises de l'Acad. Royale de Belgique 1975, Prix de l'Afrique Méditerranéenne 1975, Prix de l'Acad. Mallarmé 1976, Prix Goncourt for short story 1979, Prix de Poésie (Soc. des Gens de Lettres) 1991, Prix PEN Club Int. 1992, Prix Paul Morand, Acad. Française 1994, Prix Albert Camus 1996; Officier, Légion d'honneur, Commdr des Arts et des Lettres. *Publications include:* poetry: Fraternité de la parole 1975, Epreuves du vivant 1983, Textes pour un poème 1949–1970, 1987, Poèmes pour un texte 1970–91, Par delà les mots 1995; novels: Le Sommeil délivré 1952, Le Sixième Jour 1960, L'Autre 1969, Nefertiti et le rêve d'Akhnaton 1974, La Maison sans racines 1985, L'Enfant multiple 1989; plays: Bérénice d'Egypte, Les Nombres, Le Montreur 1981, Echec à la Reine 1984, les saisons de passage 1996; short stories: Les Corps et le temps 1979, Mondes Miroirs Magies 1988, A la Mort, A la Vie 1992, La Femme de Job 1993, Les Saisons de passage 1996, Le Jardin perdu 1997, Territoires du Souffle 1999, Le Cœur demeure 1999; essays, children's books. *Leisure interest:* collages. *Address:* c/o Flammarion, 26 rue Racine, 75006 Paris, France. *Telephone:* 1-40-51-31-00.

CHEETHAM, Anthony John Valerian, BA; British publisher; b. 12 April 1943; s. of Sir Nicolas John Alexander Cheetham; m. 1st Julia Rollason 1969 (divorced); two s. one d.; m. 2nd Rosemary de Courcy 1979 (divorced); two d.; m. 3rd Georgina Capel 1997; ed Eton Coll., Balliol Coll., Oxford; Editorial Dir Sphere Books 1968; Man. Dir Futura Publs 1973, Macdonald Futura 1979; Chair. Century Publishing 1982–85; Man. Dir Century Hutchinson 1985; Chair. and CEO Random Century Group 1989–91; Founder and CEO Orion Publishing Group (fmrly Orion Books) 1991–. *Publication:* Richard III 1972. *Leisure interests:* tennis, gardening, trees, medieval history. *Address:* Orion Publishing Group Ltd, Orion House, 5 Upper St Martins Lane, London, WC2H 9EA (Office); 20 Grove Park, London, SE5 8LH, England. *Telephone:* (20) 7240-3444 (Office); (20) 7733-8204. *Fax:* (20) 7240-4822 (Office). *E-mail:* info@orionbooks.co.uk. *Website:* www.orionbooks.co.uk.

CHEF, Genia, MA; Russian artist; b. 28 Jan. 1954, Aktyubinsk, Kazakhstan; s. of Vladimir Scheffer and Sinaida Scheffer; m. Elke Schwab 1983; ed Polygraphic Inst., Moscow, Acad. of Fine Arts, Vienna; painter, graphic and computer artist; has provided illustrations for Publs including Edgar Allan Poe, Prose and Poetry 1983, American Romantic Tales 1984, Finger World 1993, American Alphabet 1998; Fueger Gold Prize, Acad. of Fine Arts, Vienna 1993; Delfina Studio Trust Award, New York 1994. *Exhibitions:* has exhibited at numerous exhbns. of non-conformist artists, Moscow 1976–85, Galeria Maria Salvat, Barcelona 1989, Stuart Levy Fine Art, New York 1994, Smithsonian Inst., Washington DC 1994, Zimmerly Museum, Rutgers Univ., New Jersey 1995, De Saisset Museum, Santa Clara Univ., Calif. 1995, Minnesota Univ. Art Museum 1998, Russian State Museum, St. Petersburg 1999, computer-panorama for the King Ludwig II musical theatre, Fuessen, Germany 2000, 'Jesus Christ 2000' Russian State Museum, St Petersburg and Vatican Museum 2000, 'Between Earth and Heaven', Museum of Modern Art, Ostend, Belgium 2001, Palazzo Forti, Verona, Italy 2002, Freud's Dream Museum, St Petersburg 2002, 'Shock and Show' Int. Art Festival, Trieste 2002, 'Foreign Visions', Stiftung Starke, Berlin, Museum of Modern Art, Skopje, Macedonia 2003. *Publications:* Manifesto of Degeneration 1988, Manifesto of Post-Historicism 1989, Viva Canova! 1995, New Computer Renaissance 2002. *Leisure interests:* music, books, collecting insects. *Address:* Leibnizstrasse 61, 10629 Berlin, Germany. *Telephone:* (30) 3246479. *E-mail:* geniachef@gmx.de (Home).

CHEIFFOU, Amadou; Niger politician and civil servant; fmr regional official of Int. Civil Aviation Org. (ICAO); Prime Minister and Minister of Defence 1991–93; mem. Mouvement nat. pour une société de développement (MNSD). *Address:* c/o Office of the Prime Minister, Niamey, Niger.

CHEKANAUSKAS, Vitautas Edmundas; Lithuanian architect; b. 13 May 1930, Šiauliai; m. Teresa Chekanauskienė; one d.; ed Lithuanian Art Inst., Vilnius; architect, then sr architect, group man., sr projects architect, Inst. of Urban Planning 1985–90; Prof. Vilnius Acad. of Arts (fmrly. Inst. of Arts) 1974–; mem. USSR (now Russian) Acad. of Arts 1988, Int. Architects Asscn; Lenin Prize 1974, People's Architect of USSR 1975. *Major projects:* has designed exhbn pavilion in Vilnius 1967, residential dists in Vilnius 1967–72, and other projects. *Address:* Lithuanian State Arts Academy, Maironio 6, 2600 Vilnius (Office); U. Paco 13-9, 2000 Vilnius, Lithuania (Home). *Telephone:* (2) 619944 (Office); (2) 721711 (Home).

CHELI, HE Cardinal Giovanni, M.THEOL., DCnL; Italian ecclesiastic; b. 4 Oct. 1918, Turin; ed Pontifical Lateran Univ., Pontifical Acad. for Diplomacy; ordained Roman Catholic priest 1942; Second Sec., Apostolic Nunciature in Guatemala 1952–55; First Sec., Madrid 1955–62; Counsellor, Nunciature in Rome 1962–67; served Council for Public Affairs of the Church, Vatican City 1967–73; Perm. Observer to UN 1973–86; Deacon SS. Cosma e Damiano, Apostolic Nuncio 1978–; cr. HE Cardinal 1998. Pres. Emer. Pontifical Council for the Pastoral Care of Migrants and Itinerant People 1986; Kt Commdr Orden de Isabel la Católica (Spain), Ordine al Merito della Repubblica Italiana, Verdienstkreuz der Bundesrepublik Deutschland (Germany). *Pub-*

lication: L'applicazione delle Riforme Tridentine nella diocesi di Asti 1952. *Leisure interests:* tennis, mountain climbing, reading, listening to classical music. *Address:* Piazza S. Calisto 16, 00153 Rome, Italy. *Telephone:* (06) 69887392. *Fax:* (06) 69887137. *E-mail:* mc2927@mclink.it (Home).

CHELYSHEV, Yevgeny Petrovich; Russian philologist; b. 27 Oct. 1921; m.; two d.; ed Mil. Inst. of Foreign Languages; Head of Chair of Indian Languages Mil. Inst. of Foreign Languages, Head of Sector of Indian Philology, Head Div. of Literature Inst. of Oriental Sciences, USSR (now Russian) Acad. of Sciences, Corresp. mem. USSR (now Russian) Acad. of Sciences 1981, mem. 1987, Acad. Sec. Dept of Literature and Language 1991–; mem. Bureau of Indian Soc. of Philosophy, Asian Soc. in Calcutta; main research in the field of culture, comparative literary criticism, Indian philosophy; Merited Worker of Sciences of Russia; Int. Nehru Prize; Swami Vivekananda Prize. *Publications:* Modern Poetry in Hindi 1967, Contemporary Indian Literature 1981, Indian Literature Today and Yesterday 1989, Complicity in Beauty and Spirit 1991; articles in specialized periodicals. *Leisure interests:* music. *Address:* Department of Literature and Language, Russian Academy of Sciences, Leninsky prosp. 32A, 117334 Moscow, Russia. *Telephone:* (095) 938-19-36 (Office); (095) 202-66-25 (Home).

CHEMETOV, Paul; French architect; b. 6 Sept. 1928, Paris; s. of Alexandre Chemetoff and Tamara Blumine; m. Christine Soupault 1958; one s. two d.; ed Ecole Nationale Supérieure des Beaux Arts; participated in foundation of the Atelier d'urbanisme et l'architecture 1961; Prof. Ecole d'architecture, Strasbourg 1968–72; Visiting Prof. UP8 1973; exhibited in the Venice Biennial 1976; Prof. of Architecture at Ecole Nationale des Ponts et Chaussées 1977–89; mem. Directorial Cttee, then Vice-Pres. Plan Construction 1979–87; Visiting Prof. Ecole Polytechnique Fédérale, Lausanne 1993–98; mem. Acad. d'Architecture 1996; Prix d'architecture, Cercle d'études architecturales 1965, Grand Prix Nat. d'architecture 1980; Médaille d'honneur d'Architecture 1991; Officier, Légion d'honneur, Ordre Nat. du Mérite, Ordre des Arts et des Lettres. *Publications:* Architectures – Paris 1848–1914 (jtly.) 1980, Cinq projets 1979–82 (jtly.) 1983, Paris – Banlieue 1919–1939 (with B. Marrey and M. J. Dumont) 1989, La Fabrique des villes 1992, Le Territoire de L'Architecte 1995, Vingt Mille Mots pour la Ville 1996, Un architecte dans le siècle 2002; numerous articles in professional journals. *Address:* Chemetov, 4 square Masséna, 75013 Paris, France. *Telephone:* 1-45-82-85-48. *Fax:* 1-45-86-89-14. *E-mail:* cplush@compuserve.com (Home).

CHEN, Char-Nie, MB, MSc, OBE, JP, FRCPsych; British university professor and college principal; b. 19 July 1938, Fujian Prov., China; s. of the late Kam-Heng Chen and of Mei-Ai Chen-Hsu; m. Chou-May Chien 1970; one s. two d.; ed Nat. Taiwan Univ. and Univ. Coll., London; Rotating Intern, Nat. Taiwan Univ. Hosp. 1964–65, Resident Physician, Dept of Neurology and Psychiatry 1965–68; Sr House Officer, Morgannwg Hosp., Wales 1968–69; Registrar, St George's Hosp. Medical School, London 1969–71, Lecturer, Hon. Sr Registrar 1971–72, 1973–78, Sr Lecturer, Hon. Consultant Psychiatrist 1978–80; Prof. Dept of Psychiatry, Chinese Univ. of Hong Kong 1981–98, Chair. of Dept 1981–93, mem. Univ. Senate 1981, Head, Shaw Coll. 1987–94, mem. Univ. Council 1987–94; mem. Coll. Council, Hong Kong Baptist Coll. 1984–95; Pres. Hong Kong Psychiatric Asscn 1982–84, Hong Kong Soc. of Neurosciences 1983–84, 1988–89; Exec. Chair., Hong Kong Mental Health Asscn 1983–98; Pres. Pacific Rim Coll. of Psychiatrists 1988–90, Dir 1990–; Chair. Action Comm. Against Narcotics 1992–98; Pres. Hong Kong Coll. of Psychiatrists 1993–98; Fellow, Royal Coll. of Psychiatrists 1985–, Royal Australian and New Zealand Coll. of Psychiatrists 1983–, Royal Soc. of Medicine 1975–, Hong Kong Acad. of Medicine 1993–, Hong Kong Soc. of Sleep Medicine (Pres. 1993–), Hong Kong Coll. of Psychiatrists (Pres. 1994–98, Chief Examiner 1998–); mem. British Asscn for Psychopharmacology 1974–, European Sleep Research Soc. 1976–, British Medical Asscn 1979–, Collegium Internationale Neuro-psycho-pharmacologium 1981–, Hong Kong Medical Asscn 1981–, Int. Brain Research Org. 1985–, Mental Health Asscn, Hong Kong (Chair. 1983–98, Vice-Pres. 1998–); Corresp. Fellow, American Psychiatric Asscn 1991; Visiting Prof., St George's Hosp. Medical School, London 1984; JP, Hong Kong 1993–; Hon. Fellow, Hong Kong Psychological Soc. 1986–. *Publications:* over 90 scientific papers. *Leisure interests:* reading, travelling, good food. *Address:* Flat 16B, Block 3, Villa Athena, 600 Sai Sha Road, Ma On Shan, Hong Kong Special Administrative Region, People's Republic of China. *Telephone:* (852) 2633-4192. *Fax:* (852) 2633-3067.

CHEN AILIAN; Chinese dancer, educator and choreographer; b. 24 Dec. 1939, Shanghai; d. of Chen Xi Kang and Yu Xiu Ying; m. Wei Dao Ning; two d.; ed First Coll. of Chinese Dancing; teacher Beijing Coll. of Dancing 1959–63; Chief Actress, China Opera and Dancing House 1963–; now Prof. Arts Dept Nan Kai Univ., Hainan Univ., Wang Kan Arts Coll.; demonstrations and lectures in Shangdong Prov., Shaanxi Prov., Beijing Univ., Foreign Languages Inst., Post and Telegraph Inst., Light Industry Inst. and Mun. Dancers' Unions; chief dancer Chinese Art del. to USSR, USA, France, Spain, Belgium, Denmark, Finland, Sweden, Italy, Norway, Hong Kong, Germany, etc.; f. Chen Ailian Artistic Troupe 1989 (first non-governmental performing org. in China); est. Chen Ailian Dancing School, Beijing 1995; won four gold medals as a traditional dancer at 8th World Youth Festival in Helsinki 1962; Excellent Performance Award, First Nat. Dance Concert, First Prize Ministry of Culture for Dance Soirée and Princess Wenzhen. *Performances include:* The Peony Pavilion, In the Dusk of Evening, The Oriental Melody, The Lantern Dance, Water, The Sword Dance, Ball Dance, The Song of the Serfs, Women Militia in the Grassland, The Red Silk Dance. *Publications:* I Came From An

Orphanage; articles and commentaries on dance. *Leisure interests:* literature, music, traditional opera, travel, mountain climbing. *Address:* Room 101/7, 2 Nanhuadong Street, Hufang Road, Beijing 100050, People's Republic of China. *Telephone:* 3015066.

CHEN BANGZHU; Chinese politician; b. Sept. 1934, Jiujiang City, Jiangxi Prov.; ed Faculty of Civil Eng, Chonqing Construction Eng Coll.; engineer at Jilin Chemical Industrial Dist Construction Co. 1954–65; joined CCP 1975; Chief Engineer and Dept Man. No. 4 and 9 Chemical Industrial Construction Co., Ministry of Chemical Industry 1966–80; Chief Engineer, Man. Jiuhua Bldg Co. 1980–84; Mayor of Yueyang and Deputy Sec. CCP Yueyang City Cttee 1983–84; Vice-Gov. Hunan Prov. 1984–86, Gov. 1989–95; Minister of Internal Trade 1995–98; Vice-Minister State Econ. and Trade Comm. 1998–2000; Dir State Bureau of Surveying and Mapping 2000–; Alt. mem. 13th CCP Cen. Cttee 1987–92; Deputy Sec. CCP 6th Hunan Provincial Cttee 1989–; mem. 14th Cen. Cttee CCP 1992–95; mem. 14th CCP Cen. Cttee 1992–97, 15th CCP Cen. Cttee 1997–. *Address:* c/o State Bureau of Surveying and Mapping, Beijing, People's Republic of China.

CHEN BINGDE, Lt-Gen.; Chinese army officer; b. July 1941, Nantong Co., Jiangsu Prov.; ed PLA Mil. Acad. 1983–85; joined PLA 1961; joined CCP 1962; Vice-Commdr. of Army Group and Chief of Staff 1985; Pres. PLA Nanchang Infantry Acad.; PLA Infantry Command Acad.; Army Group Commdr; Chief of Staff Nanjing Mil. Area Command 1993, Vice-Commdr 1996–99; rank of Maj.-Gen. 1988, Lt-Gen. 1995–99; Chief of Staff Jinan Mil. Area Command 1999–; mem. 15th CCP Cen. Cttee 1997–. *Address:* Nanjing Military Area Command, Nanjing, Jiangsu Province, People's Republic of China.

CHEN DUN; Chinese business executive; b. Dec. 1928, Tianjin City; Vice-Minister for Coal 1985–90; Gen. Man. China Nat. Coal Corpn 1993–; mem. 7th CPPCC 1987–92, 8th 1993–. *Address:* China National Coal Corporation, 21 Hepingli Xijie Street, Beijing 100713, People's Republic of China.

CHEN FU; Taiwanese politician; fmr Minister of Foreign Affairs; apptd. mem. Kuomintang (KMT) Cen. Standing Cttee 1994–. *Address:* c/o Ministry of Foreign Affairs, 2 Chiehshou Road, Taipei 10016, Taiwan. *Telephone:* (2) 3119292. *Fax:* (2) 3144972.

CHEN GANG; Chinese composer; b. 10 March 1935, Shanghai; s. of Chen Ge-Xin and Jin Jiao-Li; m. (divorced); two d.; ed Shanghai Conservatory of Music; now Prof. of Composition, Shanghai Conservatory of Music; mem. Council of Chinese Musicians' Asscn; Art Dir Shanghai Chamber Orchestra; Guest Prof. USA, France, Canada and Hong Kong; Sec. Chinese Dramatist Asscn 1987–; Golden Record Prize (five times). *Compositions include:* Butterfly Lovers, Violin Concerto 1959, The Sun Shines on Tashikuergan, Violin Solo 1973, Morning on the Miao Mountains, Violin Solo 1975; A Moonlight Spring Night on the Flower-surrounded River, Symphonic Picture 1976, Concerto for Oboe 1985, Wang Zhaojun, Violin Concerto 1986, Chamber Music Ensemble 1989, Dragon Symphony 1991. *Leisure interests:* literature, writing. *Address:* Shanghai Conservatory of Music, 20 Fen Yang Road, Shanghai, People's Republic of China. *Telephone:* 4370689.

CHEN GUANGYI; Chinese government official; b. 7 Aug. 1933, Putian City, Fujian; s. of Chen Zhaohe and Li Muxin; m. Chen Xiuyun 1961; two s. one d.; ed China Northeast Industry Univ.; joined CCP 1959; engineer, then section chief, div. chief, deputy Dir Baiying Nonferrous Metal Industry Co., Gansu; mem. Gansu Metallurgy Industry Bureau, Gansu Prov. Planning Cttee; Gov. of Gansu Prov. 1983–86; mem. of Cen. Cttee of CCP 1985; Sec. 5th CCP Cttee, Fujian 1986; Chair. CPPCC 6th Fujian Provincial Cttee 1988; mem. CCP 12th and 13th Cen. Cttee; mem. 14th CCP Cen. Cttee 1992–97, 15th CCP Cen. Cttee 1997–; Party Cttee Sec. and Head Civil Aviation Gen. Admin. of China 1994–98; Dir Finance Cttee of 9th NPC 1998–. *Address:* c/o Standing Committee of National People's Congress, Beijing, People's Republic of China.

CHEN HOUQUN; Chinese geologist; b. 3 May 1932, Wuxi, Jiangsu Prov.; ed ed. Tsinghua Univ., Moscow Power Mechanics Inst., USSR; made original contrib. to the theoretical study of seismic hardening of concrete dams and to solving key problems of seismic resistance in maj. civil eng projects such as Xinfengjiang, Ertan and Xiaolangdi dams; presided over the compiling, editing and revising of many nat. standards, including Standard for the Anti-Seismic Design of Hydraulic Structures; built China's first large-scale 3-dimensional and 6-free-degree earthquake simulation platform; Chair. Standing Cttee, Dept of Civil Eng, Hydraulic and Constructional Eng, Chinese Acad. of Eng; Sr Engineer and Dir Eng Anti-Seismic Research Centre, China Water Conservancy and Hydroelectric Science Research Inst.; Fellow Chinese Acad. of Eng; 20 nat., ministerial and provincial awards for science and tech. *Publications:* over 100 research papers. *Address:* China Water Conservancy and Hydroelectric Science Research Institute, 20 Chegongzhuang West Road, Beijing 100044, People's Republic of China (Office). *Telephone:* (10) 68415522 (Office). *Fax:* (10) 68478065 (Home). *E-mail:* engach@mail.cae.ac.cn (Office).

CHEN HUANYOU; Chinese administrator; b. 1934, Nantong City, Jiangsu Prov.; ed Chinese People's Univ.; joined CCP 1954; mem. Standing Cttee of Jiangsu Prov. CP 1983, now Chair. People's Armament Cttee; Deputy to 8th NPC Jiangsu Prov.; Vice-Gov. Jiangsu Prov. 1984–89, Gov. 1989–94, now Chair. Standing Cttee of People's Congress; Deputy Sec. CCP Jiangsu Prov. Cttee 1986–93, Sec. CCP Jiangsu Prov. Cttee 1994–2000; mem. 14th CCP

Cen. Cttee 1992–97, 15th CCP Cen. Cttee 1997–. *Address:* 70 W Beijing Road, Nanjing, Jiangsu Province, 210000, People's Republic of China. *Telephone:* 025-663 5164.

CHEN HUIGUANG; Chinese politician; b. 1939, Yulin City, Guangxi; ed Guangxi Inst. of Coal Mining; fmr engineer; Dongluo Mining Bureau, Guangxi, successively, Engineer, Mining Technician, Head of Production Section, Deputy Head and Head 1961–; joined CCP 1965; Sec. CCP Municipal Cttee, Nanning 1983–85; Deputy Sec. CCP Cttee, Guangxi 1983–85, (Leading) Sec. 1985–88; mem. 12th CCP Cen. Cttee 1982–87; 13th CCP Cen. Cttee 1987–92; Chair. Guangxi Zhuang Autonomous Region CPPCC 1988. *Address:* 1 Minlelu Road, Nanning City, Guangxi, People's Republic of China.

CHEN JIAER; Chinese academic; b. 1 Oct. 1934, Shanghai; ed Jilin Univ.; Prof., Peking Univ. 1984–, Vice-Pres. 1984–96, Pres. 1996–99; Dir Heavy Ion Physics Research Inst. 1986–2002; Academician, Chinese Acad. of Sciences 1993, Pres. Chinese Physics Soc. 1995–; Vice-Pres. Nat. Science Foundation of China 1991–99; Pres. Beijing Asscn of Science and Tech. 1997–, Asscn of Asia Pacific Physical Socs. 1998–2001; Vice-Pres. Nat. Natural Science Foundation of China 1991–99, Pres. 1999–; mem. 4th Presidium of Depts., Chinese Acad. of Sciences 2000–02; Fellow Inst. of Physics 2001; mem. Third World Academy of Sciences (TWAS) 2002; Hon. SSc (Menlo Coll., Calif.) 1999, (Waseda Univ., Japan) 2000, (Chinese Univ. of Hong Kong) 2000, (Loughborough) 2002. *Address:* National Natural Science Foundation of China, 83 Shuangqing Road, Haidian District, 100085 Beijing (Office); Room 4–501, Bldg 12, Lanqiying, Peking University, Beijing, People's Republic of China (Home). *Telephone:* (10) 62326876 (Office); (10) 62758868 (Home). *Fax:* (10) 62327082 (Office); (10) 62758868 (Home). *E-mail:* chenjer@rose.nsfc.gov.cn (Office); chenje@pku.edu.cn (Home). *Website:* www.nsfc.gov.cn (Office).

CHEN JIANGONG; Chinese writer; b. Nov. 1949, Beihai, Guangxi Prov.; ed Peking Univ.; joined Beijing Writers' Asscn 1981; Sec. of Secr., Chinese Writers' Asscn 1995–2001, Vice-Chair. 2001–. *Publications:* A Girl with the Eyes of a Red Phoenix, Selected Novels by Chen Jiangong, No. 9 Huluba Alley, Letting Go, Curly Hair, Previous Offence. *Address:* Beijing Writers' Association, Beijing, People's Republic of China.

CHEN JINHUA; Chinese government official and business executive; b. 1931, Qingyang, Anhui; Gen. Man. China Petrochemical Corpn 1983–90; Dir State Econ. Restructuring Comm. 1990–93; Minister in charge of State Planning Comm. 1993–98; Head Co-ordination Group for Tertiary Industries 1993–98; mem. 14th Cen. Cttee CPC 1992–97; Vice-Chair. 9th Nat. Cttee of CPPCC 1998–. *Address:* National Committee of Chinese People's Political Consultative Conference, 23 Taipingqiao Street, Beijing, People's Republic of China.

CHEN JUNSHENG; Chinese government official; b. 1927, Huanan Co., Helongjiang Prov.; mem. Standing Cttee of Heilongjiang Prov. CP, Sec.-Gen. 1979–80, Deputy Sec. 1983–84; Sec. Qigihar City CP 1980–82; Sec. of the Fed. of T.U., Deputy Chair. Exec. Cttee 1984–85; Vice-Pres. Fed. T.U. 1985; Sec. Gen. State Council 1985–88; Sec. CCP Cttee of Cen. State Organs 1986–88; Head Leading Group for Econ. Devt in Poor Areas (now Leading Group for Helping the Poor through Devt) 1986–, for Comprehensive Agricultural Devt, for Housing System Reform; mem. 13th CCP Cen. Cttee 1987–92; mem. 14th CCP Cen. Cttee 1992–97; State Councillor 1988–98; Head State Flood-Control and Drought Relief H.Q.; Chair. Nat. Afforestation Cttee; Chair. Bd of Dirs. Nat. Office of Supply and Marketing Co-operatives 1995–98; Vice-Chair. Nat. Cttee of CPPCC 1998–. *Address:* National Committee of Chinese People's Political Consultative Conference, 23 Taipingqiao Street, Beijing, People's Republic of China.

CHEN KAIGE; Chinese film director; b. 1954, Beijing; m. Ni Ping 1995; ed Beijing Cinema Coll.; worker, rubber plantation, Yunnan; soldier for four years; Golden Palm Award 1993, New York Film Critics' Best Foreign Film 1993. *Films include:* The Yellow Earth (Best Film, Berlin Film Festival), Life on a String, King of the Children 1988, Farewell My Concubine 1993, The Assassin 1998, The Emperor and the Assassin 1999, Killing Me Softly 2002. *Publications:* King of the Children, The New Chinese Cinema (with Tony Raynes) 1989, Bawang bieji 1992. *Address:* William Morris Agency, 151 South El Camino Drive, Beverly Hills, CA 90212 (Office); Beijing Cinema College, Beijing, People's Republic of China.

CHEN KUIYUAN; Chinese party official; Sec. CCP Tibet Autonomous Region Cttee 1992–2000; mem. 14th CCP Cen. Cttee 1992–97, 15th CCP Cen. Cttee 1997–; Sec. CCP Henan Prov. Cttee 2000–. *Address:* Chinese Communist Party Henan Provincial Committee, Zhengzhou, Henan Province, People's Republic of China.

CHEN LI-AN, PhD; Taiwanese government official; b. 22 June 1937, Ching-tien County, Chekiang; m. four s.; one d.; ed Mass. Inst. of Tech. and New York Univ.; Eng Honeywell Co., USA 1960–63; Prof. City Univ. of New York 1968–70; Pres Ming Chi Inst. of Tech. 1970–72; Dir Dept of Technological and Vocational Educ., Ministry of Educ. 1972–74; Pres. Nat. Taiwan Inst. of Tech. 1974–77; Vice-Minister, Ministry of Educ. 1977–78; Dir Dept of Org. Affairs, Cen. Cttee, Kuomintang 1979–80; Deputy Sec.-Gen. Cen. Cttee, Kuomintang 1980–84; Chair. Nat. Science Council, Exec. Yuan 1984–88, Minister, Ministry of Econ. Affairs 1988–90, of Nat. Defence 1990; Sec. Shaoxing City 1991–; left Nat. Party 1995. *Address:* c/o Ministry of National Defence, Chieshou Hall, Chung-King S. Road, Taipei (Office); 120 Jen-Ai Road, Section 3, Taipei, Taiwan (Home).

CHEN LIANGYU; Chinese politician; b. Oct. 1946, Ningbo, Zhejiang Prov.; ed PLA Logistics Eng Inst.; joined PLA 1963, CCP 1980; designer Shanghai Pengpu Machine Bldg Factory; Sec. CCP Shanghai Electric Appliances Corpn Cttee; Vice-Dir, then Dir Veteran Cadre Dept, Shanghai Municipal Cttee –1985, Vice-Sec.-Gen., then Vice-Sec. Shanghai Municipal Cttee 1992–96; Vice-Sec., then Dist Magistrate Huangpu Dist Cttee 1985–92; Exec. Vice-Mayor of Shanghai 1996–2001, Mayor Dec. 2001–03; alt. mem. 15th CCP Cen. Cttee 1997–, Party Sec. of Shanghai 2002–. *Address:* Office of Chinese Communist Party Secretary of Shanghai, Zhongguo Gongchan Dang, Shanghai, People's Republic of China (Office).

CHEN MINGYI; Chinese administrator; b. 1940, Fuzhou City, Fujian Prov.; ed Shanghai Jiaotong Univ. 1962; joined CCP 1960; Vice-Gov. Fujian Prov. 1985–93, Gov. 1993; Deputy Sec. CCP 6th Fujian Prov. Cttee 1993–96; Chair. Standing Cttee of Fujian People's Political Consultative Conference 2001–; alt. mem. Cen. Cttee CCP 1992–; Sec. CCP Fujian Prov. Cttee 1996–2000; Deputy to 8th NPC 1996; mem. 15th CCP Cen. Cttee 1997–. *Address: c/o* Office of the Governor, Fujian Provincial People's Government, Fuzhou City, People's Republic of China.

CHEN MUHUA; Chinese politician; b. 1921, Qingtian Co., Zhejiang Prov.; ed Yanan Mil. School; joined CCP 1938; mem. 10th Cen. Cttee of CCP 1973; Minister for Econ. Relations with Foreign Countries 1977–82, also in charge of the State Family Planning Comm. 1981–82, Minister of Foreign Trade 1982–85, a Vice-Premier 1978–82; Pres. People's Bank of China 1985–88; Dir State Treasury Aug. 1985–; Chair. Council, People's Bank of China June 1985, Hon. Chair. Bd of Dir Nov. 1985–; alt. mem. Politburo 1977–87; Head Population Census Leading Group 1979–; mem. 12th CCP Cen. Cttee 1982–87, 13th CCP Cen. Cttee 1987–92; mem. 14th CCP Cen. Cttee 1992–97; State Councillor 1982–; Chair. Cen. Patriotic Sanitation Campaign Cttee Cen. Cttee 1981–; Pres. China Greening Foundation; Chinese Gov. World Bank 1985–88, Asian Devt Bank 1986–; Pres. China Women Devt Fund 1988–; Vice-Chair. NPC 7th Standing Cttee 1988–93, 8th Standing Cttee 1993–98; Pres. All-China Women's Fed. 1988–98, Hon. Pres. 1998–; Adviser Nat. Co-ordination Group for Anti-Illiteracy Work 1994–, Chinese Asscn for Promotion of the Population Culture; Hon. Pres. Int. Econ. Co-operation Soc. 1983–, Florists' Assocn 1984–; Hon. Pres. China Assocn of Women Judges 1994–, China Assocn of Women Doctors, Assocn for Import and Export Commodity Inspection. *Address:* All-China Women's Federation, 15 Jian Guo Men Nei Street, 100130 Beijing, People's Republic of China. *Telephone:* (10) 65225357 (Office). *Fax:* (10) 65136044 (Office).

CHEN NENGKUAN, DEng; Chinese physicist; b. 1923, Cili, Hu'nan Prov.; ed Tangshan Eng College, Jiaotong Univ., Yale Univ.; fmrly Research Fellow Inst. of Physics and Inst. of Atomic Energy, Chinese Acad. of Sciences; Research Fellow Chinese Atomic Energy Science Research Inst.; Vice-Dir Science and Tech. Cttee of Ministry of Nuclear Industry; mem. Technological Science Dept of Chinese Acad. of Sciences; Exec. Council mem. Chinese Nuclear Soc.; Meritorious Service Medal for work on the Devt of China's atomic and hydrogen bombs and satellites by the CCP Cen. Cttee, the State Council and the Cen. Mil. Comm. 1999. *Address:* Chinese Academy of Sciences, 52 Sanlihe Road, Beijing 100864, People's Republic of China (Office).

CHEN PEISI; Chinese comedian; b. 1953, Ningjin, Hebei; s. of Chen Qiang; worked in Nei Monggo Production and Construction Corps 1969–73; with PLA Bayi Film Studio 1973–; comic sketches in collaboration with Zhu Shimao, at successive Chinese New Year Gala Nights on Chinese Cen. TV. *Films:* Look at This Family, Inside and Outside the Law Court, Sunset Boulevard, Erzi Running a Shop, A Stupid Manager, A Chivalrous Ball-Game Star in the Capital, A Young Master's Misfortune, A Millionaire from the South China Sea, Make a Bomb 1993, Sub-Husband 1993, Her Majesty is Fine 1995. *Address:* People's Liberation Army Bayi Film Studio, Beijing, People's Republic of China (Office).

CHEN QINGTAI; Chinese politician; b. 1937, Fengrun, Hebei Prov.; ed Tsinghua Univ.; joined CCP 1956; Dir Design Dept, Vice-Chief Engineer, Chief Engineer and then Gen. Man. Automobile Factory No. 2; Gen. Man. and Chair. Dongfeng United Co.; Vice-Dir Econ. and Trade Office of State Council; Vice-Chair. State Econ. and Trade Comm. and Dir Devt Research Centre of the State Council 1993–2001, Vice-Dir 2001–. *Address:* Development Research Centre of the State Council, Beijing, People's Republic of China (Office).

CHEN QIQI; Chinese administrator; b. 26 April 1941, Guangdong Prov.; m. Prof. Zheng Sheu Xen; one s.; ed Guangdong Medical School, Medical Coll. of Italy; doctor, Guangdong Leprosy Hospital 1965–75; teacher, Guangzhou Medical School 1975–81; Vice-Mayor of Guangzhou Municipality 1985; Pres. Guangdong Red Cross; Dir China Red Cross; Vice-Pres. Guangzhou People's Asscn for Friendship with Foreign Countries. *Address:* 1 Fuqian Road, Guangzhou, Guangdong (Office); 86 Yue Hwa Road, Guangzhou, Guangdong, People's Republic of China (Home). *Telephone:* (20) 330360 (Office); (20) 3333100 (Home). *Fax:* (20) 340347.

CHEN RONG ZHEN; Chinese business executive; b. Aug. 1938, Feidong, Anhui Prov.; Dir Hefei Washing Machine Gen. Factory (later renamed Rongshida Group) 1986–; Chair. and Pres. Rongshida Group. *Address:* Rongshida Group, Hefei, Anhui Province, People's Republic of China (Office).

CHEN SHINENG; Chinese administrator; b. 1938, Jiaxing Co., Zhejiang Prov.; ed Qinghua Univ.; joined CCP 1962; Vice-Minister of Light Industry 1984–93; Gov. of Guizhou Prov. 1993; Deputy Sec., CPC 7th Guizhou Prov. Cttee 1993, Dir Cttee for Comprehensive Man.; Vice-Minister of Chem. Industry 1996. *Address: c/o* Ministry of Chemical Industry, Bldg 16, Section 4, Anhuili, Beijing 100723, People's Republic of China. *Telephone:* (10) 6491-4455. *Fax:* (10) 6421-5982.

CHEN SHUI-BIAN, LLB; Taiwanese politician and civil servant; b. 18 Feb. 1951, Taiwan; m. Wu Shu-chen; one s. one d.; ed Nat. Taiwan Univ.; Chief Attorney-at-Law, Formosa Int. Marine and Commercial Law Office 1976–89; mem. Taipei City Council 1981–85; Publr Free Time magazine 1984; Exec. mem. Taiwan Asscn for Human Rights 1984; in jail 1986–87; mem. Legislative Yuan (Parl.) 1989–94, Exec. Dir Democratic Progressive Party (DPP) Caucus 1990–93, Convener Nat. Defence Cttee 1992–94, Convener Rules Cttee 1993, mem. Judicial Cttee 1994; Chair. Formosa Foundation 1990–94; Mayor Taipei City 1994–98; Pres. of Taiwan 2000–; mem. DPP 1987–89, 1996–2000; Hon. LLD (Kyungnam Univ., Repub. of Korea) 1995; Hon. D.Econs. (Plekhanov Russian Acad. of Econs) 1995. *Publications:* Series of Justice (4 Vols), Conflict, Compromise and Progress, Through the Line Between Life and Death, The Son of Taiwan. *Address:* Office of the President, 122 Chungking South Road, Section 1, Taipei 100, Taiwan (Office). *Telephone:* (2) 2311-3731 (Office). *Fax:* (2) 2311-1604 (Office). *E-mail:* public@mail.oop .gov.tw (Office). *Website:* www.president.gov.tw (Office).

CHEN SHUPENG; Chinese scientist; b. 14 Feb. 1920, Jiangxi; s. of Chen Yuoyuan and Lee Manlian; m. Zhang Diehua 1944; one s. one d.; ed Zhejiang Univ.; research prof., Geography Inst. of Academia Sinica 1978–; mem. Dept of Earth Sciences, Academia Sinica 1980–; Pres. Geographical Soc. of China 1991; Hon. Dir Inst. of Remote Sensing Applications 1988–, Co-Chair. Space Science Application Cttee 1990–; Fellow Third World Acad. of Sciences 1992; Hon. State Prize of Science of China 1988, State Gold Prize for Environmental Science 1993. *Publications:* Selected Works in Geo-Sciences, Vols I–IV 1990–92, Dictionary of Remote Sensing (Ed.-in-Chief) 1990, Atlas of Multidisciplinary Analysis of Meteorological Satellite Imagery in China 1992, The Start of Remote Sensing and Geo-information Systems in China 1993. *Leisure interests:* travel, field sketching, Chinese painting, Beijing opera. *Address:* Institute of Geography, Building 917, Datun Road, Beijing 100101, People's Republic of China. *Telephone:* 4914240 (Office); 2561758 (Home). *Fax:* 4911544.

CHEN SUN, PhD; Taiwanese politician and economist; b. 8 Nov. 1934, Pingtu County, Shantung; m.; two s.; ed Nat. Taiwan Univ. and Univ. of Oklahoma; Assoc. Prof. of Econs Nat. Taiwan Univ. 1968–; Vice-Chair. Econ. Planning Council, Exec. Yuan 1973–77; mem. Bd of Reviewers on Humanities and Social Sciences, Nat. Science Council Exec. Yuan 1974–93, Chair. 1990–; Vice-Chair. Council for Econ. Planning and Devt Exec. Yuan 1977–84; Pres. Nat. Taiwan Univ. 1984–93, Chinese Econ. Asscn 1985–86; Councillor, Academia Sinica, Taiwan 1987–; Minister of Nat. Defence 1993–96. *Address: c/o* Ministry of National Defence, 2nd Floor, 164 Po Ai Road, Taipei, Taiwan.

CHEN SUZHI; Chinese politician; b. 1931, Shengyang City, Liaoning Prov.; ed Liaoning Univ.; joined the CCP 1949; factory Dir 1978; Vice-Gov. Liaoning in charge of industrial work 1982; alt. mem. 12th CCP Cen. Cttee 1982–87, 13th Cen. Cttee 1987; mem. Standing Cttee CCP Prov. Cttee Liaoning 1982; Dir Liaoning Prov. Trade Union Council 1986; Alt. mem. CCP 12th and 13th Cen. Cttee; mem. Standing Cttee 7th CPC Liaoning Provincial Cttee 1985–; Rep. to CCP 13th Nat. Congress; Vice-Gov. Liaoning Prov. 1988–; Deputy to 8th NPC Liaoning Prov.; Vice-Chair. Liaoning Provincial 8th People's Congress Standing Cttee 1992–, Cttee for Comprehensive Man. of Social Security; mem. NPC Internal and Judicial Affairs Cttee. *Address:* Liaoning Trade Union Offices, Shenyang, People's Republic of China.

CHEN WEI-JAO, MD; Taiwanese university president; b. 15 Nov. 1939, Taichung; s. of late Chen Wen-Chiang and of Chen Wu-Ping; m. Shiang Yang Tang 1970; one s. one d.; ed Coll. of Medicine, Nat. Taiwan Univ., Postgrad. Medical School, Tohoku Univ. Japan and School of Hygiene and Public Health, Johns Hopkins Univ. USA; Resident Dept of Surgery, Nat. Taiwan Univ. Hosp. 1966–70, Visiting Surgeon (Pediatric Surgery) 1975–, Deputy Dir 1989–91; mem. Faculty, Coll. of Medicine Nat. Taiwan Univ. 1975–, Dean 1991–93; Pres. Nat. Taiwan Univ. 1993–, also Prof. of Surgery and Public Health; Fellow in Pediatric Surgery, Tohoku Univ. Japan 1972–75; Visiting Research Assoc. Prof. Univ. of Cincinnati 1981–82; recipient of various awards. *Publications:* Story of Separation of Conjoined Twins 1980, Unilateral Occlusion of Duplicated Mullerian Ducts with Renal Anomaly (jtly.) 2000; more than 150 scientific papers on surgery, nutrition and public health. *Leisure interest:* hiking. *Address:* 7 Chung-shan S Road, Taipei 100; 1 Roosevelt Road, Sec. 4, Taipei 106, Taiwan. *Telephone:* (2) 2363-4090. *Fax:* (2) 2362-1877. *E-mail:* chenwj@ccms.ntu.edu.tw (Office).

CHEN XIEYANG; Chinese orchestral conductor; b. 4 May 1939, Shanghai; s. of Chen Dieyi and Liang Peiqiong; m. Wang Jianying 1973; ed Music High School, Shanghai Conservatory; Conductor, Shanghai Ballet 1965–84; studied with Prof. Otto Mueller, Yale Univ., USA 1981–82; Conductor, Aspen Music Festival, Group for Contemporary Music, NY, Brooklyn Philharmonia, Honolulu Symphony, Philippines State Orchestra, Hong Kong Philharmonic, Shanghai Symphony Orchestra, Cen. Philharmonic, Beijing 1981–83, Symphony Orchestra of Vilnius, Kaunas, Novosibirsk, USSR 1985, Tokyo Symphony Orchestra 1986; Music Dir Shanghai Symphony Orchestra; has made recording for Kuklos CBE, France 1983; Dir China Musicians' Asscn; Pres. Shanghai Symphonic Music Lovers' Soc.; Excellent Conducting Prize, Shanghai Music Festival 1986. *Leisure interest:* Beijing opera. *Address:* Shanghai Symphony Orchestra, 105 Hunan Road, Shanghai 200031, People's Republic of China. *Telephone:* 64333752 (Office); 62814656 (Home).

CHEN YAOBANG; Chinese politician; b. 1935, Panyu City, Guangdong Prov.; ed Cen. China Agricultural Inst.; joined CCP 1982; Vice-Sec. CCP Wuxi City Cttee; Vice-Minister of Farming, Husbandry and Fishery; Vice-Minister of Agric.; Minister of Forestry 1997–98, of Agric. 1998–2001; mem. 15th CCP Cen. Cttee 1997–. *Address:* c/o Ministry of Agriculture, Nongzhanguan Nan Li, Chaoyang Qu, Beijing 100026, People's Republic of China (Office).

CHEN YIFEI; Chinese portrait and landscape painter, fashion designer and film director; b. 1946, Zhejiang; ed Shanghai Art School, Hunter's Coll., New York; propaganda artist during Cultural Revolution 1965–68; leading artist Shanghai Inst. of Painting 1970, Head Oil Painting Dept –1980; went to New York City 1980; f. Yifei Group, Shanghai, Layefe clothes range 1998; works depict contemporary Chinese realism. *Solo exhibitions include:* New England Center for Contemporary Art, USA 1980, 1981, 1982, 1983, Hammer Gallery, New York 1983, 1986, 1988, 1990, 'Recent Paintings', Seibu Museum, Tokyo 1990, 'The Homecoming of Chen Yifei' (retrospective), Shanghai Museum 1996–97, Nat. Museum of Fine Arts, Beijing 1996–97, 'First London Exhibition', Marlborough Fine Art, London 1997, 'Paintings of Tibet', Venice Biennale 1997. *Films directed:* Old Dream on the Sea (documentary), Evening Liaison. *Address:* c/o Marlborough Gallery, 40 West 57th Street, New York, NY, U.S.A. (Office).

CHEN YONG; Chinese seismologist; b. Dec. 1942, Chongqing; ed Chinese Univ. of Science and Tech.; Assoc. Research Fellow, Research Fellow, Dir Geophysics Research Inst. of Nat. Bureau of Seismology 1965–85; Vice-Dir Nat. Bureau of Seismology 1985–96; Fellow, Chinese Acad. of Sciences; Chair. Int. Earthquake Disaster and Forecasting Cttee. *Publications:* seven monographs and over 100 essays. *Address:* National Bureau of Seismology, 61 Fuxing Lu, Beijing 100036, People's Republic of China (Office).

CHEN YUAN, BS, MA; Chinese banker; b. 13 Jan. 1945, Shanghai; s. of Chen Yun; ed China Acad. of Social Sciences, Tsinghua Univ.; Sec. CCP Cttee of Xicheng Dist, Beijing 1982–84; Dir-Gen. Dept of Commerce and Trade, Beijing Municipal Govt 1984–88; Vice-Gov. People's Bank of China 1988–98; Gov. China Devt Bank 1998–; mem. Preparatory Cttee of Hong Kong Special Admin. Region (S.A.R.), Vice-Pres. Financial Soc.; mem. Securities Comm. of the State Council. *Publications:* The Underlying Problems and Options in China's Economy, Macroeconomic Management: The Need for Deepening Reform, Collected Works. *Address:* China Development Bank, 29 Fuchengmenwai Lu, Xicheng Qu, Beijing 100037, People's Republic of China (Office). *Telephone:* (10) 68307608 (Office). *Fax:* (10) 68306541 (Office). *Website:* cdb .com.cn (Office).

CHEN YUN-TI, (Yung-ti), PhD; Chinese professor of chemistry; b. 7 Nov. 1919, Dianjiang Co., Sichuan Prov.; m. Yang Guangyu 1947; one s. one d.; ed Indiana Univ., USA; researcher, Northwestern Univ. and Chicago Univ. 1952–54; Prof., Nankai Univ. Tianjin 1954–; mem. Chinese Acad. of Sciences 1980–, 7th NPC 1988–93, 8th Standing Cttee 1993–; Vice-Dir Standing Cttee Tianjin People's Congress 1993–; Distinguished Visiting Scholar, NAS 1984; Cornell Distinguished Visiting Prof., Swarthmore Coll., USA 1988; Hon. State Prize of Science of China 1985, 1986, 1987, 1991, 1999; Chugayev Medal and Diploma, USSR Acad. of Sciences 1987. *Publications:* Correlation Analysis in Co-ordination Chemistry 1994; over 300 articles in Chinese and foreign journals. *Leisure interests:* classical music and Beijing Opera. *Address:* Department of Chemistry, Nankai University, Tianjin 300071, People's Republic of China. *Telephone:* (22) 28363645. *Fax:* (22) 22-23502458. *E-mail:* ytchen@sun.nankai.edu.cn (Office).

CHEN YUNLIN; Chinese politician; b. Dec. 1941, Heishan Co., Liaoling Prov.; ed Beijing Agric. Univ.; joined CCP 1966; Vice-Sec. CCP Qiqihar City Cttee, Mayor Qiqihar City 1983; Vice-Sec. CCP Heilongjiang Prov. Cttee 1985; Vice-Gov. Heilongjiang Prov. 1987; Deputy Dir Cen. Office for Taiwan Affairs of State Council 1994, Dir 1996–; alt. mem. CCP Cen. Cttee 1992, 1997; mem. CCP Qiqihar City Standing Cttee. *Address:* No A35 Fuwaidafie, Beijing (Office); Office for Taiwan Affairs, c/o State Council, Beijing, People's Republic of China.

CHEN ZHILI; Chinese politician and academic; b. 21 Nov. 1942, Xianyou Co., Fujian Prov.; ed Fudan Univ., Shanghai Inst. of Ceramics, Chinese Acad. of Sciences; joined CCP 1961; Visiting Scholar, Materials Research Lab., Pa State Univ., USA 1980–82; Vice-Sec. CCP Shanghai Science Comm. Cttee 1984; alt. mem. 13th CCP Cen. Cttee 1987, 14th CCP Cen. Cttee 1992; Vice-Sec. CCP Shanghai Mun. Cttee 1989–97; Vice-Minister of State Educ. Comm. 1994–98; Minister of Educ. 1998–2003; mem. 15th CCP Cen. Cttee 1997–2002, 16h CCP Cen. Cttee 2002–; Hon. Pres. Shanghai Inst. of Int. Friendship. *Address:* c/o Zhongguo Gongchan Dang (Chinese Communist Party—CCP), Beijing, People's Republic of China (Office).

CHEN ZHONGSHI; Chinese novelist; b. 1942, Xian, Shanxi Prov.; Chair. Shaanxi Prov. Writers' Assen 1993–; Vice-Chair. Chinese Writers' Assen 2001; won Mao Dun Prize for Literature (for White Deer Height) 1997. *Publications:* White Deer Height, Early Summer, Mr. Blue Gown, The Cellar 1994. *Address:* Shanxi Provincial Writers' Association, Xian, People's Republic of China.

CHEN ZHONGWEI; Chinese surgeon; b. 1 Oct. 1929, Hangzhou City, Zhejiang Prov.; s. of B. Z. Chen and E L. Hu; m. Dr. W Z. Yin 1954; one s. one d.; ed Shanghai Second Medical Coll.; succeeded in replanting the severed forearm of a worker in Shanghai—the first operation of this kind in the world 1963; Chief Orthopaedic Dept 6th People's Hosp., Shanghai 1965–82, Deputy Dir 1970–87; Vice-Pres. Nat. Soc. of Surgery, Chinese Medical Asscn 1972–; Dir Orthopaedic Dept Zhong Shan Hosp., Shanghai Medical Univ. 1982–; Pres. Int. Soc. of Reconstructive Microsurgery 1986–89; Hon. Pres. Chinese Soc. of Reconstructive Microsurgery 1986–89; Chair. Chinese Soc. for Research in Rehabilitation of Neural Disabilities 1988–; mem. Soc. Int. de Chirurgie 1975–, Scientific Council, Chinese Acad. of Science 1980–, Third World Acad. of Science 1987–, Exec. Cttee of Int. Soc. of Reconstructive Microsurgery 1988–. *Publications:* Salvage of the Forearm Following Complete Traumatic Amputation: Report, A Case 1963, 7 books, 108 papers. *Leisure interests:* tennis, motorcycle, fishing, violin. *Address:* Zhong Shan Hospital, Shanghai Medical University, 136 Medical College Road, Shanghai 200032, People's Republic of China.

CHEN ZHU; Chinese medical scientist; b. Aug. 1953, Zhenjiang, Jiangsu Prov.; ed St Louis Hosp., Univ. de Paris 7; undertook over 20 nat. key scientific research projects and int. research projects and achieved results on the treatment of leukaemia with diarsenic trioxide and its molecular mechanism, providing a rep. model for cancer research; Vice-Pres. Chinese Acad. of Sciences; Nat. Model Worker and many prizes. *Address:* Chinese Acad. of Sciences, 52 Sanlihe Road, Beijing 100864, People's Republic of China (Office). *Telephone:* (10) 68597247 (Office). *Fax:* (10) 68597258 (Office).

CHEN ZIMING; Chinese dissident; imprisoned for 13 years for role in Tiananmen Square pro-democracy demonstrations 1989, released on medical parole 1994, rearrested for staging hunger strike 1995, released 1996.

CHEN ZUOHUANG, MM, D.M.A.; Chinese orchestral conductor; b. 2 April 1947, Shanghai; s. of Chen Ru Hui and Li He Zhen; m. Zaiyi Wang 1969; one c.; ed Cen. Conservatory of Beijing, Univ. of Michigan; Musical Dir China Film Philharmonic 1974–76; Assoc. Prof., Univ of Kansas, USA 1985–87; Prin. Conductor Cen. Philharmonic Orchestra of China 1987–; Dir Wichita Symphony Orchestra 1990–; Dir Rhode Island Philharmonic Orchestra 1992–96; Artistic Dir, Conductor China Nat. Symphony Orchestra 1996–. *Address:* Wichita Symphony Orchestra, Century II Concert Hall, 225 W Douglas Ave., Suite 207, Wichita, KS 67202, USA.

CHEN ZUOLIN; Chinese politician; b. 1923, Wuwei Co., Anhui Prov.; Vice-Chair. Revolutionary Cttee, Zhejiang Prov. 1975–79; Deputy Sec. CCP Cttee, Zhejiang 1976, Sec. 1977–83; alt. mem. 11th CCP Cen. Cttee 1977, 12th Cen. Cttee 1982; Vice-Gov., Zhejiang 1979–83; Sec.-Gen. Cen. Comm. for Discipline Inspection 1985–87, Deputy Sec. 1987; Deputy Sec. CCP Cen. Discipline Inspection Comm. 1992–; mem. Presidium of 14th CCP Nat. Congress 1992, CPC Standing Cttee, Cen. Leading Group for Party Building Work, Internal and Judicial Affairs Cttee; Deputy to 8th NPC Jiangxi Prov. *Address:* Zhejiang Government Office, 28 Reuminlu Road, Hangzhou, People's Republic of China. *Telephone:* 24911.

CHEN ZUTAO; Chinese business executive; b. 1928; joined CCP 1960; Gen. Man. China Nat. Automotive Industry Corpn 1993–. *Address:* China National Automotive Industry Corporation, 46 Fucheng Lu, Haidian Qu, Beijing 100036, People's Republic of China. *Telephone:* (10) 88123968; (10) 68125556.

CHENAULT, Kenneth Irvine, JD; American financial services company executive; b. 2 June 1951, New York; s. of Hortensius Chenault and Anne N (Quick) Chenault; m. Kathryn Cassell 1977; two s.; ed Bowdoin Coll., Harvard Univ.; called to Bar, Mass. 1981; Assoc. Rogers & Wells, New York 1977–79; Consultant Bain & Co., Boston 1979–81; Dir Strategic Planning, American Express Co., New York 1981–83, Vice-Pres. American Express Travel Related Services Co. Inc., New York 1983–84, Sr Vice- Pres. 1984–86, Exec. Vice-Pres. Platinum Card/Gold 1986–88, Personal Card Div. 1988–89, Pres. Consumer Card and Financial Services Group 1990–93, Pres. (USA) 1993–95, Vice-Chair. American Express Co., New York 1995–97, Pres., COO 1997–2000, Chair., CEO 2001–; mem. Bd of Dirs Brooklyn Union Gas, Quaker Oats Co., New York Univ. Medical Center; mem. Council of Foreign Relations, New York 1988, ABA; several hon. degrees. *Address:* American Express Company, American Express Tower, World Financial Center, 200 Vesey Street, New York, NY 10285-5104, USA.

CHENEY, Lynne Vincent, PhD; American administrator and writer; b. 14 Aug. 1941, Casper, Wyo.; d. of Wayne Vincent and Edna (née Lybyer) Vincent; m. Richard B. Cheney (q.v.) 1964; two d.; ed Colorado Coll., Univ. of Wisconsin; freelance writer 1970–83; lecturer George Wash. Univ. 1972–77, Wyo. Univ. 1977–78; researcher, writer Md Public Broadcasting 1982–83; Sr Ed. Washingtonian magazine 1983–86; Chair. Nat. Endowment for Humanities (NEH) 1986–93; W H. Brady Fellow American Enterprise Inst. 1993–95, Sr Fellow 1996–; Commr US Constitution Bicentennial Comm. 1985–87; mem. Women's Forum. *Publications:* Executive Privilege 1978, Sisters 1981, Kings of the Hill (jtly) 1983, The Body Politic 1988, Telling the Truth 1995. *Address:* American Enterprise Institute, 1150 17th Street, NW, Washington, DC 20036, USA.

CHENEY, Richard B.; American politician and fmr business executive; b. 30 Jan. 1941, Lincoln, Neb.; s. of Richard H. Cheney and Marjorie Dickey Cheney; m. Lynne Vincent Cheney (q.v.); two d.; ed Univ. of Wyoming, Univ. of Wisconsin; engaged on staff of Gov. of Wis. and as a Congressional Fellow on staff of a mem. of House of Reps.; also worked for an investment advisory firm; Exec. Asst to Donald Rumsfeld 1969–71, Deputy 1971–73; Deputy Asst to the Pres. 1974–75, Chief of White House Staff 1975–77; Congressman, At-large District, Wyoming, 1978–89; Republican Whip 1987–88; Sec. of Defense 1989–93; Sr Fellow American Enterprise Inst. 1993–95; Chair. Bd and CEO Halliburton Co., Dallas 1995–2000 (Pres. 1997); Vice-Pres. of USA Jan. 2001–; fmr Chair. House Republican Policy Cttee 1980; Republican. *Address:* Office of the Vice-President, The White House, Old Executive Office Building, NW, Washington, DC 20501, USA.

CHENG ANDONG; Chinese politician; b. Oct. 1936, Huainan City, Anhui Prov.; ed univ.; mem. CCP 1980–; fmr Mayor of Pingxiang City, Jiangxi Prov., fmr Mayor of Nanchang City; Sec. CCP Xian Municipal Cttee 1990; mem. Standing Cttee CCP Shaanxi Provincial Cttee 1991; alt. mem. 14th CCP Cen. Cttee; Gov. of Shaanxi Feb. 1995–. *Address:* Office of the Governor, Xian, Shaanxi Province, People's Republic of China.

CHENG LIANCHANG; Chinese government official; b. 14 May 1931, Jilin; m. Huang Shulan; one s. one d.; ed Jilin Industrial School, People's Univ. of China; joined CCP 1950; Vice-Minister of 7th Ministry of Machine Building 1975–82; Vice-Minister, Exec. Vice-Minister of Astronautical Ind. 1982–88; Sr Engineer and Researcher 1988–; Exec. Vice-Minister of Personnel 1988–94; mem. State Educational Comm. 1988–94; Vice-Pres. Nat. School of Admin. 1994–96; Vice-Chair. Steering Cttee for Enterprise; Standing mem. 8th Nat. Cttee CPCCC 1993–97, 9th Nat. Cttee CPPCC 1998–; Prof. of China People's Univ.; Fellow World Acad. of Productivity Science 2001; First-class Award, Ministry of Astronautical Ind. 1984, State Council Award for Outstanding Contribution in High-energy Physics 1991. *Publications:* Selected Works (2 Vols), Textbook for State Public Servant Examination (20 Vols). *Leisure interest:* swimming. *Address:* Room 1501, No. 13 Building, Cuiwei Xili, Haidian District, Beijing 100036, People's Republic of China (Home); c/o Ministry of Personnel, Hepingli Zhongjie, Beijing 100013. *Telephone:* (10) 68462628 (Office); (10) 68258072 (Home); (10) 11184228. *Fax:* (10) 84223240.

CHENG SHIFA; Chinese artist; b. 1921, Songjiang Cty., Jiangsu; ed Shanghai Coll. of Fine Arts; lecturer Univ. of Hong Kong 1985; mem. Nat. Cttee Fed. Literary and Art Circles 1983, Council Shanghai br. of Artists' Asscn; Silver Medal Leipzig Int. Book Exhbn (for novel The Scholars) 1959. *Publications:* A Dream of the Red Mansion, Folk Stories of the West Lake, The Twelve Beauties, The Wild Boar Forest, The True Story of Ah Q, Gall and the Sword, Tale of the Horse-headed Fiddle.

CHENG SIWEI, MBA; Chinese politician; b. June 1935, Beijing; ed East China Chemical Eng Inst., UCLA; Vice-Chair. China Democratic Nat. Construction Asscn; mem. Standing Cttee 8th CPPCC 1993–98; Vice-Minister of Chemical Industry; Chair. China Democratic Nat. Construction Asscn 1996–; Vice-Chair. Standing Cttee of 9th NPC 1998–. *Address:* Ministry of Chemical Industry, Building 16, Section 4, Anhuili, Beijing 100723, People's Republic of China.

CHENG SIYUAN, PH.D; Chinese politician; b. 22 Aug. 1908, Binyang Co., Guangxi Prov.; m. Shi Hong 1948; ed Rome Univ., Italy; Chief Adviser to fmr Acting Pres. of Kuomintang Govt Li Zongren 1965; Vice-Chair. Standing Cttee 7th Nat. Cttee CPPCC 1988–92; Vice-Chair. Standing Cttee 8th NPC 1993–98, 9th NPC 1998–. *Publications include:* Li and Jiang and China 1952, Li Zongren's Last Years 1980, Political Life 1988, My Memories 1994, A Biography of General Bai Chongxi 1995. *Leisure interests:* swimming, reading, history. *Address:* Standing Committee, National People's Congress, Tian'anmen Square, Beijing, People's Republic of China.

CHENG WEIGAO; Chinese government official; b. 1933, Suzhou City, Jiangsu Prov.; joined CCP 1950; Deputy Sec. Henan Prov. CP Cttee 1987–90; Gov. of Henan Prov. 1988–90, of Hebei Prov. 1991–93, Deputy to 8th NPC Henan Prov.; alt. mem. 14th CCP Cen. Cttee 1992–; mem. 15th CCP Cen. Cttee 1997–; Sec. CCP Hebei Prov. Cttee 1993–98; Chair. Hebei Prov. People's Congress 1998–99. *Address:* c/o Hebei Provincial Committee of CCP, Shijiazhuang City, Hebei Province, People's Republic of China.

CHENG YANAN; Chinese sculptor; b. 15 Jan 1936, Tianjin; d. of Cheng Goliang and Liuo Shijing; m. Zhang Zuoming 1962 (died 1989); one s. one d.; ed Cen. Acad. of Fine Arts, Beijing; sculptor Beijing Architectural Artistic Sculpture Factory 1961–84, Sculpture Studio, Cen. Acad. of Fine Arts 1984–; mem. China Artists' Asscn. *Exhibitions include:* Jia Mei Shi Museum, Aomen 1986, Hong Kong 1990 and in Japan, France, Zaire, Congo, Hungary. *Address:* 452 New Building of Central Institute of Fine Arts, No 5 Shuaifuyan Lane, East District, Beijing, People's Republic of China.

CHEPIK, Sergei; Russian artist; b. 24 June 1953, Kiev; s. of Ludmilla Sabaneyeva and Mikhail Chepik; m. Marie-Aude Albert 1992; one s.; ed Shevchenko Art Inst., Kiev, Repin Art Inst., Leningrad; mem. Young Artists' Union 1978; studied at Mylnikov's Studio and held first exhbns in USSR and abroad 1978–81; moved to Paris 1988; Retrospective Exhbn: Paintings, Graphic Arts, Ceramics, Youth Palace, Leningrad 1986, One Man Show and Retrospective, Roy Miles Gallery, London 1990, Recent Works, Roy Miles Gallery, London 1993, 1994, Retrospective Exhbn Prieuré St Maurice, Senlis 1993, Graphics, Galerie Guiter, Paris 1997, major exhbn of works at the Catto Gallery, London 1998. *Group exhibitions include:* Young Painters: Nat. Exhbn of Graduation Works, Manege, Leningrad and Moscow 1979, Young Painters, Artists' Union, Leningrad 1980, Prague Biennale 1981, Russian Painting, Tokyo 1981, Zone 1981, Manege, Leningrad 1981, Young Soviet Painters,

Acad. of Arts, Moscow, Leningrad 1982, 1984, Russian Painting, Osaka, Tokyo 1982, Petersburg, Petrograd, Leningrad Manege, Leningrad 1982, Nat. Portrait Exhbn, Artists' Union, Moscow 1983, Soviet Painting Week, Tokyo 1984, Soviet Painting, Cologne 1985, Salon d'Automne, Grand Palais, Paris (Gold Medal for House of the Dead) 1988, Russian paintings, Roy Miles Gallery, London 1988, 1989, 1993, Monte Carlo Int. Exhbn of Modern Art, Rocabella (Monaco City Award for the Tree) 1989. *Solo exhibitions include* Russian Landscapes, Artists' Union, Leningrad 1985. *Leisure interests:* literature, ballet, ceramics, sculpture. *Address:* c/o The Catto Gallery, 100 Heath Street, London, NW3, England; c/o Galerie Guiter, 23 rue Guenegaud, 75006 Paris, France. *Telephone:* (20) 7435-6660 (London); 1-43-54-30-88 (Paris). *Fax:* (20) 7431-5620 (London).

CHEPURIN, Aleksandr Vasilyevich; Russian diplomatist; b. 1952; ed Moscow Inst. of Int. Relations; on staff Ministry of Foreign Affairs since 1975; various diplomatic posts abroad and in USSR Ministry of Foreign Affairs; Deputy Head, First Deputy Head Personnel Service, Ministry of Foreign Affairs of Russia 1992–93, Dir Dept of Personnel 1994–96; Amb. to Denmark 1996–99; mem. staff Ministry of Foreign Affairs 1999–. *Address:* c/o Ministry of Foreign Affairs, Smolenskaya-Sennaya 32/34, 121200 Moscow, Russia (Office).

CHER, (Cherilyn Lapierre Sarkisian); American singer and actress; b. 20 May 1946, El Centro, Calif.; d. of John Sarkisian and Georgina Holt; m. 1st Sonny Bono (divorced 1975, died 1998); one d.; m. 2nd Gregg Allman (divorced); one s.; half of singing duo Sonny and Cher; Sonny and Cher Comedy Hour (TV) 1971–75; own TV variety series and night club act; acted in play Come Back to the Five and Dime, Jimmy Dean, Jimmy Dean; has won 11 gold and 3 platinum records; Best Actress Award, Cannes Film Festival, for Mask, Acad. Award for Moonstruck 1987. *Recordings include:* I Got You Babe, The Beat Goes On, Bang Bang, You Better Sit Down Kids, We all Sleep Alone, Black Rose (album) 1980, Cher 1987, Heart of Stone 1989, It's a Man's World 1996, The Casablanca Years 1996, Believe 1998 (Grammy Award for Best Dance Recording), Strong Enough 1999, Living Proof (album) 2001. *Films include:* Good Times, Chastity, Come Back to the Five and Dime, Jimmy Dean, Jimmy Dean, Silkwood, Mask, Witches of Eastwick, Moonstruck, Suspect, Mermaids, Love and Understanding, Faithful, If these Walls could Talk, Pret-a-Porter, Tea with Mussolini. *Address:* Reprise Records, 3000 Warner Boulevard, Burbank, CA 19010; c/o ICM, 8942 Wilshire Boulevard, Beverly Hills, CA 90211, USA.

CHÉREAU, Patrice; French film, theatre and opera director; b. 2 Nov. 1944; s. of Jean-Baptiste Chéreau and Marguerite Pélicier; ed Lycée Louis-le-Grand and Faculté de Lettres, Paris; Co-Dir Théâtre national populaire (T.N.P.) 1972–81; Dir Théâtre des Amandiers, Nanterre 1982–90; Chevalier Légion d'honneur, Officier des Arts et des Lettres; numerous prizes. *Theatre productions include:* L'Intervention 1964, L'Affaire de la rue de Lourcine 1966, Les Soldats 1967, La Révolte au Marché noir 1968, Don Juan, Richard II, Splendeur et Mort de Joaquin Murieta 1970, La Finta Serva 1971, Lulu 1972, Massacre à Paris 1972, La Dispute 1973, Lear 1975, Peer Gynt 1981, Les Paravents 1983, Combats de Nègre et de Chiens 1983, La Fausse suivante 1985, Quai Ouest 1986, Dans la solitude des champs de coton 1987, 1995, Hamlet 1988, Le Retour au désert 1988, Le Temps et la Chambre 1991. *Opera productions:* L'Italiana in Algeri 1969, The Tales of Hoffmann 1974, Der Ring des Nibelungen (Bayreuth 1976–80), Lulu 1979, Lucio Silla 1984, Wozzeck 1992, Don Giovanni (Salzburg 1994–96). *Films include:* La Chair de l'Orchidée 1974, Judith Therpauve 1978, L'Homme blessé 1984, Hotel de France 1987, Le Temps et la Chambre 1993, Queen Margot 1994, Those Who Love Me Can Take The Train 1998 (César Award for Best Dir), Intimacy 2001 (Golden Bear, Berlin Film Festival). *Address:* c/o Artmédia, 10 avenue Georges V, 75008 Paris, France.

CHERESHNEV, Valery Aleksandrovich, DMed; Russian immunologist; b. 24 Oct. 1944, Khabarovsk; m.; two c.; ed Medical Inst., Perm, Russian Acad. of Sciences; researcher Medical Inst., Perm –1988; Dir Inst. of Ecology and Micro-organism Genetics, Russian Acad. of Sciences, Ural, Perm 1988–; corresp. mem. Acad. of Sciences 1990–97, mem. 1997–, Vice-Pres. Russian Acad. of Sciences, Ural Br. 1999–; Medal for Merits in Labour; Order of Friendship. *Leisure interest:* khatkha yoga. *Address:* Presidium, Ural Branch, Russian Academy of Sciences, Permovmayskaya str., 91, 620219 Yekaterinburg (Office); Institute of Ecology and Micro-organism Genetics, Golev str. 13, 614081 Perm, Russia (Office). *Telephone:* (3432) 74-02-23 (Office); (3432) 33-54-54 (Home). *E-mail:* chereshnev@prm.uran.ru (Office).

CHERESTAL, Jean-Marie; Haitian economist and politician; b. 1947, Port Salut; economist in Canada, Costa Rica, Panama, Chile; fmr Minister of Planning and of Finance; fmr Rep. to Lomé Convention; Prime Minister of Haiti 2001–02. *Address:* c/o Bureau du Premier Ministre, Villa d'Accueil, Delmas 60, Musseau, Port-au-Prince, Haiti (Office).

CHERKESOV, Col.-Gen. Victor Vasilejvich; Russian security officer and lawyer; b. 13 July 1950, Leningrad; m. Natalya Sergejvna Cherkesova (née Chaplina); two d.; ed Leningrad State Univ.; investigator Leningrad KGB Dept 1975–; Head Dept of Fed. Security Service St Petersburg and Leningrad Region 1992–98; First Deputy Dir Russian Fed. Security Service 1998–2000; Rep. of Russian Pres. to N.-W. Fed. Dist 2000–; mem. Russian Federation Security Council; Order of the Red Star 1985, Order of Honour 2000, 14 medals; Honoured Lawyer of the Russian Federation, Honourable Domestic Intelligence Officer of the Russian Federation, Honourable External Intelligence Officer of the Russian Federation. *Address:* 12, 3 liniya, Vasilievsky Ostrov, 199004 St Petersburg; Office of the Plenipotentiary Representative of the President, Shpalernaya str. 47, 193015, St Petersburg, Russia (Office). *Telephone:* (812) 323-07-74 (St Petersburg) (Office); (095) 206-65-50 (Moscow) (Office). *Fax:* (812) 323-75-87 (Office). *E-mail:* szfo@saint-petersburg.ru.

CHERMAYEFF, Peter, AB, MArch, FAIA; American architect; b. 4 May 1936, London; s. of Serge Ivan Chermayeff and Barbara Chermayeff; m. Andrea Petersen 1983; one s. one d. two step-s.; ed Harvard Univ.; co-f. Cambridge Seven Assocs. Inc. 1962, resigned 1998; co-f. Chemayeff, Solegub and Poole Inc. 1998–; Pres. International Design for the Environment Assocs., Inc. (IDEA); mem. Mass. Council on Arts and Humanities 1969–72, Bd of Advisors School of Visual Arts, Boston Univ. 1976–80, Visiting Cttee Rhode Island School of Design, Providence 1969–75; Bd Design of Consultants Univ. of Pa, Pa 1976–80; Claude M. Fuess Award, Phillips Acad., Andover 1979. *Films include:* (producer) Orange and Blue 1962, Cheetah 1971, Wildebeest 1984. *Major complete works include:* Guidelines and Standards, Mass. Bay Transportation Authority 1967, U.S. Exhibition Expo 67 Montreal 1967, New England Aquarium, Boston 1969, "Where's Boston?" exhbn and show, Boston 1975, San Antonio Museum of Art, San Antonio, Texas 1981, Nat. Aquarium, Baltimore, Maryland 1981, Ring of Fire Aquarium, Osaka, Japan 1990, Tennessee Aquarium, Chattanooga 1992, Genoa Aquarium, Italy 1992, Nivola Museum, Sardinia 1996, Lisbon Oceanarium, 1998. *work in progress:* New Bedford Aquarium, LA, Child (Rainforest) Cedar Rapids, Mammal Partition, Va. Marine Science Museum, Oberhausen Aquarium, Germany, Cala Gonone Aquarium, Sardinia, Mindelo Aquarium, São Vicente, Cape Verde. *Address:* IDEA Inc., 51 Melcher Street, Boston, MA 02210 (Office); Chermayeff, Sollogub and Poole Inc., 1030 Massachusetts Avenue, Cambridge, MA 02138, USA (Office). *Telephone:* (617) 357-5000 (Boston) (Office); (617) 492-4332 (Cambridge) (Office); (617) 357-5011 (Boston) (Home); (617) 492-3725 (Cambridge) (Home). *E-mail:* pchermayeff@csparchitects (Office); competer@492-idea.com (Office).

CHERN, Shiing-Shen, BS, MS, DSc; American (naturalized 1961) professor of mathematics; b. 26 Oct. 1911, Kashing, China; s. of Lien Chin Chern and Mei Han; m. Shih Ning Cheng 1939; one s. one d.; ed Nankai Univ., Tientsin, Tsing Hua Univ., Peking and Univ. of Hamburg, Germany; Prof. of Math., Tsing Hua Univ., Peking 1937–43; mem. Inst. for Advanced Study, Princeton, NJ, USA 1943–45; Acting Dir Inst. of Math., Academia Sinica, Nanking, China 1946–48; Prof. of Math., Univ. of Chicago, USA 1949–60, Univ. of Calif. at Berkeley 1960–79, Prof. Emer. 1979–; Dir Math. Sciences Research Inst., Berkeley 1982–84, Dir Emer. 1984–; Dir Nankai Inst. of Math., Tianjin, China 1984; mem. Academia Sinica, NAS, American Acad. of Arts and Sciences; Corresp. mem. Brazilian Acad. of Sciences; Foreign mem. Royal Soc. of London 1985–, Corresp. mem. Academia Peloritana, Messina, Sicily 1986; Assoc. founding mem. Third World Acad. of Sciences 1983; Life mem. New York Acad. of Sciences 1987; mem. American Philosophical Soc. 1989; Foreign mem. Accad. Nazionale dei Lincei, Rome 1988, Académie des Sciences, Paris 1989; Hon. mem. Indian Mathematical Soc., London Math. Soc. 1986; Hon. LLD (Chinese Univ. of Hong Kong) 1969; Hon. DSc (Univ. of Chicago) 1969, (Univ. of Hamburg, Germany) 1971, (State Univ. of New York at Stony Brook) 1985, (Univ. of Notre Dame) 1994; Dr hc (Eidgenossische Technische Hochschule, Switzerland) 1982; Hon. Dr. (Nankai Univ.) 1985; Nat. Medal of Science (USA) 1975; Chauvenet Prize (Math. Asscn of America) 1970; Steele Prize, American Math. Soc. 1983; shared Wolf Foundation Prize, Israel 1983–84. *Publications:* S. S. Chern, Selected Papers 1978, Complex Manifolds without Potential Theory 1979, Selected Papers Vols II, III, IV 1989, Exterior Differential Systems (with Bryant, Gardner, Goldschmidt and Griffiths) 1990. *Address:* University of California at Berkeley, Department of Mathematics, Berkeley, CA 94720 (Office); 8336 Kent Court, El Cerrito, CA 94530, USA (Home). *Telephone:* (510) 232-4148. *Fax:* (510) 643-5340.

CHERNIN, Peter; American film company executive; fmrly Pres. Fox Broadcasting Co.; Chair. Twentieth Century Fox Film Corpn 1992; now Chair., CEO Fox Inc.; Pres., COO Fox Newscorp. 1996–, News Corpn. 2000–. *Address:* Fox Inc., Room 5080, 10201 West Pico Boulevard, Building 100, Los Angeles, CA 90035, USA.

CHERNOBROVKINA, Tatyana Anatolyevna; Russian ballerina; b. 14 Aug. 1965; m. Dmitry Zababurin; one s.; ed Saratov School of Choreography; soloist Saratov Theatre of Opera and Ballet 1983–87; prima ballerina Moscow Stanislavsky and Nemirovich-Danchenko Musical Theatre 1987–; prize-winner 5th Moscow Int. Competition of Ballet Dancers 1985; Merited Artist of Russia 1994, People's Artist of Russia 1999. *Main ballet roles:* Odette/Odile (Swan Lake), Macha (The Nutcracker), Aurora (Sleeping Beauty), Juliet (Romeo and Juliet), Kitry (Don Quixote), Giselle (Giselle). *Address:* Moscow Musical Theatre, B. Dmitrovka str. 17, 103009 Moscow, Russia (Office). *Telephone:* (095) 229-19-57 (Office); (095) 954-14-26 (Home). *Fax:* (095) 954-14-26 (Home).

CHERNOFF, Herman, PhD; American professor of statistics; b. 1 July 1923, New York; s. of Max Chernoff and Pauline Markowitz; m. Judith Ullman 1947; two d.; ed Townsend Harris High School, City Coll. of New York, Brown and Columbia Univs.; Research Assoc., Cowles Comm. for Research in Econs. Univ. of Chicago 1947–49; Asst Prof. of Math., Univ. of Illinois 1949–51, Assoc. Prof. 1951–52; Assoc. Prof. of Statistics, Stanford Univ. 1952–56, Prof. 1956–74; Prof. of Applied Math., MIT 1974–85; Prof. of Statistics, Harvard Univ. 1985–97, Prof. Emer. 1997–; mem. NAS, American Acad. of Arts and

Sciences; Dr hc (Ohio State) 1983, (Technion) 1984, (Univ. of Rome, La Sapienza) 1995, (Athens) 1999; Townsend Harris Prize 1982, Wilks Medal 1987. *Publications:* Elementary Decision Theory (jtly with L.E. Moses) 1959, Sequential Analysis and Optimal Design 1972; numerous articles in scientific journals. *Address:* Department of Statistics SC713, Harvard University, Cambridge, MA 02138 (Office); 75 Crowninshield Road, Brookline, MA 02446, USA (Home). *Telephone:* (617) 495-5462 (Office); (617) 232-8256 (Home). *Fax:* (617) 496-8057.

CHERNOMYRDIN, Viktor Stepanovich, CandTechSc; Russian politician; b. 9 April 1938, Cherny-Otrog, Orenburg Dist; m.; two s.; ed Kuybyshev Polytechnic Inst.; Soviet Army 1957–60; operator in oil refinery 1960–67; mem. CPSU 1961–91 (mem. Cen. Cttee 1986–90); work with Orsk City Cttee 1967–73; deputy chief engineer, Dir of Orenburg gas plant 1973–78; work with CPSU Cen. Cttee 1978–82; USSR Deputy Minister of Gas Industry, Chief of All-Union production unit for gas exploitation in Tyumen Dist 1982–85; USSR Minister of Gas 1985–89; Chair. Bd Gasprom 1989–92; Deputy Prime Minister, Minister of Fuel and Energy June–Dec. 1992; Chair. Council of Ministers 1992–98; Acting Prime Minister Aug.–Sept. 1998; Deputy to USSR Supreme Soviet 1987–89; Chair. Bd All-Russian Movt Our Home – Russia 1995–2000; Special Rep. of Pres. Yeltsin on Kosovo conflict settlement 1999; mem. State Duma 1999; joined Yedinstvo (Unity) Movt 2000; Amb. to Ukraine 2001–; mem. Russian Eng Acad.; Hon. Prof. Moscow State Univ.; numerous orders and medals including Order of October Revolution, Order of Labour Red Banner, Order for Services to the Motherland. *Leisure Interests:* hunting, automobiles, playing accordion. *Address:* Russian Embassy, Vozdukhoflotsky prospekt 27, 03049 Kiev, Ukraine. *Telephone:* (44) 245-33-95 (Office); (44) 246-36-73 (Home). *Fax:* (44) 246-34-69 (Office). *E-mail:* embrus@public.icyb.kiev.ua (Office).

CHERNOV, Vladimir Kirillovich; Russian baritone; b. 1956, Belorechensk; m. Olga Chernova; one s.; ed Moscow Conservatory (pupil of Georgy Seleznev and Hugo Titz); winner of All-Union Glinka Competition, int. Competitions: Tchaikovsky (Moscow), Voci Virdiagni (Vercelli), M. Helin (Helsinki); soloist of Kirov (now Mariinsky) Theatre 1990–; debut in USA 1988 (La Bohème, Boston), in UK 1990 (Forza del Destino, Glasgow); perm. soloist of Metropolitan Opera 1990–, Wiener Staatsoper 1991–; guest singer at La Scala, Chicago Lyric Opera, Mariinsky Opera, La Monnaie (Brussels) and other theatres of Europe and America; leading parts in operas Queen of Spades, Boris Godunov, Barber of Seville, La Traviata, Eugene Onegin, Don Carlos, War and Peace, The Masked Ball, Faust, Rigoletto, Falstaff; in concerts and recitals performs opera arias, song cycles of Mahler, Tchaikovsky, romances. *Address:* c/o Columbia Artists Management Inc., 165 West 57th Street, New York, NY 10019, USA. *Telephone:* (212) 799-8721.

CHERNUKIN, Vladimir Anatolyevich; Russian banking executive; b. 31 Dec. 1968, Moscow; ed ed. Acad. of Int. Business, Acad. of Finance, Russian Fed. Govt; with Techmashexport co., Ministry of Foreign Trade 1986–87; with Chimmashexport co., Ministry of Chemical Machine Construction 1986–87; army service 1987–89; sr expert, Technomashimport Ministry of External Econ. Relations 1989–96; Vice-Pres. Dept of Credits, Vnesheconombank 1996–, mem. Bd of Dirs Vnesheconombank 1998–; Vice-Chair. 1999–2002, Chair. July 2002–. *Address:* Vneshconombank, Adademika Sakharova prosp. 9, 103810 Moscow, Russia (Office). *Telephone:* (095) 721-98-53 (Office); (095) 234-29-30 (Office).

CHERNY, Gorimir Gorimirovich; Russian scientist; b. 22 Jan. 1923, Kamenets-Podol'sky; s. of the late Gorimir Cherny and Zoja Cherny; m. 1st Augusta Gubarev 1949 (died 1986); m. 2nd Alla Sebik 1989; two d.; ed Moscow Univ.; served in Soviet Army 1941–45; worked for Cen. Inst. of Aircraft Engines 1949–58; mem. CPSU 1954–91; Prof. at Moscow Univ. 1958; Dir Univ. Research Inst. of Mechanics 1960–92; Corresp. mem. USSR (now Russian) Acad. of Sciences 1962–81, mem. 1981, Acad.-Sec. Div. of Eng, Mechanics and Control Processes 1992–97, Scientific Adviser to Presidium 1997–; Corresp. mem. Int. Acad. of Astronautics 1966, mem. 1969; Foreign mem. Nat. Acad. of Eng, USA 1998; State Prizes 1972, 1978, 1991, nine orders and various medals. *Publications:* author of numerous books and scientific articles on aerodynamics, theory of detonation and combustion, theory of gas-fired machines. *Address:* Institute of Mechanics, Moscow State University, michuzinsky prospekt 1, 117192 Moscow, Russia (Office); 1 Kudzinskaja pl., apt 365, 123272 Moscow, Russia (Home). *Telephone:* (095) 939-11-59 (Office); (095) 247-47-41 (Home); (095) 938-14-04. *Fax:* (095) 938-18-44 (Office); (095) 939-02-65. *E-mail:* ggcher@inmech.msu.zu (Office).

CHERNYSHOV, Albert Sergeyevich; Russian diplomatist (retd); b. 18 Aug. 1936, Voronezh; m.; one d.; ed Moscow Inst. of Int. Relations; diplomatic service 1959–; Asst man., attaché, Sec. Dept of External Policy Information, USSR Ministry of Foreign Affairs 1959–67; Second, First Sec. Embassy Vietnam 1967–71; Counsellor of Minister of Foreign Affairs 1973–76, Chief Counsellor 1976–81, Asst Minister 1982–87, Chief Gen. Secretariat, mem. of Bd 1987; USSR (later Russian) Amb. to Turkey 1987–94; Deputy Minister of Foreign Affairs 1994–96; Amb. to India 1996–2001; mem. staff Ministry of Foreign Affairs 2001–. *Address:* c/o Ministry of Foreign Affairs, Smolenskaya Sennaya 32/34, 121200 Moscow, Russia (Office).

CHERPITEL, Didier J.; French international organization official and investment banker; b. 24 Dec. 1944, Paris; s. of Bernard Cherpitel and Denise Cherpitel (née Lange); m. Nicole Estrangin 1973; one s. two d.; ed Inst. d'Etudes Politiques, Paris, Univ. of Paris; joined JP Morgan/Morgan Guaranty Trust 1972, various posts in Paris 1972–80, Man. Dir of Investment Banking Operations, Morgan Guaranty Pacific, Singapore 1980–83, Head of Commercial Banking Activities, Brussels 1983–84, Exec. Dir and Head of Capital Markets Activities, London 1984–88, Man. Dir Soc. de Bourse JP Morgan SA, Paris 1988–96, mem. Bd JP Morgan Europe 1994–97, Man. Dir of Pvt. Banking Activities Europe, JP Morgan, London 1977–98; mem. Bd French Stock Exchange (CBV) 1991–96; Admin. and Treas. American Chamber of Commerce in France 1991–96; Man. Dir Security Capital Markets Group Ltd, London 1998–99; Admin. Cie générale d'industrie et de participations (CGIP) 1999–; Sec.-Gen. Int. Fed. of Red Cross and Red Crescent Socs., Geneva 2000–. *Leisure interests:* travel, photography, opera, golf. *Address:* International Federation of Red Cross and Red Crescent Societies, 17 chemin des Crêts, Petit-Saconnex, 1209 Geneva; P.O. Box 372, 1211 Geneva 19, Switzerland (Office); 3 rue de Contamines, 1206 Geneva, Switzerland (Home). *Telephone:* (22) 7304344 (Office). *Fax:* (22) 7341921 (Office). *E-mail:* cherpitel@ifrc.org (Office). *Website:* www.ifrc.org (Office).

CHESHIRE, Air Chief Marshal Sir John (Anthony), KBE; British air force commander and government official; b. 4 Sept. 1942; m. Shirley Ann Stevens 1964; one s. one d.; ed Ipswich School, Worksop Coll., RAF Coll., Cranwell; specialist in air support, Special Forces until 1980; Commdr Air Wing, Brunei 1980–82, RAF Lyneham 1983–85, Plans Br. HQ Strike Command 1986–87; Defence and Air Attaché, Moscow 1988–90; Deputy Commandant RAF Staff Coll. 1991–92; Asst Chief of Staff for Policy Supreme Headquarters, Allied Powers, Europe 1992–94; Mil. Rep. to NATO HQ 1995–97; Commdr-in-Chief Allied Forces NW Europe 1997–2000; Lt-Gov. and Commdr-in-Chief of Jersey (Channel Islands) 2000–. *Address:* Office of the Lieutenant-Governor, Government House, St Helier, Jersey, JE2 7GH, Channel Islands (Office). *Website:* www.gov.je.

CHESNAKOV, Aleksei Aleksandrovich, PhD; Russian political scientist; b. 1 Sept. 1970, Baku, Azerbaijan; m.; one d.; ed Moscow State Univ.; Jr, then Sr Researcher Inst. of Mass Political Movts., Russian-American Univ. (RAU) 1991–93; researcher, then Head of Collective of Political Lectures, Centre of Political Conjunction of Russia 1993–97, Dir 1997–; mem. Presidium Ind. Assoc. Civil Soc.; Dir Centre of Social-Political Information, Inst. of Social-Political Studies, Russian Acad. of Sciences 1997–. *Publications:* numerous scientific publs on social and political problems; monographs: One Hundred Political Leaders of Russia 1993, Azerbaijan: Political Parties and Organizations 1993, Russia: Power and Elections 1996, Social and Political Situation in Russia in 1996 1997, Russia: New Stage of Neo-liberal Reforms 1998. *Address:* Institute of Social-Political Studies, Russian Academy of Sciences, Leninsky prosp. 32A, 117334 Moscow, Russia (Office). *Telephone:* (095) 938-19-10 (Office).

CHET, Ilan, PhD; Israeli professor of microbiology; b. 12 April 1939, Haifa; m. Ruth Geffen; two s. three d.; ed Hebrew Univ. of Jerusalem; teacher of microbiology (specializing in soil microbiology, fungal physiology and biological control of plant diseases), Faculty of Agric., Hebrew Univ. of Jerusalem 1965–, Assoc. Prof. of Microbiology 1975–78, Prof. 1978–, Head Dept of Plant Pathology and Microbiology 1981–83, Dean Faculty of Agric. 1986–89; mem. Senate, Hebrew Univ. of Jerusalem 1978, mem. Exec. Cttee of Hebrew Univ. 1990–92, Bd of Man. 1990–, Vice-Pres. for Research and Devt 1992–, Chair. Univ. Authority for Research and Devt 1992–2001; Pres. Weizmann Inst., Rehovot 2001–; Dir Otto Warburg Center of Biotech. in Agric., Rehovot 1983–86, 1990–92; mem. Bd Scientific Incubators Co. 1992–94, Yissum R & D Co. 1992–; Chair. Nat. Cttee for Strategic Infrastructure 1998–; Chair. Cttee for Agric. and Biotech., Nat. Council of Research and Devt 1984–86; mem. Nat. Cttee for Biotech. 1985–92, 1996–97, IUPAC Comm. on Biotech. 1986–92, Editorial Bd, European Journal of Plant Pathology 1995–; Chair. Special Projects Cttee, Int. Soc. for Plant Pathology 1989–93; External Adviser to EU 1999; panel mem. NATO 2001; numerous visiting professorships and lectureships; mem. Israeli Nat. Acad. of Sciences and Humanities 1998; Fellow American Phytopathological Soc. 1991; Dr. hc (Lund) 1991; Max-Planck Research Award 1994, Israel Prize for Agricultural Research 1996, Wolf Prize 1998 and numerous other prizes. *Publications:* Soil-Plant Interaction (co-ed.) 1986, Innovative Approaches to Plant Disease Control (ed.) 1987, Biotechnology in Plant Disease Control (ed.) 1993; numerous chapters, reviews and articles; 30 patents. *Address:* President's Office, Stone Building, Weizmann Institute, Rehovot (Office); 7 Boxer Street, Nes Ziona 74046, Israel (Home). *Telephone:* (8) 9343951 (Office); (8) 9405865 (Home). *Fax:* (8) 9344100 (Office). *E-mail:* ilan.chet@weizmann.ac.il (Office).

CHEUNG, Linus; Chinese business executive; Chief Exec. Hong Kong Telecom; Chair. Companhia de Telecomunicações de Macau 1996–. *Address:* Hong Kong Telecom, Hong Kong Telecom Tower, 39/F, Taikoo Place, 979 King's Road, Quarry Bay, Hong Kong Special Administrative Region, People's Republic of China. *Telephone:* 2888-2888. *Fax:* 2877-8877.

CHEVALIER, Roger; French aeronautical engineer; b. 3 May 1922, Marseille; s. of Louis Chevalier and Marie-Louise Assaud; m. Monique Blin 1947; two s.; ed Ecole Polytechnique and Ecole Nationale Supérieure de l'Aéronautique; Head of Dept, Aeronautical Arsenal 1948–53; Chief Engineer, Nord-Aviation 1954–60; Technical Dir Soc. pour l'Etude et la Réalisation d'Engins Balistiques (SEREB) 1960, Dir-Gen. 1967–70; mem. admin. council Onera 1972–; Vice-Pres. Gifas 1977–81; Gen. Man. Société Nationale de l'Industrie Aérospatiale (SNIAS), Exec. Senior Vice-Pres. 1976–82, Vice-Chair. 1982–87; Pres. Asscn Aéronautique et Astronautique de France; mem. Int. Astronautical Fed. (IAF) 1980–82, Pres. 1982–86; Vice-Pres. Aero-Club de France 1981; Pres. French Acad. for Aeronautics and Astronautics; Pres. Soc. d'études de réalisation et d'applications techniques (SERAT) 1985–91; Fellow, American Aeronautic and Astronautic Inst.; mem. Int. Acad. of Astronautics; Commdr Légion d'honneur; Médaille de l'Aéronautique, Prix Galabert 1966, Prix Acad. des Sciences 1967, Allan D. Emil Award 1982; Commdr Ordre nat. du mérite, Commdr of Merit (Fed. Repub. of Germany) 1987. *Leisure interests:* tennis, hunting, reading. *Address:* 4 rue Edouard Detaille, 75017 Paris, France. *Telephone:* 1-42-27-59-28.

CHEVALLAZ, Georges-André, DLitt; Swiss politician; b. 7 Feb. 1915, Lausanne; s. of Georges Chevallaz and Frida Chevallaz; m. Madeleine Roch 1945; two s.; ed Univ. of Lausanne; teacher, School of Commerce 1942–55; Dir Canton Library, Reader in Diplomatic History, Univ. of Lausanne 1955–58; Syndic de Lausanne 1957–73; Nat. Councillor 1959–73; mem. Fed. Council 1973–, Head of Finance and Customs Dept 1974–79; Vice-Pres. of Switzerland Jan.–Dec. 1979, Pres. Jan.–Dec. 1980, Head of Fed. Military (Defence) Dept 1980–83; Radical Democrat. *Publications:* Aspects de l'agriculture vaudoise à la fin de l'ancien régime 1949, Histoire générale de 1789 à nos jours 1957, 1967, 1973, 1990, Les grandes conférences diplomatiques 1964, La Suisse ou le sommeil du juste 1967, La Suisse est-elle gouvernable? 1984, Le Gouvernement des Suisses 1989, Le défi de la neutralité 1995, Les raisons de l'espoir 1999, etc. *Address:* 113 Vuillettaz, 1066 Epalinges, Switzerland. *Telephone:* (21) 784-19-19. *Fax:* (21) 784-20-29.

CHEVÈNEMENT, Jean-Pierre; French politician; b. 9 March 1939, Belfort; s. of Pierre Chevènement and Juliette Garessus; m. Nisa Grünberg 1970; two s.; ed Lycée Victor-Hugo, Besançon, Univ. de Paris, Ecole Nationale d'Admin.; joined Parti Socialiste (PS) 1964; Commercial Attaché, Ministry of Econ. and Finance 1965–68; Sec.-Gen. Centre d'études, de recherches et d'éducation socialistes 1965–71; Commercial Adviser, Jakarta, Indonesia 1969; Political Sec. Fédération socialiste de Paris 1969–70; Dir of Studies, Soc. Eres 1969–71; Nat. Sec. PS 1971–75, 1979–80, mem. Exec. Bureau 1971–81, 1986, Steering Cttee 1971–92; Deputy (Belfort) to Nat. Ass. 1973–81, 1986; Vice-Pres. Departmental Ass. of Franche-Comté; mem. Bd Dirs. Repères magazine; Minister of State, Minister of Research and Tech. 1981–82, of Industry 1982–83, of Nat. Educ. 1984–86, of Defence 1988–91, of the Interior 1997–2000; Cand. Presidential Elections 2002; First Asst to Mayor of Belfort 1977–83, 1997–, Mayor 1983–97; Pres. Conseil Régional de Franche-Comté 1981–82, mem. 1986–88, fmr Vice-Pres.; f., Pres. Citizens Movt 1992–; mem. Foreign Affairs Comm., Nat. Ass. 1986–88, Finance Comm. 1993–; Croix de la valeur militaire. *Publications:* (as Jacques Mandrin): L'énarchie ou les mandarins de la société bourgeoise 1967, Socialisme ou socialmédiocratie 1969, Clefs pour le socialisme 1973, Le vieux, la crise, le neuf 1975, Les socialistes, les communistes et les autres, Le service militaire 1977, Etre socialiste aujourd'hui 1979, Apprendre pour entreprendre 1985, Le pari sur l'intelligence 1985, Une certaine idée de la République m'amène à 1992, le Temps des citoyens 1993, Le Vert et Le Noir. Intégrisme, Pétrole, Dollar 1995, France–Allemagne: parlons franc 1996, La République contre les bien-pensants 1999. *Leisure interest:* chess. *Address:* Assemblée Nationale, 75355 Paris, France. *Telephone:* 1-45-50-39-50. *Fax:* 1-45-55-68-73 (Office).

CHEW, Geoffrey Foucar, PhD; American professor of physics; b. 5 June 1924, Washington, DC; s. of Arthur Percy Chew and Pauline Lisette Foucar; m. 1st Ruth Elva Wright 1945 (died 1971); one s. one d.; m. 2nd Denyse Mettel 1972; two s. one d.; ed George Washington Univ. and Univ. of Chicago; Research Physicist, Los Alamos Scientific Lab. 1944–46; Research Physicist, Lawrence Radiation Lab. 1948–49, Head of Theoretical Group 1967; Asst Prof. of Physics, Univ. of California at Berkeley 1949–50, Prof. of Physics 1957, now Emer. Chair. Dept of Physics 1974–78, Dean of Physical Sciences 1986–92; Asst Prof., then Assoc. Prof. of Physics, Univ. of Illinois 1950–55, Prof. 1955–56; Fellow, Inst. for Advanced Study 1956; Overseas Fellow, Churchill Coll., Cambridge 1962–63; Scientific Associate, CERN 1978–79; Prof. Miller Inst. 1981–82; Visiting Prof., Univ. of Paris 1983–84; mem. NAS, American Acad. of Arts and Sciences; Hughes Prize of American Physical Soc. 1962, Lawrence Award of US Atomic Energy Comm. 1969, Berkeley Citation (Univ. of Calif.) 1991. *Publications:* The S-Matrix Theory of Strong Interactions 1961, The Analytic S-Matrix 1966; over 100 scientific articles. *Leisure interests:* gardening, hiking. *Address:* Berkeley Laboratory, 50A-5104, Berkeley, CA 94720 (Office); 10 Maybeck Twin Drive, Berkeley, CA 94708, USA (Home). *Telephone:* 486-5010 (Berkeley Lab.); 848-1830 (Home). *Fax:* 486-6808 (Office); 848-4117 (Home). *E-mail:* gfchew@1b1.gov (Office); gfchew@mindspring.com (Home).

CHEW CHOON SENG, BMechEng, MSc; Singaporean business executive; ed Univ. of Singapore and Imperial Coll. of Science and Tech., Univ. of London; joined Singapore Airlines (SIA) 1972, co. man. assignments in Japan and Italy, regional apppointments as Sr Vice-Pres. South-West Pacific, the Americas and Europe, headed Divs of Planning, Marketing and Finance, Sr Exec. Vice-Pres. (Admin.) for Corp. Affairs, Auditing and Finance 2001–03, CEO June 2003–. *Address:* Singapore Airlines Ltd. (SIA), Airline House, 25 Airline Road, 819829 Singapore, Singapore (Office). *Telephone:* 65415880 (Office). *Fax:* 65456083 (Office). *E-mail:* publicaffairs@singaporeair.com.sg (Office). *Website:* www.singaporeair.com (Office).

CHEYSSON, Claude; French politician; b. 13 April 1920, Paris; s. of Pierre Cheysson and Sophie Funck-Brentano; m. 3rd Danielle Schwartz 1969; one s. two d. (and three c. from previous m.); ed Ecole Polytechnique and Ecole d'Administration, Paris; escaped from occupied France to Spanish prison 1943; Officer in the Free French Forces 1943–45; entered French Diplomatic Service 1948; attached to UN Mission in Palestine 1948; Head of French liaison office with Fed. German Govt, Bonn 1949–52; adviser to Prime Minister of Vietnam, Saigon 1952–54; Chef de Cabinet to French Prime Minister (Mendès-France) 1954–55; technical adviser to Minister for Moroccan and Tunisian Affairs 1955–56; Sec.-Gen. Comm. for Technical Co-operation in Africa (C.C.T.A.), Lagos 1957–62; Dir-Gen. Sahara Authority (Organisme Saharien), Algiers 1962–65; Amb. to Indonesia 1966–69; Pres. Entreprise minière et chimique and Pres. Dir-Gen. Cie des potasses du Congo 1970–73; mem. Bd Le Monde 1970–81, 1985–92; Commr for Devt Aid, Comm. of European Communities 1973–81; Minister of External Relations 1981–84; Commr for Mediterranean Policy and North-South Relations, Comm. of European Communities 1985–88; mem. European Parl. 1989–94; mem. Exec. Bd Socialist Party 1989–94; Pres. Institut Mendès-France 1987–89; Pres. Fondation Arche de la Fraternité 1989–93; Town Councillor, Bargemon, France 1983–89, 1995; Dr. hc Univ. of Louvain; Joseph Bech Prize 1978, Prix Luderitz (Namibia) 1983; Commdr, Légion d'honneur, Croix de guerre, Grand Cross, Grand Officier, Commdr from numerous cos. *Leisure interest:* skiing. *Address:* 52 rue de Vaugirard, 75006 Paris; La Belle Bastide, 83830 Bargemon, France. *Telephone:* 1-43-26-46-65 (Paris); 4-94-76-64-62 (Bargemon). *Fax:* 1-43-26-46-65.

CHHATWAL, H.E. Surbir Jit Singh, MPolSc; Indian diplomatist; b. 1 Oct. 1931, Bannu; s. of Datar Singh Chhatwal and Rattan Kaur Chhatwal; m. Neelam Singh 1962; one s. one d.; ed Agra Univ.; joined Foreign Service 1955; Ministry of External Affairs, including one year at Cambridge, UK; Third Sec., Madrid 1958–60; Under-Sec., Ministry of External Affairs, New Delhi 1960–62; First Sec., Havana, Cuba 1962–64; Deputy Sec. (Co-ordination), Ministry of External Affairs, New Delhi 1964–66; First Sec. and Acting High Commr, Ottawa, Canada 1966–68; First Indian Consul-Gen., Seoul, S. Korea 1968–71; Dir Ministry of Foreign Trade, New Delhi 1971–73; Chief of Protocol, Ministry of External Affairs, New Delhi 1973–75; High Commr in Malaysia 1975–79, in Sri Lanka 1982–85, in Canada 1985–90; Amb. to Kuwait 1979–82; Visiting Prof. Jawaharlal Nehru Univ., New Delhi 1990–91; mem. and Chair. Union Public Service Comm. 1991–96; Sec. Asscn of Indian Diplomats 1991–93, Vice-Pres. 1993–94, Pres. 1994–95; mem. Governing Council of Foundation for Aviation and Sustainable Tourism (NGO) 1993–2001; Nat. Co-Chair. Inst. of Marketing and Management, New Delhi 1994–; Life Trustee Inst. for World Congress on Human Rights 1999–; Sr Vice-Pres. and Exec. Chair. of Nat. Asscn for Older Persons; Co-ordinator (Head) think tank on int. relations Surya Foundation, New Delhi 2000–. *Leisure interests:* reading, golf. *Address:* S-168, PanchShila Park, New Delhi 110017, India. *Telephone:* (11) 601-4488. *Fax:* (11) 601-5398.

CHI HAOTIAN, Gen.; Chinese army officer; b. 1929, Zhaoyuan Co., Shandong Prov.; m. Jiang Qingping; joined army 1944, CCP 1946; Maj., unit, Nanjing Mil. Region 1958; Deputy Political Commissar, Beijing Mil. Region 1975–77; Deputy Ed.-in-Chief, People's Daily 1977–82; Deputy Chief of Staff PLA 1977–82; Political Commissar, Jinan Mil. Region 1985–87; PLA Chief of Staff Dec. 1987–; Minister of Nat. Defence 1993–2000, 2002–03, State Councillor 2000–03; Chair. Drafting Cttee for Nat. Defence Law of People's Repub. of China; mem. CCP Cen. Cttee 1985–; mem. PRC Cen. Mil. Cttee 1988–; rank of Gen. 1988; mem. 14th CCP Cen. Cttee 1992–97, 15th CCP Cen. Cttee 1997–2002, 16th CCP Cen. Cttee 2002–; mem. Cen. Mil. Comm. CCP 1992–, Vice-Chair. 1995–; mem. 8th NPC 1993–, Politburo; State Councillor 1993–; Hon. Pres. Wrestling Asscn. *Address:* c/o Ministry of National Defence, Jingshanqian Jie, Beijing 100009, People's Republic of China (Office).

CHIANG KAI-SHEK, Madame (Soong, Mayling), LLD, LHD; Chinese sociologist; b. 5 March 1897; m. (Pres.) Chiang Kai-shek 1927 (died 1975); ed Wellesley Coll., USA; first Chinese woman appointed mem. of Child Labour Comm.; inaugurated Moral Endeavour Asscn; established schools in Nanking for orphans of revolutionary soldiers; fmr mem. Legislative Yuan; served as Sec.-Gen. of Chinese Comm. on Aeronautical Affairs; Dir-Gen. New Life Movement; founded and directed Nat. Chinese Women's Asscn for War Relief and Nat. Asscn for Refugee Children; accompanied husband on mil. campaigns; Patroness Int. Red Cross Cttee; Hon. Chair. British United Aid to China Fund and United China Relief; First Hon. Mem. Bill of Rights Commemorative Soc.; first Chinese woman to be decorated by Nat. Govt of China; Hon. Chair. American Bureau for Medical Aid to China and Cttee for the promotion of the Welfare of the Blind; awards include Gold Medal of Nat. Inst. of Social Sciences; Hon. mem. numerous socs; LHD (John B. Stetson Univ., Bryant Coll., Hobart and William Smith Colls., Nebraska Wesleyan Univ.), LLD (Rutgers Univ., Goucher Coll., Wellesley Coll., Loyola Univ., Russell Sage Coll., Hahnemann Medical Coll., Univs. of Michigan and Hawaii and Wesleyan Coll., Macon); Hon. FRCS (Eng). *Publications:* Sian: A Coup d'Etat 1937, China in Peace and War 1939, China Shall Rise Again 1939, This is Our China 1940, We Chinese Women 1941, American Tour Speeches 1942–43, Little Sister Su 1943, The Sure Victory 1955, Madame Chiang Kai-shek: Selected Speeches 1958–59, Album of Reproductions of Paintings Vol. I 1952, Vol. II 1962, Religious Writings 1963, Madame Chiang Kai-shek: Selected Speeches 1965–66, Album of Chinese Orchid Paintings 1971, Album of Chinese Bamboo Paintings 1972, Album of Chinese Landscape Paintings 1973, Album of Chinese Floral Paintings 1974, Conversations with Mikhail Borodin 1977. *Address:* Lattingtown, Long Island, New York, USA.

CHIARA, Maria; Italian opera singer; b. 24 Nov. 1939, Oderzo; m. Antonio Cassinelli; ed Conservatorio Benedetto Marcello, Venice, with Maria Carbone; début as Desdemona in Otello, Doge's Palace, Venice, 1965, then Rome Opera début 1965; frequent performances in Italy, including Turandot with Plácido Domingo, Verona 1969; débuts Germany and Austria 1970; début La Scala, Milan as Micaela, Carmen 1972; début Royal Opera House, Covent Garden, London, Turandot 1973; début Metropolitan Opera, New York in La Traviata and at Lyric Opera, Chicago in Manon Lescaut 1977; sings in all maj. opera houses of Europe, USA and S. America; opened 1985/86 season at La Scala in Aïda. *Recordings include:* Aïda, Madame Butterfly, Il Segreto di Susanna and a disc of operatic arias (Decca). *Address:* c/o S. A. Gorlinsky Ltd, 33 Dover Street, London, W1X 4NJ, England (Office); Národni divadlo, Ostrovní 1, Prague 1, Nové Mesto, Czech Republic.

CHIBA, Kazuo, BEcons; Japanese businessman; b. 26 March 1925, Miyagi Pref.; m. Noriko Chiba 1954; two s.; ed Univ. of Tokyo; joined Oji Paper Co. Ltd 1950, Dir 1974, Mill Man. Kasugai Mill 1978, Man. Dir 1981, Sr Man. Dir 1985, Exec. Vice-Pres. 1987, Pres. 1989–; Blue Ribbon Medal 1990. *Leisure interests:* golf, reading. *Address:* Umegaoka 16-32, Midori-ku, Yokohama, 227 Japan. *Telephone:* (45) 9716602.

CHIBBER, Lieut.-Gen. Bakshi Krishan Nath, MSc; Indian politician; b. 10 Feb. 1936, Varanasi; s. of G. R. Chibber and Saraswati Chibber; m. Rama Chibber; one s. one d.; Adviser Govt of Bhutan 1964–67; infantry Bn Commdr 1971–73; instructor and Head of Training 1978–80; Brigade Commdr, Ferozepur 1980–82; GOC, Amritsar 1987–90, 11 Corps 1990–92; Chief of Staff, Western Command 1992–93; Security Adviser, Govt of Punjab 1993–94; Gov. of Punjab 1994–; Ugen Thogyal Medal. *Address:* c/o Punjab State Government, Chandigarh, Punjab, India.

CHIBESAKUNDA, Hon. Justice Lombe Phyllis, BL; Zambian lawyer and diplomatist; b. 5 May 1944; ed Chipembi Girls' School, Nat. Inst. of Public Admin, Lusaka; called to the Bar, Gray's Inn, UK; State Advocate Ministry of Legal Affairs 1969–72; pvt legal practice with Jacques and Partners 1972–73; mem. Nat. Ass. (Parl.) for Matero 1973; fmr Solicitor-Gen. and Minister of State for Legal Affairs; Amb. to Japan 1975–77; High Commr in UK, concurrently Amb. to the Netherlands and the Holy See 1977–81; High Court Judge, Lusaka; Chair. Industrial Court of Zambia, Perm. Human Rights Comm. (PHRC) 1998–; Chief Zambian Del., UN Law of the Sea Conf. 1975, Rep. UN Comm. on the Status of Women; Chair. Equality Cttee Sub-Cttee UN Independence Party's Women's League; f. Social Action Charity, Lusaka; Founder-mem. Link Voluntary Org.; Life mem. Commonwealth Parl. Asscn; Kt Grand Cross of the Order of Pope Pius IX 1979. *Address:* Permanent Human Rights Commission, POB 33812, Lusaka (Office); High Court of Zambia, POB 50067, Lusaka, Zambia (Office). *Telephone:* (1) 251347. *Fax:* (1) 251342. *E-mail:* phrc@zamnet.zm.

CHIBURDANIDZE, Maiya Grigorievna; Georgian chess player; b. 17 Jan. 1961, Kutaisi, Georgia; ed T'bilisi Medical Inst. 1978; Int. Grand Master 1977; Honoured Master of Sport 1978; USSR Champion 1977; World Champion 1978–91 (youngest-ever world champion aged 17); winner of numerous women's int. chess tournaments; Capt. winning Soviet team at 8th Women's Chess Olympics 1978, Georgian winning team at Chess Olympics 1994; Oscar Chess Prize 1984–87. *Address:* Georgian Chess Federation, Tbilisi, Georgia.

CHICAGO, Judy, MFA; American artist, author and educator; b. 20 July 1939, Chicago, Ill.; m. 1st Jerry Gerowitz 1961 (died 1962); m. 2nd Lloyd Hamrol 1969; m. 3rd Donald Woodman; ed Univ. of Calif., Los Angeles; taught art at Univ. of Calif. Extension, Los Angeles 1963–69, Univ. of Calif. Inst. Extension, Irvine 1966–69, Californian State Univ., Fresno (f. art programme for women) 1969–71, Calif. Inst. of the Arts, Valencia (f. first Feminist Art Programme) 1971–73; co-f. Feminist Studio Workshop and Woman's Bldg, Through the Flower Corpn, Los Angeles 1977; Presidential Appt. in Art and Gender Studies, Indiana Univ. 1999; Robb Lecturer, Univ. of Auckland 1999; Hon. DFA (Smith Coll., Northampton, Mass.) 2000; Hon. DHumLitt (Lehigh Univ., Bethlehem, Pa) 2000; numerous awards. *Exhibitions:* Womanhouse (with students of Calif. Inst. of the Arts) 1972, The Dinner Party (multi-media project) 1974–79, The Birth Project 1980–85 (units now housed in numerous public collections, with core display at Museum of Albuquerque), Powerplay, Holocaust Project: from darkness into light 1993, Resolutions: A Stitch in Time 2000, Voices from the Song of Songs, Fitzwilliam Museum, Cambridge, England 2001; retrospective: Fla State Univ. Art Museum 1999; has exhibited throughout USA, Canada, Europe, Australia and Asia. *Publications:* Through the Flower: My Struggle as a Woman Artist 1975, The Dinner Party: A Symbol of Our Heritage 1979, Embroidering Our Heritage: The Dinner Party Needlework 1980, The Birth Project 1985, Holocaust Project: From Darkness into Light 1993, The Dinner Party/Judy Chicago 1996, Beyond the Flower: The Autobiography of a Feminist Artist 1996, Women and Art: Contested Territory 1999. *Leisure interests:* cats and exercise. *Address:* Through the Flower, 101 North 2nd Street, Belen, NM 87002, USA (Office). *Telephone:* (505) 864-4080 (Office). *Fax:* (505) 864-4088 (Office). *E-mail:* throughtheflower@compuserve.com (Office). *Website:* www.judychicago.com (Office).

CHIDYAUSIKU, Godfrey; Zimbabwean judge; b. 1947; Ind. MP 1974–77; elected Zimbabwe African Nat. Union-Patriotic Front (ZANU-PF) MP 1980; Deputy Minister of Local Govt 1980, of Justice 1981; Attorney-Gen. 1982, apptd. High Court Judge 1987; Chief Justice of Zimbabwe 2001–; Chair. Constitutional Comm. 2000. *Address:* Chief Justice Chambers, CY 870, Causeway, Zimbabwe (Office). *Fax:* (4) 731867 (Office).

CHIEN, Eugene Y. H., PhD; Taiwanese politician and professor of engineering; b. 4 Feb. 1946, Taoyuan Co.; m. Wang Kuei-Jung (Gwendolyn Chien); two s. one d.; ed Nat. Taiwan Univ. and New York Univ., USA; Assoc. Prof., Prof. and Chair. Dept of Aeronautical Eng, Tamkang Univ. 1973–78, Prof. and Dean Coll. of Eng 1978–84; Mem. Legis. Yuan 1984–87, Chair. Nat. Defense Cttee, Educ. Cttee 1984–87; Minister of State, Environmental Protection Admin., Exec. Yuan 1987–91; Minister of Transportation and Communications 1991–93; Rep., Taipei Rep. Office, UK 1993–97; Sr Adviser, Nat. Security Council 1997–2000; Deputy Sec.-Gen. Office of the Pres. 2000–02; Minister of Foreign Affairs Feb. 2002–; Chair. Int. Co-operation and Devt Fund 2002–; Pres. Chinese Inst. of Environmental Eng 1988–90, Chinese Inst. of Engineers 1990–91, Sino-British Cultural and Econ. Ascn 1998–; Prof. Emer., Catholic Univ. of Honduras 2002; Hon. Fellow Cardiff Univ., UK 1998. *Leisure interests:* horse riding, reading, swimming, jogging, chess, go chess. *Address:* Ministry of Foreign Affairs, 2 Chiehshou Road, Taipei 10016 (Office); Ministry of Foreign Affairs, 2 Kaitakelan Blvd., Taipei 100, Taiwan (Office). *Telephone:* (2) 2311-9292 (Office); (2) 2348-2999 (Office). *Fax:* (2) 2314-4972 (Office). *Website:* www.mofa.gov.tw (Office).

CHIEN, Rt Rev John Chih-Tsung, MDiv, STM; Taiwanese ecclesiastic (retd); b. 23 March 1940; m. Grace Chu 1963; one s. two d.; ed Tunghai Univ., Tainan Theological Coll., Selly Oak Coll. UK and Va Theological Seminary, USA; St Andrew's, Chading; Grace Church, Tainan; Good Shepherd, Taipei; Dean, St John's Cathedral, Taipei; Bishop, Diocese of Taiwan 1988–; Trustee Tunghai Univ., St John's and St Mary's Inst. of Tech.; Procter Fellow, Episcopal Divinity School, Cambridge, Mass., USA; Hon. DD 1998. *Publications:* Ten Years' Memories of being Bishop, Dimensions of life. *Address:* 70-1 Kou Bey Li, Ta-Lin Town, Chia-yi Hsien 622, Taiwan. *Telephone:* (5) 295-45-35 (Home). *Website:* episcopal.sjsmit.edu.tw (Office).

CH'IEN KUO FUNG, Raymond, CBE, PhD, JP; Chinese business executive and politician; b. 26 Jan. 1952, Tokyo, Japan; m. Whang Hwee Leng; one s. two d.; ed schools in Hong Kong, Rockford Coll., Ill., Univ. of Pennsylvania; Group Man. Dir Lam Soon Hong Kong Group; Chair. Industry and Tech. Devt Council, Hong Kong Industrial Tech. Centre Corpn, Hong Kong/Japan Business Co-operation Cttee; mem. Exec. Council 1992–97, Exec. Council Hong Kong Special Admin. Region 1997–; mem. Bd China Centre for Econ. Research, Beijing Univ.; Hon. Adviser China Aerospace Corpn; Hon. Prof. Nanjing Univ. *Address:* Executive Council Secretariat, 1st Floor, Main Wing, Central Government Offices, Central, Hong Kong Special Administrative Region, People's Republic of China.

CHIEPE, Gaositwe Keagakwa Tibe, MBE, P.H., BSc, MA, FRSA; Botswana politician, diplomatist and educationist (retd); b. 20 Oct. 1922, Serowe; d. of the late T. and S. T. Chiepe (née Sebina); ed secondary school in Tigerloof, S. Africa and Univs. of Fort Hare and Bristol; Educ. Officer, Botswana 1948, Senior Educ. Officer 1962, Deputy Dir of Educ. 1965, Dir of Educ. 1968; High Commr in UK and Nigeria 1970–74, concurrently accredited to Sweden, Norway, Denmark, Fed. Repub. of Germany, France, Belgium and the EEC; Minister of Commerce and Industry 1974–77, of Mineral Resources and Water Affairs 1977–84, of External Affairs 1984–95, of Educ. 1995–99; Patron Botswana Forestry Soc., Botswana Soc. for the Arts; Hon. Pres. Kalahari Conservation Soc.; Hon. LLD (Bristol); Hon. DLitt (Chicago) 1994; Hon. D.Educ. (Fort Hare) 1996. *Leisure interests:* music, gardening. *Address:* P.O. Box 186, Gaborone, Botswana. *Telephone:* 352796 (Home).

CHIGIR, Mikhail Mikalayevich; Belarus politician and economist; b. 1948, Usovo, Minsk Region; m.; two c.; ed Belarus State Inst. of Nat. Econs, Moscow Inst. of Finance and Statistics; Chief Div. of Credit, State Bank of Minsk Region, Chief Moscow Regional Br. of State Bank of Minsk 1973–80; official Belarus CP 1982–86; Dir Minsk City Office USSR State Bank 1986–87; First Deputy Chair. Exec. Bd Agroprombank, Belarus Repub. 1988–91; Chair. Exec. Bd Jt-Stock Commercial Agricultural-Industrial Bank Belagroprombank 1991–94; Prime Minister of Belarus 1994–96, resgnd in opposition to Pres. Lukashenko; Presidential Cand. 1999, arrested on the eve of elections on the charges of alleged corruption, sentenced to 3 years' imprisonment on probation.

CHIHANA, Chakufwa; Malawi politician and fmr trade union leader; b. 11 March 1939; s. of Tom Chihana and Agness Chihana; one s. two d.; Pres. Alliance for Democracy opposition party; sentenced to 9 months imprisonment for anti-govt activities Dec. 1992, released June 1993; Second Vice-Pres. of Malawi and Minister of Irrigation and Water Devt 1994–96; Special Adviser Worldwide Intellectuals Asscn for African Famine Relief, Seoul, Korea 1996–; Robert F. Kennedy Memorial Human Rights Award 1993. *Address:* P.O. Box 86, Rumplii; P.O. Box 1902, Lilongwe, Malawi.

CHIHARA, Charles Seiyo, PhD; American professor of philosophy; b. 19 July 1932, Seattle, Wash.; s. of George Chihara and Mary Chihara; m. Carol Rosen 1964; one d.; ed Seattle and Purdue Univs., Univ. of Washington, Oxford Univ.; Faculty mem. Univs. of Wash. 1961–62, Ill. 1962–63, Calif. at Berkeley 1963–, Prof. 1975–, Prof. Emer.; Mellon Postdoctoral Fellowship 1964–65, Humanities Research Fellowship 1967–68, Nat. Endowment for the Humanities Fellowship 1985–86, 1994–95, Univ. of Calif. Pres.'s Research Fellowship in the Humanities 1996–97. *Publications:* Ontology and the Vicious-Circle Principle 1973, Constructibility and Mathematical Existence 1990, The Worlds of Possibility: Modal Realism and the Semantics of Modal Logic 1998. *Address:* Department of Philosophy, University of California, Berkeley, CA 94720 (Office); 567 Cragmont Avenue, Berkeley, CA 94708,

USA. *Telephone:* (510) 525-4023. *Fax:* (510) 642-4164. *E-mail:* charles1@ socrates.berkeley.edu (Office). *Website:* philosophy.berkeley.edu/chihara (Office).

CHIK, Dato' Sabbaruddin, BA, MPA; Malaysian politician; b. 11 Dec. 1941, Temerloh, Penang; ed Abu Bakar Secondary School, Temerloh, Malay Coll., Kuala Kangser, Perak, Univ. of Malaya and Inst. of Social Studies, The Hague; Asst State Sec. Negri Sembilan, Prin. Asst Sec. JPM, Dir Planning, GPU/SERU, Dir Int. Trade, Ministry of Trade and Industry, Deputy State Sec. Selangor 1966–81; Gen. Man. Pernes Trading Sdn. Bhd. 1981–82; mem. Parl. for Temerloh 1982–; Deputy Minister of Finance 1982; Minister of Culture, Arts and Tourism 1987–99; mem. UMNO Supreme Council 1984–. *Address:* c/o Ministry of Culture, Arts and Tourism, 34th–36th Floor, POB 5–7, Menaro Dato' Onn, Putra World Trade Centre, 50694 Kuala Lumpur, Malaysia.

CHIKÁN, Attila, PhD; Hungarian politician and economist; b. 4 April 1944, Budapest; m. Márta Nagy; one s. one d.; ed Karl Marx Univ. of Econ. Sciences, Budapest, Grad. School of Business, Stanford Univ.; Prof. Budapest Univ. of Econs 1968–, Prof. and Chair. 1990–; Minister of Econ. Affairs 1998–99; Rector Budapest Univ. of Econ. Sciences and Public Admin. 2000–; Chair. Council of Econ. Advisers of the Prime Minister 2000–; First Vice-Pres., Sec.-Gen. Int. Soc. for Inventory Research; Pres. Fed. of European Production and Industrial Man. Societies 1996–; Pres. Int. Fed. of Purchasing Materials and Man. 2000–01; mem. editorial bds Int. Journal of Purchasing and Materials Man., Int. Journal of Logistics 1997–, Int. Journal of Quantitative and Operations Man. 1998–. *Publications:* author or co-author of eight books. *Leisure interest:* sports. *Address:* Budapest University of Economic Sciences and Public Administration, 1093 Budapest, Fővám tér 9, Hungary (Office). *Telephone:* (1) 217-62-68. *Fax:* (1) 217-88-83. *E-mail:* chikan@rektor.bke.hu.

CHIKANE, Rev. Frank, MA; South African ecclesiastic; b. 3 Jan. 1951, Soweto; s. of James Mashi and Erenia Chikane; m. Kagiso Oglobry; three s.; ed Turfloop Univ. and Univs. of S. Africa, Durban and Pietermaritzburg; worked with Christ for All Nations 1975–76; ordained Minister 1980; part-time research officer, Inst. of Contextual Theology 1981, Gen. Sec. 1983; Gen. Sec. S. African Council of Churches 1987–94; Sr Research Fellow Univ. of Cape Town 1995–; Hon. DTheol (Groningen Univ.); Diakonia Peace Prize 1986; Star Crystal Award 1987, Third World Prize 1989. *Publications:* Doing Theology in a Situation of Conflict 1983, The Incarnation in the Life of People in South Africa 1985, Children in Turmoil: Effect of the Unrest on Township Children 1986, Kairos Document – A Challenge to Churches, No Life of my Own (autobiog.). *Leisure interests:* reading, keeping fit (mentally, spiritually, physically). *Address:* University of Cape Town, Private Bag, Rondebosch 7700; P.O. Box 4291, Johannesburg 2000; 310 Zone 7, Pimville 1808, Soweto, South Africa (Home).

CHIKAOKA, Riichiro; Japanese politician; mem. House Reps; fmr Parl. Vice-Minister of Health and Welfare; Dir Gen. Science and Tech. Agency 1996. *Address:* c/o Science and Technology Agency, 2-2-1, Kasumigaseki, Chiyoda-ku, Tokyo 100, Japan (Office). *Telephone:* (3) 3581-5271 (Office).

CHIKH, Slimane; Algerian politician; b. 13 July 1940, Beni Isguen; m.; four c.; ed Coll. Sadiki de Kharznadar, Tunis and Univ. of Algiers; Dir Inst., des Sciences politiques et de l'information, Univ. of Algiers 1975–78; Assoc. Prof., Univ. d'Aix-Marseille 1979–81; Rector Univ. of Algiers 1982–84; Prof. Univ. of Algiers 1984–88; Minister of Educ. and Training 1988–89; Assoc. Prof. Univ. Laval 1989, Institut d'Etudes Politiques, Paris 1990–91; Conseiller Présidence de la République 1992–94; Minister of Culture 1994–96, of Educ. 1996. *Address:* 8 ave de Pékin, El-Mouradia, Algiers, Algeria. *Telephone:* (2) 60-54-41.

CHIKIN, Valentin Vasilevich; Russian journalist; b. 25 Jan. 1932; ed Moscow Univ.; literary corresp. for Moscow Komsomol newspaper 1951–58; mem. CPSU 1956–91, CP of Russian Fed. 1992–; literary corresp., Deputy Ed., Ed. of Komsomolskaya Pravda 1958–71; Deputy, First Deputy Ed.-in-Chief of Sovietskaya Rossiya 1971–84; First Deputy Pres. of State Cttee on Publishing, Printing and the Book Trade 1984–86; Ed.-in-Chief of Sovietskaya Rossiya 1986–; Sec. of USSR Union of Journalists 1986–90; cand. mem. of CPSU Cen. Cttee 1986–91; mem. State Duma (CP faction) 1993–, re-elected 1995, 1999. *Address:* Sovietskaya Rossiya, ul. Pravdy 24, Moscow, Russia. *Telephone:* (095) 257-27-72.

CHIKVAIDZE, Alexander Davidovich; Georgian diplomatist; b. 19 Jan. 1932, T'bilisi; m.; two s.; ed Moscow State Univ., Acad. of Political Sciences, Diplomatic Acad.; taught int. law, Moscow State Univ., headed youth orgs. in Georgian Repub., then Head T'bilisi Region Cttee of CPSU; Chair. Rep. Cttee for Publishing and Book Trade 1976–79; fmr Vice-Consul (Cultural Affairs), Mumbai, First Sec. (Cultural Dept), Embassy of USSR in London; Consul-Gen., San Francisco 1979–83; Amb. to Kenya and to UNEP and Habitat 1983–85; Head of Sector, CPSU Cen. Cttee 1985–88; USSR Amb. to Netherlands 1988–91, Russian Amb. to the Netherlands 1991–92; Minister of Foreign Affairs of Georgia 1992–95; fmr Amb. to Greece; fmr Chair. USSR Chess Fed.; Lenin Centenary Medal. *Publication:* Western Countries' Foreign Policy on the Eve of the Second World War 1976. *Address:* c/o Ministry of Foreign Affairs, Chitadze str. 4, 380110 T'bilisi, Georgia. *Telephone:* (32) 989377. *Fax:* (32) 997249.

CHILADZE, Otar; Georgian writer; b. 20 March 1933, Signakhi, Georgia; s. of Ivane Chiladze and Tamar Chiladze; brother of Tamaz Chiladze; m. Nana

Chiladze 1956 (died 1990); one s. one d.; ed Tbilisi State Univ.; professional writer since 1950s; Sh. Rustaveli Prize 1983, State Prize of Georgia for play Labyrinth 1993. *Publications include:* The Trains and Passengers (collection of verses) 1959, Iron Bed, The Other Side, Remember about Life; A Man was Going by the Road (novel) 1973, Each Who Meets Me (novel) 1976, Iron Theatre (novel) 1983, March Cock (novel) 1987, Avelum 1996. *Address:* Av. of David Agmashenebeli 181, Apt. 6, 380012 Tbilisi, Georgia. *Telephone:* (32) 34-51-84 (Home).

CHILADZE, Tamaz; Georgian writer; b. 5 March 1931, Signakhi; s. of Ivane and Tamar Chiladze; brother of Otar Chiladze; ed Univ. of Tbilisi; first published works in 1951; mem. CPSU 1967–89; Chief Ed. Sabchota Khelovneba 1973–89; Shota Rustaveli Prize 1992, State Prize of Georgia 1997. *Publications include:* Sun Dial (poems) 1961, A Network of Stars 1961, Ponytrek 1963, The First Day 1965, Who Lives on the Stars 1970, White Smoke 1973, Memory (poems) 1978, Martyrdom of St Shushanik (essay) 1978, Herald of Spring (essay) 1985, The Ray of the Setting Sun (novel) 1993, The Cactus Garden (novel) 1993; plays: Shelter on the Ninth Floor, Murder, Role for a Beginner Actress, Bird Fair, The Day of Appointment. *Address:* 22 Simon Chickovani Street, Flat 7, Tbilisi 380071, Georgia. *Telephone:* (32) 33-49-87.

CHILINGAROV, Artur Nikolayevich, CAND. GEO. SC.; Russian polar explorer, traveller and politician; b. 25 Sept. 1939, Leningrad; m.; one s. one d.; ed Adm. Makarov Higher Marine School of Eng; worked as metalworker Baltic vessel repair plant; First Sec. Regional Comsomol Cttee in Yakutya; headed drifting station N Pole 19, organized station N Pole 22, head Bellingshausen station in Antarctica, head expedition to free scientific vessel Mikhail Somol in Antarctic, expedition on board atomic ice-breaker Sibir; Deputy Chair. USSR State Cttee on Meteorology 1986–92; counsellor, Chair. Russian Supreme Soviet on problems of Arctic and Antarctic 1991–93, Asscn of Russian Polar Researchers 1991–; mem. State Duma (Parl.) 1993–, Deputy Chair. 1994–; mem. Org. Cttee Otechestvo Movt 1999; joined Yedinstvo and Otechestvo Union; mem. Russian Acad. of Natural Sciences; Co-Chair. Russian Foundation of int. humanitarian aid and co-operation; Hero of the Soviet Union, USSR State Prizes. *Leisure interest:* football. *Address:* State Duma, Okhotny ryad 1, 103009 Moscow, Russia. *Telephone:* (095) 292-80-44. *Fax:* (095) 292-76-50 (Home).

CHILINGIRIAN, Levon, OBE, FRCM, ARCM; British violinist; b. 28 May 1948, Nicosia, Cyprus; nephew of Manoug Parikian; m. Susan Paul Pattie 1983; one s.; ed Royal Coll. of Music (RCM), London; f. Chilingirian string quartet 1971; has performed in N and S America, Africa, Australasia, Europe and Far East; Prof. RCM 1985; Musical Dir Camerata Roman of Sweden; BBC Beethoven Competition 1969, Munich Duo Competition (with Clifford Benson) 1971; Cobbett Medal 1995, Royal Philharmonic Soc. Chamber Music Award 1995; Hon. DMus (Sussex) 1992. *Recordings include:* ten Mozart quartets, last three Schubert quartets, Debussy and Ravel quartets, Schubert octet and quintet, six Bartok quartets and piano quintet, late and middle Dvořák quartets, Tippett Triple Concerto; music by Panufnik, Tavener, Pärt, Chausson, Grieg, Vierne, Hahn and Komitas (with Chilingirian Quartet). *Leisure interests:* reading, backgammon, football. *Address:* 7 Hollingbourne Road, London, SE24 9NB, England. *Telephone:* (20) 7978-9104. *Fax:* (20) 7274-5764.

CHILOSI, Alberto, PhD; Italian economist and academic; b. 14 Jan. 1942, Modena; s. of Giuseppe Chilosi and Clara Trabucchi; m. Lucia Ponzini; one s.; ed La Spezia, Univ. of Pisa, Warsaw Central School of Planning and Statistics; Asst at Univ. of Pisa 1966–69; lecturer then Assoc. Prof. of Econs Univ. Officielle du Congo 1969–72; lecturer in Theory and Policy of Econ. Devt, Univ. of Pisa 1972–81, Prof. of Econ. Policy 1981–; Pres. Asscn Italiana per lo Studio dei Sistemi Economici Comparati 1988–89. *Publications:* Growth Maximization, Equality and Wage Differentials in the Socialist Economy 1976, Kalecki 1979, Self-Managed Market Socialism with Free Mobility of Labour 1986, L'Economia del Periodo di Transizione 1992. *Leisure interests:* cycling, swimming. *Address:* Dipartimento di Scienze Economiche, Sede di Scienze Politiche, Via Serafini, 3, 56126 Pisa (Office); Via S. Andrea, 48, 56126 Pisa, Italy (Home). *Telephone:* (050) 2212439 (Office); (050) 544184 (Home). *E-mail:* chilosi@specon.unipi.it (Office). *Website:* www.dse.ec.unipi.it/chilosi (Office).

CHILUBA, Frederick J.T., MPhil; Zambian politician; b. 30 April 1943, Wusakile; s. of Jacob Titus Chiluba Nkonde and Diana Kaimba; m. Vera Chiluba (divorced); nine c.; ed Kawambwa Secondary School, and later in USA and fmr Soviet Bloc countries; shop steward 1967; fmr Chair. Zambian Congress of Trades Unions 1987–91; mem. Parl. for Nkana; Pres. of Zambia 1991–2002; Co-Founder and Leader Movt for Multiparty Democracy (MMD); Chair. African Union (AV) 2001–; charged with theft of public money Feb. 2003. *Address:* c/o Office of the President, PO Box 30208, Lusaka, Zambia (Office).

CHILVER, Baron (Life Peer) cr. 1987, of Cranfield in the County of Bedfordshire; **Henry Chilver,** MA, DSc, F.R.ENG., CIMgt, FRS; British university teacher, university administrator and business executive; b. 30 Oct. 1926, Barking, Essex; s. of A. H. Chilver; m. Claudia Grigson 1959; three s. two d.; ed Southend High School and Univ. of Bristol; Structural Engineer, British Railways 1947–48; lecturer, Univ. of Cambridge 1952–54, Univ. of Bristol 1956–61, Fellow, Corpus Christi Coll., Cambridge 1958–61; Prof. of Civil Eng, London Univ. 1961–69; Dir Centre for Environmental Studies 1967–69; Vice-Chancellor, Cranfield Inst. of Tech. 1970–89; Dir English China Clays 1973,

Chair. 1989–95; Dir ICI 1990–93, Zeneca 1993–95; Chair. RJB Mining 1993–97, Chiroscience Group PLC 1995–98, Univs. Computer Bd 1975–78, The Post Office 1980–81, Advisory Council for Applied Research and Devt 1982–85, Milton Keynes Devt Corpn 1983–92, Plymouth Devt Corpn 1996–98; Chair. Univs Funding Council 1988–91; mem. or fmr mem. various cttees of inquiry, review bodies etc.; Hon. Fellow, Corpus Christi Coll., Cambridge; hon. degrees (Leeds, Bristol, Salford, Strathclyde, Bath, Buckingham, Cranfield, Compiègne); Telford Gold Medal 1962 and Coopers Hill War Memorial Prize 1977, Inst. of Civil Engineers. *Publications:* Problems in engineering structures (with R. J. Ashby) 1958, Strength of Materials and Structures (with J. Case) 1971; papers on structural eng. and stability. *Address:* House of Lords, London, SW1A 0PW, England (Office).

CHIMUTENGWENDE, Chen (Chenhamo), MA; Zimbabwean writer and politician; b. 28 Aug. 1943, Mazowe Dist; m. Edith Matore; three s. two d.; ed Bradford Univ., UK; Exec. Dir Europe–Third World Research Centre, London 1969–74; Deputy Dir and Sr Lecturer in Mass Communications and Int. Affairs, City Univ., London 1978–79; UNESCO Consultant on Mass Communications (Broadcasting) 1979–80; Corresp. for East and Southern Africa, Inter Press Service, Rome 1980–83; Sr Lecturer, Head School of Journalism, Univ. of Nairobi 1980–82; MP 1985–; fmr Minister of Information, Posts and Telecommunications; Pres. New Africa Int. Network (NAIN) 1997–; Corresp. UNESCO's Int. Social Science Journal 1980–; Chair. Una Global Vision Ltd 1986–; Pres. UN Convention on Climate Change 1996–98; Chair. UN High Level Cttee of Ministers and Sr Officials 1997–98. *Publication:* South Africa: The Press and the Politics of Liberation 1978. *Leisure interests:* music, dancing, travelling, reading. *Address:* New Africa International Network (NAIN), 8 San Fernando, 130 Fife Avenue, Corner 5th Street, Harare (Office); 6 Duthie Road, Belgravia, Harare, Zimbabwe (Home). *Telephone:* (4) 253296 (Office); (4) 733542 (Home). *Fax:* (4) 707771 (Office). *E-mail:* NAIN@ africaonline.co.zw (Office); chen@unitedafrica.co.zw (Home). *Website:* www .nain.org.zw (Office).

CHINAMASA, Patrick Anthony, LLB; Zimbabwean politician; b. 25 Jan. 1947; m.; mem. Zimbabwe African Nat. Union–Patriotic Front (ZANU–PF); currently Minister of Justice, Legal and Parl. Affairs. *Leisure interests:* watching sport, jogging, reading. *Address:* Ministry of Justice, Legal and Parliamentary Affairs, Corner House, cnr. Samora Machel Ave. and Leopold Takawira Street, Private Bag 7751, Causeway, Harare (Office); Honeybear Lane, Borrowdale, Harare, Zimbabwe (Home). *Telephone:* (4) 777054 (Office); (4) 860006 (Home). *Fax:* (4) 772999 (Office).

CHINCHIAN, Zaven Osep, BA; Egyptian ecclesiastic; b. 1929, Aleppo, Syria; s. of Osep and Lucy Chinchian; ed Seminary of Armenian Patriarchate, Jerusalem; teacher, Secondary Dept, Nat. School, Jerusalem 1953–56, Seminary of Jerusalem 1952–56; Vicar-Gen. in Alexandria 1958–76, in New York, USA 1977–78; Primate of Diocese of the Armenian Orthodox Church in Egypt and N Africa 1979–; St George's Insignia from Russian Orthodox Church 1988. *Publications:* one literary work, a book of short stories 1959 and many articles in various magazines. *Leisure interests:* studying theology and the Writings of the Church Fathers. *Address:* 179 Rameses Avenue, P.O. Box 48, Faggala, Cairo, Egypt. *Telephone:* (2) 5901385. *Fax:* (2) 5906671.

CHINO, Tadao, BA; Japanese international banker; b. 1934; m.; two d.; ed Stanford Univ., Tokyo Univ.; joined Ministry of Finance 1960, numerous Sr posts in banking, budget and int. finance bureaux, Deputy Dir.-Gen. Banking Bureau 1987–89, Dir.-Gen. Int. Finance Bureau 1989, Vice-Minister of Finance for Int. Affairs 1991–93, Special Adviser to Finance Minister 1993; Jr official UN Econ. Comm. for Asia and Far E (ECAFE) 1964; Deputy Gov. Agric., Forestry and Fisheries Finance Corpn 1994; now Chair. Bd of Advisers, Nomura Research Inst. Ltd; Chair. Bd, Pres. Asian Devt Bank 1999–. *Address:* Asian Development Bank, 6 Asian Development Bank Avenue, Mandaluyong City 0401, Metro Manila (Office); P.O. Box 789, 0980 Manila, Philippines. *Telephone:* (2) 6324444 (Office). *Fax:* (2) 636244 (Office). *E-mail:* information@mail.asiandevbank.org (Office). *Website:* www.adb.org (Office).

CHIPMAN, John Miguel Warwick, CMG, MA, DPhil; British/Canadian administrator and academic; b. 10 Feb. 1957, Montreal; s. of Lawrence Carroll Chipman and Maria Isabel Prados; m. Lady Theresa Manners 1997; two s.; ed Westmount High School, Montreal, El Estudio, Madrid, Harvard Univ., London School of Econs and Balliol Coll. Oxford; Research Assoc. Int. Inst. of Strategic Studies (IISS), London 1983–84; Research Assoc. Atlantic Inst. for Int. Affairs, Paris 1985–87; Asst Dir for Regional Security, IISS 1987–91, Dir of Studies 1991–93, Dir IISS 1993–, Founder IISS Publ Strategic Comments; Dir Arundel House Enterprises, U.S. Office IISS, Washington, Asia Office IISS, Singapore; mem. Bd Aspen Inst. Italia; regular broadcaster on int. affairs; NATO Fellowship 1983. *Publications:* Cinquième République et Défense de l'Afrique 1986, French Power in Africa 1989; ed. and prin. contrib. to NATO's Southern Allies: Internal and External Challenges 1988; articles in journals and book chapters. *Leisure interests:* tennis, skiing, scuba diving, collecting travel books, music. *Address:* International Institute for Strategic Studies, Arundel House, 13–15 Arundel Street, London, WC2R 3DX, England. *Telephone:* (20) 7379-7676. *Fax:* (20) 7836-3108.

CHIPPERFIELD, David Alan; British architect; b. 18 Dec. 1953; s. of Alan John Chipperfield and Peggy Chipperfield (née Singleton); partner Dr Evelyn Stern; two s. one d. and one s. from previous relationship; ed Architectural Asscn; Prin. David Chipperfield Architects 1984–; Visiting Lecturer Harvard

Univ. 1987–88; Design Tutor RCA 1988–89; Visiting Prof. Univ. of Naples 1992, Univ. of Graz 1992, Ecole Polytechnique Fedérale de Lausanne 1993; Prof. Staatliche Akademie der Bildenden Künste, Stuttgart 1995–; commissions include: shops for Issey Miyake, London and Japan 1986–87, Arnolfini Gallery, Bristol 1987, pvt. museum, Tokyo 1987, Tak Design Centre, Kyoto 1989, Matsumoto Corpn HQ, Okoyama 1990, River and Rowing Museum, Henley-on-Thames 1994, Neues Museum, Berlin 1997, Bryant Park Hotel, New York 1998, Ernsting Service Centre, Munster 1998, Museum Island Masterplan, Berlin 1998, Dolce and Gabbana Stores, worldwide 1998, San Michele Cemetery, Venice 1998, Palace of Justice, Salerno 1999, Davenport Museum of Art, Iowa 1999, Ansaldo 'City of Cultures', Milan 2000; founder, Dir 9H Gallery, London; mem. RIBA; Trustee Architectural Foundation, London 1992–97; Andrea Palladio Prize 1993, RIBA Regional Award 1996, 1998, Civic Trust Award 1999, Tessenow Gold Medal Award 1999, and numerous other awards and prizes. *Publication:* Theoretical Practice 1994. *Leisure interests:* drawing, reading, swimming. *Address:* David Chipperfield Architects, 1A Cobham Mews, Agar Grove, London, NW1 9SB (Office). *Telephone:* (20) 7267-9422. *Fax:* (20) 7267-9347.

CHIRAC, Jacques René; French politician; b. 29 Nov. 1932, Paris; s. of François Chirac and Marie-Louise Valette; m. Bernadette Chodron de Courcel 1956; two d.; ed Lycée Carnot, Lycée Louis-le-Grand, Ecole Nationale d'Administration and Inst. d'Etudes Politiques, Paris; Mil. Service in Algeria; Auditor, Cour des Comptes 1959–62; Special Asst, Secr.-Gen. of Govt 1962; Special Asst, Private Office of M. Pompidou 1962–65; Counsellor, Cour des Comptes 1965–94; Sec. of State for Employment Problems 1967–68; Sec. of State for Economy and Finance 1968–71; Minister for Parl. Relations 1971–72, of Agriculture and Rural Devt 1972–73, 1973–74, of the Interior March–May 1974; Prime Minister of France 1974–1976, 1986–88; Sec.-Gen. Union des Démocrates pour la République (UDR) 1974–75, Hon. Sec.-Gen. 1975–76; Pres. Rassemblement pour la République (fmrly UDR) 1976–94, Hon. Sec.-Gen. 1977–80; mem. European Parl. 1979; Pres. Regional Council, La Corrèze 1970–79; Municipal Counsellor, Sainte-Féréole 1965–77; Mayor of Paris 1977–95; Pres. of France May 1995–; Deputy for Corrèze March–May 1967, June–Aug. 1968, March–May 1973, 1976–79, 1981–86, 1988–95; mem. Comm. on Nat. Defence, Nat. Assembly 1980–86; Prix Louise Michel 1986; Grand-Croix, Légion d'honneur, Ordre nat. du Mérite, Croix de la Valeur Militaire, Chevalier du Mérite agricole, des Arts et des Lettres, de l'Étoile noire, du Mérite sportif, du Mérite touristique, Médaille de l'Aéronautique, Grand Cross Merit of the Sovereign Order of Malta. *Publications:* Discours pour la France à l'heure du choix, La lueur de l'espérance: réflexion du soir pour le matin 1978, Une Nouvelle France, Réflexions 1 1994, La France pour Tous 1995. *Address:* Palais de l'Elysée, 55–57 rue du Faubourg Saint-Honoré, 75008 Paris, France.

CHIRICĂ, Andrei; Romanian politician; b. 14 June 1939, Ploieşti; ed Electronics and Telecommunications Coll. of Bucharest; engineer in the Radio and TV Dept 1961–68; Chief Engineer, Gen. Direction of Post and Telecommunications 1968–84, then Asst Gen. Dir for matters of research and information in telecommunications, Minister of Communications 1990–94; Pres. romtelecom 1994–95; Pres. C. A. Mobil Rom 1996–. *Publications:* specialized works. *Address:* C. A. Mobil Rom, Bucharest, Romania. *Telephone:* (1) 2033512. *Fax:* (1) 2033512.

CHISHOLM, Sam; New Zealand television executive; b. 8 Oct. 1939; s. of R. and N. Chisholm; m. 1st Ronda Chisholm 1967; one d.; m. 2nd Susan Chisholm 2002; ed King's Coll. S. Auckland; fmr sales man. for Johnson & Johnson; joined Channel 9 Melbourne 1963; Man. Dir and CEO Nine Network 1976–90, Dir Nine Network Australia 1980–93; CEO Sky TV, UK 1990, CEO and Man. Dir British Sky Broadcasting 1990–97, Dir BSkyB 1990–99; Exec. Dir News Corpn 1993–97; Dir Star TV and Foxtel 1993–97, Telstra 2000–, Australian Wool Services Ltd 2000–; Chair. Foxtel Man. 2001–; Dir Tottenham Hotspur FC 1998–2000, Victor Chang Cardiac Research Inst. 2000–. *Leisure interests:* reading, television, fishing. *Address:* Bundarbo Station, Via Jugiong, NSW 2726, Australia.

CHISSANO, Joaquim Alberto; Mozambican politician; b. 2 Oct. 1939, Chibuto; m. Marcelina Rafael Chissano; four c.; Asst Sec. to Pres., Frente de Libertação de Moçambique (FRELIMO) in charge of Educ. 1963–66, Sec. to Pres., FRELIMO 1966–69; Chief Rep. FRELIMO in Dar es Salaam 1969–74; Prime Minister, Transitional Govt of Mozambique 1974–75, Minister of Foreign Affairs 1975–86, Pres. of Mozambique and C.-in-C. of Armed Forces Nov. 1986–; Order, Augusto César Sandino (Nicaragua) 1988. *Address:* Office of the President, Avda Julius Nyerere 1780, Maputo, Mozambique. *Telephone:* (1) 491121. *Fax:* (1) 492065.

CHITANAVA, Nodari Amrosievich; Georgian politician and agricultural specialist; b. 10 March 1936, Zugdidi Region, Georgia; s. of Ambrose Chitanava and Tina Chitanava; m. Keto Dimitrovna 1964; two d.; mem. CPSU 1958–91; komsomol and party work 1959–; Second Sec. Adzhar obkom 1973–74; Minister of Agric. for Georgian SSR 1974–79; First Deputy Chair., Georgian Council of Ministers 1979–85; Party Sec. for Agric. 1985–89; Chair. Council of Ministers, Georgian SSR 1989–90; Minister of Agric. 1991–93; Dir Econ. and Social Problems Research Inst. 1993–; Chair. Georgian Economists' Soc. *Leisure interest:* spending time in the country. *Address:* Institute for Macroeconomics, 16 Zandukeli Str., 380008 Tbilisi, Atheni str. 16, Tbilisi, Georgia (Home). *Telephone:* (32) 93-12-55; (32) 99-75-15 (Office); (32) 23-37-53 (Home).

CHITTISTER, Joan D., MA, PhD; American social psychologist, author and lecturer; b. 26 April 1936, Dubois, Pa; d. of Harold C. Chittister and Loretta Cuneo Chittister; ed St Benedict Acad. Erie, Mercyhurst Coll. Erie, Univ. of Notre Dame and Pennsylvania State Univ.; elementary teacher, 1955–59, secondary teacher 1959–74; taught Pa State Univ. 1969–71; Pres. Fed. of St Scholastica 1971–78; Prioress, Benedictine Sisters of Erie 1978–90; Pres. Conf. of American Benedictine Prioresses 1974–90; Invited Visiting Fellow, St Edmund's Coll. Cambridge, UK 1995–96; mem. Exec. Bd Ecumenical and Cultural Inst. St John's Univ. Collegeville 1976–98; Exec. Dir Benetvision; mem. Bd of Dirs. Nat. Catholic Reporter 1983–2000; 10 hon. degrees and several awards, including Notre Dame Alumni Assoc. Women's Award of Achievement 1997, Distinguished Alumni Award (Penn. State Univ.) 2000. *Publications include:* Climb Along the Cutting Edge: An Analysis of Change in Religious Life 1977, Women, Church and Ministry 1983, Winds of Change: Women Challenge the Church 1986, Wisdom Distilled from the Daily 1990, The Rule of Benedict: Insights for the Ages 1992, There is a Season 1995, The Fire in these Ashes: A Spirituality of Contemporary Religious Life 1995, The Psalms: Meditations for Every Day of the Year 1996, Beyond Beijing: The Next Step for Women 1996, Passion for Life: Fragments of the Face of God 1996, Songs of Joy: New Meditations on the Psalms 1997, Light in the Darkness: New Reflections on the Psalms 1998, Heart of Flesh: A Feminist Spirituality for Women and Men 1998, In Search of Belief 1999, Gospel Days: Reflections for Every Day of the Year 1999, The Story of Ruth: Twelve Movements in Every Woman's Life 2000, The Illuminated Life: Monastic Wisdom for Seekers of Light 2000, Living Well: Scriptural Reflections for Every Day 2000, The Friendship of Women: A Spiritual Tradition 2000; numerous articles and lectures on religious life, peace and justice issues and women in church and society. *Leisure interests:* computers, music, reading. *Address:* St Scholastica Priory, 355 East 9th Street, Erie, PA 16503, USA. *Telephone:* (814) 454-4052. *Fax:* (814) 459-8066.

CHITTOLINI, Giorgio; Italian professor of medieval history; b. 9 Dec. 1940, Parma; s. of Gino Chittolini and Diva Scotti; m. Franca Leverotti 1977; one d.; Assoc. Prof. of History, Univ. of Pisa 1974–76, Univ. of Pavia 1976–79; Fellow at Villa I Tatti, Florence 1980; Prof. of Medieval History, Univ. of Parma 1981–84, Univ. of Milan 1985–; mem. Bd of Eds., Società e Storia 1979–; mem. Scientific Cttee, Istituto Storico Italo-Germanico, Trento 1989–; Pres. Centro Studi Civiltà del tardo Medioevo 1990–; mem. Int. Comm. for the History of Towns 1995. *Publications:* La formazione dello stato regionale e le istituzioni del contado 1979, Gli Sforza, la chiesa lombarda e la corte di Roma (1450–1535) 1990, Comunità, Governi e Feudi nell'Italia Centrosettentrionale 1995, Materiali di storia ecclesiastica lombarda (series ed.) 1995. *Address:* Department of History, Università Degli Studi di Milano, Via Festa del Perdono 7, 20122 Milan; Via Madre Cabrini 7, 20122 Milan, Italy. *Telephone:* (02) 58304652.

CHITTY, Sir Thomas Willes (pen name **Thomas Hinde**), Bt; British author; b. 2 March 1926, Felixstowe; s. of Sir Thomas Henry Willes Chitty; m. Susan Elspeth Hopkinson 1951; one s. three d.; ed Winchester Coll. and Univ. Coll., Oxford; served in Royal Navy 1944–47; with Shell group 1953–60; Granada Arts Fellow, Univ. of York 1964–65; Visiting lecturer, Univ. of Illinois 1965–67; Visiting Prof. Boston Univ. 1969–70; now freelance writer. *Publications include:* Mr. Nicholas 1952, For the Good of the Company 1961, The Day the Call Came 1964, High 1968, Our Father 1975, Daymare 1980; travel: The Great Donkey Walk 1977, The Cottage Book 1979, Stately Gardens of Britain 1983, A Field Guide to the English Country Parson 1983, Forests of Britain 1984, The Domesday Book: England's Heritage, then and now 1986, Courtiers: 900 years of Court Life 1986, Tales from the Pump Room: An Informal History of Bath 1988, Sir Henry and Sons (autobiog.) 1980, Capability Brown 1986, Imps of Promise: A History of the King's School Canterbury 1990, Looking-Glass Letters (ed.) (letters of Lewis Carroll) 1991, Paths of Progress, A History of Marlborough College 1992, A History of Highgate School 1993, A History of King's College School 1994, Carpenter's Children, A History of the City of London School 1995, An Illustrated History of the University of Greenwich 1996, A History of Abingdon School 1997. *Leisure interests:* eating, drinking, talking, listening, gardening, reading, travelling. *Address:* c/o Andrew Hewson, John Johnson, 45-47 Clerkenwell Green, London, EC1R 0HT (Office); Bow Cottage, West Hoathly, Sussex, RH19 4QF, England. *Telephone:* (20) 7251-0125 (Office); (1342) 810269. *E-mail:* thomas.chitty@ukgateway.net (Home).

CHITVIRA, Thongyod; Thai politician; b. Suphanburi; mem. municipality Suphanburi 1949, then mayor; mem. provincial council; mem. Nat. Ass., Commerce Minister 1975; Public Health Minister 1980; Deputy Prime Minister 1981–82, Sept.–Dec. 1990; mem. Social Action Party. *Address:* c/o Social Action Party, House of Representatives, Bangkok 10300, Thailand.

CHIU, Frederic; American pianist; ed Indiana Univ., Juilliard School; began career in Paris; has given concerts in Antwerp, Berlin, Brussels, Frankfurt, The Hague, London, Milan, Rome, Warsaw, Africa, Asia, USA; co-f. Consonances Festival, St Nazaire, France; Petscheck Award, American Pianists Asscn Fellowship and numerous other awards. *Recordings include:* Liszt transcriptions of Schubert's Schwanengesang, Chopin's Etudes and Rondeaux, Prokofiev's Lieutenant Kije Suite.

CHIU CHUANG-HUAN; Taiwanese politician; b. 25 July 1925, Changhua County; ed School of Political Science, Nat. Chengchi Univ.; Dir 3rd Dept, Ministry of Personnel, Taiwan 1965–67; Dept Dir 5th Section, Cen. Cttee,

Kuomintang 1967–68; Commr Dept of Social Affairs, Taiwan Prov. Govt 1969–72; Dir Dept of Social Affairs, Cen. Cttee, Kuomintang 1972–78; Minister without Portfolio 1976–78; Deputy Sec.-Gen., Cen. Cttee, Kuomintang 1978; Minister of the Interior 1978–81; Vice-Premier Exec. Yuan, Taiwan 1981–84; Hon. PhD (Youngnam Univ., Repub. of Korea). *Publications:* Thought Regarding Social Welfare in the Three Principles of the People, A Summary of the Chinese Social Welfare System.

CHIZEN, Bruce, BS; American business executive; ed Brooklyn Coll., City Univ. of New York; Retail Merchandising Man. (Eastern Region) Mattel Electronics 1980–83; Sales Dir (Eastern Region) Microsoft Corpn 1983–87; Founding Sr Man. Claris Corpn 1987, later Vice-Pres. Sales, Worldwide Marketing, Vice-Pres. and Gen. Man. Claris Clear Choice; joined Adobe Systems Inc. 1994, Vice-Pres. and Gen. Man. Graphics Professional Div. and Consumer Div., later Exec. Vice-Pres. Worldwide Products and Marketing, Pres. and CEO Adobe Systems Inc. 2000–; Dir Synopsys, Inc., Children's Discovery Museum of San Jose. *Address:* Adobe Systems Incorporated, 345 Park Avenue, San Jose, CA 95110-2704, U.S.A. (Office). *Telephone:* (408) 536-6000 (Office). *Fax:* (408) 537-6000 (Office). *Website:* www.adobe.com (Office).

CHIZHOV, Ludvig Aleksandrovich; Russian diplomatist (retd); b. 25 April 1936, Radornishl, Zhitomir Region; m.; one s. one d.; ed Moscow Inst. of Int. Relations; fmr mem. CPSU; attaché, Embassy, Japan 1960–65, First Sec., Counsellor, 1971–77; Third Sec., Second Sec., Second Far Eastern Dept, Ministry of Foreign Affairs 1966–70; Counsellor, Second Far Eastern Dept 1978–80; Minister Counsellor, Embassy, Japan 1980–86; Head of Pacific Ocean Countries Dept, Ministry of Foreign Affairs 1986–89; Russian Amb. to Japan 1990–96; Amb.-at-Large 1996–98; Dir 3rd European Dept, Ministry of Foreign Affairs 1998–2001, on staff of Ministry 2001–. *Leisure interests:* fishing, reading. *Address:* Ministry of Foreign Affairs, Smolenskaya-Sennaya 32/34, Moscow, Russia.

CHKHEIDZE, Peter, PhD; Georgian diplomatist; b. 22 Oct. 1941, Tbilisi; s. of the late Peter Chkheidze and Julia Chkheidze; m. Manana Chkheidze 1963; two s.; ed Tbilisi Nat. Univ., Diplomatic Acad. of USSR Ministry of Foreign Affairs and Inst. of State and Law, USSR Acad. of Sciences; various positions, Attorney Service of Repub. of Georgia 1963–75; First Sec., Dept of Int. Orgs., Ministry of Foreign Affairs of USSR 1978; First Sec., Counsellor, then Chief of Dept Perm. Mission of USSR to UN 1978–84; leading posts in nat. state and public insts. 1984–89; Chair. Ind. Trade Unions Confed. of Repub. of Georgia 1989–91; Deputy Prime Minister of Repub. of Georgia and Perm. Rep. of Govt of Georgia to USSR, later Russian Fed. 1991–92; Chargé d'Affaires in Russian Fed. 1992–93; Amb. to USA 1993–94; Perm. Rep. to UN 1993–2002; Amb. to Turkmenistan and Afghanistan 2002–; Corresp. Mem. Int. Informatization Acad. 1994–. *Publications:* various publs in fields of law and int. relations 1975–95. *Leisure interests:* literature, art, horse-riding. *Address:* 139A, Azadi str., Ashgabat 744000, Turkmenistan (Office); Inguri St 3, Apt. 52, Tbilisi 380071, Georgia. *Telephone:* (12) 344838 (Turkmenistan) (Office); (12 343568 (Turkmenistan) (Home); 33-7056 (Tbilisi). *Fax:* (12) 343248 (Turkmenistan) (Office). *E-mail:* georgia@online.tm (Office).

CHKHEIDZE, Revaz (Rezo) Davidovich; Georgian film director; b. 8 Dec. 1926, Kutaisi; m. Tinatin Gambashidze 1950; one s. two d.; studied acting at Tbilisi State Theatrical Inst. 1943–46; studied under Sergei Yutkevich and Mikhail Romm at VGIK (Film School) 1949–53; Dir Georgia film studios 1972–; Deputy USSR Supreme Soviet 1974–84; USSR People's Artist 1980; All-Union Festival Prize 1973, 1981; Lenin Prize 1986. *Films include:* Magdana's Donkey 1956 (with T. Abuladze), Our Yard 1957, A Soldier's Father 1965, Our Youth 1970, The Seedlings 1973, Your Sun, Earth 1981, Life of Don Quixote and Sancho 1989. *Address:* Larsskaya Street 5, Apt 3, 380009 Tbilisi, Georgia. *Telephone:* (32) 51-06-27 (Office); (32) 23-38-84 (Home).

CHKHEIDZE, Temur Georgyevich; Georgian theatre director; b. Nov. 1942, Tbilisi; ed Georgian Inst. of Theatre; debut as Dir 1967; with Shota Rustaveli Drama Theatre 1969–80; Artistic Dir Kote Mardzhanishvili Drama Theatre 1980–88; freelance 1988–; worked in Moscow Gorky Art Theatre 1983, St Petersburg 1991; over 40 stage productions; Lenin Prize. *Address:* Mardzhanishvili Drama Theatre, Tbilisi, Georgia (Office).

CHKHIKVADZE, Ramaz Grigorievich; Georgian actor; b. 28 Feb. 1928, Georgia; grad. Rustaveli Georgian State Drama Inst. 1951; since then with the Rustaveli Theatre, Georgia, for which he has played over 50 parts; awards include Best Leading Man at VIIIth Moscow Film Festival for film Saplings, Mardzhanishvili Prize for performance of title role in Kvarkvare, 1975; Georgian State Prize 1974, 1981; USSR State Prize 1979; USSR People's Artist 1981, Hero of Socialist Labour 1988. *Roles include:* Louis XIV (Bulgakov's Molière), Macheath (Brecht's Threepenny Opera), Adzhak (Caucasian Chalk Circle), Richard (Richard III), has also acted in several films (including role of Stalin in Victory 1985. *Address:* S. Chikovani Street 20, Apartment 5H, 380015 Tbilisi, Georgia. *Telephone:* (32) 36-45-25.

CHO, Fujio; Japanese business executive; fmr Exec. Vice-Pres. Toyota Motor Corpn., now Pres. *Address:* Toyota Motor Corporation, 1 Toyota-cho, Toyota, Aichi 471-8571, Japan (Office). *Telephone:* (565) 28-2121 (Office). *Fax:* (565) 23-5800. *Website:* www.global.toyota.com (Office).

CHO, Ramaswamy, BSc, BL; Indian journalist, playwright, actor and lawyer; b. 5 Oct. 1934, Madras (now Chennai); s. of R. Srinivasan and Rajammal Srinivasan; m. 1966; one s. one d.; ed P.S. High School, Loyola Coll., Vivekananda Coll., Madras and Madras Law Coll., Madras Univ.; started practice as lawyer, Madras High Court 1957; Legal Adviser to T.T.K. Group of Cos. 1961–; film scriptwriter and actor 1966–; theatre dir, actor and playwright 1958–; Ed. Tamil political fortnightly Thuglak 1970–; Pres. People's Union of Civil Liberties, Tamilnadu 1980–82; nominated mem. of Rajya Sabha (Parl.); has acted in 180 films, written 14 film scripts, directed 4 films; written, directed and acted in 4 TV series in Tamil; Haldi Gati Award, Maharana of Mewar, for nat. service through journalism 1985, Veerakesari Award for investigative journalism 1986, B. D. Goenka Award for Excellence in Journalism, Panchajanya Award for promotion of nationalism 1998. *Publications:* 23 plays and 10 novels in Tamil; numerous articles on politics, in English and Tamil. *Leisure interest:* photography. *Address:* 46 Greenways Road, Chennai, 600028; 35 Meena Bagh, New Delhi, 110011, India. *Telephone:* (44) 4936913, 4936914, 4936915 (Chennai); (11) 3792520 (New Delhi).

CHOI, Man-Duen, PhD, FRSC; Canadian professor of mathematics; b. 13 June 1945, Nanking, China; m. Pui-Wah Ip 1972; two s. one d.; ed Chinese Univ. of Hong Kong and Univ. of Toronto; lecturer, Dept of Math., Univ. of Calif. Berkeley 1973–76; Asst Prof. Dept of Math., Univ. of Toronto 1976–79, Assoc. Prof. 1979–82, Prof. of Math. 1982–; mem. American Math. Soc., Canadian Math Soc., Math. Asscn of America; Israel Halperin Prize 1980. *Publications:* numerous articles in mathematical journals. *Leisure interests:* yoga, stamps. *Address:* Department of Mathematics, University of Toronto, Toronto, Ont., M5S 1A1, Canada. *Telephone:* (416) 978-3415. *Fax:* (416) 978-4107.

CHOI KYU-HAH; Korean politician; b. 16 July 1919, Wonju City, Gangwon-do; m. Kee Hong 1936; two s. one d.; ed Kyung Gi High School, Seoul, Tokyo Coll. of Educ., Japan and Nat. Daedong Inst., Manchuria; Prof., Coll. of Educ., Seoul Nat. Univ. 1945–46; Dir Econ. Affairs Bureau, Ministry of Foreign Affairs 1951–52; Consul-Gen. Korean Mission, Japan 1952–57, Minister 1959; Vice-Minister of Foreign Affairs 1959–60; Amb. to Malaysia 1964–67; Minister of Foreign Affairs 1967–71; Special Pres. Asst for Foreign Affairs 1971–75; Acting Prime Minister 1975–76; Prime Minister 1976–79; Acting Pres. Oct.-Dec. 1979, Pres. 1979–80; Chief Korean del. to UN Gen. Assembly 1967, 1968, 1969; del. to numerous int. confs 1955–; Hon. LittD (Hankook Univ. of Foreign Studies, Seoul); decorations from Ethiopia, Panama, El Salvador, Malaysia, Saudi Arabia, Tunisia and Belgium; Order of Diplomatic Service Merit. *Leisure interest:* angling.

CHOJNACKA, Elisabeth, MA; French harpsichordist; b. 10 Sept. 1939, Warsaw, Poland; d. of Tadeusz Chojnacki and Edwarda Chojnacka; m. Georges Lesèvre 1966; ed Warsaw Acad. of Music, Ecole Supérieure de Musique and with Aimée van de Wiele, Paris; first recital of contemporary harpsichord, L'Arc, Paris 1971; interpreter of harpsichord works by many contemporary composers including Xenakis, Ligeti, Halffter, Donatoni, Ferrari, Bussotti, Górecki, Takemitsu etc.; many works for modern harpsichord written for her and dedicated to her; has created completely new repertoire for solo modern harpsichord; soloist with Orchestre de Paris, Cleveland and Minneapolis Orchestras 1974, Suisse Romande Orchestra 1979, Orchestre National de France 1981; Prof. of Contemporary Harpsichord, Mozarteum Acad. of Music, Salzburg 1995–; numerous tours in Europe, USA, Japan and Mexico; appearances at prin. festivals of contemporary music; master classes; collaborates with choreographer Lucinda Child 1991–; numerous recordings of classical and contemporary music; First Prize, Int. Harpsichord Competition, Vercelli, Italy 1968; Orphée Prize 1981, 2000, Grand Prix de la SACEM 1983; Chevalier Légion d'honneur, Officier des Arts et des Lettres, Croix d'Officier Ordre de Mérite pour la Pologne. *Publications:* articles in La Revue Musicale. *Leisure interests:* cinema, literature, dancing, genetics, astrophysics, theatre, ballet, paintings. *Address:* 17 rue Emile Dubois, 75014 Paris, France. *Telephone:* 1-45-89-52-82 (Office); 1-45-82-52-82. *Fax:* 1-45-65-31-90 (Office).

CHOMSKY, (Avram) Noam, MA, PhD; American theoretical linguist; b. 7 Dec. 1928, Pennsylvania; s. of William Chomsky and Elsie Simonofsky; m. Carol Schatz 1949; one s. two d.; ed Univ. of Pennsylvania; at MIT 1955–, Prof. of Modern Languages 1961–66, Ferrari Ward Prof. of Modern Languages and Linguistics 1966–, Inst. Prof. 1976–; Nat. Science Foundation Fellow, Princeton Inst. for Advanced Study 1958–59; American Council of Learned Socs. Fellow, Center for Cognitive Studies, Harvard Univ. 1964–65; mem. American Acad. of Arts and Sciences, Linguistic Soc. of America, American Philosophical Asscn, American Acad. of Political and Social Science, NAS, etc.; Corresp. Fellow, British Acad.; Hon. Fellow, British Psychological Soc. 1985, Royal Anthropological Inst.; Hon. DHL (Chicago) 1967, (Loyola Univ., Swarthmore Coll.) 1970, (Bard Coll.) 1971, (Mass.) 1973, (Maine, Gettysburg Coll.) 1992, (Amherst Coll.) 1995, (Buenos Aires) 1996; Hon. DLitt (London) 1967, (Delhi) 1972, Visva-Bharati (West Bengal) 1980, (Pa) 1984, (Cambridge) 1995; hon. degrees (Tarragona) 1998, (Guelph) 1999, (Columbia) 1999, (Connecticut) 1999, (Pisa) 1999, (Harvard) 2000, (Toronto) 2000, (Western Ontario) 2000, Kolkata (2001); George Orwell Award, Nat. Council of Teachers of English 1987, Kyoto Prize in Basic Sciences 1988, James Killian Award (MIT) 1992; Helmholtz Medal, Berlin Brandenburgische Akad. Wissenschaften 1996, Benjamin Franklin Medal, Franklin Inst., Philadelphia 1999, Rabindranath Tagore Centenary Award, Asiatic Soc. 2000, Peace Award, Turkish Publrs Asscn 2002. *Publications include:* Syntactic Structures 1957, Current Issues in Linguistic Theory 1964, Aspects of the Theory of Syntax 1965, Cartesian Linguistics 1966, Language and Mind 1968, The Sound Pattern of English (with Morris Halle) 1968, American Power and the New Mandarins 1969, At War with Asia 1970, Problems of Knowledge and

Freedom 1971, Studies on Semantics in Generative Grammar 1972, For Reasons of State 1973, The Backroom Boys 1973, Bains de Sang (trans. of Counter-revolutionary Violence) (with Edward Herman) 1974, Peace in the Middle East? 1974, Reflections on Language 1975, The Logical Structure of Linguistic Theory 1975, Essays on Form and Interpretation 1977, Human Rights and American Foreign Policy 1978, The Political Economy of Human Rights (2 Vols, with Edward Herman) 1979, Rules and Representations 1980, Lectures on Government and Binding 1981, Radical Priorities 1981, Towards a New Cold War 1982, Concepts and Consequences of the Theory of Government and Binding 1982, Fateful Triangle 1983, Knowledge of Language: Its Nature, Origins and Use 1986, Turning the Tide 1986, Barriers 1986, Pirates and Emperors 1986, On Power and Ideology 1987, Language and Problems of Knowledge 1987, Language in a Psychological Setting 1987, The Culture of Terrorism 1988, Generative Grammar 1988, Manufacturing Consent (with Edward Herman) 1988, The Chomsky Reader 1988, Necessary Illusions 1989, Language and Politics 1989, Deterring Democracy 1991, What Uncle Sam Really Wants 1992, Chronicles of Dissent 1992, Year 501 1993, Letters from Lexington 1993, The Prosperous Few and the Restless Many 1993, Language and Thought 1994, World Orders, Old and New 1994, The Minimalist Program 1995, Powers and Prospects 1996, Class Warfare 1996, The Common Good 1998, Profit over People 1998, The New Military Humanism 1999, New Horizons in the Study of Language and Mind 2000, Rogue States: The Rule of Force in World Affairs 2000, A New Generation Draws the Line 2000, Architecture of Language 2000, 9-11 2001, Understanding Power 2002, On Nature and Language 2002; numerous lectures. *Address:* Department of Linguistics and Philosophy, Massachusetts Institute of Technology, 77 Massachusetts Avenue, Cambridge, MA 02139 (Office); 15 Suzanne Road, Lexington, MA 02420, USA (Home). *Telephone:* (617) 253-7819 (Office); (781) 862-6160 (Home). *Fax:* (617) 253-9425 (Office). *E-mail:* chomsky@mit.edu (Office).

CHON CHOL HWAN, MA; South Korean banker and professor of economics; b. 6 Aug. 1938, Jeolla Buk-do Prov.; ed Seoul Nat. Univ., Victoria Univ. of Manchester, UK; Prof., Dept of Econs, Chungnam Nat. Univ. 1976–98, Dean Coll. of Econs and Man. 1991–93; mem. Monetary Bd, Bank of Korea 1983–89, Gov. Bank of Korea (Chair. Monetary Policy Cttee) 1998–2002; Pres. Soc. for Korean Econ. Devt 1995–96; Hon. PhD (Kunsan Nat. Univ.); 12th Dasan Econs Prize 1993. *Publications:* Social Justice and Economic Logic 1980, The Korean Economy 1986, An Introduction to International Economic Cooperation 1987, The Monetary History of Korea (1961–1990) 1991, Economics 1993. *Address:* c/o The Bank of Korea, 110, 3-ga, Namdaemun-no, Jung-gu, Seoul 100-794, Republic of Korea (Office).

CHONGWE, Rodger Masauso Alivas, LLB, SC; Zambian lawyer; b. 2 Oct. 1940, Chipata; m. Gwenda Fay Eaton 1967; one s. one d.; ed St Mark's Coll., Mapanza, Choma, Munali Secondary School, Lusaka, Univ. of Western Australia School of Law, Perth; Native Courts Asst and Dist Asst, Govt of Northern Rhodesia 1962–63; admitted to practise as barrister, solicitor and Proctor of the Supreme Court of Western Australia and the High Court of the Commonwealth of Australia 1968; admitted as solicitor and barrister before all courts, Zambia 1969; Asst Solicitor, Martin & Co., Lusaka 1969–70, partner 1979; partner, Mwisiya Chongwe & Co., Lusaka 1970–77; owner, RMA Chongwe & Co., Lusaka 1987–; apptd State Counsel 1985; mem. Industrial Relations Court of Zambia 1976–87; lecturer, Law Practice Inst. 1974–83, Examiner 1975–; Dir Tazama Pipelines Ltd 1974–89; Local Dir Jos Hansen & Soehne Zambia Ltd 1983–; Dir Standard Chartered Bank of Zambia Ltd 1985–; mem. Int. Bar Assn 1978–, mem. Council 1984–86; Councillor Law Assn of Zambia 1979, Vice-Chair. 1980, Chair. 1981–86, Councillor 1986–, Chair. Human Rights Cttee 1986–; Chair. African Bar Assn 1985–; mem. Council of Legal Educ. of Zambia 1982–; Commr Law Devt Comm. of Zambia 1981–; Exec. mem. Commonwealth Lawyers' Assn 1983–, Sec.-Gen. 1986, Pres. 1990–; Gov. Art Centre Foundation 1977–; Treasurer Int. Assn of Artists 1983–. *Publications:* numerous papers on legal topics, particularly concerning human rights, the legal profession and legal education. *Address:* Second Floor, Plot Number 9003, Corner Panganani and Chifinga Roads, P.O. Box 31190, Lusaka (Office); Subdivision 36, Farm Number 34A, Great East Road, Lusaka, Zambia (Home).

CHOPPIN, Purnell Whittington, MD; American scientist; b. 4 July 1929, Baton Rouge, La.; s. of Arthur Richard Choppin and Eunice Dolores (Bolin) Choppin; m. Joan H. Macdonald 1959; one d.; ed Louisiana State Univ.; Intern Barnes Hosp., St Louis 1953–54, Asst Resident 1956–57; Postdoctoral Fellow, Research Assoc., Rockefeller Univ., New York 1957–60, Asst Prof. 1960–64, Assoc. Prof. 1964–70, Prof., Sr Physician 1970–85, Leon Hess Prof. of Virology 1980–85, Vice-Pres. Acad. Programs 1983–85, Dean of Graduate Studies 1985; Vice-Pres., Chief Scientific Officer, Howard Hughes Medical Inst. 1985–87, Pres. 1987–99; Pres. Emer. 2000–; Virology 1973–82; Chair. Virology Study Section, Nat. Insts of Health 1975–78; mem. Bd of Dirs. Royal Soc. of Medicine Foundation Inc., New York 1978–93, Advisory Cttee on Fundamental Research, Nat. Multiple Sclerosis Soc. 1979–84 (Chair. 1983–84), Advisory Council Nat. Inst. of Allergy and Infectious Diseases 1980–83, Sloan-Kettering Cancer Cttee, New York 1983–84, Comm. on Life Sciences, Nat. Research Council 1982-87, Council for Research and Clinical Investigation, American Cancer Soc. 1983–85; Pres. American Soc. of Virology 1985–86; Fellow AAAS; mem. NAS (Chair. Class IV medical sciences 1983–86, Section 43 microbiology and immunology 1989–93), mem. council 2000–, mem. Governing Bd Nat. Research Council, NAS 1990–92; mem. council Inst. of Medicine 1986–92, Exec. Cttee 1988–91; mem. American

Philosophical Soc. (mem. council 1999–2001, Vice-Pres. 2000–); Assn of American Physicians, American Soc. of Microbiology, American Assn of Immunologists and other professional orgs.; numerous hon. degrees; Howard Taylor Ricketts Award, Univ. of Chicago 1978, Waksman Award for Excellence in Microbiology, NAS 1984. *Publications:* numerous articles and chapters on virology, cell biology, infectious diseases. *Leisure interests:* fly fishing and stamp collecting. *Address:* Howard Hughes Medical Institute, 4000 Jones Bridge Road, Chevy Chase, MD 20815 (Office); 2700 Calvert Street, NW, Washington, DC 20008, USA (Home).

CHOPRA, Deepak; writer. *Publications:* Return of the Rishi 1989, Quantum Healing 1990, Perfect Health 1990, Unconditional Life 1991, Creating Health 1991, Creating Affluence 1993, Ageless Body, Timeless Mind 1993, Restful Sleep 1994, Perfect Weight 1994, The Seven Spiritual Laws of Success 1995, The Path of Love 1996, How to Create Wealth 1999, Everyday Immortality: A Concise Course in Spiritual Transformation 1999, How to Know God: The Soul's Journey into the Mystery of Mysteries 2000. *Address:* Chopra Centre for Well Being, 7630 Fay Avenue, La Jolla, CA 92037, USA (Office).

CHORLEY, 2nd Baron, cr. 1945, of Kendal; **Roger Richard Edward Chorley,** FCA; British accountant; b. 14 Aug. 1930; s. of 1st Baron Chorley and Katharine Campbell Hopkinson; m. Ann Debenham 1964; two s.; ed Stowe School, Gonville and Caius Coll., Cambridge; joined Cooper Brothers & Co. (later Coopers & Lybrand) 1955, New York office 1959–60, Pakistan (Indus Basin Project) 1961, Partner 1967–89; Accounting Adviser to Nat. Bd.for Prices and Incomes 1965–68; Visiting Prof., Dept of Man. Sciences, Imperial Coll. of Science and Tech., London Univ. 1979–82; mem. Royal Comm. on the Press 1975–77, Finance Act 1960 Tribunal 1974–79, Ordnance Survey Review Cttee 1978–79, British Council Review Cttee 1979–80, Bd British Council 1981–99 (Deputy Chair. 1990–99), Top Salaries Review Body 1981–90, Ordnance Survey Advisory Bd 1983–85, House of Lords Select Cttee on Science and Tech. 1983, 1987, 1990, Select Cttee on Sustainable Devt 1994–95; elected mem. House of Lords 2001–; Chair. The National Trust 1991–96; fmr Pres. Cambridge Univ. Mountaineering Club, mem. expeditions Himalayas (Rakaposhi) 1954, (Nepal) 1957; Hon. Pres. Assn for Geographic Information 1995–; Vice-Pres. Council for Nat. Parks 1996–; Hon. Sec. Climbers' Club 1963–67; mem. Man. Cttee Mount Everest Foundation 1968–70; Pres. Alpine Club 1983–85; mem. Council Royal Geographical Soc. 1984–, Vice-Pres. 1986–87, Pres. 1987–90; mem. Finance Cttee Nat. Trust 1972–90, Exec. Cttee 1989–96; mem. Council, Royal Soc. of Arts 1987–89, City and Guilds of London Inst.; mem. Nat. Theatre Bd 1980–91; Hon. Fellow Royal Inst. of Chartered Surveyors; Hon. Fellow Central Lancs. Univ. 1993; Patron British Mountaineering Council 1996–; Hon. DSc (Reading, Kingston); Hon. LLD (Lancaster). *Leisure interest:* mountains. *Address:* 50 Kensington Place, London, W8 7PW, England (Home); House of Lords, London, SW1A 0PW.

CHORZEMPA, Daniel Walter, PhD; American pianist, organist, musicologist and composer; b. 7 Dec. 1944, Minneapolis; s. of Martin Chorzempa Sr and Henrietta Reiswig; ed Univ. of Minnesota; fmr church organist; Organ Instructor, Univ. of Minn. 1962–65; Fulbright Scholar, Cologne 1965–66; extensive piano and organ recitals in Germany, Denmark, Italy and UK 1968–; J. S. Bach Prize, Leipzig 1968. *Recordings:* major works of Liszt for Philips. *Leisure interests:* mathematics, architecture, poetry, renaissance history and literature. *Address:* 5000 Cologne 1, Grosse Budengasse 11, Germany. *Telephone:* 231271.

CHOU CHANG-HUNG, PhD; Taiwanese researcher and academic; b. 5 Sept. 1942, Tainan, Taiwan; s. of F. K. Chou and C. Y. Shih Chou; m. Ruth L. H. Yang Chou 1970; one s. one d.; ed Nat. Taiwan Univ., Taipei, Univ. of Calif., Santa Barbara, USA, Univ. of Toronto, Canada; Assoc. Research Fellow, Inst. of Botany, Academia Sinica, Taipei 1972–76, Research Fellow 1976–, Dir 1989–96; Prof. Dept of Botany, Nat. Taiwan Univ. 1976–; mem. various nat. cttees. for Int. Council of Scientific Unions (ICSU) 1974–; Sec. for Int. Affairs Academia Sinica 1988–, mem. Council Academia Sinica 1989–, Pacific Science Assn 1989; mem. Cttee for Science Educ. Ministry of Educ. 1986–, Cttee for Environmental Educ. 1991–, Cttee for Cultural and Natural Preservation Council of Agric. 1990; mem. Council Taiwan Livestock Research Inst. 1976–, Taiwan Forestry Research Inst. 1989–, Council Nat. Sustainable Devt 1997–; Dir Life Science Research Promotion Centre Nat. Science Council 1989–; Visiting Scholar, Oklahoma Univ., Univ. of Texas, Washington State Univ. 1979–80; Pres. Botanical Soc. of Repub. of China (Taiwan) 1983–84, Biological Soc. of Repub. of China (Taiwan) 1987–88; Chair. Nat. Cttee Int. Union of Biological Sciences (IUBS) 1990–, mem. Exec. Cttee of IUBS, Vice-Pres. IUBS 1997–; Chair. SCOPE Nat. Cttee; Ed. Botanical Bulletin Academia Sinica 1989–; Fellow Third World Acad. of Sciences; mem. Academia Sinica, Taipei; awards from Ministry of Educ. and Science Council of Taiwan. *Publications:* over 200 scientific papers, one univ. textbook. *Leisure interest:* listening to classical music. *Address:* 280 Yean Jiou Yuan Road, Sec. 2, Institute of Botany, Academia Sinica, Taipei, Taiwan 115. *Telephone:* (2) 2789-9590 (ext. 451); (2) 2651-0363. *Fax:* (2) 2782 7954.

CHOU CH'UEN; Taiwanese politician; founding mem. New Party Aug. 1993–; mem. Legis. Council 1995–. *Address:* New Party, 4th Floor, 65 Guang Fuh South Road, Taipei, Taiwan. *Telephone:* (2) 2756-2222.

CHOW, Sir C. K. (Chung Kong), Kt., MS, M.B.A., FIChemE; British (b. Hong Kong) business executive; b. 9 Sept. 1950; ed Univs of Wisconsin and California, Chinese Univ. of Hong Kong, Harvard Univ.; Research Engineer

Climax Chemical Co., New Mexico 1974–76; Process Engineer Sybron Asia Ltd, Hong Kong 1976–77; joined BOC Group 1977, with Hong Kong Oxygen, Hong Kong and BOC Australia 1977–84, Man. Dir Hong Kong Oxygen 1984–86, Pres. BOC Japan 1986–89, Group Man. Gases Business Devt, BOC Group PLC, UK and USA 1989–91, Regional Dir N Pacific, Tokyo and Hong Kong 1991–93, CEO Gases 1993–96, apptd. to Main Bd 1994, Man. Dir 1994–97; CEO GKN PLC 1997–2001, Brambles Industries Ltd 2001–; Dir (non-exec.) Standard Chartered PLC 1997–, Pres. 1999–2000, Deputy Pres. 2000–01; fmr Pres. Soc. of British Aerospace Cos.; mem. Governing Body London Business School. *Address:* Brambles Industries Ltd, Level 40, Gateway Building, 1 Maquarie Place, Sydney, NSW 2000, Australia (Office). *Telephone:* (2) 9256-5222 (Office). *Fax:* (2) 9256-5299 (Office).

CHOW MAN YIU, Paul; Chinese businessman; fmr Exec. Dir Sun Hung Kai Securities Ltd; CEO Hong Kong Securities Clearing Corpn 1990–91; fmr Dir Hong Kong Stock Exchange; CEO Hong Kong Stock Exchange Council 1991. *Address:* c/o The Stock Exchange of Hong Kong Ltd, 1/F One and Two Exchange Square, Central, Hong Kong Special Administrative Region, People's Republic of China.

CHOW YUN-FAT; Chinese film actor; b. 18 May 1955, Lamma Island; m. Jasmine Chow 1986; began acting career at TV station TVB, Hong Kong 1973, appearing in over 1,000 TV series. *Films include:* The Story of Woo Viet, A Better Tomorrow 1986, God of Gamblers 1989, The Killer 1989, Eighth Happiness, Once a Thief 1991, Full Contact 1992, Hard Boiled 1992, Peace Hotel 1995, Broken Arrow, Anna and the King 1999, Crouching Tiger, Hidden Dragon 2000, King's Ransom 2001, Bulletproof Monk 2001. *Address:* Chow Yun Fat International, P.O. Box 71288, Kowloon Central, Hong Kong Special Administrative Region, People's Republic of China (Office); c/o William Morris Agency, 151 El Camino Drive, Beverly Hills, CA 90212, USA.

CHOWDHURY, A. Q. M. Badruddoza, FRCPE, FRCP(CLAS), TDD; Bangladeshi head of state and practising surgeon; b. 1939; s. of the late Kafil Uddin Chowdhury; m.; one s. two d.; ed St Gregory High School, Dhaka Coll., Dhaka Medical Coll., Univ. of Wales, UK; practised as physician specializing in treatment of tuberculosis; Founding Sec.-Gen. Bangladesh Nationalist Party (BNP) 1978, fmr Deputy Leader; fmr Sr Deputy Prime Minister, Minister of Health and Family Planning, of Foreign Affairs; Pres. of Bangladesh 2001–; fmr Pres. Nat. Anti-Tuberculosis Asscn of Bangladesh, Int. Union Against Tuberculosis; led Bangladesh del. to World Health Conf., Geneva 1978, 1979 and many dels. to int. confs on tuberculosis and chest diseases; Hon. Fellow Coll. of Physicians and Surgeons (Bangladesh); Nat. TV Award 1976. *Publications:* many research papers in nat. and int. journals; essays and plays. *Address:* Office of the President, Dhaka (Office); Residence Bari Dhar, near Gulshan, Dhaka, Bangladesh (Home).

CHOWDHURY, Anwarul Karim, MA; Bangladeshi diplomatist; b. 5 Feb. 1943; m.; three c.; ed Univ. of Dhaka; Dir.-Gen. for S. and SE Asia, Foreign Ministry 1979–80, for Multilateral Econ. Co-operation 1986–90; Deputy Perm. Rep. to UN 1980–86, Perm. Rep. 1996–2001, Chair. Fifth Cttee (Admin. and Budgetary) of UN 1997–2000, High Rep. for Least Developed Countries 2002–; fmr Vice-Pres. Econ. and Social Council; UNICEF Dir for Japan, Australia and NZ 1990–93, Sec. Exec. Bd UNICEF, New York 1993–96 (Chair. Bd 1985–86). *Publications:* contribs. to journals on devt and human rights issues. *Address:* United Nations, New York, NY 10017, USA.

CHOWDHURY, Mizanur Rahman; Bangladeshi politician; b. 19 Oct. 1928, Chandpur; m. 1955; ed Feni Coll.; Headmaster, Bamoni High School 1952, Teacher, Chandpur Nuria High School 1956; Vice-Chair. Chandpur Municipality 1959; elected mem. Nat. Ass. of Pakistan 1962, 1965, 1970; Organising Sec. East Pakistan Wing, Awami League 1966, Acting Gen. Sec. 1966, 1967, organized Awami League election campaign 1970, Jt Convenor 1976; Minister of Information and Broadcasting 1972–73, Minister of Relief and Rehabilitation 1973; Minister of Posts and Telecommunications 1985–88; Prime Minister of Bangladesh 1986–88; Sr Vice-Chair. Jatiya Dal Party 1984, Gen. Sec. 1985–86. *Leisure interest:* reading. *Address:* c/o Prime Minister's Office, Old Sangsad Bhaban, Tejgaon, Dhaka, Bangladesh (Office).

CHRAÏBI, Driss; Moroccan/French novelist; b. Driss Chraïbi, 15 July 1926; s. of Haj Fatmi and Habiba Zwitten; m. 1st (dissolved); m. 2nd Sheena McCallion; five s.; ed Lycée Lyautey, Casablanca, Ecole de Chimie, Paris; various contribs to French radio; Prix France, Prix des Ecrivains de langue française, Grand Prix Atlas (Morocco), Prix Radio. *Publications:* Le Passé Simple 1954, Les Boucs 1955, Succession Ouverte 1962, Un Ami Viendra Vous Voir 1966, La Civilisation, Ma Mere! 1972, Mort au Canada 1975, Une Enquête au Pays 1981, La Mère du Printemps 1983, Naissance à l'Aube 1986, L'Inspecteur Ali 1991, Une Place au Soleil 1993, L'Homme du Livre 1995, L'Inspecteur Ali à Trinity College 1996, L'Inspecteur Ali et la C.I.A. 1997, Le Monde à Côté 2001. *Leisure interests:* music, crosswords, world travel. *Address:* 15 rue Paul Pons, 26400 Crest, France (Office); c/o Editions Denoël, 9 rue du Cherche-Midi, 75278 Paris Cedex 06. *Telephone:* (4) 75-76-74-66 (Home). *Fax:* (4) 75-76-74-66 (Home).

CHRAMOSTOVÁ, Vlasta; Czech actress and human rights activist; b. 17 Nov. 1926, Brno; m. Stanislav Milota 1971; ed Conservatoire of Music and Performing Arts, Brno; with The Free Theatre, Brno 1945, Municipal Theatre, Olomouc 1945–46, State Theatre Brno 1946–49, Theatre in Vinohrady, Prague 1950–69; mem., ensemble, Theatre behind the Gate 1970–72; banned from acting in public; signed Charter 77, Jan. 1977; appealed to artists in the West for support for Charter 77, 1977; Charter 77 activist 1977–89; sentenced to imprisonment for 3 months, sentence suspended on one-year-probation, April 1989; mem. Nat. Theatre Ensemble Prague 1990–91; joined Drama Co. of Nat. Theatre Prague 1991–; Merited Artist 1965, Czech Theatre Artists' Award 1967, Peace Prize awarded by Paul Lauritzen Foundation 1989, Hon. mem. Masaryk Democratic Movt 1990; Order of T. G. Masaryk 1998. *Publications:* Kniha pamětí (Memoirs) 1999. *Address:* Národni divadlo, Ostrovní 1, Prague 1, Nové Město; Čelakovského sady 10, Prague 2, 120 00, Czech Republic. *Telephone:* (224) 210892 (Office); (224) 225088 (Home).

CHRÉTIEN, Rt Hon Joseph Jacques Jean, PC, QC, BA, LLD; Canadian politician and lawyer; b. 11 Jan. 1934, Shawinigan; s. of Wellie Chrétien and Marie Boisvert; m. Aline Chaîné 1957; two s. one d.; ed Laval Univ., Québec; Dir, Bar of Trois-Rivières 1962; Liberal mem. House of Commons 1963–86; Parl. Sec. to Prime Minister 1965, to Minister of Finance 1966; Minister without Portfolio 1967–68, of Nat. Revenue Jan.–July 1968, of Indian Affairs and Northern Devt 1968–74; Pres. Treas. Bd 1974–76; Minister of Industry, Trade and Commerce 1976–77, of Finance 1977–79, of Justice, Attorney-Gen. of Canada and Minister of State for Social Devt 1980–82, of Energy, Mines and Resources 1982–84, Sec. of State for External Affairs, Deputy Prime Minister June–Sept. 1984; Prime Minister of Canada 1993–(2004); Legal Counsel, Lang, Michener, Laurence & Shaw, Ottawa, Toronto and Vancouver 1984–90; MP for Beauséjour 1990–93, for St. Maurice 1993–; Leader Nat. Liberal Party 1990–; Hon. LLD (Wilfred Laurier Univ.) 1981, (Laurentian Univ.) 1982, (W Ont.) 1982, (York Univ.) 1986, (Alberta) 1987, (Lakehead) 1988, (Ottawa) 1994, (Meiji) 1996; Hon. PhD (Warsaw School of Econs) 1999, (Michigan State Univ.) 1999, (Hebrew Univ.) 2000 (Memorial Univ.) 2000. *Publications:* Straight from the Heart 1985, Finding a Common Ground 1992. *Leisure interests:* skiing, fishing, golf. *Address:* Office of the Prime Minister, Langevin Block, Parliament Buildings, 80 Wellington Street, Ottawa, Ont. K1A 0A2, Canada (Office). *Telephone:* (613) 992-4211 (Office). *Fax:* (613) 941-6900 (Office). *E-mail:* pm@pm.gc.ca (Office). *Website:* www.pm.gc.ca (Office).

CHRÉTIEN, Raymond A.J., BA, LLL; Canadian diplomatist; b. 20 May 1942, Shawinigan, Quebec; s. of Maurice Chrétien and Cécile Chrétien (née Marcotte); m. Kay Rousseau; one s. one d.; ed Séminaire de Joliette and Univ. Laval; called to the Bar, Quebec 1966; mem. Legal Affairs Div., Div. External Affairs, Govt of Canada 1966–67, Policy Dir Industry, Investments and Competition 1981–82; Asst Under-Sec. for Manufacturing, Tech. and Transportation 1982–83; Insp.-Gen. 1983–85, Assoc. Under-Sec. of State for External Affairs 1988–91; Third Sec. Perm. Mission to UN, New York 1967–68; Asst Sec. Fed. and Provincial Relations Comm., Privy Council Office 1968–70, Exec. Asst to Sec., mem. Treasury Bd 1970–71; Exec. Asst to Pres., Canadian Int. Devt Agency 1971–72; First Sec. Canadian Embassy, Beirut 1972–75; First Sec., Counsellor, Canadian Embassy, Paris 1975–78; Amb. to Zaïre 1978–81, to Mexico 1985–88, to Belgium and Luxembourg 1991–94, to USA 1994–2001, to France 2000–; UN Sec.-Gen. Special Envoy to Central Africa 1996; Order of Aztec Eagle, Mexico; Hon. mem., Bar of US Court of Appeal for the Armed Forces 1988; Hon. DLitt (Brock) 1999; Hon. DJur (Laval) 2001, (State Univ. of New York) 2002. *Address:* Embassy of Canada, 35 ave Montaigne, 75008 Paris, France (Office). *Telephone:* 1-44-43-29-00. *Fax:* 1-44-43-29-99. *Website:* www.amb-canada.fr.

CHRISTENSEN, Helena; Danish model and photographer; b. Helena Christensen, 25 Dec. 1968, Copenhagen; d. of Flemming Christensen and Elsa Christensen; one s.; grad. in arithmetic and sociology course; fmr child model; began adult modelling career in Paris 1988; appeared on cover of British Vogue; has since worked as one of world's leading models in promotions for Versace, Rykiel, Chanel, Lagerfeld, Revlon, Dior, Prada etc.; has appeared on all maj. magazine covers working for photographers including Herb Ritts, Bruce Weber, Patrick DeMarchelier, Penn, Steven Meisel, Helmut Newton etc. *Leisure interests:* photography (black and white), oil/watercolour painting. *Address:* Marilyn's Agency, 4 rue de la Paix, Paris, France. *Telephone:* 1-53-29-53-53.

CHRISTENSEN, Kai; Danish architect; b. 28 Dec. 1916, Copenhagen; s. of late J. C. Christensen and Jenny Christensen; m. Kirsten Vittrup Andersen 1941 (died 1990); two d.; ed Royal Acad. of Fine Arts, Copenhagen; Dir, Technical Dept of Fed. of Danish Architects 1947–52; Man. Dir Danish Bldg Centre 1952–61; Attached to Danish Ministry of Housing 1961–86; Graphic Adviser to Govt Depts. 1986–; Chief, Scandinavian Design Cavalcade 1962–69; mem. Fed. of Danish Architects 1943, The Architectural Asscn, London 1955, life mem. 2000, Danish Cttee for Bldg Documentation 1950–79, Danish Soc. of History, Literature and Art 1969, Cttee mem. 1979, Vice-Pres. 1981, Pres. 1985–2001, Hon. Mem. 2001–; Cttee mem., Danish Soc. for Chamber Music 1989; Fellow Royal Soc. of Arts, London 1977; Sec.-Gen. Nordisk Byggedag (Scandinavian Bldg Conf.) VIII 1961, XIII 1971; Pres. Int. Conf. of Building Centres 1960, Danish Ministries Soc. of Art 1982–87; mem. Scandinavian Liaison Cttee concerning Govt Bldg 1963–72; associated Ed. Building Research and Practice/Bâtiment International (CIB magazine) 1968–85; Danish Design Council's Award for Industrial Graphics 1989; awards and prizes in public competition. *Major works:* designs for arts and crafts, graphic design, exhbns, furniture for the Copenhagen Cabinet Makers' exhbns. *Publications:* books about architecture, graphic design, humaniora and music; articles and treatises in technical magazines and daily press. *Leisure interests:* chamber music, chess, fencing. *Address:* 100 Vester Voldgade, DK-1552 Copenhagen V, Denmark. *Telephone:* (45) 33-12-13-37.

CHRISTENSEN, Søren, LLB; Danish civil servant; b. 31 Oct. 1940, Copenhagen; m. Inge Rudbeck 1964; ed Univ. of Copenhagen; sec. Secr. of Lord Mayor, Municipality of Copenhagen 1968–71, deputy office man. 1971–73; Head of Secr. Municipality of Randers 1973–78, CEO 1978–86; Perm. Under-Sec. Ministry of Finance 1986–94; Head of Danish Supreme Admin. Authority, Copenhagen 1994–97; Sec.-Gen. Nordic Council of Ministers 1997–2002. *Publication:* Info Society Year 2000 1994. *Leisure interests:* sailing, skiing. *Address:* c/o Nordic Council of Ministers, Store Strandstrasse 18, 1255 Copenhagen, Denmark.

CHRISTIE, Sir George William Langham, Kt, CH; British music administrator; b. 31 Dec. 1934; s. of John Christie, CH and Audrey Mildmay Christie; m. Patricia Mary Nicholson 1958; three s. one d.; ed Eton Coll.; Asst to Sec. of Calouste Gulbenkian Foundation 1957–62; Chair. Glyndebourne Productions 1956–99; mem. Arts Council of GB and Chair. Music Panel 1988–92; Founder Chair. of London Sinfonietta; Hon. mem. Guildhall School of Music and Drama 1991; DL; Hon. FRCM 1986; Hon. FRNCM 1986; Hon. DMus (Sussex) 1990, (Keele) 1993; Hon. DLitt (Exeter) 1994. *Address:* Old House, Moor Lane, Ringmer, E Sussex, BN8 5UR, England (Home).

CHRISTIE, Julie (Frances); British actress; b. 14 April 1940, Assam, India; d. of Frank St John Christie and Rosemary Christie (née Ramsden); ed Brighton Technical Coll. and Central School of Speech and Drama; Dr hc (Warwick) 1994; Motion Picture Laurel Award, Best Dramatic Actress 1967, Motion Picture Herald Award 1967; Fellow BAFTA 1997. *Films include:* Crooks Anonymous 1962, The Fast Lady 1962, Billy Liar 1963, Young Cassidy 1964, Darling 1964 (Acad. Award 1966), Doctor Zhivago (Donatello Award) 1965, Fahrenheit 451 1966, Far From the Madding Crowd 1966, Petulia 1967, In Search of Gregory 1969, The Go-Between 1971, McCabe & Mrs. Miller 1972, Don't Look Now 1973, Shampoo 1974, Demon Seed, Heaven Can Wait 1978, Memoirs of a Survivor 1980, Gold 1980, The Return of the Soldier 1981, Les Quarantièmes rugissants 1981, Heat and Dust 1982, The Gold Diggers 1984, Miss Mary 1986, The Tattooed Memory 1986, Power 1987, Fathers and Sons 1988, Dadah is Death (TV) 1988, Fools of Fortune 1989, McCabe and Mrs Miller 1990, The Railway Station 1992, Hamlet 1995, Afterglow 1998, The Miracle Maker (voice) 2000. *Plays:* Old Times 1995, Suzanna Andler 1997, Afterglow 1998. *Address:* c/o ICM Ltd, Oxford House, 76 Oxford Street, London, W1D 1BS, England (Office).

CHRISTIE, Linford, OBE; British athlete and business executive; b. 2 April 1960, St Andrew's, Jamaica; s. of James Christie and of the late Mabel Christie; one d.; fmr cashier Wandsworth Co-op; mem. Thames Valley Harriers; winner, UK 100m 1985, 1987, 200m 1985 (tie), 1988; winner, Amateur Athletics Asscn 100m. 1986, 1988, 200m 1988; winner, European 100m record; silver medallist, 100m, Seoul Olympic Games 1988, Winner 100m gold medal, Commonwealth Games 1990, Olympic Games 1992, World Athletic Championships 1993, Weltklasse Grand Prix Games 1994, European Games 1994; winner 100m. Zurich 1995; Capt. of British Athletics Team 1995–97; officially retd 1997; banned for two years for misuse of drugs 2000; Co-Founder (with Colin Jackson, and Man. Dir Nuff Respect sports man. co. 1992–; successful coach to prominent UK athletes including Katharine Merry; Hon. MSc (Portsmouth Univ.) 1993; Male Athlete of the Year 1988, 1992; BBC Sports Personality of the Year 1993. *Publications:* Linford Christie (autobiog.) 1989, To be Honest With You 1995, A Year in the Life of Linford Christie 1996. *Leisure interests:* cooking and gardening. *Address:* c/o Susan Barrett, Nuff Respect, The Coach House, 107 Sherland Road, Twickenham, Middx, TW9 4HB, England. *Telephone:* (20) 8891-4145. *Website:* www.nuff-respect.co.uk.

CHRISTIE, Rt. Hon. Perry Gladstone, LLB; Bahamian politician; b. 21 Aug. 1943, Nassau; s. of Gladstone L. Christie and Naomi Christie; m. Bernadette Hanna; two s. one d.; ed Govt High School and Univ. of Birmingham, UK; attorney with McKinney Bancroft and Hughes; f. own law practice Christie Ingraham & Co. (now Christie Davis & Co.); mem. Bd Dirs Broadcasting Corpn of The Bahamas 1973; mem. Progressive Liberal Party (PLP), Leader 1997–; Senator 1974; mem. House of Ass. (PLP) for Centerville and Farm Road, New Providence; served as Minister for Health, Housing and Nat. Insurance, Tourism and Agric., Trade and Industry; Prime Minister and Minister of Finance 2002–. *Address:* Office of the Prime Minister, Sir Cecil V. Wallace-Whitfield Centre, POB CB-10980, Nassau, Bahamas (Office). *Telephone:* 327-5826 (Office). *Fax:* 327-5806 (Office). *E-mail:* info@opm.gov.bs. *Website:* www.opm.gov.bs.

CHRISTIE, William Lincoln, BA; French (b. American) harpsichordist, conductor and musicologist; b. 19 Dec. 1944, Buffalo, NY; s. of William Christie and Ida Jones; ed Harvard Univ., Yale School of Music; studied harpsichord with Ralph Kirkpatrick, Kenneth Gilbert and David Fuller; moved to France 1971; mem. Five Centuries Ensemble 1971–75, René Jacobs' Concerto vocale 1976–80; f. Les Arts Florissants vocal and instrumental ensemble 1979; Prof., Conservatoire Nat. Supérieur de Musique, Paris 1982–95; conducts many leading int. orchestras; recent career highlights include: Handel's Theodora, Glyndebourne 1996, Handel's Semele, Aix-en-Provence Festival 1996, Rameau's Hippolyte et Aricie, Paris 1996/97, Lully's Thésée, Barbican, London 1998, Monteverdi's Il ritorno d'Ulisse in patria, Aix-en-Provence 2000; conducted the Berlin Philharmonie and led Le jardin des voix, new workshop for young singers, followed by European tour 2002; Chevalier Légion d'honneur 1993, Officier des Arts et des Lettres, Prix Edison, Netherlands 1981, Grand prix du disque, Prix mondial de Montreux, Switzerland 1982, Gramophone Record of the Year, UK 1984, 1995, 1997,

Deutscher Schallplattenpreis 1987, Grand prix de la Critique (best opera performance) 1987, Prix Opus, USA 1987, Prix int. de musique classique 1992, Prix Grand siècle Laurent Perrier 1997, Grammy Award for Handel's Acis and Galatea 2000, Grammy and Cannes Classical Awards for Alcina 2001; Hon.DMus (New York) 1999. *Recordings:* numerous recordings including all works for harpsichord by Rameau, works by Monteverdi, Purcell, Handel, Couperin, Charpentier, Desmarest, Mozart, etc. *Leisure interests:* gardening, old houses. *Address:* Les Arts Florissants, 2 rue Saint-Pétersbourg, 75008 Paris (Office); 81 avenue Victor Hugo, 75116 Paris (Home); Le Bâtiment, Thiré, 85210 Sainte-Hermine, France (Home). *E-mail:* w.christie@wanadoo.fr. *Website:* www.arts-florissants.com.

CHRISTMAN, Luther Parmalee, PhD; American professor of nursing and sociology; b. 26 Feb. 1915, Summit Hill, PA; s. of Elmer and Ellen (née Barnicott) Christman; m. Dorothy M. Black 1939; one s. two d.; ed Pennsylvania Hosp. School, Philadelphia, Temple, Michigan State and Thomas Jefferson Univs; Prof. of Sociology Coll. of Arts and Sciences, Vanderbilt Univ., Nashville, Tenn. 1967–72, Dir of Nursing, Dean Coll. of Nursing, Vanderbilt Univ. Hosp. 1967–72, Adjunct Prof. Vanderbilt Univ. 1991–; Vice-Pres. Nursing Affairs, Rush-Presbyterian-St Luke's Medical Center; Dean Coll. of Nursing, Rush Univ. 1971–77, Dean Emer. 1977–87; Sr Adviser Center for Nursing, American Hosp. Asscn 1989; Pvt. consulting service 1989–; Pres. Christman-Cornesky and Assocs 1990–97; Fellow Nat. League for Nursing 1950–60, American Acad. of Arts and Sciences; Visiting Fellow, NZ Nurses' Educ. and Research Foundation 1978; Dr hc HLD (Thomas Jefferson) 1980, Hon. DSc (Grand Valley State) 1998; Distinguished Alumnus Award (Temple) 1996, (Rush) 1997, (Michigan) 1999; Jesse M. Scott Award, American Nurses' Asscn 1988, Living Legend Award, American Acad. of Nursing 1995; several other awards. *Publications:* Interpersonal Behavior and Health Care (with Michael Counte) 1981, Hospital Organization and Health Care Delivery (with Michael Counte) 1981, Effects of Clinical Nursing Specialization (with Basil Georgopolous) 1990. *Leisure interest:* horticulture. *Address:* 5535 Nashville Highway, Chapel Hill, TN 37304, USA (Home). *Telephone:* (931) 364-7660. *Fax:* (931) 364-3188. *E-mail:* lchristman@united.net.

CHRISTO AND JEANNE-CLAUDE, (Christo Javacheff) and (Jeanne-Claude de Guillebon); American (naturalized) artists; b. 13 June 1935, Gabrovo, Bulgaria and Casablanca; one s.; ed Univ. of Tunis, Acad. of Fine Arts, Sofia; Christo went to Paris 1958; works include: Wrapped Objects 1958; project for Packaging of Public Building 1961; Iron Curtain Wall of Oil Barrels blocking rue Visconti, Paris; Wrapping a Girl, London 1962; Showcases 1963; Store Front 1964; Air Package and Wrapped Tree, Eindhoven, Netherlands 1966; 42,390 cu. ft. Package, Walker Art Center, Minneapolis School of Art 1966; Wrapped Kunsthalle, Bern 1968; 5,600 cu. m. Package for Kassel Documenta 4 1968; Wrapped Museum of Contemporary Art, Chicago 1969; Wrapped Coast, Little Bay, Sydney, Australia, 1 m. sq. ft. 1969; Valley Curtain, Grand Hogback, Rifle, Colorado, suspended fabric curtain 1970–72; Running Fence, Calif. 1972–76; Wrapped Roman Wall, Rome 1974; Ocean Front, Newport 1974; Wrapped Walk-Ways, Kansas City 1977–78; Surrounded Islands, Biscayne Bay, Miami, Florida 1980–83; The Pont Neuf Wrapped, Paris 1975–85; The Umbrellas, Japan-USA 1984–91; Wrapped Reichstag, Berlin 1971–95; Wrapped Trees, Fondation Beyeler and Berower Park, Riehen, Switzerland 1997–98; The Wall, 13,000 oil barrels, Gasometer, Oberhausen, Germany, indoor installation 1999; Praemium Imperiale 1995. *Fax:* (212) 966-2891.

CHRISTODOULAKIS, Nikos M.; Greek politician; ed Nat. Tech. Univ. of Athens and Univ. of Cambridge, UK; fmr mem. Euro-Communist party, linked with student uprising at Athens polytechnic 1973; Sr Research Officer, Dept of Applied Econs, Univ. of Cambridge 1984–86; Fellow European Univ. of Florence 1989–90; fmr Prof. of Econ. Analysis, Athens Univ. of Econs, Vice-Rector 1992–94; fmr Visiting Research Fellow, London Business School, Tinbergen Inst.; Prof. of Econs., Grad. School, Charles Univ., Prague 1992–93; Prof. of Econs, Univ. of Cyprus 1996; Sec.-Gen. Research and Tech. 1993–96; Econ. Adviser to Prime Minister 1996; Deputy Minister of Finance 1996–2000; Minister of Devt with portfolios of Energy, Industry, Tech., Tourism and Commerce 2000–01; Minister of Economy and Finance 2001–. *Publications include:* several books and articles on econ. policy, business cycles, growth, forecasting and econ. models. *Leisure interest:* art. *Address:* Ministry of Economy and Finance, Odos Karageorgi, Servias 10, 10562 Athens, Greece (Office). *Telephone:* (1) 08477116 (Office). *Fax:* (1) 03238657 (Office). *E-mail:* ypetho@mnec.gr (Office). *Website:* www.ypetho.gr (Office).

CHRISTODOULOU, Christodoulos, PhD; Cypriot central bank governor and politician; b. 13 April 1939, Avgorou; m.; one d.; ed Pedagogical Acad. of Cyprus, Nicosia, Pantios High School of Political Sciences, Athens and Aristotelian Univ. of Salonica, Greece, Univ. of Wales, UK; began career as school teacher 1962; joined Publs Section, Press and Information Office 1964, Dir Govt Printing Office 1968–85; Perm. Sec. Ministry of Labour and Social Insurance 1985–89; served in Ministry of Agric. and Natural Resources 1989–94; Minister of Finance 1994–99, of the Interior 1999–2002; Gov. of Cen. Bank of Cyprus May 2002–; mem. Gen. Council of Cyprus Civil Servants Trade Union 1978–, Exec. Cttee 1980–85; Chair. Br. Dirs of Govt Depts 1982–85; Chair. Bd Dirs Human Resource Devt Authority of Cyprus 1985–89; Rep. of Cyprus to ILO 1985–87; Govt Del. to Int. Labour Conf. 1985–89; del. to numerous other int. orgs including FAO, IBRD, IMF, The Commonwealth. *Leisure interests:* reading, gardening. *Address:* Central Bank of Cyprus, POB

25529, 80 Kennedy Avenue, 1395 Nicosia, Cyprus (Office). *Telephone:* (7) 22714471 (Office). *Fax:* (7) 22378151 (Office). *E-mail:* chr.c.christodoulou@centralbank.gov.cy (Office). *Website:* www.centralbank.gov.cy (Office).

CHRISTOFIDES, Manolis; Cypriot government official and lawyer; b. 1 Feb. 1941, Lefka; m.; two d.; ed Pancyprian Gymnasium and Univ. of Athens; leading mem. of Youth Org. of EOKA during Cyprus liberation struggle 1955–59; reserve officer with rank of Lt; served in area of Morphou-Lefka during Turkish invasion 1974; fmr Chair. Nicosia Bar Asscn; Chair. Cyprus Bar Council 1982–88; mem. Bd Cyprus Broadcasting Corpn 1971–79; Founding mem. Democratic Rally Party, f. party's Youth Org. (NEDISY), Chair. for 10 years, now Hon. Pres.; mem. Parl. 1981–91; Minister of Health 1993–97; Govt. Spokesperson 1997–98; Presidential Commr. 1998–; Grand Commdr of Honour (Hellenic Repub.), Grand Commdr Order of the Orthodox Kts. of the Holy Sepulchre (Patriarch of Jerusalem). *Address:* Presidential Palace, Nicosia (Office); 23 Armenias Street, Flat 502, Strovolos, Nicosia, Cyprus (Home). *Telephone:* 867429 (Office); 312312 (Home). *Fax:* 513605 (Office); 513110 (Home).

CHRISTOPHER, Ann, BA, RA, FRBS, RWA; British sculptor; b. 4 Dec. 1947, Watford, Herts.; d. of late William Christopher and of Phyllis Christopher; m. Kenneth Cook 1969; ed Watford Girls' Grammar School, Harrow School of Art, West of England Coll. of Art; works include bronze sculpture, Castle Park, Bristol 1993, Corten sculpture, Marsh Mills, Plymouth 1996, Bronze Sculpture for offices of Linklaters and Paines solicitors, London 1997, Bronze Sculpture, Great Barrington, USA 1998, Corten Sculpture, Port Marine, UK 2001; works in Redfern Gallery, London, Ann Kendall Richards Inc., New York; RBS Silver Medal for sculpture of outstanding merit 1994, Frampton Award 1996, Otto Beit Medal for Sculpture of outstanding merit 1997. *Solo exhibitions:* Redfern Gallery, London 1997, Courcoux & Courcoux 1999. *Publications:* Sculpture and Drawings 1969–89, Sculpture 1989–94. *Leisure interests:* cinema, travel, architecture. *Address:* Stable Block, Hay Street, Marshfield, Nr. Chippenham, SN14 8PF, England. *Telephone:* (1225) 891717. *Fax:* (1225) 891717.

CHRISTOPHER, Sir (Duncan) Robin (Carmichael), Kt, KBE, CMG; British diplomatist; b. 13 Oct. 1944, Sussex; m. Merril Stevenson 1980; two d.; ed Keble Coll., Oxford and Tufts Univ., USA; spent year teaching in Bolivia with VSO; teacher, Philosophy Dept, Univ. of Sussex 1969; joined FCO 1970; Second then First Sec., New Delhi 1972–76; First Sec. (Financial Relations Dept on North–South Dialogue and later News Dept as Spokesperson on Europe), FCO 1976; Deputy High Commr, Lusaka 1980–83; First Sec., FCO (Western Europe) 1983–87; on secondment to Cabinet Office 1985; Econ. and Commercial Counsellor, Madrid 1987–91; Head Southern African Dept, FCO 1991–94; Amb. to Ethiopia 1994–97, to Indonesia 1997–2000, to Argentina 2000–. *Address:* British Embassy, Dr. Luis Agote 2412/52, 1425, Buenos Aires, Argentina (Office). *Telephone:* (11) 4803-7070 (Office). *Fax:* (11) 4806-5713 (Office). *E-mail:* ukembarg@starnet.ar (Office). *Website:* www.britain.org.ar (Office).

CHRISTOPHER, Warren M.; American politician and lawyer; b. 27 Oct. 1925, Scranton, ND; s. of Ernest Christopher and Catharine Christopher; m. Marie Wyllis 1956; three s. one d.; ed Univ. of Southern California, Stanford Law School; served in USNR 1943–45; mem., O'Melveny and Myers law firm, LA 1950–67, 1969, partner 1958–67, 1969–76, 1981–93, Sr Partner 1997–; special consultant on foreign econ. problems to Under-Sec. of State George Ball 1961–65; a trade negotiator in Kennedy Admin.; Deputy Attorney-Gen. in Johnson Admin.; Deputy Sec. of State in Carter Admin. (chief negotiator for Panama Canal treaties, supervisor human rights policies abroad, negotiated for release of U.S. hostages in Iran 1980) 1977–81; Chair. comm. to review conduct of LA Police Dept in Rodney King case 1991; Sec. of State 1993–97; Past-Pres. LA Co. Bar Asscn; fmr Dir LA World Affairs Council, mem. Trilateral Comm.; several hon. degrees; Medal of Freedom 1981. *Publications:* In the Stream of History 1998, Chances of a Lifetime 2000. *Address:* O'Melveny and Myers, 1999 Avenue of the Stars, Floor 7, Los Angeles, CA 90067, USA.

CHRISTOPHERSEN, Henning, M.ECON.; Danish politician; b. 8 Nov. 1939, Copenhagen; s. of Richard Christophersen and Gretha Christophersen; m. Jytte Risbjerg Nielsen 1961; one s. two d.; ed Univ. of Copenhagen; Head of the Economic Section of the Handicrafts Council 1965–70; mem. Folketing 1971–84, mem. of Parl. Finance Cttee 1972–76, Vice-Chair. 1976–78, Minister of Foreign Affairs 1978–79; Deputy Leader, Danish Liberal Party 1972, Acting Party Leader 1977–78, Party Leader 1978–84; Deputy Prime Minister and Minister of Finance 1982–84; Vice-Pres. Comm. responsible for Budget, Financial Control, Personnel and Admin., Comm. of European Communities (now European Comm.) 1985–89, Econ. and Financial Affairs 1989–95, Co-ordination of Structural Funds 1989–92; a Vice Pres. of EC (now EU) 1993–95; currently Chair. European Inst. of Public Admin., Netherlands; mem. Bd of Dirs. Den Danske Bank, Int. Advisory Bd Creditanstalt-Bankverein, Austria, European Advisory Cttee on the Opening-up of Public Procurement, Danish Council for European Policy and the Baltic Sea Council, Sweden; Nat. Order of Merit. *Publications:* En udfordring for de Liberale, Taenker om Danmark i Det Nye Europa 1989 and numerous articles on econs. *Leisure interests:* genealogy, history and languages. *Address:* Avenue des Biches, 1930 Kraainem, Belgium.

CHROMY, Bronisław; Polish sculptor; b. 3 June 1925, Leńcze nr Lanckorona; m.; two d.; ed Acad. of Fine Arts, Cracow 1956; one-man exhbns. in Poland and abroad; int. exhbns and competitions; creator of many monuments commemorating victims of World War II; mem. Polish Acad. of Arts and Sciences, Cracow; mem. Union of Polish Artists and Designers 1970–; Meritorious Medal for Nat. Culture 1986, Commdr Cross with Star Order of Polonia Restituta 1999. *Achievements:* some works permanently in museums and pvt collections; sculptures include: Pieta Oświęcimska (Monument) 1963, Smok wawelski, Cracow 1970, Pomnik Żołniercy Polskich (Monument to Polish Soldiers), Katowice 1978, Pomnik jana Pawła II (Monument to John Paul II), Tarnów 1981, Zielonki nr Cracow 1998. *Leisure interests:* music, literature, nature. *Address:* ul. Halki 5, 30-228 Cracow, Poland.

CHRONOWSKI, Andrzej; Polish politician; b. 9 April 1961, Grybów, Nowy Sącz Prov.; m. Barbra Chronowski; two s.; ed Acad. of Mining and Metallurgy, Cracow; railway repair factory, Nowy Sącz 1987, production line specialist, head Employees' Council; mem. Solidarity Trade Union; Senator 1993–; Sec. Solidarity Senate Club Presidium 1993–97; Vice-Marshal of Senate 1997–; Chair. Nowy Sącz Region of Social Movt of Solidarity Election Action (RS AWS) 1997–; mem. Nat. Econ. Cttee, Cttee for Human Rights and Lawfulness, Cttee of Initiatives and Legislative Work. *Leisure interests:* skiing, climbing, time with family. *Address:* Biuro Senatorskie Andrzeja Chronowskiego, ul. Pijarska 17a, 33–300 Nowy S5C2 (Office); Kancelaria Senatu RP, ul. Wiejska 6, 00-902 Warsaw, Poland. *Telephone:* (22) 6941650 (Office). *Fax:* 6941650 (Office). *E-mail:* senator@chronowski.pl (Office); kolago@nw.senat.gov.pl (Office). *Website:* www.senat.gov.pl (Office).

CHRYSOSTOMOS, Archbishop; Cypriot Orthodox ecclesiastic; b. 27 Sept. 1927, Statos, Paphos; ed Univ. of Athens; Archbishop of Nova Justiniana and all Cyprus. *Address:* P.O. Box 1130, Archbishop Kyprianos Street, Nicosia, Cyprus (Office). *Telephone:* (2) 2430696 (Office). *Fax:* (2) 2432470 (Office).

CHRYSSA; American artist; b. 1933, Athens; ed Acad. Grand Shaumière, Paris and San Francisco School of Fine Arts; one-woman shows, Solomon Guggenheim Museum, New York 1961, Museum of Modern Art, New York 1963, Walker Art Centre, Minneapolis 1968, Whitney Museum of Modern Art, New York 1972, Musée d'Art Contemporain, Montreal 1974, Musée d'Art Moderne de la Ville de Paris 1979, Nat. Pinacotheque Museum Alexander Soutsos, Athens 1980, Albright-Knox Gallery, Buffalo 1982, Leo Castelli Gallery 1988 and at galleries in New York, Boston, San Francisco, Paris, Cologne, Düsseldorf, Zurich, Turin and Athens since 1961; work has also appeared in many group exhbns. and belongs to numerous public collections in USA and Europe; Guggenheim Fellowship 1973; CAVS, MIT 1979. *Address:* c/o Albright-Knox Art Gallery, 1285 Elmwood Avenue, Buffalo, New York, NY 14222, USA.

CHRZANOWSKI, Wiesław Marian; Polish politician and lawyer; b. 20 Dec. 1923, Warsaw; s. of Wiesław Chrzanowski and Izabela Chrzanowska; ed Jagiellonian Univ., Cracow, M.Curie-Skłodowska Univ., Lublin; during Nazi occupation active in resistance Movt, mem. Nat. Party (Bd bi-weekly Młoda Polska 1942–45), served Home Army 1942–44, Warsaw Uprising 1944; Pres. clandestine Law Students' Asscn 1942–43; Asst, Sr Asst Civil Law Dept in Warsaw Univ. and Cen. School of Commerce, Warsaw 1945–48; arrested and sentenced to 8 years for attempting to overthrow regime 1948–54, acquitted and rehabilitated 1956; legal counsellor 1955–72; attorney's trainee 1957–60, attorney 1981–90; researcher 1972–79, Asst Prof. 1980–88, Prof. 1988, Cooperative Research Inst.; Asst Prof. Catholic Univ. of Lublin 1982–87, Prof. 1987–, Deputy Dean Canon and Secular Law Faculty 1987–90; mem. informal information group of Primate of Poland 1965–81; mem. Social Council of Primate of Poland 1983–84; mem. Episcopal Comm. for Agric. 1982–86; mem. on behalf of Episcopate of team drawing up convention between Holy See and Poland and Law on State-Church Relations 1987–89; mem. Solidarity Trade Union 1980–89 (adviser to Nat. Comm., plenipotentiary for registration by Voivodship and Supreme Court 1980–81); mem. Labour Party 1945–46, Christian-Nat. Union 1989– (Chair. Main Bd 1989–94); Chair. Supreme Council 1995–98, 2000–01; Minister of Justice and Attorney-Gen. Jan.–Dec. 1991; Deputy to Sejm (Parl.) 1991–93, Marshal (Speaker) of Sejm 1991–93; Senator 1997–2001. *Publications:* over 100 books and articles on civil law and cooperative law, many contribs. in underground journals and Polish journals appearing abroad. *Leisure interests:* reading, history (19th and 20th century), sociology, theatre, mountain hiking. *Address:* ul. Solec 79a/82, 00-402 Warsaw, Poland. *Telephone:* (22) 629-30-88.

CHU, Steven, BA, PhD; American physicist; b. 28 Feb. 1948, St Louis; s. of Ju Chin Chu and Ching Chen Li; two s.; ed Univ. of Rochester, Univ. of Calif., Berkeley; post-doctoral fellow Univ. of Calif., Berkeley 1976–78; with Bell Labs., Murray Hill, NJ 1978–83; Head Quantum Electronics Research Dept AT&T Bell Labs., Holmdell, NJ 1983–87; Prof. of Physics and Applied Physics, Stanford Univ. 1987–, Frances and Theodore Geballe Prof. of Physics and Applied Physics 1990–, Chair. Physics Dept 1990–93; Visiting Prof. Collège de France 1990; Fellow American Physics Soc. (Chair. Laser Science Topical Group 1989), Optical Soc. of America, American Acad. of Arts and Sciences; Woodrow Wilson Fellow 1970, NSF Doctoral Fellow 1970–74; mem. NAS, Academia Sinica; awarded Herbert P. Broida Prize for laser spectroscopy 1987, King Faisal Prize for Science 1993, Schawlow Prize 1994, Meggars Award 1994, Humboldt Sr Scientist Award 1995, Science for Art Prize 1995, shared Nobel Prize for Physics 1997 for developing methods of cooling matter to very low temperatures using lasers. *Publications:* numerous papers on atomic physics and laser spectroscopy. *Address:* Department of Physics, Stanford University, Stanford, CA 94305, USA.

CHU HUY MAN, Gen.; Vietnamese politician and soldier; b. 1913, Nghe An Province; one s. three d.; Col in Viet Nam People's Army 1950; Commdr of Dien Bien Phu 1954; mem. Cen. Cttee of Lao Dong Party; promoted to Maj.-Gen., Chief Commdr in Western Highlands 1960–75; mem. Politburo of CP of Viet Nam 1976–; promoted to Gen., Dir of Political Dept of Viet Nam People's Army 1976–; Vice-Pres. Council of State 1981–86; promoted to four-star Gen. 1982; Adviser to Ministry of Defence 1986–. *Address:* 36 A Ly Nam De, Hanoi, Viet Nam.

CHU KAO-CHENG; Taiwanese politician; fmr Leader New Party; mem. for Kao-hsiung, Legisl. Council 1995–. *Address:* New Party, 4th Floor, 65 Guang Fuh South Road, Taipei, Taiwan. *Telephone:* (2) 2756-2222. *Fax:* (2) 2756-5750. *E-mail:* npncs@ms2.hinet.net (Office). *Website:* www.np.org.tw (Office).

CHU PO; Chinese politician; b. Oct. 1944, Tongcheng, Anhui Prov.; ed Tianjin Univ.; joined CCP 1969; Vice-Sec. CCP Hu'nan Prov. Cttee 1994–99; Gov. Hu'nan Prov. 1999–2001; Sec. CCP Cttee of Inner Mongolian Autonomous Region 2001. *Address:* Chinese Communist Party Committee of Inner Mongolian Autonomous Region, Huhot, Inner Mongolia, People's Republic of China (Office).

CHUA, Nam-Hai, PhD, FRS; Singaporean plant molecular and cell biologist; b. 8 April 1944; m. Suat-Choo Pearl Chua 1970; two d.; ed Univ. of Singapore and Harvard Univ.; lecturer, Dept of Biochemistry, Univ. of Singapore 1969–71; Research Assoc. Dept of Cell Biology, Rockefeller Univ. 1971–73, Asst Prof. Dept of Cell Biology 1973–77, Prof. and Head, Lab. of Plant Molecular Biology 1988–, Andrew W. Mellon Prof. 1988–; consultant Shanghai Research Centre for Life Sciences, Chinese Acad. of Science 1996–, Global Tech. Centre and Nutrition, Monsanto Co. 1997–; numerous consultancies and bd memberships. *Publications:* over 260 scientific publs. *Leisure interests:* squash, skiing. *Address:* Laboratory of Plant Molecular Biology, Rockefeller University, 1230 York Avenue, New York, NY 10021, USA. *Telephone:* (212) 327-8126.

CHUAN LEEKPAI, LLB; Thai politician; b. 28 July 1938, Muang Dist., Trang Prov.; ed Trang Wittaya School and Thammasat Univ.; studied for two years with Bar Assen of Thailand; mem. Parl. for Trang Prov. 1969–; Deputy Minister of Justice 1975; Minister of Justice and Minister, Prime Minister's Office 1976; Minister of Justice 1980; Minister of Commerce 1981, of Agric. and Co-operatives 1982–83, of Educ. 1983–86, of Public Health 1988–89, of Agric. and Co-operatives 1990–91; Deputy Prime Minister 1990, Prime Minister of Thailand 1992–95, 1997–2001; Leader Prachatipat (Democrat Party—DP); Leader of Opposition 1995–96, 1996–97, 2001–; Minister of Defence 1997–2001; Vice-Pres. Prince of Songkhla Univ. Council; 6 hon. degrees; Kt Grand Cordon of the Most Noble Order of the Crown of Thailand 1981, Kt Grand Cordon (Special Class) of the Most Exalted Order of the White Elephant 1982, Order of Sukatuna (Special Class), Raja, Philippines 1993, Kt Grand Commdr (2nd Class, Higher Grade) of the Most Illustrious Order of Chula Chom Klao 1998, Order of the Sun (Grand Cross), Peru 1999. *Address:* Prachatipat (Democratic Party), 67 Thanon Setsiri, Samsen Nai, Phyathai, 10400, Bangkok 10300, Thailand (Office). *Telephone:* (2) 278-4042 (Office). *Fax:* (2) 279-6086. *E-mail:* admin@democrat.or.th (Office). *Website:* www.democrat.or.th (Office).

CHUBAIS, Anatoly Borisovich, CEconSc; Russian politician and economist; b. 16 June 1955, Borizov, Minsk Region; m.; one s. one d.; ed Leningrad Inst. of Tech. and Eng; engineer and Asst to Chair. Leningrad Inst. of Econ. and Eng 1977–82, docent 1982–90, Deputy, then First Deputy-Chair. of Leningrad Municipal Council Jan.–Nov. 1991; Minister of Russia, Chair. State Cttee for Man. of State Property 1991–98; Deputy Prime Minister, Chair. Co-ordination Council for Privatization 1992–94; First Deputy Prime Minister 1994–96; mem. State Duma (Parl.) 1993–95; Head of Pres. Yeltsin's Admin 1996–97; First Deputy Prime Minister 1997–98, Minister of Finance March–Nov. 1997; Russian Dir, EBRD 1997–98; mem. Russian Security Council 1997–98; CEO United Energy Systems; Head Russian Fed. Interdepartmental Comm. on Co-operation with Int. Financial and Econ. Orgs and Group of Seven 1998; CEO RAO 'UES' of Russia 1998–, Dir 2000–; Co-Chair. Round Table of Russian and EU Producers 2000–; Pres. Electric Power Council of CIS 2000–; mem. Man. Bd Russian Union of Manufacturers & Entrepreneurs 2000–; mem. Govt Comm. on Co-operation with EU 2000–; Co-Chair. 'Union of Right Forces' 2001. *Leisure interests:* skiing, mountains, riding his scooter, the internet, information technology. *Address:* RAO 'Unified Energy System' of Russia, Kitaigorodsky Proyezd 7, 103074 Moscow, Russia. *Telephone:* (095) 785-43-30/ 785-43-31. *Fax:* (095) 206-80-73. *E-mail:* rao@elektra.ru (Office). *Website:* www.rao-ees.ru (Office); www.chubais.ru (Home).

CHUBUK, Ion, DrEcon; Moldovan politician; b. 20 May 1943; ed Odessa Inst. of Agric.; First Deputy Chair. Moldovan State Planning Cttee 1984–86; Head of Div. Research Inst. of Agric. 1986–89; Deputy Chair. Moldovan Agricultural-Industrial Council 1989–90; First Deputy Minister of Econs 1990–91; Deputy Prime Minister, Perm. Rep. of Moldovan Govt in USSR Council of Ministers 1991–92; First Deputy Minister of Foreign Affairs 1992–94; First Deputy Minister of Econs April–Dec. 1994; Chair. Moldovan Accountant Chamber 1994–97, Deputy Chair. Accountant Chamber 1999–; Prime Minister of Moldova 1997–99; Deputy Chair. Centrists Union 2000–. *Address:* c/o Office of the Prime Minister, Piata Marii Adunari Nationale 1, 277033 Chisinau, Moldova (Office).

CHUDAKOVA, Marietta Omarovna, DLit; Russian academic; b. 2 Jan. 1937, Moscow; m. Alexander Pavlovich Chudakov; one d.; ed Moscow State Univ.; school teacher in Moscow 1959–61; sr researcher, Div. of Manuscripts, Div. of Rare Books, Div. of Library Research All-Union Lenin's Public Library 1965–84; Ed.-in-Chief Tynyanovski sborniki 1984–; teacher Inst. of Literature 1986–, Prof. 1992–; main research on history of Russian Literature (Soviet Period), archives and literary criticism; Visiting Prof. Stanford 1989, Univ. of S. Calif. 1990, Ecole Normale Supérieure, Paris 1991, Geneva Univ. and European Inst. in Geneva 1994, Ottawa Univ. 1995, Cologne Univ. 1999; Chair. All-Russian Mikhail Bulgakov Fund; mem. Acad. Europae; Prize of Moscow Komsomol for research on Yuri Olesha 1970. *Publications:* Effendi Kapiev (biog.) 1970, Craftsmanship of Yuri Olesha 1972, Talks about Archives 1975, Poetics of Mikhail Zoshchenko 1979, Life of Mikhail Bulgakov 1988, Literature of the Soviet Past 2001; more than 350 publs in magazines on literary subjects and political essays. *Leisure interests:* rowing, skiing. *Address:* Miklukha-Maklaia str. 39, korp. 2, Apt. 380, 117485 Moscow, Russia (Home). *Telephone:* (095) 202-84-44 (Office); (095) 335-92-57 (Home). *Fax:* (095) 375-78-03 (Office). *E-mail:* marietta@online.ru (Home).

CHUDÍK, Ladislav; Slovak actor; b. 27 May 1924, Hlohovec Dist., B. Bystrica; m.; one c.; ed Comenius Univ., Bratislava, State Conservatoire, Bratislava; with Slovak Nat. Theatre, Bratislava 1944, 1951–, Nová Scéna 1946–1951; Minister of Culture 1990; tutor Conservatoire and Acad. of Musical Arts, Bratislava—VSMU; State Prize 1959, Certificate of Merit 1965, Nat. Artist 1982. *Films include:* Kapitan Dabac 1959, Piesen o sivom holubovi, Polnocna omsa, Smrt prichadza v dazdi, Putovani Jana Amose, Vylet do mladosti. *Plays include:* Macbeth, Herodes, Henry IV, Borkman. *Television includes:* Nemocnice na okraji mesta (series). *Leisure interests:* literature, poetry, gardening. *Address:* c/o Slovenské národné divadlo—SND, Gorkého 4, 81586 Bratislava, Slovakia (Office).

CHUKHRAI, Grigoriy Naumovich; Russian film director; b. 23 May 1921, Melitopol, Zaporozhye Region; s. of Naum Vladimirovich Roubanov and Klavdia Petrovna Chukhrai; m. Irina Pavlovna Penkova 1944; one s. one d.; ed All-Union State Inst. of Cinematography 1953; Soviet Army 1939–45; mem. CPSU 1944–89; Producer Mosfilm 1955–64, 1977–; Dir Experimental Film Studio 1965–76; Honoured Art Worker of RSFSR, People's Artist of USSR 1981, Lenin Prize 1961, Nika Prize 1994, Order of Red Star, Order of Patriotic War, Order of Red Banner of Labour (three times), Labour Order of Hungary, Partisan Star of Czechoslovakia. *Films:* The 41st 1956, Ballad of a Soldier 1959, The Clear Sky 1961, There Lived an Old Man and Old Woman 1964, Memory 1971, Quagmire 1978, Life is Beautiful 1980, I Will Teach You to Dream 1984, Stalin and the War 1991. *Leisure interest:* the theory of economics. *Address:* Pudovkina str. 3, Apt. 60, 119285 Moscow, Russia. *Telephone:* (095) 143 34 44. *Fax:* (095) 200-42-84.

CHUKHRAI, Pavel Grigoryevich; Russian film maker; b. 14 Oct. 1946, Bykovo, Moscow; s. of Grigoriy Chukhrai; m. Maria Zvereva; two d.; ed All-Union State Inst. of Cinematography; actor, cameraman, script-writer; mem. Union of Cinematographers, European Acad. of Cinema and TV; Lenin's Komsomol Prize 1991, All-Union Film Festival Prize 1981, four Kinoshock Festival prizes, six Russian Acad. prizes, four Golden Oven Festival prizes, Grand Prix Prague Film Festival, Jury Prize, Int. Film Festival, Japan. *Films include:* Hello Kids (actor) 1962, You Sometimes Recall (dir) 1977, Who Will Pay for Luck (script-writer) 1980, People in the Ocean (script-writer) 1980, A Cell for Canaries (script-writer, dir) 1983, Zina-Zinulya (dir) 1986, Thief (dir) 1997, Remember Me So 1999, Children From Abyss. *Address:* Bolshaya Pirogovskaya str. 53/55, apt. 177, Moscow, Russia (Home). *Telephone:* (095) 246-98-61 (Home). *Fax:* (095) 246-98-61 (Home). *E-mail:* pavel@girmet.ru (Home).

CHUN DOO-HWAN, Gen.; South Korean politician and army officer (retd); b. 18 Jan. 1931, Gyeongsang Nam-do; s. of Chun Sang-Woo and Kim Jum-Mun; m. Lee Soon-Ja; three s. one d.; ed Heedoh Primary School, Daegu, Daegu Tech. High School, Mil. Acad., Army Coll.; commissioned Second Lt 1955; Adjutant-Gen. School 1959; US Special Forces and Psychological Warfare School 1959; US Army Infantry School 1960; Acting Planning Dir, Special Warfare Bureau Army HQ, 1960–61; Domestic Affairs Sec. to Chair. of Supreme Council for Nat. Reconstruction 1961–62; Dir Personnel Admin. Bureau, Korean CIA 1963; Exec. Officer 1st Airborne Special Forces Group 1966–67; Commdr 30th Bn, Capital Garrison Command 1967–69; Sr Aide to Chief of Staff 1969–70; Commdr 29th Regt, 9th Infantry Div. (Viet Nam) 1970–71; Commdr 1st Airborne Special Forces Group 1971; Asst Dir Presidential Security Office 1976; Commanding Gen. 1st Infantry Div. 1978; Commdr Defence Security Command 1979–80; Acting Dir Korean CIA April–June 1980; Chair. Standing Cttee Special Cttee for Nat. Security Measures June 1980; promoted to full Gen. Aug. 1980; retd from army Aug. 1980; Pres. Repub. of Korea 1980–88; Pres. Democratic Justice Party 1981–87, Hon. Pres. 1987–88; in rural exile 1988–90; returned to Seoul Dec. 1990; arrested and charged with orchestrating 1979 mil. coup, Dec. 1994; on hunger strike Dec. 1994–Jan. 1995; indicted on charges of taking bribes Jan. 1996; found guilty of mutiny and treason and sentenced to death Aug. 1996; sentence commuted to life imprisonment Dec. 1996; numerous decorations. *Leisure interest:* tennis.

CHUNDER, Pratap Chandra, MA, LLB, PhD; Indian politician and lawyer; b. 1 Sept. 1919, Calcutta; s. of Nirmal and Suhasini Chunder; m. Leena Roy Chowdhury 1940; four s.; ed Univ. of Calcutta; law practice in Calcutta since

1945; mem. Senate and Law Faculty of Calcutta Univ. 1961–68; mem. Exec. Council of Rabindra Bharati Univ. 1962–68; mem. West Bengal Legislative Ass. 1962–68; Pres. West Bengal Provincial Congress Cttee 1967–69; Minister of Finance and Judiciary in State Govt 1968; mem. Working Cttee and Cen. Parl. Bd of Org. Congress 1969–76; mem. Janata Party 1977–; mem. Lok Sabha from Calcutta North East March 1977–79; Union Minister of Education, Social Welfare and Culture 1977–79; mem. Calcutta Bar Asscn; Pres. Int. Educ. Conf. UNESCO 1977–79, Indo-American Soc. 1984–92, 1997–, Writers' Guild of India 1985–, Bengali Literary Conf. 1987–, All India Buddhist Mission 1989–, Iran Soc. 1990–92, Indian Inst. of Social Welfare and Business Man. 1991–, World Bengali Conf. 1991, Soc. for the Deaf 1991–94, Bharatiya Vidya Bhavan Calcutta Agartala Region 1993–, Inc. Law Soc. 1995–98; Chair. Planning Bd, Asiatic Soc. 1998–; Patron Mahabodhi Soc. of India 1995–; fmr ed. several Bengali literary magazines; Trustee Victoria Memorial 1990–98, 1999–, Sardar V.B. Patel Memorial Trust 1991–98; Regional Grand Master of Eastern India 1990–93, Deputy Grand Master 1993–94; Hon. Citizen of New Orleans; Chair. West Bengal Heritage Comm. 2001–; Hon. DLitt, Hon. DSc and Fellow, Asiatic Soc. of Calcutta 1975; Best Playwright award, Calcutta Univ. 1965; Bhalotia Prize for Best Novel 1991; Indira Gandhi Memorial Prize for Educ. 1992; Mother Theresa Award 1998, Medal of Sofia Univ., AIFACS Award for Art 2002. *Plays:* Bubhuksa, Sahartali, Prajapati, Amlamadhor, Ajab Desh (puppet play). *Television:* Lebedeff Ki Nakiya (film). *Works:* six one-man exhbns of paintings in Calcutta and New Delhi 1982, 1984, 1985, 1987, 1999, 2001, including one in China and one in USA. *Publications:* Kautilya on Love and Morals, The Sons of Mystery, Job Charnock and his Lady Fair, In Captivity, Socialist Legality and Indian Law, Brother Vivekananda, Facets of Freemasonry, Kautilya Arthasastra, Sankha Sindur (film), Job Charnocker Bibi (film). *Leisure interests:* reading, writing, painting. *Address:* 23 Nirmal Chunder Street, Kolkata 700012, India. *Telephone:* 2368248; 2360252; 2482112 (Office).

CHUNG, Kyung-Wha; South Korean violinist; b. 26 March 1948, Seoul; sister of Chung Myung-Whun; m. Geoffrey Leggett 1984; two s.; ed Juilliard School; studied under Ivan Galamian; started career in USA; winner of Leventritt Competition 1968; European debut 1970; has played under conductors such as Abbado, Barenboim, Davis, Dorati, Dutoit, Giulini, Haitink, Jochum, Kempe, Kondrashin, Leinsdorf, Levine, Maazel, Mehta, Muti, Previn, Rattle, Rozhdestvensky and Solti; has played with maj. orchestras including all London Orchestras, Chicago, Boston and Pittsburgh Symphony Orchestra, New York, Cleveland, Philadelphia, Berlin, Israel and Vienna Philharmonics, Orchestre de Paris; has toured world; recordings for EMI; played at Salzburg Festival with London Symphony Orchestra 1973, Vienna Festival 1981, 1984, Edinburgh Festival 1981 and at eightieth birthday concert of Sir William Walton March 1982; with Hallé Orchestra, London Proms 1999. *Recordings:* Concertos by Bartók, Beethoven, Bruch, Mendelssohn, Stravinsky, Tchaikovsky, Vieuxtemps, Walton. *Leisure interests:* arts, family. *Address:* c/o Columbia Artists Management Inc., 165 West 57th Street, New York, NY 10019, USA; c/o Harrison Parrott Ltd, 12 Penzance Place, London, W11 4PA, England.

CHUNG, Myung-Whun; South Korean conductor and pianist; b. 22 Jan. 1953, Seoul; brother of Kyung-Wha Chung; ed Mannes Coll. of Music and Juilliard School, New York, USA; fmr Asst to Carlo Maria Giulini, as Assoc. Conductor, Los Angeles Philharmonic; has conducted Berlin Philharmonic, Amsterdam Concertgebouw and the maj. orchestras of London and Paris and the four main U.S. orchestras 1981–; Musical Dir Radio Orchestra of Saarbrücken 1984–89; has conducted opera at Metropolitan, New York, Geneva, San Francisco and elsewhere 1986–; Guest Conductor, Teatro Comunale, Florence 1987–; Musical Dir Opéra de la Bastille, Paris 1989–94; Conductor, Nat. Acad. of Santa Cecilia, Rome 1997–; Musical Dir Radio France Philharmonic Orchestra 2000–; and Musical Dir Philharmonic Orchestra of Asia; performs as pianist in trio with his sisters Kyung-Wha and Myung-Wha; 2nd Prize, Tchaikovsky Competition, Moscow 1974; Abbiati Prize (Italian critics); Best Conductor, Best Lyrical Production, Best French Classical Recording, Victoires de la Musique 1995. *Address:* Orchestre philharmonique de Radio France, 116 avenue du President Kennedy, 75220 Paris cedex 16, France (Office).

CHUNG, (Raymond) Arthur; Guyanese judge; b. 10 Jan. 1918, Windsor Forest, West Coast, Demerara; s. of Joseph and Lucy Chung; m. Doreen Pamela Ng-See-Quan 1954; one s. one d.; ed Modern High School, Georgetown and Middle Temple, London; land surveyor 1940; lived in England 1946–48; Asst Legal Examiner, UK Inland Revenue Dept 1947; returned to Guyana 1948; Magistrate 1954, Sr Magistrate 1960; Registrar of Deeds of the Supreme Court 1961; Judge of the Supreme Court 1962–70; First Pres. of the Repub. of Guyana 1970–80.

CHUNG, Sir Sze-yuen, Kt, GBE, G.B.M., DSc, DEng, PhD, FREng, Hon. FIMechE, FIEE, CBIM, JP; Chinese/British business executive; b. 3 Nov. 1917, Hong Kong; m. Nancy Cheung 1942 (died 1977); one s. two d.; ed Hong Kong and Sheffield Univs; consulting Eng 1952–56; Gen. Man. Sonca Industries 1956–50, Man Dir 1960–77, Chair. 1977–88; mem. Hong Kong Legis. Council 1965–74, Sr Unofficial Member 1974–78; mem. Hong Kong Exec. Council 1972–80, Sr Unofficial Member 1980–88; Chair. Fed. of Hong Kong Industries 1966–70; Chair. Hong Kong Productivity Council 1974–76; founding Chair. Hong Kong Polytechnic 1972–86, City Polytechnic of Hong Kong 1984–85, Hong Kong Univ. of Science and Tech. 1987–99, Hong Kong Hosp. Authority 1990–95; Adviser to the Govt of People's Repub. of China on Hong Kong Affairs 1992–97; f. and Pres. Hong Kong Acad. of Eng Sciences 1994–97; mem. Chinese Govt.'s Preparatory Cttee for the Est. of Hong Kong Special Admin. Region (HKSAR) 1996–97; Convenor HKSAR Exec. Council 1997–99; holder of many other public appts; Order of the Sacred Treasure (Japan); Silver Jubilee Medal 1977; Hon. DSc (Hong Kong) 1976 and other awards and distinctions; Whitworth Prize, IMechE (London) 1952; Gold Medal, Asian Productivity Org.1980. *Publications:* Hong Kong's Journey to Reunification – Memoirs of Sze-yuen Chung; articles in professional journals. *Leisure interest:* swimming. *Address:* 128 Argyle Street, 10/F, Kowloon, Hong Kong Special Administrative Region (Office); House 25, Bella Vista, Silver Terrace Road, Clear Water Bay, Kowloon, Hong Kong Special Administrative Region, People's Republic of China (Home). *Telephone:* 27610281 (Office). *Fax:* 27607493.

CHUNG MONG-JOON, MA, PhD; South Korean politician, sports administrator and business executive; b. 17 Oct. 1951, Pusan; s. of the late Chung Ju-Yung; m.; two s. two d.; ed Joongang High School, Coll. of Commerce, Seoul Nat. Univ., MIT, USA and Johns Hopkins Univ., USA; First Lt Reserve Officers Training Corps; joined Hyundai Heavy Industries 1978, Man. Dir 1980, CEO 1987, Adviser 1991–2002; Pres. Hanjin Heavy Industries & Construction Co. Ltd (HHIC) 1982–87, Chair. 1987; Chief Dir Ulsan Inst. of Tech. Foundation 1983–; elected mem. Nat. Ass. (Ind.) 1988–; f. Nat. Unity 21 party Nov. 2002; Vice-Pres. F.I.F.A. 1994–, Chair. Media Cttee 1997–; Pres. Korea Football Asscn 1993–; Co-Chair. Korean Organizing Cttee for 2002 FIFA World Cup, Korea–Japan 2002, Deputy Chair. Bureau Cttee for FIFA Youth Competitions, Organizing Cttees. for FIFA U-17 World Championship, Finland 2003, FIFA World Youth Championship, UAE2003; Chair. Modern Econ. and Social Inst. 1990; Chair Prof. Korea Univ. 1999–; mem. Bd Trustees Ulsan Univ. (Chair. 1983), Johns Hopkins Univ., Korea Univ.; Chair. Bd Asan Foundation 2001–; Hon. PhD (Myongji Univ.) 1998; Hon. LLD (Univ. of Maryland) 1999. *Publications include:* Corporate Management Ideology 1982, Relations Between the Government and the Corporate in Japan 1995. *Leisure interests:* football, tennis, golf, equestrianism, hiking. *Address:* Korea Football Association, 1-131, Shinmunro 2-Ga, Jongro-Gu, Seoul 110-062 (Office); 345-1, Pyeongchang-dong, Jongno-gu, Seoul, Republic of Korea. *Telephone:* (2) 733-6764 (Office); (2) 735-2755 (Office). *Fax:* (2) 735-2755 (Office). *Website:* www.mjchung.com (Office); www.kfa.or.kr (Office).

CHUNG SHUI MING, BSc, MBA; Hong Kong government official; b. 23 Nov. 1951, Hong Kong; two c.; ed Univ. of Hong Kong, Chinese Univ. of Hong Kong; now Chief Exec. Hong Kong Special Admin. Region Land Fund; fmr Hong Kong Affairs Adviser to Chinese Govt; Fellow Hong Kong Soc. of Accountants; mem. Exec. Council, Hong Kong Special Admin. Region July 1997–; Hong Kong Housing Soc. Exec. Cttee, Housing Authority Finance Cttee; fmr Chinese mem. Sino–British Land Comm. *Address:* Executive Council Secretariat, First Floor, Main Wing, Central Government Offices, Lower Albert Road, Central, Hong Kong Special Administrative Region, People's Republic of China.

CHUNG WON SHIK; South Korean politician; fmr Minister of Educ.; Prime Minister of South Korea 1991–92; mem. Democratic Liberal Party (DLP). *Address:* c/o Office of the Prime Minister, 77 Sejong-no, Chongno-ku, Seoul, Republic of Korea.

CHURCHILL, Caryl, BA; British playwright; b. 3 Sept. 1938, London; d. of Robert Churchill and Jan Churchill (née Brown); m. David Harter 1961; three s.; ed Trafalgar School, Montreal, Canada, Lady Margaret Hall, Oxford Univ.; first play, Downstairs, performed at Nat. Union of Students Drama Festival 1958; numerous radio plays and several TV plays. *Stage plays include:* Having a Wonderful Time (Oxford Players, 1960), Owners (Royal Court, London) 1972, Objections to Sex and Violence (Royal Court) 1975, Vinegar Tom (Monstrous Regiment toured 1976), Light Shining in Buckinghamshire (performed by Joint Stock Co., Edinburgh Festival 1976, then Royal Court), Traps (Royal Court) 1977, Cloud Nine (Joint Stock Co., Royal Court) 1979, 1980, Lucille Lortel Theater, New York 1981–83; Top Girls (Royal Court) 1982, 1983, Public Theater, New York 1983, Fen (Joint Stock Co., Almeida Theatre, London 1983, Royal Court 1983, Public Theater, New York 1983), Softcops (RSC 1984), A Mouthful of Birds (Joint Stock, Royal Court and tour 1986), Serious Money (Royal Court 1987, Wyndham Theatre 1987, Public Theater New York 1988), Icecream (Royal Court 1989, Public Theater New York 1990), Mad Forest (Cen. School of Drama, Nat. Theatre Bucharest, Royal Court 1990), Lives of the Great Poisoners (Second Stride Co. Riverside Studios, London and tour 1991), The Skriker (Nat. Theatre 1994), Thyestes (by Seneca, translation; Royal Court Theatre Upstairs 1994); Hotel (Second Stride Co., The Place) 1997, This Is A Chair (Royal Court) 1997, Blue Heart (Out of Joint, Royal Court) 1997, Far Away (Royal Court) 2000, (Albery) 2001. *Radio:* The Ants, Not . . Not . . not . . not enough Oxygen, Abortive Schreiber, Nervous Illness, Identical Twins, Perfect Happiness, Henry's Past. *Television:* The Judge's Wife, The After Dinner Joke, The Legion Hall Bombing, Fugue (jtly). *Publications:* Owners 1973, Light Shining 1976, Traps 1977, Vinegar Tom 1978, Cloud Nine 1979, Top Girls 1982, Fen 1983, Fen and Softcops 1984, A Mouthful of Birds 1986, Serious Money 1987, Plays I 1985, Plays II 1988, Objections to Sex and Violence in Plays by Women Vol. 4 1985, Ice Cream 1989, Mad Forest 1990, Lives of the Great Poisoners 1992, The Striker 1994, Thyestes 1994, Blue Heart 1997, This is a Chair 1999, Faraway 2000; anthologies. *Address:* c/o Casarotto Ramsay Ltd, National House, 60–66 Wardour Street, London W1V 3HP, England. *Telephone:* (20) 7287-4450. *Fax:* (20) 7734-9293.

CHURIKOVA, Inna Mikhailovna; actress and screenwriter; b. 5 Oct. 1945, Belibey, Bashkiria; d. of Mikhail Churikov and Yelizaveta Mantrova; m. Gleb Panfilov 1974; one s.; ed Shchepkin Theatre School; with Moscow Youth Theatre 1965–68; with Lenin Komsomol Theatre (now Lenkom), Moscow 1973–; début in films 1961; small parts in films in 1960s; Lenin Komsomol Prize 1976; RSFSR State Prize 1985; USSR People's Artist 1985; Nika Prize 1993, Triumph Prize 1994, Kinotaur Festival Prize 1994, Kamaz Festival First Prize 1994, Russian Fed. State Prize 1997, Cristal Turandot Drama Asscn Award (twice). *Plays:* The Gambler (Stanislavsky Award) 1996, The Sheep 1997, Old Women 1999, City of Millionaires 2000. *Roles in:* No Ford Through Fire (Panfilov) 1968, The Beginning 1970, May I Speak? 1976, Valentina 1981, Vassa 1983, War-Novel 1984 (Berlin Film Festival Prize), Three Girls in Blue (theatre) 1985, The Theme 1986, Mother 1991, Adam's Rib 1991 (Critics' Prize), Sorry (theatre) 1992, Casanova's Mantle 1992, The Seagull (theatre) 1994, The Year of the Dog 1994, Father Frost 2001 and many others. *Address:* Lenkom Theatre, Malaya Dmitrovka 6, Moscow, Russia. *Telephone:* (095) 137-89-67. *E-mail:* varadero@mail.ru (Home). *Website:* www .lenkom.ru (Office).

CHURKIN, Vitaly Ivanovich, PhD; Russian diplomatist; b. 21 Feb. 1952; m.; one s. one d.; ed Moscow State Inst. of Int. Relations; attaché, Translations Dept, Ministry of Foreign Affairs, Interpreter of USSR del. to SALT II Negotiations 1974–79; Third Sec. USA Dept of Ministry of Foreign Affairs 1979–82; Second Sec., First Sec., USSR Embassy, Washington, DC 1982–87; expert, Int. Dept of Cen. Cttee CPSU 1987–89; Counsellor of Ministry of Foreign Affairs 1989–90; Dir Information and Press Dept 1990–92; rank of Amb. Extraordinary and Plenipotentiary 1990; Deputy Minister of Foreign Affairs of Russia 1992–94; Amb. to Belgium 1994–97, to Canada 1998–. *Leisure interest:* tennis. *Address:* Embassy of the Russian Federation, 285 Charlotte Street, Ottawa, Ont., K1N 8L5, Canada. *Telephone:* (613) 235-4371.

CHUTE, Robert Maurice, ScD; American professor of biology (retd) and poet; b. 13 Feb. 1926, Bridgton, Maine; s. of James Cleveland and Elizabeth Davis Chute; m. Virginia Hinds 1946; one s. one d.; ed Univ. of Maine, The Johns Hopkins Univ.; Instructor and Asst Prof. Middlebury Coll. 1953–59; Asst Prof. Northridge State Coll. 1959–61; Assoc. Prof. and Chair. of Biology, Lincoln Univ. 1961; Prof. and Chair. of Biology, then Dana Prof. of Biology, Bates Coll. 1962–93, now Emer.; Fellow AAAS; Maine Arts and Humanities Award 1978, Chad Walsh Award (Beloit Poetry Journal) 1997. *Publications:* Environmental Insight 1971, Introduction to Biology 1976, Sweeping the Sky: Soviet Women Flyers in Combat 1999; poetry: Quiet Thunder 1975, Uncle George Poems 1977, Voices Great and Small 1977, Thirteen Moons/Treize Lunes 1982, Samuel Sewell Sails for Home 1986, When Grandmother Decides to Die 1989, Woodshed on the Moon—Thoreau Poems, Barely Time to Study Jesus 1996, Androscoggin Too 1997, trans.: Thirteen Moons (into Micmac Maliseet—native American) 2002. *Leisure interests:* walking, reading, films, Thoreau studies. *Address:* 85 Echo Cove Lane, Poland Spring, ME 04274, USA. *Telephone:* (207) 998-4338.

CHYNGYSHEV, Tursunbek; Kyrgyzstan politician and economist; b. 15 Oct. 1942, Naryn Dist; s. of Asanbek Chyngyshev and Saira Chyngysheva; m. Ludmila V. Chyngysheva 1968; one s. one d.; ed Kyrgyz Univ., Acad. of Social Sciences, Moscow; functionary of CP of Kyrgyzstan, Head Div. of Econs, Cen. Cttee of CP of Kirgizia; Mayor of Tokmok; participated in democratic Movt since late 1980s; State Sec. Kyrgyz SSR 1991–92, mem. USSR Cttee on Operative Man. of Nat. Econ. Aug.–Dec. 1991; Prime Minister of Kyrgyzstan 1992–93, mem. Parl. Kyrgyz Repub; Gen. Man. HENFEN Ltd; Vice-Pres. Kyrgyz Nat. Oil Co.; Pres. Asscn of Commercial Banks of Kyrgyzstan 1996–; Man. Mercury Bank; Order of Honour, Order of People's Friendship. *Address:* 4 Koyenkozov Str., Bishkek 720017, Kyrgyzstan. *Telephone:* (312) 21-78-87. *Fax:* (312) 21-78-87.

CHYNOWETH, Alan Gerald, BSc, PhD, FIEEE, FInstP; British physicist; b. 18 Nov. 1927, Harrow, Middx; s. of James Charles Chynoweth and Marjorie Fairhurst; m. Betty Freda Edith Boyce 1950; two s.; ed King's College, Univ. of London; Postdoctoral Fellow of Nat. Research Council of Canada, Chemistry Div., Ottawa 1950–52; mem. Tech. Staff, Bell Telephone Labs. 1953–60, Head, Crystal Electronics Dept 1960–65, Asst Dir Metallurgical Research Lab. 1965–73, Dir Materials Research Lab. 1973–76, Exec. Dir Electronic and Photonic Devices Div. 1976–83, Vice-Pres., Applied Research, Bell Communications Research 1983–92; Survey Dir of Nat. Acad. of Sciences Cttee on Survey of Materials Science and Eng 1971–73, Comm. on Mineral Resources and the Environment 1973–75; mem. of Nat. Materials Advisory Bd, Wash. 1975–79, NATO Special Programme Panel on Materials 1977–82, Consultant to NATO Advanced Study Inst. Panel 1982–89; mem. Materials Research Soc., Metallurgical Soc.; Alternate Dir Microelectronics and Computer Tech. Corpn 1985–92; Dir Industrial Research Inst. 1990–92; Chair. Tech. Transfer Merit Program, NJ Comm. on Science and Tech. 1992–; Consultant to EC Telecommunications Directorate 1995; Lecturer Electrochemical Soc. 1983; Co.-Ed. Optical Fiber Telecommunications 1979; Assoc. Ed. Solid State Comm. 1975–83; mem. visiting Cttee, Cornell Univ. Materials Science Centre 1973–76, Natural Sciences Advisory Bd, Univ. of Pennsylvania 1988–92, Advisory Bd Dept of Electrical Eng and CS, Univ. of Calif., Berkeley 1987–, Advisory Bd, Dept of Electrical Eng, Univ. of S. Calif. 1988–; mem. Office of Science and Tech. Policy Panel on High Performance Computing and Communications, mem. Frederik Philips Award Cttee 1998–, Corp. Achievement Award Cttee 1999–; Fellow American Physical Soc.; W. R. G. Baker Prize Award, IEEE 1967, Frederik Philips Award, IEEE 1992, George E Pake Prize,

APS 1992, Eng Leadership Recognition, IEEE 1996. *Publications:* over 60 papers in professional journals on solid state physics, 11 patents on solid state devices, Nat. Acad. of Sciences reports: Materials and Man's Needs, Materials Conservation through Technology, Resource Recovery from Municipal Solid Wastes. *Leisure interests:* travel, boating. *Address:* Telcordia Techs. Box 7040, 331 Newman Springs Road, Red Bank, NJ 07701 (Office); 6 Londonderry Way, Summit, NJ 07901, USA (Home). *Telephone:* (908) 273-4581 (Home). *E-mail:* algchy@aol.com (Office).

CIAMPI, Carlo Azeglio, LLB; Italian politician; b. 9 Dec. 1920, Livorno; s. of Pietro Ciampi and Marie Masino; m. Franca Pilla 1946; one s. one d.; ed Scuola Normale Superiore di Pisa, Pisa Univ.; served in Italian Army 1941–44; with Banca d'Italia 1946, economist Research Dept 1960–70, Head Research Dept 1970–73, Sec. Gen. 1973–76, Deputy Dir Gen. 1976–78, Dir Gen. 1978–79, Gov. 1979–93; Chair. Ufficio Italiano dei Cambi, 1979–83 (Hon. Gov. 1994–); Prime Minister 1993–94; Minister of the Treasury and the Budget 1996–98; Pres. of Italy May 1999–; Chair. IMF Interim Cttee 1998–99; mem. Bd of Govs. for Italy IBRD, IDA, IFC; mem. Cttee of Govs. EEC; mem. Bd of Dirs. Consiglio Nazionale delle Ricerche, BIS; mem. Istituto Adriano Olivetti di Studi per la Gestione dell'Economia e delle Aziende; Military Cross, Grand Officer, Order of Merit of the Italian Republic. *Publications:* Un metodo per Governare 1996. *Address:* Office of the President, Palazzo del Quirinale, 00187 Rome, Italy (Office). *Telephone:* (06) 46991 (Office).

CICHY, Leszek; Polish bank executive and mountaineer; b. 14 Nov. 1951, Pruszków; m. Maria Gierałtowska; two s.; ed Warsaw Univ. of Technology; researcher Geodesic Dept, Warsaw Univ. of Tech. 1977–90; engineer in Syria 1990–92; mem. staff Housing Investments, Warsaw 1992–93, Polski Bank Rozwoju 1993–98; Vice-Chair. Dom Inwestycyjny BRE Banku, Warsaw 1998–99, Bank Współpracy Europejskiej, Warsaw 1999–2000; Dir Kredyt Bank, Warsaw 2000–01; Vice-Chair. and Finance Dir, Capital Group ERGIS 2001–; mem. Polish Alpine Club, Chair. 1995–2000; mountaineering expeditions include Tatra, Alps, Andes, Caucasus, Karakoram and Himalaya; first person to climb Mount Everest in the winter (with partner Krzysztof Wielicki) 1980; first Pole to climb the Crown of the Earth (highest peaks on every continent) 1980–99. *Publication:* Talks about Everest (co-author) 1982. *Leisure interests:* tennis, skiing, astronomy. *Address:* ul. Na Uboczu 16/49, 02–791 Warsaw, Poland (Home).

CIECHANOVER, Aaron, MD, PhD; Israeli doctor and molecular biologist; b. Oct. 1947, Haifa; ed Hebrew Univ. of Jerusalem; mil. service as a doctor in Israeli army; studied protein degradation at biochemical level with Avram Hershko 1976–81; collaborated with Alexander Varshavsky at MIT; Dir Rappaport Family Inst. for Research in Medical Sciences and Prof. of Biochemistry, Technion–Israel Inst. of Tech.; Albert Lasker Basic Medical Research Award 2000. *Address:* Faculty of Medicine, Technion–Israel Institute of Technology, P.O. Box 9649, Bat Galim, Haifa, 31096 Israel (Office); 4-8514722 (Office). *Fax:* 4-8517008 (Office). *E-mail:* rafael@biomed.technion.ac .il (Office). *Website:* www.technion.ac.il/medicine.

CIEMNIEWSKI, Jerzy, LLD; Polish lawyer and politician; b. 2 Aug. 1939, Warsaw; m.; one s.; ed Warsaw Univ.; lecturer Warsaw Univ. 1962–68; scientific worker, State and Law Inst. of Polish Acad. of Sciences, Warsaw 1968–, lecturer 1972–; mem. Solidarity Independent Self-governing Trade Union 1980–; Assoc. Understanding Cttee of Creative and Scientific Asscns. and Teachers' Solidarity, also scientific worker Social and Labour Study Centre attached to Nat. Comm. of Solidarity 1980–81; mem. Helsinki Cttee in Poland 1983–; participant Round Table debates, mem. group for law and judicature reform, expert group for political reforms Feb.–April 1989; mem. State Election Comm. during election to the Sejm (Parl.) and Senate 1989; Under-Sec. of State in Office of the Council of Ministers, Sec. of Council of Ministers 1989–91; Deputy to Sejm 1991–98; judge Constitutional Tribunal 1998–; mem. Democratic Freedom Union 1990–94, Freedom Union 1994–; Awards of Gen. Sec. of Polish Acad. of Sciences 1974, 1976. *Publications:* numerous scientific works, mainly on constitutional law, including Ustawa o systemie konstytucyjnym SFR Jugosławii 1976, Sejm Ustawodawczy RP (1947–1952) 1978 (co-author), Studia nad rządem 1985 (co-author), System delegacki na tle ewolucji ustroju politycznego SFR Jugosławii 1988, Draft of the Constitution of the Republic of Poland (co-author) 1990. *Leisure interests:* family life, walking with dog, general history, painting. *Address:* Tribunał Konstytucyjny, al. J. Ch. Szucha 12A, 00-198 Warsaw, Poland. *Telephone:* (22) 657-45-01.

ÇILLER, Tansu, PhD; Turkish politician; b. 1945, Istanbul; m.; two c.; ed Robert Coll., Boğaziçi Univ., Univ. of Connecticut and Yale Univ.; Assoc. Prof. 1978, Prof. 1983; served on academic bds. of various univs., mainly in Dept of Econs Boğaziçi Univ.; joined True Path Party (DYP) 1990, Leader 1993–; mem. Parl. 1991; Minister of State for the Economy 1991; Prime Minister 1993–96; Deputy Prime Minister and Minister of Foreign Affairs 1996–97. *Publications:* nine publs on econs. *Address:* c/o True Path Party, Selanik Cod. 40, Kizilay, Ankara, Turkey. *Telephone:* (312) 4191818. *Fax:* (312) 4176090. *Website:* www.dyp.org.tr (Office).

CIMINO, Michael; American film writer and director; b. 1943, New York; screenplay writer for Silent Running 1972, Magnum Force 1973; screenplay writer and Dir Thunderbolt and Lightfoot 1974; producer, writer and Dir The Deer Hunter (Academy Award for Best Dir 1979) 1978; writer and Dir Heaven's Gate 1980, Prod. and Dir Year of the Dragon 1985, Dir The Sicilian

1987, The Last Temptation of Christ 1988, Desperate Hours 1990, The Sunchasers 1996, The Dreaming Place. *Address:* c/o Jeff Berg, ICM, 8942 Wilshire Blvd., Beverly Hills, CA 90211, USA.

CIMOLI, Giancarlo; Italian administrator; Chair. and Man. Dir Ferrovie dello Stato (state railways) 1996–; mem. Aspen Inst. *Address:* Ferrovie dello Stato, Piazza della Croce Rossa 1, 00161 Rome, Italy (Office). *Telephone:* (06) 84903758 (Office). *Fax:* (06) 84905186 (Office).

CIMOSZEWICZ, Włodzimierz, DJur; Polish politician and lawyer; b. 13 Sept. 1950, Warsaw; m.; one s. one d.; ed Warsaw Univ.; Asst, Sr Asst in Int. Law Inst., Warsaw Univ. 1972–85; farmer 1985–; mem. Polish United Workers' Party (PZPR) 1971–90; Deputy to Sejm (Parl.) 1989– (Vice-Chair. Cttee for Nat. and Ethnic Minorities, mem., Chair. Constitutional Cttee); Presidential Cand. Democratic Left Alliance (SLD) Presidential Election 1990; Deputy Chair. Council of Ministers and Minister of Justice and Attorney-Gen. 1993–95; Vice-Marshal (Speaker) of Sejm 1995–96; Prime Minister of Poland 1996–97; Chair. European Integration Cttee 1996–97; Minister of Foreign Affairs 2001–. *Leisure interests:* reading, hunting, crafts. *Address:* Ministry of Foreign Affairs, al. J. Ch. Szucha 23, 00-580 Warsaw, Poland (Office). *Telephone:* (22) 5239200 (Office). *Website:* www.msz.gov.pl (Office).

CIOCCA, Pierluigi, DIur; Italian banker; b. 17 Oct. 1941, Pescara; ed Univ. of Rome, Fondazione Einaudi (Univ. of Turin) and Balliol Coll. Oxford; economist, Research Dept Banca d'Italia (Bank of Italy) 1969–82; Cen. Man. for Cen. Bank Operations, Bank of Italy 1985–88, Cen. Man. for Econ. Research 1988–95; Deputy Dir-Gen. Bank of Italy 1995–; mem. Working Party 3 OECD Econ. Policy Cttee 1997–; substitute for Gov. Bank of Italy, Governing Council, European Cen. Bank 1998; mem. Financial Stability Forum 1999–. *Publications:* La nuova finanza in Italia, Una difficile meta-morfosi (1980–2000) 2000. *Address:* Banca d'Italia, Via Nazionale 91, 00184 Rome, Italy. *Telephone:* (06) 47921. *Fax:* (06) 47922983. *Website:* www.bancaditalia.it (Office).

CIORBEA, Victor; Romanian politician and jurist; b. 26 Oct. 1954, Ponor Village; s. of Vasile Ciorbea and Eugenia Ciorbea; m. 1977; one d.; ed Law School, Cluj-Napoca, Case Western Reserve Univ., Cleveland, Ohio, USA; Judge Court of Bucharest 1979–84; Prosecutor, Dept Civil Cases, Gen. Prosecutor's Office 1984–87; Asst to Lecturer Law School, Bucharest 1987–90; Pres. Free Trade Unions Fed. in Educ. 1990–96, CNSLR 1990–93, CNSLR-FRĂTIA 1993–94, Democratic Union Confed., Romania 1994–96; Prime Minister of Romania 1996–98; mem. Exec. Bd ICFTU, ETUC, CES 1993–94; rep. of Romania at OIM confs.; Vice-Pres. PNTCD; Mayor Bucharest 1996–98; Vice-Pres. Christian Democratic Nat. Peasants' Party (CDNPP) 1999–; mem. Bd Alianta Civica 1996. *Address:* CDNPP, 73231 Bucharest, Bd. Carol I 34, Romania (Office). *Telephone:* (1) 6154533 (Office). *Fax:* (1) 6143277 (Office).

CIOSEK, Stanisław, MA; Polish politician; b. 2 May 1939, Pawłowice, Radom Prov.; s. of Józef Ciosek and Janina Ciosek; m. Anna Ciosek 1969; two d.; ed Higher School of Econs, Sopot; activist in youth orgs. 1957–75; Chair. Regional Council of Polish Students' Asscn (ZSP), Gdańsk, Deputy Chair. and Chair. Chief Council, ZSP 1957–73; Chair. Chief Council of Fed. of Socialist Unions of Polish Youth (FSZMP) 1974–75; mem. Polish United Workers' Party (PZPR) 1959–90, deputy mem. PZPR Cen. Cttee 1971–80, First Sec. Voivodship Cttee PZPR and Chair. Presidium of Voivodship Nat. Council, Jelenia Góra 1975–80, mem. PZPR Cen. Cttee 1980–81, 1986–90; Deputy to Sejm 1972–85; Minister for Co-operation with Trade Unions Nov. 1980–85, for Labour, Wages and Social Affairs March 1983–84, Vice-Chair. Cttee of Council of Ministers for Co-operation with Trade Unions 1983–85; Sec. Socio-Political Cttee of Council of Ministers 1981–85; Sec. PZPR Cen. Cttee 1986–88; alt. mem. Political Bureau of PZPR Cen. Cttee 1988, mem. Political Bureau 1988–89; Sec.-Gen. Nat. Council of Patriotic Movt for Rebirth (PRON) 1988–89; Co-organizer and participant Round Table debates 1989; Amb. to USSR 1989–91, to Russia 1991–96; Foreign Policy Adviser to Pres. of Poland 1997–; Commdr's Cross, Order of Polonia Restituta. *Address:* Patac Prezydencki, ul. Krakowskie Pnedmiescie 48/50, 00-071 Warsaw (Office). *E-mail:* ciosek@prezydent.pl (Office). *Website:* www.prezydent.pl.

CIPRIANI THORNE, HE Cardinal Juan Luis; Peruvian ecclesiastic; b. 28 Dec. 1943, Lima; ordained priest 1977; Bishop 1988; Archbishop of Ayacucho 1995–99, of Lima 1999–; cr. Cardinal 2001. *Address:* Arzobispado, Plaza de Armas s/n, Apdo. 1512, Lima 100, Perú (Office); Calle Los Nogales 249, San Isidro, Lima 27. *Telephone:* (14) 427-5980 (Office); (14) 441-1977. *Fax:* (14) 427-1967 (Office); (14) 440-9134. *E-mail:* arzolimas@amauta.rcpnet.pe (Office).

CIRIANI, Henri Edouard; French architect and professor of architecture; b. 30 Dec. 1936, Lima, Peru; s. of Enrique Ciriani and Caridad Suito; m. Marcelle Espejo 1962; two d.; ed Santa Maria School, Nat. Univ. of Eng and Town Planning Inst., Lima; Asst Architect Dept of Architecture, Ministry of Devt and Public Works, Lima, Project Architect 1961–64; Pvt. Practice with Crousse and Paez 1961–63; Asst Prof. of Design, Nat. Univ. of Eng, Lima 1962–64; emigrated to France 1964; f. pvt. practice 1968; Prof. Ecole des Beaux-Arts de Paris 1969–83; Prof. of Architecture, Ecole d'Architecture de Paris-Belleville 1984; Dist Prof. Univ. Nacional de Ingeniería, Lima 1985–; Visiting Prof. Tulane Univ., New Orleans 1984, Univ. Coll., Dublin 1985, Ecole d'Architecture de Grenoble 1988, Univ. of Pennsylvania 1989 and many

others; Sir Banister Fletcher Visiting Lecturer, Univ. Coll., London 1986; lectures worldwide; Nat. Grand Prix of Architecture 1983, Equerre d'Argent 1983, Palme d'Or de l'Habitat 1988, Brunner Memorial Prize 1997, Chevalier, Légion d'honneur 1997. *Public works include:* public housing at Ventanilla Matute 1963, San Felipe 1964, Rimac Mirones 1965, Marne-la-vallée Noisy II 1980, Noisy III 1981, St Denis 1982, Evry 1985, Lognes 1986, Charcot 1991, Bercy 1994, Colombes 1995; urban landscape at Grenoble 1968–74; public facilities at St Denis Child-care Centre 1983; Cen. kitchen for St Antoine Hosp., Paris 1985; Torcy Child-care Centre 1989; Museum of the First World War, Péronne 1992; extension to Ministry of Finance Bldg, Paris 1993; Arles Archaeological Museum 1995; pvt. bldgs. at The Hague Apartment Tower 1995; retrospective exhbns. at Institut Français d'Architecture, Paris 1984, Figueira da Foz, Oporto and Lisbon 1985, New York 1985, Tokyo 1987, Lima 1996, New York 1997, Montreal 1997. *Publications:* Pratique de la pièce urbaine 1996, Paroles d'architecte (ed. by Jean Petit Lugano) 1997. *Leisure interests:* drawing, collecting postcards. *Address:* 61 rue Pascal, 75013 Paris, France (Office).

CIRICI, Cristian; Spanish architect; b. 26 Sept. 1941, Barcelona; s. of Alexandre Cirici and Cármen Cirici; m. Anna Bricall; three s.; ed Higher Tech. School of Architecture of Barcelona; partner Studio PER 1965–; partner and mem. Man. Bd BD Ediciónes de Diseño; Prof. of Projects Higher Tech. School of Architecture of Barcelona 1976–78; Visiting Prof. Washington Univ. St Louis, USA 1981, New Mexico Univ., Albuquerque; Nat. Prize for Restoration 1979, FAD Prize for the Best Decoration Work of Barcelona 1965, 1970, 1972; Prize for the Best Restoration 1979, Delta de Oro ADI-FAD 1976. *Major works:* flats, Tokio St Barcelona 1972, Casa Frances, Minorca 1977, restoration of Casa Thomas 1979, Casa Diaz-Morera 1981, industrial and commercial bldgs. in Tunel del Cadi area 1983, reconstruction of Mies Van der Rohe Pavilion, Barcelona 1987, extension of Zoological Museum of Barcelona 1989. *Publication:* Miró Otro (jtly) 1968.

CIRY, Michel; French painter, etcher and graphic artist; b. 31 Aug. 1919, La Baule; s. of Georges Ciry and Simone (née Breune) Ciry; ed Ecole des Arts Appliqués, Paris; studied music with Nadia Boulanger; religious and secular paintings and etchings; painter 1951–; Prof. School of Fine Arts Fontaine-bleau 1957–58, Académie Julian 1960; fmr mem. Conseil Supérieur de l'Enseignement des Beaux-Arts; Vice-Pres. Comité Nat. de la Gravure 1957–; numerous exhbns. in Europe and America including Paris, London, New York, Boston, Amsterdam, Rome and Berlin; works in Museums of Europe and America; has illustrated numerous books including books by Month-erlant, Green, Claudel and Mauriac; mem. Acad. des Beaux-Arts, Florence 1964–, Belgian Acad. 1988; Prix Nat. des Arts 1945, Grande médaille de vermeil de la Ville de Paris 1962, Prix de l'Ile de France 1964, Prix Eugène Carrière 1964, Lauréate Acad. des Beaux-Arts 1968; Prix Wildenstein 1968; Lauréat du Grand Prix Georges Baudry 1984; Officier, Légion d'honneur, Chevalier des Arts et des Lettres, Officier, Ordre Nat. du Mérite. *Major works:* Chemin de croix 1960–64, Stabat Mater 1960, 1961, 1963, 1965, Fièvres 1965, Christ's Passion 1955, 1957, 1960, 1964, Marie-Madeleine 1961, 1963, 1965, Saint François 1950, 1954, 1959, 1960, 1964, 1965. *Compositions include:* six sacred symphonies for choir and orchestra, several chamber works. *Publications:* twenty-four vols of autobiog., Brisons nos fers 1992. *Address:* La Bergerie, 76119 Varengeville-sur-Mer, Seine-Maritime, France.

CISNEROS, Gustavo A.; Venezuelan media executive; b. 16 Aug. 1947; m. Patricia Phelps; three c.; ed Babson Coll., Wellesley, Mass., USA; Chair. and CEO Cisneros Group (family-owned co. holding stakes in over 70 cos. in 39 countries including Venevisión, Univisión, Chilevisión, Caracol Televisión de Colombia, Playboy TV Latin America, Caribbean Communications Network, Direct TV Latin America and American Online Latin America (AOLA); Dir Panamco Bottling Co., AOL Latin America, Pueblo Int., Inc., Ibero-American Media Partners 1997–; owner Los Leones del Caracas baseball team 2001–; Co-Founder (with wife Patricia and brother Ricardo) Fundación Cisneros; charter mem. UN Information and Communications Technologies Task Force; mem. World Business Council, World Econ. Forum; mem. Int. Advisory Councils, Columbia Univ., Babson Coll.; mem. Advisory Cttee, David Rock-efeller Center for Latin American Studies, Harvard Univ.; mem. Bd of Advisers for Panama Canal; mem. Chair.'s Int. Advisory Council, Americas Soc.; mem. Bd of Overseers, Int. Center for Econ. Growth; mem. Bd Govs. Joseph H. Lauder Inst. of Man., Wharton School at Univ.of Pennsylvania; mem. Chair.'s Council, Museum of Modern Art; mem. Bd Trustees, Museum of TV and Radio. *Address:* Cisneros Group, 36 East 61st Street, New York, NY 10021, U.S.A. (Office); Edeficio Venevisión, Final Avenida La Salle, Colina de los Caobos, Caracas 1050 (Office); Fundación Cisneros, Centro Mozarteum, Final Avenida La Salle, Colina de los Caobos, Caracas 1050, Venezuela (Office). *Telephone:* (212) 708-9444 (USA) (Office); (582) 708-9697 (Venezuela) (Office). *E-mail:* info@cisneros.com (Office); info@fundacion.cisneros.org (Office). *Website:* www.cisneros.com (Office); www.venevision.net (Office).

CISNEROS, Henry G., BA, DPA; American politician; b. 11 June 1947, San Antonio; s. of J. George Cisneros and Elvira Munguia; m. Mary-Alice Perez; one s. two d.; ed Texas A&M, Harvard and George Washington Univs; Asst Dir Dept of Model Cities, San Antonio 1969–70; Asst to Exec. Vice-Pres., Nat. League of Cities, Washington, DC 1970–71; Teaching Asst Dept of Urban Studies and Planning, MIT 1972–74; Faculty mem. Public Admin. Program, Univ. of Texas 1974–87; Faculty mem. Dept of Urban Studies, Trinity Univ. 1974–87; mem. City Council, San Antonio 1975–81, Mayor 1981–89; Chair. Cisneros Asset Man. Co., Cisneros Benefit Group, Cisneros Communications

1989– ; Sec. Dept of Housing and Urban Devt 1993–97; Pres., COO Univision Communications Inc., LA 1997–2000; Chair., CEO American CityVista, San Antonio Sept. 2000–; Co-Chair. Nat. Hispanic Leadership Agenda 1988–92; Vice-Chair. Pres.'s Summit on Volunteeerism 1997; Hon. mem. American Inst. of Architects 1986; 23 hon. degrees; numerous honours and awards including Nat. Recognition Award, Mexican Govt 1985, Pres.'s Award, Nat. League of Cities 1989, Hubert Humphrey Award, Leadership Conference for Civil Rights 1994. *Publication:* San Antonio's Place in the Technology Economy 1982. *Leisure interests:* reading, going to the cinema, spending time with his family. *Address:* American CityVista, 454 Soledad, Suite 300, San Antonio, TX 78205-1555; 2002 West Houston Street, San Antonio, TX 78207, USA (Home). *Telephone:* (210) 228-9574 (Office). *Fax:* (210) 228-9914 (Office); (210) 224-7222 (Home). *Website:* www.americancityvista.com (Office).

CIUHA, Jože; Slovenian artist and painter; b. 26 April 1924, Trbovlje; s. of Jože and Amalija Ciuha; m. Radmila Novak 1962; one s. one d.; ed Acad. of Fine Arts, Ljubljana and Univ. of Rangoon, Burma (Buddhist art and philosophy); work includes painting on plexi-glass, print-making, murals, tapestry, scenography, illustrating and water colours; developed silk-screen technique; his extensive travels in Europe, Asia and S. America inspired deep interest in ancient cultures; over 100 one-man exhbns. in Europe and USA; more than 20 nat. and int. prizes. *Publications:* Petrified Smile, Conversations with Silence (based on sketchbooks from his S. American journey 1964–65), Travels to the Tenth Country (for children). *Leisure interest:* literature. *Address:* 61000 Ljubljana, Prešernova 12, Slovenia; and 4 Place de la Porte de Bagnolet, 75020 Paris, France. *Telephone:* (61) 218956 (Ljubljana).

CIULEI, Liviu; Romanian actor, scenographer and theatre, film and opera director; b. 7 July 1923, Bucharest; ed Bucharest Inst. of Architecture, Bucharest Conservatory of Music and Theatre; actor since 1945; stage Dir and scenographer since 1946; Dir "Lucia Sturdza Bulandra" Theatre, Bucharest 1962–72, Hon. Dir 1972–; Dir Guthrie Theater, Minneapolis, Minn. 1980–84; freelance Dir and direction teacher Columbia Univ., New York; acted at Bulandra, Odeon and C. Nottara theatres in Bucharest, as Puck in A Midsummer Night's Dream, Protasov in The Children Of The Sun, Treplev in The Seagull, Dunois in St Joan, Danton in Danton's Death; numerous roles in Romanian films 1951–75; State Prize 1962 for films; Grand Prize at the Int. Festival of Karlovy Vary 1960, for the film Valurile Dunării (The Waves of the Danube) as Dir and interpreter; prize for the best direction at the Int. Festival at Cannes 1965, for the film Pădurea Spînzuraţilor (The Forest of the Hanged) as Dir and interpreter. *Plays directed include:* Night Asylum, Bucharest 1960, Munich 1976, Washington, DC, Sydney 1977, Danton's Death, West Berlin 1967, Leonce and Lena, Bucharest 1970, Washington 1974, Vancouver 1976; Macbeth, Bucharest, Berlin 1968; As You Like It, Bucharest 1961, Gottingen 1968, Minneapolis 1982; The Tempest, Bucharest 1979, Minneapolis 1984; Richard II, Düsseldorf 1969; Hamlet, Washington 1978, New York 1987; A Midsummer Night's Dream, New York 1988; The Threepenny Opera, Bucharest 1964, Minneapolis 1986; Volpone, Berlin 1970; Macbeth, Munich 1973; Six Characters in Search of an Author, Washington 1988; Long Day's Journey into Night, Bucharest 1976; Bacchantes, Minneapolis 1988; Requiem for a Nun, Minneapolis 1984, etc. *Operas directed include:* Lady Macbeth of Mtsensk, The Gambler, Così fan tutte, Wozzeck, Falstaff, at Spoleto, Chicago, Washington, Cardiff, Amsterdam etc.; designer Prince Igor, Covent Garden, London 1990; numerous tours abroad with Romanian productions, including Budapest 1960, Leningrad and Moscow 1966, Florence 1969, 1970, Regensburg, Frankfurt Main, Essen 1970, Edin. Festival 1971, The Hague, Amsterdam 1972, etc. *Address:* Teatrul Bulandra, Str. Schitu Măgureanu Nr. 1, Bucharest, Romania; 400 West 119th Street, Apt. 12-0, New York, NY 10027, USA. *Telephone:* 149696 (Bucharest).

CIVILETTI, Benjamin R., LLB; American lawyer; b. 17 July 1935, Peekskill, NY; s. of Benjamin C. Civiletti and Virginia I. Civiletti; m. Gaile Lundgren 1958; two s. one d.; ed Johns Hopkins Univ., Baltimore, Md, Columbia Univ., New York, Univ. of Maryland; admitted Md Bar 1961; law clerk to judge, U.S. District Court, Md 1961–62; Asst U.S. attorney 1962–64; mem. firm, Venable, Baetjer & Howard 1964–77, 1981– (Chair. 1996–); Asst Attorney-Gen., Criminal Div., U.S. Dept of Justice 1977–79; Attorney-Gen. of USA 1979–81; Chair., Dir Healthcorp Inc.; Dir Beth. Steel Corpn, Wackenhut Corrections Corpn, MBNA America, MBNA International; Trustee Johns Hopkins Univ. Advisory Bd, Martindale-Lexus. *Leisure interests:* golf, gardening, antiques. *Address:* Venable, Baetjer & Howard, 1800 Merc Bank and Trust Building, 2 Hopkins Plaza, Baltimore, MD 21201 (Office); Venable, Baetjer & Howard, 1301 Pennsylvania Avenue, NW, Suite 1200, Washington, DC 20004, USA (Office). *Telephone:* (410) 244-7600 (Baltimore), (202) 962-4843 (Washington). *Fax:* (410) 244-7742 (Baltimore), (202) 962-8300 (Washington).

CIXOUS, Hélène, DèsSc; French professor of literature and author; b. 5 June 1937, Oran, Algeria; d. of Georges Cixous and Eve Klein; one s. one d.; ed Lycée d'Alger, Lycée de Sceaux, Sorbonne; mem. staff. Univ. of Bordeaux 1962–65; Asst lecturer, Sorbonne 1965–67; lecturer, Univ. of Paris X (Nanterre) 1967–68; helped found Univ. of Paris VIII (Vincennes) 1968, Chair. and Prof. of Literature 1968–, founder and Dir Centre d'Etudes Féminines 1974–; co-founder of journal Poétique 1969; Dr. hc (Queen's Univ., Kingston, Canada) 1991, (Edmonton, Canada) 1992, (York, UK) 1993, (Georgetown, Washington, DC, USA) 1995, (Northwestern, Chicago, USA) 1996; Prix Médicis 1969, Prix des critiques for best theatrical work of the year 1994, 2000, Amb. of Star Awards, Pakistan 1997; Southern Cross of Brazil 1989, Légion d'honneur 1994, Officier Ordre Nat. du Mérite 1998. *Theatre:* Portrait de Dora 1976, Le nom d'Oedipe 1978, La prise de l'école de Madhubaï 1984, L'Histoire terrible mais inachevée de Norodom Sihanouk, roi du Cambodge 1985, L'Indiade ou l'Inde de leurs rêves 1987, On ne part pas on ne revient pas 1991, Voile noire voile blanche 1994, L'Histoire qu'on ne connaîtra jamais 1994, La Ville Parjure ou le Réveil des Erinyes 1994, Tambours sur la digue 1999 (Molière Award 2000), Rouen la trentième nuit de mai 31 2001. *Publications include:* Le Prénom de Dieu 1967, Dedans 1969, Le Troisième corps, Les Commencements 1970, Un vrai jardin 1971, Neutre 1972, Tombe, Portrait du Soleil 1973, Révolutions pour plus d'un Faust 1975, Souffles 1975, La 1976, Partie 1976, Angst 1977, Préparatifs de noces au-delà de l'abîme 1978, Vivre l'orange 1979, Anankè 1979, Illa 1980, With ou l'art de l'innocence 1981, Limonade tout était si infini 1982, Le Livre de Promethea 1983, Manne 1988, Jours de l'An 1990, L'Ange au secret 1991, Déluge 1992, Beethoven à jamais 1993, La fiancée juive 1995, Messie 1996, Or, les lettres de mon père 1997, Osnabrück 1999, Les Rêveries de la femme sauvage 2000, Le Jour où je n'étais pas là 2000, Portrait de Jacques Derrida en jeune saint juif 2001, Benjamin à Montaigne, il ne faut pas le dire 2001, Manhattan. Lettres de la Préhistoire 2002; Essays: L'exil de James Joyce 1969, Prénoms de personne 1974, La Jeune née 1975, La venue à l'écriture 1977, Entre l'écriture 1986, L'heure de Clarice Lispector 1989, Reading with Clarice Lispector 1990, Readings, the Poetics of Blanchot, Joyce, Kafka, Lispector, Tsvetaeva 1992, Three Steps on the Ladder of Writing 1993, Photos de racines 1994, Stigmata 1998, Escaping Texts 1998. *Address:* Éditions Galilée, 9 rue Linné, 75005 Paris (Office); Centre d'études féminines, Université Paris VIII, 2 rue de la Liberté, 93526 Saint-Denis cedex 2, France.

CIZIK, Robert, BS, MBA; American business executive; b. 4 April 1931, Scranton, Pa; s. of John Cizik and Anna Paraska Cizik; m. Jane Morin 1953; three s. two d.; ed Univ. of Connecticut and Harvard Grad. School of Business Admin.; Accountant with Price, Waterhouse & Co. 1953–54, 1956; financial analyst, Exxon Co. 1958–61; joined Cooper Industries 1961, Dir Cooper Industries 1971–96, Pres. 1973–92, CEO 1975–95, Chair. Bd 1983–96; Chair. Stanadyne Automotive 1998–2000; Chair. Koppers Industries 1999–; Dir Harris Corpn 1988–99, Air Products & Chemicals 1992–2002, Temple-Inland Inc.; Advisory Dir Wingate Partners 1994–; Dir American Industrial Partners 1996–98; Proprietor Cizik Interests, Houston 1996–; Hon. LLD (Kenyon Coll.) 1983 and other awards. *Address:* Cizik Interests, Chase Tower, 600 Travis Street, Suite 3628, Houston, TX 77002, USA. *Telephone:* (713) 222-7300. *Fax:* (713) 222-7353.

CLAES, Willy; Belgian politician; b. 24 Nov. 1938, Hasselt; m. Suzanne Meynen 1965; one s. one d.; ed Univ. Libre de Bruxelles; mem. Exec. Cttee, Belgian Socialist Party, Jt Pres. 1975–77; mem. Limbourg Council 1964; mem. Chamber of Deputies 1968–; Minister of Educ. (Flemish) 1972–73, of Econ. Affairs 1973–74, 1977–81, Deputy Prime Minister 1979–81, 1988–94, Minister of Econ. Affairs, Planning and Educ. (Flemish Sector) 1988–91, of Foreign Affairs 1991–94; Sec.-Gen. NATO 1994–95; Pres. European Socialist Party; given suspended three year prison sentence for corruption Dec. 1998. *Publications include:* Tussen droom en werkelijkheid 1979, La Chine et l'Europe 1980, Livre Blanc de l'Energie 1980, Elementen voor een nieuw energiebeleid 1980, De Derde Weg: beschouwingen over de Wereldcrisis 1987. *Address:* Berkenlaan 62, B3500 Hasselt, Belgium.

CLAIR, Louis Serge; Mauritian politician; b. 1 April 1940, Rodrigues; s. of Emmanuel Clair and Willida Clair; m. Danielle Limock 1984; two c.; studied philosophy, theology and social sciences in France and TV production in Australia; Dir and Ed. L'Organisation (first local newspaper in island of Rodrigues) 1976–86; Leader Org. du Peuple Rodriguais; mem. Legis. Ass. 1982–; Minister for Rodrigues and the Outer Islands 1982–89, for Rodrigues 1989–95. *Leisure interests:* sight-seeing, gardening. *Address:* Organisation du Peuple Rodriguais, Port Mathurin, Rodrigues, Mauritius.

CLANCY, HE Cardinal Edward Bede, AC; Australian ecclesiastic; b. 13 Dec. 1923, Lithgow, NSW; s. of John Bede Clancy and Ellen Lucy Clancy; ed St Columba's Coll., Springwood, NSW, St Patrick's Coll, Manly, NSW, Pontifical Biblical Inst. and Propaganda Fide Univ., Rome; Auxiliary Bishop, Archdiocese of Sydney 1974–78; Archbishop, Archdiocese of Canberra and Goulburn 1979–83; Archbishop of Sydney 1983–. cr. HE Cardinal 1988, with the titular Church of St Maria in Vallicella; Chancellor Australian Catholic Univ. 1992–. *Leisure interest:* golf. *Address:* Catholic Archdiocese of Sydney, Archdiocesan Chancery, 13th Floor, Polding House, 276 Pitt Street, Sydney, NSW 2000, Australia. *Telephone:* (2) 9390-5100. *Fax:* (2) 9261-8312.

CLANCY, James; Canadian trade union official; b. 10 March 1950, Ont.; social worker, Toronto 1970s; Pres. Ont. Public Services Employees Union 1984–90; Pres. Nat. Union of Public and Gen. Employees 1990–; currently Gen. Vice-Pres. Canadian Labour Congress. *Address:* National Union of Public and General Employees, 15 Auriga Drive, Nepean, Ont., K2E 1B7, Canada (Office). *Telephone:* (613) 228-9800 (Office). *Fax:* (613) 228-9801 (Office). *E-mail:* national@nupge.ca (Office). *Website:* www.nupge.ca (Office).

CLANCY, Tom; American author; b. 12 March 1947, Baltimore; m. Wanda Thomas 1969; one s. three d.; ed Loyola Coll. *Publications:* The Hunt for Red October 1984, Red Storm Rising 1986, Patriot Games 1987, Cardinal of the Kremlin 1988, Clear and Present Danger 1989, The Sum of all Fears 1991, Without Remorse 1992, Submarine 1993, Debt of Honour 1994, Tom Clancy's Op Centre (with Steve Pieczenik) 1994, Reality Check 1995, Games of Statel (with Steve Pieczenik) 1996, Tom Clancy's Op Centre II (with Steve Pieczenik) 1996, Executive Orders 1996, Into the Storm (with Fred Franks Jr) 1997,

Rainbow Six 1998, Carrier 1999, The Bear and the Dragon 2000. *Address:* Red Storm Entertainment 2000 Aerial Centre, Suite 110, Morrisville, NC 27560, USA.

CLAPTON, Eric, OBE; British guitarist and songwriter; b. 30 March 1945, Ripley, Surrey; m. 1st Patti Harrison (née Boyd) 1979 (divorced 1988); one s. (deceased) by Lori Delsanto; one d.; m. 2nd Melia McEnery 2002; guitarist with groups: Roosters 1963, Yardbirds 1963–65, John Mayall's Bluesbreakers 1965–66, Cream 1966–68, Blind Faith 1969, Derek and the Dominoes 1970, Delaney and Bonnie 1970–72; solo performer 1972–; awarded six Grammys 1993; Grammy Award for best male pop vocalist 1997, Grammy Award for best pop instrumental performance 2002. *Recordings include:* Disraeli Gears 1967, Wheels of Fire 1968, Goodbye Cream 1969, Layla 1970, Blind Faith 1971, Concert for Bangladesh 1971, Eric Clapton's Rainbow Concert 1973, 461 Ocean Boulevard 1974, E.C. Was Here 1975, No Reason to Cry 1976, Slowhand 1977, Backless 1978, Just One Night 1980, Money and Cigarettes 1983, Behind the Sun 1985, August 1986, Journeyman 1989, 24 Nights 1992, Unplugged 1992, From the Cradle 1994, Pilgrim 1998, One More Car One More Rider 2002. *Compositions include:* Presence of the Lord, Layla, Badge (with George Harrison); soundtrack recordings include: Tommy 1974, The Colour of Money, Lethal Weapon, Rush; appeared in film Tommy 1974. *Address:* c/o Michael Eaton, 22 Blades Court, Deodar Road, London, SW15 2NU, England (Office).

CLARE, Anthony Ward, BAO, MD, M.PHIL.; psychiatrist and broadcaster; b. 24 Dec. 1942; s. of late Bernard J. Clare and Mary Agnes Dunne; m. Jane Carmel Hogan 1966; three s. four d.; ed Gonzaga Coll., Dublin, Univ. Coll., Dublin; Auditor Literary and Historical Soc. 1963–64; internship St Joseph's Hosp., Syracuse, NY 1967; psychiatric training, St Patrick's Hosp., Dublin 1967–69; psychiatric registrar, Maudsley Hosp., London 1970–72, Sr Registrar 1973–75; research worker, Gen. Practice Research Unit, Inst. of Psychiatry 1976–79, Sr Lecturer 1980–82; Prof. and Head of Dept of Psychological Medicine, St Bartholomew's Hosp. Medical Coll. 1983–88; Clinical Prof. of Psychiatry, Trinity Coll., Dublin 1989–2000; Medical Dir, St Patrick's Hosp., Dublin 1989–2000; Consultant Psychiatrist St Patrick's and St Edmondsbury Hosps 2000–; Chair. The Prince of Wales Advisory Group on Disability 1989–97; Hon. DSc (Univ. of Westminster) 1992, (Univ. of E Anglia 1993; Hon. DUniv (Open Univ.) 1993. *Radio appearances include:* Let's Talk About Me, In the Psychiatrist's Chair 1982–, Stop the Week, All in the Mind 1988–, Men In Crisis 2000. *TV series include:* Motives 1983, The Enemy Within 1995. *Publications:* Psychiatry in Dissent 1980, Psychosocial Disorders in General Practice 1979 (jt), Let's Talk About Me (jt) 1981, Social Work and Primary Health Care (jt) 1982, In the Psychiatrist's Chair 1984, Lovelaw 1986, Depression and How to Survive It (jt) 1993, On Men: Crisis in Masculinity 2000. *Leisure interests:* family, tennis, theatre. *Address:* St Patrick's Hospital, P.O. Box 136, James's Street, Dublin 8 (Office); Delville, Lucan, Co. Dublin, Ireland (Home). *Telephone:* (1) 677-5423 (Office). *Fax:* (1) 626–4782 (Home). *E-mail:* jcclare@indigo.ie (Home).

CLARK, Rt Hon (Charles) Joseph, PC, CC; Canadian politician; b. 5 June 1939, High River, Alberta; s. of Charles A. Clark and Grace R. Welch; m. Maureen Anne (née McTeer) 1973; one d.; ed Univ. of Alberta, Dalhousie Univ.; began career as a journalist; Nat. Pres. Progressive Conservative Party of Canada (PCP) Student Fed. 1963–65; First Vice-Pres. PCP Asscn of Alberta 1966–67; Lecturer, Univ. of Alberta 1965–67; Special Asst to Davie Fulton 1967; Exec. Asst to PCP Leader Robert Stanfield 1967–70; MP for Rocky Mountain 1972–79, for Yellowhead 1979–93; Leader of PCP 1976–83, 2000–; Prime Minister of Canada 1979–80; Sec. of State for External Affairs 1984–91, Minister responsible for Constitutional Affairs, Pres. of Queen's Privy Council 1991–93; UN Sec.-Gen.'s Special Rep. for Cyprus 1993–96; Pres. Joe Clark & Assocs.; Chair. CANOP Worldwide Corpn, SMG Canada, Canada-Korea Forum; mem. Bd Bentall Corpn, Hughes Aircraft of Canada, Inuvaluit Energy Inc. and other resource companies, Nat. History Soc. (of Canada), Pacific Council on Int. Policy, North-South Inst.; mem. Council of Freely Elected Heads of Govt, Int. Council of the Asia Soc.; Hon. LLD (New Brunswick) 1976, (Calgary) 1984, (Alberta) 1985, (Univ. of King's Coll., Concordia Univ.) 1994; mem. Alberta Order of Excellence 1983, Hon. Chief Samson Cree Nation 1992. *Publication:* A Nation Too Good To Lose 1994. *Address:* Progressive Conservative Party of Canada, 275 Slater Street, Suite 501, Ottawa, Ont. K1P 5H9 (Office); c/o Joe Clark & Associates, 30th Floor, 237 4th Avenue, SW, Calgary, Alberta, T2P 4X7, Canada. *Telephone:* (613) 238-6111 (Office); (403) 268-6863. *Fax:* (613) 238-7429 (Office); (403) 268-3100. *E-mail:* pcinfo@ pcparty.ca (Office). *Website:* www.pcparty.ca (Office).

CLARK, Colin Whitcomb, PhD, FRS, FRSC; Canadian mathematician; b. 18 June 1931, Vancouver; s. of George Savage Clark and Irene Clark (née Stewart); m. Janet Arlene Davidson 1955; one s. two d.; ed Univs of British Columbia and Washington; instructor Univ. of Calif. at Berkeley 1958–60; Asst Prof., then Assoc. Prof., Prof. of Mathematics Univ. of British Columbia 1960–94, Emer. Prof. 1994–; Regents' Prof. Univ. of Calif. at Davis 1986; Visiting Prof. Cornell Univ. 1987, Princeton Univ. 1997. *Publications include:* Dynamic Modelling in Behavioral Ecology (with M. Mangel) 1988, Mathematical Bioeconomics 1990, Dynamic State Variable Models in Ecology (with M. Mangel) 2000. *Leisure interests:* natural history, hiking, gardening. *Address:* 9531 Finn Road, Richmond, BC, V7A 2L3, Canada. *Telephone:* (604) 274-5379 (Home). *E-mail:* biec@interchange.ubc.ca (Home).

CLARK, Geoff; Australian politician and administrator; b. Warrnambool, Vic.; fmr heavyweight boxer and Australian Rules footballer; Admin. Admor Framlingham Aboriginal Trust 1979–96; Commr Aboriginal and Torres Strait Islander (ATSIC) Vic. 1996–, Chair. ATSIC 1999–; Vice-Chair. Aboriginal Provisional Govt; mem. Nat. (and Vic.) Indigenous Working Group on Native Title; participated in Australian dels to Cttee on the Elimination of Racial Discrimination, Geneva; mem. Indigenous Peoples Orgs on Int. Issues. *Leisure interests:* fishing, scuba diving, walking, training and gym workouts. *Address:* Aboriginal and Torres Strait Islander Commission, POB 17, Woden, ACT 2606, Australia (Office).

CLARK, Rt Hon. Helen Elizabeth, PC, MA; New Zealand politician; b. 26 Feb. 1950, Hamilton; m. Peter Davis; ed Epsom Girls' Grammar School and Auckland Univ.; fmr Lecturer, Dept of Political Studies, Auckland Univ. 1973–81; MP for Mount Albert 1981–96, 1999–, for Owairaka 1996–99; Minister of Housing and Minister of Conservation 1987–89, of Health 1989–90, of Labour 1989–90; Deputy Prime Minister 1989–90, Prime Minister of New Zealand Nov. 1999–, also Minister for Arts, Culture and Heritage; Deputy Leader of the Opposition 1990–93; Leader NZ Labour Party and Leader of the Opposition 1993–99; Spokesperson on Health and Labour 1990–93; mem. Labour Party 1971–; Danish Peace Foundation's Peace Prize 1986. *Leisure interests:* tennis, film, theatre, classical music, opera, cross-country skiing, trekking, reading. *Address:* Parliament House, Wellington, New Zealand (Office). *Website:* www.primeminister.govt.nz.

CLARK, Howard Charles, PhD, FRSC, FCIC; Canadian professor of chemistry and academic; b. 4 Sept. 1929, Auckland, NZ; s. of Eric Crago Clark; m. Isabel Joy Dickson-Clark 1954; two d.; ed Takapuna Grammar School, Auckland, Univs. of Auckland, Cambridge; lecturer, Univ. of Auckland 1954–55; Fellow, Univ. of Cambridge 1955–57; Asst Prof. then Prof., Univ. of British Columbia 1957–65; Assoc. Prof., Univ. of Western Ont. 1965–66; Prof. and Head of Chem., Univ. of Guelph 1967–76; Academic Vice-Pres. and Prof. of Chem. 1976–86; Pres., Vice-Chancellor Dalhousie Univ. 1986–95; Ed. Canadian Journal of Chemistry 1974–78; Chair. Int. Relations Cttee, Assoc. of Univs. and Colls. of Canada 1993–; Past Chair. Metro United Way Task Force; Co-Chair. NABST Oceans and Coasts Cttee 1993–94; Dir Corp. Higher Educ. Forum 1990–94; mem. Chem. Inst. of Canada (Pres. 1983–84), Assn of Atlantic Univs. 1986–, Assn of Univs. and Colls. of Canada 1986–, Nat. Advisory Bd on Science and Tech. 1991–94, Commonwealth Standing Cttee on Student Mobility and Higher Educ. Co-operation 1992–; Hon. DSc (Univ. of Vic.) 1989, (Univ. of Guelph) 1993; Noranda Award of Chem. Inst. of Canada 1968. *Publications:* author or co-author of over 250 articles and chapters in professional journals. *Leisure interests:* tennis, swimming, gardening. *Address:* RR#1, Moffat, Ont., L0P 1J0, Canada.

CLARK, Ian D., DPhil, MPP; Canadian government official and international civil servant; b. 15 April 1946, Antrim, UK; s. of Sidney Clark and Zella I. Stade; m. Marjorie Sweet 1968; ed Univs of British Columbia and Oxford and Harvard Univ.; Exec. Asst to Minister of Urban Affairs 1972–74; Dir then Dir-Gen. Analysis and Liaison Br. Dept of Regional Econ. Expansion 1974–79; Dir then Deputy Sec. Ministry of State for Econ. Devt 1979–82; Deputy Sec. Privy Council Office 1982–87; Deputy Minister, Dept of Consumer and Corp. Affairs 1987–89; Sec. Treas. Bd 1989–94, also Comptroller-Gen. of Canada 1993–94; Exec. Dir IMF 1994–96; Partner KPMG 1996–98; Pres. Council of Ont. Univs 1998–; Harvard Kennedy School Alumni Achievement Award 1997. *Address:* 44 Glenview Avenue, Toronto, Ont. M4R 1P6, Canada; Council of Ontario Universities, 11th Floor, 180 Dundas Street West, Toronto, Ont. M5G 1Z8 (Office). *Telephone:* (416) 979-2165 (Office); (416) 488-7784 (Home). *Fax:* (416) 979-8635 (Office); (416) 488-5916 (Home). *E-mail:* ianclark@cou.on.ca (Office). *Website:* http://www.cou.on.ca (Office).

CLARK, Johnson (John) Pepper, BA; Nigerian poet, dramatist and professor of English; b. 3 April 1935, Kiagbodo; s. of Fuludu Bekederemo Clark; m. Ebunoluwa Bolajoko Odutola; one s. three d.; ed Govt Coll. Ughelli, Univ. Coll. Ibadan, Princeton Univ.; Ed. The Horn (Ibadan) 1958; head of features, editorial writer Express Group of Newspapers, Lagos 1961–62; Research Fellow Inst. of African Studies, Univ. of Lagos 1963–64, lecturer Dept of English 1965–69, Sr lecturer 1969–72, Prof. of English 1972–80; consultant UNESCO 1965–67; Ed. Black Orpheus (journal) 1965–78; Visiting Distinguished Fellow Center for Humanities, Wesleyan Univ., Conn. 1975–76; Visiting Research Prof. Inst. of African Studies, Univ. of Ibadan 1979–80; Distinguished Visiting Prof. of English, Writer in Residence Lincoln Univ., Pa 1989; Visiting Prof. of English Yale Univ., Conn. 1990; Trustee, mem. Petroleum (Special) Trust Fund and Man. Bd, Abuja 1995–; mem. Nat. Council of Laureates (Nigeria) 1992; Nigerian Nat. Merit Award, Nigerian Nat. Order of Merit; Foundation Fellow Nigerian Acad. of Letters 1996. *Drama includes:* Song of a Goat 1961, Three Plays 1964, Ozidi 1968, The Bikoroa Plays 1985, The Wives' Revolt. *Poetry published includes:* Poems 1962, A Reed in the Tide 1965, Casualties 1970, A Decade of Tongues 1981, State of the Union 1985, Mandela and Other Poems 1988, A Lot From Paradise 1997. *Other publications:* America, Their America 1964, The Example of Shakespeare 1970, Transcription and Translation from the Oral Tradition of the Izon of the Niger Delta; The Ozidi Saga (trans.) 1977, The Hero as a Villain 1978. *Leisure interests:* walking, swimming, collecting classical European and traditional African music. *Address:* G.P.O. Box 1668, Marina, Lagos; 23 Oduduwa Crescent, GRA., Ikeja, Lagos; Okemeji Place, Funama, Kiagbodo, Burutu Local Government Area, Delta State, Nigeria. *Telephone:* (1) 497-8436 (Lagos). *Fax:* (1) 497-8463 (Lagos).

CLARK, Jonathan Charles Douglas, PhD; British historian; b. 28 Feb. 1951, London; s. of Ronald James Clark and Dorothy Margaret Clark; m. Katherine Redwood Penovich 1996; ed Cambridge Univ.; Research Fellow, Peterhouse, Cambridge 1977–81; Research Fellow, The Leverhulme Trust; Fellow All Souls Coll., Oxford 1986–95, Sr Research Fellow 1995; Joyce and Elizabeth Hall Distinguished Prof. of British History, Univ. of Kan., USA 1995–; Visiting Prof. Cttee on Social Thought, Univ. of Chicago 1993; Visiting Prof. Univ. of Northumbria 2001–; Visiting Distinguished Lecturer, Univ. of Manitoba 1999. *Publications:* The Dynamics of Change 1982, English Society 1688–1832 1985, Revolution and Rebellion 1986; The Memoirs and Speeches of James, 2nd Earl Waldegrave (Ed.) 1988, Ideas and Politics in Modern Britain (Ed.) 1990, The Language of Liberty 1660–1832 1993, Samuel Johnson 1994, Edmund Burke, Reflections on the Revolution in France (Ed.) 2000, English Society 1660–1832 (revised Edn) 2000, Samuel Johnson in Historical Context (Jt Ed.) 2002, Our Shadowed Present 2003; articles on British and American history. *Leisure interest:* history. *Address:* Hall Center for the Humanities, University of Kansas, 1540 Sunflower Road, Lawrence, KS 66045-7618, USA. *Telephone:* (785) 864-4798. *Fax:* (785) 864-3884 (Office). *E-mail:* jcdclark@ku.edu (Office).

CLARK, Rt Hon Joseph (see Clark, Rt Hon Charles Joseph).

CLARK, Lynda, QC, LLB, PhD; British lawyer and law officer; b. 26 Feb. 1949, Dundee; ed Univ. of St Andrews and Univ. of Edinburgh; lecturer Univ. of Dundee 1973–76; admitted as Advocate of the Scots Bar 1977; called to the English Bar, Inner Temple 1988, Bencher 2000; contested constituency of Fife NE (Labour Party) 1992; MP (Labour) for Edinburgh Pentlands 1997–; Advocate Gen. for Scotland 1999–; mem. Court Univ. of Edinburgh 1995–97. *Leisure interests:* reading, arts, swimming. *Address:* Office of the Advocate General for Scotland, Dover House, Whitehall, London, SW1A 2AU, England (Office). *Telephone:* (20) 7270-6720 (Office). *Fax:* (20) 7270-6813 (Office).

CLARK, Mary Higgins, BA; American author and business executive; b. 24 Dec. 1931, New York; d. of Luke Higgins and Nora Durkin; m. Warren Clark 1949 (died 1964); two s. three d.; ed Fordham Univ.; advertising Asst Remington Rand 1946; stewardess, Pan Am 1949–50; radio scriptwriter, producer Robert G. Jennings 1965–70; Vice-Pres., partner, Creative Dir, Producer Radio Programming, Aerial Communications, New York 1970–80; Chair. Bd, Creative Dir D.J. Clark Enterprises, New York 1980–; mem. American Acad. of Arts and Sciences, Mystery Writers of America, Authors League; several hon. degrees; Grand Prix de Littérature Policière, France 1980. *Publications:* Aspire to the Heavens, A Biography of George Washington 1969, Where Are the Children? 1976, A Stranger is Watching 1978, The Cradle Will Fall 1980, A Cry in the Night 1982, Stillwatch 1984, Weep No More, My Lady 1987, While My Pretty One Sleeps 1989, The Anastasia Syndrome 1989, Loves Music, Loves to Dance 1991, All Around the Town 1992, I'll Be Seeing You 1993, Remember Me 1994, The Lottery Winner 1994, Bad Behavior 1995, Let Me Call You Sweetheart 1995, Silent Night 1996, Moonlight Becomes You 1996, My Gal Sunday 1996, Pretend You Don't See Her 1997, The Plot Thickens 1997, You Belong to Me 1998, All Through the Night 1998, We'll Meet Again 1999, Before I Say Good-Bye 2000, Deck the Halls 2000, Daddy's Little Girl 2002, On the Street Where You Live 2002. *Address:* 210 Central Park S, New York, NY 10019, USA.

CLARK, Petula, CBE; British singer and actress; b. Sally Olwen, 15 Nov. 1932, Epsom; d. of Leslie Norman Clarke and Doris Olwen; m. Claude Wolff 1961; one s. two d.; started career as child singer entertaining troops during Second World War; early appearances in films under contract to Rank Organization; made numerous recordings and television appearances in both England and France; success of single Downtown started career in the US; has received two Grammy Awards and ten Gold Discs. *Films include:* Medal for the General 1944, Murder in Reverse 1945, London Town 1946, Strawberry Roan 1947, Here Come the Huggets, Vice Versa, Easy Money 1948, Don't Ever Leave Me 1949, Vote for Huggett 1949, The Huggetts Abroad, Dance Hall, The Romantic Age 1950, White Corridors, Madame Louise 1951, Made in Heaven 1952, The Card 1952, The Runaway Bus 1954, My Gay Dog 1954, The Happiness of Three Women 1955, Track the Man Down 1956, That Woman Opposite 1957, Daggers Drawn 1964, Finian's Rainbow 1968, Goodbye Mr Chips 1969, Second Star to the Right 1980. *Stage appearances:* Sound of Music 1981, Someone Like You (also wrote) 1989, Blood Brothers (Broadway) 1993, Sunset Boulevard 1995–96; nat. tour 1994–95, Sunset Boulevard 1995, 1996, New York 1998, USA tour 1998–2000. *Address:* c/o John Ashby, PO Box 288, Woking, Surrey, GU22 0YN, England.

CLARK, Sir Robert Anthony, Kt, DSC; British business executive; b. 6 Jan. 1924, London; s. of John Anthony Clark and Gladys Clark (née Dyer); m. Marjorie Lewis 1949; two s. one d.; ed Highgate School, King's Coll., Cambridge; served in Royal Navy 1942–46; qualified as lawyer with Messrs. Slaughter and May, became partner 1953; Dir Hill Samuel Bank Ltd (fmrly Philip Hill, Higginson, Erlangers Ltd, then Hill Samuel and Co. Ltd) 1962–91, Chair. 1974–87, Chief Exec. 1974–77, also Chief Exec. Hill Samuel Group 1976–80, Chair. 1980–87; IMI PLC 1980–89, Marley 1984–89, Vodafone Group PLC 1988–98, Rauscher Pierce and Clark Int. (fmrly Rauscher Pierce and Clark) 1992–; Dir Mirror Group Newspapers (now called Trinity Mirror Group) 1991, Chair. 1992–98; Dir Rover Group (fmrly BL PLC) 1977–88, Bank of England 1978–85, Shell Transport and Trading Co. 1982–94, Alfred McAlpine PLC 1957–96, SmithKline Beecham PLC 1986–95; Chair. Review Bd on Doctors' and Dentists' Remuneration 1979–86, Charing

Cross and Westminster Medical School 1982–96; Dir ENO 1983–87; Hon. DSc (Cranfield) 1982. *Leisure interests:* music, reading, collecting antiquarian books. *Address:* R,P&C International, 56 Green Street, Mayfair, London, W1Y 3RH; Munstead Wood, Godalming, Surrey GU7 1UN, England (Home). *Telephone:* (20) 7491-2434 (Office); (1483) 417867 (Home). *Fax:* (20) 7491-9081.

CLARK, Robin Jon Hawes, PhD, DSc, FRSA, FRSC, FRS; British university professor; b. 16 Feb. 1935, Rangiora, NZ; s. of Reginald Hawes Clark and Marjorie Alice Clark; m. Beatrice Rawdin Brown 1964; one s. one d.; ed Marlborough Coll., Blenheim, Christ's Coll., Christchurch, NZ, Canterbury Univ. Coll., Univ. of NZ, Univ. of Otago, NZ, Univ. Coll. London; Asst lecturer in Chemistry Univ. Coll. London 1962, lecturer 1963–71, Reader 1972–81, Prof. 1982–88, Head Dept of Chemistry 1989–99, Dean Faculty of Science 1988–89, Sir William Ramsay Prof. 1989–, mem. Council 1991–94, Fellow Univ. Coll. London 1992, mem. Senate and Acad. Council Univ. of London 1988–93; mem. Dalton Council Royal Soc. of Chem. 1985–88, Vice-Pres. 1988–90; mem. SRC Inorganic Chem. Panel 1977–80, S.E.R.C. Post-Doctoral Fellowships Panel 1983, S.E.R.C. Inorganic Chem. Panel 1993–94; Chair. Steering Cttee Int. Conferences on Raman Spectroscopy 1990–92, 11th Int. Conf. on Raman Spectroscopy, London 1988, Advisory Council, Ramsay Memorial Fellowships Trust 1989– (Trustee 1994–); mem. Council, Royal Soc. 1993–94, Royal Institution 1996–, Vice-Pres. 1997–, Sec. 1998–; Tilden 1983, Nyholm 1989, Thomas Graham 1991, Harry Hallam 1993, 2000, and Liversidge 2003; Lecturer and Medallist Royal Soc. of Chem.; Hon. Fellow Royal Soc. of NZ 1989; mem. Academia Europaea 1990, Fellow Royal Soc. 1990 (mem. Council 1993–94); UK-Canada Rutherford Lecturer 2000; Hon. FRSNZ; Hon. DSc (Canterbury, NZ) 2001; Joannes Marcus Marci Medal (Czech Spectroscopy Soc.) 1998, T. J. Sidey Medal (Royal Soc. of NZ) 2001. *Publications:* The Chemistry of Titanium and Vanadium 1968, The Chemistry of Titanium, Zirconium and Hafnium (jtly) 1973, The Chemistry of Vanadium, Niobium and Tantalum (jtly) 1973, Advances in Spectroscopy (co-ed.) Vols 1–26 1975–98, Raman Spectroscopy (co-ed.) 1988; over 450 scientific papers in learned journals on topics in transition metal chemistry and spectroscopy. *Leisure interests:* golf, cycling, long distance walking, travel, bridge, music, theatre, wine. *Address:* Christopher Ingold Laboratories, University College London, 20 Gordon Street, London, WC1H 0AJ, England. *Telephone:* (1923) 85-7899 (Home); (20) 7679-7457 (Office). *Fax:* (20) 7679-7463. *E-mail:* r.j.h.clark@ucl.ac.uk.

CLARK, Gen. Wesley; American army officer; ed US Mil. Acad., Univ. of Oxford (Rhodes Scholar); served in Viet Nam, awarded silver and bronze stars; fmr Sr mil. Asst to Gen. Alexander Haig; fmr Head Nat. Army Training Center; fmr Dir of Strategy Dept of Defense; Sr mem. American negotiating team at Bosnian peace negotiations, Dayton, OH 1995; fmr Head US Southern Command, Panama; NATO Supreme Allied Commdr in Europe (SACEUR) 1997–2000; Head US Forces in Europe 1997–2000; Consultant Stephens Group Inc. 2000–; Sr Adviser Center for Strategic and Int. Studies, Washington, DC 2000–; Hon. KBE. *Publication:* Waging Modern War: Bosnia, Kosovo and the Future of Combat 2001. *Address:* Stephens Group Inc., 111 Center Street, Little Rock, AR 72201, USA. *Website:* www.stephens.com.

CLARK, William, Jr, BA; American diplomatist; b. 12 Oct. 1930, Oakland, Calif.; s. of William Clark and Mary Edith Coady; m. Judith Lee Riley 1954; one s.; ed San Jose State Univ., Columbia Univ., Nat. War Coll.; Dir Liaison Dept U.S. Civil Admin., Naha, Japan 1970–72, U.S.-Japan Trade Officer Embassy, Tokyo, Japan 1972–74, Dir Special Trade Activities Dept of State, Washington, DC 1974–76, Nat. War Coll. 1976–77, Political Counsellor Embassy, Seoul, Rep. of Korea 1977–80, Dir Japanese Affairs, Dept of State, Washington, DC 1980–81; Minister Embassy Tokyo, Japan 1981–85, Cairo, Egypt 1985–86; Chargé d'Affaires Embassy, Egypt 1986, Deputy Asst Sec. of State, Washington, DC 1986–89; Amb. to India 1989–92; Asst Sec. of State East Asian and Pacific Affairs, Dept of State 1992–93; Sr Adviser Centre for Strategic and Int. Studies, Washington, D.C. 1993–95, 1996–; Pres. Japan Soc. 1996–; Hon. DLitt Calif. State Univ. 1992; Superior Service Award 1971, Outstanding Service Award 1972, Distinguished Service Award 1985, Meritorious Service Award 1987, Distinguished Honor Award 1989, Order of the Sacred Treasure Gold and Silver Star (Japan) 2000. *Leisure interests:* tennis, riding, skiing, golf. *Address:* 333 E. 474th Street, New York, NY 10017 (Office); 4845 W. Street NW, Washington, DC 20007, USA (Home); 420 E. 54th Street, Apartment 5–J, New York, NY 10022. *Telephone:* (212) 715-1221 (Office); (212) 319-4927 (New York) (Home); (202) 398-7160 (Washington). *E-mail:* wclark@japansociety.org (Office). *Website:* www.japansociety.org (Office).

CLARK OF WINDERMERE, Baron (Life Peer), cr. 2001, of Windermere in the County of Cumbria; **David George Clark,** PC, PhD; British politician; b. 19 Oct. 1939, Castle Douglas; s. of George Clark and Janet Clark; m. Christine Kirkby 1970; one d.; ed Univ. of Manchester, Univ. of Sheffield; fmr forester, lab. Asst and student teacher; Pres. Univ. of Manchester Union 1963–64; trainee man., USA 1964; univ. lecturer 1965–70; MP for Colne Valley 1970–74, for S. Shields 1979–; Labour spokesman on Agric. and Food 1973–74, on Defence 1980–81, on Environment 1981–86, on Environmental Protection and Devt 1986–87, on Food, Agric. and Rural Affairs 1987–92, on Defence, Disarmament and Arms Control 1992–97; Pres. Open Spaces Soc. 1979–88; mem. Parl. Ass., NATO 1981–; Chancellor of Duchy of Lancaster 1997–98; Chair. Atlantic Council of UK 1998–, Forestry Comm. 2001–; mem. House of Lords 2001–; Freeman of South Tyneside 1999. *Publications:* The

Industrial Manager 1966, Colne Valley: Radicalisation to Socialism 1981, Victor Grayson: Labour's Lost Leader 1985, We Do Not Want the Earth 1992. *Leisure interests:* walking, gardening, watching football. *Address:* House of Lords, London, SW1A 0PW, England. *Telephone:* (20) 7219-8890 (Office). *Fax:* (20) 7219-4885 (Office). *E-mail:* clarkd@parliament.uk; dr.david.clark@lineone.net (Home).

CLARKE, Aidan, PhD; Irish professor of modern history; b. 2 May 1933, Watford, England; s. of the late Austin Clarke and of Nora Walker; m. Mary Hughes 1962; two s. two d.; ed The High School, Dublin and Trinity Coll., Dublin; lecturer in Modern History and Politics, Magee Univ. Coll., Derry 1959–65; lecturer in Modern History, Trinity Coll., Dublin 1965–78, Assoc. Prof. 1978–86, Erasmus Smith's Prof. 1986–, Sr Tutor 1971–73, Registrar 1974–76, Bursar 1980–81, Vice-Provost 1981–87, 1989–91, Fellow 1970–; Chair. Irish Historical Soc. 1978–80; mem. Royal Irish Acad. 1982–, Sr Vice-Pres. 1988–89, Sec. Cttee of Polite Literature and Antiquities 1989–90, Pres. 1990–93; Hon. LittD (Dublin) 1992. *Publications include:* The Old English in Ireland 1625–42 1966, contribs. to The New History of Ireland, 111: Early Modern Ireland 1976 Prelude to Restoration in Ireland: the end of the Commonwealth, 1659-1660 1999; numerous articles and essays on early modern Irish history. *Address:* Arts Building, Trinity College, Dublin 2 (Office); 160 Rathfarnham Road, Dublin 14, Ireland (Home). *Telephone:* (1) 608-1572 (Office); (1) 490-3223 (Home). *E-mail:* aclarke@tcd.ie (Office).

CLARKE, Sir Arthur C(harles), Kt, CBE, BSc; British science writer and underwater explorer; b. 16 Dec. 1917, Minehead, Somerset; s. of Charles Wright Clarke and Nora Mary Willis; m. Marilyn Mayfield 1953 (divorced 1964); ed Huish's Grammar School, Taunton and King's Coll., London; auditor HM Exchequer and Audit Dept 1936–41; RAF 1941–46; Inst. of Electrical Engineers 1949–50; Technical Officer on first G.C.A. radar 1943; originated communications satellites 1945; Chair. British Interplanetary Soc. 1947–50, 1953; Asst Ed. Physics Abstracts 1949–50; engaged on underwater exploration on Great Barrier Reef of Australia and coast of Ceylon (Sri Lanka) 1954–; has lived in Sri Lanka since 1956; Chancellor, Univ. of Moratuwa, Sri Lanka, 1979–, Int. Space Univ. 1989–; Vikram Sarabhai Prof., Physical Research Lab., Ahmedabad 1980; extensive lecturing, radio and TV, UK and USA; Fellow King's Coll. London, Royal Astronomical Soc.; mem. Royal Asiatic Soc., British Astronomical Asscn, Science Fiction Writers of America, Astronomical Soc. of the Pacific; Hon. DSc (Beaver Coll.) 1971, (Moratuwa) 1979, Hon. DLitt (Bath) 1988, (Liverpool) 1995, (Baptist Univ. of Hong Kong) 1996; numerous prizes and awards, including UNESCO Kalinga Prize 1961; Stuart Ballantine Gold Medal, Franklin Inst. 1963; AAAS—Westinghouse Science Writing Prize 1969; AIAA Aerospace Communications Award 1974; Nebula Award 1973, 1974, 1979, John Campbell Award 1974, Hugo Award 1956, 1974, 1980, Galaxy Award 1979, IEEE Centennial Medal 1984, Marconi Int. Fellowship 1982, Vidya Jyothi Medal 1986, Science Fiction Writers of America 'Grand Master' 1986, Charles A. Lindbergh Award 1987, Assoc. Fellow, Third World Acad. of Sciences 1987, Freedom of Minehead, Somerset 1992, Von Karman Award (Int. Acad. of Astronautics) 1996, Presidential Award (Univ. of Ill.) 1997, Communications Award (Explorers Club) 2001, Von Karman Wings Award (Aerospace Historical Soc.) 2001, Paul Harris Fellow and Hon. Rotary Mem. 2001. *Film screenplay:* 2001: A Space Odyssey (with Stanley Kubrick) 1964–68. *Television work:* Arthur C. Clarke's Mysterious World 1980, World of Strange Powers 1984, Arthur C. Clarke's Mysterious Universe 1994 (all as writer and host). *Publications:* Non-fiction: Interplanetary Flight 1950, The Exploration of Space 1951, The Young Traveller in Space 1954 (published in USA as Going into Space), The Coast of Coral 1956, The Making of a Moon 1957, The Reefs of Taprobane 1957, Voice across the Sea 1958, The Challenge of the Spaceship 1960, The Challenge of the Sea 1960, Profiles of the Future 1962, Voices from the Sky 1965, The Promise of Space 1968, The View from Serendip 1977, 1984: Spring 1984, Ascent to Orbit 1984, Astounding Days: A Science Fictional Autobiography 1989, How the World Was One 1992, The Snows of Olympus 1994; with Mike Wilson: Boy Beneath the Sea 1958, The First Five Fathoms 1960, Indian Ocean Adventure 1961, The Treasure of the Great Reef 1964, Indian Ocean Treasure 1964; with R. A. Smith: The Exploration of the Moon 1954; with Editors of Life: Man and Space 1964; with the Apollo XI Astronauts: First on the Moon 1970; Report on Planet Three 1972; with Chesley Bonestell: Beyond Jupiter 1972; with Simon Welfare and John Fairley: Arthur C. Clarke's Mysterious World 1980 (also TV series), Arthur C. Clarke's World of Strange Powers 1984, Arthur C. Clarke's Chronicles of the Strange and Mysterious 1987, Arthur C. Clarke's A–Z of Mysteries 1993; with Peter Hyams: The Odyssey File 1984, "Greetings, Carbon-Based Bipeds!" 1999; Fiction: Prelude to Space 1951, The Sands of Mars 1951, Islands in the Sky 1952, Against the Fall of Night 1953, Childhood's End 1953, Expedition to Earth 1953, Earthlight 1955, Reach for Tomorrow 1956, The City and the Stars 1956, Tales from the White Hart 1957, The Deep Range 1957, The Other Side of the Sky 1958, Across the Sea of Stars 1959, A Fall of Moondust 1961, From the Oceans, From the Stars 1962, Tales of Ten Worlds 1962, Dolphin Island 1963, Glide Path 1963, Prelude to Mars 1965; with Stanley Kubrick: 2001: A Space Odyssey (novel and screenplay) 1968; The Lost Worlds of 2001 1971, 1972, Of Time and Stars 1972, The Wind from the Sun 1972, Rendezvous with Rama 1973, The Best of Arthur C. Clarke 1973, Imperial Earth 1975, The Fountains of Paradise 1979, 2010: Odyssey Two 1982, The Sentinel 1984, The Songs of Distant Earth 1986, 2061: Odyssey Three 1988, Cradle (with Gentry Lee) 1988, Rama II (with Gentry Lee) 1989, Tales from Planet Earth 1990, The Ghost from the Grand Banks 1990, The Garden of Rama (with Gentry Lee) 1991, The Hammer of God 1993, Rama Revealed (with Gentry Lee) 1993, Richter 10 (with Mike McQuay), 3001: The Final Odyssey 1997, Trigger (with Mike Kube-McDowell) 1998, The Light of Other Days (with Stephen Baxter) 2000, Greetings, Carbon-Based Bipeds! 2000, Collected Short Stories 2001. *Leisure interests:* photography, table tennis, diving. *Address:* 25 Barnes Place, Colombo 7, Sri Lanka; c/o David Higham Associates, 5 Lower John Street, Golden Square, London, W1R 3PE, England. *Telephone:* (1) 699757 (Colombo). *Fax:* (1) 698730 (Colombo).

CLARKE, Brian, FRSA; British artist; b. 2 July 1953, Oldham, Lancs.; s. of late Edward Ord Clarke and of Lilian Clarke (née Whitehead); m. Elizabeth Cecilia Finch 1972; one s.; ed Oldham School of Arts and Crafts, Burnley School of Art, The North Devon Coll. of Art and Design; Visiting Prof. Architectural Art, Univ. Coll. London 1993; mem. Council Winston Churchill Memorial Trust 1985–; Trustee and mem. Cttee Robert Fraser Foundation 1990–; Trustee The Stained Glass Museum; the subject of six books; judge, The BBC Design Awards 1990, Royal Fine Art Comm. and Sunday Times Architecture Award 1991; stage designs for Paul McCartney World Tour 1990, 1993, The Ruins of Time (Dutch Nat. Ballet) 1993; Europa Nostra award 1990, Leeds Award for Architecture, Special Award for Stained Glass 1990, The European Shopping Centre Award 1995, BDA Auszeichnung guter Bauten, Heidelberg 1996; Hon. FRIBA 1993. *Major exhibitions include:* Festival of City of London (with John Piper and Marc Chagall) 1979, Mappin Art Gallery, Sheffield 1980, RIBA, London 1981, Robert Fraser Gallery, London 1983, Seibu Museum of Art, Tokyo 1987, Hessisches Landesmuseum 1988, Deutsches Architekturmuseum Frankfurt 1980, Galerie Karsten Greve, Cologne 1989, Indar Pasricha Gallery, New Delhi 1989, Mayor Gallery, London 1990, 1993, Sezon Museum of Art, Tokyo 1990, Ingolstadt, Germany 1992, Oldham Art Gallery 1993, Tony Shafrazi Gallery, New York 1995, (with Linda McCartney) Musée Suisse du Vitrail au Château de Romont, Switzerland. *Major works:* St Gabriel's Church, Blackburn 1976, All Saints Church, Habergham 1976, Queen's Medical Centre, Nottingham 1978, Laver's & Barraud Bldg, London 1981, Olympus Optical Europa GmbH HQ Bldg, Hamburg 1981, King Khaled Int. Airport, Riyadh, Saudi Arabia 1982, Buxton Thermal Baths, Derbyshire 1987, Lake Sagami Country Club, Yamanishi, Japan (in Asscn with Arata Isozaki) 1988, New Synagogue, Darmstadt, Germany 1988, Victoria Quarter, Leeds 1989, Cibreo Restaurant, Tokyo 1990, Glaxo Pharmaceuticals, Stockley Park, Uxbridge 1990, Stansted Airport, Essex (in Asscn with Sir Norman Foster) 1991, Spindles Shopping Centre, Oldham 1991–93, España Telefónica, Barcelona 1991, Number One America Square, London 1991, 35–38 Chancery Lane, London 1991, The Carmelite, London 1992, 100 New Bridge Street, London 1992, façade of Hôtel de Ville des Bouches-du-Rhône, Marseille (with Will Alsop) 1992–94, Glass Dune, Hamburg (with Future Systems) 1992, EAM Bldg, Kassel, Germany 1992–93, New Synagogue, Heidelberg, Germany 1993, W H Smith & Sons, Abingdon 1994, SMS Lowe The Grace Bldg, New York 1994, Cliveden Hotel 1994, Schadow Arkaden, Düsseldorf 1994, Norte Shopping, Rio de Janeiro 1995, Rye Hosp., Sussex (with Linda McCartney) 1995, Pfizer Pharmaceuticals, New York 1997, Willis Corroon Bldg, Ipswich 1997, RWE Essen (refurbishment of lobby) 1997, Offenbach Synagogue 1997, Praça Norte Clock Tower 1997, Obersalbach 1997, Chicago Sinai 1997. *Design:* Hammersmith Hosp., London 1993, Crossrail, Paddington, London 1994, Q206 Berlin 1994, Frankfurter Allee Plaza, Berlin 1994, New Synagogue, Aachen 1994, Hungerford Bridge, London (with Alsop and Störmer) 1996, Center Villa-Lobos, São Paulo 1997, Future Systems Tower NEC 1997, Heidelberg Cathedral 1997, Chep Lap Kok Airport, Hong Kong 1997. *Leisure interests:* reading, hoarding. *Address:* The Tony Shafrazi Gallery, 119 Wooster Street, New York, NY 10012, USA. *Telephone:* (212) 274-9300. *Fax:* (212) 334-9499.

CLARKE, Bryan Campbell, MA, DPhil, FRS; British professor of genetics; b. 24 June 1932, Gatley, Cheshire; s. of Robert Campbell Clarke and Gladys Mary Clarke (née Carter); m. Ann Gillian Jewkes 1960; one s. one d.; ed Fay School, Southborough, Mass., Magdalen Coll. School, Oxford and Magdalen Coll., Oxford; Nature Conservancy research student, Oxford Univ. 1956–59; Asst in Zoology, Univ. of Edin. 1959–63, Lecturer 1963–69, Reader 1969–71; Prof. of Genetics, Univ. of Nottingham 1971–93, Research Prof. 1993–97, Prof. Emer. 1997–, Leverhulme Emer. Research Fellow, Inst. of Genetics 1999–; Science Research Council Sr Research Fellow 1976–81; Ed. Heredity 1978–85, Proc. of the Royal Society, series B 1988–93; Vice-Pres. Genetical Soc. 1981–83, Linnean Soc. 1984–86, Soc. for the Study of Evolution 1990–91; Chair. Terrestrial Life Sciences Cttee NERC 1984–87, Biological Sciences Panel, HEFCE 1994–96, Bd of Trustees, Charles Darwin Trust 2000–; mem. Biological Sciences Cttee, SERC 1990–93, Council of Royal Soc. 1994–96. *Publications:* Berber Village 1959; about 120 scientific publications. *Leisure interests:* painting, computing. *Address:* Linden Cottage, School Lane, Colston Bassett, Nottingham, NG12 3FD, England (Home). *Telephone:* (1949) 81243 (Home).

CLARKE, Rt Hon Charles (Rodway), PC, BA; British politician; b. 21 Sept. 1950; s. of Sir Richard Clarke and Brenda Clarke (née Skinner); m. Carol Marika Pearson 1984; two s.; ed Highgate School and King's Coll., Cambridge; Pres. Nat. Union of Students (NUS) 1975–77; various admin. posts 1977–80; Head, Office of Rt. Hon. Neil Kinnock, MP 1981–92; Chief Exec. Quality Public Affairs 1992–97; mem. Hackney London Borough Council 1980–86; MP (Labour) for Norwich S. 1997–; Parl. Under-Sec. of State, Dept for Educ. and Employment 1998–99; Minister of State, Home Office 1999–2001; Chair. Labour Party and Minister without Portfolio 2001–02; Sec. of State for Educ.

and Skills 2002–; mem. Treasury Select Cttee 1997–98. *Leisure interests:* chess, reading, walking. *Address:* Department for Education and Skills, Sanctuary Buildings, Great Smith Street, London, SW1P 3BT, England (Office). *Telephone:* (20) 7925-5000 (Office). *Fax:* (20) 7925-6000. *E-mail:* dfes .ministers@dfes.gsi.gov.uk. *Website:* www.dfes.gov.uk.

CLARKE, Christopher Simon Courtenay Stephenson, QC, FRSA; British lawyer; b. 14 March 1947, Plymouth; s. of the late Rev. John Stephenson Clarke and of Enid Courtenay Clarke; m. Caroline Anne Fletcher 1974; one s. two d.; ed Marlborough Coll. and Gonville and Caius Coll., Cambridge; called to the Bar, Middle Temple 1969; apptd. QC 1984; Recorder of the Crown Court 1990–, Deputy High Court Judge 1993–; mem. Courts of Appeal of Jersey and Guernsey 1998; Attorney of the Supreme Court of Turks and Caicos Islands 1975–; Bencher of the Middle Temple 1991; Counsel for the Bloody Sunday Inquiry 1998–; Councillor Int. Bar Asscn 1988–90; Chair. Commercial Bar Asscn 1993–95; mem. Bar Council 1993–99; Harmsworth Memorial Scholar, Middle Temple 1969; Lloyd Stott Memorial Prizeman (Middle Temple) 1969, J.J. Powell Prizeman (Middle Temple) 1969. *Leisure interest:* opera. *Address:* Brick Court Chambers, 7–8 Essex Street, London, WC2R 3LD (Office); 42 The Chase, London, SW4 0NH, England (Home). *Telephone:* (20) 7379-3550 (Office); (20) 7622-0765 (Home). *Fax:* (20) 7379-3558 (Office); (20) 7652-4555 (Home). *E-mail:* clarke@brickcourt.co.uk (Office); cscsclarke@msn.com (Home).

CLARKE, David Stuart, AO, BEcons, MBA; Australian business executive; b. 3 Jan. 1942; s. of Stuart Clarke and Ailsie Clarke; m. 1st Margaret Partridge 1964 (divorced 1994); two s.; m. 2nd Jane Graves 1995; ed Knox Grammar School and Sydney and Harvard Univs; Dir Darling & Co. Ltd (now Schroder Australia Ltd) 1966–71, Babcock Australia Holdings Ltd 1972–81, Hooker Corpn Ltd 1984–86, Reil Corpn Ltd 1986–87; Jt Man. Dir Hill Samuel Australia Ltd 1971–77, Man. Dir 1977–84, Chair. 1984–85: Dir Hill Samuel & Co. Ltd (London) 1978–84; Chair. Accepting Houses Asscn of Australia 1974–76, Sceggs Darlinghurst Ltd 1976–78; Exec. Chair. Macquarie Bank Ltd 1985–; Chair. Barlile Corpn Ltd 1986–93, NSW Rugby Union 1989–95, Wine Cttee, Royal Agricultural Soc. of NSW 1990–, Brian McGuigan Wines Ltd 1991–, Australian Wool Realization Comm. 1991–93, Menzies Research Centre 1994–97, Goodman Fielder Ltd 1995–2000, Campaign Chair. Salvation Army Educ. Foundation 1996–98; Deputy Chair. Australian Opera 1983–86, Chair. 1986–95, Chair. Opera Australia Capital Fund, Opera Australia 1996–; Pres. Harvard Club of Australia 1977–79; Dir Australian Rugby Union Ltd 1990–97, Deputy Chair. 1997–98, Chair. 1998–; mem. Exec. Cttee., Cttee. for Econ. Devt of Australia 1982–98; mem. Council Royal Agric. Soc. of New South Wales 1986– (mem. Bd 1991–), Bd of Trustees, Financial Markets Foundation for Children 1989–2000 (Hon. life mem. 2000), Sydney Advisory Bd (Chair. 1999–), The Salvation Army 1990–, Corp. Citizen's Cttee Children's Cancer Inst. of Australia 1992–, Investment Advisory Cttee, Australian Olympic Foundation 1996–, Advisory Cttee, Harvard Business School Asia 1997–, Council, Royal Humane Soc. of NSW 1999–2000; Co-convenor Cook Soc. 1988–97; Hon. Fed. Treas. Liberal Party of Australia 1987–89; Hon. DSc (Econ), Sydney Univ. *Leisure interests:* opera, skiing, tennis, golf, bridge, philately, personal computers, ballet, wine. *Address:* 5 Keltie Bay, 15 Sutherland Crescent, Darling Point, NSW 2027, Australia.

CLARKE, Edmund (Ed), PhD; Canadian banking executive; b. 1947; ed Harvard Univ., USA; fmr Fed. Deputy Minister under Pierre Trudeau, headed Nat. Energy Program 1980; corp. finance officer Merrill Lynch Canada Inc. 1984; fmr Financial Trustco Capital Ltd; CEO CT Financial Services Inc., negotiated $7-billion takeover by Toronto-Dominion (TD) Bank Financial Group 1999; Pres. and COO TD Bank Financial Group 1999–2002, CEO Dec. 2002–. *Address:* Toronto-Dominion Bank, POB 1, Toronto Dominion Centre, Toronto, M5K 1A2, Canada (Office). *Website:* www .td.com (Office).

CLARKE, Sir Ellis Emmanuel Innocent, GCMG, LLB; Trinidadian government official, lawyer and diplomatist; b. 28 Dec. 1917, Port of Spain; s. of the late Cecil E. I. Clarke and of Elma Pollard; m. Eyrmyntrude Hagley 1952; one s. one d.; ed St Mary's Coll., Port of Spain, Trinidad, London Univ. and Gray's Inn, London; pvt. law practice, Trinidad 1941–54; Solicitor-Gen. Trinidad and Tobago 1954–56; Deputy Colonial Sec. 1956–57; Attorney-Gen. 1957–61; Constitutional Adviser to the Cabinet 1961–62; Amb. to the United States 1962–73 and to Mexico 1966–73; Perm. Rep. to UN 1962–66; Rep. on Council of OAS 1967–73; Chair. of Bd, British West Indian Airways 1968–73; Gov.-Gen. and C-in-C of Trinidad and Tobago 1973–76, Pres. 1976–87; Awarded first Trinity Cross (T.C.) 1969, KStJ 1973, Hon. Master of Bench, Gray's Inn 1980. *Leisure interests:* golf, racing, cricket. *Address:* 16 Frederick Street, Port of Spain, Trinidad and Tobago.

CLARKE, Geoffrey, RA, ARCA; British artist and sculptor; b. 28 Nov. 1924; s. of John Moulding Clarke and Janet Petts; m.; two s.; ed RCA; exhbns at Gimpel Fils Gallery 1952, 1955, Redfern Gallery 1965, Taranman Gallery 1975, 1976, 1982, Yorkshire Sculpture Park 1994, Chappel Gallery 1994; touring exhbns at Christchurch Mansions, Ipswich 1994, Herbert Art Gallery, Coventry and Pallant House, Chichester 1995; retrospective Exhbn Fine Art Soc. 2000; commissioned work includes: iron sculpture, Time Life Building, New Bond Street; mosaics, Liverpool Univ. Physics Block; stained glass windows for Treasury, Lincoln Cathedral; bronze sculpture, Thorn Electric Building, Upper St Martin's Lane; three stained glass windows, high altar, cross and candle-sticks, the flying cross and crown of thorns, all for Coventry

Cathedral, screens in Royal Mil. Chapel, Birdcage Walk; other works at Newcastle Civic Centre, Churchill Coll., Aldershot, Suffolk Police HQ, All Souls, W London, The Majlis, Abu Dhabi, York House, N London, St Paul, Minn. *Address:* Stowe Hill, Hartest, Bury St Edmunds, Suffolk, IP29 4EQ, England. *Telephone:* (1284) 830319. *Fax:* (1284) 830126.

CLARKE, Graeme Wilber, MA, LittD; Australian professor of classics; b. 31 Oct. 1934, Nelson, New Zealand; s. of Wilber P. Clarke and Marjorie E (née Le May) Clarke; m. Nancy J. Jordan 1963; three s. one d.; ed Sacred Heart Coll., Auckland, NZ, Univ. of Auckland, Balliol Coll., Oxford; lecturer, Dept of Classics, Australian Nat. Univ. 1957, 1961–63, Sr Lecturer, Dept of Classics and Ancient History, Univ. of Western Australia 1964–66, Assoc. Prof., Dept of Classical Studies, Monash Univ. 1967–68, Prof. Dept of Classical Studies, Univ. of Melbourne 1969–81, Prof. Emer. 1981–; Deputy Dir Humanities Research Centre, Australian Nat. Univ. 1982–90, Dir 1991–99, Prof.Emer. 2000–; Visting Fellow Dept of History, Australian Nat. Univ. 2000–; Fellow Australian Acad. of the Humanities 1975, Soc. of Antiquaries, London 1989; Dir archaeological excavation in N Syria at Jebel Khalid 1984–. *Publications:* The Octavius of Marcus Minucius Felix 1974, The Letters of St Cyprian (4 Vols) 1984–88, Rediscovering Hellenism (ed.) 1988, Reading the Past in Late Antiquity (ed.) 1990, Identities in the Eastern Mediterranean in Antiquity (ed.) 1998, Jebel Khalid on the Euphrates. Report on Excavations 1986–1996 (Vol. I) 2001. *Leisure interest:* gardening. *Address:* Department of History, Australian National University, Canberra, ACT 0200 (Office); 62 Wybalena Grove, Cook, ACT 2614, Australia (Home). *Telephone:* (2) 6125-4789 (Office); (2) 6251-4576 (Home). *Fax:* (2) 6125-4083 (Office). *E-mail:* graeme.clarke@anu.edu.au (Office).

CLARKE, John, MA, PhD, FRS; British professor of physics; b. 10 Feb. 1942, Cambridge; s. of Victor P. Clarke and Ethel M. Clarke; m. Grethe Fog Pedersen 1979; one d.; ed Perse School, Cambridge and Univ. of Cambridge; Postdoctoral Scholar, Dept of Physics, Univ. of Calif. Berkeley 1968–69, Asst Prof. 1969–71, Assoc. Prof. 1971–73, Prof. 1973–; Luis W Alvarez Memorial Chair in Experimental Physics 1994–; Prin. Investigator, Lawrence Berkeley Nat. Lab., Berkeley 1969–; Hon. Fellow Christ's Coll., Cambridge; Visiting Fellow Clare Hall, Cambridge 1989; Fellow, AAAS, American Physical Soc., Inst. of Physics; Alfred P. Sloan Foundation Fellowship 1970–72; Adolph C. and Mary Sprague Miller Research Professorship 1975–76, 1994–95; Guggenheim Fellowship 1977–78; Calif. Scientist of the Year 1987, Fritz London Memorial Award 1987, Joseph F. Keithley Award, American Physical Soc. 1998, Comstock Prize in Physics, Nat. Acad. of Sciences 1999 and other honours and awards. *Publications:* approx. 390 publs in learned journals. *Address:* Department of Physics, University of California, Berkeley, CA 94720-7300, USA. *Telephone:* (510) 642-3069. *Fax:* (510) 642-1304.

CLARKE, (John) Neil, LLB, FCA; British business executive; b. 7 Aug. 1934; s. of late George P. Clarke and Norah M. Bailey; m. Sonia H. Beckett 1958; three s.; ed Rugby School and King's Coll. London; partner, Rowley, Pemberton, Roberts & Co. 1960–69; Charter Consolidated 1969–88, Deputy Chair. and Chief Exec. 1982–88; Dir Anglo-American Corpn of South Africa 1976–90, Consolidated Gold Fields 1982–89, Travis Perkins 1990–2002, Porvair 1994–96; Chair. Johnson Matthey 1984–90; Dir Molins 1987–91, Chair. 1989–91; Chair. Genchem Holdings 1989–, British Coal 1991–97; Chevalier, Ordre nat. du Mérite. *Leisure interests:* music, tennis, golf. *Address:* High Willows, 18 Park Avenue, Farnborough Park, Orpington, Kent, BR6 8LL, England. *Telephone:* (1689) 851651 (Office). *Fax:* (1689) 862229 (Office).

CLARKE, Rt Hon Kenneth Harry, PC, QC, BA, LLB; British politician; b. 2 July 1940; s. of Kenneth Clarke and Doris Clarke (née Smith); m. Gillian Mary Edwards 1964; one s. one d.; ed Nottingham High School and Gonville and Caius Coll., Cambridge; called to the Bar, Gray's Inn 1963; practising mem. Midland circuit 1963–79; Research Sec. Birmingham Bow Group 1965–66; contested Mansfield, Notts. in General Elections 1964, 1966, MP for Rushcliffe Div. of Notts. 1970–; Parl. Pvt. Sec. to Solicitor Gen. 1971–72; an Asst Govt Whip 1972–74, Govt Whip for Europe 1973–74; Lord Commr, HM Treasury 1974; Opposition Spokesman on Social Services 1974–76, on Industry 1976–79; Parl. Sec., Dept of Transport, later Parl. Under Sec. of State for Transport 1979–82; Minister of State (Minister for Health), Dept of Health and Social Security 1982–85; Paymaster-Gen. and Minister for Employment 1985–87; Chancellor of Duchy of Lancaster and Minister for Trade and Industry 1987–88, Minister for the Inner Cities 1987–88; Sec. of State for Health 1988–90, for Educ. and Science 1990–92, for the Home Dept 1992–93; Chancellor of the Exchequer 1993–97; mem. Parl. Del. to Council of Europe and WEU 1973–74; Chair. Alliance UniChem PLC 1997–2001, Deputy Chair. (non-exec.) 2001–; Dir Foreign and Colonial Investment Trust 1997–, Deputy Chair. British American Tobacco 1998–; Dir Ind. News and Media (V.I.C.) 1999–; Chair. Savey Asset Man. PLC 2000–; Master of Bench, Gray's Inn; Liveryman, Clockmakers' Co. 2001–; Hon. LLD (Nottingham) 1989, (Huddersfield) 1993; Hon. DUniv (Nottingham Trent) 1996. *Publication:* New Hope for the Regions 1969. *Leisure interests:* bird-watching, jazz, cricket, football. *Address:* House of Commons, London, SW1A 0AA, England. *Telephone:* (20) 7219-3000.

CLARKE, Sir Robert (Cyril), Kt, MA; British business executive; b. 28 March 1929, Eltham; s. of Robert Henry Clarke and Rose Lilian Clarke (née Bratton); m. Evelyn (Lynne) Mary Harper 1952; three s. one d.; ed Dulwich Coll. and Pembroke Coll. Oxford; trainee, Cadbury Bros. Ltd 1952; Gen. Man. John Forrest Ltd 1954; Marketing Dir Cadbury Confectionery 1957; Man. Dir

Cadbury Cakes Ltd 1962; Chair. Cadbury Cakes Ltd and Dir Cadbury Schweppes Foods Ltd 1969; Man. Dir McVitie & Cadbury Cakes Ltd 1971–74; mem. Bd United Biscuits (UK) Ltd 1974, Man. Dir UB Biscuits 1977, Chair. and Man. Dir United Biscuits (UK) Ltd and Dir United Biscuits (Holdings) PLC 1984–95, Group Chief Exec. United Biscuits (Holdings) PLC 1986–90, Deputy Chair. 1989, Chair. 1990–95; Dir (non-exec.) Thames Water PLC 1988–, Chair. 1994–99; Gov. World Econ. Forum 1990–. *Leisure interests:* reading, walking, renovating old buildings, planting trees. *Address:* c/o Thames Water PLC, 14 Cavendish Place, London, W1M 9DJ, England.

CLARKE, Sir Rupert W. J., Bt, AM, MA, MBE (Mil); Australian company director and grazier; b. Rupert William John Clarke, 5 Nov. 1919, Sydney; s. of late Rupert T.H. Clarke and Elsie F. Tucker; m. Kathleen Grant Hay 1947 (died 1999); three s. (one deceased) one d.; m. 2nd Gillian de Zoete 2000; ed Eton Coll., Magdalen Coll. Oxford, UK; Chair. United Distillers Pty Ltd 1958–88; Dir P & O Australia Ltd 1980–, Chair. 1983–96, Hon. Pres. 1996–; Chair. Nat. Australia Bank Ltd 1986–92; Consul-Gen. of Monaco; Chair. Victory Re-Insurance Co. of Australia 1956–86, Cadbury Schweppes Australia Ltd 1971–88, Morganite Australia Pty Ltd 1981–88, Legal and Gen. 1983–86; Vice-Chair. and Dir Conzinc Riotinto of Australia Ltd 1961–87; Dir Howard Florey Inst. of Experimental Physiology and Medicine (Vice-Pres. 1997–2000); Chair. Vic. Amateur Turf Club 1973–90; Dir Royal Humane Soc. of Australia 1955–99, Pres. 1992–99; Hon. Fellow Trinity Coll. Melbourne; Australian Sports Medal 2001; Commdr, Ordre des Grimaldi (Monaco) 1975, Officier, Légion d'honneur, Officier, Ordre de Léopold (Belgium). *Publication:* At War With Alex 2000. *Leisure interests:* swimming, horse breeding and racing, shooting. *Address:* Level 7, 500 Bourke Street, Melbourne 3000 (Office); 3c Ormsby Grove Melbourne 3142 (Home); Bolinda Vale, Clarkefield, Vic. 3430, Australia (Home). *Telephone:* (3) 9602-3088 (Office); (3) 9827-4929 (Home). *Fax:* (3) 9670-2629 (Office); (3) 9826-8194 (Home).

CLARKSON, Rt. Hon. Adrienne, CC, CMM, CD; Canadian Governor-General and broadcaster; b. 1939, Hong Kong; d. of William Poy; m. John Ralston Saul; ed Univ. of Toronto, Sorbonne, Paris; broadcaster with CBC TV 1965–82, 1988–98; Ont.'s Agent-Gen. in Paris 1982–87; Pres. McClelland & Stewart Publishing 1987–88; fmr Chair. Bd of Trustees, Canadian Museum of Civilization, Hull, Quebec; fmr Pres. Exec. Bd IMZ, Vienna (int. audio-visual Asscn of music, dance and cultural programmers); Gov.-Gen. of Canada Oct. 1999–; fmr Bencher of Law Soc. of Upper Canada; numerous hon. doctorates and academic distinctions. *TV includes:* Take Thirty, Adrienne at Large, The Fifth Estate, Adrienne Clarkson's Summer Festival, Adrienne Clarkson Presents, Something Special. *Publications include:* three books and numerous magazine and newspaper articles. *Address:* Rideau Hall, 1 Sussex Drive, Ottawa, Ont. K1A 0A1, Canada (Office). *Telephone:* (613) 993-8200 (Office). *E-mail:* info@gg.ca (Office). *Website:* www.gg.ca (Office).

CLARKSON, Thomas William, PhD; professor of toxicology; b. 1 Aug. 1932, Blackburn; s. of William Clarkson and Olive Jackson; m. Winifred Browne 1957; one s. two d.; ed Univ. of Manchester; Instructor, Univ. of Rochester School of Medicine, USA 1958–61, Asst Prof. 1961–62, Assoc. Prof. 1965–71, Prof. 1971–, Head of Div. of Toxicology 1980–86, J. Lowell Orbison Distinguished Service Alumni Prof. 1983–, Dir Environmental Health Sciences Center 1986–98, Chair. Dept of Environmental Medicine 1992–98; Scientific Officer, Medical Research Council, UK 1962–64; Sterling Drug Visiting Prof., Albany Medical Coll. 1989; Sr Fellowship, Weizmann Inst. of Science 1964–65; Post-Doctoral Fellow, Nuffield Foundation 1956–57 and US Atomic Energy Comm., Univ. of Rochester 1957–58; mem. Inst. of Medicine of NAS; Dir NASA Center in Space Environmental Health 1991–95; mem. La Academia Nacional de Medicina de Buenos Aires 1984; mem. Collegium Ramazzini 1983; J. Lowell Orbison Distinguished Service Alumni Prof.; Hon. Dr Med. (Umeå) 1986; Merit Award 1999 (SOT), Arthur Kornberg Award (Rochester) 1999. *Publications:* over 200 published papers; co-ed. of Reproductive and Developmental Toxicology, The Cytoskeleton as a Target for Toxic Agents, Biological Monitoring of Toxic Metals, Advances in Mercury Toxicology. *Address:* Department of Environmental Medicine, University of Rochester School of Medicine, Box EHSC, Rochester, New York, NY 14642, USA. *Telephone:* (716) 275-3911 (Office). *Fax:* (716) 256-2591. *E-mail:* tom_clarkson@urmc.rochester.edu (Office).

CLARY, David Charles, PhD, ScD, FRS, FInstP, FRSC; British professor of chemistry; b. 14 Jan. 1953, Halesworth, Suffolk; s. of Cecil Raymond Clary and Mary Mildred Clary (née Hill); m. Heather Ann Vinson 1975; three s.; ed Colchester Royal Grammar School, Sussex Univ., Corpus Christi Coll., Cambridge; researcher IBM Research Lab., San Jose, Calif. 1977–78; post-doctoral research at Manchester Univ. 1978–80; research lecturer in Chem. UMIST 1980–83; Lecturer, then Reader in Theoretical Chem. Dept of Chem., Cambridge Univ. 1983–96; Fellow Magdalene Coll., Cambridge 1983–96, Sr Tutor 1989–93, Fellow Commoner 1996–; Prof. of Chem., Dir of Centre for Theoretical and Computational Chem., Univ. Coll., London 1996–2002; Head of Mathematical and Physical Sciences, Oxford Univ. 2002–; Professorial Fellow, St John's Coll., Oxford 2002–; mem. Int. Acad. of Quantum Molecular Science 1998; Ed. Chemical Physics Letters 2000–; Annual Medal of Int. Acad. of Quantum Molecular Science 1989; medals of the Royal Soc. of Chem.: Meldola (1981), Marlow (1986) Corday-Morgan (1989), Tilden (1998), Chem. Dynamics (1998); FRS (1997), FAAAS (2002), FAPS (2002). *Achievements:* developed quantum theory for chemical reactions of polyatomic molecules. *Publications:* over 250 research papers on chemical physics and theoretical chemistry in learned journals. *Leisure interests:* family, football. *Address:* Department of Mathematical and Physical Sciences, Oxford University, 9 Parks Road, Oxford OX1 3PD, England (Office). *Telephone:* (1865) 282572. *Fax:* (1865) 282571.

CLASPER, Michael (Mike), BEng, CBE; British airlines company executive; b. 21 April 1953, Sunderland; s. of Douglas Clasper and Hilda Clasper; m. Susan Rosemary Shore 1975; two s. two d.; ed Bede School, Sunderland, St John's Coll. Cambridge; with British Rail 1974–78; joined Proctor & Gamble 1978, Advertising Dir 1985–88, Gen. Man. Proctor & Gamble Holland 1988–91, Man. Dir and Vice-Pres. Proctor & Gamble UK 1991–95, Regional Vice-Pres. Laundry Products, Proctor & Gamble Europe 1995–99, Pres. Global Home Care and New Business Devt, Proctor & Gamble, Brussels 1999–2001; Deputy CEO and Chair. Airports Bd BAA PLC 2001–03, CEO June 2003–; mem. Advisory Council on Business and the Environment 1993–99; mem. Man. Cttee Business and Environment Programme, Univ. of Cambridge Programme for Industry 2000–; mem. Man. Cttee Prince of Wales Business and Environment Programme; Fellow Inst. of Grocery Distribution; Hon. PhD (Sunderland Univ.). *Leisure interests:* swimming, cycling, skiing, tennis, golf. *Address:* BAA PLC, 130 Wilton Road, London, SW1V 1LQ, England (Office). *Telephone:* (20) 7834-9449 (Office). *Website:* www.baa.co.uk (Office).

CLATWORTHY, Robert, RA; British sculptor; b. 31 Jan. 1928; s. of E. W. and G. Clatworthy; m. 1st Pamela Gordon 1954 (divorced); two s. one d.; m. 2nd Jane Clatworthy (née Illingworth Stubbs) 1989; ed Dr. Morgan's Grammar School, Bridgwater, West of England Coll. of Art, Chelsea School of Art, The Slade; teacher, West of England Coll. of Art 1967–71; Visiting Tutor, RCA 1960–72; mem. Fine Art Panel of Nat. Council for Diplomas in Art and Design 1961–72; Governor, St Martin's School of Art 1970–71; Head of Dept of Fine Art, Central School of Art and Design 1971–75; exhbns. at Hanover Gallery, Waddington Galleries, Holland Park Open Air Sculpture, Battersea Park Open Air Sculpture, Tate Gallery (British Sculpture in the Sixties), Burlington House (British Sculptors 1972), Basil Jacobs Fine Art Ltd, Diploma Galleries, Burlington House, Photographers Gallery, Quinton Green Fine Art, Chapman Gallery 1988, 1989, 1990, Austin/Desmond Fine Art Ltd, in Asscn with Keith H. Chapman 1991, 1992, 1994, 1996, 1998, UKModernart 2001, Thompson's Gallery 2003; work in collections of Arts Council, Contemporary Art Soc., Tate Gallery, Victoria and Albert Museum, GLC, Nat. Portrait Gallery (portrait of Dame Elisabeth Frink 1985); public Sculptures; Large Bull, Alton Housing Estate, London SW15; Monumental Horse and Rider in grounds of Charing Cross Hosp. London, W6. *Address:* Moelfre, Cynghordy, Llandovery, Carmarthenshire, SA20 0UW, Wales. *Telephone:* (1550) 720201. *E-mail:* robertclatworthy@hotmail.com (Office). *Website:* www.robertclatworthy.co.uk (Office).

CLAVÉ, Antoni; Spanish painter; b. 5 April 1913, Barcelona; ed evening classes at Escuela Superior de Bellas Artes de San Jorge, Barcelona; magazine and book illustrator 1930–49; full-time painter since 1955; commenced carpet painting 1957 and metal work 1960; first one-man exhbn, Perpignan, France 1939, later in Paris, London, Oran, Gothenburg, Buenos Aires, Rome, Milan, Barcelona, Bilbao, LA, Geneva, Cologne, Luxembourg, Colmar, Toulouse, Venice and Tokyo; other exhbns.: "Thirty Years of Painting", Tokyo 1972, New York 1973, "En marge de la peinture", Centre Georges Pompidou, Paris 1978, Works 1958–78, Musée d'art moderne de la ville de Paris 1978, 1979; Musée d'Unterlinden, Colmar, peintures 1958–78, Septembre: A. H. Grafik, Stockholm, Dix Instruments étranges, gravures, Retrospective 1939–80, Museo de Arte Contemporáneo, Madrid 1980; Musée des Augustins, Toulouse, 1984, Biennale de Venise, Pavillon d'Espagne; 125 works 1958–84, paintings, sculptures, Museo de Arte Contemporáneo, Madrid, 150 lithographs and carvings; exhbns in Paris and Perpignan 1985; and at Tokyo Metropolitan Teien Museum, Osaka Modern Art Museum, Yamanashi-ken Kiyoharu Museum 1986; Matarasso Prize, Biennal São Paulo 1957, UNESCO Prize, Kamakara Museum Prize. *Major works:* illustrations for La Dame de Pique, Pushkin 1946, black lithographs Candide, Voltaire 1948, Gargantua, Rabelais 1953, La Gloire des Rois, Saint-John Perse 1976.

CLAVEL, Bernard; French writer; b. 29 May 1923, Lons-le-Saunier; s. of Henri Clavel and Héloïse Dubois; m. 2nd Josette Pratte 1982; three s. (of first marriage); ed primary school; left school aged 14 and apprenticed as pâtissier 1937; subsequently held various jobs on the land and in offices; painter and writer since age 15; has written numerous plays for radio and television and contributed to reviews on the arts and pacifist journals; Prix Eugène Leroy, Prix populiste, Prix Jean Macé, Prix Goncourt (for Les fruits de l'hiver), Grand Prix littéraire de la Ville de Paris, Prix Ardua de l'Université 1997, Prix des maisons de la presse 1998. *Publications include:* L'ouvrier de la nuit 1956, Qui m'emporte 1958, L'espagnol 1959, Malataverne 1960, La maison des autres 1962, Celui qui voulait voir la mer 1963, Le coeur des vivants 1964, Le voyage du père 1965, L'Hercule sur la place 1966, Les fruits de l'hiver 1968, Victoire au Mans 1968, L'espion aux yeux verts 1969, Le tambour du bief 1970, Le massacre des innocents 1970, Le seigneur du fleuve 1972, Le silence des armes 1974, Lettre à un képi blanc 1975, La boule de neige 1975, La saison des loups 1976, La lumière du lac 1977, Ecrit sur la neige 1977, La fleur de sel 1977, La femme de guerre 1978, Le Rhône ou la métamorphose d'un dieu 1979, Le chien des Laurentides 1979, L'Iroquoise 1979, Marie Bon Pain 1980, La bourrelle 1980, Felicien le fantôme (with Josette Pratte) 1980, Terres de Mémoire 1980, Compagnons du Nouveau-Monde 1981, Arbres 1981, Odile et le vent du large 1981, Le Hibou qui avait avalé la lune 1981, L'Homme du Labrador 1982, Harricana 1983, L'Or de la terre 1984, Le mouton noir et le loup blanc 1984, Le roi des poissons 1984, L'oie qui avait perdu le nord 1985, Miserere 1985, Bernard Clavel qui êtes-vous? 1985, Amarok 1986, Au cochon qui danse 1986, L'Angélus du soir 1988, Le grand voyage de Quick Beaver 1988, Quand j'étais capitaine 1990, Retour au pays 1990, Meurtre sur le Grandvaux 1991, La révolte à deux sous 1992, Cargo pour l'enfer 1993, Les roses de Verdun 1994, Le Carcajou 1995, Jésus le fils du charpentier 1996, Contes et légendes du Bordelais 1997, La Guinguette 1997, Le Soleil des morts 1998, Achille le singe 1998, Les Petits bonheurs 1999, Le Commencement du monde 1999, La Louve du Noirmont 2000, Le Cavalier du Baïkal 2000, Histoires de chiens 2000, Brutus 2001 and numerous essays, short stories and children's books. *Leisure interests:* sport, painting, handicraft. *Address:* Albin Michel, 22 rue Huyghens, 75014 Paris, France.

CLAVIER, Christian Jean-Marie; French actor; b. 6 May 1952, Paris; s. of Jean-Claude Clavier and Phanette Rousset-Rouard; one d. by Marie-Anne Chazel; Chevalier Ordre nat. du Mérite, Officier Ordre nat. des Arts et des lettres. *Stage appearances include:* Ginette Lacaze, La Dame de chez Maxim's, Non Georges pas ici 1972, Ma tête est malade 1976, Le Pot de terre contre le pot de vin 1977, Amours, coquillages et crustacés 1978, Le Père Noël est une ordure 1979–80, Papy fait de la résistance 1981, Double Mixte 1986–88, Un fil à la patte 1989, Panique au plaza 1995. *Films include:* Que la fête commence 1974, F. comme Fairbanks 1976, Le Diable dans la boîte 1976, L'Amour en herbe 1977, Des enfants gâtés 1977, Dîtes-lui que je l'aime 1977, Les Bronzés font du ski (also co-writer) 1979, Cocktail Molotov 1980, Je vais craquer 1980, Clara et les chics types 1980, Quand tu seras débloqué, fais-moi signe 1981, Elle voit des nains partout 1981, le Père Noël est une ordure (also co-writer) 1982, Rock and Torah 1982, la Vengeance d'une blonde 1993, les Anges gardiens (also co-writer) 1994, Les Couloirs du temps (also co-writer) 1998, Astérix et Obélix contre César 1999, The Visitors 2000, Les Misérables 2000, Astérix et Obélix: Mission Cleopatra 2002. *Television includes:* l'Été 1985, Sueurs froides 1988, Palace 1988, Si Guitry m'était conté 1989, Bougez pas j'arrive 1989, Mieux vaut courir 1989, Fantôme sur l'oreiller (co-writer 1989), Charmante soirée (co-writer 1990). *Leisure interests:* skiing, cycling, swimming. *Address:* c/o Ouille, 7 rue des Dames Augustines, 92200 Neuilly, France. *Telephone:* 1-41-34-13-34 (Office). *Fax:* 1-41-34-13-10 (Office).

CLAYBURGH, Jill, BA; American actress; b. 30 April 1944, New York; d. of Albert H. Clayburgh and Julia (Door) Clayburgh; m. David Rabe 1979; ed Sarah Lawrence Coll., Bronxville, NY; Broadway debut in The Rothschilds 1979; Best Actress Award, Cannes Film Festival and Golden Apple Award for the best film actress for An Unmarried Woman. *Stage appearances include:* In the Boom Boom Room, Design for Living. *Films for Television include:* Crowned and Dangerous 1998, My Little Assassin 1999, Leap of Faith 2002, Phenomenon 2002. *Films include:* Portnoy's Complaint 1972, The Thief Who Came to Dinner, The Terminal Man 1974, Gable and Lombard 1976, Silver Streak 1976, Semi-Tough 1977, An Unmarried Woman 1978, La Luna 1979, Starting Over 1979, It's My Turn 1980, I'm Dancing as Fast as I Can 1982, Hannah K 1983, Shy People 1987, Beyond the Ocean, Between the Lines 1990, Naked in New York 1994, Fools Rush In 1997, Going All the Way 1997, Never Again 2001. *Address:* 12424 Wilshire Boulevard, Suite 1000, Los Angeles, CA 90025, USA.

CLAYTON, Dame Barbara, DBE, PhD, MD, CBiol, FRCP, FRCPE, FRCPath, FRCPI, FMedSci; British professor of chemical pathology; b. 2 Sept. 1922, Liverpool; d. of William Clayton and Constance Clayton; m. William Klyne 1949 (died 1977); one s. one d.; ed Bromley County School for Girls, Edinburgh Univ.; consultant Hosp. for Sick Children 1959–78 (mem. Bd of Govs. 1968–78); Prof. Inst. of Child Health, Univ. of London 1970–78, Univ. of Southampton 1979–87 (Hon. Research Prof. in Metabolism 1987–); Pres. Asscn of Clinical Biochemists 1977–78, Soc. for the Study of Inborn Errors of Metabolism 1981–82 (Hon. mem. 1988), Royal Coll. of Pathologists 1984–87, Nat. Soc. for Clean Air and Environmental Protection 1995–97; Chair. Standing Cttee on Postgrad. Medical and Dental Educ. 1988–99, Health of the Nation Task Force on Nutrition 1992–95, Medical and Scientific Panel, Leukaemia Research Fund 1988–; Dean Faculty of Medicine Univ. of Southampton 1983–86; Hon. Pres. British Dietetic Asscn 1989–; mem. Royal Comm. on Environmental Pollution 1981–96, Gen. Medical Council 1983–87; Leverhulme Emeritus Fellowship 1988–90; Gov. British Nutrition Foundation, Hon. Pres. 1999–; Hon. Fellow Royal Coll. of Physicians, Ireland 1987, American Soc. of Clinical Pathologists 1987, Inst. of Biology 2000; Hon. Fellow Royal Coll. of Paediatrics and Child Health 1968;Corresp. mem.Soc. Française Pédiatric 1975; Gesellschaft für Laboritoriumsmedizin 1990; numerous named lectures including Stanley Davidson RCPE 1973; Hartley Lecture, Southampton Univ. 1990, Wilfrid Fish GDC 1995; British Nutrition Foundation Lecture 1997; Hon. DSc (Edin.) 1987, (Southampton) 1992, (London) 2000; Hon. FIBiol 2000; Jessie MacGregor Prize for MedSci RCPE 1955, 1985; Wellcome Prize (Asscn of Clinical Biochemists) 1988; Gold Medal for Distinguished Merit (British Medical Asscn) 1999. *Publications:* Clinical Biochemistry and the Sick Child (jtly) 1994, numerous publs on nutrition, pediatrics and the environment. *Leisure interests:* natural history, visiting the Arctic. *Address:* Room AC19, Level C, South Academic Block, Southampton, SO16 6YD, England. *Telephone:* (23) 8079-6800 (Office); (23) 8076-9937 (Home). *Fax:* (23) 8079-4760.

CLAYTON, Robert Norman, MSc, PhD, FRS; Canadian geochemist; b. 20 March 1930; s. of Norman Clayton and Gwenda Clayton; m. Cathleen Shelbourne Clayton 1971; one d.; ed Queen's Univ. Canada and Calif. Inst. of Tech.; Research Fellow, Calif. Inst. of Tech. 1955–56; Asst Prof. Pa State Univ. 1956–58; Asst Prof. Univ. of Chicago 1958–62, Assoc. Prof. 1962–66, Prof. Depts. of Chemistry and of the Geophysical Sciences 1966–80, Enrico Fermi Distinguished Service Prof. 1980–. *Publications:* over 200 papers in geochemical journals. *Address:* 5201 South Cornell, Chicago, IL 60615, USA.

CLEARY, Jon Stephen; Australian author; b. 22 Nov. 1917, Sydney, NSW; s. of Mathew Cleary and Ida F. Brown; m. Constantine E. Lucas 1946; two d. (one deceased); ed Marist Brothers School, NSW; various jobs, including bush-working and commercial art 1932–40; served Australian Imperial Forces, Middle East, New Britain, New Guinea 1940–45; full-time writer since 1945, except for 3 years as journalist, Australian News and Information Bureau, London and New York 1948–51; winner, ABC Nat. Play Competition 1945; Crouch Literary Prize 1951; Edgar Award for Best Crime Novel 1974; First Lifetime Award, Australian Crime Writers Soc. 1998. *Cinema:* The Siege of Pinchgut 1958, The Sundowners 1960, The Green Helmet 1960. *Television includes:* No Friend like an Old Friend (CBS) 1951, Just Let Me Be (ATV) 1958, Bus Stop (Fox) 1967. *Publications:* 51 novels and two books of short stories (1983), including You Can't See Round Corners 1948, The Sundowners 1952, The High Commissioner 1966, High Road to China 1977, Mask of the Andes 1971, Spearfield's Daughter 1982, The Phoenix Tree 1984, The City of Fading Light 1985, Dragons at the Party 1987, Now and Then, Amen 1988, Babylon South 1989, Murder Song 1990, Pride's Harvest 1991, Dark Summer 1992, Bleak Spring 1993, Autumn Maze 1994, Winter Chill 1995, Endpeace 1996, A Different Turf 1997, Five-Ring Circus 1998, Dilemma 1999, Bear Pit 2000, Yesterday's Shadow 2001, The Easy Sin 2002. *Leisure interests:* watching cricket, filmgoing, reading. *Address:* c/o HarperCollins, 23 Ryde Road, Pymble, NSW 2073, Australia.

CLEAVER, Alan Richard, MA; British couturier and business executive; b. 30 May. 1952, Northampton; s. of Terence Richard Cleaver and Miriam Elanor Tomlin; ed Wellingborough Tech. Grammar School, Northampton School of Art, Kingston Coll. of Art and RCA; worked with Michael Aukett Assoc. 1973–74; freelance stylist Maison de Marie Claire, Paris 1977–79; freelance design consultant, Paris 1976–79; Co. Designer Byblos, Italy 1980–; Man. Dir S.R.L. Milan 1986–; External Examiner/Visiting Lecturer RCA 1986–. *Leisure interests:* travel, opera, walking. *Address:* Via Vallone 11, Monte Conero, Sirolo; Bosco di San Francesco 6, Sirolo; Piazza Plebiscito 55, Ancona, Italy. *Telephone:* (071) 936203; (071) 936225; (071) 203790.

CLEAVER, Sir Anthony Brian, Kt, MA; British business executive; b. 10 April 1938, London; s. of late William Brian Cleaver and Dorothea Early Cleaver (née Peeks); m. Mary Teresa Cotter 1962 (died 1999); one s. one d.; m. 2nd Jennifer Lloyd Graham 2000; ed Berkhamsted School and Trinity Coll. Oxford; nat. service in Intelligence Corps 1956–58; joined IBM 1962, UK Sales Dir 1976–77, DP Dir, mem. Bd, IBM UK (Holdings) 1977–80, Vice-Pres. of Marketing IBM Europe 1981–82, Asst Gen. Man. IBM UK 1982–84, Gen. Man. 1984–85, Chief Exec. 1986–91, Chair. 1990–94; Chair. AEA Tech. PLC 1996–2001; Chair. Industrial Devt Advisory Bd Dept of Trade and Industry 1993–99, UKAEA 1993–96, The Strategic Partnership 1996–2000, Medical Research Council 1998–, IX Holdings Ltd 1999–, Baxi Partnership 1999–2000, SThree 2000–, UK eUniversities Worldwide Ltd 2000–, Working Links (Employment) Ltd 2002–; Pres. Involvement and Participation Asscn 1997–2002, Inst. of Man. 1998–2000; Dir Nat. Computing Centre 1977–80; Dir Gen. Accident PLC (fmrly Gen. Accident) Fire and Life Assurance Corpn 1988–98, Gen. Cable PLC 1994–98 (Chair. 1995–98), Smith and Nephew PLC 1993–; mem. Council, Templeton Coll. Oxford 1982–93, Asscn for Business Sponsorship of the Arts 1985–97; mem. Bd CEED 1985–98 (Deputy Chair. 1992–98); mem. Cttee on Standards in Public Life 1997–, British Govt Panel on Sustainable Devt 1998–2000; Chair. Bd of Govs., Birkbeck Coll. 1989–98; Fellow of British Computer Soc.; Hon. Fellow Birkbeck Coll. 1999; Hon. LLD (Nottingham) 1991, (Portsmouth) 1996; Hon. DSc (Cranfield) 1995, (City) 2001, (Hull) 2001; Global 500 Roll of Honour (UN Environment Program) 1989. *Leisure interests:* sport, especially cricket, music, especially opera and reading. *Address:* UK eUniversities Worldwide Ltd, 14 Buckingham Gate, London, SW1E 6LB (Office). *Telephone:* (20) 7932-4401 (Office). *Fax:* (20) 7932-4402 (Office). *E-mail:* acleaver@ukeu.com (Office). *Website:* www.ukeu.com (Office).

CLEESE, John Marwood, MA; British actor and writer; b. 27 Oct. 1939; s. of Reginald Cleese and Muriel Cleese; m. 1st Connie Booth 1968 (divorced 1978); one d.; m. 2nd Barbara Trentham 1981 (divorced 1990); one d.; m. 3rd Alyce Faye Eichelberger 1992; ed Clifton Sports Acad. and Downing Coll., Cambridge; started writing and making jokes professionally 1963; first appearance on British TV 1966; appeared in and co-wrote TV series: The Frost Report, At Last the 1948 Show, Monty Python's Flying Circus, Fawlty Towers, The Human Face; f. and Dir Video Arts Ltd 1972–89; appeared as Petruchio in The Taming of the Shrew, BBC TV Shakespeare cycle 1981; appeared in Cheers, for which he received an Emmy Award; guest appearances in Third Rock From the Sun; Hon. A.D. White Prof.-at-Large, Cornell Univ. 1999–; Hon. LLD (St Andrews). *Films include:* Interlude, The Magic Christian, And Now For Something Completely Different, Monty Python and the Holy Grail, Romance with a Double Bass, Life of Brian, Time Bandits, Privates on Parade, Yellowbeard 1982, The Meaning of Life 1983, Silverado 1985, Clockwise 1986, A Fish Called Wanda (BAFTA Award for Best Film Actor) 1988, Erik the Viking 1988, Splitting Heirs 1992, Mary Shelley's Frankenstein 1993, The Jungle Book 1994, Fierce Creatures 1996, The Out of Towners 1998, Isn't She Great 1998, The World Is Not Enough 1999, The Quantum Project 2000, Rat Race 2000, Pluto Nash 2000, Harry Potter and the Philosopher's Stone 2001,

Die Another Day 2002, Harry Potter and the Chamber of Secrets 2002. *Publications:* Families and How to Survive Them, Life and How to Survive It (both with Robin Skynner), The Human Face (with Brian Bates). *Leisure interests:* gluttony, sloth. *Address:* c/o David Wilkinson, 115 Hazlebury Road, London, SW6 2LX,England. *Telephone:* (20) 7371-5188. *Fax:* (20) 7371-5161.

CLEGHORN, John E., BComm, CA; Canadian banker; b. 7 July 1941, Montreal, PQ; s. of H. W Edward Cleghorn and Hazel Miriam Dunham; m. Pattie E. Hart 1963; two s. one d.; ed McGill Univ.; Clarkson Gordon & Co. (chartered accountants) 1962–64; sugar buyer and futures trader, St Lawrence Sugar Ltd, Montreal 1964–66; Mercantile Bank of Canada 1966–74; joined Royal Bank of Canada 1974, various Sr exec. positions 1975–83, Pres. 1983, Pres., COO 1986, Pres. CEO 1994–95, Chair. CEO 1995–2001; Dir Royal Bank of Canada, Royal Trust; Chancellor Wilfrid Laurier Univ. 1996–; Gov. McGill Univ.; mem. Canadian and BC Insts. of Chartered Accountants; Fellow Ordre des Comptables Agréés du Québec, Inst. of Chartered Accountants of Ont.; Hon. DCL (Bishop's Univ.) 1989, (Acadia Univ.) 1996; Hon. LLD (Wilfrid Laurier Univ.) 1991. *Leisure interests:* skiing, jogging, tennis, fishing. *Address:* Wilfred Laurier University, 75 University Avenue, Waterloo, Ont., N2L 3C5 (Office); Royal Bank of Canada, Royal Bank Plaza, 200 Bay Street, Toronto, Ont., M5J 2J5, Canada. *Telephone:* (519) 884-1970 (Office); (416) 974-4049. *Fax:* (519) 886-9357 (Office); (416) 974-7403. *Website:* www.wlu.ca (Office).

CLELAND, Joseph Maxwell, MA; American politician; b. 24 Aug. 1942, Atlanta, Ga; s. of Joseph Cleland and Juanita Kesler; ed Stetson Univ. Deland, Fla; mem. Ga Senate, Atlanta 1971–75; consultant, Comm. on Veterans Affairs, US Senate 1975–77; Admin. Veterans Affairs, Washington, DC 1977–81; Sec. of State, State of Ga 1982–95; Senator from Georgia 1997–2003; mem. Senate Armed Services Cttee 1997–2002, Cttee on Governmental Affairs 1997–2002, Cttee on Small Businesses 1997–2002, Commerce Cttee 1999–2002; mem. Nat. Comm. on Terrorist Attacks 2002–; Democrat; recipient of numerous awards and distinctions. *Address:* c/o United States Senate, 461 Dirksen Senate Office Building, Washington, DC 20510-0001, USA.

CLÉMENT, Jérôme, LenD; French government official; b. 18 May 1945, Paris; s. of Yves-André Clément and Raymonde Gornik; m. Marie-Christine Sterin 1974; one s. three d.; ed Lycées Montaigne and Louis-le-Grand, Paris, Facultés de Droit et des Lettres, Paris and Ecole Nat. d'Admin; Ministry of Culture 1974–76, 1978–80; Cour des Comptes 1976–78; Cultural Counsellor, French Embassy, Cairo 1980–81; Counsellor, Office of Prime Minister Mauroy 1981–84; Dir-Gen. Centre nat. de la cinématographie 1984–89; mem. Supervisory Bd Soc. Européenne de Programmes de Télévision (La Sept) 1986–89, Pres. 1989–; Pres. Asscn Int. des Télévisions de l'Educ. et de la Découverte 1999–2001; Pres. Arte 1991–, la Cinquième (TV channel) 1997–2000; Dir Réunion des musées nationaux, Orchestre de Paris; municipal councillor Clamart 2001–; Chevalier, Ordre nat. du Mérite, Commdr des Arts et des Lettres, Commdr Ordre du Mérite (Fed. Repub. of Germany). *Publications:* Socialisme et multinationales 1976, Cahiers de l'Atelier, Un Homme en quête de Vertu 1992, Lettres à Pierre Bérégovoy 1993, La Culture expliquée à ma fille 2000. *Leisure interests:* piano, music, painting, tennis, running. *Address:* Arte, 2a rue de la Fonderie, 67000 Strasbourg; 205 avenue Jean-Jaurès, 92140 Clamart, France (Home); Le Vieux Castel, 49350 Gennes. *Telephone:* 1-55-00-77-77 (Office).

CLEMENT, John, CBIM; British business executive; b. 18 May 1932; s. of Frederick and Alice Eleanor Clement; m. Elisabeth Anne Emery 1956; two s. one d.; ed Bishop's Stortford Coll.; Howards Dairies, Westcliff on Sea 1949–64; United Dairies London Ltd 1964–69; Asst Man. Dir Rank Leisure Services Ltd 1969–73; Chair. Unigate Foods Div. 1973; Chief Exec. Unigate PLC 1976–90, Chair. 1977–91; Dir Eagle Star Holdings 1981–86; Chair. (non-exec.) The Littlewoods Org. 1982–90; Chair. Culpho Consultants 1991–, Chair. Tuddenham Hall Foods 1991–; Dir (non-exec.) Ransomes PLC 1991–, Chair. 1993–98; Dir Anglo American Insurance Co. Ltd 1991–94, Chair. 1993–94; Dir Jarvis Hotels Ltd 1994–, Kleinwort 2nd Endowment Trust PLC (now Dresdner RCM 2nd Endowment Trust PLC) 1993–; Chair. Nat. Car Auctions Ltd 1995–; mem. Supervisory Bd Nutricia N.V.; mem. Securities and Investment Bd 1986–89; High Sheriff, Suffolk 2000–01. *Leisure interests:* tennis, shooting, sailing, bridge, rugby. *Address:* Tuddenham Hall, Tuddenham, Ipswich, Suffolk, IP6 9DD, England. *Telephone:* (1473) 785217. *Fax:* (1473) 785405.

CLEMENT, Wolfgang; German politician; b. 7 July 1940, Bochum; five d.; ed Univ. of Münster; journalist Westfälische Rundschau newspaper –1967, various positions including Deputy Ed.-in-Chief 1968–81; Research Asst Inst. for Procedural Law, Univ. of Marburg 1967–68; Press Spokesman SPD Nat. Exec., Bonn 1981–86, resngd over campaign controversy 1986; Ed.-in-Chief Hamburger Morgenpost newspaper 1986–88; Chief-of-Staff N. Rhine–Westphalia State Chancellery 1989–90, Minister without Portfolio 1990–95, Head of Ministry of Industry, Small Business, Technology and Transport 1995–96; mem. N. Rhine–Westphalia State Ass. 1993–; elected Deputy Chair. SPD Exec. for State of N. Rhine–Westphalia 1996; Premier of State of N. Rhine–Westphalia 1998–2002; Deputy Chair. SPD Nat. Exec. 1999–; Fed. Minister of Econs and Labour Oct. 2002–. *Address:* Federal Ministry of Economics and Labour, Scharnhorststrasse 34–37, 10115 Berlin, Germany (Office). *Telephone:* (1) 8886150 (Office). *Fax:* (1) 8886157010 (Office). *E-mail:* info@bmwi.bund.de (Office). *Website:* www.bmwi.de (Office).

CLEMENTE, Carmine Domenic, AB, MA, PhD; American professor of anatomy; b. 29 April 1928, Penns Grove, NJ; s. of Ermanno Clemente and Caroline (Friozzi) Clemente; m. Juliette G. Clemente 1968; ed Univ. of Pennsylvania and Univ. Coll. London; U.S. Public Health Service Fellow and Asst Instr. in Anatomy, Univ. of Pa 1950–52; Instr. in Anatomy, Univ. of Calif. Los Angeles 1952–53, Asst Prof. 1954–59, Assoc. Prof. 1959–63, Prof. and Chair. Dept of Anatomy 1963–73, Prof. of Anatomy 1973–94, Prof. Emer. 1994–; Prof. of Surgery (Anatomy), Charles R. Drew Postgrad. Medical School 1974– (mem. Bd 1985–), Dir Brain Research Inst. 1976–87; John Simon Guggenheim Memorial Scholar, Nat. Inst. for Medical Research, Mill Hill, London 1988–89, 1991; Consultant in Surgical Anatomy, Martin Luther King Hosp. Los Angeles 1971; Consultant in Research Neurophysiology, Sepulveda Veterans Admin. Hosp.; mem. numerous advisory cttees. etc.; mem. Inst. of Medicine of NAS; consultant Robert Wood Johnson Foundation, Princeton, NJ 1990–; numerous awards and distinctions. *Publications:* Ed. Gray's Anatomy 1973–; numerous books, films and some 190 scientific Publs. *Leisure interest:* philately. *Address:* Dept of Neurobiology, UCLA School of Medicine, Los Angeles, CA 90095 (Office); 11737 Bellagio Road, Los Angeles, CA 90049, USA (Home). *Telephone:* (310) 825-9566 (Office); (310) 472-1149 (Home).

CLEMENTE, Francisco; Italian painter; b. 1952, Naples; s. of Marquess Lorenzo Clemente; m. Alba Primiceri 1974; four c.; ed Univ. of Rome. *Major exhibitions include:* Venice Biennale 1980, Retrospective at the Guggenheim 1999.

CLEMENTI, David Cecil, CA; British financial executive; b. 25 Feb. 1949, Hunts.; s. of Air Vice-Marshal Creswell Montagu Clementi and Susan Clementi (née Pelham); m. Sarah Louise (Sally) Cowley 1972; one s. one d.; ed Winchester Coll., Lincoln Coll., Oxford, Harvard Business School; with Corp. Finance Div. Kleinwort Benson Ltd 1975–87, Head 1989–94; Head Kleinwort Benson Securities 1987–89; Chief Exec. Kleinwort Benson Ltd 1994–97; Vice-Chair. Kleinwort Benson Group PLC 1997; Deputy Gov. Bank of England 1997–2002; Chair. Prudential PLC 2002–. *Leisure interests:* sailing, athletics. *Address:* Prudential PLC, Laurence Pountney Hill, London, EC4R 0HH, England (Office). *Telephone:* (20) 7548-3901 (Office). *Fax:* (20) 7548-3631 (Office). *Website:* www.prudential.co.uk (Office).

CLEMENTS, Suzanne; British fashion designer; m. Inacio Ribeiro 1992; ed Cen. St Martin's Coll. of Art and Design; produced own range of knitwear; design consultant with husband, Brazil 1991–93; f. Clements Ribeiro with husband, London 1993; first collections launched Oct. 1993, numerous since; first solo show London Fashion Week March 1995; fashion shows since in Paris, Brazil, Japan; consultant to cos in UK and Italy; winners Designer of the Year New Generation Category 1996. *Address:* c/o Beverly Cable PR, 11 St Christopher's Place, London, W1V 1NG (Office); Clements Ribeiro Ltd, 413–415 Harrow Road, London W9 3QT, England. *Telephone:* (20) 8962-3060. *Fax:* (20) 8962-3061.

CLEMENTS, William Perry, Jr.; American fmr politician; b. 13 April 1917, Dallas, Tex.; s. of William P. Clements and Evelyn Cammack Clements; m. Rita Crocker Clements 1975; one s. one d. (by previous marriage); ed Highland Park High School, Dallas and Southern Methodist Univ.; founder, Chair., CEO SEDCO Inc., Dallas 1947–73, 1977, 1983–; mem. Nat. Exec. Bd, Boy Scouts of America; mem. Bd of Trustees and Bd of Govs., Southern Methodist Univ.; Deputy Sec. for Defense 1974–77; Gov. of Texas 1979–83, 1987–91; mem. Nat. Bipartisan Comm. of Cen. America 1983–84; Dept of Defense Medal for Distinguished Service with Bronze Palm. *Address:* 1901 North Akard, Dallas, TX 75201, USA.

CLEMINSON, Sir James Arnold Stacey, KBE, MC, DL; British company director; b. 31 Aug. 1921, Hull, Yorkshire; s. of Arnold Russell and Florence Stacey Cleminson; m. Helen Juliet Measor; one s. two d.; ed Bramcote and Rugby schools; served British Army, Parachute Regt 1940–46; joined Reckitt Colman Overseas 1946; Dir and later Vice-Chair. J. J. Colman Norwich 1960–69; Dir Reckitt and Colman 1969, Chair. Food Div. 1970, CEO 1973–80, Chair. 1977–86; Vice-Chair. Norwich Union 1961–92 (Dir 1979–92); Dir United Biscuits Holdings 1982–89; Pres. CBI 1984–86; Pres. Endeavour Training 1984–97; Chair. British Overseas Trade Bd 1986–90, Jeyes Hygiene PLC 1986–89, Riggs A. P. Bank 1987–91 (Dir 1985–2002); Dir Eastern Counties Newspaper Group 1986–92, J. H. Fenner PLC 1985–97 (Vice-Chair. 1993–97), Riggs Nat. Bank of Washington DC 1991–93; Pro-Chancellor Hull Univ. 1986–94; fmr Trustee, Army Benevolent Fund; Trustee Airborne Forces Security Fund, Norwich Cathedral Trust; Pres. Norfolk SSAFA 1994–2000; Hon. LLD (Hull) 1985. *Leisure interests:* fishing, shooting, golf. *Address:* Loddon Hall, Hales, Norfolk NR14 6TB, England. *Fax:* (1508) 528557 (Office).

CLEOBURY, Nicholas Randall, MA, FRCO; British conductor; b. 23 June 1950, Bromley, Kent; s. of John Cleobury and Brenda Cleobury; m. Heather Kay 1978; one s. one d.; ed King's School, Worcester and Worcester Coll., Oxford; Asst organist, Chichester Cathedral 1971–72, Christ Church, Oxford 1972–76; conductor, Schola Cantorum of Oxford 1973–76; chorus master, Glyndebourne Festival Opera 1977–79; Asst Dir BBC Singers 1977–79; Prin. Opera Conductor, Royal Acad. of Music 1980–87; Guest Conductor, Zurich Opera House 1993–; Music Dir Oxford Bach Choir 1997–; Artistic Dir Aquarius 1983–92, Cambridge Symphony Soloists 1990–92, Britten Sinfonia 1992–, Sounds New 1996–; Music Dir Broomhill 1990–94, Artistic Dir Cambridge Festival 1992; has conducted worldwide from Australia to USA 1979–; numerous recordings; Hon. RAM 1985. *Leisure interests:* cricket, food, wine, reading, theatre. *Address:* China Cottage, Church Lane, Petham,

Canterbury, Kent, CT4 5RD, England. *Telephone:* (1227) 700584. *Fax:* (1227) 700827. *E-mail:* nicholascleobury@aol.com (Home). *Website:* www .nicholascleobury.net.

CLEOBURY, Stephen John, MA, BMus, FRCM, FRCO; British conductor; b. 31 Dec. 1948, Bromley; s. of John Frank Cleobury and Brenda Julie Cleobury (née Randall); ed King's School, Worcester and St John's Coll. Cambridge; organist, St Matthew's, Northampton 1971–74; sub-organist, Westminster Abbey 1974–78; Master of Music, Westminster Cathedral 1979–82; Dir of Music, King's Coll. Cambridge 1982–; mem. Council, Royal School of Church Music 1982–; Pres. Inc. Asscn of Organists 1985–87, Cathedral Organists' Asscn 1988–90, Royal Coll. of Organists 1990–92 (Hon. Sec. 1981–90); Chief Conductor BBC Singers 1995–; recordings of solo organ works and directing choir of King's Coll. and BBC Singers; Hon. DMus (Anglia Polytechnic) 2001. *Leisure interest:* reading. *Address:* King's College, Cambridge, CB2 1ST, England. *Telephone:* (1223) 331224 (Office). *Fax:* (1223) 331890 (Office). *E-mail:* choir@kings.cam.ac.uk.

CLERCQ, Willy De, LLD, MA; Belgian politician and barrister; b. 8 July 1927, Ghent; s. of Frans De Clercq and Yvonne Catry; m. Fernande Fazzi 1953; two s. one d.; Barrister, Court of Appeal, Ghent 1951; with Gen. Secretariat of UN, New York 1952; mem. Chamber of Reps. for Ghent-Ekloo 1958–85; Deputy Prime Minister, in charge of Budget 1966–68; Deputy Prime Minister and Minister of Finance 1973–74, Minister of Finance 1973–77, Deputy Prime Minister and Minister of Finance and Foreign Trade Dec. 1981–85; Vice-Pres. Partij voor Vrijheid en Vooruitgang (PVV) 1961; Pres. PVV 1971–73, 1977–81; mem. European Parl. 1979–81, 1989–; Pres. Cttee for External Econ. Relations and Legal Affairs Cttee 1989–99; Minister of State 1985; Hon. Pres. European Liberal and Democratic Party (ELD) 1980–85; part-time Prof. Univs of Ghent and Brussels; Chair. of Interim Cttee of the IMF 1976–77, 1983–85; Commr for External Relations and Trade Policy, Comm. of European Communities 1985–89; mem. Bd Care Int., China Europe Int. Business School, Shanghai; Hon. Pres. European Movt, Belgium; Hon. Pres. Union of European Federalists; Grand Cross Order of Leopold II, Officier Légion d'honneur, Grand Cross First Class, Order of Merit (Germany) and several other honours. *Publications:* Europe, Back to the Top. *Leisure interests:* sport, travel. *Address:* Cyriel Buyssestraat 12, 9000 Ghent, Belgium (Home). *Telephone:* (2) 284-26-60 (Office); (9) 221-18-13 (Home). *Fax:* (2) 284-91-49 (Office); (9) 221-18-13 (Home); (9) 220-07-77. *E-mail:* wdeclercq@europarl.eu .int (Office); info@fazzi.be (Home). *Website:* www.wdeclercq.be (Office).

CLERMONT, Yves Wilfrid, PhD, FRSC; Canadian professor of anatomy; b. 14 Aug. 1926, Montreal; s. of Rodolphe Clermont and Fernande Primeau; m. Madeleine Bonneau 1950; two s. one d.; ed Univ. of Montreal, McGill Univ., Collège de France, Paris; Teaching Fellow, Dept of Anatomy, Faculty of Medicine, McGill Univ., Montreal 1952–53, Lecturer 1953–56, Asst Prof. 1956–60, Assoc. Prof. 1960–63, Prof. 1963–97, Chair. of Dept 1975–85, Emer. Prof. 1997–; Vice-Pres. American Asscn of Anatomists 1979–83; mem. Review Group and Advisory Group of Expanded Programme of Research in Human Reproduction, WHO, Geneva 1971–76, Royal Soc. of Canada 1972–; Ortho Prize, Canadian Soc. of Fertility 1958, Prix Scientifique de la Province de Québec 1963, Siegler Award, American Fertility Soc. 1966, Van Campenhout Award, Canadian Fertility Soc. 1986, JCB Grant Award, Canadian Asscn of Anatomists 1986, Distinguished Andrologist Award, American Asscn of Andrology 1988, Osler Teaching Award, Faculty of Medicine, McGill Univ. 1990, Serono Award American Asscn of Andrology. *Publications:* more than 140 scientific articles in journals and books in the field of biology of reproduction and cell biology. *Leisure interests:* reading history and biography, gardening, listening to classical music. *Address:* Department of Anatomy, McGill University, 3640 University Street, Montreal, Québec, H3A 2B2 (Office); 567 Townshend, St Lambert, Québec, J4R 1M4, Canada (Home). *Telephone:* (514) 398-6349 (Office); (450) 671-5606 (Home). *Fax:* (514) 398-5047. *E-mail:* clermont@med.mcgill.ca (Home); clermont@medcor.mcgill.ca (Office); clermont@medcor.mcgill.ca (Home).

CLEVELAND, Harlan, AB; American administrator, educationist and government official; b. 19 Jan. 1918, New York; s. of Stanley Matthews and Marian Phelps (van Buren); m. Lois W Burton 1941; one s. two d.; ed Princeton and Oxford Univs; served Allied Control Comm., Rome 1944–45; UNRRA, Rome and Shanghai 1946–48; Econ. Co-operation Admin., Washington 1948–51; Asst Dir for Europe, Mutual Security Agency 1952–53; Exec. Ed. The Reporter, New York 1953–55, Publr 1955–56; Dean, Maxwell Graduate School of Citizenship and Public Affairs, Syracuse Univ. 1956–61; Asst Sec. for Int. Organization Affairs, State Dept 1961–65; Amb. to NATO 1965–69; Pres., Prof. of Political Science, Univ. of Hawaii 1969–74, Pres. Emer. 1974–; Dir Aspen Program in Int. Affairs Sept. 1974–80; Chair. Weather Modification Advisory Bd 1977–78; Distinguished Visiting Tom Slick Prof. of World Peace, LBJ School of Public Affairs, Univ. of Texas 1979; Prof. of Public Affairs and Dean Hubert H. Humphrey Inst. of Public Affairs, Univ. of Minn. 1980–87, Prof. Emer. 1988–; Pres. World Acad. of Arts and Sciences 1991–2000; recipient of 23 hon. degrees; US Medal of Freedom, Woodrow Wilson Award (Princeton Univ.), Prix de Talloires; Democrat. *Publications:* The Promise of World Tensions (ed.) 1961, The Ethic of Power (co-ed.) 1962, Ethics and Bigness (co-) 1962, The Obligations of Power 1966, NATO: The Transatlantic Bargain 1970, The Future Executive 1972, The Third Try at World Order 1977; Co-author: The Overseas Americans 1960, Human Growth: An Essay on Growth, Values and the Quality of Life 1978; Energy Futures of Developing Countries (ed.) 1980, Bioresources for Development (co-ed.) 1980, The Management of Sustainable Growth (ed.) 1981, The Knowledge Executive: Leadership in an Information Society 1985, The Global Commons 1990, Birth of a New World 1993, Leadership and the Information Revolution 1997. *Leisure interests:* sailing, golf, writing. *Address:* University of Minnesota, Hubert H. Humphrey Center, 301 19th Avenue South, Minneapolis, MN 55455-0429 (Office); 46891 Grissom Street, Sterling, VA 20165-3593, USA (Home). *Telephone:* (703) 450-0428 (Home). *Fax:* (703) 450-0429 (Home). *E-mail:* harlanclev@cs.com (Home). *Website:* ourworld.cs.com/ harlancecleve/ (Home).

CLEWLOW, Warren (Alexander Morten); South African business executive and chartered accountant; b. 13 July 1936, Durban; s. of Percy Edward Clewlow; m. Margaret Brokensha 1964; two s. three d.; ed Glenwood High School, Univ. of Natal; joined Barlow Group as Co. Sec. Barlow's (OFS) Ltd 1963; Alt. Dir Barlow Rand Ltd 1974, Dir 1975; mem. Exec. Cttee with various responsibilities Barlow Group 1978–83; CEO Barlow Rand Ltd (now Barloworld) 1983–86, Deputy Chair. and Chief Exec. 1985, Chair. 1991–; Dir SA Mutual Life Assurance Soc.; Chair. Pretoria Portland Cement, Sasol Ltd, Nedbank Ltd, Nedcor Ltd; Hon. Treas. African Children's Feeding Scheme; Regional Gov. Univ. of Cape Town Foundation; Council mem. South Africa Foundation; Chair. State Pres. Econ. Advisory Council 1985; mem. Bd Asscn of Marketers; Trustee Project South African Trust, Nelson Mandela Children's Fund; Hon. Prof. Business Man. and Admin., Univ. of Stellenbosch 1986; Chair. Duke of Edinburgh's South African Foundation; Chair. The President's Award for Youth Empowerment Trust; D. Econ. hc (Natal) 1988; Businessman of the Year, Sunday Times 1984, Marketing Man of the Year, SA Inst. of Marketing 1984; Dr. G. Malherbe Award, Univ. of Natal 1986, Order for Meritorious Service (Gold Class) 1988. *Leisure interests:* tennis, horticulture, historical reading, sugar plantation farmering. *Address:* Barloworld Ltd., P.O. Box 782248, Sandton, 2146, South Africa (Office). *Telephone:* (11) 445-1000 (Office). *Fax:* (11) 444-8209. *E-mail:* marians@barloworld.com.

CLIBURN, Van (Harvey Lavan, Jr); American pianist; b. 12 July 1934, Shreveport; s. of Harvey Lavan and Rildia Bee (née O'Bryan) Cliburn; studied with mother and at Juilliard School; public appearances, Shreveport 1940; début, Houston Symphony Orchestra 1952, New York Philharmonic Orchestra 1954, 1958; concert pianist on tour US 1955–56, USSR 1958; appearances in Brussels, London, Amsterdam, Paris, etc.; Hon. H.H.D. (Baylor), MFA (Moscow Conservatory) 1989, winner first Int. Tchaikovsky Piano Competition, Moscow 1958, Arturo Toscanini Award, Classical Music Broadcaster's Asscn 1998, Kennedy Center Honor 2001. *Address:* c/o Ann Hilton, PO Box 470217, Fort Worth, TX 76147-0217 (Office); Van Cliburn Foundation, 2525 Ridgmar Boulevard, Suite 307, Fort Worth, TX 76116-4583, USA (Office).

CLIFF, Ian Cameron, OBE, MA; British diplomatist; b. 11 Sept. 1952, Twickenham; s. of Gerald Shaw Cliff and Dorothy Cliff; m. Caroline Redman 1988; one s. two d.; ed Hampton Grammar School and Univ. of Oxford; history teacher, Dr Challoner's Grammar School, Amersham 1975–79; joined Foreign Office 1979; First Sec., Khartoum 1982–85, FCO 1985–89, UK Mission to UN, New York 1989–93; Dir Exports to Middle East, Near East and N Africa, Dept of Trade and Industry 1993–96; Deputy Head of Mission, British Embassy, Vienna 1995–2001; Amb. to Bosnia and Herzegovina 2001–. *Leisure interests:* music, railways, philately. *Address:* Embassy of the UK, 8 Tina Ujevica, Sarajevo, Bosnia and Herzegovina (Office). *Telephone:* 33444429 (Office).

CLIFFORD, Max(well); British public relations executive; b. April 1943, Kingston-upon-Thames; s. of Frank Clifford and Lilian Clifford; m. Elizabeth Clifford; one d.; ed secondary modern school, South Wimbledon; worked in dept store (sacked); fmr jr reporter Merton and Morden News; fmr jr press officer EMI Records (promoted the Beatles); worked in public relations; founder Max Clifford Assocs (press and public relations consultancy) 1968–, clients have included Muhammad Ali, Geoffrey Boycott, Marlon Brando, David Copperfield, Diana Ross, O. J. Simpson, Frank Sinatra, SEAT, Laing Homes. *Address:* Max Clifford Associates Ltd, 109 New Bond Street, London, W1Y 9AA, England. *Telephone:* (20) 7408-2350. *Fax:* (20) 7409-2294.

CLIFFORD, Sir Timothy Peter Plint, Kt, BA, FRSA; British museum administrator; b. 26 Jan. 1946; s. of Derek Plint Clifford and the late Anne Clifford (née Pierson); m. Jane Olivia Paterson 1968; one d.; ed Sherborne, Dorset, Perugia Univ., Courtauld Inst., Univ. of London; Asst Keeper Dept of Paintings Manchester City Art Galleries 1968–72, Acting Keeper 1972; Asst Keeper Dept of Ceramics Victoria and Albert Museum, London 1972–76; Dir Manchester City Art Galleries 1978–84, Nat. Galleries of Scotland 1984–; mem. Cttee ICOM (UK) 1980–82, Chair. Int. Cttee for Museums of Fine Art 1980–83, mem. Exec. Cttee 1983–88; mem. Bd Museums and Galleries Comm. 1983–88, British Council 1987–92; mem. Exec. Cttee Scottish Museums Council 1984–; Vice-Pres. Turner Soc. 1984–86, 1989–; Pres. Nat. Asscn of Decorative and Fine Arts Socs. 1996–; Trustee Lake Dist Art Gallery and Museum Trust 1989–97, Royal Yacht Britannia 1998; Hermitage Devt Trust 1999–, Stichting Hermitage aan de Amstel 1999–; Patron Friends of Sherborne House 1997–; Freeman Goldsmiths Co. 1989, City of London 1989; Hon. LLD (St Andrews) 1996, Hon. DLitt (Glasgow) 2001; Special Award BIM 1991; Commendatore al Ordine della Repubblica Italiana 1999, FSA (Scotland). *Publications include:* John Crome (with Derek Clifford) 1968, The Man at Hyde Park Corner: Sculpture by John Cheere (with T. Friedmann) 1974, Vues pittoresques de Luxembourg ... par J.M.W. Turner 1977, Ceramics of Derbyshire 1750–1975 1978, J.M.W. Turner, Acquerelli e incisioni 1980, The

Nat. Gallery of Scotland: an Architectural and Decorative History (with Ian Gow) 1988, Raphael: the Pursuit of Perfection (co-author) 1994, Effigies and Ecstasies: Roman Baroque Sculpture and Design in the Age of Bernini (with A. Weston-Lewis) 1998, Designs of Desire: Architectural and Ornament Prints and Drawings 1500–1850 2000, (co-author) A Poet in Paradise: Lord Lindsay and Christian Art 2000. *Leisure interests:* bird watching, entomology. *Address:* National Galleries of Scotland, The Mound, Edinburgh, EH2 2EL, Scotland (Office). *Telephone:* (131) 556-8921 (Office). *Fax:* (131) 220-2753 (Office).

CLIFTON, James Albert, BA, MD; American physician, investigator, teacher and administrator; b. 18 Sept. 1923, Fayetteville, NC; s. of the late James A. Clifton, Sr and Flora McNair Clifton; m. Katherine Rathe 1949; two d. (and one d. deceased); ed Vanderbilt Univ.; Asst Prof. of Medicine, Univ. of Ia Coll. of Medicine 1954–58, Assoc. Prof. 1958–63, Prof. 1963–76, Roy J. Carver Prof. of Medicine 1976–90, Dir Center for Digestive Diseases 1985–90, Prof. Emer. 1991–, Interim Dean 1991–93; Chief, Div. of Gastroenterology, Univ. of Ia, Dept of Medicine 1953–71, Prof. Emer. 1991–; Chair. Dept of Medicine, Univ. of Ia Coll. of Medicine 1970–76; Pres. American Coll. of Physicians 1977–78, American Gastroenterological Asscn 1970–71; Chair. Subspecialty Bd in Gastroenterology, American Bd of Internal Medicine 1972–75, American Bd of Internal Medicine 1980–81; Pres. Univ. of Iowa Retirees Asscn 1999–2000, Emer. Faculty Asscn 2000; mem. Ludwig Inst. for Cancer Research, Zürich, Switzerland 1984–95, Central Soc. for Clinical Research, American Physiological Soc., Asscn of American Physicians, Inst. of Medicine (NAS), Royal Soc. of Medicine, London, Scientific Advisory Cttee, Health Task Force Cttee (Nat. Insts of Health), Nat. Advisory Council, Nat. Insts of Arthritis, Metabolism and Digestive Diseases (Nat. Insts of Health); consultant to numerous US medical schools; Visiting Scientist, Mount Desert Island Biological Research Lab., Bar Harbor, Maine 1964; Visiting Prof. of Medicine, St Mark's Hosp. (Univ. of London), England 1984–85; Distinguished Medical Alumnus Award, Vanderbilt Univ., Alfred Stengel Award, American Coll. of Physicians, Distinguished Medical Alumnus Award, Univ. of Iowa 2000, Distinguished Mentoring Award 2002. *Publications:* numerous scientific papers on intestinal absorption of nutrients, gastrointestinal motility and numerous publs regarding philosophy and current affairs in internal medicine. *Leisure interests:* music, photography and travel. *Address:* University of Iowa Hospital and Clinics, 4 J.C.P., Hawkins Drive, Iowa City, IA 52242 (Office); 39 Audubon Place, Iowa City, IA 52245, USA (Home). *Telephone:* (319) 356-1771 (Office); (319) 351-1561 (Home). *Fax:* (319) 353-6399 (Office); (319) 351-1561 (Home). *E-mail:* james-clifton@uiowa.edu (Office); zybumjim@home.com (Home).

CLINTON, Bill (William) Jefferson, JD; American politician; b. 19 Aug. 1946, Hope, Arkansas; s. of Roger Clinton and the late Virginia Dwire; m. Hillary Rodham (q.v.) 1975; one d.; ed Hot Springs High School, Georgetown Univ., Univ. Coll., Oxford, Yale Law School; Professor, Univ. of Arkansas Law School 1974–76; Democratic Nominee, U.S. House Third District, Arkansas 1974; Attorney-Gen., Arkansas 1977–79, State Gov. 1979–81, 1983–93; Pres. of USA 1993–2001; impeached by House of Reps. for perjury and obstruction of justice Dec. 1998; acquitted in the Senate on both counts Jan. 1999; suspended from practising law in Supreme Court 2001–(06); mem. counsel firm Wright, Lindsey & Jennings 1981–83; Chair. Southern Growth Policies Bd 1985–86; Chair. Nat. Govs.' Asscn 1987, Co-Chair. Task Force on Educ. 1990–91; Vice-Chair. Democratic Govs' Asscn 1987–88, Chair. (elect) 1988–89, Chair. 1989–90; Chair. Educ. Comm. of the States 1987; Chair. Democratic Party Affirmative Action 1975, Southern Growth Policies Bd 1980; Chair. Democratic Leadership Council 1990–91; mem. US Supreme Court Bar, Bd of Trustees, Southern Center for Int. Studies of Atlanta, Ga; Hon. Fellow Univ. Coll. Oxford 1992; Hon. DCL (Oxford) 1994; Hon. DLitt (Ulster) 1995. *Publication:* Between Hope and History 1996. *Leisure interests:* jogging, swimming, golf, reading. *Address:* 55 West 125th Street, New York, NY 10027, USA.

CLINTON, Hillary Rodham, MA, DJur; American First Lady and lawyer; b. 26 Oct. 1947, Chicago, Ill.; d. of Hugh Ellsworth and Dorothy Howell Rodham; m. Bill (William) Jefferson Clinton (q.v.) (President of USA), 1975; one d.; ed Wellesley Coll. and Yale Univ.; joined Rose Law Firm 1977, now Sr Partner; Legal Counsel, Nixon impeachment staff, House Judiciary Cttee 1974; Asst Prof. of Law, Fayetteville and Dir Legal Aid Clinic 1974–77; lecturer in Law, Univ. of Arkansas, Little Rock 1979–80; Chair. Comm. on Women in the Profession, American Bar Asscn 1987–91; Head Pres.'s Task Force on Nat. Health Reform 1993–94; newspaper columnist July 1995–; Senator from New York Jan. 2001–; Co-Chair. Children's Defense Fund 1973–74; mem. Bd Dirs. Southern Devt Bancorpn. 1986, Nat. Center on Educ. and the Econ. 1987, Franklin and Eleanor Roosevelt Inst. 1988, Children's TV Workshop 1989, Public/Pvt. Ventures 1990, Arkansas Single Parent Scholarship Fund Program 1990; Hon. LLD (Arkansas, Little Rock) 1985, (Arkansas Coll.) 1988, (Hendrix Coll.) 1992; Hon. DHL (Drew) 1996; numerous awards and distinctions including One of Most Influential Lawyers in America (Nat. Law Journal) 1988, 1991, Outstanding Lawyer-Citizen Award (Arkansas Bar Asscn) 1992, Lewis Hine Award, Nat. Child Labor Law Comm. 1993, Friend of Family Award, American Home Econs Foundation 1993, Humanitarian Award, Alzheimer's Asscn 1994, Elie Wiesel Foundation 1994, AIDS Awareness Award 1994, Grammy Award 1996, numerous other awards and prizes. *Publications:* It Takes a Village 1996, Dear Socks, Dear Buddy 1998, An

Invitation to the White House 2000, Living History (memoirs) 2003; numerous contribs to professional journals. *Leisure interests:* reading, walking, tennis. *Address:* US Senate, Washington, DC 20510, USA.

CLINTON-DAVIS, Baron (Life Peer), cr. 1990, of Hackney in the London Borough of Hackney; **Stanley Clinton Clinton-Davis,** PC, LLB; British politician, solicitor and international official; b. 6 Dec. 1928, London; s. of the late Sidney Davis and of Lily Davis; m. Frances Jane Lucas 1954; one s. three d.; ed Hackney Downs School, Bournemouth School, Mercers' School and King's Coll., London; fmr Councillor and Mayor, London Borough of Hackney; MP for Hackney Cen. 1970–83; Parl. Under-Sec. of State for Trade 1974–79; Opposition Spokesman for Trade 1979–81, for Transport, House of Lords 1990–97; Minister of State, Dept of Trade and Industry 1997–98; Deputy Opposition Spokesman for Foreign Affairs 1981–83; Commr EC for the Environment, Consumer Protection, Nuclear Safety, Forests and Transport Jan. 1985–86, for Environment, Transport and Nuclear Safety 1986–88; Chair. Refugee Council 1989–97, Advisory Cttee on Protection of the Sea (ACOPS) 1989–97, 1998–2001 (Pres. 2001–); Consultant on European affairs and law, S. J. Berwin & Co. 1989–97, European Cockpit Asscn (ECA) 1995–97; Pres. Asscn of Metropolitan Authorities 1992–97, Airfields Environment Fed. 1994–97, British Airline Pilots Asscn (BALPA) 1994–; Deputy Chair. Labour Finance and Industry Group 1993–; Fellow King's Coll. and Queen Mary and Westfield Coll., London Univ.; Labour; Dr hc (Polytechnical Inst., Bucharest) 1993; First Medal for Outstanding Services to Animal Welfare in Europe (Eurogroup for Animal Welfare) 1988, Grand Cross, Order of Leopold II, for services to EC (Belgium) 1990. *Publication:* Good Neighbours? Nicaragua, Central America and the United States (co-author) 1982. *Leisure interests:* reading political biographies, golf. *Address:* House of Lords, Westminster, London, SW1A 0PW, England. *Telephone:* (20) 7215-5501.

CLOONEY, George; American actor; b. 6 May 1961, Lexington, Kentucky; s. of Nick Clooney; m. Talia Blasam (divorced). *Television series:* E/R 1984–85, The Facts of Life 1985–86, Roseanne 1988–89, Sunset Beat 1990, Baby Talk 1991, Bodies of Evidence 1992, Sisters 1992–94, ER 1994–99. *Television films:* Combat High 1986, Fail Safe 2000. *Films:* Return of the Killer Tomatoes 1988, Red Surf 1990, Unbecoming Age 1993, From Dusk Till Dawn 1996, One Fine Day 1996, Batman and Robin 1997, The Peacemaker 1998, Out of Sight 1998, The Thin Red Line 1998, South Park: Bigger Longer and Uncut (voice) 1999, Three Kings 1999, The Perfect Storm 1999, O Brother, Where Art Thou? 2000, Spy Kids 2001, Ocean's Eleven 2001, Welcome to Collinwood 2002, Solaris 2003, Confessions of a Dangerous Mind (also Dir) 2003. *Address:* Creative Artists, 9830 Wilshire Boulevard, Beverly Hills, CA 90212, USA (Office).

CLOSE, Glenn; American actress; b. 19 March 1947, Greenwich, Conn.; d. of William Close and Bettine Close; m. 1st Cabot Wade (divorced); m. 2nd James Marlas 1984 (divorced); one d. by John Starke; ed William and Mary Coll.; joined New Phoenix Repertory Co. 1974; co-owner The Leaf and Bean Coffee House, Bozeman 1991–. *Stage appearances include:* Love for Love, The Rules of the Game, The Singular Life of Albert Nobbs, Childhood, Real Thing (Tony Award), King Lear, The Rose Tattoo, Benefactors, Death and the Maiden, Sunset Boulevard, A Streetcar Named Desire (Royal Nat. Theatre) 2002. *Films include:* The World According to Garp 1982, The Big Chill 1983, The Natural 1984, The Stone Boy 1984, Maxie 1985, Jagged Edge 1985, Fatal Attraction 1987, Dangerous Liaisons 1989, Hamlet 1989, Reversal of Fortune 1989, The House of Spirits 1990, Meeting Venus 1990, Hamlet 1990, Immediate Family 1991, The Paper 1994, Mary Reilly 1994, Serving in Silence: The Margaret Cammermeyer Story 1995, 101 Dalmatians 1996, Mars Attacks! 1996, Air Force One 1997, Paradise Road 1997, Tarzan 1999, Cookie's Fortune 1999, 102 Dalmatians 2000, The Safety of Objects 2001, Pinocchio (voice) 2002; numerous TV film appearances. *Address:* c/o Creative Artists Agency, 9830 Wilshire Boulevard, Beverly Hills, CA 90212, USA.

CLOSETS, François de; French author and journalist; b. 25 Dec. 1933, Enghien-les-Bains; s. of Louis-Xavier de Closets and Marie-Antoinette Masson; m. 1st Danièle Lebrun; one s.; m. 2nd Janick Jossin 1970; one s. one d.; ed Lycée d'Enghien, Faculté de Droit de Paris and Inst. d'Etudes Politiques, Paris; Ed. then special envoy of Agence France-Presse in Algeria 1961–65; scientific journalist, Sciences et Avenir 1964–, Acualités Télévisées 1965–68; contrib. L'Express 1968–69; Head of scientific service, TV Channel 1 1969–72; Head of scientific and tech. service of TV Channel 2 1972; contrib. to Channel 1 1974; Asst Ed.-in-Chief TF1; Co-producer l'Enjeu (econ. magazine) 1978–88; Dir of econ. affairs, TFI 1987; co-producer, Médiations magazine 1987–93; Producer, illustrator "Savoir Plus" for France 2 1992–2000, "Les Grandes Enigmes de la Science" for France 2 1992–2003; Grand Prix du reportage du Syndicat des journalistes et écrivains 1966, Prix Cazes 1974, 7 d'or du meilleur journaliste 1985, Roland Dorgelès prize 1997. *Publications:* L'Espace, terre des hommes, La lune est à vendre 1969, En danger de progrès 1970, Le Bonheur en plus 1974, La France et ses mensonges 1977, Scénarios du futur (Vol. I) 1978, Le monde de l'an 2000 (Vol. II) 1979, Le Système EPM 1980, Toujours plus 1982, Tous ensemble pour en finir avec la syndicatrie 1985, La Grande Manip 1990, Tant et Plus 1992, Le Bonheur d'apprendre, et comment on l'assassine 1996, Le compte à Rebours 1998, L'Imposture informatique 2000, La dernière liberté 2001. *Address:* France 2, 7 esplanade Henri de France, 75907 Paris Cedex 15, France.

CLOTET, Lluis; Spanish architect; b. 31 July 1941, Barcelona; s. of Jaime Clotet and Concepción Clotet; ed Higher Tech. School of Architecture; Jt f. Studio PER 1964–83; collaborator XV Triennale de Milano 1973, Festival of

Fine Architecture, Paris 1978, Transformations in Modern Architecture, MOMA, New York 1979, Forum Design, Linz 1980, Biennale de Venezia 1980, The House as Image, Louisiana Museum of Modern Art 1981, The Presence of the Past, San Francisco 1982, Ten New Buildings, ICA, London 1983, Contemporary Spanish Architecture, New York 1986; Assoc. with Ignacio Paricio 1983–; Prof. in Drawing, Barcelona Higher Tech. School in Architecture 1977–84; numerous prizes. *Major works include:* Banco España 1981–89, Water Cistern Ciutadella Park, Barcelona 1985–88, SIMON SA Bldg, Canovelles 1987–88, Museum of Art, Convent dels Angels, Barcelona (Restoration and extension plan) 1984–89, Teleport, Castellbisbal, Barcelona (plan) 1988, Sport Pavilion in Granada, 100 dwellings at the Olympic Village.

CLOUDSLEY-THOMPSON, John Leonard, MA, PhD, DSc, CBiol, FIBiol, FRES, FLS, FZS, FWAAS; British professor of zoology; b. John Leonard Thompson, 23 May 1921, Murree, India; s. of Dr. A. G. G. Thompson and Muriel Elaine (née Griffiths) Thompson; m. J. Anne Cloudsley 1944; three s.; ed Marlborough Coll., Pembroke Coll., Cambridge; war service 1940–44, commissioned 4th Queen's Own Hussars 1941 transferred to 4th County of London Yeomanry (Sharpshooters); Lecturer in zoology, King's Coll., Univ. of London 1950–60; Prof. of Zoology, Univ. of Khartoum and Keeper, Sudan Natural History Museum 1960–71; Prof. of Zoology, Birkbeck Coll., Univ. of London 1972–86, Prof. Emer. 1986–; Nat. Science Senior Research Fellow, Univ. of New Mexico, Albuquerque 1969; Leverhulme Emer. Fellowship, Univ. Coll. London 1987–89; Visiting Prof. Univ. of Kuwait 1978, 1983, Univ. of Nigeria, Nsukka 1981, Univ. of Qatar 1986; Chair. British Naturalists' Asscn 1974–83, Vice-Pres. 1985–; Chair. Biological Council 1977–82 (Medal 1985); Pres. British Arachnological Soc. 1982–85, British Soc. for Chronobiology 1985–87; Vice-Pres. Linnean Soc. 1975–76, 1977–78; Hon. mem. Royal African Soc. 1969 (Medal 1969), British Herpetological Soc. 1983 (Pres. 1991–96), Centre Int. de Documentation Arachnologique, Paris 1995; Ed.-in-Chief Journal of Arid Environments Vols 1–37 1978–97; Liveryman Worshipful Co. of Skinners 1952; Hon. Capt. FWAAS 1962, Hon. FLS 1997; Hon. DSc (Khartoum Univ.) and Silver Jubilee Gold Medal, 1981, Inst. of Biology K.S.S. Charter Award 1981, J. H. Grundy Memorial Medal, Royal Army Medical Coll. 1987, Peter Scott Memorial Award B.N.A. 1993. *Publications:* Spiders, Scorpions, Centipedes and Mites 1958, Animal Behaviour 1960, Rhythmic Activity in Animal Physiology and Behaviour 1961, Animal Conflict and Adaptation 1965, Animal Twilight 1967, Zoology of Tropical Africa 1969, The Temperature and Water Relations of Reptiles 1971, Desert Life 1974, Terrestrial Environments 1975, Insects and History 1976, Man and the Biology of Arid Zones 1977, The Desert 1977, Animal Migration 1978, Biological Clocks 1980, Tooth and Claw 1980, Evolution and Adaptation of Terrestrial Arthropods 1988, (ed.) Adaptations of Desert Organisms (25 Vols) 1989–2001, Ecophysiology of Desert Arthropods and Reptiles 1991, The Nile Quest (novel) 1994, Predation and Defence Amongst Reptiles 1994, Biotic Interactions in Arid Lands 1996, Teach Yourself Ecology 1998, The Diversity of Amphibians and Reptiles 1999. *Leisure interests:* music, photography, travel. *Address:* 10 Battishill Street, London, N1 1TE, England. *Telephone:* (20) 7359-7197 (Home).

CLOUGH, Ray William, Jr, ScD; American professor of structural engineering; b. 23 July 1920, Seattle; s. of Ray W Clough, Sr and Mildred Eva Nelson; m. Shirley Claire Potter 1942; one s. two d.; ed Univ. of Washington, Seattle, California Inst. of Tech., Pasadena, Calif. and Massachusetts Inst. of Tech., Cambridge, Mass.; served USAF 1942–46; joined Civil Eng Faculty, Univ. of Calif. as Asst Prof. of Civil Eng 1949, Assoc. Prof. 1954, Prof. 1959–, Chair. Div. of Structural Eng and Structural Mechanics 1967–70, Nishkian Prof. of Structural Eng 1983–87, Prof. Emer. 1987–; Consultant in Structural Eng, specializing in structural dynamics, computer methods of structural analysis and earthquake eng 1953–; mem. US Army Corps of Engineers Structural Design Advisory Bd 1967–; mem. NAS, Nat. Acad. of Eng; Hon. mem. American Soc. of Civil Eng 1988; Research Prize, Howard Medal, Newmark Medal, Moisieff Medal, Th. von Karman Medal (American Soc. of Civil Engineers), George W. Housner Medal 1996; Prince Philip Medal, Royal Acad. of Eng 1997. *Publication:* Dynamics of Structures (with J. Penzien) 1975, 1993. *Leisure interests:* skiing (cross-country) and hiking. *Address:* PO Box 4625, Sunriver, OR 97707-1625, USA (Home). *Telephone:* (541) 593-5064 (Home). *Fax:* (541) 593-2823 (Home).

CLOUTIER, Gilles G., CC, PhD, FRSC; Canadian engineer and physicist; b. 27 June 1928, Québec City; s. of late Philéas Cloutier and Valéda Nadeau; m. Colette Michaud 1954; two s. three d.; ed Univ. Laval, Québec and McGill Univ.; Prof. of Physics, Univ. de Montreal 1963–68; Man. of Basic Research Lab., Dir of Research and Asst Dir of Inst., Research Inst. of Hydro-Québec (IREQ) 1968–78; Pres. Alberta Research Council 1978–83; Exec. Vice-Pres. Tech. and Int. Affairs, Hydro-Québec 1983–85; Rector, Univ. de Montreal 1985–93; Pres. Conf. of Rectors and Prins. of Québec Univs. 1987–89; Chair. of Corporate Higher Educ. Forum 1992–93; Deputy Chair. Advisory Council on Science and Tech. 1998–; consultant in high tech. commercialization; mem. Bd Centre d'initiative technologique de Montreal 1985–93, Chamber of Commerce of Greater Montreal 1989–93, Asia Pacific Foundation of Canada, Bechtel Canada; mem. Bd of Trustees of Manning Awards; five hon. doctorates (Montreal, Alberta, McGill, Lyon II and Toronto Univs.); Officier Order of Québec, Chevalier Légion d'honneur 1991. *Address:* 2910 boulevard Edouard-Montpetit, Bureau 6, Montreal, H3C 3J7 (Office); 4500 Promenade Paton, Apt. 1208, Laval, Québec, H7W 4Y6, Canada (Home). *Telephone:* (514) 343-5775 (Office); (450) 687-3520 (Home). *Fax:* (450) 687-7477 (Office).

CLUFF, John Gordon (Algy); British business executive; b. 19 April 1940; s. of the late Harold Cluff and of Freda Cluff; m. Blondel Hodge 1993; three s.; ed Stowe School; army officer, served W Africa, Cyprus, Malaysia 1959–64; Chief Exec. Cluff Resources (fmrly Cluff Oil) 1971–, Chair. (and Chair. Zimbabwe) 1979–; Proprietor, The Spectator 1981–85, Chair. 1985–; Chair. Apollo Magazine Ltd 1985; Chair. and CEO Cluff Mining 1996–; Trustee Anglo-Hong Kong Trust 1989–, Stowe House Preservation Trust 1999–; Dir Centre for Policy Studies 1998–; Gov. Commonwealth Inst. 1995–, Chair. Conservative Comm. on the Commonwealth 2001; mem. Bd of Govs Stowe School 1998–. *Leisure interests:* collecting books and paintings, golf, shooting. *Address:* Cluff Mining PLC, 29 St James's Place, London, SW1A 1NR, England. *Telephone:* (20) 7495-2030 (Office).

CLUFF, Leighton Eggertsen, MD; American physician and foundation executive; b. 10 June 1923, Salt Lake City; s. of Lehi E. Cluff and Lottie (Brain) Cluff; m. Beth Allen 1944; two d.; ed Univ. of Utah; Intern, Johns Hopkins Hosp. 1949–50, Asst Resident 1951–52; Asst Resident Physician, Duke Hosp. 1950–51; Visiting Investigator, Asst Physician, Rockefeller Inst. of Medical Research 1952–54; Fellow, Nat. Foundation of Infantile Paralysis 1952–54; mem. Faculty, Johns Hopkins School of Medicine; mem. staff, Johns Hopkins Hosp. 1954–66, Prof. of Medicine 1964–66; Prof. and Chair. Dept of Medicine, Univ. of Florida 1966–76; Exec. Vice-Pres. Robert Wood Johnson Foundation 1976–86, Pres. 1986–90, Trustee Emer. 1990–; Distinguished Physician, Dept of Veterans' Affairs 1990–; Prof. Emer. of Medicine, Univ. of Fla 1990–; Dir American Social Health Asscn1991–99, 2002–, Chair. 1997–99. *Publications:* books and articles on internal medicine, infectious diseases, clinical pharmacology. *Leisure interests:* tennis, golf, fly fishing, woodworking, writing. *Address:* 8851 SW 45th Boulevard, Gainesville, FL 32608-4138, USA (Home). *Telephone:* (904) 336-0116. *Fax:* (904) 336-7821. *E-mail:* leighcluff@aol.com (Home).

CLUZEL, Jean, LenD; French politician; b. 18 Nov. 1923, Moulins; s. of Pierre Cluzel and Jeanne (née Dumont) Cluzel; m. Madeleine Bonnaud 1947; three s. one d.; ed Lycée de Vichy and Univ. of Paris; Pres. and Dir-Gen. Cluzel-Dumont 1947–71; Municipal Councillor St Pourcain/Sioule 1959–65; Admin., later Senator, Allier 1971, 1980, 1989; Conseiller Gen. Moulins-Ouest 1967, 1973, 1979, 1985; Pres. Conseil général, Allier 1970–76, 1985–92; Senator, Allier 1971, 1980, 1989; mem. l'Union Centriste, Spokesman and Vice-Pres. Comm. des Finances du Senat; Pres. Cttee for Econ. Expansion of Allier 1959–67; Pres. "Positions" and "L'Allier Demain", Fed. des Elus Bourbonnais 1972, Univ. Populaire de Bransat 1981, Comité Français pour l'Audiovisuel 1993; Dir Cahiers de l'audiovisuel 1994; Admin. France 2 1998, Singer Polignac Foundation 1999–; Council mem. Admin. du conseil mondial pour la Radio et la Télévision; Officier Légion d'honneur. *Publications:* Horizons Bourbonnais 1973, Les boutiques en colère 1975, Elu de peuple 1977, Télé Violence 1978, L'argent de la télévision 1979, Finances publiques et pouvoir local 1980, Les pouvoirs publics et la transmission de la culture 1983, Les pouvoirs publics et les caisses d'épargne 1984, Les anti-monarque de la Vème 1985, Un projet pour la presse 1986, La loi de 1987 sur l'épargne 1987, La télévision après six réformes 1988, Les finances locales decentralisées 1989, Le Sénat dans la société française 1990, Une ambition pour l'Allier 1992, Une autre bataille de France 1993, mots pour Mots 1993, Pour qui sont ces tuyaux qui sifflent sur nos têtes? 1993, Feu d'artifices pour fin de législature 1993, L'age de la télévision 1993, Lettre à mes collègues représentants du peuple 1993, Education, culture et télévision 1994, Du modèle canadien à l'appel sud-africain 1996, L'audiovisuel en Europe centrale et orientale 1996, La télévision 1996, Presse et démocratie 1997, L'indispensable Sénat 1998, A propos du Sénat et de ceux qui voudraient en finir avec lui 1999. *Address:* Institut de France, 23 quai de Conti, 75006 Paris (Office); 12 villa Dupont, 75116 Paris, France (Home).

CLWYD, Ann; British politician, journalist and broadcaster; b. 21 March 1937; d. of Gwilym Henri Lewis and Elizabeth Ann Lewis; m. Owen Dryhurst Roberts 1963; ed Holywell Grammar School, The Queen's School, Chester and Univ. Coll. Bangor; fmr BBC studio man., freelance reporter and producer; Welsh corresp. The Guardian and The Observer 1964–79; Vice-Chair. Welsh Arts Council 1975–79; mem. Royal Comm. on NHS 1976–79, Arts Council of GB 1975–80; various public and political appointments; mem. European Parl. for Mid and West Wales 1979–84; Opposition Front Bench Spokesperson on Women 1987–88, on Educ. 1987–88; Shadow Sec. of State on Overseas Devt and Co-operation 1989–92, on Wales 1992, for Nat. Heritage 1992–93; Opposition Front Bench Spokesperson on Employment 1993–94, on Foreign Affairs 1994–95; mem. Select Cttee on Int. Devt 1997–; Chair. All-Party Group on Human Rights 1997–; Chair. INDICT 1997–; mem. Parl. (Labour) for Cynon Valley 1984–. *Address:* House of Commons, London, SW1A 0AA, England; 6 Deans Court, Dean Street, Aberdare, Mid Glamorgan, CF44 7BN, Wales (Office). *Telephone:* (1685) 871394 (Office); (20) 7219-3000.

CLYDE, Baron (Life Peer), cr. 1996, of Briglands in Perthshire and Kinross; **James John Clyde,** PC, BA, LLB; British judge; b. 29 Jan. 1932, Edinburgh; m. Ann Hoblyn 1963; two s.; ed The Edinburgh Acad., Oxford Univ., Edinburgh Univ.; called to Scottish Bar 1959; QC 1971; Advocate-Depute 1973–74; Judge Courts of Appeal, Jersey and Guernsey 1979–85; a Lord of Appeal in Ordinary 1996–2001; Chair. Medical Appeal Tribunals 1974–85, Orkney Inquiry 1991–92, St George's School for Girls; Pres. Scottish Young Lawyers Asscn 1988–97, Scottish Univs. Law Inst. 1991–98; Vice-Pres. Royal Blind Asylum & School 1987–; Assessor to Chancellor Edin. Univ., mem. Univ. Court 1989–97, Vice-Chair. of Court 1993–96; Dir Edin. Acad. 1978–88;

leader UK del. to Consultative Comm. of the Bars of Europe 1981–84; Senator Coll. of Justice 1985–96; Chancellor to Bishop of Argyll and the Isles 1972–85; mem. Scottish Valuation Advisory Council 1972–96, Vice-Chair. 1980–87, Chair. 1987–96; Hon. Bencher Middle Temple 1996; Hon. Fellow Corpus Christi Coll. 1996; Trustee Nat. Library of Scotland 1977–94, St Mary's Music School 1978–91; Gov. Napier Polytechnic, later Univ. 1989–93; Hon. DLitt (Napier) 1995; Dr hc (Heriot-Watt) 1994, (Edin.) 1997. *Publication:* Armour on Valuation 3rd to 5th edns (Jt), Judicial Review (jtly). *Leisure interests:* music and gardening. *Address:* House of Lords, London, SW1A 0PW, England.

CLYNE, Michael George, AM, MA, PhD; Australian professor of linguistics; b. 12 Oct. 1939, Melbourne; s. of Dr. John Clyne and Edith Clyne; m. Irene Donohoue 1977; one d.; ed Caulfield Grammar School, Univs. of Melbourne, Bonn and Utrecht and Monash Univ.; Tutor then Sr Tutor, Monash Univ. 1962–64, Lecturer then Sr Lecturer 1965–71, Assoc. Prof. of German 1972–88, Prof. of Linguistics 1988–2000; Research Dir Language and Soc. Centre 1990–2000; Professorial Fellow in Linguistics Univ. of Melbourne 2001–, Dir Research Unit for Multilingualism and Cross-Cultural Communication 2001–; Pres. Australian Linguistic Soc. 1986–88, Vice-Pres. 1989–90; Fellow, Acad. of Social Sciences in Australia, Australian Acad. of Humanities; Hon. Life mem. Applied Linguistics Asscn of Australia 1989–; other professional memberships, appts. etc.; Hon. DPhil (Munich); Austrian Cross of Honour for Science and the Arts (1st class) 1996; Jakob- and Wilhelm-Grimm Prize 1999. *Publications include:* Transference and Triggering 1967, Perspectives on Language Contact 1972, Deutsch als Muttersprache in Australien 1981, Multilingual Australia 1982, Language and Society in the German-Speaking Countries 1984, Australia: Meeting Place of Languages 1985, An Early Start: Second Language at the Primary School 1986, Community Languages, the Australian Experience 1991, Pluricentric Languages 1992, Inter-cultural Communication at Work 1994, Developing Second Language From Primary School 1995, The German Language in a Changing Europe 1995, Background Speakers 1997, Undoing and Redoing Corpus Planning 1997, Pluricentric Languages in an Immigrant Context 1999, Dynamics of Language Contact 2003. *Leisure interests:* music, reading. *Address:* Department of Linguistics and Applied Linguistics, University of Melbourne, Melbourne, Vic. 3010 (Office); 33 Quaintance Street, Mount Waverley, Vic. 3149, Australia (Home). *Telephone:* (3) 8344-8986 (Office); (3) 9807-7180 (Home). *Fax:* (3) 8344-8990 (Office). *E-mail:* mgclyne@unimelb.edu.au (Office).

COAKLEY, Sarah Anne, MA, ThM, PhD; British professor of theology; b. 10 Sept. 1951, London; d. of F. Robert Furber and Anne McArthur; m. James Coakley 1975; two d.; ed Blackheath High School for Girls, New Hall, Cambridge and Harvard Divinity School; lecturer in Religious Studies, Lancaster Univ. 1976–90, Sr Lecturer 1990–91; Tutorial Fellow in Theology and univ. lecturer, Oriel Coll. Oxford 1991–93; Prof. of Christian Theology, The Divinity School, Harvard Univ. 1993–95, Edward Mallinckrodt, Jr Prof. of Divinity 1995–; Harkness Fellowship 1973–75; Select Preacher, Oxford Univ. 1991; Hulsean Lecturer, Univ. of Cambridge 1991–92, Hulsean Preacher 1996; Samuel Ferguson Lecturer, Manchester Univ. 1997, Riddell Lecturer, Newcastle Univ. 1999, Tate-Wilson Lecturer, Southern Methodist Univ. 1999, Prideaux Lecturer, Exeter Univ. 2000, Jellema Lecturer, Calvin Coll. 2001, Stone Lecturer, Princeton Theological Seminary 2002, Cheney Lecturer, Berkeley Divinity School of Yale 2002; Hulsean Prize, Cambridge Univ. 1977. *Publications:* Christ Without Absolutes: A Study of the Christology of Ernst Troeltsch 1988, The Making and Remaking of Christian Doctrine (co-ed. with David Pailin) 1993, Religion and the Body (ed.) 1997, Powers and Submissions: Spirituality, Philosophy and Gender 2002, Re-thinking Gregory of Nyssa (ed) 2003; contribs to Church of England Doctrine Comm. Reports 1987, 1991; articles in theological journals. *Leisure interests:* musical activities, thinking about the garden. *Address:* The Divinity School, Harvard University, 45 Francis Avenue, Cambridge, MA 02138, USA. *Telephone:* (617) 495-4518. *Fax:* (617) 496-0585.

COASE, Ronald; British professor of economics; b. 29 Dec. 1910, Willesden; s. of Henry Coase and Rosalie Coase; m. Marian Hartung 1937; ed L.S.E; Asst lecturer, lecturer, reader LSE 1935–51; Prof. Univ. of Chicago Law School 1964–82, Clifton R. Musser Prof. Emer. 1982–, also Sr Fellow in Law and Econs; winner Nobel Prize for Econs 1991; numerous hon. degrees. *Publications:* British Broadcasting: a study in Monopoly 1950, The Firm, the Market and the Law 1988, Essays on Economics and Economists 1994. *Address:* University of Chicago Law School, 1111 East 60th Street, Chicago, IL 60637; The Hallmark, 2960 Lake Shore Drive, Chicago, IL 60657, USA (Home).

COATES, Anne Voase; British film executive and producer; b. 12 Dec. 1925, Reigate, Surrey; m. Douglas Hickox (deceased); two s. one d.; ed Bartrum Gables Coll.; worked as nurse E Grinstead Plastic Surgery Hosp. *Films include:* Pickwick Papers, Grand National Night, Forbidden Cargo, To Paris With Love, The Truth About Women, The Horse's Mouth, Tunes of Glory, Don't Bother to Knock, Lawrence of Arabia (Acad. Award 1962), Becket (Acad. Award), Young Cassidy, Those Magnificent Men in their Flying Machines (co-ed.) Hotel Paradiso, Great Catherine, The Bofors Gun, The Adventurers, Friends, The Public Eye, The Nelson Affair, 11 Harrowhouse, Murder on the Orient Express, Man Friday, Aces High, The Eagle Has Landed, The Medusa Touch (producer and ed.), The Legacy, The Elephant Man, The Bushido Blade, Ragtime (co-ed.), The Pirates of Penzance, Greystoke: The Legend of Tarzan, Lord of the Apes, Lady Jane, Raw Deal, Masters of the Universe, Farewell to the King (co-ed.), Listen to Me, I Love You to Death, What About Bob?

Chaplin, In the Line of Fire (G.B.F.E. Award), Pontiac Moon, Congo, Striptease, Out to Sea, Out of Sight, Erin Brockovich 1999, Sweet November 2000, Unfaithful 2001. *Address:* 8455 Fountain Avenue, Apartment 621, Los Angeles, CA 90069 (Office); c/o The Gersh Agency, 232 North Canon Drive, Beverly Hills, CA 90210, USA. *Telephone:* (213) 654-7282 (Office).

COATES, John Henry, BA, PhD, FRS; Australian professor of mathematics; b. 26 Jan. 1945, New South Wales; s. of J. H. Coates and B. L. Lee; m. Julie Turner 1966; three s.; ed Australian Nat. Univ., Ecole Normale Supérieure, Paris, France, Cambridge Univ., UK; Asst Prof., Harvard Univ., USA 1969–72; Assoc. Prof. (with tenure), Stanford Univ., USA 1972–75; lecturer, Cambridge Univ., UK 1975–77; Prof., Australian Nat. Univ. 1977–78; Prof., Université de Paris XI (Orsay)1978–85; Prof. and Dir of Math., Ecole Normale Supérieure, Paris 1985–86; Sadleirian Prof. of Math., Cambridge Univ. 1986–, Head of Dept of Pure Math. and Math. Statistics 1991–97; Professorial Fellow Emmanuel Coll. 1975–77, 1986–; Vice-Pres. Int. Mathematical Union 1991–95; Dr. hc (Ecole Normale Supérieure) 1997. *Leisure interest:* reading. *Address:* Emmanuel College, Cambridge, CB1 2EA; 104 Mawson Road, Cambridge, CB1 2EA, England.

COATS, Daniel Ray, JD; American politician; b. 16 May 1943, Jackson, Mich.; s. of Edward R. Coats and Vera E. Coats; m. Marcia Crawford 1965; one s. two d.; ed Wheaton Coll., Ill., Univ. of Indiana; served US Army 1966–68; called to Bar of Ind. 1972; mem. Congress from 4th Dist Ind. 1981–89; Dist Rep. for Congressman Dan Quayle 1976–80; Senator from Ind. 1989–99; Amb. to Germany 2001–; lobbyist Pharmaceutical Research and Mfrs of America; mem. Bd Dirs IPALCO, Lear Siegler Services Inc., Int. Republic Inst., The Empowerment Network. *Address:* Embassy of the USA, Neustädtische Kirche 4/5, 10117 Berlin, Germany (Office). *Telephone:* (30) 83052805 (Office). *Fax:* (30) 20457574 (Office). *Website:* www.usembassy.de (Office).

COBURN, John, AM, ASTC; Australian artist; b. 23 Sept. 1925, Ingham, Queensland; s. of Edgar L. Cockburn and Alice Beatts; m. Barbara Woodward 1953 (died 1985); two s. one d.; m. Doreen Gadsby-Wells 1991; ed All Souls' School, Charters Towers and East Sydney Technical Coll.; has participated in major exhbns of Australian art in Australia and abroad, including Australian Painting, Tate Gallery 1963; first one-man exhbn Gallery of Contemporary Art, Melbourne 1957 and has since held many others in Australian cities, in Paris and Washington 1971, New York 1977, Paris, Bologna, Istanbul and Moscow 1989; art teacher, Nat. Art School, Sydney 1959–66; lived in France 1969–72 where designed many tapestries for the Aubusson workshops including two large tapestry curtains for Sydney Opera House; Head, Nat. Art School, Sydney 1972–74; Trustee, Art Gallery of NSW, Sydney 1976–80; work represented in Australian Nat. Gallery, Canberra, all Australian State galleries, Vatican Museum, Graphische Sammlung Albertina, Vienna and John F. Kennedy Center for the Performing Arts, Washington; Blake Prize for Religious Art 1960, 1977; Hon. DLitt (James Cook), Assoc. Sydney Tech. Coll. *Leisure interests:* drawing, swimming. *Address:* 4/425 Pacific Highway, Lindfield, NSW 2070, Australia.

COCHRAN, Johnnie L., Jr., BS, JD; American lawyer; b. 2 Oct. 1937, Shreveport, La.; ed Univ. of Calif. Los Angeles, Loyola Univ. and Univ. of S. Calif.; called to Bar, Calif. 1963, U.S. Dist Court (Western Dist) Tex. 1966, U.S. Supreme Court 1968; Deputy City Attorney, Criminal Div. City of LA 1963–65; Asst Dist Attorney, LA County 1978–82; fmr Adjunct Prof. of Law, Univ. of Calif. LA and Loyola Univ.; lawyer rep. U.S. Dist Court (Cen. Dist) Calif. 1990, U.S. Court of Appeals (9th Circuit) Judicial Conf. 1990; mem. Bd Dirs. LA Family Housing Corpn, Lawyers Mutual Insurance Co.; Special Counsel, Chair. Rules Cttee Democratic Nat. Convention 1984; Special Counsel, Cttee on Standard Official Conduct, Ethics Cttee 99th Congress, U.S. House of Reps.; Defence Counsel in trial on charges of murder of O.J. Simpson 1995, of Louise Woodward 1997; Fellow, American Bar Foundation; mem. American Coll. Trial Lawyers. *Address:* 4929 Wilshire Boulevard, Ste 1010, Los Angeles, CA 90010, USA.

COCHRAN, Thad; American politician; b. 7 Dec. 1937, Pontotoc, Miss.; s. of William Holmes and Emma Grace (née Berry) Cochran; m. Rose Clayton 1964; two c.; ed Mississippi Univ. and School of Law, Univ. of Dublin, Ireland; law practice in Jackson, Miss. 1965–72; Pres. Young Lawyers' section of Miss. State Bar, Chair. Miss. Law Inst.; mem. US House of Reps. 1973–78; Senator from Mississippi 1979–; Sec. Republican Conf. in US Senate 1985–90, Chair. Republican Conf., US Senate 1990–96; mem. Agric. Nutrition and Forestry Cttee, Appropriations Cttee, Govt Affairs Cttee, Rules and Admin. Cttee and Select Cttee on Indian Affairs. *Address:* 326 Russell Senate Office Building, Washington, DC 20510, USA.

COCHRAN, William, PhD, FRS, FRSE; British professor of natural philosophy; b. 30 July 1922, Scotland; s. of James Cochran and Margaret W Baird; m. Ingegerd Wall 1953; one s. two d.; ed Boroughmuir School, Edinburgh and Univ. of Edinburgh; Asst in Physics, Univ. of Edinburgh 1943–46; Research Asst, Univ. Demonstrator, Lecturer, Reader, Cavendish Lab., Cambridge 1946–64; Fellow, Trinity Hall, Cambridge 1951–64; Prof. of Physics, later of Natural Philosophy, Univ. of Edinburgh 1964–87, Dean, Faculty of Science 1978–81, Vice-Prin. 1983–87; Hon. DSc (Heriot-Watt) 1992, (Edinburgh) 1994; Guthrie Medal, Inst. of Physics 1966, Hughes Medal, Royal Soc. 1978, N.F. Potts Medal, Franklin Inst. 1985; Scott Prize, Royal Soc. of Edin. 1992; Hon. Fellow Trinity Hall, Cambridge 1982–. *Publications:* The Crystalline State, Vol. III (with H. S. Lipson) 1966, Dynamics of Atoms in Crystals 1973,

20th Century Physics (with others) 1994. *Leisure interests:* family history, Scots verse and light verse. *Address:* Department of Physics, The University, King's Buildings, Edinburgh, EH9 3JZ (Office); 3 Rustic Cottages, Colinton Road, Edinburgh, EH13 0LD, Scotland (Home). *Telephone:* (131) 441-2135 (Home).

COCKBURN, William, CBE, TD, FRSA; British business executive; b. 28 Feb. 1943; entered Post Office 1961, Personal Asst to Chair. 1971–73, Asst Dir of Planning and Finance 1973–77, Dir Cen. Finance Planning 1977–78, Dir Postal Finance 1978–79, Dir London Postal Region 1979–82, mem. Bd 1981–95, Man. Dir Royal Mail 1986–92, Chief Exec. The Post Office 1992–95; Chair. Int. Post Corpn 1994–95; Group Chief Exec., W H Smith Group PLC 1996–97; Group Man. Dir British Telecommunications PLC 1997–2001; Chair. Parity Group PLC 2001–; Deputy Chair. Business Post PLC 2002–; Dir (non-exec.) Watkins Holdings Ltd 1985–93, Lex Service PLC 1993–2002, Centrica PLC 1997–99; Dir Business in the Community 1990–, Yakara PLC 2002–; Pres. Inst. of Direct Marketing 2001–; Fellow Chartered Inst. of Transport; Freeman City of London. *Address:* Parity Group PLC, 16 St Martin's Le Grand, London, EC1A 4NA (Office); 9 Avenue Road, Farnborough, Hants. GU14 7BW, England (Home).

COCKER, Jarvis Branson; British singer; ed St Martin's Coll. of Art and Design; singer with Pulp (fmrly named Arabacus Pulp) 1981–; made videos for Pulp, Aphex Twin, Tindersticks; co-producer "Do You Remember The First Time?" (TV). *Singles include:* My Legendary Girlfriend 1991, Razzmatazz 1992, O.U. 1992, Babies 1992, Common People 1995, Disco 2000 1996. *Albums include:* It, Freaks, Separations, PulpIntro: The Gift Recordings, His 'N' Hers, Different Class 1995, This is Hardcore 1998.

COCKFIELD, Baron (Life Peer), cr. 1978, of Dover in the County of Kent; **(Francis) Arthur Cockfield,** Kt, LLB, BSc(Econ).; British business executive; b. 28 Sept. 1916; s. of late Lt Charles Cockfield and Louisa James; m. Aileen Monica Mudie 1970 (died 1992); ed Dover Grammar School, London School of Economics; called to Bar, Inner Temple 1942; Inland Revenue Dept of Civil Service 1938; Asst Sec. Bd of Inland Revenue 1945, Commr 1951–52, also Dir of Statistics and Intelligence to Bd of Inland Revenue 1945–52; Finance Dir Boots Pure Drug Co. Ltd 1953–61, Man. Dir and Chair. Exec. Man. Cttee 1961–67; mem. Nat. Econ. Devt Council (NEDC) 1962–64, 1982–83; Special Adviser on Taxation to the Chancellor of the Exchequer 1970–73; Chair. Price Comm. 1973–77; Minister of State, Treasury 1979–82; Sec. of State for Trade 1982–83, Chancellor of the Duchy of Lancaster 1983–84; Commr for Internal Market, Tax Law and Customs, Comm. of European Communities and a Vice-Pres. of the Comm. 1985–88; Adviser to Peat, Marwick McLintock 1989–93; Hon. Fellow, LSE 1972; Hon. LLD (Fordham, NY), (Sheffield) 1990, (Sussex) 2002; Dr hc (Surrey) 1989; Grand Cross Order of Leopold II (Belgium). *Publication:* The European Union: Creating the Single Market 1994. *Address:* House of Lords, London, SW1A 0PW, England.

CODRON, Michael Victor, CBE, MA; British impresario; b. 8 June 1930, London; s. of I. A. Codron and Lily Codron (née Morgenstern); ed St Paul's School, Worcester Coll., Oxford; Dir Aldwych Theatre, Hampstead Theatre, Royal Nat. Theatre; Cameron Mackintosh Prof. Oxford Univ. 1993; independent theatrical producer; has produced over 300 shows in West End, London including: The Birthday Party 1958, The Caretaker 1960, The Killing of Sister George, Little Malcolm and his Struggle against the Eunuchs, Big Bad Mouse 1966, The Boyfriend (revival) 1967, A Voyage Round My Father, The Homecoming (revival), Dr. Faustus, The Dresser, Three Sisters, Uncle Vanya, The Cherry Orchard 1989, Man of the Moment, Private Lives 1990, The Rise and Fall of Little Voice 1992, Time of My Life, Jamais Vu 1993, Kit and the Widow, Dead Funny, Arcadia, The Sisters Rosensweig 1994, Indian Ink, Dealer's Choice 1995, The Shakespeare Revue 1996, A Talent to Amuse 1996, Tom and Clem 1997, Silhouette 1997, Heritage 1997, Things We Do For Love, The Invention of Love, Alarms and Excursions 1998, Copenhagen 1999, Quartet, Comic Potential 1999, Peggy for You 2000, Blue/Orange 2001, Life After George 2002, Bedroom Farce 2002. *Film:* Clockwise 1986. *Leisure interest:* collecting Caroline of Brunswick memorabilia. *Address:* Aldwych Theatre Offices, Aldwych, London, WC2B 4DF (Office); 12 Tower Bridge Wharf, London, E1 9UR, England (Home). *Telephone:* (20) 7240-8291 (Office); (20) 7925-6243. *Fax:* (20) 7240-8467 (Office); (20) 7240-8467.

COE, Baron (Life Peer), cr. 2000, of Ranmore in the County of Surrey; **Sebastian Newbold Coe,** OBE, BSc; British athlete; b. 29 Sept. 1956, London; s. of Peter Coe and Angela Coe; m. Nicola Susan Elliott 1990; two s. two d.; ed Loughborough Univ.; competed Olympic Games, Moscow 1980, winning Gold Medal at 1500 m. and Silver Medal at 800 m. and repeated this in Los Angeles 1984; European Junior Bronze Medallist at 1500 m. 1975; European Bronze Medallist at 800 m. 1978; European Silver Medallist at 800 m. 1982; European 800 m. Champion 1986; has held world records at 800 m., 1000 m., 1500 m. and mile; est. new records at 800 m., 1000 m. and mile 1981; mem. 4 × 400 m. world record relay squad 1982; only athlete to hold world records at 800 m., 1000 m., 1500 m. and mile simultaneously; Pres. first athletes' del. to IOC, Baden-Baden 1981 and mem. first athletes' comm. set up after Congress by IOC 1981–; Conservative MP for Falmouth and Camborne 1992–97; mem. Employment Select Cttee 1992–94, Nat. Heritage Select Cttee 1995–97; Parl. Pvt. Sec. to Chancellor of Duchy of Lancaster 1994–95, to Michael Heseltine 1995–96; Jr Govt Whip 1996–97; Deputy Chief of Staff then Pvt. Sec. to William Hague, Leader of the Opposition 1997–2001; Chair. Diadora UK 1987–94, ADT Health Quest Charitable Trust 1991–; Vice-Chair.

Sports Council 1986–89, Sports Aid Trust 1987; mem. Health Educ. Authority 1987–92, Health Educ. Council (now Authority) 1986–; Vice-Patron Sharon Allen Leukemia Trust 1987–, Olympic Cttee Medical Comm. 1987–95, Sport for All Comm. 1997–; Admin. Steward, British Boxing Bd of Control 1995–; Global Adviser NIKE 2000–; Founding mem. World Sports Acad. 2000–; sports columnist, Daily Telegraph 2000–; BBC Sports Personality of 1979; Sir John Cohen Memorial Award 1981; Príncipe de Asturias Award (Spain) 1987; Hon. D.Tech. (Loughborough) 1985, Hon. DSc (Hull) 1988, Hon. LLB (Sheffield) 1991. *Publications:* Running Free (with David Miller) 1981, Running for Fitness 1983, The Olympians 1984, More Than a Game 1992, Born to Run (autobiog.) 1992. *Leisure interests:* jazz, theatre, reading, some writing. *Address:* c/o Conservative Central Office, 32 Smith Square, London, SW1P 3HH, England. *Telephone:* (20) 7218-3000 (Office). *E-mail:* blacks@parliament.uk (Office).

COELHO, Paulo; Brazilian author; b. 1947, Rio de Janeiro; fmr playwright, theatre director, hippie and popular songwriter; imprisoned for alleged subversive activities against Brazilian Govt 1974; elected mem. Brazilian Acad. of Arts 2002–. *Publications:* The Pilgrimage 1987, The Alchemist 1988, Brida 1990, The Valkyries 1992, Maktub 1994, By The River Piedra I Sat Down and Wept 1994, The Fifth Mountain 1996, The Manual of the Warrior of Light 1997, Veronica Decides to Die 1998. *Address:* c/o HarperCollins, 77–85 Fulham Palace Road, Hammersmith, London, W6 8JB, England. *Telephone:* (20) 8741-7070. *E-mail:* autor@paulocoelho.com.br (Home).

COÈME, Guy; Belgian politician; b. 21 Aug. 1946, Waremme; m.; two c.; ed Univ. of Liège; mem. Nat. Office, Parti Socialiste (PS) 1970–74, Vice-Pres. PS 1983–; Deputy Mayor, Waremme 1971–74, 1982–87; Prov. Councillor, Liège 1971–74; Deputy, Liège 1974–81, Huy-Waremme 1982–; Burgomaster, Waremme 1987–; Sec. of State for the Wallonne Region, with responsibility for the Environment and Planning 1981–82; Minister-Pres. Wallonne Regional Exec., with responsibility for Water, Rural Devt, Conservation and Admin. Feb.-May 1988; Minister of Nat. Defence 1988–92; Deputy Prime Minister and Minister of Communications and Public Services 1992–94; Pres. Soc. for the Regional Devt of Wallonne 1978; Vice-Pres. Socialist Party 1983; Admin. Soc. for Regional Investment in Wallonne 1979. *Address:* c/o Parti Socialiste, 13 boulevard de l'Empereur, 1000 Brussels, Belgium.

COEN, Enrico Sandro, PhD, FRS, FLS, CBE; British geneticist; b. 29 Sept. 1957, Southport, Lancs.; s. of Ernesto Coen and Dorothea Coen (née Cattani); m. Lucinda Poliakoff 1984; two s. one d.; ed King's Coll., Cambridge; joined John Innes Inst., Norwich 1984, Project Leader 1995–98, Deputy Head Dept of Genetics 1998–; Hon. Lecturer Univ. of E Anglia 1989, Hon. Reader 1994, Hon. Prof. 1998; Foreign Assoc. mem. NAS 2001; EMBO Medal, Rome 1996, Science for Art Prize, Paris 1996, Linnean Gold Medal, London 1997. *Publications:* The Art of Genes 1999; 80 articles in int. scientific research journals. *Leisure interests:* painting, children. *Address:* John Innes Centre, Colney Lane, Norwich, NR4 7UH (Office); 3 Waverley Road, Norwich, NR4 6SG, England (Home). *Telephone:* (1603) 452274 (Office); (1603) 506242 (Home). *Fax:* (1603) 450022. *E-mail:* enrico.coen@bbsrc.ac.uk (Office). *Website:* www.jic.bbsrc.ac.uk (Office).

COEN, Ethan; American film producer and screenwriter; b. 1958, St Louis Park, Minn.; s. of Ed Coen and Rena Coen; brother of Joel Coen (q.v.) ; m.; ed Princeton Univ.; screenwriter (with Joel Coen) Crime Wave (fmrly XYZ Murders); producer, screenplay; ed. Blood Simple 1984. *Films include:* Raising Arizona 1987, Miller's Crossing 1990, Barton Fink 1991 (Palme d'Or, Cannes Festival), The Hudsucker Proxy 1994, Fargo 1996, The Naked Man, The Big Lebowski 1998, O Brother, Where Art Thou? 2000, The Man Who Wasn't There 2001, A Fever in the Blood 2002. *Publication:* Gates of Eden 1998. *Address:* c/o U.T.A., 9560 Wilshire Boulevard, Beverly Hills, CA 90212, USA.

COEN, Joel; American film director and screenwriter; b. 1955, St Louis Park, Minn.; s. of Ed Coen and Rena Coen; brother of Ethan Coen (q.v.) ; m. (divorced); ed Simon's Rock Coll. and New York Univ.; Asst Ed. Fear No Evil, Evil Dead; worked with rock video crews; screenwriter (with Ethan Coen) Crime Wave (fmrly XYZ Murders). *Films include:* (with Ethan Coen): Blood Simple 1984, Raising Arizona 1987, Miller's Crossing 1990, Barton Fink 1991 (Palme d'Or, Cannes Festival), The Hudsucker Proxy 1994, Fargo 1996 (Best Dir Award, Cannes Int. Film Festival 1996), The Big Lebowski, O Brother, Where Art Thou? 2000, The Man Who Wasn't There 2001. *Address:* c/o U.T.A., 9560 Wilshire Boulevard, Beverly Hills, CA 90212, USA.

COETZEE, John M., MA, PhD; South African writer and academic; b. 9 Feb. 1940, South Africa; one s. one d.; ed Univ. of Cape Town, Univ. of Texas; Asst Prof. of English, State Univ. of New York 1968–71; Lecturer, Univ. of Cape Town 1972–76, Sr lecturer 1977–80, Assoc. Prof. 1981–83, Prof. of Gen. Literature 1984–; Hon. Dr. (Strathclyde) 1985, (State Univ. of New York) 1989, (Cape Town) 1995; CNA Literary Award 1977, 1980, 1983, Geoffrey Faber Prize 1980, James Tait Black Memorial Prize 1980, Booker-McConnell Prize 1983, Prix Femina Etranger 1985 (for Life and Times of Michael K), Jerusalem Prize 1987, Sunday Express Book of the Year Prize (for Age of Iron) 1990, Premio Mondello (for The Master of Petersburg) 1994, Irish Times Int. Fiction Prize (for the Master of Petersburg) 1995; Booker Prize (for Disgrace) 1999. *Publications:* Dusklands 1974, In the Heart of the Country 1977, Waiting for the Barbarians 1980, Life and Times of Michael K 1983, Foe 1986, White Writing 1988, Age of Iron 1990, Doubling the Point: Essays and Interviews (ed. by David Atwell) 1992, The Master of Petersburg 1994, Giving

Offence: Essays on Censorship 1996, Boyhood 1997, The Lives of Animals (lecture) 1999, Disgrace 1999. *Address:* P.O. Box 92, Rondebosch 7701, South Africa.

COEY, John Michael David, DSc; Irish professor of physics; b. 24 Feb. 1945, Belfast; s. of David S. Coey and Joan E Newsam; m. Wong May 1973; two s.; ed Tonbridge School, Jesus Coll. Cambridge and Univ. of Manitoba; Chargé de Recherches, CNRS, Grenoble 1974–78; lecturer/Prof. Trinity Coll. Dublin 1978–, Prof. of Experimental Physics 1987–, Head, Dept of Physics 1989–92; Visiting Scientist, IBM Research Center, Yorktown Heights, NY 1976–77, 1988, Univ. of Bordeaux 1984, Centre d'Etudes Nucléaires de Grenoble 1985–86, Johns Hopkins Univ. Applied Physics Lab. 1986, Univ. de Paris 7 1992, Univ. of Calif. San Diego 1997, Fla State Univ. 1998; co-inventor, thermopiezic analyser 1986, nitromag 1990; Chief Coordinator, Concerted European Action on Magnets 1987–94; Dir Magnetic Solutions Ltd 1994–; mem. Academic Cttee Magnetism Lab. Inst. of Physics, Beijing 1988–; mem. Royal Irish Acad., Vice-Pres. 1989; Fulbright Fellow 1997–98; Fellow American Physical Soc. 2000; DSc (hc) Inst. Nat. Polytechnique de Grenoble 1994; Charles Chree Prize and Medal, Inst. of Physics London. *Publications:* Magnetic Glasses (with K. Moorjani) 1984, Structural and Magnetic Phase Transitions in Minerals (with S. Ghose and E Salje) 1988, Rare-Earth Iron Permanent Magnets 1996, Permanent Magnetism (with R. Skomski) 1999; numerous papers on magnetic and electronic properties of solids. *Leisure interest:* gardening. *Address:* Department of Physics, University of Dublin Trinity College, Dublin 2 (Office); Hillbrook House, Castleknock, Dublin 15, Ireland (Home). *Telephone:* (1) 6081470 (Office). *E-mail:* jcoey@tcd.ie.

COFFEY, Rev. David Roy, BA; British Baptist leader and minister of religion; b. 13 Nov. 1941; s. of Arthur Coffey and Elsie Maud Willis; m. Janet Anne Dunbar 1966; one s. one d.; ed Spurgeon's Coll., London; ordained to Baptist ministry 1967; Minister Whetstone Baptist Church, Leicester 1967–72, N Cheam Baptist Church, London 1972–80; Sr Minister Upton Vale Baptist Church, Torquay 1980–88; Sec. for Evangelism, Baptist Union of GB 1988–91, Gen. Sec. 1991–; Pres. Baptist Union 1986–87; Vice-Pres. European Baptist Fed. 1995–, Pres. 1997–99; Vice-Pres. Baptist World Alliance 2000–; Free Churches Moderator and Co-Pres. Churches Together in England March 2003–. *Publications:* Build that Bridge: a Study in Conflict and Reconciliation 1986, Discovering Romans: a Crossway Bible Guide 2000. *Leisure interests:* music, soccer, bookshops, Elgar Soc. *Address:* Baptist House, PO Box 44, 129 Broadway, Didcot, Oxon., OX11 8RT, England. *Telephone:* (1235) 517700. *Fax:* (1235) 517715. *E-mail:* gen.sec@baptist.org.uk (Office). *Website:* www.baptist.org.uk (Office).

COFFEY, Shelby, III; American journalist; m. Mary Lee Coffey; ed Univ. of Virginia; with Washington Post 1968–85, latterly Asst Man. Ed. for nat. news and Deputy Man. Ed. for features; Ed. U.S. News and World Report 1985–86; Ed. Dallas Times Herald 1986; Deputy Assoc. Ed. Los Angeles Times, subsequently Exec. Ed. 1986–89, Ed. and Exec. Vice-Pres. 1989; Nat. Press Foundation Ed. of the Year 1994. *Address:* c/o Los Angeles Times, Times Mirror Co., Times Mirror Square, Los Angeles, CA 90053, USA.

COFFIN, Frank Morey; American government official and lawyer; b. 11 July 1919, Lewiston, Maine; s. of Herbert and Ruth Coffin; m. Ruth Ulrich 1942; one s. three d.; ed Bates Coll. and Harvard Univ.; admitted to Maine Bar 1947, legal practice 1947–56; mem. US House of Reps 1957–61; Man. Dir Devt Loan Fund, Dept of State 1961; Deputy Admin., Agency for Int. Devt 1961–62; Deputy Admin. for Operations 1962–64; US Rep. to Devt Assistance Cttee, Org. for European Co-operation and Devt (OECD), Paris 1964–65; US Circuit Judge, Court of Appeals for First Circuit 1965–89, Chief Judge 1972–83; Sr Judge 1989–; Adjunct Prof., Univ. of Maine School of Law 1986–89; Dir Governance Inst. 1987–; Chair. Maine Justice Action Group 1996–2001; mem. American Acad. of Arts and Sciences. *Publications:* Witness for Aid 1964, The Ways of a Judge 1980, A Lexicon of Oral Advocacy 1984, On Appeal 1994. *Leisure interests:* sculpture, painting, boating. *Address:* United States Court of Appeals, 156 Federal Street, Portland, ME 04101-4152, USA.

COFFMAN, Vance D., MS, PhD; American aerospace company executive; b. 3 April 1944; m. Arlene Coffman; two d.; ed Iowa State Univ., Stanford Univ.; joined Lockheed Corpn as guidance and control systems analyst, Space Systems Div. (led devt of several major space programmes) 1967, apptd Div. Vice-Pres. 1985, Div. Vice-Pres. and Asst Gen. Man. 1987, Div. Pres. (responsible for Hubble Space Telescope and MILSTAR satellite communications programme) 1988, Pres. Space Systems Div. Lockheed Missiles & Space Co. and Vice-Pres. Corpn, Exec. Vice-Pres. Corpn –1995; Pres. and COO Space & Strategic Missiles Sector, Lockheed Martin Corpn (following merger of Lockheed and Martin Marietta Corpns) 1995, Pres., COO and Exec. Vice-Pres. Corpn –1997, Vice-Chair. and CEO 1997–98, Chair. and CEO 1998–; mem. Bd Dirs Bristol–Myers Squibb 1998, United Negro Coll. Fund 2001, 3M Co. 2002; mem. Nat. Acad. of Eng. (NAE), Security Affairs Support Asscn; Fellow American Astronomical Soc. 1991, AIAA 1996; Hon. Dr Aerospace Eng (Embry-Riddle Univ.) 1998, Hon. DrEng (Stevens Inst. of Tech.) 1998, Hon. LLD (Pepperdine Univ.) 2000; Professional Progress in Eng. Award, Iowa State Univ. 1989, Distinguished Achievement Citation, Iowa State 1999, Rear Admiral John J. Bergen Industry Award, NY Council of the Navy League 2000, Fleet Admiral Chester W. Nimitz Award, Navy League of USA 2001, Exec. of the Year, Washington Techway 2001, Bob Hope Distinguished Citizen Award, Nat. Defense Industrial Asscn (LA Chapter) 2002. *Address:*

Lockheed Martin, 6801 Rockledge Drive, Bethesda, MD 20817-1877, USA (Office). *Telephone:* (301) 897-6000 (Office). *Website:* www.lockheedmartin.com (Office).

COHAN, Robert Paul, CBE; British choreographer; b. 27 March 1925; s. of Walter Cohan and Billie Cohan; ed Martha Graham School, New York; Partner, Martha Graham School 1950, Co-Dir Martha Graham Co. 1966; Artistic Dir Contemporary Dance Trust Ltd, London 1967–; Artistic Dir and Prin. Choreographer, London Contemporary Dance Theatre 1969–87, Founder-Artistic Dir 1987–89; Artistic Adviser, Batsheva Co., Israel 1980–89; Dir York Univ., Toronto Choreographic Summer School 1977, Gulbenkian Choreographic Summer School, Univ. of Surrey 1978, 1979, 1982 and other int. courses; Gov. Contemporary Dance Trust; Ed., Choreography and Dance (journal) 1988–; Chair. Robin Howard Foundation; with London Contemporary Dance Theatre has toured Europe, S. America, N Africa, USA; maj. works created: Cell 1969, Stages 1971, Waterless Method of Swimming Instruction 1974, Class 1975, Stabat Mater 1975, Masque of Separation 1975, Khamsin 1976, Nympheas 1976, Forest 1977, Eos 1978, Songs, Lamentations and Praises 1979, Dances of Love and Death 1981, Agora 1984, A Mass for Man 1985, Ceremony 1986, Interrogations 1986, Video Life 1986, Phantasmagoria 1987, A Midsummer Night's Dream 1993, The Four Seasons 1996, Aladdin 2000; Hon. Fellow York Univ., Toronto; Hon. DLitt (Exeter Univ.) 1993; Dr. hc (Middx) 1994; Evening Standard Award for outstanding achievement in ballet 1975; Soc. of West End Theatres Award for outstanding achievement in ballet 1978. *Publication:* The Dance Workshop 1986. *Leisure interest:* dancing. *Address:* The Place, 17 Dukes Road, London, WC1H 9AB, England. *Telephone:* (20) 7387-0161.

COHEN, Abby Joseph, BA, MS; American financial executive; b. 29 Feb. 1952, New York; d. of Raymond Joseph Cohen and late Shirley (Silverstein) Joseph; m. David M. Cohen 1973; two d.; ed Martin Van Buren High School, Cornell Univ., George Washington Univ.; Jr Economist, Fed. Reserve Bd, Washington, DC 1973–76; economist/analyst, T. Rowe Price Assocs., Baltimore, Md 1976–83; investment strategist, Drexel Burnham Lambert, New York 1983–90, BZW, New York 1990; investment strategist Goldman, Sachs & Co. 1990–, Man. Dir 1996–, Man. Partner 1998–; Chair. Inst. of Chartered Financial Analysts; mem. Bd of Govs. Nat. Economists Club, New York Soc. of Security Analysts; Vice-Chair. Asscn for Investment Man. Research; mem. Nat. Asscn of Business Economists; Trustee/Fellow Cornell Univ.; Woman Achiever (Woman of the Year) Award, YWCA, New York 1989. *Address:* Goldman, Sachs & Co., 85 Broad Street, New York, NY 10004, USA.

COHEN, Bernard Woolf, DFA; British artist; b. 28 July 1933, London; m. Jean Britton 1959; one s. one d.; ed South West Essex School of Art, St Martin's School of Art, London and Slade School of Fine Art, London; held teaching appts. at several art schools 1957–67; teacher of painting and drawing, Slade School of Fine Art 1967–73, 1977; Visiting Prof. Univ. of New Mexico 1969–70, faculty alumni 1974; guest lecturer, Royal Coll. of Art 1974–75; Visiting Artist, Minneapolis School of Art 1964, 1969, 1971, 1975, Ont. Coll. of Art 1971, San Francisco Art Inst., Univ. of Victoria, BC 1975; has lectured at several Canadian univs. since 1969; fmrly Principal lecturer (Painting), Wimbledon School of Art 1980–84; Slade Prof., Chair. of Fine Art Univ. of London 1988–2000, Prof. Emer. 2000–; Fellow, Univ. Coll. London 1992; DFA (Univ. of London, Slade School). *Exhibitions* include: one-man exhbns at various London galleries since 1953, Venice Biennale 1966, Betty Parsons Gallery, NY 1967, Hayward Gallery, London (retrospective) 1972, Studio La Città, Verona 1972, 1975, Galleria Anunciata, Milan 1973, Tate Gallery, London (print retrospective) 1976, (paintings) 1995, Gallery Omana, Osaka 1979, Flowers East, London 1998, Flowers West, Los Angeles 1999, Flowers Central London 2001; has also participated in numerous group exhbns. in London, Europe, Japan and USA since 1953. *Publications:* articles and statements in journals and catalogues. *Leisure interests:* music, cinema, travel, museums. *Address:* 80 Camberwell Grove, London, SE5 8RF, England (Home). *Telephone:* (20) 7708-4480 (Home). *Fax:* (20) 7708-4480 (Home). *E-mail:* bwc44@hotmail.com.

COHEN, Gerald Allan, MA, BPhil, FBA; Canadian academic; b. 14 April 1941, Montreal; s. of Bella Lipkin and Morrie Cohen; m. 1st Margaret Florence Pearce 1965 (divorced 1996); one s. two d.; m. 2nd Michèle Jacottet 1999; ed Morris Winchewsky Jewish School, Strathcona Acad. and McGill Univ., Montreal and New Coll. Oxford, England; lecturer in Philosophy, Univ. Coll. London 1963–78, Reader 1978–84; Chichele Prof. of Social and Political Theory and Fellow of All Souls, Oxford 1985–; Isaac Deutscher Memorial Prize 1980. *Publications:* Karl Marx's Theory of History: A Defence 1978, History, Labour and Freedom: Themes from Marx 1988, Self-Ownership, Freedom and Equality 1995, If You're an Egalitarian, How Come You're so Rich? 2000. *Leisure interests:* Guardian crossword puzzles, American popular music 1920–60, painting, architecture, the politics of India, travel, patience. *Address:* All Souls College, Oxford, OX1 4AL, England (Office). *Telephone:* (1865) 279339 (Office). *Fax:* (1865) 279299 (Office). *E-mail:* gerald.cohen@all-souls.ox.ac.uk (Office).

COHEN, (Laurence) Jonathan, MA, DLitt, FBA; British university teacher (retd); b. 7 May 1923, London; s. of Israel and Theresa Cohen; m. Gillian M. Slee 1953; three s. one d.; ed St Paul's School, London and Balliol Coll., Oxford; served Naval Intelligence to Lt, RDVR 1942–45; Asst Dept of Logic and Metaphysics, Edinburgh Univ. 1947–50; lecturer in Philosophy, Univ. of St Andrew's at Dundee 1950–57; Fellow and Praelector, Queen's Coll., Oxford

1957–90, British Acad. Reader in the Humanities 1982–84, Sr Tutor 1985–90, Fellow Emer. 1990; Commonwealth Fund Fellow, Princeton and Harvard Univs. 1952–53; Visiting Prof., Columbia Univ. 1967–68, Yale Univ. 1972–73; Fellow, Australian Nat. Univ. 1980, Visiting Prof., Northwestern Univ. Law School 1988; Hon. Prof. North Western Univ., Xian, China 1987; Pres. British Soc. for Philosophy of Science 1977–79; Co-Pres. Int. Union of History and Philosophy of Science 1987–91; Chair. Philosophy Section, British Acad. 1993–96; Sec.-Gen. ICSU 1993–96; mem. Nat. Exec. Cttee of Council for the Protection of Rural England 1992–95; mem. Nat. Cttee for Philosophy 1993–2002. *Publications:* The Principles of World Citizenship 1954, The Diversity of Meaning 1962, The Implications of Induction 1970, The Probable and the Provable 1977, The Dialogue of Reason 1986, An Introduction to the Philosophy of Induction and Probability 1989, An Essay on Belief and Acceptance 1992, Knowledge and Language 2002; (Gen. Ed.) Clarendon Library of Logic and Philosophy 1970–; numerous articles in professional journals. *Leisure interests:* gardening, walking. *Address:* The Queen's College, Oxford, OX1 4AW, England. *Telephone:* (1993) 881250.

COHEN, Leonard, OC; Canadian singer and songwriter; b. 21 Sept. 1934, Montreal; s. of Nathan B. Cohen and Marsha Klinitsky; two c.; ed McGill Univ.; f. country-and-western band, The Buckskin Boys 1951; initially wrote poetry, winning McGill Literary Award for first collection, Let Us Compare Mythologies; moved to New York in early 1960s. *Recordings include:* Songs of Leonard Cohen, Songs From A Room, Various Positions 1985, I'm Your Man 1988, The Future, Cohen Live 1994, Ten New Songs 2001. *Address:* c/o Kelley Lynch, Stranger Management Inc., 419 North Larchmont Blvd., Suite 91, Los Angeles, CA 90004, USA.

COHEN, Lyor; American music company executive; b. New York City; ed Univ. of Miami; financial officer Bank Leumi; Hip-Hop Performance Promoter, Mix Club, LA; joined Rush Entertainment 1985, later Partner; currently Pres. and CEO Island Def Jam Records. *Address:* Island Def Jam Records, 2220 Colorado Avenue, Santa Monica, CA 90404, USA (Office). *Website:* www.islanddefjam.com (Office).

COHEN, Marvin Lou, PhD; American (b. Canadian) professor of physics; b. 3 March 1935, Montreal, Canada; s. of Elmo Cohen and Molly Zaritsky; m. 1st Merrill Leigh Gardner 1958 (died 1994); one s. one d.; m. 2nd Suzy R. Locke 1996; ed Univs. of California (Berkeley) and Chicago; mem. Tech. Staff, Bell Labs., Murray Hill, NJ 1963–64; Asst Prof. of Physics, Univ. of Calif. (Berkeley) 1964–66, Assoc. Prof. 1966–68, Prof. 1969–95, Univ. Prof. 1995–; Prof. Miller Inst. Basic Research in Science, Univ. of Calif. 1969–70, 1976–77, 1988, Chair. 1977–81, Univ. Prof. 1995–, Faculty research Prof., lecturer 1997–; Chair. Gordon Research Conf. on Chem. and Physics of Solids 1972; U.S. Rep., Semiconductor Comm., Int. Union of Pure and Applied Physics 1975–81; Visiting Prof., Cambridge Univ., UK 1966, Univ. of Paris 1972–73 etc., Univ. of Hawaii 1978–79, Technion, Haifa, Israel 1987–88; Alfred P. Sloan Fellow, Cambridge Univ. 1965–67; Guggenheim Fellow 1978–79, 1990–91; Fellow, American Physics Soc. Exec. Council 1975–79, Chair. 1977–78; mem. NAS 1980, American Acad. of Arts and Sciences, Oliver E Buckley Prize Comm. 1980–81, Chair. 1981; mem. Selection Cttee for Presidential Young Investigator Awards 1983; mem. Cttee on Nat. Synchotron Radiation Facilities 1983–84; Chair. 17th Int. Conf. on the Physics of Semiconductors 1984; mem. Govt-Univ.-Industry Research Round Table 1984–, Vice-Chair. Working Group on Science and Eng Talent 1984–, Advisory Bd Texas Center for Superconductivity 1991– (mem. 1988–90); mem. Research Briefing Panels NAS on Funding and on High Temperature Superconductivity 1987, U.S.-Japan Workshop on Univ. Research 1988–89, Science Policy Bd Stanford Synchrotron Radiation Lab. 1990–92, Visiting Cttee The Ginzton Lab., Stanford Univ. 1991, American Acad. of Arts and Sciences 1993, Scientific Policy Cttee, Stanford Linear Accelerator Center 1993–95; Chair. Comstock Prize Cttee NAS; Assoc. Ed. Materials Science and Eng 1987; mem. Advisory Bd Int. Journal of Modern Physics B 1987–, Editorial Bd Perspectives in Condensed Matter Physics 1987–, AAAS 1993–, American Physical Society Lilienfeld Prize Cttee 1994–95; Oliver E Buckley Prize for solid state physics 1979; Dept of Energy Award 1981, 1990, Lawrence Berkeley Lab. Certificate of Merit 1991, Julius Edgar Lilienfeld Prize (American Physical Soc.) 1994. *Publications:* over 600 articles on research topics. *Leisure interests:* music (clarinet), running. *Address:* 201 Estates Drive, Piedmont, CA 94611 (Home); Department of Physics, University of California, Berkeley, CA 94720, USA. *Telephone:* (510) 642-4753. *Fax:* (510) 643-9473.

COHEN, Sir Philip, Kt, PhD, FRS, FRSE; British research biochemist; b. 22 July 1945, Edgware, Middx; s. of Jacob Davis Cohen and Fanny Bragman; m. Patricia T. Wade 1969; one s. one d.; ed Hendon County Grammar School and Univ. Coll. London; SRC/NATO Postdoctoral Fellow, Univ. of Washington, Seattle 1969–71; lecturer in Biochemistry, Univ. of Dundee 1971–77, Reader 1977–81, Prof. of Enzymology 1981–84, Royal Soc. Research Prof. 1984–; Dir MRC Protein Phosphorylation Unit 1990–; Dir Wellcome Trust Biocentre 1997–; Fellow, Univ. Coll. London 1993, Acad. of Medical Sciences 1998; Hon. Fellow Royal Coll. of Pathologists 1998; mem. Discovery Advisory Bd SmithKline Beecham Pharmaceutical Co. 1993–97; mem. European Molecular Biology Org. 1982, Academia Europaea 1990; Croonian Lecturer, Royal Soc. 1998; Hon. DSc (Abertay) 1998, (Strathclyde) 1999; Anniversary Prize, Fed. of European Biochemical Socs. 1977, Colworth Medal 1977, CIBA Medal and Prize 1991, British Biochemical Soc.; Prix Van Gysel, Belgian Royal Acads of Medicine 1992; Bruce Preller Prize, Royal Soc. of Edin. 1993, Louis Jeantet Prize for Medicine 1997, Pfizer Award for Innovative Science in Europe 1999, Sir Hans Krebs Medal, Fed. of European Biological Socs 2001; Bristol-Myers Squibb Distinguished Achievement Award for Metabolic Research 2002. *Publications:* Control of Enzyme Activity 1976; over 430 articles in scientific journals. *Leisure interests:* bridge, golf, ornithology, picking wild mushrooms, cooking. *Address:* School of Life Sciences, MSI/WTB Complex, University of Dundee, Dow Street, Dundee, DD1 5EH (Office); Inverbay II, Invergowrie, Dundee, DD2 5DQ, Scotland (Home). *Telephone:* (1382) 344238 (Office); (1382) 562328 (Home). *Fax:* (1382) 223778; (1382) 223778 (Office). *E-mail:* p.cohen@dundee.ac.uk (Office).

COHEN, Ra'anan, BA; Israeli politician; b. 1937, Iraq; m.; four c.; ed Tel-Aviv Univ.; army service; mem. Knesset 1984–; served on Immigration and Absorption, Labour and Welfare, State Control, Finance, Anti-Drug Abuse, Knesset, Foreign Affairs and Defence Cttees.; Chair. Meretz Parl. group 1992–99; Chair. of House of Reps. of Histadrut 1994–98; mem. Meretz leadership; Sec. Israel Ahat; Chair. Beit Or Aviva (org. for the rehabilitation of drug addicts); Minister of Trade and Industry 1999–2001, Minister without Portfolio March 2001–. *Address:* The Knesset, Jerusalem, Israel (Office); Israel Ahat, Ramat-Gan, Tel Aviv. *E-mail:* amuta@ehudbarak.co.il (Office).

COHEN, Robert; British cellist and conductor; b. 15 June 1959, London; s. of Raymond Cohen and Anthya Rael; m. Rachel Smith 1987; four s.; ed Purcell School and Guildhall School of Music, cello studies with William Pleeth, André Navarra, Jacqueline du Pré and Mstislav Rostropovich; started playing cello at age of 5; Royal Festival Hall début (Boccherini Concerto), aged 12; London recital début, Wigmore Hall, aged 17; Tanglewood Festival, USA 1978; recording début (Elgar concerto) 1979; concerts USA, Europe and Eastern Europe 1979; since 1980, concerts world-wide with maj. orchestras and with conductors who include Muti, Abbado, Dorati, Sinopoli, Otaka, Mazur, Davis, Marriner and Rattle; Dir Charleston Manor Festival, E Sussex 1989–; regular int. radio broadcasts and many int. TV appearances; plays on the "Ex-Roser' David Tecchler of Rome cello dated 1723; conductor, various chamber orchestras 1990–, symphony orchestras 1997–; Visiting Prof. Royal Acad. of Music 1998–; Prof. of Advanced Cello Studies Conservatorio della Svizzera Italiana di Lugano 2000–; Fellow of the Purcell Scholl for Young Musicians 1992–; winner Young Concert Artists Int. Competition, NY 1978, Píatigorsky Prize, Tanglewood Festival 1978; winner UNESCO Int. Competition, Czechoslovakia 1981. *Recordings include:* Elgar concerto (new Elgar concerto 1993), Dvořák concerto, Tchaikovsky Rococo Variations, Rodrigo Concierto en modo Galante, Beethoven Triple concerto, Grieg sonata, Franck sonata, Virtuoso Cello Music record, Dvořák Complete Piano trios with Cohen Trio, Schubert String Quintet with Amadeus Quartet, Complete Bach solo cello Suites, Howard Blake Diversions, Bliss Concerto 1992, Walton Concerto 1995, Britten Cello Suites 1997, Morton Feldman Concerto 1998, Britten Cello Symphony 1998, Sally Beamish Cello Concerto River 1999, HK Gruber Cello Concerto 2003. *Television:* Bach Sarabandes (BBC), Elgar Cello Concerto (BBC). *Leisure interests:* photography, computers, playing sports with my children. *Address:* Robert Cohen Music Office, 15 Birchwood Avenue, London, N10 3BE, England (Office). *Telephone:* (20) 8444-1065 (Office). *Fax:* (20) 8365-2563 (Office). *E-mail:* office@robertcohen.info (Office). *Website:* www.robertcohen.info (Office).

COHEN, Stanley, BA, PhD; American professor of biochemistry (retd.); b. 17 Nov. 1922, Brooklyn, New York; s. of Louis Cohen and Fruma Feitel; m. 1st Olivia Larson 1951; m. 2nd Jan Elizabeth Jordan 1981; three s.; ed Brooklyn and Oberlin Colls., Univ. of Michigan; Teaching Fellow, Dept of Biochemistry, Univ. of Mich. 1946–48; Instructor, Depts. of Biochemistry and Pediatrics, Univ. of Colo School of Medicine, Denver 1948–52; Postdoctoral Fellow, American Cancer Soc., Dept of Radiology, Washington Univ., St Louis 1952–53; Research Prof. of Biochem. American Cancer Soc. Nashville 1976–; Asst Prof. of Biochemistry, Vanderbilt Univ. School of Medicine, Nashville 1959–62, Assoc. Prof. 1962–67, Prof. 1967–86, Distinguished Prof. 1986–2000, Distinguished Prof. Emer. 2000–; mem. Editorial Bds Excerpta Medica, Abstracts of Human Developmental Biology, Journal of Cellular Physiology; mem. NAS, American Soc. of Biological Chemists, Int. Inst. of Embryology, American Acad. of Arts and Sciences; Hon. DSc (Chicago) 1985; Nobel Prize for Physiology and Medicine 1986, and many other prizes and awards. *Leisure interests:* camping, tennis. *Address:* 11306 East Limberlost Road, Tucson, AZ 85749 (Home); Department of Biochemistry, Vanderbilt University School of Medicine, 607 Light Hall, Nashville, TN 37232, USA. *Telephone:* (615) 322-3318 (Office). *Fax:* (615) 322-4349 (Office).

COHEN, Stanley, MD; American pathologist; b. 4 June 1937, New York; s. of Herman Joseph Cohen and Eva Lapidus; m. Marion Doris Cantor 1959; two s. one d.; ed Stuyvesant High School, Columbia Coll. and Columbia Univ. Coll. of Physicians and Surgeons; Internship and Residency, Albert Einstein Medical Center and Harvard-Mass. Gen. 1962–64; Instructor, Dept of Pathology, New York Univ. Medical Center 1965–66; Captain, MC, USA, Walter Reed Inst. of Research 1966–68; Assoc. Prof., State Univ. of New York at Buffalo 1968–72, Assoc. Dir, Center for Immunology 1972–74, Prof. of Pathology 1972–74; Assoc. Chair. Dept of Pathology, Univ. of Conn. Health Center 1976–80, Prof. of Pathology 1974–87; Prof., Chair. Bd Hahnemann Univ., Philadelphia 1987–94; Chair. Dept of Pathology, Hahnemann Medical Center 1986–94; Prof., Chair. Univ. Medicine and Dentistry, N J. Medical Center 1994–; Kinne Award 1954; Borden Award 1961; Parke-Davis Award in Experimental Pathology 1977; Outstanding Investigator Award, Nat. Cancer Inst. 1986; Co-Chair. Int. Lymphokine Workshop 1979, 1982 and 1984. *Publications:* 175 scientific articles on cellular immunity; ed. 7 books including Mechanisms of Cell-Medicated Immunity 1977, Mechanisms of Immunopathology 1979, The Biology of the Lymphokines 1979, Interleukins, Lymphokines and Cytokines 1983, Molecular Basis of Lymphatic Action 1986, The Role of Lymphatics in the Immune Response 1989. *Leisure interests:* music, photography, karate. *Address:* University of Medicine Dentistry-New Jersey, Medical School, Newark, NJ 07103 (Office); 79 Ettl Circle, Princeton, NJ 08540-2334, USA (Home).

COHEN, Stanley Norman, BA, MD; American professor of genetics; b. 17 Feb. 1935, Perth Amboy, NJ; s. of Bernard and Ida (Stolz) Cohen; m. Joanna Lucy Wolter 1961; one s. one d.; ed Rutgers Univ., New Brunswick, NJ and Univ. of Pennsylvania School of Medicine, Philadelphia, Pa; intern, The Mount Sinai Hosp., New York 1960–61; Asst Resident in Medicine, Univ. Hosp., Ann Arbor, Mich. 1961–62; Clinical Assoc., Arthritis and Rheumatism Branch, Nat. Inst. of Arthritis and Metabolic Diseases 1962–64; Sr Resident in Medicine, Duke Univ. Hosp., Durham, NC 1964–65; American Cancer Soc. Postdoctoral Research Fellow, Dept of Molecular Biology and Dept of Developmental Biology and Cancer, Albert Einstein Coll. of Medicine, Bronx, New York 1965–67; Asst Prof. 1967–68; Asst Prof. of Medicine, Stanford Univ. School of Medicine 1968–71, Head, Div. of Clinical Pharmacology 1969–78, Assoc. Prof. of Medicine 1971–75, Prof. of Genetics 1977 and Prof. of Medicine 1975–, Chair. Dept of Genetics 1978–86, K.-T. Li Prof. of Genetics 1993–; mem. of various scientific orgs including NAS; Fellow American Acad. of Arts and Sciences, Chair. Genetics Section 1988–91; Fellow American Acad. of Microbiology; Kinyoun Lecturer 1981; Trustee Univ. of Pa 1997–2002; Burroughs Wellcome Scholar Award 1970, Mattia Award, Roche Inst. for Molecular Biology 1977, Wolf Prize in Medicine 1981, Marvin J. Johnson Award, American Chemical Soc. 1980, Albert Lasker Basic Medical Research Award 1980, Distinguished Graduate Award Univ. of Pa School of Medicine 1986, Nat. Medal of Science 1988, Cetus Award 1988, Nat. Biotech. Award 1989, Nat. Medal of Tech. 1989, American Chem. Soc. Special Award 1992, Helmut Horten Research Award 1993; Lemelson-MIT Prize 1996; Guggenheim Fellow 1975, Josiah Macy Jr Foundation Faculty Scholar 1975–76; Fellow AAAS. *Address:* Department of Genetics M-322, Stanford University School of Medicine, Stanford, CA 94305-5120, USA.

COHEN, Sydney, CBE, MD, PhD, FRCPath, FRS; British professor of medicine; b. 18 Sept. 1921, Johannesburg, S. Africa; s. of Morris and Pauline Cohen; m. 1st June Bernice Adler 1950 (died 1999); one s. one d.; m. 2nd Deirdre Maureen Ann Boyd 1999; ed King Edward VII School, Witwatersrand Univ., Johannesburg, Univ. of London; Emergency Medical Service, UK 1944–46; lecturer, Dept of Physiology, Univ. of Witwatersrand 1947–53; mem. Scientific Staff, Nat. Inst. for Medical Research, London 1954–60; Reader, Dept of Immunology, St Mary's Hosp., London 1960–65; Prof. of Chemical Pathology, Guy's Hosp. Medical School, London 1965–86, now Prof. Emer.; mem. MRC 1974–76, Chair. Tropical Medicine Research Bd 1974–76, Royal Soc. Assessor 1983–85; Chair. WHO Scientific group on Immunity to Malaria 1976–81; mem. Council, Royal Soc. 1981–83; Nuffield Dominion Fellow in Medicine 1954; Founding Fellow, Royal Coll. of Pathologists 1964; Hon. DSc (Witwatersrand) 1987. *Publications:* papers and books on immunology and parasitic infections. *Leisure interests:* golf, gardening, forestry. *Address:* 8 Gibson Place, St. Andrews, KY16 9JE, Scotland (Home); Hafodfraith, Llangurig, SY18 6QG, Wales (Home). *Telephone:* (1334) 476568 (Home).

COHEN, William Sebastian, BA, LLB; American politician and business executive; b. 28 Aug. 1940, Bangor, Maine; s. of Reuben and Clara (née Hartley) Cohen; two s.; ed Bangor High School, Bowdoin Coll., Boston Univ. Law School; admitted to Maine Bar, Mass. Bar, Dist of Columbia Bar; partner Prairie, Cohen, Lynch, Weatherbee and Kobritz 1966–72; Asst Attorney, Penobscot County, Maine 1968–70, instructor Univ. of Maine at Orono 1968–72; mem. Bd of Overseers, Bowdoin Coll. 1973–85; City Councillor, Bangor 1969–72, Mayor 1971–72; elected to Congress 1972, re-elected 1974, 1976, Senator from Maine 1979–96; fmr mem. numerous cttees. and subcttees.; Sec. of Defense 1997–2001; Founder and CEO The Cohen Group 2001–; Fellow of John F. Kennedy Inst. of Politics, Harvard 1972; award for Distinguished Public Service, Boston Univ. Alumni Assocn 1976, L. Mendel Rivers Award, Non-Commissioned Officers' Assocn 1983, President's Award, New England Assocn of School Superintendents 1984, Silver Anniversary Award, Nat. Collegiate Athletic Assocn 1987, Nat. Assocn Basketball Coaches, US 1987, numerous other awards. *Publications:* Of Sons and Seasons 1978, Roll Call 1981, Getting the Most Out of Washington 1982 (with Prof. Kenneth Lasson), The Double Man 1985 (with Senator Gary Hart), A Baker's Nickel 1986, Men of Zeal (with Senator George Mitchell) 1988, One-Eyed Kings 1991, Murder in the Senate (with Thomas B. Allen) 1993. *Leisure interests:* poetry, sport. *Address:* The Cohen Group, 600 13th Street, NW, Suite 640, Washington, DC 20005-3096 (Office); Secretary of Defense, The Pentagon, Washington, DC 20301, USA. *Telephone:* (202) 697-5737.

COHEN, Yitzhak; Israeli politician; b. 1951; m.; ten c.; army service; fmr Deputy Mayor of Ashkelon and Sec.-Gen. of El Hama'ayan (Shas-affiliated educational inst.); mem. Knesset (Parl.) 1996–; mem. of Labour and Social Affairs and Finance Cttees.; Minister of Religious Affairs 1999–2001. *Address:* The Knesset, Jerusalem, Israel (Office). *Telephone:* (2) 5311170 (Office). *Fax:* (2) 6535469 (Office).

COHEN-TANNOUDJI, Claude Nessim, PhD; French academic; b. 1 April 1933, Constantine; s. of Abraham Cohen-Tannoudji and Sarah Sebbah; m. Jacqueline Veyrat 1958; two s. one d.; ed Ecole Normale Supérieure; Research Assoc. CNRS 1962–64; Maître de Conférences, then Prof. Faculté des Sciences, Paris 1964–73; Prof. Coll. de France 1973–; mem. Acad. des Sciences; Foreign Assoc. NAS; Fellow, American Physical Soc.; Foreign Hon. mem. American Acad. of Arts and Sciences; Dr. hc (Uppsala); recipient of several awards including Ampère Prize (Acad. des Sciences) 1980, Lilienfeld Prize (American Physical Soc.), Charles Townes Award (Optical Soc. of America) 1993; Harvey Prize (Technion, Haifa); CNRS Gold Medal 1996; Nobel Prize for Physics 1997; Commdr Ordre nat. du Mérite; Officier Légion d'honneur. *Publications:* in collaboration: Optique et Electronique Quantiques 1965, Mécanique Quantique (2 Vols) 1973, Photons et Atomes, Introduction à l'Electrodynamique Quantique 1987, Processus d'Interaction entre Photons et Atomes 1988, Atoms in Electromagnetic Fields 1994, Lévy Statistics and Laser Cooling. How rare events bring atoms to rest 2001. *Leisure interest:* music. *Address:* Laboratoire Kastler Brossel, 24 rue Lhomond, 75231 Paris Cedex 05 (Office); 38 rue des Cordelières, 75013 Paris, France (Home). *Telephone:* 1-47-07-77-83 (Office); 1-45-35-02-18 (Home). *Fax:* 1-44-32-34-34 (Office). *E-mail:* cct@lkb.ens.fr (Office).

COHN, Mildred, MA, PhD; American professor of biochemistry and biophysics; b. 12 July 1913, New York City; d. of Isidore M. Cohn and Bertha Klein; m. Henry Primakoff 1938 (deceased); one s. two d.; ed Hunter Coll. and Columbia Univ.; Cornell Univ. Medical Coll., New York 1938–46; Washington Univ. Medical School, St Louis, Mo. 1946–60; Prof. of Biophysics and Biophysical Chem., Univ. of Pa School of Medicine 1961–75, Prof. of Biochemistry and Biophysics 1975–82; Benjamin Rush Prof. of Physiological Chem. 1978–82, Prof. Emer. 1982–; Visiting Prof. Univ. of Calif., Berkeley 1981, Johns Hopkins Univ. Medical School 1982–91; Career Investigator, American Heart Asscn 1964–78; Sr mem. Inst. for Cancer Research 1982–85; mem. American Acad. of Arts and Sciences, NAS, American Philosophical Soc.; Hon. ScD (Women's Medical Coll. of Pennsylvania) 1966, (Radcliffe Coll.) 1978, (Washington Univ.) 1981, (Brandeis, Hunter Coll., Univ. of Pennsylvania) 1984, (N Carolina) 1985, (Miami) 1990; Hon. PhD (Weizmann Inst. of Science) 1988; Cresson Medal, Franklin Inst. 1975, Garvan Medal, American Chem. Soc, 1963, Nat. Medal for Science 1982, Chandler Medal, Columbia Univ. 1986, Distinguished Service Award, Coll. of Physicians, Phila 1987, Remsen Award, Maryland Section, American Chemical Soc. 1988, Pa Gov.'s Award for Excellence in Science 1993, Stein-Moore Award, Protein Soc. 1997, Oesper Award, Univ. of Cincinnati 2000 and several other awards. *Publications:* over 150 articles in professional journals, etc. *Leisure interests:* hiking, writing, history of science. *Address:* Department of Biochemistry and Biophysics, University of Pennsylvania School of Medicine, 242 Anat-Chem Philadelphia, PA 19104-6059 (Office); 226 W Rittenhouse Square #1806, Philadelphia, PA 19103, USA (Home). *Telephone:* (215) 898-8404 (Office); (215) 546-3449 (Home). *Fax:* (215) 898-4217.

COHN, Norman, MA, DLitt, FBA; British author and historian; b. 12 Jan. 1915, London; s. of August Cohn and Daisy Cohn (née Reimer); m. Vera Broido 1941; one s.; ed Gresham's School, Holt and Christ Church Oxford; served in Queen's Royal Regt and Intelligence Corps 1940–46; lecturer in French, Glasgow Univ. 1946–51; Prof. of French, Magee Univ. Coll. (then associated with Trinity Coll. Dublin), Ireland 1951–60; Prof. of French, King's Coll., Durham Univ. 1960–63; changed career to become Dir Columbus Centre, Sussex Univ. and Gen. Ed. of Centre's Studies in Persecution and Extermination 1966–80; Professorial Fellow, Sussex Univ. 1966–73, Astor-Wolfson Prof. 1973–80, Prof. Emer. 1980–; Visiting Prof. King's Coll., London 1986–89; Adviser, Montreal Inst. for Genocide Studies 1986–; Adviser, Center for Millennial Studies, Boston Univ. 1999–; Hon. LLD (Concordia, Canada); Anisfield-Wolf Award in Race Relations 1967. *Publications:* Gold Khan and other Siberian Legends 1946, The Pursuit of the Millennium: Revolutionary Millenarians and Mystical Anarchists of the Middle Ages 1957, Warrant for Genocide: the Myth of the Jewish World-conspiracy and the Protocols of the Elders of Zion 1967, Europe's Inner Demons: an Enquiry Inspired by the Great Witch-hunt 1975, Cosmos, Chaos and the Ancient Roots of Apocalyptic Faith 1993, Noah's Flood: The Genesis Story in Western Thought 1996. *Leisure interests:* walking, looking at pictures, butterfly-watching. *Address:* Orchard Cottage, Wood End, Ardeley, Herts., SG2 7AZ, England. *Telephone:* (1438) 869-247.

COHN, Paul Moritz, PhD, FRS; British professor of mathematics (retd); b. 8 Jan. 1924, Hamburg, Germany; s. of James and Julia (née Cohen) Cohn; m. Deirdre S. Sharon 1958; two d.; ed Trinity Coll., Cambridge; Chargé de Recherches, Nancy, France 1951–52; lecturer, Univ. of Manchester 1952–62; Visiting Prof., Yale Univ. 1961–62; Reader, Queen Mary Coll., London 1963–67; Visiting Prof, Univ. of Chicago 1964; Visiting Prof., Rutgers State Univ., 1967–68Prof. and Head, Dept of Math., Bedford Coll., London 1967–84; Prof., Univ. Coll., London 1984–89, Astor Prof. of Mathematics 1986–89, Prof. Emer. and Hon. Research Fellow 1989–; Pres. London Mathematical Soc. 1982–84; mem. Math. Cttee, SRC 1977–80, Council, Royal Soc. 1985–87, Nat. Cttee for Math. 1985–89 (Chair. 1988–89); L.R. Ford Award 1972, Berwick Prize 1974. *Publications include:* Free Rings and Their Relations 1971 (2nd Edn 1985, Algebra 1, 2 1974, 1982, Algebra (2nd Edn in 3 Vols) 1982–90, Algebraic Numbers and Algebraic Functions 1991, Elements of Linear Algebra 1994, Skew Fields 1995, Introduction to Ring Theory 2000, Classic Algebra 2000, Basic Algebra 2002, Further Algebra 2003; research papers in algebra. *Leisure interest:* language in all its forms, genealogy. *Address:*

Department of Mathematics, University College London, Gower Street, London, WC1E 6BT, England (Office). *Telephone:* (20) 7679-4459 (Office). *Fax:* (20) 7383-5519 (Office). *E-mail:* pmc@math.ucl.ac.uk (Office).

COHN-BENDIT, (Marc) Daniel; German politician; b. 4 April 1945, Montauban, Tarn-et-Garonne, France; m. Ingrid Voigt 1997; one c.; ed Odenwaldschule, Germany, Univ. de Paris X-Nanterre; student movt.'s spokesman, Paris 1968; deported from France May 1968; nursery school teacher, Frankfurt 1968–73; co-f. German students' group Revolutionärer Kampf, Bockenheim 1970; co-f. cultural magazine Pflasterstrand 1970, Ed.-in-Chief 1978–84; Deputy Mayor of Frankfurt 1989–97; elected MEP (Greens) 1994, (Ecology Greens) 1999; Vice-Pres. Parl. Comm. on Culture, Youth, Media and Sport 1994–95, mem. Foreign Affairs Comm.; Rapporteur on regional co-operation between states of fmr Yugoslavia 1996, Chair. Del. to Jt EU-Turkey Parl. Comm.; Adviser to Joschka Fischer, Vice-Chancellor and Minister of Foreign Affairs 1998–; mem. German Green Party 1984, French Green Party 1998–; co-f. Forum Européen de Prévention Active des Conflicts 1994; presenter monthly literary programme Literaturclub, Swiss German TV 1995; f. monthly Eurospeed 1997; Dr. hc (Catholic Univ. of Tilburg, Netherlands) 1997. *Documentary films:* (writer) A chacun son allemagne 1976, Nous l'avons tant aimée, la révolution (four films) 1983, C'est la vie (full-length film) 1990, Angst im Rüchen hat jeder von uns 1992. *Publications include:* La Révolte étudiante 1968, Le Grand bazar 1976, Nous l'avons tant aimée, la révolution 1987; co-author numerous other books. *Leisure interest:* football. *Address:* c/o Parlement Européen, 97–113 rue Wiertz, 1047 Brussels, Belgium (Office).

COHN-SHERBOK, Dan, PhD, DD, MAHL, MLitt; American rabbi and university professor; b. 1 Feb. 1945, Denver, Colo; s. of Bernard Sherbok and Ruth Sherbok; m. Lavinia C. Heath 1976; ed Williams Coll., Hebrew Union Coll. and Univ. of Cambridge; rabbi in USA, UK, Australia and South Africa 1968–74; Univ. lecturer in Theology, Univ. of Kent 1975–97, Dir Centre for Study of Religion and Society 1982–90; Visiting Prof. of Judaism, Univ. of Wales at Lampeter 1995–97, Prof. 1997–; Visiting Prof. Univ. of Essex 1993–94, Middx Univ. 1994–, Univ. of St Andrews 1995–96, St Andrew's Biblical Theological Coll. Moscow 1996, Univ. of Wales, Bangor, Univ. of Vilnius 1999, Univ. of Durham 2002; Fellow, Hebrew Union Coll., Acad. of Jewish Philosophy; Hon. DD (Hebrew Union Coll., Jewish Inst. of Religion) 1995. *Publications:* The Jewish Heritage 1988, The Crucified Jew 1992, The Jewish Faith 1993, Not a Nice Job for a Nice Jewish Boy 1993, Judaism and Other Faiths 1994, The Future of Judaism 1994, The American Jew 1994, Jewish and Christian Mysticism 1994, Modern Judaism 1995, Jewish Mysticism 1995, The Hebrew Bible 1996, Biblical Hebrew for Beginners 1996, The Liberation Debate 1996, Atlas of Jewish History 1996, Medieval Jewish Philosophy 1996, Fifty Key Jewish Thinkers 1996, The Jewish Messiah 1997, After Noah: Animals and the Liberation of Theology 1997, Understanding the Holocaust 1999, Jews, Christians and Religious Pluralism 1999, Messianic Judaism 2000, Interfaith Theology 2001, Holocaust Theology: A Reader 2001, Anti-Semitism 2002; Judaism: History, Belief, Practice 2003. *Leisure interests:* keeping cats, walking, drawing cartoons. *Address:* Department of Theology and Religious Studies, University of Wales, Lampeter, Ceredigion, SA48 7ED, Wales. *Telephone:* (1570) 424968 (Office); (1570) 424968. *Fax:* (1570) 423641 (Office).

COINTAT, Michel; French politician and agronomist; b. 13 April 1921, Paris; s. of Lucien Cointat and Marie-Louise Adam; m. Simone Dubois 1942; two s.; ed Ecole Nat. des Eaux et Forêts; Insp. of water and forests, Uzès, Gard 1943–49; Insp. forests of Haute-Marne 1950–58; Dir Gen. Soc. for Devt of waste ground and scrub lands of the East 1948–61, Pres. 1961–71; Dir du Cabinet, Ministry of Agriculture 1961–62, Dir Gen. of Production and Supply 1962–67; Pres. Special Agricultural Cttee to EEC 1965; Minister of Agriculture 1971–72, of External Trade 1980–81; Deputy Rassemblement pour la République (fmrly Union Démocratique pour la République) for Ille-et-Vilaine 1967–71, 1981–93; mem. European Parl. 1968–71, 1974–79; Mayor of Fougères 1971–83; Pres. Financial Comm. in Regional Council of Brittany; Pres. Special Comm. to examine proposed land law; Dir Editions Ufap 1975–83; Questeur (Admin. Official) Assemblée Nat. 1988–90; Pres. Paneurope France 1990–92; Pres. Echanges et consultations techniques internationaux 1997–; mem. Acad. d'agriculture de France 1987–, Pres. 1996–; mem. Acad. de l'art de vivre 1994–, Pres. 2000–; Légion d'honneur, Officier Ordre nat. du Mérite, Commdr du Mérite agricole, Officier des Palmes académiques, Chevalier Economie nationale, Grand Officier du Mérite (Fed. Repub. of Germany), Grand Officier Ordre de Victoria, Commdr du Mérite Italien, Grand Officier Ordre de la Haute-Volta, Grand Officier du Rio Branco, Mérite Européen. *Publications:* about 500 articles on agric., forestry, fishing and related subjects; collections of poems: Souvenirs du temps perdu 1957, Poèmes à Clio 1965, Les heures orangées 1974, les Moments inutiles 1983, le Neveu de Jules Ferry: Abel 1987, 1789: Sept députés bretons à Versailles 1988, Souvenirs de l'Uzège 1992, Poèmes en fleurs 1996, Fleurs en fêtes 1997, Rivarol 2001, Les Couloirs de l'Europe 2001. *Address:* Ecti, 101–109 rue Jean-Jaurès, 92300 Levallois-Perret (Office); 89 rue du Faubourg Saint-Denis, 75010 Paris, France (Home).

COKER, Peter Godfrey, RA, ARCA; British artist; b. 27 July 1926, London; m. Vera J. Crook 1951; one s. (deceased); ed St Martin's School of Art, Royal Coll. of Art; has participated in numerous group shows including Tate Gallery 1958, 1992, Royal Coll. of Art 1952–62, Royal Acad. Bicentenary Exhbn 1968, British Painting 1952–77, Royal Acad. and at other galleries in UK, Austria and Canada; works in numerous perm. collections in UK including Tate Gallery, Arts Council, Chantrey Bequest, Victoria & Albert Museum, British Museum, Nat. Portrait Gallery, Nat. Maritime Museum, Stedelijk Museum, Ostend, Berardo Collection, Sintra, Portugal; Arts Council Award 1976. *One-man exhibitions include:* Zwemmer Gallery, 1956, 1957, 1959, 1964, 1967, Thackeray Gallery, London 1970, 1972, 1974, 1975, 1976, 1978, Gallery 10, London 1980, 1982, 1984, 1986, 1988, Flying Colours Gallery, Edinburgh 1990. *Retrospective exhibitions:* Royal Acad. 1979, Abbot Hall, Kendal and travelling 1992–93, Chris Beetles Gallery, London 2001, 75th Birthday Display, Tate Britain 2001, Major Retrospective (1949–1992), Chris Beetles Gallery, London 2002. *Publication:* Etching Techniques 1976, Peter Coker RA, biography and catalogue raisonné 2002. *Leisure interests:* 19th-century French painters, Neoclassicism. *Address:* The Red House, Mistley, Manningtree, Essex, CO11 1BX, England.

COLANINNO, Roberto; Italian business executive; b. 16 Aug. 1943, Mantua; began career with Fiamm SpA, fmr Chief Exec.; f. jtly Sogefi SpA (finance co.); mem. Bd of several regional and nat. banks in Italy including Mediobanco; CEO Olivetti & Co. –2001; Chair. and CEO Telecom Italia –2001; Cavaliere del Lavoro. *Address:* c/o Olivetti SpA, Via G. Jervis 77, 10015 Ivrea, Italy (Office).

COLASUONNO, HE Cardinal Francesco; Italian ecclesiastic; b. 2 Jan. 1925, Grumo Appula; ordained priest 1947; Archbishop, See of Tronto, Truentum 1975; also apptd. Apostolic Nuncio in Italy and San Marino 1975; cr. Cardinal Feb. 1998. *Address:* Apostolic Nunciature, Via Po, 27–29, 0198 Rome, Italy.

COLCLEUGH, D. W. (Dave), PhD; Canadian business executive; b. Fort Erie, Ont.; m.; two c.; ed Univs. of Toronto and Cambridge; research engineer DuPont Canada, Kingston 1963–68, polymer tech. supervisor, Fibres Div. 1968–73, tech. superintendent, Explosives Div., North Bay 1973–75, Tech. and Planning Man., Explosives Div., Montreal 1975–79, Rubber Industry Man., Tyre and Industrial Div. 1979–82, Man. of Gen. Products, Mississauga 1982–85, prin. consultant Corp. Planning Div., Wilmington April–Dec. 1985, Gen. Man. of Finishes, Toronto 1985–89, Dir of Corp. Planning and Devt April–Nov. 1989, Vice-Pres. of Mfg and Eng 1989–92, Sr Vice-Pres. with responsibility for Fibres and Intermediates, Eng Polymers Units and Mfg and Eng 1992–94; Vice-Pres., Gen. Man. of Nylon, DuPont Asia-Pacific 1994–95, Pres. 1995–97; Pres., CEO DuPont Canada Inc. 1997–, Chair of Bd 1998–. *Address:* Office of the President and Chief Executive Officer, DuPont Canada Inc., P.O. Box 2200, Mississauga, Ont., L5M 2H3, Canada.

COLE, Natalie Maria, BA; American singer; b. 6 Feb. 1950, Los Angeles; d. of Nathaniel Adam Cole (Nat 'King' Cole) and Maria Hawkins; m. 1st Marvin J. Yancy 1976 (divorced); m. 2nd Andre Fisher (divorced); ed Univ. of Massachusetts; recordings of albums and singles 1975–; recipient of several Grammys and other music awards. *Albums include:* Inseparable 1975, Natalie 1976, Unpredictable 1977, Thankful 1977, Live 1978, I Love You So 1979, We're The Best Of Friends 1979, Don't Look Back 1980, Happy Love 1981, I'm Ready 1983, Unforgettable – A Tribute to Nat 'King' Cole (with Johnny Mathis) 1983, Dangerous 1985, Everlasting 1987, Good To Be Back 1989, Unforgettable 1991, Too Much Weekend 1992, Take A Look 1993, Holly and Ivy 1994, Stardust (two Grammy Awards), Magic of Christmas 1999. *Address:* c/o Jennifer Allen, PMK, 8500 Wilshire Boulevard, Suite 700, Beverly Hills, CA 90211, USA.

COLE-HAMILTON, David John, PhD, CChem, FRSC, FRSE; British professor of chemistry; b. 22 May 1948, Bovey Tracey; s. of AM Cole-Hamilton and the late MM Cartwright; m. Elizabeth A. Brown 1973; two s. two d.; ed Haileybury & Imperial Service Coll. and Univ. of Edinburgh; Research Asst and temporary lecturer, Imperial Coll. London 1974–78; lecturer, Univ. of Liverpool 1978–83, Sr lecturer 1983–85; Irvine Prof. of Chemistry St Andrew's Univ. 1985–, Chair. of Chem. 1985–90; Tilden Lecturer, Royal Soc. of Chem. 2000–01; Sir Edward Frankland Fellowship 1985; Corday Morgan Medal and Prize 1983; Industrial Award for Organo-metallic Chem. 1998. *Publications:* 270 articles on homogeneous catalysis and organometallic chemistry. *Address:* School of Chemistry, University of St Andrews, St Andrews, Fife, KY16 9ST (Office); St Rule, Boarhills, By St Andrews, Fife, KY16 8PP, Scotland (Home). *Telephone:* (1334) 463805 (Office). *Fax:* (1334) 463808. *E-mail:* djc@st-and.ac.uk (Office).

COLEGATE, Isabel, FRSL; British writer; b. 10 Sept. 1931, London; d. of Arthur Colegate and Winifred Colegate; m. Michael Briggs 1953; two s. one d.; ed Runton Hill School, Norfolk; literary agent Anthony Blond Ltd, London 1952–57; Dr hc (Bath) 1988. *Publications include:* The Blackmailer 1958, A Man of Power 1960, The Great Occasion 1962, Statues in a Garden 1964, The Orlando Trilogy 1968–72, News From the City of the Sun 1979, The Shooting Party 1980 (W H. Smith Literary Award; filmed 1985), A Glimpse of Sion's Glory 1985, Deceits of Time 1988, The Summer of the Royal Visit 1991, Winter Journey 1995, A Pelican in the Wilderness 2002, Hermits Solitaries and Recluses 2002. *Address:* c/o Peters, Fraser and Dunlop, Drury House, 34–43 Russell Street, London, WC2B 5HA, England. *Telephone:* (20) 7344-1000. *Fax:* (20) 7836-9539.

COLEMAN, Norm, BA, JD; American politician and lawyer; b. Brooklyn; m. Laurie Coleman; one s. one d.; ed Hofstra Univ., Univ. of Iowa; served in Office of Attorney-Gen. of Minn. in various positions including Chief Prosecutor and Solicitor-Gen. of State of Minn. 1976–93; elected Mayor of St Paul (as

Conservative Democrat) 1993, re-elected 1997 (as Republican); Republican Cand. for Gov. of Minn. 1998; Senator from Minnesota 2003–. *Leisure interests:* playing basketball with his daughter, juggling, Bob Dylan's music. *Address:* Office of the Senator from Minnesota, US Senate, Senate Buildings, Washington, DC 20150, USA (Office).

COLEMAN, Ornette; American jazz musician; b. 9 March 1930, Fort Worth; s. of Randolph Coleman and Rosa Coleman; m. Jayne Cortez (divorced 1964); one s.; player alto and tenor saxophone, trumpet, violin, bassoon; developed Harmoldic music theory; has appeared in numerous maj. festivals world-wide including JVC Jazz Festival, New York 1991; has toured in Japan, Europe, Africa; Guggenheim Foundation Fellow 1967, 1974; Praemium Imperiale, Japan Art Asscn 2001. *Film:* Ornette: Made in America 1986. *Music: Recordings include:* Something Else 1958, The Shape of Jazz to Come 1959, Live at the Tivoli 1965, Paris concert Nov 4 1965, Live in Milano 1968, New York is Now 1968, Dancing in Your Head 1976, At the Golden Circle, Stockholm 1987, Naked Lunch 1992, Sound Museum: Hidden Man 1996, Sound Museum: Three Museum 1996; *Compositions include:* Music of Ornette Coleman (works for string quartet and woodwind quintet), Skies of America and over 100 compositions for small jazz group and larger ensembles. *Address:* c/o Polygram Group, Distribution Verve Records Worldwide, Plaza 825, 8th Avenue, New York, NY 10019-7416, USA (Office).

COLEMAN, Robert John, MA, JD; British civil servant and lawyer; b. 8 Sept. 1943; m. Malinda Tigay Cutler 1966; two d.; ed Devonport High School for Boys, Plymouth, Jesus Coll. Oxford and Univ. of Chicago Law School; Lecturer in Law, Univ. of Birmingham 1967–70; called to the Bar 1969; in practice as barrister-at-law, London 1970–73; Admin., subsequently Prin. Admin., EC 1974–82, Deputy Head of Div. 1983, Head of Div. 1984–87, Dir Public Procurement 1987–90, Dir Approximation of Laws, Freedom of Establishment and Freedom to Provide Services, the Professions 1990–91, Dir-Gen. Transport, European Comm. 1991–99; Dir-Gen. Health and Consumer Protection 1999–; mem. School of Man. Advisory Bd, Univ. of Bath 2001–. *Publications:* articles in professional journals. *Address:* 114 rue des Deux Tours, 1210 Brussels, Belgium. *Telephone:* (2) 218-38-65.

COLEMAN, Sidney, PhD; American physicist and teacher; b. 7 March 1937, Chicago; s. of Harold Coleman and Sadie (Shanas) Coleman; m. Diana Teschmacher 1982; ed Illinois Inst. of Tech. and California Inst. of Tech.; mem. Physics Dept, Harvard Univ. 1961–, Prof. 1969–, Donner Prof. of Science 1980–; Trustee Aspen Center for Physics; Fellow American Physical Soc., NAS, American Acad. of Arts and Sciences; J. Murray Lack Award (NAS) 1989, Distinguished Alumnus Award (Calif. Inst. of Tech.), Dirac Medal (Int. Centre for Theoretical Physics) 1990, Dannie Heineman Prize (A.P.S.) 2000. *Publications:* numerous tech. papers on high-energy physics; Aspects of Symmetry 1985. *Address:* Physics Department, Harvard University, Cambridge, MA 02138; 1 Richdale Avenue, Unit 12, Cambridge, MA 02140-2610, USA (Home). *Telephone:* (617) 496 8346 (Univ.); (617) 495-2807 (Home). *Fax:* (617) 496-8396. *E-mail:* coleman@physics.harvard.edu (Office).

COLEMAN, Terry (Terence Francis Frank), LLB, FRSA; British reporter and author; b. 13 Feb. 1931; s. of Jack Coleman and D. I. B. Coleman; m. 1st Lesley Fox-Strangeways Vane 1954 (divorced); two d.; m. 2nd Vivien Rosemary Lumsdaine Wallace 1981; one s. one d.; ed 14 schools and Univ. of London; fmr Reporter Poole Herald; fmr Ed. Savoir Faire; fmr Sub-Ed. Sunday Mercury, Birmingham Post; Reporter then Arts Corresp. The Guardian 1961–70, Chief Feature Writer 1970–74, 1976–79, New York Corresp. 1981, Special Corresp. 1982–89; Special Writer with Daily Mail 1974–76; Assoc. Ed. The Independent 1989–91; Columnist The Guardian 1992–; Feature Writer of the Year, British Press Awards 1982, Journalist of the Year (What the Papers Say Award) 1988. *Publications:* The Railway Navvies 1965 (Yorkshire Post Prize for best first book of the year), A Girl for the Afternoons 1965, Providence and Mr Hardy (with Lois Deacon) 1966, The Only True History: collected journalism 1969, Passage to America 1972, An Indiscretion in the Life of an Heiress (Hardy's first novel) (Ed.) 1976, The Liners 1976, The Scented Brawl: collected journalism 1978, Southern Cross 1979, Thanksgiving 1981, Movers and Shakers: collected interviews 1987, Thatcher's Britain 1987, Empire 1994, W G. Grace: a biography 1997, Nelson: the Man and the Legend (biog.) 2001. *Leisure interests:* cricket, opera and circumnavigation. *Address:* c/o Peters, Fraser and Dunlop, 34–43 Russell Street, London, WC2B 5HA, England. *Telephone:* (20) 7720-2651 (Home).

COLERIDGE, David Ean; British insurance executive; b. 7 June 1932; s. of Guy Cecil Richard Coleridge and Katherine Cicely Stewart Smith; m. Susan Senior 1955; three s.; ed Eton Coll.; with Glanvill Enthoven 1950–57; joined R. W Sturge & Co. 1957, Dir 1966–95; Chair. A. L. Sturge (Holdings) Ltd (now Sturge Holdings PLC) 1978–95; mem. Cttee of Lloyd's Underwriting Agents Asscn 1974–82, Chair. 1981–82; mem. Council and Cttee of Lloyd's 1983–86, 1988–92; Deputy Chair. Lloyd's 1985, 1988, 1989, Chair. 1991–92; Dir Wise Speke Holdings Ltd 1987–94, Ockham Holdings PLC (now Highway Insurance PLC) 1996– (Chair. 1995). *Leisure interests:* golf, racing, gardening, family. *Address:* Spring Pond House, Wispers, nr Midhurst, West Sussex, GU29 0QH; 37 Egerton Terrace, London, SW3 2BU, England. *Telephone:* (1730) 813277; (20) 7581-1756 (London). *Fax:* (20) 7591-0637 (London).

COLERIDGE, Nicholas David; British publisher, journalist and author; b. 4 March 1957; s. of David Ean Coleridge (q.v.) and Susan (Senior) Coleridge; m. Georgia Metcalfe 1989; three s. one d.; ed Eton, Trinity Coll., Cambridge; Assoc. Ed. Tatler 1979–81; columnist Evening Standard 1981–84; Features Ed. Harpers and Queen 1985–86, Ed. 1986–89; Editorial Dir Condé Nast Publs 1989–91, Man. Dir 1992–, Vice-Pres. Condé Nast Int. 1999–; Chair. British Fashion Council 2000–; mem. Council RCA 1995–2000; Young Journalist of the Year, British Press Awards 1983, Mark Boxer Award for Editorial Excellence 2001. *Publications:* Tunnel Vision 1982, Around the World in 78 Days 1984, Shooting Stars 1984, The Fashion Conspiracy 1988, How I Met My Wife and Other Stories 1991, Paper Tigers 1993, With Friends Like These 1997, Streetsmart 1999, Godchildren 2002. *Address:* Rignell Farm, Barford St Michael, Oxon. OX15 0PN; 38 Princedale Road, London, W11 4NL, England. *Telephone:* (20) 7221-4293.

COLES, Anna L. Bailey, PhD; American professor of nursing; b. (Anna Louise Bailey), 16 Jan. 1925, Kansas City; d. of Lillie Mai Buchanan and Gordon A. Bailey; m. 1953 (divorced 1980); three d.; ed Freedmen's Hosp. School of Nursing, Washington, DC, Avila Coll., Kansas City, Mo. and Catholic Univ. of America; Instructor, Veterans Admin. Hosp., Topeka, Kan. 1950–52; Supervisor, Veterans Admin. Hosp., Kansas City 1952–58; Asst Dir In-Service Educ., Freedmen's Hosp. 1960–61, Admin. Asst to Dir 1961–66, Assoc. Dir Nursing Service 1966–67, Dir of Nursing 1967–69; Prof. and Dean, Howard Univ. Coll. of Nursing 1968–86, Dean Emer. 1986–, retd 1986; Dir Minority Devt, Univ. of Kansas School of Nursing 1991–95; Pres. Societas Docta, Inc. 1996–99; mem. Inst. of Medicine; Meritorious Public Service Award, DC 1968; Distinguished Alumni Award, Howard Univ.; Lifetime Achievement Award Asscn of Black Nursing Faculty in Higher Educ. 1993; numerous other awards. *Publications:* articles in professional journals; contrib. to Fundamentals of Stroke Care 1976; Nurses, an Encyclopedia of Black America 1981. *Leisure interests:* reading, outdoor cooking and travelling. *Address:* 15107 Interlachen Drive, #205, Silver Spring, MD 20906, USA. *Telephone:* (301) 598-3680 (Home). *Fax:* (301) 598-3680 (Home).

COLES, Sir (Arthur) John, GCMG; British diplomatist; b. 13 Nov. 1937; s. of Arthur S. Coles and Doris G. Coles; m. Anne M. S. Graham 1965; two s. one d.; ed Magdalen Coll. School, Brackley and Magdalen Coll. Oxford; joined HM Diplomatic Service 1960; Middle Eastern Centre for Arabic Studies, Lebanon 1960–62; Third Sec. Khartoum 1962–64; Asst Political Agent, Trucial States (Dubai) 1968–71; Head of Chancery, Cairo 1975–77; Counsellor, UK Perm. Mission to EEC 1977–80; Head of S. Asian Dept FCO 1980–81; Pvt. Sec. to Prime Minister 1981–84; Amb. to Jordan 1984–88; High Commr in Australia 1988–91; Deputy Under-Sec. of State, FCO 1991–94; Perm. Under-Sec. of State and Head of HM Diplomatic Service 1994–97; Dir B.G. PLC 1998–; Visiting Fellow All Souls Coll. Oxford 1998–99; Trustee Imperial War Museum 1999–; Chair. Sight Savers Int. 2001, Atlantic Coll. Council 2001–. *Publications:* British Influence and the Euro 1999, Making Foreign Policy: A Certain Idea of Britain 2000. *Leisure interests:* walking, cricket, bird-watching, reading, music. *Address:* Kelham, Dock Lane, Beaulieu, Hants., SO42 7YH, England.

COLES, John Morton, MA, PhD, ScD, FBA, FSA, FRSA; archaeologist; b. 25 March 1930, Canada; s. of John L. Coles and Alice M. Brown; m. 1st Mona Shiach 1958 (divorced 1985); two s. two d.; m. 2nd Bryony Orme 1985; ed Univs. of Toronto, Edinburgh and Cambridge; Univ. Lecturer and Reader, Univ. of Cambridge 1960–80, Prof. of European Prehistory 1980–86; Fellow, Fitzwilliam Coll. Cambridge 1963–; mem. Academia Europaea 1989–, Royal Comm. on Ancient and Historical Monuments of Scotland 1992–2002, Discovery Programme Ireland 2001–; Hon. Prof. Exeter Univ.; Dr. hc (Uppsala) 1997; Europa Prize for Prehistory 2000; Grahame Clark Medal, British Acad. 1995, ICI Medal (jtly.), British Archaeological Awards 1998, Gold Medal, Soc. of Antiquaries of London 2002. *Publications:* The Archaeology of Early Man (with E Higgs) 1969, Field Archaeology in Britain 1972, Archaeology by Experiment 1973, The Bronze Age in Europe (with A. Harding) 1979, Experimental Archaeology 1979, Prehistory of the Somerset Levels (with B. Orme) 1980, The Archaeology of Wetlands 1984, Sweet Track to Glastonbury (with B. Coles) 1986, Meare Village East: the excavations of A. Bulleid and H. St George Gray 1932–1956 1987, People of the Wetlands (with B. Coles) 1989, Images of the Past 1990, From The Waters of Oblivion 1991, Arthur Bulleid and the Glastonbury Lake Village 1892–1992 (with A. Goodall and S. Minnitt) 1992, Fenland Survey (with D. Hall) 1994, Rock Carvings of Uppland 1995, Industrious and Fairly Civilised: the Glastonbury Lake Village (with S. Minnitt) 1995, Enlarging the Past (with B. Coles) 1996, Lake Villages of Somerset (with S. Minnitt) 1996, Changing Landscapes: the ancient Fenland (with D. Hall) 1998, Patterns in a Rocky Land: Rock Carvings in South-West Uppland, Sweden 2000; numerous papers on European prehistory, field archaeology, experimental archaeology, wetland archaeology. *Leisure interests:* music, travel, wetlands. *Address:* Fursdon Mill Cottage, Thorverton, Devon, EX5 5JS, England. *Telephone:* (1392) 860125. *Fax:* (1392) 861095. *E-mail:* johnmcoles@aol.com (Home).

COLES, Robert Martin, AB, MD; American child psychiatrist; b. 12 Oct. 1929, Boston, Mass.; s. of Philip W Coles and Sandra (Young) Coles; m. Jane Hallowell 1960; three s.; ed Harvard Coll. and Columbia Univ.; Intern, Univ. of Chicago clinics 1954–55; Resident in Psychiatry, Mass. Gen. Hosp., Boston 1955–56, McLean Hosp., Belmont 1956–57; Resident in Child Psychiatry, Judge Baker Guidance Center, Children's Hosp., Roxbury, Mass. 1957–58, Fellow 1960–61; mem. psychiatric staff, Mass. Gen. Hosp. 1960–62; Clinical Asst in Psychiatry, Harvard Univ. Medical School 1960–62; Research Psychiatrist in Health Services, Harvard Univ. 1963–, lecturer in Gen. Educ. 1966–, Prof. of Psychiatry and Medical Humanities, Harvard Univ. Medical School 1977–; numerous other professional appts; mem. American Psychiatric Asscn; Fellow, American Acad. of Arts and Sciences etc.; awards include Pulitzer Prize for Vols II and III of Children of Crisis 1973, Sara Josepha Hale Award 1986. *Publications:* Harvard Diary 1988, Times of Surrender: Selected Essays 1989, The Spiritual Life of Children; numerous books and articles in professional journals. *Leisure interests:* tennis, bicycle riding, skiing. *Address:* Harvard Health Services, Harvard University, 75 Mt. Auburn Street, Cambridge, MA 02138 (Office); 81 Carr Road, Concord, MA 01742, USA (Home). *Telephone:* (617) 495-3736 (Office); (617) 369-6498 (Home).

COLGAN, Michael Anthony, BA; Irish theatre, film and television producer; b. 17 July 1950, Dublin; s. of James Joseph Colgan and Josephine Patricia (née Geoghegan) Colgan; m. Susan Mary FitzGerald 1975; one s. two d.; ed Trinity Coll. Dublin; Theatre Dir Abbey Theatre, Dublin 1974–78; Co. Man. Irish Theatre Co., Dublin 1977–78; Man. Dublin Theatre Festival 1978–80, Artistic Dir 1981–83, mem. Bd of Dirs. 1983–; Artistic Dir Gate Theatre, Dublin 1984–; Exec. Dir Little Bird Films, Dublin and London 1986–; co-founder Belacqua Film Co. 1998, Blue Angel Film Co. 1999; Artistic Dir Parma Festival, Italy 1997; mem. Irish Arts Council 1989–93; Gov. Dublin City Univ. 1998–2001; Hon. LLD (Trinity Coll. Dublin) 2000; Arts Award, Irish Independent 1985, 1987, Nat. Entertainment Award 1996, People of the Year Award 1999. *Plays produced:* I'll Go On (Samuel Beckett), Dublin, Paris, London, Edin., Bari, Jerusalem, Brussels, Amsterdam, Chicago, New York; Juno and the Paycock (Sean O'Casey), Dublin, Jerusalem, Edin., New York; Salome (Oscar Wilde), Dublin, Edin., Charleston, SC; Three Sisters, Dublin and Royal Court Theatre, London; Molly Sweeney (Brian Friel), Dublin, London and New York; The Beckett Festival, Dublin, New York, London; The Pinter Festival, Dublin; Waiting For Godot and Krapp's Last Tape (Samuel Beckett) on tour in USA 2000, The Pinter Festival, New York 2001, The Homecoming (Harold Pinter), Dublin, London 2001, Krapp's Last Tape, Dublin, London, One for the Road (Harold Pinter), London 2001, Port Authority (Conor McPherson) Dublin, London 2001. *Television:* Two Lives (exec. producer) for RTÉ 1986, Troubles (two two-hour films) for LWT 1996. *Film:* Beckett on Film (co-producer): all 19 of Beckett's plays filmed using internationally known dirs. and actors. *Leisure interests:* Schubert, Beckett, New York City. *Address:* Gate Theatre, Cavendish Row, Dublin 1 (Office); 25 Orwell Park, Dublin 6, Ireland (Home). *Telephone:* (1) 874-4368 (Office). *Fax:* (1) 874-5373 (Office). *E-mail:* info@gate-theatre.ie (Office).

COLLARD, Jean Philippe; French solo pianist; b. 27 Jan. 1948, Mareuil-sur-Aÿ (Marne); s. of Michel Collard and Monique (Philipponnat) Collard; m. 2nd Ariane de Brion; one s., one d. and two s. from a previous marriage; ed Conservatoire National de Musique de Paris; Chevalier des Arts et des Lettres, Chevalier Ordre nat. du Mérite; Chevalier Légion d'honneur 2003. *Recordings include:* music by Bach, Brahms, Debussy, Fauré, Franck, Rachmaninov, Ravel, Saint-Saëns, Schubert, Chopin, Mozart. *Leisure interests:* windsurfing, tennis. *Address:* Caroline Martin Musique, 126 rue Vieille du Temple, 75003 Paris, France. *Telephone:* 1-42-74-49-01 (Office). *Fax:* 1-40-46-93-77. *E-mail:* caroline.martin.musique@wanadoo.fr (Office).

COLLENETTE, David Michael, PC, BA; Canadian politician; b. 24 June 1946, London, England; s. of David H. Collenette and Sarah M. Collenette; m. Penny Collenette 1975; one s.; ed Glendon Coll., York Univ.; fmrly worked in life insurance, plastics and exec. recruitment; fmr Exec. Vice-Pres. Mandrake Man. Consultants; elected to House of Commons 1974, 1980, 1993; fmr Minister of State (Multiculturalism), Parl. Sec. to Postmaster-Gen. and to Pres. of Privy Council; Minister of Nat. Defence and Minister of Veterans Affairs 1993–96, of Transport July 1997–; mem. Liberal Party. *Leisure interests:* squash, soccer, swimming, classical music and theatre. *Address:* Transport Canada, 330 Sparks Street, Ottawa, Ont., K1A 0N5 (Office); House of Commons, Ottawa, Ont., K1A 0A6, Canada. *Telephone:* (613) 995-4988 (Office). *Fax:* (613) 995-4988 (Office). *E-mail:* mintc@tc.gc.ca (Office). *Website:* www.tc.gc.ca (Office).

COLLETTE, Toni; Australian actress; b. 1 Dec. 1972, Sydney; m. Dave Galafassi 2003; ed Nat. Inst. for Dramatic Art, Sydney. *Films include:* Spotswood 1991, Muriel's Wedding 1994, This Marching Girl Thing 1994, Arabian Knight (voice) 1995, Lilian's Story 1995, Cosí 1996, The Pallbearer 1996, Emma 1996, Clockwatchers 1997, The James Gang 1997, Diana & Me 1997, The Boys 1997, Velvet Goldmine 1998, 8 1/2 Women 1999, The Sixth Sense 1999, Shaft 2000, Hotel Splendide 2000, Changing Lanes 2002, Dirty Deeds 2002, About a Boy 2002, The Hours 2003, Japanese Story 2003. *Leisure interests:* yoga, mental and spiritual retreats in India, climbing Tibetan Himalayas.

COLLEY, Linda Jane, PhD, FRHistS, FBA; British professor of history; b. 13 Sept. 1949; d. of Roy Colley and Marjorie Colley (née Hughes); m. David Nicholas Cannadine (q.v.) 1982; one d. (deceased); ed Bristol and Cambridge Univs; Eugenie Strong Research Fellow, Girton Coll., Cambridge 1975–78; Fellow Newnham Coll., Cambridge 1978–79, Christ's Coll., Cambridge 1979–81; Asst Prof. of History Yale Univ. 1982–85, Assoc. Prof. 1985–90, Prof. of History 1990–92, Richard M. Colgate Prof. of History 1992–98, Dir Lewis Walpole Library 1982–96; Prof. School of History, LSE 1998–2003, Leverhulme Personal Research Prof., European Inst. 1998–2003; Shelby M.C. Davis 1958 Prof. of History, Princeton Univ. 2003–; mem. Bd British Library; mem. Advisory Bd Tate Britain, Paul Mellon Centre for British Art; Anstey Lecturer Univ. of Kent 1994; William Church Memorial Lecturer, Brown Univ. 1994, Distinguished Lecturer in British History, Univ. of Texas at Austin 1995, Trevelyan Lecturer Cambridge Univ. 1997, Wiles Lecturer,

Queen's Univ. Belfast, Prime Minister's Millennium Lecture 2000, Raleigh Lecture, British Acad. 2002, Nehru Lecture 2002, Bateson Lecture, Oxford 2003; Wolfson Prize 1993. *Publications:* In Defiance of Oligarchy: The Tory Party 1714–60 1982, Namier 1989, Crown Pictorial: Art and the British Monarchy 1990, Britons: Forging the Nation 1707–1837 1992 (Wolfson Prize 1993); Captives: Britain, Empire and the World 1600–1850 2002; numerous articles and reviews in UK and American learned journals. *Leisure interests:* travel, looking at art. *Address:* Dept of History, Princeton Univ., 129 Dickinson Hall, Princeton, NJ 08544–1017, USA; c/o Curtis Brown, Haymarket House, 28–29 Haymarket, London, SW1 4SP, England.

COLLIER, Lesley Faye, CBE; British ballet dancer; b. 13 March 1947; d. of Roy Collier and Mavis Collier; twin s.; ed The Royal Ballet School, White Lodge, Richmond; joined Royal Ballet 1965, prin. dancer 1972–95, répétiteur 2000–; has danced most prin. roles in the Royal repertory; ballet mistress Royal Ballet School 1995–99, mem. Classical Ballet Staff 1999–2000; Evening Standard Ballet Award 1987. *Address:* Royal Ballet, Royal Opera House, Covent Garden, London, WC2E 9DD, England.

COLLIGNON, Stefan Colin, PhD; German economist; b. 11 Dec. 1951, Munich; s. of Klaus Collignon and Rosemarie Collignon; m. Judith Zahler 1984; ed Institut d'Etudes Politiques, Paris, Free Univ. of Berlin, Univ. of Dar es Salaam, Tanzania, Queen Elizabeth House, Oxford, UK, London School of Econs; Financial Analyst, First Nat. Bank in Dallas, Paris 1975–76; teacher, Lindi Secondary School, Deutscher Entwicklungsdienst (German Volunteer Service), Tanzania 1977–79; Man. Dir and Chair. Dorcas Ltd, London 1981–88; Dir Research and Communication, Asscn for the Monetary Union of Europe, Paris 1989–98; lecturer, Institut d'Etudes Politiques, Paris 1990–95, Free University, Berlin 1997–2000; Pres. Asscn France-Birmanie 1990–; Prof. of European Political Economy, LSE 2001–. *Publications:* Droits de l'Homme, Monnaie et développement économique 1992, Europe's Monetary Future (Vol. I) 1994, The Monetary Economics of Europe: Causes of the EMS Crisis (Vol. II) 1994, European Monetary Policy (ed.) 1997, Exchange Rate Policies in Emerging Asian Countries 1999; numerous articles and book chapters on monetary union. *Address:* London School of Economics, Houghton Street, London WC2A 2AE, England. *Website:* www.stefancollignon.de (Home).

COLLINS, Billy; American poet and professor of English; b. 1941, New York; Prof. of English Lehman Coll., City Univ. of New York; conducts summer poetry workshops Univ. Coll. Galway, Ireland; Library of Congress's Poet Laureate Consultant in Poetry 2001, U.S. Poet Laureate 2001–02; Fellow, New York Foundation for the Arts, Nat. Endowment for the Arts, Guggenheim Foundation; Literary Lion, New York Public Library 1992. *Publications:* Pokerface 1977, Video Poems 1980, The Apple that Astonished Paris 1988, Questions About Angels 1991, The Art of Drowning 1995, Picnic, Lightning 1998, Taking Off Emily Dickinson's Clothes 2000, Sailing Alone Around the Room: New and Selected Poems 2001; poems in many anthologies, including The Best American Poetry 1992, 1993, 1997 and periodicals, including Poetry, American Poetry, Review, American Scholar, Harper's, Paris Review and The New Yorker. *Address:* c/o Lehman College, 250 Bedford Park Boulevard West, Business Office, Shuster Hall Building, Bronx, New York, NY 10468, U.S.A. (Office). *Website:* www.lehman.cuny.edu (Office).

COLLINS, Bob; Australian politician; b. Newcastle, NSW; m.; three c.; worked as extension officer, NT Dept of Agric., market gardener, Arnhem Land, tech. officer, Wildlife Research Div., CSIRO 1967–77; elected as mem. for Arnhem, House of Reps. 1977, subsequently mem. for Arafura; Parl. Leader Australian Labor Party 1981–86; elected Senator for NT 1987–98; Minister for Shipping, Aviation Support and Minister Assisting the Prime Minister for Northern Australia 1990–92, for Transport and Communications 1992–93, for Primary Industries and Energy 1993–96; Shadow Minister for Primary Industries and for Northern Australia and Territories 1996–97. *Address:* c/o ALP, GPO Box 2026, Darwin, NT 0801, Australia.

COLLINS, Christopher Douglas, FCA; British business executive; b. 19 Jan. 1940, Welwyn; s. of Douglas Collins and Patricia Collins; m. Susan Lumb 1976; one s. one d.; ed Eton Coll.; articled clerk, Peat Marwick Mitchell 1958–64; Man. Dir Goya Ltd 1968–83, Dir 1975–80; amateur steeplechase jockey 1965–75; rep. of GB in three-day equestrian events 1974–80; Steward, Jockey Club 1980–81; mem. Horse Race Betting Levy Board 1982–84; Chair. Aintree Racecourse Ltd 1983–88, Nat. Stud 1986–88; joined Hanson PLC 1989, Dir 1991, Vice-Chair. 1995, Deputy Chair. 1997, Chair. 1998–; Chair. Forth Ports PLC 2000–; Dir Old Mutual PLC 1999–, The Go-Ahead Group PLC 1999–, Alfred McAlpine PLC 2000–. *Leisure interests:* riding, skiing. *Address:* 1 Grosvenor Place, London, SW1X 7JH, England. *Telephone:* (20) 7245-1245. *Fax:* (20) 7235-3455.

COLLINS, Francis S., MD, PH.D; American research scientist; ed Univ. of Virginia, Yale Univ., Univ. of North Carolina at Chapel Hill; Fellowship in Human Genetics Yale Univ.; fmr staff mem. Howard Hughes Medical Inst., Univ. of Mich. Medical Center, Ann Arbor 1984; with research team identified gene for cystic fibrosis 1989, for neurofibromatosis 1990, for Huntington disease 1993; Dir Nat. Human Genome Research Inst., Head Human Genome Project; mem. Inst. of Medicine, NAS; co-recipient Gairdner Foundation Int. Award for work on Cystic Fibrosis 1990. *Address:* National Human Genome Research Institute, 31 Center Drive, Room 4609, Bethesda, MD 20892-0001, USA (Office).

COLLINS, Gerard; Irish politician; b. 16 Oct. 1938, Abbeyfeale, Co. Limerick; s. of the late James J. Collins and Margaret Collins; m. Hilary Tattan; ed Univ. Coll. Dublin; fmr vocational teacher; mem. Dáil 1967–; Acting Gen. Sec. Fianna Fáil Party 1964–67; Parl. Sec. to Minister for Industry and Commerce and to Minister for the Gaeltacht 1969–70; Minister for Posts and Telegraphs 1970–73; mem. Consultative Ass. of Council of Europe 1973–75; Limerick Co. Council 1974–77; Minister for Justice 1977–81, 1987–89, for Foreign Affairs March–Dec. 1982, 1989–93; Chair. Parl. Cttee on EEC Affairs 1983–87; mem. European Parl. 1994–, Leader Fianna Fáil Group, Vice-Pres. Union for Europe Group, Pres. European Parl. Del. to S. Asia and South Asian Asscn for Regional Co-operation (SAARC); Chair. of the EU-South Africa Interparliamentary Del. *Address:* The Hill, Abbeyfeale, Co. Limerick, Ireland (Home); 6F 365, European Parliament, 97–113 rue Wiertz, 1047 Brussels, Belgium (Office). *Telephone:* (2) 284-56-22 (Office); (68) 32441. *Fax:* (2) 284-96-22 (Office). *E-mail:* gcollins@europarl.eu.int (Office). *Website:* www.europarl.ep.ec (Office).

COLLINS, Jackie; British novelist; sister of Joan Collins (q.v.). *Mini-series:* Hollywood Wives (ABC TV), Lucky Chances (NBC TV), Lady Boss (NBC TV). *Screenplays:* Yesterday's Hero, The World is Full of Married Men, The Stud. *Publications:* The World is Full of Married Men 1968, The Stud 1969, Sunday Simmons and Charlie Brick 1971, Lovehead 1974, The World is Full of Divorced Women 1975, Lovers and Gamblers 1977, The Bitch 1979, Chances 1981, Hollywood Wives 1983, Lucky 1985, Hollywood Husbands 1986, Rock Star 1988, Lady Boss 1990, American Star 1993, Hollywood Kids 1994, Vendetta–Lucky's Revenge 1996, Thrill 1998, LA Connections (four-part serial novel) 1998, Dangerous Kiss 1999, Hollywood Wives: The New Generation 2001, Lethal Seduction 2001. *Address:* c/o Simon and Schuster, 1230 Avenue of the Americas, New York, NY 10020, USA. *Fax:* (310) 278-6517.

COLLINS, James Franklin; American diplomatist; b. 4 June 1939, Aurora, Illinois; Dir for Intelligence Policy, Nat. Security Council, Washington; Deputy Exec. Sec. Europe and Latin America, US Dept of State, Washington; Vice-Counsel Izmir, Turkey; Political Counsellor Amman, Jordan; Deputy Chief of Mission, American Embassy Moscow 1990–93, Co-ordinator for Regional Affairs for New Ind. States, US Dept of State 1993–94, Sr Co-ordinator Office of Amb.-at-Large for New Ind. States 1994–97; Amb. to Russia 1997–2001; retd 2001; sr int. adviser Akin, Gump, Strauss, Hauer & Feld 2001–. *Address:* 5125 Edgemoor Lane, Bethesda, MD 28014, USA (Home). *E-mail:* jcollins@akingump.com (Office); jfcollins@aol.com (Home).

COLLINS, Joan, OBE; British actress; b. 23 May 1933, London; d. of Joseph William and Elsa (née Bessant) Collins; sister of Jackie Collins (q.v.); m. 1st Maxwell Reed (divorced); m. 2nd Anthony Newley (divorced); one s. one d.; m. 3rd Ronald S. Kass 1972 (divorced); one d.; m. 4th Peter Holm 1985 (divorced 1987); m. 5th Percy Gibson 2002. *Films include:* I Believe in You 1952, Our Girl Friday 1953, The Good Die Young 1954, Land of the Pharaohs 1955, The Virgin Queen 1955, The Girl in the Red Velvet Swing 1955, The Opposite Sex 1956, Island in the Sun 1957, Sea Wife 1957, The Bravados 1958, Seven Thieves 1960, Road to Hong Kong 1962, Warning Shot 1966, The Executioner 1969, Quest for Love 1971, Revenge 1971, Alfie Darling 1974, The Stud 1979, The Bitch 1980, The Big Sleep, Tales of the Unexpected, Neck 1983, Georgy Porgy 1983, Nutcracker 1984, Decadence 1994, In the Bleak Midwinter 1995, Hart to Hart 1995, Annie: A Royal Adventure 1995, The Clandestine Marriage 1998, The Flintstones–Viva Rock Vegas 1999, Joseph and the Amazing Technicolor Dreamcoat 1999, These Old Broads 2000. *Television:* TV appearances include Dynasty (serial) 1981–89, Cartier Affair 1985, Sins 1986, Monte Carlo 1986, Tonight at 8.30 1991, Pacific Palisades (serial) 1997, Will and Grace (USA) 2000. *Plays include:* The Last of Mrs Cheyne, London 1979–80, Private Lives London 1990, Broadway 1991, Love Letters, USA tour 2000. *Publications:* Past Imperfect 1978, The Joan Collins Beauty Book 1980, Katy, A Fight for Life 1982, Prime Time 1988, Love and Desire and Hate 1990, My Secrets 1994, Too Damn Famous 1995, Second Act 1996, My Friends' Secrets 1999. *Leisure interests:* cinema, antiques, reading, collecting. *Address:* c/o Paul Keylock, 16 Bulbecks Walk, South Woodham Ferrers, Essex, CM3 5ZN, England. *Fax:* (20) 7360-8306 (Office); (2145) 328625 (Home).

COLLINS, Sir John (Alexander), Kt.; British business executive; b. 10 Dec. 1941; s. of John Constantine Collins and Nancy Isobel Mitchell; m. Susan Mary Hooper 1965; ed Campbell Coll., Belfast, Reading Univ.; with Shell Int. Chemicals 1964, seconded to Kenya, Nigeria, Colombia, U.K. 1964–89, Supply and Marketing Co-ordinator and Dir Shell Int. Petroleum Co. Ltd 1989–90, Chair. and CEO Shell UK 1990–93; CEO Vestey Group 1993–2001; Deputy Chair. (non-exec.) and Dir (non-exec.) Dixons Group PLC 2001–02, Chair. 2002–; Chair. Cantab Pharmaceuticals 1996–99, Nat. Power 1997–2000; Dir BSkyB 1994–97, N. M. Rothschild & Sons 1995–, London Symphony Orchestra 1997–, Peninsular & Oriental Steam Navigation Co. Ltd 1998–, Stoll Moss Theatres Ltd 1999–2000; Chair. Advisory Cttee on Business and the Environment 1991–93; mem. Prime Minister's Advisory Cttee for Queen's Awards for Export, Tech. and Environmental Achievement 1992–99; Gov. Wellington Coll. 1995–99. *Leisure interests:* opera, theatre, sailing, riding, golf, tennis, the New Forest. *Address:* Dixons Group PLC, 29 Farm Street, London, W1J 5RL, England (Office). *Website:* www.dixons-group-plc.co.uk (Office).

COLLINS, Joseph Jameson; American communications executive; b. 27 July 1944, Troy, New York; s. of Mark Francis Collins and Olive Elizabeth Collins (née Jameson); m. Maura McManmon 1972; one s. three d.; with American TV and Communications Corpn 1964–84, 1988–90, fmrly Chair., CEO; Pres. HBO 1984–88; Chair., CEO Time Warner Cable 1990–. *Address:* Time Warner Cable, 290 Harbor Drive, Stamford, CT 06902, USA.

COLLINS, Larry, BS; American author; b. John L. Collins Jr, 14 Sept. 1929, Hartford, Conn.; s. of John L. Collins and Helen Cannon Collins; m. Nadia Hoda Sultan 1966; two s.; ed Loomis Inst., Windsor, Conn. and Yale Univ.; Advertising Dept, Proctor and Gamble, Ohio 1951–53; U.S. Army Supreme HQ, Paris 1953–55; Correspondent, United Press Paris 1956, Rome 1957, Middle East, Beirut 1957–59, Newsweek Magazine, Beirut 1959–61, Chief of Bureau, Newsweek, Paris 1961–65; Deauville Film Festival Literary Award 1985, Mannesmann—Talley Literary Prize 1989. *Publications:* Is Paris Burning? 1965, Or I'll Dress you in Mourning 1968, O Jerusalem 1972, Freedom at Midnight 1975, The Fifth Horseman 1980, Fall from Grace 1985, Maze 1989, Black Eagles 1993, Le Jour du Miracle: D-Day Paris 1994, Tomorrow Belongs to Us 1998. *Leisure interests:* tennis, skiing. *Address:* La Biche Niche, 83350 Ramatuelle, France. *Telephone:* 4-94-97-15-68. *Fax:* 4-94-97-86-16. *E-mail:* larcollins@aol.com (Home).

COLLINS, Michael; American fmr astronaut and museum official; b. 31 Oct. 1930, Rome, Italy; m. Patricia M. Finnegan 1957; one s. two d.; ed U.S. Military Acad. and Harvard Univ.; commissioned by USAF, served as experimental flight test officer, AF Flight Test Center, Edwards AF Base, Calif.; selected by NASA as astronaut Oct. 1963; backup pilot for Gemini VII mission 1965; pilot of Gemini X 1966; command pilot, Apollo XI mission for first moon landing July 1969; Asst Sec. for Public Affairs, Dept of State 1970–71; Dir Nat. Air and Space Museum 1971–78, Under-Sec. Smithsonian Inst. 1978–80; Maj.-Gen. USAF Reserve; Vice-Pres. LTV Aerospace and Defense Co. 1980–85; Pres. Michael Collins Assocs. 1985–; Fellow, Royal Aeronautical Soc., American Inst. of Aeronautics and Astronautics; mem. Int. Acad. of Astronautics, Int. Astronautical Fed.; Exceptional Service Medal (NASA), DSM (NASA), Presidential Medal of Freedom, DCM (USAF), DFC, F.A.I. Gold Space Medal. *Publications:* Carrying the Fire 1974, Flying to the Moon and Other Strange Places 1976, Liftoff 1988, Mission to Mars 1990.

COLLINS, Pauline, OBE; British actress; b. 3 Sept. 1940, Exmouth, Devon; d. of William Henry Collins and Mary Honora Callanan; m. John Alderton; two s. one d.; ed Convent of the Sacred Heart, Hammersmith, Cen. School of Speech and Drama; Dr hc (Liverpool Polytechnic) 1991. *Stage appearances:* A Gazelle in Park Lane (stage debut, Windsor 1962), Passion Flower Hotel 1965, The Erpingham Camp 1967, The Happy Apple 1967, 1970, The Importance of Being Earnest 1968, The Night I Chased the Women with an Eel 1969, Come as You Are 1970, Judies 1974, Engaged 1975, Confusions 1976, Rattle of a Simple Man 1980, Romantic Comedy 1983, Woman in Mind, Shirley Valentine (Olivier Award for best actress, London, Tony, Drama Desk and Outer Critics' Circle awards, New York) 1988, 1989, Shades 1992. *Films:* Shirley Valentine (Evening Standard Film Actress of the Year 1989, BAFTA Best Actress Award 1990) 1989, City of Joy 1992, My Mother's Courage 1997, Paradise Road 1997, Mrs Caldicott's Cabbage War 2002. *Television appearances include:* Sarah in series Upstairs Downstairs, Thomas and Sarah, Forever Green, No Honestly, Tales of the Unexpected, Lond Distance Information 1979, Knockback 1984, Tropical Moon over Dorking, The Ambassador 1998, Man and Boy 2002. *Publication:* Letter to Louise 1992.

COLLINS, Phil, LVO; British pop singer, drummer and composer; b. 30 Jan. 1951, Chiswick, London; s. of Greville Collins and June Collins; m. 1st 1976 (divorced); one s. one d.; m. 2nd Jill Tavelman 1984 (divorced 1995); one d.; m. 3rd Orianne Cevey 1999; one s.; ed Barbara Speake stage school; former child actor appearing as the Artful Dodger in London production of Oliver; joined rock group Genesis as drummer 1970, lead singer 1975–96; albums with Genesis include: Selling England by the Pound 1973, Invisible Touch 1986, We Can't Dance 1991; has also made own solo albums, including No Jacket Required, But Seriously, Face Value, Hello I Must be Going, Dance into the Light 1996, Hits 1998, Testify 2002; appeared in films Buster 1988, Frauds 1993; Trustee Prince of Wales's Trust 1983–; awards include: Grammy (seven), Ivor Novello (six), Brit (four), Variety Club of GB (two), Silver Clef (two) and Elvis awards; Acad. award for You'll be in my Heart from film Tarzan 1999.

COLLINS, Susan M., BA; American politician; b. 7 Dec. 1952, Caribou, Maine; ed St Lawrence Univ.; Prin. Adviser on Business Affairs to Senator Bill Cohen; Commr Maine Dept of Professional and Financial Regulation; Staff Dir Senate Sub-Cttee on Oversight Govt Man. 1981–87; Chair. Maine Cabinet Council on Health Care Policy; Republican Cand. for Gov. of Maine 1994; Dir New England Operations, US Small Business Admin; Exec. Dir Center Family Business, Hudson Coll., Bangor; Senator from Maine 1997–, mem. Cttee on Health, Educ., Labor and Pensions 1997–, Sub-Cttee on Children and Families 1997–, Sub-Cttee on Public Health and Safety 1997–, Cttee on Govt Affairs 1997–, Chair. Perm. Sub-Cttee on Investigation 1997–, mem. Special Cttee on Ageing; Outstanding Alumni Award, St Lawrence Univ. 1992. *Address:* Office of the Senator from Maine, US Senate, Senate Buildings, Washington, DC 20510, USA (Office).

COLLINSON, Patrick, CBE, PhD, FBA, FRHistS, FAHA; British professor of history; b. 10 Aug. 1929, Ipswich; s. of William Cecil Collinson and Belle Hay Collinson (née Patrick); m. Elizabeth Albinia Susan Selwyn 1960; two s. two d.; ed King's School, Ely, Pembroke Coll., Cambridge and Univ. of London; Research Asst, Univ. Coll. London 1955–56; Lecturer in History, Univ. of Khartoum, Sudan 1956–61; Lecturer in Ecclesiastical History, King's Coll.

London 1961–69; Prof. of History, Univ. of Sydney, Australia 1969–75; Prof. of History, Univ. of Kent at Canterbury 1976–84; Prof. of Modern History, Univ. of Sheffield 1984–88; Regius Prof. of Modern History, Univ. of Cambridge 1988–96, now Emer.; Visiting Prof. Univ. of Richmond, VA 1999; Assoc. Visiting Prof. Univ. of Warwick 2000–; Fellow Trinity Coll., Cambridge 1988–; Chair. Advisory Ed. Bd Journal of Ecclesiastical History 1982–93; Pres. Ecclesiastical History Soc. 1985–86, Church of England Record Soc. 1991–; mem. Council British Acad. 1986–89; Ford's Lecturer in English History, Oxford Univ. 1979; Hon. DUniv (York) 1988, Hon. DLitt (Kent) 1989, (Trinity Coll. Dublin) 1992, (Sheffield) 1994, (Oxford) 1997, (Essex) 2000; Medlicott Medal, Historical Asscn 1998. *Publications:* The Elizabethan Puritan Movement 1967, Archbishop Grindal 1519–1583: the Struggle for a Reformed Church 1979, The Religion of Protestants: the Church in English Society 1559–1625 (The Ford Lectures 1979) 1982, Godly People: Essays on English Protestantism and Puritanism 1984, English Puritanism 1984, The Birthpangs of Protestant England: religious and cultural change in the 16th and 17th centuries 1988, Elizabethan Essays 1993, A History of Canterbury Cathedral (jtly) 1995, The Reformation in English Towns (jtly) 1998, A History of Emmanuel College, Cambridge (jtly) 1999, (ed) Short Oxford History of the British Isles: The Sixteenth Century 2002. *Leisure interests:* mountain walking, music. *Address:* Trinity College, Cambridge, CB2 1TQ (Office); The Winnats, Cannonfields, Hathersage, Hope Valley, Derbyshire, S32 1AG, England (Home). *Telephone:* (1223) 338400 (Office); (1433) 650333 (Home). *Fax:* (1433) 650918.

COLLMAN, James Paddock, PhD; American professor of chemistry; b. 31 Oct. 1932, Beatrice, Neb.; s. of Perry G. Collman and Frances Dorothy Palmer; m. Patricia Tincher 1955; four d.; ed Univs. of Nebraska and Illinois; Instructor, Univ. of NC 1958–59, Asst Prof. 1959–62, Assoc. Prof. 1962–66, Prof. of Organic and Inorganic Chem. 1966–67; Prof., Stanford Univ. 1967–, George A. and Hilda M. Daubert Prof. of Chem. 1980–; mem. NAS, American Acad. of Arts and Sciences; Alfred P. Sloan Foundation Fellow 1963–66; Nat. Science Foundation Sr Postdoctoral Fellow 1965–66; Guggenheim Fellow 1977–78, 1985–86; Churchill Fellow (Cambridge) 1977–; Dr. hc (Univ. of Nebraska) 1988, (Univ. de Bourgogne) 1988; American Chemical Soc. (ACS) Award in Inorganic Chem. 1975, Calif. Scientist of the Year Award 1983, Arthur C. Cope Scholar Award (ACS) 1986, Pauling Award 1990, ACS Award for Distinguished Service in the Advancement of Inorganic Chem. 1991, LAS Alumni Achievement Award, Coll. of Liberal Arts and Sciences Univ. of Ill. 1994, Marker Lecturer Medal 1999. *Publications:* Principles and Applications of Organo-transition Metal Chemistry (with Louis S. Hegedus) 1980, 1987, Naturally Dangerous 2001; and 300 scientific papers. *Leisure interest:* fishing. *Address:* Department of Chemistry, Stanford University, Stanford, CA 94305, USA (University); 794 Tolman Drive, Stanford, CA 94305-5080, USA (Home). *Telephone:* (650) 725-0283 (University); (650) 493-0934 (Home). *Fax:* (650) 725-0259 (Office). *E-mail:* jpc@stanford.edu (Office).

COLLOMB, Bertrand Pierre Charles, PhD; French business executive; b. 14 Aug. 1942, Lyon; s. of Charles Collomb and Hélène Traon; m. Marie-Caroline Collomb 1967; two s. one d.; ed Ecole Polytechnique, Paris, Univ. of Texas, Austin, U.S.A; worked with French Govt, f. and man. Center for Man. Research, Ecole Polytechnique 1972–75; joined Lafarge Coppée as Regional Man. 1975, later Pres. and CEO Ciments Lafarge France; CEO Orsan (Biotechnology Co. of the Lafarge Group) 1983; CEO Lafarge Corp. 1987–88; Vice-Chair. and CEO Lafarge 1989, Chair. and CEO 1989–; Pres. of Afep (Asscn of French Private Businesses) 2001–; Vice-Pres. L'Entreprise pour L'Environnement; mem. of ERT (Round Table of European Industrialists); Officier, Légion d'honneur. *Leisure interests:* horse riding, tennis, hunting. *Address:* Lafarge, 61 rue des Belles Feuilles - BP 40, 75782 Paris Cedex 16 (Office); 4 rue de Lota, 75116 Paris, France (Home). *Telephone:* 1-44-34-11-11 (Office); 1-45-53-02-86 (Home). *Fax:* 1-44-34-12-00. *E-mail:* bertrand.collomb@lafarge.com (Office). *Website:* www.lafarge.com.

COLLOR DE MELLO, Fernando; Brazilian politician; b. 1949, Rio de Janeiro; m. 1st Lilibeth Monteiro de Carvalho 1975 (divorced 1981); two s.; m. 2nd Rosane Malta 1984; ed Univ. of Brasília; joined family media group becoming Pres. in 1978; Mayor of Maceió, Alagoas state 1979; Fed. Deputy from Alagoas 1982; Gov. of Alagoas 1986; formed Nat. Reconstruction Party 1989; Pres. of Brazil 1990–92; found guilty of official misconduct and removed from office by the Senate Dec. 1992; charged with corruption June 1993; banned from political activity until year 2000; brought to trial Dec. 1994; acquitted of all charges by High Court Dec. 1994.

COLLUM, Hugh Robert, FCA; British business executive; b. 29 June 1940, Tavistock; m. Elizabeth Noel Stewart 1965; two d.; ed Eton Coll.; with Coopers & Lybrand 1959–64; Finance Dir Courage Ltd 1973–81; Deputy Finance Dir, Cadbury Schweppes PLC 1981–83, Finance Dir 1983–86; Finance Dir, Beecham PLC 1987–89, Exec. Vice-Pres. and Chief Financial Officer, SmithKline Beecham PLC 1989–98; Chair. Hundred Group of Finance Dirs 1990–92; Chair.. Chiroscience Group PLC 1998–99; Deputy Chair. Celltech Group PLC 2000–; Chair. British Nuclear Fuels PLC 1999–; Dir (non-exec.) Sedgwick Group PLC 1987–92, M & G Group PLC 1992–98, Ladbroke Group PLC 1994–96, Whitehead Mann Group PLC 1997–, Safeway PLC 1997–, Invensys PLC 1998–2002, South African Breweries PLC 1999–2002, Barclays Private Bank Advisory Board 2001–; mem. Cadbury Cttee on Financial Aspects of Corporate Governance 1991–95; Founding Soc. Award 2002. *Leisure interests:* sport, opera. *Address:* 65 Buckingham Gate, London, SW1W

6AP (Office); Clinton Lodge, Fletching, East Sussex, TN22 3ST, England (Home). *Telephone:* (20) 7222-9717 (Office); (1825) 722952 (Home). *Fax:* (20) 7799-3224 (Office); (1825) 723967 (Home).

COLMAN, Sir Michael Jeremiah, 3rd Bt, cr. 1907; British business executive; b. 7 July 1928, London; s. of Sir Jeremiah Colman, 2nd Bt and Edith Gwendolyn Tritton; m. Judith Jean Wallop (née William-Powlett) 1955; two s. three d.; ed Eton; Capt. Yorks Yeomanry 1967; Dir Reckitt and Colman PLC 1970–95, Chair. 1986–95; First Church Estates Commr 1993–99; Dir Foreign and Colonial Ventures Advisors Ltd 1988–99; Trade Affairs Bd Chemical Industries Asscn 1978–84, Council 1983–84; Council Mem. Royal Warrant Holders Asscn 1977–, Pres. 1984; mem. Gen. Council and Investment Cttee, King Edward's Hosp. Fund for London 1978–; Assoc. of Trinity House, mem. Lighthouse Bd 1985–94, Younger Brother 1994; mem. Bd UK Centre for Econ. and Environmental Devt 1985–99, Chair. 1996–99; mem. of the Court of Skinners' Co. 1985– (Master 1991–92); mem. Council of Scouts Asscn 1985–2000; Assoc. Trustee, St Mary's Hosp., London 1988–2000; Hon. LLD (Hull) 1993. *Leisure interests:* farming, shooting, forestry, golf. *Address:* Malshanger, Basingstoke, Hants., RG23 7EY (Home); 40 Chester Square, London, SW1W 9HT, England. *Telephone:* (1256) 780241 (Home).

COLMAN, Peter Malcolm, PhD, FAA, FTSE; Australian medical research scientist; b. 3 April 1944; s. of Clement Colman and Kathleen Colman; m. Anne Elizabeth Smith 1967; two s.; ed Univ. of Adelaide; Post-Doctoral Fellow Univ. of Oregon 1969–72, Deutsche Forschungsgemeinschaft, Max Planck Inst., Munich 1972–75; Queen Elizabeth II Fellow Univ. of Sydney 1975–77; consultant Univ. of Utah 1977; Prin. Investigator Nat. Health and Medical Research Council, Univ. of Sydney 1977–78, Officer, Commonwealth Scientific and Industrial Research (CSIRO) 1978–89; Non-Exec. Dir Biota Holdings Ltd 1985–91; Professorial Assoc., Univ. of Melbourne 1988–98, Professorial Fellow 1998–; Chief of Div. CSIRO Div. of Biomolecular Eng 1989–97; Dir Biomolecular Research Inst. 1991–2000; Adjunct Prof. La Trobe Univ. 1998–2001; Sr Prin. Research Fellow (NHMRC), Walter and Eliza Hall Inst. of Medical Research, Div. Head 2001–; Fellow Australian Acad. of Tech. Sciences and Eng.; Royal Soc. Victorian Medal 1986, Lemberg Medallist and lecturer, Australian Biochemical Soc. 1988, Burnet Medal, Australian Acad. of Science 1995, Australia Prize 1996. *Achievements:* co-discoverer of neuraminidase inhibitors as medicines for influenza virus infection. *Leisure interest:* music. *Address:* 74 Hotham Street, East Melbourne, Vic. 3002, Australia (Home).

COLOMBANI, Jean-Marie; French journalist; b. 7 July 1948, Dakar, Senegal; m. Catherine Sénès 1976; five c.; ed Lycée Hoche, Versailles, Lycée La Pérouse, Nouméa, New Caledonia, Univ. of Paris II-Assas, Univ. of Paris I Panthéon-Sorbonne, Inst. d'Etudes Politiques, Paris and Inst. d'Etudes Supérieures de Droit Public; journalist, ORTF, later Office of FR3, Nouméa 1973; Ed. Political Service, Le Monde 1977, Head of Political Service 1983, Ed.-in-Chief 1990, Deputy Editorial Dir 1991; Man. Dir S.A.–Le Monde March–Dec. 1994, Chair. of Bd and Dir of Publs Dec. 1994–; Chair. Advisory Council, Midi-Libre Group 2000–. *Publications:* Contradictions: entretiens avec Anicet Le Poro 1984, L'utopie calédonienne 1985, Portrait du président ou le monarque imaginaire 1985, Le mariage blanc (co-author) 1986, Questions de confiance: entretiens avec Raymond Barre 1987, Les héritiers (co-author), La France sans Mitterrand 1992, La gauche survivra-t-elle aux socialistes? 1994, Le Double Septennat de François Mitterrand, Dernier Inventaire (jtly) 1995, De la France en général et de ses dirigeants en particulier 1996, Le Résident de la République 1998, La Cinquième ou la République des phratries (jtly) 1999, Les infortunes de la Republique 2000, Tous Américains? 2002. *Leisure interest:* cinema. *Address:* Le Monde, 21 bis rue Claude Bernard, 75005 Paris (Office); 5 rue Joseph Bara, 75006 Paris, France (Home).

COLOMBO, Emilio; Italian politician; b. 11 April 1920; ed Rome Univ.; took active part in Catholic youth orgs.; fmr Vice-Pres. Italian Catholic Youth Asscn; Deputy, Constituent Assembly 1946–48, Parl. 1948–; Under-Sec. of Agriculture 1948–51, of Public Works 1953–55; Minister of Agriculture 1955–58, of Foreign Trade 1958–59, of Industry and Commerce 1959–60, March-April 1960, 1960–63, Feb.-May 1972; Prime Minister 1970–72; Minister without Portfolio in charge of Italian representation of UN 1972–73; Minister of Finance 1973–74, of the Treasury 1974–76, of Foreign Affairs 1980–83, 1992–93, of Budget and Econ. Planning 1987–88, of Finance 1988–89; 1976–80 (Pres. 1977–79); Pres. Nat. Cttee for Nuclear Research 1961; mem. Cen. Cttee Christian Democratic Party 1952, 1953. *Address:* Via Aurelia 239, Rome, Italy.

COLOMBO, John Robert, BA; Canadian editor, author and consultant; b. 24 March 1936, Kitchener, Ont.; m. Ruth F. Brown 1959; two s. one d.; ed Kitchener-Waterloo Collegiate Inst., Waterloo Coll. and Univ. Coll., Univ. of Toronto; editorial Asst Univ. of Toronto Press 1957–59; Asst Ed. The Ryerson Press 1960–63; Consulting Ed. McClelland & Stewart 1963–70, Ed.-at-Large 1963–; Gen. Ed. The Canadian Global Almanac 1992–2000; Centennial Medal 1967; Hon. DLitt (York Univ., Toronto) 1998; Order of Cyril and Methodius 1979; Esteemed Kt of Mark Twain 1979; Harbour Front Literary Prize 1985. *Publications:* over 150 books of poetry, prose, reference, science fiction anthologies and translations including Colombo's Canadian Quotations 1974, Colombo's Canadian References 1976, Colombo's Book of Canada 1978, Canadian Literary Landmarks 1984, 1,001 Questions about Canada 1986, Off Earth 1987, Colombo's New Canadian Quotations 1987, Mysterious Canada

1988, Extraordinary Experience 1989, Songs of the Great Land 1989, Mysterious Encounters 1990, The Dictionary of Canadian Quotations 1991, Mackenzie King's Ghost 1991, UFOs over Canada 1991, Dark Visions 1992, Worlds in Small 1992, The Mystery of the Shaking Tent 1993, Walt Whitman's Canada 1993, Luna Park 1994, Voices of Rama 1994, Canadian Global Almanac 1995, Close Encounters of the Canadian Kind 1995, Ghost Stories of Ontario 1995, Haunted Toronto 1996, Iron Curtains 1996, The New Consciousness 1997, Semi Certainties 1998, Weird Stories 1999, Ghosts in our Past 2000, The UFO Quote Book 2000, 1000 Questions about Canada 2001, Famous Lasting Words 2001, Only in Canada 2002, The Penguin Book of Canadian Jokes 2002, The Penguin Treasury of Popular Canadian Poems and Songs 2002. *Leisure interest:* reading. *Address:* 42 Dell Park Avenue, Toronto, Ont., M6B 2T6, Canada. *Telephone:* (416) 782-6853. *Fax:* (416) 782-0285. *E-mail:* jrc@ca.inter.net (Office). *Website:* www.colombo.ca (Home).

COLOMBO, Umberto, ScD; Italian public enterprise executive; b. 20 Dec. 1927, Livorno; s. of Eugenio Colombo and Maria Eminente Colombo; m. Milena Piperno 1951; two d.; ed Univ. of Pavia, Mass. Inst. of Tech., USA; Dir Montedison's G. Donegani Research Centre 1967–70, Dir-Gen. for Research and Corp. Strategies, Montedison 1971–78; Chair. Italian Atomic Energy Comm. 1979–82; Chair. ENEA (Italian Nat. Agency for New Tech., Energy and the Environment) 1982–93; Pres. European Science Foundation 1991; Minister for Univs. and Scientific Research 1993–94; Hon. Trustee Aspen Inst. of Humanistic Studies; fmr mem. Council, UN Univ.; fmr Chair. European Communities' Cttee on Science and Tech. (CODEST), UN Advisory Cttee on Science and Tech. for Devt, OECD Cttee on Scientific and Tech. Policy, European Industrial Research Man. Asscn; mem. Accademia Nazionale dei Lincei; Foreign mem. Swiss, Swedish, Japanese and U.S. Acads. of Eng Sciences, American Acad. of Arts and Sciences, Fellowship of Eng (UK); Conrad Schlumberger Prize 1958, Roncaglia Mari Prize 1977, Honda Prize for Ecotechnology 1984. *Publications:* (Co-Author): Beyond the Age of Waste 1976, WAES Report Italy 1978, La Speranza Tecnologica 1979, Il Secondo Pianeta 1982, Scienza e Tecnologia verso il XXI Secolo 1988, La Frontiere della Tecnologica 1990. *Leisure interests:* music, farming. *Address:* ENEA, Viale Regina Margherita 125, 00198 Rome (Office); Via San Martino ai Monti 26 *bis*, 00184 Rome, Italy (Home). *Telephone:* (06) 8541007 (Office); (06) 4827265 (Home).

COLOMER VIADEL, Vicente; Spanish professor; b. 30 April 1946, Valencia; s. of Antonio Colomer de Figueroa and Vicenta Viadel Haro; m. Carmen Zafra García 1981; two d.; ed Colegio Blay de Valencia, Colegio Cervantes de Valencia, Univ. Complutense de Madrid; Assoc. Prof. of Electricity and Magnetism, Univ. Complutense de Madrid 1978–79; Asst Prof., Univ. of Córdoba 1979, Head of Physics Dept 1979–84, Prof. 1980–, Rector 1984–90; Visiting Scientist, MIT 1980; Visiting Prof. Univ. de Paris-Sud 1983; Pres. Roger Garaudy 1992–; Dir Torre Calahorra Centre; Premio Extraordinario de doctorado; Visitante distinguido Univ. Córdoba, Argentina. *Publications:* 50 scientific papers on plasma physics and electromagnetism. *Leisure interests:* reading, travelling, solving mathematical problems. *Address:* Torre Calahorra, Puente Ramano s/n. 14009 Córdoba; Profesor Julian Rivera Tarraco 1 (El Brillante), 14012 Córdoba, Spain. *Telephone:* 293929; 282078. *Fax:* 202677.

COLSON, Charles Wendell, JD; American lay preacher and author; b. 16 Oct. 1931, Boston; s. of Wendell Colson and Inez Ducrow; m. 1st Nancy Billings 1953; two s. one d.; m. 2nd Patricia Hughes 1964; ed Brown Univ. and George Washington Univ.; Asst to Asst Sec. Navy 1955–56; admin. Asst to Senator L. Saltonstall 1956–61; Sr partner, Gadsby & Hannah 1961–69; Special Counsel to Pres. Nixon 1969–72; partner, Colson & Shapiro, Washington, DC 1973–74; received seven month gaol sentence for role in Watergate scandal; Assoc. Fellowship House, Washington 1975–76, Prison Fellowship 1976–; Distinguished Sr Fellow Coalition for Christian Colls. and Univs. 1997; Trustee Gordon Conwell Theological Seminary; recipient of several hon. degrees; Templeton Prize 1993 and other awards. *Radio:* "Breakpoint" (daily radio commentary). *Publications:* Born Again 1975, Life Sentence 1979, Crime and The Responsible Community 1980, Loving God 1983, Who Speaks for God? 1985, Kingdoms in Conflict 1987, Against the Night 1989, The God of Stones and Spiders 1990, Why America Doesn't Work (with J. Eckerd) 1991, The Body 1992, A Dance with Deception 1993, A Dangerous Grace 1994, Gideon's Torch 1995, Burden of Truth 1997, Evangelicals and Catholics Together (with R. Neuhaus) 1995, How Now Shall We Live (with N. Pearcey) 1999, Chuck Colson Speaks 2000, Answers to Your Kids' Questions 2000, Justice that Restores 2001. *Leisure interests:* writing, fishing. *Address:* Prison Fellowship, P.O. Box 17500, Washington, DC 20041, USA. *Telephone:* (703) 478-0100. *Fax:* (703) 834-3658.

COLSON, Elizabeth Florence, PhD; American anthropologist; b. 15 June 1917, Hewitt, Minn.; d. of Louis Henry Colson and Metta Damon Colson; ed Wadena Public High School, Univ. of Minnesota, Radcliffe Coll.; Sr Research Officer Rhodes-Livingstone Inst. 1946–47, Dir 1948–51; Sr lecturer Manchester Univ., UK 1951–53; Assoc. Prof. Goucher Coll. 1954–55; Assoc. Prof. and Research Assoc., Boston Univ. 1955–59; Prof. Brandeis Univ. 1959–63; Prof. Univ. of Calif., Berkeley 1964–84, Prof. Emer. June 1984–; Lewis Henry Morgan Lecturer, Univ. of Rochester 1973; Visiting Prof. Univ. of Zambia 1987; mem. NAS, American Acad. of Arts and Science; Fellow Center for Advanced Study in the Behavioral Sciences, Stanford Univ.; Fairchild Fellow Calif. Inst. of Technology; Hon. Fellow Royal Anthropological Soc., UK; Rivers Memorial Medal; Dr. hc (Brown, Rochester, Univ. of Zambia); Distinguished

Lecture, American Anthropological Asscn 1975; Faculty Research Lecture, Univ. of Calif. Berkeley 1983; Malinowski Distinguished Lecture, Soc. for Applied Anthropology 1984; Distinguished Africanist Award, AAAS 1988. *Publications:* Seven Tribes of British Central Africa, 1951, The Makah 1953, Marriage and the Family among the Plateau Tonga 1958, Social Organization of the Gwembe Tonga 1962, Social Consequences of Resettlement 1971, Tradition and Contract 1974, Autobiographies of three Pomo Women 1974; (with Thayer Scudder) Secondary Education and the Formation of an Elite 1980, People in Upheaval (Jt) 1987, (with Thayer Scudder) For Prayer and Profit 1988; (with Lenore Ralstrom and James Anderson) Voluntary Efforts in Decentralized Management 1983, The History of Nampeyo 1991. *Address:* c/o Department of Anthropology, University of California, Berkeley, CA 94720, USA. *Telephone:* (510) 642-3391; (510) 526-3743 (Home). *E-mail:* colson@sscl.berkeley.edu (Home).

COLTRANE, Robbie; British actor; b. 31 March 1950, Glasgow; m. Rhona Irene Gemmel 2000; one s. one d.; ed Glasgow School of Art; co-producer, Young Mental Health (documentary) 1973; co-writer and Dir Jealousy (BBC) 1992; Peter Sellers Comedy Award, Evening Standard 1990, Best Actor, Royal TV Soc. 1993, Best Actor, Broadcasting Press Guild 1993, Best Actor TV Series, British Acad. of Film and TV Arts 1993, 1994, 1995, Best Actor, Monte Carlo TV Festival 1994, Fipa d'Or for Best Actor, Nice Film and TV Festival 1995, Best Actor Film or Miniseries Nat. Cable Ace Awards (USA) 1996, Best Actor TV Series, Royal TV Soc.1996, Goldener Gong for Best Actor, German TV 1996. *Films include:* Mona Lisa, Subway Riders, Britannia Hospital, Defence of the Realm, Caravaggio, Eat The Rich, Absolute Beginners, The Fruit Machine, Slipstream, Nuns On The Run, Huckleberry Finn, Bert Rigby, You're A Fool, Danny, Champion of the World, Henry V, Let It Ride, The Adventures of Huckleberry Finn, Goldeneye, Buddy, Montana, Frogs for Snakes, Message in a Bottle, The World is Not Enough 1999, On the Nose 2000, From Hell 2000, Harry Potter and the Philosopher's Stone 2001, Harry Potter and the Chamber of Secrets 2002. *Stage appearances include:* Waiting for Godot, End Game, The Bug, Mr Joyce is Leaving, The Slab Boys, The Transfiguration of Benno Blimpie, The Loveliest Night of the Year, Snobs and Yobs, Your Obedient Servant (one-man show) 1987, Mistero Buffo 1990. *Television appearances include:* The Comic Strip Presents . . . ., Five Go Mad In Dorset, The Beat Generation, War, Summer School, Five Go Mad on Mescalin, Susie, Gino, Dirty Movie, The Miner's Strike, The Supergrass (feature film), The Ebb-tide, Alice in Wonderland, The Young Ones, Kick Up the Eighties, The Tube, Saturday Night Live, Lenny Henry Show, Blackadder, Tutti Frutti, Coltrane in a Cadillac, Cracker, Boswell and Johnson's Tour of the Western Isles 1990, The Plan Man 2003. *Publications:* Coltrane in a Cadillac 1992, Coltrane's Planes and Automobiles 1999. *Leisure interests:* sailing, film, vintage cars, music, art. *Address:* c/o CDA, 19 Sydney Mews, London, SW3 6HL, England. *Telephone:* (20) 7581-8111.

COLUMBUS, Chris; American film director and screenplay writer; b. 10 Sept. 1958, Spangler, Pa; s. of Alex Michael Columbus and Mary Irene Puskar; m. Monica Devereux 1983; two d.; ed New York Univ. Film School; wrote for and developed TV cartoon series Galaxy High School; f. own production co. 1942 Productions. *Screenplays include:* Reckless 1983, Gremlins 1984, The Goonies 1985, The Young Sherlock Holmes 1985, Only the Lonely 1991, Little Nemo: Adventures in Slumberland (jtly) 1992, Nine Months 1995. *Films directed include:* Adventures in Babysitting 1987, Heartbreak Hotel 1988, Home Alone 1990, Only the Lonely 1991, Home Alone 2: Lost in New York 1992, Mrs Doubtfire 1993, Nine Months (also producer) 1995, Jingle All the Way (also producer) 1996, Stepmom (also producer) 1998, (producer) Monkey Bone 1999, Bicentennial Man (also producer) 1999, Harry Potter and the Philosopher's Stone (also producer) 2001, Harry Potter and the Chamber of Secrets (also producer) 2002. *TV directed includes:* Amazing Stories, Twilight Zone, Alfred Hitchcock Presents (series). *Address:* c/o Beth Swofford, CAA, 9830 Wilshire Boulevard, Beverly Hills, CA 90212, USA.

COLVILLE OF CULROSS, 4th Viscount, cr. 1902; 14th Baron (Scotland), cr. 1604; 4th Baron (UK), cr. 1885; **John Mark Alexander Colville,** QC, MA; British judge; b. 19 July 1933; s. of the late Viscount Colville of Culross and Kathleen Myrtle Gale; m. 1st Mary Elizabeth Webb-Bowen 1958 (divorced 1973); four s.; m. 2nd Margaret Birgitta, Viscountess Davidson (née Norton) 1974; one s.; ed Rugby School, New Coll. Oxford; called to Bar, Lincoln's Inn 1960, Bencher 1986, QC 1978, a Recorder 1990–93, Circuit Judge 1993–99; Minister of State, Home Office 1972–74; UK Rep., UN Human Rights Comm. 1980–83, mem. UN Working Group on Disappeared Persons 1980–84 (Chair. 1981–84), Special Rapporteur on Human Rights in Guatemala 1983–86, mem. UN Human Rights Cttee 1996–; Dir Securities and Futures Authority (fmrly Securities Asscn) 1987–93; Chair. Mental Health Act Comm. 1983–88, Alcohol Educ. and Research Council 1984–90, Parole Bd for England and Wales 1988–92; author of reports for Govt on Prevention of Terrorism Act and Northern Ireland Emergency Powers Act 1986–93; Chair. Norwich Information and Tech. Centre 1983–85; Dir Rediffusion TV Ltd 1961–68, British Electric Traction Co. Ltd 1968–72, 1974–84 (Deputy Chair. 1980–81); mem. CBI Council 1982–84; Gov. BUPA 1990–93; mem. Royal Co. of Archers (Queen's Body Guard for Scotland); Hon. Fellow New Coll. Oxford; Hon. DCL (East Anglia). *Address:* House of Lords, London, SW1A 0PW, England.

COLVIN, Sir Howard Montagu, Kt, CVO, CBE, MA, FBA, FRHistS, FSA; British architectural historian; b. 15 Oct. 1919; s. of late Montagu Colvin; m. Christina E. Butler 1943; two s.; ed Trent Coll. and Univ. Coll. London (UCL); served in RAF 1940–46; Asst lecturer, UCL 1946–48; Fellow, St John's Coll.

Oxford 1948–87, now Emer., Tutor in History 1948–78, Librarian 1950–84; Reader in Architectural History, Univ. of Oxford 1965–87; Fellow, UCL 1974; mem. Historic Bldgs. Council for England 1970–84, Historic Bldgs. and Monuments Comm. 1984–85, Historic Bldgs. Advisory Cttee 1984–2001, Royal Comm. on Ancient and Historical Monuments of Scotland 1977–89, Royal Comm. on Historical Manuscripts 1981–88, Royal Fine Art Comm. 1962–72, Royal Comm. on Historical Monuments, England 1963–76, etc.; Hon. FRIBA; Hon. FSA (Scotland); Wolfson Literary Award 1978; D. Univ. (York) 1978. *Publications include:* The White Canons in England 1951, A Biographical Dictionary of English Architects 1660–1840 1954, The History of the King's Works (gen. and part author) 1963–82, A History of Deddington 1963, Building Accounts of King Henry III 1971, Unbuilt Oxford 1983, Calke Abbey, Derbyshire 1985, The Canterbury Quadrangle, St John's College, Oxford 1988, All Souls: an Oxford college and its buildings (with J. S. G. Simmons) 1989, Architecture and the After-Life 1991, A Biographical Dictionary of British Architects 1600–1840 1995, Essays in English Architectural History 1999; catalogues; articles in learned journals. *Leisure interest:* gardening. *Address:* 50 Plantation Road, Oxford, OX2 6JE, England. *Telephone:* (1865) 557460.

COLVIN, Marie Catherine, BA; American journalist; b. 12 Jan. 1956, New York; d. of William Joseph Colvin and Rosemarie Marrow; m. Patrick Bishop 1989 (divorced); ed Yale Univ.; with United Press Int. (UPI), New York and Washington, DC 1982–84, Paris Bureau Chief 1984–86; Middle East Corresp. Sunday Times, London 1986–96, Foreign Affairs Corresp. 1996–; Woman of the Year (for work in Timor-Leste), Women of the Year Foundation, London 2000, Courage in Journalism Award, Int. Women's Media Foundation, USA 2000, Journalist of the Year, USA Foreign Corresps.' Asscn 2001, Foreign Reporter of the Year, UK Press Awards 2001. *Television:* Behind the Myth: Yasser Arafat (BBC documentary). *Leisure interests:* sailing, reading. *Address:* c/o Sunday Times Foreign Desk, 1 Pennington Street, London, E1 9XW, England (Office). *Telephone:* (20) 7782-5701 (Office). *Fax:* (20) 7782-5050 (Office). *E-mail:* mariecolvin@hotmail.com (Home).

COLWELL, Rita Rossi, PhD; American professor of microbiology; b. 23 Nov. 1934, Mass.; d. of Louis Rossi and Louise DiPalma; m. Jack H. Colwell 1956; two d.; ed Purdue Univ. and Univ. of Wash.; Research Asst Drosophila Genetics Lab. Purdue Univ. 1956–57; Dept of Microbiology,Univ. of Wash. 1957–58; Predoctoral Assoc. Univ. of Washington 1959–60, Asst Research Prof. 1961–64; Asst Prof. of Biology Georgetown Univ. 1964–66, Assoc. Prof. 1966–72; Prof. of Microbiology Univ. of Md 1972–; Founding Dir Center of Marine Biotech. Univ. of Md 1987–91, Founding Dir Biotech. Inst. 1987–91, Pres. 1991–98; Dir Nat. Science Foundation 1998–; numerous professional appointments; 22 hon. doctorates; Gold Medal, Canterbury (UK) 1990, Purkinje Gold Award (Prague) 1991, MD Pate, Civic Award 1991, Barnard Medal, Col Univ. 1996; Gold Medal, Univ. of Calif. (LA) 2000; numerous other awards; elected to US Nat. Acad. of Science. *Publications:* 16 books, over 600 articles in journals, book chapters, abstracts. *Leisure interests:* gardening, sailing, jogging. *Address:* National Science Foundation, 4201 Wilson Boulevard, Suite 1205, Arlington, VA 22230 (Office); 5010 River Hill Road, Bethesda, MD 20816, USA (Home). *Telephone:* (703) 292-8000 (Office); (301) 229-5129 (Home). *Fax:* (703) 292-9232 (Office); (301) 320-2795 (Home). *E-mail:* rcolwell@nsf.gov (Office); colwell@umbi.umd.edu (Office). *Website:* www.nsf.gov (Office).

COMANECI, Nadia; Romanian gymnast; b. 12 Nov. 1961, Oneşti, Bacău County; d. of Gheorghe and Stefania-Alexandria Comaneci; m. Bart Connor 1996; ed Coll. of Physical Educ. and Sports, Bucharest; overall European champion Skien 1975, Prague 1977, Copenhagen 1979; overall Olympic champion, Montreal 1976, first gymnast to be awarded a 10; overall World Univ. Games Champion, Bucharest 1981; gold medals European Championships, Skien 1975 (vault, asymmetric bars, beam), Prague 1977 (bars), Copenhagen 1979 (vault, floor exercises), World Championships, Strasbourg 1978 (beam), Fort Worth 1979 (team title), Olympic Games, Montreal 1976 (bars, beam), Moscow (beam, floor), World Cup, Tokyo 1979 (vault, floor); World Univ. Games, Bucharest 1981 (vault, bars, floor and team title); silver medals European Championships, Skien 1975 (floor), Prague 1977 (vault), World Championships, Strasbourg 1978 (vault), Olympic Games, Montreal 1976 (team title), Moscow 1980 (individual all-round, team title), World Cup, Tokyo 1979 (beam); bronze medal Olympic Games, Montreal 1976 (floor); retd May 1984, Jr team coach 1984–89; granted refugee status in USA 1989; with Bart Connor Gymnastics Acad.; performs as dancer, gymnastics entertainer and promotes commercial products; Contributing Ed., "International Gymnast" magazine; UN Spokesperson for Int. Year of Volunteers 2001; Sportswomen of the Century Prize, Atheletic Sports Category 1999; Govt Excellence Diploma 2001. *Website:* www.radiocomaneci.com.

COMBS, Sean (Puff Daddy, P Diddy); American rap artist, producer and fashion designer; b. 1970, Harlem, New York; began career at Uptown (R & B label); talent spotter for artistes such as Jodeci and Mary J. Blige (q.v.); producer for Ma$e, Sting, MC Lyte, Faith Evans, The Lox, Mariah Carey (q.v.), the late Notorious BIG; f. Bad Boy Entertainment label; remixed and reworked songs by artists including Jackson 5, Sting, Goldie, Trent Reznor and The Police; co-producer (with Jimmy Page) of soundtrack to film Godzilla; created fashion collection under name Sean John 2001, opened flagship store in Manhattan 2002; charged with gun possession Dec. 1999, acquitted of gun possession and bribery 2001. *Recordings include:* I'll Be Missing You (with Faith Evans, Grammy Award for Best Rap Performance by a Duo or Group

1998), Been Around the World 1997, Roxanne, Can't Nobody Hold Me Down 1997, Victory 1998, Come With Me 1998, It's All About the Benjamins 1998, P.E. 2000. *Albums include:* No Way Out (Grammy Award for Best Rap Album 1998) 1997, Forever 1999. *Albums produced include:* Honey by Mariah Carey, Life After Death and Mo Money Mo Problems by Notorious Big, Cold Rock a Party by MC Lyte, Cupid by 112, Feel So Good by Ma$e.

COMENDANT, Grigory Ivanovich; Ukrainian ecclesiastic; b. 1946, Ukraine; ed Hamburg Theological Seminary; minister, Sr minister of Ukraine 1971–90; Chair. Union of Evangelic Christian Baptists 1990–; Chair. Bd of Union of Evangelic Christian Baptists, Pres. Fed. of Union of Evangelic Christian Baptists 1992–. *Address:* Union of Evangelic Christian Baptists, Trechsvyatski per. 3, 109028 Moscow, Russia. *Telephone:* (095) 917-51-61.

COMISKEY, Brendan, MSc, DD; Irish ecclesiastic; b. 13 Aug. 1935, Tasson, Co. Monaghan; ed Ireland and USA, post-graduate educ. Catholic Univ. of America, Lateran Univ., Rome, Trinity Coll. Dublin; teacher and Dean Damien High School, La Verne, Calif; Chair. of Dept Washington (DC) Theological Union; elected Prov., Anglo-Irish Prov. of the Congregation of the Sacred Hearts and Sec.-Gen. Conference of Maj. Religious Superiors 1974; Auxiliary Bishop of Dublin 1979–84, Bishop of Ferns 1984–2002; Chair. Bishops' Comm. for Communications; Pres. Catholic Communications Inst. of Ireland; mem. Nat. Episcopal Conf., Bishops' Comm. for Ecumenism, Comm. for Youth; Chaplain Int. Council of Alliance of Catholic Kts. 1999; Patron Wexford Festival Opera; Trustee St Patrick's Coll., Maynooth; Freeman Wexford Town 1990; Conventual Chaplain ad Honorem of Order of Malta. *Address:* c/o Bishop's House, Wexford, Ireland.

COMOLLI, Jean-Dominique, M.ECON.SC; French business executive and fmr public servant; b. 25 April 1948, Bougie, Algeria; s. of Ivan Comolli and Jacqueline Courtin; m. Catherine Delmas 1968; two s. one d.; ed Inst. d'Etudes Politiques, Paris, Ecole Nat. d'Admin; civil servant, Budget Dept, Ministry of Economy, Finance and Budget 1977–81, Minister of the Budget's Tech. Adviser to Cabinet, then Prime Minister's Tech. Adviser to Cabinet 1981–86, Asst Dir Budget Dept 1986–88, Prin. Pvt. Sec. to Minister of the Budget 1988–89, Dir.-Gen. Customs and Indirect Duties, Ministry of the Budget 1989–95; Chair. and CEO Soc. Nat. d'Exploitation Industrielle des Tabacs et Allumettes (Seita) 1993–99; Co-Chair. ALTADIS (cr. out of merger of Seita and Tabacalera) 1999–; Chevalier, Légion d'honneur, Chevalier, Ordre nat. du Mérite. *Address:* Altadis, 182–188 avenue de France, 75639 Paris Cedex 13 (Office); 23 avenue de l'Observatoire, 75006 Paris, France (Home). *Telephone:* 1-44-97-65-65 (Office). *Fax:* 1-44-97-62-43 (Office). *E-mail:* jean-dominique.comolli@altadis.com (Office). *Website:* www.altadis.com (Office).

COMPAGNON, Antoine Marcel Thomas; French university professor and writer; b. 20 July 1950, Brussels, Belgium; s. of Gen. Jean Compagnon and Jacqueline Terlinden; ed Lycée Condorcet, The Maret School, Washington, DC, USA, Prytanée Militaire, La Flèche, Ecole Polytechnique, Paris, Ecole Nationale des Ponts et Chaussées, Paris, Univ. of Paris VII; with Fondation Thiers and Research Attaché, Centre National de la Recherche Scientifique 1975–78; Asst Lecturer, Univ. of Paris VII 1975–80; Asst Lecturer, Ecole des Hautes Etudes en Sciences Sociales, Paris 1977–79; Lecturer, Ecole Polytechnique, Paris 1978–85; teacher at French Institute, London 1980–81; Lecturer, Univ. of Rouen 1981–85; Prof. of French, Columbia Univ., New York 1985–91; Visiting Prof., Univ. of Pa 1986, 1990; Prof., Univ. of Le Mans 1989–90; Blanche W Knopf Prof. of French and Comparative Literature, Columbia Univ. New York 1991–; Prof. Univ. of Paris IV-Sorbonne 1994–; Sec. Gen. Int. Asscn of French Studies 1989–; Guggenheim Fellow 1988; Visiting Fellow, All Souls Coll. Oxford 1994; Fellow American Acad. of Arts and Sciences 1997; Chevalier des Palmes académiques. *Publications:* La Seconde Main ou le travail de la citation 1979, Le Deuil antérieur 1979, Nous, Michel de Montaigne 1980, La Troisième République des lettres, de Flaubert à Proust 1983, Ferragosto 1985, critical edn of Marcel Proust, Sodome et Gomorrhe 1988, Proust entre deux siècles 1989, Les Cinq Paradoxes de la modernité 1990, Chat en poche: Montaigne et l'allégorie 1993, Connaissez-vous Brunetière? 1997, Le Démon de la théorie 1998; numerous articles on French literature and culture. *Address:* Columbia University, New York, NY 10027 (Office); 29 Claremont Avenue, New York, NY 10027, USA; 36 rue de Moscou, 75008 Paris, France (Home). *Telephone:* (212) 854-5528 (Office); (212) 222-2550 (Home, New York); 1-43-87-71-48 (Home, Paris). *Fax:* (212) 854-5863 (Office). *E-mail:* compagnon@columbia.edu (Office).

COMPAORÉ, Blaise; Burkinabè politician and army officer; fmr second in command to Capt. Thomas Sankara whom he overthrew in a coup in Oct. 1987; Chair. Popular Front of Burkina Faso and Head of Govt Oct. 1987–, Interim Head of State June–Dec. 1991, Pres. of Burkina Faso Dec. 1991–. *Address:* Office of the President, 03 BP 7030, Ouagadougou 03, Burkina Faso. *Telephone:* 30-66-30 (Office). *Fax:* 31-49-26. *Website:* www.primature.gov.bf (Office).

COMPER, Francis Anthony (Tony), BA; Canadian banker; b. 24 April 1945, Toronto, Ont.; m. Elizabeth Comper 1971; ed Univ. of Toronto; Vice-Pres., Systems Devt Bank of Montreal 1978–82, Sr Vice-Pres., Personal Banking 1982, Sr Vice-Pres. and Sr Operations Officer, Treasury Group 1982–84 and Man., London, UK Branch 1984–86 and Sr Marketing Officer, Corp. and Govt Banking 1986–87, Exec. Vice-Pres., Operation 1987–89, Chief Gen. Man. and COO 1989–90, Pres., COO and Dir 1990–99, Pres. CEO and Dir 1999, Chair., CEO and Dir 1999–; Chair. Capital Campaign for the Univ.

of Toronto 1997–2002; Hon. Chair. Bd of Govs. The Yee Hong Centre for Geriatric Care; Dir Harris Bancorp, Inc., Harris Trust and Savings Bank, Toronto, C. D. Howe Inst., C. D. Howe Memorial Foundation, Canadian Club, BMO Nesbitt Burns Inc., Catalyst, NY; Hon. D.Hum.Lit. (Mount Saint Vincent); Human Relations Award, Council of Christians and Jews 1998. *Leisure interests:* golf, tennis, theatre, arts, reading. *Address:* Bank of Montreal, First Bank Tower, First Canadian Place, Toronto, Ont., M5X 1A1, Canada (Office). *Telephone:* (416) 867-7650 (Office); (416) 923-1161 (Home). *Fax:* (416) 867-7061.

COMPTON, Rt Hon John George Melvin, PC, L.L.B.; Saint Lucia politician; b. 1926, Canouan, St Vincent and the Grenadines; m.; five c.; ed London School of Econs; called to the Bar (Gray's Inn); pvt. practice in St Lucia 1951–; ind. mem. Legis. Council 1954; joined Labour Party 1954; Minister for Trade and Production 1957; Deputy Leader Labour Party 1957–61; resgnd 1961; formed Nat. Labour Movt 1961 (later became United Workers' Party); Leader, United Workers' Party 1964; Chief Minister of St Lucia 1964, Premier 1967–79, Prime Minister Feb.-July 1979, 1982–96, also Minister of Foreign Affairs, Planning and Finance 1982–88, of Planning, Finance, Statistics, Devt and Home Affairs 1988–92, of Finance, Planning and Devt 1992–96, Sr Minister 1996–97. *Address:* P.O. Box 149, Castries, Saint Lucia.

CONDE CONDE, Mario; Spanish businessman; b. 14 Sept. 1948, Tuy, Pontevedra; m. Lourdes Arroyo; two s.; ed Univ. of Deusto; Head State Law Dept, Toledo 1973, Head of Studies Gen. State Admin. Ministry of Finance 1974–76; Man. Dir and Co. Sec. various family cos. 1976–81; set up own law firm 1981; Vice-Pres. and Man. Dir Antibióticos SA Group 1983–87; Pres. Penibérica SA 1984–87, Inst. of Biology and Serum Therapy IBAS SA 1985–87; Vice-Pres. Alergia e Inmunología SA 1986–87; Pres. Banco Español de Crédito (Banesto) 1987–93; Pres. Unión y el Fénix Español SA, La Corporación Industrial y Financiera de Banesto; mem. Bd Hidroeléctrica Española, Petróleos del Mediterráneo (Petromed); mem. Admin. Bd and Exec. Bd Montedison; Perm. mem. Gen. Comm. for Codification; Gov. Foundation for the Support of Culture; Mercurio de oro "ad personam" 1987, Encomienda de Número de la Orden del Mérito Agrícola; indicted on charges of embezzling funds 1996, convicted March 1997, sentenced to six years' imprisonment, charged with fraud Dec. 1997, sentenced to ten years' imprisonment for fraud March 2000. *Publication:* El Sistema 1994.

CONDE de SARO, Francisco Javier, M.L.; Spanish diplomatist; b. 13 March 1946, Madrid; s. of Francisco Javier Conde and María Jesús de Saro; m. Ana Martínez de Irujo; one s. two d.; ed Univ. of Madrid, Diplomatic School, Madrid; Dir-Gen. for Int. Econ. Relations, Ministry of Foreign Affairs 1971; Asst Dir-Gen. for Int. Relations, Directorate of Maritime Fisheries 1976; Dir of Political Affairs for Africa and Asia, Ministry of Foreign Affairs 1978; counsellor Ministry of Transport, Tourism and Communications 1978; Econ. and Commercial Counsellor, Spanish Embassy, Rabat 1979–83, Buenos Aires 1983–86; Dir-Gen. Juridical and Institutional Co-ordination, Sec. of State for EU, Ministry of Foreign Affairs 1986–90, Sec.-Gen. 1994; Amb. of Spain to Algeria 1990–94; Perm. Rep. to NATO 1996–2000; Perm. Rep. to EU 2000–; Kt Commdr of Civil Merit (Spain), of Isabel la Católica (Spain), of Mayo Order (Argentina), of Order of the Lion (Senegal); Kt of Order of El Ouissam El Mohammadi (Morocco); Grand Cross for Naval Merit (Spain), Grand Cross of Merit (Austria). *Address:* 52 Boulevard du Régent, 1000 Brussels (Office); 26 Drève des Rhododendrons, 1170 Brussels, Belgium (Home). *Telephone:* (2) 509-86-01/2/3 (Office); (2) 660-20-12 (Home). *Fax:* (2) 511-26-30 (Office).

CONDON, Baron (Life Peer), cr. 2001, of Langton Green in the County of Kent; **Paul Leslie Condon,** Kt, QPM, DL, CCMI (CIMgt), FRSA; British police officer; b. 1 Jan. 1946, Dorset; m.; two s. one d.; ed St Peter's Coll. Oxford; joined Metropolitan Police 1967, Insp. 1975–78, Chief Insp. 1978–81; Superintendent, Bethnal Green 1981–82; Staff Officer to Commr as Superintendent, then as Chief Superintendent 1982–84; Asst Chief Constable of Kent 1984–87; Deputy Asst Commr Metropolitan Police 1987–88, Asst Commr 1988–89; Chief Constable of Kent 1989–92; Commr, Metropolitan Police 1993–2000; Dir Anti-Corruption Unit, Int. Cricket Council 2000–; Dir (non-exec.) Securicor PLC 2000–. *Address:* c/o ICC, The Clock Tower, Lord's Cricket Ground, London, NW8 8QN, England.

CONDOR, Sam Terence, BA; Saint Christopher and Nevis politician and businessman; b. 4 Nov. 1949; m.; one s. two d.; ed Ruskin Coll., Oxford, Univ. of Sussex, UK; printer, Saint Christopher and Nevis Govt Printery 1967–82; Sr Clerk, Inland Revenue Dept 1980–82; Man. Dir Quality Foods Ltd 1986–95; MP 1989–; Deputy Prime Minister, Minister of Trade, Industry, Caricom Affairs, Youth, Sports and Community Devt 1995–99, Deputy Prime Minister, Minister of Foreign Affairs, Int. Trade and Caricom Affairs, Community and Social Devt and Gender Affairs 2000–01; Deputy Prime Minister and Minister of CARICOM Affairs, Int. Trade, Labour, Social Security, Telecommunications and Tech. 2001–; Vice-Chair. Young Labour 1980–82, Deputy Leader Saint Christopher and Nevis Labour Party 1990–; mem. Saint Christopher and Nevis Tourist Bd 1975–78; Nat. Football Player 1969–72, Man. and Coach Nat. Football Team 1986–88; Margaret Marsh Prize for Most Outstanding Overseas Student, Ruskin Coll. 1979–80. *Address:* Office of Deputy Prime Minister and Minister of Foreign Affairs, Church Street, P.O. Box 186, Basseterre (Office); North Pelican Drive, Bird Rock, Saint Christopher, Saint Christopher and Nevis, West Indies (Home). *Telephone:* 465-2521 (Office); 465-1545 (Home). *Fax:* 465-1778 (Office). *E-mail:* mintica@caribsurf.com (Office).

CONLON, James, BMus; American conductor; b. 18 March 1950, New York; s. of Joseph and Angeline Conlon; m. Jennifer Ringo; two d.; ed High School of Music and Art, New York and Juilliard School; fmr faculty mem. Juilliard School of Music; since making début with New York Philharmonic has conducted every major U.S. orchestra and many leading European orchestras; Conductor New York Philharmonic Orchestra 1974–, Metropolitan Opera, New York 1976–; début at Metropolitan Opera 1976, Covent Garden 1979, Paris Opéra 1982, Lyric Opera of Chicago 1988, La Scala, Milan 1993–, Kirov Opera 1994–; Music Dir Cincinnati May Festival 1979–, Berlin Philharmonic Orchestra 1979–, Rotterdam Philharmonic Orchestra 1983–91; Musical Adviser to Dir Paris Opera 1995– (Prin. Conductor 1996–); conducted opening of Maggio Musicale, Florence 1985; Chief Conductor, Cologne Opera 1989; Gen. Music Dir City of Cologne 1990–; has conducted at major int. music festivals and with numerous leading orchestras; numerous recordings of works by Mozart, Liszt, Poulenc etc; Grand Prix du Disque for recording of Poulenc Piano Concertos (Erato); Officier, des Arts et des Lettres 1996–. *Address:* Shumen Associates, 120 W 58th Street, New York, NY 10019, USA.

CONNELL, HE Cardinal Desmond; Irish ecclesiastic; b. 24 March 1926, Dublin; ordained priest 1951; Archbishop of Dublin 1988–; cr. Cardinal 2001. *Address:* Archbishop's House, Drumcondra, Dublin 9, Republic of Ireland (Office). *Telephone:* (1) 8373732 (Office). *Fax:* (1) 8369796 (Office).

CONNELL, Elizabeth, BMus; Irish opera singer; b. 22 Oct. 1946, Port Elizabeth, South Africa; d. of the late (Gordon) Raymond Connell and (Maud) Elizabeth Connell (née Scott); ed Univ. of the Witwatersrand and Johannesburg Coll. of Educ., SA and London Opera Centre; début at Wexford Festival, Ireland as Varvara in Katya Kabanova 1972; Australian Opera 1973–75; English Nat. Opera 1975–80; début Royal Opera House, Covent Garden, London as Viclinda in I Lombardi 1976; Ortrud in Lohengrin, Bayreuth Festival 1980; Electra in Idomeneo, Salzburg Festival 1984; début Metropolitan Opera, New York as Vitellia in La Clemenza di Tito 1985; début Vienna State Opera as Elisabeth in Tannhäuser 1985; début Glyndebourne, England as Electra in Idomeneo 1985; début La Scala, Milan as Ortrud in Lohengrin 1981; sang full range of dramatic mezzo repertoire until 1983 when moved into dramatic soprano field; sings worldwide, freelance in opera, oratorio, concert and recital work; Maggie Teyte Prize 1972. *Leisure interests:* reading, theatre, concerts, cooking, embroidery, writing and composing. *Address:* c/o Connaught Artists' Management, 2 Molasses Row, Plantation Wharf, London, England (Office).

CONNELLY, Jennifer; American actress; b. 12 Dec. 1970; d. of Gerard Connelly and Eileen Connelly; m. Paul Bettany 2002; one s. with David Dugan; ed Saint Ann's School, Brooklyn, Yale Univ. and Stanford Univ.; fmr. model. *Films include:* Once Upon A Time in America 1984, Il mondo dell'orrore di Dario Argento 1985, Seven Minutes in Heaven 1985, The Valley 1985, Phenomena 1985, Labyrinth 1986, Inside the Labyrinth 1986, Some Girls 1988, Etoile 1988, The Hot Spot 1990, Career Opportunities 1991, The Rocketeer 1991, Of Love and Shadows 1994, Higher Learning 1995, Far Harbor 1996, Mulholland Falls 1996, Inventing the Abbotts 1997, Dark City 1998, Requiem for a Dream 2000, A Beautiful Mind (Acad. Award, BAFTA Award and Golden Globe Award for Best Supporting Actress 2002) 2001, Pollock 2001, The Hulk 2003. *TV appearances include:* Tales of the Unexpected 1984, The $treet 2001. *Single:* Monologue of Love (in Japanese). *Leisure interests:* hiking, camping, swimming, bike riding, quantum physics, philosophy. *Address:* c/o International Creative Management, 8942 Wilshire Boulevard, Beverly Hills, CA 90211, USA (Office).

CONNERY, Sir Sean, Kt; Scottish actor; b. 25 Aug. 1930; s. of Joseph and Euphamia Connery; m. 1st Diane Cilento 1962 (divorced 1974); one s. one step-d.; m. 2nd Micheline Boglio Roquebrun 1975; served in Royal Navy; Dir Tantallon Films Ltd 1972–; Hon.D.Litt. (Heriot-Watt) 1981, (St Andrew's) 1988; Acad. Award, Best Supporting Actor 1988; Fellow, Royal Scottish Acad. of Music and Drama 1984; Freeman City of Edinburgh 1991; mem. Scottish Nat. Party 1992–; Commdr des Arts et des Lettres 1987, American Cinematique Award 1991, Rudolph Valentino Award 1992, Nat. Board of Review Award, Légion d'honneur, BAFTA Lifetime Achievement Award 1990, BAFTA Fellowship 1998; numerous awards and prizes. *Films include:* No Road Back 1955, Time Lock 1956, Action of the Tiger 1957, Another Time, Another Place, Hell Drivers, 1958, Darby O'Gill and the Little People 1959, Tarzan's Greatest Adventure 1959, On the Fiddle 1961, The Longest Day 1962, The Frightened City 1962, Woman of Straw 1964, Marnie 1964, The Hill 1965, A Fine Madness 1966, Shalako 1968, The Molly Maguires 1968, The Red Tent 1969, The Anderson Tapes 1970, The Offence 1973, Zardoz 1974, Murder on the Orient Express 1974, Ransom 1974, The Wind and the Lion 1975, The Man Who Would Be King 1975, Robin and Marian 1976, A Bridge Too Far 1977, The Great Train Robbery 1978, Meteor 1978, Cuba 1979, Outland 1981, The Man with the Deadly Lens 1982, The Untouchables 1986, The Name of the Rose 1987, The Presidio 1988, Rosencrantz and Guildenstern are Dead, A Small Family Business, Indiana Jones and the Last Crusade 1989, Hunt for Red October 1989, The Russia House 1989 (BAFTA Award 1990), Mutant Ninja Turtles 1990, Highlander 2 1990, Medicine Man 1992, Rising Sun 1993, A Good Man in Africa 1994, First Knight 1994, Just Cause 1994, The Rock 1996, Dragonheart 1996, The Avengers 1998, Entrapment 1999, Playing By Heart 1999, Finding Forrester 2000; as James Bond in Dr. No 1963, From Russia with Love 1964, Goldfinger 1965, Thunderball 1965, You Only Live Twice 1967, Diamonds are Forever 1971, Never Say Never Again 1983.

Publication: Neither Shaken Nor Stirred 1994. *Leisure interests:* golf, tennis, reading. *Address:* c/o Creative Artists Agency Inc., 9830 Wilshire Boulevard, Beverly Hills, CA 90212, USA (Office).

CONNICK, Harry, Jr.; American jazz musician, actor and singer; b. 1968, New Orleans, La.; m. Jill Goodacre 1994; ed New Orleans Center for the Creative Arts, Hunter Coll. and Manhattan School of Music; studied with Ellis Marsalis; Grammy Award. *Albums include:* Harry Connick Jr 1987, 20 1989, We Are In Love 1991, Lofty's Roach Soufflé 1991, Blue Light, Red Light 1991, Eleven 1992, 25 1992, When My Heart Finds Christmas 1993, She 1994, Star Turtle 1996, To See You 1997, Come By Me 1999; contrib. to music for film When Harry Met Sally; composed music for Thou Shalt Not (Broadway) 2001. *Films include:* Memphis Belle, Little Man Tate 1991, Independence Day, Excess Baggage, Hope Floats; Band Leader Harry Connick's Big Band. *Address:* Wilkins Managment Inc., 323 Broadway, Cambridge, MA 02139 (Office); Columbia Records, c/o Anita Nanko, 51/12, 550 Madison Avenue, P.O. Box 4450, New York, NY 10101, USA.

CONNOLLY, Billy; British comedian, actor, playwright and presenter; b. 24 Nov. 1942; m. 1st Iris Connolly (dissolved 1985); one s. one d.; m. 2nd Pamela Stephenson 1990; three d.; worked as apprentice welder; performed originally with Gerry Rafferty and The Humblebums; first play, The Red Runner, staged at Edinburgh Fringe 1979; Hon. DLitt (Glasgow) 2001. *Theatre:* The Great Northern Welly Boot Show, The Beastly Beatitudes of Balthazar B 1982. *Television includes:* Androcles and the Lion 1984, Return to Nose and Beak (Comic Relief), South Bank Show Special (25th Anniversary Commemoration) 1992, Billy, Billy Connolly's World Tour of Scotland (6 part documentary) 1994, The Big Picture 1995, Billy Connolly's World Tour of Australia 1996, Erect for 30 Years 1998, Billy Connolly's World Tour of England, Ireland and Wales 2002, Gentleman's Relish. *Films include:* Absolution 1979, Bullshot 1984, Water 1984, The Big Man 1989, Pocahontas 1995, Treasure Island (Muppet Movie) 1996, Deacon Brodie (BBC Film) 1996, Mrs Brown 1997, Ship of Fools 1997, Paws 1997, Still Crazy 1998, Debt Collector 1998, Boon Docksaints 1998, Beautiful Joe 2000, An Everlasting Piece 2000, The Man Who Sued God, White Oleander, Gabriel and Me 2002; numerous video releases of live performances including Bite Your Bum 1981 (Music Week and Record Business Award 1982), An Audience with Billy Connolly 1982. *Albums include:* The Great Northern Welly Boot Show (contains no. 1 hit DIVORCE), Pick of Billy Connolly (Gold Disc) 1982. *Publications include:* Gullible's Travels 1982. *Address:* c/o Tickety-boo Limited, The Boathouse, Crabtree Lane, London, SW6 6TY, England. *Telephone:* (20) 7610-0122. *Fax:* (20) 7610-0133. *E-mail:* tickety-boo@tickety-boo.com (Home). *Website:* www.billyconnolly.com.

CONNOR, Joseph E., AB, MS; American international official and accountant; b. 23 Aug. 1931, New York; s. of Joseph E. Connor; m. 1st Cornelia B. Camarata 1958 (died 1983); two s. one d.; m. 2nd Sally Howard Johnson 1992; ed Univ. of Pittsburgh and Columbia Univ.; joined Price Waterhouse & Co., New York 1956, Partner 1967–, Man. Partner, Western region, Los Angeles 1976–78, Chair. Policy Bd 1978–88, Chair. World Firm 1988–92; Pres. ICC 1990–92; Under-Sec. Gen. UN, New York 1994–; Distinguished Prof. of Business, Georgetown Univ. 1992–94; Consultant Foreign Direct Investment Program, US Dept of Commerce; Chair. US Council for Int. Business 1987–. *Address:* United Nations, United Nations Plaza, New York, NY 10021, USA.

CONNORS, James Scott (Jimmy); American tennis player; b. 2 Sept. 1952, Belleville, Ill.; s. of James Scott Connors I and Gloria Thompson Connors; m. Patti McGuire 1978; one s. one d.; ed Univ. of California at Los Angeles; amateur player 1970–72, professional since 1972; Australian Champion 1974; Wimbledon Champion 1974, 1982; USA Champion 1974, 1976, 1978, 1982, 1983; SA Champion 1973, 1974; WCT Champion 1977, 1980; Grand Prix Champion 1978; commentator for NBC; played Davis Cup for USA 1976, 1981; ranked World Number 1 for a record 157 weeks; won 109 tournament titles; BBC Overseas Sports Personality 1982. *Leisure interest:* golf. *Address:* Tennis Management Inc., 109 Red Fox Road, Belleville, IL 62223; RHB Ventures, 1320 18th Street, NW, Suite 100, Washington DC 20036, USA.

CONOMBO, Joseph Issoufou; Burkinabè fmr politician; b. 9 Feb. 1917, Kombissiri, Upper Volta (now Burkina Faso); s. of Ousman Conombo and Tassombedo Timpoko; m. 2nd Genevieve Nuninger di Illfurth 1978; two s. three d.; ed Ecole Primaire et Supérieure, Bingerville, Ecole Normale "William Ponty", Dakar, Senegal; participated in World War II; Co-founder of Union Voltaïque 1946; medical practitioner 1946–48; Consultant to Union Française 1948–51; Del. to Assemblée Nat. in Paris 1951–59; mem. Nat. Ass. 1952–80; Mayor of Ouagadougou 1960–65; Dir-Gen. for Public Health 1966–68; Minister of Foreign Affairs 1971–73; Prime Minister 1978–80; Sec. Gen. for Overseas Relations Asscn Seuloguin-Developpement, Kombissiri Prov.; mem. Rassemblement Démocratique Africain 1959–80; Pres. Upper Volta Red Cross Soc. 1961–80. *Publications:* M'Ba Tinga 1989, Souvenirs de guerre d'un Tirailleur Sénégalais 1989, Bouda François Timpiga de Manga 1995. *Address:* 2033 Avenue de la Liberté, BP 613, Ouagadougou, Burkina Faso. *Telephone:* 334912.

CONQUEST, (George) Robert (Acworth), CMG, OBE, MA, DLitt, FBA, FRSL; British/American author and scholar; b. 15 July 1917, Malvern, England; s. of Robert F.W. Conquest and Rosamund A. Acworth; m. 1st Joan Watkins 1942 (divorced 1948); two s.; m. 2nd Tatiana Milhailova 1948 (divorced 1962); m. 3rd Caroleen Macfarlane 1964 (divorced 1978); m. 4th Elizabeth Neece 1979; ed Winchester Coll., Univ. of Grenoble and Magdalen Coll. Oxford; mil. service 1939–46; HM Foreign Service 1946–56; Sydney and Beatrice Webb Research Fellow, London School of Econs 1956–58; Visiting Poet, Univ. of Buffalo 1959–60; Literary Ed. The Spectator 1962–63; Sr Fellow, Columbia Univ. Russian Inst. 1964–65; Fellow, Woodrow Wilson Int. Center, Washington, DC 1976–77; Sr Research Fellow, Hoover Inst. Stanford Univ. 1977–79, 1981–; Distinguished Visiting Fellow, Heritage Foundation 1980–81; Adjunct Fellow Center for Strategic and Int. Studies 1983–. *Publications:* Power and Policy in the USSR 1961, The Great Terror 1968, V.I. Lenin 1972, Kolyma: The Arctic Death Camps 1978, The Harvest of Sorrow 1986, New and Collected Poems 1988, Tyrants and Typewriters 1989, The Great Terror Reassessed 1990, Stalin: Breaker of Nations 1991, Demons Don't 1999, Reflections on a Ravaged Century 1999. *Address:* c/o Hoover Institution, Stanford, CA 94305; 52 Peter Coutts Circle, Stanford, CA 94305, USA (Home). *Telephone:* (650) 723-1647. *Fax:* (650) 723-1687.

CONRAD, Donald Glover, BS, MBA; American insurance company executive; b. 23 April 1930, St Louis; s. of Harold Armin and Velma Glover (Morris) Conrad; m. M. Stephania Shimkus 1980; one d. one step-d.; one s. two d. by previous marriage; ed Wesleyan and Northwestern Univs. and Univ. of Michigan; with Exxon Co. 1957–70; Financial Adviser, Esso Natural Gas, The Hague, Netherlands 1965–66, Treasurer Esso Europe, London 1966–70; Sr Vice-Pres. Aetna Life & Casualty Co., Hartford, Conn. 1970–72, fmr Exec. Vice-Pres. and Dir; Dir Terra Nova Insurance Co., Federated Investors Inc.; owner Hartford Whalers Hockey Club 1988–92; US Senate Vice-Chair. Ind. Energy Corpn 1989–; Sr Adviser to the Pres., World Bank 1995–; mem. Bd and Exec. Cttee, American Council for the Arts. *Address:* The World Bank, 1818 H Street, NW, Washington, DC 20433, USA (Office). *Telephone:* (202) 477-1234 (Office). *Fax:* (202) 477-6391 (Office). *E-mail:* pic@worldbank.org (Office). *Website:* www.worldbank.org (Office).

CONRAD, Kent, MBA; American politician; b. 12 March 1948, Bismarck, ND; m. Lucy Calautti 1987; one d.; ed Univ. of Missouri, Stanford Univ. and George Washington Univ.; Asst to tax Commr State of ND Tax Dept Bismarck 1974–80, tax Commr 1981–86; Senator from North Dakota 1987–; Chair. Budget Cttee 2001–; Democrat. *Address:* US Senate, 530 Hart Senate Office Bldg, Washington, DC 20510-0001, USA.

CONRAN, Jasper Alexander Thirlby; British fashion designer; b. 12 Dec. 1959, London; s. of Sir Terence Conran (q.v.) and Shirley Conran (q.v.); ed Bryanston School, Dorset, Parsons School of Art and Design, New York; Fashion Designer, Man. Dir Jasper Conran Ltd 1978–; designer of lines for Debenhams 1997–; theatre costumes, Jean Anouilh's The Rehearsal, Almeida Theatre 1990, My Fair Lady 1992; Sleeping Beauty, Scottish Ballet 1994, The Nutcracker Sweeties, Birmingham Royal Ballet 1996, Edward II 1997, Arthur 2000; Fil d'Or (Int. Linen Award) 1982, 1983, British Fashion Council Designer of the Year Award 1986–87, Fashion Group of America Award 1987, Laurence Olivier Award for Costume Designer of the Year 1991, British Collections Award (in British Fashion Awards) 1991. *Address:* Jasper Conran Ltd, 6 Burnsall Street, London, SW3, England. *Telephone:* (20) 7352-3572.

CONRAN, Shirley Ida; British designer and author; b. 21 Sept. 1932; d. of Ida and W Thirlbey Pearce; m. 1st Sir Terence Conran (q.v.) (divorced 1962); two s.; m. 2nd; m. 3rd; ed St Paul's Girls' School and Portsmouth Art Coll.; Press Officer, Asprey Suchy (jewellers) 1953–54; Publicity Adviser to Conran Group Cos. 1955; org. and designed several kitchen and design exhbns.; ran Conran Fabrics Ltd 1957; started Textile Design Studio 1958; Home Ed., Daily Mail 1962, Women's Ed. 1968; Women's Ed. The Observer Colour Magazine and contrib. to Woman's Own 1964; Fashion Ed. The Observer 1967, columnist and feature writer 1969–70; columnist Vanity Fair 1970–71, Over 21 1972; has made numerous TV and radio appearances. *Publications:* Superwoman 1974, Superwoman Yearbook 1975, Superwoman in Action 1977, Futures 1979, Lace 1982, The Magic Garden 1983, Lace 2 1984, Savages (novel) 1987, Down with Superwoman 1990, The Amazing Umbrella Shop 1990, Crimson 1991, Tiger Eyes 1994, The Revenge of Mimi Quinn 1998. *Leisure interests:* long distance swimming, yoga. *Address:* c/o Simon & Schuster UK Ltd, Africa House, 64–78 Kingsway, London, WC2B 6AH, England (Office).

CONRAN, Sir Terence Orby, Kt; British designer and retailing executive; b. 4 Oct. 1931, Esher, Surrey; s. of Rupert Conran and Christina Halstead; m. 1st Brenda Davison (divorced); m. 2nd Shirley Conran (q.v.) (divorced 1962); two s.; m. 3rd Caroline Herbert 1963 (divorced 1996); two s. one d.; m. 4th Vicki Davis 2000; ed Bryanston School and Cen. School of Art and Design, London; Chair. Conran Holdings Ltd 1965–68; Jt Chair. Ryman Conran Ltd 1968–71; Chair. Habitat Group Ltd 1971–88, Habitat/Mothercare PLC 1982–88; Chair. Habitat France SA 1973–88, Conran Stores Inc. 1977–88, J. Hepworth & Son Ltd 1981–83 (Dir 1979–83), Richard Shops 1983; Chair. Storehouse PLC 1986–90, CEO 1986–88, non-exec. Dir 1990; Chair. The Conran Shop Ltd 1976–, Conran Roche 1980–, Jasper Conran 1982–, Butlers Wharf 1984–90, Bibendum Restaurant 1986–, Benchmark Ltd 1989–, Blueprint Café 1989–, Terence Conran Ltd 1990–, Conran Holdings 1990–, The Conran Shop SNC 1990–, Le Pont de la Tour 1991–, Quaglino's Restaurant Ltd 1991–, The Butler's Wharf Chop House Ltd 1992–; CD Partnership 1993–, Conran Restaurants Ltd 1994–, Bluebird Store Ltd 1994–, Mezzo Ltd 1995–, Conran Shop Marylebone 1995–, Conran Shop Germany 1996–, Coq d'Argent Ltd 1997–, Orrery Ltd 1997–; Vice-Pres. FNAC 1985–89; Dir Conran Ink Ltd 1969–, The Neal Street Restaurant 1972–89, Electra Risk Capital 1981–84,

Conran Octopus Ltd 1983–, Heal & Son Ltd 1983–87, Savacentre 1986–88, British Home Stores 1986–88, Michelin House Investment Co. Ltd 1989–; f. Conran Foundation, Butler's Wharf; launched Content by Conran range of furniture for Christie Tyler 2003; mem. Royal Comm. on Environmental Pollution 1973–76; mem. Council, Royal Coll. of Art 1978–81, 1986–; mem. Advisory Council, Victoria & Albert Museum 1979–83, Trustee 1984–90; Trustee Design Museum 1989–, Chair. 1992–; mem. Creative Leaders' Network; Dr hc (RCA) 1996, Hon. DLitt (Portsmouth) 1996; RSA Bicentenary Medal 1982, Commdr Ordre des Arts et des Lettres 1991 and other awards for design. *Publications:* The House Book 1974, The Kitchen Book 1977, The Bedroom & Bathroom Book 1978, The Cook Book (with Caroline Conran) 1980, The New House Book 1985, The Conran Directory of Design 1985, The Soft Furnishings Book 1986, Plants at Home 1986, Terence Conran's France 1987, Terence Conran's D.I.Y. by Design 1989, D.I.Y. in the Garden 1991, Terence Conran's Toys and Children's Furniture 1992, Terence Conran's Kitchen Book 1993, The Essential House Book 1994, Terence Conran on Design 1996, The Essential Garden Book 1998, Easy Living 1999, Chef's Garden 1999, Terence Conran on Restaurants 1999, Terence Conran on London 2000; Q and A: A Sort of Autobiography 2001, Terence Conran on Small Spaces 2001. *Leisure interests:* gardening, cooking. *Address:* 22 Shad Thames, London, SE1 2YU, England. *Telephone:* (20) 7378-1161. *Fax:* (20) 7403-4309. *Website:* www.conran.com.

CONROY, Pat, BA; American author; b. 26 Oct. 1945, Atlanta, Ga; s. of Col Donald Conroy and Frances (Peg) Dorothy Conroy; m. 1st Barbara Bolling 1969 (divorced 1977); m. 2nd Lenore Gurewitz 1981 (divorced 1995); one s. five d.; ed The Citadel; all novels have been filmed, with the film Conrack based on his non-fiction work The Water Is Wide; Ford Foundation Leadership Devt Grant 1971, Nat. Endowment for the Arts Award for Achievement in Educ. 1974, SC Hall of Fame, Acad. of Authors 1988, Golden Plate Award, American Acad. of Achievement 1992, Ga Comm. on the Holocaust Humanitarian Award 1996, Lotos Medal of Merit for Outstanding Literary Achievement 1996 and many others. *Publications:* non-fiction: The Boo 1970, The Water Is Wide 1972; novels: The Great Santini 1976, The Lords of Discipline 1980, The Prince of Tides 1986, Beach Music 1995; screenplays: Invictus 1988 (TV film), The Prince of Tides (with Becky Johnson) 1991, Beach Music 1997. *Address:* c/o Doubleday, 1540 Broadway, New York, NY 10036, USA.

CONSAGRA, Pietro; Italian sculptor; b. 4 Oct. 1920, Mazara; two s. two d.; ed Acad. of Fine Arts, Palermo; Works in following museums: Tate Gallery, London; Nat. Museum and Middleheim Park, Antwerp; Museums of Modern Art, São Paulo, Paris, Rome, New York, Buenos Aires, Caracas, Zagreb, Helsinki; Guggenheim Museum, New York; Art Inst., Chicago; Carnegie Inst., Pittsburgh; Inst. of Fine Arts, Minneapolis and Houston; Grand Prize for Sculpture, Venice Biennale 1960; Prize for Metalwork, Sao Paulo Biennial 1955, Einaudi Prize, Venice Biennale 1956, Hon. mention, Int. Exhibition, Pittsburgh 1958, Prix de la Critique, Brussels 1958, Carnegie Int. Prize 1958, 1st Prize, Morgan's Painting Prize, Rimini 1959, Antonio Feltrinelli Prize for Sculpture, Accademia dei Lincei, Rome 1984, Gold Medal of the Italian Republic for Art and Culture, Rome 2001. *One-man shows:* Rome 1947, 1949, 1951, 1959, 1961 1966, 1972, 1976, 1989; Milan 1965, 1969, 1971, 1980, 1986, 1996, 2001; Venice 1948; Brussels 1958; Paris 1959; Zürich 1961; São Paulo Biennial 1955, 1959; Venice Biennale 1956, 1960, 1972, 1982, New York 1962, 1967, Buenos Aires 1962, Boston 1963, Documenta Kassel, 1959, 1964, Rotterdam 1967, Verona 1977, L'Hermitage, St Petersburg 1991, Darmstadt 1997, Palermo 1998, Bolzano 2000; work included in permanent collections of galleries and museums in Rome, Houston, New York, Washington, Cologne, Stuttgart, Hannover, Paris, St Petersburg, Venice and Lugano. *Publication:* Vità mia (autobiog., Literary Prize, Mondello, Palermo) 1980. *Address:* Via Cassia 1162, 00189 Rome; Via Solferino 3, 20121 Milan, Italy. *Telephone:* 86460319. *Fax:* 86460319. *E-mail:* pietroconsagra@archivioconsagra.it.

CONSALVI, Simón Alberto; Venezuelan diplomatist; b. 7 July 1929; m.; two c.; ed Univ. Central de Venezuela; mem. Nat. Congress 1959–64, 1974–; Amb. to Yugoslavia 1961–64; Dir Cen. Office of Information for the Presidency 1964–67; Pres. Nat. Inst. of Culture and Art 1967–69; Dir Nat. Magazine of Culture; Int. Ed. El Nacional newspaper 1971–74; Minister of State for Information 1974; Perm. Rep. to UN 1974–77; Pres. UN Security Council 1977; Minister of Foreign Affairs 1977–79, 1985–88; Amb. to USA 1990–94; fmr Sec.-Gen. of Presidency; mem. Nat. Congress Foreign Relations Comm. *Publications:* El Perfil y la sombra 1997; numerous articles and assays. *Address:* c/o Ministerio de Relaciones Exteriores, Casa Amoville, esq. Principal, Caracas, Venezuela.

CONSIDINE, Frank William; American business executive; b. 15 Aug. 1921, Chicago; s. of Frank J. Considine and Minnie Regan; m. Nancy Scott 1948; ed Loyola Univ. Chicago; partner, F.J. Hogan Agency, Chicago 1945–47; Asst to Pres. Graham Glass Co. Chicago 1947–51; owner, F.W. Considine Co., Chicago 1951–55; Vice-Pres. Metro Glass Div. Kraftco, Chicago 1955–60; Vice-Pres. and Dir Nat. Can Corpn (now American Nat. Can Co.), Chicago 1961–67, Exec. Vice-Pres. 1967–69, Pres. 1969–88, CEO 1973–88, Chair. 1983–90, Hon. Chair. and Chair. Exec. Cttee 1990–; Vice-Chair. Triangle Industries Inc. (parent Corpn) 1985–88; mem. Bd of Dirs. Encyclopaedia Britannica, First Chicago Corpn, First Nat. Bank of Chicago, Helene Curtis Industries Inc., Ill. Power Co., Schwitzer Inc., Scotsman Industries, Maytag Co., Tribune Co., IMC Fertilizer Group Inc.; Hon. LLD (Loyola) 1986, Hon. LHD (Northwestern) 1987. *Address:* c/o American National Can Co., 8770 W Bryn Mawr, Chicago, IL 60631, USA.

CONSTÂNCIO, Vitor Manuel; Portuguese banker; b. 12 Oct. 1943, Lisbon; s. of António Francisco Constâncio and Ester Ribeiro Vieira Constâncio; m. Maria José Constâncio 1968; one s. one d.; ed Instituto Superior de Ciências Económicas e Financeiras, Lisbon and Bristol Univ.; Asst Prof. Faculty of Econs 1965–73 and 1989–; Dir of Global Planning Studies, Planning Research Centre 1973; Sec. of State for Planning and Budget 1974–75; Head of Econ. Research Dept, Banco de Portugal 1975; mem. Parl. 1976, 1980-82, 1987–89; Chair. Parl. Comm. of Econ. and Finance 1976; Pres. of Comm. formed to negotiate with EEC 1977; Vice-Gov. Banco de Portugal 1977 and 1979–85, Gov. 1985, Adviser 1989–95; Minister of Finance and Planning 1978; Sec.-Gen. Socialist Party 1986–89; mem. Council of State 1996–; Prof. of Econs Tech. Univ. of Lisbon 1989–; mem. Bd Banco BPI 1995–2000; Gov. Banco de Portugal 2000–. *Address:* Office of the Governor, Banco de Portugal, Rua do Ouro 27, 1100-150 Lisbon, Portugal (Office). *Telephone:* (21) 3213200 (Office). *Fax:* (21) 3215407 (Office). *E-mail:* info@bporthgal.pt (Office). *Website:* www .bportugal.pt (Office).

CONSTANT, Paule, DèsSc; French author; b. 25 Jan. 1944, Gan; d. of Yves Constant and Jeanne Tauzin; m. Auguste Bourgeade 1968; one s. one d.; ed Univ. of Bordeaux and Univ. of Paris (Sorbonne); Asst Lecturer in French Literature, Univ. of Abidjan 1968–75; Maître-assistant, then Maître de Conférences in French Literature and Civilization, Univ. of Aix-Marseille III 1975–90, Inst. of French Studies for Foreign Students 1986–95; Prof. Université Aix–Marseille III 1995–; diarist, Revue des Deux Mondes, Paris; Prix Valéry Larbaud 1980, Grand Prix de l'Essai, Acad. Française 1987, Prix François Mauriac 1990, Grand Prix du Roman, Acad. Française 1990, Prix Goncourt 1998; Chevalier, Légion d'honneur, France; Ordre de l'Educ. Nat. de Côte d'Ivoire. *Publications:* novels: Ouregano 1980, Propriété privée 1981, Balta 1983, White Spirit 1989, Le Grand Ghâpal 1991, La Fille du Gobernator 1994, Confidence pour confidence 1998; Un monde à l'usage des demoiselles (essay) 1987. *Leisure interest:* bibliophile (18th and 19th century works on educ.). *Address:* Institut d'études françaises pour étudiants étrangers, 23 rue Gaston de Saporta, 13100 Aix-en-Provence; 29 rue Cardinale, 13100 Aix-en-Provence, France. *Telephone:* (4) 42-38-45-08.

CONSTANTINE II, former King of the Hellenes; b. 2 June 1940; m. Princess Anne-Marie of Denmark 1964; three s. two d.; ed Anavryta School and Law School, Athens Univ.; Military Training 1956–58; visited United States 1958, 1959; succeeded to throne March 1964; left Greece Dec. 1967; deposed June 1973; Monarchy abolished by Nat. Referendum Dec. 1974; deprived of Greek citizenship, remaining property in Greece nationalized April 1994; won ruling in European Court of Human Rights for compensation; Gold Medal, Yachting, Olympic Games, Rome 1960. *Address:* 4 Linnell Drive, Hampstead Way, London, NW11, England.

CONSTANTINESCU, Emil, PhD, DSc; Romanian politician, jurist and geologist; b. 19 Nov. 1939, Tighina (now Repub. of Moldova); s. of Ion Constantinescu and Maria Constantinescu; m. Nadia Ileana Bogorin; one s. one d.; ed Bucharest Univ.; practising lawyer 1960–61; lecturer and sr lecturer Bucharest Univ. 1966–90, Prof. of Mineralogy 1990–, Vice-Pres. 1991–92, Pres. 1992–96, Hon. Chair. of Senate 1996–; Visiting Prof. Duke Univ. NC USA 1991–92; Chair Nat. Romanian Council of Univ. Rectors 1992–96; mem. Steering Cttee of European Univs Assoc. (CRE) 1992–98, Int. Assoc. of Univ. Presidents (IAUP) 1994–96, Founder mem. Univ. Solidarity 1990; Pres. Civic Acad. 1990–92; Acting Chair. Romanian Anti-Totalitarian Forum 1991; Pres. Democratic Convention 1992–96; Pres. of Romania 1996–2000; Gen. Sec. Romanian Geological Soc. 1987–93, 1990–93; Hon. mem. Geological and Mineralogical Socs. of America, UK, Germany, SA, Japan, Greece; Hon. mem. Nat. Geographical Soc. of USA and Geographical Soc. of France; Hon. DSc, Univs. of Athens, Liège, Montréal, Delhi, Beijing, Ankara, Chişinău, Astana, Maribor, Bangkok, Sofia, ENS Paris; Romanian Acad. Award in Geology 1980, Aristide Calvany Award for Peace, Democracy and Human Devt Paris 1997, Award for Democracy of Democratic Center Washington, DC 1998, European Statesman of the Year Award New York 1998, European Coudenhove-Kalergi Award for Contrib. to Devt of Europe and Free Movt of Ideas, Bern 1998, American Bar Asscn Award 1999, Palmas Académicas from Acad. of Brazil 2000; awards and medals from Acad. des Sciences Inst. de France, Univs of Paris-Sorbonne, Prague, Amsterdam, Bratislava, Szeged, São Paulo. *Publications:* 12 books and over 60 articles in scientific journals. *Address:* Bd. Magheru 28–30, Bucharest 701591, Romania. *Telephone:* 2023904 (Office); 2229100 (Home). *Fax:* 2023932 (Office); 2229038 (Home). *E-mail:* cabinet_ec@ aspec.ro (Office). *Website:* www.constantinescu.ro (Office).

CONTAMINE, Claude Maurice; French television executive; b. 29 Aug. 1929, Metz, Moselle; s. of late Henry Contamine and Marie-Thérèse Dufays; m. Renée Jaugeon (deceased); one s.; ed Lycée Malherbe, Caen, Facultés de Droit, Caen and Paris and Ecole Nat. d'Administration; public servant until 1964; Asst Dir-Gen. ORTF and Dir of TV 1964–67; Pres. Dir-Gen. Union générale cinématographique (UGC) 1967–71; Consul-Gen. Milan 1971–72; Asst Dir-Gen. in charge of external affairs and co-operation, ORTF 1973–74; Minister plenipotentiary 1974; mem. Haut Conseil de l'Audiovisuel 1973–80; Pres. France-Régions (FR3) 1975–81; Conseiller Maître, Cour des Comptes 1981; Pres. Télédiffusion de France (TDF) 1986; Pres. Dir-Gen. Société nat. de programme Antenne 2 1986–89; Rapporteur général European TV and Film Forum 1990–; Pres. Conservatoire Européen d'Ecriture Audiovisuelle 1996–2002; mem. Conseil Supérieur de la Magistrature 1998–2002; Officier, Légion d'honneur, Commdr Ordre nat. du Mérite, Officier des Arts et des Lettres. *Address:* 12 rue de Bassano, 75116 Paris, France.

CONTAMINE, Philippe, DèsSc; French university professor; b. 7 May 1932, Metz; s. of Henry Contamine and Marie-Thérèse Dufays; m. Geneviève Bernard 1956; two s. one d.; ed Lycée Malherbe, Caen, Lycée Louis-le-Grand, Paris, Sorbonne; History and Geography teacher, Lycée, Sens 1957–60, Lycée Carnot, Paris 1960–61; Asst Prof. of Medieval History, Sorbonne 1962–65; Asst lecturer, lecturer then Prof. of Medieval History, Univ. of Nancy 1965–73; Prof. of Medieval History, Univ. of Paris (Nanterre) 1973–89; Prof. of Medieval History, Univ. of Paris (Sorbonne) 1989–2000, Prof. Emer. 2000–; Dir Dept of History 1976–79; Sec. to Soc. de l'histoire de France 1984–; Pres. Nat. Soc. of Antique Dealers 1999; mem. Institut de France (Académie des Inscriptions et Belles-Lettres, Pres. 2000) 1990, Acadaemia Europea 1993; Corresp. Fellow Royal Historical Soc. 1993; Pres. Soc. Nat. des Antiquaires de France 1999; Commdr. des Palmes académiques, Officier des Arts et des Lettres. *Publications:* La Guerre de cent ans 1968, Guerre, Etat et Société à la fin du Moyen Age 1972, La Vie quotidienne en France et en Angleterre pendant la guerre de cent ans 1976, La guerre au Moyen Age 1980, La France aux XIVe et XVe siècles 1981, La France de la fin du XVe siècle (co-ed.) 1985, L'Etat et Les Aristocraties (Ed.) 1989, L'histoire militaire de la France 1992, Des pouvoirs en France 1300–1500 1992, L'Economie Mediévale 1993, De Jeanne d'Arc aux guerres d'Italie 1994, La Noblesse au royaume de France de Philippe Le Bel à Louis XII 1997, Guerre et concurrence entre les Etats européens du XIVe au XVIIIe siècle (Ed.) 1998, Autour de Marguerite d'Ecosse: reines, princesses et dames du XVe siècle (Ed.) 1999. *Address:* 1 rue Victor Cousin, 75005 Paris; 11–15 rue de l'Amiral Roussin, 75015 Paris, France.

CONTE, Arthur; French politician, journalist and broadcasting executive; b. 31 March 1920, Salses, Pyrénées-Orientales; s. of Pierre Conte and Marie-Thérèse Parazols; m. Colette Lacassagne 1951 (died 2001); one s. one d.; ed Montpellier Univ.; foreign leader writer, Indépendant de Perpignan 1945; later worked for Paris Match; subsequently leader-writer for Les Informations and contrib. to Le Figaro, Historia, Les Nouvelles Littéraires; Sec. Socialist Party Fed. for Pyrénées-Orientales; Deputy to Nat. Assembly 1951–62, 1968–72; Sec. of State for Industry and Commerce 1957; Mayor of Salses 1947–72; Del. to Assembly of Council of Europe 1956–62; Pres. WEU Assembly 1961–62; Chair. and Dir-Gen. ORTF 1972–73; Chevalier, Légion d'honneur. *Publications:* La légende de Pablo Casals, Les étonnements de Mister Newborn, Les promenades de M. Tripoire, Les hommes ne sont pas des héros, La vigne sous le rempart, Yalta ou le partage du monde, Bandoung, tournant de l'histoire, sans de Gaulle, Lénine et Staline, Les frères Burns, Hommes libres, L'épopée mondiale d'un siècle (5 Vols), Le premier janvier 1900, Le premier janvier 1920, Le premier janvier 1940, Le premier janvier 1960, Le premier janvier 1983, L'aventure européenne (2 Vols), L'homme Giscard, L'Après-Yalta, Karl Marx face à son temps, Les dictateurs du vingtième siècle, Les présidents de la cinquième république, Les premiers ministres de la Ve république, Verdun, Le 1er janvier 1789 1988, Billaud Varenne, géant de la Révolution 1989, Joffre 1991, L'epopée coloniale de la France 1992, Nostalgies françaises 1993, Au village de mon enfance 1994, L'epopée des chemins de fer français 1996, C'était la IVe République 1998, La drôle de guerre 1999, Les paysans de France 2000, Soldats de France 2001, Ma terre de toujours 2002. *Leisure interest:* golf. *Address:* 94 avenue de Suffren, 75015 Paris, France. *Telephone:* 1-47-83-23-45.

CONTÉ, Gen. Lansana; Guinean politician and army officer; fmr mil. Commdr of Boké Region, W Guinea; Pres. Repub. of Guinea after mil. coup, April 1984–, also Minister of Defence, Security, Planning Co-operation and Information and Pres. Council of Ministers; Chair. Comité militaire de redressement nat. (CMRN) April 1984–90, Comité transitoire de redressement nat. (CTRN) 1991–92. *Address:* Office du Président, Conakry, Guinea.

CONTI, Most Rev Mario Joseph, PhL, STL, FRSE; British ecclesiastic; b. 20 March 1934, Elgin; s. of Louis Joseph Conti and Josephine Quintilia Panicali; ed Blairs Coll., Aberdeen, Pontifical Scots Coll. and Gregorian Univ., Rome; ordained Priest 1958; apptd. Curate St Mary's Cathedral, Aberdeen 1959, apptd. Parish Priest St Joachim's Wick 1962; Bishop of Aberdeen 1977–2002; Archbishop of Glasgow 2002–; Pres.-Treas. Scottish Catholic Int. Aid Fund 1978–84; Pres. Nat. Liturgy Comm. 1981–85, Nat. Comm. for Christian Doctrine and Unity 1985–; Vice-Pres. Comm. for Migrant Workers and Tourism 1978–84, Scottish Catholic Heritage Comm. 1980–; mem. Council for Promotion of Christian Unity (Rome) 1984–, Int. Comm. for English in the Liturgy 1978–87, Pontificial Comm. for Cultural Heritage of the Church, Rome 1994–; Convener, Action of Churches Together in Scotland 1990–93; Co-Moderator of Jt Working Group, RC Church and World Council of Churches 1995; Chaplain to British Asscn of the Order of Malta 1995–2000, Conventual Chaplain Grand Cross 2001–; mem. Historic Bldgs. Council of Scotland 2000; Hon. DD (Aberdeen) 1989; Order of Merit of the Italian Repub. 1982, Kt Commdr of Holy Sepulchre 1989. *Publications:* occasional articles and letters in nat. and local press. *Leisure interests:* walking, travel, swimming, music and the arts. *Address:* Curial Offices, 196 Clyde Street, Glasgow, G1 4JY, Scotland (Office); 40 Newlands Rd, Glasgow G43 1JD (Home). *Telephone:* (141) 226-5898 (Office). *Fax:* (141) 225-2600 (Office). *E-mail:* curia@rcag.org.uk (Office). *Website:* www.rcag.org.uk (Office).

CONTI, Tom; British actor and director; s. of Alfonso Conti and Mary McGoldrick; m. Kara Wilson 1967; one d.; ed Royal Scottish Acad. of Music; West End Theatre Managers' Award; Royal Television Soc. Award, Variety Club of Great Britain Award 1978, Tony Award of New York 1979. *London theatre includes:* Savages (Christopher Hampton) 1973, The Devil's Disciple (Shaw) 1976, Whose Life is it Anyway? (Brian Clarke) 1978, They're Playing Our Song (Neil Simon/Marvin Hamlisch) 1980, Romantic Comedy (Bernard Salde), An Italian Straw Hat 1986, Two Into One, Treats 1989, Jeffrey Bernard is Unwell 1990, The Ride Down Mt. Morgan 1991, Present Laughter (also Dir) 1993, Chapter Two 1996, Jesus My Boy 1998. *Films include:* Flame, Full Circle, Merry Christmas Mr. Lawrence, Reuben, American Dreamer, Saving Grace, Miracles, Heavenly Pursuits, Beyond Therapy, Roman Holiday, Two Brothers Running, White Roses, Shirley Valentine, Someone Else's America, Crush Depth, Something to Believe In 1996, Out of Control 1997, The Enemy 2000. *Television work includes:* Madame Bovary, Treats, The Glittering Prizes, The Norman Conquests, The Beate Klarsfield Story, Fatal Dosage, The Quick and the Dead, Blade on the Feather, The Wright Verdicts, Deadline. *Directed:* Last Licks, Broadway 1979, Before the Party 1980, The Housekeeper 1982, Treats 1989, Present Laughter 1993, Last of the Red Hot Lovers 1999. *Leisure interest:* music. *Address:* Artists Independent Network, 32 Tavistock St, London, WC2E 7PB, England. *Telephone:* (20) 7352-7722.

CONTOGEORGIS, George, MA, PhD; Greek professor of political science; b. 14 Feb. 1947; s. of Dimitri Contogeorgis and Elia Contogeorgis; m. Catherine Kampourgiannidou 1972; two d.; ed Univ. of Athens, Univ. of Paris II, Ecole Pratique des Hautes Etudes, Ecole des Hautes Etudes en Sciences Sociales; Prof. of Political Science, Panteion Univ. Athens 1983–, Rector 1984–90; Gen. Dir ERT SA (Hellenic Broadcasting Corpn) 1985, Pres.-Gen. Dir 1989; Minister, Ministry of the Presidency (State Admin., Communication, Media), Govt Spokesman 1993; Dir European Masters Programme in Political Science; Founder mem. and Sec.-Gen. Greek Political Sciences Asscn 1975–80; leader writer in Athenian daily newspapers; mem. High Council and Research Council, European Univ. Florence 1986–94; mem. High Council, Univ. of Europe, Paris and Centre of Regional Studies, Montpellier; Visiting Prof. Inst. d'Etudes Politiques, Paris, Univ. Libre de Bruxelles, Univ. Catholique de Louvain, Univs. of Montpellier, Tokyo, etc.; Prof. Franqui Chair. Univ. of Brussels; mem. Council Pôle Sud, Political Science Review, Revue Internationale de Politique Comparée; mem. French Political Science Asscn, I.P.S.A. and other int. asscns. *Publications:* The Theory of Revolution in Aristotle 1975, The Popular Ideology. Socio-political Study of the Greek Folk Song 1979, Political System and Politics 1985, Social Process and Political Self-government: The Greek City-State Under the Ottoman Empire 1982, The Local Government in the State 1985, Nuclear Energy and Public Opinion in Europe 1991, History of Greece 1992, Système de communication et système d'échange: La télévision 1993, After Communism (in collaboration) 1993, Greek Society in 20th Century 1995, Democracy in the Technological Society 1995, Society and Politics 1996, The Greek Cosmosystem 1997, New World Order 1998, Identité cosmosystémique ou identité nationale? Le Paradigme hellénique 1999, Le Citoyen dans la cité 2000. *Leisure interest:* water sports. *Address:* Panteion University of Athens, 136 Sygrou Avenue, Athens 176 71 (Office); 7 Tassopoulou Street, Athens 153 42, Greece (Home). *Telephone:* (1) 9201743 (Office); (1) 6399662 (Home); 6081780 (Home). *Fax:* (4) 9201743 (Office); (1) 6081780. *E-mail:* contogeo@panteion.gr (Office). *Website:* www.panteion.gr (Office).

CONWAY, John Horton, MA, PhD, FRS; British mathematician; b. 26 Dec. 1937, Liverpool; m. Diana Conway; three s. six d.; ed Gonville and Caius Coll., Cambridge; Lecturer in Pure Math., Cambridge Univ. –1973, Reader in Pure Math. and Math. Statistics 1973–83, Prof. of Math. 1983–87; John von Neumann Distinguished Prof. of Math., Princeton Univ. 1986–; Fellow Sidney Sussex Coll., Cambridge 1964–70, Gonville and Caius Coll., Cambridge 1970–87; Hon. Fellow Gonville and Caius Coll. 1999; Hon. DSc (Liverpool) 2001; Polya Prize London Math. Soc. 1987, Frederic Esser Nemmers Prize, Northwestern Univ. 1999, Steele Prize, American Math. Soc. 1999, Joseph Priestley Award, Dickinson Coll. 2001. *Publications:* Regular Algebra and Finite Machines 1971, On Numbers and Games 1976, Atlas of Finite Groups 1985, The Book of Numbers 1996, The Sensual Quadratic Form 1998. *Address:* Department of Mathematics, Fine Hall, Princeton University, Washington Road, Princeton, NJ 08544 (Office); 71 College Road W., Princeton, NJ 08540, USA (Home). *Telephone:* (609) 258-6468 (Office); (609) 683-0206 (Home). *Fax:* (609) 921-0353 (Home). *E-mail:* conway@math.princeton.edu (Office).

COOBAR, Abdulmegid; Libyan politician; b. 1909; ed Arabic and Italian schools in Tripoli and privately; with Birth Registration Section, Tripoli Municipal Council and later its Section Head, Adviser on Arab Affairs for the Council 1943–44; resigned from Govt Service 1944; mem. Nat. Constitutional Assembly 1950 and mem. Cttee to draft the Libyan Constitution; MP for Eastern Gharian 1952–55, Pres. of Parl. Assembly 1952–55; Deputy Prime Minister and Minister of Communications 1955–56; again elected for Eastern Gharian to the new Chamber of Deputies 1955, Pres. 1956; mem. of Council of Viceroy 1956; Deputy Prime Minister and Minister of Foreign Affairs 1957; Prime Minister 1957–60, concurrently Minister for Foreign Affairs 1958–60; Independence Award (1st Class).

COOK, Sir Alan Hugh, Kt, MA, PhD, ScD, FRS, FRSE, FInstP; British professor of natural philosophy; b. 2 Dec. 1922, Felstead; s. of Reginald Thomas Cook and Ethel Cook (née Saxon); m. Isabell Weir Adamson 1948; one s. one d.; ed Westcliff High School, Corpus Christi Coll., Cambridge; scientist Nat. Physical Lab., Teddington 1952–69; First Prof. of Geophysics, Univ. of Edinburgh 1969–72; Jacksonian Prof. of Natural Philosophy, Univ. of Cambridge 1972–90; Master of Selwyn Coll., Cambridge 1983–93; Visiting Fellow, Jt Inst. for Lab. Astrophysics, Univ. of Colorado 1965–66; Visiting Prof. Univ. of

Calif. at Los Angeles, Berkeley and San Diego 1981–82, Center for Theological Enquiry, Princeton 1993; Ed. Geophysical Journal 1958–85, Notes and Records of the Royal Soc. 1996–; Pres. Royal Astronomical Soc. 1977–79; Foreign Fellow Acad. Nazionale Lincei, Rome; CV Boys Prize, Inst. of Physics 1967; Charles Chree Medal and Prize, Inst. of Physics 1993; Humphrey Davy Lecture, Royal Soc. 1994. *Publications:* Gravity and the Earth 1969, Global Geophysics 1970, Interference/Electromagnetic Waves 1971, Physics of the Earth and Planets 1973, Celestial Masers 1977, Interiors of the Planets 1980, The Motion of the Moon 1988, Gravitational Experiments in the Laboratory 1993, Observational Foundations of Physics 1994, Edmond Halley 1997 and many contribs. to learned journals. *Leisure interests:* travel, painting, listening to music. *Address:* 8 Wootton Way, Cambridge, CB3 9LX, England. *Telephone:* (1223) 356887. *E-mail:* ahc.13@cam.ac.uk (Home).

COOK, Beryl, OBE; British artist; b. 10 Sept. 1926, Egham, Berks.; d. of Adrian S. Barton-Lansley and Ella M. Farmer-Francis; m. John V. Cook 1948; one s.; ed Kendrick Girls School, Reading; Kate Greenaway Medal 1980. *Exhibitions:* Plymouth Arts Centre 1975, 1995, Whitechapel Art Gallery 1976, Walker Art Gallery, Liverpool 1979, Musée de Cahors 1981, Chelmsford Museum 1982, Glasgow 1992, New York 1992; retrospective travelling exhbns., Plymouth, Stoke On Trent, Preston, Nottingham, Edinburgh 1988–89, Blackpool, Durham, Hartlepool, Stoke On Trent 1998. *Publications:* The Works 1978, Private View 1980, Seven Years and a Day (illustrations) 1980, One Man Show 1981, Bertie and the Big Red Ball (illustrations) 1982, My Granny (illustrations) 1983, Beryl Cook's New York 1985, Beryl Cook's London 1988, Mr Norris Changes Trains (illustrations) 1990, Bouncers 1991, The Loved One (illustrations) 1993, Happy Days 1995, Illustrations for Folio Soc.'s Edn of The Prime of Miss Jean Brodie 1998, Happy Days 1999, Illustrations for Cruising 2000, Beryl Cook The Bumper Edition 2000. *Leisure interests:* reading, travel. *Address:* 8 Alfred Street, The Hoe, Plymouth, Devon PL1 2RP, England.

COOK, Brian (Robert) Rayner, BA, ARCM (Hons); British professional singer (baritone); b. 17 May 1945, London; s. of Robert Cook and Gladys Soulby; m. Angela M. Romney 1974; one s. one d.; ed Univ. of Bristol, Royal Coll. of Music and privately with Alexander Young (vocal studies) and Helga Mott (repertoire); church organist and choirmaster at age 15; major conducting début (opera) 1966; professional singing début 1967; has appeared as soloist in oratorio, recitals, music-theatre and opera throughout the UK, Europe, USA, Canada, S. America, the Middle East, the Far East and N Africa and has broadcast frequently in UK, Europe and many other countries; has given first performances of various works written for him by distinguished composers; Dir singers' workshops, jury mem. int. singing competitions and specialist adjudicator; Visiting Tutor in Vocal Studies and Postgrad. Examiner, Birmingham Conservatoire 1980–99; fmrly Tutor Welsh Coll. of Music and Drama, Cardiff; Specialist Univ. Music Assessor, Higher Educ. Funding Councils of England and Wales 1994–95; Kathleen Ferrier Memorial Scholarship 1969 and many other major singing prizes. *Recordings include:* opera, oratorio and songs by Schütz, Charpentier, Adam, Fauré, Dvořák, Nielsen, Orff, Camilleri, Parry, Elgar, Delius, Butterworth, Vaughan Williams, Holst, Havergal Brian, Coates, Poston, Rubbra, Cruft, Walton, Ferguson and Williamson. *Television:* Professional solo debut (BBC) 1970; has since appeared in televised concerts in many European countries in works ranging from Mozart's Requiem to Mahler's 8th Symphony. *Leisure interests:* news, current affairs and scientific devts., practical healing, colour photography, major comedy figures of the 20th century, historic recordings, messing about in boats. *Address:* The Quavers, 53 Friars Avenue, Friern Barnet, London, N20 0XG, England. *Telephone:* (20) 8368-3010.

COOK, Christopher Paul, MA; British artist and poet; b. 24 Jan. 1959, Great Ayton, N Yorks.; s. of E. P. Cook and J. Leyland; m. Jennifer Jane Mellings 1982; two s.; ed Univ. of Exeter, Royal Coll. of Art; Italian Govt scholar to Accad. di Belle Arti, Bologna 1986–89; Fellow in Painting Exeter Coll. of Art 1989–90; guest artist Stadelschule, Frankfurt 1991; Visiting Fellow Ruskin School, Univ. of Oxford 1992–93; Distinguished Visiting Artist Calif. State Univ., Long Beach 1994; Visiting Artist to Banaras Hindu Univ., Varanasi, India 1994, 1996; Reader in Painting Univ. of Plymouth 1997–; Prizewinner John Moores Liverpool XXI 1999, Arts Council of England Award 2000. *Solo exhibitions include:* Camden Arts Centre 1985, Cleveland Gallery, Middlesbrough 1989, Museum van Rhoon, Rotterdam 1992, Northern Centre for Contemporary Art 1993, Helmut Pabst Gallery, Frankfurt 1995, Haugesund Kunstforening, Norway 1997, De Beyerd Museum, Breda 1999, Heidelberger Kunstverein 1999, Bundanon Trust, NSW 2000, Hirschl Contemporary Art, London 2000, Ferens Gallery, Hull 2001, Towner Gallery, Eastbourne 2001, Koraalberg Gallery, Antwerp 2002. *Publications:* Dust on the Mirror 1997, For and Against Nature 2000. *Leisure interest:* the outdoors. *Address:* c/o Hirschl Contemporary Art, 5 Cork St, London, England. *Telephone:* (7779) 587950.

COOK, Gordon Charles, MD, DSc, MRCS, FRCP, FRACP, FLS FRCPE; British physician; b. 17 Feb. 1932, Wimbledon; s. of Charles F. Cook and Kate (née Kraninger, then Grainger) Cook; m. Elizabeth J. Agg-Large 1963; one s. three d.; ed Wellingborough Grammar School, Kingston-upon-Thames, Raynes Park Grammar Schools and Royal Free Hospital School of Medicine, Univ. of London; junior appts Royal Free Hosp., Brompton Hosp. and Royal Northern Hosp. 1958–60; medical specialist, captain, RAMC and Royal Nigerian Army 1960–62; Lecturer in Medicine, Royal Free Hosp. School of Medicine 1963–65, 1967–69, Makerere Univ. Coll., Uganda 1965–67; Prof. of Medicine, Univ. of

Zambia 1969–74, Univ. of Riyadh, Saudi Arabia 1974–75; Visiting Prof. of Medicine, Univs of Basrah and Mosul, Iraq 1976; Sr Lecturer in Clinical Tropical Medicine, London School of Hygiene and Tropical Medicine 1976–97; Consultant Physician, Univ. Coll. London Hosps. and Hosp. for Tropical Diseases, London 1976–97; Prof. of Medicine and Chair. Clinical Sciences Dept, Univ. of Papua New Guinea 1978–81; Hon. Sr Lecturer in Medicine Univ. Coll. London 1981–2002 (Visiting Prof. 1999–); Hon. Consultant Physician, St Luke's Hosp. for the Clergy 1988–; Visiting Prof. of Medicine, Doha, Qatar 1989; Hon. Lecturer in Clinical Parasitology, Medical Coll. of St Bartholomew's Hosp., London 1992–; Sr Research Fellow, Wellcome Centre for the History of Medicine 1997–2002; Chair. Erasmus Darwin Foundation, Lichfield 1994–; Chair. Medical Writers Group, Soc. of Authors 1997–99; Vice-Pres. Royal Soc. of Tropical Medicine and Hygiene 1991–93, Pres. 1993–95; Vice-Pres., History of Medicine Section, Royal Soc. of Medicine 1994–96, Pres., 2003–; Fellowship of Postgrad. Medicine, Vice-Pres. 1996–2000, Pres. 2000–; Examiner, Royal Coll. of Physicians, Univs of London and Makerere, Uganda; Ed. Journal of Infection 1995–97; mem. Editorial Bd Transactions of Royal Soc. of Tropical Medicine, The Postgrad. Medical Journal; mem. Jt Cttee on Higher Medical Training, Exec. Cttee and examiner Faculty of History and Philosophy of Medicine and Pharmacy, The Worshipful Soc. of Apothecaries 1997–; mem. of council, History of Medicine section, Royal Soc. of Medicine 1999–; Trustee, Overseas Devt Admin. and Bookpower; mem. Code of Practice Cttee, Asscn of British Pharmaceutical Industry; mem. Asscn of Physicians of GB and Ireland 1973–; numerous other medical and scientific socs; Trustee Educational Low-Priced Sponsored Texts (ELST) 1996–; Charlotte Brown Prize, Cunning and Legg Awards (Royal Free Hosp. School of Medicine), Frederick Murgatroyd Memorial Prize, Royal Coll. of Physicians, London 1973, Hugh L'Etang Prize, Royal Soc. of Medicine 1999; Monckton Copeman lecturer, Soc. of Apothecaries 2000. *Publications:* Acute Renal Failure (jtly) 1964, Tropical Gastroenterology 1980, Communicable and Tropical Diseases 1988, Parasitic Disease in Clinical Practice 1990, From the Greenwich Hulks to Old St Pancras: a history of tropical disease in London 1992; Ed. 100 Clinical Problems in Tropical Medicine (jtly) 1987, Travel-associated Disease 1995, Gastroenterological Problems from the Tropics 1995, Manson's Tropical Diseases (21st Edn) 2003; over 500 papers on physiology, gastroenterology, tropical medicine, nutrition and medical history. *Leisure interests:* cricket, walking, medical and scientific history, African and Pacific artefacts. *Address:* Infectious Diseases Unit, Windeyer Building, 46 Cleveland Street, London, W1P 6DB (Office); 11 Old London Road, St Albans, Herts., AL1 1QE, England (Home). *Telephone:* (20) 7679-9271 (Office); (1727) 869000 (Home). *Fax:* (20) 7679-9311 (Office). *E-mail:* g.cook@ucl.ac.uk (Office).

COOK, Michael John, AO, LLB; Australian diplomatist; b. 28 Oct. 1931, Burma; s. of H.J.M. Cook and Maureen H. Taylor; m. 1st Helen Ibbitson 1957 (divorced 1970); one s. three d.; m. 2nd Catriona Matheson 1970; one s. one d.; ed Geelong Grammar School, Univ. of Melbourne, Canberra Univ. Coll. and Imperial Defence Coll.; joined Australian Dept of Foreign Affairs 1954; Amb. to Vietnam 1973–74; CEO Pvt. Office of Prime Minister 1979–81; Dir-Gen. Office of Nat. Assessments 1981–89; Amb. to USA 1989–93; Distinguished Visiting Fellow Menzies Centre, Univ. of London 1993–94. *Leisure interests:* tennis, history, Bach. *Address:* 126 Loudoun Road, London, NW8 0ND, England.

COOK, Peter Frederick Chester, AADip, RIBA, BDA, FRSA, MEASA; British architect and professor of architecture; b. 22 Oct. 1936, Southend-on-Sea; s. of late Maj. Frederick William Cook and Ada Alice Cook (née Shaw); m. 1st Hazel Aimée Fennell 1960 (divorced 1990); m. 2nd Yael Reisner 1990; one s.; ed Bournemouth Coll. of Art, Architectural Asscn (A.A.), London; Architectural Asst, James Cubitt & Partners, London 1960–62; Asst Architect, Taylor Woodrow Design Group, London 1962–64; taught at A.A. 1964–89; Partner, Archigram Architects 1964–75, Cook and Hawley Architects, London 1976–; Bartlett Prof. of Architecture, Bartlett School of Architecture and Planning, Univ. Coll. London 1990–, Chair. Bartlett School of Architecture 1990–; Prof. of Architecture, HBK Frankfurt, Germany 1984–; visiting critic many schools of architecture USA and abroad; Visiting Prof. Oslo Architecture School 1982–83, RI School of Design 1981, 1984; Architect of "Plug-in-City", "Instant City", etc., of the Lutlowplatz Housing, Berlin 1990 (with Christine Hawley) and the Kunsthaus, Graz (with Colin Fournier); under construction; works featured in several books; Graham Foundation Award 1970, Monte Carlo Competition 1st Prize 1970, Landstuhl Housing Competition 1st Prize 1980, LA Prize (AIA) 1988, Int. Competition for Historic Museum 1st Prize, Austria 1995, Jean Tschumi Prize (U.I.A.) 1996, Int. Competition for Kunsthaus, Graz 1st Prize, Austria 2000, Grand Prize of the Buenos Aires Biennale 2001, Royal Gold Medal of the Royal Inst. of British Architects (RIBA) 2000 (as mem. of Archigram). *Exhibitions include:* Venice Biennale 1996–2000, Archigram Travelling Exhbn 1995– (Vienna, Paris, Zurich, Hamburg, Manchester, New York, Pasadena, San Francisco, Seattle, Milan, Brussels, Buenos Aires, Los Angeles, Rotterdam); various exhibitions at Deutsches Architektus Museum, Frankfurt, Aldes Gallery, Berlin, Architekturcentrum, Vienna, Centre Pompidou, Paris, Yamagiwa and GA Galleries, Tokyo; "Form Zero" now touring. *Publications:* Primer 1996, The Power of Contemporary Architecture 1999, The Paradox of Contemporary Architecture 2001, The City as Inspiration 2001. *Leisure interests:* listening to music, talking to young architects, restaurants. *Address:* Bartlett School of Architecture and Planning, University College London, 22 Gower Street, London WC1H 0QB (Office); 54 Compayne Gardens, London, NW6 3RY, England (Home). *Telephone:* (20)

7679-7504 (Univ.); (20) 7372-3784 (Home). *Fax:* (20) 7679-4831 (Univ.). *E-mail:* peter.cook@ucl.ac.uk (Office); architecture@ucl.ac.uk; c.mountford@ucl.ac.uk. *Website:* www.bartlett.ucl.ac.uk.

COOK, Rt Hon Robert (Robin) Finlayson, PC, MA, MP; British politician; b. 28 Feb. 1946; s. of the late Peter Cook and of Christina Cook (née Lynch); m. 1st Margaret K. Whitmore 1969 (divorced 1998); two s.; m. 2nd Gaynor Regan 1998; ed Aberdeen Grammar School and Univ. of Edinburgh; Tutor-Organiser with Workers' Educ. Asscn 1970–74; Labour MP for Edin. Cen. 1974–83, for Livingston 1983–; Chair. Scottish Asscn of Labour Student Orgs 1966–67; Sec. Edin. City Labour Party 1970–72; mem. Edin. Corpn 1971–74, Chair. Housing Cttee 1973–74; an Opposition Treasury Spokesman 1980–83; Opposition Spokesman on Trade 1986–87; Opposition Front Bench Spokesman on European and Community Affairs 1983–86, on Health and Social Security 1987–89, on Health 1989–92, on Trade and Industry 1992–94, on Foreign and Commonwealth Affairs 1994–97; Chair. Labour Party 1996–97; Sec. of State for Foreign and Commonwealth Affairs 1997–2001; Pres. of the Council and Leader of the House of Commons 2001–03; Chair. Party of European Socialists 2001–; Chair. Modernisation of the House of Commons Select Cttee; Labour's Campaign Co-ordinator 1984–86; mem. Tribune Group. *Leisure interests:* eating, reading, talking. *Address:* House of Commons, London, SW1A 0AA, England. *Telephone:* (20) 7219-4040.

COOK, Stephen Arthur, PhD, FRSC, OM, FRS; Canadian/American university professor; b. 14 Dec. 1939, Buffalo, NY; s. of Gerhard A. Cook and Lura Cook; m. Linda Craddock 1968; two s.; ed Univ. of Michigan and Harvard Univ.; Asst Prof. of Math., Univ. of Calif. at Berkeley 1966–70; Assoc. Prof. of Computer Science, Univ. of Toronto, Canada 1970–75, Prof. 1975–85, Univ. Prof. 1985–; E.W.R. Staecie Memorial Fellowship 1977–78; Killam Research Fellow, Canada Council 1982–83; mem. NAS, American Acad. of Arts and Science; Turing Award, Assoc. Computing Machinery 1982; Killam Prize 1997, CRM/Fields Inst. Prize 1999. *Publications:* numerous articles in professional journals on theory of computation. *Leisure interest:* sailing. *Address:* Department of Computer Science, University of Toronto, Toronto, Ont., M5S 3G4 (Office); 6 Indian Valley Crescent, Toronto, Ont., M6R 1Y6, Canada (Home). *Telephone:* (416) 978-5183 (Office). *Fax:* (416) 978-1931 (Office). *E-mail:* sacook@cs.toronto.edu (Office). *Website:* www.cs.toronto.edu/dcs/people/faculty/sacook.html (Office).

COOKE, (Alfred) Alistair; American (b. British) writer and broadcaster; b. 20 Nov. 1908, Manchester, England; s. of Samuel Cooke and Mary Elizabeth Byrne; m. 1st Ruth Emerson 1934; m. 2nd Jane White Hawkes; one s. one d.; ed Jesus Coll., Cambridge, Yale and Harvard Univs; Film Critic, BBC 1934–37; London Coresp. Nat. Broadcasting Co. 1936–37; Special Coresp. on American Affairs, The Times 1938–41; Commentator on American Affairs BBC 1938–, wrote and narrated America: a Personal History of the United States, BBC 1972–73; American feature writer, Daily Herald 1941–44; UN Coresp. The Manchester Guardian (now The Guardian) 1945–48, Chief Coresp. in USA 1948–72; host T.V. Masterpiece Theatre 1971–92; Hon. Fellow Jesus Coll. Cambridge 1989; Hon. LLD (Edinburgh, Manchester), Hon. LittD (St Andrew's) 1975, Hon. DLit (Cambridge) 1988; Peabody Award 1952, 1972, Writers' Guild Award for Best Documentary 1972, Dimbleby Award 1973, four Emmy Awards (Nat. Acad. of TV Arts and Sciences, USA) 1973, Benjamin Franklin Award 1973, Medal for Spoken Language (American Acad. of Arts and Letters) 1983; Hon. KBE 1973; BAFTA Award 1991. *Publications:* Garbo and the Night Watchmen (ed.) 1937, Douglas Fairbanks 1940, A Generation on Trial: USA v. Alger Hiss 1950, One Man's America (English title Letters from America) 1952, Christmas Eve 1952, A Commencement Address 1954, The Vintage Mencken (ed.) 1955, Around the World in Fifty Years 1966, Talk about America 1968, Alistair Cooke's America 1973, Six Men 1977, The Americans: Fifty Letters from America on Our Life and Times 1979, Above London (with Robert Cameron) 1980, Masterpieces 1982, The Patient has the Floor 1986, America Observed: The Newspaper Years of Alistair Cooke 1989, Fun and Games with Alistair Cooke 1994, Memories of the Great and the Good 1999. *Leisure interests:* biography, music, playing golf, watching tennis. *Address:* 1150 Fifth Avenue, New York, NY 10128; Nassau Point, Cutchogue, NY 11935, USA.

COOKE, Sir Howard (Felix Hanlan), ON, GCMG, GCVO, CD; Jamaican politician, schoolteacher and insurance company executive; b. 13 Nov. 1915; s. of David Brown Cooke and Mary Jane Minto; m. Ivy Sylvia Lucille Tai 1939; two s. one d.; teacher, Mico Training Coll. 1936–38; Headmaster, Belle-Castle All-Age School 1939–50; teacher, Port Antonio Upper School 1951, Montego Bay Boys' School 1952–58; Br. Man. Standard Life Insurance Co. Ltd 1960–71; Unit Man. Jamaica Mutual Life Assurance Co. Ltd 1971–81; Br. Man. Alico Jamaica 1982–91; mem. West Indies Fed. Parl. 1958–62, Senate 1962–67, House of Reps. 1967–80; Govt Minister 1972–80; Gov.-Gen. of Jamaica 1991–; Sr Elder United Church of Jamaica and Grand Cayman; lay pastor and fmr Chair. Cornwall Council of Churches; mem. Ancient and Accepted Order of Masons; Special Plaque for Distinguished Services (CPA) 1980. *Leisure interests:* gardening, cricket, football, reading. *Address:* Office of the Governor-General, King's House, Hope Road, Kingston 10, Jamaica, West Indies (Office). *Telephone:* 927-6424 (Office).

COOKE, Jean Esme Oregon, RA; British artist; b. 18 Feb. 1927, Lewisham, London; d. of Arthur Oregon Cooke and Dorothy E. Cranefield; m. John Bratby 1953 (divorced 1977, died 1992); three s. one d.; ed Blackheath High School, Cen. School of Arts and Crafts, Camberwell, City & Guilds School, Goldsmiths' Coll. School of Art and Royal Coll. of Art (royal scholar); pottery workshop 1950–53; lecturer in Painting, Royal Coll. of Art 1964–74; mem. Council, Royal Acad. 1983–85, 1992–94, 2001–02; Academic Bd Blackheath School of Art 1986–; Gov. Cen. School of Art and Design 1984; mem. tertiary educ. Bd Greenwich 1984; Life Pres. Friends of Woodlands Art Gallery 1990–; numerous solo shows in London and throughout Britain 1963–; works exhibited annually at Royal Acad. and in other group exhbns; work included in collections of Tate Gallery, Usher Gallery, Lincoln, Royal Acad., Royal Coll. of Art, Brinsley Ford, Lincoln Coll., St Hilda's Coll., Oxford, Govt Art Collections Fund, Australia, HM The Queen; made TV film for BBC Portrait of John Bratby 1978. *Publications:* Contemporary British Artists, The Artist 1980, The Artist's Garden 1989, Seeing Ourselves: Women's Self-Portraits (Frances Borzello). *Leisure interests:* ungardening, talking, shouting, walking along the beach, reading. *Address:* 7 Hardy Road, Blackheath, London, SE3 7NS, England. *Telephone:* (20) 8858-6288.

COOKE OF THORNDON, Baron (Life Peer) cr. 1996, of Wellington in New Zealand and of Cambridge in the County of Cambridgeshire; **Robin Brunskill Cooke,** Kt., KBE, PC, MA, PhD, QC; New Zealand judge; b. 9 May 1926, Wellington; s. of Hon. Philip Brunskill Cooke, MC and Valmai Digby Gore; m. Phyllis Annette Miller 1952; three s.; ed Victoria Univ. Coll., Wellington, Clare Coll. and Gonville & Caius Coll., Cambridge; called to Bar 1954; practised at NZ Bar 1955–72; Judge of Supreme Court 1972–76, of Court of Appeal 1976–86, now of Hong Kong Court of Final Appeal, Supreme Court of Fiji, Court of Appeal of Samoa; Visiting Fellow All Souls Coll., Oxford 1990; Chair. Comm. of Inquiry into Housing 1970–71; Ed.-in-Chief The Laws of NZ; Lord of Appeal 1996–2001; Life mem. Lawasia; comm. mem. Int. Comm. of Jurists 1993–; Special status mem. American Law Inst. 1993–; Research Fellow Gonville & Caius Coll. 1952–56, Hon. Fellow 1982; Distinguished Visiting Fellow, Victoria Univ. of Wellington 1997–; Hon. Bencher, Inner Temple 1985; Sultan Azlan Shah Law Lecturer, Malaysia 1990, Peter Allan Memorial Lecturer, Hong Kong 1994, Hamlyn Lecturer, UK 1996; Patron Wellington Cricket Asscn 1995–; Hon. Fellow Legal Research Foundation, NZ 1993; Hon. LLD (Vic. Univ. of Wellington) 1989, (Cambridge) 1990; Hon. DCL (Oxford) 1991; Yorke Prize 1954. *Publications:* Ed.: Portrait of a Profession (Centennial Book of NZ Law Soc.) 1969, Turning Points of the Common Law 1997; articles in law reviews. *Leisure interests:* The Times crossword, watching cricket, Shakespeare. *Address:* 4 Homewood Crescent, Karori, Wellington 6005, New Zealand (Home); Lords of Appeal Corridor, House of Lords, London SW1A 0PW, England (Office). *Telephone:* (4) 476-8059 (Home); (20) 7219-3202 (Office). *Fax:* (20) 7219-6156 (Office).

COOKSON, Richard Clive, PhD, FRSC, FRS; British chemist; b. 27 Aug. 1922, Hexham, Northumberland; s. of Clive and Marion (James) Cookson; m. Ellen Fawaz 1948; two s.; ed Harrow School and Trinity Coll. Cambridge; Research Fellow, Harvard Univ. 1948; Research Chemist, Glaxo Labs. Ltd 1949–51; Lecturer, Birkbeck Coll. London 1951–57; Prof. of Chem. Univ. of Southampton 1957–85, Prof. Emer. 1985–; Dir Cookson Chemicals Ltd 1986–94; Chair. Tocris Cookson Ltd 1994–. *Publications:* research papers. *Address:* Northfield House, Stratford Tony Road, Coombe Bissett, Salisbury, Wilts., SP5 4JZ, England.

COOLEY, Denton Arthur, BA, MD; American surgeon; b. 22 Aug. 1920, Houston, Tex.; s. of Ralph C. Cooley and Mary Fraley Cooley; m. Louise Goldsborough Thomas 1949; five d.; ed Univ. of Texas and Johns Hopkins Univ. School of Medicine; Intern Johns Hopkins School of Medicine, Baltimore 1944–45, Instructor surgery 1945–50; Sr Surgical Registrar Thoracic Surgery, Brompton Hospital for Chest Diseases, London 1950–51; Assoc. Prof. of Surgery Baylor Univ. Coll. of Medicine, Houston 1954–62, Prof. 1962–69; Surgeon-in-Chief (founder) Texas Heart Inst., Houston 1962–; Clinical Prof. of Surgery, Univ. of Texas Medical School, Houston 1975–; served as Capt., Chief Surgical Service, Army Medical Corps, Linz, Austria 1946–48; has performed numerous heart transplants; implanted first artificial heart 1969; mem. numerous socs and asscns; Hon. Doctorem Medicinae (Turin) 1969; Hon. Fellow Royal Coll. of Physicians and Surgeons 1980, Royal Coll. of Surgeons 1984, Royal Australasian Coll. of Surgeons 1986; Hoktoen Gold Medal 1954, Grande Médaille, Univ. of Ghent, Belgium 1963, René Leriche Prize, Int. Surgical Soc. 1965–67, Billings Gold Medal, American Medical Asscn 1967, Semmelweis Medal 1973, St Francis Cabrini Gold Medal (first recipient) 1980, Theodore Roosevelt Award, Nat. Collegiate Athletic Asscn 1980, Presidential Medal of Freedom 1984, Nat. Medal of Tech., US Dept of Commerce 1998; Knight Commdr, Order of Merit of Italian Repub., Order of the Sun, Peru and others. *Publications:* Surgical Treatment of Congenital Heart Disease 1966, Techniques in Cardiac Surgery 1975, 1984, Techniques in Vascular Surgery 1979, Essays of Denton A. Cooley—Reflections and Observations 1984; over 1,000 scientific articles. *Leisure interests:* golf, ranching. *Address:* Texas Heart Institute, PO Box 20345, 6621 Fannin Street, Houston, TX 77225-0345, USA (Office). *Telephone:* (713) 791-4900 (Office).

COOLIDGE, Martha; American film director, producer and writer; b. 17 Aug. 1946, New Haven, Conn.; d. of Robert Tilton Coolidge and Jean McMullen; m. Michael Backes; one s.; ed Rhode Island School of Design, Columbia Univ. and New York Univ. Inst. of Film and TV Grad. School; producer, Dir and writer of award-winning documentaries including Passing Quietly Through, David: Off and On, Old Fashioned Woman; wrote and produced daily children's TV show Magic Tom, Canada; author of original story filmed as The Omega Connection; Blue Ribbon Award, American Film Festival for first feature film Not a Pretty Picture. *Films include:* Bimbo, The

City Girl, Valley Girl, Joy of Sex, Glory Days, Real Genius, Plain Clothes, Rambling Rose, Lost in Yonkers, Angie, Three Wishes, Out to Sea. *Television includes:* The Twilight Zone, Sledge Hammer (pilot), House and Home (pilot), Trenchcoat in Paradise (film), Bare Essentials, Crazy in Love, Introducing Dorothy Dandridge 1999, If These Walls Could Talk II 2000, The Ponder Heart 2000, Flamingo Rising 2001–. *Leisure interest:* breeding Paso-Fino horses. *Address:* c/o Beverly Magid Guttman Associates, 118 South Beverly Drive, Suite 201, Beverly Hills, CA 90212, USA.

COOMBS, Douglas Saxon, CNZM, PhD, MSc, FRSNZ; New Zealand professor of geology; b. 23 Nov. 1924, Dunedin; s. of Leslie D. Coombs and Nellie Véra Coombs; m. Anne G. Tarrant 1956; two s. one d.; ed King's High School, Dunedin, Univ. of Otago, Emmanuel Coll., Cambridge; Asst Lecturer in Geology, Univ. of Otago 1947–48, Lecturer 1949, 1952–55, Prof. 1956–90, Prof. Emer. 1990–; 1851 Exhbn Scholar, Emmanuel Coll., Cambridge 1949–52; Visiting Prof. Pa State Univ. 1960, Yale Univ. 1967–68, Geneva Univ. 1968, 1975, Univ. of Calif. at Santa Barbara 1982; Vice-Pres. Int. Mineralogical Asscn 1974–86; Chair. Bd of Govs, King's High School 1979–88; Life Fellow Mineralogical Soc. of America 1961; Foreign Assoc. NAS 1977; Fellow Japan Soc. for Promotion of Science 1988; Hon. Fellow Geological Soc. of London 1968, Geological Soc. of America 1983; Hon. mem. Mineralogical Soc. of Great Britain and Ireland 1986; Hon. DSc (Geneva); McKay Hammer Award, Geological Soc. of NZ 1961, Hector Medal, Royal Soc. of NZ 1969. *Publications:* numerous scientific papers, especially on very low-grade metamorphism. *Leisure interest:* genealogy. *Address:* Geology Department, University of Otago, P.O. Box 56, Dunedin (Office); 6 Tolcarne Avenue, Dunedin, New Zealand (Home). *Telephone:* (3) 479-7505 (Office); (3) 467-5699 (Home). *Fax:* (3) 479-7527 (Office). *E-mail:* doug.coombs@stonebow.otago.ac.nz; coombs@earthlight.co.nz.

COOMBS, Philip H.; American educator and economist; b. 15 Aug. 1915, Holyoke, Mass.; s. of Chas and Nellie Coombs; m. Helena Brooks 1941; one s. one d.; ed Holyoke Public Schools, Amherst Coll., Univ. of Chicago and Brookings Inst.; Instructor in Econs, Williams Coll., Mass. 1940–41; Economist, Office of Price Admin. 1941–42; mem. US Army and Econ. Adviser, Office of Strategic Services and US Air Force 1942–45; Econ. Adviser to Dir of Office of Econ. Stabilization 1945–46; Deputy Dir Veterans Emergency Housing Program 1946–47; Prof. of Econs, Amherst Coll. 1947–49; Econ. Adviser to Gov. Chester Bowles, Conn. 1949–50; Exec. Dir President Truman's Materials Policy Comm. (Paley Comm.) 1951–52; Sec. and Dir of Research, Fund for Advancement of Educ. (Ford Foundation) 1952–61, Program Dir, Educ. Div., Ford Foundation 1957–61; Asst Sec. of State for Educational and Cultural Affairs, Dept of State 1961–62; Fellow Council on Foreign Relations 1962–63; Founding Dir Int. Inst. for Educational Planning (UNESCO), Paris 1963–68, Dir of Research 1969–70; Visiting Prof., Harvard Univ. Grad. School of Educ. 1969–70; Co-founder (with James Perkins) of Int. Council for Educational Devt 1970–1995, Vice-Chair. 1970–90, Chair. 1990–95; Faculty mem. Inst. of Social and Policy Studies, Yale Univ. 1970–72; Visiting Scholar, Univ. of London Inst. of Educ. 1983–86; Hon. Visiting Prof., Beijing Normal Univ., People's Republic of China 1987, 1988; mem. Council on Foreign Relations; Hon. LHD (Amherst Coll.) 1962; LLD (Brandeis Univ. and Monmouth Coll.); Legion of Merit 1944; Sociedad de Alfonso X el Sabio, Spain 1969, Orden Andres Bello (First Class) Venezuela 1987. *Publications:* The Fourth Dimension of Foreign Policy 1964, Education and Foreign Aid 1965, The World Educational Crisis—A Systems Analysis 1968, Managing Educational Costs 1972, New Paths to Learning: for Rural Children and Youth 1973, Attacking Rural Poverty: How Nonformal Education Can Help 1974, Education for Rural Development: Case Studies for Planners 1975, Meeting the Basic Needs of the Rural Poor: The Integrated, Community-Based Approach 1980, Future Critical World Issues in Education 1981, New Strategies for Improving Rural Family Life 1981, The World Crisis in Education: The View from the Eighties 1985, Cost Analysis: A Tool for Educational Policy and Planning 1987, The Spanish University Reform—An Assessment Report 1987, A Strategy to Improve the Quality of Mexican Higher Education 1992, A Productive Future for the Benemérita Universidad Autónoma de Puebla (Mexico) 1994, Report of External Evaluation of the Univ. do Vale do Paraiba (UNIVAP). *Leisure interests:* sailing, fishing, swimming, reading, touring, house repairs, community service. *Address:* 317 West Main Street, #6105, Chester, CT 06412, USA (Home). *Telephone:* (860) 526-9908. *Fax:* (860) 526-9923. *E-mail:* phcoombs1@aol.com (Home).

COOMBS, Stephen; British pianist; b. 11 July 1960; s. of Geoffrey Samuel Coombs and Joan Margaret Jones; ed Royal Northern Acad. of Music, RAM; debut at Wigmore Hall 1975; has given concerts and masterclasses in Britain, France, Germany, Italy, Hungary, Portugal, Switzerland, Scandinavia, Korea, Thailand, the Philippines, Hong Kong, USA; has appeared in festivals at Cheltenham, Salisbury, Snape Maltings Proms, Henley, the Three Choirs, Radley, Bath, Lichfield, Cardiff, Spoleto, Italy, St. Nazaire, France, Sintra, Portugal; visiting lecturer Univ. of Cen. England 1994–96; Founder and Artistic Dir 'Pianoworks' Int. Piano Festival, London 1998–99; Dir of Instrumental Studies, Blackheath Conservatoire of Music and the Arts 2001–; Gold Medal, First Int. Liszt Concourse, Hungary 1977, Worshipful Co. of Musicians/Maisie Lewis Award 1986 and numerous other awards and prizes. *Recordings include:* Two Piano Works of Debussy 1989, Ravel Works for Two Pianos 1990, Mendelssohn Two Double Piano Concertos 1992, Arensky Piano Concerto in F Minor and Fantasy on Russian Folk Songs 1992, Bortkiewicz Piano Concerto No. 1 1992, Arensky Suites for Two Pianos 1994, Glazunov

Complete Piano Works 4 Vols 1995, Glazunov Piano Concertos Nos. 1 & 2 1996, Goedicke Concertstück 1996, Reynaldo Hahn Piano Concerto 1997, Massenet Piano Concerto 1997, Bortkiewicz Piano Works 1997, Liadov Piano Works 1998, Milhaud Works for Two Pianos 1998, Arensky Piano Works 1998, Scriabin Early Piano Works 2001, Hahn Piano Quintet 2001, Verne Piano Quintet 2001. *Leisure interests:* genealogy, pubs, reading. *Address:* c/o Wordplay, 35 Lizban Street, Blackheath, London, SE3 8SS, England.

COOPER, Christopher W. (Chris); American actor; b. 9 July 1949, Kansas City; s. of Charles Cooper and Mary Ann Cooper; m. Marianne Leone 1983; one s.; ed Stephens Coll. Univ. of Missouri; Broadway debut in Of the Fields Lately 1980; London stage debut 1980; stage appearances include The Balled of Soapy Smith, A Different Moon (off-Broadway productions) 1983, Cobb, The Grapes of Wrath, Sweet Bird of Youth, Love Letters; TV appearances include Lonesome Dove (series) 1990, Return to Lonesome Dove (series) 1993; Cowboy Hall of Fame Award for Best Actor 1991. *Films include:* Bad Timing 1980, Matewan 1987, Lonesome Dove 1990, Thousand Pieces of Gold 1991, Guilty by Suspicion 1991, City of Hope 1991, This Boy's Life 1993, Pharaoh's Army 1995, Money Train 1995, Lone Star 1996, A Time to Kill 1996, Horton Foote's Alone 1997, Breast Men 1997, The Horse Whisperer 1998, Great Expectations 1998, October Sky 1999, American Beauty (Award for Outstanding Performance of a Cast in a Motion Picture, Screen Actors Guild 2000) 1999, The Patriot 2000, Me Myself and Irene 2000, The Bourne Identity 2002, The Ring 2002, Adaptation (Awards for Best Supporting Actor: Nat. Board of Review, Broadcast Film Asscn, LA Critics' Asscn, Golden Globe 2003, Acad. Award 2003) 2002, Seabiscuit 2003, Interstate 60 2003.

COOPER, Emmanuel, OBE,PhD; British ceramic potter, writer and critic; b. 12 Dec. 1938, Chesterfield; s. of Fred Cooper and Kate Elizabeth Cooper (née Cook); ed Clay Cross Tupton Hall Grammar School, Dudley Training Coll., Bournemouth and Hornsey Schools of Art; est. own studio in London 1965; part-time teacher Middx Polytechnic (now Univ.) –1998; Ed. Ceramic Review 1998; Visiting Prof. of Ceramics and Glass RCA 2000–; mem. Crafts Council Index, Visual Art and Architecture Panel, Arts Council 2000–; mem. Council Craft Potters Asscn, Arts Council of England 2000–. *Exhibitions:* Contemporary Applied Art, London 1998, Beaux Art, Bath 1996, 2000. *Publications:* People's Art: Visual Art and Working Class Culture 1992, Fully Exposed: The Male Nude in Photography 1996, Ten Thousand Years of Studio Pottery 2000, (ed) Lucie Rie 2002. *Leisure interests:* theatre, film, art. *Address:* 38 Chalcot Road, London, NW1 8LP, England. *Telephone:* (20) 7722-9090 (Home). *Fax:* (20) 7916-3462 (Home). *E-mail:* emmanuel.cooper@lineone.net.

COOPER, Imogen; British concert pianist; b. 28 Aug. 1949, London; d. of the late Martin Du Pré Cooper and of Mary Stewart; m. John Batten 1982; ed Paris Conservatoire and in Vienna with Alfred Brendel; TV début at Promenade Concerts, London 1975, has appeared regularly since then; first British pianist and first woman pianist in South Bank Piano series, Queen Elizabeth Hall, London; broadcasts regularly for BBC; performs with New York, Berlin, Vienna and LA Philharmonic orchestras and with Boston, London, Sydney, Melbourne and Concertgebouw Symphony orchestras; gives solo recitals worldwide. *Recordings include:* Schubert's Schwannengesang, Winterreise, Die Schöne Mullerin and Schumann's Heine Lieder and Kerner Lieder (with Wolfgang Holzmair), Mozart's Concerto for two pianos K.365 (with Alfred Brendel), Schubert four-hand piano music with Anne Queffélec and "The Last Six Years" of Schubert's piano music; Premier Prix, Paris Conservatoire 1967, Mozart Memorial Prize 1969; Hon. Mus.D. (Exon) 1999. *Leisure interests:* visual arts, reading, walking, architecture. *Address:* c/o Van Walsum Management Ltd, 4 Addison Bridge Place, London, W14 8XP, England. *Telephone:* (20) 7371-4343. *Fax:* (20) 7371-4344.

COOPER, Jilly; British writer; b. 21 Feb. 1937, Essex; d. of Brig. W.B. Sallitt, OBE and Mary Elaine Whincup; m. Leo Cooper 1961; one s. one d.; ed Godolphin School, Salisbury; reporter Middx Ind. 1957–59; account exec.; copy writer; publr.'s reader; receptionist; puppy fat model; switchboard wrecker; temp. typist 1959–69; columnist The Sunday Times 1969–82, Mail on Sunday 1982–87; Lifetime Achievement Award, British Book Awards 1998. *Publications:* 35 books, include: Class 1979, Intelligent and Loyal 1980, Animals in War 1983, The Common Years 1984, Riders 1985, Rivals 1988, Polo 1991, The Man who Made Husbands Jealous, Araminta's Wedding 1993, Apassionata 1996, How to Survive Christmas 1996, Score! 1999, Pandora 2002. *Leisure interests:* merry-making, mongrels, music, wild flowers. *Address:* c/o Vivienne Schuster, Curtis Brown, 4th Floor, Haymarket House, 28-29 Haymarket, London, SW1Y 4SP, England. *Telephone:* (20) 7396-6600 (Office). *Fax:* (20) 7396-0110 (Office). *E-mail:* cb@curtisbrown.co.uk.

COOPER, Leon N., DSc, PhD; American professor of physics; b. 28 Feb. 1930, New York; s. of Irving Cooper and Anna Zola; m. Kay Anne Allard 1969; two d.; ed Columbia Univ.; mem. Inst. for Advanced Study 1954–55; Research Assoc., Univ. of Ill. 1955–57; Asst Prof., Ohio State Univ. 1957–58; Assoc. Prof. Brown Univ. 1958–62, Prof. 1974, Thomas J. Watson Sr Prof. of Science 1974–, Dir Center for Neural Science 1978–90, Inst. for Brain and Neural Systems 1991–, Brain Science Program 2000–; Visiting Lecturer, Varenna, Italy 1955; Visiting Prof., Brandeis Summer Inst. 1959, Bergen Int. School of Physics, Norway 1961, Scuola Internazionale Di Fisica, Erice, Italy 1965, L'Ecole Normale Supérieure, Centre Universitaire Int., Paris 1966, Cargèse Summer School 1966, Radiation Lab., Univ. of Calif., Berkeley 1969, Faculty of Sciences, Quai St Bernard, Paris 1970, 1971, Brookhaven Nat. Lab. 1972; Consultant for various industrial and educational orgs.; Chair. of Math.

Models of Nervous System Fondation de France 1977–83; mem. Conseil supérieur de la Recherche Univ. René Descartes, Paris 1981–88; mem. Defence Science Bd 1989–93; Nat. Science Foundation Post-doctoral Fellow 1954–55; Alfred P. Sloan Foundation Research Fellow 1959–66; John Simon Guggenheim Memorial Foundation Fellow 1965–66; Fellow, American Physical Soc., American Acad. of Arts and Sciences; Sponsor, American Fed. of Scientists; mem. NAS, American Philosophical Soc.; Hon. DSc (Columbia, Sussex), 1973, (Illinois, Brown) 1974, (Gustavus Adolphus Coll.) 1975, (Ohio State Univ.) 1976, (Univ. Pierre et Marie Curie, Paris) 1977; Comstock Prize, NAS 1968; Nobel Prize 1972; Award in Excellence (Columbia Univ.) 1974; Descartes Medal, Acad. de Paris, Univ. René Descartes 1977; John Jay Award (Columbia Coll.) 1985. *Publications:* An Introduction to the Meaning and Structure of Physics 1968, Structure and Meaning 1992, How We Learn, How We Remember 1995; numerous scientific papers. *Leisure interests:* skiing, music, theatre. *Address:* Box 1843, Department of Physics and Neuroscience, Brown University, Providence, RI 02912-1843, USA (Office).

COOPER, Richard Newell, PhD; American professor of economics and fmr public official; b. 14 June 1934, Seattle, Wash.; s. of Richard W. Cooper and Lucile Newell; m. 1st Carolyn Cahalan 1956 (divorced 1980); m. 2nd Ann Lorraine Hollick 1982 (divorced 1994); m. 3rd Jin Chen 2000; two s. one d.; ed Oberlin Coll., London School of Econs, UK, Harvard Univ.; Sr Staff Economist, Council of Econ. Advisers 1961–63; Deputy Asst Sec. of State for Monetary Affairs 1965–66; Prof. of Econs, Yale Univ. 1966–77, Provost 1972–74; Under-Sec. of State for Econ. Affairs 1977–81; Maurits C. Boas Prof. of Econs Harvard Univ. 1981–; Dir Rockefeller Bros. Fund 1975–77, Schroders Bank and Trust Co. 1975–77, Warburg-Pincus Funds 1986–98, Center for Naval Analysis 1992–95, Phoenix Cos 1983–, Circuit City Stores 1983–, CNA Corpn 1997–, Inst. for Int. Econs 1983–, Fed. Reserve Bank of Boston 1987–92 (Chair. 1990–92); Chair. Nat. Intelligence Council 1995–97; consultant to U.S. Treasury, Nat. Security Council, World Bank, IMF, U.S. Navy; Marshall Scholarship (UK) 1956–58; Fellow American Acad. of Sciences 1974; Hon. LLD (Oberlin Coll.) 1958, Dr. hc (Paris II) 2000; Nat. Intelligence Medal 1996. *Publications:* The Economics of Interdependence 1968, Economic Policy in an Interdependent World 1986, The International Monetary System 1987, Stabilization and Debt in Developing Countries 1992, Boom, Crisis and Adjustment (co-author) 1993, Environment and Resource Policies for the World Economy 1994, Trade Growth in Transition Economies (ed.) 1997, What The Future Holds (ed.) 2002. *Address:* Center for International Affairs, Harvard University, 1033 Massachusetts Avenue, Cambridge, MA 02138 (Office); 33 Washington Avenue, Cambridge, MA 02140, USA (Home). *Telephone:* (617) 495-5076 (Office). *Fax:* (617) 495-8292 (Office). *E-mail:* rcooper@fas.harvard.edu (Office). *Website:* www.economics.harvard.edu (Office).

COOR, Lattie Finch, PhD; American academic; b. 26 Sept. 1936, Phoenix, Ariz.; s. of Lattie F. Coor and Elnora (née Witten) Coor; m. Elva Wingfield 1994; three c. from a previous marriage; ed N Arizona Univ., Washington Univ., St Louis, American Coll., Greece; admin. Asst to Gov. of Mich. 1961–62; Asst to Chancellor, Washington Univ., St Louis 1963–67, Asst Dean, Grad. School of Arts and Sciences 1967–69, Dir Int. Studies 1967–69, Asst Prof. of Political Science 1967–76, Vice-Chancellor 1969–74, Univ. Vice-Chancellor 1974–76; Pres., Univ. of Vt, Burlington 1976–89; Pres. Ariz. State Univ. 1990–2002, Pres. Emer. 2002–, Prof. of Public Affairs; consultant for Dept of Health, Educ. and Welfare; special consultant to US Commr for Educ. 1971–74; Chair., Cttee on governmental relations, American Council on Educ. 1976–80; Dir New England Bd of Higher Educ. 1976–; mem. Pres.'s Comm., Nat. Coll. Athletic Asscn, Nat. Asscn State Univs. and Land Grant Colls. (Chair. Bd 1991–92). *Address:* Arizona State University, Administration Building, Tempe, AZ 85287-2203, USA (Office). *E-mail:* Lattie.Coor@asu.edu (Office).

COORE, David Hilton, BA, BCL, QC, MP; Jamaican politician; b. 22 Aug. 1925, St Andrew; s. of Clarence Reuben Coore and Ethlyn Maud Hilton; m. Rita Innis 1949; three s.; ed Jamaica Coll., McGill Univ., Exeter Coll., Oxford; practised as barrister-at-law in Jamaica 1950–72; mem. Legis. Council 1960–62; Opposition Spokesman on Finance 1967–72; Chair. People's Nat. Party 1969–78; mem. Parl. 1972–; Deputy Prime Minister 1972–78, also Minister of Finance 1972–78, of Planning 1977–78, of Foreign Affairs and Foreign Trade 1989, of Legal Affairs and Attorney Gen. 1993–95; Leader Govt Business 1989; Chair. Bd of Govs. Caribbean Devt Bank 1972–73, Inter-American Devt Bank 1973–74; Queen's Counsel 1961. *Leisure interests:* reading, swimming, golf. *Address:* c/o Ministry of Legal Affairs, 12 Ocean Boulevard, Kingston Mall, Kingston 10, Jamaica.

COPE, Jonathan, CBE; British ballet dancer; b. 1963; m. Maria Almeida, one s. one d.; ed Royal Ballet School; joined Royal Ballet 1982, Soloist 1985–86, Prin. 1987–90, 1992–; set up property devt business 1990–92. *Leading roles (with Royal Ballet) include:* Prince in Swan Lake, The Sleeping Beauty and The Nutcracker, Romeo and Juliet (partnering Sylvie Guillem and Darcey Bussell, q.v.), Solor in La Bayadère, Albrecht in Giselle, Le Baiser de la Fée, The Prince of the Pagodas, Cinderella, Palemon in Ondine, Serenade, Agon, Apollo, Opus 19/The Dreamer, The Sons of Horus, Young Apollo, Galanteries, The Planets, Still Life at the Penguin Café, The Spirit of Fugue, Concerto, Gloria, Requiem, A Broken Set of Rules, Pursuit, Piano, Grand Pas Classique, Monotones, Crown Prince Rudolph in Mayerling, Woyzeck in Different Drummer, Second Friend in The Judas Tree, Beliaev in A Month in the Country, Birthday Offering, La Valise, Air Monotones II, Fox in Renard,

Fearful Symmetries, Symphony in C (partnering Sylvie Guillem), Duo Concertant, If This Is Still a Problem, Des Grieux in Manon, Illuminations. *Address:* The Royal Ballet, Royal Opera House, Covent Garden, London, WC2E 9DD, England. *Telephone:* (20) 7240-1200. *Fax:* (20) 7212-9121.

COPE, Wendy Mary, MA, FRSL; British writer; b. 21 July 1945, Erith; d. of Fred Stanley Cope and Alice Mary Cope (née Hand); ed Farringtons School, St Hilda's Coll., Oxford Univ., Westminster Coll. of Educ., Oxford; primary school teacher, London 1967–86; professional writer 1986–; Hon. DLitt (Southampton); Cholmondeley Award for Poetry 1987, Michael Braude Award, American Acad. of Arts and Letters 1995. *Publications:* Making Cocoa for Kingsley Amis (poetry) 1986, Serious Concerns (poetry) 1992, If I Don't Know (poetry) 2001. *Leisure interest:* music. *Address:* c/o Faber and Faber, 3 Queen Square, London, WC1N 3AU, England. *Telephone:* (20) 7465-0045.

COPPEL, Ronald Lewis, AM, FCA; Australian stock exchange official and accountant; b. 19 Dec. 1933, Belfast; s. of Marcus Coppel and Mabel Coppel; m. Valerie K. Bentley 1960; one s. one d.; ed Royal Belfast Academical Inst. and Belfast Coll. of Tech.; partner, Coppel & Coppel (chartered accountants), Belfast 1957–63; Sr Accountant, C.P. Bird & Assocs. Perth, W Australia 1963–67; partner, Crowther, Bird & Spillsbury (public accountants), Perth 1967–70; Gen. Man. The Stock Exchange of Perth Ltd 1970–74; Exec. Dir Australian Associated Stock Exchanges 1974–87; Exec. Dir and Deputy Man. Dir Australian Stock Exchange Ltd 1987–94; Chair. ASX Settlement Transfer and Clearing Corpn Ltd 1994–; mem. Accounting Standards Review Bd 1986–90. *Leisure interests:* current affairs, walking, music, theatre. *Address:* 137 Koola Avenue, Killara, NSW 2071, Australia. *Telephone:* (2) 9498-6185 (Office). *Fax:* (2) 9498-2814 (Office). *E-mail:* tanagra@island.com.au.

COPPENS, Yves; French professor of palaeoanthropology and prehistory; b. 9 Aug. 1934, Vannes; s. of René Coppens and Andrée Coppens; m. Françoise Le Guennec 1959; ed Univ. of Rennes, Univ. of Paris (Sorbonne); Research Asst CNRS, Paris 1956–69; Assoc. Prof., then Prof. Nat. Museum of Natural History 1969–83; Prof. of Palaeoanthropology and Prehistory, Collège de France 1983–; mem. Acad. of Sciences 1985–, Nat. Acad. of Medicine 1991–, Royal Acad. of Sciences (Belgium) 1992–; Dr. hc (Bologna Univ.) 1988, (Liège Univ.) 1992; prizes include Silver Medal CNRS, Kalinga Prize for Popularization of Science (UNESCO) 1984, Glaxo Prize 1978; Chevalier, Légion d'honneur, Officier, Ordre Nat. du Mérite, Officier des Palmes Académiques, Officier, des Arts et des Lettres, Officier, Ordre Nat. Tchadien. *Publications:* over 400 scientific papers; ed., author or jt author of over 20 books on palaeontology, anthropology and prehistory. *Address:* Musée de l'Homme, Palais de Chaillot, place du Trocadéro, 75116 Paris (Office); Collège de France, 11 place Marcelin Berthelot, 75005 Paris, Cedex 5; 4 rue du Pont-aux-Choux, 75003 Paris, France (Home). *Telephone:* 1-44-27-10-23.

COPPERFIELD, David; American magician; b. Kotkin, 1956, Metuchen, NJ; ed Fordham Univ.; Prof. of Magic, New York Univ. 1974; appeared in musical Magic Man 1974; presenter, The Magic of ABC; performer, Dir, producer, writer, The Magic of David Copperfield 1978–; creator, founder, Project Magic 1982; levitated across Grand Canyon 1984; walked through Great Wall of China 1986; escaped from Alcatraz prison 1987; made Statue of Liberty disappear 1989; went over Niagara Falls 1990; made Orient Express disappear 1991; introduced flying illusion 1992; escaped from burning ropes 13 storeys above ground, Caesar's Palace 1993; appearances in Taiwan 1987, Mexico City 1987, Hong Kong, Singapore, Kuala Lumpur, Brazil 1988, Germany 1993; first UK tour 1994; European tour 1995; Golden Rose Award, Montreux Film Festival 1987; recipient of numerous Emmy awards and nominations; Bambi award 1993, etc. *Film:* Terror Train 1980.

COPPERWHEAT, Lee; British fashion designer; s. of Terence Copperwheat and Diana Frances Brooks; ed Tresham Coll., Northampton, London Coll. of Fashion; fmrly tailor with Aquascutum; est. design room and fmr man. of sampling and production Passenger sportswear; freelance design projects for numerous clients; fmr teacher menswear tailoring Brighton Univ.; fmr lecturer St Martin's School of Art, London; formed Copperwheat Blundell with Pamela Blundell (q.v.); Young Designer of the Year 1994 (with Pamela Blundell). *Address:* Copperwheat Blundell, 14 Cheshire Street, London, E2 6EH, England.

COPPOLA, Francis Ford; American film director and writer; b. 7 April 1939, Detroit, Michigan; s. of Carmine and Italia Coppola; m. Eleanor Neil; two s. (one deceased) one d.; ed Hofstra Univ., Univ. of California; theatre direction includes Private Lives, The Visit of the Old Lady, San Francisco Opera Co. 1972; Artistic Dir Zoetrope Studios 1969–; owner Niebaum-Coppola Estate, Napa Valley; Cannes Film Award for The Conversation 1974; Director's Guild Award for The Godfather; Acad. Award for Best Screenplay for Patton, Golden Palm (Cannes) 1979 for Apocalypse Now, also awarded Best Screenplay, Best Dir and Best Picture Oscars for The Godfather Part II; U.S. Army Civilian Service Award; Commdr Ordre des Arts et des Lettres. *Films include:* Dementia 13 1963, This Property is Condemned 1965, Is Paris Burning? 1966, You're a Big Boy Now 1967, Finian's Rainbow 1968, The Rain People 1969, Patton 1971, The Godfather 1972, American Grafitti 1973, The Conversation 1974, The Godfather Part II 1975, The Great Gatsby 1974, The Black Stallion (produced) 1977, Apocalypse Now 1979, One from the Heart 1982, Hammett (produced) 1982, The Escape Artist 1982, The Return of the Black Stallion 1982, Rumble Fish 1983, The Outsiders 1983, The Cotton Club 1984, Peggy Sue Got Married 1986, Gardens of Stone 1986, Life without Zoe 1988, Tucker: The Man and His Dream 1988, The Godfather Part III 1990,

Dracula 1991, My Family/Mi Familia 1995, Don Juan De Marco 1995, Jack 1996, The Rainmaker 1997, The Florentine 1999, The Virgin Suicides 1999, Grapefruit Moon 2000, The Two Fridas, Assassination Tango (producer), Supernova, Megalopolis; exec. producer The Secret Garden 1993, Mary Shelley's Frankenstein 1994, Buddy 1997, The Third Miracle 1999, Goosed 1999, Sleepy Hollow 1999, Monster, Jeepers Creepers, No Such Thing, Pumpkin. *Address:* Zoetrope Studios, 916 Kearny Street, San Francisco, CA 94133; c/o CAA, 9830 Wilshire Boulevard, Beverly Hills, CA 90212, USA.

COPPS, Sheila Maureen, PC, BA; Canadian politician; b. 27 Nov. 1952, Hamilton, Ont.; d. of Victor Kennedy and Geraldine Florence (Guthro) Copps; m. Austin Thorne; one d.; ed Univ. of Western Ont., Univ. of Rouen, France, McMaster Univ.; journalist, Ottawa Citizen 1974–76, Hamilton Spectator 1977; Constituency Asst to Leader Liberal Party Ont. 1977–81; MP for Hamilton Centre 1981–84; Deputy Leader Fed. Liberal Party; Deputy Prime Minister 1993–97, Minister of the Environment 1993–96, Minister of Canadian Heritage 1996–. *Publication:* Nobody's Baby 1986. *Address:* House of Commons 5095, Ottawa, Ont., K1A 0A6 (Office); Ministry of Canadian Heritage, Immeuble Jules Léger, 15 rue Eddy, Hull, Québec, K1A 1K5, Canada. *Telephone:* (819) 997-7788. *Fax:* (819) 994-1267. *E-mail:* min_copps@pch.gc.ca (Office). *Website:* www.pch.gc.ca (Office).

CORBALLY, John Edward, PhD; American university administrator; b. 14 Oct. 1924, South Bend, Wash.; s. of John E. and Grace Williams Corbally; m. Marguerite Walker 1946; one s. one d.; ed Univs of Washington and California, Berkeley; High School Teacher and principal, State of Wash. 1947–53; Coll. of Educ. Faculty, Ohio State Univ. 1955–61, Dir Personnel Budget 1959–61, Exec. Asst to Pres. 1961–64, Vice-Pres. for Admin. 1964–66, Vice-Pres. for Academic Affairs and Provost 1966–69; Chancellor and Pres. Syracuse Univ. 1969–71; Pres. Univ. of Illinois 1971–79, Pres. Emer. 1979–, Distinguished Prof. of Higher Educ. 1979–82, Prof. Emer. 1982–; Dir John D. and Catherine T. MacArthur Foundation 1979–, Pres. 1980–89, Chair. 1995–; Consultant Heidrik & Struggles 1989–90; Chair. Nat. Council on Educational Research 1973–79; Hon. LLD (Univ. of Md 1971, Blackburn Coll. 1972, Ill. State Univ. 1977, Univ. of Akron 1978, Ohio State Univ. 1980). *Publications:* co-author: Educational Administration: The Secondary School 1961, School Finance 1962, An Introduction to Educational Administration 1984. *Leisure interests:* gardening, travel. *Address:* 1507 151st Place, SE Mill Creek, WA 98012, USA.

CORBETT, Gerald Michael Nolan, MA, MSc; British business executive; b. 7 Sept. 1951, Hastings, Sussex; s. of the late John Michael Nolan Corbett and of Pamela Muriel Corbett (née Gay); m. Virginia Moore Newsum; one s. three d.; ed Tonbridge School, Prembroke Coll. Cambridge and the London Business School; with Boston Consulting Group 1975–82; Group Financial Controller Dixons Group PLC 1982–86, Corp. Finance Dir 1986–87; Group Finance Dir Redland PLC 1987–94, Grand Metropolitan PLC 1994–97; Dir (non-exec.) MEPC PLC 1995–98, Burmah Castrol PLC 1998–2000; CEO Railtrack PLC 1997–2000; Chair. Woolworths Group PLC 2001–; Chair. Bd of Govs Abbots Hill School 1997–2002; Foundation Scholar, Pembroke Coll., Cambridge 1972–75, William Pitt Prize 1974, London Business School Prize 1979. *Leisure interests:* tennis, skiing, fishing, golf, country pursuits. *Address:* Woolworths Group PLC, Woolworth House, 242–246 Marylebone Road, London, NW1 6JL (Office); Holtsmere End Farm, Redbourn, Herts., AL3 7AW, England (Home). *Telephone:* (20) 7706-5524 (Office); (1582) 792336 (Home). *Fax:* (20) 7479-5328 (Office); (1582) 722718 (Home). *E-mail:* gerald.corbett@woolworths.co.uk (Office). *Website:* www.woolworthsgroupplc.com.

CORBETT, Michael McGregor, BA, LLB; South African judge; b. 14 Sept. 1923, Pretoria; s. of Alan Frederick Corbett and Johanna Sibella McGregor; m. Margaret Murray Luscombe 1949; two s. two d.; ed Univ. of Cape Town, Trinity Coll. Cambridge, England; enlisted in SA Army 1942, active service 1943–44; admitted as advocate and commenced practice at Cape Bar, Cape Town 1948, appointed QC 1961–, Judge of Cape Prov. Div. of Supreme Court 1963, Judge of Appeal 1974, Chief Justice of SA 1989–96; Hon. LLD (Cape Town) 1982, (OFS) 1990, (Rhodes) 1990, (Pretoria) 1993, (Witwatersrand) 1994, (Stellenbosch) 1996; Hon. Bencher Lincoln's Inn 1991; Hon. Fellow Trinity Coll. Cambridge 1992; Hon. mem. American Bar Asscn 1997; Order for Meritorious Service 1996; Pres. of Convocation Medal, Univ. of Cape Town 1998. *Publications:* The Quantum of Damages in Bodily and Fatal Injury Cases (jtly) 1960, The Law of Succession in South Africa (jtly) 1980. *Leisure interests:* tennis, walking. *Address:* 18 Ladies Mile Extension, Constantia, Cape Town 7806, South Africa (Home).

CORBO, Vittorio, PhD; Chilean economist; b. 22 March 1943, Iquique; s. of Gerardo Corbo and Maria Lioi; m. Veronica Urzua 1967; one s. one d.; ed Universidad de Chile and Mass. Inst. of Tech.; Asst Prof. Concordia Univ. 1972–74, Assoc. Prof. 1974–78, Prof. of Econs 1979–81; Prof. Inst. of Econs Pontificia Univ. Católica de Chile 1981–84, 1991–; Sr adviser, IBRD 1984–87, Div. Chief. 1987–91; Vice-Pres. Int. Econ. Asscn 2000–; econ. adviser, Santander Group 1991–; Visiting Prof. Georgetown Univ., Washington, DC 1985–91. *Publications:* Inflation in Developing Countries 1974, Monetary Policy in Latin America in the 1990s 2000. *Leisure interest:* the sky. *Address:* Instituto de Economía, Pontificia Universidad Católica de Chile, Casilla 114–D, Alameda 340, Santiago, Chile. *E-mail:* vcorbo@rdc.cl (Home). *Website:* www.puc.cl.

CORBY, Sir (Frederick) Brian, Kt, MA, FIA; British company executive and actuary; b. 10 May 1929, Raunds, Northants.; s. of Charles Walter and Millicent Corby; m. Elizabeth Mairi McInnes 1952; one s. two d.; ed Kimbolton School and St John's Coll., Cambridge; joined Prudential Assurance Co. Ltd 1952, Asst Gen. Man. (Overseas) 1968–73, Deputy Gen. Man. 1974–75, Gen. Man. 1976–79, Chief Actuary 1980–81, Group Gen. Man., Prudential Corpn PLC 1979–82, CEO 1982–90, Chair. 1990–95; Chief Gen. Man. Prudential Assurance Co. Ltd 1982–85, Chair. 1985–90; Deputy Pres. CBI 1989–90, Pres. 1990–92; Pres. Nat. Inst. for Econ. and Social Research 1994–; Vice-Pres. Inst. of Actuaries 1979–83; Chair. South Bank Bd 1990–98; Deputy Chair. British Insurance Asscn 1984–85; Chair. Asscn of British Insurers 1985–87; Dir Bank of England 1985–93, Pan-Holding 1993–, Montanaro Small Cos. Investment Trust PLC (Chair.) 1995–99, Mid-Ocean Reinsurance 1995–98, Brockbank Holdings Ltd (Chair.) 1995–99, Moorfield Estates PLC (Chair.) 1996–2000, XL Capital 1998–, Nat. Asscn of Security Dealers, Inc. 2000–; Chancellor Univ. of Herts. 1992–96. *Publications:* articles in Journal of Inst. of Actuaries. *Leisure interests:* reading, golf, gardening. *Address:* Fairings, Church End, Albury, Ware, Herts., SG11 2JG, England.

CORCUERA CUESTA, José Luis; Spanish politician; b. 2 July 1945, Pradoluengo, Burgos Prov.; m.; two d.; joined Partido Socialista Obrero Español 1973; joined Unión Gen. de Trabajadores (UGT) 1973, Org. Sec. Metalworking Fed., UGT, later Gen. Sec. 1977; mem. UGT Exec. Cttee 1980–85, Exec. Sec. Fed. Exec. Cttee 1986, Sec. for Inst. Policy 1988; Deputy for Vizcaya 1979, 1982–94; Minister of the Interior 1989–93. *Address:* c/o PSOE, Ferraz 68 y 70, 28008 Madrid, Spain.

CORDEN, Warner Max, AC, MComm, MA, PhD, FBA, FASSA; Australian professor of international economics; b. 13 Aug. 1927, Breslau, Germany (now Wrocław, Poland); s. of the late Ralph S. Corden; m. Dorothy Martin 1957; one d.; ed Melbourne Boys High School, Univ. of Melbourne and LSE; Lecturer, Univ. of Melbourne 1958–61; Nuffield Reader in Int. Econ. and Fellow of Nuffield Coll., Oxford 1967–76; Professorial Fellow, Australian Nat. Univ. 1962–67, Prof. of Econs 1976–88; Chung Ju Yung Prof. of Int. Econ., Paul H. Nitze School of Advanced Int. Studies, Johns Hopkins Univ. 1989–2002; Professorial Fellow, Univ. of Melbourne 2002–; Visiting Prof., Univ. of Calif. (Berkeley) 1965, Univ. of Minn. 1971, Princeton Univ. 1973, Harvard Univ. 1986; Sr Adviser, IMF 1986–88; Pres. Econ. Soc. of Australia and New Zealand 1977–80; mem. Group of Thirty 1982–90; Foreign Hon. mem. American Econ. Asscn 1986; Distinguished Fellow, Econ. Soc. of Australia 1995; Hon. Dr. (Melbourne) 1995; Bernard Harms Prize 1986. *Publications:* The Theory of Protection 1971, Trade Policy and Economic Welfare 1974, 1997, Inflation, Exchange Rates and the World Economy 1977, 1985, Protection, Growth and Trade 1985, International Trade Theory and Policy 1992, Economic Policy, Exchange Rates and the International System 1994, The Road to Reform 1997, Too Sensational: On the Choice of Exchange Rate Regimes 2002. *Address:* Dept of Economics and Commerce, University of Melbourne, Melbourne, Victoria 3010, Australia (Office). *Telephone:* (3) 8344-5296 (Office). *Fax:* (3) 8344-6899 (Office). *E-mail:* m.corden@unimelb.edu.au (Office).

CORDOBA, José ("Pepe"); Mexican public servant; b. Paris, France; ed Sorbonne, Paris, Stanford Univ., USA; naturalized Mexican 1985; Chef de Cabinet, Pres.'s Office 1988–. *Address:* Oficina del Presidente, Los Pinos, Puerta 1, Col. San Miguel Chapultepec, 11850 México, DF, Mexico.

CORDOVEZ, Diego; Ecuadorean diplomatist and lawyer; b. 3 Nov. 1935, Quito; s. of Luis Cordovez-Borja and Isidora Zegers de Cordovez; m. Maria Teresa Somavia 1960; one s.; ed Univ. of Chile; admitted to Bar 1962; foreign service of Ecuador until 1963; joined UN as Econ. Affairs Officer 1963; political officer on special missions to Dominican Repub. 1965, Pakistan 1971; Dir UN Econ. and Social Council Secr. 1973–78, Asst Sec.-Gen. for Econ. and Social Matters, UN 1978–81; Special Rep. of UN Sec.-Gen. on Libya–Malta dispute 1980–82; Sec.-Gen.'s rep. on UN Comm. of Inquiry on hostage crisis in Tehran 1980; Sr officer responsible for efforts to resolve Iran/Iraq war 1980–88; Under-Sec.-Gen. for Special Political Affairs 1981–1988; Special Envoy to Grenada 1983; UN Mediator, Afghanistan 1982–88, Rep. for implementation of Geneva Accords 1988–89; Minister for Foreign Affairs 1988–92; Pres. World Trade Center (Ecuador) 1993–98; Special Counsel LeBoeuf, Lamb, Greene and Macrae 1993–98; Special Adviser to UN Sec. Gen. for Cyprus 1997–99, for Latin American Affairs 1999–, Pres. Andean Centre for Int. Studies 2000; mem. American Soc. of Int. Law; Order of Merit (Ecuador), Légion d'honneur, Grand Cross (Spain, Portugal, Brazil, Argentina, Chile, Peru, Colombia, Venezuela). *Publications:* UNCTAD and Development Diplomacy 1971, Out of Afghanistan: The Inside Story of the Soviet Withdrawal (jtly) 1995, Nuestra Propuesta Inconclusa (Ecuador - Perú: Del Inmovilismo al Acuerdo de Brasilia) 2000. *Leisure interests:* reading, carpentry. *Address:* Calle Afganistán N41–90, El Bosque, Quito, Ecuador. *Fax:* (5932) 244-0289. *E-mail:* mail@diegocordovez.com (Home).

CORELL, Hans, LLB; Swedish diplomatist and lawyer; b. 7 July 1939, Västermo; s. of Alf Corell and Margit Norrman; m. Inger Peijfors 1964; one s. one d.; ed Univ. of Uppsala; court clerk, Eksjö Dist Court and Göta Court of Appeal 1962–67; Asst Judge, Västervik Dist Court 1968–72; Legal Adviser, Ministry of Justice 1972, 1974–79; Additional mem. and Assoc. Judge of Appeal, Svea Court of Appeal 1973; Asst Under-Sec. Div. for Constitutional and Admin. Law, Ministry of Justice 1979–81; Judge of Appeal 1980; Under-Sec. for Legal Affairs, Ministry of Justice 1981–84; Amb. and Under-Sec. for Legal and Consular Affairs, Ministry of Foreign Affairs 1984–94; mem. Perm. Court of Arbitration, The Hague 1990–; Under-Sec.-Gen. for Legal Affairs,

The Legal Counsel of the UN 1994–; Hon. LLD (Stockholm) 1997; William J. Butler Human Rights Medal (Cincinnati) 2001. *Publications:* Sekretesslagen (co-author) 1992, Proposal for an International War Crimes Tribunal for the Former Yugoslavia (CSCE Report) (co-author) 1993; various legal publs. *Leisure interests:* art, music (Piper of the Caledonian Pipes and Drums of Stockholm 1975–84), ornithology. *Address:* UN Secretariat, Room S-3427, New York, NY 10017 (Office); 249 East 48th Street, New York, NY 10017, USA (Home). *Telephone:* (212) 963-5338 (Office); (212) 753-1160 (Home). *E-mail:* corell@un.org (Office). *Website:* www.un.org/law.

CORELLI, Franco; Italian tenor; b. 8 April 1921, Ancona; ed Pesaro Conservatory, Maggio Musicale, Florence; first appearance as Don José in Carmen, Spoleto 1951; appeared in Spontini's La Vestale, La Scala, Milan 1954, Teatro San Carlo, Naples 1955, Cavaradossi, Covent Garden, London 1956, Rome 1957, 1958, Naples 1958, La Scala (with Maria Callas) 1960; Metropolitan Opera début as Manrico in Il Trovatore 1961; has sung maj. parts in Andrea Chénier, La Bohème, Turandot, Tosca, Ernani, Aïda, Don Carlos, Forza del Destino, Cavalleria Rusticana, I Pagliacci, etc.; performs regularly on American TV; recital tour with Renata Tebaldi; 1st Prize Spoleto Nat. Competition. *Address:* c/o Teatro alla Scala, Via Filodrammatici 2, Milan, Italy.

COREN, Alan, MA; British editor, author and broadcaster; b. 27 June 1938, London; s. of Samuel Coren and Martha Coren; m. Anne Kasriel 1963; one s. one d.; ed East Barnet Grammar School, Wadham Coll., Oxford, Univ. of California, Berkeley and Yale Univ.; Asst Ed. Punch 1963–66, Literary Ed. 1966–69, Deputy Ed. 1969–77, Ed. 1977–87; Ed. The Listener 1988–89; TV critic, The Times 1971–78, Columnist 1988–; Columnist, Daily Mail 1972–76, Mail on Sunday 1984–92, Sunday Express 1992–96; contrib. to Observer, Listener, Sunday Times, Atlantic Monthly, TV Guide, Tatler, Times Literary Supplement, London Review of Books, Daily Telegraph, The Spectator, Playboy, Guardian; Commonwealth Fellowship 1961–63; Rector St Andrew's Univ. 1973–76; Hon. DLitt (Nottingham) 1993, British Soc. of Magazine Eds. Ed. of the Year 1986. *Publications:* The Dog it was that Died 1965, All Except the Bastard 1969, The Sanity Inspector 1974, The Collected Bulletins of Idi Amin 1974, Golfing for Cats 1975, The Further Bulletins of Idi Amin 1975, The Arthur Books (12 novellas) 1976–80, The Lady from Stalingrad Mansions 1977, The Peanut Papers 1977, The Rhinestone as Big as the Ritz 1979, Tissues for Men 1980, The Cricklewood Diet 1982, Bumf 1984, Something for the Weekend 1986, Bin Ends 1987, Seems Like Old Times 1989, More Like Old Times 1990, A Year in Cricklewood 1991, Toujours Cricklewood? 1993, Sunday Best 1993, Animal Passions 1994, A Bit on the Side 1995, The Alan Coren Omnibus 1996, The Cricklewood Dome 1998, The Cricklewood Tapestry 2000. *Leisure interests:* bridge, tennis, riding. *Address:* c/o Robson Books, 10 Blenheim Court, Brewery Road, London, N7 9NY, England.

COREY, Elias James, PhD; American professor of chemistry; b. 12 July 1928, Methuen, Mass.; s. of Elias J. Corey and Tina Hasham; m. Claire Higham 1961; two s. one d.; ed Mass. Inst. of Tech.; Instructor in Chem., Univ. of Ill. 1951–53, Asst Prof. of Chem. 1953–55, Prof. 1956–59; Prof. of Chem., Harvard Univ. 1959–68, Chair. Dept of Chem. 1965–68, Sheldon Emery Prof. 1968–; Alfred P. Sloan Foundation Fellow 1955–57, Guggenheim Fellow 1957, 1968–69; mem. American Acad. of Arts and Sciences 1960–68, NAS 1966; Hon. AM, Hon. DSc; Pure Chem. Award of American Chemical Soc. 1960, Fritzsche Award of American Chemical Soc. 1967, Intra-Science Foundation Award 1967, Harrison Howe Award, American Chemical Soc. 1970, Award for Synthetic Organic Chem. 1971, CIBA Foundation Award 1972, Evans Award, Ohio State Univ. 1972, Linus Pauling Award 1973, Dickson Prize in Science, Carnegie Mellon Univ. 1973, George Ledlie Prize, (Harvard) 1973, Remsen Award, Arthur C. Cope Award 1976, Nichols Medal 1977, Buchman Memorial Award (Calif. Inst. of Tech.) 1978, Franklin Medal 1978, Scientific Achievement Award Medal 1979, J. G. Kirkwood Award (Yale) 1980, C. S. Hamilton Award (Univ. of Nebraska) 1980, Chemical Pioneer Award (American Inst. of Chemists) 1981, Rosenstiel Award (Brandeis Univ.) 1982, Paul Karrer Award (Zurich Univ.) 1982, Medal of Excellence (Helsinki Univ.) 1982, Tetrahedron Prize 1983, Gibbs Award (American Chem. Soc.) 1984, Paracelsus Award (Swiss Chem. Soc.) 1984, V. D. Mattia Award (Roche Inst. of Molecular Biology) 1985, Wolf Prize in Chemistry (Wolf Foundation) 1986, Silliman Award (Yale Univ.) 1986, U.S. Nat. Medal of Science 1988, Japan Prize 1989, Nobel Prize for Chemistry 1990 and numerous others. *Publications:* approx. 700 chemical papers. *Leisure interests:* outdoor activities and music. *Address:* Department of Chemistry, Harvard University, 12 Oxford Street, Cambridge, MA 02138-2902 (Office); 20 Avon Hill Street, Cambridge, MA 02140, USA (Home). *Telephone:* (617) 495-4033 (Office); (617) 864-0627 (Home).

CORFIELD, Sir Kenneth (George), Kt, CE, FEng, FIEE, FIMechE; British company executive and engineer; b. 27 Jan. 1924, Rushall; s. of Stanley Corfield and Dorothy Elizabeth Corfield (née Mason); m. Patricia Jean Williams 1960; one d.; ed Elmore Green High School, South Staffs. Coll. of Advanced Tech.; Tech. Officer, ICI Ltd 1947–50; Chief Exec., KG Corfield Ltd, camera Mfrs 1950–61; Exec. Dir Parkinson Cowan Ltd 1962–67; Vice-Pres., Dir ITT Europe Inc. 1967–70; Man. Dir Standard Telephones and Cables Ltd 1970–85, Deputy Chair. 1974–79, Chair. and CEO 1979–85; Chair. Standard Telephones and Cables (N Ireland) 1974–85; Vice-Pres. Int. Standard Electric Corpn, ITT Sr Officer in UK 1974–84; Chair. Nat. Econ. Devt Cttee for Ferrous Foundries Industry 1975–78; Vice-Chair. British Inst. of Man. 1978–84; Vice-Pres. Inst. of Marketing 1980–; Chair. Eng Council 1981–85, Distributed Information Processing Ltd 1987–, Octagon Investment Man. 1987–96, Gandolfi Ltd 1987–, Tanks Consolidated Investments 1990–, Linhof & Studio Ltd 1993–; Dir Midland Bank Group 1979–91, Britoil 1982–88, Vice-Pres. Eng Employers Fed. –1985; mem. Pres.'s Cttee and Council, CBI –1985; mem. Council, Inst. of Dirs. 1981–85 (Pres. 1984–85); mem. Advisory Council, Science Museum 1975–83, Trustee 1984–92; mem. Advisory Council for Applied Research and Devt 1981, Nat. Econ. Devt Cttee for Electronics 1981; Hon. FIEE; Hon. Fellow, Sheffield City Polytechnic 1983, Wolverhampton Polytechnic 1986; Dr. hc (Surrey), (Open Univ.) 1985, Hon. DSc (City Univ.) 1981, (Bath) 1982, (Queen's, Belfast) 1982, (Loughborough) 1982, (Aston) 1985, Hon. LLD (Strathclyde) 1982, Hon. DSc (Eng) Univ. of London 1982, Hon. DEng (Bradford) 1983. *Publications:* Report on Product Design for NEDC 1979, No Man an Island 1982, Patterns of Change: Collected Essays 1983. *Leisure interests:* shooting, photography, cinema, music. *Address:* 10 Chapel Place, Rivington Street, London, EC2A 3DQ, England.

CORISH, Patrick Joseph, MA, DD; Irish historian (retd); b. 20 March 1921, Co. Wexford; s. of Peter William Corish and Brigid Mary O'Shaughnessy; ed St Peter's Coll., Wexford and Nat. Univ. of Ireland (NUI) (St Patrick's Coll., Maynooth and Univ. Coll., Dublin); ordained as Priest 1945; Prof. of Ecclesiastical History Pontifical Univ., Maynooth 1947–75; Prof. of Modern History, Maynooth, NUI 1975–88; mem. Royal Irish Acad. 1956; Sec. Catholic Record Soc. of Ireland 1948; ed. Soc.'s journal Archivium Hibernicum 1948–77; mem. Irish Manuscripts Comm. 1949; Domestic Prelate 1967. *Publications:* A History of Irish Catholicism (ed. and contrib.) 1967–71, The Catholic Community in the Seventeenth and Eighteenth Centuries 1981, The Irish Catholic Experience 1985, Maynooth College: a bicentenary history 1995. *Leisure interest:* gardening. *Address:* St Patrick's College, Maynooth, Co. Kildare, Ireland. *Telephone:* (1) 6285222. *Fax:* (1) 6289063.

CORMAN, Roger William, AB, AFM; American film director and producer; b. 5 April 1926, Detroit, Mich.; m. Julie Ann Halloran; two s. two d.; ed Stanford Univ. Calif., Oxford Univ., England; Dir Five Guns West 1955; Founder, Pres. New World Pictures 1970–83, Concorde-New Horizons Corpn 1983–; distributed films including: Cries and Whispers, Amarcord, Fantastic Planet, The Story of Adele H, Small Change, The Tin Drum; mem. Producers' Guild of America, Directors' Guild of America; Dr. hc (American Film Inst.); Lifetime Achievement Award, L.A. Film Critics 1997; 1st Producers of Century Award, Cannes Film Festival 1998; Award of Venice Film Festival. *Films as producer or director include:* The Day the World Ended 1956, The Fall of the House of Usher 1960, The Little Shop of Horrors 1960, The Pit and the Pendulum 1961, The Intruder 1962, The Raven 1963, Masque of the Red Death 1964, The Secret Invasion 1964, The Wild Angels 1966, The Saint Valentine's Day Massacre 1967, The Trip 1967, Bloody Mama 1970, Gas-s-s 1970, Von Richthofen and Brown 1971, Frankenstein Unbound 1989, Grand Theft Auto, I Never Promised You a Rose Garden, Avalanche, Deathsport, Piranha, Rock 'n' Roll High School, Deathrace 2000, Nightfall, Roger Corman Presents (13 horror/science fiction films for TV), Two to Tango, Time Trackers, Heroes Stand Alone, Bloodfist, Silk 2, Haunted Symphony, Midnight Tease. *Film appearances include:* The Silence of the Lambs, The Godfather Part II, Philadelphia, Apollo 13, Scream 3, The Independent, A Galaxy Far Far Away. *Publication:* How I Made 100 Films in Hollywood and Never Lost a Dime (autobiog.) 1990. *Address:* c/o Concorde-New Horizons Corpn, 11600 San Vicente Blvd., Los Angeles, CA 90049, USA.

CORNEA, Doina; Romanian philologist; b. 30 May 1929, Braşov; m.; one d.; ed Faculty of Philology, Univ. of Cluj; Asst Lecturer in French Literature, Univ. of Cluj; dismissed for writing an open letter to Those Who Haven't Ceased to Think 1982; 30 other open letters followed 1983–89; held for interrogation for five weeks Nov. 1987; under house arrest 1988–89; mem. Romanian Nat. Salvation Front 1989–90, Memory Foundation; founder mem. of Social Dialogue Group (G.D.S.) 1989, of Civil Alliance; co-founder of Antitotalitarian Forum of Romania 1990; Dr. hc (Brussels) 1989; int. awards for activities in furtherance of human rights; Officier, Légion d'honneur 1999; Thorolf Rafto Human Rights Award, Norway 1989, Steaua României, Mare Cruce 2000, Magyar Köztársasági Érdemrend Tisztikeresztje 2002. *Art exhibition:* Painting Exhbn, Cluj 1981. *Publications:* Liberté? 1990, Opened Letters and Other Texts 1991, translations from French, Fata Nevazuta a Lucrurilor 1990–99 1999, La face cachée des choses 2000. *Address:* Str. Alba Iulia Nr. 16, Cluj-Napoca 3400, Romania. *Telephone:* (64) 198460. *Fax:* (64) 433623.

CORNEILLE (see Beverloo, Cornelis Van).

CORNELIS, François; Belgian oil company executive; b. 25 Oct. 1949, Uccle, Brussels; m. Colette Durant 1973; two s. two d.; ed Univ. of Louvain; joined Petrofina SA as a systems engineer, subsequently Co-ordinator of Supply and Refining Operations, Brussels, Supply and Shipping Man., Petrofina, UK, London, Vice-Pres., Special Asst to Pres., American Petrofina, Dallas, Tex., USA 1983–84, Gen. Man. and Asst to Pres., Petrofina 1984–86, Exec. Dir, Office of the Chair. 1986–90, CEO Vice-Chair. 1990–; Vice-Chair. Total Fina 1999–. *Address:* Total Fina SA, Rue de l'Industrie 52, 1040 Brussels, Belgium.

CORNELL, Eric Allin, BS, PhD; American physicist; s. of Allin Cornell and Elizabeth Cornell née Greenberg; m. Celeste Landry; one d.; ed Stanford Univ., MIT; Research Asst Stanford Univ. 1982–85, MIT 1985–90; Teaching Fellow Harvard Extension School 1989; Post-doctoral research, Jt Inst. for Lab. Astrophysics (JILA), Boulder 1990–92, Fellow 1994–; Asst Prof. Adjoint Dept of Physics, Univ. of Colo at Boulder 1992–95, Prof. Adjoint 1995–, Fellow

1994–; Sr Scientist Nat. Inst. of Standards and Tech. (NIST), Boulder 1992–, Fellow 1994–; Fellow American Physical Soc. 1997–, Optical Soc. of America 2000–; mem. Nat. Acad. of Sciences 2000; numerous awards including Dept of Commerce Gold Medal 1996, Fritz London Prize in Low Temperature Physics 1996, King Faisal Int. Prize in Science 1997, I. I. Rabi Prize 1997, Lorentz Medal, Royal Netherlands Acad. of Arts and Sciences 1998, Benjamin Franklin Medal in Physics 1999, Nobel Prize in Physics (Jt recipient) 2001. *Address:* Joint Institute for Laboratory Astrophysics (JILA), University of Colorado, Campus Box 440, Boulder, CO 80309-0440, USA (Office). *Telephone:* (303) 492-6281 (Office). *Fax:* (303) 492-5235 (Office). *E-mail:* cornell@ jila.colorado.edu (Office). *Website:* www.colorado.edu (Office).

CORNESS, Sir Colin (Ross), Kt, MA; British business executive; b. 9 Oct. 1931, Chorlton; s. of the late Thomas Corness and Mary Evlyne Corness; ed Uppingham School, Magdalene Coll., Cambridge, Grad. School of Business Admin., Harvard; Dir Taylor Woodrow Construction Ltd 1961–1964; Man. Dir Redland Tiles Ltd 1965–70, Group Man. Dir Redland PLC 1967–82, Deputy Chair. and Man. Dir 1974–77, Chair. 1977–95; CEO 1977–91; Chair. Nationwide Bldg Soc. 1991–96; Dir Chubb and Son PLC 1974–84, W.H. Smith and Son Holdings PLC 1980–87, SE Region, Nat. Westminster Bank PLC 1982–86, Courtaulds PLC 1986–91, Gordon Russell PLC 1985–89, Bank of England 1987–95, S. G. Warburg Group PLC 1987–95, Unitech PLC 1987–95, Union Camp Corpn 1991–99, Chubb Security PLC 1992–97, Glaxo Wellcome PLC 1994–97 (Chair. 1995–97), Taylor Woodrow PLC 1997–2001; Chair. Bldg Centre 1974–77; mem. Econ. Devt Cttee for Bldg 1980–84, Industrial Devt Advisory Bd 1982–84, UK Advisory Bd of the British-American Chamber of Commerce 1987–; Trustee, Uppingham School 1996–99; Hon. DBA Kingston 1994. *Leisure interests:* travel, music, tennis. *Address:* c/o Glaxo Wellcome PLC, 34 Berkeley Square, London, W1X 6JT, England.

CORNFORTH, Sir John Warcup, Kt, AC, CBE, DPhil, FRS; Australian research scientist; b. 7 Sept. 1917, Sydney; s. of J. W. Cornforth and Hilda Eipper; m. Rita H. Harradence 1941; one s. two d.; ed Univs. of Sydney and Oxford; Scientific Staff, Medical Research Council 1946–62; Dir Milstead Lab. of Chemical Enzymology, Shell Research Ltd 1962–75; Assoc. Prof. Univ. of Warwick 1965–71; Visiting Prof. Univ. of Sussex 1971–75; Royal Soc. Prof. Univ. of Sussex 1975–82; Corresp. mem. Australian Acad. of Science 1977–; Foreign Assoc. US Nat. Acad. of Sciences 1978–; Foreign mem. Royal Netherlands Acad. of Sciences 1978–; Foreign Hon. mem. American Acad. 1973–; Hon. Fellow St Catherine's Coll., Oxford 1976–, RSC 2001; Hon. Prof. Beijing Medical Univ. 1986–; Hon. DSc (ETH Zurich) 1975, (Oxford, Dublin, Liverpool, Warwick Univs.) 1976, (Aberdeen, Hull, Sussex, Sydney Univs.) 1977, (Kent) 1995; Corday-Morgan Medal, Chem. Soc. 1953, Flintoff Medal, Chem. Soc. 1966, Ciba Medal, Biochem. Soc. 1966, Stouffer Prize 1967, Davy Medal, Royal Soc. 1968, Ernest Guenther Award, American Chemical Soc. 1969, Prix Roussel 1972, Nobel Prize for Chemistry 1975, Royal Medal, Royal Soc. 1976, Copley Medal, Royal Soc. 1982. *Publications:* The Chemistry of Penicillin (part author) 1949 and numerous papers on chemical and biochemical topics. *Leisure interests:* tennis, gardening, chess. *Address:* Saxon Down, Cuilfail, Lewes, East Sussex, BN7 2BE, England.

CORNILLET, Thierry Pierre Fernand, D. ÈS SC.POL.; French politician; b. 23 July 1951, Montélimar, Drôme; s. of Col Jean-Baptiste Cornillet and Inès Genoud; m. Marie-France Rossi 1983; one s. one d.; ed Lycée Alain Borne, Montélimar, Univs. of Lyon II, Lyon III and Paris I—Panthéon Sorbonne; Head of Dept, Office of Dir of Civil Security at Ministry of Interior 1977–81; Head of Dept, Office of Minister of External Trade, then of Admin. Reform 1980–81; Export Man., Lagarde S.A., Montélimar 1981–83; Dir Office of Deputy Mayor of Nancy 1983–85; Legal Adviser to Jr Minister, Ministry of Interior 1985–86, Chef de Cabinet 1986–88; Head of Dept, Cie nationale du Rhône 1988–93; Municipal Councillor, Montélimar 1983, Mayor 1989–; mem. Gen. Council of Drôme 1985–93, Vice-Chair. 1992–93; mem. and Sec. Regional Council of Rhône-Alpes 1986, Vice-Pres. 1999–; Deputy from Drôme for Union pour la démocratie française et du Centre (UDF) 1993–97; Vice-Chair. Parti Radical 1988–97, Chair. 1997–; mem. European Parl. 1999–; Sec. Assemblée nationale 1993–95; Chevalier Ordre nat. du Mérite. *Address:* European Parliament, 97–113 rue Wiertz, 1047 Brussels, Belgium.

CORNISH, (Robert) Francis, CMG, LVO; British diplomatist; b. 18 May 1942, Bolton; m. Alison Jane Dundas 1964; three d.; ed Charterhouse School, Royal Mil. Acad., Sandhurst; commissioned 14th/20th King's Hussars and served in Libya, UK and Germany, becoming Adjutant 1966; joined HM Diplomatic Service 1968, served in Kuala Lumpur and Jakarta before becoming Head, Greek Desk, London; First Sec. (EEC), Bonn 1976–80; apptd. Asst Pvt. Sec. to Prince of Wales 1980, also worked for Princess of Wales –1983; High Commr to Brunei 1983–86; Dir of Public Diplomacy, Washington, DC and Head, British Information Services, New York 1986; Head News Dept FCO, London and Spokesman for the Foreign Sec. 1990–93; Sr British Trade Commr, Hong Kong 1993, first Consul-Gen. Hong Kong 1997; Sr Directing Staff Royal Coll. of Defence Studies 1998; Amb. to Israel 1998–2001. *Leisure interests:* farming, riding, hill walking. *Address:* c/o Foreign and Commonwealth Office, King Charles Street, London, SW1A 2AH; Coombe Farm, West Monkton, Somerset, TA2 8RB, England (Home).

CORNISH, William Rodolph, LLD, BCL, FBA; Australian barrister; b. 9 Aug. 1937, S. Australia; s. of Jack R. Cornish and Elizabeth E. Cornish; m. Lovedy E. Moule 1964; one s. two d.; ed St Peter's Coll., Adelaide, Adelaide Univ. and Oxford Univ., England; Lecturer in Law, LSE 1962–68; Reader in Law, Queen

Mary Coll., London Univ. 1969–70; Prof. of English Law, LSE 1970–90; Prof. of Law, Cambridge Univ. 1990–95, Dir Centre for Euro Legal Studies 1991–94, Herchel Smith Prof. of Intellectual Property Law, Univ. of Cambridge 1995–; Fellow, Magdalene Coll. 1990–, Pres. 1998–2001; Academic Dir British Law Centre, Warsaw Univ. 1992–; Hon. QC 1997. *Publications:* The Jury 1968, Intellectual Property 1981, Encyclopaedia of UK and European Patent Law (with others) 1978, Law and Society in England 1750–1950 1989; numerous articles in legal periodicals. *Address:* Magdalene College, Cambridge, CB3 0AG, England. *Telephone:* (1223) 330081. *Fax:* (1223) 330086. *E-mail:* ipunit@cam.ac.uk (Office).

CORNWELL, Andrew, MSc; British politician and journalist; b. 30 Sept. 1966, London; ed LSE; financial journalist 1988–98; mem. Bd London Pensions Fund Authority 2000–; European Media Officer BOND (British Overseas NGOs for Devt) 2001; currently Chair. Green Party of England and Wales. *Address:* Green Party, 1a Waterlow Road, London, N19 5NJ, England (Office). *Telephone:* (20) 7272-4474 (Office). *Fax:* (20) 7272-6653 (Office). *E-mail:* chair@greenparty.org.uk (Office). *Website:* www.greenparty.org.uk (Office).

CORNWELL, David John Moore (pseudonym John le Carré); British writer; b. 19 Oct. 1931, Poole, Dorset; s. of Ronald Thomas Archibald Cornwell and Olive Glassy; m. 1st Alison Ann Veronica Sharp 1954 (divorced 1971); three s.; m. 2nd Valerie Jane Eustace 1972; one s.; ed St Andrew's Preparatory School, Pangbourne, Sherborne School, Berne Univ. and Lincoln Coll., Oxford; teacher, Eton Coll. 1956–58; in Foreign Service (Second Sec., Bonn, then Political Consul Hamburg) 1959–64; Hon. Fellow Lincoln Coll. Oxford; Hon. D. Litt. (Exeter) 1990, (St Andrews) 1996, (Southampton) 1997, (Bath) 1998; Somerset Maugham Award 1963, James Tait Black Award 1977. *Publications:* Call for the Dead 1961 (filmed as The Deadly Affair 1967), Murder of Quality 1962 (filmed), The Spy Who Came in From the Cold 1963 (filmed), The Looking Glass War 1965, A Small Town in Germany 1968, The Naive and Sentimental Lover 1971, Tinker, Tailor, Soldier, Spy 1974 (made into TV series), The Honourable Schoolboy 1977 (made into TV series), Smiley's People 1979 (made into TV series), The Quest for Karla (collected edn of previous three titles) 1982, The Little Drummer Girl 1983 (filmed), A Perfect Spy 1986, The Russia House 1989 (filmed), The Secret Pilgrim 1991, The Night Manager 1993, Our Game 1995, The Tailor of Panama 1996 (filmed), Single and Single 1999, The Constant Gardener 2001. *Address:* c/o David Higham Associates, 5–8 Lower John Street, Golden Square, London, W1F 9HA, England. *Telephone:* (20) 7434-5900. *Fax:* (20) 7437-1072.

CORNYN, John, LLM; American politician; b. 2 Feb. 1952, Houston, Tex.; s. of John Cornyn and Gale Cornyn; ed Trinity Univ. and St. Mary's School of Law, San Antonio, Univ. of Va. Law School; Dist Court Judge, San Antonio 1984–90; elected to Texas Supreme Court 1990, re-elected 1996; Attorney-Gen. of Texas 1997–2003; Senator from Texas 2003–; mem. Bush-Cheney Transition Advisory Cttee 2000; St Mary's Distinguished Law School Grad. 1994; Trinity Univ. Distinguished Alumnus 2001; Outstanding Texas Leader Award, John Ben Shepperd Foundation of Texas 2000, James Madison Award, Freedom of Information Foundation of Texas 2001. *Address:* Office of the Senator from Texas, US Senate, Senate Buildings, Washington, DC 20510, USA (Office).

COROPCEAN, Brig. Gen. Ion; Moldovan army officer; b. 11 March 1960, Liveden' vill; s. of Ștefan Coropcean; m. Valentina Coropcean; one s. one d.; ed Poltava Mil. Air Defence High School, Mil. Air Defence Acad.; cadet 1977–81, Air Defence Platoon Commdr 1981–84, Air Defence Battery Commdr 1984–87, Air Defence Bn Commdr, Air Defence Acad. 1987–88, Chief of Staff and Deputy Commdr Air Defence Regt 1991–92, Deputy Commdr Air Defence Brigade 1992–97, Commdr Mil. Coll. 1997–98, Chief of Staff Nat. Army, Deputy Minister of Defence 1998–; Medal of Courage, Medal of Mil. Merit. *Leisure interests:* books, football, literature. *Address:* ȘOS. Hincești 84, MD2021 Chișinău (Office); str. Alba Julia 200/1, Ap. 100, MD2071 Chișinău, Republic of Moldova (Home). *Telephone:* (2) 799460 (Office); (2) 514874 (Home). *Fax:* (2) 234434 (Office). *E-mail:* coropcei@md.pims.org (Office).

CORR, Edwin Gharst, MA; American diplomatist and university professor; b. 6 Aug. 1934, Edmond, Okla; s. of E. L. Corr and Rowena Gharst; m. Susanne Springer 1957; three d.; ed Univ. of Okla and Texas; officer Dept of State, Foreign Office 1961–62; sent to Mexico 1962–66; Dir Peace Corps, Cali, Colombia 1966–68; Panama Desk Officer, Dept of State 1969–71; Program Officer InterAmerican Foundation 1971; Exec. Asst to Amb., American Embassy, Bangkok 1972–75; Counsellor Political Affairs, American Embassy, Ecuador 1976; Deputy Chief of Mission 1977–78; Deputy Asst Sec. Int. Narcotics Matters, State Dept 1978–80; Amb. to Peru 1980–81, Bolivia 1981–85, El Salvador 1985–88; State Dept Diplomat-in-Residence, Univ. of Okla 1988–90, Prof. of Political Science 1990–96, Dir Energy Inst. of the Americas 1996–2001, Assoc. Dir of Int. Program Center 1996–; Nat. Order of Merit (Ecuador) 1978, Condor of the Andes (Bolivia) 1985, US Pres.'s Meritorious Service Award 1985, US State Dept Distinguished Honor Award 1988, Jose Matias Delgado Decoration (El Salvador) 1988. *Publications:* The Political Process in Colombia 1971, Low-Intensity Conflict: Old Threats in a New World (co-editor) 1992, The Search for Security: The US Grand Strategy in the 21st Century (co-editor) 2002; numerous articles in English and Spanish. *Leisure interests:* ranching, reading, public speaking, writing, exercise. *Address:* International Programs Center, University of Oklahoma,

Norman, OK 73019 (Office); 1617 Jenkins Street, Norman, OK 73072, USA (Home). *Telephone:* (405) 325-1396 (Office); (405) 321-7036 (Home). *Fax:* (405) 325-7454 (Office). *E-mail:* ecorr@ou.edu.

CORREA, Charles M., MArch; Indian architect and planner; b. 1 Sept. 1930, Secunderabad; s. of Carlos Marcos Correa and Ana Florinda de Heredia; m. Monika Sequeira 1961; one s. one d.; ed Univ. of Michigan and MIT; Pvt. Practice 1958–; Chief Architect New Bombay 1971–74; Chair., Nat. Comm. on Urbanization; Hon. Fellow, American Inst. of Architecture 1977, Finnish Assen of Architects 1992, RIBA 1993, American Acad. of Arts and Sciences 1993; Hon. Dr. (Univ. of Mich.) 1980; Padma Shri, Pres. of India 1972; RIBA Gold Medal 1984, Gold Medal, Indian Inst. of Architects 1987, Gold Medal, Int. Union of Architects 1990, Praemium Imperiale for Architecture, Japan Art Assen 1994, Aga Khan Award for Architecture 1998. *Major works include:* Mahatma Gandhi Memorial Museum, Sabarmati Ashram, Ahmedabad, Kovalam Beach Devt, Kerala, Kanchanjunga apartments, Mumbai, Cidade de Goa, Dona Paula, New India Centre, Delhi, Performing Arts Centre, Kala Acad., Goa, Previ low-income housing, Peru, Bharat Bhavan, Bhopal, Jawahar Kala Kendra, Jaipur, Nat. Crafts Museum, Delhi, British Council, Delhi, IUCCA, Pune Univ. *Publication:* The New Landscape 1985, Housing and Urbanisation 1999. *Leisure interests:* model railways, old films, swimming. *Address:* 9 Mathew Road, Mumbai 400004 (Office); Sonmarg, Nepean Sea Road, Mumbai 400006, India (Home). *Telephone:* (22) 3633307 (Office); (22) 3633306 (Home).

CORREIA, Carlos; Guinea-Bissau politician; mem. Partido Africano da Independência da Guiné e Cabo Verde (PAIGC); fmr Minister of State for Rural Devt and Agric.; Prime Minister of Guinea-Bissau 1991–94, 1997–98; fmr Perm. Sec. Council of State; currently Gov. for Guinea Bissau, African Devt Bank. *Address:* c/o Ministry of the Economy and Finance, CP 67, Avda 3 de Agosto, Bissau, Guinea-Bissau.

CORRELL, A.D. (Pete), MS; American paper industry executive; b. 28 April 1941, Brunswick, Ga.; s. of Alston Dayton Correll and Elizabeth Correll (née Flippo); m. Ada Lee Fulford 1963; one s. one d.; ed Univs of Georgia and Maine (Orono); tech. service engineer, Westvaco 1963–64; instructor, Univ. of Maine (Orono) 1964–67; various positions in pulp and paper man., Weyerhaeuser Co. 1967–77; Div. Pres., Paperboard, Mead Corpn 1977–80, Group Vice-Pres. 1980–83, Sr Vice-Pres., Forest Products 1983–88; Sr Vice-Pres., Pulp and Printing Paper, Ga Pacific Corpn 1988–89, Exec. Vice-Pres., Pulp and Paper 1989–91, Pres., COO 1991–93, CEO 1993–, Chair. 1993–; mem. Bd of Dirs. Univ. of Maine Pulp and Paper Foundation (Vice-Pres.), Engraph Inc., Trust Co. Bank of Atlanta, Trust Co. of Ga, Atlanta Chamber of Commerce, Atlanta Symphony Orchestra, Robert W. Woodruff Arts Center. *Address:* Georgia-Pacific Corporation, PO Box 105605, 133 Peachtree Street, NE, Atlanta, GA 30303-1808, USA. *Telephone:* (404) 521-4000.

CORRIGAN, E. Gerald, PhD; American banker and economist; b. 3 June 1941, Waterbury, Conn.; ed Fairfield and Fordham Univs; Group Vice-Pres. (Man. and Planning) Fed. Reserve Bank of New York 1976–80, Pres. 1985–93; Special Asst to Chair., Bd of Govs. Fed. Reserve System 1979–80; Pres. Fed. Reserve Bank of Minneapolis 1981–84; Chair. int. advisers, Goldman Sachs & Co. 1994–96, Man. Dir 1996–, now partner, Man. Dir; Chair. Bd of Dirs Russian-American Enterprise Fund 1993–; Trustee, Macalester Coll., St Paul, Minn. 1981–, Jt Council Econ. Educ. 1981–, Fairfield Univ., Fairfield, Conn. 1985–; mem. Trilateral Comm. 1986–; Pres. BRI 1991–; Chair. Basle Cttee on Banking Supervision (1st American in that post) 1991–. *Address:* Goldman Sachs & Co., 85 Broad Street, New York, NY 10004, USA.

CORRIGAN, (Francis) Edward, PhD, FRS; British professor of mathematics; b. 10 Aug. 1946, Birkenhead; s. of late Anthony Corrigan and of Eileen Corrigan (née Ryan); m. Jane Mary Halton 1970; two s. two d.; ed St Bede's Coll., Manchester, Christ's Coll. Cambridge; Addison Wheeler Fellow, Durham Univ. 1972–74; CERN Fellow, CERN Geneva 1974–76; lecturer Univ. of Durham 1976, Reader 1987, Prof. of Math. 1992–99; Prof. of Math. and Head of Dept Univ. of York 1999–; Visiting Prof., Centre for Partide Theory, Univ. of Durham 1999–; Life mem. Clare Hall, Cambridge; Editor-in-Chief, Journal of Physics A 1999–; Adrian-Daiwa Prize 1998. *Publications:* over 80 articles in learned journals and conf. proceedings. *Leisure interests:* music, squash, walking. *Address:* University of York, Mathematics, Heslington, York, YO10 5DD (Office); 177 Fossway, York YO31 8SQ, England (Home). *Telephone:* (1904) 433774 (Office). *Fax:* (1904) 433071.

CORRIGAN-MAGUIRE, Mairead; Northern Irish human rights activist; b. 27 Jan. 1944, Belfast; d. of Andrew Corrigan and Margaret Corrigan; m. 2nd Jackie Maguire 1981; two s. three step-c.; ed St Vincent's Primary School, Belfast, Miss Gordon's Commercial Coll.; works as shorthand typist; Co-Founder and Chair. Community of the Peace People 1980–81, Hon. Life Pres.; Hon. LLD (Yale Univ.) 1976; Jt recipient of Nobel Peace Prize for launching the Northern Ireland Peace Movt (later renamed Community of the Peace People) 1976, Carl von Ossietzky Medal for Courage (Berlin Section, Int. League of Human Rights). *Leisure interests:* swimming, walking. *Address:* Community of the Peace People, 224 Lisburn Road, Belfast, BT9 6GE, Northern Ireland (Office). *Telephone:* (28) 9066-3465 (Office). *Fax:* (28) 9068-3947 (Office). *E-mail:* peacepeople@gn.apc.org (Office).

CORRIPIO AHUMADA, HE Cardinal Ernesto; Mexican ecclesiastic; b. 29 June 1919, Tampico; ordained priest 1942; Titular Bishop of Zapara 1953–56; Bishop of Tampico 1956–67; Archbishop of Antequera 1967–76, of Puebla de

los Angeles 1976–77; Archbishop of Mexico City and Primate of Mexico 1977–94, Archbishop Emer. 1994–; cr. Cardinal 1979; mem. Sacred Congregation for the Sacraments and Divine Worship, Pontifical Comm. for Latin America; entitled L'Immacolata al Tiburtino. *Address:* Calle nato 54, Col. Ampliación Tepepan, 16629 México, DF, Mexico. *Telephone:* (5) 6751606.

CORSARO, Frank Andrew; American theatre and opera director; b. 22 Dec. 1924, New York; s. of Joseph and Marie (née Quarino) Corsaro; m. Mary Cross Bonnie Lueders 1971; one s.; ed Yale Univ.; began career as actor 1948, appearing since in productions including Mrs. McThing, Broadway 1951; first film appearance in Rachel 1967; Dir of numerous plays including A Hatful of Rain, Broadway 1955–56, The Night of the Iguana 1961–62, Tremonisha 1975, 1600 Pennsylvania Avenue 1976, Cold Storage, Lyceum 1977–, Whoopee! 1979, Knockout 1979; directed and acted in numerous TV productions; one-man art show 1976; Dir numerous operas with New York City Opera 1958–, Washington Opera Soc. 1970–74, St Paul Opera 1971, Houston Grand Opera 1973–77, Assoc. Artistic Dir 1977–; Artistic Dir, The Actors Studio 1988–; Drama Dir Juilliard Opera Centre 1989, Artistic Dir, Vocal Arts Dept, Juilliard School 1988; Plays. *Theatre:* productions include La Traviata, Madame Butterfly, Faust, Manon Lescaut, A Village Romeo and Juliet, L'Incoronazione di Poppea, The Angel of Fire, Hugh the Drover, Rinaldo, Love for Three Oranges (Glyndebourne 1983), La Fanciulla del West (Deutsches Oper Berlin 1983), Rinaldo (Metropolitan Opera 1983), Fennimore and Gerda (Edinburgh Festival 1983), Where the Wild Things Are, Higgeldy, Piggeldy, Pop (Glyndebourne 1985), Alcina (Spitalfields 1985), (LA Opera Centre 1986), L'Enfant et les Sortilèges, L'Heure espagnole, Glyndebourne Festival 1987, Hansel and Gretel (Houston, Toronto, Zurich 1997–98), Kuhlhandel (Juilliard 1998). *Publications include:* L'histoire du soldat (adaptation), La Bohème (adaptation), A Piece of Blue Sky (play), Maverik 1978, Libretto: Before Breakfast (music by Thomas Pasatieri), Libretto: Heloise and Abelard (music by Steven Paulus), Kunma (novel). *Leisure interests:* painting, piano playing, writing. *Address:* 60 Lincoln Plaza, New York, NY 10023 (Office); 33 Riverside Drive, New York, NY 10023, USA (Home). *Telephone:* (212) 799-5000 extn. 261 (Office); (212) 874-1048. *Fax:* (212) 724-0263 (Office).

CORSTEN, Severin, DPhil; German librarian; b. 8 Dec. 1920, Heinsberg/Rheinland; s. of Leo and Gertrud (née Heusch) Corsten; m. Dr. Margret Loenartz 1952; one s. two d.; ed Univ. of Bonn; Librarian, Library of Ministry of Foreign Affairs, Bonn 1954–63; Deputy Dir Universitäts- und Stadtbibliothek, Cologne 1963–71, Dir 1971–85; Hon. Prof. Univ. of Cologne 1975–; Kt of the Papal Order of St Gregory; Verdienstkreuz am Bande des Verdienstordens. *Publications:* Das Domanialgut im Amt Heinsberg 1953, Die Anfänge des Kölner Buchdrucks 1955, Das Heinsberger Land im frühen Mittelalter 1959, Die Bibliothek des Auswärtigen Amtes 1961, Die Kölnische Chronik von 1499 1982, Studien zum Kölner Frühdruck 1985, Der Buchdruck im 15. Jahrhundert, (Vols 1, 2) 1988–93, Untersuchungen zum Buch-und Bibliothekswesen 1988, Handbuch der historischen Buchbestände in Deutschland (Vols 3, 4) 1992–93. *Leisure interest:* music. *Address:* Breslauer Strasse 14, 53175 Bonn, Germany. *Telephone:* (228) 375320.

CORTAZZI, Sir (Henry Arthur) Hugh, GCMG, MA; British diplomatist (retd); b. 2 May 1924, Sedbergh, Yorks. (now Cumbria); s. of F. E. M. Cortazzi and M. Cortazzi; m. Elizabeth Esther Montagu 1956; one s. two d.; ed Sedbergh School, Univ. of St Andrews and Univ. of London; served RAF 1943–48; joined Foreign Office 1949; Third Sec., Singapore 1950–51; Second Sec., Tokyo 1951–54; Foreign Office, London 1954–58; First Sec., Bonn 1958–60, Tokyo 1961–65 (Head of Chancery 1963); Foreign Office 1965–66; Counsellor (Commercial), Tokyo 1966–70; Royal Coll. of Defence Studies 1971; Minister (Commercial), Washington 1972–75; Deputy Under-Sec. of State FCO 1975–80; Amb. to Japan 1980–84 (retd); apptd. Dir Hill Samuel and Co. Ltd (later Hill Samuel Bank Ltd) 1984–91, Foreign and Colonial Pacific Investment Trust 1984–98, G. T. Japan Investment Trust 1984–99, Thornton Pacific Investment Trust SA 1986–2002; Adviser to Mitsukoshi Dept Store, Tokyo, Japan 1984–; Sr Adviser NEC Corpn, Japan 1992–98, Dai-Ichi Kangyo Bank, Japan 1992–99, Bank of Kyoto 1992–99, Wilde Sapte, solicitors 1992–99; mem. Econ. and Social Research Council 1984–90; Hon. DUniv (Stirling); Yamagata Banto Prize, Osaka 1990; Grand Cordon, Order of the Sacred Treasure (Japan) 1995. *Publications:* trans. of Japanese short stories by Keita Genji 1972, A Diplomat's Wife in Japan: Sketches at the Turn of the Century (Ed.) 1982, Isles of Gold: Antique Maps of Japan 1983, Higashi No Shimaguni, Nishi No Shimaguni 1984, Dr. Willis in Japan (1862–1877) 1985, Mitford's Japan (Ed.) 1985, Zoku Higashi No Shimaguni, Nishi No Shimaguni (Ed.) 1987, Victorians in Japan: in and around the Treaty Ports 1987, Kipling's Japan (Ed.) 1988, The Japanese Achievement, A Short History of Japan and Japanese Culture 1990, Britain and Japan 1859–1991: Themes and Personalities 1991, Modern Japan: a concise survey 1993; A British Artist in Meiji Japan (Ed.) 1991, Building Japan 1868–1876 1991, 1991, Caught In Time: Japan (Ed.)1995, Japan and Back and Places Elsewhere: A Memoir 1998, Japan Experiences (Ed.) 2001, Biographical Portraits Vol. IV (Ed.) 2002. *Leisure interests:* the arts, especially literature and Japanese studies. *Address:* Ballsocks, Vines Cross, Heathfield, East Sussex, TN21 9ET, England (Home).

CORTES, Joaquín; Spanish dancer; b. 1970, Madrid; joined Spanish Nat. Ballet 1985, Prin. Dancer 1987–90; now appears in own shows, blending gypsy dancing, jazz blues and classical ballet; appeared in Pedro Almodóvar's film The Flower Of My Secret.

CORTI, Mario A., MBA, DEcon; Swiss business executive; b. 22 Oct. 1946, Lausanne; m.; ed Univ. of Lausanne, Harvard Business School, USA; Corp. Planner Kaiser Aluminium & Chemical Corpn, Oakland, Calif. 1972–76; Dir and Deputy Head Banking Dept Swiss Nat. Bank, Zürich 1977–86, mem. Cooke Cttee; Amb. and Del. of Swiss Govt for Trade Agreements, Deputy Dir, Fed. Office for Foreign Econ. Affairs, Bern 1986–90; joined Nestlé AG 1990, Sr Vice-Pres. and Chief Admin. Officer, Glendale, Calif. 1991–93, Exec. Vice-Pres. and Chief Financial Officer, Glendale 1994–95, Exec. Vice-Pres. and Chief Financial Officer, Vevey, Switzerland 1996–2001; mem. Bd Swissair Group (fmrly SAirGroup) 2000–, Chair. and CEO 2001–; mem. Bd Swiss-American Chamber of Commerce 1997–, Industrie-Holding 1998–2000, Swiss Soc. of Chemical Industries 1998–, Montreux Palace Hotel 2001–; mem. Admission Bd Swiss Stock Exchange 1996–; mem. Swiss Business Fed. 1997–, Crédit Suisse Group Int. Advisory Bd 1999–, Bd of Overseers Harvard Business School 2000–; lecturer on Swiss Foreign Econ. Policy, Univ. of Bern 1988–90. *Address:* c/o Swissair, Zürich Airport, 8058 Zürich, Switzerland (Office). *Telephone:* (1) 812-12-12 (Office). *Fax:* (1) 810-80-46 (Office). *Website:* www.sairgroup.com (Office).

CORWIN, Norman; American writer-producer-director of radio, television, stage and cinema; b. 3 May 1910, Boston, Mass.; s. of Samuel H. Corwin and Rose Ober; m. Katherine Locke 1947; one s. one d.; Newspaperman 1929–38; writer, director, producer for Columbia Broadcasting System 1938–48; Chief, Special Projects, UN Radio 1949–53; mem. Faculty of Theatre Arts Univ. of Calif., LA; Regents Lecturer Univ. of Calif., Santa Barbara; Visiting Prof. School of Journalism, Univ. of Southern Calif. 1981, Prof. 1989–; writer in residence, Univ. of N Carolina; Patten Memorial Lecturer, Indiana Univ. 1981; Co-Chair. Scholarship Cttee of Acad. of Motion Picture Arts and Sciences Chair. Writers Exec. Cttee, mem. Bd of Govs. 1979–88, Chair. Documentary Awards Comm. 1967–82, 1985–94, Sec. Acad. Foundation 1983–88; mem. Bd of Dirs. Writers Guild of America, Selden Ring Journalism Award 1994–, Bette Davis Foundation 1997–; Trustee Filmex; writer, Dir and host TV series, Norman Corwin Presents, Westinghouse Broadcasting Co.; radio series More by Corwin, Nat. Public Radio 1996–97; Sec. Acad. of Arts and Sciences Foundation 1983; First Vice-Pres. Acad. of Motion Picture Arts and Sciences 1988; Stasheff Lecturer, Univ. of Mich. 1984; papers acquired by Thousand Oaks Library Foundation 1993; subject of 90-minute TV documentary 1995; three hon. degrees; Peabody Medal, Edward Bok Medal, Award of American Acad. of Arts and Sciences 1942, American Newspaper Guild Page One Award 1944, 1945, Wendell Wilkie One-World Award 1946, PEN Award 1986, inducted Radio Hall of Fame 1993, Dupont Award, Columbia Univ. 1996, ICON Award, Bradbury Creativity Award 2001 and other awards. *Films:* The Blue Veil, The Grand Design, Lust for Life, The Story of Ruth, Yamashita, The Tiger of Malaya, Scandal at Scourie. *Cantatas:* The Golden Door, Yes Speak Out Yes (commissioned by UN 1968). *Stage plays:* The Rivalry, The World of Carl Sandburg, The Hyphen, Cervantes, Together Tonight 1975, The Strange Affliction 1995, Fifty Years After 14 August (on surrender of Japan) 1995. *Radio:* No Love Lost, The Curse of 589, The Secretariat 1998, Our Lady of the Freedoms and Some of Her Friends, The Writer with the Lame Left Hand (Cervantes) 1999, Memos to a New Millennium 2000, College Collage 2002. *Publications:* They Fly through the Air 1939, Thirteen by Corwin 1942, More by Corwin 1944, On a Note of Triumph (both as a book and album of recordings) 1945, Untitled and Other Dramas 1947, Dog in the Sky 1952, Overkill and Megalove 1962, Prayer for the 70's 1969, Holes in a Stained Glass Window 1978, Jerusalem Printout 1978, Greater than the Bomb 1981, A Date with Sandburg 1981, Trivializing America 1984, Network at Fifty 1984, CONartist 1993, Norman Corwin's Letters 1994, Years of the Electric Ear 1994, Limericks, Freebies and Never Once Drunk 1999, Message for the Millennium 2000, The Huntington 2002. *Leisure interests:* mineralogy, music, painting, chess. *Address:* School of Journalism, University of Southern California, University Park, Los Angeles, CA 90089-1695 (Office); Suite 302, 1840 Fairburn Avenue, Los Angeles, CA 90025-4958, USA. *Telephone:* (310) 475-3179 (Office). *Fax:* (310) 475-3179 (Office). *E-mail:* corwin@usc.edu (Office).

CORY, Hon. Peter, BA; Canadian judge; b. 25 Oct. 1925, Windsor, Ont.; s. of Andrew Cory and Mildred Cory (née Beresford Howe); m. Edith Nash 1947; three s.; ed Univ. of Windsor, 6th Bomber Group, RCAF 1943–46; called to Bar of Ont. 1950; created QC 1963; Bencher, Law Soc. of Upper Canada 1971–74; Trial Div., Supreme Court of Canada 1974; apptd to Court of Appeal, Ont. 1981; apptd to Supreme Court of Canada 1989, Judge 1989–99, retd 1999; apptd by British and Irish Govts to lead investigations into suspected collusion of intelligence services and IRA in six cross-border Irish killings Aug. 2002; fmr Pres. Advocates Soc., York Co. Law Asscn; fmr Chair. Ont. Civil Liberties Section, Canadian Bar Asscn, fmr mem. Council. *Leisure interests:* tennis, squash. *Address:* POB 50, First Canadian Place, Toronto, Ont., M5X 1B8, Canada (Office).

CORZINE, Jon Stevens, MBA; American banker and politician; b. 1 Jan. 1947, Taylorville, Ill.; s. of Roy Allen Corzine and Nancy June (née Hedrick) Corzine; m. Joanne Dougherty 1968; two s. one d.; ed Univs. of Chicago and Illinois; bond officer Continental Ill. Nat. Bank 1970; Asst Vice-Pres. Banc-Ohio Corpn 1974–75; joined Goldman, Sachs & Co. 1975, Vice-Pres. 1977, partner 1980–98, man. consultant 1985–94, Co-Head Fixed Income Div. 1988–94, Sr Partner, Chair. Man. Cttee, CEO 1994–99, now Co-Chair.; Senator from NJ Jan. 2001–; mem. Bd Dirs NY Philharmonic 1996–, Public

Securities Asscn (Vice-Chair. 1985, Chair. 1986). *Address:* One Gateway Center, 11th Floor, Newark, NJ 07102 (Office); US Senate, Washington, DC 20510, USA (Office).

COSBY, Bill, MA, EdD; American actor; b. 12 July 1937, Philadelphia; s. of William Cosby and Anna Cosby; m. Camille Hanks 1964; five c. (one s. deceased); ed Temple Univ. and Univ. of Mass.; served USNR 1956–60; Pres. Rhythm and Blues Hall of Fame 1968–; recipient of four Emmy Awards and eight Grammy Awards. *Films include:* Hickey and Boggs 1972, Man and Boy 1972, Uptown Saturday Night 1974, Let's Do It Again 1975, Mother, Jugs and Speed 1976, Aesop's Fables, A Piece of Action 1977, California Suite 1978, Devil and Max Devlin 1979, Leonard: Part VI 1987, Ghost Dad 1990, The Meteor Man 1993, Jack 1996, 4 Little Girls. *Television:* The Bill Cosby Show 1969, 1972–73, I Spy, The Cosby Show 1984–92, Cosby Mystery Series 1994–; recitals include: Revenge, To Russell, My Brother, With Whom I Slept, Top Secret, 200 M.P.H., Why Is There Air, Wonderfulness, It's True, It's True, Bill Cosby is a Very Funny Fellow: Right, I Started Out as a Child, 8:15, 12:15, Hungry, Reunion 1982, Bill Cosby . . . Himself 1983, Those of You With or Without Children, You'll Understand; Exec. Producer A Different Kind of World (TV series) 1987–93; Presenter Kids Say the Darndest Things 1998–, As I Was Saying 1997. *Publications:* The Wit and Wisdom of Fat Albert 1973, Bill Cosby's Personal Guide to Power Tennis, Fatherhood 1986, Time Flies 1988, Love and Marriage 1989, Childhood 1991, Little Bill Series 1999, Congratulations! Now What? 1999. *Address:* c/o The Brokaw Co., 9255 Sunset Boulevard, Los Angeles, CA 90069, USA.

COSGRAVE, Liam; Irish politician; b. 13 April 1920, Templeogue, Co. Dublin; s. of the late William T. Cosgrave (Pres. of the Exec. Council of the Irish Free State, 1922–32) and Louise Flanagan; m. Vera Osborne 1952; two s. one d.; ed Synge Street Christian Brothers' Schools, Dublin, St Vincent's Coll., Castleknock, Co. Dublin and Kings Inns; called to the Bar 1943; Sr Counsel 1958; served in Army; TD, Dublin Co. 1943–48, Dún Laoghaire and Rathdown 1948–81; Leader, Fine Gael Party 1965–77; Parl. Sec. to the Prime Minister and to Minister for Industry and Commerce 1948–51; Minister for External Affairs 1954–57; Prime Minister 1973–77; Minister for Defence 1976; Chair. and Leader of first Irish Del. to UN Gen. Ass. 1956; Hon. LLD (Duquesne Univ., St John's Univ.) 1956, (De Paul Univ.) 1958, (Nat. Univ. of Ireland and Dublin Univ.) 1974; Kt Grand Cross of Pius IX (Ordine Piano). *Address:* Beechpark, Templeogue, Co. Dublin, Ireland.

COSGROVE, Art, BA, PhD; Irish university president; b. 1 June 1940, Newry, Co. Down, NI; m. Emer Sweeney 1968; nine c.; ed Abbey CBS, Newry, Co. Down, NI and Queen's Univ., Belfast, NI; mem. academic staff Univ. Coll. Dublin 1963–, Sr Lecturer Dept of Medieval History 1976, Assoc. Prof. and Acting Head of Dept 1990, apptd. Chair. Combined Depts. of History 1991, Pres. Univ. Coll. Dublin 1994–; Visiting Prof. History Dept, Univ. of Kansas 1974; LLD hc (Queen's Univ., Belfast) 1995. *Publications:* Studies in Irish History presented to R. D. Edwards (jtly.) 1979, Late Medieval Ireland 1370–1541 1981, Parliament and Community (jtly.) 1981, Marriage in Ireland 1985, A New History of Ireland II: Medieval Ireland 1169–1534 1987, Dublin Through the Ages 1988. *Address:* Office of the President, University College Dublin, Belfield, Dublin 4, Ireland (Office). *Telephone:* 7161666 (Office). *Fax:* 7161170 (Office). *E-mail:* president@ucd.ie (Office). *Website:* www.ucd.ie (Office).

ĆOSIĆ, Dobrica; Serbia and Montenegro (Serbian) writer and politician; b. 29 Dec. 1921, Velika Drenova; m. Božica Ćosić; one d.; ed Belgrade Univ., Higher Party School; war service 1941–45; worked as journalist, then as freelance writer; corresp. mem. Serbian Acad. of Arts and Sciences 1970, mem. 1976; left League of Communists of Yugoslavia (LCY), prosecuted; resumed active political activity 1980s; Pres. of Repub. of Yugoslavia (now Serbia and Montenegro) 1992–93. *Publications:* The Sun is Far 1951, Roots 1954, Sections 1961, Fairy Tale 1965, The Time of Death (Vols 1–4) 1972–79, The Time of Evil: Sinner (Vols 1–4) 1985, Apostate 1986, Believer 1990, The Time of Power 1995; studies and essays: Hope and Fear 2001, Real and Possible 2001, Serbian Question (Vols 1–4) 2002, Writer's Notes (Vols 1–4) 2002. *Address:* Serbian Academy of Sciences and Arts, Knez Mikhailova str. 35, Belgrade (Office); Branka Djonovića 6, Belgrade, Serbia and Montenegro (Home). *Telephone:* (11) 3342400 (Office); (11) 663437 (Home). *Telex:* (11) 182825 (Office). *E-mail:* sasapres@bib.sanu.ac.yu (Office).

COSMOS, Jean; French playwright; b. Jean Louis Gaudrat, 14 June 1923, Paris; s. of Albert Gaudrat and Maria Maillebuau; m. Alice Jarrousse 1948; one s. two d.; ed Inst. St Nicholas, Igny, Coll. Jean-Baptiste Say, Paris; songwriter 1945–50, writer for radio 1952–60, for TV 1964–; mem. Comm. Soc. des auteurs dramatiques 1971–; co-librettist Goya 1996 (opera); TV, Soc. des auteurs et compositeurs prizes 1970; Chevalier Légion d'honneur, Officier des Arts et des Lettres. *Plays:* author or adapter of numerous plays for the theatre including la Fille du roi 1952, Au jour le jour 1952, les Grenadiers de la reine 1957, Macbeth 1959, 1965, le Manteau 1963, la Vie et la Mort du roi Jean 1964, Arden de Faversham 1964, Monsieur Alexandre 1965, la Bataille de Lobositz 1969, Major Barbara 1970, le Marchand de Venise 1971, Sainte Jeanne des Abattoirs 1972, Ce sacré Bonheur 1987; author of numerous TV plays including les Oranges (Albert Ollivier prize) 1964, le Pacte 1966, Un homme, un cheval 1968, la Pomme oubliée (after Jean Anglade), l'Ingénu (after Voltaire), Bonsoir Léon, la Tête à l'envers, le Trêve, le Coup Monté, Aide-toi, Julien Fontanes, magistrat (TV Series 1980–89), La Dictée 1984; with Jean Chatenêt: 16 à Kerbriant, Ardéchois coeur fidèle (Critics' choice)

1975, Les Yeux Bleus, la Lumière des Justes (after Henri Troyat); with Gilles Perrault: le Secret des dieux, la Filière, Fabien de la Drôme, seven-part serial of Julien Fontanes, Magistrat, regular contrib. to les Cinq dernières minutes. *Films include:* Bonjour toubib 1959 La vie et rien d'autre 1989, Le Colonel Chabert 1994, La fille de d'Artagnan 1994, Capitaine Conan 1996, Le bossu 1997, Laissez-passer 2002, Effroyables jardins 2003. *Address:* c/o Artmédia, 20 avenue Rapp, 75007 Paris (Office); 57 rue de Versailles, 92410 Ville d'Avray, France (Home).

COSSIGA, Francesco, LLD; Italian politician; b. 26 July 1928, Sassari; m. Giuseppa Sigurani 1960; two s.; joined Democrazia Cristiana (DC) 1945, Provincial Sec. 1956–58, mem. Nat. Council 1956–85; MP for Sassari 1958–85; Under-Sec. of State for Defence 1966–70; Minister for Public Admin. 1974–76, of the Interior 1976–78; Prime Minister 1979–80; Pres. of Senate 1983–85; Pres. of Italy 1985–92; Life-term Senator (Ind. Group) 1992–; Dr. hc (Oxford) 1987. *Address:* c/o Palazzo Giustiniani, Via della Dogana Vecchia 29, 00186 Rome, Italy. *Telephone:* (06) 67062012. *Fax:* (06) 67063658.

COSSONS, Sir Neil, Kt, OBE, MA, FSA; British foundation executive; b. 15 Jan. 1939, Nottingham; s. of Arthur Cossons and Evelyn Cossons (née Bettle); m. Veronica Edwards 1965; two s. one d.; ed Henry Mellish Grammar School, Nottingham, Univ. of Liverpool; Curator of Tech., Bristol City Museum 1964; Deputy Dir, City of Liverpool Museums 1969; Dir Ironbridge Gorge Museum 1971; Dir Nat. Maritime Museum, Greenwich 1983; Dir Science Museum, London 1986–2000; Commr Historic Buildings and Monuments Comm. for England (English Heritage) 1989–95, 1999–2000, Chair. 2000–; mem. Royal Coll. of Art Council 1989–, Design Council 1990–94, British Waterways Bd 1995–2001; mem. Council Foundation for Mfg and Industry 1993–98; Fellow and Past Pres. of the Museums Asscn; Comité scientifique, Conservatoire National des Arts et Métiers 1991–2000; Hon. Fellow RCA; Hon. D.Soc.Sc. (Birmingham) 1979; Hon. DUniv (Open Univ.) 1984, (Sheffield Hallam) 1995, (York) 1998; Hon. DLitt (Liverpool) 1989, (Bradford) 1991, (Nottingham Trent) 1994, (Univ. of West of England) 1995, (Bath) 1997; Hon. DSc (Leicester) 1995, (Nottingham) 2000; Hon. DArts (De Montfort) 1997; Companion, Inst. of Man. 1996; Norton Medlicott Medal (Historical Asscn) 1991, President's Medal (Royal Acad. of Eng) 1993. *Publications:* Industrial Archaeology of the Bristol Region (with RA Buchanan) 1968, Industrial Archaeology 1975, Transactions of the First International Congress on the Conservation of Industrial Monuments (Ed.) 1975, Rees's Manufacturing Industry (Ed.) 1975, Ironbridge—Landscape of Industry (with H. Sowden) 1977, The Iron Bridge—Symbol of the Industrial Revolution (with BS Trinder) 1979, The Management of Change in Museums (Ed.) 1985, Making of the Modern World (Ed.) 1992, Perspectives on Industrial Archaeology (Ed.) 2000. *Leisure interests:* travel, industrial archaeology. *Address:* English Heritage, 23 Savile Row, London, W1S 2ET (Office); The Old Rectory, Rushbury, Shropshire, SY6 7EB, England (Home). *Telephone:* (20) 7973-3334 (Office); (1694) 771603 (Home). *Fax:* (20) 7973-3379 (Office); (1694) 771703 (Home). *E-mail:* neil.cossons@english-heritage.org.uk (Office).

COSTA, Antonio Maria, PhD; Italian economist; b. 16 June 1941, Mondovi; s. of Francesco Costa and Maria Costa; m. Patricia Agnes Wallace 1971; two s. one d.; ed Univ. of California, Berkeley, Acad. of Sciences of the USSR and Univ. of Turin; Visiting Prof. of Econs, Moscow Univ. and Acad. of Sciences of the USSR 1965–67; Instructor of Econs, Univ. of Calif., Berkeley 1968–70; Prof. of Econs, New York Univ., 1976–83; Sr Econ. Adviser to the UN 1970–83; Special Counsellor in Econs to the Sec.-Gen. of OECD 1983–87; Dir Gen. Econ. and Financial Affairs, EC 1987–92; Sec.-Gen. EBRD, London, UK 1992–2001; Dir-Gen. UN Office for Drug Control and Crime Prevention, Vienna, Austria 2002–. *Publications:* articles on econs and politics. *Leisure interest:* work. *Address:* United Nations Office for Drug Control and Crime Prevention, Vienna International Centre, PO Box 500, A-1400 Vienna, Austria. *Telephone:* (1) 26060-4266 (Office). *Fax:* (1) 26060-5819 (Office). *E-mail:* odccp@odccp.org. *Website:* www.unodc.org.

COSTA, Gabriel Arcanjo Ferreira da, BLL; São Tomé e Príncipe politician and lawyer; b. 11 Dec. 1954; lawyer and magistrate; mem. Parl. (Juventude Movimento Libertação de São Tomé e Príncipe) in first Ass. following nat. independence 1975–98; Counsellor for Legal and Political Affairs to Pres. Trovoada 1991–95, Head of Cabinet of Pres. 1996–98; State Minister of Justice, Admin. Reform and Local Admin. –1998; Special Rep. of Exec. of CPLP for Guinea-Bissau 1998–2000; Amb. to Portugal, Morocco and Spain 2000–02; Prime Minister of São Tomé e Príncipe 2002. *Address:* c/o Office of the Prime Minister, Rua Município, CP 302, São Tomé, São Tomé e Príncipe (Office).

COSTA, Manuel Pinto da; São Tomé e Príncipe politician; b. 5 Aug. 1937, Água Grande; Founded Movement for the Liberation of São Tomé e Príncipe (MLSTP) 1972; Sec.-Gen., MLSTP, based in Gabon 1972–75, Pres. 1978; Pres. of São Tomé e Príncipe 1975–91; Minister of Agric., Land Reform and Defence 1975–78, of Labour and Social Security 1977–78, of Territorial Admin. 1978–82, of Defence and Nat. Security 1982–86, fmr Minister of Planning and Econs; Prime Minister 1978–88; visited China and N Korea Dec. 1975; Dr. hc (Berlin); José Marti Medal, Cuba. *Address:* c/o Office of the President, C.P. 38, São Tomé, São Tomé e Príncipe.

COSTA-GAVRAS, Constantiy; French (Greek-born) film director and film script writer; b. Constantiy Gavras, 13 Feb. 1933, Arcadia; s. of Panayotis and Panayota Gavras; m. Michele Ray 1968; three c.; ed Sorbonne, Inst. d'Etudes Cinématiques, Paris; worked as Asst to film Dirs. Yves Allegret, Jacques Demy, René Clair, René Clément; Pres. Cinémathèque Française 1982–87; Chevalier, Légion d'honneur, Commdr Arts et Lettres, Officier Ordre Nat. du Mérite; Prix Académie Française for Life Achievement 1998. *Films directed include:* The Sleeping Car Murder (also writer) 1965 (MWA Award), Un Homme de Trop 1966 (Moscow Film Festival Prize), Z (co-writer) 1969 (Jury Award, Cannes, Award for Best Foreign-Language Film), L'Aveu (co-writer) 1970, State of Siege (co-writer) 1973 (Louis Delluc Prize), Section Spéciale (co-writer) 1975 (Best Dir, Cannes), Clair de Femme (writer) 1979, Missing (co-writer) 1982 (Gold Palm, Cannes, Academy Award, best screenplay, British Acad. best screenplay), Hanna K (co-writer) 1983, Family Business (writer) 1985, Betrayed 1988 (ACLUF Award), Music Box 1989 (Golden Bear, Berlin), The Little Apocalypse (Dir and co-writer) 1993, Mad City 1996; directed opera Il Mondo della Luna (Joseph Haydn), Teatro San Carlo, Naples 1994, Amen 2001. *Publication:* Etat de Siège: The making of the film. *Leisure interests:* theatre, opera, books. *Address:* c/o Artmédia, 20 avenue Rapp,75007, Paris, France. *Telephone:* 1-44-41-13-73 (Office). *Fax:* 1-44-41-13-74 (Office). *E-mail:* kgprod@wanadoo.fr (Office).

COSTA PEREIRA, Renato Claudio; Brazilian aviation official and international organization official; b. 30 Nov. 1936; m.; ed Brazilian Air Force Academy; Personnel Commdr, Belo Horizonte Air Force Base 1961–67; Officer, Brazilian Air Force Gen. Personnel Command 1967–70, Instructor Officer, Brazilian Air Force Improvement Officer School 1970–74; Pilot Instructor, Brazilian Air Force Acad. 1974–77; Man. and Co-ordinator of Research and Devt project 1978–84; Dir Flight Protection Inst. 1984–85; Logistics Adviser to Minister of Aeronautics 1985–87; Chief, Brazilian Air Comm., London, England 1987–89; Sec. of Planning and Contracting, Secr. of Econ. and Finance, Ministry of Aeronautics 1989–90; Dir Operations Sub-Dept, Civil Aviation Dept 1990–92, Dir Planning Sub-Dept 1990–94; Pres. Latin American Comm. of Civil Aviation 1990–97, responsible for establishing the basis for the enlargement of the Comm. to a Pan-American body in 1997; Pres. Brazilian Govt agency for int. air navigation affairs 1990–97; Sec.-Gen. Int. Civil Aviation Org. 1997–. *Address:* International Civil Aviation Organization, 999 University Street, Montreal, Quebec, H3A 5H7, Canada (Office). *Telephone:* (514) 954-8219 (Office). *Fax:* (514) 954-6077 (Office). *E-mail:* icaohq@icao.int (Office). *Website:* www.icao.int (Office).

COSTEDOAT, Gen. Pierre-Jacques; French army officer; b. 27 Jan. 1942, Casablanca, Morocco; s. of René Costedoat and Marguerite Bosc; m. Anne-Marie Delamare 1965; four d.; ed Saint-Cyr-Coëtquidan mil. acad.; Second Lt, 74th Artillery Regt 1964, Lt 1966; Capt., 1st Artillery Regt 1972, then Battery CO; Maj., 11th Artillery Regt 1977, Lt-Col 1981, Col 1984; attended as auditeur Centre des hautes études militaires and Institut des hautes études de défense nationale 1987–88; CO 93rd Mountain Artillery Regt, then Staff 1988–89, at Direction Générale de la Sécurité extérieure (DGSE) 1989–95; Brig. 1992; CO Saint-Cyr Coëtquidan Mil. Acad. 1995–98; rank of Maj.-Gen. 1995; Asst Gen. Sec. of Nat. Defence 1998–2000; Gen. de corps 1998–; Mil. Gov. of Paris, Commdr of Ile-de-France, Officer Gen. Paris Zone of Defence 2000–; Officier Légion d'honneur, Commdr Ordre nat. du Mérite. *Leisure interests:* skiing, tennis, golf. *Address:* Etat-major, QG des loges, BP 201, 00488 armées (Office); 2 boulevard des Invalides, 75007 Paris, France (Office). *Telephone:* 1-44-42-39-65 (Office). *Fax:* 1-44-42-37-44 (Office). *E-mail:* gmp@gmp.terre.defense.gouv.fr (Office).

COSTELLO, Elvis; British singer and songwriter; b. Declan Patrick Aloysius McManus, 25 Aug. 1954, London; s. of Ross McManus and Lillian McManus (née Costello); m. 1st Mary Costello 1974; one s.; m. 2nd Cait O'Riordan 1986; formed Elvis Costello and the Attractions 1977; concert appearances, UK and USA 1978–; Dir S Bank Meltdown 1995. *Film:* Americathon 1979. *Music:* Albums include: My Aim is True 1977, This Year's Model 1978, Armed Forces 1979, Get Happy 1980, Trust 1981, Almost Blue 1981, Taking Liberties, Imperial Bedroom 1982, Goodbye Cruel World 1984, Punch the Clock 1984, The Best Of 1985, Blood and Chocolate 1986, King of America 1986, Spike 1989, Mighty Like the Rose 1991, The Juliet Letters (with Brodsky Quartet) 1993, Brutal Youth (with Steve Nieve, Pete Thomas, Bruce Thomas and Nick Lowe) 1994, Kojak Variety 1995, All This Useless Beauty 1996, Extreme Honey 1997, Painted from Memory 1998 (Grammy Award 1999), For the Stars (with Anne Sofie von Otter) 2001, When I Was Cruel 2002; Singles include: Alison 1977, Watching the Detectives 1977, Crawling to the USA 1978, Radio, Radio 1978, Stranger in the House 1978, Girls Talk 1979, Oliver's Army 1979, (I Don't Want To Go To) Chelsea 1979, Accidents Will Happen 1979, Good Year for the Roses 1981, Boy With a Problem 1982, Every Day I Write the Book 1983, Pills and Soap 1983, The People's Limousine 1985, Little Atoms 1996, She 1999. *Address:* c/o Rick Gersean, Warner Bros. Records, 3300 Warner Boulevard, Burbank, CA 91510, USA.

COSTELLO, Peter Howard, BA, LLB; Australian politician; b. 14 Aug. 1957; s. of R. J. Costello and M. A. Costello; m. Tanya Costello 1982; one s. two d.; ed Carey Grammar School, Monash Univ.; solicitor, Mallesons, Melbourne 1981–84; tutor (part-time) Monash Univ. 1984–86; mem. Victorian Bar 1984–90; MP for Higgins, Victoria, 1990–; Shadow Minister for Corp. Law Reform and Consumer Affairs 1990–92; Shadow Attorney-Gen. and Shadow Minister for Justice 1992–93, for Finance 1993–94; Deputy Leader of the Opposition and Shadow Treas. 1994–96; Deputy Leader Liberal Party 1996–, Commonwealth of Australia Treas. 1996–; mem. Liberal Party. *Publication:* Arbitration in Contempt (jtly.) 1986; articles for periodicals and journals. *Leisure interests:* swimming, football, reading. *Address:* Parliament House, Canberra, ACT 2600, Australia.

COSTELLOE, Paul; Irish fashion designer and artist; b. 23 June 1945, Dublin; m. 1982; six s. one d.; ed Blackrock Coll. Dublin, design coll. in Dublin and Chambre Syndical Paris; design asst Jacques Esterel, Paris 1969–71; designer, Marks & Spencer 1972; chief house designer, A. Rinascente, Milan 1972–74; designer, Anne Fogerty, New York, Pennaco, New York and Trimfit, Philadelphia 1974–79; established own design house, Paul Costelloe Int. Ltd, in conjunction with business partner Robert Eitel 1979–; merchandise sold in UK, Ireland, Europe, Scandinavia and N America under Paul Costelloe Collection and Dressage labels; opened flagship store, Knightsbridge 1994; designer of new British Airways uniform 1994; Hon. DLitt (Ulster) 1996; Fil d'Or award, Int. Linen Council, 1987, 1988, 1989; British Designer of the Year 1989 and other awards. *Leisure interests:* rugby, tennis, golf. *Address:* 30 Westminster Palace Gardens, Artillery Row, London, SW1P 1RR (Office); 27 Cheval Place, London, SW7 1EW, England. *Telephone:* (20) 7233-2210; (20) 7589-9484 (London). *Fax:* (20) 7233-2230 (Office); (20) 7589-9481 (London).

COSTNER, Kevin; American actor; b. 1955; m. Cindy Silva (divorced); one s. two d.; one s. by Bridget Rooney; ed California State Univ. Fullerton; directing début in Dances with Wolves 1990 (Acad. Award for Best Picture 1991). *Films include:* Frances 1982, The Big Chill 1983, Testament 1983, Silverado 1985, The Untouchables 1987, No Way Out 1987, Bull Durham 1988, Field of Dreams 1989, Revenge 1989, Robin Hood: Prince of Thieves 1990, JFK 1991, The Bodyguard 1992, A Perfect World 1993, Wyatt Earp 1994, The War 1994, Waterworld 1995, Tin Cup 1996, The Postman 1997, Message in a Bottle 1998, For Love of the Game 1999, Thirteen Days 2000, 3000 Miles to Graceland 2001, Dragonfly 2002; co-producer Rapa Nui, China Moon 1993, exec.-producer Rapa Nui 1994. *Leisure interest:* golf. *Address:* TIG Productions, Producers' Building 5, 4000 Warner Boulevard, Burbank, CA 91523; c/o William Morris Agency, 151 El Camino Drive, Beverly Hills, CA 90212, USA.

COT, Jean-Pierre; French politician, international organization official and academic; b. 23 Oct. 1937, Geneva, Switzerland; s. of Pierre Cot and Luisa Phelps; m.; three c.; Prof., then Dean, Faculty of Law, Amiens 1968; Prof. of Int. Law and Political Sociology, Univ. of Paris I (Panthéon-Sorbonne) 1969, Dir Disarmament Research and Study Centre (CEREDE); mem. Steering Cttee, Parti Socialiste (PS) 1970, 1973, mem. Exec. Bureau 1976; Mayor of Coise-Saint-Jean-Pied-Gauthier 1971–95; Deputy (Savoie) to Nat. Ass. 1973–81; Gen. Councillor, Savoie 1973–81; PS Nat. Del. for matters relating to the European Communities 1976–79; mem. European Parl. 1978–79, 1984–99, Pres. Budget Cttee 1984–87, Chair. Socialist Group 1989–94, Vice-Pres. 1997–99; Judge Int. Tribunal for the Law of the Sea 2002–; Minister-Del. for Co-operation, attached to Minister for External Relations 1981–82; mem. Exec. Council UNESCO 1983–84. *Publication:* A l'épreuve du pouvoir: le tiers-mondisme, pour quoi faire? 1984 and numerous works on int. law and political science. *Address:* Coise-Saint-Jean-Pied-Gauthier, 73800 Montmélian, France (Home).

COTE, David M., BBA; American business executive; ed Univ. of New Hampshire; various man. positions General Electric –1996, Corp. Sr Vice-Pres., Pres. and CEO General Electric Appliances 1996–99; Pres., CEO and Chair. TRW, Cleveland 1999–2002; apptd Pres. and CEO Honeywell Feb. 2002, apptd Chair. Bd July 2002, currently Chair. and CEO; mem. Nat. Security Telecommunications Advisory Cttee; Hon. LLD (Pepperdine Univ.) 2001. *Address:* Honeywell, 101 Columbia Road, Morristown, NJ 07962, USA (Office). *Telephone:* (973) 455-2000 (Office). *Fax:* (973) 455-4807 (Office). *Website:* www.honeywell.com (Office).

COTRUBAŞ, Ileana; Romanian opera and concert singer (retd); b. 1939, Galaţi; d. of Maria and Vasile Cotrubaş; m. Manfred Ramin 1972; ed Conservatorul Ciprian Porumbescu, Bucharest; Lyric soprano range; début as Yniold in Pelléas et Mélisande at Bucharest Opera 1964; Frankfurt Opera 1968–70; Glyndebourne Festival 1968; Salzburg Festival 1969; Staatsoper Vienna 1969; Royal Opera House, Covent Garden 1971; Lyric Opera of Chicago 1973; Paris Opera 1974; La Scala, Milan 1975; Metropolitan Opera, New York 1977; operatic roles include Susanna, Pamina, Norina, Gilda, Traviata, Manon, Antonia, Tatyana, Mimi, Mélisande; concerts with all major European orchestras; Lieder recitals at Musikverein Vienna, Royal Opera House, Covent Garden, Carnegie Hall, New York, La Scala; First Prize, Int. Singing Competition, Hertogenbosch, Netherlands 1965, First Prize, Munich Radio Competition 1966; Austrian Kammersängerin 1981; Grand Officer, Order of Sant'Iago da Espada (Portugal) 1990; Hon. Citizen of Bucharest 1995. *Recordings:* Bach Cantatas, Mozart Masses, Brahms Requiem, Mahler Symphonies 2, 8; complete operas including Le Nozze di Figaro, Die Zauberflöte, Hänsel und Gretel, Calisto, Louise, L'Elisir d'amore, Les Pêcheurs de perles, La Traviata, Rigoletto, Alzira, Manon. *Publication:* Opernwahrheiten 1998.

COTTA, Michèle, LèsL, DrèsScPol; French journalist; b. 15 June 1937, Nice; d. of Jacques Cotta and Helène Scoffier; m. 1st Claude Tchou (divorced); one s. (deceased) one d.; m. 2nd Phillipe Barret 1992; ed Lycée de Nice, Faculté de Lettres de Nice and Inst. d'études politiques de Paris; Journalist with L'Express 1963–69, 1971–76; Europ I 1970–71, 1986; political diarist, France-Inter 1976–80; Head of political service, Le Point 1977–80, Reporter 1986; Chief Political Ed. RTL 1980–81; Pres. Dir-Gen. Radio France 1981–82; Pres. Haute Autorité de la Communication Audiovisuelle 1982–86; Producer Faits de Société on TF1 1987, Dir of Information 1987–92, Pres. Sofica Images Investissements 1987; producer and presenter La Revue de presse, France 2 1993–95; political ed. Nouvel Economiste 1993–96; producer and presenter Polémiques, France 2 1995–99, Dir-Gen. France 2 1999–; editorial writer RTL 1996–99; mem. Conseil économique et social; Chevalier, Légion d'honneur, Officier, Ordre nat. du mérite. *Publications:* La collaboration 1940–1944, 1964, Les elections présidentielles 1966, Prague, l'été des Tanks 1968, La Vième République 1974, Les miroirs de Jupiter 1986, Les Secrets d'une Victoire 1995. *Address:* 70 boulevard Port Royal, 75005 Paris, France (Home). *Telephone:* 1-49-22-20-16 (Office); 1-49-22-20-17 (Office); 6-09-48-10-00. *E-mail:* michele.cotta@groupe-ab.fr (Office); mcotta@noos.fr (Home).

COTTERILL, Rodney Michael John, PhD, DSc; British/Danish biophysicist; b. 27 Sept. 1933, Bodmin, UK; s. of Herbert Cotterill and Aline Le Cerf; m. Vibeke Nielsen 1959; two d.; ed Cowes and Newport High Schools, Isle of Wight, Univ. Coll. London, Yale Univ. and Emmanuel Coll. Cambridge; RAF 1952–54; Assoc. Scientist, Argonne Nat. Lab. 1962–67; Prof. Tech. Univ. of Denmark (now Danish Tech. Univ.) 1967–; Visiting Prof. Tokyo Univ. 1978, 1985; Fellow, Royal Danish Acad. of Sciences and Letters, Danish Acad. of Tech. Sciences, Inst. of Physics (UK); Kt, Order of the Dannebrog 1979 (First Class 1994); Ellen and Hans Hermer Memorial Prize 1978, James Arthur Lecturer (American Museum of Natural History, New York) 2003. *Publications:* The Cambridge Guide to the Material World 1985, Computer Simulation in Brain Science (ed.) 1988, No Ghost in the Machine 1989, Models of Brain Function (ed.) 1989, Neural Network Dynamics (co-ed.) 1992, Brain and Mind 1994, Autism, Intelligence and Consciousness 1994, Enchanted Looms 1998, Biophysics 2002 ; articles on topics in physics, biology and medicine. *Leisure interests:* sailing, choral singing, writing. *Address:* Biophysics, Danish Technical University, Building 307, 2800 Lyngby, Denmark (Office). *Telephone:* 45-25-32-03 (Office). *Fax:* 45-93-23-99 (Office). *E-mail:* rodney.cotterill@fysik.dtu.dk (Office). *Website:* info.fysik.dtu.dk/brainscience/people/rodney (Office).

COTTI, Flavio; Swiss politician; b. 18 Oct. 1939, Muralto, m. Renata Naretto; one d.; ed Univ. of Freiburg; barrister and public notary in Locarno 1965–75; mem. Locarno Communal Council 1964–75; mem. of cantonal Parl. of Ticino 1967–75; mem. of Govt, canton of Ticino, Head Dept of Home Affairs, Econ. Affairs, Justice and Mil. Matters 1975–83; mem. Nat. Council 1983–86; mem. Fed. Council Dec. 1986–; Head Fed. Dept of Home Affairs 1987–93; Dept of Foreign Affairs 1993–99; Pres. of Swiss Confed. 1991 and 1998; Pres. Bd of Dirs., Ticino Cantonal Tourist Office 1976–84; Pres. Christian Democratic People's Party (CDPP) of Ticino 1981, CDPP of Switzerland 1984; Chair. OSCE 1996; Pres. of Int. Advisory Bd CS Group 1999–; mem. of Bds of Fiat SpA 2000–, Jakobs Foundation 1999–, Georg Fischer. *Address:* c/o Christian Democratic People's Party, Klaraweg 6, Postfach 5835, 3001 Bern, Switzerland.

COTTINGHAM, Robert; American artist; b. 26 Sept. 1935, Brooklyn, New York; s. of James and Aurelia Cottingham; m. Jane Weismann 1967; three d.; ed Brooklyn Tech. High School, Pratt Inst.; army service 1955–58; Art Dir with Young and Rubicam Advertising Inc., New York 1959–64, Los Angeles 1964–68; left advertising to paint 1968–; taught at Art Centre Coll. of Design, Los Angeles 1969–70; moved to London 1972–76; returned to USA 1976–; Nat. Endowment for the Arts 1974–75; numerous one-man exhbns. 1968–; works in many public galleries in USA and also in Hamburg Museum, Tate Gallery, London and Utrecht Museum; MacDowell Colony Residency 1993, 1994; Walter Gropius Fellowship, Huntington Museum of Art 1992; mem. Nat. Acad. of Design. *Publications:* numerous print publs (lithographs, etchings). *Leisure interests:* travel, music, history. *Address:* PO Box 604, Blackman Road, Newtown, CT 06470, USA. *Telephone:* (203) 426-4072.

COTTON, Frank Albert, PhD; American chemist; b. 9 April 1930, Philadelphia, Pa; s. of Albert Cotton and Helen M. Taylor; m. Diane Dornacher 1959; two d.; ed Drexel Inst. of Tech., Temple and Harvard Univs.; Asst Prof. Mass. Inst. of Tech. (MIT) 1955–60, Assoc. Prof. 1960–61, Prof. 1961–71; Robert A. Welch Distinguished Prof., Texas A & M Univ. 1971–; Dir Lab. for Molecular Structure and Bonding 1983–; Consultant Union Carbide, New York 1964–; mem. Nat. Science Bd 1986–92; mem. NAS (Chair. Physical Sciences 1985–88), American Acad. of Arts and Sciences, Göttingen Acad. of Sciences, Royal Danish Acad. of Sciences and Letters, Indian Acad. of Sciences, Indian Nat. Science Acad., Royal Soc. of Edin., Academia Europaea, Russian Acad. of Sciences, Royal Soc. of London, Institut de France, Academie des Sciences; numerous hon. degrees; American Chem. Soc. Awards in Inorganic Chem. 1962, 1974, Baekeland Award (NJ section) 1963, Dwyer Medal (Univ. of NSW) 1966, Centenary Medal (Chemical Soc. London) 1974, Nichols Medal (New York section) 1975, Harrison Howe Award (Rochester section) 1975, Edgar Fahs Smith Award (Philadelphia section) 1976, Pauling Medal (Oregon and Puget Sound Sections) 1976, Kirkwood Medal (Yale Univ.) 1978, Willard Gibbs Medal (Chicago Section, ACS) 1980, Nyholm Medal (Royal Soc. Chem.) 1982, Nat. Medal of Science 1982, Award in Physical and Mathematical Sciences (New York, Acad. Sciences), T. W. Richards Medal (New England Section, American Chem. Soc.), King Faisal Int. Prize in Science 1990, Chemical Sciences Award, NAS, Gold Medal American Inst. of Chemists 1998, Lavoisier Medal, Soc. Française de Chimie 2000, Award in Organometallic Chemistry (ACS) 2001. *Publications:* Advanced Inorganic Chemistry (with G. Wilkinson, FRS, M. Bochmann, C.A. Murillo) 6th Edn 1999, Chemical Applications of Group Theory 3rd Edn 1990, Chemistry, An Investigative Approach 2nd Edn 1973, Basic Inorganic Chemistry (with G. Wilkinson, P. Gaus) 3rd Edn 1995, Multiple Bonds between Metal Atoms (with R. A. Walton) 2nd Edn 1993, approx. 1,465 research papers. *Leisure *interests:* equitation, conservation. *Address:* Department of Chemistry, Texas A & M University, College Station, TX 77843 (Office); 4101 Sand Creek Road, Bryan, TX 77808, USA (Home). *Telephone:* (979) 845-4432 (Office); (979) 589-2501 (Home).

COTTON, Hon. Sir Robert Carrington, KCMG, AO, F.C.P.A.; Australian politician; b. 29 Nov. 1915, Broken Hill, NSW; s. of H. L. Carrington and Muriel Cotton; m. Eve MacDougall 1937; one s. two d.; ed St Peter's Coll., Adelaide; fmr Federal Vice-Pres. Liberal Party of Australia; State Pres. NSW 1957–60, Acting Pres. 1965; Senator for NSW 1965–78; leader Del. of Fed. Parl. to meetings of IPU in Majorca and Geneva 1967; Minister of State for Civil Aviation 1969–72, Minister of Mfg Industry, Science and Consumer Affairs Nov.-Dec. 1975, of Industry and Commerce 1975–77; Consul-Gen., New York 1978–81; Amb. to USA 1982–85; Chair. Kleinwort Benson Australian Income Fund (New York) 1986–; Deputy Chair. Allders Int. Pty Ltd; Dir Reserve Bank of Australia 1981–83; Hill and Knowlton Inc. 1986–91, Capital Television Holdings Ltd, Thomson—CSF Pacific Holdings Pty Ltd 1997–; Chair. Australian Taiwan Business Council 1987–89, Australian Photonics Cooperative Research Centre, Nat. Gallery of Australia Foundation 1991–94, Australian Medical Asscn Enquiry 1986–87. *Leisure interests:* photography, writing. *Address:* Apartment 11, Southern Cross Gardens, 2 Spruson Street, Neutral Bay, NSW 2089, Australia.

COTTON, William (Bill) Frederick, Kt, CBE, FRTS; British television administrator; b. 23 April 1928; s. of the late William (Billy) Edward Cotton and Mabel Hope; m. 1st Bernadine Maud Sinclair 1950 (died 1964); three d.; m. 2nd Ann Corfield (née Bucknall) 1965 (divorced 1989); one step-d.; m. 3rd Kathryn Mary Burgess (née Ralphs) 1990; ed Ardingly Coll.; Jt Man. Dir Michael Reine Music Co. 1952–56; BBC-TV producer, Light Entertainment Dept 1956–62, Asst Head of Light Entertainment 1962–67, Head of Variety 1967–70, Head of Light Entertainment Group 1970–77; Controller BBC 1 1977–81; Deputy Man. Dir TV, BBC 1981–82; Dir of Programmes, TV and Dir of Devt, BBC 1982; Man. Dir, TV, BBC 1984–87; Chair. BBC Enterprises 1982–87; Dir Noel Gay Org. 1988–97, Chair. Noel Gay TV 1988–97; Non-exec. Dir Alba PLC 1988–; Deputy Chair. Meridian Broadcasting 1992–96 (Chair. 1996–2001); Dir Billy Marsh Assocs. 1998–; Vice-Pres. Marie Curie Cancer Care (fmrly Marie Curie Foundation) 1990–; Vice-Pres. Royal Television Soc. 1984–92, Pres. 1992–95; Fellow BAFTA 1998; Hon. DA (Bournemouth) 2000. *Publication:* Double Bill: 80 Years of Entertainment. *Leisure interest:* golf. *Address:* c/o Billy Marsh Associates, 187 North Gower Street, London, NW1 2NB; Summer Hill, The Glebe, Studland, Swanage, Dorset, BH19 3AS, England.

COTTRELL, Sir Alan (Howard), Kt, PhD, ScD, FEng, FRS; British scientist and professor of physical metallurgy; b. 17 July 1919, Birmingham; s. of Albert and Elizabeth Cottrell; m. Jean Elizabeth Harber 1944 (died 1999); one s.; ed Moseley Grammar School, Univ. of Birmingham, Univ. of Cambridge; lecturer in Metallurgy, Univ. of Birmingham 1943–49, Prof. of Physical Metallurgy 1949–55; Deputy Head, Metallurgy Div., AERE, Harwell, Berks. 1955–58; Goldsmiths' Prof. of Metallurgy, Cambridge Univ. 1958–65; Deputy Chief Scientific Adviser (Studies), Ministry of Defence 1965–67, Chief Adviser 1967; Deputy Chief Scientific Adviser to HM Govt 1968–71, Chief Scientific Adviser 1971–74; Master, Jesus Coll., Cambridge 1974–86, Vice-Chancellor, Cambridge Univ. 1977–79; Part-time mem. UKAEA 1962–65, 1983–87; Dir Fisons PLC 1979–80; mem. Advisory Council on Scientific Policy 1963–64, Cen. Advisory Council for Science and Technology 1967–, Exec. Cttee British Council 1974–87, Advisory Council, Science Policy Foundation 1976–, UK Perm. Security Comm. 1981–92; Hon. mem. American Soc. for Metals 1972, Fellow 1974; Hon. mem. The Metals Soc. 1977, Japan Inst. of Metals 1981; Foreign Assoc. NAS, USA 1972, Nat. Acad. of Eng, USA 1976; Foreign Hon. mem. American Acad. of Arts and Sciences 1960; Fellow Royal Soc., (Vice-Pres. 1964, 1976, 1977), Royal Swedish Acad. of Sciences 1970; Academia Europaea 1991; Hon. Fellow Christ's Coll., Cambridge 1970 (Fellow 1958–70), Jesus Coll., Cambridge 1986, Imperial Coll., London 1991, Inst. of Metals 1989; Hon. DSc (Columbia) 1965, (Newcastle) 1967, (Liverpool) 1969, (Manchester) 1970, (Warwick) 1971, (Sussex) 1972, (Bath) 1973, (Strathclyde and Aston in Birmingham) 1975, (Cranfield Inst. of Tech.) 1975, (Oxford) 1979, (Essex) 1982, (Birmingham) 1983; Hon. DEng (Tech. Univ. of Nova Scotia) 1984; ScD (Cambridge) 1976; LLD (Cambridge) 1981; Rosenhain Medal, Inst. of Metals, Hughes Medal, Royal Soc. 1961, Réaumur Medal, Soc. Française de Métallurgie 1964; Inst. of Metals (Platinum) Medal 1965, James Alfred Ewing Medal, ICE 1967, Holweck Medal, Soc. Française de Physique 1969, Albert Sauveur Achievement Award, American Soc. for Metals 1969, James Douglas Gold Medal, American Inst. of Mining, Metallurgy and Petroleum Engineers 1974, Rumford Medal, Royal Soc. 1974, Harvey Prize (Technion, Israel) 1974, Acta Metallurgica Gold Medal 1976, Guthrie Medal and Prize, Inst. of Physics 1977, Gold Medal, American Soc. for Metals 1980, Brinell Medal, Royal Swedish Acad. of Eng Sciences 1980, Kelvin Medal, ICE 1986, Hollomon Award, Acta Metallurgica 1990, Copley Medal, Royal Soc. 1996, Von Hippel Award, Materials Res. Soc. 1996. *Publications:* Theoretical Structural Metallurgy 1948, Dislocations and Plastic Flow in Crystals 1953, The Mechanical Properties of Matter 1964, Theory of Crystal Dislocations 1964, An Introduction to Metallurgy 1967, Portrait of Nature 1975, Environmental Economics 1978, How Safe is Nuclear Energy? 1981, Introduction to the Modern Theory of Metals 1988, Chemical Bonding in Transition Metal Carbides 1995, Concepts in the Electron Theory of Alloys 1998 and scientific

papers in various learned journals. *Leisure interests:* music, fly-fishing. *Address:* 40 Maids Causeway, Cambridge, CB5 8DD, England. *Telephone:* (1223) 363806.

COUCHEPIN, François; Swiss lawyer; b. 19 Jan. 1935, Martigny; s. of Louis Couchepin and Andrée Couchepin; m. Anne Marie Cottier 1957; six c.; ed Univ. of Lausanne; legal practitioner at law firm of Rodolphe Tissières 1959–64; own legal practice in Martigny 1964–; elected to Cantonal Council of Canton Valais 1965, re-elected 1969, 1973, 1977; Sec. Radical Group 1965–77, Pres. 1977–79; Head, French Section, Cen. Language Service, Fed. Chancellery 1980; Vice-Chancellor responsible for gen. admin. of Fed. Chancellery 1981; Chancellor of the Swiss Fed. 1991–99; mem. Defence Staff; mem. numerous comms. *Address:* c/o Federal Chancellery, Bundeshaus-West, 3003 Berne, Switzerland.

COUCHEPIN, Pascal; Swiss politician; b. 5 April 1942, Martigny; m.; three c.; ed Lausanne Univ.; elected mem. local council Martigny 1968; Deputy Mayor of Martigny 1976, Mayor 1984–88; elected to the Nat. Council 1979; Chair. Parl. Group, Liberal Democrat Party—LDP 1989–96; fmr Chair. Nat. Council's Cttee for Science and Research; fmr Chair. Fed. Dept of Justice and Police section of the Control Cttee; elected to Federal Council 1998; Vice-Pres. of the Swiss Confederation 2002, Pres. of the Swiss Confederation 2003–; Head of Fed. Dept of Econ. Affairs 1998–2002, of Home Affairs 2003–; fmr Gov. IBRD, EBRD. *Address:* Federal Department of Home Affairs, Bundeshaus, Inselgasse, 3003 Bern, Switzerland (Office). *Telephone:* 313229111 (Office). *Fax:* 313227901 (Office). *E-mail:* info@gs-edi.admin.ch (Office). *Website:* www.edi.admin.ch (Office).

COUPLES, Frederick Stephen (Fred); American golfer; b. 3 Oct. 1959, Seattle, Wash.; m. Thais Couples; one s. one d.; ed Univ. of Houston; turned professional 1980; mem. US Ryder Cup Team 1989, 1991, 1993, 1995, 1997; mem. Pres.'s Cup 1994, 1996, 1998; won Kemper Open 1984, Tournament Players Championship 1984, Byron Nelson Golf Classic 1987, Nissan Los Angeles Open 1990, Federal Express St Jude Classic BC Open, Johnnie Walker World Championship 1991, Nissan Los Angeles Open, Nestlé Int., Masters 1992, Honda Classic 1993, Buick Open 1994, World Cup 1994, Dubai Desert Classic, Johnnie Walker Classic 1995, The Players' Championship 1996, Bob Hope Chrysler Classic 1998, Memorial Tournament 1998; PGA Tour Player of the Year 1991, 1992; Arnold Palmer Award 1992. *Leisure interests:* tennis, all sports, antiques, bicycling, vintage cars. *Address:* c/o PGA Tour, 100 Avenue of the Champions, P.O. Box 109601, Palm Beach Gardens, FL 33410, USA.

COURANT, Ernest David, PhD; American (naturalized) physicist; b. 26 March 1920, Göttingen, Germany; s. of Richard Courant and Nina Runge; m. Sara Paul 1944; two s.; ed Swarthmore Coll. and Univ. of Rochester, USA; Scientist Nat. Research Council (Canada), Montreal 1943–46; Research Assoc. in Physics, Cornell Univ. 1946–48; Physicist Brookhaven Nat. Lab., Upton, NY 1948–60, Sr Physicist 1960–89, Distinguished Scientist Emer. 1990–; Prof. (part-time) Yale Univ. 1961–67, State Univ. of NY, Stony Brook 1967–85; Visiting Prof. Univ. of Mich. 1989–; Hon. Prof. Univ. of Science and Tech. of China, Hefei 1994; co-discoverer of Strong-focusing principle, particle accelerators; mem. NAS 1976; Fellow AAAS 1981; Hon. DSc (Swarthmore Coll.) 1988; Pregel Prize, New York Acad. of Sciences 1979, Fermi Prize 1986, R. R. Wilson Prize 1987. *Publications:* various articles; contrib. to Handbuch der Physik 1959, Annual Review of Nuclear Science 1968. *Address:* 40 West 72nd Street, New York, NY 10023, USA (Home). *E-mail:* ecourant@msn.com (Home).

COURIER, Jim; American tennis player; b. 17 Aug. 1970, Sanford Fla; ed Nick Bollettieri Tennis Acad.; coached by José Higueras; winner, French Open 1991, 1992, Indian Wells (doubles) 1991; runner-up, US Open 1991, ATP World Championship 1991; winner Australian Open 1992–93, Italian Open 1993; runner-up French Open 1993, Wimbledon 1993; winner of 23 singles titles and six doubles titles and over 16 million dollars in prize money at retirement in May 2000. *Address:* International Management Group, Suite 300, 1 Erieview Place, Cleveland, OH 44114; US Tennis Association, 70 West Red Oak Lane, White Plains, NY 10604, USA.

COURRÈGES, André; French couturier; b. 9 March 1923, Pau (Pyrénées-Atlantiques); s. of Lucien Courrèges and Céline Coupe; m. Jacqueline Barrière 1966; one d.; ed Ecole Supérieure Technique; studied eng; moved to Paris and spent year as fashion designer 1945; went to Balenciaga's workrooms 1948 and served 11 years apprenticeship; f. Société André Courrèges 1961, Founder Dir, then Chair. and Man. Dir 1966; Founder Dir and Admin, Sport et Couture Amy Linker 1969; Founder Dir Société Courrèges Design 1981; launched his "Couture-Future" 1967; "Couture-Future" distributed by stores all over the world and by 45 exclusive boutiques in 10 countries including USA, Canada, Japan, Australia. *Leisure interests:* Basque pelota, physical fitness, rugby. *Address:* 40 rue François 1er, 75008 Paris (Office); 27 rue Delabordère, 92200 Neuilly-sur-Seine, France (Home).

COURT, Hon. Sir Charles (Walter Michael), Kt, AK, KCMG, OBE (MIL.), FCA, FCIS, FASA; Australian politician (retd); b. 29 Sept. 1911, Crawley, Sussex, England; s. of late W. J. Court and Rose R. Court; m. 1st Rita Steffanoni 1936 (died 1992); five s.; m. 2nd Judith Butt 1997; ed Perth Boys' School, WA; Founder Partner, Hendry, Rae & Court, chartered accountants 1938–70; served Australian Imperial Forces 1940–46, rising to rank of Lt-Col; Liberal mem. Legis. Ass. for Nedlands, Parl. WA 1953–82, Deputy Leader of Opposition 1956–59; Minister for Railways 1959–67, for Industrial Devt and the NW 1959–71, for Transport 1965–66; Deputy Leader of Opposition 1971–72, Leader 1972–74; Premier, State Treas., Minister Co-ordinating Econ. and Regional Devt, WA 1974–82; State Registrar (W Australia) Inst. of Chartered Accountants in Australia 1946–52; Senator Jr Chamber Int. 1971; Nat. Pres. Order of Australia Asscn 1986–89; Hon. Col W Australia Univ. Regt 1969–74, S.A.S. Regt (A.M.F.) 1976–80; Fellow Inst. of Chartered Accountants in Australia, Inst. of Chartered Secs. and Admins.; Life mem. Australian Soc. of CPA; Life mem. Inst. of Chartered Accountants 1982; Patron or Vice-Patron numerous musical, sporting and other bodies; Hon. FAIM 1980; Hon. LLD (W Australia) 1969; Hon. DTech (WA Inst. of Tech.); Dr hc (Murdoch Univ. of WA) 1995; Hon. DLitt (Edith Cowan Univ.) 1999; Mfrs' Export Council Award 1969, Industrial Design Council of Australia Award 1978 and numerous other awards; Knight of the Order of Australia; First Class Order of the Sacred Treasure, Japan; Kt Commdr, Order of Merit, Italy; Order of Brilliant Star, Taiwan. *Publications:* Charles Court: The Early Years and many papers on industrial, economic and resource development matters. *Leisure interests:* music, various cultural and sporting interests. *Address:* 18 Peel Parade, Coodanup, WA 6210, Australia (Home). *Telephone:* (8) 9535-5983 (Home). *Fax:* (8) 9535-5641.

COURT, Rev. Margaret, MBE; Australian tennis player; b. 16 July 1942, Albury, NSW; d. of Lawrence Smith and Maud Smith; m. Barry Court 1967; one s. three d.; ed Albury High School; amateur player 1960–67; professional 1968–77; Australian champion 1960, 1961, 1962, 1963, 1964, 1965, 1966, 1969, 1970, 1971, 1973; French champion 1962, 1964, 1969, 1970, 1973; Wimbledon champion 1963, 1965, 1970; US champion 1962, 1965, 1969, 1970, 1973; holds more major titles in singles, doubles and mixed doubles than any other player in history; won two Grand Slams, in mixed doubles 1963 and singles 1970; played Federation Cup for Australia 1963, 1964, 1965, 1966, 1968, 1969, 1971; ordained a Pentecostal minister in 1991, f. the Victory Life Centre, Perth 1996; Int. Tennis Hall of Fame 1979, Australian Tennis Hall of Fame 1993, Show Court One at Melbourne Park renamed Margaret Court Arena as a tribute on eve of Australian Open Jan. 2003. *Publications:* The Margaret Smith Story 1964, Court on Court 1974, Winning Faith (with Barbara Oldfield) 1993, Winning Words 1999, Our Winning Position 2003. *Address:* 21 Lowanna Way, City Beach, Perth, WA 6010, Australia.

COURTENAY, Sir Thomas (Tom) Daniel, Kt, KBE; British actor; b. 25 Feb. 1937; s. of the late Thomas Henry Courtenay and Annie Eliza Quest; m. 1st Cheryl Kennedy 1973 (divorced 1982); m. 2nd Isabel Crossley 1988; ed Kingston High School, Hull, Univ. Coll. London, Royal Acad. of Dramatic Art; started acting professionally 1960; Fellow Univ. Coll. London; Hon. DLitt (Hull); Best Actor Award, Prague Festival 1968, TV Drama Award (for Oswald in Ghosts) 1968, Golden Globe Award for Best Actor 1983, Drama Critics' Award and Evening Standard Award 1980, 1983, BAFTA Award for Best Actor 1999. *Films include:* The Loneliness of the Long Distance Runner 1962, Private Potter 1962, Billy Liar 1963, King and Country 1964, Operation Crossbow 1965, King Rat 1965, Doctor Zhivago 1965, The Night of the Generals 1967, The Day the Fish Came Out 1967, A Dandy in Aspic 1968, Otley 1969, One Day in the Life of Ivan Denisovitch 1970, Catch Me a Spy 1971, The Dresser 1983, The Last Butterfly 1990, Redemption (TV) 1991, Let Him Have It 1991, Old Curiosity Shop (TV) 1995, The Boy from Mercury 1996, A Rather English Marriage (TV) 1998, Whatever Happened to Harold Smith 1999, Last Orders 2002. *Plays include:* Billy Liar 1961–62, The Cherry Orchard 1966, Macbeth 1966, Hamlet 1968, She Stoops to Conquer 1969, Charley's Aunt 1971, Time and Time Again (Variety Club of GB Stage Actor Award) 1972, Table Manners 1974, The Norman Conquests 1974–75, The Fool 1975, The Rivals 1976, Clouds 1978, Crime and Punishment 1978, The Dresser (Drama Critics Award and Evening Standard Award for Best Actor) 1980, 1983, The Misanthrope 1981, Andy Capp 1982, Jumpers 1984, Rookery Nook 1986, The Hypochondriac 1987, Dealing with Clair 1988, The Miser 1992, Moscow Stations, Edinburgh 1993, London 1994, New York 1995, Poison Pen, Manchester 1993, Uncle Vanya, New York 1995, Art, London 1996, King Lear, Manchester 1999. *Publication:* Dear Tom: Letters from Home (memoirs) 2000. *Leisure interests:* playing the flute, watching sport. *Address:* c/o Jonathan Altaras Associates, 13 Shorts Gardens, London, WC2H 9AT, England.

COUTARD, Raoul; French film maker; b. 1924, Paris; with French mil. Information Service, Vietnam, subsequently civilian photographer for Time and Paris-Match; worked in photographic labs. during 2nd World War; f. production co. making documentary films; cameraman with French New Wave dirs. including Godard and Truffaut; later with Costa-Gavras. *Films include:* Au bout de souffle, Shoot the Pianist, Lola, Jules et Jim, Baie des Anges, Les Carabiniers, Alphaville, La Peau Douce, Pierrot Le Fou, La 317ème Section, Weekend, Sailor from Gibraltar, The Bride Wore Black, Z, Carmen, Dangerous Moves, La Garce, Let Sleeping Cops Lie, Bethune: The Making of a Hero.

COUTAZ, Bernard Edouard; French music industry executive; b. 30 December 1922, Saint-Auban-sur-l'Ouvèze (Drôme); s. of Edouard Coutaz and Louise Barlatier; ed Faculté catholique de Lyon; journalist, Bayard Presse 1954–60; f. Harmonia Mundi (recording co.) 1958, Edns. Bernard Coutaz (books on music) 1987, Diffusion livres d'Harmonia Mundi 1987, Chair., CEO SA Harmonia Mundi, Man. holding co. Mas de vert 1960–;

Chevalier Légion d'honneur, Officier des Arts et des Lettres. *Address:* Harmonia Mundi, Mas de vert, B.P. 150, 13631 Arles (Office); 23 rue Baudanoni, 13200 Arles, France (Home).

COUTINHO, Vice-Adm. António Alba Rosa; Portuguese naval officer (retd); b. 14 Feb. 1926, Lisbon; s. of António Rodrigues Coutinho and Ilda dos Prazeres Alva Rosa Coutinho; m. Maria Candida Maldonado 1950; three s. one d.; ed Portuguese Naval Acad., Lisbon Univ., Scripps Inst. of Oceanography, USA; commissioned in Portuguese Navy 1947; served on board naval vessels and attended naval courses 1948–54; Hydrographic Engineer, Chief of Hydrographic Mission, Angola 1959–61; in prison in Zaire 1961; several commissions and naval courses 1962–64; Dir of Dredging Services, Mozambique 1964–72; Commdg Officer of Frigate Admiral P. Silva 1973–74; mem. Portuguese Armed Forces Movt 1974, mem. Mil. Junta 1974–75, mem. Supreme Revolutionary Council March-Nov. 1975; Pres. Angola Gov. Junta 1974, High Commr in Angola 1974–75; accused of violating human rights Jan. 1977, acquitted by supreme discipline council July 1977, forced to retire by navy chief of staff Aug. 1977, reintegrated on active duty by decision of supreme mil. court Feb. 1978, retd (on his own request) Dec. 1982; Distinguished Services Medal, Mil. Merit; Knight Aviz Order; Commdr Order of Henry the Navigator; Vasco da Gama Naval Medal; Kt of Spanish Naval Merit. *Leisure interests:* big game hunting, angling, sailing. *Address:* Rua Carlos Malheiro Dias 18, 3° esq., 1700 Lisbon, Portugal. *Telephone:* 883638.

COUTO, Mia; Mozambican writer and journalist; b. 1955, Beira; fmr Dir Mozambique Information Agency; columnist Notícias daily newspaper. *Publications:* Voices Made Night 1986, Every Man is a Race 1994 and other collections of short stories. *Address:* c/o Notícias, Rua Joaquim Lapa 55, CP 327, Maputo, Mozambique (Office).

COUTTS, Ronald Thomson, PhD, DSc, FRSC, F.R.S.(C.); Canadian professor of medicinal chemistry; b. 19 June 1931, Glasgow, Scotland; s. of Ronald Miller Coutts and Helen Alexanderina Crombie; m. Sheenah Kirk Black 1957; two s. one d.; ed Woodside Secondary School, Glasgow, Univ. of Strathclyde, Glasgow Univ. and Chelsea Coll., London; lecturer in Medicinal Chem. Sunderland Tech. Coll., England 1959–63; Asst then Assoc. Prof. Univ. of Saskatchewan, Canada 1963–66; Prof. Univ. of Alberta 1966–97, Distinguished Univ. Prof. 1984–, Pres. Faculty Asscn 1978–79, mem. Bd of Govs. 1982–85, Hon. Prof. of Psychiatry 1979–, Prof. Emer. 1997–; McCalla Prof. Univ. of Alberta 1985–86; Pres. Xenotox Services Ltd 1978–; Scientific Ed. Canadian Journal of Pharmaceutical Sciences 1967–72; mem. Ed. Bd Asian Journal of Pharmaceutical Sciences 1978–85; Ed. Journal of Pharmacological Methods 1984–98; Ed. Bd Chirality 1989–95; Pres. Asscn of Faculties of Pharmacy of Canada 1994–96; Fellow, Pharmaceutical Soc. of GB, Canadian Inst. of Chemistry, American Asscn of Pharmaceutical Scientists; McNeil Research Award 1982; McCalla Prof. Univ. of Alberta 1985–86; Canadian Coll. of Neuropsychopharmacology Medal 1992; Innovation in Neuropsychopharmacology Research Award 1999. *Publications:* over 340 research manuscripts and reviews; several textbooks and chapters in textbooks. *Leisure interests:* golf, cross-country skiing, squash and music (playing and listening). *Address:* University of Alberta, Faculty of Pharmacy and Pharmaceutical Sciences, Edmonton, Alta., T6G 2N8 (Office); 4724-139 Street, Edmonton, Alta., Canada (Home). *Telephone:* (780) 492-5594 (Office); (780) 436-4313 (Home).

COUTURE, Pierre-François; French business executive and civil servant; b. 15 May 1946, Grenoble; s. of André Couture and Françoise Couture (née Dubourguez); brother of Xavier Couture (q.v.); m. 2nd Jocelyne Kerjouan; one s.; three c. from previous m.; ed Ecole Nat. d'Admin., Inst. d'Etudes Politiques, Paris, Univ. of Paris II; Dir Industry and Energy Dept, Ministry of the Econ. and Finance 1974–78, mem. Oil Co. Audit Programme 1979; Dir of Budgets Ministries of Finance and Justice and Office of the Prime Minister 1978–79; Gen. Sec. Exploration and Production Div., Cie Française des Pétroles 1979–81; Tech. Adviser Ministry of the Budget 1981–83; Tech. Adviser Ministry of Industry 1983–84, Dir of Gas, Electricity and Coal 1983–1990; Adviser to Chair. of La Poste 1996; Special Adviser to Industry Sec. in charge of Postal Services and Telecommunications, Ministry of the Economy, Finance and Industry 1997–99; Chair. Enterprise Minière et Chimique (EMC) 1999–; mem. Bd Dirs. Charbonnages de France, France Télécom; Chair. Viet Nam Cttee, Medef Int.; Chevalier, Ordre Nat. du Mérite, Chevalier, Légion d'honneur. *Leisure interests:* travel, mountain sports, golf. *Address:* Enterprise Minière et Chimique, 62 rue Jeanne d'Arc, 75013 Paris, France (Office). *Telephone:* 1-44-06-52-00 (Office). *Fax:* 1-53-82-05-32 (Office). *E-mail:* pf.couture@mail.groupe-eme.com (Office). *Website:* www.groupe-emc.com (Office).

COUVE DE MURVILLE, Most Rev. Maurice Noël Léon, MA, MPhil, STL; British ecclesiastic; b. 27 June 1929, St Germain-en-Laye, France; s. of Noël Couve de Murville and Marie Souchon; ed Downside School, Trinity Coll., Cambridge, Inst. Catholique, Paris and School of Oriental and African Studies, London; ordained priest for diocese of Southwark 1957; Curate, St Anselm's, Dartford, Kent 1957–60; Priest-in-Charge, St Francis, Moulsecoomb 1961–64; Catholic Chaplain Univ. of Sussex 1961–77, Univ. of Cambridge 1977–82; Sr Catholic Chaplain Univ. of Cambridge 1977–82; Archbishop of Birmingham (RC) 1982–99; Order of Malta Grand Cross Conventual Chaplain ad honorem 1982; DUniv (Open) 1994, Hon. DD (Birmingham) 1996. *Publications:* Catholic Cambridge (with Philip Jenkins) 1983, John Milner 1752–1826 1986, Karl Leisner 1988, Pierre Toussaint 1995, Marcel

Callo 1999, Junípero Serra 2000. *Leisure interests:* gardening, local history. *Address:* 53 North Parade, Horsham, West Sussex, RH12 2DE, England (Home).

COUZENS, Sir Kenneth (Edward), KCB; British public official; b. 29 May 1925; s. of Albert and May (née Biddlecombe) Couzens; m. Muriel Eileen Fey 1947; one s. (deceased) one d.; ed Portsmouth Grammar School, Univ. of London and Caius Coll., Cambridge; served in RAF 1943–47; Inland Revenue 1949–51; Private Sec. to Financial Sec., HM Treasury 1952–55, to Chief Sec. 1962–63; Asst Sec. Treasury 1963–69; Under-Sec. Civil Service Dept 1969–70, Treasury 1970–73; Deputy Sec. Incomes Policy and Public Finance 1973–77; Second Perm. Sec. (Overseas Finance), Treasury 1977–82; Vice-Chair. Monetary Cttee of the EEC 1981–82; Perm. Under-Sec. of State, Dept of Energy 1982–85; mem. UK Advisory Bd, Nat. Econ. Research Associates 1986–98; Deputy Chair. British Coal 1985–88; Chair. Coal Products Ltd 1988–92; Dir Crédit Lyonnais Capital Markets 1989–98, Chair. 1991–96 (non-exec. Vice-Chair. 1996–98); Commr, Local Govt Comm. for England 1993–95. *Address:* Coverts Edge, Woodsway, Oxshott, Surrey, KT22 0ND, England. *Telephone:* (1372) 843207.

COVENEY, James, DUniv, BA; British professor of French; b. 4 April 1920, London; s. of James and Mary Coveney; m. Patricia Yvonne Townsend 1955; two s.; ed St Ignatius Coll. and Univs. of Reading and Strasbourg; served in Welch Regt, Royal West Kent Regt and RAF as Pilot (Flight-Lt), World War II; Lecturer, Univ. of Strasbourg 1951–53; Lecturer in medieval French, Univ. of Hull 1953–58; Asst Dir, Civil Service Comm. 1958–59; UN Secretariat, New York 1959–61; NATO Secretariat 1961–64; Sr Lecturer, Head of Modern Languages, Univ. of Bath 1964–68, Prof. of French 1969–85, now Prof. Emer.; Visiting Prof. Ecole Nat. d'Admin., Paris 1974–85, Univ. of Buckingham 1974–86, Bethlehem Univ. 1985; Consultant, Univ. of Macau 1988, Int. Communications, Inc., Tokyo 1991–94; Corresp. mem. Acad. des Sciences, Agric., Arts et Belles-lettres, Aix-en-Provence 1975; Chevalier, Ordre des Palmes Académiques 1978; Officier, Ordre Nat. du Mérite 1986. *Publications:* La Légende de l'Empereur Constant 1955; Co-author: Glossary of French and English Management Terms 1972, Le français pour l'ingénieur 1974, Guide to French Institutions 1978, French Business Management Dictionary 1993. *Address:* 40 Westfield Close, Bath, BA2 2EB, England. *Telephone:* (1225) 316670. *Fax:* (1225) 400090.

COWEN, Brian, BCL; Irish politician; b. 10 Jan. 1960, Tullamore; s. of the late Bernard Cowen and of Mary Cowen; m. Mary Molloy 1990; two d.; ed Univ. Coll. Dublin and Inc. Law Soc. of Ireland; solicitor; mem. Offaly Co. Council 1984–93; mem. Dáil 1984; Minister for Labour 1991–92, for Transport, Energy and Communications 1992–94, for Health and Children 1997–2000, for Foreign Affairs 2000–; fmrly Opposition Spokesperson on Agric. and Food; mem. Fianna Fáil. *Leisure interests:* sport, reading, music. *Address:* Department of Foreign Affairs, 80 Saint Stephen's Green, Dublin 2 (Office); Ballard, Tullamore, Co. Offaly, Ireland. *Telephone:* (1) 4780822 (Office). *Fax:* (1) 4082400 (Office). *Website:* www.irlgov.ie/iveagh (Office).

COWEN, Rt. Hon. Sir Zelman, PC, AK, GCMG, GCVO, QC; Australian academic; b. 7 Oct. 1919, Melbourne; s. of late Bernard Cowen and of Sara Granat; m. Anna Wittner 1945; three s. one d.; ed Scotch Coll., Melbourne, Univ. of Melbourne, Univ. of Oxford; served in Royal Australian Naval Volunteer Reserve 1940–45; consultant to Mil. Govt in Germany 1947; Australian Dominion Liaison Officer to Colonial Office 1951–66; Dean of Faculty of Law, Prof. of Public Law, Univ. of Melbourne 1951–66; Vice-Chancellor, Univ. of New England, NSW 1967–70, Univ. of Queensland 1970–77; Gov.-Gen. of Australia 1977–82; Provost of Oriel Coll., Oxford 1982–90; Pro-Vice Chancellor of Oxford Univ. 1988–90; Chair. John Fairfax Holdings Ltd 1992–94 (Dir 1994–96); Visiting Prof., Univ. of Chicago 1949, Harvard Law School and Fletcher School of Law and Diplomacy 1953–54, 1963–64, Univ. of Utah 1954, Ill. 1957–58, Wash. 1959, Univ. of Calcutta, India 1975; Menzies Scholar in Residence, Univ. of Va, 1983; Pres. Adult Educ. Asscn of Australia 1968–70; mem. and (at various times) Chair. Victorian State Advisory Cttee to Australian Broadcasting Comm.; mem. Devt Corpn of NSW 1969–70, Bd of Int. Asscn for Cultural Freedom 1970–75; Academic Gov. of Bd of Govs., Hebrew Univ. of Jerusalem 1969–77, 1982–; mem. Club of Rome 1974–77; Pres. Australian Inst. of Urban Studies 1973–77; Chair. Bd of Govs., Utah Foundation 1975–77; Law Reform Commr, Commonwealth of Australia 1976–77; Chair. Australian Vice-Chancellor's Cttee 1977, Australian Studies Centre Cttee (London) 1982–90, Press Council (UK) 1983–88, Nat. Council of Australian Opera 1983–, Victoria League for Commonwealth Friendship 1986–89, of Trustees, Visnews Ltd 1986–91, Bd of Dirs., Sir Robert Menzies Memorial Foundation 1990–97, Australian Nat. Acad. of Music 1995–2000; Dir Australian Mutual Provident Soc. 1982–90; mem. Nat. Council of Australian Opera (Chair. 1983–95); Trustee Sydney Opera House 1969–70, Queensland Overseas Foundation 1976–77, Sir Robert Menzies Memorial Trust (UK), Winston Churchill Memorial Trust (UK), Van Leer Inst. of Jerusalem (Chair. 1988–95, Hon. Chair. 1995–); Pres. Order of Australia Asscn 1992–95; Nat. Pres. Australia-Britain Soc. 1993–95; Foreign Hon. Mem. American Acad. of Arts and Sciences; Fellow, Royal Soc. of Arts, Acad. of Social Sciences in Australia, Australian Coll. of Educ., Australian and NZ Asscn for the Advancement of Science (now Hon. Fellow), Australian Nat. Acad. of Music 2000; Hon. Fellow New Coll., Oxford, Univ. House, Australian Inst. of Architects, Australian Acad. of Social Sciences, Australian Coll. of Educ., Univ. House of Australia, Nat. Univ., Australian Acad. of Technological Sciences, Royal Australasian Coll. of Physicians, Royal Australian Coll. of Medical Administrators, Royal Australian Coll. of Obstetricians and Gynaecologists, Australian Acad. of the Humanities, Australian Soc. of Accountants, Australian Inst. of Chartered Accountants, Australian Coll. of Rehabilitation Medicine; Hon. Master, Gray's Inn Bench 1976, QC of the Queensland Bar, mem. Victorian Bar and Hon. Life mem. NSW Bar Asscn; Hon. Fellow, Trinity Coll., Dublin, Oriel Coll., Oxford; Hon. LLD (Univs. of Hong Kong, Queensland, Melbourne, WA, Turin, Australian Nat. Univ., Tasmania, Victoria Univ. of Tech.), Hon. DLitt (Univs. of New England, Sydney, Oxford, James Cook Univ. of N Queensland), Hon. DHL (Hebrew Union Coll., Cincinnati), (Univ. of Redlands, Calif.), Hon. DUniv (Newcastle, Griffith, Sunshine Coast Univ. Coll. Queensland), Hon. DPhil (Hebrew Univ. of Jerusalem, Univ. of Tel Aviv); Kt, Order of Australia, Kt Grand Cross, Order of St Michael and St George, Royal Victorian Order, KStJ, Kt Grand Cross, Order of Merit, Italy. *Publications:* Specialist Editor, Dicey: Conflict of Laws 1949, Australia and the United States: Some Legal Comparisons 1954, (with P. B. Carter) Essays on the Law of Evidence 1956, American-Australian Private International Law 1957, Federal Jurisdiction in Australia 1959 (with Leslie Zines), Matrimonial Causes Jurisdiction 1961, The British Commonwealth of Nations in a Changing World 1964, Sir John Latham and Other Papers 1965, Sir Isaac Isaacs 1967, 1993, The Private Man (A.B.C. Boyer Lectures 1969), Individual Liberty and the Law (Tagore Law Lectures 1975), The Virginia Lectures 1984, Reflections on Medicine, Biotechnology and the Law (Pound Lectures, Neb. Univ.) 1986, A Touch of Healing (3 Vols) 1986. *Leisure interests:* music, performing and visual arts. *Address:* 4 Treasury Place, East Melbourne, Vic. 3002, Australia (Office). *Telephone:* (3) 96500299 (Office). *Fax:* (3) 96500301 (Office). *E-mail:* zelman.cowen@dpmc.gov.au (Office).

COWLEY, Alan Herbert, PhD, FRS; British professor of chemistry; b. 29 Jan. 1934, Manchester; s. of the late Herbert Cowley and Dora Cowley; m. Deborah Elaine Cole 1975; two s. three d.; ed Univ. of Manchester; Postdoctoral Fellow, then Instr. Univ. of Fla, USA 1958–60; Tech. Officer, Exploratory Group, ICI (Billingham Div.), UK 1960–61; Asst Prof. of Chem., Univ. of Tex. at Austin 1962–67, Assoc. Prof. 1967–70, Prof. 1970–84, George W. Watt Centennial Prof. of Chem. 1984–88, Richard J.V. Johnson Regent's Prof. of Chem. 1989–91, Robert A. Welch Prof. of Chem. 1991–; Sir Edward Frankland Prof. of Inorganic Chem., Imperial Coll., London 1988–89; Vice-Chair. Bd of Trustees, Gordon Research Confs. 1993–94 (Chair. 1994–95)mem. Editorial Bd Inorganic Chemistry 1979–83, Chemical Reviews 1984–88, Polyhedron 1984–2000, Journal of American Chem. Soc. 1986–91, Journal of Organometallic Chemistry 1987–, Organometallics 1988–91, Dalton Trans 1997–2000, Inorganic Syntheses 1983–; Guggenheim Fellowship 1976–77; Centenary Medal and Lectureship, Royal Soc. of Chem. 1986; Chemical Pioneer Award, American Inst. of Chemists 1994, Von Humboldt Prize 1996, Chevalier, Ordre des Palmes Académiques and several other awards. *Publications:* more than 450 articles in learned journals. *Leisure interests:* squash, sailing, classical music, literature. *Address:* Department of Chemistry and Biochemistry, University of Texas at Austin, Austin, TX 78712, USA. *Telephone:* (512) 471-7484. *Fax:* (512) 471-6822. *E-mail:* cowley@mail.utexas.edu. *Website:* cowley@mail.utexas.edu.

COWLEY, John Maxwell, PhD, FAA, FRS; American professor of physics; b. 18 Feb. 1923, Australia; s. of Alfred E. Cowley and Doris R. Cowley; m. Roberta Beckett 1951; two d.; ed Univ. of Adelaide and MIT, USA; Research Officer, Commonwealth Scientific and Industrial Research Org., Australia 1945–62; Chamber of Mfrs Prof. of Physics, Univ. of Melbourne 1962–70; Galvin Prof. of Physics, Arizona State Univ., USA 1970–94, Dir Facility for High Resolution Electron Microscopy 1983–90, Regents' Prof. 1988–94, Prof. Emer. 1994–; Fellow American Physical Soc.; Hon. DSc (Northwestern Univ.) 1995; BE Warren Award, American Crystallographic Asscn 1976, Distinguished Award, Electron Microscopy Soc. of America 1979, Ewald Award, Int. Union of Crystallography 1987. *Publications:* Diffraction Physics 1975, Modulated Structures—1979 (Ed.) 1979, Electron Diffraction Techniques (Ed.) 1992, approximately 400 scientific articles in journals. *Leisure interests:* painting and hiking. *Address:* Department of Physics and Astronomy, Box 871504, Arizona State University, Tempe, AZ 85287-1504, USA. *Telephone:* (480) 965-6459. *Fax:* (480) 965-7954. *E-mail:* cowleyj@asu.edu (Office).

COWLEY, Roger Arthur, FRS, FRSE, FRSC; British professor of physics; b. 24 Feb. 1939, Essex; s. of C. A. Cowley; m. Sheila Joyce Wells 1964; one s. one d.; ed Brentwood School and Univ. of Cambridge; Fellow of Trinity Hall, Cambridge 1962–64; Research Officer. Atomic Energy of Canada Ltd 1964–70; Prof. of Physics, Univ. of Edinburgh 1970–88; Dr. Lee's Prof. of Experimental Philosophy and Fellow of Wadham Coll., Univ. of Oxford 1988–, Chair. of Physics 1993–96, Chair. of Physics Dept 1999–2002; Max Born Medal and Prize 1973, Holweck Medal and Prize 1990. *Publications:* over 350 scientific publs. *Address:* Oxford Physics Clarendon Laboratory, Parks Road, Oxford, OX1 3PU (Office); Tredinnock, Harcourt Hill, Oxford, OX2 9AS, England (Home). *Telephone:* (1865) 272224 (Office); (1865) 247570 (Home). *E-mail:* r.cowley@physics.ox.ac.uk (Office).

COWLING, Maurice John, MA; British academic; b. 6 Sept. 1926, London; s. of Reginald Frederick Cowling and May Cowling (née Roberts); m. P. M. Gale (née Holley) 1996; ed Battersea Grammar School, Jesus Coll., Cambridge; served in British and Indian Armies 1944–47; Fellow Jesus Coll., Cambridge 1950–53, 1961–63, Peterhouse, Cambridge 1963–93, Emer. 1993–; on editorial staff The Times and Daily Express 1955–59; County Councillor, Cambs. 1966–70; Literary Ed. The Spectator 1970–71, Dir Politeia 1998–; Visiting Prof. Adelphi Univ. 1993–97. *Publications include:* The Nature and Limits of Political Science 1963, Mill and Liberalism 1963, 1867: Disraeli, Gladstone and Revolution 1967, The Impact of Labour 1971, The Impact of Hitler 1975, Religion and Public Doctrine in Modern England (Vol. 1) 1981, (Vol. 2) 1985, (Vol. 3) 2001, A Conservative Future 1997. *Address:* c/o Peterhouse, Cambridge, CB2 1RD, England (Office); 9A Redcliffe Caswell Bay, Swansea, SA3 3BT, Wales (Home). *Telephone:* (1792) 367934.

COWPER-COLES, Sherard Louis, CMG, LVO; British diplomatist; b. 8 Jan. 1955; s. of Sherard Hamilton Cowper-Coles and Dorothy Short; m. Bridget Cowper-Coles; four s. one d.; ed Tonbridge School, Hertford Coll. Oxford; joined FCO 1977; Third, then Second Sec., Cairo 1980–83; First Sec. Planning Office, FCO 1983–85, Pvt Sec. to Perm. Under-Sec. of State 1985–87; First Sec., Washington 1987–91; Asst Security Policy Dept, FCO 1991–93, Head Hong Kong Dept 1994–97; Counsellor, Paris 1997–99; Prin. Pvt Sec. to Sec. of State for Foreign and Commonwealth Affairs 1999–2001; Amb. to Israel 2001–; Hon. Fellow Hertford Coll. Oxford. *Address:* British Embassy, 192 Rehov Hayarkon, Tel-Aviv 63405, Israel (Office). *Telephone:* 3-7251244 (Office). *Fax:* 3-5271572 (Office). *E-mail:* sherard.cowper-coles@fco.gov.uk (Office). *Website:* www.britemb.org.il (Office).

COX, Archibald, AB, LLB, LLD; American lawyer; b. 17 May 1912, Plainfield, NJ; s. of Archibald Cox and Frances B. Perkins; m. Phyllis Ames 1937; one s. two d.; ed St Paul's School, Concord and Harvard Univ.; admitted to Mass. Bar 1937; in practice with Ropes, Gray, Best, Coolidge and Rugg, Boston 1938–41; Attorney, Office of Solicitor-Gen., US Dept of Justice 1941–43; Assoc. Solicitor, Dept of Labor 1943–45; lecturer on Law, Harvard Univ. 1945–46, Williston Prof. of Law 1946–76; Carl M. Loeb Univ. Prof. 1976–84, Prof. Emer. 1984–; Visiting Prof. of Law, Boston Univ. 1984–97; Chair. Wage Stabilization Bd 1952, Advisory Panel to Senate Cttee on Educ. and Labour 1958–59; Solicitor-Gen. of US 1961–65; Prosecutor, Watergate Investigation 1973; Pitt Prof. of American History and Insts., Cambridge Univ. 1974–75; Chair. Common Cause 1980–93; mem. American Bar Asscn, American Acad. of Arts and Sciences, Bd of Overseers, Harvard Univ. 1962–65. *Publications:* Cases on Labor law 1948, Law and the National Labor Policy 1960, Civil Rights, the Constitution and the Courts 1967, The Warren Court 1968, The Role of the Supreme Court in American Government 1976, Freedom of Expression 1981, The Court and the Constitution 1987 and articles in legal periodicals. *Address:* Harvard Law School, Cambridge, MA 02138 (Office); 78 Condon Point Road, Brooksville, ME 04617, USA (Home). *Telephone:* (617) 495-3133 (Office); (207) 326-8242.

COX, Barry Geoffrey, BA, FRTS; British executive and journalist; b. 25 May 1942, Guildford; m. 1st Pamela Doran 1967 (divorced 1977); m. 2nd Kathryn Kay 1984 (divorced 1992); two s. two d.; ed Tiffin School, Kingston, Surrey and Magdalen Coll. Oxford; reporter, The Scotsman 1965–67; feature writer, Sunday Telegraph 1967–70; producer/Dir World in Action, Granada TV 1970–74; The London Programme, London Weekend TV 1974–77, Head of Current Affairs 1977–81, Controller of Features and Current Affairs 1981–87, Dir of Corp. Affairs 1987–94, Special Adviser to Chief Exec. 1994–95; Dir Ind. TV Asscn 1995–98; Deputy Chair. Channel 4 1999–; Consultant to United Broadcasting and Entertainment 1998–2001, Ind. TV News 1998–; Chair. of Bd Oval House 2001–; mem. Council Inst. of Educ. 2000–. *Publications:* Civil Liberties in Britain 1975, The Fall of Scotland Yard 1977. *Leisure interests:* tennis, walking, theatre. *Address:* Channel 4 Television Corporation, 124 Horseferry Road London, S.W.1, England (Office). *Website:* bagecox@aol.com.

COX, Brian Denis; British actor, director and writer; b. 1 June 1946; s. of Charles Mcardle Campbell Cox and Mary Ann Gillerine (née Mccann); m. Caroline Burt 1968 (divorced 1987); one s. one d.; ed London Acad. of Music and Dramatic Art. *Stage appearances include:* debut at Dundee Repertory 1961; Royal Lyceum, Edin. 1965–66, Birmingham Repertory 1966–68, As You Like It, Birmingham and Vaudeville (London debut) 1967, Peer Gynt, Birmingham 1967, When We Dead Awaken, Edin. Festival 1968, In Cele-bration, Royal Court 1969, The Wild Duck, Edin. Festival 1969, The Big Romance, Royal Court 1970, Don't Start Without Me, Garrick 1971, Mir-andolina, Brighton 1971, Getting On, Queen's 1971, The Creditors, Open Space 1972, Hedda Gabler, Royal Court 1972; Playhouse, Nottingham: Love's Labour's Lost, Brand, What The Butler Saw, The Three Musketeers 1972; Cromwell, Royal Court 1973; Royal Exchange, Manchester: Arms and the Man 1974, The Cocktail Party 1975; Pilgrims Progress, Prospect Theatre 1975, Emigres, Nat. Theatre Co., Young Vic 1976; Olivier Theatre: Tambur-laine the Great 1976, Julius Caesar 1977; The Changeling, Riverside Studios 1978; Nat. Theatre: Herod, The Putney Debates 1978; On Top, Royal Court 1979, Macbeth, Cambridge Theatre and tour of India 1980, Summer Party, Crucible 1980, Have You Anything to Declare?, Manchester then Round House 1981, Danton's Death, Nat. Theatre Co., Olivier 1982, Strange Inter-lude, Duke of York (Drama Magazine Best Actor Award 1985) 1984 and Nederlander, New York 1985, Rat in the Skull, Royal Court (Drama Magazine and Olivier Best Actor Awards 1985) 1984 and New York 1985, Fashion, The Danton Affair, Misalliance, Penny for a Song 1986, The Taming of the Shrew, Titus Andronicus 1987, The Three Sisters 1989, RSC and Titus Andronicus on tour, Madrid, Paris, Copenhagen (Olivier Award for Best Actor in a Revival and Drama Magazine Best Actor Award for RSC 1988) 1988, Frankie and Johnny in the Claire-de-Lune, Comedy 1989, Richard III, King Lear, nat. and world tour 1990–91, The Master Builder, Edin. 1993, Riverside 1994, St. Nicholas, Bush Theatre 1997, New York (Lucille Lortel Award 1998) 1998, Skylight, Los Angeles 1997, Dublin Carol, Old Vic and Royal Court 2000.

Plays directed: Edin. Festival: The Man with a Flower in his Mouth 1973, The Stronger 1973; Orange Tree, Richmond: I Love My Love 1982, Mrs Warren's Profession 1989; The Crucible, Moscow Art Theatre, London and Edin. 1989, The Philanderer, Hampstead Theatre Club (world premier of complete version) (Int. Theatre Inst. Award 1990) 1991. *Films include:* Nicholas and Alexandra 1971, In Celebration 1975, Manhunter 1986, Shoot for the Sun 1986, Hidden Agenda 1990, The Cutter 1994, Braveheart 1995, Rob Roy 1995, Chain Reaction 1996, The Glimmer Man 1996, The Long Kiss Goodnight 1996, Desperate Measures 1997, Food for Ravens 1997, Poodle Spring 1997, The Boxer 1998, The Corruptor 1998, Mad About Mamba 1998, The Minus Man 198, Rushmore 1998, The Biographer 2000, Saltwater 201, LIE 2001, Morality Play, Affairs of the Necklace. *TV appearances include:* Churchill's People: The Wallace 1972, The Master of Ballantrae 1975, Henry II in The Devil's Crown 1978, Thérèse Raquin 1979, Dalhousie's Luck 1980, Bothwell 1980, Bach 1981, Pope John Paul II 1984, Florence Nightingale 1985, Beryl Markham: A Shadow in the Sun 1988, Secret Weapon 1990, Acting in Tragedy (BBC Masterclass) 1990, The Lost Language of Cranes 1992, The Cloning of Joanna May 1992, The Big Battalions 1992, The Negotiator 1994, Witness for Hitler 1995, Blow Your Mind See A Play 1995, Nuremberg 2001. *Publications include:* Salem to Moscow: An Actor's Odyssey 1991, The Lear Diaries 1992. *Leisure interests:* keeping fit, tango. *Address:* c/o Conway van Gelder, 18–21 Jermyn Street, London, SW1Y 6HP, England (Office). *Telephone:* (20) 7287-0077 (Office).

COX, Sir David (Roxbee), Kt, PhD, FRS; British statistician; b. 15 July 1924, Birmingham; s. of Sam R. Cox and Lilian (née Braines) Cox; m. Joyce Drummond 1948; three s. one d.; ed Handsworth Grammar School, Bir-mingham and St John's Coll. Cambridge; with Royal Aircraft Establishment 1944–46; Wool Industries Research Asscn 1946–50; Statistical Lab., Univ. of Cambridge 1950–55; with Dept of Biostatistics, Univ. of N Carolina 1955–56, Birkbeck Coll., London 1956–66; Bell Telephone Labs. 1965; Prof. of Stat-istics, Imperial Coll. of Science and Tech., London 1966–88; Warden Nuffield Coll., Oxford 1988–94; Science and Eng Research Council Sr Research Fellow 1983–88; Ed. Biometrika 1966–91; Pres. Int. Statistics Inst. 1995–97; Fellow Imperial Coll., Birkbeck Coll. London; Hon. Fellow St John's Coll. Cambridge, Inst. of Actuaries, Nuffield Coll. Oxford, British Acad.; Hon. DSc (Reading, Bradford, Heriot Watt, Helsinki, Limburg, Queen's, Kingston, Ont., Waterloo, Neuchâtel, Padua, Minn., Toronto, Abertay Dundee, Crete, Bor-deaux 2, Athens Univ. of Econs, Harvard, Elche, Rio de Janeiro); Hon. Foreign mem.: U.S. Acad. of Arts and Sciences, Royal Danish Acad., NAS, American Philosophical Soc., Indian Acad. of Sciences; Guy Medals in silver and gold, Royal Statistical Soc., Weldon Medal, Univ. of Oxford, Deming Medal, ASQC, Kettering Medal and Prize, Gen. Motors Cancer Research Foundation, Max Planck Prize. *Publications:* several books on statistics, articles in Journal of the Royal Statistical Soc., Biometrika etc. *Address:* c/o Nuffield Coll., Oxford, OX1 1NF, England.

COX, George Edwin; British business executive; b. 28 May 1940; s. of George Herbert Cox and Beatrice Mary Cox; m. 1st Gillian Mary Mannings (divorced 1996); two s.; m. 2nd Lorna Janet Peach 1996; two d.; ed Quintin School, Queen Mary Coll., Univ. of London; began career in aircraft industry, in factory man. and in precision eng; Man. Dir Butler Cox (I.T. Consultancy and Research Co.) 1977; Chief Exec. then Chair. PE Int.; fmr UK Chief Exec. Unisys Ltd, Head of Service Activities across Europe, then Chair.; Dir-Gen. Inst. of Dirs Sept. 1999–; mem. Bd Shorts 2000–; Chair. Merlin (Medical Emergency Relief Int.) 2001–; Dir (non-exec.) Bradford & Bingley PLC); fmr Dir Inland Revenue 1996–99, LIFFE 1995–2002; Visiting Prof. Man. School, Royal Holloway, Univ. of London 1995–. *Leisure interest:* rowing, gliding, theatre. *Address:* Institute of Directors, 116 Pall Mall, London SW1Y 5ED, England (Office). *Telephone:* (20) 7451-3116 (Office).

COX, Pat; Irish European Union official and politician; m.; six c.; ed Trinity Coll., Dublin; lecturer Dept of Econs, Inst. of Public Admin., Dublin and Univ. of Limerick (frly. NIHE) 1974–82; TV Current Affairs Reporter for 'Today Tonight' 1982–86; Gen. Sec. Progressive Democrats 1985–, MEP for Munster 1989–, Deputy Leader European Liberal Democrats (ELDR) 1994–98, Pres. 1998–; Pres. European Parl. Jan 2002–; mem. Dáil Éireann (Irish Parl.) for Cork S. Cen. Nov. 1992–. *Address:* Office of the President, European Parlia-ment, 97–113 rue Wiertz, 1047 Brussels, Belgium (Office). *Telephone:* (2) 284-21-11 (Office). *Fax:* (2) 284-69-74 (Office). *Website:* www.europarl.eu.int (Office).

COX, Paul; Netherlands film director and author; b. 16 April 1940, Venlo, The Netherlands; s. of W Cox; two s. one d.; ed Melbourne Univ.; settled in Australia 1965; photographic exhbns. in Australia, The Netherlands, Ger-many, Japan, India and USA; taught photography and cinematography for several years; f. Illumination Films with Tony Llewellyn-Jones and Bernard Eddy 1977; directed: (shorts) Mantuta 1965, Time Past 1966, Skindeep 1968, Marcel 1969, Symphony 1969, Mirka 1970, Phyllis 1971, Island 1975, We are All Alone My Dear 1975, Ways of Seeing 1977, Ritual 1978; (feature length) The Journey 1972, Illuminations 1976, Inside Looking Out 1977, Kostas 1978, Lonely Hearts 1981, Man of Flowers 1983, Death and Destiny (A Journey into Ancient Egypt) 1984, My First Wife 1984, Cactus 1986, Vincent 1988, Island 1989, Golden Braid 1990, A Woman's Tale 1991, The Nun and the Bandit 1992, Exile 1993, Lust and Revenge 1996, The Hidden Dimension 1997, Molokai – the true story of Father Damien 1998, Innocence 1998, The Diaries of Vaslav Nijinsky 2001; (documentaries) Calcutta 1970, All Set Backstage 1974, For A Child Called Michael 1979, The Kingdom of Nek Chand 1980,

Underdog 1980, Death and Destiny 1984, Handle with Care 1985; (for Children's TV) The Paper Boy 1985, The Secret Life of Trees 1986, The Gift 1988, Exile 1993; numerous awards and prizes. *Publications:* Home of Man (jtly.), Human Still Lives of Nepal, I Am 1997, Reflections 1998. *Address:* Illumination Films, 1 Victoria Avenue, Albert Park, Vic. 3206, Australia. *Telephone:* (3) 9690-5266 (Office). *Fax:* (3) 9696-5625.

COX, Philip Sutton, AO, BArch, PhD; Australian architect; b. 1 Oct. 1939, Killara, Sydney; s. of Ronald Albert Cox and Lilian May Cox; m. Virginia Louise Gowing 1972; two d.; ed Sydney Church of England Grammar School, Sydney Univ.; worked in New Guinea 1962; apptd. Tutor in Architecture, Univ. of Sydney 1963; est. Ian McKay & Philip Cox pvt. practice with Ian McKay 1963; est. Philip Cox and Assocs. 1967; Architect Sydney Olympics, Stage I; Tutor in Architecture, Univ. of NSW 1971, 1973, 1978, Prof. 1989–; Founding mem. The Australian Acad. of Design 1990–; Life Fellow Royal Australian Inst. of Architects, Chair. Educ. Bd, Fed. Chapter; Vice-Chair. Architecture and Design Panel, Visual Arts Bd, Australia Council; Vice-Pres. Cancer Patients Assistance Soc. of NSW; Fellow Australian Acad. of Humanities; mem. R.I.B.A.; Hon. FAIACommonwealth Scholarship 1956; numerous awards and prizes including Royal Australian Inst. of Architects Gold Medal and Merit Awards, Commonwealth Asscn of Architects Sir Robert Matthew Award, Blacket Award, Sir John Sulman Medal. *Publications:* several books including The Australian Homestead (with Wesley Stacey) 1972, Historic Towns of Australia (with Wesley Stacey) 1973, Restoring Old Australian Houses and Buildings, an Architectural Guide (with others) 1975, Australian Colonial Architecture (with Clive Lucas), The Functional Tradition (with David Moore) 1987. *Leisure interests:* gardening, swimming, walking, painting. *Address:* Cox Richardson Architects and Planners, 204 Clarence Street, Sydney, NSW 2000, Australia (Office). *Telephone:* (2) 9267-9599 (Office); (2) 9267-9599 (Home). *Fax:* (2) 9264-5844 (Office); (2) 9264-5844 (Office). *E-mail:* sydney@cox.com.au (Office); www.cox.com.au (Office).

COX, Robert W., MA; Canadian academic; ed McGill Univ., Montréal; fmr Asst. Dir-Gen. ILO; fmr. Dir Int. Inst. for Labour Studies, Geneva, Switzerland; fmr Prof. of Political Science, Grad. Inst. of Int. Studies, Geneva; Prof. of Int. Org., Columbia Univ., New York 1972–77; Visiting Prof. Yale Univ., Univ. de Laval, Québec, Univ. of Toronto, Univ. of Denver; Programme Co-ordinator on Multilateralism and the UN System, United Nations Univ., Tokyo; currently Prof. Emer., Dept of Political Science, York Univ., Toronto. *Publications include:* The Anatomy of Influence 1975, Production, Power and World Order 1987, International Political Economy: Understanding Global Disorder 1995, Approaches to World Order 1996, The New Realism (ed.) 1997, Counter-Hegemony and Foreign Policy (co-author) 2001, Political Economy of a Plural World—Critical Reflections on Power, Morals and Civilizations 2002. *Address:* Department of Political Science, Faculty of Arts, S652 Ross Building, York University, 4700 Keele Street, Toronto, Ont., M3J 1P3, Canada (Office). *Telephone:* (416) 736-5265 (Office). *Fax:* (416) 736-5700 (Office). *Website:* www .yorku.ca/polisci (Office).

COX, Stephen Joseph; British artist; b. 16 Sept. 1946, Bristol; s. of Leonard John Cox and Ethel Minnie May McGill; m. Judith Atkins 1970; two d.; ed St Mary Redcliffe, Bristol, West of England Coll. of Art, Bristol and Cen. School of Art and Design, London; lives and works in London, Italy, India and Egypt; works in collections of Tate Gallery, Victoria and Albert Museum, British Museum, Arts Council of GB, British Council, Walker Art Gallery, Liverpool, Henry Moore Centre for Sculpture, Leeds City Gallery, Fogg Museum, USA, Groningen Museum, Netherlands, Peter Ludwig Collection, Fed. Repub. of Germany, Uffizi Gallery, Florence, Fattoria di Celle, Pistoia, Palazzo del Commune, Spoleto, Santa Maria della Scala, Slena, Regione di Aosta and pvt. collections in USA and Europe; numerous public sculptures in England including St Paul's Cathedral Church, Harringay, St. Nicholas, Newcastle upon Tyne, St Luke's, Chelsea, India, Egypt and Australia; Consultant sculptor, Rajiv Gandhi Samadhi, Delhi; Sr Research Fellow, Wimbledon School of Art 1995–96; Gold Medal Indian Triennale, Arts Council Major Awards 1978, 1980, British Council Bursaries 1978, 1979, Hakone Open Air Museum Prize, Japan 1985, Goldhill Sculpture Prize, Royal Acad. 1988. *Solo exhibitions include:* London (Lisson Gallery, Nigel Greenwood Gallery, Tate Gallery, Royal Botanic Gardens, Michael Hue-Williams Fine Art, Dulwich Picture Gallery), Bath Festival Artsite, Bristol (Arnolfini Gallery), Nottingham (Midland Group Gallery), Oxford (Museum of Modern Art), Glyndebourne Festival Opera, Amsterdam, Bari, Milan, Rome, Spoleto (1982 Festival), Florence, Geneva, Basle, Paris, Cairo, New Delhi, Santa Maria della Scala, Srena, Museo Archaelogico, Aosta, Culture Gallery, New York. *Group exhibitions include:* Paris Biennale 1977, British Sculpture in 20th Century, Whitechapel Art Gallery, London 1981, Venice Biennale 1982, 1986, New Art, Tate Gallery, London 1983, Int. Garden Festival, Liverpool 1984, Int. Survey of Painting and Sculpture 1984, M.O.M.A., New York, Forty Years of Modern Art 1945–85, Tate Gallery (new display 1992), Origins, Originally and Beyond, Sydney Biennale, Prospekt '86, Frankfurt, 19th Sculpture Biennale, Middlehiem, Belgium, British Art in the 1980s, Museum of Modern Art, Brussels, 20th Century British Sculpture, Schloss Ambross, Innsbruck, Austria, 'Sculpture and the Divine', Winchester Cathedral, 'Encounters', Nat. Gallery London. *Address:* 154 Barnsbury Road, Islington, London, N1 0ER, England. *Telephone:* (20) 7278-4184.

COX, Warren Jacob, BA, MArch, FAIA; American architect; b. 28 Aug. 1935, New York; s. of Oscar Sydney Cox and Louise Bryson (Black) Cox; m. Claire Christie-Miller 1975; one s. one d.; ed The Hill School, Yale Univ., Yale Univ.

School of Architecture; partner Hartman-Cox Architects, Washington DC 1965–; Visiting Architectural Critic, Yale Univ. 1966, Catholic Univ. of America 1967, Univ. of Va 1976; Dir Center for Palladian Studies in America 1982–; lecturer numerous architectural schools and insts.; juror for design awards programs; mem. Editorial Bd Guide to the Architecture of Washington, DC 1965, 1974; AIA Architectural Firm Award 1988, AIA Nat. Honor Awards 1970, 1971, 1981, 1983, 1989, 1994, Louis Sullivan Prize 1972 and over 100 other awards. *Work includes:* Euram Bldg, Nat. Perm. Bldg, Sumner Square, Market Square, Mount Vernon Coll. Chapel, Folger Shakespeare Library Additions, Immanuel Presbyterian Church, Concert Hall Redesign, Kennedy Center, Renovation of the Nat. Archives, Patent Office Bldg and Lincoln and Jefferson Memorials, Washington, DC; Winterthur Museum New Exhbn Bldg, Wilmington, Del.; Chrysler Museum, Norfolk, Va; John Carter Brown Library Addition, Providence, RI; H.E.B. Corp. HQ, San Antonio, Tex.; Nat. Humanities Center, Raleigh, NC; U.S. Embassy, Malaysia; Law School, Washington Univ.; Law School, Tulane Univ.; Library, Addition and Residence Hall, Georgetown Univ. Law Center, Washington; Library, Case Western Reserve Univ., Cleveland, Ohio; Law Library, Univ. of Conn., Hartford, Conn., Fed. Courthouse, Corpus Christi, Tex., Divinity School Addition, Duke Univ., Durham, NC, City and County Courthouses, Lexington, Ky, McIntire School of Commerce and Special Collections Library, Univ. of VA, Charlottesville, VA, Jefferson Library, Charlottesville, VA. *Publication:* Hartman-Cox Architects/Master Architects Series. *Leisure interests:* architectural history, automobile racing, shooting, golden retriever dogs, farming, book collecting. *Address:* Hartman-Cox Architects, 1074 Jefferson Street, NW, Washington, DC 20007 (Office); 3111 N Street, NW, Washington, DC 20007 (Home); Kennersley, P.O. Box 1, Church Hill, MD 21623, USA (Home). *Telephone:* (202) 333-6446 (Office); (202) 965-0615 (Home). *Fax:* (202) 333-3802 (Office).

COX, Winston A., MSc(Econs); Barbadian banker and international organization official; m.; five c.; ed Univ. of the West Indies, Inst. of Social Studies, Netherlands; joined Cen. Bank of Barbados 1974, Adviser to Gov. 1982–87, Gov. 1997; Dir of Finance, Ministry of Finance 1987–91; mem. Exec. Bd IBRD 1994–97; Gov. Cen. Bank of Barbados 1997–99; Deputy Sec.-Gen. of the Commonwealth Sept. 2000–. *Address:* Commonwealth Secretariat, Marlborough House, Pall Mall, London, SW1Y 5HX, England (Office). *Telephone:* (20) 7839-3411 (Office). *Fax:* (20) 7930-0827 (Office). *E-mail:* coxw@ commonwealth.int.

COX ARQUETTE, Courteney; American actress; b. 15 June 1964, Birmingham, Ala; d. of Richard Lewis and Courteney (Bass-Copland) Cox; m. David Arquette 1999; modelling career New York; appeared in Bruce Springsteen music video Dancing in the Dark 1984. *Films:* Down Twisted 1986, Masters of the Universe 1987, Cocoon: The Return 1988, Mr. Destiny 1990, Blue Desert 1990, Shaking the Tree 1992, The Opposite Sex 1993, Ace Ventura, Pet Detective 1994, Scream 1996, Commandments 1996, Scream 2 1997, The Runner 1999, Alien Love Triangle 1999, Scream 3 1999, The Shrink Is In 2000, 3000 Miles to Graceland 2001, Get Well Soon 2001, Alien Love Triangle 2001. *Television series:* Misfits of Science 1985–86, Family Ties 1987–88, The Trouble with Larry 1993, Friends 1994–. *Television films include:* Roxanne: The Prize Pulitzer 1989, Till We Meet Again 1989, Curiosity Kills 1990, Morton and Hays 1991, Topper 1992, Sketch Artist II: Hands That See 1995. *Address:* c/o Creative Artists Agency, 9830 Wilshire Boulevard, Beverly Hills, CA 90212, USA.

COZ, Steve; American editor and publishing executive; b. 26 March 1957, Grafton, Mass.; s. of Henry Coz and Mary Coz; m. Valerie Virga 1987; ed Harvard Univ.; freelance writer various US publs 1979–82; reporter Nat. Enquirer, Fla 1982–95, Ed.-in-Chief 1995–; American celebrity analyst BBC Radio 1995–96; Edgar Hoover Memorial Award for Distinguished Public Service 1996; Haven House Award of Excellence for Outstanding Reporting on Domestic Violence Issues 1996. *Address:* American Media Inc., 5401 NW Broken Sound Boulevard, Boca Raton, FL 33487, USA.

CRABTREE, Robert H., MA, DSc, DPhil; British/American professor of chemistry; b. 17 April 1948, London; s. of Arthur Crabtree and Marguerite M. Vaniere; ed Brighton Coll. and Univs. of Oxford and Sussex; Attaché de Recherche, CNRS, France 1975–77; Asst Prof. of Chem. Yale Univ. 1977–82, Assoc. Prof. 1982–85, Prof. 1985–; A.P. Sloan Fellow 1981; Dreyfus Teacher-Scholar 1982; Corday-Morgan Medal 1984; Royal Soc. of Chem. Organometallic Chem. Award 1991, American Chem. Soc., Organometallic Chem. Award 1993. *Publication:* The Organometallic Chemistry of the Transition Metals 1994. *Leisure interest:* travel. *Address:* 97 Fairwood Road, Bethany, CT 06524, USA.

CRADOCK, Rt. Hon. Sir Percy, PC, GCMG; British diplomatist; b. 26 Oct. 1923; m. Birthe Marie Dyrlund 1953; joined FCO 1954; First Sec. Kuala Lumpur, Malaya 1957–61, Hong Kong 1961–62, Beijing 1962–63; Foreign Office 1963–66; Counsellor and Head of Chancery, Beijing 1966–68, Chargé d'affaires 1968–69; Head of FCO Planning Staff 1969–71; Asst Under-Sec. of State and Head of Cabinet Office Assessments Staff 1971–76; Amb. to GDR 1976–78, concurrently Leader UK Mission to Comprehensive Test Ban Negotiations, Geneva 1977–78; Amb. to People's Repub. of China 1978–83: Leader of Negotiating Team with China over Hong Kong 1982–83; Deputy Under-Sec. with special responsibility for negotiations with China over Hong Kong 1983–85; Foreign Policy Adviser to the Prime Minister 1984–92; Dir South China Morning Post 1996–2000; Hon. Fellow St John's, Cambridge

1982. *Publications:* Experiences of China 1993, In Pursuit of British Interests 1997, Know Your Enemy: How the Joint Intelligence Committee Saw the World 2002. *Address:* c/o The Reform Club, 104 Pall Mall, London, SW1, England.

CRAGG, Anthony Douglas, MA, CBE; British sculptor; b. 9 April 1949, Liverpool; s. of Douglas R. Cragg and Audrey M. Rutter; m. 1st Ute Oberste-Lehn 1977; two s.; m. 2nd Tatjana Verhasselt 1990; one s. one d.; ed Cheltenham and Wimbledon Schools of Art and Royal Coll. of Art; teacher, Düsseldorf Kunstakademie 1978–, Prof. and Co-Dir 1988–; Prof. Hochschule der Künste (HdK), Berlin 2001–; Turner Prize 1988; Chevalier des Arts et des Lettres 1992. *Solo exhibitions include:* Lisson Gallery 1979, 1980, 1985, 1991, 1992, Whitechapel Gallery, London 1981, Kanrasha Gallery, Tokyo 1982, 1984, 1989, 1990, Kunsthalle, Bern 1983, Palais de Beaux-Arts, Brussels 1985, Staatsgalerie Moderner Kunst, Munich 1985, Musée d'Art Contemporain, Paris 1985, Brooklyn Museum 1986, Hayward Gallery, London 1986, Houston Contemporary Art Museum 1991, Wiener Secession, Vienna 1991, IVAM, Valencia 1992, Studio Barnabo, Venice 1993, Musée des Beaux-Arts, Nantes, 1994, Stadtgalerie, Saarbrücken 1994, Museo Nacional Centro de Arte Reina Sofia, Madrid 1995, Henry Moore Foundation, Halifax 1996, MNAM, Centre Georges Pompidou, Paris 1996, Whitechapel Art Gallery 1997, Art Gallery of New South Wales, Sydney 1997, Lenbachhaus, Munich 1998, Galerie der Stadt, Stuttgart 1999, Tate Gallery, Liverpool 2000. *Group exhibitions include:* Venice Biennale 1980–86, São Paulo Bienale 1983, Sydney Bienale 1984, 1990; work on perm. display Tate Modern, London 2000–. *Leisure interests:* walking, geology. *Address:* c/o Tate Modern, Bankside, London, SE1 9T6, England; Marienburgerstr. 24, 42277 Wuppertal Germany. *Telephone:* (202) 551350. *Fax:* (202) 5513512. *E-mail:* tcragg@wtal.de.

CRAIG, David Parker, AO, DSc, FRS, FRSA, FAA; Australian professor of chemistry; b. 23 Nov. 1919, Sydney; s. of Andrew Hunter Craig and Mary Jane Parker; m. Veronica Bryden-Brown 1948; three s. one d.; ed Univ. of Sydney and Univ. Coll. London; Capt., Australian Imperial Force 1941–44; Lecturer in Chem., Univ. of Sydney 1944–46, Prof. of Physical Chem. 1952–56; Turner and Newall Research Fellow 1946–49; Lecturer in Chem., Univ. Coll. London 1949–52, Prof. 1956–67, Visiting Prof. 1968–; Prof. of Chem., Australian Nat. Univ. 1967–85, Prof. Emer. 1985–, Dean, Research School of Chem. 1970–73, 1977–81; Firth Visiting Prof., Univ. of Sheffield 1973; Visiting Prof., Univ. Coll. Cardiff 1975–89; Visiting Foreign Prof., Univ. of Bologna 1984; part-time mem. Exec. CSIRO 1980–85; Pres. Australian Acad. of Science 1990–94; Fellow, Univ. Coll. London; Hon. DSc (Sydney), (Bologna); Hon. FRSC; H. G. Smith Memorial Medal, Leighton Medal. *Publications:* Excitons in Molecular Crystals—Theory and Applications (co-author) 1968, Molecular Quantum Electrodynamics: An Introduction to Radiation-Molecule Interactions (co-author) 1984; original papers on chemistry in scientific journals. *Leisure interest:* tennis. *Address:* 199 Dryandra Street, O'Connor, ACT 2602, Australia. *Telephone:* (2) 6125-2839 (Office); (2) 6249-1976 (Home). *Fax:* (2) 6125-3216 (Office). *E-mail:* david.craig@anu.edu.au (Office).

CRAIG, George; American publishing executive; Dir Production, Honeywell Computers Scotland 1965–74; Vice-Chair. and Group Man. Dir William Collins, UK 1974–87; Pres. and CEO Harper & Row Publrs. Inc. (now HarperCollins Publs), New York 1987–96; mem. Bd of Dirs. The News Corpn Ltd; mem. Editorial Advisory Bd Publrs. Weekly Int. *Address:* c/o HarperCollins Publishers, 10 East 53rd Street, New York, NY 10022, USA. *Telephone:* (212) 207-7000. *Fax:* (212) 207-7759.

CRAIG, Ian Jonathan David, PhD; British astrophysicist; b. 30 Aug. 1950, Sheffield; s. of Ronald W Craig and Beatrice I. Craig; m. Fiona M. Jardine 1979; one s. one d.; ed Chesterfield Coll. of Tech. and Westfield and Univ. Colls. London; Research Fellow, Dept of Astronomy, Univ. of Glasgow 1974–76, 1977–79; Research Assoc. Inst. for Plasma Research, Stanford Univ. 1976–77; lecturer in Math. Univ. of Waikato, NZ 1979–85, Sr Lecturer 1985–93, Assoc. Prof. 1993–; research astronomer, Inst. for Astronomy, Univ. of Hawaii 1990–91; guest investigator on Skylab 1977; mem. Int. Astronomical Union. *Publications include:* Inverse Problems in Astronomy—A Guide to Inversion Strategies For Remotely Sensed Data (with J. C. Brown) 1986. *Leisure interests:* cycling, swimming, skiing, windsurfing; wood: growing it, working it and burning it. *Address:* Department of Mathematics, University of Waikato, Private Bag, Hamilton (Office); 25 Cranwell Place, Hamilton, New Zealand (Home).

CRAIG, Larry Edwin, BA; American politician; b. 20 July 1945, Council, Ida; s. of Elvin Craig and Dorothy Craig; m. Suzanne Thompson 1983; two s. one d.; ed Univ. of Idaho and George Washington Univ.; farmer, rancher, Midvale area, Ida; mem. Ida Farm Bureau 1965–79; mem. N.R.A., Future Farmers of America; Pres. Young Republican League, Ida 1976–77; mem. Ida Republican Exec. Cttee 1976–78; mem. Ida Senate 1974–80; mem. 97th–101st Congresses from 1st Dist of Ida 1981–91; Senator from Idaho 1991–; Republican. *Leisure interest:* gardening. *Address:* United States Senate, 520 Hart Senate Office Building, Washington, DC 20510-0001, USA (Office). *Telephone:* (202) 224-2752 (Office). *Website:* craig.senate.gov (Office).

CRAIG, Mary, MA; British author and broadcaster; b. 2 July 1928, St Helens, Lancs.; d. of William Joseph Clarkson and Anne Mary Clarkson; m. Francis John Craig 1952 (died 1995); four s. (one deceased); ed Notre Dame Convent, St Helens, Liverpool Univ., St Anne's Coll. Oxford Univ.; N-W Organizer, Sue Ryder Trust 1962–68; TV Critic, Catholic Herald 1971–76; presenter and features writer (freelance) with BBC Radio 1969–77; interviewer, Thames TV, Southern TV (freelance); freelance journalist and book reviewer; The Christopher Book Award (for Blessings), USA 1979, John Harriott Award 1993 and other awards; Officer's Cross of Order of Polonia Restituta 1987. *Publications:* Longford 1978, Woodruff at Random 1978, Blessings 1979, Man from a Far Country 1979, Candles in the Dark 1983, The Crystal Spirit 1986, Spark from Heaven 1988, Tears of Blood: A Cry for Tibet 1992, Kundun: The Dalai Lama, His Family and His Times 1997, The Last Freedom: A Journal 1997, Waiting for the Sun: A Peasant Boy in Occupied Tibet 1999, His Holiness the Dalai Lama (anthology, ed.) 2001; *for children:* Pope John Paul II 1982, Mother Teresa 1984, Lech Wałęsa 1989. *Leisure interests:* reading modern history and biography, logic puzzles, listening to music, playing the piano, travel. *Address:* 1 Lodge Gardens, Penwood, Burghclere, nr Newbury, Berks., RG20 9EF, England (Home); c/o Peters Fraser and Dunlop, Drury House, 34-43 Russell Street, London WC2B 5HA. *Telephone:* (20) 7344-1000.

CRAIG, Michael; British actor; b. 27 Jan. 1929, Poona, India; appeared in The Homecoming, New York 1967–68; frequent appearances on stage in Australia; actor and scriptwriter for TV plays and films in Australia; TV appearances in UK. *Films include:* The Love Lottery, Passage Home, The Black Tents, To the Night, Eyewitness, House of Secrets, High Tide at Noon, Campbell's Kingdom, The Silent Enemy, Nor the Moon by Night, The Angry Silence, Doctor in Love, The Mysterious Island, Payroll, No My Darling Daughter, A Life for Ruth, The Iron Maiden, Captive City, Summer Flight, Of a Thousand Delights, Life at the Top, Modesty Blaise, Funny Girl, Royal Hunt of the Sun, Twinky, Country Dance, Royal Hunt of the Sun, The Second Mrs Anderson, Inn of the Damned, A Sporting Proposition, The Irishman, Turkey Shoot, Stanley, The Timeless Land, Appointment with Death. *Address:* c/o Shanahans, P.O. Box 478, King's Cross, Sydney, NSW 2033, Australia.

CRAIG-MARTIN, Michael, MFA; Irish artist; b. 28 Aug. 1941, Dublin; s. of Paul F. Craig-Martin and Rhona Gargan Craig-Martin; m. Janice Hashey 1963 (divorced); one d.; ed Yale Univ.; lecturer British Acad. of Art 1966–69; artist in residence King's Coll., Cambridge 1970–72; Sr Lecturer Goldsmith's Coll., Univ. of London 1974–88, Millard Prof. of Fine Art 1994–; Trustee Tate Gallery 1989–99; Dr. hc (San Francisco Art Inst.) 2001. *Exhibitions include:* "The New Art", Hayward Gallery, London 1972, Retrospective 1968–1989, Whitechapel Art Gallery, London, 1989, "Always Now", Kunstverein, Hanover 1998, São Paulo Bienal 1998, Kunstverein, Stuttgart 1999, Waddington Gallery 2000. *Designs include:* Costume design for M-Piece, Mark Baldwin Dance Co., Queen Elizabeth Hall, London 1988. *Telephone:* (20) 7437-8611. *Fax:* (20) 7734-4146.

CRAIG OF RADLEY, Baron (Life Peer), cr. 1991, of Helhoughton in the County of Norfolk; **Marshal of the RAF David Brownrigg Craig**, GCB, OBE, MA, FRAeS; British air force officer; b. 17 Sept. 1929, Dublin, Ireland; s. of Maj. Francis Brownrigg Craig and Olive Craig; m. Elizabeth June Derenburg 1955; one s. one d.; ed Radley Coll. and Lincoln Coll., Oxford; commissioned in RAF 1951, Commanding Officer RAF Cranwell 1968–70; ADC to The Queen 1969–71; Dir Plans and Operations, HQ Far East Command 1970–71, Commanding Officer RAF Akrotiri 1972–73, ACAS (Ops) Ministry of Defence 1975–78, Air Officer Commanding No. 1 Group RAF Strike Command 1978–80, Vice-Chief of the Air Staff 1980–82, Air Officer, C-in-C, RAF Strike Command and C-in-C UK Forces 1982–85, Chief of Air Staff 1985–88, Chief of Defence Staff 1988–91; Air ADC to The Queen 1985–88; Chair. Council of King Edward VII Hosp. (Sister Agnes) 1998–; Deputy Chair. RAF Benevolent Fund 1996–; mem. House of Lords Select Cttee on Science and Tech. 1993–99; Convenor Cross-bench Peers 1999–; Pres. RAF Club 2002–; Hon. Fellow Lincoln Coll. Oxford 1984; Hon. DSc (Cranfield). *Leisure interests:* fishing, shooting, golf. *Address:* c/o House of Lords, London, SW1A 0PW, England. *E-mail:* craigd@parliament.uk (Office).

CRAIK, Fergus Ian Muirden, PhD, FRSC; British/Canadian professor of psychology; b. 17 April 1935, Edinburgh; s. of George Craik and Frances Crabbe; m. Anne Catherall 1961; one s. one d.; ed George Watson's Boys' Coll., Edinburgh and Univs. of Edinburgh and Liverpool; mem. scientific staff, MRC Unit for Research on Occupational Aspects of Ageing, Univ. of Liverpool 1960–65; lecturer in Psychology, Birkbeck Coll. London 1965–71; Assoc. Prof. then Prof. of Psychology, Univ. of Toronto 1971–, Chair. Dept of Psychology 1985–90; Sr Scientist, Rotman Research Inst. 2000–; Fellow, Center for Advanced Study in Behavioral Sciences, Stanford Univ. 1982–83; Killam Research Fellowship 1982–84; Guggenheim Fellowship 1982–83; Fellow, Soc. of Experimental Psychologists, Canadian Psychological Asscn, American Psychological Asscn; D. O. Hebb Award; William James Fellow Award, Killam Prize for Science 2000. *Publications:* Levels of Processing in Human Memory (ed. with L. S. Cermak) 1979, Aging and Cognitive Processes (ed. with S. Trehub) 1982, Varieties of Memory and Consciousness (ed. with H. L. Roediger III) 1989, The Handbook of Aging and Cognition (ed. with T. A. Salthouse) 1992, 2000, The Oxford Handbook of Memory (ed. with E. Tulving) 2000. *Leisure interests:* reading, walking, tennis, music. *Address:* Rotman Research Institute of Baycrest Centre, 3560 Bathurst Street, Toronto, Ont., M6A 2E1, Canada (Office). *Telephone:* (416) 785-2500 extn. 3526 (Office). *Fax:* (416) 785-2862 (Office).

CRAINZ, Franco, MD, FRCOG; Italian university professor; b. 18 May 1913, Rome; s. of the late Silvio Crainz and Ada Fanelli Crainz; ed Rome Univ.; Prof. and Head of Dept, School for Midwives, Novara 1956–64; Prof. and Head, Dept of Obstetrics and Gynaecology, Univ. of Cagliari 1964–66, of Messina 1966–67, of Bari 1967–72; Prof. of Obstetrics and Gynaecology, Rome Univ. 1972–88, Prof. Emer. 1988–; Vice-Pres. Italian Soc. of the History of Medicine; Hon. Pres. Italian Soc. of Obstetrics and Gynaecology (Pres. 1977–80); Hon. mem. European Soc. of Gynaecology and of the Austrian, Portuguese, Romanian, Spanish and Swiss socs.; Corresp. mem. German Soc.; Fellow ad eundem, Royal Coll. of Obstretricians and Gynaecologists. *Publications:* An Obstetric Tragedy–The Case of HRH the Princess Charlotte Augusta 1977, The Birth of an Heir to the 5th Duke of Devonshire 1989, Dr. Matthew Baillie 1995, The Pregnant Madonna in Christian Art (with J. Dewhurst) 2001; over 100 medical papers. *Leisure interests:* history of medicine, music, archaeology, history, gardening. *Address:* Via P. Mascagni 124, 00199 Rome, Italy. *Telephone:* (06) 8610433.

CRAMOND, William Alexander, AO, OBE, MD, FRCPsych, FRANZCP, FRACP, FRSE; British/Australian professor of clinical psychiatry; b. 2 Oct. 1920, Aberdeen; s. of W J. Cramond, MBE and May Battisby; m. Bertine J. C. Mackintosh 1949; one s. one d.; ed Robert Gordon's Coll. Aberdeen and Univ. of Aberdeen; Physician Supt, Woodilee Hosp. Glasgow 1955–61; Dir of Mental Health, S. Australia 1961–65; Foundation Prof. of Mental Health, Univ. of Adelaide 1963–71; Prin. Medical Officer in Mental Health, Scottish Home and Health Dept 1971–72; Foundation Dean, Faculty of Medicine, Univ. of Leicester 1972–75; Prin. and Vice-Chancellor, Univ. of Stirling 1975–80; Dir of Mental Health, Health Comm. NSW 1980–83; Prof. of Clinical Psychiatry, Univ. of Sydney 1980–83, The Flinders Univ. of S. Australia 1983–92; Emer. Prof. 1993–; Chair. Bd of Dirs. SA Mental Health Services 1993–95; Hon. DUniv (Stirling). *Leisure interests:* reading, theatre. *Address:* 28 Tynte Street, North Adelaide, South Australia 5006, Australia. *Telephone:* (8) 8267-1600.

CRANBORNE, Viscount; **Rt Hon Robert Michael James Gascoyne-Cecil,** PC, DL; British politician; b. 30 Sept. 1946; s. of 6th Marquess of Salisbury; m. Hannah Ann Stirling 1970; two s. three d.; ed Eton Coll., Oxford Univ.; MP for Dorset S. 1979–87; mem. House of Lords 1992–; Parl. Under-Sec. of State for Defence 1992–94; Lord Privy Seal 1994–97; Shadow Leader of House of Lords 1997–98; sits in House of Lords as Lord Gascoyne-Cecil 1999–; fmr Pres. Herts. Agric. Soc.; DL Dorset 1987; mem. Conservative Party. *Address:* Manor House, Cranborne, Wimborne, Dorset, BH21 5PP, England. *Telephone:* (1725) 517781 (Office). *Fax:* (1725) 517764 (Office).

CRANBROOK, 5th Earl of (cr. 1892); **5th Viscount (cr.1878) Gathorne Gathorne-Hardy,** MA, PhD, CBiol, DL; British biologist; b. 20 June 1933, London; m. Caroline Jarvis 1967; two s. one d.; ed Eton Coll., Corpus Christi Coll. Cambridge and Univ. of Birmingham; lecturer, Sr lecturer in Zoology, Univ. of Malaya 1961–70; Ed. Ibis (journal of British Ornithologists' Union) 1973–80; mem. Royal Comm. on Environmental Pollution 1981–92; Trustee, Natural History Museum 1982–86; mem. Natural Environment Research Council 1982–88; mem. Nature Conservancy Council 1990–91; Chair. English Nature 1991–98, ENTRUST 1996–2002; Dir (non-exec.) Anglian Water 1989–98; mem. Broads Authority, Harwich Haven Authority 1988–98; mem. Bd Foundation for European Environmental Policy 1987–98, Chair. 1990–98; Vice-Pres. Nat. Soc. for Clean Air and Environmental Protection; also partner in family farming business in Suffolk; Chair. Inst. for European Environmental Policy 1990–; Chair. Int. Trust for Zoological Nomenclature 2001–; Hon. DSc (Aberdeen) 1989, (Cranfield) 1996; Hon. Johan Bintang Sarawak 1997. *Publications:* Mammals of Borneo 1965, Riches of the Wild: Mammals of South East Asia 1987, Belalong: a tropical rain forest (jtly) 1994, Wonders of Nature in South East Asia 1997, Ballad of Jerjezang (jtly) 2001, Swiftlets of Borneo (jtly) 2002. *Leisure interest:* walking. *Address:* Glemham House, Great Glemham, Saxmundham, IP17 1LP, England. *Telephone:* (7775) 755825. *Fax:* (1728) 663339 (Home). *E-mail:* lordcranbook@greatglemhamfarms.co.uk (Office).

CRANDALL, Robert Lloyd, BA; American business executive; b. 6 Dec. 1935, Westerly, RI; s. of Lloyd Evans Crandall and Virginia (née Beard) Crandall; m. Margaret Jan Schmults 1957; two s. one d.; ed William and Mary Coll., Univ. of Rhode Island, Wharton School, Univ. of Pennsylvania; Dir of Credit and Collections, then Vice-Pres. Data Services TWA 1967–73; COO 1973–85 and Sr Vice-Pres. (Finance), American Airlines 1973–74, Sr Vice-Pres. Marketing 1974–80, Dir 1976–, Pres. 1980–95, Chair., CEO Jan. 1985–; Pres., Chair. and CEO AMR Corpn 1985–98; Dir of several cos. *Leisure interests:* skiing, tennis, running, reading. *Address:* c/o AMR Corporation, 4333 Amon Carter Boulevard, Fort Worth, TX 76155, USA.

CRANE, Peter Robert, PhD, FRS, FIBiol; British professor of paleontology; b. 18 July 1954, Kettering; s. of Walter Robert Crane and Dorothy Mary Crane (née Mills); m. Elinor Margaret Hamer 1986; one s. one d.; ed Reading Univ.; lecturer Dept of Botany, Reading Univ. 1978–82; post-doctoral research scholar, Dept of Biology, Ind. Univ. 1981–82; Curator Dept of Geology, The Field Museum, Chicago 1982–92, Vice-Pres. Center for Evolutionary and Environmental Biology 1992–93, Vice-Pres. Academic Affairs and Dir The Field Museum 1994–99; mem. Paleontological Soc. (Pres. 1998–2000); Dir Royal Botanic Gardens, Kew 1999–; Foreign Assoc. Nat. Acad. of Sciences, USA 2001; Foreign mem. Royal Swedish Acad. of Sciences 2002; Bicentenary Medal, Linnean Soc. 1984, Schuchert Award 1993. *Publication:* (ed jtly) The Origins of Angiosperms and their Biological Consequences 1987, (ed jtly) The Evolution, Systematics and Fossil History of the Hamamelidae Vols 1 and 2 1989; (jtly) The Origin and Diversification of Land Plants 1997. *Address:* Royal Botanic Gardens, Kew, Richmond, Surrey, TW9 3AB, England.

CRANFIELD, Rev. Charles Ernest Burland, MA, FBA; British professor of theology; b. 13 Sept. 1915, London; s. of Charles Ernest Cranfield and Beatrice Mary Cranfield (née Tubbs); m. Ruth Elizabeth Gertrude Bole 1953; two d.; ed Mill Hill School, Jesus Coll., Cambridge and Wesley House, Cambridge; research in Basle until outbreak of Second World War; Probationer in Methodist Church 1939; ordained 1941; Minister in Shoeburyness 1940–42; Chaplain to the Forces (from end of hostilities worked with German Prisoners of War, was first staff chaplain to POW Directorate in War Office) 1942–46; Minister in Cleethorpes 1946–50; admitted to Presbyterian Church of England (now part of United Reformed Church) 1954; Lecturer in Theology, Univ. of Durham 1950–62, Sr Lecturer 1962–66, Reader 1966–78, Prof. of Theology (personal) 1978–80, Emer. Prof. 1980–; Jt Gen. Ed., new series of International Critical Commentary 1966–; Hon. DD (Aberdeen) 1980; Burkitt Medal for Biblical Studies 1989. *Publications:* The First Epistle of Peter 1950, The Gospel according to Saint Mark 1959, I and II Peter and Jude 1960, A Critical and Exegetical Commentary on the Epistle to the Romans, Vol. 1 1975, Vol. 2 1979, Romans: a Shorter Commentary 1985, The Bible and Christian Life: a Collection of Essays 1985, If God Be For Us: a Collection of Sermons 1985, The Apostles' Creed: a Faith to Live By 1993, On Romans and Other New Testament Essays 1998. *Address:* 30 Western Hill, Durham City, Durham, DH1 4RL, England. *Telephone:* (191) 384-3096.

CRANFIELD, Thomas L., BA; Irish banker and civil servant; b. 3 Feb. 1945, Dublin; m.; three d.; ed Univ. Coll. Dublin; personal admin. in American biomedical eng co., Dublin 1970–73; Head of Div. EIB (Luxembourg) 1973–90; Deputy Registrar European Court of Justice (Luxembourg) 1990–2000; Dir.-Gen. Office for Official Publs of the EU 2000–. *Address:* Office for Official Publications of the European Union, 2 rue Mercier, 2985 Luxembourg (Office). *Telephone:* 2929-1 (Office). *Fax:* 2929-44691 (Office). *E-mail:* ThomasL.Cranfield@cec.eu.int (Office).

CRANHAM, Kenneth Raymond; British actor; b. 12 Dec. 1944, Dunfermline, Scotland; s. of Ronald Cranham and Margaret McKay Fergusson; m. Fiona Victory; two d.; ed Tulse Hill School, London, Royal Acad. of Dramatic Art (RADA), Nat. Youth Theatre; Bancroft Gold Medal, RADA 1966. *Cinema includes:* Two Men Went to War, Born Romantic, Shiner, Gangster No. 1, Women Talking Dirty, The Last Yellow, Under Suspicion, Chocolat, The Clot, Oliver, Brother Sun Sister Moon, Joseph Andrews. *Theatre includes:* RSC: School for Scandal, Ivanov, The Iceman Cometh; Nat. Theatre: Flight, An Inspector Calls, Kick for Touch, Cardiff East, From Kipling to Vietnam, The Caretaker, Strawberry Fields; Royal Court: Saved, Ruffian on the Stair, The London Cuckolds; W End: Loot, Comedians, Entertaining Mr Sloane, The Novice, Doctor's Dilemma, Paul Bunyan (Royal Opera House); Broadway: Loot, An Inspector Calls. *Radio:* The Barchester Chronicles, New Grub Street, Sons and Lovers. *Television includes:* Night Flight, Without Motive, The Murder of Stephen Lawrence, Our Mutual Friend, Oranges are Not the Only Fruit, Rules of Engagement, The Contractor, The Birthday Party, Lady Windermere's Fan, Thérèse Raquin, 'Tis a Pity She's a Whore, Merchant of Venice, The Caretaker, The Dumb Waiter, La Ronde, The Sound of Guns, Sling Your Hook. *Leisure interests:* vernacular music, art, food, travel, some people. *Address:* c/o Markham & Froggatt Ltd, 4 Windmill Street, London, W1P 1HF, England (Office). *Telephone:* (20) 7636-4412 (Office).

CRANSTON, David Alan, CBE; British administrator and fmr army officer; b. 20 Oct. 1945; s. of Stanley Cranston and Mary Cranston (née Fitzherbert); m. Pippa Ann Reynolds 1968; three d.; ed Strathallan School, Perthshire, Royal Mil. Acad., Sandhurst; served in Army 1966–95, retd with rank of Brig.; with Personal Investment Authority 1995–97, Royal Bank of Scotland Group 1997–2000, Dir.-Gen. Nat. Asscn of Pension Funds 2000–01; Dir (non-exec.) Nat. Australia Life Co. Ltd; Chair. British Biathlon Union 1996–. *Leisure interests:* gardening, reading, sport. *Address:* c/o National Association of Pension Funds, 4 Victoria Street, London, SW1H 0NX, England (Office).

CRAPO, Michael Dean, JD, BA; American politician and lawyer; b. 20 May 1951, Idaho Falls; s. of George Lavelle Crapo and Melba Crapo (née Olsen); m. Susan Diane Hasleton 1974; two s. three d.; ed Brigham Young, Utah and Harvard Univs; called to Bar Calif. 1977, Idaho 1979; law clerk to US Court of Appeals San Diego 1977–78; assoc. attorney Gibson, Dunn & Crutcher 1978–79; attorney Holden, Kidwell, Hahn & Crapo 1979–92, partner 1983–92; mem. Idaho State Senate 1984–93, Asst majority leader 1987–88, Pres. Pro Tempore 1989–92; mem. U.S. House of Reps. from 2nd Idaho Dist 1992–99; Senator from Idaho Jan. 1999–; mem. numerous cttees and bds; Republican; recipient of numerous awards. *Leisure interests:* backpacking, skiing. *Address:* US Senate, 11 Russell Senate Building, Washington, DC 20510, USA. *Telephone:* (202) 224-6142 (Office).

CRAVEN, Sir John Anthony, Kt, BA; Canadian/British merchant banker; b. 23 Oct. 1940; m. 2nd Jane Frances Stiles-Allen 1970; three s.; one s. one d. from 1st m.; ed Michaelhouse, S. Africa, Jesus Coll., Cambridge, Queen's Univ., Kingston, Ont.; with Clarkson & Co., Toronto 1961–64, Wood Gundy Bankers 1964–67; Dir S. G. Warburg & Co. 1967–73, Vice-Chair. 1979; Chief Exec. White Weld & Co. Ltd 1973–78; Founder and Chair. Phoenix Securities Ltd 1981–89; CEO Morgan Grenfell Group 1987–89, Chair. 1989–97; mem. Bd Man. Dirs. Deutsche Bank AG, Frankfurt 1990–96, Supervisory Bd Société Générale de Surveillance Holding, Geneva 1989–98; Chair. (non-exec.) Tootal Group 1985–91, Lonmin PLC 1997–; Dir Securities and Investment Bd 1990–93; Dir Rothmans Int. PLC 1991–99; Dir (non-exec.) Reuters 1997–, Robert Fleming Holdings Ltd 1999–2000; Dir Gleacher & Co. Ltd

2000–, Fleming Family & Partners Ltd 2000–, Ducati Motor Holdings SpA 1999–; mem. Ont. Inst. of Chartered Accountants, Canadian Inst. of Chartered Accountants. *Leisure interests:* hunting, shooting, skiing. *Address:* c/o Gleacher & Co. Ltd, Cleveland House, 33 King Street, 3rd Floor, London, SW1Y 6RJ, England (Office).

CRAVEN, Wes, MA; American director, screenplay writer and actor; b. 2 Aug. 1939, Cleveland, Ohio; ed Wheaton Coll., Johns Hopkins Univ.; fmr Prof. of Humanities; began film career at film production house, became Asst to Co. Pres. working on post-production; Asst Ed. to Sena Cunningham; mem. Dirs Guild of America. *Films include:* The Last House on the Left (also screenplay and ed.) 1972, The Hills Have Eyes (also screenplay and ed.) 1976, You've Got to Walk It Like You Talk It or You'll Lose That Beat, Deadly Blessing (also co-writer) 1979, Swamp Thing (also screenplay) 1980, The Hills Have Eyes II (also screenplay) 1983, Invitation To Hell 1984, A Nightmare on Elm Street (also screenplay) 1984, Deadly Friend (co-writer) 1986, The Serpent and the Rainbow 1988, A Nightmare on Elm Street III (co-writer, co-exec. producer) 1986, Shocker (also screenplay and co-exec. producer) 1989, The People Under the Stars (also screenplay and co-exec. producer) 1991, Wes Craven's New Nightmare (also screenplay and actor) 1994, Vampire in Brooklyn 1995, The Fear (actor), Scream 1998, Scream 2 1999, Music of the Heart 1999 (dir), Scream 3, Carnival of Souls (exec. producer), Alice (producer). *TV includes:* (films) A Stranger in our House (co-writer) 1978, Invitation to Hell 1982, Chiller 1983, Casebusters 1985, A Little Peace and Quiet 1987, Wordplay 1987, Chameleon 1987, Her Pilgrim Soul 1987, Shatterday 1987, Dealer's Choice 1987, The Road Not Taken 1988, Night Visions (also co-writer and exec. producer) 1990, Nightmare Café (exec. producer) 1991, Laurel Canyon (exec. producer), Body Bags (actor); (series) Twilight Zone, Crimebusters. *Address:* c/o Joe Quenqua, PMK, 1775 Broadway, Suite 701, New York, NY 10019, USA.

CRAWFORD, Bryce, Jr., PhD; American professor of chemistry; b. 27 Nov. 1914, New Orleans, La.; s. of Bryce Low Crawford and Clara Hall Crawford; m. Ruth Raney 1940; two s. one d.; ed Stanford Univ.; Nat. Research Council Fellow, Harvard Univ. 1937–39; Instructor, Yale Univ. 1939–40; Asst Prof., Univ. of Minn. 1940–43, Assoc. Prof. 1943–46, Prof. 1946–82, Regents' Prof. 1982–85, Prof. Emer. 1985–, Chair. Dept of Chem. 1955–60, Dean, Graduate School 1960–72; Fulbright Prof., Oxford Univ. 1951, Tokyo Univ. 1966; Ed. Journal of Physical Chem. 1970–80; Chair. Council of Graduate Schools 1962–63; Pres. Asscn of Graduate Schools 1970, Graduate Record Examinations Bd 1968–72; mem. NAS (Council 1975–78), Home Sec. 1979–87; mem. American Acad. of Arts and Sciences 1977; American Chem. Soc. (Bd of Dirs. 1969–77), Coblentz Soc., American Philosophical Soc.; Fellow, American Physical Soc.; Presidential Certificate of Merit 1946; Guggenheim Fellowships 1950, 1972; Fulbright Professorship 1951, 1966; Minn. Award, American Chem. Soc. 1969, Pittsburgh Spectroscopy Award 1977, Ellis Lippincott Award 1978, Priestley Medal 1982. *Publications:* articles in scientific journals. *Address:* Dept of Chemistry, University of Minnesota, 207 Pleasant Street SE, Minneapolis, MN 55455 (Office); 1545 Branston, St Paul, MN 55108, USA (Home). *Telephone:* (612) 625-5394. *E-mail:* crawford@chemsun .chem.umm.edu (Office).

CRAWFORD, Cindy; American fashion model; b. 1966; m. 1st Richard Gere 1991 (divorced); m. 2nd Rande Gerber 1998; one s. one d.; promoted Revlon (cosmetics) and Pepsi Cola; presented own fashion show on MTV (cable and satellite); has appeared on numerous covers for magazines; model for numerous fashion designers; has released several exercise videos; face of Kelloggs Special K 2000; spokesperson for eStyle.com, Omega watches, 24 Hr. Fitness. *Film:* Fair Game 1995. *Publications:* Cindy Crawford's Basic Face 1996, About Face (for children) 2001. *Address:* c/o Wolf-Kasteler, 132 S. Rodeo Drive, Suite 300, Beverly Hills, CA 90212, USA.

CRAWFORD, Sir Frederick William, Kt, DL, DEngDSc, CCIM, FREng, FIEEE, FIEE, FInstP, FIMA; British scientist; b. 28 July 1931, Birmingham; s. of William Crawford and Victoria Maud Crawford; m. Béatrice Madeleine Jacqueline Hutter 1963; one s. (deceased) one d.; ed George Dixon Grammar School, Birmingham, Univ. of London, Univ. of Liverpool; Research Trainee, J. Lucas Ltd 1948–52; scientist, Nat. Coal Bd Mining Research Establishment 1956–57; Sr Lecturer in Electrical Eng, Birmingham Coll. of Advanced Tech. 1958–59; Stanford Univ., Calif 1959–82; Prof. (Research), Inst. for Plasma Research 1964–67, Assoc. Prof. 1967–69, Prof. 1969–82, Chair. 1974–80; Dir Centre for Interdisciplinary Research 1973–77; Visiting Prof., Math. Inst. 1977–78, Visiting Fellow, St Catherine's Coll., Oxford 1977–78, 1996–97; Vice-Chancellor, Aston Univ. 1980–96; U.S. Nat. Cttee, Union Radio-Scientifique Internationale 1975–81, Chair. Int. Comm. 1978–81, UK Rep. 1982–84; Chair. Int. Scientific Cttee, Int. Conf. on Phenomena in Ionised Gases 1979–81; mem. US-UK Educ. Comm. 1981–84, British North-American Cttee 1987–, Franco-British Council 1987–98; Chair. Birmingham Civic Soc. 1983–88, Criminal Cases Review Comm. 1996–; High Sheriff, W Midlands Co. 1995; Hon. DSc (Buckingham) 1996; Freeman, City of London 1986; Master, Worshipful Co. of Engineers 1996, Co. of Information Technologists 2000; Hon. Bencher, Inner Temple 1996. *Publications:* numerous publs on higher educ. and plasma physics. *Address:* Criminal Cases Review Commission, Alpha Tower, Suffolk Street Queensway, Birmingham, B1 1TT (Office); 47 Charlbury Road, Oxford, OX2 6UX, England (Home). *Telephone:* (121) 633-1800 (Office). *E-mail:* f.w.crawford@btinternet.com (Home).

CRAWFORD, James Richard, SC, DPhil, FBA; Australian professor of international law; b. 14 Nov. 1948, Adelaide; s. of James Crawford and Josephine Bond; m. 1st Marisa Luigina Ballini 1971 (divorced 1990); m. 2nd Patricia Hyndman 1992 (divorced 1998); four d.; m. 3rd Joanna Gomula 1998; one s.; ed Brighton High School and Univs of Adelaide and Oxford; lecturer, Sr lecturer, Reader, Prof. of Law, Univ. of Adelaide 1974–86; mem. Australian Law Reform Comm. 1982–84, part-time 1984–90; Challis Prof. of Int. Law, Univ. of Sydney 1986–92, Dean, Faculty of Law 1990–92; Whewell Prof. of Int. Law, Univ. of Cambridge 1992–; Dir Lauterpacht Research Centre for Int. Law 1997–; barrister, Sr Counsel (NSW, Australia) 1997; mem. UN Int. Law Comm. 1992. *Publications:* The Creation of States in International Law 1979, The Rights of Peoples (ed. 1988), Australian Courts of Law (3rd Edn) 1993, The International Law Commission Articles on State Responsibility 2002, International Law as an Open System 2002. *Leisure interests:* reading, cricket, walking. *Address:* Lauterpacht Research Centre for International Law, 5 Cranmer Road, Cambridge, CB3 8AL, England. *Telephone:* (1223) 335358. *Fax:* (1223) 311668. *E-mail:* jrc1000@hermes.cam.ac.uk (Office). *Website:* www.law.cam.ac.uk\rcil (Office).

CRAWFORD, Michael, OBE; British actor and singer; b. (as Michael Dumbell-Smith), 19 Jan. 1942; ed St Michael's Coll., Bexley, Oakfield School, Dulwich; actor 1955–; films for Children's Film Foundation; hundreds of radio broadcasts; appeared in original productions of Noyes Fludde and Let's Make an Opera by Benjamin Britten; has toured in UK, USA and Australia. *Stage roles include:* Travelling Light 1965, the Anniversary 1966, No Sex Please, We're British 1971, Billy 1974, Same Time, Next Year 1976, Flowers for Algernon 1979, Barnum 1981–83, 1984–86, Phantom of the Opera, London (Olivier Award for Best Actor in a Musical) 1986–87, Broadway (Tony Award for Best Actor in a Musical) 1988, Los Angeles 1989, The Music of Andrew Lloyd Webber (concert tour), USA, Australia, UK 1991–92, EFX, Las Vegas 1995–96, Dance of the Vampires, Broadway 2003. *Films include:* Soap Box Derby 1950, Blow Your Own Trumpet 1954, Two Living One Dead 1962, The War Lover 1963, Two Left Feet 1963, The Knack 1965, A Funny Thing Happened on the Way to the Forum 1966, The Jokers 1966, How I Won the War 1967, Hello Dolly 1969, The Games 1969, Hello Goodbye 1970, Alice's Adventures in Wonderland 1972, The Condorman 1980. *TV appearances include:* Sir Francis Drake (series) 1962, Some Mothers Do 'Ave 'Em (several series), Chalk and Cheese (series), Sorry (play) 1979. *Publication:* Parcel Arrived Safely: Tied with String (autobiog.) 2000. *Address:* c/o ICM Ltd, Oxford House, 76 Oxford Street, London, W1D 1BS, England. *Telephone:* (20) 7636-6565. *Fax:* (20) 7323-0101.

CRAWFORD, Michael Hewson, MA, FBA; British university teacher; b. 7 Dec. 1939, Twickenham, Middx; s. of Brian Hewson Crawford and Margarethe Bettina Crawford (née Nagel); ed St Paul's School, London and Oriel Coll. Oxford; Research Fellow, Christ's Coll. Cambridge 1964–69; Univ. Lecturer, Cambridge 1969–86; Jt Dir Excavations of Fregellae 1980–86, Valpolcevera Project 1987–94, Velleia Project 1994–95, S. Martino Project 1996–; Chair. British Epigraphy Soc. 1996–99; Visiting Prof. Pavia Univ. 1983, 1992, Ecole Normale Supérieure, Paris 1984, Padua Univ. 1986, Sorbonne, Paris 1989, San Marino Univ. 1989, Milan Univ. 1990, L'Aquila Univ. 1990, Ecole des Hautes Etudes, Paris 1997, Ecole des Hautes Etudes en Sciences Sociales, Paris 1999; Prof. of Ancient History, Univ. Coll. London 1986–; Foreign mem. Istituto Lombardo, Reial Academia de Bones Lletres; mem. Academia Europaea; Joseph Crabtree Orator 2000; Trustee, Entente Cordiale Scholarships 2000; Officier des Palmes Académiques 2001; Archer Huntington Medal of the American Numismatic Society 2002. *Publications:* Roman Republican Coinage 1974, The Roman Republic 1978, La Moneta in Grecia e a Roma 1981, Sources for Ancient History 1983, Coinage and Money under the Roman Republic 1985, L'Impero romano e la struttura economica e sociale delle province 1986, Medals and Coins from Budé to Mommsen (with C. Ligota and J. B. Trapp) 1990, Antonio Agustín between Renaissance and Counter-reform 1993, Roman Statutes (Ed.) 1995, Historia Numorum (with N.K. Rutter et al.) 2001. *Address:* Department of History, University College London, Gower Street, London, WC1E 6BT, England. *Telephone:* (20) 7679-7396.

CRAWLEY, Frederick William, CBE, FCIB; British banker; b. 10 June 1926, London; s. of William Crawley and Elsie Crawley; m. Ruth E. Jungman 1951; two d.; entered Lloyds Bank 1942, Chief Accountant 1969, Asst Gen. Man. 1973, Exec. Dir Lloyds Bank Int. 1975, Asst Chief Gen. Man. 1977, Deputy Chief Gen. Man. 1978–82, 1983–84, Vice-Chair. and CEO Lloyds Bank Calif. 1982–83, Chief Gen. Man. Lloyds Bank PLC 1984–85, Deputy Group Chief Exec. 1985–87; Chair. Black Horse Agencies Ltd 1985–88; Deputy Chair. Girobank PLC 1991, Chair. 1991–94; Chair. Betta Stores PLC 1990–92, Alliance & Leicester Bldg Soc. 1991–94, Legal and Gen. Recovery Investment Trust PLC 1994–98; Dir Lloyds Bank 1984–88, Lloyds Devt Capital Ltd 1987–92, FS Assurance Ltd 1988–89, FS Investment Mans. Ltd 1988–89, FS Investment Services Ltd 1988–89, Barratt Devts Ltd 1988–96, Alliance & Leicester Estate Agents Ltd 1988–92, Legal and Gen. Bank Ltd 1997–2001; Consultant Anglo-Airlines Ltd 1988–92; Hon. Treas. RAF Benevolent Fund 1988–, Deputy Chair. RAF Benevolent Fund Enterprises Ltd 1988–; Fellow St Andrew's Man. Inst. 1996–97; Assoc. Royal Aeronautical Soc. 1984–. *Leisure interests:* aviation, shooting, photography. *Address:* 4 The Hexagon, Fitzroy Park, London, N6 6HR, England. *Telephone:* (20) 8341-2279 (Office); (20) 8341-2279 (Home). *Fax:* (20) 8341-2279 (Office); (20) 8341-2279 (Home).

CRAXTON, John Leith, RA; British artist; b. 3 Oct. 1922; s. of the late Harold Craxton and Essie Craxton; ed Betteshanger, Kent, Westminster

School of Art, London, Cen. School of Art, London, Goldsmiths' Coll., London; has designed sets for Royal Ballet, London; works exhibited in Tate Gallery, London, Victoria and Albert Museum, London, British Museum, London, Gallery of Modern Art, Edin., Nat. Museum of Wales, Arts Council, British Council, British Govt Picture Collection, Nat. Gallery, Melbourne, Metropolitan Museum, NY; HM Consular Corresp., Hania, Crete 1992–. *Solo exhibitions include:* Leicester Galleries, London 1944, 1951, 1954, 1956, 1961, 1966, St George's Gallery, London 1945, Galerie Gasser, Zürich 1946, British Council, Athens 1946, 1949, 1985, Mayor Gallery, London 1950, Crane Gallery, Manchester 1955, Whitechapel Art Gallery 1967, Hamet Gallery, London 1971, Christopher Hull Gallery, London 1982, 1985, 1987, 1993, Chrysostomos Gallery, Hania, Crete 1985, Pallant Gall. Chichester 1998–99. *Leisure interests:* music, museums, motorbikes, seafood. *Address:* Moshon 1, Hania, Crete, Greece (Office); c/o Allie Mayne, Royal Academy of Arts, Burlington House, Piccadilly, London, W1V 0DS; 14 Kidderpore Avenue, London, NW3 7SU, England.

CREAN, Simon, LLB; Australian trade union official; b. 26 Feb. 1949, Melbourne; s. of Frank Crean and Mary Crean; m. Carole Lamb 1973; two d.; ed Middle Park Cen. School, Melbourne High School and Monash Univ.; Research Officer, Federated Storemen and Packers' Union of Australia 1970–74, Asst Gen. Sec. 1974–79, Gen. Sec. 1979–85; Minister of Science and Tech. 1990–91, of Employment, Educ. and Training 1993–96; Man. Opposition Business, Shadow Minister for Industry and Regional Devt 1996–98, Shadow Treas. and Deputy Leader of the Opposition 1998–2001, Leader of the Opposition 2001–; Deputy Leader of the Australian Labor Party 1998–2001, Leader 2001–; Pres. Australian Council of Trades Unions 1985–90; mem. House of Reps. (for Hotham, Vic.) 1990–; mem. Econ. Planning Advisory Council, Nat. Labor Consultative Council, ILO Governing Body, Qantas Bd, Transport Industry Advisory Council, Business Educ. Council. *Leisure interest:* tennis. *Address:* 401 Clayton Road, Clayton, Vic. 3168, Australia.

CREECH, Rt. Hon. Wyatt (W. B.), BA; New Zealand politician, accountant and vineyard developer; b. Oct. 1946, Oceanside, Calif., USA; m. Danny (Diana) Creech; three s.; ed Massey and Victoria Univs.; mem. Martinborough Council 1980–86; MP for Wairarapa 1988–; Minister of Revenue, Customs, in Charge of the Public Trust Office and responsible for Govt Superannuation Fund 1990–91, Minister of Revenue, in Charge of the Public Trust Office and responsible for Govt Superannuation Fund and Sr Citizens, Assoc. Minister of Finance and Social Welfare 1991–93, Minister of Revenue and Employment, Deputy Minister of Finance 1993–96, Minister of Educ., for Courts, for Ministerial Services and Leader of the House 1996–98, Deputy Prime Minister 1998–99; Shadow Minister of State 2001–; Assoc. Spokesperson for Foreign Affairs and Trade; Deputy Leader Nat. Party 1997–2001; Chair. Cabinet Social Policy Cttee, Cabinet Legislation Cttee; mem. Nat. Party. *Leisure interests:* gardening, outdoor pursuits, wine tasting. *Address:* Parliament Buildings, Wellington, New Zealand (Office).

CREED, Martin; British artist; b. 21 Oct. 1968, Wakefield; s. of John Creed and Gisela Grosscurth; partner Paola Pivi; ed Slade School of Fine Art, London. *Art Exhibitions:* 18 solo exhbns and projects in Europe and N America including Martin Creed Works, Southampton City Art Gallery, Art Now, Tate Britain Gallery 2000; numerous group exhbns world-wide; *Works include:* Work No. 11 (Arts Council Collection) 1989, Work No. 79 (later shown at Intelligence: New British Art 2000, Tate Gallery) 1993, Work No. 81, Work No. 88, Everything is Going to Be Alright 1999, Work No. 143 (installed on face of Tate Britain Gallery) 2000, Work No. 200 1998, Work No. 227: The Lights Going On and Off (Turner Prize) 2001. *Music:* sings with punk band owada. *Address:* c/o GBE, 436 West 15th Street, New York, NY 1011, USA. *E-mail:* mail@martincreed.com. *Website:* www.martincreed.com.

CREEL MIRANDA, Santiago; Mexican politician and lawyer; b. 11 Dec. 1954, Mexico City; ed Univ. Nacional Autónoma de México, Univ. of Michigan, USA; lawyer, pvt. law firm; fmr Sec. Vuelta periodical; f. Este País magazine; fmr Prof. Autonomous Tech. Inst. of Mexico, Head Acad. Dept; Citizen Adviser to Gen. Council, Fed. Electoral Inst. 1994–96, Fed. Deputy 1997–; joined Nat. Action Party (PAN), cand. for Head Govt of Fed. Dist 1999; Sec. of the Interior 2000–; mem. Mexican Bar, Coll. of Lawyers, Mexican Acad. of Human Rights, Lawyers' Cttee for Human Rights. *Address:* Secretariat of State for the Interior, Bucareli 99, 1°, Col. Juárez, 06069 México, DF, Mexico (Office). *Telephone:* (5) 592-1141 (Office). *Fax:* (5) 546-5350 (Office). *Website:* www.gobernacion.gob.mx (Office).

CREELEY, Robert White, MA; American writer and professor of English; b. 21 May 1926, Arlington, Mass.; s. of Oscar Slade and Genevieve (Jules) Creeley; m. 1st Ann McKinnon 1946 (divorced 1955); two s. one d.; m. 2nd Bobbie Louise Hall 1957 (divorced 1976); three d.; m. 3rd Penelope Highton 1977; one s. one d.; ed Univ. of New Mexico and Harvard Univ.; Instructor Black Mountain Coll. 1954–55; Visiting Lecturer Univ. of New Mexico, Albuquerque 1961–62, Lecturer in English 1963–66, Visiting Prof. 1968–69, 1978, 1979, 1980; lecturer Univ. of BC, Vancouver 1962–63; Prof. of English, State Univ. of NY, Buffalo 1967–, Gray Prof. of Poetry and Letters 1978–89, Dir Poetics Program 1991–92; Capen Prof. of Poetry and the Humanities 1989–; Visiting Prof., San Francisco State Coll. 1970–71; Bicentennial Chair. of American Studies, Helsinki Univ. 1988–89; Ed. Black Mountain Review 1954–57; American Field Service 1944–45; mem. American Acad. of Arts and Letters; D. H. Lawrence Fellow 1960, Guggenheim Fellow 1964, 1971; Rockefeller Grantee 1965; SUNY Distinguished Prof. 1989; Hon. DLitt (Univ. of New Mexico) 1993; Levinson Prize of Poetry Magazine 1960, Blumenthal-Leviton Award of Poetry Magazine 1965, Union League Civic and Arts Foundation Prize, Poetry Magazine 1967, Shelley Memorial Award of Poetry Soc. of America 1981, Nat. Endowment for the Arts Grant in Writing 1982, DAAD Grant 1983, 1987, Leone D'Oro Premio Speciale 1985, Frost Medal, Poetry Soc. of America 1987, State Poet of NY 1989–91, Horst Bienek Lyric Prize (Munich) 1993, Lila Wallace-Reader's Digest Writers Award 1995, Bollingen Prize 1999, Chancellor's Medal, State Univ. of NY 1999, American Book Award, Columbus Foundation 2000, Golden Rose Award, New England Poetry Club 2001, Lannan Literacy Lifetime Achievement award 2001. *Publications:* Le Fou 1952, The Immoral Proposition 1953, The Kind of Act of 1953, The Gold Diggers 1954, revised edn 1965, All That is Lovely in Men 1955, If You 1956, The Whip 1957, A Form of Women 1959, For Love, Poems 1950–60 1962, The Island 1963, Words 1967, Numbers 1968, Pieces 1969, The Charm 1969, A Quick Graph 1970, The Finger 1970, St Martins 1971, A Day Book 1972, Listen 1972, A Sense of Measure 1973, His Idea 1973, Contexts of Poetry 1973, Thirty Things 1974, Backwards 1975, Presences (with Marisol) 1976, Selected Poems 1976, Mabel: A Story 1976, Myself 1977, Hello 1978, Was That a Real Poem and Other Essays 1979, Corn Close 1979, Later 1979, Robert Creeley and Charles Olson: The Complete Correspondence, Vols 1 & 2, 1980, vol. 3 1981, vol. 4 1982, vol. 5 1983, vol. 6 1985, Vols 7 and 8 1987, vol. 9 1990, Mother's Voice 1981, Echoes 1982, Collected Poems 1945–75, 1983, Mirrors 1983, The Collected Prose 1984, Memory Gardens 1986, The Company 1988, Collected Essays 1989, Windows 1990, Autobiography 1990, Echoes 1994, So There, Poems 1976–1983 1998, Life & Death 1998; Edited: New American Story (with Donald M. Allen) 1965, The New Writing in the USA (with Donald M. Allen) 1967, Selected Writings of Charles Olson 1967, Whitman: Selected Poems 1972, The Essential Burns 1989, Selected Poems (revised) 1991, Selected Poems of Charles Olson 1993, Tales out of School, Selected Interviews 1993, Echoes 1994, Life and Death 1998, I So There, poems 1976–83 1998, Day Book of a Virtual Poet 1998. *Address:* State University of New York at Buffalo, Clemens 313, Buffalo, NY 14260-0001, USA (Office). *Telephone:* (716) 645-2575 (Office). *E-mail:* creeley@acsu.buffalo.edu (Office).

CREMONA, Hon. John Joseph, K.M., LLD, DLitt, PhD, DJur; Maltese jurist, historian and writer; b. 6 Jan. 1918, Gozo; s. of Dr. Antonio Cremona and Anne Camilleri; m. Beatrice Barbaro Marchioness of St George 1949; one s. two d.; ed Malta, Rome, London, Cambridge and Trieste Univs.; Crown Counsel 1947; Lecturer in Constitutional Law, Royal Univ. of Malta 1947–65; Attorney Gen. 1957–64; Prof. of Criminal Law, Univ. of Malta 1959–65; Prof. Emer. 1965–; Pres. of Council 1972–75; Crown Advocate-Gen. 1964–65; Vice Pres. Constitutional Court and Court of Appeal 1965–71; Judge, European Court of Human Rights 1965–92, Vice-Pres. 1986–92; Pro-Chancellor, Univ. of Malta 1971–74; Chief Justice of Malta, Pres. of the Constitutional Court, the Court of Appeal and the Court of Criminal Appeal 1971–81; mem. UN Cttee on Elimination of Racial Discrimination 1984–88, Chair. 1986–88; Judge, European Tribunal in Matters of State Immunity 1986–92, Vice-Pres. 1986–92; fmr Acting Gov.-Gen., Acting Pres. of Malta; Chair. Human Rights Section, World Asscn of Lawyers; Chair. Public Broadcasting Services Ltd 1996–98; Pres. Malta Human Rights Asscn; Vice-Pres. Int. Inst. of Studies Documentation and Information for the Protection of the Environment 1980–; mem. Int. Inst. of Human Rights 1992; mem. Editorial Bd several human rights journals in Europe and America; Fellow, Royal Historical Soc.; Hon. Fellow, LSE; Hon. mem. Real Academia de Jurisprudencia y Legislación (Madrid); Kt of Magisterial Grace, Sovereign Mil. Order of Malta; Kt Grand Cross Order of Merit (Italy); Kt Grand Cross, Constantine St George; Kt Order of St Gregory the Great; Kt Most Venerable Order of St John of Jerusalem; Companion of the Nat. Order of Merit (Malta); Chevalier, Légion d'honneur. *Publications include:* The Treatment of Young Offenders in Malta 1956, The Malta Constitution of 1835 1959, The Legal Consequences of a Conviction in the Criminal Law of Malta 1962, The Constitutional Development of Malta 1963, From the Declaration of Rights to Independence 1965, Human Rights Documentation in Malta 1966, Selected Papers (1946–89) 1990, The Maltese Constitution and Constitutional History 1994, Malta and Britain: The Early Constitutions 1996; three volumes of poetry; articles in French, Italian, German, Portuguese and American law reviews. *Address:* Villa Barbaro, Main Street, Attard, Malta. *Telephone:* 440818.

CRÉPEAU, Paul-André, CC, OQ, QC, LPh, LLL, BCL, DenD; Canadian professor of law; b. 20 May 1926, Gravelbourg, Sask.; s. of J. B. Crépeau and Blanche Provencher; m. Nicole Thomas 1959; two s. one d.; ed Univs. of Ottawa, Montreal, Oxford and Paris; Pres. Civil Code Revision Office 1965–77; Prof. of Civil Law 1966–94, McGill Univ., Wainwright Chair. of Civil Law 1976–94; Dir Inst. of Comparative Law 1975–84, now Prof. Emer.; Dir Québec Research Centre of Private and Company Law 1975–96; Pres. Int. Acad. of Comparative Law 1990–98; LLD hc (Ottawa) 1971, (York) 1984, (Dalhousie) 1989, (Strasbourg) 1990, (Montréal) 1994; Chevalier Ordre nat. du Mérite (France) 2002; Kt, Order of St John, Jerusalem (Malta): Killam Award 1984–85, 1985–86; Gov. Gen. Prize for Law 1993. *Publications:* La responsabilité civile du médecin et de l'établissement hospitalier 1956, Rapport sur le Code civil 1978, Code civil, Edition historique et critique 1966–1980 1981, L'intensité de l'obligation juridique 1989, L'Affaire Daigle et la Cour Suprême du Canada ou la Méconnaissance de la tradition civiliste en Mélanges Brière 1993, Lecture du message législatif in Mélanges Beetz 1995, Abuse of Rights in the Civil Law of Quebec in Aequitas and Equity 1997, Les Principes d'Unidroit et le Code civil du Québec: Valeurs partagées? 1998, La Réforme du Droit civil canadien: une certaine conception de la Recodification 2001. *Leisure interests:* reading, gardening. *Address:* Québec Research Centre of Private and Comparative Law, 3647 Peel Street, Montréal, Qué. H3A 1X1 (Office); 5 Place du Vésinet, Montréal, Qué., H2V 2L6, Canada (Home). *Telephone:* (514) 398-2770 (Office); (514) 272-5941 (Home). *Fax:* (514) 398-7145.

CRESPIN, Régine; French soprano; b. 23 Feb. 1927, Marseilles; d. of Henri and Marguerite Crespin (née Meirone); m. Lou Bruder 1962; ed Conservatoire Nat. d'Art Dramatique; Singer, Opéra, Paris; has sung in prin. concert houses, Europe and America; Prof. of Music, Higher Nat. Conservatory of Music 1976–92; Commdr Légion d'honneur, Grand Officier Ordre national du Mérite, Commdr Ordre des Arts et Lettres. *Publication:* A la scène, à la ville (memoirs) 1997. *Address:* 3 avenue Frochot, 75009 Paris, France.

CRESSON, Edith; French politician; b. 27 Jan. 1934, Boulogne-sur-Seine; d. of Gabriel and Jacqueline Campion; m. Jacques Cresson 1959; two d.; Nat. Sec. Parti Socialiste; Youth Organizer, Parti Socialiste 1975; Mayor, Châtellerault 1983–97, Deputy Mayor 1997–; Gen. Counsellor Chatellerault-Ouest 1982–; mem. European Parl. 1979–81; Minister of Agric. 1981–83, of Foreign Trade and Tourism 1983–84, of Industrial Redeployment and Foreign Trade 1984–86, of European Affairs 1988–90; Prime Minister of France 1991–92; Pres. L'Association démocratique des français de l'étranger 1986; Pres. SISIE 1992–94; European Commr for Educ., Research, Science and Devt 1994–99; mem. Nat. Ass. for Vienne 1986–88; mem. Nat. Secr. Parti Socialiste 1987; Pres. Fondation des écoles de la deuxième chance 2002–; Dr hc (Weizmann Inst., Open Univ., UK); Chevalier Légion d'honneur. *Publication:* Avec le soleil 1976, Innover ou subir 1998. *Address:* 10 avenue George V, 75008 Paris (Office); Mairie, 86108 Châtellerault cedex, France.

CRESSWELL, Peter, PhD, FRS; British professor of immunobiology and biology; b. 6 March 1945; s. of Maurice Cresswell and Mary Cresswell; m. Ann K. Cooney 1969; two s.; ed Univ. of Newcastle, London Univ., Harvard Univ.; fmrly Chief Div. of Immunology, Duke Univ. Medical Center; Prof. of Immunobiology and Biology, investigator, Howard Hughes Medical Inst., Yale Univ. School of Medicine 1991–; research into mechanisms regulating generation of complexes of peptides with Major Histocompatability Complex (MHC) molecules, essential in the immune response. *Address:* Section of Immunobiology, Howard Hughes Medical Institute, Yale University School of Medicine, 333 Cedar Street, New Haven, CT 06520, USA (Office). *Telephone:* (203) 7855-176 (Office). *E-mail:* peter.cresswell@yale.edu. *Website:* info.med.yale.edu/ysm (Office).

CRETNEY, Stephen Michael, QC, MA, DCL, FBA; British professor of law; b. 25 Feb. 1936, Witney, Oxon.; s. of Fred Cretney and Winifred Cretney; m. Rev. Antonia L. Vanrenen 1973; two s.; ed Manchester Warehousemen and Clerks' Orphan Schools, Cheadle Hulme and Magdalen Coll., Oxford; Partner, Macfarlanes (Solicitors), London 1964–65; Lecturer, Kenya School of Law, Nairobi 1966–67, Southampton Univ. 1968–69; Fellow and Tutor in Law, Exeter Coll., Oxford 1969–78; mem. Law Comm. for England and Wales 1978–83; Prof. of Law (Dean of Faculty 1984–88), Univ. of Bristol 1984–93; Fellow All Souls Coll. Oxford 1993–2001, Emer. Fellow 2001–. *Publications:* Enduring Powers of Attorney (4th Edn) 1996, Principles of Family Law (7th Edn) 2002, Law, Law Reform and the Family 1998, Family Law (4th Edn) 2000, Family Law in the 20th Century: A History 2003. *Leisure interests:* cooking, taking snapshots. *Address:* All Souls College, Oxford, OX1 4AL (Office); The Rectory, 3 Drake's Farm, Peasemore, Berks., RG20 7DF, England (Home). *Telephone:* (1865) 279379 (Office); (1635) 248925 (Home). *Fax:* (1865) 279299 (Office); (1635) 248191 (Home). *E-mail:* stephen.cretney@all-souls.ox.ac.uk (Office); Smcretney@aol.com (Home).

CREWE, Albert Victor, PhD; American physicist and professor; b. 18 Feb. 1927, Bradford, England; s. of Wilfred and Edith Fish (née Lawrence) Crewe; m. Doreen Crewe; one s. three d.; ed Liverpool Univ.; Asst Lecturer, Liverpool Univ. 1950–52, lecturer 1952–53; Research Assoc. Chicago Univ. 1955–56, Asst Prof. of Physics 1956–59, Assoc. Prof. 1959–63; Dir Particle Accelerator Div., Argonne Nat. Lab. 1958–61, Dir 1961–67; Prof. Dept of Physics and Biophysics Enrico Fermi Inst. 1963–71, Univ. of Chicago 1963–71, Dean, Physical Sciences Div. 1971–81, William E. Wrather Distinguished Service Prof. 1977–96, Prof. Emer. 1996–; Pres. Orchid One Corpn 1987–90; constructed England's first diffusion cloud chamber with Dr W. H. Evans at Liverpool Univ.; directed construction of large magnetic spectrometer for Chicago Univ.'s synchrocyclotron; consultant Sweden, Argentina; directed much of design and construction of Argonne's Zero Gradient Synchrotron; as Dir Argonne Nat. Lab., developed relationships with U.S. Atomic Energy Comm., Argonne Univ. and Chicago Univ., expressed in Tripartite Agreement; invented the scanning transmission electron microscope; obtained first atom images 1971; Fellow, American Physical Soc., American Nuclear Soc.; mem. NAS, American Acad. of Arts and Sciences, Scientific Research Soc. for America, Electron Microscopy Soc. of America, Chicago Area Research and Devt Council (Chair. 1964), Gov.'s Science Advisory Cttee for State of Ill.; artist mem. Palette and Chisel Acad. of Fine Arts, Chicago; Hon. Fellow, Royal Microscopical Soc. 1984; Immigrant's Service League's Annual Award for Outstanding Achievement in the Field of Science 1962; "Industrial Research Man of the Year 1970"; Michelson Medal (Franklin Inst.) 1978; Ernst Abbe Award, New York Microscope Soc. 1979; Duddell Medal, Inst. of Physics, UK 1980; hon. degrees awarded by (Univ. of Missouri) 1972, (Lakeforest Coll.) 1972, (Elmhurst Coll.) 1973, (Univ. of Liverpool) 2001. *Art exhibitions:* Quadrangle Club (Univ. of Chicago) 1999, "Tactility", Aldo Castillo Gallery, Chicago 2000. *Leisure interests:* sculpture, painting. *Address:* Enrico Fermi Institute, University of Chicago, 5640 South Ellis Avenue, Chicago, IL 60637 (Office); 8 Summit Drive, Dune Acres, Chesterton, IN 46304, USA (Home). *Telephone:* (773) 702-7821 (Office); (219) 787-5018 (Home). *E-mail:* crewe@midway.uchicago.edu (Office); avdbc@attbi.com (Home).

CRICHTON, (John) Michael (pseudonym Jeffrey Hudson and John Lange, jt pseudonym with Douglas Crichton as Michael Douglas), AB, MD; American writer, film director and fmr physician; b. 23 Oct. 1942, Chicago; s. of John Henderson Crichton and Zula Miller; ed Harvard Univ., Harvard Medical School; Lecturer in anthropology Cambridge Univ. 1965; Post-Doctoral Fellow Salk Inst., La Jolla 1969–70; Visiting Writer MIT 1988; creator and co-exec. producer TV series ER 1994–; mem. Acad. of Motion Picture Arts and Sciences, Author's Guild, Writers' Guild of America, Bd of Trustees Western Behavioral Sciences Inst., La Jolla 1986–91, Bd of Overseers Harvard Univ. 1990–96, Author's Guild Council 1995–, Assn of American Medical Writers Award 1970, Acad. of Motion Pictures Arts and Sciences Tech. Achievement Award 1995, Writers' Guild of American Award 1995 and several others. *Films directed:* Pursuit, The Great Train Robbery, Coma, Looker, Runaway, Physical Evidence. *Publications:* (as Michael Douglas) Dealing: or, The Berkeley to Boston Forty-Brick Lost-Bag Blues 1972; (as Jeffrey Hudson) A Case of Need 1968, The Andromeda Strain 1969; (as John Lange) Odds On 1966, Scratch One 1967, Easy Go 1968, Zero Cool 1969, The Venom Business 1969, Drug of Choice 1970, Grave Descend 1970, Five Patients: The Hospital Explained 1970, Binary 1972, The Terminal Man 1972, Westworld (screenplay) 1973, The Great Train Robbery 1975, Eaters of the Dead 1976, Congo 1980, Looker (screenplay) 1981, Electronic Life: How to Think About Computers 1983, Runaway (screenplay) 1984, Sphere 1987, Travels 1988, Jurassic Park 1990, Rising Sun 1992, Disclosure 1994, Jasper Johns 1994, The Lost World 1995, The Terminal Man 1995, Airframe 1996, Timeline 1999. *Address:* Constant Productions, 2118 Wilshire Avenueblvd, #433, Santa Monica, CA 90403, USA.

CRICHTON-BROWN, Sir Robert, KCMG, CBE, TD; Australian business executive; b. 23 Aug. 1919, Melbourne; s. of late L. Crichton-Brown; m. Norah I. Turnbull 1941; one s. one d.; ed Sydney Grammar School; Man. Dir Security and Gen. Insurance Co. Ltd 1952; Chair. Security Life Assurances Ltd 1961–85, NEI Pacific Ltd 1961–85, Edward Lumley Ltd (Group), Australia 1974–89 (Man. Dir 1952–82, Dir 1989–), The Commercial Banking Co. of Sydney Ltd 1976–82, Commercial and General Acceptance Ltd 1977–82, Westham Dredging Co. Pty Ltd 1975–85, Rothmans of Pall Mall (Australia) Ltd 1981–85 (Exec. Chair. 1985–88); Vice-Chair. Nat. Australia Bank Ltd 1982–85, Custom Credit Corpn Ltd 1982–85; Dir Daily Mail & General Trust Ltd (UK) 1979–95, The Maritime Trust; Exec. Chair. Rothmans Int. PLC 1985–88; Underwriting mem. Lloyd's 1946–97; Dir Royal Prince Alfred Hosp. 1970–84; Fed. Pres. Inst. of Dirs. in Australia 1967–80; Fed. Hon. Treas. Liberal Party of Australia 1973–85; Nat. Co-ordinator, Duke of Edinburgh's Award Scheme in Australia 1980–85; mem. or official of numerous professional and charitable orgs. in Australia; mem. Australia's winning Admiral's Cup Team (Balandra) 1967; winner, Sydney-Hobart Yacht Race (Pacha) 1970. *Leisure interest:* sailing. *Address:* Edward Lumley Holdings Ltd, 99 Bishopsgate, London, EC2M 3XD, England (Office). *Telephone:* (20) 7588-3188 (Office). *Fax:* (20) 7588-3472 (Office).

CRICK, Francis Harry Compton, OM, FRS, PhD; British neuroscientist; b. 8 June 1916, Northampton; s. of late Harry Crick and Annie Elizabeth Wilkins; m. Odile Speed 1949; one s. (by previous marriage) two d.; ed Univ. Coll., London and Cambridge Univ.; Scientist, Admiralty, 1940–47; Medical Research Council (MRC) Student, Strangeways Lab. Cambridge 1947–49; MRC Lab. of Molecular Biology, Cambridge 1949–77; Kieckhefer Distinguished Research Prof., The Salk Inst., La Jolla, Calif. 1977–, Pres. 1994–95; Adjunct Prof. of Psychology, Univ. of Calif., San Diego; Fellow, Churchill Coll., Cambridge 1960–61, Hon. Fellow 1965; Fellow Univ. Coll., London 1962; Fellow AAAS 1966; Fellow, Indian Nat. Science Acad. 1982; Foreign Assoc. NAS 1969; Assoc. Académie Française 1978; mem. German Acad. of Science 1969; Foreign mem. American Phil. Soc., Philadelphia 1972; Hon. Fellow, Caius Coll., Cambridge 1976; Foreign Hon. mem. American Acad. of Arts and Sciences 1962; Hon. mem. American Soc. Biological Chem. 1963, Hellenic Biochemical and Biophysical Soc. 1974; Hon. MRIA 1964; Hon. FRSE 1966; Hon. Fellow Inst. of Biology 1995; Hon. Fellow Tata Inst. of Fundamental Research, Bombay 1996; Nobel Prize for Medicine (with J. D. Watson and M. H. F. Wilkins 1962; Royal Medal, Royal Soc. 1972; Copley Medal, Royal Soc. 1975, Michelson-Morley Award, Cleveland, USA 1981; numerous memorial lectures and other awards. *Publications:* Of Molecules and Men 1967, Life Itself 1981, What Mad Pursuit 1988, The Astonishing Hypothesis 1994; numerous papers and articles on molecular and cell biology and on neurobiology. *Leisure interests:* gardening, swimming. *Address:* The Salk Institute for Biological Studies, P.O. Box 85800, San Diego, CA 92186–5800 (Office); 1792 Colgate Circle, La Jolla, CA 92037, USA (Home).

CRICK, Ronald Pitts, FRCS, FRCOPHTH; British ophthalmic surgeon; b. 5 Feb. 1917, Toronto, Canada; s. of Owen John Pitts Crick and Margaret Daw; m. Jocelyn Mary Grenfell Robins 1941; four s. one d.; ed Latymer Upper School, London, King's Coll. Hosp. Medical School, London; surgeon, Merchant Navy 1939–40; Surgeon-Lt, RDVR 1940–46; Ophthalmic Registrar, King's Coll. Hosp. 1946–48; Surgical First Asst, Royal Eye Hosp., London 1947–50, Surgeon 1950–69; Ophthalmic Surgeon, Belgrave Hosp. for Children 1950–66; Ophthalmic Surgeon, King's Coll. Hosp. 1950–82, Hon. Ophthalmic Surgeon 1982–; Recognized Teacher in Ophthalmology, Univ. of London 1960–82, Lecturer Emer., School of Medicine and Dentistry, King's Coll. 1982–; Chair. Ophthalmic Training Cttee, SE Thames Regional Health Authority 1973–82; Fellow and Vice-Pres. Ophthalmology Section, Royal Soc. of Medicine 1964; Charter mem. Int. Glaucoma Congress of American Soc. of Contemporary Ophthalmology 1977–; f. Int. Glaucoma Asscn 1974, Chair. 1974–2000, Pres. 2000–; Co-Ed. Glaucoma Forum (quarterly journal); Open Science Scholarship, King's Coll. Hosp. Medical School 1934; Fellow Royal Coll. of Ophthalmologists; Sir Stewart Duke-Elder Glaucoma Award (Int. Glaucoma Congress) 1985; Alim Memorial Lecturer, Ophthalmological Soc. of Bangladesh 1991. *Publications:* All About Glaucoma (with W. Leydhecker) 1981, A Text Book of Clinical Ophthalmology (with with P. T. Khaw) 2002; numerous articles in ophthalmic books and journals. *Leisure interests:* natural history, motoring, sailing, designing ophthalmic instruments. *Address:* International Glaucoma Association, King's College Hospital, Denmark Hill, London, SE5 9RS (Office); 10 Golden Gates, Sandbanks, Poole, Dorset, BH13 7QN, England. *Telephone:* (20) 7737-3265 (Office); (1202) 707560 (Home). *Fax:* (20) 7346-5929 (Office); (1202) 701560 (Home). *E-mail:* info@iga.org.uk (Office). *Website:* www.iga.org.uk/home.htm (Office).

CRICKHOWELL, Baron (Life Peer), cr. 1987, of Pont Esgob in the Black Mountains and County of Powys; **(Roger) Nicholas Edwards,** PC, MA; British politician; b. 25 Feb. 1934; s. of late Ralph Edwards and Marjorie Ingham Brooke; m. Ankaret Healing 1963; one s. two d.; ed Westminster School, Trinity Coll., Cambridge; mem. Lloyd's 1965–2002; MP for Pembroke 1970–87; Opposition Spokesman on Welsh Affairs 1975–79; Sec. of State for Wales 1979–87; Chair. Nat. Rivers Authority 1989–96, ITNET PLC 1997–; Pres. Univ. of Wales, Cardiff 1988–98, Contemporary Art Soc. for Wales 1988–93; Dir HTV Ltd 1987–2002 (Chair. 1997–2002), Associated British Port Holdings PLC 1988–99; mem. Cttee Automobile Asscn 1997–98; mem. Conservative Party; Hon. LLD. *Publications:* Opera House Lottery 1997, Westminster, Wales and Water 1999. *Leisure interests:* gardening, fishing. *Address:* 4 Henning Street, London, SW11 3DR, England; Pont Esgob Mill, Fforest Coal Pit, Nr. Abergavenny, Mon., NP7 7LS, Wales.

CRISP, Sir (Edmund) Nigel (Ramsay), Kt, KCB, MA; British civil servant; b. 14 Jan. 1952; s. of Edmund Theodore Crisp and Dorothy Shephard Crisp (née Ramsay); m. Siân Elaine Jenkins 1976; one s. one d.; ed Uppingham School and St John's Coll., Cambridge; Deputy Dir Halewood Community Council 1973; Production Man. Trebor 1978; Dir Cambs. Community Council 1981; Unit Gen. Man. E. Berks. Health Authority 1986; Chief Exec. Heatherwood and Wexham Park Hosps 1988; Chief Exec. Oxford Radcliffe Hosps NHS Trust 1993–96; Regional Dir S. Thames 1977–98, London 1999–2000; Perm. Sec. Dept of Health and Chief Exec. NHS 2000–. *Leisure interest:* the countryside. *Address:* Richmond House, 79 Whitehall, London, SW1A 2NS, England (Office).

CRISTIANI BURKARD, Alfredo; Salvadorean politician and businessman; b. 1948; m. Margarita Cristiani; ed Georgetown Univ., Washington, DC, USA; fmr exec. in family pharmaceutical, coffee and cotton businesses; Leader, Republican Nationalist Alliance (ARENA) 1985; mem. Nat. Ass. 1988–; Pres. of El Salvador 1989–94. *Address:* National Assembly, San Salvador, El Salvador.

CROCKER, Chester Arthur, PhD; American government official; b. 29 Oct. 1941, New York; s. of Arthur Crocker and Clare Crocker; m. Saone Baron 1965; three d.; ed Ohio State Univ., Johns Hopkins Univ.; editorial asst Africa Report 1965–66, News Ed. 1968–69; lecturer American Univ. 1969–70; staff officer Nat. Security Council 1970–72; Dir Master of Science, Foreign Service Program, Georgetown Univ. 1972–78, Dir African Studies, Center for Strategic and Inst. Studies 1976–81; Asst Sec. of State for African Affairs 1981–89; James R. Schlesinger Prof. of Strategic Studies, Georgetown Univ. 1989–; Chair. African Working Group, Reagan Campaign 1980; Chair. Bd U.S. Inst. of Peace; Int. Consultant; mem. Bd Ashanti Goldfields, ASA Ltd, Nat. Defense Univ.; Presidential Citizen's Medal, Sec. of State's Distinguished Service Award. *Publications:* South Africa's Defense Posture 1982, South Africa into the 1980s 1979, High Noon in Southern Africa 1992, African Conflict Resolution 1995, Managing Global Chaos 1996, Herding Cats: Multiparty Mediation in a Complex World 1999, Turbulent Peace: The Challenges of Managing International Conflict 2001, and numerous articles. *Address:* Room 813, Intercultural Center, School of Foreign Service, Georgetown University, Washington, DC 20057, USA (Office). *Telephone:* (202) 687-5074 (Office). *Fax:* (202) 687-2315 (Office). *E-mail:* crockerc@georgetown.edu (Office).

CROCKER, Ryan C., BA; American diplomatist; b. 19 June 1949, Spokane, WA; s. of Carol Crocker; m. Christine Crocker; ed Whitman Coll. and Princeton Univ.; diplomatic positions in Iran 1972–74, Qatar 1974–76, Iraq 1978–80, Lebanon 1981–84; Deputy Dir Office of Arab-Israeli Affairs 1985–87; Political Counselor, American Embassy, Cairo 1987–90; Dir State Dept's Iraq–Kuwait Task Force Aug. 1990; Amb. to Lebanon 1990–93, to Kuwait 1994–97, to Syria 1998–; rank of Career Minister 1999; Presidential Distinguished Service Award 1994, Dept of Defense Medal for Distinguished Civilian Service 1997, Presidential Meritorious Service Award 1999, State Dept Award for Valor, Three Superior Honor Awards, American Foreign Service Asscn Rivkin Award. *Address:* American Embassy, BP 29, 2 rue al-Mansour, Damascus, Syria (Office). *Telephone:* (11) 3333232 (Office). *Fax:* (11) 2247938 (Office).

CROCKETT, Andrew Duncan, MA; British banker; b. 23 March 1943, Glasgow; s. of Andrew Crockett and Sheilah Stewart; m. Marjorie Hlavacek 1966; two s. one d.; ed Queens' Coll. Cambridge and Yale Univ.; with Bank of England 1966–72, Exec. Dir 1989–93; with IMF 1972–89; Gen. Man. BIS 1994–2003; Chair. Financial Stability Forum 1999–; Monetary Policy Adviser to IMF 2002–. *Publications:* Money: Theory, Policy, Institutions 1973, International Money: Issues and Analysis 1977; contribs. to professional journals. *Leisure interests:* reading, golf, tennis. *Address:* Bank for International Settlements, Centralbahnplatz 2, 4002 Basel, Switzerland. *Website:* www.bis.org (Office).

CROFF, Davide; Italian banker; b. 1 Oct. 1947; ed in Venice, Pembroke Coll. Oxford; Asst Prof. of Political Econ., Univ. of Padua 1971–72; Research Dept Officer Banca d'Italia, Rome 1974–79; Foreign and Financial Affairs Dept Fiat SpA, Turin 1979–83, in charge of Int. Treasury Dept 1982, Finance Man. 1983–86, Sr Vice-Pres. 1986–89; CEO Finance and Int., Banca Nazionale del Lavoro, Rome 1989–90, Man. Dir 1990–. *Address:* Banca Nazionale del Lavoro, Via Vittorio Veneto 119, 00187 Rome, Italy (Office). *Telephone:* (06) 47021 (Office). *Fax:* (06) 47027298 (Office). *E-mail:* press.bnl@bnl.it (Office). *Website:* www.bnl.it (Office).

CROHAM, Baron (Life Peer), cr. 1978, of the London Borough of Croydon; **Douglas Albert Vivian Allen,** GCB; British civil servant; b. 15 Dec. 1917, Surrey; s. of Albert Allen and Elsie Maria Allen (née Davies); m. Sybil Eileen Allegro 1941 (died 1994); two s. one d.; ed Wallington County Grammar School and London School of Econs; Asst Prin., Bd of Trade 1939; served Royal Artillery 1940–45; Prin., Bd of Trade 1945, Cabinet Office 1947, Treasury 1948; Asst Sec., Treasury 1949–58; Under-Sec., Ministry of Health 1958–60, Treasury 1960–62; Third Sec., Treasury 1962–64; Deputy Under-Sec. of State, Dept of Econ. Affairs 1964–66, Second Perm. Under-Sec. of State 1966, Perm. Under-Sec. of State 1966–68; Perm. Sec., Treasury 1968–74; Head Home Civil Service, Perm. Sec. Civil Service Dept 1974–77; Chair. Econ. Policy Cttee, OECD 1972–77, Deputy Chair. BNOC 1978–82, Chair. 1982–86; Adviser to Gov., Bank of England 1978–83; Dir (non-exec.) Pilkington PLC 1978–92; Trustee, Anglo-German Foundation 1977–, Chair. 1982–98; Pres. Inst. of Fiscal Studies 1978–92; Chair. Inst. of Man. Econ. and Social Affairs Cttee 1982–85, Trinity Insurance 1988–92; Dir (non-exec.) Guinness Peat Group 1983–87, Chair. 1983–86; Dir (non-exec.) Guinness Mahon and Co. Ltd 1989–92. *Leisure interests:* woodwork, bridge. *Address:* 9 Manor Way, South Croydon, Surrey, England (Home). *Telephone:* (20) 8688-0496 (Home).

CROMME, Gerhard, DJur; German business executive; b. 25 Feb. 1943, Vechta/Oldenburg; m.; four d.; ed Münster, Lausanne, Paris and Harvard Univs.; joined Compagnie de Saint-Gobain 1971, latterly Deputy Del.-Gen. for Fed. Repub. of Germany and Chair. Man. Dir. Man. Bd VEGLA/Vereinigte Glaswerke GmbH, Aachen; Chair. Man. Bd Krupp Stahl AG, Bochum 1986; mem. Exec. Bd Fried. Krupp GmbH, Essen 1988 (now Fried. Krupp AG Hoesch-Krupp), CEO 1989–99; CEO ThyssenKrupp AG 1999–2001, Chair. Supervisory Bd. 2001–; Chair. and mem. several supervisory bds. and advisory councils. *Address:* ThyssenKrupp AG, August-Thyssen Str. 1, 40211 Düsseldorf, Germany (Office). *Telephone:* (211) 824-0 (Office). *Fax:* (211) 824-36000 (Office).

CRONENBERG, David; Canadian film director; b. 15 March 1943, Toronto; ed Univ. of Toronto; has directed fillers and short dramas for TV. *Films include:* Stereo 1969, Crimes of the Future 1970, The Parasite Murders/Shivers 1974, Rabid 1976, Fast Company 1979, The Brood 1979, Scanners 1980, Videodrome 1982, The Dead Zone 1983, The Fly 1986, Dead Ringers 1988, The Naked Lunch 1991, eXistenZ 1998 (Silver Berlin Bear 1999), Spider 2002; directed: (shorts) Transfer 1966, From the Drain 1967; acted in Nightbreed 1990, The Naked Lunch (wrote screen-play), Trial by Jury, Henry and Verlin, To Die For 1995, Extreme Measures 1996, The Stupids 1996; Dir, writer, producer, actor Crash (Cannes Jury Special Prize 1997) 1996. *Publications:* Crash 1996, Cronenberg on Cronenberg 1996. *Address:* David Cronenberg Productions Ltd, 217 Avenue Road, Toronto, Ont., M5R 2J3, Canada; c/o John Burnham, William Morris Agency, 151 South El Camino Drive, Beverly Hills, CA 90212, USA.

CRONIN, Anthony; Irish author; b. 23 Dec. 1928, Co. Wexford; s. of John Cronin and Hannah Barron; m. Thérèse Campbell 1955; two d.; ed Blackrock Coll., Univ. Coll., Dublin and Kings Inns, Dublin; Assoc. Ed. The Bell 1952–54; Literary Ed. Time and Tide 1956–58; Visiting lecturer in English, Univ. of Montana, USA 1966–68; writer-in-residence, Drake Univ., Ia 1968–70; columnist, Irish Times 1973–80; cultural and artistic adviser to the Prime Minister of Ireland 1980–83, 1987–92; Martin Toonder Award for contrib. to Irish literature 1983. *Publications:* Poems 1958, The Life of Riley 1964, A Question of Modernity 1966, Dead as Doornails 1976, Identity Papers 1980, New and Selected Poems 1982, Heritage Now 1982, An Irish Eye 1985, No Laughing Matter, The Life and Times of Flann O'Brien 1989, The End of the Modern World 1989, Relationships 1994, Samuel Beckett: The Last Modernist 1996, The Minotaur and Other Poems 1999, Anthony Cronin's Personal Authology 2000. *Leisure interests:* reading, walking, travelling, watching horse-racing. *Address:* 30 Oakley Road, Dublin 6, Ireland. *Telephone:* 4970490. *Fax:* 4970490.

CRONIN, James Watson, PhD; American professor of physics; b. 29 Sept. 1931, Chicago, Ill.; s. of James Farley Cronin and Dorothy Watson Cronin; m. Annette Martin 1954; one s. two d.; ed Southern Methodist Univ., Univ. of Chicago; Nat. Science Foundation Fellow 1952–55; Assoc. Brookhaven Nat. Lab. 1955–58; Asst Prof. of Physics, Princeton Univ. 1958–62, Assoc. Prof.

1962–64, Prof. 1964–71; Prof. of Physics, Univ. of Chicago 1971–; Loeb Lecturer in Physics, Harvard Univ. 1976, lecturer Nashima Foundation 1993; mem. NAS, American Acad. of Arts and Sciences, American Physical Soc.; Hon. DSc (Leeds) 1996; Research Corpn Award 1968; Ernest O Lawrence Award 1977; John Price Wetherill Medal, Franklin Inst. 1975; shared Nobel Prize for Physics 1980 with Prof. Val Fitch (q.v.) for work on elementary particles; Nat. Medal of Science 1999. *Publications:* numerous articles on physics. *Address:* Enrico Fermi Institute, University of Chicago, 5630 South Ellis Avenue, Chicago, IL 60637 (Office); 5825 South Dorchester Avenue, Chicago, IL 60637, USA. *Telephone:* (312) 962-7102 (Office).

CRONKITE, Walter Leland, Jr; American television correspondent; b. 4 Nov. 1916, St Joseph, Missouri; s. of the late W. L. Cronkite and of Helene Fritsche; m. Mary Elizabeth Maxwell 1940; one s. two d.; ed Univ. of Texas; News writer and Editor, Scripps-Howard & United Press, Houston, Kansas City, Dallas, Austin, El Paso and New York; United Press War Corresp. 1942–45, later Foreign Corresp., Chief Corresp. Nuremberg War Crimes Trials, Bureau Man., Moscow 1946–48; lecturer 1948–49; CBS, news corresp. 1950–81; Anchorman and Man. Ed., CBS Evening News with Walter Cronkite 1962–81, CBS News Special Corresp. 1981–, mem. Bd of Dirs. CBS Inc.; Chair. The Cronkite Ward Co. 1993–; several hon. degrees; Emmy Award (several times), Acad. TV Arts and Sciences 1970, George Polk Journalism Award 1971, Jefferson Award 1981, Presidential Medal of Freedom 1981, George Foster Peabody Award 1981, Distinguished Service Award from the Nat. Asscn of Broadcasters 1982, Trustees' Award from the Nat. Acad. of Television Arts and Sciences 1982. *Television:* The Cronkite Reports (miniseries, Discovery Channel) 1994–96, Cronkite Remembers (mini-series, CBS and Discovery Channel) 1996. *Publications:* Eye on the World 1971, Challenges of Change 1971; co-author South by Southeast 1983, North by Northeast 1986, Westwind 1990, A Reporter's Life 1996, Around America 2001. *Leisure interest:* yachting. *Address:* c/o CBS Inc., 51 West 52nd Street, New York, NY 10019, USA.

CRONYN, Hume, OC; Canadian actor and director; b. 18 July 1911, London, Ont.; s. of Hume Blake and Frances A. Cronyn (née Labatt); m. Jessica Tandy 1942 (died 1994); one s. two d.; ed Ridley Coll., St Catharine's, Ont., McGill Univ., New York School of Theatre, Mozarteum, Salzburg and American Acad. of Dramatic Art, New York; after amateur experience with an acting group in Montréal, joined Cochran's Stock Co., Wash., DC; professional début in Up Pops the Devil 1931; made first film, Shadow of a Doubt 1943; Dir several Actor's Lab. productions 1946–57; staged (with Norman Lloyd) and co-starred in Phoenix Theatre's production Madam Will You Walk 1953; staged successful production of The Fourposter 1952, on tour 1951–53; inaugurated NBC radio series The Marriage 1953; has appeared in numerous plays and has toured extensively with his productions; has appeared in many maj. U.S. TV drama series; TV films include To Dance With the White Dog 1993, Alone 1996, Twelve Angry Men 1997, Sea People 1998; mem. Bd Dirs. Stratford Festival (first actor) 1978; nominated for Acad. Award for performance in The Seventh Cross 1944; Hon. LLD (Univ. of Western Ont.) 1974; Comoedia Matinee Club's Award for The Fourposter 1952, American Theatre Wings' Antoinette Perry Play Award (The Fourposter) 1952, Barter Theatre Award 1961, Delia Austria Medal, New York Drama League (Big Fish Little Fish) 1961, Antoinette Perry (Tony) Award and won Variety New York Drama Critics Poll for Polonius (Hamlet) 1964, Herald Theater Award for Tobias (A Delicate Balance), LA Drama Critics Circle Award for Best Actor (Caine Mutiny Court Martial) 1972, 1972–73 Obie Award (Krapp's Last Tape), Brandeis Univ. Creative Arts Awards for distinguished achievement 1978, LA Critics' Award (Gin Game) 1979, elected to American Hall of Fame 1979, Kennedy Center Honor 1986, Nat. Medal Arts 1990; Antoinette Perry Lifetime Achievement Award (with Jessica Tandy) 1994. *Films include:* Cleopatra 1963, Rollover 1981, Garp 1981, Impulse 1983, Cocoon 1985, Batteries Not Included 1987, Age Old Friends 1990, Cocoon: The Return, The Pelican Brief 1994, Camilla, Marvin's Room 1996, Alone 1999. *Publications:* A Terrible Liar (autobiog.) 1991, Birdhouse Contributions (poetry) 1993, Voices of Oppression (jtly.) 1995. *Address:* ICM Samuel L. Cohn, 40 West 57th Street, New York, NY 10019 (Office); 63–23 Carlton Street, Rego Park, New York, NY 11374, USA.

CROSBIE, John Carnell, PC, OC, QC, BA, LLB; Canadian politician; b. 30 Jan. 1931, St John's, Newfoundland; s. of Chesley A. Crosbie and Jessie (Carnell) Crosbie; m. Jane Furneaux; two s. one d.; ed St Andrew's Coll., Aurora, Ont., Queen's Univ., Ont., Dalhousie Law School, Univ. of London, LSE; called to Newfoundland Bar 1957; Prov. Minister of Municipal Affairs and Housing 1966, mem. Newfoundland House of Ass. 1966, 1971–76; Minister of Finance, Econ. Devt, Fisheries, Inter-Govt Affairs, Mines and Energy and Pres. of the Treasury Bd, Leader of House of Ass. 1975; mem. House of Commons 1976–93; Minister of Finance 1979, of Justice and Attorney-Gen. of Canada 1984–86, of Transport 1986–89, of Int. Trade 1989–91, of Fisheries and Oceans and the Atlantic Canada Opportunities Agency 1991–93; Counsel to Patterson Palmer Hunt Murphy 1994–; Chancellor Memorial Univ. of Newfoundland 1994–; Dir Bell Canada Int., Atlantic Inst. of Market Studies and other Canadian corpns.; Hon. Consul of Mexico to Newfoundland and Labrador 1996–; mem. Progressive Conservative Party; Officer of Order of Canada 1998. *Publication:* No Holds Barred 1997. *Leisure interests:* reading, tennis, salmon and trout fishing. *Address:* Scotia Centre, 235 Water Street, P.O. Box 610, St John's, Newfoundland, A1C 5L3 (Office); P.O. Box 23119, St John's, Newfoundland, A1B 4J9, Canada (Home). *Telephone:* (709) 7266124 (Office);

(709) 8953308 (Home). *Fax:* (709) 7220483 (Office); (709) 8953343 (Home). *E-mail:* jcrosbie@pattersonpalmer.ca (Office); jane.crosbie@hf.sympatico.ca (Home). *Website:* www.pattersonpalmer.ca (Office).

CROSBY, James Robert; British business executive; b. 14 March 1956; m.; four c.; ed Lancaster Royal Grammar School and Brasenose Coll., Oxford; joined Scottish Amicable 1977, Investment Dir, Fund Man. 1983–, later Gen. Man.–1994; Man. Dir Halifax Life 1994–96, Financial Services and Insurance Dir Halifax PLC 1996–99, CEO Halifax Group PLC Jan. 1999–, Group CEO HBOS PLC (after merger of Halifax PLC and Bank of Scotland) 2001–; Fellow, Faculty of Actuaries (FFA) 1980. *Address:* HBOS PLC, PO Box 5, The Mound, Edinburgh, EH1 1YZ, Scotland (Office). *Website:* www.hbosplc.com (Office).

CROSS, George Alan Martin, PhD, FRS; British professor of molecular parasitology; b. 27 Sept. 1942, Cheshire; s. of George Bernard Cross and Beatrice Mary Cross (née Horton); one d.; ed Cheadle Hulme School, Downing Coll. Cambridge; Scientist, Biochemical Parasitology, MRC 1969–77; Head, Dept of Immunochem. and Molecular Biology, Wellcome Foundation Research Labs. 1977–82; André and Bella Meyer Prof. of Molecular Parasitology, Rockefeller Univ. 1982–, Dean Grad. and Postgrad. Studies 1995–99; Leeuwenhoek Lecturer, The Royal Soc. 1998; Fleming Prize, Soc. for Gen. Microbiology 1978, Chalmers Medal, Royal Soc. of Tropical Medicine and Hygiene 1983, Paul Ehrlich and Ludwig Darmstaedter Prize 1984. *Leisure interests:* sailing, tennis. *Address:* The Rockefeller University, 1230 York Avenue, New York, NY 10021, USA. *Telephone:* (212) 327-7571. *Fax:* (212) 327-7845. *E-mail:* george.cross@rockefeller.edu (Office). *Website:* tryps .rockefeller.edu (Office).

CROSSLAND, Sir Bernard, Kt, CBE, DSc, MRIA, FEng, FRS; British professor of mechanical engineering; b. 20 Oct. 1923, Sydenham; s. of Reginald F. Crossland and Kathleen M. Crossland (née Rudduck); m. Audrey Elliot Birks 1946; two d.; ed Simon Langton's Grammar School, Derby Tech. Coll. and Nottingham Univ. Coll.; eng apprentice, Rolls-Royce, Derby 1940–41, Tech. Asst 1943–45; Asst Lecturer, Lecturer, Sr Lecturer in Mech. Eng, Univ. of Bristol 1946–59; Prof. and Head, Dept of Mechanical and Industrial Eng, Queen's Univ., Belfast 1959–82, Dean, Faculty of Eng 1964–67, Pro-Vice–Chancellor 1978–82, Special Research Prof. 1982–84, Emer. Prof. 1984–; Consulting Engineer 1984–; Chair., N Ireland Manpower Council 1981–86; Pres. Inst. of Mechanical Engineers 1986–87, Past Pres. 1987–91; Pres. The Welding Inst. 1995–98; mem. Industrial Devt Bd for N Ireland 1982–87, N Ireland Econ. Council 1981–85; mem. Agricultural and Food Research Council 1981–87, Engineering Council 1983–88; Chair. Postgrad. Advisory Bd to Dept of Educ. for N Ireland 1982–95, Bd for Engineers Registration 1983–86, Hazards Forum 1991–93, Bilsthorpe Colliery Accident Public Hearing 1994; Non-exec. Dir Gilbert Assocs. (Europe) Ltd 1991–94; Assessor of King's Cross Underground Fire Investigation; Founder Fellow Irish Acad. of Eng 1998; Thomas Lowe Gray Lecture, Inst. of Mechanical Eng 1999; Hon. mem. ASME; Hon. Fellow Welding Inst., Inst. of Engineers of Ireland, Inst. of Mechanical Engineers, Inst. of Structural Engineers; Hon. DSc (Ireland) 1984, (Dublin) 1985, (Edin.) 1987, (Aston) 1988, (Queen's Univ., Belfast) 1988, (Cranfield Inst. of Tech.) 1989, Hon. D. Eng (Bristol) 1992, (Limerick) 1993, (Liverpool) 1993; Hon. Fellowship (Univ. of Luton) 1994; George Stephenson Research Prize and Thomas Hawksley Gold Medal of Inst. of Mech. Eng, Kelvin Medal of Inst. of Civil Eng 1992, James Watt Int. Medal, Inst. of Mech. Eng 1999, Cunningham Medal, Royal Irish Acad. 2001. *Publications:* An Introduction to Mechanics of Machines 1964, Explosive Welding of Metals 1982, Industry's Needs in the Education and Training of Engineers (report); numerous papers on high-pressure eng and explosive welding in int. journals. *Leisure interests:* walking, reading, travel. *Address:* The Queen's University, Belfast, BT7 1NN (Office); 16 Malone Court, Belfast, BT9 6PA, Northern Ireland (Home). *Telephone:* (28) 9038-0860 (Office); (28) 9066-7495 (Home). *Fax:* (28) 9038-1753 (Office).

CROSSLEY, Paul Christopher Richard, CBE, MA; British concert pianist and music director; b. 17 May 1944, Dewsbury; s. of the late Frank Crossley and Myra Crossley (née Barrowcliffe); ed Silcoates School, Wakefield, Mansfield Coll.; has performed all over world as concert pianist; Artistic Dir London Sinfonietta 1988–94; Hon. Fellow Mansfield Coll., Oxford 1991; 15 maj. films on twentieth-century composers. *Recordings include:* Liszt: A Recital 1983, Adams: Eros Piano 1991, Debussy: Complete Piano Music 1993, Lutoslawski: Piano Concert 1995, Takemitsu: Quotation of Dream 1998, Takemitsu: Complete Piano Music 2000. *Leisure interests:* reading and mahjong. *Address:* c/o Connaught Artists Management, 2 Molasses Row, Plantation Wharf, London, SW11 3UX, England (Office). *Telephone:* (20) 7738-0017 (Office). *Fax:* (20) 7738-0909 (Office). *E-mail:* classicalmusic@ connaughtartists.com (Office).

CROWE, Cameron; American film director and screenplay writer; b. 13 July 1957, Palm Springs, Calif.; ed California State Univ., San Diego; writer Rolling Stone magazine. *Screenplays include:* Fast Times at Ridgemont High 1982, The Wild Life (also co-producer) 1984, Say Anything (also Dir) 1989, Singles (also Dir) 1992; Dir, producer Jerry Maguire 1996, Almost Famous 2000, Vanilla Sky 2001; acted in American Hot Wax 1978; creative consultant on TV series Fast Times 1986. *Address:* c/o Columbia Tristar, 10202 Washington Boulevard, Culver City, CA 90232, USA (Office).

CROWE, Martin David, MBE; New Zealand cricketer; b. 22 Sept. 1962, Auckland; s. of David Crowe and Audrey Crowe; m. Simone Curtice 1991 (separated 1996); ed Auckland Grammar School; right-hand batsman, slip fielder; played for Auckland 1979–80 to 1982–83, Cen. Dists. 1983–84 to 1989–90 (Capt. 1984–85 to 1989–90), Somerset 1984–88, Wellington 1990–91 to 1994–95 (Capt. 1993–94); played in 77 Tests for NZ 1981–82 to 1995–96, 16 as Capt., scoring 5,444 runs (average 45.36) with 17 hundreds, including NZ record 299 v. Sri Lanka, Wellington, Feb. 1991); scored 19,608 first-class runs (71 hundreds); toured England 1983, 1986, 1990 and 1994; 143 limited-overs internationals; Exec. Producer Sky TV cricket broadcasts; Wisden Cricketer of the Year 1985, NZ Sportsman of the Year 1991; selected World Cup Champion Cricketer 1992. *Publication:* Out on a Limb 1996. *Leisure interests:* tennis, golf, wine. *Address:* P.O. Box 109302, Newmarket, Auckland, New Zealand.

CROWE, Russell; New Zealand actor; b. 7 April 1964; m. Danielle Spencer 2003; Variety Club Award (Australia) 1993, Film Critics Circle Award 1993, Best Actor Seattle Int. Film Festival 1993, Man. Film and TV Awards, Motion Pictures Exhibitors Asscn 1993, LA Film Critics Asscn 1999, Nat. Bd of Review 1999, Nat. Soc. of Film Critics 1999, Acad. Award for Best Actor 2000. *Films include:* The Crossing 1993, The Quick and the Dead 1995, Romper Stomper 1995, Rough Magic 1995, Virtuosity 1995, Under the Gun 1995, Heaven's Burning 1997, Breaking Up 1997, LA Confidential 1997, Mystery Alaska 1999, The Insider 1999, Gladiator 2000, Proof of Life 2000, A Beautiful Mind (Golden Globe, BAFTA Award and Screen Actors' Guild Award for Best Actor) 2001. *Address:* ICM, 8942 Wilshire blvd, Beverly Hills, CA 90211, USA (Office); c/o Bedford & Pearke Management Ltd, PO Box 171, Cameray, NSW 2062, Australia.

CROZIER, Adam Alexander, BA; British business executive; b. 26 Jan. 1964; s. of Robert Crozier and Elinor Crozier; m. Annette Edwards 1994; two d.; ed Heriot-Watt Univ., Edin.; with Pedigree Petfoods, Mars (UK) Ltd 1984–86; with Daily Telegraph 1986–88; joined Saatchi & Saatchi 1988, Dir 1990, Media Dir 1992, Vice-Chair. 1994, Jt Chief Exec. 1995–99; Chief Exec. Football Asscn 2000–02; Chief Exec. Royal Mail Group 2003–. *Leisure interests:* football, golf, his children. *Address:* Royal Mail Group PLC, 148 Old Street, London, EC1V 9HQ, England (Office). *Website:* www.royalmailgroup .com (Office).

CROZIER, Brian Rossiter (John Rossiter); British writer and journalist; b. 4 Aug. 1918, Kuridala, Queensland, Australia; s. of R. H. Crozier and Elsa (McGillivray) Crozier; m. 1st Mary Lillian Samuel 1940 (died 1993); one s. three d.; m. 2nd Jacqueline Marie Mitchell 1999; ed Lycée, Montpellier, Peterborough Coll., Harrow, Trinity Coll. of Music, London; music and art critic, London 1936–39; reporter and sub-ed., Stoke On Trent, Stockport, London 1940–41; aeronautical inspection 1941–43; sub-ed., Reuters 1943–44, News Chronicle 1944–48, sub-ed. and writer Sydney Morning Herald, Australia 1948–51; corresp., Reuters-AAP 1951–52; features ed., Straits Times, Singapore 1952–53; leader writer and corresp., The Economist 1954–64; BBC commentator, English, French and Spanish overseas services 1954–66, Chair. Forum World Features 1965–74; Ed., Conflict Studies 1970–75; Co-founder and Dir Inst. for the Study of Conflict 1970–79, Consultant 1979–; Columnist, Now!, London 1980–81, Nat. Review, New York 1978–90 (contributing ed. 1982–), The Times 1982–84, The Free Nation, London 1982–89; Adjunct Scholar, The Heritage Foundation 1983–95; Distinguished Visiting Fellow, Hoover Inst., Stanford, Calif., USA 1996–2001. *Art Exhibitions:* London 1948, Sydney 1949–50. *Publications:* The Rebels 1960, The Morning After 1963, Neo-Colonialism 1964, South-East Asia in Turmoil 1965, The Struggle for the Third World 1966, Franco 1967, The Masters of Power 1969, The Future of Communist Power (in U.S.A.: Since Stalin) 1970, De Gaulle (vol. I) 1973, (vol. II) 1974, A Theory of Conflict 1974, The Man Who Lost China (Chiang Kai-shek) 1977, Strategy of Survival 1978, The Minimum State 1979, Franco: Crepúsculo de un hombre 1980, The Price of Peace 1980, Socialism Explained (co-author) 1984, This War Called Peace (co-author) 1984, The Andropov Deception (novel) (under pseudonym John Rossiter) 1984, The Grenada Documents (ed.) 1987, Socialism: Dream and Reality 1987, The Gorbachev Phenomenon 1990, Communism: Why Prolong its Death Throes? 1990, Free Agent: The Unseen War 1993, The KGB Lawsuits 1995, Le Phénix rouge (co-author) 1995, The Rise and Fall of the Soviet Empire 1999 and contribs to journals in numerous countries. *Leisure interests:* taping stereo, piano. *Address:* 18 Wickliffe Avenue, Finchley, London, N3 3EJ, England (Home). *Telephone:* (20) 8346-8124 (Home). *Fax:* (20) 8346-4599.

CRUICKSHANK, Donald Gordon, MBA, LLD, CA; British government official and financial administrator; b. 17 Sept. 1942; s. of Donald C. Cruick-shank and Margaret Morrison; m. Elizabeth B. Taylor 1964; one s. one d.; ed Univ. of Aberdeen and Manchester Business School; consultant, McKinsey & Co. 1972–77; Gen. Man. Sunday Times, Times Newspapers 1977–80; Pearson PLC 1980–84; Man. Dir Virgin Group 1984–89; Chair. Wandsworth Health Authority 1986–89; Chief Exec. Nat. Health Service in Scotland 1989–93; Dir-Gen. of Telecommunications 1993–98; Chair. Action 2000 1997–2000; Chair. UK Banking Review 1998–2000; Chair. SMG PLC 1999–, London Stock Exchange 2000–03. *Leisure interests:* sport, golf, opera. *Address:* SMG PLC, 200 Renfield Street, Glasgow, G2 3PR, England. *Telephone:* (141) 300-3300. *Website:* www.smg.plc.uk (Office).

CRUISE, Tom (Thomas Cruise Mapother IV); American actor; b. 3 July 1962, Syracuse, NY; m. 1st Mimi Rogers 1987 (divorced 1990); m. 2nd Nicole Kidman 1990 (divorced 2001); one adopted d. one adopted s. *Films include:* Endless Love 1981, Taps 1981, All the Right Moves 1983, Losin' It 1983, The Outsiders 1983, Risky Business 1983, Legend 1984, Top Gun 1985, The Color

of Money 1986, Rain Man 1988, Cocktail 1989, Born on the Fourth of July 1989, Daytona, Rush, Days of Thunder 1990, Sure as the Moon 1991, Far and Away 1992, A Few Good Men 1992, The Firm 1993, Interview with the Vampire 1994, Jerry Maguire 1996, Mission Impossible 1996, Eyes Wide Shut 1997, Magnolia 1999 (Golden Globe 2000), Mission Impossible 2 (also producer) 2000, Vanilla Sky (also producer) 2001, Minority Report 2002, Space Station 3D (voice) 2002; producer Without Limits 1998. *Address:* C/W Productions, c/o Paramount Studios, 5555 Melrose Avenue, Hollywood, CA 90038, USA (Office).

CRUMB, George, BM, MM, DMA; American composer; b. 24 Oct. 1929, Charleston, W Va; s. of George Henry and Vivian Reed; m. Elizabeth Brown 1949; two s. one d.; ed Mason Coll. of Music, Univ. of Illinois, Univ. of Michigan, Hochschule für Musik (Berlin); Prof., Univ. of Colorado 1959–63; Creative Assoc., State Univ. of New York at Buffalo 1963–64; Prof., Univ. of Pa 1971–, Annenberg Prof. 1983–; Pulitzer Prize for Music 1968, Koussevitsky Int. Recording Award 1971, Prince Pierre de Monaco Prize 1989, Edward MacDowell Colony Medal, Peterborough 1995. *Publications:* Ancient Voices of Children, Black Angels, Eleven Echoes of Autumn, 1965, Songs, Drones and Refrains of Death, Makrokosmos Vols I–III, Music for a Summer Evening, Five Pieces for Piano, Night of the Four Moons, Night Music I, Echoes of Time and the River, Four Nocturnes, Star-child, Dream Sequence, Celestial Mechanics, Apparition, A Little Suite for Christmas 1979, Gnomic Variations, Pastoral Drone, Processional, A Haunted Landscape, The Sleeper, An Idyll for the Misbegotten, Federico's Little Songs for Children, Zeitgeist, Easter Dawning for Carillon, Eine Kleine Mitternachtmusik 2002, Unto the Hills 2002, Otherworldly Resonances 2002. *Leisure interest:* reading. *Address:* Music Building, University of Pennsylvania, PA 19104 (Office); 240 Kirk Lane, Media, PA 19063, USA. *Telephone:* (215) 565-2438.

CRUMPTON, Michael Joseph, CBE, PhD, FRS, FMedSci; British biochemist and immunologist; b. 7 June 1929; s. of Charles E. Crumpton and Edith Crumpton; m. Janet Elizabeth Dean 1960; one s. two d.; ed Poole Grammar School, Univ. Coll., Southampton and Lister Inst. of Preventive Medicine, London; joined scientific staff Microbiological Research Establishment, Porton, Wilts. 1955–60; Deputy Dir Research Labs., Imperial Cancer Research Fund Labs., London 1979–91, Dir 1991–93; Dir Imperial Cancer Research Tech. Ltd 1989–99 (COO 1993–94); Visiting Scientist Fellowship, Nat. Insts. of Health, Bethesda, Md, USA 1959–60; Research Fellow, Dept of Immunology, St Mary's Hosp. Medical School, London 1960–66; mem. scientific staff Nat. Inst. for Medical Research, Mill Hill 1966–79, Head of Biochemistry Div. 1976–79; Visiting Fellow, John Curtin School for Medical Research, Australian Nat. Univ., Canberra 1973–74; mem. Cell Bd MRC 1979–83, Science Council, Celltech Ltd 1980–90, EMBO 1982–, WHO Steering Cttee for Encapsulated Bacteria 1984–91 (Chair. 1988–91), Sloan Cttee Gen. Motors Research Foundation 1986–88 (Chair. 1988), Council Royal Inst. 1986–90 (mem. Davy Faraday Lab. Comm. 1985–90, Chair. 1988–90), MRC 1986–90, Royal Soc. 1990–92, Scientific Advisory Comm., Lister Inst. 1986–91, MRC AIDS Directed Prog. Steering Cttee 1987–91, Scientific Cttee Swiss Inst. for Experimental Cancer Research 1989–96; Chair. Scientific Advisory Bd Biomedical Research Centre, Univ. of British Columbia 1987–91, Health and Safety Exec., Dept of Health Advisory Comm. on Dangerous Pathogens 1991–99; Dir (non-exec.) Amersham Int. PLC 1990–97, Amersham Pharmacia Biotech Ltd 1997–2001, Amersham Pharmacia Biotech Inc. 2001–; mem. Governing Body British Postgraduate Medical Foundation 1987–95, Academia Europaea 1996–, Governing Body Imperial Coll. 1994; mem. numerous Editorial Bds.; Hon. Fellow Royal Coll. of Pathologists; Hon. mem. American Association of Immunology 1995; Biochemistry Soc. Visiting Lecturer, Australia 1983; Trustee EMF Biological Research Trust 1995–, Breakthrough Breast Cancer 1997–. *Publications:* numerous scientific papers. *Leisure interests:* gardening, reading. *Address:* 33 Homefield Road, Radlett, Herts., WD7 8PX, England. *Telephone:* (1923) 854675. *Fax:* (1923) 853866.

CRUTZEN, Paul Josef; Netherlands professor of atmospheric chemistry; b. 1933, Amsterdam; s. of the late Josef Crutzen and Anna Crutzen; m.; three d.; ed Stockholm Univ.; fmr Dir Atmospheric Chemistry Div. Max-Planck Inst. for Chem.; now with Scripps Inst. of Oceanography, Univ. of Calif. at San Diego; mem. Swedish Acad. of Sciences, Royal Swedish Acad. of Eng Sciences, Academia Europaea; Foreign Assoc. mem. NAS; shared Nobel Prize in Chem. 1995; German Environmental Prize 1994, Tyler Environment Prize, Volvo Environmental Prize. *Publications include:* Atmospheric Change; An Earth System Perspective (with T.E. Graedel) 1993. *Address:* Max-Planck Institute for Chemistry, Jon.-Joachim-Becher-Weg 27, 55128 Mainz (Office); Am Fort Gonsenheim 36, 55122 Mainz, Germany (Home); (6131) 305333 (Office); (6131) 381094 (Home). *Fax:* (6131) 305577. *E-mail:* air@mpch-mainz.mpgde (Office).

CRUYFF, Johan; Netherlands footballer and professional football manager; b. 25 April 1947, Amsterdam; one s.; played for Ajax 1964–73; top scorer in Dutch League, with 33 goals 1967; capped 48 times, scored 33 int. goals and captained Netherlands 1974 World Cup final; retd 1978; started playing again, signed for Los Angeles Aztecs; played for Washington Diplomats 1979–80, for Levante, Spain 1981, then for Ajax and Feyenoord 1982; Man. Ajax 1985–87, winning European Cup Winners' Cup 1987; Man. Barcelona, winning Cup Winners' Cup 1989, European Cup 1992, Spanish League title

1991, 1992, 1993, Spanish Super Cup 1992; left Barcelona in 1996; f. Cruyff Foundation (for disabled sportspeople), Johan Cruyff Univ. (to assist retd sportspeople) 1998; European Footballer of the Year 1971, 1973–74.

CRUZ, Celia; Cuban singer; b. 21 Oct. 1929, Havana; d. of Simón Cruz and Catalina Alfonso; m. Pedro Knight 1962; performed salsa music with various artists including: La Sonora Matancera, Ray Barretto, Willie Colón and Tito Puente; Grammy award for Latin Tropical Performance (with Ray Barretto) 1974; Nat. Medal of Arts 1994. *Films:* Salsa 1988, Fires Within 1991, The Mambo Kings 1992, The Perez Family 1995, Damas del Swing, Las 1997, Alma no tiene color, El 1997, Yo Soy, del Son a la Salsa 1997. *Television includes:* The 1997, Summer Video Jams 1999.

CRUZ, Penélope; Spanish actress; b. 28 April 1974, Madrid; d. of Eduardo and Encarna Cruz Sánchez; ed National Conservatory, Madrid. *Films:* Live Flesh, Belle Epoque 1992, Jamón, Jamón 1992, La Celestina 1996, Open Your Eyes 1997, The Hi-Lo Country 1998, Talk of Angels 1998, The Girl of Your Dreams (Goya Award) 1998, All About My Mother 1999, Woman on Top 1999, All the Pretty Horses 2000, Captain Corelli's Mandolin 2001, Blow 2001, Vanilla Sky 2001, Fanfan La Tulipe 2003. *Address:* c/o Pedro Almodóvar, El Deseo SA, Ruiz Perelo 15, Madrid 28028, Spain (Office).

CRUZ-DIEZ, Carlos; Venezuelan painter; b. 17 Aug. 1923; ed School of Plastic and Applied Arts, Caracas; Dir of Art. Venezuelan subsidiary of McCann-Erickson Advertising Agency 1946–51; Teacher, History of Applied Arts, School of Arts, Caracas 1953–55; in Barcelona and Paris working on physical qualities of colour now named Physichromies 1955–56; opened studio of visual arts and industrial design, Caracas 1957; Prof. and Asst Dir School of Arts, Caracas 1959–60; moved to Paris 1960; Pres. for Life Carlos Cruz-Diez Museum of Print and Design Foundation, Caracas; First one-man exhbn, Caracas 1947, later in Madrid, Genoa, Turin, London, Paris, Cologne, Munich, Oslo, Brussels, Ostwald Museum, Dortmund, Bottrop (Fed. Repub. of Germany), New York, Bogotá, Rome, Venice and Essen; Retrospective exhbns at Signals, London and Galerie Kerchache, Paris 1965, Galerie Denise René, Paris 1994, Städtisches Museum, Gelsenkirchen, Museo de Arte Moderno, Bogotá and Museo de Arte Moderno J. Soto, Ciudad Bolívar 1998, represented at numerous group exhbns; works exhibited in Museo de Bellas Artes, Caracas, Victoria and Albert Museum, Tate Gallery, London, Casa de las Américas, Havana, Städtisches Museum, Leverkusen, Germany, Museum of Modern Art, NY, Museum of Contemporary Art, Montréal, Museum des 20. Jahrhunderts, Vienna, Univ. of Dublin, Museo Civico di Torino, Wallraf-Richartz Museum, Cologne, Musée de Grenoble, Centre Georges Pompidou, Musée d'Art Moderne, Paris, Neue Pinakothek, Munich; Grand Prix at 3rd Biennale, Córdoba, Argentina; Prix Int. de Peinture à la IX Biennale de São Paulo; Orden Andres Bello (Venezuela) 1981; Officier des Arts et des Lettres (France) 1985. *Publications:* My Reflection on Colour 1989, Interactive Random Chromatic Experience (software) 1995. *Address:* 23 rue Pierre Semard, 75009 Paris, France. *E-mail:* carlos@cruz-diez.com (Office). *Website:* www.cruz-diez.com (Office).

CRVENKOVSKI, Branko; Macedonian politician and engineer; b. 12 Oct. 1962, Sarajevo; m.; one s. one d.; ed Skopje Univ.; computer engineer SEMOS Co. 1987–90; Chair. Social-Democratic Union of Macedonia (SDUM) 1990–92, Pres. 1991–; Chair. Cabinet of Ministers (Prime Minister) Repub. of Macedonia 1992–98, 2002–. *Address:* Office of the Prime Minister, Ilindenska bb, 1000 Skopje (Office); Bihačka 8, 1000 Skopje, Macedonia. *Telephone:* (2) 115389 (Office). *Fax:* (2) 112561 (Office). *E-mail:* office@primeminister.gov .mk (Office). *Website:* www.primeminister.gov.mk (Office).

CRVENKOVSKI, Stevo; Macedonian politician and film director; b. 18 March 1947, Skopje; ed Acad. of Theatre, Film, Radio and TV, Belgrade; film Dir Vardarstudio (Skopje), later concurrently Dir 1970–92; in independence movt since 1990; Deputy Chair. Macedonian Govt 1992–93; Minister of Foreign Affairs 1993–96; Amb. to UK 1997–. *Address:* Macedonian Embassy, 10 Harcourt House, 19A Cavendish Square, London, W1M 9AD, England (Office). *Telephone:* (20) 7499-5152 (Office). *Fax:* (20) 7499-2864 (Office). *E-mail:* mkuk@btinternet.com (Office).

CRYSTAL, Billy; American actor and comedian; b. 14 March 1947, Long Beach, NY; s. of Jack Crystal and Helen Crystal; m. Janice Crystal (née Goldfinger); two d.; ed Marshall Univ., Nassau Community Coll., New York Univ.; mem. of the group 3's Company; solo appearances as a stand-up comedian; TV appearances include: Soap 1977–81, The Billy Crystal Hour 1982, Saturday Night Live 1984–85, The Love Boat, The Tonight Show; TV films include: Breaking up is Hard to do 1979, Enola Gay, The Men, The Mission, The Atomic Bomb 1980, Death Flight; Emmy Award for Outstanding Writing 1991. *Films include:* The Rabbit Test 1978, This is Spinal Tap 1984, Running Scared 1986, The Princess Bride 1987, Throw Momma from the Train 1987, When Harry Met Sally . . . 1989, City Slickers 1991, Mr Saturday Night (also Dir Producer, co-screen-play writer) 1993, Forget Paris 1995, Hamlet, Father's Day, Deconstructing Harry, My Giant 1998, Analyze This 1998, The Adventures of Rocky & Bullwinkle 2000, Monsters Inc. 2001, Mike's New Car 2002, Analyze That 2002. *Publication:* Absolutley Mahvelous 1986. *Address:* Wilkinson and Lipsman Public Relations, 8170 Beverly Hills, Suite 205, Los Angeles, CA 90048; CAA, 9830 Wilshire Boulevard, Beverly Hills, CA 90212, USA.

CSABA, László, PhD, DrSci, DrHab; Hungarian economist and professor of economics; b. 27 March 1954, Budapest; s. of Ede Csaba and Márta Biró; m.

Gabriella Ónody 1980; one s. one d.; ed Univ. of Budapest, Hungarian Acad. of Sciences; Fellow Inst. for World Econs, Budapest 1976–87; economist/ researcher, then Sr Economist Kopint-Datorg Econ. Research 1988–2000; Hon. Prof. of Int. Econs, Coll. of Foreign Trade, Budapest Univ. of Econs 1991–97, Prof. 1997–; Prof. of Econs and European Studies, Cen. European Univ. 2000–; Head Doctoral Programme, Univ. of Debrecen 1999–; Vice-Pres. European Asscn for Comparative Econs 1990–94, 1996–98, Pres. 1999–2000; mem. Econs Cttee Hungarian Acad. of Sciences 1986–, Co-Chair. 1996–99, 2000–02, Chair. 2003–(05); Visiting Prof. Bocconi Univ., Milan 1991, Helsinki Univ. 1993, Europa Univ., Viadrina, Frankfurt 1997, Freie Univ. Berlin 1998–2000, Cen. European Univ. 1998; mem. ed. bds of various journals. *Publications:* Eastern Europe in the World Economy 1990, The Capitalist Revolution in Eastern Europe 1995; ed. six books; over 190 articles and chapters in books published in 18 countries. *Leisure interests:* classical music, travel, soccer. *Address:* Department of International Relations and European Studies, Central European University, Nador u. 9, 1051 Budapest (Office); Dohány u. 94, 1074 Budapest, Hungary (Home). *Telephone:* (1) 327-30-17 (Office); (1) 327-32-43 (Home). *E-mail:* csabal@ceu.hu (Office). *Website:* www .ceu.hu (Office).

CSÁNYI, Sándor, MSc, PhD; Hungarian banker; b. 20 March 1953, Jászárokszállás; m.; five c.; ed Inst. of Finance and Accounting, Budapest Univ. of Econ. Sciences; Fiscal Dept Ministry of Finance 1974–83, Secr. 1983–84; Dept Head of Ministry of Agric. and Food 1984–86, of Hungarian Credit Bank Co. 1986–89; Deputy CEO Commercial and Credit Bank Co. 1989–92, Pres. 1992–; Chair. and CEO OTP Bank-Nat. Savings and Commercial Bank Ltd, Budapest; Vice-Pres. Bd Hungarian Bankers Asscn; mem. Bd Europay, Matáv, Mol; Global Leader of Tomorrow World Econ. Forum, Davos 1996. *Leisure interests:* tennis, fishing. *Address:* Nádor u. 16, 1051 Budapest, Hungary (Office). *Telephone:* (1) 353-1444 (Office). *Fax:* (1) 312-6858 (Office). *E-mail:* otpbank@otpbank.hu (Office). *Website:* www.otpbank.hu (Office).

CSÁSZÁR, Ákos; Hungarian mathematician; b. 26 Feb. 1924, Budapest; s. of Károly Császár and Gizella Szücs; m. Klára Cseley; ed Budapest Univ.; Prof. Loránd Eötvös Univ. Budapest 1957–94, Prof. Emer. 1994–; Dir Inst. of Mathematics, Loránd Eötvös Univ. 1983–86; Visiting Prof. Technische Universität Stuttgart 1975, Università di Torino 1979, Technische Universität Graz 1983; fmr mem. Editorial Bd, Periodica Mathematica Hungarica, Studia Mathematica Hungarica; Chief Ed. Acta Mathematica Hungarica 1996, Annales Univ. Scientiarum Budapestinensis Sectio Mathematica; Gen. Sec. János Bolyai Mathematical Soc. 1966–80, Pres. 1980–90, Hon. Pres. 1990–; corresp. mem. Hungarian Acad. of Sciences 1970, full mem. 1979–; Kossuth Prize 1963; Bolzano Medal (Prague) 1981, Arany János Prize 1999. *Publications:* Foundations of General Topology 1960, General Topology 1974, Valós analízis (Real Analysis) 1983 (2 Vols); articles in int. mathematical periodicals. *Leisure interests:* music, botany, bridge. *Address:* 1052 Budapest, Párizsi utca 6/a, Hungary. *Telephone:* (1) 318-5172.

CSIKÓS-NAGY, Béla; Hungarian economist; b. 9 Sept. 1915, Szeged; s. of Dr. József Csikós-Nagy and Jolán Jedlicska; m. Dr. Livia Kneppó 1944; two d.; ed Szeged Univ. and Univ. of Pécs; joined Hungarian CP 1945; Chair. Hungarian Bd of Prices and Materials 1957–84; Exec. Co-Chair. Council of Industrial Policy 1984–90; lecturer on Price Theory at Karl Marx Univ. of Econ. Sciences, Budapest 1959–90, title of Univ. Prof. 1964, Dr. of Econ. Sc. 1967; Under-Sec. of State 1968–84; Pres. Hungarian Econ. Asscn 1970–90, Hon. Chair. 1994–; mem. Exec. Cttee Int. Econ. Asscn 1971–77, 1983–86; Hon. Prof. Univ. of Vienna, mem. Oxford Energy Club 1977, Corresp. mem. Austrian Acad. of Sciences; mem. Hungarian Acad. of Sciences 1982–; Hon. Chair. Int. Soc. of Econs; Pres. Hungarian Bridge Fed. 1983–90; Hungarian State Prize 1970, Banner Order of Hungarian People's Repub. *Publications:* Pricing in Hungary 1968, General and Socialist Price Theory 1968, Hungarian Economic Policy 1971, Socialist Economic Policy 1973, Socialist Price Theory and Price Policy 1975, Towards a New Price Revolution 1978, On Hungarian Price Policy 1980, Economic Policy 1982, The Price Law in Socialist Planned Economy 1983, Topical Issues of Hungarian Price Policy 1985, Socialist Market Economy 1987, Price and Power (with Peter S. Elek) 1995, Hungarian Economic Policy in the 20th Century 1996, Economics in the World of Globalization 2002. *Leisure interest:* patience (card game). *Address:* Bp. V. Sas-u.25.VI.em., Budapest 1245, Pf. 1044 (Office); Budapest XII, Varosmajor u. 26/c, Hungary (Home). *Telephone:* 331-6906 (Office); 3554-081 (Home). *Fax:* 331-6906 (Office).

CSIKSZENTMIHALYI, Mihaly, PhD; American professor of psychology; b. 29 Sept. 1934, Fiume, Italy; s. of Alfred Csikszentmihályi and Edith (Jankovich de Jessenice) Csikszentmihályi; m. Isabella Selega 1961; two s.; ed Univs. of Illinois and Chicago; went to USA in 1956; Assoc. Prof. and Chair., Dept of Sociology and Anthropology, Lake Forest Coll. 1965–71; Prof. of Human Devt, Univ. of Chicago 1971, Chair. Dept of Behavioral Sciences 1985–87; Davidson Prof. of Man., Drucker School of Man., Claremont Grad. Univ. 1999–; mem. Bd of Advisers, Encyclopaedia Britannica 1985–; Consultant, The JP Getty Museum, Malibu 1985–; Sr Fulbright Scholar, Brazil 1984, New Zealand 1990; Fellow American Acad. of Arts and Sciences, American Acad. of Political and Social Sciences, Hungarian Acad. of Sciences, Nat. Acad. of Educ., Nat. Acad. of Leisure Sciences, World Economic Forum, Center for Advanced Study in the Behavioral Sciences; DSc hc (Lake Forest Coll.) 1999, (Colorado Coll.) 2002, (Rhode Island School of Design) 2003. *Publications:* Beyond Boredom and Anxiety 1975, The Creative Vision 1976, The Meaning of Things 1981, Being Adolescent 1984, Optimal Experience 1988, Flow—The Psychology of Optimal Experience 1990, Television and the Quality of Life 1990, The Art of Seeing 1990, Talented Teenagers 1993, The Evolving Self 1993, Creativity 1996, Finding Flow in Everyday Life 1997, Flow in Sport 1999, Becoming Adult 2000, Good Work 2001, Good Business 2003; contrib. to several other books. *Leisure interests:* mountain climbing, chess and history. *Address:* 1021 North Dartmouth Avenue, Claremont, CA 91711 (Office); 700 East Alamosa Drive, Claremont, CA 91711, USA (Home). *Telephone:* (909) 607-3307 (Office); (909) 621-7345 (Home). *Fax:* (909) 621-8543 (Office). *E-mail:* miska@cgu.edu (Office).

CSOÓRI, Sándor; Hungarian poet and writer; b. 3 Feb. 1930, Zámoly, Co. Fejér; ed Új hang (monthly) 1955–56; Contrib. to Irodalmi Újság (monthly) 1954–55; drama critic Mafilm Studio 1968; joined opposition Movt 1980; participated in political discussions of Monor 1985 and Lakitelek 1987; founding mem. Hungarian Democratic Forum 1987, presidium mem. 1988–92; Chair. Illyés Gyula Foundation 1990–94; Pres. World Fed. of Hungarians 1991–; Attila József Prize 1954, Herder Prize 1981, Kossuth Prize 1990, Eeva Joenpelto Prize 1995. *Publications:* selected poems: Fölröppen a madár (Up Flies the Bird) 1954, Ördögpille (Demon Butterfly) 1957, Elmaradt lázálom (Postponed Nightmare) 1980, Knives and Nails 1981, Hóemléke (Memory of Snow) 1983, Várakozás a tavaszban (Waiting in the Spring) 1983, Menekülés a magányból (Escape from Loneliness) 1962, Hattyúkkal ágyútűzben (In Cannon Fire with Swans) 1995, Ha volna életem (If I Had a Life) 1996; sociographies: Tudósítás a toronyból (Report From the Tower) 1963, Kubai utinapló (Cuban Travel Diary) 1965; essay volumes: Faltól falig (From Wall to Wall) 1968, Nomád napló (Nomadic Diary) 1979, Félig bevallott élet (Half Confessed Life) 1984, Készülődés a számadásra (Preparation for Final Reckoning) 1987, Nappali hold (Daytime Moon) 1991, Tenger és diólevél I. II. (The Sea and Nut Leaves) 1994, Száll a alá poklokra (Descent into Hell) 1997; Film scripts: Tízezer nap (Ten thousand days), Földobott kő (The thrown-up stone), 80 huszár (Eighty Hussars), Tüske a köröm alatt (A Thorn under the Fingernail), Hószakadás (Snow-Storm), Nincs idö (No Time Left). *Address:* 1068 Budapest, Benczúr u. 15, Hungary.

CUBAS GRAU, Raúl; Paraguayan politician; b. 23 Aug. 1943, Asunción; m. Mirta Gusinsky de Cubas; two d.; ed Universidade Católica do Rio de Janeiro; worked as engineer ANDE 1967–73; Commercial Dir CIE SRL 1977–79; Dir CONCRET-MIX SA 1970–88; Legal Rep. 14 de Julio SA 1980–1993; Dir COPAC VIAL SA 1987–91; Legal Rep. of consortium OCHO A S.A.C.I.–14 Julio S.A.–CONPASA 1992; Exec. Minister of State for Ministry of Econ. and Social Planning and Devt 1994–96; Minister of Finance 1996; Pres. of Paraguay 1998–99.

CUBITT, Sir Hugh (Guy), Kt, CBE, FRICS, JP, DL, FRSA; British fmr business executive; b. 2 July 1928, London; s. of late Col the Hon. Guy Cubitt and Rosamond M. E. Cholmeley; m. Linda I. Campbell 1958; one s. two d.; ed Royal Naval Colls. Dartmouth and Greenwich; RN 1942–53; partner, Rogers, Chapman & Thomas 1958–67, Cubitt & West 1962–79; Chair. The Housing Corpn 1980–90, Lombard North Cen. PLC 1980–91; Commr English Heritage 1988–94; Chair. Anchor Group of Housing Assocs. 1991–98; Chair. Rea Brothers Group PLC 1996–98; Dir PSIT PLC 1962–97; Dir Nat. Westminster Bank 1977–90, mem. UK Advisory Bd 1990–91; Gov. Peabody Trust 1991–2003 (Chair. 1998–2003); mem. Westminster City Council 1963–78; Lord Mayor of Westminster 1977–78; Pres. London Chamber of Commerce 1988–91; High Sheriff of Surrey 1983–84; Chair. Rea Bros. Group PLC 1995–98; Hon. Fellow Royal Acad. of Music; Chief Hon. Steward, Westminster Abbey 1997–2002; other professional and civic appts. *Leisure interests:* country sports, travel, photography, painting. *Address:* Chapel House, West Humble, Dorking, Surrey, RH5 6AY, England. *Telephone:* (1306) 882994. *Fax:* (1306) 886825 (Home). *E-mail:* cubitt@peabody.org.uk (Home).

CUCKNEY, Baron (Life Peer), cr. 1995, of Millbank in the City of Westminster; **John Graham Cuckney,** Kt, MA; British business executive; b. 12 July 1925, India; s. of late Air Vice-Marshal E. J. Cuckney; m. 2nd Muriel Boyd 1960; ed Shrewsbury School, Univ. of St Andrews; Civil Asst, Gen. Staff, War Office 1949–57; Dir of various industrial and financial cos. 1957–72 incl. Lazard Bros. & Co. 1964–70, J. Bibby & Sons 1970–72; Chair. Standard Industrial Trust 1966–70, Mersey Docks and Harbour Bd 1970–72, Bldg Econ. Devt Cttee 1976–79; Ind. mem. Railway Policy Review Cttee 1966–67; Special mem. Hops Marketing Bd 1971–72; Chief Exec. (Second Perm. Sec.), Property Services Agency 1972–74; Sr Crown Agent and Chair. of Crown Agents for Oversea Govts. and Administrations 1974–78; Chair. (part-time) Int. Mil. Services Ltd 1974–85, Port of London Authority 1977–79, The Thomas Cook Group Ltd 1978–87; Dir Midland Bank PLC 1978–88; Dir Royal Insurance PLC 1979, Deputy Chair. 1982–85, Chair. 1985–94; Dir Brooke Bond Liebig Ltd (now Brooke Bond Group PLC) 1978–84, Vice-Chair. 1980–81, Chair. 1981–84; Dir John Brown PLC 1981–86, Deputy Chair. 1982–83, Chair. 1983–86; Chair. Westland Group PLC 1985–89, The Orion Publishing Group Ltd 1994–97; Dir and Deputy Chair. TI Group PLC 1985–90; Dir Brixton Estate PLC 1985–96, Lazard Brothers & Co. Ltd 1988–90; Dir Investors in Industry Group PLC (now 3i Group PLC) 1986–92, Chair. 1987–92; Dir Glaxo Holdings PLC 1990–95 (Vice-Chair. 1993–95); Chair. Int. Maritime Bureau 1981–85; Founder Chair. Maxwell Pensioners' Trust 1992–95; Adviser to Sec. of State for Social Security on the Maxwell pensions affair 1992–95; Elder Brother of Trinity House 1980; Hon. D. Sc. (Bath) 1991; Hon. LL.D. (St Andrews) 1993. *Address:* House of Lords, London, SW1A 0PW, England. *Telephone:* (20) 7219-3000.

CUEVAS, José Luis; Mexican painter; b. 26 Feb. 1934, México, DF; s. of Alberto Cuevas and María Regla; m. Bertha Riestra 1961; three d.; ed Univ. de México, School of Painting and Sculpture 'La Esmeralda', Mexico; over forty one-man exhbns. in New York, Paris, Milan, Mexico, Buenos Aires, Toronto, Los Angeles, Washington, etc.; group exhbns. all over N and S America, Europe, India and Japan; works are in Museum of Modern Art, Solomon R. Guggenheim Museum, Brooklyn Museum (New York), Art Inst. Chicago, Phillips Collection, Washington, DC, Museums of Albi and Lyons, France, etc.; has illustrated following books: The Worlds of Kafka and Cuevas 1959, The Ends of Legends String, Recollections of Childhood 1962, Cuevas por Cuevas (autobiog.) 1964, Cuevas Charenton 1965, Crime by Cuevas 1968, Homage to Quevedo 1969, El Mundo de José Luis Cuevas 1970, Cuaderno de Paris 1977, Zarathustra 1979, Les Obsessions Noirs 1982, Letters to Tasenda 1982; First Int. Award for Drawing, São Paulo Bienal 1959, First Int. Award, Mostra Internazionale di Bianco e Nero de Lugano, Zürich 1962, First Prize, Bienal de Grabado, Santiago, Chile 1964, First Int. Prize for engraving, first Biennial of New Delhi, India 1968, Nat. Fine Arts Award Mexico 1981. *Publications:* Cuevas por Cuevas 1964, Cuevario 1973, Confesiones de José Luis Cuevas 1975, Cuevas por Daisy Ascher 1979. *Address:* Galeana 109, San Angel Inn, México 20, DF, Mexico; c/o Tasende Gallery, 820 Prospect Street, La Jolla, CA 92037, USA. *Telephone:* 548-78-20; 548-90-54 (both México, DF).

CUEVAS CANCINO, Francisco; Mexican diplomatist; b. 7 May 1921, Mexico City; m. Ana Hilditch 1946; two s. one d.; ed Free School of Law, Mexico City, McGill Univ., Montréal, Ottawa, London and Columbia Univs; Third Sec., London 1946–49; served UN Secr. 1950–53; Adviser to Minister of Foreign Affairs 1954; Asst Dir of Int. Orgs., Ministry of Foreign Affairs and Head, Tech. Assistance Programme in Mexico 1956–57; Legal Counsellor, Perm. Mission of Mexico at UN 1959–60; Dir Centre for Int. Studies, Mexico City 1961; Alt. Rep. of Mexico at UN 1962, Perm. Rep. 1965–70, 1978; Perm. Del. of Mexico to UNESCO, Paris 1970–76, mem. Exec. Bd UNESCO 1971–74; Consul Gen., Paris 1977; mem. Mexican del. to UN Gen. Ass. 1955–70; Amb. to EEC 1981–83, to UK 1983–86, to Austria 1986–90; Perm. Rep. to UNIDO and IAEA 1986–. *Publications:* books on law, international affairs and history. *Address:* Secretariat of State for Foreign Affairs, Ricardo Flores Magón, 1 Tlatelolco, 06995, México DF, Mexico.

CUEVAS SALVADOR, José María, LLB; Spanish trade union official; b. 29 June 1935, Madrid; m. Pilar Tello; four c.; ed Univ. Complutense, Madrid and Univ. of Navarra; worked for family bldg materials business; Man. Dir Sarrió, SA 1977–, now Vice-Pres.; Vice-Chair. and mem. Bd Dirs VISCOFAN, SA; Chair. Spanish Nat. Paper and Cardboard Asscn 1976; promoted and f. Spanish Confed. of Employers' Orgs (CEOE) 1977, mem. Bd Dirs 1977, Sec.-Gen. 1978, Chair. 1984–; Chair. CEOE Labour and Social Affairs Comm. 1978; Vice-Pres. Union of Industrial and Employers' Confeds of Europe (UNICE) 1996–; Dir Uppermost Council Official Chambers of Commerce, Industry and Navigation 1998–. *Address:* Oficina del Presidente, CEOE, Diego de León 50, 28006 Madrid, Spain (Office). *Telephone:* (91) 5663400 (Office). *Fax:* (91) 5644247. *E-mail:* comunicacion@ceoe.es (Office). *Website:* www.ceoe.es (Office).

CUI NAIFU; Chinese politician; b. 8 Oct. 1928, Beijing; s. of Cui Yu Lian and Chang Wei Fung Cui; m. 1955; one s. one d.; joined CCP 1948; Dir Propaganda Dept and Dean of Studies, Lanzhou Univ.; Vice-Chair. Lanzhou Univ. Revolutionary Cttee; Vice-Minister of Civil Affairs 1981, Minister 1982–93; mem. 12th Cen. Cttee CCP 1982–87, 13th Cen. Cttee CCP 1987–92, 14th Cen. Cttee 1992–97; mem. 8th NPC 1993–98, NPC Deputy Jiangxi Prov.; Deputy Head, Group for Resettlement of Ex-Servicemen and Retired Officers 1983–88, Head 1988–; Research Soc. for Theory of Civil Admin. and Social Welfare 1985; Chair. China Org. Comm. of UN Decade of Disabled Persons 1986; Hon. Pres. China Asscn of Social Workers 1991–; Deputy Dir China Org. Comm. of Int. Decade of Natural Disaster Reduction 1991–; Pres. China Charity Fed. 1994–; Hon. Dir China Welfare Fund for the Handicapped 1985–; Hon. Pres. China Asscn for the Blind and Deaf Mutes 1984. *Leisure interest:* calligraphy. *Address:* No. 9, Xi Huang Cheng Gen Street, Beijing 100032, People's Republic of China. *Telephone:* 66017240. *Fax:* 66017240.

CULHANE, John Leonard, PhD, CPhys, FInstP, FRS; Irish university professor; b. 14 Oct. 1937, Dublin; s. of late John Thomas Culhane and Mary Agnes Culhane (née Durkin); m. Mary Brigid Smith 1961; two s.; ed Univ. Coll. Dublin, Univ. Coll. London; lecturer in Physics Univ. Coll. London 1967–69, 1970–76, Reader 1976–81, Prof. 1981–; research scientist Lockheed Palo Alto Lab. 1969–70; Dir Mullard Space Science Lab. Univ. Coll. London 1983–, Head Dept of Space and Climate Physics 1993–; UK Del. and Vice-Pres. European Space Agency Science Programme Cttee 1989–94; Chair. British Nat. Space Centre Space Science Programme Bd 1989–92, COSPAR Comm. 1994–, European Space Science Cttee, European Space Foundation 1997–; mem. Advisory Panel European Space Agency Space Science Dept 1995–, UK Particle Physics and Astronomy Research 1996–2000; Foreign mem. Norwegian Acad. of Sciences and Letters 1996; Hon. DSc (Wrocław) 1996. *Publications:* X-Ray Astronomy, over 270 papers on Solar and Cosmic X-Ray Astronomy, X-Ray Instrumentation and Plasma Spectroscopy. *Leisure interests:* music, motor racing. *Address:* 24 Warnham Road, Horsham, W Sussex, RH12 2QU, England. *Telephone:* (1483) 274111 (Office). *E-mail:* jlc@mssl.ucl.ac.uk (Office).

CULKIN, Macaulay; American actor; b. 26 Aug. 1980, New York; s. of Christopher "Kit" Culkin and Pat Culkin; m. Rachel Milner 1998; ed St

Joseph's School of Yorkville, New York and George Balanchine's School of Ballet, New York. *Films include:* Rocket Gibraltar 1988, Uncle Buck 1989, See You In The Morning 1989, Jacob's Ladder 1990, Home Alone 1990, My Girl 1991, Only the Lonely 1991, Home Alone 2: Lost in New York 1992, The Nutcracker, The Good Son 1993, The Pagemaster, Getting Even With Dad, Richie Rich 1995, Body Piercer 1998. *Play:* Madame Melville, Vaudeville Theatre, London 2000. *Address:* c/o Brian Gersh, William Morris Agency, 151 S El Camino Drive, Beverly Hills, CA 90212, USA.

CULLEN, Michael John, MA, PhD; New Zealand politician; b. 1945, London, England; m. Anne Lowson Collins; two d.; ed Christ's Coll. Christchurch, Canterbury Univ. and Univ. of Edinburgh; Asst Lecturer, Canterbury Univ., Tutor Univ. of Stirling, Sr Lecturer in History, Univ. of Otago (Dunedin) and Visiting Fellow, Australian Nat. Univ. 1968–81; mem. Parl. 1981–; Minister of Social Welfare 1987–90; Assoc. Minister of Finance 1987–88, of Health 1988–90, of Labour 1989–90; Opposition Spokesperson on Finance 1991, Deputy Leader of Opposition 1996–; fmr Minister for Accident Insurance, Leader of the House; Treas., Minister of Finance and of Revenue 1999–; mem. Labour Party. *Leisure interests:* music, reading, house renovation, golf. *Address:* Parliament House, Wellington, New Zealand. *Telephone:* 470-6551. *Fax:* 495-8442.

CULLINAN, Brendan Peter; Irish judge; b. 24 July 1927, Dublin; s. of Patrick J. Cullinan and Elizabeth Kitchen; one s. (one deceased) two d.; ed Christian Bros. School, Dublin, Univ. Coll. Dublin, Nat. Univ. of Ireland, King's Inns, Dublin and Irish Mil. Coll.; mil. service 1946–65; mem. Irish contingent, Equestrian Games of XVIth Olympiad, Stockholm 1956; called to Irish Bar 1963; legal officer, army Legal Service, Dublin 1963–65; seconded to Inst. of Public Admin. Dublin for service in Zambia and designated under Overseas Service Aid Scheme (OSAS) of Ministry of Overseas Devt (now Overseas Devt Admin.), London 1965–68; lecturer, Sr Lecturer and Acting Head of Law School, Lusaka, Zambia 1965–68; legal officer, Army Legal Service, Dublin 1968–69; Resident Magistrate and Deputy Registrar, High Court, Lusaka 1969–70; Sr Resident Magistrate and Registrar 1970–73; admitted to practice as legal practitioner in Zambia 1971; Puisne Judge Dec. 1973; called to Bar, Lincoln's Inn, London 1977; frequently Acting Judge of Supreme Court, Lusaka 1976–80; Judge of Supreme Court 1980; Dir of Legal Services Corpn Lusaka 1982–83; Puisne Judge of Supreme Court of Fiji, Lautoka and Suva 1984–87; Chief Justice of Lesotho 1987–95, Judge of Court of Appeal (ex officio) and Chair. Judicial Services Comm. *Leisure interests:* golf, swimming, gardening. *Address:* 16 Oak Park Gardens, London, S.W.19, England. *Telephone:* (20) 8785-2260.

CULLINAN, Edward Horder, CBE, RA; British architect; b. 17 July 1931, London; s. of Edward Revil Cullinan and Dorothea Joy Horder; m. Rosalind Sylvia Yeates 1961; one s. two d.; ed Ampleforth Coll., Cambridge Univ., Architectural Asscn, Univ. of Calif., Berkeley, USA; with Denys Lasdun 1958–65; est. Edward Cullinan Architects 1965; numerous professorships include Bannister Fletcher Prof. London Univ. 1978–79; Graham Willis Prof., Sheffield Univ. 1985–87; George Simpson Prof., Univ. of Edinburgh 1987–; designed and built Horder House, Hampshire 1959–60, Minster Lovell Mill, Oxfordshire 1969–72, Parish Church of St Mary, Barnes 1978–84, Lambeth Community Care Centre 1979–84, R.M.C. Int. H.Q. 1985–90, Visitor Centre and Landscape at Fountains Abbey and Studley Royal 1988–92, Media Bldg Cheltenham Art Coll. 1990–94, Library St John's Coll. Cambridge 1991–94, Faculty of Divinity, Cambridge Univ. 1995–2000, Archaeolink Visitor Centre, Aberdeenshire 1996–97, Faculty of Math., Cambridge Univ. 1996–, Dock-lands Campus, Univ. of E London 1996–99, Downland Gridshell, Weald & Downland Open Air Museum 1997–2002, Greenwich Millennium School and Health Centre 1998–2001, Bristol Harbourside Masterplan 2000–, Singapore Man. Univ. 2000–; represented at Royal Acad. Summer Exhbn and many others; Financial Times Architecture at Work Award 1991 and many other awards and prizes. *Publications:* Edward Cullinan Architects 1984, Edward Cullinan Architects 1995, Master Plan for the University of North Carolina at Charlotte 1995; contribs. to journals. *Leisure interests:* horticulture, cycling, surfing, Arctic and Sahara travel, history, building, geography. *Address:* 1 Baldwin Terrace, London, N1 7RU, England. *Telephone:* (20) 7704-1975.

CUMING, Frederick George Rees, RA, ARCA; British painter; b. 16 Feb. 1930; s. of Harold Cuming and Grace Cuming; m. Audrey Lee Cuming 1962; one s. one d.; ed Univ. School, Bexley Heath, Sidcup Art School, Royal Coll. of Art; travelling scholarship to Italy; exhbns in Redfern, Walker, New Grafton, Thackeray and Fieldborne Galleries; works in collections including Dept of the Environment, Treasury, Chantrey Bequest, RA, Kendal Museum, Scunthorpe Museum, Bradford, Carlisle, Nat. Museum of Wales, Brighton and Hove Museum, Maidstone Museum, Towner Gallery, Eastbourne, Monte Carlo Museum, Farringdon Trust, Worcester Coll. Oxford, St John's Coll. Oxford, W. H. Smith, Thames TV, Nat. Trust Foundation for Art; works in galleries in Canada, France, Germany, Greece, Holland; Grand Prix, Art Contemporaine, Monte Carlo. *Group exhibitions include:* RA, John Moore's London Group. *Solo exhibitions include:* Thackeray Gallery, Chichester, Lewes, Eastbourne, Guildford, Durham, Chester, Folkestone, Canterbury, New York, Dallas, San Francisco, Florida. *Publication:* Figure in a Landscape. *Leisure interests:* tennis, golf, snooker, reading, music, travelling. *Address:* The Gables, Wittersham Road, Iden, Nr. Rye, E Sussex, TN31 7WY, England. *Telephone:* (1797) 280322. *Website:* www.fredcumingra.com (Office).

CUMMINGS, Constance, CBE; British actress; b. Constance Halverstadt, 15 May 1910, Seattle, USA; d. of Dallas Vernon Halverstadt and Kate Cummings; m. Benn Wolfe Levy 1933 (died 1973); one s. one d.; ed St Nicholas Girls' School, Seattle; first appeared on the stage in Sour Grapes 1932, since then in many stage, film and TV roles; mem. Arts Council 1965–70; Chair. of Arts Council Young People's Theatre Panel 1965–74; mem. Royal Soc. of Arts 1975; mem. Council, English Stage Co. 1978–; Antoinette Perry Award for Best Actress (in Wings). *Plays include:* Emma Bovary, The Taming of the Shrew, Romeo and Juliet, St Joan, Lysistrata, Coriolanus, Long Day's Journey into Night, The Cherry Orchard, The Bacchae, Mrs. Warren's Profession, Wings (USA) 1978–79, Hay Fever 1980, Chalk Garden (New York) 1982, (London) 1992, The Old Ladies (BBC TV) 1983, Eve 1984, The Glass Menagerie 1985, Fanny Kemble at Home 1986, Crown Matrimonial 1987, Tête-à-Tête 1990, The Chalk Garden 1992, Uncle Vanya 1996. *Films include:* Busman's Honeymoon 1940, Blithe Spirit 1945, John and Julie 1955, The Intimate Stranger 1956, The Battle of the Sexes 1959, Sammy Going South 1962, In the Cool of the Day 1963. *Leisure interests:* needlework, gardening, music. *Address:* Cote House Farm, Aston, Oxon.; 68 Old Church Street, London, SW3 6EP, England. *Telephone:* (20) 7352-0437.

CUNHAL, Alvaro; Portuguese politician; b. 10 Nov. 1913, Coimbra; s. of Avelino Cunhal and Mercedes Cunhal; ed Lisbon Univ.; mem. Portuguese Communist Party 1931–; Sec.-Gen. Fed. Communist Youth Movts. 1935; mem. PCP Cen. Cttee 1936–, Cen. Cttee Secr. 1942–49, 1960–92; active in party reorganization and devt of links with int. communist movt 1942–49; imprisoned for political activities 1937–38, 1940, 1949–60 (escaped from gaol 1960); Sec.-Gen. PCP 1961–92, Chair. Nat. Council 1992–96; Minister without Portfolio 1974–75; elected MP 1975, 1976, 1979, 1980, 1983, 1985, 1987; mem. Council of State 1983–91; mem. many PCP dels. abroad. *Publications:* numerous vols concerning Portuguese social and econ. history and political tracts; novels under the pseudonym Manuel Tiago. *Leisure interests:* drawing and painting. *Address:* Partido Comunista Português, Rua Soeiro Pereira Gomes, 3, 1699 Lisbon, Portugal.

CUNLIFFE, Jonathan Stephen, CB, MA; British civil servant; b. 2 June 1953; s. of Ralph Cunliffe and Cynthia Cunliffe; m. Naomi Brandler 1984; two d.; ed St Marylebone Grammar School, London and Manchester Univs.; joined Civil Service 1980, various posts in Depts of Environment and Transport 1980–90; Head Public Sector Pay Div., HM Treasury 1990–92, Head Int. Financial Insts Div. 1992–94, Treasury Debt and Reserves Man. Div. 1994–96, Deputy Dir Macroeconomic Policy and Prospects and Head of Treasury European Monetary Union (EMU) team 1996–98, Deputy Dir, then Dir Int. Finance, later Macroeconomic Policy and Int. Finance 1998–2001, 2002–, Man. Dir Finance Regulation and Industry, HM Treasury 2001–02; Alt. Dir EBRD 1992–94; Alt. mem. EU Monetary Cttee responsible for Debt and Reserves Man. 1996–98. *Leisure interests:* tennis, cooking, walking. *Address:* HM Treasury, Parliament Street, London, SW1P 3AG, England (Office).

CUNNINGHAM, Edward Patrick, MAgrSc, PhD, MRIA; Irish professor of animal genetics and international public servant; b. 4 Aug. 1934, Dublin; s. of Eugene Cunningham and Kathleen Moran; m. Catherine Dee 1965; four s. two d.; ed Clongowes Wood Coll., Univ. Coll. Dublin and Cornell Univ., Ithaca, NY, USA; Housemaster, Albert Agricultural Coll. Dublin 1956–57; Research and Teaching Asst, Univ. Coll. Dublin 1957–58, Cornell Univ. 1960–62; Research Officer, The Agricultural Inst., Dublin 1962, Head Dept of Animal Breeding and Genetics 1970, Deputy Dir Agricultural Inst. 1980–88; Prof. of Animal Genetics, Trinity Coll., Dublin 1974–; Dir Animal Production and Health Div., FAO, Rome 1990–93, Dir Screwworm Emergency Centre for N Africa 1990–92; Jt Founder and Chair. Identigen Ltd 1997–; Visiting Prof. Agricultural Univ. of Norway 1968–69, Econ. Devt Inst., IBRD 1988; mem. Royal Irish Acad., Royal Swedish Acad. of Agriculture and Forestry, Royal Norwegian Acad. of Science and Letters, Russian Acad. of Agricultural Sciences, Acad. d'Agriculture de France; A. M. Leroy Fellowship 1991; DAgric hc (Agric. Univ., Norway) 1997; ScD hc (Dublin Univ.) 1997; Ordre du Mérite Agricole; Golden Egg Int. Award, Verona 1983; Boyle Medal, Royal Dublin Soc. 1996. *Publications:* Animal Breeding Theory 1969, Development Issues in the Livestock Sector 1992. *Leisure interests:* farming, history. *Address:* Department of Genetics, Trinity College, Dublin 2 (Office); Vesington House, Dunboyne, Co. Meath, Ireland (Home). *Telephone:* (1) 608 1064 (Office); (1) 825 5350 (Home). *Fax:* (1) 679 8558 (Office); (1) 825 5350 (Home). *E-mail:* epcnngham@tcd.ie (Office). *Website:* www.tcd.ie (Office).

CUNNINGHAM, Rt Hon John A. (Jack), PC, DL, PhD, MP; British politician; b. 4 Aug. 1939, Newcastle upon Tyne; s. of Andrew Cunningham; m. Maureen Cunningham 1964; one s. two d.; ed Jarrow Grammar School and Bede Coll., Univ. of Durham; former Research Fellow in Chem. Univ. of Durham; school teacher; trades union officer; mem. Parl. for Whitehaven, Cumbria 1970–83, for Copeland 1983–; Parl. Pvt. Sec. to Rt Hon James Callaghan 1972–76; Parl. Under-Sec. of State, Dept of Energy 1976–79; Opposition Spokesman on Industry 1979–83, on Environment 1983–89, Shadow Leader of the House and Campaigns Co-ordinator 1989–92, Opposition Spokesman on Foreign and Commonwealth Affairs 1992–94, on Trade and Industry 1994–95, on Nat. Heritage 1995–97; Minister of Agric., Fisheries and Food 1997–98, for the Cabinet Office and Chancellor of the Duchy of Lancaster 1998–99; DL (Cumbria) 1991; mem. Labour Party. *Leisure interests:* fell walking, fly fishing, gardening, theatre, classical and folk music, reading, Newcastle United Football Club, listening to other people's opinions. *Address:* House of Commons, London, SW1A 0AA, England.

CUNNINGHAM, Merce; American choreographer and dancer; b. 16 April 1919, Centralia, Wash.; s. of Mr. and Mrs. C. D. Cunningham; ed Cornish School, Seattle and Bennington Coll. School of Dance; soloist with Martha Graham Dance Co. 1939–45; began solo concerts 1942; mem. faculty School of American Ballet, New York 1948, 1950–51; formed own company 1953; opened own dance school in New York 1959; Hon. mem. American Acad. and Inst. of Arts and Letters 1984; Guggenheim Fellowships 1954, 1959; MacArthur Fellowship 1985; Hon. DLitt (Univ. of Ill.) 1972; Hon. DFA, Wesleyan Univ., Conn. 1995; Dr. hc (Western Australian Acad. of Performing Arts) 2001; Dance Magazine Award 1960, Soc. for Advancement of The Dance in Sweden Gold Medal 1964, Gold Star for Choreographic Invention Paris 1966, New York State Award 1975, Capezio Award 1977, Wash. State Award 1977, Samuel H. Scripps American Dance Festival Award 1982, Mayor of New York's Award of Honor for Arts and Culture 1983, Kennedy Center Honors 1985, Laurence Olivier Award 1985, Algur H. Meadows Award (Southern Methodist Univ., Dallas) 1987, Digital Dance Premier Award 1990, Nat. Medal of Arts 1990, Medal of Honor, Universidad Complutense of Madrid 1993, Dance and Performance Award, London 1993, Golden Lion of Venice Biennale 1995, Nellie Cornish Arts Archievement Award, Seattle 1996; Wexner Prize, Ohio State Univ. 1993, Premio Internazionale "Gino Tani" 1999, Nijinsky Special Prize, Monaco 2000, Dorothy and Lillian Gish Prize 2000; Ordre des Arts et des Lettres 1982, Légion d'honneur 1989. *Plays:* An Alphabet (Edinburgh Festival 2001, Western Australia Int. Festival, Perth 2002). *Television productions include:* "Dance in America" Event for TV 1977; Points in Space (BBC-TV) 1986. *Works include:* The Seasons 1947, 16 Dances for Soloist and Company of Three 1951, Septet 1953, Minutiae 1954, Springweather and People 1955, Suite for Five 1956, Nocturnes 1956, Antic Meet 1958, Summerspace 1958, Rune 1959, Crises 1960, Aeon 1961, Story 1963, Winterbranch 1964, Variations V 1965, How to Pass, Kick, Fall and Run 1965, Place 1966, Scramble 1967, RainForest 1968, Walkaround Time 1968, Canfield 1969, Second Hand 1970, Tread 1970, Signals 1970, Un Jour ou Deux 1973, Sounddance 1975, Rebus 1975, Torse 1976, Squaregame 1976, Travelogue 1977, Inlets 1977, Fractions 1978, Exchange 1978, Locale 1979, Duets 1980, Channels/Inserts 1981, Gallopade 1981, Trails 1982, Quartet 1982, Coast Zone 1983, Roaratorio 1983, Pictures 1984, Doubles 1984, Phrases 1984, Native Green 1985, Arcade 1985, Grange Eve 1986, Points in Space 1986, Carousal 1987, Five Stone Wind 1988, Cargo X 1989, Field and Figures 1989, Inventions 1989, August Pace 1989, Polarity 1990, Neighbors 1991, Trackers 1991, Beach Birds 1991, Loosestrife 1991, Change of Address 1992, Enter 1992, Doubletoss 1993 CRWDSPCR 1993, Breakers 1994, Ocean 1994, Ground Level Overlay 1995, Windows 1995, Rondo 1996, Installations 1996, Scenario 1997, Pond Way 1998, Biped 1999, Interscape 2000, Way Station 2001, Loose Time 2002. *Publications:* Changes: Notes on Choreography 1969, The Dancer and the Dance, Conversations with Jacqueline Lesschaeve 1985, Other Animals (drawings and journals) 2002. *Leisure interest:* drawing. *Address:* Cunningham Dance Foundation, 55 Bethune Street, New York, NY 10014, USA (Office). *Telephone:* (212) 255-8240 (Office). *Fax:* (212) 633-2453 (Office). *E-mail:* info@merce.org (Office). *Website:* www.merce.org (Office).

CUNNINGHAM, Michael, MA; American novelist; b. 1952, Cincinnati, Ohio; ed Stanford Univ., Calif.; fmr bartender; joined Univ. of Ia Writers Workshop 1978; writer for Carnegie Corpn; now Adjunct Asst Prof., Columbia Univ. *Publications:* Golden States 1984, A Home at the End of the World 1990, Flesh and Blood 1995, The Hours 1998 (Pulitzer Prize, PEN/Faulkner Award for Fiction 1999). *Address:* Columbia University, Creative Writing Center, Room 415, 2970 Broadway, New York, NY 10027-6939, USA (Office).

CUNNINGHAM, William Hughes, MBA, PhD; American professor of marketing; b. 5 Jan. 1944, Detroit, Mich.; m.; one s.; ed Michigan State Univ.; Asst Prof. of Marketing, Univ. of Texas at Austin 1971–73, Assoc. Prof. 1973–79, Prof. 1979–, Foley's/Sanger Harris Prof. of Retail Merchandising 1982–83, Dean, Coll. of Business Admin./Grad. School of Business 1983–85, Regents Chair in Higher Educ. Leadership 1985–92, James L. Bayless Chair. for Free Enterprise 1988–; Pres. Univ. of Texas at Austin 1985–92; Chancellor, Univ. of Texas System 1992–2000, Lee Hage and Joseph D. Jamail Regents Chair in Higher Educ. Leadership 1992–2000; Dir numerous cos.; Hon. LLD (Michigan State Univ.) 1993 and other distinctions. *Publications:* with others: The Personal Force in Marketing 1977, Consumer Energy Attitudes and Behavior in the Southwest 1977, Effective Selling 1977, Métodos Efectivos de Ventas 1980, Marketing: A Managerial Approach 1987, Grondslagen van het Marketing Management 1984, Introduction to Business 1988, Business in a Changing World 1992. *Leisure interests:* golf, tennis, raquetball, horseback riding. *Address:* University of Texas, East Austin, TX 78713 (Office); 1909 Hills Oak Court, Austin, TX 78703, USA (Home). *Telephone:* (512) 499-0488 (Home). *E-mail:* wcunningham@mail.utexas.edu (Office).

CUNY, Jean-Pierre, MSc; French business executive; b. 8 April 1940, Menton; s. of Robert Cuny and Marie-Louise Marchal; m. Anne-Marie Fousse 1968; two d.; ed Ecole Centrale, Paris and Mass. Inst. of Tech.; engineer Serete 1968, Information Man. 1973; Project Man. CGA 1976; Cost Controller Placoplatre 1977, Production Dir 1978, Marketing Dir 1982, Gen. Man. 1985, Chair. and CEO 1986, Dir BPB PLC (parent co. of Placoplatre) 1988, Deputy Chair. Gypsum Div. 1988, CEO 1994–99; Pres. Eurogypsum 1996–99; Chair.

Saint Elvi Finance 2000–; Chair. and CEO Bigot Mécanique 2002–; Chevalier, Légion d'honneur. *Leisure interests:* skiing, theatre, reading, music, film. *Address:* 50 Avenue de Saxe, 75015 Paris, France. *Telephone:* 1-47-83-54-13.

CUOMO, Andrew, BA, JD; American politician; s. of Mario Cuomo (q.v.); m. Kerry Cuomo; one d.; ed Fordham Univ., Albany Law School; fmr Asst Dist Attorney, Manhattan; fmr partner Blutrich, Falcone and Miller, NY; Chair. NY Comm. on the Homeless 1991–93; Asst Sec. Community Planning and Devt, Dept of Housing and Urban Devt 1993–97, Sec. of Housing and Urban Devt 1997–2001; numerous awards and prizes. *Address:* c/o Department of Housing and Urban Development, 451 7th Street, SW, Washington, DC 20410, USA.

CUOMO, Mario Matthew, LLB; American state governor; b. 15 June 1932, Queen's County NY; s. of Andrea and Immaculata Cuomo; m. Matilda Raffa; two s. (including Andrew Cuomo, q.v.) three d.; ed St John's Coll. and St John's Univ.; admitted to NY Bar 1956, Supreme Court Bar 1960; Confidential Legal Asst to Hon. Adrian P. Burke, NY State Court of Appeals 1956–58; Assoc., Corner, Weisbrod, Froeb and Charles, Brooklyn 1958–63, partner 1963–75; Sec. of State, NY 1975–79; Lt-Gov. of New York State 1979–82, Gov. 1983–95; partner Wilkie Farr and Gallagher 1995–; mem. Faculty St John's Univ. Law School 1963–75; Counsel to community groups 1966–72; Democrat; NY Rapallo Award, Columbia Lawyers' Assdn 1976, Dante Medal, Italian Govt./ American Assdn of Italian Teachers 1976, Silver Medallion, Columbia Coalition 1976, Public Admin. Award, C. W. Post Coll. 1977. *Publications:* Forest Hills Diary: The Crisis of Low-Income Housing 1974, Maya 1984, Lincoln on Democracy (jtly) 1990, The New York Idea 1994, Common Sense 1995, Reason to Believe 1995, The Blue Spruce 1999; articles in legal journals. *Address:* Wilkie, Farr and Gallagher, 787 7th Avenue, New York, NY 10019 (Office); 50 Sutton Place South, New York, NY 10022, USA.

CUPITT, Rev. Don, MA; British ecclesiastic and university lecturer; b. 22 May 1934, Oldham; s. of Robert Cupitt and Norah Cupitt; m. Susan Marianne Day 1963; one s. two d.; ed Charterhouse, Trinity Hall, Cambridge, Westcott House, Cambridge; ordained 1959; Vice-Prin., Westcott House, Cambridge 1962; Dean of Emmanuel Coll., Cambridge 1966–91; Stanton Lecturer, Univ. of Cambridge 1968–71; lecturer, Univ. of Cambridge 1973–96; Life Fellow Emmanuel College 1996; Fellow of the Jesus Seminar 2001; Hon. DLitt (Bristol) 1985. *Television documentaries:* Who Was Jesus? 1977, The Sea of Faith (series) 1984. *Publications:* Christ and the Hiddenness of God 1971, Crisis of Moral Authority 1972, The Leap of Reason 1976, The Debate about Christ 1979, Jesus and the Gospel of God 1979, Taking Leave of God 1980, The World to Come 1982, The Sea of Faith 1984, Only Human 1985, Life Lines 1986, The Long-Legged Fly 1987, The New Christian Ethics 1988, Radicals and the Future of the Church 1989, Creation out of Nothing 1990, What is a Story? 1991, The Time Being 1992, After All 1994, The Last Philosophy 1995, Solar Ethics 1995, After God: The Future of Religion 1997, Mysticism after Modernity 1997, The Religion of Being 1998, The Revelation of Being 1998, The New Religion of Life in Everyday Speech 1999, The Meaning of It All in Everyday Speech 1999, Kingdom Come in Everyday Speech 2000, Philosophy's Own Religion 2000, Reforming Christianity 2001, Emptiness and Brightness 2001, Is Nothing Sacred? 2002, Life, Life 2003, Radical Theology 2003. *Leisure interests:* hill-walking, the arts. *Address:* Emmanuel College, Cambridge, CB2 3AP, England. *Telephone:* (1223) 334200. *Fax:* (1223) 334426. *E-mail:* susancupitt@waitrose.com (Home).

CURA, José; Argentine singer (tenor); b. 1962, Rosario, Santa Fe; ed Univ. of Rosario, School of Arts, Teatro Colon, Buenos Aires; vocal studies with Horacio Amauri, Argentina and Vittorio Terranova, Italy; appearances at leading int. opera houses 1992–; Premio Abbiatti, Italian Critics' Award, Premio Carrara, Cultura Millenaria 1997, XII Premio Internazionale di Arte e Cultura Cilea 1997. *Opera includes:* Makropoulos Affair, Le Villi, Fedora, Stiffelio, Iris, Samson et Dalila, Carmen, Cavalleria Rusticana, Norma, Tosca, La Gioconda, I Pagliacci, Otello, Aida; *Recordings include:* Le Villi, Iris, Argentine Songs, Puccini Arias, Samson et Dalila, Otello, I Pagliacci, Manon Lescaut. *Address:* c/o Royal Opera House Contracts, Covent Garden, London WC2E 9DD, England (Office).

CURIEN, Hubert, DèsSc; French politician and scientist; b. 30 Oct. 1924, Cornimont, Vosges; s. of Robert Curien; m. Anne-Perrine Dumézil 1949; three s.; ed Lycée d'Epinal, Coll. de Remiremont, Lycée Saint-Louis, Ecole Normale Supérieure and Faculté des Sciences, Paris; Prof., Faculté des Sciences, Paris 1956–95; Scientific Dir Centre Nat. de la Recherche Scientifique (CNRS) 1966–69, Dir-Gen. 1969–73, Gen. Del. of Scientific and Tech. Research 1973–76, Pres. Admin. Council, Institut de biologie physico-chimique 1975–2000; Pres. Centre Nat. Etudes Spatiales 1976–84; Minister of Research and Technology 1984–86, 1988–93; Pres. Scientific Council of Defence 1986–93; Pres. European Science Foundation 1979–84; Vice-Pres. Soc. of French Engineers and Sciences 1987–89; Chair. Council, European Space Agency 1981–84; Chair. Council, CERN, European Lab. for Particle Research 1994–96; Pres. Acad. Europaea 1994–97; Pres. Acad. des Sciences 2000–02; fmr Pres. Soc. Française de Minéralogie et Cristallographie; Prize, Acad. des Sciences, Honda Prize 1998; Grand Officier, Légion d'honneur, Commdr, Ordre nat. du Mérite, Commdr, Palmes académiques; Military Medal. *Publications:* scientific articles on solid state physics and mineralogy. *Address:* 24 rue des Fossés Saint-Jacques, 75005 Paris, France (Home). *Telephone:* 1-46-33-26-36 (Home).

CURRAN, Charles E., STD; American professor of moral theology and ecclesiastic; b. 30 March 1934, Rochester, NY; s. of John F. Curran and Gertrude L. Beisner; ed St Bernard's Coll. Rochester, Gregorian Univ. Rome and Accademia Alfonsiana, Rome; ordained Roman Catholic priest 1958; Prof. of Moral Theology, St Bernard's Seminary, Rochester, NY 1961–65; Asst Prof., Assoc. Prof., Prof. of Moral Theology, Catholic Univ. of America, Washington, DC 1965–89; Sr Research Scholar, Kennedy Center for Bio-Ethics, Georgetown Univ. 1972; External Examiner in Christian Ethics, Univ. of W.I. 1982–86; Visiting Prof. of Catholic Studies Cornell Univ. 1987–88; Visiting Brooks and Firestone Prof. of Religion, Univ. of S. Calif 1988–90; Visiting Eminent Scholar in Religion, Auburn 1990–91; Elizabeth Scurlock Univ. Prof. of Human Values, Southern Methodist Univ. 1991–; Pres. Catholic Theological Soc. of America 1969–70, Soc. of Christian Ethics 1971–72; American Theological Soc. 1989–90; Dr. hc (Charleston, W Va) 1987, (Concordia Coll., Portland, Ore.) 1992; J. C. Murray Award (Catholic Theol. Soc.) 1972, Building Bridges Award, New Ways Ministry 1992, Presidential Award Coll. Theology Soc. 2003. *Publications:* Catholic Social Teaching 1891–Present: A Historical, Theological and Ethical Analysis, The Origins of Moral Theology in the United States: Three Different Approaches, The Catholic Moral Tradition Today: a Synthesis; numerous books, articles, lectures and addresses. *Leisure interests:* reading, golf, swimming. *Address:* Southern Methodist University, 317 Dallas Hall, POB 750317, Dallas, TX 75275-0317, USA (Office); 4125 Woodcreek, Dallas, TX 75220 (Home). *Telephone:* (214) 768-4073 (Office); (214) 352–8974 (Home). *Fax:* (214) 768-4129. *E-mail:* ccurran@mail.smu.edu (Office).

CURRIE, James McGill, MA; British civil servant and European Union official; b. 17 Nov. 1941, Kilmarnock; s. of the late David Currie and of Mary Currie (née Smith); m. Evelyn Barbara MacIntyre 1968; one s. one d.; ed St Joseph's High School, Kilmarnock, Blairs Coll., Aberdeen, Royal Scots Coll., Valladolid, Univ. of Glasgow; Admin. trainee Scottish Office, Edinburgh 1968–72; Prin. Scottish Educ. and Devt Depts 1972–77; Asst Sec. Scottish Industry Dept 1977–82; Transport and Environment Counsellor UK Perm. Representation to EC 1982–86; Dir of Programmes Directorate-Gen. XVI Regional Policy 1987–88; Chief of Staff to Competition Policy Commr Sir Leon Brittan 1989–93; Deputy Head of Del., Washington, DC 1993–96; Dir-Gen. (Customs and Indirect Taxation), EC 1996–97, (Environment, Nuclear Safety and Civil Protection) 1997–2001; Visiting Prof. of Law, Georgetown Law Center, Washington, USA 1997–; Non-Exec. Dir Royal Bank of Scotland 2001–; Hon. DLitt (Glasgow) 2001. *Leisure interests:* golf, guitar, good food, tennis. *Address:* Flat 7, 54 Queens Gate Terrace, London, SW7 5PJ, UK (Home).

CURRIE-JONES, Edwina, MA, MSc; British politician, writer and broadcaster; b. 13 Oct. 1946, Liverpool; d. of the late Simon Cohen; m. 1st Raymond F. Currie 1972 (divorced 2001); two d.; m. 2nd John Jones 2001; ed Liverpool Inst. for Girls, St Anne's Coll., Oxford, London School of Econs; teacher and lecturer in econs, econ. history and business studies 1972–81; mem. Birmingham City Council 1975–86; Conservative MP for Derbyshire S. 1983–97; Parl. Pvt. Sec. to Sec. of State for Educ. and Science 1985–86; Parl. Under-Sec. of State for Health 1986–88; mem. Parl. Select Cttee on Social Services 1983–86; Jt Chair. Conservative Group for Europe 1995–97; Vice-Chair. European Movt 1995–99; Jt Chair. Future of Europe Trust 1995–97; Speaker of the Year, Asscn of Speakers' Clubs 1990, 1994 Campaigner of the Year, The Spectator/Highland Park Parliamentarian of the Year Awards. *Radio presenter:* Late Night Currie, BBC 1998–. *Publications:* Life Lines 1989, What Women Want 1990, Three Line Quips 1992, A Parliamentary Affair (novel) 1994, A Woman's Place (novel) 1996, She's Leaving Home (novel) 1997, The Ambassador (novel) 1999, Chasing Men (novel) 2000, This Honourable House (novel) 2001, Diaries (1987–92) 2002. *Leisure interests:* keeping fit, family, theatre. *Address:* c/o Curtis Brown, Haymarket, London, SW1Y 4SP, England (Office); c/o Little, Brown (UK) Ltd, Brettenham House, Lancaster Place, London, WC2E 7EN, England. *Telephone:* (20) 7396-6600 (Office).

CURRIE OF MARYLEBONE, Baron (Life Peer), cr. 1996, of Marylebone, in the City of Westminster; **David Anthony Currie,** M.SOC.SC., DLitt, PhD; British university professor; b. 9 Dec. 1946, London; s. of Kennedy Moir Currie and Marjorie (née Thompson); m. 1st Shaziye Gazioglu 1965 (divorced); two s.; m. 2nd Angela Mary Piers Dumas 1995; ed Battersea Grammar School, Univs of Manchester, Birmingham, London; economist Hoare Govett 1971–72, Sr Economist Econ. Models 1972; Lecturer in Econs Queen Mary Coll., Univ. of London 1972–79, Reader 1979–81, Prof. 1981–88; Prof. of Econs London Business School 1988–, Dir Centre for Econ. Forecasting 1988–95, Research Dean 1989–92, Deputy Prin. 1992–95; Deputy Dean External Relations 1999–2000; Dean City Univ.'s Cass Business School 2001–; Houblon-Norman Research Fellow Bank of England 1985–86, Visiting Scholar IMF 1987; mem. Advisory Bd to Research Councils 1992–93, Retail Price Index Advisory Cttee 1992–93, Treasury's Panel of Ind. Forecasters 1992–95; Trustee Joseph Rowntree Reform Trust 1991–2002; Dir Int. Schools of Business Man.; Gov. London Business School 1989–95, 1997–2000; OFGEM Man. Bd 1999–2001; Dir Abbey Nat. PLC 2001–02; Chair. Ofcom (communications regulator) July 2002–; Chair. Coredeal MTS 2002. *Publications:* Advances in Monetary Economics 1985, The Operation and Regulation of Financial Markets (jtly) 1986, Macroeconomic Interactions Between North and South (jtly) 1988, Macroeconomic Policies in an Interdependent World (jtly) 1989, Rules, Reputation and Macroeconomic Policy Co-ordination (jtly) 1993, European Monetary Union: Problems in the Transition to a Single

European Currency (jtly) 1995, North-South Linkages and International Macroeconomic Policy (jtly) 1995, The Pros and Cons of EMU 1997, Will the Euro Work? 1998. *Leisure interests:* music (playing the cello), literature, swimming. *Address:* City University's Cass Business School, Barbican Centre, London, EC2Y 8HB, England. *Telephone:* (20) 7040-8601 (Office). *Fax:* (20) 7040-8899 (Office). *E-mail:* dcurrie@city.ac.uk.

CURTEIS, Ian Bayley; British playwright; b. 1 May 1935, London; m. 1st Dorothy Joan Armstrong 1964; two s.; m. 2nd Joanna Trollope 1985; two step-d.; m. 3rd Lady Grantley; two step-s.; ed London Univ.; Dir and actor in theatres throughout UK and BBC TV script reader 1956–63; BBC and ATV staff Dir (drama) 1963–67; Chair. Cttee on Censorship, Writers' Guild of Great Britain 1981–85, Pres. of Guild 1998–2001. *Plays for TV:* Beethoven, Sir Alexander Fleming (BBC entry, Prague Festival 1973), Mr. Rolls and Mr. Royce, Long Voyage Out of War (trilogy), The Folly, The Haunting, Second Time Round, A Distinct Chill, The Portland Millions, Philby, Burgess and Maclean (British entry, Monte Carlo Festival 1978), Hess, The Atom Spies, Churchill and the Generals (Grand Prize for Best Programme of 1981, New York Int. Film and TV Festival), Suez 1956, Miss Morison's Ghosts (British entry Monte Carlo Festival), BB and Lord D.; writer of numerous television series; screenplays: La Condition humaine (André Malraux), Lost Empires (adapted from J. B. Priestley), Eureka, Graham Greene's The Man Within (TV) 1983, The Nightmare Years (TV) 1989, The Zimmerman Telegram 1990, Yalta 1991, The Choir (BBC 1), The Falklands Play 2002; numerous articles and speeches on the ethics and politics of broadcasting. *Plays for radio:* Eroica 2000, Love 2001, After the Break, The Falklands Play 2002. *Publications:* Long Voyage Out of War (trilogy) 1971, Churchill and the Generals 1980, Suez 1956, 1980, The Falklands Play 1987. *Leisure interest:* avoiding television. *Address:* 2 Warwick Square, London, SW1V 2AA; Markenfield Hall, North Yorks., HG4 3AD, England. *Telephone:* (20) 7821-8606 (Home); (1765) 603411.

CURTIS, David Roderick, AC, MB, BS, PhD, FRACP, FAA, FRS; Australian professor of pharmacology; b. 3 June 1927, Melbourne; s. of E. D. Curtis and E. V. Curtis; m. Lauris Sewell 1951; one s. one d.; ed Melbourne High School, Univ. of Melbourne and Australian Nat. Univ., Canberra; resident medical positions 1950–53; Research Scholar, Australian Nat. Univ. 1954–56, Research Fellow 1956–57, Fellow 1957–59, Sr Fellow 1959–62, Professorial Fellow 1962–65, Prof. of Pharmacology 1966–68, Prof. of Neuropharmacology 1968–73; Prof. and Head, Dept of Pharmacology, John Curtin School of Medical Research, Australian Nat. Univ. 1973–89, Dir and Howard Florey Prof. of Medical Research 1989–92, Univ. Fellow 1993–95, Emer. Prof. 1993–; Visiting Fellow, John Curtin School 1995–; Burnet Lecturer 1983; Pres. Australian Acad. of Science 1986–90; Chair. Inaugural Australia Prize Cttee 1989–90. *Publications:* scientific papers on various topics concerned with neurophysiology and neuropharmacology. *Leisure interests:* gardening, turning wood, wombling. *Address:* 7 Patey Street, Campbell, ACT 2612, Australia. *Telephone:* (2) 6248-5664. *Fax:* (2) 6248-5664.

CURTIS, Jamie Lee; American actress; b. 22 Nov. 1958, Los Angeles, Calif.; d. of Tony Curtis (q.v.) and Janet Leigh; m. Christopher Guest; one c.; ed Choate School, Conn., Univ. of the Pacific, Calif. *Films include:* Halloween, The Fog, Terror Train, Halloween II, Road Games, Prom Night, Love Letters, Trading Places, The Adventures of Buckaroo Banzai: Across the 8th Dimension, Grandview, USA, Perfect, 8 Million Ways to Die, Amazing Grace and Chuck, A Man in Love, Dominick and Eugene, A Fish Called Wanda, Blue Steel, My Girl, Forever Young, My Girl 2, True Lies 1994 (Golden Globe Award for Best Actress in a musical or comedy), House Arrest 1996, Fierce Creatures 1996, Halloween H20 1998, Virus 1999, The Tailor of Panama (also Dir) 2000, Daddy and Them, Halloween H2K: Evil Never Dies. *Television includes:* She's In The Army Now, Dorothy Stratten: Death of a Centrefold, Operation Petticoat, The Love Boat, Columbo, Quincy, Charlie's Angels, Anything but Love (Dir), Money on the Side, As Summers Die, Mother's Boys, Drowning Mona (Dir) 2000. *Publications:* When I Was Little 1993, Today I Feel Silly and Other Moods That Make My Day 1999. *Address:* c/o Rick Kurtzmann, CAA, 9830 Wilshire Blvd., Beverly Hills, CA 90212, USA.

CURTIS, Richard Whalley Anthony, BA, CBE; British screenplay writer; b. 8 Nov. 1956; s. of Anthony J. Curtis and Glynness S. Curtis; two s. one d. by Emma Vallencey Freud; ed Harrow School, Christ Church, Oxford; co-f. and producer Comic Relief 1985–2000. *Films include:* The Tall Guy 1988, Four Weddings and a Funeral 1994, Bean 1997, Notting Hill 1999, Bridget Jones's Diary (co-writer) 2001. *TV includes:* Not the Nine O'Clock News 1979–83, Blackadder 1984–89, Mr Bean 1989–95, Bernard and the Genie 1993, The Vicar of Dibley 1994–. *Leisure interests:* TV, films, pop music. *Address:* c/o Anthony Jones, Peters, Fraser & Dunlop, Drury House, 34–43 Russell Street, London, WC2B 5HA, England.

CURTIS, Tony (Bernard Schwarz); American film actor; b. 3 June 1925, New York; s. of Manuel and Helen (née Klein) Schwarz; m. 1st Janet Leigh 1951 (divorced 1962); two d.; m. 2nd Christine Kaufmann 1963 (divorced 1967); two d.; m. 3rd Leslie Allen 1968; two s.; m. 4th Lisa Deutsch 1993; ed New School of Social Research; served in U.S. Navy; Kt Order of the Repub. of Hungary 1996. *Films include:* Houdini 1953, Black Shield of Falworth 1954, So This is Paris? 1954, Six Bridges to Cross 1955, Trapeze 1956, Mister Cory 1957, Sweet Smell of Success 1957, Midnight Story 1957, The Vikings 1958, Defiant Ones 1958, Perfect Furlough 1958, Some Like It Hot 1959, Spartacus 1960, The Great Imposter 1960, Pepe 1960, The Outsider 1961, Taras Bulba

1962, Forty Pounds of Trouble 1962, The List of Adrian Messenger 1963, Captain Newman 1963, Paris When It Sizzles 1964, Wild and Wonderful 1964, Sex and the Single Girl 1964, Goodbye Charlie 1964, The Great Race 1965, Boeing, Boeing 1965, Arriverderci, Baby 1966, Not with My Wife You Don't 1966, Don't Make Waves 1967, Boston Strangler 1968, Lepke 1975, Casanova 1976, The Last Tycoon 1976, The Manitou 1978, Sextette 1978, The Mirror Crack'd 1980, Venom 1982, Insignificance 1985, Club Life 1986, The Last of Phillip Banter 1988, Balboa, Midnight, Lobster Man from Mars, The High-Flying Mermaid, Prime Target, Center of the Web, Naked in New York, The Reptile Man, The Immortals 1995, The Celluloid Closet 1995, Louis et Frank 1997, Brittle Glory 1997. *Television includes:* Third Girl from the Left 1973, The Persuaders 1971–72, The Count of Monte Cristo 1976, Vegas 1978, Mafia Princess 1986, Christmas in Conneticut 1992, A Perry Mason Mystery: The Case of the Grimacing Governor, Elvis Meets Nixon. *Publications:* Kid Andrew Cody and Julie Sparrow 1977, Tony Curtis: An Autobiography 1993. *Leisure interest:* painting. *Address:* c/o William Morris Agency, 151 South El Camino Drive, Beverly Hills, CA 90212, USA (Office).

CUSACK, John; American actor; b. 28 June 1966, Evanston, Ill.; s. of Richard Cusack and Nancy Cusack; mem. Piven Theatre Workshop, Evanston from age 9–19; f. New Criminals Theatrical Co., Chicago. *Films:* (actor): Class 1983, Sixteen Candles 1984, Grandview USA 1984, The Sure Thing 1985, Journey of Natty Gann 1985, Better Off Dead 1985, Stand By Me 1985, One Crazy Summer 1986, Broadcast News 1987, Hot Pursuit 1987, Eight Men Out 1988, Tapeheads 1988, Say Anything 1989, Fatman and Little Boy 1989, The Grifters 1990, True Colors 1991, Shadows and Fog 1992, Roadside Prophets 1992, The Player 1992, Map of the Human Heart 1992, Bob Roberts 1992, Money for Nothing 1993, Bullets Over Broadway 1994, The Road to Wellville 1994, City Hall 1995, Anastasia 1997, Con Air 1997, Hellcab 1997, Midnight in the Garden of Good and Evil 1997, This is My Father 1998, The Thin Red Line 1989, Pushing Tin 1998, Being John Malkovich 1999, America's Sweethearts 2001, Live of the Party 2000, Serendipity 2001, Max 2002, Adaptation 2002; (actor, dir, writer): Grosse Pointe Blank 1997; (producer, actor): Arigo 2000; (actor, writer): High Fidelity 1997, The Cradle Will Rock 1999. *Address:* 1325 Avenue of the Americas, New York, NY 10019, USA (Office).

CUSACK, Sinead Mary; Irish actress; b. 1948; d. of late Cyril Cusack and Maureen Kiely; m. Jeremy Irons 1977; two s.; numerous appearances in TV drama. *Films include:* Alfred the Great, Tamlyn, Hoffman 1969, David Copperfield 1970, Revenge 1971, The Devil's Widow 1971, Horowitz in Dublin Castle, The Last Remake of Beau Geste 1977, Rocket Gibraltar, Venus Peter, Waterland, God on the Rocks 1992, Bad Behaviour 1993, The Cement Garden 1993, The Sparrow, Flemish Board, Stealing Beauty. *Theatre includes:* Lady Amaranth in Wild Oats, Lisa in Children of the Sun, Isabella in Measure for Measure, Celia in As You Like It, Evadne in The Maid's Tragedy, Lady Anne in Richard III, Portia in The Merchant of Venice, Ingrid in Peer Gynt, Kate in The Taming of the Shrew, Beatrice in Much Ado About Nothing, Lady Macbeth in Macbeth, Roxanne in Cyrano de Bergerac (all for RSC), Virago in A Lie of the Mind 2001, Oxford Festival, Gate Theatre, Dublin, Royal Court etc. *Address:* c/o Curtis Brown Group, 4th Floor, Haymarket House, 28–29 Haymarket, London, SW1Y 4SP, England.

CUSHING, Sir Selwyn (John), KNZM, CMG, FCA; New Zealand business executive and airline executive; b. 1 Sept. 1936; s. of Cyril John Cushing and Henrietta Marjory Belle Cushing; m. Kaye Dorothy Anderson 1964; two s.; ed Hastings High School, Univ. of New Zealand; partner Esam Cushing and Co., Hastings 1960–86; Dir Brierly Investments Ltd 1986–93, Chair., CEO 1999–; Deputy Chair. Air New Zealand 1988, now Chair.; Chair. Carter Holt Harvey Ltd 1991–93, Electricity Corpn of NZ 1993–97. *Leisure interests:* cricket, music. *Address:* Air New Zealand, Quay Tower, 29 Customs Street W, Private Bag 92007, Auckland (Office); 1 Beaston Road, Hastings, New Zealand. *Telephone:* (9) 366-2400 (Office). *Fax:* (9) 366-2401 (Office). *Website:* www .airnz.co.nz (Office).

CUSSLER, Clive (Eric), PhD; American novelist; b. 1931; s. of Eric Cussler and Amy Hunnewell; m. Barbara Knight 1955; three c.; owner Bestgen & Cussler Advertising, Newport Beach, Calif. 1961–65; Copy Dir Darcy Advertising, Hollywood, Calif. and Instr. in Advertising Communications, Orange Coast Coll. 1965–67; Advertising Dir Aquatic Marine Corpn, Newport Beach, Calif. 1967–79; Vice-Pres. and Creative Dir of Broadcast, Meffon, Wolff and Weir Advertising, Denver, Colo 1970–73; Chair. Nat. Underwater and Marine Agency; Fellow New York Explorers Club, Royal Geographical Soc.; Lowel Thomas Award, New York Explorers Club. *Publications:* The Mediterranean Caper 1973, Iceberg 1975, Raise the Titanic 1976, Vixen O-Three 1978, Night Probe 1981, Pacific Vortex 1983, Deep Six 1984, Cyclops 1986, Treasure 1988, Dragon 1990, Sahara 1992, Inca Gold 1994, Shock Wave 1995, Sea Hunters 1996, Flood Tide 1997, Clive Cussler and Dirk Pitt Revealed 1997, Serpent 1998, Atlantis Found 1999, Blue Gold 2000, Valhalla Rising 2001, Fire Ice 2002, Sea Hunters II 2002. *Leisure interest:* discovering shipwrecks, collecting classic cars. *Address:* c/o Putnam Publishing Group, 200 Madison Avenue, New York, NY 10016, USA.

CUTAYAR, Egidio; Egyptian banker; b. 22 Dec. 1937, Alexandria; m.; one d.; joined Barclays Bank Int. 1961, Asst Rep., Milan 1970, Asst Man. Banca Barclays Castillini SpA, Milan 1975, Man. 1976, Asst Gen. Man. Europe Barclays Bank PLC Head Office, London 1986, Sr Gen. Man., Milan, Vice-Chair. Barclays Financial Services Italia SpA, Milan 1986, Jt Man. Dir

Banque du Caire Barclays Int. SAE, Cairo 1988–, Vice-Chair. Loans and Participations Cttee Hellenic Mutual Fund Man. Co. SA, Greece 1979, Vice-Pres. Egyptian British Businessmen Asscn, Dir Barclays Leasing Int., Milan 1978, Bd mem. Hellenic Investment Bank, Hellenic Mutual Fund Man. Co. SA, Greece 1979, Italian Chamber of Commerce, Egyptian British Friendship Soc., mem. American Chamber of Commerce, German Chamber of Commerce. *Address:* Banque du Caire Barclays International SAE, 12 Midan El Sheikh Youssef, Garden City, Cairo, Egypt. *Telephone:* (2) 354 0686.

CUTHBERT, Alan William, MA, ScD, FRS, FMedSci; British professor of pharmacology; b. 7 May 1932, Peterborough; s. of the late Thomas William Cuthbert and Florence Mary Cuthbert (née Griffin); m. Harriet Jane Webster 1957; two s.; ed Deacons Grammar School, Peterborough, Leicester Coll. of Tech., Univs. of St Andrew's and London; Reader in Pharmacology, Univ. of Cambridge 1973–79, Sheild Prof. of Pharmacology 1979–99; Master, Fitzwilliam Coll. Cambridge 1991–99; Deputy Vice-Chancellor, Univ. of Cambridge 1995–99; Chair. Editorial Bd British Journal of Pharmacology 1974–82; Vice-Pres. Ephar 1997–; Foreign Sec. British Pharmacological Soc. 1997–2000, Hon. mem. 2000; mem. Academia Europaea, Acad. Royale de Médecine de Belgique; Fellow, Jesus Coll. Cambridge 1968–91, Hon. Fellow 1991–; Master Fitzwilliam Coll. Cambridge 1990–99 (Hon. Fellow 1999); Gov. De Montfort Univ. 1998–; Hon. DSc, Hon. LLD. *Publications:* numerous articles on physiology, pharmacology and biology. *Leisure interests:* painting, sculpture, photography, gardening, travel. *Address:* Department of Medicine, University of Cambridge, Addenbrooke's Hospital, Hills Road, Cambridge, CB2 3QQ (Office); 7 Longstanton Road, Oakington, Cambridge CB4 5BB, England (Home). *Telephone:* (1223) 336853 (Office); (1223) 233676 (Home). *Fax:* (1223) 336846 (Office). *E-mail:* awc1000@cam.ac.uk (Office). *Website:* www.med.cam.ac.uk.

CUTLER, Walter Leon, MA; American diplomatist; b. 25 Nov. 1931, Boston, Mass.; s. of Walter Leon Cutler and Esther Dewey; m. 1st Sarah Gerard Beeson 1957 (divorced 1981); two s.; m. 2nd Isabel Kugel Brookfield 1981; ed Wesleyan Univ. and Fletcher School of Int. Law and Diplomacy; Vice-Consul, Yaoundé, Cameroon 1957–59; Staff Asst to Sec. of State 1960–62; Political-Econ. Officer, Algiers 1962–65; Consul, Tabriz, Iran 1965–67; Political-Mil. Officer, Seoul, Repub. of Korea 1967–69; Political Officer, Saigon, Repub. of Viet Nam 1969–71; Special Asst, Bureau of Far Eastern Affairs, Dept of State 1971–73, mem. Sr Seminar on Foreign Policy 1973–74, Dir Office of Cen. Africa 1974–75; Amb. to Zaïre 1975–79, to Iran 1979; Deputy Asst Sec. of State for Congressional Relations 1979–81; Amb. to Tunisia 1981–83, to Saudi Arabia 1983–87, 1988–89; Pres. Meridian Int. Center, Washington, DC 1989–; Sr Advisor Trust Co. of the West, LA 1990–; Research Prof. of Diplomacy, Georgetown Univ. 1987–88; Special Emissary for Sec.-Gen. of UN, New York 1994; mem. Council on Foreign Relations, New York, American Acad. of Diplomacy, Washington Inst. of Foreign Affairs; Wilbur J. Carr Award 1989, Dir-Gen.'s Cup, Dept of State 1993; Order of the Leopard (Repub. of Zaïre) 1979; King Abdulaziz Decoration (Saudi Arabia) 1985. *Leisure interests:* sports, ornithology. *Address:* Meridian International Center, 1630 Crescent Place, NW, Washington, DC 20009-4004, USA.

CUTTS, Simon; British artist, poet and publisher; b. 30 Dec. 1944, Derby; s. of George Tom Cutts and Elizabeth Purdy; m. 1st Annira Uusi-Illikainen (divorced 1973); one s.; m. 2nd Margot Hapgood (died 1985); ed Herbert Strutt Grammar School, Belper, Derbyshire, Nottingham Coll. of Art, Trent Polytechnic; travel and miscellaneous employment including The Trent Bookshop, Nottingham 1962–69; Jt Ed. Tarasque Press 1964–72; publishing, lecturing and writing 1972–74; Dir and Co-Partner Coracle Press Books (now Coracle Production and Distribution) 1975–87; Dir, Coracle Press Gallery 1983–86; Dir Victoria Miro Gallery 1985–; org. of exhbns in Europe and New York. *Publications:* numerous publs including Quelques Pianos 1976, Pianostool Footnotes 1983, Petits-Airs for Margot 1986, Seepages 1988. *Leisure interests:* walking, running, cooking, eating, drinking and the nostalgia of innocence. *Address:* Victoria Miro, 21 Cork Street, London, W1 (Office); 4/16 Courtfield Gardens, London, SW5, England (Home). *Telephone:* (20) 7734-5082 (Office); (20) 7370-4301 (Home).

CYWIŃSKA, Izabella, MA; Polish theatre producer and director; b. 22 March 1935, Kamień; d. of Andrzej Cywiński and Elżbieta Łuszczewska; m. Janusz Michałowski 1968; ed Warsaw Univ., State Acad. of Drama, Warsaw; Asst, Rural Architecture Faculty, Warsaw Univ. of Tech. 1956–58; Stage Dir, Theatre in Cracow-Nowa Huta 1966–68, Polski Theatre, Poznań 1966–68; Dir and Artistic Man. Wojciech Bogusławski Theatre, Kalisz 1969–73, Nowy Theatre, Poznań 1973–88; Vice-Pres. Understanding Cttee of Creative Circles, Poznań 1980–81; Minister of Culture and Art 1989–91; founder and Vice-Pres. Culture Foundation 1991–93; artistic Dir 50th Anniversary of the Revolt in the Warsaw Ghetto; mem. Polish Stage Artists' Asscn, Presidential Council for Culture 1992–95, Gen. Ass. European Cooperation Foundation, Brussels; First Prize for "Beauty", Int. TV Festival, Plovdiv, Bulgaria 1997; All-Poland Drama Festivals, Kalisz 1970, 1973, 1980, Opole 1976, Wrocław 1976, Minister of Culture and Art Award (2nd class) 1977; Kt.'s Cross of Polonia Restituta Order , Medal Kalos Kagathos, Gold Cross of Merit, Nat. Educ. Comm. Medal and other decorations; Nat. Broadcasting Council of Poland Award 1999, Special Prix Europa Award 2000, Willy Brandt Award, Prix Europa Int. TV Festival, Berlin 2000. *Plays directed include:* Iphigenie auf Tauris 1968, The Morals of Mrs. Dulska 1970, The Death of Tarelkin 1973, I giganti della montagna 1973, Lower Depths 1974, They 1975, Wijuny 1976, Bath-house 1978, Judas from Karioth 1980, The Accused: June '56 1981,

Enemy of the People 1982, Dawn 1986, Virginity 1986, Cemeteries 1988, Tartuffe 1989, Antygona in New York 1993, Hanemann 2002; also Dir in USA and USSR, I Leave You 2003. *TV film:* Frédéric's Enchantment (about Chopin) 1998, Purym's Miracle 1999. *Television production include:* God's Lining (TV series) 1997, Beauty (TV theatre) 1998, Second Mother 1999, Touch (TV theatre) 2001, Marilyn Mongol (TV theatre) 2002, Bar World (TV theatre) 2003. *Publication:* Nagłe zastępstwo 1992. *Leisure interests:* foreign travel, politics. *Address:* ul. Piwna 7A m. 5, 00-265 Warsaw, Poland (Home). *Telephone:* (22) 635-32-33. *Fax:* (22) 635-32-33; (22) 635-32-33 (Home). *E-mail:* cywinska@hoga.pl (Home).

CZERWIŃSKA, Anna, PharmD; Polish mountaineer; b. 10 July 1949, Warsaw; ed Acad. of Medicine, Warsaw; mem. staff CEFARM, Warsaw 1977–79, Centre of Rehabilitation STOCER 1980–83, Children's Hosp., Dziekanów Leśny 1984–87; Dir own firm Anamax–Import-Export, Warsaw 1989–; mountaineering expeditions include Tatra, Alps, Karakoram, Himalayas (female teams), Mount Everest (solo) 2000 (oldest woman to reach summit); solo climbing the length of the Tatra ridge 1991; first Polish woman to climb the Crown of the Earth (highest peaks on every continent) 1995–2000;

has reached the summit of six of the world's 8000m peaks. *Publications:* Twice Matterhorn (with Krystyna Palmowska) 1980, Difficult Mountain Rakaposhi 1982, Broad Peak – Only Two 1988, Nanga Parbat – Ill-Fated Mountain 1989, Threat Around K2 1990, Crown of the Earth 2000. *Leisure interests:* do-it-yourself, gardening; mountain biking, white-water rafting. *Address:* Anamax–Import-Export, ul. Łomiańska 10 m. 4, 01-685 Warsaw, Poland (Office). *Telephone:* (22) 8332093 (Office).

CZIBERE, Tibor; Hungarian politician and engineer; b. 16 Oct. 1930, Tapolca; s. of Jozsef Czibere and Maria Loppert; m. Gabriella Nagy 1956; two d.; ed Tech. Univ. of Heavy Industry, Miskolc; engineer with Ganz-MÁVAG Machine Works 1956; rejoined Miskolc Univ. and active as lecturer 1963, Prof. and fmr Dean of Mechanical Eng Faculty 1968, Rector 1978–86, Prof. 1986–88, 1989–; Minister of Culture 1988–89; Corresp. mem. Hungarian Acad. of Sciences 1976, mem. 1985–, mem. of Parl. 1983–85, 1988–90; Vice-Pres. Nat. Council of Patriotic People's Front 1985–89; Kossuth Prize 1962, Labour Order of Merit 1971, Star Order of the People's Repub. 1986, Szetgyörgyi Albert Prize 1996. *Address:* University of Miskolc, 3515-Miskolc-Egyetemváros, Hungary. *Telephone:* (46) 365-111.

D

DA COSTA, Manuel Saturnino; Guinea-Bissau politician; Sec. Gen. Partido Africano da Independência da Guiné e Cabo Verde (PAIGC); Prime Minister 1994–97. *Address:* c/o Partido Africano da Independência da Guiné e Cabo Verde, C.P. 106, Bissau, Guinea-Bissau.

DA CRUZ POLICARPO, HE Cardinal José; Portuguese ecclesiastic; b. 26 Feb. 1936, Alvorninha, Caldas da Rainha; ed Seminário Major de Cristo-Rei, Pontifícia Universidade Gregoriana, Rome; ordained priest 1961; Lecturer Catholic Univ. of Portugal 1970, Auxiliary Prof. 1971, Prof. (Extraordinary) 1977, Prof. (Ordinary) 1986, Dir Faculty of Theology 1974–80, 1985–88; Bishop 1978; Auxiliary Bishop of Lisbon 1978–97; Coadjutor 1997; Patriarch 1998; Pres. Portuguese Episcopal Conf. 1999–; cr. Cardinal 2001; mem. Higher Council, Catholic Univ. of Portugal, Pres. Comm. 1985–87, Rector 1988–92, 1992–96, Chancellor 1998–; Hon. Assoc. Portuguese Acad. of History 2000–. *Publications:* José Policarpo 1999, Palavra e Vida 2000. *Address:* Cúria Patriarcal, Campo di Sta Clara, 1100-473 Lisbon, Portugal (Office). *Telephone:* (21) 8810500 (Office); (21) 9457310 (Home). *Fax:* (21) 8810530 (Office); (21) 9457329 (Home). *E-mail:* gab.patriarca@patriarcado-lisboa.pt (Office). *Website:* www.patriarcado-lisboa.pt (Office).

DA CRUZ VILAÇA, José Luís, DEcon; Portuguese judge, lawyer and professor of law; b. 20 Sept. 1944, Braga; s. of Fernando da Costa Vilaça and Maria das Dores G. Cruz Vilaça; m. Marie-Charlotte Opitz 1995; two s. two d. (three c. from previous m.); ed Univs. of Coimbra, Paris and Oxford; Asst Faculty of Law, Univ. of Coimbra 1966, Prof. of Fiscal Law and Community Law 1979; mil. service, Naval Legal Dept 1969–72; mem. Parl. 1980–86; Sec. of State for Home Affairs 1980, for Presidency of Council of Ministers 1981, for European Affairs 1982; Advocate-Gen. Court of Justice of EC 1986–89; Full Prof. and Dir Inst. for European Studies, Lusiada Univ. Lisbon 1988; Pres. Court of First Instance of EC 1989–95; Chair. Disciplinary Bd of EC; Partner PLMJ and Assocs, Lisbon; Sec.-Gen. Portuguese Asscn of European Law (APDE); Visiting Prof. Univ. Nova de Lisboa; Gran Croce del Ordine di Merito (Italy), Grand-Croix de la Couronne de Chêne (Luxembourg). *Publications:* A empresa cooperativa 1969, L'économie portugaise face à l'intégration économique européenne 1978, Introdução ao estudo da Economia 1979, Modelo económico da CEE e modelo económico português 1984, As consêquencias da adesão de Portugal à CEE no sector cultural 1984, The Court of First Instance of the European Communities: A Significant Step Towards the Consolidation of the European Community as a Community Governed by the Rule of Law 1993, Y-a-t-il des limites matérielles à la révision des traités instituant les communautés européennes? 1993, The Development of the Community Judicial System Before and After Maastricht 1994, La procédure en référé comme instrument de protection juridictionnelle des particuliers en droit communautaire 1998, An Exercise on the Application of Keck & Nithoreard in the Field of Free Provision of Services 1999, Código da Unión Europeia 2001. *Leisure interests:* tennis, gardening, literature. *Address:* PLMJ–A. M. Pereira e Associados, Avenida da Liberdade 224, 1250-148 Lisbon, Portugal (Office). *Telephone:* (21) 3197321 (Office). *Fax:* (21) 3197319 (Office). *E-mail:* jcv@plmj.pt (Office).

DA SILVA, Luis Inácio (Lula) (see Lula Da Silva, Inácio).

DAANE, James Dewey; American banker and educator; b. 6 July 1918, Grand Rapids, Mich.; s. of Gilbert L. and Mamie (née Blocksma) Daane; m. 1st Blanche M. Tichenor 1941 (divorced); one d.; m. 2nd Onnie B. Selby 1953 (deceased); m. 3rd Barbara W McMann 1963; two d.; ed Duke Univ. and Harvard Univ.; with Fed. Reserve Bank of Richmond 1939–60, Monetary Economist 1947, Asst Vice-Pres. 1953, Vice-Pres., Dir, Research Dept, 1957; Chief, IMF Mission to Paraguay 1950–51; Vice-Pres., Econ. Adviser, Fed. Reserve Bank of Minneapolis May-July 1960; Asst to Sec. of U.S. Treasury, Prin. Adviser to Under-Sec. for Monetary Affairs 1960–61; Deputy Under-Sec. of Treasury for Monetary Affairs and Gen. Deputy to Under-Sec. for Monetary Affairs 1961–63; mem. Bd of Govs., Fed. Reserve System 1963–74; Vice-Chair. Commerce Union Bank 1974–78; Vice-Chair. Tennessee Valley Bancorp 1975–78; Chair. Int. Policy Cttee, Sovran Financial Corpn/Cen. South 1978–87; Dir Nat. Futures Asscn, Ill. 1983; Chair. money market Cttee S Sovran Bank 1988–90; Frank K. Houston Prof. of Banking and Finance, Grad. School of Man., Vanderbilt Univ. 1974–85, Valere Blair Potter Prof. of Banking and Finance 1985–89, Prof. Emer. 1989–; Alan R. Holmes Prof. of Econs Middlebury Coll. 1991–99; Dir Whittaker Corpn 1977–89, Chicago Bd of Trade 1979–82; mem. American Finance Asscn, American Econ. Asscn. *Address:* Vanderbilt University, Owen Graduate School of Management, 401 21st Avenue, South Nashville, TN 37203 (Office); 102 Westhampton Place, Nashville, TN 37205, USA (Home).

DACHEVILLE, Colette (pseudonym Stéphane Audran); French actress; b. 8 Nov. 1932, Versailles; d. of Corneille Dacheville and Jeanne Rossi; m. 1st Jean-Louis Trintignant; m. 2nd Claude Chabrol 1964; one s.; ed Lycée Lamartine, Paris, Cours Charles Dullin; studied drama under Tania Balachova and Michel Vitold; Commdr Légion d'honneur. *Films include:* Les bonnes femmes 1959, L'oeil du malin 1961, Landru 1962, Ligne de démarcation 1966, Champagne Murders 1966, Les biches 1968 (Best Actress, Berlin), La femme infidèle 1968, La peau de torpedo 1969, La dame dans l'auto avec les lunettes et un fusil 1969, Le boucher 1970 (Best Actress, San Sebastián), La rupture 1970, Aussi loin que l'amour 1970, Juste avant la nuit 1971, Without Apparent Motive 1971, Un meurtre est un meurtre 1972, Dead

Pigeon on Beethoven Street 1972, Discreet Charm of the Bourgeoisie 1972 (Best Actress, Soc. of Film and TV Arts), Les noces rouges 1973, Comment réussir dans la vie quand on est con et pleurnichard 1973, Le cri du coeur 1974, Ten Little Indians 1974, B Must Die 1974, The Black Bird 1975, Vincent, François, Paul and Others 1975, Folies bourgeoises 1976, Silver Bears 1976, Devil's Advocate 1976, Violette Nozière 1978, Le Soleil en face 1979, The Big Red One 1980, Coup de Torchon 1981, Boulevard des assassins 1982, Le choc 1982, On ira tous au paradis, Le sang des autres 1983, Poulet au vinaigre 1984, Babette's Feast 1988 (Best Actress, Taormina), La Cage aux Folles III: The Wedding, Manika: The Girl Who Lived Twice 1989, Quiet Days in Clichy 1989, Betty 1991. *TV appearances in:* Brideshead Revisited 1981, Mistral's Daughter 1984, The Sun Also Rises 1984, Poor Little Rich Girl 1986, Tecx 1989, Cry No More My Lady. *Address:* c/o 2F De Marthod, 11 rue Chanez, Paris 75016, France. *Telephone:* 47431314.

DACKO, David; Central African Republic politician; b. 24 March 1930, M'Baiki; ed Ecole Normale, Brazzaville; Minister of Agriculture, Stockbreeding, Water and Forests, Cen. African Govt Council 1957–58; Minister of Interior, Economy and Trade, Cen. African Provisional Govt 1958–59; Premier, Cen. African Repub. 1959–66, Minister of Nat. Defence, Guardian of the Seals 1960–66; Pres. of Cen. African Repub. 1960–66 (deposed by mil. coup); mem. Mouvement pour l'Evolution Sociale de l'Afrique Noire (MESAN); under house arrest for several years; appointed Personal Adviser to Pres. (later Emperor) 1976; Pres. of restored Repub. 1979–81; ousted in coup Sept. 1981; Pres. UDEAC 1979; Ind. Cand., Presidential Elections Oct. 1992; Head Provisional Nat. Political Council March–May 1993; Founder, Leader Mouvement pour la Démocratie et le Développement (MDD) 1993–; Cand., Presidential Elections 1999. *Address:* Mouvement pour la Démocratie et le Développement, Bangui, Central African Republic.

DACOSTA, Claude Antoine; Republic of Congo politician and agronomist; Prime Minister of the Congo 1992–93; Chair. Devt Cttee 1993.

DACRE, Paul Michael, BA; British newspaper editor; b. 14 Nov. 1948, London; s. of Peter Dacre and Joan Dacre (née Hill); m. Kathleen Thomson 1973; two s.; ed Univ. Coll. School, London, Leeds Univ.; reporter, feature writer, Assoc. Features Ed., Daily Express 1970–76, Washington and New York Corresp. 1976–79; New York Bureau Chief, Daily Mail 1980, News Ed., London 1981–85, Asst Ed. (News and Foreign) 1986, Asst Ed. (Features) 1987, Exec. Ed. 1988, Assoc. Ed. 1989–91, Ed. 1992–, Ed.-in-Chief Assoc. Newspapers 1998–; Ed. Evening Standard 1991–92; Dir Associated Newspaper Holdings 1991–, Daily Mail & General Trust PLC 1998–, Teletext Holdings Ltd 2000–; mem. Press Complaints Comm. 1998–. *Address:* Daily Mail, Northcliffe House, 2 Derry Street, London, W8 5TT, England. *Telephone:* (20) 7938-6000. *Fax:* (20) 7937-7977.

DADDAH, Moktar Ould, LenD; Mauritanian politician; b. 20 Dec. 1924, Boutilmit; ed secondary school, Senegal and Paris; interpreter; studied law; with firm Boissier Palun, Dakar; territorial councillor 1957; Premier, Islamic Repub. of Mauritania 1958–78; Pres. of the Repub. 1961–78; under house arrest 1978–79; left Mauritania, sentenced in absentia to hard labour for life Nov. 1980; Pres. Org. Commune Africaine et Malgache 1965; Chair. OAU 1971–72; fmr Sec.-Gen. Parti du Peuple Mauritanien.

DAFA, Bader Omar Al-, MA; Qatari diplomatist; m. Awatef Mohamed Al-Dafa; three c.; ed Western Michigan Univ., School of Advanced Int. Studies, Johns Hopkins Univ., USA; Diplomatic Attaché, Ministry of Foreign Affairs 1976; Amb. to Spain 1982–88, to Egypt (also Perm. Rep. to Arab League) 1988–93, to France (non-resident, accred. to Greece and Switzerland) 1993–95, to Russia (also accred. to Finland, Latvia, Lithuania and Estonia) 1995–98; Dir of European and American Affairs, Ministry of Foreign Affairs 1998–2000; Amb. to USA 2000–. *Address:* Embassy of Qatar, 4200 Wisconsin Avenue, NW, Washington, DC 20016, USA (Office). *Telephone:* (202) 274-1603 (Office). *Fax:* (202) 237-0061 (Office). *E-mail:* washington@mofa.gov.qa.

DAFALLAH, Gizouli; Sudanese politician and physician; b. Dec. 1935, Blue Nile Prov.; two d.; ed Khartoum Medical Coll.; Chair. Alliance of the Nat. Forces April 1985 (after overthrow of Pres. Gaafar al-Nemery in coup); Chair. Doctors' Union; Prime Minister of Sudan 1985–86. *Address:* c/o Office of the Prime Minister, Khartoum, Sudan.

DAFFA, Ali Abdullah al-, PhD; Saudi Arabian professor of mathematics; b. Anayza; ed Stephen F. Austin State Univ., East Texas State Univ., Vanderbilt Univ.; Asst Prof. King Fahd Univ. of Petroleum and Minerals, Dhahran 1972, Assoc. Prof. 1977, Chair. Dept of Math. Sciences 1974–77, Dean Coll. of Sciences 1977–84, Prof. 1980–; Visiting Prof. King Saud Univ., Riyadh 1979–82, Harvard Univ. 1983; Pres. Union of Arab Mathematicians and Physicists 1979–81, 1986–88; mem. Royal Acad. of Research on Islamic Civilization, Jordan, Scientific Council of the Islamic Foundation for Science, Tech. and Devt, Jeddah, Arab Scientific Soc., Baghdad; mem. Bd King Faisal Centre for Islamic Studies and Research; mem. editorial Bd Encyclopaedia of Islamic Civilization; hon. mem. Acad. of Arabic Language; Fellow Islamic Acad. of Sciences. *Publications:* 36 books and more than 250 articles on math. and history of science. *Address:* King Fahd University of Petroleum and

Minerals, Dhahran 31261, Saudi Arabia (Office). *Telephone:* (3) 860-0000 (Office). *Fax:* (3) 860-3306 (Office). *E-mail:* rector@kfupm.edu.sa (Office). *Website:* www.kfupm.edu.sa (Office).

DAFOE, Willem; American actor; b. 22 July 1955, Appleton, Wis.; s. of William Dafoe; ed Wisconsin Univ. *Films include:* The Loveless 1981, New York Nights 1981, The Hunger 1982, Communists are Comfortable (and three other stories) 1984, Roadhouse 66 1984, Streets of Fire 1984, To Live and Die in LA 1985, Platoon 1986, The Last Temptation of Christ 1988, Saigon 1988, Mississippi Burning 1989, Triumph of the Spirit 1989, Born on the 4th of July 1990, Flight of the Intruder 1990, Wild at Heart 1990, The Light Sleeper 1991, Body of Evidence 1992, Far Away, So Close 1994, Tom and Viv 1994, The Night and the Moment 1994, Clear and Present Danger 1994, The English Patient 1996, Basquiat 1996, Speed 2: Cruise Control 1997, Affliction 1997, Lulu on the Bridge 1998, eXistenZ 1998, American Psycho 1999, Shadow of the Vampire 2000, Bullfighter 2000, The Animal Factory 2000, Edges of the Lord 2001, The Reckoning 2001, Spider-Man 2002, Auto Focus 2002.

DAFT, Douglas (Doug) N.; Australian business executive; b. 1944; joined Coca-Cola Co., Australia 1969, Pres. Cen. Pacific Div. 1984, N Pacific Div. 1988, Pres. Coca-Cola (Japan) Co. 1988, Pres. Pacific Group, Atlanta 1991, Head Middle and Far East and Africa Groups, Head Schweppes Div. 1999, Chair., CEO 2000–. *Address:* The Coca-Cola Company, One Coca-Cola Place, Atlanta, GA 30313, USA (Office).

DAGAN, Maj.-Gen. Meir; Israeli army officer; b. 1947; army officer, Head of Rimon undercover unit, Gaza Strip, early 1970s, mem. 143 Div., Yom Kippur War 1973, Commdr in S Lebanon 1982, Special Asst to Army Chief of Staff 1987–93, retd from army 1995; joined Mossad 1995, Deputy Dir 1995–97, Counter-Terrorism Adviser to Prime Minister 1997–2000, Head of Israeli negotiating team Nov. 2001, Head of Mossad Oct. 2002–; several citations for bravery during army service. *Address:* Mossad, c/o Ministry of Defence, Kaplan Street, Hakirya, Tel-Aviv 67659, Israel.

DAGHESTANI, Fakhruddin, PhD; Jordanian civil servant and engineer; m.; six c.; ed Univ. of Missouri; lecturer Coll. of Eng, Univ. of Missouri 1961–67, at IBM, Rochester, Minn. 1968–71; Dir Mechanical Eng Dept, Royal Scientific Soc. (RSS) 1971–76, Vice-Pres. 1976–83, Acting Pres. 1983–84, Pres. 1984–86, Adviser and Prin. Researcher 1986–91, Dir Centre for Int. Studies 1991–93; Dir Gen. Natural Resources Authority 1993–96, Mineral Investment Co. 1996–; mem. Scientific Council IFSTAD 1984–86, Exec. Cttee COMSTECH 1986–94; mem. Arab Fed. of Scientific Research 1983–86; Founding Fellow Islamic Acad. of Sciences, mem. Council 1986–99; mem. Bd of Govs. RSS, Telecommunications Corpn, Natural Resources Authority, Jordan Electricity Authority, Arab Potash Co., Nat. Petroleum Co. and Jordan Phosphate Mining Co.; mem. Bd Faculties of Grad. Studies and Scientific Research, Jordan Univ.; mem. Editorial Bd Journal of the Islamic Acad. of Sciences; fmr mem. Editorial Bd Islamic Thought and Scientific Creativity (journal) 1990–95. *Publications:* Ed. and Co-Ed. 11 books, author of over 40 technical papers on applied mechanics. *Address:* PO Box 419, Jubaiha 11941, Jordan (Office).

DAGHESTANI, Najib Abu Al Alaa, MSc; Syrian engineer and technical and investment analyst; b. 26 June 1940, Damascus; s. of Kazem Daghestani and Inaam Al Azem; m. Moira Beaton 1972 (divorced 1987); two s.; ed Enfield Coll. of Tech. London and Univ. of Strathclyde; geotechnical engineer, UK 1968–72; counterpart to ILO expert, geotechnical engineer (Ministry of Communication), Syria 1972–74; civil and material engineer Saudi Arabia 1974–78; project man., Jt gen. man. Sultanate of Oman 1978–81; contracts man. Libya 1981–82; promotion and devt man. (Middle East and Africa) Cyprus, UAE, Saudi Arabia, Yemen 1982–86; consultant, Daghestani Eng Services, Portugal 1996–. *Publication:* Ground Engineering 1970. *Leisure interests:* water sports, hiking, painting, reading. *Address:* 62 Mahdi Ben Barakeh Avenue, Damascus, Syria; PO Box 428, 8500 Portimão, Portugal. *Telephone:* (11) 3334544 (Damascus), (282) 424050 (Portimão).

DAGWORTHY PREW, Wendy Ann, BA; British fashion designer and professor of fashion; b. Wendy Ann Dagworthy, 4 March 1950, Gravesend; d. of Arthur S. Dagworthy and Jean A. Stubbs; m. Jonathan W. Prew 1973; two s.; ed Medway Coll. of Design and Hornsey Coll. of Art; founder, designer and Dir Wendy Dagworthy Ltd (design co.) 1972–; Dir London Designer Collections 1982; consultant to CNAA Fashion/Textiles Bd 1982–; Course Dir Fashion BA Hons Degree, Cen. St Martin's Coll. of Art and Design 1989–; Prof. of Fashion and Head of School of Fashion and Textiles, Royal Coll. of Art 1998–; Judge, Royal Soc. of Arts Bd; judge of art and design projects for various mfrs; participating designer in Fashion Aid and many charity shows; exhibited seasonally in London, Milan, New York and Paris; Lecturer and External Assessor at numerous polytechnics and colls of art and design; frequent TV appearances; Fil d'Or Int. Linen Award 1986. *Leisure interests:* dining out, cooking, reading, painting, drawing. *Address:* Royal College of Art, Kensington Gore, London SW7 3EU (Office); 18 Melrose Terrace, London, W6, England (Home). *Telephone:* (20) 7590-4444 (Office); (20) 7602-6676 (Home). *Fax:* (20) 7590-4360 (Office). *E-mail:* w.dagworthy@rca.ac.uk (Office). *Website:* www.rca.ac.uk (Office).

DAHAB, Field Marshal Abdul-Rahman Swar al-; Sudanese politician and army officer; b. 1934, Omdurman; m.; two s. three d.; joined Sudanese Mil. Acad. 1954; trained at mil. acads in Jordan, Britain and Egypt; Minister of Defence, C-in-C Sudanese Army March 1985–86; led mil. coup April 1985; Chair. Transitional Mil. Council 1985–86; rank of Field Marshal 1987. *Address:* c/o Ministry of Defence, Khartoum, Sudan.

DAHAN, Nissim; Israeli politician and academic; b. 1954, Morocco; m.; nine c.; ed Porat Yossef Talmudic Coll.; completed mil. service; mem. Knesset (Parl.) 1996–; mem. of Finance, Econs, Foreign Affairs and Defence Cttees 2001–; Deputy Minister of Finance 1999–2000; Minister of Health (Shas Party); mem. Cttee for the Establishment of Ganei Modi'in, Jerusalem Devt Authority; Dir Orgs and Insts Dept of the Ministry of Religious Affairs. *Address:* Ministry of Health, PO Box 1176, 2 Ben-Tabai Street, Jerusalem 91010, Israel (Office). *Telephone:* (2) 6708511 (Office). *Fax:* (2) 6796491 (Office). *E-mail:* ndahan@knesset.gov.il (Office).

DAHL, Birgitta, BA; Swedish politician; b. 20 Sept. 1937, Råda; d. of Anna-Brita Axelsson and Sven Dahl; m. Enn Kokk; one s. two d.; ed Univ. of Uppsala; teacher, clerical officer, Scandinavian Inst. of African Studies, Uppsala 1960–65; Sr Admin. Officer, Dag Hammarskjöld Foundation 1965–68, Swedish Int. Devt Authority 1965–82; mem. Parl. 1968–2002; fmr mem. Bd of Dirs Nat. Housing Bd; mem. Advisory Council of Foreign Affairs; del. to UN Gen. Ass.; mem. Exec. Cttee Social Democratic Party 1975–96; Minister with special responsibility for Energy Issues, Ministry of Energy 1982–86, for the Environment and Energy 1987–90, for the Environment 1990–91; Spokesperson on Social Welfare; Chair. Environment Cttee of Socialist Int. 1986–93, Confed. of Socialist Parties of EC 1990–94, Chair. High Level Advisory Bd on Sustainable Devt to Sec.-Gen. 1996–97; Speaker of Riksdag (Swedish Parl.) 1994–2002; Sr Adviser Global Environment Facility (GEF) 1998–; Grand Cross of the White Rose (Finland) 2002, Cross of Terra Mariana (Estonia) 2002, Das Grosse Goldene Ehreinzeiche (Austria) 2002, Quorum Merueve Laboris (Sweden) 2003. *Address:* Idroftsgatan 12, 75335 Uppsala, Sweden (Home). *Telephone:* (18) 211793 (Home). *Fax:* (18) 211793 (Home). *E-mail:* 34dahl@telia.com.

DAHL, Robert Alan, PhD; American professor of political science; b. 17 Dec. 1915, Inwood, Iowa; s. of Peter I. Dahl and Vera Lewis Dahl; m. 1st Mary Louise Barlett 1940 (died 1970); three s. one d.; m. 2nd Ann Goodrich Sale 1973; ed Univ. of Washington, Div. of Econ. Research, Nat. Labor Relations Bd and Yale Univ.; Man. Analyst, US Dept of Agric. 1940; Economist, Office of Production Man., OPACS and War Production Bd 1940–42; US Army 1943–45; with Yale Univ., successively Instructor, Asst Prof., Assoc. Prof. and Sterling Prof. of Political Science 1964–86; Chair. Dept of Political Science 1957–62; Ford Research Prof. 1957; Lecturer in Political Science, Flacso, Santiago, Chile 1967; Guggenheim Fellow 1950 and 1978; Fellow, Center for Advanced Study in the Behavioral Sciences 1955–56 and 1967; Pres. American Political Science Asscn 1967; Fellow American Acad. of Arts and Sciences, American Philosophical Soc., NAS; fmr Trustee, Center for Advanced Study in the Behavioral Sciences; fmr mem. Educ. Advisory Bd, Guggenheim Foundation; Hon. LLD (Mich.) 1983, (Alaska) 1987, (Harvard) 1996; Hon. DHumLitt (Georgetown) 1993; Woodrow Wilson Prize 1963, Talcott Parsons Prize 1977 and other prizes; Bronze Star Medal with Cluster, Cavaliere of Repub. of Italy. *Publications:* Congress and Foreign Policy 1950, Domestic Control of Atomic Energy (with R. Brown) 1951, Politics, Economics and Welfare (with C. E. Lindblom) 1953, A Preface to Democratic Theory 1956, Social Science Research on Business (with Haire and Lazarsfeld) 1959, Who Governs? 1961, Modern Political Analysis 1963, Political Oppositions in Western Democracies 1966, Pluralist Democracy in the United States 1967, After the Revolution 1970, Polyarchy: Participation and Opposition 1971, Regimes and Opposition 1972, Democracy in the United States 1972, Size and Democracy (with E. R. Tufte) 1973, Dilemmas of Pluralist Democracy 1982, A Preface to Economic Democracy 1985, The Control of Nuclear Weapons: Democracy v. Guardianship 1985, Democracy, Liberty and Equality 1986, Democracy and the Critics 1989, Towards Democracy: A Journey 1997, Reflections (1940–1997) 1997, On Democracy 1999, Politica e Virtú 2001, How Democratic is the American Constitution 2002, Intervista sul Pluralismo 2002. *Leisure interests:* tennis, sailing, fly-fishing. *Address:* 17 Cooper Road, North Haven, CT 06473, USA (Home). *Telephone:* (203) 288-3126. *Fax:* (203) 432-6196.

DAHL, Sophie; British fashion model; b. 1978; granddaughter of Patricia Neal (q.v.) and the late Roald Dahl; discovered as a model by Isabella Blow who saw her crying in the street; has worked with fashion photographers Nick Knight, David La Chapelle, Karl Lagerfeld, David Bailey, Enrique Badulescu, Herb Ritts and Ellen Von Unwerth; has appeared in ID, The Face, Arena, Elle, Esquire, Scene magazines and advertising campaigns for Lainey Keogh, Bella Freud, Printemps, Nina Ricci, Karl Lagerfeld, Oil of Ulay, Hennes; music videos for U2, Elton John and Duran Duran; contribs to The Telegraph, The Sunday Times, Tatler and Elle magazine; cameo appearance in films Mad Cows and Best 1999; stage appearance in The Vagina Monologues, The Old Vic 1999; judge Orange Prize for Fiction 2003. *Publication:* The Man with the Dancing Eyes 2003. *Address:* c/o Storm Model Management, 5 Jubilee Place, London, SW3 3TD, England. *Telephone:* (20) 7352-2278.

DAHLBECK, Eva; Swedish actress and author; b. 8 March 1920, Nacka; d. of Edvard Dahlbeck and Greta Österberg; m. Col Sven Lampell 1944; two s.; ed Royal Dramatic Theatre School, Stockholm. *Films include:* The Counterfeit Traitor 1961, Biljett till Paradiset 1961, För att inte tala om alla dessa Kvinnor 1964, Alskande par 1964, Kattorna 1965, Les créatures 1965, Den Röda Kappan 1966. *Plays include:* Candida 1961, Ända älskar vi varavdra

1963, Tchin-Tchin 1963, The Balcony 1964, Doctors of Philosophy 1964. *Publications:* Dessa mina minsta (play) 1955, Hem till Kaos (novel) 1964, S'is'ta Spegeln (novel) 1965, Den S'junde Natten (novel) 1966, Domen (novel) 1967, Med Seende Ögon (novel) 1972, Hjrätslagen (novel) 1974, Saknadens Dal (novel) 1976, Maktspråket 1978, I Våra Tomma Rum 1980. *Leisure interests:* reading, music.

DAHLFORS, John Ragnar, MCE; Swedish civil engineer; b. 31 Dec. 1934, Stockholm; s. of Mats Dahlfors and Astrid Dahlfors; m. 1st Anita Roger 1962 (dissolved); one s. two d.; m. 2nd Ing-Britt Schlyter 1998; ed Royal Inst. of Tech., Stockholm; engineer with Gränges AB Liberia project 1962–66, Sales Man. Gränges Hedlund AB 1967–68, Pres. 1970–74, Tech. Man. Gränges Construction AB 1969, Pres. Gränges Aluminium AB 1974–78; Pres. Boliden AB 1978–86; man. consultant at Sevenco; mem. Bd, Nordea Funds, ABA of Sweden, Perten Instruments, EIAB, Vemdalsfjäll, ACB Group, Mailbox Etc; mem. Swedish Acad. of Eng Sciences. *Leisure interests:* sailing, golf, tennis, hunting. *Address:* Sevenco, Warfinges Väg 27, 10425 Stockholm (Office); Sävstigen 1, 133 35 Saltsjöbaden, Sweden (Home). *Telephone:* (8) 61-95-200 (Office); (8) 71-72-800 (Home). *Fax:* (8) 13-02-88 (Office); (8) 71-76-798 (Home). *E-mail:* john.dahlfors@telia.com (Home).

DAHLIE, Bjorn; Norwegian Olympic skier; b. 19 June 1967; partner Vilde; two s.; winner of a record total of 29 medals (gold, silver and bronze) 1991–99, including eight Gold Olympic medals; retd 2001. *Publication:* Gulljakten (autobiog.). *Leisure interest:* hunting.

DAHLLÖF, Urban Sigurd, DPhil; Swedish professor emeritus; b. 11 Nov. 1928, Göteborg; s. of Sigurd Dahllöf and Karin Hansson; m. Tordis Larsson 1950; two s. one d.; ed Uppsala Univ. and Univ. of Stockholm; Research Asst, Stockholm School of Educ. 1956–60, Asst Prof. 1963–66; Asst Prof., Univ. of Göteborg 1960–62, Assoc. Prof. 1966–72, Prof. of Educ. 1972–76; Prof. of Educ., Uppsala Univ. 1976–93; Project Leader (part-time) Mid-Sweden Univ. Coll. 1991–96; Research Dir (part-time) Univ. of Trondheim 1991–96; Adjunct Prof. Møre Research/Volda Coll., Volda, Norway 1994–99; Head of Bureau, Nat. Bd of Educ., Stockholm 1962–63, Office of the Swedish Chancellor of the Univs, Stockholm 1973–75; Visiting Prof., Univ. of Melbourne 1984; Sr Consultant, Interior Univ. Soc., Prince George, BC 1988; Chair. Study Group on Evaluation in Higher Educ., OECD, Paris 1988–90; Chair. Swedish School Research Cttee 1978–80, Swedish Secondary School Planning Cttee 1979–81; Pres. Swedish Psychological Asscn 1966–68; Hon. Rector Mid-Sweden Univ. Coll. 1997; mem. Swedish Royal Acad. of Sciences, Swedish Acad. of Letters, History and Antiquities; Hon. mem. Swedish Psychological Asscn; Sidney Suslow Award for Outstanding Research, Asscn for Int. Research 1989. *Publications include:* Demands on the Secondary School 1963, Ability Grouping, Content Validity and Curriculum Process Analysis 1971, Reforming Higher Education and External Studies in Sweden and Australia 1977, Regional Universities in a Comparative Western Perspective 1988, Dimensions of Evaluation in Higher Education (jtly) 1991, New Universities and Regional Context (jtly) 1994, Expanding Colleges and New Universities (jtly) 1996, Towards the Responsive University (jtly) 1998, Tertiary Education and Regional Development in Cross-National Perspective 1999, Municipal Study Centres for Higher Education in Sweden (jtly) 2000. *Leisure interest:* train timetables. *Address:* Department of Education, Box 2109, 750 02 Uppsala (Office); Östra Ågatan 17, 753 22 Uppsala, Sweden (Home). *Telephone:* (18) 471-16-68 (Office); (18) 14-16-94 (Home). *Fax:* (18) 471-16-51 (Office). *E-mail:* urban.dahllof@ped.uu.se (Office).

DAHRENDORF, Baron (Life Peer), cr. 1993, of Clare Market in the City of Westminster; **Ralf (Gustav) Dahrendorf,** KBE, FBA, DPhil, PhD; British (b. German) sociologist, politician and university administrator; b. 1 May 1929, Hamburg; s. of Gustav Dahrendorf and Lina Witt; m. Ellen Joan de Kadt 1980; ed Hamburg Univ. and London School of Econs; Asst, Univ. of Saar, Saarbrücken 1954, Privatdozent in sociology 1957; Fellow, Center for Advanced Study in the Behavioral Sciences, Palo Alto, USA 1957–58; Prof. of Sociology, Hamburg 1958, Tübingen 1960, Constance 1966 (on leave since 1969); Visiting Prof. at several European and US Univs; Vice-Chair. Founding Cttee Univ. of Constance 1964–66, First Dean Faculty of Social Science 1966–67; Adviser on educational questions to the Land Govt of Baden-Württemberg 1964–68; mem. German Council of Educ. 1966–68; Chair. Comm. on Comprehensive Univ. Planning 1967–68; mem. Free Democratic Party (FDP) 1967, Fed. Exec. 1968–74; mem. Land Diet of Baden-Württemberg and Vice-Chair. FDP Parl. Party 1968–69; mem. Fed. Parl. (Bundestag) and Parl. Sec. of State in Foreign Office 1969–70; mem. Comm. of the European Communities 1970–74; Chair. Royal Univ. of Malta Comm. 1972–74; mem. Hansard Soc. Comm. for Electoral Reform 1975–76, Royal Comm. on Legal Services 1976–78, Cttee to Review the Functioning of Financial Insts 1977–80; Dir European Centre for Research and Documentation in Social Sciences 1966–82, LSE 1974–84; BBC Reith Lecturer 1974; Visiting Scholar, Russell Sage Foundation, New York 1986–87; Warden, St Antony's Coll. Oxford 1987–97; Chair. Delegated Powers Select Cttee 2002–; Pres. German Sociological Soc. 1967–70; Hon. Presidium Anglo-German Soc. 1973–; Chair. Social Science Council of the European Science Foundation 1976–77, Newspaper Publishing 1992–93; Trustee Ford Foundation 1976–88; Chair. Bd Friedrich-Naumann-Stiftung 1982–87; Dir (non-exec.) Bankges. Berlin (UK) PLC 1996–2001; mem. Council, British Acad. 1980–81, Vice-Pres. 1982–84; mem. German PEN Centre 1971–; Foreign Assoc., NAS 1977; Foreign mem. American Philosophical Soc., Phila 1977; Hon. mem. Royal Irish Acad. 1974; Foreign Hon. mem. American Acad. of Arts and Sciences 1975; Hon. mem. Royal Coll. of Surgeons 1982; Fellow Imperial Coll., London 1974, Royal Soc. of Arts 1977, British Acad. 1977; Hon. Fellow LSE 1973; Hon. DLitt (Reading) 1973, (Malta) 1992, Hon. DSc (Ulster) 1973, (Bath) 1977, Hon. DUniv (Open Univ.) 1974, (Surrey) 1978, Hon. DHL (Kalamazoo Coll.) 1974, (Maryland) 1978, (Johns Hopkins Univ.) 1982, Hon. LittD (Trinity Coll., Dublin) 1975, Hon. Dr (Univ. Catholique de Louvain) 1977, (Univ. of Buenos Aires) 1993, Hon. LLD (Wagner Coll., Staten Island, New York, Columbia Univ., NY, York, Ontario Univs, Westminster, UK, Manchester, UK) Dr Social Sc. (Queen's Belfast), (Birmingham); Hon. DPolSci (Bologna) 1991; Dr hc (Urbino) 1993, (Univ. René Descartes) 1994; Hon. PhD (Univ. of Haifa) 1994; Journal Fund Award for Learned Publications 1966; Agnelli Prize 1992; Grand Croix de l'Ordre du Mérite du Sénégal 1971, Grand Croix de l'Ordre du Mérite du Luxembourg 1974, Grosses Bundesverdienstkreuz mit Stern und Schulterband (FRG) 1974, Grosses goldenes Ehrenzeichen am Bande (Austria) 1975, Grand Croix de l'Ordre de Léopold II (Belgium) 1975, Theodor Heuss Prize 1997, Garrigues Walker Prize 1998. *Publications include:* Marx in Perspective 1953, Industrie- und Betriebssoziologie 1956, Homo Sociologicus 1958, Soziale Klassen und Klassenkonflikt 1957 and 1959, Die angewandte Aufklärung 1963, Gesellschaft und Demokratie in Deutschland 1965, Pfade aus Utopia 1967, Essays in the Theory of Society 1968, Konflikt und Freiheit 1972, Plädoyer für die Europäische Union 1973, The New Liberty: Survival and Justice in a Changing World (Reith Lectures) 1975, A New World Order? (Ghana Lectures 1978) 1979, Life Chances (also in German) 1979, On Britain (BBC TV Lectures) 1982/83, Reisen nach innen und aussen 1984, Law and Order 1985, The Modern Social Conflict 1988, Reflections on the Revolution in Europe 1990, History of the London School of Economics and Political Science 1895–1995 1995, Liberale und Andere: Portraits 1995, After 1989: Morals, Revolution and Civil Society 1997, Liberal und Unabhängig, Gerd Bucerius und Seine Zeit 2000, Universities After Communism 2000, Über Grenzen 2002. *Address:* House of Lords, London, SW1A 0PW, England.

DAI AILIAN; Chinese choreographer and dancer; b. 1916, Trinidad, W Indies; m. Ye Qianyu (divorced); studied in London 1931; worked with Modern Dance Co. of Ernst and Lotte Berk; studied at Jooss-Leeder Dance School and with Anton Dolin, Margaret Craske, Marie Rambert; went to China 1941; teacher Nat. Opera School, Nat. Inst. of Social Educ. and Yucai School; since 1949 has been leader dance team attached to N China Univ., Cen. Theatrical Inst., leader Cen. Song and Dance Ensemble, Artistic Dir dance drama troupe, Cen. Experimental Opera Theatre; Pres. Beijing Dancing Acad., China Ballet Soc., China Labanotation Soc.; Hon. Chair. Chinese Dancers' Asscn; Adviser Cen. Ballet; mem. Int. Jury, Int. Youth Festival, Bucharest 1953, Moscow 1957, Choreography Competition, Turin 1983, 3rd USA Int. Ballet Competition, Jackson 1986, 2nd Int. Ballet Competition 1987, New York, 3rd Int. Ballet Competition, Paris 1988, 3rd Tokyo Ballet Competition for Asia and Pacific 1987, New York Int. Ballet Competition 1990; Chair. China Nat. Ballet Competition 1984, New York 1987, Chair. of Jury, 1st Shanghai Int. Ballet Competition 1998; Lecture-demonstrations on Chinese Ethnic Folk Dance at CEO China Forum, Beijing, UNESCO, Paris, Dartington Coll. of Arts, Devon 1988–89; Lecture-demonstrations on Chinese Dance History, Univ. of Calif., Univ. of San Francisco, Asian Museum, Inst. of Arts, USA 1993; Sr Consultant, China Asscn for the Advancement of Int. Friendship; Cttee mem. Int. Dance Council UNESCO, Vice-Chair. 1982–86, 1986; Consultant London Chinese Cultural Centre 1989, Int. Folk Arts Org. Mödling, Austria 1990; Hon. Chair. Chinese Dancers' Asscn 1991–; mem. Int. Labanotation Council; Lecture on Labanotation in China, Laban Centre, London 1988; Patron Language of Dance Centre, London 1992, Laban Inst., Univ. of Surrey 1992; mem. Cttee China Int. Cultural Exchange Centre; mem. Beijing Int. Soc.; mem. Standing Cttee CPPCC; mem. Presidium 6th CPPCC Nat. Cttee 1983, 8th 1993–; Fellow Hong Kong Acad. of Arts 1996; Guest Lecturer Univs. of Toronto, Ottawa and Vancouver, Canada 1997; Hon. mem. China Fed. of Literary and Art Circles 1996. *Works include:* Lotus Dance, The Old Carries the Young, Flying Apsaras, The Women Oil-drillers' Dance, Tears of Pear Blossoms. *Address:* Apt. 2-16 Hua Qiao Gong Yu, Hua Yuan Cun, Hai Dian, Beijing 100044, People's Republic of China. *Telephone:* (10) 68414163.

DAI BINGGUO; Chinese diplomatist; b. 1941, Yinjiang Co., Guizhou Prov.; ed Sichuan Univ.; joined CCP 1973; Dir Dept of USSR and Eastern European Affairs, Ministry of Foreign Affairs; Vice-Minister of Foreign Affairs; Dir Int. Liaison Dept of CCP Cen. Cttee 1997–; mem. 15th CCP Cen. Cttee 1997–. *Address:* International Liaison Department of Chinese Communist Party Central Committee, Beijing, People's Republic of China.

DAI XIANGLONG; Chinese banker and economist; b. Oct. 1944, Yizheng City, Jiangsu Prov.; ed Cen. Inst. of Finance and Banking; mem. CCP 1973–; Deputy Section Chief, People's Bank of China (PBC), Jiangsu Prov. Br. 1978; Deputy Section Chief and Deputy Head of Dept Agricultural Bank of China (ABC), Jiangsu Br., Vice-Gov. 1983; Sec. CCP Group, Communications Bank of China (CBC), also Gen. Man. and Vice-Chair. Bd CBC 1989; Chair. Bd China Pacific Insurance Co. Ltd 1990–93; Vice-Gov. People's Bank of China 1993–95, Gov. 1995–2003; alt. mem. 14th CCP Cen. Cttee 1992–97; mem. 15th CCP Cen. Cttee 1997–2002, 16th CCP Cen. Cttee 2002–. *Address:* c/o People's Bank of China, 32 Chengfang Jie, Xicheng Qu, Beijing 100800, People's Republic of China (Office).

DAIANU, Daniel, PhD; Romanian economist and politician; b. 30 Aug. 1952, Bucharest; ed Acad. of Econ. Studies, Bucharest, Acad. of Sciences, Bucharest and Harvard Business School; Visiting Scholar Russian Research Center,

Harvard Univ. 1990–92; Deputy Minister of Finance Feb.–Aug. 1992; Chief Economist Cen. Bank of Romania 1992–97; Minister of Finance 1997–98; currently Prof. of Econs, Acad. of Econ. Studies, Bucharest; Visiting Scholar, Woodrow Wilson Center, Washington, DC 1992, IMF, Washington, DC 1993; Visiting Sr Fellow NATO Defense Coll., Rome 1995; Visiting Prof. Berkeley Univ. 1999; Acad. of Sciences Highest Award for Econs 1994. *Publications:* Transformation of Economies as a Real Process 1998, Economic Vitality and Viability 1996. *Leisure interests:* reading, football, basketball. *Address:* Negro Voda Street, Block C3, Floor 3, apt. 9, Sector 3, Bucharest, Romania. *Telephone:* (1) 2300723. *Fax:* (1) 2315530. *E-mail:* ddaianu@hotmail.com (Home).

DAIBER, Hans Joachim, DPhil; German professor of Arabic; b. 1 April 1942, Stuttgart; s. of Otto Daiber and Martha Daiber; m. Helga Brosamler 1971; one s. one d.; ed Theological Seminaries of Maulbronn and Blaubeuren, Univs of Tübingen and Saarbrücken; lecturer in Arabic, Univ. of Heidelberg 1975–77; Prof. of Arabic, Free Univ. Amsterdam 1977–95; Prof. of Oriental Philology and Islam, Univ. of Frankfurt am Main 1995–; Special Visiting Prof., Univ. of Tokyo 1992; Visiting Prof. Int. Inst. of Islamic Thought and Civilization, Kuala Lumpur 2001; mem. Royal Netherlands Acad. of Arts and Sciences; mem. German Oriental Inst., Beirut 1973–75, German Oriental Soc., American Oriental Soc., Oosters Genootschap, Soc. Int. pour l'étude de la philosophie médiévale, Union Européenne d'Arabisants et d'Islamisants; ed. Aristoteles Semitico-Latinus, Islamic Philosophy, Theology and Science, German 'Habilitation' 1973. *Publications:* Die arabische Übersetzung der Placita philosophorum 1968, Ein Kompendium der aristotelischen Meteorologie in der Fassung des Hunain Ibn Ishaq 1975, Das theologisch-philosophische System des Muammar Ibn Abbad as-Sulami 1975, Gott, Natur und menschlicher Wille im frühen islamischen Denken 1978, Aetius Arabus 1980, The Ruler as Philosopher: a new interpretation of al-Farabi's view 1986, Wasil Ibn Ata' als Prediger und Theologe 1988, Catalogue of Arabic Manuscripts in the Daiber Collection (Vol. I) 1988, (Vol. II) 1996, Naturwissenschaft bei den Arabern im 10 Jahrhundert nach Christus 1993, Neuplatonische Pythagorica in arabischem Gewande 1995, The Islamic Concept of Belief in the 4th/10th Century 1995, Bibliography of Islamic Philosophy (Vols I-II) 1999; numerous articles in journals on Islamic philosophy, theology, history of sciences, Greek heritage in Islam. *Address:* University of Frankfurt am Main, Department of Oriental Studies, PB 111932, 60054 Frankfurt am Main (Office); Am Hüttenhof 10, 40489 Düsseldorf, Germany (Home). *Telephone:* (211) 403714 (Home); (69) 798-22131. *Fax:* (69) 798-24964 (Office); (211) 403725 (Home). *E-mail:* daiber@em.uni-frankfurt.de (Office). *Website:* www.rz.uni-frankfurt.de/fb9/orientalistik (Office).

DAICHES, David, CBE, MA, DPhil, PhD, FRSL, FRSE; British writer and university professor; b. 2 Sept. 1912, Sunderland; s. of Salis and Flora (née Levin) Daiches; m. 1st Isobel J. Mackay 1937 (died 1977); one s. two d.; m. 2nd Hazel Neville 1978 (died 1986); ed George Watson's Coll., Edin., Edin. Univ. and Balliol Coll., Oxford; Bradley Fellow, Balliol Coll., Oxford 1936–37; Asst Prof. of English, Univ. of Chicago 1940–43; Second Sec. British Embassy, Washington 1944–46; Prof. of English, Cornell Univ. 1946–51; Univ. Lecturer in English, Cambridge Univ. 1951–61, Fellow of Jesus Coll., Cambridge 1957–62; Dean, School of English Studies, Univ. of Sussex 1961–67, Prof. of English 1961–77, Prof. Emer. 1977–; Dir Inst. for Advanced Studies in the Humanities, Edin. Univ. 1980–86, Gifford Lecturer 1983; Sr Fellow, Nat. Humanities Center, USA 1987–88; Hon. LittD (Brown, Edin., Sussex, Glasgow and Guelph Univs); Dr hc (Sorbonne, Bologna); Hon. DUniv (Stirling); many awards and prizes. *Publications:* 45 books including: The Novel and the Modern World 1939, A Study of Literature 1948, Robert Burns 1950, Two Worlds 1956, Critical Approaches to Literature 1956, Literary Essays 1956, Milton 1957, A Critical History of English Literature 1960, More Literary Essays 1968, Scotch Whisky 1969, Sir Walter Scott and his World 1971, A Third World (autobiog.) 1971, Robert Burns and his World 1971, Prince Charles Edward Stuart 1973, Robert Louis Stevenson and his World 1973, Was 1975, Moses 1975, James Boswell and His World 1976, Scotland and the Union 1977, Glasgow 1977, Edinburgh 1978, Fletcher of Saltoun: Selected Political Writings and Speeches (ed.) 1979, Literature and Gentility in Scotland 1982, God and the Poets 1984, Edinburgh: A Traveller's Companion 1986, A Weekly Scotsman and Other Poems 1994. *Leisure interests:* music, talking. *Address:* 22 Belgrave Crescent, Edinburgh, EH4 3AL, Scotland.

DAINBA GYAINCAN; Chinese government official; b. 1940, Lhasa, Tibet; joined CCP 1964; Mayor of Lhasa Municipality 1993–. *Address:* Government of Xizang Autonomous Region, Lhasa City, People's Republic of China.

DAINTITH, Terence Charles, MA; British professor of law; b. 8 May 1942, Coulsdon; s. of Edward Daintith and Irene M. Parsons; m. Christine Bulport 1965; one s. one d.; ed Wimbledon Coll. and St Edmund Hall, Oxford; called to Bar, Lincoln's Inn 1966; Assoc. in Law, Univ. of Calif. Berkeley 1963–64; lecturer in Constitutional and Admin. Law, Univ. of Edin. 1964–72; Prof. of Public Law, Univ. of Dundee 1972–83, Dir Centre for Petroleum and Mineral Law Studies 1977–83; Prof. of Law, European Univ. Inst., Florence 1981–87, External Prof. 1988–; Prof. of Law, Univ. of London 1988–, Dir Inst. of Advanced Legal Studies 1988–95, Dean Univ. of London Insts of Advanced Study 1991–94, School of Advanced Study 1994–2001; Prof. of Law, Univ. of Western Australia 2002–; Additional Bencher, Lincoln's Inn 2000; Ed. Journal of Energy and Natural Resources Law 1983–92; mem. Academia Europaea (Chair. Law Cttee 1993–96, Social Sciences Section 1996–98); Hon. LLD (De Montfort) 2001. *Publications:* The Economic Law of the United Kingdom 1974, United Kingdom Oil and Gas Law (with G. D. M. Willoughby) 1977, Energy Strategy in Europe (with L. Hancher) 1986, The Legal Integration of Energy Markets (with S. Williams) 1987, Law as an Instrument of Economic Policy 1988, Harmonization and Hazard (with G. R. Baldwin) 1992, Implementation of EC Law in the United Kingdom 1995, The Executive in the Constitution (with A. C. Page) 1999. *Address:* Institute of Advanced Legal Studies, 17 Russell Square, London, WC1B 5DR, England (Office); Law School, University of Western Australia, Nedlands, WA 6907, Australia (Office). *Telephone:* (20) 7862-5844 (London) (Office). *Fax:* (20) 7862-5850 (London) (Office).

DAJANY, Musa I. R., MA, LLB; Jordanian broadcasting executive; b. 1924, Jerusalem; m. Nadia Dajany 1947; one s. three d.; Chief Announcer, Near East Arab Broadcasting Station 1944, Controller of Programmes, Palestine Broadcasting Dept 1946, Head of Programmes Operations 1952, Deputy Dir of Programmes, Cyprus 1956; Controller of Programmes, Jordan Broadcasting Dept 1957; Asst Dir Bahrain Broadcasting 1958; Expert in Radio Production, Libyan Broadcasting Dept 1959; Controller of Special Programmes, Kuwait Broadcasting 1960; Information Adviser, Arab Student Aid Int., USA 1989; currently Adviser and Man. Dir The Broadcasters Est.; Prize from Japan Broadcasting NHK; Independence Decoration. *Publications:* Fifty Years with Arab Broadcasting 1996; articles on various topics in Arabic press. *Leisure interests:* reading, theatre, music. *Address:* PO Box 5517, Zahran, Amman 11183, Jordan. *Telephone:* (6) 5534815. *Fax:* (6) 695273.

DALAI LAMA, The (Tenzin Gyatso), temporal and spiritual head of Tibet; Fourteenth Incarnation; Tibetan; b. 6 July 1935, Taktser, Amdo Prov., NE Tibet; s. of Chujon Tsering and Tsering Dekyi; born of Tibetan peasant family in Amdo Prov.; enthroned at Lhasa 1940; rights exercised by regency 1934–50; assumed political power 1950; fled to Chumbi in S Tibet after abortive resistance to Chinese State 1950; negotiated agreement with China 1951; Vice-Chair. Standing Cttee CPPCC, mem. Nat. Cttee 1951–59; Hon. Chair. Chinese Buddhist Asscn 1953–59; Del. to Nat. People's Congress 1954–59; Chair. Preparatory Cttee for the 'Autonomous Region of Tibet' 1955–59; fled Tibet to India after suppression of Tibetan national uprising 1959; Dr of Buddhist Philosophy (Monasteries of Sera, Drepung and Gaden, Lhasa) 1959; Supreme Head of all Buddhist sects in Tibet (Xizang); Memory Prize 1989, Congressional Human Rights Award 1989, Nobel Peace Prize 1989, Freedom Award (USA) 1991. *Publications:* My Land and People 1962, The Opening of the Wisdom Eye 1963, The Buddhism of Tibet and the Key to the Middle Way 1975, Kindness, Clarity and Insight 1984, A Human Approach to World Peace 1984, Freedom in Exile (autobiog.) 1990, The Good Heart 1996, Ethics for the New Millennium 1998, Art of Happiness (jtly) 1999, A Simple Path: Basic Buddhist Teachings by His Holiness the Dalai Lama 2000, Stages of Meditation: Training the Mind for Wisdom 2001, The Spirit of Peace 2002. *Leisure interests:* gardening, mechanics. *Address:* Thekchen Choeling, McLeod Ganj 176219, Dharamsala, Himachal Pradesh, India.

DALBERTO, Michel; French pianist; b. 2 June 1955, Paris; s. of Jean Dalberto and Paulette Girard-Dalberto; ed Lycée Claude Bernard, Lycée Racine, Conservatoire National Supérieur de Musique, Paris; prin. teachers at Conservatoire: Vlado Perlemuter, Jean Hubeau; started professional career 1975; concerts in maj. musical centres and at int. festivals; Artistic Dir Festival des Arcs 1991–; Pres. of the Jury Clara Haskil Competition 1991–; Chevalier Ordre nat. du Mérite; Clara Haskil Prize 1975; First Prize Leeds Int. Pianoforte Competition 1978; Acad. Charles Cros Award 1980 and Acad. Disque Français Award 1984, for recordings; Diapason d'Or Award for Best Concerto Recording 1991. *Recordings:* albums: Schubert Piano Music (complete recordings), French Mélodies (with Barbara Hendricks), Debussy Preludes, Mozart Concerti. *Leisure interests:* skiing, scuba diving, vintage cars. *Address:* c/o IMG Artists, Lovell House, 616 Chiswick High Road, London, W4 5RX, England. *E-mail:* knaish@imgworld.com (Office).

DALBORG, Hans Folkeson, MBA, PhD; Swedish banker; b. 21 May 1941, Säter; m. Anna Ljungqvist 1965; one s. two d.; ed Univ. of Uppsala and Stockholm School of Econs; teacher and admin. Stockholm School of Econs 1967–72; joined Skandia 1972, Deputy Man. Dir responsible for int. business 1981–83, Pres. and COO Skandia Int. Insurance Corpn 1983–89, Sr Exec., Vice-Pres., COO Skandia Group and CEO Skandia Int. Insurance Corpn 1989–91; Pres. and CEO Nordbanken AB 1991–97; Pres., Group CEO MeritaNordbanken PLC 1998–, Vice Chair. 2000–. *Address:* Nordbanken AB, Kungsgt. 10, 105 71 Stockholm, Sweden (Office). *Telephone:* (8) 614-70-00 (Office). *Fax:* (8) 20-08-46 (Office); (8) 614-78-10. *Website:* www.nb.se (Office).

DALDRY, Stephen, BA; British theatre and film director; b. 2 May 1961, Dorset; s. of the late Patrick Daldry and of Cherry Daldry (née Thompson); m. Lucy Daldry 2001; ed Huish Grammar School, Taunton, Univ. of Sheffield; trained with Il Circo di Nando Orfei, Italy; f. Metro Theatre Co., Artistic Dir 1984–86; Assoc. Artist, Crucible Theatre, Sheffield 1986–88; Artistic Dir Gate Theatre, London 1989–92; Artistic Dir English Stage Co., Royal Court Theatre, London 1992–99, Assoc. Dir 1999–; Dir Stephen Daldry Pictures 1998–; Cameron Mackintosh Visiting Prof. of Contemporary Theatre, Oxford Univ. 2002; BAFTA Award for Billy Elliot 2000. *Films:* Eight 1998, Via Dolorosa 1999, Dancer (Dir) 2000, Billy Elliot (Dir) 2000, The Hours 2002. *Producer:* Six Degrees of Separation, Oleanna, Damned for Despair (Gate) 1991, An Inspector Calls (Royal Nat. Theatre) 1992, (Aldwych) 1994, (Garrick) 1995, (NY) 1995, (Playhouse) 2001, Machinal (Royal Nat. Theatre) 1993,

The Kitchen (Royal Court) 1995, Via Dolorosa (Royal Court) 1998, (NY) 1999, Far Away (Royal Court) 2000, (Albery) 2001, Judgement Day, Ingoldstadt, Figaro Gets Divorced, Rat in the Skull. *Address:* c/o Working Title Films, 77 Shaftesbury Avenue, London W1V 8HQ, England (Office). *Telephone:* (20) 7307-3000 (Office). *Fax:* (20) 7307-3002 (Office).

DALE, Jim; British actor; b. James Smith, 15 Aug. 1935; m.; three s. one d.; ed Kettering Grammar School; music hall comedian 1951; singing, compering, directing 1951–61; first film appearance 1965; appeared in nine Carry On films; later appeared with Nat. Theatre and Young Vic; appeared in London's West End in The Card 1973; host, Sunday Night at the London Palladium (TV show) 1994; with Young Vic appeared on Broadway in The Taming of the Shrew and Scapino 1974; Broadway appearances: Barnum (Tony Award) 1980, Joe Egg 1985, Me and My Girl 1987–88, Candide 1997; other stage appearances include: Privates on Parade (New York), Travels With My Aunt (off-Broadway) 1995, Fagin in Oliver! (London Palladium) 1995–97; lyricist for film Georgy Girl. *Films include:* Lock Up Your Daughters, The Winter's Tale, The Biggest Dog in the World, National Health, Adolf Hitler—My Part in his Downfall, Joseph Andrews, Pete's Dragon, Hot Lead Cold Feet, Bloodshy, The Spaceman and King Arthur, Scandalous, Carry On Cabby, Carry On Cleo, Carry On Jack, Carry On Cowboy, Carry On Screaming, Carry On Spying, Carry On Constable, Carry On Doctor, Carry On Don't Lose Your Head, Carry On Follow That Camel, Carry On Columbus 1992, Hunchback of Notre Dame 1997. *Address:* c/o Sharon Bierut, CED, 257 Park Avenue South, New York, NY 10010, USA; c/o Janet Glass, 28 Berkeley Square, London, W1X 6HD, England.

D'ALEMA, Massimo; Italian politician and journalist; b. 20 April 1949, Rome; Sec. Partito Democratico della Sinistra (PDS), re-named Democratici di Sinistra (DS) 1998, Pres. 2000–; mem. Camera dei Deputati for Apulia; fmr mem. Progressisti Federativo; fmr mem. Budget Comm.; Prime Minister of Italy 1998–2000; Pres. Fondazione Italianieuropei 2000–. *Address:* Via delle Botteghe Oscure 4, 00186 Rome, Italy. *Telephone:* (06) 67111. *Fax:* (06) 6711596. *E-mail:* ufficio.stampa@democraticidisinistra.it. *Website:* www .dsonline.it.

DALES, Sir Richard Nigel, Kt, KCVO, CMG, MA; British diplomatist; b. 26 Aug. 1942, Woodford, Essex; s. of the late Maj. K. Dales and of O. M. Dales; m. Elizabeth M. Martin 1966; one s. one d.; ed Chigwell School, Essex and St Catharine's Coll. Cambridge; joined Foreign Office 1964; Third Sec. Yaoundé, Cameroon 1965–67; with FCO, London 1968–70; Second Sec., later First Sec., Copenhagen 1970–73; Asst Pvt. Sec. to Sec. of State for Foreign and Commonwealth Affairs 1974–77; Head of Chancery, Sofia 1977–81; FCO 1981–82; Head of Chancery, Copenhagen 1982–86; Deputy High Commr in Zimbabwe 1986–89; Head of Southern Africa Dept FCO 1989–91; seconded to Civil Service Comm. 1991–92; High Commr in Zimbabwe 1992–95; Dir (Africa and Commonwealth), FCO 1995–98; Amb. to Norway 1998–2002. *Leisure interests:* music, walking, reading. *Address:* 521 Bunyan Court, Barbican, London, EC2Y 8DH, England. *Telephone:* (7919) 184083 (Home). *E-mail:* richardandelizabeth@fsmail.net (Home).

D'ALESSANDRO, Dominic, BSc; Italian financial services executive; b. Molise; m. Pearl D'Alessandro; two s. one d.; ed Loyola Coll., Montréal; accountant, Coopers & Lybrand 1968–75; with Genstar Ltd 1975–81, Dir of Finance, Dhahran, Saudi Arabia, subsequently Gen. Man., Dhahran, later Vice-Pres. Materials and Construction Group, San Francisco; with Royal Bank of Canada 1981–88, Vice-Pres. and Controller, then Exec. Vice-Pres. for Finance –1988; Pres. and CEO Laurentian Bank of Canada 1988–94; Pres. and CEO Manulife Financial 1994–; Dir American Council of Life Insurance; mem. Bd The Hudson's Bay Co., TransCanada PipeLines; mem. Business Council on Nat. Issues; fmr Chair. Bd Canadian Life and Health Insurance Asscn; Fellow Inst. Chartered Accountants 1993; Co-Chair. Corp. Fund for Breast Cancer Research Campaign 1996; Campaign Chair. for the Salvation Army, Ont. Cen. Div., for Greater Toronto United Way Campaign 1998; Dr hc (Concordia Univ.) 1998; Bronze Medal, Inst. of Chartered Accountants 1971; Man. Achievement Award, McGill Univ. 1999, Arbour Award, Univ. of Toronto 1999, CEO Award of Excellence in Public Relations, Canadian Public Relations Soc. 2001. *Address:* Manulife Financial, 200 Bloor Street East, Toronto, Ont., M4W 1E5, Canada (Office). *Telephone:* (416) 926-3000 (Office). *Website:* www.manulife.com (Office).

DALEY, Richard Michael; American politician and lawyer; b. 24 April 1942, Chicago, Ill.; s. of the late Richard J. Daley and of Eleanor Guilfoyle; m. Margaret Corbett 1972; one s. (and one s. deceased), two d.; ed De La Salle High School, Providence Coll. RI and DePaul Univ. Chicago; Asst Corpn Counsel, City of Chicago 1969; Del. Ill. Constitutional Convention 1970; briefly formed law practice with Raymond F. Simon; subsequently joined father's law firm; mem. Ill. State Senate 1972; State Attorney, Cook Co., Ill. 1980–89; Mayor of Chicago 1989–; Democrat. *Leisure interests:* cinema, reading. *Address:* Office of the Mayor, City Hall, Room 507, 121 N LaSalle Street, Chicago, IL 60602-1202, USA.

DALEY, William M., BA, LLD; American politician and lawyer; m. Loretta Daley; three c.; ed Loyola Univ., John Marshall Law School; called to Ill. Bar 1975; fmrly with Daley and George, Chicago; partner Mayer, Brown and Platt; Vice-Chair. Amalgamated Bank, Chicago 1989, Pres., COO 1990–93; Sec. Dept of Commerce, Washington 1997–2000; mem. Bd of Dirs Electronic Data System Corpn, Texas 2001–; fmr Special Counsel to Pres. for NAFTA; St

Ignatius Award for Excellence in the Practice of Law, World Trade Award, World Trade Center, Chicago 1994. *Address:* Electronic Data Systems, 5400 Legacy Drive, Plano, TX 75024, USA (Office).

DALGARNO, Alexander, PhD, FRS, MRIA; British professor of astronomy; b. 5 Jan. 1928, London; s. of William Dalgarno and Margaret Dalgarno; m. 1st Barbara Kane 1957 (divorced 1972); two s. two d.; m. 2nd Emily Izsák 1972 (divorced 1987); ed Univ. Coll. London; mem. Faculty, Applied Math., Queen's Univ., Belfast 1951–67; Prof. of Astronomy, Harvard Univ. 1967–77, Chair. Dept of Astronomy 1971–76, Dir Harvard Coll. Observatory 1971–72, Phillips Prof. of Astronomy 1977–; mem. Smithsonian Astrophysical Observatory 1967–; Ed. Astrophysical Journal Letters 1973–2002; Hon. DSc (Queen's, Belfast) 1972, (York) 2000; Medal of Int. Acad. of Quantum Molecular Science 1969, Hodgkins Medal, Smithsonian Inst. 1977, Davisson-Germer Prize, American Physical Soc. 1980; Meggers Award, Optical Soc. of America 1986, Gold Medal, Royal Astronomical Soc. 1986, Spiers Medal, Royal Soc. of Chem., Fleming Medal, American Geophysical Union 1995, Hughes Medal, Royal Soc. 2002. *Publications:* numerous scientific papers in journals. *Address:* Harvard-Smithsonian Center for Astrophysics, 60 Garden Street, Cambridge, MA 02138 (Office); 27 Robinson Street, Cambridge, MA 02138, USA (Home). *Telephone:* (617) 495-4403 (Office); (617) 354-8660 (Home). *Fax:* (617) 495-5970 (Office). *E-mail:* adalgarno@cfa.harvard.edu (Office).

DALGLISH, Kenneth (Kenny) Mathieson, MBE; British football manager; b. 4 March 1951, Glasgow; played for Celtic, Scottish League champions 1972–74, 1977, Scottish Cup Winners 1972, 1974, 1975, 1977, Scottish League Cup winners 1975; played for Liverpool, European Cup winners 1978, 1981, 1984, FA Cup winners 1986, 1989, League Cup winners 1981–84, Man. 1986–91; Man. Blackburn Rovers 1991–97, Newcastle United 1997–98; Dir of Football Operations, Celtic 1999–2000; 102 full caps for Scotland scoring 30 goals; Freeman of Glasgow; Footballer of the Year 1979, 1983, Manager of the Year (three times). *Address:* c/o Celtic Football Club, Celtic Park, Glasgow, G40 3RE, Scotland (Office).

DALITZ, Richard Henry, PhD, FRS, CPhys, FInstP; British research physicist (retd); b. 28 Feb. 1925, Dimboola, Australia; s. of Frederick W. Dalitz and Hazel Blanche (née Drummond) Dalitz; m. Valda Suiter 1946; one s. three d.; ed Tooronga Rd. Cen. School and Scotch Coll., Melbourne, Ormond Coll., Univ. of Melbourne and Trinity Coll., Cambridge; Research Asst in Physics, Univ. of Bristol 1948–49; Lecturer in Math. Physics, Univ. of Birmingham 1949–55; Reader 1955–56; Prof. of Physics, Enrico Fermi Inst. for Nuclear Studies, Univ. of Chicago 1956–66; Royal Soc. Research Prof., Univ. of Oxford 1963–90, Prof. Emer. 1990–; Foreign mem. Polish Acad. of Sciences 1980; Foreign Fellow Nat. Acad. of Sciences (India) 1990; Fellow, All Souls Coll., Oxford 1964–90, Fellow Emer. 1990–; Foreign Assoc. NAS 1991; Corresp. mem. Australian Acad. of Sciences 1978; Hon. DSc (Melbourne) 1991; Maxwell Medal, Inst. of Physics, London 1966, Bakerian Lecture and Jaffe Prize, Royal Soc. 1969, Hughes Medal, Royal Soc. 1975, J. Robert Oppenheimer Memorial Prize, Univ. of Miami 1980, Royal Medal, Royal Soc. 1982, Harrie Massey Prize (jtly, Inst. of Physics, London and Australian Inst. of Physics) 1990. *Publications:* Strange Particles and Strong Interactions 1962, Nuclear Interactions of the Hyperons 1965, Nuclear Energy Today and Tomorrow (co-author) 1971, A Breadth of Physics (co-author) 1988, The Collected Papers of P. A. M. Dirac 1924–1948 1995, Selected Scientific Papers of Sir Rudolf Peierls (co-ed.) 1997, The Foundations of Newtonian Scholarship (co-ed.) 1999; numerous papers on theoretical physics, in scientific journals. *Leisure interests:* study of the history of the Wends and their emigrations to the New World, travelling hopefully and finding out why. *Address:* Department of Theoretical Physics, University of Oxford, 1 Keble Road, Oxford, OX1 3NP, England. *Telephone:* (1865) 273966 (Office). *Fax:* (1865) 273947 (Office). *E-mail:* r.dalitz@physics.ox.ac.uk (Office).

DALLARA, Charles H., MA, PhD, MALD; American international finance official; b. 1948, Spartanburg, NC; m. 1st Carolyn Gault; one s. one d.; m. 2nd Peixin Li; ed Univ. of S Carolina and Fletcher School of Law and Diplomacy; int. economist, US Treasury Dept 1976–79; Special Asst to Under-Sec. for Monetary Affairs 1979–80; Guest Scholar Brookings Inst. 1980–81; Special Asst to Asst Sec. for Int. Affairs 1981–82; Alt. Exec. Dir IMF 1982–83; Deputy Asst Sec. for Int. Monetary Affairs, US Treasury Dept 1983–85; Exec. Dir IMF 1984–89; Asst Sec. for Policy Devt and Sr Advisor for Policy 1988–89; Asst Sec. for Internal Affairs 1989–93; Man. Dir JP Morgan 1991–93; Man. Dir Inst. of Int. Finance 1993–. *Address:* IIF, 2000 Pennsylvania Avenue, Suite 8500, Washington, DC 20006 (Office); 12196 Goldenchair Court, Oak Hill, VA 20171, USA (Home). *Telephone:* (202) 857-3604 (Office). *Fax:* (202) 833-1194 (Office). *E-mail:* cdallara@iif.com (Office).

DALLE, François Léon Marie-Joseph, LenD; French business executive; b. 18 March 1918, Hesdin; s. of Joseph and Jeanne (Dumont) Dalle; four s. two d.; ed Saint-Joseph de Lille, Faculty of Law, Paris; fmr advocate, Court of Appeal, Paris 1941–42; Plant Man., then Asst Gen. Man., Monsavon Co. 1945–48, Marketing Man., L'Oréal 1948–50, Asst Gen. Man. 1950–57, Pres., Dir-Gen. L'Oréal 1957–84, Pres. Strategy Cttee 1984–90; Pres. L'Oréal Soc. 1957–84; Pres. Saipo 1957–; Dir Philips (France), Banque Nat. de Paris 1973–82, Editions Masson, Union des Annonceurs, Dir and mem. Bd Nestlé SA 1975– (Vice-Pres. 1986–90), fmr Dir Lancôme; Vice-Pres. Institut Pasteur 1970–78; Hon. Dir 1978–; Pres. Exec. Cttee Humanisme et Entreprise 1968; mem. staff, Conseil Nat. du Patronat Français 1968, Exec. Council 1972–75; Founder and Pres. Asscn Entreprise et Progrès 1969, mem. Exec. Cttee 1971–;

mem. Grandes Entreprises Françaises Asscn (AGREF) 1977–82; mem. Futuribles Int. Asscn, INSEAD, council Centre d'Etudes Littéraires et Scientifiques Appliquées (CELSA), (Pres. 1989–); founder and Pres. Institut de l'Entreprise 1975–; fmr Pres. Mennen-France, Dir Centre Européen d'Educ. Permanente; Pres. Comm. Nat. de l'Industrie 1984; Lauréat de la faculté de droit de Paris; Commdr. Légion d'honneur, Ordre nat. du Mérite, Médaille de la Résistance, Commdr des Palmes académiques, Commendatore della Repubblica Italiana. *Publications:* L'entreprise du futur (with Jean Bounine Cabalé) 1971, Quand l'entreprise s'éveille à la conscience sociale (with Jean Bounine Cabalé) 1975, Dynamique de l'auto-reforme de l'entreprise (with Nicolas Thiéry) 1976, L'education en entreprise: contre le chômage des jeunes (jtly) 1993, Le Sursaut (jtly) 1994, L'aventure l'Oréal 2001. *Leisure interests:* writing, hunting. *Address:* Villa Clairefontaine, 14 chemin du Nant d'Argent, 1223 Cologny, Geneva, Switzerland.

DALLI, Hon. John, FCCA, CPA, MBIM; Maltese politician and accountant; b. 5 Oct. 1948, Qormi; s. of Carmelo Dalli and Emma Bonnici; m. Josette Callus; two d.; ed Malta Coll. of Arts, Science and Tech.; posts in financial admin. and gen. man., Malta and Brussels; Man. Consultant; MP, Nationalist Party 1987–; Parl. Sec. for Industry 1987–90; Minister for Econ. Affairs 1990–92, of Finance 1992–96, 1998–; Shadow Minister and Opposition Spokesman for Finance 1996–98. *Address:* Ministry of Finance, Cavalier House, 158 Old Mint Street, Valletta, CMR 02, Malta. *Telephone:* 232646, 251349. *Fax:* 240205 (Office); 446146 (Home); 242609. *E-mail:* johndalli@magnet.com (Office); john.s.dalli@kemmunet.net.mt (Home).

D'ALMEIDA, Armindo Vaz; São Tomé e Príncipe politician; Prime Minister 1995–96. *Address:* c/o Office of the Prime Minister, Praça Yon Gato, CP 302, São Tomé, São Tomé e Príncipe.

DALRYMPLE, Frederick Rawdon, AO; Australian diplomatist; b. 6 Nov. 1930, Sydney, s. of Frederick Dalrymple and Evelyn Dalrymple; m. Ross E. Williams 1957; one s. one d.; ed Sydney Church of England Grammar School and Univs of Sydney and Oxford; Lecturer in Philosophy, Univ. of Sydney 1955–57; joined Dept of External Affairs 1957, served in Bonn, London 1959–64; Alt. Dir Asian Devt Bank, Manila 1967–69; Minister, Djakarta 1969–71; Amb. to Israel 1972–75, to Indonesia 1981–85, to USA 1985–89, to Japan 1989–93; Chair. ASEAN Focus Group Pty Ltd 1994–2001; Visiting Prof. Univ. of Sydney 1994–2002; Hon. Fellow Univ. of Sydney 2003. *Publications:* Looking East and West from Down Under 1992; Continental Drift: Australia's Search for a Regional Identity 2003. *Leisure interests:* reading, golf. *Address:* 34 Glenmore Road, Paddington, NSW 2021, Australia. *E-mail:* rdalrymple@econ.usyd.edu.au (Office); rdalrymp@ozemail.com.au (Home). *Website:* www.usyd.edu.au, aseanfocus.com (Office).

DALTON, Grant; New Zealand yachtsman; b. 1957; m. Nicki Dalton; one s. one d.; fmr accountant; trainee sailmaker 1977; first participation in Whitbread round the world race (now the Volvo Ocean Race) on board Dutch Flyer II 1981–82, Lion New Zealand 1985–86; skipper Fischer & Peykel 1989–90, New Zealand Endeavour 1993–94 (race winner), Wor 60 1997–98 (Merit Cup), Club Med Catamaran, The Race (winner) March 2001, Nautor Challenge Team, Volvo Ocean Race 2001; other races include Sydney-Hobart race (four times), Fastnet Race (five times), Admirals' Cup 1985, Americas Cup, Fremantle, Australia 1987.

DALTON, Timothy; British actor; b. 21 March 1946; ed Royal Acad. of Dramatic Art; joined Nat. Youth Theatre; first London appearance at Royal Court Theatre; toured with Prospect Theatre Co.; guest artist with RSC. *Film appearances include:* The Lion in Winter, Le Voyeur (France), Cromwell, Wuthering Heights, Mary Queen of Scots, Permission to Kill, The Man Who Knew Love (Spain), Sextette, Agatha 1978, Flash Gordon 1979, Chanel Solitaire 1980, The Doctor and the Devils 1985, Brenda Starr, role of Ian Fleming's James Bond in The Living Daylights 1987 and Licence to Kill 1989, Hawks 1987, The King's Whore 1989, The Rocketeer 1990, The Informant 1996, The Reef 1996, The Beautician and the Beast 1996, Made Men 1998, Cleopatra 1998, Possessed 1999, Timeshare 2000, American Outlaws 2001, Looney Tunes – Back in Action 2002. *Stage appearances include:* King Lear, Love's Labour's Lost, Henry IV, Henry V (all with Prospect Theatre Co.), Romeo and Juliet (RSC), The Samaritan, Black Comedy and White Liars, The Vortex, The Lunatic, The Lover and the Poet 1980, The Romans 1980, Henry IV, Part I (RSC) 1981, Antony and Cleopatra 1986, The Taming of the Shrew 1986, A Touch of the Poet 1988. *Television appearances include:* Centennial 1979, Jane Eyre, The Master of Ballantrae, Mistral's Daughter 1984, Florence Nightingale 1984, Sins 1985, Framed 1992, Scarlett 1994, Salt Water Moose 1995, Cleopatra 1998, Possessed 1999, Time Share 2000. *Address:* c/o ICM, Oxford House, 76 Oxford Street, London, W1D 1BS, England. *Telephone:* (20) 7636-6565. *Fax:* (20) 7323-0101 (Office).

DALY, Brendan; Irish politician; b. 2 Feb. 1940, Cooraclare, Co. Clare; m. Patricia Carmody; two s. one d.; ed Kilrush Co. Boys' School; mem. Dáil 1973–; Minister of State, Dept of Labour 1980–81; Minister for Fisheries and Forestry March–Dec. 1982, for the Marine 1987–89, for Defence Feb.–Nov. 1991, for Social Welfare 1991–92; Minister of State, Dept of Foreign Affairs 1992–93; elected to Seanad Éireann 1993, re-elected 1997, 2002; mem. Northern Ireland Peace Forum 1994; mem. Irish Parl. Foreign Affairs Cttee 1993–; mem. Fianna Fáil. *Address:* Cooraclare, Kilrush, Co. Clare, Republic of Ireland (Home). *Telephone:* (65) 9059040. *Fax:* (65) 9059218. *E-mail:* brendan.daly@oireachtas.irlgov.ie.

DALY, HE Cardinal Cahal Brendan, MA, DD, DHumLitt, DTheol; Northern Irish ecclesiastic; b. 1 Oct. 1917, Loughguile, Co. Antrim; s. of Charles Daly and Susan Connolly; ed St Malachy's Coll., Belfast, Queen's Univ., Belfast, St Patrick's Coll., Maynooth, Institut Catholique, Paris; ordained priest 1941; Classics Master St Malachy's Coll. 1945–46; Lecturer in Scholastic Philosophy, Queen's Univ., Belfast 1946–63, Reader 1963–67; Bishop of Ardagh and Clonmacnois 1967–82; Bishop of Down and Connor 1982–90; Archbishop of Armagh and Primate of All Ireland 1990–96, Archbishop Emer. 1996–; cr. Cardinal 1991; Chancellor St Patrick's Pontifical Univ., Maynooth 1990–96; mem. Congregation for Clergy, for Evangelization of the Peoples; mem. Pontifical Council for the Union of Christians; Hon. DD (Queen's Univ. of Belfast) 1990, (St John's, New York); Hon. Dr of Law (Sacred Heart Univ., CT), (Notre Dame Univ., Indiana), (Exeter); Hon. DLitt (Trinity Coll., Dublin); Hon. LLD (Nat. Univ. of Ireland). *Publications:* Morals, Law and Life 1962, Natural Law Morality Today 1965, Violence in Ireland and Christian Conscience 1973, Theologians and the Magisterium 1977, Peace and the Work of Justice 1979, Communities Without Consensus: The Northern Irish Tragedy 1984, Renewed Heart for Peace 1984, Cry of the Poor 1986, The Price of Peace 1991, Tertullian: the Puritan and his Influence 1993, Moral Philosophy in Britain from Bradley to Wittgenstein 1996, Steps on my Pilgrim Journey 1998, The Minding of Planet Earth 2000, contrib. to various philosophical works. *Address:* 23 Rosetta Avenue, Ormeau Road, Belfast, BT7 3HG, Northern Ireland. *Telephone:* (28) 9064-2431. *Fax:* (28) 9049-2684.

DALY, John Patrick; American golfer; b. 28 April 1966, Carmichael, Calif.; m. Cherie Daly; two c.; ed Univ. of Arkansas; turned professional 1987; won Missouri Open 1987, Ben Hogan Utah Classic 1990, PGA Championship, Crooked Stick 1991, BC Open 1992, BellSouth Classic 1994, British Open 1995, Dunhill Cup 1993, 1998, BMW Int. Open 2001. *Recording:* My Life (album). *Leisure interests:* sports, writing lyrics, playing the guitar. *Address:* c/o PGA America, 100 Avenue of the Champions, Palm Beach Gardens, FL 33418, USA.

DALY, Robert Anthony; American business executive; b. 8 Dec. 1936, Brooklyn, New York; s. of James Daly and Eleanor Daly; m. Carole Bayer Sager; two s. one d.; one step-s.; ed Brooklyn Coll.; Dir business affairs, then Vice-Pres. business affairs, then Exec. Vice-Pres. CBS TV Network 1955–80; Pres. CBS Entertainment Co. 1977–; Chair. and Co-CEO Warner Bros, Burbank, Calif. 1980, Chair., CEO 1982–99, Chair. and Co-CEO 1994; Chair. and Co-CEO Warner Music Group 1995–99 (resgnd); Man. Gen. Partner, Chair. and CEO LA Dodgers baseball team 1999–; mem. Bd Dirs. American Film Inst., Museum of TV and Radio; mem. Acad. of Motion Picture Arts and Sciences, Nat. Acad. of TV Arts and Sciences; Hon. DFA (American Film Inst.) 1999; Hon. DHumLitt (Trinity Coll.) 2001. *Address:* Los Angeles Dodgers, 1000 Elysian Park Avenue, Los Angeles, CA 90012-1199, USA.

DAM, Kenneth W., JD; American lawyer and university professor; b. 10 Aug. 1932, Marysville, Kan.; s. of Oliver W. Dam and Ida L. Dam; m. Marcia Wachs 1962; one s. one d.; ed Univs of Kansas and Chicago; law clerk, Mr Justice Whittaker, US Supreme Court 1957–58; Assoc., Cravath, Swaine & Moore, New York 1958–60; Asst Prof., Univ. of Chicago Law School 1960–61, Assoc. Prof. 1961–64, Prof. 1964–71, 1974–76, Harold J. & Marion F. Green Prof. of Int. Legal Studies 1976–85; Max Pam Prof. of American and Foreign Law 1992–2001; Provost, Univ. of Chicago 1980–82; Consultant, Kirkland & Ellis, Chicago 1961–71, 1974–80, 1993–; Exec. Dir Council on Econ. Policy 1973; Asst Dir for Nat. Security and Int. Affairs, Office of Man. and Budget 1971–73; Deputy Sec. of State 1982–85; Deputy Sec. US Treasury 2001–; Vice-Pres., Law and External Relations, IBM Corpn 1985–92; Pres., CEO United Way America 1992; Dir Alcoa 1987–; Trustee Brookings Inst. 1989–2001, Council on Foreign Relations 1992–2001, Chicago Council on Foreign Relations 1992–2001; mem. American Acad. of Arts and Sciences, American Acad. of Diplomacy, American Bar Asscn, American Law Inst.; Chair. German-American Academic Council. *Publications:* Federal Tax Treatment of Foreign Income (with L. Krause) 1964, The GATT: Law and International Economic Organization 1970, Oil Resources: Who Gets What How? 1976, Economic Policy Beyond the Headlines (with George P. Shultz) 1978, The Rules of the Game: Reform and Evolution in the International Monetary System 1982, Cryptography's Role in Securing the Information Society 1996 (co-ed.); numerous articles on legal and economic issues. *Address:* Treasury Department, 1500 Pennsylvania Avenue, Washington, DC 20220 (Office); University of Chicago Law School, 1111 East 60th Street, Chicago, IL 60637, USA.

DAM-JENSEN, Inger; Danish opera singer; b. 13 March 1964, Copenhagen; m. Morten Ernst Lassen; ed Royal Danish Acad. of Music, Danish Opera School; studied with Kirsten Buhl Møller; started career 1992; operatic roles include Zdenka (Arabella), Ophelia (Hamlet), Norina (Don Pasquale), Sophie (Der Rosenkavalier), Adina (L'elisir d'amore), Susanna (Le Nozze di Figaro), Musetta (La Bohème) for Royal Danish Opera, Despina (Così fan Tutte) and Blondchen (Die Entführung aus dem Serail) for Royal Opera House, Covent Garden, Sifare (Mitridate) for Geneva Opera; concert appearances with numerous orchestras including Danish Radio Symphony, New York Philharmonic, Berlin Philharmonic, Czech Philharmonic and Gabrieli Consort; has performed at BBC Promenade Concerts and Edin. Festival. *Recording:* Mahler's Fourth Symphony. *Address:* c/o Harrison Parrott Ltd, 12 Penzance Place, London, W11 4PA, England (Office); Hollændervej 4A, 1855 Frederiksberg C, Denmark (Home). *Telephone:* 26-17-40-59 (Denmark) (Office); 33-23-40-59 (Home). *Fax:* 33-23-40-59 (Office). *E-mail:* inger@danlassen.dk (Home).

D'AMATO, Alfonse M., BA, LLB; American politician and lawyer; b. 1 Aug. 1937, Brooklyn, New York; m. Penelope Ann Collenburg 1960 (divorced); two s. two d.; ed Syracuse Univ.; Receiver of Taxes, Town of Hempstead 1971–72, Supervisor, Hempstead 1972–78, Presiding Supervisor 1978–81; Senator from NY State 1981–98, on Banking, Housing and Urban Affairs Cttee (Chair. 1995) and Finance Cttee; lawyer, Fox News 1999–; Republican. *Publications:* Power, Pasta and Politics (autobiog.) 1995. *Address:* George Publishing Company, 1633 Broadway, 41st Floor, New York, NY 10019 (Office); Island Park, NY 11558, USA (Home).

DAMON, Matt; American actor; b. 8 Oct. 1970, Cambridge, Mass.; numerous awards for Good Will Hunting including Acad. Award for Best Writing, Screenplay written directly for Screen, Silver Berlin Bear Award for Outstanding Single Achievement 1997. *Films include:* Mystic Pizza 1988, Rising Son (TV) 1990, School Ties 1992, Geronimo: An American Legend 1993, The Good Old Boys (TV) 1995, Courage Under Fire 1996, Glory Daze 1996, Chasing Amy 1997, The Rainmaker 1997, Good Will Hunting (also co-writer) 1997, Saving Private Ryan 1998, Rounders 1998, Dogma 1999, The Talented Mr Ripley 1999, Titan A.E. (voice) 1999, All the Pretty Horses 1999, The Legend of Baggar Vance 2000, Finding Forrester 2000, Ocean's Eleven 2001, The Majestic (voice) 2001, Gerry (also writer) 2002, Spirit: Stallion of the Cimarron (voice) 2002, The Third Wheel 2002, The Bourne Identity 2002, Confessions of a Dangerous Mind 2003. *Address:* Creative Artists Agency, 9830 Wilshire Boulevard, Beverly Hills, CA 90212, USA (Office).

DANCE, Charles; British actor; b. 10 Oct. 1946, Rednal, Worcs.; s. of late Walter Dance and Eleanor Perks; m. Joanna Haythorn 1970; one s. one d.; formerly worked in industry; with RSC 1975–80, 1980–85; Best Actor, Paris Film Festival 1990. *Television appearances include:* The Fatal Spring, Nancy Astor, Frost in May, Saigon–The Last Day, Thunder Rock (drama), Rainy Day Women, The Jewel in the Crown (nominated for Best Actor BAFTA Award), The Secret Servant, The McGuffin, The Phantom of the Opera 1989, Rebecca 1996, In the Presence of Mine Enemies 1997, Murder Rooms 1999, Justice in Wonderland 2000, Nicholas Nickleby 2001. *Films include:* For Your Eyes Only, Plenty, The Golden Child, White Mischief, Good Morning Babylon, Hidden City, Pascali's Island 1988, China Moon 1990, Alien III 1991, Limestone 1991, Kabloonak (Best Actor, Paris Film Festival 1991), Century, Last Action Hero, Exquisite Tenderness 1993, Short Cut to Paradise 1993, Undertow 1994, Michael Collins, Space Truckers 1996, Goldeneye, The Blood Oranges, What Rats Won't Do, Hilary and Jackie 1998, Don't go Breaking my Heart 1999, Jurij 1999, Dark Blue World 2000, Gosford Park 2001, Ali G in da House 2001, Black and White, Swimming Pool 2002. *Theatre:* Coriolanus (title role) (RSC) 1989, Irma La Douce, Turning Over, Henry V, Three Sisters 1998, Good 1999, Long Day's Journey Into Night 2001, The Play What I Wrote 2002. *Radio:* The Heart of the Matter 2001, The Charge of the Light Brigade 2001. *Address:* c/o ICM, Oxford House, 76 Oxford Street, London, W1D 1BS, England. *Telephone:* (20) 7636-6565.

D'ANCONA, Hedy, DSc; Netherlands politician; b. 1 Oct. 1937; former journalist and broadcaster; mem. Senate 1974; State Sec. for Female Emancipation 1981–82; mem. European Parl. 1984–89; Minister of Welfare, Public Health and Culture 1989–94; mem. Partij van de Arbeid. *Address:* c/o Partij van de Arbeid, Nicolaas Witsenkade 30, 1017 ZT Amsterdam; P.O. Box 1310, 1000 BH Amsterdam, Netherlands.

DANCZOWSKA, Kaja; Polish violinist; b. 25 March 1949, Cracow; one d.; ed State Higher Music School in Kraków, Moscow Conservatory; studied violin under teachers E. Uminska and David Oistrakh; Prof. Acad. of Music, Kraków 1977–; Prof. at courses of interpretation in Poland and abroad 1984–; Ordinary Prof. 1997; mem. of jury int. violin competitions in Poznań, Munich, New York and Tokyo 1986–; participation in the major violin festivals; co-operation with the greatest conductors and orchestras; recordings for Wifon, Polskie Nagrania, Deutsche Grammophon, Philips; numerous awards include four prizes in Int. Violin Competition 1967–75, Queen Elizabeth Prize, Brussels 1976 (Silver Medal), Individual Prize of Minister of Culture and Art 1991, Prize of Minister of Culture and Art 1998; Excellence in Teaching Award, USA 1998, Polish Culture Foundation Award 1998; Officer's Cross, Order of Polonia Restituta 2001. *Leisure interests:* film, literature. *Address:* Academy of Music, ul. św. Tomasza 43, 31-027 Kraków, Poland (Office). *Fax:* (12) 4222343 (Office).

DANDAVATE, Madhu; Indian politician and fmr professor of physics; b. 21 Jan. 1924, Ahmed Nagar, Maharashtra; ed Royal Inst. of Science, Bombay; participated in Independence Movt, later in Quit India Movt 1942; leader of passive resistance in Goa Campaign 1955; took part in Samyukta Maharashtra Movt for formation of Maharashtra state; joined Praja Socialist Party (PSP) 1948, Chair. Maharashtra State Unit of PSP, later Jt Sec. of All-India PSP; participated in Land Liberation Movt 1969; associated with Maharashtra Citizens' Defence Cttee during conflicts with People's Repub. of China and Pakistan; mem. Maharashtra Legis. Council 1970–71; mem. Lok Sabha from Rajapur 1971–79, 1980–; Vice-Prin. and Head of Physics Dept, Siddhartha Coll. of Arts and Science, Bombay –1971; mem. Janata Party 1977–; Minister of Railways 1977–80, of Finance 1989–90. *Publications:* Gandhiji's Impact on Socialist Thinking, Three Decades of Indian Communism, Evolution of Socialist Policies, Kashmir—a Test for Secularism, Myth and Mystery of Congress Socialism, Bharatiya Swarajwad (in Marathi), Marx and Gandhi, Echoes in Parliament. *Address:* Sharadashram, Bhawani Shankar Road, Dadar, Mumbai 400028, India.

DANELIUS, Hans Carl Yngve; Swedish diplomatist and lawyer; b. 2 April 1934, Stockholm; s. of Sven Danelius and Inga (née Svensson) Danelius; m. Hanneke Schadee 1961; three s. one d.; ed Dept of Legal Studies, Stockholm Univ.; law practice in Swedish courts 1957–64; mem. Secr., European Comm. of Human Rights, Strasbourg 1964–67, mem. European Comm. of Human Rights 1983–99; Asst Judge, Svea Court of Appeal 1967–68; Adviser, Ministry of Justice 1968–71; Deputy Head, Legal Dept, Ministry for Foreign Affairs 1971–75, Head 1975–84, rank of Amb. 1977–84; Amb. to Netherlands 1984–88; Judge, Supreme Court of Sweden 1988–2001; Pres. Council on Legislation 2001–; arbitrator, Int. Centre for Settlement of Investment Disputes (ICSID) 1999–; mem. Perm. Court of Arbitration at the Hague 1982–; mem. Court of Conciliation and Arbitration of Org. for Security and Co-operation in Europe (OSCE) 1995–; mem. Constitutional Court of Bosnia and Herzegovina 1996–2002; Chief Ed. Svensk Juristtidning (Swedish Law Journal) 1973–84; Dr hc (Stockholm) 1988; Swedish and foreign decorations. *Publications:* Mänskliga Rättigheter (Human Rights) 1975, The United Nations Convention Against Torture 1988, Mänskliga Rättigheter i Europeisk Praxis (Human Rights in European Practice) 1997; numerous articles in Swedish and foreign journals. *Address:* Supreme Court, Box 2066, 10312 Stockholm (Office); Roslinvägen 33, 16851 Bromma, Sweden (Home). *Telephone:* (8) 61-76-400 (Office); (8) 37-34-91 (Home). *Fax:* (8) 56-43-34-84.

DANELIYA, Georgy Nikolayevich; Georgian film director; b. 25 Aug. 1930, Tbilisi; m. Galina Daneliya; one s. one d.; ed Moscow Inst. of Architecture, Higher Courses of Film Direction; worked Inst. for City Designing; Prof. All-Russian Inst. of Cinematography 1975–85; film Dir studio Mosfilm; State Prizes of USSR and Russia; USSR People's Artist; more than 70 prizes in int. film festivals. *Films include:* Serezha 1960, I am Wailing About Moscow 1963, Thirty Three 1965, Don't Grieve 1969, Aphonya 1975, Mimino 1978 (Gold Prize Avelino Festival, Italy), Autumn Marathon 1979 (Grand Prix San Sebastian Festival, Spain, Grand Prix Chambourci Festival, France), Gentlemen of Luck 1981, Tears were Dropping 1982, Kin-Dza-Dza 1987, Passport 1989, White Dance 1992, Nastya 1993, On the First Breath or Heads or Tails? 1995. *Address:* Makarenko 1/19 apt. 15, 103062 Moscow, Russia. *Telephone:* (095) 921-43-74.

DANES, Claire; American film actress; b. 12 April 1979, New York; d. of Chris Danes and Carla Danes; ed performing arts school, NY and Lee Strasberg Studio; first acting roles in off-Broadway theatre productions: Happiness, Punk Ballet and Kids on Stage. *Films:* Dreams of Love (debut) 1992, Thirty (short) 1993, The Pesky Suitor (short), Little Women 1994, Romeo and Juliet 1996, To Gillian on Her 37th Birthday 1996, Polish Wedding, U-Turn 1997, The Rainmaker 1997, Les Misérables 1998, The Mod Squad 1999, Brokedown Place 1999, Monterey Pop 2000, Dr T and the Women 2000, Flora Plum 2000, The Cherry Orchard 2002, Igby Goes Down 2002, The Hours 2002, Terminator 3: Rise of the Machines 2003. *Television includes:* My So-Called Life (series), No Room for Opal (film), The Coming Out of Heidi Leiter.

DANFORTH, John Claggett, AB, BD, LLB; American politician and lawyer; b. 5 Sept. 1936, St Louis; s. of Donald and Dorothy Danforth; m. Sally B. Dobson 1957; one s. four d.; ed Princeton and Yale Univs.; admitted to NY Bar 1963, Mo. Bar 1966; Davis Polk and others, law firm 1963–66, Bryan Cave and others, law firm 1966–68, 1995–; Attorney-Gen. of Mo. 1969–76; Senator from Missouri 1976–95; mem. Senate Cttees on Finance, Commerce, Science and Transportation, Select Cttee on Intelligence; Head of Special Envoy to Sudan 2001–; ordained priest, Episcopal Church 1964; Asst or assoc. rector of churches in New York City, St Louis, Jefferson City; assoc. rector Church of the Holy Communion, Univ. City, Mo. 1995–; Hon. Assoc. St Alban's Church, Washington; awards include Presidential World Without Hunger Award, Legislative Leadership Award of Nat. Comm. against Drunk Driving, Brotherhood and Distinguished Missourian awards of Nat. Conf. of Christians and Jews. *Publication:* Resurrection: The Confirmation of Clarence Thomas 1994. *Address:* Bryan Cave LLP, 1 Mel Nor Lane, Suite 3600, St Louis, MO 63125, USA.

DANIEL, Jean, LèsL; French journalist and author; b. 21 July 1920, Blida, Algeria; s. of Jules Bensaïd and Rachel Bensimon; m. Michèle Bancilhon 1965; one d.; ed Sorbonne, Paris; Cabinet of Felix Gouin, Pres. Council of Ministers 1946; Founder and Dir Caliban (cultural review) 1947–51; Prof. of Philosophy, Oran 1953; Asst Ed.-in-Chief, subsequently Ed.-in-Chief, L'Express 1955–64; Corresp., New Repub., Washington 1956–65; Assoc., Le Monde 1964; Ed.-in-Chief Le Nouvel Observateur 1964–, Ed. Dir 1965–, Dir 1978–; Admin. Louvre Museum 1992–99; Dir Monde des débats 2001; mem. Comité Nat. d'Ethique; Officier, Légion d'honneur, Croix de Guerre, Commdr Arts et Lettres, Commdr Ordre Nat. du Mérite. *Publications:* L'Erreur 1953, Journal d'un journaliste, Le Temps qui reste 1973, Le Refuge et la source 1977, L'Ere des ruptures 1979, De Gaulle et l'Algérie 1985, Les religions d'un président 1988, Cette grande lueur à l'Est 1989, La Blessure suivi de le Temps qui vient 1992, L'ami anglais 1994, Voyage au bout de la Nation (essay) 1995, Dieu, est-il fanatique? 1996, Avec le temps. Carnets 1970–1998 1998 (Prix Méditerranée 1999), Soleils d'Hiver 2001. *Leisure interest:* tennis. *Address:* Le Nouvel Observateur, 10–12 place de la Bourse, 75081 Paris Cedex 02, France. *Telephone:* 1-44-88-34-10. *Fax:* 1-44-88-37-34.

DANIEL, Sir John Sagar, Kt, MAEd.Tech, ATh, DèsSc; British/Canadian educationist; b. 31 May 1942, Banstead, UK; s. of John Edward Daniel Sagar and Winifred Sagar; m. Kristin Anne Swanson 1966; one s. two d.; ed Christ's

Hosp., Sussex, St Edmund Hall, Univ. of Oxford, Univ. of Paris, Concordia Univ., Montréal; Assoc. Prof. Ecole Polytechnique, Univ. de Montréal 1969–73; Dir des Etudes, Télé-Univ., Univ. de Québec 1973–77; Vice-Pres. Athabasca Univ., Alberta 1977–80; Academic Vice-Rector Concordia Univ. 1980–84; Pres. Laurentian Univ., Sudbury 1984–90; Vice-Chancellor Open Univ., UK 1990–2001; Pres. Open Univ., USA 1999–2001; Asst Dir-Gen. for Educ., UNESCO 2001–; mem. Council of Foundation, Int. Baccalaureate 1992– (Vice-Pres. 1996–99), British North American Cttee 1995–; mem. Council Open Univ., Hong Kong 1996–, CBI 1996–; Trustee Carnegie Foundation for the Advancement of Teaching 1993–; Forum Fellow, World Econ. Forum, Switzerland 1998; Fellow, Open Univ. (UK); Hon. Fellow St Edmund Hall, Oxford; Hon. DLitt (Deakin Univ., Australia), (Univ. of Lincs. and Humberside) 1996; Hon. DSc (Coll. Mil. Royale, Saint-Jean), (Open Univ. of Sri Lanka) 1994, (Univ. de Paris VI); Hon. D.Ed. (CNAA); Hon. LLD (Waterloo, Canada), (Univ. of Wales); Hon. DUniv (Univs. of Athabasca, Portugal, Humberside, Anadolu Univ., Turkey, Sukhothai Thammathirat Open Univ., Thailand, Télé-université, Université du Québec, Canada, Univ. of Derby, Open Univ., Hong Kong, New Bulgarian Univ.); Hon. D.Hum.Lit. (Thomas Edison State Coll., USA, Richmond, American Int. Univ. in London); Individual Award of Excellence, Commonwealth of Learning 1995, Morris T. Keeton Award, Council for Adult and Experiential Learning (USA) 1999; Officier, Ordre des Palmes Académiques; Queen's Jubilee Medal (Canada). *Publications:* over 200 articles and books including Learning at a Distance: A World Perspective 1982, Developing Distance Education (jtly) 1988, Mega-universities and Knowledge Media: Technology Strategies for Higher Education 1996. *Leisure interests:* walking, boating, reading. *Address:* Education Sector, UNESCO, Place de Fontenoy, 75352 Paris 07.SP/1, France (Office). *Telephone:* 1-45-68-10-46 (Office). *E-mail:* j.daniel@unesco.org (Office). *Website:* www.unesco.org (Office).

DANIEL, Paul Wilson, CBE; British conductor; b. 5 July 1958; m. Joan Rodgers (q.v.) 1988; two d.; mem. music staff English Nat. Opera (ENO), London 1982–87, Music Dir 1997–; Music Dir Opera Factory 1987–90, Opera North, Leeds 1990–97; Prin. Conductor English Northern Philharmonia 1990–97; has conducted all the maj. London orchestras and most of the regional UK orchestras and orchestras in USA, Germany, Netherlands, France and Australia; Olivier Award for Outstanding Achievement in Opera 1997, Gramophone Award for English Music Series 1999. *Operas conducted include:* (ENO) The Mask of Orpheus, Akhnaten, Tosca, Rigoletto, Carmen, Figaro's Wedding, King Priam, Flying Dutchman, From the House of the Dead, Tales of Hoffman, Falstaff, Manon, Othello, Boris Godunov, La Traviata, The Carmelites, Nixon in China, The Silver Tassie, War and Peace, Lulu, The Trojans; (Opera North) Ariane et Barbe-Bleue, Attila, King Priam, Don Giovanni, Der Ferne Klang, Boris Godunov (also at BBC Proms 1992), Rigoletto, Don Carlos, Wozzeck, Gloriana, Baa Baa Black Sheep (world premiere), Playing Away, Il Trovatore, Pelléas et Mélisande, Jenůfa, Luisa Miller; (Royal Opera Covent Garden) Mitridate; has also conducted opera productions in Nancy, Munich, Brussels, Geneva. *Address:* c/o English National Opera, London Coliseum, St Martin's Lane, London, WC2N 4ES (Office); c/o Ingpen and Williams, 26 Wadham Road, London, SW15 2LR, England.

DANIELL, Robert F.; American business executive; m.; ed Boston Univ. Coll. of Industrial Tech.; joined Sikorsky as design engineer 1956, programme man. for S-61, S-62 and S-58 commercial helicopter programmes 1968, Commercial Marketing Man. 1971, Vice-Pres. (Commercial Marketing) 1974, Vice-Pres. (Marketing) 1976, Exec. Vice-Pres. 1977, later Pres. and CEO until 1982; Vice-Pres. United Technologies Corpn 1982, Sr Vice-Pres. (Defense Systems) 1983, Pres., COO and Dir 1984–92, CEO 1986–94, Chair. 1987–97; Dir Travelers Corpn, Hartford, Shell Oil Co., Houston; Fellow, Univ. of Bridgeport; Hon. DSc (Bridgeport); Hon. LLD (Trinity Coll. and Boston Univ.). *Address:* c/o United Technologies Corporation, United Technologies Building, One Financial Plaza, Hartford, CT 06101, USA.

DANIELS, Jeff; American actor; b. 19 Feb. 1955, Athens, Ga; ed Cen. Michigan Univ.; apprentice Circle Repertory Theatre, New York; f. Purple Rose Theatre Co., Chelsea, Mich. *Theatre:* The Farm 1976, Brontosaurus 1977, My Life 1977, Feedlot 1977, Lulu 1978, Slugger 1978, The Fifth of July 1978, Johnny Got His Gun 1982 (Obie Award), The Three Sisters 1982–83, The Golden Age 1984, Redwood Curtain 1993, Short-Changed Review 1993, Lemon Sky. *Films include:* Ragtime 1981, Terms of Endearment 1983, The Purple Rose of Cairo 1985, Marie 1985, Heartburn 1986, Something Wild 1986, Radio Days 1987, The House on Carroll Street 1988, Sweet Hearts Dance 1988, Grand Tour 1989, Checking Out 1989, Arachnophobia 1990, Welcome Home, Roxy Carmichael 1990, Love Hurts 1990, The Butcher's Wife 1992, Gettysburg 1993, Speed 1994, Dumb and Dumber 1994, Fly Away Home 1996, Two Days in the Valley 1996, 101 Dalmatians 1996, Trial and Error 1997, Pleasantville 1998, All the Rage 1999, My Favorite Martian 1999, Chasing Sleep 2000, Escanaba in da Moonlight 2000, Super Sucker 2002, Blood Work 2002, The Hours 2002, Gods and Generals 2002. *Television includes:* (films) A Rumor of War 1980, Invasion of Privacy 1983, The Caine Mutiny Court Martial 1988, No Place Like Home 1989, Disaster in Time 1992, Redwood Curtain 1995, Teamster Boss: The Jackie Presser Story; (specials) Fifth of July, The Visit (Trying Times). *Plays (author):* Shoeman 1991, The Tropical Pickle 1992, The Vast Difference 1993, Thy Kingdom's Coming 1994, Escanaba in da Moonlight 1995.

DANIELS, (John) Eric; American banker; b. 14 Aug. 1951, Montana; fmr COO Citigroup Consumers Bank and Head Travelers Life & Annuity; Founder and CEO Zona Financiera –2001; Head of Lloyds TSB UK Retail Banking 2001–03, CEO April 2003–. *Address:* Lloyds TSB Bank PLC, 71 Lombard Street, London, EC3P 3BS, England (Office). *Telephone:* (20) 7626-1500 (Office). *Website:* www.lloydstsb.com (Office).

DANIELS, Mitchell E.; American government official and business executive; m. Cheri Daniels; four d.; ed Princeton Univ., Georgetown Univ.; Chief of Staff to Richard Luger, Mayor of Indianapolis 1971–82; Exec. Dir Nat. Republican Senatorial Cttee 1983–84; Asst to fmr Pres. Ronald Reagan, also liaison with local officials; apptd Pres. and CEO Hudson Inst. 1987; Pres. N American Pharmaceutical Operations, Eli Lilly and Co. –1997, Sr Vice-Pres. of Corp. Strategy and Policy 1997–2001; Dir Office of Man. and Budget (OMB), US Admin. Jan. 2001–. *Address:* Office of Management and Budget, Eisenhower Executive Office Building, (7th Street and Pennsylvania Avenue, NW), Washington, DC 20503, USA (Office). *Telephone:* (202) 395-3000 (Office). *Fax:* (202) 395-3888 (Office). *Website:* www.whitehouse.gov/omb (Office).

DANIELS, William Burton, PhD, MS; American professor of physics; b. 21 Dec. 1930, Buffalo, NY; s. of William C. Daniels and Sophia P. Daniels; m. Adriana A. Braakman 1958; two s. one d.; ed Univ. of Buffalo and Case Inst. (now Case-Western Reserve Univ.); Asst Prof. of Physics, Case Tech. 1957–59; Research Scientist, Union Carbide Corpn 1959–61; Asst Prof. Princeton Univ. 1961–63, Assoc. Prof. 1963–66, Prof. of Mechanical Eng 1966–72; Unidel Prof. of Physics, also of Astronomy, Univ. of Del. 1972–2000, Unidel Prof. Emer. 2001–, Chair. Physics Dept 1977–80; Fellow, American Physical Soc.; John Simon Guggenheim Memorial Fellow 1976–77; Humboldt Sr Award 1982, 1992. *Publications:* more than 100 articles on the physics of solids at high pressures. *Leisure interests:* sailing, mountaineering. *Address:* Physics Department, University of Delaware, Newark, DE 19716 (Office); 283 Dallam Road, Newark, DE 19711, USA (Home). *Telephone:* (302) 451-2667 (Office). *Fax:* (302) 831-1637. *E-mail:* Family.Daniels@yahoo.com.

DANILOV, Yuri Mikhailovich; Russian judge; b. 1 Aug. 1950, Mukachevo, Ukraine; m.; three c.; ed Voronezh State Univ.; fmr metalworker in Lugansk; People's Judge Povorinsk Dist Court, Voronezh Region 1971–80; mem. Voronezh Regional Court 1980–83, Chair. 1985–89; instructor Voronezh Regional CP Cttee 1983–85; First Deputy Head Dept of Gen. Courts, USSR Ministry of Justice 1989–91, Deputy Minister of Justice 1991–92; Chief Jurist, Vice-Pres. Int. Food Exchange 1992–93; Deputy Chair. State Cttee on Anti-Monopoly Policy and Support of New Econ. Structures; Chair. Comm. on Stock Exchanges 1993–94; Judge Constitutional Court of Russian Fed. 1994–; Merited Jurist of Russian Fed. *Address:* Constitutional Court of Justice of the Russian Federation, Ilyinka str. 21, 103132 Moscow, Russia (Office). *Telephone:* (095) 206-16-29 (Office).

DANILOV-DANILYAN, Victor Ivanovich, DEcon; Russian politician; b. 9 May 1938, Moscow; m.; three s.; ed Moscow State Univ.; jr researcher, engineer, sr engineer, Computation Cen., Moscow State Univ. 1960–64; researcher, leading engineer, Head of lab., Cen. Inst. of Math. and Econs, USSR Acad. of Sciences 1964–76; Head of lab., Prof., All-Union Research Inst. of System Studies, USSR Acad. of Sciences 1976–80; Head of lab., Chair. Acad. of Nat. Econ., USSR Council of Ministers 1980–91; Deputy Minister of Nature and Environment of USSR Aug.–Nov. 1991; Minister of Ecology and Natural Resources, Russian Fed. 1991–96; Chair. State Cttee on Ecology, Russian Fed. Aug. 1996–; Pres.-Rector Int. Industrial Ecology and Political Univ. (MNEPU) 1991–; mem. State Duma (parl.) 1993–96; founder and author, ecological programme of Kedr (Cedar) Movt 1994; mem. Russian Acad. of Natural Sciences. *Address:* MNEPU, Krasnokazarmennaya str. 14, 111250 Moscow, Russia (Office). *Telephone:* (095) 273-55-48 (Office).

DANIÑO ZAPATA, Roberto Enrique; Peruvian politician and lawyer; ed Catholic Univ. of Peru, Harvard Univ., USA; fmr Sec.-Gen. Ministry of Economy, Finance and Trade; fmr Pres. Foreign Investment and Tech. Agency, Chair. Foreign Public Debt Comm.; founding Gen. Counsel Inter-American Investment Corpn, Washington, DC, Chair. Inter-American Devt Bank's External Review Group for Pvt. Sector Operations; Partner int. law firm Wilmer, Cutler & Pickering, Head Latin American Practice Group 1996–2001; Pres. Council of Ministers (Prime Minister) of Peru 2001–; fmr mem. Bd Newbridge Andean Partners, Royal & SunAlliance/Fenix, Cementos Pacasmayo, Sindicato Pesquero, Violy, Byorum & Partners, The Mountain Inst., The Infant Nutrition Fund; fmr mem. The Coca-Cola Co. Latin American Advisory Bd, Americas Soc. Chair.'s Council, Carnegie Endowment's G-50 Bd. *Address:* Office of the Prime Minister, Ucayali 363, Lima, Peru (Office). *Telephone:* (1) 4273860 (Office). *Fax:* (1) 4323266 (Office).

DANINOS, Pierre; French writer; b. 26 May 1913, Paris; m. 1st Jane Marrain 1942; m. 2nd Marie-Pierre Dourneau 1968; one s. two d.; ed Lycée Janson de Sailly; began as journalist 1931; liaison agent to the British Army, Flanders 1940; Columnist for Le Figaro. *Plays:* Un certain M. Blot, Daninos pot pourri. *Publications:* Le sang des hommes 1940, Les carnets du bon Dieu (Prix Interallié) 1947, Sonia, les autres et moi (Prix Courteline) 1952, Les carnets du Major Thompson 1954, Vacances à tous prix 1958, Un certain Monsieur Blot 1960, Le jacassin 1962, Snobissimo 1964, Le 36e dessous 1966, Les touristocrates 1974, Made in France 1977, La composition d'histoire 1979, Le veuf joyeux 1981, La galerie des glaces 1983, La France dans tous ses états 1985, Profession: Écrivain 1988, Candidement vôtre 1992, 40 ans de vacances

1993, Vous écrivez encore? 1999, Les derniers carnets du Major Thompson 2000. *Leisure interests:* loafing, tennis, collecting British hobbies, life. *Address:* 15 rue Chauveau, 92200 Neuilly-sur-Seine, France.

DANKWORTH, John Philip William, CBE, FRAM; British musician; b. 20 Sept 1927, London; m. Cleo Laine (q.v.) 1958; one s. one d.; ed Monoux Grammar School, Royal Acad. of Music; f. large jazz orchestra 1953; with Cleo Laine f. Wavendon Stables (performing arts centre) 1970; Pops Music Dir London Symphony Orchestra 1985–90; Hon. Fellow Leeds Coll. of Music; numerous record albums, most recent include Echoes of Harlem, Misty, Symphonic Fusions, Moon Valley; Hon. MA (Open Univ.) 1975; Hon. DMus (Berklee School of Music) 1982, (York Univ.) 1993; Variety Club of GB Show Business Personality Award (with Cleo Laine) 1977, ISPA Distinguished Artists Award 1999, Bob Harrington Lifetime Achievement Award (with Cleo Laine) 2001, BBC British Jazz Awards Lifetime Achievement Award (with Cleo Laine) 2002. *Compositions include:* Improvisations (with Matyas Seiber) 1959, Escapade (commissioned by Northern Sinfonia Orchestra) 1967, Tom Sawyer's Saturday, for narrator and orchestra (commissioned by Farnham Festival) 1967, String Quartet 1971, Piano Concerto (commissioned by Westminster Festival) 1972, Grace Abounding (for Royal Philharmonic Orchestra) 1980, The Diamond and the Goose (for City of Birmingham Choir and Orchestra) 1981, Reconciliation (for Silver Jubilee of Coventry Cathedral) 1987, Woolwich Concerto (clarinet concerto for Emma Johnson) 1995, Double Vision 1997, Dreams '42 (string quartet for Kidderminster Festival) 1997, Objective 2000 (for combined orchestras of the Harpur Trust Schools) 2000, Mariposas (piano and violin concerto, written for Peter Fisher) 2001 (orchestrated for London Chamber Ensemble 2002). *Film scores include:* Saturday Night and Sunday Morning, Darling, The Servant, Morgan, Accident, Gangster No. 1. *Publication:* Sax from the Start 1996, Jazz in Revolution 1998. *Leisure interests:* driving, household maintenance. *Address:* The Old Rectory, Wavendon, Milton Keynes, MK17 8LT, England. *Fax:* (1908) 584414. *Website:* www.quarternotes.com.

DANNEELS, HE Cardinal Godfried; Belgian ecclesiastic; b. 4 June 1933, Kanegem, Bruges; ordained priest 1957; Bishop of Antwerp 1977; Archbishop of Malines-Brussels 1979–; Castrene Bishop of Belgium 1980–; Pres. Episcopal Conf. of Belgium, Pax Christi Int.; mem. Synod of Bishops, Sacred Congregation for Evangelization, Council for the Public Affairs of the Church, Congregation of Catholic Educ., Congregation of Divine Worship, Secr. for Non-believers, Congregation for the Oriental Churches; cr. Cardinal 1983. *Address:* Aartsbisdom, Wollemarkt 15, 2800, Mechelen, Belgium. *Telephone:* (15) 216-501. *Fax:* (15) 209-485. *E-mail:* aartsbisdom@kerknet.be (Office).

DANSEREAU, Pierre, CC, GOQ, DSc, FRSC; Canadian professor of ecology; b. 5 Oct. 1911, Montréal; s. of J.-Lucien Dansereau and Marie Archambault; m. Françoise Masson 1935; ed Collège Sainte-Marie, Montréal, Institut Agricole d'Oka, Univ. of Geneva, Switzerland; Asst Dir of Tech. Services, Montréal Botanical Garden 1939–42; Dir Service de Biogéographie, Montréal 1943–50; Assoc. Prof. of Botany, Univ. of Mich., Ann Arbor, USA 1950–55; Dean of Faculty of Science and Dir of Botanical Inst., Univ. of Montréal 1955–61; Asst Dir and Head, Dept of Ecology, The New York Botanical Garden, Bronx, 1961–68; Prof., Inst. of Urban Studies, Univ. of Montréal 1968–71; Prof. and Scientific Dir, Centre de Recherches Ecologiques de Montréal, Univ. of Québec 1971–72, Prof. of Ecology attached to Centre de Recherches en Sciences de l'Environnement 1972–76, Hon. Prof. and Prof. of Ecology in Master's Programme in Environmental Sciences 1976–, doctoral programme 1987–, Prof. Emer. 1989–; many visiting professorships; Commonwealth Prestige Fellowship, Univ. of NZ 1961; numerous hon. degrees; 1st Prize (Prix David) Québec, science section 1959, Massey Medal, Royal Canadian Geographical Soc. 1974, Molson Prize 1974, Canada Council 1975, Izaak Walton Killam Prize, Canada Council 1985, Lawson Medal, Canadian Botanical Asscn 1986, Dawson Medal, Royal Soc. of Canada 1995, Grand Officier, Ordre nat. du Québec 1992, Canadian Science and Engineering Hall of Fame 2001. *Films:* An Ecologist's Notebook (6 half-hour films in English and French), Ecology Close-up (6 15-minute films in English and French) 1979–83, 3 films about his life, work and ideas have been made by the Nat. Film Bd of Canada and Univ. of Québec 2000–01. *Publications:* Biogeography: an ecological perspective 1957, Contradictions & Biculture 1964, Dimensions of Environmental Quality 1971, Inscape and Landscape 1973, La terre des hommes et le paysage intérieur 1973, Harmony and Disorder in the Canadian Environment 1975, EZAIM: Écologie de la Zone de l'Aéroport International de Montréal – Le cadre d'une recherche écologique interdisciplinaire 1976, Essai de classification et de cartographie écologique des espaces 1985, Les dimensions écologiques de l'espace urbain 1987, Interdisciplinary perspective on production-investment-control processes in the environment 1990, L'envers et l'endroit: le désir, le besoin et la capacité 1994, Postface: la voie forestière, la vérité biologique, la vie durable 1994, Biodiversity, ecodiversity, sociodiversity 1997, A ética ecologica e a educação para o desenvolvimento sustentável: a mensagem de Pierre Dansereau 1999. *Leisure interests:* swimming, travel, theatre. *Address:* Université du Québec à Montréal, B.P. 8888, Succ. Centre-Ville, Montréal, Québec, H3C 3P8 (Office); 205 chem. Côte-Sainte-Catherine, apt. 104, Outremont, Montréal, Québec, H2V 2A9, Canada (Home). *Telephone:* (514) 987-3000 (Office). *Fax:* (514) 987-4054 (Office). *E-mail:* dansereau.pierre@uqam.ca (Office).

DANSON, Ted; American actor; b. 29 Dec. 1947, San Diego, Calif.; s. of Edward Danson and Jessica McMaster; m. 1st Randall L. Gosch 1970 (divorced 1977); m. 2nd Cassandra Coates 1977 (divorced); two d.; m. 3rd Mary Steenburgen (1995); ed The Kent School, Connecticut and Stanford and Carnegie-Mellon Univs.; teacher, The Actor's Inst. Los Angeles 1978; star, NBC-TV series Cheers (American Comedy Award 1991) 1982–93; CEO Anasazi Productions (fmrly Danson/Fauci Productions). *Films include:* The Onion Field 1979, Body Heat 1981, Creepshow 1983, A Little Treasure 1985, A Fine Mess 1986, Just Between Friends 1986, Three Men and a Baby 1987, Cousins 1989, Dad 1989, Three Men and a Little Lady 1990, Made in America 1992, Getting Even With Dad 1993, Pontiac Moon 1993, Gulliver's Travels (TV) 1995, Loch Ness 1996, Homegrown 1998, Thanks of a Grateful Nation 1998, Saving Private Ryan 1998, Becker 1998, Mumford 1999. *Theatre includes:* The Real Inspector Hound 1972, Comedy of Errors. *Television:* Actor and producer of TV films including: When the Bough Breaks 1986, We Are The Children 1987; exec. producer TV films: Walk Me to the Distance 1989, Down Home 1989, Mercy Mission: The Rescue of Flight 771 1993, On Promised Land 1994; other appearances in TV dramas, etc. *Address:* c/o Josh Liberman, Creative Artists Agency, 9830 Wilshire Boulevard, Beverly Hills, CA 90212, USA.

DANTON, J. Periam, MA, PhD; American professor and librarian; b. 5 July 1908, Palo Alto, Calif.; s. of George Henry and Annina Periam; m. Lois King 1948 (divorced 1973); one s. one d.; ed Leipzig, Columbia and Chicago Univs and Oberlin and Williams Colls.; served in NY Public Library 1928–29; Williams Coll. Library 1929–30, American Library Asscn 1930–33; Librarian and Assoc. Prof. Colby Coll. Library 1935–36, Temple Univ. 1936–46; Del. Int. Fed. of Library Asscns. meetings 1939, 1964, 1966–72; Visiting Prof., Univs. of Chicago 1942 and Columbia 1946; Lt, Lt-Commdr, USNR 1942–45; Prof. Librarianship, Calif. Univ. 1946–76, Dean, School of Librarianship 1946–61, Prof. Emer. 1976–; Pres. Asscn American Library Schools 1949–50; Fulbright Research Scholar (Univ. Göttingen) 1960–61, (Vienna) 1964–65; Guggenheim Fellow 1971–72; US Dept of State, American Specialist, Ethiopia 1961; Ford Foundation Consultant on Univ. Libraries in Southeast Asia 1963; UNESCO Library Consultant, Jamaica 1968; Dir US Dept of State—American Library Asscn Multi-Area Group Librarian Program 1963–64; Guest Lecturer Univ. Toronto 1963, Hebrew Univ. Jerusalem 1965, 1985, Univs Belgrade, Ljubljana and Zagreb 1965, Univ. of British Columbia 1968, McGill Univ. 1969, Univ. of N Carolina 1977, Univ. of Tex. 1978, Southern Ill. Univ. 1979; mem. Bd of Eds Asscn of Coll. and Research Libraries Monographs 1966–70, Library Quarterly 1968–90, International Library Review 1968–75; Hon. mem. Vereinigung Österreichischer Bibliothekare, Verein Deutscher Bibliothekare; Hon. Research Fellow, Univ. of London 1974–75; Berkeley Citation 1976. *Publications:* Library Literature, 1921–32 1934, Education for Librarianship 1949, United States Influence on Norwegian Librarianship 1890-1940 1957, The Climate of Book Selection: Social Influences on School and Public Libraries 1959, Book Selection and Collections: A Comparison of German and American University Libraries 1963, Jamaica: Library Development 1968, Index to Festschriften in Librarianship 1970, Between M.L.S. and Ph.D.: A Study of Sixth-Year Specialist Programs in Accredited Library Schools 1970, The Dimensions of Comparative Librarianship 1973, Index to Festschriften in Librarianship 1967–75, 1978. *Leisure interests:* classical music, swimming, travel. *Address:* School of Information Management and Systems, 104 South Hall #4600, Berkeley, CA 94720-4600; 500 Vernon Street #402, Oakland, CA 94610, USA (Home). *Telephone:* (510) 642-1464; (510) 642-0924 (Office); (510) 653-4802 (Home). *Fax:* (510) 642-5814.

DANTZIG, George Bernard, PhD; American professor of operations research and computer science; b. 8 Nov. 1914, Portland, Ore.; s. of Tobias and Anja G. Dantzig; m. Anne Shmuner 1936; two s. one d.; ed Univs of Maryland, Michigan and California (Berkeley); Statistician, US Bureau of Labor Statistics 1937–39; Chief, Combat Analysis Branch, USAF HQ Statistical Control 1941–46; Math. Adviser, USAF HQ 1946–52; Research Mathematician, Rand Corpn, Santa Monica, Calif. 1952–60; Chair. Operations Research Center and Prof., Univ. of Calif. (Berkeley) 1960–66; Prof. of Operations Research and Computer Science, Stanford Univ. 1966–97, Prof. Emer. 1997–; Int. Inst. for Applied Systems Analysis, Head of Methodology Project 1973–74; mem. NAS, Nat. Acad. of Eng; Fellow, American Acad. of Arts and Sciences; Hon. mem. Inst. Electrical and Electronics Engineers; numerous Hon. degrees; Nat. Medal of Science, USA 1975, Harvey Prize (Technion, Israel) 1985, Silver Medal Operational Research Soc. (GB) 1986, COORS American Ingenuity Award 1989, Pender Award, Univ. of Pa 1995. *Publications:* Linear Programming and Extensions 1963, Compact City (with Thomas L. Saaty) 1973; over 150 published technical papers. *Leisure interests:* planning future cities, writing science fiction. *Address:* Department of Management Science and Engineering, Stanford University, Stanford CA 94305-4023 (Office); 821 Tolman Drive, Stanford, CA 94305, USA (Home). *Telephone:* (650) 493-0578. *E-mail:* george-dantzig@worldnet.att.net (Office and Home).

DANTZIG, Rudi Van; Netherlands choreographer; b. 4 Aug. 1933, Amsterdam; s. of Murk van Dantzig and Berendina Hermina Homburg; ed High School and Art Coll.; took ballet lessons with Sonia Gaskell; joined Sonia Gaskell's co. Ballet Recital (later Netherlands Ballet), soloist 1959; won Prix de la Critique (Paris) for choreography in Night Island 1955; with Netherlands Dance Theatre 1959–60, artistic Dir and prin. choreographer Netherlands Nat. Ballet 1968–91; has also worked for London Dance Theatre, Ballet Rambert, The Royal Ballet, Harkness Ballet (New York), Bat-Dor (Tel Aviv), Ballet d'Anvers (Antwerp), Nat. Ballet of Washington, Royal Danish Ballet, American Ballet Theater, Nat. Ballet of Canada, Ballets of Munich and

Cologne, Viennese Opera Ballet, Royal Winnipeg Ballet, Houston Ballet, Hungarian State Ballet, Finnish Opera Ballet, Pacific South-West Ballet (Seattle), Paris Opera Ballet, Royal NZ Ballet, Cape Town Ballet (SA), Lyriki Skini Ballet (Athens, Royal Ballet of Stockholm, Classical Ballet of Israel); Officer Oranje-Nassau 1969, Verdienstkreuz (Germany). *Choreography for:* Night Island 1955, Jungle 1961, Monument for a Dead Boy 1965, Romeo and Juliet 1967, Moments 1968, Epitaaf 1969, Astraal 1969, The Ropes of Time 1970, On Their Way 1970, Painted Birds 1971, Are Friends Delight or Pain 1972, The Unfinished 1973, Orpheus 1974, Ramifications 1974, Blown in a Gentle Wind (with Wade Walthall, for Rudolf Nureyev) 1975, Ginastera 1976, Gesang der Jünglinge 1977, Vier letzte Lieder 1978, Ulysses (for Nureyev) 1979, Life (with Toer van Schayk) 1979, Voorbÿ Gegaan 1979, About a Dark House 1978, Dialogues 1980, Underneath My Feet 1981, Room at the Top 1982, No-Mans Land 1982, I Just Simply Hold my Breath 1983, In Praise of Folly 1983, For We Know Not What We Are Doing 1986, To Bend or to Break 1987, Sans armes, Citoyens! 1987 (for the Paris Opera), Swan Lake (with Toer van Schayk) 1988, Archangels Paint Red the Sky 1990, Memories from the Lower Depths 1991, Refuge 1994, Tables d'Amour 1995. *Publications:* Nureyev, Aspects of the Dancer, Spectrum jaarboek 1979, Voorbÿ Gegaan—the making of a Pas-de-deux, Olga de Haas: A Memory, For a Lost Soldier (novel) 1986, Rudolf Nureyev, The Trail of a Comet 1993, Abyss (short stories) 1996; articles in Ballet and Modern Dance; film appearances in Van Dantzig—Portrait of a Choreographer (by Jan Vrÿman), The Making of a Ballet. *Leisure interests:* literature, politics. *Address:* Het Nationale Ballet, Het Muziektheater, Waterlooplein 22, 1011 PG Amsterdam (Office); Emma-Straat 27, Amsterdam, Netherlands (Home). *Telephone:* 551-82-25 (Office); 679-83-31 (Home).

DAOUD, HE Cardinal Ignace Moussa I; Syrian ecclesiastic; b. 18 Sept. 1930, Meskané, Homs; ordained priest 1954; Bishop of Le Caire dei Siri 1977, of Homs dei Siri 1994; Patriarch 1998–2001; Prefect of the Congregation for Oriental Churches; cr. Cardinal 2001; Pres. Pontifical Council for Oriental Churches 2001–. *Address:* c/o Syrian Catholic Patriarchate, rue de Damas, PO Box 116-5087, Beirut, Lebanon (Office).

DAOUDI, Riad, PhD; Syrian lawyer, professor of law and international arbitrator; b. 22 July 1942, Damascus; s. of Rashad Daoudi and Adallat Daoudi; m. Viviane Collin 1978; two s. one d.; ed Institut des Hautes Etudes Internationales, Paris; Prof. of Int. Law, Damascus Law School 1978–91; Asst Dean for Academic Affairs, Faculty of Law, Univ. of Damascus 1980–82; lawyer, mem. Syrian Bar 1982–; Registrar, Judicial Tribunal of Org. of Arab Petroleum Exporting Countries (OAPEC) 1983–, now lawyer, legal adviser, registrar Judicial Tribunal of OAPEC; Legal Adviser to Ministry of Foreign Affairs 1991–; mem. UN Int. Law Comm. 2002–(07); Lauréat, best doctoral thesis, Univ. of Paris 1977–78. *Publications:* Parliamentary Immunities: Comparative Study in Arab Constitutions (in Arabic) 1982, Peace Negotiations – Treaty of Versailles (textbook for law students, in Arabic) 1983, Arab Commission for Human Rights, An Encyclopedia of Public International Law (in English) 1985; articles and contribs to books on int. affairs and int. law. *Leisure interests:* tennis, reading. *Address:* The Judicial Tribunal of the OAPEC, PO Box 20501, Safat 13066, Kuwait (Office); Dam Zoukak Al Sakhar Salim Al Sharah Street, Hadjar Building, 3rd Floor, Syria (Home). *Telephone:* 4818289 (Office); (11) 6622266 (Home). *Fax:* 4818274 (Office); (11) 3319229 (Home).

DARBINYAN, Armen Razmikovich, Cand. Econ.; Armenian politician and university rector; b. 23 Jan. 1965, Gyumri, Armenia; m.; one d.; ed Moscow State Univ.; lecturer, Moscow State Univ. 1986–89; sr expert, Head of Dept, Perm. Mission of Armenia to Russian Fed., Plenipotentiary Rep., Intergovt. Comm. on Debts of Vnesheconombank 1989–92; Dir-Gen. Armenian Foreign Trade Co. Armenintorg 1992–94; First Deputy Chair. Cen. Bank of Armenia 1994–97; Minister of Finance 1997, of Finance and Econs 1997–98; Prime Minister of Armenia 1998–99; Minister of Nat. Economy 1999–2000; Chair. Fund for Devt, Yerevan 2000–; Chair. Bd Trustees, Int. Center for Human Devt 2000–; Rector Russian-Armenian State Univ. 2001–; mem. Russian Acad. of Natural Sciences; Commdr World Order of Science, Education and Culture 2002. *Publications:* Role of the State in Countries with Transition Economies, Economic Development: Prospects and Role of the Diaspora, From Stability to Economic Growth. *Leisure interests:* music and composing songs. *Address:* 19 str. Sayat Nova, 375001 Yerevan, Armenia. *Telephone:* (1) 58-26-38 (Office). *Fax:* (1) 52-70-82 (Office). *E-mail:* adarbinian@ichd.org (Office). *Website:* www.ichd.org (Office).

DARBOVEN, Hanne; German artist, writer and musician; b. 29 April 1941, Munich; ed Hochschule für Bildende Künste, Hamburg; has participated in numerous group exhbns. of contemporary art in galleries in Europe, USA, Canada and also São Paulo Biennale 1973 and Venice Biennale 1982. *Solo exhibitions include:* Düsseldorf 1967, 1968, 1970, 1971, 1975, Munich 1969, Cologne 1970, 1980, Amsterdam 1970, 1972, 1974, 1975, 1976, Leo Castelli Gallery, New York 1973, 1974, 1976, 1977, 1978, 1980, 1982 and in Paris, Brussels, Oxford, Turin, Milan, Bologna, Zürich, Basle, Houston, etc. *Compositions:* series of pieces for solo instruments, chamber and full orchestra. *Publications:* books including: El Lissitzky, Hosmann, Hamburg und Yves Gevaert 1974, Atta Troll Kunstmuseum 1975, Baudelaire, Heine, Disecpolo, Maizi, Flores, Kraus: Pour écrire la liberté 1975, New York Diary 1976, Ein Jahrhundert, Vol. 1 1971–77, Schreibzeit 1999. *Leisure interest:* keeping goats. *Address:* Am Burgberg 26, 21 Hamburg 90, Germany. *Telephone:* (40) 7633033.

D'ARCEVIA, Bruno; Italian painter and sculptor; b. 21 Oct. 1946, Arcevia, Ancona; s. of Benedetto Bruni and Amelia Filippini; m. Maria Falconetti 1972; one s. one d.; worked in France and Venezuela 1975–78; co-f. Nuova Maniera Italiana Movt 1982–83; one of 20 Italian artists included in ArToday review, London 1996; Gold San Valentino award, named Marchigiano dell'Anno 1998; Commendatore Ordine della Repubblica Italiana. *Solo exhibitions include:* Mayer Swarz Gallery, Beverly Hills, LA 1988–90, Koplin Gallery, Santa Monica, Calif. 1993, Caldwell-Snyder Gallery, San Francisco and New York 1996–, Heroic Quests, Hopkins Hall Gallery, Ohio State Univ. Coll. of the Arts 2000 and Caldwell Snyder Gallery, San Francisco 2000. *Group exhibitions include:* Profili, Rome 1990. *Leisure interests:* underwater fishing. *Address:* Via dei Campi Sportivi 2A, 00197 Rome (Office); Via Luigi Angeloni 29, 00149 Rome, Italy (Home). *Telephone:* (06) 8070185 (Office); (06) 5503637 (Home). *Fax:* (06) 8070185.

D'ARCY, Margaretta; Irish playwright and author; m. John Arden 1957; five c. (one deceased); Artistic Dir Corrandulla Arts and Entertainment Club 1973–, Galway Women's Entertainment 1982, Galway Women's Sceal Radio, Radio Pirate-Woman 1986; Arts Council Playwriting Award (with John Arden) 1972, Women's Int. Newsgathering Service, Katherine Davenport Journalist of the Year Award 1998. *Plays produced:* The Happy Haven 1961, Business of Good Government 1962, Ars Longa Vita Brevis 1964, The Royal Pardon 1966, Friday's Hiding 1967, The Hero Rises Up 1969, The Island of the Mighty 1974, The Non-Stop Connolly Show 1975, Vandaleur's Folly 1978, The Little Gray Home in the West 1978, The Making of Muswell Hill 1979 (all with John Arden), A Pinprick of History 1977. *Radio includes:* Keep Those People Moving 1972, The Manchester Enthusiasts 1984, Whose Is the Kingdom? 1988, A Suburban Suicide 1994 (all with John Arden). *Television documentary:* Profile of Sean O'Casey (with John Arden) 1973. *Publications:* Tell Them Everything (Prison Memoirs) 1981, Awkward Corners (with John Arden) 1988, Galway's Pirate Women, a Global Trawl 1996. *Address:* c/o Casarotto Ramsay, 60–66 Wardour Street, London, W1V 3HP, England. *Telephone:* (20) 7287-4450. *Fax:* (20) 7287-9128.

DARGIE, Sir William Alexander, Kt, CBE, FRSA, FRAS; Australian artist and administrator; b. 4 June 1912, Melbourne; s. of late A. Dargie and of Adelaide Dargie; m. Kathleen Howitt 1937; one s. one d.; official war artist with Australian Imperial Forces, Royal Australian Air Force, Royal Australian Navy; Head. Nat. Gallery, Vic. Art School 1946–53; Chair. Commonwealth Art Advisory Bd 1969–73; mem. Interim Council, Nat. Gallery, Canberra 1968–73, Nat. Capital Planning Advisory Cttee 1970–73, Aboriginal Arts Advisory Cttee 1969–71, Council, Nat. Museum of Vic. 1978–83; Trustee, Native Cultural Reserve, Port Moresby, Papua New Guinea 1969–75, Museum and Art Gallery, Papua New Guinea 1970–73; Chair. Bd of Trustees, McLelland Gallery 1981–87; has painted portraits of HM Queen Elizabeth II, HRH Duke of Gloucester, HRH the late Princess Royal, HRH the late Princess Marina, HRH Princess Alexandra and many individuals distinguished in arts, sciences and politics in Australia, NZ and UK; exhibitor, Royal Acad. and Royal Soc. of Portrait Painters; MA (hc); Woodward and McPhillimy Awards 1940, Archibald Prize (eight times) NSW, MacKay Prize 1942. *Leisure interests:* tennis, folklore, material culture of Melanasia. *Address:* 19 Irilbarra Road, Canterbury, Vic. 3126, Australia. *Telephone:* (3) 9836-3396.

DARLING, Rt Hon Alistair (Maclean), PC; British politician and lawyer; b. 28 Nov. 1953; m. Margaret McQueen Vaughan 1986; one s. one d; ed Loretto School, Musselburgh, Aberdeen Univ.; fmr advocate; admitted to Faculty of Advocates 1984; mem. Lothian Regional Council 1982–87 (Chair. Transport Cttee 1986–87), Lothian and Borders Police Bd 1982–86; Gov. Napier Coll., Edinburgh 1982–87; MP (Labour) for Edin. Cen. 1987–; Shadow Chief Sec. to HM Treasury 1996–97; Chief Sec. to HM Treasury 1997–98; Sec. of State for Social Security 1998–2001, for Work and Pensions 2001–02, for Transport 2002–. *Address:* Department for Transport, Eland House, Bressenden Place, London, SW1E 5DU, England. *Telephone:* (20) 7890-3000. *Fax:* (20) 7276-0818. *Website:* www.dft.gov.uk.

DARMAN, Richard Gordon, MBA; American government official and investor; b. 10 May 1943, Charlotte; m. Kathleen Emmet 1967; three s.; ed Harvard Univ.; Deputy Asst Sec. Dept of Health, Educ. and Welfare, Washington, DC 1971–72; Asst to Sec., Dept of Defense 1973, Special Asst to Attorney-Gen. 1973; Asst Sec. Dept of Commerce 1976–77; Asst to Pres. 1981–85; Deputy Sec. Treasury Dept 1985–87; Dir Office of Man. and Budget (Cabinet post) 1988–93; Man. Dir, Partner The Carlyle Group 1993–; Prof. JFK School of Govt, Harvard Univ. 1998–2002; Prin. Dir ICF Inc., Washington, DC 1975, 1977–80; Lecturer in Public Policy and Man., Harvard Univ. 1977–80; Man. Dir Shearson Lehman Brothers Inc., New York 1987–88; Asst to fmr Pres. Reagan 1981–85; Vice-Chair. Del. to UN Conf. on Law of Sea 1977; mem. Ocean Policy Cttee, NAS 1978–80, Bd of Dirs. Frontier Ventures Corpn 1993–, Telcom Ventures, Sequana Therapeutics, The New England Funds, Council on Excellence in Govt 1995–, AES Corpn 2002–; Ed. Harvard Educ. Review 1970, Contributing Ed. US News and World Report 1987–88; Dir Smithsonian Nat. Museum of American History 2000–; Trustee Brookings Inst. 1987–88. *Publication:* Who's in Control? 1996. *Address:* The Carlyle Group, 1001 Pennsylvania Avenue, NW, Washington, DC 20004-2505, USA.

DARMON, Marco; French lawyer; b. 26 Jan. 1930, Tunis, Tunisia; m. Elsa Lévy 1958; one s. one d.; magistrate in Brittany 1957–59; joined Ministry of Justice 1959; Tech. Counsellor, Office of the Keeper of the Seals 1973–74;

subsequently Vice-Pres. Tribunal de Grande Instance, Paris; Asst Dir Office of Keeper of the Seals 1981–82; Pres. of Chamber, Cour d'Appel, Paris; Dir of Civil Affairs and of the Seal of Ministry of Justice 1982; Advocate-Gen., European Court of Justice, Luxembourg 1984–94.

DARNTON, Robert Choate, DPhil; American professor of history; b. 10 May 1939, New York; s. of the late Byron Darnton and Eleanor Darnton; m. Susan Lee Glover 1963; one s. two d.; ed Harvard Univ., Oxford Univ., UK; reporter, The New York Times 1964–65; Jr Fellow, Harvard Univ., 1965–68; Asst Prof., subsequently Assoc. Prof., Prof., Princeton Univ. 1968–, Shelby Cullom Davis Prof. of European History 1984–, Dir Program in European Cultural Studies 1987–95; fellowships and visiting professorships including: Ecole des Hautes Etudes en Sciences Sociales, Paris 1971, 1981, 1985, Netherlands Inst. for Advanced Study 1976–77, Inst. for Advanced Study, Princeton 1977–81, Oxford Univ. (George Eastman Visiting Prof.) 1986–87, Collège de France, Wissenschafts-Kolleg zu Berlin 1989–90, 1993–94; Pres. Int. Soc. for Eighteenth-Century Studies 1987–91, American Historical Asscn 1999–2000; mem. Bd of Dirs., Voltaire Foundation, Oxford, Social Science Research Council 1988–91; mem. Bd of Trustees Center for Advanced Study in the Behavioral Sciences 1992–96, Oxford Univ. Press, USA 1993–, The New York Public Library 1994–2000; mem. various editorial bds; Fellow American Acad. of Arts and Sciences, American Philosophical Soc., American Antiquarian Soc.; Adviser, Wissenschafts-Kolleg zu Berlin 1994–; Foreign mem. Academia Europaea, Acad. Royale de Langue et de Littérature Françaises de Belgique; Guggenheim Fellow 1970; Corresp. Fellow British Acad. 2001; Dr hc (Neuchâtel) 1986, (Lafayette Coll.) 1989, (Univ. of Bristol) 1991; Leo Gershoy Prize, American Historical Asscn 1979, MacArthur Prize 1982, Los Angeles Times Book Prize 1984, Prix Médicis 1991, Prix Chateaubriand 1991, Nat. Book Critics Circle Award 1996; Officier Ordre des Arts et des Lettres 1995, Chevalier Légion d'Honneur 2000. *Television series:* Démocratie (co-ed.), France 1999. *Publications:* Mesmerism and the End of the Enlightenment in France 1968, The Business of Enlightenment 1979, The Literary Underground of the Old Regime 1982, The Great Cat Massacre 1984, The Kiss of Lamourette 1989, Revolution in Print (co-ed.) 1989, Edition et sédition 1991, Berlin Journal, 1989–1900 1991, Gens de lettres, gens du livre 1992, The Forbidden Best-Sellers of Pre-Revolutionary France 1995, The Corpus of Clandestine Literature 1769–1789 1995, Démocratie (co-ed.) 1998, J.-P. Brissot: His Career and Correspondence 1779–1787 2001. *Leisure interests:* squash, travel. *Address:* Department of History, Princeton University, Princeton, NJ 08540 (Office); 6 McCosh Circle, Princeton, NJ 08540, USA (Home). *Telephone:* (609) 258-4169 (Office); (609) 924-6905 (Home). *Fax:* (609) 258-5326 (Office).

DARRIEUX, Danielle; French actress; b. 1 May 1917, Bordeaux; d. of Jean and Marie-Louise (née Witkowski) Darrieux; m. 3rd Georges Mitsinkides 1948; one s.; ed Paris Univ.; First appeared in films 1931, in theatre 1937; numerous TV film appearances; Chevalier, Légion d'honneur, Commdr, Ordre des Arts et des Lettres, César d'honneur 1985, Prix de l'Amicale des Cadres de l'Industrie Cinématographique 1987. *Films include:* Le bal, Mayerling, Un mauvais garçon, Battement de coeur, Premier rendez-vous, Ruy Blas, Le plaisir, Madame de ..., Le rouge et le noir, Bonnes à tuer, Le salaire du péché, L'amant de Lady Chatterley, Typhon sur Nagasaki, La ronde, Alexander the Great, Marie Octobre, L'homme à femmes, Les lions sont lâchés, Le crime ne paie pas, Le diable et les dix commandements, Le coup de grâce, Patate, Greengage Summer, Les demoiselles de Rochefort, 24 heures de la vie d'une femme, Divine, L'année sainte, En haut des marches, Le lieu du crime, Corps et biens, Quelques jours avec moi, Bille en tête, le Jour des rois, les Mamies, Ça ira mieux demain 2000, 8 Femmes 2002. *Plays:* La robe mauve de Valentine 1963, Gillian 1965, Comme un oiseau 1965, Secretissimo 1965, Laurette 1966, CoCo 1970, Ambassador (musical) 1971, Folie douce 1972, Les Amants terribles 1973, Boulevard Feydau 1978, L'intoxe 1981, Gigi 1985, Adorable Julia 1987, Adelaïde 90 1990, George et Margaret 1992, Les Mamies 1992, Harold et Maude 1995, Ma petite fille, mon amour 1998, Une Douche écossaise 1998, Oscar et la dame en rose 2003. *Address:* Agence Nicole Cann, 1 rue Alfred de Vigny, 75008 Paris, France.

DARWISH, Mahmoud; Palestinian poet, politician and journalist; b. 1942, Birwa; ed schools in Galilee, Moscow Univ., USSR; journalist in Haifa, Israel; mem. Israeli Communist Party (Rakah) 1961–71; fmr Chief Ed. Al-Karmil periodical, then Al-Ittihad newspaper; left Israel for exile in Lebanon 1971; Ed. Shu'un Filistiniyya (Palestinian Affairs) 1972; Dir Palestinian Liberation Org. (PLO) Research Centre, Beirut 1975–82; mem. PLO Exec. 1987–93; Lotus Prize, Union of Afro-Asian Writers 1969, Mediterranean Prize 1980, Ibn Sina Prize 1982, Lenin Peace Prize 1983. *Publications:* Asafir Bila Ajniha (Bird Without Wings) 1960, Awraq al-Zaytun (Olive Leaves) 1964, Ashiq Min Filastin (A Lover from Palestine) 1966, Uhibbuki aw la Uhibikki (I Love You, I Love You Not) 1972, Qasidat Bayrut (Ode to Beirut) 1982, Madih al-Zill al-Ali (A Eulogy for the Tall Shadow) 1983, Sareer El Ghariba (Bed of a Stranger) 1988, Why Did You Leave the Horse Alone? 1994. *Address:* c/o Kegan Paul, P.O. Box 256, London, WC1B 3SW, England (Office).

DASCHLE, Thomas Andrew, BA; American politician; b. 9 Dec. 1947, Aberdeen, S Dakota; m. Linda Hall Daschle; one s. two d.; ed S Dakota State Univ.; served to 1st Lt, USAF 1969–72; Chief Legis. Aide and then Field Coordinator to US Senator 1973–77; mem. 96th–97th Congresses from 1st S Dakota Dist, 98th Congress 1977–87; Senator from S Dakota 1987–; Senate Minority Leader Congress 1995–2001, 2002–, Majority Leader 2001–02;

Democrat; numerous awards including Distinguished Service Award, Nat. Rural Electric Cooperation Asscn 2000. *Address:* US Senate, 509 Hart Senate Building, Washington, DC 20510-0001, USA.

d'ASCOLI, Bernard Jacques-Henri Marc; French concert pianist; b. 18 Nov. 1958, Aubagne; one s.; ed Marseille Conservatoire; became blind 1962; took up music 1970; youngest Baccalauréat matriculate of France 1974; first public appearances on both piano and organ 1974; elected as most talented French artist of the year (Megève) 1976; began int. professional career 1982, following débuts at maj. London concert halls with Royal Philharmonic Orchestra and first recording; toured Australia with Chamber Orchestra of Europe 1983; début Amsterdam Concertgebouw 1984, USA, with Houston Symphony Orchestra 1985, Musikverein, Vienna 1986, Henry Wood Promenade Concerts, London 1986, Tokyo Casals Hall and Bunka Kaikan Hall 1988, with Boston Symphony Orchestra 1992; recordings of Chopin and Schumann (with Schidlof Quartet); first prize Int. Maria Casals competition, Barcelona 1979; prizewinner, Leipzig Bach competition and Warsaw Chopin competition 1980; 3rd prize, Leeds Int. piano competition 1981. *Leisure interests:* reading, swimming, humane sciences. *Address:* c/o Van Walsum Management, 4 Addison Bridge Place, London, W14 8XP (Office); c/o Transart (MC) Ltd., 8 Bristol Gardens, London, W9 2JG, England.

DASGUPTA, Sir Partha Sarathi, Kt, PhD, FBA; Indian/British professor of economics and philosophy; b. 17 Nov. 1942, Dacca; s. of the late Prof. Amiya Dasgupta and Shanti Dasgupta; m. Carol M. Meade 1968; one s. two d.; ed Univs of Delhi and Cambridge; Lecturer in Econs LSE 1971–75, Reader 1975–78, Prof. of Econs 1978–85; Prof. of Econs Univ. of Cambridge and Fellow, St John's Coll. Cambridge 1985– (Frank Ramsey Prof. of Econs 1994–); Prof. of Econs and Prof. of Philosophy and Dir of Program on Ethics in Society, Stanford Univ. 1989–92; Chair. Beijer Int. Inst. of Ecological Econs, Stockholm; Pres. European Econ. Assn. 1999, Royal Econ. Soc. 1998–2001; mem. Pontifical Acad. of Social Science; Hon. mem. American Econ. Asscn; Foreign Hon. mem. American Acad. of Arts and Sciences; Foreign mem. Royal Swedish Acad. of Sciences; Foreign Assoc. NAS; Fellow, Third World Acad. of Sciences, Econometric Soc.; Hon. Fellow, LSE; Dr hc (Wageningen Univ.) 2000; Volvo Environment Prize 2002. *Publications:* Human Well-Being and the Natural Environment 2002; books and articles on econs of environmental and natural resources, technological change, normative population theory, political philosophy, devt planning and the political economy of destitution. *Leisure interests:* cinema, theatre, reading. *Address:* Faculty of Economics and Politics, Sidgwick Avenue, Cambridge, CB3 9DD (Office); 1 Dean Drive, Holbrook Road, Cambridge, England. *Telephone:* (1223) 212179.

DASH-YONDON, Budragchaagiin, PhD; Mongolian politician; b. 17 Feb. 1946, Huvsgul; s. of Jugnaa Budragchaa and Sengee Chogjmoo; m. Choijamts Batjargal; one s. two d.; ed Mongolian State Univ., State Univ. of Kiev, USSR; Prof., Mongolian State Univ. 1968–74; officer at Scientific and Educational Dept, MPRP Cen. Cttee 1978–79; Vice-Chancellor, Higher Party School, MPRP Cen. Cttee 1979–85; Deputy Head and Head of Dept, MPRP Cen. Cttee 1985–90; First Sec.-Gen., MPRP Ulan Bator City Party Cttee 1990–91; MPRP Sec.-Gen. 1991–96; Political Adviser to Pres. 1997–. *Leisure interests:* reading, chess. *Address:* Mongolian People's Revolutionary Party, Baga toiruu 37/1, Ulaanbaatar-11, Mongolia.

DASSAULT, Serge; French engineer; b. 4 April 1925, Paris; s. of the late Marcel Dassault and Madeleine Minckès; m. Nicole Raffel 1950; three s. one d.; ed Lycée Janson-de-Sailly, Ecole Polytechnique, Ecole Nat. Supérieure de l'Aéronautique, Centre de Perfectionnement dans l'Administration des Affaires, Inst. des Hautes Etudes de la Défense Nationale; Dir of Flight Testing, Avions Marcel Dassault 1955–61, Export Dir 1961–63; Dir-Gen. Société Electronique Marcel Dassault 1963–67, Pres. Dir-Gen. 1967–86; Admin. Avions Marcel Dassault-Breguet Aviation 1967, Pres. Dir-Gen. 1986–2000, Adviser, Hon. Pres. 2000–; Vice-Pres. Société de Gestion de Participations Aéronautiques (SOGEPA); Admin. Dassault Belgique Aviation 1968; Town Councillor, Corbeil-Essonnes 1983–95, Mayor 1995–; Regional Councillor, Ile de France 1986–95; Gen. Councillor Essonne 1988–, Pres. Departmental Cttee RPR de l'Essonne 1998–; mem. Comité de direction du Groupement des industries électroniques 1968, Groupement des Industries Françaises Aéronautiques et Spatiales 1968; Hon. Pres. Fondation des Œuvres Sociales de l'Air 1968; Commissaire Général des Salons Internationaux de l'Aéronautique et de l'Espace 1974–93; Chief Engineer Armaments 1974; Pres. Asscn Française pour la Participation dans les Entreprises 1972; Chair. working group, Participation active dans l'entreprise, Nat. Council, Patronat Français 1985; Pres. of Section Asscn européenne des constructeurs de matériel spatial (AECMA) 1987–, Groupement des Industries Françaises Aéronautiques et Spatiales (Gifas) 1993–97, Council of French Defence Industry 1994–96; Chevalier, Légion d'honneur, Médaille de l'Aéronautique, Officier de l'Ordre national du Mérite ivoirien. *Publications:* La Gestion participative, J'ai choisi la vérité 1983. *Leisure interests:* golf, hunting, fishing. *Address:* Dassault Industries, 9 rond-point des Champs-Elysées-Marcel Dassault, 75008 Paris; Mairie, place Galignani, 91100 Corbeil-Essonnes, France (Office). *Telephone:* 1-47-41-79-21.

DASSIN, Jules; American film director; b. 18 Dec. 1911, Middletown, Conn.; s. of Samuel and Berthe (née Vogel) Dassin; m. 1st Béatrice Launer (divorced); one s. (deceased) two d.; m. 2nd Melina Mercouri 1966 (died 1994); ed Morris High School; attended drama school in Europe 1936; Asst Dir to Alfred

Hitchcock 1940; films directed in USA include Brute Force 1947, Naked City 1948, Thieves' Highway 1949, Night and the City 1950; settled in France 1954 and directed Rififi (also acted) 1954, Celui qui doit mourir 1956, Never on Sunday (also acted) 1960, Phaedra 1961, Topkapi 1963, 10.30pm Summer 1966, Up Tight 1968, Promise at Dawn 1970, The Rehearsal 1974, A Dream of Passion 1978; plays directed include: Ilya, Darling, Medicine Show, Magdalena, Joy to the World, Isle of Children, Two's Company, Heartbreak House, Threepenny Opera, Sweet Bird of Youth, A Month in the Country, Who's Afraid of Virginia Woolf?, The Road to Mecca, Death of A Salesman; Director's Prize, Cannes Film Festival 1955 for Rififi; Commdr Légion d'honneur, Commdr Ordre des Arts et Lettres. *Address:* Melina Mercouri St 8, Athens 11521, Greece. *Telephone:* (1) 7232300; (1) 3315601 (Office). *Fax:* (1) 7232042; (1) 3315600 (Office). *E-mail:* mmf@internet.gr (Office).

DÄUBLER-GMELIN, Herta, DJur; German politician; b. 12 Aug. 1943, Bratislava, Slovakia; m. Wolfgang Däubler 1969; one s. one d.; ed Univs. of Tübingen and Berlin; mem. Social Democratic Party of Germany (SPD) 1965–, Chair. Tübingen Dist br. 1971–72, State Chair. Asscn of Social Democrat Women Baden-Württemberg 1971–76, mem. State Exec. Baden-Württemburg, elected to Fed. Exec. Cttee 1979, Deputy Chair. Bundestag Parl. Group 1983, 1991–93, elected mem. Party Presidium 1984, 1997, Deputy Chair. 1988–, legal adviser to Parl. Group 1994, elected to Party Exec. Cttee 1997; Fed. Minister of Justice 1998–; Chair. working group on Equality for Women 1983, Bundestag Legal Affairs Cttee 1980–83, Legal Policy Working Group 1994; Dr hc (Freie Univ. Berlin). *Publications:* numerous books, articles in political journals and newspapers. *Address:* Ministry of Justice, Heinemannstrasse 6, 53175 Bonn; Geierweg 20, 72114 Dusslingen, Germany. *Telephone:* (228) 580 (Bonn). *Fax:* (228) 584525 (Bonn).

DAUD, Datuk Sulaiman bin Haj, BDS; Malaysian politician; b. 4 March 1933, Kuching, Sarawak; m.; four c.; ed Otago Univ., New Zealand and Univ. of Toronto; teacher 1954–56; Dental Officer, State Govt of Sarawak 1963–68; State Dental Officer, Brunei 1971; Political Sec. Ministry of Primary Industries 1972; Minister for Land and Mineral Resources, Sarawak 1973–74; mem. Parl. 1974–; Deputy Minister of Land Devt 1974–75, of Land and Mines 1975–76, of Land and Regional Devt 1976–77, of Health 1978–81; Minister of Fed. Territory March 1981; Minister of Educ. July 1981, of Sport, Youth and Culture 1984–86, of Land and Regional Devt 1986–89; Minister in the Prime Minister's Dept 1989–90; Vice-Pres. Party Pesaka Bumiputra Bersatu, Sarawak; other public appts and leader of Malaysian dels to int. confs; Johan Bintang Sarawak, Panglima Negara Nintang Sarawak. *Address:* c/o Parti Pesaka Bumiputra Bersatu, Jalan Satok/Kulas, 93400 Kuching, Sarawak, Malaysia.

DAUDISS, Imants; Latvian politician and diplomatist; b. 15 Aug. 1945, Riga; m.; one d.; ed Ivanovo Inst. of Chem. Eng; Head of lab., Riga chemical eng plant 1968–70; Head of Dept, Sec., Riga Comsomol City Cttee 1970–76; Sec. Riga Dist CP Cttee 1976–80; First Deputy Chair. State Publishing, Printing and Book Sale Cttee 1980–86; Sec., Head of Dept Riga City CP Cttee 1986–89; Sec. of Presidium, Supreme Soviet Latvian SSR 1989–90; Sec. Supreme Council Latvian Repub. 1989–93; Sec. Saeima (Parl.) 1993–97; Amb. to Russia 1998–2001, to UK 2001–. *Address:* Latvian Embassy, 45 Nottingham Place, London, W1U 5LY, England. *Telephone:* (20) 7312-0042. *E-mail:* embassy@embassyoflatvia.co.uk.

DAUGNY, Bertrand, L.ÈS SC.; French business executive and engineer; b. 5 Jan. 1925, Paris; s. of Pierre-Marie Daugny and Suzanne Hauser; m. 1st Nicole Wolff (deceased); one s. one d.; m. 2nd Elisabeth Joussellin 1958; two d.; ed Faculté des Sciences, Paris and Ecole Supérieure d'Electricité; engineer, later Head of Dept Cie Française Thomson-Houston 1948–54; Founder, Electronic Dept, Avions Marcel Dassault 1954, Admin. Deputy and Man. Dir Electronique Marcel Dassault (now Dassault Electronique) 1963, Admin. and Man. Dir 1967, Vice-Chair. and Man. Dir Electronique Serge Dassault 1983–86; Chair. and CEO Dassault Electronique 1986–99; mem. Bd of Dirs. Dassault Industries 1990–99, Dassault Aviation 1991–99, Dassault Automatismes et Télécommunications 1991–99; Commdr Légion d'honneur, Médaille Militaire, Chevalier Ordre nat. du Mérite, Croix de Guerre, Médaille Aéronautique. *Address:* 38 boulevard de la Saussaye, 92200 Neuilly-sur-Seine, France.

DAUNT, Sir Timothy Lewis Achilles, KCMG; British diplomatist; b. 11 Oct. 1935; s. of L.H.G. Daunt and Margery Daunt (née Lewis Jones); m. Patricia Susan Knight 1962; one s. two d.; ed Sherborne School, St Catharine's Coll., Cambridge; mil. service with King's Royal Irish Hussars 1954–56; entered diplomatic service 1959; Ankara 1960; Foreign Office 1964; Nicosia 1967; Pvt. Sec. to Perm. Under-Sec. of State, FCO 1970; with Bank of England 1972; mem. UK Mission, New York 1973; Counsellor OECD, Paris 1975; Head of S European Dept, FCO 1978–81; Assoc. Centre d'études et de recherches internationales, Paris 1982; Minister and Deputy Perm. Rep. to NATO, Brussels 1982–85; Asst Under-Sec. of State (Defence), FCO 1985–86; Amb. to Turkey 1986–92; Deputy Under-Sec. of State (Defence), FCO 1992–95; Lt-Gov. Isle of Man 1995–2000; Chair. British Inst. of Archaeology, Ankara 1995–, Anglo-Turkish Soc. 2001–. *Address:* 20 Ripplevale Grove, London, N1 1HU, England (Home). *Telephone:* (20) 7697-8177. *E-mail:* daunt@ripplevale .fsnet.co.uk (Office and Home) (Office).

DAUSSET, Jean Baptiste Gabriel, MD; French doctor; b. 19 Oct. 1916, Toulouse; s. of Henri Pierre Jules Dausset and Elisabeth Brullard; m. Rosa Mayoral Lopez 1962; one s. one d.; ed Lycée Michelet, Faculty of Medicine, Paris; internship, Paris hosps 1941; Asst Faculty of Medicine, Univ. of Paris 1946; Dir Lab., Nat. Blood Transfusion Centre 1950–63; Chief, Immunohaematology Lab., Inst. de Recherches sur les Leucémies et les Maladies du Sang, Paris 1961; Chief Biologist Service d'Hématologie-Serologie-Immunologie, Hôpital Saint-Louis, Paris 1963; Dir of Research Unit on Immunogenetics of Human Transplantation, of Inst. Nat. de la Santé et la Recherche Médicale 1968–84; Prof. of Immunohaematology, Head Dept, Faculty of Medicine, Univ. of Paris 1968–77; Prof. of Experimental Medicine, Collège de France 1978–87; mem. French Acads. of Science and Medicine 1977–87; Dir Human Polymorphism Study Centre 1984–; mem. NAS, Washington 1980; shared Nobel Prize for Physiology and Medicine 1980 with Dr Baruj Benacerraf and Dr George Snell for work on histocompatibility antigens; Honda Prize 1987; Grand Croix Légion d'honneur, Commdr des Palmes Académiques, Grand Croix Ordre Nat. du Mérite; numerous other awards. *Publications:* Immuno-hématologie biologique et clinique 1956, Clin d'œil à la vie 1998, numerous articles. *Leisure interest:* modern art. *Address:* CEPH, 27/29 rue Juliette Dodu, 75010 Paris (Office); 44 rue des Ecoles, 75005 Paris, France (Home). *Telephone:* 1-53-72-51-50 (Office). *E-mail:* dausset@cephb.fr (Office).

DAUZIER, Pierre Marie, BA, LLB; French advertising executive; b. 31 Jan. 1939, Périgueux; s. of late Maurice Dauzier and of Marie Faucher; m. Erle Fleischmann 1968; one s. one d.; ed Ecole Bossuet, Lycée Henri IV, Univs. of Clermont-Ferrand and Paris and Inst. of Higher Advertising Studies; Account Exec. Havas Conseil (Advertising Agency) 1963–65, Sr Account Exec. 1965–66, Head, Commercial Dept 1966–68, Man. 1968–70, Gen. Man. 1972–75, Chair. Supervisory Bd 1975–79, Chair. of Man. Bd of Dirs. 1979, Chair. and CEO 1982, Hon. Pres. 1982–86; Man. Rep. at Needham Harper & Steers, New York 1970–72, Gen. Man. 1972–75, Pres. and CEO Univas 1975–79, Chair. and CEO 1980–82; Gen. Man. Havas 1982–86, Chair. and CEO 1986–98; Chair. and CEO Information & Publicité 1986–93; Chair. and CEO Eurocom 1988–89, CLMM (Cie Luxembourgeoise Multi Média) 1994–97; Deputy Chair. Supervisory Bd ODA 1994; Chevalier, Ordre Nat. du Mérite, Officier Légion d'honneur, Officier de Mérite agricole. *Publication:* Le Marketing de l'apocalypse 1998. *Address:* 68 rue du Faubourg Saint-Antoine, 75012 Paris, France (Office).

DAVENPORT, (Arthur) Nigel, MA; British actor; b. 23 May 1928, Shelford, Cambridge; s. of Arthur Henry Davenport and Katherine Lucy Davenport (née Meiklejohn); m. 1st Helena White 1951 (died 1978); one s. one d.; m. 2nd Maria Aitken 1972 (divorced); one s.; ed Cheltenham Coll. and Trinity Coll. Oxford; entered theatrical profession 1951; worked mainly in theatre 1951–61; frequent TV appearances; Pres. British Actors' Equity Asscn 1986–92. *Plays include:* A Taste of Honey (Broadway) 1960, Murder is Easy (Duke of York's) 1993, Our Betters (Chichester) 1997; Nat. tours: King Lear 1986, The Old Country 1989, Sleuth 1990, The Constant Wife 1994–95, Brideshead Revisited 1995, On That Day 1996. *Films include:* Look Back in Anger 1958, Peeping Tom 1960, In the Cool of the Day 1963, The Third Secret 1964, A High Wind in Jamaica 1965, Life at the Top 1965, Sands of the Kalahari 1965, Where the Spies Are 1965, A Man for All Seasons 1966, Play Dirty 1968, Sebastian/Mr Sebastian 1968, The Strange Affair 1968, Royal Hunt of the Sun 1969, Sinful Davey 1969, Virgin Soldiers 1969, The Last Valley 1970, The Mind of Mr Soames 1970, No Blade of Grass 1970, Mary Queen of Scots 1971, Villain 1971, Living Free 1972, Charlie One-Eye 1973, La Regenta, Phase IV 1974, The Island of Dr Moreau 1977, Stand Up Virgin Soldiers 1977, The Omega Connection 1979, Zulu Dawn 1979, Nighthawks 1981, Chariots of Fire 1981, Strata 1982, Greystoke 1984, Caravaggio 1986, Without a Clue 1988, The Cutter 1992, Hotel Shanghai 1995, La Revuelta de El Coyote 1997, David Copperfield 1999, Mumbo Jumbo 2000. *Television includes:* South Riding, The Prince Regent, Howard's Way 1987–88, 1990, Trainer 1991, The Treasure Seekers 1996, The Opium Wars 1996, Longitude 1999. *Leisure interests:* gardening, travel.

DAVENPORT, Lindsay; American tennis player; b. 8 June 1976, Palos Verdes, Calif.; d. of Wink Devenport and Ann Davenport; ed Murriela Valley High School; turned professional 1993; career wins include: Lucerne 1993, 1994, Brisbane 1994, singles and doubles (with Jana Novotna, q.v., Bausch & Lomb Championships 1997, Bank of the West 1998, Toshiba Classic 1998, Acura Invitational 1998, US Open 1998, European Championships 1998, Toray Pan Pacific (doubles) 1999, Sydney Int. 1999, Wimbledon 1999 (singles and doubles), Advanta Championships, Philadelphia 1999, Chase Championships, New York 1999, Australian Open 2000, Indian Wells 2000, seven singles titles in 2001; mem. Olympic Team 1996, gold medallist singles 2000; mem. US Fed. Cup Team 1993–2000, 2002. *Leisure interests:* watching hockey, sports in general, music, crosswords, going to the beach. *Address:* US Tennis Association, 70 West Red Oak Lane, White Plains, NY 10604, USA.

DAVENPORT, Paul Theodore, PhD; Canadian university president; b. 24 Dec. 1946, Summit, NJ; s. of Theodore Davenport and Charlotte Lomax Paul; m. Josette Brotons 1969; one s. two d.; ed Stanford Univ. and Univ. of Toronto; Assoc. then full Prof. Dept of Econs McGill Univ. 1973; Assoc. Dean, Faculty of Grad. Studies and Research, McGill Univ. 1982–86; Vice-Prin. (Planning and Computer Services), McGill Univ. 1986–89; Pres., Vice-Chancellor Univ. of Alberta 1989–94, Univ. of Western Ont. 1994–; Chair. Asscn of Univs and Collsof Canada 1997–99, Council of Ont. Univs 1999–2001; Hon. LLD (Alta) 1994, (Toronto) 2000; Chevalier Légion d'Honneur 2001. *Publication:* Reshaping Confederation: The 1982 Reform of the Canadian Constitution (ed. with R. Leach) 1984. *Leisure interests:* biking, Impressionist painting, modern jazz, photography. *Address:* Office of the President, Stevenson-Lawson

Building, University of Western Ontario, London, Ont., N6A 5B8 (Office); 1836 Richmond Street, London, Ont., N6A 4B6, Canada (Home). *Telephone:* (519) 661-3106 (Office); (519) 660-0178 (Home). *Fax:* (519) 661-3139. *E-mail:* pdavenpo@uwo.ca (Office). *Website:* www.uwo.ca (Office).

DAVEY, Grenville, BA; British sculptor and artist; b. 28 April 1961, Launceston, Cornwall; ed Exeter Coll., Goldsmith's Coll., London; Research Fellow in Drawing, Univ. of E London 1997–; Visiting Prof., London Inst.; Turner Prize (Tate Gallery) 1992; Art and Architecture Award, Royal Soc. of Arts 1995. *One-man exhibitions include:* Lisson Gallery, London 1987, Primo Piano, Rome 1989, Stichting De Appel Foundation, Amsterdam 1990, Galerie Crousel-Robelin Bama, Paris 1991, Galleria Franz Paludetto, Turin 1992, Chisenhale Gallery, London 1992, Château Rochechouart and Crypt, Limoges 1993, Henry Moore Foundation 1994, Museum of Modern Art, Vienna 1996, Kunstverein, Hanover 1996, Odense, Denmark 1999, Yorks Sculpture Park 1999. *Group exhibitions include:* Centre Nat. d'Art Contemporain de Grenoble 1988, Fondation Cartier, Paris 1989, Galeria Grita Insam, Vienna 1989, Nat. Museum of Modern Art, Tokyo 1989–90, Leeds City Art Gallery 1990, Hayward Gallery, London 1990, Fundació Caixa de Pensions, Barcelona 1991, Palacio Velázquez, Madrid 1991–92, Whitechapel Art Gallery, London 1992, Tate Gallery, London 1992, Killerton House, Exeter 1993, Peggy Guggenheim Collection, Venice 2002, John Hansard Gallery, Southampton 2002. *Leisure interests:* work, walking. *Address:* University of East London, 4–6 University Way, London, E16 2RD, England (Office). *Telephone:* (20) 8223-3433 (Office).

DAVEY, Kenneth George, OC, PhD, FRSC; Canadian professor, scientist and educator; b. 20 April 1932, Chatham, Ont.; s. of William Davey and Marguerite (Clark) Davey; m. Jeannette Isabel Evans 1959 (separated 1989); one s. two d.; ed McKeough Public School, Chatham, Chatham Collegiate Inst., Univ. of Western Ontario, Cambridge Univ., UK; NRC Fellow (Zoology), Univ. of Toronto 1958–59; Drosier Fellow, Gonville and Caius Coll., Cambridge 1959–63; Assoc. Prof. of Parasitology, McGill Univ., Montréal 1963–66, Dir Inst. of Parasitology 1964–74, Prof. of Parasitology and Biology 1966–74; Prof. of Biology, York Univ., Toronto 1974–, Chair. of Biology 1974–81, Dean of Science 1982–85, Distinguished Research Prof. of Biology 1984–, Vice-Pres. (Academic Affairs) 1986–91, Prof. Emer. 2000–; Ed. Int. Journal of Invertebrate Reproduction and Devt 1979–85, Canadian Journal of Zoology 1995–; Assoc. Ed. Encyclopedia of Reproduction 1996–; mem. Bd of Dirs Huntsman Marine Lab. 1978–80, 1982–85, Pres. and Chair. of Bd 1977–80; Pres. Biological Council of Canada 1979–82, Canadian Soc. of Zoologists 1981–82; Sec. Acad. of Science, Royal Soc. of Canada 1979–85; mem. Council, Royal Canadian Inst. 1996—(Pres. 2000–02), mem. Nat. Council on Ethics in Human Research (Pres. 2002–03); Fellow Entomological Soc. of Canada; Hon. DSc (Western Ont.) 2002; Gold Medal 1981 (Entomological Soc. of Canada), Fry Medal (Canadian Soc. of Zoologists) 1987, Gold Medal (Biological Council of Canada) 1987, Distinguished Biologist Award (Canadian Council of Univ. Biology Chairs) 1992, Hitschfeld Award (Canadian Asscn Univ. Research Admins) 1997. *Publications:* Reproduction in Insects 1964; 200 articles on insect endocrinology. *Leisure interests:* handweaving, food and wine. *Address:* Department of Biology, York University, 4700 Keele Street, Toronto, Ont., M3J 1P3 (Office); 96 Holm Crescent, Thornhill, Ont., L3T 5J3, Canada (Home). *Telephone:* (416) 736-2100 (Office); (905) 882-5077 (Home). *Fax:* (416) 736-5698. *E-mail:* davey@yorku.ca (Office).

DAVID, Clive; American music company executive and producer; b. New York City; lawyer, CBS 1960, Vice-Pres. and Gen. Man. 1966; with Columbia Records –1973, joined Bell Records, Arista Records 1974, later Pres.; Founder and Owner J Records 2000–; currently Chair. RCA Music Group; producer for Dido, Aretha Franklin (q.v.), Sarah McLachlan, Whitney Houston (q.v.), Billy Joel (q.v.), Janis Joplin, Alicia Keys, Santana, Carlos Santana, Patti Smith and Bruce Springsteen (q.v.). *Publication:* Clive—Inside the Record Business (autobiog.) 1974. *Address:* RCA Records, 1540 Broadway, New York, NY 10036, USA (Office). *E-mail:* info@rcarecords.com (Office). *Website:* www.jrecords.com (Office).

DAVID, François Paul; French civil servant; b. 5 Dec. 1941, Clermont-Ferrand; s. of Jean David and Rose David (née Cabane); m. Monique Courtois 1967; two s.; ed French Lycée, London, Faculté de Lettres, Paris, Ecole nat. d'admin.; mem. staff Dept of Foreign Econ. Relations, Ministry of Finance 1969–73, Head Agric. Policy Office 1976–78; Commercial Counsellor, Embassy in the UK 1974–76; Tech. Adviser Office of Minister of Foreign Trade 1978–80; Asst Dir Ministry of Economy, Finance and Budget 1981–84, Deputy Dir 1984–86, Dir Office of Jr Minister in charge of Foreign Trade at Ministry of Economy, Finance and Privatization 1986–87, Dir Dept of Foreign Econ. Relations 1987–89; Dir-Gen. Int. Affairs, Aérospatiale 1990–94; Chair. and CEO Compagnie française d'assurance pour le commerce extérieur (Coface) 1994–; mem. European Advisory Bd Schroder Salomon Smith Barney 2001–; Chair. Union de Berne 1997–99, Club d'information et de réflexion sur l'économie mondiale (Cirem) 1999–; Commdr, Légion d'honneur, Chevalier, Ordre nat. du Mérite, Officier du Mérite agricole. *Publications:* Le Mythe de l'exportation 1971, Autopsie de la Grande-Bretagne 1976, Le Commerce international à la dérive 1982, La Guerre de l'export 1987, Relations économiques internationales: La politique commerciale des grandes puissances face à la crise 1989, Jacques Cœur, l'aventure de l'argent 1990. *Leisure interests:* tennis, karate. *Address:* Coface, 12 cours Michelet, 92065 Paris-la-Défense (Office); 6 rue Auguste Bartholdi, 75015 Paris, France (Home).

DAVID, George Alfred Lawrence, MBA; American business executive; b. 7 April 1942, Bryn Mawr, Pa; s. of Charles Wendell David and Margaret Simpson; m. Barbara Osborn 1965; one s. two d.; ed Harvard Univ. and Univ. of Virginia; Asst Prof. Univ. of Va, Charlottesville 1967–68; Vice-Pres. Boston Consulting group 1968–75; Sr Vice-Pres. (Corp. Planning and Devt) Otis Elevator Co., New York 1975–77, Sr Vice-Pres. and Gen. Man. Latin American Operations, West Palm Beach, Fla 1977–81, Pres. N American Operations, Farmington, Conn. 1981–85, Pres. and CEO Otis Elevator Co. 1985–89; Exec. Vice-Pres. and Pres. (Commercial/Industrial) United Technologies Corpn (parent co.) 1989–92, Pres., COO 1992–, CEO 1994–, Chair. 1997–, mem. Bd Dirs. Inst. Int. Econs, Washington 1996–. *Address:* c/o Otis Elevator Co., 10 Farm Springs Road, Farmington, CT 06032-2526 (Office); United Technologies Corporation, 1 Financial Plaza, Suite 22, Hartford, CT 06103-2608, USA.

DAVID, Jacques-Henri; French business executive; b. 17 Oct. 1943, Ygrande (Allier); s. of André David and Suzanne Dupeyrat; m. Isabelle Lamy 1967; one d.; ed Lycée Louis-le-Grand, Paris, Ecole Polytechnique, Inst. d'Etudes Politiques, Paris and Ecole Nat. Supérieure de la Statistique et des Études Économiques (Insee), Paris; Admin. Insee 1967–68; Head, econometric studies service, Banque de France 1969–75; Deputy Sec.-Gen. Conseil Nat. du Crédit 1973–75; Prof. Inst. d'Etudes Politiques 1975; Insp. of Finance, Ministry of Econ. and Finance 1975–79; Adviser, Office of Minister of Econ. 1979, Deputy Dir 1980, Dir 1980–81; Sec.-Gen. Conseil Nat. du Crédit 1981–84; Finance Dir Cie Saint-Gobain 1984–86, Dir-Gen. 1986–89; Pres. Banque Stern 1989–92; Pres. Centre de Recherche pour l'expansion de l'économie (Rexecode) 1989–96, Ipécode 1989; Dir-Gen. Compagnie Gen. des Eaux 1993–95; Pres. CEPME 1995–99, Sofaris 1996–99, Bank for Devt of Small and Medium-Sized Businesses 1997–99; Pres. Dir.-Gen. Deutsche Bank in France 1999–; mem. Social and Econ. Council 1996–; Chevalier Légion d'honneur, Officier Ordre nat. du Mérite. *Publications:* La Politique monétaire 1974, Réévaluation et verité des bilans 1977, La Monnaie et la politique monétaire 1984, Crise financière et relations monétaires internationales 1985, Le Financement des opérations à risque dans les PME 1997. *Leisure interests:* piano, skiing, tennis, yachting. *Address:* Deutsche Bank, 3 avenue de Friedland, 75008 Paris, France (Office). *E-mail:* jacques-henri.david@db.com (Office).

DAVID-WEILL, Michel; French banking executive; b. 23 Nov. 1932, Paris; s. of late Pierre David-Weill and of Berthe Haardt; m. Hélène Lehideux 1956; four d.; ed Lycée français, New York and Inst. d'études politiques, Paris; Lazard Frères & Co. LLC, NY 1961–65, Sr Partner 1977–; Gen. Partner Lazard Frères & Cie, Paris 1965, Maison Lazard & Cie 1976–; Gen. Partner and Chair. Lazard Partners Ltd Partnership 1984–; Chair. Lazard Brothers & Co. Ltd, London 1990–92, Deputy Chair. 1992; Chair. Eurafrance 1972–; mem. Man. Bd, Sovac 1972–, Chair. 1982–95; Pres. Lazard (after merger of Lazard Bros. Paris, London and NY) 2000–02, Chair. Jan. 2002–; mem. Bd of Dirs, Danone, later Vice-Chair.; mem. Man. Bd Publicis; Dir La France SA, La France IARD, La France-Vie, La France Participations et Gestion, SA de la Rue Impériale de Lyon, Fonds Partenaires-Gestion (FPG), Fiat SpA, Pearson PLC, Euralux, Exor Group, ITT Corp., The Dannon Co. Inc., NY Stock Exchange 1995–; Chair. Artistic Council, Réunion des Musées Nationaux, Paris, Metropolitan Museum Council, New York, New York Hosp. Morgan Library; mem. Inst. (Acad. des Beaux Arts, Paris); Officier, Légion d'honneur, Officier, Ordre Nat. du Mérite, Commdr des Arts et des Lettres. *Address:* c/o Lazard, 121 boulevard Haussmann, 75008 Paris (Office); Institut de France, 23 quai Conti, 75006 Paris, France.

DAVIDE, Hilario G., Jr, BSc, BL; Philippine chief justice; b. 20 Dec. 1935, Colawin, Argau, Cebu; s. of Hilario P. Davide, Sr and Virginia Jimenea Perez; ed Univ. of the Philippines; Pvt. Sec. to Vice-Gov. then to Gov. of Cebu 1959–63; Faculty Mem. Coll. of Law, Southwestern Univ., Cebu City 1962–68; Del. to Constitutional Convention 1971, Chair. Cttee on Duties and Obligations of Citizens and Ethics of Public Officials; Minority Floor Leader 1978–79; mem. interim Batasang Pambansa Ass. representing Region VII 1978–84; Chair. Comm. on Elections 1988–90, Presidential Fact Finding Comm. 1990–91; Assoc. Justice of the Supreme Court 1991–98, Sr Assoc. Justice Oct.-Nov. 1998, Chief Justice 1998–; Hon. Pres. World Jurist Asscn of the World Peace Through Law Centre; mem. Advisory Council of Eminent Jurists, UNEP, Regional Office for Asia and the Pacific; Hon. LLD (Southwestern Univ.) 1999, (Far Eastern Univ.) 2001, (Univ. of the Philippines) 2001, (Angeles Univ. Foundation) 2001, (De La Salle Univ.) 2001; Hon. DH (Univ. of Cebu) 2000, (Ateneo de Manila Univ.) 2001, (Univ. of the Visayas) 2001; Service to the Nation Award 1987, Outstanding Kts of Columbus Award 1995, Nat. Maagap Award, Organized Response for the Advancement of Soc. (ORAS) 1998, Millennium Medal of Merit, Order of the Kts of Rizal 2000, Rajah Humabon Award 2001, Grand Perlas Award, Philippine Foundation Inc. 2001, Rule of Law Award, Chief Justice Techankee Foundation 2001, Chino Roces Foundation Freedom Award 2001, Rizal Peace Award, Univ. of S Philippines 2001. *Address:* Office of the Chief Justice, Supreme Court of the Philippines, Padre Faura Street, Ermita, Manila 1000, The Philippines (Office). *Telephone:* (632) 523-0679 (Office). *E-mail:* infos@supremecourt.gov.ph (Office). *Website:* www.supremecourt.gov.ph (Office).

DAVIDOVICH, Bella; American (USSR born) pianist; b. 16 July 1928, Baku, Azerbaijan; m. Julian Sitkovetsky 1950 (died 1958); one s.; ed Moscow Conservatory; studied with Konstantin Igumnov and Jakob Flier; First Prize, Chopin Competition, Warsaw 1949; soloist with Leningrad Philharmonic for

28 consecutive seasons; toured Europe; went to USA 1978; mem. faculty Juilliard School, NY 1983–; became US citizen 1984; has performed with world's leading conductors in USA, Europe and Japan; Prof., Juilliard School; Deserving Artist of the Soviet Union. *Leisure interests:* opera, literature, film. *Address:* c/o Agnes Bruneau, 155 West 68th Street, No. 1010, New York, NY 10023, USA (Office).

DAVIDSON, Basil Risbridger, MC; British historian; b. 9 Nov. 1914, Bristol; s. of Thomas Davidson and Jessie Davidson; m. Marion Ruth Young 1943; three s.; served British Army 1940–45, Lt-Col 1945; journalist with The Economist, The Star, The Times, New Statesman, Daily Herald, Daily Mirror, 1938–62; Visiting Prof. in African History, Univ. of Ghana 1964, Univ. of Calif., LA (UCLA) 1965; Regent's Lecturer in African History, UCLA 1971; Montague Burton Visiting Prof. of Int. Relations, Univ. of Edin. 1972; Hon. Research Fellow, Univ. of Birmingham 1974; Simon Sr Research Fellow, Univ. of Manchester 1975–76; Agnelli Visiting Prof., Univ. of Turin 1990; Hon. Fellow, SOAS (Univ. of London) 1989; Hon. DLitt (Univ. of Ibadan) 1975, (Dar es Salaam) 1985, (Univ. of Western Cape, SA) 1997; Hon. DUniv (Open Univ.) 1980, (Edin.) 1981; Mil. Cross, Bronze Star, US Army; Zasluge za Narod, Yugoslav Army; Freeman City of Genoa 1945; Haile Selassie Award for African Research 1970; Medalha Amílcar Cabral 1976; Grand Officer, Order of Prince Henry the Navigator (Portugal) 2002. *Publications:* principal works: Old Africa Rediscovered 1959, Black Mother—The African Slave Trade 1961 (revised 1980), The African Past 1964, History of West Africa to 1800 1965, History of East and Central Africa to the Late Nineteenth Century 1967, Africa in History: Themes and Outlines 1967, The Africans: A Cultural History 1969, The Liberation of Guiné 1969 (revised 1981), In the Eye of the Storm: Angola's People 1972, Black Star 1973, Can Africa Survive? 1975, Africa in Modern History, The Search for a New Society 1978, Special Operations Europe—Scenes from the anti-Nazi War 1980, The People's Cause: A History of Guerrillas in Africa 1981, Modern Africa 1982, Africa (TV series) 1984, The Story of Africa 1984, The Fortunate Isles 1988, The Black Man's Burden 1992, The Search for Africa—History, Politics, Culture 1994, West Africa Before the Colonial Era: A History to 1850 1998. *Leisure interests:* planting trees, watching wild birds. *Address:* 21 Deanery Walk, Avonpark Village, Limpley Stoke, Bath, BA2 7JQ, England (Home).

DAVIDSON, Donald Herbert, PhD; American professor of philosophy; b. 6 March 1917, Springfield, Mass.; s. of Clarence H. Davidson and Grace C. Anthony; m. 3rd Marcia Cavell 1984; one d.; ed Harvard Univ.; Asst in Philosophy, Harvard Univ. 1941–42, 1946; Instructor, Queen's Coll., New York 1947–50; Asst Prof. Stanford Univ. 1951–56, Assoc. Prof. 1956–60, Prof. 1960–67; Prof. Princeton Univ. 1967–70, lecturer with the rank of Prof. 1970–75; Prof. Rockefeller Univ. 1970–76; Prof. Univ. of Chicago 1976–81; Prof. Univ. of Calif., Berkeley 1981–, Willis S. Marion Slusser Prof. of Philosophy 1986; numerous visiting professorships; Ed. Synthese Library 1966–; Consulting Ed. Behaviorism 1972–, Philosophia 1970–, Dialectica 1982–; mem. American Philosophical Asscn, Pres. 1985–86; mem. American Acad. of Arts and Sciences, American Philosophical Soc., Norwegian Acad. of Science and Letters; Corresp. Fellow, British Acad.; FAAA; Hon. DLitt (Oxford) 1995; Hon. PhD (Stockholm) 1999; Hegel Prize 1991. *Publications include:* Decision-Making: An Experimental Approach (with Patrick Suppes) 1957, Reasons and Causes 1963, Essays on Actions and Events 1982, Inquiries into Truth and Interpretation 1984, Plato's Philebus 1990, Structure and Content of Truth 1990, Subjective, Intersubjective, Objective 2001, numerous essays and articles in philosophical journals. *Leisure interests:* gliding, skiing, music. *Address:* Department of Philosophy, University of California, Berkeley, CA 94720, USA. *Telephone:* (510) 642-2722 (Office). *Fax:* (510) 642-4164 (Office). *E-mail:* davidson@socrates.berkeley.edu (Office).

DAVIDSON, Janet Marjorie, ONZM, MA, DSc, FRSNZ; New Zealand archaeologist and ethnologist; b. 23 Aug. 1941, Lower Hutt; s. of Albert Dick Davidson and Christine Mary Davidson (née Browne); m. Bryan Foss Leach 1979; one d.; ed Hutt Valley High School and Univ. of Auckland; Field Assoc. Bernice P. Bishop Museum, Honolulu 1964–66; E. Earle Vaile Archaeologist Auckland Inst. and Museum 1966–79; Hon. lecturer in Anthropology, Univ. of Otago 1980–86; ethnologist Nat. Museum of NZ 1987–91; Curator (Pacific Collections) Museum of NZ Te Papa Tongarewa 1991–; extensive archaeological field work in NZ and the Pacific; Rhodes Visiting Fellow, Lady Margaret Hall, Oxford 1974–76. *Publications:* Archaeology on Nukuaro Atoll 1971, The Prehistory of New Zealand 1984, numerous articles on the archaeology and prehistory of New Zealand and various Pacific Islands. *Leisure interests:* music, theatre, opera, ballet, cooking. *Address:* Museum of New Zealand, Box 467, Wellington 1 (Office); 5 Hillview Crescent, Paparangi, Wellington 4, New Zealand (Home).

DAVIDSON, John Macdonald, AM, BArch, LFRAIA, RIBA; Australian architect; b. 21 Oct. 1926, Sydney; s. of the late John H. Davidson and of Daisy Macdonald; m. Helen M. King 1954; two s. one d.; ed Geelong Coll. and Univ of Melbourne; Assoc. Godfrey and Spowers (architects) 1954–61, Partner, later Dir 1961, Chair. Godfrey and Spowers Australia Pty Ltd 1979–91; Pres. Royal Australian Inst. of Architects 1978–79; mem. Expert Panel in Architecture (COPQ) 1978–; mem. Int. Council, Int. Union of Architects (UIA) 1981–85, Vice-Pres. UIA 1985–87; Chair. Metropolitan Strategy Consultative Cttee 1984–89, South Yarra Collaborative Pty Ltd 1983–89; Partner, Catalyst Design Group 1992–; Hon. FAIA. *Publication:* The Awarding and Administration of Architectural Contracts 1961. *Leisure interests:* music, art, writing, fly fishing. *Address:* 4/6 Lennox Street, Hawthorn, Vic. 3122; 252 Church Street, Richmond, Vic. 3121, Australia. *Telephone:* (3) 9428-6352. *Fax:* (3) 9428-6897.

DAVIE, Alan, CBE, DA, HRSA, RWA; British painter, jazz musician and jeweller; b. 1920, Grangemouth, Stirlingshire; s. of James W. Davie and Elizabeth Turnbull; m. Janet Gaul 1947; one d.; ed Edinburgh Coll. of Art, Edinburgh Moray House Coll. of Educ.; Gregory Fellowship, Leeds Univ. 1956–59; Sr Fellow RCA Lectures Colour Conf. Bristol 1991; Visiting Prof. Univ. of Brighton 1993–; Hon. mem. Royal Scottish Acad. 1977; Hon. DLitt (Heriot-Watt Univ.) 1994, (Univ. of Herts.) 1995; Saltire Award, Mosaic Scotland 1976. *Exhibitions include:* first one-man exhbn Edin. 1946; numerous one-man exhbns in Europe and USA 1949–, at Gimpel Galleries in London, New York and Zürich 1949–98, ACA Gallery, New York 1993, 1997, Cohon Gallery, Chicago, Brighton Univ. 1993, FIAC, Paris 1994, 1995, Porto, Almada, Portugal 1994–95, Pallant House, Chichester, Mappin Gallery, Sheffield 1996, Inverness Gallery 1997, Art Fair, Nice 1997, Pier Arts Centre, Orkney 1998; rep. at Dunn Int. Exhbn, London 1963; Prize for the best foreign painter at his one-man exhbn at the 7th Bienal de São Paulo, Brazil 1963; Gulbenkian Painting and Sculpture of a Decade Exhbn, Tate Gallery, London 1964; several exhbns at the Salon de Mai; Exhbn Paintings 1956–88, touring Scotland, Helsingborg 1988; retrospective exhbns Edin. Festival, RSA Galleries 1972; Exhbn Tapestries, Paris 1977; retrospective exhbn McLellan Gallery, Glasgow, Talbot Rice Gallery, Edinburgh 1992, British Council touring exhbn, Edinburgh, Brussels, S America 1992–95, Australia 1995–97; Kilkenny Castle, Ireland 1993, Barbican Gallery, London 1993, Chicago 1994; tapestry design executed by Tapestry Workshop, Victoria, Australia, exhibited London 1995; retrospective exhbn of drawings, Scottish Nat. Gallery of Modern Art, Brighton Univ. 1997, of oils and gouache, ACA Gallery, New York 1997, mixed exhbn Pallant House, Chichester, Ricard Gallery, New York 1997, Scottish Art 1945–2000, Aberdeen, Dundee 1999; exhbn Works on Paper, Faggionata Fine Arts Gallery, London 1998; retrospective Scottish Nat. Gallery of Modern Art 2000, Cobra Museum, Netherlands 2001; tapestry design for Edin. Hosp., woven by Dovecote Studio 2002. *Work includes:* first public music recital, Tate Gallery and Gimpel Fils, London 1971; four recordings 1972–86; music concerts 1972, concerts and broadcasts 1974. *Publications:* Monograph: Alan Davie 1992, The Quest for the Miraculous, Alan Davie 1993, Alan Davie Drawings 1997. *Leisure interests:* gliding, music, photography, underwater swimming. *Address:* Gamels Studio, Rush Green, Hertford, SG13 7SB, England. *Telephone:* (1920) 463684. *Fax:* (1920) 484406.

DAVIES, A. Michael, MA, FCA; British company director; b. 23 June 1934; s. of Angelo Henry Davies and Clarice Mildred Davies; m. Jane Priscilla Davies 1962; one s. (deceased) one d.; ed Shrewsbury School, Queens' Coll., Cambridge; Chair. Tozer Kemsley & Millbourne 1982–86, Bredero Properties 1986–94, Worth Investment Trust 1987–95, Calor Group 1989–97 (Dir 1987–97), Perkins Foods 1987–2001, Berk 1988–95, Wiltshier 1988–95, Nat. Express Group PLC 1991–, Simon Group 1993–, Corporate Services Group 1999–2002; Deputy Chair. T.I. Group 1990–93 (Dir 1984–93), Manpower 1987–91, AerFi 1993–2000; Dir Imperial Group 1972–82, Littlewoods Org. 1982–88, TV-am 1982–88, British Airways 1983–2002, Worcester Group 1991–92. *Address:* Little Woolpit, Ewhurst, Cranleigh, Surrey, GU6 7NP; 7 Lowndes Close, London, S.W.1, England. *Telephone:* (1483) 277344.

DAVIES, David, BA; British designer; ed Kingston Coll. of Art; with designer Stuart Baron launched own multi-disciplinary design consultancy David Davies Assocs 1982, now Creative and Man. Dir Davies/Baron; work includes retail and graphic identity for Next, creation of all brand identities for British Airways and int. store design for Valentino, Italy; consultant to many leading cos. including British Airways, Royal Bank of Scotland, Marks & Spencer, Mothercare, Malaysia Airlines, Sonae (Portugal), Coin (Italy), Austrian Airlines, Air NZ; has designed lines of clothing, furniture and products for the 'Davies' label; consultant to Marks & Spencer Home Furnishings; Channel 4 TV commission to create design series Eye to Eye.

DAVIES, Sir David E. N., Kt, CBE, PhD, DSc, FIEE, FREng, FRS; British electrical engineer; b. 28 Oct. 1935, Cardiff; s. of D. E. Davies and Sarah Samuel; m. 1st Enid Patilla 1962 (died 1990); two s.; m. 2nd Jennifer E. Rayner 1992; ed Univ. of Birmingham; Lecturer, then Sr Lecturer in Electrical Eng, Univ. of Birmingham 1961–67; Asst Dir Research Dept, British Railways Bd 1967–71; Visiting Industrial Prof. of Electrical Eng Loughborough Univ. 1969–71; Prof. of Electrical Eng Univ. Coll. London 1971–88, Pender Prof. of Electrical Eng 1985–88, Vice-Provost Univ. Coll. 1986–88; Vice-Chancellor Loughborough Univ. of Tech. 1988–93; Chief Scientific Adviser, Ministry of Defence 1993–99; Chair. Defence Scientific Advisory Council 1992–93; Pres. Inst. of Electrical Engineers 1994–95; Vice-Pres. Royal Acad. of Eng 1995–96, Pres. 1996–2001; Chair. Railway Safety 2000–; Dir Strategy Ltd 1974–79, Gaydon Tech. 1986–88, Loughborough Consultants 1988–93, Inst. Consumer Ergonomics 1988–93, ERA Tech. 1997–, Lattice PLC 2000–02; Hon. Fellow Univ. of Wales, Coll. of Cardiff 2001; Hon. DSc (Birmingham) 1994, (Loughborough) 1994, (South Bank) 1994, (Bradford) 1995, (Surrey) 1996, (Warwick) 1997, (Bath) 1997, (Heriot-Watt) 1999, (UMIST) 2000, (Wales) 2002; Rank Prize for Optoelectronics 1984; IEEE Centennial Medal 1984, IEE Faraday Medal 1987 and other awards. *Publications:* about 120 publications on antennas, radar and fibre optics. *Address:* Railway Safety, Evergreen House, 160 Euston Road, London, NW1 2DX, England (Office). *Telephone:* (20) 7904-7701 (Office). *Fax:* (20) 7557-9071 (Office).

DAVIES, David Reginald, DPhil; American X-ray crystallographer and researcher; b. 22 Feb. 1927, Camarthen, Wales; s. of Theophilus Howel Davies and Gwladys Evelyn Evans (Hodges) Davies; m. 1st Cynthia Margaret Seaman 1951 (divorced 1981); two d.; m. 2nd Monica Walters 1985; ed Magdalen Coll., Oxford, England, California Inst. of Tech., Pasadena, USA; Research Assoc., Albright & Wilson Ltd, Birmingham, England 1954–55; Visiting Scientist Nat. Inst. of Health, Bethesda, Md, USA 1955–61, Chief, Section on Molecular Structure 1961–; Visiting Scientist, MRC Lab. Molecular Biology 1963–64; mem. American Acad. of Arts and Sciences, NAS, American Soc. of Biological Chemists, American Crystallographic Asscn, Biophysical Soc. (Council 1960–65, 1973–78), Protein Soc.; Visiting Scientist Max Planck Inst., Heidelberg 1972–73; Presidential Meritorious Exec. Award 1982, Presidential Rank Award 1988, Stein and Moore Award, Protein Soc. 1998. *Publications:* articles in scientific journals. *Leisure interests:* tennis, sailing. *Address:* National Institutes of Health, NIDDK, Laboratory of Molecular Biology, 9000 Rockville Pike, Bethesda, MD 20892; 4224 Franklin Street, Kensington, MD 20895, USA (Home). *Telephone:* (301) 496-4295 (Office). *Fax:* (301) 496-0201 (Office). *E-mail:* david.davies@nih.gov (Office).

DAVIES, Edward Brian, BA, DPhil, FRS; British professor of mathematics; b. 13 June 1944, Cardiff; m. Jane Christine Phillips 1968; one s. one d.; ed Oxford Univ.; Lecturer in Math., Oxford Univ. 1970–81; Prof. of Math., King's Coll., London 1981–; Fellow of King's Coll. 1996; Sr Berwick Prize, London Math. Soc. 1998. *Publications:* four academic books and more than 180 research papers. *Leisure interests:* philosophy, science. *Address:* Department of Mathematics, King's College, Strand, London, WC2R 2LS, England (Office). *Fax:* (20) 7848-2017 (Office). *E-mail:* e.brian.davies@kcl.ac.uk (Office). *Website:* www.mth.kcl.ac.uk/staff/eb_davies.html (Office).

DAVIES, Emrys Thomas, CMG; British diplomatist (retd); b. 8 Oct. 1934, London; s. of Evan William Davies and Dinah Davies (née Jones); m. Angela Audrey May 1960; one s. two d.; ed Parmiter's Foundation School, London, Univs of Tours and Grenoble, France, School of Slavonic Studies, Cambridge Univ., School of Oriental and African Studies, London Univ. Inst. of Fine Arts, Hanoi; served in RAF 1953–55; joined HM Diplomatic Service 1955, Attaché, Chargé d'Affaires Office, Peking 1956–59, Northern Dept (Soviet and E European Affairs), FCO 1959–60, Third Sec. British Political Residency, Bahrain 1960–62, mem. UK Del. UN Gen. Ass. (Econ. Cttee) 1962, Desk Officer, Econ. Affairs, UN Dept, FCO 1962–63, Asst Political Adviser Govt of Hong Kong 1963–68, First Sec. (Political), High Comm., Ottawa 1968–72, Asst Head N American Dept, FCO 1972–74, Asst Head Financial Relations Dept, FCO 1974–76, Commercial Counsellor, Embassy Peking (Chargé 1976 and 1978) 1976–78, NATO Defense Coll., Rome 1979, Deputy High Commr, Ottawa 1979–82, Overseas Inspector HM Diplomatic Service 1982–84, Deputy Head UK Del. (and Counsellor Econ. and Financial Affairs) OECD Paris 1984–87, Amb. to Vietnam 1987–90, High Commr in Barbados, Grenada, St Vincent, St Lucia, Dominica, Antigua and St Kitts 1990–94; Head UK Del. to EC Monitor Mission to fmr Yugoslavia, Zagreb 1995, Sarajevo 1998–99; Sec.-Gen. Tripartite Comm. for Restitution of Monetary Gold, Brussels 1995–98, Appointments Adviser to Welsh Office 1997–. *Leisure interests:* golf, visual arts, walking, reading. *Address:* Edinburgh House, 8 Alison Way, St Paul's Hill, Winchester, Hampshire, SO22 5BT, England. *Telephone:* (1962) 853627. *Fax:* (1962) 853627.

DAVIES, (Evan) Mervyn, CBE, JP, FCIB; British banking executive; b. 21 Nov. 1952; s. of Richard Aled Davies and Margaret Davies; m. Jeanne Marie 1979; one s. one d.; ed Rydal School, North Wales, Harvard Business School; Man. Dir, UK Banking and Sr Credit Officer, Citibank 1983–93; joined Standard Chartered Bank PLC with responsibility for Global Account Man. 1993, Head of Corp. and Investment Banking, Singapore –1997, mem. Bd Dirs 1997–, Group Exec. Dir responsible for Group-wide Tech. and Operations in Hong Kong, China and NE Asia 1997–2001, Group CEO, London Nov. 2001–; mem. Hong Kong Exchange Fund Cttee, Singapore British Business Council; mem. Exec. Cttee Hong Kong Community Chest –2001; fmr Chair. Hong Kong Youth Arts Festival; Dir Visa Int. Asia Pacific Regional Bd –2001; Chair. British Chamber of Commerce, Hong Kong 2000–01. *Leisure interests:* sport, art, antiques, opera, reading. *Address:* Standard Chartered Bank PLC, 1 Aldermanbury Square, London, EC2V 7SB, England (Office). *Telephone:* (20) 7280-7088 (Office). *Fax:* (20) 7600-2546 (Office). *Website:* www.standardchartered.com (Office).

DAVIES, Gavyn, OBE, BA; British economist; b. 27 Nov. 1950; s. of W. J. F. Davies and M. G. Davies; m. Susan Jane Nye 1989; two s. one d.; ed St John's Coll., Cambridge and Balliol Coll., Oxford; Econ. Adviser, Policy Unit, 10 Downing Street 1974–79; economist Phillips and Drew 1979–81; Chief UK Economist Simon & Coates 1981–86, Goldman Sachs 1986–93, partner 1988–2001, Head of Investment Research (London) 1991–93, Chief Int. Economist and Head of European Investment Research 1993–97, Chair. Investment Research Dept 1999–2001, Advisory Dir 2001–; Vice-Chair. BBC 2001, Chair. 2001–; Visiting Prof. of Econs LSE 1988–98; Prin. Econs Commentator, The Independent 1991–99; mem. HM Treasury's Ind. Forecasting Panel 1993–97; Chair. Govt Inquiry into the Future Funding of the BBC 1999; Hon. Fellow Aberystwyth Univ. 2002; Hon. DScS (Southampton) 1998; Hon. LLD (Nottingham) 2002. *Leisure interest:* Southampton Football Club. *Address:* Chairman's Office, Room 2462, BBC, Broadcasting House, Portland Place, London, W1A 1AA, England (Office). *Telephone:* (20) 7765-5802 (Office).

DAVIES, Sir Graeme John, Kt, FREng, FRSE, MA, BE, PhD; British university vice-chancellor; b. 7 April 1937, New Zealand; s. of Harry J. Davies and Gladys E. Davies; m. Florence I. Martin 1959; one s. one d.; ed Univ. of Auckland; lecturer Univ. of Cambridge 1962–77, Fellow, St Catharine's Coll. 1967–76; Prof. Dept of Metallurgy, Univ. of Sheffield 1977–86; Vice-Chancellor, Univ. of Liverpool 1986–91; Chief Exec. Univs. Funding Council 1991–93, Polytechnics and Colls Funding Council 1992–93, Higher Educ. Funding Council for England 1992–95; Prin., Vice-Chancellor Univ. of Glasgow 1995–2003; Vice-Chancellor Univ. of London 2003–; Freeman City of London, Freeman and Burgess Holder City of Glasgow; Hon. Fellow Royal Soc. of NZ, Trinity Coll. of Music 1995; Hon. DSc (Nottingham) 1995; Hon. D.Met. (Sheffield) 1995; Hon. LLD (Liverpool) 1991, (Strathclyde) 2000; Hon. DEng (Manchester Metropolitan) 1996, (Auckland) 2003. *Publications:* Solidification and Casting 1973, Textures and Properties of Materials 1976, Hot Working and Forming Processes 1980, Superplasticity 1981, Essential Metallurgy for Engineers 1985. *Leisure interests:* cricket, birdwatching, The Times crossword. *Address:* Coulter Mains, Coulter, nr Biggar, ML12 6PR, Scotland.

DAVIES, Sir Howard John, Kt, MA, MSc; British administrative official; b. 12 Feb. 1951; s. of Leslie Davies and Marjorie Davies; m. Prudence Keely 1984; two s.; ed Manchester Grammar School, Merton Coll. Oxford and Stanford Grad. School of Business; Foreign Office 1973–74; Pvt. Sec. to British Amb. in Paris 1974–76; HM Treasury 1976–82; McKinsey & Co. Inc. 1982–87; Controller, Audit Comm. 1987–92; Dir GKN PLC 1990–95; Dir-Gen. Confed. of British Industry (CBI) 1992–95; Deputy Gov., Bank of England 1995–97, Dir (non-exec.) 1998–; Chair. Financial Services Authority (fmrly Securities and Investments Bd) 1997–2003; Dir LSE Oct. 2003–; mem. NatWest Int. Advisory Bd 1992–95; Deputy Chair. Rowntree Cttee Enquiry 1993; Pres. Age Concern England 1994–98; Chair. Employers' Forum on Age 1996–; Trustee, Tate 2002–. *Leisure interests:* cricket, writing for publication. *Address:* London School of Economics, Houghton Street, London, WC2A 2AE, England. *Telephone:* (20) 7405-7686 (Office). *Website:* www.lse.ac.uk (Office).

DAVIES, John Arthur, MA, PhD, FRSC; Canadian research scientist; b. 28 March 1927, Prestatyn, Wales; s. of Francis J. Davies and Doris A. Edkins; m. Florence Smithson 1950; three s. three d.; ed St Michael's Coll. High School and Univ. of Toronto; Asst, later Assoc. Research Officer, Atomic Energy of Canada 1950–65, Sr Research Officer 1965–70, Prin. Research Officer 1970–85; Part-time Prof. of Eng Physics, McMaster Univ. 1970–92, Dir McMaster Accelerator Lab. 1989–92, Prof. Emer. 1992–; Adjunct Prof., Dept of Electrical Eng, Univ. of Salford, UK 1972–92; Visiting Prof., Nobel Inst. of Physics, Stockholm, Sweden 1962, Univ. of Aarhus, Denmark 1964–65, 1969–70, 1994, Univ. of Osaka, Japan 1972; mem. Royal Danish Acad. of Arts and Sciences, Böhmische Physical Soc., Chemical Inst. of Canada; Hon. DSc (Royal Roads Mil. Coll.) 1984, (Univ. of Salford) 1993; Noranda Award (Chem. Inst. of Canada) 1965; First T. D. Callinan Award (Electrochem. Soc.) 1968, W. B. Lewis Medal 1998. *Publications:* co-author of over 250 research articles and five books in the fields of ion implantation, ion channelling and ion beam analysis. *Leisure interests:* canoeing, cross-country skiing. *Address:* Box 224, 7 Wolfe Avenue, Deep River, Ont., K0J 1P0, Canada (Home). *Telephone:* (613) 584-2301 (Home). *E-mail:* davies@magma.ca (Home).

DAVIES, Jonathan, MBE; British rugby union player; b. 24 Oct. 1962, Trimsaran, Carmarthenshire; s. of the late Leonard Davies and of Diana Davies (née Rees); m. 1st Karen Marie Davies 1984 (died 1997); two s. one d.; m. 2nd Helen Jones 2002; ed Gwendraeth Grammar School; rugby union outside-half; played for the following rugby union clubs: Trimsaran, Neath, Llanelli; turned professional in 1989; with Cardiff 1995–97; played for Welsh nat. team (v. England) 1985, World Cup Squad (6 appearances) 1987, Triple Crown winning team 1988, tour NZ (2 test appearances) 1988, 29 caps, sometime Capt.; also played for Barbarians Rugby Football Club; rugby league career; played at three-quarters; Widnes (world record transfer fee) 1989, Warrington 1993–95 (free transfer); reverted to rugby union in 1995; Welsh nat. team; British nat. team, tour NZ 1990, 6 caps, fmr Capt.; retd from playing 1997; writer and commentator on Rugby Union and League. *Publication:* Jonathan (autobiog.) 1989. *Leisure interest:* all sports. *Address:* c/o Cardiff Rugby Football Club, Cardiff Arms Park, Westgate Street, Cardiff, Wales.

DAVIES, Kay Elizabeth, CBE, MA, DPhil; British geneticist; b. Kay Elizabeth Partridge, 1 April 1951, Stourbridge; d. of Harry Partridge and Florence Partridge; m. Stephen Graham Davies 1973 (divorced); one s.; ed Somerville Coll. Oxford; Guy Newton Jr Research Fellow, Wolfson Coll. Oxford 1976–78; Royal Soc. European Postdoctoral Fellow, Service de Biochimie, Centre d'études nucléaires de Saclay, Gif-sur-Yvette, France 1978–80; Cystic Fibrosis Research Fellow, Biochem. Dept, St Mary's Hosp. Medical School, London 1980–82, MRC Sr Research Fellow, 1982–84; MRC Sr Research Fellow, Nuffield Dept of Clinical Medicine, John Radcliffe Hosp., Oxford 1984–86, MRC External Staff 1986–89, Molecular Genetics Group, Inst. of Molecular Medicine 1989–92, MRC Research Dir, Royal Postgrad. Medical School 1992–94, Head of Molecular Genetics Group, Inst. of Molecular Medicine 1994–95; Prof. of Molecular Genetics, Univ. of London 1992–94; Prof. of Genetics, Dept of Biochem., Univ. of Oxford 1995–97, Dr Lee's Prof. of Anatomy 1998–; Hon. Dir MRC Functional Genetics Unit, Oxford 1999–; Co-Dir Oxford Centre for Gene Function 2001–; Univ. Research Lecturer, Nuffield Dept of Clinical Medicine, John Radcliffe Hosp. 1989–92; Fellow Green Coll. Oxford 1989–92, 1994–95; Fellow Keble Coll. Oxford 1995–; Fellow Hertford Coll. Oxford 1997–; Wellcome Trust Award 1996, SCI Medal

1999, Feldberg Foundation Prize 1999, Gaetano Conte Prize in Basic Myology 2002. *Publications:* 293 papers in scientific journals. *Leisure interests:* tennis, music, general keep-fit. *Address:* Department of Human Anatomy and Genetics, University of Oxford, South Parks Road, Oxford, OX1 3QX, England. *Telephone:* (1865) 272179 (Office). *Fax:* (1865) 272420 (Office). *E-mail:* kay.davies@anat.ox.ac.uk (Office). *Website:* www.anat.ox.ac.uk (Office).

DAVIES, Laura, CBE; British golfer; b. 5 Oct. 1963, Coventry; d. of David Thomas Davies and Rita Ann Davies (née Foskett); turned professional 1985; victories include Belgian Open 1985, British Women's Open 1986, US Women's Open 1987, AGF Biarritz Open 1990, Wilkinson Sword English Open 1995, Irish Open 1994, 1995, French Masters 1995, LPGA Championship 1996, Danish Open 1997, Chrysler Open 1998, 1999, WPGA Championship 1999, Compaq Open 1999, TSN Ladies World Cup of Golf (Individual) 2000, WPGA Int. Matchplay 2001, Norwegian Masters 2002; rep. England in World Team Championship, Taiwan 1992, Europe in Solheim Cup 1990, 1992, 1994; Rookie of the Year 1985; Order of Merit winner 1985, 1986, 1992; Rolex Player of the Year 1996. *Publication:* Carefree Golf 1991. *Leisure interests:* fast cars, all sports, shopping. *Address:* c/o Women's Professional Golf European Tour, The Tytherington Club, Dorchester Way, Tytherington, Macclesfield, SK10 2JP, England. *Website:* www.lauradavies.co.uk (Office).

DAVIES, Nicholas Barry, BA, DPhil, FRS; British biologist; b. 23 May 1952, Liverpool; s. of Anthony Barry Davies and Joyce Margaret Davies (née Parrington); m. Jan Parr 1979; two d.; ed Merchant Taylors' School, Crosby, Pembroke Coll., Cambridge, Wolfson Coll., Oxford; Demonstrator in Zoology, Edward Grey Inst., Oxford Univ. 1976–79; Jr Research Fellow, Wolfson Coll., Oxford 1977–79; Demonstrator, Dept of Zoology, Cambridge Univ. 1979–84, Lecturer 1984–92, Reader 1992–95, Prof. of Behavioural Ecology 1995–; Fellow, Pembroke Coll., Cambridge 1979–; Pres. Int. Soc. for Behavioural Ecology 2000; Corresp. Fellow, American Ornithologists' Union 1999, German Ornithological Soc. 2000; Scientific Medal, Zoological Soc. of London 1987, Cambridge Univ. Teaching Prize 1995, William Bate Hardy Prize, Cambridge Philosophical Soc. 1995, Medal of Assen for Study of Animal Behaviour 1996, Frink Medal, Zoological Soc. of London 2001. *Publications:* Dunnock Behaviour and Social Evolution 1992, An Introduction to Behavioural Ecology (co-author), Behavioural Ecology: an Evolutionary Approach (co-ed.), Cuckoos, Cowbirds and Other Cheats 2000. *Leisure interests:* bird-watching, mountains, music. *Address:* Department of Zoology, University of Cambridge, Downing Street, Cambridge, CB2 3EJ, England (Office). *Telephone:* (1223) 334405 (Office). *Fax:* (1223) 336676 (Office). *E-mail:* n.b .davies@zoo.cam.ac.uk (Office).

DAVIES, Sir Peter Maxwell, Kt (see Maxwell Davies, Sir Peter).

DAVIES, Rodney Deane, CBE, DSc, FRSCPhys; British radio astronomer; b. 8 Jan. 1930, Balaklava, S Australia; s. of Holbin James Davies and Rena Irene (née March) Davies; m. Valda Beth Treasure 1953; two s. (one deceased), two d.; ed Univs of Adelaide and Manchester; Research Officer Radio Physics Div., CSIRO Sydney 1951–53; Lecturer Univ. of Manchester 1953–63, Sr Lecturer 1963–67, Reader 1967–76, Prof. of Radio Astronomy 1976–97, Prof. Emer. 1997–; Sec. Royal Astronomical Soc. 1978–86, Pres. 1987–89; Dir Nuffield Radio Astronomy Labs, Jodrell Bank 1988–97. *Publications:* Radio Studies of the Universe (with H. P. Palmer) 1959, Radio Astronomy Today (with H. P. Palmer and M. I. Large) 1963. *Leisure interests:* fell-walking, gardening. *Address:* University of Manchester, Jodrell Bank Observatory, Jodrell Bank, Macclesfield, Cheshire, SK11 9DL; Park Gate House, Fulshaw Park Road, Wilmslow, Cheshire, SK9 1QG, England. *Telephone:* (1477) 571321 (Office); (1625) 523592 (Home). *Fax:* (1477) 571618. *E-mail:* rdd@jb.man.ac.uk (Office). *Website:* www.jb.man.ac.uk (Office).

DAVIES, Rt Hon Ron(ald), PC; British politician; b. 6 Aug. 1946; s. of the late Ronald Davies; m. 1st Anne Williams; m. 2nd Christina Elizabeth Rees 1981; one d.; m. 3rd Lynne Hughes 2002; ed Bassaleg Grammar School, Portsmouth Polytechnic, Univ. Coll. of Wales, Cardiff; schoolteacher 1968–70; Workers' Educ. Asscn Tutor/Organiser 1970–74; Further Educ. Adviser, Mid-Glamorgan Local Educ. Authority 1974–83; mem. Rhymney Valley Dist Council 1969–84 (fmr Vice-Chair.); MP for Caerphilly 1983–2001; Opposition Whip 1985–87; Labour Spokesman on Agric. and Rural Affairs 1987–92, on Wales 1992–97; Sec. of State for Wales 1997–98; elected leader of Labour Group in Nat. Ass. for Wales Sept. 1998, resgnd Oct. 1998; mem. Nat. Ass. for Wales for Caerphilly 1999–2003 (resgnd), Chair. Econ. Devt Cttee 1999–2003; Highest Order, Gorsedd of the Bards 1998. *Publications:* pamphlets on Welsh devolution. *Leisure interests:* walking, gardening, sport. *Address:* Bedwas Community Council Offices, Newport Road, Bedwas, CF83 8YB, Wales (Office). *Telephone:* (29) 2085-2477 (Office). *Fax:* (29) 2086-6022 (Office).

DAVIES, Ryland; British opera and concert singer (tenor); b. 9 Feb. 1943, Cwm Ebbw Vale, Monmouthshire (now Gwent); s. of Joan and Gethin Davies; m. 1st Anne Howells (q.v.) 1966 (divorced 1981); m. 2nd Deborah Jane Rees 1983; one d.; ed Royal Manchester Coll. of Music (Fellow 1971); voice teacher Royal Northern Coll. of Music (RNCM) 1987–94, Royal Coll. of Music, London 1999–; Dir Opera Productions RNCM Mananan Festival, Clonter Opera Trust; début as Almaviva in The Barber of Seville, Welsh Nat. Opera 1964, subsequent appearances including Tamino in The Magic Flute 1974, Yenick in Bartered Bride 1989; Glyndebourne Festival Chorus 1964–66, taking parts including Belmonte in The Abduction from the Seraglio, Ferrando in Così fan tutte, Flamand in Capriccio, Lysander in A Midsummer Night's Dream, The Prince in Love of Three Oranges, Lensky in Eugene Onegin, Tichone in Katya Kabanova, Basilio/Curzio in Le nozze di Figaro, Auctioneer in The Rake's Progress; appearances with Scottish Opera as Ferrando and as Fenton in Falstaff, Tamino in The Magic Flute and as Nemorino in L'Elisir d'Amore; with Sadler's Wells Opera as Almaviva, Essex in Britten's Gloriana; with Royal Opera as Hylas in The Trojans, Don Ottavio in Don Giovanni, Ferrando, Cassio in Otello, Nemorino in L'Elisir d'Amore, Ernesto in Don Pasquale, Lysander in A Midsummer Night's Dream and Almaviva; with English Nat. Opera as Eisenstein in Die Fledermaus, Basilio in Le nozze di Figaro, Rev. H. Adams in Peter Grimes, Albazar in Turk in Italy, L'Aumonier in Dialogues des Carmelites, Gaudenzio in La Bohème; overseas appearances include Salzburg Festival, at San Francisco, Chicago, Paris, at Metropolitan Opera, New York, Hollywood Bowl, Paris Opera, Geneva, Brussels, Lyons, Amsterdam, Mannheim, Israel, Buenos Aires, Stuttgart, Nice, Nancy, Philadelphia, Berlin, Hamburg; returned to Covent Garden 1994, 2002, Welsh Nat. Opera 1994, New York Metropolitan Opera 1994, 1995, 2001, Glyndebourne 1997, New Israeli Opera 1997, Chicago Lyric Opera 1998, 2003, Santa Fe Opera 1998, 1999, New Israeli Opera 1998, Netherlands Opera 1998, 1999, 2002, English Nat. Opera 1999, Houston Grand Opera 2002, Japan 2002, Florence 2002; Boise Mendelsohn Foundation Scholarship 1964; Fellow Welsh Coll. of Music and Drama 1996; Hon. Fellow Royal Manchester Coll. of Music 1971; Ricordi Opera Prize, Royal Manchester Coll. of Music 1963, Imperial League of Opera Prize, Royal Manchester Coll. of Music 1963, First John Christie Award, Glyndebourne 1965. *Recordings include:* The Abduction from the Seraglio, L'Amore dei Tre Re (Montemezzi), La Navarraise (Massenet), The Trojans, Saul, Così fan tutte, Thérèse (Massenet), Monteverdi Madrigals, Idomeneo, The Seasons (Haydn), Messiah, L'Oracolo (Leone), Judas Maccabaeus, Pulcinella, Il Matrimonio Segreto, Lucia di Lammamoor, Otello, Mozart's Requiem, C Minor Mass, Credo Mass, Coronation Mass, Messe Solonelle; Idipus Rex (Shepherd), Il Trovatore (Ruiz), Don Carlo (Conte di Lerma), Le nozze di Figaro (Basilio/Curzio), Esclarmonde (Massenet). *Video films include:* Don Pasquale, A Midsummer Night's Dream, Die Entführung aus dem Serail, Love of Three Oranges, Trial by Jury, Katya Kabanova. *Television:* Merry Widow, Capriccio (BBC, Glyndebourne), A Goodly Manner for a Song (STV), On Wenlock Edge (BBC Wales, Glyndebourne), Dido and Aeneas (BBC, Glyndebourne), Mass in C Minor. *Achievements:* played rugby for Wales Schoolboys, 2 caps 1957–58, Wales Boys Clubs under-18s 1959–60. *Leisure interests:* art, cinema, sport. *Address:* c/o IMG Artists, Lovell House, 616 Chiswick High Road, London, W4 5RX, England. *Telephone:* (20) 8233-5800 (Office).

DAVIES, Stephen Graham, MA, DPhil; British research chemist; b. 24 Feb. 1950; s. of Gordon W. J. Davies and June M. Murphy; m. Kay E. Partridge 1973; one s.; ICI Postdoctoral Fellow, Oxford 1975–77; NATO Postdoctoral Fellow, Oxford 1977–78; Attaché de Recherche, CNRS, Paris 1978–80; Fellow, New Coll. Oxford 1980–; Univ. lecturer in Chem. Univ. of Oxford 1980–; Dir Oxford Asymmetry Ltd 1991–; mem. of various cttees, editorial bds; Hickinbottom Fellowship 1984; Pfizer Award for Chem. 1985, 1988, Corday Morgan Medal 1984, Royal Soc. of Chem. Award for Organometallic Chem. 1989, Bader Award, Royal Soc. of Chem. 1989. *Publications:* Organometallic Chemistry: Applications to Organic Chemistry 1982; more than 250 papers in learned journals. *Leisure interest:* chemistry. *Address:* Dyson Perrins Laboratory, University of Oxford, South Parks Road, Oxford, OX1 3QY, England. *Telephone:* (1865) 275646. *Fax:* (1865) 275633.

DAVIES, (Stephen) Howard, FRSA; British theatre and film director; b. 26 April 1940; s. of Thomas Davies and of the late (Eileen) Hilda Bevan; m. Susan Wall (divorced); two d.; ed Christ's Hosp. and Univs of Durham and Bristol; Theatre Dir, Assoc. Dir Bristol Old Vic 1971–73; founder mem. Avon Touring Co.; Asst Dir RSC 1974, Assoc. Dir 1976–86; Founder and Dir The Warehouse RSC (productions include Piaf, Good, Les Liaisons Dangereuses) 1977–82; freelance Dir 1974–76; Assoc. Dir Nat. Theatre (productions include The Shaughraun, Cat on a Hot Tin Roof, The Secret Rapture) 1987–88, Royal Nat. Theatre (productions include Hedda Gabler, The Crucible, Piano, A Long Day's Journey Into Night) 1989–; Dir Who's Afraid of Virginia Woolf? 1996, The Italian Girl in Algiers, ENO 1997, The Iceman Cometh 1998, Vassa 1999, Battle Royal 1999, All My Sons (Olivier Award for Best Dir 2001) 2000, Private Lives 2001; Evening Standard Award, 2 Olivier Awards. *Television:* Armadillo (BBC TV) 2001. *Leisure interests:* travel, hill-walking, watching rugby, film, painting. *Address:* c/o Royal National Theatre, South Bank, London, SE1 9PX, England. *Telephone:* (20) 7452-3333. *Fax:* (20) 7620-1197. *Website:* www.nationaltheatre.org.uk.

DAVIES, Susan Elizabeth, OBE; British gallery director (retd); b. 14 April 1933, Iran; d. of late Stanworth Adey and Joan Charlsworth; m. John R. T. Davies 1954; two d.; ed Nightingale Bamford School, New York, Eothen School, Surrey and Triangle Secretarial Coll.; Municipal Journal 1953–54; Artists' Placement Group 1966–67; ICA 1967–70; Founder and Dir The Photographers' Gallery, London 1971–91; photography consultant and writer 1991–; Hon. FRPS 1986; Progress Medal, Royal Photographic Soc. 1982; Kulturpreis, German Photographic Soc. 1990. *Leisure interests:* jazz, gardening, grandchildren. *Address:* 53/55 Britwell Road, Burnham, Bucks., SL1 8DH, England. *Telephone:* (1628) 662677. *Fax:* (1628) 662677. *E-mail:* sue .ristic@virgin.net (Home). *Website:* jazzrescue.com (Office).

DAVIES, Terence; British screenwriter and film director; b. 1945, Liverpool; ed Coventry Drama School and Nat. Film School; articled clerk in shipping office; later worked for 12 years in an accountancy practice. *Films:* Children 1977, Madonna and Child 1980, Death and Transfiguration 1983, Distant

Voices, Still Lives (Int. Critics Prize, Cannes Film Festival) 1988, Movie Masterclass 1990, The Long Day Closes 1992, The Neon Bible 1995, The House of Mirth 2000. *Radio:* The Walk to the Paradise Garden (BBC Radio 3) 2001. *Publications:* Hallelujah Now, A Modest Pageant. *Address:* c/o Nigel Britten Management, Riverbank House, 1 Putney Bridge Approach, Fulham, London, SW6 3JD; Flat 7, Block Q, Peabody Buildings, Duchy Street, London, SE1 8DX, England (Home). *Telephone:* (20) 7384-3842 (Office). *Fax:* (20) 7384-3862 (Office). *E-mail:* nbm.office@virgin.net (Office).

DAVIGNON, Viscount Etienne, LLD; Belgian business executive; b. 4 Oct. 1932, Budapest, Hungary; m. Françoise de Cumont 1959; one s. two d.; Head of Office of Minister of Foreign Affairs 1963, Political Dir 1969–76; Chair. Governing Bd, Int. Energy Agency 1974–76; Commr for Industry and Int. Markets, Comm. of European Communities 1977–81, Vice-Pres. for Industry, Energy and Research Policies 1981–85; CEO SIBEKA 1986–; Chair. Société Générale de Belgique 1988–, Exec. Chair. Bd of Dirs. 1989–, Vice-Chair. 2001–; Chair. Spaak Foundation; Vice-Chair. Union Minière 1993–; Vice-Pres. Tractebel, Fortis, ACCOR, Petrofina 1990; mem. Advisory Bd, BASF 1998–, Pechiney; participated in EU reform appeal 2001; Hon D.Hum.Litt. (American Coll. in Paris) 1988. *Leisure interests:* golf, skiing, tennis. *Address:* Société Générale de Belgique, Rue Royale 30, 1000 Brussels (Office); 12 avenue des Fleurs, 1150 Brussels, Belgium. *Telephone:* (2) 507-03-82 (Office). *Fax:* (2) 507-03-00 (Office).

DAVIS, Sir Andrew, Kt, CBE; British conductor; b. 1944; m. Gianna Rolandi 1989; one s.; ed Royal Coll. of Music, King's Coll., Cambridge; studied conducting with Franco Ferrara, Rome; continuo player with Acad. of St Martin-in-the-Fields and English Chamber Orchestra; Festival Hall début conducting BBC Symphony Orchestra Nov. 1970; Asst Conductor Philharmonia Orchestra 1973–77, Prin. Guest Conductor Royal Liverpool Philharmonic Orchestra 1974–77; Music Dir Toronto Symphony 1975–88, Conductor Laureate 1988–; Musical Dir Glyndebourne Festival Opera 1988–2002; Chief Conductor BBC Symphony Orchestra 1989–2000, Conductor Laureate 2000–, tours with orchestra: Far East 1990, Europe 1992, Japan 1993, 1997, USA 1995, 1998, South America 2001, Far East and Australia 2002; Prin. Guest Conductor Royal Stockholm Philharmonic 1995–99; Musical Dir. Chicago Lyric Opera 2000–; has conducted London Philharmonic, London Symphony, Royal Philharmonic, Boston, Chicago, Cleveland, Los Angeles Philharmonic, New York Philharmonic, Pittsburg Symphony, Orchestre Nat. de France, Frankfurt Radio Orchestra, Royal Concertgebouw Orchestra, Tonhalle Orchestra, Stockholm Philharmonic Orchestra, Israel Philharmonic, Bavarian Radio Symphony and Berlin Philharmonic orchestras, London Sinfonietta, Dallas Symphony and Dresden Staatskapelle orchestras; has conducted at Glyndebourne Festival Opera, Covent Garden Opera, Metropolitan Opera, Washington, DC, Chicago Lyric Opera, Bavarian State Opera, Paris Opéra, La Scala, Milan, Sir Henry Wood Promenade Concerts, maj. British and European music festivals; tours of People's Republic of China 1978, Europe 1983 with Toronto Symphony Orchestra; recordings for CBS include Duruflé's Requiem (Grand Prix du Disque 1978), cycle of Dvořák symphonies and, for EMI, Tippett's The Mask of Time (won a Gramophone Record of the Year Award 1987, Grand Prix du Disque 1988); currently recording for Teldec Classics (has completed Vaughan Williams symphony cycle). *Leisure interest:* medieval stained glass. *Address:* c/o Askonas Holt Ltd, Lonsdale Chambers, 27 Chancery Lane, London, WC2A 1PF, England. *Telephone:* (20) 7400-1700. *Fax:* (20) 7400-1799. *E-mail:* info@askonasholt.co.uk (Office).

DAVIS, Carl, BA; American composer and conductor; b. 28 Oct. 1936, New York; s. of Isadore Davis and Sara Davis; m. Jean Boht 1971; two d.; ed New England Conservatory of Music, Bard Coll.; Asst Conductor, New York City Opera 1958; Assoc. Conductor, London Philharmonic Orchestra 1987–88; Prin. Conductor, Bournemouth Pops 1984–87; Prin. Guest Conductor Munich Symphony Orchestra 1990–; Artistic Dir and Conductor, Royal Liverpool Philharmonic Orchestra, Summer Pops 1993–2000; Guest Conductor Hallé Orchestra, Birmingham Symphony Orchestra, Scottish Symphony Orchestra; Hon. Fellowship (Liverpool Univ.) 1992; Hon. Dr of Arts (Bard, New York) 1994; Hon. DMus (Liverpool) 2002; Chevalier des Arts et des Lettres 1983, Special Achievement Award for Music for Television and Film 2003. *Musical theatre:* Diversions (Obie Prize Best Review) 1958, Twists (Arts Theatre London) 1962, The Projector and Cranford (Theatre Royal Stratford East), Pilgrim (Edinburgh Festival), The Wind in the Willows, Peace (Opera North), Alice in Wonderland (Hammersmith) 1987, The Vackees (Haymarket) 1987, The Mermaid. *Incidental music for theatre includes:* Prospect Theatre Co., Nat. Theatre, RSC. *Ballet:* A Simple Man 1987, Lipizzaner 1988, Liaisons Amoureuses (Northern Ballet Theatre) 1988, Madly, Badly, Sadly, Gladly, David and Goliath, Dances of Love and Death (London Contemporary Dance Theatre), The Picture of Dorian Gray (Sadler's Wells Royal Ballet), A Christmas Carol (Northern Theatre Ballet) 1992, The Savoy Suite (English Nat. Ballet) 1993, Alice in Wonderland (English Nat. Ballet) 1995, Aladdin (Scottish Ballet) 2000, Pride and Prejudice: First Impressions (Central Ballet School Tour) 2002. *Music for TV includes:* The Snow Goose 1971, The World at War (Emmy Award) 1972, The Naked Civil Servant 1975, Our Mutual Friend 1978, Hollywood 1980, Churchill: The Wilderness Years 1981, Silas Marner 1985, Hotel du Lac 1986, The Accountant (BAFTA Award) 1989, The Secret Life of Ian Fleming 1989, Separate but Equal 1991, The Royal Collection 1991, A Year in Provence 1992, Fame in the 20th Century: Clive James 1992, Ghengis Cohn 1993, Thatcher: The Downing Street Years 1993,

Pride and Prejudice 1995, Oliver's Travels 1995, Eurocinema: The Other Hollywood 1995, Cold War 1998–99, Good Night Mr Tom 1998, The Great Gatsby 2000, The Queen's Nose, An Angel for May. *Operas for TV:* The Arrangement, Who Takes You to The Party?, Orpheus in the Underground, Peace. *Film music:* The Bofors Gun 1969, The French Lieutenant's Woman (BAFTA award) 1981, Champions 1984, The Girl in a Swing 1988, Rainbow 1988, Scandal 1988, Frankenstein Unbound 1989, The Raft of the Medusa 1991, The Trial 1992, Voyage 1993, Widow's Peak 1994, Topsy Turvy 2000; series of Thames Silents including Napoleon 1980, 2000, The Wind, The Big Parade, Greed, The General, Ben Hur, Intolerance, Safety Last, The Four Horsemen of the Apocalypse 1992, Wings 1993, Waterloo 1995, Phantom of the Opera 1996. *Concert works:* Music for the Royal Wedding, Variations on a Bus Route, Overture on Australian Themes, Clarinet Concerto 1984, Lines on London Symphony 1984, Fantasy for Flute and Harpsichord 1985, The Searle Suite for Wind Ensemble, Fanfare for Jerusalem 1987, The Glenlivet Fireworks Music 1988, Norwegian Brass Music 1988, Variations for a Polish Beggar's Theme 1988, Pigeons Progress 1988, Jazz Age Fanfare 1989, Everest 1989, Landscapes 1990, The Town Fox (text by Carla Lane) 1990, A Duck's Diary 1990, Paul McCartney's Liverpool Oratorio (with Paul McCartney) 1991. *Recordings include:* Napoleon 1983, Christmas with Kiri (with Kiri Te Kanawa) 1986, Beautiful Dreamer (with Marylin Horne) 1986, The Silents 1987, Ben Hur 1989, A Simple Man 1989, The Town Fox and Other Musical Tales (text by Carla Lane) 1990, Paul McCartney's Liverpool Oratorio 1991, Leeds Castle Classics, Liverpool Pops at Home 1995. *Publications:* sheet music of television themes. *Leisure interests:* reading, gardening, playing chamber music, cooking. *Address:* c/o Paul Wing, 3 Deermead, Little Kings Hill, Great Missenden, Bucks., HP16 0EY (Office); 8 Smith Street, London, SW3 4LL, England. *Telephone:* (1494) 890511; (20) 7730-9477. *Fax:* (1494) 890522 (Office). *E-mail:* admin@threefoldmusic.co.uk (Office). *Website:* www.carl-davis.com (Office).

DAVIS, Sir Colin Rex, Kt, CBE, CH; British musician; b. 25 Sept. 1927, Weybridge, Surrey; s. of Reginald George Davis and Lilian Colbran; m. 1st April Cantelo 1949 (dissolved 1964); one s. one d.; m. 2nd Ashraf Naini 1964; three s. two d.; ed Christ's Hospital and Royal Coll. of Music; Asst Conductor, BBC Scottish Orchestra 1957–59; Conductor, Sadler's Wells Opera House 1959, Musical Dir 1961–65; Chief Conductor, BBC Symphony Orchestra 1967–71, Chief Guest Conductor 1971–75; Artistic Dir Bath Festival 1969; Musical Dir Royal Opera House, Covent Garden 1971–86; Prin. Guest Conductor, Boston Symphony Orchestra 1972–84; Prin. Guest Conductor, London Symphony Orchestra 1975–95, Prin. Conductor 1995–; Prin. Guest Conductor, New York Philharmonic Orchestra 1998–; Music Dir and Prin. Conductor, Bavarian State Radio Orchestra 1983–92; Hon. Conductor Dresden Staatskapelle 1990–; Hon. DMus (Keele) 2002, (RAM) 2002; Grosser Deutscher Schallplattenpreis 1978; Grammy Award 'Opera Recording of the Year' 1980, Royal Philharmonic Soc. Gold Medal 1995; Commendatore of the Repub. of Italy 1976, Officier, Légion d'honneur 1999, Commdr.'s Cross of the Order of Merit, Fed. Repub. of Germany 1987, Commdr Ordre des Arts et des Lettres 1990, Order of the Lion of Finland (Commdr 1st Class) 1992; Bayerischen Verdiensterden 1993, Distinguished Musician Award (ISM) 1996, Grammy Award 'Best Orchestral Recording' 1997, Sibelius Birth Place Medal 1998, Freedom of the City of London 1992, Maximiliansorden (Bavaria) 2000, Best Classical Album and Best Opera Recording (for Les Troyens), Grammy Awards 2002. *Leisure interests:* reading, tree-planting, knitting. *Address:* c/o Alison Glaister, 39 Huntingdon Street, London, N1 1BP, England. *Telephone:* (20) 7609-5864. *Fax:* (20) 7609-5866. *E-mail:* aglaister@rexx.demon.co.uk (Office).

DAVIS, Crispin Henry Lamert, MA; British business executive; b. 19 March 1949; s. of the late Walter Patrick Davis and of Jane Davis (née Lamert); m. Anne Richardson 1970; three d.; ed Charterhouse, Oriel Coll., Oxford; joined Procter & Gamble 1970; Man. Dir Procter & Gamble Co., Germany 1981–84; Vice-Pres. Food Div., Procter & Gamble USA 1984–90; European Man. Dir United Distillers 1990–92, Group Man. Dir 1992–94; CEO Aegis PLC 1994–99; Chief Exec. Reed Elsevier 1999–; mem. Finance Cttee, National Trust 2000–. *Leisure interests:* sport, gardening, art. *Address:* Reed Elsevier PLC, 25 Victoria Street, London, SW1H 0EX (Office); Hills End, Titlarks Hill, Sunningdale, Berks., SL5 0JD, England (Home). *Telephone:* (20) 7222-8420 (Office); (1344) 291233 (Home). *Fax:* (20) 7227-5799. *E-mail:* crispin.davis@reedelsevier.co.uk. *Website:* www.reed-elsevier.com.

DAVIS, Rt. Hon. David (Michael), PC, MSc; British politician and business executive; b. 23 Dec. 1948; s. of Ronald Davis and Elizabeth Davis; m. Doreen Margery Cook 1973; one s. two d.; ed Warwick Univ., London Business School and Harvard Univ.; joined Tate & Lyle Transport 1974, Man. Dir Tate and Lyle 1980–82, Strategic Planning Dir Tate and Lyle PLC 1984–87, Dir (non-exec.) 1987–90; Conservative MP for Boothferry 1987–97, for Haltemprice and Howden 1997–; Asst Govt Whip 1990–93; Parl. Sec. Office of Public Service and Science, Cabinet Office 1993–94; Minister of State, FCO 1994–97; Chair. House of Commons Public Accounts Cttee 1997–; cand. Conservative Party leadership election 2001; Chair. Conservative Party 2001–02; Shadow Sec. of State for the Office of the Deputy Prime Minister 2002–; Chair. Fed. of Conservative Students 1973–74; Chair. Financial Policy Cttee, Confed. of British Industry 1977–79. *Publications:* BBC Guide to Parliament, How to Turn Round a Business; numerous articles on business and politics. *Leisure* *interests:* writing, mountaineering. *Address:* House of Commons, London, SW1A 0AA, England (Office). *Telephone:* (20) 7219-4183 (Office). *E-mail:* davisd@parliament.uk.

DAVIS, Don H., MBA; American business executive; ed Texas A & M Univ.; joined Allen-Bradley Co. 1963, Pres. 1989; fmrly Exec. Vice-Pres., COO Rockwell Automation and Semiconductor Systems, Pres. Automation, Rockwell Int. Corpn 1993, Sr Vice-Pres. 1993, Pres., COO 1995–97, Pres., CEO 1997–98, Chair., CEO 1998–; Dir Ingram Micro Inc., Sybron Corpn; mem. Bd numerous orgs. *Address:* Rockwell International Corporation, 777 East Wisconsin Avenue, Suite 1400, Milwaukee, WI 53202, USA (Office).

DAVIS, Geena, BFA; American actress; b. 21 Jan. 1957, Wareham, Mass.; m. 1st Richard Emmolo 1981 (divorced 1983); m. 2nd Jeff Goldblum (q.v.) (divorced 1990); m. 3rd Renny Harlin 1993 (divorced); m. 4th Reza Jarrahy 2001; one d.; ed Boston Univ.; mem. Mount Washington Repertory Theatre Co.; worked as a model. *Films include:* Tootsie 1982, Fletch 1984, Transylvania 6-5000 1985, The Fly 1986, Beetlejuice 1988, The Accidental Tourist 1988 (Acad. Award for Best Supporting Actress), Earth Girls are Easy 1989, Quick Change 1990, The Grifters, Thelma and Louise 1991, A League of Their Own 1992, Hero 1992, Angie 1994, Speechless (also producer) 1994, Cutthroat Island 1995, The Long Kiss Goodnight 1996, Stuart Little 1999, Stuart Little 2 2002. *TV appearances include:* Buffalo Bill, Sara, Family Ties, Remington Steele, Secret Weapons (TV film), The Geena Davis Show 2000. *Address:* c/o ICM, 8942 Wilshire Boulevard, Beverly Hills, CA 90211, USA.

DAVIS, Gray, JD, BA; American politician; b. 26 Dec. 1942; m. Sharon Ryer 1983; ed Stanford and Columbia Univs.; Chief of Staff to Gov. of Calif. 1974–81, State Rep. 1982–86, State Controller 1986–94, Lt Gov. 1994–99, Gov. of Calif. 1999–; mem. various bds; f. Calif. Foundation for the Protection of Children; Democrat. *Address:* Governor's Office, State Capitol, Sacramento, CA 95814-4906, USA.

DAVIS, James Othello, MD, PhD; American physician; b. 12 July 1916, Tahlequah, Okla; s. of Zemry Davis and Villa (Hunter) Davis; m. Florrilla L. Sides 1941; one s. one d.; ed Univ. of Missouri and Washington Univ. School of Medicine, St Louis, Mo.; Intern and Fellow, Barnes Hospital, St Louis 1946; Investigator, Gerontology Unit, Nat. Heart Inst., Bethesda, Md and Baltimore City Hosp. 1947–49; Investigator, Lab. of Kidney and Electrolyte Metabolism 1949–57; Chief, Section on Experimental Cardiovascular Disease, Nat. Heart Inst., Bethesda, Md 1957–66; Prof. and Chair. Dept of Physiology, Univ. of Mo. School of Medicine 1966–82, Prof. Emer. 1982–; discovered and defined the important relationship of the renin-angiotensin system to the control of aldosterone secretion; mem. NAS and numerous other professional socs and orgs; James O. Davis Distinguished Lecturership in Cardiovascular Science est. in his honour 1995; several awards and honours. *Publications:* more than 260 scientific publications. *Leisure interests:* trout fishing, travel, tennis. *Address:* 612 Maplewood Drive, Columbia, MO 65203-1764, USA. *Telephone:* (573) 443-7878 (Home).

DAVIS, John Horsley Russell, PhD, FBA; British professor of social anthropology; b. 9 Sept. 1938; s. of William Russell Davis and Jean Davis (née Horsley); m. Dymphna Gerarda Hermans 1981; three s.; ed Univ. Coll. Oxford and Univ. of London; Lecturer, Sr Lecturer, Reader in Social Anthropology, then Prof. Univ. of Kent 1966–90 (f. Centre for Social Anthropology and Computing 1983); Prof. of Social Anthropology, Univ. of Oxford 1990–95; Fellow, All Souls Coll. Oxford 1990–95, Warden 1995–; Chair. European Asscn of Social Anthropologists 1993–94; Pres. Royal Anthropological Inst. 1997–2001. *Publications:* Land and Family in Pisticci 1973, People of the Mediterranean 1977, Libyan Politics: Tribe and Revolution 1987, Exchange 1992. *Leisure interests:* gardens, music. *Address:* All Souls College, Oxford, OX1 4AL, England. *Telephone:* (1865) 279300. *E-mail:* jd@mukh.asc.ox.ac.uk. *Website:* www.all-souls.ox.ac.uk.

DAVIS, Judy; Australian actress; b. 23 April 1956, Perth; m. Colin Friels; one s. one d. *Films include:* My Brilliant Career, High Tide, Kangaroo, A Woman Called Golda, A Passage to India, Impromptu, Alice, Barton Fink, Where Angels Fear To Tread, Naked Lunch, Husbands and Wives, The Ref, The New Age, Children of the Revolution, Blood and Wine, Absolute Power, Deconstructing Harry, Celebrity, Gaudi Afternoon, Me and My Shadows, Life with Judy Davis (TV) 2001 (Golden Globe). *Address:* c/o Shanahan Management Pty Ltd, P.O. Box 478, King's Cross, NSW 2011, Australia.

DAVIS, Leonard Andrew; Australian engineer and business executive; b. 3 April 1939, Port Pirie; s. of Leonard Harold Davis and Gladys Davis; m. Annette Brakenridge 1963; two d.; ed S. Australian Inst. of Tech.; Man. Dir Pacific Coal 1984–89; Group Exec. CRA Ltd 1989–91; Mining Dir RTZ Corpn 1991–94; Man. Dir, Chief Exec. CRA Ltd 1994–95; Deputy Chief Exec., COO RTZ–CRA 1996; CEO Rio Tinto 1996–2000, Deputy Chair. 2000–; Hon. DSc 1998. *Address:* Rio Tinto PLC, 6 St James's Square, London, SW1Y 4LD, England; Rio Tinto Ltd, 35th Floor, 55 Collins Street, Melbourne, Vic. 3000, Australia. *Telephone:* (20) 7930-2399 (London) (Office); (3) 9283-3333 (Melbourne) (Office). *Fax:* (20) 7930-3249 (London) (Office).

DAVIS, Nathaniel, PhD; American diplomatist and professor of humanities; b. Nathaniel Davis, 12 April 1925, Boston, Mass.; s. of Harvey Nathaniel Davis and Alice Marion Rohde; m. Elizabeth Kirkbride Creese 1956; two s. two d.; ed Phillips Exeter Acad., Brown Univ., Fletcher School of Law and Diplomacy, Cornell Univ., Middlebury Coll., Columbia Univ., Univ. Central de Venezuela; Asst in History, Tufts Univ. 1947; Lecturer in History, Howard

Univ. 1962–65, 1966–68; Third Sec., US Embassy, Prague 1947–49; Vice-Consul, Florence 1949–52; Second Sec., Rome 1952–53, Moscow 1954–56; Deputy Officer-in-Charge, Soviet Affairs, Dept of State 1956–60; First Sec., Caracas 1960–62; Special Asst to Dir of Peace Corps 1962–63, Deputy Assoc. Dir 1963–65; Minister to Bulgaria 1965–66; Sr Staff, Nat. Security Council, White House 1966–68; Amb. to Guatemala 1968–71, to Chile 1971–73; Dir-Gen. US Foreign Service 1973–75; Asst Sec. of State for African Affairs April–Dec. 1975; Amb. to Switzerland 1975–77; State Dept Adviser, Naval War Coll. 1977–83; Alexander and Adelaide Hixon Emer. Prof. of Humanities, Harvey Mudd Coll., Claremont, Calif. 1983–; Lecturer Naval War Coll., San Diego 1991–; Del., Democratic Nat. Convention 1988, 1992, 1996, 2000; Fulbright Scholar 1996–97; mem. Exec. Bd Calif. Democratic Party. American Acad. of Diplomacy 1990–; Hon. LLD (Brown Univ.) 1970; Hartshorn Premium 1942, Caesar Misch Premium 1942; Cinco Aguilas Blancas Alpinism Award 1962, US Navy's Distinguished Public Service Award 1983, Elvira Roberti Award for Outstanding Leadership, LA County Democratic Party 1995, Prism Award for Public Service, Claremont Democratic Club 1999. *Publications:* The Last Two Years of Salvador Allende 1985, Equality and Equal Security in Soviet Foreign Policy 1986, A Long Walk to Church: A Contemporary History of Russian Orthodoxy 1995. *Leisure interests:* skiing, mountain climbing, white water canoeing, water-colour painting. *Address:* Harvey Mudd College, 301 E 12th Street, Claremont, CA 91711-5990 (Office); 1783 Longwood Avenue, Claremont, CA 91711, USA (Home). *Telephone:* (909) 607-3384 (Office); (909) 624-5293 (Home). *Fax:* (909) 607-7600 (Office); (909) 621-8360.

DAVIS, Sir Peter (John), Kt, FRSA; British business executive; b. 23 Dec. 1941, Heswall, Cheshire; s. of John Stephen Davis and Adriaantje Davis (née de Baat); m. Susan J. Hillman 1968; two s. one d.; ed Shrewsbury School, Inst. of Marketing; man. trainee, The Ditchburn Org., Lytham, Lancs. 1959–65; Gen. Foods Ltd, Banbury, Oxon. 1965–72; Marketing Dir Key Markets 1973; Man. Dir David Grieg and Group Man. Dir Key Markets, David Grieg 1975–76; Departmental Dir (non-foods) J. Sainsbury PLC 1976, mem. Bd responsible for marketing 1977, Asst Man. Dir Buying and Marketing and Dir Sava Centre 1979–86; Dir then Deputy Chair. Homebase Ltd 1983–86; Group CEO J. Sainsbury PLC 2000–; Dir Shaws Supermarkets, USA 1984–86; Deputy Chief Exec. Reed Int. PLC 1986, Chief Exec. 1986–94, Chair. 1990–94, CEO and Deputy Chair. of Reed Elsevier 1993 (following merger Jan. 1993), Co-Chair. 1993–94; Vice-Pres. Chartered Inst. of Marketing 1991–; Chair. Nat. Advisory Council for Educ. and Training Targets 1993–97, Basic Skills Agency 1991–97, New Deal Task Force 1997–2000; Deputy Chair. Business in the Community 1991–97 (Chair. 1997–2002); Founder and Bd mem. Marketing Council 1994–; Dir (non-exec.) Granada Group 1987–91; Dir British Satellite Broadcasting (BSB) 1988–90; Dir (non-exec.) Boots Co. 1991–2000, Prudential Corpn 1994–95 (Group Chief Exec. 1995–2000, 2001), UBS AG 2001–; Trustee Royal Opera House 1994–, Victoria and Albert Museum 1994–96; mem. Royal Opera House Bd 2000–, Royal Opera House Foundation 2001; Hon. LLD (Exeter) 2000. *Leisure interests:* sailing, opera, reading, wine. *Address:* J. Sainsbury PLC, 33 Holborn, London, EC1N 2HT, England (Office). *Telephone:* (20) 7695-6000 (Office). *Fax:* (20) 7695-2740 (Office). *E-mail:* spjd@tao.sainsburys.co.uk (Office). *Website:* www.j-sainsbury.co.uk (Office).

DAVIS, Raymond Jr., PhD; American nuclear chemist; b. 14 Oct. 1914, Washington, DC; s. of Raymond Davis and Ida Rogers Davis; m. Anna Marsh Torrey 1948; three s. two d.; ed Univ. of Maryland and Yale Univ.; Dow Chemical Co. 1937–38; served USAF 1942–46; Monsanto Chemical Co. (Mound Lab.) 1946–48; Brookhaven Nat. Lab. 1948–84; Research Prof., Dept of Physics and Astronomy, Univ. of Pa 1985–; Boris Pregel Prize (with O. A. Schaeffer, New York Acad. of Sciences) 1957, Comstock Award (NAS) 1978, American Chem. Soc. Award for Nuclear Chem. 1979, Tom Banner Prize (American Physical Soc.) 1988, W.K.H. Panofsky Prize (American Physical Soc.) (jtly) 1991, Beatrice Tinsley Prize (American Astronomical Soc.) 1994, George Ellory Hale Prize (American Astronomical Soc.) 1996, Bruno Pontecorvo Prize 1999, Wolf Prize in Physics (shared) 2000, Nobel Prize in Physics 2002. *Publications:* Several articles on neutrinos and lunar rock study. *Leisure interests:* sailing and tennis. *Address:* Department of Physics and Astronomy, University of Pennsylvania, Philadelphia, PA 19104 (Office); 28 Bergen Lane, Blue Point, NY 11715, USA (Home). *Telephone:* (215) 898-8176 (Office); (516) 363-6521 (Home). *E-mail:* rdavis@systec.com (Office).

DAVIS, Steve, OBE; British snooker player; b. 22 Aug. 1957, Plumstead, London; s. of Harry George Davis and Jean Catherine Davis; m. Judith Lyn Greig 1990; two s.; ed Alexander McLeod Primary School, Abbey Wood School, London; became professional snooker player 1978; has won 73 titles; in 99 tournament finals (2002); in list of top 16 players for record 20 seasons; major titles include: UK Professional Champion 1980, 1981, 1984, 1985, 1986, 1987; Masters Champion 1981, 1982, 1988, 1997; Int. Champion 1981, 1983, 1984; World Professional Champion 1981, 1983, 1984, 1987, 1988, 1989; winner Asian Open 1992, European Open 1993, Welsh Open 1994; mem. Bd World Professional Billiards and Snooker Asscn 1993–; regular snooker presenter on BBC TV; BBC Sports Personality of the Year 1989, BBC TV Snooker Personality of the Year 1997. *Television:* Steve Davis and Friends (chat show). *Publications:* Steve Davis, World Champion 1981, Frame and Fortune 1982, Successful Snooker 1982, How to Be Really Interesting 1988, Steve Davis

Plays Chess 1996. *Leisure interests:* collecting R & B and soul records, chess, Tom Sharpe books. *Address:* 10 Western Road, Romford, Essex, RM1 3JT, England. *Telephone:* (1708) 782200. *Fax:* (1708) 723425 (Office).

DAVIS, Sir Thomas Robert Alexander Harries, KBE, MD; Cook Islands politician (retd) and university chancellor; b. 11 June 1917, Ruatonga, Rarotonga; s. of Sydney Thomes Davis and Maryanne Harries; m. 1st Myra Lydia Henderson 1940; three s.; m. 2nd Pa Tepaeru Ariki 1979; m. 3rd Carla Cassata 2000; one d.; ed Otago Univ. and Medical School, Univ. of Sydney, Harvard School of Public Health; Medical Officer and Surgeon Specialist, Cook Islands Medical Service 1945–48; Research mem. Dept of Nutrition, Harvard School of Public Health 1952; Head of Dept of Environmental Medicine, Arctic Aero-medical Laboratory, Fairbanks, Alaska 1955–56; US Army Medical Research Laboratory, Fort Knox, Ky 1956–61; Dir of Research, US Army Research Inst. of Environmental Medicine 1961–63; employed by Arthur D. Little, Inc. 1963–71; returned to Cook Islands 1971, formed Democratic Party; also runs medical practice in Rarotonga; Prime Minister of Cook Islands 1978–87 (numerous other portfolios); Chancellor South Seas Univ. 2000–; Chair. Team Cook Islands, Volvo around the world Yacht Race; designed and built two Polynesian canoes 1991–95; Fellow, Royal Soc. of Tropical Medicine and Hygiene, Royal Soc. of Medicine; mem. NZ Medical Asscn, Cook Islands Medical and Dental Asscn, Visitors' Bd of Dirs, Bishop Museum, Hawaii; Chair. Voyaging Canoe Building Cttee, Library and Museum Devt Cttee; Pres. Library, Museum Soc. 1991–92; Hon. mem. Alaska Territorial Medical Asscn; Patron Rarotonga Sailing Club, Auatiu Sports Club; Silver Jubilee Medal 1977, Order of Merit, Fed. Repub. of Germany, Papua New Guinea Independence Medal, Cook Islands Sports Achievement Award 1999, Pacific Islander of the Century, Achievers magazine 1999. *Publications:* Doctor to the Islands 1954, Makutu 1956, Island Boy 1992, Vaka 1992 and over 100 scientific and other publications. *Leisure interests:* big game fishing, ham radio, music, planting vegetables, yachting, traditional canoeing. *Address:* P.O. Box 116, Aremango, Rarotonga, Cook Islands. *Telephone:* 27400. *Fax:* 27401. *E-mail:* davis@gatepoly.co.ck (Office).

DAVISON, Alan, PhD, DIC, FRS; British professor of chemistry; b. 24 March 1936, Ealing; ed Univ. Coll. of Swansea, Imperial Coll. of Science and Tech.; lecturer in chem., Harvard Univ. 1962–64; Asst Prof. MIT 1964–67, Assoc. Prof. 1967–74, Prof. of Inorganic Chem. 1974–; maj. research interests: Technetium and Rhenium chem., radiopharmaceutical chem. and bioinorganic chem.; Alfred P. Sloan Foundation Fellow 1967–69; Hon. Fellowship, Univ. Coll. of Swansea 1990; Herbert M. Stauffer Award for Outstanding Laboratory Paper 1990, Paul C. Aebersold Award for Outstanding Achievement in Basic Science applied to Nuclear Medicine 1993. *Publications:* numerous publs articles and papers published. *Address:* Department of Chemistry, Massachusetts Institute of Technology, Cambridge, MA 02139 (Office); 80 Cass Street, West Roxbury, MA 02132, USA (Home). *Telephone:* (617) 253-1794 (Office). *Fax:* (617) 258-6989 (Office). *E-mail:* adavison@mit.edu (Office). *Website:* www.mit.edu/chemistry (Office).

DAVISON, Edward Joseph, BASc, MA, PhD, ScD, FIEEE, FRSC, ARCT; Canadian professor of engineering; b. 12 Sept. 1938, Toronto; s. of Maurice J. Davison and Agnes E. Quinlan; m. Zofia M. Perz 1966; four c.; ed Royal Conservatory of Music, Toronto and Univs. of Toronto and Cambridge, UK; Asst Prof. Dept of Electrical Eng, Univ. of Toronto 1964–66, 1967–68, Assoc. Prof. 1968–74, Prof. Dept of Electrical Eng 1974–, Univ. Prof. Dept of Electrical and Computer Eng 2001–; Asst Prof. Univ. of Calif., Berkeley 1966–67; Pres. IEEE Control Systems Soc. 1983 (Distinguished mem. 1984–); Chair. Int. Fed. of Automatic Control (IFAC) Theory Cttee 1987–90, mem. IFAC Council 1991–93, 1993–96, Vice-Chair. IFAC Tech. Bd 1991–93, Vice-Chair. IFAC Policy Cttee 1996–99; Dir Electrical Eng Assocs Ltd, Toronto 1977–, Pres. 1997–; Consulting Engineer Asscn of Professional Engineers of Prov. of Ont. 1979–; Killam Research Fellowship 1979, 1981, E.W.R. Steacie Research Fellowship 1974, Athlone Fellowship 1961; Hon. Prof. Beijing Inst. of Aeronautics and Astronautics 1986; mem. Russian Acad. of Nonlinear Sciences 1998–; IEEE Centennial Medal 1984, IFAC Quazza Medal 1993, IFAC Outstanding Service Award 1996, Hendrik W Bode Lecture Prize (IEEE Control Systems Soc.) 1997. *Publications:* more than 400 research papers in numerous journals. *Leisure interests:* backpacking, skiing. *Address:* Department of Electrical Engineering, University of Toronto, Toronto, Ont., M5S 1A4, Canada. *Telephone:* (416) 978-6342. *Fax:* (416) 978-0804. *E-mail:* ted@control.utoronto.ca (Office). *Website:* www.control.utoronto.ca/people/profs/ted/ted.htm/ (Office).

DAVISON, Ian Frederic Hay, BScC, FCA; British business executive and accountant (retd); b. 30 June 1931; s. of late Eric Hay Davison and Inez Davison; m. Maureen Patricia Blacker 1955; one s. two d.; ed Dulwich Coll., LSE and Univ. of Michigan, USA; mem. Inst. of Chartered Accountants (mem. Council 1975–99); Man. Partner Arthur Andersen & Co., Chartered Accountants 1966–82; Ind. mem. NEDC for Bldg Industry 1971–77; mem. Price Comm. 1977–79; Chair. Review Bd for Govt Contracts 1981; Chief Exec. and Deputy Chair. Lloyd's 1983–86; Dept of Trade Insp., London Capital Securities 1975–77; Insp. Grays Bldg Soc. 1978–79; Chair. Accounting Standards Cttee 1982–84; Chair. The Nat. Mortgage Bank PLC 1992–2000, Roland Berger Ltd 1996–98; Chair. Dubai Financial Services Authority 2002–; Chair. Rutter Investment Man. 2002–; Chair. (non-exec.) MDIS (fmrly McDonnell Information Systems) 1993–99, Newspaper Publrs (Dir 1986–94) 1993–94; Chair. Monteverdi Trust 1979–84, Sadler's Wells Foundation 1995–, Pro Provost RCA 1996–, Crédit Lyonnais Capital Markets 1988–91, Charte-

rail 1991–92; Chair. Nat. Council for One-Parent Families 1991–; Dir Morgan Grenfell Asset Man. 1986–88, Midland Bank PLC 1986–88, Storehouse PLC 1988–96 (Chair. 1990–96), Chloride PLC 1988–98, Cadbury Schweppes PLC 1990–2000, CIBA PLC 1991–96; Trustee, Victoria and Albert Museum 1984–93; Dir and Trustee, Royal Opera House, Covent Garden 1984–86; Trustee, SANE 1996– (Chair. 2000–02); Gov. LSE 1982–. *Publication:* Lloyd's: A View of the Room 1987. *Leisure interests:* music, theatre, bell-ringing. *Address:* 40 Earlham Street, London, WC2H 9LH, England.

DAVISON, Rt Hon Sir Ronald Keith, GBE, CMG, PC, LLB; New Zealand judge and lawyer; b. 16 Nov. 1920, Kaponga; s. of the late Joseph James Davison and Florence Minnie Davison; m. Jacqueline May Carr 1948; two s. (one deceased) one d.; ed Te Kuiti Dist High School, Auckland Univ.; served in Army, reaching rank of Lt, 1940–46; Flying Officer, RNZAF, Europe; called to bar 1948; partner, Milne, Meek and Davison 1948–53; pvt. practice 1953–; QC 1963–; Chief Justice of NZ 1978–89; Chair. Legal Aid Bd 1969–78; Chair. Environmental Council 1969–74; Chair. Aircrew Industrial Tribunal 1971–78; Chair. Montana Wines Ltd 1972–78; mem. Auckland Dist Law Soc. Council 1959–65, Pres. 1965–66; Dir, NZ Insurance Co. Ltd 1975–78; mem., Auckland Electric Power Bd 1958–71; mem., NZ Law Soc. Council 1964–66; fmr mem. Torts and Gen. Law Reform Cttee; Church Advocate, Auckland Diocese 1973–78; Vicar's Warden, St Mark's Church, Remuera 1974–78. *Leisure interests:* golf, fishing. *Address:* 1 Lichfield Road, Parnell, Auckland, New Zealand. *Telephone:* (9) 3020493.

DAVYDOV, Mikhail Ivanovich, DrMed; Russian clinical oncologist; b. 11 Oct. 1947, Konotop, Sumy region, Ukraine; s. of Ivan Ivanovich Davydov and Asmar Tamrazovna Davydova; m. Irina Borisovna Zborovskaya; one s.; ed Moscow 1st Sechenov Inst. of Medicine; researcher, Sr Researcher, Head of Lab., Head of Div., Deputy Dir Moscow Blokhin Oncological Scientific Centre, Russian Acad. of Medicine, Dir Research Inst. of Clinical Oncology 1980–, Prof. 1986–; mem. Int. Soc. of Surgeons, American and European Soc. of Surgeons, New York Acad. of Sciences; corresp. mem. Russian Acad. of Medicine; numerous decorations including Merited Worker of Science of Russia 1996. *Publications:* over 300 scientific publns on oncological surgery, including 3 monographs and 6 methodical films. *Leisure interests:* boxing, sports, hunting, classical and retro music. *Address:* Moscow Blokhin Oncological Scientific Centre, Russian Academy of Medical Sciences, Kashirskoye shosse 24, 115475 Moscow, Russia (Office). *Telephone:* (095) 324-11-14 (Office).

DAVYDOV, Oleg Dmitriyevich; Russian politician; b. 25 May 1940, Moscow; m.; three c.; ed Moscow Inst. of Construction Eng; staff mem. Inst. Hydroproject 1953–63; counsellor on foreign econ. activities in USSR Trade Missions in Finland, Libya and other countries, supervised construction of energy plants abroad; Deputy Chair. USSR State Cttee on Econ. Relations 1985–88, Deputy Minister of Foreign Econ. Relations 1988–91; mem. Bd of Dirs. and Exec. Bd NIPEC Oil Corpn, consultant Dagwig Bureau Consulting Co. 1991–92; First Deputy Minister of Foreign Econ. Relations of Russia Jan.–Sept. 1993, Minister 1993–97; Deputy Prime Minister 1994–97; First Deputy Chair. Co-ordinating Cttee, Interdepartmental Council for Mil. Tech. Policy (KMS) 1996–97; Counsellor Immatrom Voyma Co. 1997–; Chief Consultant Moscow Centre of Social, Political and Econ. Studies 1998–.

DAWAGIV, Luvsandorj; Mongolian diplomatist; b. 15 May 1943, Uyanga soum, Uburkhangai aimak (Prov.); s. of Luvsandorj Doljin and Dolgorgiv Seree; m. Maya Jagdal 1971; one s. two d.; ed Moscow State Inst. of Int. Relations, Diplomatic Acad., Moscow; joined Foreign Service of Mongolia in 1971; Attaché, London 1974; Deputy Head, Head of Dept 1984–90; Head of European and American Dept 1990–; Amb. to USA 1991–95; Head of Law, Treaty and Archives Dept 1995–; Deputy Dir First Dept (Asia and America) 1996–97, Ministry of External Relations; Dir 1997–2001; Amb. to Thailand 2001–; Order of Polar Star (Mongolia) 1991. *Leisure interests:* hunting, travelling. *Address:* Embassy of Mongolia, 90/3 Soi Areesamphan I, Thanon Phaholyothin, Phyathai, Bangkok 10400, Thailand (Office); Peace Avenue 7a, Ulan Bator 13, Mongolia. *Telephone:* (2) 278-5792 (Office); (1) 311311. *Fax:* (2) 278-4927 (Office); (1) 322127. *E-mail:* mongemb@loxinfo.co.th (Office).

DAWE, Donald Bruce, AO, MLitt, PhD; Australian writer; b. 15 Feb. 1930, Geelong; s. of Alfred John Dawe and Mary Ann Amelia Dawe; m. Gloria Desley Dawe (née Blain) 1964 (died 1997); two s. two d.; ed Northcote High School, Univs of Melbourne, New England and Queensland; Educ. Section, RAAF 1959–68; teacher, Downlands Sacred Heart Coll., Toowoomba, Queensland 1969–71; Lecturer, Sr Lecturer, Assoc. Prof., Faculty of Arts, Univ. of Southern Queensland 1971–93; Hon. DLitt (Univ. of Southern Queensland) 1995, (Univ. of NSW) 1997; Ampol Arts Award 1967, Patrick White Award 1980; Philip Hodgins Memorial Medal for Literary Excellence 1997. *Publications:* Condolences of the Season: Selected Poems 1971, Over Here, Hark! and Other Stories 1983, Essays and Opinions 1990, Mortal Instruments 1995, Sometimes Gladness: Collected Poems 1954–97 1997, A Poet's People 1999. *Leisure interests:* gardening, watching Australian Rules football. *Address:* 30 Cumming Street, Toowoomba, Queensland 4350, Australia. *Telephone:* (7) 4632-7525.

DAWKINS, (Clinton) Richard, FRS; British biologist; b. 26 March 1941, Nairobi, Kenya; s. of Clinton John Dawkins and Jean Mary Vyvyan (née Ladner) Dawkins; m. Hon. Lalla Ward 1992; one d. (by previous m.); Asst Prof. of Zoology Univ. of Calif., Berkeley 1967–69; Lecturer Oxford Univ. 1970–89, Reader in Zoology 1989–96, Charles Simonyi Prof. of the Public Understanding of Science 1996–; Fellow New College, Oxford 1970–; Hon. DLitt (St Andrews) 1995, (ANU) 1996; Hon. DSc (Westminster) 1997, (Hull) 2001; numerous awards including Nakayama Prize 1994, Int. Cosmos Prize 1997, Kistler Prize 2001. *Television includes:* Nice Guys Finish First, BBC 1985, The Blind Watchmaker, BBC 1986, Break the Science Barrier, Channel 4 1994, Royal Institution Christmas Lectures, BBC 1992. *Publications include:* The Selfish Gene 1976, The Extended Phenotype 1982, The Blind Watchmaker (RSL Prize 1987, LA Times Literature Prize 1987) 1986, River Out of Eden 1995, Climbing Mount Improbable 1996, Unweaving the Rainbow: Science, Delusion and the Appetite for Wonder 1998, A Devil's Chaplain (essays) 2003. *Leisure interest:* human intercourse. *Address:* Oxford University Museum, Parks Road, Oxford, OX1 3PW, England. *E-mail:* richard.dawkins@new.ox.ac.uk.

DAWKINS, Hon. John Sydney, BEc, RDA; Australian politician, economist and business adviser; b. 2 March 1947, Perth; m. 1st (divorced); one s. one d.; m. 2nd Maggie Dawkins 1987; one d. one step-s.; ed Scotch Coll., Roseworthy Agricultural Coll.; fmr mem. Senate, Univ. of W Australia; worked for Bureau of Agricultural Econs and Dept of Trade and Industry 1971–72; MP, House of Reps., Seat of Tangney, WA 1974–75, Seat of Fremantle, WA 1977–94; Minister for Finance and Minister Assisting the Prime Minister for Public Service Matters 1983–84, Minister for Trade and Minister Assisting the Prime Minister for Youth Affairs 1984–87, for Employment, Educ. and Training 1987–91, Treasurer 1991–93; Chair. Cairns Group of Agricultural Exporting Countries 1985–87, OECD Ministerial Council 1993, John Dawkins and Co. 1994–, Medical Corpn of Australasia 1997–, Elders Rural Services Ltd 1998–, mem. Bd Sealcorp Holdings, Fred Hollows Foundation, Indian Ocean Centre; fmr mem. Nat. Exec., Australian Labor Party, Party Vice-Pres. 1982–83; Australian Govt Special Investment Rep. 1994–95; Press Officer, WA Trades and Labor Council 1976–77; Hon. DUniv (Univ. of S Australia, Queensland Univ. of Tech.) 1997. *Leisure interests:* farming, viticulture, travel. *Address:* 25th Floor, 91 King William Street, Adelaide, SA 5000 (Office); 75 Church Terrace, Walkerville, SA 5081, Australia (Home). *Telephone:* (8) 82123667. *Fax:* (8) 82124228 (Office). *E-mail:* john.dawkins@sealcorp.com.au (Office).

DAWSON, Sir Daryl Michael, AC, KBE, CB, LLM; Australian judge; b. 12 Dec. 1933, Melbourne; s. of Claude Charles Dawson and Elizabeth May Dawson; m. Mary Louise Thomas 1971; ed Canberra High School and Melbourne and Yale Univs.; admitted to Bar, Vic. 1957; lecturer, Council of Legal Educ. 1962–74; mem. Ormond Coll. Council 1965–73 (Chair. 1992–93); QC 1971; mem. Victoria Bar Council 1971–74; admitted to Tasmania Bar 1972; Solicitor-Gen. State of Vic. 1974–82; mem. Australian Motor Sport Appeal Court 1974–86; Judge, High Court of Australia 1982–97; Judge, Hong Kong Court of Final Appeal 1997–; Adjunct Prof. Monash Univ. 1998–; Professorial Fellow Univ. of Melbourne 1998–; Fulbright Scholar 1955. *Leisure interest:* gardening. *Address:* P.O. Box 147, East Melbourne, Vic. 3002, Australia. *Telephone:* (3) 9417-2818. *Fax:* (3) 9417-4499.

DAWSON, Sandra Jane Noble, BA, CIMgt; British college principal and professor of management studies; b. 4 June 1946, Bucks.; d. of Wilfred Denyer and Joy Denyer (née Noble); m. Henry R. C. Dawson 1969; one s. two d.; ed Dr Challoner's Grammar School, Amersham, Univ. of Keele; research officer Govt Social Survey 1968–69; research officer, then lecturer, sr lecturer Industrial Sociology Unit, Dept of Social and Econ. Studies, Imperial Coll. of Science, Tech. and Medicine 1969–90, Prof. of Organizational Behaviour, Man. School 1990–95; KPMG Prof. of Man. Studies and Dir Judge Inst. of Man. Studies, Univ. of Cambridge 1995–, also Fellow Jesus Coll. 1995–99; Master Sidney Sussex Coll., Cambridge 1999–; Chair Riverside Mental Health Trust 1992–95; Dir (non.-exec.) Riverside Health Authority 1990–92, Cambridge Econometrics 1996–, Fleming Claverhouse Investment Trust 1996–; mem. Research Strategy Bd, Offshore Safety Div., Health and Safety Exec. 1991–95, Strategic Review Group, Public Health Lab. Service 1994–99, Sr Salaries Review Body 1997–, Econ. and Social Research Council Research Priorities Bd 2000–; Hon. Fellow Jesus Coll. Cambridge; Fellow City & Guilds of London Inst. 1999; Hon. DLitt (Keele) 2000;Hon. DSc; Anglian Businesswoman of the Year 2000. *Publications include:* Analysing Organisations 1986, Safety at Work: The Limits of Self Regulation 1988, Managing the NHS 1995, Policy Futures for UK Health 2000, papers on man. in learned journals. *Leisure interests:* music, walking, family. *Address:* Judge Institute of Management Studies, Trumpington Street, Cambridge, CB2 1AG; Sidney Sussex College, Cambridge, CB2 3HU, England. *Telephone:* (1223) 339590 (Judge Institute); (1223) 338800 (Sidney Sussex College). *E-mail:* s.dawson@jims.cam.ac.uk (Office).

DAWSON, Thomas C., II, MBA; American economist; b. 9 March 1948, Washington, DC; s. of Allan Duval Dawson and Jane Dodge Dawson; m. Moira Jane Haley 1974; two s. one d.; ed Stanford Univ., Woodrow Wilson School of Public and Int. Affairs, Princeton Univ.; fmrly economist, US Consulate Gen., Rio de Janeiro for US State Dept; fmr Consultant, McKinsey and Co.; Deputy Asst Sec. for Developing Nations, Treasury Dept 1981–84; Asst Sec. for Business and Consumer Affairs, Treasury Dept 1984–85; fmr Deputy Asst to the Pres. and Exec. Asst to Chief of Staff, the White House; fmr Special Asst to Asst Sec. for Int. Affairs, Treasury Dept; Exec. Dir IMF 1989–93, Dir External Relations Dept 1999–; First Vice-Pres. Merrill Lynch and Co. 1993–94, Dir 1995–. *Address:* International Monetary Fund, 700 19th Street,

NW, Washington, DC 20431 (Office); 50 Portland Road, Summit, NJ 07901, USA (Home). *Telephone:* (202) 623-7300 (Office). *Fax:* (202) 623-6278 (Office). *E-mail:* publicaffairs@imf.org (Office). *Website:* www.imf.org (Office).

DAY, Sir Derek (Malcolm), KCMG; British diplomatist; b. 29 Nov. 1927, London; s. of late Alan W. Day; m. Sheila Nott 1955; three s. one d.; ed Hurstpierpoint Coll. and St Catharine's Coll. Cambridge; RA 1946–48; entered diplomatic service 1951; served Tel Aviv 1953–56, Rome 1956–59, Washington, DC 1962–66, Nicosia 1972–75; Amb. to Ethiopia 1975–78; Asst Under-Sec. of State FCO 1979, Deputy Under-Sec. of State 1980, Chief Clerk 1982–84; High Commr in Canada 1984–87; Commr Commonwealth War Graves Comm. 1987–92; Vice-Chair. British Red Cross 1988–94; Dir Monenco Ltd, Canada 1988–92; Chair. Crystal Palace Sports and Leisure Ltd 1992–97; mem. Defence Medical Services Clinical Research Cttee 1995– (Chair. 1999); Gov. Hurstpierpoint Coll. 1987–97; Gov. Bethany School 1987–2000. *Address:* Etchinghill, Goudhurst, Kent, TN17 1JP, England. *Telephone:* (1580) 211114 (Home). *E-mail:* dandsday@virgin.net (Home).

DAY, Doris ((Doris von Kappelhoff)); American actress and singer; b. 3 April 1924, Cincinnati, Ohio; d. of Frederick Wilhelm and Alma Sophia von Kappelhoff; m. 1st Al Jorden 1941 (divorced 1943); one s.; m. 2nd George Weilder 1946 (divorced 1949); m. 3rd Marty Melcher 1951 (died 1968); m. 4th Barry Comden 1976 (divorced 1981); professional dancing appearances, Doherty and Kappelhoff, Glendale, Calif.; singer Karlin's Karnival, radio station WCPO; singer with bands, Barney Rapp, Bob Crosby, Fred Waring, Les Brown; singer and leading lady, Bob Hope radio show (NBC) 1948–50, Doris Day Show (CBS) 1952–53; singer for Columbia Records 1950–; with Warner Bros. film studio; Laurel Award, Leading New Female Personality in Motion Picture Industry 1950, Top Audience Attractor 1962, American Comedy Lifetime Achievement Award 1991. *Recordings:* albums: You're My Thrill 1949, Tea for Two 1950, Lullaby of Broadway 1951, On Moonlight Bay 1951, I'll See You in My Dreams 1951, By the Light of the Silvery Moon 1953, Young Man with a Horn 1954, Day Dreams 1955, Day in Hollywood 1955, Young at Heart 1955, Love Me or Leave Me 1955, Most Happy Fella 1956, Day by Day 1957, Hooray for Hollywood Vols I and II 1959, Cuttin' Capers 1959, Day by Night 1959, Boys and Girls Together 1959, Hot Canaries 1959, Lights Cameras Action 1959, Listen to Day 1960, Show Time 1960, What Every Girl Should Know 1960, I Have Dreamed 1961, Bright and Shiny 1961, You'll Never Walk Alone 1962, Duet 1962, The Best of Doris Day 2002; singles: Day by Day 1949, Sugarbush 1952, Secret Love 1954, The Black Hills of Dakota 1954, If I Give My Heart to You 1954, Ready Willing and Able 1955, Whatever Will Be Will Be (Que Sera Sera) 1956, Move Over Darling 1964. *Films include:* Romance on the High Seas 1948, My Dream is Yours 1949, Young Man With a Horn 1950, Tea for Two 1950, West Point Story 1950, Lullaby of Broadway 1951, On Moonlight Bay 1951, I'll See You in My Dreams 1951, April in Paris 1952, By the Light of the Silvery Moon 1953, Calamity Jane 1953, Lucky Me 1954, Yankee Doodle Girl 1954, Love Me or Leave Me 1955, The Pajama Game 1957, Teacher's Pet 1958, The Tunnel of Love 1958, It Happened to Jane 1959, Pillow Talk 1959, Please Don't Eat the Daisies 1960, Midnight Lace 1960, Lover Come Back 1962, That Touch of Mink 1962, Jumbo 1962, The Thrill of It All 1963, Send Me No Flowers 1964, Do Not Disturb 1965, The Glass Bottom Boat 1966, Caprice 1967, The Ballad of Josie 1968, Where Were You When the Lights Went Out? 1968, With Six You Get Egg Roll 1968, Sleeping Dogs, Hearts and Souls 1993, That's Entertainment III 1994. *Television includes:* The Doris Day Show 1968–72, The Pet Set 1972. *Address:* c/o Columbia Records, 550 Madison Avenue, New York, NY 10022 (Office); c/o Doris Day Animal League, 227 Massachusetts Avenue, NE, Washington, DC 20002, USA.

DAY, Sir (Judson) Graham, Kt, LLB; Canadian business executive; b. 3 May 1933; s. of Frank C. Day and Edythe G. (née Baker) Day; m. Leda A. Creighton 1958; one s. two d.; ed Queen Elizabeth High School, Halifax, NS and Dalhousie Univ., Halifax; pvt. law practice, Windsor, NS 1956–64; Canadian Pacific Ltd, Montréal and Toronto 1964–71; Deputy Chair. Org. Cttee for British Shipbuilders and Deputy Chair. and Chief Exec. desig., British Shipbuilders 1975–76; Prof. of Business Studies and Dir Canadian Marine Transportation Centre, Dalhousie Univ. 1977–81; Vice-Pres. Shipyards and Marine Devt, Dome Petroleum Ltd 1981–83; Chair. and CEO British Shipbuilders 1983–86; Chair. The Rover Group (fmrly BL) PLC 1986–91, CEO 1986–88; Dir Cadbury Schweppes PLC 1988–93, Chair. 1989–93; Deputy Chair. MAI 1989–93; Chair. British Aerospace 1991–92; Chair. PowerGen 1990–93, Dir 1990–93; Special Consultant to Ashurst Morris Crisp 1994–; Dir The Laird Group PLC 1985–, Bank of NS (Canada) 1989–, NOVA Corpn of Alberta 1990–; Dir (non-exec.) Ugland Int. Holdings (Deputy Chair. 1997–); Pres. Inc. Soc. of British Advertisers 1991–93; Fellow Univ. of Wales, Coll. of Cardiff 1992–; Dr. hc (Humberside) 1992 and numerous other hon. degrees. *Leisure interests:* reading, lakeside chalet in Canada. *Address:* 18 Avon Street, P.O. Box 423, Hantsport, NS, B0P 1P0, Canada.

DAY, Peter, DPhil, FRS; British scientist and academic; b. 20 Aug. 1938, Wrotham, Kent; s. of Edgar Day and Ethel Hilda Day (née Russell); m. Frances Mary Elizabeth Anderson 1964; one s. one d.; ed Maidstone Grammar School, Wadham Coll., Oxford; Cyanmid European Research Inst., Geneva 1962; Jr Research Fellow St John's Coll., Oxford 1963–65, Tutor 1965–91; Departmental Demonstrator Univ. of Oxford 1965–67, Lecturer in Inorganic Chemistry 1967–89; Oxford Univ. Prof. Associé de Paris-Sud 1975; Guest Prof. Univ. of Copenhagen 1978, Visiting Fellow ANU 1980; Du Pont Lecturer Indiana Univ. 1988; Sr Research Fellow SRC 1977–82; mem. Neutron Beam

Research Cttee Science and Eng Research Council 1983–88, Chem. Cttee 1985–88, Molecular Electronics Cttee 1987–88, Nat. Cttee on Superconductivity 1987–88, Materials Comm. 1988–90, Medicines Comm. 1998–; Vice-Pres. Dalton Div. Royal Soc. of Chemistry 1986–88; Dir Inst. Laue-Langevin, Grenoble 1988–91; Dir Royal Inst. and Davy Faraday Research Lab. 1991–98, Fullerian Prof. of Chemistry 1994–; Visiting Prof. Univ. Coll., London 1991, Royal Inst. Research Fellow 1995–; mem. Academia Europaea, Treas. 2000–; Hon. Foreign mem. Indian Acad. of Science; Hon. Fellow Wadham Coll. 1991, St John's Coll. 1996; Royal Soc. Bakerian Lecturer 1999; Hon. Fellow Univ. Coll. London 2003; Hon. DSc (Newcastle), (Kent); Corday-Morgan Medal 1971, Solid State Chem. Award 1986; Daiwa Adrian Prize 1999. *Publications:* Physical Methods in Advanced Inorganic Chemistry (jtly) 1968, Electronic States of Inorganic Compounds 1974, Emission and Scattering Techniques 1980, Electronic Structure and Magnetism of Inorganic Compounds (Vols 1–7) 1972–82, The Philosopher's Tree 1999; numerous papers on inorganic chem. in learned journals. *Leisure interest:* driving slowly through rural France. *Address:* The Royal Institution of Great Britain, 21 Albemarle Street, London, W1S 4BS (Office); 16 Dale Close, Oxford, OX1 1TU, England (Home). *Telephone:* (20) 7409-2992 (Office). *Fax:* (20) 7629-3569 (Office).

DAY, Peter Rodney, PhD; American (b. British) agricultural scientist; b. 27 Dec. 1928, Chingford, Essex; s. of Roland Percy Day and Florence Kate (née Dixon); m. Lois Elizabeth Rhodes 1950; two s. one d.; ed Chingford County High School and Birkbeck Coll., Univ. of London; John Innes Inst. 1946–63; Assoc. Prof., Ohio State Univ., Columbus, USA 1963–64; Chief, Genetics Dept, Conn. Agricultural Experiment Station, New Haven 1964–79; Dir Plant Breeding Inst., Cambridge, UK 1979–87; Dir Biotechnology Center for Agriculture and the Environment, Rutgers Univ., NB 1987–, Rutgers Univ. Prof. of Genetics 1987–; Special Professorship, Univ. of Nottingham 1981–87; Sec. Int. Genetics Fed. 1984–93; Pres. British Soc. for Plant Pathology 1985; Chair. Cttee on Managing Global Genetic Resources, NAS, USA 1986–94; mem. Exec. Cttee, Norfolk Agricultural Station 1980–1987, Cttee on Genetic Experimentation, Int. Council of Scientific Unions 1984–93, Bd of Trustees, Int. Centre for Maize and Wheat Improvement, 1986–92, panel mem. Int. Food Biotech. Council 1988–90; Fellow American Phytopathological Soc.; Commonwealth Fund Fellow, Univ. of Wis. 1954–56; John Simon Guggenheim Memorial Fellow, Univ. of Queensland 1972; non-resident Fellow Noble Foundation, Ardmore, Okla 1991–97; Frank Newton Prize, Birkbeck Coll., Univ. of London 1950. *Publications:* Fungal Genetics (with J. R. S. Fincham) 1963, Genetics of Host-Parasite Interactions 1974; more than 100 scientific papers. *Leisure interests:* music, Scottish country dancing. *Address:* Biotechnology Center for Agriculture and the Environment, Foran Hall, Cook College, Rutgers University, 59 Dudley Road, New Brunswick, NJ 08901-8520 (Office); 394 Franklin Road, North Brunswick, NJ 08902, USA (Home). *Telephone:* (732) 932-8165 (Office). *Fax:* (732) 932-6535. *E-mail:* day@aesop.rutgers.edu (Office). *Website:* njaes.rutgers.edu/~biotech (Office).

DAY, Stockwell Burt; Canadian politician; b. 16 Aug. 1950, Barrie, Ont.; s. of Stockwell Day and Gwendolyn Day (née Gilbert); m. Valorie Martin 1971; three s.; auctioneer, Alberta 1972–74; Dir Teen Challenge Outreach Ministries, Edmonton, Alberta 1974–75; contractor, Commercial Interiors, Alberta 1976–78; School Admin., Asst Pastor, Bentley (Alberta) Christian Centre 1978–85; mem. Legis. Ass. Alberta, Legislature, Edmonton 1986–, Govt Whip 1989–92, Govt House Leader 1994–97; Minister of Labour 1992–96, of Family and Social Services 1996–97; Prov. Treas., Acting Premier 1997–2000; Leader Canadian Alliance (fed. opposition party) 2000–. *Leisure interests:* tennis, roller blading, backpacking, reading. *Address:* The Canadian Alliance, Government of Alberta, Suite 600, 833 Fourth Avenue, SW, Calgary, AB, T2P 3T5, Canada (Office). *Telephone:* (403) 269-1990 (Office). *Fax:* (403) 269-4077 (Office). *Website:* www.canadianalliance.ca (Office).

DAY-LEWIS, Daniel; Irish actor; b. 20 April, London; s. of the late Cecil Day-Lewis and of Jill Balcon; m. Rebecca Miller 1996; two s.; one s. by Isabelle Adjani; ed Sevenoaks School, Sherington, SE London, Bedales and Bristol Old Vic Theatre School. *Films include:* My Beautiful Laundrette, A Room with a View, Stars and Bars, The Unbearable Lightness of Being, My Left Foot 1989 (Acad. Award for Best Actor, BAFTA Award, Best Actor), The Last of the Mohicans 1991, In the Name of the Father 1993, The Age of Innocence 1992, The Crucible 1995, The Boxer 1997, Gangs of New York (Screen Actors Guild Award for Best Actor 2003, BAFTA Award for Best Actor in a Leading Role 2003) 2002. *Plays include:* Class Enemy, Funny Peculiar, Bristol Old Vic; Look Back in Anger, Dracula, Little Theatre, Bristol and Half Moon Theatre, London; Another Country, Queen's Theatre; Futurists, Nat. Theatre; Romeo, Thisbe, RSC, Hamlet 1989. *Television includes:* A Frost in May, How Many Miles to Babylon?, My Brother Jonathan, Insurance Man. *Address:* c/o Julian Belfrage Associates, 46 Albemarle Street, London, W1S 4DF, England.

DAYTON, Mark; American politician; b. 26 Jan. 1947, Minneapolis; two s.; ed Yale Univ.; science teacher NY City Public Schools 1969–71; counsellor and admin. for a social service agency, Boston 1971–75; legis. asst to Walter Mondale, Senator of Minn. 1975–77; mem. staff Office of Gov. Rudy Perpich 1977–78; Commr of Econ. Devt, State of Minn. 1978–82, Commr of Energy and Econ. Devt 1982–86; Candidate for Senate 1982; elected Minn. State Auditor 1990–94; held key positions in election campaign of Senator Paul Wellstone 1995–96; Senator from Minn. 2001–, mem. Agric. Cttee, Armed Services Cttee, Rules Cttee, Governmental Affairs Cttee. *Address:* Office of the Senator from Minnesota, US Senate, Senate Buildings, Washington, DC 20510, USA (Office).

DÉ, Shobha; Indian author and journalist; b. 7 Jan. 1948, Satara, India; m. 1st (divorced); m. 2nd Dilip Dé 1984; four d. two s; ed Queen Mary's School, Bombay; fmr model; later copy-writer; launched India's first gossip magazine Stardust; also launched magazines Society, Celebrity and TV soap-opera Swabhimaan 1995. *Publications:* English-language novels: Socialite Evenings 1989, Strange Obsessions 1993, Snapshots, Small Betrayals (short stories), articles and columns in newspapers and magazines. *Leisure interests:* music, dancing, movies, reading. *Address:* c/o Penguin Books India, 11 Community Centre, Panchsheel, Park, New Delhi 110017, India. *Telephone:* (11) 6494401. *Fax:* (11) 6494403.

de BEAUCÉ, Thierry; French government official; b. 14 Feb. 1943, Lyon; s. of Bertrand Martin de Beauce and Simone de la Verpillère; two d.; ed Univ. of Paris and Ecole Nat. d'Admin; civil admin., Ministry of Cultural Affairs 1968–69; seconded to Office of Prime Minister 1969–73; Tech. Adviser, Pvt. Office of Pres. of Nat. Ass. 1974; seconded to Econ. Affairs Directorate, Ministry of Foreign Affairs 1974–76; Cultural Counsellor, Japan 1976–78; Second Counsellor, Morocco 1978–80; Vice-Pres. for Int. Affairs Société Elf Aquitaine 1981–86; Dir-Gen. of Cultural, Scientific and Tech. Relations, Ministry of Foreign Affairs 1986–87; State Sec. attached to Minister of Foreign Affairs 1988–91; Adviser to Pres. on African Affairs 1991–94; Vice-Pres. Conf. on Yugoslavia 1992; Amb. to Indonesia 1995–97; Dir of Int. Affairs, Vivendi 1997–; Chevalier, Légion d'honneur. *Publications:* Les raisons dangéreuses (essay) 1975, Un homme ordinaire (novel) 1978, L'Ile absolue (essay) 1979, Le désir de guerre 1980, La chute de Tanger (novel) 1984, Nouveau discours sur l'universalité de la langue française 1988, Le livre d'Esther 1989, La République de France 1991, La Nonchalence de Dieu 1995. *Address:* Vivendi, 52 rue d'Anjou, 75008 Paris (Office); 73 avenue F. D. Roosevelt, Paris 8, France (Home). *Telephone:* 1-45-63-22-37 (Home).

De BENEDETTI, Carlo; Italian company chairman; b. 14 Nov. 1934, Turin; m. Margherita Crosetti 1960; three s.; ed Turin Polytechnic; with Compagnia Italiana Tubi Metallici Flessibili 1959; Chair. and CEO Gilardini 1972–76; Dir Euromobiliare Finance Co. 1973–, Vice-Chair. 1977–; f. Compagnia Industriali Riunite (CIR) 1976, Vice-Chair. and CEO 1976–95, Chair. 1995–; f. Finco 1976 (renamed Cofide–Compagnia Finanziaria De Benedetti 1985), Vice-Chair. and CEO 1976–91, Chair. 1991–; Vice-Chair. and CEO Olivetti & Co. SpA 1978–83, Chair. and CEO 1983–96, Hon. Chair. 1996–99; Dir SMI SpA 1983–; Chair. Cerus (Paris) 1986–; Chair. Sogefi; f. CDB Web Tech 2000, Exec. Chair. 2000–; f. Rodolfo Debenedetti Foundation 1998, Chair. 1998–; Vice-Chair. European Round Table of Industrialists, Brussels; Vice-Pres. Confindustria 1984–; mem. Int. Council, Morgan Guaranty Trust 1980–; Chair. Fondiara 1989–; controlled Editore Arnoldo Mondadori 1990, half-share 1991–; Co-Chair. Council for USA and Italy; mem. Bd of Dirs Valeo, Pirelli, Gruppo Editoriale L'Espresso; mem. European Advisory Cttee, NY Stock Exchange, Int. Council, Centre for Strategic and Int. Studies, Int. Advisory Council, China Int. Trust and Investment Corpn, Beijing, Royal Swedish Acad. of Eng Science, Italian Council, European Inst. of Business Admin; under house arrest after questioning on corruption charges Nov. 1993, released Nov. 1993; sentenced to six years and four months' imprisonment, sentence reduced to four and a half years July 1996; cleared of fraud charges connected with collapse of Banco Ambrosiano Veneto Aug. 1998; Hon. LLD (Wesleyan Univ., Conn., USA) 1986; Cavaliere del Lavoro 1983, Officier, Légion d'honneur 1987. *Publications:* L'Avventura della Nuova Economia 2000, lectures and articles in business journals. *Address:* CIR SpA, Via Ciovassino 1, 20121 Milan, Italy. *Telephone:* 02722701. *Fax:* 0272270200 (Office).

DE BERNIÈRES, Louis, MA; British writer; b. Louis Henry Piers de Bernière-Smart, 8 Dec. 1954, London; s. of Maj. Reginald Piers Alexander de Bernière-Smart; ed Bradfield Coll., Manchester Univ., Leicester Polytechnic, Inst. of Educ., London Univ.; landscape gardener 1972–73; teacher and rancher, Colombia 1974; philosophy tutor 1977–79; car mechanic 1980; English teacher 1981–84; bookshop asst 1985–86; supply teacher 1986–93. *Publications:* The War of Don Emmanuel's Nether Parts 1990, Señor Vivo and the Coca Lord 1991, The Troublesome Offspring of Cardinal Guzman 1992, Captain Corelli's Mandolin 1994 (film 2001), The Book of Job 1999, Red Dog 2001. *Leisure interests:* music, literature, golf, fishing, carpentry, gardening, cats. *Address:* c/o Lavinia Trevor Agency, 7 The Glasshouse, 49A Goldhawk Road, London, W12 8QP, England (Office). *Telephone:* (20) 8749-8481 (Office).

DE BONIS, Donato; Italian ecclesiastic; b. 13 April 1930, Potenza; s. of Domenico De Bonis and Maria Vincenzina De Bonis; ed Lateran Univ.; ordained priest 1953; at the service of the Holy See 1953–; Prelate, Inst. for Religious Works 1989; Bishop, Kts. of Malta 1993; Gen. Treas. of Apostolic Admin. *Address:* Vatican City, 00193 Rome, Italy.

de BONO, Edward Francis Charles Publius, DPhil, PhD; British author and academic; b. 19 May 1933; s. of the late Prof. Joseph de Bono and of Josephine de Bono (née O'Byrne); m. Josephine Hall-White 1971; two s.; ed St Edward's Coll., Malta, Royal Univ. of Malta and Christ Church, Oxford; Research Asst, Univ. of Oxford 1958–60, Jr Lecturer in Medicine 1960–61; Asst Dir of Research, Dept of Investigative Medicine, Cambridge Univ. 1963–76, Lecturer in Medicine 1976–83; Dir Cognitive Research Trust, Cambridge 1971–; Sec.-Gen. Supranational Independent Thinking Org. (SITO) 1983–; f. Edward de Bono Nonprofit Foundation; Hon. Registrar St Thomas' Hosp. Medical School, Harvard Medical School; Hon. Consultant Boston City Hosp. 1965–66; Chair. Council, Young Enterprise Europe 1998–;

creator of two TV series: The Greatest Thinkers 1981, de Bono's Thinking Course 1982; planet DE73 named edebono after him. *Publications:* The Use of Lateral Thinking 1967, The Five-Day Course in Thinking 1968, The Mechanism of Mind 1969, Lateral Thinking: a textbook of creativity 1970, The Dog Exercising Machine 1970, Technology Today 1971, Practical Thinking 1971, Lateral Thinking for Management 1971, Children Solve Problems 1972, Po: Beyond Yes and No 1972, Think Tank 1973, Eureka: a history of inventions 1974, Teaching Thinking 1976, The Greatest Thinkers 1976, Wordpower 1977, The Happiness Purpose 1977, The Case of the Disappearing Elephant 1977, Opportunities: a handbook of Business Opportunity Search 1978, Future Positive 1979, Atlas of Management Thinking 1981, de Bono's Thinking Course 1982, Conflicts: a better way to resolve them 1985, Six Thinking Hats 1985, Letter to Thinkers 1987, I am Right You are Wrong 1990, Positive Revolution for Brazil 1990, Six Action Shoes 1991, Serious Creativity 1992, Teach Your Child to Think 1992, Water Logic 1993, Parallel Thinking 1994, Teach Yourself to Think 1995, Mind Pack 1995, Edward de Bono's Textbook of Wisdom 1996, How to be More Interesting 1997, Simplicity 1998, New Thinking for the New Millennium 1999, Why I Want to be King of Australia 1999, The Book of Wisdom 2000, The de Bono Code 2000 and numerous publs in Nature, Lancet, Clinical Science, American Journal of Physiology. *Leisure interests:* travel, toys, thinking. *Address:* Cranmer Hall, Fakenham, Norfolk, NR21 9HX, England (Home); L2 Albany, Piccadilly, London, W1V 9RR. *Website:* www.edwarddebono.com (Office).

DE BONT, Jan; cinematographer and director; b. 22 Oct. 1943, Netherlands; ed Amsterdam Film Acad. *Cinematography:* Turkish Delight, Keetje Tippel, Max Heuelaar, Soldier of Orange, Private Lessons (American debut) 1981, Roar, I'm Dancing as Fast as I Can, Cujo, All the Right Moves, Bad Manners, The Fourth Man, Mischief, The Jewel of the Nile, Flesh and Blood, The Clan of the Cave Bear, Ruthless People, Who's That Girl, Leonard Part 6, Die Hard, Bert Rigby—You're A Fool, Black Rain, The Hunt for Red October, Flatliners 1990, Shining Through 1992, Basic Instinct, Lethal Weapon 3, 1992. *TV (photography):* The Ray Mancini Story, Split Personality (episode of Tales from the Crypt). *Films directed:* Speed (debut) 1994, Twister, Speed 2: Cruise Control (also screenplay and story), The Haunting. *Address:* c/o David Gersh, The Gersh Agency, 232 North Canon Drive, Beverly Hills, CA 90210, USA.

DE BORTOLI, Ferruccio; Italian journalist; b. 20 May 1953, Milan; s. of Giovanni De Bortoli and Giancarla Soresini; m. Elisabetta Cordani 1982; one s. one d.; ed Univ. of Milan; journalist 1973–; mem. editorial staff, Corriere d'Informazione 1975–78; Econs Corresp. Corriere della Sera 1978–85; Ed.-in-Chief, L'Europeo (magazine) 1985–86; Ed.-in-Chief, Econs Section, Corriere della Sera 1987–93; Deputy Ed. Corriere della Sera 1993–96, Ed. 1997–. *Leisure interests:* reading, music, skiing. *Address:* Via Solferino 28, 20122 Milan (Office); Via Donatello 36, 20131 Milan, Italy (Home). *Telephone:* 0262827560 (Office). *Fax:* 0229009705 (Office). *E-mail:* fdebortoli@corriere.it (Office). *Website:* www.corriere.it (Office).

de BREE, Jr., Simon; Netherlands business executive; b. 14 April 1937, Koudekerke; s. of Cornelis de Bree and Leintje Minderhoud; m. Judith Rijkée 1963; one s. one d.; ed Univ. of Tech. Delft; research scientist, DSM NV 1966–69, Acquisition Dept 1969–73, Sales and Marketing, Plastics Div. 1973–80, Man. Polymers Group 1980–83, Pres. Polymers Group 1983–86; mem. Man. Bd DSM NV 1986–93, Chair. Man. Bd 1993–; Kt, Order of Netherlands Lion. *Leisure interests:* skiing, skating, cycling. *Address:* DSM NV, P.O. Het Overloon 1, 6411 TE Heerlen, The Netherlands. *Telephone:* (45) 578-2423. *Fax:* (45) 574-0680.

de BROGLIE, Prince Gabriel Marie Joseph Anselme; French administrator; b. 21 April 1931, Versailles; s. of Prince Edouard de Broglie and Princess Hélène Le Bas de Courmont; m. Diane de Bryas 1953; one s. one d.; ed Ecole Saint-Martin de France, Faculté de droit de Paris and Inst. d'études politiques; Auditor Conseil d'Etat 1960, Counsel 1967; Legal Adviser to Sec.-Gen., Interdepartmental Cttee on matters of European econ. co-operation 1964; Tech. Adviser, Ministry of Social Affairs 1966–68, to Prime Minister 1968–69, Minister of State for Cultural Affairs 1970; Sec.-Gen. Office de Radiodiffusion-Télévision Française 1971, Asst Dir-Gen. 1973; Dir Radio-France 1975–79, Dir-Gen. 1977–79; Pres. Inst. nat. de l'audiovisuel 1979–1981; mem. Haut Conseil de l'Audiovisuel 1972; Pres. Univ. Radiophonique et Télévisuelle Int. 1976–87, Hon. Pres. 1987; Vice-Pres., later Pres. TV Historical Cttee 1980; Pres. Comm. Nat. de la Communication et des Libertés 1986–89; Pres. Soc. des Bibliophiles Français; mem. Acad. des Sciences Morales et Politiques 1997, L'Académie française 2001–; Commdr, Légion d'honneur, Ordre nat. du Mérite, Commdr des Arts et Lettres. *Publications include:* Le Général de Valence ou l'insouciance et la gloire 1972, Ségur sans cérémonie, ou la gaieté libertine 1977, L'histoire politique de la Revue des Deux Mondes 1979, L'Orléanisme, la ressource libérale de la France 1981, Une image vaut dix mille mots 1982, Madame de Genlis (Gobert Prize) 1985, Le français, pour qu'il vive 1986, Guizot (Amb.'s Prize) 1990, Le XIXᵉ siècle, l'éclat et le déclin de la France 1995, Mac Mahon 2000. *Leisure interest:* books. *Address:* Institut de France, 23 quai Conti, 75006 Paris; 96 rue de Grenelle, 75007 Paris, France (Home).

De BURGH, Chris; British singer and songwriter; b. 15 Oct. 1948, Argentina; m. Diane Patricia Morley; two s. one d.; ed Trinity Coll. Dublin. *Albums include:* Far Beyond These Castle Walls 1975, Spanish Train & Other Stories 1975, End Of A Perfect Day 1977, Crusader 1979, Eastern Wind 1980, Best Moves 1981, Man On The Line 1984, Very Best of 1984, Into the Light

(including No. 1 UK hit song The Lady In Red) 1986, Beautiful Dreams 1995, The Love Songs Album 1997, Quiet Revolution 1999, Notes From Planet Earth—The Ultimate Collection 2001, Timing is Everything 2002. *Address:* Kenny Thomson Management, 754 Fulham Road, London, SW6 5SH, England. *Telephone:* (20) 7731-7074. *Fax:* (20) 7736-8605. *E-mail:* ktmuk@dircon .co.uk (Office).

de CASTELLA, (François) Robert, MBE, BSc; Australian athlete, biophysicist, company director and consultant; b. 27 Feb. 1957, Melbourne; s. of Rolet François de Castella and Ann M. Hall; m. Gayelene J. Clews 1980 (divorced 1998); two s.; ed Xavier Coll., Kew, Monash Univ. and Swinburne Inst. of Tech.; winner, Fukuoka Marathon (world's fastest for out-and-back course) 1981; Marathon Champion, Commonwealth Games, Brisbane 1982; winner Rotterdam Marathon 1983; World Marathon Champion, Helsinki 1983; winner Boston Marathon 1986; winner Commonwealth Games 1986; Dir Australian Inst. of Sport 1990–95; Chair. Health Promotions Bd ACT (Healthpact) 1996–; Dir Decorp Pty Ltd 1995–, Action Potential 1996–98, RWM Publs 1996–, Leisure Australia 1999–; Man. Dir SmartStart (Australia) Pty Ltd 1997–; mem. Bd Australian Sports Comm. –1999, Bd. Sports Australian Hall of Fame 1997–; Australian of the Year 1983. *Publications:* de Castella on Running 1984, Deek, Australia's World Champion 1984, Smart Sport 1996. *Leisure interests:* music, relaxation, motorcycling, tennis, golf, Scuba diving. *Address:* Smart Start (Australia) Pty Ltd, P.O. Box 3808, Weston, ACT 2611, Australia. *Telephone:* (2) 6288-0361. *Fax:* (2) 6287-1461. *E-mail:* deck@smartstart.com.au (Office). *Website:* smartstart.com.au (Office).

DE CECCO, Marcello, BA, LLB; Italian professor of economics; b. 17 Sept. 1939, Rome; s. of Vincenzo de Cecco and Antonietta de Cecco; m. Julia Maud Bamford; two s.; ed Univ. of Parma, Cambridge Univ., UK; Asst Lecturer, Univ. of E Anglia, England 1967–68; Prof. of Econs, Univ. of Siena 1968–79, European Univ. Inst., Florence 1979–86, Univ. of Rome 'La Sapienza' 1986–, Prof. of Monetary Econs 1989–; Exec. Dir Monte dei Paschi di Siena 1978–83; Dir Crediop, Rome 1979–81, Italian Int. Bank, London 1980–83; Visiting Scholar, IMF 1994; fmr mem. Inst. for Advanced Study, Princeton Univ., Center for Int. Affairs and Center for European Studies, Harvard Univ. *Publications:* Money and Empire 1976, International Economic Adjustment 1981, Changing Money 1985, A European Central Bank 1990. *Address:* Dipartimento di Economia Pubblica, Via Castro Laurenziano 9, Rome, Italy. *Telephone:* (06) 49766358.

DE CHASTELAIN, Gen. A(lfred) John G(ardyne) D(rummond), OC, CMM, CH, CD, BA; Canadian army officer and diplomatist; b. 30 July 1937, Bucharest, Romania; emigrated to Canada 1955, naturalized 1962; s. of Alfred George Gardyne de Chastelain and Marion Elizabeth de Chastelain (née Walsh); m. Mary Ann Laverty 1961; one s. one d.; ed Fettes Coll., Edin., UK, Mount Royal Coll., Calgary, Royal Mil. Coll. of Canada, Kingston, British Army Staff Coll., Camberley; commissioned 2nd Lt, 2nd Bn, Princess Patricia's Canadian Light Infantry (PPCLI) 1960, Capt., aide-de-camp to Chief of Gen. Staff, Army HQ 1962–64, Co. Commdr, 1st Bn, PPCLI, FRG 1964–65, Co. Commdr, Edmonton, rank of Maj., later with 1st Bn, UN Force, Cyprus 1968; Brigade Maj., 1st Combat Group, Calgary 1968–70, Commdg Officer, 2nd Bn, PPCLI, Winnipeg 1970–72, rank of Lt-Col., Sr Staff Officer, Quartier Gen. Dist, Québec 1973–74, rank of Col, Commdr Canadian Forces Base, Montréal 1974–76, Deputy Chief of Staff, HQ UN Forces, Cyprus and Commdr Canadian Contingent 1976–77, rank of Brig.-Gen. and apptd. Commdt Royal Mil. Coll. of Canada, Kingston 1977–80, command of 4th Canadian Mechanized Brigade Group, FRG 1980–82, Dir.-Gen. Land Doctrine and Operations, Nat. Defence Headquarters, Ottawa 1982–83, rank of Maj.-Gen. 1983, Deputy Commdr Mobile Command, St Hubert, Québec 1983–86, rank of Lt-Gen. and apptd. Asst Deputy Minister (Personnel) Nat. Defence HQ, Ottawa 1986–88, Vice-Chief, Defence Staff 1988–89, rank of Gen. and apptd. Chief of the Defence Staff 1989–93; Amb. to USA 1993; reapptd. Chief of the Defence Staff 1994–95; mem. Int. Body on the Decommissioning of Arms in Northern Ireland 1995–96, Chair. Business Cttee and Co-Chair. Strand Two Talks, Northern Ireland Peace Process (leading to the Good Friday Agreement) 1996–98, Chair. Independent Int. Comm. on Decommissioning, 1997–; Col of the Regiment PPCLI 2000–; Pres. Dominion of Canada Rifle Asscn 1986–93; mem. Royal Canadian Legion, Royal Canadian Mil. Inst.; Past First Nat. Vice-Pres. Boy Scouts of Canada; mem. St Andrews Soc. of Montreal, Royal Scottish Country Dance Soc.; Hon. DMilSc (Royal Mil. Coll. of Canada) 1996, Hon. LLD (Royal Roads Univ.); Canadian Forces Decoration 1968, Commendation Medal of Merit and Honour (Greece) 1991, Vimy Award 1992, Commdr OSJ 1991, US Legion of Merit 1995. *Publications:* articles on int. diplomacy. *Leisure interests:* bagpipes, Scottish country dancing, fishing and painting. *Address:* Independent International Commission on Decommissioning, Rosepark House, Upper Newtownards Road, Belfast, BT4 3NX, Northern Ireland (Office); 170 Acacia Avenue, Ottawa, Ont., K1M 0R3, Canada (Home). *Telephone:* (28) 9048-8600 (Office); (613) 744-7300 (Home). *Fax:* (28) 9048-8601 (Office); (613) 744-0777 (Home). *E-mail:* chairman@iol.ie (Office); ajgd.dec@sympatico.ca (Home).

DE CLERCK, Stefaan; Belgian politician; b. 12 Dec. 1951, Kortryk; two s. three d.; M.P. 1991, 1998–2001; Minister of Justice 1995; Pres. Christelijke Volksparteit (CVP) 1999–; Mayor of Kortryk 2001–. *Address:* Christelijke Volkspartij, 89 Wetstraat, 1040 Brussels (Office); Damkaai, 8500 Kortryk, Belgium (Home). *Telephone:* (2) 238-38-14 (Office); (56) 20-46-33 (Home). *Fax:*

(2) 230-43-60 (Office); (56) 25-89-99 (Home). *E-mail:* sdeclerck@cvp.be (Office); stefaan.d.clerck@pandora.be (Home). *Website:* www.cvp.be (Office); www.stef-kortryk.com (Home).

De CONCINI, Dennis, LLB; American politician and lawyer; b. 8 May 1937, Tucson, Ariz.; s. of Evo and Ora De Concini; one s. two d.; ed Univ. of Arizona and Univ. of Arizona Coll. of Law; Committeeman, Pima County 1958–76; worked with family law practice 1963–65; special counsel to Gov. of Ariz. 1965, Admin. Asst to Gov. 1965–67; Partner, DeConcini & McDonald, law firm 1968–73; Pima County Attorney 1972–76; Admin., Ariz. Drug Control District 1975–76; fmr mem. Ariz. Democratic Exec. Cttee, Vice-Chair. 1964, 1970; Senator from Arizona 1977–95, mem. judiciary Cttee, appropriations Cttee, Rules Cttee, Special Select Cttee on Indian Affairs, Veterans' Affairs Cttee; mem. Select Cttee on Intelligence, Senate Caucus on Int. Narcotics Control; consulting practice Parry, Romani, De Concini & Symms Assocs., Washington, DC 1995–, DeConcini, McDonald, Yetwin & Lacy, Tuscon 1995–; Dir Nat. Center for Missing and Exploited Children 1995–; mem. Académie Française 1993–; Chair. Comm. on Security and Co-operation in Europe; served US Army 1959–60, Judge Advocate Gen. Corps. 1964–67; mem. or fmr mem. Pima County Bar Asscn, Ariz. Bar Asscn, American Bar Asscn, American Judicature Soc., American Arbitration Asscn, Nat. District Attorneys' Asscn; mem. Ariz. County Attorneys' and Sheriffs' Asscn, Sec.-Treas. 1975, Pres. 1976. *Leisure interests:* golf, boating, jogging. *Address:* 517 C Street, NE, Washington, DC 20002; 2525 E Broadway, Suite 111, Tucson, AZ 85716, USA. *Telephone:* (202) 547-4000 (Washington) (Office); (520) 325-9600 (Tucson) (Office). *Fax:* (202) 543-5044 (Washington) (Office); (520) 327-9744 (Tucson) (Office). *E-mail:* prdands@aol.com (Office). *Website:* www.lobbycongress.com (Office).

DE CUENCA Y CUENCA, Luis Alberto; Spanish philologist, poet, translator and writer; b. 1950, Madrid; ed Universidad Autónoma de Madrid; Prof. Philology Inst. of Council for Scientific Research, then Publs Dir; literary critic for several Publs including El País; Dir Biblioteca Nacional (Nat. Library) 1996–2000; Premio Nacional de Literatura Infantil y Juvenil 1989. *Publications include:* El cantar de Valtario (The Song of Valtario) (translation), El héroe y sus máscaras (The Hero and his Masks). *Address:* c/o Biblioteca Nacional, Paseo de Recoletos 20, 28071 Madrid, Spain. *Telephone:* (1) 5807800. *Fax:* (1) 5775634.

DE DEO, Joseph E. (Joe), BA; American advertising executive; b. 18 Sept. 1937, Newark; s. of Joseph De Deo and Clara Veneziano; m. Esther Ellen Dadigan 1969; one s.; ed The Delbarton School, Princeton Univ.; joined Young and Rubicam (Y & R) as man. trainee, New York 1961, Account Exec. 1963, Account Supervisor 1967, Vice-Pres. 1968, Chair. Australian operations, opening agencies Sydney, then Adelaide and Melbourne 1969–79, Sr Vice-Pres. and Area Dir for Asia/Pacific Region 1971, set up Y & R cos. Tokyo 1972, Hong Kong 1974, Chair. UK group, London and Regional Dir for UK, France, Belgium and Netherlands 1974–77, Area Dir for Europe and the Middle East 1977–80, Pres. Y & R Europe 1980–90, Pres. and CEO Young and Rubicam Advertising Worldwide 1990–92, Vice-Chair., Chief Creative Officer Young & Rubicam Inc., NY 1992–93, Corp. Vice-Chair. 1993–. *Leisure interests:* skiing, reading, antique collecting. *Address:* Young & Rubicam Inc., 285 Madison Avenue, New York, NY 10017, USA.

de DUVE, Christian René, MD, MSc; Belgian scientist; b. 2 Oct. 1917, Thames Ditton, England; s. of Alphonse de Duve and Madeleine Pungs; m. Janine Herman 1943; two s. two d.; ed Univ. of Louvain; Prof. of Physiological Chem., Univ. of Louvain Medical School 1947–85, Prof. Emer. 1985–; Prof. of Biochemical Cytology, Rockefeller Univ., New York City 1962–88, Prof. Emer. 1988–; founder-mem., Pres. Int. of Cellular and Molecular Pathology, Brussels 1974–91; mem. Royal Acad. of Medicine (Belgium), Royal Acad. of Belgium, American Chem. Soc., Biochem. Soc., American Soc. of Biological Chem., Pontifical Acad. of Sciences, American Soc. of Cell Biology, Deutsche Akad. der Naturforschung, Leopoldina, Koninklijke Akad. voor Geneeskunde van België, etc.; Foreign mem. American Acad. of Arts and Sciences, Royal Soc., London, Royal Soc. of Canada; Foreign assoc. NAS, USA; Hon. DSc (Keele Univ.) 1981, Dr. hc (Rockefeller) 1997 and numerous other hon. degrees; Prix des Alumni 1949; Prix Pfizer 1957; Prix Francqui 1960; Prix Quinquennal Belge des Sciences Médicales 1967; Gairdner Foundation Int. Award of Merit (Canada) 1967; Dr. H. P. Heineken Prijs (Netherlands) 1973; Nobel Prize for Medicine 1974. *Leisure interests:* tennis, skiing, bridge. *Address:* c/o Rockefeller University, 1230 York Avenue, New York, NY 10021, U.S.A. (Office). ICP, 75 Avenue Hippocrate, 1200 Brussels, Belgium.

de FERRANTI, Sebastian Basil Joseph Ziani, DL; British electrical engineer; b. 5 Oct. 1927, Alderley Edge, Cheshire; s. of the late Sir Vincent de Ferranti and Lady Dorothy H. C. de Ferranti (née Wilson); brother of the late Basil Ziani de Ferranti, MP, MEP; m. 1st Mona Helen Cunningham 1953; one s. two d.; m. 2nd Naomi Angela Rae 1983 (died 2001); ed Ampleforth Coll.; served 4th/7th Dragoon Guards 1947–49; Brown Boveri, Switzerland and Alsthom, France 1948–50; Transformer Dept, Ferranti Ltd 1950, Dir 1954–82, Man. Dir 1958–75, Chair. 1963–82; Dir GEC PLC 1982–97; Pres. BEAMA 1969–70, Manchester and Region Centre for Educ. in Science, Educ. and Tech. 1972–78; Chair. Int. Electrical Asscn 1970–73; Vice-Pres. RSA 1980–84; Commr Royal Comm. for Exhbn of 1851 1984–97; Dir Nat. Nuclear Corpn 1984–88; mem. Nat. Defence Industries Council 1969–77; Trustee, Tate Gallery 1971–78; Chair. North-West Civic Trust 1983–88; Chair. Hallé Concerts Soc. 1988–96, Pres. 1997–; High Sheriff of Cheshire 1988–89; Hon.

mem. Royal Northern Coll. of Music 1997, mem. Bd of Govs 1988–2000; Hon. Fellow, UMIST; Granada Guildhall Lecture 1966; Royal Inst. Discourse 1969; Louis Blériot Lecture, Paris 1970; Faraday Lecture 1970, 1971; DL; Hon. DSc (Cranfield Inst. of Tech.) 1973, (Salford Univ.), Hon. LLD (Manchester) 1998. *Address:* Henbury Hall, Macclesfield, Cheshire, SK11 9PJ, England (Home). *Telephone:* (1625) 422101.

DE FONBLANQUE, John, CMG, MA, MSc,; British diplomatist; b. 20 Dec. 1943, Fleet, Hants; s. of Maj.-Gen. E. B. De Fonblanque and Elizabeth De Fonblanque; m. Margaret Prest 1984; one s.; ed Ampleforth School, King's Coll., Cambridge, London School of Econs; joined FCO 1968, Second Sec. Jakarta 1969–72, Second, later First Sec. to EC, Brussels 1972–77; Prin. HM Treasury 1977–80; FCO 1980–83; Asst Sec. Cabinet Office 1983–86; Head of Chancery, New Delhi 1986, Counsellor (Political and Institutional) Mission to EC, Brussels 1988, Asst Under-Sec. of State Int. Orgs. then Dir Global Issues 1994–98, Dir (Europe) FCO 1998–99, Head Del. to OSCE with rank of Amb. 1999–. *Leisure interest:* mountain walking. *Address:* United Kingdom Delegation to the Organisation for Security and Co-operation in Europe, Jaurèsgasse 12, 1030 Vienna (Office); Himmelstrasse 49, 1190 Vienna, Austria (Home). *Telephone:* (1) 716133301 (Office); (1) 3202556 (Home). *Fax:* (1) 716133900 (Office); (1) 320255618 (Home). *E-mail:* John.DeFonblanque@vienna.mail.fco.gov.uk (Office).

DE GENNES, Pierre-Gilles, PhD; French professor; b. 24 Oct. 1932, Paris; s. of Robert De Gennes and Yvonne Morin-Pons; ed Ecole Normale; Research Engineer, Commissariat Energie Atomique 1955–59; Prof. Univ. Orsay 1961–71; Prof. of Solid State Physics, Coll. de France 1971–; Dir Ecole de Physique et Chimie industrielles 1976–; Wolf Prize 1990, Nobel Prize for Physics 1991. *Publications:* Superconductivity of Metals and Alloys 1966, The Physics of Liquid Crystals 1974, Scaling Concepts in Polymer Physics 1979, Simple Views on Condensed Matter 1992, Les objets fragiles 1994. *Leisure interests:* hiking, windsurfing and drawing. *Address:* Collège de France, 11 place Marcelin-Berthelot, 75231 Paris (Office); 10 rue Vauquelin, 75005 Paris, France (Home). *Telephone:* 1-44-27-12-11 (Office); 1-40-79-45-00 (Home). *Fax:* 1-44-27-11-09 (Office). *Website:* www.college-de-france.fr (Office).

DE GIORGI, HE Cardinal Salvatore; Italian ecclesiastic; b. 6 Sept. 1930, Vernole; ordained priest 1953; Bishop 1973, Archbishop, See of Oria 1978, of Foggia 1981, of Taranto 1987, of Palermo 1996; cr. Cardinal Feb. 1998. *Address:* Curia Arcivescovile, Corso Vittorio Emanuele 461, 90134 Palermo, Italy.

DE GRAAF, Thom Carolus; Netherlands politician and fmr civil servant; b. 11 June 1957, Amsterdam; m.; two c.; ed Catholic Univ. of Nijmegen; fmr Lecturer in Constitutional Law, Catholic Univ. of Nijmegen; civil servant, Ministry of Interior 1985–94; Deputy Dir for Police Affairs 1991–94; fmr Mun. Councillor, Leiden; mem. De Koning Cttee on Constitutional Reform 1992–93; joined Democraten 66 (D66) 1977, Sec. Nat. Bd 1986–90, Chair. D66 Parl. Group 1997–, now Leader D66; mem. Parl. 1994–. *Leisure interests:* history, poetry, tennis, ice skating. *Address:* Democraten 66, P.O. Box 20018, 2500 EA The Hague (Office); Blaux Karper 2, 2318 NN Leiden, Netherlands (Home). *Telephone:* (70) 3182627 (Office); (71) 5232057 (Home). *Fax:* (70) 3183626 (Office). *E-mail:* Th.dGraaf@tk.parlement.nl (Home). *Website:* www.d66.nl (Office); www.thomdegraaf.nl (Home).

DE GRAVE, Franciscus (Frank) Hendrikus Gerardus, DJur; Dutch politician; b. 27 June 1955, Amsterdam; m.; two c.; ed Univ. of Groningen; Int. Sec. J.O.V.D. youth org. 1977–78, Nat. Pres. 1978–80; mem. Volkspartij voor Vrihoid en Democratie (VVD) parl. group 1977–81; Asst Sec. to Man. Bd AMRO bank 1980–82; Amsterdam City Councillor 1982–86; mem. First Chamber of Parl. 1982–90; Councillor for Finances and Deputy Mayor, Amsterdam City Council 1990–94, Acting Mayor Jan.–June 1994; Sec. of State for Social Security and Employment 1996–98; Minister of Defence 1998–; mem. Vaste Comm. for Defence 1982–86, Bd Vereniging Nederlandse Gemeenten; Commr R.A.I., Bank Nederlandse Gemeenten and Amsterdam Arena. *Address:* Ministry of Defence, Plein 4, P.O. Box 20701, 2500 ES The Hague, Netherlands (Office). *Telephone:* (70) 3187320 (Office). *Fax:* (70) 3187264 (Office). *Website:* www.mindef.nl (Office).

DE HAAN, Hendrik, PhD; Netherlands professor of international economics; b. 8 April 1941, Nijmegen; m. Adriana Annie Kramer 1966; two s. one d.; ed Univ. of Groningen, Netherlands, Catholic Univ. of Louvain, Belgium; Prof. of Int. Econs, Univ. of Groningen 1971–; consultant to UNCTAD 1975; consultant-expert to UN on econ. and social consequences of the arms race 1977, 1982, 1987; consultant to UN on relationship between disarmament and Devt 1985–87; Foreign Policy Adviser to Christian Democratic Party 1989–. *Publications:* Het Moderne Geldwezen (Modern Money), several other books on econ. topics, numerous articles in scientific journals. *Address:* Department of Economics, P.O. Box 800, 9700 AV Groningen (Office); Hoofdstraat 173, 9827 PB Lettelbert, Netherlands (Home). *Telephone:* (50) 633710 (Office). *Fax:* (50) 637337.

de HAVILLAND, Olivia Mary; American (b. British) actress; b. 1 July 1916, Tokyo, Japan; d. of Walter Augustus de Havilland and Lilian Augusta (née Ruse); m. 1st Marcus Aurelius Goodrich 1946 (divorced 1953); one s.; m. 2nd Pierre Paul Galante 1955 (divorced 1979); one d.; ed Saratoga Grammar School, Notre Dame Convent, Los Gatos Union High School; stage début in A Midsummer Night's Dream 1934, film début in screen version 1935; Pres.

Cannes Film Festival 1965; on lecture tours in USA 1971–80; mem. Bd of Trustees of American Coll. in Paris 1970–71, of American Library in Paris 1974–81; mem. Altar Guild, Lay Reader, American Cathedral in Paris 1971–81; Dr. hc (American Univ. of Paris) 1994; numerous awards include: Acad. Award 1946, 1949, New York Critics Award 1948, 1949, Look Magazine Award 1941, 1946, 1949, Venice Film Festival Award 1948, Filmex Tribute 1978, American Acad. of Achievement Award 1978, American Exemplar Medal 1980, Golden Globe 1988. *Films include:* Captain Blood 1935, Anthony Adverse 1936, The Adventures of Robin Hood 1938, Gone with the Wind 1939, Hold Back the Dawn 1941, Princess O'Rourke 1942, To Each His Own (Acad. Award) 1946, The Dark Mirror 1946, The Snake Pit 1947, The Heiress (Acad. Award) 1949, My Cousin Rachel 1952, Not as a Stranger 1954, The Proud Rebel 1957, The Light in the Piazza 1961, Lady in a Cage 1963, Hush Hush Sweet Charlotte 1964, The Adventurers 1968, Airport '77 1976, The Swarm 1978, The Fifth Musketeer. *Plays:* Romeo and Juliet 1951, Candida 1951–52, A Gift of Time 1962. *Television includes:* Noon Wine 1966, Screaming Woman 1972, Roots, The Next Generations 1979, Murder is Easy 1981, Charles and Diana: A Royal Romance, 1982, North and South II 1986, Anastasia 1986 (Golden Globe Award), The Woman He Loved 1987. *Publications:* Every Frenchman Has One 1962, Mother and Child (contrib.) 1975. *Leisure interests:* crossword puzzles, reading tales of mystery and imagination, painting on Sunday. *Address:* B.P. 156-16, 75764 Paris Cedex 16, France.

DE HOOP, Adrianus Teunis, PhD; Netherlands professor of electromagnetic theory and applied mathematics; b. 24 Dec. 1927, Rotterdam; ed Delft Univ. of Tech.; Research Asst, Delft Univ. of Tech. 1950–52, Asst Prof. 1953–56, Assoc. Prof. 1957–60, Prof. 1960–96, Lorentz Chair Prof. Emer. 1996–; Reserve Officer, Royal Netherlands Navy 1952–53; Research Asst, Univ. of Calif., Los Angeles 1956–57; Visiting Research Scientist, Philips Research Labs., Eindhoven 1976–77, Consultant 1977–89; mem. Royal Netherlands Acad. of Arts and Sciences 1989, Royal Flemish Acad. of Arts and Sciences of Belgium 1998, Visiting Scientist Schlumberger Oilfield Services, Ridgefield, USA 1982–; Hon. PhD (Ghent) 1982; awards from Stichting Fund for Science, Tech. and Research 1986, 1989, 1990, 1993, 1994, Gold Research Medal, Royal Inst. of Eng 1989, Heinrich Hertz Medal, IEEE 2001, URSI Balthasar van der Pol Gold Research Medal 2002. *Publications:* Handbook of Radiation and Scattering of Waves 1995, numerous articles in journals. *Leisure interest:* playing the piano. *Address:* Faculty of Information Technology and Systems, Delft University of Technology, Mekelweg 4, 2628 CD Delft (Office); Korenmolen 17, 2661 LE Bergschenhoek, Netherlands (Home). *Telephone:* (15) 2785203 (Office); (10) 5220049 (Home). *Fax:* (15) 2786194. *E-mail:* a.t.dehoop@its.tudelft.nl (Office).

DE IRALA, Xabier; Spanish airline executive; b. 1946, New York; ed La Salle Univ., Philippines; CEO and other positions, Gen. Electric, Spain 1971–86, CEO Gen. Electric, Portugal 1986–87, Financial Dir Gen. Electric, England 1987–88, Vice-Pres. Gen. Electric, CGR, France 1988–90; Exec. Vice-Pres., CEO, Asea Brown Boveri España 1990–96; Chair., CEO Iberia July 1996–; Chair. Bd of Govs. IATA; Chair. Fitur; Pres. Spain-Philippines Jt Business Cttee; Pres. Exceltur; mem. Advisory Bd, E.S.C. Bordeaux, Bd of Dirs., Italtel, Italy; Officier, Légion d'honneur. *Leisure interests:* chess, mountaineering. *Address:* IBERIA, Líneas Aéreas de España, SA, Velázquez 130, 28006 Madrid, Spain (Office). *Telephone:* (91) 5877010 (Office). *Fax:* (91) 6523039 (Office). *E-mail:* Presidencia@iberia.es (Office). *Website:* www.iberia.com (Office).

De JAGER, Cornelis; Netherlands astrophysicist; b. 29 April 1921, Den Burg, Texel; s. of Jan de Jager and Cornelia Kuyper; m. Duotje Rienks 1947; two s. two d.; ed Univ. of Utrecht; Asst in Theoretical Physics, Univ. of Utrecht 1946; Asst in Astronomy, Univ. of Leiden; Asst Astronomy Inst., Utrecht; Assoc. Prof. of Stellar Astrophysics, Univ. of Utrecht 1957, Ordinary Prof. in Gen. Astrophysics 1960–86; Extraordinary Prof., Univ. of Brussels and founder, Space Research Lab., Utrecht Astronomy Inst., Brussels 1961; Man. Dir Utrecht Astronomy Inst. 1963–78, Chair. Inst. Council 1978–83; Asst Gen. Sec. Int. Astronomical Union 1967–70, Gen. Sec. 1970–73; Pres. Netherlands Astronomy Comm. 1975–83; mem. Exec. Council Cttee on Space Research (COSPAR) 1970–72, Pres. 1972–78, 1982–86; mem. Exec. Council, ICSU 1970–82, Vice-Pres. 1976–78, Pres. 1978–80; Chair. Skepsis (for critical evaluation of the paranormal) 1987–97, European Council of Sceptical Orgs 1995–2001, Council of Chancellors of Global Foundation 2001–; Aggregate Prof., Univ. of Brussels 1970–86; mem. Royal Netherlands Acad. of Art and Sciences (Foreign Sec. 1985–90), Royal Belgium Acad. of Art and Sciences, Acad. Europe (Paris and London); Assoc. mem. Royal Astronomical Soc. (London); Corresp. mem. Soc. Royale de Science, Liège; mem. Int. Acad. Astronautics, Chair. Basic Sciences Section 1984–92; Foreign mem. Deutsche Akademie Leopoldina, Halle; Foreign Fellow Indian Nat. Scientific Acad.; Hon. mem. Netherlands Soc. of Astronomy and Meteorology 1996; Dr hc (Univ. of Wrocław, Poland) 1975, (Observatoire de Paris) 1976; Yuri Gagarin Medal (USSR) 1984, J. Janssen Medal (France) 1984, Ziolkowski Medal, USSR Acad. of Sciences; Kt, Order of the Dutch Lion 1983; Gold Medal Royal Astronomical Soc., London 1988; Hale Medal, American Astronomical Soc. 1988; COSPAR Medal for Int. Co-operation in Space Science 1988, Silver Medal Royal Netherlands Acad. Arts and Sciences, Gold Medal Netherlands Soc. Astronomy and Meteorology, In Praise of Reason Award CSICOP, Buffalo, NY 1990, Von Karman Award of Int. Acad. of Astronautics 1993. *Publications:* about 550 publs including: The Hydrogen Spectrum of the Sun 1952, Structure and Dynamics of the Solar Atmosphere 1959, The Solar Spectrum 1965, Solar Flares and Space Research (with Z. Svestka) 1969, Sterrenkunde 1969, Reports on Astronomy 1970, 1973, Highlights in Astronomy 1970, Ontstaan en Levensloop van Sterren (with E. van den Heuvel), 2nd edn 1973, Image Processing Techniques in Astronomy (with H. Nieuwenhuyzen) 1975, The Brightest Stars 1980, Instabilities in evolved super- and hyper-giants 1992, Bolwerk van de Sterren 1993, Tien Opmerkelijke Sterrekundige Ontdekkingen 1995, Kannibalen bij de grenzen van het heelal 1996, Solar Flares and Collisions Between Current-carrying Loops (jtly) 1996, Van het Clijf tot Den Hoorn (jtly) 1998. *Leisure interests:* birds, plants, jogging, history. *Address:* Molenstraat 22, 1791 DL Den Burg, Texel, Netherlands (Home). *Telephone:* (222) 320816, (620) 420611. *E-mail:* jager01@planet.nl (Home).

de JONGH, Eduard S.; Netherlands art historian; b. 7 June 1931, Amsterdam; m. Lammijna Oosterbaan 1977; two s. one d.; ed Baarns Lyceum and Univ. of Utrecht; journalist and art critic, Het Parool and Vrij Nederland 1954–74; Librarian, Inst. for Art History, Univ. of Utrecht 1963–66; Ed. Openbaar Kunstbezit (radio course) 1963–73; Ed. Simiolus (art history quarterly) 1966–77; mem. staff, Centrum Voortgezet Kunsthistorisch Onderzoek, Univ. of Utrecht 1966–73; Asst Prof. Inst. for Art History, Univ. of Utrecht 1973–76, Prof. of Art History 1976–89, Prof. Emer. 1989–; Ed. Kunstschrift 1990–; Visiting scholar, Getty Center for History of Art and Humanities 1987; mem. Royal Netherlands Acad.; foreign mem. Royal Belgian Acad.; Karel van Mander Award. *Publications:* Zinne- en minnebeelden in de schilderkunst van de zeventiende eeuw 1967, Tot Lering en Vermaak: Betekenissen van Hollandse genrevoorstellingen uit de zeventiende eeuw 1976, Still Life in the Age of Rembrandt 1982, Portretten van echt en trouw: Huwelijk en gezin in de Nederlandse kunst van de zeventiende eeuw 1986, Kunst en het vruchtbare misverstand 1993, Faces of the Golden Age: Seventeenth-Century Dutch Portraits 1994, Kwesties van betekenis: Thema en motief in de Nederlandse schilderkunst van de zeventiende eeuw 1995, Mirror of Everyday Life: Genre Prints in The Netherlands 1550–1700 (with Ger Luijten) 1997, Questions of Meaning: Theme and Motif in Dutch Seventeenth-Century Painting 2000, Dankzij de tiende muze: 33 Opstellen uit Kunstschrift 2000; many articles on iconological and art theoretical subjects. *Address:* Frederik Hendrikstraat 29, 3583 VG Utrecht, Netherlands.

DE KEERSMAEKER, Baroness; **Anne Teresa;** Belgian choreographer; b. 11 June 1960, Wemmel; one s. one d.; ed Mudra, School of Maurice Béjart, Brussels and Tisch School of the Arts, New York Univ.; presented first work, Asch in Brussels 1980; Founder, Artistic Dir Rosas Dance Co. 1983–; Rosas became co.-in-residence, Théâtre de la Monnaie, Brussels with herself as resident choreographer 1992; directed opera Bluebeard (Bartók) 1997; Artistic Dir at P.A.R.T.S. school 1995–; has also directed work for video; recipient of numerous int. dance awards; Dr. hc (Free Univ. of Brussels) 1999. *Choreographic works:* Asch 1981, Fase: four movements to music of Steve Reich 1982, Rosas danst Rosas 1983, Elena's Aria 1984, Bartók/Aantekeningen 1986, Verkommenes Ufer/Medeamaterial/Landschaft mit Argonauten 1987, Mikrokosmos-Monument/Selbstporträt mit Reich und Riley (und Chopin ist auch dabei)/Im zart fliessender Bewegung-Quatuor Nr. 4 1987, Ottone, Ottone 1988, Stella 1990, Achterland 1990, Erts 1992, Mozart/Concert Arias, un moto di gioia 1992, Toccata 1993, Kinok 1994, Amor Constante más allá de la muerte 1994, Erwartung/Verklärte Nacht 1995, Woud 1996, Just Before 1997, Three Solos for Vincent Dunoyer 1997, Duke Bluebeard's Castle 1998, Drumming 1998, Quartett 1999, I Said I 1999, In Real Time 2000, Rain 2001, Small hands (out of the lie of no) 2001, (but if a look should) April me 2002, Once 2002. *Films:* Hoppla! 1989, Achterland 1994, Rosas danst Rosas 1997. *Address:* Rosas VZW, Van Volxemlaan 164, 1190 Brussels, Belgium (Office). *Telephone:* (2) 344-55-98 (Office). *Fax:* (2) 343-53-52 (Office). *E-mail:* mail@rosas.be (Office). *Website:* www.rosas.be (Office).

de KLERK, Albert; Netherlands organist and composer; b. 4 Oct. 1917; ed Amsterdamsch Conservatorium under Dr. Anthon van der Horst; Organist St Joseph's Church, Haarlem 1934–; City Organist Haarlem 1956–82; Dir of Catholic Choir, Haarlem 1946–91; Prof. of Organ and Improvization, Sweelinck Conservatorium, Amsterdam 1964–85; numerous gramophone records for Telefunken, C.B.S., E.M.I.-Bovema, etc.; Prix d'Excellence, Amsterdam 1941, Prix du Disque, Prix Edison (for Die Kleinorgel) 1962, Netherlands Choir Music Prize 1991. *Compositions:* several works for organ including three concertos for organ and orchestra, chamber-music and liturgical music (seven masses). *Address:* Crayenesterlaan 22, Haarlem, Netherlands.

de KLERK, Frederik Willem, LLB; South African politician; b. 18 March 1936, Johannesburg; s. of J. de Klerk; m. 1st Marike Willemse 1959 (divorced 1998); two s. one d.; m. 2nd Elita Georgiadis 1998; ed Monument High School, Krugersdorp, Potchefstroom Univ.; in law practice 1961–72; mem. House of Ass. 1972; Information Officer Nat. Party, Transvaal 1975; Minister of Posts and Telecommunications and of Social Welfare and Pensions 1978, subsequently Minister of Posts and Telecommunications and of Sport and Recreation 1978–79, of Mines, Energy and Environmental Planning 1979–80, of Mineral and Energy Affairs 1980–82, of Internal Affairs 1982–85, of Nat. Educ. and Planning 1984–89; Acting State Pres. of South Africa Aug.–Sept. 1989, State Pres. of South Africa 1989–94; Exec. Deputy Pres., Govt of Nat. Unity 1994–96; Leader of the Official Opposition 1996–97; mem. Nat. Party, Transvaal Leader 1982–89, Leader 1989–97; also fmr Chair. of the Cabinet and C-in-C of the Armed Forces; fmr Chair. Council of Ministers; shared Nobel Prize for Peace with Nelson Mandela (q.v.) 1993; Jt winner Houphouet Boigny

Prize (UNESCO) 1991; Asturias Prize 1992, Liberty Medal (SA) 1993; seven Hon. doctorates. *Publications:* The Last Trek: A New Beginning (autobiog.) 1999, various articles and brochures for the Nat. Party Information Service. *Leisure interests:* golf, reading. *Address:* Private Bag X999, Cape Town 8000, South Africa (Office). *Telephone:* (21) 4182202 (Office). *Fax:* (21) 4182626 (Office). *E-mail:* fwdeklerk@mweb.co.za (Home). *Website:* www.fwdklerk.org .za (Office).

DE KORTE, Rudolf Willem, Dr rer. nat; Netherlands politician; b. 8 July 1936, The Hague; m.; two c.; ed Maerlant Gymnasium, The Hague, Leiden Univ., Harvard Business School; employed in industry, Hong Kong 1964–66, Ethiopia 1967–68; Gen. Sales Man. Unilever-Emery NV 1969–71, Dir 1972–77; Sec. People's Party for Freedom and Democracy (VVD) 1971–78; MP 1977, Minister for Home Affairs March–July 1986, Deputy Prime Minister and Minister for Econ. Affairs 1986–89; mem. (VVD) Lower House of Parl. 1989–; mem. Wassenaar Municipal Council 1978–82. *Address:* c/o Tweede Kamer der Staten-Generaal, P.O. Box 20018, 2500 EA The Hague, Netherlands.

de la BILLIÈRE, Gen. Sir Peter (Edgar de la Cour), KCB, KBE, DSO, MC, DL; British army officer (retd); b. 29 April 1934, Plymouth; s. of Surgeon Lt-Commdr Claude Dennis Delacour de Labillière and Frances Christing Wright Lawley; m. Bridget Constance Muriel Goode 1965; one s. two d.; ed Harrow School, Staff Coll., Royal Coll. of Defence Studies; joined King's Shropshire Light Infantry 1952; commissioned, Durham Light Infantry; served Japan, Korea, Malaya (despatches 1959), Jordan, Borneo, Egypt, Aden, Gulf States, Sudan, Oman, Falkland Islands; Commdg Officer, 22 Special Air Service (SAS) Regt 1972–74; Gen. Staff Officer 1 (Directing Staff), Staff Coll. 1974–77; Commdr British Army Training Team, Sudan 1977–78; Dir SAS and Commdr SAS Group 1978–83; Commdr British Forces, Falkland Islands and Mil. Commr 1984–85; Gen. Officer Commdg Wales 1985–87; Col Comdt. Light Div. 1986–90; Lt-Gen. Officer commanding SE Dist 1987–90; Commdr British Forces in Middle East Oct. 1990–91; rank of Gen. 1991 after Gulf War, Ministry of Defence Adviser on Middle East 1991–92; retd from army June 1992; Pres. SAS Asscn 1991–96, Army Cadet Force 1992–99; mem. Council Royal United Services Inst. 1975–77; Chair. Jt Services Hang Gliding 1986–88; Cdre Army Sailing Asscn 1989–90; Commr Duke of York's School 1988–90; Freeman City of London 1991; Hon. Freeman Fishmongers' Co. 1991; Trustee Imperial War Museum 1992–99; Dir (non-exec.), Middle East and Defence Adviser, Robert Fleming Holdings 1992–99; Chair. Meadowland Meats 1994–2002; Jt Chair. Dirs. FARM Africa 1995–2001 (mem. Bd 1992–2001); DL Hereford and Worcester 1993; Trustee Naval and Mil. Club 1999–; Hon. DSc (Cranfield) 1992; Hon. DCL (Durham) 1993; Legion of Merit Chief Commdr (USA), Order of Abdul Aziz 2nd Class (Saudi Arabia), Meritorious Service Cross (Canada), Kuwait Decoration of the First Class, Order of Qatar Sash of Merit. *Publications:* Storm Command: a personal story 1992, Looking for Trouble (autobiog.) 1994. *Leisure interests:* family, squash, apiculture, farming, sailing. *Address:* c/o Naval and Military Club, 4 St James's Square, London, SW1Y 4JU, England.

DE LA CROIX DE CASTRIES, Henri René Marie Augustin; French insurance business executive and fmr civil servant; b. 15 Aug. 1954, Bayonne (Basses-Pyrénées); s. of François de La Croix de Castries and Gisèle de La Croix de Castries (née de Chevigné); m. Anne Millin de Grandmaison 1984; one s. two d.; ed Ecole Saint-Jean-de-Passy, Coll. Stanislas, Faculté de droit, Paris, Ecole nat. d'admin.; Deputy Insp., then Insp. of Finance 2nd class, Treasury 1984, Deputy Sec.-Gen. Interministerial Cttee on Industrial Restructuring 1984–85, Head Office of Capital Goods 1985–88, of Foreign Exchange and Balance of Payments 1988–89; Man. Finance Dept, AXA (insurance group) 1989–90, Sec.-Gen. 1991–93, Man. Dir 1993–2000, SEVP, mem. Exec. Cttee AXA 2000–, CEO 2000–; Chair. Bd of Dirs Equitable Cos. (USA). Chevalier, Ordre nat. du Mérite 1996, Chevalier, Légion d'Honneur 2001. *Address:* AXA, 25 avenue Matignon, 75008 Paris (Office); 17 rue du Cherche-Midi, 75006 Paris (Home); Château de Gastines, 49150 Fougeré, France (Home). *Telephone:* (1) 40-75-47-70 (Office). *Fax:* (1) 40-75-48-11 (Office). *E-mail:* henri.decastries@axa.com (Office). *Website:* www.Axa.com (Office).

DE LA HOYA, Oscar; American boxer; b. 4 Feb. 1973, Los Angeles; s. of Joel De La Hoya and the late Cecilia De La Hoya; m. Millie Corretjer; fmr amateur boxer, 223 victories (163 knockouts), only 5 losses; turned professional after winning gold medal lightweight Barcelona Olympics 1992; Int. Boxing Fed. (IBF) lightweight title 1995; World Boxing Council (WBC) super lightweight title (over Julio Cesar Chavez) 1996; WBC welterweight title (over Pernell Whitaker) 1997; lost WBC welterweight belt to Felix Trinidad in a majority decision in 1999; lost to Sugar Shane Mosley in 2000 in his 2nd career defeat; has won major titles in five weight divisions: 130, 135, 140, 147 and 154 pounds; WBC Boxer of the Decade 2001; f. Oscar de la Hoya Foundation; owner Golden Boy Promotions LLC; currently pursuing singing career. *Album:* Oscar (topped Billboard's Latin Dance charts for several weeks). *Address:* Oscar de la Hoya Foundation, 633 West 5th Street, Suite 6700, Los Angeles, CA 90071, USA. *Website:* www.oscardelahoya.com (Office).

DE LA MADRID HURTADO, Miguel; Mexican politician and lawyer; b. 1934, Colima; m. Paloma C. de la Madrid; five c.; ed Harvard Univ., USA; successively with Bank of Mexico, Petróleos Mexicanos (PEMEX) (Asst Dir of Finances 1970–72); Dir Public Sector Credit, later Under-Sec., Ministry of Finance; Sec. for Planning and Fed. Budget, Govt of Mexico 1979–80;

Institutional Revolutionary Party (PRI) cand. to succeed López Portillo as Pres. of Mexico Sept. 1981; Pres. of Mexico 1982–88; Pres. Nat. Asscn of Lawyers 1989–, Mexican Inst. of Culture 1989–; Dir-Gen. Fondo de Cultura Económica 1990–2000. *Publications:* Elementos de Derecho Constitucional, La Politica de la Renovacion, El Ejercicio de las Facultades Presidenciales, Una Vision de America Latina. *Leisure interests:* music, reading, films, golf. *Address:* Parras 46, Barrio Sta. Catarina, Deleg. Coyoacán, 04010 México, DF, Mexico. *Telephone:* (55) 5658-4459. *Fax:* (55) 5658-7979 (Office).

DE LA PEÑA, Javier, MS; Spanish petrochemical industry executive; b. 13 May 1940, Cortes, Navarra; s. of Juan-Jesus de la Peña and Julia de la Peña; m. Katherine Zegarra 1969; one s. three d.; ed Univ. of Valencia and Univ. of Kansas, USA; joined Phillips Petroleum group 1965, Dept of Eng (Okla) and Int. Dept (New York), USA 1965–67, Marketing, Phillips Calatrava Ventas, Madrid 1967–68, Man. in charge of Projects for Latin America (New York) 1968–70, Marketing Man. Phillips Calatrava Ventas, Madrid 1970–72, Gen. Man. 1972–74, Devt Man. Phillips Petroleum Chemicals, Brussels 1975–77, Vice-Pres., Devt and Licensing 1978–82, Vice-Pres. and Man. Dir for Petrochemicals (Olefins and Aromatics) of Phillips Petroleum Chemicals 1982–85; Vice-Pres. REPSOL PETROLEO, SA, in charge of Petrochemical Group; REPSOL Rep. in Asscn of European Petrochemical Producers 1985; Pres. REPSOL QUIMICA, SA 1986; Fulbright Scholar 1963–64. *Leisure interests:* sports, piano and music.

DE LA QUADRA-SALCEDO Y FERNANDEZ DEL CASTILLO, Tomás, PhD; Spanish politician; b. 1946, Madrid; m.; two c.; ed Complutense Univ. of Madrid; Asst Lecturer in Admin. Law, Faculty of Law, Complutense Univ. of Madrid 1977–81 (Temporary Lecturer 1968), in Audiovisual Media, Information Sciences Faculty 1981–; mem. Lawyers' Asscn of Madrid 1968–; Minister of Territorial Admin. 1982–85, of Justice 1985–93; Pres. Council of State 1985. *Publications:* various articles and books. *Address:* c/o PSOE, Ferraz 68 y 70, 28008 Madrid, Spain. *Telephone:* (1) 582 0444. *Fax:* (1) 582 0422.

de la RENTA, Oscar; Dominican Republic fashion designer; b. 22 July 1932, Santo Domingo; m. 1st Françoise de Langlade 1967 (died 1983); one adopted s.; m. 2nd Anne E de la Renta 1989; ed Santo Domingo Univ., Academia de San Fernando, Madrid; staff designer, under Cristobal Balenciaga, AISA couture house, Madrid; Asst to Antonio Castillo, Lanvin-Castillo, Paris 1961–63; designer, Elizabeth Arden couture and ready-to-wear collection, New York 1963–65; designer and partner, Jane Derby Inc. New York 1965; after her retirement firm evolved into Oscar de la Renta, Inc. which was purchased by Richton Int. 1969; Chief Exec. Richton's Oscar de la Renta Couture, Oscar de la Renta II, Oscar de la Renta Furs, Oscar de la Renta Jewelry and mem. Bd of Dirs. Richton Int. 1969–73; f. Oscar de la Renta, Ltd 1973, CEO 1973–; couturier for Balmain, Paris Nov. 1993–; produces about 80 different product lines including high-fashion clothing, household linens, accessories and perfumes for shops in USA, Canada, Mexico and Japan; owner, Oscar de la Renta shop, Santo Domingo 1968–; recipient of numerous fashion awards; Caballero, Order of San Pablo Duarte, Order of Cristobal Colon. *Address:* Oscar de la Renta Ltd, 550 7th Avenue, 8th Floor, New York, NY 10018, USA.

de la RÚA, Fernando; Argentine politician; b. 15 Sept. 1937, Córdoba; s. of Antonio de la Rúa and Eleonora Bruno de la Rúa; m. Inés Pertiné; two s. one d.; ed Liceo General Paz, Córdoba, Universidad Nacional de Córdoba; joined Unión Cívica Radical (UCR) as a student; mem. staff Ministry of Interior 1963–66; cand. for Vice-Pres. 1973, Senator for Fed. Capital 1973–76, 1983–96; visiting lecturer univs. in USA, Mexico and Venezuela during mil. dictatorship; f. Centro de Estudios Para la República (now Fundación de estudios sobre temas politicos), Buenos Aires 1982; Mayor of Buenos Aires 1996–99; Leader ALIANZA coalition; Pres. of Argentina 1999–2001; Prof. of Criminal Law, Univ. of Buenos Aires; Founder mem. Consejo Argentino para las Relaciones Internacionales. *Leisure interests:* gardening, birds, nature, reading. *Address:* c/o Casa de Gobierniero, Balcarce 50, 1064 Buenos Aires, Argentina (Office).

de la TOUR, Frances; British actress; b. 30 July 1944, Bovingdon, Herts.; d. of Charles de la Tour and Moyra (née Fessas) de la Tour; m. Tom Kempinski 1972 (divorced 1982); one s. one d.; ed Lycée français de Londres, Drama Centre, London; Hon. Fellow Goldsmiths Coll., Univ. of London 1999. *Stage appearances include:* with RSC: As You Like It 1967, The Relapse 1969, A Midsummer Night's Dream 1971, The Man of Mode 1971, Antony and Cleopatra 1999; Small Craft Warnings (Best Supporting Actress, Plays and Players Award) 1973, The Banana Box 1973, As You Like It (Oxford Playhouse) 1974, The White Devil 1976, Hamlet (title role) 1979, Duet for One (Best Actress, New Standard Award, Best Actress, Critics Award, Best Actress, Soc. of W End Theatres—SWET Award) 1980, Skirmishes 1981, Uncle Vanya 1982, Moon for the Misbegotten (Best Actress, SWET Award) 1983, St Joan (Royal Nat. Theatre) 1984, Dance of Death (Riverside Studios) 1985, Brighton Beach Memoirs (Royal Nat. Theatre) 1986, Lillian 1986, Façades 1988, King Lear 1989, When She Danced (Olivier Award) 1991, The Pope and the Witch 1992, Greasepaint 1993, Les Parents Terribles (Royal Nat. Theatre) 1994, Three Tall Women 1994–95, Blinded by the Sun (Royal Nat. Theatre) 1996, The Play About the Baby (Almeida Theatre) 1998, The Forest (Royal Nat. Theatre) 1998–99, Fallen Angels (Apollo) 2000–01 (Best Actress, Royal Variety Club), The Good Hope and Sketches by Harold Pinter (Royal Nat. Theatre) 2001–02, Dance of Death (Lyric) 2003. *Films include:* Rising Damp (Best Actress, Standard Film Award) 1980, The Cherry Orchard

1998, Love Actually 2002. *Television appearances include:* Rising Damp 1974, 1976, Cottage to Let 1976, Flickers 1980, Skirmishes 1982, Duet for One 1985, Partners 1986, Clem 1986, A Kind of Living (series) 1987/88, Downwardly Mobile (series) 1994, Cold Lazarus 1996, Tom Jones 1997, The Egg 2002. *Address:* c/o Claire Maroussas, ICM, Oxford House, 76 Oxford Street, London, W1N 0AX, England. *Telephone:* (20) 7636-6565. *Fax:* (20) 7323-0101 (Office).

DE LAGUNA, Frederica, PhD; American anthropologist; b. 3 Oct. 1906, Ann Arbor, Mich.; d. of Theodore and Grace Andrus de Laguna; ed Phoebe Anna Thorne School, Bryn Mawr, Pa, Bryn Mawr Coll. and Columbia Univ.; on staff of Univ. of Pa Museum 1931–34; US Soil Conservation Service 1935–36; Lecturer, Bryn Mawr Coll. 1938–41, Asst Prof. 1941–42, 1946–49, Assoc. Prof. 1949–55, Prof. of Anthropology 1955–75; USNR 1942–45; Chair. Dept of Sociology and Anthropology, Bryn Mawr Coll. 1950–67, Chair. Dept of Anthropology 1967–72, R. Kenan Jr Prof. 1974–75, Prof. Emer. 1975–; Bryn Mawr Coll. European Fellowship 1927; Columbia Univ. Fellowship 1930–31; Nat. Research Council Fellow 1936–37; Rockefeller Post-War Fellow 1945–46; Viking Fund Fellow 1949, Social Science Research Council Faculty Fellow 1962–63; Hon. Fellow Rochester (New York) Museum of Arts and Sciences 1941; Fellow AAAS, American Anthropological Asscn (Pres. 1966–67); Fellow and Hon. Life mem. Arctic Inst. of N America; mem. NAS; Hon. Life Mem. Alaska Anthropological Asscn (Hon. Pres. 1991–), Asscn for Northern Studies (Japan); Hon. DHumLitt (Alaska); Lindback Award for Distinguished Teaching 1975, Distinguished Service Award, American Anthropological Asscn 1986, Fiftieth Anniversary Award, Soc. for American Archaeology 1988, Alaska Anthropology Asscn Award for Lifetime Contribs. 1993, American Book Award, Before Columbus Foundation 1995. *Publications:* The Archaeology of Cook Inlet, Alaska 1934, The Eyak Indians of the Copper River Delta, Alaska (with Kaj Birket-Smith) 1938, The Prehistory of Northern North America as Seen from the Yukon 1947, Chugach Prehistory: The Archaeology of Prince William Sound, Alaska 1956, The Story of a Tlingit Community 1960, Selected Papers from the American Anthropologist 1888–1920 (ed.) 1960, Archeology of the Yakutat Bay Area, Alaska (jtly.) 1964, Under Mount Saint Elias: The History and Culture of the Yakutat Tlingit 1972, Voyage to Greenland: A Personal Initiation into Anthropology 1977, The Tlingit Indians, by George Thornton Emmons (ed.) 1991, Tales from the Dena 1995, Travels Among the Dena 2001; novels: The Thousand March: Adventures of an American Boy with Garibaldi 1930, The Arrow Points to Murder 1937, Fog on the Mountain 1938; contribs. to learned journals. *Address:* The Quadrangle, Apt. 1310, 3300 Darby Road, Haverford, PA 19041-1067, USA. *Telephone:* (610) 658-2298.

De LAURENTIIS, Dino; Italian film producer; b. Agostine de Laurentiis, 8 Aug. 1919, Torre Annunziata, Naples; s. of Aurelio and Giuseppina (née Salvatore) De Laurentiis; m. 1st Silvana Mangano 1949; one s. (deceased) three d.; m. 2nd Martha Schumacher; two d.; founded Real Ciné, Turin 1941; Exec. Producer Lux Film 1942; acquired Safir Studios and f. Teatri della Farnesina 1948; co-founder Ponti-De Laurentiis SpA 1950; Prin. De Laurentis Entertainment Group Inc. 1986–88, Prin., founder Dino De Laurentiis Co. 1988–95, now consultant to co.; numerous awards and prizes include Oscars for La Strada 1957 and Le Notti di Cabiria and 1958, Golden David Awards for Le Notti di Cabiria (Cannes Palme d'Or) 1958, The Tempest 1959, The Great War 1960, Tutti a Casa 1961, A Difficult Life 1962, The Bible 1966, Bandits in Milan 1968, Silver Ribbon (Italian Film Critics) for La Strada 1957, Venice Golden Lion for La Strada 1957, Muhomatsu No Issho 1958, The Great War 1960, Venice Silver Lion for Europa 51 1952, Golden Globe Awards for War and Peace 1956 and Best of Enemies 1963, Cavaliere del Lavoro, Irving Thalberg Memorial Award 2001. *Films produced include:* La Figlia del Capitano, Il Bandito, Molti Sogni per la Strada, Anna, Bitter Rice, La Strada, Le Notti di Cabiria, Ulysses, War and Peace, The Tempest, This Angry Age, Europa 51, The Gold of Naples, The Great War, Five Branded Women, I Love You Love, The Best of Enemies, Barabbas, To Bed or Not to Bed, The Bible, The Three Faces of a Woman, Barbarella, A Man Called Sledge, Waterloo, The Valachi Papers, Serpico, Mandingo, Three Days of the Condor 1974, Death Wish 1974, Lipstick 1976, Buffalo Bill and the Indians 1976, Drum 1976, King Kong 1976, The Shootlist 1976, King of the Gypsies 1978, The Brink's Job 1978, The Great Train Robbery 1978, Hurricane 1979, Flash Gordon 1980, Ragtime 1981, Conan the Barbarian 1982, Dead Zone 1983, Firestarter 1984, The Bounty 1984, Dune 1984, Year of the Dragon 1985, Manhunter 1985, Blue Velvet 1986, Trick or Treat 1986, King Kong Lives 1986, Crimes of the Heart 1986, Weeds 1987, Dracula's Widow 1987, Adult Education 1987, The Desperate Hours, Kuffs, Once Upon a Crime, Body of Evidence, Army of Darkness, Unforgettable, Assassins, Bound, Breakdown, U-571, Hannibal 2001. *Television:* Sometimes They Come Back 1991, Slave of Dreams 1995, Solomon and Sheba 1995. *Address:* Dino de Laurentiis Company, 100 Universal City Plaza, Universal City, CA 91608, USA (Office). *Telephone:* (818) 777-2111 (Office). *Fax:* (818) 866-5566 (Office). *Website:* www.dinodelaurentiis.it (Office).

de los ANGELES, Victoria; Spanish soprano singer; b. Victoria Gómez Cima, 1 Nov. 1923, Barcelona; m. Enrique Magriñá 1948 (deceased); two s.; ed Univ. and Conservatoire of Barcelona; Barcelona début 1945, Paris Opera and La Scala, Milan 1949, Royal Opera House, Covent Garden, London 1950, Metropolitan Opera House, New York 1951, Vienna State Opera 1957; numerous appearances at other opera houses, concert tours and recordings; Dr hc (Barcelona); 1st Prize, Geneva Int. Competition 1947; Cross of Lazo de

Dama of the Order of Isabel the Catholic, Condecoración Banda de la Orden Civil de Alfonso X (El Sabio), Spain and numerous other orders and decorations.

De LUCCHI, Michele; Italian architect; b. 8 Nov. 1951, Ferrara; s. of Alberto De Lucchi and Giuliana Zannini; ed Liceo Scientifico Enrico Fermi, Padua, Faculty of Architecture, Univ. of Florence; founder mem., Cavart (avant-garde design and architecture group) 1973–76; Asst Prof., Univ. of Florence 1976–77; worked with Gaetano Pesce, Superstudio, Andrea Branzi, Ettore Sottsass 1977–80; Consultant, Centrokappa Noviglio, Milan 1978; Consultant, Olivetti Synthesis, Massa 1979–, Olivetti SpA, Ivrea 1984–; freelance designer, several furniture mfrs 1979–; founder mem., Int. Designer Group Memphis 1981–. *Publication:* Architetture Verticali 1978. *Leisure interest:* travel photography. *Address:* Via Cenisio 40, 20154 Milan, Italy (Home). *Telephone:* (02) 314636 (Home).

de MADARIAGA, Isabel, PhD, FBA, FRHistS; British professor of Russian studies; b. 27 Aug. 1919, Glasgow, Scotland; d. of Salvador de Madariaga and Constance Archibald; m. Leonard B. Schapiro 1943 (divorced 1976); ed Ecole Internationale, Geneva, Switzerland, Headington School for Girls, Oxford, Instituto Escuela, Madrid, London Univ.; BBC Monitoring Service 1940–43; Cen. Office of Information London 1943–47; Econ. Information Unit., Treasury 1947–48; Editorial Asst, Slavonic and East European Review 1951–64; Part-time Lecturer in History, LSE 1953–66; Lecturer in History, Univ. of Sussex 1966–68; Sr Lecturer in Russian History, Lancaster Univ. 1968–71; Reader in Russian Studies, School of Slavonic and East European Studies, London Univ. 1971–81, Prof. 1981–84, Prof. Emer. 1984–; Corresp. mem. Royal Acad. of History, Spain. *Publications:* Britain, Russia and the Armed Neutrality of 1780 1963, Opposition (with G. Ionescu) 1965, Russia in the Age of Catherine the Great 1981, Catherine II: A Short History 1990, Politics and Culture in Eighteenth-Century Russia 1998; many scholarly articles. *Leisure interest:* music. *Address:* 25 Southwood Lawn Road, London, N6 5SD, England. *Telephone:* (20) 8341-0862.

de MAIZIÈRE, Lothar; German politician and lawyer; b. 2 March 1940, Nordhausen; m.; three d.; mem. Christian Democratic Union, Leader 1989–90; Deputy Prime Minister and Spokesman on Church Affairs 1989–90; Prime Minister German Democratic Republic and Minister of Foreign Affairs March–Oct. 1990; Minister without Portfolio 1990–91, Deputy Chair. CDU, Chair Brandenburg CDU Oct.-Dec. 1990, 1991; leader Lutheran Church Council; resgnd as CDU deputy 1991. *Publication:* Anwalt der Einheit 1996. *Address:* Am Kupfergraben 6/6A, 10117 Berlin, Germany.

de MAIZIÈRE, Gen. Ulrich; German army officer (retd); b. 24 Feb. 1912, Stade; s. of Walther de Maizière and Elisabeth Dückers; m. Eva Werner 1944; two s. two d.; ed Humanistisches Gymnasium, Hanover; army service 1930, commissioned 1933; Battalion and Regimental Adjutant, 50th Infantry Reg.; Gen. Staff Coll., Dresden 1940; during Second World War Gen. Staff Duties with 18th Motorized Infantry Div., G3 and Chief of Staff of 10th Mechanized Div., wounded 1944, at end of war Deputy Chief of Operations Div. Army Gen. Staff; prisoner-of-war 1945–47; dealer in books and sheet music 1947–51; Office of Fed. Commr for Nat. Security Affairs 1951; Col and Chief of Ops. Branch, Fed. Armed Forces Staff 1955; Commdr of Combat Team A1 and Commdr 2nd Brigade 1958; Deputy Commdr 1st Armoured Infantry Div. 1959; Commdt Fed. Armed Forces School for Leadership and Character Guidance 1960–62, Fed. Armed Forces Command and Staff Coll. 1962–64; Chief of Army Staff 1964–66; Chief of Fed. Armed Forces Staff 1966–72; Hon. Pres. Clausewitz Gesellschaft; Freiherr-von-Stein-Preis 1964, Commdr Legion of Merit 1965, 1969, Grand Officier, Légion d'honneur 1969; two Iron Crosses (2 kl) 1939 and (1kl) 1944, Grosses Bundesverdienstkreuz mit Stern und Schulterband 1970, Hermann-Ehlers-Preis 1986. *Publications:* Landesverteidigung im Rahmen der Gesamtverteidigung 1964, Soldatische Führung heute 1966, Bekenntnis zum Soldaten 1971, Führen im Frieden 1974, Verteidigung in Europa—Mitte 1975, In Der Pflicht (autobiog.) 1989. *Leisure interests:* classical music, literature, contemporary history. *Address:* 53177 Bonn, Tulpenbaumweg 20, Germany. *Telephone:* (228) 9524459. *Fax:* (228) 9524459.

DE MARCO, Guido, KUOM, BA, LLD, MP; Maltese head of state; b. 22 July 1931, Valletta; s. of Emmanuele de Marco and Giovanna Raniolo; m. Violet Saliba; one s. two d.; ed St Aloysius Coll. and Royal Univ. of Malta; Crown Counsel 1964–66; MP (Nationalist Party) 1966–99; Deputy Prime Minister 1987–96, Minister for Internal Affairs and Justice 1987–91, of Foreign Affairs 1991–96, 1998–99; Shadow Minister and Opposition Spokesman on Foreign Affairs 1996–98; Pres. of Malta 1999–; Pres. Gen. Ass. of UN 1990–91; Medal Order of Diplomatic Service Merit 1991, Grand Cross Order of Merit (Portugal) 1994, Chevalier Grand Cross Order of Merit (Italy) 1995, Hon. mem. Most Distinguished Order of St Michael and St George 2000, Collare dell'Ordine al Merito Melitense, Order Stara Planina with Ribbon (Bulgaria) 2001, Collar Estoniani Order of the Cross of Terra Mariana 2001, Grand Cross Special Class Order of Merit (FRG) 2001. *Publications:* A Presidency With a Purpose 1991, A Second Generation United Nations 1995, Malta's Foreign Policy in the Nineties 1996. *Leisure interests:* reading and travel. *Address:* Office of the President, The Palace,Valletta CMR 02, Malta. *Telephone:* 21221221. *Fax:* 21241241.

de MARIA y CAMPOS, Mauricio, MA; Mexican international civil servant and economist; b. 13 Oct. 1943, Mexico DF; s. of Mauricio de María y Campos and Teresa Castello; m. Patricia Meade 1981; two s. one d.; ed Nat. Univ. of

Mexico, Univ. of Sussex, UK; Head Planning and Policy Unit Mexican Nat. Science and Tech. Council 1971–72; Deputy Dir Evaluation Dept Tech. Transfer Ministry of Trade and Industry 1973–74, Dir Gen. Foreign Investment 1974–77, Vice-Minister Industrial Devt 1982–89; Dir Gen. Tax Incentives and Fiscal Promotion Ministry of Finance 1977–82; Exec. Vice-Pres. Banco Mexicano SOMEX 1989–92; Deputy Dir Gen. UNIDO 1992–93, Dir Gen. 1993–97; Amb. at Large and Special Adviser on UN Affairs, Ministry of Foreign Affairs 1998–2001; Amb. to Lesotho 2002–; mem. Int. Club of Rome 1998– (Pres. of Mexican Chapter 1998–); Grand Commendateur Ordre nat. du Mérite, Order of Francisco de Miranda (Venezuela); Great Decoration in Gold on the Sash (Austria); Grand Ordre du Mono (Togo). *Publications:* Challenges and Opportunities for Scientific and Technological Collaboration Between the EEC and Mexico 1990, The Transformation of the Mexican Automobile Industry during the 1980s 1992; various Publs on industrial and technological policy and on regional Devt. *Leisure interests:* classical music, writing, reading, swimming, jogging, dancing, journalism. *Address:* Mexican Embassy, c/o American Embassy, 254 Kingsway, P.O.B. 333, Maseru 100, Lesotho.

DE MELO, Eurico; Portuguese politician and chemical engineer; b. Sept. 1925; worked in the Textile industry; taught Textile Chem. at Faculty of Engineering, Oporto; mem. Popular Democratic Party (PPD, now PSD) 1974–; Chair. District Political Cttee of Braga; Civil Gov. of Braga 1975–76; Minister of the Interior 1980–81, of State and of Internal Admin. 1986–87; Deputy Prime Minister and Minister of Defence 1987–90; mem. Social Democratic Party (PSD) Nat. Political Cttee. *Address:* c/o Partido Social Democrata, Rua de São Caetano 9, 1296 Lisbon Codex, Portugal.

DE MEURON, Pierre, DipArch; Swiss architect; b. 1950, Basel; ed Swiss Fed. Tech. Univ. (ETH), Zurich; Asst to Prof. Dolf Schnebli, ETH, Zurich 1977; f. architectural practice Herzog & De Meuron (with Jacques Herzog, q.v. 1978; Prof. of Architecture and Design, ETH 1999–; Visiting Prof. Harvard Univ., Cambridge, Mass. 1989, Tulane Univ., New Orleans 1991; (all jtly with Jacques Herzog) Architecture Prize, Berlin Acad. of Arts 1987, Andrea Palladio Int. Prize for Architecture, Vicenza, Italy 1988, Pritzker Architecture Prize 2001. *Principal works include:* Blue House, Oberwil 1979–80, Photostudio Frei, Weil am Rhein 1981–82, Sperrholz Haus, Bottmingen 1984–85, Apartment Bldg, Hebelstr. 11, Basel 1984–88, Wohn- und Geschäftshaus Schwitter, Basel 1985–98, Goetz Art Gallery, Munich 1989–92, Wohn- und Geschäftshauss Schützenmattstr., Basel 1992–93, Dominus Winery, Napa Valley, Yountville, Calif. 1995–97, Tate Gallery Extension (Tate Modern), Bankside, London 1995–99, Cultural Centre and Theatre, Zurich 1996, Ricola Marketing Bldg, Laufen 1998. *Works in progress include:* Prada Headquarters, NY, De Young Museum, San Francisco, Walker Art Center Extension, Minneapolis; projects in England, France, Germany, Italy, Spain and Japan. *Address:* Herzog & De Meuron Architekten, Rheinschanze 6, Basel, 4056, Switzerland (Office). *Telephone:* (61) 3855758 (Office). *Fax:* (61) 3855757 (Office). *E-mail:* hdemarch@access.ch (Office).

DE MEYER, Jan Carl Hendrika Oswald, DJur; Belgian judge; b. 21 Feb. 1921, Malines; s. of Oswald De Meyer and Anna Maria Gysbrechts; m. Rita Smets 1949 (died 1986); one s. four d.; ed St Rombout's Coll. Malines, Faculté St Louis, Brussels and Univ. of Louvain; mem. Bar at Malines 1944–48, 1952–86; Substitute Auditor, Council of State 1948–49, mem. Coordination Office 1949–52, Assessor 1962–80; lecturer, Univ. of Louvain 1951–56, Ordinary Prof. 1956–86, Prof. Emer. 1986–, Head, Dept of Political and Social Sciences 1964–67, Dean, School of Law 1971–74; mem. Belgian Senate 1980–81; Judge, European Court of Human Rights 1986–98. *Address:* Kerselarenweg 1, B-3020 Herent; Faculteit Rechtsgeleerdheid, Tiensestraat 41, 3000 Louvain, Belgium. *Telephone:* (32) 16226384.

DE MICHELIS, Gianni; Italian politician and professor of chemistry; b. 26 Nov. 1940, Venice; Prof. of Chem., Univ. of Padua; Lecturer in Chem., Univ. of Venice; Nat. Chair. Unione Goliardica Italiana 1962–64; Councillor, Venice 1964–76; mem. Cen. Cttee Italian Socialist Party (PSI) 1969–76, mem. Nat. Exec. 1976–; MP for Venice 1976–; fmr Minister for State-owned Industries; Minister of Labour and Social Security 1986–87; Deputy Prime Minister 1988–89; Minister of Foreign Affairs 1989–92; Deputy Leader PSI 1992; charged with fraud May 1995; sentenced to 4 years imprisonment for corruption July 1995; on trial for siphoning cash from Third World projects 1996. *Address:* c/o Socialisti Italiani, Via del Corso 476, 00186 Rome, Italy.

DE MIRANDA, João Bernardo; Angolan politician; b. 18 July 1951; m.; Dir of Information, Rádio Nacional de Angola 1977–80; Ed.-in-Chief Jornal de Angola newspaper 1980–84; Sec. Movimento Popular de Libertação de Angola (MPLA) Ideological Area (Prov. of Luanda); Head of Political and Legal Affairs Div., MPLA Cen. Cttee 1985–89, Head of Information and Propaganda Dept 1989–91; Vice-Minister of Information 1991; Vice-Minister of Foreign Relations 1991–99, Minister of Foreign Affairs 1999–. *Publications include:* Nambuangongo. *Address:* Ministry of Foreign Affairs, Avda Comandante Gika 8, CP 1500, Luanda, Angola (Office). *Telephone:* (2) 323250 (Office). *Fax:* (2) 393246. *E-mail:* webdesigner@mirex.ebonet.net. *Website:* www.mirex.ebonet.net.

De MITA, Luigi Ciriaco; Italian politician; b. 2 Feb. 1928, Fusco, Avellino; fmr mem. Catholic Action; mem. Chamber of Deputies for Benevento-Avellino-Salerno 1963, 1972–; Nat. Counsellor Partito Democrazia Cristiana (Christian Democrats) (DC) 1964, later Political Vice-Sec.; Under-Sec. for the Interior; Minister of Industry and Commerce 1973–74, of Foreign Trade

1974–76; Minister without Portfolio with responsibility for the Mezzogiorno 1976–79; Sec.-Gen. DC 1982–88, Pres. 1989, 1991–92; Prime Minister of Italy 1988–89; Head Parl. Comm. for Constitutional Reform –1993. *Address:* c/o Partito Democrazia Cristiana, Piazza del Gesù 46, 00186 Rome, Italy.

DE MONTEBELLO, Comte Philippe, BA; French art historian and museum director; b. 16 May 1936, Paris; m. Edith Bradford Myles 1961; ed Harvard Univ., Inst. of Fine Arts, New York Univ., USA; Curatorial Asst, later Asst Curator, Assoc. Curator, Dept of European Paintings, Metropolitan Museum of Art 1963–69, Vice-Dir for Curatorial and Educational Affairs 1974–77, Acting Dir 1977–78, Dir. 1978–99, Dir and CEO 1999–; Dir Museum of Fine Arts, Houston, Tex. 1969–74; Gallatin Fellow, New York Univ. 1981; Hon. LLD (Lafayette Coll.) 1979, Hon. DHumLitt (Bard Coll., New York) 1981, Hon. DFA (Iona Coll., New Rochelle) 1982; Kt Commdr, Pontifical Order of St Gregory the Great 1984; Chevalier, Légion d'honneur 1991; Nat. Inst. of Social Sciences Gold Medal 1989, Spanish Inst. Gold Medal Award 1992, Distinguished Alumnus Award, New York Univ. 1998 and other awards. *Publications:* Peter Paul Rubens (monograph) 1968 and numerous articles, dictionary entries and introductions to exhbn catalogues. *Leisure interests:* chess, tennis, music. *Address:* Metropolitan Museum of Art, 1000 Fifth Avenue, New York, NY 10028 (Office); 1150 Fifth Avenue, 4B, New York, NY 10028, USA (Home). *Telephone:* (212) 570-3902 (Office); (212) 289-4475 (Home). *Fax:* (212) 650-2102 (Office).

DE MORNAY, Rebecca; American film and television actress; b. 29 Aug. 1961, Los Angeles, Calif.; m. Bruce Wagner 1989 (divorced 1991); ed in Austria and at Lee Strasberg Inst. in Los Angeles; apprenticed at Zoetrope Studios. *Theatre includes:* Born Yesterday 1988, Marat/Sade 1990. *Films include:* One from the Heart 1982, Risky Business 1983, Testament 1983, The Slugger's Wife 1985, Runaway Train 1985, The Trip to Bountiful 1985, Beauty and The Beast 1987, And God Created Woman 1988, Feds 1988, Dealers 1989, Backdraft 1991, The Hand that Rocks the Cradle (Best Actress, Cognac Crime Film Festival 1992), Guilty as Sin 1993, The Three Musketeers 1993, Never Talk to Strangers, The Winner 1996, Thick as Thieves 1998, Table for One 1998, The Right Temptation 1999, Night Ride Home 1999, Range of Motion 2000, A Girl Thing 2001. *Television appearances include:* The Murders in the Rue Morgue 1986, By Dawn's Early Light 1990, An Inconvenient Woman 1992, Blind Side 1993, Getting Out 1994, The Shining 1996, The Con 1997, Night Ride Home 1999, The Conversion (Dir) 1996, ER 1999, Salem Witch Trials 2002.

DE NIRO, Robert; American actor; b. 17 Aug. 1943, New York; s. of the late Robert De Niro and of Virginia Admiral; m. Diahnne Abbott 1976; one s. one d.; two c. by Toukie Smith; f. and Pres. Tri Beca Productions 1989–; co-cr. We Will Rock You (musical) 2002; Commdr Ordre des Arts et des Lettres; Lifetime Achievement Award, Gotham Awards 2001. *Films include:* The Wedding Party 1969, Jennifer On My Mind 1971, Bloody Mama, Born to Win 1971, The Gang That Couldn't Shoot Straight 1971, Bang the Drum Slowly 1973, Mean Streets 1973, The Godfather, Part II 1974 (Acad. Award for Best Supporting Actor), The Last Tycoon, Taxi Driver 1976, New York, New York, 1900 1977, The Deer Hunter 1978, Raging Bull (Acad. Award Best Actor) 1980, True Confessions 1981, The King of Comedy 1982, Once Upon a Time in America 1984, Falling in Love 1984, Brazil 1984, The Mission 1985, Angel Heart 1986, The Untouchables 1987, Letters Home from Vietnam, Midnight Run 1988, We're No Angels 1989, Stanley and Iris 1989, Goodfellas 1989, Jacknife 1989, Awakenings 1990, Fear No Evil 1990, Backdraft 1990, Cape Fear 1990, Guilty of Suspicion 1991, Mistress 1992, Night and the City 1992, Mad Dog and Glory 1992, This Boy's Life 1993, Mary Shelley's Frankenstein 1993, A Bronx Tale (also Dir, co-produced) 1993, Sleepers 1996, The Fan 1996, Marvin's Room 1996,, Great Expectations 1997, Jackie Brown 1998, Ronin 1998, Analyze This 1999, Flawless 1999 (also producer), The Adventures of Rocky and Bullwinkle (also producer) 1999, Meet the Parents (also producer) 2000, Men of Honor 2000, 15 Minutes 2001, The Score 2001, Showtime 2002, City By the Sea 2002, Analyze That 2002, City By the Sea 2003; producer Thunderheart 1992, Entrophy 1999, Conjugating Niki 2000, Prison Song 2001, About a Boy 2002. *Address:* CAA, 9830 Wilshire Boulevard, Beverly Hills, CA 90212, USA.

de NOINVILLE, Guillaume; French business executive; b. 8 May 1960, Paris; s. of Christian Durey de Noinville and Béatrice Gallimard; m. Claire de Laguiche; three s. one d.; ed Inst. d'Etudes Politiques, Paris; Finance and Control Dept, Bull Group, Paris 1984–86; Treas. Electrolux France, Senlis 1986–92, Man. Dir Electrolux Financement (leasing co.), Senlis 1992–96, Chief Finance Officer Electrolux France 1994–, Belgium 1998–, Pres.-Dir Gen. Electrolux France SA 2001–. *Address:* Electrolux France S.A., BP 139, 43 avenue Félix Louat, 60307 Senlis Cedex (Office); 8 rue du Gué d'Orient, 95470 Saint-Witz, France (Home). *Telephone:* (3) 44-62-26-39 (Office). *Fax:* (3) 44-62-21-89 (Office). *E-mail:* guillaume.de-noinville@electrolux.fr (Office). *Website:* www.electrolux.com (Office).

DE OLIVEIRA MACIEL, Marco Antônio, LLB, MA; Brazilian politician and lawyer; b. 21 July 1940, Recife; s. of José do Rego Maciel and Carmen Sylvia Cavalcanti de Oliveira Maciel; m. Anna Maria Ferreira; one s. two d.; ed Catholic Univ. of Pernambuco, Pernambuco Univ.; Adviser to Pernambuco State Govt 1964–66; Prof. of Public Int. Law, Catholic Univ. of Pernambuco 1966–; State Deputy, Pernambuco Legis. Ass., Govt Leader 1967–71; Regional Sec. ARENA Party 1969–70, Second Nat. Sec. 1972, First Sec. 1974–75; Fed. Deputy 1971–79, Pres. Chamber of Deputies 1977–79; Gov. Pernambuco State 1979–82; Fed. Senator for PDS Party 1982; Minister for

Educ. 1985–86; Minister Chief of Staff of Pres. 1986; Pres. Provisional Nat. Comm. Partido da Frente Liberal (PFL) 1984–85, Nat. Pres. 1987, Fed. Senator for PFL 1990, mem. Nat. Council, Leader PFL in Senate 1990; Minority Leader in Senate 1990–, Govt Leader 1991–92; Vice-Pres. of Brazil 1994–; mem. Pernambuco Section Brazilian Bar Asscn, Brazilian Acad. of Political and Moral Sciences 1993–, Argentinian Law Asscn; numerous honours including Grand Cross, Order of Rio Branco, Brasilia Order of Merit, Légion d'honneur (France), Grand Cross, Order of Infante Dom Henrique (Portugal), Grand Cross, Order of May (Argentina) 1979, Cross of Merit (FRG), Ordre nat. du Mérite (France), City of Recife Medal of Merit. *Publications:* numerous Publs on politics and educ. *Address:* Office of the Vice-President, Palácio do Planalto, 4° andar, 70150-900 Brasília, DF, Brasil (Office). *Telephone:* (61) 411-1573 (Office). *Fax:* (61) 323-1461 (Office). *E-mail:* casacivil@planalto.gov.br (Office). *Website:* www.planalto.gov.br (Office).

DE PALACIO DEL VALLE-LERSUNDI, Loyola; Spanish politician; b. 16 Sept. 1950, Madrid; ed Univ. Complutense de Madrid; Tech. Sec. Gen. Fed. of Press Asscns 1979–82; First Gen. Pres. Nuevas Generaciones 1977–78; Senator Vice-Pres. Popular Group 1986–89; mem. Nat. Exec. Cttee Partido Popular (PP) 1988–89; Deputy for Segovia 1988–; Vice-Pres. parliamentary PP; Minister of Agric., Fisheries and Food 1996–99; Vice-Pres. of EC and Commr for Relations with European Parl., Transport and Energy Sept. 1999–. *Address:* Commission of the European Communities, 200 rue de la Loi, 1049 Brussels, Belgium (Office). *Telephone:* (2) 299-11-11 (Office). *Fax:* (2) 295-01-38 (Office). *Website:* europa.eu.int (Office).

DE PALMA, Brian, MA; American film director; b. 11 Sept. 1940, Newark, NJ; s. of Anthony Fredrick De Palma and Vivienne (née Muti) De Palma; m. Gale Ann Hurd 1991; one d.; ed Sarah Lawrence Coll., Bronxville and Columbia Univ. *Films include:* (short films) Icarus 1960, 660124: The Story of an IBM Card 1961, Wotan's Wake 1962; (feature length) The Wedding Party 1964, The Responsive Eye (documentary) 1966, Murder à la Mode 1967, Greetings 1968, Dionysus in '69 (co-Dir) 1969, Hi Mom! 1970, Get to Know Your Rabbit 1970, Sisters 1972, Phantom of the Paradise 1974, Obsession 1975, Carrie 1976, The Fury 1978, Home Movies 1979, Dressed to Kill 1980, Blow Out 1981, Scarface 1983, Body Double 1984, Wise Guys 1985, The Untouchables 1987, Casualties of War 1989, Bonfire of the Vanities 1990, Raising Cain 1992, Carlito's Way 1993, Mission Impossible 1996, Snake Eyes 1998, Mission to Mars 2000, Femme Fatale 2002. *Address:* Paramount Pictures, Lubitsch Annex #119, 5555 Melrose Avenue #119, W Hollywood, CA 90038, USA.

DE PALMA, Rossy; Spanish actress; b. Rosa Elena García, Palma de Mallorca; fmrly singer with punk band Peor Imposible; fashion model in Spain and for John-Paul Gaultier, Paris. *Films include:* Law of Desire, Women on the Verge of a Nervous Breakdown, Kika, Las Hetairas, Prêt à Porter.

DE PERETTI, Jean-Jacques; French politician; b. 21 Sept. 1946, Clermont-Ferrand; three c.; ed Inst. des Hautes Etudes Internationales; Asst Lecturer, St-Maur Faculty of Law and Univs. of Orléans and Paris I 1969–84; Chargé de Mission, Cabinet of Pierre Messmer 1972; Dir de Cabinet to Pres. of Paris Region 1974; Chargé de Mission to André Bord, Sec.-Gen. of Union des Démocrates pour la République (UDR) 1976; Chargé de Mission, Cabinet of Antoine Rufenacht, Sec. of State to Prime Minister; Sec. of State to Minister for Industry, Trade and Craft Trades; Man. Exec. IBM until 1986; Adviser to Prime Minister Jacques Chirac 1986; Mayor of Sarlat 1989–; fmr mem. Regional Council and Deputy to Nat. Ass. for Dordogne Dept's 4th constituency; Departmental Councillor for Dordogne 1992–; Nat. Sec. Rassemblement pour la République (RPR) 1990–93, Deputy Sec.-Gen. 1994–95; Minister for Overseas France May–Nov. 1995; Minister-Del. to Prime Minister with responsibility for Overseas France 1995–97; mem. Regional Council of Aquitaine; mem. Hudson Inst. *Address:* 11 rue Barbert de Jouy, 75007 Paris (Office); Mairie, 24200 Sarlat-la-Canéda, France. *Telephone:* (5) 53-31-53-30 (Office). *Fax:* (5) 53-31-08-04 (Office). *E-mail:* jjpc@wanadoo.fr (Office).

DE PERIO-SANTOS, Rosalinda, BS, LLB; Philippine diplomatist and lawyer; b. 18 Oct. 1939; d. of José T. De Perio and Soledad M. Molina; m. (husband deceased); one d.; ed Univ. of the Philippines, Far Eastern Univ., Columbia Univ., New York and Northwestern Univ., IL, USA; Adviser Philippines Mission to UN, New York 1962–64; Vice-Consul Consulate-Gen., New York 1964–66; Consul Consulate-Gen., Chicago, USA 1966–72; Minister Counsellor and Consul-Gen. Brasilia, Brazil 1981–83; Perm. Rep. to UN (and other int. orgs) Geneva, Switzerland 1986–89; Amb. to Israel and Amb.(non-resident) to Cyprus and Jordan 1993–; Colombo Plan Fellow 1961, Rockefeller Fellow, Carnegie Endowment for Int. Peace, Columbia Univ., NY 1961–62, Hague Acad. Int. Fellow 1974 Outstanding Zambaleña 1986, Outstanding Woman Lawyer, CIRDA 1987. *Address:* Embassy of the Philippines, Textile Centre Building, 13th Floor, 2 Rehov Kaufmann, POB 50085, Tel-Aviv 68012, Israel (Office). *Telephone:* 3-5175263 (Office). *Fax:* 3-5102229 (Office). *E-mail:* filembis@netvision.net.il (Office).

DE PEYER, Gervase, FRCM; British clarinettist and conductor; b. 11 April 1926, London; s. of Esme Everard Vivian de Peyer and Edith Mary Bartlett; m. 1st Sylvia Southcombe 1950 (divorced 1971); one s. two d.; m. 2nd Susan Rosalind Daniel 1971 (divorced 1979); m. 3rd Katia Perret Aubry 1980; ed King Alfred's School, London, Bedales School and Royal Coll. of Music, London; served HM Forces 1945, 1946; studied in Paris 1949; int. soloist 1949–; Founder mem. Melos Ensemble 1950–72; Prin. Clarinet, London Symphony Orchestra 1955–72; Founder and Conductor Melos Sinfonia of

Washington 1992; Dir London Symphony Wind Ensemble; fmr Assoc. Conductor Haydn Orchestra of London; solo clarinettist, Chamber Music Soc. of Lincoln Center, NY 1969–; fmr Resident Conductor Victoria Int. Festival, BC, Canada; Co-founder and Artistic Dir Innisfree Music Festival, Pa, USA; mem. Faculty, Mannes Coll. of Music, NY; also conductor; recording artist with all maj. companies (most recorded solo clarinettist in the world); gives recitals and master classes throughout the world; Gold Medallist Worshipful Co. of Musicians 1948, Charles Gros Grand Prix du Disque 1961, 1962, Plaque of Honor for Acad. of Arts and Sciences of America for recording of Mozart concerto 1962. *Leisure interests:* theatre, good food, anything dangerous, travel, sport. *Address:* Porto Vecchio 109, 1250 S Washington Street, Alexandria, VA 22314, USA; 42 Tower Bridge Wharf, St Katherine's Way, London, E1 9UR, England. *Telephone:* (703) 739-0824 (USA); (20) 7265-1110 (UK). *Fax:* (703) 739-0572 (USA); (20) 7265-1110 (UK).

DE PRÉMONVILLE, Myrène Sophie Marie; French designer; b. 1 April 1949, Hendaye; d. of Jean-Marie de Prémonville and Monique Arnault; m. (divorced); one d.; gained degree in decorative arts; Asst, Pronostyl 1970–75; freelance designer 1975–83; f. Myrène de Prémonville SARL 1983, Myrène de Prémonville SA 1986. *Leisure interests:* art, cinema, travel. *Address:* 180 rue de Grenelle, 75007 Paris, France. *Telephone:* 47-05-44-10.

de RACHEWILTZ, Igor, PhD, FAHA; Italian historian and philologist; b. 11 April 1929, Rome; s. of Bruno Guido and Antonina Perosio; m. Ines Adelaide Brasch 1956; one d.; ed St Gabriel's Coll., Rome Univ. and ANU; Research scholar ANU 1956–60, Sr Lecturer Faculty of Asian Studies 1963–65, Fellow Inst. of Advanced Studies 1965–67, Sr Fellow 1967–94, Visiting Fellow 1995–; Lecturer in Asian Civilization, Canberra Univ. Coll. 1960–62; Visiting Prof. Bonn Univ. 1979, Rome Univ. 1996, 1999, 2001, 2002; mem. Sonderforschungsbereich 12, 1979–; Vice-Pres. Int. Asscn for Mongol Studies 1992–2002; Hon. Pres. Int. Centre for Genghis Khan Studies, Mongolia; Kt Order of Merit of Italian Repub. 1998; Hon. DLitt (Univ. Rome La Sapienza) 2001. *Publications:* The Hsi-yu lu by Yeh-lü Ch'u-ts'ai 1962, Papal Envoys to the Great Khans 1971, Index to the Secret History of the Mongols 1972, The Preclassical Mongolian Version of the Hsiao-ching 1982, The Secret History of the Mongols 1971–86, Repertory of Proper Names in Yüan Literary Sources 1988–96, text edn and word-index of Erdeni-yin tobci 1990–91, In the Service of the Khan 1993, Le matériel mongol du Houa i i iu de Houng-ou (1389): Commentaires 1995, The Mongolian Tanjur version of the Bodhicaryāvatāra 1996; numerous articles on Sino-Mongolian topics, medieval history and Altaic philology. *Leisure interests:* botany, travel. *Address:* c/o Division of Pacific and Asian History, Australian National University, Canberra ACT 0200; 9 Ridley Street, Turner, ACT 2612, Australia (Home). *Telephone:* (2) 6125-3171; (2) 6248-0557 (Home). *Fax:* (2) 6125-5525. *E-mail:* ider@coombs .anu.edu.au (Office). *Website:* rspas.anu.edu.au/pah (Office).

de RIVOYRE, Christine Berthe Claude Denis, LèsL; French author and journalist; b. 29 Nov. 1921, Tarbes, Hautes-Pyrénées; d. of François de Rivoyre and Madeleine Ballande; ed Insts. du Sacré-Coeur of Bordeaux and Poitiers, Faculté des lettres de Paris and School of Journalism, Syracuse Univ., NY; journalist with Le Monde 1950–55; Literary Ed. of Marie-Claire 1955–65; mem. Haut comité de la langue française 1969–, Jury of Prix Médicis 1970–; Chevalier, Légion d'honneur, Chevalier des Arts et des Lettres; Prix Interallié (for Le petit matin) 1968; Prix des Trois Couronnes (for Boy) 1973; Grand Prix de la ville de Bordeaux 1973; Grand Prix littéraire Prince Rainier de Monaco 1982; Prix Paul Morand 1984. *Publications:* L'alouette au miroir 1956, La mandarine 1957, La tête en fleurs 1960, La glace à l'ananas 1962, Les sultans 1964, Le petit matin 1968, Le seigneur des chevaux (with Alexander Kalda) 1969, Fleur d'agonie 1970, Boy 1973, Le voyage à l'envers 1977, Belle alliance 1982, Reine-mère 1985, Crépuscule taille unique 1989, Racontez-moi les flamboyants 1995, Le Petit matin 1998. *Address:* Editions Grasset, 61 rue des Saints-Péres, 75006 Paris (Office); Onesse-Laharie, 40110 Morcenx, France.

DE ROMILLY, Jacqueline, DèsSc; French academic; b. 26 March 1913, Chartres; d. of Maxime David and Jeanne Malvoisin; m. Michel Worms de Romilly 1940 (divorced 1973); ed Ecole Normale Supérieure, Univ. of Paris; Prof. of Ancient Greek, Univ. of Lille 1949–57, Univ. of Paris-Sorbonne 1957–73; Prof. Coll. de France 1973–84, Hon. Prof. 1984; mem. Acad. des Inscriptions et Belles Lettres, Inst. de France 1975–, Acad. Française 1988–; Corresp. mem. 8 Acads.; several French Acad. Prizes; Grand Officier Légion d'honneur, des Palmes académiques, Ordre des Arts et des Lettres; Grand Croix Ordre nat. du mérite; Commdr Order of the Phoenix (Greece); Insignia of Honour for Science and Art (Austria). *Publications:* L'enseignement en détresse 1984, Sur les chemins de Ste. Victoire 1987, Ouverture à coeur 1990, Pourquoi la Grèce? 1992, Les Oeufs de Pâques 1993, Lettres aux Parents sur les Choix Scolaires 1993, Tragédies grecques au fil des ans 1995, Rencontres avec la Grèce antique 1995, Alcibiade ou les dangers de l'ambition 1995, Jeux de lumière sur l'Hellade 1996, Hector 1997, Le Trésor des savoirs oubliés 1998, Laisse flotter les rubans 1999, La Grèce antique contre la violence 2000, Héros tragiques, héros lyriques 2001, Thucydides and Greek Tragedy, Sous des dehors si calmes 2002 and about twenty books on classical Greek literature. *Address:* 12 rue Chernoviz, 75016 Paris, France. *Telephone:* 1-42-24-59-07.

de ROSNAY, Joël, DèsSc; French biologist; b. 12 June 1937, Mauritius; s. of Gaëtan de Rosnay and Natacha Koltchine; m. Stella Jebb 1959; one s. two d.; ed MIT; Dir of Applied Research, Inst. Pasteur 1975–84; Dir of Devt and Int.

Relations, Cité des sciences et de l'industrie de La Villette 1988–97, Dir of Strategy 1996–99, Dir of Evaluation 1999–; Columnist Europe 1 1987–95; Chevalier Légion d'honneur, Officier Ordre nat. du Mérite; Prix de l'Information Scientifique, Acad. des Sciences 1990. *Publications:* Les origines de la vie 1965, Le macroscope 1975, La révolution biologique 1982, Branchez-vous 1985, L'avenir du vivant 1988, L'avenir en direct 1989, Les rendez-vous du futur 1991, L'homme symbiotique 1995, La plus belle histoire du monde (contrib.) 1996. *Leisure interests:* skiing, surfing. *Address:* 146 rue de l'Université, 75007 Paris; Cité des Sciences et de l'Industrie de la Villette, 30 avenue Corentin Cariou, 75019 Paris, France.

de RUITER, Hendrikus; Netherlands business executive; b. 3 March 1934, The Hague; m. Theodora O. van der Jagt 1957; one s. two d.; ed Technological Univ. of Delft; Research Chemist, Koninklijke/Shell Laboratorium Amsterdam (KSLA) 1956; Chief Technologist, Berre Refinery, Compagnie de Raffinage Shell-Berre 1965–67; returned to KSLA 1967; joined Shell Int. Petroleum Co. Ltd (SIPC), London 1969; Man. Dir Shell Co. of Thailand and Pres. Société Shell du Laos 1972; Coal Production and Trading Co-ordinator, SIPC 1975; Pres. Shell Int. Trading Co. 1979; Dir Shell Internationale Petroleum Maatschappij BV 1981; Man. Dir NV Koninklijke Nederlandsche Petroleum Maatschappij; mem. Presidium, Bd of Dirs, Shell Petroleum NV and Man. Dir The Shell Petroleum Co. Ltd 1983–; mem. Supervisory Bd AEGON NV (Vice-Chair. 1993–, Heineken NV 1993–, Koninklijke Ahold NV (Chair.) 1994–, Wolters Kluwer NV (Chair.) 1994–, Royal Dutch Petroleum Co. 1994–, Beers NV (Chair) 1995–2002, Coris Group PLC (fmrly Hoogovens Group BV) (Vice-Chair.) 1995–2002, Koninklijke Vopak NV (fmrly Koninklijke Pakhoed NV) 1995–2002; Dir Shell Petroleum NV 1994–, The Shell Petroleum Co. Ltd 1994–, Chair. Univar NV (fmrly part of Koninklijke Vopak) 2002–; Kt Order of the Netherlands Lion 1987. *Address:* c/o Royal Dutch Petroleum Company, Carel van Bylandtlaan 30, PO Box 162, 2501 AN The Hague, Netherlands. *Telephone:* (70) 3774504.

DE SANCTIS, Roman William, MD; American cardiologist; b. 30 Oct. 1930, Cambridge Springs, Pa; s. of Vincent De Sanctis and Marguerita De Sanctis; m. Ruth A. Foley 1955; four d.; ed Univ. of Arizona, Harvard Medical School; Resident in Medicine Mass. Gen. Hosp. 1958–60, Fellow in Cardiology 1960–62, Dir Coronary Care Unit 1967–80, Dir Clinical Cardiology 1980–98, Dir Emer. 1998–; Physician 1970–; mem. Faculty of Medicine, Harvard Medical School 1964–, Prof. 1973–98, James and Evelyn Jenks and Paul Dudley White Prof. of Medicine 1998–; U.S. Navy Consultant and Asst to Attending Physician to U.S. Congress 1956–58; Master, American Coll. of Physicians 1995; Fellow, American Coll. of Cardiology, Inst. of Medicine; Distinguished Clinical Teaching Award, Harvard Medical School 1980; Gifted Teacher Award (American Coll. of Cardiologists), Hon. DSc (Wilkes Coll., Univ. of Ariz.). *Publications:* author and co-ed. of over 130 scientific papers. *Leisure interests:* travel, music, golf. *Address:* Massachusetts General Hospital, 15 Parkman Street, Suite 467, Boston, MA 02114 (Office); 5 Thoreau Circle, Winchester, MA 01890, USA (Home). *Telephone:* (781) 7262889 (Office); (617) 729-1453 (Home). *Fax:* (617) 726-5271.

de SAVARY, Peter John; British entrepreneur; b. 11 July 1944, Essex; m. 3rd Lucille Lana Paton; three d. (and two d. from previous m.); ed Charterhouse; commercial activities in finance, energy, leisure and property; British challenger for The Americas Cup 1983, 1987; Chair. The Carnegie Club, Scotland 1994–; Chair. Carnegie Abbey, Rhode Island; Chair. Cherokee Plantation, SC; Tourism Personality of the Year (English Tourist Bd) 1988. *Leisure interests:* sailing, carriage driving, riding. *Address:* Skibo Castle, Dornoch, Sutherland, IV25 3RQ, Scotland.

de SCHOUTHEETE de TERVARENT, Baron Philippe; Belgian diplomatist; b. 21 May 1932, Berlin, Germany; m. Bernadette Joos de Ter Beerst 1956; two s.; joined Belgian diplomatic service; served Paris 1959–61, Cairo 1962–65, Madrid 1968–72, Bonn 1972–76; Chef de Cabinet to Minister of Foreign Affairs 1980–81; Amb. to Spain 1981–85; Political Dir 1985–87; Perm. Rep. to EU 1987–97; Guest Prof. Univ. of Louvain la Neuve 1990–; Rep. of order of Malta to EC 2000–; Special Adviser EC 2000–; mem. Bd. of Dirs Centre for European Policy Studies, Acad. Royale de Belgique; Adolphe Bentinck Prize 1997; Grand Officer, Order of Leopold. *Publications:* La coopération politique européenne 1986, Une Europe pour tous 1997, The Case for Europe 2000. *Address:* Avenue de Broqueville 99, 1200 Brussels, Belgium.

DE SOTO, Alvaro; Peruvian diplomatist; b. 16 March 1943, Argentina; m. Irene Philippi 1985 (divorced); two s. one d.; ed Int. School, Geneva, Catholic Univ. Lima, San Marcos Univ. Lima, Diplomatic Acad. Lima and Inst. of Int. Studies Geneva; Acting Dir Maritime Sovereignty Div. Ministry of Foreign Affairs 1975–78; Deputy Perm. Rep. of Peru at UN, Geneva 1978–82; Special Asst to UN Sec.-Gen. 1982–86; Asst Sec.-Gen. and Exec. Asst to UN Sec.-Gen. 1987–91; Personal Rep. of UN Sec.-Gen. in El Salvador Peace Negotiations 1990–91; Asst Sec.-Gen. UN Office for Research and Collection of Information 1991; Sr Political Adviser to UN Sec.-Gen. 1992–94; Asst Sec.-Gen. for Political Affairs 1995–99, Under-Sec.-Gen., Special Adviser to Sec.-Gen. on Cyprus 1999–2000; Special Rep. of the Sec.-Gen. for Cyprus and Chief of Mission UNFICYP (UN Peace-Keeping Force in Cyprus) 2000–. *Address:* UNFICYP, Department of Peace-Keeping Operations, Room S-3727-B, United Nations, New York, NY 10017, USA (Office). *Telephone:* (212) 963-8079 (Office). *Fax:* (212) 963-9222 (Office). *E-mail:* desoto@un.org (Office). *Website:* www.un.org/Depts/dpko.

DE SOTO, Guillermo Fernández; Colombian politician and international organization official; b. 1956; ed Univ. of Bogotá, Georgetown Univ., USA; Under-Minister of Foreign Affairs 1980, Minister 1998–2002; f. Groupe de Contadora; Intermediate Sec. Groupe de Rio; Dir Chamber of Commerce, Bogota 1993–98; Sec.-Gen. Andean Community 2002–. *Address:* Comunidad Andina, Ave. Paseo de la República 3895, esq. Aramburú, San Isidro, Lima 27, Peru (Office). *Telephone:* (1) 4111400 (Office). *Fax:* (1) 2213329 (Office). *E-mail:* contacto@comunidadandina.org. *Website:* www.comunidadandina.org (Office).

DE SOTO, Hernando; Peruvian economist; b. 2 June 1941, Arequipa; ed Institut Universitaire de Hautes Etudes Internationales, Geneva, Switzerland; fmr economist for GATT; fmr Pres. Exec. Cttee, Copper Exporting Countries Org. (CIPEC); fmr Man. Dir Universal Eng Corpn; a fmr prin. Swiss Bank Corpn Consultant Group; fmr Gov. Cen. Reserve Bank, Peru; Personal Rep. and Chief Adviser to Pres. Alberto Fujimori –2000; currently Pres. Inst. for Liberty and Democracy (ILD), Lima; Sir Antony Fisher Int. Memorial Award – Atlas 1990, 2001, one of five 'Leaders for the New Millennium' chosen by Time magazine 1999. *Publications:* The Other Path 1986, The Mystery of Capital: Why Capitalism Triumphs in the West and Fails Everywhere Else 2000. *Address:* Instituto Libertad y Democracia, Av. Del Parque Norte 829, San Isidro, Lima 27, Peru (Office). *Telephone:* (1) 2254131 (Office). *Fax:* (1) 4759559 (Office). *E-mail:* postmaster@ild.org.pe (Office). *Website:* www.ild.org.pe (Office).

de THÉ, Guy Blaudin, MD, PhD; French cancer research specialist; b. 5 May 1930, Marseilles; s. of François Blaudin de Thé and Madeleine du Verne; m. Colette Pierrard de Maujoux 1958 (died 1991); one s. two d.; ed Faculty of Medicine, Marseilles, Univ. of Paris, Sorbonne; Research Asst Duke Univ. Medical Center, USA 1961–63; Visiting Scientist, Laboratory of Viral Oncology, Nat. Cancer Inst., NIH, USA 1963–65; Head of Unit of Electron Microscopy, CNRS 1965–67; Chief, Unit of Biological Carcinogenesis, WHO Int. Agency for Research on Cancer, Lyons 1967–78; Dir of Research Faculty of Medicine A. Carrel, Lyon and Cancer Research Inst., Villejuif, Paris 1979–90, CNRS 1990–; Head Unit of Epidemiology of Oncogenic Viruses and Prof. Pasteur Inst., Paris 1990–97, Prof. Emer. 1998–; Visiting Prof. Faculty of Public Health, Harvard Univ. 1981–85; Fogarty Scholar-in-Residence, NIH, Bethesda USA 1992–96; Gen. Sec., then Pres. Int. Asscn of Retrovirology 1998–99; mem. Scientific Council, Ligue nat. française contre le cancer 1972–74; mem. Nat. Acad. Médecine, Soc. française de Microbiologie, American Soc. for Cell Biology, American Asscn for Cancer Research, AAAS, European Asscn for Cancer Research; Corresp. mem. Inst. de France Acad. des Sciences; Scientific Prize, Acad. of Sciences 1971, Medical Research Foundation 1979, Collège de France 1981, Silver Medal, CNRS 1981, Life Sciences Inst. Paris 1991; Officier, Ordre nat. du Mérite. *Publications:* many publs on the cell virus relationship in avian and murine leukaemia viruses and role of viruses in human tumours (Burkitt's lymphoma in Africa, Nasopharyngeal carcinoma in South-East Asia); Retroviruses and Central Nervous Degenerative Diseases; Sur la piste du cancer (popular scientific book) 1984, Modes de vie et cancers 1988. *Leisure interest:* arts. *Address:* Institut Pasteur, Département des rétrovirus, 28 rue Dr Roux, 75015 Paris (Office); 14 rue Le Regrattier, 75004 Paris, France (Home). *Telephone:* 1-45-68-89-30 (Office); 1-43-54-01-22 (Home). *Fax:* 1-45-68-89-31 (Office); 1-40-51-05-15 (Home). *E-mail:* dethe@pasteur.fr (Office).

de VAUCLEROY, Baron Gui, LLD, MEconSc; Belgian business executive; b. 28 Sept. 1933, Dendermonde; ed Univ. of Louvain; Research Asst Centre for Social Studies 1957–59; joined Delhaize Le Lion 1960, mem. Exec. Cttee 1967, Vice-Pres. Exec. Cttee 1984, CEO and Pres. Exec. Cttee 1990–98, Chair. Bd Dirs 1999–; Chair. Fed. of Enterprises in Belgium 1999–2002; Vice-Pres. Union of Industrial Employers Europe 2000–02; Commdr de l'Ordre de Léopold, Grand Officier de l'Ordre de Léopold II. *Address:* Delhaize Group, Rue Osseghem 53, PO Box 60, Molenbeek-Saint-Jean, Brussels 1080 (Office); Avenue Baron Albert d'Huart 137, 1950 Kraainem, Belgium (Home). *Telephone:* (2) 412-21-14 (Office). *Fax:* (2) 412-21-18 (Office).

DE VICENZO, Roberto; Argentine golfer; b. 14 April 1923, Buenos Aires; professional golfer since 1938; won more than 230 tournaments worldwide; won Argentine PGA and Open 1944; subsequently won Argentine PGA six more times by 1952 and Open eight more times in 1974; represented Argentina in numerous World Cups, twice individual winner; also winner, Chilean, Colombian, Brazilian and Panama Opens; first appeared in Britain 1948; winner, British Open, Hoylake 1967; Hon. mem. St Andrews World Golf Hall of Fame 1989.

de VIRION, Tadeusz Józef; Polish diplomatist and lawyer; b. 28 March 1926, Warsaw; s. of Jerzy de Virion and Zofia de Virion; m. Jayanti de Virion 1985; one d.; ed Warsaw Univ.; served in Home Army during Nazi occupation 1943–45, took part in Warsaw Uprising 1944; qualified as judge 1948; qualified as attorney 1950, since then on Warsaw Bar, counsel for the defence in criminal cases; judge State Tribunal 1989–90 (resgnd), 1993–2002; Amb. to UK 1990–93 (also Accred to Ireland until Oct. 1991); Hon. and Devotional Kt of Sovereign Order of Kts. of Malta 1980 and Commdr Cross with Star 'Pro Merito Meliteusi', Commdr Cross of Polonia Restituta, Gold Cross of Merit, Home Army's Cross. *Address:* ul. Zakopiańska 17, 03-934 Warsaw, Poland. *Telephone:* (22) 617-88-80.

DE VRIES, Bert, DEcon; Netherlands politician; b. 29 March 1938; ed Groningen Univ. and Amsterdam Free Univ.; fmrly worked in tax service, with Philips and as lecturer, Erasmus Univ. Rotterdam; mem. Parl. 1982–; Parl. Leader, Christian Democratic Appeal 1982; Minister of Social Affairs and Employment 1989–94. *Address:* c/o Christian Democratic Appeal, Dr. Kuyperstraat 5, 2514 BA The Hague, Netherlands.

DE WAAL, Marius Theodorus, BSc, B.ING.; South African business executive; b. 12 March 1925, Paarl Dist; s. of Pieter de Waal; m. Kitty du Plessis 1949; three s. one d.; ed Univs. of Stellenbosch, Delft and Harvard Advanced Man. Programme, Swansea; town engineer, Bellville 1947–60; with Industrial Devt Corpn of SA Ltd 1961–90; Chair. Iscor Ltd 1988–95, Transnet 1990–, Siemens Ltd; Dir SA Reserve Bank, BMW; Hon. DEng, Hon. DComm, Hon. DBA. *Leisure interest:* tennis. *Address:* Transnet Ltd, PO Box 72501, Parkview 2122, South Africa.

de WAART, Edo; Netherlands conductor; b. 1 June 1941, Amsterdam; s. of M. de Waart and J. Rose; one s. (and one d. from 1st marriage); ed Amsterdam Music Lyceum; Asst Conductor, Concertgebouw Orchestra, Amsterdam 1966; Perm. Conductor, Rotterdam Philharmonic 1967, Musical Dir and Prin. Conductor 1973–79; Prin. Guest Conductor, San Francisco Symphony Orchestra 1975–77, Music Dir 1977–85; Music Dir Minn. Orchestra 1986–95; Artistic Dir, Netherlands Radio Philharmonic Orchestra 1989–; Prin. Guest Conductor, Santa Fe Opera 1991–92; Chief Conductor, Dutch Radio Philharmonic Orchestra 1989–; Artistic Dir and Chief Conductor, Sydney Symphony Orchestra 1993–; First Prize Dimitri Mitropoulos Competition, New York 1964. *Address:* c/o Harrison & Parott Ltd., 12 Penzance Place, London, W11 4PA, England (Office); RFO No. 8—Muziekcentrum Van, de Omroep Postbus 10, 1200 JB Hilversum, Netherlands; Sydney Symphony Orchestra, PO Box 4338, Sydney, NSW 2001, Australia.

DE WEERDT, Hon. Mark Murray, QC, MA, LLB; Canadian judge and lawyer (retd); b. 6 May 1928, Cologne, Germany; s. of Hendrik Eugen de Weerdt and Ina Dunbar Murray; m. Linda Anne Hadwen 1956; four s.; ed Glasgow Univ., UK and Univ. of BC, Vancouver; Constable, Royal Canadian Mounted Police 1950–52; barrister and solicitor, BC 1956–70, 1973–81, NWT 1958–81; Crown Attorney, NWT 1958–63; City Solicitor, Yellowknife, NWT 1959–71; Magistrate and Juvenile Court Judge, NWT 1971–73; Gen. Solicitor, Insurance Corpn of BC 1974–76; Sr Counsel, Dept of Justice of Canada, Vancouver 1976–79, Gen. Counsel and Dir 1979–81; Sr Judge of the Supreme Court of the NWT 1981–96; Justice of Appeal, Court of Appeal of the NWT 1981–97, Court of Appeal of the Yukon Territory 1981–97; Chair. Judicial Council of the NWT 1981–96; mem. Nat. Council Canadian Foundation for Human Rights; Dir Canadian Inst. for the Admin. of Justice; mem. Canadian Bar Asscn, Pension Appeals Bd 2000; QC (Canada) 1968; mem. Nat. Council Int. Comm. of Jurists (Canadian Sec.), Advisory Council, Canadian Human Rights Inst., The Osgoode Soc., The Selden Soc.; Commemorative Medal 1992, Public Service Award, Commr of NWT 1997. *Leisure interest:* general reading. *Address:* 5459 Crown Street, Vancouver, BC, V6N 4K1, Canada (Home).

DEACON, Richard, CBE, RA, MA; British sculptor; b. 15 Aug. 1949, Bangor, Wales; s. of Group Capt. Edward William Deacon and the late Joan Bullivant Winstanley; m. Jacqueline Poncelet 1977 (divorced 2001); one s. one d.; ed Somerset Coll. of Art, St Martin's School of Art, RCA, Chelsea School of Art; toured S America 1996–97; Prof. Ecole Nat. Supérieure des Beaux-Arts, Paris 1998–; Vice-Chair. Baltic Centre for Contemporary Art Trust 1999–; mem. British Council, Arts Council of England Architecture Advisory Group 1996–99; Visiting Prof. Chelsea School of Art 1992–; Trustee Tate Gallery 1992–97; Turner Prize 1987; Chevalier Ordre des Arts et des Lettres 1999. *Works include:* What Could Make Me Feel This Way?, Struck Dumb, Double-talk, Body of Thought No 2, The Back of My Hand, Distance No Object No 2, Dummy, Under My Skin, Breed, Skirt, Laocoon, After, Moor, Let's Not Be Stupid, No Stone Unturned, Building From the Inside, Can't See the Wood for the Trees. *Exhbns. include:* Whitechapel Art Gallery (a retrospective) 1989, Hanover Kunstverein 1993, Orangerie in the Herrenhäuser Gärten, Hanover 1993, Tate Gallery, Liverpool 1999, Dundee Contemporary Art 2001. *Leisure interests:* swimming, walking. *Address:* c/o Lisson Gallery, 67 Lisson Street, London, NW1 5DA, England.

DEAN, Christopher, OBE; British ice skater; b. 27 July 1958, Nottingham; s. of the late Colin Dean and Mavis (née Pearson) Dean; m. 1st Isabelle Duchesnay 1991 (divorced 1993); m. 2nd Jill Ann Trenary 1994; two s.; police constable 1974–80; British Ice Dance Champion (with Jayne Torvill, q.v., 1978–83, 1994; European Ice Dance Champion (with Jayne Torvill) 1981, 1982, 1984, 1994; World Ice Dance Champion (with Jayne Torvill) 1981–84, World Professional Champions 1984–85, 1990, 1995–96; Olympic Ice Dance gold medal (with Jayne Torvill) 1984, Olympic Ice Dance bronze medal (with Jayne Torvill) 1994; choreographed Encounters for English Nat. Ballet 1996, Stars on Ice in USA 1998–99, 1999–2000; Hon. MA (Nottingham Trent) 1994, BBC Sports Personality of the Year (with Jayne Torvill) 1984, Figure Skating Hall of Fame (with Jayne Torvill) 1989. *Ice Dance:* World tours with own and int. companies of skaters 1985, 1988, 1994, 1997, also tours of Australia and New Zealand 1991, UK 1992, 1997–98, Japan 1996, USA and Canada 1997–98. *Television:* Path to Perfection (ITV video) 1984, Fire & Ice (also video) 1986, Bladerunners (BBC documentary), The Artistry of Torvill & Dean (ABC TV) 1994, Face the Music 1995, Torvill & Dean, The Story So Far (biographical video) 1996, Bach Sixth Cello Suite (with Yo-Yo Ma) 1996. *Publications:* Torvill and Dean's Face the Music and Dance (with Jayne Torvill) 1993, Torvill and Dean: An Autobiography (with Jayne Torvill) 1994,

Facing the Music (with Jayne Torvill) 1995. *Leisure interests:* theatre, ballet, fast cars. *Address:* c/o Sue Young, PO Box 32, Heathfield, East Sussex, TN21 0BW, England (Office). *Telephone:* (1435) 867825 (Office); (1273) 330798.

DEAN, Graham, BA; British artist; b. 5 Dec. 1951, Birkenhead; s. of Leslie Dean and Dorothy Dean; m. Denise Warr 1989; one s. one d.; ed Laird School of Art, Birkenhead, Bristol Polytechnic; Abbey Award in Painting, British School, Rome 1992. *Major exhibitions include:* Corpus Christi Coll., Oxford 1979, Liverpool Acad. 1980, Basle Art Fair 1987, Oriel Gallery, Cardiff 1988, Austin Desmond Fine Art, London 1988, Nerlino Gallery, New York 1989–90, British School, Rome 1992, Jill George Gallery, London 1984, 1995, Kunsthaus, Lübeck, 1995, Williams Museum and Art Gallery, Brighton Museum and Art Gallery 1995, 1996, Victoria Art Gallery, Bath 1999, Stephen Lacey Gallery, London 2000, 2001. *Dance:* collaborations with Darshan Singh Bhuller, including No Go Zone, White Picket Fence. *Films:* several independent shorts and videos, including Solsbury Hill (with Peter Gabriel). *Publications:* The Green Room and Other Paintings 1995, Straight to Red 1999, Light Sweet Crude 2001. *Leisure interests:* tennis, supporting Liverpool football club. *Address:* c/o Stephen Lacey Gallery, 1 Crawford Passage, Ray Street, London, EC1R 3DP (Office); 17 Norfolk Road, Brighton, East Sussex, BN1 3AA, England (Home). *Telephone:* (20) 7837-5507 (Office); (1273) 731872 (Home). *Fax:* (1273) 731872 (Home). *E-mail:* info@stephenlaceygallery.co.uk (Office); graham.dean1@virgin.net (Home). *Website:* www .stephenlaceygallery.co.uk (Office); www.grahamdean.com (Home).

DEAN, Howard, BA, MD; American state governor; b. 17 Nov. 1948; s. of Howard Brush Dean and Andrea Maitland; m. Judith Steinberg; one s. one d.; ed Yale Univ. and Albert Einstein Coll. of Medicine; Intern, then resident in internal medicine, Medical Center Hosp. Vermont 1978–82; internal medicine specialist medical practice in Shelburne, Vt; mem. Vermont House of Reps. 1983–86, Asst minority leader 1985–86; Lt Gov. State of Vermont 1986–91; Gov. of Vermont 1991–2003; Democrat. *Address:* c/o Office of the Governor, Pavilion Office Building, 109 State Street, Montpelier, VT 05609-0001 (Office); 325 South Cove Road, Burlington, VT 05401-5447, USA.

DEAN, Hon. John Gunther, PhD; American diplomatist; b. 24 Feb. 1926, Germany; s. of Dr Joseph and Lucy Dean; m. Martine Duphénieux 1952; two s. one d.; ed Harvard Coll., Harvard and Paris Univs; entered Govt Service 1950; diplomatic posts in France, Belgium, Viet Nam, Laos, Togo, Mali and in US Dept of State; Dir Pacification Program in Mil. Region 1, Viet Nam 1970–72; Deputy Chief Mission, American Embassy, Laos 1972–74; Amb. to Khmer Repub. 1974–75, to Denmark 1975–78, to Lebanon 1978–81, to Thailand 1981–85, to India 1985–88; mem. Bd of dirs of corpns and academic insts in USA, Europe and Asia 1990–; Personal Rep. of Dir-Gen. of UNESCO for Cambodia 1989–99; numerous US and foreign decorations. *Address:* 29 boulevard Jules Sandeau, 75116 Paris, France. *Telephone:* 1-45-04-71-84. *Fax:* 1-45-04-78-57. *E-mail:* johnmartinedean@aol.com (Home).

DEAN, Stafford Roderick; British opera and concert singer; b. 20 June 1937, Surrey; s. of Eric E. Dean and Vera S. Bathurst; m. 1st Carolyn J. Lambourne 1963; four s.; m. 2nd Anne E. Howells 1981; one s. one d.; ed Epsom Coll., Royal Coll. of Music and privately with Howell Glynne and Otakar Kraus; Opera for All 1962–64; Glyndebourne Chorus 1963–64, Prin. début as Lictor in L'Incoronazione di Poppea 1963; under contract to Sadler's Wells Opera/English Nat. Opera 1964–70; Royal Opera House, Covent Garden 1969–, début as Masetto in Don Giovanni; int. début as Leporello in Don Giovanni, Stuttgart 1971; guest appearances with Metropolitan Opera, New York, Chicago Lyric, San Francisco, Berlin, Munich, Hamburg, Cologne, Frankfurt, Vienna, Paris, Turin operas etc.; specializes in Mozart bass repertoire; bass soloist in world premiere of Penderecki Requiem, Stuttgart 1984; concert appearances in choral works by Beethoven, Shostakovich, Verdi. *Leisure interests:* family life, garden. *Address:* c/o IMG Artists, Lovell House, 616 Chiswick High Road, London, W4 5RX, England. *Telephone:* (20) 8233-5800. *Fax:* (20) 8233-5801.

DEAN, Winton (Basil), MA, FBA; British musicologist and author; b. 18 March 1916, Birkenhead; s. of Basil Dean and Esther (née Van Gruisen) Dean; m. Hon. Thalia Mary Shaw 1939 (died 2000); one s. (two d. deceased) one adopted d.; ed Harrow, King's Coll., Cambridge; mem. Music Panel, Arts Council of GB 1957–60; Ernest Bloch Prof. of Music, Univ. of Calif., Berkeley, USA 1965–66, Regent's Lecturer 1977; mem. Council, Royal Musical Asscn 1965–98 (Vice-Pres. 1970–98, Hon. mem. 1998–); mem. Vorstand, GF Händel-Gesellschaft, Halle 1980– (Vice-Pres. 1991–99, Hon. mem. 1999), Kuratorium, Göttinger Händel-Gesellschaft 1982–97, Hon. mem. 1997–; Hon. mem. RAM; Corresp. mem. American Musicological Soc.; Hon. MusDoc (Cambridge) 1996; City of Halle Handel Prize 1995. *Publications:* Bizet 1948, Carmen 1949, Handel's Dramatic Oratorios and Masques 1959, Shakespeare and Opera 1964, Georges Bizet, His Life and Work 1965, Handel and the Opera Seria 1969, The New Grove Handel 1982, Handel's Operas 1704–1726 (with J. M. Knapp) 1987, Essays on Opera 1990, (co-ed.) Handel's Opera Giulio Cesare in Egitto 1999; maj. contribs to New Oxford History of Music, vol. VIII 1982 and Grove's Dictionary of Music and Musicians, 5th and 6th edns 1954, 1980. *Leisure interests:* shooting, naval history. *Address:* Hambledon Hurst, Godalming, Surrey, GU8 4HF, England. *Telephone:* (1428) 682644.

DEANE, Derek, OBE; British artistic director; b. Derek Shepherd, 18 June 1953, Cornwall; s. of William Gordon Shepherd and Margaret Shepherd; ed Royal Ballet School; with Royal Ballet Co. 1972–89, reaching rank of Premier

Dancer; Asst Dir Rome Opera 1990–92; Artistic Dir English Nat. Ballet 1993–2001. *Leisure interests:* tennis, gardening, reading, dinner parties, theatre, performing arts, travel. *Address:* c/o English National Ballet, Markova House, 39 Jay Mews, London, SW7 2ES, England.

DEANE, Phyllis Mary, MA, FBA; British professor of economic history and economic historian; b. 13 Oct. 1918; d. of John Edward Deane and Elizabeth Jane Brooks; ed Chatham County School, Hutcheson's Girls' Grammar School, Glasgow and Univ. of Glasgow; Carnegie Research Scholar 1940–41; Research Officer, Nat. Inst. of Econ. and Social Research 1941–45; Colonial Research Officer 1946–48; Research Officer, Colonial Office 1948–49; Dept of Applied Econs, Cambridge Univ. 1950–61, Lecturer, Faculty of Econs and Politics 1961–71, Reader in Econ. History 1971–81, Prof. 1981–83, now Prof. Emer.; Fellow of Newnham Coll. 1961–83, Hon. Fellow 1983; Ed. Economic Journal 1968–75; Pres. Royal Econ. Soc. 1980–82; Hon. D.Litt. (Glasgow) 1989. *Publications:* The Future of the Colonies (with Julian Huxley) 1945, The Measurement of Colonial National Incomes 1948, Colonial Social Accounting 1953, British Economic Growth 1688–1959 (with W. A. Cole) 1962, The First Industrial Revolution 1965, The Evolution of Economic Ideas 1978, The State and the Economic System 1989, The Life and Times of J. Neville Keynes 2001, papers and reviews in econ. journals. *Leisure interests:* walking, gardening. *Address:* 4 Stukeley Close, Cambridge, CB3 9LT, England.

DEANE, Seamus Francis, PhD; Irish professor of English and American literature; b. 9 Feb. 1940; s. of Winifred Deane and Frank Deane; m. Marion Treacy 1963; three s. one d.; ed Queen's Univ., Belfast, Cambridge Univ.; Fulbright and Woodrow Wilson Scholar, Visiting Lecturer, Reed Coll., Portland, Ore. 1966–67; Visiting Lecturer, Univ. of Calif., Berkeley 1967–68; Visiting Prof. 1978; Lecturer, Univ. Coll., Dublin 1968–77, Sr Lecturer 1978–80, Prof. of English and American Literature 1980–93; Visiting Prof., Univ. of Notre Dame, Indiana 1977, Keough Prof. of Irish Studies 1993–; Walker Ames Prof., Univ. of Washington, Seattle 1987, Jules Benedict Distinguished Visiting Prof., Carleton Coll., Minn. 1988; Dir Field Day Theatre Co. 1980–; mem. Royal Irish Acad. 1982; Hon. DLitt (Ulster) 1999; AE Memorial Award for Literature 1972; Ireland/America Fund Literary Award 1988; Guardian Fiction Prize 1996; Irish Times Int. Fiction Prize 1997, Irish Times Irish Literature Prize 1997; Ruffino Antico Fattore Int. Literary Award (Florence, Italy) 1998. *Publications:* Celtic Revivals 1985, Short History of Irish Literature 1986, Selected Poems 1988, The French Revolution and Enlightenment in England 1789–1832 1988, Field Day Anthology of Irish Writing 550–1990 1991, Reading in the Dark 1996, Strange Country 1997. *Address:* Institute of Irish Studies, 1145 Flanner Hall, University of Notre Dame, IN 46556, USA.

DEANE, Hon. Sir William Patrick, AC, KBE, BA, LLB, QC; Australian Governor-General and fmr judge; b. 4 Jan. 1931, St Kilda; s. of the late C. A. Deane, MC and Lillian Hussey; m. Helen Russell 1965; one s. one d.; ed St Joseph's Coll. Sydney, Sydney Univ. and Trinity Coll. Dublin, Ireland; Teaching Fellow in Equity, Univ. of Sydney 1956–61; barrister 1957; Justice, Supreme Court, NSW 1977, Fed. Court of Australia 1977–82; Pres. Australian Trade Practices Tribunal 1977–82; Justice, High Court of Australia 1982–95, Gov.-Gen. of Australia 1996–2001; KStJ; Hon. LLD (Sydney, Griffith, Notre Dame, Trinity Coll., Univ. of NSW); Hon. DUniv (Southern Cross, Australian Catholic Univ., Queensland Univ. of Tech., Univ. of W Sydney); Hon. D.Sacred.Theol. (Melbourne Coll. of Divinity). *Address:* c/o PO Box 4168, Manuka, 2603, Australia. *Telephone:* (2) 6239-4716 (Office). *Fax:* (2) 6239-4916 (Office).

DEARING, Baron (Life Peer), cr. 1998, of Kingston upon Hull in the County of the East Riding of Yorkshire; **Ronald Ernest Dearing,** Kt, CB, BScEcon., CBIM, FInstM; British public servant and business executive; b. 27 July 1930, Hull; s. of E. H. A. and M. T. (née Hoyle) Dearing; m. Margaret Patricia Riley 1954; two d.; ed Malet Lambert High School, Doncaster Grammar School, Hull Univ., London Business School; Ministry of Labour and Nat. Service 1946–49; Ministry of Power 1949–62; Treasury 1962–64; Ministries of Power and Tech. and Dept of Trade and Industry 1965–72; Regional Dir Dept of Trade and Industry 1972–74; Under-Sec. Dept of Industry 1974–76, Deputy Sec. for Nationalized Industry Matters 1976–80, Chair. of Nationalized Industries' Chair.'s Group 1983–84; Deputy Chair. Post Office 1980–81, Chair. 1981–87; Chair. CNAA 1987–88, Review Cttee on Accounting Standards 1987–88, Co. Durham Devt Co. 1987–90, Polytechnics and Colls Funding Council 1988–92, Financial Reporting Council 1990–93, Northern Devt Co. 1990–94, Higher Educ. Funding Council (England) 1992–93, Schools Curriculum and Assessment Authority 1993–96, Camelot Group PLC 1993–95, Nat. Cttee of Inquiry into Higher Educ. 1996–97, Write Away 1996–2000, Cttee on Church of England Schools 2000–02, Ufi Ltd 1999–2001, Higher Educ. Policy Inst. 2002–; Pres. Inst. of Direct Marketing 1994–97; Chancellor Univ. of Nottingham 1993–2000; mem. Cadbury Cttee on Financial Aspects of Corporate Governance 1991–92; Dir (non-exec.) Whitbread 1987–90, Prudential Corpn 1987–91, IMI PLC, British Coal 1988–91, Thorn Ericsson Ltd, SDX Business Systems Ltd; Fellow of London Business School, Nottingham Univ.; Hon. Fellow Sunderland Univ., Royal Acad. of Eng; Hon. degrees include Hon. DScEcon. (Hull) 1986, Hon. DTech (CNAA), Hon. DCL (Durham) 1992, Hon. LLD (Nottingham) 1993, (Exeter) 1998. *Leisure interests:* gardening, reading, car boot sales. *Address:* House of Lords, London, SW1A 2PW, England (Office).

DEARLOVE, Sir Richard (Billing), Kt., KCMG, OBE, BA; British diplomatist; b. 23 Jan. 1945; m. Rosalind McKenzie 1968; two s. one d.; ed Monkton Combe School, Kent School, Conn., USA, Queens' Coll., Cambridge; joined the Foreign Office 1966, postings to Nairobi 1968–71, Prague 1973–76, FCO, London 1971–73, 1976–80, 1984–87, First Sec. Paris 1980–84, Counsellor UK Mission to the UN (UKMIS), Geneva 1987–91, Washington 1991–93; Dir of Personnel and Admin., Secret Intelligence Service (SIS) 1993–94, Dir of Operations 1994–99, Asst Chief 1998–99, Chief 1999–. *Address:* PO Box 1300, London, SE1 1BD, England (Office).

DEASY, Austin, TD; Irish politician; b. 26 Aug. 1936, Dungarvan, Co. Waterford; s. of Michael Deasy and Geraldine Deasy; m. Catherine Keating 1961; two s. two d.; ed Dungarvan Christian Brothers' School and Univ. Coll., Cork; former secondary school teacher; mem. Waterford Co. Council and Dungarvan Urban Council 1967–; mem. Seanad Éireann 1973–77; mem. Dáil Éireann (Parl.) 1977–, Vice-Chair. Foreign Affairs Cttee 1997–; Minister for Agric. 1982–87; Leader, Irish Del. to Council of Europe 1997–; mem. Fine Gael. *Leisure interests:* golf, gardening, horse-racing. *Address:* Kilrush, Dungarvan, Co. Waterford, Ireland. *Telephone:* (58) 43003. *Fax:* (58) 45315.

DEAVER, Michael Keith, BA; American fmr government official; b. 11 April 1938, Bakersfield, Calif.; m. Carolyn Deaver; two c.; ed San José State Univ.; worked as Cabinet Sec. and Asst to Ronald Reagan as Gov. of Calif. in 1960s; active in Reagan's presidential campaign 1980; Deputy Chief of Staff, White House, Washington, DC 1981–85; set up own lobbying firm 1985; later convicted of lying to Congress about his lobbying activities; Republican.

DeBAKEY, Michael Ellis, BS, MD, MS; American surgeon; b. 7 Sept. 1908, Lake Charles, Louisiana; s. of Shaker M. DeBakey and Raheeja Zorba DeBakey; m. 1st Diana Cooper 1936 (died 1972); four s.; m. 2nd Katrin Fehlhaber 1975; one d.; ed Tulane Univ., New Orleans; Instructor Tulane Univ. 1937–40, Asst Prof. of Surgery 1940–46, Assoc. Prof. 1946–48; War Service, Colonel, ultimately Dir Surgical Consultant Div., Office of the Surgeon Gen. 1942–46; US Army Surgical Consultant to Surgeon-Gen. 1946–; Prof. and Chair. Dept of Surgery, Baylor Coll. of Medicine, Houston, Texas 1948–93, Distinguished Service Prof. 1968–, Vice-Pres. for Medical Affairs and CEO 1968–69, Pres. 1969–79, Chancellor 1979–96, Olga Keith Wiess Prof. of Surgery 1981–, Chancellor Emer. 1996–; Dir Nat. Heart and Blood Vessel Research and Demonstration Center, Baylor Coll. of Medicine 1976–84; Dir DeBakey Heart Center 1985–; Surgeon-in-Chief, Ben Taub Gen. Hosp. 1963–93; Sr Attending Surgeon, Methodist Hosp., Houston; consultant surgeon to many hosps in Texas and Walter Reed Army Hosp. in Washington, DC; Hon. Chair. American Hosp. of Moscow, Russia; implanted first partial artificial heart in human April 1966; mem. Nat. Advisory Heart Council 1957–61, Program Planning Cttee and Cttee on Training, Nat. Insts of Health, 1961–, Nat. Advisory Council on Regional Medical Programs, Dept of Health, Educ. and Welfare 1965–, Advisory Council, Inst. for Advanced Research in Asian Science and Medicine, Brooklyn, New York 1978–, Advisory Council, Nat. Heart, Lung and Blood Inst. 1957–61, 1974–77, 1982–86, Tex. Science and Tech. Council 1984–86; Chair. Pres. Comm. on Heart Disease, Cancer and Stroke 1964–66; Pres. Southern Surgical Assen 1989–90; Hon-Pres. Int. Soc. for Rotary Blood Pumps 1993, 1998; editorial bds of numerous medical journals and ed. of Year Book of General Surgery, Vascular Surgery in World War II, Medical History of World War II, vol. II: General Surgery; ed. Journal of Vascular Surgery 1983–88; Fellow Biomaterials Science and Eng, Soc. for Biomaterials 1994–; mem. numerous American and foreign medical socs and asscns and holder of numerous advisory appointments; more than 50 hon. degrees; US Army Legion of Merit 1945 and many American and foreign awards including Albert Lasker Award for Clinical Research 1963, Presidential Medal of Freedom with Distinction 1969, Encyclopaedia Britannica Lifetime Achievement Award 1980, American Surgical Assen Distinguished Service Award 1981, Theodore E. Cummings Memorial Prize for Outstanding Contribs in Cardiovascular Disease 1987, Nat. Medal of Science 1987, American Legion Distinguished Service Award 1990, Foundation for Biomedical Research Lifetime Achievement Award 1991, American Task Force for Lebanon Jacobs Award 1991, Nat. Foundation for Infectious Diseases Maxwell Finland Award 1992, Royal Coll. of Physicians and Surgeons of USA Hon. Distinguished Fellow 1992, Commdr's Cross, Order of Merit (Germany) 1992, Order of Independence Medal (First Class), UAE 1992, Acad. of Athens 1992, Ellis Island Medal of Honor 1993, Giovanni Lorenzini Foundation Prize for the Advancement of Biomedical Sciences 1994, American Heart Assen Lifetime Achievement Award 1994, Russian Mil. Acad. Boris Petrovsky Int. Surgeon's Award, First Laureate of the Petrovsky Gold Medal 1997, Common Wealth Trust Award in Science and Invention 1997, John P. McGovern Compleat Physician Award 1999; Texas State and House Resolutions honouring Dr DeBakey for 50 years of medical practice in Texas 1999; Children Uniting Nations Global Peace and Tolerance Lifetime Achievement Award 1999, American Philosophical Soc. Jonathan Rhoads Medal 2000, Library of Congress Bicentennial Living Legend Award 2000, Villanova Univ. Mendal Medal Award 2001, NASA Invention of the Year Award 2001, Hon. Fellow and Medal of Merit for Distinguished Achievements in Cardiovascular Educ. and Research, Int. Acad. of Cardiovascular Sciences 2002, Lindbergh-Carrel Prize 2002; and other honours. *Publications:* numerous chapters in medical textbooks and a number of books including: The Living Heart 1977, The Living Heart Diet 1984, The New Living Heart

1997, over 1,600 articles. *Address:* Baylor College of Medicine, 1 Baylor Plaza, Houston, TX 77030, USA (Office). *Telephone:* (713) 790-3185 (Office). *Fax:* (713) 790-2176 (Office).

DEBBASCH, Charles, DenD; French professor of public law; b. 22 Oct. 1937, Tunis, Tunisia; s. of Max Debbasch; m. Odile Peyridier 1959; three s. two d.; tutorial Asst 1957; junior lecturer, law faculty, Aix-en-Provence Univ. 1959–62, Prof. of Law, Grenoble Univ. 1962–63, Aix-en-Provence 1963–67; Chair of Public Law, Faculty of Law and Econ. Sciences, Aix-en-Provence 1967, Dir Centre of Research into Legal Admin. 1966–, Centre of Research and Study on Mediterranean Societies 1969–71; Head of Research Comm., Ministry of Educ. 1968–69; Dir Teaching and Research Unit attached to faculty of Law and Pol. Sciences, Aix-Marseille Univ. 1966, Dean, Faculty of Law and Pol. Sciences 1971–73; Pres. Nat. Asscn of Pres. of Univs. specializing in law and politics and Deans of law faculties 1971–78; Prof. Coll. of Europe, Bruges 1975–81; Pres. Consultative Cttee public law univs. 1978; tech. adviser Gen. Secr. French presidency 1978–81; Pres. Fondation Vasarely 1981–91; Dir and Dir-Gen. of Press Group, Dauphiné Libéré 1984–89; Pres. Agence générale d'information 1985–89; Pres. Supervisory Council of Dauphiné Libéré 1989–94, Observatoire int. de la démocratie 1994–; Dir Inst. Int. du droit des médias 1989–; Officier, Ordre nat. du Mérite, Chevalier, Légion d'honneur, Chevalier des Palmes Académiques, Grand Officer of the Aztec Eagle (Mexico), Commdr Order of Tunisian Repub., Officer of Merit, Senegal. *Publications:* Procédure administrative contentieuse et procédure civile 1962, La République tunisienne 1962, Institutions administratives 1975, Traité du droit de la radio-diffusion 1967, Le Droit de la radio et de la télévision 1970, L'Administration au pouvoir 1970, L'Université désorientée 1971, Droit administratif 1973, Science administrative 1980, la France de Pompidou 1974, Introduction à la politique 1982, Contentieux administratif 1985, Les Chats de l'émirat 1976, Institutions et droit administratifs (3 Vols, 1980–99), L'Etat civilisé 1979, L'Elysée dévoilé 1982, Lexique de politique 1984, Les constitutions de la France 1983, Droit constitutionnel 1986, Les Associations 1985, La Ve République 1985, La Disgrace du socialisme 1985, La réussite politique 1987, La Cohabitation froide 1988, Le Droit de l'audiovisuel 1988, La société française 1989, Les Grands arrêts du droit de l'audiovisuel 1991, Mémoires du Doyen d'Aix-en-Provence 1996, Droit des médias 1999, Droit administratif des biens 1999, La Constitution de la Ve République 2000, contrib. to numerous other works. *Address:* Centre de recherches administratives, Université de Droit, d'Economie et des Sciences, 3 avenue Robert Schuman, 13628 Aix-en-Provence (Office); 25 avenue Mozart, 75116 Paris, France (Office). *Telephone:* 4-42-17-29-29 (Aix); 1-45-20-45-72 (Paris). *E-mail:* debbasch.charles@wanadoo.fr (Home).

DEBONO, Giovanna, BA; Maltese politician; b. 25 Nov. 1956; d. of the late Coronato Attard and of Anna Attard (née Tabone); m. Anthony Debono; one s. one d.; ed Univ. of Malta; teacher Educ. Dept 1981–87; MP, Nationalist Party 1987–; Parl. Sec. Ministry for Social Devt 1995–96; Minister for Gozo 1998–. *Address:* Ministry for Gozo, St Francis Square, Victoria, CMR 02, Gozo, Malta. *Telephone:* 561482. *Fax:* 561755.

DEBRAY, Régis; French author and government official; b. 2 Sept. 1940, Paris; s. of Georges Debray and Janine Alexandre; m. Elisabeth Burgos 1968; one d.; ed Ecole normale supérieure de la rue d'Ulm; colleague of Che Guevara, imprisoned in Bolivia 1967–70; Co-Ed., Comité d'études sur les libertés 1975; Adviser on foreign affairs to François Mitterrand; responsible for Third World Affairs, Secr.-Gen. of Presidency of Repub. 1981–84; Office of Pres. of Repub. 1984–85, 1987–88; Maître des requêtes, Conseil d'Etat 1985–93; Sec.-Gen. Conseil du Pacifique Sud 1986–; Prix Fémina 1977. *Publications:* La Critique des armes 1973, La Guerilla du Che 1974, Entretiens avec Allende 1971, Les Epreuves du fer 1974, L'Indésirable 1975, La Neige brûle 1977, Le Pouvoir intellectuel en France 1979, Le Scribe, Critique de la raison politique, La Puissance et les rêves 1984, Les Empires contre l'Europe 1985, Comète, ma comète 1986, Eloges 1986, Masques 1987, Que vive la République 1988, A demain de Gaulle 1990, Cours de médiologie générale 1991, Christophe Colomb, le visiteur de l'aube: les traités de Tordesillas 1992, Vie et Mort de l'Image: une histoire du regard en Occident 1992. *Address:* Editions Gallimard, 5 rue Sébastien Bottin, 75007 Paris, France.

DEBRÉ, Bernard André Charles Robert, DenM; French politician and surgeon; b. 30 Sept. 1944, Toulouse; s. of the late Michel Debré and Anne-Marie Lemaresquier; m. Véronique Duron 1971; three s. one d.; ed Lycée Janson de Sailly and Faculté de Médecine, Paris; hosp. doctor 1965–1980; hosp. surgeon 1980; Prof. Faculté de Médecine, Paris 1985; Head of Urology, Hôpital Cochin 1990; other professional appointments; Deputy (RPR) to Nat. Assembly 1986–94; Mayor of Amboise 1992–2001; Minister of Cooperation 1994–95; mem. of French Cttee of Ethics 1986–88; Chevalier, Légion d'Honneur and numerous foreign decorations. *Publications:* La France malade de sa santé 1983, Un traité d'urologie (4 vols) 1985, Le voleur de vie (la bataille du Sida) 1989, L'illusion humanitaire 1997, Le retour de Mwami 1998, La grande transgression 2000 (Prix Louis Pauwels 2001), Le suicide de France (jtly) 2002, Avertissement aux Malades, aux Médicins et aux Elus (ed.) 2002, articles in French and foreign journals. *Leisure interests:* travel, collecting antique plates, sports. *Address:* Hôpital Cochin, 27 rue du Faubourg, Saint Jacques, 75014 Paris (Office); 30 rue Jacob, 75006 Paris, France (Home). *Telephone:* 1-58-41-27-50 (Office); 1-43-25-51-41 (Home); 6-85-30-45-73. *Fax:* 1-58-41-27-55 (Office).

DEBRÉ, Jean-Louis, DenD; French politician and magistrate; b. 30 Sept. 1944, Toulouse; s. of the late Michel Debré (fmr Prime Minister of France) and of Anne-Marie Lemaresquier; m. Ann-Marie Engel 1971; two s. one d.; ed Lycée Janson-de-Sailly, Inst. d'Etudes Politiques, Faculté de Droit, Paris and Ecole Nat. de la Magistrature; Asst Faculté de Droit, Paris 1972–75; Adviser, Office of Jacques Chirac 1974–76; Deputy Public Prosecutor, Tribunal de Grande Instance, Evry 1976–78; Magistrate, Cen. Admin. of Ministry of Justice 1978; Chef de Cabinet to Minister of Budget 1978; Examining Magistrate, Tribunal de Grande Instance, Paris 1979; RPR Deputy to Nat. Ass. 1986–95, 1997–, Pres. RPR Group 1997–; Town Councillor, Evreux 1989; Conseiller Gén. Canton de Nonancourt 1992–; Deputy Sec.-Gen. and Spokesman for Gaullist Party 1993; Minister of the Interior 1995–97; Vice-Pres. Gen. Council of the Euro 1998–; Mayor of Evreux 2001–; Pres. of Nat. Ass. 2002–; Chevalier du Mérite Agricole, Grand-croix l'Ordre d'Isabelle la catolique (Spain). *Publications:* Les idées constitutionnelles du Général de Gaulle 1974, La constitution de la Ve République 1974, Le pouvoir politique 1977, Le Gaullisme 1978, La justice au XIXe 1981, Les républiques des avocats 1984, Le curieux 1986, En mon for intérieur 1997, Pièges 1998, Le Gaulisme n'est pas une nostalgie 1999. *Leisure interests:* riding, tennis. *Address:* Assemblée nationale, 75355 Paris (Office); Hôtel de ville, 7 place du Général de Gaulle, 27000 Evreux; 126 rue de l'Université, 75007 Paris, France (Home).

DEBREU, Gerard, DSc; American (b. French) professor of economics and mathematics; b. 4 July 1921, Calais; s. of Camille and Fernande (née Decharne) Debreu; m. Françoise Bled 1945; two d.; ed Ecole Normale Supérieure, Paris and Univ. of Paris; naturalized US citizen 1975; Research Assoc. CNRS 1946–48; Cowles Comm. for Research in Econs, Univ. of Chicago 1950–55; Assoc. Prof. of Econs, Cowles Foundation for Research in Econs, Yale Univ. 1955–61; Prof. of Econs, Univ. of Calif., Berkeley 1962–, also of Mathematics 1975–, Faculty Research Lecturer 1984–85, Class of 1958 Chair. 1986, Prof. Emer. 1985–; Guggenheim Fellow, Visiting Prof., Univ. of Louvain, Belgium 1968–69; Overseas Fellow, Churchill Coll. Cambridge, UK 1972; several visiting professorships; Frisch Memorial Lecturer, Fifth World Congress of Econometric Soc., Cambridge, Mass. 1985; mem. Editorial Bd Journal Econ. Theory 1972–, Games and Econ. Behaviour 1989–; Assoc. Ed. Int. Econ. Review 1959–69; mem. Advisory Bd Journal of Math. Econs 1974–; Corresp. The Mathematical Intelligencer 1983–84; mem. Editorial Bd Journal of Complexity 1985, Econ. Theory 1991–; Fellow AAAS, American Acad. of Arts and Sciences; mem. NAS (Chair. Section of Econ. Sciences 1982–85, mem. Cttee on Human Rights 1984–90, Class V Chair. (Behavioral and Social Sciences), mem. Council 1993–96), American Philosophical Soc.; Pres. Econometric Soc. 1971; Distinguished Fellow, American Econ. Asscn 1982; (Pres. 1990); Foreign Assoc. French Acad. of Sciences; Dr hc (Bonn, Lausanne, Northwestern Univ., Toulouse, Yale, Bordeaux, Keio (Japan)); Nobel Prize for Econ. Sciences 1983; Officier, Légion d'honneur, Commdr de l'Ordre Nat. du Mérite. *Publications:* Theory of Value: An Axiomatic Analysis of Economic Equilibrium 1959, Mathematical Economics: Twenty Papers of Gerard Debreu 1983. *Address:* Department of Economics, University of California, 549 Evans Hall, Berkeley, CA 94720-3880, USA. *Telephone:* (510) 642-7284; (510) 642-1966. *Fax:* (510) 642-6615.

DEBY, Idriss; Chadian politician; fmr C-in-C of Armed Forces; fmr mil. adviser to Pres. Hissène Habré (q.v.), overthrew him in coup Dec. 1990; Chair. Interim Council of State, Head of State 1990–91; Pres. of Chad March 1991–, also C-in-C of Armed Forces. *Address:* Office of the President, 74, N'Djamena, Chad. *Telephone:* 51-44-37. *Fax:* 51-45-01.

DECAUX, Alain; French historian and TV producer; b. 23 July 1925, Lille; s. of Francis Decaux and Louise Tiprez; m. 1st Madeleine Parisy 1957; one d.; m. 2nd Micheline Pelletier 1983; one s. one d.; ed Lycée Faidherbe, Lille, Lycée Janson-de-Sailly, Paris and Univ. of Paris; journalist 1944–; historian 1947–; Minister Del. attached to the Minister for Foreign Affairs: Francophone Countries 1988–91; cr. radio programme La tribune de l'histoire with André Castelot, Colin-Simard and later Jean-François Chiappe 1951; cr. TV programmes: La caméra explore le temps with Stellio Lorenzi and André Castelot 1956, Alain Decaux raconte 1969, L'histoire en question 1981, Le dossier d'Alain Decaux 1985; f. magazine L'histoire pour tous 1960; Pres. Groupement syndical des auteurs de télévision 1964–66, 1971–72; Vice-Chair. Société des auteurs et compositeurs dramatiques 1965–67, 1969–71, Chair. 1973–75; Dir Société Técipress 1967–91; Vice-Chair. Syndicat nat. des auteurs et compositeurs 1968–73; Admin. Librairie Plon 1969–72; Dir Historia Magazine 1969–71; worked on various periodicals, including Les nouvelles littéraires, Le Figaro littéraire, Historia, Histoire pour tous, Miroir de l'histoire, Lecture pour tous; Chair. Centre d'animation culturelle des Halles et du Marais (Carré Thorigny) 1971–73; mem. Conseil supérieur des lettres 1974; mem. Man. Cttee Centre nat. des lettres 1974–75; Minister of Francophone Affairs 1988–91; Policy Co-ordinator, French Overseas TV 1989; elected to Académie Française 1979; Chair. Centre d'action culturelle de Paris 1981–; Chair. Société des amis d'Alexandre Dumas 1971; Pres. Coll. des conservateurs du Château de Chantilly 1998–; Prix d'histoire, Académie Française 1950, Grande médaille d'or, Ville de Versailles 1954, Grand prix du disque for Révolution française 1963, Prix Plaisir de lire 1968, Oscar de la télévision et de la radio 1968, 1973, Prix de la Critique de Télévision 1972, médaille de vermeil de la Ville de Paris 1973, Prix littéraire de la Paulée de Meursault 1973; Grand Offcier Légion d'honneur, Grand Officier Ordre National du Mérite, Commdr Ordre des Arts et des Lettres. *Publications:*

Louis XVII 1947, Letizia, mère de l'empereur 1949, La conspiration du général Malet 1952, La Castiglione, dame de cœur de l'Europe 1953, La belle histoire de Versailles 1954, De l'Atlantide à Mayerling 1954, Le prince impérial 1957, Offenbach, roi de Second Empire 1958, Amours Second Empire 1958, L'énigme Anastasia 1960, Les heures brillantes de la Côte d'Azur, Les grands mystères du passé 1964, Les dossiers secrets de l'histoire 1966, Grands secrets, grandes énigmes 1966, Nouveaux dossiers secrets 1967, Les Rosenberg ne doivent pas mourir (play) 1968, Grandes aventures de l'histoire 1968, Histoire des Françaises (2 vols) 1972, Histoire de la France et des Français (with André Castelot, 13 vols) 1970–74, Le cuirassé Potemkine (co-writer, play) 1975, Blanqui 1976, Les face à face de l'histoire 1977, Alain Decaux raconte (4 vols) 1978, 1979, 1980, 1981, L'Histoire en question (2 vols) 1982–83, Notre-Dame de Paris (co-writer, play) 1978, Danton et Robespierre (co-writer, play) 1979, Un homme nommé Jésus (co-writer, play) 1983, Victor Hugo (biog.) 1984, Les Assassins 1986, Le Pape pélerin 1986, Destins fabuleux 1987, Alain Decaux raconte l'Histoire de France aux enfants 1987, L'Affaire du Courrier de Lyon 1987, Alain Decaux raconte la Révolution Française aux enfants 1988, La Liberté ou la mort (co-writer) 1988, La Révolution racontée aux enfants 1988, Alain Decaux raconte Jésus aux enfants 1991, Jésus était son nom 1991 (play), Le Tapis rouge 1992, Je m'appelais Marie-Antoinette (co-writer, play) 1993, Histoires Extraordinaires 1993, Nouvelles histoires extraordinaires 1994, L'abdication 1995, C'était le XXe siècle 1996, Alain Decaux raconte la Bible aux enfants 1996, Monaco et ses princes 1997, La course à l'abîme 1997, La Guerre absolue 1998, De Staline à Kennedy 1999, De Gaulle, celui qui a dit non (co-writer) 1999, Morts pour Vichy 2000, L'Avorton de Dieu: une vie de Saint Paul 2003. *Address:* 86 boulevard Flandrin, 75116 Paris, France.

DeCRANE, Alfred C., Jr; American business executive; b. 11 June 1931, Cleveland, Ohio; s. of Alfred Charles DeCrane and Verona (Marquard) DeCrane; m. Joan Elizabeth Hoffman 1954; one s. five d.; ed Notre Dame and Georgetown Univs; attorney, Texaco Inc., Houston and New York 1959, Asst to Vice-Chair. 1965, to Chair. 1967, Gen. Man. Producing Dept, Eastern Hemisphere 1968, Vice-Pres. 1970, Sr Vice-Pres. and Gen. Counsel 1976, mem. Bd of Dirs. 1977–96, Exec. Vice-Pres. 1978–83, Pres. 1983–86, Chair. of Bd 1987–96, CEO 1993–96; Hon. Dir American Petroleum Inst.; mem. Bd of Dirs, Corn Products Int., Harris Corpn; mem. Advisory Bd Morgan Stanley Int.; mem. Bd of Trustees Univ. of Notre Dame; Hon. DHL (Manhattanville Coll.) 1990, Hon. JD (Univ. of Notre Dame) 2002. *Address:* Two Greenwich Plaza, PO Box 1247, Greenwich, CT 06836, USA. *Telephone:* (203) 863-6580.

DÉDÉYAN, Charles, DèsL; French university professor; b. 4 April 1910, Smyrna, Turkey; s. of Prince and Princess Dédéyan (née Emma Elisabeth Ekisler); m. Phyllis Sivrisarian 1938; four s. one d.; ed Coll. Notre Dame de Ste Croix, Neuilly and Sorbonne; mem. French Resistance in Brittany World War II; Reader in French Literature, Univ. of Rennes 1942; Prof. of French and Comparative Literature, Univ. of Lyon 1945; Prof. of Comparative Literature at the Sorbonne 1949–79, Prof. Emer. 1979–; Sec.-Gen. Int. Fed. of Modern Languages and Literatures 1946–54; Dir Inst. of Comparative Modern Literature, Sorbonne 1955–68, 1971; Ed. Encyclopédie permanente Clartés 1961 and Revue des Etudes Gaulliennes; Decorations from World War II; Prix de la Pensée Française 1946, Prix France Allemagne 1966, Grand Prix du Rayonnement français, Académie Française 1967; Officier, Légion d'honneur, Commdr des Palmes Académiques, Commdr Ordre Pontifical de Saint-Sylvestre, Ufficiale al Merito della Repubblica Italiana, Kt of Malta 2002. *Publications:* La "Sophonisbe" de Mairet 1945, Montaigne chez ses amis anglo-saxons 1946, Essai sur le journal de voyage de Montaigne 1946, Le journal de voyage de Montaigne 1947, Argile 1947, Studies on Marivaux, Stendhal, Du Fail, Balzac, V. Hugo 1950–53, Le thème de Faust dans la littérature européenne 1954–67, Madame de Lafayette, La nouvelle Héloïse, Stendhal et les Chroniques italiennes 1955, Voltaire et la pensée anglaise 1956, Le "Gil Blas" de Le Sage 1956, 1965, Gérard de Nerval et l'Allemagne 1957–59, L'Angleterre dans la pensée de Diderot 1959, Dante en Angleterre 1958–66, "Le Roman Comique" de Scarron 1959, Rilke et la France 1961, L'influence de Rousseau sur la sensibilité européenne à la fin du XVIIIe siècle 1961, Stendhal chroniqueur 1962, Victor Hugo et l'Allemagne 1963, 1965, 1967, L'Italie dans l'œuvre romanesque de Stendhal 1963, Le cosmopolitisme littéraire de Charles Du Bos 1968–70, Racine et sa "Phèdre" 1968, Le nouveau mal du siècle de Baudelaire à nos jours 1968–72, Une guerre dans le mal des hommes 1971, Chateaubriand et Rousseau 1972, Le cosmopolitisme européen sous la Révolution et l'Empire 1976, L'Arioste en France 1975–76, Lamartine et la Toscane 1978, Giorgione dans les lettres françaises 1979, Le drame romantique en Europe 1982, Dante dans le romantisme anglais 1983, Le roman comique de Scarron 1983, Le critique en voyage 1985, Diderot et la pensée anglaise 1986, Montesquieu ou l'Alibi persan 1987, Le retour de Salente ou Voltaire et l'Angleterre 1988, La nouvelle Héloïse ou l'éternel retour 1990, Montesquieu ou les lumières d'Albion 1990, Télémaque ou la liberté de l'esprit 1991, Polyeucte ou le cœur et la grâce 1992, Lorelei ou l'enchanteur enchanté 1993, De l'Amadis est née l'Astrée 1994, Quand Guarini franchit les Alpes 1995, N'allez pas au théâtre 1997, En écoutant Stendhal 1997, Stendhal captivé et captif ou le mythe de la prison 1998, Le critique en voyage: esquisse d'une histoire littéraire comparée 1998. *Leisure interests:* fine arts, masterpieces of the great painters, old books. *Address:* 90 bis rue de Varenne, 75007 Paris; Manoir de La Motte, 35780 La Richardais, France. *Telephone:* 1-01-45-51-07 (Paris); 2-99-88-52-50 (La Richardais).

DEECH, Dame Ruth Lynn, DBE, MA, FRSM; British university administrator and lawyer; b. 29 April 1943, London; d. of Josef Fraenkel and Dora Rosenfeld; m. John Deech 1967; one d.; ed St Anne's Coll. Oxford and Brandeis Univ. USA; called to Bar, Inner Temple 1967; Legal Asst Law Comm. 1966–67; Asst Prof. Univ. of Windsor Law School, Canada 1968–70; Fellow and Tutor in Law, St Anne's Coll. Oxford 1970–91, Vice-Prin. 1988–91, Prin. 1991–; mem. Oxford Univ. Hebdomadal Council 1986–2000; Chair. Oxford Univ. Admissions Cttee 1993–97, 2000–03; Gov. Oxford Centre for Hebrew and Jewish Studies 1994–2000; Chair. Human Fertilization and Embryology Authority 1994–2002; Pro-Vice-Chancellor, Oxford Univ. 2001–; mem. Human Genetics Comm. 2000–02, European Acad. of Sciences and Arts 2001–; Rhodes Trustee 1997–; Visiting Prof. Osgoode Hall Law School, Canada 1978; Hon. Fellow, Soc. for Advanced Legal Studies 1997; Hon. Bencher, Inner Temple 1996–; Gov. BBC 2002–. *Publications:* Divorce Dissent 1994; articles on family law, property law, autobiog. etc. *Leisure interests:* music, after-dinner speaking. *Address:* St Anne's College, Oxford, OX2 6HS, England. *Telephone:* (1865) 274820. *Fax:* (1865) 274895.

DEEDES, Baron (Life Peer), cr. 1986, of Aldington in the County of Kent; **William Francis Deedes,** KBE, PC, MC, DL; British politician and newspaper editor; b. 1 June 1913, Aldington, Kent; s. of (Herbert) William Deedes; m. Evelyn Hilary Branfoot 1942; two s. (one deceased) three d.; ed Harrow School; journalist with Morning Post 1931–37; war corresp. on Abyssinia 1935; served in war of 1939–45, Queen's Westminsters (12 King's Royal Rifle Corps); MP (Conservative) for Ashford Div. of Kent 1950–74; Parl. Sec., Ministry of Housing and Local Govt 1954–55; Parl. Under-Sec. Home Dept 1955–57; DL, Kent 1962; Minister without Portfolio (Information) 1962–64; mem. Advisory Cttee on Drug Dependence 1967–74; Chair. Select Cttee on Immigration and Race Relations 1970–74; Ed. Daily Telegraph 1974–86, mem. editorial staff 1986–; Hon. DCL (Kent) 1988; Special Award, British Press Awards 1992. *Publication:* Dear Bill: W. F. Deedes Reports (autobiog.) 1997. *Address:* New Hayters, Aldington, Kent, TN25 7DT, England. *Telephone:* (1233) 720269.

DEFLASSIEUX, Jean Sébastien; French banker; b. 11 July 1925, Cap d'Ail; s. of Alexis Deflassieux and Thérèse Dalmasso; m. 1st Christiane Orabona 1950 (deceased); one s.; m. 2nd Huguette Dupuy 2000; ed HEC, Law Faculty, Paris, London School of Econs, Ecole d'organisation scientifique du travail; analyst, Div. of financial studies, Crédit Lyonnais 1948–54; attached to Cabinet of Jean Filippi (Sec. of State for the Budget) 1956–57 and of Arthur Conte (Sec. of State for Industry) 1957; Insp. of Paris br. offices, Crédit Lyonnais 1958; Sub-Dir Haute Banque 1959–69, Dir of External Commerce 1969–72, of Int. Affairs 1972, in charge of the Cen. Man. of Int. Affairs 1978–82; Adviser to Prime Minister Pierre Mauroy 1981–84; Gen. Admin. 1982, Chair. and CEO Crédit Lyonnais 1982–86, Hon. Chair. 1986–; Chair. Banque des Echanges Internationaux, Paris 1987–96, Monacŕedit (Monaco) 1980–99, Banque AIG, Paris 1991–94; Dir Arab Banking Corpn Int. Bank PLC, London 1991–, and of other banks and cos.; Del. Gen. Radio Alpazur NRJ Menton 1998; Pres. European League for Econ. Co-operation (French Section) 1983; Pres. (French Section) Int. Vienna Council (East–West) 1985–96; Commdr, Légion d'Honneur, Commdr Ordre Nat. du Mérite, Croix de Guerre 1939–45, Palmes Académiques. *Leisure interest:* history. *Address:* 9 boulevard du Jardin exotique, 98000 Monaco (Home); 41 rue Vineuse, 75116 Paris (Home); Credit Lyonnais, 19 boulevard des Italiens, 75002 Paris, France. *Telephone:* 7-93-50-06-28 (Monaco) (Home); 1-47-04-37-10 (Paris) (Home); 1-42-95-11-11 (Paris) (Office).

DEGENERES, Ellen; American actress; b. 26 Jan. 1958, New Orleans. *Films include:* Wisecracks 1991, Coneheads 1993, Mr Wrong 1996, Doctor Doolittle (voice) 1998, Goodbye Lover 1999, EdTV 1999, The Love Letter 1999, Reaching Normal 1999, If These Walls Could Talk 2000. *TV includes:* (series) Duet 1988–89, Open House 1989, Laurie Hill 1992, Ellen 1994–98 (also producer), The Ellen Show 2001.

DEGUARA, Louis, MD; Maltese politician and doctor; b. 18 Sept. 1947, Naxxar; m. Maria Fatima Mallia; one s. one d.; ed St Aloysius Coll., Birkikara, Univ. of Malta; medical practitioner 1973; fmrly houseman St Luke's, Sir Paul Boffa and Gozo General Hospitals, Prin. Medical Officer of Health, Northern Region; Gen. Practitioner 1977–; MP, Nationalist Party 1981–; Parl. Sec. Ministry for Social Devt 1995–96; Shadow Minister and Opposition Spokesman for Health 1996–98; Minister of Health 1998–. *Address:* Ministry of Health, Palazzo Castellania, 15 Merchant Street, Valletta, CMR 02, Malta. *Telephone:* 224071. *Fax:* 252574.

DEHAENE, Jean-Luc; Belgian politician; b. 7 Aug. 1940, Montpellier, France; m. Celie Verbeke 1965; four c.; ed Univ. of Namur; adviser to various Govt ministries 1972–81; Minister of Social Affairs and Institutional Reforms 1981–88; Deputy Prime Minister and Minister of Communications and Institutional Reforms 1988–92; Prime Minister of Belgium 1992–99; Vice-Pres. of EU Special Convention on a European Constitution 2001–. *Address:* Special Convention on a European Constitution, European Union, 200 rue de la Loi, 1049 Brussels, Belgium.

DEHEM, Roger Jules, PhD, FRSC; Belgian professor of economics; b. 24 July 1921, Wemmel; s. of Charles Dehem and Elise (née Masschelein) Dehem; m. Gertrude Montbleau 1950; two s. four d.; ed Univ. of Louvain; Lecturer McGill Univ. 1947–49, Prof. Univ. of Montréal 1948–58; Prin. Admin. OEEC 1958–59; Economist Adv. Fabrimétal, Brussels 1959–60; Prof. Economics Laval Univ., Québec 1961–95, Prof. Emer. 1995–; Fellow Rockefeller Foundation 1946–48; Pres. Canadian Econ. Asscn 1973–74. *Publications:* L'efficacité sociale du système économique 1952, Traité d'analyse économique 1957, L'utopie de l'économiste 1969, L'équilibre économique international 1970, De l'étalon sterling à l'étalon dollar 1972, Précis d'économique internationale 1982, Histoire de la pensée économique 1984, Les Economies capitalistes et socialistes 1988, Capitalismes et Socialismes 1989. *Address:* 2000 rue Chapdelaine, Ste.-Foy, Québec, G1V 1M3, Canada (Home). *Telephone:* (418) 681-9593.

DEHENNIN, Baron Herman, LLD; Belgian diplomatist; b. 20 July 1929, Lier; s. of Alexander Dehennin and Flora Brehmen; m. Margareta-Maria Donvil 1954; two s.; ed Catholic Univ. of Leuven; Lt in Royal Belgian Artillery 1951–53; entered Diplomatic Service 1954, Second Sec. The Hague 1956–59, First Sec. New Delhi 1960–63, Commercial Counsellor, Madrid 1964–65, Chargé d'Affaires, Congo 1965–66, Amb. to Rwanda 1966–70, EC Minister of Belgium in Washington, DC 1970–74, Deputy Admin. to Dir-Gen. Foreign Econ. Relations, Brussels 1974–77, Grand Marshal of the Belgian Royal Court 1981–85; Amb. to Japan 1978–81, to USA 1985–90, to UK 1991–94; Pres. Special Olympics 1995–; Grand Cross of Order of Leopold, Grand Cross of Order of the Crown. *Leisure interests:* jogging, hiking, tennis, fishing, hunting, reading (history and philosophy).

DEHMELT, Hans Georg, Dr rer. nat; American physicist; b. 9 Sept. 1922, Görlitz, Germany; s. of Georg Dehmelt and Asta Klemmt; m. Diana Dundore 1989; one s. from a previous m.; ed Gymnasium Zum Grauen Kloster, Berlin, Breslau Tech. Univ., Göttingen Univ. and Inst. of Hans Kopfermann; served as private in German army 1940–46, POW 1945–46; Deutsche Forschungs-Gemeinschaft Fellow, Inst. of Hans Kopfermann 1950–52; co-discovered nuclear quadrupole resonance 1949; postdoctoral work in microwave spectroscopy lab., Duke Univ., USA 1952–55; Visiting Asst Prof., Univ. of Washington, Seattle 1955–56, Asst Prof. 1956–58, Assoc. Prof. 1958–61, Prof. 1961–, also research physicist; with others, achieved the most precise electron magnetic moment determination to date, through work on geonium 1976–; became US citizen 1961; Fellow American Physical Soc.; mem. NAS, American Acad. of Arts and Sciences; Dr rer. nat hc (Ruprecht Karl Univ., Heidelberg) 1986, Hon. DSc (Chicago) 1987; Davisson-Germer Prize, American Physical Soc. 1970, Alexander von Humboldt Prize 1974, Award in Basic Research, Int. Soc. of Magnetic Resonance 1980, Count Rumford Prize, American Acad. of Arts and Sciences 1985, Nobel Prize in Physics 1989 for measurement on isolated Subatomic particle and atomic particle at rest, Nat. Medal of Science 1995. *Publication:* Radiofrequency Spectroscopy of Stored Ions 1967. *Address:* Department of Physics, PO Box 35-1560, University of Washington, Seattle, WA 98195-1560; 1600 43rd Avenue E, Seattle, WA 98112-3205, USA (Home). *Website:* www.phys.washington.edu/~dehmelt (Office).

DEICHTER, Avraham; Israeli state security official; served in Sayeret Matkal commando unit; Deputy Head Shin Bet (nat. intelligence agency) –2000, Head 2000–. *Address:* c/o Ministry of Public Security, P.O. Box 18182, Building 3, Rinjat Hamemshala, Jerusalem 91181, Israel (Office). *Telephone:* (2) 5308003 (Office). *Fax:* (2) 5847872 (Office). *E-mail:* mops@netvision.net.il (Office).

DEIGHTON, Len; British author; b. 1929, London. *Publications:* The Ipcress File 1962 (also film), Horse under Water 1963, Funeral in Berlin 1964 (also film), Où est le Garlic 1965, Action Cook Book 1965, Cookstrip Cook Book (USA) 1966, Billion Dollar Brain 1966 (also film), An Expensive Place to Die 1967, Len Deighton's London Dossier (guide book) 1967, The Assassination of President Kennedy (co-author) 1967, Only When I Larf 1968 (also film), Bomber 1970 (also radio dramatization), Declarations of War (short stories) 1971, Close-Up 1972, Spy Story 1974 (also film), Yesterday's Spy 1975, Twinkle, Twinkle, Little Spy 1976, Fighter: the True Story of the Battle of Britain 1977, SS-GB 1978, Airshipwreck (co-author) 1978, Blitzkrieg 1979, Battle of Britain (co-author) 1980, XPD 1981, Goodbye Mickey Mouse 1982, Berlin Game 1983, Mexico Set 1984, London Match 1985, Winter: a Berlin Family 1899–1945 1987, Spy Hook 1988, ABC of French Food 1989, Spy Line 1989, Spy Sinker 1990, Basic French Cookery Course 1990, Mamista 1991, City of Gold 1992, Violent Ward 1993, Blood, Tears and Folly 1993, Faith 1994, Hope 1995, Charity 1996. *Address:* c/o Jonathan Clowes Ltd, 10 Iron Bridge House, Bridge Approach, London, NW1 8BD, England.

DEINEKIN, Gen. Piotr Stepanovich, DrMilSc; Russian army officer; b. 14 Dec. 1937, Morozovsk, Rostov Region; m.; three c.; ed Balashov Military Aviation School, Yuri Gagarin Air Force Acad., Gen. Staff Acad.; pilot, army air force 1957–69, Commdr aviation Regt, div. 1969–82, Deputy Commdr Army Air Force 1982–85, Commdr 1985–90, First Vice-C-in-C of USSR Air Force 1990, C-in-C and Deputy Minister of Defence of USSR (now Russia) 1991–97; Head Pres.'s Admin. Dept on the Cossack Problem 1998–; Hero of Russian Fed. 1997. *Address:* Staraya pl. 4, entr. 1, Moscow, Russia. *Telephone:* (095) 206-35-73 (Office).

DEISS, Joseph; Swiss politician; b. 18 Jan. 1946, Fribourg; m. Elizabeth Mueller; three s.; ed Coll. Saint-Michel, Fribourg, Univ. of Fribourg, Kings Coll. Cambridge, UK; Lecturer (part-time) of Political Economy, Univ. of Fribourg 1973–83, Prof. Extraordinary 1984–99, Sr Faculty mem. Dept of Social and Econ. Science 1996–98; Deputy, Great Council of Fribourg 1981–91, Pres. 1981. Nat. Adviser 1991–99; Vice-Pres. Comm. on Foreign Policy, Nat. Council 1995–96; Pres. Comm. on Revision of the Fed. Constitution 1996; Adviser to Head of Fed. Dept of Foreign Affairs March 1999–2002; Head of Fed. Dept of Econ. Affairs 2003–; Pres. Banque Raiffeisen

du Haut-Lac 1996–99; Chair. of Bd Schuhmacher AG, Schmitten 1996–99. *Address:* Federal Department of Economic Affairs, Bundeshaus Ost, 3003 Bern, Switzerland (Office). *Telephone:* 313222007 (Office). *Fax:* 313222194 (Office). *E-mail:* info@gs-evd.admin.ch. *Website:* www.evd.admin.ch.

DEKKER, W.; Netherlands business executive; b. 26 April 1924, Eindhoven; joined Philips, SE Asia Regional Bureau 1948, Man. 1956–59, with Indonesian Philips co. 1948–66, Man. Far East Regional Bureau 1959–66, Gen. Man. Philips in Far East, Tokyo 1966–72, mem. Bd British Philips 1972, Chair. and Man. Dir 1972–76, mem. Bd of Man. N.V. Philips' Glœilampenfabrieken 1976–82, Pres. 1982, Chair. 1982–94; mem. Supervisory Bd Dresdner Bank, Germany, AMRO Bank, Netherlands; mem. Int. Advisory Bd Allianz Versicherungs AG, Germany, Volvo, Sweden; mem. Bd Fiat, Italy; mem. Int. Advisory Cttee Chase Manhattan Bank, New York; mem. Advisory Bd Montedison, Italy; mem. Advisory Cttee for Investments of Foreign Cos. in the Netherlands to Minister of Econ. Affairs; mem. Atlantic Advisory Council, United Technologies Corp., USA; Chair. Supervisory Bd Maatschappij voor Industriële Projecten; mem. European Advisory Cttee New York Stock Exchange; mem. Special Advisory Group, UNIDO; Prof. of Int. Man., Univ. of Leiden; mem. Tinbergen Inst., Rotterdam; Co-founder European Roundtable of Industrialists 1983, Chair. 1988–; Hon. LLD (Univ. of Strathclyde) 1976, Dr. hc (Tech. Univ. of Delft) 1987; Hon. CBE; Goldenes Ehrenzeichen für Verdienste um das Land Wien (Vienna); Commdr, Order of Orange Nassau; Commdr, Order of Belgian Crown; Kt, Order of Dutch Lion; Commdr Légion d'honneur; Cavaliere di Gran Croce dell'Ordine al Merito, Italy.

DEL CASTILLO VERA, Pilar; Spanish politician and academic; b. 31 July 1952, Nador (Marruecos); m. Guillermo Gortázar; two c.; ed Universidad Complutense de Madrid, Univ. of Ohio, U.S.A.; Lecturer in Constitutional Law, subsequently Prof. of Political Science and Admin., Universidad Nacional de Educación a Distancia (UNED) 1986–; wrote policy papers for Fundación para el Análisis y los Estudios Sociales (FAES); Tech. Adviser Centro de Investigaciones Sociológicas (CIS) 1987–88, Pres. 1996–2000; Minister of Educ., Culture and Sport 2000–; fmr Ed. Nueva Revista de Política, Cultura y Arte; mem. Associación Nacional e Internacional de Ciencia Política; Fulbright Scholar. *Publications:* Financiación de los partidos y candidatos en las democracias occidentales, Cultura Política, Comportamiento político y electoral. *Address:* Ministry of Education, Culture and Sport, Alcala 34, 28071 Madrid, Spain (Office). *Telephone:* (91) 5221100 (Office). *Fax:* (91) 5213575 (Office). *Website:* www.mec.es (Office).

DEL PONTE, Carla, LLM; Swiss lawyer; b. 9 Feb. 1947, Lugano; ed Univs. of Berne and Geneva; in pvt. practice, Lugano 1975–81; Investigating Magistrate, then Public Prosecutor, Lugano 1981–94; Attorney-Gen. and Chief Prosecutor of Switzerland 1994–2000, mem. Fed. Comm. on White-Collar Crime 1994–99; Chief Prosecutor Int. Criminal Tribunals of the former Yugoslavia and Rwanda 1999–. *Address:* Office of the Chief Prosecutor, United Nations War Crimes Tribunals, Churchillplein 1, P.O. Box 13888, 2501 The Hague, The Netherlands (Office). *Telephone:* (70) 416-5233 (Office). *Fax:* (70) 416 5355 (Office). *Website:* www.un.org/icty (Office).

DEL TORO, Benicio; Puerto Rican actor, director and writer; b. 19 Feb. 1967, Santurce, Puerto Rico; s. of Gustavo Del Toro and the late Fausta Sanchez Del Toro; ed Univ. of California at San Diego, Circle in the Square Acting School, Stella Adler Conservatory. *Films:* Big Top Pee-wee 1988, Christopher Columbus: The Discovery 1992, Fearless 1993, Money for Nothing 1993, China Moon 1994, The Usual Suspects 1995, Swimming With Sharks 1995, Cannes Man 1996, The Funeral 1996, Basquiat 1996, The Fan 1996, Joyride 1997, Excess Baggage 1997, Fear and Loathing in Las Vegas 1998, Snatch 2000, Traffic (Acad. Award for Best Supporting Actor) 2000, The Way of the Gun 2000, The Pledge 2001, Bread and Roses 2001, The Hunted 2002. *Website:* www.beniciodeltoro.com.

DEL VALLE ALLIENDE, Jaime; Chilean politician and lawyer; b. 2 July 1931, Santiago; m. Paulina Swinburn Pereira; four c.; ed Escuela de Derecho de la Universidad Católica de Chile; taught at Catholic Univ. Law School from 1955, appt. Dir 1969, Dean 1970; various posts in Supreme Court 1958–64; Public Prosecutor 1964–74; Pro-Rector, Pontificia Univ. Católica de Chile 1974; Dir-Gen. nat. TV channel 1975–78; mem. Bd Colegio de Abogados 1981–, Pres. 1982–83; Minister of Justice Feb.–Dec. 1983; Minister of Foreign Affairs 1983–87. *Address:* c/o Ministerio de Asuntos Exteriores, Palacio de la Moneda, Santiago, Chile. *Telephone:* 6982501.

DELACÔTE, Jacques; conductor; s. of Pierre Delacôte and Renée Wagner Delacôte; m. Maria Lucia Alvares-Machado 1975; ed Music Conservatoire, Paris, Acad. of Music, with Prof. Hans Swarowsky, Vienna; was Asst of Darius Milhaud and Leonard Bernstein; among the orchestras conducted: Orchestre de Paris, Orchestre Nat. de France, New York Philharmonic, Vienna Philharmonic, Vienna Symphony, Israel Philharmonic, Orchestre Nat. de Belgique, London Symphony, San Francisco, Cleveland, Scottish Chamber, Scottish Nat. Opera, RIAS Berlin, WDR Cologne, SF Stuttgart, SWF Baden-Baden, Bavarian Radio, Munich, English Chamber, BBC, London, London Philharmonic, Royal Philharmonic, London, Japan Philharmonic, Yomiuri Symphony, Royal Opera House Covent Garden (including Far East tour, Korea and Japan), English Nat. Opera, Opernhaus Zürich, Teatro Real Madrid, Teatro Liceo, Barcelona, La Fenice, Venice, Vienna State Opera, Deutsche Oper Berlin, Pittsburgh Opera, Welsh Nat. Opera, Opéra de Paris, Teatro Colón Buenos Aires, Canadian Opera Co., Royal State Opera Copenhagen, State Opera Hamburg, State Opera Munich, Chicago Lyric Opera; also recordings with EMI, Philips London and Tring London; 1st Prize and Gold Medal Mitropoulos Competition, New York 1971. *Festivals include:* Flandernfestival, Macerata Festival, Klangbogen Vienna, Dresden Musiktage. *Leisure interest:* chess. *Address:* Dr. Hilbert Maximilianstr. 22, 80539 Munich, Germany.

DELANÖE, Bertrand Jacques Marie; French politician; b. 30 May 1950, Tunis, Tunisia; s. of Auguste Delanöe and Yvonne Delanöe (née Delord); ed Institution Sainte-Marie, Rodez, Univ. of Toulouse; mem., Conseil de Paris 1977–, Socialist Député 1981–86, Senator 1995–, Mayor of Paris March 2001–; Pres. of Paris Socialist Group 1993–; mem. Cttee of Dirs., Parti Socialiste 1979–, Party Spokesman 1981–83, mem. Exec. Bureau 1983–87, 1997–; Pres. France-Egypt Friendship Group 1981–86. *Publication:* Pour l'honneur de Paris 1999. *Address:* Hôtel de Ville, 75196 Paris RP, France (Office).

DELAY, Florence; French writer and university lecturer; b. 19 March 1941, Paris; d. of the late Jean Delay and of Marie Madeleine Delay (née Carrez); ed Lycée Jean de la Fontaine, Paris, Sorbonne; Lecturer in Gen. and Comparative Literature Univ. of Paris III 1972–; Theatre Critic Nouvelle Revue française 1978–85; mem. Prix Fémina jury 1978–81, Editorial Bd Critique magazine 1978–96, Reading Cttee Gallimard publrs. 1979–86; mem. Acad. française 2000–; Commdr des Arts et des Lettres; Grand prix du roman de la Ville de Paris 1999. *Publications:* Minuit sur les jeux 1973, Le Aïe aïe de la corne de brume 1975, Graal théâtre vol. I 1977, vol. II 1981, L'Insuccès de la fête 1980, Riche et légère (Prix Fémina) 1983, Course d'amour pendant le deuil 1986, Petites formes en prose après Edison (essays) 1987, Les Dames de Fontainebleau (essays) 1987, Partition rouge 1989, Hexaméron 1989, Etxemendi (Prix François Mauriac) 1990, Semaines de Suzanne 1991, Catalina 1994, La Fin des temps ordinaires 1996, La Séduction brève (essays) 1997, Dit Nerval 1999, L'Evangile de Jean (transl. of Gospel of John) 2001. *Address:* c/o Gallimard, 5 rue Sébastien Bottin, 75007 Paris (Office); 58 rue Monsieur le Prince, 75006 Paris, France (Home).

DELAY, Tom; American politician; b. 1947, Laredo, Tex.; m. Christine DeLay; one d.; ed Baylor Univ., Univ. of Houston; owned and operated small business in Tex. 1970s; elected to Texas House of Reps 1978; mem. US Congress from 22nd Dist Texas, held various positions in House of Reps including Republican Conf. Sec., Deputy Whip, Chair. Republican Study Cttee, Majority Whip –2003, Majority Leader 2003–, mem. Appropriations Cttee; mem. Advisory Bd Child Advocates of Fort Bend County; Taxpayers Friend Award, Nat. Taxpayers Union; Golden Bulldog Award, Watchdog of the Treasury; Nat. Security Leadership Award, Peace Through Strength Coalition *. Address:* Office of the Majority Leader, 2370 Rayburn House Office Building, Washington, DC 20515, USA (Office). *Website:* TomDeLay.house .gov (Office).

DELEBARRE, Michel Stephane Henry Joseph; French politician; b. 27 April 1946, Bailleul (Nord); s. of Stéphane Delebarre and Georgette Deroo; m. Janine Debeyre 1969; one d.; Asst Sec.-Gen. Cttee for the Expansion of the Nord-Pas de Calais area 1968–71, Sec.-Gen. 1971–74; Cabinet Dir for Pres. of Nord-Pas de Calais Regional Council 1974–78; Gen. Del. for Devt for City of Lille 1977–80; Sec.-Gen. City of Lille 1980; Pres. regional fund for contemporary art 1982; mem. of Cabinet of Prime Minister 1981–82; Cabinet Dir 1982–84; unassigned prefect 1983; Minister of Labour, Employment and Professional Training 1984–86; Socialist Mem of Parl. for Nord 1986, 1988–93, 1997–98; mem. Exec. Bd Socialist Party 1987; Minister of Transport and Marine Affairs 1989; Minister of State, Minister of Town and Physical Planning 1990–91; Minister of State, Minister of Civil Service and Public Admin. Enhancement 1991–92; Adviser for Urban and Regional Planning; Chair. Cttee of Experts advising Lionel Jospin, Leader Socialist Party 1995; First Deputy Pres., Regional Council for Nord-Pas de Calais 1986, 1992–98; Mayor of Dunkirk 1989–; Pres. Urban Community of Dunkirk 1995–, Regional Council of Nord-Pas de Calais 1998–, L'Union nationale des féderations d'organismes d'HLM 1999–; mem. Nat. Council of Evaluation 1999–. *Address:* Conseil Régional Nord-Pas de Calais, Hôtel de Région, Centre Rihour, 59555 Lille Cedex; Hôtel de Ville, place Charles Valentin, 59140 Dunkirk, France.

DELGADO, Alvaro; Spanish artist; b. 9 June 1922, Madrid; m. Mercedes Gal Orendain; one s.; ed pupil of Vazquez Diaz 1936–39, Benjamin Palencia 1939–42; mem. Real Acad. de Bellas Artes, Real Acad. de San Fernando; Acad. Delegado de la Calcografia; Commdr Order of Ethiopia; First Prize, Concurso Nacional de Carteles Para Teatro 1939; First Prize, Proyecto Para Figurines y Decorados 1940; Cuba Prize for Painting, IIa Bienal Arte Hispano Americano 1952; Grand Prize for Painting, Bienal de Arte Mediterraneo, Alejandria 1955; Grand Prize for Painting, Exposición Int., Alicante 1960; Primera Medalla de Dibujo, Exposición Nacional Bellas Artes 1960; Gold Medal, Salon Nacional del Grabado 1962; Vocal del Patronato del Museo del Prado, Madrid 1970. *Leisure interest:* constant travel. *Address:* Biarritz 5, Parque de las Avenidas, Madrid 28028, Spain.

DELIBES, Miguel, DIur; Spanish writer and university teacher; b. 17 Oct. 1920, Valladolid; s. of Adolfo Delibes and Maria Delibes; m. Angeles de Castro 1946 (died 1974); seven c.; ed School of Higher Studies, Bilbao, Univ. of Valladolid, School of Journalism, Bilbao; Prof. Univ. of Valladolid 1945–85; Dir El Norte de Castilla (newspaper) 1956–62; mem. Real Acad. de la Lengua 1973; Dr hc (Madrid, Valladolid, Saarbrücken); recipient Premio Nacional de

Narrativa 1955, 1999, Premio de la Crítica 1962, Premio Nadal, Premio Nacional de Literatura, Premio Príncipe de Asturias, Premio Nacional de las Letras 1991, Miguel de Cervantes Prize 1993. *Publications include:* La sombra del ciprés es alargada 1948, El camino 1950, Las ratas 1962, El libro de la caza menor 1964, Cinco horas con Mario 1966, Parábola del náufrago 1969, El disputado voto del señor Cayo 1978, Los santos inocentes 1981, El tesoro 1985, Pegar la hebra 1990, El conejo 1991, Señora de rojo sobre fondo gris 1991, El último coto 1992, Diario de un jubilado 1995, El hereje 1998, Madera de héroe 2002. *Leisure interests:* hunting, fishing, tennis. *Address:* Calle Dos de Mayo 10, 47004 Valladolid, Spain. *Telephone:* 983/300250.

DeLILLO, Don; American writer; b. 20 Nov. 1936; Award in Literature, American Acad. and Inst. of Arts and Letters 1984, Jerusalem Prize for the Freedom of the Individual in Soc. 1999, William Dean Howells Medal 2000. *Publications:* Americana 1971, End Zone 1972, Great Jones Street 1973, Ratner's Star 1976, Players 1977, Running Dog 1978, The Names 1982, White Noise 1985 (Nat. Book Award 1985), Libra 1988 (Int. Fiction Prize 1989), Mao II 1991 (Pen Faulkner Award 1992), Underworld 1997, The Body Artist 2000. *Address:* c/o Wallace Literary Agency, 177 E 70th Street, New York, NY 10021, USA.

DELL, Michael S.; American business executive; b. 1965, Houston, Tex.; s. of Alexander Dell and Lorraine Dell; m. Susan Lieberman 1989; two d.; ed Univ. of Texas 1983–84; Founder, Chair. and CEO Dell Computer Corpn (fmrly PC's Ltd), Austin, Tex. 1984–; Entrepreneur of the Year Award (Inc. magazine) 1990, JD Power Customer Satisfaction Award 1991, 1993; CEO of the Year (Financial World magazine) 1993. *Address:* Dell Computer Corporation, 1 Dell Way, Round Rock, TX 78682-0001, USA (Office).

DELLA CASA-DEBELJEVIC, Lisa (see Casa-Debeljevic, Lisa Della).

DELL'OLIO, Louis; American fashion designer; b. 23 July 1948, New York; ed Parsons School of Design, New York; Asst designer to Dominic Rompello of Teal Traina, New York 1969–71; Chief Designer, Georgini div. of Originala, New York 1971–74; design collaborator with Donna Karan (q.v.), Anne Klein & Co. 1974–93; Chief Designer 1984–93; mem. Fashion Designers of America; Coty Awards 1977, 1981.

DELON, Alain; French actor; b. 8 Nov. 1935, Sceaux; m. Nathalie Delon (divorced); one s.; one s. one d. by Rosalie Van Breemen; with French Marine Corps 1952–55; independent actor-producer under Delbeau (Delon-Beaume) Productions 1964–; Pres., Dir-Gen. Adel Productions 1968–87, Leda Productions 1987–; numerous TV appearances; Chevalier, Légion d'honneur, Commdr des Arts et des Lettres. *Films include:* Christine 1958, Faibles femmes 1959, Le chemin des écoliers 1959, Purple Noon 1959, Rocco and His Brothers 1960, Eclipse 1961, The Leopard 1962, Any Number Can Win 1962, The Black Tulip 1963, The Love Cage 1963, L'insoumis 1964, The Yellow Rolls Royce 1964, Once a Thief 1964, Les centurions 1965, Paris brûle-t-il? 1965, Texas Across the River 1966, Les adventuriers 1966, Le samourai 1967, Histoires extraordinaires 1967, Diaboliquement votre 1967, Adieu l'ami 1968, Girl on a motorcycle 1968, La piscine 1968, Jeff 1968, Die Boss, Die Quietly 1969, Borsalino 1970, Madly 1970, Doucement les basses 1970, Le cercle rouge 1971, L'assassinat de Trotsky 1971, La veuve Couderc 1971, Un flic 1972, Le professeur 1972, Scorpio 1972, Traitement de choc 1972, Les granges brûlées 1973, Deux hommes dans la ville 1973, Borsalino & Co. 1973, Les seins de glace 1974, Creezy 1975, Zorro 1975, Le gitan 1975, Mr. Klein 1975, Le gang 1977, Mort d'un pourri 1977, Armaguedon 1977, L'homme pressé 1977, Attention, les enfants regardent 1978, Le toubib 1979, Trois hommes à abattre 1980, Pour la peau d'un flic 1981, Le choc 1982, Le battant 1982, Un Amour de Swann 1984, Notre Histoire (César, Best Actor 1985) 1984, Parole de flic 1985, Le passage 1986, Ne réveillez pas un flic qui dort, Nouvelle Vague 1989, Dancing Machine 1990, Le Retour de Casanova 1992, Un Crime 1993, L'Ours en peluche 1994, Le Jour et La Nuit 1996, Une Chance sur deux 1998, Les Acteurs 2000. *Stage performances:* 'Tis Pity She's a Whore 1961, 1962, Les yeux crevés 1967, Variations énigmatiques 1996. *Leisure interests:* swimming, riding, boxing. *Address:* c/o Leda Productions, 4 rue Chambiges, 75008 Paris, France.

DELORS, Jacques Lucien Jean; French politician and economist; b. 20 July 1925, Paris; s. of Louis Delors and Jeanne Rigal; m. Marie Lephaille 1948; one s. (deceased) one d. (Martine Aubry) ed Lycée Voltaire, Paris, Lycée Blaise-Pascal, Clermont-Ferrand, Univ. of Paris; Head of Dept, Banque de France 1945–62, attached to staff of Dir-Gen. of Securities and Financial Market 1950–62, mem. Gen. Council 1973–79; mem. Planning and Investments Section, Econ. and Social Council 1959–61; Head of Social Affairs Section, Commissariat général du Plan 1962–69; Sec.-Gen. Interministerial Cttee for Vocational Training and Social Promotion 1969–73; Adviser to Jacques Chaban-Delmas 1969, Chargé de mission 1971–72; Assoc. Prof. of Co. Man., Univ. of Paris IX 1973–79; f. Club Echange et Projets 1974; Dir Labour and Soc. Research Centre 1975–79; Parti Socialiste Nat. Del. for int. econ. relations 1976–81; elected mem. European Parl. 1979, Chair. Econ. and Monetary Cttee 1979–81; Minister for the Economy and Finance 1981–83, for the Economy, Finance and Budget 1983–84; Mayor of Clichy 1983–84; Pres. Comm. of the European Communities (now European Commission) 1985–94, Commr for Forward Planning and Legal Service, for Gen. Admin. and Co-ordination of Structural Funds 1985–89; Pres. Int. Comm. on Educ. for the Twenty-First Century, UNESCO 1992–99; Pres. Conseil d'admin. Collège d'Europe, Bruges 1995–99, Conseil de l'emploi, des revenus et de la cohésion sociale (CERC) 2000–; f. Notre Europe 1996; hon. degrees from 24 univs. in

Europe, USA and Canada; Officier, Légion d'honneur. *Publications:* Les indicateurs sociaux 1971, Changer 1975, En sortir ou pas (jtly) 1985, La France par l'Europe (jtly) 1988, Le Nouveau concert Européen 1992, Our Europe: The Community and National Development 1993, Pour Entrer dans le XXIᵉ Siècle 1994, Combats pour l'Europe 1996; numerous articles; reports for UN on French planning (1966) and long-term planning (1969). *Address:* Association Notre Europe, 41 boulevard des Capucines, 75002 Paris, France (Office). *Telephone:* 1-44-58-97-97 (Office). *Fax:* 1-44-58-97-99 (Office). *E-mail:* notreeurope@notre-europe.asso.fr. *Website:* www.notre-europe.asso.fr (Office).

DELPY, Julie; French film actress; b. 21 Dec. 1969, Paris; ed New York Univ. Film School. *Films include:* Detective 1985, Mauvais Sang 1986, La Passion Béatrice 1987, L'Autre Nuit 1988, La Noche Oscura 1989, Europa Europa 1991, Voyager 1991, Warszawa 1992, Young and Younger 1993, The Three Musketeers 1993, When Pigs Fly 1993, The Myth of the White Wolf 1994, Killing Zoe 1994, Mesmer 1994, Trois Couleurs Blanc 1994, Trois Couleurs Rouge 1994, Before Sunrise 1995, An American Werewolf in Paris 1997, The Treat 1998, LA Without a Map 1998, Blah, Blah, Blah (Dir), The Passion of Ayn Rand 1999. *Television includes:* ER. *Address:* c/o The William Morris Agency, 151 El Camino Drive, Beverley Hills, CA 90212, USA.

DeLUISE, Dom; American comedian and actor; b. 1 Aug. 1933, Brooklyn, New York; m. Carol Arthur; three s.; ed Tufts Coll.; spent two seasons with Cleveland Playhouse; TV debut on the Garry Moore Show. *Theatre includes:* Little Shop of Horrors, Die Fledermaus (New York Metropolitan Opera), Peter and the Wolf. *Films include:* Fail Safe, Blazing Saddles, Hot Stuff (also Dir), The Best Little Whorehouse in Texas. *Television includes:* (series): The Entertainers, The Dean Martin summer Show, Dom DeLuise Show, The Barrum-Bump Show, The Glenn Campbell Goodtime Show, The New Candid Camera, Fievel's American Tails (voice); (films): Evil Roy Slade, Only With Married Men, Happy (also exec. producer), Don't Drink the Water, The Tin Soldier. *Address:* The Artist Group, c/o Robert Malcolm, 10100 Santa Monica Boulevard, Los Angeles, CA 90067, USA (Office).

DELVALLE HENRIQUEZ, Eric Arturo; Panamanian politician; b. 2 Feb. 1937; m. Mariela Díaz de Delvalle; one s. two d.; ed Colegio Javier, Panama City, Louisiana State Univ. and Soulé Coll. of Accountancy; fmr Chair. and Dir of several pvt. commercial enterprises; mem. Bd of Dirs. Inst. for Econ. Promotion 1963; mem. Games Control Bd 1960–64; Del. to Nat. Ass. 1968; Vice-Pres. Nat. Ass. 1968; Leader, Repub. Party; Vice-Pres. of Panama 1984, Pres. 1985–88 (removed from office for alleged drug-trafficking).

DEMARCO, Richard, OBE, FRSA; British professor of European cultural studies; b. 9 July 1930, Edinburgh; s. of Carmine Demarco and Elizabeth Valentine Fusco; m. Anne C. Muckle 1957; ed Holy Cross Acad., Edin. Coll. of Art, Moray House Coll. and Royal Army Educ. Corps; art master, Duns Scotus Acad., Edin. 1956–67; Vice-Chair. Founding Cttee and Vice-Chair. Bd Dirs Traverse Theatre, Edin. 1963–67; Dir Sean Connery's Scottish Int. Educ. Trust (SIET) 1972–74; Dir Richard Demarco Gallery 1966–, European Youth Parliament 1993–; Trustee Kingston-Demarco European Cultural Foundation 1993–95, Dir Demarco European Art Foundation 1993–; Prof. of European Cultural Studies, Kingston Univ. 1993–2000, Prof. Emer. 2001–; Artistic Adviser European Youth Parl. 1992–; Consultant to Ministries of the Environment and Culture, Malta 1999; mem. Royal Scottish Soc. of Painters in Watercolours; Hon. Fellow, Royal Incorporation of Architects; Hon. LLD (Dundee); Cavaliere della Repubblica Italiana, Chevalier des Arts et des Lettres (France). *Publications:* The Artist as Explorer 1978, The Road to Meikle Seggie 1978, A Life in Pictures 1994, Art = Wealth 1995. *Leisure interest:* exploring the road to Meikle Seggie in the footsteps of Roman legionnaires, Celtic saints and scholars, respectful of the Rule of St Benedict. *Address:* Demarco European Art Foundation, Building 2, New Parliament House, 5 Regent Road, Edinburgh, EH7 5BL; 23A Lennox Street, Edinburgh, EH4 1PY, Scotland (Home). *Telephone:* (20) 8547-7027 (Kingston); (131) 557-0707 (Edinburgh); (131) 343-2124 (Home). *Fax:* (20) 8547-8246 (Kingston); (131) 557-5972 (Edinburgh); (131) 343-3124 (Home).

DEMAS, William Gilbert, MA; Trinidadian civil servant and economist; b. 14 Nov. 1929, Port-of-Spain; s. of late Herman and Audrey (née Walters) Demas; m. Norma Taylor 1958; one d.; ed Queen's Royal Coll., Trinidad and Emmanuel Coll., Cambridge; Adviser to W Indies Trade Comm., UK 1957–58; Head, Econ. Planning Div., Govt of Trinidad and Tobago 1959–66; Perm. Sec. Ministry of Planning and Devt 1966–68; Econ. Adviser to the Prime Minister 1968–69; Sec.-Gen. Commonwealth Caribbean Regional Secr. 1970–74; Pres. Caribbean Devt Bank 1974–88; Dir Cen. Bank; Chair. Multi-Sectoral Planning Task Force (Trinidad and Tobago) 1985–; Humming Bird Gold Medal (for public service). *Publications:* Economics of Development in Small Countries 1965, Planning and the Price Mechanism in the Context of Caribbean Economic Integration 1966. *Leisure interests:* films, listening to all kinds of music.

DEMBY, Albert Joe, PhD; Sierra Leonean politician; Vice-Pres. of Sierra Leone 1996–2002; Deputy Leader Sierra Leone People's Party (SLPP). *Address:* Sierra Leone People's Party, 29 Rawdon Street, Freetown, Sierra Leone (Office).

DEMEL, Herbert, PhD; Austrian business executive; b. 14 Oct. 1953, Vienna; ed Vienna Tech. Univ.; Robert Bosch GmbH, Stuttgart 1984–90; Audi AG,

Ingolstadt 1990–, mem. Man. Bd in charge of Research and Devt 1993, Speaker of Man. Bd and CEO responsible for Research and Devt and Sales and Marketing 1994, Chair. Man. Bd 1995–97.

DEMERITTE, Richard C., CA, FAIA, FCGA, FBIM, FRSA; Bahamian diplomat and chartered accountant; b. 27 Feb. 1939, Nassau; s. of Richard and Miriam (née Whitfield) Demeritte; m. Ruth Smith 1966; one s. (deceased) two d.; ed Eastern Secondary School, Bahamas School of Commerce, Metropolitan Coll., London and Century Univ., USA; Deputy Treas. Treasury Dept 1956–79; Auditor-Gen. Commonwealth of the Bahamas 1980–84, 1988–96; High Commr in UK 1984–87; Amb. to EEC 1986–88, to Belgium, France, Fed. Repub. of Germany 1987–88; Man. Partner Richard C. Demeritte & Co., Chartered Accountants 1997–; Pres. Certified Gen. Accountants Asscn of the Bahamas (and mem. Council), Caribbean Asscn of Certified Gen. Accountants, Universal and Financial Business Consultants 1996–; fmr Pres. Asscn of Int. Accountants, now mem. Council; mem. Council Bahamas Inst. of Chartered Accountants; mem. Council Bahamas Inst. of Chartered Accountants; Fellow Certified Gen. Accountants, Canada 1996. *Leisure interests:* golf, chess, billiards, gardening, research, computer technology. *Address:* P.O. Box CB-11001, Cable Beach, West Bay Street, Nassau, Bahamas. *Telephone:* 327-5729 (Office); 327-8193 (Home). *Fax:* 327-0288 (Office); 327-8861 (Home). *E-mail:* demerite@bahamas.net.bs (Office).

DEMESSINE, Michelle; French politician; b. 18 June 1947, Frelinghien (Nord); m.; one c.; ed Valentine Labbé Tech. Lycée, Lille; worked as sec. 1964–75; elected as union del. 1968, apptd. mem. Département Exec. Cttee of Conféd. Générale du Travail 1973; Dept Br. Sec. Union des Femmes Françaises 1976–90, now Hon. Chair.; joined Parti Communiste Français (PCF) 1970, elected mem. Nord Département Cttee 1977, mem. PCF Bureau 1977–; mem. Regional Econ. and Social Cttee 1983–95; Senator for Nord 1992–97; Vice-Chair. Social Affairs Cttee, study group on combating drug trafficking and addiction, fact-finding mission on women in public life; municipal councillor for Houplines 1995–; Sec. of State for Tourism 1997–2002; elected to Senate Sept. 2001–. *Publication:* Femmes d'ici (co-author) 1985. *Address:* Senat, 15 rue de Vaugirard, 75291 Paris Cedex 0, France (Office). *Website:* www.senat.fr (Office).

DEMETEROVÁ, Gabriela; Czech violinist; b. 17 May 1971, Prague; ed Prague Conservatoire, Acad. of Fine Arts, Prague; has performed with leading Czech orchestras in France, Germany, UK, USA; Stringed Autumn Prague 2001, Int. Music Festival Český Krumlov Honour to Baroque 2001; winner Jaroslav Kocián Competition, Yehudi Menuhin Competition 1993. *Recordings include:* selection from Biber's Biblical Sonatas 1996, Di Italian Baroque and numerous recordings for Czech Radio. *Leisure interests:* cycling, computer games, horse riding. *Address:* Bilkova 21, Prague 1,110 00, Czech Republic. *E-mail:* demeterovag@volny.cz; ars@arskoncert.cz (Office). *Website:* www.GabrielaDemeterova.com.

DEMIDOVA, Alla Sergeyevna; Russian actress; b. 29 Sept. 1936, Moscow; d. of S. Demidov and A. Kharchenko; m. Vladimir Valutsky 1961; ed Moscow Univ. and Shchukin Theatre School; acted with Taganka Theatre, Moscow 1964–; in films since 1957–; f. own Little Theatre "A" 1993; People's Artist of RSFSR 1984, USSR State Prize 1977, President's Prize 2002. *Film roles include:* Olga (Day Stars) 1968, Maria Spiridonova (The Sixth of July) 1968, Zhenya (A Degree of Risk) 1969, Julia von Meck (Tchaikovsky) 1970, Lesya Ukrainka (I Come to You) 1972, Arkadina (The Seagull), 1975, Liza (The Mirror) A. Tarkovsky, 1975, the Soothsayer (The Little Scarlet Flower) 1978, Pashenka (Father Sergius) 1978, Duchess of Marlborough (A Glass of Water) TV 1979, Lebiadkina (Demons) 1993, Empress (Invisible Travellers) 1999. *Theatre roles include:* Ranevskaya (Cherry Orchard), Gertrud (Hamlet), Fedra (Fedra M. Tsvetaeva), Melentyeva (Wooden Horses); has also performed Akhmatova's Requiem and Poem Without Hero. *Publications:* works on the art of theatre including The Second Reality, The Shadows behind the Mirrors, The Running Line of My Memory 2000 and numerous articles. *Leisure interests:* philosophy, painting, gardening, her animals (two dogs and a cat). *Address:* Tverskaya str. 8, korp. 1 Apt. 83, 103009 Moscow, Russia. *Telephone:* (095) 229-04-17. *Fax:* (095) 229-04-17. *E-mail:* valutsky@yandex.ru.

DEMIN, Col.-Gen. Yuri Georgiyevich, DJurSc; Russian lawyer; b. 1945, Voronezh; m.; one d.; ed Higher KGB School, USSR Council of Ministers; involved in drafting of Fed. Security Service law 1994–95; Head of Legal Dept, Fed. Security Service of Russian Fed. 1995–97; Deputy Prosecutor-Gen., Chief Mil. Prosecutor 1997–2000; First Deputy Minister of Justice 2000–. *Publications:* (monographs) Diplomatic Missions 1995, Status of Diplomatic Missions and their Personnel 1995 and numerous articles. *Address:* Ministry of Justice, B. Karetny per. IDA, 101434 Moscow, Russia (Office). *Telephone:* (095) 209-77-44 (Office). *Fax:* (095) 209-66-95 (Office).

DEMIREL, Süleyman; Turkish politician and engineer; b. 1924; ed Istanbul Technical Univ.; researcher in irrigation and electrification, Bureau of Reclamation 1949–50; Engineer, Electrical Survey Admin.; Head of Dams Dept 1954–55; Exchange Fellowship scholar, several pvt. cos. and public depts. USA 1954–55; Dir-Gen. Hydraulic Works, Turkey 1955–60; pvt. contractor, engineer and Lecturer, Middle East Tech. Univ. 1962–64; Chair. Justice Party (AP) 1965–80; Isparta Deputy 1965–80; Deputy Prime Minister Feb.-Oct. 1965; Prime Minister (led AP Govt) 1965–71, (four coalition govts.) 1977–78; Opposition Leader 1978–80; Prime Minister 1979–80; banned from politics 1980–87; Chair. True Path Party (DYP) 1987–93; Deputy for Isparta

1987–93; Prime Minister 1991–93; Pres. of Turkey 1993–2000. *Address:* c/o Office of the President, Cumhurbaş-Kanlığı Köşkü, Cankaya, Ankara, Turkey.

DEMJÁN, Sándor; Hungarian business executive; b. 14 May 1943, Börvely; m.; ed Coll. for Trading and Catering, Budapest; Sr Man. Sales Dept. ÁFÉSZ Gorsium, Székesfehérvár 1968–73; f. SKÁLA Dept Store Chain and SKÁLA-COOP, CEO SKÁLA Jt Venture 1973–86; Founder and Chair. Magyar Hitel Bank, CEO 1986–90; Founder and Partner Cen. European Devt Corpn (CEDC) 1990–91; Founder and Pres. Polus Investment Co. Inc., Toronto, Canada 1991–; f. Gránit Pólus Investment & Devt Co.; Founder and co-Chair. Bd Trigranit Devt Co. 1996; f. WestEnd City Centre, Budapest 1999; co-Founder and co-Chair. (with George Soros, q.v., Int. Man. Centre 1988; Chair. Bd United Way 1995–98; Co-Chair. Nat. Asscn of Enterpreneurs and Employers (Vosz) 1997; est. first Corpn in fmr USSR (KAMAZ); adviser to Govt of Tatarstan; Pres. MLL Professional Football Sub-Alliance 2000; Man of the Year 1986, 1988, Entrepreneur of the Year 1996, Most Influential Businessman of the Decade 2000, Most Successful Real Estate Developer of the Year 2002; State of Hungary Award 1980; Planetary Consciousness, Hungarian Business Award 1998. *Leisure interests:* fishing, playing chess. *Address:* TriGranit Development Corporation, Váci út 3, 1062 Budapest, Hungary (Office). *Telephone:* 1-374-6502 (Office). *Fax:* 1-374-6505 (Office). *E-mail:* info@trigranit.com (Office). *Website:* www.trigranit.com (Office).

DEMME, Jonathan; American director, producer and writer; b. 22 Feb. 1944, Rockville Centre, NY; m. Joanne Howard; two c.; ed Univ. of Florida; worked in publicity Dept United Artists, Embassy Pictures, Pathe Contemporary Films; writer for Film Daily 1966–68. *Films directed:* Hot Box (also co-screenwriter), Caged Heat 1974, Crazy Mama 1975, Fighting Mad 1976, Citizens Band 1977, Last Embrace 1979, Melvin and Howard 1980, Swing Shift 1983, Something Wild 1986, Married to the Mob 1988, Swimming to Cambodia, The Silence of the Lambs (Acad. Award for Best Film 1992), Cousin Bobby 1992, Philadelphia 1993, Mandela 1996, That Thing You Do 1996, Beloved 1998, Storefront Hitchcock 1998, The Truth About Charlie 2002; exec. producer Devil in a Blue Dress 1995; Who am I this Time (for TV) 1982, Stop Making Sense (documentary) 1984, Konbir (video) 1989, Konbir: Burning Rhythms of Haiti (recording) 1989; producer Miami Blues 1990. *Address:* c/o Bob Bookman, Creative Artists Agency, 9830 Wilshire Boulevard, Beverly Hills, CA 90212-1804; Clinica Estetico, 127 W 24th Street #7, New York, NY 10011-1914, USA.

DEMPSEY, Noel, BA; Irish politician; b. Jan. 1953, Trim, Co. Meath; m. Bernadette Rattigan; two s. two d.; ed St Michael's Christian Bros.' School, Trim, Univ. Coll., Dublin, St Patrick's Coll., Maynooth; fmr career guidance counsellor; Nat. Sec. Local Authority Mems. Asscn 1984–89; Chair. Meath Co. Council 1986–87; fmr mem. numerous local Govt cttees.; mem. Dáil Éireann Feb. 1987–; mem. Dáil Public Accounts Cttee 1987–89, 1990–92; fmr Chair. Backbench Cttee on Tourism, Transport and Communications; fmr Sec. Backbench Cttee on the Environment; fmr Dir Midland East Regional Tourism Org.; Minister of State at Depts. of Taoiseach, Defence and Finance, Govt Chief Whip 1992–94; fmr Opposition Spokesperson on Environment; Fianna Fáil Co-ordinator on Forum for Peace and Reconciliation; Nat. Treasurer Fianna Fáil; Minister for the Environment and Local Govt June 1997–. *Leisure interests:* Gaelic football, reading, golf. *Address:* Department of the Environment and Local Government, Custom House, Dublin 1 (Office); Newtown, Trim, County Meath, Ireland (Home). *Telephone:* (1) 8882479 (Office); (46) 31146 (Home). *Fax:* (1) 8882576 (Office). *E-mail:* minister@environ.irlgov.ie (Office). *Website:* www.environ.ie (Office).

DEMSZKY, Gábor; Hungarian politician and sociologist; b. 4 Aug. 1952, Budapest; s. of Rudolf Demszky and Irén Király; m. Vera Révai (divorced); four c.; ed Eötvös Loránd Univ.; contrib. to periodical Világosság (Lucidity) 1977; Founder Paupers Relief Fund 1979; Founder AB Independent Publishing House 1980; Ed. illegal Hirmondó (Courier) 1983; Founding-mem. Network of Free Initiative and Alliance of Free Democrats 1989; mem. Parl. 1989–90 (resgnd), 1998; Chair. Cttee of Nat. Security 1990; mem. Exec. Bd Alliance of Free Democrats 1994–; Pres. of Alliance 2000–01; Founder Children's Rescue Soc.; negotiator in Moscow talks on Soviet troops withdrawal and on Hungary's leaving the Warsaw Pact; Mayor of Budapest 1990–; Vice-Pres. Standing Conf. of Local and Regional Authorities, Council of Europe 1992–94; Congress of Local and Regional Authorities 1994–96, Pres. Alliance of Free Democracy 2000; Freedom to Publish Prize, Int. Asscn of Publishers 1984. *Leisure interests:* jogging, sailing, riding, water-skiing, fishing. *Address:* 1052 Budapest, Városház utca 9/11, Hungary. *Telephone:* (1) 327-1022.

DEMUS, Jörg; Austrian concert pianist; b. 2 Dec. 1928, St Pölten, Lower Austria; s. of Dr Otto and Erika (Budik) Demus; ed Vienna State Acad. of Music and studies with various musicians; début at age 14; mem. Gesellschaft der Musikfreunde, Vienna; débuts in London and Switzerland 1950, tour of Latin America 1951, Paris 1953, New York 1955, Japan 1961; has composed music for piano, songs, chamber music, opera; has performed in almost all important musical centres; has made over 450 LP records and CDs; Dr hc (Amherst Univ.) 1981; Premier Busoni at Int. Piano Competition, Bolzano 1956; Harriet Cohen Bach-Medal 1958; Hon. Prof. of Austria 1977; Beethoven Ring, Vienna Beethoven Soc. 1977; Mozart Medal, Mozartgemeinde, Vienna 1979; several Edison Awards and Grand Prix du Disque; Schumann Award, Zwickau, E Germany, 1986. *Publications:* Abenteuer der Interpretation

(essays), co-author of a book on Beethoven's piano sonatas. *Leisure interests:* antiques, nature, collecting and restoring historic keyboard instruments. *Address:* c/o Mr Roland Sölder, Lyra Artists Management, Döblinger Hauptstrasse 77A/10, 1190 Vienna, Austria (Office). *Telephone:* (1) 3687472 (Office); (1) 3681226 (Home). *Fax:* (1) 3687473 (Office).

DENARD, Col Bob (Robert); French mercenary; b. Gilbert Bourgeaud, 1929, nr Bordeaux; m. Amina Denard; two c.; joined French colonial army, quartermaster to a commando Regt Indo-China, Algeria; charged with an assassination attempt on Pierre Mendès-France 1954, acquitted 1955; mercenary for Moise Tshombe's breakaway Congo State of Katanga 1960; mercenary activities Biafra, Gabon, Yemen 1960s; backed coup to depose Pres. Abdallah of the Comoros Repub. 1976 (after Abdallah had declared independence from France 1975), Pres. Soilih installed; Minister of Defence Comoros Govt of Pres. Soilih (as Col Said Mustapha M'hadju); undertook failed coup attempt against Mathieu Kérékou (q.v.)'s regime Benin 1977; supported reinstatement of Pres. Abdallah following the assassination of Pres. Soilih 1978, apptd. Chief of the Presidential Guard; took refuge in South Africa following charges of responsibility for the assassination of Pres. Abdallah 1989; charged with involvement in abortive coup in Benin 1991, received five-year sentence in absentia, prison term commuted to suspended sentence 1993; returned to France Feb. 1993; launched attempted coup in Comoros Sept. 1995; arrested by French special forces who put down coup Oct. 1995, released from prison Aug. 1996; on trial after assassination of Pres. Abdallah May 1999; acquitted of charges May 1999.

DENCH, Dame Judith (Judi) Olivia, DBE; British actress; b. 9 Dec. 1934, York; d. of Reginald Arthur and Eleanora Olave (née Jones) Dench; m. Michael Williams 1971 (died 2001); one d.; ed The Mount School, York, Central School of Speech Training and Dramatic Art; performed in Old Vic seasons 1957–61, appearing in parts including Ophelia (Hamlet), Katherine (Henry V), Cecily (The Importance of Being Earnest), Juliet (Romeo and Juliet), appeared with Old Vic Co. at two Edin. Festivals, Venice, on tour to Paris, Belgium and Yugoslavia and on tour to USA and Canada; appearances with RSC 1961–62, including parts as Anya (The Cherry Orchard), Titania (A Midsummer Night's Dream), Dorcas Bellboys (A Penny for a Song), Isabella (Measure for Measure); on tour to W Africa with Nottingham Playhouse 1963; mem. Bd Nat. Theatre 1988–91; subsequent roles include Irina (The Three Sisters) and Doll Common (Alchemist), Oxford Playhouse 1964–65, title-role in Saint Joan and Barbara (The Astrakhan Coat), Nottingham Playhouse 1965, Amanda (Private Lives), Lika (The Promise) 1967, Sally Bowles (Cabaret) 1968, Grace Harkaway (London Assurance) 1970, 1972, Barbara Undershaft (Major Barbara) 1970; Assoc. mem. RSC 1969–, appearing as Bianca (Women Beware Women), Viola (Twelfth Night), Hermione and Perdita (Winter's Tale), Portia (Merchant of Venice), Duchess (Duchess of Malfi), Beatrice (Much Ado About Nothing), Lady Macbeth (Macbeth), Adriana (Comedy of Errors), also on tour with RSC to Japan and Australia 1970, Japan 1972; other performances include Vilma (The Wolf), Oxford and London 1973, Miss Trant (The Good Companions), 1974, Sophie Fullgarney (The Gay Lord Quex) 1975, Nurse (Too True to be Good) 1975, 1976, Millament (Way of the World) 1978, Cymbeline 1979, Juno and the Paycock 1980–81, Lady Bracknell (The Importance of Being Earnest) 1982, Deborah (A Kind of Alaska) 1982, Pack of Lies 1983, Mother Courage 1984, Waste 1985, Mr and Mrs Nobody 1986, Antony and Cleopatra 1987, Entertaining Strangers 1987, Hamlet 1989, The Cherry Orchard 1989, The Sea 1991, The Plough and the Stars 1991, Coriolanus 1992, The Gift of the Gorgon 1993, The Seagull (Royal Nat. Theatre) 1994, The Convent 1995, Absolute Hell (Royal Nat. Theatre) 1995, A Little Night Music (Royal Nat. Theatre) 1995, Amy's View (Royal Nat. Theatre) 1997, (New York) 1999, Filumena 1998, The Royal Family 2001, The Breath of Life (Theatre Royal, Haymarket) 2002; Dir Much Ado About Nothing 1988, Look Back in Anger 1989, The Boys from Syracuse 1991; mem. Bd, Nat. Theatre 1988–; Prin. Royal Scottish Acad. of Music and Drama 2001–; Hon. Fellow Royal Holloway Coll. London, Hon. DLitt (Warwick) 1978, (York) 1983, (Keele) 1989, (Birmingham) 1989, (Loughborough) 1991, (Open Univ.) 1994, (London) 1994, (Oxford) 2000; Dr hc (Surrey) 1996; numerous awards including Paladino d'Argentino (Venice Festival Award for Juliet) 1961, Best Actress of Year (Variety London Critics for Lika in The Promise) 1967, Most Promising Newcomer (British Film Acad. for Four in the Morning) 1965, Best Actress of the Year (Guild of Dirs for Talking to a Stranger) 1967, Soc. West End Theatre Award (for Lady Macbeth) 1977, Best Actress New Standard Drama Awards (for Juno and the Paycock) 1980, (for Lady Bracknell in The Importance of Being Earnest and Deborah in A Kind of Alaska) 1983, (for Cleopatra in Antony and Cleopatra) 1987, Olivier Award for Best Actress in Antony and Cleopatra 1987; BAFTA Award for Best Television Actress 1981, for Best Supporting Actress (for A Room with a View) 1987 and (for A Handful of Dust) 1988, Golden Globe and BAFTA Best Actress Award for Mrs Brown. *Films include:* A Study in Terror 1965, He Who Rides a Tiger 1966, Four in the Morning 1966, A Midsummer Night's Dream (RSC Production) 1968, The Third Secret 1978, Dead Cert, Wetherby 1985, Room with a View 1986, 84 Charing Cross Road 1987, A Handful of Dust 1988, Henry V 1989, Goldeneye 1995, Mrs Brown 1996, Tea with Mussolini 1998, Shakespeare in Love (Acad. Award for Best Supporting Actress) 1998, The World is Not Enough 1999, Chocolat 2000, Iris BAFTA Award for Best Actress 2002) 2001, The Shipping News 2001, The Importance of Being Earnest 2002, Die Another Day 2002. *TV appearances in:* Major Barbara, Pink String and Sealing Wax, Talking to a Stranger, The Funambulists, Age of Kings, Jackanory, Hilda Lessways, Luther, Neighbours, Parade's End, Marching

Song, On Approval, Days to Come, Emilie, Comedy of Errors, Macbeth, Langrishe Go Down, On Giants' Shoulders, Love in a Cold Climate, A Fine Romance, The Cherry Orchard, Going Gently, Saigon—Year of the Cat 1982, Ghosts 1986, Behaving Badly 1989, Absolute Hell, Can You Hear Me Thinking?, As Time Goes By, Last of the Blonde Bombshells (BAFTA Best Actress). *Publications:* Judi Dench: A Great Deal of Laughter (biog.), Judi Dench: With a Crack in Her Voice 1998. *Leisure interests:* painting, drawing, swimming, sewing, catching up with letters. *Address:* c/o Julian Belfrage Associates, 46 Albemarle Street, London, W1X 4PP, England.

DENENBERG, Herbert Sidney, PhD, JD, BS, LLM; American consumer reporter, lawyer and educator; b. 20 Nov. 1929, Omaha, Neb.; s. of David Aaron Denenberg and Fannie Molly (Rothenberg) Denenberg; m. Naomi Glushakow 1958; ed Omaha Cen. High School, Johns Hopkins and Creighton Univs, Harvard Law School and Univ. of Pennsylvania; lawyer, Denenberg & Denenberg, Attorneys-at-Law 1954–55; lawyer, US Army Judge Advocate Gen. Corps. 1955–58; Prof., Wharton School, Univ. of Pa 1962–71; Insurance Commr, State of Pa 1971–74; Special Adviser to Gov. of Pa on Consumer Affairs 1974; Commr, Pa Public Utilities Comm. 1974–75; Consumer Reporter, WCAU-TV (NBC), Philadelphia 1975–98; Consumer Columnist Philadelphia Daily News 1979–81, Philadelphia Journal 1981–82, Delaware Co. Daily and Sunday Times 1987–89, Burlington Co. Daily Times 1987–89, Reading Eagle 1989–, Doylestown Patriot 1987–89 and other newspapers; Consumer and Investigative Reporter Harron Cable Update, 2nd Tri-State Media Network Cable System 1999–2000, WLVT (PBS) 2001–; Adjunct Prof. of Information Science and Tech., Cabrini Coll. 2000–; mem. Advisory Bd The People's Doctor 1988–91; Consultant to US Dept of Labor, Small Business Admin., US Dept of Transportation, Legislature of Nev. and Wis.; Trustee Center for Proper Medication Use; mem. Inst. of Medicine (NAS); Hon. LLD (Allentown Coll.) 1989, Hon. DHL (Spring Garden Coll.) 1992; 40 Emmy awards for investigative and consumer reports; numerous awards from Nat. Press Club, Consumer Fed. of America and Nat. Acad. of TV Arts and Sciences, B'nai B'rith Beber Award, Consumer Fed. of America Outstanding Media Service Award; American Bd of Trial Advocates Award of Achievement for Excellence in Legal Reporting and Analysis 1996. *Publications include:* Risk and Insurance (textbook) 1964, Insurance, Government and Social Policy (textbook) 1969, Herb Denenberg's Smart Shopper's Guide 1980, The Shopper's Guidebook 1974, Life Insurance And/Or Mutual Funds 1967, Mass Marketing of Property and Liability Insurance 1970, The Insurance Trap 1972, Getting Your Money's Worth 1974, Cover Yourself 1974, Shopper's Guide to Medical Equipment 1990, A Consumer's Guide to Herbal Medicines 1999, hundreds of articles, Govt reports and statutes. *Leisure interests:* reading, photography. *Address:* PO Box 7301, St David's, PA 19087-7301, USA (Office). *Telephone:* (610) 687-0293 (Office); (610) 687-0293 (Home). *Fax:* (610) 687-0229. *E-mail:* hdenenberg@aol.com (Office). *Website:* thedenenbergreport.org (Office).

DENEUVE, Catherine (Catherine Dorléac); French actress; b. 22 Oct. 1943, Paris; d. of Maurice Dorléac and Renée Deneuve; m. David Bailey 1965 (divorced); one s. by Roger Vadim; one d. by Marcello Mastroianni; ed Lycée La Fontaine, Paris; film début in Les petits chats 1959; Pres., Dir-Gen. Films de la Citrouille 1971–79; f. Société Cardeva 1983; Co-Chair UNESCO Campaign to protect the World's Film Heritage 1994–; Hon. Golden Bear, Berlin Film Festival, Arts de l'Alliance française de New York Trophy 1998. *Films include:* Les portes claquent 1960, L'homme à femmes 1960, Le vice et la vertu 1962, Et Satan conduit le bal 1962, Vacances portugaises 1963, Les parapluies de Cherbourg 1963 (Palme d'Or, Festival de Cannes 1964), Les plus belles escroqueries du monde 1963, La chasse à l'homme 1964, Un monsieur de compagnie 1964, La Costanza della Ragione 1964, Repulsion 1964, Le chant du monde 1965, La vie de château 1965, Liebes Karusell 1965, Les créatures 1965, Les demoiselles de Rochefort 1966, Belle de jour 1967 (Golden Lion at Venice Festival 1967), Benjamin 1967, Manon 70 1967, Mayerling 1968, La chamade 1966, Folies d'avril 1969, Belles d'un soir 1969, La sirène du Mississippi 1969, Tristana 1970, Peau d'âne 1971, Ça n'arrive qu'aux autres 1971, Liza 1971, Un flic 1972, L'évènement le plus important depuis que l'homme a marché sur la lune 1973, Touche pas la femme blanche 1974, La femme aux bottes rouges 1975, La grande bourgeoisie 1975, Hustle 1976, March or Die 1977, Coup de foudre 1977, Ecoute, voir . . . 1978, L'argent des autres 1978, A nous deux 1979, Ils sont grands ces petits 1979, Le dernier métro 1980, Je vous aime 1980, Le choix des armes 1981, Hôtel des Amériques 1981, Le choc 1982, L'africain 1983, The Hunger 1983, Le bon plaisir 1984, Paroles et musiques 1984, Le lieu du crime 1986, Pourvu que ce soit une fille 1986, Drôle d'endroit pour une rencontre 1989, La reine blanche 1991, Indochine 1992 (César award for Best Actress 1993), Ma saison préférée 1993, La Partie d'Échecs 1994, The Convent 1995, les Cent et une nuits 1995, les Voleurs 1995, Généalogie d'un crime 1997, Place Vendôme 1998, Le Vent de la nuit 1999, Belle-Maman 1999, Pola x 1999, Time Regained 1999, Dancer in the Dark 2000, Je centre à la maison 2001, Absolument fabuleux 2001, 8 Femmes 2002. *Address:* c/o Artmédia, 20 avenue Rapp, 75007 Paris, France.

DENG LIQUN; Chinese politician; b. 1914, Guidong Co., Hunan Prov.; m. Luo Liyun; one s.; ed Beijing No. 26 Middle School; mem. CCP 1936–; Dir Educ. Dept Marxism-Leninism Inst.; Dir Propaganda Dept CCP Jibei Pref. Cttee; Deputy Dir Gen. Office of Finance and Econ. Comm. of North-East China; Dir Policy Research Office of CCP Liaoning Provincial Cttee; after founding of People's Repub. of China in 1949 served as Chair. Cultural and Educ. Cttee of Xinjiang Regional People's Cttee; Dir Propaganda Dept of Xinjiang Bureau under CCP Cen. Cttee; Ed. and Deputy Ed.-in-Chief, Red Flag; branded as counter-revolutionary revisionist and purged during Cultural Revolution; Vice-Pres. Acad. of Social Sciences 1978; Dir Policy Research Section under CCP Cen. Cttee 1981; Adviser to Soc. for Study of Econ. of Minority Areas 1981, to Soc. of Labour Science 1982, to Soc. for Study of Workers' Political and Ideological Work; Dir CCP Cen. Cttee Propaganda Dept 1982–85; mem. 12th CCP Cen. Cttee 1982, also mem. Secr. 1982–87; Vice-Chair. Nat. Cttee for Promoting Socialist Ethics 1983; Head, CCP Cen. Leading Group for Educ. of Cadres 1985; mem. CCP Cen. Advisory Comm. 1987; Deputy Head, CCP Cen. Cttee Party Bldg Group 1990–; Deputy Head, CCP Cen. Cttee Leading Group for Party History Work 1994–; Hon. Pres. Soc. for Studies on Party Mems. 1991–. *Address:* c/o Central Committee of Chinese Communist Party, Beijing, People's Republic of China.

DENG NAN; Chinese administrator; b. Oct. 1945, Guang'an, Sichuan Prov.; d. of the late Deng Xiaoping (fmr Gen. Sec., CCP and fmr Chair., Gen. Mil. Comm., CCP) and of Zhuo Lin; joined CCP 1978; Vice-Minister in charge of State Science and Tech. Comm. 1991–98; Vice-Minister of Science and Tech. 1998–. *Address:* Ministry of Science and Technology, 15B Fuxing Lu, Haidian Qu, Beijing 10015, People's Republic of China (Office). *Telephone:* (10) 68515050 (Office). *Fax:* (10) 68515006 (Office). *Website:* www.most.gov.cn (Office).

DENG PUFANG; Chinese politician; b. 1943; s. of late Deng Xiaoping and Zhuo Lin; ed Beijing Univ.; Deputy Dir-in-Chief of the Welfare Fund for Handicapped 1984, Dir-in-Chief, 1985–; Ed.-in-Chief Spring Breeze (Journal) 1984–; visited France by invitation of Danielle Mitterrand, Aug. 1985; Vice-Chair. of China Organizing Comm. of UN's Decade of Disabled Persons 1986–90, Chair. 1990–; Vice-Chair. Cttee for Coordination of Work for the Disabled; Pres. Chinese Fed. for the Disabled 1988–; Advisor China Assen for Int. Friendly Contacts 1991–; alt. mem. 15th CCP Cen. Cttee 1997. *Address:* China Welfare Fund for Handicapped, Beijing, People's Republic of China.

DENG YAPING, MA; Chinese table tennis player; b. Feb. 1973, Zhengzhou, He'nan Prov.; ed Quinghua Univ. Beijing, Univ. of Nottingham; mem. of Chinese women's table tennis team 1988; won over 20 gold medals in various world championships; top-ranked female table tennis player 1991–98; mem. Sports Cttee of IOC; has co-chaired Chinese Olympic Cttee and Sports Assen of China; Chinese Sports Personality of the Century 1999, mem. Laurens World Sports Acad. *Address:* c/o State General Bureau for Physical Culture and Sports, 9 Tiyuguan Road, Chongwen District, Beijing, People's Republic of China.

DENG YOUMEI; Chinese writer; b. 1931, Tianjin; messenger in CCP-led New 4th Army 1945; entered Cen. Research Inst. of Literature 1952; in political disgrace 1957–77; Sec. Chinese Writers' Assen 1985–96, Vice-Chair. 1996–. *Publications:* On the Precipice, Our Army Commander, Han the Forger, Tales of Taoranting Park, Snuff Bottles, Na Wu, Moon Over Liangshan Mountain. *Address:* Chinese Writers' Association, 25 Dongtucheng Road, Beijing 100013, People's Republic of China. *Telephone:* (10) 64261554.

DENHAM, Susan Gageby, BA, LLM; Irish judge; b. 22 Aug. 1945, Dublin; d. of R. J. D. Gageby and Dorothy Lester; m. Brian Denham 1970; three s. one d. (and one s. deceased); ed Alexandra Coll. Dublin, Trinity Coll. Dublin, King's Inns, Dublin and Columbia Univ. New York; called to Irish Bar 1971; mem. Midland Circuit 1971–91; called to Inner Bar 1987; Judge, High Court 1991–92, Supreme Court 1992–; Pro-Chancellor Univ. of Dublin Trinity Coll. 1996–; Chair. Working Group on a Courts Comm. 1995–98; Chair. Cttee on Court Practice and Procedure Courts Service Bd; Hon. Sec. Cttee on Judicial Conduct and Ethics; Bencher King's Inns. *Leisure interests:* horses, gardens. *Address:* The Supreme Court, The Four Courts, Dublin 7, Ireland. *Telephone:* (1) 8725555 (Ext. 533).

DENHARDT, David Tilton, PhD, FRSC; American professor of biological sciences; b. 25 Feb. 1939, Sacramento, Calif.; s. of David B. Denhardt and Edith E. Tilton; m. Georgetta Louise Harrar 1961; one s. two d.; ed Swarthmore Coll., Pa and Calif. Inst. of Tech., Pasadena; Instructor Biology Dept, Harvard Univ. 1964–66, Asst Prof. 1966–70; Assoc. Prof. Biochemistry Dept, McGill Univ., Montréal 1970–76, Prof. 1976–80; Dir Cancer Research Lab. and Prof. of Biochem., Microbiology and Immunology, Univ. of W Ont. 1980–88; Chair. Biological Sciences, Rutgers Univ. 1988–95, Dir Bureau of Biological Research 1988–95, Prof. of Biological Sciences 1988–, Chair. Biology Dept 1988–95; ed. Journal Virology 1977–87, GENE 1985–93, Experimental Cell Research 1994–; Assoc. Ed. Journal of Cell Biochemistry 1994–; mem. numerous bds.; Fellow American Acad. of Microbiology 1993. *Leisure interests:* travel, reading, canoeing, skiing, camping. *Address:* Nelson Biological Laboratories, Rutgers University, 604 Allison Road, Piscataway, NJ 08854-8000, USA (Office). *Telephone:* (732) 445-4569 (Office); (908) 704-0279 (Home). *Fax:* (732) 445-0104. *E-mail:* denhardt@biology.rutgers.edu (Office).

DENHOLM, Sir Ian (John Ferguson), Kt, CBE, JP, DL; British shipowner; b. 8 May 1927, Glasgow; s. of Sir William and Lady Denholm (née Ferguson); m. Elizabeth Murray Stephen 1952; two s. two d.; ed Loretto School, Midlothian; Chair. Denholm Group of Companies 1974–98; Deputy Chair. P & O Steam Navigation Co. 1980–83; Pres. Chamber of Shipping of UK 1973–74; Chair. North of England Protecting & Indemnity Assen 1976–78, Murray Group Investments Trusts 1985–93, Dir P & O 1974–83, Fleming Mercantile Investment Trust PLC 1984–94; Murray Man. Ltd 1985–92; Pres. Gen. Council of British Shipping 1988–89, BIFA 1990–91, BIMCO 1991–93;

mem. Nat. Ports Council 1974–77, Scottish Transport Group 1975–82, London Bd of Bank of Scotland 1982–91, West of Scotland Bd of Bank of Scotland 1991–95; DL Renfrewshire 1980; Hon. Norwegian Consul in Glasgow 1975–97. *Leisure interest:* fishing. *Address:* Newton of Belltrees, Lochwinnoch, Renfrewshire, PA12 4JL, Scotland. *Telephone:* (1505) 842406.

DENIAU, Jean François, DenD, LèsL; French politician, diplomatist and writer; b. 31 Oct. 1928, Paris; s. of Marc Deniau and Marie-Berthe Loth-Simmonds; m. 1st Dominique de Mirbeck 1958; one s. one d.; m. 2nd Frédérique Dupuy 1971; ed Inst. d'Etudes Politiques de Paris, Ecole Nat. d'Admin; Ecole Nat. d'Admin. 1950–52; Finance Insp. 1952–55; Sec.-Gen. Inter-Ministerial Cttee on European Econ. Co-operation 1955–56; Del. to OEEC 1955–56; Del. to Inter-Govt Conf. on the Common Market and Euratom 1956; Head of Mission, Cabinet of Pres. of Counsel 1957–58; Tech. Adviser, Ministry of Industry and Commerce 1958–59; Dir Comm. on countries seeking Asscn with EEC 1959–61; Head of Del., Conf. with States seeking membership of EEC 1961–63; Dir External Econ. Relations, Ministry of Finance and Econ. Affairs (France) 1963; Amb. to Mauritania 1963–66; Pres. Comm. Franco-Soviétique pour la télévision en couleur; mem. Combined Comm. of EEC, ECSC and Euratom 1967–73; Commr for Devt Aid, European Communities 1969–73; Sec. of State for Foreign Affairs 1973–74, for Agricultural and Rural Devt 1974, for Agric. 1975–76; Amb. to Spain 1976–77; Sec. of State for Foreign Affairs 1977–78; Minister of Foreign Trade 1978–80; Minister Del. to the Prime Minister in Charge of Admin. Reforms 1980–81; lost seat in Nat. Ass. 1981, re-elected Deputy for Cher 1986, 1988–97; MEP 1979–86, Vice-Pres. Political Comm., Vice-Pres. Sub-Comm. on Human Rights; Pres. Conseil Général, Cher 1981–85, re-elected 1985, 1988, 1993–98; Pres. Féd. Nat. des Clubs Perspective et Réalité 1982–84; Vice-Pres. Nat. Ass. Comm. on Foreign Affairs, 1986; elected to Acad. Française 1992; mem. Marine Acad. 1999–; Grand Prix de Littérature, Acad. Française 1990; Commdr Légion d'honneur, Croix de guerre. *Publications:* La mer est ronde (Prix de la Mer) 1976, L'Europe interdite 1977, Deux heures après minuit 1985, La Désirade 1988, Un héros très discret 1989, L'empire nocturne 1990, Ce que je crois 1992, Le secret du Roi des Serpents 1993, Mémoires de 7 Vies Vol. I Les temps aventureux 1994, Vol. II Croire et oser 1997, L'Atlantique mon désert 1996, Le bureau des secrets perdus 1998, Tadjoura 1999, Histoire de courage 2000, La bande à Suzanne 2000, L'île Madame 2001, Dictionnaire amoureux de la mer 2002. *Leisure interest:* sailing. *Address:* 3 avenue Octave Gréard, 75007 Paris, France. *Telephone:* 1-44-38-41-58. *Fax:* 1-44-38-43-33. *Website:* www.jeanfrancois-deniau.org (Home).

DENISOV, Andrei Ivanovich; Russian politician and diplomatist; b. 3 Oct. 1952, Kharkov, Ukraine; m. Natalya Denisova; one d.; ed ed. Moscow Inst. of Int. Relations; joined Ministry of Foreign Affairs 1992, various diplomatic posts in ministry and abroad, Dir Dept of Econ. Co-operation 1997–2000, Deputy Minister of Foreign Affairs responsible for int. econ. co-operation Dec. 2001–; Amb. to Egypt 2000–01. *Address:* Ministry of Foreign Affairs, Smolenskaya-Sennaya str. 32/34, 121200 Moscow, Russia (Office). *Telephone:* (095) 244-29-89 (Office). *Fax:* (095) 244-29-78 (Office). *E-mail:* adenisov@mid.ru (Office).

DENISSE, François-Jean; French astronomer; b. 16 May 1915, Saint-Quentin, Aisne; s. of Jean Julien Denisse and Marie Nicolas; m. Myriam Girondot 1948; two d.; ed Ecole Normale Supérieure; Teacher at Lycée, Dakar 1942–45; Attaché at CNRS 1946–47; Guest Worker, Nat. Bureau of Standards, USA 1948–49; Head of Research of CNRS at Ecole Normale Supérieure 1950–51, Dir of Studies, Inst. des Hautes Etudes, Dakar 1952–53; Asst Astronomer, Paris Observatory 1954–56, Astronomer 1956–63, Dir 1963–68; Chair. of Bd of Nat. Space Research Centre 1968–73; Dir Institut Nationale d'Astronomie et de Géophysique 1968–71; Pres. Bureau des Longitudes 1974–75; mem. Atomic Energy Comm. 1970–75, Head of Research at the Ministry of Univs. 1976–81; Pres. Council of the European Southern Observatory 1977–81; Pres. Cttee for Space Research (COSPAR) 1978–82; mem. Acad. des Sciences 1967, Int. Acad. of Astronautics 1968–, Royal Astronomical Soc.; Commdr, Légion d'honneur, Commdr, Ordre national du Mérite. *Leisure interest:* golf. *Address:* 48 rue Monsieur Le Prince, 75006 Paris, France (Home). *Telephone:* 1-43-29-48-74.

DENKTAŞ, Rauf R.; Cypriot politician; b. 27 Jan. 1924, Ktima, Paphos; s. of Judge M. Raif Bey; m. Aydin Munir 1949; two s. (one deceased) two d.; ed The English School, Nicosia and Lincoln's Inn, London; law practice in Nicosia 1947–49; Jr Crown Counsel 1949, Crown Counsel 1952; Acting Solicitor-Gen. 1956–58; Pres. Fed. of Turkish Cypriot Asscns. 1958–60; Pres. Turkish Communal Chamber 1960, re-elected 1970; Pres. 'Turkish Federated State of Cyprus' 1975–83; Pres. 'Turkish Repub. of Northern Cyprus' Nov. 1983–. *Publications:* Secrets of Happiness 1943, Hell Without Fire 1944, A Handbook of Criminal Cases 1955, Five Minutes to Twelve 1966, The AKRITAS Plan 1972, A Short Discourse on Cyprus 1972, The Cyprus Problem 1973, A Discourse with Youth 1981, The Cyprus Triangle 1982. *Leisure interests:* reading, writing, sea sports, shooting, photography. *Address:* The Office of the President, 'Turkish Republic of Northern Cyprus', Lefkoşa, via Mersin 10, Turkey. *Telephone:* (22) 83141. *Fax:* (22) 75281. *E-mail:* pressdpt@brimnet.com (Office).

DENNEHY, Brian; American actor; b. 9 July 1939, Bridgeport, Conn.; m. 2nd Jennifer Dennehey; three c. (from previous marriage); ed Chaminade High School, Columbia and Yale Univs.; served with U.S. Marine Corps for five years; numerous stage appearances; Tony Award (Best Actor in a Drama

for Death of a Salesman) 1999. *Films include:* Semi-Tough 1977, F.I.S.T. 1978, Foul Play 1978, Butch and Sundance: the Early Days 1979, 10 1979, Little Miss Marker 1980, Split Image 1982, First Blood 1982, Never Cry Wolf 1983, Gorky Park 1983, Twice in a Lifetime 1985, Silverado 1985, Cocoon 1985, F/X 1986, Legal Eagles 1986, Best Seller 1987, The Belly of an Architect 1987, Return to Snowy River 1988, Cocoon: The Return, The Last of the Finest, Presumed Innocent, FX2, Gladiator, Seven Minutes, Midnight Movie 1993, Gilligan's Island 1997, Tommy Boy, The Stars Fell on Henrietta, Romeo and Juliet, Deep River, Finders Keepers, Looking for Mr. Goodbar. *Television appearances include:* Big Shamus, Little Shamus, Star of the Family, Birdland 1993, numerous TV films. *Address:* c/o Susan Smith and Associates, 121 North San Vicente Boulevard, Beverly Hills, CA 90211, USA. *Telephone:* (213) 852-4777 (Office).

DENNETT, Daniel Clement, DPhil; American philosopher, university professor and author; b. 28 March 1942, Boston; s. of Daniel C. Dennett, Jr and Ruth M. Leck; m. Susan Bell 1962; one s. one d.; ed Phillips Exeter High School, Harvard Univ., Oxford Univ.; Asst Prof. of Philosophy, Univ. of Calif., Irvine 1965–70, Assoc. Prof. 1971; Assoc. Prof., Tufts Univ. 1971–75, Prof. 1975–85, Distinguished Arts and Sciences Prof., Dir Center for Cognitive Studies, Tufts 1985–; Visiting Prof., Harvard 1973–74, Pittsburgh 1975, Oxford 1979, Ecole Normale Supérieure, Paris 1985; Visiting Fellow, All Souls Coll. Oxford 1979; John Locke Lecturer, Oxford 1983, Gavin David Young Lecturer, Adelaide, Australia 1984; Woodrow Wilson Fellow 1963, Guggenheim Fellow 1973, 1986, Fulbright Fellow 1978; Fellow Center for Advanced Study in Behavioral Sciences 1979, American Acad. of Arts and Sciences 1987. *Publications:* Content and Consciousness 1969, Brainstorms 1978, The Mind's I (with Douglas Hofstadter) 1981, Elbow Room 1984, The Intentional Stance 1987, Consciousness Explained 1991, Darwin's Dangerous Idea 1995, Kinds of Minds 1996, Brainchildren 1998, Freedom Evolves 2003; numerous articles in professional journals. *Leisure interests:* sculpture, farming, cider-making, sailing, choral singing. *Address:* Center for Cognitive Studies, Tufts University, Medford, MA 02155, USA (Office). *Telephone:* (617) 627-3297 (Office). *Fax:* (617) 627-3952 (Office).

DENNIS, Bengt, MA; Swedish banker; b. 5 Jan. 1930, Grengesberg; m. Turid Stroem 1962; one s. one d.; ed Columbia Univ., NY; econ. journalist 1959–67; Head of Dept, Ministry of Finance 1967–70; Under-Sec. of State, Ministry of Commerce 1970–76; Amb., Ministry of Foreign Affairs 1977–80; Ed.-in-Chief, Dagens Nyheter 1981–82; Gov. Cen. Bank of Sweden 1982–92; Chair. Bd of Dirs. BIS 1990–93; Sr Adviser Skandinaviska Enskilda Banken 1994–2001; Man. Dir Bengt Dennis Consulting AB 2002–. *Leisure interests:* sailing, skiing, skating. *Address:* Vasagatan 36, 4 tr., Box 415, 10128 Stockholm (Office); Maria Sandels Gränd 3, 11269 Stockholm, Sweden. *Telephone:* (8) 613-08-50 (Office); (8) 651-04-32 (Home). *Fax:* (8) 613-08-68 (Office). *E-mail:* bengt.dennis@bdco.biz (Office).

DENNIS, Donna Frances; American sculptor and teacher; b. 16 Oct. 1942, Springfield, Ohio; d. of Donald P. Dennis and Helen Hogue Dennis; ed Carleton Coll., Northfield, Minn., Paris and New York; teaching positions at Skowhegan School 1982, Boston Museum School (Visiting artist) 1983, State Univ. of NY, Purchase Coll. 1984–86, 1988–, School of Visual Arts, New York 1983–90, Princeton Univ. (Visiting Artist) 1984, State Univ. of NY Purchase Coll. (Assoc. Prof.) 1990–96, Prof. 1996–; perm. comms: Dreaming of Faraway Places: The Ships Come to Washington Market, PS 234, New York, Klapper Hall, Queens Coll., CUNY 1995, American Airlines Terminal, JFK Int. Airport, NY 1996, I.S. 5, Queens, NY 1997, Terminal One, JFK Int. Airport, NY 2001; Fellow Nat. Endowment for the Arts 1977, 1980, 1986, 1994; recipient of several awards, including John Simon Guggenheim Fellowship 1979, Distinguished Achievement Award, Carleton Coll. 1989, Bard Award, City Club of New York 1989, Bessie Award for Set Design 1992, NEA Fellowship (4 times), Pollock-Krasner Award 2001. *Solo exhibitions include:* West Broadway Gallery, New York 1973, Holly Solomon Gallery, New York 1976, 1980, 1983, 1998, Contemporary Arts Center, Cincinnati 1979, Locus Solus Gallery, Genoa 1981, Neuberger Museum, State Univ. of NY, Purchase Coll. 1985, Univ. Gallery, Univ. of Mass. at Amherst 1985, Brooklyn Museum, New York 1987, Richard Green Gallery, New York 1987, Del. Art Museum, Wilmington 1988, Muhlenberg Coll. Center for the Arts, Allentown, Pa 1988, Madison Art Center, Madison, Wis. 1989, Indianapolis Museum of Art 1991–98, Sculpture Center, New York 1993, Dayton Art Inst., Dayton, Ohio 2003. *Group exhibitions include:* Walker Art Center, Minneapolis 1977, Biennial Exhbn Whitney Museum 1979, Hirshhorn Museum, Washington, DC 1979, 1984, Developments in Recent Sculpture, Whitney Museum 1981, Venice Biennale 1982, 1984, New Art at the Tate, Tate Gallery, London 1983, Storm King Art Center, Mountainville, NY 1991, 42nd St Art Project 1994, Katonah Museum, NY 1994, Neuberger Museum, State Univ. of NY, Purchase Coll. 1997, Asheville Art Museum, Asheville, NC 1998. *Publication:* 26 Bars (with Kenward Elmslie) 1987. *Leisure interest:* reading fiction. *Address:* 131 Duane Street, New York, NY 10013, USA. *Telephone:* (212) 233-0605.

DENNIS, Michael Mark, LLM; Canadian property developer; b. 4 March 1942, Toronto; ed Osgoode Hall Law School and Univ. of Calif. (Berkeley); Asst Prof. Osgoode Hall Law School 1965–67; Consultant, Nat. Planning Comm. Philippines 1968–69; Chair. Fed. Govt Task Force on Housing 1970–72; Special Asst to Mayor of Toronto 1973; Commr of Housing City of Toronto 1974–79; Exec. Vice-Pres. Olympia & York Properties (USA) 1985–; Exec. Dir

Olympia & York Canary Wharf Ltd 1987–90. *Publication:* Programs in Search of a Policy (with Susan Fish) 1973. *Leisure interests:* literature, travel, sports, music. *Address:* 101 Woodlawn Avenue, W Toronto, Ont., M4V 1G6, Canada.

DENNISTON, Rev. Robin Alastair, MA, MSc, PhD; British publisher and ecclesiastic; b. 25 Dec. 1926, London; s. of late Alexander Guthrie Denniston and Dorothy Mary Gilliat; m. 1st Anne Alice Kyffin Evans 1950 (died 1985); one s. two d.; m. 2nd Dr Rosa Susan Penelope Beddington 1987 (died 2001); ed Westminster School and Christ Church, Oxford; Ed. Collins 1950–59; Man. Dir Faith Press 1959–60; Ed. Prism 1959–61; Promotion Man. Hodder & Stoughton Ltd 1960–64, Editorial Dir 1966, Man. Dir 1968–72, also Dir Mathew Hodder Ltd and subsidiary cos; Deputy Chair. George Weidenfeld & Nicolson (and subsidiary cos) 1973; Chair. (non-exec.) A. R. Mowbray & Co. 1974–88; Chair. Sphere Books 1975–76, Thomas Nelson & Sons (and subsidiary cos) 1975, Michael Joseph Ltd 1975, George Rainbird Ltd 1975; Dir Thomson Publs Ltd 1975, Hamish Hamilton Ltd 1975, (non-exec.) W. W. Norton 1989–; Academic Publr Oxford Univ. Press 1978, Sr Deputy Sec. to the Dels. 1984–88, Oxford Publr 1984–88; Student of Christ Church 1978; ordained Deacon 1978, Priest 1979; Hon. Curate Parish of Clifton-on-Teme 1978; New with S Hinksey 1985; Non-Stipendiary Minister, Great with Little Tew 1987–90, Burntisland and St Columba's Aberdour, Fife 1990–93; Priest-in-charge Great with Little Tew and Over Worton with Nether Worton 1995–2002. *Publications:* The Young Musicians 1956, Partly Living 1967, Part Time Priests? (ed.) 1960 (co-ed.) Anatomy of Scotland 1992, Churchill's Secret War: Diplomatic Decrypts, the Foreign Office and Turkey 1942–4 1997, Trevor Huddleston: A Life 1999. *Leisure interests:* music, farming, walking. *Address:* The Vicarage, Great Tew, Oxon., OX7 4AG; 112 Randolph Avenue, London, W9 1PQ, England.

DENNY, Floyd Wolfe, Jr, MD; American professor of paediatrics; b. Floyd Wolfe Denny, Jr, 22 Oct. 1923, South Carolina; s. of Floyd W. Denny and Marion P. Denny; m. Barbara Horsefield 1946; two s. one d.; ed Wofford Coll. and Vanderbilt Univ. School of Medicine; Asst Prof. of Pediatrics, Univ. of Minn. 1951–53, Vanderbilt Univ. 1953–55; Asst Prof. of Pediatrics and Preventive Medicine, Case Western Reserve Univ. 1955–60, Assoc. Prof. of Preventive Medicine 1960; Prof. of Pediatrics, Univ. of NC 1960–, Alumni Distinguished Prof. of Pediatrics 1973–, Chair. Dept of Pediatrics 1960–81, Dir Program on Health Promotion and Disease Prevention 1985–93; Lasker Award; Hon. DSc (Wofford Coll.) 1985. *Publications:* over 100 articles in medical journals on rheumatic fever, streptococcal infections, acute respiratory infections and sarcoidosis. *Leisure interests:* gardening, reading. *Address:* 358, Wing C, CB No. 7225, University of North Carolina, Chapel Hill, NC 27599 (Office); Building 1, Apt. 308, Carolina Meadows, Chapel Hill, NC 27514, USA (Home). *Telephone:* (919) 966-2504 (Office); (919) 929 2359 (Home). *Fax:* (919) 966-3852 (Office).

DENNY, Robyn (Edward M. F.), ARCA; British artist; b. 3 Oct. 1930, Abinger, Surrey; s. of Sir Henry Denny, Bt and Joan, Lady Denny; m. 1st Anna Teasdale (divorced); m. 2nd Marjorie Abéla; two s. one d.; ed Clayesmore School, Dorset, St Martin's School of Art and Royal Coll. of Art, London; first one-man exhbns. in London at Gallery One and Gimpel Fils 1958; has since given one-man exhbns. throughout Europe and USA; retrospective exhbn Tate Gallery, London 1973; has represented Britain at Biennales in Paris, Tokyo, Milan, Brussels, USA and Australia and at 33rd Venice Biennale; works in numerous public collections; has received many public commissions for site specific works; teaching assignments have included Slade School, Univ. of London and Minn. Inst. of Fine Art; fmr adviser, Arts Council of GB, Inst. of Contemporary Arts, London; recipient of several awards and prizes. *Publications:* articles and criticism in int. publs. *Address:* Unit 4B, 24–28 Wilds Rents, London, SE1 4QG, England.

DENTON, Charles Henry, BA, FRSA, FRTS; British television executive; b. 20 Dec. 1937; s. of Alan Charles Denton and Mary Frances Royle; m. Eleanor Mary Player 1961; one s. two d.; ed Reading School and Univ. of Bristol; worked as deckhand 1960; trainee advertising 1961–63; with BBC 1963–68; freelance TV producer Granada, ATV and Yorkshire TV cos 1969–70; Dir Tempest Films Ltd 1969–71; Man. Dir Black Lion Films 1979–81; Head of Documentaries ATV 1974–77, Controller of Programmes 1977–81; Dir of Programmes Cen. Ind. TV 1981–84; Dir Cen. Ind. Television PLC 1981–87; Chief Exec. Zenith Productions 1984–93, Chair. Zenith North Ltd 1988–93; Head of Drama BBC 1993–96; Chair. Action Time Ltd 1988–93, Producers' Alliance for Cinema and TV (PACT) 1991–1993, Cornwall Film 2001–; Gov. BFI 1992–99; mem. Arts Council of England 1996–98; mem. Bd Film Council 1999–2002. *Leisure interests:* walking, music. *Address:* Cornwall Film, Pydar House, Pydar Street, Truro, Cornwall, TR1 1EA, England. *Telephone:* (1872) 322886. *Website:* www.cornwallfilm.com.

DENTON, Derek Ashworth, MM, BS, FAA, FRACP, FRCP, FRS; Australian research physiologist; b. 27 May 1924, Launceston, Tasmania; s. of A. A. Denton; m. Dame Margaret Scott 1953; two s.; ed Launceston Grammar School and Univ. of Melbourne; Haley Research Fellow, Walter & Eliza Hall Inst. of Medical Research 1948; Overseas Nat. Health and Medical Research Council (NH & MRC) Fellow, Cambridge 1952–53; Medical Research Fellow, later Sr Medical Research Fellow, Nat. Health and Medical Research Council 1949–63, Prin. Research Fellow, Admin. Head and Chief Scientist 1964–70; Dir and originating Bd mem. Howard Florey Inst. of Experimental Physiology and Medicine 1971–89, Emer. Dir 1990–; Visiting Prof., British Heart Foundation and Balliol Coll. Oxford, UK; Adjunct Scientist, Southwest

Foundation for Biomedical Research, San Antonio, Tex., USA; Dir The David Syme Co. Ltd 1984–, Australian Ballet Foundation 1983–, Sydney Dance Co. 1994–; First Vice-Pres. Int. Union of Physiological Sciences 1983–89; Chair. Nominating Cttee of Council, Int. Union of Physiological Sciences 1986–89; Chair. Cttee to Review Comms. of Int. Union of Physiological Sciences 1986–95; Foreign Medical mem. Royal Swedish Acad. of Sciences; mem. Jury of Basic and Clinical Medical Awards, Albert and Mary Lasker Foundation 1979–89; Hon. Foreign Fellow, American Acad. of Arts and Sciences; Hon. Foreign mem. American Physiology Soc.; OECD Examiner of Science and Tech. Policy of Govt of Sweden; Foreign Assoc. NAS (USA), French Acad. of Science, Inst. of France 2000. *Publications:* The Hunger for Salt 1982, The Pinnacle of Life 1993, 300 articles and reviews. *Leisure interests:* tennis, fishing, ballet, music, wine. *Address:* 816 Orrong Road, Toorak, Vic. 3142, Australia (Home). *Telephone:* (3) 8344-5639 (Office); (3) 9827-2640 (Home).

DENTON, Frank Trevor, MA, FRSC; Canadian economist; b. 27 Oct. 1930, Toronto; s. of Frank W. Denton and Kathleen M. Davies; m. Marilyn J. Shipp 1953; three s. one d.; ed Univ. of Toronto; economist, Prov. Govt of Ont. 1953–54, Fed. Govt of Canada 1954–59, 1961–64, Philips Electronics Industries Ltd 1959–60, Senate of Canada Cttee staff 1960–61; Dir of Econometrics, Dominion Bureau of Statistics 1964–68; Consultant, Econ. Council of Canada 1964–68; Prof. of Econs, McMaster Univ. 1968–96, Prof. Emer. 1996–; Dir McMaster Program for Quantitative Studies in Econs and Population 1981–96; various other consulting appts.; Fellow, American Statistical Asscn, Royal Statistical Soc.; mem. Int. Statistical Inst., Int. Union for Scientific Study of Population. *Publications:* Growth of Manpower in Canada 1970; Co-author: Population and the Economy 1975, Working-Life Tables for Canadian Males 1969, Historical Estimates of the Canadian Labour Force 1967, The Short-Run Dynamics of the Canadian Labour Market 1976, Unemployment and Labour Force Behaviour of Young People: Evidence from Canada and Ontario 1980, Pensions and the Economic Security of the Elderly 1981; Co-ed.: Independence and Economic Security in Old Age 2000; numerous monographs, articles, technical papers in economics, statistics, demography. *Address:* Department of Economics, McMaster University, Hamilton, Ont., L8S 4M4 (Office); 382 Blythewood Road, Burlington, Ont., L7L 2G8, Canada (Home). *Telephone:* (905) 525-9140 ext. 24595 (Office); (905) 639-9361 (Home). *Fax:* (905) 521-8232. *E-mail:* dentonf@mcmaster.ca (Office).

DENTON, Richard Michael, MA, PhD, DSc, FMedSci, FRS; British biochemist; b. 16 Oct. 1941, Sutton Coldfield; s. of the late Arthur Benjamin Denton and of Eileen Mary Denton (née Evans); m. Janet Mary Jones 1965; one s. two d.; ed Wycliffe Coll., Stonehouse, Glos., Christ's Coll., Cambridge; Lecturer in Biochemistry Univ. of Bristol 1973–78, Reader 1978–87, Prof. (Personal Chair) 1987–, Head of Biochemistry Dept 1995–2000, Chair. Medical Sciences 2000–, Dean of Medical and Veterinary Sciences 2003–; MRC Research Fellowship 1984–88, mem. Council MRC 1999–, Chair. MRC Training and Career Devt Bd 2002–; Founder Fellow Acad. of Medical Sciences 1998. *Publications:* over 220 research papers in various int. research journals, with maj. topic the molecular basis of the control of metabolism by insulin and other hormones. *Leisure interests:* family, fell walking, keeping fit, cooking. *Address:* University of Bristol School of Medical Sciences, University Walk, Bristol, BS8 1TD, England (Office). *Telephone:* (117) 928-8097 (Office). *Fax:* (117) 928-8274 (Office). *E-mail:* r.denton@bristol.ac.uk (Office). *Website:* www.bch.bris.ac.uk (Office).

DÉON, Michel; French writer; b. 4 Aug. 1919, Paris; s. of Paul Déon and Alice de Fossey; m. Chantal d'Arc 1963; one s. one d.; ed Lycée Janson-de-Sailly and Faculty of Law, Paris; journalist with l'Action française, Marie-Claire 1942–56; publisher 1954; writer 1956–; mem. Acad. Française 1978–, Acad. of Sciences, Portugal; Dr. hc (Nat. Univ. of Ireland); Commdr, Légion d'Honneur 2002; Officier des Arts et des Lettres; Prix Interallié 1970, Grand Prix du Roman 1973, Grand Prix Jean Giono 1996. *Plays:* Ma Vie n'est plus un Roman, Ariane ou L'oubli. *Publications:* novels: Je ne veux jamais l'oublier 1950, La Corrida 1952, Le Dieu pâle 1954, Les trompeuses espérances 1956, Les gens de la nuit 1957, Tout l'amour du monde 1959, Un parfum de jasmin 1966, Les poneys sauvages 1970, Un taxi mauve 1973, Le jeune homme vert 1976, Mes arches de Noé 1978, Un déjeuner de soleil 1981, Louis XIV par lui-même 1983, Je vous écris d'Italie 1984, Bagages pour Vancouver 1985, La Montée du Soir, Ma Vie n'est plus un Roman (drama) 1987, Un Souvenir 1990, Le Prix de l'amour 1992, Parlons en . . . 1993, Ariane ou L'oubli (drama) 1992, Pages grecques (essays) 1993, Une longue amitié 1995, Je me suis beaucoup promené 1995, La Cour des Grands 1996, Madame Rose, Pages françaises 1999, Taisez-vous . . . J'entends venis un ange 2001. *Leisure interests:* shooting, sailing, bibliophile. *Address:* The Old Rectory, Tynagh, Co. Galway, Ireland; 5 rue Sébastien Bottin, 75007, Paris, France. *Telephone:* (090) 97-45-143 (Ireland). *Fax:* (090) 97-45-376 (Ireland).

DEPARDIEU, Gérard; French actor and vineyard owner; b. 27 Dec. 1948, Chateauroux; s. of René Depardieu and Alice Depardieu (née Marillier); m. Elisabeth Guignot 1970; one s. one d.; ed Ecole communale, Cours d'art dramatique de Charles Dullin and Ecole d'art dramatique de Jean Laurent Cochet; Pres. Jury, 45th Cannes Int. Film Festival 1992; Chevalier, Ordre nat. du Mérite, Chevalier Légion d'honneur, Chevalier des Arts et des Lettres; numerous nat. and int. awards. *Appeared in short films:* Le Beatnik et le minet 1965, Nathalie Granger 1971. *Films include:* Les gaspards 1973, Les valseuses 1973, Pas si méchant que ça 1974, 1900 1975, La dernière femme 1975, Sept morts sur ordonnance 1975, Maîtresse 1975, Barocco 1976, René la Canne 1976, Les plages de l'Atlantique 1976, Baxter vera Baxter 1976,

Dites-lui que je l'aime 1977, Le camion 1977, Préparez vos mouchoirs 1977, Rêve de singe 1977, Le sucre 1978, Buffet froid 1979, Loulou 1979, Le dernier métro 1980 (César award Best Actor, France), Le choix des armes 1981, La femme d'à côté 1981, La chèvre 1981, Le retour de Martin Guerre 1981 (Best Actor Award, American Society of Film Critics), Danton 1981, Le grand frère 1982, La lune dans le caniveau 1983, Les compères 1983, Fort Saganne 1983, Tartuffe (also Dir) 1984, Rive Droite, Rive Gauche 1984, Police 1984, One Woman or Two 1985, Jean de Florette 1985, Tenue de soirée 1985, Rue du départ 1986, Les fugitifs 1986, Sous le Soleil de Satan 1986, Camille Claudel 1987, Drôle d'endroit pour une rencontre 1988, Je veux rentrer à la maison 1988, Trop belle pour toi 1988, Cyrano de Bergerac 1989 (César award Best Actor), Uranus 1990, Green Card (Golden Globe for Best Comedy Actor), Mon Père ce héros 1991, 1492: Conquest of Paradise 1991, Tous les matins du monde 1991, Germinal 1992, A Pure Formality 1993, Le Colonel Chabert 1993, La Machine 1994, Elisa, Les Cents et Une Nuits, Les Anges Gardiens, Le Garçu (all 1994), Bogus, Unhook the Stars, Secret Agent 1995, Vatel 1997, The Man in the Iron Mask 1997, Les Portes du Ciel 1999, Astérix et Obélix 1999, Un pont entre deux rives (also Dir) 1999, Vatel 1999, Les Acteurs 2000, Chicken Run 2000, Le Placard 2001, 102 Dalmatians 2001, Astérix et Obélix: Mission Cleopatra 2002. *Plays include:* Boudu sauvé des eaux 1968, Les Garçons de la bande 1969, Une fille dans ma soupe 1970, Galapagos 1971, Saved 1972, Home 1972, Ismé 1973, Isaac 1973, La Chevauchée sur le lac de Constance 1974, les Gens déraisonnables sont en voie de disparition 1977, Tartuffe (also Dir) 1983, Lily Passion 1986, Les portes du ciel 1999, Œdipus Rex 2001, Le Carnaval des animaux 2001. *Television includes:* L'Inconnu 1974, Le Comte de Monte Cristo 1998, Balzac 1999, Bérénice 1999, Les Misérables 2000. *Publication:* Lettres volées 1988. *Address:* Artmédia, 20 avenue Rapp, 75007 Paris, France.

DEPARDON, Raymond; French photographer; b. 6 July 1942, Villefranche-sur-Saône; s. of Antoine Depardon and Marthe Bernard; m. Claudine Nougaret 1987; two s.; ed primary school in Villefranche; apprentice to Louis Foucherand, Paris 1958, Asst 1959; copy then photographic reporter, Dalmas agency 1960; co-founder Gamma agency 1967; mem. Magnum Agency, Paris and New York 1978; one-man Exhbn Correspondance new yorkaise, San Clemente, Paris 1984, Lausanne 1985; participant in group exhbns. in Paris, New York etc.; recipient of several film awards. *Films include:* Ian Pallach, Tibesti Tou (short) 1974, Numéros zéro 1977, Reporters 1981, Faits divers: les Années déclic 1983, Empty Quarter 1985, Urgences 1987, La Captive du désert 1990, La Colline des Anges 1993, Délits flagrants 1994, Sida propos 1995, Afriques: Comment ça va avec la douleur 1995, Paris 1998, Muriel Leferle 1999, Profils paysans l'approche 2001. *Publications:* photographic albums: Tchad 1978, Notes 1979, Correspondance new yorkaise 1981, Le Désert américain 1983, San Clemente 1984, Les Fiancées de Saigon 1986, Hivers 1987, Depardon cinéma 1993, Return to Vietnam (with Jean-Claude Guillebaud) 1994, La Ferme du Garet 1995, La Porte des Larmes (with Jean-Claude Guillebaud) 1995, En Afrique 1995, Voyages 1998, Silence rompu 1998, Corse 2000, Détours (Nadar Prize) 2000, Errances 2000, Rêves de déserts 2000. *Address:* Magnum, 19 rue Hégésippe Moreau, 75018 Paris (Office); 18 bis rue Henri Barbusse, 75005 Paris, France (Home).

DEPP, Johnny; American actor; b. 9 June 1963, Owensboro, Ky; m. Lori Anne Allison (divorced); partner Vanessa Paradis; one d. one s.; fmr rock musician; TV appearances include 21 Jump Street. *Films include:* A Nightmare on Elm Street 1984, Platoon 1986, Slow Burn 1986, Cry Baby 1990, Edward Scissorhands 1990, Benny and Joon 1993, What's Eating Gilbert Grape 1993, Arizona Dream 1993, Ed Wood 1994, Don Juan de Marco 1994, Dead Man 1995, Nick of Time 1995, Divine Rapture, The Brave 1997 (also writer and Dir), Donnie Brasco 1997, Fear and Loathing in Las Vegas 1998, The Astronaut's Wife 1998, The Source 1999, The Ninth Gate 1999, The Libertine 1999, Just to Be Together 1999, Sleepy Hollow 1999, Before Night Falls 2000, The Man Who Cried 2000, Chocolat 2000, Blow 2001, From Hell 2001, Lost in La Mancha 2002, Once Upon a Time in Mexico 2002. *Address:* 9100 Wilshire Boulevard, Suite 725, East Beverly Hills, CA 90212, USA.

DERANT LAKOUÉ, Enoch; Central African Republic politician; fmr mem. Mouvement pour la Libération du Peuple Centrafricain (MLPC—Liberation Movement of the Central African People party); Founder and Pres. Parti social-démocrate (PSD) early 1990s; Prime Minister of Cen. African Repub. March–Oct. 1993; Presidential cand. 1993, 1999; Founder Co-ordination of Opposition Political Parties; Dir BERETEC/CENTRAFRIQUE, Bangui. *Address:* Parti social-démocrate (PSD), BP 543, Bangui, Central African Repubic (Office).

DERBEZ BAUTISTA, Luis Ernesto, PhD; Mexican politician and economist; b. 1 April 1947, Mexico City; ed San Luis Potosí Autonomous Univ., Univ. of Oregon and Iowa State Univ., USA; economist, IBRD (World Bank), responsible for regional areas including Chile 1983–86, Cen. America 1986–89, Africa 1989–92, Western and Cen. Africa 1992–94, India, Nepal and Bhutan 1994–97 (also dir multilateral econ. assitance and structural adjustment programmes in Chile, Costa Rica, Honduras and Guatemala); ind. consultant World Bank Mexico City Office and Inter-American Devt Bank, Washington DC 1997–2000; Econ. Adviser and Co-ordinator of Econ. Affairs to Pres. elect of Mexico 2000; fmr Sec. for Economy; Sec. of State for Foreign Affairs 2002–; fmr Prof. Grad. School of Business Man., Istituto Tecnológico y de Estudios Superiores de Monterrey (also Dir Econometric Studies Unit and Econs Dept); fmr Vice-Rector Univ. of the Americas, Cholula, Mexico; fmr Visiting Prof. Johns Hopkins Univ. School of Int. Studies, USA. *Address:* Secretariat of State for Foreign Affairs, Av. Ricardo Flores Magón 1, Tlatelolco, 06995 México, DF, Mexico (Office). *Telephone:* (55) 5782-3982 (Office). *Fax:* (55) 5782-4109 (Office). *E-mail:* comment@sre.gob.mx (Office). *Website:* www.sre.gob.mx (Office).

DERBYSHIRE, Sir Andrew George, Kt, MA, AADip, FRIBA, FRSA; British architect; b. 7 Oct. 1923; s. of late Samuel Reginald and Helen Louise Puleston (née Clarke) Derbyshire; m. Lily Rhodes (née Binns); three s. one d.; ed Chesterfield Grammar School, Queens' Coll., Cambridge, Architectural Asscn, London; Admiralty Signals Establishment and Bldg Research Station 1943–46; Farmer and Dark (Marchwood and Belvedere power stations) 1951–53; W Riding Co. Architect's Dept 1953–55; Asst City Architect, Sheffield 1955–61; mem. Research Team, RIBA Survey of Architects' Offices 1960–62; mem. Robert Matthew, Johnson-Marshall and Partners 1961–, Chair. 1983–89, Pres. RMJM Group 1989–98; involved with Devt of Univ. of York 1962–; Cen. Lancs. New Town, NE Lancs. Impact Study, Univ. of Cambridge, W Cambridge Devt and New Cavendish Lab., Preston Market and Guildhall, London Docklands Study, Hillingdon Civic Centre, Cabtrack and Minitram feasibility studies, Suez Master Plan Study, Castle Peak Power Station, Hong Kong, Harbour reclamation and urban devt, Hong Kong; mem. RIBA Council 1950–72, 1975–81, Sr Vice-Pres. 1980–81; mem. Bldg Industry Communications Research Cttee 1964–66; mem. Ministry of Transport Urban Research and Devt Group 1967; mem. Inland Transport Research and Devt Council 1968; mem. Dept of the Environment Planning and Transport Research Advisory Council 1971–76; mem. Comm. on Energy and the Environment 1978–81; mem. (part-time) Cen. Electricity Generating Bd 1973–84; mem. of Bd, Property Services Agency 1975–79; mem. Bd London Docklands Devt Corpn and Chair. of Planning Cttee 1983–88; mem. Construction Industry Sector Group of NEDC 1988–92; mem. Construction Industry Council, Chair. Research Cttee 1989–94; Chair. Art for Architecture Project, RSA 1994–98; Hoffman Wood Prof. of Architecture, Univ. of Leeds 1978–80; External Prof., Dept of Civil Eng., Univ. of Leeds 1981–85; Gresham Coll. Prof. of Rhetoric 1990–92; Hon. Fellow Inst. of Structural Eng. 1992, Inst. of Advanced Architectural Studies, Univ. of York 1994; Hon. DUniv (York) 1972. *Publications:* The Architect and His Office 1962 and numerous articles on planning, energy conservation and scientific research. *Leisure interests:* family, garden. *Address:* 4 Sunnyfield, Hatfield, Herts., AL9 5DX, England (Home). *Telephone:* (1707) 265903. *Fax:* (1707) 275874. *E-mail:* andrewderby@btinternet.com (Home).

DERIPASKA, Oleg Vladimirovich; Russian businessman; b. 2 April 1963, Dzerdjinsk, Gorky Region; ed Moscow State Univ., Plekhanov Acad. of Nat. Econs; Financial Dir Jt Stock Mil. Investment and Trade Co. 1990–92; Dir Gen. Rosaluminproduct 1992–93; Dir Krasnoyarskaluminproduct 1993; Dir-Gen. Aluminproduct 1993–94; Dir Sayany Aluminium Plant 1994; Vice-Pres. Russian Union of Businessmen and Entrepreneurs 1999–. *Address:* Sibizsky Aluminy Group, Mashkova Btz. 11, Building 2, 103064 Moscow, Russia (Office). *Telephone:* (095) 720-49-10 (Office).

DERN, Laura; American actress; b. 10 Feb. 1967, Los Angeles; d. of Bruce Dern and Diane Ladd; ed Lee Strasberg Inst., Royal Acad. of Dramatic Art, London; film debut aged 11 in Foxes 1980. *Films include:* Teachers 1984, Mask 1985, Smooth Talk 1985, Blue Velvet 1986, Haunted Summer 1988, Wild at Heart 1990, Rambling Rose 1991, Jurassic Park 1993, A Perfect World 1993, Devil Inside, Citizen Ruth 1996, Bastard Out of Carolina 1996, October Sky 1999, Dr T and the Women 2000, Daddy and Them 2001, Focus 2001, Novocaine 2001, Jurassic Park III 2001, I Am Sam 2001. *Television appearances include:* Happy Endings, Three Wishes of Billy Greer, Afterburn, Down Came a Blackbird, The Siege at Ruby Ridge, The Baby Dance, A Season for Miracles, The West Wing (episode), Within These Walls, Damaged Care; Dir The Gift 1994.

DERNESCH, Helga; Austrian opera singer; b. 3 Feb. 1939, Vienna; m. Werner Kramm; two c.; ed Vienna Conservatory; sang many operatic roles in Berne 1961–63, Wiesbaden 1963–66, Cologne 1966–69; freelance guest appearances at all maj. opera houses in Europe 1969–; regular appearances at Bayreuth Festival 1965–69, at Salzburg Easter Festival 1969–73; since 1979 has sung as mezzo-soprano; regular appearances at San Francisco Opera 1982–; début Metropolitan Opera, New York 1985; has sung in operas and concerts throughout Europe, N and S America, Japan; many recordings. *Leisure interests:* films, people, literature. *Address:* Salztorgasse 8/11, 1013 Vienna (Office); Neutorgasse 2/22, 1013 Vienna, Austria.

DERR, Kenneth T., MBA; American business executive; b. 1936; m. Donna Mettler 1959; three c.; ed Cornell Univ.; with Chevron Corpn (formerly Standard Oil Co. of Calif.) 1960–, Vice-Pres. 1972–85; Pres. Chevron USA Inc. 1978–84; Head, merger program, Chevron Corpn and Gulf Oil Corpn 1984–85; Vice-Chair. Chevron Corpn 1985–88, Chair. 1989–99, CEO 1989–99; mem. Bd of Dirs. Citicorp, AT&T, Potlatch Corpn; Dir American Petroleum Inst., now Chair. *Address:* c/o Chevron Corporation, P.O. Box 7643, 575 Market Street, San Francisco, CA 94105, USA.

DERRIDA, Jacques; French philosopher; b. 15 July 1930, El Biar, Algiers, Algeria; s. of Aimé Derrida and Georgette Safar; m. Marguérite Aucouturier 1957; two s.; ed Ecole Normale Supérieure, Paris; taught at Sorbonne 1960–64, at Ecole Normale Supérieure 1965–84; Hon. DLitt (Cambridge) 1992. *Publications:* La voix et le phénomène 1967, De la grammatologie 1967, L'écriture et la différence 1967, Marges 1972, La dissémination 1972, GLAS 1974, La vérité en peinture 1979, La carte postale 1980, Psyché 1987, De l'esprit 1987, Mémoires—Pour Paul De Man 1988, Du droit à la philosophie 1990, Mémoires d'aveugle 1990, Le problème de la genèse dans la philosophie de Husserl 1990, L'autre cap 1991, Donner le temps 1991, Qu'est-ce que la poésie? 1991, Spectres de Marx 1993, Politiques de l'amitié 1994, Mal d'Archive 1995, Adieu à Emmanuel Levinas 1997, De l'hospitalité 1997, Demeure: Fiction and Testimony 1998, Donner La Mort 1999, The Work of Mourning 2001, Papier Machine 2001. *Address:* Ecole des Hautes Etudes en Sciences Sociales, 54 boulevard Raspail, 75006 Paris, France.

DERSHOWITZ, Alan Morton, LLB; American professor of law; b. 1 Sept. 1938; s. of Harry Dershowitz and Claire Ringel; m. Carolyn Cohen; two s. one d.; ed Brooklyn Coll. and Yale Univ.; admitted to DC Bar 1963, Mass. Bar 1968, US Supreme Court 1968; Law clerk to Chief Judge David Bazelon, US Court of Appeal 1962–63, to Justice Arthur Goldberg, US Supreme Court 1963–64; mem. Faculty, Harvard Coll. 1964–, Prof. of Law 1967–; Fellow, Center for Advanced Study of Behavioral Sciences 1971–72; consultant to Dir Nat. Inst. for Mental Health (NIMH) 1967–69, (Pres.'s Comm. on Civil Disorders) 1967, (Pres.'s Comm. on Causes of Violence) 1968, (Nat. Asscn for Advancement of Colored People Legal Defense Fund) 1967–68, Pres.'s Comm. on Marijuana and Drug Abuse 1972–73, (Ford Foundation Study on Law and Justice) 1973–76; rapporteur, Twentieth Century Fund Study on Sentencing 1975–76; Guggenheim Fellow 1978–79; mem. Comm. on Law and Social Action, American Jewish Congress 1978; Dir American Civil Liberties Union 1968–71, 1972–75, Asscn of Behavioral and Social Sciences, NAS 1973–76; Chair. Civil Rights Comm. New England Region, Anti-Defamation League, B'nai B'rith 1983; Hon. MA (Harvard Coll.) 1967; Hon. LLD (Yeshiva) 1989. *Publications:* Psychoanalysis, Psychiatry and the Law 1967, Criminal Law: Theory and Process 1974, The Best Defense 1982, Reversal of Fortune: Inside the von Bülow Case 1986, Taking Liberties: A Decade of Hard Cases, Bad Laws and Bum Raps 1988, Chutzpah 1991, Contrary to Popular Opinion 1992, The Abuse Excuse 1994, The Advocate's Devil 1994, Reasonable Doubt 1996, The Vanishing American Jew 1997, Sexual McCarthyism 1998, Just Revenge 1999, The Genesis of Justice 2000, Supreme Injustice 2001, Letters to a Young Lawyer 2001, Shouting Fire 2002; articles in legal journals. *Address:* Harvard Law School, 1575 Massachusetts Avenue, Cambridge, MA 02138-2801, USA.

DERVIŞ, Kemal, BSc, PhD; Turkish economist and politician; b. 1949, Istanbul; ed LSE, UK, Princeton Univ., USA; Lecturer in Econs. Middle Eastern Tech. Univ. 1973; Adviser on issues of econ. and int. relations to Prime Minister Bülent Ecevit 1973–76; Lecturer in Int. Relations and Econs Princeton Univ. 1977; mem. Research Dept, World Bank 1978–82, Head of Industrial Strategy and Policy, Global Industry Dept 1982–86, Sr Economist of Europe, Middle East and N. African Affairs 1986–87, Head of Cen. Europe Div. 1987–96, Vice-Pres. in charge of Middle East and Africa Region 1996–2000, Vice-Pres. in charge of Poverty Reduction and Econ. Man. 2000–01; Minister of Econ. Affairs 2001–02; Minister of State 2002; mem. Cumhuriyet Halk Partisi—CHP (Republican People's Party) 2002–; *Publications include:* General Equilibrium Models for Development Policy (co-author); numerous articles on econ. policy and devt econs. *Address:* c/o Cumhuriyet Halk Partisi—CHP, Çevre Sok. 38, Ankara, Turkey (Office).

DERYABIN, Yuri Stepanovich; Russian diplomatist (retd); b. 3 Jan. 1932, Karachelka, Kurgan Region; m.; two d.; ed Moscow Inst. of Int. Relations; diplomatic service 1954–; Third, then Second Sec. Dept of Scandinavian Countries, Ministry of Foreign Affairs 1959–62; Second Sec. Embassy, Norway 1962–65, First Sec. USSR Embassy, Finland 1968–73, Counsellor 1973–75; Counsellor-Envoy 1980–83; Deputy Chief Second European Dept, Ministry of Foreign Affairs 1986–87; Chief Dept of Problems of Security and Cooperation in Europe 1987–90; Deputy Minister of Foreign Affairs 1991–92; Russian Amb. to Finland 1992–96; Deputy Sec., Security Council of Russia 1997–98; Head Centre for N European Research, Inst. of Europe, Russian Acad. of Sciences 1999–. *Address:* Institute of Europe, Centre for North European Research, Mokhovaya Str. 11, Korp. 38, 103873 Moscow, Russia. *Telephone:* (095) 201-67-55.

DERYCKE, Erik, LLM; Belgian politician and lawyer; b. 28 Oct. 1949, Waregem; m.; two c.; ed Rijksuniversiteit Gent; barrister in Kortrijk 1972–; Provincial Councillor for W Flanders 1975–84; Rep. for Kortrijk, Belgian Chamber of Reps. 1984; Municipal councillor for Waregem 1989; Sec. of State for Science Policy 1990–91; Minister for Devt Aid and Deputy Minister for Science Policy 1991–92; Sec. of State for Devt Aid 1992–95; Minister for Foreign Affairs and Devt Co-operation March–June 1995; Minister for Foreign Affairs 1995–99; Hon. Pres. Socialist Party of Waregem; mem. Socialist Party Bureau. *Address:* c/o Ministry of Foreign Affairs, 2 rue des Quatre Bras, 1000 Brussels, Belgium.

DERZHAVIN, Mikhail Mikhailovich; Russian actor; b. 15 June 1936, Moscow; m. Roksana Babayan; one s.; ed Moscow Shchukin Theatre School; with Moscow Lenkom Theatre 1959–67; actor Malaya Bronnaya Theatre 1967–69; with Moscow Satire Theatre 1969–. *Films include:* Womaniser, Impotent. *Theatre roles include:* Master of Ceremonies in Goodbye, Master of Ceremonies, Bear in Ordinary Miracle, lead role in Tartuffe, A Piece for Two; two-man variety shows with A. Shirvindt (q.v.). *Leisure interest:* fishing. *Address:* Moscow Satire Theatre, Triumphalnaya pl. 2, 103050 Moscow, Russia (Office). *Telephone:* (095) 299-63-05 (Office).

DESAI, Anita; Indian author and professor; b. 24 June 1937; d. of Toni Nimé and D.N. Mazumdar; m. Ashvin Desai 1958; two s. two d.; ed Queen Mary's School, Delhi and Miranda House, Univ. of Delhi; Prof. of Writing, MIT 1993–; Winifred Holtby Prize, Royal Soc. of Literature 1978, Sahitya Adad. Prize 1978, Hadassah Prize, New York 1988, Alberto Moravia Prize, Italy 1999; Padma Sri 1989, Neil Gunn Award for Int. Writing 1994. *Film:* In Custody 1994. *Television:* The Village By the Sea, BBC 1994. *Publications:* Cry, The Peacock 1963, Voices in the City 1965, Bye-Bye Blackbird 1971, Where Shall We Go This Summer? 1973, Fire on the Mountain 1978, Games at Twilight 1979, Clear Light of Day 1980, The Village by the Sea 1983, In Custody (filmed 1994) 1984, Baumgartner's Bombay 1988, Journey to Ithaca 1995, Fasting, Feasting 1999, Diamond Dust and Other Stories 2000. *Address:* c/o Deborah Rogers Ltd, 20 Powis Mews, London, W11 1JN, England.

DESAI, Baron (Life Peer), cr. 1991, of St Clement Danes in the City of Westminster; **Meghnad Jagdishchandra Desai,** PhD; British (b. Indian) economist; b. 10 July 1940, Baroda; s. of Jagdishchandra Desai and Mandakini Desai (née Majmundar); m. Gail Wilson 1970 (separated 1995); one s. two d.; ed Univ. of Bombay, Univ. of Pennsylvania, USA; Assoc. Specialist, Dept of Agricultural Econs, Univ. of Calif. at Berkeley, USA 1963–65; Lecturer, LSE 1965–77, Sr Lecturer 1977–80, Reader 1980–83, Prof. of Econs 1983–; Head Devt Studies Inst. 1990–95; Dir Centre for the Study of Global Governance, LSE 1992–; Consultant at various times to FAO, UNCTAD, Int. Coffee Org., World Bank, UNIDO, Ministries of Industrial Devt and Educ., Algeria, British Airports Authority and other bodies; Co-Ed. Journal of Applied Econometrics 1984–; mem. Editorial Bds Int. Review of Applied Econs and several other journals; mem. Council, Royal Econ. Soc. 1988; mem. Exec. Cttee Asscn of Univ. Teachers in Econs 1987– (Pres. 1987–90); mem. Univ. of London Senate representing LSE 1981–89; Chair. Econ. Research Div., LSE 1983–; mem. Nat. Exec. of Council for Academic Freedom and Democracy 1972–83, Speaker's Comm. on Citizenship 1989–, Berndt Carlson Trust; mem. or fmr mem. Governing Body of Courtauld Inst., British Inst. in Paris, Cen. School of Arts, Polytechnic of N London; Chair. Holloway Ward (Islington Cen.) Labour Party 1977–80; Chair. Islington S and Finsbury Labour Party 1986–92, Pres. 1992–; Dr hc (Kingston Univ.) 1992; Hon. DSc (Econs) (E London) 1994; Hon. DPhil (London Guildhall) 1996. *Publications:* Marxian Economic Theory 1974 (trans. in several languages), Applied Econometrics 1976, Marxian Economics 1979, Testing Monetarism 1981, Marx's Revenge 2001; ed. several books; numerous papers and contribs to books and journals. *Leisure interests:* reading, politics. *Address:* Centre for the Study of Global Governance, London School of Economics, Houghton Street, London, WC2A 2AE (Office); 606 Collingwood House, Dolphin Square, London, SW1V 3NF, England (Home). *Telephone:* (20) 7955-7489 (Office); (20) 7798-8673 (Home). *Fax:* (20) 7955-7591. *E-mail:* m.desai@lse.ac.uk (Office).

DESAI, Nitin Dayalji, BA, MSc; Indian international official, economist and civil servant; b. 5 July 1941, Bombay; s. of Dayalji M. Desai and Shantaben Desai; m. Aditi Gupta 1979; two s.; ed Univ. of Bombay and London School of Econs; Lecturer in Econs Univ. of Liverpool 1965–67, Univ. of Southampton 1967–70; consultant, Tata (India) Econ. Consultancy Services 1970–73; consultant/adviser, Planning Comm. Govt of India 1973–85; Sr Adviser, Brundtland Comm. 1985–87; Special Sec. Planning Comm. India 1987–88; Sec./Chief Econ. Adviser, Ministry of Finance 1988–90; Deputy Under-Sec.-Gen. UNCED, Geneva 1990–92; Under-Sec.-Gen. of Dept for Policy Co-ordination and Sustainable Devt UN 1993–97, Under-Sec.-Gen. for Econ. and Social Affairs 1997–. *Address:* United Nations, Room DC2–2320, New York, NY 10017 (Office); 330 East 33 Street Apt. 12M, New York, NY 10016, USA (Home). *Telephone:* (212) 532-0028 (Home).

DESAILLY, Jean; French actor; b. 24 Aug. 1920, Paris; m. Ginette Nicolas (divorced); two d.; ed Paris Ecole des Beaux Arts; Pensionnaire, Comédie Française 1942–46; mem. Renaud-Barrault Company 1947–68; Dir Théâtre Jacques Hébertot 1972–; mem. Council for Cultural Devt 1971–73; Co-Dir, Théâtre de la Madeleine 1980–; mem. du Haut Comité de la langue française 1969–; numerous TV appearances; Chevalier, Légion d'honneur, Officier, Ordre nat. du Mérite, Chevalier, Palmes Académiques, Commdr, Arts et Lettres. *Plays include:* La nuit du diable, Le bossu, Malatesta, Le procès, On ne badine pas avec l'amour, Le château, Madame Sans-Gène, Tête d'or, La cerisaie, Le marchand de Venise, Comme il vous plaira, Hamlet, Andromaque, Le soulier de satin, Il faut passer par les nuages, Le mariage de Figaro, Brève rencontre, Un ami imprévu, Double jeu, Le légume, Dis-moi Blaise, Amphitryon 38 1976, Un ennemi du peuple 1977, Le Cauchemar de Bella 1978, Siegfried 1980, Arsenic et vieilles dentelles 1981, La dixième de Beethoven 1982, Sodome et Gomorrhe 1982, L'amour fou 1983, Les oeufs de l'autruche 1984, Un otage 1984, Comme de mal entendu 1985, Le silence éclaté 1986, Les Pieds dans l'eau 1987, La Foire d'empoigne 1988, Le HE Cardinal d'Espagne 1993; Co-Dir Tout dans le jardin. *Films include:* Le père Goriot, La symphonie pastorale, Le point du jour, Occupe-toi d'Amélie, Si Versailles m'était conté, Les grandes manoeuvres, Maigret tend un piège, Les grandes familles, Le baron de l'écluse, Plein soleil, La mort de belle, Un soir sur la plage, Les sept péchés capitaux, Les amours célèbres, L'année du bac, La peau douce, Le doulos, Les deux orphelines, Le franciscain de Bourges, L'Ardoise, Comptes à rebours, L'assassinat de Trotsky, Un flic, L'ironie du sort, Le professionnel 1981, Le fou du roi 1984, Le Radeaux de la Méduse 1998. *Address:* c/o Babette Pouget, 9 Square Villaret de Joyeuse, 75017 Paris, France.

DESAILLY, Marcel David; French footballer; b. 7 Sept. 1968, Nima-Accra, Ghana; defender with Nantes Atlantique 1986–92, with Olympique de Marseille 1992–93 (winner European Cup 1993), with AC Milan, Italy

1993–98 (winner European Super Cup 1994, European Cup 1995, Champion of Italy 1994, 1996), with Chelsea, England 1998–; first selected for French nat. team 1993, winner World Cup 1998, Euro 2000; Capt. of France Dec. 2000–; Capt. of Chelsea July 2001–; Chevalier, Légion d'honneur. *Address:* Chelsea Football Club, Stamford Bridge, Fulham Road, London, SW6 1HS, England (Office). *Telephone:* (20) 7385-5545 (Office). *Fax:* (20) 7381-4831 (Office).

DESARIO, Vincenzo, BA; Italian banker; b. 11 June 1933, Barletta; m.; three c.; ed Univ. of Bari; joined Banca d'Italia (Bank of Italy), Foggia br. 1960; Banking Supervision Inspectorate, Bank of Italy head office, Rome 1968; Cen. Man. for Banking and Financial Supervision, Bank of Italy 1983; Bank of Italy Del. to Interbank Deposit Protection Fund 1991; Deputy Dir-Gen. Bank of Italy 1993–94, Dir-Gen. 1994–. *Address:* Banca d'Italia, Via Nazionale 91, 00184 Rome, Italy. *Telephone:* (06) 47921. *Fax:* (06) 47922983. *Website:* www.bancaditalia.it (Office).

DESCHAMPS, Didier Claude; French footballer; b. 15 Oct. 1968, Bayonne (Pyrénées-Atlantiques); m. Claude Deschamps; one s.; ed St Bernard private school, Bayonne, Nantes Football Acad.; amateur player Aviron Bayonnais; professional, 1st Div. 1986–; played for FC Nantes 1989, Olympique de Marseille (OM), FC des Girondins de Bordeaux, OM 1989–94, Juventus (Turin, Italy) 1994–99, Chelsea (UK) 1999–2000, Valencia (Spain) 2000–01; played for French nat. team 1989–2000, Capt. and player, Euro 92, Tournoi de France 1997, Capt. of winning team of World Cup 1998 and Euro 2000; most capped player (France) (103 appearances); fmr Man. Club de Football de Concarneau; Sports Dir and Coach AS Monaco 2001–; 1,000 m. nat. record holder 1980; French Footballer of the Year 1996, Médaille de la ville de Bayonne 1998, Chevalier Légion d'honneur. *Address:* Monaco Association Sportive, 7 avenue des Castelans, 98000 Monaco (Office). *Website:* www.asm-foot.mc (Office).

DESCHÊNES, Hon. Jules, CC, QC, LLD, FRSC; Canadian judge; b. 7 June 1923, Montréal; s. of Wilfrid Deschênes and Berthe (née Bérard) Deschênes; m. Jacqueline Lachapelle 1948; three s. two d.; ed Ecole St-Jean Baptiste Montréal, Coll. André-Grasset, Coll. de Montréal and Seminaire de Philosophie, Univ. of Montréal; called to Bar of Québec 1946; QC 1961; practised as barrister and solicitor 1946–72; Sr Partner Deschênes, de Grandpré, Colas, Godin & Lapointe 1966–72; Justice, Court of Appeal, Québec 1972–73; Chief Justice, Superior Court of Québec 1973–83; Lecturer in Private Int. Law, Univ. of Montréal 1962–69; mem. Exec. Cttee Canadian Judicial Council 1977–83; Pres. Comm. of Inquiry on War Criminals 1985–86; Consultant, U.N. Centre for Social Devt and Humanitarian Affairs, Vienna 1983–85; Judge, Int. Criminal Tribunal for the fmr Yugoslavia 1993–97; Pres. World Asscn of Judges' Cttee on Expanding Jurisdiction of Int. Court of Justice 1977–82, Québec Bar Admission School 1988–90, Royal Soc. of Canada 1990; mem. Council, World Peace Through Law Center 1980–82; mem. Int. Law Asscn, Int. Comm. of Jurists, Canadian Council on Int. Law; Hon. LLD (Concordia) 1981, (McGill) 1989; Gold Medal Canadian Inst. for the Admin. of Justice 1985; Kt Order of Malta 1978. *Publications:* The Sword and the Scales 1979, Les plateaux de la balance 1979, L'école publique confessionnelle au Québec 1980, Ainsi parlèrent les Tribunaux . . . Conflits linguistiques au Canada 1968–80 1981, Justice et Pouvoir 1984, Ainsi parlèrent les Tribunaux II 1985, co-author L'Université; son rôle, le rôle de ses composantes, les relations entre ses composantes 1969, Maîtres chez eux 1981, Judicial Independence: The Contemporary Debate 1985, Sur la ligne de feu (autobiog.) 1989 and over 100 articles.

D'ESCOTO BROCKMANN, Miguel; Nicaraguan politician; b. 5 Feb. 1933, Hollywood, USA; s. of Miguel D'Escoto Muñoz and Rita Brockmann Meléndez; ed Instituto Pedagógico La Salle, Managua, Nicaragua, St Mary's Coll., Moraga, Calif., Manhattan Coll., New York, State Univ. of New York, Columbia Univ., Sur le ligne de Feu, New York; Sub-Dir Dept of Social Communications, Maryknoll, New York, USA 1962–63; worked for Brazilian and Mexican church in slums of Belo Horizonte, Rio de Janeiro, Brazil and Mexico DF 1963–69, Dir 1970–79; Founder and Pres. Fundación Nicaragüense Pro-Desarrollo Comunitario Integral, León, Nicaragua 1973; became involved with Frente Sandinista de Liberación Nacional from 1975; f. Grupo de los 12, a group of professionals and intellectuals supporting the Sandinista Front 1977; Minister of Foreign Affairs 1979–90; elected mem. of Sandinista Ass. 1980. *Address:* c/o Ministerio del Exterior, Detrás de Los Ranchos, Managua, JR, Nicaragua.

DESHPANDE, Shashi, BA, MA, BL; Indian author; b. 19 Aug. 1938, Dharwad; d. of Adya Rangacharya and Sharada Adya; m. D. H. Deshpande 1962; two s.; ed Univs. of Bombay and Mysore; fmrly worked for a law journal and magazine; full-time writer 1970–; mem. Sahitya Akademi Bd for English 1989–94; Thirumathi Rangammal Prize, Sahitya Akademi Award for a Novel, Nanjangud Thirumalamba Award. *Translation:* Forgive Us Our Sins (play, from Kannada into English). *Film Script:* Drishti. *Publications:* The Dark Holds No Terrors 1980, Roots and Shadows 1983, That Long Silence 1988, The Binding Vine 1993, A Matter of Time 1996, The Intrusion and Other Stories 1994, Small Remedies 2000. *Leisure interests:* reading, music. *Address:* 409 41st Cross, Jayanagar V Block, Bangalore 560041, India. *Telephone:* (80) 6636228. *Fax:* (80) 6641137. *E-mail:* shashid@vsnl.com (Home).

DESJOYEAUX, Michel; French yachtsman; b. 16 July 1965; m. (divorced); three c.; began racing at age 18; set fastest time ever and became first man to achieve a solo, non-stop navigation of the world in less than 100 days (93

days 4 hours approx.); winner Whitbread 1985–86, Triangle du Soleil 1986, Twostar (with Jean Maurel) 1992, Solitaire du Figaro 1990, 1998, Leg 2 of Mini Transat 1991, Transat AG2R 1992, Figaro French Championships 1996, 1998, Multihull Trophy 1994, Spi Ouest 1997, Leg 1 of Transat AG2R (with Frank Cammas) 1998, Grand Prix de Fécamp (with Alain Gautier) 1999, Grand Prix de la Trinité (with Alain Gautier) 2000, Vendée Globe 2001 and others; transatlantic sprint Route du Rhum 2002; pioneered the swing keel early 1990s. *Publication:* L'enfant de la vallée des fons 2001. *Address:* Mer Agitée S.A.R.L., Port La Forêt, 29940 La Forêt Fouesnant, France (Office). *Telephone:* (2) 98-56-82-85 (Office). *Fax:* (2) 98-56-81-69 (Office). *E-mail:* meragiteesarl@aol.com (Office). *Website:* www.michel-desjoyeaux.com (Office).

DESKUR, HE Cardinal Andrzej Maria; Polish ecclesiastic; b. 29 Feb. 1924, Sancygniów; ordained 1950; consecrated Bishop (Titular See of Thenae) 1974, Archbishop 1980; cr. Cardinal 1985; Hon. Chair. Pontifical Council for Social Communications; Pres. Pontifical Acad. of the Immaculate Conception; mem. Congregation for Devotion to God and Discipline of Sacraments, Congregation for Canonization, Pontifical Council for Ministry of Health Service Staff, Pontifical Comm. of the Holy See. *Address:* Palazzo S. Carlo, 00120 Città del Vaticano, Rome, Italy. *Telephone:* (06) 69883597.

DESLONGCHAMPS, Pierre, FCIC, OC, OQ, PhD, FRSC, FRS; Canadian professor of chemistry; b. 8 May 1938, St-Lin, Québec; s. of Rodolphe Deslongchamps and Madeleine Magnan; m. 1st Micheline Renaud 1960 (divorced 1975); two s.; m. 2nd Shirley E. Thomas 1976 (divorced 1983); m. 3rd Marie-Marthe Leroux 1987; ed Montréal Univ., Univ. of New Brunswick; Postdoctoral Fellow Harvard Univ. 1965–66; Asst Prof. Montréal Univ. 1966–67, Asst Prof. Sherbrooke Univ. 1967–68, Assoc. Prof. 1968–72, Prof. 1972–; A. P. Sloan Fellowship 1970–72, E. W. R. Steacie Fellowship 1971–74; mem. Canadian Cttee of Scientists and Scholars 1993–, Société française de Chimie 1995, Foreign Assoc. mem. Acad. des Sciences de Paris 1995; fellow numerous academic socs.; AAAS; Fellow Guggenheim Foundation, 1979; several hon. degrees; Scientific Prize of Québec 1971, E. W. R. Steacie Prize 1974, Médaille Vincent (ACFAS) 1975, Izaak Walton Killam Memorial Scholarships 1976–77, Merck, Sharp and Dohme Lectures Award (CIC) 1976, Médaille Parizeau (ACFAS) 1979, Marie-Victorin Prize 1987, Alfred Bader Award (CSC) 1991, Canada Gold Medal for Science and Eng 1993, R. U. Lemieux Award for Organic Chem. (Chemical Soc. for Chem.) 1994. *Publications:* over 220 publs in the area of organic synthesis and the development of the concept of stereoelectronic effects in organic chemistry, Stereoelectronic Effects in Organic Chemistry 1983. *Leisure interests:* reading, fishing, hunting, canoeing. *Address:* Département de chimie, Institut de Pharmacologie, Université de Sherbrooke, Sherbrooke, Québec, J1H 5N4 (Office); 161 de Vimy, Sherbrooke, Québec J1J 3M6, Canada (Home). *Telephone:* (819) 564-5300 (Office); (819) 563-8788 (Home). *Fax:* (819) 820-6823 (Office). *E-mail:* pierre.deslongchamps@usherbrooke.ca (Office).

DESMAREST, Thierry Jean Jacques; French business executive and mining engineer; b. 18 Dec. 1945, Paris; s. of Jacques Desmarest and Edith Desmarest (née Barbe); m. Annick Geraux 1972; one s. two d.; ed Ecole Nat. Supérieure des Mines de Paris, Ecole Polytechnique; qualified mining engineer; worked as engineer with Mines Directorate, New Caledonia 1971–73, Dir of Mines and Geology 1973–75; Tech. Advisor Ministry of Industry 1975–78, of Econ. 1978–80; mem. Bd dirs. Total Algeria 1981–83, Dir for Latin America and W Africa 1983–87, for the Americas, France, Far East and Dir Man. and Econ. Div. 1988–89, CEO Total Exploration Production 1989–95, mem. Exec. Cttee 1989–95, Pres. and CEO Total Group (now Total Fina Elf, Pres. 1999–) 1995–; Pres. Elf Aquitaine 2000–; mem. Supervisory Bd Paribas 1995; Dir Asscn française des entreprises privées 2001–; Man. of the Year 1999, Nouvel Economiste. *Leisure interest:* skiing. *Address:* Total Fina Elf, 2 place de la Coupole, La Défense 6, 92078 Paris-la-Défense cedex, France (Office).

DESMEDT, John E., MD, PhD; Belgian neurologist; b. 19 Feb. 1926, Wavre; Prof. and Dir Brain Research Unit, Univ. of Brussels 1962–, fmr Chair. Dept of Physiology and Pathophysiology Medical Faculty; Pres. Int. Fed. for Clinical Neurophysiology 1985–; mem. Acad. Royale de Médecine de Belgique, Acad. Royale de Belgique; foreign mem. Accademia Nazionale dei Lincei (Italy), Acad. Nat. de Médecine (France); Fellow, New York Acad. of Sciences, Royal Soc. of Medicine, AAAS and mem. or hon. mem. of numerous other professional socs., int. scientific orgs. etc.; Francqui Prize 1972, Dautrebande Prize for Pathophysiology 1979, Maisin Prize (Fonds Nat. de la Recherche Scientifique) 1985; Dr. hc (Palermo) 1975, (Strasbourg) 1981; Grand Officier, Ordre de Léopold. *Publications:* New Developments in Electromyography and Clinical Neurophysiology (3 Vols) 1973, Motor Control Mechanisms in Health and Disease 1983. *Leisure interests:* horse-riding, jogging, fishing. *Address:* Brain Research Unit, University of Brussels, 20 rue Evers, Brussels 1000, Belgium. *Telephone:* (2) 538-08-44. *Fax:* (2) 538-29-05.

DESMOND, Richard Clive; British publishing and media executive; b. 8 Dec. 1951; s. of Cyril Desmond and Millie Desmond; m. Janet Robertson 1983; one s.; Advertisement Exec. Thomson Newspapers 1967–68; Group Advertisement Man. Beat Publs Ltd 1968–74; f. Northern & Shell Network 1974 (Chair. 1974–); launched Int. Musician (magazine) 1974; Demonde Advertising 1976–89; Publr Next, Fitness, Cook's Weekly, Venture, Penthouse, Bicycle, Stamps, Electric Blue, Rock CD, Guitar, For Woman, Attitude, Arsenal, Liverpool; f. Fantasy Channel 1995, OK! Magazine 1993–, OK! TV 1999–;

owner Express Newspapers 2000–. *Leisure interest:* drums. *Address:* Express Newspapers, Ludgate House, 245 Blackfriars Road, London, SE1 9UX, England (Office). *Telephone:* (20) 7928-8000 (Office). *Fax:* (20) 7922-7577 (Office). *E-mail:* ed98@cityscape.co.uk (Office).

DESPIĆ, Aleksandar, DrPhysChem; Serbia and Montenegro (Serbian) electrochemist; b. 6 Jan. 1927, Belgrade; s. of Ranko Despić and Vukosava Despić (née Kalimančić); m. Zorica Vukadinović 1954 (died 2002); ed Belgrade Univ., London Univ.; served World War II; teacher, Prof. of Physical Chem. Belgrade Univ. 1951–92; worked in Pa Univ. 1957–59, 1967–68; Chair. Serbian Chemical Soc. 1973–77, Union of Chemical Socs of Yugoslavia 1978–81; mem. Serbian Acad. of Sciences and Arts, Vice-Pres., Pres. 1994–99; mem. Croatian and Slovenian Acads of Sciences and Arts, European Acad. of Sciences and Arts; Hon. Chair. Serbian Chemical Soc. 1979–; Chair. Exec. Bd Museum of Science and Tech. in Belgrade, Foundation for Devt of Scientific and Artistic Youth; Head of Div. of Surface Tech. and Energy Inst. of Tech. Sciences, Serbian Acad. of Sciences; October Prize 1968, 7 July Prize 1990, Karić Award 1999. *Publications:* over 180 scientific works, 22 invention patents, over 15 monographs and textbooks including On Theory of Mechanisms of Chemical Reactions 1965, On Theory of Dendritic Growth 1968, Aluminium-Air Battery with Salt Solution 1976, Electrochemical Deposition of Alloys and Composites 1995, numerous articles in Yugoslavian and foreign scientific periodicals. *Address:* Serbian Academy of Sciences and Arts, Knez Mihailova str. 35, 11000 Belgrade, Serbia and Montenegro. *Telephone:* (11) 323-9492 (Home). *Fax:* (11) 638-792. *E-mail:* adespic@eunet.yu (Home).

DESYATNIKOV, Leonid Arkadievich; Russian composer; b. 1955, Kharkov, Ukraine; ed Leningrad State Conservatory; mem. Composers' Union 1979–; Golden Sheep Prize 2000. *Works include:* opera: Poor Lisa; ballet: Love Song in Minor; tango-operita: Astor Piazzola's Maria de Buenos Aires (Grammy Award); symphony: Sacred Winter; film scores: Sunset 1990, Lost in Siberia 1991, Capital Punishment 1992, Touch 1992, Moscow Nights 1994, Katia Izmailova 1994, Hammer and Sickle 1994, Giselle's Mania 1995, The Prisoner of the Mountains 1996, The One Who is More Tender 1996, Moscow 2000, His Wife's Diary 2000. *Address:* Nepokorennykh prosp. 16, korp. 1, apt. 177, 195220 St. Petersburg, Russia (Home). *Telephone:* (812) 545-20-98 (Home).

DETREKŐI, Ákos, DSc; Hungarian civil engineer and university rector; b. 27 Nov. 1939, Budapest; m.; two c.; ed Tech. Univ., Budapest; Asst Faculty of Civil Eng, Tech. Univ., Budapest 1963–68, Sr Asst 1968–72, Lecturer Dept of Geodesy 1963–78, Dept of Photogrammetry 1978–, Assoc. Prof. 1972–80, Prof., Head of Dept 1980–, Dean Faculty of Civil Eng 1986–90, Rector 1997–; Lecturer Technische Univ., Dresden 1980–83; now Hon. Pres. Hungarian Humboldt Soc., Hungarian Soc. of Surveying, Remote Sensing and Cartography 1994–; mem. Hungarian Acad. of Sciences Cttee of Geodesy 1975 (Chair. 1990–97), Hungarian Council for Space Research 1995–; Fasching Antal Medal 1988, Lazar Deák Medal 1993, Szent-Györgyi Albert Prize 1996, Humboldt Medal 1996. *Publications:* one book and numerous contribs. and articles. *Leisure interest:* music. *Address:* Department of Photogrammetry, Budapesti Műszaki és Gazdaságtudományi Egyetem, Müegyetem rkp. 3, 1521 Budapest Nagybányai u. 43/B, Budapest, Hungary (Office). *Telephone:* (1) 4631187 (Office). *Fax:* (1) 4633084 (Office).

DETTORI, Lanfranco, MBE; Italian flat race jockey; b. 15 Dec. 1970, Milan; s. of 13-times Italian champion jockey Gianfranco Dettori and Iris Maria Niemen; m. Catherine Allen 1997; has ridden races in England, France, Germany, Italy, USA, Dubai, Australia, Hong Kong and other countries in the Far East 1992–; 1,000 rides and 215 wins in UK 1995; horses ridden include Lamtarra, Barathea, Vettori, Mark of Distinction, Balanchine, Moonshell, Lochsong, Classic Cliché, Dubai Millennium, Daylami, Sakhee; maj. race victories include St Leger (twice), The Oaks (twice), The Breeders Cup Mile, Arc de Triomphe (twice), French 2,000 Guineas (twice), English 1,000 Guineas, Queen Elizabeth II Stakes, Prix L'Abbaye, The Japan Cup (twice), The Dubai World Cup; rode winners of all seven races at Ascot on 28 Oct. 1996; survived air crash 2000; launched signature range of food 2001; Jockey of the Year 1994, 1995, BBC Sports Personality of the Year 1996, Int. Sports Personality of the Year, Variety Club 2000. *Publication:* A Year in the Life of Frankie Dettori 1996. *Leisure interests:* golf, wine, cooking. *Address:* c/o Peter Burrell, Classic Management, 53 Stewart's Grove, London, SW3 6PH, England (Office). *Telephone:* (20) 7352-4448. *Fax:* (20) 7352-9697 (Office). *E-mail:* pburrell@classicmanagement.com (Office).

DETWEILER, David Kenneth, V.M.D., MS; American professor of physiology; b. 23 Oct. 1919, Philadelphia, Pa; s. of David Rieser Detweiler and Pearl I. (Overholt) Detweiler; two s. four d.; ed Univ. of Pennsylvania; Asst Instructor Veterinary School, Univ. of Pa 1942–43, Instructor 1943–45, Assoc. Instructor 1945–47, Asst Prof. 1947–51, Assoc. Prof. 1951–62, Prof. of Physiology and Head of Physiology Lab. 1962–90, Dir Comparative Cardiovascular Studies Unit 1960–90, Prof. Emer. 1990–; Guggenheim Fellow 1955–56; mem. Inst. of Medicine, NAS; mem. Nat. Acads. of Practice 1989; Hon. DSc (Ohio State Univ.) 1966; Hon. MVD (Vienna) 1968; Hon. DMV (Turin) 1969; Gaines Award and Medal, American Veterinary Asscn 1960; Distinguished Veterinarian Award, Pa Veterinary Medical Asscn 1989; elected to Hon. Roll American Veterinary Asscn 1990; D. K. Detweiler Prize for Cardiology established by German-speaking group of World Veterinary Medicine Asscn 1982; David K. Detweiler Conf. Room dedicated in School of Veterinary Medicine, Univ. of Pa 1993, School's Centennial Medal 1994,

Certificate of Appreciation for Drug Evaluation and Research Seminar Program, Food and Drug Admin. 1998. *Publications:* some 170 publications on cardiology and cardiovascular physiology. *Leisure interests:* art, music, languages. *Address:* Waverly Heights, Apt. A212, 1400 Waverly Road, Gladwyne, PA 19035, USA (Home). *Telephone:* (610) 645-8964. *Fax:* (610) 645-8719.

DEUBA, Sher Bahadur, MA; Nepalese politician; b. 12 June 1946, Angra, Dadeldhura Dist; ed Tribhuvan Univ.; Chair. Far Western Students Cttee Kathmandu 1965; served a total of nine years imprisonment for political activities 1966–85; Founder mem. Nepal Students' Union 1970; Research Fellow, LSE 1988–90; active in Popular Movt for Restoration of Democracy in Nepal 1991; mem. Parl. 1991–; Minister of Home Affairs; Leader, Parl. Party, Nepali Congress 1994; Prime Minister 1995–97, 2001–02, Minister of Foreign Affairs and Defence 2001–02. *Address:* c/o Office of the Prime Minister, Central Secretariat, Singha Durbar, Kathmandu, Nepal.

DEUKMEJIAN, George, JD; American state governor; b. 6 June 1928, Albany, NY; s. of C. George and Alice (née Gairdan) Deukmejian; m. Gloria M. Saatjian 1957; one s. two d.; ed Siena Coll. and St John's Univ.; admitted to NY State Bar 1952, Calif. Bar 1956, Supreme Court Bar 1970; partner Riedman, Dalessi, Deukmejian & Woods, Long Beach, Calif. –1979; mem. Calif. Ass. 1963–67, Calif. Senate (Minority Leader) 1967–79; Attorney-Gen., Calif. 1979–82; Gov. of California 1983–90; partner Sidley and Austin 1991–2000; Republican. *Address:* 5366 East Broadway, Long Beach, CA 90803-3549, USA (Office).

DEUTCH, John, PhD; American professor of chemistry; b. 27 July 1938, Brussels, Belgium; s. of Michael J. and Rachel Fischer Deutch; m. Pat Lyons; three s.; ed Amherst Coll. and MIT; Systems Analyst, Office of Sec. for Defense 1961–65; Fellow, N.A.S./N.R.C. Nat. Bureau of Standards 1966–67; Asst Prof. Princeton Univ. 1967–70; mem. Faculty, MIT 1970–, Prof. of Chemistry 1971–; Chair. Dept of Chem. 1976–77, Dean, School of Science 1982–85, Provost 1985–90, Inst. Prof. 1990–; Dir of Energy Research, Dept of Energy 1977–79, Acting Asst Sec. 1979, Under-Sec. 1979–80; Under Sec. for Acquisition and Tech. Dept of Defense 1993–94, Deputy Sec. 1994–95; Dir CIA 1995–96; mem. White House Science Council 1985–89; mem. Bd of Dirs. Citicorp, CMS Energy, Parkin-Elmer Corpn, Schlumberger, Science Applications Inc.; other professional and public appts.; mem. American Physics Soc., American Chem. Soc., American Acad. of Arts and Sciences, Council on Foreign Relations, President's Foreign Intelligence Advisory Cttee 1990–94, Trilateral Comm. 1991; Sloan Fellow 1969–71; Guggenheim Fellow 1974; DSc hc (Amherst Coll.) 1978; DPhil hc (Lowell) 1986; recipient of awards from Dept of State and Dept of Energy. *Publications:* research articles. *Address:* Massachusetts Institute of Technology, 77 Massachusetts Avenue, Cambridge, MA 02139, USA.

DEUTEKOM, Cristina; opera singer; b. 28 Aug. 1938, Amsterdam; one d.; first maj. appearance at Munich State Opera 1966, then at Vienna Festwochen; sang at Metropolitan Opera, New York 1967; has sung in all the maj. opera houses in Europe, especially Italy and USA; specializes in bel canto operas by Rossini, Bellini and Donizetti and the great Verdi operas; recordings for EMI, Decca and Philips; Grand Prix du Disque 1969, 1972. *Leisure interests:* driving round the world, singing, shopping (especially for shoes).

DEV, Kapil (see Kapil Dev).

DEVAN NAIR, Chengara Veetil; Singaporean politician and trade unionist (retd); b. 5 Aug. 1923, Malacca, Malaysia; s. of I.V.K. Nair and Sri Devi; m. Avadai Dhanam 1953; three s. one d.; ed Victoria Secondary School, Singapore; teacher, St Andrew's School, Singapore 1949–51; Gen. Sec. Singapore Teachers' Union 1949–51; detained 1951–53; Convenor and mem. Cen. Exec. Cttee, People's Action Party (PAP) 1954–56; Sec. Singapore Factory and Shopworkers Union 1954–56; detained 1956–59; Political Sec. Ministry of Educ. 1959–60; Chair. Prisons Inquiry Comm. 1960; Chair. Adult Educ. Bd 1960–64; Sec. Nat. Trades Union Congress (NTUC) and Dir of its Research Unit, Singapore 1964–65; mem. House of Reps., Malaysia 1964–69; Founder and First Sec.-Gen. Democratic Action Party, Malaysia 1964–69; Dir NTUC Research Unit 1969–81; Sec.-Gen. NTUC 1969–79, Pres. 1979–81; Pres. ICFTU Asian Regional Org. 1975–81; MP for Anson, Singapore 1979, re-elected 1980; resgnd as MP and Pres. NTUC Oct. 1981; Pres. of Repub. of Singapore 1981–85; Consultant to AFL-CIO 1985–87; Fellow Inst. of Advanced Study, Ind. Univ., USA 1985–87; Fellow Southeast Asia Program Cornell Univ., USA; Hon. DLitt (Univ. of Singapore) 1976; Public Service Star, Singapore 1963. *Publications:* Singapore Socialism that Works, Who Lives if Malaysia Dies?, Tomorrow—the Peril and the Promise, Asian Labour and the Dynamics of Change, Not By Wages Alone, Singapore: Reflective Essays, Singapore: The Promise and the Breach. *Leisure interests:* swimming, reading, music. *Address:* 176 Buckingham Drive, Hamilton, Ont., L9C 2G7, Canada. *Telephone:* (905) 575-0739. *Fax:* (905) 575-7973.

DEVANEY, John Francis, CEng, FIEE, FIMechE; British business executive; b. 25 June 1946; s. of the late George Devaney and Alice Ann Devaney; two s. one d.; ed St. Mary's Coll., Blackburn and Univ. of Sheffield; worked for Perkins Engines 1968–69, mfg positions in Peterborough 1968–76, Project Man., Ohio, USA 1976–77, Pres. 1983–88, Group Vice-Pres. European Components Group, Peterborough 1988, Group Vice-Pres. Enterprises Group, Toronto, Canada 1988–89; Chair., CEO and Group Vice-Pres. Kelsey-Hayes Corpn, Detroit, Mich., USA 1989–92; Man. Dir Eastern Electricity PLC (later

Eastern Group PLC) 1992, CEO 1993, Exec. Chair. 1995–98; Dir EXEL Logistics (formed with merger of Nat. Freight Corpn with Ocean Group) 1996, Chair. 2000–02; Chair. Marconi PLC Dec. 2002–; Founder and Chair. British Energy; Chair. Liberata –2002; Dir and fmr Chair. EA Technology; Dir (non-exec.) HSBC (fmrly Midland Bank) 1994–, British Steel 1998–; Pres. Electricity Asscn 1994–95, Inst. for Customer Services 1998–. *Leisure interests:* skiing, golf, tennis, sailing. *Address:* Marconi PLC, Head Office, 4th Floor, Regents Place, 338 Euston Road, London, NW1 3BT, England (Office). *Telephone:* (20) 7493-8484 (Office). *Fax:* (20) 7493-1974 (Office). *Website:* www .marconi.com (Office).

DEVE GOWDA, Haradanahalli Dodde Gowda; Indian politician; b. 18 May 1933, Haradan ahalli; Chennamma Deve Gowda; m.; four s. two d.; ed Govt polytechnic inst.; trained as civil engineer; ran contracting business; elected to Karnataka State Legis. in 1960s; imprisoned during state of emergency in 1970s; Minister of Public Works and Irrigation, Karnataka until 1980; Chief Minister of Karnataka 1995–96; fmr mem. Lok Sabha; leader multiparty United Front 1996; Prime Minister, Minister of Home and Agric., Science and Tech., Personnel and Atomic Energy 1996–97. *Address:* 5 Safdarjung Lane, New Delhi 110011, India. *Telephone:* (11) 3794499.

DEVERS, Gail, BA; American athlete; b. 19 Nov. 1966, Seattle; m. Ron Roberts 1988 (divorced 1992); ed Univ. of California; holds record for most World Championship gold medals won by a woman (5): 100m, (1993), 100m hurdles (1993, 1995, 1999), 4x100m relay (1997); Olympic champion 100m (1992, 1996); Olympic gold medal 4x100m relay (1996); US champion 100m hurdles (seven times); est. Gail Devers Foundation. *Address:* Elite International Sports and Management, 1034 South Brentwood Boulevard, Suite 1530, Saint Louis, MO 03117-1215, USA (Office). *Website:* www.gaildevers .com.

DEVESI, Sir Baddeley, GCMG, GCVO; Solomon Islands politician and administrator; b. 16 Oct. 1941, East Tathiboko, Guadalcanal; s. of Mostyn Tagabasoe Norua and Laisa Otu; m. June Marie Barley 1969; four s. three d. (one d. deceased); ed St Mary's School, Maravovo, King George VI School, Solomon Islands, Ardmore Teachers' Training Coll., Auckland, New Zealand; Teacher, Melanesian Mission schools, Solomon Islands 1965–66; elected mem. British Solomon Islands Legis. and Exec. Councils 1967–68; Lecturer, Solomon Islands Teachers' Coll. 1970–72; Asst Sec. for Social Services 1972, Internal Affairs 1972; Dist Officer, S. Malaita 1973–75; Perm. Sec. Ministry of Works and Public Utilities 1976, Ministry of Transport and Communications 1977; Gov.-Gen. of Solomon Islands 1978–88; Minister for Foreign Affairs and Trade Relations 1989–91; Deputy Prime Minister and Minister for Home Affairs 1990–92, for Health and Medical Sciences 1992; Deputy Prime Minister and Minister for Transport, Works, Communications and Aviation 1996–2000; Chancellor, Univ. of S Pacific 1980–83; KStJ; Hon. DUniv. *Leisure interests:* swimming, lawn tennis, cricket, reading, snooker. *Address:* c/o Office of Deputy Prime Minister, Honiara, Solomon Islands.

DEVI, V. S. Rama, MA, LLM; Indian politician and lawyer; b. 15 Jan. 1934, Chebrolu; d. of V. V. Subbiah and Venkataratnamma; m. V. S. Ramavatar; one s. two d.; advocate Andhra Pradesh High Court 1959, various roles in Legis. Dept, then Special Sec. 1985; mem. Secr. of Law Comm. and Indian Govt 1985; Sec. Legis. Dept, Ministry of Law 1989–92; officiating Chief Election Commr 1990; Gov. of Himachal Pradesh 1997–1999 of Karnataka 1999–; Judicial mem. Customs, Excise and Gold Control Appellate Tribunal 1982–83; Sec.-Gen. Rajya Sabha. *Publications:* 20 books. *Address:* Raj Bhavan, Bangalore, India (Office). *Telephone:* (80) 2254101 (Office). *Fax:* (80) 2258150 (Office).

DeVITO, Danny; American actor and director; b. 17 Nov. 1944, New Jersey; m. Rhea Perlman 1982; two s. two d.; ed American Acad. of Dramatic Arts, Wilfred Acad. of Hair and Beauty Culture; Golden Globe Award for Taxi 1979, Emmy Award 1981. *Stage appearances include:* The Man with a Flower in his Mouth, Down the Morning Line The Line of Least Existence, The Shrinking Bride, Call me Charlie, Comedy of Errors, Merry Wives of Windsor, Three by Pirandello, One Flew Over the Cuckoo's Nest. *Films include:* Lady Liberty, Scalawag, Hurry Up or I'll be 30, One Flew Over the Cuckoo's Nest, Deadly Hero, Car Wash, The Van, The World's Greatest Lover, Goin' South, Going Ape, Terms of Endearment, Romancing the Stone, Johnny Dangerously, Head Office, Jewel of the Nile, Wiseguys, Ruthless People, My Little Pony (voice), Tin Men, Throw Momma from the Train (also Dir), Twins, War of the Roses (also Dir), Other People's Money 991, Batman Returns 1992, Hoffa (also Producer, Dir) 1992, Renaissance Man 1994, Junior 1994, Get Shorty (also Co-Producer), Matilda (also Dir, Co-Producer), Mars Attacks 1997, The Rainmaker 1997, LA Confidential 1997, Man on the Moon 1999; Producer Feeling Minnesota 1996, Gattaca 1997, Living Out Loud 1998, The Virgin Suicides 1999, Stretch Armstrong 1999, Pittsburgh 1999, Hospitality Suite 1999, Man On the Moon 1999, Drowning Mona 2000, Screwed 2000, Heist 2001, What's the Worst That Could Happen? 2001, Death to Smoochy 2002, Austin Powers in Goldmember 2002. *Television includes:* Taxi (also Dir), Mary (Dir only), Valentine, The Rating Game (Dir), All the Kids Do It, A Very Special Christmas Party, Two Daddies? (voice), The Selling of Vince DeAngelo (Dir), Amazing Stories (also Dir), The Simpsons (voice). *Address:* c/o Fred Specktor, Creative Artists Agency, 9830 Wilshire Boulevard, Beverly Hills, CA 90212, USA.

DEVLIN, Dean; American actor, screenplay writer and producer; b. 27 Aug. 1962; George Pal Memorial Award 1998. *Film produced:* The Patriot 2000. *Films written and produced:* Stargate 1994 (Best Picture, Acad. of Science Fiction, Fantasy and Horror Films, Readers' Choice Award, Sci-Fi Universe magazine), Independence Day 1996 (Best Picture, Acad. of Science Fiction, Fantasy and Horror Films, People's Choice Best Picture), Godzilla 1998. *Film screenplay:* Universal Solider 1992. *Films acted in:* My Bodyguard 1980, The Wild Life 1984, Real Genius 1985, City Limits 1985, Martians Go Home 1990, Moon 44 1990, Total Exposure 1991. *TV series:* The Visitor (creator, exec. producer) 1997. *TV appearances in:* North Beach 1985, Rawhide 1985, Hard Copy 1987, Generations 1989; guest appearances in: LA Law, Happy Days, Misfits of Science. *Address:* c/o Creative Artists Agency, 9830 Wilshire Boulevard, Beverly Hills, CA 90212; Astaire East, 3rd Floor, 10202 W Washington Boulevard, Culver City, CA 90232, USA (Office). *Telephone:* (310) 244-4300 (Office).

DEVLIN, Stuart Leslie, AO, CMG; Australian goldsmith, silversmith and designer; b. 9 Oct. 1931, Geelong; s. of Richard and Jesse Devlin; m. 1st Kim Hose 1962; m. 2nd Carole Hedley-Saunders 1986; ed Gordon Inst. of Tech., Geelong, Royal Melbourne Inst. of Tech. and Royal Coll. of Art; art teacher, Victoria Educ. Dept 1950–58, Royal Coll. of Art 1958–60; Harkness Fellow, New York 1960–62; Lecturer, Prahan Tech. Coll., Melbourne 1962; Inspector of Art in Tech. Schools, Victoria Educ. Dept 1964–65; working as goldsmith, silversmith and designer in London 1965–; exhbns of gold and silver in numerous cities in UK, USA, Australia, Middle East, etc.; has executed many commissions for commemorative coins in gold and silver for various countries; designed and made cutlery for State Visit to Paris 1972, Duke of Edinburgh Trophy for World Driving Championship 1973, silver to commemorate opening of Sydney Opera House 1973, Grand National Trophy 1975 and Regalia for Order of Australia 1975–76; Centrepiece for Royal Engineers to commemorate their work in Northern Ireland 1984; Bas-relief portrait HRH Princess of Wales for Wedgwood 1986; devised and executed Champagne Diamond Exhbn 1987; designed and made Sydney 2000 Olympic coins 1997; designed and made Millennium Commemorative dishes for Goldsmiths' Co. and Information Technologists' Co. 2000; granted Royal Warrant (goldsmith and jeweller to HM Queen Elizabeth II) 1982; mem. Court of Wardens, Goldsmiths' Co. 1992, Prime Warden, 1996–97; Vice-Chair. Intergraph Graphics Users' Group, UK 1996–98; Hon. Dr of Arts (Royal Melbourne Inst. of Tech.) 2000. *Leisure interests:* work, wind-surfing, tennis. *Address:* Highwater House, Kingston Gorse, West Sussex, BN16 1SQ, England. *Telephone:* (1903) 858939.

DEVONSHIRE, 11th Duke of, cr. 1694, Baron Cavendish, Earl of Devonshire, Marquess of Hartington, Earl of Burlington, Baron Cavendish (UK); **Andrew Robert Buxton Cavendish,** KG, PC, MC; British landowner; b. 2 Jan. 1920; s. of 10th Duke of Devonshire and Lady Mary Cecil; m. Hon. Deborah Vivian Freeman-Mitford 1941; one s. two d.; ed Eton and Trinity Coll. Cambridge; served Coldstream Guards 1939–45; Conservative parl. cand. 1945, 1950; succeeded father 1950; Pres. Bldg Socs. Asscn 1954–61; Parl. Under-Sec. of State for Commonwealth Relations 1960–62; Minister of State, Commonwealth Relations Office 1962–64 and for Colonial Affairs 1963–64; Chancellor of Manchester Univ. 1965–86; Steward, Jockey Club 1966–69; mem. Horserace Totalisator Bd 1977–86; Trustee, Nat. Gallery 1960–68; Pres. Royal Hosp. and Home, Putney 1954–91, Lawn Tennis Asscn 1955–61, Royal Nat. Inst. for Blind 1979–85, Nat. Asscn for Deaf Children 1978–95; Vice-Pres. London Library 1993–; Chair. Grand Council, British Empire Cancer Campaign 1956–81, Thoroughbred Breeders' Asscn 1978–81; Hon. LLD (Manchester, Sheffield, Liverpool, Newfoundland). *Publication:* Park Top: A Romance of the Turf 1976. *Address:* Chatsworth, Bakewell, Derbyshire DE45 1PP; 4 Chesterfield Street, London, W1J 5JF, England. *Telephone:* (1246) 582204; (20) 7499-5803. *Fax:* (1246) 582937 (Office).

DEVRIES, William Castle, MD; American surgeon; b. 19 Dec. 1943, Brooklyn; s. of Hendrik Devries and Cathryn L. Castle; seven c.; ed Univ. of Utah; intern Duke Univ. Medical Center 1970–71; Resident in cardiovascular and thoracic surgery 1971–79; Asst Prof. of Surgery, Univ. of Utah –1984; Chief of Thoracic Surgery, Salt Lake Hosp., Va –1984; Pres. De Vries & Assocs. 1988–99; Surgeon Hardin Memorial Hosp., Elizabethtown, Ky 1999–; mem. American Medical Asscn, Soc. of Thoracic Surgeons. *Address:* Hardin Memorial Hospital, 913 N Dixie Avenue, Elizabethtown, KY 42701, USA (Office).

DEWEY, John Frederick, MA, PhD, DSc, ScD, FRS, FGS; British professor of geology; b. 22 May 1937, London; s. of John Edward Dewey and Florence Nellie Mary Dewey; m. Frances Mary Blackhurst 1961; one s. one d.; ed Bancroft's School, Univ. of London; lecturer, Univ. of Manchester 1960–64, Univ. of Cambridge 1964–70; Prof. Univ. of Albany, NY 1970–82; Prof. Univ. of Durham 1982–86; Prof. of Geology, Univ. of Oxford 1986–2000, Fellow Univ. Coll. 1986–; Prof. of Geology, Univ. of Calif. Davis 2000–; mem. Academia Europaea 1990; Foreign mem. NAS 1997; Lyell Medal, Geological Soc. of London, T.N. George Medal, Univ. of Glasgow, Penrose Medal, Geological Soc. of America, Arthur Holmes Medal, European Union of Geosciences, Wollaston Medal, Geological Soc. of London, Fourmarie Medal, Belgian Acad. of Sciences. *Publications:* 138 papers in scientific journals. *Leisure interests:* skiing, tennis, cricket, model railways, watercolour painting, British music 1850–1950. *Address:* University College, Oxford, OX1 4BH, England; Department of Geology, University of California, Davis, CA 95616 (Office); 748 Elmwood Drive, Davis, CA 95616, USA (Home). *Telephone:* (530) 754-7472 (Office); (530) 757-7519 (Home). *E-mail:* dewey@ geology.ucdavis.edu (Office).

DEWINE, R. Michael, BS, JD; American politician; b. 5 Jan. 1947, Springfield, Ohio; s. of Richard DeWine and Jean DeWine; m. Frances Struewing 1967; four s. four d.; ed Miami Univ. Oxford, Ohio and Ohio Northern Univ.; admitted to Bar, Ohio 1972, US Supreme Court 1977; Asst prosecuting attorney, Green County, Xenia, Ohio 1973–75, prosecuting attorney 1977–81; mem. Ohio Senate 1981–82; mem. US House of Reps. 1983–90; Lt-Gov. of Ohio 1991–94; Senator from Ohio 1995–; Republican. *Address:* US Senate, 140 Russell State Building, Washington, DC 20510-0001 (Office); 2587 Conley Road, Cedarville, OH 45314-9525, USA (Home).

DEWOST, Jean-Louis; French European Community official; b. 6 Sept. 1937, Dunkirk; s. of Emmanuel Dewost and Colette Ruyssen; m. Agnès Huet 1967; one s. two d.; ed Univ. de Paris, Inst. d'Etudes Politiques de Paris and Ecole Nat. d'Admin; Jr official, Conseil d'Etat 1967–69; Asst Man. Industrial Affairs, European Org. for Devt and Construction of Space Vehicle Launchers (CECLES/ELDO) 1962–72, Dir Finance and Econ. Planning 1972–73; Maître des Requêtes, Conseil d'Etat 1972, Conseiller d'Etat 1986, Pres. de la Section Sociale, 2001–; legal adviser EC Council Legal Service 1973–85, Jurisconsulte 1986–87; Dir-Gen. EC Legal Service 1987–2001; Prof. Inst. d'Etudes Politiques, Paris; Chevalier, Légion d'honneur, Officier, Ordre nat. du Mérite, Grand Officier, Order of White Rose of Finland. *Publications:* several Publs on law and EC law. *Leisure interests:* tennis, swimming, opera. *Address:* Conseil d'Etat, 75100 Paris, France (Office). *Telephone:* (2) 296-24-12 (Office). *Fax:* (2) 296-30-86 (Office).

DEXTER, Colin, OBE, MA (Cantab.), MA (Oxon.); British author; b. 29 Sept. 1930, Stamford, Lincs.; s. of Alfred Dexter and Dorothy Dexter; one s. one d.; ed Stamford School, Christ's Coll., Cambridge; nat. service (Royal Signals) 1948–50, taught Classics 1954–66; Sr Asst Sec. Oxford Delegacy of Local Examinations 1966–88; Gold Dagger, Crime Writers' Asscn (twice), Silver Dagger (twice), Cartier Diamond Dagger, Freedom of the City of Oxford 2001. *Publications:* Last Bus to Woodstock 1975, Last Seen Wearing 1977, The Silent World of Nicholas Quinn 1977, Service of All the Dead 1979, The Dead of Jericho 1981, The Riddle of the Third Mile 1983, The Secret of Annexe 3 1986, The Wench is Dead 1989, The Jewel that was Ours 1991, The Way through the Woods 1992, Morse's Greatest Mystery and Other Stories 1993, The Daughters of Cain 1994, Death is Now my Neighbour 1996, The Remorseful Day 1999. *Leisure interests:* reading, music, crosswords (fmr nat. crossword champion). *Address:* 456 Banbury Road, Oxford, OX2 7RG, England.

DHANABALAN, Suppiah, BA; Singaporean company director; b. 8 Aug. 1937; m. Tan Khoon Hiap 1963; one s. one d.; ed Victoria School and Univ. of Malaya; Asst Sec. Ministry of Finance 1960–61; Sr Industrial Economist, Deputy Dir (Operations and Finance) Econ. Devt Bd 1961–68; Vice-Pres., Exec. Vice-Pres. Devt Bank of Singapore 1968–78, Chair. 1998–; MP 1976–96; Sr Minister of State, Ministry of Nat. Devt 1978–79, Ministry of Foreign Affairs 1979–80; Minister of Foreign Affairs 1980–88, Culture 1981–84, Community Devt 1984–86, Nat. Devt 1987–92, of Trade and Industry 1992–93; Chair. Parameswara Holdings 1994–; Sr Adviser, Nuri Holdings (S) Pte. Ltd 1994–99; Chair. Singapore Airlines Ltd 1996–98; Chair. Temasek Holdings (Pte.) Ltd 1996–. *Leisure interests:* reading, golf. *Address:* Development Bank of Singapore, 6 Shenton Way, DBS Building, Tower One, Singapore 068809. *Telephone:* 68785101. *Fax:* 62218026. *E-mail:* sdhana@dbs.com (Office). *Website:* www.dbs.com (Office).

DHANAPALA, Jayantha C. P., MA; Sri Lankan diplomatist; b. 30 Dec. 1938, Colombo; m. Maureen Elhart; one s. one d.; ed Univ. of Peradeniya, Univ. of London, England, American Univ., Washington, DC, USA; corp. exec. in pvt sector 1962–65; diplomatic appointments in People's Repub. of China, UK and USA 1965–77; Dir Non-Aligned Movt Div., Ministry of Foreign Affairs 1978–80, Additional Foreign Sec. 1992–95; Deputy High Commr to India 1981–83; Amb. and Perm. Rep. to UN, Geneva, Switzerland 1984-87, Dir UN Inst. for Disarmament Research 1987–92; Amb. to USA (also Accred to Mexico) 1995–97; UN Under-Sec.-Gen. for Disarmament Affairs Feb. 1998–; Pres. Review and Extension Conf. of Treaty on the Non-Proliferation of Nuclear Weapons 1995; Rep. of UN to Conf. on Disarmament; mem. Canberra Comm., Australia; Diplomat-in-Residence, Center for Non-Proliferation Studies, Monterey Inst. of Int. Studies, Calif., USA, 'Jit' Trainor Award for Distinction in the Conduct of Diplomacy. *Publications include:* China and the Third World 1984, Nuclear War, Nuclear Proliferation and Their Consequences (jtly.) 1985. *Address:* United Nations, United Nations Plaza, New York, NY 10017, U.S.A. *Telephone:* (212) 963-1232 (Office). *Fax:* (212) 963-4879 (Office).

DHANARAJAN, Dato' Gajaraj (Raj), PhD; Malaysian educationalist; ed Univ. of Madras, India, Univ. of London, Univ. of Aston, UK; research officer and lecturer, School of Biological Sciences, Univ. of Science, Malaysia, Assoc. Prof. of Distance Educ. and Deputy Dir Centre for Off-Campus Studies; Assoc. Dir (Academic) Open Learning Inst. of Hong Kong (now Open Univ. of Hong Kong) 1989–91, Dir 1991–95, Prof. 1992–95, Prof. Emer. 1995–; Pres. and CEO The Commonwealth of Learning, Vancouver 1995–; fmr Sec.-Gen. Asian Asscn of Open Univs.; fmr educational adviser Int. Union for the Conservation of Nature; Hon. Fellow Coll. of Preceptors, London 1996–; several hon. degrees; Asian Asscn of Open Univs. Meritorious Service Award 1997; Order of Chivalry, State of Penang 1994. *Address:* The Commonwealth of Learning,

1285 West Broadway, Suite 600, Vancouver, BC, V6H 3X8, Canada (Office). *Telephone:* (604) 775-8200 (Office). *Fax:* (604) 775-8210 (Office). *E-mail:* gdhan@col.org (Office). *Website:* www.col.org/gdhan (Office).

DHANIN CHEARAVANONT; Thai business executive; b. Bangkok; ed secondary school, Shantou, China and commercial school, Hong Kong; Chair. CP (Charoen Pokphand) Group (conglomerate of 250 cos. involved in agri-business, petrochemicals, motorcycles, autoparts, telecommunications, etc.) and owner of TM Int. Bank, Shanghai (first foreign-owned bank with head office in China); adviser to Chinese Govt during Hong Kong negotiations with Britain. *Address:* CP Group, C.P. Tower, 313 Silom Road, Bangrak, Bangkok 10500, Thailand. *Telephone:* (662) 638-2000. *Fax:* (662) 638-2676. *E-mail:* pr@cpthailand.com. *Website:* www.cpthailand.com.

DHAR, Bansi, F.I.M.A., A.M.P.; Indian business executive; b. 7 March 1930, Delhi; s. of late Murli Dhar and Swaroop Devi; m. 1st Urmila Bansidhar 1953 (deceased); m. 2nd Suman Bansidhar 1976; three s.; ed Delhi Univ., Harvard Univ.; trainee, Eng Dept DCM Ltd 1952, various man. appts., Chair. of Bd and Man. Dir DCM Shriram Industries Ltd 1990–; Chair. Bd Daurala Organics Ltd, Indital Tintoria Ltd, DCM Hyundai Ltd, Hindustan Vacuum Glass Ltd, DCM Remy Ltd; mem. Bd Dirs. several cos.; mem. Exec. Cttee, Fed. Indian Chambers of Commerce and Industry (and fmr Pres.), Indian Chemical Mfrs Asscn; Vice-Chair. Shriram Scientific and Industrial Research Foundation; Dir Indian Trade Promotion Org.; Chair. Delhi Asscn of the Deaf; Pres. Delhi Badminton Asscn; fmr Pres. All India Org. of Employers, Indian Sugar Mills Asscn, Delhi Factory Owners Asscn, Indian Council of Arbitration; Fellow All India Man. Asscn Indian Inst. of Chemical Engineers; Hon. DLitt (Agra). *Leisure interests:* badminton, gardening, philately, photography, Indian classical music, theatre, bridge. *Address:* DCM Shriram Industries Ltd, Kanchenjunga Building, 18 Barakhamba Road, New Delhi 110001 (Office); 27 Sardar Patel Marg., New Delhi 110021, India (Home). *Telephone:* (11) 3314641 (Office); (11) 6113472 (Home). *Fax:* (11) 3315424 (Office); (11) 6875715 (Home). *E-mail:* shriram@del2.vsnl.net.in (Office).

DHARMASAKTI, Sanya; Thai judge and business executive; b. 5 April 1907, Bangkok; s. of Phaya Dharmsaravedya and Lady Dharmasaravedya; m. Panga Benjati 1935; two s.; ed Bangkok and London, UK; fmr Chief Justice of Thailand; fmr Rector, Thammasat Univ.; Prime Minister 1973–75; Pres. Privy Council 1976, Councillor 1998–; Hon. Pres. Siam Cement Corpn 1998–; Pres. World Fellowship of Buddhists 1984–88; Order of Chuala Chom Klao 1973, Order of the Nine Gems, 1997. *Leisure interests:* gardening, reading, walking. *Address:* 15 Sukhumvit Road, Soi 41, Bangkok; Office of the Privy Councillor, Grand Palace, Bangkok, Thailand (Office). *Telephone:* (2) 251-1151 (Office); (2) 259-8765 (Home). *Fax:* (2) 258-8893 (Home).

DHARSONO, Gen. Hartono; Indonesian politician and army officer; fmr Sec. Gen. of ASEAN; arrested Nov. 1984, sentenced to 10 years' imprisonment 1986, reduced to 7, released Sept. 1990; launched Forum for the Purification of People's Sovereignty (FPPS) 1991.

d'HAUTERIVES, Arnaud Louis Alain; French artist; b. 26 Feb. 1933, Braine (Aisne); s. of Louis and Germaine (née Hincelin) d'Hauterives; m. Renée Delhaye 1959; two s. one d.; ed Ecole des Beaux Arts, Reims, Ecole Supérieure des Beaux Arts, Paris; started painting as a career 1957; illustrator of some art books; Jt Pres. Soc. Int. des Beaux Arts 1985, Hon. Pres. La Critique Parisienne 1984–; Pres. Acad. des Beaux Arts 1987–92, Life Sec. 1996–; mem. Inst. de France (Vice-Pres. 1987), Acad. des Sciences d'outre mer, Russian Acad. of Fine Arts (Dir 1998–); exhbns in France, Belgium, USA, China, Japan, Italy, Spain, USSR; academician Académie Royale des Beaux Arts de San Fernando; mem. Académie de Marseille; Hon. mem. Cercle de Lamer; Officier Légion d'honneur, des Palmes Académiques, Officier Ordre nat. du Mérite, Ordre des Arts et des Lettres; Premier Grand Prix de Rome 1957, Prix de la Critique 1967. *Leisure interests:* lithography, gliding. *Address:* Académie des Beaux Arts, 23 Quai de Conti, 75006 Paris, France. *Telephone:* 1-44-41-43-20. *Fax:* 1-44-41-43-21.

DHLOMO, Oscar Dumisani, D.ED.; South African politician; b. 28 Dec. 1943, Umbumbulu, Natal; s. of late Isaac Dhlomo; m. Nokukhanya V. Ntshingila 1966; three s. one d.; ed Sibusiswe Secondary School, Amanzimtoti Coll., Univ. of SA and Univ. of Zululand; teacher, Umlazi 1967–72; secondary school headmaster, Umlazi 1973–74; Lecturer in Educ., Univ. of Zululand 1974–77; mem. KwaZulu Legislative Ass. 1978–90; Sec.-Gen. Inkatha 1978–90; Minister of Educ. and Culture, KwaZulu Govt until 1990; First Chair. KwaZulu Nat. Jt Exec. Authority 1988–89; Chair. Bd KwaZulu Training Trust, Emandleni-Matleng Training Camp; Co-Convenor, Kwa-Zulu-Natal Indaba, Chair. 1988–90; Dir Devt Bank of Southern Africa 1990–; Founder, Exec.-Chair. Inst. for Multiparty Democracy 1991–; Dir Standard Bank Investment Corpn 1991–, Anglovaal Ltd 1991–, The Natal Witness Printing and Publishing Co. (Pty) Ltd 1991–, Shell SA (Pty) Ltd 1992–, Southern Life 1990– and several other cos.; mem. Buthelezi Comm. 1982. *Publications:* co-author of two books on social studies, educ. papers. *Leisure interests:* music, reading. *Address:* c/o Development Bank of Southern Africa, 1258 Lever Road, Midrand, P.O. Box 1234, Halfway House 1685 (Office); Private Bag X04, Ulundi 3838, South Africa. *Website:* www.dbsa.org (Office).

DHOLAKIA OF WALTHAM BROOKS, Navnit Dholakia, Baron (Life Peer), cr. 1997, of Waltham Brooks in the Co. of West Sussex, OBE, DL, BSc; British politician; b. 4 March 1937, Tabora, Tanganyika (now Tanzania); m. two d.; ed P. P.Inst., Bhavnagar, Gujerat, India, Brighton Tech. Coll., UK; fmr magistrate, mem. Bd of Visitors, HM Prison Lewes; Deputy Lt W Sussex 1999; Pres. Liberal Democrat party 2000–, Spokesperson on Home Affairs; Chair. Nat. Asscn for the Care and Resettlement of Offenders (NACRO); mem. Council, Howard League for Penal Reform; mem. Governing Body, Commonwealth Inst.; mem. Man. Bd, Policy Research Inst. on Ageing and Ethnicity; mem. House of Lord Appointments Comm.; Trustee Mental Health Foundation, Pallant House Gallery, Chichester, British Empire and Commonwealth Museum, Bristol; Asian of the Year 2000. *Address:* House of Lords, London, SW1A 0PW, England (Office). *Telephone:* (20) 7219-5203 (Office). *E-mail:* dholakian@parliament.uk (Office).

DI BELGIOJOSO, Lodovico Barbiano; Italian architect; b. 1 Dec. 1909, Milan; s. of Alberico Barbiano and Margherita (née Confalonieri) di Belgiojoso; m. Carolina Cicogna Mozzoni 1934; two s. two d.; ed School of Architecture, Milan; Architect 1932–; Prof. of Architecture 1949; Prof. Venice Univ. Inst. of Architecture 1956–63; Prof. of Architectural Composition, School of Architecture, Milan Polytechnic 1963; pvt. practice with Peressutti and Rogers in town planning, architecture, interior decoration and industrial design; mem. Nat. Council of Italian Town Planning Inst.; mem. Acad. di S. Luca, Rome. *Works include:* houses, factories, pavilions; Italian Merchant Navy Pavilion, Paris Int. Exhbn 1937; health resort for children, Legnano 1939; Post Office, Rome 1939; monument to the dead in German concentration camps, Milan cemetery 1946; U.S. Pavilion at Triennale 1951; Olivetti Showroom, Fifth Avenue, New York and Labyrinth at the Tenth Triennale 1954; restoration and re-arrangement of Castello Sforzesco Museums 1956; skyscraper Torre Velasca, Milan 1957; Canadian Pavilion, Venice Biennale; collaborator Italian Pavilion, Brussels Exhbn 1958; Hispano Olivetti Building, Barcelona 1965; consultant motorways throughout Italy 1970; Messina Univ. 1973; Gratosoglio housing Devt, Milan 1976; Renovation of Royal Palace as Museum, Milan 1978, Galleria Sabanda Museum, Turin 1983, Stock Exchange, Milan 1985, 19th century Bldg for offices, Milan 1986; Designer, Extension of Law Courts, Messina 1988; Extension of Messina Univ. 1989. *Publications:* (in collaboration with Banfi, Peressutti and Rogers): Piano regolatore della Val d'Aosta 1937, Piano A.R. 1946, Stile 1936, etc. *Leisure interests:* arts, poetry. *Address:* Studio Architetti B.B.P.R., 2 via dei Chiostri, 20121 Milan (Office); 8 via Perugia, 20121 Milan, Italy. *Telephone:* 86463085 (Office); 784362 (Home).

DI PIETRO, Antonio; Italian lawyer and politician; b. 2 Oct. 1950, Montenero di Bisaccia; m. 1st Isabella Ferrara; one s.; m. 2nd Susanna Mazzoleni 1995; ed Statale Univ. Milan, Pavia Univ.; studied law at evening classes; fmrly worked as factory hand, Germany; fmr police officer; fmr magistrate, Bergamo; prosecutor, Milan 1984–94; uncovered bribery of officials, Milan March 1992, led Operation Clean Hands exposing high levels of political corruption in Italy 1992–94; univ. teacher and parl. consultant 1995–96; Minister of Public Works 1996–97; elected to Senate 1997; MEP 1999–. *Publications:* Memoria 1999, Intervista su Tangentopoli 2000, Mani Pulite–La Vera Storia 2002. *Address:* European Parliament, 97–113 rue Wiertz, 1047 Brussels, Belgium. *E-mail:* adipietro@europarl.eu.int (Office). *Website:* www.antoniodipietro.org (Office).

DI ROSA, Antonio, BSc; Italian journalist; b. 17 April 1951, Messina; s. of Calogero Rossetti and Anna Rossetti; partner; one s. two d.; began career at Giornale di Calabria 1974–78; moved to Gazzetta del Popolo 1978, Deputy Head Home News 1979–81, Head 1981–84; joined La Stampa 1984, Head Home News April–July 1988; Deputy Cen. Ed.-in-Chief Corriere della Sera 1988, Cen. Ed.-in-Chief 1993, Deputy Ed. Jan. 1996–; Premio Senigallia 1983. *Leisure interests:* books, cinema, travel. *Address:* Corriere della Sera, Via Solferino 28, 20121 Milan (Office); Via G. Morelli 1, Milan, Italy (Home). *Telephone:* (02) 6339 (Office); (02) 781199. *Fax:* (02) 29009668 (Office). *Website:* www.corriere.it (Office).

DI RUPO, Elio, DSc; Belgian politician; b. 1951, Morlanwelz; ed Univ.of Mons; researcher, Chef de Cabinet, Budget and Energy Minister, Walloon Region 1982–85; Communal Councillor, Mons 1982–2000; MP 1987–89, MEP 1989–1991; Pres. of Energy Comm.; Senator 1991–95; Minister of Educ. 1992–94, Deputy Prime Minister and Minister of Communications and Public Enterprises 1994–95, Deputy Prime Minister and Minister for Economy and Telecommunications 1995–1999; Minister-Pres. of Wallonia 1999–2000; Mayor of Mons 2001–; Pres. Socialist Party (PS) 2000–. *Address:* Parti Socialiste, 13 boulevard de l'Empereur, 1000 Brussels, Belgium (Office). *Telephone:* (2) 548-32-11 (Office). *Fax:* (2) 548-33-90 (Office). *E-mail:* elio@dirupa.net (Office). *Website:* www.ps.be (Office).

DIA, Mamadou; Senegalese politician; b. 18 July 1910, Kombole; ed William Ponty School, Dakar; Councillor, Senegal 1946–52; Grand Councillor, French West Africa 1952–57; Founder mem. Bloc Démocratique Sénégalais (BDS), later Sec.-Gen; Senator for Senegal 1949–55; Deputy to Nat. Ass., Paris 1956–59; Deputy to Legis. Ass., Senegal 1959; Vice-Pres., Council of Ministers, Senegal 1957–58, Pres. 1958–59; Vice-Pres., Mali Fed. 1959–60; Pres. Council of Ministers, Senegal 1960–62, concurrently Minister of Defence and Security 1962; Govt overthrown Dec. 1962, sentenced to life detention May 1963, sentence reduced to 20 years imprisonment 1972, released 1974; political rights restored 1976; co-founder and Ed. of Ande Soppi (periodical) July 1977; Chevalier, Palmes académiques. *Publications:* Réflexions sur l'économie de l'Afrique noire 1953, Contributions à l'étude du mouvement

coopératif en Afrique noire 1957, L'économie africaine 1957, Nations africaines et solidarité mondiale 1960, Africa's Management in the 1990s and beyond 1996.

DIAB, Rashid, MFA, PhD; Sudanese painter, printmaker and art critic; b. 1957, Wad Medani, Gezira Prov.; ed School of Fine and Applied Arts, Khartoum; travelled to Madrid on scholarship from Spanish govt to undertake grad. degrees in fine and applied art; produced over 20 solo exhbns in Africa, Europe and the Middle East; participated in numerous group exhibitions, winning prizes in Cuba and Taiwan; Founder and Dir Medani Galeria, Madrid, Spain; f. Arts Gallery in Khartoum. *Address:* Office of the Director, Medani Galeria, Madrid, Spain (Office).

DIABRE, Zephirin, MBA, PhD; Burkinabè international civil servant; b. 26 Aug. 1959, Ouagadougou; ed Ecole Supérieure de Commerce, Bordeaux, France, Univ. of Bordeaux; Prof. of Business Admin. 1987–89; Man. Dir Burkina Brewery 1989–92; Minister for Trade, Industry and Mining 1992–94, for Economy, Finance and Planning 1994–96; Chair. Council of Econ. and Social Affairs 1996–97; Visiting Scholar, Harvard Inst. for Int. Devt, Fellow of Weatherhead Center for Int. Affairs, USA 1997–98; Assoc. Admin. UNDP, New York 1999–; Officier, Ordre Nat. du mérite, Burkina Faso, Chevalier, Légion d'honneur. *Address:* Office of the Associate Administrator, United Nations Development Programme, 1 United Nations Plaza, New York, NY 10017, USA (Office). *Telephone:* (212) 906-5788 (Office).

DIACK, Lamine; Senegalese international sports official and politician; b. b. 7 June 1933; m.; 15 c.; long jump record holder, France and W. Africa 1957–60; football coach, Foyer France Senegal football team 1963–64; Pres. African Amateur Athletic Confed. (AAAC) 1963–64; Technical Dir Senegal Nat. Football Team 1964–68; Gen. Commr for State Sport 1969–70, Sec. of State for Youth and Sport 1970–73; mem. Exec. Cttee Supreme Council for Sport in Africa (SCSA) 1973–87; Pres. ASC DIARAAF football team 1974–78, 1994–; mem. Nat. Olympic Cttee of Senegal 1974–, Pres. 1985–; Gen. Sec. Senegalese Athletic Fed. 1974–78, Pres. 1974–78, Hon. Pres. 1978–; mem. Int. Olympic Cttee 1999–; Vice-Pres. Int. Asscn of Athletics Feds (IAAF) 1976–91, Sr Vice-Pres. 1991–99, Pres. 1999–; Chair. City Council (Mayor) of Dakar 1978–80; mem. Nat. Ass. of Senegal (Parl.) 1988–93, Sr Vice-Pres. (Deputy Speaker) 1988–93; Chair. of Bd, Soc. Nat. des Eaux (SONES) 1995–2001; numerous awards including Grand Officier de l'Etoile Equatoriale (Gabon), Commdr Order of Good Hope (S. Africa), Chevalier, Légion d'Honneur (France), Chevalier de l'Ordre Nat. du Lion (Senegal), Olympic Order, IAAF Order of Merit. *Address:* Office of the President, International Association of Athletics Federations, 17 rue Princesse Florestine, BP 359, Monaco, MC 98007, Monaco (Office). *Telephone:* (377) 9310888 (Office). *Fax:* (377) 93159515 (Office). *E-mail:* president@iaaf.org (Office). *Website:* www.iaaf.org (Office).

DIALLO, Absa Claude, BA; Senegalese diplomatist; b. 1942, Hanoi, Vietnam; ed Univ. of Dakar and Nat. School of Admin. Senegal; Head, Geographical Div. Office of Political, Cultural and Social Affairs, Ministry of Foreign Affairs 1964; Adviser, Office of Minister for Foreign Affairs 1965–72; Minister-Counsellor, Bonn (also Accred to Austria and Switzerland) 1972–77; Perm. Del. of Senegal at UNESCO 1977–80; roving Amb. 1980–81; Dir of Political and Cultural Affairs, Ministry of Foreign Affairs 1981–88; Perm. Rep. to UN 1988–91, to UN Security Council 1988–89; Chair. UN Cttee on the Exercise of the Inalienable Rights of the Palestinian People 1988–91; UN ad hoc Cttee on Cambodia 1988–90; Amb. to Sweden 1992–93, to Norway 1993, to Russia 1993–95 (also Accred to Bulgaria, Romania, Hungary, Ukraine, Poland, Czech Repub., Slovakia); Amb. and Perm. Rep. to UN and other int. orgs. in Geneva 1996–. *Address:* c/o Ministry of Foreign Affairs and Sengalese Abroad, place de l'Indépendance, Dakar, Senegal.

DIAMANTOPOULOU, Anna; Greek politician; b. 1959, Kozani; m.; one c.; ed Aristotle Univ. of Thessaloniki, Panteion Univ. of Athens; civil engineer 1981–85; Lecturer, Insts. of Higher Technological Educ. 1983–85; Man. Dir of regional devt co.; Prefect of Kastoria 1985–86; Sec.-Gen. for Adult Educ. 1987–88; Sec.-Gen. for Youth 1988–89; mem. Cen. Cttee of PASOK 1991–99; Pres. of Hellenic Org. of Small and Medium-Sized Enterprises and Handicrafts (EOMMEX); Sec.-Gen. for Industry 1994–96; mem. of Parl. for Kozani 1996–99; Deputy Minister for Devt 1996–99; EU Commr for Employment and Social Affairs 1999–; mem. Forum for Co-operation of Balkan Peoples, Int. Women's Network; Chevalier, Légion d'Honneur 2002. *Address:* Commission of the European Communities, 200 rue de la Loi, 1049 Brussels, Belgium (Office). *Telephone:* (2) 298-2000 (Office). *Fax:* (2) 298-2099 (Office). *Website:* europa.eu.int (Office).

DIAMOND, Abel J., OC, DEng, M.ARCH, MA, FRAIC ARIBA, RCA; Canadian architect; b. 8 Nov. 1932, S. Africa; s. of Jacob Diamond and Rachel Zipporah Diamond (née Werner); m. Gillian Mary Huggins 1959; one s. one d.; ed Univs. of Cape Town, Oxford and Pennsylvania; Asst Prof. of Architecture and Architectural Asst to Louis Kahn, Philadelphia 1963–64; Assoc. Prof., Univ. of Toronto 1964–69; Prof., Univ. of York 1969–72; Adjunct Prof., Univ. of Texas at Arlington 1980–81; Sr Partner A. J. Diamond, Donald Schmitt and Co. 1975–; Chair. Nat. Capital Comm., Design Advisory Comm., Ottawa; Advisory Bd, School of Architecture, Univ. of Toronto 1987–; Commr Ont. Human Rights Comm. 1986–89; Bd of Govs., Mount Sinai Hosp., Toronto 1987–; Graham Prof. of Architecture, Univ. of Pa 1996–; mem. Royal Acad. of Arts (Canada), RIBA, Canadian Inst. of Planners, American Inst. of Planners; Hon. Fellow AIA; Hon. DEng (Dalhousie) 1996; numerous design prizes including Toronto Arts Award 1990, Order of Ont. 1998, Royal Architectural Inst. Gold Medal 2001. *Works include:* Ontario Medical Asscn HQ 1970, Univ. of Alberta Long Range Plan 1970, Alcan HQ Office, Toronto 1972, Montreal 1978, Cleveland 1982, Queen's Univ. Housing, Kingston, Ont. 1976, Citadel Theatre, Edmonton, Alberta 1976 (with B. Myers and R. L. Wilkin), Nat. Ballet School Stage Training Facility, Toronto 1983, Burns Bldg Renovation, Calgary 1983, Berkeley Castle Renovation, Toronto 1983, Metro Toronto Central YMCA 1984, Ont. Arts Council HQ Offices, Toronto 1985, Four Seasons HQ Offices, Toronto 1985, Imperial Theatre, St John, NB 1988, Earth and Sciences Center, Univ. of Toronto 1988, Curtiss Hall, Toronto 1988, Sunny Brook Hosp., Newcastle Town Hall 1989, York Univ. Student Centre 1991, Lois Hancsey Aquatic Center 1991, Jerusalem City Hall 1992, Richmond Hill Cen. Library 1992, HQ Toronto Historic Bd 1993, Israeli Foreign Ministry, Jerusalem 1996, 'Alumbrera', Mustique 2000, Garland House, Toronto. *Leisure interest:* watercolour painting. *Address:* 2 Berkeley Street, Suite 600, Toronto, Ont., M5A 2W3, Canada (Office). *Telephone:* (416) 862-8800.

DIAMOND, Jared Mason, PhD; American biologist; b. 10 Sept. 1937, Boston; s. of Louis K. Diamond and Flora K. Diamond; m. Marie M. Cohen 1982; ed Harvard Coll., Univ. of Cambridge, UK; Fellow Trinity Coll., Univ. of Cambridge 1961–65, Jr Fellow Soc. of Fellows, Harvard Coll. 1962–65; Assoc. in Biophysics, Harvard Medical School 1965–66; Assoc. Prof. of Physiology, Univ. of Calif. Medical School, Los Angeles 1966–68, Prof. 1968–; Research Assoc. Dept of Ornithology American Museum of Natural History; mem. NAS, Fellow American Acad. of Arts and Sciences; Burr Award of Nat. Geographical Soc., Nat. Medal Sciences 1999. *Publications:* contrib. Discover magazine; The Avifauna of the Eastern Highlands of New Guinea 1972, Ecology and Evolution of Communities 1975, Community Ecology 1985, Guns, Germs and Steel: The Facts of Human Societies (Pulitzer Prize, Cosmos Prize) 1998, several hundred research papers on physiology, ecology and ornithology. *Address:* Department of Physiology, University of California at Los Angeles Medical School, 10833 Le Conte Avenue, Los Angeles, CA 90095, USA.

DIAMOND, Baron (Life Peer), cr. 1970, of the City of Gloucester; **John Diamond,** FCA; British politician; b. 30 April 1907, Leeds; s. of Solomon Diamond and Henrietta Beckerman; m.; two s. two d.; ed Leeds Grammar School; Chartered Accountant; Labour MP for Blackley, Manchester 1945–51, for Gloucester 1957–70; mem. Gen. Nursing Council and Chair. of its Finance and Gen. Purposes Cttee 1947–53; Hon. Treas. Fabian Soc. 1950–64; Dir Sadler's Wells Trust 1957–64; Hon. Treas. Labour Cttee for Europe 1961–64; Chief. Sec. to the Treasury 1964–70; mem. Cabinet 1968–70; Hon. Treas. The European Movt; Deputy Chair. of Cttees, House of Lords 1974; Chair. Royal Comm. on Distribution of Income and Wealth 1974–79, Prime Minister's Advisory Cttee on Business Appointments of Crown Servants 1975–88; Privy Councillor; Chair. Industry and Parl. Trust 1977–82; Trustee, SDP (Social Democratic Party) 1981–82, Leader SDP in House of Lords 1982–88; LLD hc (Leeds) 1978. *Publications:* Public Expenditure in Practice 1975, Socialism the British Way (jtly) 1948. *Leisure interests:* music, reading the classics, gardening. *Address:* House of Lords, London, SW1A 0AA (Office); Aynhoe, Doggetts Wood Lane, Chalfont St Giles, Bucks., HP8 4TH, England (Home). *Telephone:* (1494) 763229 (Home).

DIAMOND, Neil Leslie; American pop singer and composer; b. 24 Jan. 1941, Brooklyn; m. Marcia Murphey 1975, two c. (and two c. from previous m.); ed New York Univ.; frmly. with Bang Records, Uni, MCA Records, Los Angeles; now recording artist with Columbia Records; guest artist, TV network shows; numerous albums 1966–; 19 platinum albums; 28 Gold albums; composer of film scores, Jonathan Livingston Seagull (Grammy Award) 1973, Every Which Way but Loose 1978, The Jazz Singer (also actor) 1980. *Singles include:* Solitary Man, Cherry, Cherry, Kentucky Woman, I'm a Believer, September Morn, Sweet Caroline, Holly Holy, A Little Bit Me, A Little Bit You, Longfellow Serenade, Song Sung Blue, America, I Am, I Said. *Address:* c/o Columbia Records, 2100 Colorado Avenue, Santa Monica, CA 90404, USA.

DIANOV, Yevgeniy Mikhailovich; Russian physicist; b. 31 Jan. 1936, Tula; m. Helen Zagorovskaya 1968; one s. one d.; ed Moscow State Univ.; researcher, Lebedev Inst. USSR Acad. of Sciences 1960–72, Sr researcher 1972–80, Head of Lab. 1980–83; Head of Lab. Gen. Physics Inst. of USSR Acad. of Sciences 1983–85, Head of Dept of Gen. Physics 1985–88; Prof. Physical-Technical Inst. 1985–88; Deputy Dir of Gen. Physics Inst. Acad. of Sciences of Russia 1988–93, Dir Fibre Optics Research Centre, Gen. Physics Inst. 1993–; Corresp. mem. USSR (now Russian) Acad. of Sciences 1987, mem. 1994; USSR State Prize 1974, Popov Prize, USSR Acad. of Sciences 1988, Russian Fed. State Prize 1998. *Publications:* over 500 papers on quantum electronics. *Leisure interests:* jogging, reading. *Address:* Fibre Optics Research Centre, General Physics Institute, RAS, 38 Vavilova Street, 119991 Moscow (Office); Leninsky Prospekt 13, Apt. 139, 117071 Moscow, Russia (Home). *Telephone:* (095) 135-05-66 (Office); (095) 237-32-76 (Home). *Fax:* (095) 135-81-39; (502) 224-71-34.

DIARRA, Seydou Elimane; Côte d'Ivoirian politician and diplomatist; b. 1933; won scholarship to study agric. in France; fmr head of state-run agric. co-operation and insurance body, Abidjan; fmr head of govt org. in charge of cocoa; fmr African Rep. to Int. Coffee Org; fmr Amb. to Brazil, EU and UK; pres. cocoa exporting business; Prime Minister of Côte d'Ivoire 1999–2000,

Jan. 2003–. *Address:* Office of the Prime Minister, boulevard Angoulvant, 01 BP 1533, Abidjan 01, Côte d'Ivoire (Office). *Telephone:* 20-31-50-00 (Office). *Fax:* 20-22-18-33 (Office).

DIAS, H.E. Cardinal Ivan; Indian ecclesiastic; b. 14 April 1936, Mumbai; ordained priest 1958; Bishop of Rusubisir with title of Archbishop 1982; Archbishop of Mumbai (fmrly Bombay) 1996–; cr. Cardinal 2001. *Address:* Archbishop's House, 21 Nathalal Parekh Marg, Mumbai 400001, India (Office). *Telephone:* (22) 2021093 (Office). *Fax:* (22) 2853872 (Office).

DIAS FERREIRA LEITE, Maria Manuela, BEcons; Portuguese politician; b. 3 Dec. 1940, Lisbon; ed Instituto Superior de Ciências Económicas e Financeiras, Tech. Univ. of Lisbon; researcher Calouste Gulbenkian Foundation 1964–73; Asst Public Finance and Econs, Instituto Superior de Economia e Gestão (ISEG) 1966–79; Dir Dept of Statistics, Inst. of State Holdings (IPE) 1975–77; Co-ordinator Finance Group, Research Bureau, Banco de Portugal 1977–86; Dir-Gen. Public Accounting, Ministry of Finance 1986–90; Sec. of State of Budget 1990–91; Sec. of State attached to Minister and of Budget 1991–93; with Ministry of Educ. 1993–95; MP 1991–95, 1995–2000; Vice-Pres. of Parl. Group, Social Democratic Party (PSD) 1996–2001, Pres. Sept. 2001; Minister of State and of Finance April 2002–. *Address:* Ministry of Finance, Av. Infante D. Henrique 1, 1149-009 Lisbon, Portugal (Office). *Telephone:* (1) 218816820 (Office). *Fax:* (1) 218816862 (Office). *E-mail:* gab .mef@mf.gov.pt (Office). *Website:* www.min-financas.pt (Office).

DIAZ, Cameron; American actress; b. 30 Aug. 1972, Long Beach, Calif.; d. of Emilio Diaz and Billie Diaz; fmr model; Boston Soc. of Film Critics Best Supporting Actress 2001, Chicago Film Critics Best Supporting Actress 2002. *Films include:* The Mask 1994, The Last Supper 1995, Feeling Minnesota 1996, She's the One 1996, Head Above Water 1996, Keys to Tulsa 1997, My Best Friend's Wedding 1997, A Life Less Ordinary 1997, Fear and Loathing in Las Vegas 1997, There's Something About Mary 1998, Very Bad Things 1998, Being John Malkovich 1999, Invisible Circus 1999, Any Given Sunday 1999, Charlie's Angels 2000, Things You Can Tell Just by Looking at Her 2000, Shrek (voice) 2001, Vanilla Sky 2001, The Sweetest Thing 2002, Gangs of New York 2002, Charlie's Angels: Full Throttle 2003. *Address:* c/o International Creative Management, 8942 Wilshire Boulevard, Beverly Hills, CA 90211, USA.

DIBA, Farah (see Pahlavi, Farah Diba).

DIBDIN, Michael John, MA; British writer; b. 21 March 1947, Wolverhampton; s. of Frederick John Dibdin and Peigi Taylor; m. 1st Benita Mitbrodt 1971 (divorced 1986); m. 2nd Sybil Sheringham 1987 (divorced 1995); m. 3rd Kathrine Beck 1997; two d.; ed Friends' School, Lisburn, N Ireland, Univs. of Sussex and Alberta, Canada; CWA Gold Dagger Award 1988, Grand Prix des Romans Policiers 1994. *Publications:* The Last Sherlock Holmes Story 1978, A Rich Full Death 1986, Ratking 1988, The Tryst 1989, Vendetta 1990, Dirty Tricks 1991, Cabal 1992, The Dying of the Light 1993, Dead Lagoon 1994, Dark Spectre 1995, Così fan Tutti 1996, A Long Finish 1998, Blood Rain 1999, Thanksgiving 2000, And Then You Die 2002, Medusa 2003. *Leisure interests:* wine, music, travel. *Address:* c/o Pat Kavanagh, Peters, Fraser & Dunlop, 503/4 The Chambers, Chelsea Harbour, London, SW10 0XF, England. *Telephone:* (20) 7344-1000.

DIBELA, Sir Kingsford, GCMG; Papua New Guinea politician and teacher; b. 16 March 1932; s. of Norman Dibela and Edna Dalauna; m. Winifred Tomalarina 1952; two s. four d.; ed St Paul's Primary School, Dogura; qualified as primary school teacher, teacher 1949–63; Pres. Weraura Local Govt Council 1963–77; MP 1975–82, Speaker of Nat. Parl. 1977–80; Gov.-Gen. 1983–89; K.St.J. *Leisure interests:* golf, sailing and cricket. *Address:* P.O. Box 113, Port Moresby, Papua New Guinea.

DIBIAGGIO, John A., DDS, MA; American university administrator; b. 11 Sept. 1932, San Antonio; s. of Ciro DiBiaggio and Acidalia DiBiaggio; m. Nancy Cronemiller 1989; one s. two d. (from previous marriage); ed E Mich. Univ., Univ. of Detroit and Univ. of Mich.; gen. dentistry practice, New Baltimore, Mich. 1958–65; Asst Prof. School of Dentistry, Univ. of Detroit 1965–67; Asst Dean Student Affairs, Univ. of Ky 1967–70; Prof., Dean, School of Dentistry, Va Commonwealth Univ. Richmond 1970–76; Vice-Pres. for Health Affairs, Exec. Dir Health Center, Univ. of Conn. Farmington 1976–79; Pres. Univ. of Conn. Storrs 1979–85, Mich. State Univ. E Lansing 1985–92, Tufts Univ., Medford, Mass. 1992–; mem. Bd American Automobile Asscn, Kaman Corpn; mem. numerous comms. and professional socs.; Trustee American Cancer Soc. Foundation 1993– (Pres. 1999); 11 hon. degrees; Order of Merit (Italy), Pierre Fauchard Gold Medal Award 1987, 1989. *Publications:* Applied Practice Management: A Strategy for Stress Control (with others) 1979; articles in professional journals. *Leisure interest:* tennis. *Address:* Tufts University, Office of the President, Medford, MA 02155, USA (Office). *Telephone:* (617) 627-3300 (Office). *Fax:* (617) 627-3555 (Office). *E-mail:* President@Tufts.edu (Office).

DiCAPRIO, Leonardo; American actor; b. 11 Nov. 1974, Hollywood; s. of George DiCaprio and Irmelin DiCaprio. *Films include:* Critters III 1991, Poison Ivy 1992, This Boy's Life 1993, What's Eating Gilbert Grape 1993, The Quick and the Dead 1995, The Basketball Diaries 1995, Total Eclipse 1995, Marvin's Room 1996, William Shakespeare's Romeo and Juliet 1996, Titanic 1997, Man in the Iron Mask 1998, Celebrity 1998, The Beach 2000, Don's Plum 2001, Gangs of New York 2002, Catch Me If You Can 2002. *TV series* *include:* Parenthood 1990, Growing Pains 1991. *Address:* c/o Birken Productions Inc., PO Box 291958, Los Angeles, CA 90029, USA (Office). *Website:* www.leonardodicaprio.com (Office).

DICHTER, Misha, BS; American concert pianist; b. 27 Sept. 1945, Shanghai, China; s. of Leon Dichter and Lucy Dichter; m. Cipa Dichter 1968; two s.; ed Juilliard School of Music under Rosina Lhevinne; winner, Silver Medal, Tchaikovsky Int. Competition, Moscow 1966; since then has performed with leading orchestras and at festivals and given recitals worldwide; also performs with wife as piano duo; Grand Prix du Disque Liszt 1999. *Publications:* articles in New York Times, Ovation and Keyboard magazines. *Leisure interests:* tennis, jogging, drawing, sketching. *Address:* c/o Connie Shuman, CAMI, Mushalla Division, 165 West 57th Street, New York, NY 10019, USA (Office).

DICKIE, Brian James; British opera director; b. 23 July 1941; s. of the late Robert Kelso and of Harriet Elizabeth (née Riddell) Dickie; m. 1st Victoria Teresa Sheldon (née Price) 1968; two s. one d.; m. 2nd Nancy Gustafson 1989; ed Trinity Coll., Dublin; Admin. Asst Glyndebourne Opera 1962–66; Admin. Glyndebourne Touring Opera 1967–81; Opera Man. Glyndebourne Festival Opera 1970–81, Gen. Admin. 1981–89; Artistic Dir Wexford Festival 1967–73; Artistic Adviser Théâtre Musical de Paris 1981–87; Gen. Dir Canadian Opera Co. 1989–93; Artistic Counsellor Opéra de Nice 1994–97; Gen. Dir EU Opera 1997–99, Chicago Opera Theater 1999–; Chair. London Choral Soc. 1978–85, Theatres Nat. Cttee Opera Cttee 1976–85; Vice-Chair. Theatres Nat. Cttee 1980–85; Vice-Pres. Theatrical Man. Asscn 1983–85; mem. Bd Opera America 1991–93. *Address:* Chicago Opera Theater, 70 East Lake Street, Suite 540, Chicago, IL 60601 (Office); 405 Edgemere Way North, Naples, FL 33999 (Home); 2000 N Lincoln Park West, Apt 412, Chicago, IL 60614, USA. *Telephone:* (312) 7048420 (Office); (773) 3276471. *Fax:* (312) 7048421 (Office).

DICKIE, Lloyd M., PhD, FRSC; Canadian ecologist; b. 6 March 1926, Kingsport, NS; s. of Ebenezer Cox Dickie and Pearl (née Sellars) Dickie; m. Marjorie C. Bowman 1952; one s. two d.; ed Acadia Univ., Yale Univ., Univ. of Toronto; research scientist, Fisheries Research Bd, NB 1951–62, Great Lakes Inst., Toronto 1962–65; Dir Marine Ecology Lab., Bedford Inst. Oceanography, Dartmouth, NS 1965–74; Chair. and Prof. of Oceanography, Dalhousie Univ., Halifax 1974–77, Dir Inst of Environmental Studies, Dalhousie Univ. 1974–76; Research Scientist, Marine Ecology Lab. and Marine Fish Div., Bedford Inst. of Oceanography, Dartmouth, NS 1976–87, Sr Research Scientist Biological Sciences Br., Dept of Fisheries and Oceans 1987–93, participant in Ocean Production Enhancement Network 1991–92, Scientist Emer. 1994–; Oscar-Sette Memorial Award (American Fish Soc.) 1991. *Publications:* Ad Mare: Canada Looks to the Sea (with R. W Stewart) 1971, The Biomass Spectrum: A Predator-Prey Theory of Aquatic Production (jtly.) 2001, some 80 scientific papers. *Address:* c/o Bedford Institute of Oceanography, P.O. Box 1006, Dartmouth, NS, B2Y 4A2 (Office); 7 Lakewood Court, Dartmouth, NS, B2X 2R6, Canada (Home). *Telephone:* (902) 426-7368 (Office); (902) 435-1545 (Home).

DICKINSON, Angie (pseudonym of Angeline Brown); American actress; b. 30 Sept. 1931, Kulm, ND; ed Immaculate Heart Coll., Glendale Coll. *Films include:* Lucky Me 1954, Man With the Gun, The Return of Jack Slade, Tennessee's Partner, The Black Whip, Hidden Guns, Tension at Table Rock, Gun the Man Down, Calypso Joe, China Gate, Shoot Out at Medicine Bend, Cry Terror, I Married a Woman, Rio Bravo, The Bramble Bush, Ocean's 11, A Fever in the Blood, The Sins of Rachel Cade, Jessica, Rome Adventure, Captain Newman MD, The Killers, The Art of Love, Cast a Giant Shadow, The Chase, The Poppy is Also a Flower, the Last Challenge, Point Blank, Sam Whiskey, Some Kind of a Nut, Young Billy Young, Pretty Maids All in a Row, The Resurrection of Zachary Wheeler, The Outside Man, Big Bad Mama, Klondike Fever, Dressed to Kill, Charlie Chan and the Curse of the Dragon Queen, Death Hunt, Big Bad Mama II, Even Cowgirls Get the Blues, The Maddening, Sabrina, The Sun–The Moon and The Stars, Pay It Forward, Sealed with a Kiss 1999, The Last Producer 2000, Duets 2000, Pay it Forward 2000, Big Bad Love 2001, Ocean's Eleven 2001. *Television series:* Police Woman, Cassie & Co. *Television films:* The Love War, Thief, See the Man Run, The Norliss Tapes, Pray for the Wildcats, A Sensitive Passionate Man, Overboard, The Suicide's Wife, Dial M for Murder, One Shoe Makes it Murder, Jealousy, A Touch of Scandal, Stillwatch, Police Story: The Freeway Killings, Once Upon a Texas Train, Prime Target, Treacherous Crossing, Danielle Steel's Remembrance; mini-series: Pearl, Hollywood Wives, Wild Palms.

DICKSON, Jennifer, CM, RA, LLD; Canadian artist, photographer and lecturer; b. 17 Sept. 1936, S. Africa; d. of the late John L. Dickson and Margaret J. (Turner) Dickson; m. Ronald A. Sweetman 1962; one s.; ed Goldsmiths' Coll. School of Art, Univ. of London; Assoc. Atelier 17 (graphic workshop), Paris 1960–65; teacher, Brighton Coll. of Art 1961–68, Univ. of W Indies, Jamaica 1968, Univ. of Wis. 1972, Saidye Bronfman Centre, Montreal 1970–71, 1982–83, Ohio Univ., Athens 1973, 1979, Univ. of S Ill. 1973, Calif. State Univ., Sacramento 1974, Denison Univ. 1976, Univ. of Ottawa 1980–83 (Sessional Instructor 1980-85); lecturer, History of Art, Montreal Museum of Fine Arts 1988–91; visiting artist at many univs, colls. etc.; has held more than 55 one-woman exhbns in six countries and participated in more than 350 group exhbns; works in numerous public collections in Canada, USA, UK, Europe, New Zealand, Australia and S Africa including Nat. Gallery of Canada, Metropolitan Museum, New York, British Museum, London and Hermitage Museum, Leningrad; Fellow, Royal Soc. of Painter-Etchers and

Engravers; Hon. LLD (Univ. of Alberta) 1988; awards include Prix de Jeunes Artistes pour Gravure, Biennale de Paris 1963, Special Purchase Award, World Print Competition, San Francisco Museum of Art 1974, Biennale Prize, 5th Norwegian Int. Print Biennale 1981. *Exhibitions include:* The Last Silence: Pavane for a Dying World, Canadian Museum of Contemporary Photography 1993. *Publications:* The Hospital for Wounded Angels 1987, The Royal Academy Gardener's Journal 1991, Water Song 1997, Garden Capricci 1999, Sanctuary: A Landscape of the Mind 2000 and suites of original prints and photographs, Nature and Artifice 2003. *Leisure interests:* historic gardens, opera, films. *Address:* 20 Osborne Street, Ottawa, Ont., K1S 4Z9, Canada. *Telephone:* (613) 233-2315 (Studio); (613) 730-2083 (Home). *Fax:* (613) 730-1818 (Home). *E-mail:* ronsweetman@canada.com.

DICKSON, Robert George Brian, PC, CC, LLB, DCnL, CD; Canadian lawyer; b. 25 May 1916, Yorkton, Sask.; s. of Thomas Dickson and Sarah Elizabeth Gibson; m. Barbara Melville 1943; three s. one d.; ed Regina Collegiate Inst., Univ. of Manitoba and Manitoba Law School; served with Royal Canadian Artillery 1940–45; called to Man. Bar 1940; Lawyer, Aikins, MacAuley & Co. 1945–63; Lecturer, Man. Law School 1948–54; apptd. to Court of Queen's Bench, Man. 1963, Court of Appeal 1967, Justice, Supreme Court of Canada 1973–84, Chief Justice of Canada 1984–90, Deputy Gov.-Gen.; Life Bencher, Law Soc., Man.; Hon. Bencher, Lincoln's Inn 1984, Law Soc. of Upper Canada 1997; Hon. Prof., Univ. of Man. 1985; Chancellor, Diocese of Rupert's Land, Anglican Church of Canada 1960–71; mem. Bd of Trustees, the Sellers Foundation; KStJ 1985; Hon. Fellow, American Coll. of Trial Lawyers; Hon. LLD (Man.) 1973, (Sask.) 1978, (Ottawa) 1979, (Queen's) 1980, (Dalhousie) 1983, (York) 1985, (BC) 1986, (Toronto) 1986, (Laurentian) 1986, (Yeshiva) 1987, (McGill) 1987, (Carleton) 1988, (Mount Allison) 1989, (Brock) 1990, (Winnipeg) 1991, (Western) 1992, (Law Soc. of Upper Canada) 1993, (Univ. of Victoria) 1993; Commdr, Ordre nat. du Mérite 1994, Kt Marshall Mil. and Hospitaller Order of St Lazarus of Jerusalem 1996, Vimy Award 1997. *Leisure interest:* riding.

DIDDLEY, Bo; American blues singer; b. Otha Ellas Bates, later known as Ellas McDaniel, 28 Dec. 1928, McComb, Mississippi; m. Ethel Mae Smith 1946 (divorced); one c.; m. 2nd Kay McDaniel; two c.; fmr boxer; began singing career in blues clubs of Chicago; has performed with Billy Boy Arnold, Otis Spann, Chuck Berry and Jimmie Vaughan; Ed.'s Lifetime Achievement Award, Guitar Player Magazine 1990. *Singles include:* Bo Diddley, Bo Diddley's A Gunslinger, Diddley Daddy, Bo's A Lumberjack, Pretty Thing, Hey Good Lookin' Who Do You Love? *Albums include:* The Black Gladiator 1971, Where It All Begins, A Man Amongst Men, Got Another Bag of Tricks 1973, Another Dimension 1975, I'm a Man 1977. *Address:* Atlantic Records, 1290 Avenue of the Americas, New York, NY 10104, U.S.A. (Office).

DIDION, Joan, BA; American writer; b. 5 Dec. 1934, Sacramento; d. of Frank Reese Didion and Eduene (née Jerrett) Didion; m. John G. Dunne 1964; one d.; ed Univ. of California, Berkeley; Assoc. Features Ed. Vogue magazine 1956–63; fmr columnist Saturday Evening Post, fmr contributing Nat. Review; now freelance writer; First Prize Vogue's Prix de Paris 1956, Morton Dauwen Zabel Prize (American Asscn of Arts and Letters) 1978, Edward McDowell Medal 1996. *Publications: novels* Run River 1963, Play It as It Lays 1970, A Book of Common Prayer 1977, Democracy 1984, The Last Thing He Wanted 1996. *Essays:* Slouching Towards Bethlehem 1969, The White Album 1978, After Henry 1992. *Non-fiction:* Salvador 1983, Miami 1987, After Henry 1992, Political Fictions 2001. *Screenplays for films:* The Panic in Needle Park 1971, A Star is Born 1976, True Confessions 1981, Up Close and Personal 1996. *Address:* c/o Janklow & Nesbit, 445 Park Avenue, New York, NY 10022-2606, USA.

DIEKMANN, Michael; German business executive; b. 23 Dec. 1954, Bielefeld; m.; three c.; ed Göttingen Univ.; Financial Dir Diekmann/Thieme GBR 1983–86, Pres. 1987–88; Exec. Asst to Head of Hamburg Regional Office, Allianz Versicherungs-AG 1988–89, Head of Sales, Hamburg Harburg office 1990, Head of Hanover office 1991–92, Head of Customer Relationship Man. for pvt customers, Munich 1993, mem. Exec. Bd of Man. of regional office for N. Rhine-Westphalia as Head of Sales 1994–95, Dir Allianz Insurance Man. Asia Pacific Pte Ltd, Singapore 1996–97, mem. Bd of Man. Allianz AG, Munich responsible for Asia-Pacific region 1998, responsible for Asia-Pacific, Cen. and Eastern Europe, Middle East, Africa and Group Man. Devt 2000, responsible for the Americas and Group Human Resources 2002–03, CEO Allianz-Dresdner May 2003–. *Address:* Allianz-Dresdner AG, Königinstrasse 28, 80802 Munich, Germany (Office). *Website:* www.allianz.com (Office).

DIENER, Theodor Otto, DSc; American plant virologist; b. 28 Feb. 1921, Zürich, Switzerland; s. of Theodor E. Diener and Hedwig R. Baumann; m. Sybil Mary Fox 1968; three s. (from previous m.); ed Swiss Fed. Inst. of Tech., Zürich; Plant Pathologist, Swiss Fed. Agricultural Research Station, Waedenswil 1948–49; Asst Prof. of Plant Pathology Rhode Island State Univ., Kingston, USA 1950; Asst-Assoc. Plant Pathologist, Wash. State Univ., Prosser 1950–59; Research Plant Pathologist, Plant Virology Lab., Agricultural Research Service, US Dept of Agric., Beltsville, Md 1959–88; Collaborator, Agricultural Research Service, US Dept of Agric., Beltsville, Md 1988–97; Prof., Center for Agric. Biotech. and Dept of Botany, Univ. of Md, College Park 1988–, Acting Dir Center for Agric. Biotech. 1991–92; Distinguished Univ. Prof. 1994–; Distinguished Prof. Univ. of Md Biotech. Inst. 1998–99, Distinguished Prof. Emer. 1999–; discovered and named viroids, smallest known agents of infectious disease; mem. NAS, American Acad. of

Arts and Sciences, Leopoldina (German Acad. of Nat. Scientists); Fellow NY Acad. of Sciences, American Phytopathological Soc.; Campbell Award, American Inst. of Biological Sciences 1968; Superior Service Award, US Dept of Agric. 1969, Distinguished Service Award 1977; Alexander von Humboldt Award (Fed. Repub. of Germany) 1975; Wolf Prize (Israel) 1987, E. C. Stakman Award, Univ. of Minn. 1988; Nat. Medal of Science (USA) 1987; Science Hall of Fame, Agricultural Research Service, US Dept of Agriculture 1989. *Publications:* Viroids and Viroid Diseases 1979, Ed. The Viroids 1987; ed. numerous chapters in scientific books and more than 200 scientific papers. *Leisure interest:* private pilot. *Address:* Center for Agricultural Biotechnology, University of Maryland, College Park, MD 20742 (Office); 11711 Battersea Drive, PO Box 272, Beltsville, MD 20705, USA (Home). *Telephone:* (301) 405-7659 (Office). *Fax:* (301) 504-5449 (Office). *E-mail:* diener@umbi.umd.edu (Office).

DIENSTBIER, Jiří; Czech politician, journalist and writer; b. 20 April 1937, Kladno; s. of Jiří Dienstbier and Anna Dienstbierová; m. 4th J. Melenová 1999; one s. three d.; ed Charles Univ., Prague; Czechoslovak Broadcasting 1959, foreign correspondent in Far East, USSR, Germany, France, UK, Yugoslavia 1960–68, USA 1968–69; dismissed from broadcasting 1970; worked in archives of an Eng company; expelled from Czechoslovak CP and Journalists' Union 1969; signed Charter 1977, spokesman 1979; sentenced to three years in prison 1979–82; boilerman 1982–89; spokesman for Charter 77 1985–86; ed. of Čtverec (The Square), a periodical on int. politics 1979–; Co-Founder of Lidové Noviny (The People's Newspaper) 1988–; Czechoslovak Minister for Foreign Affairs 1989–92; mem. Council of State 1990–92, Deputy Prime Minister CFSR 1990–92, Deputy to House of People Fed. Ass. 1990–92, Chair. Council of the Civic Movt 1991–; Chair. Free Democrats Party (fmrly Civic Movt) 1993–95 (merged with Liberal Nat. Social Party 1995); Chair. Liberal Nat. Social Party 1995–96 (left Party 1997); Chair. Czech Council on Foreign Relations; mem. Comm. on Global Governance; mem. UN Cttee for Solving Global Problems 1995–; Special Envoy to Gen. Ass. of UN 1995; lecturer 1998–; Special Rapporteur of the UN Comm. on Human Rights for Bosnia and Herzegovina, Croatia and Yugoslavia 1998–2001; Visiting Prof. Claremont Grad. Univ., California (USA) 1997–98, Univ. of North Carolina, Chapel Hilll (USA) 1999, Charles Univ. Prague 2001; Dr hc (Univ. de Bourgogne) 1993; Humanist of the Year (USA) 1979; Grand Cross of Order for Merit (Order of Kt's of Malta) 1990, Francesco Cossiga Medal (Italy) 1991, Pro Merito Medal, Parl. Ass. Council of Europe 1991, Hero of Freedom of the Press in the World, IPI (Boston, USA) 2000. *Publications include:* The Night Began at Three in the Morning 1967, Before We Roast Young Pigs 1976, Christmas Present 1977, Guests 1978, Charter 77 – Human Rights and Socialism 1981, Dreaming of Europe 1990, From Dreams to Reality 1999; Kosovo Shades over Balkans 2002, Tax on Blood 2002, stage plays, articles and essays in Samizdat. *Leisure interests:* reading, music, history. *Address:* Apolinářská 6, 12800 Prague 2, Czech Republic. *Telephone:* (2) 2161-0109; (2) 2492-3321 (Home). *Fax:* (2) 2925-34. *E-mail:* j.dienstbier@embassy.mzv.cz (Office); j@dienstbier.cz (Home).

DIEPGEN, Eberhard; German politician; b. 13 Nov. 1941, Berlin; m. Monika Adler 1975; one s. one d.; ed Free Univ. of Berlin; joined CDU 1962, later Chair., W Berlin CDU; mem. Berlin Chamber of Deputies 1971–81; mem. Bundestag (Parl.) as W Berlin Rep. 1980–81; Mayor of Berlin 1984–89, 1991–2001; Senator for Justice 2000–; Chair. Supervisory Bd Berlin Brandenburg Flughafen Holding GmbH 1996–; Grosses Bundesverdienstkreuz mit Stern 1994. *Leisure interests:* soccer, European history. *Address:* c/o Berliner Rathaus, 10173 Berlin, Germany.

DIEZ CANESCO TERRY, Raúl; Peruvian politician; b. 23 Jan. 1948, Lima; ed San Ignacio de Loyola Univ.; fmr Pres. Dir Corpac; elected Frente Democrático mem. Parl. for Lima 1990; cand. for Mayor of Lima 1993; Acción Popular party cand. for Pres. 1995; fmr Vice-Minister of Tourism; First Vice-Pres. and Minister of Industry, Tourism, Integration and Int. Trade Negotiations 2001–. *Address:* Ministry of Industry, Tourism, Integration and International Trade Negotiations, Calle 1 Oeste, Urb. Corpac, San Isidro, Lima 27, Peru (Office). *Telephone:* (1) 2243347 (Office). *Fax:* (1) 2243264 (Office). *Website:* www.mitinci.gob.pe (Office).

DIFORIO, Robert G., BA; American publishing executive; b. 19 March 1940, Mamaroneck, NY; s. of Richard John Diforio Sr and Mildred Kuntz; m. Birgit Rasmussen 1983; one s. one d.; ed Williams Coll., Mass. and Harvard Business School's Advanced Man. Programme; Vice-Pres. Kable News Co. 1970; Vice-Pres. and Sales Man. New American Library (NAL) 1972, Sr Vice-Pres. and Marketing Dir 1976, Pres. and Publisher 1980–81, CEO and Chair. Bd NAL/E. P. Dutton 1983–89; Prin. D4EO Literary Agency Inc. 1991–; Sr Ptnr D4EO Allen O'Shea Literary Partners LLC 2001–. *Leisure interests:* reading, children, golf, investing. *Address:* 7 Indian Valley Road, Weston, CT 06883, USA (Office). *Telephone:* (203) 544-7180 (Office); (203) 544-7182 (Home). *Fax:* (203) 544-7160 (Office). *E-mail:* d4eo@optonline.net (Office). *Website:* www.d4eo .com (Office).

DIJOUD, Paul Charles Louis; French politician; b. 25 July 1938, Neuilly-sur-Seine; s. of Jules-Raoul Dijoud and Andrée Claquin; m. Catherine Cochaux 1968 (divorced 1983); one s. one d.; m. 2nd Maryse Dolivot 1988; ed Lycée Condorcet, Faculté de Droit de Paris, Inst. d'Etudes politiques de Paris; Student at Ecole Nat. d'Admin. 1964–66; Commercial attaché, Dept of external econ. relations in Ministry of Econ. and Finance; elected to Nat. Ass. 1967, 1968, 1973, 1978, defeated 1981; Asst Sec.-Gen. Ind. Republican Party

1967–69; Conseiller Général for canton of Embrun 1968–88; Pres. Ind. Republican Exec. Cttee for Provence-Côte d'Azur 1968–88; Mayor of Briançon 1971–83; Sec. of State attached to Prime Minister's Office 1973–74, later to Minister of Cultural Affairs and the Environment, to Minister of Employment with Responsibility for Immigrant Workers 1974, Secretary of State for Sport 1977, for Overseas Depts. and Territories 1978; Commercial Adviser to Cen. Admin., Ministry of Economy and Finance 1981; Man. Dir Cie Commerciale Sucres et Denrées 1982–84; Pres. Comidex 1984; Pres. Conseil d'administration du parc national des Ecrins 1973; Plenipotentiary Minister 1988; Amb. to Colombia 1988–91, to Mexico 1992–94; Minister of State with responsibility for the principality of Monaco 1994–97; Amb. to Argentina 1997–; Chevalier Légion d'honneur. *Address:* French Embassy, Cerrito 1399, Buenos Aires, Argentina (Office). *Telephone:* (11) 4819-2930 (Office). *Fax:* (11) 4393-1235 (Office). *E-mail:* ambafr@impsat1.com.ar (Office). *Website:* www .embafrancia-argentina.org (Office).

DILEITA, Dileita Mohamed; Djibouti politician and diplomatist; b. 12 March 1958, Tadjourahle; ed Centre for Vocational Training (CFA), Médéa, Algeria; fmrly Amb. to Ethiopia; Prime Minister of Djibouti March 2001–. *Address:* Office of the Prime Minister, B.P. 2086, Djibouti (Office). *Telephone:* 351494 (Office). *Fax:* 355049 (Office).

DILENSCHNEIDER, Robert, MA; American business executive; b. 21 Oct. 1943, New York; s. of Sigmund J. Dilenschneider and Martha Witucki; m. Janet Hennessey 1969; two s.; ed Univ. of Notre Dame and Ohio State Univ.; Account Supervisor, Hill and Knowlton Inc., New York 1967–70, Vice-Pres. 1970–73, Sr Vice-Pres. 1973–80, Exec. Vice-Pres., Chicago 1980–84, Pres. and COO, Chicago 1984–86, Pres. and CEO Hill and Knowlton, New York 1986–91; Prin. The Dilenschneider Group Inc., New York 1991–; mem. U.S. Japan Business Council, Public Relations Soc. of America, Int. Public Relations Asscn; mem. Advisory Bd New York Hosp., Cornell Medical Center, Coll. of Business Admin. at Univ. of Notre Dame; recipient, New York's Big Apple Award. *Publications:* Power and Influence: A Briefing for Leaders 1991, On Power 1993. *Address:* Dilenschneider Group Inc., 200 Park Avenue, New York, NY 10166, USA.

DILIBERTO, Oliviero; Italian politician and professor of law; b. 13 Oct. 1956, Cagliari; s. of Marco Diliberto and Mariadonella Reale; m. Gabriella Serreti 1997; ed in Cagliari, Rome, Frankfurt and Paris; Prov. Sec. Juvenile Fed. of Italian Communist Party 1978; mem. Prov. Sec.'s Office, Italian Communist Party 1982; mem. Nat. Sec.'s Office, Reconstructed Communism Party 1994; Dir Liberazione (party journal) 1994, leader Parl. Group 1995, now Pres. Progressive Parl. Group; fmrly mem. Third Perm. Cttee on Foreign and EC Affairs, Ninth Perm. Cttee on Transport, Post and Telecommunications; Minister of Justice 1998–2001; Prof. of Roman Law, Univ. of Cagliari; currently Prof. of Roman and Levantine Law, Univ. of Rome 'La Sapienza'. *Address:* Piazzale Aldo Moro 5, 00185 Rome, Italy.

DILKS, David Neville, BA, FRSL, FCGI; British professor of international history and university administrator; b. 17 March 1938, Coventry; s. of Neville Ernest and Phyllis Dilks; m. Jill Medlicott 1963; one s.; ed Royal Grammar School, Worcester, Hertford Coll. and St Antony's Coll., Oxford; Asst lecturer, lecturer LSE 1962–70; Prof. of Int. History, Univ. of Leeds 1970–91, Chair. School of History 1974–79, Dean Faculty of Arts 1975–77; Vice-Chancellor Univ. of Hull 1991–99; Visiting Fellow All Souls' Coll., Oxford 1973; Chair. and Founder Commonwealth Youth Exchange Council 1968–73; mem. Advisory Council on Public Records 1977–85, Inst. of Contemporary British History 1986–, Univs Funding Council 1988–91; Trustee Edward Boyle Memorial Trust 1982–96, Imperial War Museum 1983–91, Lennox-Boyd Trust 1984–91, Royal Commonwealth Soc. Library Trust 1987–91; Pres. Int. Cttee for the History of the Second World War 1992–2000; Liveryman, Goldsmiths' Co. 1984; Dr hc (Russian Acad. of Sciences) 1996; Curzon Prize, Univ. of Oxford 1960; Prix du rayonnement de la langue française 1994; Médaille de Vermeil, Acad. Française. *Publications:* Curzon in India (Vols 1 & 2) 1969, 1970, The Diaries of Sir Alexander Cadogan (ed.) 1971, Retreat from Power (ed.) 1981, Neville Chamberlain: Pioneering & Reform, 1869–1929 1984, Barbarossa 1941–The Axis, The Allies and World War–Retrospect, Recollection, Revision (jtly), Grossbritannien und der deutsche Widerstand (jtly) 1994; and numerous articles in learned journals. *Leisure interests:* ornithology, steam railways, organ music, Bentley cars. *Address:* Wits End, Long Causeway, Leeds, LS16 8EX, West Yorks., England (Home). *Telephone:* (113) 267-3466 (Home). *Fax:* (113) 261-1240 (Home).

DILLANE, Stephen; actor; b. 1957; partner Naomi Wirthner; one c.; ed Univ. of Exeter, Bristol Old Vic Drama School; journalist local newspaper; following drama school, worked in repertory Coventry, Manchester and Chester; Tony Award for Best Leading Actor (The Real Thing) 2000. *Films:* Hamlet 1990, Welcome to Sarajevo 1997. *Television:* The Secret Garden 1987, Hostages 1993, The Rector's Wife 1993, The Widowing of Mrs. Holroyd 1995, Anna Karenina (mini-series) 2000. *Plays:* (Royal Nat. Theatre) The Beaux's Strategem, Dancing at Lughnasa, Long Day's Journey into Night, Angels in America, Millennium Approaches, Perestroika; Hush (Royal Court); Endgame (Donmar Warehouse); Hamlet (Gielgud Theatre).

DILLARD, Annie, MA; American author; b. 30 April 1945, Pittsburgh, Pa; d. of Frank Doak and Gloria Lambert; m. 1st R. H. W. Dillard 1965; m. 2nd Gary Clevidence 1979 (divorced); m. 3rd Robert D. Richardson, Jr 1988; one d. two step.-d.; ed Hollins College; contributing editor, Harper's Magazine 1974–85; Distinguished Visiting Prof. Wesleyan Univ. 1979–83, Adjunct Prof.

1983–, writer in residence 1987–; mem. Bd of Dirs. Writers' Conf. 1984– (Chair. 1991–); mem. Nat. Cttee on US–China Relations 1982–; Pulitzer Prize (for Pilgrim at Tinker Creek) 1975, Nat. Endowment for the Arts (Literature) Grant 1981, John Simon Guggenheim Memorial Grant 1985, Gov. of Conn.'s Award 1993, The Campion Award 1994, The Milton Prize 1994, American Arts and Letters Award in Literature 1998. *Publications:* Tickets for a Prayer Wheel (poetry), Pilgrim at Tinker Creek (prose) 1974, Holy the Firm 1978, Living by Fiction 1982, Teaching a Stone to Talk 1982, Encounters with Chinese Writers 1984, An American Childhood 1987, The Writing Life 1989, The Living (novel) 1992, The Annie Dillard Reader 1994, Mornings Like This (poetry) 1995, For the Time Being 1999. *Leisure interests:* soup kitchens in Key West, Fla and Chapel Hill, NC. *Address:* c/o Timothy Seldes, Russell and Volkening, 50 W 29th New York, NY 10001-4227, USA.

DILLER, Barry; American entertainment executive; b. 2 Feb. 1942, San Francisco; s. of Michael Diller and Reva (née Addison) Diller; Vice-Pres. of prime-time TV, ABC network 1971–74; Chair. Bd Paramount Pictures Corpn 1974–84; Pres. Gulf and Leisure Time Group 1983–84; Chair. and CEO Fox Inc. 1984–92; Chair. and CEO TCF Holdings Inc. 1984–85, QVC Network 1992–95, Silver King Communications 1995–98; Chair. Home Shopping Network (HSN) 1995–98; Chair. and CEO USA Interactive (USAI), USA Networks Inc., New York 1998–2001, Chair. 2001–; Chair. and CEO Vivendi Universal Entertainment (VUE) 2002–03; mem. Bd Dirs. News Corp Ltd, Washington Post Co., Coca-Cola Co., Conservation Int., Channel 13/WNET; Trustee, New York Univ.; mem. American Film Inst., Variety Clubs Int., Hollywood Radio and TV Soc., Acad. of Motion Picture Arts and Sciences. *Address:* USA Networks Inc., 152 West 57th Street, 42nd Floor, New York, NY 10019, USA (Office). *Telephone:* (212) 314-7400 (Office). *Fax:* (212) 314-7399 (Office). *Website:* www.usanetworks.com (Office).

DILLER, Elizabeth, BArch; American artist and university professor; ed The Cooper Union School of Architecture; co-f. (with Ricardo Scofidio, q.v., Diller & Scofidio (D + S), New York 1979, cr. installations and electronic media projects; taught at The Cooper Union School of Architecture 1981–90; Assoc. Prof. of Architectural Design, Princeton Univ. 1990–, Dir Grad. Studies 1993–; Jt recipient (with Ricardo Scofidio) fellowships from Graham Foundation for Advanced Study in the Fine Arts 1986, New York Foundation for the Arts 1986, 1987, 1989, Chicago Inst. for Architecture and Urbanism 1989, Tiffany Foundation Award for Emerging Artists 1990, Progressive Architecture Award (for Slow House) 1991, Chrysler Award for Achievement and Design 1997. *Publications:* (with Ricardo Scofidio) Flesh 1995, Back to the Front: Tourisms of War. *Address:* Princeton University School of Architecture, 5116 Architecture, Princeton, NJ 08544-0001, USA (Office).

DILLON, Matt; American actor; b. 18 Feb. 1964, New Rochelle, NY; s. of Paul Dillon and Mary Ellen Dillon.; several TV appearances. *Films include:* Over the Edge 1979, Little Darlings 1980, My Bodyguard 1980, Liar's Moon 1982, Tex 1982, The Outsiders 1983, Rumble Fish 1983, The Flamingo Kid 1984, Target 1985, Rebel 1985, Native Son 1986, The Big Town (The Arm) 1987, Kansas 1988, Drugstore Cowboy 1989, A Kiss Before Dying 1991, Singles 1992, The Saint of Fort Washington, Mr. Wonderful 1993, Golden Gate 1994, To Die For 1995, Frankie Starlight 1995, Beautiful Girls 1996, Grace of My Heart 1996, Albino Alligator 1996, In and Out 1997, Wild Things 1998, There's Something About Mary 1998, One Night at McCool's 2000, Deuces Wild 2000, City of Ghosts 2002. *Address:* William Morris Agency, ICM 151 S. El Camino Drive, Beverly Hills CA 90212, USA.

DILNOT, Andrew, CBE, BA; British economist and university administrator; ed Olchfa Comprehensive School, Swansea, St. John's Coll., Oxford; joined Inst. of Fiscal Studies 1981, Dir 1991–2002; Prin. St. Hugh's Coll., Oxford Oct. 2002–; visiting lecturer numerous univs. in UK and abroad; regular contrib. to broadcast and printed media, including BBC Radio 4 programmes Analysis and More or Less; mem. Social Security Advisory Cttee, Govt Evidence Based Policy Panel; mem. Council, Royal Econ. Soc.; mem. Council, Queen Mary and Westfield Coll. *Address:* Office of the Principal, St Hugh's College, Oxford, OX2 6LE, England (Office). *Telephone:* (1865) 274900 (Office). *Fax:* (1865) 274912 (Office). *E-mail:* andrewdilnot@st-hughs.ox.ac.uk (Office). *Website:* www.st-hughs.ox.ac.uk (Office).

DIMAS, Pyrros; Greek weightlifter; b. Pirro Ohima, 13 Oct. 1971, Himarra, Albania; m. Anastasia Sdougkou; two d. one s.; light-heavyweight lifter; emigrated to Greece 1991; gold medal Barcelona Olympic Games 1992, Atlanta Olympic Games 1996, Sydney Olympic Games 2000; World Championship title 1993, 1995, 1998; European Championship title 1995; world record in the snatch (85kg category); major in the Greek army; Greek Athlete of the Year 1992, 1993, 1995, 1996; Top Athlete in the 1995 World Championship. *Leisure interests include:* video games, backgammon, cinema. *Address:* c/o The Hellenic Weightlifting Federation, 43 Sygrou Av. 117, 43 Athens, Greece (Office). *Website:* www.pyrros.gr (Office).

DIMBLEBY, David, MA; British broadcaster; b. 28 Oct. 1938, London; s. of the late Richard Dimbleby and of Dilys Thomas; m. 1st Josceline Gaskell 1967 (dissolved 2000); one s. two d.; m. 2nd Belinda Giles 2000; one s.; ed Charterhouse, Christ Church, Oxford, Univs of Paris and Perugia; presenter and interviewer BBC Bristol 1960–61; Chair. Dimbleby and Sons Ltd 1986–2001, fmrly Man. Dir 1967; Richard Dimbleby Award BAFTA 1998. *Broadcasts include:* Quest (religious programme), What's New? (children's science), People and Power 1982–83; General Election Results Programmes 1979, 1983, 1987, 2001, various programmes for the Budget, by-elections,

local elections etc.; presenter Question Time BBC 1993–. *Documentary films include:* Ku-Klux-Klan, The Forgotten Million, Cyprus: The Thin Blue Line 1964–65, South Africa: The White Tribe 1979 (Royal TV Soc. Supreme Documentary Award), The Struggle for South Africa 1990 (US Emmy Award, Monte Carlo Golden Nymph), US-UK Relations: An Ocean Apart 1988, David Dimbleby's India 1997; live commentary on many public occasions including: State Opening of Parliament, Trooping the Colour, Wedding of HRH Prince Andrew and Sarah Ferguson, HM The Queen Mother's 90th Birthday Parade (Royal TV Soc. Outstanding Documentary Award), Funeral of Diana, Princess of Wales 1997, Memorial services including Lord Olivier (Royal TV Soc. Outstanding Documentary Award). *Publication:* An Ocean Apart (with David Reynolds) 1988. *Address:* 14 King Street, Richmond, Surrey, TW9 1NF, England.

DIMBLEBY, Jonathan; British broadcaster, journalist, author and farmer; b. 31 July 1944; s. of the late Richard Dimbleby and of Dilys Thomas; m. Bel Mooney 1968; one s. one d.; ed Univ. Coll. London; reporter, BBC Bristol 1969–70, BBC Radio, World at One 1970–71; reporter, This Week, Thames TV 1972–78, 1986–88, TV Eye 1979; reporter, Yorkshire TV, Jonathan Dimbleby in Evidence: The Police (series), The Bomb 1980, The Eagle and the Bear 1981, The Cold War Game 1982, The American Dream 1984, Four Years On – The Bomb 1984; Assoc. Ed./Presenter, First Tuesday 1982–86; Presenter/Ed. Jonathan Dimbleby on Sunday, TV-am 1985–86, On the Record, BBC TV 1988–93, Charles: the Private Man, the Public Role, Central TV 1994, Jonathan Dimbleby, London Weekend Television (LWT) 1995–; Presenter, Any Questions?, BBC Radio 4 1987–, Any Answers? 1989–, main presenter of Gen. Election coverage, ITV 1997; writer/presenter The Last Governor, BBC 1997; An Ethiopian Journey, LWT 1998, A Kosovo Journey, LWT 2000, Michael Heseltine – A Life in the Political Jungle, LWT 2000; Pres. Voluntary Service Overseas 1999–, Soil Asscn 1997–, Royal Soc. for the Protection of Birds 2001–, Bath Festivals Trust 2003; Vice-Pres. Council for Protection of Rural England 1997–; Trustee Richard Dimbleby Cancer Fund, One World Broadcasting Trust, Forum for the Future; Richard Dimbleby Award 1974. *Publications:* Richard Dimbleby 1975, The Palestinians 1979, The Prince of Wales: A Biography 1994, The Last Governor 1997. *Leisure interests:* music, sailing, tennis, farming, riding. *Address:* c/o David Higham Associates, Ltd, 5 Lower John Street, London, W1R 4HA, England. *Telephone:* (20) 7437-7888.

DIMÉNY, Imre, DR. AGR.SC.; Hungarian agropolitician and agronomist; b. 3 Aug. 1922, Komolló; s. of János Dimény and Anna Illyés; m. Margit Erzsébet Buzgó 1947; one d.; agronomic engineer; rural, county and ministry official 1945–55; Dept Head, later Vice-Pres. Nat. Planning Bureau 1955–62; Alt. mem. Cen. Cttee and Leader Agricultural Dept Hungarian Socialist Workers' Party 1962–66; Minister of Agric. and Food 1967–75; Prof., Univ. of Horticulture, Budapest 1975–95, Rector 1975–86, Prof. Emer. 1995–; mem. Hungarian Acad. of Sciences 1982–; Dr hc (Univ. of Agricultural Sciences Gödöllő) 1994, (Univ. of Horticulture and Food Industry, Pannon Univ. of Agric.) 1997, (Univ. of Agricultural Sciences, Debrecen) 1999. *Leisure interests:* reading, gardening. *Address:* Szent István University, Faculty of Food Sciences, 1118 Budapest XI, Villányi út 35–41 (Office); 1026 Budapest, Szilágyi Erzsébet fasor 79, 111/2, Hungary (Home). *Telephone:* (1) 356-6580.

DIMITROV, Aleksander; Macedonian politician and lawyer; b. 29 Nov. 1949, Skopje; ed Skopje Univ.; mem. Man. Bd, Air Service Skopje, Sec. Forum for Int. Relations; ed. Forum (newspaper) 1969–72; ed. Mlad Borac (newspaper) 1972–78; Sec. Council for Foreign Relations 1979–82; Under-Sec. Cttee for Int. Relations 1982–92; Dir for Int. Affairs, Dir Office of Palair 1993–96; Minister of Foreign Affairs 1998–2001. *Address:* c/o Ministry of Foreign Affairs, Dame Grueva 14, 9100 Skopje, Macedonia.

DIMITROV, Philip; Bulgarian politician; b. 31 March 1955, Sofia; s. of Dimitar Vassilev Dimitrov and Katherine Philipov Dimitrov; m. Elena Valentinova Gueorgieva-Dimitrova 1988; ed St Kliment Ohridsky Univ., Sofia; fmr lawyer; leader Bulgarian Union of Democratic Forces; Prime Minister of Bulgaria 1991–92; Vice-Chair. Bulgaria Jt Parl. Cttee, EU 1995–97; Perm. Rep. to UN, New York 1997–98; Amb. to USA 1998–2002; Truman-Reagan Freedom Award for contrib. to overcoming communism 1999. *Publication:* For They Lived Lord 1991. *Address:* c/o Ministry of Foreign Affairs, Al. Zhendov St 2, 1113 Sofia, Bulgaria (Office).

DIMITROVA, Ghena; Bulgarian opera singer; b. 6 May 1941, Beglej; ed Bulgarian State Conservatoire (with Christo Brumbarov); début as Abigaille in Nabucco, Sofia Opera; Singer Laureate, Int. Competition, Treviso, Italy for interpretation of Amelia, Un Ballo in Maschera 1972; appearances France, Italy and Spain, early 1970s; appeared in Cen. and S. America and at Bolshoi, Moscow 1975–78; début Vienna Opera 1978; début Verona in La Gioconda 1980, several subsequent appearances there 1980–; début London, concert performance of La Gioconda at Barbican 1983; in Turandot, La Scala 1983; Macbeth, Salzburg Festival 1984; début Royal Opera House, Covent Garden in Turandot 1984; appears in opera houses of Vienna, Munich, Paris, Hamburg, Berlin, Madrid, Barcelona, Naples, Zürich, Rome, NY, San Francisco, Chicago; opened La Scala 1985/86 season in Aida; Gold Medal and First Prize, Fourth Int. Competition for Young Singers, Sofia 1970; People's Artist 1979; Golden Archer and Giovanni Zenatello Prizes (Rome and Verona) 1981; has recorded Nabucco and Oberto, Conte di San Bonifacio and discs of opera arias and Puccini arias. *Address:* c/o Stafford Law, 6 Barham Close, Weybridge, KT13 9PR, England (Office).

DIMOVSKA, Dosta; Macedonian politician; b. 17 Feb. 1954, Skopje; ed Skopje Univ.; teacher Georgi Dimitrov School, Skopje 1980–98; Asst, Asst Prof. Faculty of Philosophy, Skopje Univ. 1981–91; mem. Parl. 1991–95; mem. of staff BS Stock Holding Co. 1995–97, Kisela Voda, Skopje 1998; Chair. Cttee on Inter-Ethnic Relations; Deputy Prime Minister, Minister of Internal Affairs 1998–2001; Vice-Pres. Internal Macedonian Revolutionary Org.-Democratic Party for Macedonian Nat. Unity (IMRO-DPMNU) 1991, 1995. *Publications:* two Vols of poetry, essays and political reviews. *Address:* IMRO-DPMNU, 1000 Skopje, Petar Drapshin br. 36, Macedonia (Office). *Telephone:* (2) 111441 (Office). *Fax:* (2) 211586 (Office).

DINCERLER, M. Vehbi; Turkish politician; b. 2 Aug. 1940, Gaziantep; s. of Esat and Şefika Dincerler; m.; three s. one d.; ed Depts of Eng, Istanbul Tech. Univ., Business Inst., Istanbul Univ., Graduate School, Univ. of Syracuse, NY; worked for State Planning Org.; joined Project Studies for Turkey at World Bank, studied economy of Ireland; academic at Middle East Tech. Univ., Gaziantep Campus; mem. Nat. Ass. 1983–, Minister of Educ., Youth and Sports 1983–85, Minister of State 1985–87; Chair. Nat. Ass. Foreign Relations Cttee 1988–90; Minister of State 1989–91; mem. Constitutional Cttee 1991–, N Atlantic Ass.; Motherland Party. *Leisure interests:* music, social activities. *Address:* Ahmet Hasim Cad. 67/U Dikmen, Ankara, Turkey, 06460. *Telephone:* (312) 4415361. *Fax:* (312) 4381555.

DINE, James; American artist; b. 16 June 1935, Cincinnati, Ohio; m. Nancy Minto 1957; three s.; ed Cincinnati Art Acad.; first one-man Exhbn Reuben Gallery, New York 1960; work appears in many public collections including Guggenheim Museum, Moderna Museet, Stockholm, Museum of Modern Art, New York, Dallas Museum of Fine Arts, Tate Gallery and Whitney Museum of Modern American Art. *Solo exhibitions include:* Palais des Beaux Arts, Brussels 1963, 1970, Sidney Jannis Gallery, New York 1963, 1964, 1967, Robert Fraser Gallery, London 1965, 1966, 1969, Stedelijk Museum, Amsterdam (drawings) 1967, Museum of Modern Art, Munich 1969, Berlin Festival, Sonnabend Gallery, New York and Whitney Museum of American Art, New York 1970; Exhbn of Designs for A Midsummer Night's Dream, Museum of Modern Art, New York 1967. *Group exhibitions include:* Painting and Sculpture of a Decade, Tate Gallery, London 1964, Venice Biennale 1964, A Decade of American Drawings 1965, Young America 1965 and Art of the United States 1670-1966 1966 (all three at Whitney Museum of American Art), U.S. Pavilion, Expo 1967, Montreal and Hayward Gallery, London 1969. *Publications:* Welcome Home, Lovebirds 1969 (also illustrator); co-author and illustrator The Adventures of Mr. and Mrs. Jim & Ron 1970; illustrator The Poet Assassinated 1968, Drawing from the Glypothek 1993. *Address:* c/o The Pace Gallery, 32 East 57th Street, New York, NY 10022, USA.

DING FENGYING; Chinese party official; b. 1943, Luotian Co., Hubei Prov.; ed Huazhong Teachers Coll.; joined CCP 1961; Chair. Hubei Branch, Chinese Women's Fed. 1973; Vice-Chair. Revolutionary Cttee, Hubei Prov. 1978–79; alt. mem. 12th CCP Cen. Cttee 1982–87; First Sec. CCP Cttee, Huangguang Pref. 1983–; Deputy Sec. CCP Cttee, Hubei Prov. 1986, mem. CPC 5th Hubei Prov. Cttee 1988–, Sec. Comm. for Discipline Inspection, Hubei Prov. 1988–; mem. CCP Cen. Discipline Inspection Comm. 1992–. *Address:* Hubei Dangwei, 1 Beihuanlu Road, Shuiguohu, Wuchang City, Hubei Province, People's Republic of China. *Telephone:* 813351.

DING GUANGEN; Chinese state official; b. Sept. 1929, Wuxi Co., Jiangsu Prov.; ed Jiaotong Univ. of Shanghai; joined CCP. 1956; Deputy Sec.-Gen. Standing Comm. NPC 1983–85; Minister of Railways 1985–88; Vice-Minister State Planning Comm. 1988; Dir Taiwan Affairs Office 1988; mem. 12th CCP Cen. Cttee 1985–87, 13th CCP Cen. Cttee 1987–92; Sec. Secr. 14th CCP Cen. Cttee 1992–; alt. mem. Political Bureau 1987, mem. 1992–; Head United Front Work Dept of CCP 1990–92; Head CCP Propaganda Dept 1992–; Head Cen. Leading Group for Propaganda and Thought 1994–; mem. Secr. 15th CCP Cen. Cttee 1997–. *Address:* Central Committee of the Chinese Communist Party, Zhongnanhai, Beijing, People's Republic of China.

DING GUANGXUN, Bishop K. H.; Chinese theologian and church leader; b. 20 Sept. 1915; ed St Johns Univ., Shanghai and New York Union Theological Seminary, ordained 1942, Sec. Student Christian Movt of Canada, Student World Christian Fed., Geneva; returned to China 1951; Pres. Nanjing Theological Seminary 1952, consecrated Bishop 1955; Vice-Chair. Three-Self Patriotic Cttee Movt of the Protestant Churches of China 1961, Chair. 5th Cttee 1980–97, Hon. Chair. 1997–; Pres. Christian Council of China; Hon. Pres. Chinese People's Asscn for Peace and Disarmament 1985–; a Deputy Chair. CPPCC 1989–; Vice-Chair. CPPCC 7th Nat. Cttee 1989–93, Religious Cttee 1991–; Vice-Chair. CPPCC 8th Nat. Cttee 1993–98, 9th Nat. Cttee 1998–; Chinese Religious Peace Cttee 1994–; Sec. of Secr. CCP Cen. Cttee 1992–. *Address:* Nanjing Theological Seminary, Nanjing 210029; 378 Mo Chou Road, Nanjing 210004, People's Republic of China.

DING HENGGAO, Gen.; Chinese politician and scientist; b. 1931, Nanjing Co., Jiangsu Prov.; m. Nie Lili (d. of Marshal Nie Rongzhen); ed Nanjing Univ. and in USSR; Minister of State Comm. of Science, Tech. and Industry for Nat. Defence 1985, Party Cttee Sec. 1989–; rank of Lt-Gen. PLA 1988, Gen. 1994; mem. 13th CCP Cen. Cttee 1989–92, 14th CCP Cen. Cttee 1992–, Nat. Leading Group for Science and Tech. Chinese Acad. of Eng, Minister in charge of Comm. of Science, Tech. and Industry for Nat. Defence 1993–96. *Address:* 1 - South Building, Aimin Street, Xicheng District, Beijing 100034, People's Republic of China. *Telephone:* (10) 66056357. *Fax:* (10) 66738111. *E-mail:* engach@mail.cae.ac.cn (Office).

DING JIEYIN; Chinese sculptor; b. 4 Feb. 1926, Yinxian, Zhejiang; d. of Ding Yong-sen and Gao Yu-ding; m. Hong Bo 1952; one d.; ed Cen. Acad. of Fine Arts, Beijing; Asst Researcher, Sculpture Studio, Cen. Acad. of Fine Arts; Ed. China Sculpture; Chief Ed. supplement Chinese Art, New Evening newspaper, Hong Kong; Vice-Dir Longshan Art Acad., Rizhao 1992–; mem. China Artists' Asscn; about 60 pieces of sculpture; works exhibited at China Art Gallery, Beijing 1991, 1992 and commissioned by various cities. *Publications:* Clay Figures in the Temples of Da Tong 1982, The Art of Colour Clay Sculpture in Jin Ancestral Temple 1988; articles in Meishu, Art Research, People's Daily and Chinese Art supplement, New Evening (Hong Kong). *Leisure interests:* literature, basketball. *Address:* Xiao-Wei-Hu-Tong 68, Beijing 100005, People's Republic of China. *Telephone:* 5136377.

DING SHISUN; Chinese university administrator and mathematician; b. 5 Sept. 1927, Shanghai; s. of Ding Rounong and Liu Huixian; m. Gui Linlin 1956; two s.; ed Math. Dept, Tsing-hua Univ.; Asst Tsing-hua Univ. 1950–52; joined staff Beijing Univ. 1952, promoted to Prof. of Math. 1979, Vice-Chair. Math. Dept 1978–80, Chair. 1981–82, Pres. Beijing Univ. 1984–89; Pres. Math. Soc. of Beijing 1986–88; Vice-Pres. Chinese Math. Soc. 1988–91; visited Math. Dept, Harvard Univ., USA 1983; specializes in fields of algebra and number theory; Exec. Vice-Chair. China Democratic League Cen. Cttee 1987, Chair. 1997; mem. CPPCC 8th Nat. Cttee 1993–98; Vice-Chair. Educ. and Culture Cttee; Vice-Chair. Standing Cttee of 9th NPC 1998–; Hon. Dr. (Soka, Japan) 1985; Hon. DSc (Nebraska) 1988. *Publications:* several books and papers. *Leisure interest:* classical music. *Address:* Mathematics Department, Beijing University, Haidian, Beijing, 100871, People's Republic of China.

DING WENCHANG, Maj.-Gen.; Chinese party official and army officer; b. 1933, Suxian Co., Anhui Prov.; joined CCP 1956; Dir Political Dept, PLA Air Force 1988, Political Commissar 1992–, Party Cttee Sec.; rank of Maj.-Gen. 1988, Gen. of Air Force 1996; mem. 14th CCP Cen. Cttee 1992–97; mem. 15th CCP Cen. Cttee 1997–. *Address:* Political Department of Air Force, Beijing, People's Republic of China.

DING XIAQI; Chinese mathematician and research professor; b. 25 May 1928, Yiyang Co., Hunan Prov.; m. Luo Peizhu 1957; three d.; ed Dept of Math., Wuhan Univ.; Research Asst, Assoc., Assoc. Prof., Prof. Inst. of Math., Acad. Sinica 1951–79; Research Prof., Inst. of Systems Sciences, Acad. Sinica 1979–91; Research Prof., Inst. of Applied Math., Acad. Sinica 1991–; Prof. Dir Wuhan Inst. of Math., Acad. Sinica 1985–94, Dr. Wuhan Inst. of Mathematical Physics; Academician, Chinese Acad. of Sciences 1991–; mem. Cttee Math. Soc. of China; Standing mem. Cttee of Chinese Soc. of Systems Eng; Prize Award, Nat. Science Conf., Beijing 1978, Prize of Chinese Acad. of Sciences 1978, 1st Class Prize, Chinese Acad. of Science 1988, 2nd Class Prize Natural Science Prize of People's Repub. of China 1989. *Publications:* more than 80 papers on PDE, functions spaces, number theory and numerical analysis; 4 monographs. *Leisure interests:* mathematics. *Address:* Institute of Applied Mathematics, Academia Sinica, Beijing 100080, People's Republic of China. *Telephone:* 6256293910 (Office); 62561754 (Home). *Fax:* 62541689.

DINI, Lamberto; Italian politician and banker; b. 1 March 1931, Florence; m.; one d.; ed Univ. of Florence, Univs. of Minnesota and Michigan, USA; economist, IMF, Washington DC, then various posts to Deputy Dir Africa Dept 1959–76, mem. Bd Exec. Dirs. 1976–78, now Alt. Gov. for Italy; joined Banca d'Italia (cen. bank) as Asst Gen. Man. 1979, later Gen. Man.; mem. Monetary Cttee of EU, Bd Dirs. BIS; Minister of the Treasury 1994–95; Prime Minister of Italy 1995–96; Minister of Foreign Affairs 1996–2001; currently Deputy Speaker of Senate; Leader Rinnovamento Italiano; Vice-Pres. European Liberal, Democrat and Reform party; Fulbright Scholar. *Address:* Rinnovamento Italiano, Via di Ripetta 142, 00186 Rome, Italy. *Website:* www .rinnovamento.it.

DINI AHMED, Ahmed; Djibouti politician; b. 1932, Obock; Vice-Pres., Territorial Ass., French Somaliland (now Repub. of Djibouti) 1959–60; Minister of Production 1963–64, of the Interior 1967–72; joined Ligue Populaire Africaine pour l'Indépendance 1972; Pres. Nat. Ass. of French Territory of the Afars and the Issas May–June 1977, of Repub. of Djibouti June–July 1977; Prime Minister July–Dec. 1977; Pres. Front pour la restauration de l'unité et de la démocratie (insurgent Movt) 1992–94, split into two factions March 1994; leader of faction favouring a continuation of mil. activities.

DINKINS, David, BS; American politician and lawyer; b. 10 July 1927, Trenton, NJ; m. Joyce Burrows 1953; one s. one d.; ed Howard Univ., Washington, DC and Brooklyn law school; joined Harlem law firm 1956; elected to New York State Ass. 1965; Pres. Bd of Elections, New York 1972; City Clerk, New York 1975–85; Manhattan Borough Pres. 1986; contested Democratic Primary, defeating Mayor Edward Koch Sept. 1989; Mayor of New York 1990–93; Prof. Columbia Univ.'s School of Int. and Public Affairs 1993. *Leisure interest:* tennis. *Address:* Columbia University, Morningside Heights, New York, NY 10027, USA.

DINWIDDY, Bruce Harry, MA; British diplomatist; b. 1 Feb. 1946; s. of the late Thomas Lutwyche Dinwiddy and Ruth Dinwiddy (née Abbott); m. Emma Victoria Llewellyn 1974; one s. one d.; ed Winchester Coll., New Coll. Oxford; economist, Govt. of Swaziland, Overseas Devt. Inst. (ODI) Nuffield Fellow 1967–70, Research Officer 1970–73; entered FCO 1973, Cen. and Southern African Dept 1973–4, Second Sec. Mission CSCE, Geneva 1974, Hong Kong and Indian Ocean Dept 1974–75; Del. to Mutual and Balanced Force Reductions (MBFR) negotiations, Vienna 1975–77; Perm. Under Sec.'s Dept, FCO

London 1977–81, Personnel Operations Dept 1983–84, Asst Head, Personnel Policy Dept 1985–86, 2001–02; Head of Chancery in Cairo, Egypt 1981–83; Counsellor on loan to Cabinet Office 1986–88; CDA/SWP, Ebenhausen 1989; Embassy Counsellor in Bonn, Germany 1989–91; Deputy High Commr in Ottawa, Canada 1992–95; Head of African Dept (Southern) FCO 1995–98; Commr (non-resident) British Indian Ocean Territory 1996–98; High Commr in Dar es Salaam, Tanzania 1998–2001; secondment to Standard Chartered Bank 2001–02; Gov. of Cayman Islands 2002–. *Publication:* Promoting African Enterprise 1974. *Leisure interests:* golf, lawn tennis, music, travel. *Address:* Office of the Governor, 4th Floor, Government Administration Building, Elgin Avenue, George Town, Grand Cayman, Cayman Islands (Office). *Telephone:* 244-2402 (Office). *Fax:* 945-4131 (Office). *E-mail:* tgo@gov .ky (Office). *Website:* www.gov.ky.

DION, Céline, OQ; Canadian singer; b. 30 March 1968, Charlemagne, Québec; d. of Adhémar Dion and Thérèse Dion; m. René Angélil 1994; one s.; became first Canadian to win Gold Disc in France with single D'amour ou d'amitié which sold over 700,000 copies 1983; winner, Eurovision song contest, Dublin 1988; performed anthem The Power of the Dream at opening ceremony of Olympic Games, Atlanta 1996; winner, Gold Medal, Yamaha World Song Festival, Tokyo 1982, Female Vocalist of the Year, Juno Awards 1991, 1992, 1993 and many other awards; Medal of Arts (France) 1996. *Albums include:* Unison (including single Where Does My Heart Beat Now) released 1990, Dion chante Plamondon 1991, Sleepless in Seattle 1993, The Colour of My Love 1993, D'eux 1995 (best-selling French-language album of all time) 1995, Falling Into You 1996, Let's Talk About Love 1998, These are Special Times 1998 (Grammy and Juno Awards 1999), All the Way 1999, A New Day Has Come 2002. *Singles include:* Beauty and the Beast (Acad. Award for Best Song Written for a Motion Picture or TV 1992, Grammy Award 1993), If You Asked Me To, Nothing Broken But My Heart, Love Can Move Mountains, When I Fall In Love, The Power of Love, Misled, Think Twice, Because You Loved Me, My Heart Will Go On (Grammy Award 1999), Immortality 1998, Treat Her Like a Lady 1998, That's the Way, It Is 1999, The First Time I Ever Saw Your Face 2000. *Publications:* All the Way 2000, My Story, My Dreams 2001. *Leisure interests:* skiing, water-skiing, roller-blading, miniature cups, crystal objects, tea pots, cuddly frogs, looking after son, golf. *Address:* Les Productions Feeling, 2540 boulevard Daniel-Johnson, Porte 755, Laval, Québec H7T 2S3, Canada.

DION, Hon. Stéphane, PC, MSc; Canadian politician and academic; b. 1955; m.; one d.; ed Laval Univ., Inst. d'études politiques de Paris; Prof. of Political Science, Univ. of Montreal 1984–96; Minister of Intergovernmental Affairs and Pres. Queen's Privy Council for Canada 1996–; Guest Scholar, Brookings Inst., Washington, DC 1990–91, Laboratoire d'économie publique de Paris 1994–95; Research Fellow, Canadian Centre for Man. Devt 1990–91; Co-Ed. Canadian Journal of Political Science 1990–93; mem. Aid to Scholarly Publs Cttee of Social Sciences Fed. of Canada, Advisory Council of Inst. of Inter-governmental Relations, Queen's Univ. *Address:* Privy Council Office, Lan-gevin Block, 8th Floor, Intergovernmental Affairs, 66 Slater Street, Ottawa, Ont., K1A 0A3, Canada.

DIOP, Abdoulaye; Senegalese politician; ed Lycée El Hadj Malick Sy de Thiès, Univ. of Dakar and Ecole Nat. d'Admin et de Magistrature; Asst to Prin. Paymaster, Thiès 1980–81; Rate Collector Commune de Fatick 1981–84, Commune de Mbour 1984–87, Commune de Pikine 1987–90; Tax Collector Dakar Centre 1990–93; Tax and Rate Collector, Ville de Dakar 1993–95, Dakar Urban Community 1993–95; Sr Banking Exec., Treas.-Gen. and Dir of Treasury and Public Finance 1995–98; Minister Del., Ministry of Economy and Finance 2000, Minister of Economy and Finance 2001–; mem. Observ-atoire des finances locales de Cotonou 1996–; Comm. de réforme des textes de la décentralisation; Pres. Tech. Cttee responsible for Reform of Local Finance in Senegal; Chevalier, Ordre nat. du Lion de la République du Sénégal 1996. *Address:* Ministry of Economy and Finance, PO 4017, Dakar, Senegal (Office). *Telephone:* 822-41-95 (Office). *Fax:* 822-28-69 (Office). *Website:* www.finances .gouv.sn (Office).

DIOP, Iba Mar; Senegalese professor of medicine; b. 17 May 1921, St Louis; m.; six c.; ed African School of Medicine and Pharmacy, Univ. of Bordeaux; Head of Clinic Dakar Faculty of Medicine and Pharmacy 1965, Asst Prof. 1970, Prof. 1975, Dean 1976; specialist in infectious diseases; Pres. Asscn of African Faculties and Schools of Medicine 1977–81; Fellow Islamic Acad. of Sciences, mem. Council and Vice-Pres. 1994–98, Acting Pres. 1999; mem. Medical Comm., IOC, Acad. Nat. de Médecine, France, African Acad. of Sciences 1988, Founding Mem. and Sec. Senegal Acad. of Sciences and Techniques; Founding Pres. then Hon. Pres. Int. Union Against Venereal Diseases; Sec. Medical Soc. of French-speaking Black Africa 1962, Vice-Pres. 1963, Pres. 1977, now mem.; mem. French-speaking Soc. for Infectious Pathology 1971, Int. Therapeutic Union 1975; Fellow Third World Acad. of Sciences, mem. Council 1992; UNO Medal (Congo) 1961, Commdr, Ordre des Palmes Académiques 1985, Officier, Légion d'honneur 1983, Médaille Orange, Croix Rouge Française 1968, Officier, Ordre des Palmes Académ-iques (Togo) 1980, Commdr, Ordre Nat. de la Côte d'Ivoire 1982, Chevalier, Ordre Nat. du Cameroun 1983, Officer, Nat. Order of Cen. Africa 1983, Médaille de la Ville de Paris 1985, Commdr, Congo Order of Merit 1985, First Laureate Alfred Quenum Prize for Africa, WHO, First Laureate Mohamed El Fasi Prize, Laureate Third World Acad. of Sciences; Hon. Dean UCAD. *Publications:* over 300 Publs on infectious and tropical diseases. *Address:* Clinique Fann Hock, Rue 70 x 55, B.P. 15504, Dakar-Fann, Senegal (Office).

DIOP, Majmout; Senegalese politician and pharmacist; b. 30 Sept. 1922, St Louis; ed Ecole Africaine de Médecine et de Pharmacie (Dakar), Paris Univ. and African Inst., Univ. of Moscow; Hospital pharmacist, Senegal and Gabon 1947–50; Pres. Senegalese students' Asscn in France 1951; studied Marxism at Bucharest 1953–56; Sec.-Gen. Parti africain de l'indépendance (PAI) 1957–; exiled from Senegal 1961–76; engaged in research in political sociology at Inst. of Human Sciences, Mali 1968–76; dispensary pharmacist, Dakar 1977–. *Publications:* Contribution à l'Etude des problèmes politiques en Afrique Noire 1959, Classes et idéologies de classe au Sénégal 1963, Notes sur la classe ouvrière sénégalaise 1965, Histoire des classes sociales dans l'Afrique de l'Ouest (Vol. I) 1971, (Vol. II) 1972, Etude sur le Salariat 1975, Essai sur l'esclavage en Afrique de l'Ouest (to be published); and many articles in reviews and journals. *Address:* Parti africain de l'indépendance (PAI), P.O. Box 820, Maison du Peuple Guediewaye, Dakar (Office); 153 Avenue du Président Lamine Gueye, Dakar (Office); 210 HCM, Guediawaye, Dakar, Senegal (Home). *Telephone:* 837-01-36 (Office).

DIOP, Pape Bouba; Senegalese footballer; b. 28 Jan. 1978, Dakar; began career as midfielder with Espoir Dakar, then Diaraaf Dakar 1997–98, Vevey-Sports 1999–2000, Neuchâtel Xamax July–Dec. 2000, Grasshoppers Zurich, Switzerland Jan.–Dec. 2001, Racing Club de Lens, France Jan. 2002–; mem. Senegal nat. football team June 2000–, took part in African Nations Cup, Feb. 2002, top scorer for Senegal nat. football team in World Cup 2002. *Address:* c/o Racing Club de Lens, Avenue Alfred Maes, BP 236, 62304 Lens Cedex, France (Office).

DIOUF, Abdou, LenD, LèsL; Senegalese politician; b. 7 Sept. 1935, Louga; m. 1963; ed Lycée Faidherbe, St Louis, Dakar and Paris Univs.; Dir of Tech. Co-operation and Minister of Planning Sept.–Nov. 1960; Asst Sec.-Gen. to Govt 1960–61; Sec.-Gen. Ministry of Defence June–Dec. 1961; Gov. Sine-Saloum Region 1961–62; Dir de Cabinet of Minister of Foreign Affairs 1962–63, of Pres. of Repub. 1963–65; Sec.-Gen. to Pres.'s Office 1964–68; Minister of Planning and Industry 1968–70; Prime Minister 1970–80; Pres. of Senegal 1981–2000, of Confed. of Senegambia 1982–89; Chair. OAU 1985–86; mem. Nat. Ass. for Longa Département 1973–; mem. Sengalese Progressive Union (U.P.S.) 1961–, later Asst Sec.-Gen.; fmr Asst Sec.-Gen. Parti socialiste sénégalais (P.S.), now Chair.; Jt winner Africa Prize for Leadership 1987. *Address:* Parti socialiste sénégalais, Maison du Parti, Colobane, BP 12010, Dakar, Senegal (Office). *Telephone:* 824-06-73. *Fax:* 825-50-54. *E-mail:* ps@ telecomplus.sn (Office). *Website:* www1.telecomplus.sn/ps (Office).

DIOUF, Jacques, PhD; Senegalese international civil servant and agrono-mist; b. 1 Aug. 1938, Saint-Louis; m. Aïssatou Seye 1963; one s. four d.; ed Lycée Faidherbe, Saint-Louis, Ecole Nat. d'Agriculture, Paris/Grignon, Ecole Nat. d'Application d'Agronomie Tropicale, Paris/Nogent and Sorbonne, Paris; Exec. Sec. African Groundnut Council, Lagos 1965–71; Exec. Sec. West African Rice Devt Asscn, Monrovia 1971–77; Sec. of State for Science and Tech., Govt of Senegal, Dakar 1978–83; mem. Nat. Ass., Chair. Foreign Relations Cttee and elected Sec., Dakar 1983–84; Sec. Gen. Banque centrale des états de l'Afrique de l'ouest, Dakar 1985–90; Perm. Rep. of Senegal to UN 1991–93; Dir-Gen. FAO 1994–; led Senegalese dels to UN Confs on Science and Tech., Vienna 1979 (Chair. of 1st Comm.), Industrial Devt, New Delhi 1980, New and Renewable Energy Sources, Nairobi (Vice-Chair.) 1981, Peaceful Use of Space, Vienna 1982; African Rep., Consultative Group on Int. Agricultural Research, Washington; mem. Bd of Dirs. ISNAR, The Hague, IITA Lagos, IIRSDA Abidjan, ICRAF, Nairobi, Int. Foundation for Science, Stockholm, African Capacity Building Foundation, Harare, World Inst. for Devt Econs Research, Helsinki, Council of African Advisers of the World Bank, Washington DC; Chair. SINAES, Dakar; mem. Consultative Cttee on Medical Research, WHO, Geneva; Grand Commdr, Order of the Star of Africa (Liberia) 1977, Award for Services to Education (France) 1979, Commdr Order of Agricultural Merit (Canada) 1995, Grand Cross Order of Merit in Agriculture, Fisheries and Food (Spain) 1996, Order of Solidarity (Cuba) 1998, Commdr, Légion d'honneur 1998, Grand Cross Order of May for Merit (Argentina) 1998, Two Niles Decoration (Sudan), 2000; numerous hon. doctorates. *Publications:* La détérioration du pouvoir d'achat de l'Arachide 1972, Les fondements du dialogue scientifique entre les civilisations Euro-occidentale et Négro-Africaine 1979, The Challenge of Agricultural Develop-ment in Africa 1989. *Leisure interests:* reading, music, sports. *Address:* Food and Agriculture Organization of the United Nations, Viale delle Terme di Caracalla, 00100 Rome, Italy (Office). *Telephone:* (06) 57051 (Office). *Fax:* (06) 57053152 (Office). *E-mail:* telex-room@fao.org (Office). *Website:* www.fao.org (Office).

DIPICO, Manne Emsley, BA; South African civil servant and trade unionist; b. 21 April 1959, Kimberley; ed Univ. of Fort Hare; joined African Nat. Congress (ANC) 1982; Nat. Educ. Co-ordinator Nat. Union of Mineworkers; Azanian Students' Org. (AZASO) rep. for United Democratic Front (UDF) Exec. Border Region, AZASO Treas. Univ. of Fort Hare; mem. UDF N Cape 1985–86; detained Ciskei 1984, detained under state of emergency, Kimberley 1986, arrested and sentenced to five years for furthering the aims of a banned org. through terrorist activities 1987–90, released before end of sentence; Regional Sec. ANC 1991–92, Regional Chair. N Cape 1992–; Regional Elections Co-ordinator 1993–94; Premier N Cape Prov. Legislature 1994–. *Address:* Private Bag X5016, Kimberley 8301 (Office); 5248 Magashula Street, P.O. Mankurwane, Galeshawe-Kimberley 8345, South Africa (Home). *Telephone:* (53) 8309300 (Home). *Fax:* (53) 8332122 (Office). *E-mail:* cmatlhacko@pancmail.ncape.gov.za (Office).

DIRCEU DE OLIVEIRA E SILVA, José; Brazilian politician and lawyer; b. 16 March 1946, Passa Quatro; m. 1st Clara Becker (divorced); m. 2nd Maria Rita Garcia de Andrade; one s. two d.; fmr student leader; organized protest of 100,000 people against Brazilian mil. dictatorship 1967; jailed 1968, released 1969 in exchange for kidnapped US Amb. Charles Elbrick; went into exile in Cuba where he received guerrilla training; returned permanently to Brazil 1975; assumed false identity (Carlos Henrique Gouveia de Melo) in Cruzeiro do Oeste, Paraná, became a shopkeeper; amnestied 1979; Co-Founder (with Luiz Inácio Lula da Silva, q.v.) Workers' Party (PT), later Gen. Sec., Leader 1994, Pres. 1995–; elected State Deputy 1986, Deputy Fed. Parl. 1990, 1997, 1999, 2001–; Gov. State of São Paulo 1994; Chief Adviser to Pres.-elect Luiz Inácio Lula da Silva, q.v.; Chief of Cabinet 2003–. *Address:* Office of the Civilian Cabinet, Palácio do Planalto, 4° Andar, Praça dos Três Poderes, 70150 Brasília, DF, Brazil (Office). *Telephone:* (61) 411-1573 (Office). *Fax:* (61) 323-1461 (Office). *E-mail:* ccivilinfo@planalto.gov.br (Office). *Website:* www .presidencia.gov.br/casacivil (Office).

DIRKSEN, Gebhard, DJur; German banker and lawyer; b. 29 June 1929, Göttingen; s. of Wilhelm and Magdalene (née Güthenke) Dirksen; m. Renate Pöhl 1971; one s. two d.; ed at schools in Gutersloh/Westfalen and Univs. of Mainz, Freiburg and Göttingen; articled in Göttingen, Hanover and Celle; Deputy Chair. Bd of Dirs Norddeutsche Landesbank Girozentrale 1959–94. *Address:* Westpreussenufer 4, 30659 Hannover, Germany. *Telephone:* 6478746.

DISANAYAKA, Heen Banda, BA; Sri Lankan banker; b. 28 Aug. 1937, Talawa; m. Wasantha Wijekoon 1963; one s. two d.; ed Univ. of Sri Lanka; Dir-Gen. of Customs 1976; Alt. Exec. Dir Asian Devt Bank 1987; Deputy Sec. to Treasury 1989; Gov. Cen. Bank of Sri Lanka 1992–95, also fmr Chair. of Monetary Bd; Alt. Dir IMF, Washington DC 1996–98. *Leisure interest:* organic farming. *Address:* 84/1 Old Kottawa Road, Mirihana, Nugegoda, Sri Lanka. *Telephone:* 852199.

DISNEY, Anthea; British business executive; b. 13 Oct. 1946, Dunstable; d. of Alfred Leslie and Elsie Wale; m. Peter Robert Howe 1984; ed Queen's Coll.; New York corresp. London Daily Mail 1973–75, Features Ed. 1975–77, New York Bureau Chief 1977–79; columnist London Daily Express, New York 1979–84; Managing Ed. New York Daily News 1984–87; Ed. Sunday Daily News 1984–87; Ed. US magazine 1987–88; Ed.-in-Chief Self magazine 1988–89; magazine developer Murdoch magazines 1989–90; exec. producer A Current Affair, Fox TV 1990–91; Ed.-in-Chief TV Guide magazine 1991–95; Editorial Dir Murdoch Magazines 1994–95; Pres. and CEO HarperCollins Publrs. 1996–97; Chair., CEO News America Publishing 1997–; Exec. Vice-Pres. of Content, News Corpn 1999–. *Address:* News Corporation, Suite 300, 1211 Avenue of the Americas, New York, NY 10036, USA.

DISTEL, Sacha; French singer and songwriter; b. 29 Jan. 1933, Paris; s. of Léon and Andrée (née Ventura) Distel; m. Francine Bréaud 1963; two s.; ed Lycée Claude-Bernard, Paris; voted best guitarist by Jazz Hot magazine and in critics poll 1957, 1958, 1959; acted in films, Les Mordus 1960, Nous irons à Deauville 1962, La Bonne Soupe 1964, Le Voyou 1970, Sans mobile apparent 1971; has sung more than 200 songs in French, English, Italian, German; TV presenter in France, England and Germany; producer of TV shows Sacha Show, Top à Sacha Distel 1973, Sacha's in Town (UK) 1972; producer and performer La Belle Vie TV programme 1984–85; Chevalier des Arts et des Lettres 1987, Chevalier, Légion d'honneur 1997, numerous awards. *Publication:* Les Pendules à l'heure 1985. *Leisure interests:* swimming, skiing and tennis. *Address:* c/o Charley Marouani, 37 rue Marbeuf, 75008 Paris, France.

DITZ, Johannes; Austrian industrial executive and fmr. politician; fmr Austrian People's Party politician; CEO Österreichische Industrieholding AG (ÖIAG) (Govt holding co.); Chair. Austrian Airlines, Telekom Austria; Chair. Supervisory Bd OMV (oil and gas co.); Vice-Chair. Supervisory Bd Böhler-Uddeholm AG. *Address:* c/o Austrian Airlines, Fontanastr. 1, 1107 Vienna, Austria (Office). *Telephone:* (1) 176-6 (Office). *Fax:* (1) 688-55-05. *E-mail:* public.relations@aua.com (Office). *Website:* www.aua.com (Office).

DIVINSKY, Ferdinand, DSc; Slovak biochemist and university administrator; b. 17 Aug. 1947, Bratislava; m.; two c.; ed Tech. Univ., Bratislava; researcher, Slovakoform 1970–72; teacher Comenius Univ., Bratislava 1972–2002, Rector 2002–; short-term research studies in UK 1986–87, 1991, Belgium, USA, Germany 1991; Hon. Sr Research Fellow, King's Coll. London, UK; Jubilee Medal, Charles Univ., Prague 1998. *Publications include:* numerous scientific papers. *Leisure interests:* literature, nature. *Address:* Comenius University, Šafárikovo nám. c. 6, 818 06 Bratislava 16, Slovakia (Office). *Telephone:* (2) 52921594 (Office). *Fax:* (2) 52963836 (Office). *E-mail:* ferdinand.divinsky@rec.uniba.sk. *Website:* www.uniba.sk (Office).

DIXIT, Avinash Kamalakar, BSc, BA, PhD; American economist; b. 8 June 1944, Bombay, India; s. of Kamalakar Ramachandra Dixit and Kusum Dixit; ed Bombay Univ., Cambridge Univ., MIT; Fellow, Balliol Coll., Oxford 1970–74; Prof., Univ. of Warwick 1974–80; Prof., Princeton Univ. 1981–; Vice-Pres. American Econ. Asscn 2002; Fellow, Econometric Soc. 1977, Vice-Pres. 2000, Pres. 2001; Guggenheim Fellowship 1992; Fellow, American Acad. of Arts and Sciences 1992. *Publications:* Theory of International Trade (co-author) 1980, Thinking Strategically (co-author) 1991, Investment under Uncertainty (co-author) 1994. *Address:* Department of Economics, Princeton University, Princeton, NJ 08544 (Office); 36 Gordon Way, Princeton, NJ 08540, USA (Home). *Telephone:* (609) 258-4013 (Office). *Fax:* (609) 258-6419 (Office). *E-mail:* dixitak@princeton.edu (Office). *Website:* www.princeton.edu/ ~dixitak/home (Office).

DIXIT, Jyotindranath, MA; Indian diplomatist; b. 8 Jan. 1936, Madras; m. Vijaya Sundaram 1958; three s. two d.; ed Univ. of Delhi; served in different capacities in Indian embassies in Mexico, Chile, Bhutan, Japan, Austria 1958–69; at Ministry of External Affairs dealing with China, Pakistan and UN Affairs 1961–63, 1969–72; first Amb. (acting) to Bangladesh 1972–75; Minister Indian Embassy, Washington, USA 1975–78; Chief Spokesman on Foreign Policy, Govt of India 1978–82; Amb. to Afghanistan 1982–85, to Pakistan 1989; High Commr to Sri Lanka 1985–89, to Pakistan 1989–91; Foreign Sec. to the Govt of India 1991–94. *Publication:* Self in Autumn (poems) 1982. *Leisure interests:* reading, swimming, rowing, hiking. *Address:* AJH-102-A, Aryun rang, DLF Dunkirk Enclave phase 1, Gurgaon-122002, Haryana, India.

DIXON, Sir (David) Jeremy, Kt, RIBA; British architect; b. 31 May 1939; s. of late Joseph L. Dixon and Beryl M. Braund; m. Fenella Clemens 1964 (separated 1990); one s. two d.; ed Merchant Taylors' School and Architectural Asscn School of Architecture; Prin. in pvt. practice with Fenella Dixon 1975–90; formed partnership of Jeremy Dixon/BDP with William Jack (for extension to Royal Opera House, Covent Garden) Prin.1983–90; Prin. Jeremy Dixon, Edward Jones 1990–; other projects include Piazzale Roma, Venice, grove of fountains Somerset House (with Edward Jones); Tate Gallery restaurant; Nat. Portrait Gallery extension; shop for Clifton Nurseries; Northants. county offices; housing projects in London; study centre for Darwin Coll., Cambridge; work for J. Sainsbury PLC, Henry Moore Foundation; Chair. RIBA Regional Awards Group 1991–. *Leisure interests:* walking in English landscape, contemporary sculpture and painting, music. *Address:* Unit 6c, 44 Gloucester Avenue, London, NW1 8JD, England (Office).

DIXON, Frank James, MD; American medical scientist; b. 9 March 1920, St Paul, Minnesota; s. of Frank James and Rose Augusta (née Kuhfeld) Dixon; m. Marion Edwards 1946; two s. one d.; ed Univ. of Minnesota, US Naval Hospital, Great Lakes, Illinois; Research Asst, Dept of Pathology, Harvard Medical School 1946–48; Instructor, Dept of Pathology, Washington Univ. Medical School 1948–50; Asst Prof. Dept of Pathology 1950–51; Prof. and Chair. Dept of Pathology, Univ. of Pittsburgh School of Medicine 1951–61, Chair. Biomedical Research Depts 1970–74; Chair. Dept of Experimental Pathology, Scripps Clinic and Research Foundation 1961–74, Dir Research Inst. 1974–86, Dir Emer. 1986–; mem. NAS, Asscn American Physicians, AAAS and numerous other professional orgs; Harvey Society Lecturer 1962; mem. numerous editorial bds and advisory cttees.; Pahlavi Lecturer, Ministry of Science and Higher Educ., Iran 1976; Hon. DrSc (Medical Coll. of Ohio, Univ. of Washington); Theobald Smith Award in Medical Sciences from AAAS 1952, Parke-Davis Award from the American Soc. for Experimental Pathology 1957, Award for Distinguished Achievement from Modern Medicine 1961, Martin E. Rehfuss Award in Internal Medicine 1966, Von Pirquet Medal from Annual Forum on Allergy 1967, Bunim Gold Medal from the American Rheumatism Asscn 1968, Mayo Soley Award from the Western Soc. for Clinical Research 1969, Gairdner Foundation Award 1969, Dickson Prize in Medicine, Univ. of Pittsburgh 1975, Albert Lasker Basic Medical Research Award 1975, Homer Smith Award in Renal Physiology, New York Heart Asscn 1976, Rous-Whipple Award of the American Asscn of Pathologists 1979, First award in Immunology from Kaiser Permanente Medical Group, LA, Calif. 1979, Distinguished Service Award, Lupus Foundation 1987, Paul Klemperer Award 1989, Jean Hamburger Award 1990. *Publications:* Ed. Advances in Immunology and over 450 papers. *Leisure interests:* running, tennis, art collecting. *Address:* Scripps Research Institute, 10550 North Torrey Pines Road, La Jolla, CA 92037-1000 (Office); 2355 Avenida de la Playa, La Jolla, CA 92037, USA (Home). *Telephone:* (858) 784-8100.

DIXON, Kenneth Herbert Morley, CBE, DL, BA(Econs), FRSA; British business executive; b. 19 Aug. 1929, Stockport; s. of Arnold Morley Dixon and Mary Jolly; m. Patricia Oldbury Whalley 1955; two s.; ed Cranbrook School, Sydney, Manchester Univ., Harvard Business School; joined Rowntree & Co. Ltd 1956, Dir 1970, Chair. UK Confectionery Div. 1973–78; Deputy Chair. Rowntree Mackintosh Ltd 1978–81; Group Chair. Rowntree Mackintosh PLC (now Rowntree PLC) 1981–89; Vice-Chair. Legal and General Group 1986–94; Deputy Chair. Bass PLC 1990–96; mem. Council Inc. Soc. of British Advertisers 1971–79, Council Cocoa, Chocolate and Confectionery Alliance 1972–79, Council Advertising Asscn 1976–79, CBI Cos. Cttee 1979–84, Council CBI 1981–90, BIM Econ. and Soc. Affairs Cttee 1980–84, Food and Drink Fed. Exec. Cttee 1986–89 (mem. Council 1986–87); mem. Council York Univ. 1983–2001, Pro-Chancellor 1987, Chair. 1990–2001; Trustee Joseph Rowntree Foundation 1996–, Deputy Chair. 1998–2001, Chair. 2001–; Dr. hc (York Univ.) 1993, (Open) 1997. *Leisure interests:* reading, music, fell walking. *Address:* Joseph Rowntree Foundation, The Homestead, Water End, York, YO30 6WP, England. *Telephone:* (1904) 615901. *Fax:* (1904) 620072. *E-mail:* info@jrf.org.uk. *Website:* www.jrf.org.uk.

DIXON, Richard Newland, ScD, PhD, CChem, FRSC, FRS; British professor of chemistry; b. 25 Dec. 1930, Borough Green; s. of Robert T. Dixon and Lilian Dixon; m. Alison M. Birks 1954; one s. two d.; ed Judd School, Tonbridge, King's Coll. London and St Catharine's Coll. Cambridge; Scientific Officer, UKAEA Aldermaston 1954–56; Postdoctoral Fellow, Univ. of Western Ont. 1956–57, Nat. Research Council, Ottawa 1957–59; ICI Fellow, Univ. of

Sheffield 1959–60, Lecturer in Chem. 1960–69; Prof. of Chem., Univ. of Bristol 1969–96, Alfred Capper Pass Prof. of Chem. 1990–96, Prof. Emer. 1996–, Leverhulme Emer. Fellow 1996–98, Univ. Sr Research Fellow 1996–, Dean, Faculty of Science 1979–82, Pro-Vice Chancellor 1989–92; Dir (non-exec.) United Bristol Healthcare NHS Trust 1994–, Vice-Chair. 1995–; Sorby Research Fellow, Royal Soc. 1964–69; mem. Council, Faraday Div. Royal Soc. of Chem. 1985–98 (Vice-Pres. 1989–98), Cttees of SERC, 1980–83, 1987–90; Hallam Lecturer, Univ. of Wales 1988, Liversidge Lecturer, Royal Soc. of Chem. 1993; Harkins Lecturer, Univ. of Chicago, USA 1993; Corday Morgan Medal, Royal Soc. of Chem. 1968, Spectroscopy Medal, Royal Soc. of Chem. 1985. *Publications:* Spectroscopy and Structure 1965, Theoretical Chemistry, Vol. I 1972, Vol. II 1974, Vol. III 1977; numerous research articles in scientific journals. *Leisure interests:* mountain walking, photography, gardening, theatre-going. *Address:* School of Chemistry, University of Bristol, Cantock's Close, Bristol, BS8 1TS (Office); 22 Westbury Lane, Coombe Dingle, Bristol, BS9 2PE, England (Home). *Telephone:* (117) 9287661 (Office); (117) 9681691 (Home). *Fax:* (117) 9251295. *E-mail:* r.n.dixon@bris.ac.uk (Office).

DIZ, Adolfo César, CPA, DEcon, MA, DPhil; Argentine economist; b. 12 May 1931, Buenos Aires; s. of Agustín Diz and Elisa Aristizábal; m. Martha Solari 1959; five s.; ed Univ. de Buenos Aires and Univ. of Chicago; Instructor of Statistics, Univ. de Buenos Aires 1951–55, 1958–59; Prof. of Statistics, Univ. Nacional de Tucumán 1959–60, Dir Inst. de Econ. Research 1959–65, Prof. of Statistics and Econometrics 1960–61, 1964, Prof. of Monetary Theory 1962, 1965–66; Exec. Dir Int. Monetary Fund (IMF) 1966–68; Envoy extraordinary and Minister plenipotentiary, Argentine Financial Rep. in Europe 1969–73; Dir Center for Latin American Monetary Studies 1973–76; Pres. Banco Central de la República Argentina 1976–81; Dir Per Jacobsson Foundation 1976–; Econ. Consultant 1981–; mem. Nat. Acad. of Econ. Sciences; mem. of Argentine Socs., American Econ. Asscn and Econometric Soc. *Publications:* Money and Prices in Argentina 1935–62, in Varieties of Monetary Experience (Ed. D. Meiselman), Money Supply Models (in Spanish) and numerous economic articles. *Address:* Callao Avenida 2049-P6 (1024), Buenos Aires, Argentina. *Telephone:* (11) 4815-2418 (Office); (11) 4813-6036. *Fax:* (11) 4815-2418. *E-mail:* acdiz@overnet.com.ar (Home).

DJERASSI, Carl, AB, PhD; American chemist, educator and author; b. 29 Oct. 1923, Vienna; s. of Dr Samuel Djerassi and Dr Alice Friedmann; m. 1st Virginia Jeremiah (divorced 1950); m. 2nd Norma Lundholm (divorced 1976); one s. one d. (deceased); m. 3rd Diane W. Middlebrook 1985; ed Kenyon Coll. and Univ. of Wisconsin; Research Chemist, Ciba Pharmaceutical Co., Summit, NJ 1942–43, 1945–49; Assoc. Dir of Research, Syntex, SA, Mexico City 1949–51, Research Vice-Pres. 1957–60, Pres. Syntex Research 1968–72; Assoc. Prof. of Chem., Wayne State Univ., Detroit 1952–54, Prof. 1954–59, Stanford Univ. 1959–; Pres. of the Bd Zoecon Corpn (renamed Sandoz Crop Protection Corpn) 1968–83, Chair. 1968–88; f. Djerassi Foundation Resident Artists Program; Royal Chemical Soc. Centenary Lecturer 1964; Royal Swedish Acad. of Eng Sciences thirteenth Chemical Lecturer 1969; Swedish Pharmaceutical Soc. Scheele Lecturer 1972; mem. Editorial Bd Journal of the American Chemical Society 1968–76, Journal of Organic Chemistry 1955–58, Tetrahedron 1958–92, Steroids 1963–, Proceedings of NAS 1964–70; mem. NAS Bd on Science and Tech. for Int. Devt 1967–76, Chair. 1972–76; mem. American Pugwash Cttee 1967–1981; mem. NAS, NAS Inst. of Medicine, Brazilian Acad. of Sciences, American Acad. of Arts and Sciences; Foreign mem. German Acad. of Natural Scientists (Leopoldina), Royal Swedish Acad. of Sciences 1973, Bulgarian Acad. of Sciences 1979, Royal Swedish Acad. of Eng Sciences 1984; Hon. Fellow Royal Chemical Soc. 1968, American Acad. of Pharmaceutical Science; numerous hon. degrees; Award in Pure Chem. 1958, Baekeland Medal 1959, Fritzsche Medal 1960, Creative Invention Award 1973, Award in the Chem. of Contemporary Technological Problems 1983, Esselen Award for Chem. in the Public Interest 1989, American Chemical Soc.; Intra-Science Research Award 1969, Freedman Foundation Patent Award 1971, Chemical Pioneer Award 1973, Perkin Medal 1975, American Inst. of Chemists; Nat. Medal of Science 1973 (for synthesis of first oral contraceptive), Wolf Prize in Chem. 1978, Bard Award in Medicine and Science 1983, Roussel Prize (Paris) 1988, NAS Award for the Industrial Application of Science 1990, Nat. Medal of Tech. 1991, Priestley Medal (American Chem. Soc.) 1992, Nevada Medal 1992, Thomson Gold Medal (Int. Mass Spectrometry Soc.) 1994, Prince Mahidol Award (Thailand) 1996, Willard Gibbs Medal 1997, Othmer Gold Medal, Chem. Heritage Foundation 2000, Erasmus Medal, Academia Europea 2003. *Plays:* An Immaculate Misconception 1998, Oxygen (with Roald Hoffman) 2000, Calculus 2002, EGO 2003. *Publications:* (author or co-author) Optical Rotatory Dispersion 1960, Steroid Reactions 1963, Interpretation of Mass Spectra of Organic Compounds 1964, Structure Elucidation of Natural Products by Mass Spectrometry (2 Vols) 1964, Mass Spectrometry of Organic Compounds 1967, The Politics of Contraception 1979, 1981, The Futurist and Other Stories (fiction) 1988, Cantor's Dilemma (novel) 1989–, Steroids Made It Possible (autobiog.) 1990, The Clock Runs Backward (poetry) 1991, The Pill, Pygmy Chimps and Degas' Horse (autobiog.) 1992, Bourbaki Gambit (novel) 1994, From the Lab into the World (collected essays) 1994, Marx, deceased (novel) 1996, Menachem's Seed (novel) 1997, NO (novel) 1998, This Man's Pill (memoir) 2001; numerous scientific articles, also poems, memoirs and short stories. *Leisure interests:* skiing, modern art, opera, theatre. *Address:* Department of Chemistry, Stanford University, Stanford, CA 94305-5080, USA (Office). *Telephone:* (650) 723-2783 (Office). *E-mail:* djerassi@stanford.edu (Office). *Website:* www.djerassi.com (Office).

DJIMASTA, Koibla; Chadian politician; mem. Union pour la démocratie et la République (UDR); Prime Minister of Chad 1995–97. *Address:* c/o Union pour la démocratie et la République, N'Djamena, Chad.

DJOHAR, Said Ahmed; Comoran politician; leader Union comorienne pour le progrès (UDZIMA); Acting Pres. of the Comoros Nov. 1989–March 1990; elected Pres. 1990–95; stripped of exec. power; returned to Comoros Jan. 1996; Interim Pres. Jan.–March 1996; Pres. Cand. March 1996.

DJOUSSOUF, Abbass; Comoran politician; leader Forum pour le redressement national (FRN); Prime Minister of Comoros 1998–99. *Address:* c/o Office of the Prime Minister, Moroni, Comoros.

DJUKANOVIĆ, Milo; Serbia and Montenegro (Montenegrin) politician and economist; b. 15 Feb. 1962, Nikšić, ed Titograd Univ.; joined League of Communists of Yugoslavia (LCY) 1979 (mem. Cen. Cttee 1986–89) later named Democratic Party of Socialists (DPS); Prime Minister of the Repub. of Montenegro 1991–97, Nov. 2002–; Pres. of the Repub. of Montenegro 1997–2002. *Address:* Office of the Prime Minister, Podgorica, Jovana Tomaševića bb, Serbia and Montenegro (Office). *Fax:* (81) 52833 (Office); (81) 52246 (Office).

DLAMINI, Barnabas Sibusiso; Swazi politician; Minister of Finance 1984–93; fmr Exec. Dir IMF; Prime Minister of Swaziland July 1996–. *Address:* Office of the Prime Minister, Government House, P.O. Box 395, Mbabane, Swaziland (Office). *Telephone:* 4042251 (Office). *Fax:* 4043943 (Office). *E-mail:* ppcu@realnet.co.sz (Office).

DLAMINI, Prince Bhekimpi Alpheus; Swazi politician, soldier and administrator; served with Eighth Army in World War II; mem. Swazi Nat. Council, participated in constitutional talks 1963; Asst Minister of Admin. 1966, then Deputy Minister, Deputy Prime Minister's Dept; Prime Minister of Swaziland 1983–86; found guilty of treason and sentenced to 15 years' imprisonment March 1988; granted pardon July 1988.

DLAMINI, Obed Mfanyana; Swazi politician; b. 4 April 1937, Mhlosheni Area, Shiselweni Dist; ed Sincen Primary School, Hlatikulu Primary School, Swaziland Nat. High School, U.N.I.S.A; teacher and Boarding Master, Manzini Nazarene High School 1961–64; cost clerk, later Asst Personnel Officer, Roberts Construction (Swaziland) (Pty) Ltd 1964–66; clerk, Standard Chartered Bank of Swaziland 1966, Asst Man. Admin. –1981; fmr Training and Ind. Relations Man. Swaziland Fruit Canners (Pty) Ltd; fmr Gen. Sec. Swaziland Fed. of Trade Unions, mem. Labour Advisory Bd, Training and Localization Council, Wages Advisory Bd, Man. Training Council, Regional Educ. Advisory Bd, Workers' Educ. Group; Prime Minister of Swaziland 1989–93; Senator 1993–; Pres. Ngwane Nat. Liberatory Congress (CNNLC); Chair. Swazi Democratic Alliance 1999–. *Leisure interests:* soccer, wrestling, tug-of-war, jazz, music. *Address:* Ngwane National Liberatory Congress, Ilanga Centre, Martin Street, Manzini; The Senate, Mbabane, Swaziland. *Telephone:* 5053935 (Office).

DLAMINI, Sotsha; Swazi politician; fmr Asst Police Commr. –1984; Prime Minister of Swaziland 1986–89. *Address:* c/o Office of the Prime Minister, Mbabane, Swaziland.

DLAMINI-ZUMA, Nkosazana C., MB, CH.B.; South African politician and doctor; b. 27 Jan. 1949; m.; four c.; ed Amanzintoti Training Coll., Univ. of Zululand, Univ. of Natal, Univ. of Bristol, Univ. of Liverpool; Research Technician Medical School, Univ. of Natal 1972; Vice-Pres. SA Students Org. 1975–76; Chair. ANC Youth Section GB 1977–78; House Officer Frenchay Hosp. Bristol 1978–79; House Officer Canadian Red Cross Memorial Hosp., Berks. 1979–80; Medical Officer-Pediatrics Mbabane Govt Hosp. Swaziland 1980–85; Pediatric attachment Wittington Hosp. 1987–89; Vice Chair. Regional Political Cttee of ANC GB 1978–88, Chair. 1988–89; ANC Health Dept Lusaka 1989–90; Research Scientist Medical Research Council, Durban 1991–94; Minister of Health 1994–99, of Foreign Affairs 2001–; Dir Health Refugee Trust, Health and Devt Org., England 1988–90; Chair. S. Natal Region Health Cttee of ANC 1990–92; mem. Exec. Cttee S. Natal Region of ANC 1990–93; Chair. S. Natal Region ANC Women's League 1991–93; Pres. World Conf. Against Racism 2001; mem. Steering Cttee National AIDS Coordinating Cttee 1992–; mem. Bd Centre for Social Devt Studies Univ. of Natal, Durban 1992–; Trustee Health Systems Trust 1992–. *Address:* Ministry of Foreign Affairs, Union Buildings, East Wing, Government Avenue, Pretoria 0002 (Office); 602 Stretten Bay, St Andrews Street, Durban 4001, South Africa (Home). *Telephone:* (12) 3510005 (Office). *Fax:* (12) 3510253 (Office).

DLOUHÝ, Vladimír, CSc; Czech politician and economist; b. 31 July 1953, Prague; m. 1st (divorced 1999); m. 2nd Eliška Břízoá 2001; one s. one d.; ed Prague School of Econs, Charles Univ. Prague and Catholic Univ., Louvain; fmr teacher, Prague School of Econs; scientist, Inst. of Econ. Forecasting, Czechoslovak Acad. of Sciences 1983–89, latterly Deputy Dir; Deputy Prime Minister and Chair. State Planning Comm. 1989–90; Minister of the Economy 1990–92; Minister of Trade and Industry of Czech Repub. 1992–97; Int. Adviser, Goldman Sachs 1997–; Adviser to Exec. Man., ABB 1997–; mem. Civic Democratic Alliance 1991–98, Vice-Pres. March–Oct. 1992, Deputy Chair. 1993–97; mem. State Defence Council 1993; Chair. Council of Customs Union 1994–97, Bd of Supervisors Stock Co. Unipetrol 1996–97; Deputy Chair. Bd of Supervisors, Volkswagen-Skoda Group, Mladá Boleslav 1994–95; mem. Parl. 1996–98; mem. Bd of Supervisors, Foundation Bohemiae

1992–2001; mem. Bd of Dirs. Cofinec 1997–2000; Grand Croix, Ordre de Léopold II (Belgium). *Publications:* Ekonometrický model čs. obchodní bilance 1985, Models of Disequilibrium and Shortage in Centrally Planned Economies 1989; articles in Czechoslovak and int. econ. journals. *Leisure interest:* music. *Address:* Pachtův palác, Anenské náměstí 4, 110 00 Prague 1, Czech Republic. *Telephone:* (2) 2163-5351. *Fax:* (2) 2163-5350.

DMITRIEV, Alexander Sergeevich; Russian conductor; b. 19 Jan. 1935, Leningrad; m.; one s.; ed Leningrad Choir School, Leningrad State Conservatory, Vienna Akad. für Musik und darstellende Kunst; Conductor Karelian Radio and TV Symphony Orchestra 1961, Prin. Conductor 1962–71; Prin. Conductor Maly Opera and Ballet Theatre, St Petersburg 1971–77, (and Music Dir) Symphony Orchestra of St Petersburg Philharmonia 1977–; Prin. Conductor Stavanger Symphony Orchestra (Norway) 1990–98; Merited Worker of Arts of Karelian ASSR 1967, People's Artist of Russia 1976, USSR People's Artist; Prize 2nd USSR Competition for Conductors 1966. *Recordings include:* Handel's Messiah, Haydn's Schöpfung, Schubert's Symphony Nos. 1–9, Tchaikovsky's Symphonies 4, 5, 6, Rachmaninov's Symphony No. 2, Debussy's 3 Nocturnes, Ravel's Valses nobles et sentimentales, Ma Mère l'Oye, Saeverud's Peer Gynt, Symphony dolorosa, Balakirev's Piano Concerto, Medtner's Piano Concerto No. 1, Rachmaninov's Piano Concerto No. 3, Britten's Violin concerto. *Address:* Symphony Orchestra, St Petersburg Philharmonic Society, Mikhailovskaya str. 2, St Petersburg 091011, Russia (Office). *Telephone:* (812) 114-64-17 (Office). *Fax:* (812) 311-21-26 (Office). *E-mail:* dmitriev@mail.spbnit.ru; alexanderdmitriev@hotmail.com.

DMITRIEV, Andrey Viktorovich; Russian diplomatist; b. 10 April 1941, Moscow; m.; one s. one d.; ed Moscow State Pedagogic Inst. of Foreign Languages, Diplomatic Acad.; mem. staff UN Secr., NY 1969–76, USSR Embassy, Brazil 1978–82, Peru 1987–89, USSR then Russian Embassy, Nicaragua 1989–92, Amb. to Nicaragua 1995–99, Dir Latin American Dept Ministry of Foreign Affairs, Moscow 1999–2001, Amb. to Cuba (also Accred to Barbados) 2001–. *Address:* Embajada de la Rusia, 5A Avenida, N6402, entre 62–66, Miramar, Havana, Cuba (Office). *Telephone:* (7) 33-10-85 (Office). *Fax:* (7) 33-10-38 (Office).

DMITRIYEVA, Tatyana Borisovna, MD, DMedSc; Russian psychiatrist and politician; b. 21 Dec. 1951, Ivanovo; d. of Boris Alexandrovich Gareyev and Julia Fedorovna Gareyeva; m. Andrey Sergeyevich Dmitriyev; ed Ivanovo Inst. of Medicine; psychiatrist Ivanovo Region Psychiatric Hosp. 1975–76; jr, sr researcher All-Union Serbsky Nat. Research Centre for Social and Forensic Psychiatry 1976–86, Head of Clinical Dept, Deputy Dir 1986–90, Dir 1990–; concurrently Prof., Head of Chair. Moscow Sechenov Acad. of Medicine; Minister of Public Health of Russian Fed. 1996–98; mem. Russian Acad. of Medical Sciences; Russian Acad. of Medical Sciences V. S. Gulevich Prize for the Best Medical Work on Medical Biological Chemistry 2001. *Publications:* Mental Health of the Population of Russia 2001, Manual on Social Psychiatry 2001, Social Stress and Mental Health 2001, Alliance of Law and Mercy: On Human Rights Protection in Psychiatry 2001; numerous articles in scientific journals. *Leisure interests:* reading fiction, horse riding, travel. *Address:* Serbsky Research Centre, Kropotkinsky per. 23, 119992 Moscow (Office); Apt 21, Bldg 2, house 2/1, Malaya Tulskaya ul., 113191 Moscow, Russia. *Telephone:* (095) 201-52-62 (Office). *Fax:* (095) 201-72-31 (Office). *E-mail:* center@serbsky.ru (Office).

DMITRIYEVSKY, Anatoly Nikolayevich; Russian engineer; b. 6 May 1937; m.; one s. one d.; ed Gubkin Moscow Inst. of Oil and Gas; Sr teacher Gubkin Moscow Univ. of Oil and Gas; Pro-rector, Chair Algerian Nat. Inst. of Oil, Gas and Chem.; Dir Oil and Gas Research Inst., Russian Acad. of Sciences 1987–; Pres. Union of Scientific and Eng Org. of Russia; mem. of Bd Int. Gas Union; mem. Russian Acad. of Sciences 1991; USSR State Prize 1986, State Prize of Russia 1998. *Publications include:* Lithological System and Genetic Analysis of Oil and Gas Sedimentary Basins 1982, Fundamental Basis of Oil and Gas Geology 1991. *Leisure interests:* tennis, mountain skiing, photography. *Address:* Oil and Gas Research Institute, Gubkina str. 3, 117701 Moscow, Russia. *Telephone:* (095) 135-73-71 (Office). *Fax:* (095) 135-54-65 (Office). *E-mail:* a.dmitrievsky@ogri.ru (Office).

DO MUOI; Vietnamese politician; b. 1917, Hanoi; joined Movt against French colonial rule 1936; imprisoned by French; escaped in 1945 and took part in anti-Japanese uprising in Ha Dong Prov.; political and mil. leader in provs. of Red River delta during struggle against French 1951–54; Alt. mem. Cen. Cttee Communist Party of Viet Nam (CPV) 1955–60, mem. 1960–; Alt. mem. Political Bureau CPV 1976–82, now mem. Gen. Sec. of Cen. Cttee CPV 1987–; Deputy to Nat. Ass. 2nd, 4th, 5th, 6th, 7th and 8th Legislatures; Minister of Commerce 1969; Deputy Prime Minister and Minister of Bldg 1976–87; Vice-Chair. Council of Ministers in charge of Economy 1987–; Prime Minister 1988–91; Sec. Gen. CPV 1991–98; Vice-Chair. Nat. Defence Council 1989; Order of the October Revolution (USSR) 1987 and several Vietnamese decorations. *Address:* Communist Party of Viet Nam, 1 Hoang Van Thu, Hanoi; Council of Ministers, Hanoi, Viet Nam.

DO NASCIMENTO, HE Cardinal Alexandre; Angolan ecclesiastic; b. 1 March 1925, Malanje; s. of Antonio André do Nascimento and Maria Ana Alves da Rocha; ed Gregoriana Univ., Rome, Faculty of Laws, Lisbon; ordained priest 1952; Bishop of Malanje 1975; Archbishop of Lubango 1977–86, of Luanda 1986–2001; Archbishop Emer. of Luanda 2001–; Apostolic Admin. of Onjiva; mem. Sacred Congregation for the Propagation of the Faith and the Evangelization of the People; cr. Cardinal 1983; Pres. Caritas

Internationalis; Preacher, Retreat of the Holy Father and the Roman Curia 1984; mem. Sacred Congregation Pro Culto Divino 1985, Congregation Pro Institutione Catholica; Hon. mem. Acad. das Ciéncias (Lisbon), Acad. da Historia; Dr hc (Lisbon) 2000; Golden Medal for Human Rights Portuguese Ass. *Publications:* Caminhos da Esperanca 1992, Livro de Ritmos (poetry), Discursos e Mensagens 2002. *Leisure interests:* reading, music. *Address:* Rua Américo Júlio Carvalho 97–99, Bairro Azul, Luanda, Angola. *Telephone:* (2) 350755. *Fax:* (2) 351751. *E-mail:* dalexnascimento@snet.co.ao.

DO NASCIMENTO, Edson Arantes (see Pelé).

DOBBINS, James F., BA; American diplomatist; b. 1942, New York; m. Toril Kleivdal; two s.; ed Georgetown Univ. School of Foreign Service; U.S. naval officer; mem. Policy Planning Staff, State Dept, Washington DC 1969–71, Deputy Asst Sec. 1982–85, Prin. Deputy Asst Sec. 1989–90, Acting Asst Sec. for European and Canadian Affairs 1991, Special Asst to Pres., Nat. Security Council Staff 1996–99, Special Adviser to Pres. for Kosovo and Dayton Implementation 1999–2000, Asst Sec. of State for European Affairs 2000–01; mem. U.S. Mission to OECD 1967–68, U.S. del. to Vietnam Peace Talks 1968; Political Officer, U.S. Embassy, Paris 1969; mem. U.S. Mission to UN 1973–75, Political-Military Officer U.S. Embassy, London 1978–81; Deputy Chief of Mission, Bonn 1985–89; Amb. to the EC 1991–93; Special Envoy to Afghanistan Nov. 2001–; Sr Fellow, Rand Corpn 1993; mem. Council on Foreign Relations 1995–96; two Superior Honor Awards, three Presidential Awards, six Sr Performance Awards, Dept of the Army Decoration for Dist Civilian Service, Armed Forces Expeditionary Medal, Nat. Defense Service Medal, Expeditionary Medal, Repub. of Viet Nam. *Address:* c/o National Security Council, Eisenhower Executive Office Building, 17th Street and Pennsylvania Avenue NW, Washington, DC 20504, USA (Office).

DOBBS, Mattiwilda; American singer; b. 11 July 1925, Atlanta Ga; d. of John Wesley Dobbs and Irene Thompson Dobbs; m. 1st Luis Rodríguez García 1953 (died 1954); m. 2nd Bengt Janzon 1957 (died 1997); ed Spelman Coll., Atlanta and Columbia Univ.; studied with Lotte Leonard 1946–50; Marian Anderson scholarship, soloist at Mexico Univ. Festival 1947; studied at Mannes Music School and Berkshire Music Center 1948, with Pierre Bernac, Paris 1950–52; 1st Voice Prize, Geneva Int. Competition 1951; concert tour Netherlands, France and Sweden 1952; début La Scala (Milan) in L'Italiana in Algeri 1953; sang at Glyndebourne 1953, 1954, 1956, 1961, Royal Opera House, Covent Garden (London) 1954, 1955, 1956, 1959, San Francisco Opera 1955, Metropolitan Opera (New York) 1956–64; Stockholm Royal Opera 1957–71; Hamburg State Opera 1961–63; concert appearances in Europe, USA, Mexico, Israel, Australia, New Zealand and USSR; Order of the North Star (Sweden). *Address:* 1101 South Arlington Ridge Road, Apt. 301, Arlington, VA 22202, USA. *Telephone:* (703) 892-5234.

DOBBS, Michael John, PhD, MALD, MA; British author; b. 14 Nov. 1948; two s.; ed Christ Church, Oxford and Fletcher School of Law and Diplomacy, USA; UK Govt Special Adviser 1981–87; Chief of Staff, UK Conservative Party 1986–87, Jt Deputy Chair. 1994–95; Deputy Chair. Saatchi & Saatchi 1983–91; BBC TV presenter 1999–2001. *Publications:* House of Cards 1989, Wall Games 1990, Last Man to Die 1991, To Play the King 1993, The Touch of Innocents 1994, The Final Cut 1995, Goodfellowe MP 1997, The Buddha of Brewer Street 1998, Whispers of Betrayal 2000, Winston's War 2002. *Address:* 12 Onslow Court, Drayton Gardens, London, SW10 9RL, England. *Telephone:* (07836) 201967 (mobile). *E-mail:* michldobbs@aol.com (Office).

DOBESCH, Gerhard, DPhil; Austrian professor of Roman history, archaeology and epigraphy; b. 15 Sept. 1939, Vienna; s. of Dr. Carl Dobesch and Gustave Dobesch; ed Univ. of Vienna; lecturer in Ancient History 1967–73; Prof. of Greek and Roman History, Univ. of Graz 1973–76; Prof. of Roman History, Archaeology and Epigraphy, Univ. of Vienna 1976–; corresp. mem. Austrian Archaeological Inst. 1972–, mem. 1998–; corresp. mem. Austrian Acad. of Sciences 1980, mem. 1984–. *Publications:* Caesars Apotheose zu Lebzeiten und sein Ringen um den Königstitel 1966, Der panhellen: Gedanke und der Philippos des Isokrates 1968, Wurde Caesar zu Lebzeiten in Rom als Staatsgott anerkannt?, 1971, Nochmals zur Datierung des grossen Senatskonsultes 1971, Nikolaos von Damaskus und die Selbstbiographie des Augustus 1978, Die Kelten in Österreich nach den ältest 1980, Die Kimbern in den Ostalpen und die Schlacht bei Noreia 1982, Zu Caesars Sitzenbleiben vor dem Senat 1988, Zur Einwanderung die Kelten in Oberitalien 1989, Caesar als Ethnograph 1989, Zu zwei Daten d. Gesch. Galliens 1989, Europa in d. Reichskonzeption 1989, Autonomie des Menschen und Werthaftigkeit in der Antike 1990, Die Kelten als Nachbarn der Etrusker 1992, J. K. Newman u. Catull 1992, 100 Jahre Kleinasiat. Komm. 1993, Principis dignationem 1993; Vom äusseren Proletariat zum Kulturträger 1994, Phokion und der Korinthische Bund 1994, Aus der Vor-und Nachgeschichte der Markomannenkriege 1994, Das europäische "Barbaricum" und die Zone der Mediterrankultur 1995, Der Ostalpenraum als Kultur- und Machtgrundlage in keltischer und römischer Zeit 1996, Würdigung Fritz Schachermeyr 1996, Die römische Kaiserzeit–eine Fortsetzung des Hellenismus? 1996; Zu Virunum als Namen der Stadt auf dem Magdalensberg 1997, Ende und Metamorphose des Etruskertums 1998, Der Weltreichsgedanke bei Caesar 1998, Mitherausgeber: Adolf Wilhelm, Kleine Schriften: Abt. II, Teil III 2000 Teil IV 2002, Einige merkwürdige Überlieferungen über Caesar 2000, Urgeschichtliches Eisen in der Sicht des Althistorikers 2000, Caesars monarchische Ideologie 2000, Ausgewählte Schriften (2 Vols) 2001, Caesars Volcae Tectosages in Mitteleuropa 2001, Caesar, Commentarii über den gallischen Krieg, Buch 1,

Kapitel 1: eine Sensation, Wiener Humanistische Blätter 42 2001; numerous specialist articles. *Leisure interests:* literature, art history. *Address:* Universität Wien, Institut für Alte Geschichte, Dr. Karl Lueger-Ring 1, 1010 Vienna (Office); Spitalgasse 29/10, 1090 Vienna, Austria (Home). *Telephone:* 4277-40520 (Office); 407 95 22 (Home). *Fax:* 4277-9405 (Office). *E-mail:* gerhard.dobesch@univie.ac at (Office).

DOBRETSOV, Nikolai Leontyevich, D.GEOL.; Russian geologist; b. 15 Jan. 1936; m.; five c.; ed Leningrad Inst. of Mines; chief Altai Mining expedition, Jr then Sr researcher; Head of Lab. Inst. of Geology and Geophysics, Siberian br. of USSR (now Russian) Acad. of Sciences in Novosibirsk; Head of Lab. Inst. of Tectonics and Geophysics, USSR Acad. of Sciences in Khabarovsk; Dir Buryat Inst. of Geology, Chair. Presidium of Buryat Research Cen. Siberian br. of USSR Acad. of Sciences, Dir-Gen. United Inst. of Geology, Geophysics and Mineralogy; Corresp. mem. USSR (now Russian) Acad. of Sciences 1984, mem. 1987, mem. Presidium 1991–; now Pres. of Siberian Br. 2002–, Vice-Pres. Russian Acad. of Sciences. *Publications include:* Introduction to Global Petrology 1980, Global Petrological Processes 1981, Deep-level Geodynamics 1994; papers on tectonics and petrography. *Leisure interests:* books, fishing. *Address:* United Institute of Geology, Geophysics and Mineralogy, Prospect Acad. Koptyuga 3, 630090 Novosibirsk, Russia (Office).

DOBRODEYEV, Oleg Borisovich, CAND.HIST.SC.; Russian television producer; b. 28 Nov. 1959, Moscow; m.; one s.; ed Moscow State Univ.; mem. of staff Inst. of USA and Canada 1982–83; ed. of TV programme Vremya, USSR Cen. TV, later Deputy Ed.-in-Chief 1983–90; Ed.-in-Chief of news programme Vesti; Ed.-in-Chief Information TV Agency (ITA) 1990–91, Ostankino Co. 1991–93; Ed.-in-Chief Information Service, NTV Co., later Vice-Pres. 1993–2000, Dir.-Gen. NTV Co. 1997–2000; Chair. All-Russian State TV-Radio Co. (RTR) 2000–; Order of Honour 1999. *Leisure interest:* reading people's memoirs. *Address:* All-Russian State TV-Radio Co., Yamskogo Polya 5th str. 19/21, 125040 Moscow, Russia (Office). *Telephone:* (095) 234-8600 (Office); (095) 214-4978 (Office). *Fax:* (095) 214-2347 (Office). *E-mail:* vgtrk2@ space/ru (Office). *Website:* www.vesty-rtr.com (Office).

DOBRYNIN, Anatoliy Fedorovich, MSc; Russian diplomatist (retd); b. 16 Nov. 1919, Krasnaya Gorka, Moscow Region; m.; one d.; ed S Ordzhonikidze Moscow Aviation Inst., Higher Diplomatic School, Ministry of Foreign Affairs; engineer at aircraft plant, Second World War; joined diplomatic service 1946; Counsellor, later Minister-Counsellor, Soviet Embassy, Washington 1952–55; Asst Minister of Foreign Affairs 1955–57; Under-Sec.-Gen. for Political and Security Council Affairs UN 1957–59, Head American Dept, USSR Ministry of Foreign Affairs 1959–61; Amb. to USA 1962–86; Adviser to Pres. Gorbachev (q.v.) 1988–91; Consultant to Russian Ministry of Foreign Affairs 1995–; mem. CPSU 1945–, Cand. mem., CPSU Cen. Cttee 1966–71, mem. 1971–90, Sec. Cen. Cttee for Foreign Affairs 1986–88; Head Int. Dept 1986–88; Deputy of USSR Supreme Soviet 1986–89; Hero of Socialist Labour 1982, Order of Lenin (five times). *Publication:* In Confidence (memoirs) 1995. *Address:* c/o Ministry of Foreign Affairs, Smolenskaya Sennaya 32/34, Moscow, Russia.

DOBRZANSKI, Stanislaw; Polish business executive and politician; b. 22 March 1949, Hrubieszów; m.; two c.; ed Maria Sklodowska-Curie Univ., Lublin; Vice-Dir Nat. Library, Warsaw 1982–85; Dept Dir Ministry of Culture and Art; Dir agency of Wschodni Bank Cukrownictwa; Under-Sec. of State, Office of the Council of Ministers 1993–96; Minister of Nat. Defence 1996–97; Pres. Polskie Sieci Elektroenergetyczne S.A. 2001–. *Address:* Polskie Sieci Elektroenergetyczne S.A., ul. Mysia 2, 00-456 Warsaw, Poland (Office). *Telephone:* (22) 6931580 (Office). *Fax:* (22) 6931087 (Office). *E-mail:* stanislaw .dobrzanski@pse.pl (Office). *Website:* www.pse.pl (Office).

DOBSON, Rt Hon Frank (Gordon), PC, BSc(Econs); British politician; b. 15 March 1940; s. of the late James William Dobson and Irene Shortland Dobson; m. Janet Mary Alker 1967; two s. one d.; ed Archbishop Holgate Grammar School, York, LSE; admin. appointments with Cen. Electricity Generating Bd 1962–70, Electricity Council 1970–75; mem. Camden Borough Council 1971–76, Leader 1973–75; Asst Sec. Comm. for Local Admin. 1975–79; MP for Holborn and St Pancras South 1979–83, for Holborn and St Pancras 1983–; Opposition Spokesman on Educ. 1981–83, on Health 1983–87, on Energy 1989–92, on Employment 1992–93, on Transport and London 1993–94, on Environment and London 1994–97; Sec. of State for Health 1997–99; Labour candidate for Mayoralty of London 2000; Shadow Leader of the House of Commons 1987–89; Gov. LSE 1986–, Inst. of Child Health 1987–92; Labour. *Address:* House of Commons, London, SW1A 0AA; 22 Great Russell Mansions, Great Russell Street, London, WC1B 3BE, England. *Telephone:* (20) 7242-5760.

DOBSON, Michael William Romsey, MA; British banking and finance executive; b. 13 May 1952, London; s. of Sir Denis (William) Dobson; m. Frances de Salis 1998; one d.; ed Eton Coll., Trinity Coll. Cambridge; joined Morgan Grenfell 1973, banker Morgan Grenfell New York 1978–80, Man. Dir 1984–85, Chief Exec. Morgan Grenfell Asset Management 1987–88, Deputy CEO 1988–89, CEO Morgan Grenfell Group (now Deutsche Morgan Grenfell) 1989–97; mem. Bd of Man. Dirs Deutsche Bank AG 1996–2000 (responsible for investment banking 1996–98, for asset man. 1998–2000), mem. Advisory Bd; f. Beaumont Capital Man. Ltd 2000 (acquired by Schroders PLC 2001); Non-Exec. Dir Schroders PLC April–Nov. 2001, CEO 2001–; Non-Exec. Dir Gen. Enterprise Man. Services Ltd. *Address:* Schroders PLC, 31 Gresham Street, London, EC2V 7QA, England (Office). *Telephone:* (20) 7658-6962 (Office). *Fax:* (20) 7658-3476 (Office). *E-mail:* michael.dobson@schroders.com (Office). *Website:* www.schroders.com (Office).

DOCHANASHVILI, Guram; Georgian writer; b. 1939, Tbilisi, Georgia; s. of Petre Dochanashvili and Gulnara Emukhvari; m.; one d.; ed Tbilisi State Univ.; worked in Dept of Archaeology Inst. of History Georgian Acad. of Sciences 1962–75; Head. Div. of Prose Mnatobi (magazine) 1975–85; Deputy Dir Gruzia Film Studio 1985–; Ivane Dzhavakhishvili Medal, Tbilisi State Univ. 1984, State Prize of Georgia 1994. *Publications include:* There, Behind the Mountain 1966. *Address:* c/o Georgian Union of Writers, Machabeli str. 13, 380000 Tbilisi, Georgia.

DOCHERTY, David, BA, PhD; British broadcasting executive; b. 10 Dec. 1956, Scotland; s. of David Docherty and Anna Docherty; m. Kate Stuart-Smith 1992; two d.; ed Univ. of Strathclyde, LSE; Research Fellow Broadcasting Research Unit, London 1984–88; Dir of Research Broadcasting Standards Council 1988–89; Head of Broadcasting Analysis BBC TV 1990–92, Head of TV Planning and Strategy BBC Network TV 1992–96, Dir of Strategy and Channel Devt BBC Broadcast 1996–97, Deputy Dir of TV BBC Broadcast 1997–, Dir New Services, BBC Bd of Man. 1999; Man. Dir of Broadband Content, Telewest Communications 2000–; Chair. Bd of Govs. Univ. of Luton 2001–; mem. Bd BBC America UKTV. *Publications:* The Last Picture Show?: Britain's Changing Film Audience 1987, Keeping Faith?: Channel 4 and Its Audience 1988, Running the Show: 21 Years of London Weekend Television 1990, Violence in Television Fiction 1991, The Spirit Death 2000, The Killing Jar 2002, The Fifth Season 2003. *Leisure interest:* writing. *Address:* Flextech Television, 160 Great Portland Street, London, W1W 5QA (Office); Serge Hill, Abbots Langley, Herts., WD5 0RY, England (Home); 160 Great Portland Street, London, W1W 5AA, England. *Telephone:* (20) 7299-5000.

DOCTOROW, Edgar Lawrence, AB; American novelist; b. 6 Jan. 1931, New York; s. of David Richard and Rose (Levine) Doctorow; m. Helen Esther Setzer 1954; one s. two d.; ed Kenyon Coll., Gambier, Ohio; served with US army 1953–55; Ed. New American Library, New York 1960–64; Ed.-in-Chief Dial Press., New York 1964–69, Publr 1969; writer-in-residence Univ. of Calif., Irvine 1969–70; mem. faculty Sarah Lawrence Coll., Bronxville, NY 1971–78; mem. Authors Guild (Dir), American P.E.N. (Dir), Writers Guild of America East, Century Asscn; Creative Writing Fellow Yale School of Drama 1974–75; Creative Artists Program Service Fellow 1973–74; Visiting Sr Fellow Council on Humanities, Princeton Univ. 1980; Gluckman Prof. of American and English Letters, New York Univ. 1982–; Guggenheim Fellow 1973; Hon. LHD (Kenyon Coll.) 1976, (Hobart Coll.) 1979; Arts and Letters Award (American Acad. and Nat. Inst. Art) 1976, Nat. Book Critics Circle Award 1976, 1990, Guggenheim Fellow 1973, American Book Award 1986, Howells Medal, American Acad. of Arts and Letters 1990, PEN/Faulkner Prize 1990, Nat. Humanities Medal 1998, Commonwealth Award 2000. *Publications:* Welcome to Hard Times 1960, Big as Life 1966, The Book of Daniel 1971, Ragtime 1975, Drinks before Dinner (play) 1975, Loon Lake 1980, Lives of the Poets: Six Stories and a Novella 1984, World's Fair 1985, Billy Bathgate 1988, The Waterworks 1994, Poets and Presidents: Selected Essays 1994, City of God 2000. *Address:* English Department, New York University, 19 University Place, 2nd Floor, New York, NY 10003; c/o Random House Publishers, 210 E 50th Street, New York, NY 10022, USA (Office).

DODD, Christopher J., BA, JD; American politician; b. 27 May 1944, Willimantic, Conn.; s. of Thomas J. and Grace (Murphy) Dodd; ed Providence Coll., RI and Univ. of Louisville, Ky; Volunteer with Peace Corps, Dominican Repub. 1966–68; admitted to Conn. Bar 1973; mem. House of Reps. 1975–81 from 2nd Dist Conn.; Senator from Connecticut 1980–; Democrat; numerous awards. *Address:* US Senate, 448 Russell Senate Building, Washington, DC 20510-0001, USA.

DODD, John Newton, MSc, PhD; New Zealand physicist; b. 19 April 1922, Hastings; s. of John H. Dodd and Eva E. Weeks; m. Jean P. Oldfield 1950; three s. one d.; ed Otago Boys' High School and Univs. of Otago and Birmingham; lecturer, Sr Lecturer, Reader in Physics, Otago Univ. 1952–65, Prof. of Physics 1965–88 (Beverly Prof. 1968–88); Pres. Royal Soc. of NZ 1989–94; 1851 Exhibition Scholarship; Nuffield Fellowship; Hector Medal (RSNZ), NZ Commemoration Medal 1990. *Publications:* Einstein (with A. E. Musgrave), Atoms and Light Interactions 1991; scientific papers in field of atomic and optical physics. *Leisure interests:* music, gardening, reading, theatre, snooker, croquet. *Address:* 13 Malvern Street, Dunedin, New Zealand. *Telephone:* 4679757.

DODD, Lois; American artist; b. 22 April 1927, Montclair, NJ; one s.; ed Montclair High School, Cooper Union; a founder, Tanager Gallery 1952–62; mem. Bd of Govs. Skowhegan School of Painting and Sculpture 1980– (Chair. 1986–88); mem. Nat. Acad. of Design 1988–, American Acad. of Arts and Letters 1998–; American Acad. and Inst. of Arts and Letters Award 1986, Hassam, Speicher, Betts and Symons Purchase Prize 1991, Nat. Acad. of Design Leonilda S. Gervas Award 1987, Henry Ward Ranger Purchase Award 1990. *Exhibitions include:* Tanager Gallery, New York 1954–62, Green Mountain Gallery, New York 1969–76, Fischbach Gallery, New York 1978–2002, Alexandre Gallery, New York 2003–, Caldbeck Gallery, Rockland, Maine 1990–; works in perm. collections including: Bryn Mawr Coll., Pa, Dartmouth Coll., NH, Colby Coll. Art Museum, Maine, Farnsworth Museum, Maine, Montclair Art Museum, NJ, Kalamazoo Art Center, Mich., Nat. Acad.

of Design, New York, Wadsworth Atheneum, Hartford, Conn., Whitney Museum, New York, Museo dell'Arte, Udine, Italy. *Address:* 30 East 2nd Street, New York, NY 10003, USA (Home). *Telephone:* (212) 254-7159 (Office). *Fax:* (212) 254-7159 (Office).

DODGE, David A., PhD; Canadian banker; b. Toronto; ed Queen's Univ., Princeton Univ., USA; fmr Asst Prof. of Econs, Queen's Univ.; Assoc. Prof. of Canadian Studies and Int. Econs, School of Advanced Int. Studies, Johns Hopkins Univ., USA; Dir Int. Econs Programme, Inst. for Research on Public Policy 1979–80; fmr fed. public servant, Sr positions in Cen. Mortgage and Housing Corpn, Anti-Inflation Bd, Dept of Employment and Immigration, Dept of Finance; fmr Deputy Minister of Finance; mem. Bd of Dirs. Bank of Canada 1992–97; Sr Fellow Faculty of Commerce, Univ. of BC; Visiting Prof. Dept of Econs, Simon Fraser Univ. 1997–98; Deputy Minister of Health 1998–2001; Gov., Chair. Bd of Dirs Bank of Canada. *Address:* Bank of Canada, 234 Wellington Street, Ottawa, Ont., K1A 0G9, Canada (Office). *Telephone:* (613) 782-8383 (Office); (613) 782-8111. *Fax:* (613) 782-7003 (Office).

DODIN, Lev Abramovich; Russian stage director; b. 14 May 1944, Leningrad; m. Tatyana Borisovna Shestakova (q.v.) 1972; ed Leningrad Theatre Inst.; lecturer in drama, Leningrad Theatre Inst., 1963–83; with Leningrad Youth Theatre 1967– (now Chief Dir), Dir of Leningrad Maly Drama Theatre 1983–; Prof., St Petersburg Acad. of Dramatic Art; USSR State Prize 1986, State Prize of Russia 1992, Triumph Prize 1992, Ubu Prize, Italy 1993, 1995, Stanislavsky Prize 1996, Premio Europa, Italy 2000; RSFSR Merited Artist 1986, People's Artist of Russian Fed., Order of Literature and Arts, France 1994. *Productions include:* The Robber (K. Čapek) 1974, The Gentle One (Dostoyevsky) 1980, The House (F. Abramov) 1980, Brothers and Sisters (F. Abramov) 1985, Lord of the Flies 1986, Stars in the Morning Sky (A. Galin) 1988, Gaudeamus 1990, The Demons (Dostoyevsky) 1992, Claustrophobia (V. Yerofeev) 1994, The Cherry Orchard (A. Chekhov) 1994, Play With No Title (A. Chekhov) 1966, Chevengur (A. Platonov) 1999, Molly Sweeney (Brian Friel) 2000. *Operas include:* Elektra (R. Strauss) 1995, Lady Macbeth of Mtsensk (Franco Abbiati Prize for best musical performance, Italy 1998) (D. Shostakovich) 1998, Mazeppa (Tchaikovsky) 1999, The Queen of Spades (Tchaikovsky) 1998–2001. *Address:* Maly Drama Theatre, Rubinstein Str. 18, St Petersburg, Russia. *Telephone:* (812) 113-21-08. *Fax:* (812) 113-33-66 (Office). *E-mail:* stronin@mail.convey.ru (Office).

DOER, Gary Albert; Canadian politician; b. 31 March 1948, Winnipeg, Man.; m. Ginny Devine; two d.; first elected to Man. Legis. Ass. (MLA) as MP for Concordia 1986, Minister of Urban Affairs 1986–88, Minister of Crown Investments 1987–88, Minister of Man. Telephone Systems 1987–88, also Minister responsible for Man. Liquor Control Comm.; Leader New Democrats 1988–, Leader of the Opposition 1990–99, Premier of Man., Pres. Exec. Council and Minister of Fed.-Provincial Relations 1999–; fmr Pres. Man. Govt Employees' Asscn; fmr Deputy Supt, Vaughan St Detention Centre; Vice Pres.-Man. Special Olympics, Pres. Boys' and Girls' Club of Winnipeg; mem. Bd Winnipeg Blue Bombers, Prairie Theatre Exchange, Niagara Inst., Univ. of Man. *Leisure interest:* waterskiing. *Address:* Office of the Premier, Legislative Building, 204 Broadway, Winnipeg, Man. R3C 0V8, Canada (Office). *Telephone:* (204) 945-3714 (Office). *Fax:* (204) 949-1484 (Office). *Website:* www.gov.mb.ca (Office).

DOERING, William von Eggers, PhD; American professor of chemistry; b. 22 June 1917, Fort Worth, Tex.; s. of Carl Rupp Doering and Antoinette Mathilde von Eggers; m. 1st Ruth Haines 1947 (divorced 1954); two s. one d.; m. 2nd Sarah Cowles 1969 (divorced 1981); ed Shady Hill School, Mass., Belmont Hill School, Mass. and Harvard Univ.; with Office of Scientific Research and Devt 1941, Nat. Defense Research Cttee 1942, Polaroid Corpn 1943 (all in Cambridge, Mass.); Instructor, Columbia Univ. 1943–45, Asst Prof. 1945–48, Assoc. Prof. 1948–52; Prof. Yale Univ. 1952–56, Whitehead Prof. of Chem. 1956–67; Prof. Harvard Univ. 1967–68, Mallinckrodt Prof. of Chem. 1968–86, Prof. Emer. 1986–; Chair. Council for a Liveable World, Washington, DC 1964–73, Pres. 1973–78; U.S. Dir People's Repub. of China-USA Chem. Graduate Program 1982–86; mem. NAS, American Acad. of Arts and Sciences; Hon. Prof. Fudan Univ., Shanghai 1980; Hon. DSc (Texas Christian Univ.); Hon. D. Nat. Sci. (Karlsruhe) 1987; John Scott Award 1945, American Chem. Soc. Award in Pure Chem. 1953, A. W von Hoffman Medal (Gesellschaft Deutscher Chemiker) 1962, William C. De Vane Medal 1967, Theodore William Richards Medal 1970, James Flack Norris Award 1989 and other awards from American Chem. Soc.; Robert A. Welch Award in Chemistry 1990; Kosolapoff Award, Auburn Univ. 1995. *Publications:* Quinine 1944, Tropolone 1950, Tropylium Ion 1954, Carbenes 1954, Bullvalene 1962, Thermal Rearrangements 1966. *Leisure interests:* music, theatre, tennis, hiking. *Address:* Harvard University, Dept of Chemistry, 12 Oxford Street, Cambridge, MA 02138 (Office); 53 Francis Avenue, Cambridge, MA 02138, USA (Home). *Telephone:* (617) 495-4263 (Office).

DOĞAN, Aydın; Turkish media executive; b. 1936, Kelkit; m.; ed Istanbul High Economy and Commerce Acad.; started business operations while still at school, f. his first industrial co. 1974; Pres. Doğan Group; owner eight newspapers including Hürriyet and Milliyet and two TV stations; fmr mem. Ass. and Admin. Bd Istanbul Chamber of Commerce, Bd mem. Union of Chambers and Stock Markets; Chair. Newspaper Owners' Union 1986–96; f. Aydın Doğan Foundation 1996; Hon. DHumLitt (Girne American Univ.) 1999, Dr. hc (Aegean Univ.) 2000; State Superior Services Medal 1999. *Address:*

Aydın Doğan Vakfı, Hürriyet Medya Towers, 34544 Güneşli, Istanbul, Turkey (Office). *Telephone:* (212) 677-0760 (Office). *Fax:* (212) 677-0762 (Office). *E-mail:* advakfi@hurriyet.com.tr (Office).

DOGRAMACI, Ihsan, MD, LLD, LHD, FRCP, FAAP; Turkish paediatrician and educator; b. 3 April 1915, Erbil; s. of Ali Dogramaci and Ismet Kirdar; m. Ayser Hikmet Suleyman 1941; two s. one d.; ed Istanbul, Harvard and Washington Univs.; Asst Prof. of Paediatrics, Ankara Univ. 1947–49, Assoc. Prof. 1949–54, Prof. and Head of Dept 1954–63; Dir Inst. of Child Health, Ankara 1958–81; Prof. of Paediatrics and Head of Dept, Hacettepe Faculty of Medicine 1963–81, Dean of Faculty June–Nov. 1963; Pres. Ankara Univ. 1963–65; Chair. Bd of Trustees Middle East Tech. Univ. 1965–67; Pres. Hacettepe Children's Medical Centre, Ankara 1965–81; Rector, Hacettepe Univ. 1967–75; Pres. UNICEF Exec. Bd 1967–70; Pres. Int. Paediatric Asscn 1968–77, Dir-Gen. 1977–93, Hon. Pres. 1992–; Pres.and Chair. Bd of Trustees, Bilkent Univ. 1985–, Pres. Bilkent Univ. 1992–; Pres. Union of Middle-Eastern and Mediterranean Paediatric Socs 1971–73, Int. Children's Center, Ankara 1980–, Higher Educ. Council of Turkey 1981–92; mem. of Standing Conf. of Rectors and Vice-Chancellors of the European Univs 1969–81; Hon. Pres. Int. Conf. for Higher Educ. 1992–; Hon. Fellow, American Acad. Pediatrics 1959; Hon. mem. American Pediatric Soc., Deutsche Gesellschaft für Kinderheilkunde 1973, Soc. de Pédiatrie de Paris 1958, British Paediatric Asscn 1964, Finnish Paediatric Asscn 1971, etc.; Corresp. mem. Acad. Nat. de Médecine, France 1973; Hon. LLD (Nebraska) 1965; Dr. hc (Nice) 1973; hon. degrees also from Univs. of Glasgow, Anatolia, Bosporus, Baghdad, Marmara, Ain Shams, Soka, Devlet Tib (Baku), E Mediterranean, De Montfort, Istanbul and Osmangazi; Fellow, Royal Coll. of Physicians London 1971, Founder Hon. Fellow Royal Coll. of Paediatrics and Child Health London 1996; Grand Officier, Duarte, Sánchez y Mella 1976, Officier, Légion d'honneur 1978, Christopherson Award 1986, Commdr, Order of the Lion of Finland (First Class), Commdr Order of Merit of Poland 1989, Gran Cruz Placa de Plata de la Orden Heráldica de Cristóbal Colón (Dominican Rep.) 1990, Léon Bernard Foundation Prize (WHO) 1981, Maurice Pate Award (UNICEF) 1995, State Medal for Outstanding Merit 1995, State Medal (Romania) 1997, Health-For-All Gold Medal (WHO) 1997, First Rank Order of Independence (Azerbaijan) 1998. *Publications:* Annenin Kitabi–Mother's Handbook on Child Care 1952–2000, Premature Baby Care 1954; ed. Turkish Journal of Paediatrics. *Address:* Bilkent University Board of Trustees, PO Box 126 Bahçelievler, 06502 Ankara, Turkey. *Telephone:* (312) 266 4596. *Fax:* (312) 2664678. *E-mail:* ihsand@bilkent.edu.tr (Office).

DOHNÁNYI, Christoph von (see von Dohnányi, Christoph).

DOHNÁNYI, Klaus von (see von Dohnányi, Klaus).

DOI, Takako; Japanese politician; b. 30 Nov. 1928, Kobe; ed Doshisha Univ.; fmr univ. lecturer on Japanese constitution; mem. Lower House (Diet) 1969–; Leader, Japan Socialist Party (JSP) 1986–91; Speaker, House of Reps. 1993–96; Chair Social Democratic Party of Japan 1996–. *Leisure interest:* singing. *Address:* Social Democratic Party of Japan, 1-8-1 Nagata-cho, Chiyoda-ku, Tokyo 100-0014, Japan. *Telephone:* (3) 3580-1171. *Fax:* (3) 3580-0691. *E-mail:* sdpjmail@omnics.co.jp (Office). *Website:* www.omnics.co.jp/politics/SDPJ/SDPJ-E.html (Office).

DOJE CEDAIN; Chinese government official; b. 1924; m. Gesang Zhuoga; ed Beijing Normal Univ.; Gov. of Xizang (Tibet) Autonomous Region 1983–85; Researcher, Inst. of Research on World Religions, Chinese Acad. of Social Sciences 1985–; Adviser United Front Work Dept under CCP Cen. Cttee 1986–; mem. Standing Cttee 6th NPC 1986–88, Standing Cttee 7th 1988–93, 8th 1993–; Vice-Chair. Educ., Science, Culture and Public Health Cttee under the NPC 1986; Deputy Head China-Spain Friendship Group 1986. *Address:* Chinese Academy of Social Sciences, 5 Jianguomen Nei Da Jie, Beijing, People's Republic of China.

DOJEI CERING; Chinese government official; b. 1939, Xiahe Co., Gansu Prov.; worked in Tibet 1959; joined CCP 1960; country magistrate in Tibet 1962; mem. Tibet Autonomous Region CCP 1974–90; mem., Standing Cttee Tibet CCP 1977–90; First Sec., Xigaze Municipality CCP 1979–82; Vice-Chair. Tibet Autonomous Region 1983–85, Acting Admin. Head 1986–88, Chair. 1988–90; deputy for Tibet Autonomous Region, 7th NPC 1988–; Vice-Minister of Civil Affairs 1990–93, Minister 1993–; Vice-Chair. China Cttee Int. Decade for Nat. Disaster Reduction; mem. 8th NPC 1993; mem. 14th CCP Cen. Cttee 1992–97, 15th CCP Cen. Cttee 1997–; Dir Leading Group for Placement of Demobilized Army Officers 1993–; Deputy Head Leading Group for the Work of Supporting the Army, Giving Preferential Treatment to the Families of Armymen and Martyrs, supporting the Govt and Cherishing the People, State Council Leading Group on Boundary Delimitation. *Address:* Ministry of Civil Affairs, 147 Beiheyan Dajie, Dongcheng Qu, Beijing100721, People's Republic of China (Office). *Telephone:* (10) 65135333 (Office). *Fax:* (10) 65135332 (Office).

DOKTOR, Martin; Czech canoeist; b. 21 May 1974, Polička; s. of Josef Doktor and Zuzana Doktorová; m. Kateřina Svobodová 2000; one s.; ed Charles Univ., Prague; silver medals 500m and 1000m Canoeing World Championships, Duisburg, Germany; gold medals 500m and 1000m Olympic Games, Atlanta, USA 1996; silver medals 200m and 1000m, gold medal 500m Canoeing World Championships, Dartmouth, Canada 1997; silver medal 500m, gold medal 1000m European Championships, Plovdiv, Bulgaria 1997; World Cup winner 1998; gold medal 200m World Championships, Szeged,

Hungary 1998, silver medal 1000m; World Cup winner 1999; silver medals 200m, 500m and 1000m European Championships, Zagreb, Croatia 1999; silver medal 200m and 500m, bronze medal 1000m Canoeing World Championships, Milan, Italy 1999; gold medal 1000m, bronze medal 200m European Championships 2000; World Cup winner 2000; bronze medal 1000m European Championships, Italy 2001; silver medal 1000m World Championships, Poland 2001; World Cup winner 2002; Best Czech Sportsman of the Year 1996. *Publications:* Story of the Defeated Champion 2000, Technique and Tactics of Paddling in Flat Water Canoes 2001. *Leisure interests:* skiing, music, cycling, golf. *Address:* Sluneční 627, 533 04 Sezemice, Czech Republic (Home); Račice 64, 411 08 Štětí. *Telephone:* (46) 6931717 (Office); (41) 6811872 (Home). *Fax:* (46) 6931717 (Office); (41) 6810400 (Home). *E-mail:* prosport@pce.cz (Office); md@martindoktor.cz (Home). *Website:* www.martindoktor.cz (Home).

DOLAN, Charles F.; American cable television executive; b. 16 Oct. 1926, Cleveland, Ohio; m. Helen Burgess; three s. three d.; ed John Carroll Univ.; served in USAF; jtly. with wife est. co. producing and distributing sports and industrial films; subsequently f. Teleguide Inc. (providing information services via cable to New York hotels) and Sterling Manhattan Cable (first urban cable TV co. in USA), Home Box Office Inc.; Founder and Chair. Cablevision Systems Corp. 1985–; co-owner Madison Square Garden Properties 1995–; Dir Cold Spring Harbor Lab., St Francis Hosp., Long Island; Chair. Nat. Acad. of TV Arts and Sciences; a Man. Dir of Metropolitan Opera, New York; Trustee Fairfield Univ., Conn.; mem. Bd of Govs. Nat. Hockey League. *Address:* Cablevision Systems Corporation, 1111 Stewart Avenue, Bethpage, NY 11714-3581, USA.

DOLAN, James; American business executive; m.; five c.; fmrly Asst Gen. Man. Cablevision Chicago, Vice-Pres. for Advertising Sales Cablevision; Man. WKNR-AM radio station, Cleveland; Corpn Dir Advertising Rainbow Programming Holdings, CEO 1992–95; CEO, Pres. Cablevision Systems Corpn 1995–. *Leisure interests:* yachting, music. *Address:* Cablevision Systems Corporation, 1111 Stewart Avenue, Bethpage, NY 11714, USA.

DOLBY, Ray M., BS, PhD; American engineer and inventor; b. 1933, Portland, OR; m. Dagmar Dolby; ed Stanford Univ., Cambridge Univ., UK; mem. staff Ampex Corpn 1949–57; Consultant to UK Atomic Energy Authority 1961; UN adviser in India 1963–65; Founder and Chair. Dolby Laboratories Inc., London 1965–, opened further offices and labs in San Francisco 1976, inventor Dolby noise-reduction units, Dolby 'A' system sold to recording studios, work on noise-reduction for tape cassettes and 8-track cartridge led to Dolby 'B' system 1971, now adopted world-wide, and adapted for cinema 1978; holder of more than 50 US patents; Fellow Audio Eng. Soc., British Kinematograph, Sound and TV Soc.; Hon. mem. Soc. of Motion Picture and TV Engineers; Hon. OBE 1986; Hon. Fellow Pembroke Coll., Cambridge 1983, Hon. DSc (Cambridge), Dr hc (York) 1999; Audio Eng. Soc. Gold Medal, Soc. of Motion Picture and TV Engineers Samuel L. Warner Memorial Award, Alexander M. Poniatoff Gold Medal, Progress Medal, Acad. of Motion Picture Arts and Sciences, Scientific and Eng. Award 1979, Acad. Award 1989, Emmy Award, Nat. Acad. of TV Arts and Sciences 1989, US Nat. Medal of Tech. 1997, IEEE Masaru Ibuka Consumer Electronics Award 1997, American Electronic Asscn Medal of Honor 1997. *Publications include:* contribs to papers on video tape recording, long wavelength X-ray analysis and noise reduction. *Address:* c/o Dolby Laboratories, Wootton Bassett, Wiltshire, SN4 8QJ, England (Office). *Website:* www.dolby.com (Office).

DOLCE, Domenico; Italian fashion designer; b. 13 Aug. 1958, Polizzi Generosa, nr Palermo, Sicily; s. of Saverio Dolce; designer, father's atelier, then Asst in a Milan atelier; with Stefano Gabbana (q.v.) opened fashion consulting studio 1982, selected to take part in New Talents show, Milano Collezioni 1985; f. Dolce & Gabbana 1985, first maj. women's collection 1985, knitwear 1987, beachwear 1989, men's wear 1990, women's fragrance, D&G line 1992, men's fragrance, home collection 1994, jeans line, eyewear 1996; opened boutiques Milan, Hong Kong, Singapore, Taipei, Seoul, London; Woolmark Award 1991, Perfume Acad. Int. Prize for Best Feminine Fragrance of Year 1993, Best Masculine Fragrance of Year 1995. *Address:* Dolce & Gabbana, Via Santa Cecilia 7, 20122 Milan, Italy (Office). *Telephone:* (02) 54-10-81-52 (Office). *Fax:* (02) 76-02-06-00 (Office). *Website:* www.dolcegabbana.it (Office).

DOLE, Elizabeth Hanford, MA, JD; American administrator; b. 29 July 1936, Salisbury, NC; d. of John Van Hanford and Mary E. Cathey; m. Robert J. Dole (q.v.) 1975; ed Duke and Harvard Univs. and Univ. of Oxford; called to Bar, Dist of Columbia 1966; Staff Asst to Asst Sec. for Educ., Dept of Health, Educ. and Welfare 1966–67; practising lawyer, Washington, DC 1967–68; Assoc. Dir Legis. Affairs, then Exec. Dir Pres.'s Comm. for Consumer Interests 1968–71; Deputy Asst Office of Consumer Affairs, The White House, Washington, DC 1971–73; Commr Fed. Trade. Comm. 1973–79; Asst to Pres. for Public Liaison 1981–83; Sec. of Transport 1983–87; Trustee Duke Univ. 1974–88; mem. Visiting Comm., John F. Kennedy School of Govt 1988–; Sec. of Labor 1989–90; Pres. American Red Cross 1991–98; Cand. for Republican presidential nomination 1999; Senator from N Carolina 2003–; mem. Comm. Harvard School of Public Health 1992–, Bd of Overseers, Harvard Univ. 1989–95; numerous awards. *Address:* Office of the Senator from North Carolina, Suite B34, Dirksen Building, US Senate, Washington, DC 20510, USA. *Telephone:* (202) 2246342.

DOLE, Robert J.; American politician; b. 22 July 1923, Russell, Kan.; s. of Doran R. Dole and Bina Dole; m. 2nd Elizabeth Hanford Dole (q.v.) 1975; one d.; ed Russell public schools, Univ. of Kansas and Washbourn Municipal Univ.; mem. Kansas Legislature 1951–53; Russell County Attorney 1953–61; mem. House of Reps. 1960–68; US Senator from Kansas 1969–96; Senate Majority Leader 1995–96; Senate Republican Leader 1987–96; House Majority Leader 1985–87, Minority leader 1987; Chair. Republican Nat. Cttee 1971–72; Vice-Presidential Cand. 1976, Presidential Cand. 1996; mem. of counsel Verner, Liipfert, Bernhard, McPherson and Hand, Alston and Bird 2003–; Chair. Senate Finance Cttee 1981–84; Pres. Dole Foundation 1983–99; Dir Mainstream Inc.; Adviser, US Del. to FAO Conf., Rome 1965, 1974, 1977; mem. Congressional del. to India 1966, Middle East 1967; mem. US Helsinki Comm., del. to Belgrade Conf. 1977; Chair. International Comm. on Missing Persons 1997–; Trustee, William Allen White Foundation, Univ. of Kan.; mem. Nat. Advisory Cttee, The John Wesley Colls.; mem. American Bar Asscn; mem. Nat. Advisory Cttee on Scouting for the Handicapped, Kan. Asscn for Retarded Children, Advisory Bd of United Cerebral Palsy, Kan.; Hon. mem. Advisory Bd of Kidney Patients Inc.; Presidential Medal of Freedom 1997; Distinguished Service Award 1997; Republican. *Publication:* Great Political Wit (co.ed.) 1999, Great Presidential Wits 2001. *Leisure interests:* politics, watching the news. *Address:* Alston & Bird LLP, 10th Floor, North Building, 601 Pennsylvania Avenue, NW, Washington, DC 20004-2601, USA. *Website:* www.bobdole.org.

DOLGEN, Jonathan L., JD; American film executive; b. 27 April 1945, NY; ed Cornell Univ., New York. Univ. Law School; lawyer Fried, Frank, Harris, Shriver & Jacobson 1969–76; Asst Gen. Counsel then Deputy Gen. Counsel Columbia Pictures Industries 1976–85, Sr Vice-Pres. World Business Affairs 1979, Exec. Vice-Pres. 1980; Pres. Columbia's Pay Cable & Home Entertainment Group 1983; Sr Exec. Vice-Pres. Fox Inc. 1985–90; Pres. TV Div. Twentieth Century Fox Inc. 1985–88, Pres. 1988–93; Chair. Twentieth TV 1988–90; Pres. Columbia Pictures 1990–94, Pres. Columbia Pictures, Culver City 1991–; Chair. and CEO Viacom Entertainment Group 1994–; f. Friends of Cornell Univ. Arts Center, founder mem. Educ. First; mem. Alumni Council New York Univ. Law School; mem. Bd Dirs Sony Pictures; Fellow Claremont Univ. Center and Grad. School. *Address:* Viacom Entertainment Group, 1515 Broadway, New York, NY 10036-8901, USA (Office).

DOLGUSHIN, Nikita Aleksandrovich; Russian choreographer; b. 8 Nov. 1938, Leningrad; s. of Aleksandr Pavlovich and Vera Ivanonva Kazanskaya; m. Alexsandra Anatolievna Baranova; ed Leningrad School of Choreography; soloist, Kirov (now Maryinsky) Theatre of Opera and Ballet 1959–61; leading dancer, Novosibirsk Theatre of Opera and Ballet 1961–66, 1968–83; soloist, Leningrad Maly Opera and Ballet Theatre; Head of Ballet Chair, St Petersburg Conservatory (SPB) 1983–, Artistic Dir, head of ballet co., State Theatre of SPB Conservatory; fmr Prof., Paris Univ. of Dance; Chevalier Order of Catherine the Great; Dr h.c. Univ. Towson (USA); USSR People's Artist, Kt of Ballet (Spirit of Dance); Laureate of Int. Competition (Varna). *Leading roles include:* Satire (Spartacus), Albert (Giselle), Romeo (Romeo and Juliet), Prince (Nutcracker), Prince Igor (Yaroslavna). *Films:* Nikita Dolgushin Philosophy of Dance the Place in History, Masked Ball. *Publications:* numerous articles in Ballet magazine 1960–90. *Address:* St Petersburg State Conservatory, Teatralnaya pl. 3, St Petersburg, Russia. *Telephone:* (812) 311-66-74 (Office); (812) 314-56-44 (Home). *Fax:* (812) 311-81-65 (Office). *E-mail:* theatre@comset.net (Office).

DOLL, Sir (William) Richard (Shaboe), Kt, CH, OBE, FRS, FMedSci, MD, DSc, FRCP; British epidemiologist and medical researcher; b. 28 Oct. 1912, Hampton; s. of William and Kathleen Doll; m. Joan Faulkner (née Blatchford) 1949; one s. one d.; ed Westminster School and St Thomas's Hospital Medical School, Univ. of London; military service 1939–45; with Medical Research Council's Statistical Research Unit 1948–69, Dir 1961–69; mem. Advisory Cttee on Medical Research WHO 1963, Council of Int. Epidemiological Asscn 1961, Scientific Cttee Int. Agency for Cancer Research 1965–70, 1975–78, Hebdomadal Council, Oxford Univ. 1975–81, Comm. on Environment and Health, WHO 1990–91; Regius Prof. of Medicine, Oxford 1969–79, Warden Green Coll. 1979–83; Hon. mem., Imperial Cancer Research Fund, Cancer Studies Unit, Radcliffe Infirmary, Oxford 1983–; mem. Royal Comm. on Environmental Pollution 1973–79, Comm. on Energy and the Environment 1978–81; Senior mem. Inst. of Medicine; Foreign Hon. mem. Norwegian Acad. of Sciences 1976, New York Acad. of Arts and Sciences 1977; Hon. FRCS, FRCOG, FRCR, FRCGP; Emer. Fellow Academia Europaea; Hon. Assoc. Physician Central Middx Hospital 1949–69; Foreign Assoc. Nat. Acad. of Sciences, USA 2001; Hon. DSc (Newcastle) 1969, (Belfast) 1972, (Reading) 1973, (Newfoundland) 1973, (Stony Brook) 1988, (Harvard) 1988, (London) 1988, (Oxford) 1989, (Oxford Brookes) 1994, (Kingston) 1996; DM (Tasmania) 1975, (Birmingham) 1994, (Bergen) 1996; David Anderson Berry Prize, Royal Soc. of Edinburgh (jointly) 1958, Bisset Hawkins Medal, Royal Coll. of Physicians, London 1962, UN Award for Cancer Research 1962, Rock Carling Fellow, Nuffield Provincial Hospitals Trust, London 1967, Gairdner Award 1970, Buchanan Medal, Royal Soc. 1972, Presidential Award, New York Acad. of Sciences 1975, Prix Griffuel, Paris 1975, John Snow Award, Epidemiology Section, American Public Health Asscn 1976, Gold Medal, Royal Inst. of Public Health 1977, Charles S. Mott Prize for Prevention of Cancer 1979, Nat. Award, American Cancer Soc. 1981, Gold Medal, BMA 1983, Wilhelm Conrad Röntgen Prize, Accademia dei Lincei 1984, Johann-Georg-Zimmermann Preis, Hanover 1985, Founders' Award, Chemical Inst. of Toxicology 1986,

Royal Medal, Royal Soc. 1986, Alton Ochsner Award (jtly) 1988, Helmut Horten Award (jtly) 1991, first Prince Mahidol Award (Bangkok) 1992, Richard T. Hewitt Award 1999, Dr Nathan Davis Int. Award, American Medical Asscn 2001. *Publications:* Articles on causes of cancer, aetiology of lung cancer, leukaemia, epidemiology, effects of ionizing radiations, oral contraceptives, treatment of gastric ulcers, etc. *Leisure interests:* conversation, good food. *Address:* 12 Rawlinson Road, Oxford, OX2 6UE, England. *Telephone:* (1865) 558887. *Fax:* (1865) 558817.

DOLLERY, Sir Colin (Terence), Kt, FRCP, FMedSci; British physician; b. 14 March 1931; s. of Cyril Robert Dollery and Thelma Mary Dollery; m. Diana Myra Stedman 1958; one s. one d.; ed Lincoln School and Univ. of Birmingham; House Officer, Queen Elizabeth Hosp. Birmingham, Hammersmith Hosp. and Brompton Hosp. 1956–58; Medical Registrar, Hammersmith Hosp. 1958–60, Sr Registrar and Tutor in Med. 1960–62; Consultant Physician 1962–2000; Lecturer in Medicine, Royal Postgrad. Medical School, Univ. of London 1962–65, Prof. of Clinical Pharmacology 1965–87, Prof. of Medicine 1987–91, Dean 1991–96, Pro-Vice-Chancellor for Medicine 1992–96; Sr Consultant Research and Devt., SmithKline Beecham PLC 1996–2000, GlaxoSmithKline 2001–; Dir (non-exec.) Larson-Davis, Inc. 1998–99, Discovery Partners, Inc. 2001–, Predict, Inc. 2001–; mem. MRC 1982–84, Univ. Funding Council (fmrly Univ. Grants Cttee) 1984–91; hon. mem. Asscn of American Physicians; Chevalier, Ordre Nat. du Mérite. *Publications:* The Retinal Circulation 1971, Therapeutic Drugs 1991; papers in scientific journals. *Leisure interests:* travel, amateur radio, work. *Address:* 101 Corringham Road, London, NW11 7DL, England. *Telephone:* (20) 8458-2616.

DOLLFUS, Audouin, D. ÈS SC.; French astronomer; b. 12 Nov. 1924, Paris; s. of Charles Dollfus and Suzanne Soubeyran; m. Catherine Browne 1959; four c.; ed Univ. de Paris; joined Observatoire de Meudon (astrophysical div. of Observatoire de Paris) 1946, Head of Lab. for Physics of the Solar System; Astronomer, Observatoire de Paris 1965, now Emer.; Pres. Observatoire de Triel 1994–; mem. Int. Acad. of Astronautics (Trustee 1975–81), Société Astronomique de France (Pres. 1979–81), Aéro-club de France (Trustee 1995–99), French Asscn for the Advancement of Science (Pres. 1993–95); Hon. mem. Royal Astronomical Soc. of Canada, Astronomy and Geophysics Soc. of USSR; Assoc. Royal Astronomical Soc., London, Soc. French Explorers, Explorers Club USA, Soc. Philomatique de Paris, NY Acad. of Science; Grand Prix Acad. des Sciences (Paris), Int. Award Galabert for Astronautics, Diploma Tissandier (Int. Fed. Astronautics). *Achievements:* pioneered balloon astronomy, discovered Janus (10th satellite of planet Saturn) 1966. *Publications:* 350 scientific publications on astrophysics. *Leisure interest:* ballooning (holds three official world records with gas balloons: duration, distance, altitude). *Address:* Observatoire, 92195 Meudon (Office); 77 rue Albert Perdreaux, 92370 Chaville, France. *Telephone:* 1-47-50-97-43.

DOLOGUELE, Anicet G.; Central African Republic politician; fmr Finance and Budget Minister; Prime Minister of Cen. African Repub., Minister of the Economy, Finance, Planning and Int. Co-operation 1999–2001; currently Gen. Man. Banque de développement des états de l'Afrique centrale. *Address:* Banque de développement des états de l'Afrique centrale, Place du Gouvernement, B.P. 1177, Brazzaville, Republic of the Congo (Office).

DOLZHENKO, Irina Igorevna; Russian opera singer (mezzo-soprano); b. 23 Oct. 1955, Tashkent, Uzbekistan; m.; one d.; mem. children's troupe, Stanislavsky and Nemirovich-Danchenko Music Theatre, Moscow –1996; soloist Bolshoi Theare 1996–; sang with Swedish Royal Opera, Deutsche Oper, Berlin, Theatre Colon, Buenos Aires, New Israeli Opera, Tel-Aviv; recitals in Japan, S Korea, USA, Australia, Europe; People's Artist of Russia. *Operatic roles include:* Amneris in Aida, Adalgisa in Norma, Amelfa in The Golden Cockerel, Morozova in Oprichnik, Cherubino in Marriage of Figaro, Azucena in Il Trovatore, Ulrica in Un Ballo in Maschera. *Address:* c/o Bolshoi Theatre of Russia, Teatralnaya pl. 1, 13009 Moscow, Russia (Office). *Telephone:* (095) 719-79-30 (Home).

DOMARKAS, Juozas; Lithuanian conductor; b. 28 July 1936, Varkaliai, Plunge Dist; m. (wife deceased); two s.; ed Klaipeda Simkus College of Music, Lithuanian Acad. of Music, Leningrad State Conservatory; Asst conductor, Vilnius Band 1957–60; Artistic Dir and Chief Conductor Lithuanian Nat. Orchestra (NLO) 1964–; participated in numerous nat. and int. festivals; teacher, Sr teacher, Assoc. Prof. Lithuanian Acad. of Music 1968–93, Chair and Prof. 1993–; Grand Duke Gediminas First Order and Award 1998. *Address:* Lietuvos Nacionaline Filharmonija, Ausros Vartu 5, LT-2001, Vilnius (Office); Jogalios 16-5, LT-2001 Vilnius, Lithuania (Home). *Telephone:* (2) 62-70-47 (Office); (2) 62-84-61 (Home). *Fax:* (2) 62-28-59 (Office).

DOMB, Cyril, MA, PhD, FRS; British/Israeli professor of physics; b. London; s. of Joel Domb and Sarah (née Wulkan) Domb; m. Shirley Galinsky 1957; three s. three d.; ed Hackney Downs School, London, Pembroke Coll., Cambridge; Fellow, Clarendon Lab., Oxford 1949–52; Univ. Lecturer in Mathematics, Cambridge 1952–54; Prof. of Theoretical Physics, London Univ. 1954–81; Prof. of Physics, Bar Ilan Univ., Israel 1981–89, Prof. Emer. 1989–; Academic Pres. Jerusalem Coll. of Technology 1985–94; Rayleigh Prize 1947, Max Born Prize 1981. *Publications:* Co-operative Phenomena in Crystals, in Advances in Physics 1960, Clerk Maxwell and Modern Science (ed.) 1963, Phase Transitions and Critical Phenomena, Vols 1–6 (with M. S. Green), Vols 7–20 (ed. with J. L. Lebowitz), Memories of Kopul Rosen (ed.) 1970, Challenge–Torah views on science and its problems (ed. with A. Carmell) 1976, The Critical Point 1996; scientific papers. *Leisure interests:* walking,

swimming. *Address:* c/o Department of Physics, Bar Ilan University, 52 900 Ramat Gan, Israel; 28 St Peter's Court, Queen's Road, London, NW4 2HG, England.

DOMBROVSKIS, Valdis; Latvian politician; b. 5 Aug. 1971; ed Latvian Univ., Riga Tech. Univ., Maincas Univ. and Merilendas Univ.; Minister of Finance Nov. 2002–. *Address:* Ministry of Finance, Smilsu iela 1, 1050 Riga, Latvia (Office). *Website:* www.fm.gov.lv (Office).

DOMENICI, Pete V., BS, LLB; American senator; b. 7 May 1932, Albuquerque; s. of Cherubino Domenici and Alda Domenici; m. Nancy Burk 1958; two s. six d.; ed Univs. of Albuquerque, New Mexico, Denver; elected to Albuquerque City Comm. 1966, Chair. 1967; mem. Nat. League of Cities Revenue and Finance Steering Cttee and the Resolutions Cttee of the 1969 Annual Conf. of Mayors; served on Governor's Policy Bd for Law Enforcement and on Middle Rio Grande Conf. of Govts.; US Senator from New Mexico 1972–; Chair. Senate Budget Cttee 1981, 1995–2001, Senate Indian Affairs Cttee; Republican; several hon. degrees; Public Sector Leadership Award 1996; numerous other awards. *Leisure interests:* hunting, fishing. *Address:* US Senate, 328 Hart Senate Office Building, Washington, DC 20510-0001 (Office); 120 3rd Street, NE, Washington, DC 20002 (Home); 135 East 50th Street, 5L, New York, NY 10022, USA (Home).

DOMINGO, Plácido, FRCM; Spanish opera singer; b. 21 Jan. 1941, Madrid; s. of the late Plácido and Pepita (Embil) Domingo; m. Marta Ornelas; three s.; ed Nat. Conservatory of Music, Mexico City; operatic début at Monterrey, Mexico 1961; début at Metropolitan Opera, New York, 1968; British début in Verdi's Requiem at Festival Hall 1969; Covent Garden début in Tosca 1971, returned to sing in Aida, Carmen 1973, La Bohème 1974, Un Ballo in Maschera 1975, La Fanciulla del West; has taken leading roles in about 50 operas; with New York City Opera 1965–; Artistic Dir Washington Opera 1994–, LA Opera 2000–; Artistic Adviser and Prin. Guest Conductor Los Angeles Opera; Fellow, Royal N Coll. of Music; recent engagements include Tosca (conducting), Romeo and Juliet at Metropolitan Opera, New York, NY, Aida, Il Trovatore in Hamburg, Don Carlos in Salzburg; I vespri siciliani and La forza del destino in Paris, Turandot in Barcelona, Otello in Paris, London, Hamburg and Milan, Carmen in Edin., Turandot at the Metropolitan; New York stage début in My Fair Lady 1988 (213 performances by 2000); Dr hc (Royal Coll. of Music) 1982, (Univ. Complutense de Madrid) 1989; Commdr Légion d'honneur; Hon. KBE 2002; eight Grammy Awards. *Films include:* Madame Butterfly with Von Karajan, La Traviata 1982, Carmen 1984, Otello 1986. *Recordings include:* Aida, Un Ballo in Maschera, Tosca. *Publication:* My First Forty Years (autobiog.) 1983. *Address:* c/o Vincent and Farrell Associates, Suite 740, 8th Avenue, New York, NY 10001, USA.

DOMINGO SOLANS, Eugenio, DEcon; Spanish international banker, economist and university professor; b. 26 Nov. 1945, Barcelona; ed Univ. of Barcelona, Autonomous Univ. of Madrid; Prof. of Public Finance, Univ. of Barcelona 1968–70, Autonomous Univ. of Madrid 1970–; economist, Banco Atlántico 1970, 1973–77, 1978–79; economist, Research Group, Econ. and Social Devt Plan 1970–73; Econ. Adviser, Ministry of Econs 1977–78; Man. Research Dept, Inst. of Econ. Studies 1979–86; Asst Pres. Banco Zaragozano 1986–91; mem. Bd BZ Gestión 1987–91, Banco Zaragozano 1988–94, Banco de Toledo 1988–94 (Sec. Bd 1990–94); mem. Governing Council and Exec. Comm., Banco de España 1994–98; Prof. of Monetary Policy and Spanish Tax System, Univ. Coll. of Financial Studies, Madrid 1996–; mem. Exec. Bd and Governing Council, European Cen. Bank 1998–; Businessmen's Soc. Award 1994. *Address:* Universidad Autónoma de Madrid, Carretera de Colmenar Km. 15, Cantoblanco 28049, Madrid, Spain (Office). *Telephone:* (91) 3975000 (Office). *Fax:* (91) 3974123 (Office). *Website:* www.uam.es (Office).

DOMINIAN, Jacobus, MBE, DSC, F.R.C.P.(E.), F.R.C.PSY.; British psychiatrist; b. 25 Aug. 1929, Athens, Greece; s. of Charles Dominian and Mary Scarlato; m. Edith Mary Smith 1955; four d.; ed St Mary's School, Bombay, Stamford Grammar School, England, Fitzwilliam Coll., Cambridge, Exeter Coll., Oxford and Inst. of Psychiatry, London; Sr House Officer United Oxford Hosps. 1955–58; Registrar Maudsley Hosp., London 1958–61, Sr Registrar 1961–64; Sr Consultant Psychiatrist Cen. Middx Hosp., London 1965–88, Hon. Consultant 1988–; Dir One Plus One (Marriage and Partnership Research) 1971–; Hon. DSc (Lancaster) 1976. *Publications:* Christian Marriage 1967, Marital Breakdown 1968, Depression 1976, Proposals for a New Sexual Ethic 1976, Authority 1976, Marital Pathology 1980, Marriage, Faith and Love 1981, The Capacity to Love 1985, Sexual Integrity: the answer to AIDS 1987, Passionate and Compassionate Love–A Vision for Christian Marriage 1991, The Everyday God (with Edmund Flood) 1993, Marriage 1995, One Like Us: a psychological interpretation of Jesus 1998, Let's Make Love 2001. *Leisure interests:* swimming, theatre, music and reading. *Address:* 10 Harley Street, London, W1 (Office); Pefka, The Green, Croxley Green, Rickmansworth, Herts., WD3 3JA, England. *Telephone:* (1923) 720972.

DOMINO, Fats; American blues singer; b. Antoine Domino, 26 Feb. 1928, New Orleans, La.; fmr factory worker; began singing career in local clubs; Hall of Fame Grammy Award 1997, Lifetime Achievement Grammy Award 1997, Nat. Medal of Arts 1998. *Singles include:* The Fat Man, Goin' Home, Going To The River, Please Don't Leave Me, Don't You Know, Ain't That A Shame, Bo Weevil, I'm In Love Again, My Blue Heaven, Blueberry Hill, Walking to New Orleans, My Girl Josephine, Let The Four Winds Blow, Red Sails In The Sunset. *Albums include:* Here Comes Fats Domino 1963, Fats Domino 1966, Trouble in Mind, Fats is Back 1968, Sleeping on the Job 1978, The Fat Man

1995, Live at Gilleys 1999, Live! Collector's Edition 2000. *Address:* SMS Records, 14134 NE Airport Way, Portland, OR 97230 (Office); c/o Atlantic Records, 1290 Avenue of the Americas, New York, NY 10104, USA.

DOMITIEN, Elisabeth; Central African Republic politician; fmr mem. Mouvement d'évolution sociale de l'Afrique noire (MESAN), Vice-Pres. 1975–79; Prime Minister of Central African Repub. 1975–76.

DOMLJAN, Žarko; Croatian politician; b. 14 Sept. 1932, Imotski; m. Iva Marijanovic; one d.; ed Zagreb Univ., Music Coll.; mem. Croatian Nat. Theatre Orchestra 1955–57; Ed.-in-Chief, Deputy Dir, Editorial Dept of Lexicographical Inst. 1968–86; Ed.-in-Chief Yugoslav Encyclopedia of Art and Encyclopedia of Croatian Art 1985–96, Life of Art Journal 1967–73; research advisor Inst. of Art History 1987–90; mem. and Pres. Parl. of Croatian Repub. 1990–92; mem. Chamber of Reps. of Croatian Parl. 1992, Vice Pres. 1992–; Chair. Foreign Policy Bd; mem. State Council of Defence and Nat. Security and of Presidential Council. *Publications:* Architect Hugo Erlich 1979, Modern Architecture in Yugoslavia 1986. *Leisure interests:* tennis, mountain trekking. *Address:* Kukuljevićeva 32, 10000 Zagreb, Croatia (Home). *Telephone:* (1) 4851011 (Office).

DOMMISSE, Ebbe, BA, MSc; South African newspaper editor; b. 14 July 1940, Riversdale; s. of Jan Dommisse and Anna Dommisse; m. Dalène Laubscher 1963; two s. one d.; ed Paarl Boys High School, Univ. of Stellenbosch and Grad. School of Journalism, Columbia Univ.; reporter, Die Burger, Cape Town 1961, Chief sub-ed. 1968, News Ed. 1971; Asst Ed. and political commentator, Beeld, Johannesburg (founder mem. of new Johannesburg daily) 1974; Asst Ed. Die Burger 1979, Sr Asst Ed. 1984, Ed. 1990–; Exec. mem. Nasionale Koerante; Trustee Helpmekaarfonds; mem. Akad. vir Wetenskap en Kuns; Nieman Travel Fellowship 1987. *Publications:* with Alf Ries: Broedertwis 1982, Leierstryd 1990. *Leisure interests:* reading, the arts, ecology, tennis. *Address:* Die Burger, 40 Heerengracht, P.O. Box 692, Cape Town 8000, South Africa (Office). *Telephone:* (21) 4062222.

DOMOTO, Hisao; Japanese painter; b. 1928; ed Kyoto Acad. of Fine Arts; studied in France, Italy and Spain 1952; settled in Paris 1955; abandoned traditional Japanese style and exhibited abstract paintings Salon des Indépendants, Salon de Mai, Paris 1956, 1957; rep. at Rome/New York Art Foundation first Exhbn Rome, "Otro Arte" Exhbn Madrid, Facchetti and Stadler Galleries, Paris 1957; one-man Exhbn Martha Jackson Gallery, New York 1959; First Prize, Acad. of Japan 1951 and 1953; First Prize of Musée d'Art Moderne for foreign painters in Paris 1958.

DONABEDIAN, Avedis, BA, MD; American professor of public health and physician; b. 7 Jan. 1919, Beirut, Lebanon; s. of Samuel Donabedian and Maritza (née Der Hagopian) Donabedian; m. Dorothy Salibian 1945; three s.; ed Friends' Boys' School, Ramallah (Palestine), American Univ. of Beirut and Harvard Univ. School of Public Health, USA; Teaching Fellow in Pharmacology, American Univ. of Beirut 1938–40; Physician, then Acting Supt, English Mission Hosp., Jerusalem 1945–47; Instructor in Physiology, Clinical Asst in Venereology, American Univ. of Beirut 1948–50, Physician, then Dir Univ. Health Service 1951–54; Medical Assoc., Medical Care Evaluation Studies, United Community Services of Metropolitan Boston, Mass., USA 1955–57; Research Assoc., then Visiting Lecturer, Harvard School of Public Health 1955–57; Asst Prof., then Assoc. Prof. of Preventive Medicine, New York Medical Coll. 1957–61; Assoc. Prof. of Public Health Econs, then Prof. of Public Health Econs, then Prof. of Medical Org., Univ. of Mich. School of Public Health 1961–79; Nathan Sinai Distinguished Prof. of Public Health, Univ. of Mich. 1979–89, Prof. Emer. 1989–; mem. Inst. of Medicine; Hon. Pres. Avedis Donabedian Foundation 1990–; Hon. Fellow Royal Coll. of Gen. Practitioners, London 1991; Hon. mem. Nat. Acad. of Mexico 1992; several awards including Award in Recognition of a Distinguished Career in Health Services Research, Asscn for Health Services Research 1985, Baxter American Foundation Prize 1986, Ernest A. Codman Award (Jt Comm. on Accreditation of Healthcare Orgs.) 1997, Sedgwick Memorial Medal, American Public Health Asscn 1999. *Publications:* A Guide to Medical Care Administration: Vol. II, Medical Care Appraisal 1969, Aspects of Medical Care Administration 1973, Benefits in Medical Care Programs 1976, The Definition of Quality and Approaches to its Assessment 1980, The Criteria and Standards of Quality 1982, The Methods and Findings of Quality Assessment and Monitoring 1985. *Leisure interests:* gardening, photography, languages, literature and music. *Address:* Department of Health Management and Policy, School of Public Health, The University of Michigan, 109 South Observatory Street, Ann Arbor, MI 48109; 1739 Ivywood Drive, Ann Arbor, MI 48103, USA (Home). *Telephone:* (734) 764-5432 (Office); (734) 665-4565. *Fax:* (734) 764-4338.

DONAGHY, Rita, OBE, BA; British public servant; b. 9 October 1944, Bristol; d. of William Scott Willis and Margaret Brenda Howard; m. 1st James Columba Donaghy 1968 (divorced 1985, died 1986); m. 2nd Ted (Edward) Easen-Thomas; ed Univ. of Durham; Asst Registrar, then Perm. Sec. of Students' Union, Univ. of London Inst. of Educ. 1968–2000; Pres. Nat. and Local Govt Officers' Asscn (NALGO) 1989–90, TUC 2000; mem. Low Pay Comm. 1997–2000; Chair. Advisory, Conciliation and Arbitration Service (ACAS) 2000–; mem. Cttee on Standards in Public Life (Wicks Cttee) 2000; Dr hc (Open Univ.) 2002. *Leisure interests:* theatre, gardening, reading. *Address:* ACAS, Brandon House, 180 Borough High Street, London, SE1 1LW (Office); 35 Lyndhurst Grove, London, SE15 5AN, England (Home). *Tele-*

phone: (20) 7210-3670 (Office); (20) 7703-4573 (Home). *Fax:* (20) 7210-3664 (Office); (20) 7703-4573 (Home). *E-mail:* rdonaghy@acas.org.uk (Office); ritadonaghy@waitrose.com (Home). *Website:* www.acas.org.uk (Office).

DONAHUE, Thomas Michael, PhD; American professor and atmospheric scientist; b. 23 May 1921, Healdton, Okla; s. of Robert E. Donahue and Mary J. Lyndon; m. Esther McPherson 1950; three s.; ed Rockhurst Coll. and Johns Hopkins Univ.; Asst Prof., Prof. of Physics, Univ. of Pittsburgh 1951–74, Dir Space Research Lab. 1966–74; Prof. of Atmospheric and Oceanic Science Univ. of Mich. 1974–87, Edward H. White II Distinguished Univ. Prof. of Planetary Science 1987–94, Prof. Emer. 1994–; Prof. of Physics 1989–94, Dir Program for the Integrated Study of Global Change 1990–94; mem. Visiting Cttee Max Planck Soc., Lindau; mem. NAS, Chair. Space Science Bd 1982–88, liaison to Nat. Research Council in Geophysics 1997–2001, Chair. sec. of Geophysics 2002–; mem. NASA Advisory Council 1982–88; Chair. Science Steering Group, Pioneer Venus Mission 1974–93; Chair. Cttee on Solar Terrestrial Research 1972–75; Chair. Atmospheric Sciences Advisory Panel 1968–72; mem. Cttee on Atmospheric Science 1960–72, Rocket Research Cttee 1966–69, Geophysics Research Forum (fmrly Bd) 1972–75, 1982–, Climate Bd 1979–82, Physical Science Cttee 1972–76, Solar System Exploration Cttee 1980–82; Chair. Cttee for US–USSR Workshop on Planetary Sciences 1988–91, Space Science in the 21st Century Study 1985–88, Space Telescope Inst. Visiting Cttee 1987–89, Cttee on Public Affairs, American GEO Physical Union 1990–93; participated in Voyager Missions to Outer Planets 1977, Galileo Mission to Jupiter 1995, Cassini Mission to Saturn; Henry Russel Lectureship, Univ. of Mich. 1986; mem. NASA Science Center Assessment Study 1987–88; Fellow, American Physical Soc., AAAS, American Geophysical Union (Pres. Solar Planetary Relations Section 1974–76); mem. American Astronomical Soc., Bd of Trustees, Upper Atmosphere Research Corpn 1968–80 (Chair. 1972), Univ. Space Research Corpn for Atmospheric Research 1976–83 (Sec. 1978–89, Vice-Chair. 1980-83), Int. Acad. of Astronautics 1987–; mem. ARECIBO Advisory Bd 1971–75, 1987–89 (Chair. 1989); Hon. DSc (Rockhurst Coll.) 1981; NASA Public Service Award 1977, Distinguished Public Service Medal 1980; Henry Arctowski Medal (NAS) 1981, Fleming Medal, American Geophysical Union 1981, winner Space Science Award, American Inst. of Aeronautics and Astronautics 1987, Space Science Award (Nat. Space Club) 1989, Attwood Award (Coll. of Eng, Mich. Univ.) 1994; Guggenheim Fellow (at Observatoire de Meudon, France) 1960. *Publications:* numerous scientific papers. *Leisure interests:* tennis, wine, music (classical and traditional), Irish history. *Address:* Space Research Building, University of Michigan, 2455 Hayward Avenue, Ann Arbor, MI 48109 (Office); 1781 Arlington Boulevard, Ann Arbor, MI 48104-4105, USA (Home). *Telephone:* (734) 971-3577 (Home); (734) 763-2390. *Fax:* (734) 764-5137. *E-mail:* tmdonahue@umich.edu (Office).

DONALD, Sir Alan (Ewen), KCMG, BA, LLM; British diplomatist (retd); b. 5 May 1931, Inverurie, Aberdeenshire, Scotland; s. of Robert T. Donald and Louise Turner; m. Janet H.T. Blood 1958; four s.; ed Aberdeen Grammar School, Fettes Coll. Edinburgh and Trinity Hall, Cambridge; mil. service 1949–50; joined Foreign (later Diplomatic) Service 1954; Third Sec. Beijing 1955–57; Pvt. Sec. to Parl. Under Sec. of State, Foreign Office 1958–61; UK Del. to NATO, Paris 1961–64; First Sec. Beijing 1964–66; Counsellor, Athens 1971–73; Political Adviser to Gov. of Hong Kong 1974–77; Amb. to Zaire, Rwanda and Burundi 1977–80; to People's Republic of Congo 1978–80, to Indonesia 1984–86, to People's Repub. of China 1988–91; Asst Under-Sec. (Asia/Pacific), Foreign and Commonwealth Office 1980–84; Adviser on Chinese Affairs Rolls-Royce 1991–99; Dir Fleming Far Eastern Investment Co. 1991–97, China Fund Inc. 1992–2003, Batey, Burn Ltd 1992–98, HSBC China Fund Ltd 1994–2000, Fleming Asian Investment Co. 1997–2001; Adviser to Willis, Faber and Dumas Ltd 1994–; Hon. LLD (Aberdeen) 1991. *Leisure interests:* music, military history, water colour sketching, films. *Address:* Applebys, Chiddingstone Causeway, nr Tonbridge, Kent, TN11 8JH, England. *Telephone:* (1892) 870598. *Fax:* (1892) 870490. *E-mail:* aedchidd@aol .com (Home).

DONALD, Athene Margaret, PhD, FRS; British professor of experimental physics; b. 15 May 1953, London; d. of Walter Griffith and Annette Marian Tylor; m. Matthew J. Donald 1976; one s. one d.; ed Camden School for Girls, London and Girton Coll., Cambridge; postdoctoral researcher, Cornell Univ. 1977–81; Fellow Robinson Coll., Univ. of Cambridge 1981–, Science and Eng Research Council Research Fellow 1981–83, Royal Soc. Research Fellow 1983–85, lecturer 1985–95, reader 1985–98, Prof. of Experimental Physics 1998–; mem. Governing Council, Inst. of Food Research 1999–; Samuel Locker Award in Physics, Birmingham Univ. 1989, Charles Vernon Boys Prize, Inst. of Physics 1989, Rosenhain Medal and Prize, Inst. of Materials 1995. *Publications:* Liquid Crystalline Polymers (jtly) 1992, Starch: Structure and Function (jtly) 1997, Starch: Advances in Structure and Function (jtly) 2001; numerous articles in scientific journals. *Address:* Department of Physics, Cavendish Laboratory, University of Cambridge, Madingley Road, Cambridge, CB3 0HE, England (Office). *Telephone:* (1223) 337382 (Office). *Fax:* (1223) 363263. *E-mail:* amd3@cam.ac.uk (Office). *Website:* www.phy.cam .ac.uk.

DONALDSON, Charles Ian Edward, MA, FBA, FRSE, FAHA; British/ Australian professor of English; b. 6 May 1935, Melbourne, Australia; s. of Dr. William Edward Donaldson and Elizabeth (née Weigall) Donaldson; m. 1st Tamsin Jane Procter 1962 (divorced 1990); one s. one d.; m. 2nd Grazia Maria Therese Gunn 1991; ed Melbourne Grammar School, Melbourne Univ.,

Magdalen Coll., Oxford, Merton Coll., Oxford; Sr Tutor in English, Melbourne Univ. 1958; Fellow and lecturer in English, Wadham Coll., Oxford 1962–69; CUF Lecturer in English, Oxford Univ. 1963–69; Prof. of English, ANU 1969–91, Dir, Humanities Research Centre 1974–90; Regius Prof. of Rhetoric and English Literature Edin. Univ. 1991–95; Grace 1 Prof. of English and Fellow, King's Coll., Cambridge Univ. 1995–2002, Convenor King's Coll. Research Centre 1997–2000, Dir Centre for Research in the Arts, Social Sciences and Humanities 2001–; visiting appointments at Univ. of Calif., Santa Barbara 1967–68, Gonville and Caius Coll., Cambridge 1985, Cornell Univ. 1988, Folger Shakespeare Library 1988, Melbourne Univ. 1991. *Publications:* The World Upside Down: Comedy From Jonson to Fielding 1970, Ben Jonson: Poems (ed.) 1975, The Rapes of Lucretia: A Myth and its Transformations 1982, Jonson and Shakespeare (ed.) 1982, Transformations in Modern European Drama 1983, Seeing the First Australians (ed., with Tamsin Donaldson) 1985, Ben Jonson 1985, Shaping Lives (Co-Ed.) 1992, Jonson's Walk to Scotland 1993, The Death of the Author and the Life of the Poet 1995, Jonson: Selected Poems (ed.) 1995, Jonson's Magic Houses 1997. *Address:* King's College, Cambridge, CB2 1ST (Office); 11 Grange Road, Cambridge, CB3 9AS, England (Home). *Telephone:* (1223) 765275 (Office); (1223) 321683 (Home). *Fax:* (1223) 765276 (Office). *E-mail:* id202@cus.cam.ac.uk (Office). *Website:* www.crassh.cam.ac.uk (Office).

DONALDSON, Dame (Dorothy) Mary, GBE, JP; British fmr local government official; b. 29 Aug. 1921, Wickham, Hants.; d. of late Reginald George Gale Warwick and Dorothy Alice Warwick; m. John Francis Donaldson (now Lord Donaldson of Lymington, q.v., 1945; one s. two d.; ed Portsmouth High School of Girls, Wingfield Morris Orthopaedic Hosp., Middlesex Hosp., London; Chair. Women's Nat. Cancer Control Campaign 1967–69; Vice-Pres. British Cancer Council 1970; served on numerous other medical and community bds. and Cttees.; Alderman, City of London (Ward of Coleman Street) 1975–91, Sheriff 1981–82, first woman Lord Mayor of London 1983–84; Chair. Interim Licensing Authority for In-vitro Fertilization and Human Embryology 1985–91; Chair. Council responsible for Ombudsman in Banking 1985–94; mem. Press Complaints Comm. 1991–94; F.C.R.O.G. ad eundem 1991; mem. City of London Corpn; Hon. Fellow, Girton Coll.; Hon. DSc (City Univ.) 1983; Order of Oman 1982; Order of Bahrain 1984; Grand Officier, Ordre nat. du mérite (France) 1984; Pres.'s Medal of Inst. of Public Relations 1984. *Leisure interests:* sailing, gardening, skiing. *Address:* 5 Kingsfield, Lymington, SO41 3QY, England (Home); 171 Andrewes House, Barbican, London, EC2Y 8BA. *Telephone:* (20) 7588-6610 (Home).

DONALDSON, Roger; New Zealand (b. Australian) film director; b. 15 Nov. 1945, Ballarat, Australia; emigrated to NZ aged 19; established still photography business, then started making documentary films. *Television:* Winners and Losers (series of short dramas). *Films include:* Sleeping Dogs (also producer), Smash Palace (also producer), The Bounty, Marie, No Way Out, Cocktail, Cadillac Man (also producer), White Sands, The Getaway, Species, Dante's Peak, The Guide, 13 Days.

DONALDSON, Samuel Andrew, BA; American journalist; b. 11 March 1934, El Paso, Texas; s. of Samuel A. Donaldson and Chloe Hampson; m. 1st Billie K. Butler 1963; three s. one d.; m. 2nd Janice C. Smith 1983; ed Univ. of Tex., El Paso and Univ. of S Calif.; radio/TV news reporter/anchorman, WTOP, Washington 1961–67; Capitol Hill/corresp., ABC News, Washington 1967–77, White House Corresp. 1977–89, Chief White House Corresp. 1998–99, anchor Prime Time Live 1989–98, co-anchor 20/20 Live, ABC 1998–, anchor SamDonaldson@abcnews.com 1999–, The Sam Donaldson Show, ABC Radio Network 2001–; panellist This Week With David Brinkley 1981–96; co-anchor This Week With Sam Donaldson and Cokie Roberts 1996–2002; Broadcaster of the Year Award, Nat. Press Foundation 1998 and numerous other awards. *Publication:* Hold on Mr President 1987. *Address:* ABC, 1717 Desales Street, NW, Washington, DC 20036, USA (Office). *E-mail:* samdonaldson@abcnews.com (Office).

DONALDSON, Simon Kirwan, DPhil, FRS; British professor of mathematics; b. 20 Aug. 1957, Cambridge; s. of Peter Donaldson and Jane Stirland; m. Ana Nora Hurtado 1986; two s. one d.; ed Sevenoaks School, Kent, Pembroke Coll., Cambridge, Worcester Coll., Oxford; Jr Research Fellow, All Souls Coll., Oxford 1983–85; Wallis Prof. of Math., Oxford Univ. 1985–98; Fellow St Anne's Coll., Oxford 1985–98, Hon. Fellow 1998; Prof. of Pure Math. Imperial Coll., London Univ. 1998–; Hon. Fellow Pembroke Coll., Cambridge 1992; Fields Medal 1986, Craoford Prize 1994. *Publications:* The Geometry of Four-manifolds (with P. B. Kronheimer) 1990, Floer Homology Groups in Yang-Mills Theory 2002; numerous papers in mathematical journals. *Leisure interest:* sailing. *Address:* Room 674, Huxley Building, Department of Mathematics, Imperial College, 180 Queen's Gate, London, SW7 2BT, England. *Telephone:* (20) 7594-8559. *Fax:* (20) 7594-8517 . *E-mail:* s.donaldson@ic.ac.uk. *Website:* www.ma.ic.ac.uk.

DONALDSON, William H., MBA; American business executive and financial official; ed Yale Univ., Harvard Business School; rifle platoon Commdr and later aide-de-camp to Commanding Gen. 1st Provisional Marine Air Ground Task Force, US Marine Corps 1953–55; Co-Founder Donaldson, Lufkin & Jenrette 1959, CEO 1959–73; Under-Sec. of State 1973–75; fmr Counsel to Vice-Pres. Rockefeller; Co-Founder Grad. School of Man., Yale Univ.1975, first Dean and William S. Beinecke Prof. of Man. 1975–80; f. Donaldson Enterprises investment co. 1981, Chair. 2001–; Chair. and CEO New York Stock Exchange 1990–95; Chair., Pres. and CEO Aetna Inc. –2001; Commr

and Chair. Securities and Exchange Comm. 2002–. *Address:* Securities and Exchange Commission, 450 Fifth Street, NW, Washington, DC 20001, USA (Office). *Telephone:* (202) 942-2900 (Office). *Website:* www.sec.gov.

DONALDSON OF LYMINGTON, Baron (Life Peer), cr. 1988, of Lymington in the County of Hampshire; **John Francis Donaldson,** Kt; British lawyer and judge; b. 6 Oct. 1920, London; s. of late M. Donaldson and E. M. H. Maunsell; m. Dorothy M. Warwick (now Dame Mary Donaldson, GBE (q.v.)) 1945; one s. two d.; ed Charterhouse and Trinity Coll., Cambridge; called to the Bar, Middle Temple 1946; Judge of the High Court of Justice, Queen's Bench Div. 1966–79; Pres. Nat. Industrial Relations Court (NIRC) 1971–74; Pres. British Maritime Law Asscn 1979–95; Lord Justice of Appeal 1979–82; Chair. Advisory Council on Public Records 1982–92; Master of the Rolls 1982–92; Chair. Financial Law Panel 1992–2002, Inquiry into Coastal Pollution from Merchant Shipping 1993–94, Lord Donaldson's Assessment (Derbyshire) 1995, Review of Salvage and Intervention and their Command and Control 1999, Review of the Five-year Strategy for Her Majesty's Coastguard; Pres. British Insurance Law Asscn 1979–81, Chartered Inst. of Arbitrators 1980–83; Dr hc (Essex) 1983, Hon. LLD (Sheffield) 1984, (Nottingham Trent) 1992, (Southampton) 1998. *Leisure interest:* sailing, reading. *Address:* House of Lords, London, SW1A 0PW, England. *Telephone:* (1590) 675716 (Home).

DONATH, Helen; American opera and concert singer; b. 10 July 1940, Corpus Christi, Tex.; d. of Jimmy Erwin and Helen Hamauei; m. Klaus Donath 1965; one s.; ed Roy Miller High School, Del Mar Coll., Texas; studied with Paola Novikova, later with husband Klaus Donath (by whom all song-recitals are accompanied); début at Cologne Opera House 1962, at Hanover Opera House 1963–68, Bayerische Staatsoper, Munich 1968–72; guest appearances in London (Covent Garden), Vienna, Milan, San Francisco, Lisbon, New York, etc.; has given concerts in all maj. European and American cities; over 100 recordings 1962–; Pope Paul Medal, Salzburg 50 Year Anniversary Medal, Bratislava Festival Award, Deutscher Schallplatten-preis and Grosses Lob for her first song recital recording, Lower Saxony Prize for Culture 1990. *Major roles include:* Pamina in Die Zauberflöte, Zerlina in Don Giovanni, Eva in Die Meistersinger, Sophie in Der Rosenkavalier, Susanna in Le Nozze di Figaro, Anne Trulove in the Rake's Progress, Ilia in Idomeneo, Micaela in Carmen. *Leisure interests:* family, gardening, cooking, swimming, filming. *Address:* c/o Shaw Concerts, 1900 Broadway, New York, NY 10023, USA (Office); Bergstrasse 5, D-3002 Wedemark 1, Germany.

DONDELINGER, Albert Marie Joseph, DJur; Luxembourg banker; b. 22 March 1934, Redange, Attert; s. of Jean Dondelinger and Simone Lamborelle; m. Francine Dondelinger-Gillen; three d.; ed Coll. St Michel, Brussels, Catholic Univ. of Louvain, Belgium; Alt. Gov. for Luxembourg, IBRD 1967–76; mem. European Monetary Cttee 1971–76, Bd of Belgium-Luxembourg Exchange Inst. 1972–76; Adviser to Group of Twenty and Assoc. mem. IMF Interim Cttee 1972–76; mem. Bd European Monetary Co-operation Fund and mem. Govs. Cttee, EEC Cen. Banks 1973–76; Govt Commr to State Savings Bank 1974–76; Co-Chair. Comm. for Financial Affairs of Conf. for Int. Econ. Co-operation (North-South Dialogue, Paris) 1975–76; Chair. Luxembourg Bankers' Asscn 1977–78; Man. Dir and Chair. Exec. Bd, Banque Internationale à Luxembourg 1977–90, Hon. Chair. 1990–; ind. economic and business man. consultant 1990–; Pres. European League for Econ. Co-operation (Luxembourg Bureau); Vice-Pres. Foundation Prince Henri-Princesse Maria Teresa; Vice-Chair. SOS-Sahel; Pres. Cercle Artistique de Luxembourg; mem. Bd Inst. Régional Intracommunautaire; mem. Inst. Int. d'Etudes Bancaires 1978–; Commdr Order of Couronne de Chêne (Luxembourg), Commdr Order of the Crown (Belgium), the Nat. Order (Ivory Coast), Officier, Ordre Nat. du Mérite, Order of Merit (Luxembourg). *Publication:* Le secret bancaire au Grand-Duché de Luxembourg 1972. *Leisure interests:* photography, bibliophily, golf, skiing, swimming.

DONDOUX, Jacques; French telecommunications engineer and politician; b. 16 Nov. 1931; s. of Marcel Dondoux and Suzanne Durand; m. Sigrid Liberge; two c.; ed Ecole supérieure des télécommunications; engineer, Centre nat. d'études des télécommunications (CNET) 1956–68, Asst Dir 1968–71, Dir 1971–74; Production Dir Gen. Telecommunications Directorate 1974–75; Special Adviser, Postal Services and Telecommunications Inspectorate 1975–81, Telecommunications Dir-Gen. 1981–86; Mayor of Saint-Agrève 1995–; Minister of State attached to Minister for the Economy, Finance and Industry, with responsibility for Foreign Trade 1997–99; mem. Econ. and Social Council 1999–; Commdr Légion d'honneur, Chevalier ordre nat. du Mérite, Chevalier, Palmes académiques. *Address:* Irest, 98 rue de Sèvres, 75007 Paris (Office); 49 rue de Boulainvilliers, 75016 Paris, France (Home).

DONDUKOV, Alexander Nikolayevich, DTechSc; Russian politician and engineer; b. 29 March 1954, Kuybyshev (now Samara); engineer, sr engineer, leading constructor Moscow Machine Construction Bureau (designers' office), Moscow 1977–85; Deputy Chief Constructor 1985, Chief Constructor 1991, Head, Gen. Constructor Moscow Machine Construction factory Skorost' 1991–93; Chair. Bd of Dirs, Gen. Constructor A. S. Yakovlev Machine Designers' Office 1993–2000, 2001–; mem. Govt Council for Industrial Policy 1994–; mem. Congress of Russian Intelligentsia 1994–; Minister of Industry, Science and Tech., Russian Fed. 2000–02. *Address:* A. S. Yakovlev Machine Designers' Bureau, Leningradsky prosp. 68, 123315 Moscow A–47, Russia (Office). *Telephone:* (095) 157-57-37 (Office).

DONE, Kenneth Stephen, AM; Australian artist; b. 29 June 1940, Sydney; s. of Clifford Wade Done and Lillian Maureen Done; m. Judith Ann Walker; one s. one d.; ed Katoomba and Mosman High Schools, Nat. Art School, Sydney; Creative Dir Advertising Samuelson Talbot, Sydney, J. Walter Thompson 1960–78; Chair. Ken Done Group of Cos. 1979–; Goodwill Amb. UNICEF Australia; Paul Harris Fellow, Rotary Int.; Hon. Fellow Design Inst. of Australia; Hon. Fellow Design Inst. of Australia 1999; NSW Tourism Award 1986, Rotary Award for Excellence 1993, Spirit of Australia Award 1993, Cannes Gold Lion Award, Export Hero Award, Westpac Banking Corpn 1999, Life Fellow Medal Powerhouse Museum 2002. *Exhibitions include:* numerous solo and group exhbns. throughout Australia 1978–, numerous solo exhbns. throughout Japan 1986–, other solo exhbns. in Seoul, Rep. of Korea 1991, Paris 1996, 2000, Manila, Philippines 1997, Los Angeles 2000, London 2000, San Francisco 2001, Stockholm 2001, Pusan Korea 2001; group exhbns in Baltimore 1997, San Francisco 2001, London 2002, Korea 2002. *Publications:* Ken Done: Paintings and Drawings 1975–87, Craftsman House 1992, Ken Done Paintings (1990–1994) 1994, Ken Done: The Art of Design 1994, Ken Done's Sydney, 20 Years of Painting 1999. *Leisure interests:* golf, swimming, diving, travelling. *Address:* 17 Thurlow Street, Redfern, NSW 2016, Australia (Office). *Telephone:* (2) 9698-8555. *Fax:* (2) 9319-3374. *E-mail:* gallery@done .com.au (Office). *Website:* www.done.com.au (Office).

DONEN, Stanley; American film producer and director; b. 13 April 1924, Columbia, SC; s. of Mortie and Helen Donen; ed Univ. of South Carolina; Lifetime Achievement Award, Acad. of Motion Picture Arts and Sciences 1998, Golden Eddie Award, American Cinema Eds. 1988, Lifetime Achievement Award, Palm Beach Int. Film Festival 1999 . *Films include:* (Dir) Fearless Fagan, Give the Girl a Break, Royal Wedding, Love is Better Than Ever, Deep in My Heart, Seven Brides for Seven Brothers, Funny Face, Kiss Them for Me; co-Dir Singin' in the Rain, It's Always Fair Weather, On the Town; (producer-Dir) Pajama Game, Indiscreet, Damn Yankees, Once More with Feeling, Surprise Package, The Grass is Greener, Charade, Arabesque, Two for the Road, Bedazzled, Staircase, The Little Prince, Lucky Lady, Movie, Movie, Saturn 3, Blame it on Rio 1984, Red Shoes 1993, The Seven Deadly Sins, Love Letters 1999. *Address:* c/o LaGrange Group, 11828 La Grange Avenue, Los Angeles CA 90025, USA.

DONG FURENG; Chinese economist; b. 26 July 1927, Ningbo, Zhejiang Prov.; s. of Dong Junmin and Zhao Jueying; m. Liu Ainian 1957; one s. one d.; ed Wuhan Univ. and Moscow Nat. Inst. of Econs of the Soviet Union; Teacher Dept of Econs, Wuhan Univ. 1950–52, Lecturer 1957–58; Asst Researcher Econs Inst., Chinese Acad. and Deputy Head Group on Balance of Nat. Economy 1959–77; Deputy Dir Econs Inst., Chinese Acad. of Social Sciences 1978–85, Dir 1985–88, Hon. Dir 1988–; Sr Researcher and Vice-Chair. Academic Cttee Inst. of Econs 1979–85; Prof., Beijing Univ. 1979–, Wuhan Teachers' Coll. 1980–, Wuhan Univ. 1986–, Chinese People's Univ.; Deputy to NPC of People's Republic of China 1988–, mem. Standing Cttee of NPC 1988–98, Vice-Chair. Financial and Econ. Cttee of NPC 1988–98; mem. Academic Cttee Inst. of Marxism and Mao Zedong Thought, Chinese Acad. of Social Sciences 1980–88; Gen. Sec. Union of Chinese Socs. for Econ. Research 1981–87; Vice-Pres. Grad. School of Chinese Acad. of Social Sciences 1982–85; mem. Academic Senate of Chinese Acad. of Social Science 1982–85; Chair. Acad. Cttee Inst. of Econs 1985–88; Econ. Consultant, China Int. Trust and Investment Corpn (CITIC), Dir CITIC Research Int. 1991–93; Consultant, Environment Protection Cttee, State Council 1991–98, Environment Protection Bureau 1991–98; mem. Nat. Cttee of CPPCC 1998–2003, also Vice-Chair. CPPCC Econ. Cttee; mem. Int. Advisory Bd Centre for Devt Research, Univ. of Bonn 1999–; Academic Advisor Ritsumeikan Univ. Japan 1998–; Short-term Consultant, The World Bank 1985; Visiting Prof. St Antony's Coll. and Wolfson Coll., Univ. of Oxford 1985, Duisberg Univ. 1988; Chief Ed. Journal of Econ. Research 1985–88; Officier, Ordre des Palmes Académiques 1987. *Publications:* Dynamic Analysis of the Soviet National Income 1959, Problems of the Socialist Reproduction and the National Income 1980, Socialist Economic Institution and its Superiority (ed.) 1981, Theoretical Problems of the Chinese Economy in the Great Transformation 1981, On Sun Yefang's Socialist Economic Theory 1983, Selected Works of Dong Fureng 1985, On Economic Development Strategies 1988, Industrialization and China's Rural Modernization 1992, Reform and Development—On the Chinese Economy in the Great Transformation 1995, On Economic Reform 1995, On China's Economy 1996, Studies on Economic Development 1997, On Socialist Market Economy 1998, Talking on Economy 1998, Essays on Market Economy 1999–, The Chinese Economy: Approaching a Market Economy 2001, Arguments For and Against Developing a Stock Market 2002, A Dialectical View of the Market Economy 2002; Studies on the Chinese Economy (Co-Ed. with Peter Nolan) and over 40 books and 120 essays on the Chinese economy. *Leisure interests:* arts, reading, music. *Address:* Institute of Economics (CASS), 2 Beixiaojie, Yuetan, Beijing 100836, People's Republic of China (Office). *Telephone:* (10) 68030264 (Office); (10) 68176200 (Home). *Fax:* (10) 68032473 (Office); (10) 68176200 (Home). *E-mail:* dongfr@public.gb .com.cn (Home).

DONG JICHANG; Chinese party official; b. 1930, Hancheng Co., Shaanxi Prov.; joined CCP 1949; alt. mem. 12th CCP Cen. Cttee 1982–87, mem. 13th Cen. Cttee 1987–; Deputy Sec. CCP Cttee, Shaanxi Prov. 1983–90, a Vice-Chair. 1990–; Sec. CCP Cttee, Xian 1984; Vice-Chair. Shaanxi Prov. Cttee of CPPCC 1990–; Pres. Econ. Promotion Asscn for Lonhai-Lanxin Area 1987–. *Address:* Shaanxi Provincial Chinese Communist Party, Xian, Shaanxi, People's Republic of China.

DONG KEJUN; Chinese woodcut artist; b. 18 Feb. 1939, Chongqing, Sichuan; s. of Dong Xueyuan and Gue Ximing; m. Lü Hengfen 1969; one s.; Dir of Chinese Artistic Asscn; Standing Dir Chinese Woodcut Asscn; Vice-Chair. Guizhow Artistic Asscn; Chair. Guiyang Artistic Asscn; Vice-Pres. Acad. of Painting and Calligraphy; mem. Standing Cttee of Guizhou br. of Chinese People's Political Consultative Conf.; Vice-Chair. Guizhou Prov. Br. Artists' Assoc. 1988–; Chair. Artists' Assoc. Guiyang Br. 1988–; council mem. Artists' Assoc. 1988–; works on view at nat. exhbns. 1965–, also in Japan, USA, France, Sweden, Germany, Africa and Australia; Prizewinner, 9th Nat. Woodcut Exhbn 1986. *Works include:* Spring Returns to the Miao Mountain 1979, A Close Ball 1979, An Illustration of the Continuation of Feng Xuefeng's Fables (a hundred pieces) 1980, Company 1981, Go Back Drunkenly 1982, Lively Spring 1983, The Miao Nat. Sisters in Their Splendid Costume 1985, Contemporary Totem-1 1986, Mountain Breath 1986, A White Cottage 1987, Sunny Rain 1988, A Hundred Pieces of Coloured Inkwash Drawings 1991–92, The Big Sleep 1993, The Bird Market 1993, Illusion 1993, Eagle 1994, Man and Horse 1995, Going to Market 1995. *Publications:* Dong Kejun Woodcut Works, Selected Paintings of Dong Kejun 1992, Selected Chinese Coloured Inkwash Paintings 1995. *Leisure interests:* literature, music, film and dance. *Address:* Guiyang Artistic Asscn, 27 Road Shizi, Guiyang, Guizhou Prov., People's Republic of China.

DONG ZHENG; Chinese research professor and physician; b. 3 Nov. 1926, Gaoyang Co., Hebei Prov.; s. of Dong Mingxun and Dong Wangshi; m. Li Qun 1953; two s.; ed Bethune Medical Univ., Northwest China Univ.; Chief Physician, Inst. of Acupuncture and Moxibustion 1955–70; 2nd Nat. Training Course of Traditional Medicine 1958–59; Research Prof. and Dir Dept of Medicine, Guanganmen Hosp. 1983–95; Research Prof. Tung Shin Hosp., Malaysia 1993; mem. Acupuncture and Moxibustion Asscn, Traditional Chinese Medicine Research Asscn, Specialist Group, China Scientific and Tech. Asscn; specializes in use of combined Chinese traditional medicine and Western medicine; has conducted studies of asthma, eczema, emphysema, bronchitis, allergic diseases, immunopathy, diseases of connective tissues and nerve system, multiple sclerosis, polymyositis, dermatomyositis, myotonic muscular dystrophy; Advanced Worker medal 1977. *Publications:* Male Sex Disorders 1959, A Short Course in Acupuncture and Moxibustion 1960, A Short Course in Traditional Chinese Herbs 1960, The Surface of the Body connects with the Viscera 1992, External Qigong in the Treatment of Disease, Smoking is Harmful to Health; and numerous articles concerning connection between Yinyang theory and modern medicine, effect of external Qigong on human body. *Leisure interests:* traditional Chinese painting, Chinese qigong and taiji box. *Address:* Guanganmen Hospital, Academy of Traditional Medicine, Bei-xin-Ge, Guang An Men, Beijing 100053; Apt 1301, 78 Maliandou Road, Xuan Wu area, Beijing, People's Republic of China. *Telephone:* (10) 8800-1137 (Office); (10) 6335-5009 (Home).

DONIGI, Peter Dickson, CBE, LLB; Papua New Guinea diplomatist and lawyer; b. 19 Dec. 1950; m.; five c.; ed Univ. of Papua New Guinea; pvt. legal practice 1981–98; Amb. and Special Envoy to UN 1991–92, Perm. Rep. to UN 1998–; Amb. to Germany (also Accred to Holy See) 1992–95; mem. Council Commonwealth Lawyers' Asscn 1991–; fmr Pres. Papua New Guinea Law Soc.; Commonwealth Fellow 1991. *Publications:* Indigenous or Aboriginal Rights to Property: A Papua New Guinea Experience. *Address:* Permanent Mission of Papua New Guinea to the United Nations, 201 East 42nd Street, Suite 405, New York, NY 10017, USA (Office). *Telephone:* (212) 557-5001 (Office). *Fax:* (212) 557-5009 (Office). *E-mail:* png@un.int (Office).

DONLEAVY, James Patrick; American author; b. 23 April 1926, New York City; s. of Patrick and Margaret Donleavy; m. 1st Valerie Heron (divorced 1969); one s. one d.; m. 2nd Mary Wilson Price (divorced 1989); one s. one d.; ed Preparatory School, New York and Trinity Coll., Dublin; served in the USN during the Second World War; Brandeis Univ. Creative Arts Award, Evening Standard Drama Award, American Acad. and Nat. Inst. of Arts and Letters Award, AAAL Grantee 1975, Worldfest Houston Gold Award 1992, Cine Golden Eagle Writer and Narrator 1993. *Publications:* (novels) The Ginger Man 1955, A Singular Man 1963, The Beastly Beatitudes of Balthazar B 1968, The Onion Eaters 1971, A Fairy Tale of New York 1973, The Destinies of Darcy Dancer, Gentleman 1977, Schultz 1979, Leila 1983, Wrong Information is Being Given Out at Princeton 1998; (short stories and sketches) Meet My Maker the Mad Molecule 1964, An Author and His Image 1997; (novella) The Saddest Summer of Samuel S. 1966; also: The Unexpurgated Code: A Complete Manual of Survival and Manners 1975, De Alfonce Tennis, The Superlative Game of Eccentric Champions. Its History, Accoutrements, Rules, Conduct and Regimen. A Legend 1984, J. P. Donleavy's Ireland: In All Her Sins and in Some of Her Graces 1986, A Singular Country 1989, The History of the Ginger Man 1993, The Lady Who Liked Clean Rest Rooms 1995, Wrong Information is Being Given Out at Princeton 1998; (plays) The Ginger Man 1959, Fairy Tales of New York 1960, A Singular Man 1964, The Saddest Summer of Samuel S. 1968, The Plays of J. P. Donleavy 1972, The Beastly Beatitudes of Balthazar B. 1981, Are You Listening Rabbi Low 1987, That Darcy, That Dancer, That Gentlemen 1990, A Letter Marked Personal 2001. *Leisure interests:* De Alfonce Tennis, dry stone walling. *Address:* Levington Park, Mullingar, Co. Westmeath, Ireland.

DONNELLAN, Declan; British theatre and opera director; b. 4 Aug. 1953, Manchester; ed Univ. of Cambridge; called to Bar (Middle Temple) 1978; freelance theatre productions include Don Giovanni (Scottish Opera Go Round), A Masked Ball (Opera 80), Rise and Fall of the City of Mahagonny (Wexford Festival), Macbeth and Philoctetes (Nat. Theatre of Finland); co-f. Cheek By Jowl (production co.) 1981, Artistic Dir 1981–; productions with Cheek By Jowl include Racine's Andromache, Corneille's The Cid, Twelfth Night, A Midsummer Night's Dream, Hamlet, As You Like It, Measure for Measure, Martin Guerre 1996, Much Ado About Nothing 1998 and his own trans. of Musset's Don't Fool With Love and The Blind Men; also wrote and directed Lady Betty and Sara Sampson; Assoc. Dir Nat. Theatre (NT) 1989–97; work for NT includes Fuente Ovejuna 1989, Peer Gynt, Sweeney Todd 1993, Angels in America, Perestroika 1993, School for Scandal 1998; writer and Dir The Big Four (Channel Four TV); Dir Mahoganny (opera) 1995; Hay Fever, Savoy 1999, Falstaff, Salzburg Festival 2001; recipient of six Olivier Awards, Time Out Award (with Nick Ormerod) for Angels in America 1992, Observer Award for Outstanding Achievement. *Address:* Cheek by Jowl Theatre Company, Alford House, Aveline Street, London, SE11 5DQ, England. *Telephone:* (20) 7793-0153 (Office). *Fax:* (20) 7735-1031 (Office). *Website:* www.cheekbyjowl.com (Office).

DONNELLY, Christopher Nigel, BA, TD; British defence and foreign affairs specialist; b. 10 Nov. 1946, Rochdale, Lancs.; s. of the late Anthony Donnelly and Dorothy M. Morris; m. Jill Norris 1971; one s. one d.; ed HE Cardinal Langley School, Middleton, Lancs. and Univ. of Manchester; Instr. Royal Mil. Acad. Sandhurst (RMAS) 1969–72; Sr Lecturer, Soviet Studies Research Center, RMAS 1972–79, Dir 1979–89; Territorial Army Officer (Int. Corps) 1970–93; Adjunct Prof. Carnegie Mellon Univ. 1985–89, Georgia Tech. Univ. 1989–93; Special Adviser for Cen. and E European Affairs to Sec.-Gen. of NATO 1989–. *Publications:* Red Banner 1989, War and the Soviet Union 1990, Gorbachev's Revolution 1991. *Leisure interests:* shooting, fishing. *Address:* Office of the Secretary-General, HQ NATO, Avenue Leopold III, 1110 Brussels, Belgium. *Telephone:* (2) 707-45-21. *Fax:* (2) 707-35-86. *E-mail:* donnelly@hq.nato.int (Office).

DONNER, Andreas Matthias, DIur; Netherlands jurist; b. 15 Jan. 1918; s. of Jan Donner and Golida van den Burg; m. Dina A. Mulder 1946; three s. six d.; ed Amsterdam Free Univ.; Legal Adviser Assoc. of Christian Schools in the Netherlands 1941–45; Prof. of Constitutional Law, Free Univ. of Amsterdam 1945–58; Pres. Court of Justice of the European Communities 1958–64, Judge 1964–79, alt. Pres. of First Chamber; Prof. Constitutional Law Univ. of Groningen 1979–85, Prof. Emer. 1985–; mem. European Court of Human Rights 1986–88; fmr Pres., Royal Netherlands Acad. of Arts and Sciences; Hon. DrIur (Louvain, Edin., Freiburg). *Publications:* Nederlands Bestuursrecht (Netherlands Administrative Law) 5th Edn 1986, Handboek van het Nederlandse Staatsrecht 11th Edn 1983. *Address:* c/o University of Groningen, Broerstraat 5, P.O. Box 72, 9700 AB Groningen, Netherlands. *Telephone:* (50) 639111.

DONNER, Clive; British film and theatre director; b. 21 Jan. 1926, London; s. of Alex Donner and Deborah Donner (née Taffel); m. Jocelyn Rickards 1971; Asst film editor, Denham Studios 1942; freelance film director 1950–; work has included feature films and documentary films for British television and direction of theatrical productions in London and New York. *Films include:* (as ed.) Scrooge 1951, Genevieve 1952, The Purple Plain 1955; (as Dir) The Secret Place 1952, Some People (Best Film, Barcelona Festival) 1962, The Caretaker (Silver Bear, Berlin Film Festival) 1963, Nothing but the Best (Best Film, Barcelona Festival) 1963, What's New Pussycat? (Jean Georges Auroil/Paul Gibson Award) 1965, Here We Go Round the Mulberry Bush 1967, Alfred the Great 1969, Best Kept Secret (Silver Award, Motor Neurone Asscn) 1986, Stealing Heaven 1988, Boheme. *Plays directed include:* The Formation Dancers 1964, plays by Shakespeare and Pinter, Nottingham Playhouse 1970–71, The Front Room Boys, Royal Court Theatre 1971, Kennedy's Children, Arts Head Theatre, Arts Theatre, Golden Theater, New York 1975. *TV programmes directed:* Rogue Male (Int. Emmy Award) 1976, She Fell Among Thieves 1977, Oliver Twist 1981, The Scarlet Pimpernel 1982, A Christmas Carol 1984, Charlemagne 1994. *Leisure interests:* classical music (particularly opera), popular music, reading, walking anywhere from the streets of London to the Australian sea shore. *Address:* 20 Thames Reach, 80 Rainville Road, London, W6 9HS, England. *Telephone:* (20) 7385-5580. *Fax:* (20) 7385-2423 (Home).

DONNER, Jörn Johan, BA; Finnish film director, writer, politician and diplomatist; b. 5 Feb. 1933, Helsinki; s. of Dr. Kai Donner and Greta von Bonsdorff; m. 1st Inga-Britt Wik 1954 (divorced 1962); m. 2nd Jeanette Bonnier 1974 (divorced 1988); m. 3rd Bitte Westerlund 1995; five s. one d.; ed Helsinki Univ.; worked as writer and film Dir in Finland and Sweden, writing own film scripts; contrib. and critic to various Scandinavian and int. journals; CEO Jörn Donner Productions 1966–; Dir Swedish Film Inst., Stockholm 1972–75, Exec. Producer 1975–78, Man. Dir 1978–82; Chair. Bd Finnish Film Foundation, 1981–83, 1986–89, 1992–95; mem. Bd Marimekko Textiles and other cos.; mem., Helsinki City Council 1969–1972, 1984–92; MP 1987–95; Vice-Chair. Foreign Affairs Cttee 1991–95; Chair. Finnish EFTA Parliamentarians 1991–95; Consul-Gen. of Finland, Los Angeles 1995–96; mem. European Parl. 1996–99; Opera Prima Award Venice Film Festival 1963, Vittorio de Sica Prize, Sorrento 1978, Acad. Award for Producer of Best Foreign Language Picture (Fanny and Alexander) 1984. *Films:* A Sunday in September 1963, To Love 1964, Adventure Starts Here 1965, Rooftree 1967,

Black on White 1968, Sixty-nine 1969, Portraits of Women 1970, Anna 1970, Images of Finland 1971, Tenderness 1972, Baksmalla 1974, Three Scenes (with Ingmar Bergman), The Bergman File 1975–77, Men Can't Be Raped 1978, Dirty Story 1984, Letters from Sweden 1987, Ingmar Bergman, a Conversation 1998, The President 2000. *Television:* host of talk show (Sweden and Finland) 1974–95. *Publications:* 48 books including: Report from Berlin 1958, The Personal Vision of Ingmar Bergman 1962. *Leisure interests:* fishing, cooking. *Address:* Pohjoisranta 12, 00170 Helsinki (Office); Pargasövägen 208, 10600 Ekenäs, Finland (Home). *Telephone:* (9) 1356060 (Office); (19) 202033, (9) 1357112 (Home). *Fax:* (9) 1357568 (Office); (19) 202150 (Home). *E-mail:* j.donner@surfnet.fi (Home).

DONNER, Richard; American director and producer; b. 24 April 1930, New York; actor off-Broadway; collaborated with Dir Martin Ritt on TV adaptation of Somerset Maugham's Of Human Bondage; moved to Calif. and began directing commercials, industrial films and documentaries. *Films include:* X-15 1961, Salt and Pepper 1968, Twinky 1969, The Omen 1976, Superman 1978, Inside Moves 1981, The Toy 1982, Ladyhawke 1985, The Goonies 1985, Lethal Weapon 1987, Scrooged 1988, Lethal Weapon 2 1989, Radio Flyer 1991, The Final Conflict (exec. producer) 1991, The Lost Boys (exec. producer) 1991, Delirious (exec. producer) 1991, Lethal Weapon 3 1992, Free Willy (co-exec. producer) 1993, Maverick 1994, Assassins 1995, Free Willy 3: The Rescue, Lethal Weapon 4 1998, Blackheart (producer) 1999, Conspiracy Theory. *Television includes:* (films) Portrait of a Teenage Alcoholic, Senior Year, A Shadow in the Streets, Tales from the Crypt presents Demon Knight (co-exec. producer), Any Given Sunday 1999, X-Men 2000 (exec. producer); (series episodes) Have Gun Will Travel, Perry Mason, Cannon, Get Smart, The Fugitive, Kojak, Bronk, Lucas Tanner, Gilligan's Island, Man From U.N.C.L.E., Wild Wild West, Twilight Zone, The Banana Splits, Combat, Two Fisted Tales, Conspiracy Theory. *Address:* The Donners Company, 9465 Wilshire Boulevard, #420, Beverly Hills, CA 90212; c/o CAA, 9830 Wilshire Boulevard, Beverly Hills, CA 90212, USA. *Telephone:* (310) 777-4600 (Office). *Fax:* (310) 777-4610 (Office).

DONOGHUE, Denis, PhD; Irish literary critic; b. 1 Dec. 1928; ed Univ. Coll., Dublin; Admin. Office, Irish Dept of Finance 1951–54; Asst Lecturer, Univ. Coll., Dublin 1954–57, Coll. lecturer 1957–62, 1963–64, Prof. of Modern English and American Literature 1965–79; Visiting Scholar, Univ. of Pa 1962–63; Univ. Lecturer, Cambridge Univ. and Fellow, King's Coll. 1964–65; Henry James Prof. of Letters, New York Univ. 1979–; mem. Int. Cttee of Asscn of Univ. Profs. of English; BBC Reith Lecturer 1982; Hon. DLitt. *Publications:* The Third Voice 1959, Connoisseurs of Chaos 1965, The Ordinary Universe 1968, Emily Dickinson 1968, Jonathan Swift 1969, Yeats 1971, Thieves of Fire 1974, Sovereign Ghost: studies in Imagination 1978, Ferocious Alphabets 1981, The Arts Without Mystery 1983, We Irish: Essays on Irish Literature and Society 1987, Walter Pater: Lover of Strange Souls 1995, The Practice of Reading 1998, Words Alone: The Poet T. S. Eliot 2000, Adam's Curse: Reflections on Literature and Religion 2001; contribs. to reviews and journals and ed. of three vols. *Address:* English Department, New York University, 726 Broadway (7th Floor), New York, NY 10003, USA; Gaybrook, North Avenue, Mount Merrion, Dublin, Ireland. *E-mail:* dd1@nyu.edu (Office).

DONOHOE, Amanda; British actress; b. 1962; ed Francis Holland School for Girls, London, Cen. School of Speech & Drama, London; mem. Royal Exchange Theatre, Manchester; Broadway debut, Uncle Vanya 1995. *Films include:* Foreign Body, Castaway, The Lair of the White Worm, The Rainbow, Tank Malling, Diamond Skulls (Dark Obsession), Paper Mask, The Madness of King George, Liar Liar, Writer's Block, I'm Losing You. *Television includes:* (series): LA Law (Golden Globe Award); (films): Married to Murder, Shame, It's Nothing Personal (also co-exec. producer), The Substitute, Shame II: The Secret (also co-exec. producer); (special): Game, Set and Match. *Plays include:* The Graduate 2001.

DONOHOE, Peter Howard, BMus, ARCM, FRNCM; British pianist; b. 18 June 1953, Manchester; s. of Harold Donohoe and Marjorie Donohoe (née Travis); m. Elaine Margaret Burns 1980; one d.; ed Royal Manchester Coll. of Music Chetham's School of Music, Univ. of Leeds; teachers include Derek Wyndham and Yvonne Loriod, Paris; professional solo pianist 1974–; appears several times each season with major symphony orchestras in London and rest of UK and performs regularly at the Promenade Concerts 1979–; performances with the LA Philharmonic, Chicago, Pittsburgh, Cincinnati, Dallas, Detroit and Cleveland orchestras and in Europe with Berlin Philharmonic and Symphony, Leipzig Gewandhaus, Dresden Philharmonic, Swedish Radio and Radio France Philharmonic orchestras and Maggio Musicale Fiorentino; has also performed at Edin. Festival, Schleswig-Holstein Music Festival and Festival of the Ruhr; recordings include Messiaen's Turangalila Symphony (EMI) 1986, Dominic Muldowney Piano Concerto 1986 and Tchaikovsky's Piano Concerto No. 2 1986 (Gramophone magazine's Concerto of the Year) 1988, Brahms Piano Concerto No. 1, Liszt, Berg and Bartok Sonatas, Beethoven, Diabelli Variations and Sonata Opus 101, Rachmaninov Preludes; Founder, Artistic Dir British Piano Concerto Foundation; Vice-Pres. Birmingham Conservatoire of Music; Hon. DMus (Birmingham) 1992, (Univ. of Central England); Hon. DLitt (Warwick) 1996; winner Moscow Int. Tchaikovsky Competition 1982. *Leisure interests:* golf, helping young musicians, jazz. *Address:* c/o Askonas Holt Ltd, Lonsdale Chambers, 27 Chancery Lane, London, WC2A 1PF, England (Office).

DOOB, Joseph Leo, MA, PhD; American professor of mathematics; b. 27 Feb. 1910, Cincinnati, Ohio; s. of Leo and Mollie Doerfler Doob; m. Elsie Haviland Field 1931 (died 1991); two s. one d.; ed Harvard Univ.; Univ. of Illinois 1935–78, Prof. of Math. 1945–78, Prof. Emer. 1979–; mem. NAS, American Acad. of Arts and Sciences; Foreign Assoc. French Acad. des Sciences; Nat. Medal of Science. *Publications:* Stochastic Processes, Classical Potential Theory and its Probabilistic Counterpart, Measure Theory. *Leisure interest:* recorder. *Address:* 101 West Windsor Road, No. 1104, Urbana, IL 61801-6663, USA (Home).

DOODY, Margaret Anne, DPhil; Canadian professor of English; b. 21 Sept. 1939, St John, NB; d. of Rev. Hubert Doody and Anne Ruth Cornwall; ed Centreville Regional High School, NB, Dalhousie Univ., Halifax, Lady Margaret Hall, Oxford; Instructor in English 1962–64; Asst Prof., English Dept Vic. Univ. 1968–69; lecturer, Univ. Coll. of Swansea, Wales 1969–77; Visiting Assoc. Prof. of English, Univ. of Calif. at Berkeley 1976–77, Assoc. Prof. 1977–80; Prof. of English, Princeton Univ. 1980–89; Andrew W Mellon Prof. of Humanities and Prof. of English, Vanderbilt Univ., Nashville 1989–99, Dir Comparative Literature 1992–99; John and Barbara Glynn Family Prof. of Literature, Univ. of Notre Dame 2000–; Commonwealth Fellowship 1960–62; Canada Council Fellowship 1964–65; Imperial Oil Fellowship 1965–68; Guggenheim Foundation Fellowship 1978; Hon. LLD (Dalhousie) 1985; Rose Mary Crawshay Prize 1986. *Play:* Clarissa (co-writer), New York 1984. *Publications:* A Natural Passion: A Study of the Novels of Samuel Richardson 1974, Aristotle Detective 1978, The Alchemists 1980, The Daring Muse 1985, Frances Burney: The Life in the Works 1988, Samuel Richardson: Tercentenary Essays (ed. with Peter Sabor) 1989, The True Story of the Novel 1996, Anne of Green Gables (ed. with Wendy Barry and Mary Doody Jones) 1997, Aristotle e la giustizia poetica 2000. *Leisure interests:* travel, looking at ancient paintings and mosaics, reading detective fiction, swimming in the sea, music (Mozart, bluegrass). *Address:* English Department, University of Notre Dame, Notre Dame, IN 46556 (Office); 435 Edgewater Drive, Mishawaka, IN 46545, USA (Home). *Telephone:* (219) 631-9723 (Office); (219) 257-7927 (Home). *E-mail:* Doody.y@md.edu (Home); margaret.doody.1@nd.edu.

DOOGE, James Clement Ignatius, ME, MSc; Irish engineer and politician; b. 30 July 1922, Birkenhead, England; s. of Denis Patrick and Veronica Catherine (née Carroll) Dooge; m. Veronica O'Doherty 1946 (died 1991); two s. three d.; ed Christian Brothers' School, Dún Laoghaire, Univ. Coll., Dublin, Iowa, USA; Jr Civil Engineer, Irish Office of Public Works 1943–46; Design Engineer, ESB 1946–58; Prof. of Civil Eng, Univ. Coll., Cork 1958–70, Univ. Coll., Dublin 1970–81, 1982–84, now Prof. Emer.; Minister for Foreign Affairs 1981–82; Leader Irish Senate 1983–87; consultant UN specialized agencies, EC; Pres. Royal Irish Acad. 1987–90, Int. Asscn for Hydrological Sciences 1975–79; mem. Exec. Bureau Int. Union for Geodesy and Geophysics 1979–87; Pres. ICSU 1993–96; mem. Royal Acad. of Eng; Hon. Agric. Science Degree 1978, Hon. DTech 1980, Hon. DSc (Birmingham), Hon. ScD (Dublin) 1988, Hon. DEng (Edin.) 2000, Hon. Dr (Kraków) 2000, (Madrid) 2001; Horton Award 1959, Bowie Medal (American Geophysical Union) 1986; Kettle Plaque 1948, 1985 and Mullins Medal 1951, 1962 (Inst. of Engineers of Ireland), John Dalton Medal 1998, Int. Prize for Meteorology 1999. *Address:* Centre for Water Resources Research, University College, Earlsfort Terrace, Dublin 2 (Office); 2 Belgrave Road, Monkstown, Co. Dublin, Ireland (Home). *Telephone:* 7167499 (Office); 2805515 (Home). *Fax:* 7167399 (Office); 2806583 (Home).

DOOKERAN, Winston, BA, MSc; economist; b. 24 June 1943, Trinidad and Tobago; m. Shirley Dookeran; one s.; ed Univ. of Manitoba, Canada, London School of Econs; Lecturer in Econs Univ. of the West Indies 1971–81; MP Trinidad and Tobago 1981–91; Minister of Planning and Mobilization, Vice-Chair. Nat. Planning Comm. 1986–91; Dir Price-Waterhouse Man. Consultants and to the Caribbean Govs. 1992–95; Fellow Center for Int. Affairs, Harvard Univ. 1993–95; Sr Economist UN Econ. Comm. for Latin America and the Caribbean 1995–97; Gov. Cen. Bank of Trinidad and Tobago 1997–2002; Visiting Scholar Weatherhead Center for Int. Affairs Harvard Univ.; Hon. LLD (Univ. of Man.) 1991. *Publications:* ed. Choices and Change: Reflections on the Caribbean 1996, The Caribbean Quest: Directions for Structural Reforms in a Global Economy 1999 (co-ed.). *Address:* Systematics Studies Ltd, St Augustine, Trinidad (Office). *Telephone:* (868) 645-8466 (Office); (868) 640-5694 (Home). *Fax:* (868) 645-8467 (Office). *E-mail:* wdookeran@wcfia.harvard.edu (Office); wdookeran@tstt.net.tt (Home). *Website:* www.winstondookeran.com (Home).

DOOLITTLE, James H., BA; American communications executive; ed High Point Coll.; System Man. American TV and Communications Corpn 1970–72, Regional Man. 1972–77, E Div. Man. of NC and mid-states regions 1977–80, Vice-Pres. Eastern Operations 1980–82, Sr Vice-Pres. Cable Operations 1982–84, Exec. Vice-Pres. 1984–85, with Pres.'s office 1985–87, Exec. Vice-Pres., COO 1987–; Pres. Time Warner Cable 1998–, Glenn Britt 1999–. *Address:* Time Warner Cable, 290 Harbor Drive, Stamford, CT 06902, USA.

DORAN, Sean; Irish/Australian artistic director; b. 1958, Derry; ed Univ. of E Anglia and Goldsmiths Coll. London, UK; dir music-theatre co., Bloomsbury, London 1988; Chief Exec. UK Year of Literature and Writing, NI 1995; Artistic Dir Belfast Festival, NI 1997–99; Dir Perth Int. Arts Festival, Australia 1999–2003; Artistic Dir ENO, London 2003–. *Address:* English

National Opera, St Martin's Lane, London, WC2N 4ES, England (Office). *Telephone:* (20) 7836-0111 (Office). *Fax:* (20) 7240-0581 (Office). *Website:* www.eno.org (Office).

DORAZIO; Italian artist; b. 1927, Rome; ed Rome, Paris; played maj. role in the revival of Italian Futurist and Abstractionist tradition, published manifesto Forma I 1947; has exhibited throughout Europe, USA, S. America and Australia; est. Fine Arts Dept of School of Fine Arts, Univ. of Pa 1960–61, Prof. 1960–69; included in main avant-garde exhbns. of 1950s and 1960s; Venice Biennale Prize 1960, Paris Biennale Prize 1961, Prix Kandinsky 1961, Premio Int. Lissone 1965, Int. Prize, Cracow 1970. *Solo exhibitions include:* Venice Biennale 1960, 1966, Düsseldorf 1961, San Marino Int. 1967, Bennington, USA, Cologne, Berlin 1969, Museum of Modern Art, Belgrade 1970, Marlborough Galleries in Rome 1964, 1968, 1972, New York 1965, 1969, London 1966.

DORDA, Abuzed Omar, BA; Libyan politician and diplomatist; b. 4 April 1944, Rhebat; m.; six c.; ed Benghazi Univ.; teacher 1965–70; Gov. Misurata Prov. 1970–72; Minister of Information and Culture 1972–74, Under-Sec., Ministry of Foreign Affairs 1974–76, Minister of Municipalities 1976–79, Sec. Gen. People's Cttee for Economy 1979–82, for Agric. 1982–86, for the Municipality of Al-Jabal Al-Gharbi 1986–90, Sec. of the Gen. People's Cttee. (Prime Minister) 1990–94, Asst Sec. 1994–95; Perm. Rep. to UN 1997–. *Address:* Permanent Mission of Libya to the UN, 309–315 East 48th Street, New York, NY 10017, U.S.A. (Office).

DORE, Ronald Philip, CBE, BA; British university professor; b. 1 Feb. 1925, Bournemouth; s. of Philip H. B. Dore and Elsie C. King; m. Nancy MacDonald 1957; one s. one d.; one s. with Maria Paisley; ed School of Oriental and African Studies, London Univ.; Asst Prof. then Assoc. Prof., Univ. of BC 1956–60; Reader, LSE 1961, Hon. Fellow 1980; Prof., LSE and SOAS 1964–69; Prof. and Fellow, Inst. of Devt Studies, Sussex Univ. 1970–81; Tech. Change Centre, London 1982–86; Dir Japan-Europe Industry Research Centre, Imperial Coll., London 1986–91; Research Assoc., Centre for Econ. Performance, LSE and Political Science 1991–; Visiting Prof. Imperial Coll. of Science, Tech. and Medicine, London Univ. 1982, of Sociology, Harvard Univ. 1987; Adjunct Prof., MIT 1989–94; mem. British Acad. 1975–; Foreign Hon. Fellow, American Acad. of Arts and Sciences 1978, Hon. Foreign Fellow Japan Acad. 1986–; Japan Foundation Prize 1977; Order of the Rising Sun (Third Class) Japan. *Publications:* City Life in Japan 1958, Land Reform in Japan 1959, Education in Tokugawa Japan 1965, British Factory/Japanese Factory 1973, The Diploma Disease 1976, Shinohata Portrait of a Japanese Village 1978, Flexible Rigidities, Industrial Policy and Structural Adjustment in Japanese Economy 1986, Taking Japan Seriously: A Confucian Perspective on Leading Economic Issues 1987, Japan and World Depression, Then and Now (Essays) (Jt Ed.) 1987, How the Japanese Learn to Work (with Mari Sako) 1988, Corporatism and Accountability: Organized Interests in British Public Life (Jt Ed.) 1990, Will the 21st Century be the Age of Individualism? 1991, The Japanese Firm: the Source of Competitive Strength (Jt Ed.) 1994, Japan, Internationalism and the UN 1997, Stockmarket Capitalism, Welfare Capitalism: Japan and Germany versus the Anglo-Saxons 2000, Social Evolution, Economic Development and Culture 2001, Selected Writings of Ronald Dore 2002. *Address:* 157 Surrenden Road, Brighton, East Sussex, BN1 6ZA, England. *Telephone:* (1273) 501-370 (Home).

DORENSKY, Sergey Leonidovich; Russian pianist and piano teacher; b. 3 Dec. 1931, Moscow; m. Nina Tserevitinova; one s.; ed Moscow State Conservatory (pupil of Grigory Ginzburg); winner Int. Competitions Warsaw 1955, Rio de Janeiro 1958; concert tours in USSR, Brazil, Japan, Italy, Germany, Australia, NZ, S Korea; teacher Moscow Conservatory 1957–, Prof. 1981, Dean Piano Faculty 1978–97; Vice-Pres. Russian Chopin Soc., Russian Rachmaninov Soc.; mem. jury of more than 75 maj. int. competitions, including Tchaikovsky (Moscow), Van Cliburn (Fort Worth), Mozart (Salzburg), UNISA (Pretoria); mem. Russian Acad. of Arts 1995; People's Artist of Russia 1988, Order of Friendship 1997. *Address:* Bryusov per. 8/10, Apt. 75, 103009 Moscow, Russia (Home). *Telephone:* (095) 229-22-24 (Home).

DORFF, Stephen; American actor; b. 29 July 1973, Atlanta, Georgia; started acting aged 9. *Films:* The Gate 1987, The Power of One 1992, An Ambush of Ghosts 1992, Judgment Night 1993, Rescue Me 1993, BackBeat 1993, S.F.W. 1994, Reckless 1995, Innocent Lies 1995, I Shot Andy Warhol 1996, The Audition 1996, Space Truckers 1997, City of Industry 1997, Blood and Wine 1997, Blade 1998, Entropy 1999, Quantum Project 2000, Cecil B. Demented 2000, The Last Minute 2001, Zoolander 2001, All For Nothin' 2002, Deuces Wild 2002, Riders 2002, FearDotCom 2002, Den of Lions 2002. *Television films:* In Love and War 1987, Hiroshima Maiden 1988, The Absent-Minded Professor 1988, I Know My First Name is Steven 1989, Always Remember I Love You 1989, Do You Know the Muffin Man? 1989, A Son's Promise 1990, Earthly Possessions 1999. *Television series:* What a Dummy 1990. *Address:* 9350 Wilshire Boulevard, Suite 4, Beverly Hills, CA 90212, USA.

DORFMAN, Ariel; Chilean writer; b. Argentina; Research Prof. of Literature and Latin American Studies, Duke Univ., NC 1992–; won Time Out and Olivier Prize for Death and the Maiden. *Publications include:* Death and the Maiden (play, also screenplay), My House is on Fire (short stories), Konfidenz, Reader (play), The Nanny and Iceberg (novel) 1999.

DORGAN, Byron Leslie, MBA; American politician; b. 14 May 1942, Dickinson, ND; s. of Emmett P. Dorgan and Dorothy (Bach) Dorgan; m.

Kimberly Olsen Dorgan; four c. (one deceased); ed Univ. of North Dakota, Univ. of Denver; Exec. Devt trainee, Martin Marietta Corpn, Denver 1966–67; Deputy Tax Commr, then Tax Commr, State of ND 1967–80; Democrat mem. 97th–101st Congress from N Dakota 1981–93, mem. Ways and Means Cttee 1981–93; Senator from N Dakota 1993–, Asst Democratic Floor Leader 1996–99; Chair. Democratic Policy Cttee 1999–; mem. Cttee on Commerce, Science and Transportation, Cttee on Indian Affairs. *Address:* US Senate, 713 Hart Senate Office Bldg, Washington, DC 20510-0001, USA. *E-mail:* senator@dorgan.senate.gov.

DORIN, Bernard J., GCVO; French diplomatist; b. 25 Aug. 1929, Beauvais; s. of Gen. Robert Dorin and Jacqueline Dorin (née Goumard); m. Christine du Bois de Meyrignac 1971; two s. two d.; ed Univs. of Paris, Lyon, Harvard, Institut d'Etudes Politiques, Paris, Ecole Nat. d'Admin; Attaché Embassy, Ottawa 1957–59; Political Directorate Ministry of Foreign Affairs 1959–63, Adviser to Sec.-Gen. 1963–64; Tech. Adviser to Pvt. Office of Minister of Information 1964–66, of Minister Del. with responsibility for Scientific Research and Nuclear and Space Questions 1966–67, of Minister of Nat. Educ. 1967–68, of Minister with responsibility for Scientific Research 1968–69; Chargé de Mission responsible to the Personnel and Gen. Admin. Dir Ministry of Foreign Affairs 1970–71; Amb. to Haiti 1972–75; Head Francophone Affairs Dept Ministry of Foreign Affairs 1975–78, of American Div. 1981–84; Amb. to S. Africa 1978–81, to Brazil 1984–87, to Japan 1987–90, to UK 1991–93; Ambassadeur de France dignitaire 1992–; Conseiller d'Etat 1993–97; Officier Légion d'honneur, Officier Ordre nat. du Mérite; Chevalier Order of Malta. *Publications:* Appelez-moi Excellence. *Leisure interests:* mountaineering, heraldry, naive painting. *Address:* 39 avenue de Saxe, 75007 Paris (Office); 96 rue de Grenelle, 75007 Paris, France (Home). *Telephone:* 1-44-49-95-95 (Office). *Fax:* 1-44-49-09-54 (Office).

DORIN, Françoise Andrée Renée; French actress, novelist and playwright; b. 23 Jan. 1928, Paris; d. of late René Dorin and of Yvonne Guilbert; m. Jean Poiret (b. Poiré) (divorced); one d.; at Théâtre des Deux-Ânes, then du Quartier Latin (Les Aveux les plus doux 1957), then La Bruyère (Le Chinois 1958); Presenter TV programme Paris-Club 1969; playwright and author 1967–; Chevalier, Légion d'honneur, Officier, Ordre nat. du Mérite, Arts et Lettres; trophée Dussane 1973, Grand Prix du théâtre (for L'Etiquette) 1981. *Songs include:* Que c'est triste Venise, N'avoue jamais, Faisons l'humour ensemble, Les miroirs truqués 1982. *Plays include:* Comme au théâtre 1967, La Facture 1968, Un sale égoiste, Les Bonshommes 1970, Le Tournant 1973, Le Tube 1974, L'Autre Valse 1975, Si t'es beau, t'es con 1976, Le Tout pour le tout 1978, L'Intoxe 1980, Les Cahiers Tango 1987, Et s'il n'en restait qu'un 1992; lyrics for Vos gueules les mouettes 1971, Monsieur Pompadour 1972, L'Etiquette 1983, Les jupes-culottes 1984, La valise en carton (musical comedy) 1986, L'âge en question 1986, La Retour en Toupaine 1993, Monsieur de Saint-Futile (Vaudeville) 1996, Soins intensifs 2001. *Publications:* novels include Virginie et Paul, La Seconde dans Rome, Va voir Maman, Papa travaille 1976, Les lits à une place 1980, Les miroirs truqués 1982, Les jupes-culottes 1984, Les corbeaux et Les renardes 1988, Nini patte-en-l'air 1990, Au nom du père et de la fille 1992, Pique et Coeur 1993, La Mouflette 1994, Les Vendanges tardives 1997, La Courte paille 1999, Les Julottes 2001. *Address:* c/o Artmédia, 20 avenue Rapp, 75007 Paris, France.

DORIVAL, Bernard, DèsSc; French professor and writer; b. 14 Sept. 1914, Paris; s. of André Dorival and Suzanne Beurdeley; m. Claude de la Brosse 1944; three s. one d.; ed Lycées Carnot and Condorcet, Paris and Ecole normale supérieure; Prof. Ecole du Louvre 1941–; Curator Musée Nat. d'Art Moderne, Paris 1941–65, Chief Curator 1967–68; Curator Musée Nat. des Granges de Port-Royal 1955–68; Chargé de recherches at Centre Nat. de la Recherche Scientifique 1968–72; Prof. Univ. of Paris (Sorbonne) 1972–83, Prof. Emer. 1983–; mem. Société Royale d'Art et Archéologie de Belgique; Chevalier, Légion d'honneur, Officier des Arts et des lettres. *Publications:* La peinture française 1942, Les étapes de la peinture française contemporaine 1943–46, Du côté de Port-Royal 1946, Les peintres du XXe siècle 1955, L'école de Paris au Musée National de l'Art Moderne 1961, Robert Delaunay 1975, Sonia Delaunay 1980; monographs on Cézanne, Philippe de Champaigne, Jean-Baptiste de Champaigne and Rouault, 2 Vols (with Isabelle Ronalt); numerous works on painting. *Address:* 78 rue Notre-Dame-des-Champs, 75006 Paris, France (Home). *Telephone:* 1-43-54-69-12.

DORMAN, David W., BA; American telecommunications executive; b. 1954; ed Georgia Inst. of Tech.; began career in software devt, sales and marketing; joined Sprint Business 1981, Pres. 1990–94; CEO Pacific Bell 1994–96, later becoming Exec. Vice-Pres. SBC Communications; Chair., Pres. and CEO PointCast Network 1996–99; CEO Concert (global jt venture between AT&T Corpn and British Telecom) 1999–2000; Pres. AT&T Corpn. Dec. 2000–, mem. Bd of Dirs Feb. 2002–, Chair. and CEO July 2002–; mem. Bd 3Com Corpn, ETEK Dynamics Ltd, Sabre, Science Applications Int. Corpn (SAIC), Scientific-Atlanta Inc., Int. Advisory Bd, British American Business Council; mem. Bd of Dirs Atlanta Symphony Orchestra; mem. Pres. Clinton's Advisory Cttee on High Performance Computing and Communications, Information Tech. and Next Generation Internet. *Address:* Office of the President, AT&T Corporation, 6th Floor, 32 Avenue of the Americas, New York, NY 10013, USA (Office). *Website:* www.att.com (Office).

DORMANDY, John Adam, DSc, MD, FRCS; British surgeon; b. 5 May 1937, Hungary; s. of Paul Szeben and Clara Szeben; m. Klara Dormandy 1982; one s. one d.; ed St Paul's School, London and London Univ.; Resident in Surgery,

St George's Hosp. Medical School 1963–65, Lecturer in Applied Physiology 1970–74, Sr Lecturer in Surgery 1975–80, Prof. of Vascular Sciences 1995–; Consultant Vascular Surgeon, St James' and St George's Hosp. 1973–; Pres. of Section of Clinical Medicine, Royal Soc. of Medicine 1978; Pres. Venous Forum 1984; Chair. Int. Soc. of Haemorheology 1982; Examiner in Physiology, Royal Coll. of Surgeons 1984, Hunterian Prof. 1970; Hamilton Bailey Prize in Surgery 1973; Fahreus Medal 1983. *Publications:* numerous articles in books and scientific journals. *Leisure interests:* tennis, skiing. *Address:* Department of Vascular Surgery, St George's Hospital, St James' Wing, Blackshaw Road, London SW17 0QT (Office); 82 East Hill, London, SW18 2HG, England (Home). *Telephone:* (20) 876- 8346. *Fax:* (20) 8682-2550. *E-mail:* dormandyjohn@aol.com (Home).

DORMANN, Jürgen; German business executive; b. 1940; began career with Hoechst AG 1963, Finance and Accounting Dir 1987–94, Chair. Man. Bd 1994–2002, apptd Chair. Bd of Dirs 1999, oversaw merger of Hoechst AG with Rhone-Poulenc SA to create Aventis SA, Chair. Aventis SA 1999–2002; Dir ABB Asea Brown Boveri Ltd 1999–, Chair. Dec. 2001–, CEO 2002–; Dir IBM (Int. Business Machines) 1996–, mem. Audit Cttee; mem. Supervisory Bd Allianz AG 1999–; mem. European Chemical Industry Council 2000–. *Address:* Office of the Chief Executive, ABB Asea Brown Boveri Ltd, Oberhausener Strasse 33, 40472 Ratingen, Germany (Office). *Website:* www.abb .com (Office).

DORMENT, Richard, MA, M.PHIL., PhD; American art critic; b. 15 Nov. 1946, Montclair, NJ; s. of James Dorment and Marguerite Dorment (née O'Callaghan); m. 1st Kate S. Ganz 1970 (dissolved 1981); one s. one d.; m. 2nd Harriet Mary Waugh 1985; ed Georgetown Prep. School, Princeton and Columbia Univs.; Asst Curator European Painting Phila Museum of Art 1973–76; Curator Alfred Gilbert: Sculptor and Goldsmith Exhbn, RA, London 1985–86; art critic Country Life 1986; Co-Curator James McNeill Whistler Exhbn, Tate Gallery 1994–95; art critic Daily Telegraph 1986–; reviewer for New York Review of Books, Times Literary Supplement, Literary Review; contrib. to Burlington Magazine; Hawthornden Prize for Art Criticism in Britain 1992; Critic of the Year, British Press Awards 2000. *Publications:* Victorian High Renaissance (Exhbn catalogue contrib.) 1976, Alfred Gilbert 1985, British Painting 1750–1900: A Catalogue of British Paintings in the Philadelphia Museum of Art 1986, Alfred Gilbert: Sculptor and Goldsmith 1986, James McNeill Whistler (with Margaret MacDonald) 1994. *Address:* 10 Clifton Villas, London, W9 2PH, England (Home).

DORN, Dieter; German theatre director; b. 31 Oct. 1935, Leipzig; ed Theaterhochschule, Leipzig and Max-Reinhardt-Schule, Berlin; actor, producer and Dir in Hannover 1958–68; Dir in Essen and Oberhausen 1968–70; Dir at Deutsches Schauspielhaus, Hamburg 1971, Burgtheater, Vienna 1972, 1976; Dir at Staatliche Schauspielbühnen, Berlin 1972–75, Salzburg Festival 1974, 1982, 1986; Chief Dir Münchner Kammerspiele (producing works by Lessing, Goethe, Büchner, Shakespeare etc.) 1976–83, Man. (Intendant) 1983–; has also directed opera productions in Vienna, Munich, Kassel and at Salzburg and Ludwigsburg festivals; mem. Akademie der Künste, Berlin, Bayerische Akademie der Schönen Künste; numerous prizes. *Address:* Münchner Kammerspiele, Hildegardstrasse 1, 80539 Munich, Germany. *Telephone:* 237210.

DORONINA, Tatyana Vasiliyevna; Russian actress; b. 12 Sept. 1933, Leningrad; d. of Vasiliy Ivanovich Doronin and Anna Ivanovna Doronina; m. Robert Dimitrievich Takhnenko; ed Studio School of Moscow Art Theatre; Leningrad Lenin Komsomol State Theatre 1956–59; Leningrad Maxim Gorky State Bolshoi Drama Theatre 1959–66; Moscow Art Theatre 1966–71; Moscow Mayakovski Theatre 1971–83; Moscow Arts Theatre 1983–, Artistic Dir Moscow Gorky Arts Theatre 1987–; works as actress and stage Dir; People's Artist of the USSR 1981. *Main roles include:* theatre: Zhenka Shulzhenko (Factory Girl by Volodin), Lenochka (In Search of Happiness by Rozov), Sophia (Wit Works Woe by Griboyedov), Nadya Rozoyeva (My Elder Sister by Volodin), Nadezhda Polikarpovna (The Barbarians by Gorky), Lushka (Virgin Soil Upturned by Sholokov), Nastasya Filippovna (The Idiot by Dostoyevsky), Valka (Irkutsk Story by Arbuzov), Oxana (Loss of the Squadron by Korneichuk), Masha (Three Sisters by Chekhov), Grushenka (Brothers Karamazov by Dostoyevsky), Arkadina (The Seagull by Chekhov); films: Nadya (Elder Sister by Volodin), Natasha (Again about Love by Radzinskiy), Zoya (First Echelon), Klava (Horizon), Nika (Roll Call), Shura (Stepmother); also acted in TV films. *Address:* Moscow Gorky Arts Theatre, 22 Tverskoi Blvd, 119146 Moscow, Russia. *Telephone:* (095) 203-74-66.

DORR, Noel, MA, BComm; Irish diplomatist; b. 1 Nov. 1933, Limerick; s. of John Dorr and Bridget Clancy; m. Caitríona Doran 1983; ed St Nathy's Coll., Ballaghderreen, Nat. Univ. of Ireland, Georgetown Univ., Washington, DC; Third Sec., Dept of Foreign Affairs, Dublin 1960–62, Embassy, Brussels 1962–64, First Sec. Embassy, Washington, DC 1964–70, Dept of Foreign Affairs, Dublin 1970–72, Counsellor (Press and Information) 1972–74, Asst Sec. and Political Dir 1974–77, Deputy Sec. and Political Dir 1977–80, Perm. Rep. to UN 1980–83; Amb. to UK 1983–87; Sec. Dept of Foreign Affairs 1987–95; Personal Rep. of Minister for Foreign Affairs, EU Intergovernmental Conference 1996–. *Leisure interests:* reading, swimming. *Address:* Department of Foreign Affairs, Iveagh House, 76–78 Harcourt Street, Dublin 2, Ireland.

DORRELL, Rt Hon Stephen James, PC, BA; British politician; b. 25 March 1952; s. of Philip Dorrell; m. Penelope Anne Wears Taylor 1980; three s. one d.; ed Uppingham School, Brasenose Coll. Oxford; Conservative MP for Loughborough 1979–97, for Charnwood 1997–, Parl. Pvt. Sec. to Sec. of State for Energy 1983–87, Asst Govt Whip 1987–88, a Lord Commr of Treasury 1988–90, Parl. Under-Sec. of State, Dept of Health 1990–92, Financial Sec. to Treasury 1992–94; Sec. of State for Nat. Heritage 1994–95, for Health 1995–97; Shadow Sec. for Educ. and Employment 1997–98; Bd mem. Christian Aid 1985–87. *Leisure interests:* aviation, reading. *Address:* House of Commons, London, SW1A 0AA, England. *Telephone:* (20) 7219-4472. *Fax:* (20) 7219-5838 (Office). *E-mail:* dorrells@parliament.uk (Office).

DORSEN, Norman, BA, LLB; American professor of law and civil libertarian; b. 4 Sept. 1930, New York; s. of Arthur Dorsen and Tanya Stone; m. Harriette Koffler 1965; three d.; ed Bronx High School of Science, Columbia Coll., Harvard Law School and London School of Econs; law clerk to Chief Judge Calvert Magruder, US Court of Appeals, First Circuit 1956–57, to Justice John M. Harlan, US Supreme Court 1957–58; pvt. law practice, New York 1958–60; Assoc. Prof. of Law, New York Univ. Law School 1961–65, Prof. 1965–78, Stokes Prof. 1978–, Counselor to the Pres.; mem. Bd of Dirs. American Civil Liberties Union 1965–91, Gen. Counsel 1969–76, Pres. 1976–91; Founding Pres. Soc. of American Law Teachers 1972–74, Pres. US Asscn of Constitutional Law; Vice-Chair. US Dept of Health, Educ. and Welfare Review Panel on New Drug Regulation 1975–76, Chair. 1976–77; mem. Bd of Dirs Lawyers Comm. for Human Rights 1978–, Chair. 1995–2000; Bd Dirs Thomas Jefferson Center for Protection of Free Expression 1990–; Dir Global Law School Program 1994–, Chair. 1996–2002; mem. Council on Foreign Relations; Chair., US Treasury Citizens' Panel on Allegations regarding Good O'Boys Round-up; consultant Americans for Religious Liberty; Fellow American Acad. of Arts and Sciences; Founder and Editorial Dir I.CON, The Int. Journal of Constitutional Law; Hon. LLD (Ripon Coll., John Jay Coll. of Criminal Justice); Minister of Justice's Medal (France) 1983, Eleanor Roosevelt award for Human Rights, various awards for civil rights and as legal educator. *Publications include:* books: Political and Civil Rights in the US (with others) 1967, Frontiers of Civil Liberties 1968, ACLU Handbooks Series (Gen. Ed.) 1971–95, Disorder in the Court (co-author) 1973, The Evolving Constitution 1987, Human Rights in Northern Ireland (with others) 1991, Democracy and the Rule of Law (Co-Ed.) 2001, The Unpredictable Constitution (Co-Ed.) 2002, Comparative Constitutionalism 2003; articles on constitutional law and civil liberties. *Leisure interests:* country living, aerobics. *Address:* 40 Washington Square South, New York, NY 10012 (Office); 146 Central Park West, New York, NY 10023, USA (Home). *Telephone:* (212) 998-6233 (Office). *Fax:* (212) 995-4030 (Office). *E-mail:* norman .dorsen@nyu.edu (Office).

DORST, Tankred; German author; b. 19 Dec. 1925, Sonneberg; s. of Max Dorst and Elisabeth Dorst; m. Ursula Ehler-Dorst; mem. German PEN Centre, Bayerische Akad. der schönen Künste, Deutsche Akad. der darstellenden Künste, Deutsche Akad. für Sprache und Dichtung; several prizes including Gerhart Hauptmann Prize, Georg-Büchner Prize 1990. *Film as director and screenwriter:* Eisenhans. *Plays:* around 40 plays including Toller, Eiszeit, Merlin oder das wüste Land, Herr Paul, Was sollen wir tun, Fernando Krapp hat mir diesen Brief geschrieben, Die Legende vom Armen Heinrich; Karlos, Korbes; several opera libretti. *TV programmes (writer and director):* Klaras Mutter, Mosch. *Publications:* Plays (Vols 1–7). *Address:* Karl Theodor Strasse 102, 80796 Munich, Germany. *Fax:* (89) 3073256.

DORUK, Mustafa, PhD; Turkish professor of engineering; b. 23 Feb. 1932; ed School of Eng Yildiz, Technische Hochschule, Darmstadt, Germany; Asst Prof. Dept of Metallurgical Eng, Middle East Tech. Univ., Turkey 1963–70, Assoc. Prof. 1970–76, Prof. 1976, Chair. of Dept 1965–69, of Dept of Metallurgical and Materials Eng 1988–97; Asst Pres. and Acting Pres. Middle East Tech. Univ. 1974–77, Dean Faculty of Eng 1978–85; UN Scholar, U.C.L.A. 1972–73; Visiting Prof. Technische Hochschule, Darmstadt 1979; mem. Structure and Materials Panel of NATO/AGARD, Int. Congress on Corrosion, Founding mem. Corrosion Asscn of Turkey; mem. Chamber of Turkish Metallurgical Engineers; Fellow Islamic Acad. of Sciences; Hon. Senator, Technical Univ. Darmstadt. *Publications:* over 50 Publs. *Address:* Islamic Academy of Sciences, P.O. Box 830036, Amman, Jordan (Office). *Telephone:* 5522104 (Office). *Fax:* 5511803 (Office).

DOS SANTOS, HE Cardinal Alexander José Maria, O.F.M.; Mozambican ecclesiastic; b. 18 March 1924, Inhambane; ordained 1953, elected to Church in Lourenço Marques (now Maputo) 1974, consecrated Bishop 1975; Archbishop of Maputo 1976–; cr. Cardinal 1988. *Address:* Paço Arquiepiscopal, Avenida Eduardo Mondlane 1448, C.P. 258, Maputo, Mozambique. *Telephone:* (1) 426240. *Fax:* (1) 421873.

DOS SANTOS, Fernando da Piedade Dias (Nandó); Angolan politician; b. 1952, Luanda; ed Instituto Industrial de Luanda; involved with Grupo Boa Esperança from 1970 (pro-independence); nat. service, Portuguese colonial army 1973–74; deserted to join guerilla forces of Movimento Popular de Libertação de Angola (MPLA); mem. staff FAPLA (Armed Forces of MPLA), rank of Major 1984, Col 1986, Maj.-Gen. 1992; Insp., Corpo do Polícia Popular de Angola—CPPA (People's Police Force of Angola) 1976–78, Head of 1st Command Div. 1978–79, Head of Political Dept and Personnel Section in Nat. Directorate 1979–81, Nat. Dir of People's Police 1984–86; Deputy Head Nat. Political Directorate, Ministry of the Interior 1981–84, Nat. Dir of Personnel 1982–84, Deputy Minister of State Security 1984, Deputy Minister of the Interior 1984, also Head of Information Services 1990, Deputy Minister of the

Interior responsible for Internal Order 1995–99, Minister of the Interior 1999–2002; elected Deputy People's Ass. 1986–; Commdr-Gen. and Gen. Commr of Nat. Police (Polícia Nacional) 1995–; Co-ordinator Exec. Cttee of Inter-Ministerial Comm. of Process of Peace and Reconciliation 2001, Nat. Comm. for Social and Productive Reintegration of Demobilised Troops and Displaced Persons 2002; Prime Minister of Angola Dec. 2002–. *Address:* Office of the Prime Minister, c/o Ministry of the Interior, Avda 4 de Fevereiro, Luanda, CP 2723, Angola (Office).

DOS SANTOS, José Eduardo; Angolan politician; b. 28 Aug. 1942, Luanda; s. of Eduardo Avelino dos Santos and Jacinta José Paulino; ed Liceu Salvador Correia; joined Movimento Popular de Libertação de Angola (MPLA) 1961; went into exile 1961 and was a founder mem. and Vice-Pres. of MPLA Youth based in Léopoldville, Congo (now Kinshasa, Democratic Repub. of Congo); first Rep., MPLA, Brazzaville 1961; sent with group of students for training in Moscow 1963; graduated as Petroleum Engineer, Inst. of Oil and Gas, Baku 1969; then mil. course in telecommunications; returned to Angola and participated in war against Portuguese 1970–74; Second in Command of Telecommunications Services, MPLA Second Politico-Military Region, Cabinda; mem. Provisional Readjustment Cttee, Northern Front 1974; mem. MPLA Cen. Cttee and Political Bureau 1974–; Chair. MPLA; Minister of Foreign Affairs, Angola 1975; Co-ordinator, MPLA Foreign Relations Dept 1975; Sec. Cen. Cttee for Educ., Culture and Sport, then for Nat. Reconstruction, then Economic Devt and Planning 1977–79; First Deputy Prime Minister, Minister of Planning and Head of Nat. Planning Comm. 1978–79; Pres. of Angola 1979– and Chair. of Council of Ministers 1979–, also Prime Minister 1999–2002; C-in-C of FAPLA (Armed Forces of MPLA). *Address:* Gabinete do Presidente, Luanda, Angola.

DOS SANTOS, Manuel, B.SC.(Econs); Mozambican diplomatist; b. 7 May 1944; s. of Armando Augusto dos Santos and Luisa Chapassuca; m. Dabanga Diana dos Santos 1966; mem. Mozambique Liberation Front Exec. Cttee 1967–77, Nat. Treasurer, Sec. for Econ. Affairs 1967–73; mem. FRELIMO-Cen. Cttee 1967–91; Public Relations Officer to Prime Minister's Office 1974–75; Dir Foreign Trade at Ministry for Industry and Trade 1975–76; Gen. Sec. Ministry of Foreign Affairs 1977–78; Minister for Internal Trade 1978–80; Amb. to Tanzania 1980–83; Amb. and Perm. Rep. of Mozambique to UN 1983–89; Pres. Econ. and Soc. Council UN 1986; mem. Nat. Ass. 1972–; fmr Deputy Minister for Foreign Affairs 1989. *Address:* c/o Ministry for Foreign Affairs, Avda. Julius Nyerere 4, Maputo, Mozambique. *Telephone:* 744061.

DOSHI, Balkrishna Vithaldas, ARIBA; Indian architect; b. 26 Aug. 1927, Pune (Poona); s. of Vithaldas Gokuldas and Radhaben Vithaldas; m. Kamala Savailal Parikh 1955; three d.; ed Sir J.J. Coll. of Arts, Bombay; Sr Designer, Le Corbusier Studio, Paris 1951–55; Prin., Vastu-Shilpa Architecture and Planning Firm, Ahmedabad 1956–77; f. mem. and First Hon. Dir School of Architecture, Ahmedabad 1962–72, School of Planning, Ahmedabad 1972–81; Dean, Centre for Environmental Planning and Tech. 1972–79, Dean Emer. 1981–; founder and Hon. Dir Kanoria School of Arts Ahmedabad 1984–; Vice-Pres. Council of Architecture, Govt of India 1973–74; mem. Advisory Bd, Architecture and Urbanism Publishing Co., Tokyo 1972–, Bldg Inst., London 1972–76, Int. Jury Panel, Competition for Urban Environment in Developing Countries, Manila 1975–76; Sr Partner, Messrs. Stein Doshi & Bhalla, New Delhi, Ahmedabad 1977–; f. mem.-trustee and Dir Vastu-Shilpa Foundation for Studies and Research in Environmental Design, Ahmedabad 1978–; Chair. Centre for Environmental Planning and Tech., Study Cell 1978–81; Chair. Panel of Juries, Int. Architectural Design Competition for the Indira Gandhi Nat. Centre for Arts 1987–; Fellow, Indian Inst. of Architects; Hon. Fellow, AIA 1971, Acad., Int. Acad. of Architecture 1989; awards include Padmashree award, Govt of India 1976; Pan Pacific Architectural Citation award, Hawaii Chapter of AIA 1981, Baburao Mhatre Gold Medal (Indian Inst. of Architects) 1988, Architect of the Year Award 1991. *Major works include:* Campus for Centre for Environmental Planning and Tech., Ahmedabad 1966, townships for Gujarat State Fertilizer Co. Ltd, Baroda 1968, Electronics Corpn of India Ltd, Hyderabad 1972, Dept of Atomic Energy, Govt of India, Kota 1972, Indian Farmers' Fertilizer Co-op. Ltd, Kalol 1973, Indian Inst. of Man., Bangalore 1977, Nat. Inst. of Fashion Tech., New Delhi 1989, Kharghar Node, New Bombay 1992, Office Complex for Bharat Diamond Bourse, Bombay, Husain-Doshi Gufa Museum 1992. *Publications:* numerous articles and contributions to architectural journals. *Leisure interests:* photography, studies of philosophy. *Address:* 14, Shree Sadma Society, Navrangpura, Ahmedabad 380009, India. *Telephone:* (79) 491610 (Office); (79) 429344 (Home).

DOSHI, Vinod, MSc (ENG.); Indian business executive; b. 20 March 1932; s. of Lalchand Hirachand and Lalitabai Doshi; ed Albion Coll., Mich., USA and Univ. of Mich.; man. trainee, Cooper Eng Ltd (now amalgamated with Walchandnagar Industries Ltd) 1958, Dir in charge of operations 1960, Man. Dir 1970–75; Vice-Chair. and Man. Dir Walchandnagar Industries Ltd 1975, now Chair.; mem. Bd of Dirs. The Premier Automobiles Ltd 1972–, Chair. of Bd 1982–; Chair. and Dir numerous cos.; mem. or fmr mem. of numerous Govt bodies etc. *Leisure interests:* colour photography, music and sound recording, amateur theatre and commercial cinema. *Address:* L. B. Shastri Marg, Kurla, Mumbai, 400070, India (Office). *Telephone:* (22) 5115190 (Office). *Fax:* (22) 5144000 (Office).

DOST, Shah Mohammad; Afghanistan politician; b. 1929, Kabul; ed Kabul Univ.; mem. People's Democratic Party of Afghanistan 1963, mem. Cen. Cttee 1979; fmr Deputy Foreign Minister and Foreign Minister of the Democratic Rep. of Afghanistan; mem. Revolutionary Council; Minister of State for Foreign Affairs 1986–88; Perm. Rep. to U.N. 1988–90; Order of People's Friendship. Address: c/o Ministry of Foreign Affairs, Shah Mahmoud Ghazi Street, Shar-i-Nau, Kabul, Afghanistan.

DOSTAM, Gen. Abdul Rashid; Afghanistan politician and guerrilla leader; b. 1954, Khowja Dokoh, Juzjan Prov.; fmr plumber; with Oil and Gas Exploration Enterprise 1979; undertook mil. training in USSR 1980; Commdr pro-Soviet Jozjani Dostum Militia, N. Afghanistan 1980–92; Defence Minister in Pres. Najibullah's Govt (1986–92); allied with Gulbuddin Hekmatyar's Pashtun warriors and Shi'ite guerrillas following transition of power 1992; est. Itehad Shamal/Northern Unity org. which controlled most N Afghanistan provs. 1993–97; fled to Turkey when Taliban occupied Mazar-i-Sharif 1997; returned to fight with Northern Alliance (NA) against Taliban 2001; Leader of Jonbesh-i Melli-i Islami (Nat. Islamic Movt), Uzbek military wing of NA; f. Balkh Air (airline); awarded 'Hero of the Repub. of Afghanistan' medal by Pres. Najibullah.

DOTRICE, Roy; British actor; b. 26 May 1925, Guernsey, Channel Islands; s. of Louis Dotrice and Neva Wilton; m. Kay Newman 1946; three d.; ed Dayton and Intermediate Schools, Guernsey; air gunner, RAF 1940; POW 1942–45; acted in repertory 1945–55; formed and directed Guernsey Theatre Co. 1955; TV Actor of the Year Award 1968. Films include: The Heroes of Telemark 1965, A Twist of Sand 1968, Lock up Your Daughters 1969, Buttercup Chain, Tomorrow, One of Those Things 1971, Nicholas and Alexandra 1971, Amadeus, The Corsican Brothers 1983, The Eliminators 1985, Shaka Zulu 1985, Young Harry Houdini 1986, Camila, L-Dopa, The Lady Forgets, The Cutting Edge, The Scarlet Letter, Swimming with Sharks. Stage appearances include: Royal Shakespeare Co. 1957–65 (playing Caliban, Julius Caesar, Hotspur, Firs, Puntila, Edward IV, etc.); World War 2½, New Theatre, London 1966; Brief Lives (one-man play), Criterion (over 400 performances, world record for longest-running solo performance) 1969, toured England, Canada, USA 1973, Mayfair (over 150 performances) 1974; Broadway season 1974; Australian tour 1975; Peer Gynt, Chichester Festival 1970; One At Night, Royal Court 1971; The Hero, Edinburgh 1970; Mother Adam, Arts 1971; Tom Brown's Schooldays, Cambridge 1972; The Hollow Crown, seasons in USA 1973 and 1975, Sweden 1975; Gomes, Queen's 1973; The Dragon Variation, Duke of York's 1977; Australian tour with Chichester Festival 1978; Passion of Dracula, Queen's 1978; Oliver, Albery 1979; Mr. Lincoln (one-man play), New York 1980, Fortune 1981, A Life, New York 1981, Henry V, Stratford, Conn. 1981, Falstaff (American Shakespeare Co.) 1982, Kingdoms, Broadway 1982, Churchill, Washington and Los Angeles 1983, The Genius, Los Angeles 1984, Enemy of the People, New York 1985, Hay Fever, New York and Washington 1985–86, The Homecoming 1991, New York, The Best of Friends, New York 1993, The Woman In Black, USA 1995, Moon for the Begotten (Tony Award) 2000. TV appearances include: Dear Liar, Brief Lives, The Caretaker (Emmy Award), Imperial Palace, Misleading Cases, Clochemerle, Dickens of London, Stargazy on Zummerdown; numerous American TV appearances including Remington Steel, Hart to Hart, Family Reunion, Magnum P.I., Fairy Tale Theatre, Beauty and the Beast, Tales of Gold Monkey, The Wizard, A Team, Tales from the Dark Side, Beauty and the Beast, Going to Extremes, The Good Policeman, Madigan Man. Leisure interests: baseball, fishing, riding. Address: 98 St Martin's Lane, London, W.C.2, England. Telephone: (20) 7836-7054.

DOTY, Paul Mead, BS, MA, PhD; American biochemist and specialist in science policy and arms control; b. 1 June 1920, Charleston, W Va; s. of Paul Mead and Maud Stewart Doty; m. 1st Margaretta Elenor Grevatt 1942 (divorced 1953); one c.; m. 2nd Helga Boedtker 1954 three d.; ed Pennsylvania State Coll., Columbia and Cambridge Univs.; Instructor and Research Assoc. Polytechnic Inst., Brooklyn 1943–45, Asst Prof. Chemistry 1945–46; Asst Prof. Chem., Univ. de Notre Dame 1947–48; Asst Prof. Harvard 1948–50, Assoc. Prof. Chem. 1950–56, Prof. 1956, Pres. Science Advisory Cttee 1961–65, Mallinckrodt Prof. of Biochem. 1968–88, Prof. of Public Policy 1988–90, Prof. Emer. of Biochem. 1988–, Prof. Emer. of Public Policy 1990–; Sr Fellow Harvard 1973–91; Dir of Center for Science and Int. Affairs, Harvard Univ. 1973–85; Consultant to the Arms Control and Disarmament Agency, Nat. Security Council; mem. Gen. Advisory Cttee on Arms Control 1977–81; mem. Bd MITRE Corpn 1975–92, Int. Science Foundation 1993–97; Founder, Ed. Int. Security 1975–85; Sr Fellow, Aspen Inst. Berlin (mem. Bd 1973–); Fellow, American Acad. of Arts and Science, NAS, Philosophical Soc., Rockefeller Fellow, Cambridge Univ. 1946–47. Leisure interests: reading, travel, computing. Address: c/o John F. Kennedy School of Government, Harvard University, 79 JFK Street, Cambridge, MA 02138 (Office); 4 Kirkland Place, Cambridge, MA 02138, USA (Home). Telephone: (617) 864-6679 (Home). Fax: (617) 864-3739 (Home).

DOUGLAS, Barry, OBE; Irish concert pianist; b. 23 April 1960, Belfast, Northern Ireland; s. of Barry Douglas and Sarah Jane (née Henry) Douglas; m. Deirdre O'Hara; two s. one d.; ed Royal Coll. of Music, London; pvt. study with Maria Curcio; London début, Wigmore Hall 1981; toured Europe 1986–; regularly performs in USA; other concerts in Japan, USSR, Australia, Iceland, Czechoslovakia; recital début in Carnegie Hall, New York 1988; Artistic Dir Camerata Ireland; winner of Tchaikovsky Piano Competition, Moscow 1986; Hon. FRCM; Hon. DMus (Belfast); Diploma Royal Coll. of Music, Emmy Award for Concerto, (Channel 4 TV programme) 1993, Dia-

pason d'Or for Reger/Strauss recording 1998. Recordings include: Tchaikovsky Concertos Nos. 1, 2 and 3, Sonata in G, Brahms Concerto No. 1, Piano Quintet in F Minor, Liszt concertos and Sonata in B Minor, Beethoven, Mussorgsky, Prokofiev, Rachmaninov Concerto No. 2, Berg, Reger, Strauss, Debussy, Britten, Corigliano. Leisure interests: driving, reading, food and wine. Address: c/o IMG Artists, Lovell House, 616 Chiswick High Road, London, W4 5RX, England.

DOUGLAS, Denzil; Saint Christopher and Nevis politician; Prime Minister of Saint Christopher and Nevis, Minister of Finance, of Nat. Security, of Information, of Planning and of Foreign Affairs 1995–2001; Prime Minister and Minister of Finance, Devt Planning and Nat. Security 2001–; Chair. Bd Caribbean Devt Bank 2002–. Address: Office of the Prime Minister, Basseterre, Saint Christopher and Nevis (Office).

DOUGLAS, James Buster; American boxer; b. 7 April 1960, Columbus, Ohio; s. of Billy Douglas and Lula Douglas; m. (separated); two c.; ed Coffeyville Jr Coll., Kansas, Sinclair Community Coll., Ohio and Mercyhurst Coll., Erie, Pa; 30 wins, four losses, one draw; became world heavyweight champion, on defeating Mike Tyson (q.v.) in Tokyo Feb. 1990; lost world title fight to Evander Holyfield (q.v.) Oct. 1990; returned to boxing June 1996. Address: c/o Lawrence Nallie, 465 Waterbury Court, Suite A, Gahanna, OH 43230, USA (Office).

DOUGLAS, James H. (Jim), BA; American state official; b. 1951, Springfield; m. Dorothy Douglas; two s.; ed Middlebury Coll.; mem. House of Reps., Vt 1972–79, Majority Whip 1975–77, Majority Leader 1977–79; Exec. Asst to Gov. of Vt 1979–80; Sec. of State, Vt 1980–93, State Treas. 1994–2002, Gov. of Vt 2003–; fmr Pres. Nat. Asscn of Secs. of State, Addison Co. Chamber of Commerce, Porter Medical Center; mem. Republican Town Cttee. Address: Office of the Governor, Pavilion Office Building, 109 State Street, Montpelier, VT 05609, USA (Office). Website: www.jimdouglas.org/bio.shtml (Office).

DOUGLAS, Kirk, AB; American actor; b. 9 Dec. 1916, Amsterdam, NY; s. of Harry and Bryna (née Sanglel) Danielovitch; m. 1st Diana Dill (divorced 1950); two s.; m. 2nd Anne Buydens 1954; two s.; ed St Lawrence Univ. and American Acad. of Dramatic Arts; Pres. Bryna Productions 1955–; Dir Los Angeles Chapter, UN Asscn; Acad. Awards 1948, 1952, 1956; New York Film Critics Award, Hollywood Foreign Press Award, Commdr, des Arts et Lettres 1979, Commdr, Légion d'honneur 1985, Presidential Medal of Freedom 1981, American Film Inst.'s Lifetime Achievement Award 1991, Kennedy Center Honors 1994, Hon. Acad. Award 1996, Lifetime Achievement Award Screen Actors' Guild 1999, Golden Bear, Berlin Film Festival 2000, Nat. Medal of Arts 2002. Broadway stage appearances: Spring Again, Three Sisters, Kiss and Tell, The Wind is Ninety, Alice in Arms, Man Bites Dog, The Boys of Autumn (not on Broadway). TV work includes: Queenie (mini series) 1987, Touched by an Angel (series) 2000. Films include: The Strange Love of Martha Ivers, Letter to Three Wives, Ace in the Hole, The Bad and the Beautiful, 20,000 Leagues under the Sea, Ulysses, Lust for Life, Gunfight at O.K. Corral, Paths of Glory, The Vikings, Last Train from Gun Hill, The Devil's Disciple, Spartacus, Strangers When We Meet, Seven Days in May, Town without Pity, The List of Adrian Messenger, In Harms Way, Cast a Giant Shadow, The Way West, War Waggon, The Brotherhood, The Arrangement, There Was a Crooked Man, Gunfight 1971, Light at the Edge of the World, Catch Me a Spy, A Man to Respect 1972, Cat and Mouse, Scalawag (Dir) 1973, Once Is Not Enough 1975, Posse (producer, actor) 1975, The Moneychangers (TV) 1976, Holocaust 2000 1977, The Fury 1977, Villain 1978, Saturn 3 1979, The Final Countdown 1980, The Man from Snowy River, Tough Guys 1986, Oscar, Welcome to Veraz, Greedy 1994, Diamonds 1999, Family Jewels 2002. Publications: The Ragman's Son: An Autobiography 1988, Dance with the Devil (novel) 1990, The Secret (novel) 1992, The Gift (novel) 1992, Last Tango in Brooklyn (novel) 1994, Climbing the Mountain: My Search for Meaning 1997, The Broken Mirror (novel) 1997, My Stroke of Luck 2002. Address: Warren Cowan Associates, 8899 Beverly Boulevard, Suite 412, Beverly Hills, CA 90048-2427 (Office); The Bryna Company, 141 S El Camino Drive, Beverly Hills, CA 90212, USA (Office). Telephone: (310) 274-5294 (Office). Fax: (310) 274-2537 (Office).

DOUGLAS, Margaret Elizabeth, OBE; British broadcasting executive; b. 22 Aug. 1934, London; d. of Thomas Mincher Douglas and Dorothy Douglas (née Jones); m. Terence Lancaster 2000; ed Parliament Hill Grammar School; joined BBC 1951, fmrly sec., then researcher, dir and producer in current affairs TV, Chief Asst to Dir-Gen. 1983, Chief Political Adviser 1987–93; Supervisor of Parl. Broadcasting, Palace of Westminster 1993–99. Address: Flat 49, The Anchor Brewhouse, 50 Shad Thames, London, SE1 2LY, England (Home). Telephone: (20) 7403-3568 (Home). Fax: (20) 7403-3568 (Home).

DOUGLAS, Michael Kirk, BA; American actor and film producer; b. 25 Sept. 1944, New Brunswick, NJ; s. of Kirk Douglas (q.v.); m. Diandra Mornell Luker 1977 (divorced); one s.; m. 2nd Catherine Zeta Jones (q.v.) 2000; one s. one d.; appeared in TV series Streets of San Francisco; f. Further Films; Acad. Award for Best Actor (for Wall Street) 1988, Spencer Tracey Award 1999; UN Messenger of Peace 2000. Film appearances: It's My Turn, Hail Hero! 1969, Summertime 1971, Napoleon and Samantha 1972, Coma 1978, Running 1979, Star Chamber 1983, Romancing the Stone (also producer) 1984, A Chorus Line 1985, Jewel of the Nile 1985, Fatal Attraction 1987, Wall Street 1987, Heidi 1989, Black Rain 1989, The War of the Roses 1990, Shining Through 1990, Basic Instinct 1992, Falling Down 1993, Disclosure 1994, The American President 1995, The Ghost and the Darkness (also exec. producer) 1996, The Game 1997, A Perfect Murder 1998, One Day in September (voice) 1999, Traffic 2000, Wonder Boys 2000, One Night at McCool's 2000, Don't Say a Word 2001, A Few Good Years 2002, It Runs in the Family 2003, Monkeyface 2003. *Films produced include:* One Flew Over the Cuckoo's Nest (Academy Award for Best Film 1975), The China Syndrome, Starman (exec. producer), Flatliners 1990, Stone Cold 1991, Eyes of an Angel (exec. producer) 1991, Radio Flyer 1992, Made in America (co-exec. producer) 1993, Face/Off (exec. producer) 1997, The Rainmaker 1997, One Night at McCools 2000, Godspeed, Lawrence Mann 2002. *Address:* c/o Creative Artists Agency Inc., 9830 Wilshire Boulevard, Beverly Hills, CA 90212, USA. *Website:* www.michaeldouglas.com (Office).

DOUGLAS, Sir Roger Owen, Kt; New Zealand politician and accountant; b. 5 Dec. 1937, Auckland; s. of Norman V. and Jennie Douglas; m. Glennis June Anderson 1961; one s. one d.; ed Auckland Grammar School, Auckland Univ.; entered House of Reps. as Labour mem. for Manukau 1969 (now Manurewa); Minister of Broadcasting 1973–75, of the Post Office 1973–74, of Housing (with State Advances, Housing Corpn) 1974–75; Minister of Finance and Minister in Charge of the Inland Revenue Dept and of Friendly Socs. 1984–87, of Finance 1988, of Police and Immigration 1989–90; Dir Brierley Investments 1990–98 (Chair. (interim) 1998); John Fairfax Ltd 1997–99, Aetna Health (NZ) Ltd 1997–99, Tasman Inst. 1997–; fmr Pres. Auckland Labour Regional Council, Manukau Labour Cttee; Max Schmidheiny Freedom Prize, Switzerland 1995, Ludwig Erhard Foundation Prize, Germany 1997. *Publications:* There's Got to be a Better Way 1980, Toward Prosperity 1987, Unfinished Business 1993, Completing the Circle 1996; several papers on int. and econ. affairs. *Leisure interests:* cricket, rugby, rugby league, reading. *Address:* 411 Redoubt Road, R.D. Papatoetoe, Auckland, New Zealand. *Telephone:* (9) 2636928 (Office); (9) 2639596 (Home). *Fax:* (9) 2636938 (Office). *E-mail:* rdouglas@xtra.co.nz (Office).

DOURI, Akram J. M. al-; Iraqi diplomatist; Head of Iraqi Interests Section in USA. *Address:* Iraqi Interests Section, c/o Embassy of Algeria, 1801 P Street, NW, Washington, DC 20036, USA (Office). *Telephone:* (202) 483-7500 (Office). *Fax:* (202) 462-5066 (Office). *E-mail:* iraqiint@aol.com.

DOUSTE-BLAZY, Philippe Jean Georges Marie, DenM; French politician and doctor; b. 1 Jan. 1953, Lourdes; s. of Louis Douste-Blazy and Geneviève Béguère; m. Marie-Yvonne Calazel 1977; ed Lycée Pierre de Caousou, Toulouse and Univ. Paul Sabatier, Toulouse; Intern, Toulouse hosps. 1976–82; Head of Cardiology Clinics and Asst to Toulouse hosps. 1982–86; Univ. Prof. 1988–; Dir Arcol 1988–; Mayor of Lourdes 1989–2000, of Toulouse 2001–; mem. European Parl. 1989; Regional Councillor for Midi-Pyrénées 1992; Deputy to Nat. Ass. (Union pour la Démocratie Française) 1993, 1997–2001; Minister of Social Affairs, of Health and the City 1993–95; Minister of Culture 1995–97; Pres. Union pour la démocratie française group, Nat. Ass. 1998–; mem. New York Acad. of Sciences and numerous medical orgs. *Leisure interests:* classical music, golf. *Address:* Assemblée nationale, 75355 Paris (Office); Hôtel de ville, 31000 Toulouse (Office); 1 rue de Bagnères, 65100 Lourdes, France (Home).

DOVE, Rita Frances, BA, MFA; American author and professor of English; b. 28 Aug. 1952, Akron, Ohio; d. of Ray Dove and Elvira Dove (née Hord); m. Fred Viebahn 1979; one d.; ed Miami Univ. Ohio, Univ. of Tübingen, Germany and Univ. of Iowa; Asst Prof. Ariz. State Univ., Tempe 1981–84, Assoc. Prof. 1984–87, Prof. 1987–89; Prof. Univ. of Va, Charlottesville 1989–93, Commonwealth Prof. of English 1993–; US Poet Laureate 1993–95; Consultant in Poetry, Library of Congress 1993–95; Writer-in-Residence, Tuskegee Inst. Ala 1982; poetry panellist, Nat. Endowment for Arts, Washington, DC 1984–86 (Chair. 1985); Judge Pulitzer Prize in Poetry 1991 (Chair. of jury 1997), Nat. Book Award in Poetry 1991 and other awards; mem. numerous editorial bds; numerous hon. degrees; numerous prizes and awards including Lavan Younger Poet award Acad. of American Poets 1986, Pulitzer Prize (for Thomas and Beulah) 1987, Great American Artist Award, NAACP 1993, Golden Plate Award, American Acad. of Achievement 1993, Charles Frankel Prize/Nat. Humanities Medal 1996, Duke Ellington Lifetime Achievement Award in the Lliterary Arts, Ellington Fund in Washington, DC 2001. *Publications include:* The Yellow House on the Corner (poetry) 1980, Museum (poetry) 1983, Fifth Sunday (short stories) 1985, Thomas and Beulah (poetry) 1986, Grace Notes (poetry) 1989, Through the Ivory Gate (novel) 1992, Selected Poems 1993, The Darker Face of the Earth (verse drama) 1994, Mother Love (poetry) 1995, The Poet's World (essays) 1995, Evening Primrose (poetry) 1998, On the Bus with Rosa Parks (poetry) 1999, Best American Poetry (Ed.) 2000. *Leisure interests:* playing the viola da gamba, classical voice training, ballroom dancing. *Address:* Department of English, University of Virginia, Charlottesville, VA 22903, USA. *Telephone:* (804) 924-6618 (Office).

DOVER, Sir Kenneth James, Kt, MA, DLitt, FRSE, FBA; British classical scholar; b. 11 March 1920, Croydon; s. of Percy Henry James and Dorothy Valerie Anne (Healey) Dover; m. Audrey Ruth Latimer 1947; one s. one d.; ed St Paul's School, Balliol and Merton Colls., Oxford; served Royal Artillery 1940–45; Fellow and Tutor of Balliol Coll., Oxford 1948–55; Prof. of Greek, Univ. of St Andrews 1955–76, Chancellor 1981–; Pres. Corpus Christi Coll. Oxford 1976–86, Hon. Fellow 1986–; Visiting Lecturer, Harvard Univ. 1960; Visiting Prof. Univ. of Calif., Berkeley 1967; Prof.-at-Large Cornell Univ. 1983–88; Prof. Stanford Univ. 1987–92; FBA 1966–, Pres. 1978–81; Hon. Fellow, Balliol Coll. 1977–, Merton Coll. 1980–, Pres. Hellenic Soc. 1971–74, Classical Asscn 1975; Foreign mem. Royal Netherlands Acad. 1979–; Foreign

Hon. mem. American Acad. of Arts and Sciences 1979–; Hon. LLD (Birmingham) 1979, Hon. DLitt (Bristol and London) 1980, (Liverpool) 1983, (Durham) 1984, Hon. LLD and DLitt (St Andrews) 1981, Hon. DHL (Oglethorpe) 1984; Kenyon Medal, British Acad. 1993. *Publications:* Greek Word Order 1960, Clouds (Aristophanes) 1968, Lysias and the Corpus Lysiacum 1968, (with A. W. Gomme and A. Andrewes) Historical Commentary on Thucydides, vol. IV 1970, vol. V 1981, Theocritus, Select Poems 1971, Aristophanic Comedy 1972, Greek Popular Morality in the Time of Plato and Aristotle 1974, Greek Homosexuality 1978, The Greeks 1980, Ancient Greek Literature (with M. L. West and others) 1980, Greek and the Greeks 1987, The Greeks and their Legacy 1989, Frogs (Aristophanes) 1993, Marginal Comment 1994, The Evolution of Greek Prose Style 1997. *Leisure interests:* gardening, historical linguistics. *Address:* 49 Hepburn Gardens, St Andrews, Fife, KY16 9LS, Scotland. *Telephone:* (1334) 473589.

DOWELL, Sir Anthony James, Kt, CBE; British ballet dancer; b. 16 Feb. 1943, London; s. of Arthur H. Dowell and Catherine E. Dowell; ed Royal Ballet School; Prin. dancer, The Royal Ballet 1966, Sr Prin. dancer 1967–; joined American Ballet Theatre 1978; cr. roles in the following ballets: The Dream 1964, Romeo and Juliet 1965, Shadow Play 1967, Monotones 1969, Triad 1972, Manon 1974, A Month in the Country 1976; narrator in Oedipus Rex, Metropolitan Opera House, New York 1981; cr. role of Prospero in Nureyev's The Tempest, Royal Opera House, London 1982; Asst to Dir Royal Ballet 1984–85, Dir 1986–2001; Dir new productions of Swan Lake, Ondine and The Sleeping Beauty for Royal Ballet; designed costumes for Thais pas de deux (Frederick Ashton), In the Night (Jerome Robbins) and Symphony in C (George Balanchine) for Royal Ballet; Critics' Circle Award 2001, De Valois Award for outstanding achievement in dance 2002. *Address:* c/o The Royal Ballet, Covent Garden, London, WC2E 7QA, England. *Telephone:* (20) 7240-1200.

DOWELL, John Derek, PhD, CPhys, FInstP, FRS; British professor of elementary particle physics; b. 6 Jan. 1935, Ashby-de-la-Zouch; s. of William E. Dowell and Elsie D. Dowell; m. Patricia Clarkson 1959; one s. one d.; ed Coalville Grammar School, Leics. and Univ. of Birmingham; Research Fellow, Univ. of Birmingham 1958–60; Research Assoc. CERN, Geneva 1960–62; Lecturer, Univ. of Birmingham 1962–70, Sr Lecturer 1970–74, Reader 1974–80, Prof. of Elementary Particle Physics 1980–97, Poynting Prof. of Physics 1997–2002, Emer. Prof. 2002–; Visiting Scientist, Argonne Nat. Lab. USA 1968–69; Scientific Assoc. CERN 1973–74, 1985–87; Chair. SERC Particle Physics Cttee 1981–85; mem. CERN Scientific Policy Cttee 1982–90, 1993–96; mem. European Cttee for Future Accelerators 1989–93, BBC Science Consultative Group 1992–94, DESY Extended Scientific Council 1992–98; Chair. CERN LEP Cttee 1993–96; mem. CERN Research Bd 1993–96; Chair. ATLAS Collaboration Bd 1996–98; mem. UK Particle Physics and Astronomy Research Council 1994–97; mem. Court of Univ. of Warwick 1993–2001; mem. Council, Royal Soc. 1997–98, also Vice-Pres.; mem. American Physical Soc.; mem. RAE Physics Panel, Higher Educ. Funding Council 2001; Rutherford Medal and Prize, Inst. of Physics 1988. *Publications:* numerous papers in physics journals. *Leisure interests:* piano, amateur theatre, skiing. *Address:* School of Physics and Astronomy, University of Birmingham, Birmingham, B15 2TT (Office); 57 Oxford Road, Moseley, Birmingham, B13 9ES, England (Home). *Telephone:* (121) 414-4658 (Office); (121) 449-3332. *Fax:* (121) 414-6709 (Office). *E-mail:* jdd@hep.ph.bham.ac.uk (Office).

DOWLING, John Elliott, PhD; American professor of biology and neurobiologist; b. 31 Aug. 1935, Rhode Island; s. of Joseph Leo Dowling and Ruth W (Tappan) Dowling; m. 1st Susan Kinney (divorced 1974); two s.; m. 2nd Judith Falco 1975; one d.; ed Harvard Univ.; Instructor, Harvard Univ. 1961, Asst Prof. 1961–64; Assoc. Prof., Johns Hopkins Univ. 1964–71; Prof. of Biology, Harvard Univ. 1971–87, Assoc. Dean 1980–84, Master, Leverett House 1981–98, Maria Moors Cabot Prof. of Natural Science 1987–2001, Pres. of Corpn Marine Biological Lab. 1998–, Llura and Gordon Gund Prof. of Neurosciences 2001–; mem. NAS, American Acad. of Arts and Sciences, American Philosophical Soc.; Hon. MD (Lund, Sweden) 1982; Friedenwald Medal 1970, Retinal Research Award 1981, Prentice Medal 1991, Von Sallman Prize 1992, Helen Keller Prize 2000, Llura Liggett Gund Award 2001. *Publications:* The Retina: An Approachable Part of the Brain 1987, Neurons and Networks 1992, Creating Mind: How the Brain Works 1998; 226 publs in professional journals and ed. of 5 Vols. *Leisure interests:* sailing, squash and music. *Address:* The Biological Laboratories, Harvard University, 16 Divinity Avenue, Cambridge, MA 02138 (Office); 135 Charles Street, Boston, MA 02114, USA (Home). *Telephone:* (617) 495-2245 (Office); (617) 720-4522 (Home). *Fax:* (617) 496-3321 (Office). *E-mail:* dowling@mcb.harvard.edu (Office).

DOWLING, Patrick Joseph, CBE, BE, PhD, FICE, FCGI, F.R.ENG., FRS; Irish university vice-chancellor; b. 23 March 1939, Dublin; s. of John Dowling and Margaret McKittrick; m. Grace Lobo 1966; one s. one d.; ed Christian Bros. School, Dublin, Univ. Coll. Dublin and Imperial Coll. London; Sr demonstrator in Civil Eng Univ. Coll. Dublin 1960–61; Bursar in Structural Steelwork, Imperial Coll. London 1961–62, research on Steel Bridge Decks 1962–65; bridge engineer British Constructional Steelwork Asscn 1965–68; Research Fellow, Imperial Coll. London 1968–74, Reader in Structural Steelwork 1974–79, Prof. of Steel Structures 1979–94, British Steel Prof. and Head, Dept of Civil Eng 1985–94; Vice-Chancellor and Chief Exec., Univ. of Surrey Oct. 1994–; partner Chapman and Dowling Consulting Engineers

1981–94; Chair. Surrey Satellite Tech. Ltd 1994–; Chair. Engineeing Council 2001–; Pres. Inst. of Structural Engineers 1994–95; Fellow Imperial Coll. 1997, D.L Surrey 1999; Hon. LL.D (Nat. Univ. of Ireland) 1995; Dr. (Vilnius Tech. Univ. Lithuania) 1996, (Ulster) 1998; Telford Premium, Inst. of Civil Engs. 1976; Gustave Trasenster Medal, Asscn des Ingénieurs Sortis de l'Univ. de Liège 1984; several awards from Inst. of Structural Engineers. *Publications:* Steel Plated Structures 1977, Buckling Shells in Offshore Structures 1982, Structural Steel Design 1988, Constructional Steel Design 1992; over 200 refereed papers. *Leisure interests:* travelling, sailing, reading, good company. *Address:* University of Surrey, Guildford, Surrey, GU2 7XH, England. *Telephone:* (1483) 689249. *Fax:* (1483) 689518. *E-mail:* a.roberts@surrey.ac.uk (Office). *Website:* www.surrey.ac.uk (Office).

DOWLING, Vincent; American (b. Irish) actor, director, producer and playwright; b. 7 Sept. 1929, Dublin; s. of Mai Kelly Dowling and William Dowling; m. 1st Brenda Doyle 1952 (deceased); m. 2nd Olwen Patricia O'Herlihy 1975; one s. four d.; ed St Mary's Coll., Rathmines, Dublin, Rathmines School of Commerce, Brendan Smith Acad. of Acting; with Standard Life Insurance Co., Dublin 1946–50; Brendan Smith Productions, Dublin 1950–51; Roche-David Theatre Productions 1951–53; actor, Dir, Deputy Artistic Dir, Lifetime Assoc., Abbey Theatre, Dublin 1953–76, Artistic Dir 1987–89; Producing Dir Great Lakes Shakespeare Festival, Cleveland, Ohio 1976–84; Artistic and Producing Dir Solvang Theaterfest 1984–86; Prof. of Theatre, Coll. of Wooster, Ohio 1986–87; Producing Dir, Abbey Theatre 1989–90; founding Dir Miniature Theatre of Chester 1990–; Co-founder, Jacob's Ladder Trail Business Asscn; several distinguished visiting professorships at univs. in USA; Hon. DFA (Westfield State Coll., Mass. John Carroll Univ., Cleveland, Ohio, Coll. of Wooster, Ohio 1999); European Artist's Prize, Loyola Univ. 1969; Outstanding Producer, Cleveland Critics Circle Award 1982 for The Life and Adventures of Nicholas Nickelby; Irishman of the Year 1982; Wild Geese Award 1988, Loyola Mellon Humanitarian Award 1989, Walks of Life Award, Irish American Archives Soc. of Cleveland 2000. *Film appearances:* My Wife's Lodger 1953, Boyds Shop 1959, Johnny Nobody 1963, Young Cassidy 1965. *Original plays:* The Fit-Ups 1978, Acting is Murder 1986, A Day in the Life of an Abbey Actor 1990, Wilde About Oscar, Another Actor at the White House (one-man show), The Upstart Crow (A Two-Person Play about Will Shakespeare) 1995, 4 P's (one-man autobiographical). *Radio:* role of Christy Kennedy (for 17 years) in The Kennedys of Castlerosse, Radio Éireann; writer, narrator Festival Scrapbook, Radio WCLV, Cleveland, Ohio 1980-84. *T.V.* Dir and producer The Playboy of the Western World (Emmy Award) Public Broadcasting Service, USA 1983, One Day at a Time, ABC Television 1998. *Publication:* Astride the Moon (autobiog.) 2000. *Leisure interests:* fly-fishing, collecting paintings and sculpture, canoeing, travel abroad on house-swaps, old films. *Address:* 322 East River Road, Huntington, MA 01050, USA. *Telephone:* (413) 667-3906. *Fax:* (413) 667-3906. *E-mail:* newlo@compuserve.com (Home).

DOWN, Sir Alastair Frederick, Kt, OBE, MC, TD, CA; British oil executive; b. 23 July 1914, Kirkcaldy, Fife, Scotland; s. of Frederick Edward Down and Margaret Isobel Hutchison; m. Bunny Mellon 1947; two s. two d.; ed Marlborough Coll.; British Petroleum (then Anglo-Iranian Oil Co.) 1938–; Army Service 1940–45; with BP in Iran 1945–47, London 1947–54; Chief Rep. of BP, Canada 1954, later Pres. The British Petroleum Co. of Canada Ltd, BP Canada Ltd, BP Refinery Canada Ltd, BP Exploration Co. of Canada Ltd; Man. Dir The British Petroleum Co. Ltd 1962–75, Deputy Chair. 1969–75; Chair., Burmah Oil Co. Ltd 1975–83, Chief Exec. 1975–80; Chair. British-North American Research Asscn 1980–84, London American Energy, N.V., 1981–; Dir TRW Inc., Ohio 1977–, Scottish American Investment Co. Ltd, Edin. 1980–, Royal Bank of Canada, Montreal, 1981–; mem. Soc. of Chartered Accountants of Scotland; Chair. Council of Marlborough Coll.; Fellow, British Inst. of Man.; Kt Commdr Order of Orange Nassau 1946; Businessman of the Year Award 1980; Cadman Memorial Medal, Inst. of Petroleum 1981. *Leisure interests:* golf, fishing, shooting. *Address:* Greystones, 91 Newland, Sherborne, Dorset, DT9 3AG, England.

DOWNER, Alexander John Gosse, BA; Australian politician and fmr diplomatist; b. 9 Sept. 1951; s. of Sir Alexander Downer; m. Nicola Robinson 1978; one s. three d.; ed Geelong Grammar School, Victoria, Radley Coll. and Univ. of Newcastle-upon-Tyne, UK; mem. Australian Diplomatic Service 1976–81, Australian Mission to European Communities, Embassy to Belgium and Luxembourg 1977–80; Sr Foreign Affairs Rep., S Australia 1981; Political Adviser to Prime Minister 1982–83; Dir Australian Chamber of Commerce 1983–84; Liberal Mem. House of Reps for Mayo, S Australia 1984–; Shadow Minister for Arts, Heritage and Environment 1987, for Housing, Small Business and Customs 1988–89, for Trade and Trade Negotiations 1990–92, for Defence 1992–93; Fed. Shadow Treas. 1993–94; Leader Liberal Party 1994–95; Shadow Minister for Foreign Affairs 1995–96; Minister for Foreign Affairs 1996–. *Leisure interests:* reading, music, tennis, golf. *Address:* Department of Foreign Affairs and Trade, Locked Bag 40, QVT, Canberra, ACT 2600 (Office); 76 Mount Barker Road, Stirling, SA 5152, Australia (Home). *Telephone:* (2) 6277-7500 (Office). *Fax:* (2) 6273-4112 (Office).

DOWNES, Sir Edward (Thomas), Kt, CBE, FRCM; British conductor; b. 17 June 1924; studied with Herman Scherchen; professional conducting debut in UK with Carl Rosa Co.; conductor at Royal Opera House, Covent Garden 1952–69; Musical Dir Australian Opera 1972–76; Prin. Conductor, BBC Northern Symphony Orchestra, subsequently BBC Philharmonic Orchestra 1980–91; Chief Conductor, Netherlands Radio Orchestra until 1983; Assoc.

Music Dir and Prin. Conductor, Royal Opera House, Covent Garden 1991–; regular appearances abroad as guest conductor; Hon. D. Mus. (Birmingham) 1994; Evening Standard Opera Award for production of Verdi's Attila at Covent Garden 1991. *Address:* Royal Opera House, Covent Garden, London, WC2E 7QA, England. *Telephone:* (20) 7240-1200.

DOWNEY, Sir Gordon (Stanley), KCB, B.SC.ECON.; British public servant; b. 26 April 1928, London; s. of Stanley William and Winifred Downey; m. Jacqueline Goldsmith 1952; two d.; ed Tiffin's School, London School of Econs; comm. Royal Artillery 1946–48; Ministry of Works 1951; entered Treasury 1952; Asst Private Sec. to Chancellor of Exchequer 1955–57; Asst Sec. 1965, Under-Sec. 1972; Head of Cen. Unit., Treasury 1975; Deputy Sec. 1976; Deputy Head of Cen. Policy Review Staff (on secondment) 1978–81; Comptroller and Auditor-Gen. 1981–87; Special Adviser to Ernst and Young 1988–90; Complaints Commr for Securities Asscn 1989–90; Chair. Delegacy, King's Coll. Medical and Dental School 1989–91; Chair. Financial Intermediaries, Mans. and Brokers Regulatory Asscn (FIMBRA) 1990–93, Personal Investment Authority 1992–93; Parl. Commr for Standards 1995–98; Readers' Rep. The Independent 1990–95; mem. Bd, Business Performance Group, LSE 1989–94; Hon. Fellow King's Coll. London. *Leisure interests:* reading, tennis, visual arts. *Address:* 137 Whitehall Court, London, SW1A 2EP, England. *Telephone:* (20) 7321-0914.

DOWNEY, James, OC, PhD; Canadian professor of English and administrator; b. 20 April 1939; s. of Ernest and Mimy Ann (Andrews) Downey; m. Laura Ann Parsons 1964; one s. one d.; ed Memorial Univ. of Newfoundland, Univ. of London; Asst Prof. of English, Carleton Univ. 1966–69, Assoc. Prof. 1969–75, Prof. 1975–80, Chair. Dept of English 1972–75, Acting Dean, Faculty of Arts 1975, Dean 1976–78, Vice-Pres. (Acad.) 1978–80, Pres. pro tempore 1979; Pres. and Vice-Chancellor Univ. of New Brunswick 1980–90, Prof. of English 1980; Pres. and Vice-Chancellor Univ. of Waterloo 1993–99; Co-Chair. Comm. on Excellence in Educ. in NB 1991–92; Fellow, Univ. of Georgia 1985; Hon. D. Hum. Litt. (Maine) 1987; Hon. D.Litt (Newfoundland) 1991; Hon. LLD (New Brunswick) 1991, (Toronto) 1998. *Publications:* The Eighteenth Century Pulpit 1969, Fearful Joy 1974 (co-ed.). *Address:* c/o Office of the President, University of Waterloo, Waterloo, Ont., N2L 3G1; 272 Mary Street, Waterloo, Ont., N2J 1S6, Canada.

DOWNEY, Robert, Jr; American actor; b. 4 April 1965, New York; s. of Robert Downey and Elsie Ford; m. Deborah Falconer; one c.; sentenced to probation for possession of cocaine; imprisoned for further drugs offence breaching terms of probation Dec. 1997; released to serve 6 months at rehabilitation centre 1998; imprisoned again Aug. 1999, freed Aug. 2000, charged with drugs possession Dec. 2000. *Films include:* Pound (début) 1970, Firstborn, Weird Science, To Live and Die in LA, Back to School, The Pick-Up Artist, Johnny B. Good, True Believer, Chances Are, Air America, Soapdish, Chaplin (BAFTA Award), Heart and Souls, Short Cuts, The Last Party, Natural Born Killers, Only You, Restoration, Mussolini: The Untold Story (TV mini-series), Danger Zone, Home for the Holidays, Richard III, Bliss Vision 1997, The Gingerbread Man 1997, Two Girls and a Guy 1998, In Dreams 1999, Friends & Lovers 1999, Wonder Boys 2000. *Television includes:* Ally McBeal 2000, Black and White 2000.

DOWNIE, Leonard, Jr, MA; American newspaper editor; b. 1 May 1942, Cleveland, Ohio; s. of Leonard Downie Sr and Pearl Evenheimer; m. 1st Barbara Lindsey 1960 (divorced 1971); two s.; m. 2nd Geraldine Rebach 1971 (divorced 1997); one s. one d.; m. 3rd Janice Galin 1997; ed Ohio State Univ.; joined The Washington Post 1964, became investigative reporter in Washington, specializing in crime, housing and urban affairs; helped to supervise coverage of Watergate affair; Asst Man. Ed. Metropolitan News 1974–79; London Corresp. Washington Post 1979–82, Nat. Ed. 1982–84, Man. Ed. 1984–91; Exec. Ed. 1991–; Dir LA Times–Washington Post News Service 1991–, Int. Herald Tribune 1996–2002; Alicia Patterson Foundation Fellow 1971–72; Hon. LLD, Ohio State Univ.; two Washington-Baltimore Newspaper Guild Front Page Awards, American Bar Asscn Gavel Award for legal reporting, John Hancock Award for business and financial writing. *Publications:* Justice Denied 1971, Mortgage on America 1974, The New Muckrakers 1976, The News About the News (with Robert G. Kaiser) 1993. *Leisure interests:* ballet, classical music, travel, sports. *Address:* The Washington Post, 1150 15th Street, NW, Washington, DC 20071, USA (Office). *Telephone:* (202) 334-7512 (Office).

DOWNIE, Robert Silcock, MA, BPhil, FRSE, FRSA; British emer.professor of moral philosophy; b. 19 April 1933, Glasgow; s. of Robert M. Downie and Margaret M. Brown; m. Eileen Dorothea Flynn 1958; three d.; ed Glasgow Univ., Queen's Coll., Oxford; Tutor, Worcester Coll., Oxford 1958–59; Lecturer in Moral Philosophy, Glasgow Univ. 1959–68, Sr Lecturer 1968–69, Prof. 1969–, Emeritus Prof.; Visiting Prof. Syracuse Univ., USA 1963–64, Dalhousie Univ., Nova Scotia 1976, Durham Univ. 2000. *Publications:* Government Action and Morality 1964, Respect for Persons 1969, Roles and Values 1971, Education and Personal Relationships 1974, Caring and Curing 1980, Healthy Respect 1987, Health Promotion: Models and Values 1990, The Making of a Doctor 1992, The Healing Arts 1994, Francis Hutcheson: Selected Writings 1994, Palliative Care Ethics 1996, Medical Ethics 1996, Clinical Judgement 2000. *Leisure interest:* music. *Address:* Department of Philosophy, Glasgow University, Glasgow, G12 8QQ, Scotland. *Telephone:* (141) 339-8855 Ext. 4273. *Fax:* (141) 330-4112.

DOWNING, Wayne; American government official; fmr U.S. Army Officer, retd as four-star gen.; headed 1996 inquiry into bomb attack on U.S. airforce personnel in Saudi Arabia; Dir and Deputy Nat. Security Adviser, Office for Combating Terrorism Oct. 2001–. *Address:* National Security Council, Old Executive Office Bldg, 17th Street and Pennsylvania Ave., NW, Washington, DC 20504, USA (Office).

DOWSON, Duncan, CBE, FRS, FEng, FIMechE, FRSA, FCGI; British professor of mechanical engineering; b. 31 Aug. 1928, Kirbymoorside, York; s. of Wilfrid Dowson and Hannah Dowson; m. Mabel Strickland 1951; one s. (and one s. deceased); ed Lady Lumley's Grammar School, Pickering and Univ. of Leeds; Research Eng Sir W.G. Armstrong Whitworth Aircraft Co. 1953–54; lecturer in Mechanical Eng, Univ. of Leeds 1954, Sr Lecturer 1963–65, Reader 1965–66, Prof. of Eng Fluid Mechanics and Tribology 1966–93, now Prof. Emer. 1993–, Hon. Fellow and Research Prof. 1998–2001; Hon. Prof. Univ. of Hong Kong 1992–, Univ. of Bradford 1996–; External Prof. Univ. of Loughborough 2001–; Dir Inst. of Tribology, Dept of Mech. Eng 1967–87, Head, Dept of Mech. Eng 1987–93, Pro-Vice-Chancellor 1983–85, Dean for Int. Relations 1987–93; Pres. Inst. of Mechanical Engineers 1992–93; Chair. Yorks. Region, Royal Soc. of Arts 1992–97; Foreign mem. Royal Swedish Acad. of Eng Sciences; Life Fellow, American Soc. of Mechanical Eng (ASME); Hon. Fellow American Soc. of Lubrication Engs. (ASLE), Inst. of Mechanical Engineers; James Clayton Memorial Lecturer, Inst. of Mechanical Engineers 2000; Hon. DTech (Chalmers Univ. of Tech. Göteborg) 1979; Hon. DSc (Inst. Nat. des Sciences Appliquées, Lyon) 1991, (Liège) 1996; Hon. DEng (Waterloo, Canada) 2001; James Clayton Fund Prize, Thomas Hawksley Gold Medal, Tribology Gold Medal 1979, James Alfred Medal 1988, Sarton Medal (Belgium) 1998; recipient of numerous awards from Inst. of Mech. Eng, ASME, ASLE etc. *Publications:* Elastohydrodynamic Lubrication: the fundamentals of roller and gear lubrication (jtly) 1966, History of Tribology 1979, An Introduction to the Biomechanics of Joints and Joint Replacement (jtly) 1981, Ball Bearing Lubrication: The Elastohydrodynamics of Elliptical Contacts (jtly) 1981; papers in professional journals. *Leisure interest:* genealogy. *Address:* School of Mechanical Engineering, University of Leeds, LS2 9JT (Office); Ryedale, 23 Church Lane, Adel, Leeds, LS16 8DQ, England. *Telephone:* (113) 233-2153 (Office); (113) 267-8933. *Fax:* (133) 242-4611 (Office); (113) 281-7039 (Home). *E-mail:* d.dowson@leeds.ac.uk (Office); DDRyedale@aol.com (Home).

DOWSON, Graham Randall; British business executive; b. 13 Jan. 1923, Westcliff-on-Sea, Essex; s. of the late Cyril James Dowson and Dorothy Celia Dowson (née Foster); m. 1st Fay Valerie Weston 1954 (divorced 1974); two d.; m. 2nd Denise Joy Shurman 1975; ed City of London School, Ecole Alpina, Switzerland; war service 1939–45, Pilot, Squadron Leader RAF 1941–46; Sales, US Steel Corpn (Columbia Steel), LA 1946–49; Mid-South Network (MBS), Radio USA 1949–52; Dir A. C. Nielsen Co., Oxford 1953–58, Southern TV Ltd, London 1958–74, Paravision (UK) Ltd 1988–90, Grovewood Securities PLC 1990–91; Dir Rank Org. 1960, Deputy Chief Exec. 1972, Chief Exec. 1974–75; Partner Graham Dowson and Assocs 1975–; Chair. Mooloya Investments 1975–78, Erskine House Investments 1975–83, Pincus Vidler Arthur Fitzgerald 1979–83, Dowson Shurman (fmrly Dowson Salisbury Assocs Ltd) 1988–, Nash Industries PLC 1988–89; Chair. and Chief Exec., Teltech Marketing Services Ltd 1984–87; Dir Carron Holdings Ltd 1976–, Carron Investments Ltd 1976–, Nimslo Ltd 1979–87 (Dir 1978), PPR Securities Ltd 1976–82, RCO Holdings PLC 1979–, Filmbond PLC 1985–88, Fairhaven Int. 1988–95; Deputy Chair. Nimslo Int. Ltd, Nimslo European Holdings Ltd, Nimslo Corpn 1979–88, Nat. Playing Fields Assscn 1974–; Jt Pres. British Section, European League for Econ. Co-operation 1972–83, Jt Pres. 1983; Chair. Migraine Trust 1985–88, Premier Speakers 1987–; mem. Court of Common Council, Corpn of London 1993–95. *Leisure interest:* sailing. *Address:* 193 Cromwell Tower, Barbican, London, EC2Y 8DD, England. *Telephone:* (20) 7221-6420 (Office); (20) 7588-0396 (Home). *Fax:* (20) 7221-6312 (Office); (20) 7638-4112 (Home). *E-mail:* snic@gdowson.fsnet.co.uk (Home).

DOWSON, Sir Philip (Manning), Kt, CBE, PPRA, RIBA; British architect; b. 16 Aug. 1924, Johannesburg, S Africa; s. of Robert Dowson and Ina Cowen; m. Sarah Crewdson 1950; one s. two d.; ed Gresham's School, Univ. Coll., Oxford, Clare Coll., Cambridge; Lt RDVR 1943–47; Cambridge 1947–50; Architectural Assscn 1950–53; joined Ove Arup & Partners 1953; Founder, Architectural Partner, Arup Assocs 1963; Sr Partner, Ove Arup Partnership 1969–90, Consultant 1990–; Pres. Royal Acad. of Arts 1993–99; mem. Royal Fine Art Comm. 1971–97, Craft Advisory Cttee 1972–75; Hon. FAIA; Hon. Fellow, Duncan of Jordanstone Coll. of Art 1985, RCA 1989, Clare Coll., Cambridge 1992; Gov. St Martin's School of Art 1975–80; Trustee, Thomas Cubitt Trust 1978–98, Royal Botanic Gardens, Kew 1983–95, The Armouries, HM Tower of London 1984–89, Nat. Portrait Gallery 1993–99, Coram Foundation 1993–99; Hon. Dr of Art (De Montfort Univ.) 2000; Royal Gold Medal for Architecture 1981. *Works include:* urban and univ. devt and coll. bldgs: Oxford, Cambridge, Birmingham, Leicester; housing; schools; new uses for old bldgs; bldgs for music and industrial and office devts. *Publications:* articles in technical press. *Leisure interest:* sailing. *Address:* c/o Royal Academy of Arts, Burlington House, Piccadilly, London, W1V 0DS, England.

DOYLE, Brian André, BA, LLB; Zambian (b. British) judge; b. 10 May 1911, Moulmein, Burma; m. Nora Slattery 1937 (died 1992); one s. one d.; ed Douai School and Trinity Coll., Dublin; Magistrate, Trinidad and Tobago 1937; Resident Magistrate Uganda 1942; Solicitor-Gen. Fiji 1948; Attorney-Gen.

1949; Attorney-Gen. N Rhodesia 1956, Attorney-Gen. and Minister of Legal Affairs 1959–65; Justice of Appeal, Zambia 1965; Chief Justice of Zambia 1969–75; Dir Law Devt Comm. 1975–79; Judge Botswana Court of Appeal 1973–79, 1988–91; Chair. Delimitation Comm., Botswana 1981–82. *Leisure interests:* fishing, golf. *Address:* 26 Choumert Square, Peckham Rye, London, SE15 4RE, England.

DOYLE, Frederick Bernard, BSc, MBA, CEng, FICE, FIWEM, CIM; British civil engineer; b. 17 July 1940, Manchester; s. of James Hopkinson and Hilda Mary (née Spotsworth) Doyle; m. Ann Weston 1963; two s. one d.; ed St Bede's Coll., Manchester, Victoria Univ. of Manchester, Harvard Business School; Resident Civil Engineer, British Rail 1961–65; Man. Consultant, Arthur D. Little Inc. 1967–72; with Booker McConnell Ltd 1973–81, Sec. to Exec. Cttee 1973, Dir Eng Div. 1974, Chair. Gen. Eng Div. 1976, Chair. and Chief Exec. Booker McConnell Eng Ltd 1979, Dir of parent co. 1979; Chief Exec. Social Democratic Party 1981–83, Welsh Water Authority 1983–87; Dir Public Sector Operations, MSL Int. 1988–90, Dir 1994–96, Man Dir 1997–99; Man. Dir Hamptons 1990–92; Gen. Man. Bristol and West Bldg Soc. 1992–94; Head of Public Sector Practice, Hoggett Bowers Exec. Search and Selection 1999–2000; Dir KPMG Search and Selection 2001–; crew member Times Clipper Round the World Yacht Race 2000; NATO Fellowship 1965. *Leisure interests:* walking, theatre, reading, travel, sailing. *Address:* KPMG Search & Selection, 2 Cornwall Street, Birmingham, B3 2DL (Office); 38A West Road, Bromsgrove, Worcs., B60 2NQ, England (Home). *Telephone:* (121) 232-3000 (Office); (1527) 873565 (Home). *Fax:* (121) 232-3609 (Office). *E-mail:* bernard.doyle@kpmg.co.uk (Office); aandbdoyle@aol.com (Home). *Website:* www.kpmg.co.uk (Office).

DOYLE, James Edward, JD; American state official and lawyer; b. 23 Nov. 1945, Washington; s.of James E. Doyle and Ruth Doyle (née Bachhuber); m. Jessica Laird 1966; two s.; ed Sanford Univ., Univ. of Wis., Harvard Univ.; volunteer Peace Corps, Tunisia 1967–69; Attorney DNA Legal Services, Ariz. 1972–75; Partner Jacobs & Doyle, Madison, Wis. 1975–77; Dist Attorney Dane Co., Madison 1977–83; Partner Doyle & Ritz, Madison 1983–90; Counsel Lawton & Cates, Madison 1990–91; Attorney-Gen. State of Wis. 1991–2002; Gov. of Wis. 2002–; mem. ABA, Wis. Bar Assscn, 7th Circuit Bar Assscn. *Address:* Office of the Governor, 115 East State Capitol, Madison, WI 53702, USA (Office).

DOYLE, Noreen, MBA; American/Irish banker; b. 1949; ed Coll. of Mount St Vincent, Tuck School of Business, Dartmouth Coll.; began career with Morgan Guaranty Trust; joined Bankers Trust 1974, Client Man., New York and Houston, Div. Man. for multinat. cos, New York, Man. Dir for distribution of structured financings, New York, responsible for European affairs, London 1990–92; joined EBRD and set up syndication business 1992, responsible for credit and market risks 1997–2001, First Vice-Pres. and Head of Banking 2001–, mem. Exec. Cttee. *Address:* c/o EBRD, One Exchange Square, London, EC2A 2EH, England (Office). *Website:* www.ebrd.com (Office).

DOYLE, Roddy; Irish writer; b. 1958, Dublin; m. Bellinda Doyle; two s. *Publications:* The Commitments 1987 (film 1991), The Snapper 1990 (filmed 1992), The Van 1991, Paddy Clarke Ha Ha Ha (Booker Prize) 1993, The Woman Who Walked into Doors 1996, A Star Called Henry 1999, The Giggler Treatment 2000, Rory and Ita 2002. *Address:* c/o Patti Kelly, Viking Books, 375 Hudson Street, New York, NY 10014, USA (Office).

DRABBLE, Margaret, CBE; British author; b. 5 June 1939, Sheffield; d. of the late J. F. Drabble and Kathleen (née Bloor) Drabble; sister of A. S. Byatt; m. 1st Clive Swift 1960 (divorced 1975); two s. one d.; m. 2nd Michael Holroyd (q.v.) 1982; ed Newnham Coll., Cambridge; Chair., Nat. Book League 1980–82; Ed. The Oxford Companion to English Literature 1979–2000; Vice-Patron, Child Psychotherapy Trust 1987–; Hon. mem. American Acad. of Arts and Letters 2002; Hon. Fellow, Sheffield City Polytechnic 1989; Hon. DLitt (Sheffield) 1976, (Bradford) 1988, (Hull) 1992; E. M. Forster Award, American Acad. of Arts and Letters 1973. *Publications:* A Summer Bird-Cage 1963, The Garrick Year 1964, The Millstone 1965 (John Llewelyn Rhys Memorial Prize 1966), Jerusalem the Golden 1967, The Waterfall 1969, The Needle's Eye 1972, Arnold Bennett: A Biography 1974, The Realms of Gold 1975, The Genius of Thomas Hardy (ed.) 1976, The Ice Age 1977, For Queen and Country: Britain in the Victorian Age 1978, A Writer's Britain 1979, The Middle Ground (novel) 1980, The Oxford Companion to English Literature (ed.) 1985, 2000, The Radiant Way (novel) 1987, A Natural Curiosity 1989, Safe as Houses 1990, The Gates of Ivory 1991, Angus Wilson: A Biography 1995, The Witch of Exmoor (novel) 1996, The Peppered Moth (novel) 2001, The Seven Sisters (novel) 2002. *Leisure interests:* walking and talking. *Address:* c/o PFD, Drury House, 34-43 Russell Street, London, WC2B 5HA, England. *Telephone:* (20) 7344-1000.

DRACH, Ivan Fyodorovich; Ukrainian politician and writer; b. 17 Oct. 1936, Telizhentsy, Kiev Oblast; m. Mariya Drach; one s. one d.; ed Univ. of Kiev, Moscow State Univ.; worked as school teacher; Corresp. for Literaturnaya Ukraina and Witczyna newspapers 1961–87; scriptwriter Dovzheniev Studio 1964–87; mem. Bd, Sec. Union of Ukrainian Writers 1989–92; joined CP 1959, resgnd 1990; Founder mem. Narodny Rukh (Ukrainian nationalist opposition Movt), Leader, then co-Chair. 1989–92; Chair. Bd Ukraina Soc. 1992–; mem. Ukrainian Supreme Soviet 1990–; mem. Ukrainian World Co-ordination Council 1992–99; Chair. State Cttee of Information Policy, TV and Radio 2001; Ukrainian State Prize 1976, USSR State Prize 1983, Yaroslav Mudry Order 1996. *Publications include:* Sun Flower 1962,

Ballads of Everyday Life 1967, I Come to You 1970, Poems 1972, The Kievan Sky 1976, The Sun and the Word (poetry) 1978, Green Gates 1980, Dramatic Poems 1982, Grigory Skovoroda 1984, Temple of Sun 1988. *Address:* Gorky str. 18, Apt. 7, 252005 Kiev, Ukraine. *Telephone:* (44) 228-87-69.

DRACHEVSKY, Leonid Vadimovich; Russian diplomatist and politician; b. 5 April 1942, Alma-Ata; m.; three c.; ed Mendeleyev Inst. of Chemical Tech., Diplomatic Acad. Ministry of Foreign Affairs; Deputy Chair. State Cttee of Sport, RSFSR 1986–90, First Deputy Chair. Cttee of Sport, USSR 1990–91; on staff Ministry of Foreign Affairs since 1992; Consul (rank of Counsellor) Gen. Consulate of Russian Fed., Barcelona, Spain 1992; Head of Div., Dir Dept on Problems of CIS 1993–94; Dir First Dept of CIS Countries 1994–96; Amb. to Poland 1996–98; Deputy Minister of Foreign Affairs 1998–99; Minister for Relations with CIS Cos. 1999–2000; Plenipotentiary Rep. of Russian Pres. to Siberian Fed. Dist 2000–. *Address:* Office of the Plenipotentiary Representative of the President, Derzhavina str. 18, 630091 Novosibirsk, Russia. *Telephone:* (3832) 21-95-31 (Novosibirsk), (095) 206-72-71 (Moscow) (Office). *Fax:* (3832) 17-06-31 (Office). *E-mail:* sfo@sfo.nso.ru (Office). *Website:* www .sfo.nsk.su (Office).

DRAGHI, Mario; Italian civil servant, European Union official and international banker; Exec. Dir IBRD 1984–90; Adviser to Bank of Italy 1990; Prof. of Econs Florence Univ., Italy; Dir-Gen. Ministry of the Treasury and of the Budget 1991–2001; mem. Econ. and Financial Cttee EEC (now EU) 1991– (Chair. 2000–); Dir ENI –2001; Vice-Chair. Goldman Sachs Int., London, UK Jan. 2002–; mem. Group of Seven deputies 1991–; mem. Bd of Trustees, Princeton Inst. for Advanced Study. *Address:* Goldman Sachs International, Peterborough Court, 133 Fleet Street, London, EC4A 2BB, England (Office). *Telephone:* (20) 7774-1000. *Website:* www.gs.com.

DRAGILA, Stacy; American pole vaulter; b. Stacy Mikaelson, 25 March 1971, Auburn, CA; m. Brent Dragila; ed Placer High School, Yuba Community Coll., Idaho State Univ.; first and only women's pole vault world champion; US Outdoor Champion 1996, 1997, 1999, 2000, 2001, 2002; US Indoor Champion 1996, 1997, 1998, 1999, 2000, 2001; World Indoor Champion 1997; World Champion 1999, 2001; gold medallist Olympic Games 2000; Goodwill Games and IAAF Grand Prix Final Champion 2001; Asst Coach Idaho State Univ. track team; Jesse Owens Award 2000, 2001, IAAF Women's Athlete of the Year 2001. *Address:* c/o USA Track and Field, 1 RCA Dome, Suite 140, Indianapolis, IN 46225, USA. *Website:* www.stacydragila.com (Office).

DRAKE, Frank Donald, B.ENG.PHYS., MA, PhD; American astronomer; b. 28 May 1930, Chicago; s. of Richard C. Drake and Winifred Thompson Drake; m. 1st Elizabeth B. Bell 1953 (divorced 1977); three s.; m. 2nd Amahl Shakhashiri 1978; two d.; ed Cornell and Harvard Univs.; USN 1952–55; Harvard Radio Astronomy Project 1955–58; Ewen-Knight Corpn 1957–58; Scientist, Head Scientific Services and Telescope Operations on Nat. Radio Astron. Observatory 1958–63; Chief, Lunar and Planetary Science Section, Jet Propulsion Laboratory 1963–64; Prof. of Astronomy, Cornell Univ. 1964–85, Goldwin Smith Prof. of Astronomy 1976–85; Dir Arecibo Ionospheric Observatory 1966–68; Assoc. Dir Center for Radiophysics and Space Research, Cornell Univ. 1967–75; Chair. Dept of Astronomy, Cornell Univ. 1968–71; Dir Nat. Astronomy and Ionosphere Center 1971–81; Prof. of Astronomy, Univ. of Calif., Santa Cruz 1984–95, Prof. Emer. 1995–, Dean Div. of Natural Sciences 1984–88; Pres. Astronomical Soc. of the Pacific 1988–90; mem. AAAS, NAS 1972, The Explorers Club, Advisory Bd The World Book Encyclopedia, Int. Astronomical Union, Int. Scientific Radio Union, American Astronomical Soc.; Fellow, American Acad. of Arts and Sciences; Pres. SETI Inst. 1984–2000, Chair. Bd of Trustees 2000–. *Publications:* Intelligent Life in Space 1962, Murmurs of Earth 1979, (with Dava Sobel) Is Anyone Out There? 1992; and over 135 papers and articles. *Leisure interests:* snorkelling, horticulture, lapidary. *Address:* SETI Institute, 2035 Landings Drive, Mountain View, CA 94043, USA (Office). *Telephone:* (650) 961-6633 (Office). *Fax:* (650) 961-7099 (Office). *E-mail:* drake@seti.org (Office).

DRAPER, Kenneth, MA, RA; British painter and sculptor; b. 19 Feb. 1944, Killamarsh, Sheffield; s. of Albert Draper and Dorothy Rosa Anne Lamb; m. 1st Heather Lieven Beste 1965 (divorced); one s.; m. 2nd Nadiya Jinnah 1972 (divorced); partner Jean Macalpine; ed Chesterfield Coll. of Art, Kingston School of Art, RCA; solo exhbns. include Redfern Gallery, London 1969, Warwick Arts Trust, London 1981, Galerie Nouvelles Images, Den Haag, Holland 1984, Austin Desmond, London 1991, Adelson Gallery, New York 1993, Friends Room, RA 1993, Hart Gallery, London 1994, 1996, 1998, Peter Bartlow Gallery, Chicago 1995; *group exhbns. include:* British Sculptors 1972, RA 1972, Silver Jubilee Exhbn Contemporary British Sculpture, Battersea Park 1977, The British Art Show, Mappin, Sheffield 1980, British Sculpture in the Twentieth Century, Whitechapel Art Gallery 1981; work in public collections of Arts Council of GB, Contemporary Arts Soc., Courtauld Inst., London, Ashmolean Museum, Oxford, Usher Gallery, Lincoln; Mark Rothko Memorial Award 1971. *Leisure interests:* reading, chess, sport, travel. *Address:* Carrer D'es Port 2, Apto. 6, 07720 Es Castell, Minorca, Balearic Is., Spain. *Telephone:* (971) 353457. *Fax:* (971) 353457.

DRAPER, William Henry, III, MBA; American government official; b. 1 Jan. 1928, White Plains, NY; s. of William Henry Draper and Katherine Baum; m. Phyllis Culbertson 1953; one s. two d.; ed Yale and Harvard Univs; with Inland Steel Co., Chicago 1954–59; Draper, Gaither & Anderson, Palo Alto, Calif. 1959–62; Pres. Draper & Johnson Investment Co. Palo Alto 1962–65; founder, gen. partner, Sutter Hill Capital Co., Palo Alto 1965–70, Sutter Hill Ventures, Palo Alto 1970–81; Pres., Chair. Export-Import Bank US, Washington, DC 1981–86; Admin., CEO UNDP 1986–93; Man. Dir Draper Int., San Francisco 1994–; numerous directorships etc.; Trustee Yale Univ. 1991–98, George Bush Library Foundation 1993–; Chair. World Affairs Council, N Calif. 2000–02; Republican; Hon. LLD (Southeastern Univ.). *Address:* Draper Richards, 50 California Street, Suite 2925, San Francisco, CA 94111-4726 (Office); 91 Tallwood Court, Atherton, CA 94027-6431, USA (Home). *E-mail:* bill@draperrichards.com.

DRAŠKOVIĆ, Vuk; Serbia and Montenegro (Serbian) politician, journalist and writer; b. 29 Nov. 1946, Mezha Banat Region, Vojvodina; m. Danika Drašković (née Bošković); ed Belgrade Univ.; moved to Herzegovina; as student took part in demonstrations 1968; mem. staff Telegraph Agency of Yugoslavia TANJUG 1969–78, worked in Lusaka, Zambia; dismissed from post of correspondent for disinformation 1978; Adviser Council of Trade Unions of Yugoslavia 1978–80; Ed. Rad (newspaper) 1980–85; freelance journalist and writer 1985–; Founder and Pres. Serbian Renewal Movt (SRM) 1990–; candidate for Presidency of Yugoslavia 1990, 1992, of Serbia 1997; mem. Nat. Ass.; detained, released from detention July 1993; leader of mass protests against Pres. Milošević from Nov. 1996; Vice-Prime Minister of Yugoslavia 1998–99 (resgnd). *Publications:* 8 books, including novels: Judge, Knife, Prayer 1, Prayer 2, Russian Consul, Night of the General, Polemics, Answers; numerous articles and collections of articles. *Address:* Srpski pokret obnove, Belgrade, Serbia and Montenegro. *Telephone:* (11) 635281. *Fax:* (11) 628170. *Website:* www,spo.org.yu.

DRAVINS, Dainis, PhD; Swedish professor of astronomy; b. 10 Sept. 1949, Lund; m. Christina (née Hedqvist) Dravins 1982; one s.; ed Lund and Uppsala Univs. and Calif. Inst. of Tech., Calif., USA; Prof. of Astronomy, Lund Univ. 1984–; mem. Royal Swedish Acad. of Sciences 1987; Foreign mem. Latvian Acad. of Sciences 1992. *Publications:* numerous articles on astronomy. *Address:* Lund Observatory, Box 43, 22100 Lund, Sweden. *Telephone:* (46) 2227297; (46) 2227000. *Fax:* (46) 2224614 (Office). *E-mail:* dainis@astro.lu.se (Office). *Website:* www.astro.lu.se/~dainis (Office).

DRAY, William Herbert, MA, DPhil, LLD, FRSC; Canadian professor of philosophy; b. 23 June 1921, Montreal, PQ; s. of William J. Dray and Florence E. Jones; m. Doris K. Best 1943; one s. one d.; ed Univ. of Toronto and Balliol and Nuffield Colls. Oxford; RCAF 1941–46, Active Reserve (Wing Commdr, retd) 1956–66; lecturer in Philosophy, Univ. of Toronto 1953–55, Asst Prof. to Prof. 1955–68; Prof. Trent Univ. 1968–76, Chair. Dept of Philosophy 1968–73; Prof. of Philosophy with cross-appt. to History, Univ. of Ottawa 1976–86, Prof. Emer. 1986–; visiting appts. at Ohio State Univ. 1959, Case Inst. 1966, Harvard Univ. 1967, 1973, Stanford Univ. 1962, Duke Univ. 1973; ACLS Fellowship 1960–61, Canada Council Fellowship 1971, 1978, Killam Research Fellowship 1980–81, Nat. Humanities Center Fellowship 1983–84; Molson Prize of the Canada Council 1986. *Publications:* Laws and Explanation in History 1957, Philosophy of History 1964, 1993, Philosophical Analysis and History (ed.) 1966, Perspectives on History 1980, Substance and Form in History (ed., with L. Pompa) 1981, La philosophie de l'histoire et la pratique historienne d'aujourd'hui (ed. with D. Carr et al.) 1982, On History and Philosophers of History 1989, History as Re-enactment 1995, The Principles of History: R. G. Collingwood (ed. with W. J. van der Dussen) 1999. *Address:* Apt. 818, 32 Clarissa Drive, Richmond Hill, Ont., L4C 9R7, Canada. *Telephone:* (905) 883-1995. *E-mail:* whdray@aol.com (Home).

DREIFUSS, Ruth; Swiss politician; b. 9 Jan. 1940, St Gall; ed Ecole d'Etudes Sociales, Geneva and Univ. of Geneva; Sec. 1958–59; Ed. Coopération, Swiss Union of Cooperatives, Basle 1961–64; Asst Sociologist, Centre Psycho-Social Universitaire, Geneva 1965–68; Asst in Nat. Accounting, Faculty of Econ. and Social Sciences, Univ. of Geneva 1970–72; civil servant, Swiss Devt Agency Fed. Ministry of Foreign Affairs 1972–81; Sec. Swiss Fed. of Trade Unions 1981–93; elected to Swiss Fed. Council March 1993, Vice-Pres. 1998; Head, Fed. Dept of Home Affairs April 1993–; Pres. of Switzerland 1999; Dr. hc (Haifa) 1999, (Jerusalem) 2000. *Address:* Federal Department of Home Affairs, Bundeshaus, Inselgasse, 3003 Berne, Switzerland (Office). *Telephone:* (31) 3228002 (Office). *Fax:* (31) 3227901 (Office). *E-mail:* info@gs-edi .admin.ch (Office). *Website:* www.edi.admin.ch (Office).

DRELL, Sidney David; American professor of physics; b. 13 Sept. 1926, Atlantic City, NJ; s. of Tulla and Rose White Drell; m. Harriet Stainback 1952; one s. two d.; ed Princeton Univ. and Univ. of Illinois; Research Assoc. Univ. of Illinois 1949–50; Physics Instructor Stanford Univ. 1950–52; Research Assoc. MIT 1952–53, Asst Prof. 1953–56; Assoc. Prof. Stanford Univ. 1956–60, Prof. of Physics 1960–63, Lewis M. Terman Prof. and Fellow 1979–84; Prof. Stanford Linear Accelerator Center 1963–, Deputy Dir 1969–98, Exec. Head of Theoretical Physics 1969–86; Prof. Emer. 1998–; Sr Fellow Hoover Inst. 1998–; Adjunct Prof. Dept of Eng and Public Policy, Carnegie Mellon Univ. 1989–96; Visiting Scientist and Guggenheim Fellow, CERN 1961–62; Visiting Prof. and Loeb Lecturer, Harvard Univ. 1962, 1970; Consultant to Los Alamos Scientific Lab. 1956–, Office of Science and Tech., Exec. Office of the Pres. 1960–73; consultant Arms Control and Disarmament Agency 1969–81, Office of Tech. Assessment, US Congress 1975–91, Office of Science and Tech. Policy 1977–82, Nat. Security Council 1973–81; Consultant, Senate Select Cttee on Intelligence 1978–83; Co-Dir Stanford Centre for Int. Security and Arms Control 1984–89; consultant House Armed Services Cttee 1990–91, Senate Select Cttee on Intelligence 1990–93; Chair. Int. Advisory Bd Inst. of Global Conflict and Cooperation, Univ. of Calif. 1990–93; mem. High Energy Physics

Advisory Panel to DOE 1974–86 (Chair. 1974–82); mem. JASON Div. (Mitre Corpn) 1960–; mem. Bd The Arms Control Asscn, Washington 1971–93; mem. Council on Foreign Relations 1980–; mem. Advisory Cttee MIT Physics Dept 1974–90; mem. Pres.'s Science Advisory Cttee 1966–70; Visiting Schrodinger Prof., Theoretical Physics, Univ. of Vienna 1975; mem. Bd of Trustees, Inst. for Advanced Study, Princeton, NJ 1974–83; Bd Gov. Weizmann Inst. of Science, Rehovoth, Israel 1970–; Bd Dir Annual Reviews Inc. 1976–97; mem. numerous advisory cttees and editorial bds including MIT Lincoln Lab. Advisory Bd 1985–90, Aspen Strategy Group 1984–91, Carnegie Comm. on Science, Tech. and Govt 1988–93, Scientific and Academic Advisory Cttee on Nat. Labs, Univ. of Calif. 1988–92, Pres.'s Foreign Intelligence Advisory Bd 1993–, Comm. on Maintaining US Nuclear Weapons Expertise 1999; Chair. Pres.'s Council on the Nat. Labs 1992–99; Fellow American Physical Soc. (Pres. 1986); mem. NAS, American Acad. of Arts and Sciences, American Philosophical Soc. 1987–, Academia Europaea; Guggenheim Fellow, Rome 1972; Richtmeyer Memorial Lecturer to American Asscn of Physics Teachers 1978; Visiting Fellow, All Souls Coll., Oxford Univ. 1979; Danz Lecturer, Univ. of Washington 1983; I. I. Rabi Visiting Prof. Columbia Univ. 1984; Hans Bethe Lecturer, Cornell Univ. 1988, Brickwedde Lecturer, Johns Hopkins Univ.; Hon. DSc (Univ. of Ill., Chicago Circle) 1981; E. O. Lawrence Memorial Award 1972, Univ. of Ill. Alumni Award for Distinguished Service in Eng 1973, Leo Szilard Award for Physics in the Public Interest 1980, MacArthur Fellowship Award 1984–89, Univ. of Ill. Achievement Award 1988, Hilliard Roderick Prize in Science, Arms Control and Int. Security (AAAS) 1993, Co-recipient Ettore Majorana-Erice Science for Peace Prize 1994, Woodrow Wilson Award for Distinguished Achievement in the Nation's Service, Princeton Univ. 1994, Gian Carlo Wick Commemorative Award ICSC World Lab. 1996, Distinguished Assoc. Award of US Dept of Environment 1997, I. Ya. Pomeranchuk Prize (Moscow) 1998, Linus Pauling Lecturer and Medallist, Stanford Univ. 1999–2000, Presidential Medal, Univ. of Calif. 2000, one of 10 scientists honoured by U.S. Reconnaissance Office as Founders of National Reconnaissance as a Space Discipline 2000, Enrico Fermi Award 2000, Nat. Intelligence Distinguished Service Medal 2001, William O. Baker Award, Security Affairs Support Asscn 2001, Heinz R. Pagels Human Rights of Scientists Award 2001. *Publications:* Relativistic Quantum Mechanics, Relativistic Quantum Fields (both with J. D. Bjorken) and numerous papers on theoretical physics; Facing the Threat of Nuclear Weapons 1983 (updated 1989), The Reagan Strategic Defense Initiative: A Technical, Political and Arms Control Assessment (co-author) 1984, Sidney Drell on Arms Control 1988, Reducing Nuclear Danger (co-author) 1993, In the Shadow of the Bomb: Physics and Arms Control 1993, The New Terror: Facing the Threat of Biological and Chemical Weapons (co-ed.) 1999. *Leisure interests:* music, reading. *Address:* Stanford Linear Accelerator Center, 2575 Sand Hill Road, Mail Stop 80, Menlo Park, CA 94025 (Office); 570 Alvarado Row, Stanford, CA 94305, USA (Home). *Telephone:* (650) 926-2664 (Office). *Fax:* (650) 926-4500 (Office). *E-mail:* drell@slac.stanford.edu (Office).

DRENTH, Pieter Johan Diederik, PhD; Netherlands professor of work and organizational psychology and psychodiagnostics; b. 8 March 1935, Appelscha; s. of Gerrit Drenth and Froukje Wouda; m. Maria Annetta Elizabeth de Boer 1959; three s.; ed Vrije Univ., Amsterdam; served in Royal Dutch Navy 1955–60; Research Fellow Social Science Research Div., Standard Oil Co., New York 1960–61; Sr lecturer in Psychometrics and Industrial Psychology, Vrije Univ., Amsterdam 1962–67, Prof. of Work and Organizational Psychology and Psychodiagnostics 1967–; Vice-Chancellor 1983–87; Dean Faculty of Psychology and Educ. 1998–2001; Visiting Prof. Washington Univ. St Louis 1966, Univ. of Washington, Seattle 1977; Pres. Royal Netherlands Acad. of Arts and Sciences 1990–96, ALLEA (European Network of Acads. of Science) 2000–; mem. Royal Netherlands Acad. of Arts and Sciences 1980; mem. Supervisory Bd Shell-Nederland B.V.; Dr. hc (Ghent) 1980, (Paris V) 1996; Heymans Award for Outstanding Contrib. to Psychology 1986, Kt Order of the Lion 1991, Aristotle award for outstanding contribs. to European psychology 1995, Commdr Order of Oranje Nassau 1996. *Publications:* Mental Tests and Cultural Adaptation (Ed.) 1972, Inleiding in de testtheorie 1976, Decisions in Organizations 1988, Advances in Organizational Psychology (Ed.) 1988, New Handbook Work and Organizational Psychology (Ed.) 1989, Testtheorie 1990, Gardening in Science 1996, numerous scientific papers and psychological tests. *Leisure interests:* cycling, music, literature. *Address:* Vrije Universiteit, Faculty of Psychology and Education, V.d. Boechorststraat 1, 1081 BT Amsterdam; Royal Netherlands Academy of Arts and Sciences, Kloveniersburgswal 27-29, 1000 GC Amsterdam (Office); Pekkendam 6, 1081 HR Amsterdam, Netherlands (Home). *Telephone:* (20) 5510754 (Office); (20) 6449109 (Home). *Fax:* (20) 6447938 (Home); (20) 6204941. *E-mail:* president@allea.org (Office); pjdd@xs4all.nl (Home).

DRESE, Claus Helmut, DPhil; German theatre director; b. 25 Dec. 1922, Aachen; s. of Karl Drese and Helene Drese; m. Helga Lautz 1950; two c.; studied German studies, philosophy and history in Cologne, Bonn and Marburg; Theatre Literary Man., Mannheim 1952–59; Theatre Dir, Heidelberg 1959–62, Wiesbaden 1962–68, Cologne 1968–75, Zurich 1975–; Dir Vienna State Opera 1986–91. *Publications:* various contribs. to newspapers, radio and television.

DRETSKE, Frederick Irwin, PhD; American philosopher; b. 9 Dec. 1932, Ill.; s. of Hattie Walschlager and Frederick E Dretske; m. 1st Virginia Lord 1954; m. 2nd Brenda Peters 1965; m. 3rd Judith Fortson 1988; one s. one d.; ed Purdue Univ., Univ. of Minnesota; Asst Prof. to Prof., Univ. of Wis. 1960–90; Prof. of Philosophy Stanford Univ. 1990–98, Sr Research Scholar, Duke Univ. 1999–; American Council of Learned Socs. Fellowship 1965, Nat. Endowment for the Humanities Fellowships 1975, 1985, Fellow Center for Advanced Study in the Behavioral Sciences Stanford Univ. 1988; Pres. American Philosophical Asscn (Cen. Div.) 1984–85. *Publications:* Seeing and Knowing 1969, Knowledge and the Flow of Information 1981, Explaining Behavior 1988, Naturalizing the Mind 1995, Perception, Knowledge and Belief 2000. *Leisure interests:* carpentry, travel. *Address:* 1410 Bivins Street, Durham, NC 27707, USA (Home). *Telephone:* (919) 490-4641 (Home). *Fax:* (919) 401-0207 (Home). *E-mail:* fred.dretske@mindspring.com (Home).

DREW, John Sydney Neville, MA, AM, MBA; British academic; b. 7 Oct. 1936, Hornchurch; s. of late John Drew and Kathleen Wright; m. Rebecca Usher 1962; two s. one d.; ed King Edward's School, Birmingham, St John's Coll. Oxford, Tufts Univ. and London Business School; HM Diplomatic Service 1960–73; Dir of Marketing and Exec. Programmes, London Business School 1973–79; Dir of Corp. Affairs, Rank Xerox 1979–84; Dir of European Affairs, Touche Ross Int. 1984–86; Head, UK Offices, Comm. of EC 1987–93; Dir Durham Inst., Visiting Prof. of European Business, Durham Univ. 1997–, now Chair. Durham Inst.; Dir Europa Times 1993–94, Change Group Int. 1996–; Deputy Chair. Enterprise Support Group 1993–94; Pres. Inst. of Linguists 1993–99, EUROTAS 1998–, Hon. Fellow; Assoc. Fellow, Templeton Coll. Oxford 1982–86; Visiting Prof. Imperial Coll. London 1987–91, Open Univ. 1992–; Hon. Ed. European Business Journal 1987–2002; Hon. MBA (Northumbria) 1991. *Publications:* Doing Business in the European Community 1979, Networking in Organizations 1986, Developing an Active Company Approach to the European Market 1988, Readings in International Enterprise (Ed.) 1995; articles on European integration and personal devt. *Leisure interests:* travel, golf, personal and inner devt. *Address:* 49 The Ridgeway, London, NW11 8QP, England (Home). *Telephone:* (20) 8455-5054 (Office). *Fax:* (20) 8455-4516 (Office). *E-mail:* profdrew@eurotas.org (Office).

DREWS, Juergen, MD; German research director and physician; b. 16 Aug. 1933, Berlin; s. of Walter Drew and Lotte Grohnert; m. Dr. Helga Eberlein 1963; three d.; ed Berlin, Innsbruck, Heidelberg and Yale Univs.; Prof. of Medicine, Univ. of Heidelberg 1973–; Head, Chemotherapy Section, Sandoz Research Inst., Vienna 1976–79, Head, Sandoz Research Inst. 1979–82, Int. Pharmaceutical R&D, Sandoz, Basel 1982–85; Dir Pharmaceutical Research, F. Hoffmann-La Roche Ltd, Basel 1985–86, Chair. Research Bd and mem. Exec. Cttee 1986–90, Pres. Int. R&D and mem. Exec. Cttee Roche Group, Hoffmann-La Roche Inc., Nutley, NJ 1991–95, Pres. global research, mem. exec. Cttee 1996–97; Chair. Int. Biomedicine Man. Partners, Basel 1998–mem. Dean's Council, Yale Univ. School of Medicine 1993–. *Publications:* Chemotherapie 1979, Immunpharmakologie, Grundlagen und Perspektiven 1986, Immunopharmacology 1990, Die verspielte Zukunft 1998, In Quest of Tomorrow's Medicines 1999; more than 200 scientific papers. *Leisure interests:* skiing, climbing, literature, piano. *Address:* c/o Hoffmann-La Roche Inc., Nutley, NJ 07110, USA.

DREXLER, Millard S.; American business executive; b. 1944, Bronx, New York; m.; worked part-time in garment industry, New York; Pres., CEO Ann Taylor Co.; Exec. Vice-Pres. Merchandising, Pres. Gap Stores Div. Gap Inc., San Bruno, Calif. 1983–, now Pres., mem. Bd of Dirs. The Gap Inc., San Bruno, Pres., CEO The Gap Inc., San Francisco 1995–2002; Chair. and CEO J. Crew Group Inc. 2003–. *Leisure interest:* novels by John Grisham. *Address:* J. Crew Group Inc., 770 Broadway, New York, NY 10013, USA (Office). *Telephone:* (212) 2092500. *Fax:* (212) 2092666. *Website:* www.jcrew.com.

DREYFUS, George, AM; composer; b. 22 July 1928, Wuppertal, Germany; two s. one d.; ed Vienna Acad. of Music; Composer-in-residence, Tienjin, China 1983, Shanghai 1987, Nanjing 1991; Henry Lawson Award 1972, Prix de Rome 1976, Mishkenot Sha'ananim, Jerusalem 1980, Don Banks Fellowship 1992, Grosses Bundesverdienstkreuz (Germany). *Compositions include:* Garni Sands, The Gilt-Edged Kid (operas); Symphonies Nos. 1 & 2; Symphonie Concertante 1977; Jingles . . . & More Jingles; Reflections in a Glasshouse; The Illusionist; The Grand Aurora Australis Now Show; Galgenlieder; Songs Comic & Curious; Music in the Air; From within Looking out; The Seasons; Ned Kelly Ballads; Quintet after the Notebook of J.-G. Noverre; Sextet for Didjeridoo & Wind Instruments; Old Melbourne; several pieces for young people; The Sentimental Bloke (musical) 1985, Lifestyle 1988, Song of Brother Sun 1988 (choral pieces), Rathenau (opera) 1993, Die Marx Sisters (opera) 1994; more than 100 scores for film and TV including The Adventures of Sebastian the Fox 1963, Rush 1974, Great Expectations 1986. *Publications:* The Last Frivolous Book (autobiog.) 1984, Being George–And Liking It! 1998. *Leisure interests:* swimming, gardening. *Address:* 3 Grace Street, Camberwell, Vic. 3124, Australia. *Telephone:* (3) 9809-2671 (Home). *Fax:* (3) 9809-2671 (Home).

DREYFUSS, Richard Stephan; American actor; b. 29 Oct. 1947, New York; s. of Norman Dreyfuss and Gerry D. Student; m. Jeramie Dreyfuss 1983; two s. one d.; ed San Fernando Valley State Coll.; alternative mil. service Los Angeles County Gen. Hosp. 1969–71; mem. American Civil Liberties Union Screen Actors Guild, Equity Asscn, American Fed. of TV and Radio Artists, Motion Picture Acad. Arts and Sciences; Golden Globe Award 1978, Acad. Award for Best Actor in The Goodbye Girl 1978. *Stage appearances include:* Julius Caesar 1978, The Big Fix (also producer) 1978, Othello 1979, Death and the Maiden 1992, The Prisoner of Second Avenue 1999. *Films include:* American Graffitti 1972, Dillinger 1973, The Apprenticeship of Duddy Kravitz 1974, Jaws 1975, Inserts 1975, Close Encounters of the Third Kind 1976, The Goodbye Girl 1977, The Competition 1980, Whose Life Is It Anyway? 1981, Down and Out in Beverly Hills 1986, Stakeout 1988, Moon over Parador 1989, Let it Ride, Always 1989, Rosencrantz and Guildernstern are Dead, Postcards from the Edge 1990, Once Around 1990, Randall and Juliet 1990, Prisoners of Honor 1991, What About Bob? 1991, Lost in Yonkers 1993, Another Stakeout 1993, The American President, Mr Holland's Opus 1995, Mad Dog Time 1996, James and the Giant Peach (voice) 1996, Night Falls on Manhattan 1997, The Call of the Wild 1997, Krippendorf's Tribe 1998, A Fine and Private Place 1998, The Crew 2000, The Old Man Who Read Love Stories 2000, Who is Cletis Tout? 2001; TV movie Oliver Twist 1997; Dir, producer Nuts 1987, Hamlet (Birmingham) 1994. *Publication:* The Two Georges (with Harry Turtledove) 1996. *Address:* William Morris Agency, 151 S. El Camino Drive, Beverly Hills, CA 90212, USA.

DRINAN, Robert Frederick, MA, LLM, ThD; American politician, professor and writer; b. 15 Nov. 1920, Boston; s. of James J. Drinan and Ann Flanagan; ed Boston Coll., Georgetown Univ. and Gregorian Univ., Rome; ordained Jesuit Priest 1953; Dean Boston Coll. Law School 1956–70; mem. U.S. Congress from Mass. 1971–81; Prof. Georgetown Univ. Law Center 1980–; mem. ABA, Chair. Section on Individual Rights and Responsibilities 1990–91; Fellow, American Acad. of Arts and Sciences; 21 hon. degrees from American univs. *Publications:* Religion, the Courts and Public Policy 1963, Democracy, Dissent and Disorder 1969, Vietnam and Armaggedon 1970, Honor the Promise 1977, Beyond the Nuclear Freeze 1983, God and Caesar on the Potomac 1985, Cry of the Oppressed 1987, Stories from the American Soul 1990, The Fractured Dream 1991, The Mobilization of Shame: A Global View of Human Rights 2001. *Address:* Georgetown University Law Center, 600 New Jersey Avenue, NW, Washington, DC 20001-2022, USA (Office). *Telephone:* (202) 662-9073 (Office). *Fax:* (202) 662-9412 (Office). *E-mail:* drinan@law.georgetown.edu (Office).

DRISS, Rachid; Tunisian diplomatist and journalist; b. 27 Jan. 1917, Tunis; m. Jeanine Driss 1953; one s.; ed Sadiki Coll., Tunis; joined Neo-Destour party 1934; journalist exiled in Cairo and with Pres. Bourguiba founder mem. Bureau du Maghreb Arabe; returned to Tunisia 1955; Ed. El Amal; Deputy, Constitutional Ass. 1956; Minister of Posts, Telegraph and Telephones 1957–64; mem. Nat. Ass. 1959, 1969; Amb. to the USA and Mexico 1964–69; mem. Political Bureau of Council of the Repub. 1969–; Perm. Rep. to UN 1970–76; Vice-Pres. Econ. and Soc. Council 1970, Pres. 1971, 1972; mem. Conseil Constitutionnel 1987–92; Special Emissary of Arab League to Kuwait and Iraq 1992; Founder, Pres. Asscn des études internationales 1981–, Arab Bd for Child Devt; Pres. Higher Comm. on Human Rights and Fundamental Freedoms 1991–2000; Dir Etudes Internationales (quarterly); Grand Cordon de l'Ordre de l'Indépendance de la République Tunisienne and many foreign decorations. *Publications:* From Bab Souika to Manhattan 1980, Diaries from the Maghreb Office in Cairo 1981, A l'aube la lanterne 1981, From Djakarta to Carthage 1985, Errances (poems) 1990, Feuilles d'insomnie (novel) 1990, Report on Human Rights in Tunisia 1992, Au gré du Calame (poems) 1996, Reflets d'un combat (history of Tunisian Nat. Movt 1997. *Address:* Rue St Cyprien, 2016 Carthage, Tunisia. *Telephone:* (71) 791663 (Office); (71) 746846 (Home). *Fax:* (71) 796593 (Office). *E-mail:* aeitunis@planet.tn (Office).

DRIVER, Minnie (Amelia); British actress; b. 31 Jan. 1970, London; d. of Charles Driver and Gaynor Churchward (née Millington); ed Bedales School, Hants.; Best Newcomer, London Circle of Film Critics 1997, Best Actress, London Circle of Film Critics 1998. *Television appearances include:* God on the Rocks 1990, Mr Wroe's Virgins 1993, The Politician's Wife 1995. *Films include:* Circle of Friends 1995, Goldeneye 1995, Baggage 1996, Big Night 1996, Sleepers 1996, Grosse Point Blank 1997, Good Will Hunting 1997, The Governess 1998, Hard Rain 1998, At Sachem Farm 1998, Trespasser (voice) 1998, An Ideal Husband 1999, Tarzan (voice) 1999, South Park: Bigger, Longer and Uncut 1999, Slow Burn 2000, Beautiful 2000, Return to Me 2000, The Upgrade 2000, High Heels and Lowlifes 2001, D.C. Smalls 2001. *Play:* Sexual Perversity in Chicago, Comedy Theatre, London 2003. *Address:* c/o Lou Coulson, 1st Floor, 37 Berwick Street, London, W1V 3LF, England. *Telephone:* (20) 7734-9633.

DRNOVŠEK, Janez, DEcon; Slovenian politician; b. 17 May 1950, Celje; ed Llubljana Univ., Maribor Univ.; worked as Dir Zagorje Construction Co., Chief Exec. Trbovlje br. of Ljubljanska Bank, adviser on econ. affairs in Yugoslavian Embassy, Egypt; elected to Slovenian Parl. (Skupščina) of Yugoslavia 1986; Slovenian mem. of Collective Presidency of Yugoslavia 1989; Pres. of Presidency 1989–90; Head of Non-Aligned Movt, Chair. Summit Conf. Sept. 1989; one of initiators of introduction of multi-party system in Yugoslavia; Founder and Pres. Liberal Democracy of Slovenia (LDS) party 1991–; Leader of Ind. Movt; Prime Minister of Slovenian Repub. 1992–May 2000, Nov. 2000–02; President of Slovenia 2002–; Hon. Citizen Mexico City 1998, Texas 1999; Hon. DJur (Boston Univ.) 1994, Dr hc (Univ. Illinois, Wesleyan); American Studies Foundation award 1998, Diálogo Europeo award (Spain) 1998. *Publications:* Escape from Hell 1996; numerous articles on loans, monetary policy and int. financial relations. *Leisure interests:* swimming, cycling, reading, jogging, tennis. *Address:* Office of the President, Erjavčeva 17, 1000 Ljubljana (Office); V Murglah 77, 1000 Llubljana, Slovenia (Home). *Telephone:* (1) 4781205 (Office). *Fax:* (1) 4781357 (Office). *E-mail:* janez.drnovsek@gov.si (Office). *Website:* www.up-rs.si (Office).

DRONKE, (Ernst) Peter (Michael), MA, FBA; British medieval Latin scholar and author; b. 30 May 1934; s. of A. H. R. Dronke and M. M. Dronke (née Kronfeld); m. Ursula Miriam Brown 1960; one d.; ed Victoria Univ., NZ and Magdalen Coll. Oxford; Research Fellow, Merton Coll. Oxford 1958–61; Lecturer in Medieval Latin, Cambridge Univ. 1961–79, Reader in Medieval Latin Literature 1979–89, Prof. 1989–2001, Emer. Prof. 2001–, Fellow of Clare Hall 1964–2001; Visiting Prof. of Medieval Studies, Westfield Coll. London 1981–86; Carl Newell Jackson Lecturer, Harvard Univ. 1992; Corresp. Fellow, Real Academia de Buenas Letras, Royal Dutch Acad., Medieval Acad. of America, Austrian Acad. of Sciences; Hon. Pres., Int. Courtly Literature Soc.; Co-Ed. Mittellateinisches Jahrbuch 1977–; Premio Internazionale Ascoli Piceno 1988. *Publications:* Medieval Latin and the Rise of European Love-Lyric (2 Vols) 1965–66, The Medieval Lyric 1968, Poetic Individuality in the Middle Ages 1970, Fabula 1974, Abelard and Heloise in Medieval Testimonies 1976, Barbara et antiquissima carmina (with Ursula Dronke) 1977, Bernardus Silvestris, Cosmographia (Ed.) 1978, Introduction to Francesco Colonna, Hypnerotomachia 1981, Women Writers of the Middle Ages 1984, The Medieval Poet and his World 1984, Dante and Medieval Latin Traditions 1986, Introduction to Rosvita, Dialoghi Drammatici 1986, A History of Twelfth-Century Western Philosophy (Ed.) 1988, Hermes and the Sibyls 1990, Latin and Vernacular Poets of the Middle Ages 1991, Intellectuals and Poets in Medieval Europe 1992, Verse with Prose: From Petronius to Dante 1994, Nine Medieval Latin Plays 1994, Hildegard of Bingen, Liber divinorum operum (Jt Ed.) 1996, Sources of Inspiration 1997, Dante's Second Love (lectures) 1997, Introduction to Alessandro nel medioevo occidentale 1997, Growth of Literature: the Sea and the God of the Sea (with Ursula Dronke) 1998, Etienne Gilson's Letters to Bruno Nardi (Ed.) 1998, Hildegard of Bingen: The Context of Her Thought and Art (Jt Ed.) 1998, Imagination in the Late Pagan and Early Christian World 2003; essays in learned journals and symposia. *Leisure interests:* music, film and Brittany. *Address:* 6 Parker Street, Cambridge, CB1 1JL, England.

DROSSOYIANNIS, Anthony; Greek politician and fmr army officer; b. 1922, Athens; m.; one s.; ed Mil. Acad.; during 2nd world war, active service in Greece and with Ieros Lochos (Sacred Battalion) in Middle East under Allied Command, took part in liberation of Samos 1943, of islands of Aegean and Dodecanese as Commdr of commando units of Ieros Lochos 1944; subsequently in Third Army Corps and Instructor, Mil. Acad. until 1947, Co. Commdr of Tactical Staff and Deputy Commdr of a commando unit, Civil War 1947–50, served with commando and infantry units 1950–67 rank of Bn Commdr; banished and imprisoned several times during mil. dictatorship; promoted to rank of Lt-Gen. after return to democracy; MP 1985; Asst Minister of Defence 1981–84, Alternate Minister of Defence 1984–86, Minister of Public Order 1986–88; Gold Medal of Bravery with Mil. Cross, Medal of Merit (several times). *Address:* 42 Pipinou Street, 112 51, Athens, Greece.

DROZDOVA, Margarita Sergeyevna; Russian ballerina; b. 7 May 1948, Moscow; ed Moscow Choreographic School, State Inst. of Theatre Art (GITIS); danced with Stanislavsky Musical Theatre Ballet Co., Moscow 1967–91, coach 1991–; mem. CPSU 1980–91; Anna Pavlova Award, Paris 1968; RSFSR State Prize 1980, People's Artist of USSR 1986. *Roles include:* Odette-Odile, Gayané, The Commissar (M. Bronner's 'Optimistic Tragedy'), Medora (A. Adam's 'Corsaire'), Swanilda (Delibes' 'Coppélia'), Cinderella (Prokofiev). *Address:* Stanislavsky and Nemirovich Danchenko Musical Theatre, Pushkinskaya str. 17, Moscow, Russia. *Telephone:* (095) 299-31-36 (Home).

DRUBICH, Tatyana Lusienovna; Russian actress; b. 7 June 1960, Moscow; m. Sergey Soloviev (divorced); one d.; ed Third Moscow Medical Inst.; worked as a nurse then as a physician; actress 1972–; Head of Russian Rep. of German chemical factory Dr. Weigert 1992–. *Films include:* 15th Spring (debut) 1972, 100 Days after Childhood 1975, Disarray 1978, Particularly Dangerous 1978, The Rescuer 1979, The Direct Heiress 1982, Selected 1983, Tester 1984, Black Monk 1986, Keep Me, My Talisman 1986, Assa 1987, Black Rose – an Emblem of Sorrow, White Rose – an Emblem of Love 1989, Hey, Fools 1996, Moscow 2000. *Address:* Seleznevskaya str. 30, korp. 3, Apt. 77, 103473 Moscow, Russia. *Telephone:* (095) 281-60-82.

DRUCKER, Daniel Charles, PhD; American engineer; b. 3 June 1918, New York; s. of Moses Abraham Drucker and Henrietta Weinstein; m. Ann Bodin 1939 (died 2000); one s. one d.; ed Columbia Univ., New York; Instructor Cornell Univ., Ithaca, NY 1940–43; Supervisor Armour Research Foundation 1943–45; Asst Prof. Ill. Inst. of Tech., Chicago 1946–47; Assoc. Prof., then Prof. Brown Univ., Providence, R. I. 1947–64, Chair. Div. of Eng 1953–59, L. Herbert Ballou Univ. Prof. Brown Univ. 1964–68; Pres. Soc. for Experimental Stress Analysis 1960–61, American Acad. of Mechanics 1972–73, American Soc. of Mechanical Eng 1973–74, Int. Union of Theoretical and Applied Mechanics 1980–84, Vice-Pres. 1984–88; Pres. American Soc. for Eng Educ. 1981–82; Dean of Eng, Univ. of Ill. at Urbana-Champaign 1968–84; Graduate Research Prof. of Eng Sciences, Univ. of Fla 1984–94, Grad. Research Prof. Emer. 1994–; mem. Nat. Acad. of Eng; Foreign mem. Polish Acad. of Sciences; mem. Nat. Science Bd 1988–94; Hon. mem. Ill. Soc. of Professional Engineers; Fellow American Acad. of Arts and Sciences, American Acad. of Mechanics, American Soc. of Civil Engineers, American Soc. for Eng Educ., American Soc. of Mechanical Engineers (also Hon. mem.), Soc. for Experimental Mechanics (also Hon. mem.); Fellow, AAAS; Guggenheim Fellow 1960–61, NATO Sr Science Fellow 1968, Charter Fellow, American Soc. for Eng Educ. 1983; Murray Lecturer, Soc. for Experimental Stress Analysis 1967, Marburg Lecturer, American Soc. for Testing and Materials 1966; Hon. DEng (Lehigh,

Univ. Bethlehem, Pa) 1976; Dr. hc Technion, Israel Inst. of Tech. 1983; Hon. Dr.Sc. (Brown Univ.) 1984, (Northwestern Univ.) 1985, (Univ. of Illinois) 1992; M. M. Frocht Award, Soc. for Experimental Stress Analysis, 1971, Illig Medal, Columbia Univ. 1938, Lamme Medal, American Soc. for Eng Educ. 1967, von Karman Medal, American Soc. of Civil Eng 1966, Thomas Egleston Medal, Columbia Univ. School of Eng and Applied Science 1978, Gustave Trasenster Medal, Univ. of Liège, Belgium 1979, William Prager Medal, Soc. of Eng Science 1983, Timoshenko Medal, American Soc. of Mechanical Engineers 1983, John Fritz Medal, Founder Eng Socs. 1985, 1986, Thurston Lecturer and Distinguished Lecturer, American Soc. of Mechanical Engineers 1987–89, Nat. Medal of Science 1988, ASME Medal 1992, American Soc. for Eng Educ. Hall of Fame 1993, Daniel C. Drucker Medal, American Soc. of Mechanical Engineers 1997, Panetti-Ferrari Int. Prize and Gold Medal, Accad. delle Scienze di Torino 1999. *Publications:* Introduction to the Mechanics of Deformable Bodies 1967; and over 200 tech. articles. *Address:* 231 Aerospace Engineering Building, University of Florida, Gainesville, FL 32611, USA. *Telephone:* (352) 392-9699. *Fax:* (352) 392-7303 (Office). *E-mail:* dcd@aero.ufl.edu (Office).

DRUCKER, Michel; French television journalist; b. 12 Sept. 1942, Vire (Calvados); s. of Abraham Drucker and Lola Schafler; m. Danielle Savalle (Dany Saval) 1973; ed Lycée Emile-Maupas, Vire; sports reporter, ORTF 1964, presenter variety programmes 1966, producer and presenter Sport en Fête, football commentator 1969; commentator World Cup Football Championships 1970, 1974, 1978; presenter (Radio-Télé-Luxembourg – RTL) C'est vous 1974–, Les Rendez-vous du dimanche 1975–1981, Stars 1981, Champs-Elysées 1982–85, (Europe 1) Studio 1 1983, (Antenne 2) Champs-Elysées, 1987–90, (TF1) Stars 90 1990–94, Ciné Stars 1991–94, (France 2) Studio Gabriel 1994–97, Faites la fête 1994–98, Drucker & Co., Stars & Co. 1997–98, Vivement dimanche, Vivement dimanche prochain, Tapis rouge 1998–; Chevalier Légion d'honneur, Chevalier des Arts et des Lettres, Sports Journalist of the Year, Télémagazine 1971, 1972, 1973, Prix Triomphe de la télévision à la Nuit du cinéma 1973, 7 d'Or for Best Variety Programme Presenter 1987, Prix Gémeaux de la francophonie, Quebec, Canada 2000. *Publications:* La Balle au bond (autobiog.) 1973, La Coupe du monde de football 1974, La Chaîne (novel) 1979, November des amours 1984, Hors antenne, conversation avec Maurice Achard 1987, Les Numéros 1. Tous les grands du football français 1987. *Leisure interests:* tennis, cycling, football, skiing, flying. *Address:* Production DMD, 21 rue Jean Mermoz, 75008 Paris (Office); Pavillon Gabriel, 9 avenue Gabriel, 75008 Paris, France (Home).

DRUCKER, Peter Ferdinand, LLD; American management consultant, teacher and writer; b. 19 Nov. 1909, Vienna, Austria; s. of Adolph and Caroline Drucker; m. Doris Schmitz 1937; one s. three d.; ed Gymnasium, Vienna and Univ. of Frankfurt; Prof. of Political Philosophy, Bennington Coll., Bennington, Vt 1942–49; Prof. of Man., Grad. School of Business Admin., New York 1950–72; Clarke Prof. of Social Science, Claremont Grad. School, Claremont, Calif. 1971–2002; Prof. and Lecturer in Oriental Art, Pomona Coll., Claremont 1980–85; Godkin Lecturer, Harvard Univ. 1994; Man. Consultant (own firm) 1945–; Fellow, AAAS, American Acad. of Man., Int. Acad. of Man.; Hon. Fellow, BIM; 25 hon. degrees from univs in USA, UK, Japan, Belgium, Czech Repub., Spain and Switzerland; Britannica Award 1987, Distinguished Leadership Medal, Nat. Acad. of Man. 2001, N. S. President's Medal of Freedom 2002. *Publications:* The End of Economic Man 1939, The Future of Industrial Man 1942, Concept of the Corporation 1946, The New Society 1950, The Practice of Management 1954, America's Next Twenty Years 1957, Landmarks of Tomorrow 1959, Managing for Results 1964, The Effective Executive 1966, The Age of Discontinuity 1969, Technology, Management and Society 1970, The New Markets and other essays 1971, Management: Tasks, Responsibilities, Practices 1974, The Unseen Revolution: How Pension Fund Socialism came to America 1976, People and Performance 1977, Management, an Overview 1978, Adventures of a Bystander 1979, Song of the Brush, Japanese Paintings 1979 (co-author), Managing in Turbulent Times 1980, Toward the Next Economics and other essays 1981, The Changing World of the Executive 1982, The Last of All Possible Worlds (fiction) 1982, The Temptation to Do Good (fiction) 1984, Innovation and Entrepreneurship 1985, Frontiers of Management 1986, The New Realities 1989, Managing the Non-Profit Organization 1990, Management for the Future 1991, Social Ecology 1992, Post Capitalist Society 1993, Managing in a Time of Great Change 1995, Drucker on Asia: A Dialogue with Tsao Nagauchi 1997, Peter Drucker on the Profession of Management 1998, Management Challenges for the 21st Century 1999, The Essential Drucker 2001, Managing in the Next Society 2002, A Functioning Society 2002; and educational films and on-line teaching devices. *Leisure interests:* Japanese art, history of work and of tech. *Address:* c/o Claremont Graduate School, Claremont, CA 91711, USA (Office).

DRUMMOND, Sir John Richard Gray, Kt, CBE, MA, FRSA, FRCM; British arts administrator; b. 25 Nov. 1934; s. of late Capt. A.R.G. Drummond and of Esther Pickering; ed Canford School, Trinity Coll. Cambridge; joined BBC 1958, Asst Head, Music and Arts, Controller of Music 1985–91, Controller Radio 3 1987–91, Dir BBC Promenade Concerts 1985–95; Dir Edin. Int. Festival 1978–83, European Arts Festival 1992; Vice-Chair. British Arts Festivals Asscn 1981–83 (Vice-Pres. 1994–); Pres. Kensington Soc. 1985–2001; Chair. Nat. Dance Co-ordinating Cttee 1986–95; Gov. Royal Ballet 1986–2000; mem. Theatres Trust 1989–99, Chair. 1998–2001; Chevalier, Légion d'honneur. *Programmes produced include:* Tortelier Master

Classes 1964, Leeds Piano Competition 1966, Diaghilev 1967, Kathleen Ferrier 1968, Music Now 1969, Spirit of the Age 1975, The Lively Arts 1976–78. *Publications:* A Fine and Private Place (with Joan Bakewell) 1977, The Turn of the Dance (with N. Thompson) 1984, Speaking of Diaghilev 1997, Tainted by Experience (autobiog.) 2000. *Leisure interests:* architecture, bookshops, ceramics. *Address:* 5 Walker's Lane, Lewes, East Sussex, BN7 2JR, England. *Telephone:* (1273) 474995 (Home).

DRUON, Maurice Samuel Roger Charles; French author; b. 23 April 1918, Paris; s. of René Druon and Léonilla Samuel-Cros; m. Madeleine Marignac 1968; ed Lycée Michelet, Ecole des Sciences Politiques, Faculté des Lettres de Paris; War Corresp. Allied Armies 1944–45; mem. Académie Française 1966, Perpetual Sec. 1986–99; Minister for Cultural Affairs 1973–74; mem. French Parl. 1978–81, mem. European Parl. 1979–80, mem. Académie Royale du Maroc 1980, assoc. mem. Académie d'Athènes 1981; mem. Franco-British Council 1973–74; Pres. Assn France-Italie; Assoc. mem. Lisbon Acad. of Sciences, Brazilian Acad.; hon. mem. Romanian Acad. 1996; Dr. hc (York Univ., Ont.) 1987, (Boston) 1997; Prix Goncourt for novel Les grandes familles 1948, Prix de Monaco 1966; Hon. KBE; Grand-Croix, Légion d'honneur, Commdr des Arts et Lettres, Commdr, Order of Phoenix (Greece), Commdr Ordre de la République de Tunisie, Grand Cross of Merit (Italy), Grand Officier ordre du Lion du Sénégal, Grand Cross of the Aztec Eagle (Mexico), Grand Officier, Order of Merit (Malta), Ordre du Mérite culturel (Monaco), Ordre de l'Honneur de Grèce, du Ouissam Alaouite, Grand Cross of the Christ (Portugal), Grand Officier Orden de Mayo (Argentina). *Film script:* Les grandes familles 1958. *Television scripts:* Les rois maudits 1972, Les grandes familes 1991. *Publications:* Lettres d'un Européen 1943, Le chant des partisans 1943, La dernière brigade 1946, La fin des hommes (3 Vols Les grandes familles 1948, La chute des corps 1950, Rendez-vous aux enfers 1951), La volupté d'être 1954, Les rois maudits 1955–77 (7 Vols Le roi de fer, La reine étranglée, Les poisons de la couronne, La loi des mâles, La louve de France, Le lis et le lion, Quand un Roi perd la France), Tistou les pouces verts 1957, Alexandre le Grand 1958, Des seigneurs de la plaine à l'hôtel de Mondez 1962, Les mémoires de Zeus (2 Vols L'aube des dieux 1963, Les jours des hommes 1967), Bernard Buffet 1964, Paris, de César à St Louis 1964, Le pouvoir 1965, Les tambours de la mémoire 1965, Le bonheur des uns ... 1967, Discours de réception à l'Académie française 1968, L'avenir en désarroi 1968, Vézelay, colline éternelle 1968, Nouvelles lettres d'un européen 1943–70, Une église qui se trompe de siècle 1972, La parole et le pouvoir 1974, Oeuvres complètes 1974–79, Attention la France 1981, Réformer la démocratie 1982, La culture et l'état 1985, Lettre aux français sur leur langue et leur âme 1994, Circonstances 1997 (Prix Saint-Simon), Circonstances Politiques 1998, Circonstances Politiques II 1999, Le Bon français 1999 (Prix Agrippa d'Aubigné 2000), La France aux ordres d'un cadavre; plays: Mégarée 1942, Un voyageur 1953, La Contessa 1962. *Leisure interests:* riding, travel. *Address:* Académie Française, 23 quai Conti, 75006 Paris (Office); 81 rue de Lille, 75007 Paris (Home); Abbaye de Faise, 33570 Les Artigues de Lussac, France (Home).

DRURY, Very Rev. John Henry, MA; British ecclesiastic and university administrator; b. 23 May 1936, Clacton; s. of Henry Drury and Barbara Drury; m. Clare Nineham 1972; two d.; ed Bradfield Coll. and Trinity Hall, Cambridge; Curate, St John's Wood Church, London 1963; Chaplain, Downing Coll. Cambridge 1966; Chaplain and Fellow, Exeter Coll. Oxford 1969; Canon of Norwich Cathedral 1973; lecturer, Univ. of Sussex 1979; Dean, King's Coll. Cambridge 1981; Dean, Christ Church, Oxford 1991–; Hussey Lecturer Univ. of Oxford 1997; Hon. Fellow Exeter Coll., Oxford 1992, Trinity Hall, Cambridge 1997. *Publications:* Angels and Dirt 1972, Luke 1973, Tradition and Design in Luke's Gospel 1976, Parables in the Gospels 1985, Critics of the Bible 1724–1873 1989, The Burning Bush 1990, Painting the Word 1999. *Leisure interests:* drawing, walking, carpentry. *Address:* The Deanery, Christ Church, Oxford, OX1 1DP, England. *Telephone:* (1865) 276161. *Fax:* (1865) 276238. *E-mail:* jan.bolongaro@christ-church.ox.ac.uk (Office).

DRUT, Guy Jacques; French politician and athlete; b. 6 Dec. 1950, Oignies (Pas de Calais); s. of Jacques Drut and Jacqueline Wigley; m. 2nd Véronique Hardy 1984; one d. and one d. by first m.; ed Lycée de Douai, Lycée d'Henin-Liétard, Lycée Roubaix, Ecole Normale Supérieure d'Education Physique et Sportive and Inst. Nat. des Sports; French Jr record-holder, 110m hurdles, pole vault and decathlon; French 110m hurdles champion 1970–76, 1981; European 100m hurdles champion, Rome 1974; European 110m hurdles record, Rome 1974; world record, Berlin 1975; Silver Medal, 110m hurdles, Munich Olympics 1972, Gold Medal, Montreal Olympics 1976; Bronze Medal, 50m hurdles, European Championships 1981; retd from competition 1981; Chief of Staff to Prime Minister Jacques Chirac 1975–76; mem. Nat. Council UDR, Cen. Cttee RPR; Deputy Mayor of Paris responsible for Youth and Sport 1985–89; RPR Deputy from Seine-et-Marne to Nat. Ass. 1986–95; Town Councillor, Meaux 1989–92; Regional Councillor, Ile-de-France 1992–; Mayor of Coulommiers 1992–; Minister of Youth and Sport May–Nov. 1995, Minister del. 1995–97; elected Deputy for Seine-et-Marne (Groupe du Rassemblement pour la République) 1997–; mem. IOC 1996–; Chevalier, Ordre Nat. du Mérite. *Publications:* L'or et l'argent 1976, Jacques Chirac: la victoire du sport (jtly) 1988, J'ai deux mots à vous dire 1997. *Leisure interests:* golf, hunting. *Address:* Mairie, 77120 Coulommiers; Assemblée nationale, 75355 Paris, France. *Telephone:* 1-64-75-80-02 (Office). *Fax:* 1-64-75-03-53 (Office).

DRYSDALE, Andrew; South African journalist; b. 19 Oct. 1935, Dui-welskloof, Transvaal; s. of Andrew Patarson Drysdale; ed Parktown High School; fmr Ed. The Argus; Fellow, Harvard Univ., USA. *Leisure interests:* golf, tennis. *Address:* P.O. Box 56, Cape Town 8000, South Africa.

DRYUKOV, Anatoly Matveyevich; Russian diplomatist; b. 4 Sept. 1936, Voronezh; m.; two d.; ed Moscow Inst. of Int. Relations; diplomatic service 1960–; attaché Embassy, Pakistan 1962–64; mem. Dept of South-East Asia, USSR Ministry of Foreign Affairs 1964–66; mem. Secr. of Deputy Minister 1966–69; First Sec. Embassy, Zambia 1969–73; Asst Deputy Minister 1973–78, expert, Deputy Chief Dept of South-East Asia 1978–86, Deputy Chief Dept of Socialist Countries of Asia 1986–87; with Embassy, Singapore 1987–90; Chief Main Dept of Staff and higher educ. establishments of USSR Ministry of Foreign Affairs 1990–91; Russian Amb. to India 1991–96, Gen. Insp. Ministry of Foreign Affairs 1996–98; Amb. to Armenia 1998–. *Address:* Russian Embassy, Pionerskaya str. 72, 375015 Erevan, Armenia. *Telephone:* (2) 52-45-22, 52-45-24. *Fax:* (2) 52-13-78.

D'SOUZA, Most Rev. Eugene, BA, BEd; Indian ecclesiastic (retd); b. 15 Nov. 1917, Nagpur; s. of Ignatius Charles D'Souza; mem. Congregation of Missionaries of St Francis de Sales 1935; ordained priest 1944; consecrated first native Bishop of Nagpur 1951, first Archbishop 1953; est. St Francis de Sales Coll. of Arts & Science and St Charles Seminary, Nagpur 1956; Archbishop of Bhopal 1963–94, Archbishop Emer. 1994; est. Bhopal School of Social Sciences, Univ. Coll., Univ. of Bhopal 1965; est. Asha Niketan, Rehabilitation Centre for handicapped and deaf children 1967; mem. Catholic Bishops' Conf. of India, mem. Standing Cttee 1953–; mem. Governing Bd St John's Medical Coll., Bangalore; active participant Vatican Council II and several int. conventions; Nat. Award for Distinguished Service in Educ. and Rehabilitation of the Handicapped 1976. *Address:* Assumption Villa, Asha Niketan, Assumption Parish, E/6, Arera Colony, Bhopal, MP 462 016, India. *Telephone:* (755) 564966.

D'SOUZA, Wilfred, MB, BS, FRCS, FRCSE; Indian politician and surgeon; b. 23 April 1927, Anjuna, Bardez; s. of the late Tito Fermino and Alina Anamaria; m. Grace Goodwin; two c.; ed Grant Medical Coll. Univ. of Bombay; surgeon, Goa Medical Coll. Hosp. 1963–67; Consulting Surgeon, Hospicio Hosp., Margao and Asilo Hosp., Mapusa 1963–67; Consulting Surgeon, CMM Hosp., Panjim and Holy Cross Hosp., Mapusa 1969–96; elected to Goa, Daman and Diu Ass. 1974, 1980; elected to Legis. Ass. (after Goa became State in Repub. of India) 1989, 1994, 1999, 2002; Pres. Goa Pradesh Congress Cttee 1977–80; Minister for Public Health, Public Works Dept, Govt of Goa 1981–83, Science and Tech. Planning 1990; Leader of Opposition 1990–91; Deputy Chief Minister, Govt of Goa 1991–93, Chief Minister 1993–94, 1998; currently Deputy Chair., Planning Bd, Chair. Cttee on Public Undertakings, mem.Public Accounts Cttee; Pres.Goa unit of Nationalist Congress Party; mem. Asscn of Surgeons of India; Hon. Fellow Int. Coll. of Surgeons; Commdr Grand Cross of the Order of Infante Dom Henrique (Portugal); Dr B. C. Roy Award for Eminent Medical Man and Statesman (India), Silver Elephant Award (India), Son of India Award. *Address:* c/o Dias Bldg, Ormuz Road, Panjim, Goa (Office); 359 Mussavaddi, Saligao, Bardez, Goa, India (Home). *Telephone:* (832) 2224964 (Office); (832) 2278000 (Home). *E-mail:* willie@goatelecom.com.

du CANN, Col Rt Hon Sir Edward Dillon Lott, PC, KBE, MA, FRSA; British politician and businessman; b. 28 May 1924, Beckenham; s. of late C. G. L. du Cann and Janet du Cann (née Murchie); m. 1st Sallie Murchie 1962 (divorced 1989); one s. two d.; m. 2nd Jenifer Patricia Evelyn (Lady Cooke) née King 1990 (died 1995); ed Woodbridge School, Suffolk and St John's Coll., Oxford; MP 1956–87; Founder and Chair. Unicorn Group of Unit Trusts 1957–62, 1964–72; Founder mem. Asscn Unit Trust Mans. 1961, Chair. 1961; Econ. Sec. to the Treasury 1962–63; Minister of State, Bd of Trade 1963–64; Chair. of Conservative Party 1965–67, Pres. 1981–82; Chair. 1922 Cttee 1972–84; First Chair. Select Cttee on Public Expenditure 1971–73, Public Accounts Cttee 1974–79; mem. Cttee of Privileges 1972–87; First Chair. Treasury and Civil Service Cttee 1979–83, Liaison Cttee of Select Cttee Chairs. 1979–83; Vice-Chair. British-American Parl. Group 1977–81; Pres. of Conservative Parl. European Community Reform Group 1985–87; Founder Chair. All-Party Maritime Affairs Parl. Group 1984–87; First Chair. Public Accounts Comm. 1984–87; led Parl. del. to USA 1978, 1979, first British Parl. del. to China 1982; Chair. Keyser Ullmann Ltd 1972–75, Cannon Assurance Ltd 1972–80, Lonrho PLC 1984–91 (Dir 1972–92); Dir Martins Bank 1967–69, Barclays Bank (London Bd) 1969–72; Visiting Fellow, Univ. of Lancaster Business School 1970–82; Patron, Asscn of Insurance Brokers 1973–77, Human Ecology Foundation 1987; Gov. Hatfield Coll., Durham Univ. 1988–92; Master Fruiterers Co. 1990; Pres. Inst. of Freight Forwarders 1988–89; Hon. Vice-Pres. British Insurance Brokers Asscn 1978–; Chair. Templeton Foundation Awards Ceremony 1984 (mem. Panel of Judges 1984); mem. of Man. Council of the GB-SasaKawa British-Japanese Foundation 1984–93; First Hon. Freeman Borough of Taunton Deane 1977; Admiral, House of Commons Yacht Club 1974–87; Hon. Col 155 Regiment (Wessex) Volunteers 1972–82, Hon. Life mem. of the Inst. of RCT, Commonwealth Parl. Asscn, Taunton Racecourse. *Publications:* Investing Simplified 1959, The Case for a Bill of Rights 1975, How to Bring Government Expenditure under Parliamentary Control 1979, A New Competition Policy 1984, Hoist the Red Ensign 1987, Two Lives 1995, The Wellington Caricatures 2000. *Leisure*

interests: sailing, gardening, walking the dog. *Address:* 6 Old Pye House, 15–17 St Ann's Street, London, SW1P 2DE, England; Pervolia, Lemona, 8545 Paphos, Cyprus.

DU DAOZHENG; Chinese journalist; b. Nov. 1923, Dingxiang Co., Shanxi Prov.; s. of Du Xixiang and Qi Luaying; m. Xu Zhixian 1950; one s. four d.; ed Middle School, Dingxiang, Shanxi and Beijing Marx-Lenin Coll.; joined CCP 1937; Chief of Hebei and Guangdong Bureau, Xinhua News Agency 1949–56; Ed.-in-Chief Yangchen Wanbao 1956–69; Dir Home News Dept, Xinhua News Agency 1977–82; Ed.-in-Chief Guangming Daily 1982; Dir Media and Publs Office 1987–88; Hon. Pres. Newspaper Operation and Man. Assoc. 1988–; Deputy 7th NPC 1988–; Dir State Press and Publs Admin. 1988–89; winner of the Nat. News Prize 1979. *Publications:* Explore Japan (co-author), Interviews with Famous Chinese Journalists. *Leisure interest:* photography.

DU MINGXIN; Chinese composer and university professor; b. Aug. 1928, Qianjiang Co., Hubei Prov.; ed Tchaikovsky State Conservatoire USSR 1954–58; Prof. of Composition, Cen. Conservatory of Music 1978–; Exec. Dir Chinese Musicians' Asscn; mem. 11th CPPCC 1997–. *Compositions include:* Great Wall Symphony, Luoshen Symphony, two violin concertos, two piano concertos, music (with others) for ballets Mermaid, The Red Detachment of Women, piano trio, string quartet. *Address:* Central Conservatory of Music, 43 Baojia Street, Beijing 100031, People's Republic of China.

DU PLESSIS, Christian; British opera singer; b. 2 July 1944, Vryheid, South Africa; ed Potchefstroom and Bloemfontein Univs; début in Pretoria 1967; British début in Andrea Chenier at Theatre Royal, Drury Lane 1970; prin. baritone, English Nat. Opera 1973–81; USA début in Les Pêcheurs de Perles, Texas 1984; Covent Garden début in Rigoletto 1984; recipient, Ernest Oppenheimer Bursary 1968, 1969, 1970; maj. roles with cos. in UK, USA, France, Holland, Hong Kong, Ireland); maj. recordings for Opera Rara, EMI, Decca and ABC Dunhill; retd 1988. *Leisure interest:* Dir of Fine Arts gallery. *Address:* c/o Performing Arts, 1 Hinde Street, London, W1M 5RH, England.

DU PLESSIS, Daniel Jacob, MB, CH.B., MCh, FRCS; South African surgeon and university vice-chancellor; b. 17 May 1918, Paarl; s. of Daniel J. du Plessis and Louisa M. (Carstens) du Plessis; m. Louisa S. Wicht 1946; two s.; ed Paarl Boys' High School, Univs. of Cape Town and the Witwatersrand; Capt. S. African Medical Corps 1942–46; postgraduate studies, Cape Town, Johannesburg, Oxford and London 1946–52; Surgeon, Univ. of Cape Town and Groote Schuur Hosp. 1952–58; Prof. of Surgery, Univ. of the Witwatersrand, Johannesburg 1958–77, Vice-Chancellor 1978–83; Nuffield Scholarship 1951–52, Carnegie Fellowship 1963; Hon. Fellowship American Coll. of Surgeons 1974, American Surgical Asscn 1981, Asscn of Surgeons of GB and Ireland 1979, Coll. of Surgeons of SA 1982; Pres. Southern Transvaal Br., Medical Asscn of SA 1986–87; mem. Advisory Council for Univs. and Technikons 1984–92; Hon. Life Vice-Pres. Surgical Research Soc. of SA, Asscn of Surgeons of SA 1984; Chair. of Council, B. G. Alexander Nursing Coll. 1985–95; Natalspruit (now Bonalesedi) Nursing Coll. 1986–92; mem. Council, Medical Univ. of Southern Africa 1986–94, Johannesburg Coll. of Educ. 1986–92, Univ. of Transkei 1989–92; mem. Bd of Govs., American Coll. of Surgeons 1988–(94); Trustee, SA Blood Transfusion Service 1985–; Hon. LLD (Witwatersrand) 1984; Hon. MD (Cape Town) 1986; Hon. PhD (Medical Univ. of Southern Africa) 1995; Paul Harris Rotary Award 1983; Order for Meritorious Service (Gold) 1989. *Publications:* Principles of Surgery 1968, Synopsis of Surgical Anatomy 1975; and articles in professional journals. *Leisure interests:* walking, reading. *Address:* 17 Chateau Road, Richmond, Johannesburg 2092, South Africa (Home).

DU QINGLIN; Chinese politician; b. Nov. 1946, Panshi Co., Jilin Prov.; joined CCP 1966; Sec. Communist Youth League Jilin City Cttee 1978; Vice-Sec. Communist Youth League Jilin Provincial Cttee, mem. Communist Youth League Cen. Cttee 1979; Vice-Sec. CCP Changchun City Cttee 1984; Vice-Sec. CCP Jilin Provincial Cttee 1988; Vice-Sec. CCP Hainan Provincial Cttee 1992–98, Sec. 1998–2001; alt. mem. 14th CCP Cen. Cttee 1992–97; Chair. Standing Cttee of Hainan Provincial People's Congress 1993–2001; mem. 15th CCP Cen. Cttee 1997–2002, 16th CCP Cen. Cttee 2002–; Minister of Agric. 2001–. *Address:* Ministry of Agriculture, 11 Nongzhanguan Nanli, Beijing 100026, People's Republic of China. *Telephone:* (10) 64192316. *E-mail:* webmaster@agri.gov.cn (Office). *Website:* www.agri.gov.cn (Office).

DU RUNSHENG; Chinese politician and economist (retd); b. 8 Aug. 1913, Taigu, Shanxi; ed Beijing Teachers Univ.; involved in revolutionary activities in early 1930s; Commdr guerrilla forces Taihang Mountains; mem. of a border region Govt, Deputy Gov. Taihang Pref. 1937–45; Sec.-Gen. Cen.-Plains Bureau, CPC 1946–49; Sec.-Gen. Cen.-South Bureau, CPC, Vice-Chair. Land Reform Cttee of Cen.-South Region 1949; Sec.-Gen. Cen. Dept of Rural Work, CPC and Deputy Dir Agric. and Forestry Office of State Council 1953; Sec.-Gen. Acad. of Sciences 1956–79; in disgrace during Cultural Revolution 1967–76; Deputy Dir State Agric. Comm. in charge of Policy Study on Rural Reform 1979–82; Dir Rural Policy Research Office of Secr., CPC and Pres. Rural Devt Research Centre, State Council; in charge of Policy Study on Rural Econ. Reform and Devt 1982; Pres. Soc. of Land Econ. 1994–; mem. Cen. Advisory Cttee, CPC 1983–; Deputy Head Leading Group for Educ. of Cadres, CCP Cen. Cttee 1985–; Deputy to NPC, mem. Finance and Econ. Cttee, NPC 1983–88; mem. Leading Group for Finance and Economy of CCP Cen. Cttee 1988–89; Pres. China Agricultural Econs Soc. 1988–; Vice-Chair. Nat. Agricultural Zoning Cttee 1983–; Deputy Head Leading Group for Devt of Rural Energy 1984–; Dir Rural Policy Research Centre of CPC Cen. Cttee 1988;

Pres. Friendship Asscn for the Mentally Handicapped 1993–; a Vice-Pres. Chinese Fed. for the Disabled 1993–; Hon. Prof. Beijing Agricultural Univ. 1949–; Guest Prof. Chinese People's Univ. *Publications:* Rural Economic Reform in China (collection of articles) 1985, many articles on rural Devt in China. *Leisure interest:* tennis. *Address:* State Council's Research Center for Rural Development, 9 Xihuangchenggen Nanjie, Beijing 100032, People's Republic of China. *Telephone:* 665254.

DU TIEHUAN; Chinese government official; Asst Dir PLA Gen. Political Dept 1993–94; Political Commissar Ji'nan Mil. Region 1994–96; Political Commissar, Beijing Mil. Area Command 1996–; mem. 15th CCP Cen. Cttee 1997–; rank of Gen. 2000. *Address:* Political Commissar's Office, Beijing Military Area Command, Beijing, People's Republic of China.

DU YUZHOU; Chinese government official; b. 1942, Qiqihar, Heilongjiang; ed Qinghua Univ.; joined CCP 1965; technician, Changde Textile Machinery Plant, Hunan 1968–70, Deputy Workshop Head, then Deputy Section Chief 1970–73; engineer, Deputy Dir then Dir Design Inst. of Ministry of Textile Industry 1978–85; Vice-Minister of Textiles 1985–93; Vice-Chair., Chair. Chinese Gen. Asscn of Textile Industry, Dir State Admin. for Textile Industry 1993–. *Address:* State Administration for Textile Industry, 12 East Changan Street, Beijing 100742, People's Republic of China.

DUBAI, Ruler of (see Maktoum, Rashid al-).

DUBENETSKY, Yakov Nikolayevich; Russian economist and banker; b. 26 Oct. 1938, Stayki, Belarus; m.; one s.; ed Moscow State Univ.; Deputy Chair. Stroybank of the USSR 1985–87; First Deputy Chair. Bank for Industry and Construction of the USSR (Pomstroybank of the USSR) 1987–91; Chair. Bd Russian Jt Stock Investment and Commercial Bank for Industry and Construction (Pomstroybank of Russia) 1991–99; Chair. Bd Bank Asscn Russia 1995–; Vice-Pres. Asscn of Russian Banks 1995–; Co-Chair. Round Table of Russian Business 2000–; mem. Political Consultative Council of Pres. of Russian Fed. 1996–, Nat. Banking Council 1996–, Int. Acad. of Man. 1997–, Bd for finance and economy, Rosneftegazstroi 2001–. *Address:* Association of Russian Banks, Skatertny per. 20, Bldg 1, 103009 Moscow, Russia. *Telephone:* (095) 291-66-30. *Fax:* (096) 291-66-66. *E-mail:* arb@arb.ru (Office).

DUBININ, Sergey Konstantinovich, DEcon; Russian business executive; b. 10 Dec. 1950, Moscow; m.; two c.; ed Moscow State Univ.; Docent, Researcher, Prof. Moscow State Univ. 1974–91; mem. Pres. Mikhail Gorbachev's admin. 1991; Deputy Chair. Russian State Cttee for co-operation with CIS 1992–93; First Deputy Minister of Finance, Acting Minister of Finance 1993–94; First Deputy Chair. Exec. Bd Commercial Bank Imperial 1994–95; mem. Exec. Bd Jt Stock co. Gazprom 1995, Deputy Chair. Bd Gazprom Co. 1998–2001; Deputy CEO Unified Power Grids of Russia (RAO ES) 2001–; Chair. Cen. Bank of Russia 1995–98; Russian Rep. to IBRD 1996–98; Chair. Interstate Monetary Cttee CIS 1996–98, Supervisory Bd Sberbank and Vneshtorgbank; 850th Anniversary of Moscow Govt Award 1998. *Publications:* books on public, int. and corp. finance and finance markets; numerous articles on scientific research. *Leisure interests:* art, classical music, theatre, sports. *Address:* 101 Bldg 3 pr-t Vernadskogo, 119526 Moscow, Russia. *Telephone:* (095) 220-4445 (Office). *Fax:* (095) 925-2952 (Office). *E-mail:* baldihina@rao .elektra.ru (Office). *Website:* www.rao-ees.ru (Office).

DUBININ, Yuri Vladimirovich, D.HIST.SC.; Russian diplomatist (retd); b. 7 Oct. 1930, Nalchik; m. Liana Khatchatrian 1953; three d.; ed Moscow Inst. for Int. Relations; mem. CPSU 1954–91; Asst in Embassy in France 1955–56, with UNESCO Secr., Paris 1956–59; mem. Apparat USSR Ministry of Foreign Affairs 1959–63, 1969–78, now Prof. Inst. of Int. Relations; First Sec., Embassy Counsellor, Embassy in France 1963–69; Amb. to Spain 1978–86, to USA 1986–90, to France 1990–91; Perm. Rep. to UN 1986; Prof. of Political Science, George Washington Univ., USA 1991; Amb.-at-Large 1991–94; Deputy Minister of Foreign Affairs 1994–99; Amb. to Ukraine 1996–99; Head of Russian Del. on negotiations with Estonia 1991, with Ukraine 1992–94; Hon. Prof. Slaviansky Univ., Kiev, Ukraine 1999; mem. Int. Ecological Acad. Kiev 1997, Int. Acad. of Spiritual Unity of Peoples of the World 2001; numerous honours and awards including Orders of the Red Banner 1971, 1980, 1988, Order of Honour 1996, Order of Merit (Ukraine); planet named Dubinin by Int. Astronomical Soc. 1999. *Publications:* U.S.S.R.–France: Experience of Co-operation 1979, Soviet-Spanish Relations 1983, Representing Perestroika in the West 1989, Diplomatic Truth: Memoirs of the Ambassador to France 1997, Ambassador, Ambassador! Memoirs of the Ambassador to Spain 1999. *Address:* Bolshoy Palashevsky per. 3, App. 34, 123104 Moscow, Russia. *Telephone:* (095) 203-27-49. *Fax:* (095) 203-27-49.

DUBOIS, Jacques-Emile, PhD; French professor of chemistry; b. 13 April 1920, Lille; s. of Paul Dubois and Emilienne Chevrier; m. Bernice Claire Shaaker 1952; one s. one d.; ed Univs of Lille and Grenoble; CNRS researcher, Univ. of Grenoble 1943, lecturer 1945, Asst Prof. 1947; Mem. Liberation Cttee, Isère 1944; Ramsay Fellow, Univ. Coll., London 1948–50; Scientific Adviser to French Cultural Counsellor, London 1948–50; Prof. of Physical Chem. and Petrochem. and Dir of Chem. Inst., Univ. of Saar 1949–57, Dean of Science Faculty 1953–57; Prof. of Physical Organic Chem., Univ. of Paris 1957–, now Prof. Emer.; Research Fellow, Columbia Univ., New York 1956; Guest Prof. of Physical Chem., Univ. of Saar 1958; Scientific Adviser to French Minister of Educ. 1962–63; Jt Dir of Higher Educ. 1963–65; Dir of Research for Ministry of Defence 1965–77; Co-Dir Curie Foundation 1977–80; Dir

French Nat. Univ. Agency for Scientific and Tech. Documentation and Information (AUDIST) 1978–81; Scientific Dir Cie Générale d'Electricité 1979–83; Chair. IUPAC Interdivisional Cttee on Machine Documentation 1970–77; Founding Pres., Asscn for Research and Devt in Chem. Informatics (ARDIC) 1971–; Vice-Pres. French Physical Chem. Soc. 1972–74, Pres. 1974–76; Vice-Pres. CNIC (Nat. Centre for Chemical Information) 1972–89; French Nat. Del. to CODATA, Vice-Chair. 1980–88, Chair. CODATA Artificial Intelligence and Graphics Task Group 1988–, Pres. CODATA Int. 1994–98 (Pres. CODATA France 2001–); mem. Directorate Nat. Research Council 1963–71, 1975–; mem. Council French Chemical Soc. 1965–67, Faraday Soc.; Dr hc (Regensburg); Commdr, Légion d'honneur, Commdr Ordre nat. du Mérite, Médaille de la Résistance, Commdr des Palmes académiques, Jecker Prize and Berthelot Medal (Acad. of Sciences), Le Bel and Ancel Prizes (French Chemical Soc.), Stas Medal (Belgian Chemical Soc.), Grand Prix Technique, City of Paris 1975, Bruylants Chair. and Medal (Louvain Univ.) 1982, Grand prix du Festival d'Angers 1986, CAOC Medal 1991, Herman Skolnik Award for Chemical Information 1992. *Publications:* (Co-Ed.) Data and Knowledge in a Changing World 1996, works in field of kinetics, fast reaction rates, electro-chemistry, automation applied to chemistry and author of the DARC topological system used for on-line information systems and for computer-assisted design in chem. *Leisure interest:* skiing. *Address:* 100 rue de Rennes, 75006 Paris, France (Home). *Telephone:* 1-42-22-45-16 (Home). *Fax:* 1-45-49-27-46 (Home).

DUBOWITZ, Victor, MD, PhD, FRCP, FRCPCH, DCH; British professor of pediatrics; b. 6 Aug. 1931, Beaufort West, S. Africa; s. of the late Charley Dubowitz and Olga Schattel; m. Lilly M. S. Sebok 1960; four s.; ed Cen. High School, Beaufort West and Univs of Cape Town and Sheffield; intern, Groote Schuur Hospital, Cape Town 1955; Sr House Officer, Queen Mary's Hosp. for Children 1957–59; Research Assoc. Royal Postgraduate Medical School 1958–59; Lecturer in Clinical Pathology, Nat. Hosp. for Nervous Diseases, London 1960; Lecturer in Child Health, Univ. of Sheffield 1961–65, Sr Lecturer 1965–67, Reader 1967–72; Research Assoc. Inst. for Muscle Disease and Asst Paediatrician, Cornell Medical Coll., New York 1965–66; Prof. of Pediatrics, Royal Postgraduate Medical School, Univ. of London 1972–96, Prof. Emer. 1996–; Consultant Paediatrician, Hammersmith Hosp. 1972–96; Dir Jerry Lewis Muscle Research Centre, Royal Postgrad. Medical School 1975–96; Pres. European Pediatric Neurology Soc. 1994–97; World Muscle Soc. 1995–, Medical Art Soc. 1996–2000; Curator of Art, Royal Coll. of Paediatrics and Child Health; Dir of Therapeutic Studies, European Neuromuscular Centre (ENMC), The Netherlands 2000–; recipient of several awards etc. *Publications:* The Floppy Infant 1969, Muscle Biopsy: A Modern Approach (with M. H. Brooke) 1973, 1985, Gestational Age of the Newborn (with L. M. S. Dubowitz) 1977, Muscle Disorders in Childhood 1978, The Neurological Assessment of the Pre-term and Full-term Newborn Infant (with L. M. S. Dubowitz) 1981, 1999, A Colour Atlas of Muscle Disorders in Childhood 1989, A Colour Atlas of Brain Disorders in the Newborn (with L. de Vries, L. Dubowitz and J. Penock) 1990, Muscle Disorders in Childhood 2 1995; Ed.-in-Chief Neuromuscular Disorders, European Journal of Paediatric Neurology. *Leisure interests:* sculpting, hiking, photography, antique glass. *Address:* 25 Middleton Road, Golders Green, London, NW11 7NR, England (Home). *Telephone:* (20) 8455-9352 (Home). *Fax:* (20) 8905-5922 (Home).

DUBY, Jean Jacques, PhD; French mathematician and scientist; b. 5 Nov. 1940, Paris; s. of Jean Duby and Lucienne (née Lacomme) Duby; m. Camille Poli 1963; one d.; ed Ecole Normale Supérieure, Paris; research staff mem., Thomas J. Watson Research Center, USA 1963–64; Systems Engineer IBM France 1965–66, Man. Application Systems IBM Mohansic Lab. 1974–75, Exec. Asst to Vice-Chair. IBM Corpn 1975–76, Br. Office Man. IBM France 1977–78, Special Assignment IBM Communications Div. 1979, Dir Switching Systems IBM Europe 1980–82, Dir Science and Tech. IBM France 1986–88, Group Dir Science and Tech. IBM Europe 1988–91; Man. Grenoble Scientific Centre 1967–69; Assoc. Prof. European Systems Research Inst. and Univ. of Geneva 1970–71; Project Man. Paris Stock Exchange 1972–73; Scientific Dir CNRS 1982–86; Scientific Dir Union d'assurances de Paris (UAP) 1991–97; Pres. Inst. Nat. de recherche sur les transports et leur sécurité 1992–96; Chair. Bd of Dirs. Ecole Normale Supérieure de Cachan 1994–2000; Dir-Gen. Ecole Supérieure d'Electricité 1995–; Professeur des universités 1999–; Chair. Scientific Council of Bouygnes Télécom 2001–; Officier Ordre Nat. du Mérite (France), Chevalier Ordre Nat. de la Côte d'Ivoire. *Leisure interests:* skiing, mountaineering. *Address:* Ecole supérieure d'électricité, Plateau de Moulon, 91192 Gif-sur-Yvette, France (Office). *E-mail:* jean-jacques.duby@ supelec.fr (Office).

DUBYNA, Oleh; Ukrainian politician and engineer; b. 20 March 1959, Elizavetovka, Dniepropetrovsk region; m.; one s.; ed Dnieprodzerzhinsk Industrial Inst., Dnieprodzerzhinsk State Tech. Univ.; employee Dniepr Metallurgic plant 1976, master, Sr master, then engineer 1986–93, Head of Bureau, Deputy Head of Div., First Deputy Dir-Gen. 1996–98; teacher Dnieprodzerzhinsk Polytech. Higher School 1985–86; Asst to Dir, then Deputy Dir-Gen. Dniepr br. of Intermontage Kam – Soviet-Swiss Joint Venture DEMOS 1993–96; Deputy Head, Chair. Bd of Dirs., Dir-Gen. Alchevsk Metallurgic plant 1998–99; Dir-Gen. Kryvoy Rog State Ore-Metallurgic plant, Krivorozhstal 1999–; Deputy Prime Minister for Econ. Policy 2000–01; First Deputy Prime Minister 2001–02. *Address:* c/o Cabinet of Ministers, Hrushevskogo str. 12/2, 252008 Kiev, Ukraine (Office).

DUCHOVNY, David; American film actor; b. 7 Aug. 1960, New York; s. of Amram Duchovny and Meg Duchovny; m. Tea Leoni (q.v.) 1997; ed Yale and Princeton Univs; stage appearances include off-Broadway plays, The Copulating Machine of Venice, California and Green Cockatoo; writer and Dir of various episodes of The X-Files; Golden Globe for Best Actor in Drama Series 1996. *Films include:* Working Girl 1988, New Year's Day 1989, Bad Influence 1990, Julia Has Two Lovers 1990, The Rapture 1991, Don't Tell Mom the Babysitter's Dead 1991, Denial 1991, Beethoven 1992, Chaplin 1992, Red Shoe Diaries 1992, Ruby 1992, Venice, Venice 1992, Kalifornia 1993, Apartment Zero, Close Enemy, Loan, Independence Day, Playing God 1997, The X-Files 1998, Return To Me 2000, Evolution 2001, Zoolander 2001, Full Frontal 2002. *Television includes:* Twin Peaks 1990, The X-Files 1993–, Life With Bonnie 2002. *Address:* 20th Century Fox Film Corporation, PO Box 900, Beverly Hills, CA 90213, USA (Office).

DUCKWORTH, Marilyn, OBE; New Zealand writer; b. Marilyn Rose Adcock, 10 Nov. 1935, Auckland; d. of Cyril John Adcock and Irene Robinson; sister of Fleur Adcock ; m. 1st Harry Duckworth 1955 (divorced 1964); m. 2nd Ian Macfarlane 1964 (dissolved 1972); m. 3rd Daniel Donovan 1974 (died 1978); m. 4th John Batstone 1985; four d.; ed Queen Margaret Coll., Wellington and Victoria Univ., Wellington; 10 writers' fellowships 1961–96 including Katherine Mansfield Fellowship, Menton 1980, Fulbright Visiting Writer's Fellowship, USA 1987, Victoria Univ. Writing Fellowship 1990, Hawthornden Writing Fellowship, Scotland 1994, Sargeson Writing Fellowship, Auckland 1995, Auckland Univ. Literary Fellowship 1996; NZ Literary Fund Award for Achievement 1963, NZ Book Award for Fiction 1985. *Plays:* Home to Mother, Feet First. *Publications:* thirteen novels including A Gap in the Spectrum 1959, A Barbarous Tongue 1963, Disorderly Conduct 1984, Married Alive 1985, Pulling Faces 1987, A Message from Harpo 1989, Unlawful Entry 1992, Seeing Red 1993, Leather Wings 1995, Studmuffin 1997, Swallowing Diamonds 2003; short stories: Explosions on the Sun 1989; poems: Other Lovers' Children; memoir: Camping on the Faultline. *Leisure interest:* playing the violin. *Address:* 41 Queen Street, Mt. Victoria, Wellington 6001, New Zealand. *Telephone:* (4) 384-9990 (Home). *Fax:* (4) 384-9990 (Home).

DUCORNET, Rikki, BA; American/French writer; b. 19 April 1943, USA; s. of Gerard De Gré and Muriel Harris; one s.; Novelist-in-Residence, Univ. of Denver 1988–; Lannan Literary Fellowship 1993. *Publications:* (novels) The Stain 1984, Entering Fire 1986, The Fountains of Neptune 1989, The Jade Cabinet 1993, Phosphor in Dreamland 1995; (short fiction) The Word Desire 1997. *Address:* Department of English, University of Denver, Denver, CO 80208, USA.

DUCZMAL JAROSZEWSKA, Agnieszka; Polish conductor; b. 7 Jan. 1946, Krotoszyn; m.; one s. two d.; ed Acad. of Music, Poznań; creator and Dir Radio Amadeus Chamber Orchestra 1968–; Asst conductor Poznań Nat. Philharmonic 1971–72, conductor of Poznań Opera 1972–81; performs in Europe, N and S America and Asia; over 20 recordings including live concerts for TV and performances for radio; won award at first Nat. Competition for Conductors, Katowice 1970, Silver Medal of Herbert von Karajan at the Meeting of Young Orchestras, West Berlin 1976, La Donna del Mondo Award of St Vincent Int. Culture Centre, Rome 1982, Commdr's Cross Order of Polonia Restituta 1998. *Leisure interests:* dogs, literary classics, gardening, mountaineering. *Address:* Polish Radio Amadeus Chamber Orchestra, al. Marcinkowskiego 3, 61-745 Poznań, Poland (Office). *Telephone:* (61) 851-66-86 (Office). *Fax:* (61) 851-66-87 (Office). *E-mail:* agnieszka.duczmal@amadeus .pl.

DUDA-GRACZ, Jerzy; Polish painter; b. 20 March 1941, Częstochowa; s. of Adam Duda-Gracz and Pelagia Stepniewska; m. Wilma Dudek 1969; one d.; ed Acad. of Fine Arts in Kraków 1968; lecturer, Acad. of Fine Arts in Kraków, Silesian Univ. and European Acad. of Arts, Warsaw; mem. Union of Polish Artists and Designers 1979–90; Prof. Silesian Univ., Katowice; about 180 one-man and about 360 group exhbns in Poland, Europe, America and Asia; perm. exhbn Duda-Gracz Author's Gallery, Częstochowa; works in perm. collections include: Nat. Museum Warsaw, Kraków, Poznań, Wrocław, Gdańsk, Uffizi Gallery Florence, A Pushkin Museum Moscow; numerous awards including Silver Cross of Merit 1977, Prime Minister Prize (2nd Class) 1979, Minister of Culture and Art Prize (1st Class) 1985, Minister of Foreign Affairs Prize (1st Class) 1988, Grand Cross Order of Polonia Restituta 2000. *Paintings include:* (series) Polish Pictures and Portraits 1968–80, Polish Motives, Polish Landscapes 1980–83, Jurassic Pictures 1984–90, Aristocrat and Historian Pictures 1984–90, Provincial Pictures 1986–, Golgota of Jasna Góra 2000–2001, For Chopin (pictures for all Chopin's compositions) 1999–2003. *Leisure interest:* reading books (especially diaries). *Address:* ul. Daszyńskiego 24, 40-834 Katowice, Poland (Home).

DUDAU, Nicolae; Moldovan politician and diplomatist; b. 19 Dec. 1945, Grineuts; m. Galina Dudeu; one d.; ed Higher CPSU School, Moscow, Chișinău Tech. Univ.; employee Chișinău tractor Mfg factory 1963–75; army service 1964–67; various admin. posts in orgs. in Chișinău 1975–90; Deputy Chair. Chișinău City Planning Cttee 1990–91; First Sec. Chișinău City CP Cttee 1990–91; Exec. Dir Int. Charity Foundation 1991–93; Minister-Counsellor Moldovan Embassy and Russian 1993–94; First Deputy Minister of Foreign Affairs 1997–98, Minister of Foreign Affairs 2001–; Amb. to Belarus 1998–2001. *Address:* Ministry of Foreign Affairs, str. 31 August 1989 80, 2012 Chișinău, Moldova (Office). *Telephone:* (2) 23-39-40 (Office). *Fax:* (2) 23-23-02 (Office). *E-mail:* massmedi@mfa.un.md (Office).

DUDBRIDGE, Glen, PhD, FBA; British academic; b. 2 July 1938, Clevedon, Somerset; s. of George Victor Dudbridge and Edna Kathleen Dudbridge (née Cockle); m. Sylvia Lo Fung-young 1965; one s. one d.; ed Bristol Grammar School, Magdalene Coll. Cambridge and New Asia Coll. of Advanced Chinese Studies, Hong Kong; Research Fellow, Magdalene Coll. 1965; Lecturer in Modern Chinese, Oxford Univ. 1965–85; Prof. of Chinese, Cambridge Univ. 1985–89; Shaw Prof. of Chinese, Oxford Univ. 1989–; Fellow, Wolfson Coll. Oxford 1966–85, Emer. Fellow 1985–; Fellow, Magdalene Coll. Cambridge 1985–89; Fellow, Univ. Coll. Oxford 1989–; Visiting Prof., Yale Univ., USA 1972–73, Univ. of Calif., Berkeley, USA 1980, 1998; Hon. mem. Chinese Acad. of Social Sciences 1996. *Publications:* The Hsi-yu chi (a study of antecedents to the sixteenth-century Chinese novel) 1970, The Legend of Miao-shan 1978, The Tale of Li Wa (study and critical edition of a Chinese story from the ninth century) 1983, Religious Experience and Lay Society in T'ang China (A reading of Tai Fu's Kuang-I Chi) 1995, Sanguo Dian Lüe Ji Jiao 1998, Lost Books of Medieval China 2000. *Address:* Institute for Chinese Studies, Walton Street, Oxford, OX1 2HG, England. *Telephone:* (1865) 280389. *Fax:* (1865) 280435.

DUDERSTADT, James Johnson, PhD; American professor of engineering and university president; b. 5 Dec. 1942, Madison, Iowa; s. of Mack Henry Duderstadt and Katharine Sydney Johnson Duderstadt; m. Anne Marie Lock 1964; two d.; ed Yale Univ., California Inst. of Tech.; US Atomic Energy Comm. Postdoctoral Fellow, California Inst. of Tech. 1968; Asst Prof. of Nuclear Eng, Univ. of Mich. 1969, Assoc. Prof. 1972, Prof. 1976–81, Dean Coll. of Eng 1981, Provost and Vice-Pres. for Academic Affairs 1986, Pres. 1988–96, Pres. Emer. and Prof. of Scientific Eng 1996–; Dir Millennium Project 1996–; mem. US Nat. Science Bd 1985–96 (Chair. 1991–94), NAE Council 1997–, of Advisory Councils of Cornell Univ. and MIT, Nat. Acad. of Eng; Compton Award, American Nuclear Soc. 1985, Lawrence Award, US Dept of Energy 1986. *Publications:* Nuclear Reactor Analysis (with L. J. Hamilton) 1976, Transport Theory (with W. R. Martin) 1979, Inertial Confinement Fusion (with G. A. Moses) 1982, numerous tech. pubns on nuclear reactor theory, radiation transport, statistical mechanics and kinetic theory, plasma physics and computer simulation. *Address:* Millennium Project, The University of Michigan, 2001 Media Union, Ann Arbor, MI 48109, USA. *Telephone:* (313) 647-7300. *Fax:* (313) 647-6814.

DUDLEY, Hugh Arnold, CBE, ChM, FRCS, FRACS; British professor of surgery; b. 1 July 1925, Dublin; s. of Walter Dudley and Ethel Smith; m. Jean Bruce Lindsay Johnston 1947; two s. one d.; ed Edin. and Harvard Univs; Lecturer in Surgery, Edin. Univ. 1954–58; Sr Lecturer in Surgery, Aberdeen Univ. 1958–63; Foundation Prof. of Surgery, Monash Univ., Melbourne 1963–72; Prof. of Surgery, St Mary's Hosp., London 1973–88, Prof. Emer. 1988–; Ed. Operative Surgery 1976–94, Consulting Ed. 1994–; Chair. Ethics Cttee, Army Personnel Research Establishment 1989–94, Chemical and Biological Research Establishment, Porton Down 1988–96 (mem. Council 1992–94); fmr Pres. of Surgical Research Soc. of Australasia and of GB and Ireland, of Biological Eng Soc. and of British Journal of Surgery Soc.; Hon. Fellow American Surgical Asscn 1986, SA Coll. of Surgeons 1987. *Publications:* Principles of General Surgical Management 1958, Communication in Medicine and Biology 1977; Ed. Emergency Surgery 1979, 1986, Guide for House Surgeons 1974, 1982, 1987, Practical Procedures for House Officers 1988, The People's Hosp. of North East Scotland (jtly) 1992. *Leisure interest:* surgical history. *Address:* Glebe Cottage, Haughs of Glass, Huntly, Aberdeenshire, AB54 4XH, Scotland (Home). *Telephone:* (1466) 700376. *E-mail:* hugh .dudley@aol.com (Home).

DUE, Ole; Danish lawyer; b. 10 Feb. 1931, Korsør; s. of H. P. Due and Jenny Due (née Jensen); m. Alice Maud Halkier Nielsen 1954; three s. one d.; ed Univ. of Copenhagen; civil servant Ministry of Justice Copenhagen 1955, Head of Div. 1970, Head of Dept 1975, Acting Appeal Court Judge 1978; Judge Court of Justice, EEC 1979–94, Pres. 1988–94; Arbitrator OSCE Court of Conciliation and Arbitration 1995–; Chair. Danish Inst. of Int. Affairs; Hon. Bencher Gray's Inn, London, King's Inns, Dublin; Hon. Prof. (Copenhagen Univ.); Hon. Dr. (Stockholm Univ.); Grand Cross, Order of Dannebrog, Ordre de la Couronne (Belgium), Ordre de la Couronne de Chêne (Luxembourg). *Publications include:* articles on Community law, private int. law and legal technique. *Address:* University of Copenhagen, Institute of Legal Science, A, Skindergade 14, 3rd Floor, 1159 Copenhagen K, Denmark. *Telephone:* 35-32-31-20. *Fax:* 35-32-40 00.

DUERR, Hans-Peter Emil, PhD; German physicist; b. 7 Oct. 1929, Stuttgart; s. of Dr Rupert Duerr and Eva Duerr (née Kraepelin); m. Carol Sue Durham 1956; two s. two d.; ed Univs of Stuttgart and California, Berkeley; Research Asst Dept of Physics, Berkeley 1956–57, Max-Planck Inst. für Physik, Göttingen and Munich 1958–62; Visiting Assoc. Prof., Berkeley and Inst. of Math. Sciences, Madras, India 1962–63; Visiting Prof., Berkeley 1968–69; Prof. Univ. of Munich 1969; mem. Directorate Max-Planck Inst. für Physik, Munich, Chair. 1971–72, 1977–80, 1987–92, Vice-Chair. 1981–86, 1993–95, Emer. 1997–; Man. Dir Max-Planck-Inst. für Physik und Astrophysik 1978–80; mem. Bd Vereinigung Deutscher Wissenschaftler 1980–86, mem. Advisory Bd 1986–91, Chair. Bd 1991–; Chair. Advisory Cttee Wissenschaftszentrum Munich 1984–; mem. Bd Greenpeace Germany 1985–91, Co-Chair. Exec. Cttee 1988–89; Chair. Bd Global Challenges Network 1987–; mem. Pugwash Council 1987–, Club of Rome 1991–; mem. Bd Int. Foundation for the Survival and Devt of Humanity 1988–93, Moscow, Chair. Bd German br., Munich 1988–93; mem. Bd and Scientific Advisory Cttee Internationale Akademie für Zukunftsfragen, Vienna 1990–; Chair. Kuratorium Umweltakademie-Umwelt und Man., Oberpfaffenhofen, 1990–; mem. Kuratorium E.F.-Schumacher-Gesellschaft 1980–, City Energy Cttee, Munich 1983–, Int. Advisory Council Econ. Devt of Hainan, China 1990–93, Council Int. Network of Engineers and Scientists for Global Responsibility, Hamburg 1991–, Ständiges Wissenschaftsforum der Sozialdemokratie, Bonn 1994–, Scientific Advisory Cttee Institut für Zukunftsstudien und Technologiebewertung, Berlin 1995– and other cttees and advisory bds; Pres. Bd of Trustees European Trust for Natural and Cultural Wealth, Prague; mem. Bd Dir Bulletin of Atomic Scientists, Chicago 1993–, Academia Scientarium et Artium Europaea, Salzburg; Advisory Cttee Int. Judicial Org. for Environment and Devt (IJO) 1991–, Advisory Council Int. Center of Integrative Studies, New York 1993–, Scientific Advisory Bd Potsdam Inst. for Climate Impact Research; Trustee Muhammad Abdus Salam Foundation, London 1994–, Comm. on Globalization 2001; mem. Deutsche Akademie der Naturforscher Leopoldina Halle; Dr hc (Oldenburg) 2002; Right Livelihood Award 1987, Waldemar von Knoeringen Award 1989, Natura Obligat Medal 1991, Elise and Walter Haas Int. Award 1993, 'München leuchtet' Gold Medal 1996. *Publications:* more than 300 publs on nuclear physics, elementary particle physics, gravitation, epistemology, peace and disarmament, energy, ecology, econs, politics. *Address:* Max-Planck-Institut für Physik, Foehringer Ring 6, 80805 Munich (Office); Grasmeierstrasse 14c, 80805 Munich, Germany (Home). *Telephone:* (89) 32354280 (Office); (89) 32197844 (Home). *Fax:* (89) 32354304 (Office); (89) 32197845 (Home). *E-mail:* hpd@mppmu.mpg.de (Office). *Website:* www.mppmu.mpg.de (Office).

DUFF, Michael James, PhD; British professor of physics; b. 28 Jan. 1949, Manchester; s. of Edward Duff and Elizabeth Duff (née Kaylor); m. Lesley Yearling 1984; one s. one d.; ed De La Salle Coll., Salford, Queen Mary Coll. and Imperial Coll., London Univ.; Post-doctoral Fellowships in Theoretical Physics, Int. Centre for Theoretical Physics, Trieste, Italy, Oxford Univ., King's Coll. and Queen Mary Coll., London Univ., Brandeis Univ., USA 1972–79; Faculty mem. Imperial Coll. London 1979–88, Sr Physicist, CERN, Geneva 1984–87; Prof. of Physics, Texas A&M Univ., USA 1988–92, Distinguished Prof. of Physics 1992–; Oskar Klein Prof. of Physics, Univ. of Mich. 1999–; Dir Mich. Center for Theoretical Physics 2000–; Fellow American Physical Soc. *Publications:* Observations on Conformal Anomalies 1977, Kaluza-Klein Supergravity 1986, Strings Solitons 1994, The World in Eleven Dimensions 1999; numerous articles on unified theories of the elementary particles. *Leisure interests:* soccer, watercolours, golf. *Address:* 3425 Randall Laboratory, Department of Physics, University of Michigan, Ann Arbor, MI 48109 (Office); 846 Arboretum Drive, Saline, MI 48176, USA (Home). *Telephone:* (734) 944 3623 (Home); (734) 936 0662 (Office). *E-mail:* mduff@umich .edu (Office). *Website:* feynman.physics.lsa.edu/~mduff (Office).

DUFFEY, Joseph Daniel, PhD; American administrator and professor; b. 1 July 1932, Huntington, West Virginia; s. of Joseph I. Duffey and Ruth Wilson Duffey; m. Anne Wexler 1974; four s.; ed Marshall Univ., Andover Newton Theological School, Yale Univ. and Hartford Seminary Foundation; Assoc. Prof. and Acting Dean, Hartford Seminary Foundation 1960–70; Adjunct Prof. and Fellow, Calhoun Coll. 1970–74; Gen. Sec. and Spokesman American Asscn of Univ. Prof., Washington, DC 1974–76; Asst Sec. of State, US Dept of State 1977; Chair. Nat. Endowment for the Humanities, US Govt 1977–82; Chancellor Univ. of Mass. 1982–, Pres. 1990–91; Pres. American Univ. Washington 1991–93; Head US Information Agency 1993–98; Sr Exec. Chair. Int. Univ. Project, Sylvan Learning System, Washington 1999–; Order of Leopold II (Belgium) 1979, Tree of Life Award, American Jewish Congress 1984. *Publications:* Lewis Mumford's Quest 1979, US Global Competitiveness 1988, Looking Back and Looking Forward: The US and the World Economy 1989. *Address:* Sylvan Learning System, 1000 Lancaster Street, Baltimore, MD 21202 (Office); Apt 311, 2801 New Mexico Avenue, NW, Washington, DC 20007-3913, USA (Home). *Telephone:* (410) 843-6707 (Office); (202) 965-1044 (Home). *Fax:* (202) 965-1098 (Office); (202) 965-1098 (Home). *E-mail:* jduffey@ speakeasy.org (Office).

DUFFIELD, Dame Vivien Louise, DBE, MA; British philanthropist; b. 26 March 1946; d. of Sir Charles Clore and Francine Halphen; m. John Duffield 1969 (divorced 1976); one s. one d.; ed Cours Victor Hugo, Paris, Lycée Français de Londres; Heathfield School, Lady Margaret Hall, Oxford; Dir Royal Opera House Trust 1985–2001, Royal Opera House 1990–2001; Vice-Chair. Great Ormond Street Hosp. Wishing Well Appeal 1987, Royal Marsden Hosp. Cancer Appeal 1990; mem. NSPCC Centenary Appeal Cttee 1983, Financial Devt Cttee 1985; mem. Royal Ballet Bd 1990–, Gov. Royal Ballet 2002–; Trustee Dulwich Collection Picture Gallery 1993–2002; Gov. South Bank Bd 2002–; Hon. DLitt (Buckingham) 1990; Hon. DPhil (Weizmann Inst.) 1985, (Hebrew Univ.) 1998; Hon. RCM 1987. *Leisure interests:* skiing, opera, ballet, shooting. *Address:* c/o Clore Foundation, 3 Chelsea Manor Studios, Flood Street, London, SW3 5SR, England. *Telephone:* (20) 7351-6061.

DUFFY, Francis Cuthbert (Frank), CBE, PhD, MArch; British architect; b. 3 Sept. 1940, Berwick-upon-Tweed; s. of the late John Austin Duffy and Annie Margaret Duffy (née Reed); m. Jessica Duffy; three d.; ed Architectural Asscn School, London, Univ. of California at Berkeley and Princeton Univ., USA; Asst Architect Nat. Bldg Agency 1964–67; consultant to JFN Assocs., New York 1968–70; est. JFN Assocs. in London 1971–74; Co-f. DEGW 1974, partner 1974–89, Chair. 1989–99, Sr Consultant with title of Founder 1999–; Harkness Fellow 1967–71; Visiting Prof. MIT 2001–(04); Pres. RIBA 1993–95, Architects' Council of Europe 1994; est. DEGW's combination of maj. interior

design and architectural work (e.g. Boots The Chemists, Nottingham; Apicorp, Saudi Arabia) and strategic consultancy to int. corp. clients (e.g. IBM, BP, Lloyds Bank, Goldman Sachs, Fidelity). *Publications:* Planning Office Space 1966, The ORBIT Studies 1981–85, The Changing Workplace 1982, The Changing City 1989, The New Office 1997, Architectural Knowledge 1998. *Leisure interests:* reading, writing, talking, drawing. *Address:* DEGW North America LLC, 589 Eighth Avenue, 12th Floor, New York, NY 10018 (Office); Apt. 21A, 310 East 46th Street, New York, NY 10017, USA (Home); Threeways, The Street, Walberswick, Nr Southwold, Suffolk, IP18 6TZ, England (Home). *Telephone:* (212) 290-1601 (Office); (212) 973-0552 (Home, USA); (1502) 723814 (Home, England). *Fax:* (212) 290-1619 (Office). *E-mail:* fduffy@ degwna.com (Office). *Website:* www.degw.com (Office).

DUFFY, Maureen Patricia, BA, FRSL; British author; b. 1933; d. of Grace Rose Wright; ed Trowbridge High School for Girls, Sarah Bonnell High School for Girls, King's Coll., London Univ.; staged pop art exhbn with Brigid Brophy 1969; Chair. Greater London Arts Literature Panel 1979–81, Authors Lending and Copyright Soc. 1982–94, Copyright Licensing Agency 1996–99 (Vice-Chair. 1994–96); Pres. Writers' Guild of GB 1985–88 (Jt Chair. 1977–78); Co-Founder Writers' Action Group 1972–79; Vice-Pres. European Writers Congress 1992–, Beauty without Cruelty 1975–, British Copyright Council 1998– (Vice-Chair. 1981–86, Chair. 1989–98, Vice-Pres. 1998–); Fellow, King's Coll. London; Hon. Pres. Authors Lending and Copyright Soc. 2002; Fellow King's College 2002; CISAC Gold Medal for Literature 2002. *Publications:* That's How It Was 1962, The Single Eye 1964, The Microcosm 1966, The Paradox Players 1967, Lyrics for the Dog Hour (poetry) 1968, Wounds 1969, Rites (play) 1969, Love Child 1971, The Venus Touch 1971, The Erotic World of Faery 1972, I Want to Go to Moscow 1973, A Nightingale in Bloomsbury Square (play) 1974, Capital 1975, Evesong (poetry) 1975, The Passionate Shepherdess 1977, Housespy 1978, Memorials of the Quick and the Dead (poetry) 1979, Inherit the Earth 1980, Gorsaga 1981 (adapted for TV 1988), Londoners: An Elegy 1983, Men and Beasts 1984, Collected Poems 1949–84 1985, Change 1987, A Thousand Capricious Chances: Methuen 1889–1989 1989, Illuminations 1991, Occam's Razor 1993, Henry Purcell (biog.) 1994, Restitution 1998, England: The making of a myth from Stonehenge to Albert Square 2001. *Address:* 18 Fabian Road, London, SW6 7TZ, England. *Telephone:* (20) 7385-3598. *Fax:* (20) 7385-2468.

DUFOIX, Georgina, DèsScEcon; French politician; b. 16 Feb. 1943, Paris; d. of Alain Negre and Antoinette Pallier; m. Antoine Dufoix 1963; two s. two d.; ed Lycée de Nîmes and Univs. of Montpellier and Paris-Sorbonne; mem. Man. Cttee Parti Socialiste 1979; Sec. of State for Family Affairs 1981–83, for Family Affairs, Population and Immigrant Workers 1983–84; Minister for Social Affairs and Nat. Solidarity 1984–86; Conseiller-gén. for Gard 1982, Socialist Deputy 1986–88; Sec. of State for Family Affairs, for Women's Rights and for Repatriates May–June 1988; Chargée de mission auprès du Président 1988–92; Pres. Admin. Council, French Red Cross 1989–92; Del. Fight against Drugs 1989–93; mem. bd, UNRISD; Communications Co. Vera; mem. Governing Bd War-torn Soc. Project, Geneva. *Leisure interest:* her vineyard. *Address:* 35 rue des Blancs-Manteaux, 75004 Paris, France (Home). *Telephone:* (1) 40-27-00-82 (Office).

DUFOUR, Bernard, MSc; French aviation official; b. 14 Feb. 1933, France; s. of Jean Dufour and Denise Dufour (née Penot); m. Bernadette de Villepin 1956; five c.; ed Ecole Ozanam, Limoges, Lycée Janson de Sailly, Paris, Ecole Ste Geneviève, Ecole Polytechnique; Engineer Sud Aviation 1956–61, Dir helicopter production 1961–64, St Nazaire 1964–65, Toulouse 1965–76, Usine Belfort Alsthom 1977–89, GEC Alsthom (Electromechanical Div.) 1989–94; Dir Gen. ALSTOM Electromécanique 1989–94; Pres., CEO SNECMA 1994–96; Chevalier, Ordre nat. du Mérite, Légion d'honneur, Tudor Vladiminescu (Romania), Médaille Aéronautique. *Leisure interests:* cycling, riding, sailing, skiing. *Address:* 4 rue Henri Heine, 75016 Paris, France. *Telephone:* 1-45-25-22-78.

DUFOURCQ, Bertrand Charles Albert, LenD; French diplomatist; b. 5 July 1933, Paris; s. of Norbert Dufourcq and Marguerite-Odette Latron; m. Elisabeth Lefort des Ylouses 1961; two s. two d.; ed Lycées Montaigne and Louis-le-Grand, Paris, Faculté de Droit, Paris, Inst. d'Etudes Politiques, Paris and Ecole Nat. d'Admin.; Sec. for Foreign Affairs 1961; Chef de Cabinet to Prefect/Admin.-Gen. of City of Algiers 1961; Ministry of Foreign Affairs 1962; Cultural Counsellor, Tokyo 1964; Counsellor for Foreign Affairs 1967; various posts at Ministry of Foreign Affairs and Ministry of Industrial and Scientific Devt 1967–69; Head of Cultural, Scientific and Tech. Service, Embassy, Moscow 1969–72; Ministry of Foreign Affairs 1972–76, 1978–79; Amb. to People's Repub. of Congo 1976–78; European Dir Ministry of External Relations 1979–84; Dir Office of M. Claude Cheysson 1984; special attachment to Minister of External Relations 1984–85; Admin. Ecole Nat. d'Admin. 1980–83; Amb. to Vatican 1985–88; Dir of Political Affairs, Ministry of Foreign Affairs 1988–91; Amb. to USSR 1991, to Russia 1992 (also Accred to Mongolia 1991–92), to Germany 1992–93; Sec.-Gen. Ministry of Foreign Affairs 1993–98; Prés. Fondation de France 2000–; Prés. Centre du Musique Baroque de Versailles 1998–; Commdr Légion d'honneur, Ordre nat. du Mérite, Amb. de France. *Address:* 48 rue Madame, 75006 Paris, France (Home).

DUGGER, John Scott; American artist and designer; b. 18 July 1948, Los Angeles, Calif.; s. of Dr. James Attwood Dugger, MD and Julian Marie Riddle; ed Loy Norrix High School, Kalamazoo, Mich., Gilmore Inst. of Art, Mich.,

School of the Art Inst. of Chicago, Ill.; created Perennial (first Ergonic Sculpture), Paris 1970; Delegation Leader, Soc. for Anglo-Chinese understanding Delegation to China 1972; Founder-Dir Banner Arts, London 1976; mem. Exec. Cttee Art Services Grants Ltd (Artists' Housing Charity) 1980–85; Chair. Asscn of Space Artists, London 1984, 1985; Vice-Chair. Int. Artists Asscn, UK Cttee 1986–87; maj. works include Documenta 5, People's Participation Pavilion, Kassel, Fed. Repub. of Germany 1972, Monumental Strip-Banner Installation, Trafalgar Square, London 1974, Sports Banner Exhbn, Inst. of Contemporary Arts, London 1980; Original Art Banners commissioned for HM the Queen's 60th Birthday, Buckingham Palace 1986, Tibet Mountainscape Banner for His Holiness the XIV Dalai Lama—Int. Year of Tibet 1991; Int. Certified Master Fabric Craftsman, I.F.A.I. (Industrial Fabric Asscn) 1992; works on display at Arts Council of GB, Tate Gallery, London; Maj. Award, Arts Council of GB 1978, Calouste Gulbenkian Foundation Awards 1979, 1980, Int. Achievement Award 1993. *Leisure interests:* oriental art, mountaineering, martial arts.

DUHALDE MALDONADO, Eduardo Alberto; Argentine politician; b. 5 Oct. 1941, Lomas de Zamora, Prov. of Buenos Aires; s. of Tomas Duhalde and María Esther Maldonado; m. Hilda Beatriz González 1971; one s. four d.; fmr mem. staff Legal Dept Lomas de Zamora Town Council; Pres. Exec. Cttee Partido Justicialista of Lomas de Zamora 1973; Mayor Lomas de Zamora 1974–76, removed from post following mil. coup, re-elected 1983; elected Nat. Deputy for Prov. of Buenos Aires 1987, First Vice-Pres. Chamber of Deputies 1987–89; Vice-Pres. of Argentina, Pres. Senate 1989–91; Gov. Prov. of Buenos Aires 1991–99; Partido Justicialista cand. presidential elections 1999; Pres. Congreso Nacional del Partido Justicialista; Pres. of Argentina 2002–03; f. Office for Drug Addiction Prevention and Assistance, Lomas de Zamora 1984, Comm. on Drug Addiction, Chamber of Deputies; Dr hc (Genoa) 1992, (Universidad Hebrea Argentina) 1999, (Universidad del Salvador) 1999; Orden de Boyacá, Colombia, Orden Cruceiro do Sul, Brazil, Orden del Quetzal, Guatemala, Orden de Bernardo O'Higgins, Chile. *Publications:* La revolución productiva (with Carlos Saúl Menem, q.v.) 1987, Los políticos y las Drogas 1988, Hacia un mundo sin drogas 1994, Política, familia, sociedad y drogas 1997. *Leisure interests:* fishing, chess, folk music, reading, watching football. *Address:* c/o Office of the President, Balcarce 50, 1064 Buenos Aires, Argentina (Office).

DUIGAN, John, MA; Australian film director, screenwriter and author; b. England; ed Univ. of Melbourne; fmr lecturer, Univ. of Melbourne and Latrobe Univ.; co-Dir Vietnam (TV mini-series); wrote and Dir TV documentaries: Fragments of War: The Story of Damien Parer 1988, Bitter Rice 1989. *Films include:* Trespassers, Mouth to Mouth, Winter of Our Dreams 1981, Far East, The Year My Voice Broke 1987 (Australian Acad. Award for Best Dir), Romero (Dir only), Flirting 1991, Wide Sargasso Sea 1993, Sirens (actor, Dir only) 1994, The Journey of August King, The Leading Man (Dir only) 1996, Lawn Dogs (Dir only), Molly 1999, The Parole Officer 2001. *Publications:* novels: Badge, Players, Room to Move.

DUISENBERG, Willem Frederik (Wim), PhD; Netherlands economist; b. 9 July 1935, Heerenveen; m. Gretta Nieuwenhuizen 1987; two s. one d.; ed State Univ. of Groningen; Scientific Asst, State Univ., Groningen 1961–65; with IMF 1965–69; Special Adviser to Governing Bd, De Nederlandsche Bank NV 1969–70; Prof. of Macroecons, Univ. of Amsterdam 1970–73; Minister of Finance 1973–77; mem. of Parl. 1977–78; mem., Vice-Chair. Exec. Bd Rabobank Nederland 1978–81; Pres. De Nederlandsche Bank 1982–97 (Exec. Dir 1981–82); Pres. European Monetary Inst. 1997–98, European Cen. Bank 1998–(2003); Chair. Netherlands Cancer Inst. 1997–; Gov. IMF 1982–97; Commdr Order of the Netherlands Lion, Commdr, Order of Orange-Nassau; decorations from Belgium, France, Luxembourg, Portugal, Senegal, Sweden, Germany. *Publications:* Economic Consequences of Disarmament 1965, The IMF and the International Monetary System 1966, The British Balance of Payments 1969, Some Remarks on Imported Inflation 1970. *Address:* European Central Bank, Kaiserstrasse 29, 60311, Frankfurt, Germany (Office). *Telephone:* (69) 13440 (Office). *Fax:* (69) 13446000 (Office). *E-mail:* info@ecb .int (Office). *Website:* www.ecb.int (Office).

DUKAKIS, Michael Stanley; American politician; b. 3 Nov. 1933, Brookline, Mass.; s. of Dr. Panos Dukakis and Euterpe Dukakis; m. Katharine Dickson; one s. two d.; ed Brookline High School, Swarthmore Coll., Harvard Law School; Army service in Korea 1955–57; mem. Town Meeting, Brookline 1959, Chair. Town Cttee 1960–62; Attorney Hill & Barlow, Boston 1960–74; alt. Del. Democratic Nat. Convention 1968; mem. Mass. House of Reps. for Brookline 1962–70, later Chair. Cttee on Public Service and mem. Special Comm. on Low Income Housing; f. a research group for public information 1970; moderator of TV public affairs debate programme The Advocates; Gov. of Massachusetts 1975–79, 1983–91; teacher Fla Atlantic Univ., Boca Raton 1992; Democratic Cand. for Pres. 1988; lecturer and Dir of Inter-Governmental Studies, John F. Kennedy School of Govt, Harvard Univ. 1979–82; Distinguished Prof. Northeastern Univ., Boston; Vice Chair. AmTrack Reform Bd 1998–; Gold Medal, City of Athens, Greece 1996. *Publication:* Creating the Future: Massachusetts comeback and its promise for America (with Rosabeth Moss Kanter) 1988. *Address:* Department of Political Science, Northeastern University, 303 Meserve Hall, Boston, MA 02115 (Office); 650 Kelton Avenue, Apartment 302, Los Angeles, CA 90024, USA (Home).

DUKAKIS, Olympia, MA; American actress; b. 20 June 1931; m. Louis Zorich; three s.; ed Boston Univ.; teacher of drama at New York Univ. grad.

programme for 15 years; founding mem. The Charles Playhouse, Boston, Whole Theatre, Montclair, NJ; appeared in more than 100 regional theatre productions; subsequently appeared in off-Broadway shows including Mann Ish Mann, The Marriage of Bette and Boo, Titus Andronicus, Peer Gynt, The Memorandum, The Curse of the Starving Class, Electra; has appeared in Broadway productions of Abraham Cochrane, The Aspern Papers, The Night of the Iguana, Who's Who in Hell, Mike Nichols' Social Security; numerous TV appearances; mem. Bd Nat. Museum of Women in the Arts, Washington, DC and other arts orgs; Acad. Award for Best Supporting Actress for Moonstruck 1988; recipient of two Obie Awards. *Films include:* The Idolmaker, John Loves Mary, Death Wish, Rich Kids, Made for Each Other, Working Girl, Moonstruck, Dad, Look Who's Talking, Steel Magnolias, In the Spirit, Look Who's Talking Too, The Cemetery Club, Digger, Over the Hill, Look Who's Talking Now, Naked Gun 33¹/₃, The Final Insult (cameo), I Love Trouble, Jeffrey, Mighty Aphrodite, Mr Holland's Opus, Picture Perfect, My Beautiful Son 2001, Ladies and The Champ 2001, And Never Let Her Go 2001, The Intended 2002. *Television includes:* Tales of the City (series). *Address:* William Morris Agency, 151 S El Camino Drive, Beverly Hills, CA 90212; 222 Upper Mountain Avenue, Montclair, NJ 07043, USA (Home).

DUKE, Robin Chandler; American diplomatist; b. 1923; m. Angier Biddle Duke (deceased); writer N.Y. Journal American 1940s; fmr mem. Bd Dirs. American Home Products, Rockwell Int., Int. Flavors and Fragrances; Dir U.S.–Japan Foundation, Lucile and David Packard Foundation, UN Asscn of USA 2000–; fmr Vice-Chair. and mem. Advisory Bd Inst. of Int. Educ.; Chair. Del. to 21st Session of UNESCO 1980, Amb. 1980; Amb. to Norway 2000–01; mem. Council on Foreign Relations; Fellow Acad. of Arts and Social Sciences; f. Population Action Int. *Address:* c/o Department of State, 2201 C Street, NW, Washington, DC 20520, U.S.A.

DUKES, Alan M., MA; Irish politician; b. 22 April 1945, Dublin; s. of James Dukes and Margaret Moran; m. Fionnuala Corcoran 1968; two d.; ed Scoil Colmcille and Colaiste Mhuire, Dublin and Univ. Coll., Dublin; Chief Econ., Irish Farmers Asscn 1967–72; Dir Irish Farmers Asscn, Brussels 1973–76; Personal Adviser to Commr of EEC 1977–80; mem. Dáil Éireann for Kildare 1981–2002; Opposition Spokesperson on Agric. March–Dec. 1982; Minister of Agric. 1981–82, for Finance 1982–86, for Justice 1986–87; Leader and Pres. Fine Gael 1987–90; mem. Council of State 1987–90; Minister for Transport, Energy and Communications 1996–97; Opposition Spokesperson on Environment and Local Govt; Pres. Irish Council of the European Movt 1987–91, Chair. 1997–2000; Vice-Pres. Int. European Movt 1991–96; Adjunct Prof. of Public Admin., Man. Univ. of Limerick 1991–; Vice-Pres. European People's Party 1987–96; Chair. Jt Olreachtas Cttee on Foreign Affairs 1995–96. *Address:* Dáil Éireann, Dublin 2, Ireland. *Telephone:* (1) 6183729. *Fax:* (1) 6184159.

DULBECCO, Renato; American virologist; b. 22 Feb. 1914, Cantanzaro, Italy; s. of Leonardo and Maria Dulbecco; m. 1st Giuseppina Salvo 1940 (divorced 1963); m. 2nd Maureen Muir 1963; two d. (and one s. deceased); ed Univ. of Turin; Asst Prof. of Pathology, Univ. of Turin 1940–46, of Experimental Embryology 1947; Research Assoc. Dept of Bacteriology, Indiana Univ. 1947–49; Sr Research Fellow Calif. Inst. of Tech. 1949–52, Assoc. Prof. 1952–53, Prof. 1954–63; Sr Fellow, Salk Inst. for Biological Studies 1963–72; Asst Dir of Research, Imperial Cancer Research Fund Labs (London) 1972–74, Deputy Dir 1974–77; Distinguished Research Prof., Salk Inst., La Jolla, Calif. 1977–, Pres. 1989–92, Pres. Emer. 1993–; Chair. Int. Physicians for Prevention Nuclear War Inst., American-Italian Foundation for Cancer Research; mem. American Asscn for Cancer Research, NAS, American Acad. of Arts and Sciences; Foreign mem. Royal Soc., London 1974, Accad. Nazionale dei Lincei; Hon. mem. Accademia Ligure di Scienze e Lettere; Trustee, La Jolla Co. Day School; Hon. LLD (Glasgow) 1970, Hon. DSc (Yale) 1968, Dr hc (Vrije Univ., Brussels) 1978; several awards, including Ehrlich Prize, Lasker Award 1964, Ludovic Gross Horwitz Prize 1973, Selman A. Waksman Award in Microbiology, NAS, 1974, Nobel Prize in Medicine (Physiology) 1975; Mandel Gold Medal (Czechoslovak Acad. of Sciences) 1982. *Address:* Salk Institute, PO Box 85800, San Diego, CA 92186-5800 (Office); 7525 Hillside Drive, La Jolla, CA 92037-3941, USA (Home). *Telephone:* (858) 453-4100 (Office). *Fax:* (858) 458-9741 (Office). *E-mail:* Dulbecco@salk.edu (Office).

DULLES, HE Cardinal Avery, AB, PhL, STD; American theologian; b. 24 Aug. 1918, Auburn, NY; s. of the late John Foster Avery and Janet Pomeroy Avery; ed Harvard Univ.; ordained priest 1956; McGinley Prof. of Theology, Fordham Univ. 1988–; Prof. Emer. Catholic Univ. of America 1988–; cr. Cardinal 2001; SJ. *Publications:* numerous books include: The Splendor of Faith: The Theological Vision of Pope John Paul II 1999, The New World of Faith 2000; articles on theological matters. *Address:* School of Religion and Religious Education, Fordham University, Fordham Road, Bronx, New York, NY 10458, USA (Office). *Website:* www.fordham.edu/theology (Office).

DUMAS, Jean-Louis Robert Frédéric, LenD; French business executive; b. 2 Feb. 1938, Paris; s. of Robert Dumas and Jacqueline Hermès; m. Rena Gregoriadès 1962; one s. one d.; ed Lycée Janson-de-Sailly, Faculté de Droit de Paris and Inst. d'Etudes Politiques, Paris; Asst buyer, Bloomingdales, New York 1963; joined gen. man. Hermès 1964, Dir, Gen. Man. 1971–78, Chair. and Man. Dir Hermès, Holding Hermès 1978–95, Pres. Groupe Hermès 1995–, Man., Artistic Dir Hermès Int. 1995–; Pres. Castille investissements 1997; Pres. Sport-Soie 1978; Vice-Pres. Comité Colbert 1978–88, Pres.

1988–91; Dir Orfèvrerie Christofle 1988, Gaumont 1991; Nat. adviser on foreign trade 1973–; Officier, Légion d'honneur, Officier des Arts et des Lettres. *Leisure interests:* photography, watercolour paintings. *Address:* Hermès, 24 rue du Faubourg St Honoré, 75008 Paris, France (Office). *Telephone:* 1-40-17-47-17 (Office).

DUMAS, Pierre, LèsD; French politician; b. 15 Nov. 1924, Chambéry; m. 2nd Janine Berenfeld 1992; one d.; ed Ecole Libre des Sciences Politiques; Sales Man. Box Co., La Rochette; Deputy 1958–62, 1967, 1968, 1969–73; Sec. of State for Public Works April–Oct. 1962, Sec. of State for Relations with Parl., responsible for Tourism 1962–67; Sec. of State to Prime Minister, in charge of Tourism 1967–68; Sec. of State for Social Affairs 1968–69; Head French Del. ECOSOC, UN, New York and Geneva 1973–77; Senator 1986–95; Pres. Soc. française pour le Tunnel Routier du Fréjus 1962–2000; Pres. Office Nat. des Forêts 1973–83; Mayor of Chambéry 1959–77, 1983–89; Rassemblement pour la République; Commdr, Légion d'honneur, Médaille de la Résistance. *Address:* 1 place de la Libération, 73000 Chambéry (Office); 22 rue Benoît Molin, 73000 Chambéry, France (Home). *Telephone:* (4) 79-85-79-66 (Office). *Fax:* (4) 79-70-35-06 (Office).

DUMAS, Rhetaugh Etheldra Graves, MS, PhD, RN, FAAN; American health and higher education administrator, nurse and psychologist; b. 26 Nov. 1928, Natchez, Miss.; d. of Rhetaugh Graves and Josephine (Clemmons) Graves Bell; sister of Wade H. Graves and Norman Bell, Jr; m. A. W. Dumas, Jr 1950; one d.; ed Dillard Univ., New Orleans, Yale Univ. School of Nursing and Union Grad. School, Yellow Springs, Ohio; Dir Student Health Center, Dillard Univ. 1957–59; Yale-New Haven Hosp. 1960; Instructor in Psychiatric Nursing, Dillard Univ. 1961; Research Asst and Instructor Yale Univ. School of Nursing 1962–65, Asst Prof. 1965–66, Assoc. Prof. 1966–72; Dir of Nursing, Conn. Medical Health Center, Yale-New Haven Medical Center 1966–72; Chief, Psychiatric Nursing Educ. Br., Div. of Manpower and Training 1972–75; Deputy Dir Div. of Manpower and Training Programs, Nat. Inst. of Mental Health 1976–79; Deputy Dir Nat. Inst. of Mental Health, Alcohol, Drug Abuse and Mental Health Admin., US Public Health Service 1979–81; Dean Univ. of Mich. School of Nursing, Ann Arbor 1981, Prof. 1981, Vice-Provost for Health Affairs, Univ. of Mich. 1994–97, Cole Prof., School of Nursing 1994–, Vice-Provost Emer. 1997–, Dean Emer. 1997–; Pres. American Acad. of Nursing 1987–89; Pres. Nat. League of Nursing 1997–99; mem. NAS Inst. of Medicine; Hon. DHumLitt (Yale) 1989 and several other hon. degrees and awards. *Publications:* The Dilemmas of Black Females in Leadership; numerous articles in professional journals and book chapters. *Leisure interests:* reading, music, singing. *Address:* The University of Michigan, 400 N Ingalls Street, Room 4320, Ann Arbor, MI 48109-2003 (Office); 6 Eastbury Court, Ann Arbor, MI 48105, USA (Home). *Telephone:* (734) 936-6213 (Office); (734) 668-6103 (Home). *Fax:* (734) 764-4546 (Office); (734) 761-6195 (Home). *E-mail:* rhetaugh@Umich.edu (Office).

DUMAS, Roland, LenD; French politician, lawyer and journalist; b. 23 Aug. 1922, Limoges; s. of Georges and Elisabeth (née Lecanuet) Dumas; m. 2nd Anne-Marie Lillet 1964; two s. one d.; ed Lycée de Limoges, Univs. of Paris and London; called to the Bar, Paris 1950 and has practised as a lawyer ever since; journalist with AGEFI, Socialiste Limousin; Political Dir La Corrèze républicaine et socialiste 1967–; mem. Nat. Ass. 1956–58, 1967–68, 1981–83, 1986–93, Vice-Pres. 1968; Minister for European Affairs 1983–84; for Foreign Affairs 1984–86, 1988–93; Govt spokesman July–Dec. 1984; Pres. Nat. Ass. Comm. on Foreign Affairs 1986–87; Chair. Constitutional Court 1995–99, resgnd March 2000; imprisoned for involvement in 'Elf Affair' (financial scandal) May 2001, acquitted Jan. 2003; Officier, Légion d'honneur, Croix de guerre, Croix du combattant volontaire, Grand-Croix de l'ordre d'Isabelle la Catholique (Spain), Ordre du Mérite (Germany). *Publications:* J'ai vu vivre la Chine, Les Avocats, Le Droit de l'information et de la presse, Plaidoyer pour Roger-Gilbert Lecomte, Le droit de la Propriété Littéraire et Artistique. Le peuple assemblé 1989, Le fil et la pelote—Mémoires 1996. *Address:* 19 quai de Bourbon, 75004 Paris, France.

DUMASY, Lise, DèsL; French professor of literature; b. 18 June 1954, Taza, Morocco; ed Ecole Normale Supérieure, Sèvres; schoolteacher 1978–80; research engineer CNRS 1980, seconded to Inst. de France 1984; teacher Mannheim Univ. 1987–88; Sr lecturer Univ. Stendhal (Grenoble-III) then Prof. 1992, Head Dept of French Language, Literature and Civilization 1992–95, mem. Scientific Council 1997, Prin. 1999–. *Address:* Bureau de la Présidente, Université Stendhal (Grenoble-III), BP 25, 38040 Grenoble Cedex 9, France (Office).

DUMMETT, Sir Michael Anthony Eardley, Kt, MA, DLitt; British professor of philosophy; b. 27 June 1925, London; s. of George Herbert Dummett and Mabel Iris Dummett (née Eardley-Wilmot); m. Ann Chesney 1951; three s. two d.; ed Sandroyd School, Winchester Coll., Christ Church, Oxford; served army 1943–47; Asst Lecturer in Philosophy, Univ. of Birmingham 1950–51; Prize Fellow, All Souls Coll., Oxford 1950–57, Research Fellow 1957–61; Harkness Foundation Fellow, Univ. of Calif., Berkeley 1955–56; Reader in Philosophy of Mathematics, Oxford Univ. 1961–74; Sr Research Fellow, All Souls Coll., Oxford 1974–79, Sub-Warden 1974–76; Visiting Lecturer Univ. of Ghana 1958, Stanford Univ., Calif., USA 1960–66, Univ. of Minn. 1968, Princeton Univ. 1970, Rockefeller Univ., New York 1973; William James Lecturer in Philosophy, Harvard Univ. 1976; Wykeham Prof. of Logic, Univ. of Oxford 1979–92; Fellow, New College, Oxford 1979–92, Emer. Fellow 1992–98, Hon. Fellow 1998–; Fellow, British Acad. 1967–84 (resgnd); Sr

Fellow 1995–; Emer. Fellow, All Souls College, Oxford 1979–; Chair. Jt Council for the Welfare of Immigrants 1970–71; mem. unofficial cttee of inquiry into events in Southall, 1979–80, Shadow Bd Barclays Bank 1981; Foreign Hon. mem. American Acad. of Arts and Sciences; Hon. PhD (Nijmegen) 1983; Hon. DLitt (Caen) 1993, (Aberdeen) 1993; Lakatos Award 1994, Rolf Schock Prize in Philosophy and Logic 1995. *Publications:* Frege: Philosophy of Language 1973, The Justification of Deduction 1973, Elements of Intuitionism 1977, Truth and other Enigmas 1978, Immigration: where the Debate goes wrong 1978, Catholicism and the World Order 1979, The Game of Tarot 1980, Twelve Tarot Games 1980, The Interpretation of Frege's Philosophy 1981, Voting Procedures 1984, The Visconti-Sforza Tarot Cards 1986, Ursprünge der Analytischen Philosophie 1988, The Logical Basis of Metaphysics 1991, Frege and other Philosophers 1991, Frege: Philosophy of Mathematics 1991, Grammar and Style 1993, The Seas of Language 1993, Origins of Analytical Philosophy 1993, Il Mondo e l'Angelo 1993, I Tarocchi Siciliani 1995, A Wicked Pack of Cards 1996, Principles of Electoral Reform 1997, A History of the Occult Tarot 1870–1970 2002. *Leisure interests:* history of card games and playing cards. *Address:* New College, Oxford, OX1 3BN (Office); 54 Park Town, Oxford, OX2 6SJ, England (Home). *Telephone:* (1865) 279555 (Office); (1865) 558698. *Fax:* (1865) 558698.

DUMONT, Dame Ivy, DBE, DPA; Bahamian civil servant, politician and Governor-General; b. 1930, Roses, Long Island; m. Reginald Dumont; two c.; fmr teacher; worked in public admin. then in human resources devt in pvt. sector; fmr Sec.-Gen. Free Nat. Movt; Senator and Cabinet Minister 1992–2000; Chair. Public Service Comm. –2001; Acting Gov.-Gen. Nov.–Dec. 2001, Gov.-Gen. of the Bahamas Jan. 2002–; Founding mem. Bahamas Union of Teachers. *Address:* Government House, P.O. Box N-8301, Nassau, The Bahamas (Office).

DUNAWAY, Dorothy Faye; American actress; b. 14 Jan. 1941, Bascom, Florida; d. of John and Grace Dunaway; m. 1st Peter Wolf 1974; m. 2nd Terry O'Neill 1981; one s.; ed Univs. of Florida and Boston; spent three years with Lincoln Center Repertory Co. in New York, appearing in A Man For All Seasons, After the Fall and Tartuffe; Off-Broadway in Hogan's Goat 1965; appeared at the Mark Taper Forum, LA in Old Times, as Blanche du Bois in A Streetcar Named Desire 1973, The Curse of an Aching Heart 1982; Acad. Award Best Actress for Network. *Films include:* Hurry Sundown 1967, The Happening 1967, Bonnie and Clyde 1967, The Thomas Crown Affair 1968, A Place For Lovers 1969, The Arrangement 1969, Little Big Man 1970, Doc 1971, The Getaway 1972, Oklahoma Crude 1973, The Three Musketeers 1973, Chinatown 1974, Three Days of the Condor 1975, The Towering Inferno 1976, Voyage of the Damned 1976, Network 1976, The Eyes of Laura Mars 1978, The Champ 1979, The First Deadly Sin 1981, Mommie Dearest 1981, The Wicked Lady 1982, Supergirl 1984, Barfly 1987, Burning Secret 1988, The Handmaid's Tale 1989, On a Moonlit Night 1989, Up to Date 1989, Scorchers 1991, Faithful 1991, Three Weeks in Jerusalem, The Arrowtooth Waltz 1991, Double Edge, Arizona Dream, The Temp, Dun Juan DeMarco 1995, Drunks, Dunston Checks In, Albino Alligator, The Chamber, Fanny Hill 1998, Love Lies Bleeding 1999, The Yards 1999, Joan of Arc 1999, The Thomas Crown Affair 1999, The Yards 2000, Stanley's Gig 2000, Yellow Bird 2001, Changing Hearts 2002, Rules of Attraction 2002, Mid-Century 2002, The Calling 2002. *Television includes:* After the Fall 1974, The Disappearance of Aimee 1976, Hogan's Goat, Mommie Dearest 1981, Evita!–First Lady 1981, 13 at Dinner 1985, Beverly Hills Madame 1986, The Country Girl, Casanova, The Raspberry Ripple, Cold Sassy Tree, Silhouette, Rebecca, Gia 1998, Running Mates 2000, The Biographer 2002. *Publication:* Looking For Gatsby (autobiog., with Betsy Sharkey) 1995. *Address:* c/o Ed Limato, ICM, 8942 Wilshire Boulevard, Beverly Hills, CA 90211, USA.

DUNBAR, Adrian; British actor; b. Enniskillen, N Ireland; m. Anna Nygh; one d.; one step s.; ed Guildhall School of Music and Drama, London. *Films include:* The Fear, A World Apart, Dealers, My Left Foot, Hear My Song 1992, The Crying Game 1993, Widows' Peak 1994, Richard III 1995, The Near Room 1996, The General 1998, Wild About Harry 2000, Shooters 2000, The Wedding Tackle 2000, How Harry Became a Tree 2001, Triggerman 2002, Darkness 2002. *Stage appearances include:* Ourselves Alone (Royal Court Theatre) 1985, King Lear (Royal Court). *Television appearances include:* Reasonable Force (BBC TV), Cracker.

DUNCAN, Daniel Kablan; Côte d'Ivoirian politician; b. 1943, Ouelle; ed Inst. Commercial, Nancy and Inst. de Commerce Int. Paris; Ministry of Economy and Finance 1970; in-house training, IMF, Washington, DC 1973; joined Cen. Bank of W African States (BCEAO); with Caisse Nat. de Prévoyance Sociale; returned to BCEAO HQ, Dakar 1989; Minister Del. responsible for Econ., Finance and Planning, Office of Prime Minister 1990–93; Prime Minister of Côte d'Ivoire 1993–2000; also fmr Minister of Economy, Finance and Planning, Minister of Planning and Industrial Devt. *Address:* c/o Office of the Prime Minister, boulevard Angoulvant, 01 BP 1533, Abidjan 01, Côte d'Ivoire.

DUNCAN SMITH, Rt. Hon. (George) Iain, PC; British politician; b. 9 April 1954; s. of the late Group Capt. W. G. G. Duncan Smith and of Pamela Mary Duncan Smith (née Summers); m. Elizabeth Wynne Fremantle; two s. two d.; ed HMS Conway (Cadet School), Royal Mil. Acad. Sandhurst; served in Scots Guards 1975–81; Dir GEC (later Marconi) 1981–88, Bellwinch PLC 1988–89; Publishing Dir Jane's Information Group 1989–92; Conservative Party cand. for Bradford W, gen. elections 1987; Vice-Chair. Fulham Conservative Asscn

1991; MP for Chingford 1992–97, for Chingford and Woodford Green 1997–; mem. Select Cttee on Health 1994–95, on Standards and Privileges 1996–97; Vice-Chair. Conservative European Affairs Cttee 1996–97; Shadow Sec. of State for Social Security 1997–99, for Defence 1999–2001; Leader Conservative Party and Leader of the Opposition 2001–; Freeman City of London. *Publications:* pamphlets on social security, European and defence issues. *Leisure interests:* family, painting, fishing, cricket, tennis, shooting, opera, reading. *Address:* Conservative Party, 32 Smith Square, London SW1P 3HH (Office); House of Commons, London SW1A 0AA, England (Office). *Telephone:* (20) 7222-9000 (Office). *Fax:* (20) 7222-1135 (Office). *Website:* www .conservatives.com (Office).

DUNHAM, Archie W., BEng, MBA; American business executive; b. 1938; m. Linda Dunham; three c.; ed Univ. of Okla.; with US Marine Corps 1960–64; Pres. and CEO Conoco Inc. 1996–2002, Chair. 1999–2002, Chair. ConocoPhillips (following merger between Conoco and Phillips) 2002–; Dir American Petroleum Inst., Energy Inst. of the Americas, Nat. Bd, Smithsonian Inst., US–Russia Business Council; Dir Louisiana-Pacific Corpn, Phelps Dodge Corpn, Union Pacific Corpn, Greater Houston Partnership, Memorial Hermann Healthcare System; Chair. Nat. Assn of Mfrs; Chair. and fmr Pres. Houston Grand Opera; mem. Bretton Woods Cttee, Business Round Table, The Business Council; Gov. The Houston Forum; mem. Bd of Visitors M.D. Anderson Cancer Center; mem. Texas Gov.'s Business Council, Comm. on Nat. Energy Policy, Nat. Infrastructure Advisory Council, Marine Corps Heritage Foundation; Trustee George Bush Presidential Library Foundation, Houston Symphony, United Way of the Texas Gulf Coast; Dr. h.c. (Okla) 1999; B'nai B'rith Int. Achievement Award 2000, Ellis Island Medal of Honor 2001, Horatio Alger Award 2001. *Address:* Office of the Chairman, ConocoPhillips, 600 North Dairy Ashford, POB 2197, Houston, TX 77252-2197, USA (Office). *Telephone:* (281) 293-1000 (Office). *Website:* www.conocophillips.com (Office).

DUNHAM, Katherine; American dancer and choreographer; b. 22 June 1909, Ill.; m. 1st Jordis McCoo 1931 (divorced); m. 2nd John Thomas Pratt 1941 (died 1986); one d.; ed Chicago and Northwestern Univs.; début, Chicago World's Fair 1934; with Chicago Opera Co. 1935–36; Julius Rosenwald Travel Fellowship 1936–37; Dance Dir Labor Stage 1939–40; has appeared in numerous films 1941–; founded Katherine Dunham School of Cultural Arts and Katherine Dunham Dance Co. 1945; numerous tours and personal appearances in N and S. America and Europe. *Publications:* Journey to Accompong 1946, Form and Function in Primitive Dance, Form and Function in Educational Dance, A Touch of Innocence 1959, Island Possessed 1969, Kasamance 1974. *Address:* 532 North 10th Street, East St Louis, IL 62201, USA.

DUNKEL, Arthur, BScEcon; Swiss consultant and fmr international civil servant; b. 28 Aug. 1932, Lisbon, Portugal; one s. one d.; ed French Lycée, Lisbon, Business School, Lausanne, Coll. St Michel, Fribourg, Univ. of Lausanne; joined Swiss Fed. Office for Foreign Econ. Affairs, Berne 1956, Head, section for OECD matters 1960–64, for co-operation with developing countries 1964–71, for world trade policy 1971–73; Perm. Rep. to GATT 1973–76; Del. of Fed. Council for Trade Agreements with rank of Amb. 1976–80; Dir-Gen. GATT 1980–93; Vice-Chair. and Rapporteur UNCTAD Inter-Governmental Group on Supplementary Financing 1968, Rapporteur UNCTAD Bd 1969, Chair. Cttee on Balance-of-Payments Restrictions 1972–75; Chair. UN Conf. on New Wheat Agreement 1978; Asst Lecturer, Inst. of Journalism, Univ. of Fribourg 1974–78; Sr Lecturer on Int. Econs, Univs of Geneva and Fribourg 1983–; Arthur Dunkel Consultancy 1993–; mem. Bd of Dirs various cos.; Pres. Swiss Trade Initiative for the Middle East and N Africa; Hon. Dr (Fribourg) 1980, (Basle) 1992; Freedom Prize, Max Schmidheiny Foundation (Switzerland) 1989, Consumers for World Trade Award (USA) 1990, Fed. of Swiss Industrial Holding Cos Award 1993, Max-Petitpierre Award (Switzerland) 1993, Médaille d'Or, Foundation Jean Monnet for Europe (Switzerland) 1995. *Address:* 56 rue du Stand, 1204 Geneva (Office); 32a rue de St Jean, 1203 Geneva, Switzerland (Home). *Telephone:* (22) 3101706 (Office); (22) 3455860 (Home). *Fax:* (22) 3101705 (Office). *E-mail:* STI2@iprolink.ch (Office).

DUNLOP, Frank, BA, CBE; British theatre director; b. 15 Feb. 1927, Leeds; s. of Charles Norman Dunlop and Mary Aarons; ed Kibworth Beauchamp Grammar School, Univ. Coll. London, Old Vic School, London; served RAF 1946–49; f. and Dir Piccolo Theatre Co. 1954–; Assoc. Dir Bristol Old Vic 1955–59; Dir Plays W End of London and Mermaid Theatre 1959–; Theatre Dir Brussels, including Theatre Nat. Belge 1959–; Dir Nottingham Playhouse 1961–64; f. Dir Pop Theatre 1966–; Assoc. Dir and Admin. Nat. Theatre London 1967–71; Founder and Dir Young Vic Theatre 1970–78, 1980–83; Theatre Dir USA (Broadway, LA) 1974–; Dir Edin. Festival 1983–91; Fellow Univ. Coll., London 1979; Hon. DUniv (Heriot-Watt) 1989, (Edin.) 1990. *Publication:* Scapino 1975. *Leisure interests:* work and doing nothing. *Address:* c/o Piccolo Theatre Co., 13 Choumert Square, London, SE15 4RE, England; c/o E. Nives, Suite 417, 1775 Broadway, New York, NY 10019, USA. *Telephone:* (20) 7252-8515 (London); (212) 265-8787 (USA). *Fax:* (20) 7358-9291 (London); (212) 265-8873 (USA).

DUNLOP, John T., AB, PhD, LLD, DCS; American industrial relations expert and economist; b. 5 July 1914, Placerville, Calif.; s. of John Dunlop and Antonia Dunlop (née Forni); m. Dorothy Webb 1937; two s. one d.; ed Univs of California and Cambridge, England; Instructor Harvard Univ. 1938, Assoc. Prof. 1945, Chair. Wertheim Cttee on Industrial Relations 1945–, Prof. 1950–,

Chair. Dept of Econs 1961–66, Dean Faculty of Arts and Sciences 1970–73; Chair. Bd for Settlement of Jurisdictional Disputes 1948–57; mem. Atomic Energy Labor Relations Panel 1948–53; mem. Sec. Labor's Advisory Cttee on Labor–Management Relations in Atomic Energy Installations 1954–57; mem. Kaiser Steelworkers' Comm. 1960–68, Presidential Railroad Comm. 1960–62, Missiles Sites Labor Comm. 1961–67; Chair. Nat. Manpower Policy Task Force 1968–69; mem. President's Nat. Comm. on Productivity 1970–73, Chair. 1973–75; Chair. Manpower Inst. 1970–73; Dir Cost of Living Council 1973–74; Co-ordinator President's Labor–Man. Cttee 1974–76; US Sec. of Labor 1975–76; Chair. Construction Industry Joint Conf. 1959–68; mem. Construction Industry Collective Bargaining Comm. 1969–71; Chair. US Labor Man. Group 1970–76; Chair. Construction Industry Stabilization Cttee 1971–73, mem. 1973–74; Chair. Pay Advisory Cttee 1979–80; Chair. Comm. on Future of Worker–Man. Relations 1993–95, Int. Competition Policy Advisory Cttee to Attorney Gen. 1997–2000; Pres. Industrial Relations Research Assocn 1960, Int. Industrial Relations Research Assocn 1973–76; mem. American Acad. of Arts and Sciences, American Philosophical Soc., Inst. of Medicine; Louis K. Comstock Award, Nat. Electrical Contractors' Assocn 1974, Housing Hall of Fame 1986, Murray-Green-Meany Award 1987; Hon. Life Mem. Nat. Acad. of Arbitrators 1991; Workplace Legacy Award, W.J. Usery Centre for the Workplace 1999, Industrial Relations Research Assocn Lifetime Achievement Award 2000, Gold Medal Award, Nat. Policy Assocn 2000. *Publications:* Wage Determination under Trade Unions 1944, Cost Behavior and Price Policy 1943, Collective Bargaining: Principles and Cases (with James J. Healy) 1949, The Wage Adjustment Board. (with Arthur D. Hill) 1950, The Theory of Wage Determination (Ed.) 1957, Industrial Relations Systems 1958, 1993, Industrialism and Industrial Man 1960, Potentials of the American Economy (Ed.) 1961, Economic Growth in the United States (Ed.) 1961, Automation and Technological Change (Ed.) 1962, Frontiers of Collective Bargaining (Ed.) 1967, Labor and the American Community (with Derek Bok) 1970, Inflation and Incomes Policies: the Political Economy of Recent U.S. Experience 1974, Industrialism and Industrial Man Reconsidered 1975, The Lessons of Wage and Price Controls—The Food Sector 1978, Business and Public Policy 1980, Dispute Resolution, Negotiation and Consensus Building 1984, The Management of Labor Unions 1990, Mediation and Arbitration of Employment Disputes (with A. Zack) 1997, A Stitch in Time, Lean Retailing and the Transformation of Manufacturing—Lessons from Apparel and Textile Industries (with others) 1999. *Leisure interest:* walking. *Address:* 208 Littaner Center, Harvard University, Cambridge, MA 02138 (Office); 509 Pleasant Street, Belmont, MA 02478, USA. *Telephone:* (617) 495-4157 (Office). *Fax:* (617) 495-7730 (Office).

DUNMORE, Helen; British poet and novelist; b. 1952, Yorks.; m.; one s. one d. one step-s.; Hon. Fellow Royal Soc. of Literature; Poetry Book Soc. Choice (for The Raw Garden), Poetry Soc.'s Alice Hunt Bartlett Award (for The Sea Skater), Signal Poetry Award (for Secrets) 1995, McKitterick Prize (for Zennor in Darkness) 1994, Orange Prize for Women Writers of Fiction (for A Spell of Winter) 1996. *Publications:* (poetry): The Sea Skater, The Raw Garden, Secrets, Out of the Blue, New and Selected Poems; (novels): Zennor in Darkness, Burning Bright, A Spell of Winter, Talking to the Dead 1996, Love of Fat Men (short stories) 1998, Your Blue-Eyed Boy 1998, With Your Crooked Heart 1999, Ice Cream (short stories) 2000, The Siege 2001; also children's novels. *Leisure interests:* family life and friendships. *Address:* c/o Caradoc King, A. P. Watt Ltd, 20 John Street, London, WC1N 2DR, England. *Telephone:* (20) 7405-6774. *Fax:* (20) 7831-2154.

DUNN, Douglas Eaglesham, FRSL; British poet; b. 23 Oct. 1942; s. of William D. Dunn and Margaret McGowan; m. 1st Lesley B. Wallace 1964 (died 1981); m. 2nd Lesley Jane Bathgate 1985; one s. one d.; ed Univ. of Hull; full-time writer 1971–91; Writer-in-residence Duncan of Jordanstone Coll. of Art and Dundee Dist Libraries 1987–; Fellow in Creative Writing, Univ. of St Andrews 1989–91, Prof. 1991–; Dir St Andrews Scottish Studies Inst. 1992–, Head School of English 1994–99; Hon. Visiting Prof. Dundee Univ. 1987–89; Hon. Fellow, Humberside Coll. 1987; Hon. LLD (Dundee) 1987; Hon. DLitt (Hull) 1995; Somerset Maugham Award (for Terry Street) 1972, Faber Memorial Prize (for Love or Nothing) 1976, Hawthornden Prize (for St Kilda's Parliament) 1982, Whitbread Poetry Award and Whitbread Book of the Year (for Elegies) 1986; Cholmondeley Award 1989. *Publications:* Terry Street 1969, The Happier Life 1972, New Poems 1972–73 (ed.) 1973, Love or Nothing 1974, A Choice of Byron's Verse (ed.) 1974, Two Decades of Irish Writing (criticism) 1975, The Poetry of Scotland (ed.) 1979, Barbarians 1979, St Kilda's Parliament 1981, Europa's Lover 1982, A Rumoured City: New Poets from Hull (ed.) 1982, To Build a Bridge: A Celebration of Humberside in Verse (ed.) 1982, Elegies 1985, Secret Villages (short stories) 1985, Selected Poems 1986, Northlight 1988, New and Selected Poems 1989, Poll Tax: The Fiscal Fake 1990, Andromache 1990, The Essential Browning (ed.) 1990, Scotland. An Anthology (ed.) 1991, Faber Book of Twentieth Century Scottish Poetry (ed.) 1992, Dante's Drum-Kit 1993, Boyfriends and Girlfriends (short stories) 1995, Oxford Book of Scottish Short Stories (ed.) 1995, The Donkey's Ears, The Year's Afternoon 2000, 20th Century Scottish Poems (ed.) 2000. *Leisure interests:* playing the clarinet and saxophone, listening to jazz, gardening, philately. *Address:* School of English, The University, St Andrews, Fife, KY16 9AL, Scotland (Office). *Telephone:* (1334) 462666 (Office). *Fax:* (1334) 462655 (Office). *E-mail:* ded@st-andrews.ac.uk (Office).

DUNN, John Montfort, BA, FBA, FSA; British professor of political theory; b. 9 Sept. 1940, Fulmer; s. of Brig. Henry G. M. Dunn and Catherine M. Kinloch;

m. 1st Susan D. Fyvel 1965; m. 2nd Judith F. Bernal 1971; m. 3rd Ruth Ginette Scurr 1997; two s. (one deceased) one d.; ed Winchester Coll., Millfield School, King's Coll. Cambridge and Harvard Univ.; Grad. School of Arts and Sciences; Official Fellow in History, Jesus Coll. Cambridge 1965–66; Fellow, King's Coll. Cambridge 1966–, Coll. lecturer, Dir of Studies in History 1966–72; Lecturer in Political Science, Univ. of Cambridge 1972–77, Reader in Politics 1977–87, Prof. of Political Theory 1987–; Visiting Lecturer, Univ. of Ghana 1968–69; Chair. Section P. (Political Studies), British Acad. 1994–97, Bd of Consultants, Kim Dae-Jung Peace Foundation for the Asia-Pacific Region 1994–. *Publications:* The Political Thought of John Locke 1969, Modern Revolutions 1972, Dependence and Opportunity (with A. F. Robertson) 1973, Western Political Theory in the Face of the Future 1979, Political Obligation in its Historical Context 1980, Locke 1984, The Politics of Socialism 1984, Rethinking Modern Political Theory 1985, The Economic Limits to Modern Politics (ed.) 1990, Interpreting Political Responsibility 1990, Storia delle dottrine politiche 1992, Democracy: the unfinished journey (ed.) 1992, Contemporary Crisis of the Nation State? (ed.) 1994, The History of Political Theory 1995, Great Political Thinkers (21 Vols) (co-ed.) 1997, The Cunning of Unreason 2000, Pensare la Politica 2002. *Leisure interests:* watching birds and animals, opera, travel. *Address:* King's College, Cambridge, CB2 1ST (Office); The Merchant's House, 31 Station Road, Swavesey, Cambridge, CB4 5QJ, England (Home). *Telephone:* (1223) 331258 (Office); (1954) 231451 (Home). *Fax:* (1223) 331315. *E-mail:* jmd24@cam.ac.uk (Office).

DUNN, Baroness (Life Peer), cr. 1990, of Hong Kong Island in Hong Kong and of Knightsbridge in the Royal Borough of Kensington and Chelsea; **Lydia Selina Dunn;** Hong Kong business executive; b. 29 Feb. 1940; d. of Yenchuen Yeh Dunn and Chen Yin Chu; m. Michael David Thomas, C.M.G., Q.C. 1988; ed St Paul's Convent School, Coll. of Holy Names, Oakland, Calif., USA and Univ. of California, Berkeley; Exec. Dir John Swire & Sons Ltd 1996–; Dir John Swire & Sons (HK) Ltd 1978–, Swire Pacific Ltd 1981–, Cathay Pacific Airways Ltd 1985–97 (Adviser to Bd 1997–), Volvo 1991–93 (mem. Int. Advisory Bd 1985–91), Christie's Int. PLC 1996–98, Christie's Fine Art 1998–2000, Marconi PLC (fmrly GEC) 1997–2002; Deputy Chair. Hong Kong & Shanghai Banking Corpn 1992–96 (Dir 1981–96), HSBC Holdings PLC (fmrly Hong Kong and Shanghai Banking Corpn Holdings–London) 1992–96 (Dir 1990–); mem. Hong Kong Legis. Council 1976–88 (Sr mem. 1985–88); mem. Hong Kong Exec. Council 1982–95 (Sr mem. 1988–95); Chair. Lord Wilson Heritage Trust 1993–95; mem. Hong Kong/Japan Business Co-operation Cttee 1983–95, Chair. 1988–95; mem. Hong Kong/U.S. Econ. Co-operation Cttee 1984–93; Chair. Hong Kong Trade Devt Council 1983–91; Hon. Fellow London Business School 2000; Hon. LLD (Chinese Univ. of Hong Kong) 1984, (Univ. of Hong Kong) 1991, (Univ. of BC, Canada) 1991, (Leeds) 1994; Hon. DSc (Buckingham) 1995; Prime Minister of Japan's Trade Award 1987, U.S. Sec. of Commerce's Award to Peace and Commerce 1988. *Publication:* In the Kingdom of the Blind 1983. *Leisure interest:* study of antiques. *Address:* John Swire & Sons Ltd, Swire House, 59 Buckingham Gate, London, SW1E 6AJ, England.

DUNST, Kirsten Caroline; American actress; b. 30 April 1982, Point Pleasant, NJ; d. of Klaus Dunst and Inez Dunst; ed Notre Dame High School; began career at age of four as model, Elite agency; first roles in TV commercials; has appeared in more than 40 films and 10 TV guest appearances. *Films include:* The Bonfire of the Vanities 1990, High Strung 1991, Interview with the Vampire 1994 (MTV Award for Best Breakthrough Performance, Saturn Award for Best Young Actress), Little Women 1994, Jumanji 1995, Mother Night 1996, Wag the Dog 1997, Small Soldiers 1998, Strike! 1998, The Virgin Suicides 1999, Drop Dead Georgeous 1999, Luckytown Blues 2000, Bring It On 2000, Crazy/Beautiful 2001, The Cat's Meow 2001, Spiderman 2002. *TV appearances include:* Sisters 1991, Star Trek: The Next Generation 1993, ER (several episodes) 1996, The Outer Limits 1997, Stories From My Childhood 1998. *Address:* c/o William Morris Agency, 151 El Camino Drive, Beverly Hills, CA 90210, USA (Office).

DUNSTAN, (Andrew Harold) Bernard, RA; British artist; b. 19 Jan. 1920, Teddington; s. of the late Dr A. E. Dunstan; m. Diana M. Armfield 1949; three s.; ed St Paul's School, Byam Shaw School and Slade School; has exhibited at Royal Acad. since 1945; exhibits regularly at Agnews, London; numerous one-man exhbns; works in many public and pvt. collections including Museum of London, Nat. Portrait Gallery, Nat. Gallery of NZ; Past Pres. Royal West of England Acad.; mem. New English Art Club; Chair. Artists' Gen. Benevolent Inst. 1987–91; Trustee RA 1989–95. *Publications:* Learning to Paint 1970, Painting in Progress 1976, Painting Methods of the Impressionists 1976, The Paintings of Bernard Dunstan 1993, Ruskin's Elements of Drawing (Ed.) 1991. *Leisure interest:* music. *Address:* 10 High Park Road, Kew, Richmond, Surrey, TW9 4BH, England. *Telephone:* (20) 8876-6633.

DUNSTAN, Gordon Reginald, CBE, MA, FSA; British university professor (retd); b. 25 April 1917, Plymouth; s. of Frederick John Menhennet Dunstan and Winifred Amy Orchard; m. Ruby Maud Fitzer 1949; two s. one d.; ed Leeds Univ.; Minor Canon, St George's Chapel, Windsor Castle 1955–59; Minor Canon, Westminster Abbey 1959–67; Canon Theologian, Leicester Cathedral 1966–82; Prof. of Moral and Social Theology, King's Coll., London Univ. 1967–82, Prof. Emer. 1982–; Hon. Research Fellow, Univ. of Exeter 1982–; Chaplain to HM the Queen 1976–87; Founder Fellow Acad. of Medical Sciences 1998; mem. Nuffield Council on Bioethics 1990–95; Vice-Pres. London Medical Group and Inst. of Medical Ethics 1985–2001; Pres. Tavistock Inst. of Medical Psychology 1991–; Hon. DD (Exeter) 1973, Hon. LLD (Leicester) 1986; Hon. FRSM 1984, Hon. MRCP 1987, Hon. FRCP 1995, Hon. mem. British Paediatric Asscn 1990, Hon. FRCOG 1991, Hon. FRCGP 1993, Hon. FRCPH 1997. *Publications:* The Family Is Not Broken 1962, The Register of Edmund Lacy, Bishop of Exeter 1420–1455, 5 Vols 1963–72, A Digger Still 1968, Not Yet the Epitaph 1968, The Sacred Ministry 1970, The Artifice of Ethics 1974, A Moralist in the City 1974, Consent in Medicine (co-ed. with M. J. Seller) 1983, The Moral Status of the Human Embryo (co-ed. with M. J. Seller) 1988, Biomedical Ethics: An Anglo-American Dialogue (co-ed. with D. Callahan) 1988, Doctors' Decisions: Ethical Conflicts in Medical Practice (co-ed. with E. A. Shinebourne) 1989, The Human Embryo: Aristotle and the Arabic and European Traditions (ed.) 1990, Euthanasia: Life, Death and the Medical Duty 1996. *Leisure interests:* small islands, *domus* and *rus*. *Address:* Maple Dene, 10–14 St Agnes Road, Moseley, Birmingham, B13 9PW, England. *Telephone:* (1392) 276015.

DUNWOODY, Richard, MBE; British jockey (retd) and business executive; b. 18 Jan. 1964, Belfast, Northern Ireland; s. of George Dunwoody and Gillian Dunwoody (née Thrale); m. (divorced); ed Rendcomb Coll.; rode winner Grand Nat. (West Tip) 1986, (Minnehoma) 1994, Cheltenham Gold Cup (Charter Party) 1988, Champion Hurdle (Kribensis) 1990; Champion Nat. Hunt Jockey 1992–93, 1993–94, 1994–95; at retirement in 1999 held record for most wins (1,699, record later broken); Group Man. Partner, Dunwoody Sports Marketing 2002; Nat. Hunt Jockey of the Year 1990, 1992–95; Champion of Champions 2001. *Publications:* Hell For Leather (with Marcus Armytage), Dual (with Sean Magee), Hands and Heels (with Marcus Armytage), Obsessed. *Leisure interests:* motor sport, rugby, football, running. *Address:* c/o Dunwoody Sports Marketing, The Litten, Newtown Road, Newbury, Berks., RG14 7BB, England (Office). *Telephone:* (1635) 582880 (Office). *Fax:* (1635) 845811 (Office). *E-mail:* richard.d@du-mc.co.uk (Home).

DUPLAT, Jean-Louis; Belgian judge; Pres. Tribunal de Commerce –1989; Chair. Belgian Banking and Finance Comm. 1989–2000. *Address:* Commission Bancaire et Financière, 99 ave Louise, 1050 Brussels, Belgium.

DUQUESNE, Antoine; Belgian politician and barrister; b. 3 Feb. 1941, Ixelles; ed Athénée Royal of Liège, Univ. of Liège; Asst Lecturer in Law, State Univ. of Liège 1965–71; barrister in Liège 1965–75; Chef de Cabinet for various ministers 1973–87; Asst Gen. Sec. of Comité Nat. de Formation et de Perfectionnement Professionel dans les Métiers et Négoces 1975–77; Gen. Admin. of Comité Nat. de Coordination et de Concertation de la Formation Permanente des Classes moyennes 1977–82; Man. of Caisse Nat. de Crédit Professionel (C.N.C.P.) 1983–88; Minister of Nat. Educ. 1987–88; Barrister in Marche-en-Famenne 1988–; Senator and mem. Comms. on Social Affairs, Educ. and Science and Chair. Comm.of Agric. and the Self-Employed 1988–91; town councillor of Manhay 1989–, Mayor 1995–; Chair. Parti Réformateur Libéral (PRL) 1990–92; Deputy and mem. of Comms. of Revision of the Constitution and of Justice 1991–99; Provincial Chair. PRL for Luxembourg 1994–; Vice-Chair. of House of Reps. 1995–99; Chair. Comm. of Justice 1996–98; Chair. Comm. for Foreign Relations 1999; Minister of the Interior 1999–; mem. Conseil régional wallon 1991–95, Conseil de la Communauté française 1991–95; Grand Officer, Order of Leopold 1999. *Publications:* numerous legal articles. *Address:* Ministry of the Interior, 60–62 rue Royale, 1000 Brussels, Belgium (Office); Al Maison 3, 6960 Harre-Manhay, Belgium (Home). *Telephone:* (2) 504-85-11 (Office). *Fax:* (2) 504-85-00 (Office). *E-mail:* cab.affint@mibz.fgov.be (Office). *Website:* mibz.fgov.be (Office).

DUQUESNE, Jacques Henri Louis, LenD; French journalist and author; b. 18 March 1930, Dunkirk; s. of Louis Duquesne and Madeleine Chevalier; m. Edith Dubois 1954; one s. one d.; ed Coll. Jean-Bart, Dunkirk and Faculté de Droit, Paris; reporter, La Croix 1957–64; Deputy Dir Panorama Chrétien 1964–70, head of investigations 1967; Asst Ed.-in-Chief, L'Express 1970–71; Co-founder and Asst Ed.-in-Chief, Le Point 1972–74, Ed.-in-Chief 1974–77, Pres.-Dir-Gen. 1985–90; Dir-Gen. La Vie Catholique group of Publs 1977–79; news reporter, Europe No. 1 1969–, La Croix 1983–, Midi Libre 1997–; Chair. Bd L'Express 1997–; Dir Editions du Seuil; mem. Jury, Prix Interallié 1986–; Chevalier, Légion d'honneur. *Publications:* L'Algérie ou la guerre des mythes 1959, Les 16–24 ans 1964, Les prêtres 1965, Les catholiques français sous l'occupation 1966, Demain une Eglise sans prêtres 1968, Dieu pour l'homme d'aujourd'hui 1970, La gauche du Christ 1972, Les 13–62 ans 1974, La grande triche 1977, Une voix, la nuit 1979, La rumeur de la ville 1981, Maria Vadamme 1983, Alice Van Meulen 1985, Saint-Eloi 1986, Au début d'un bel été 1988, les Vents du Nord m'ont dit 1989, Catherine Courage 1990, Jean Bart 1992, Laura C. 1994, Jésus 1994, Théo et Marie 1996, les Années Jean-Paul II 1996 (jtly.), Le Dieu de Jésus 1997, Le Bonheur en 36 vertus, Romans du Nord 1999, Les Héritières 2000, Pour comprendre la guerre d'Algérie 2001. *Address:* 13 rue de Poissy, 75005 Paris, France (Home).

DURACK, David Tulloch, MB, DPhil, FRCP, FRACP, FACP; American professor of medicine; b. 18 Dec. 1944, W Australia; s. of Reginald W. Durack and Grace E. Tulloch; m. Carmen E. Prosser 1970; three s. one d.; ed Scotch Coll. Perth and Univs. of W Australia and Oxford; Rhodes Scholar; intern Radcliffe Infirmary, Oxford; further training at Royal Postgrad. Medical School, London; fmr Chief, Div. of Infectious Diseases and Int. Health, Duke Univ. 1977–, Prof. 1982; Chair. Dept of Medicine and Chief, Div. of Infectious Diseases, Health Care Int. (Scotland) 1994–95; now Vice-Pres. Corp. Medical Affairs, Becton Dickinson 1999–. *Publications:* co-ed. of medical textbooks; more than 190 articles and 30 textbook chapters. *Leisure interest:* flying (multi-engine, instrument-rated pilot). *Address:* Becton Dickinson Technologies, PO Box 12016, RTP, NC 27709–2016 (Office); 1700 Woodstock Road, Durham, NC 27705–5232, USA (Home). *Telephone:* (919) 597-6492 (Office); (919) 401-4848 (Home). *Fax:* (919) 549-7572 (Office). *E-mail:* david.durack@bd.com (Office); dtd@daviddurack.com (Home).

DURAFOUR, Michel André François; French politician and writer; b. 11 April 1920, St-Etienne, Loire; s. of Antoine Durafour and Olga Durafour (née Gaillard); m. Maryse Forissier 1973; one s. one d.; ed Lycée de St Etienne and Law Faculty of Paris Univ.; assignment in office of Minister of Information 1944–46; journalist, writer, Deputy Mayor 1947–65, Mayor of St-Etienne 1965–77; mem. Senate for Loire, Independent 1965–67; Deputy to Nat. Assembly for St-Etienne N-E, N-W 1967–68, 1973–74, 1978–81; Minister of Labour 1974–76, Minister attached to PM with responsibility for Econ. and Finance 1976–77, of the Civil Service and Admin. Reform 1988–91, of State 1989–91; mem. Secr. Parti Radical-Socialiste; mem. Nat. Bureau of Mouvement Réformateur 1971–; Chair. Groupe des Réformateurs (Social Democratic group) in Nat. Assembly 1973–74; Pres. Comm. de la Production et des échanges de l'Assemblée Nat.; Assoc. Prof. Univ. of Paris IX 1980–81; Prof. Univ. of Lyon III 1981; Pres. Conseil Régional (Rhône-Alpes) 1980–81, Regional Councillor and Gen. Chair. Budget 1986–88; mem. Senate for Loire, Social Democratic group 1983–88; Vice-Prés. de la Commission des Affaires Culturelles du Sénat 1985, de la Commission des Finances du Sénat 1986–88; Ministre d'Etat in charge of civil service and admin. reforms 1988–91; Conseiller d'Etat (on special service) 1992–96; Grand Prix du Théâtre for Les Démoniaques 1950; Grand Prix du Roman d'Aventure for Agnès et les vilains Messieurs 1963. *Publications:* Les Démoniaques 1950, Notre rêve qui êtes aux cieux (film entitled Les fruits sauvages), Bettina Colonna, Les hommes sont comme ça, Le juif du ciel, Les moutons du ciel, Agnès et les vilains Messieurs (under pseudonym Pierre Jardin), Dites-le avec des pastèques, Pascaline, La Baïonnette de Mirabeau and others. *Address:* c/o Éditions Jean-Claude Lattès, 17 rue Jacob, 75006 Paris (Office); 62 rue de Ponthieu, 75008 Paris, France.

DURÁN, Roberto; Panamanian boxer; b. 16 June 1951, Chorrillo; m. Felicidad Durán; four c.; professional boxer March 1967–2002; first fighter to win world titles at four different weights; won world lightweight title from Ken Buchanan June 1972; equalled the record number of championship defences (12) before relinquishing title to box as welterweight from Feb. 1979; won World Boxing Council version of world welterweight title from Ray Leonard, Montreal June 1980: lost it to Leonard, New Orleans Nov. 1980, retained it 1989; won WBC version of world middleweight title against Ian Barkley, Atlantic City Feb. 1989, relinquished it to challenge Ray Leonard to WBC super-middleweight title: lost to Leonard, Las Vegas Dec. 1989; exempt from all taxes, receives monthly pension for life from Govt. *Leisure interest:* cars. *Address:* Nuevo Reperto El Carmen, Panama.

DURÁN-BALLÉN, Sixto; Ecuadorean politician; b. 14 July 1921, Boston, Mass., USA; s. of Sixto E Durán Ballén and Maria E Durán Ballén; m. Josephine Villa Lobos 1945; three s. six d.; ed Sturens Inst. of Tech., NJ, Columbia Univ. and Univ. of Wisconsin; practised as architect; Sub-Dir of Regional Planning for Tungurahua 1949–68; fmr Mayor of Quito; official of Inter-American Devt Bank, Washington DC 1956; mem. Chamber of Deputies 1984–; f. Partido Unidad Republicana 1992; Pres. of Ecuador 1992–96; mem. Partido Conservador Ecuatoriano (PCE), MP 1998–; Ambassador to U.K. 2001–; Chevalier Légion d'honneur, Commdr Order of Orange-Nassau (Netherlands), Order of San Carlos (Colombia), Order of Tidor Vladimirescu (First Class) (Romania), Order of Francisco Miranda (Venezuela). *Address:* Embassy of Ecuador, Flat 3B, 3 Hans Crescent, Knightsbridge, London, SN1X 0LS, England (Office). *Telephone:* (20) 7584-1367 (Office). *Fax:* (20) 7823-9701 (Office). *E-mail:* embajada@ecuador.freeserve.co.uk (Office).

DURAND, Claude; French publisher; b. 9 Nov. 1938, Livry-Gargan (Seine-et-Oise); s. of Félix Durand and Suzanne Durand (née Thuret); m. Carmen Perea 1965; two s.; ed Ecole normale d'instituteurs de Versailles; fmr schoolteacher; Literary Dir Editions du Seuil 1965–78; Gen. Man. Editions Grasset 1978–80; Chair. and CEO Librairie Arthème Fayard 1980–, Librairie Stock 1991–98; Chair. Bd of Dirs. Inst. Mémoire de l'édition contemporaine 1990–93, Deputy Chair. 1993–; Chevalier, Légion d'honneur, Chevalier, Ordre nat. du Mérite, Commdr des Arts et des Lettres. *Publication:* La Nuit zoologique (novel, Prix Médicis) 1979. *Address:* Librairie Fayard, 75 rue des Saints-Pères, 75006 Paris (Office); 46 rue de Naples, 75008 Paris, France (Home).

DURANT, Isabelle; Belgian politician; b. 4 Sept. 1954, Brussels; ed Univ. Coll. London; registered nurse; teacher 1981–89; mem. of Ecologist Party (AGALEV) 1989–, Attaché of Ecologist Parl. Group at Regional Council of Brussels 1992–94; Federal Sec. and Spokeswoman for ECOLO-AGALEV 1994–99; mem. Fed. Office of ECOLO-AGALEV 1995–99; Co-ordinator of Etats généraux de l'Ecologie politique (EGEP) 1996–; Deputy Prime Minister and Minister for Mobility and Transport 1999–2003. *Address:* c/o Ministry of Transport, Wetstraat 63–65, rue de la Loi, 1040 Brussels, Belgium (Office).

DURANTE, Viviana Paola; Italian ballerina; b. 8 May 1967, Rome; joined Royal Ballet Co., London 1984, became soloist 1987, prin. 1989, guest artist 1997, 1999; guest ballerina American Ballet Theater, Teatro della Scala Milan, K-Ballet Japan; Premio Positano Award (Italy) 1991, Evening Standard Award, Time Out Award. *Principal parts include:* Ondine, Juliet, Nikiya (La Bayadère), Odette-Odile (Swan Lake), Aurore (Sleeping Beauty), Cinderella, Princess Rose (Prince of Pagodas), Anastasia, Marie Vetsera (Mayerling), Excelsior 2001; also roles in My Brother and My Sisters, Requiem, Don Quixote, Manon, Nutcracker, Rhapsody, Capriccio, Anna Karenina, Carmen, Symphonic Variations. *Video Films:* Mayerling, Sleeping Beauty. *Leisure interests:* yoga, reading, life. *Address:* Royal Ballet Company, Royal Opera House, Covent Garden, London, WC2E 9DD, England.

DURÃO BARROSO, José Manuel, MPolSci; Portuguese politician; b. 23 March 1956, Lisbon; m.; three c.; ed Univs. of Lisbon and Geneva; lecturer, Faculty of Law, Univ. of Lisbon, Dept of Political Science, Univ. of Geneva; Visiting Scholar, Univ. of Georgetown, Washington, DC; mem. Parl. 1985–; fmr Sec. of State for Home Affairs and for Foreign Affairs and Co-operation; Minister of Foreign Affairs 1992–95; mem. Nat. Council Social Democratic Party (PSD), Leader 1999–; Vice-Pres. EPP 1999–; Prime Minister of Portugal March 2002–; Chair. Comm. for Foreign Affairs 1995–96; Head Dept. of Int. Relations, Univ. Lusíada 1995–99; Visiting Prof. Georgetown Univ. 1996–98; decorations from Brazil, Germany, Japan, Morocco, Netherlands, Portugal, Spain, UK. *Publications:* Governmental System and Party System (co-author) 1980, Le Système Politique Portugais face à l'Intégration Européenne 1983, Política de Cooperação 1990, A Política Externa Portuguesa 1992–93, A Política Externa Portuguesa 1994–95, Uma Certa Ideia de Europa 1999, Uma Ideia para Portugal 2000; several studies on political science and constitutional law in collective works, encyclopaedias and int. journals. *Address:* Presidência do Conselho de Ministros, Rua da Imprensa à Estrela 2, 1249-064 Lisbon (Office); Social Democratic Party, Rua de São Caetano 9, 1249-087 Lisbon Codex, Portugal. *Telephone:* (21) 3952140 (Office). *Fax:* (21) 3979520 (Office). *E-mail:* presidente@psd.pt (Office). *Website:* www.psd.pt (Office).

DURBIN, Richard Joseph, JD; American politician; b. 21 Nov. 1944, East St Louis, Ill.; s. of William Durbin and Ann Durbin; m. Loretta Schaefer 1967; one s. two d.; ed Georgetown Univ.; called to Bar, Ill. 1969; legal practice 1969–; Chief legal counsel to Lt Gov. Paul Simon of Ill. 1969; mem. staff, minority leader, Ill. State Senate 1972–77, parliamentarian 1969–77; Assoc. Prof. Medical Humanities, S Ill. Univ. 1978–; mem. 98th–103rd Congress 1983–97; Senator from Ill. 1997–; mem. Select Cttee on Ethics 1999 and numerous other cttees; Democrat. *Address:* United States Senate, 332 Dirksen Senate Office Building, Washington, DC 20510-0001, USA.

DURDYNETS, Gen. Vasyl Vasylyevich; Ukrainian lawyer and army officer; b. 27 Sept. 1937, Romochevytsya; m.; one d.; ed Lvov State Univ.; Sec., First Sec. Lvov Regional Comsomol Cttee, Deputy Head of Section Central Comsomol Cttee, Moscow, Head of Section Central Cttee of Lvov Regional CP 1960–73; Deputy Head of Dept of Admin., CP Cen. Cttee 1973–78; Deputy Minister, then First Deputy Minister of Internal Affairs 1978–91; People's Deputy 1991–94, Head Cttee of Defence and Nat. Safety 1991–92, mem. 1997–, First Deputy Speaker of Parl. 1992–94; First Deputy Head Co-ordination Cttee for Fighting Corruption and Organized Crime 1994–95, Head 1995–99; Vice-Prime Minister, First Vice-Prime Minister 1995–99, Acting Prime Minister June–July 1997; Dir Nat. Bureau of Investigations 1997–99; Minister for Emergency Situations and Protection of the Population from the Consequences of the Chernobyl Catastrophe 1999–; mem. Supreme Econ. Council 1997; Hon. Prof. Acad. of Internal Affairs 1997; ICDO Medal, Int. Civil Defence Org. (Switzerland) 2000, 14 nat. awards. *Address:* Ministry for Emergency Situations and Protection of the Population from the Consequences of Chernobyl, 01030 Kiev, 55 O. Gonchara Str., Ukraine (Office). *Telephone:* (44) 247-30-01 (Office). *Fax:* (44) 226-34-37 (Office).

DURHAM, Sir Kenneth, Kt, BSc, CBIM; British company director; b. 28 July 1924, Blackburn, Lancs.; s. of the late George Durham and Bertha Durham (née Aspin); m. Irene Markham 1946; one s. one d.; ed Queen Elizabeth Grammar School, Blackburn, Univ. of Manchester; Flight Lt in RAF 1943–46; joined Atomic Research Establishment, Harwell, then Unilever Research Lab., Port Sunlight 1950, Head of Lab. 1961; Head of Lab., Colworth 1965; Chair. BOCM Silcock Ltd 1971; Dir Unilever Ltd and Unilever NV 1974–86; Vice-Chair. Unilever Ltd (now Unilever PLC) 1978–82, Chair. 1982–86; Dir British Aerospace Ltd 1980–90, Deputy Chair. 1986–90; Dir Woolworth Holdings (now Kingfisher, PLC) 1985–90, Chair. 1986–90; Dir Morgan Grenfell Holdings 1986–90; Chair. Trade Policy Research Centre 1982; Vice-Pres. Liverpool School of Tropical Medicine 1982–, Help the Aged 1986–; Gov. London Business School 1982; Advisory Council Chase Manhattan Bank NA 1983; mem. Int. Advisory Cttee of United Technologies Corpn 1983; Chair. Econ. and Financial Policy Cttee, CBI 1983–86; Trustee Leverhulme Trust 1974; Hon. FBA 1997; Hon. DSc (Loughborough) 1984; Order of Orange Nassau (Netherlands) 1985. *Publications:* Surface Activity and Detergency 1960, various scientific papers. *Leisure interests:* walking, golf.

DURIE, Sir David Robert Campbell, KCMG, MA, CIMgt, FRSA; British diplomatist; b. 21 Aug. 1944, Glasgow; s. of the late F. R. E. Durie; m. Susan Frances Weller; three d.; ed Univ. of Oxford; served in various British Govt depts. 1966–91; Minister and Deputy UK Perm. Rep. to EU 1991–95; Dir-Gen. for Enterprise and Regions, Dept Trade and Industry 1995–2000; Gov. and C-in-C Gibraltar 2000–03; KStJ. *Leisure interests:* exercise, culture, family. *Address:* c/o The Convent, Main Street, Gibraltar (Office).

DURKAN, Mark; Irish politician; b. 26 June 1960, Derry; s. of Brendan Durkan and Isobel Durkan (née Tinney); m. Jackie Durkan; ed St Columb's Coll., Derry, Queen's Univ., Belfast, Magee Coll., Derry; Deputy Pres. Union of Students in Ireland 1982–84; Asst to John Hume, MP 1984–98; Chair. Social Democratic and Labour Party (SDLP) 1990–95, Leader 2001–; elected to Derry City Council 1993–2002; mem. Forum for Peace and Reconciliation, Dublin 1994–96; elected to NI Forum for Political Dialogue 1996; SDLP Negotiator in inter-party discussions 1996–98; mem. NI Ass. 1998–2002 (Ass. suspended Oct. 2002); Minister of Finance 1999–2001, Deputy First Minister 2001–02; mem. NI Housing Council 1993–95, Western Health and Social Services Council 1993–2000. *Address:* Constituency Office, 7b Messines Terrace, Derry, BT48 7QZ, Northern Ireland (Office). *Telephone:* (28) 7136-0700 (Office). *Fax:* (28) 7136-0808 (Office). *E-mail:* m.durkan@sdlp.ie (Office).

DURLACHER, Nicholas John, CBE, BA; British business executive; b. 20 March 1946, Plaxtol; s. of John Sidney Durlacher and Alma Gabriel Adams; m. Mary McLaren 1971; one s.; ed Stowe School, Buckingham, Magdalene Coll., Cambridge; fmrly Chair. London Int. Financial Futures and Options Exchange; Chair. Securities and Futures Authority 1995–2000; Ennismore European Smaller Companies Fund 1998–; Chair. FFastFill PLC 2000–02; Chair. Elexon Ltd 2000–; Quilter Global Enhanced Income Trust PLC 2000–; Dir UFJ Int. PLC; Trustee Brain and Spine Foundation. *Leisure interests:* skiing, golf, tennis. *Address:* Elexon Ltd, 4th Floor, 350 Euston Road, London, NW1 3AW (Office); 10 Rutland Street, London, SW7 1EH, England (Home). *Telephone:* (20) 7380-4251 (Office). *Fax:* (20) 7380-0407 (Office). *E-mail:* nick .durlacher@elexon.co.uk (Office). *Website:* www.elexon.co.uk (Office).

DUROV, Lev Konstantinovich; Russian actor; b. 23 Dec. 1931, Moscow; m. Irina Nikolayevna Kirichenko; one d.; ed Studio School of Moscow Art Theatre; actor and stage Dir Cen. Children's Theatre 1954–63, Lenkom Theatre 1963–67, Malaya Bronnaya Theatre 1967–; Theatre-School of Contemporary Plays 1993–; as stage Dir produced over 20 theatre productions; in cinema since 1953; People's Artist of Russian Fed. 1982, USSR People's Artist 1990. *Plays include:* Chebutykin, Medvedenko, Molière, Sganarelle, Yago, Zhevakin, Alyosha. *Films include:* Farewell, Leap Year, Don't be Afraid, I'm with You, Three Musketeers, Success, Orphan of Kazan. *Address:* Frunzenskaya nab. 3b, Apt. 206, 119146 Moscow, Russia (Home). *Telephone:* (095) 242-43-46 (Home).

DÜRR, Heinz; German industrialist; b. 16 July 1933, Stuttgart; s. of Otto Dürr; m. Heide Dürr; three d.; ed Tech. Hochschule, Stuttgart; Man. and Man. Dir Dürr AG (fmrly Otto Dürr GmbH), Stuttgart 1957–80, Chair. Supervisory Bd 1980–; Chair. Exec. Bd AEG Aktiengesellschaft, Berlin and Frankfurt 1980–90; mem. Daimler-Benz AG, Stuttgart 1986–90; Chair.Exec. Bd Deutsche Bundesbahn, Deutsche Reichsbahn 1991–94, Deutsche Bahn AG 1994–97, Supervisory Bd Deutsche Bahn AG 1997–99, Carl-Zeiss-Stiftung (Commr) 1999–, Krone GmbH 1999–; Chair. Fed. of Metal Working Industries in Baden-Württemberg and mem. Presidium Fed. of Metal and Electrical Industry Employers' Asscns. 1975–80; mem. European Advisory Bd, Schroder, Salomon, Smith Barney 2001 and seven supervisory bds.; DrIng hc (Rhine-Westphalian Tech. Univ., Aachen) 1996. *Leisure interests:* tennis, golf, theatre, jazz, cross-country skiing. *Address:* Charlottenstrasse 57, 10117 Berlin, Germany. *Telephone:* (30) 20945200 (Office). *Fax:* (30) 20945205 (Office).

DURR, Hon. Kent D. Skelton; South African fmr politician, fmr diplomatist and business executive; b. 28 March 1941, Cape Town; s. of Dr. John M. Durr and Diana Skelton; m. Suzanne Wiese 1966; one s. two d.; ed SA Coll. School, Cape Town Univ.; Dir family publishing co. 1966–68; Founder and later Man. Dir Durr Estates 1968–84; Chair. Clean Diesel Technologies Inc. 1995–97, Fuel-Tech NV 1995–97; Exec. Chair. Commonwealth Investment Guarantee Agency Ltd 1997; elected to Prov. Council of Cape 1974, MP for Maitland 1977–91, Deputy Minister (Trade and Industry) 1984–86, (Finance) 1984–88; Minister of Budget and Public Works 1988–89; Cabinet Minister of Trade and Industry and Tourism 1989–91; Amb. to UK 1991–94, High Commr in UK 1994–95; Chair. Commonwealth Investment Guarantee Agency 1995–99, Nasdaq Listed Cos, USA 1995–99; mem. Parl. and Senate, African Christian Democratic Party 1999–; Chair. Darling Wildlife (Cattle and Game) 1999–; Freeman City of London 1995. *Leisure interests:* field sports, mountaineering, conservation, game farming. *Address:* Houses of Parliament, PO Box 15, Cape Town 8000 (Office); Darling Wildlife, P.O. Box 289, Yzerfontein 7351, Cape, South Africa. *Telephone:* (21) 4033803 (Office); (21) 6853908 (Home). *Fax:* (21) 4619690 (Office); (2245) 12352 (Home). *E-mail:* kdurr@acdp.za.com (Office).

DURRANT, Jennifer Ann; British artist; b. 17 June 1942, Brighton; d. of Caleb John Durrant and Winifred May Durrant (née Wright); m. William A. H. Henderson 1964 (divorced 1976); m. 2nd Richard Alban Howard Oxby 2000; ed Varndean Grammar School for Girls, Brighton, Brighton Coll. of Art and Crafts, Slade School of Fine Art, Univ. Coll., London; part-time art teacher various colls. 1965–74; part-time Lecturer on Painting, St Martin's School of Art, London 1974–87, RCA 1979–, Chelsea School of Art 1987–, Royal Acad. Schools 1991–; Exhbn Selector, Northern Young Contemporaries, Whitworth Gallery, Manchester, TV SW Arts; Painting Faculty mem. The British School at Rome 1979–83; Newham Hosp. Comm. (in Asscn with Greater London Arts Asscn and King Edward's Hosp. Fund), Towner Art Gallery, Eastbourne; Abbey Minor Travelling Scholarship 1964; Artist-in-Residence, Somerville Coll., Oxford 1979–80; works in collections of Arts Council of GB, British Council, Contemporary Art Soc., Tate Gallery, London, Museum of Fine Arts, Boston, USA, Neue Galerie, Aachen etc. and in pvt. collections; Arts Council Award 1976, Arts Council Maj. Award 1978, Greater London Arts Asscn Award 1980, Athena Art Award 1988. *Solo exhibitions include:* Univ. of Surrey, Guildford 1975, Arnolfini Gallery, Bristol 1979, Museum of Modern Art, Oxford 1980, Nicola Jacobs Gallery, London 1982,

1985, Arcade Gallery, Harrogate 1983, Northern Centre for Contemporary Art, Sunderland 1986; Serpentine Gallery, London 1987, Newlyn-Orion, Penzance 1988, Lynne Stern Assocs, London 1989. *Group exhibitions include:* London, Liverpool, Reykjavik, Boston, USA, Edmonton, Canada, New York, Aachen, Fed. Repub. of Germany, Pittsburg, USA, Birmingham, Stoke on Trent, Sheffield 1988, Newcastle 1989, London, Lincoln 1990. *Leisure interests:* classical music, including opera, archaeology, visiting museums, looking at paintings and sculpture. *Address:* 9–10 Holly Grove, London, SE15 5DF, England. *Telephone:* (20) 7639-6424.

DURRANT, (Mignonette) Patricia, CD, OJ, BA; Jamaican diplomatist and United Nations official; b. 30 May 1943; ed Univ. of West Indies (UWI), Univ. of Cambridge, UK; Admin. Officer, Ministry of Agric. 1964–70; First Sec. Ministry of Foreign Affairs 1971–72, Prin. Asst Sec. 1972–74; Minister-Counsellor, Mission to OAS, Washington, DC 1974–77; Asst Dir Political Div., Ministry of Foreign Affairs 1977–81, Deputy Dir 1981–83; Deputy Perm. Rep. to UN, New York 1983–87, Perm. Rep. 1995–; Pres. UN High-Level Cttee on Tech. Co-operation among Developing Countries 1999–2001, Rep. of Jamaica to UN Security Council 2000–01; currently Chair. UN Preparatory Cttee for the Special Session on Children, Chair. Consultative Cttee for the UN Devt Fund for Women (UNIFEM) and Vice-Chair. Open-Ended Working Group on the Reform of the UN Security Council; Amb. to FRG (and non-resident Amb. to Israel, the Netherlands, Switzerland and the Holy See) 1987–92; Dir.-Gen. Ministry of Foreign Affairs and Foreign Trade 1992–95; Order of Distinction in the Rank of Commdr 1992, Order of Jamaica 2000; Distinguished Grad. Award, Univ. of West Indies 1998, Distinguished Achievement Award, World Asscn of fmr UN Interns and Fellows (WAFUNI). *Address:* Permanent Mission of Jamaica to the United Nations, 767 Third Avenue, 9th Floor, New York, NY 10017, USA (Office). *Telephone:* (212) 935-7509 (Office). *Fax:* (212) 935-7607 (Office). *E-mail:* jamaica@un.int (Office). *Website:* www.un.int/ jamaica (Office).

DUSSAULT, René, LLL, PhD, FRSC; Canadian judge; b. 23 Nov. 1939, Québec; s. of Daniel Dussault and Madeleine Pelletier; m. Marielle Godbout 1967; two s.; ed Laval Univ. and London School of Econs and Political Science; lecturer in Law, Laval Univ. 1966–70; legal counsel, Québec Health and Welfare Inquiry Comm.; Special Adviser to Minister of Social Affairs of Québec 1970–73; Chair. Québec Professions Bd 1973–77; Deputy Minister of Justice, Québec 1977–80; Prof. Nat. School of Public Admin. 1981–89; Laskin Chair in Public Law, Osgoode Hall Law School 1983–84; legal consultant, Kronström, McNicoll & Assocs., Québec City; Judge, Québec Court of Appeal 1989–; Co-Chair. Royal Comm. on Aboriginal Peoples 1991–96; Hon. LLD (York) 1992, (Dalhousie) 1997; Québec Interprofessional Council Prize 1991; Québec Bar Asscn Medal 1987, Vanier Medal, Inst. of Public Admin. of Canada 1998, Touchstone Award, Canadian Bar Asscn 2001. *Publications:* Le contrôle judiciaire de l'administration au Québec 1969, Traité de droit administratif, Vols I & II 1974 (also co-author of subsequent Vols), Administrative Law: A Treatise, Vols I-V 1985–90. *Address:* 300 Boulevard Jean-Lesage (R. 438), Québec, PQ G1K 8K6 (Office); 1332 James-LeMoine Avenue, Sillery, PQ G1S 1A3, Canada (Home). *Telephone:* (418) 649-3425 (Office); (418) 527-6332 (Home). *Fax:* (418) 643-4154 (Office). *E-mail:* rdussault@ justice.gouv.qc.ca (Office).

DUTILLEUX, Henri; French composer; b. 22 Jan. 1916, Angers; s. of Paul and Thérèse (née Koszul) Dutilleux; m. Geneviève Joy 1946; ed Conservatoire Nat. de Musique, Paris; career devoted to music 1945–; Dir service Créations Musicales Radiodiffusion française 1945–63; Prof. of Composition Ecole Normale de Musique, Paris 1961–, Pres. 1969–74; Assoc. Prof. Conservatoire Nat. Supérieur de Musique, Paris 1970–71; fmr mem. UNESCO Music Council; Hon. mem. American Acad. and Inst. of Arts and Letters, Accad. di Santa Cecilia, Royal Acad. of Music, London; Assoc. mem. Royal Acad. of Belgium; Hon. mem. RAM, London; 1st Grand Prix de Rome 1938, Grand Prix du Disque 1957, 1958, 1966, 1968, 1976, 1978 and 1984, Grand Prix Nat. de la Musique 1967, Prix de la Ville de Paris 1974, Koussevitzky Int. Recording Award 1976, World Record Award (Montreux) 1983; Prix Int. Maurice Ravel 1987, Grand Prix, Music Council UNESCO 1987, Praemium Imperiale Japan 1994; Grand Officier, Légion d'honneur, Commdr Ordre Nat. du Mérite, des Arts et des Lettres, du Mérite Culturel de Monaco. *Compositions:* Sonata for Piano 1948, First Symphony 1951, Le Loup (Ballet) 1953, Second Symphony (Le Double) 1959, Métaboles (for orchestra) 1964, Cello Concerto: Tout un monde lointain 1970, Figures de Résonances (for two pianos) 1971, Preludes for Piano 1974, Ainsi la Nuit (for string quartet) 1976, Timbres, Espace, Mouvement (for orchestra) 1978, 3 Strophes sur le nom de Sacher (for cello) 1981, L'Arbre des Songes (violin concerto) 1985, Le Jeu des contraires (for piano) 1988, Mystère de l'instant (for 24 strings and cimbalom) 1989, Les Citations (for oboe, harpsichord, double-bass and percussion) 1991, The Shadows of Time (for orchestra) 1997. *Publications:* Mystère 1997, Mémoire des sons 1997. *Address:* 12 rue St-Louis-en-l'Isle, 75004 Paris, France. *Telephone:* 1-43-26-39-14.

DUTOIT, Charles E., OC; Swiss conductor and music director; b. 7 Oct. 1936, Lausanne; s. of Edmond Dutoit and Berthe Dutoit (née Laederman); one s. one d.; ed Conservatoire of Lausanne and Geneva, Accademia Musicale Chigiana, Siena, Italy, Conservatorio Benedetto Marcello, Venice, Italy and Berks. Music Center, Tanglewood, USA; Assoc. Conductor Berne Symphony Orchestra 1964, Music Dir 1966–77; Music Dir Radio Zurich Orchestra, Nat. Symphony Orchestra of Mexico, Gothenberg Symphony Orchestra, Sweden, Montreal Symphony Orchestra 1977–2002, Prin. Guest Conductor Minn.

Orchestra 1983–84, 1985–86; Artistic Dir and Prin. Conductor Philadelphia Orchestra summer season Mann Music Center 1990–2000, Saratoga Springs 1990–; Music Dir Orchestre Nat. de France 1990–2001; Prin. Guest Conductor NHK Symphony Orchestra, Tokyo 1996–, Music Dir 1998–; over 125 recordings since 1980, winning over 40 int. awards; operatic début at Covent Garden (conducting Faust) 1983; DMus hc (Montreal) 1984, (Laval) 1985; Grand Prix de l'Académie du disque français, High Fidelity Int. Record Critics' Award, Montreux Record Award, Grand Prix du Prés. de la République (France), Japan Record Acad. Award, Artist of the Year (Canada Music Council) 1982, Commdr Ordre des Arts et des Lettres. *Address:* c/o Orchestre Symphonique de Montréal, Place des Arts 260 Boulevard Maisonneuve Ouest, Montréal, Québec H2X 1Y9, Canada.

DUȚU, Alexandru, PhD; Romanian historian and author; b. 2 Sept. 1928, Bucharest; s. of Nicolae Duțu and Elisabeta Negoescu; m. Angela Dăscălescu 1958 (died 1986); one d., one s.; ed Coll. of Modern Philology and Coll. of Law; researcher, Inst. for South East European Studies 1963–90, Dir 1990–97; Prof., Int. School for Political Sciences 1990–; Dir French-Romanian Seminar (Bucharest) 1990–95; Dir Centre for the Study of European Mentalities 1994–; Visiting Prof., E.H.E.S.S. (Paris) 1990, Collège de France 1995; ed. Revue des études sud-est européennes; Deputy Ed. Synthesis; Deputy Ed. Mentalities 1984–; Prize of the Romanian Acad., of the Int. Asscn for South-East European Studies; Fellowship Great Britain 1968–69, USA 1986; Vice-Chair. Int. Asscn for Comparative Literature 1979–85; mem. Scientific Council of Coll. of European Citizenship (Council of Europe) 1997–; mem. French, Austrian, Spanish socs. for the study of 18th century culture; mem. Romanian Writers' Union; Corresp. mem. Foundation for Hellenic Culture; Chevalier des Palmes Académiques 1997. *Publications:* Shakespeare in Romania, 1964, Les livres de sagesse dans la culture roumaine 1971, Romanian Humanists and the European Culture 1977, European Intellectual Movements and the Modernization of the Romanian Culture 1981, Humanisme, baroque, lumières—l'exemple roumain 1984, The Human Dimension of History. Trends in the History of Mentalities 1986, L'état des lieux en sciences sociales 1993, Culture et Politique 1995, Y a-t-il une Europe orthodoxe? 1997, 'Political Models and National Identities in 'Orthodox Europe' 1998. *Leisure interests:* skiing, travelling. *Address:* Calea 13 Septembrie 13, C.P. 22.159, Bucharest (Office); Str. C. C. Arion 6, 78144 Bucharest, Romania (Home). *Telephone:* (1) 3144996 (Office). *Fax:* (1) 3124134.

DUVAL, David Robert; American professional golfer; b. 9 Nov. 1971, Jacksonville, Fla; s. of senior PGA Tour golfer Bob Duval; ed Georgia Tech.; became professional golfer 1993; mem. Walker Cup team 1991, Pres.'s Cup team, 1996, 1998, Ryder Cup team 1999; winner Nike Wichita Open 1993, Nike Tour Championship 1993, Michelob Championship at Kingsmill 1997, 1998, Walt Disney World/Oldsmobile Classic 1997, the Tour Championship 1997, Tucson Chrysler Classic 1998, Shell Houston Open 1998, NEC World Series of Golf 1998, Mercedes Championship 1999, Bob Hope Chrysler Classic 1999, the Players Championship 1999, BellSouth Classic 1999, Ryder Cup 1999, Open Championship, Royal Lytham, UK 2001; Collegiate Player of the Year 1993, Dave Williams Award 1993, Jasper Award, Jacksonville 1996. *Leisure interests:* reading, fly fishing, surfing, skiing, baseball. *Address:* c/o PGA of America, Box 109601, 100 Avenue of Champions, Palm Beach Gardens, FL 33410, USA (Office).

DUVALIER, Jean-Claude; Haitian politician; b. 3 July 1951, Port-au-Prince; s. of late Pres. François Duvalier and late Simone (née Ovide) Duvalier; m. Michele Bennett 1980 (divorced 1990); one s.; ed Coll. of St Louis de Gonzague, Port-au-Prince and faculty of law, Univ. of Haiti; named political heir to Pres. François Duvalier Jan. 1971; Life Pres. 1971–86 (overthrown in coup); now living in Mougins, France; extradition requested by Haitian Govt Dec. 1998.

DUVALL, Robert; American actor; b. 5 Jan. 1931, San Diego; s. of William H. Duvall; m. 1st Gail Youngs (divorced); m. 2nd Sharon Brophy 1991; ed Principia Coll. Ill.; student, Neighborhood Playhouse, New York; Acad. Award for Best Actor in Tender Mercies 1984; recipient of other film awards. *Films include:* To Kill a Mockingbird 1963, Captain Newman, MD 1964, The Chase 1965, Countdown 1968, The Detective 1968, Bullitt 1968, True Grit 1969, The Rain People 1969, M*A*S*H 1970, The Revolutionary 1970, The Godfather 1972, Tomorrow 1972, The Great Northfield, Minnesota Raid 1972, Joe Kidd 1972, Lady Ice 1973, The Outfit 1974, The Conversation 1974, The Godfather Part II 1974, Breakout 1975, The Killer Elite 1975, Network 1976, The Eagle Has Landed 1977, The Greatest 1977, The Betsy 1978, Apocalypse Now 1979, The Great Santini 1980, True Confessions 1981, Angelo My Love (actor and Dir) 1983, Tender Mercies 1983, The Stone Boy 1984, The Natural 1984, The Lightship 1986, Let's Get Harry 1986, Belizaire the Cajun 1986, Colors 1988, Convicts, Roots in a Parched Ground, The Handmaid's Tale 1990, A Show of Force 1990, Days of Thunder, Rambling Rose 1991, Newsies 1992, The New Boys 1992, Stalin 1992, The Plague, Geronimo, Falling Down 1993, The Paper 1994, Wrestling Ernest Hemingway 1994, Something To Talk About, The Stars Fell on Henrietta, The Scarlet Letter, A Family Thing (also co-producer), Phenomenon 1996, The Apostle 1997, Gingerbread Man 1997, Deep Impact, A Civil Action 1999, Gone In Sixty Seconds 2000, A Shot at Glory (also producer) 2000, The 6th Day 2000, Apocalypse Now: Redux 2001, John Q 2002, Assassination Tango (also producer) 2002; Dir films We're Not the Jet Set, Assassination Tango 2002; several TV films and appearances. *Stage*

appearances include: A View from the Bridge 1965 (Obie Award), Wait Until Dark 1966, American Buffalo. *Address:* c/o William Morris Agency, 151 S. El Camino Drive, Beverly Hills, CA 90212, USA.

DUVALL, Shelley; American actress and producer; b. 7 July 1949, Houston, Tex.; f. TV production co. Think Entertainment. *Films include:* (actress): Brewster McCloud, McCabe and Mrs. Miller, Thieves Like Us, Nashville, Buffalo Bill and the Indians, Three Women (Cannes Festival Prize 1977), Annie Hall, The Shining, Popeye, Time Bandits, Frankenweenie, Roxanne, Suburban Commando, Frogs!, The Underneath, Portrait of a Lady, Twilight of the Ice Nymphs, Rocket Man, Changing Habits, Alone 1997, Home Fries 1998, Space Cadet, Big Monster on Campus, The 4th Floor, Dreams in the Attic, Manna From Heaven 2001. *Television includes:* (actress): Bernice Bobs Her Hair, Lily, Twilight Zone, Mother Goose Rock 'n' Rhyme, Faerie Tale Theatre (Rumpelstiltskin, Rapunzel), Tall Tales and Legends (Darlin' Clementine); (exec. producer): Faerie Tale Theatre, Tall Tales and Legends, Nightmare Classics, Dinner at Eight (film), Mother Goose Rock 'n' Rhyme, Stories from Growing Up, Backfield in Motion (film), Bedtime Stories, Mrs. Piggle-Wiggle.

DUVERGER, Maurice; French political scientist; b. 5 June 1917, Angoulême; s. of Georges and Anne (née Gobert) Duverger; m. Odile Batt 1949; ed Bordeaux Univ.; contrib. to Le Monde 1946–; Prof. of Political Sociology, Paris Univ. 1955–85, Prof. Emer. 1985–; Founder and Pres. Inst. of Research into Insts. and Cultures of Europe (IRICE); MEP 1989–95; mem. American Acad. of Arts and Sciences; Grand Officier Légion d'honneur, Commdr ordre nat. du Mérite. *Publications:* Les partis politiques 1951, Demain, la république. . . 1959, De la dictature 1961, La Sixième république et le régime présidentiel 1961, Introduction to the Social Sciences 1964, Introduction à la politique 1964, La démocratie sans le peuple 1967, Institutions politiques 1970, Janus: les deux faces de l'Occident 1972, Sociologie de la politique 1973, La monarchie républicaine 1974, Lettre ouverte aux socialistes 1976, L'autre coté des choses 1977, Echec au roi 1978, Les orangers du lac Balaton 1980, La République des Citoyens 1982, Bréviaire de la cohabitation 1986, La Cohabitation des Français 1987, La nostalgie de l'impuissance 1988, Le Lièvre libéral et la tortue européenne 1990, Europe des hommes 1994, L'Europe dans tous ses Etats 1995, A la recherche du droit perdu 2001. *Leisure interest:* theatre. *Address:* Presses universitaires de France, 6 avenue Reille, 75014 Paris (Office); IRICE, 1 rue Descartes, 75005 Paris; 24 rue des Fossés-Saint-Jacques, 75005 Paris (Home); Mas du Grand Côté, 13100 Le Tholonet, France (Home).

DUWAISAN, Khalid Abdulaziz al-, BA(COMM.); Kuwaiti diplomatist; b. 15 Aug. 1947; s. of Abdulaziz Saud Al-Duwaisan and Sabeka Abdullah Al-Duwaisan; m. Dalal Al-Humaizi 1980; one s. one d.; ed Cairo Univ., Univ. of Kuwait; joined Ministry of Foreign Affairs 1970, Diplomatic Attaché 1974, Embassy, Washington, DC 1975; Amb. to Netherlands 1984 (also Accred to Romania 1988); Chair. Kuwaiti del. for supervision of demilitarized zone between Iraq and Kuwait and Chief Co-ordinator Comm. for Return of Stolen Property 1991; Amb. to UK 1993– (also Accred to Repub. of Ireland, Norway, Sweden and Denmark); Hon. GCVO (UK). *Leisure interests:* tennis, swimming. *Address:* Kuwaiti Embassy, 2 Albert Gate, London, SW1X 7JU (Office); 22 Kensington Palace Gardens, London, W.8, England (Home). *Telephone:* (20) 7590-3400 (Office); (20) 7221-7374 (Home). *Fax:* (20) 7823-1712. *E-mail:* kuwait@dircon.co.uk (Office). *Website:* www.kuwaitinfo.org.uk (Office).

DVOŘÁK, Tomáš; Czech athlete; b. 11 May 1972, Zlín; s. of Petr Dvořák and Hana Dvořák; m. Gabriela Dvořák; two d.; decathlete; bronze medal, Olympic Games, Atlanta 1996, gold medal, European Cup 1995, 1999 (world record of 8,994 points, since broken), gold medal, World Championships, Athens 1997, Seville 1999, Edmonton 2001; Athlete of the Year, Czech Repub. 1999, Jim Thorpe All-Around Award. *Leisure interests:* cooking, gardening, family, music. *Address:* Stadion Juliska, 160 00 Prague 6, Czech Republic (Office). *Telephone:* (2) 20203812 (Office).

DVORSKÝ, Peter; Slovak opera singer; b. 25 Sept. 1951, Partizánske, Topol'čany Dist; s. of Vendelín Dvorský and Anna Dvorská; m. Marta Varšová 1975; two d.; ed State Conservatoire, Bratislava; studied with R. Carossi and M. di Luggo, Milan 1975–76; opera soloist, Slovak Nat. Theatre, Bratislava 1972–96, 1999; sang at Metropolitan Opera, New York 1977, Covent Garden, London 1978, Bolshoi Theatre, Moscow 1978, La Scala, Milan 1979; regularly at Bratislava, Vienna State Opera, Covent Garden, La Scala, New York Metropolitan Opera, Munich, Berlin, Prague, Geneva and Paris; also in many other cities throughout the world; numerous radio and TV performances; many recordings; Chair. Council of Slovak Music Union 1991–; Pres. Harmony Foundation 1991–; performed charity concerts after floods in Czech Repub. 2002; awards include Tchaikovsky Competition, Geneva (5th Prize 1974, 1st Prize 1975), Leoš Janáček Memorial Medal 1978, Giuseppe Verdi Medal 1979, Artist of Merit 1981, Nat. Artist 1984, Kammersänger, Vienna 1986, Francisco Cilea Prize 1991, Wilhelm Furtwängler Prize 1992. *Leisure interests:* hunting, music, piano, family. *Address:* J. Hronca 1a, 841 02 Bratislava, Slovakia (Office).

DWEK, Raymond Allen, DPhil, DSc, FRS, FRSC, CBiol, FIBiol; British scientist and university professor; b. 10 Nov. 1941, Manchester; s. of Victor Joe Dwek and Alice Liniado; m. Sandra Livingstone 1964; two s. two d.; ed Carmel Coll., Manchester Univ., Lincoln Coll., Oxford, Exeter Coll., Oxford; research lecturer in Physical Chem., Christ Church, Oxford 1966–68, in Biochem. 1975–76; lecturer in Inorganic Chem., Christ Church, Oxford 1968–75, in

Biochem., Trinity Coll., Oxford 1976–84; Fellow Exeter Coll., Oxford 1974–88, Professorial Fellow 1988–; Dir Glycobiology Inst., Univ. of Oxford 1988–, Prof. of Glycobiology 1988–, Head of Dept of Biochem. 2000–; Dir for Grad. Training 1998–; mem. Oxford Enzyme Group 1971–88; founder mem. Oxford Oligosaccharide Group 1983; Oxford Univ. Non-exec. Dir and founder Glycosciences Ltd (fmrly Glycosystems Ltd); Dir and f. scientist IgX, Oxford 1998; Dir United Therapeutics 2002–; Visiting Royal Soc. Research Fellow Weizmann Inst., Rehovot, Israel 1969; Royal Soc. Locke Research Fellow 1974–76; Visiting Prof. Duke Univ., NC; Hon. Life/Founder mem. Swedish Biophysical Soc. 1979–; mem. European Molecular Biological Org. (EMBO) 1988–; Scientific Advisory Bd, Hepatitis Foundation USA 1994–; Judge, Millennium Fund Competition, The Daily Telegraph 1994; Boyce Thompson Distinguished Lecturer, Cornell Univ., USA 1997; Scientific Adviser to the Pres., Ben Gurion Univ., Negev, Israel; Dr hc (Catholic Univ. of Louvain) 1996; Hon. PhD (Ben-Gurion Univ., Israel) 2001; Wellcome Trust Award for Research in Biochem. Related to Medicine 1994, Scientific Leadership Award Hepatitis B Foundation, Philadelphia, Delaware Valley Coll. Centennial Award 1997, Commdr Nat. Romanian Order for Merit 2000. *Publications:* books: Nuclear Magnetic Resonance (NMR) in Biochemstry 1973, Physical Chemistry Principles and Problems for Biochemists (jtly) 2002, NMR in Biology (jtly) 1977, Biological Spectrosocopy (jtly) 1984; numerous scientific articles and patents. *Leisure interests:* family, patent law, sport, listening to music. *Address:* Glycobiology Institute, South Parks Road, Oxford, OX1 3QU (Office); Exeter College, Oxford, OX1 3DP, England. *Telephone:* (1865) 275344 (Office). *Fax:* (1865) 275771. *E-mail:* raymond.dwek@exeter.ox.ac.uk (Office). *Website:* www.bioch .ox.ac.uk/glcob (Office).

DWORKIN, Andrea; American author; b. 26 Sept. 1946, Camden, NJ, USA; d. of Harry Spiegel and Sylvia Spiegel; ed Bennington Coll.; has worked as a waitress, receptionist, factory worker. *Publications:* Woman Hating 1974, Out Blood: Prophecies and Discourses on Sexual Politics (Essays) 1976, The New Woman's Broken Heart 1980, Take Back the Night: Women on Pornography 1980, Pornography: Men Possessing Women 1981, Right-wing Women 1983, Ice and Fire (novel) 1986, Letters from a War Zone 1976–1987, 1989, Mercy 1990, Life and Death 1996, Scapegoat 2000.

DWORKIN, Ronald Myles, FBA; American professor of law; b. 11 Dec. 1931; s. of David Dworkin and Madeline Talamo; m. Betsy Celia Ross 1958 (died 2000); one s. one d.; ed Harvard Coll., Oxford Univ., UK, Harvard Law School; Legal Sec. to Judge Learned Hand 1957–58; Assoc., Sullivan & Cromwell, New York 1958–62; Assoc. Prof. of Law, Yale Law School 1962–65, Prof. 1965–68, Wesley N. Hohfeld Prof. of Jurisprudence 1968–69; Prof. of Jurisprudence, Oxford Univ. 1969–98, now Emer., Fellow Univ. Coll. 1969–98, now Emer.; Quain Prof. of Jurisprudence, Univ. Coll., London 1998–; Visiting Prof. of Philosophy, Princeton Univ. 1974–75; Prof. of Law, New York Univ. Law School 1975–; Prof.-at-Large, Cornell Univ. 1976–80; Visiting Prof. of Philosophy and Law, Harvard Univ. 1977, of Philosophy 1979–82; mem. Council, Writers and Scholars Educational Trust 1982–, Programme Cttee, Ditchley Foundation 1982–; Co-Chair. US Democratic Party Abroad 1972–76; Fellow American Acad. of Arts and Sciences 1979; Hon. Queen's Counsel; Hon. LLD (Williams Coll.) 1981, (John Jay Coll. of Criminal Justice) 1983, (Claremont Coll.) 1987, (Kalamazoo Coll.) 1987. *Publications:* Taking Rights Seriously 1977, The Philosophy of Law (Ed.) 1977, A Matter of Principle 1985, Law's Empire 1986, Philosophical Issues in Senile Dementia 1987, A Bill of Rights for Britain 1990, Life's Dominion 1993, Freedom's Law 1996, Sovereign Virtue 2000; articles in legal and philosophical journals. *Address:* 17 Chester Row, London, SW1W 9JF, England.

DWURNIK, Edward; Polish painter; b. 19 April 1943, Radzymin; m.; one d.; ed Acad. of Fine Arts, Warsaw; over 150 one-man exhbns. (retrospective) including Warsaw 1971, 1974, 1975, 1977, 1980, 1990, 2001, Toruń 1980, Wrocław 1987, Bydgoszcz 1997, Bytom 1997; exhbns. abroad: Darmstadt 1977, Moscow 1978, Groteborg 1981, Eindhoven 1985, Lingen 1986, London 1987, 1991–92, Stuttgart (retrospective) 1994; Norwid Prize for Exhbn in Warsaw 1980; Coutts Contemporary Art Foundation Award, Zurich 1992; numerous Polish and int. awards. *Paintings include:* (series) Hitch-hiking 1966; The Way to the East 1989–91, From December to June 1990–94, Blue 1992–, Diagonal 1996, XXIII 1998–, XXV 2000–; (pictures) Together 1975, Tiurma 1987, the Constitution of 3rd May 1989, Europa 2000. *Leisure interests:* driving, travelling, opera, films, music (heavy metal). *Address:* ul. Podgorska 5, 02-921 Warsaw, Poland. *Telephone:* (22) 8429879. *Fax:* (22) 8429879.

DY NIEN, Nguyen; Vietnamese politician; b. 9 Dec. 1935, Thanh Hoa; m.; three d.; ed Banaras Hindu Univ., India; mem. Nat. Liberation Movt 1951; joined Ministry of Foreign Affairs 1954, Deputy Dir, then Dir 1980–83, Asst Minister 1984–86, Deputy 1987–2000, Minister of Foreign Affairs 2000–; elected mem. Cen. Cttee Communist Party of Viet Nam 1991–; Pres. Viet Nam Nat. Comm. for UNESCO 1987; Pres. Nat. Cttee for Overseas Vietnamese 1995. *Address:* Ministry of Foreign Affairs, 1 Ton That Dam, Ba Dinh District, Hanoi, Viet Nam (Office). *Telephone:* (4) 8458201 (Office). *Fax:* (4) 8445905 (Office). *Website:* www.mofa.gov.vn (Office).

DYACHENKO, Tatyana Borisovna; Russian politician; b. 17 Jan. 1960, Sverdlovsk; d. of fmr Pres. Boris Yeltsin (q.v.) and Naina Yeltsin; two s.; m. 2nd Valentin Borisovich Yumashev; one d.; ed Moscow State Univ.; engineer Construction Bureau Salut 1982–94, Construction Bureau Zarya Urala, Moscow 1994–95; mem. Boris Yeltsin Election Campaign 1996; counsellor to Pres. Yeltsin 1997–99. *Leisure interest:* tourism.

DYADKOVA, Larissa; Russian singer; b. 9 March 1952, Zelenodolsk; m. Alexandre Kogan 1985; one d.; ed Leningrad Conservatory class of J. Levando; soloist Mariinsky Theatre 1978–; toured with Mariinsky Theatre in European countries, guest soloist Metropolitan Opera, La Scala, Communale Theatre, Florence, Deutsche Oper Berlin, Arena di Verona, San Francisco Opera, New Israeli Opera. *Concert appearances:* performs Verdi's Requiem in concerts, vocal series by Mussorgsky and Mahler, cantatas by Prokofiev; works with conductors Levine, Rostropovich, Mehta, Abbado, Temirkanov, Gergiev. *Address:* Mariinsky Theatre, Teatralnaya pl. 1, St Petersburg, Russia (Office). *Telephone:* (812) 114-30-39. *Fax:* (812) 114-30-39.

DYAKOV, Dumitru; Moldovan politician and journalist; b. 10 Feb. 1952, Kargopole, Kurgan Region, Russia; m.; two d.; ed Belarus State Univ.; Sec. Comsomol Cttee, Moldovan State TV and Radio; corresp., Komsomolskaya Pravda in Moldova –1976; on Comsomol Cen. Cttee, on Moldovan CP Cen. Cttee; Head TASS Bureau in Romania 1989–93; Sec. Moldovan Embassy, Moscow 1993–94; mem. Parl. 1994–; Chair. Parl. Comm. on Foreign Policy 1994–95; Deputy Speaker 1995–97, Speaker 1998–2000; f. Alliance for Democratic and Flourishing Moldova 1998; founder Chair. Democratic party 2000. *Address:* Parliament Buildings, Stefan Chelmari prosp. 105, 277073 Chişinău, Moldova. *Telephone:* (2) 23-35-28 (Office).

DYBKJAER, Lone, MChemEng; Danish politician; b. Lone Vincents, 23 May 1940, Copenhagen; m. Poul Nyrup Rasmussen (q.v.); two d.; ed Rungsted Statsskole, Tech. Univ. of Denmark; Sec., Acad. of Tech. Sciences 1964–66, Medico-Tech. Cttee 1966–70; Head Information Secr., Tech. Univ. of Denmark 1970–77; Adviser, Geotechnical Inst. 1978–79; mem. Folketing (Parl.) 1973–77, 1979–94; Chair. Parl. Energy Cttee, 1984–87, Tech. Cttee 1984–88, Parl. nine-mem. Cttee on Tech. Bd 1986–88; Social Liberal Party Spokesperson on Energy, Labour Market and Environmental Questions 1979–87, 1990–94, on Foreign Affairs 1987–88; Minister of the Environment 1988–90; MEP 1994–, First Vice-Chair. Cttee on Devt and Co-operation (responsible for human rights) 1999–2002, mem. Cttee on Women's Rights and Equal Opportunities 1999–, Cttee on Constitutional Affairs 2002–; ACP-EU Ass. 2002–; Bird Life Prize 1993; Cyclist of the Year 1989; Gold Medal for Conservation of Bldgs. 1991. *Publications:* Tête à tête with a Modern Politician 1998, Strange Parliament 1999, Digital Denmark 1999. *Leisure interests:* tennis, reading, family life. *Address:* ASP 10G 116, European Parliament, rue Wiertz, 1047 Brussels, Belgium (Office); c/o Det radikale Venstre, Christiansborg, 1240 Copenhagen K, Denmark (Office); Allégade 6A, 2000 Frederiksberg, Denmark (Home). *Telephone:* (2) 284-7391 (Belgium) (Office); 33-3-4-56 (Denmark) (Office). *Fax:* (2) 284-9391 (Belgium) (Office); 33-13-72-51 (Denmark) (Office). *E-mail:* ldybkjaer@europarl.eu.int (Office); rvlody@ft.dk (Office). *Website:* www.lone-dybkjaer.dk (Office).

DYDUCH, Marek; Polish politician and lawyer; b. 27 Aug. 1957, Swidnica; s. of Hipolit Dyduch and Krystyna Dyduch; m. Dorota Dyduch; one d. one s.; ed Wrocław Univ.; Chair. Local Council 1982–83; Vice-Chair. Exec. Bd, Union of Polish Socialist Youth (ZSMP) 1983–86, Chair. 1986–91; mem. Polish United Workers' Party (PZPR) 1982–; mem. Prov. Nat. Council, Walbrzych 1984–88; Deputy to the Sejm (Parl.) 1993–; mem. Social Democracy of the Repub. of Poland (SdRP) 1990–99, Democratic Left Alliance (after party reorganization) 1999–, Sec.-Gen. 2002–; Sec. of State Ministry of the Treasury 2001–02; Bronze Cross of Merit 1989. *Leisure interests:* tennis, skiing, local and global social phenomena, history, science-fiction. *Address:* National Council of Democratic Left Alliance, ul. Rozbrat 44A, 00-419 Warsaw, Poland (Office). *Telephone:* (22) 6292554 (Office). *Fax:* (22) 6212592 (Office). *E-mail:* mdyduch@sld.org.pl (Office). *Website:* www.dyduch.pl (Office).

DYER, Alexander Patrick, BS, MBA; American business executive; b. 30 Aug. 1932, Santa Rosa, Calif.; s. of John Dyer and late Amie M. Moore; m. Shirley Shine 1954; one s. (and one s. deceased); ed US Mil. Acad. and Harvard Business School; Exec. Vice-Pres. Air Products and Chemicals, BOC Group PLC 1987–89, Man. Dir Gases and CEO 1989–93, Deputy Chair. 1993–95, CEO 1993–96; Deputy Chair. Bunzl PLC 1996– (Chair. 1993–96); Dir BWAY Corpn. *Leisure interests:* golf, skeet, antique collecting. *Address:* Bunzl PLC, 110 Park Street, London, W1K 6NX, England (Office); 1803 Apple Tree Lane, Bethlehem, PA 18105, USA (Home). *Telephone:* (20) 7495-4950 (Office); (610) 691-5522 (Home). *Fax:* (20) 7495-2527 (Office); (610) 866-5102 (Home). *E-mail:* apdyer 1954@aol.com (Home).

DYKE, Greg(ory), BA; British television executive; b. 20 May 1947; s. of David Dyke and Denise Dyke; partner Sue Howes; one s. one d.; one step-s. one step-d.; ed Hayes Grammar School, Univ. of York and Harvard Business School; reporter on local paper; researcher, London Weekend Television (LWT) 1977, later founding producer, The Six O'Clock Show; joined TV-AM 1983; Dir of Programmes, TVS 1984–87; Dir of Programmes, LWT 1987–90, Man. Dir 1990; Group Chief Exec. LWT (Holdings) PLC 1991–94; Chair. Ind. TV Asscn 1992–94; Chair. GMTV 1993–94; Chair. CEO Pearson TV 1995–99; Chair. Channel 5 Broadcasting 1997–99; Dir Gen. BBC 2000–; Dir BSkyB 1995, Phoenix Pictures Inc., New York, Pearson PLC 1996–99 and others; Dir (non-exec.) Manchester United Football Club 1997–99; Trustee Science Museum 1996–, English Nat. Stadium Trust 1997–99. *Leisure interests:*

tennis, theatre, football, cinema. *Address:* Director-General, BBC, Broadcasting House, Portland Place, London, W1A 1AA, England (Office). *E-mail:* greg.dyke@bbc.co.uk (Office). *Website:* www.bbc.co.uk (Office).

DYKHOVICHNY, Ivan Vladimirovich; Russian film director; b. 16 Oct. 1947, Moscow; m.; ed Shchukin Higher Theatre School and Acad. of Cinematography; actor Taganka Theatre 1970–81; film Dir Mosfilm Studios 1984–96; Chief Dir All-Russian TV 1998–2000; winner All-Union Film Festival, All-European Festival of Cameramen's Art. *Films include:* Tester, Black Monk, Red Series, A Mass, Female Role, Music for December. *Television scriptwriting includes:* Catch 22. *Address:* Stary Petrovsko-Razumovsky proyezd 6/8, korp. 3, Apt. 110, 125083 Moscow, Russia. *Telephone:* (095) 214-48-61.

DYLAN, Bob; American composer and singer; b. Robert Zimmerman, 24 May 1941, Duluth, Minn.; m. Sarah Lowndes (divorced 1978); four c. one adopted d.; ed Univ. of Minnesota; best known for composition and interpretation of pop, country and folk music; self-taught on harmonica, guitar, piano, auto-harp; performer numerous tours and concerts 1960–66, 1971, 1974, 1975, 1976, 1978–80, 1981; devised and popularized folk-rock 1965; f. new group The Travelling Wilburys 1988; Hon. DMus (Princeton) 1970, Commdr Ordre des Arts et des Lettres, named to Rock and Roll Hall of Fame 1988. *Films include;* (actor) Eat the Document, Pat Garrett and Billy the Kid, Renaldo and Clara (also directed), Hearts of Fire 1986 and Concert for Bangladesh. *Singles include:* Blowin' in the Wind, Don't Think Twice It's All Right, A Hard Rain's A-gonna Fall, She Belongs to Me, It's All over Now Baby Blue, The Times They Are A-changing, Just Like a Woman, I'll Be Your Baby Tonight, I Shall Be Released, Lay, Lady, Lay, If Not for You, Mr. Tambourine Man, Like a Rolling Stone, Simple Twist of Fate, Forever Young, Mozambique, Hurricane, Knockin' on Heaven's Door, Gotta Serve Somebody, etc. *Albums include:* Blonde on Blonde, The Freewheelin' Bob Dylan, Highway 61 Revisited, Nashville Skyline, New Morning, Blood on the Tracks, Desire, Slow Train Coming, Infidels, Empire Burlesque, Knocked out Loaded, Down in the Groove 1988, Dylan and the Dead (with Grateful Dead) 1989, Oh Mercy 1989, Blonde on Blonde, Under The Red Sky 1990, Vol. 3 (with Travelling Wilburys) 1990, The Bootleg Series 1990, Good as I Been to You 1992, World Gone Wrong 1993, Unplugged 1995, Time Out of Mind (Grammy Award 1998) 1998, Love and Theft 2001. *Publications:* Tarantula 1966, 1971, Writings and Drawings 1973, The Songs of Bob Dylan 1966–1975, Lyrics 1962–1985, Drawn Blank 1994; Highway 61 Revisited (interactive CD-ROM). *Address:* P.O. Box 870, New York, NY 10276; c/o Columbia Records, 550 Madison Avenue, New York, NY 10022, USA.

DYSON, Freeman John, FRS; American physicist; b. 15 Dec. 1923, Crowthorne, England; s. of late Sir George Dyson and Lady Mildred (Atkey) Dyson; m. 1st Verena Huber 1950 (divorced 1958); m. 2nd Imme Jung 1958; one s. five d.; ed Cambridge and Cornell Univs; Fellow of Trinity Coll., Cambridge 1946; Warren Research Fellow, Birmingham Univ. 1949; Prof. of Physics, Cornell Univ. 1951–53; Prof., Inst. for Advanced Study, Princeton 1953–94, Prof. Emer. 1994–; Chair. Fed. of American Scientists 1962; mem. NAS 1964–; Foreign Assoc. Acad. des Sciences, Paris 1989; Hon. DSc (City Univ., UK) 1981 (Oxford) 1997; Gifford Lecturer, Aberdeen 1985; Heineman Prize, American Inst. of Physics 1965, Lorentz Medal, Royal Netherlands Acad. 1966, Hughes Medal, Royal Soc. 1968, Max Planck Medal, German Physical Soc. 1969, Harvey Prize, Israel Inst. of Tech. 1977, Wolf Prize (Israel) 1981, Matteucci Medal, Rome 1990, Fermi Award (USA) 1994, Templeton Prize 2000. *Publications:* Disturbing the Universe 1979, Weapons and Hope 1984, Origins of Life 1986, Infinite in All Directions 1988, From Eros to Gaia 1992, Imagined Worlds 1997, The Sun, The Genome and the Internet 1999; papers in The Physical Review, Journal of Mathematical Physics, etc. *Address:* Institute for Advanced Study, Princeton, NJ 08540 (Office); 105 Battle Road Circle, Princeton, NJ 08540, USA. *Telephone:* (609) 734-8055 (Office). *Fax:* (609) 951-4489 (Office). *E-mail:* dyson@ias.edu (Office).

DYSON, James, CBE, FCSD, MDes; British designer; b. 2 May 1947; s. of Alec Dyson and Mary (née Bolton) Dyson; m. Deirdre Hindmarsh 1967; two s. one d.; ed Gresham's School, Royal Coll. of Art; Dir Rotork Marine 1970–74; Man. Dir Kirk Dyson 1974–79; developed and designed Dyson Dual Cyclone vacuum cleaner 1979–93; f., Chair. Prototypes Ltd (now Dyson Research) 1979–, Dyson Appliances Ltd 1992–; Chair. Bath Coll. of Higher Educ. 1990–92, Design Museum 1999–; mem. Design Council 1997–, Council RCA 1998–; Hon. Fellow Liverpool John Moores Univ., Hon. MEID (Inst. of Eng Designers) 1997; numerous hon. doctorates including Hon. DLitt (Staffordshire) 1996; Hon. DSc (Oxford Brookes) 1997, (Huddersfield) 1997, (Bradford) 1998; numerous design awards and trophies. *Publications include:* Doing a Dyson 1996, Against the Odds (autobiog.) 1997. *Leisure interests:* running, garden design, music, fishing, cricket, tennis. *Address:* Dyson Appliances Ltd., Tetbury Mill, Malmesbury, Wilts., SN16 0RP (Office); Kingsmead Hill, Little Somerford, Wilts., SN15 5JN, England (Home). *Telephone:* (1666) 827200 (Office); (1666) 828282 (Home). *Fax:* (1666) 827321 (Home). *Website:* www.dyson.co.uk (Office).

DYVIK, Helge Julius Jakhelln, DPhil; Norwegian professor of general linguistics; b. 23 Dec. 1947, Bodø; s. of late Einar Dyvik and Harriet Dyvik (née Jakhelln); m. 1st Eva Sætre 1973 (divorced 1994); one s. one d.; m. 2nd Martha Thunes 2001; ed Univ. of Bergen, Univ. of Durham, UK; Research Asst (Old Norse), Univ. of Bergen 1974–75, Lecturer 1976, Project Asst (Old Norwegian syntax) 1976–81, Research Fellow (Vietnamese syntax project) 1981–83, Prof.

of Gen. Linguistics 1983–; Pres. Nordic Asscn of Linguists 1993–1998; mem. Norwegian Language Council 2000–, Programme Cttee for Nordic Council of Ministers' Research Programme on Language Tech. 2000– (Chair. 2002–); Fridtjof Nansen Award for Eminent Research, Norwegian Acad. of Letters and Science 1987. *Publications:* Grammatikk og Empiri 1981, Categories and Functions in Vietnamese Classifier Constructions 1983, Semantic Mirrors 1998. *Leisure interests:* play reading, choral singing. *Address:* Department of Linguistics and Comparative Literature, Linguistic Studies Section, University of Bergen, Sydnespl. 7, 5007 Bergen (Office); Straumevn. 13, 5042 Bergen Fjøsanger, Norway (Home). *E-mail:* helge.dyvik@lili.uib.no (Office). *Website:* www.hg.uib.no/li/lili/slf/ans/Dyvik (Office).

DZAIDDIN BIN HAJI ABDULLAH, Mohamed; Malaysian judge; b. 16 Sept. 1937, Arau, Perlis; m. Puan Noriah Binti Tengku Ismael; two c.; ed Sultan Abdul Hamid Coll. Alor Setar; journalist The Malay Mail 1956; joined police service as Insp.; called to Bar, Middle Temple, London, UK 1966; advocate and solicitor in Kota Bharu and Kuala Lumpur; juridicial commr (part-time) 1979–81; apptd High Court Judge, Criminal Div. of Kuala Lumpur High Court 1982–84, Penang High Court 1984–93; Supreme Court Judge (renamed Fed. Court Judge) 1993–2000; Chief Justice of the Fed. Court Dec. 2000–; fmr Chair. Kelantan Bar Cttee; Vice-Pres. Malaysian Bar 1981–82; elected Pres. ASEAN Law Asscn 1997. *Address:* Chief Justice's Chambers, Federal Court of Malaysia, Bangunan Sultan Abdul Samad, Jalan Raja, 50506 Kuala Lumpur, Malaysia (Office). *Telephone:* (3) 26939011. *Fax:* (3) 26932582. *E-mail:* halijah@kehakiman.gov.my. *Website:* www.kehakiman.gov.my.

DZASOKHOV, Aleksandr Sergeyevich, CandHistSc; Russian politician; b. 3 April 1934, Ordzhonikidze, North-Ossetian ASSR; m. Farisa Borissovna 1959; two s.; ed North Caucasian Mining-Metallurgical Inst. and CPSU Higher Party School; mem. CPSU 1957–91; First Sec. Ordzhonikidze Komsomol City Cttee 1957–61; Sec. of USSR Cttee of Youth Orgs 1961–64; leader of young Soviet specialists to Cuba 1964–65; First Sec., Pres. of USSR Youth Orgs 1965–67; Deputy Chair., Chair. of Soviet Cttee for Solidarity with Countries of Asia and Africa 1965–86; USSR Amb. to Syria 1986–88; First Sec. of North Ossetian CPSU Dist Cttee (Obkom) 1988–90; USSR People's Deputy 1989–91; Chair. Cttee of USSR Supreme Soviet on Int. Affairs 1990–91; mem., Sec. of Cen. Cttee CPSU, mem. of CPSU Politburo 1990–91; People's Deputy of Russia, mem. Supreme Soviet of Russian Fed. 1992–93; Chair. Sub-Cttee on Asia and the Pacific; mem. State Duma (Parl.) 1993–98; elected Pres. of Repub. of N Ossetia (Alania) 1998–; Deputy Chair. Inter-Parl. Group of Russian Fed. 1993, Chair. 1996–2001; mem. Acad. of Creative Endeavours. *Publications:* several books on problems of post-colonialism in third-world countries, including Formation and Evolution of the Post-colonial World 1999. *Address:* House of Soviets, Office of the President, Svobody pl. 1, 362038 Vladikavkaz, North Ossetia-Alania, Russia. *Telephone:* (8672) 53-35-24. *Fax:* (8672) 75-36-56. *E-mail:* president@rno.ssc.ac.ru (Office).

DZHANIBEKOV, Maj.-Gen. Vladimir Aleksandrovich; Russian cosmonaut (retd); b. 13 May 1942, Iskander, Tashkent Region, Uzbekistan; m. Lilya Munirovna Dzhanibekova; two d.; ed Yeisk High Mil. Aviation School; mem. CPSU 1970–91; mil. pilot-instructor 1965–70; mem. Cosmonauts' team 1970–; 5 space flights including Soviet-Mongolian on spaceship Salut 6-Soyuz 39; Commdr Cosmonauts' team Yuriy Gagarin Centre of Cosmonauts' Training 1985–88; Head Dept of Theoretical and Research Educ. of Cosmonauts 1988–98; Hero of Soviet Union 1978, 1981; Hero of Mongolian Repub. 1981; Officier Légion d'honneur 1982. *Leisure interest:* painting. *Address:* Yuriy Gagarin Centre for Cosmonauts' Training, Zvezdny Gorodok, Moscow Region, Russia. *Telephone:* (095) 526-28-70.

DZHEMILEV, Mustafa (Abdul-Dzhemil); Ukrainian (Crimean Tatar) activist; b. 13 Nov. 1943, Ayserez, Crimea; m. Safinar Dzhemileva; three c.; suffered continual harrassment from Soviet authorities when he attempted to form a youth movt in Tashkent 1962–; subsequently, imprisonment or exile for activity: 1966–67, 1969–72, 1974–75, 1975–77, 1979–82, 1983–86; continued to organize Crimean Tatar protest actions in Cen. Asia and Moscow; returned to Crimea 1989; Chair. Crimean Tatar Majlis 1991–; Pres. Crimea Foundation 1998–; mem. Ukrainian Parl. 1998–; political observer Business magazine; Dr hc (Seljuk Univ., Higher Tech. Inst. Gebze, Turkey); Nansen Medal UNHCR1998, Pylyp Orlyk Int. Award 2000, Yaroslav Mudryi Medal 2001, Hon. Prize of Parliament of Ukraine 2002. *Leisure interest:* studying informative websites. *Address:* ul. Shmidta 25, Simferopol, Crimea (Office); 6th Microrayon 100, Bakhchesaray, Crimea, Ukraine (Home). *Telephone:* (652) 2275259 (Office); (652) 5443758 (Home). *Fax:* (652) 2274372 (Office). *E-mail:* MCemiloglu@ttt.Crimea.com (Home).

DZHIGARKHANIAN, Armen Borisovich; Armenian/Russian stage and film actor; b. 3 Oct. 1935, Erevan; m. Tatiana Vlasova 1967; one s.; ed Erevan Theatre Inst.; actor with Stanislavsky Russian Drama Theatre in Yerevan 1955–67; with Moscow Lenin Komsomol Theatre 1967–69, with Mayakovsky Theatre 1969–96, with Dzhigarkhanian Theatre 1996–; Armenian SSR State Prize 1975, 1979; RSFSR People's Artist 1973, USSR People's Artist 1985, Stanislavsky Award 2001. *Films:* has appeared in a number of films. *Roles include:* Levinson in Fadeev's Thunder, Stanley in Tennessee Williams' Streetcar Named Desire, Socrates and Nero in Radzinsky's Chats with Socrates and the Theatre in the time of Nero and Seneca, Big Daddy in Tennessee Williams' Cat on a Hot Tin Roof, Nelson in Rattigan's Vivat Regina!, Max in Pinter's Homecoming, Krapp in Beckett's Krapp's Last Tape,

Domenic in E. D. Phillippo's Philoumena Marturano. *Leisure interests:* reading, listening to classical music, playing with pet Siamese cat. *Address:* 37 Starokonysheny per., Apt. 9, 121002 Moscow, Russia. *Telephone:* (095) 930-23-07 (Office); (095) 203-30-79 (Home); (214) 772-7464 (Dallas, U.S.A.). *Fax:* (095) 930-03-47 (Office).

DZHORBENADZE, Avtandil Khristoforovich, DrMed; Georgian politician; b. 1951, Chibati, Lanchkhut region; s. of Khristophor Dzhorbenadze and Mariam Kamaladze; m. Nino Vepkhadze; two s.; ed Tbilisi State Inst. of Med. 1974; intern Tbilisi clinical hosp. #1 1975, roentgenologist, sec. CP Cttee, Deputy Chief Doctor 1978–86; therapeutist Tbilisi polyclinic #29 1975–76; practitioner mil. unit in Georgia 1976–78; First Deputy Head, then Head Tbilisi City Dept of Public Health 1986–92; Deputy Minister of Public Health and Social Security 1992–93; Minister of Public Health 1993–99, of Labour, Public Health and Social Security 1999–2001; Minister of State and Head of the State Chancellery of Georgia Dec. 2001–. *Publications:* over 30 scientific Publs. *Address:* Office of State Minister, Ingorkva 7, 380034 Tbilisi, Georgia (Office). *Telephone:* (32) 98-97-93 (Office).

DZIUBA, Andrzej Franciszek (Franciszek Wieczyński), DD; Polish ecclesiastic and university professor; b. 10 Oct. 1950, Pleszew; s. of Stanisław Dziuba and Ludwika Szlachciak; ed Primatial Priests' Seminary, Gniezno, Pontifical Theological Faculty, Poznań, Catholic Univ. Lublin, Acad. Alfonsiana, Rome and Univ. Italiana per Stranieri, Perugia; ordained priest, Gniezno 1975; Asst parish priest and catechist, Łobżenica 1975–76; studies in Lublin 1976–79, Rome 1979–81; Sec. to Primate of Poland 1981–98, Dir Secr. 1984–98; Asst parish priest, St Martin's Church, Warsaw 1981–98, St Barbara's Church, Warsaw 1998–; Prof. Catholic Univ. Lublin 1989–, Acad. of Catholic Theology, Warsaw 1995–99, Primatial Priest's Seminary, Gniezno 1998–, Cardinal S. Wyszyński Univ. 1999–; Hon. Chaplain to His Holiness Pope John Paul II 1990, Prelate 1996; Primate of Poland Foundation in GB 1991; Canon Metropolitan Chapter of Warsaw 1998; Theological Counsellor to Primate of Poland 1998–; Hon. Conventual Chaplain of Order of Malta 1998–; Kt Commdr of Equestrian Order of Holy Sepulchre of Jerusalem 1996, Cross with Gold Star of Merit of Holy Sepulchre of Jerusalem 1996, Kt Ecclesiastical Grace of Sacred Mil. Constantinian Order 1999. *Publications:* Mikołaj z Mościsk, teolog moralista XVII w. 1985, Jan Azor, teolog-moralista 1988, Informator Katolicki 89/90 1990, Droga Krzyżowa 1991, Różaniec święty 1992, Kościół katolicki w Polsce. Informator 1993, Jezus nam przebacza. Przygotowanie do sakramentu pojednania 1994, Matka Boża z Guadalupe 1995, Kościół katolicki w Polsce. Informator 1995, Orędzie moralne Jezusa Chrystusa 1996 Dynamika wiary 1997, Kościół katolicki w Polsce. Informator 1997, Droga krzyżowa 1998, Biography of HE Cardinal Józef Glemp 1998, Cardinal Stefan Wyszyński Primate of Poland. A Life-Sketch 2000, U źródeł Bożej Mądrości. Życie i nauka Jezusa Chrystusa 2000, Spowiedź małżeńska. Życie małżeńskie a sakramentalna posługa pokuty i pojednania 2002; numerous articles on moral theology, church history, Catholic social sciences. *Address:* ul. Nowogrodzka 49/11, 00-695 Warsaw, Poland. *Telephone:* (22) 6213510. *Fax:* (22) 6358745.

DZIUBA, Ivan Mykhailovych; Ukrainian literary critic; b. 26 July 1931, Mykolaivka, Ukraine; s. of Mykhailo Dzyuba and Olga Dzyuba; m. Marta Lenets 1963; one d.; ed Donetsk Pedagogical Inst.; Ed. various journals and publs published by Ukrainian State Publishing House; published An Ordinary Man or a Petit-Bourgeois as well as numerous samizdat articles in 1960s; expelled from Writers' Union 1972 after publication of Internationalism or Russification? (numerous edns.); arrested 1972, sentenced to 5 years' imprisonment 1973; recanted and released Nov. 1973; Writers' Union membership restored 1980s; mem. Ukrainian Acad. of Sciences 1992–, mem. Presidium 1997–; Academician-Sec. Dept of Literature, Language and Arts 1996–; Minister of Culture Dec. 1992–94; Sr Researcher, T. Shevchenko Inst. of Literature 1994–; Ed.-in-Chief Suchasnist (magazine) 1991–, Encyclopaedia of Modern Ukraine 1998–; head of Cttee Tazas Shevchenko Nat. Ukrainian Award; freelance literary corresp. 1982–; O. Biletski Prize 1987, Laureate, Shevchenko's Award 1991, Int. Antonovich Prize 1992, V. Zhabotinsky Prize 1996, Vernadsky Prize 2001. *Publications:* 20 books including Between Politics and Literature 1998, Thirst 2001 and numerous articles on history and devt of Ukrainian literature and writers of former USSR. *Leisure interests:* gardening, mushrooming. *Address:* 54 Volodymyrska Street, Kiev

01030 (Office); Antonova str. 7, Apt. 60, 03186 Kiev, Ukraine (Home). *Telephone:* (44) 235-09-81 (Office); (44) 248-41-77 (Home). *Fax:* (44) 228-11-93 (Office). *E-mail:* shevcom@ukr.net (Office).

DZIWISZ, Stanisław, ThD; Polish Roman Catholic ecclesiastic; b. 27 April 1939, Raba Wyżna; ed Primatial Priest Seminary, Kraków, Metropolitan Ecclesiastic Seminary, Kraków, Pontifical Acad. of Theology, Kraków; ordained priest 1963; Asst Parish Priest, Maków Podhalański 1963–65; Chaplain to Archbishop of Kraków Karol Wojtyła (now Pope John Paul II) 1966–78; lecturer Higher Inst. of Catechism, Kraków 1966–78; ed. Kraków Curie Notificationes e Curia Metropolitana Cracoviensi 1966–78; Personal Sec. to Pope John Paul II 1978–, Prelate 1985, Apostolic Protonotary, Canon of Cathedral Chapter, Lviv and Metropolitan Chapter, Kraków 1997; Bishop and Prefetto aggiunto 1998; Vice-Chair. John Paul II Foundation 1985–. *Publication:* Kult św. Stanisława biskupa w Krakowie do Soboru Trydenckiego (Cult of Saint Stanislaus, Bishop of Kraków until Trent Synod) 1978. *Address:* Palazzo Apostolico, 00120 Città del Vaticano, Vatican City (Office).

DZUMAGULOV, Apas Dzumagulovich; Kyrgyzstan politician; b. 19 Sept. 1934, Arashan, Kyrgyz SSR; m.; three s.; ed Moscow Gubkin Inst. of Oil; mem. CPSU 1962–91; worked at Complex S., Geological Expedition USSR Acad. of Sciences 1958–59; Sr geologist oil field Changar-Tash, Head. Cen. Research Lab., Chief Geologist Drilling Div., Chief Engineer Oil Co. Kyrghizneft Osh Dist 1959–73; Head Industrial-Transport Div. Cen. Cttee CP of Kyrgyz SSR 1973–79; Sec. Cen. Cttee CP of Kirgyzia 1979–85; First Sec. Issyk-Kul Dist Cttee 1985–86; Chair. Council of Ministers Kyrgyz SSR 1986–91; Chair. Org. Cttee, then Chair. Regional Soviet of Deputies, Head of Admin. Chuysk Region 1991–93; Deputy to USSR Supreme Soviet 1984–89; USSR People's Deputy 1989–91; People's Deputy of Kyrgyzstan; mem. Revision Comm. CPSU 1986–91; Prime Minister of Kyrgyz Repub. 1993–97; Amb. to Germany, Scandinavian countries and Vatican City 1998–. *Address:* Embassy of Kyrgyzstan, 1058S Berlin, Otto-Suhr-Allee 146, Germany (Office). *E-mail:* 101477.1160@compuserve.com (Office).

DŽUNOV, Todor, DSc; Macedonian professor of law and jurist; b. 11 Oct. 1931, Vatasha, Kavadarci; m. Granka Džunov 1958; ed Univ. of 'Cyril and Metodius', Skopje; Asst, Faculty of Law, Skopje 1956, Reader 1964, Assoc. Prof. 1969, Prof. 1974–94, Dean, Faculty of Law 1981–83; Rector, Univ. of 'Cyril and Metodius', Skopje 1985–88; Justice of the Constitutional Court 1994, Pres. 2000–; Pres. Research Council of Macedonia 1973–80; mem. and Chief of dels. of interstate bodies for scientific and tech. co-operation with Greece, USA and UK; mem. del. on succession issues on fmr Repub. of Yugoslavia; 11th of October Award 1980, Gold Award, Faculty of Law, Skopje 2001, Gold Award, Faculty of Philosophy, Univ. of 'Cyril and Metodius', Skopje, State Medal for Labour, State Medal for People Merit. *Publications:* more than 100 titles including Private International Law (textbook), International Legal Regulation of the Use of Rivers and Lakes of Common Interest Out of Navigation 1964, International Regulation of the Use of Waters 1979, Collection of Laws on the Private International Law 1984, Foreign Policy of SFRY and Non-Alignment 1989. *Address:* Constitutional Court, 12 Udarka brig. 2, 1000 Skopje (Office); Partizanski odredi No. 8/25, 1000 Skopje, Republic of Macedonia (Home). *Telephone:* (2) 163063 (Office); (2) 130163 (Home). *Fax:* (2) 119355 (Office). *E-mail:* tdzunov@usud.gov.mk (Office).

DZURINDA, Mikuláš, PhD; Slovak politician; b. 4 Feb. 1955, Spišský Štvrtok; m.; two c.; ed Univ of Transport and Communications, Žilina, econ. researcher Transport Research Inst., Žilina 1979–80; information tech. officer Czechoslovak Railways Regional Directorate, Bratislava 1980–88, Head of Automated Control Systems Dept 1988–91; Deputy Minister of Transport and Postal Service of Slovak Repub. 1991–92, 1994; Vice-Chair. for Econ. Christian Democratic Movt 1993–2000; spokesman of Slovak Democratic Coalition 1997–98, Chair. 1998–; Prime Minister of Slovak Repub. 1998–2002, 2002–; f. Slovak Democratic and Christian Union 2000, Chair. 2000–; mem. Nat. Council of Slovak Repub. (NCSR) 1992–; Vittorino Colombo Award (Italy) 2000. *Publications:* Where There's a Will There's a Way. *Leisure interests:* family, sport, running a marathon. *Address:* Government Office of the Slovak Republic, Nám. Slobody 1, 813 70 Bratislava 1, Slovakia (Office). *Telephone:* (2) 572-95111 (Office). *Fax:* (2) 544-15484 (Office). *E-mail:* premier@government.gov.sk. *Website:* www.premier.gov.sk (Office).

EABORN, Colin, FRS; British scientist and professor of chemistry; b. 15 March 1923, Cheshire; s. of Tom Stanley Eaborn and Caroline Eaborn; m. Joyce Thomas 1949; ed Ruabon Grammar School, Clwyd, Univ. Coll. of N Wales, Bangor; worked at Univ. of Leicester 1947–62 (Asst Lecturer 1947–50, Lecturer 1950–57, Reader in Chem. 1957–62); at Univ. of Sussex 1962–, Prof. of Chem. 1962–88, Emer. Prof. 1988–, Dean of School of Molecular Sciences 1964–68, 1978–79, Pro-Vice Chancellor (Science) 1968–73; Research Assoc., Univ. of Calif. at Los Angeles 1950–51; Robert A. Welch Visiting Scholar, Rice Univ., Tex. 1961–62, Erskine Fellow, Univ. of Canterbury, NZ 1965; Distinguished Prof. of Chem., New Mexico State Univ. 1973, Commonwealth Fellow and Visiting Prof. of Chem., Univ. of Victoria, BC, Canada 1976, Riccoboni Lecturer, Univ. of Padua 1977; Gilman Lecturer, Iowa State Univ. 1978; Hon. Sec., Chemical Soc. 1964–71; mem. Council Royal Soc. 1978–80, 1988–89; Regional Ed., Journal of Organometallic Chem. 1963–95, mem. Editorial Advisory Bd Organometallics 1999–2002; Hon. Fellow Univ. of Wales, Bangor 2000; Hon. DSc (Sussex) 1990; F. S. Kipping Award for Organosilicon Chem. (American Chem. Soc.) 1964, Award for Organometallic Chem. 1974, Ingold Medal 1976, Award for Main Group Chemistry 1989 (all Royal Soc. of Chem.). *Publications:* Organosilicon Compounds 1960, The Synthesis and Reactions of the Carbon-Silicon Bond (in Organometallic Compounds of the Group IV Elements, Pt. 1) 1968; over 500 research papers in scientific journals. *Address:* School of Chemistry, Physics and Environmental Science, University of Sussex, Brighton, BN1 9QJ, England (Office). *Telephone:* (1273) 678124. *Fax:* (1273) 677196. *E-mail:* c.eaborn@susx.ac.uk (Office).

EAGLEBURGER, Lawrence Sidney, MS; American government official; b. 1 Aug. 1930, Milwaukee, Wis.; s. of late Dr Leon S. and Helen M. Eagleburger; m. Marlene Ann Heinemann 1966; three s.; ed Univ. of Wisconsin; joined US foreign service 1957; Third Sec., Tegucigalpa, Honduras 1957–59; Dept of State 1959–62; Second Sec., Belgrade, Yugoslavia 1962–65; Dept of State 1965–66; mem. Nat. Security Council staff 1966–67; Special Asst to Under-Sec. of State 1967–68; Exec. Asst to Asst to Pres. for Nat. Security Affairs 1969; Politicial Adviser, US Mission to NATO 1969–71; Deputy Asst Sec. of Defense, Internal Security Affairs 1971–72, Acting Asst Sec. of Defense, Internal Security Affairs 1973, Exec. Asst to Sec. of State 1973–77; Deputy Asst to Pres. for Nat. Security Operations 1973; Deputy Under-Sec. of State for Man., Exec. Asst to Sec. of State 1975–77; Amb. to Yugoslavia 1977–81; Asst Sec. of State for European Affairs 1981–82, Under-Sec. of State for Political Affairs 1982–84; Deputy Sec. of State 1989–92 (Envoy to Israel during Gulf Conflict 1991); Acting Sec. of State Aug.–Dec. 1992, Sec. of State Dec. 1992–Jan. 1993; Prof. (part-time) Univ. of S Carolina 1984 (Distinguished Visiting Prof. of Int. Studies 1984), Univ. of Va (part-time) 1993–; Pres. Kissinger Assocs. Inc. July 1984–; mem. Bd ITT Corpn 1984–, Josephson Int. Mutual Life Insurance Co. of NY, LBS Bank; Hon. LLD (S Carolina) 1985, (George Washington Univ.) 1986; President's Award for Distinguished Civil Service, Dept of Defense Distinguished Service Medal; Hon. KBE 1995. *Address:* c/o University of Virginia, University Station, P.O. Box 9011, Charlottesville, VA 22906, USA.

EAGLETON, Terence Francis, PhD; British professor of English literature; b. 22 Feb. 1943, Salford, Lancs.; s. of Francis Paul Eagleton and Rosaleen Riley; m. 1st Elizabeth Rosemary Galpin 1966 (divorced 1976); two s.; m. 2nd Willa Murphy; one s.; ed Trinity Coll., Cambridge; Fellow in English Jesus Coll., Cambridge 1964–69; Tutorial Fellow Wadham Coll., Oxford 1969–89; lecturer in Critical Theory and Fellow of Linacre Coll., Oxford 1989–92; Thomas Warton Prof. of English Literature and Fellow of St Catherine's Coll., Oxford Oct. 1992–2001; Prof. of Cultural Theory, Univ. of Manchester 2001–; Dr hc (Nat. Univ. of Ireland), (Santiago di Compostela); Hon. DLitt (Salford). *Films:* screenplay for Wittenstein. *Plays:* St Oscar 1989, Disappearances 1998. *Publications:* Criticism and Ideology 1976, Marxism and Literary Criticism 1976, Literary Theory: an Introduction 1983, The Function of Criticism 1984, The Ideology of the Aesthetic 1990, The Crisis of Contemporary Culture 1993, Heathcliff and the Great Hunger 1995, The Illusions of Postmodernism 1996, Literary Theory 1996, Crazy John and the Bishop and other Essays on Irish Culture 1998, The Idea of Culture 2000, The Gatekeeper (autobiog.) 2001, Sweet Violence: The Idea of the Tragic 2002. *Leisure interest:* Irish music. *Address:* Department of English, Manchester University, Manchester, M13 9PL, England (Office).

EAGLING, Wayne John; Canadian ballet dancer, choreographer and artistic director; s. of Eddie Eagling and Thelma Eagling; ed P. Ramsey Studio of Dance Arts, Royal Ballet School; Sr Prin. Royal Ballet 1975–91; Artistic Dir Dutch Nat. Ballet 1991–. *Ballets:* has danced lead roles in Sleeping Beauty, Swan Lake, Cinderella and other major classics; created roles include: Young Boy in Triad, Solo Boy in Gloria, Ariel in The Tempest, Woyzeck in Different Drummer; choreographed The Hunting of the Snark and Frankenstein, The Modern Prometheus, Ruins of Time 1993, Symphony in Waves 1994, Alma Mahler (for La Scala, Milan) 1994, Duet 1995, Lost Touch 1995, Nutcracker and Mouseking (with Toer van Schayk) 1996, The Last Emperor (for Hong Kong Ballet) 1998, Magic Flute (with Toer van Schayk) 1999, Le Sacré du Printemps 2000. *Publication:* The Company We Keep (with Ross MacGibbon and Robert Jude) 1981. *Leisure interests:* golf, scuba diving, tennis. *Address:* Dutch National Ballet, Het Muziektheater, Waterlooplein 22, 1011 PG Amsterdam (Office); Postbus 16486, 1001 RN Amsterdam, Netherlands. *Telephone:* (20) 5518138. *Fax:* (20) 5518070. *E-mail:* info@het-nationale-ballet.nl (Office).

EAMES, Baron (Life Peer), cr. 1995, of Armagh in the County of Armagh; **Most Rev. Robert Henry Alexander Eames,** PhD; British ecclesiastic; b. 27 April 1937; s. of William E. Eames and Mary E. T. Eames; m. Ann C. Daly 1966; two s.; ed Methodist Coll., Belfast, Queen's Univ., Belfast and Trinity Coll., Dublin; Research Scholar and Tutor, Faculty of Laws, Queen's Univ., Belfast 1960–63; Curate Asst, Bangor Parish Church 1963–66; Rector, St Dorothea's, Belfast 1966–74; Examining Chaplain to Bishop of Down 1973; Rector, St Mark's, Dunelda 1974–75; Bishop of Derry and Raphoe 1975–80; Bishop of Down and Dromore 1980–86; Archbishop of Armagh and Primate of All Ireland 1986–; Select Preacher, Oxford Univ. 1986–87, Cambridge Univ. 1989; Irish Rep., Anglican Consultative Council 1984, mem. Standing Cttee 1985; Chair. Archbishop of Canterbury's Comm. on Communion and Women in the Episcopate 1988–, Comm. on Inter-Anglican Relations 1988–, Anglican Int. Doctrinal Comm. (USA) 1991; Gov. Church Army 1985–; Hon. LLD (Queen's Univ. Belfast) 1989, (Trinity Coll. Dublin) 1992, (Lancaster) 1994; Dr hc (Cambridge) 1994; Hon. DD (Exeter) 1999. *Publications:* A Form of Worship for Teenagers 1965, The Quiet Revolution – Irish Disestablishment 1970, Through Suffering 1973, Thinking through Lent 1978, Through Lent 1984, Chains to be Broken 1992; and contributions to New Divinity, Irish Legal Quarterly, Criminal Law Review, Northern Ireland Legal Quarterly, Univ. Review and The Furrow. *Leisure interests:* sailing, rugby, football, reading. *Address:* The See House, Cathedral Close, Armagh, BT61 7EE, Northern Ireland. *Telephone:* (28) 3752-7144 (Office); (28) 3752-2851 (Home). *Fax:* (28) 3752-7823 (Office). *E-mail:* archbishop@armagh.anglican.org (Office). *Website:* ireland.anglican.org.

EANES, Gen. António dos Santos Ramalho; Portuguese politician and army officer; b. 25 Jan. 1935, Alcains; s. of Manuel dos Santos Eanes and Maria do Rosario Ramalho; m. Maria Manuela Duarte Neto Portugal 1970; two s.; ed High School, Castelo Branco, Higher Inst. of Applied Psychology, Lisbon Faculty of Law; enlisted in Army School 1953; Commissioned to Portuguese India 1958–60, Macao 1960–62, Mozambique 1962–64, Operations Officer of Light Infantry Battalion, Mozambique 1966–67, Information Officer, Portuguese Guinea (Guinea-Bissau) 1969–73, Angola 1973–74; Physical Education Instructor, Mil. Acad. 1968; Dir of Dept of Cultural and Recreational Affairs 1973; rank of Second Lt 1957, Lt 1959, Capt. 1961, Maj. 1970, Gen. 1978; involved in leadership of mil. movts finally contesting mil. apparatus and colonial wars 1968–74; after April Revolution named to first 'Ad-hoc' Cttee for mass media June 1974; Dir of Programmes of Portuguese TV June–Sept. 1974, Chair. of Bd of Dirs of TV co., resigned after accusation of 'probable implication' in abortive counter-coup March 1975, cleared after inquiry; rank of Lt-Col; mem. Cttee restructuring 5th Div., Gen. Staff Armed Forces; Army Chief of Staff (with temporary rank of Gen.) 1975–76; mem. of Mil. Cttee of Council of Revolution; responsible for Constitutional Law approved Dec. 1975; Col 1976; Pres. of Portugal 1976–86; Chair. of Council of Revolution; C-in-C of Armed Forces 1976–80, 1980–81; Leader, Portuguese Democratic Renewal Party 1986–87; mem. Council of State; War Cross 2nd class, Silver Medal for Distinguished Services with Palm, Silver Medal for Exemplary Behaviour, Commemorative Medal of the Portuguese Armed Forces, Degree of Kt of Mil. Order of Avis. *Address:* c/o Partido Renovador Democrático, Travessa do Fala Só 9, 1200 Lisbon, Portugal. *Telephone:* 323997.

EARL, Robert I.; American business executive; b. 1952; f. President Entertainment (theme restaurants) 1977, sold co. to Pleasurama PLC, joined Pleasurama man. team, Man. Hard Rock Cafe PLC 1987–93; CEO and Dir Planet Hollywood Int. 1993–2000, Chair. Bd 1998–. *Address:* Planet Hollywood International Inc., 8669 Commodity Circle, Orlando, FL 32819, USA (Office). *Telephone:* (407) 363-7827 (Office). *Fax:* (407) 352-7310 (Office). *E-mail:* general_information@planethollywood.com (Office).

EASLEY, Michael F., JD, BA; American state official; b. 1950, Rocky Mount, NC; m. Mary Pipines; one s.; ed Univ. of NC, NC Cen. Univ.; Dist Attorney, 13th Dist, NC 1982–91; pvt. practice, Southport, NC 1991–93; Attorney-Gen. 1993–; Gov. of NC 2000–; Pres. NC Conf. of Dist Attorneys; mem. NC Dist Attorneys Asscn; Public Services Award, US Dept of Justice 1984. *Leisure interests:* hunting, sailing, woodwork. *Address:* Office of the Governor, 20301 Mail Service Center, Raleigh, NC 27699-0301, USA (Office).

EASON, Henry, CBE, JP, BCom; British banking administrator; b. 12 April 1910, Middlesbrough; s. of late H. and F. J. Eason; m. Florence Isobel Stevenson 1939 (died 1992); one s. two d.; ed Yarm and King's Coll., Univ. of Durham; Barrister, Gray's Inn; Lloyds Bank Ltd until 1939; RAF (Wing Commdr), Second World War (twice Mentioned in Despatches); Sec.-Gen. Inst. of Bankers 1959–71, Vice-Pres. 1969–75; Hon. Fellow 1971. *Leisure interests:* golf, travel, reading. *Address:* 12 Redgate Drive, Hayes Common, Bromley, Kent, BR2 7BT, England (Home).

EAST, Rt Hon Paul Clayton, PC, QC, LLM; New Zealand politician and lawyer; b. 1946, Opotiki; s. of Edwin Cuthbert East and Edith Pauline Addison East; m. Marilyn Therese Kottmann 1972; three d.; ed Univ. of

Virginia School of Law, Univ. of Auckland School of Law, King's Coll.; law clerk, Morpeth Gould & Co., Auckland 1968–70; partner, East Brewster Solicitors, Rotorua 1974–; fmr Rotorua City Councillor and Deputy Mayor; Nat. Party MP for Rotorua 1978–96; Attorney-Gen., Minister responsible for Serious Fraud Office and Audit Dept 1990–97, Leader of the House 1990–93, Minister of Crown Health Enterprises 1991–96, for State Services 1993–97, for Defence and War Pensions 1996–97, for Corrections 1996–97; High Commr in UK (also accred to Nigeria and Ireland) 1999–2002. *Leisure interests:* fishing, skiing, golf. *Address:* 23 Sophia Street, PO Box 608, Rotorua, New Zealand. *E-mail:* pauleastnz@hotmail.com (Home).

EASTCOTT, Harry Hubert Grayson, MS, FRCS, FRCOG; British surgeon; b. 17 Oct. 1917, Montreal, Canada; s. of Henry George Eastcott and Gladys Eastcott (née Tozer); m. Doreen Joy Mittell 1941; four d.; ed Latymer School, London and Medical Schools at St Mary's Hosp., London, Middlesex Hosp., London and Harvard; Jr resident appointments 1941–43; Surgeon Lt RDVR 1944–46; Sr Surgical Registrar St Mary's Hosp., London 1947–50, Asst Dir Surgical Unit of Medical School 1950–54, Consultant Surgeon 1955–82, Emer. 1982–; Consultant Surgeon Royal Masonic Hosp., London 1964–80; King Edward VII Hosp. for Officers, London 1965–87; in Surgery and Vascular Surgery RN 1957–82; Pres. Medical Soc., London 1976 (Sec. 1963, Trustee 1987), Section of Surgery, Royal Soc. of Medicine 1977 (Sec. 1963), United Services Section 1980–82, Int. Vascular Symposium, London 1981; Sr Vice-Pres. Royal Coll. of Surgeons 1982 (mem. Ct. of Examiners 1964–70, mem. Council 1971–83, Jr Vice-Pres. 1981–83, mem. Court of Patrons 1997); fmr Examiner in Surgery Univs. of London, Cambridge, Lagos and Queen's, Belfast; Hunterian Professorship R.C.S. 1953; Editorial Sec. British Journal of Surgery 1972–78; Hon. mem. Soc. for Vascular Surgery, USA 1974, Purkinje Soc., Czechoslovakia 1984, Int. Union of Angiology 1995, European Soc. for Vascular Surgery 1995; Hon. mem. and Hippocratic Orator Hellenic Medical Soc. 1986; several memorial lectures; Hon. FACS 1977, Hon. FRACS 1978, Hon. Fellow American Surgical Asscn 1981; Fothergillian Gold Medal (Medical Soc. of London) 1974, Cecil Joll Prize (Royal Coll. of Surgeons) 1983, Galen Medal of Worshipful Soc. of Apothecaries 1993, Leriche Prize (Int. Surgical Soc.) 2001. *Publications:* Arterial Surgery 1969, 1973, 1993, A Colour Atlas of Operations upon the Internal Carotid Artery 1984; contrib. to Lancet. *Leisure interests:* music, travel, aeronautics, gardening. *Address:* 16 White Cross Road, Haddenham, Bucks., HP17 8BA, England. *Telephone:* (1844) 290629. *Fax:* (1844) 292003 (Home). *E-mail:* hhgevasc@clara.net (Office).

EASTMAN, Dean Eric, PhD; American physicist, science policy consultant and data processing executive; b. 21 Jan. 1940, Oxford, Wis.; m. Ella Mae Staley 1979; Research Staff mem. IBM, Yorktown Heights, NY 1963–74, Man. Surface Physics and Photo-emission 1971–82, Dir Advanced Packaging Tech. Lab. and Sr Man. III-V Semi-conductor Packaging Tech. & Systems Dept and GaAs Devices and Tech. Dept 1982–85, STD Dir of Devt and Product Assurance 1985–86, IBM Research Vice-Pres. of System Tech. and Science 1986–94, IBM Dir Hardware Devt Re-Eng 1994–95, IBM Server Group Vice-Pres. Devt Re-Eng and Tech. Strategy 1996–98; Prof. of Physics Univ. of Chicago 1998–; Govt Adviser to numerous science orgs.; Fellow American Physical Soc.; mem. NAS, Nat. Acad. of Eng; IBM Fellow 1974–; APS Oliver E. Buckley Prize 1980. *Publications:* numerous articles on solid state physics in professional journals. *Address:* Department of Physics, University of Chicago, 5801 S. Ellis Avenue, Chicago, IL 60637 (Office); 806 Pines Bridge Road, Ossining, NY 10562, USA (Home).

EASTMAN, Ernest, MIA; Liberian politician and diplomatist; b. 27 March 1930, Monrovia; s. of H. Nathan Eastman and Adeliue Payne; m. Salma Mohammedali; four s. five d.; ed Coll. of West Africa, Oberlin Coll., Ohio, Columbia Univ., New York; Dir Bureau of Afro-Asian Affairs (Dept of State) 1957–64; Under-Sec. of State for Admin. 1964–67; Under-Sec. of State 1968–72; Amb. to East Africa (Kenya, Lesotho, Madagascar, Tanzania, Uganda, Zambia) 1972–74; Amb. to the Far East (Japan, Repub. of Korea, Democratic People's Repub. of Korea, Philippines, Indonesia, India) 1974–77; Sec.-Gen. Mano River Union (Economic and Customs Union for the Repubs of Liberia, Sierra Leone and Guinea) 1977–83; Minister of Foreign Affairs 1983–85; mem. special missions to the Presidents of Dahomey, Niger, Guinea, Ivory Coast, Gambia and USA; mem. official del. to several int. confs of the OAU, UN and Non-Aligned Movement; several decorations including Kt Great Band, Humane Order of African Redemption, several European and African decorations. *Publications:* A History of the State of Maryland in Liberia 1957; many newspaper articles on int affairs. *Address:* c/o Ministry of Foreign Affairs, POB 9002, Monrovia, Liberia.

EASTMAN, John; American lawyer; b. 1940, New York; s. of late Lee Eastman; brother-in-law of Sir Paul McCartney (q.v.); m. Jodie Eastman; one s. one d.; ed Stanford Univ. and Univ. of New York; worked for Senate Commerce Cttee 1963; Office of US Attorney, New York; took part in Robert Kennedy's 1968 presidential election campaign; with father founded Eastman & Eastman (law firm); specializes in contract and copyright law; represents many leading showbusiness and media personalities. *Leisure interests:* collecting pictures, 19th-century English literature.

EASTON, David, BA, PhD, FRSC; professor of political science; b. 24 June 1917, Toronto; s. of Albert Easton and Mary Easton; m. Sylvia Johnstone 1942 (died 1990); one s.; ed Univ. of Toronto and Harvard Univ.; Teaching Fellow Dept of Govt Harvard Univ. 1944–47; Asst Prof. Dept of Political Science Univ. of Chicago 1947–53, Assoc. Prof. 1953–55, Prof. 1955–, Andrew MacLeish Distinguished Service Prof. 1969–82, Prof. Emer. 1982–; Sir Edward Peacock Prof. of Political Science Queen's Univ., Kingston, Ont. 1971–80; Distinguished Prof. of Political Science Univ. of Calif., Irvine 1981–; Pres. American Political Science Asscn 1968–69; Int. Cttee on Social Science Documentation 1969–71; Chair. Bd of Trustees Acad. of Ind. Scholars 1979–81; Co-Chair. Western Center, American Acad. of Arts and Sciences 1984–90, Vice-Pres. of Acad. 1984–90; Fellow Center for Advanced Study in the Behavioral Sciences, Stanford 1957–58, American Acad. of Arts and Sciences 1962–; Ford Prof. of Governmental Affairs 1960–61; David Easton Award est. by American Political Science Foundation (Foundations of Political Theory Section) 1996; Distinguished Faculty Lecturership for Research, Univ. of Calif., Irvine 1997; Hon. LLD (McMaster) 1970, (Kalamazoo) 1972; Hon. DPhil (Freie Universität, Berlin) 2001; Int. Alexander von Humboldt Research Prize 1995, Lauds and Laurels Distinguished Research Award, Univ. of Calif., Irvine 1995, Public Policy Studies Org. Thomas R. Dye Service Award 1997. *Publications:* The Political System: An Inquiry into the State of Political Science 1953, A Framework for Political Analysis 1965, A Systems Analysis of Political Life 1965, Varieties of Political Theory (Ed.) 1966, Children in the Political System: Origins of Political Legitimacy (with J. Dennis) 1969, The Analysis of Political Structure 1990, Divided Knowledge: Across Disciplines, Across Cultures (Co-Ed.) 1991, The Development of Political Science (Ed. with others) 1991, Regime and Discipline (Ed. with others) 1995; plus several reports of educ. cttees. chaired by him. *Address:* University of California, School of Social Sciences, Irvine, CA 92697, USA. *Telephone:* (949) 824-6132. *Fax:* (949) 824-8762; (949) 854-5180. *E-mail:* d2easton@orion.oac.uci.edu (Office).

EASTON, Sheena; British singer; b. 27 April 1959, Bellshill; m. Tim Delarm 1997; two c.; ed Royal Scottish Acad. of Music and Drama; career launched by appearance on TV show The Big Time; has collaborated with Prince; Grammy Award for Best New Artist 1981. *Singles include:* 9 to 5, Modern Girl, For Your Eyes Only (theme of James Bond film), Sugar Walls, U Got the Look (with Prince). *Albums include:* Take My Time 1981, You Could Have Been with Me 1981, Madness, Money and Music 1982, Best Kept Secret 1983, A Private Heaven 1984, The Lover in Me 1988, Greatest Hits (jtly.) 1989, Me gustas tal como eres (Grammy Award for Mexican-American Performance) 1984. *Television appearances include:* Miami Vice (series), Body Bags, The Highlander, The Adventure of Brisco County Jr, Outer Limits 1995, Chicken Soup for the Soul 1999. *Musical:* Man of La Mancha. *Address:* c/o Harriet Wasserman Management, 18122 Hatteras Street, Tarzana, CA 91356, USA.

EASTWOOD, Clint; American actor and film director; b. 31 May 1930, San Francisco; s. of Clinton and Ruth Eastwood; m. 1st Maggie Johnson 1953 (divorced); one s. one d.; one d. by Frances Fisher 1993; m. 2nd Dina Ruiz 1996; one d.; ed Los Angeles City Coll.; worked as lumberjack, Ore.; army service; appeared in TV series Rawhide 1959–65; owner Malpaso Productions 1969–; Co-Chair. UNESCO Campaign to protect the world's film heritage; mem. Nat. Arts Council 1973; Mayor of Carmel 1986–88; Fellow BFI 1993; Légion d'honneur, Commdr des Arts et des Lettres; Irving G. Thalberg Award 1995, Lifetime Achievement Awards American Film Inst. 1996, Screen Actors Guild 2003. *Films include:* Revenge of the Creature 1955, Francis in the Navy 1955, Lady Godiva 1955, Tarantula 1955, Never Say Goodbye 1956, The First Travelling Saleslady 1956, Star in the Dust 1956, Escapade in Japan 1957, Ambush at Cimarron Pass 1958, Lafayette Escadrille 1958, A Fistful of Dollars 1964, For a Few Dollars More 1965, The Good, the Bad and the Ugly 1966, The Witches 1967, Hang 'Em High 1968, Coogan's Bluff 1968, Where Eagles Dare 1969, Paint Your Wagon 1969, Kelly's Heroes 1970, Two Mules for Sister Sara 1970, The Beguiled 1971, Play Misty for Me (also Dir) 1971, Dirty Harry 1971, Joe Kidd 1972, High Plains Drifter (also Dir) 1973, Magnum Force 1973, Breezy (Dir) 1973, Thunderbolt and Lightfoot 1974, The Eiger Sanction (also Dir) 1975, The Outlaw Josey Wales (also Dir) 1976, The Enforcer 1976, The Gauntlet (also Dir) 1978, Every Which Way But Loose 1978, Escape from Alcatraz 1979, Bronco Billy (also Dir) 1980, Any Which Way You Can 1980, Firefox (also Dir) 1982, Honky Tonk Man (also Dir) 1982, Sudden Impact (also Dir) 1983, Tightrope 1984, City Heat 1984, Pale Rider 1985 (also Dir), Heartbreak Ridge 1986 (also Dir), Bird 1988 (Golden Globe Award for Best Dir 1989), The Dead Pool 1988, Pink Cadillac 1989, White Hunter, Black Heart (also Dir) 1989, The Rookie (also Dir) 1990, Unforgiven (also Dir) (Acad. Awards for Best Film and Best Dir 1993) 1992, In the Line of Fire 1993, A Perfect World (also Dir) 1993, The Bridges of Madison County (also Dir, Producer) 1995, The Stars Fell on Henrietta (Co-Producer only), Absolute Power (also Dir) 1997, True Crime 1998; Dir Midnight in the Garden of Good and Evil 1997, Space Cowboys (also Dir) 2000, Blood Work (also Dir, producer) 2002. *Address:* c/o Leonard Hirshan, William Morris Agency, 151 S El Camino Drive, Beverly Hills, CA 90212, USA.

EATON, Fredrik Stefan, OC, BA, LLD; Canadian business executive and fmr diplomatist; b. 26 June 1938, Toronto; s. of the late John David Eaton and Signy Hildur Stephenson; m. Catherine Martin 1962; one s. one d.; ed New Brunswick Univ.; joined The T. Eaton Co. Ltd and held various positions in Victoria, London, Toronto 1962–67, Dir 1967–69, Chair., Pres., CEO 1977–88, Chair. 1988–91; Pres., Dir Eaton's of Canada (parent co. of the other Eaton cos.) 1969–77, Chair. Exec. Cttee 1994–97; High Commr in UK 1991–94; Chancellor Univ. of New Brunswick 1993–; Chair. White Raven Capital Corpn; Order of Ontario; Hon. LLD (New Brunswick) 1983; Man. Award 1987 (McGill Univ.). *Leisure interests:* art, music, reading, shooting, yachting.

Address: White Raven Capital Corporation, 55 St Clair Avenue West, Suite 260, Toronto, Ont., M4V 2Y7, Canada (Office). *Telephone:* (416) 929-3942 (Office). *Fax:* (416) 925-4339 (Office).

EATON, George, FCA; Irish chartered accountant; b. 11 Jan. 1942, Cork; s. of Thomas J. V. Eaton and Catherine Hannon; m. Ellen Patricia O'Grady 1966; one d.; ed Christian Brothers Coll., Cork, The Inst. of Chartered Accountants, Ireland; with Touche Ross, Chartered Accountants, Cork 1960–66; Chief Accountant, Seafield Fabrics, Youghal 1966–67; Deputy Man. Dir General Textiles 1967–75; Chair. Portuguese Irish Chamber of Commerce 1987–89; Pres. The Chambers of Commerce of Ireland 1985–87; Hon. Consul of Hungary 1990–. *Publication:* Introducing Ireland 1989. *Leisure interests:* history, genealogy, reading, book collecting. *Address:* Custume Place, Athlone, Ireland. *Telephone:* (902) 78531. *Fax:* (902) 74691. *E-mail:* eatond@iol.ie (Office).

EATON, Robert J., BS; American motor industry executive and engineer; b. 13 Feb. 1940, Buena Vista; s. of Gene Eaton and Mildred Eaton; m. Connie Drake 1964; two s.; ed Univ. of Kansas; joined Gen. Motors (Chevrolet Motor Div.) 1963, transferred to Eng staff 1971, Exec. Engineer 1974, Chief Engineer, Corp. Car Programs 1976, Asst Chief Engineer and Dir of Reliability at Oldsmobile 1979, Vice-Pres. in charge of Tech. Staffs 1986, Pres. Gen. Motors Europe 1988–92; COO Chrysler Motors Corporation 1992–93, Chair., CEO 1993–2000, now Co.-Chair., Co.-CEO DaimlerChrysler –2000; Chair. Bd Dirs. Saab Auto 1990–; mem. Bd Dirs. Group Lotus 1986–; mem. Industrial Advisory Bd Stanford Univ.; Fellow, Soc. of Automotive Engineers, Eng Soc. of Detroit; mem. Nat. Acad. of Eng; Chevalier du Tastevin 1989. *Leisure interests:* skiing, golf, hunting. *Address:* c/o Daimler Chrysler, 12000 Chrysler Drive, Highland Park, MI 48288, USA.

EATWELL, Baron (Life Peer), cr. 1992, of Stratton St Margaret in the County of Wiltshire; **John Leonard Eatwell,** PhD; British academic; b. 2 Feb. 1945; s. of Harold Jack Eatwell and Mary Eatwell; m. Hélène Seppain 1970 (divorced); two s. one d.; ed Headlands Grammar School, Swindon, Queens' Coll. Cambridge, Harvard Univ., USA; Teaching Fellow Grad. School of Arts and Sciences, Harvard Univ. 1968–69; Research Fellow Queens' Coll. Cambridge 1969–70; Fellow Trinity Coll. Cambridge 1970–96, Asst Lecturer Faculty of Econs and Politics, Cambridge Univ. 1975–77, Lecturer 1977–, Pres. Queens' Coll. 1997–; Visiting Prof. of Econs New School for Social Research, New York 1982–96; Econ. Adviser to Neil Kinnock, Leader of Labour Party 1985–92; Opposition Spokesman on Treasury Affairs and on Trade and Industry, House of Lords 1992–93, Prin. Opposition spokesman on Treasury and Econ. Affairs 1993–97; Trustee Inst. for Public Policy Research 1988–95, Sec. 1988–97, Chair. 1997–; Dir (non-exec.) Anglia TV Group 1994–2001, Cambridge Econometrics Ltd 1996–; Chair. Extemporary Dance Theatre 1990, Crusaid 1993–98, British Screen Finance Ltd 1997–2000 and assoc. cos; Gov. Contemporary Dance Trust 1991–95; Dir Arts Theatre Trust, Cambridge 1991–98, Bd, Securities and Futures Authority 1997–; mem. Bd Royal Opera House 1998–2002; Chair. Royal Ballet 1998–2001, Commercial RadioCos Asscn 2000–, British Library 2001–; mem. Regulatory Decisions Cttee, FSA 2001–; Dir Cambridge Endowment for Research in Finance 2002–. *Publications:* An Introduction to Modern Economics (with Joan Robinson) 1973, Whatever Happened to Britain? 1982, Keynes's Economics and the Theory of Value and Distribution (ed. with Murray Milgate) 1983, The New Palgrave: A Dictionary of Economics, 4 Vols 1987, The New Palgrave Dictionary of Money and Finance, 3 Vols 1992 (both with Murray Milgate and Peter Newman), Transformation and Integration: Shaping the Future of Central and Eastern Europe (jtly) 1995, Global Unemployment: Loss of Jobs in the '90s (ed.) 1996, Not "Just Another Accession": The Political Economy of EU Enlargement to the East (jtly) 1997, Global Finance at Risk: the Case for International Regulation (with L. Taylor) 2000, Hard Budgets, Soft States 2000, Social Policy Choices in Central and Eastern Europe 2002, International Capital Markets (with L. Taylor) 2002; articles in scientific journals. *Leisure interests:* classical and contemporary dance, Rugby Union football. *Address:* The President's Lodge, Queens' College, Cambridge, CB3 9ET, England. *Telephone:* (1223) 335556. *Fax:* (1223) 335555. *E-mail:* president@quns.cam.ac.uk (Office).

EBASHI, Setsuro, MD, PhD; Japanese biophysicist and pharmacologist; b. 31 Aug. 1922, Tokyo; s. of Haruyoshi Ebashi and Hisaji Ebashi; m. Fumiko Takeda 1956; ed Univ. of Tokyo; Prof. of Pharmacology, Faculty of Medicine, Univ. of Tokyo 1959–83, Prof. of Biophysics, Faculty of Science 1971–83, Prof. Emer. 1983–; Prof. Nat. Inst. for Physiological Sciences 1983–86, Dir-Gen. 1985–91, Prof. Emer. 1993–; Pres. Okazaki Nat. Research Inst. 1991–93; Visiting Prof. Univ. of Calif. 1963, Harvard Univ. 1974; Pres. Int. Union of Pure and Applied Biophysics 1978–81, Int. Union of Pharmacology 1990–94; mem. Japan Acad., Sec.-Gen. 2000; Foreign mem. Royal Soc., Academia Europaea; Foreign Assoc. NAS; Asahi Prize 1968; Imperial Prize, Japan Acad. 1972; Int. Prize for Biology 1999; Peter Harris Award 1986; Order of Cultural Merit (Bunka-Kunsho) 1975, Grand Cordon of Order of the Sacred Treasure 1995. *Publications:* articles in scientific journals. *Address:* 17-503, Nagaizumi Myodaiji, Okazaki 444-0864, Japan (Home). *Telephone:* (564) 53-7345. *Fax:* (564) 52-3719. *E-mail:* ebashi@nips.ac.jp (Home).

EBBERS, Bernard J.; American (b. Canadian) communications executive; b. 27 Aug. 1941, Edmonton, Alberta, Canada; m. Linda Piggott 1968 (divorced); one d.; ed Mississippi Coll., Clinton, Miss., USA; jr high school science teacher and physical educ. coach, then man. of a clothing warehouse; registered his first co. Master Corpn hotel business 1974; f. Best Western hotel chain; invested in telecommunications co. Long Distance Discount Service (LDDS – renamed LDDS Communications Inc. 1993, WorldCom Inc. 1995, later MCI WorldCom Inc.), Jackson, Miss. 1983, CEO 1985, Pres., Chair. and CEO 1998–2002, co. filed for bankruptcy July 2002; mem. Promise Keepers (Christian men's org.); Trustee Miss. Coll. *Address:* Joshua Management, Brookhaven, MS, USA.

EBEN, Petr; Czech composer; b. 22 Jan. 1929, Žamberk; s. of Vilém Eben and Marie Ebenová-Kahlerová; m. Šárka Ebenová (née Hurníková) 1953; three s.; ed Acad. of Music Arts, Prague; Music Dir, TV, Prague 1954; début as pianist, Prague 1954; lecturer, Inst. for Musicology, Charles Univ., Prague 1955–, Assoc. Prof. –1990; Prof. of Composition, Acad. of Music, Prague 1990–96; lecturer at Royal Northern Coll. of Music (RNCM), Manchester, UK 1978, Sr lecturer in theory of music 1988; Pres. Prague Spring music festival 1990–96; mem. Union of Composers, Prague; Pres. Czech Soc. for Spiritual Music, Endowment of Prague Nat. Theatre; Hon. Fellow RNCM 1992; Chevalier Ordre des Arts et des Lettres; Order of Cyril and Methodius; Dr hc (Charles Univ.) 1994; Czech Music Fund Prize 1991, 1992, Stamitz-Preis, Künstlergilde 1993, Medal of Merit 2002. *Compositions include:* (church opera) Jeremiáš; (ballet) Curses and Blessings; (oratorios) Apologia Socratus, Sacred Symbols, Oratorium Anno Domini 2000; (symphonic works) Vox clamantis, Prague Nocturne, Night Hours, Improperia; (concertos) for organ and orchestra, for piano and orchestra; (music for organ) Sunday Music, Laudes, Mutationes, Faust, Job, Biblical Dances, Labyrinth of the World and Heart's Paradise 1997, Chagall Windows (for trumpet and organ); (cantatas) Pragensia, Bitter Earth; also song cycles, piano trio, string quartet, quintets, many choral works. *Recording:* The Music of Petr Eben with Dagmar Pecková 1999. *Publications:* Score-Reading and Playing (co-author); contributions to journals. *Address:* Academy of Music Arts, Malostranské nám. 12, 110 00 Prague 1, Czech Republic (Office). *Telephone:* (257) 534205 (Office). *Fax:* (257) 530405 (Office).

EBERHART, Richard, MA, LittD; American poet; b. 5 April 1904, Austin, Minn.; s. of the late Alpha La Rue Eberhart and Lena Lowenstein; m. Helen Elizabeth Butcher 1941; one s. one d.; ed Univ. of Minnesota, Dartmouth Coll., St John's Coll., Cambridge, England and Harvard Univ.; USNR World War II, rose to Lt-Commdr; Asst Man. Butcher Polish Co. 1946, now Hon. Vice-Pres. and mem. of Bd of Dirs.; Master of English, St Mark's School, Southborough, Mass. 1933–41, Cambridge School, Kendal Green, Mass. 1941–42; Visiting Prof. of English and Poet in Residence, Univ. of Washington 1952–53; Prof. of English, Univ. of Connecticut 1953–54; inaugural Visiting Prof. of English, Poet in Residence, Wheaton Coll., Norton, Mass. 1954–55; Resident Fellow in Creative Writing, Christian Gauss Lecturer, Princeton 1955–56; Prof. of English, Poet in residence, Dartmouth 1956–, Class of 1925 Prof. 1968–70, Emer. 1970–; Distinguished Visiting Prof., Univ. of Fla, Gainesville 1974–, Visiting Prof. 1975–86; Adjunct Prof., Colombia Univ. 1975; Regents' Prof., Univ. of Calif., Davis 1975; Fla Amb. of the Arts 1984–; Hon. Fellow, St John's Coll. Cambridge 1986; mem. Advisory Cttee on Arts for Nat. Cultural Center, Washington (now John F. Kennedy Center for Performing Arts) 1959; Consultant in Poetry, Library of Congress 1959–61; mem. Nat. Inst. Arts and Letters (now American Acad. and Inst. of Arts and Letters) 1960 (mem. American Acad. 1982), Peace Corps Mission to Kenya 1966, American Acad. Arts and Sciences 1967; Founder and Pres. Poets' Theatre Inc., Cambridge, Mass. 1951; Fellow of Acad. of American Poets 1969; Consultant in American Letters 1963–66; London Poetry Int. 1973, Third World Congress of Poets, Baltimore 1976; Hon. Pres. Poetry Soc. of America 1972; Hon. DLit (Dartmouth) 1954, (Skidmore) 1966, (Wooster) 1969, (Colgate) 1974; Hon. DHL (Franklin Pierce) 1978, (St Lawrence Univ.) 1985; Harriet Monroe Memorial Prize 1950, Shelley Memorial Prize 1951, Bollingen Prize 1962, Pulitzer Prize 1966, Nat. Book Award 1977, Pres.'s Medallion, Univ. of Fla 1977; Poet Laureate of New Hampshire 1979; New York quarterly Poetry Award 1980, Diploma of World Acad. of Arts and Culture, Repub. of China 1981, Sarah Jolepha Hale Award 1982; honoured by proclamation of Richard Eberhart Day (Rhode Island 14 July 1982, Dartmouth Coll. 14 Oct. 1982), Robert Frost Medal, Poetry Soc. of America 1986. *Publications:* A Bravery of Earth 1930, Reading the Spirit 1937, Song and Idea 1942, Poems New and Selected 1944, Burr Oaks 1947, Brotherhood of Men 1949, An Herb Basket 1950, Selected Poems 1951, Undercliff 1953, Great Praises 1957, Collected Poems 1930–60 1960, Collected Verse Plays 1962, The Quarry 1964, Selected Poems 1930–65 1965, New Directions 1965, Thirty One Sonnets 1967, Shifts of Being 1968, Fields of Grace 1972, Collected Poems 1930–1976 1976, Collected Poems 1930–1986 1986, Poems to Poets 1976, To Eberhart from Ginsberg 1976, Survivors 1979, Of Poetry and Poets (criticism) 1979, Ways of Light 1980, New Hampshire/Nine Poems 1980, Four Poems 1980, A Celebration 1980, Chocorua 1981, Florida Poems 1981, The Long Reach 1984, Negative Capability 1986, Maine Poems 1988, New and Collected Poems 1990. *Leisure interests:* cruising on coast of Maine and swimming. *Address:* 80 Lyme Road, Apartment 161, Hanover, NH 03755, USA.

EBERLE, Adm. Sir James Henry Fuller, GCB; British naval officer (retd); b. 31 May 1927, Bristol; s. of Victor Fuller Eberle, MC and Joyce Mary Eberle; m. Ann Patricia Thompson 1950 (died 1988); one s. two d.; ed Clifton Coll. and Royal Naval Coll., Dartmouth; served in Second World War at home, East Indies and Pacific 1944–45; served in Korean War, HMS Belfast and Fleet Staff Officer 1952–53; Sr officer, 100 Minesweeping Squadron 1958–59; Capt.

HMS Intrepid 1968–70; Defence Fellow, Univ. Coll., Oxford 1970; promoted Rear-Adm. 1971; Flag Officer, Carriers and Amphibious Ships and Commdr NATO Striking Group Two 1975–76; mem. Admiralty Bd 1977–78; Commdr-in-Chief Fleet, Allied C-in-C Eastern Atlantic, C-in-C Channel 1979–80; C-in-C Naval Home Command 1981–82; retd 1983, rank of Adm.; Dir Royal Inst. of Int. Affairs 1984–90; Dir UK-Japan 2000 Group 1986–98; Chair. UK Asscn of Harriers and Beagles 1998–; mem. Bd Countryside Alliance 2002–; Hon. LLD (Bristol) 1989, (Sussex) 1992; Freeman of Bristol 1946, London 1982. *Publications:* Management in the Armed Forces 1972, Jim, First of the Pack 1982, Britain's Future in Space 1988. *Leisure interests:* tennis, field sports. *Address:* Lower Abbotsleigh, Blackawton, Devon, TQ9 7AF, England (Home). *Telephone:* (1548) 521-202 (Home). *Fax:* (1548) 521-633 (Home). *E-mail:* admiraljim@lineone.net (Home).

EBERT, Peter; British (naturalized) opera director; b. 6 April 1918, Frankfurt am Main, Germany; s. of late Carl Ebert and Lucie Oppenheim; m. 1st Kathleen Havinden 1944; two d.; m. 2nd Silvia Ashmole 1951; five s. three d.; ed Salem School, Germany and Gordonstoun, Scotland; Intendant, Stadttheater Bielefeld, Germany 1973–75, Wiesbaden State Theatres 1975–77; Dir of Productions, Scottish Opera 1965–76, Gen. Admin. 1977–80; Producer, Guild Opera Co., Los Angeles 1962–76; Hon. DMus (St Andrews) 1979. *Leisure interest:* building walls. *Address:* Col di Mura, Lippiano, 06010, Italy. *Telephone:* (075) 8502102. *Fax:* (075) 8502102.

EBTEKAR, Masumeh, MA, PhD, DSc; Iranian politician and women's organization official; b. 1960, Tehran; m.; two c.; ed Shahid Beheshti Univ. and Tarbiat Modarres Univ., Tehran; Ed.-in-Chief Keyhan Int. (English daily newspaper) 1981–83; Editorial Dir Farzaneh Journal of Women's Studies and Research; Founding-mem. Centre for Women's Studies and Research 1986–; Dir Women's NGO Co-ordination Office, Tehran 1994–; Pres. Network of Women's NGOs in the Islamic Repub. of Iran 1995–; Faculty mem. School of Medical Science, Tarbiat Modarres Univ. 1989–95, Asst Prof. 1995–; Vice-Pres. and Head of the Org. for the Protection of the Environment (first female Vice-Pres. of Iran) Aug. 1997–; Del., Vice-Chair. or Chair. of many int. confs on women. *Publications include:* numerous contribs to int. journals. *Address:* c/o Office of the President, Palestine Avenue, Azerbaijan Intersection, Tehran, Iran (Office).

ECCLESTON, Christopher; British actor; b. 16 Feb. 1964, Salford; s. of Joseph Ronald Eccleston and Elsie Lavinia Eccleston. *Films include:* Let Him Have It 1991, Shallow Grave 1995, Jude 1996, Elizabeth 1998, A Price Above Rubies 1998, Heart 1999, Old New Borrowed Blue 1999, Existenz 1999, Gone in 60 Seconds 2000, The Invisible Circus 2001, The Others 2001, I am Dina 2002, 28 Days Later 2002. *Theatre includes:* Miss June 2000. *Television appearances:* Cracker 1993–94, Hearts and Minds 1995, Our Friends in the North 1996, Hillsborough 1996, Strumpet 2001, Flesh and Blood (Best Actor, Royal TV Soc. Awards 2003) 2002. *Leisure interest:* supporting Manchester United Football Club. *Address:* Hamilton Asper Management, Ground Floor, 24 Hanway Street, London, W1P 9DD, England. *Telephone:* (20) 7636-1221. *Fax:* (20) 7636-1226.

ECCLESTONE, Bernard (Bernie), BSc; British business executive; b. Oct. 1930; m. 1st; one d.; m. 2nd Slavica Ecclestone; two d.; ed Woolwich Polytechnic, London; est. car and motorcycle dealership, Midweek Car Auctions, Bexley, Kent; racing-car driver for short period (Formula 3); owner Connaught racing team 1957; Man. Jochen Rindt; set up Brabham racing team 1970; owner Formula One Holdings, now controls Formula One Constructors' Asscn, representing all the top car-racing teams; CEO Formula One Admin. Ltd; Vice-Pres. in charge of Promotional Affairs, Fed. Int. de l'Automobile (FIA) (racing's int. governing body). *Address:* Formula One Administration Limited, 6 Prince's Gate, London, SW7 1QJ, England. *Website:* www.formula1.com.

ECEVIT, Bülent, BA; Turkish politician and journalist; b. 28 May 1925, Istanbul; s. of the late Prof. Fahri Ecevit, MP and Nazli Ecevit; m. Rahşan Ecevit 1946; ed Robert Coll., Istanbul, Ankara, London and Harvard Univs; Govt official 1944–50, Turkish Press Attaché's Office, London 1946–50; Foreign News Ed., Man. Ed., later Political Dir Ulus (Ankara) 1950–61, Political Columnist, Ulus 1956–61; mem. Parl. (Republican People's Party) 1957–60, 1961–80; mem. Constituent Ass. 1961; Minister of Labour 1961–65; Political Columnist Milliyet 1965; Sec.-Gen. Republican People's Party 1966–71, Chair. 1972–80; Prime Minister Jan.–Nov. 1974, June–July 1977, 1978–79 (resigned Oct. 1979), 1998–2002; Deputy Prime Minister and Minister of State 1997–98; detained after coup Sept. 1980, released Oct. 1980, imprisoned by mil. régime Dec. 1981–Feb. 1982, rearrested April 1982, imprisoned again Aug.–Oct. 1982; Chair. Democratic Left Party Jan. 1989–; mem. Turkish Philosophical Soc., Turkish Language Asscn, Ankara Journalists' Asscn. *Publications:* Ortanin Solu (Left of Centre) 1966, Bu Düzen Değismelidir (The System Must Change) 1968, Atatürk ve Devrimcilik (Atatürk and Revolution) 1970, Sohbet (Conversations), Demokratik Sol (Democratic Left) 1974, Dis Politika (Foreign Policy) 1975, Işçi-Köylü Elele (Workers and Peasants Together) 1976, Şiirler (Poems) (German, Russian, Serbian, Danish and Romanian trans.) 1976; Translations into Turkish: Gitanjali (R. Tagore) 1941, Straybirds (R. Tagore) 1943, Cocktail Party (T. S. Eliot) 1963. *Leisure interests:* art and literature. *Address:* Demokratik Sol Parti (DSP) (Democratic Left Party), Fevzi Çakma Cad. 17, Ankara; Or-an

Şehri 69/5, Ankara, Turkey (Home). *Telephone:* (312) 2124950 (Office). *Fax:* (312) 2123474 (Office). *E-mail:* akguvercinist@dsp.org.tr (Office). *Website:* www.dsp.org.tr (Office).

ECHANDI JIMÉNEZ, Mario, LLD; Costa Rican politician and diplomatist; b. 1915, San José; s. of Alberto Echandi and Josefa Jiménez; ed Univ. de Costa Rica; legal career 1938–47; Sec.-Gen. Partido Unión Nacional 1947; Amb. to USA 1950–51, 1966–68; Minister for Foreign Affairs 1951–53; Pres. of Costa Rica 1958–62; defeated candidate in Pres. election 1970. *Address:* San José, Costa Rica.

ECHAVARRI, Luis Enrique, MSc; Spanish industry executive and international organization official; b. 1950; m.; two c.; ed Univ. of Madrid; Project and Nuclear Plants Man., Westinghouse Electric, Madrid; Man. Lemóniz, Sayago and Almaraz nuclear power plants; Tech. Dir Consejo de Seguridad Nuclear (Spanish nuclear regulatory comm.), Commr, Man. Dir; Dir-Gen. OECD Nuclear Energy Agency 1997–; rep. of Spain at int. fora on nuclear energy, including Int. Atomic Energy Agency and EU. *Address:* Organisation for Economic Co-operation and Development Nuclear Energy Agency, Le Seine Saint-Germain, 12 boulevard des Iles, 92130 Issy-les-Moulineux, France (Office). *Telephone:* 1-45-24-10-10 (Office). *Fax:* 1-45-24-11-10 (Office). *E-mail:* nea@nea.fr (Office).

ECHENOZ, Jean (Maurice Emmanuel); French author; b. 26 Dec. 1947, Orange, Vaucluse; s. of Marc Echenoz and Annie Languin; one s.; professional writer 1979–; Grand prix du roman de la Ville de Paris 1997. *Novels:* Le Méridien de Greenwich 1979 (Prix Fénéon 1980), Cherokee 1983 (Prix Médicis 1983), L'Equipée malaise 1986, L'Occupation des sols 1988, Lac 1989 (Grand Prix du Roman de la Société des Gens de Lettres 1990, European Literature Prize, Glasgow 1990), Nous trois 1992, Les Grandes Blondes 1995 (Prix Novembre 1995), Un An 1997, Je m'en vais 1999 (Prix Goncourt 1999), Jérôme Lindon 2001, Samuel (trans. of bible, jtly) 2001, Au piano 2003. *Address:* c/o Editions de Minuit, 7 rue Bernard-Palissy, 75006 Paris, France.

ECHEVARRIA, Most Rev. Javier, PhD; Spanish ecclesiastic; b. 14 June 1932; ed Univ. of Madrid, Pontifical Univ. of St Thomas, Rome, Pontifical Lateran Univ., Rome; moved to Rome 1950; ordained priest 1955; lecturer in Moral Theology, Collegio Romano della Santa Croce 1960, Collegio Romano di Santa Maria 1964; apptd. personal sec. to Josemaría Escrivá (founder of Opus Dei) 1957, mem. Gen. Council Opus Dei 1966–75, Sec.-Gen. 1975–82, Vicar-Gen. 1982–94, Prelate of Opus Dei 1994–; consecrated Bishop 1995; Consultant Sacred Congregation for the Clergy 1995–; mem. Supreme Tribunal of the Apostolic Signatura 2001–, Sacred Congregation for the Causes of Saints 2002–. *Publications:* Memoria del Beato Josemaría Escrivá 2000, Itinerarios de vida cristiana 2001, Para servir a la Iglesia 2001. *Address:* Curia of the Prelature, 73 Viale Bruno Buozzi, 00197 Rome, Italy. *Telephone:* (06) 808961. *Fax:* (06) 808964.

ECKHARDT, Sándor; Hungarian oncologist; b. 14 March 1927, Budapest; s. of Sándor Eckhardt and Irén Huszár; m. Mária Petrányi; three s.; ed Semmelweis Medical Univ. Budapest; specialist in internal medicine 1955; training course of malignant diseases in children, Villejuif, France 1969; MRC Fellow, Chester Beatty Inst., London, 1961; Eleanor Roosevelt Cancer Research Fellow, Bethesda 1964–65; Chair. Drug Devt Program, Hungary 1966–70; Dir Nat. Inst. of Oncology, Budapest 1971–92; Prof. Clinical Oncology, Postgrad. Univ. Medical School, Budapest 1977–; mem. Hungarian Acad. of Sciences 1984–; Chair. Trial Centre of East European countries and Program Co-ordinator of drug research 1979–98; mem. Union Int. Contre le Cancer (UICC) Exec. Cttee 1978–86, Treas. 1986–90, Pres. 1990–94, Past Pres. 1994–98; Sec. Gen. 14th Int. Cancer Congress 1982–86; adviser WHO Cancer Unit 1971–98; mem. Medical Advisory Cttee WHO Euro Office, Copenhagen 1974–82; mem. Scientific Council Int. Agency for Research on Cancer 1976–80, Chair. 1979–82; mem. American Asscn of Cancer Research 1976–, Medical Acad. of Moscow 1979–, European Soc. of Medical Oncology 1985–; American Soc. of Clinical Oncology 1987–, Chief Ed. Antitumour Drug Therapy, Budapest 1977–86; Clinical ed. Oncology 1978–84, Onkologie 1980–86, Current Medical Chem. 2002; Labour Order of Merit 1975, State Prize 1985, Széchenyi Prize 1994. *Publications:* include Drug Therapy of Cancer (WHO Geneva) 1973; Dibromodulcitol 1982; Drug Development in Eastern Europe 1987; co-ed. Proceedings of the 14th International Cancer Congress, Budapest (13 Vols) 1986, Cancer Surveys 1994, Ann. Oncol. 1999, 7 Surg. Oncol. 2000. *Address:* National Institute of Oncology, 1525 Budapest, Ráth György utca 7/9, Hungary (Office). *Telephone:* (1) 224-8751 (Office). *Fax:* (1) 224-8620 (Office); (1) 224-8741 (Office). *E-mail:* eckhardt@oncol.hu (Office).

ECO, Umberto, PhD; Italian author and university professor; b. 5 Jan. 1932, Alessandria, Piedmont; s. of Giulio Eco and Giovanna Bisio; m. Renate Ramge 1962; one s. one d.; ed Liceo Plana, Alessandria, Univ. degli Studi, Turin; cultural ed. Italian TV (RAI), Milan 1954–59; mil. service 1958–59; Sr Nonfiction Ed., Bompiani, Milan 1959–75; Asst Lecturer in Aesthetics, Univ. of Turin 1956–63, Lecturer 1963–64; Lecturer, Faculty of Architecture, Univ. of Milan 1964–65; Prof. of Visual Communications, Univ. of Florence 1966–69; Prof. of Semiotics, Milan Polytechnic 1970–71; Assoc. Prof. of Semiotics, Univ. of Bologna 1971–75, Prof. 1975–, Dir Inst. of Communications Disciplines 1993–, f. School of Arts 2000; Visiting Prof. New York Univ. 1969–70, 1976, Northwestern Univ. 1972, Yale Univ. 1977, 1980, 1981, Columbia Univ. 1978, 1984; Columnist on L'Espresso 1965; Ed. VS 1971–; mem. Academia Europaea 1998–; Chevalier de la Légion d'honneur, Ordre pour le Mérite, Cavaliere di Gran Croce (Italy); Hon. DLitt (Glasgow) 1990, (Kent) 1992 and numerous other hon. degrees; Medici Prize 1982, McLuhan Teleglobe Prize 1985, Crystal Award (World Econ. Forum) 2000; Prince of Asturias Prize for Communication and the Humanities 2000. *Publications:* Il Problema Estetico in San Tommaso 1956 (as The Aesthetics of Thomas Aquinas 1988), Sviluppo dell'Estetica Medioevale 1959 (as Art and Beauty in the Middle Ages 1986), Opera Aperta 1962, Diario Minimo 1963, Apocalittici e Integrati 1964, L'Oeuvre Ouverte 1965, La Struttura Assente 1968, Il Costume di Casa 1973, Trattato di Semiotica Generale 1975, A Theory of Semiotics 1976, The Role of the Reader 1979, Il Nome della Rosa (novel) 1981, Semiotics and the Philosophy of Language 1984, Sette anni di desiderio 1977–83 1984, Faith in Fakes 1986, Art and Beauty in the Middle ages, Il pendolo di Foucault 1988, The Open Work 1989, The Limits of Interpretation 1990, Misreadings 1993, How to Travel with a Salmon and Other Essays 1994, The Search for the Perfect Language 1995, The Island of the Day Before (novel) 1995, Serendipities 1997, Kant and the Platypus 1999, Bandolino (novel) 2000, Experiences in Translation 2000, Five Moral Pieces 2001. *Address:* Scuola Superiore Studi Umanistici, Via Marsala 26, Bologna, Italy. *Telephone:* (051) 2917111 (Office). *E-mail:* sssub@dsc.unibo.it (Office).

EDBERG, Stefan; Swedish tennis player; b. 19 Jan. 1966, Vastervik; m. Annette Edberg; one s. one d.; won Jr Grand Slam 1983, Milan Open 1984, San Francisco, Basle and Memphis Opens 1985, Gstaad, Basle and Stockholm Opens 1986, Australian Open 1986, 1987, Wimbledon 1988, 1990, finalist 1989, US Open 1991, Masters 1989, German Open 1992, US Open 1992; winner (with Anders Jarryd) Masters and French Open 1986, Australian and US Opens 1987; semi-finalist in numerous tournaments; mem. Swedish Davis Cup Team 1984, 1987; retd in 1996 having won 60 professional titles and more than 20 million dollars in prize money; f. Stefan Edberg Foundation to assist young Swedish tennis players; Adidas Sportsmanship Award (four times). *Leisure interest:* golf. *Address:* c/o ATP Tour 200, ATP Tour Boulevard, Ponte Vedra Beach, FL 32082, USA.

EDDERY, Patrick James John; Irish jockey; b. 18 March 1952, Newbridge, Co. Galway; s. of Jimmy Eddery and Josephine Eddery; m. Carolyn Jane (née Mercer) 1978; one s. two d.; winner of over 4,400 races in UK (second only to Gordon Richards in number of wins in UK); first win on Alvaro at Epsom 1969; has ridden 100 winners in a year 28 times 1973–; first jockey in Britain to ride seven winners in a day 1992; rode for Peter Walwyn 1972–80; Champion Jockey 1974–77, 1986, 1988–91, 1996; Champion Jockey in Ireland 1982; rode winner of the Oaks 1974, 1979, 1996, 2002, the Derby, on Grundy 1975, on Golden Fleece 1982, Quest for Fame 1990, Prix de l'Arc de Triomphe 1980, 1985–87, St Leger (four times); owner of stud farm; Flat Jockey of the Year 1990, 1991, 1996. *Leisure interests:* tennis, golf, snooker, swimming. *Address:* Musk Hill Farm, Nether Winchendon, Aylesbury, Bucks., HP18 0DT, England (Home). *Telephone:* (1844) 290282 (Home). *Fax:* (1844) 291180 (Office).

EDDINGTON, Roderick (Rod) Ian, M.ENG.SC., DPhil; Australian airline executive; b. 2 Jan. 1950, Perth; s. of Gilbert Maxwell Eddington and April Mary Eddington; m. Young Sook Park 1994; one s. one d.; ed Christ Church Grammar School, WA, Univ. of Western Australia, Oxford Univ.; joined Cathay Pacific Airways Ltd 1979, various positions Hong Kong, Korea and Japan, Deputy Man. 1990–92, Man. Dir and CEO 1992–96; Dir News Ltd (Australian arm of News Corpn) 1997–2000, Deputy Chair. 1998–2000; Exec. Chair. Ansett Australia 1997–2000; CEO British Airways (BA) 2000–; Dir John Swire & Sons Pty Ltd 1997–; mem. Bd of Man. Fremantle Football Club 1998–2000; Rhodes Scholar 1974. *Leisure interests:* cricket, bridge, football. *Address:* British Airways, Waterside, P.O. Box 365, Harmondsworth, UB7 0GB, England (Office). *Telephone:* (845) 779-9977 (Office). *Website:* www.britishairways.com (Office).

EDDY, Don, MFA; American artist; b. 4 Nov. 1944, Long Beach, Calif.; m. Leigh Behnke 1995; one d.; ed Fullerton Jr Coll., Univ. of Hawaii, Honolulu, Univ. of California at Santa Barbara; represented in numerous public collections; subject of two monographs and an electronic book about his work. *Exhibitions:* solo exhbns at Ewing Krainin Gallery, Honolulu 1968, Molly Barnes Gallery, LA 1970, 1971, Esther Bear Gallery, Santa Barbara 1970, Galerie ME Thelen, Essen/Cologne 1970, French and Co., New York 1971, Galerie Petit, Paris 1973, Nancy Hoffman Gallery, New York 1974, 1976, 1979, 1983, 1986, 1990, 1992, 1994, 1996, 1998, 2000, 2002, Williams Coll. Museum of Art, Williamstown, Mass. 1975, The Art Gallery, Miami-Dade Community Coll., Miami 1976, Univ. of Hawaii at Manoa, Honolulu 1982, Scarabb Gallery, Cleveland, Ohio 1994, The Huntington Museum of Art, West Virginia 1996; has participated in numerous group exhbns 1970–; retrospective exhbn Duke Univ. Museum of Art 2000, Boca Raton Museum of Art 2000, New Orleans Contemporary Art Center 2000. *Address:* 543 Broadway, New York, NY 10012, USA (Office). *Telephone:* (212) 925-3124 (Office). *Fax:* (212) 925-2302 (Office).

EDELMAN, Eric S., PhD; American diplomatist; m. Patricia Davis; two s. two d.; ed Cornell Univ., Yale Univ.; mem. US Del. to West Bank/Gaza Autonomy Talks 1980–81; watch officer, State Dept Operations Center 1981–82; staff officer, Secr. Staff 1982; Special Asst to Sec. of State 1982–84; with Office of Soviet Affairs, Dept of State 1984–86; Head, External Political Section, American Embassy, Moscow 1987–89; Special Asst (European Affairs) to Under-Sec. of State for Political Affairs 1989–90; Asst Deputy Under-Sec. of Defense for Soviet and East European Affairs, Office of Sec. of Defense 1990–93; Deputy Chief of Mission, Prague 1994–96; Exec. Asst to Deputy Sec.

of State; Amb. to Finland 1998–2001; Nat. Security Adviser, Office of the Vice-President 2001–; Award for Distinguished Civilian Service 1993, Superior Honor Award 1989, 1990, 1995. *Address:* Office of the Vice-President, Eisenhower Executive Office Building, Washington, DC 20501, USA (Office). *Telephone:* (202) 456-2326 (Office).

EDELMAN, Gerald Maurice, MD, PhD; American molecular biologist and neuroscientist; b. 1 July 1929, New York; s. of Edward and Anna Freedman Edelman; m. Maxine Morrison 1950; two s. one d.; ed Ursinus Coll., Univ. of Pennsylvania and The Rockefeller Univ.; Medical House Officer, Mass. Gen. Hospital 1954–55; Capt., US Army Medical Corps. 1955–56; Asst Physician, Hospital of The Rockefeller Univ. 1957–60; Asst Prof. and Asst Dean of Grad. Studies, The Rockefeller Univ, 1960–63, Assoc. Prof. and Assoc. Dean of Grad. Studies 1963–66, Prof. 1966–74; Vincent Astor Distinguished Prof. 1974–92, Assoc. Neurosciences Research Program, Scientific Chair. 1980; Dir Neurosciences Inst., Neurosciences Research Program 1981–; mem. The Scripps Research Inst. La Jolla, Calif., Chair. Dept of Neurobiology 1992–, Chair. Dept of Neurobiology 1992–; mem. Biophysics and Biophysical Chemistry Study Section, NIH 1964–67, Scientific Council, Centre for Theoretical Studies 1970–72, The Harvey Society 1974–, Pres. 1975–76; mem. NAS American Acad. of Arts and Sciences, American Philosophical Soc., Genetics Soc., American Chem. Soc., American Soc. of Biological Chemists, American Asscn of Immunologists, American Soc. for Cell Biology, Soc. for Developmental Biology, Alpha Omega Alpha Hon. Medical Soc., Council on Foreign Relations, AAAS; Foreign mem. Acad. des Sciences; Fellow, NY Acad. of Sciences; Trustee, Rockefeller Brothers Fund 1972–82; Non-Res. Fellow and mem. Bd of Trustees, Salk Inst. for Biological Studies; Fellow, New York Acad. of Medicine; mem. Bd of Overseers Faculty of Arts and Sciences, Univ. of Pa; mem. Bd Scientific Overseers, The Jackson Laboratory; mem. Bd of Trustees, Carnegie Inst. of Washington, mem. Advisory Cttee; mem. Advisory Bd, The Basel Inst. for Immunology 1970–77, Chair. 1975–77; mem. Bd of Governors, Weizmann Inst. of Science, Israel; Hon. mem. Japanese Biochemical Soc., Pharmaceutical Soc. of Japan; Hon. DSc (Univ. of Pa) 1973, (Adolphus Coll., Minn.) 1975, (Georgetown) 1989, (Tulane) 1991, (Miami) 1995, (Adelphi) 1995; Hon. ScD (Ursinus Coll.) 1974, (Williams Coll.) 1976; Hon. MD (Siena) 1974; Dr hc (Paris, Cagliari) 1989, (Naples) 1990; Annual Alumni Award, Ursinus Coll. 1969, Eli Lilly Award in Biological Chem., American Chemical Soc. 1965, Spencer Morris Award, Univ. of Pa 1954, Nobel Prize for Physiology or Medicine 1972 (with R. Porter Albert Einstein Commem. Award of Yeshiva Univ. 1974, Buchman Memorial Award, Calif. Inst. of Tech. 1975, Rabbi Shai Shaknai Mem. Prize in Immunology and Cancer Research, Hebrew Univ.-Hadassah Medical School, Jerusalem 1977, Regents Medal of Excellence, New York 1984, Cécile and Oskar Vogt Award (Düsseldorf) 1988, Distinguished Grad. Award, Univ. of Pa 1990, Medal of the Presidency of the Italian Repub. 1999 and many other awards and prizes. *Publications:* Neural Darwinism 1987, Topobiology 1988, The Remembered Present 1989, Bright Air, Brilliant Fire 1992, A Universe of Consciousness 2000; over 500 articles in professional journals. *Leisure interests:* violin, chamber music. *Address:* Department of Neurobiology, SBR 14, The Scripps Research Institute, 10550 North Torrey Pines Road, La Jolla, CA 92037-1000, USA. *Telephone:* (858) 784-2600. *Fax:* (858) 784-2646.

EDELMAN, Marek; Polish politician and doctor; b. 1921, Warsaw; ed Acad. of Medicine; mem. Jewish Socialist Party (Bund) and Jewish Fighting Org. (ŻOB); participant, then Commdr Warsaw Ghetto Uprising 1943; soldier Home Army, participant Warsaw Uprising 1944; co-f. Cttee for Defence of Workers 1976; interned 1981–82; mem. Solidarity Self-governing Ind. Trade Union, Civic Cttee attached to Lech Wałęsa (q.v.), Democratic Union (UD), later Freedom Union (UW); White Eagle Order 1998. *Publications:* The Bund's Role in the Defence of the Warsaw Ghetto 1945, The Ghetto Fights 1946. *Address:* Regionalna Rada Unii Wolności, ul. Piotrkowska 157, 90-440 Łódź, Poland (Office).

EDELSTEIN, Victor Arnold; French couturier and artist; b. 10 July 1945, London; m. Anna Maria Succi 1973; trainee designer Alexon 1962, Asst Designer and Pattern Cutter to Biba 1967, designer Salvador 1971, Christian Dior 1975; f. Victor Edelstein Ltd 1978–93; designed ballet of Rhapsody in Blue for Rambert Dance Co. 1989; pantomime Cinderella, Richmond Theatre 1991, black pas de deux, Swan Lake, Covent Garden 1991; exhbns include Sotheby's, London 1996, Hopkins Thomas Gallery, Paris 1999. *Leisure interests:* opera, gardening, collecting old master drawings, skiing.

EDELSTEIN, Yuli; Israeli politician; b. 1958, Ukraine; m.; two c.; ed Moscow Inst. for Teacher Training; fmr Hebrew teacher, Moscow; emigrated to Israel 1987; fmr teacher Melitz Centre for Jewish-Zionist Educ., School for Educational Inst., Jerusalem; Adviser to Opposition Leader Benjamin Netanyahu 1993–94; a founder of Yisrael Ba-Aliya party 1995; headed party's election campaign; mem. Knesset (Parl.) 1996–, Minister of Immigrant Absorption 1996–99, Deputy Minister 2000–; Deputy Speaker Knesset 1999–2001. *Address:* c/o Ministry of Immigration and Absorption, P.O. Box 883, 2 Rehov Kaplan, Kiryat Ben-Gurion, Jerusalem 91006 (Office); Alon Shvut, Israel (Home). *Telephone:* (2) 6752691 (Office). *Fax:* (2) 5669244 (Office). *E-mail:* sar@moia.gov.il (Office). *Website:* www.moia.gov.il (Office).

EDGAR, David Burman, BA; British writer; b. 26 Feb. 1948, Birmingham; s. of Barrie Edgar and Joan Edgar (née Burman); m. Eve Brook 1979 (died 1998); two s.; ed Oundle School, Manchester Univ.; Fellow in Creative Writing, Leeds Polytechnic 1972–74; Resident Playwright, Birmingham

Repertory Theatre 1974–75; Lecturer in Playwrighting, Univ. of Birmingham 1975–78, Dir of Playwriting Studies 1989–, Prof. 1995–99; UK/US Bicentennial Arts Fellow resident in USA 1978–79; Literary Consultant, RSC 1984–88; Bd mem., Birmingham Repertory Theatre 1985–; Fellow Birmingham Polytechnic 1991; Hon. Sr Research Fellow, Univ. of Birmingham 1988–92, Hon. Prof. 1992–; Hon. MA (Bradford) 1986; DUniv (Surrey) 1993, (Birmingham) 2002; Soc. of West End Theatres Best Play Award 1980, New York Tony Best Play Award 1981. *Plays:* Dick Deterred 1974, O Fair Jerusalem 1975, Saigon Rose 1976, Blood Sports 1976, Destiny (for RSC) 1976, Wreckers 1977, The Jail Diary of Albie Sachs (for RSC) 1978, Mary Barnes 1978–79, Teendreams 1979, Nicholas Nickleby (adaptation for RSC) 1980, Maydays (for RSC) 1983, Entertaining Strangers 1985, That Summer 1987, The Shape of the Table 1990, Dr Jekyll and Mr Hyde (adaptation for RSC) 1991, Pentecost 1994, Other Place 1994, Young Vic 1995, Albert Speer (adaptation for Nat. Theatre) 2000, The Prisoner's Dilemma 2001. *TV Plays:* I Know What I Meant 1974, Baby Love 1974, Vote for Them 1989, Buying a Landslide 1992, Citizen Locke 1994. *Radio:* Ecclesiastes 1977, A Movie Starring Me 1991. *Film:* Lady Jane 1986. *Publications:* Destiny 1976, Wreckers 1977, Teendreams 1979, Maydays 1983, Plays One 1987, Heartlanders 1989, Pentecost 1995, State of Play (ed.) 1999, Albert Speer 2000, The Prisoner's Dilemma 2001. *Leisure interests:* fine art, cookery, writing letters. *Address:* c/o Alan Brodie Representation, 211 Piccadilly, London, W1V 9LD (Office). *Telephone:* (20) 7917-2871 (Office). *Fax:* (20) 7917-2872 (Office).

EDGAR, James; American politician; b. 22 July 1946, Vinita, Okla; m. Brenda Smith; one s. one d.; ed Eastern Ill. Univ., Univ. of Ill. and Sangamon State Univ.; key Asst to Speaker, Ill. House of Reps. 1972–73; aide to Pres. Ill. Senate 1974, to House Minority Leader 1976; mem. Ill. House of Reps. 1977–91; Dir Legis. Affairs, Gov. of Ill. 1979–80; Sec. of State of Ill. 1981–91; Gov. of Illinois 1991–99; Chair. Nat. Govt's Asscn Comm. Econ. Devt and Tech. Innovation 1991, Strategic Planning Review Task Force 1991; Distinguished Fellow, Inst. of Govt and Public Affairs, Univ. of Ill. 1999–; Republican. *Address:* University of Illinois Institute of Government and Public Affairs, 1007 W Nevada Street, Apartment MC-037, Urbana, IL 61801, USA.

EDGE (THE), (David Evans); Irish musician; b. 8 Aug. 1961; s. of Garvin Evans and Gwenda Evans; m. Morleigh Steinberg 2002; ed Mount Temple School; guitarist and founder mem. U2 1978–; toured Australasia, Europe and USA 1980–84, Live Aid Wembley 1985, Self Aid Dublin, A Conspiracy of Hope (Amnesty Int. Tour) 1986, world tour of 100 performances Europe and USA 1987, toured Australia 1989, New Year's Eve concert Point Depot Dublin (broadcast live to Europe and USSR) 1989, World tour 1992–93, Dublin Concert 1993; Gold disc for War (USA), Platinum disc for Under a Blood Red Sky (UK), Band of the Year (Rolling Stone Writers' poll) 1984, (Readers' poll) 1986, Grammy Awards: Album of the Year (The Joshua Tree) 1987, Best Rock Performance (Desire) 1989, Best Video (Where the Streets Have No Name) 1989, Best Live Act BPI Awards 1993, Best Int. Group, Brit Awards 2001, Outstanding Contrib. to the Music Industry, Brit Awards 2001. *Films:* Rattle of Hum 1988. *Albums include:* Boy 1980, October 1981, War 1983, Under a Blood Red Sky 1983, The Unforgettable Fire 1984, The Joshua Tree 1987, Rattle and Hum 1988, Achtung Baby 1991, Zooropa 1993, Pop 1997, All That You Can't Leave Behind 2000. *Singles include:* With or Without You, I Still Haven't Found What I'm Looking For and Where the Streets Have No Name (all reached number 1 in US charts) 1987, Desire (first UK number 1 single) 1988, Stay 1993 (UK number 1 single), Discotheque 1997 (entered UK charts at number 1), Sweetest Thing 1998, Beautiful Day 2000, Stuck in a Moment You Can't Get Out Of 2001. *Address:* c/o Regine Moylet Publicity, 9 Ivebury Court, 325 Latimer Road, London, W10 6RA, England. *Telephone:* (20) 8969-2600. *Fax:* (20) 7221-8532.

EDGLEY, Michael Christopher, MBE; Australian entrepreneur; b. 17 Dec. 1943, Melbourne; s. of the late Eric Edgley and of Edna Edgley (née Luscombe); m. Jeni King 1972; one s. three d.; ed Trinity Coll., Perth; Chair. Edgley Ventures Pty Ltd 1962–, promoting a wide range of cultural, artistic and sporting events throughout Australia, NZ, the UK and Asia; Citizens of the Year Award for WA 1976. *Leisure interests:* jogging, tennis. *Address:* Edgley International, 2 Chapel Street, Richmond, Vic. 3121, Australia.

EDINBURGH, HRH The Prince Philip, Duke of, Prince of the United Kingdom of Great Britain and Northern Ireland, Earl of Merioneth, Baron Greenwich, KG, KT, OM, GBE; b. 10 June 1921, Corfu, Greece; s. of Prince Andrew of Greece and Denmark and Princess Alice of Battenberg; m. HRH Princess Elizabeth (now HM Queen Elizabeth II, q.v.) 20 Nov. 1947; children: Prince Charles Philip Arthur George, Prince of Wales (q.v.), b. 14 Nov. 1948, Princess Anne Elizabeth Alice Louise, The Princess Royal (q.v.), b. 15 Aug. 1950, Prince Andrew Albert Christian Edward, Duke of York (q.v.), b. 19 Feb. 1960, Prince Edward Antony Richard Louis, Earl of Wessex (q.v.), b. 10 March 1964; ed Cheam, Salem and Gordonstoun Schools, Royal Naval Coll., Dartmouth; renounced right of succession to thrones of Greece and Denmark, naturalized British subject 1947, adopting surname Mountbatten; served Royal Navy 1939–51, served in Indian Ocean, Mediterranean, North Sea, Pacific Ocean during Second World War; Personal ADC to King George VI 1948–52; PC 1951–; ranks of Adm. of the Fleet, Field Marshal, Marshal of the Royal Air Force, Captain-Gen. Royal Marines 1953–; Chancellor, Univs. of Wales 1948–76, Edinburgh 1952–, Salford 1967–91, Cambridge 1977–; Pres., Patron or Trustee numerous orgs including: Nat. Playing Fields Asscn 1948–, Nat. Maritime Museum 1948–, London Fed. of Clubs for Young People (now called London Youth) 1948–, City & Guilds of London Inst. 1951–, Cen. Council of Physical Recreation 1951–, Design Council 1952–, RSA 1952–, English-Speaking Union of the Commonwealth 1952–, Outward Bound Trust 1952–, Trinity House 1952–, Guild of Air Pilots and Air Navigators 1952–, RCA 1955–, Commonwealth Games Fed. 1955–90, Duke of Edinburgh's Award Scheme 1956–, Duke of Edinburgh's Commonwealth Study Confs 1956–, Royal Agric. Soc. of the Commonwealth 1958–, Voluntary Service Overseas 1961–, World Wildlife Fund UK 1961–82, Int. Equestrian Fed. 1964–86, Maritime Trust 1969–, British Commonwealth Ex-Services League 1974–, Royal Acad. of Eng 1976–, British Trust for Ornithology 1987–; Pres. World Wide Fund for Nature 1981–96, Pres. Emer. 1997–; numerous awards, decorations and hon. degrees worldwide. *Publications:* 12 publications 1957–94. *Address:* Buckingham Palace, London, SW1A 1AA, England.

EDMONDS, David, BA; British civil servant; b. 6 March 1944, Grapenhall; s. of Albert Edmonds and Gladys Edmonds; m. Ruth Edmonds (née Beech) 1964; two s. two d.; ed Helsby Co. Grammar School, Univ. of Keele; with Ministry of Housing 1966–70, with Dept of the Environment 1970–84; Chief Exec. The Housing Corpn 1984–91; Man. Dir Group Services NatWest Group 1991–98; Dir-Gen. Oftel (Office of Telecommunications) 1998–; mem. Bd English Partnerships 2000–, Chair. Property, Planning and Projects Cttee 2000–; mem. Council and Treasurer Keele Univ. 1997–; mem. (non-exec.) Bd Ofcom 2002–. *Leisure interests:* opera, golf, art, walking. *Address:* Oftel, 50 Ludgate Hill, London, EC4M 7JJ, England (Office). *Telephone:* (20) 7634-8801 (Office). *Fax:* (20) 7634-8940 (Office). *E-mail:* david.edmonds@oftel.gov.uk (Office). *Website:* www.oftel.gov.uk (Office).

EDMONDS, John Walter, MA; British trade union official; b. 28 Jan. 1944, London; s. of Maude Rose Edmonds and Walter Edgar Edmonds; m. Janet Linden 1967; two d.; ed Oriel Coll. Oxford; Research Asst, GMB (fmrly General, Municipal and Boilermakers' Union) Trade Union 1965, Deputy Research Officer 1967, Regional Organizer 1968, Nat. Officer 1972, Gen. Sec. 1986–May 2003; fmr mem. Council Advisory, Conciliation and Arbitration Service (ACAS), Forestry Comm.; mem. Nat. Employment Panel (fmrly New Deal Task Force) –2002; Dir (non-exec.) Carbon Trust, Environment Agency 2002–; Hon. Trustee Nat. Soc. for the Prevention of Cruelty to Children; Hon. LLD (Sussex). *Leisure interests:* cricket, carpentry. *Address:* 50 Graham Road, Mitcham, Surrey, CR4 2HA, England (Home). *Telephone:* (20) 8648-9991 (Home).

EDSTRÖM, Jan-Erik, MD; Swedish professor of molecular genetics; b. 21 April 1931; s. of Erik Edström and Vera (née Henriksson) Edström; m. 1st Karin Ivarsson 1955 (divorced 1968); three s.; m. 2nd Elisabet Ericson 1980; two s. two d.; Assoc. Prof. of Histology, Univ. of Gothenburg 1962–64; Prof. of Histology, Univ. of Umeå 1964–65, Karolinska Inst., Stockholm 1965–79, Research Assoc. 2000–; Sr Scientist, European Molecular Biology Lab., Heidelberg 1979–85; Prof. of Molecular Genetics, Univ. of Lund 1985–2000; mem. Royal Acad. of Science 1986; MD hc (Karolinska Inst.) 1968. *Publications:* publs on molecular genetics. *Address:* Nybodagatan 7, X, 17142 Solna, Sweden. *Telephone:* (8) 7287558 (Office).

EDWARD, David Alexander Ogilvy, CMG, QC, MA, LLD, FRSE; British judge; b. 14 Nov. 1934, Perth; s. of John O. C. Edward and Margaret I. MacArthur; m. Elizabeth Young McSherry 1962; two s. two d.; ed Sedbergh School, Univ. Coll., Oxford and Edinburgh Univ.; advocate 1962–, Clerk Faculty of Advocates 1967–70, Treas. 1970–77; Pres. Consultative Cttee, Bars and Law Socs. of the EEC 1978–80; Salvesen Prof. of European Insts. and Dir Europa Inst., Univ. of Edin. 1985–89, Hon. Prof. 1990; Judge of the Court of First Instance of the European Communities 1989–92, Judge, Court of Justice of the EC 1992–; Pres. Scottish Council for Int. Arbitration; fmr Specialist Adviser to House of Lords Select Cttee on the EEC; fmr Chair. Continental Assets Trust PLC; fmr Dir Adam & Co. PLC, Harris Tweed Asscn Ltd; fmr mem. Law Advisory Cttee British Council, Panel of Arbitrators, Int. Centre for Settlement of Investment Disputes; fmr mem. Gründungssenat, Europa.-Univ. Viadrina, Frankfurt/Oder; fmr Trustee, Nat. Library of Scotland; Trustee Trier Acad. of European Law, Industry and Parl. Trust, Hopetoun House Trust, Carnegie Trust for the Univs. of Scotland; Hon. Bencher, Gray's Inn; Hon. Fellow Univ. Coll. Oxford; Hon. LLD (Univ. of Edin.) 1993, (Aberdeen) 1997, (Napier) 1998; Hon. DIur (Saarland) 2001, (Münster) 2001. *Publications:* The Professional Secret, Confidentiality and Legal Professional Privilege in the EEC 1976, European Community Law: an introduction (with R. C. Lane) 1995; articles in legal journals. *Address:* European Communities Court of Justice, 2925 Luxembourg (Office). *Telephone:* 43-03-22-03 (Office). *Fax:* 43-03-20-40 (Office). *E-mail:* david.edward@curia.eu.int (Office).

EDWARDES, Sir Michael (Owen), Kt, BA, FBIM; British company executive; b. 11 Oct. 1930, South Africa; s. of Denys Owen Edwardes and Audrey Noel Edwardes (née Copeland); m. 1st Mary Margaret Finlay 1958 (divorced, died 1999); three d.; m. 2nd Sheila Ann Guy 1988; ed St Andrew's Coll., Grahamstown, SA, Rhodes Univ., SA; joined Chloride Group in SA as management trainee 1951, mem. Man. Bd 1969, Chief Exec. 1972, Exec. Chair. 1974–77, Deputy Chair. (non-exec.) 1977–82, Chair. (non-exec.) 1982–88 (acting Chief Exec. 1985–87); Chair. and Chief Exec. BL PLC 1977–82; Dir (non-exec.) Hill Samuel Group PLC 1980–87, Standard Securities 1984–87, Minerals and Resources Corpn 1984–, Flying Pictures Ltd 1987–; Chair. Mercury Communications Ltd 1982–83, ICL PLC 1984; Chair. and Chief Exec. Dunlop Holdings 1984–85; Chair. Charter Consolidated PLC 1988–96, Tryhorn Investments Ltd 1987–, Porth Group PLC 1991–95, ARC

Int. Ltd 1991–93; Exec. Dir Minorco 1984, Strand Partners 1994–, Syndicated Services Co. Inc. 1995–; Deputy Chair. R. K. Carvill Int. Holdings Ltd 1988–; Dir (non-exec.) Int. Man. Devt Inst., Washington 1978–94, Hi-Tec Sports 1993–; Pres. Comité des Constructeurs d'Automobiles du Marché Commun 1979–80; Trustee Thrombosis Research Inst. 1991–; mem. Nat. Enterprise Bd 1975–77, CBI Council 1974 (mem. President's Cttee 1981–), Review Cttee for Queen's Award for Industry; Hon. Fellow, Inst. of Mechanical Engineers; Hon. DIur Rhodes Univ., SA 1980; Young Businessman of the Year 1975. *Publication:* Back From the Brink 1983. *Leisure interests:* water skiing, sailing, squash, tennis.

EDWARDS, Anthony; American actor; b. 19 July 1962, Santa Barbara, Calif.; ed Royal Acad. of Dramatic Art, London; joined Santa Barbara Youth Theatre, in 30 productions aged 12–17; working in commercials aged 16; stage appearance in Ten Below, New York 1993; Screen Actors Guild Award 1996, 1998, 1999, Golden Globe 1998. *Films include:* Fast Times at Ridgemont High 1982, Heart Like a Wheel 1982, Revenge of the Nerds 1984, The Sure Thing 1985, Gotcha! 1985, Top Gun 1985, Summer Heat 1987, Revenge of the Nerds II 1987, Mr. North 1988, Miracle Mile 1989, How I Got into College 1989, Hawks 1989, Downtown 1990, Delta Heat, The Client 1994, Us Begins with You 1998, Don't Go Breaking My Heart 1999, Jackpot 2001. *Television includes:* (series) It Takes Two 1982–83, Northern Exposure 1992–93, ER 1994–2002, Soul Man, Rock Story 2000; (films) The Killing of Randy Webster 1981, High School USA 1983, Going for the Gold: The Bill Johnson Story 1985, El Diablo 1990, Hometown Boy Makes Good 1990, In Cold Blood 1996; (specials) Unpublished Letters, Sexual Healing. *Address:* c/o United Talent Agency, 9560 Wilshire Boulevard, Suite 500, Beverly Hills, CA 90212, USA.

EDWARDS, Blake; American film director and screen writer; b. William Blake McEdwards, 26 July 1922, Tulsa, Okla; m. Julie Andrews 1969; ed high school; served US Coast Guard Reserve World War II; wrote for radio shows Johnny Dollar, Line-Up; writer and creator of Richard Diamond; creator TV shows Dante's Inferno, Peter Gunn, Mr. Lucky. *Writer and co-producer:* Panhandle 1947, Stampede 1948. *Writer:* All Ashore 1952, Sound Off 1952, Cruisin' Down the River 1953, Drive a Crooked Road 1954, My Sister Eileen (musical version) 1955, Operation Mad Ball 1957, Notorious Landlady 1962. *Writer and director* Bring Your Smile Along 1955, He Laughed Last 1955, Mr Cory 1956, This Happy Feeling 1958. *Films directed:* Operation Petticoat 1959, High Time 1960, Breakfast at Tiffany's 1961, Days of Wine and Roses 1962, The Carey Treatment 19723. *Producer, co-writer, director:* The Soldier in the Rain 1963, The Pink Panther 1964, A Shot in the Dark 1964, What Did You Do in the War, Daddy? 1966, Peter Gunn 1967, The Party 1968, Darling Lili 1969, Wild Rovers 1971, The Tamarind Seed 1974, The Return of the Pink Panther 1975, The Pink Panther Strikes Again 1976, Revenge of the Pink Panther 1978, 10 1979, S.O.B. 1980, Victor/Victoria 1981, Trail of the Pink Panther 1982, Curse of the Pink Panther 1983, The Man Who Loved Women 1983, Micki and Maude 1984, That's Life 1986, Blind Date 1986, Sunset 1988, Skin Deep 1989, Switch 1991, Son of the Pink Panther 199. *Producer and director:* Experiment in Terror 1962. *Co-writer and director:* The Great Race 1964. *Writer, director and co-producer:* Victor/Victoria (stage musical), Broadway 1995. *Address:* CAA, 9830 Wilshire Boulevard, Beverly Hills, CA 90212 (Office); Blake Edwards Co., Suite 501, 10520 Wilshire Boulevard, Apt. 1002, Los Angeles, CA 90024, USA (Office).

EDWARDS, Christopher Richard Watkin, MD, FRCP, FRCPE, FMedSci, FRSE; British university vice-chancellor; b. 12 Feb. 1942; s. of Thomas Archibald Watkin Edwards and Beatrice Elizabeth Ruby Watkin Edwards; m. Sally Amanda Kidd 1968; two s. one d.; ed Marlborough Coll., Christ's Coll. Cambridge; lecturer in Medicine, St Bartholomew's Hosp., London 1969–75, Sr Lecturer and MRC Sr Research Fellow 1975–80, Hon. Consultant Physician 1975–80; Moncrieff Arnott Prof. of Clinical Medicine, Univ. of Edin. 1980–95, Dean Faculty of Medicine 1991–95, Provost Faculty Group of Medicine and Veterinary Medicine 1992–95; Prin. and Prof. of Medicine Imperial Coll. of Science and Medicine, Univ. of London 1995–2000; Vice-Chancellor Univ. of Newcastle 2001–; mem. MRC 1991–95; Gov. Wellcome Trust 1994–; Co-founder FMedSci 1998; Hon. DSc (Aberdeen) 2000. *Publications:* Clinical Physiology (Ed.) 1984, Essential Hypertension as an Endocrine Disease 1985, Endocrinology 1986, Recent Advances in Endocrinology Metabolism, Vol. 3 (Ed.) 1989, Davidson's Principles and Practice of Medicine (Ed.) 1995; over 400 scientific papers and communications. *Leisure interests:* running, reading, golf, skiing, painting. *Address:* University of Newcastle, 6 Kensington Terrace, Newcastle upon Tyne, NE1 7RU, England (Office). *Telephone:* (191) 222-6064 (Office). *Fax:* (191) 222-6828 (Office). *E-mail:* c.edwards@ncl.ac.uk (Office).

EDWARDS, Edwin Washington, LLD; American politician; b. 7 Aug. 1927, Marksville, La.; s. of Clarence W. Edwards and Agnes Brouillette Edwards; m. 1st Elaine Schwartzenburg 1949 (divorced 1989); two d. two s.; m. 2nd Candace Picou 1994; ed Louisiana State Univ.; naval cadet 1945–46; practised law in Crowley, La. 1949–80, Sr partner in law firm of Edwards, Edwards and Broadhurst; practised in Baton Rouge, La. 1980–; pvt. practice 1988–; mem. Crowley City Council 1954–62, La. State Senate 1964–66; House of Reps 1965–72, Public Works Cttee 1965–68, Whip to La. and Miss. Dels, Judiciary Cttee and Cttee on Internal Security; Gov. of Louisiana 1972–80, 1984–88, 1992–96; convicted of racketeering, conspiracy and extortion May 2000; sentenced to 10 years' imprisonment 2001; Chair. Interstate Oil Compact Comm. 1974, Ozarks Regional Comm. 1974, Educ. Comm. of Task Force on State, Institutional and Fed. Responsibilities 1975; mem. Nat.

Resources and Environmental Man. Cttee of Southern Govs' Conf., Rural and Urban Devt Cttee of Nat. Govs' Conf.; mem. Crowley Chamber of Commerce, Crowley Industrial Foundation, American Legion; Democrat.

EDWARDS, Gareth Owen, MBE; British rugby union player (retd) and businessman; b. 12 July 1947; s. of Thomas Granville Edwards and Annie-Mary Edwards; m. Maureen Edwards 1972; two s.; ed Pontardawe Tech. School, Millfield School, Cardiff Coll. of Educ.; Welsh Secondary Schools Rugby int. 1965–66; English Schools 200 yards hurdles champion 1966 (UK under-19 record-holder); Welsh nat. team: 53 caps 1967–78, Capt. 13 times, youngest captain (aged 20) 1968; played with following clubs: Cardiff 1966–78, Barbarians 1967–78, British Lions 1968, 1971, 1974; Jt Dir Euro-Commercials (South Wales) Ltd 1982–, Players (UK) Ltd 1983–88; Chair. Hamdden Ltd 1991–; Chair. Regional Fisheries Advisory Cttee, Welsh Water Authority 1983–89. *Publications:* Gareth – An Autobiography 1978, Rugby Skills 1979, Rugby Skills for Forwards 1980, Gareth Edwards on Fishing 1984, Gareth Edwards on Rugby 1986, Gareth Edwards' 100 Great Rugby Players 1987. *Leisure interests:* fishing, golf. *Address:* Hamdden Ltd, Plas y Ffynnon, Cambrian Way, Brecon, Powys, LD3 7HP; 211 West Road, Nottage, Porthcawl, Mid-Glamorgan, CF36 3RT, Wales. *Telephone:* (1874) 614657 (Brecon); (1656) 785669 (Porthcawl).

EDWARDS, Huw; British news broadcaster and journalist; b. 1961, Llangennech, Wales; m.; four c.; ed Univ. of Cardiff; began career as reporter with local radio station Swansea Sound; joined BBC training scheme, Cardiff 1985, becoming parl. reporter, Political Corresp. BBC News, London 1988, Chief Political Corresp. BBC News 24, Presenter BBC One O'Clock, Six O'Clock and Breakfast News 1994–, 10 O'Clock News Sept. 2002–. *Other television and radio work includes:* Newsnight, Panorama, Songs of Praise; classical music programmes on BBC Two and Radio 3 and Radio 4. *Address:* c/o BBC Television Centre, Wood Lane, London, W12 7RJ, England (Office). *Website:* www.bbc.co.uk (Office).

EDWARDS, James Burrows, DMD, F.A.C.D., F.I.C.D.; American university president and oral surgeon; b. 24 June 1927, Hawthorne, Fla; s. of O. M. Edwards and Bertie R. Hieronymus Edwards; m. Ann Norris Darlington 1951; one s. one d.; ed Coll. of Charleston, Univ. of Louisville and Univ. of Pa Graduate Medical School; oral surgery residency, Henry Ford Hosp., Detroit, Mich. 1958–60; dentistry practice, specializing in oral and maxillofacial surgery, Charleston, SC 1960–; Clinical Assoc. in Oral Surgery, Coll. of Dental Medicine, Medical Univ., SC 1967–77, Clinical Prof. of Oral Surgery and Community Dentistry 1977–82, Prof. of Oral and Maxillofacial Surgery 1982, Pres. of Univ. 1982–99, Pres. Emer. 1999–; Fellow American Coll. of Dentists, Int. Coll. of Dentists; mem. Federation Dentaire Internationale, British Asscn of Oral and Maxillofacial Surgeons, Int. Soc. of Oral and Maxillofacial Surgeons and numerous dental orgs in US; Chair. of Charleston County Republican Cttee 1964–69; Chair. of First Congressional District Republican Cttee 1970; mem. SC Statewide Steering Cttee for Republican Party; mem. SC State Senate 1972–74; Governor of South Carolina 1975–78; US Sec. of Energy 1981–82; mem. Bd of Dirs Wachovia Bank of SC, Phillips Petroleum Co., William Benton Foundation, Brendle's Inc., SCANA Corpn, Encyclopaedia Britannica Inc., Imo Delaval Inc., Harry Frank Guggenheim Foundation and numerous others; several hon. degrees. *Leisure interests:* hunting, fishing, sailing, water skiing. *Address:* c/o Office of the President, Medical University of South Carolina, 268 Calhoun Street, Charleston, SC 29425, USA.

EDWARDS, (James) Griffith, CBE, FMedSci; British psychiatrist; b. 3 Oct. 1928, India; s. of the late J. T. Edwards and Constance Amy Edwards (née McFadyean); m. 1st 1969 Evelyn Morrison (divorced 1981); one s. two d. (one deceased); m. 2nd France Susan Stables 1981; ed Andover Grammar School, Balliol Coll., Oxford; Dir Addiction Research Unit 1967–94; fmrly Chair. Nat. Addiction Centre; Prof. of Addiction Behaviour, Inst. of Psychiatry, Univ. of London 1979–94, Emer. Prof. 1994–; Ed. Addiction 1978–96, Ed.-in-Chief 1996–. *Publications:* papers on scientific and clinical aspects of addiction including Alcohol: the Ambiguous Molecule 2000. *Address:* c/o National Addiction Centre, Institute of Psychiatry, King's College London, De Crespigny Park, London, SE5 8AF; 32 Crooms Hill, London, SE10 8ER, England (Home). *Telephone:* (20) 8858-5631 (Home). *E-mail:* p.davis@iop.kcl.ac.uk (Office); grifsu@crooms.freeserve.co.uk (Home).

EDWARDS, John Coates, MA, CMG, JP; British diplomatist; b. 25 Nov. 1934, Tunbridge Wells, Kent; s. of Herbert J. Edwards and Doris M. Edwards (née Starzacher); m. Mary Harris 1959; one s. one d.; ed Skinners' Company School, Tunbridge Wells and Brasenose Coll. Oxford; Lt RA 1953–55; Colonial Office 1960–62; Nature Conservancy Council 1962–64; Ministry of Overseas Devt 1965–68, 1976–78; First Sec. Bangkok and Perm. Rep. to ECAFE 1968–71; Head, E Africa Devt Div. British High Comm. Nairobi 1972–75; Head, British Devt Div. in the Caribbean, Barbados and UK; Dir Caribbean Devt Bank 1978–81; Head, W Indian and Atlantic Dept FCO 1981–84; Deputy High Commr in Kenya 1984–88; High Commr in Lesotho 1988–91, in Botswana 1991–94; Head UK Del., EC Monitoring Mission in Fmr Yugoslavia 1995–99. *Leisure interests:* birdwatching, fishing. *Address:* Fairways, Back Lane, Ightham, Sevenoaks, Kent, TN15 9AU, England. *Telephone:* (1732) 883556.

EDWARDS, John Hilton, MB, BChir, FRS, FRCP; British consultant in genetics and professor of genetics; b. 26 March 1928, London; s. of the late Harold Clifford Edwards and of Ida Margaret Edwards; m. Felicity Clare Toussaint 1956; two s. two d.; ed Univ. of Cambridge, Middlesex Hospital,

London; Medical Officer, Falklands Islands Dependancy Survey 1952–53; MRC Unit on Population Genetics, Oxford 1958–60; Geneticist, Children's Hospital of Philadelphia, Pa 1960–61; Lecturer, Univ. of Birmingham, subsequently Sr Lecturer and Reader, 1961–67, Prof. of Human Genetics 1969–79; Investigator, New York Blood Center 1967–68; Consultant in Human Genetics, Univ. of Iceland 1967–, in Clinical Genetics, Nat. Health Service; Hon. Consultant Paediatrician, Birmingham Regional Bd 1967–79; Prof. of Genetics, Univ. of Oxford 1979–95, Prof. Emer. 1995–; Visiting Prof. of Paediatrics, Cornell Univ., Ithaca, NY, USA 1967–68. *Publications:* Outline of Human Genetics 1978; numerous publications on paediatrics, clinical genetics and mathematical genetics. *Leisure interests:* gliding, skiing, walking. *Address:* c/o Biochemistry Dept, South Parks Road, Oxford (Office); 78 Old Road, Headington, Oxford, England (Home). *Telephone:* (1865) 760430 (Home). *E-mail:* jhe@bioch.ox.ac.uk (Office); jheox@ntlworld.com (Home). *Website:* www.bioch.ox.ac.uk/~jhe (Office).

EDWARDS, John Reid, BS, JD; American politician and lawyer; b. 10 June 1953; s. of Wallace R. Edwards and Catherine Edwards; m. Mary Elizabeth Anania; one s. (deceased) two d.; ed N Carolina Univ., Univ. of N Carolina at Chapel Hill; called to Bar NC 1977, Tenn. 1978; Assoc. Dearborn and Ewing, Nashville 1978–81; trial lawyer, Wade Smith 1981; Assoc. Tharrington Smith and Hargrove, Raleigh 1981–83, partner 1984–92; partner Edwards and Kirby, Raleigh 1993–99; own practice 1993; Senator for N Carolina 1999–; Dir Urban Ministries, Raleigh 1996–97; mem. NC Acad. of Trial Lawyers (Vice-Pres. Bd of Govs.), NC Bar Asscn, Banking, Housing and Urban Affairs, Governmental Affairs, Small Business and Y2K Cttees; Fellow American Coll. of Trial Lawyers. *Address:* US Senate, 225 Dirkson Senate Building, Washington, DC 20510-0001, USA (Office). *Telephone:* (202) 224-3154 (Office). *Fax:* (202) 228-1374 (Office).

EDWARDS, Jonathan, CBE; British athlete; b. 10 May 1966, London; s. of Andrew David Edwards and Jill Caulfield; m. Alison Joy Briggs 1990; two s.; ed West Buckland, Devon; bronze medal, World Championships 1993; gold medal, Fifth Athletics World Championships, Gothenburg 1995 (twice breaking own world record for triple jump, clearing 18.29m), Edmonton 2001; silver medal, Olympic Games, Atlanta 1996, World Championships 1997, 1999; gold medal European Championships 1998, European Indoor Championships 1998, Goodwill Games 1998, Olympic Games 2000, World Championships 2001, Commonwealth Games 2002; Sports Fellowship, Univ. of Durham 1999; British Sportsman of the Year 1995, IAAF Athlete of the Year 1995, BBC Sports Personality of the Year 1995, British Male Athlete of the Year 1995, 2000, 2001. *Publication:* A Time to Jump 2000. *Address:* c/o Jonathan Marks, MTC, 20 York Street, London, W1U 6PU, England. *Telephone:* (20) 7935-8000. *Fax:* (20) 7935-8066. *E-mail:* info@mtc-uk.com (Office). *Website:* www.mtc-uk.com (Office).

EDWARDS, Jorge; Chilean writer and diplomatist; b. 29 July 1931, Santiago; ed Univ. of Chile, Princeton Univ.; diplomatist 1957–73; Amb. to Cuba 1970; Advisory Minister in Paris 1971–73; Literary Prize of the City of Santiago 1961, 1991, Atenea Prize of Univ. of Concepción (Chile), Essay Prize of the City of Santiago 1991, Cervantes Prize for Literature 2000. *Publications:* (novels) El patio 1952, Gente de la ciudad 1962, Las máscaras 1967, Temas y variaciones 1969, Fantasmas de carne y hueso 1992, El peso de la noche 1965, Los convidados de piedra 1978, El museo de cera 1981, La mujer imaginaria 1985, El anfitrión 1988, El origen del mundo 1996.

EDWARDS, Kenneth John Richard, PhD; British university vice-chancellor (retd); b. 12 Feb. 1934; s. of John Edwards and Elizabeth M. Edwards; m. Janet M. Gray 1958; two s. one d.; ed Market Drayton Grammar School, Univ. of Reading and Univ. Coll. of Wales, Aberystwyth; Fellow, Univ. of Calif. 1961–62; ARC Fellow, Welsh Plant Breeding Station, Aberystwyth 1962–63, Sr Scientific Officer 1963–66; Lecturer in Genetics, Univ. of Cambridge 1966–84, Head, Dept of Genetics 1981–86; Lecturer, St John's Coll. Cambridge 1971–84, Fellow 1971–87, Tutor 1981–84; Sec.-Gen. of Faculties, Univ. of Cambridge 1984–87; Vice-Chancellor, Univ. of Leicester 1987–99; Chair. Cttee of Vice-Chancellors and Prins 1993–95; mem. Marshall Aid Commemoration Comm. 1991–98, Council ACU 1994–99; Chair. Governing Body, Inst. of Grassland and Environmental Research 1994–99; Pres. Asscn of European Univs 1998–2001; Visiting Lecturer, Birmingham 1965; Visiting Prof., Buenos Aires 1973; Leverhulme Research Fellow, Univ. of Calif. 1973; Hon. LLD (Belfast) 1994, (Leicester) 1999; Hon. DSc (Reading) 1995, (Loughborough) 1995, (Warwick) 2000; Dr hc (Cluj, Romania) 1997, (Maribor, Slovenia) 1999, (Olomouc, Czech Repub.) 2002. *Publications:* Evolution in Modern Biology 1977; articles on genetics in scientific journals. *Leisure interests:* music, gardening. *Address:* 10 Sedley Taylor Road, Cambridge, England. *Telephone:* (1223) 245680 (Home). *E-mail:* kenneth.edwards@ntlworld.com (Home).

EDWARDS, Peter Philip, PhD, FRS, FRSC; British professor of inorganic chemistry; b. 30 June 1949; s. of the late Ronald Goodlass and of Ethel Mary Edwards; m. Patricia Anne Clancy 1970; two s. one d.; ed Univ. of Salford; Fulbright Scholar and NSF Fellow, Baker Lab. of Chem., Cornell Univ. 1975–77; Science and Eng Research Council/NATO Fellow and Ramsay Memorial Fellow, Inorganic Chem. Lab., Oxford Univ. 1977–79; demonstrator in Inorganic Chem., Jesus Coll., Cambridge Univ. 1979–81, Dir of Studies in Chem. 1979–91, lecturer, Univ. Chem. Labs. 1981–91; Visiting Prof. Cornell Univ. 1983–86; Nuffield Science Research Fellow 1986–87; Co-Founder and Co-Dir. Interdisciplinary Research Centre in Superconductivity

1988; BP Venture Research Fellow 1988–90; Prof. of Inorganic Chem. Univ. of Birmingham 1991–, of Chem. and of Materials 1999–, Head of School of Chemistry 1996–99; Royal Soc. Leverhulme Trust Sr Research Fellow 1996–97; Vice-Pres. Dalton Division Royal Soc. of Chem. 1995; Corday Medal 1985, Tilden Medal 1992, Liversidge Medal 1999. *Publications:* The Metallic and Non-Metallic States of Matter (jtly) 1985, Metal-Insulator Transitions Revisited 1995. *Leisure interests:* exercise, sports. *Address:* School of Chemistry, University of Birmingham, Edgbaston, Birmingham, B15 2TT, England (Office). *Telephone:* (121) 414-4379 (Office). *Fax:* (121) 414-4442. *E-mail:* p.p.edwards@bham.ac.uk (Office). *Website:* www.chem.bham.ac.uk.

EDWARDS, Philip Walter, PhD, FBA; British professor of English literature; b. 7 Feb. 1923, Barrow-in-Furness; s. of the late R. H. Edwards and B. Edwards; m. 1st Hazel Valentine 1947 (died 1950); m. 2nd Sheila Wilkes 1952; three s. one d.; ed King Edward's High School, Birmingham, Univ. of Birmingham; Lecturer in English, Univ. of Birmingham 1946–60; Prof. of English Literature, Trinity Coll. Dublin 1960–66; Visiting Prof., Univ. of Mich. 1964–65; Prof. of Literature, Univ. of Essex 1966–74; Visiting Prof., Williams Coll., Mass. 1969; Visiting Fellow, All Souls Coll., Oxford 1970–71; King Alfred Prof. of English Literature, Univ. of Liverpool 1974–90; Visiting Prof., Univ. of Otago, New Zealand 1980, Int. Christian Univ., Tokyo 1989. *Publications:* Sir Walter Raleigh 1953, The Spanish Tragedy (ed.) 1959, Shakespeare and the Confines of Art 1968, Massinger, Plays and Poems (ed. with C. Gibson) 1976, Pericles Prince of Tyre (ed.) 1976, Threshold of a Nation 1979, Hamlet Prince of Denmark (ed.) 1985, Shakespeare: A Writer's Progress 1986, Last Voyages 1988, The Story of the Voyage 1994, Sea-Mark: The Metaphorical Voyage, Spenser to Milton 1997, The Journals of Captain Cook (ed.) 1999. *Leisure interest:* calligraphy. *Address:* High Gillinggrove, Gillinggate, Kendal, Cumbria, LA9 4JB, England. *Telephone:* (1539) 721298. *E-mail:* pedwards@gilling.edi.co.uk (Home).

EDWARDS, Robert Geoffrey, CBE, MA, PhD, FRS; British professor of human reproduction; b. 27 Sept. 1925; s. of Samuel Edwards and Margaret Edwards; m. Ruth Eileen Fowler 1956; five d.; ed Manchester Cen. High School and Univs of Wales and Edinburgh; Research Fellow, Calif. Inst. of Tech. 1957–58; scientist, Nat. Inst. of Medical Research, Mill Hill 1958–62; Glasgow Univ. 1962–63; Dept of Physiology, Univ. of Cambridge 1963–89; Ford Foundation Reader in Physiology 1969–85; Prof. of Human Reproduction, Univ. of Cambridge 1985–89, Prof. Emer. 1989–; Fellow, Churchill Coll. Cambridge, now Extraordinary Fellow; Scientific Dir Bourn Hallam Clinics, Cambs. and London; Chair. European Soc. of Human Reproduction and Embryology 1984–86; Visiting Scientist, Johns Hopkins Univ. 1965, Univ. of NC 1966, Free Univ. Brussels 1984; Hon. Pres. British Fertility Soc. 1988–; Life Fellow, Australian Fertility Soc.; Chief Ed. Human Reproduction 1986–; Hon. mem. French Soc. for Infertility; Hon. Citizen of Bordeaux; Hon. FRCOG; Hon. MRCP; Hon. DSc (Hull, York, Free Univ. Brussels); Gold Medal, Spanish Fertility Soc. 1985; King Faisal Award 1989. *Publications:* A Matter of Life (with P. C. Steptoe) 1980, Conception in the Human Female 1980, Mechanisms of Sex Differentiation in Animals and Man (with C. R. Austin), Human Conception in Vitro (with J. M. Purdy) 1982, Implantation of the Human Embryo (with J. M. Purdy and P. C. Steptoe) 1985, In Vitro Fertilization and Embryo Transfer (with M. Seppälä) 1985, Life Before Birth 1989; numerous articles in scientific and medical journals. *Leisure interests:* farming, politics, music. *Address:* Duck End Farm, Dry Drayton, Cambridge, CB3 8DB, England. *Telephone:* (1954) 780602.

EDWARDS, Robert John, CBE; British journalist; b. 26 Oct. 1925, Farnham, Surrey; s. of Gordon and Margaret (née Grain) Edwards; m. 1st Laura Ellwood 1952 (dissolved 1972); two s. two d.; m. 2nd Brigid Segrave 1977; ed Ranelagh School; Ed. Tribune 1951–55; Deputy Ed. Sunday Express 1957–59; Ed. Daily Express 1961–62, 1963–65; Ed. Evening Citizen (Glasgow) 1962–63; Ed. Sunday People (fmrly The People) 1966–72; Ed. Sunday Mirror 1972–84; Dir Mirror Group Newspapers 1976–86, Sr Group Ed. 1984–85, Non-exec. Deputy Chair. 1985–86; Chair. London Press Club Scoop of the Year Awards Panel 1998–; Ombudsman to Today newspaper 1990–95. *Publication:* Goodbye Fleet Street 1988. *Leisure interest:* boating. *Address:* Tregeseal House, Nancherrow, St Just, Penzance, TR19 7PW, England. *Telephone:* (1736) 787060. *Fax:* (1736) 786617. *E-mail:* edwardsrj@aol.com (Home).

EDWARDS, (Roger) Nicholas (see Crickhowell, Baron).

EDWARDS, Sir Sam(uel Frederick), Kt, FRS, FInstP, F.I.M.A., FRSC, CChem, CPhys, C.MATH.; British physicist and administrator; b. 1 Feb. 1928, Swansea; s. of Richard and Mary Jane Edwards; m. Merriell E. M. Bland 1953; one s. three d.; ed Swansea Grammar School, Gonville and Caius College, Cambridge, Harvard Univ.; member, Inst. for Advanced Study, Princeton 1952–53; staff mem. Birmingham Univ. 1953–58, Manchester Univ. 1958–72; Prof. of Theoretical Physics, Manchester Univ. 1963–72; John Humphrey Plummer Prof. of Physics, Cambridge Univ. 1972–84, Cavendish Prof. 1984–95, Pro Vice-Chancellor 1992–95, Prof. Emer. 1995–; mem. Council, Inst. of Physics 1967–73, Vice-Pres. of Inst. 1970–73, Chair. Publ Div. 1970–73; mem. Science Bd, Science Research Council 1970–73, mem. Physics Cttee 1968–70, Polymer Science Cttee 1968–73, Chair. Physics Cttee 1970–73, Science Research Council 1973–77; Dir Lucas Industries 1981–93, Steetley PLC 1985–92; mem. Council European Physical Soc. 1969–71, Univ. Grants Cttee 1971–73, Scientific Advisory Council, Min. of Defence 1973–81, 1988– (Chair. 1978–81), Advisory Bd for the Research Councils, Dept of Ed.

and Science 1973–77, Metrology and Standards Requirements Bd, Dept of Industry 1974–77, Advisory Council on Research and Devt, Dept of Energy 1974–77 (Chair. 1983–88), UK Del. NATO Science Cttee 1974–78, Senatsausschuss für Forschungspolitik und Forschungsplanung der Max Planck Gesellschaft 1975–77, Council Inst. of Mathematics and its Applications 1976– (Pres. 1980–81), European Council for Research and Devt 1975–79, Scientific Advisory Cttee Allied Corpn 1980–84; Chair. Council BAAS 1977–82, Pres. 1988–89, Council Royal Soc. 1981–83 (Vice-Pres. 1982–83); Chief Scientific Adviser, Dept of Energy 1983–88; Chair. Sr Advisory Group of Unilever PLC 1992–96; mem. Research Advisory Group BP 1993–97; Fellow Gonville and Caius Coll., Cambridge 1972–; Foreign mem. Acad. des Sciences 1989, NAS 1996; Hon. Fellow Inst. of Physics, French Physical Soc., BAAS 2002; Hon. mem. European Physical Soc.; Hon. DTech (Loughborough) 1975; Hon. DSc (Edin., Salford, Bath, Birmingham, Wales, Strasbourg, Sheffield, Dublin, Leeds), (Swansea) 1994, (E Anglia) 1995, (Cambridge) 2001, (Mainz) 2002; Maxwell, Guthrie Medals and Prizes, Inst. of Physics 1974, 1987, Founders' Polymer Prize 2001, American Physical Soc. Prize for High Polymer Physics 1982, Davy Medal, Royal Soc. 1984, Gold Medallist, Inst. of Math. 1986, Gold Medallist Rheology Soc. 1990, LVMH Science pour l'Art Prize 1993, Boltzmann Medal, IUPAP 1995, Royal Medal, Royal Soc. 2001. *Publications:* Technological Risk 1980, Theory of Polymer Dynamics (with M. Doi) 1986, Networks of Liquid Crystal Polymers (with S. Aharoni) 1994. *Address:* Cavendish Laboratory, Cambridge, CB3 9LU (Office); 7 Penarth Place, Cambridge, CB3 9LU, England (Home). *Telephone:* (1223) 337259 (Office); (1223) 366610 (Home). *Fax:* (1223) 337000 (Office). *E-mail:* sfe11@phy.cam.ac.uk (Office). *Website:* www.poco.phy.cam.ac.uk/~sfe11/Welcome.htm (Office).

EDWARDS, Sian; British conductor; b. 27 Aug. 1959; ed Royal Northern Coll. of Music, Manchester; studied with Sir Charles Groves, Norman Del Mar and Neeme Järvi and with Prof. I.A. Musin, Leningrad Conservatoire 1983–85; won first Leeds Conductors' Competition 1984; has worked with many leading orchestras in UK including London Philharmonic (LPO), Royal Liverpool Philharmonic, Royal Scottish Orchestra, City of Birmingham Symphony, Hallé, BBC Philharmonic, English Chamber orchestras and London Sinfonietta; also with LA Philharmonic Orchestra, The Cleveland Orchestra, The Ensemble Modern, Rotterdam Philharmonic Orchestra and other orchestras; operatic debut, Mahagonny, Scottish Opera 1986; other operatic productions include La Traviata and L'Heure Espagnole (Glyndebourne) 1987–88, Katya Kabanova, New Year (Glyndebourne Touring Opera) 1988–90, The Knot Garden, Rigoletto, Il Trovatore (Royal Opera House, Covent Garden) 1988–91, world premiere Greek (Mark Anthony Turnage), Munich Biennale 1988, Edin. Festival 1988, The Gambler (ENO) 1990, Khovanshchina (ENO) 1994, Mahagonny 1995, La Clemenza di Tito 1998, Eugene Onegin 2000, Peter Grimes (ENO) 2001, Don Giovanni, Danish Royal Opera 2001, The Death of Klinghoffer, La Damnation de Faust, Finnish Nat. Opera 2001; Music Dir ENO 1993–95. *Recordings include:* Tchaikovsky orchestral music (Royal Liverpool Philharmonic Orchestra) and Peter and the Wolf, Young Person's Guide to the Orchestra, Tchaikovsky's 5th symphony (LPO). *Address:* c/o Ingpen and Williams Ltd, 26 Wadham Road, London, SW15 2LR (Office); 70 Twisden Road, London, NW5 1DN, England. *Telephone:* (20) 8874-3222 (Office).

EELSEN, Pierre Henri Maurice, LenD; French administrator and company executive; b. 12 July 1933, Montmorency, Val-d'Oise; s. of Maurice Eelsen and Jacqueline Robert; m. 1st; two s. one d.; m. 2nd Danièle Mesle, 1980; one s.; ed Lycée Jacques-Decour, Paris, Univ. de Paris; at Renault 1958–84, responsible for econ. studies Renault Eng 1959, attached to Dir of Relations 1965, Head Dept Agric. Machinery 1967, attached to Gen. Secretariat 1969, Asst to Sec.-Gen. 1971, Jt Sec.-Gen. 1975, Gen. Del. 1979, mem. Exec. Cttee 1981; Head Dept Int. Affairs Chambre syndicale des constructeurs d'automobiles 1962; mem. European Econ. and Social Cttee 1982–84; Pres. Nat. Asscn for Devt of Overseas depts 1982–85; Admin. Ecole nat. d'admin. 1983; Pres.-Dir-Gen. Air Inter 1984–90; Pres. Agence Nationale pour le Développement de l'Education Permanente (ADEP) 1985–91, Centre national d'enseignement à distance 1988–, Admin. council Institut régional d'admin. de Nantes 1988, French Div. of Centre européen de l'entreprise publique 1989, Chambre Syndicale des Transporteurs Aériens 1986–90; Pres. Nord-Pas de Calais Développement 1991–94, Observatoire Nat. du Tourisme 1991–96, L'Institut européen de recherche et de formation supérieure du tourisme 1992–94; Man. Ed Consultants 1994–; Vice-Pres. Airport Div. SEN (Vinci Group) 1999–2002; Chair. Sogindo 2002–; Commdr, Ordre nat. du Mérite, Officier, Légion d'honneur. *Address:* Sogindo, 52 rue Guynemer, 92404 Courbevoie Cedex (Office); 33 rue Lhomond, 75005 Paris (Home); Domaine de Camarat, 83350 Ramatuelle, France (Home). *Telephone:* 1-46-91-74-53 (Office). *Fax:* 1-46-91-74-60 (Office); 1-43-31-20-37 (Home). *E-mail:* JC.Roulot@sogindo.fr (Office).

EFI, Hon. Taisi Tupuola Tufuga; Samoan politician; b. 1938; s. of Tupua Tamasese Mea'ole; ed St Joseph's Coll., Apia, Western Samoa and Victoria Univ., Wellington, NZ; elected to Western Samoan Parl. 1965–91; Minister of Works, Civil Aviation, Marine and Transport 1970–73; Prime Minister 1976–82, fmr Minister of Foreign Affairs, Local and Dist Affairs and Police; Jt Leader Samoa Nat. Devt Party (SNDP). *Address:* Samoa National Development Party, P.O. Box 1233, Apia, Samoa. *Telephone:* 23543. *Fax:* 20536.

EFIMOV (see Yefimov).

EFSTATHIOU, George Petros, BA, PhD, FRS; British professor of astrophysics; b. 2 Sept. 1955, London; s. of Petros Efstathiou and Christina Parperi; m. 1st Helena Jane Smart 1976 (divorced 1997); m. 2nd Yvonne Nobis 1998; two s. one d.; ed Somerset Comprehensive School, London, Keble Coll., Oxford, Univ. of Durham; Research Asst, Univ. of Calif., Berkeley 1979–80, Univ. of Cambridge 1980–83, Jr Research Fellow King's Coll., Cambridge 1980–84, Sr Research Fellow 1984–88, Asst Dir of Research, Inst. of Astronomy, Cambridge 1984–88; Savilian Prof. of Astronomy and Fellow New Coll., Oxford 1988–97; Prof. of Astrophysics, Univ. of Cambridge 1997–, Fellow King's Coll. 1997–; Bappu Medal and Prize, Astronomical Soc. of India 1988, Maxwell Medal and Prize, Inst. of Physics 1990, Bodossaki Foundation Prize for Astrophysics 1994, Robinson Price in Cosmology, Royal Soc. 1997. *Publications:* articles in astronomical journals. *Leisure interests:* running, playing guitar. *Address:* Institute of Astronomy, Madingley Road, Cambridge, CB3 0HA, England (Office). *Telephone:* (1223) 337530 (Office); (1223) 574001 (Home). *Fax:* (1223) 339910 (Office). *E-mail:* gpe@ast.cam.ac.uk.

EGAN, HE Cardinal Edward Michael, DD, JCD; American ecclesiastic; b. 2 April 1932, Oak Park, Ill.; s. of Thomas J. Egan and Genevieve Costello Egan; ed StMary of the Lake Seminary, Mundelein, Ill., Pontifical N American Coll., Vatican City, Pontifical Gregorian Univ., Rome, Italy; ordained priest 1957; curate at Holy Name Cathedral Parish 1958, later Asst Chancellor Archdiocese of Chicago and Sec. to HE Cardinal Albert Meyer; Asst Vice-Rector and Repetitor of Moral Theology and Canon Law, Pontifical N American Coll., Vatican City 1960; Sec. to HE Cardinal John Cody 1964, later Co-Chancellor Archdiocese of Chicago; Judge, Tribunal of the Sacred Roman Rota 1971–85; fmr Prof. of Canon Law, Vatican City, Pontifical Gregorian Univ., Rome; fmr Prof. of Civil and Criminal Procedure, Studium Rotale; fmr Commr Congregation for the Sacraments and Divine Worship; fmr Consultor Congregation of the Clergy; consecrated Bishop 1985; Auxiliary Bishop of New York and Vicar for Educ. 1985; Third Bishop of Bridgeport 1988–2000; Archbishop of New York 2000–; cr. Cardinal 2001; Pres. and Chair. Bd Trustees Catholic Near East Welfare Asscn; Trustee Ratisbonne Inst., Jerusalem, Israel, St Thomas More Coll., NH, Sacred Heart Univ., Fairfield, CT, Nat. Shrine of the Immaculate Conception, Washington, DC, Catholic Univ. of America, Washington, DC 2000–; Dr hc (St John's Univ., New York, Thomas More Coll., Western Connecticut State Univ.). *Address:* 1011 First Avenue, New York, NY 10022-4134, USA (Office). *Telephone:* (212) 371-1000 (Office). *Fax:* (212) 826-6020 (Office).

EGAN, Sir John Leopold, Kt, MScEcon, DL, FRAeS, FIC, FIMI, FCIT, FCIPS; British business executive; b. 7 Nov. 1939, Rawtenstall, Lancs.; s. of James Edward Egan; m. Julia Emily Treble 1963; two d.; ed Bablake School, Coventry, Imperial Coll., London, London Business School; petroleum engineer, Shell Int. 1962–66; Gen. Man. AC-Delco Replacement Parts Operation, Gen. Motors Ltd 1968–71; Man. Dir Unipart, Parts and Service Dir, Leyland Cars 1971–76; Corp. Parts Dir Massey Ferguson 1976–80; Chair. Jaguar Cars Ltd 1980–84, Chair and Chief Exec., Chief Exec. and Man. Dir Jaguar PLC 1984–85, Chair. and Chief Exec. Jaguar PLC 1985–90; Chief Exec. BAA PLC 1990–99, Dir 1990–; Dir Legal & Gen. Group 1987–97, Chair. 1993–97, Pres. 1998–; Chair. MEPC PLC 1998–2000, Inchcape PLC 2000–, Harrison Lovegrove Ltd 2000–, Qinetiq 2001–02, Asite 2001–; Deputy Pres. CBI 2001–02, Pres. 2002–; mem. Bd Dirs Foreign and Colonial Investment Trust 1985–97, British Tourist Authority 1994–97; Pres. Inst. of Man. 2000–01; Sr Fellow RCA; Hon. Prof., Dept of Eng, Univ. of Warwick 1990; Dr hc (Cranfield Inst.) 1986, Hon. DTech (Loughborough) 1987, Hon. LLD (Bath) 1988; Castrol Gold Medal, Inst. of Motor Industry Award 1982, Int. Gold Medal, Inst. of Production Engineers, City and Guilds of London Hon. Insignia Award for Tech. 1987 and several other awards. *Leisure interests:* skiing, squash, walking, music. *Address:* Inchcape PLC, 22A St James's Square, London, SW1Y 5LP, England (Office). *Telephone:* (20) 7546-0022. *Fax:* (20) 7533-9117. *E-mail:* contact@inchcape.com. *Website:* www.inchcape.com.

EGELUND, Niels; Danish diplomatist; b. 4 July 1946, Copenhagen; ed Coll. of Europe, Bruges, Belgium, Univ. of Aarhus; joined Foreign Service 1972, postings Washington, DC, Bonn; Amb., Under-Sec. of State, Political Dir 1992–93; Chief Adviser to Prime Minister on Foreign and Defence Policy 1993–99; Perm. Rep. to NATO 1999–; Commdr Order of Dannebrog and various other decorations. *Address:* Permanent Mission of Denmark, North Atlantic Treaty Organization, Blvd. Léopold III, 1110 Brussels, Belgium (Office). *Telephone:* (2) 707-6100 (Office). *Fax:* (2) 707-6115 (Office).

EGERTON, Sir Stephen Loftus, KCMG, MA; British fmr diplomatist and business consultant; b. 21 July 1932, Indore, India; s. of William Egerton and Angela D. Egerton (née Bland); m. Caroline Cary-Elwes OBE 1958; one s. one d.; ed Eton Coll., Trinity Coll., Cambridge; served with 60th Rifles 1951–53; joined Foreign Office 1956; served in Lebanon, Kuwait, Baghdad, New York, Tripoli, Rio de Janeiro; Amb. to Iraq 1980–82; Asst Under-Sec. of State for Middle Eastern Affairs FCO 1982–86; Amb. to Saudi Arabia 1986–89, to Italy 1989–92, to Albania (non-resident) May–July 1992; consultant, Enterprise Oil PLC 1992–2002; Dir St Andrew's Trust, Lambeth Palace 1994–99, Trustee 1999–; Pres. Soc. for Libyan Studies 1995–98; Vice-Pres. British School of Archaeology in Iraq and Mesopotamia 1995–; Vice-Chair. Keats-Shelley Memorial Asscn (London and Rome); Coordinator Int. Links Group, Norwich Cathedral 2000–; First Class, Order of Feisal bin Abdul Aziz 1987; Grand Cross of Merit of the Italian Repub. 1990. *Leisure interests:* conversation, topiary, travel. *Address:* 32 Poplar Grove, London, W6 7RE (Office); Pear Tree Cottage, Seething, Norfolk, NR15 1AL, England (Home). *Telephone:* (20) 7602-7876.

EGGLETON, Arthur C. (Art); Canadian politician; fmr accountant; mem. Toronto City Council and Metropolitan Toronto Council 1969–93; Mayor of Toronto 1980–91; MP 1993–; Pres. Treas. Bd and Minister responsible for Infrastructure 1993–96; Minister for Int. Trade 1996–97, of Nat. Defence 1997–; Civic Award of Merit, Toronto 1992. *Address:* Ministry of National Defence, Major-General George R. Pearkes Building, 101 Colonel By Drive, Ottawa, Ont., K1A 0K2, Canada.

EGILSSON, Ólafur; Icelandic diplomatist and lawyer; b. 20 Aug. 1936, Reykjavik; s. of Egill Kristjánsson and Anna Margrjet Thurídur Ólafsdóttir Briem; m. Ragna Sverrisdóttir Ragnars 1960; one s. one d.; ed Commercial College of Iceland and Iceland Univ.; journalist with newspapers Vísir 1956–58, Morgunbladid 1959–62; Publishing Exec. 1963–64; Head, NATO Regional Information Office, Reykjavik 1964–66; Gen.-Sec. Icelandic Asscn for Western Co-operation 1964–66; Political Div., Icelandic Foreign Ministry 1966–69; First Sec., then Counsellor, Icelandic Embassy, Paris 1969–71; Deputy Perm. Rep. OECD, UNESCO and Council of Europe 1969–71; Deputy Perm. Rep. N Atlantic Council, Deputy Head, Icelandic Del. to EEC, Counsellor, Embassy in Brussels 1971–74; Counsellor, then Minister Counsellor, Political Div. of Foreign Ministry 1974–80; Chief of Protocol (with rank of Amb.) 1980–83; Acting Prin. Pvt. Sec. to Pres. of Iceland 1981–82; Deputy Perm. Under Sec. and Dir-Gen. for Political Affairs, Foreign Ministry 1983–87; Amb. to UK (also accred to Ireland, Netherlands and Nigeria) 1986–89; Amb. to USSR, later Russia 1990–94; Amb. to Denmark (also accred to Japan, Italy, Israel, Lithuania and Turkey) 1994–96; in charge of Arctic co-operation 1996–98 (also accred to Holy See, Turkey, Australia and NZ); Amb. to China 1998– (also accred to Australia, Japan, Repub. of Korea, NZ and Viet Nam); Chair. Bd of Govs Icelandic Int. Devt Agency 1982–87; Exec. mem. Bible Soc. of Iceland 1977–87, History Soc. 1982–88; Commdr Icelandic Order of the Falcon and decorations from Finland, France, Norway, Spain, Sweden and Luxembourg. *Publications:* Co-author: Iceland and Jan Mayen 1980, NATO's Anxious Birth – The Prophetic Vision of the 1940s 1985; Ed. Bjarni Benediktsson 1983. *Leisure interests:* history, skiing, music (classical, opera). *Address:* Icelandic Embassy, Landmark Tower 1, 802, 8 North Dongsanhuan Lu, Beijing 100600, People's Republic of China (Office). *Telephone:* (10) 65907795 (Office). *Fax:* (10) 65907801 (Office). *E-mail:* icemb.beijing@utn.stjr.is.

EGLI, Alphons, DJur; Swiss politician; b. 8 Oct. 1924, Lucerne; s. of Gotthard Egli; m.; three c.; ed legal studies in Zurich, Berne and Rome; private legal practice in Lucerne 1952–82; mem. Lucerne Municipal Council 1963–67, Lucerne Cantonal Parl. 1967–75; mem. Council of States 1975; Leader, Christian Democratic Group 1979; Fed. Councillor 1982–; Head, Fed. Dept of the Interior 1982–85, 1986, Pres. of Swiss Confed. and Head of State Jan.–Dec. 1986. *Address:* c/o Federal Chancellery, Bundeshaus-West, Bundesgasse, 3003 Berne, Switzerland.

EGLIN, Colin Wells, BSc; South African politician and quantity surveyor; b. 14 April 1925, Cape Town; s. of Carl Eglin and Elsie May Wells; m. 1st Joyce Eglin 1949 (died 1997); three d.; m. 2nd Raili Eglin 2000; ed De Villiers Graaff High School and Univ. of Cape Town; army service in Egypt and Italy 1943–45; mem. Pinelands Municipal Council 1951–54, Cape Prov. Council 1954–58; mem. Parl. 1958–61, 1974–; Leader Progressive Party 1970–75, Progressive Reform Party 1975–77, Progressive Federal Party 1977–79, 1986–88; Official Opposition Leader 1977–79, 1986–87; Chief DP Constitutional Negotiator 1991–96; Co-Chair. Transitional Exec. Council 1993–94; mem. Man. Cttee Constitutional Ass. 1994–96; Vice-Pres. Liberal Int. 1990–; Sec.-Gen. Org. of African Liberal Parties 1995–99; Democratic Party Spokesman on Foreign Affairs 1989–; Partner, Bernard James and Partners (Quantity Surveyors) 1952–; Hon. LLD (Cape Town) 1997; Parliamentarian of the Century, Leadership Magazine Jan. 2000, Ramon Trias Fargas Memorial Award 2002. *Publications:* Betrayal of Coloured Rights, Forging Links in Africa, Priorities for the Seventies, New Deal for the Cities, Africa – A Prospect of Reconciliation, Pacesetter for Political Change, Security Through Negotiation. *Leisure interests:* golf, travel. *Address:* National Assembly, P.O. Box 15, Cape Town 8000 (Office); 28 Southern Cross Drive, Constantia 7806, South Africa (Home). *Telephone:* (21) 4033511 (Office); (21) 7940584 (Home). *Fax:* (21) 4613782 (Office). *E-mail:* coleglin@netactive.co.za (Home).

EGLINTON, Geoffrey, DSc, PhD, FRS; British professor of organic geochemistry; b. 1 Nov. 1927, Cardiff; m. Pamela J. Coupland 1955; two s. one d. (deceased); ed Sale Grammar School and Univ. of Manchester; Postdoctoral Fellow, Ohio State Univ. 1952; Lecturer in Organic Chem., Univ. of Glasgow 1954–64; Visiting Fellow, Univ. of Calif. (Berkeley) 1964; Sr Lecturer in Organic Chem., Univ. of Glasgow 1964–67, Reader 1967; Sr Lecturer in Organic Geochem. and Head, Organic Chem. Unit, Univ. of Bristol 1967; Reader in Organic Geochem. 1968–73; Prof. and Head of Organic Geochem. Unit 1973–93, Prof. Emer. 1993–; Dir Biogeochemistry Centre 1991–97, Sr Research Fellow 1995–; Visiting Scholar Woods Hole Oceanographic Inst., Mass. 1986, Adjunct Scientist 1991–; Geochemistry Fellow of Geochemical Soc. and European Asscn for Geochemistry 1996; Melvin Calvin Lectureship (Univ. of Calif., Berkeley) 1985; H. Burr Steinbach Visiting Scholar, Woods Hole Oceanographic Inst. 1986; NASA Gold Medal 1973, Hugo Muller Silver Medal (Chem. Soc.) 1974, Alfred E. Treibs Medal 1981, Major Edward Fitzgerald Coke Medal of the Geological Soc. 1986; Harold C. Urey Award, European Asscn of Geochemists 1997; Royal Medal, Royal Soc. 1997, Martin Gold Medal, Chromatographic Soc. 1999, Goldschmidt Medal, Geochemical Soc. 2000. *Publications:* over 500 articles and books. *Leisure interests:* hiking, sailing. *Address:* Oldwell, 7 Redhouse Lane, Westbury-on-Trym, Bristol, BS9 3RY, England (Home). *Telephone:* (117) 968 3833 (Home).

EGON, Nicholas; British painter; b. 15 Nov. 1921, Brno, Czechoslovakia; m. 1st Diana Horton 1948; m. 2nd Matti Xylas 1980; ed pvt. tutors, Birkbeck Coll., London Univ., Oxford Univ.; served with army in Middle East 1942–46; taught painting and history of art, Sir John Cass Coll., lectured at Nat. Gallery, London and Oxford and Cambridge 1946–50; portraits, landscapes and abstracts in nat., royal and pvt. collections, USA, UK, France, Italy, Greece, Spain, Jordan, Saudi Arabia, Morocco, Oman and Switzerland; Chair. of Patrons, Centre for Hellenic Studies, King's Coll., London Univ. 1989–. *Solo exhibitions:* 10 exhbns in London 1950–90. *Publications:* Some Beautiful Women (portraits) 1952, Paintings of Jordan 1986. *Leisure interests:* travel, history, music, archaeology. *Address:* Villa Aëtos, Katakali, 20100 Corinthia (Studio); Deinokratous 81, 115 21 Athens, Greece; 34 Thurloe Square, London, SW7 2SR, England. *Telephone:* (741) 33442 (Corinthia); (1) 7291774 (Athens); (20) 7589-0700 (London). *Fax:* (741) 33640 (Corinthia); (1) 7294748 (Athens); (20) 7589-0620 (London).

EGOYAN, Atom, OC, BA; film director; b. 19 July 1960, Cairo; s. of Joseph Egoyan and Shushan Devletian; m. Arsinée Khanjian; one c.; ed Univ. of Toronto; Dir Ego Film Arts, Toronto 1982–; films shown at int. film festivals around the world; Dr hc (Trinity Coll., Univ. of Toronto, Univ. of Victoria, Brock Univ., Ont., Coll. of Art and Design, Univ. of British Columbia); Chevalier, Ordre des Arts et des Lettres. *Exhibitions:* Notorious, Museum of Modern Art, Oxford, Return to the Flock, Irish Museum of Modern Art, Early Development, Le Fresnoy, USA, Venice Biennale, Close, Venice Biennale, Hors d'Usage, Musée d'Art Contemporain de Montréal. *Films:* writer, dir and producer feature films: Next of Kin 1984 (Gold Ducat award, Mannheim Int. Film Week 1984), Family Viewing 1987 (Int. Critics Award 1988, Best Feature Film Award, Uppsala, Prix Alcan, Festival du Nouveau Cinéma, Montreal), Speaking Parts 1989 (Best Screenplay Prize, Vancouver Int. Film Festival), The Adjuster 1991 (Special Jury Prize, Moscow Film Festival, Golden Spike Award, Valladolid Film Festival), Calendar 1993 (prize at Berlin Int. Film Festival), Exotica 1994 (Int. Film Critics Award, Cannes Film Festival 1994, Prix de la Critique award for Best Foreign Film 1994), The Sweet Hereafter 1997 (Grand Prix, Int. Critics Prize, Cannes Film Festival 1997), Elsewhereless 1998, Dr Ox's Experiment 1998, Felicia's Journey 1999, Krapp's Last Tape 2000, Ararat 2001. *Operas:* Salome, Canadian Opera Co. 1996, Houston Grand Opera 1997, Elsewhereless 1998, Dr Ox's Experiment 1998, Salome (new production), Canadian Opera Co. 2002. *Leisure interest:* classical guitar. *Address:* Ego Film Arts, 80 Niagara Street, Toronto, Ont., M5V 1C5, Canada. *Telephone:* (416) 703-2137 (Office). *Fax:* (416) 504-7161 (Office). *E-mail:* admin@egofilmarts.com (Office). *Website:* www.egofilmarts.com (Office).

EGUIAGARAY UCELAY, Juan Manuel, BA, PhD; Spanish politician; b. 25 Dec. 1945, Bilbao; m.; one s.; ed Univ. of Deusto, Univ. of Nancy, France; mem. PSE-PSOE (Workers' Socialist Party of Spain) 1977–; councillor Town Council, Bilbao 1979, Provincial Deputy, Vizcaya 1979–81, mem. Juntas Generales Vizcaya 1979–83, Deputy and Spokesman for Socialist Party of Basque Parl. 1980–88, mem. Exec. Cttee PSE-PSOE 1979–, Vice-Sec. Gen. Basque Socialists 1985–88, Govt Del. for Autonomous Community of Murcia, then for Autonomous Community of the Basque Country 1988–89; Exec. Sec. PSOE Fed. Exec. Comm. 1990; Minister for Public Admin. 1991–93, of Industry and Energy 1993–96; Nat. Deputy for Murcia 1996–; Fed. Sec. for the Economy (34th Fed. Congress of PSOE), fmrly PSOE Nat. Parl. Spokesman and PSOE Nat. Parl. Spokesman for Econ. Affairs; Vice-Chair. Cttee on Econ., Trade and Tax Affairs; Prof. of Econs Univ. de Deusto. *Address:* Congreso de los Diputados, Plaza de las Cortes 9, 28014 Madrid, Spain. *Telephone:* (1) 3907639. *Fax:* (1) 4201648 (Office). *E-mail:* juan.eguiagaray@diputado.congreso.es (Office).

EHLE, Jennifer; British actress; ed Cen. School of Speech and Drama. *Plays include:* Summerfolk (Royal Nat. Theatre), The Relapse (RSC), The Painter of Dishonour (RSC), Richard III (RSC) 1996, Tartuffe (Playhouse), The Real Thing (Albery) 1999, (Broadway) 2000. *Television:* Melissa, Pride and Prejudice (BAFTA Best Actress Award), Beyond Reason, Pleasure, Self Catering, The Maitlands, Micky Love, The Camomile Lawn. *Films:* This Year's Love, Bedrooms and Hallways 1998, Wilde 1998, Paradise Road, Backbeat, Sunshine 2000, Possession 2002. *Address:* c/o ICM, 76 Oxford Street, London, W1N 0AX, England. *Telephone:* (20) 7636-6565.

EHLERMANN, Claus-Dieter, DrIur; German lawyer; b. 15 June 1931, Scheessel; s. of Kurt Ehlermann and Hilde (née Justus) Ehlermann; m. Carola Grumbach 1959; two d.; ed Univs of Marburg/Lahn and Heidelberg, Univ. of Michigan Law School, Ann Arbor; Research Asst Fed. Constitutional Court, Karlsruhe 1959–61; Legal Adviser, Legal Service of the Comm. of European Communities 1961–73, Dir and Deputy Financial Controller 1973–77, Dir-Gen. of the Legal Service 1977–87; Spokesman of the Comm. of the European Communities and of its fmr Pres. Jacques Delors (q.v.) 1987–90, Dir-Gen. of Directorate-Gen. for Competition 1990–95; Prof. of Econ. Law, European Univ. Inst., Florence; fmr mem. Appellate Body of WHO, Geneva; Hon. Prof. Univ. of Hamburg; Hon. Bencher, Gray's Inn, London; Hon. DrIur 1999.

Publications: numerous documents on the European Community and its legal order. *Leisure interests:* reading, skiing. *Address:* Istituto Universitario Europeo, Badia Fiesolana, Via dei Roccettini 9, 50016 San Domenico di Fiesole (Firenze), Italy; Centre William Rappard, Rue de Lausanne 154, Case postale, 1211 Geneva 21, Switzerland; 51 avenue du Val des Seigneurs, 1150 Brussels, Belgium (Home). *Telephone:* (055) 4685798 (Italy); (2) 7622127 (Home). *Fax:* (055) 4685776 (Italy); (2) 7711993 (Home). *E-mail:* claus .ehlermann@iue.it (Office); carola.ehlermann@planetinternet.be (Home). *Website:* www.iue.it/rsc/eco-pol/competition.htm (Office); www.iue.it/law/ehlermann/index.htm (Home).

EHRLICH, Paul Ralph, MA, PhD; American population biologist; b. 29 May 1932, Philadelphia, Pa; s. of William and Ruth (Rosenberg) Ehrlich; m. Anne Fitzhugh Howland 1954; one d.; ed Univs of Pennsylvania and Kansas; Assoc. investigator, USAF research project, Alaska and Univ. of Kansas 1956–57; Research Assoc. Chicago Acad. of Sciences and Univ. of Kansas Dept of Entomology 1957–59; mem. Faculty, Stanford Univ. 1959, Prof. of Biology 1966–, Bing Prof. of Population Studies 1976–; Pres. Centre for Conservation Biology 1988–; Corresp. NBC News 1989–92; Fellow AAAS; mem. NAS, European Acad. of Sciences and Arts 1992; Hon. mem. Int. Soc. for Philosophical Enquiry 1991; Hon. DHumLitt (Univ. of the Pacific) 1970; Crafoord Prize, Royal Swedish Acad. of Sciences 1990, UNEP Sasakawa Environment Prize 1994, Blue Planet Prize, Asahi Glass Foundation 1999 and many other awards for work in ecology, evolution and conservation. *Publications:* How to Know the Butterflies 1961, Population Resources, Environment 1970, 1972 (both with A. H. Ehrlich), The Population Bomb 1968, 1971, How to be a Survivor (with R. L. Harriman) 1971, co-ed.: Man and the Ecosphere (with J. P. Holdren and R. W. Holm) 1971, Global Ecology (with J. P. Holdren) 1971, Human Ecology (with A. H. Ehrlich and J. P. Holdren) 1973, Ark II (with D. Pirages) 1974, The Process of Evolution (with R. W. Holm and D. R. Parnell) 1974, The End of Affluence (with A. H. Ehrlich) 1974, Biology and Society (with R. W. Holm and I. Brown) 1976, The Race Bomb (with S. Feldman) 1977, Ecoscience: Population, Resources, Environment (with A. H. Ehrlich and J. P. Holdren) 1977, Introduction to Insect Biology and Diversity (with H. V. Daly and J. T. Doyen) 1978, The Golden Door: International Migration, Mexico and the U.S. (with D. L. Bilderback and A. H. Ehrlich) 1979, Extinction: The Causes and Consequences of the Disappearance of Species (with A. H. Ehrlich) 1981, Machinery of Nature 1986, Earth (with A. H. Ehrlich) 1987, The Birder's Handbook (with D. Dobkin and D. Wheye) 1988, New World/New Mind (with R. Ornstein) 1989, The Population Explosion (with A. H. Ehrlich) 1990, Healing the Planet (with A. H. Ehrlich) 1991, Birds in Jeopardy 1992, The Stork and the Plow (with A. H. Ehrlich and G. C. Daily) 1995, Betrayal of Science and Reason (with A. H. Ehrlich) 1996, Human Natures 2000, Wild Solutions 2001 and other books; over 800 scientific and popular articles. *Leisure interest:* collecting primitive art. *Address:* Department of Biological Sciences, Stanford University, Stanford, CA 94305, USA. *Telephone:* (650) 723-3171.

EHRLICH, Robert L., Jr, BA, JD; American state official and lawyer; b. 25 Nov. 1957, Baltimore, Md; s.of Bob Ehrlich and Nancy Ehrlich; m. Kendel Sibiski; one c.; ed Gilman School, Princeton Univ., Wake Forest Univ.; assoc. Ober, Kaler, Grimes and Shriver 1982–92, counsel 1992–94; mem. House of Dels for Md 1987–94; Republican mem. US House of Reps 1995–2002; Gov. of Md 2003–; Outstanding Young Marylander, Md Jaycees 1995, Legislator of the Year, Biotech. Industry Org., Spirit of Enterprise Award, US Chamber of Commerce, Guardian of Small Business, Nat. Fed. of Ind. Business 1987–90, Fed. Official of the Year, Nat. Industries for the Blind. *Address:* Office of the Governor, State House, Annapolis, MD 21401, U.S.A. (Office).

EHRLICH, S(aul) Paul, Jr, M.P.H., MD; American physician; b. 4 May 1932, Minn.; s. of S. Paul Ehrlich and Dorothy E. Fiterman; m. Geraldine McKenna 1959; three d.; ed Univs of Minnesota and Calif.; Staff Physician, Grants and Training Branch, Nat. Heart Inst., Nat. Insts of Health, Bethesda 1959–60; Chief, Epidemiology Field Training Station, Heart Disease Control Program, Wash., DC 1961–66, Deputy Chief Heart Disease Control Program 1966–67; Lecturer in Epidemiology, School of Public Health, Univ. of Calif. 1961–63; Clinical Assoc. Prof., Dept of Community Medicine and Int. Health, Georgetown Univ. School of Medicine, Wash., DC 1967–92; Adjunct Prof. of Int. Health, Univ. of Texas; Deputy Dir Pan American Health Org., Washington 1979–83; Assoc. Dir for Bilateral Programs, Office of Int. Health, 1967–68; Deputy Dir Office of Int. Health 1968–69; Acting Dir Office of Int. Health, Dept of Health, Educ. and Welfare Dec. 1969–70, Dir 1970–77; Asst Surgeon-Gen., USPHS 1970, Acting Surgeon-Gen. 1973–77, Deputy Surgeon-Gen. 1976–77; US Rep. to World Health Org. (WHO) 1969–72, 1973–76; Diplomate, American Bd of Preventive Medicine; Chair. Exec. Bd of WHO 1972; Sr Adviser American Asscn of World Health 1984–86, Health Consultant 1984–; US Public Health Service (USPHS) Meritorious Service Medal 1994, Dept of Health, Educ. and Welfare Sec.'s Special Citation 1975, USPHS Distinguished Service Medal 1977, USPHS Outstanding Service Medal 1983. *Publications:* articles on Chronic Disease Control, Coronary Disease Risk Factors and the Relationship of the Stroke to Other Cardiovascular Diseases. *Address:* 1132 Seaspray Avenue, Delray Beach, FL 33483-7140, USA (Home). *Telephone:* (561) 276-5705 (Home). *Fax:* (561) 276-2303 (Home). *E-mail:* spehrlich@webtv.net (Home).

EHRLICH, Thomas, LLB; American university president and professor of law; b. 4 March 1934, Cambridge, Mass.; s. of William Ehrlich and Evelyn Seltzer; m. Ellen Rome Ehrlich 1957; two s. one d.; ed Harvard Coll. and Harvard Law School, Cambridge, Mass.; law clerk, US Court of Appeals, New York 1959–60; Assoc., Foley, Sammond & Lardner law practice, Milwaukee, Wis. 1960–62; Special Asst to Legal Adviser, Dept of State, Washington, DC 1962–65, to Under-Sec. of State George W. Ball 1964–65; Prof., Stanford Univ. Law School, Stanford, Calif. 1965–71, Dean and Richard E. Lang Prof. 1971–75; Pres. Legal Services Corpn, Washington, DC 1976–79; Dir Int. Devt Co-operating Agency, Washington, DC 1979–80; Guest Scholar, The Brookings Inst. 1981; Provost and Prof. of Law, Univ. of Pa, Phila, Pa 1982–87; Pres. Ind. Univ. 1987–94; Visiting Prof. Stanford Law School 1994–99; Distinguished Univ. Scholar, Calif. State Univ., San Francisco 1995–2000; Sr Scholar Carnegie Foundation for the Advancement of Tech. 1997–; Arbitrator, US–France Int. Aviation Dispute, Geneva, Switzerland; mem. American Asscn for Higher Educ., American Bar Asscn Special Comm. on Professional Standards, Council of Ten (Council of Pres., Big Ten Univs), Council on Foreign Relations, Exec. Cttee American Soc. of Int. Law, Bd of Dirs Center for Law and Social Policy and many other bodies; Hon. LLD (Villanova) 1979, (Notre Dame) 1980, (Univ. of Pa) 1987, (Indiana). *Publications:* The International Legal Process (with Abram Chayes and Andreas F. Lowenfeld), (3 Vols) 1968, Supplement 1974, New Directions in Legal Education (with Herbert L. Packer) 1972, International Crises and the Role of Law, Cyprus 1958–67 1974, International Law and the Use of Force (with Mary Ellen O'Connell) 1993, The Courage to Inquire 1995, The Future of Philanthropy and the Nonprofit Sector in a Changing America (ed. with Charles T. Clotfelter) 1999, Higher Education and Civic Responsibility 2000, Educating Citizens (with Anne Colby, Elizabeth Beaumont and Jason Stephens) 2003; numerous articles, reviews and other publs. *Address:* Carnegie Foundation for the Advancement of Teaching, 555 Middefield Road, Menlo Park, CA 94025, USA. *Telephone:* (650) 566-5137 (Office).

EIBL-EIBESFELDT, Irenäus, DPhil; Austrian professor of zoology; b. 15 June 1928, Vienna; s. of Anton and Maria (von Hauninger) Eibl-Eibesfeldt; m. Eleonore Siegel 1950; one s. one d.; ed Univs of Vienna and Munich; Research Assoc., Biol. Station, Wilhelminenberg, nr Vienna 1946–48, Max Planck Inst. of Behavioural Physiology 1951–69; Head of ind. research unit on human ethology, Max Planck Inst. 1970–96. Emer. Researcher and Head Human Ethology Film Archive 1996–; lecturer Univ. of Munich 1963, Prof. 1970; Hon. Scientific Dir Int. Inst. for Submarine Research, Vaduz 1957–70; Head Ludwig-Boltzmann-Inst. for Urban Ethology, Vienna 1992–; mem. Humanwissenschaftliches Zentrum, Ludwig-Maximilians-Univ., Munich 1997, Deutsche Akad. der Naturforscher 1977; founding mem. and Pro-Dekan European Acad. of Arts and Sciences; Pres. Int. Soc. for Human Ethology 1985–93; Corresp. mem. Deutsche Akad. der Naturforscher Leopoldina; Dr hc (Salamanca) 1994; Wilhelm Bölsche Gold Medal 1971, Burda Prize for Communications Research 1980, Philip Morris Research Prize 1988, Gold Medal of Honour (City of Vienna) 1989, Bundesverdienstkreuz (Germany) 1995, Schwenk'scher Umweltpreis 1996, Haackert Medal 1997, Bayerischer Verdienstorden 1997, Jahrespreis von STAB, Zurich 1997, Österreichisches Ehrenkreuz für Wissenschaft und Kunst 1998 and many others. *Publications:* Galapagos, die Arche Noah im Pacific 1960, Im Reich der tausend Atolle 1964, Grundriss der vergleichenden Verhaltensforschung 1967, Liebe und Hass 1970, Die ko-Buschmanngesellschaft 1972, Der vorprogrammierte Mensch 1973, Menschenforschung auf neuen Wegen 1976, Der Hai: Legende eines Mörders (with H. Hass) 1977, Die Malediven: Paradies im Indischen Ozean 1982, Die Biologie des menschlichen Verhaltens, Grundriss der Humanethologie 1984, Der Mensch – das riskierte Wesen 1988, Human Ethology 1989, Das verbindende Erbe 1991, Und grün des Lebens goldner Baum 1992, Im Banne der Angst (co-author) 1992, Wider die Misstrauensgesellschaft 1994, In der Falle des Kurzzeitdenkens 1998. *Leisure interests:* skin diving, skiing, arts. *Address:* Humanethologisches Filmarchiv der Max Planck Gesellschaft, Von-der-Tann-Strasse 3-5, 82348 Andechs (Office); Fichtenweg 9, 82319 Starnberg, Germany (Home). *Telephone:* (8152) 373157/373159. *Fax:* (8152) 373170. *E-mail:* eibl@erl.ornithol.mpg.de (Office).

EICHEL, Hans; German politician; b. 24 Dec. 1941, Kassel; m.; two c.; ed Univs of Marburg and Berlin; fmr schoolmaster; mem. Kassel City Council 1968–75, Chair. Social Democratic Party (SDP) Group 1970–75; mem. Nat. Exec. of Young Socialists 1969–72; Chief Mayor of Kassel 1975–91; mem. SDP Nat. Exec. and Spokesman on Local Govt 1984; Chair. SDP Asscn Hesse 1989; Minister-Pres. of Hesse 1991–99; Federal Minister of Finance 1999–. *Address:* Ministry of Finance, Wilhelmstr. 97, 10117 Berlin, Germany (Office). *Telephone:* (30) 22420 (Office). *Fax:* (30) 22423260 (Office).

EICHELBAUM, Rt Hon Sir (Johann) Thomas, GBE, PC; New Zealand judge; b. 17 May 1931, Koenigsberg, Germany; s. of Dr Walter Eichelbaum and Frida M. Eichelbaum; m. Vida Beryl Franz 1956; three s.; ed Hutt Valley High School and Victoria Univ. Coll.; admitted solicitor 1953, barrister 1954; Partner, Chapman Tripp & Co. 1958–78; QC 1978; barrister 1978–82; Pres. NZ Law Soc. 1980–82; Judge, High Court of NZ 1982; Chief Justice of NZ 1989–99; Judge of Appeal, Fiji 1999–; Non-Perm. Judge, Court of Final Appeal Hong Kong 2000–; Hon. LLD (Vic. Univ. of Wellington) 1998. *Publications:* Mauet's Fundamentals of Trial Techniques (Ed.-in-Chief) 1989, Introduction to Advocacy (Consulting Ed.) 2000. *Leisure interests:* reading, walking. *Address:* 27 Tainui Street, Raumati Beach 6010, New Zealand. *E-mail:* thoseich@actrix.gen.nz (Home).

EICHHORN, Lisa; American film actress; b. 2 April 1952, Glen Falls, NY; ed Queen's Univ. Ontario, St Peter's Coll. Oxford and Royal Acad. of Dramatic Art. *Films include:* Yanks 1979, The Europeans 1979, Why Would I Lie? 1980,

Cutter and Bone (Cutter's Way) 1981, The Weather in the Streets 1983, Wildrose 1984, Opposing Force (Hell Camp) 1987, Grim Prairie Tales, Moon 44 1989, King of the Hill 1993, The Vanishing 1993, Mr 247 1994, A Modern Affair, Judas Kiss 1998, The Talented Mr Ripley 1999, Goodbye Lover 1999, Boys and Girls 2000. *Stage appearances include:* roles in British Shakespearean productions, A Doll's House, A Golden Boy, The Speed of Darkness, The Summer Winds, The Common Pursuit, The Hasty Heart, Pass/Fair, Arms and the Man, Misfits 1996.

EIFMAN, Boris Yakovlevich; Russian balletmaster; b. 22 July 1946, Rubtsovsk, Altai Region; s. of Yankel Borisovich Eifman and Klara Markovna Kuris; m. Valentina Nikolayevna Morozova; one s.; ed Kishinev School of Choreography, Leningrad State Conservatory; balletmaster Leningrad School of Choreography 1970–77; concurrently ballet productions in professional theatres including Firebird (Kirov Theatre 1975); Founder and Artistic Dir Leningrad Ensemble of Ballet (now St Petersburg Ballet Theatre Boris Eifman) 1977; Chevalier des Arts et des Lettres 1999; People's Artist of Russia 1995, Golden Baton Prize 1995, 1996, 1997, Triumph Prize 1996, Golden Mask Prize 1996, 1999, Russian State Prize 1999. *Ballets include:* Before Firebird – Gayaney 1972, Idiot (Tchaikovsky's 6th Symphony) 1980, Marriage of Figaro 1982, The Legend 1982, Twelfth Night 1984, The Duel (after Kuprin) 1986, Master and Margarita (after Bulgakov) 1987, Thérèse Raquin 1991, Requiem (Mozart) 1991, Tchaikovsky 1993, Don Quixote or Madman's Fantasy (Minkus) 1994, Brothers Karamazov (after Dostoyevsky) 1995, Red Giselle 1997, My Jerusalem 1998, Russian Hamlet 1999, Don Juan 2001. *Address:* St Petersburg Ballet Theatre Boris Eifman, Liza Chaikina str. 2, St Petersburg, 197198, Russia. *Telephone:* (812) 232-23-70 (Office); (812) 164-01-88 (Home). *Fax:* (812) 232-23-70 (Office).

EIGEN, Manfred, Dr rer. nat; German physical chemist; b. 9 May 1927, Bochum; s. of Ernst Eigen and Hedwig Feld; m. Elfriede Müller; one s. one d.; ed Georg-August-Univ. zu Göttingen; Max-Planck Inst. of Physical Chem., Göttingen, as Asst, later as Prof. and Head of Dept 1953–, Dir 1964; Hon. Prof. Technical Univ., Göttingen 1971–; Pres. Studienstiftung des Deutschen Volkes 1983–; mem. Akad. der Wissenschaften, Göttingen; Foreign Assoc. mem. Nat. Acad. of Sciences, USA; Foreign mem. Royal Soc., UK, Acad. Française 1978; Hon. Dr Univ. of Washington, St Louis Univ., Harvard Univ. and Cambridge Univ. and numerous other hon. degrees; Foreign hon. mem. American Acad. of Arts and Sciences; Otto Hahn Prize 1967; Nobel Prize for Chem.(jt recipient) for investigation of extremely rapid chemical reactions by means of disturbing the (molecular) equilibrium by the action of very short energy pulses 1967. *Address:* Georg-Dehio-Weg 14, 37075, Germany.

EINARSSON, Sveinn; Icelandic theatre director and author; b. 18 Sept. 1934, Reykjavik; s. of Einar Ól Sveinsson and Kristjana Thorsteinsdóttir; m. Thora Kristjánsdóttir 1964; one d.; ed Univ. of Stockholm and Sorbonne, Paris; Artistic Dir Reykjavik Theatre Co. 1963–72 (Hon. mem. 1991); Prin. Reykjavik Theatre School 1963–70; Gen. Man. and Artistic Dir Nat. Theatre of Iceland 1972–83; Head of Programme Production, Icelandic State TV 1989–93; Counsellor, Ministry of Culture 1983–89, 1993–; Chair. Icelandic Nat. Comm. for UNESCO 1995–; Artistic Dir Reykjavik Arts Festival 1998–2001; Vice-Pres. Int. Theatre Inst. 1979–81; mem. (part-time) Faculty, Univ. of Iceland 1970–; now freelance director and author; has directed about 80 productions (including opera) on stage and TV in Iceland and other Nordic countries and UK; productions also presented in Germany, Venezuela, Canada, the Baltic States and Korea (Theatre of Nations); several appointments with the Council of Europe: Chair. several cultural cttees; Vice-Pres. Nordic Theatre Union 1975–82; mem. Exec. Bd UNESCO 2001–; hon. mem. of several socs etc.; Officer, Order of White Rose of Finland, Order of Merit (Norway), Children's Book of Year Award 1986, Clara Lachmann Prize 1990, First Prize, Short Story Competition, 50th Anniversary of Repub. of Iceland 1994, Jón Sigurdsson Prize 1997. *Plays:* Egg of Life 1983, I'm Gold and Treasures 1984, Bukolla 1991, Bandamannasaga 1992, The Amlodi Saga 1996, The Daughter of the Poet 1998, Edda 2000. *Television:* (plays) A Stop on My Way 1971, Time is in No Harmony with Me 1993. *Publications include:* on theatre: Theatre By the Lake 1972, My Nine Years Down There 1987, Íslensk Leiklist (History of Icelandic Theatre, Vol. I) 1991, Vol. II 1996, My Eleven Years Up There 2000; novel: The Electricity Man 1998; children's books: Gabriella in Portugal 1985, Dordingull 1994. *Leisure interests:* music, skiing. *Address:* Ministry of Culture, Solvholsgata 4, 101 Reykjavik (Office); Tjarnargata 26, 101 Reykjavik, Iceland (Home). *Telephone:* 551-4032 (Home); 560-9524 (Office). *Fax:* 562 3068 (Office). *E-mail:* sveinn.einarsson@mrn.stjr .is.

EINIK, Michael, MBA; American diplomatist; b. 1949, New York; ed Univ. of Miami, George Washington Univ., Washington, DC; joined Dept of State 1972; Econ./Commercial Officer Brasilia, then San Salvador; with Bureau of Econ. and Business Affairs, Dept of State; staff Asst to Asst Sec. of State; worked in Office of Fuels and Energy during 1970s oil crisis; Petroleum Officer, Embassy, Nigeria 1981; served in Econ. Section, Moscow; Prin. Officer, Consulate-Gen., Zagreb representing US in both Croatia and Slovenia 1988–92; Chief of Personnel, European Bureau 1992–94; Deputy Chief of Mission, Bucharest; Amb. to Macedonia 1999–. *Address:* American Embassy, Ilindenska bb, 91000 Skopje, Macedonia (Office). *Telephone:* (91) 116180 (Office). *Fax:* (91) 118105 (Office). *E-mail:* usis@usemb-skopje.mpt .com.mk (Office).

EIRIKSSON, Gudmundur, LLM, BS, AB; Icelandic judge; b. 26 Oct. 1947, Winnipeg, Canada; s. of Rev. Eirikur Sverrir Brynjolfsson and Gudrun Gudmundsdottir; m. Thorey Vigdis Olafsdottir 1973; one s. three d.; ed Rutgers Coll., USA, King's Coll., Univ. of London, UK, Columbia Univ., USA; Law of the Sea Officer and Consultant, UN, New York 1974–77; Asst Legal Adviser, Legal Adviser, Ministry of Foreign Affairs, Iceland 1977–96, Amb. 1988–96; Rep. of Iceland to Third UN Conf. on Law of the Sea 1978–82; mem. UN Int. Law Comm. 1987–96; Judge, Int. Tribunal for the Law of the Sea 1987–; Visiting Scholar Univ. of Va Law School, USA 1984–85; lecturer Univ. of Iceland 1987–96; Visiting Prof. of Law, Univ. of New Mexico School of Law 1994–95; Pres. Council of N Atlantic Salmon Conservation Org. 1984–88; Grand Kt, Order of the Icelandic Falcon. *Address:* International Tribunal for the Law of the Sea, Wexstrasse 4, 20355 Hamburg, Germany.

EISELE, Lt-Gen. Manfred S.; German army officer; b. 17 March 1938, Wilhelmshaven; s. of Wilhelm Eisele and Gertrud Eisele-Meyer; m. Elke Krümpelmann 1962; two d.; ed Blankenese High School, Mil. Acad., Gen. Staff Acad., Hamburg, USA Command and Gen. Staff Coll. and Royal Coll. of Defence Studies; Commdg Officer, Artillery-Bn 125, Bayreuth 1977–78; Chef de Cabinet/Chief of Gen. Staff, Bonn 1978–80; Head of Public Information, Ministry of Defence 1980–81; Commdg Officer, Mechanized Infantry Brigade 17, Hamburg 1984–88; Chief, Combat Requirements Brigade, Supreme HQ Allied Forces Europe (SHAPE), Mons, Belgium 1988–91; Dir Politico-Military Affairs, Ministry of Defence, Bonn 1991–92; Commdg Officer, 12th Panzer Div. Würzburg 1992–94, Armed Forces Office, Bonn 1994; Asst Sec.-Gen. UN Dept of Peace-Keeping Operations 1994; Bundesverdienstkreuz, Legion of Merit, USA, Grand Cross, Rider of Vadar, Bulgaria; Dag Hammarskjöld Medal. *Publications:* Die Vereinten Nationen und das Internationale Krisenmanagement (preface by Kofi Annan) 2000. *Leisure interests:* international politics, history, music, sport. *Address:* Ravensburgstrasse 2B, 97209 Veitshöchheim, Germany. *Telephone:* (931) 9500055. *Fax:* (931) 9500042. *E-mail:* E.u.M.Eisele@t-online.de (Home).

EISEN, Herman N(athaniel), AB, MD; American immunologist and microbiologist; b. 15 Oct. 1918, Brooklyn, NY; s. of Joseph M. Eisen and Lena M. (Karush) Eisen; m. Natalie Aronson 1948; three s. two d.; ed New York Univ.; Prof. of Medicine (Dermatology), Washington Univ., St Louis 1955–61, Prof. of Microbiology and Head of Dept 1961–73; Dermatologist-in-Chief, Barnes Hosp. 1995–61, 1978–90; Prof. of Immunology, MIT 1973–89, Whitehead Inst. Prof. of Immunology 1982–89, Prof. Emer. 1989–; mem. Bd Scientific Advisors Mass. Gen. Hospital, Boston 1977–, Boston Children's Hospital 1976–, Howard Hughes Medical Inst., Sharp & Dohme Research Laboratories, Rahway 1976–; Harvey Lecturer 1964; Consultant to Surgeons-Gen. of Public Health Service, Dept of the Army; Chair. Study Section for Allergy and Immunology, Nat. Insts of Health 1964–68; mem. editorial bds of Journal of Immunology, Bacteriological Reviews, Physiological Reviews, Proceedings of the Nat. Acad. of Sciences of USA; mem. Bd, Merck, Sharpe and Dohme, Howard Hughes Medical Inst.; mem. American Soc. for Clinical Investigation (Vice-Pres. 1963–64), American Asscn of Immunologists (Pres. 1968–69), American Soc. for Biological Chemists, American Asscn of Physicians, Inst. of Medicine, NAS, American Acad. of Arts and Sciences; New York Univ. Medical Science Achievement Award 1978, Dupont Award, Clinical Ligand Soc. 1987, Outstanding Investigator Award, Nat. Cancer Inst. 1986, Behring-Heidelberger Award, American Asscn of Immunologists 1993. *Publications:* Methods in Medical Research Vol. 10 (Ed.) 1964, Microbiology (co-author) 1967–90, Immunology 1974–90, Contemporary Topics in Molecular Immunology Vol. 5 (Ed.) 1976; over 200 scientific articles. *Leisure interests:* landscape gardening, tennis. *Address:* Center for Cancer Research, Massachusetts Institute of Technology, BE 17R, 128 77 Massachusetts Avenue, Cambridge, MA 02139-4307 (Office); 9 Homestead Street, Waban, MA 02168, USA (Home). *Telephone:* (617) 253-6406. *Fax:* (617) 258-6172. *E-mail:* hneisen@mit.edu (Office).

EISENBERG, Leon, MD, MA; American physician and professor of psychiatry; b. 8 Aug. 1922, Philadelphia; s. of Morris Eisenberg and Elizabeth Sabreen; m. 1st Ruth Bleier 1947 (divorced 1967); m. 2nd Carola Guttmacher 1967; one s. one d.; ed Univ. of Pennsylvania, Mt. Sinai Hosp., New York, Sheppard Pratt Hosp., Baltimore, Johns Hopkins Hosp., Baltimore; Capt. US Army Medical Corps 1948–50; Instructor in Psychiatry and Pediatrics, Johns Hopkins Medical School 1954, Asst Prof. 1955–58, Assoc. Prof. 1958–61, Prof. of Child Psychiatry 1961–67; Chief of Psychiatry Massachusetts Gen. Hosp. 1967–74; Prof. of Psychiatry, Harvard Medical School 1967–93, Chair. of Exec. Cttee, Dept of Psychiatry 1974–80, Presley Prof., Dept of Social Medicine and Health Policy 1980–93, Prof. Emer. 1993–; Royal Soc. of Medicine Visiting Prof. 1983; Queen Elizabeth II Lecturer, Canadian Pediatric Soc. 1986; Consultant, Div. of Mental Health, WHO 1980; Lilly Lecturer, Royal Coll. of Psychiatrists 1986; Dir WHO/Harvard Collaborating Center for Research and Training in Psychiatry 1986–; mem. Inst. of Medicine NAS 1974–; WHO expert advisory panel on Mental Health 1984–; Consultant, Child Mental Health, Pan American Health Org., Uruguay 1991; William Potter Lecturer, Thomas Jefferson Univ. 1992; mem. American Acad. of Arts and Sciences; Hon. ScD (Manchester) 1973, (Mass.) 1991; Hon. Fellow Royal Coll. of Psychiatrists 1985; Theobald Smith Award 1979, Aldrich Award 1980, Samuel T. Orton Award 1980, Dale Richmond Award, A.A.P. 1989, Special Presidential Commendation, American Psychiatric Asscn 1992; numerous other awards. *Publications:* many medical publs. *Leisure interests:* classical music, theatre, reading. *Address:* Harvard Medical School, Department of

Social Medicine, 641 Huntington Avenue, Boston, MA 02115; 9 Clement Circle, Cambridge, MA 02138, USA. *Telephone:* (617) 432-1710 (Office); (617) 868-0112 (Home). *Fax:* (617) 432-2565 (Office); (617) 432-2565. *E-mail:* leon_eisenberg@hms.harvard.edu (Home).

EISENHOWER, John Sheldon Doud, BS, MA; American author and diplomatist; b. 3 Aug. 1922, Denver, Colo; s. of the late Gen. Dwight D. Eisenhower (President of the USA 1953–61) and Mamie (Doud) Eisenhower; m. 1st Barbara Jean Thompson 1947 (divorced 1986); one s. three d.; m. 2nd Joanne Thompson 1990; ed Stadium High School, Tacoma, Wash., US Military Acad., West Point, Columbia Univ. and Armored Advance Course and General Staff Coll., US Army; 2nd Lt, US Army 1944, assigned to First Army, Second World War; Instructor in English, US Mil. Acad., West Point 1948–51; served as Battalion Operations Officer, Div. Asst Operations Officer and Div. Intelligence Officer, 3rd Div., Korea; Joint War Plans Div., Army Staff, Pentagon 1957–58; Asst Staff Sec. in White House 1958–61; researcher and editor on Eisenhower memoirs The White House Years; Amb. to Belgium 1969–71; Consultant to President Nixon; Chair. Interagency Classification Review Cttee 1972–73; Brig.-Gen. US Army Reserve 1974; mem. Nat. Archives Advisory Cttee 1974–77; Chair. Pres.'s Advisory Cttee on Refugees 1975; , Order of the Crown (Belgium); Legion of Merit, Bronze Star, Army Commendation Ribbon, Combat Infantry Badge, Grand Cross. *Publications:* The Bitter Woods 1969, Strictly Personal 1974, Allies 1981, So Far From God 1989, Intervention! 1993, Agent of Destiny 1997, Yanks 2001. *Leisure interest:* aviation. *Address:* PO Box 778, Kimberton, PA 19442, USA (Home).

EISENMAN, Peter David, PhD, MS, FAIA; American architect; b. 11 Aug. 1932, Newark; s. of Herschel I. Eisenmann and Sylvia H. Heller; m. 1st Elizabeth Henderson 1963 (divorced 1990); one s. one d.; m. 2nd Cynthia Davidson 1990; one c.; ed Cornell Univ., Columbia Univ., Cambridge Univ.; Founder Inst. of Architecture and Urban Studies, New York 1967, Dir 1967–82; Architect-in-Residence American Acad., Rome 1976; with Eisenmann/Robertson Architects, New York 1980–88; Eisenmann Architects 1988–; commissioned to design Berlin Holocaust Memorial; Kea Prof. Univ. of Md 1978; Charlotte Davenport Prof., Yale Univ. 1980, Louis I. Kahn Prof. of Architecture 2001–; Arthur Rotch Prof., Harvard Univ. 1982–85; Irwin Chanin Distinguished Prof. 1986–; Louis H. Sullivan Research Prof.of Architecture, Univ. of Ill. 1987–93; John Williams Prof. of Architecture, Univ. of Ark. 1997; Arnold W. Brunner Memorial Prize in Architecture, American Acad. and Inst. of Arts and Letters 1984. *Principal works include:* Pvt. Residences Princeton, NJ, Hardwick, Vt, Lakeville and Cornwall, Conn. 1968–76, Housing, Koch-Friedrichstrasse, Berlin 1980–86, Wexner Center for Visual Arts, Columbus, Ohio 1983–89, Columbus Convention Centre 1988–93, Univ. of Cincinnati Coll. of Design, Art, Architecture and Planning 1988–96, Koizumi Sangyo Bldg, Tokyo 1989–90, Emory Univ. Art Centre 1991–95, Rebstock Park, Frankfurt, Germany 1991–95, Max Reinhardt Haus, Berlin 1992–, Haus Immendorff, Düsseldorf, Germany 1993–94, Jewish Museum, San Francisco 1996–, Library UN Complex, Geneva 1996–, Staten Island Inst. of Arts and Sciences 1997–, Holocaust Memorial, Berlin 1998–, City of Culture, Santiago de Compostela, Spain 1999–. *Address:* Eisenmann Architects, 41 W 25th Street, New York, NY 10010-2021, USA (Office).

EISENSTADT, Shmuel Noah, MA PhD; Israeli professor of sociology; b. 10 Sept. 1923, Warsaw, Poland; s. of Michael Eisenstadt and Rosa Baruchin; m. Shulamit Yaroshevski 1948; two s. one d.; ed Hebrew Univ. of Jerusalem and London School of Econs and Political Science; Chair. Dept of Sociology, Hebrew Univ., Jerusalem 1951–69, Prof. of Sociology 1959, Dean, Faculty of Social Sciences 1966–68; Fellow, Center for Advanced Studies in the Behavioral Sciences, Stanford Univ., USA 1955–56; Visiting Prof., Univ. of Oslo 1958, Univ. of Chicago 1960, Harvard Univ. 1966, 1968–69, 1975–80, Michigan 1970, Chicago 1971, Zürich 1975, Stanford 1984, 1986, 1987, 1988; Carnegie Visiting Prof., Mass. Inst. of Technology 1962–63; Simon Visiting Prof., Univ. of Manchester 1977; Research Fellow, Hoover Inst. 1986; Tanner Lecturer on Human Values, Univ. of Calif. 1988; Distinguished Visiting Prof., Univ. of Alberta, Canada 1989; Prof. Univ. of Chicago Cttee on Social Thought 1990–93; Max Weber Prof., Univ. of Heidelberg; Visiting Prof. Univ. of Erfurt 1998–2000; currently Rose Isaacs Prof. Emer. of Sociology, Hebrew Univ. of Jerusalem; Chair. Council on Community Relations, Israel 1962–64, Israeli Sociological Soc. 1969–72; mem. Advisory Bd Int. Encyclopedia of the Social Sciences; mem. Scientific Cttee Centro Gino Germani, Rome; Sr Fellow, Wilson Center for Int. Exchange, Washington 1996, 1998; Hon. Resident Fellow, Inst. of Sociology, Chinese Acad. of Social Sciences 2000; Foreign Fellow American Anthropological Asscn; Fellow Netherlands Inst. of Advanced Studies 1973; mem. Israel Acad. of Sciences and Humanities, Int. Sociological Soc., American Sociological Asscn; Foreign mem. American Philosophical Soc.; Foreign Hon. mem. American Acad. of Arts and Sciences; Foreign Assoc. NAS; Hon. Research Fellow, ANU 1977; Hon. Fellow Open Univ. Tel-Aviv, LSE; Dr hc (Helsinki) 1986, (Duke) 2002; Hon. LLD (Harvard), Hon. DHumLitt (Hebrew Union Coll. Jewish Inst. of Religion); Hon. DPhil (Tel-Aviv); McIver Award, American Sociological Asscn 1964, Rothschild Prize in the Social Sciences 1969, Israel Prize in the Social Sciences 1973, Int. Balzan Prize in Sociology 1988, Max Planck Research Award 1994, Amalphi Prize in European Sociology 2001, Humboldt Research Award 2002. *Publications:* The Absorption of Immigrants 1954, From Generation to Generation 1956, Essays on Sociological Aspects of Economical and Political Development 1961, The Political Systems of Empires 1963, (new edn with

special introduction) 1993, Essays on Comparative Institutions 1965, Modernization, Protest and Change 1966, Israeli Society 1968, The Protestant Ethic and Modernization 1968, Political Sociology of Modernization (in Japanese) 1968, Comparative Perceptives on Social Change (Ed.) 1968, Charisma and Institution Building: Selections from Max Weber (Ed.) 1968, Ensayos sobre el Cambio social y la Modernización (Spanish) 1969, Modernização e Mudança Social (Portuguese) 1969, Political Sociology (Ed.) 1970, Social Differentiation and Stratification 1971, Collection of Essays in Japanese 1971, Tradition, Change and Modernity 1973, Collection of Essays in Spanish 1973, Post-traditional Societies (Ed.) 1974, The Form of Sociology: Paradigms and Crises (with M. Curelaru) 1976, Macrosociology (with M. Curelaru) 1977, Revolutions and Transformation of Societies 1978, Patrons, Clients and Friends (with L. Roniger) 1984, Transformation of Israeli Society 1985, Origins and Diversity of Axial Age Civilizations (Ed.) 1986, Society, Culture and Urbanization (with A. Shachar) 1987, The Origins of the State Reconsidered (with M. Abitbol and N. Chazan) 1986, European Civilization in Comparative Perspective 1987, Center Formation, Protest Movements and Class Structure in Europe and the U.S. (with L. Roniger and A. Seligman) 1987, Patterns of Modernity I and II 1987, Kulturen der Achsenzeit (trans.) 1987, Die Transformation der Israelichen Gesellschaft (trans.) 1987, The Early State in African Perspective 1988, Knowledge and Society: Studies in the Sociological Culture, Past and Present (Co-Ed. with I. Silber) 1988, Japanese Models of Conflict Resolution (Co-Ed. with Eyal Ben-Ari) 1990, Martin Buber on Intersubjectivity and Cultural Creativity (Ed.), Jewish Civilization – The Jewish Historical Experience in a Comparative Perspective 1992, The Political Systems of Empires 1993, Power, Trust and Meaning 1995, Japanese Civilization–A Comparative View 1996, Modernità, Modernizzazione e Oltré 1997, Paradoxes of Democracy: Fragility, Continuity and Change 1999, Fundamentalism, Sectarianism and Revolutions 2000, Die Vielfalt der Moderne 2000, Public Spheres and Collective Identities (Co-Ed. with W. Schluchter and B. Wittrock), Multiple Modernities (Ed.) 2002, Fundamentalism and Modernity (in Hebrew) 2002. *Address:* The Hebrew University, Mount Scopus, Jerusalem (Office); 30 Radak Street, Jerusalem, Israel (Home). *Telephone:* 2-5605222 (Office); 2-5632467. *Fax:* 2-5619293 (Office).

EISNER, Michael Dammann, BS; American entertainment executive; b. 7 March 1942, Mt Kisco, NY; s. of Lester Dammann and Margaret Dammann; m. Jane Breckenridge 1967; three s.; ed Lawrenceville School, Denison Univ.; Sr Vice-Pres., Prime-Time Production and Devt, ABC Entertainment Corpn 1973–76; Pres. and COO Paramount Pictures Corpn 1976–84; Chair. and CEO The Walt Disney Co. 1984–; Chevalier, Légion d'honneur. *Leisure interests:* spectator sports. *Address:* Walt Disney Co., 500 South Buena Vista Street, Burbank, CA 91521-0006, USA. *Telephone:* (818) 560-1000.

EISNER, Thomas, BA, PhD; American professor of biology; b. 25 June 1929, Berlin, Germany; s. of Hans E. Eisner and Margarete Heil-Eisner; m. Maria L. R. Löbell 1952; three d.; ed High School and Preparatory School, Montevideo, Uruguay, Champlain Coll., Plattsburgh, NY and Harvard Univ; Research Fellow in Biology, Harvard Univ. 1955–57; Asst Prof. of Biology, Cornell Univ. 1957–62, Assoc. Prof. 1962–66, Prof. of Biology 1966–76, Jacob Gould Schurman Prof. of Chemical Ecology 1976–, Dir Cornell Inst. for Research in Chemical Ecology 1992–; Sr Fellow Cornell Center for the Environment 1994–; Consultant, World Environment and Research Programme MacArthur Foundation 1987–92; Lalor Fellow 1954–55, Guggenheim Fellow 1964–65, 1972–73; mem. Nat. Council for Nature Conservancy 1969–74, Council Fed. American Scientists 1977–81, External Scientific Advisory Cttee, MBL, Woods Hole 1989–91, 1996–99; foreign mem. Royal Soc. 1997; Dir National Audubon Soc. 1970–75; Pres. American Soc. of Naturalists 1988; mem. NAS 1969, American Philosophical Soc. 1986, Akademie Naturforscher Leopoldina 1986; Fellow, American Acad. of Arts and Sciences 1969, Animal Behavior Soc. 1971, American Entomological Soc. 1987, Zero Population Growth (Dir 1969–70); Chair. Biology Section, AAAS 1980–81, mem. Cttee for Scientific Freedom and Responsibility 1980–87, Chair. Subcttee on Science and Human Rights 1981–87; mem. Steering Cttee on Consequences of Nuclear War 1983–87, Scientific Advisory Council, World Wildlife Fund 1983–90, NAS Cttee on Human Rights 1987–90, Advisory Council, Monell Chemical Senses Center 1988–2000, World Resources Inst. 1988–95; mem. Task Force for the 90s, AIBS 1990–99, Scientific Advisory Council, Xerces Soc. (Pres. 1992–), Scientific Advisory Cttee, Cttee for Nat. Inst. for the Environment 1991–, Entomology Soc. of America Standing Cttee on Fellows 1993–94, Bd of Dirs Union of Concerned Scientists 1993–; Chair. Advisory Council, Center for Biodiversity and Conservation, American Museum of Natural History 1995–99; Hon. PhD (Würzburg, Zürich, Göteborg, Drexel); Newcomb-Cleveland Prize (with E. O. Wilson) of AAAS 1967, Founders Memorial Award of Entomological Soc. of America 1969, Prof. of Merit, Cornell Univ. 1973, Archie F. Carr Medal 1983, four awards for film Secret Weapons, BBC TV 1984, Procter Prize 1986, Karl Ritter von Frisch Medal 1988, Centennial Medal, Harvard Univ. 1989, Tyler Prize 1990, Esselen Award 1991, Silver Medal, Int. Soc. of Chemical Ecology 1991, Nat. Medal of Science 1994, Green Globe Award 1997, John Wiley Jones Award 1999; numerous other awards. *Publications:* over 400 technical papers and nine books on animal behaviour, chemical ecology, comparative physiology, chemical communication in animals, conservation. *Leisure interests:* photography, cinematography, orchestra conducting, piano. *Address:* Department of Neurobiology and

Behavior, Division of Biological Sciences, W347 Mudd Hall, Cornell University, Ithaca, NY 14853, USA. *Telephone:* (607) 255-4464. *Fax:* (607) 255-6186.

EITAN, Lt-Gen. Raphael; Israeli army officer; b. 1929, Tel Adashim; m.; four c.; ed Tel Aviv and Haifa Univs.; joined Palmach when 17; Deputy Co. Commdr 1948; various posts with paratroops 1950–53; Commdr Paratroop Unit, Sinai campaign 1956; Deputy Commdr Paratroop Brigade 1958, Commdr 1964–67; Commdr Jordan Valley Brigade 1967–68; Chief Paratroop and Infantry Officer, rank of Brig.-Gen. 1968–73; Commdr Div. on Golan Heights, rank of Maj.-Gen., Yom Kippur War 1973–74; CO Northern Command 1974–77; Chief of Gen. Staff Br. 1977–78; Chief of Gen. Staff 1978–83; mem. Ministerial Defence Cttee 1990–; Minister of Agric. and Rural Devt 1990–91, 1996–99; Deputy Prime Minister, Minister of Environment 1996–99. *Address:* c/o Ministry of Agriculture, P.O. Box 7011, 8 Arania Street, Tel Aviv 61070, Israel.

EIZENSTAT, Stuart Elliot, LLB; American diplomatist, lawyer and government official; b. 15 Jan. 1943, Chicago; s. of Leo Eizenstat and Sylvia Eizenstat; m. Frances Taylor 1967; two s.; ed Univ. of North Carolina and Harvard Univ.; admitted Ga Bar 1967, DC Bar 1981; mem. White House staff 1967–68; mem. nat. campaign staff for Hubert M. Humphrey 1968; law clerk, US Dist Court, Ga 1968–70; partner, Powell, Goldstein, Frazer & Murphy, Washington, DC 1970–77, 1981–93, Chair. Washington Office 1991–93; Asst to Pres. of USA for Domestic Affairs and Policy 1977–81, Dir Domestic Policy Staff 1977–81; Amb. to EU 1993–96; Under-Sec. of Commerce for Int. Trade 1996–97; Special Envoy Property Restitution in Cen. Europe 1993–96, Dept of State Property Claims in Cen. Europe 1995–97; Under-Sec. of Econ., Business and Agricultural Affairs 1997–99; Deputy Sec. of Treasury 1999–2001; Alt. Gov. IBRD 1998–99; State Dept Special Envoy on Property Claims in Cen. Europe; Special Rep. of Pres. and Sec. of State on Holocaust Issues 1999–2001; Adjunct Lecturer, J. F. Kennedy School of Govt Harvard Univ. 1981–93; Guest Scholar, Brookings Inst. Washington 1981; Dir of Int. Trade and Finance, Covington & Burling 2001–; mem. Presidential Task Force on US Int. Broadcasting 1991; mem. Bd of Dirs Hercules Inc. Wilmington, Israel Discount Bank of New York, P.S.I. Holdings Inc. Indianapolis; numerous other public appointments; Democrat; hon. degrees (Yeshiva Univ.) 1996, (North Carolina) 2000, (Jewish Theological Seminary) 2000; numerous awards including Leadership Award, Secr. of State 1999, B'nai B'rith Leadership Award 2000, Washington Inst. for Jewish Leadership and Values award for leadership 2001. *Publications include:* The Path to History (with A. Young) 1973, Environmental Auditing Handbook 1984, The American Agenda: Advice to the 41st President (co-ed.) 1988; articles in newspapers and professional journals. *Leisure interest:* tennis. *Address:* Covington & Burling, 1201 Pennsylvania Avenue, NW, Washington, DC 20004 (Office); 9107 Brierly Road, Chevy Chase, MD 20815-5654, USA (Home).

EKANGAKI, Nzo; Cameroonian politician; b. 22 March 1934, Nguti; ed Bali Coll., Hope Waddle Training Inst., Calabar, Nigeria and Univs of Ibadan, Nigeria, London, Oxford and Bonn; served in several posts in Cameroon Admin. 1959–60; Deputy Minister of Foreign Affairs 1962–64; Minister of Public Health and Population 1964–65, of Labour and Social Welfare 1965–72; Sec.-Gen. Org. of African Unity 1972–74; Adviser to Presidency, Yaoundé 1985–; Sec.-Gen. Kamerun Nat. Democratic Party (KNDP) 1962–66; mem. of Political Bureau, Cameroon Nat. Union Party (CNU) 1966–75; mem. Parl. S Cameroon 1961–62, mem. first Nat. Federal Assembly 1962–65, 1965–71; del. to many int. confs, to WHO Conf., Geneva 1964, to several Int. Labour Confs; rep. on many missions abroad. *Publications:* An Introduction to East Cameroon 1956, To the Nigerian People 1958. *Address:* c/o Presidency of the Republic, Yaoundé, Cameroon.

EKEUS, Carl Rolf; Swedish diplomatist; b. 7 July 1935, Kristinehamn; s. of Axel Eriksson and Margit Johansson; m. Kerstin C. Oldfelt 1970; three s. three d.; ed Univ. of Stockholm; law practice, Karlstad 1959–62; Legal Div. Ministry of Foreign Affairs 1962–63; Sec. Swedish Embassy, Bonn 1963–65; First Sec. Nairobi 1965–67; Special Asst to Minister of Foreign Affairs 1967–73; First Sec., Counsellor, Perm. Mission to UN, New York 1974–78; Counsellor, The Hague 1978–83; Amb. and Perm. Rep. to Conf. on Disarmament, Geneva 1983–89, Chair. Cttee on Chemical Weapons 1984, 1987; Amb. and Head of Swedish Del. to CSCE, Vienna 1989–93; Chair. Cttee on Principles Chapter of Charter of Paris 1991; Chair. CSCE Vienna Group 1993; Exec. Chair. UN Special Comm. on Iraq 1991–97; Amb. to USA 1997–2000; Chair. Stockholm Int. Peace Research Inst. 2000–; OSCE High Commr on Nat. Minorities 2001–; mem. Canberra Comm. on the Elimination of Nuclear Weapons, advisory Bd Center for Non-Proliferation, Monetary Inst., Tokyo Forum on Non-Proliferation and Disarmament; mem. advisory Bd of UN Sec.-Gen. on Disarmament Matters 1999, Bd Dirs Nuclear Threat Initiative 2001, Bd Atel and Margaret At-son Johnson Foundation 2001–; mem. Royal Acad. of War Science, Stockholm 2001; Hon. LLD (California Lutheran Univ.) 1999; Wateler Peace Prize, Carnegie Foundation 1997. *Publications:* reports as Special Investigator on the submarine question 1980–2001, Sweden's security policy 1969–89 2002; several articles on foreign policy, int. economy, nuclear non-proliferation, disarmament and arms control, chemical weapons, European security, Iraq and weapons of mass destruction. *Leisure interests:* piano playing, tennis. *Address:* High Commission on National Minorities, Prinsessegracht 22, 2514 AP The Hague, Netherlands (Office); Stockholm International Peace Research Institute, Signalistgatan 9, 169 70 Solna (Office); Rådmansgatan 57, 11360 Stockholm, Sweden (Home). *Telephone:*

(70) 3125500 (The Hague) (Office); (8) 312653 (Home). *Fax:* (70) 3635910 (The Hague) (Office). *E-mail:* rekeus@hcnm.org (Office). *Website:* www.sipri.se (Office); www.osce.org/hcnm (Office).

EKSTEEN, Jacobus Adriaan, MA; South African diplomatist, broadcasting executive (retd) and political consultant; b. 31 Oct. 1942, Volksrust; s. of Jacobus Adriaan and Helena Barendina Hendrika (née Baard) Eksteen; m. Ria Hofmeyr 1991; three s. (previous marriage); ed Univs of Pretoria and South Africa; entered Civil Service 1961; mem. SA legal team at Int. Court of Justice in South West Africa (Namibia) 1966; Third Sec., Second Sec., then First Sec., Embassy, USA 1968–73; served in Head Office of Dept of Foreign Affairs as Head of UN and South West Africa sections 1973–76; Counsellor and Deputy Perm. Rep. at SA Perm. Mission to UN 1976, Minister 1978, Acting Perm. Rep. 1977–79, Perm. Rep. and Amb. 1979–81; Head of Planning Div., Ministry of Foreign Affairs 1981–83; mem. SA Del. to Patent Cooperation Treaty, Washington 1970, to INTELSAT Conf., Washington 1971, to UN Gen. Assembly 1972, 1979, 1981; involved in all discussions on Namibia 1977–83; presented South Africa's case in UN Security Council Aug. 1981; Dir-Gen. (desig.) South African Broadcasting Corp. 1983, Dir-Gen. 1984–88; SA Rep. in Namibia 1990–91; Amb. and Perm. Rep. to UN and Special Agencies in Geneva 1992–95; Amb. to Turkey (also accred to Azerbaijan, Kyrgyzstan, Turkmenistan, Uzbekistan) 1995. *Leisure interests:* reading, walking, stamp collecting, hunting. *Address:* c/o Ministry of Foreign Affairs, Union Buildings, East Wing, Government Avenue, Pretoria 0002, South Africa.

EKWENSI, Cyprian; Nigerian author and pharmacist; b. 26 Sept. 1921, Minna, Northern Nigeria; ed Govt Coll., Ibadan, Achimota Coll., Ghana, School of Forestry, Ibadan, Higher Coll., Yaba, Chelsea School of Pharmacy, Univ. of London, Iowa Univ.; Lecturer in Biology, Chem. and English, Igbobi Coll., Lagos 1947–49; Lecturer, School of Pharmacy, Lagos 1949–56; Pharmacist, Nigerian Medical Service 1956; Head of Features, Nigerian Broadcasting Corpn 1956–61; Dir of Information, Fed. Ministry of Information, Lagos 1961–66; Dir of Information Services, Enugu 1966; Chair. East Cen. State Library Board, Enugu 1971–75; Man. Dir Star Printing and Publishing Co. Ltd 1975–79, Niger Eagle Press 1981–; Visiting Lecturer, Iowa Univ.; mem. Pharmaceutical Socs of GB and Nigeria, Nigerian Arts Council, Soc. of Nigerian Authors, Inst. Public Relations Nigeria and UK; Dag Hammarskjöld Int. Award for Literary Merit 1968. *Publications:* When Love Whispers, Ikolo the Wrestler 1947, The Leopard's Claw 1950, People of the City 1954, Passport of Mallam Ilia, The Drummer Boy 1960, Jagua Nana 1961, Burning Grass, An African Night's Entertainment, Yaba Round about Murder 1962, Beautiful Feathers 1963, Great Elephant Bird, Rainmaker 1965, Lokotown, Juju Rock, Trouble in Form VI, Iska, Boa Suitor 1966, Coal Camp Boy 1973, Samankwe in the Strange Forest 1974, Samankwe and the Highway Robbers, Restless City, Christmas Gold 1975, Survive the Peace 1976, Divided We Stand 1980, Motherless Baby 1980, Jaguanana's Daughter 1986, For a Roll of Parchment 1986, Beneath the Convent Wall 1987, Restless City and Xmas Gold, Behind the Convent Wall 1988, Death at Mile Two 1988, Lagos Love Deal 1988, Masquerade Time 1991, King Forever 1992. *Leisure interests:* photography, Adire Tie-Dye. *Address:* Hillview Crescent, Independence Layout, P.O. Box 317, Enugu, Nigeria (Home).

EKWUEME, Alex Ifeanyichukwu, BArch, LLB, MA, PhD; Nigerian politician, architect and lawyer; b. 21 Oct. 1932, Oko; s. of the late Lazarus Ibeabuchi Ekwueme and Agnes Nkwodumma Ekwueme; ed King's Coll., Lagos, Univ. of Washington, Seattle, Univ. of Strathclyde, Glasgow, Nigerian Law School, Lagos; est. Ekwueme Associates (architects) 1958; fmr Pres. Nigerian Inst. of Architects, Architectural Registration Council of Nigeria; Vice-Pres. candidate with Alhaji Shehu Shagari in Presidential elections Aug. 1979; Vice-Pres. of Nigeria 1979–83; detained 1983, released July 1986; fmr mem. Nat. Exec. of banned Nat. Party of Nigeria; mem. Nat. Constitutional Conf. 1994–95; Chair. All-Nigeria Politicians Summit Conf. 1995; Founding Chair. and Chair. Bd of Trustees People's Democratic Party 1998–; Fulbright Scholar 1952; Grand Commdr Order of the Niger 1988–; several hon. doctorates. *Leisure interests:* reading, lawn tennis. *Address:* Oko, Anambra State, Nigeria. *Telephone:* (42) 454815. *Fax:* (42) 456667; (42) 254757 (Office).

EL ADM, Khaled Charles, BSc; Egyptian library consultant and information adviser; b. 29 April 1957, Alexandria; ed St Mark's Coll., Faculty of Science and Technology, Paris, Alexandria Univ.; scientific reporter, Al-Ahram daily newspaper; Exec. Vice-Pres. Egyptian Scientific Clubs 1971–84; library science consultant and reference librarian, pvt. and govt sectors 1979–; Project Man., Solid Waste Project, El-Mokattam Dist, Cairo 1987; f. 43 scientific clubs in Egypt 1972–83, Cultural Heritage Asscn in Africa 1982, Nubian and Historical Heritage Asscn 1990; mem. Alexandria Planetarium project cttee 1982, numerous int. library science and other asscns. *Publications:* 34 scientific and library science articles in Arab and foreign journals. *Leisure interests:* landscape photography, history of the ancient world, tennis, basketball, volleyball, reading, classical music, plastic arts. *Address:* P.O. Box 37, Ibrahimieh (21321), Alexandria; P.O. Box 421, Ibrahimieh (21321) Alexandria, Egypt. *Telephone:* (3) 5975238.

EL FASSI, Abbas; Moroccan politician; b. 18 Sept. 1940, Berkane; m.; four c.; ed Univ. Mohammed V, Rabat; Minister of Housing 1977–81, of Handicrafts and Social Affairs 1981–85, of Social Devt, Solidarity, Employment and Professional Training 2000–02, Minister of State 2002–; Amb. to France (also accred to Tunisia) 1990–94; Gen. Sec. Istiqlal Party 1998–; mem. Bd of Dirs

Caisse Nat. de Sécurité Sociale, Entraide Nationale, Social Devt Agency. *Address:* c/o Ministry of Social Development, Solidarity, Employment and Professional Training, Rabat (Office); 12 rue Larbi Ouazzani, Rabat, Morocco (Home).

EL GOULLI, Salah Eddine, DIur; Tunisian business executive and fmr diplomatist; b. 22 June 1919, Sousse; m. M. J. Zeineb Larre 1958; one d.; ed Univ. of Paris (Sorbonne); Consul Gen., Marseilles 1956–57; Minister, Embassy, Washington, DC 1958–61; Amb. to Belgium (also accred to Netherlands, Luxembourg, EEC), to UN 1969–70, to USA (also accred to Venezuela and Mexico) 1970–73, to Netherlands 1976–78; Adviser to Minister of Foreign Affairs 1973–75, 1979–81; Pres. Philips Electronics Tunisia 1981–90, World Trade Centre, Tunis 1990–; Grand Cordon of the Repub. of Tunisia 1963, Grand Cross of Leopold 1964, Grand Cross Crown of Belgium 1969, Grand Cross Chêne 1964, Grand Cross Nassau, Luxembourg 1969. *Publications:* lectures on political and econ. matters in USA, Europe and Middle East; numerous articles in European and Tunisian press. *Leisure interests:* golf, reading, swimming. *Address:* 2 rue des Roses, 2070 La Marsa, Tunisia. *Telephone:* 774-307. *Fax:* 707-639. *E-mail:* wtct@planet.tn (Office).

ELARABY, Nabil A., JSD, LLM; Egyptian diplomatist and international arbitrator; b. 15 March 1935; m.; two s. one d.; ed Cairo Univ., New York Univ. Law School; fmr Rep. of Egypt to various UN bodies, including Gen. Ass., Security Council, ECOSOC, Comm. on Human Rights, Conf. on Disarmament; Legal Adviser to Egyptian del. to UN Middle East Peace Conf., Geneva 1973–75; Dir Legal and Treaties Dept, Ministry of Foreign Affairs 1976–78, 1983–87; Amb. to India 1981–83; led Egyptian del. to Taba talks 1986–89; Deputy Perm. Rep. to UN, New York 1978–81, Perm. Rep. 1991–99; Perm. Rep., UN Office at Geneva 1987–91; Judge, Judicial Tribunal of Org. of Arab Petroleum Exporting Countries (OAPEC) 1990–; mem. Int. Law Comm. 1994–2001; Partner Zaki Hashem and Partners 1998; mem. International Court of Justice 2001–; apptd by ICC as Arbitrator in a dispute concerning Suez Canal 1989; mem. Governing Bd Stockholm Int. Peace Research Inst.; Commr UN Compensation Comm., Geneva 1999–2001; Visiting Scholar, Robert F. Wagner Grad. School of Public Service, New York Univ. 1992–93; fmr chair. numerous UN cttees and working groups. *Leisure interest:* tennis. *Address:* International Court of Justice, 1 Peace Palace, Carnegieplein 2, 2517 KJ The Hague, Netherlands (Office). *Telephone:* (70) 3022422 (Office). *Website:* www.icj-cij.org (Office).

ELBEGDORJ, Tsahiagiyn; Mongolian politician; b. 30 March 1963, Zereg Som, Hovd Prov.; m.; two c.; machinist Erdenet copper mine 1981–82; army service 1982; mil. reporter Mil. School, Lvov, Ukraine 1983–88; journalist Ulaan-Od (Ministry of Defence newspaper) 1988–90; mem. Co-ordinating Council of Mongolian Democratic Union (MDU) 1989, leader 1990; deputy to People's Great Hural 1990–92, also mem. State Little Hural; mem. State Great Hural 1992–94, 1996, Vice-Chair. July 1996–; mem. Gen. Council Mongolian Nat. Democratic Party 1994, Leader 1996–, also Leader Democratic Union coalition in State Great Hural; Prime Minister of Mongolia April–Dec. 1998. *Address:* Mongolian National Democratic Party, Chingisiyn Örgön Chölöö 1, Ulan Bator, Mongolia. *Telephone:* 372810. *Fax:* 372810.

ELDER, Mark Philip, CBE, MA; British conductor; b. 2 June 1947; s. of John Elder and Helen Elder; m. Amanda Jane Stein 1980; one d.; ed Bryanston School and Corpus Christi Coll., Cambridge; music staff Wexford Festival 1969–70; Chorus Master and Asst Conductor Glyndebourne 1970–71; music staff Covent Garden 1970–72, Staff Conductor Australian Opera 1972–74, English Nat. Opera 1974, Assoc. Conductor 1977, Music Dir 1979–93; Prin. Guest Conductor London Mozart Players 1980–83, BBC Symphony Orchestra 1982–85, City of Birmingham Symphony Orchestra 1991–95; Music Dir Rochester Philharmonic Orchestra, NY 1989–94, Hallé Orchestra Sept. 2000–; Olivier Award for Outstanding Contribution to Opera 1990. *Address:* c/o Ingpen & Williams, 26 Wadham Road, London, SW15 2LR, England.

ELDER, Murdoch George, DSc, MD, FRCS, FRCOG; British professor of obstetrics and gynaecology; b. 4 Jan. 1938, Kolkata, India; s. of the late A. J. Elder and L. A. C. Elder; m. Margaret McVicker 1964; two s.; ed Edinburgh Acad. and Edinburgh Univ.; lecturer, Royal Univ. of Malta 1969–71; Sr Lecturer and Reader, Univ. of London, Charing Cross Hosp. Medical School 1971–78; Prof. of Obstetrics and Gynaecology, Univ. of London at Hammersmith Hosp. 1978–98; Dean, Royal Postgrad. Medical School Inst. of Obstetrics and Gynaecology 1985–95; Chair. Div. of Paediatrics, Obstetrics and Gynaecology, Imperial Coll. School of Medicine, Univ. of London 1996–98; Visiting Prof. UCLA 1984, 1986, 1997, Univ. of Singapore 1987, Univ. of Natal 1988; consultant to WHO and other int. orgs etc.; mem. WHO Scientific and Ethics Research Group; External Examiner to Univs of Edin., Cambridge, Oxford, London, Leeds, Bristol, Glasgow, Dundee, Malta, Malaya, Malaysia, Helsinki, Rotterdam, Cape Town, Singapore; Hon. Fellow Imperial Coll. School of Medicine; Silver Medal, Hellenic Obstetrical Soc. 1984, Bronze Medal, Helsinki Univ., 1996. *Publications include:* Human Fertility Control (co-author) 1979, Preterm Labor (co-ed.) 1981 and 1996, Obstetrics and Gynaecology 2002; more than 240 original publs in field of biochemistry of reproduction and clinical high-risk obstetrics. *Leisure interests:* travel, golf. *Address:* Easter Calzeat, Broughton, Biggar, ML12 6HQ, Scotland. *Telephone:* (1899) 830359. *E-mail:* melder@eastercalzeat.fsnet.co.uk (Home).

ELDIN, Gérard; French civil servant and banker; b. 21 March 1927, Cannes; s. of Charles and Elise Eldin; m. Marie-Cécile Bergerot 1960; two s. two d.; ed Bethany Coll., USA, Univ. d'Aix-en-Provence and Ecole Nationale d'Admi-

nistration; Insp. of Finances 1954–58; served in the Treasury 1958–63; Adviser to Minister of Finance and Econ. Affairs 1963–65; Deputy Dir Dept of Planning 1965–70; Deputy Sec.-Gen. OECD 1970–80; Deputy Gov. Crédit Foncier de France 1980–86; Chair. Foncier-Investissement 1982–86, Crédit-Logement 1986–87, 1995–96; Chair. Banque centrale de compensation 1987–90; Chair. Foncier-court terme Sicav 1988–96; Chair. and CEO Société d'études immobilières et d'expertises foncières (Foncier-Expertise) 1990–96; Dir Compagnie foncière de France 1980–93, Société immobilière Paix-Daunou 1987–93, Société des Immeubles de France 1993–2000; Chevalier Légion d'honneur, Commdr Ordre nat. du Mérite. *Leisure interests:* singing, local history, archaeology. *Address:* 32 rue des Archives, 75004 Paris, France (Home). *Telephone:* 1-44-54-09-83 (Home).

ELDON, David Gordon, FCIB, JP; British banker; b. 14 Oct. 1945, Inverness; s. of Leslie Eldon and Mary Eldon; m. Maria (Monsé) Martinez-Col 1975; two s. one d.; ed Duke of York's Royal Mil. School; with Commercial Banking Co. of Sydney 1964–68; with the HSBC Bank Middle East 1968–79; joined Hongkong and Shanghai Banking Corpn as Man. Special Projects 1979, Sr Man. Int. Corporate Accounts 1987–88, CEO Malaysia 1988–90, Gen. Man. Malaysia 1990–92, Gen. Man. Int. 1992–94, Exec. Dir 1994–96, CEO 1996–99, Chair. 1999–; Deputy Man. Dir The Saudi British Bank 1984–87; Chair. Resource Man. Bd Hong Kong Arts Devt Council 1993–; Pres. Soc. for the Relief of Disabled Children 1993–; Dir Hang Seng Bank Ltd 1996 (Chair. (non-exec.) 1997–), HSBC Bank Australia Ltd (non-exec.) 1993, HSBC Investment Bank Asia Holdings Ltd 1994–2002, Swire Pacific Ltd 1996–, HSBC Holdings PLC 1999–; Vice-Chair. Hong Kong Gen. Chamber of Commerce 2002–; Chair. Exec. Cttee of The Community Chest, Council Hong Kong Acad. for Performing Arts 1993–; Steward Hong Kong Jockey Club 1996–. *Address:* Group Public Affairs, The Hongkong and Shanghai Banking Corporation Ltd, Level 34, HSBC Main Building, 1 Queen's Road Central, Hong Kong Special Administrative Region, People's Republic of China. *Telephone:* 28221370. *Fax:* 25960646.

ELDON, Stewart Graham, CMG, OBE; British diplomatist; b. 18 Sept. 1953; m. Christine Eldon; one s. one d.; entered FCO 1976, UK Mission New York 1976, Asst Desk Officer, UN Dept, FCO 1977–78, Third (later Second) Sec., British Embassy, Bonn 1978–82, Head of Section, FCO Repub. of Ireland Dept 1982–83, Minister of State, FCO 1983–86, First Sec., Chancery, UK Mission, New York 1986–90, Deputy Head, Middle East Dept, FCO 1990–91, seconded to Cabinet Office 1991–93, Centre for Int. Affairs, Harvard Univ. 1993–94, Political Counsellor, UK Del. to NATO/WEU 1994–97, Dir of Confs, FCO 1997–98, Deputy Perm. Rep. UK Mission, New York 1998–2002; Amb. to Ireland April 2003–. *Address:* Embassy of the United Kingdom, 29 Merrion Road, Dublin 4, Ireland (Office). *Telephone:* (1) 2053719 (Office). *Fax:* (1) 2053885 (Office). *Website:* www.britishembassy.ie (Office).

ELFMAN, Danny; American film music composer; b. 29 May 1953; lead singer, rhythm guitarist and chief songwriter for Oingo Bongo (eight-piece rock band); Music for films including: Fast Times at Ridgemont High, Weird Science, Ghostbusters II, Something Wild; numerous scores for TV programmes. *Film scores include:* Pee-Wee's Big Adventure, Batman, Dick Tracy, Midnight Run, Darkman, Edward Scissorhands, Beetlejuice, Article 99, Nightbreed, Batman Returns, Sommersby, March of the Dead Theme (Army of Darkness) 1993, The Nightmare Before Christmas 1993, Black Beauty 1994, Dolores Claiborne 1995, To Die For 1995, Dead Presidents 1995, Mission Impossible 1996, The Frighteners 1996, Mars Attacks! 1996, Men In Black 1997, Good Will Hunting, Scream 2, My Favorite Martian, Psycho, Sleepy Hollow.

ELIASSON, Jan, MA; Swedish international official and diplomatist; b. 17 Sept. 1940, Göteborg; s. of John H. Eliasson and Karin Eliasson (née Nilsson); m. Kerstin Englesson 1967; one s. two d.; ed School of Econs, Göteborg; entered Swedish Foreign Service 1965; Swedish OECD Del., Paris 1967; at Swedish Embassy, Bonn 1967–70; First Sec. Swedish Embassy, Washington 1970–74; Head of Section, Political Dept, Ministry for Foreign Affairs, Stockholm 1974–75; Personal Asst to the Under-Sec. of State for Foreign Affairs 1975–77; Dir Press and Information Div., Ministry for Foreign Affairs 1977–80, Asst Under-Sec., Head of Div. for Asian and African Affairs, Political Dept 1980–82; Foreign Policy Adviser, Prime Minister's Office 1982–83; Amb., Under-Sec. for Political Affairs, Stockholm 1983–87; Perm. Rep. of Sweden to UN, New York 1988–92; Chair. UN Trust Fund for SA 1988–92; Personal Rep. to UN Sec.-Gen. on Iran-Iraq 1988–92; Vice-Pres. ECOSOC 1991–92; Under-Sec.-Gen. for Humanitarian Affairs, UN 1992–94; Chair. Minsk Conf. on Nagornyi Karabakh 1994; State Sec. for Foreign Affairs 1994–2000; Amb. to USA 2000–; Sec. to Swedish Foreign Policy Advisory Bd 1983–87; Expert, Royal Swedish Defence Comm. 1984–86; Dir Inst. for East–West Security Studies, New York 1989–93; Dir Int. Peace Acad. 1989–2001; Dr hc (American Univ. Washington, DC) 1994, (Gothenburg) 2001. *Leisure interests:* art, literature, sports. *Address:* c/o Ministry of Foreign Affairs, Gustav Adolfstorg 1, 10339 Stockholm, Sweden; Embassy of Sweden, 1501 M Street, NW, Washington, DC 20005, USA (Office). *Telephone:* (202) 467-2611 (Office); (202) 966-9297 (Home). *Fax:* (202) 467-2699 (Office).

ELIASSON, Olafur; Danish artist; b. 1967, Copenhagen; ed Royal Acad. of Arts, Copenhagen; lives and works in Berlin; Edstrand Foundation Prize, Sweden 1998. *Solo exhibitions include:* Lukas & Hoffmann, Cologne 1994, Forumgallereit, Malmö 1994, Neugerriemschneider, Berlin 1995, 1998, Künstlerhaus, Stuttgart 1995, Hamburger Kunstverein 1995, Galleria Emi

Fontana, Milan 1996, Galeri Andreas Brändström, Stockholm 1996, Kunstmuseet, Malmö 1996, Kunsthalle Basel, Basel 1997, Denmark Sonnenfenster, Copenhagen 1997, Kunsthalle Vien, Vienna 1997, Museum for Contemporary Art, Leipzig 1998, Arhus Kunstmuseum 1998, Bildmuseet, Umea, Sweden 1998, Galerie Enja Wonnenberger, Kiel 1998, Bonakdar Jancou Gallery, New York 1998, Kjarvalstadir Museum, Reykjavik (catalogue) 1998, Galerie Peter Kilchmann, Zurich 1998, Dundee Contemporary Art, Dundee, Scotland 1999, De Appel Foundation, Amsterdam (jtly with Job Koelewijn) 1999, Frankfurter Kunstverein, Frankfurt 1999, Kunstverein Wolfsburg, Wolfsburg 1999, 2000, Marc Foxx, Los Angeles 1999, Castello di Rivoli, Turin 1999, Galleri Ingólfsstraeti, Reykjavik 1999, Neue Galerie Graz (catalogue), Graz, Austria 2000, CCA, Kitakyushu, Japan 2000, Irsih Museum of Modern Art, Dublin 2000, The Art Inst. of Chicago 2000, IASPIS, Stockholm 2000, Museum of Modern Art, New York 2001, ZKM Center for Art and Media, Karlsruhe (catalogue) 2001, Inst. of Contemporary Art, Boston (catalogue) 2001, Kunsthaus Bregenz, Austria (catalogue) 2001, Musée d'Art Moderne de la Ville de Paris 2002, Venice Bienale 2003. *Group exhibitions include:* Hamburger Bahnhof, Berlin 2000, Kunsthalle Basel, Basel 2000, Louisiana Museum, Humblebæk, Denmark 2000, SMAK, Ghent, Belgium, Serpentine Gallery, London, Kiasma, Helsinki 2000, Kunstmuseum Bern, Bern 2001, Museum Morsbroich, Leverkusen, Germany 2001, AXA Gallery, New York 2002, Paula Cooper Gallery, New York 2002. *Projects include:* Inst. of Contemporary Art, Boston 2002, Tate Modern 2003–(04). *Address:* c/o Royal Academy of Arts, School of Visual Arts, Kgs. Nytorv 1, Postboks 3014, 1021 Copenhagen K, Denmark (Office); c/o Tate Modern, Bankside, London, SE1 9TG, England (Office). *Telephone:* 33-74-46-00 (Copenhagen) (Office). *Fax:* 33-74-46-66 (Copenhagen) (Office). *E-mail:* bk@kunstakademiet.dk (Office). *Website:* www.kunstakademiet.dk (Office).

ELIEL, Ernest L., PhD, FAAS; American professor of chemistry; b. 28 Dec. 1921, Cologne, Germany; s. of Oskar Eliel and Luise Tietz; m. Eva Schwarz 1949; two d.; ed Univs of Edinburgh, Havana and Illinois; Asst Laboratorios Vieta-Plasencia 1943–46; Instructor to Assoc. Prof., Univ. of Notre Dame 1948–60, Prof. 1960–72, Head Dept of Chem. 1964–66; W. R. Kenan Jr Prof. of Chem., Univ. of N Carolina, Chapel Hill 1972–93, Prof. Emer. 1993–; Nat. Science Foundation Senior Post-doctoral Fellow, Harvard Univ. 1958, Calif. Inst. of Technology 1958–59, ETH, Zürich 1967–68; Guggenheim Fellow 1975–76, 1983–84; mem. Nat. Acad. of Sciences, American Acad. of Arts and Sciences, American Chemical Soc. (Chair. Bd 1987–89, Pres. 1992); Hon. DSc (Duke Univ.) 1983, (Notre Dame) 1990, (Babes-Boljai Univ., Cluj, Romania) 1993; Lavoisier Medal 1968, N Carolina Award in Science 1986, Priestley Medal 1996, NAS Award for Chemistry in Service to Society 1997 and other awards. *Publications:* Stereochemistry of Carbon Compounds 1962, Conformational Analysis (co-author) 1965, Elements of Stereochemistry 1969, Stereochemistry of Organic Compounds (co-author) 1994, Basic Organic Stereochemistry (co-author) 2001; and over 300 articles in professional journals; co-editor: Topics in Stereochemistry 1967–94. *Leisure interests:* photography, travel, swimming, hiking. *Address:* Department of Chemistry CB#3290, University of North Carolina, Chapel Hill, NC 27599-3290 (Office); 345 Carolina Meadoes Villa, Chapel Hill, NC 27517, USA (Home). *Telephone:* (919) 962-6198 (Office); (919) 929-7966 (Home). *Fax:* (919) 962-2388 (Office). *E-mail:* eliel@email.unc.edu (Office); eliel@mindspring.com (Home).

ELINSON, Jack, PhD; American professor of sociomedical sciences; b. 30 June 1917, New York; s. of Sam Elinson and Rebecca Block Elinson; m. May Gomberg 1941; three s. one d.; ed Coll. of the City of New York and George Washington Univ.; scientific aide, US Govt Food and Drug Admin., Soil Conservation Service, Nat. Bureau of Standards 1937–41; statistician, War Dept 1941–42; Social Science Analyst, Dept of Defense, Armed Forces Information and Educ. Div., Attitude Research Br. 1942–51; Sr Study Dir Nat. Opinion Research Center, Univ. of Chicago 1951–56; Prof. of Sociomedical Sciences, Columbia Univ. 1956–86, Prof. Emer. 1986–; Visiting Prof. of Behavioral Sciences, Univ. of Toronto 1969–75, Distinguished Visiting Prof., Inst. for Health Care Policy, Rutgers Univ. 1986–89, Distinguished Sr Scholar 1990–; Visiting Prof. Graduate Program in Public Health, Robert Wood Johnson Medical School 1986–; Consultant, Medical and Health Research Asscn of New York City 1986–96; Service Fellow, Nat. Center for Health Statistics, US Public Health Service 1977–81; mem. Inst. of Medicine, NAS 1990; numerous professional appointments; Exceptionally Distinguished Achievement Award, American Assocn. for Public Opinion Research 1993 and many other honours and distinctions. *Publications:* Chronic Illness in a Rural Area (with R. E. Trussell) 1959, Family Medical Care under Three Types of Health Insurance (with J. J. Williams and R. E. Trussell) 1962, Public Image of Mental Health Services (with E. Padilla and M. E. Perkins) 1967, Health Goals and Health Indicators (with A. Mooney and A. E. Siegmann) 1977, Sociomedical Health Indicators (with A. E. Siegmann) 1979, Assessment of Quality of Life in Clinical Trials of Cardiovascular Therapies (with N. K. Wenger, M. E. Mattson and C. D. Furberg) 1984; articles in professional journals. *Leisure interests:* grandchildren, genealogy. *Address:* c/o Columbia University, Mailman School of Public Health, Department of Sociomedical Sciences, 722 West 168th Street, New York, NY 10032 (Office); 1181 E Laurelton Parkway, Teaneck, NJ 07666, USA. *Telephone:* (212) 305-4027 (Office); (201) 836-9222. *Fax:* (212) 305-0315 (Office); (212) 836-5758 (Home). *E-mail:* je7@columbia.edu (Office); jelinson@juno.com (Home).

ELIZABETH II, (Elizabeth Alexandra Mary), Queen of Great Britain and Northern Ireland and of Her other Realms and Territories (see under Reigning Royal Families at front of book for full titles); b. 21 April 1926, London; d. of HRH Prince Albert, Duke of York (later HM King George VI) and Duchess of York (later HM Queen Elizabeth The Queen Mother); succeeded to The Throne following Her father's death, 6 Feb. 1952; married, 20 Nov. 1947, HRH The Prince Philip, Duke of Edinburgh (q.v.), b. 10 June 1921; children: Prince Charles Philip Arthur George, Prince of Wales (q.v.) (heir apparent), b. 14 Nov. 1948; Princess Anne Elizabeth Alice Louise, The Princess Royal (q.v.), b. 15 Aug. 1950; Prince Andrew Albert Christian Edward, Duke of York (q.v.), b. 19 Feb. 1960; Prince Edward Antony Richard Louis, Earl of Wessex (q.v.), b. 10 March 1964. *Address:* Buckingham Palace, London, SW1A 1AA; Windsor Castle, Berkshire, SL4 1NJ, England; Palace of Holyroodhouse, Edinburgh, Scotland; Balmoral Castle, Aberdeenshire, AB35 5TB, Scotland; Sandringham House, Norfolk, PE35 6EN, England.

ELLEMANN-JENSEN, Uffe, MA; Danish politician; b. 1 Nov. 1941; s. of Jens Peter Jensen; m. Alice Vestergaard 1971; two s. two d.; ed Univ. of Copenhagen; Danish Defence staff 1962–64; Sec. Meat Producers' Asscn 1964–67; journalist on Berlingske Aftenavis 1967–70; econ. and political corresp. Danish television 1970–75; Ed.-in-Chief and mem. Bd daily newspaper Borsen 1975–76; mem. Parl. 1977–2001 (Liberal); Party spokesperson, political affairs 1978–82; Chair. Parl. Market Cttee 1978–79; mem. Exec. Cttee Liberal Party 1979, Chair. 1984–98; mem. Bd Cen. Bank 1978–81, 1996–99, Index Figures' Bd 1979–81, Inter-Parl. Union 1979–82; Minister of Foreign Affairs 1982–93; Vice-Pres. European Liberal Party 1985–95, Pres. 1995–2000; Chair. Foreign Policy Soc., Denmark 1993–, Baltic Devt Forum 1998–, Danish Centre for Int. Studies and Human Rights 2002–; Dir Reuters Founders Share Co. Ltd 2000–; Trustee Int. Crisis Group 1999–; Robert Schuman Prize 1987. *Publications:* De nye millionaerer (The New Millionaires) 1971, Det afhaengige samfund (The Dependent Society) 1972, Hvad gør vi ved Gudenåen (We Ought to Do Something About Gudenåen) 1973, Den truede velstand (The Threatened Wealth) 1974, Økonomi (Economy) 1975, Da Danmark igen sagde ja til det falles (When Denmark Repeated its Yes to Europe) 1987, Olfert Fischer 1991, Et lille land – og dog (A Small Country – And Yet) 1991, Din egen dag er kort (Short is Your Own Day) 1996, Ude med snøren (Going Fishing) 2001, Østen for solen (East of the Sun) 2002; numerous articles in newspapers and periodicals. *Leisure interests:* fishing, hunting, opera. *Address:* PO Box 1127, 1009 Copenhagen K, Denmark. *E-mail:* uffe@ellemann.dk (Home).

ELLIOTT, Rev. Charles Middleton, MA, DPhil; British ecclesiastic; b. 9 Jan. 1939, Wakefield; s. of Joseph William Elliott and Mary Evelyn Elliott; m. Hilary Margaret Hambling 1962; three s. one d. (deceased); ed Repton, Lincoln and Nuffield Colls Oxford and Scholae Cancellarii, Lincoln; lecturer in Econs Univ. of Nottingham 1962–65; Reader in Econs Univ. of Zambia 1965–69; Asst Sec. Jt Cttee on Soc., Devt and Peace, Vatican/WCC, Geneva 1969–72; Sr Lecturer in Econs Univ. of E Anglia 1972–77; Prof. of Devt Studies, Univ. of Wales 1977–82; Dir Christian Aid 1982–84; Benjamin Meaker Prof. Univ. of Bristol 1985–86; Visiting Prof. King's Coll. London 1987–88; Prebendary of Lichfield Cathedral 1987–96; Fellow, Chaplain and Dean, Trinity Hall, Cambridge 1990–, Affiliated Lecturer in Theology, Univ. of Cambridge 1991–, in Social and Political Sciences 1993–; Sec. Inst. of Contemporary Spirituality 1988–92; Pres. Feed the Minds 1991–; Chair. Univ. Bd of Electors to Livings 1997–; Collins Religious Book Prize 1985. *Publications:* Patterns of Poverty in the Third World 1975, Praying the Kingdom 1985, Praying through Paradox 1987, Comfortable Compassion 1987, Signs of Our Times 1988, Sword and Spirit: Christianity in a Divided World 1989, Memory and Salvation 1995, Strategic Planning for Churches: An Appreciative Approach 1997, Locating the Energy for Change: An Introduction to Appreciative Inquiry 1999; numerous articles in learned journals. *Leisure interests:* walking, gardening, fly-fishing, sailing. *Address:* Trinity Hall, Cambridge, CB2 1TJ (Office); 11 Perowne Street, Cambridge, CB1 2AY, England. *Telephone:* (1223) 332525 (Office); (1223) 69233 (Home). *Fax:* (1223) 332537 (Office). *E-mail:* cme13@hermes.cam.ac.uk (Office). *Website:* www .trinhall.cam.ac.uk.

ELLIOTT, Sir John Huxtable, Kt, FBA; British professor of history; b. 23 June 1930, Reading, Berks.; s. of Thomas Charles Elliott and Janet Mary Payne; m. Oonah Sophia Butler 1958; ed Eton Coll. and Trinity Coll., Cambridge; Asst Lecturer in History, Univ. of Cambridge 1957–62, Lecturer 1962–67; Prof. of History, King's Coll., Univ. of London 1968–73; Prof., School of Historical Studies, Inst. for Advanced Study, Princeton, NJ 1973–90; Regius Prof. of Modern History, Oxford Univ. and Fellow of Oriel Coll., Oxford 1990–97; Fellow, Trinity Coll., Cambridge 1954–67, Royal Acad. of History, Madrid, American Acad. of Arts and Sciences, American Philosophical Soc, King's Coll., Univ. of London 1998; Hon. Fellow Trinity Coll., Cambridge 1991, Oriel Coll., Oxford 1997; mem. Scientific Cttee, Prado Museum 1996; Commdr of the Order of Alfonso X, El Sabio 1984, Commdr Order of Isabel la Católica 1987, Grand Cross of the Order of Alfonso X, El Sabio 1988, Grand Cross of Order of Isabella Católica 1996, Cross of Sant Jordi (Catalonia) 1999; Dr hc (Universidad Autónoma de Madrid) 1983, (Genoa) 1992, (Portsmouth) 1993, (Barcelona) 1994, (Warwick) 1995, (Brown) 1996, (Valencia) 1998, (Lleida) 1999; Visitante Ilustre of Madrid 1983, Wolfson Literary Award for History and Biography 1986, Medal of Honour, Universidad Int. Menéndez y Pelayo 1987, Gold Medal for Fine Arts (Spain) 1991, Eloy Antonio de Nebrija Prize (Univ. of Salamanca) 1993, Prince of Asturias Prize in Social Sciences 1996, Gold Medal, Spanish Inst., New York 1997, Balzan Prize for History 1500–1800 1999. *Publications:* Imperial Spain, 1469–1716 1963, The Revolt of the Catalans 1963, Europe Divided, 1559–1598 1968, The Old World and the New, 1492–1650 1970, ed. (with H. G. Koenigsberger) The Diversity of History 1970, A Palace for a King (with J. Brown) 1980, Memoriales y Cartas del Conde Duque de Olivares 1978–80, Richelieu and Olivares 1984, The Count-Duke of Olivares 1986, Spain and Its World 1500–1700 1989, The Hispanic World (ed.) 1991, The World of the Favourite (co-ed.) 1999, The Sale of the Century (with J. Brown) 2002. *Leisure interest:* looking at paintings. *Address:* 122 Church Way, Iffley, Oxford, OX4 4EG, England. *Telephone:* (1865) 716703.

ELLIOTT, Marianne, OBE, D. PHIL., FRHistS; Irish historian; b. 25 May 1948, N Ireland; d. of Terence J. Burns and Sheila O'Neill; m. Prof. Trevor Elliott 1975; one s.; ed Dominican Convent, Fort William, Belfast, Queen's Univ. Belfast and Lady Margaret Hall, Oxford; French Govt research scholar in Paris 1972–73; other research in Ireland, UK, France, Netherlands and USA; Lecturer in History, W London Inst. of Higher Educ. 1975–77; Research Fellow, Univ. Coll. Swansea 1977–82; Visiting Prof. Ia State Univ. 1983, Univ. of S Carolina 1984; Research Fellow, Univ. of Liverpool 1984–87; Simon Fellow, Univ. of Manchester 1988–89; lecturer Birkbeck Coll., Univ. of London 1991–93; Andrew Geddes and John Rankin Prof. of Modern History, Univ. of Liverpool 1993–, Dir Inst. of Irish Studies 1997–; mem. Opsahl Comm. on Northern Ireland 1993, Encounter 1998–; Leo Gershoy Award for History 1983; Sunday Independent/Irish Life Award for Biography 1989, James Donnelly Sr Award for History (American Conf. for Irish Studies) 1991. *Publications:* Partners in Revolution. The United Irishmen and France 1982, Watchmen in Sion. The Protestant Idea of Liberty 1985, The People's Armies (translation) 1987, Wolfe Tone. Prophet of Irish Independence 1989, A Citizens' Inquiry: The Report of the Opsahl Commission on Northern Ireland 1993, The Catholics in Ireland. A History 2000. *Leisure interests:* running, swimming, hill-walking, gardening. *Address:* Institute of Irish Studies, University of Liverpool, Liverpool, L69 3BX, England. *Telephone:* (151) 794 - 3831. *Fax:* (151) 794 - 3836. *E-mail:* lindam@liv.ac.uk (Office).

ELLIOTT, Michael, CBE, DSc, CChem, PhD, FRSC, FRS; British organic research chemist; b. 30 Sept. 1924, London; s. of Thomas W. and Isobel C. (Burnell) Elliott; m. Margaret O. James 1950; two d.; ed The Skinners' Co. School, Tunbridge Wells, Univ. of Southampton and King's Coll., London; Scientific Officer Dept of Insecticides and Fungicides, Rothamsted Experimental Station 1948–53, Sr Scientific Officer 1953–61, Prin. Scientific Officer 1961–70, Sr Prin. Scientific Officer 1970–79, Deputy Chief Scientific Officer 1979–84, Head of Dept of Insecticides and Fungicides and Deputy Dir Rothamsted Experimental Station 1979–84; Visiting Lecturer, Univ. of Calif. (Berkeley) 1969, 1974; Visiting Prof., Imperial Coll., London 1979–85; Fellow, King's Coll., London 1984–; consultant on chem. of insecticides 1984–; Visiting Research Scientist, Pesticide Chem. and Toxicology Lab., Univ. of Calif. (Berkeley) 1985–88; Lawes Trust Sr Fellow, Rothamsted Experimental Station 1989–; Foreign Assoc. NAS 1996; Hon. DSc (Southampton) 1985; Mullard Medal, Royal Soc. 1982, Wolf Foundation Prize in Agriculture 1989, Prix de la Fondation de la Chimie 1989, The SCI Environment Medal 1993 and other awards and prizes. *Publications:* more than 200 scientific articles. *Leisure interest:* photography. *Address:* 45 Larkfield, Ewhurst, Cranleigh, Surrey, GU6 7QU, England. *Telephone:* (1483) 277506. *E-mail:* elliott161@aol.com.

ELLIOTT, Osborn, AB; American journalist; b. 25 Oct. 1924, New York City; s. of John and Audrey N. (Osborn) Elliott; m. 1st Deirdre M. Spencer 1948 (divorced 1972); three d.; m. 2nd the fmr Mrs. Inger A. McCabe; one step s. two step d.; ed The Browning School (NY), St Paul's School (Concord) and Harvard Univ.; served with USNR 1944–46; Reporter NY Journal of Commerce 1946–49; Contributing Ed. Time 1949–52, Assoc. Ed. 1952–55; Senior Business Ed. Newsweek 1955–59, Man. Ed. 1959–61, Ed., Editor-in-Chief, Pres., CEO, Chair. of Bd 1961–76; Deputy Mayor for Econ. Devt, New York 1976–77; Dean Graduate School of Journalism, Columbia Univ., New York 1979–86; Prof. Columbia Univ. 1979–94; fmr Dir Washington Post Co.; fmr Trustee, American Museum of Natural History, Asia Soc., Lincoln Center Theatre, New York Public Library, St Paul's School, Winston Churchill Foundation of the US Ltd; mem. Council on Foreign Relations, Pulitzer Prize Bd 1979–86; mem. Bd of Overseers of Harvard Coll. 1965–71; Chair. Citizens' Cttee for New York City 1975–80, 1990–; mem. Bd New Yorkers for Children 1999–; Organizer Save Our Cities! Save Our Children! march, Washington, DC May 1992; Fellow American Acad. of Arts and Sciences; numerous awards and hon. degrees. *Publications:* Men at the Top 1959, The World of Oz 1980, The Negro Revolution in America (ed.) 1964. *Leisure interests:* boating, fishing. *Address:* 84 Water Street, Stonington, CT 06378, USA. *Telephone:* (860) 535-5999 (Home). *Fax:* (860) 535-4970 (Home).

ELLIOTT, Sir Roger (James), Kt, MA, DPhil, FRS; British physicist and publisher; b. 8 Dec. 1928, Chesterfield; s. of James Elliott and Gladys Elliott (née Hill); m. Olga Lucy Atkinson 1952; one s. two d.; ed Swanwick Hall School, Derbyshire and New Coll., Oxford; Research Assoc. Univ. of Calif., Berkeley 1952–53; Research Fellow, Atomic Energy Research Est., Harwell 1953–55; lecturer, Univ. of Reading 1955–57; Lecturer, Oxford Univ. 1957–65, Reader 1965–74, Fellow, St John's Coll. 1957–74 (now Hon. Fellow), New Coll. 1974–96 (now Emer.), Wykeham Prof. of Physics 1974–89, Prof. of Physics 1989–96, now Emer. Prof.; Del. Oxford Univ. Press 1971–88, Chair. Computer Bd 1983–87, Sec. to Dels and Chief Exec. 1988–93; mem. Bd Blackwell Ltd 1996–, Chair. 1999–2002; Visiting Prof. Univ. of Calif., Berkeley 1960–61; Miller Visiting Prof. Univ. of Ill., Urbana 1966; Visiting Distinguished Prof. Fla State Univ. 1981, Mich. State Univ. 1997–2000; Physical Sec. and Vice-Pres. Royal Soc. (London) 1984–88; Treas. Publrs Asscn 1990–92, Pres. 1992–93; Chair. ICSU Press 1997–, Disability Information Trust 1998–2001; mem. Bd (part-time) UKAEA 1988–94, British Council 1990–98; Hon. DSc (Paris) 1983, Bath (1991), (Essex) 1993; Maxwell Medal (Physical Soc.) 1968, Guthrie Medal 1989. *Publications:* Magnetic Properties of Rare Earth Metals 1972, Solid State Physics and its Applications 1973; articles in learned journals. *Address:* 11 Crick Road, Oxford, OX2 6QL, England (Home). *Telephone:* (1865) 273997. *Fax:* (1865) 273947.

ELLIS, Alice Thomas (see Haycraft, Anna Margaret).

ELLIS, Charles Richard, MA; American publishing executive; b. 20 July 1935, New York; s. of Charles Ellis and Ruth Allen; m. 1st Nathalie Likwas 1957 (divorced 1963); one s.; m. 2nd Jeanne Laurent 1963; four step-s.; ed Princeton and Columbia Univs; teacher, Barnard School, New York 1958–63; Man. Scientific Research Assocs Chicago 1963–68; Exec. Ed. DC Heath, Boston 1968–70; Chair. and Man. Dir DC Heath Ltd, UK 1970–75; Co-Man. Dir Pergamon Press, UK 1975–78; Marketing Dir Elsevier Publishing, Amsterdam 1978–81; Pres. Elsevier Scientific Publishing Co. New York 1981–88; Exec. Vice-Pres. John Wiley & Sons, New York 1988–90, Pres., CEO 1990–97, Sr Adviser 1998–; Pres. Bd of Trustees, Princeton Univ. Press. 1987–; Chair. Asscn of American Publrs 1992–94; Vice-Chair. Int. Publrs Asscn 1996–; Chevalier des Arts et des Lettres. *Address:* John Wiley & Sons, 605 Third Avenue, New York, NY 10158 (Office); 300 East 54th Street, New York, NY 10022, USA (Home). *Telephone:* (212) 850-6000 (Office). *Fax:* (212) 850-6088 (Office).

ELLIS, Gavin Peter; New Zealand journalist; b. 6 March 1947, Auckland; s. of Peter Fisher Dundass Ellis and Catherine Ellis (née Gray); m. 1st Janine Laurette Sinclair 1969; m. 2nd Jennifer Ann Lynch 1991; one s.; ed Mount Roskill Grammar School and Auckland Univ.; on staff of Auckland Star paper 1965–70; public relations consultant 1970–71; joined New Zealand Herald 1972, Asst Ed. 1987–96, Ed. 1996–99, Ed.-in-Chief 1999–; Brittain Memorial Fellow 1980; Chair. New Zealand Section, Commonwealth Press Union; mem. New Zealand Knowledge Wave Trust; Trustee New Zealand Herald Foundation. *Leisure interests:* medieval history, opera. *Address:* 46 Albert Street, Auckland, New Zealand. *Telephone:* (9) 379-5050. *Fax:* (9) 373-6406. *E-mail:* gavin_ellis@herald.co.nz (Office); gavin.ellis@xtra.co.nz (Home). *Website:* www.nzherald.co.nz (Office).

ELLIS, George Francis Rayner, FRAS, PhD; British/South African professor of astrophysics and applied mathematics; b. 11 Aug. 1939, Johannesburg; s. of George Rayner Ellis and Gwen Hilda (née MacRobert) Ellis; m. 1st Sue Parkes 1963; one s. one d.; m. 2nd Mary Wheeldon 1978; ed Michaelhouse, Univ. of Cape Town and Cambridge Univ.; Fellow Peterhouse, Cambridge 1965–67; Asst Lecturer, lecturer Cambridge 1967–73; Prof. of Applied Math., Univ. of Cape Town 1974–88, 1990–; Prof. of Cosmic Physics, SISSA, Trieste 1988–92; G. C. MacVittie Visiting Prof. of Astronomy, Queen Mary Coll., London 1987–; Chair. GR1O Scientific Cttee 1988; mem. Int. Cttee on Gen. Relativity and Gravitation; Pres., Int. Soc. of Gen. Relativity and Gravitation 1989–92; mem. Cttee (and Vice-Pres.) Royal Soc. of SA 1990–, Pres. 1992–96; Founding mem., mem. Council, Acad. of Science of SA 1995–97, 2000–; Fellow Inst. of Maths and its Applications; Chair. Quaker Service, West Cape 1976–86, Quaker Peacework Cttee 1978–86, 1990–95, SA Inst. of Race Relations, West Cape 1985–87; Clerk SA Yearly Meeting of Quakers 1986–88; Fellowship of Univ. of Cape Town; Hon. DSc (Haverford Coll.) 1996, (Natal Univ.) 1998; Herschel Medal of Royal Soc. of SA, Gravity Research Foundation 1st Prize 1979, Star of South Africa Medal 1999. *Publications:* The Large Scale Structure of Space-Time (with S. W. Hawking, q.v.) 1973, The Squatter Problem in the Western Cape (with J. Maree, D. Hendrie) 1976, Low Income Housing Policy (with D. Dewar) 1980, Flat and Curved Space-Times (with R. Williams) 1988, Before the Beginning 1993, The Renaissance of General Relativity and Cosmology (co-ed.) 1993, The Dynamical Systems Approach to Cosmology (co-ed.) 1996, The Density of Matter in the Universe (with P. Coles) 1996, On the Moral Nature of the Universe: Cosmology, Theology and Ethics (with N. Murphy) 1996. *Leisure interests:* climbing, gliding. *Address:* Department of Mathematics and Applied Mathematics, University of Cape Town, Rondebosch 7700, Cape Town (Office); 3 Marlow Road, Cape Town 7700, South Africa (Home). *Telephone:* (21) 6502340 (Office); (21) 7612313 (Home). *Fax:* (21) 6502334 (Office); (21) 7976349 (Home). *E-mail:* ellis@maths.uct.ac.za (Office); mmellis@iafrica.com (Home).

ELLIS, John Martin, PhD; American professor; b. 31 May 1936, London, England; s. of John Albert Ellis and Emily Ellis; m. Barbara Rhoades 1978; two s. two d. one step-d.; ed City of London School and Univ. Coll., London; Royal Artillery 1954–56; Tutorial Asst in German, Univ. of Wales, Aberystwyth 1959–60; Asst Lecturer in German, Univ. of Leicester 1960–63; Asst Prof. of German, Univ. of Alberta, Canada 1963–66; Assoc. Prof. of German Literature, Univ. of Calif., Santa Cruz 1966–70, Prof. 1970–94, Prof. Emer. 1994, Dean Graduate Div. 1977–86; Literary Ed. Heterodoxy 1992–; Sec.-Treas. Asscn of Literary Scholars and Critics 1994–2001; Guggenheim Fellowship, Nat. Endowment for the Humanities Sr Fellowship; Nat. Asscn of Scholars' Peter Shaw Memorial Award (for Literature Lost). *Publications include:* Narration in the German Novelle 1974, The Theory of Literary Criticism: A Logical Analysis 1974, Heinrich von Kleist 1979, One Fairy Story Too Many: The Brothers Grimm and Their Tales 1983, Against Deconstruction 1989, Language, Thought and Logic 1993, Literature Lost: Social

Agendas and the Corruption of the Humanities 1997. *Leisure interests:* birdwatching, golf. *Address:* 144 Bay Heights, Soquel, CA 95073, USA. *Telephone:* (831) 476-1144. *Fax:* (831) 476-1188. *E-mail:* john.ellis@earthlink .net (Office).

ELLIS, Jonathan Richard (John), MA, PhD, FRS, FInstP; British physicist; b. 1 July 1946, Hampstead; s. of Richard Ellis and Beryl Lilian Ellis (née Ranger); m. Maria Mercedes Martinez Rengifo 1985; one s. one d.; ed Highgate School, King's Coll., Univ. of Cambridge; Post-doctoral Research Fellow, Stanford Linear Accelerator Center 1971–72; Richard Chase Tolman Fellow, Calif. Inst. of Technology 1972–73; Research Fellow, CERN 1973–74, Staff mem. 1974–, Leader, Theoretical Physics Div. 1988–94, Sr Staff Physicist 1994–, now Adviser to CERN Dir.-Gen. on relations with non-member states; Dr hc (Southampton) 1994; Maxwell Medal (Royal Soc.) 1982. *Publications:* over 500 scientific publs. *Leisure interests:* literature, music, travel, hiking, cinema. *Address:* Theory Division, CERN, CH-1211 Geneva 23 (Office); 5 Chemin du Ruisseau, Tannay, 1295 Mies, Vaud, Switzerland (Home). *Telephone:* (22) 7674142 (Office); (22) 7764858 (Home). *Fax:* (22) 7673850 (Office); (22) 7764858 (Home). *E-mail:* john.ellis@cern.ch (Office). *Website:* www.cern .ch.

ELLIS, Osian Gwynn, CBE, FRAM; British harpist; b. 8 Feb. 1928, Ffynnon-groew, Flintshire, Wales; s. of Rev. T. G. Ellis; m. Rene Ellis Jones 1951; two s.; ed Denbigh Grammar School, Royal Acad. of Music; Prin. Harpist London Symphony Orchestra 1960–94; mem. Melos Ensemble; Prof. of Harp Royal Acad. of Music 1959–89; recitals and concerts worldwide; radio and TV broadcasts; works written for him include harp concertos by Hoddinott 1957, Mathias 1970, Jersild 1972, Robin Holloway 1985, Rhian Samuel 2000, solos and chamber music by Gian Carlo Menotti 1977, William Schuman 1978 and music by Britten: Suite for Harp 1969, Canticle V 1974, Birthday Hansel 1975, Folk Songs for voice and harp 1976; Hon. DMus (Wales) 1970; Grand Prix du Disque, French Radio Critics' Award and other awards. *Publication:* Story of the Harp in Wales 1991. *Address:* Arfryn, Ala Road, Pwllheli, Gwynedd, LL53 5BN, Wales. *Telephone:* (1758) 612501.

ELLIS, Reginald John, PhD, FRS; British professor of biological sciences; b. 12 Feb. 1935, Newcastle-under-Lyme; s. of Francis Gilbert Ellis and Evangeline Gratton Ellis; m. Diana Margaret Warren 1963; one d.; ed Highbury Grove Grammar School, London and King's Coll., Univ. of London; Agricultural Research Council Fellow, Dept of Biochemistry, Univ. of Oxford 1961–64; Lecturer, Depts of Botany and Biochemistry, Univ. of Aberdeen 1964–70; Sr Lecturer, Univ. of Warwick 1970–73, Reader 1973–76, Prof. of Biological Sciences 1976–96, Prof. Emer. 1996–; Sr Research Fellow, Science and Eng Research Council 1983–88; mem. European Molecular Biology Org. 1986–; Sr Visiting Research Fellow, St John's Coll. Oxford 1992–93; Academic Visitor, Oxford Centre for Molecular Sciences 1996–2000; Tate & Lyle Award 1980. *Publications:* 160 papers on plant and microbial biochemistry in the scientific literature; Chloroplast Biogenesis (ed.) 1984, Molecular Chaperones (ed.) 1990, The Chaperonins (ed.) 1996, Molecular Chaperones Ten Years On (ed.) 2000. *Leisure interests:* landscape photography, fell walking. *Address:* Department of Biological Sciences, University of Warwick, Coventry, West Midlands, CV4 7AL (Office); 44 Sunningdale Avenue, Kenilworth, Warwicks. CV8 2BZ, England (Home). *Telephone:* (2476) 523509 (Office); (1926) 856382 (Home). *E-mail:* jellis@bio.warwick.ac.uk (Office).

ELLIS, Richard Salisbury, DPhil, FRS, FInstP; British professor of astronomy; b. 25 May 1950, Colwyn Bay, Wales; s. of the late Capt. Arthur Ellis and of Marion Ellis; m. Barbara Williams 1972; one s. one d.; ed Univ. Coll. London, Oxford Univ.; researcher, Durham Univ. 1974–81, lecturer 1981–83, Prof. of Astronomy 1985–93; Sr Research Fellow Royal Greenwich Observatory 1983–85; Plumian Prof., Cambridge Univ. 1993–99; Dir Inst. of Astronomy, Cambridge Univ. 1994–99; Prof. of Astronomy, Calif. Inst. of Tech. 1999–2002, Steele Prof. of Astronomy 2002–; Dir Palomar Observatory 2000–02, Caltech Optical Observatories 2002–; Visiting Prof. Durham Univ. 1994–, Cambridge Univ. 2000–; Fellow Royal Astronomical Soc.; mem. American Astronomical Soc., Astronomical Soc. of the Pacific; Fellow Univ. Coll. London 1998; Hon. DSc (Durham) 2002; Bakerian Prize, Royal Soc. 1998. *Publications:* numerous articles in scientific journals; Observational Tests of Cosmological Inflation 1991, Large Scale Structure in the Universe 1999. *Leisure interests:* skiing, photography. *Address:* Astronomy Department, Mail Stop 105-24, California Institute of Technology, Pasadena, CA 91125, USA (Office). *Telephone:* (626) 395-2598 (Office); (626) 676-5530 (Home). *Fax:* (626) 568-9352 (Office). *E-mail:* rse@astro.caltech.edu (Office). *Website:* www.astro .caltech.edu/~rse/.

ELLISON, Harlan Jay; American author; b. 27 May 1934, Cleveland; s. of Louis Laverne Ellison and Serita (née Rosenthal) Ellison; m. 1st Charlotte Stein 1956 (divorced 1959); m. 2nd Billie Joyce Sanders 1961 (divorced 1962); m. 3rd Lory Patrick 1965 (divorced 1965); m. 4th Lori Horwitz 1976 (divorced 1977); m. 5th Susan Toth 1986; ed Ohio State Univ.; part-time actor, Cleveland Playhouse 1944–49; f. Cleveland Science-Fiction Soc. 1950 and Science-Fantasy Bulletin; served US Army 1957–59; ed. Rogue magazine, Chicago 1959-60, Regency Books, Chicago 1960–61; lecturer at colls and univs; voice-overs for animated cartoons; book critic, LA Times 1969–82; Editorial Commentator Canadian Broadcasting Co. 1972–78; Instructor Clarion Writers Workshop, Michigan State Univ. 1969–77; Pres. The Kilimanjaro Corpn 1979–; TV writer for Alfred Hitchcock Hour, Outer Limits, The Man from U.N.C.L.E., Burkes Law; Film writer for The Dream Merchants,

The Oscar, Nick the Greek, Best By Far, Harlan Ellison's Movie; scenarist: I, Robot 1978, Bug Jack Barron 1982–83; creative consultant, writer and dir The Twilight Zone 1984–85; conceptual consultant Babylon 5 1993–98; mem. American Writers Guild and American Science Fiction Writers; Hugo Awards 1967, 1968, 1973, 1974, 1975, 1977, 1986; Special Achievement Awards 1968–72, Certificate of Merit, Trieste Film Festival 1970, Edgar Allan Poe Award, Mystery Writers 1974, 1988, American Mystery Award 1988, Bram Stoker Award, Horror Writers Asscn 1988, 1990, 1994; World Fantasy Award 1989, Georges Mélièes Award for cinematic achievement 1972, 1973, PEN Award for journalism 1982; Americana Annual American Literature: Major Works 1988, World Fantasy 1993 Life Achievement Award, two Audie Awards, Audio Publishers Asscn 1999 and numerous other awards. *Publications include:* Dangerous Visions (ed.) 1967, The Glass Teat 1970, The Other Glass Teat 1975, A Boy and His Dog (novella) 1975, Strange Wine 1978, Stalking the Nightmare 1982, An Edge in My Voice 1985, The Essential Ellison 1987, Angry Candy (short stories) 1988, Harlan Ellison's Watching 1989, The Harlan Ellison Hornbook 1990, Harlan Ellison's Movie 1990, Mefisto in Onyx 1993, Mind Fields (33 stories inspired by the art of Jacek Yerka) 1994, Robot: The Illustrated Screenplay 1994, City on the Edge of Forever (screenplay) 1995, Slippage 1996, Edgeworks: The Collected Ellison (4 vols) 1996–97, Repent, Harlequin 1997, Troublemakers 2001. *Leisure interests:* shooting pool, supporting progressive and environmental agendas and causes. *Address:* c/o HERC, PO Box 55548, Sherman Oaks, CA 91413-0548, USA.

ELLISON, Lawrence, J., BS; American computer software executive; b. 1944; with Amdahl Inc., Calif. 1967–71; Pres. Omex Corpn, Systems Div. 1972–77; with Oracle Corpn, Calif. 1977–, Pres., CEO 1978–, mem. Bd of Dirs; mem. Bd of Dirs Apple Computer Inc. 1997. *Address:* Oracle Corporation, 500 Oracle Parkway, Redwood City, CA 94065-1675, USA.

ELLMAN, Michael, M.SC.(ECON.), PhD; British economist; b. 27 July 1942, Ripley, Surrey; m. Patricia Harrison 1965; one s. one d.; ed Cambridge Univ. and London School of Econs; lecturer Glasgow Univ. 1967–69; Research Officer then Sr Research Officer, Dept of Applied Econs, Cambridge Univ. 1969–75; Assoc. Prof. Amsterdam Univ. 1975–78, Prof. of Econs 1978–; Fellow Tinberg Inst.; Kondratieff Prize 1998. *Publications:* Planning Problems in the USSR 1973, Socialist Planning 1989, The Destruction of the Soviet Economic System (ed. with V. Kontovovich) 1998. *Leisure interests:* walking, cycling. *Address:* Department of Economics, Universiteit van Amsterdam, Roetersstraat 11, 1018 WB Amsterdam, Netherlands (Office). *Telephone:* (20) 5254235 (Office). *Fax:* (20) 5254254 (Office). *E-mail:* m.j.ellman@uva.nl (Office).

ELLROY, James; American writer; b. 4 March 1948, Los Angeles, Calif.; m. Helen Knode. *Publications:* Brown's Requiem 1981, Clandestine 1982, The Black Dahlia 1987, The Big Nowhere 1988, L.A. Confidential 1990, White Jazz 1992, American Tabloid (Novel of the Year, Time Magazine) 1995, My Dark Places (Book of the Year, Salon.com) 1996, The Cold Six Thousand 2001. *Address:* c/o Warner Books Publicity Dept, 1271 Avenue of the Americas, New York, NY 10020, USA (Office).

ELLWOOD, Peter Brian, CBE, FCIB, FRSA; British banker; b. 15 May 1943, Bristol; s. of the late Isaac Ellwood and Edith Ellwood (née Trotter); m. Judy Ann Windsor 1968; one s. two d.; ed King's School, Macclesfield; joined Barclays Bank 1961; worked in London and Bristol; in charge of Barclaycard operations 1983; Chief Exec. Barclaycard 1985; Chief Exec. Cen. Retail Services Div. Barclays Bank; Dir On-Line Card Services Ltd, Barclays Bank (UK) Ltd; Chief. Exec. Retail Banking, TSB Bank PLC; Dir TSB Group PLC 1990–95, Chief Exec. 1992–95; Deputy Chief Exec. Lloyds TSB Group PLC 1995–97, Chief Exec. 1997–(2003); Chair. Visa Europe, Middle East and Africa 1992–96, Visa Int. 1994–99, Industrial Soc. 2001–; fmr Chair. United Dominions Trust (UDT); Dir (non.-exec.) Sears PLC 1994–96, Royal Philharmonic Orchestra 1996–; Trustee Royal Theatre, Northampton; mem. Court Univ. Coll. Northampton (fmrly Nene Coll.) 1989–; Hon. LLD (Leicester) 1994; Dr hc (Univ. of Cen. England) 1995. *Leisure interests:* music, theatre. *Address:* c/o Lloyds TSB Group PLC, 71 Lombard Street, London, EC3P 3BS, England. *Telephone:* (20) 7356-2072 (Office). *Fax:* (20) 7356-2049.

ELMANDJRA, Mahdi, PhD; Moroccan university professor; b. 13 March 1933, Rabat; s. of M'Hamed Elmandjra and Rabia Elmrini; m. Amina Elmrini 1956; two d.; ed Lycée Lyautey, Casablanca, Putney School, Vermont, USA, Cornell Univ., London School of Economics and Faculté de Droit, Univ. de Paris; Head of Confs, Law Faculty, Univ. of Rabat 1957–58; Adviser, Ministry of Foreign Affairs and to Moroccan Del. to UN 1958–59; Dir-Gen., Radiodiffusion Télévision Marocaine 1959–60; Chief of African Div., Office of Relations with Mem. States, UNESCO 1961–63; Dir Exec. Office of Dir-Gen. of UNESCO 1963–66; Asst Dir-Gen. of UNESCO for Social Sciences, Human Sciences and Culture 1966–69; Visiting Fellow, Centre of Int. Studies, London School of Econs and Political Science 1970; Asst Dir-Gen. of UNESCO for Pre-Programming 1971–74; Special Adviser to Dir-Gen. of UNESCO 1975–76; Prof. Univ. Mohamed V, Rabat 1977–; Co-ordinator, Conf. on Tech. Co-operation between Developing Countries (UNDP) 1979–80; Senior Adviser, UN Int. Year of Disabled Persons 1980–81; mem. Consultative Cultural Council of the Inst. of the Arab World (Paris); fmr Pres. World Future Studies Fed. (WFSF), Futuribles Int.; mem. Club of Rome, Acad. of the Kingdom of Morocco; Vice-Pres. Asscn Maroc-Japon; mem. World Acad. of Art and Science, Exec. Cttee, Soc. for Int. Devt, Exec. Cttee, African Acad. of Sciences,

Pugwash Conferences, Founding Pres. Moroccan Asscn of Human Rights, Acad. of the Kingdom of Morocco; Officier des Arts et des Lettres (France), Order of the Rising Sun (Japan) and numerous other decorations; Master Jury Aga Khan Award for Architecture 1986, Albert Einstein Int. Foundation Medal for Peace 1990. *Publications:* Africa 2000 1980, The New Age of Culture and Communication 1981, The Future of Humor 1982, Maghreb 2000 1982, L'Interpellation du Tiers Monde 1982, Les Aspects économiques du dialogue Euro-Arabe 1982, Information and Sovereignty 1983, The Conquest of Space: Political, Economic and Socio-Cultural Implications 1984, Casablanca 2000 1984, Development and Automation 1985, Communications, Information and Development 1985, Tomorrow's Habitat 1985, Learning Needs in a Changing Society 1986, Media and Communications in Africa 1986, The Future of International Cooperation 1986, The Financing of Research and Development in the Third World 1986, Maghreb et Francophonie 1988, Three Scenarios for The Future of International Cooperation 1988, The Place of Arab Culture in the World of Tomorrow 1988, Social Change and Law 1988, China in the 21st Century 1989, Fusion of Science and Culture: Key to the 21st Century 1989, Human Rights and Development 1989, How to Construct a Positive Vision of the Future 1990, Gulf Crisis: Prelude to the North-South Confrontation 1990, Western Discrimination in the Field of Human Rights 1990, Africa: The Coming Upheaval 1990, La Première Guerre Civilisationnelle 1991, Retrospective des Futurs 1992, Nord-Sud: Prélude à l'Ere Post-coloniale 1992, The Agreements Concerning Gaza and Jericho 1993, Biodiversity: Cultural and Ethical Aspects 1994, Cultural Diversity: Key to Survival in the 21st Century 1994, The New Challenges Facing the United Nations 1995, Dialogue de la Communication 1996, Al Quds (Jerusalem): Symbole et mémoire 1996, La décolonisation culturelle: défi majeur du 21e siècle 1996, Immigration as a Cultural Phenomenon 1997, The Path of a Mind 1997, Communication Dialogue 2000, Reglobalization of Globalization 2000. *Leisure interests:* reading, swimming, music, writing. *Address:* BP 53, Rabat, Morocco. *Telephone:* 774-258. *Fax:* 757-151. *E-mail:* elmandjra@elmandjra.org (Home). *Website:* www.elmandjra.org (Home).

ELMER, Michael B.; Danish lawyer; b. 26 Feb. 1949, Copenhagen; s. of Poul Chr. B. Elmer and Etly (née Andersson) Elmer; pnr Annette Andersen; ed Univ. of Copenhagen; civil servant Ministry of Justice 1973–76, 1977–82, Head of Div. 1982–87, 1988–91, Deputy Perm. Sec., Head of Community Law and Human Rights Dept 1991–94; Assoc. Prof. Univ. of Copenhagen 1975–85; Deputy Judge, Hillerød 1976–77; Asst Public Prosecutor 1980–81; Judge Court of Ballerup 1981–82; external examiner Danish law schools 1985–; High Court Judge (a.i.) Eastern High Court, Copenhagen 1987–88; Vice-Pres. (a.i.) Danish Maritime and Commercial Court, Copenhagen 1988, Vice Pres. 1997–; Rep. EC Court of Justice, Luxembourg 1991–94; Advocate-Gen. EC Court of Justice 1994–97; mem. governing council UNIDROIT, Rome 1999–; int. commercial arbitrator; Chair. and mem. numerous govt and int. orgs and cttees; Kt, Order of Dannebrog, Grand Cross, Order of Merit (Luxembourg). *Publications:* several books and articles on civil law (especially property law), penal law and community law. *Leisure interests:* travelling, collecting antiques. *Address:* Sø-og Handelsretten, Bredgade 70, 1260, Copenhagen (Office); Stockholmsgade 25, I.T.H., 2100, Copenhagen, Denmark (Home). *Telephone:* 33-47-92-22 (Office); 35-55-49-63 (Home). *Fax:* 33-14-56-77 (Office). *E-mail:* michael@elmer.as (Home).

ELS, Theodore Ernest (Ernie); South African golfer; b. 17 Oct. 1969, Johannesburg; s. of Nils Els and Hettie Els; m. Leizl Els; one s. one d.; wins include South African Open 1992, 1996, US Open, 1994, 1997, Toyota World Matchplay Championships 1994, 1995, 1996, South African PGA Championship 1995, Byron Nelson Classic 1995, Buick Classic 1996, 1997, Johnny Walker Classic 1997, Bay Hill Invitational 1998, Nissan Open 1999, Int. presented by Quest 2000, Standard Life Loch Lomond 2000, Open Championship 2002, Genuity Championship 2002, British Open 2002, fourth World Match Play title 2002; mem. Dunhill Cup Team 1992–2000, World Cup Team 1992, 1993, 1996, 1997, 2001; mem. President's Cup 1996, 1998, 2000; f. Ernie Els Foundation to help disadvantaged children 1999; South African Sportsman of the Year 1994, Lifetime Membership European Tour 1998. *Leisure interests:* movies, reading, sport. *Address:* 46 Chapman Road, Klippoortjie 1401, South Africa.

ELSÄSSER, Hans Friedrich, Dr rer. nat; German astronomer; b. 29 March 1929, Aalen/Württemberg; s. of Jakob Elsässer and Margarete Elsässer-Vogelgsang; m. Ruth Abele 1953; two s. one d.; ed Univ. of Tübingen; Asst Prof., Univ. of Tübingen 1957, Univ. of Göttingen 1959; Prof. of Astronomy, Univ. of Heidelberg 1962–; Dir State Observatory, Heidelberg-Königstuhl 1962–75; Dir Max Planck Inst. for Astronomy, Heidelberg-Königstuhl 1968–, Calar Alto Observatory, Spain; mem. Acad. of Sciences of Heidelberg, Halle, Helsinki and Vienna; planet Elsässer named after him; Comendador de la Orden de Isabel la Católica (Spain), Bundesverdienstkreuz. *Publications:* about 150 articles in astronomical journals and three textbooks, two with H. Scheffler. *Leisure interest:* tennis. *Address:* Max-Planck-Institut für Astronomie, Königstuhl, 69117 Heidelberg, Germany. *Telephone:* (6221) 528200.

ELSON, Bill; American music agent; Head, Music Div. Int. Creative Man. (ICM); clients have included Janis Joplin, the Doors, Jefferson Airplane, Def Leppard, Paul McCartney, Bob Dylan, Metallica.

ELSTEIN, David Keith, MA; British broadcasting executive; b. 14 Nov. 1944; s. of the late Albert Elstein and Millie Cohen; m. Jenny Conway 1978; one s.; ed Haberdashers' Aske's School, Gonville and Caius Coll. Cambridge; producer (BBC) The Money Programme, Panorama, Cause for Concern, People in Conflict 1964–68; (Thames TV) This Week, The Day Before Yesterday, The World At War 1968–72; (London Weekend) Weekend World 1972; Ed. This Week (Thames TV) 1974–78; f. Brook Productions 1982; Exec. Producer A Week in Politics 1982–86, Concealed Enemies 1983; Man. Dir Primetime TV 1983–86; Dir of Programmes Thames TV 1986–92; Head of Programmes BSkyB 1993–96; Chief Exec. Channel 5 Broadcasting 1996–2000; Chair. Nat. Film and TV School 1996–2002, British Screen Advisory Council 1997–, Civilian Content 2001–03, Xios Transcast Corpn; Chair. (non-exec.) Really Useful Theatres 2001–; Deputy Chair. Silicon Media Group 2001–; Visiting Prof. Stirling Univ. 1995–; Visiting Prof. in Broadcast Media, Oxford Univ. 1998–99, Westminster Univ. 2001–. *Publication:* The Political Structure of UK Broadcasting 1949–1999 (Oxford Lectures). *Leisure interests:* theatre, cinema, bridge, politics, reading. *Address:* British Screen Advisory Council, 13 Manette Street, London, W1D 4AW, England. *E-mail:* bsac@bsacouncil.co.uk.

ELTIS, Walter Alfred, MA, DLitt; British economist; b. 23 May 1933, Warnsdorf, Czechoslovakia; s. of Rev. Martin Eltis and Mary Schnitzer; m. Shelagh M. Owen 1959; one s. two d.; ed Wycliffe Coll., Emmanuel Coll. Cambridge and Nuffield Coll. Oxford; Research Fellow in Econs Exeter Coll., Oxford 1958–60; Lecturer in Econs, Univ. of Oxford 1961–88; Fellow and Tutor in Econs, Exeter Coll. Oxford 1963–88, Fellow Emer. 1988–; Econ. Dir Nat. Econ. Devt Office 1986–88, Dir-Gen. 1988–92; Chief Econ. Adviser to the Pres. of Bd of Trade 1992–95; Visiting Reader in Econs, Univ. of W Australia 1970–71; Visiting Prof. Univ. of Toronto 1976–77, European Univ. Florence 1979, Univ. of Reading 1992–; Gresham Prof. of Commerce, Gresham Coll. London 1993–96. *Publications:* Growth and Distribution 1973, Britain's Economic Problem: Too Few Producers (with R. Bacon) 1976, The Classical Theory of Economic Growth 1984, Keynes and Economic Policy (with P. Sinclair) 1988, Classical Economics, Public Expenditure and Growth 1993, Britain's Economic Problem Revisited 1996, Condillac: Commerce and Government (ed. with S. M. Eltis) 1998, Britain, Europe and EMU 2000. *Leisure interests:* chess, music. *Address:* Danesway, Jarn Way, Boars Hill, Oxford, OX1 5JF, England. *Telephone:* (1865) 735440.

ELTON, Sir Arnold, Kt, CBE, MS, FRCS, FRSM; British surgeon; b. 14 Feb. 1920; s. of late Max Elton and Ada Elton; m. Billie Pamela Briggs 1952; one s.; ed Univ. Coll., London, Univ. Coll. Hosp. Medical School, London; House Surgeon, House Physician, Casualty Officer Univ. Coll. Hosp. 1943–45; Sr Surgical Registrar, Charing Cross Hosp. 1947–51; Consultant Surgeon Harrow Hosp. 1951–70, Mount Vernon Hosp. 1960–70, Wellington Hosp.; Consultant Surgeon Northwick Park Hosp. and Clinical Research Centre 1970–85 (now Consulting Surgeon); Surgeon Emer. Clementine Churchill Hosp.; First Chair. Medical Staff Cttee Northwick Park Hosp., Chair. Surgical Div. and Theatre Cttee; mem. Ethical Cttee Northwick Park Hosp., Govt Working Party on Breast Screening for Cancer 1985–; Surgical Tutor Royal Coll. of Surgeons 1970–82; Nat. Chair. Conservative Medical Soc. 1975–92 (Chair. European Group, Pres. 1992–97, Pres. Emer 1997–, European Rep. 1994–), Ed. European Bulletin 1994–, Chair. Educ. and Research Div.; examiner Gen. Nursing Council, Royal Coll. of Surgeons 1971–83; Medical Dir and Deputy Chair. Medical Marketing Int. Group PLC; medical adviser Virgin Fitness Clubs, adviser H.C.A. Group of Hosps.; Exec. Dir Healthy Living (UK) Ltd, Healthy Living (Durham) Ltd, Universal Lifestyle Ltd, Medical Consulting Services Ltd; Chair. Int. Medical and Scientific Fundraising Cttee, British Red Cross, Medical and Science Div., World Fellowship Duke of Edinburgh Award; Fellow Asscn of Surgeons of GB, Int. Coll. of Surgeons; f. mem. British Asscn of Surgical Oncology; mem. Court of Patrons Royal Coll. of Surgeons 1986–, Int. Medical Parliamentarians Org. (Chair UK Div.), European Soc. of Surgical Oncology, World Fed. of Surgical Oncological Socs. (mem. Council and adviser on int. affairs), European Fed. of Surgeons, Tricare Europe Preferred Provider Network (US Armed Forces and Families), Breast and Thyroid Surgery 1997–; Devt Consultant Ridgeford Properties Ltd 2001; Health Exec. Bovis Land Lease Ltd 2000–; Medical Consultant and Advisor Keltbray Ltd 2003–; mem. Nat. Events Cttee of Imperial Cancer Research Fund; Gosse Research Scholarship; Queen's Jubilee Medal for Community Services. *Publications:* various medical publs. *Leisure interests:* tennis, music, cricket. *Address:* The Consulting Rooms, Wellington Hospital, Wellington Place, London, NW8 9LE; 58 Stockleigh Hall, Prince Albert Road, London, NW8 7LB, England (Home). *Telephone:* (20) 7935-4101. *Fax:* (20) 7483-0297. *Website:* www.medicalnet.co.uk/Sir Arnold Elton (Office).

ELTON, Benjamin Charles (Ben), BA; British author and performer; b. 3 May 1959; s. of Prof. Lewis Richard Benjamin Elton and Mary Elton (née Foster); m. Sophie Gare 1994; ed Godalming Grammar School, South Warwickshire Coll. of Further Educ., Manchester Univ.; first professional appearance Comic Strip Club 1981; numerous tours as 'stand-up comic' 1986–. *Film (writer and director:* Maybe Baby 2000; (actor) Much Ado About Nothing 1993. *Television (writer):* Happy Families 1985, Filthy Rich and Catflap 1986; (jtly): The Young Ones 1983, Blackadder II 1987, Blackadder the Third 1988, Blackadder Goes Forth 1989, The Thin Blue Line 1995–96; The Ben Elton Show 1998; (writer and performer): Friday Live 1987–88, Saturday Live 1987, The Man from Auntie 1990, 1994, Stark 1993. *Theatre (writer and director):* Gasping 1990, Silly Cow 1991, Popcorn 1997, Blast from The Past 1998, The Beautiful Game 2000, We Will Rock You (musical) 2002. *Publications:* (novels) Stark 1989, Gridlock 1991, This Other Eden 1993, Popcorn 1996, Inconceivable 1999, Dead Famous 2001; (plays) Gasping 1990, Silly Cow

1991, Popcorn 1996, Blast from the Past 1998, High Society 2002. *Leisure interests:* walking, reading, socializing. *Address:* c/o Phil McIntyre, 2nd Floor, 35 Soho Square, London, W1D 3QX, England.

ELTON, 2nd Baron, cr. 1934, of Headington; **Rodney Elton,** MA, TD; British politician and company director; b. 2 March 1930, Oxford; s. of the late Godfrey Elton, 1st Baron and Dedi Hartmann; m. 1st Anne Frances Tilney 1958 (divorced 1979); one s. three d.; m. 2nd Susan Richenda Gurney 1979; ed Eton Coll. and New Coll., Oxford; fmr Capt. Queen's Own Warwicks. and Worcs. Yeomanry; fmr Maj. Leics. and Derbyshire Yeomanry; farming 1957–73; Asst Mastership in History Loughborough Grammar School 1962–67, Fairham Comprehensive School for Boys 1967–69; contested Loughborough div. of Leics. 1966, 1970; Lecturer Bishop Lonsdale Coll. of Educ. 1969–72; Opposition Whip House of Lords 1974–76, a Deputy Chair. of Cttees. 1997–; Deputy Speaker 1999–; an Opposition Spokesman 1976–79; Parl. Under-Sec. of State for N Ireland 1979–81, Dept of Health and Social Security 1981–82, Home Office 1982–84, Minister of State 1984–85; Minister of State Dept of Environment 1985–86; Chair. Financial Intermediaries' Mans' and Brokers' Regulatory Assen (FIMBRA) 1987–90; Dir Andry Montgomery Ltd 1977–79, Deputy Chair. 1978–79, 1986–; Dir Overseas Exhbns Ltd 1977–79, Bldg Trades Exhbn Ltd 1977–79; mem. Panel on Takeovers and Mergers 1987–90; Chair. Independent Enquiry into Discipline in Schools (Report 1989); Chair. Intermediate Treatment Fund 1990–93; Chair. DIVERT Trust 1993–2000, Pres. 2000–; Quality and Standards Cttee, City and Guilds of London Inst. 1999–; Deputy Chair. Assen of Conservative Peers 1986–93; Vice-Pres. Inst. of Trading Standards Admins 1990–; mem. House of Lords Select Cttee on the Scrutiny of Delegated Powers 1993–97; mem. council Rainer Foundation 1990–96, City and Guilds of London Inst. 1991–97; Licensed Lay Minister, Church of England 1998–; fmr Trustee City Parochial Foundation and Trust for London; Conservative; Hon. Vice-Pres. Inst. of Trading Standards Officers. *Leisure interest:* painting. *Address:* House of Lords, London, SW1A 0PW, England. *Telephone:* (20) 7219-3165. *Fax:* (20) 7219-5979 (Office). *E-mail:* elton@parliament.uk (Office).

ELVIN, Herbert Lionel, MA; British educationalist; b. 7 Aug. 1905, Buckhurst Hill, Essex; s. of the late Herbert Henry Elvin of Mary Jane Elvin; m. Mona Bedortha Dutton 1934 (died 1997); one s.; ed Trinity Hall, Cambridge and Yale Univ; Fellow of Trinity Hall, Cambridge and mem. of Faculty of English, Cambridge, 1930–45; temporary civil servant, Air Ministry 1940–42, Ministry of Information (American Div.) 1942–45; Prin., Ruskin Coll., mem. Faculty of English, Oxford 1945–50; mem. Univ. Grants Cttee 1946–50; Dir Dept of Educ., UNESCO 1950–56; Prof. Educ. (Tropical Areas) London Univ., Inst. of Educ. 1956–58; Dir Inst. of Educ., London Univ. 1958–73; Chair. Commonwealth Educ. Liaison Cttee 1965–73; mem. Govt of India Educ. Comm. 1965–66; Hon. Fellow, Trinity Hall, Cambridge 1979, London Univ. Inst. of Educ. 1992; Emer. Prof. of Educ. (London). *Publications:* Men of America 1941, An Introduction to the Study of Poetry 1949, Education and Contemporary Society 1965, The Place of Commonsense in Educational Thought 1977, The Educational Systems in the European Community (ed.) 1982, Encounters with Education 1987. *Leisure interest:* reading, athletics. *Address:* 4 Bulstrode Gardens, Cambridge, CB3 0EN, England. *Telephone:* (1223) 358309.

ELVIN, Violetta (Violetta Prokhorova); British ballerina; b. 3 Nov. 1925, Moscow; d. of Vassili Prokhorov and Irena T. Grimusinskaya; m. 1st Harold Elvin 1944 (divorced 1952); m. 2nd Siegbert J. Weinberger 1953; m. 3rd Fernando Savarese 1959; one s.; ed Bolshoi Theatre School, Moscow; Mem. Bolshoi Theatre Ballet 1942, evacuated to Tashkent 1943; ballerina, Tashkent State Theatre; rejoined Bolshoi Theatre as soloist 1944; joined Sadler's Wells Ballet, Royal Opera House, Covent Garden (now the Royal Ballet) as guest soloist 1946 and later as regular mem., prima ballerina 1951–56 (concluded her stage career); guest artist, Stanislavsky Theatre, Moscow 1944, Sadler's Wells Theatre 1947; guest prima ballerina, La Scala 1952–53; guest artist, Cannes 1954, Copenhagen 1954, Teatro Municipal, Rio de Janeiro 1955, Festival Hall 1955; guest prima ballerina, Royal Opera House, Stockholm 1956; Dir Ballet Co. San Carlo Opera, Naples 1985–87. *Film appearances:* The Queen of Spades, Twice Upon a Time, Melba. *Leisure interests:* reading, walking, swimming. *Address:* Marina di Equa, 80066 Seiano, Bay of Naples, Italy. *Telephone:* (81) 8798520.

ELWES, Cary; British actor; b. 26 Oct. 1962, London; s. of Dominic Elwes and Tessa Kennedy; ed Harrow School; stage debut in Equus 1981. *Films include:* Another Country 1984, Oxford Blues 1984, The Bride 1985, Lady Jane 1986, Maschenka 1987, The Princess Bride 1987, Glory 1989, Days of Thunder 1990, Hot Shots! 1990, Leather Jackets 1991, Bram Stoker's Dracula 1992, Robin Hood: Men in Tights 1992, The Crush 1993, Rudyard Kipling's Jungle Book 1994, The Chase 1994, Twister 1996, Liar Liar 1997, Kiss the Girls 1997, The Informant 1997, Quest for Camelot (voice) 1998, Cradle Will Rock 1999, Shadow of the Vampire 2000, Wish You Were Dead 2000. *Address:* c/o Michael Gruber, William Morris Agency, 151 South El Camino Drive, Beverly Hills, CA 90212, USA.

ELWORTHY, Sir Peter (Herbert), Kt; New Zealand business executive and farmer; b. 3 March 1935, Timaru; s. of Harold Herbert Elworthy and June Mary Elworthy (née Batchelor); m. Fiona Elizabeth McHardy 1960; two s. two d.; ed Christ's Coll., Lincoln Agric. Coll.; Chair. Ravensdown Co-op 1977–82, Timaru Port Co. 1988–89, NZ Advisory Cttee on Overseas Aid 1988–89 (mem. 1986–89), NZ Farmlands Ltd 1989–92, Electricity Distribution Reform Unit

1990–92, The Power Co. 1990–97, Rural Electrical Reticulation Council 1990–96, Southland Electric Power Supply 1990–97, QEII Nat. Trust 1987–93, NZ Rural Property Trust 1988–89, Opihi (SC) River Devt Co. 1992–; Sky City Ltd (Auckland) 1992–, NZ Rural Properties Ltd 1992–, Seabil (NZ) Ltd 1994–96, Salvation Army Inaugural Community Support Cttee 1994–96; Pres. NZ Deer Farmers Asscn 1974–81, Federated Farmers of NZ 1984–87; Dir Reserve Bank of NZ 1985–99, Landcorp 1986–88, BP NZ Ltd 1986–, Ascot Man. Corp. (NZ) Ltd 1991–94, Enerco NZ Ltd 1992–95, Huttons Kiwi Ltd 1992–96, Skellerup Group Ltd 1993–96; Trustee Lincoln Univ. Foundation 1989–, Waitaingi Foundation 1990–2001, NZ Inst. of Econ. Research Inc. 1991–2001, Alan Duff Charitable Foundation 1994–2001; Fellow NZ Inst. of Agric. Sciences; Patron Int. Organic Agric. Conf., Lincoln 1994–; Nuffield Scholarship, UK 1970; Hon. DComm (Lincoln) 2002; McMeekan Memorial Award 1978, Bledisloe Award, Lincoln 1987, NZ Commemoration Medal 1990. *Leisure interests:* riding, fishing, flying, tennis, reading. *Address:* Craigmore Farm, Maungati, 2RD, Timaru, New Zealand. *Telephone:* (3) 6129809. *Fax:* (3) 6129825 (Office). *E-mail:* sir.peter@craigmore.com (Office). *Website:* www.craigmore.com (Office).

ELYAKOV, Georgy Borisovich, D.CHEM.SC.; Russian chemist; b. 13 Sept. 1929, Kostroma; m. Lyudmila Elyakova 1960; two d.; ed Moscow Univ.; mem. CPSU 1965–91; worked in Cen. Mil. Tech. Inst., USSR Ministry of Defence 1952–55; sr researcher Far East br. of USSR Acad. of Sciences 1955–69; f. and head of lab. of chem. of natural physiologically active compounds, Inst. of Biologically Active Compounds, Far East br. of USSR Acad. of Sciences 1959–64; Dir Pacific Inst. of Bioorganic Chem. 1964–2002, Scientific Head 2002–; Corresp. mem. USSR (now Russian) Acad. of Sciences 1970, mem. 1987; Vice-Pres. Russian Acad. of Sciences, Chair. Far East Div. 1991–2001; mem. Int. Soc. of Toxinologists; Hon. Citizen of Vladivostok 1999; Hon. mem. Korean Foundation; M. M. Shemyakin Prize, Russian Acad. of Sciences 1995. *Publications:* over 200 works on biologically active compounds (biosynthesis, structure and elucidation of biological functions); synthesis of principally new antibiotics and antioxidants. *Leisure interests:* driving, hunting, computers. *Address:* Pacific Institute of Bioorganic Chemistry, Far East Division of Russian Academy of Sciences, 690022 Vladivostok, Russia (Office). *Telephone:* (4232) 31-14-30 (Office); (095) 938-17-55 (Moscow). *Fax:* (4232) 31-40-50 (Office). *E-mail:* piboc@eastnet.febras.ru (Office).

EMAN, Jan Hendrik Albert (Henny); Aruban politician and lawyer; Leader Arubaanse Volkspartij (AVP); Prime Minister of Aruba and Minister of Gen. Affairs 1986–89, 1993–2001. *Address:* Arubaanse Volkspartij (AVP), Oranjestad, Aruba (Office). *Telephone:* (8) 33500 (Office). *Fax:* (8) 37870 (Office).

EMANUEL, Elizabeth Florence, MA, DesRCA, FCSD; British fashion designer; b. 5 July 1953, London; d. of Samuel Charles Weiner and Brahna Betty Weiner; m. David Leslie Emanuel 1975 (separated 1990); one s. one d.; ed City of London School for Girls, Harrow Coll. of Art; opened London salon 1978; designed wedding gown for HRH Princess of Wales 1981, costumes for Andrew Lloyd Webber's Song and Dance 1982, sets and costumes for ballet Frankenstein, The Modern Prometheus, Royal Opera House London, La Scala Milan 1985, costumes for Stoll Moss production of Cinderella 1985, costumes for film Diamond Skulls 1990, The Changeling 1995, uniforms for Virgin Atlantic Airways 1990, Britannia Airways 1995; launched int. fashion label Elizabeth Emanuel 1991; launched Bridal Collection for Berkertex Brides UK Ltd 1994; launched bridal collection in Japan 1994; opened new shop and design studio 1996; launched own brand label (with Richard Thompson) 1999. *Publication:* Style for All Seasons (with David Emanuel) 1982. *Leisure interests:* ballet, cinema, writing, environmental and conservation issues. *Address:* 49 Dorset Street, London, W1H 3FH, England. *Telephone:* (20) 7266-1055.

EMBUREY, John Ernest; British cricketer; b. 20 Aug. 1952, Peckham, London; s. of John Emburey and Rose (née Ruff) Emburey; m. 2nd Susan Elizabeth Ann Booth 1980; two d.; ed Peckham Manor Secondary School; right-hand late-order batsman, off-break bowler, slip or gully fielder; teams: Middx 1973–95, Western Prov. 1982–84, Northants. 1996–98 (player/chief coach and man.); 64 Tests for England 1978–1995, two as capt., scoring 1,713 runs (average 22.5) and taking 147 wickets (average 38.4); scored 12,021 runs (seven hundreds) and took 1,608 wickets in first-class cricket; toured Australia 1978–80, 1986–88, West Indies 1981, 1986, India 1981/82, 1992/93, Pakistan 1987, New Zealand 1988, Sri Lanka 1982, 1993; 61 one-day ints (seven as capt.); mem. seven County Championships winning teams with Middx (1976, 1977, 1980, 1982, 1985, 1990, 1993), Gillette Cup 1977, 1980, Benson and Hedges Cup 1983, 1986, Sunday League Winners' trophy 1991, Natwest Trophy 1994, 1998. retd from playing 1997; Lead coach and man. Middx Co. Cricket Club 2001–; Sky TV commentator 1988–; Wisden Cricketer of the Year 1984. *Publications:* Emburey – A Biography 1987, Spinning in a Fast World 1989. *Leisure interests:* golf, fishing, reading. *Address:* c/o Middlesex County Cricket Club, Lord's Cricket Ground, London, NW8 8QN, England. *Telephone:* (20) 7289-1300 (Office).

EMERTON, Rev. John Adney, MA, DD, FBA; British ecclesiastic and academic; b. 5 June 1928, Winchmore Hill; s. of Adney Spencer Emerton and Helena Mary Emerton (née Quin); m. Norma Elizabeth Bennington 1954; one s. one d.; ed Minchenden Grammar School, Southgate, Corpus Christi Coll., Oxford and Wycliffe Hall, Oxford; ordained deacon 1952, priest 1953; Asst Lecturer in Theology, Birmingham Univ. 1952–53; curate, Birmingham

Cathedral 1952–53; Lecturer in Hebrew and Aramaic, Univ. of Durham 1953–55; Lecturer in Divinity, Univ. of Cambridge 1955–62; Fellow, St Peter's Coll. and Reader in Semitic Philology, Univ. of Oxford 1962–68; Regius Prof. of Hebrew, Univ. of Cambridge 1968–95, Prof. Emer. 1995–; Fellow St John's Coll. Cambridge 1970–; Sec. Int. Org. for Study of Old Testament 1971–89, Pres. 1992–95; Hon. Canon, St George's Cathedral, Jerusalem 1984–; mem. Ed. Bd Vetus Testamentum 1971–97; Visiting Fellow, Inst. for Advanced Studies, Hebrew Univ. of Jerusalem 1983; visiting professorship at Univ. of Toronto; Corresp. mem. Göttingen Akad. der Wissenschaften 1990; Hon. DD (Edin.) 1977; Burkitt Medal for Biblical Studies, British Acad. 1991. *Publications:* The Peshitta of the Wisdom of Solomon 1959, The Old Testament in Syriace – The Song of Songs 1966; articles in journals. *Address:* 34 Gough Way, Cambridge, CB3 9LN, England.

EMERY, Alan Eglin Heathcote, MD, PhD, DSc, FRCP, F.R.C.P.(E.), , FLS, FRSE, FRSA; British physician and professor of human genetics; b. 21 Aug. 1928, Manchester; s. of Harold Heathcote Emery and Alice Eglin; m. 2nd Marcia Lynn Miller 1988; three s. three d. from previous m.; ed Manchester Grammar School, Chester Coll., Manchester Univ. and Johns Hopkins Univ., USA; Postdoctoral Research Fellow, Johns Hopkins Univ., Baltimore 1961–64; Lecturer, then Reader in Medical Genetics, Manchester Univ. 1964–68; Foundation Prof. and Chair., Dept of Human Genetics, Univ. of Edin. 1968–83, Prof. Emer. and Hon. Fellow 1983–; Hon. Visiting Fellow, Green Coll., Oxford 1985–; Research Dir European Neuromuscular Centre and Chair. Research Cttee 1990–99, Chief. Scientific Adviser 1999–; Pres. British Clinical Genetics Soc. 1980–83; Visiting Prof. Univs of New York, Heidelberg, UCLA, Padua, Beijing, Duke, Cape Town, Warsaw, Royal Postgrad. Medical School, London, etc.; Harveian, Boerhave, Jenner Lecturer, etc.; mem. Scientific Cttee Int. Congress on Neuromuscular Diseases 1990, 1994, 1998, 2000; mem. Exec. Cttee Research Group on Neuromuscular Diseases of World Fed. of Neurology 1996–, Exec. Bd World Muscle Soc. 1999–; Adviser, Asian and Oceanian Myology Centre, Tokyo 2000–; Vice-Pres. Muscular Dystrophy Campaign of Great Britain 1999–; Pres. Section Medical Genetics, Royal Soc. of Medicine 2001–; mem. Royal Soc. of Literature; Hon. FRS (SA); Hon. Fellow Univ. of Edin. 1990–, Gaetano Conte Acad. (Italy) 1991; Hon. mem. Dutch Soc. of Genetics 1999, Asscn of British Neurologists 1999; Hon. MD (Naples, Würzburg); Int. Award for Genetic Research (USA), Gaetano Conte Prize for Clinical Research 2000, Pro Finlandiae Gold Medal for contribs to Neuroscience 2000, Lifetime Achievement Award, WFN 2002. *Exhibition:* annual one-man exhbn of paintings, Oxford. *Publications:* Psychological Aspects of Genetic Counselling 1984, Introduction to Recombinant DNA (2nd edn with S. Malcolm) 1995, Methodology in Medical Genetics, (2nd edn) 1986, Principles and Practice of Medical Genetics (2nd edn) 1991, Elements of Medical Genetics (8th edn) 1992, Duchenne Muscular Dystrophy (2nd edn) 1993, The History of a Genetic Disease: Duchenne Muscular Dystrophy or Meryon's Disease 1995, Diagnostic Criteria for Neuromuscular Disorders (2nd edn) 1997, Neuromuscular Disorders; Clinical and Molecular Genetics 1998, Muscular Dystrophy: The Facts (2nd edn) 2000, The Muscular Dystrophies 2001, Medicine and Art (with M. L. H. Emery) 2003; 300 scientific papers. *Leisure interests:* marine biology, oil painting, fly fishing. *Address:* Peninsula Medical School, Department of Neurology, Royal Devon and Exeter Hospital, Exeter, EX2 5DW (Office); 2 Ingleside Court, Upper West Terrace, Budleigh Salterton, Devon, EX9 6NZ, England (Home). *Telephone:* (1395) 445847. *E-mail:* enmc@euronet.nl (Office).

EMERY, Lin, BA; American sculptor; b. 20 May 1928, New York City; d. of Cornell Emery and Jean Weill; m. S. B. Braselman 1962 (deceased); one s.; ed Univs of Chicago and Sorbonne, Paris; worked in studio of Ossip Zadkine, Paris 1950; 46 solo exhbns in US museums and galleries 1957–98; int. exhbns in Tokyo, Hong Kong, Manila, Sofia, Paris, London, Berlin, Brisbane, Kyoto and Frankfurt 1961–98; public sculpture erected in Civic Center, New Orleans 1966–70, Fidelity Center, Oklahoma City 1972, Humanities Center, Columbia, SC 1974, Federal Plaza, Houma, La. 1997, Marina Centre, Singapore 1986, City of Oxnard, Calif. 1988, Osaka Dome, Japan 1997, Mitre Corpn, Alexandra, Va 2001, Schiffer Publishing Co., Atglen PA 2002, Sterling Corpn, Las Colinas TX 2002, etc.; Visiting Prof. Tulane School of Architecture, New Orleans 1969–70, Newcomb School of Art, New Orleans 1980; Visiting Artist and lecturer Art Acad. of Cincinnati, La. State Univ., Univ. of New Orleans, Univ. of Tex. at Austin, Univ. of Maine 1985–88; Chair. 9th Int. Sculpture Conf. 1976, Co-Chair. Mayor's Steering Cttees, New Orleans 1979–80; Studio Chair. Coll. Art Asscn 1979; mem. Bd Contemporary Arts Center, New Orleans 1997–; mem. Loyola Univ. Visiting Cttee 1996–99; adviser, Artists Guild, New Orleans 1997–99; mentor, Center for Creative Arts, New Orleans 1998; Mayor's Award for Achievement in the Arts, La. 1980, Lazlo Aranyi Award for Public Art, Va 1990, Delgado Award for Artistic Excellence, La. 1997, Grand Prix for Public Sculpture (Japan) 1997, Gov.'s Arts Award, LA 2001. *Retrospective exhbns:* New Orleans Museum of Art 1997, Masur Museum, Monroe LA 2001, Meadows Museum, Shreveport LA 2002. *Address:* 7520 Dominican Street, New Orleans, LA 70118, USA. *Telephone:* (504) 866-7775. *Fax:* (504) 866-0144. *E-mail:* lin@linemery.com (Office).

EMIN, Tracey; British artist; b. 1964, Margate; ed John Cass School of Art, London, Maidstone Coll. of Art, Royal Coll. of Art; f. Tracey Emin Museum, London 1996; Int. Award for Video Art, Baden-Baden 1997, Video Art Prize, Südwest Bank, Stuttgart 1997. *Exhibitions include:* White Cube Gallery, London 1992, Minky Manky 1995, My Major Retrospective, Part of What

Made Me What I Am, Loose Ends 1998, Personal Effects 1998, Made in London 1998, Sweetie 1999, Temple of Diana 1999, Now its my Turn to Scream 1999, Art in Sacred Places 2000, What do you Know About Love 2000. *Films include:* Why I Never Became a Dancer. *Publications:* Exploration of the Soul 1995, Always Glad to See You 1997, Tracey Emin: Holiday Inn 1998, Tracey Emin on Pandaemonium 1998, Absolute Tracey 1998. *Leisure interests:* writing poetry, watching sunsets. *Address:* c/o White Cube, 44 Duke Street, St James's, London, SW1Y 6DD (Office); The Tracey Emin Museum, 221 Waterloo Road, London, SE1, England. *Telephone:* (20) 7930-5373 (Office); (20) 7261-1116. *Fax:* (20) 7930-9973 (Office).

EMINEM (Marshall Bruce Mathers III (Slim Shady)); American rap artist; b. 17 Oct. 1972, St Joseph, MO; m. Kim Mathers 1999 (divorced); one d.; moved to Detroit, aged 12; dropped out of high school to join local rap groups Basement Productions, D12; released debut album The Infinite on ind. label FBT; after releasing Slim Shady EP, made guest appearances with Kid Rock and Shabbam Shadeeq, leading to deal with Dr Dre's Aftermath Records; Founder and owner Slim Shady record label; MTV Annual American Music Awards Best Hip Hop Artist 2000, 2002, three Grammy Awards 2001, Best Pop/Rock Male Artist 2002, MTV Europe Music Awards Best Male Act 2002, Best Hip Hop Act 2002, Brit Award for Best Int. Male Solo Artist 2003. *Albums include:* The Infinite 1997, The Slim Shady LP 1999, The Marshall Mathers LP 2000 (Best Album, MTV Awards, Grammy Award for Best Rap Album 2003) 2002. *Singles include:* The Slim Shady EP 1998, Just Don't Give a F*** 1999, My Name is 1999, Guilty Conscience 1999, The Real Slim Shady 2000, The Way I Am 2000, Stan 2000, Without Me 2002, Lose Yourself (Acad. Award for Best Music (song in film 8 Mile) 2003. *Collaborations include:* Dr Dre, D12, Missy Elliott, Dido. *Film:* 8 Mile 2002. *Address:* c/o Interscope Records, 220 Colorado Avenue, Santa Monica, CA 90404, USA (Office).

EMMANUELLI, Henri Joseph; French politician; b. 31 May 1945, Eaux-Bonnes, Pyrénées-Atlantiques; s. of the late Louis Emmanuelli and of Julie Chourre; m. Antonia Gonzalez 1967; one s. one d.; ed Lycée Louis-Barthou, Pau, Institut d'études politiques de Paris; mem. staff Banque de l'Union Parisienne, then Compagnie financière de banque 1969–78; Deputy for Landes 1978–82, 1986–93, 1993–97, 2000–; Chair. Conseil général, Landes 1982–98, 2000–; Sec. of State for Overseas Territories and Depts 1981–83, for Budget 1983–86; Chair. Finance Comm. of Nat. Ass. 1991–93, Pres. Nat. Ass. 1992–93, Pres. Comm. for Finances, Gen. Econs and Planning 1997, 2000–; mem. Nat. Secr. Parti Socialiste 1987–, Leader 1994–95. *Publication:* Plaidoyer pour l'Europe 1992, Citadelles interdites 2000. *Leisure interests:* skiing, swimming. *Address:* Assemblée nationale, 75355 Paris; Parti Socialiste, 10 rue de Solférino, 75333 Paris Cedex, France; 22-24 rue Victor Hugo, 40000 Mont-de-Marsan (Office). *E-mail:* presidence@cg40.fr (Office); hemmanuelli@assemblee-nationale.fr (Office).

EMMENS, Clifford Walter, PhD, DSc, F.S.S., CBiol, FIBiol, FAA; Australian university professor; b. 9 Dec. 1913, London; s. of Walter J. Emmens and Narcissa L. Pugh; m. Muriel E. Bristow 1937; two s. two d.; ed Purley County School and Univ. Coll., London; demonstrator in Zoology, Univ. Coll., London 1936–37; research biologist MRC 1937–48, seconded to Ministry of Home Security and RAF 1941–46; Head Dept of Veterinary Physiology, Univ. of Sydney 1948–78, seconded part-time as officer-in-charge, CSIRO Sheep Biology Lab., later Div. of Animal Physiology 1952–54; Chair. various cttees of CSIRO, Nat. Health and Medical Research Council etc.; Fellow Inst. of Biology; mem. numerous professional socs; Hon. Fellow Australian Coll. of Veterinary Scientists; Hon. Dr of Veterinary Science; Oliver Bird Medal and Prize (UK) 1961; Istituto Spallanzani Medal (Italy) 1964. *Publications:* author and co-author of numerous books and more than 200 scientific papers. *Leisure interests:* aquarium keeping, history of science. *Address:* 603/22 Sutherland Street, Cremorne, NSW 2090, Australia.

EMMERICH, Roland; director, screenplay writer and executive producer; b. 10 Nov. 1955, Stuttgart, Germany; ed film school in Munich; film produced as a student The Noah's Ark Principle shown at 1984 Berlin Film Festival and sold to more than twenty countries; f. Centropolis Film Productions. *Films:* Making Contact (Joey) (dir only), Ghost Chase, Eye of the Storm (producer only), Moon 44, Universal Soldier, Stargate, Independence Day, The Thirteenth Floor (producer only), The Patriot. *TV:* (series) The Visitor (producer) 1997. *Address:* c/o Creative Artists Agency, 9830 Wilshire Boulevard, Beverly Hills, CA 90212, USA.

EMMOTT, William John (Bill), BA; British journalist; b. 6 Aug. 1956; s. of Richard Emmott and Audrey Emmott; m. 1st Charlotte Crowther 1982 (divorced); m. 2nd Carol Barbara Mawer 1992; ed Latymer Upper School, Hammersmith and Magdalen and Nuffield Colls. Oxford; Brussels corresp. The Economist 1980–82, Econs corresp. 1982–83, Tokyo corresp. 1983–86, Finance Ed. 1986–89, Business Affairs Ed. 1989–93, Ed.-in-Chief 1993–; Editorial Dir Economist Intelligence Unit. May–Dec. 1992; Hon. LLD (Warwick) 1999; Hon. DLitt (City) 2001. *Publications:* The Pocket Economist (with R. Pennant-Rea, q.v.) 1983, The Sun Also Sets 1989, Japanophobia 1993, Kanryo no Taizai 1996, The Economist, 20:21 Vision: The Lessons of the 20th Century for the 21st (ed.) 2002. *Leisure interests:* cricket, dog-walking, journalism. *Address:* The Economist, 25 St James's Street, London, SW1A 1HG, England. *Telephone:* (20) 7830-7061. *Fax:* (20) 7839-2968. *E-mail:* be@economist.com (Office). *Website:* www.economist.com (Office).

EMOVON, Emmanuel Uwumagbuhunmwun, PhD; Nigerian professor of chemistry and government minister; b. 24 Feb. 1929, Benin City; s. of late Gabriel A. Emovon and Oni Emovon; m. Princess Adesuwa C. Akenzua 1959; three s. three d.; ed Baptist School, Benin City, Edo Coll., Benin City, Univ. Coll., Ibadan, Univ. Coll., London Univ., UK; Lecturer in Chem., Univ. Coll. Ibadan 1959; Prof. of Chem., Univ. of Benin 1971; Vice-Chancellor Univ. of Jos 1978; Fed. Minister of Science and Tech. 1985–89; Co-ordinator, Sheda Science and Tech. Complex 1990–; invested Chief Obayagbona of Benin 1991; fmr mem. numerous govt cttees and bds; fmr external examiner; Fellow Science Asscn of Nigeria, Nigerian Acad. of Science; nat. mem. ICSU 1986. *Publications:* numerous scientific papers. *Leisure interest:* photography, gardening, long and table tennis, cricket and football. *Address:* Sheda Science and Technology Complex, Ministry of Science and Technology, P.M.B. 186, Garki, Abuja, Nigeria. *Telephone:* (9) 5233918 (Office); (9) 2340667 (Home). *Fax:* (9) 5233919.

EMPEY, Sir Reginald Norman Morgan, Kt, BSc, OBE; British politician; b. 26 Oct. 1947; s. of Samuel Frederick Empey and Emily Winifred Empey (née Morgan); m. Stella Ethna Donnan 1977; one s. one d.; ed The Royal School, Armagh, Queen's Univ., Belfast; publicity officer, Ulster Young Unionist Council 1967–68, Vice-Chair. 1968–72; Chair. Vanguard Unionist Party 1974–75; mem. E Belfast Northern Ireland Constitutional Convention 1975–76; Deputy Lord Mayor 1988–89, Lord Mayor of Belfast 1989–90, 1993–94; mem. Belfast East, NI Ass. 1998–2002 (Ass. suspended Oct. 2002); Minister of Enterprise, Trade and Investment 1999–2002; mem. Belfast City Council 1985–, Ulster Unionist Council 1987– (Hon. Sec. 1990–96, Vice-Pres. 1996–); Bd mem. Police Authority for Northern Ireland 1992–, European Cttee of the Regions for NI 1994–; mem. Ulster Unionist Party. *Leisure interests:* gardening, walking. *Address:* Knockvale House, 205 Sandown Road, Belfast, BT5 6GX, Northern Ireland.

ENAHORO, Chief Anthony, C.FR.; Nigerian politician, journalist, newspaper publisher and company director; b. 22 July 1923, Uromi Ishan, Bendel State; s. of late Chief Okotako Enahoro and Princess Inibokun Okoje; m. Helen Ediae 1954; four s. one d.; ed Govt Schools Uromi and Owo, King's Coll. Lagos; journalist 1942–52; Ed. Southern Nigerian Defender 1944–45, Daily Comet 1945–49; Assoc. Ed. West African Pilot; Ed.-in-Chief Nigerian Star 1950–52; foundation mem. Action Group Party, later Acting Gen. Sec. and Fed. Vice-Pres.; Chair. Uromi Dist Council and Ishan Div. Council; mem. Western House of Assembly and Fed. House of Reps and Party Chief Whip 1951–54; Dir Nat. Coal Bd 1953–54; Minister of Home Affairs, Transport, Information and Midwest Affairs and Leader of the House (Western Region) 1954–59; Fed. MP and Opposition Spokesman on Foreign Affairs, Internal Affairs and Legislature Affairs 1959–63; moved motion for self-govt and attended all constitutional talks preceding independence in 1960; detained during Emergency period Western Region 1962, fled to Britain, extradited and imprisoned in Nigeria for treasonable felony; released by mil. govt 1966; Leader, Midwest State del. to Constitutional Conf. and mem. Constitutional Cttee 1966; Fed. Commr for Information, Culture, Youth, Sports, Co-operatives and Labour 1967–75; mem. Nat. Democratic Coalition (NADECO); Fed. Commr for Special Duties 1975; Pres. World Black and African Festival of Arts and Culture 1972–75; State Chair. Nat. Party of Nigeria 1978–80; Chair. Cttees Edo State Movt 1981–, Nigerian Shippers Council 1982; detained Aug.–Dec. 1994; Hon. DSc (Benin) 1972. *Publication:* Fugitive Offender (autobiog.). *Leisure interests:* golf, reading, travel. *Address:* Rainbow House, 144 Upper Mission Road, P.M.B. 1425, Benin City, Nigeria. *Telephone:* 200803 (Office); 243770 (Home).

ENDARA GALIMANY, Guillermo; Panamanian politician and lawyer; b. May 1936, Panamá; m. 1st (died 1989); m. 2nd Ana Mae Díaz 1990; ed Tulane Univ., Univ. of Panamá, New York Univ. School of Law; labour lawyer; fmr Prof. of Business Law, Univ. of Panamá; aide to fmr Pres. of Panamá, Arnulfo Arias Madrid; leader Alianza Democrática Oposicionista y Civilista (ADOC); mem. Nat. Democratic Coalition (NADECO); Pres. of Panamá 1989–94. *Address:* c/o Oficina del Presidente, Palacio Presidencial, Valija 50, Panamá 1, Panama.

ENDELEY, E. M. L., OBE; Cameroonian politician and medical doctor; b. 10 April 1916, Buea (then in Nigeria); s. of late Chief Mathias Liffafe Endeley and of Mariana Mojoko Liombe; m. 1st Ethel Mina Green (divorced 1961); m. 2nd Fanny Ebenye Njoh 1965; nine s. three d.; ed Buea Govt School, Catholic Mission, Bojongo, Govt Coll. Umuahia, Higher Coll., Yaba; qualified as doctor 1942; entered govt service 1943; served Lagos, Port Harcourt, etc.; in charge of Cottage Hospital, Buea; trade union leader 1947; formed Cameroons Nat. Fed. (afterwards Kamerun Nat. Congress) 1949; mem. House of Reps and Council of Ministers 1952–54, Minister without Portfolio, Minister of Labour; First Premier, Southern Cameroons 1955–59; Pres. Bakweri Co-op. Marketing Union 1955; led South Cameroons del. to Constitutional Conf., London 1957; first Premier of South Cameroons 1958–59; Leader of the Opposition 1959–61; Leader Nat. Convention Party (later Cameroon People's Nat. Convention Party), West Cameroon 1961–66; Asst Treas. and mem. Cameroon Nat. Union (now Cameroon People's Democratic Movt) Political Bureau 1966–74, mem. Cen. Cttee 1975–; mem. Nat. Ass., Yaoundé 1973–; Chair. House Cttee on Production, Town Planning, Agric., Stockfarming, Rural and Civil Eng. *Leisure interests:* mountaineering, gardening, wild game hunting, farming. *Address:* P.O. Box 5, Buea, Southwest Province, Cameroon. *Telephone:* 32-42-26.

ENDERBY, John Edwin, CBE, PhD, FRS; British scientist; b. 16 Jan. 1931, Grimsby; s. of late Thomas Edwin Enderby and Rheita Rebecca Hollinshead Enderby; m. Susan Bowles; one s. two d.; one s. (deceased) one d. from previous marriage; ed Chester Grammar School, Westminster Coll., Birbeck Coll., Univ. of London; lecturer then Reader Univ. of Sheffield 1960–69; Prof. and Head of Dept Univ. of Leicester 1969–76; Prof. of Physics Univ. of Bristol 1976–81; H. H. Wills Prof. 1981–96, Prof. Emer. 1996–, Head of Dept, Dir H. H. Wills Lab. 1981–94; Directeur-Adjoint Inst. Laue-Langevin, Grenoble, France (on secondment) 1985–88; Ed. Proc. of the Royal Soc. 'A' 1989–93; Ed.-in-Chief Journal of Physics: Condensed Matter 1997–2001; Physical Sec. and Vice-Pres. of the Royal Soc. 1999–; mem. Council PPARC 1994–98; Chief Scientific Adviser, Inst. of Physics Publishing 2002; Distinguished Argonne Fellow (USA); Hon. Fellow, Birbeck Coll., Univ. of London 2001; Hon. DSc (Loughborough) 1998; Guthrie Medal and Prize, Inst. of Physics 1995. *Publications:* numerous papers on liquids in learned journals. *Leisure interests:* travel, woodwork, music, reading. *Address:* H. H. Wills Physics Laboratory, Tyndall Avenue, Bristol, BS8 1TL (Office); 7 Cotham Lawn Road, Bristol, BS6 6DU, England (Home). *Telephone:* (117) 928-8737 (Office); (117) 973-3411 (Home). *Fax:* (117) 925-5624.

ENDZIŅŠ, Aivars, DrIur; Latvian lawyer; b. 8 Dec. 1940, Rīga; m.; two s.; ed Univ. of Latvia, Moscow State Univ.; lecturer, Assoc. Prof., Univ. of Latvia 1972–90, 1996–97; Assoc. Prof. Police Acad. 1998–, Prof. 2002–; mem. Supreme Council, Presidium Supreme Council 1990–93; mem. Saeima (Parl.), Vice-Chair. Legal Affairs Cttee 1993–96; Acting Chair., then Chair. Constitutional Court 1996–; mem. Parl. Ass., Council of Europe 1995–96; Assoc. mem. Democracy Through Law Comm. (Venice Comm.) 1992–95, mem. 1995–, mem. Bureau 1991–2001; Order of Three Stars 2001. *Publications:* more than 60 academic publs. *Leisure interests:* fishing, hunting. *Address:* Constitutional Court, J. Alunāna iela 1, Rīga 1010 (Office); No. 31 Drustu St, Rīga 1002, Latvia (Home). *Telephone:* 722-1412 (Office); 793-4654 (Home). *Fax:* 722-0572 (Office). *E-mail:* aivars.e@satv.tiesa.gov.lv (Office). *Website:* www.satv.tiesa.gov.lv (Office).

ENESTAM, Jan-Erik, MPolSci; Finnish politician; b. 12 March 1947, Västanfjärd; m. Solveig V. Dahlqvist 1979; three c.; tourism researcher, Åland Provincial Govt 1972–74; researcher, Finnish Tourist Bd 1974; Head of Office, Åland Provincial Govt 1974–78; Municipal Man. Västanfjärd 1978–83; Project Man. Nordic Council of Ministers 1983–91; mem. Regional Policy Advisory Bd 1987–91; mem. Parl. 1991–; Chair. Västanfjärd Municipal Council 1989–96; Special Adviser to Minister of Defence 1990–91; Minister of Defence and Minister at Ministry of Social Affairs (Equality) and Health Jan.–April 1995; Minister of the Interior 1995–99, Minister of Defence, Nordic Cooperation and Foreign Affairs (Adjacent Areas) 1999–2003; Deputy Chair. Cen. Fed. of Fishing Industry 1986–94; Vice-Pres. Svenska Folkpartiet – SFP (Swedish People's Party) Parl. Group 1991–94, Chair. SFP 1998–; Commdr, Order of the White Rose of Finland 1996, Kt (Third Class), Order of Grand Duke Gediminas (Lithuania) 1997, Cross of Merit with Clasp, Armour Guild; Medal for Mil. Merit 1995, Medal of Merit, Cen. Chamber of Commerce of Finland. *Leisure interests:* literature, cross-country skiing, swimming, football, canoeing, cooking. *Address:* Svenska Folkpartiet – SFP, Simonsgatan 8A, PB 430, 00101 Helsinki, Finland (Office). *Telephone:* (9) 6931968 (Office). *Fax:* (9) 693070 (Office). *E-mail:* info@sfp.fi (Office). *Website:* www.sfp.fi.

ENGEL, Johannes K.; German journalist and editor; b. 29 April 1927, Berlin; s. of Karl and Anna (née Helke) Engel; m. Ruth Moter 1951; one s. one d.; journalist Int. News Service and Der Spiegel magazine 1946–, Office Man., Frankfurt am Main 1948, Dept Head 1951, Ed.-in-Chief, Hamburg 1961. *Address:* Kirchenredder 7, 22339 Hamburg, Germany. *Telephone:* 30071 (Office).

ENGELBRECHT, Jüri; Estonian physicist and mathematician; b. 1 Aug. 1939, Tallinn; m.; two c.; ed Tallinn Tech. Univ.; Sr lecturer Tallinn Tech. Univ.; Sr researcher, head of Dept, Deputy Dir Inst. of Cybernetics Estonian Acad. of Sciences 1968–94; part-time assoc., then Prof. Tallinn Tech. Univ. 1974–92, 1994–; Adjunct Prof. Helsinki Univ. of Tech.; mem. Estonian Acad. of Sciences 1990, Pres. 1994–; Chair. Estonian Cttee for Mechanics 1991–; mem. numerous socs and cttees; Ed.-in-Chief Proc. of the Estonian Acad. of Sciences 1991–95; ed. Research Reports in Physics 1988–93; mem. Ed. Bd Prikladnaya Mekhanika and several other journals; mem. Estonian Soc. for Physics, New York Acad. of Sciences, European Acad. of Sciences and Arts, Accademia Peloritana dei Pericolanti (Italy), Latvian Acad. of Sciences, Hungarian Acad. of Sciences, Gothenburg Royal Soc. of Sciences and Arts, World Innovation Foundation; Dr hc (Budapest); Estonian Science Prize, Humboldt Research Award 1993; Kt White Rose 1st Class (Finland), Coat of Arms 4th Class (Estonia), Lion Grand Cross (Finland). *Publications:* Nonlinear Deformation Waves 1981, Nonlinear Wave Processes of Deformation in Solids 1983, Nonlinear Evolution Equations 1986, An Introduction to Asymmetric Solitary Waves 1991, Nonlinear Dynamics and Chaos 1993, Nonlinear Wave Dynamics: Complexity and Simplicity 1997; and over 200 scientific articles. *Address:* Institute of Cybernetics, Tallinn Technical University, Akadeemia tee 21, Tallinn EE12617, Estonia. *Telephone:* (2) 644-21-29 (Office). *Fax:* (2) 645-18-05. *Website:* www.akadeemia.ee (Office).

ENGELL, Hans; Danish politician and newspaper editor; b. 8 Oct. 1948, Copenhagen; s. of Knud Engell Andersen; ed Coll. of Journalism; journalist for Berlingske newspaper consortium 1968–78; Head of Press Service of Conservative People's Party 1978–82; mem. Parl. 1984–, Minister for Defence

1982–87, of Justice 1989–93; Chair. Conservative Parl. Group 1987–89; Leader Conservative People's Party 1995–97; Ed.-in-Chief Ekstra Bladet 2000–. *Address:* Ekstra Bladet, Rådhuspladsen, 1785 Copenhagen (Office); Puggaardsgade 13, 1573 Copenhagen, Denmark. *Telephone:* 33-47-23-02 (Office). *Fax:* 33-47-14-10-00 (Office). *E-mail:* hans.engell@eb.dk (Office).

ENGHOLM, Björn, DIPL.-POL.; German politician; b. 9 Nov. 1939, Lübeck; m.; two d.; ed Acad. of Econs and Politics, Hamburg and Univ. of Hamburg; apprentice printer 1959–62, Journeyman's Certificate 1962; joined SPD 1962, mem. governing Bd 1984–; lecturer and freelance journalist 1964–69; mem. Bundestag 1969–82; Parl. State Sec. Ministry of Educ. and Science 1977–81, Minister 1981–82, Opposition Leader Landstag of Schleswig-Holstein 1983–88, Minister-Pres. 1988–93; Chair. SDP 1990–93. *Address:* Jürgen-Wullenwever-Str. 9, 23566 Lübeck, Germany.

ENGL, Walter L., Dr rer. nat, FIEEE; German professor of engineering; b. 8 April 1926, Regensburg; ed Technical Univ. of Munich; Siemens Instrument and Control Div. 1950–63, latterly Head of Research Div.; Prof. Tech. Univ. of Aachen 1963–91, Dean Faculty of Eng 1968–69; Visiting Prof. Univ. of Arizona 1967, Stanford Univ. 1970, Univ. of Tokyo 1972, 1980; Hon. Prof. Univ. of Kiel 1992; mem. Acad. of Science of North Rhine-Westphalia; mem. Int. Union of Radio Science; Foreign Assoc. mem. Eng Acad. of Japan; VDE-Ehrenring (highest award of German Electrical Engineers Soc.). *Publications:* 100 publs. *Address:* Zum Heider Busch 5, 52134 Herzogenrath, Germany (Home). *E-mail:* w.l.engl@post.rwth-aachen.de (Home).

ENGLAND, Richard, BArch; Maltese architect, university professor and artist; b. 3 Oct. 1937; s. of Edwin England Sant Fournier and Ina Desain; m. Myriam Borg Manduca 1962; one s. one d.; ed St Edward's Coll., Univ. of Malta, Politecnico, Milan, Italy; student-architect in Gio Ponti's studio, Milan 1960–62; Dir England & England, Architects 1962–; Dean Faculty of Architecture, Head Dept of Architecture, Univ. of Malta 1987–89; Prof. Int. Acad. of Architecture 1987–, Academician 1991–; subject of several monographs; Fellow Inst. of Professional Designers (London), Foundation for Int. Studies, Malta; Hon. Prof. Univ. of Ga, Inst. of Advanced Studies, Univ. of NY, Univ. of Malta, Univ. of Buenos Aires; Hon. Fellow Univ. of Bath, England, American Inst. of Architects 1999; Hon. mem. World Forum of Young Architects, Colegio de Arquitectos, Jalisco, Mexico; Officer, Nat. Order of Merit (Malta) 1993; Dr hc (Univ. of Architecture, Civil Eng and Geology, Sofia, Bulgaria); Interarch 1985 and 1991 Laureate Prizes, Commonwealth Asscn of Architects Regional Awards 1985, 1987, Gold Medal City of Toulouse 1985, Comité des Critiques d'Architecture Silver Medal 1987, USSR Biennale Laureate Prize 1988, IFRAA Prize (USA) 1991, Int. Prize, Costa Rica Biennale 1996, Gold Medal, Belgrade Architectural Triennale 2000. *Works include:* Univ. of Malta Extension, Cen. Bank of Malta, Malta Parl., St James Cavalier Centre for Creativity, Valletta; various commercial bldgs, hotels and banks in Malta and the Middle East. *Publications:* Walls of Malta 1973, White is White 1973, Contemporary Art in Malta 1974, Carrier-Citadel Metamorphosis 1974, Island: A Poem for Seeing 1980, Uncaged Reflections: Selected Writings 1965–80, In Search of Silent Spaces 1983, Octaves of Reflection 1987, Eye to I (selected poems) 1994, Sacri Luogi 1995, Mdina, Citadel of Memory 1996, Fraxions 1996, Gozo – Island of Oblivion 1997, Transfigurations: Places of Prayer (with Linda Schubert) 2000, Viaggio in Italia: Travel Sketches 2000, Gabriel Caruana Ceramics 2001. *Leisure interests:* music and art in general. *Address:* England & England Architects, 26/1 Merchants Street, Valletta, VLT10 (Office); 8 Oleander Street, The Gardens, St Julians, STJ 12, Malta (Home). *Telephone:* 21240894/21245187 (Office); 21350171 (Home). *Fax:* 21241174 (Office); 21354263 (Home). *E-mail:* myriame@onvol.net (Home).

ENGLER, John Mathias, JD; American politician; b. 12 Oct. 1948, Mt Pleasant, Mich.; s. of Mathias Engler and Agnes Neyer; m. Michele Engler; three d.; ed Mich. State Univ. and Thomas M. Cooley Law School; mem. Mich. House of Reps 1971–78; mem. Mich. Senate 1979–90, Republican leader 1983, majority leader 1984–90; state senator 1979–90; Gov. of Michigan 1990–2003; Hon. LLD (Alma Coll.) 1984, (W Mich.) 1991. *Address:* c/o Office of the Governor, State Capitol Building, PO Box 30013, Lansing, MI 48909, USA (Office).

ENGLISH, Bill, BA, BComm; New Zealand politician; b. 1961; m.; six c.; ed Otago Univ., Victoria Univ. of Wellington; fmr policy analyst and farmer; MP for Wallace 1990–93, for Clutha-Southland 1993–; Parl. Under-Sec. for Health and Crown Health Enterprises 1993–96, Minister of Crown Health Enterprises, Assoc. Minister of Educ., Minister of Health 1996–99 and Assoc. Minister of Revenue 1997–99, Minister of Finance (including Responsibility for Govt Superannuation Fund) and of Revenue 1999, Assoc. Treas. 1998–99; currently Leader New Zealand New Nat. Party, Leader of the Opposition. *Leisure interests:* rugby, running. *Address:* Parliament Buildings, Wellington, New Zealand (Office).

ENGLISH, Joseph Thomas, MD; American psychiatrist; b. 21 May 1933, Philadelphia, Pa; s. of Thomas J. English and Helen Gilmore English; m. Ann Carr Sanger 1969; two s. one d.; ed Jefferson Medical Coll.; Resident in Psychiatry, Inst. of Pa Hospital, Philadelphia 1959–61, Nat. Inst. of Mental Health, Bethesda, Md 1961–62; Chief Psychiatrist, US Peace Corps. 1962–66; Dir Office of Econ. Opportunity, Office of the Pres. 1966–68; Admin., Health Services and Mental Health Admin. US Dept of Health, Educ. and Welfare 1968–70; Pres. New York City Health and Hosps Corpn 1970–73; Adjunct Prof. Cornell Univ. School of Medicine 1975–; Assoc. Dean and Prof. of

Psychiatry, New York Medical Coll. 1979–; Chair. Dept of Psychiatry, St Vincent's Hosp., New York 1973–; Visiting Fellow, Woodrow Wilson Nat. Fellowship Foundation 1979–; Trustee Sarah Lawrence Coll. 1986–90, Menninger Foundation 1993–; Pres. American Psychiatric Asscn 1992–93, mem. World Psychiatric Soc. (Chair. section on religion and psychiatry 1994–); mem. Joint Comm. Accreditation Hosps 1984–86, Vice-Chair. 1986–88, Chair. 1988–89, Commr 2002–; numerous awards. *Address:* St Vincent's Hospital and Medical Center, 203 West 12th Street, New York, NY 10011-7762, USA. *Telephone:* (212) 604-8252. *Fax:* (212) 604-8794.

ENGLISH, Sir Terence Alexander Hawthorne, KBE, MA, FRCS, FRCP; British surgeon; b. 3 Oct. 1932, Pietermaritzburg, South Africa; s. of Arthur Alexander English and the late Mavis Eleanor Lund; m. 1st Ann Margaret Smart Dicey; two s. two d.; m. 2nd Judith Milne 2002; ed Witwatersrand Univ. and Guy's Hosp. Medical School, London; Intern, Demonstrator in Anatomy, Junior Surgical Registrar, Guy's Hosp. 1962–65; Resident Surgical Officer, Bolingbroke Hosp. 1966; Surgical Registrar, Brompton Hosp. 1967; Sr Surgical Registrar, Nat. Heart and London Chest Hosps 1968–72; Research Fellow, Cardiac Surgery, Ala Univ. 1969; Consultant Cardiothoracic Surgeon to Papworth and Addenbrooke Hosps 1973–95; Dir British Heart Foundation Heart Transplant Research Unit, Papworth Hosp. 1980–89; Consultant Cardiac Adviser, Humana Hosp. Wellington, London 1983–89; Master of St Catharine's Coll. Cambridge 1993–2000; Pres. Int. Soc. for Heart Transplantation 1984–85; Pres. Royal Coll. of Surgeons 1989–92; mem. Jt Consultants Cttee 1989–92, Standing Medical Advisory Cttee 1989–92, Audit Comm. 1993–99; Pres. BMA 1995–96; Gov. The Leys School 1993–2001; Hon. Fellow St Catharine's Coll., Cambridge, St Hugh's Coll., Cambridge, Worcester Coll., Oxford, King's Coll., London; Hon. FRCP and FRCS (Canada); Hon. FRACS; Hon. FRCA; Hon. FACS; Hon. FRCS (Ireland); Hon. FRCS (Glasgow); Hon. DSc (Sussex, York); Hon. MD (Nantes), (Mahidol, Bangkok); Man. of the Year, Royal Asscn for Disability and Rehabilitation 1980, Clement Price Thomas Award, Royal Coll. of Surgeons 1986. *Achievement:* Performed Britain's first successful heart transplant in 1979. *Publications:* over 100 articles in scientific journals. *Leisure interests:* reading, hill walking, South African history. *Address:* The Principal's Lodgings, St Hilda's College, Oxford, OX4 1DY, England (Home). *Telephone:* (1865) 798509. *E-mail:* tenglish@free.uk.com (Home).

ENGSTRÖM, Odd, BA; Swedish politician; b. 20 Sept. 1941, Skillingmark, Värmland Co.; m. Gunilla Engström; one s. one d.; ed Univ. of Uppsala; Admin. Officer, Cabinet Office 1965–67, Ministry of Finance 1967–68; Prin. Admin. Officer, Nat. Bd of Health and Welfare 1968–70; Deputy Asst Under-Sec., Asst Under- Sec. Ministry of Finance 1970–77; Sec. to Parl. Group, Social Democratic Party 1977–82; Under-Sec. of State, Cabinet Office 1982–84; Dir of Finance, Stockholm City Admin. 1984–86; Dir-Gen. Nat. Audit Bureau 1986; Political Adviser, Cabinet Office 1986–88; Minister with responsibility for the Budget, Ministry of Finance 1988–89; Deputy Prime Minister 1989–91, MP 1991–93; Chair. Bank Support Group 1993–; Dir-Gen. Ministry of Finance 1993–.

ENHSAYHAN, Mendsayhany, PhD; Mongolian politician; fmrly worked as economist; fmr Chief of Staff to Pres. Ochirbat; Prime Minister of Mongolia 1996–98; Pres. Premier Int. Inc. 1998–; mem. Democratic Alliance. *Address:* Pease Avenue 11A, Ulan Bator 210648, Mongolia (Office); c/o Great Hural, Ulan Bator, Mongolia. *Telephone:* (1) 312635 (Office); (1) 321733 (Home). *Fax:* (1) 312608 (Office). *E-mail:* premier@magicnet.mn (Office). *Website:* www.premiermongolia.com (Office).

ENKHBAYAR, Nambaryn; Mongolian politician and writer; b. 1 June 1958, Ulan Bator; s. of Baljinnyam Nambar and Radnaa Budkhand; m. Onon Tsolmon 1986; two s. one d.; ed High School No. 3, Ulan Bator, Literature Inst., Moscow; Ed. and Interpreter, Sec. and Head of Dept, Mongolian Writers' Union 1980–90; Vice-Pres. and Ed., Mongolian Interpreters' Union 1990–92; First Vice-Chair. Culture and Art Devt Cttee 1990–92; Minister of Culture 1992–96; Leader of the Opposition 1997–2000; mem. Parl. 1997–; Leader, Mongolian People's Revolutionary Party (MPRP) 1997–; Prime Minister of Mongolia 2000–; World Bank Adviser on Asian Culture and Buddhist Religion 1998–; Govt of Mongolia Polar Star 1996; MPRP Politician of the Year 1997; Govt of Mongolia Star of the Flag for Work Achievements 2001. *Publications:* translated several classic Russian novels; About Mongolian Arts, Literature and Emptiness 1989, On the Indicators of Development from the Buddhist Point of View 1998, Some Thoughts on the Relationship between Buddhist Philosophy and Economics 1998, To Develop or Not to Develop 1998. *Leisure interests:* reading, tennis, basketball, volleyball. *Address:* Office of the Prime Minister, Government House, Ulan Bator 12 (Office); Ikh Tenger, Suite 50-3, Ulan Bator, Mongolia (Home). *Telephone:* (11) 328329 (Office). *Fax:* (11) 310011 (Office). *E-mail:* erdenebaatar@pmis.gov.mn (Office); enkhbayar@pmis.gov.mn (Home). *Website:* www.pmis.gov.mn (Office).

ENKHSAIKHAN, Jargalsaihany, PhD; Mongolian diplomatist; b. 4 Sept. 1950, Ulan Bator; m. 1st Tuul Myagmarjavyn 1976 (divorced 1993); m. 2nd Batgerel Budjavyn 1994; two s. four d.; ed Moscow State Inst. for Int. Relations; Sec. of Legal Dept, Ministry of Foreign Affairs 1974–79; Mongolian Rep. at UN Conf. on Law of the Sea 1976–82; Sec. Mongolian Mission to UN, NY 1979–86; Acting Head Legal and Policy Planning Depts Ministry of Foreign Affairs 1986–88; Minister-Counsellor Mongolian Embassy, Moscow 1988–92; Adviser to Pres. of Mongolia 1992–93; Exec. Sec. to Mongolian Nat. Security Council, Nat. Security Adviser to Pres. of Mongolia 1994–96; Perm.

Rep. to UN 1996–; Rapporteur Legal (Sixth) Cttee of UN Gen. Ass. 1983, Vice-Chair. 1984, Chair. 1998; Vice-Chair. Special Cttee on Non-Use of Force in Int. Relations 1983; Chair. Group of Land-Locked States at UN 1997–; Vice-Pres. 52nd session UN Gen. Ass. 1997; Vice-Chair. Disarmament Comm. 1997; Mongolian State Order of the Polar Star 1991. *Publications:* articles on int. relations and int. law. *Leisure interest:* reading. *Address:* Permanent Mission of Mongolia to the UN, 6 East 77th Street, New York, NY 10021, USA (Office). *Telephone:* (212) 861-9460 (Office). *Fax:* (212) 861-9464 (Office). *E-mail:* mongolia@un.int (Office). *Website:* www.un.int/mongolia (Office).

ENNACEUR, Mohamed, PhD; Tunisian diplomatist, politician and lawyer; b. 21 March 1934, El Djem; m. Siren Möenstre; three s. two d.; ed Univ. of Tunis, Univ. of Paris (Sorbonne); fmrly practised as lawyer; Gov. of Sousse 1972–3; Minister of Labour and Social Affairs 1974–77, 1979–85; Pres. Econ. and Social Council of Tunisia 1985–91; Amb., Perm. Rep. of Tunisia to UN and other int. orgs, Geneva 1991–96; barrister 1997–; Chair. World Employment Conf. (ILO) 1976, 71st session of Int. Labour Conf. (ILO) 1985, 49th session of Human Rights Comm. (UN) 1993; Pres. Inst. Social-Consult; Ed. Tunisian Social Law Review; Hon. KBE, Grand Cordon of Order of Independence, Grand Cordon of Order of the Repub.; several awards and decorations from France, Britain, Germany, Belgium, Netherlands, Luxembourg, Ivory Coast. *Publications:* Human Rights after the Vienna Conference 1993; articles on labour law, human rights and social policy in Int. Studies Review, Tunisian Social Law Review, Int. Review of the Red Cross and other publs. *Leisure interests:* sports, music. *Address:* 10 rue du Mali, 1002 Tunis (Office); 15 rue Othman Kaak, 2026 Sidi Bousaid, Tunisia (Home). *Telephone:* (1) 848439 (Office); (1) 741127 (Home). *Fax:* (1) 847943 (Office). *E-mail:* social.consult@planet.tn (Office); med.ennaceur@planet.tn (Home).

ENO, Brian Peter George St John Baptiste de la Salle; British composer, artist and keyboardist; b. 15 May 1948, Woodbridge, Suffolk; s. of late William Arnold Eno and Maria Alphonsine Eno (née Buslot); m. 1st Sarah Grenville 1967; one d.; m. 2nd Anthea Norman-Taylor 1988; two c.; ed St Mary's Convent, St Joseph's Coll., Ipswich School of Art, Winchester Coll. of Art; founder mem. Roxy Music 1971–73; worked with guitarist Robert Fripp 1975–76; invented 'ambient music' 1975; Visiting Prof. RCA 1995–; Hon. Prof. of New Media, Berlin Univ. of Art 1998–; f. Long Now Foundation 1996; Hon. DTech (Plymouth) 1995; BRIT Award for Best Producer 1994, Grammy Award for Producer of Best Record of the Year 2000. *Exhibitions:* over 75 exhbns of video, light and sound artworks worldwide. *Recordings:* singles include: Seven Deadly Finns 1974; co-writer Talking Heads hit single Once In A Lifetime 1981; albums include: Here Come The Warm Jets 1974, Taking Tiger Mountain (By Strategy), Discreet Music, Another Green World, Music for Airports, Music for Films, Apollo, Before And After Science, Ambient 4 On Land, Neroli, The Drop and Drawn from Life; three albums with David Bowie 1977–79; three albums with Talking Heads 1978–80; My Life In The Bush of Ghosts (with David Byrne); co-producer U2 The Unforgettable Fire 1984, Joshua Tree 1987, Achtung Baby 1991, Zooropa 1993, All that You Can't Leave Behind 2000; Bright Red (Laurie Anderson) 1995, Outside (David Bowie) 1996. *Publications include:* A Year with Swollen Appendices 1996. *Address:* c/o Opal Ltd, 4 Pembridge Mews, London, W11 3EQ, England. *Telephone:* (20) 7221-4933. *Fax:* (20) 7727-5404.

ENOKSEN, Hans; Greenlandic politician; b. 1956; mem. Siumut Party, Chair. 2001; mem. Parl. 1995–; Minister for Fisheries, Hunting and Settlements 2001–; Prime Minister, Greenland Home Rule Govt Dec. 2002–. *Address:* Greenland Home Rule Government, POB 1015, 3900 Nuuk, Greenland (Office). *Telephone:* 396000 (Office). *Fax:* 325002 (Office). *Website:* www.homerule.gl (Office).

ENOKSEN, Odd Roger; Norwegian politician; b. 25 Sept. 1954, Andøy; m. 1st Turid Pettersen; m. 2nd Anne Kari Spjelkavik; four c.; ed Kleiva Coll. of Agric.; Leader of Andøy Centre Party 1975–78; Leader Enoksen Torvprodukter A/S 1985–90; Admin. Leader Andøytorv A/S 1990–93; mem. Centre Party's Exec. Cttee 1993–95; mem. Storting 1993–97; Leader Nordland Centre Party 1996–98; First Deputy Leader Centre Party 1997–99, Leader 1999–; Minister of Local Govt and Regional Devt 1999–2000; Leader Cttee of Industry 1997–99; mem. Extended Foreign Cttee 1997–99. *Address:* Senterpartiet, Kristian Augustsgt. 7B, 0130 Oslo, Norway (Office). *Telephone:* 22-24-68-00 (Office). *Fax:* 22-24-95-45 (Office).

ENRILE, Juan Ponce (see Ponce Enrile, Juan).

ENSIGN, John E., DMV; American politician and fmr veterinarian; b. 25 March 1958, Roseville, Calif.; s. of Mike Ensign and Sharon Ensign; m. Darlene Sciaretta; one s.; ed Ore. State Univ., Colo. State Univ.; owner of animal hosp. in Las Vegas; Gen. Man. Gold Strike Hotel and Casino 1991, Nevada Landing Hotel and Casino 1992; mem. US Congress from 1st Dist, Nev. 1994–98, mem. Ways and Means Cttee, Sub-Cttee on Health, Sub-Cttee on Human Resources, Comm. on Resources 1995–98; cand. for Senate 1998–99; Senator from Nevada 2000–. *Address:* Office of the Senator from Nevada, US Senate, Senate Buildings, Washington, DC 20510, USA (Office).

ENTHOVEN, Marius, MSc; Netherlands civil servant and international official; b. 23 Nov. 1940, Baarn; s. of Emil S. Enthoven and Anna G. Schouten; m. Lidwine Kolfschoten 1965; four d.; ed Delft Tech. Univ., Princeton Univ.; scientist with Dutch Aerospace Labs (NLR) 1967–72; Head Noise Abatement Dept Ministry for Environment 1972–77, Dir Scientific Affairs 1977–80, Chief Insp. Environmental Protection 1980–88, Dir-Gen. Environmental Protec-

tion 1988–94; Dir-Gen. Environment, Nuclear Safety and Civil Protection, Directorate-Gen. XI, European Comm. 1994–97; Special Adviser to Sec.-Gen., European Comm. 1997–98; Dir NIB Capital Bank, Netherlands 1998–; Kt Order of the Dutch Lion. *Publications:* books and articles on environmental man. issues. *Leisure interests:* literature, theatre, music, tennis. *Address:* NIB Capital Bank, P.O. Box 380, 2501 BH The Hague, Netherlands. *Telephone:* (70) 3425496 (Office). *Fax:* (70) 3459129 (Office).

ENTOV, Revold Mikhailovich, PhD; Russian economist; b. 23 March 1931, Kiev; m. Galina Gorvitz 1962; one s. one d.; ed Kharkov Univ. and Inst. for World Econ. and Int. Relations (IMEMO); Asst Prof. Bashkirian Agricultural School 1954–57; research worker, IMEMO 1961, now Head of Section; Prof. Univ. of Moscow 1970–; mem. Comm. Evaluating Projects of Econ. Reform in USSR (now Russia) 1990–91; mem. Russian Acad. of Sciences 1994; USSR State Prize 1977. *Publications:* Public Credit of the U.S. 1967, Theories of Prices 1982, Movements of Capital and the Profit Rate 1987; numerous articles on econ. theory and the U.S. econ. *Leisure interest:* history of psychology. *Address:* Institute for World Economy and International Relations, 117859 Moscow, Profsoyuznaya 23 (Office); 113149 Moscow, Azovskaya 4, Apt 44, Russia. (Home). *Telephone:* (095) 128-29-07 (Office); (095) 310-17-67 (Home).

ENTREMONT, Philippe; French pianist and conductor; b. 7 June 1934, Reims; s. of Jean and Renée (Monchamps) Entremont; m. Andrée Ragot 1955; one s. one d.; ed Institution Notre-Dame à Reims, Conservatoire National Supérieur de Musique de Paris; has performed with all maj. orchestras of world 1953–; Pres. of Acad. Int. de Musique Maurice Ravel, Saint-Jean-de-Luz 1973–80; Musical Dir and Permanent Conductor, Vienna Chamber Orchestra 1976–; Dir New Orleans Symphony Orchestra 1980–86; Prin. Conductor Denver Symphony Orchestra 1986–88, Paris Orchestre Colonne 1987–90, Netherlands Chamber Orchestra 1993–, Israel Chamber Orchestra 1995–; Dir American Conservatory Fontainebleau 1994; Prin. Guest Conductor Shanghai Broadcasting Symphony Orchestra 2001–; Officier Ordre nat. du Mérite, Officier, Légion d'honneur, Commdr des Arts et Lettres; Österreichisches Ehrenkreuz für Wissenschaft und Kunst; Harriet Cohen Piano Medal 1951, Grand Prix Int. Concours Marguerite Long-Jacques Thibaud 1953, 4 Grand Prix du Disque Awards, Edison Award 1968; Grammy Award 1972. *Leisure interest:* golf. *Address:* c/o Bureau de concerts Dominique Lierner, 17 rue du 4 septembre, 75002 Paris (Office); 10 rue de Castiglione, 75001 Paris, France. *Telephone:* 42-86-06-08. *Fax:* 42-86-86-61 (Home).

ENTWISTLE, John Nicholas McAlpine; British solicitor and consultant; b. 16 June 1941, Southport, Lancs.; s. of Sir Maxwell Entwistle and Lady (Jean) Entwistle; m. Phillida Burgess; one s. one d.; ed Uppingham School, Rutland; qualified as solicitor 1963; Asst Attorney, Shearman & Sterling, New York, USA 1963–64; partner, Maxwell Entwistle & Byrne 1966–91; mem. Liverpool City Council 1968–71; Nat. Vice-Chair. The Bow Group 1967–68; Parl. cand. (Conservative) for Huyton 1970; Consultant Solicitor, Davies Wallis Foyster 1992–; Lloyds underwriting mem. 1971–2000; Founder Dir Merseyside TEC 1990–91; Dir (non-exec.) Rathbone Brothers PLC 1992–98; Deputy Dist Chair. Appeals Service 1992; Chair. Liverpool Chamber of Commerce & Industry 1992–94; Founder Chair. NW Chambers of Commerce Asscn 1993–97; Pres. British Chambers of Commerce 1998–2000; mem. Chancellor of Exchequer's Standing Cttee on preparation for EMU 1998–2000; mem. Council, Britain in Europe 1999–; Home Sec.'s rep. for appointments to Merseyside Police Authority 1994–2000; Chair. several pvt. property cos; Trustee Nat. Museums & Galleries on Merseyside 1990–97; mem. Nat. Trust NW Regional Cttee 1992–98, Parole Bd 1994–2000, Disciplinary Cttee, Mortgage Compliance Bd 1999–, Criminal Injuries Compensation Appeals Panel 2000–; part-time immigration adjudicator; DL for Merseyside 1992–. *Leisure interests:* collecting and painting pictures, gardening, fishing and shooting. *Address:* Low Crag, Crook, nr Kendal, Cumbria, LA8 8LE, England. *Telephone:* (15395) 68715 (Office); (15395) 68268 (Home). *Fax:* (15395) 68769 (Office). *E-mail:* jentwistle@nascr.net (Office).

ENYA (Eithne Casado); Irish singer and composer; b. Eithne Ní Bhraonáin, 17 May 1961, Gweedore, Donegal; d. of Leon Ó Braonáin and Máire Bean Uí Bhraonáin; m. Sergio Casado 2002; keyboard and background vocals with family group Clannad (traditional Irish music) for two years; later started to write and record with Nicky and Roma Ryan with whom she f. Aigle Music; wrote music for film The Frog Prince and soundtrack for the BBC TV series The Celts (with Nicky and Roma Ryan); performed at Queen's 50th Wedding Anniversary Royal Variety Performance 1997, birthday celebrations of King Gustav of Sweden and privately for Pope John Paul II; has sold over 60 million worldwide; three Grammy Awards, six World Music Awards including Best-Selling Artist in the World 2001, Ivor Novello Award 1998, Echo Award (Berlin), four Best-Selling Int. Artist Awards (Japan), and numerous other int. awards. *Music:* singles: Evening Falls 1988, Orinoco Flow (No. 1 single) 1988, Oíche Chiún 1989, Storms in Africa 1989, Caribbean Blue 1991, Exile 1991, How Can I Keep 1991, Book of Days 1992, The Celts 1992, Marble Halls 1994, Anywhere Is 1995, Enya 1996, On My Way Home 1996, Enya 1997, Only If 1997, (3 Track EP) 1997, May It Be 2001, Only Time 2001, Wild Child 2001, From Singing; albums include: Watermark 1988, Shepherd Moons 1991, The Memory of Trees 1995, Paint the Sky with Stars 1997, A Day Without Rain 2000. *Leisure interests:* watercolour painting, watching classic films, gardening. *Address:* 'Manderley', Victoria Road, Killiney, Co. Dublin, Ireland.

ENZENSBERGER, Hans Magnus, DPhil; German poet and writer; b. 11 Nov. 1929, Kaufbeuren; m. 1st Dagrun Averaa Christensen; one d.; m. 2nd Maria Alexandrowna Makarowa 1986; m. 3rd Katharina Bonitz; one d.; ed Univs of Erlangen, Freiburg im Breisgau, Hamburg and Paris; Third Programme Ed., Stuttgart Radio 1955–57; Lecturer, Hochschule für Gestaltung, Ulm 1956–57; Literary Consultant to Suhrkamp's (publrs), Frankfurt 1960–; mem. 'Group 47', Ed. Kursbuch (review) 1965–75, Publr 1970–90; Ed. TransAtlantik (monthly magazine) 1980–82; Publr and Ed., Die Andere Bibliothek 1985–; Artistic Dir Renaissance Theatre Berlin 1995–; Hugo Jacobi Prize 1956, Kritiker Prize 1962, Georg Büchner Prize 1963, Premio Pasolini 1982, Heinrich Böll Prize 1985, Kultureller Ehrenpreis der Stadt München 1994, Heinrich-Heine Prize, Düsseldorf 1997 and others; Ordre pour le Mérite 2000. *Publications:* poetry: Verteidigung der Wölfe 1957, Landessprache 1960, Blindenschrift 1964, Poems for People Who Don't Read Poems (English edn) 1968, Gedichte 1955–1970 1971, Mausoleum 1975; essays: Clemens Brentanos Poetik 1961, Einzelheiten 1962, Politik und Verbrechen 1964; also: Deutschland, Deutschland unter Anderen 1967, Das Verhör von Habana (play) 1970, Freisprüche 1970, Der kurze Sommer der Anarchie (novel) 1972, Gespräche mit Marx und Engels 1973, Palaver 1974; Ed. Museum der Modernen Poesie 1960, Allerleirauh 1961, Andreas Gryphius Gedichte 1962, Edward Lears kompletter Nonsense (trans.) 1977, Raids and Reconstruction (essays, English edn), Der Untergang der Titanic (epic poem) 1978, Die Furie des Verschwindens 1980, Politische Brosamen 1982, Critical Essays 1982, Der Menschenfreund 1984, Ach Europa! 1987, Mittelmass und Wahn 1988, Requiem für eine romantische Frau 1988, Der Fliegende Robert 1989, Zukunftsmusik (poems) 1991, Die grosse Wanderung 1992, Aussichten auf den Bürgerkrieg 1993, Diderots Schatten 1994, The Palace (libretto) 1994, Civil War (English edn) 1994, Selected Poems (English edn) 1994, Kiosk (poems) 1995, English edn 1997, Voltaires Neffe (play) 1996, Der Zahlenteufel 1997, The Number Devil (English edn) 1998, Zickzack 1997, Wo warst du, Robert? (novel) 1998, Where were you, Robert? (English edn) 2000, Leichter als Luft (poems) 1999, English edn 2001, Mediocrity and Delusion (English edn) 1992. *Address:* c/o Suhrkamp-Verlag, Lindenstr. 29, 60325 Frankfurt am Main, Germany.

ENZI, Michael Bradley, MBA; American politician; b. 1 Feb. 1944, Bremerton, Wash.; s. of Elmer Enzi and Dorothy Bradley; m. Diana Buckley 1969; one s. two d.; ed George Washington Univ. and Denver Univ.; Pres. NZ Shoes, Inc. Gillette, Wyoming 1969–96, NZ Shoes of Sheridan, Inc. Wyoming 1983–91; Acting Man. Dunbar Well Services, Gillette 1985–97; Chair. Bd Dirs First Wyoming Bank, Gillette 1978–88; Dir Black Hill Corpn 1992–96; Mayor of Gillette 1975–82; mem. Wyoming House of Reps Cheyenne 1987–91, Wyoming State Senate 1991–96; Senator from Wyoming 1997–; Republican; Distinguished Eagle Scout. *Publication:* Harvard Journal on Legislation 1998. *Leisure interests:* fishing, fly tieing, canoe making, reading. *Address:* United States Senate, 290 Senate Russell Office Building, Washington, DC 20510, (Office); 431 Circle Drive, Gillette, WY 82716, USA (Home). *Telephone:* (202) 224-3424 (Office). *Fax:* (202) 228-0359 (Office). *E-mail:* senator@enzi .senate.gov (Office). *Website:* www.enzi.senate.gov (Office).

EÖTVÖS, Peter; German (b. Hungarian) composer, conductor and professor of music; b. 2 Jan. 1944, Székelyudvarhely, Hungary; s. of László Eötvös and Ilona Szücs; m. 1st Piroska Molnár 1968; one s.; m. 2nd Pi-Hsien Chen 1976; one d.; m. 3rd Maria Mezei 1995; ed Budapest Acad. and Musikhochschule, Cologne; played in Stockhausen's Ensemble, Cologne 1966–76; composer and producer at WDR Electronic Music Studio, Cologne 1971–79; Conductor and Musical Dir Ensemble. Intercontemporain, Paris 1979–91; Prin. Guest Conductor BBC Symphony Orchestra, London 1985–88; First Guest Conductor, Budapest Festival Orchestra 1992–95; Chief Conductor Netherlands Radio Chamber Orchestra 1994–; Prof. Musikhochschule Karlsruhe, Germany 1992–98, Cologne 1998–; f. Int. Eötvös Inst. for Young Conductors; mem. Akad. der Kunst, Berlin, Szechenyi Acad. of Art, Budapest, Sächsische Acad. der Künste, Dresden; Officier, Ordre des Arts et des Lettres 1986; Bartok Award, Budapest 1997, Stephan Kaske Prize, Munich 2000. *Compositions include:* (for orchestra) Chinese Opera, Shadows, Psychokosmos, Atlantis, Zeropoints, Two Monologues, Replica; (for ensemble) Intervalles-Intérieures, Windsequenzen, Steine, Triangel; (for string quartet) Korrespondenz; (for vocal ensemble) Three comedy madrigals; (for percussion) Psalm 151, (for musical theatre/opera) Radames, Harakiri, Three Sisters, As I Crossed a Bridge of Dreams. *Leisure interests:* pipe, jazz, walking. *Address:* c/o Harrison-Parrott, 12 Penzance Place, London, W11 4PA, England; Naarderweg 56, NL-1261 BV Blaricum, Netherlands. *Telephone:* (35) 5335940. *Fax:* (35) 5313265. *E-mail:* eotvospeter@hotmail.com (Home). *Website:* www.eotvospeter.com (Home).

EPERON, Alastair David Peter, FRSA; British corporate affairs consultant; b. 17 Nov. 1949, Kent; s. of Stanley A. Eperon and Patricia Woodrow; m. Ruth Tabbenor 1976; two d.; ed Ramsden School for Boys, Orpington, Kent; worked as journalist; Press Officer, Surrey Co. Council 1972-74; Head of Public Affairs, The Housing Corpn 1974–78; Sr Consultant, Shandwick 1978–80; Dir, then Deputy Man. Dir Ogilvy & Mather Public Relations, then Chief Exec. Ogilvy & Mather Corporate Financial 1980–86; Dir McAvoy Wreford Bayley 1986–, Man. Dir 1988–89, Chief Exec. McAvoy Bayley 1989–91; Dir Valin Pollen Int. 1989–90; Dir of Group Corporate Affairs, The Boots Co. PLC 1991–; Deputy Chair. British Retail Consortium; Chair. CBI Distributive Trades Panel, Advisory Bd, The Foundation; Dir Business in the Community; Fellow Inst. of Public Relations. *Leisure interests:* gardening,

countryside. *Address:* The Boots Company PLC, Group Headquarters, Nottingham, NG90 4HQ, England. *Telephone:* (115) 968-7023. *Fax:* (115) 968-7161. *E-mail:* alastair.eperon@boots-plc.com (Office).

EPHRON, Nora, BA; American author and scriptwriter; b. 19 May 1941, New York; d. of Henry Ephron and Phoebe (née Wolkind) Ephron; m. 1st Dan Greenburg (divorced); m. 2nd Carl Bernstein (divorced); two s.; m. 3rd Nicholas Pileggi; ed Wellesley Coll.; reporter, New York Post 1963–68; freelance writer 1968–; Contributing Ed. and columnist, Esquire Magazine 1972–73, Sr Ed. 1974–78; Contributing Ed., New York Magazine 1973–74; mem. American Writers' Guild, Authors' Guild, PEN, Acad. of Motion Picture Arts and Sciences. *Film appearances:* Crimes and Misdemeanors, Husbands and Wives. *Screenplays:* Silkwood (with Alice Arlen) 1983, Heartburn 1986, When Harry Met Sally... 1989, Cookie 1989 (co-exec. producer, co-screenwriter), My Blue Heaven 1990, This is My Life 1992 (dir, screenwriter, with Delia Ephron), Sleepless in Seattle (also dir) 1993, Mixed Nuts (also dir), Michael (also dir) 1996, You've Got Mail (also dir) 1998, Red Tails in Love: a Wildlife Drama in Central Park (also producer and dir) 2000, Hanging Up (also producer) 2000. *Publications:* Wallflower at the Orgy 1970, Crazy Salad 1975, Scribble, Scribble 1978, Heartburn 1983, Nora Ephron Collected 1991, Big City Eyes 2000. *Address:* c/o Sam Cohn International Creative Management, 40 West 57th Street, New York, NY 10019, USA.

EPSTEIN, Emanuel, PhD; American professor of plant nutrition and plant physiologist; b. 5 Nov. 1916, Duisburg, Germany; s. of Harry Epstein and Bertha Epstein (née Löwe); brother of Gabriel Epstein (q.v.); m. Hazel M. Leask 1943; two c. (one deceased); ed Univ. of California (Davis and Berkeley); served US Army 1943–46; Plant Physiologist, US Dept of Agric., Beltsville, Md 1950–58; Lecturer and Assoc. Plant Physiologist, Univ. of California (Davis) 1958–65, Prof. of Plant Nutrition and Plant Physiologist 1965–87, Prof. Emer. (active) 1987–, Prof. of Botany 1974–87, Prof. Emer. (active) 1987–; Faculty Research Lecturer 1980; Consultant to govt agencies, private orgs and publrs at various times; Guggenheim and Fulbright Fellowships; mem. NAS; Pres. Pacific Div., AAAS 1990–91; Gold Medal, Pisa (Italy) Univ. 1962; Charles Reid Barnes Life Membership Award, American Soc. of Plant Physiologists 1986, Univ. of Calif. (Davis) Coll. of Agricultural and Environmental Sciences Award of Distinction 1999, Cal Aggie Alumni Asscn Citation for Excellence 1999. *Publications:* Mineral Nutrition of Plants: Principles and Perspectives 1972, The Biosaline Concept: An Approach to the Utilization of Underexploited Resources (co-ed.) 1979, Saline Agriculture: Salt-Tolerant Plants for Developing Countries (co-ed.) 1990; research papers, reviews and articles. *Leisure interests:* hiking, photography and history. *Address:* Department of Land, Air and Water Resources, Soils and Biogeochemistry, University of California, Davis, CA 95616-8627, USA. *Telephone:* (530) 752-0197. *Fax:* (530) 752-1552. *E-mail:* eqepstein@ucdavis.edu (Office). *Website:* lawr .ucdavis.edu (Office).

EPSTEIN, Gabriel, A.A.DIP., FRIBA; British architect and planning consultant; b. 25 Oct. 1918, Duisburg, Germany; s. of Harry Epstein and Bertha Epstein (née Löwe); brother of Emanuel Epstein (q.v.); m. Josette A. Glonneau 1955; two s. one d.; ed schools in Germany, Belgium and Israel and Architectural Asscn School of Architecture, London; officer in Royal Engineers in World War II; Partner, Shepheard, Epstein & Hunter 1955–86; Prof. of Architecture and Dir of Inst. of Public Bldgs and Design, Univ. of Stuttgart 1978–88; Prof. Centre for Infrastructure Planning, Univ. of Stuttgart 1984–; consultant and mem. competition juries London, Stuttgart, Paris, Brussels, Leipzig, Berlin, Munich, etc. 1992–96; Pres. Architectural Asscn, London 1963–64, Franco-British Union of Architects 1976–77; mem. Berlin Acad. of Arts and Letters; mem. Soc. des Architectes Diplômés par le Gouvernement; Hon. DLitt (Lancaster); four Civic Trust Awards for Univ. and Housing Work 1966–82, two Ministry Medals for Good Design in Housing 1968, 1976, Int. Prize for Architecture for London Housing 1983. *Art exhibitions include:* several exhbns of drawings and paintings, Galerie Arcade Colette, Palais Royal, Paris 1990s. *Works include:* master plan and bldgs, Univ. of Lancaster; master plans for Open Univ. (UK), Univ. of Tlemcen (Algeria) and Univ. of Ghana; town-planning consultant for London Docks (Wapping) 1976–81, for New Univ., Paris Region 1992, for European Parl. Complex, Brussels 1992, 2003; many housing projects in London and schools and colleges in England 1950–85; School of Architecture and Eng, Cen. Library and several other bldgs for Univ. of Louvain-la-Neuve, Belgium 1970–80. *Publications:* Planning Forms for Twentieth Century Cities 1976, Well-Being In Cities: The Low Energy City 1979, Energy Use and City Form 1981. *Leisure interest:* painting. *Address:* 3 rue André Mazet, 75006 Paris, France. *Telephone:* 1-43-25-89-59. *Fax:* 1-43-26-57-42.

EPSTEIN, Matthew; American opera administrator; ed Univ. of Pennsylvania; Artistic Dir Brooklyn Acad. of Music 1987–91; consultant for the opera cos of Chicago and Santa Fe; Artistic Dir Welsh Nat. Opera 1991–94, Vice-Pres. Columbia Artists Man. 1973–. *Address:* c/o Columbia Artists Management, 165 West 57th Street, New York, NY 10019, USA.

EPSTEIN, Sir (Michael) Anthony, Kt, CBE, MD, DSc, PhD, FRCPath, FRS; British virologist; b. 18 May 1921, London; ed St Paul's School, London, Trinity Coll., Cambridge and Middlesex Hosp. Medical School, London; House Surgeon, Middlesex Hosp. and Addenbrooke's Hosp., Cambridge 1944; commissioned RAMC 1945–47; Asst Pathologist, Bland Sutton Inst., Middlesex Hosp. Medical School 1948–65; Berkeley Travelling Fellow and French Govt Exchange Scholar, Inst. Pasteur, Paris 1952–53; Visiting Investigator, Rockefeller Inst., New York 1956; Reader in Experimental Pathology, Middlesex Hosp. Medical School and Hon. Consultant in Experimental Virology, Middlesex Hosp. 1965–68; Prof. of Pathology, Univ. of Bristol 1968–85, Head of Dept and Hon. Consultant Pathologist, Avon Area Health Authority (Teaching) 1968–82; Emer. Prof. of Pathology, Univ. of Bristol at Nuffield Dept of Clinical Medicine, Univ. of Oxford 1985–; Extraordinary Fellow, Wolfson Coll., Oxford 1986–2001, Hon. Fellow 2001–; mem. MRC Cell Bd 1979–84, Chair. 1982–84; Chair. CRC/MRC Jt Cttee for Inst. of Cancer Research 1982–87; mem. MRC 1982–86, Chair. MRC Tropical Medicine Research Bd 1985–88, Medical and Scientific Advisory Panel, Leukaemia Research Fund 1982–85, Council of Royal Soc. 1983–85, 1986–91; mem. UK Co-ordinating Cttee on Cancer Research 1983–87, Scientific Advisory Cttee, The Lister Inst. of Preventive Medicine 1984–86; Scientific Adviser, Charing Cross Medical Research Centre 1984–87; Foreign Sec. and Vice-Pres. Royal Soc. 1986–91, MRC Assessor 1987–91; mem. Expert Working Party on Bovine Spongiform Encephalopathy, Dept of Health 1988, mem. Exec. Bd Int. Council of Scientific Unions 1990–93, Chair. Cttee for Science in Cen. and Eastern Europe 1992–95; mem. Exec. Council European Science Foundation 1990–93; Special Rep. of Dir.-Gen., UNESCO, for Science in Russia, Moscow 1992; mem. Programme Advisory Group, World Bank China Key Studies Project 1992–96; Jt Founder Ed. Int. Review of Experimental Pathology 1962–86; Fellow Univ. Coll. London 1991; Hon. Prof. Zhongshan Medical Univ., People's Repub. of China 1981, Chinese Acad. of Preventive Medicine 1988; Hon. Fellow Queensland Inst. of Medical Research 1983; Hon. mem. Belgian Soc. for Study of Cancer 1979, Pathological Soc. 1987; Hon. FRSE 1991; Hon. FRCP 1986; Hon. Fellow Royal Coll. of Pathologists of Australasia 1995; Hon. MD (Edin.) 1986, (Charles Univ., Prague) 1998; Hon. DSc (Birmingham) 1996; Leeuwenhoek Prize Lecturer, Royal Soc. 1983; Markham Skerritt Prize (Univ. of Bristol) 1977, Paul Ehrlich and Ludwig Darmstaedster Prize and Medal (Frankfurt) 1973, Bristol-Myers Award (New York) 1982, Prix Griffuel (Paris) 1986, Gairdner Foundation Int. Award (Toronto) 1988, S. Weiner Distinguished Visitor Award (Univ. of Manitoba) 1988, Royal Medal, The Royal Soc. 1992. *Scientific achievement:* discovered first human cancer virus Epstein-Barr virus (EBV) 1964. *Publications:* over 240 scientific papers in int. journals; numerous studies on EBV and other viruses; author and ed. of five scientific books. *Address:* Nuffield Department of Clinical Medicine, Oxford University, John Radcliffe Hospital, Headington, Oxford, OX3 9DU, England. *Telephone:* (1865) 221334. *Fax:* (1865) 222901.

ERAKAT, Saeb, MA, PhD; Palestinian politician and journalist; b. 1955, Jerusalem; ed San Francisco State Univ., USA and Bradford Univ., UK; fmr journalist Al Quds daily; Lecturer of Political Science An-Najah Univ. 1983, fmr Sec.-Gen. Arab Studies Soc.; mem. negotiating team Oslo Peace Process 1995; Head Palestinian Negotiation Steering and Monitoring Cttee 1996, currently Chief Palestinian Peace Negotiator; elected mem. Palestinian Legis. Council, Jericho 1996; currently Minister of Local Government, Palestinian Nat. Authority (PNA). *Publications include:* eight books and numerous articles on foreign policy. *Address:* Ministry of Local Government, Jericho, Palestinian Autonomous Areas (Office). *Telephone:* (2) 2321260 (Office). *Fax:* (2) 2321240 (Office). *Website:* www.p-ol.com/~molg (Office).

ERBAKAN, Necmettin; Turkish politician; b. 1926, Sinop; ed Inst. of Mechanics, Technical Univ. of Istanbul and Technische Universität, Aachen, Germany; Asst lecturer, Inst. of Mechanics, Tech. Univ. of Istanbul 1948–51, Prof. 1954–66; Engineer, Firma Deutz 1951–54; Chair. Industrial Dept, Turkish Asscn of Chambers of Commerce 1966–68, Chair. of Asscn 1968; mem. Nat. Ass. 1969–80; f. Nat. Order Party 1970 (disbanded 1971); Chair. Nat. Salvation Party Oct. 1973 (disbanded 1981); Deputy Prime Minister and Minister of State Jan.–Sept. 1974; Deputy Prime Minister 1975–77, July–Dec. 1977; detained 1980–81; now leader Refah Partisi (Welfare Party, f. 1983); Prime Minister of Turkey 1996–98; sentenced to 28 months' imprisonment for fraud March 2002. *Address:* c/o Office of the Prime Minister, Basbakanlik, Ankara, Turkey.

ERBSEN, Claude Ernest, BA; American journalist; b. 10 March 1938, Trieste, Italy; s. of Henry M. Erbsen and Laura Erbsen; m. 1st Jill J. Prosky 1959; m. 2nd Hedy M. Cohn 1970; two s. one d.; ed Amherst Coll. Mass.; reporter and printer, Amherst Journal Record 1955–57; staff reporter, El Tiempo, Bogotá 1960; with Associated Press (AP) in New York and Miami 1960–65; reporter to Chief of Bureau, AP Brazil 1965–69; Exec. Rep. for Latin America, AP 1969–70; Business Man. and Admin. Dir AP-Dow Jones Econ. Report, London 1970–75; Deputy Dir AP World Services, New York 1975–80, Vice-Pres., Dir 1987–; Vice-Pres., Dir AP-Dow Jones News Services 1980–87; mem. Bd Dirs World Press Inst. St Paul; mem. Int. Press Inst., Council on Foreign Relations; San Giusto d'Oro award, City of Trieste 1995. *Leisure interests:* reading, travel, folk art. *Address:* Associated Press, 50 Rockefeller Plaza, New York, NY 10020-1605 (Office); 27 Stratton Road, Scarsdale, NY 10583-7556, USA (Home). *Telephone:* (212) 621-1750 (Office).

ERÇEL, Gazi; Turkish banker; b. 20 Feb. 1945, Gelibolu; m. Zeynel Erçel; one d.; ed Ankara Univ., Vanderbilt Univ., Tenn.; bank examiner Ministry of Finance 1967–77; Deputy Dir-Gen. of Treasury 1977–82; Asst to Exec. Dir IMF, Washington DC 1982–86; Dir-Gen. of Treasury and Foreign Trade 1987–89; Gov. Cen. Bank of Turkey 1996–2001; Cen. Banker of the Year Award, Global Finance, Prague 2000. *Address:* c/o Türkiye Cumhuriyet Merkez Bankasi AS, Istiklal Cad. 10, 06100 Ulus, Ankara, Turkey. *Website:* www.tcmb.gov.tr (Office).

ERDEM, Kaya; Turkish government official; b. 1928, Zonguldak; s. of Hilmi and Pakize Erdem; m. Sevil Şibay 1956; two d.; ed High School of Commerce, Univ. of Marmara; mem. faculty, Anatolian Univ. 1959–65; Finance Dir Sugar Corpn 1960–62; Asst Dir-Gen. State Treasury 1963–72; mem. Cttee for Reorganization of State Econ. Enterprises 1971–72; Dir-Gen. State Treasury 1972–73; Chief Financial Counsellor, Turkish Embassy, London 1973–76; Sec.-Gen. Ministry of Finance 1978–80; Minister of Finance 1980–82, Deputy Prime Minister, Minister of State 1983–89; prominent in drafting and implementation of econ. stabilization programme 1980. *Publications:* State Economic Enterprise 1966; and numerous articles on cost and managerial accountancy. *Leisure interests:* bridge, tennis. *Address:* c/o Office of the Deputy Prime Minister, Basbakan yard. ve Devlet Bakani, Bakanlıklar, Ankara, Turkey.

ERDENECHULUUN, Luvsangiin; Mongolian diplomatist and politician; b. 10 Oct. 1948, Ulan Bator; s. of Sonomyn Luvsan and Lhamsurengiin Baimanhand; m. Sukh-Ochiryn Solongo 1969; two s. one d.; ed State Inst. of Int. Relations, Moscow and Diplomatic Acad. Moscow; officer, Dept of Int. Relations, Ministry of Foreign Affairs 1972–80; First Sec. Perm. Mission of Mongolia at UN 1980–84; Head, Press and Information Dept Ministry of Foreign Affairs 1985–86, Head, Dept of Int. Orgs 1988–90; Deputy Perm. Rep. to UN 1990, Perm. Rep. 1992–96; adviser to Pres. of Mongolia 1996–97; Minister of Foreign Affairs 2000–; scholar of int. relations 1998–; Distinguished Service Medal, Order of Polar Star. *Address:* Ministry of Foreign Affairs, Peace Avenue Building 7A, Ulan Bator, Mongolia (Office). *Telephone:* 311311 (Office). *Fax:* 322127 (Office). *E-mail:* mongmer@magicnet.mn (Office). *Website:* www.extmin.mn (Office).

ERDOGAN, Recep Tayyip, BA; Turkish politician; b. 1954, Rize; m.; four c.; ed Marmara Univ., Istanbul; professional footballer 1969–80; elected Chair. Nat. Salvation Party Youth Org. early 1970s; Chair. Istanbul Br. Welfare Party 1985; Mayor of Metropolitan Istanbul 1994–98, tenure of office ended by court decree 1998, convicted of having read a provocative poem in public, imprisoned for four months and banned for life from holding public office; mem. Virtue Party 1998–2001; Founder and Chair. AK Partisi – AKP (Justice and Development Party), ruling party in Turkey following 2002 elections, constitutional ban preventing him from holding public office overturned Jan. 2003; Prime Minister of Turkey March 2003–; Founder Democratization and Action Movt. *Address:* Office of the Prime Minister, Başbakanlik, Bakanliklar, Ankara (Office); AK Partisi, Genel Merkezi Ceyhun Atif Kansu Cad., No. 202 Balgat, Ankara, Turkey (Office). *Telephone:* (312) 4189056 (Office). *Fax:* (312) 4180476 (Office). *E-mail:* info@basbakanlik.gov.tr (Office). *Website:* www.basbakanlik.gov.tr (Office); www.akparti.org.tr (Office).

ERDŐS, André; Hungarian diplomatist; b. 1941, Algiers; s. of Gusztáv Erdős and Márta Czeichner; m. Katalin Pintér 1965; one d.; ed Moscow State Inst. for Int. Relations, Budapest School of Political Sciences; joined Hungarian Ministry of Foreign Affairs 1965; Attaché, Morocco 1968–72; staff mem. CSCE Dept Ministry of Foreign Affairs 1972–78; assigned to Perm. Mission of Hungary at UN, New York 1978–83; del. to UN Gen. Ass. 1984, 1985, 1989; Adviser to Minister of Foreign Affairs of Hungary 1984–86; Head of Hungary's del. to Vienna CSCE follow-up meeting 1986–89; Perm. Rep. to UN 1990–94, 1997–2001; Pres. UN Disarmament and Int. Security Comm. 2001–; Hungarian rep. UN Security Council 1992–93; Deputy State Sec. for Multilateral Affairs, Ministry of Foreign Affairs 1994–97; Hon. Prof. Budapest Inst. for Grad. Int. and Diplomatic Studies 1999; Middle Cross of Order of Merit, Hungary. *Publications:* Co-operation in the United Nations between Socialist and Developing Countries 1981, Soviet-German Relations 1939–41 1984, The Circumstances of the Birth of the 1941 Soviet-German Non-Aggression Pact 1987, Geography vs. Political Reality at the United Nations 2001; numerous articles on int. affairs. *Leisure interests:* philately, numismatics, collecting postcards, making video movies. *Address:* 227 East 52nd Street, New York, NY 10022, USA. *Telephone:* (212) 752-0209. *Fax:* (212) 755-5395. *E-mail:* titkarsag.new@humisny.org.

ERDRICH, Karen Louise, MA; American writer and poet; b. 7 June 1954, Little Falls, Minn.; d. of Ralph Louis Erdrich and Rita Joanne (Gourneau) Erdrich; m. Michael Anthony Dorris 1981 (died 1997); six c. (one s. deceased); ed Dartmouth Coll., Johns Hopkins Univ.; Visiting Poetry Teacher, ND State Arts Council 1977–78; Teacher of Writing, Johns Hopkins Univ., Baltimore 1978–79; Communications Dir, Ed., Circle-Boston Indian Council 1979–80; Textbook Writer Charles Merrill Co. 1980; mem. PEN (mem. Exec. Bd 1985–90); Guggenheim Fellow 1985–86; numerous awards including Nelson Algren Award 1982, Pushcart Prize 1983, Nat. Magazine Fiction Award 1983, 1987, First Prize O. Henry Awards 1987. *Publications:* Imagination (textbook) 1981, Jacklight (poems) 1984, Love Medicine (novel; trans. in more than 18 languages; won numerous awards including Nat. Book Critics' Circle Award for best work of fiction 1984) 1984, The Beet Queen 1986, Tracks 1988, The Crown of Columbus (jtly) 1991, The Bingo Palace 1994, The Bluejay's Dance 1995, Tales of Burning Love 1996, The Antelope Wife 1998, The Birchbark House 1999, The Last Report on the Miracles at Little No Horse (novel) 2001; short stories, children's stories, essays and poems published in magazines. *Address:* c/o Andrew Wylie Agency, 250 West 57th Street, Suite 2114, New York, NY 10107-2199, USA. *Telephone:* (212) 246-0069. *Fax:* (212) 586-8953 (Office). *E-mail:* mail@wylieagency.com (Office).

EREDIAUWA, Omo N'Oba N'Edo Uku-Akpolokpolo, Oba of Benin, BA; Nigerian traditional monarch; b. 24 June 1923; ed Edo Coll., Benin, Govt Coll.,

Ibadan, Yaba Coll., Lagos, Cambridge Univ., England; followed career in Civil Service; retd 1973 as Perm. Sec. in Fed. Ministry of Health; Civil Commr for Bendel State 1975–77; succeeded to throne of Benin March 1979–99; mem. Council of State 1979–. *Address:* The Palace, Box 1, Benin City, Bendel State, Nigeria. *Telephone:* (52) 240001.

ERGEN , Charles (Charlie) W., BS, MBA; American business executive; m.; ed Univ. of Tenn., Babcock Grad. School, Wake Forest Univ.; f. EchoStar Communications Corpn 1980, now Chair. and CEO, f. Dish Network (subsidiary of EchoStar Communications Corpn) 1996, Pres. 1998–; Home Satellite TV Asscn Star Award 1988, Rocky Mountain News Business Person of the Year 1996, 2001. *Address:* Office of the Chairman, EchoStar Communications, 5701 S Santa Fe Drive, Littleton, CO 80120, USA (Office). *Website:* www.dishnetwork.com (Office).

ERGIN, Mehmet, PhD; professor of physical chemistry; b. Yozgat; m.; two c.; ed Ankara Gazi High School, Ankara Univ., Glasgow Univ.; researcher Nuclear Chem. Lab., Atomic Energy Comm., Acting Dir 1963–66, fmr Pres.; research and training at IAEA Labs., Vienna; researcher Inst. for Physics and Chem., Asscn for Meat Research, Fed. Repub. of Germany, then Dept of Chem., Glasgow Univ.; lecturer, Asst Prof., then Prof. of Physical Chem. Dept of Chem., Hacettepe Univ.; Exec. Sec. Turkish Scientific and Research Council (TUBITAK) 1974, Deputy Sec. Gen. for Planning and Coordination 1985–87, Pres. 1987–90; Fellow Islamic Acad. of Sciences, Vice-Pres. 1986–99, Sec. Gen. 1999–; mem. Bd of trustees and Visiting Lecturer Faith Univ., Istanbul. *Address:* Islamic Academy of Sciences, P.O. Box 830036, Amman, Jordan (Office). *Telephone:* 5522104 (Office). *Fax:* 5511803 (Office).

ERH DONGQIANG; Chinese photographer; b. Shanghai; m. (divorced); freelance photo-journalist 1981–; Co-Founder, with Tess Johnston, Old China Hand Press 1993; work appears in China Tourism monthly, airline magazines and other publs; noted for pictures of architecture, especially images of Shanghai; has turned his home into pvt. Folk Art Museum containing memorabilia from old Shanghai and Southern China. *Publications:* with Tess Johnston: A Last Look, Near to Heaven. *Address:* c/o Old China Hand Press, Hong Kong Special Administrative Region, People's Republic of China.

ERICKSON, Arthur Charles, CC, BArch, FRAIC, ARCA; Canadian architect; b. 14 June 1924, Vancouver; s. of the late Oscar and of Myrtle Erickson (née Chatterson); ed Univ. of British Columbia, McGill Univ.; travel study in Mediterranean countries and N Europe 1950–53; private practice 1953–62; Asst Prof. Univ. of Oregon 1955–56; Instructor and Asst Prof. Univ. of British Columbia 1957–60, Assoc. Prof. 1961; Canada Council Fellowship for architectural research in Asia 1961; with Erickson, Massey 1963–72; Prin. Arthur Erickson Architects 1972–91, Pres. and CEO Arthur Erickson Architectural Corpn 1991–; mem. many architectural insts and asscns; mem. Science Council of Canada on Urban Devt 1971, Bd Canadian Conf. of the Arts 1972, Canadian Council on Urban Research, Bd of Trustees, Inst. for Research on Public Policy, fmr mem. Design Council of Portland Devt Comm.; mem. Int. Cttee of Museum of Modern Art, Americas Soc.; Life mem. Vancouver Art Gallery; Hon. Fellow Royal Architectural Inst. of Scotland 1987; Hon. FCAE; Hon. Fellow CAM Foundation; Hon. FAIA 1978; Hon. FRIBA 2001; Hon. DEng, (Nova Scotia Technical Coll.) 1971; Hon. LLD (Simon Fraser Univ.) 1973, (McGill Univ.) 1975, (Univ. of Manitoba) 1978, (Lethbridge Univ.) 1981; Hon. DLitt (British Columbia) 1985; won First Prize in competition for Simon Fraser Univ., First Prize for design of Canadian Pavilion at Expo '70, Osaka, Pan Pacific Citation, American Inst. of Architects, Hawaiian Chapter 1963, Molson Prize, Canada Council for the Arts 1967, Architectural Inst. of Japan Award for Best Pavilion Expo '70, Royal Bank of Canada Award 1971, American Architectural Fraternity 1973, Auguste Perret Award, Int. Union of Architects 1974, Canadian Housing Design Council Awards for Residential Design 1975, President's Award of Excellence, American Soc. of Landscape Architects 1979, Grande Médaille d'Or Académie d'Architecture de France 1984, Gold Medal, Royal Architectural Inst. of Canada 1984, Gold Medal, American Inst. of Architects 1986. *Major projects include:* M and B Bldg, Simon Fraser Univ. Vancouver, Museum of Anthropology, Vancouver, Vancouver Courts and Art Gallery, Roy Thomson Hall, Toronto, Bank of Canada, Ottawa, Lethbridge Univ., Alberta, Napp Labs, Cambridge, UK, California Plaza, San Diego Convention Center, Fresno City Hall, California Plaza, Tacoma Museum of Glass. *Publications:* The Architecture of Arthur Erickson 1975, Seven Stones by Edith Iglauer, The Architecture of Arthur Erickson 1988. *Leisure interests:* reading, writing, music, skiing, scuba. *Address:* 1672 West 1st Avenue, Vancouver, BC, V6J 1G1, Canada. *Telephone:* (604) 737-9801 (Office). *Fax:* (604) 737-9092 (Office). *E-mail:* atelier@lynx.bc.ca (Office). *Website:* arthurerickson.com (Office).

ERIKSSON, Göran Olof, MA; Swedish theatre director, author and translator; b. 7 March 1929; s. of Walfrid Eriksson and Ebba Renck; m. 1st Lill-Inger Ingman 1953; m. 2nd Jane Friedmann 1982; one s. one d.; ed Uppsala Univ.; Literary Ed. Göteborgs Handels-och Sjöfarts-Tidning 1956–62; Chief Cultural Ed. Stockholms-Tidningen 1962–66; theatre critic, Dagens Nyheter 1966–68; Dir Stockholms Stadsteater 1967–69, 1975–90; Prin. Dramatiska Institutet 1969–73; Artistic Leader, Ländsteatern i Dalarna 1974–77; now freelance author and dir; Swedish Theatre Critics' Award 1985; Elsa Thulin Prize 1990. *Publications:* I samma plan (essays) 1966; plays: Volpone 1969, Pariserliv 1975, En Skandal i Wien 1978, Freden 1987; essays; radio plays; trans. of about 100 plays by Shakespeare, Molière, Racine, Beckett, etc.

ERIKSSON, Per-Olof, M.SC.ENG.; Swedish business executive; b. 1 March 1938, Seglora; s. of Gunhild Eriksson and Herbert Eriksson; m. Helena Eriksson Joachimsson 1962; two s. one d.; ed Royal Inst. of Tech., Stockholm; Dir and Head of Production and Materials Control, Sandvik Coromant 1975; Pres. Seco Tools AB 1976; Pres. and CEO Sandvik AB 1984–94; mem. Bd Sandvik AB, Skanska AB, SKF AB, Custos AB, Volvo AB, Sv. Handelsbanken AB, Swedish Steel AB, Preem Petroleum AB, Sphinx-Gustavsberg NV; Chair. Swedish Nat. Grid; Hon. DTech. *Leisure interests:* orienteering, skiing, hunting and sailing. *Address:* Sandvik AB, S-811 81 Sandviken; Hedåsvägen 57, S-811 61 Sandviken, Sweden (Home). *Telephone:* 26-26-10-01 (Office); 26-27-02-02 (Home).

ERIKSSON, Sven-Goran; Swedish football manager; b. 5 Feb. 1948, Torsby; m. Ann-Christine Petterson 1977 (divorced); two c.; player with Degerfors 1975, Man. 1976–79, IFK Gothenburg 1979–82, Benfica 1982–84, 1989–92, AS Roma 1982–87, Fiorentina 1987–89, Sampdoria 1992–97, Lazio 1997–2001; Coach England Nat. Team 2001– (11 wins, 9 draws and 3 matches lost by the end of 2002); Prince's Plaque (Swedish Govt Award) 2001, BBC Sports Coach of the Year 2001. *Publication:* Sven-Goran Eriksson on Football 2001. *Address:* c/o Football Association Headquarters, Soho Square, London, England (Office). *Telephone:* (20) 7724 1182 (Office). *Website:* www.the-fa.org (Office).

ERKEBAYEV, Abdygany Erkibayevich, D.PHIL.SC.; Kyrgyzstan politician; b. 1953, Kara-Tent, Osh Region; m.; two s. one d.; ed Kyrgyz State Univ.; Jr researcher, Inst. of World Literature USSR Acad. of Sciences 1976–82; Sr teacher Kyrgyz Women's Pedagogical Inst. 1982–85; Deputy Ed. Kyrgyzstan Madanyaty (newspaper), Dir Inst. of Language and Literature Kyrgyz Acad. of Sciences 1985–90; Deputy Supreme Soviet Kyrgyz SSR 1990–91; Minister of Press and Information Kyrgyz Repub. 1991–92; Vice-Prime Minister 1992–93; Head, Osh Region Admin. 1993–95; mem. Ass. of People's Repub. of Zhogorku Kenesh, Chair. Cttee on Social Problems 1995–, Chair. Zhogorku Kenesh 2000–; Chair. Interparl. Cttee of Russia, Belarus, Kazakhstan, Kyrgyzstan (Union of Four); Co-Chair. Union of Democratic Forces; mem. Nat. Acad. of Sciences Kyrgyz Repub. *Publications:* 8 books and over 150 articles and reviews on problems of literature, arts and politics. *Address:* Zhogorku Kenesh, House of Government, 720003 Bishkek, Kyrgyzstan. *Telephone:* (312) 22-55-23 (Office).

ERLANDE-BRANDENBURG, Alain; French museum curator; b. 2 Aug. 1937, Luxeuil-les-Bains; s. of Gilbert Erlande and Renée Pierra; m. Anne-Bénédicte Mérel 1980; four c.; Curator Musée de Cluny and Musée d'Ecouen 1967, Chief Curator 1981; Dir of Studies Ecole pratique des hautes études 1975; Prof. Ecole du Louvre; Assoc. Prof. Ecole Nationale des Chartes 1991–2000; Asst Dir Musées de France 1987–92; Head Musée Nat. du Moyen-Age 1991–94; Curator Musée Nat. de la Renaissance, Château d'Ecouen; Pres. Soc. française d'archéologie; Dir French Archives, Ministry of Culture and the French Language 1994–98; Pres. French Soc. of Archaeology 1985–94, Nat. Soc. of French Antique Dealers 1995–; Commdr, Ordre nat. du Mérite; Officier, Légion d'honneur; Commdr des Arts et des Lettres. *Publications:* Paris monumental 1974, Le roi est mort 1975, Les rois retrouvés 1977, La Dame à la licorne 1978, La cathédrale d'Amiens 1982, L'abbaye de Cluny 1982, L'art gothique 1984, Chartres 1986, La conquête de l'Europe 1260–1380 1987, La cathédrale 1989, Notre-Dame de Paris 1991, Quand les cathédrales étaient peintes 1993, Histoire de l'architecture française: Du Moyen Age à la Renaissance 1995, De pierre, d'or et de felu: la création artistique au Moyen Age 1999, Trois abbayes cisterciennes en Provence, Senanque, Silvacane, Le Thoronet, Paris, le 8e jour 2000, Le Sacre de l'artiste. La création au Moyen Age 2000. *Address:* Musée Nationale de la Renaissance, Château d'Ecouen, 95440 Ecouen (Office); 10 bis rue du Pré-aux-clercs, 75007 Paris; Impasse de l'abbaye, 77120 Beautheil, France. *Telephone:* 1-34-38-38-58 (Office); 1-44-45-95-38 (Home). *Fax:* 1-34-38-38-78 (Office); 1-45-44-95-38 (Home).

ERLEN, Hubertus; German business executive; b. 7 July 1943, Troppau; ed Tech. Univ., Berlin; with Volkswagen 1971–72; joined Schering AG 1978, CEO 2001–, Chair. Bd Dirs Schering Berlin, Inc., USA; mem. Bd Dirs Medrad, Inc., USA; mem. Supervisory Bd B. Braun Melsungen AG. *Address:* Schering AG, Müllerstrasse 178, 13353 Berlin, Germany (Office). *Telephone:* (30) 4681111 (Office). *Website:* www.schering.de (Office).

ERLO, Louis Jean-Marie (pseudonym of Louis Camerlo); French theatre director; b. 26 April 1929, Lyons; one s.; ed Ecole de la Martinière and Ecole Nat. Professionnelle, Lyons; Asst producer, Opéra de Lyon 1951, producer 1953, Dir 1969–; Dir Opéra-Studio, Paris 1973–79; mem. Conseil de développement culturel 1971–73; Dir Aix-en-Provence Festival 1982; has produced operas in many of the maj. houses of Europe and in San Francisco and Buenos Aires and also for TV (especially works by Wagner); Chevalier, Légion d'honneur, Ordre nat. du Mérite, Commdr des Arts et des Lettres. *Address:* Théâtre de l'Opéra, 69001 Lyon, France.

ERNAUX, Annie; French writer; b. Annie Duchesne, 1 Sept. 1940, Lillebonne, Seine-Maritime; d. of the late Alphonse Duchesne and Blanche Dumenil; m. Philippe Ernaux 1964 (divorced); two s.; ed Lycée Jeanne-d'Arc, Rouen, Univs of Rouen, Bordeaux and Grenoble; teacher of literature 1966–2000; Prix Renaudot 1984. *Publications:* Les armoires vides 1974, La femme gelée 1984, La place 1984, Une femme 1988, Passion simple 1992, La honte 1997, Je ne suis pas sortie de ma nuit 1997, L'événement 2000, Se perdre 2001, L'occupation 2002, L'écriture comme un couteau 2003. *Address:* 23 rue des Lozères, 95000 Cergy, France. *Fax:* 1-30-31-27-74. *E-mail:* a .ernaux@infonie.fr (Home).

ERNI, Hans; Swiss painter; b. 21 Feb. 1909, Lucerne; m. Doris Kessler 1949; one s. two d.; ed Académie Julien, Paris and Vereinigte Staatsschulen für freie und angewandte Kunst, Berlin; mem. Groupe Abstraction-Création, Paris; mem. SWB; exhbns Lucerne, Paris, Basel, Oxford, Liverpool, London, Cambridge, Leicester, Zürich, Milan, Rotterdam, Prague, Stockholm, Chicago, New York, Rome, Copenhagen, Tokyo, San Francisco, Los Angeles, Washington, Mannheim, Cologne; abstract mural picture Swiss section Triennale Milan, frescoes Lucerne; great mural Switzerland for Swiss Nat. Exhbn Zürich 1939; Great Murals Exposition internationale de l'Urbanisme et de l'Habitation Paris 1947, Mural in Bernese Hosp. Montana; mem. Alliance Graphique Int.; great mural at the Musée Ethnographique, Neuchâtel 1954; has illustrated bibliophile edns of classics by Plato, Pindar, Sophocles, Virgil, Buffon, Renard, Valéry, Homer (Odyssey), Albert Schweitzer (La Paix), Voltaire (Candide), Paul Eluard, etc.; murals for int. exhbn in Brussels 1958; mosaics for the Abbey of St Maurice 1961, for Swiss TV and Radio bldg, Berne 1964; engraved glass panels 'Day and Night' and 'Towards a Humanistic Future' for the Société des Banques Suisses, Geneva, 1963; exhbns in Japan and Australia 1963, 1964, Pro Juventute stamps 1965; murals in Rolex Foundation, Union de Banques Suisses, Sion 1966, for Swissair Zürich and La Placette Geneva 1967; exhbns in Chicago, New York, Geneva 1966–68; Int. Prize at the Biennale del Mare 1953. *Publications:* Wo steht der Maler in der Gegenwart? 1947, Erni en Valais 1967, Israel Sketchbook 1968. *Leisure interest:* art. *Address:* 6045 Meggen, Lucerne, Switzerland. *Telephone:* (41) 371382.

ERNST, Richard R., DrScTech; Swiss professor of physical chemistry; b. 14 Aug. 1933, Winterthur; s. of Robert Ernst and Irma Brunner; m. Magdalena Kielholz 1963; one s. two d.; ed Edgenössische Technische Hochschule, Zürich; Scientific Collaborator, Physical-Chem. Lab., ETH, Zürich 1962–63; Scientist, Varian Associates, Palo Alto, Calif., USA 1963–68; tutor, then Asst Prof., Assoc. Prof., ETH, Zürich 1968–76, Prof. of Physical Chem. 1976–98; mem. editorial bd various journals on magnetic resonance; Pres. Research Council of ETH, Zürich 1990–94; Vice-Pres. Bd Spectrospin AG, Fällanden 1989–; Fellow American Physical Soc.; mem. Schweizer Chemikerverband, Int. Soc. of Magnetic Resonance, Schweizerische Chemische Gesellschaft, Deutsche Akad. der Naturforscher Leopoldina, Academia Europaea, Schweizerische Akad. der Technischen Wissenschaften, NAS, Royal Soc. London; Dr hc (ETH-Lausanne) 1985, (Zürich) 1994, (Antwerp) 1997, (Babes-Bolyai) 1998, (Montpellier) 1999, (Allahabad) 2000, (Prague) 2002; Hon. Dr rer. nat (Munich Tech. Univ.) 1989; several awards including Benoist Prize 1986, John Gamble Kirkwood Medal, Yale Univ. 1989, Ampere Prize 1990, Wolf Prize for Chem., Jerusalem 1991, Nobel Prize for Chem. 1991. *Leisure interests:* music, Tibetan art. *Address:* Laboratorium für Physikalische Chemie, ETH Hönggerberg HCI, 8093 Zürich (Office); Kurlistr. 24, 8404 Winterthur, Switzerland (Home). *Telephone:* (52) 2427807 (Home); (1) 6324368 (Office). *Fax:* (1) 6321257 (Office). *E-mail:* ernst@nmr.phys.chem.ethz.ch.

EROĞLU, Derviş, PhD; Turkish-Cypriot politician; b. 1938, Ergazi Magosa Dist; four c.; ed Univ. of Istanbul; fmr urologist, Ankara; mem. Parl. 1976–; Chair. Ulusal Birlik Partisi (Nat. Unity Party) 1981–; Prime Minister 'Turkish Repub. of Northern Cyprus' 1985–93, 1996–. *Address:* Office of the Prime Minister, Lefkoşa (Nicosia), Mersin 10 (Office); National Unity Party, 9 Atatürk Meydanı, Lefkoşa (Nicosia), Mersin 10, 'Turkish Republic of Northern Cyprus'. *Telephone:* (22) 83141 (Office); (22) 73972. *Fax:* (22) 75281 (Office). *E-mail:* pressdpt@brimnet.com (Office).

ERRÁZURIZ OSSA, HE Cardinal Francisco Javier; Chilean ecclesiastic; b. 5 Sept. 1933, Santiago; ordained priest 1961; Archbishop 1991; Archbishop of Valparaíso 1996–98, of Santiago 1998–; cr. Cardinal 2001. *Address:* Casilla-30 D, Erasmo Escala 1884, Santiago, Chile (Office). *Telephone:* (2) 6963275 (Office); (2) 2744830 (Home). *Fax:* (2) 6989137 (Office); (2) 2092251 (Home).

ERRERA, Gérard; French diplomatist; b. 30 Oct. 1943, Brive; s. of Paul Errera and Bella Montekio; m. Virginie Bedoya-Calvo; three c.; ed Inst. d'Etudes Politiques and Ecole Nat. d'Admin. Paris; First Sec. Washington, DC 1971–75; Special Adviser to Minister of Foreign Affairs 1975–77, 1980–81; Political Counsellor, Madrid 1977–80; Consul-Gen. San Francisco 1982–85; Dir of Int. Relations, French Atomic Energy Comm. and Gov. for France, IAEA 1985–90; Amb. to Conf. on Disarmament, Geneva 1991–95; Amb. and Perm. Rep. to NATO, Brussels 1995–98; Deputy Sec.-Gen. and Dir-Gen. of Political Affairs, Ministry of Foreign Affairs 1998–2002; Amb. to UK 2002–; Chevalier, Légion d'honneur; Officier de l'Ordre nat. du Mérite. *Leisure interests:* skiing, tennis, guitar. *Address:* Embassy of France, 58 Knightsbridge, London, SW1X 7JT, England; Ministry of Foreign Affairs, 37 quai d'Orsay, 75007 Paris, France. *Telephone:* (20) 7073-1000. *Fax:* (20) 7073-1003. *E-mail:* gerard .errera@diplomatie.gouv.fr. *Website:* www.ambafrance-uk.org.

ERRINGTON, Stuart Grant, CBE, MA, JP, DL; British financier and business executive; b. 23 June 1929, Liverpool; s. of Sir Eric Errington Bt and of the late Lady (Marjorie) Errington; m. Anne Baedeker 1954; two s. one d.; ed Rugby School, Trinity Coll., Oxford; nat. service 1947–49; Man., Ellerman Lines Ltd 1952–59; various positions, to Jt Man. Dir, Astley Industrial Trust Ltd 1959–70; various positions, to Chair. and Chief Exec., Mercantile Credit Co. Ltd (now Mercantile Group PLC) 1970–89; Dir Barclays Merchant Bank (Barclays Bank UK) 1979–86, Kleinwort Overseas Investment Trust PLC

1982–98, Municipal Mutual Insurance 1989–, Northern Electric PLC 1989–96, Nationwide Bldg Soc. (mem. 1989–97, Vice-Chair. 1995–97), Associated Property Owners 1998–; Chair. Equipment Leasing Asscn 1976–78, Finance Houses Asscns 1982–84, Europe Fed. of Leasing Asscns 1978–80; Chair. Nat. Asscn of Citizens' Advice Bureaux 1989–94; Chair. Berks. and Oxfordshire Magistrates' Courts Cttee 1999–; mem. Council Royal Holloway, London Univ. 1989– (Vice-Chair. 1995–). *Leisure interests:* fishing, golf, reading. *Address:* Earleywood Lodge, Ascot, Berks., SL5 9JP, England. *Telephone:* (1344) 621977. *Fax:* (1344) 625778.

ERRÓ, Gudmundur (pseudonym of Gudmundsson); Icelandic artist; b. 19 July 1932, Olafsvik; s. of Gudmundur Einarsson and Soffia Kristiansdottir; m. Bat Yosef 1958 (divorced 1969); one c.; ed Reykjavik, Oslo and Florence Art Acads.; painter since 1956, over 135 personal exhbns worldwide (six retrospective including Jeu de Paume, Paris 1999) and has participated in over 250 jt exhbns; Gold Medal (Sweden), Falcon Medal (Iceland), Officier d'arts et lettres. *Leisure interests:* travelling (Far East), food, Cuban cigars. *Address:* 39 rue Fondary, 75015 Paris, France. *Telephone:* 1-45-75-26-33. *Fax:* 1-45-75-26-33.

ERSBØLL, Niels, LLM; Danish diplomatist; b. 9 April 1926, Copenhagen; m. Birgitte Ullerup; two s. five d.; joined Ministry of Foreign Affairs 1955, Head of Div. 1964–67, Dir Secr. for Econ. Affairs 1967–73, State-Sec. for Econ. Affairs 1977–78; Embassy Sec. Del. to NATO, Paris 1958–60, Mission to EFTA and GATT, Geneva 1963–64, Amb. Perm. Rep. to EC, Brussels 1973–77; served in the EFTA Secr., Geneva 1960–63; Chair. Govt Bd Int. Energy Agency 1978–80; Sec.-Gen. EU (fmrly EC) Council, Brussels 1980–94; Hon. KCMG; numerous mil. awards. *Address:* Rungstedvej 36, 2970 Hørsholm, Denmark; Gachard, Montfaucon, 46240 La Bastide Murat, France.

ERSHAD, Lt-Gen. Hossain Mohammad; Bangladeshi politician and fmr army officer; b. 1 Feb. 1930, Rangpur; s. of the late Maqbul Hussain and of Begum Majida Khatun; m. Raushan Ershad 1956; one s. one adopted d.; ed Univ. of Dhaka, Officers' Training School, Kohat, Pakistan; first appointment in 2nd East Bengal Regt 1952; several appointments in various units including Adjutant, East Bengal Regt Centre, Chittagong 1960–62; completed staff course, Quetta Staff Coll. 1966; promoted Lt-Col 1969; Commdr 3rd East Bengal Regt 1969–70, 7th East Bengal Regt 1971–72; Adjutant-Gen. Bangladesh Army; promoted Col 1973; attended Nat. Defence Coll., New Delhi, India 1975; promoted Brig. 1975, Maj.-Gen. 1975; Deputy Chief of Army Staff 1975–78, Chief 1978–86; rank of Lt-Gen. 1979; led mil. takeover in Bangladesh March 1982; Chief Martial Law Administrator and Pres. Council of Ministers 24 March 1982, adopted title of Prime Minister Oct. 1982, of Pres. of Bangladesh Dec. 1983, elected Pres. of Bangladesh Oct. 1986, resigned Dec. 1990; also Minister of Defence 1986–90, of Information 1986–88; fmrly in charge of several ministries including Home Affairs; Chief Adviser Bangladesh Freedom Fighters' Asscn; Chair. Bangladesh Olympic Asscn, Bangladesh Lawn Tennis Fed.; UN Population Award 1987; sentenced to ten years' hard labour on charges of keeping unlicensed firearms, acquitted after appeal 1995; sentenced to a further ten years' imprisonment for illegally amassing money 1992, to seven years' imprisonment for graft 1993, now on bail. *Leisure interests:* golf, writing poems, art, literature and oriental music. *Address:* Diplomatic Area, Gulshan, Dhaka, Bangladesh.

ERSKINE, Peter; British telecommunications executive; fmr European Vice-Pres. of Sales and Customer Service, Mars; fmr Sr Vice-Pres. of Sales and Marketing, UNITEL; sr positions with British Telecommunications (BT) 1993–, including Dir BT Mobile, Pres. and CEO Concert and Man. Dir BT Cellnet 1998–2001; CEO mmO2 2001–. *Address:* O2, Wellington Street, Slough, SL1 1YP, England (Office). *Telephone:* (1753) 628000 (Office).

ERSKINE, Ralph, CBE, ARIBA, AMTPI, SAR; British architect; b. 24 Feb. 1914, Mill Hill, London; s. of George Erskine and Mildred Erskine (née Gough); m. Ruth Monica Francis 1939; one s. two d.; ed Friends' School, Saffron Walden, Essex, Regent Street Polytechnic, London and Konst. Akad., Stockholm; own practice in Sweden 1939–, br. office in Byker, Newcastle-upon-Tyne 1969–; engaged in city renewals plans, new library for Stockholm Univ., town planning, designs for flats, pvt. houses, housing estates, industrial bldgs, churches, shopping centres and homes for the elderly; designed Hall of Residence, Clare Coll., Cambridge, England; studies and research in architectural problems on bldg in subarctic regions; sketches: town site, Resolute, NWT, Canada; Guest Prof. at Tech. School, Zürich; lectures in Netherlands, Japan, Canada, Sweden, Finland, Poland, Denmark, Switzerland, Austria, Germany, Norway, Russia, England, France, Italy and America; has participated in exhbns in Sweden, Canada, Netherlands, Denmark, Norway and Switzerland; foreign mem. Royal Swedish Acad. of Arts; Hon. AIA, DTech (Lund Univ.) 1970; Hon. DLitt (Heriot Watt Univ., Edin.) 1982; Kasper Salin Prize (Sweden), Ytong Prize 1974; medal: litteris et artibus 1980; Gold Medal (Royal Architecture Inst. of Canada) 1982; Wolf Prize for Architecture 1984; Royal Gold Medal (RIBA) 1987. *Publications:* contrib. to architectural magazines. *Leisure interests:* skiing, skating, sailing, swimming. *Address:* Box 156, Gustav III's väg 4, 17802 Drottingholm, Sweden. *Telephone:* 7590352.

ERWA, Lt-Gen. Elfaith Mohamed; Sudanese diplomatist; b. 11 May 1950, Khartoum; m. Kawther Amin Mohamed 1973; seven c.; ed Sudan Military Coll.; fmr pilot; Adviser to Pres. of Repub. 1989–90; State Minister in the Presidency for Nat. Security 1990–95, for Nat. Defence 1995–96; Perm. Rep. to UN July 1996–; Order of Bravery. *Leisure interests:* flying, reading, computers. *Address:* Permanent Mission of Sudan to the UN, 655 Third Avenue, Suite 500-10, New York, NY 10017, USA. *Telephone:* (212) 573-6033. *Fax:* (212) 573-6160. *E-mail:* sudan@un.int (Office).

ERWIN, Alexander, B.ECON.; South African politician, academic and trade union official; b. 17 Jan. 1948; ed Durban High School, Univ. of Natal; lecturer Dept of Econs, Univ. of Natal 1971–78; visiting lecturer Centre of Southern African Studies, Univ. of York 1974–75; Gen. Sec. Trade Union Advisory and Co-ordinating Council 1977–79; Gen. Sec. Fed. of SA Trade Unions 1979–81; Br. Sec. Nat. Union of Textile Workers 1981–83; Educ. Sec. Fed. of SA Trade Unions 1983–85; Educ. Sec. Congress of SA Trade Unions 1986–88; Nat. Educ. Officer Nat. Union of Metalworkers 1988–93; Interim Exec. mem. ANC S Natal Region 1989; Exec. mem. ANC Western Areas Br. 1990–91; fmr mem. Devt and Reconstruction Cttee, Natal Peace Accord; fmr Congress of SA Trade Unions rep. at Nat. Econ. Forum; fmr Ed. ANC Reconstruction and Devt Programme; Deputy Minister of Finance 1994; Minister of Trade and Industry 1996–99, 1999–; Dr hc 1997. *Address:* c/o Ministry of Trade and Industry, 11th Floor, Prinsloo Street, Pretoria 0002, South Africa. *Telephone:* (12) 3101371 (Office). *Fax:* (12) 3227851 (Office). *E-mail:* nmoono@dti.pwv .gov.za (Office). *Website:* www.dti.pwv.gov.za (Office).

ERZEN, Jale Nejdet, MFA, PhD; Turkish art historian, artist and writer; b. 12 Jan. 1943, Ankara; d. of Necdet Erzen and Selma Erzen; ed Art Center Coll. of Design, LA, Istanbul Tech. Univ.; taught part-time at various univs in Turkey; lectured widely in USA, Italy and France; mem. staff Faculty of Architecture Middle East Tech. Univ. 1974–, Prof. of History of Art and Aesthetics 1992–; Founder and Ed. Boyut Fine Arts Journal 1980–85; Founder, Pres. SANART Asscn of Aesthetics and Visual Culture; Gen. Sec. Int. Asscn of Aesthetics 1995–98; adviser, Int. Asscn for Applied Aesthetics 1998–2001; works in pvt. and state collections in Turkey and Europe; Consultant Istanbul Biennale 1992, Istanbul Contemporary Museum 1992–93, Ankara Contemporary Museum 2000–01; Fullbright Fellow, Lawrence Univ., Wis. 1985; Japan Soc. for the Promotion of Science Fellowship 2003–; also consultant for various architectural journals; Chevalier, Ordre des Arts et des Lettres 1991; Best Critic Award, Istanbul Art Fair 2000, High Performance Award, Middle East Tech. Univ. 2000. *Exhibitions:* solo and group exhbns LA Arts Asscn and in France and Italy; exhibits regularly in Ankara and Istanbul; work in collections in Europe, USA and in nat. and pvt. collections in Turkey. *Video:* Exhbn of Suleiman the Magnificent, Grand Palais, Paris (with Stephane Yerasimos) 1989. *Publications include:* books on Ottoman architect Sinan, and Turkish artists Sabri Berkel, Erol Akyavas, Mehmet Aksoy; various articles on aesthetics, modern art, Ottoman architecture, environmental aesthetics. *Leisure interests:* gardening, horse-riding, poetry. *Address:* Faculty of Architecture, Middle East Technical University, Inönu blvd, 06531 Ankara (Office); Sanart, Kenedi Cad. 42, Kavaklidere, 06660 Ankara, Turkey (Home). *Telephone:* (312) 2102215 (Office); (312) 4464761 (Home). *Fax:* (312) 2101249 (Office). *E-mail:* erzen@arch.metu.edu .tr (Office). *Website:* www.metu.edu.tr (Office).

ESAKI, Leo, PhD; Japanese scientist; b. 12 March 1925, Osaka; s. of Soichiro Esaki and Niyoko Ito; m. 1st Masako Araki 1959; one s. two d.; m. 2nd Masako Kondo 1986; ed Univ. of Tokyo; with Sony Corpn 1956–60, conducted research on heavily-doped germanium and silicon which resulted in the discovery of tunnel diode; with IBM Corpn, USA 1960–92, IBM Fellow 1967–92, IBM T. J. Watson Research Center, New York, 1960–92, Man. Device Research 1962–92; Dir IBM-Japan 1976–92, Yamada Science Foundation 1976–; Pres. Univ. of Tsukuba, Ibaraki, Japan 1992–98; Chair. Science and Tech. Promotion Foundation of Ibaraki 1998–; Dir-Gen. Tsukuba Int. Congress Center 1999–; Pres. Shibaura Inst. of Tech. 2000–; Sir John Cass Sr Visiting Research Fellow, London Polytechnic 1981; at IBM pioneered (with co-workers) research on superlattios and quantum wells, triggering wide spectrum of experimental and theoretical investigations leading to emergence of new class of transport and optoelectronic devices; mem. Japan Acad. 1975, American Philosophical Soc. 1991, Max-Planck Gesellschaft 1984; Foreign Assoc. NAS 1976, American Nat. Acad. of Engineering 1977; Nishina Memorial Award 1959, Asahi Press Award 1960, Toyo Rayon Foundation Award 1961, Morris N. Liebmann Memorial Prize 1961, Stuart Ballantine Medal, Franklin Inst. 1961, Japan Acad. Award 1965, Nobel Prize for Physics 1973, Order of Culture, Japanese Govt 1974, US-Asia Inst. Science Achievement Award 1983, American Physical Soc. Int. Prize for New Materials (with others) 1985, IEEE Medal of Honor 1991, Japan Prize 1998, Grand Cordon Order of Rising Sun (First Class) 1998. *Publications:* numerous articles in professional journals. *Address:* Shibaura Institute of Technology, 3-9-14 Shibaura, Minato-ku, Tokyo 108 (Office); 12-6 Sanban-cho, Chiyoda-ku, Tokyo 102, Japan (Home). *Telephone:* (3) 5476-3137 (Office); (3) 3262-1788 (Home). *Fax:* (3) 5476-3175 (Office). *E-mail:* leoesaki@sic.shibaura-it.ac.jp (Office).

ESCHENBACH, Christoph; German conductor and concert pianist; b. 20 Feb. 1940, Breslau (now Wrocław, Poland); ed Musikhochschulen, Cologne and Hamburg; Musical Dir of Philharmonic Orchestra, Ludwigshafen 1979–83; Chief Conductor Tonhalle Orchestra, Zürich 1982–86; Co-Artistic Dir Pacific Music Festival 1992–98; Artistic Dir Schleswig-Holstein Music Festival 1999–2002; Musical Dir Houston Symphony Orchestra 1988–99 (Conductor Laureate 1999–), Ravinia Festival 1994–; Prin. Conductor NDR Symphony Orchestra 1998–; Musical Dir Orchestre de Paris 2000–, Philadelphia Orchestra 2003–; has appeared as conductor Boston Symphony, Chicago Symphony, Houston Symphony, LA Philharmonic, New York Philharmonic, Philadelphia Orchestra, San Francisco Symphony (US conducting

debut 1975), Berlin Philharmonic, Danis Nat. Radio Orchestra, Hamburg NDR Symphony Orchestra, Kirov Orchestra, all five London orchestras, Orchestra de Paris, Vienna Philharmonic; as pianist with Atlanta Symphony, Radio Orchestras of Munich and Stuttgart, Israel Philharmonic and Israel Chamber Orchestras, NHK Orchestra Tokyo; operatic engagements include Bayreuth, Houston Grand Opera, NY Metropolitan Opera, Hessian State Theatre, Darmstadt (operatic conducting debut 1978); festivals include Bayreuth, Ravinia Festival and Schleswig-Holstein Musical Festival; Officer's Cross with Ribbon, German Order of Merit 1990, Commdr's Cross 1993, Officer's Cross with Star of the German Order of Merit 2002, Chevalier de la Légion d'honneur 2002; 1st Prize, Steinway Piano Competition 1952, Munich Int. Competition 1962, Clara Haskil Competition 1965, Leonard Bernstein Award 1993. *Address:* c/o M. L. Falcone, Public Relations, 155 West 68th Street, New York, NY 10023, USA. *Telephone:* (212) 580-4302. *Fax:* (212) 787-9638 (Office).

ESCHENMOSER, Albert, DrScNat; Swiss chemist; b. 5 Aug. 1925, Erstfeld; s. of Alfons Eschenmoser and Johanna Eschenmoser (née Oesch); m. Elizabeth Baschnonga 1954; two s. one d.; ed Collegium Altdorf, Kantonsschule St Gallen, Swiss Federal Inst. of Technology, Zürich; Privatdozent, Organic Chem., Swiss Fed. Inst. of Technology 1956, Assoc. Prof. of Organic Chem. 1960, Prof. Organic Chem. 1965; Prof. Skaggs Inst. for Chemical Biology, La Jolla, Calif. 1996, now Prof. Emer.; Foreign Hon. mem. American Acad. of Arts and Sciences 1966, Pharmaceutical Soc. for Japan 1999; Foreign Assoc. Nat. Acad. of Sciences, USA 1973; mem. Deutsche Akademie der Naturforscher Leopoldina (Halle) 1976; Foreign mem. Royal Soc. 1986, Pontifical Acad. (Vatican) 1986, Akad. der Wissenschaften (Göttingen) 1986, Academia Europaea 1988, Croatian Acad. of Sciences and Arts 1994; Hon. FRSC (London) 1981; Hon. mem. Gesellschaft Oesterreichischer Chemiker, Vienna 1997; Hon. Dr rer. nat (Fribourg) 1966; Hon. DSc (Chicago) 1970, (Edin.) 1979, (Bologna) 1989, (Frankfurt) 1990, (Strasbourg) 1991, (Harvard) 1993, (TSRI La Jolla, Calif.) 2000; Kern Award, Swiss Fed. Inst. of Technology 1949, Werner Award, Swiss Chemical Soc. 1956, Ruzicka Award, Swiss Fed. Inst. of Technology 1958, ACS Fritzsche Award 1966, Marcel Benoist Prize (Switzerland) 1973, R. A. Welch Award in Chem. (Houston, Texas) 1974, Kirkwood Medal (Yale) 1976, A.W.v. Hofmann-Denkmünze, GDCh 1976, Dannie-Heinemann Prize (Akademie der Wissenschaften, Göttingen) 1977, Davy Medal (Royal Soc., London) 1978, Tetrahedron Prize (Pergamon Press) 1981, G. Kenner Award (Univ. of Liverpool) 1982, ACS Arthur C. Cope Award 1984, Wolf Prize in Chem. (Israel) 1986, Cothenius Medal (Akad. Leopoldina) 1991, Nakanishi Prize, Chemical Soc. of Japan 1998; Orden pour le mérite für Wissenschaften und Künste (Bonn) 1992, Österreich. Ehrenzeichen für Wissenschaft und Kunst (Vienna) 1993, Paracelsus Prize (New Swiss Chemical Soc.) 1999, Grande Médaille d'Or, Acad. des Sciences, Paris 2001, A. I. Oparin Medal, Int. Soc. Origin of Life 2002, ACS Roger Adams Award 2003. *Publications:* numerous articles on organic synthesis in professional journals. *Address:* Laboratorium für Organische Chemie, ETH Hönggerberg HCI-H309, 8093 Zürich (Office); Bergstrasse 9, 8700 Küsnacht (ZH), Switzerland (Home). *Telephone:* (1) 6322893 (Office); (1) 9107392 (Home). *Fax:* (1) 6321043 (Office).

ESCOBAR CERDA, Luis; Chilean economist; b. 10 Feb. 1927; m. 2nd Helga Koch 1973; five c.; ed Univ. de Chile and Harvard Univ.; Dir School of Econs, Univ. de Chile 1951–55, Dean of Faculty of Econs 1955–64; Minister of Econ. Devt and Reconstruction 1961–63; mem. Inter-American Cttee for Alliance for Progress 1964–66; Exec. Dir Int. Monetary Fund 1964–66, 1968–70, IBRD 1966–68; Special Rep. for Inter-American Orgs IBRD 1970–75; Trustee of Population Reference Bureau 1968–73; mem. Advisory Cttee on Population and Devt OAS 1968–73, Council Soc. for Int. Devt 1969–72; Deputy Exec. Sec. Joint Bank/Fund Devt Cttee 1975–79; Prof. Georgetown Univ. 1975–79, George Washington Univ. 1977, Dept of Econs, American Univ. 1978–79; CEO private banks 1979–84; Minister of Finance 1984–85; Amb. to UN and Int. Orgs. in Geneva 1986–90; Consultant on Econ. and Financial Matters 1990–; Prof. Univ. of Chile 1990–, Dean, Faculty of Business Admin., Iberoamerican Univ. for Sciences and Tech. 1997–2001; Acad. mem. for Life and Extraordinary Prof., Univ. of Chile; Vice-Pres. Partido Radical Social Demócrata 1994–95; Gold Medal for Best Graduate in Econs, Univ. of Chile. *Publications:* The Stock Market 1959, Organization for Economic Development 1961, A Stage of the National Economic Development 1962, Considerations on the Tasks of the University 1963, Organizational Requirements for Growth and Stability 1964, The Role of the Social Sciences in Latin America 1965, The Organization of Latin American Government 1968, Multinational Corporations in Latin America 1973, International Control of Investments 1974, External Financing in Latin America 1976, 1978, Mi Testimonio 1991, Financial Problems of Latin American Economic Integration 1992, Globalization and Challenges of Globalization 2000–01; articles in newspapers. *Leisure interests:* reading, tennis, skiing. *Address:* 1724 Sánchez Fontecilla, Santiago 10, Chile. *Telephone:* (2) 2080227. *Fax:* (2) 6716920. *E-mail:* escobarcerda@yahoo.com (Home).

ESCOBEDO, Helen (Elena), ARCA; Mexican sculptor; b. 28 July 1934, Mexico City; d. of Manuel G. Escobedo and Elsie Fulda Escobedo; m. 1st Fredrik Kirsebom (divorced 1982); one s. one d.; m. 2nd Hans-Jürgen Rabe 1995; ed Univ. of Motolinia, RCA, London; Dir of Fine Arts Nat. Univ. of Mexico 1961–74, Dir of Museums and Galleries 1974–78; Tech. Dir Nat. Museum of Art, Mexico 1981–82; Dir Museum of Modern Art, Mexico 1982–84; mem. Espacio Escultórico design team 1978–79; Guggenheim

Fellowship; Assoc. mem. Acad. Royale de Belgique; Fonca Stipendium 2000–03; Tlatilco Prize for Sculpture, Int. Water Sculpture Competition Prize, New Orleans World Fair 1983, Order of the Lion (Finland). *Solo shows:* Museo de Arte Moderno, Mexico City 1975, Nat. Art Museum, Helsinki 1991, Museo Rufino Tamayo 1992, Winnipeg Art Gallery, Canada 1996, Museo Universitario Mexico City 2001. *Designs include:* Gateway to the Wind, Olympic Highway 68, Mexico City, 1968, Signals, Auckland Harbour 1971, Rain Towers, New Orleans 1984, The Great Cone, Jerusalem 1986, Seaview, Arlington House, London 1989. *Publication:* Mexican Monuments, Strange Encounters 1989. *Leisure interests:* reading, writing. *Address:* Delbrückstr. 10, 14193 Berlin, Germany (March–Sept.); 1A Cerrada de San Jerónimo 19, Mexico 10200 DF, Mexico (Oct.–Feb.). *Telephone:* (30) 89542148 (Berlin); (55) 5595-0941 (Mexico). *Fax:* (30) 89542149 (Berlin); (55) 5683-4699 (Mexico). *E-mail:* helenescobedo@yahoo.com (Home). *Website:* www.arts-history.mx/hescobedo (Office); www.helen-excobedo.com (Home).

ESCOVAR SALOM, Ramón; Venezuelan politician; b. 1926, Lara State; mem. Nat. Congress 1947; Minister of Justice; Rep. to Lara State Legis. Ass.; mem. Senate; Sec.-Gen. of the Presidency 1974–75; Minister of Foreign Affairs 1975–77; Amb. to France 1986–89; Attorney-Gen. of Venezuela 1989–93; Prosecutor Int. Tribunal investigating crimes committed in fmr Yugoslavia 1993–94; Minister of the Interior 1994; Perm. Rep. to UN 1999–2001. *Address:* c/o Ministry of Foreign Affairs, Edif. MRE, Avda Urdaneta, Esq. Carmelitas, Caracas 1010, Venezuela.

ESKÉNAZI, Gérard André, MBA; French business executive; b. 10 Nov. 1931, Paris; s. of Roger Eskénazi and Léone Blanchard; m. Arlette Gravelin 1964; three s. one d.; ed studies in law and business admin.; joined Banque de Paris et des Pays-Bas (now Banque Paribas) 1957, Pres. Cie Financière de Paribas 1978–82; Chair. of Bd and Chair. Exec. Cttee of Pargesa SA 1985–90; Deputy Chair. and Pres. Groupe Bruxelles Lambert SA 1982–90; Chair. Parfinance 1986–90; Deputy Chair. Banque Bruxelles Lambert 1982–90; Deputy Chair. Banque Internationale à Luxembourg 1984–90; Chair. Compagnie Industrielle Pallas (COMIPAR) 1991–95; now Chair. Naviter 1999–; mem. Bd Schneider 1981–97, Petrofina 1986–90, Cie Financière Paribas 1988–90; Chevalier, Légion d'honneur and Ordre nat. du mérite. *Leisure interest:* horse riding. *Address:* Naviter, 68 rue de Faubourg Saint-Honoré, 75008 Paris (Office); 7 rue Maurice Ravel, 92210 St Cloud, France (Home). *Telephone:* 1-53-05-28-30 (Office).

ESKOLA, Antti Aarre, PhD; Finnish professor of social psychology; b. 20 Aug. 1934, Urjala; m. Riti Laakso 1958; one s. one d.; ed Univ. of Helsinki; Prof. of Sociology, Univ. of Turku 1965; Prof. of Social Psychology, Univ. of Tampere 1966–97, Prof. Emer. 1997–; Research Prof., Acad. of Finland 1982–87; mem. Finnish Acad. of Science and Letters 1983. *Publications:* Social Influence and Power in Two-Person Groups 1961, Blind Alleys in Social Psychology 1988; several other studies, textbooks, essay collections and a novel. *Address:* Department of Sociology and Social Psychology, 33014, University of Tampere, Finland.

ESMENARD, Francis; French publisher; b. 8 Dec. 1936, Paris; s. of Robert Esmenard and Andrée Michel; one s.; Pres., Dir-Gen. Éditions Albin Michel 1982–, Paris; Vice-Pres. Nat. Publishing Syndicat 1979–; Prés. du Directoire 1999–. *Leisure interests:* tennis, golf, skiing. *Address:* Éditions Albin Michel, 22 rue Huyghens, 75014 Paris, France (Office). *Telephone:* 1-42-79-10-00. *Fax:* 1-43-27-21-58.

ESPERT ROMERO, Nuria; Spanish actress and director; b. 11 June 1935, Hospitalet (Barcelona); m. Armando Moreno 1955; two d.; professional actress since 1947; first maj. success in Medée aged 19; created her own co. 1959; has appeared in works by Calderón, Shakespeare, O'Neill, Lope, De Vega, Genet, Lorca, Espriu, Valle Inclán, Sartre etc.; Dir The House of Bernarda Alba (Lorca) with Glenda Jackson and Joan Plowright, London 1986 (Evening Standard Drama Award); has also directed operas Madame Butterfly, Elektra, Rigoletto, La Traviata and Carmen at Covent Garden and in Scotland, Brussels, Israel and Japan; Artistic Dir Turandot, Liceo Theater, Barcelona 1999; more than 100 Spanish honours and awards; 17 int. awards. *Theatre includes:* The Seagle 1997, Master Class 1998, Who's Afraid of Virginia Woolf 1999, 2000, Medee 2002. *Publications:* numerous int. theatre publications. *Leisure interests:* resting, thinking, reading. *Address:* Pavia 2, 28013 Madrid, Spain. *Telephone:* (91) 7154958. *Fax:* (91) 3511177.

ESPINASSE, Jacques Paul, MBA; French business executive; b. 12 May 1943, Ales; s. of Gustave Espinasse and Andrée Bernadel; m. Daniele Samat 1964; one s. one d.; ed Univ. of Michigan; financial analyst, London and Brussels 1967–70; Consultant, Science Man. Int. 1970–73; Head, Control Dept Renault Véhicules Industriels 1973–78, Commercial Man. in charge of export in Europe 1979; Head, Int. Treasury Dept Régie Renault 1980; Financial Officer, Sommer Allibert 1981–82; Chief Financial Officer CEP Communication 1982–85; Chief Financial Officer Havas 1985–87, Exec. Vice-Pres. 1987–93; Consultant 1994–; Dir-Gen. Télévision par satellite (TPS) 1999–2002; Chief Financial Officer Vivendi Universal 2002–; Chevalier Ordre nat. du Mérite. *Leisure interest:* golf. *Address:* 29 boulevard Suchet, 75016 Paris, France. *Telephone:* 1-45-27-86-65. *Fax:* 1-45-24-23-78.

ESPINOZA VENEGAS, Samuel; Mexican ecclesiastic; ed St Andrew's Seminary and Universidad Autónoma de Baja Calif., Mexico; teacher of sociology and history; Anglican Bishop of Western Mexico 1980–, Primate of Mexico 1997–. *Leisure interest:* reading. *Address:* Fco. J. Gamboa 255,

Guadalajara, Jalisco (Office); Apdo 2-366, 44280 Guadalajara, Jalisco (Office); Av. Ley 2735, Lire, Vallarta, S.H. Guadalajara, Jalisco, Mexico (Home). *Telephone:* (36) 16-44-13 (Office); (36) 15-20-73 (Home). *Fax:* (36) 16-44-13 (Office). *E-mail:* diocte@vianet.com.mx (Office).

ESPY, Mike; American politician; b. 1953, Yazoo City, Miss.; m. (divorced); one s. one d.; ed Howard Univ., Washington, DC, Univ. of Santa Clara Law School, Calif.; fmrly attorney with Cen. Miss. Legal Services and Asst Sec. of public lands div. of Miss.; Asst Attorney-Gen., Miss. 1984–85; elected to US House of Reps 1986; fmr mem. House Agric. Cttee, Budget Cttee and Select Cttee on Hunger; Sec. of Agric. 1993–94; mem. Nat. Rifle Asscn. *Address:* c/o US Department of Agriculture, 14th Street and Independence Avenue, SW, Washington, DC 20520, USA.

ESQUIVEL, Manuel, PC; Belizean politician and teacher; b. 2 May 1940, Belize City; s. of John Esquivel and Laura Esquivel; m. Kathleen Levy 1971; one s. two d.; ed Loyola Univ., USA, Univ. of Bristol, England; teacher at St John's Jr Coll., Belize City –1984; f. United Democratic Party 1973, Chair. 1976–82; fmr Councillor, Belize City Council; mem. Senate 1979–84; Prime Minister of Belize 1984–89, 1993–98, also Minister of Finance, fmrly of Defence and of Econ. Devt; Leader of the Opposition 1989–93; Dr hc (Loyola Univ., USA) 1986. *Address:* c/o United Democratic Party, 19 King Street, P.O. Box 1143, Belize City, Belize.

ESSAAFI, M'Hamed; Tunisian diplomatist; b. 26 May 1930, Kelibia; m. Hedwige Klat 1956; one s. one d.; ed Sorbonne, Paris; First Sec., London 1956; Counsellor, then Minister Plenipotentiary, Ministry of Foreign Affairs 1960–64; Amb. to UK 1964–69; Sec.-Gen. Ministry of Foreign Affairs 1969–70, 1976–78; Amb. to USSR 1970–74, to FRG 1974–76, to Belgium, Luxembourg and EEC 1978–79; Perm. Rep. to UN Jan.–Aug. 1980; UN Sec.-Gen.'s Special Rep. for Humanitarian Affairs in SE Asia 1980–81; Chef de Cabinet of UN Sec.-Gen. Jan.–June 1982; UN Under-Sec.-Gen. and Disaster Relief Co-ordinator 1982–92; Grand Officier, Ordre de la République tunisienne; Chevalier, Ordre de l'Indépendance. *Address:* rue de la Mosquée BH20, La Marsa, Tunis, Tunisia (Home).

ESSBERGER, Ruprecht; German television director and writer; b. 8 March 1923, Berlin; s. of Eduard Essberger and Hedwig Schülthes; m. 1st Alexandra Massenberg 1949 (divorced 1962); two s.; m. 2nd Merle Insanali 1969; one d.; ed Univs of Hamburg and Göttingen; Asst TV Dir North German Rundfunk 1950, TV Dir 1953; freelance TV dir and writer 1957–; Bundesverdienstkreuz 1989; Golden Screen, Golden Rose and Golden Camera awards. *Television includes:* Familie Schölermann 1955–60, Das Fernsehgericht tagt 1960–78, Ehen vor Gericht 1970–83, 1989–96, Verkehrsgericht 1983–95. *Leisure interests:* music, sailing. *Address:* Agnesstrasse 2, 22301 Hamburg, Germany.

ESSENHIGH, Adm. Sir Nigel, KCB; British naval officer; b. 1944; m. Susie Essenhigh; ed Royal Coll. of Defence Studies; joined Royal Navy 1963, qualified as Prin. Warfare Officer, specializing in navigation 1972, served in variety of ships, Commdr Type 42 Destroyers HMS Nottingham and HMS Exeter; Hydrographer of the Navy, Chief Exec. UK Hydrographic Office, with rank of Rear Adm.; several appointments at Ministry of Defence including Asst Chief of Defence Staff (Programmes); promoted to Adm., C-in-C Fleet; C-in-C E Atlantic (NATO) and Commdr Allied Naval Forces N (NATO); First Sea Lord and Chief of Naval Staff 2001–02; Fellow Nautical Inst., Royal Inst. of Navigation; mem. Hon. Co. of Master Mariners; Younger Brother Trinity House; Aide-de-camp. *Address:* c/o Ministry of Defence, Main Building, Whitehall, London, SW1A 2HB, England (Office).

ESSEX, David Albert, OBE; British singer, actor and composer; b. 23 July 1947, London; s. of Albert and Doris Cook (née Kemp); m. Maureen Annette Neal 1971; one s. one d.; ed Shipman Secondary School, E London; started in music industry 1965; TV debut on Five O'Clock Club; has since made numerous TV appearances in UK, Europe and USA, including own BBC series 1977, The River BBC1 Series 1988; appeared on stage in repertory and later in Godspell 1971, Evita 1978, Childe Byron, Mutiny! (also wrote music) 1985, with Sir Peter Hall's Co. in She Stoops to Conquer tour and Queen's Theatre, London 1993–94; wrote score for Russian All Stars Co.'s Beauty and the Beast 1995–96; first concert tour of UK 1974, subsequent tours 1975 (including Europe, USA and Australia), 1976, 1977, 1978, 1979 (including Europe and USA), 1980, 1987, 1988, 1989/90 (World Tour); Amb. for Voluntary Service Overseas 1990–92; Pres. Stanstead Park Cricket Club; numerous gold and silver discs for LP and single records in Europe and USA; voted Best Male Singer and Outstanding Music Personality in Daily Mirror poll 1976; Variety Club of GB Award for Show Business Personality of the Year (joint) 1978 ASCAP Award 1989, BASCA Award for Composer 1994. *Films include:* Assault, All Coppers Are . . . 1971, That'll Be The Day (Variety Club Award) 1973, Stardust 1974, Silver Dream Racer 1979, Shogun Mayeda 1991. *Albums include:* Rock On 1974, All the Fun of the Fair 1975, Out on the Street 1976, Gold and Ivory 1977, Imperial Wizard 1979, Hot Love 1980, Be Bop the Future 1981, Stage Struck 1982, The Whisper 1983, This One's For You 1984 (all solo); Under Different Skies (album of musicians from developing countries); War of the Worlds (with Jeff Wayne, Richard Burton and others), From Alpha to Omega (with Cat Stevens) 1978, Silver Dream Racer (film soundtrack: composer/producer) 1979, Centre Stage 1986, Touching the Ghost 1989, David Essex Greatest Hits 1991, Cover Shot 1993, Back to Back 1994. *Leisure interests:* motorcycling, cricket, squash, flying helicopters. *Address:* c/o London Management, 2–4 Noel Street, London, W1V 3RB, England. *Telephone:* (20) 7287-9000. *Fax:* (20) 7287-3036.

ESSNER, Robert Alan, MA; American pharmaceutical industry executive; b. 1948; ed Miami Univ., Oxford, Ohio and Univ. of Chicago; with Sandoz Pharmaceutical Corpn 1978–86, Vice-Pres. 1986–87; Pres. Sandoz Consumer HealthCare Group 1987; joined American Home Products (AHP) 1989, Pres. Wyeth-Ayerst Labs 1993–97, Pres. Wyeth-Ayerst Pharmaceuticals 1997–2000, Exec. Vice-Pres., mem. Bd of Dirs, AHP 1997–, Pres. and COO 2000–01, Pres. and CEO May 2001–. *Address:* American Home Products, 5 Giralda Farms, Madison, NJ 07940-0874, USA (Office). *Website:* www.ahp .com (Office).

ESSWOOD, Paul Lawrence Vincent, ARCM; British counter-tenor singer and conductor; b. 6 June 1942, Nottingham; s. of Alfred W. Esswood and Freda Garatt; m. 1st Mary L. Cantrill 1966 (divorced 1990); two s.; m. 2nd Aimée Désirée Blattmann 1990; one s. one d.; ed West Bridgford Grammar School and Royal Coll. of Music; Lay Vicar, Westminster Abbey 1964–71; Prof. Royal Coll. of Music 1973–85, Royal Acad. of Music 1985–; Co-founder, Pro Cantione Antiqua – A Cappella 1967; opera debut, L'Erismena, Univ. of Calif., Berkeley 1968; debut at La Scala, Milan with Zürich Opera in L'Incoronazione di Poppea and Il Ritorno d'Ulisse 1978; Scottish opera debut in Dido and Aeneas 1978; world premiere, Penderecki's Paradise Lost, Chicago Lyric Opera 1979, Philip Glass's Akhnaton, Stuttgart 1984, Herbert Will's Schlafes Bruder, with Zurich Opera 1996; world première, Schnittke's Faust Cantata, Vienna, 1986; Handel's Riccardo Primo, Covent Garden, 1991; has appeared at many maj. int. festivals; specialist in performance of baroque music and has made many recordings of works by Bach, Handel, Purcell, Monteverdi, Cavalli, Britten (Abraham and Isaac), folksongs etc.; Prof. at 'Maîtrise de Notre Dame', Paris, conducting debut at Chichester Festival with Purcell's The Fairy Queen 2000, Kraków, Poland 2001; Hon. RAM 1990; Handel Prize (Germany) 1992. *Leisure interests:* gardening, apiculture. *Address:* Jasmine Cottage, 42 Ferring Lane, Ferring, West Sussex, BN12 6QT, England. *Telephone:* (1903) 504480. *Fax:* (1903) 504480. *Website:* www.themusickecompanye.com.

ESSY, Amara, LLM; Côte d'Ivoirian diplomatist; b. 20 Dec. 1944, Bouake; m. Lucie Essy 1971; three s. three d.; Chief of Div. of Econ. Relations 1970; First Counsellor, Ivory Coast Embassy, Brazil 1971–73, Ivory Coast Mission to the UN 1973–75; Perm. Rep. to the UN Office, Geneva 1975–81, to UNIDO, Vienna 1975–81; Amb. to Switzerland 1978–81; Perm. Rep. to the UN (and non-resident Amb. to Argentina and Cuba), New York 1981–91; Pres. UN Security Council 1990–91; Minister of Foreign Affairs 1990–98; Pres. 49th Session UN Gen. Ass. 1994–95; Minister of State, Minister of Foreign Affairs in charge of Int. Co-operation 1998–99; Sec.-Gen. OAU Sept. 2001–(05); participated in the following UN confs: Law of the Sea (Caracas, Geneva, New York), Int. Women's Year (Mexico City), Econ. Co-operation among Developing Countries, UNCTAD (Nairobi, Manila) and of the codification of int. law; meetings of the Econ. and Social Council and Comm. on Human Rights. *Address:* Organization of African Unity, P.O.B. 3243, Addis Ababa, Ethiopia. *Telephone:* (1) 517700. *Fax:* (1) 513036. *Website:* www.oau-oua.org.

ESTEFAN, Gloria Maria; American singer and composer; b. 1 Sept. 1957, Havana, Cuba; d. of Jose Fajardo and Gloria García; m. Emilio Estefan 1979; one s. one d.; ed Univ. of Miami; went to USA 1959; American Music Award 1987. *Albums include:* Primitive Love 1986, Let it Loose 1987, Cuts Both Ways 1990, Coming Out of the Dark 1991, Greatest Hits 1992, Mi Terra 1993, Destiny 1996; performed songs at Olympic Games, Seoul, S Korea 1988, World Series Baseball, St Louis 1987, Pan American Games 1988, Superbowl Halftime, Minneapolis 1992, Hold Me, Thrill Me, Kiss Me 1994, Destiny 1996, Gloria! 1998, Santo Santo 1999, Alma Caribeño: Caribbean Soul 2000. *Singles include:* Anything for You 1987, Live for Loving You 1991, Can't Forget You 1991, Coming Out of the Dark 1991, Always Tomorrow 1992, Go Away 1993. *Address:* c/o Epic Records, 550 Madison Avenue, New York, NY 10022 (Office); Estefan Enterprises Inc., 6205 Bird Road, Miami, FL 33155, USA.

ESTERHÁZY, Péter; Hungarian writer and essayist; b. 14 April 1950; s. of Mátyás Esterházy and Lili Mányoky; m. Gitta Reén; two s. two d.; ed Budapest Univ.; full-time writer since 1978; Füst Milán, Déry, Kossuth, József Attila, Krúdy, Aszu, Márai, Magyar Irodalini Díj, Vilenica awards, Österreichische Staatspreis für europäische Literatur. *Publications:* short stories: Pápai vizeken ne kalózkodj! 1977; novels: Fancsikó és Pinta 1976, Termelési regény 1979, Függő 1981, Ki szavatol a lady biztonságáért? 1982, Kis magyar pornográfia 1984, A sziv segédigéi 1985, Bevezetés a szépirodalomba 1986, Tizenhét hattyúk (as Csokonai Lili) 1987, Hrabal könyve 1990, Hahn-Hahn grófnő pillantása (The Glance of Countess Hahn-Hahn Down the Danube) 1991, Egy nő (She Loves Me) 1995, Harmonia caelistis 2000; essays: A kitömött hattyú 1988, Az elefántcsonttoronyból 1991, A halacska csodálatos élete 1991, Egy kékharisnya följegyzéseiből 1994, Egy kék haris 1996. *Leisure interests:* football, mathematics. *Address:* c/o Hungarian Writers Federation, 1062 Budapest, Bajza-utca 18, Hungary. *Telephone:* (1) 322-8840.

ESTES, Richard; American painter; b. 14 May 1932, Kawanee, Ill.; s. of William and Maria Estes; ed Chicago Art Inst. *Exhibitions include:* biannual, first with Allan Stone Gallery, then Marlborough Gallery, New York 1968–; travelling retrospective, The Urban Landscale, Hirshhorn, Museum of Fine Arts, Boston, Nelson Atkins 1978–79, Tokyo, Osaka, Hiroshima 1990. *Address:* c/o Marlborough Gallery, 40 West 57th Street, New York, NY 10019 (Office); 300 Central Park West, New York, NY 10024-1513; PO Box 685, Northeast Harbour, ME 04662, USA (Home).

ESTES, William K., PhD; American behavioural scientist; b. 17 June 1919, Minneapolis, Minn.; s. of Dr. George D. Estes and Mona Kaye; m. Katherine Walker 1942; two s.; ed Univ. of Minnesota; Medical admin. officer US Army 1944–46; Faculty mem. Indiana Univ. 1946–62; Prof. of Psychology Stanford Univ. 1962–68; Ed. Journal of Comparative and Physiological Psychology 1962–68, Psychological Review 1977–82, Psychological Science 1990–94; Prof., Rockefeller Univ. 1968–79; Prof., Harvard Univ. 1979–89, Prof. Emer. 1989–; Prof. Indiana Univ. 1999–; Pres. Experimental Div., American Psychological Asscn 1958; Chair. Office of Scientific and Eng Personnel, Nat. Research Council 1982–85; Chair., Cttee on Contribs. of the Behavioral and Social Sciences to the Prevention of Nuclear War, NAS 1985–89; Guggenheim Fellow 1985–86; Chair. Psychonomic Soc. 1972, Soc. for Math. Psychology 1984; mem. Soc. of Experimental Psychologists, NAS, American Acad. of Arts and Sciences, etc.; Distinguished Scientific Contrib. Award of American Psychological Asscn 1962, Warren Medal for Psychological Research 1963, Gold Medal for Lifetime Achievement in Psychological Science (American Psychological Foundation) 1992, Nat. Medal of Science (USA) 1997. *Publications:* An Experimental Study of Punishment 1944, Modern Learning Theory (with S. Koch and others) 1954, The Statistical Approach to Learning Theory 1959, Studies in Mathematical Learning Theory (with R. R. Bush) 1959, Stimulus Sampling Theory (with E. Neimark) 1967, Learning Theory and Mental Development 1970, Handbook of Learning and Cognitive Processes (ed.) 1975, Models of Learning, Memory and Choice 1982, Statistical Models in Behavioral Research 1991, Classification and Cognition 1994. *Leisure interest:* music. *Address:* Psychology Building, Indiana University, Bloomington, IN 47405, USA (Office).

ESTEVE-COLL, Dame Elizabeth, DBE, BA, FRSA; British fmr museum director and university chancellor; b. 14 Oct. 1938; d. of P. W Kingdon and Nora Kingdon; m. José Alexander Timothy Esteve-Coll 1960 (died 1980); ed Birkbeck Coll., Univ. of London; librarian, London Borough of Merton, Kingston Coll. of Art, Kingston Polytechnic 1968–77; Head, Dept of Learning Resources, Kingston Polytechnic 1977–82; Univ. Librarian Univ. of Surrey, Chair. Arts Cttee 1982–85; Chief Librarian, Nat. Art Library, Victoria & Albert Museum 1985–87; Dir Victoria & Albert Museum 1988–95; Vice-Chancellor Univ. of E Anglia 1995–97; Chancellor, Univ. of London 2001–; Assoc. Library Asscn; Hon. LittD (E Anglia) 1997; Hon. DLitt (Hull) 1998. *Publication:* The Victoria and Albert Museum (with others) 1992. *Address:* c/o Coldham Hall, Tuttington, Aylsham, Norfolk, NR11 6TA, England. *Telephone:* (1263) 735465. *Fax:* (1263) 735465.

ESTEVEZ, Emilio; American actor; b. 12 May 1962, New York; s. of Martin Sheen (q.v.); m. Paula Abdul 1992 (divorced 1994); one s. one d. *Films include:* Tex 1982, Nightmares 1983, The Outsiders 1983, The Breakfast Club 1984, Repo Man 1984, St Elmo's Fire 1984, That was then . . . This is Now 1985, Maximum Overdrive 1986, Wisdom 1986 (also wrote and directed), Stakeout 1987, Men at Work 1989, Freejack 1992, Loaded Weapon 1993, Another Stakeout 1993, Champions II 1993, Judgement Night 1993, D2: the Mighty Ducks 1994, The Jerky Boys (co-exec. producer only), Mighty Ducks 3, Mission Impossible 1996, The War at Home 1996, The Bang Bang Club 1998, Killer's Head 1999, Sand 2000, Rated X 2000. *Address:* c/o UTA, 5th Floor, 9560 Wilshire Boulevard, Beverly Hills, CA 90212, USA.

ESTIER, Claude; French journalist and politician; b. 8 June 1925, Paris; s. of Henri Ezratty and Lucie Bernerbe; ed Lycée Carnot, Paris; Political Ed. Le Populaire 1947; Ed. L'Observateur, France-Observateur, then Le Nouvel Observateur 1950–; Ed. Le Monde 1955–58; Ed.-in-Chief Libération 1958–64, Dir 1968; mem. Nat. Assembly 1967–68, 1981–86; Pres. Comm. for Foreign Affairs 1983–86; mem. Paris City Council 1971–89; Nat. Press Sec. Socialist Party 1971–79; Editorial Dir L'Unité (Socialist Party Weekly) 1972–86; MEP 1979–81; Senator 1986; Chair. Senate Socialist Group 1988–; Chevalier, Légion d'honneur. *Publications:* Pour l'Algérie 1963, L'Egypte en révolution 1965, Journal d'un Fédéré 1969, La plume au poing 1977, Mitterrand Président 1981, Véridique histoire d'un Septennat (with Véronique Neiertz) 1987, De Mitterand à Jospin: Trente ans de campagnes présidentielles 1995, Dix ans qui ont changé le monde 2000. *Address:* Palais du Luxembourg, 75291 Paris cedex 06, France.

ESTLEMAN, Loren Daniel, BA; American writer; b. 15 Sept. 1952, Ann Arbor, Mich.; s. of Leauvett C. Estleman and Louise A. Estleman; m. Deborah Ann Green 1993; one step-s. one step-d.; ed Eastern Mich., Univ.; police reporter, Ypsilanti Press 1972–73; Ed.-in-Chief, Community Foto News 1975–76; Special Writer, Ann Arbor News 1976; staff writer, Dexter Leader 1977–80; full-time novelist 1980–; Vice-Pres. Western Writers of America 1998–2000, Pres. 2000–02; Western Writers of America Spur Award, Best Historical Novel 1981, Spur Award, Best Short Fiction 1986, 1996, Private Eye Writers of America Shamus Award, Best Novel 1984, Shamus Award, Best Short Story 1985, 1988, Mich. Foundation of the Arts Award for Literature 1987, Mich. Library Asscn Authors Award 1997, Spur Award, Best Western Novel 1999, Western Heritage Award, Outstanding Western Novel 1999, Western Heritage Award, Outstanding Short Story 2000. *Publications:* (novels) The Oklahoma Punk 1976, The Hider, Sherlock Holmes vs. Dracula 1978, The High Rocks 1979, Dr. Jekyll and Mr. Holmes, Stamping Ground, Motor City Blue 1980, Aces and Eights, Angel Eyes, The Wolfer 1981, Murdock's Law, The Midnight Man 1982, Mister St John, The Glass Highway 1983, This Old Bill, Sugartown, Kill Zone, The Stranglers 1984, Every Brilliant Eye, Roses Are Dead, Gun Man 1985, Any Man's Death 1986, Lady Yesterday 1987, Bloody Season, Downriver 1988, Silent Thunder, Peeper

1989, Sweet Women Lie, Whiskey River 1990, Sudden Country, Motown 1991, King of the Corner 1992, City of Widows 1994, Edsel 1995, Stress 1996, Never Street, Billy Gashade 1997, The Witchfinder, Journey of the Dead, Jitterbug 1998, The Rocky Mountain Moving Picture Association 1999, The Hours of the Virgin 1999, White Desert 2000, The Master Executioner 2001, Sinister Heights 2002, Something Borrowed, Something Black 2002, Black Powder, White Smoke 2002; (non-fiction) The Wister Trace 1987; (collections) General Murders 1988, The Best Western Stories of Loren D. Estleman 1989, People Who Kill 1993; (anthologies) P.I. Files 1990, Deals with the Devil 1994, American West 2001. *Leisure interests:* collecting books, antiques, typewriters, records and old films on tape and DVD, hunting. *Address:* 5552 Walsh Road, Whitmore Lake, MI 48189, USA. *Website:* www.lorenestleman.com (Office).

ESTRADA, Joseph Marcelo Ejercito; Philippine politician; b. 19 April 1937, Tondo, Manila; Mayor of San Juan 1969–85; mem. Senate 1987, Vice-Pres. 1992; Chair. Partido ng Masang Pilipino (PMP); Pres. of the Philippines 1998–2001; impeached for corruption by Congress Nov. 2000, on trial in Senate 2002. *Address:* c/o Office of the President, Malacanang Palace Compound, J. P. Laurel Street, San Miguel, Metro Manila, Philippines.

ESZTERHAS, Joseph A.; American scriptwriter; b. 23 Nov. 1944, Csakanydoroszlo, Hungary; s. of Stephen Eszterhas and Maria Biro; m. 1st Geraldine Javer 1972 (divorced 1994); one s. one d.; m. 2nd Naomi Baka 1994; one s.; ed Ohio State Univ.; reporter, Plain Dealer, Cleveland; staff writer, Man. Ed. Rolling Stone, San Francisco 1971–75; screenwriter 1975–; writer and producer, Checking Out 1980, Betrayed 1989; recipient of various awards. *Publications:* novels: Thirteen Seconds: Confrontation at Kent State 1970, Charlie Simpson's Apocalypse 1974, Nark! 1974, Fist 1977; screenplays: Fist 1978, Flashdance 1983, Jagged Edge 1985, Big Shots 1987, The Music Box 1990, Basic Instinct 1991, Sliver 1993, Showgirls 1995, Telling Lies in America 1997, Original Sin 1997, One Night 1997. *Leisure interest:* reading.

ETAIX, Pierre; French film director and actor; b. 23 Nov. 1928, Roanne; s. of Pierre and Berthe (née Tacher) Etaix; m. 2nd Annie Fratellini 1969 (deceased); ed Lycée de Roanne; apprenticed as stained-glass designer; Asst film producer 1949–55; small part in Robert Bresson's Pickpocket 1959; leading role in Jacques Tati's Jour de Fête, Paris Olympia 1960; directed first short film Rupture 1961; other short films; Heureux anniversaire 1962 (Acad. Award ('Oscar') for best short film 1963), Insomnie (First Prize, Oberhausen Festival 1965); full-length films: Le soupirant 1963 (Prix Louis Delluc, Prize for best humorous film, Moscow Festival 1963), Yoyo 1964 (Grand Prix de l'OCIC, Grand Prix pour la Jeunesse, Cannes 1965), Tant qu'on a la santé 1966 (Coquille d'Argent, San Sebastián Festival), Le grand amour 1969 (Grand Prix du Cinéma Français, Grand Prix de l'OCIC 1969), Les clowns 1970, Pays de cocagne 1971, Sérieux comme le plaisir 1975, Max mon amour 1986, L'âge de Monsieur est avancé (Dir, wrote screenplay, actor); Chevalier, Ordre nat. du Mérite, Ordre des Arts et des Lettres. *Achievement:* creator (with Amie Fratellini) of the first circus school in France 1973. *Publications:* Le carton à chapeau 1981, Dactilographisme 1982, Croquis de Jerry Lewis 1983, Stars System (jtly) 1986, Criticons la caméra 2001. *Address:* Editions du Seuil, 27 rue Jacob, 75261 Paris cedex 06, France (Office).

ETAYO MIQUEO, José Javier; Spanish professor of mathematics; b. 28 March 1926, Pamplona; s. of Nicolás Etayo and María Miqueo; m. Laura Gordejuela 1956; four s.; ed Univs of Valladolid, Zaragoza and Madrid; Prof. Univ. of Madrid 1952–61; Full Prof. Univ. of Zaragoza 1961–63; Full Prof. of Math. Univ. Complutense of Madrid 1963–91, Prof. Emer. 1991–; Vice-Dean Faculty of Sciences, Univ. of Madrid 1971–75; Pres. Real Soc. Matemática Española 1976–82; mem. Consejo Superior de Investigaciones Científicas 1969, Spanish Cttee Int. Math. Union 1979–85; mem. Real Acad. de Ciencias Exactas, Fisicas y Naturales de Madrid 1983–, Gen. Sec. 1992–. *Publications:* gen. math. and geometry textbooks, various math. research papers, especially in differential geometry. *Leisure interests:* reading, music, theatre, cinema. *Address:* Real Academia de Ciencias Exactas, Fisicas y Naturales, Calle Valverde 22, 28004 Madrid (Office); Avenida Reina Victoria, 70, 4B, 28003 Madrid, Spain (Home). *Telephone:* (91) 7014230/31 (Office); (91) 5541173 (Home). *Fax:* (91) 7014232 (Office). *E-mail:* secretaria.racefyn@insde.es.

ETCHEGARAY, HE Cardinal Roger, D.IUR.UTR.; French ecclesiastic; b. 25 Sept. 1922, Espelette; s. of Jean-Baptiste Etchegaray and Aurélie Dufau; ed Petit Séminaire, Ustaritz and Grand Séminaire, Bayonne; ordained priest 1947, served diocese of Bayonne 1947–60; asst Sec., then Sec.-Gen. French Episcopal Conf. 1961–70, Pres. 1975–81; Archbishop of Marseilles 1970–84; Pres. Council of European Episcopal Confs 1971–79; Prelate, Mission of France 1975–81; Titular Bishop of Porto-Santa Rufina; cr.Cardinal 1979; Pres. Comm. Justice and Peace 1984–; Pres. Council Cor Unum 1984–95; Special Papal Emissary to Togo 1993; Pres. Cttee for Grand Jubilee of Year 2000; Officier, Légion d'honneur, Commdr, Ordre nat. du Mérite, Grand Cross Nat. Order (FRG), Grand Cross Nat. Order of Hungary. *Publications:* Dieu à Marseille 1976, J'avance comme un âne 1984, L'évangile aux couleurs de la vie 1987, Jésus, vrai homme, vrai Dieu 1997. *Address:* Piazza San Calisto, Vatican City.

ETCHEGARAY AUBRY, Alberto; Chilean politician and civil engineer; b. 5 May 1945; s. of Alberto Etchegaray and Odette Etchegaray; m.; five s., two d.; Univ. Prof. of Business Admin.; Dir Dept of Studies, Unión Social de Empresarios Cristianos; co-ordinator of visit of Pope John Paul II to Chile; Dir Hogar de Cristo; mem. Council, Semanas Sociales de Chile (initiative of Episcopal Conf. of Chile); Minister of Housing and Urban Devt 1990–94; Pres. Nat. Council against Poverty 1994–98; Dir Cía. Seg. de Vida la Construcción SA; Pres. Fundación Nacional para la Superación de la Pobreza 1997–2000, Dir 2000–; Dir Banco del Desarollo. *Publication:* Poverty in Chile: The Challenge of Equity and Social Intergration. *Address:* Canada 185-A, Providencia, Santiago, Chile. *Telephone:* (2) 204-1917 (Office). *Fax:* (2) 269-0718 (Office). *E-mail:* domet@ctcreuna.cl (Office).

ETCHEVERRY, Guillermo Jaim, MD; Argentine university rector and biologist; Titular Prof. and Dir Dept of Cellular Biology and Histology, Faculty of Medicine, Univ. of Buenos Aires 1986–90, Rector Univ. of Buenos Aires May 2002–; Prin. Investigator, CONICET, IBRO/UNESCO, John Simon Guggenheim Memorial Foundation; mem. Nat. Acad. of Educ., Argentina Acad. of Communication Arts and Sciences; Corresp. mem. Acad. of Medical Sciences of Córdoba; Bernardo Houssay Prize 1987, Master of Medicine, Argentina 2001. *Address:* University of Buenos Aires, Calle Viamonte 430/444, 1053 Buenos Aires, Argentina (Office). *Telephone:* (11) 4511-8120 (Office). *Website:* www.uba.ar (Office).

ETCHEVERRY, Michel Adrien; French actor; b. 16 Dec. 1919, Saint-Jean-de-Luz; s. of Paul and Marie (née Manton) Etcheverry; m. Jacqueline Hebel 1947; one s. one d.; ed Teacher Training Coll., Gironde, Conservatoire d'Art Dramatique, Bordeaux, Conservatoire National Supérieur d'Art Dramatique; began career as teacher, Saint-Sulpice-de-Faleyrens 1940; actor with Louis Jouvet 1945–51, appearing in productions including L'école des femmes, Knock, Le Diable et le bon Dieu, Pygmalion, L'alouette, Le journal d'Anne Frank, L'annonce faite à Marie; Assoc. mem. Comédie-Française 1961–63, mem. 1963–, appearing in productions including Nicomède, Cinna, Polyeucte, L'avare, Marie Stuart, Le maître de Santiago, Le HE Cardinal d'Espagne, La reine morte, Le Cid, Le carrosse du Saint Sacrement, La Rabouilleuse, La soif et la faim, L'otage, L'école des femmes, Dom Juan, Malatesta, Le bourgeois gentilhomme, Georges Dandin, Un fil à la patte, L'impromptu de Marigny, C'est la guerre Monsieur Gruber, La nostalgie, Camarade, Le légataire universel, Le médecin malgré lui, La Célestine, La nuit des rois, Cinna, Monsieur le Trouhadec saisi par la débauche, La poudre aux yeux, On ne badine pas avec l'amour, Meurtre dans la cathédrale, Les Fausses Confidences (producer); Pres. French Actors' Union 1959, Membre du Droit 1963; Chevalier, Légion d'honneur, Officier des Arts et des Lettres. *Films include:* Le fils de Caroline Chérie, Notre-Dame de Paris, Le salaire du péché, C'est arrivé à Aden, Michel Strogoff, Recours en grâce, Vers l'extase, Le passage du Rhin, Le puits aux 3 vérités, Le petit garçon de l'ascenseur, Amours célèbres, Mathias Sandorf, Le tigre se parfume à la dynamite, Paris brûle-t-il?, Perceval le Gallois, I ... comme Icare; numerous TV appearances including Les loups, La dévotion à la croix, Quatre-vingt treize, L'île mystérieuse, Un bourgeois de Calais, Cinna, Le Cid, Le roi Lear, Le fil rouge, Un bourgeois de Paris, Georges Dandin, Le Maître de Santiago, Le deuil sied à Electre, Le légataire universel, Le jeu de l'amour et du hasard 1976. *Address:* 47 rue du Borrégo, 75020 Paris, France.

ETEKI MBOUMOUA, William-Aurélien, LIC. EN DROIT; Cameroonian politician; b. 20 Oct. 1933, Douala; s. of Joseph Mboumoua and Mana Katta; m. Naimi Bessy Eyewe; one s. one d.; ed Ecole Nat. de la France d'Outre-mer, Paris; Prefect for Nkam 1959, for Sanage Maritime 1960–61; Minister of Educ., Youth and Culture 1961–68; mem. Exec. Council, UNESCO 1962–68, Pres. of Conf., UNESCO 1968–70; Special Adviser, with rank of Minister, to Pres. of United Republic of Cameroon 1971–74, 1978–80; Minister charged with Special Functions at the Presidency 1978; Co-Minister in charge of Missions 1980–84, Minister of Foreign Affairs 1984–87; Sec.-Gen. OAU 1974–78; Special Rep. of UN Sec.-Gen. on Small Arms Proliferation in West Africa, mem. Eminent Persons Group on curbing illicit trafficking in Small Arms and Light Weapons 1999; Nat. Pres. Cameroon Red Cross Soc. 1994–; mem. Ind. Comm. for implementation of proposals in UNDP document Proposals for Africa in this Millennium 1999, Jury du Prix UNESCO Ville pour la Paix; Commdr des Palmes académiques, Grand Officier de l'Ordre de la Valeur and many other decorations. *Publications:* Un certain humanisme 1970, Démocratiser la culture 1974; and many articles on education and African culture. *Leisure interests:* literature, poetry, painting, tennis, football, swimming. *Address:* PO Box 631, Yaoundé (Office); PO Box 1155, Yaoundé, Cameroon (Home). *Telephone:* 2224177 (Office); 2202592 (Home). *Fax:* 2224177 (Office); 2202592 (Home). *E-mail:* crol-Rcam@iccnet_cm (Office).

ETIANG, Hon. Paul Orono, BA; Ugandan diplomatist; b. 15 Aug. 1938, Tororo; s. of Kezironi Orono and Mirabu Adacat Adeke Achon; m. Zahra A. Foum 1967; two s. two d.; ed Busoga Coll. and Makerere Univ. Coll.; District Officer, Provincial Admin. 1962–64; Asst Sec., Ministry of Foreign Affairs 1964–65, Third Sec. 1965–66; Second Sec., Uganda Embassy, Moscow 1966–67; First Sec. Uganda Mission to UN 1967–68; High Commr to UK 1969–71; Chief of Protocol and Marshal of Diplomatic Corps, Uganda 1971–; Perm. Sec. Ministry of Foreign Affairs 1971–73, Acting Minister of Foreign Affairs May–Oct. 1973; Minister of State for Foreign Affairs 1973–74, Minister of State 1974–76, of Transport and Communications 1976–78, of Transport 1978–79, for Regional Co-operation 1988–89, of Commerce 1989–91, of Information 1996, Third Deputy Prime Minister 1996–98, also Minister of Labour and Social Services 1996, Minister of Disaster Preparedness and Refugees 1998; MP 1996–; Asst Sec.-Gen. OAU 1978–87. *Leisure interests:* billiards, badminton, music, theatre. *Address:* c/o P.O. Box 7089, Kampala, Uganda (Office).

ETO, Takami; Japanese politician; b. 1925, Miyazaki Pref.; fmr mem. Miyazaki Prefectural Ass., elected mem. House of Reps for 1st Constituency Miyazaki Prefecture 1969; fmrly Dir House of Reps Rules and Admin. Cttee, Parl. Vice-Minister of Agric., Forestry and Fisheries; Deputy Chair. Liberal Democratic Party Policy Research Council, Chair. Diet Affairs Cttee 1984; Minister of Construction 1985–86, of Transport 1989–90; Dir-Gen. Man. and Co-ordination Agency Aug.–Nov. 1995; now Pres. Shisuikai Policy Group, Sr Advisors Research Comm. on Comprehensive Agric.; Liberal Democratic Party; Grand Cordon Order of the Rising Sun 1998. *Address:* 718 2-1-2, Nagata Cho, Chiyoda-ku, Tokyo 100-8982 (Office); c/o Liberal Democratic Party, 1-11-23, Nagata Cho, Chiyoda-ku, Tokyo 100, Japan. *Telephone:* (3) 3508-7468 (Office). *Fax:* (3) 3591-3063 (Office). *E-mail:* g00741@shugiin.go.jp (Office).

ETOUNGOU, Simon Nko'o; Cameroonian diplomatist and politician; b. 14 Feb. 1932; ed secondary and post-secondary schools and diplomatic training in France; Head of Office in Ministry of Econ. Planning 1956–57; Cabinet Attaché, Ministry of Finance 1958–59; First Sec., Cameroon Embassy, Paris 1960; Minister-Counsellor 1960–61; Amb. to Tunisia 1961–64; led numerous Cameroon dels 1963–64; concurrently Amb. to Algeria July–Nov. 1964, to USSR 1964–65; Minister of Foreign Affairs 1965–66, 1968–70, Minister of Finance 1966–68; Amb. to Belgium, Netherlands and Luxembourg and Perm. Rep. to EEC 1971–79; Amb. to Algeria 1985–88, to France 1988–96; Kt of Nat. Order of Merit (Cameroon) and decorations from Senegal, Tunisia, FRG and Gabon. *Address:* c/o Ministry of Foreign Affairs, Yaoundé, Cameroon.

ETROG, Sorel, CM; Canadian sculptor; b. 29 Aug. 1933, Jassy, Romania; s. of Moshi Etrog and Toni Etrog; ed Jassy High School and Tel Aviv Art Inst.; Brooklyn Museum Art School Scholarship 1958; first one-man show 1958; Canadian rep. Venice Biennale 1966; comms. include Los Angeles Co. Museum 1966, Canadian Pavilion, Expo 67, Olympic Centre, Toronto 1972, Bow Valley Square, Calgary 1975, SunLife Canada, Toronto 1984, Olympic Park, Seoul 1988; works now in numerous public collections including Nat. Gallery of Canada, Tate Gallery, London, Musée d'Art Moderne, Paris, Museum of Modern Art, New York, Stratford Shakespeare Festival Theatre, Stratford, Ont., etc.; designer and illustrator of books; wrote and directed film Spiral (CBC) 1975; mem. Royal Canadian Acad., Arts and Letters Club; Hon. Fellow, Univ. Coll. of Swansea 1990; Chevalier des Arts et des Lettres. *Solo exhibitions include:* Montreal, Toronto, New York, Paris, London, Chicago, Los Angeles, Geneva, Amsterdam, Venice, Milan, Rome. *Publications:* Dream Chamber 1982, Hinges (play) 1983, The Kite 1984, Images from the Film Spiral 1987. *Address:* Box 67034, 2300 Yonge Street, Toronto, Ont., M4P 1E0, Canada. *Telephone:* (416) 480-0109. *Fax:* (416) 480-2914.

ETTL, Harald; Austrian politician; b. 7 Dec. 1947, Gleisdorf, Styria; m.; two c.; ed Higher Fed. Teaching and Experimental Coll. for Textile Industry, Vienna; Asst to Works Man. Eybl carpet factory, Ebergassing; Sec., subsequently Cen. Sec. Textile, Garment and Leather Workers' Trade Union, Chair. 1984–; Minister for Health and the Civil Service 1989–92; fmr Chair. Gen. Accident Insurance Scheme; Pres. Accident Insurance Cttee, Fed. of Austrian Social Insurance Bodies; Chair. Working Group for Integration in Austrian Trade Union Confed. *Address:* Textile, Garment and Leather Workers' Trade Union, Hohenstaufengasse 10, 1010 Vienna I, Austria (Office). *Telephone:* (1) 534-44 (Office). *Fax:* (1) 534-44-498 (Office). *E-mail:* tbl@tbl.oegb.or.at (Office).

ETZWILER, Donnell Dencil, BA, MD; American paediatrician; b. 29 March 1927, Mansfield, Ohio; s. of Donnell S. Etzwiler and Berniece J. Etzwiler; m. Marion Grassby Etzwiler 1952; one s. three d.; m. 2nd Helen B. Etzwiler 1989; ed Indiana and Yale Univs; service in USNR 1945–46; Intern, Yale-Grace New Haven Community Hosp. 1953–54; Resident, New York Hosp., Cornell Medical Center 1954–55, NIH Fellowship in Metabolism 1955–56; Instructor, Cornell Univ. Medical Coll., New York 1956–57; Clinical Prof., Univ. of Minn. School of Medicine 1957–98, Prof. Emer. 1998–; Paediatrician, Park Nicollet Medical Center, Minn. 1957–96; Medical Dir, Camp Needlepoint 1960–85; Paediatrician, Project Hope, Peru 1962; Founder, Pres. Int. Diabetes Center 1967–96, Pres. Emer. 1996–; Vice-Pres. Int. Diabetes Fed. 1979–85; Commr, Nat. Comm. on Diabetes 1975–76; Pres. American Diabetes Asscn 1976–77; Dir Diabetes Collaborating Center, WHO 1985–, Chair. 1988–94; Founder and mem. Bd Compass Project Foundation, Pres. 1998–; mem. Bd, Park Nicollet Medical Foundation 1960–96, Diabetes Research Educational Foundation 1983–93, Inst. Research and Educ. 1996–2000; Co-Dir Int. Diabetes Programme (Russia) 1989–; Fellow, All India Inst. of Diabetes, Bombay 1979, Inst. of Medicine, NAS 1982; Hon. mem. American Dietetic Asscn 1980, American Asscn of Diabetes Educators 1993, Russian Nat. Diabetes Fed. 1995; Banting Medal 1977, Upjohn Award 1983, Beckton Dickinson Camp Award 1979, Diabetes in Youth Award, American Diabetes Asscn 1976, NIH Certificate of Approval 1993, Peace Award (Russia) 1994, Charles H. Best Medal for Distinguished Service (American Diabetes Asscn) 1994, Circle of Leadership Award (American Diabetes Asscn) 1998, Shotwell Award 2000. *Publications:* Education Management of the Patient with Diabetes 1973, Diabetes Manual; Health Education for Living Program 1976, Living Well With Diabetes 1985; Ed. First International Workshop on Diabetes and Camping 1974, How to Live with Diabetes (in Russian) 1991, Staged Diabetes Management 1999, Detection and Treatment of Type 2 Diabetes and Dysmetabolic Syndrome X in Children and Adolescents 2002; over 200 scientific

articles in medical journals. *Leisure interests:* tennis, photography, travel. *Address:* 7611 Bush Lake Drive, Minneapolis, MN 55438, USA. *Telephone:* (952) 942-8489. *Fax:* (952) 944-2537. *E-mail:* dretzwiler@aol.com (Office).

EUBANK, Chris; British middleweight boxer; b. 8 Aug. 1966, Dulwich; m.; four c.; WBC Int. Middleweight Boxing Champion March–Nov. 1990 two defences; WBO Middleweight Boxing Champion Nov. 1990–Aug. 1991 three defences; WBO World Super-Middleweight Boxing Champion Sept. 1991–March 1995 fourteen defences, lost title to Steve Collins, Cork Sept. 1995, failed to regain title against Joe Calzaghe, Sheffield Oct. 1997; unsuccessful fights for WBO Cruiserweight title against Carl Thompson, Manchester April 1998, Sheffield July 1998; Patron Breakthrough; Amb. for the Int. Fund for Animal Welfare; spokesperson for the Nat. Soc. for the Prevention of Cruelty to Children. *Address:* 9 The Upper Drive, Hove, East Sussex, BN3 6GR, England.

EUSTACE, Arnhim; Saint Vincent and the Grenadines politician and economist; b. 1946; economist specializing in fiscal man.; fmr Minister of Finance; Prime Minister of Saint Vincent and the Grenadines 2000–01; Pres. New Democratic Party (NDP) 2000–. *Address:* c/o New Democratic Party, Murray Road, P.O. Box 1300, Kingstown, Saint Vincent and the Grenadines.

EVAN, Gerard, BA, PhD; British scientist; b. 1955, London; s. of Robert Evan and Gwendoline Evan (née Groom); m.; one s. one d.; ed Univ. of Oxford, Univ. of Cambridge, Univ. of California; Fellow Dept of Microbiology and Immunology, Univ. of Calif. at San Francisco (UCSF) 1982–84; Head of Lab. Ludwig Inst. for Cancer Research, Cambridge 1984–88; Head of Lab. Imperial Cancer Research Fund 1988–99; Gerson and Barbara Bass Bakar Distinguished Prof. of Cancer Biology, UCSF 1999–; mem. Scientific Advisory Bd EISAI London Research Labs 1994–, Oxagen Inc. 1997–, ESBA Tech 1998–; Consultant Cantab Pharmaceuticals Ltd 1994–99, Ontogeny Inc., Boston 1998–, Cambridge Antibody Tech. Inc. 1998–, Amersham/Nycomed 1998–; mem. Scientific Review Bd DNAX 1998–; Fellow Acad. of Medical Sciences 1999; Research Fellowship Downing Coll. Cambridge 1984; Pfizer Prize in Biology 1995, Napier Research Prof. of Cancer Biology of Royal Soc. 1996, Joseph Steiner Prize of Swiss Oncological Soc. 1997. *Radio includes:* participation in numerous science programmes for BBC. *Publications:* numerous academic publs. *Leisure interests:* sailing, music, white water rafting, hiking, skiing. *Address:* UCSF Cancer Center and Cancer Research Institute, University of California at San Francisco, 2340 Sutter Street, San Francisco, CA 94143 (Office); 728 Marin Drive, Mill Valley, CA 94941, USA (Home). *Telephone:* (415) 514 1570 (Office); (415) 514 0878. *E-mail:* gevan@cc.ucsf.edu (Office).

EVANGELISTA, Linda; Canadian fashion model; b. St Catherine, Toronto; m. Gerald Marie (divorced 1993); face of Yardley Cosmetics; numerous catwalk fashion shows. *Address:* c/o Elite Model Management, 40 Parker Street, London, WC2B 5PH, England; Elite Model Management Corporation, 111 E 22nd Street, Floor 2, New York, NY 10010, USA. *Telephone:* (20) 7333-0888 (London).

EVANGELOU, Alecos C.; Cypriot politician and lawyer; b. 23 July 1939, Kato Lakatamia; s. of Costas Evangelou and Theano A. Tsiappa; m. Nicoulla Protopapa 1965; one s. two d.; ed English School, Nicosia and Gray's Inn, London; called to the Bar, Gray's Inn, London 1967; worked in Nicosia Dist Admin., later at Ministry of Finance 1957–72; law officer, Attorney, Office of Attorney-Gen. 1972–93; fmr Chair. Appropriate Authority for Intellectual Property; fmr Pres. Supreme Sports Tribunal; Minister of Justice and Public Order 1993–97; now Sr Partner Alecos Evangelou and Co. (law firm); del. to several UN, European and Commonwealth confs; Chair. two Commonwealth Ministerial Confs; Chair. Cyprus Radio-TV Authority 1998–; Deputy Gov. American Biographical Inst., Inc. *Leisure interest:* gardening. *Address:* PO Box 29238, Nicosia 1623 (Office); 36 Makariou III Ave., Kaimakli, Nicosia 1021, Cyprus (Home). *Telephone:* (22) 879999 (Office); (22) 466130 (Home). *Fax:* (22) 879990 (Office).

EVANS, Sir (Christopher) Paul, Kt, PhD; British scientist and civil servant; b. 25 Dec. 1948, Newport; s. of Colwyn Evans and Margery Evans; m. Margaret Beckett 1971; two d.; ed St Julian's High School, Newport, Trinity Coll., Cambridge; with Dept of the Environment, subsequently of the Environment, Transport and the Regions, then Dept for Transport, Local Govt and the Regions, now Office of the Deputy Prime Minister 1975–; Private Sec. to Perm. Sec. 1978–80, Prin. 1980, Asst Sec. 1985, Under-Sec. 1993; Dir Urban Policy Unit 1997–2001; Strategic Dir of Regeneration, London Borough of Southwark 2001–. *Address:* Regeneration Department, Council Offices, Chiltern House, Portland Street, London, SE17 2ES, England (Office). *Telephone:* (20) 7525-5501 (Office). *E-mail:* paul.evans@southwark.gov.uk (Office).

EVANS, Daniel Jackson, MS; American politician; b. 16 Oct. 1925, Seattle, Wash.; s. of Daniel Lester and Irma Evans (née Ide); m. Nancy Ann Bell 1959; three s.; ed Roosevelt High School, Seattle and Univ. of Washington; USNR 1943–46; Lt on active duty Korean War 1951–53; Asst Man. Mountain Pacific Chapter, Assoc. Gen. Contractors 1953–59; State Rep. King County 1956–64; Partner, Gray and Evans, structural and civil engineers 1959–64; Gov. Washington State 1965–77; Chair. Western Govs Conf. 1968–69, Nat. Govs Conf. 1973–74; Senator from Washington 1983–89; now involved with environmental work; mem. Advisory Comm. on Intergovernmental Relations 1972, Trilateral Comm. 1973; Keynote Speaker Republican Nat. Convention 1968; mem. Pres.'s Vietnamese Refugee Comm. 1974; mem. Nat. Center for

Productivity and Quality of Working Life 1975–76; mem. Carnegie Council on Policy Studies in Higher Educ. 1977; Trustee Urban Inst. 1977, The Carnegie Foundation for the Advancement of Teaching 1977; Pres. Evergreen State Coll. 1977–83; Consultant Daniel J. Evans & Assocs., Seattle; Dir Puget Sound Power and Light, Tera Computer Co., Burlington Northern/Santa Fe, Inc., Flow Int., WA Mutual Bank; Regent Univ. of Wash. 1993–; Republican; several hon. degrees; Nat. Municipal League Distinguished Citizen Award 1977. *Leisure interests:* skiing, sailing, mountain climbing. *Address:* Daniel J. Evans & Assocs., 1111 3rd Avenue, Suite 3400, Seattle, WA 98101, USA.

EVANS, David (see The Edge).

EVANS, Donald L., BEng, MBA; American politician and oil executive; b. 27 July 1946, Houston; m. Susie Marinis; three c.; ed Univ. of Texas at Austin; joined Tom Brown Inc. 1975, Pres. 1979, later Chair. and CEO; Advisor George W. Bush's political campaigns 1978–, Nat. Finance Chair. 1999, Chair. Bush–Cheney campaign 2000; Sec. of Commerce 2001–; mem. Univ. of Texas System Bd of Regents 1995–2001, Chair. 1997–2001; Chair. United Way of Midland 1981, Pres. 1989; Chair. Beefeaters Ball, Midland Cerebral Palsy Center; mem. YMCA of Midland Metropolitan Bd 1988–94, Bd of Govs, Bynum School, Bd The Gladney Fund, Midland Chamber of Commerce, Exec. Cttee Young Life, Bd Scleroma Research Foundation, Young Presidents Org., Omicron Delta Kappa Soc., Texas Cowboys; Trustee Memorial Hosp. and Medical Center; driving force behind Native Vision programme for 10,000 Native American children; Hon. DHumLitt (Univ. of S Carolina) 2001; Midland Jaycees Distinguished Service Award and Boss of the Year 1980, Univ. of Texas at Austin Distinguished Alumnis Awards (School of Eng) 1997, 2002, (McCombs School of Business) 2002, Nat. Foreign Trade Council World Trade Award 2002. *Leisure interest:* golf. *Address:* Department of Commerce, Room 5852, 14th Street and Constitution Avenue, NW, Washington, DC 20230 (Office); 900 Whann Avenue, McLean, VA 22101, USA (Home). *Telephone:* (202) 482-2112 (Office). *Fax:* (202) 487-7420 (Office). *E-mail:* bvosburgh@doc.gov (Office). *Website:* www.doc.gov (Office).

EVANS, Gareth John, AO, QC, LLB, MA; Australian politician; b. 5 Sept. 1944, Melbourne; s. of the late Allan O. Evans and of Phyllis Evans (née Le Boeuf); m. Merran Anderson 1969; one s. one d.; ed Univ. of Melbourne, Magdalen Coll., Oxford; Lecturer and Sr Lecturer in Law, Univ. of Melbourne 1971–76; mem. Australian Reform Comm. 1975; Barrister-at-Law 1977–; Senator for Victoria 1978–96; 'Shadow' Attorney-Gen. 1980–83; Attorney-Gen. 1983–84; Minister for Resources and Energy, Minister Assisting the Prime Minister and Minister Assisting the Minister for Foreign Affairs 1984–87; Minister for Transport and Communications 1987–88, for Foreign Affairs 1988–96; Deputy Leader of Govt in the Senate 1987–93, Leader 1993–96; MP for Holt, Vic. 1996–99; Deputy Leader of Opposition, 'Shadow' Treas. 1996–98; Pres. and Chief Exec. Int. Crisis Group 2000–; Co-Chair. Int. Comm. on Intervention and State Sovereignty 2000–; Australian Humanist of the Year 1990, ANZAC Peace Prize 1994, Grawemeyen Award for Ideas Improving World Order 1995. *Publications:* Labor and the Constitution 1972–75 (Ed.) 1977, Law, Politics and the Labor Movement (Ed.) 1980, Labor Essays 1980, 1981, 1982 (co-ed.), Australia's Constitution – Time for Change? 1983 (co-author), Australia's Foreign Relations 1991 (co-author), Co-operating for Peace 1993. *Leisure interests:* reading, golf, football, travel, opera. *Address:* International Crisis Group, 149 avenue Louise, 1050 Brussels, Belgium (Office). *Telephone:* (2) 502-90-38 (Office). *Fax:* (2) 502-50-38 (Office). *E-mail:* gevans@crisisweb.org (Office); garethmp@aol.com (Home). *Website:* www.crisisweb.org (Office).

EVANS, Gwynfor, MA, LLD; Welsh politician; b. 1 Sept. 1912, Barry; s. of Dan and Catherine (née Richard) Evans; m. Rhiannon Prys Thomas 1941; four s. three d.; ed Barry County School, Univ. Coll. of Wales, Aberystwyth, St John's Coll., Oxford; qualified as solicitor 1939; Hon. Sec. Heddychwyr Cymru (Welsh Pacifist Movement) 1939–45; Chair. Union of Welsh Independents 1954; MP (Plaid Cymru), Carmarthen 1966–70, 1974–79; Pres. Plaid Cymru (Welsh Nationalist Party) 1945–81, Hon. Pres. 1982–; mem. Carmarthen Co. Council 1949–74; past mem. Welsh Broadcasting Council; Fellow, Univ. Coll. Aberystwyth, Trinity Coll. Carmarthen; Hon. LLD (Univ. of Wales) 1973; Cymmrodoriom Medal 1986. *Publications:* Plaid Cymru and Wales 1950, Rhagom i Ryddid 1964, Aros Mae 1971, Wales Can Win 1973, Land of My Fathers 1974, A National Future for Wales 1975, Diwedd Prydeindod, Bywyd Cymro 1982, Seiri Cenedl 1986, Welsh Nation Builders 1988, Pe Bai Cymru'n Rhydd 1989, Fighting for Wales 1991, Heddychiaeth Gristnogol Yng Nghymru 1991, For the Sake of Wales 1996, The History of Wales 2000, Gwlad o Hud 2000, The Fight for Freedom 2000. *Address:* Talar Wen, Pencarreg, Llanybydder, Camarthenshire, Wales. *Telephone:* (1570) 480907.

EVANS, Harold Matthew, MA; American (b. British) publisher, fmr newspaper editor and writer; b. 28 June 1928, Manchester, England; s. of the late Frederick and Mary Evans; m. 1st Enid Parker 1953 (divorced 1978); one s. two d.; m. 2nd Tina Brown 1982; one s. one d.; ed Durham Univ.; Commonwealth Fund Fellow, Univ. of Chicago 1956–57; Ed. Sunday Times, London 1967–81, The Times 1981–82; mem. Bd Times Newspapers Ltd, Dir 1978–82; Int. Press Inst. 1974–80; Dir Goldcrest Films and Television 1982–85; Ed.-in-Chief Atlantic Monthly 1984–86, Contributing Ed. 1986–, Editorial Dir and Vice-Chair. 1998–; Ed. Dir U.S. News and World Report 1984–86, Contributing Ed. 1986–, Editorial Dir and Vice-Chair. 1998–; Vice-Pres. and Sr Ed. Weidenfeld and Nicolson 1986–87; Adviser to Chair. Condé Nast Publications 1986–; Founding Ed.-in-Chief, Condé Nast Traveler 1986–90; Pres. and Publr Random House Adult Trade Group 1990–97; Editorial Dir Mortimer Zuckerman's media properties 1997–; Editorial Dir and Vice-Chair. New York Daily News Inc. 1998–99, Fast Co. 1998–; author Little, Brown and Co., NY 2000–; Fellow, Soc. Industrial Artists, Inst. of Journalists; Hon. Visiting Prof. of Journalism City Univ. 1978–; Hon. DCL (Durham) 1998; Dr hc (Stirling); Journalist of the Year Prize 1973; Int. Ed. of the Year Award 1975, Inst. of Journalists Gold Medal Award 1979; Design and Art Dir, Pres.'s Award 1981, Ed. of Year Award, Granada 1982, Hood Medal, Royal Photographic Soc. 1981, Press Photographers of GB Award 1986; Gold Award for Achievement, British Press Awards 2000, World Press Freedom Hero, Int. Press Inst. 2000. *Publications:* Active Newsroom 1964, Editing and Design, Newsman's English 1970, Newspaper Design 1971, Newspaper Headlines 1973, Newspaper Text 1973, We Learned to Ski (co-author) 1974, Freedom of the Press 1974, Pictures on a Page 1978, Suffer the Children (co-author), How We Learned to Ski 1983, Good Times, Bad Times 1983, Front Page History 1984, The American Century 1998. *Leisure interests:* music, table tennis, skiing. *Address:* Little, Brown and Co., 1271 Avenue of the Americas, New York, NY 10020, USA (Office). *E-mail:* hevans@usnews.com (Office).

EVANS, John David Gemmill, PhD, MRIA; British professor of philosophy; b. 27 Aug. 1942, London; s. of John Desmond Evans and Babette Evans; m. Rosemary Ellis 1974; ed St Edward's School, Oxford, Queen's Coll., Cambridge; Research Fellow, Sidney Sussex Coll., Cambridge 1964–65, Fellow and Lecturer 1965–78; Visiting Prof., Duke Univ., NC 1972–73; Dean of Arts Faculty, Queen's Univ., Belfast 1986–89, Prof. of Logic and Metaphysics 1978–, Dir of School of Philosophical and Anthropological Studies 1987–95; Bd mem. Arts Council of NI 1991–94; Council mem. Royal Inst. of Philosophy 1991–98; Chair. UK Nat. Cttee for Philosophy 1994–; mem. Exec. Cttee Int. Fed. of Philosophical Socs (FISP) 1988–, Aristotelian Soc. 1998–2001, Bureau Centrale, Asscn Int. des Professeurs de Philosophie 2000–. *Publications:* Aristotle's Concept of Dialectic 1977, Aristotle 1987, Moral Philosophy and Contemporary Problems 1987, Teaching Philosophy on the Eve of the Twenty-First Century 1997. *Leisure interests:* mountaineering, astronomy, travel, gardening. *Address:* 57 Ballynagarrick Road, Carryduff, Belfast BT8 8JD, Northern Ireland.

EVANS, Leo Henry 'Rusty', BA, B.ADMIN.; South African diplomatist; b. 12 Dec. 1943, Durban; s. of John Evans and Dorothy Redstone; m. 1st Kathleen Barbour 1967 (divorced 1989); three s. one d.; m. 2nd Gerda van Tonder 1989; one d.; ed Christian Brothers' Coll. Kimberley and Univs of Natal and S Africa; entered Dept of Foreign Affairs 1966; Third Sec. Lisbon 1967–70; Consul, Rio de Janeiro 1972; Consul-Gen. São Paulo 1976–78; Minister, Washington, DC 1980, London 1982; Dir Ministry of Foreign Affairs 1986, Chief Dir 1988, Deputy Dir-Gen. Africa 1989, Deputy Dir-Gen. Overseas Countries 1991; Dir-Gen. Dept of Foreign Affairs 1992–97; Dir Int. Govt Relations and Public Affairs Consultancy, Karoo Oranje Landbou Kooperasie 1998–; Order of Dom Infante Henriques (Portugal). *Leisure interests:* yachting, hunting. *Address:* P.O. Box 1846, Groenloof 0027, South Africa (Office). *E-mail:* gevans@fort.co.za (Home).

EVANS, Lloyd Thomas, AO, MAgrSci, DPhil, DSc, FRS; Australian botanist and agriculturist; b. 6 Aug. 1927, Wanganui, New Zealand; s. of Claude Evans and Gwendolyn Fraser; m. Margaret Newell 1954; two s. two d. (one deceased); ed Wanganui Collegiate School, Univ. of Canterbury, New Zealand and Brasenose Coll., Oxford; Rhodes Scholar 1951–54; Commonwealth Fund Fellow, Calif. Inst. of Tech. 1954–56; Research Scientist, Div. of Plant Industry, Commonwealth Scientific and Industrial Research Org. (CSIRO) 1956–, Chief 1971–78, now Hon. Research Scientist; NAS Pioneer Research Fellow, US Dept of Agric., Beltsville, USA 1963–64; Overseas Fellow, Churchill Coll., Cambridge 1969–70; Visiting Fellow, Wolfson Coll., Cambridge 1978; Pres. Australian Soc. of Plant Physiologists 1971–73, Australian and New Zealand Asscn for the Advancement of Science 1976–77, Australian Acad. of Science 1978–82 (Fellow); mem. Bd of Trustees, Int. Foundation for Science, Stockholm 1982–87, Int. Rice Research Inst., Philippines 1984–89, Int. Centre for Improvement of Wheat and Maize 1990–95; mem. Norwegian Acad. of Science and Letters; Foreign Fellow Indian Nat. Acad. of Agricultural Science; Hon. mem. Royal Soc., NZ, Royal Agric. Soc., England; Hon. LLD (Canterbury) 1978; Bledisloe Medal 1974, Farrer Medal 1979, other awards and prizes. *Publications:* Environmental Control of Plant Growth 1963, The Induction of Flowering 1969, Crop Physiology 1975, Day-length and the Flowering of Plants 1975, Wheat Science – Today and Tomorrow 1981, Policy and Practice: Essays in Honour of Sir John Crawford 1987, Crop Evolution, Adaptation and Yield 1993, Feeding the Ten Billion: Plants and Population Growth 1998; over 200 research papers. *Leisure interests:* chopping wood, Charles Darwin, tennis. *Address:* 3 Elliott Street, Campbell, Canberra, ACT 2612, Australia. *Telephone:* (62) 477815. *E-mail:* Lloyd.Evans@csiro.au.

EVANS, Martin John, PhD, ScD, FRS, FMedSci; British professor of mammalian genetics; b. 1 Jan. 1941, Stroud, Glos.; s. of Leonard Wilfred Evans and Hilary Joyce Evans (née Redman); m. Judith Clare Williams 1966; two s. one d.; ed St Dunstan's Coll. Catford and Christ's Coll. Cambridge; Research Asst Dept of Anatomy and Embryology, Univ. Coll. London 1963–66, Asst Lecturer 1966–69, Lecturer 1969–78; Univ. Lecturer, Dept of Genetics, Univ. of Cambridge 1978–91, Reader in Mammalian Genetics 1991, Prof. of Mammalian Genetics 1994–99; Dir, School of Biosciences and Prof. of Mammalian Genetics, Univ. of Cardiff 1999–; Hon. Fellow, St Edmund's Coll. Cambridge 2002; Albert Lasker Award for Basic Medical Research 2001. *Publications:* 75 scientific publs. *Leisure interests:* family, walking, Norfolk terriers. *Address:* Cardiff School of Biosciences, Biomedical Sciences Building, Cardiff University, Museum Avenue, PO Box 911, Cardiff, CF10 3US, Wales (Office). *Telephone:* (29) 2087-4120 (Office). *Fax:* (29) 2087-4116. *E-mail:* EvansMJ@ cardiff.ac.uk. *Website:* www.cf.ac.uk/biosi.

EVANS, Nicholas; British writer; b. Bromsgrove, Worcs.; pnr Charlotte Gordon Cumming; three s. one d.; ed Oxford Univ.; fmr journalist Evening Chronicle, Newcastle-upon-Tyne, producer documentaries for London Weekend TV, writer and producer films for TV and cinema. *Film:* Just Like a Woman 1991. *Television:* producer arts documentaries on David Hockney, Francis Bacon, Patricia Highsmith, David Lean, etc. *Publications:* The Horse Whisperer 1995 (film 1998), The Loop 1998, The Smoke Jumper 2001. *Leisure interests:* tennis, skiing, books, cinema. *Address:* c/o A. P. Watt, 20 John Street, London, WC1N 2DR, England (Office).

EVANS, Sir Richard (Harry), Kt, CBE; British aerospace industry executive; b. 1942, Blackpool; m.; three d.; ed Royal Masonic School, Herts.; joined Ministry of Transport and Civil Aviation 1960, moving to Ministry of Tech. –1967; Govt Contracts Officer Ferranti, Manchester 1967–69; Contracts Officer Mil. Aircraft Div., British Aircraft Corpn (BAC, later British Aerospace, BAe) 1969–78, Commercial Dir 1978–79, Dir Sepecat 1979, Dir-in-Charge, BAe India 1979–81, Asst Man. Dir BAe Warton Div. 1981–83, Deputy Man. Dir 1983–86, Deputy Man. Dir British Aerospace Mil. Aircraft Div. 1986–87, Marketing Dir British Aerospace PLC 1987–88, Chair. British Aerospace Defence Cos. 1988–90, CEO 1990–98, Chair. BAE Systems (British Aerospace PLC renamed following merger with Marconi Electric Systems) 1998–; Dir Panavia Aircraft GmbH 1981–; mem. Supervisory Bd Airbus Industrie 1992–; Dir (non-exec.) United Utilities PLC 1997–, Chair. 2000–; Dir NatWest PLC 1998–2000; Pres. Soc. of British Aerospace Cos. (SBAC) 1992; Hon. mem. NSPCC Council. *Leisure interests:* golf, classic cars. *Address:* BAE Systems PLC, 6 Carlton Gardens, London, SW1Y 5AD, England (Office). *Telephone:* (1252) 373232 (Office). *Fax:* (1252) 383121. *Website:* www .baesystems.com (Office).

EVANS, Richard John, MA, DPhil, LittD, FBA, FRSL; British historian; b. 29 Sept. 1947, Woodford, Essex; s. of the late Ieuan Trefor Evans and of Evelyn Evans (née Jones); m. Elín Hjaltadóttir 1976 (divorced 1993); partner Christine L. Corton; two s.; ed Forest School, London, Jesus Coll., Oxford, St Antony's Coll., Oxford; Lecturer in History, Stirling Univ. 1972–76; Lecturer in European History, Univ. of E Anglia 1976–83, Prof. 1983–89; Prof. of History, Birkbeck Coll., Univ. of London 1989–98; Vice-Master Birkbeck Coll. Univ. of London 1993–98, Acting Master 1997; Prof. of Modern History, Cambridge Univ. 1998–; Fellow Gonville and Caius Coll., Cambridge 1998; Visiting Assoc. Prof. of European History, Col Univ., New York 1980; Fellow Royal Historical Soc., Alexander von Humboldt Foundation, Free Univ. of Berlin 1981; Fellow Humanities Research Centre, ANU, Canberra, Australia 1986; Hon. Fellow Jesus Coll., Oxford 1998; Stanhope Historical Essay Prize 1969, Wolfson Literary Award for History 1987, William H. Welch Medal, American Asscn for the History of Medicine 1988, Hamburg Civic Medal for Arts and Sciences 1993, Fraenkel Prize in Contemporary History 1994. *Publications:* The Feminist Movement in Germany 1894–1933 1976, The Feminists 1977, Society and Politics in Wilhelmine Germany (ed.) 1978, Death in Hamburg 1987, Comrades and Sisters 1987, Rethinking German History 1987, In Hitler's Shadow 1989, Kneipengespräche im Kaiserreich 1989, Proletarians and Politics 1990, Rituals of Retribution 1996, Rereading German History 1997, In Defence of History 1997, Tales from the German Underworld 1998, Lying about Hitler 2001. *Leisure interests:* gardening, music (playing the piano), reading, travelling. *Address:* Gonville and Caius College, Cambridge, CB2 1TA, England.

EVANS, Sir Richard Mark, KCMG, KCVO, MA; British diplomatist (retd); b. 15 April 1928, British Honduras (now Belize); s. of the late Edward Walter Evans and Anna Margaret Kirkpatrick Evans; m. 1st Margaret Elizabeth Sessinger 1960 (divorced 1970); m. 2nd Rosemary Grania Glen Birkett 1973; two s.; ed Dragon School, Oxford, Repton School and Magdalen Coll., Oxford; Third Sec., Peking 1955–57, Second Sec., London 1958–62, First Sec., Peking 1962–64, First Sec. (Commercial), Berne 1964–68, First Sec., London 1968–70, Head of Nr. Eastern Dept, FCO 1970–72 and Far Eastern Dept 1972–74, Counsellor (Commercial), Stockholm 1975–77, Minister (Econ.), Paris 1977–79, Asst, then Deputy Under-Sec., FCO 1979–83, Amb. to People's Repub. of China 1984–88; Dir New Asian Land Fund 2000–; Fellow Emer., Wolfson Coll., Oxford 1995–. *Publication:* Deng Xiaoping and the Making of Modern China 1993. *Leisure interests:* music, reading, travel. *Address:* Sevenhampton House, Sevenhampton, Highworth, Wilts., SN6 7QA, England.

EVANS, Robert; American actor and film producer; b. 29 June 1930, Harlem, New York; s. of Josh Evans; m. 1st Ali McGraw (divorced); one s.; m. 2nd Phyllis George 1978 (divorced); child radio actor in more than 300 radio productions; partner women's clothing firm Evan-Picone 1952–67; ind. producer at 20th Century-Fox 1966–76; Vice-Pres. (Production) Paramount Pictures Corpn 1966–69, Vice-Pres. (Worldwide Production) 1969–71, Exec. Vice-Pres. 1971–76; resgnd to be ind. producer. *Films include:* (actor) The Man of 1000 Faces 1957, The Sun Also Rises 1957, The Fiend Who Walked the West 1958, The Best of Everything 1959, (producer) Chinatown 1974, Marathon Man 1976, Black Sunday 1977, Players 1979, Popeye 1980, Urban Cowboy 1980, Cotton Club 1984, The Two Jakes 1989, Sliver 1993, Jade, The

Phantom, The Saint, The Out of Towners, The Kid Stays in the Picture 2003. *Publication:* The Kid Stays in the Picture 1994. *Address:* 242 North Beverly Drive, Beverly Hills, CA 90210, USA.

EVANS, Robert John Weston, PhD, FBA; British historian; b. 7 Oct. 1943, Leicester; s. of T. F. Evans and M. Evans; m. Kati Robert 1969; one s. one d.; ed Dean Close School, Cheltenham and Jesus Coll., Cambridge; Research Fellow, Brasenose Coll. Oxford 1968–97; Univ. Lecturer in Modern History of East-Central Europe, Oxford 1969–90, Reader 1990–92, Prof. of European History 1992–97, Regius Prof. of Modern History 1997–; ed. English Historical Review 1985–95; Fellow Austrian Acad. of Sciences 1997; Hon. Fellow Hungarian Acad. of Sciences 1995; Wolfson Literary Award for History 1980, Anton Gindely-Preis (Austria) 1986, František Palacký Medal (Czechoslovakia) 1991. *Publications:* Rudolf II and His World 1973; The Making of the Habsburg Monarchy 1979, The Revolutions in Europe 1848–9 (Ed.) 2000. *Address:* Oriel College, Oxford, OX1 4EW (Office); Rowan Cottage, 45 Sunningwell, Abingdon, Oxon., OX13 6RD, England (Home). *Telephone:* (1865) 277265 (Coll.).

EVANS, Stephen Nicholas, OBE, BA; British diplomatist; b. 29 June 1950; s. of Vincent Morris Evans and Doris Mary Evans (née Braham); m. Sharon Ann Holdcroft 1975; one s. two d.; ed King's Coll., Taunton, Bristol Univ.; Lt in Royal Tank Regt 1971–74; joined FCO 1974, language student (Vietnamese), SOAS, London 1975, FCO 1976, First Sec., Hanoi 1978–80, FCO 1980–82, language training (Thai), Bangkok 1982–83, First Sec., Bangkok 1983–86, FCO 1986–90, First Sec. (Political), Ankara 1990, Counsellor (Econ., Commercial, Aid), Islamabad 1993–96, seconded to UN Special Mission to Afghanistan 1996–97, Counsellor and Head of OSCE and Council of Europe Dept, FCO 1997–98, Counsellor and Head of South Asian Dept 1998–. *Leisure interests:* cycling, golf, history. *Address:* c/o Foreign and Commonwealth Office, King Charles Street, London, SW1A 2AH, England (Office). *Telephone:* (20) 7270-3000 (Office).

EVANS, Sir (William) Vincent (John), GCMG, MBE, QC, BCL, MA; British barrister-at-law; b. 20 Oct. 1915, London; s. of the late Charles Evans and Elizabeth Jenkins; m. Joan Symons 1947; one s. two d.; ed Merchant Taylors' School, Northwood and Wadham Coll. Oxford; Called to the Bar, Lincoln's Inn 1939; mil. service 1939–46, legal adviser, British Mil. Admin. Cyrenaica, rank of Lt-Col 1945–46; Asst Legal Adviser, Foreign Office 1947–54; Legal Counsellor, Perm. Mission of UK at UN, New York 1954–59; Deputy Legal Adviser, Foreign Office 1960–68; Legal Adviser, FCO 1968–75; UK Rep. on European Cttee on Legal Cooperation, Council of Europe 1965–75, Chair. 1969–71; UK Rep. on Council of Europe Steering Cttee on Human Rights 1976–80, Chair. 1979–80; mem. Human Rights Cttee (Int. Covenant on Civil and Political Rights) 1977–84; Judge, European Court of Human Rights 1980–91; mem. Perm. Court of Arbitration 1987–97; Dir (Chair.) Bryant Symons & Co. Ltd 1964–85; mem. Council of Man., British Inst. of Int. and Comparative Law; Vice-Pres. Bd of Govs British Inst. of Human Rights; Vice-Pres. Hon. Soc. of Cymmrodorion; Hon. Fellow, Wadham Coll. Oxford; Hon. Bencher, Lincoln's Inn; Dr hc (Essex) 1986. *Address:* 4 Bedford Road, Moor Park, Northwood, Middx, HA6 2BB, England. *Telephone:* (1923) 824085.

EVANS OF PARKSIDE, Baron (Life Peer), cr. 1997, of St Helens in the County of Merseyside; **John Evans;** British politician and engineer; b. 19 Oct. 1930; s. of the late James Evans and Margaret Evans (née Robson); m. Joan Slater 1959; two s. one d.; ed Jarrow Cen. School; apprentice marine fitter 1946–49, 1950–52; nat. service, Royal Engineers 1949–50; engineer, Merchant Navy 1952–55; joined Amalgamated Union of Eng Workers (later Amalgamated Eng Union) 1952; joined Labour Party 1955; worked as fitter in ship-building, steel and eng industries 1955–65, 1968–74; mem. Hebburn Union Dist Council 1962, Leader 1969, Chair. 1972; Sec./Agent Jarrow Co-operative Labour Party 1965–68; Labour MP for Newton 1974–83, for St Helens, North 1983–97; Asst Govt Whip 1978–79; Opposition Whip 1979–80; Parl. Pvt. Sec. to Leader of Labour Party 1980–83; Opposition Spokesman on Employment 1983–87; MEP 1975–78; Chair. Regional Policy, Planning and Transport Cttee 1976–78; mem. Labour Party Nat. Exec. Cttee 1982–96. *Leisure interests:* watching football, reading, gardening. *Address:* House of Lords, Westminster, London, SW1 0PW (Office); 6 Kirkby Road, Culcheth, Warrington, Cheshire, WA3 4BS, England (Home). *Telephone:* (20) 7219-6541 (Office).

EVANS OF TEMPLE GUITING, Baron (Life Peer), cr. 2000, of Temple Guiting in the County of Gloucestershire; **Matthew Evans,** CBE, BSc Econs, FRSA; British publishing executive; b. 7 Aug. 1941; s. of the late George Ewart Evans and Florence Ellen Evans; m. 1st Elizabeth Amanda Mead 1966 (divorced 1991); two s.; m. 2nd Caroline Michel 1991; two s. one d.; ed Friends' School, Saffron Walden and LSE; bookselling 1963–64; with Faber & Faber 1964–, Man. Dir 1972–93, Chair. 1981–; Chair. Nat. Book League 1982–84, English Stage Co. 1984–90; mem. Council, Publishers' Asscn 1978–84; Gov. BFI 1982–97; Vice-Chair. 1996–97; Chair. Library and Information Comm. 1995–99; Chair. Museums, Libraries and Archives Council 2000–02; Dir Which? Ltd 1997–; mem. Arts Council Nat. Lottery Advisory Panel 1997–99, Univ. for Industry Advisory Group 1997, Royal Opera House Working Group 1997, Arts and Humanities Research Bd 1998–; mem. Franco-British Soc. 1981–; founder mem. Groucho Club (Dir 1982–97); Hon. FRCA 1999; Hon. FLA 1999. *Leisure interest:* cricket. *Address:* Faber & Faber, 3 Queen Square, London, WC1N 3AU, England. *Telephone:* (20) 7465-0045. *Fax:* (20) 7465-0034.

EVATT, Elizabeth Andreas, AC, LLM; Australian lawyer; b. 11 Nov. 1933, Sydney; d. of Clive R. Evatt and Marjorie M. Evatt (née Andreas); m. Robert Southan 1960; one d.; ed Univ. of Sydney and Harvard Univ.; called to Bar, Inner Temple; Chief Judge Family Court of Australia 1976–88; Deputy Pres. Conciliation and Arbitration Comm. 1973–89, Australian Industrial Relations Comm. 1989–94; Pres. Australian Law Reform Comm. 1988–93, mem. 1993–94; mem. UN Cttee on Elimination of Discrimination Against Women 1984–92, Chair. 1989–91; Chancellor, Univ. of Newcastle 1988–94; reviewed Aboriginal and Torres Strait Islander Heritage Protection Act 1984; Hearing Commr (part-time), Human Rights and Equal Opportunity Comm.1995–98; mem. UN Human Rights Cttee 1993–2001, World Bank Admin. Tribunal 1998–; Australian Human Rights Medal 1995. *Address:* Unit 2003, 184 Forbes Street, Darlinghurst, NSW 2010, Australia. *Fax:* (2) 9331-6734 (Home). *E-mail:* eevatt@bigpond.net.au (Office); eevatt@post.harvard.edu (Office).

EVE, Trevor John; British actor; b. 1 July 1951; s. of Stewart Frederick Eve and Elsie Eve (née Hamer); m. Sharon Patricia Maughan 1980; two s. one d.; ed Bromsgrove School, Kingston Art Coll., Royal Acad.of Dramatic Art; Patron Childhope International. *Theatre includes:* Children of a Lesser God (Olivier Award for Best Actor 1982) 1981, The Genius 1983, High Society 1986, Man Beast and Virtue 1989, The Winter's Tale 1991, Inadmissible Evidence 1993, Uncle Vanya (Olivier Award for Best Supporting Actor 1997) 1996. *Television includes:* Shoestring 1980, Jamaica Inn, A Sense of Guilt 1990, Parnell and the Englishwoman 1991, A Doll's House 1991, The Politician's Wife 1995, Black Easter 1995, Under the Sun 1997, Evilstreak 1999, David Copperfield 1999, Waking The Dead 2000, 2001, 2002. *Films include:* Hindle Wakes, Dracula, A Wreath of Roses, The Corsican Brothers, Aspen Extreme, Psychotherapy, The Knight's Tale, The Tribe, Appetite, Possession; (producer for Projector Productions): Alice Through the Looking Glass 1998, Cinderella, Twelfth Night 2002. *Leisure interests:* golf, tennis. *Address:* c/o ICM Ltd, Oxford House, 76 Oxford Street, London, W1N 0AX, England. *Telephone:* (20) 7434-1110 (Office); (20) 7636-6565. *Fax:* (20) 7323-0101.

EVENO, Bertrand; French publishing executive; b. 26 July 1944, Egletons; s. of Jean-Jacques Eveno and Suzanne Gavoille; m. 2nd Brigitte Pery 1984; five d. (three d. from previous m.); ed Lycée Condorcet and Law Faculty, Paris; Treasury Inspector 1973–77; Tech. Consultant to Health Minister 1977–78; Cabinet Dir for Minister of Culture and Communication 1978–81; mem. Atomic Energy Comm. Control Bd 1981–83; Deputy Gen. Man. André Shoe Co. 1984–86; Chair. Editions Fernand Nathan 1987–2000; Pres. Conseil d'admin., Fondation nationale de la photographie 1981–95; Gens d'Image 1986–2000; Chair. Larousse-Nathan Int. 1988–90, Le Robert dictionaries 1989–2000, Editions Masson 1995–98; Dir-Gen. Groupe de la Cité 1988–2000, Presses de la Cité 1991–95; Pres., Dir-Gen. Larousse-Bordas 1996–2000; Pres., Dir-Gen. Havas Educ. et Référence 1999–; Dir Anaya Groupe 1999–2000; Pres. Agence France Presse 2000–; Zellidja Scholarship 1961. *Publication:* monograph on Willy Ronis in Les grands photographes 1983. *Address:* Agence France Presse, 11–25 place de la Bourse, BP 20, 75061 Paris Cédex 02 (Office); 80 rue de Rennes, 75006 Paris, France (Home). *Telephone:* 1-40-41-46-46. *Fax:* 1-40-41-46-32. *Website:* www.afp.com (Office).

EVENSEN, Jens, LLD; Norwegian diplomatist, lawyer and politician; b. 5 Nov. 1917, Oslo; s. of Jens Evensen and Victoria Bjerkaas; m. Sylvei Brun Lie 1943; two s.; ed law schools and Harvard Univ., USA; Jr partner, law firm 1942–45; Legal Counsel to Solicitor-Gen. 1948–49; Advocate, Supreme Court 1951; Rockefeller Fellowship 1952–53; Dir-Gen. Legal Dept, Ministry of Foreign Affairs 1961–73; Chair. Norwegian Petroleum Council 1965–75, Fishery Limits Comm. 1967–69, many other cttees; Amb. for negotiating Trade Agreement with European Communities 1972; Minister of Commerce 1973–74, of Law of the Sea 1974–79; Chair. Norwegian Del. to Third UN Law of the Sea Conf. 1973, Vice Pres. UN Conf. on the Law of the Sea; Amb., Int. Law Adviser, Ministry of Foreign Affairs 1979–; Ad hoc Judge, Int. Court of Justice 1980–82, Judge 1985–94; Assoc. mem. Inst. de Droit Int. 1971; mem. Perm. Court of Arbitration 1978, Int. Law Comm. 1979. *Leisure interests:* sailing, skiing. *Address:* Linlandvn. 15, 1390 Vollen Asker, Oslo, Norway (Home). *Telephone:* 798515 (Home).

EVERED, David Charles, MD, FRCP, FIBiol; British scientific administrator and physician; b. 21 Jan. 1940, Beaconsfield; s. of the late Thomas C. Evered and Enid C. Evered; m. 1st Anne Lings 1964 (died 1998); one s. two d.; m. 2nd Sheila Pusinelli 2000; ed Cranleigh School, Surrey and Middlesex Hosp. Medical School; jr hosp. appointments London and Leeds 1964–70; First Asst in Medicine, Wellcome Sr Research Fellow and Consultant Physician, Univ. of Newcastle-upon-Tyne and Royal Vic. Infirmary 1970–78; Dir The Ciba Foundation, London 1978–88; Second Sec., MRC, London 1988–96, Consultant 1996–; mem. Council Int. Agency for Research into Cancer 1988–96, Royal Postgrad. Medical School 1994–96, Bd Hammersmith Hosps Nat. Health Service (NHS) Trust 1995–96, numerous cttees, socsand other professional bodies; Chair. NOC NHS Trust 1998–2001; Special Adviser Int. Agency for Research on Cancer, WHO, Lyon, France 2001–03. *Publications:* Diseases of the Thyroid 1976, Atlas of Endocrinology (with R. Hall and R. Greene) 1979 1990, Collaboration in Medical Research in Europe (with M. O'Connor) 1981; numerous papers in professional journals. *Leisure interests:* reading, history, tennis, music. *Address:* Whitehall Cottage, Whitehall Lane, Checkendon, South Oxfordshire, RG8 0TR, England. *E-mail:* david_evered@hotmail.com (Home).

EVERETT, Rupert; British actor; b. 29 May 1960, Norfolk; ed Ampleforth School and Cen. School for Speech and Drama, London; apprenticed with Glasgow Citizen's Theatre 1979–82; has modelled for Versace, Milan; sometime image of Opium perfume for Yves Saint Laurent. *Stage appearances include:* Another Country 1982, The Vortex 1989, Private Lives, The Milk Train Doesn't Stop Here Anymore, The Picture of Dorian Gray 1993, The Importance of Being Earnest 1996, Some Sunny Day 1996. *Films include:* A Shocking Accident 1982, Another Country 1984, Dance with a Stranger 1985, The Right Hand Man 1985, Duet for One 1986, Chronicle of Death Foretold 1987, Hearts of Fire 1987, Haunted Summer 1988, The Comfort of Strangers 1990, Inside Monkey Zetterland 1992, Pret à Porter 1994, The Madness of King George 1995, Dunstan Checks In, My Best Friend's Wedding 1997, A Midsummer Night's Dream 1998, B Monkey 1998, An Ideal Husband 1999, Inspector Gadget 1999, The Next Best Thing 2000, Unconditional Love 2002, The Importance of Being Earnest 2002. *Television includes:* Arthur the King, The Far Pavilions 1982, Princess Daisy 1983. *Publications:* Hello Darling, Are You Working? 1992, The Hairdressers of St Tropez 1995. *Address:* c/o William Stein, ICM, 8942 Wilshire Boulevard, Beverly Hills, CA 90211, USA.

EVERITT, Anthony Michael, BA; British academic, writer and fmr administrative official; b. 31 Jan. 1940; s. of the late Michael Everitt and Simone de Vergriette; ed Cheltenham Coll. and Corpus Christi Coll. Cambridge; lecturer, Nat. Univ. of Iran, SE London Coll. of Further Educ., Birmingham Coll. of Art, Trent Polytechnic 1963–72; Art Critic, The Birmingham Post 1970–75, Drama Critic 1974–79, Features Ed. 1976–79; Dir Midland Group Arts Centre, Nottingham 1979–80, E Midlands Arts Asscn 1980–85; Chair. Ikon Gallery, Birmingham 1976–79, Birmingham Arts Lab. 1977–79; Vice-Chair. Council of Regional Arts Asscns 1984–85; mem. Drama Panel, Arts Council of GB 1974–78, Regional Cttee 1979–80; mem. Cttee for Arts and Humanities, Council for Nat. Academic Awards 1986–87, Performing Arts Cttee 1987–92; mem. Gen. Advisory Council, IBA 1987–90; Deputy Sec.-Gen. Arts Council of GB 1985–90, Sec.-Gen. 1990–94; Visiting Prof. in Visual and Performing Arts, Nottingham Trent Univ.; Hon. Fellow Dartington Coll. of Arts. *Publications:* Abstract Expressionism 1974, In from the Margins 1997, Joining In 1997, The Governance of Culture 1997, The Creative Imperative 2001, Cicero: A Turbulent Life 2000, Cicero: The Life and Times of Rome's Greatest Politician (USA), New Voices 2003, Citizens: Towards a Citizenship Culture (contrib.); contribs to newspapers and journals. *Address:* Westerlies, Anchor Hill, Wivenhoe, Essex, CO7 9BL, England.

EVERLING, Ulrich, DJur; German judge; b. 2 June 1925, Berlin; s. of Emil Everling; m. Lore Schwerdtfeger 1953; two s. two d.; ed Zehlendorfer Gymnasium, Berlin and Univ. of Göttingen; lawyer, Fed. Ministry of Econs 1953–80, Head of Dept of European Policy 1970–80; Lecturer, Hon. Prof. of European Law, Univ. of Münster 1971–80, Univ. of Bonn 1981–; Judge, Court of Justice of the European Communities 1980–88; Dr hc 2001. *Publications:* Die europäische Wirtschaftsgemeinschaft: Kommentar zum Vertrag (co-author) 1960, Das Niederlassungsrecht im Gemeinsamen Markt 1964, Das europäische Gemeinschaftrecht im Spannungsfeld von Politik und Wirtschaft, Ausgewählte Aufsätze 1964–1984 1986, Buchpreisbindung im deutschen Sprachraum und Europäisches Gemeinschaftrecht 1997, Unterwegs zur Europäischen Union, Ausgewählte Aufsätze 1985–2000 2001; numerous articles on European law and policy. *Address:* Dahlienweg 5, 53343 Wachtberg, Germany. *Telephone:* (228) 324177. *Fax:* (228) 324898.

EVERT, Chris(tine) Marie; American tennis player; b. 21 Dec. 1954, Fort Lauderdale, Fla; d. of James Evert and Colette Evert; m. 1st John Lloyd 1979 (divorced 1987); m. 2nd Andy Mill 1988, three s.; ed St Thomas Aquinas High School, Fort Lauderdale; amateur player 1970–72; professional 1972–1989; Wimbledon Singles Champion 1974, 1976, 1981; French Champion 1974, 1975, 1979, 1980, 1983, 1985, 1986; US Open Champion 1975, 1976, 1977, 1978, 1980, 1982; Italian Champion 1974, 1975, 1980; South African Champion 1973; Colgate Series Champion 1977, 1978; World Champion 1979; played Wightman Cup for USA 1971–73, 1975–82, 1984–85; won 1,000th singles victory (first ever player) Australian Open Dec. 1984; played Federation Cup for USA 1977–82; ranked No. 1 in the world for seven years; won 1,309 matches in her career; holds 157 singles titles and 18 Grand Slam titles (third best in history); Pres. Women's Tennis Assen (WTA) 1975–76, 1983–91; Founder Chris Evert Charities for needy and drug-abusive mothers and their children 1989; Host and Organizer Annual Chris Evert Pro-Celebrity Tennis Classic 1989–; Pnr and coach, Evert Tennis Acad., Boca Raton, Fla; owner Evert Enterprises/IMG, Boca Raton, Fla 1989–; Dir and mem. Bd Pres.'s Council on Physical Fitness and Sports 1991–; NBC TV sports commentator and host for numerous TV shows; mem. Bd Ounce of Prevention Fund of Florida, Make-A-Wish Foundation of S Florida, Florida Sports Foundation, United Sports Foundation of America, Save the Children, American AIDS Asscn, Women's Sports Foundation, The Don Shula Foundation, Nat. Cttee to Prevent Child Abuse, The Buoniconti fund, Palm Beach Co. Sports Authority; Sports Illustrated Sportsman of the Year Award 1976, WTA Sportsmanship Award 1979 and Player Service Award 1981, 1986, 1987, named Greatest Woman Athlete of the Last 25 Years (Women's Sports Foundation) 1985, voted by Korbel One of Top 10 Romantic People of 1989, Flo Hyman Award 1990, Providencia Award 1991, Nat. High School Hall of Fame 1992, March of Dimes Lifetime Achievement Award 1993, Madison Square Garden Walk of Fame 1993, Int. Tennis Hall of Fame 1995, bi-colour hybrid tea rose named for her by Spring Hill Nurseries Co. 1996, Int. Tennis Fed. Chartrier Award 1997, named by ESPN as One of Top 50 Athletes of the

20th Century 1999. *Publications:* Chrissie (autobiog.) 1982, Lloyd on Lloyd (with John Lloyd) 1985. *Leisure interests:* Visiting Paris and the Great Barrier Reef in Hamilton Island. *Address:* Evert Enterprises/IMG, 7200 West Camino Real, Suite 310, Boca Raton, FL 33433, USA. *Telephone:* (561) 394-2400 (Office).

EVERT, Militiades; Greek politician; b. 1939, Athens; m. Lisa Evert (née Vanderpool); two d.; ed Econ. Univ. of Athens; MP 1974–; Mayor of Athens 1986–90; Minister of Health and Welfare 1989–90, to the Prime Minister 1990–91; Leader New Democracy Party 1993. *Address:* c/o New Democracy Party, Odos Rigillis 18, 10674 Athens, Greece (Office). *Website:* www.nd.gr (Office).

EVES, Ernie, QC; Canadian politician; b. 1946, Windsor; m.; one s. (deceased) one d.; ed Univ. of Toronto, Osgoode Hall Law School, York Univ.; first elected as MPP for Parry Sound, Ont. Legislature 1981, fmr Vice-Chair. Priorities, Policy and Communications Bd of Cabinet, fmr Vice-Chair. Man. Bd of Cabinet, fmr Govt House Leader, fmr Minister of Community and Social Services, fmr Minister of Skills Devt, Deputy Premier and Minister of Finance, Ont. 1995–2001, Leader Ont. Progressive Conservative Party March 2002–, MPP for Dufferin-Peel-Wellington-Grey May 2002–, Premier of Ont. April 2002–; Founder and Sec. Treas. Big Brothers' Asscn of Parry Sound; mem. Advisory Bd Embassy of Hope; f. Justin Eves Foundation. *Address:* Office of the Premier, Legislative Building, Queen's Park, Toronto, Ont. M7A 1A1, Canada (Office). *Telephone:* (416) 3325-1941 (Office). *Fax:* (416) 325-7578 (Office). *Website:* www.infogo.gov.on.ca (Office).

EVIN, Claude; French politician; b. 29 June 1949, Le Cellier, Loire-Atlantique; s. of André Evin and Jeanne Lecommandeur; m. Françoise Guillet 1971; three d.; Sec. St-Nazaire Section, Parti Socialiste 1975–77, mem. Loire-Atlantique Fed. Cttee of Socialist Party 1975–, mem. Nat. Cttee 1991–; Mun. Councillor and Deputy Mayor of St-Nazaire 1977–; Deputy to Nat. Ass. 1978–88, 1997–; MP Ass. of Council of Europe; Chair. Nat. Ass. Cultural, Family and Social Affairs Cttee 1981–86; mem. Social Security Audit Comm. 1985; Vice-Pres. Nat. Ass. 1986–88; Minister-Del. attached to Minister of Social Affairs and Employment with responsibility for Social Protection May–June 1988; Minister of Solidarity, Health and Social Protection 1988–91; Conseiller régional Pays de la Loire 1992–98; mem. Econ. and Social Council 1994–97, Parl. Ass., Council of Europe. *Address:* 30 rue du Bois Savary, 44600 St-Nazaire, France. *Telephone:* (2) 51-10-10-51. *Fax:* (2) 51-10-10-50.

EVISON, Frank Foster, OBE, PhD, FRSNZ; New Zealand professor of geophysics; b. 20 March 1922, Christchurch; s. of Sidney Roger Evison and Beatrice Maud Evison; m. Edith Joan Hutton 1949 (died 1990); one s. two d.; ed Christchurch West High School, Wellington Coll., Vic. Univ. of Wellington, Imperial Coll. of Science and Tech., London Univ.; RNZAF 1942–45; physicist/geophysicist, NZ Dept of Scientific and Industrial Research 1945–60, superintendent Seismological Observatory 1960–64, Dir Geophysics Div. 1964–67; Prof. of Geophysics, Vic. Univ. of Wellington 1967–88, Chair. Inst. of Geophysics 1971–88, Prof. Emer. and Hon. Fellow 1988–; discovered the 'Evison Wave' 1955; Chair. Int. Symposium on Earthquake Prediction, UNESCO, Paris 1979; Sec. Int. Comm. on Earthquake Prediction 1979–83; Co-Chair. Int. Comm. on Earthquake Hazards 1983–87; Fulbright Fellow, Univ. of Minn. 1964; Nuffield Fellow, Cambridge Univ. 1957–58, Japan SPS Research Fellow, Kyoto Univ. 1980. *Publications:* 70 scientific papers on seismology, earthquake hazard, tectonophysics, applied geophysics, seismogenesis, earthquake forecasting. *Leisure interests:* hill- and bush-walking, skiing, music. *Address:* Institute of Geophysics, Victoria University of Wellington, P.O. Box 600, Wellington (Office); 1 Glen Road, Kelburn, Wellington, New Zealand (Home). *Telephone:* (4) 4636454 (Office); (4) 4759231 (Home). *Fax:* (4) 4955186 (Office); (4) 4759231 (Home). *E-mail:* frank.evison@vuw.ac.nz (Office). *Website:* www.geo.vuw.ac.nz (Office).

EVORA, Cesaria; Cape Verdean singer; b. 27 Aug. 1941, Mindelo, Sao Vicente. *Albums include:* La Diva aux pieds nus 1988, Distino di Belita 1990, Mar Azul 1991, Miss Perfumado 1992, Sodade les plus belles mornas de Cesaria 1994, Cesaria 1995, Cabo Verde 1997, Best of Cesaria Evora 1998, Café Atlantico 1999, Cesaria Evora Remixes 1999, Sao Vicente de Longe 2002. *Website:* www.cesaria-evora.com.

EVREN, Gen. Kenan; Turkish army officer and fmr Head of State; b. 1918, Alaşehir, Manisa; s. of Naciye Evren and Hayrullah Evren; m.; three d.; ed Military Acad., War Coll.; Artillery Officer 1938; served in Korea; Chief of Staff of the Land Forces, then Deputy Chief of Staff of the Armed Forces; Commdr Fourth Army (Aegean Army), Izmir 1976; rank of Gen. 1974; Chief of the Land Forces 1977; Chief of Staff of the Armed Forces 1978; led coup deposing civilian Govt Sept. 1980; Head of State and Chair. Nat. Security Council 1980–82, Pres. of Turkey 1982–89; Head, Turkish mil. del. to USSR 1975; est. cultural foundation; numerous decorations. *Achievements:* building Marmaris High School, opened 2000. *Leisure interests:* oil painting, education. *Address:* Beyaz Ev Sokak 27, Armutalan, Marmaris, Turkey. *Telephone:* (252) 4171300. *E-mail:* kev@marmariskoleji-kiz.com (Office).

EWEN, Paterson; Canadian artist and teacher of fine art; b. 7 April 1925, Montreal, Québec; four s.; ed Montreal Museum of Fine Arts, School of Art and Design, McGill Univ., Montreal; solo exhbns in Toronto 1969–; exhbns in New Brunswick 1975, New Jersey, USA 1975, Calgary 1980, Basel, Switzerland 1978, Denmark 1980–81, FRG 1981, Luxembourg 1981, Belgium 1981, Japan

1981, Venice, Italy 1982, London 1982, Vancouver 1992, 1995, New York 1993, 1994; group exhbns New York 1993, Vancouver 1994; Assoc. Prof. Univ. of Western Ont. 1972–87, Prof. Emer. 1987–; Hon. DLitt (Western Ont.) 1989; Hon. LLD (Concordia Univ., Montreal) 1989; Nat. Award, Banff Centre School of Fine Arts 1987, Toronto Arts Award 1988, Chalmers Award for Visual Arts 1995. *Publications:* (catalogues) Carmen Lamanna at the Owens Art Gallery 1975, Paterson Ewen: Recent Works 1977, Paterson Ewen Phenomena, paintings, 1971–1987 1987, Paterson Ewen: the Montreal Years 1987, Paterson Ewen 1993. *Address:* 1015 Wellington Street, London, Ont., N6A 3T5, Canada (Home).

EWING, Maria Louise; American opera singer; b. 27 March 1950, Detroit; d. of Norman I. Ewing and Hermina M. Veraar; m. Sir Peter Hall 1982 (divorced 1989); one d.; ed Cleveland Inst. of Music; début at Metropolitan Opera, New York singing Cherubino in The Marriage of Figaro 1976, closely followed by débuts with major US orchestras including New York Philharmonic and at La Scala Milan; performs regularly at Glyndebourne including the Barber of Seville, L'Incoronazione di Poppea and Carmen; repertoire also includes Pelléas et Mélisande, The Dialogues of the Carmelites, Così fan Tutte, La Perichole, La Cenerentola, The Marriage of Figaro (Susanna); performed Salome, Covent Garden 1988, Carmen, Earl's Court, London 1989, Tosca, Los Angeles 1989, Salome, Washington 1990, Madame Butterfly, Los Angeles, Tosca, Seville, Salome, Covent Garden 1992, Tosca, Los Angeles, Chicago, Salome, San Francisco, The Trojans, Metropolitan New York 1993, Madame Butterfly, Tosca, Vienna, The Trojans, Metropolitan, New York 1993/94; also appears as concert and recital singer; début Promenade Concerts, London 1987, Lady Macbeth of Mtzensk with Metropolitan Opera 1994. *Leisure interests:* home and family. *Address:* c/o David Godfrey, Mitchell-Godfrey Management, 48 Gray's Inn Road, London, WC1X 8LT, England (Office); c/o Herbert Breslin, 119 West 57th Street, Room 1505, New York, NY 10019, USA. *Telephone:* (20) 7831-3027 (London) (Office). *Fax:* (20) 7831-5277 (London) (Office). *E-mail:* davidgodfrey@mariaewing.com (Office).

EWING, Winifred Margaret, LLB, MA, FRSA; Scottish politician and solicitor; b. Winifred Margaret Woodburn, 10 July 1929, Glasgow; d. of George Woodburn and Christina B. Anderson; m. Stewart Martin Ewing 1956; two s. one d.; ed Queen's Park School, Univ. of Glasgow, Peace Palace, The Hague; practising solicitor 1956–; mem. Parl. for Hamilton 1967–70, for Moray and Nairn 1974–79; mem. European Parl. 1975–, for the Highlands and Islands of Scotland 1979–99, mem. for Highlands and Islands, Scottish Parl. 1999–; Pres. Scottish Nat. Party, European Free Alliance 1991–; Vice-Pres. European Democratic Alliance 1984, Animal Welfare Intergroup (European Parl.) 1989–99; Chair. Cttee on Youth, Culture, Educ., Information and Sport, European Parl. 1984–; Sec. Glasgow Bar Asscn 1961–67, Pres 1970–71; mem. Exec. Cttee Scottish Co. for Devt and Industry 1972–; Freeman of Avignon; Dr hc (Open Univ.) 1993; Hon. LLD (Glasgow) 1995; Comptroller, Scottish Privileges of Veero. *Leisure interests:* hill walking, collecting paintings, singing. *Address:* Goodwill, Milton Duff, Elgin, Moray IV30 3TL, Scotland (Home). *Telephone:* (1343) 541144. *Fax:* (1343) 540011.

EYADÉMA, Gen. (Etienne) Gnassingbe; Togolese politician and army officer; b. 26 Dec. 1937, Pya, Lama Kara District; served with French Army 1953–61 in Indo-China, Dahomey, Niger and Algeria; commissioned 1963; Army Chief of Staff 1965–; led army coup Jan. 1967; Pres. of Togo April 1967– and Minister of Defence 1967, 1981–91; f. Rassemblement du Peuple Togolais, Paris 1969, Pres. 1969, mem. Political Bureau; Chair. ECOWAS 1980–81, OAU 2000–01; Grand Officier, Ordre Nat. de Mono, Mil. Cross, Chevalier, Légion d'honneur (France). *Leisure interest:* hunting. *Address:* Palais Présidentiel, avenue de la Marina, Lomé, Togo (Office). *Telephone:* 21-27-01 (Office). *Fax:* 21-18-97 (Office). *E-mail:* presidence@republicoftogo.com (Office). *Website:* www.republicoftogo.com (Office).

EYCKMANS, Luc A. F., MD, PhD; Belgian professor of medicine; b. 23 Feb. 1930, Antwerp; s. of Robert Eyckmans and Alice van Genechten; m. Godelieve Cornelissen 1957; four s. three d.; ed Univ. of Leuven; Fellowship in Tropical Medicine, Antwerp 1956–57; Hosp. Physician, Kisantu (fmr Belgian Congo) 1957–60; Fellowship in Infectious Diseases, Dallas and Cornell, New York 1961–64, in Tropical Medicine, Bahia, Brazil 1964; Lector in Infectious Diseases and Physician, Univ. of Leuven 1965–72; Prof. of Medicine (Infectious Diseases), Univ. of Antwerp 1973–76, Dir Inst. of Tropical Medicine "Prince Leopold" 1976–95; Visiting Prof. Univ. of Antwerp 1977–95, Univ. of Leuven 1989–95; Exec. Dir and mem. Bd Francqui Foundation 1993–; mem. Royal Acad. of Overseas Sciences (Belgium), Acad. Europaea; Corresp. mem. Acad. Nat. de Médicine, Paris; Grand Officer, Order of the Crown (Belgium); Dr hc (Lille). *Publications:* 130 contributions to professional journals and chapters in scientific publs. *Leisure interest:* hiking. *Address:* Fondation Francqui, Rue Defacqz 1, 1000 Brussels (Office); Wildenhoge 26, B 3020 Winksele, Belgium (Home). *Telephone:* (2) 539-33-94 (Office); (16) 22-05-96 (Home). *Fax:* (2) 537-29-21 (Office).

EYRAUD, Francis Charles, LenD, DES; French business executive; b. 16 Aug. 1931, Saint-Bonnet, Hautes Alpes; s. of Charles Eyraud and Francine Villaron; m. Simone Desmé 1967; two s. one d.; ed Coll. du Rondeau Montfleury, Grenoble, Faculté de Droit, Lettres, IEP, Paris; ENA promotion, Alexis de Tocqueville 1958; civil admin. of finance 1960; Prof. Centre de Formation des Finances 1961; in charge of practical studies, Faculté de Droit 1962; special mission to USA 1965; Chef de Bureau 1967; civil admin. 1968; Deputy Dir 1973; judicial agent of Treasury 1979–; Prés.-Dir Gén. Société

Nationale d'Exploitation Industrielle des Tabacs et Allumettes (SEITA) 1981–87; Man. Dir CORESTA 1982, Vice-Pres. 1984–86, Pres. 1986; Paymaster of Seine-Maritime and of Haute-Normandie 1988–96, of Yvelines 1996–98; Officier Légion d'honneur, Commdr Ordre nat. du Mérite, Officier des Palmes académiques; Commdr des Arts et des Lettres and other decorations. *Publications:* Cours de Législation Financière 1965. *Address:* 33 rue Saint-Augustin, 75002 Paris, France (Home). *Telephone:* 1-47-42-50-67 (Home).

EYRE, Ivan; Canadian artist and professor emeritus; b. 15 April 1935, Tullymet, Sask.; s. of Thomas Eyre and Kay Eyre; m. Brenda Fenske 1957; two s.; mem. Faculty, Univ. of Manitoba, Winnipeg 1959–93, Head, Drawing Dept 1974–78, Prof. of Drawing and Painting 1975–93, Prof. Emer. 1994–; works represented in permanent collections at Winnipeg Art Gallery, Nat. Gallery, Ottawa, Edmonton Art Gallery, Montreal Museum of Fine Arts, Assiniboine Park Pavilion Gallery, Winnipeg, Man. etc.; Canada Council Sr Fellow 1966–77; Founder mem. Winnipeg Art Gallery 1996; mem. Royal Canadian Acad. of Arts; subject of book (Ivan Eyre) by George Woodcock and of various documentary films; Queen's Silver Jubilee Medal 1977, Academic of Italy with Gold Medal 1980, Jubilee Award, Univ. of Manitoba Alumni Asscn 1982, Queen's Golden Jubilee Medal 2002. *One-man exhibitions:* one-man shows at Nat. Gallery of Canada, Ottawa, many other Canadian galleries, Frankfurter Kunstkabinett, W Germany, Canada House, London, Canadian Cultural Centre, Paris, France, Talbot-Rice Galleries, Edin., Scotland 1982, 49th Parallel Gallery, New York 1988; has participated in group shows in Colombia, Spain, USA, Hong Kong Art Fair 1993, Taejon, S Korea, Expo '93 and all the major cities of Canada. *Address:* 1098 Des Trappistes Street, Winnipeg, Manitoba R3V 1B8, Canada. *Telephone:* (204) 261-8171. *Fax:* (204) 261-8171.

EYRE, Sir Richard, Kt, CBE, DLit; British theatre, film and television director; b. 28 March 1943, Barnstaple, Devon; m. Sue Birtwistle 1973; one d.; ed Sherborne School and Cambridge Univ.; directed his first production, The Knack, at the Phoenix Theatre, Leicester 1965; Asst Dir Phoenix Theatre 1967; Assoc. Dir Royal Lyceum, Edinburgh 1967–70, Dir of Productions 1970–72; Artistic Dir Nottingham Playhouse 1973–78; Producer-Dir Play for Today for BBC 1978–80; Assoc. Dir Nat. Theatre (now called Royal Nat. Theatre) 1980–86, Artistic Dir 1988–97; BBC Gov. 1995–; Cameron Mackintosh Visiting Professorship, St Catherine's Coll. Oxford 1997; Visiting Prof. of Drama, Univ. of Warwick 1999, Univ. of Sheffield 2000; Hon. Fellow Goldsmiths Coll. 1993, King's Coll. London 1994; Hon. mem. Guildhall School of Music and Drama 1996; Officier des Arts et des Lettres 1998; Hon. DLitt (Nottingham Trent) 1992, (S Bank) 1994; Hon. BA (Surrey) 1998; Dr hc Royal Scottish Acad. of Drama 2000; Patricia Rothermere Award 1995, STV Award for Best Dir 1969, 1970, 1971, Evening Standard Award for Best Dir 1982, Soc. of West End Theatres Award for Best Dir 1982, Time Out Award Best Dir 1986, Vittorio de Sica Award 1986, Special Award, Evening Standard Awards for Drama 1988, for Best Dir 1997, Special Award for running Nat. Theatre 1997, Critics Circle Award 1996/97, Laurence Olivier Award for Outstanding Achievement 1997, South Bank Show Award for Outstanding Achievement 1997, Director's Guild Award for Outstanding Achievement 1997, Tokyo Award for the Insurance Man 1987, BAFTA Award. *Plays directed include:* Hamlet (Royal Court) 1980, Guys and Dolls (Olivier 1982, Soc. of West End Theatres and Evening Standard Awards for Best Dir 1982), The Beggar's Opera, Schweyk in the Second World War (Nat. Theatre) 1982, The Government Inspector (Nat. Theatre) 1985, Futurists (Nat. Theatre) (Time Out Award for Best Dir) 1986, Kafka's Dick (Royal Court) 1986, High Society (W End) 1987, The Changeling 1988, Bartholomew Fair 1988, Hamlet 1989, The Voysey Inheritance 1989, Racing Demon 1990, Richard III (Nat. Theatre, also nat. and int. tour) 1990, Napoli Milionaria 1991, Murmuring Judges 1991, White Chameleon 1991, The Night of the Iguana 1992, Macbeth 1993, The David Hare Trilogy – Racing Demon, Murmuring Judges, The Absence of War 1993 (Racing Demon, New York 1995), Johnny on a Spot 1994, Sweet Bird of Youth 1994, Skylight 1995, 1996 (New York 1996), La Grande Magia 1995, The Prince's Play 1996, John Gabriel Borkman 1996, Guys and Dolls 1996, 1997, King Lear 1997, Amy's View 1997 (New York 1999), The Invention of Love 1997, The Judas Kiss 1998 (New York 1998), The Novice 2000, The Crucible (New York) 2002, Vincent in Brixton 2002. *Films:* The Ploughman's Lunch (Evening Standard Award for Best Film) 1983, Loose Connections 1984, Laughterhouse (Venice Film Festival Award for Best Film) 1984, Iris (Special Mention for Excellence in Filmmaking Award, Nat. Bd of Review 2001, Humanitas Screenwriting Award for screenplay 2002) 2001. *Radio:* Macbeth (BBC Radio 3) 2000. *Television:* Waterloo Sunset, Comedians 1974, The Imitation Game 1980, Pasmore 1981, The Cherry Orchard, Country 1982, Past Caring, The Insurance Man (Tokyo World TV Festival Special Prize 1986) 1986, "V", Tumbledown (Italia RAI Prize 1988, BAFTA Award for Best TV Single Drama, Royal TV Soc. Award for Best Single Drama 1989) 1987, Suddenly Last Summer 1993, The Absence of War (BBC) 1995, King Lear (BBC) (Peabody Award 1998) 1998, Changing Stages: A Personal View of 20th-Century Theatre (writer and presenter on BBC 2) 2000. *Opera:* La Traviata, Covent Garden 1994, Le Nozze di figaro, Aix-en-Provence, France 2001. *Publication:* Utopia and Other Places (memoirs) 1993, The Eyre Review

1998, Changing Stages (with Nicholas Wright) 2000, Angel (radio play) 2001, Iris (screenplay) 2002. *Address:* c/o Judy Daish Associates Ltd, 2 St Charles Place, London, W10 6EG, England. *Telephone:* (20) 8964-8811. *Fax:* (20) 8964-8966.

EYRE, Richard Anthony, MA; British television executive; b. 3 May 1954; s. of Edgar Gabriel Eyre and Marjorie Eyre (née Corp); m. Sheelagh Colquhoun 1977; one s. one d.; ed King's Coll. School, Wimbledon, Lincoln Coll., Oxford Univ.; media buyer Benton & Bowles 1975–79, media planner 1980–84; TV airtime salesman Scottish TV 1979–80; Media Dir Aspect 1984–86, Bartle Bogle Hegarty 1986–91; Chief Exec. Capital Radio PLC 1991–97, ITV 1997–2000, Pearson TV 2000–01; Dir of Strategy and Content, RTL Group 2000–01; Non-Exec. Chair. RDF Media 2001–; Adviser to 19 Group 2002–. *Address:* RDF Media, The Gloucester Building, Kensington Village, Avonmore Road, London, W14 8RF, England (Office). *Telephone:* (20) 7013-4000 (Office). *Fax:* (20) 7013-4001. *Website:* www.rdfmedia.com.

EYSKENS, Mark, LLD, DEcon; Belgian politician; b. 29 April 1933, Louvain; m. Ann Rutsaert 1962; two s. three d.; ed Catholic Univ. of Louvain, Columbia Univ.; Prof. Catholic Univ. of Louvain; Econ. Adviser, Ministry of Finance 1962–65; mem. of Parl. 1977–; Sec. of State for the Budget and Regional Economy and Minister of Co-operation 1976–80; Minister of Finance 1980–81; Prime Minister 1981; Minister for Econ. Affairs 1981–85, for Finance 1985–88, of Foreign Affairs 1989–92, Minister of State 1998–; Chair. Council of EC Ministers of Finance 1987; Gov. IMF, IBRD 1980–81, 1985–88; mem. Council of Europe 1995–; Pres. Royal Acad. of Sciences, Letters and Fine Arts, Centre for European Culture, Inst. for European Policy; Vice-Pres. Royal Inst. for Int. Relations, Ass. of WEU 1995–; Observer European Convention 2002–; Benelux-Europe Prize; numerous Belgian and foreign distinctions. *Publications include:* Algemene economie 1970, Economie van nu en straks 1975, Une planète livrée à deux mondes 1980, La source et l'horizon, Le redressement de la société européenne 1985, Economie voor iedereen 1987, Vie et mort du Professeur Mortal 1989, Affaires étrangères 1992, Le Fleuve et l'océan, L'Affaire Titus 1998, Democratie tussen Spinen Web 1999, Het verdriet van het werelddorp 2000, Leven in tijden van Godsverdenistering 2001. *Leisure interests:* painting, literature, music. *Address:* Graaf de Grunnelaan 17, 3001 Heverlee-Leuven, Belgium (Office). *Fax:* (1) 640-60-18 (Home). *E-mail:* m.eyskens@skynet.be (Office). *Website:* www.eyskens.com.

EYTON, Anthony John Plowden, RA, RWS, R.W.A.; British artist; b. 17 May 1923, Teddington, Middx; s. of the late Capt. John Seymour Eyton and Phyllis Annie Tyser; m. Frances Mary Capell 1960 (divorced); three d.; ed Twyford School, Canford School and Camberwell School of Art; part-time teacher, Camberwell Art School 1955–86, Royal Acad. Schools 1963–99; mem. Royal Cambrian Acad.; Hon. mem. Pastel Soc.; several awards and prizes. *Exhibitions:* St George's Gallery 1955, New Art Centre 1959, 1961, 1968, New Grafton Gallery 1973, William Darby Gallery 1975, Browse & Darby 1978, 1981, 1985, 1987, 1990, 1993, 1996, 2000 South London Art Gallery (retrospective) 1980, Imperial War Museum 1983, Austin Desmond Fine Art Gallery 1990, A.T. Kearney Ltd 1997, Prince of Wales Inst. of Architecture 1998, King's Road Gallery 2002. *Leisure interest:* gardening. *Address:* c/o Browse and Darby Ltd, 19 Cork Street, London, W1X 1HB, England (Office). *Telephone:* (20) 7734-7984 (Office).

EYZAGUIRRE GUZMAN, Nicolás, PhD; Chilean international organization official and politician; b. 1952; ed Harvard Univ.; Exec. Dir IMF 1998; Minister of Finance 2000–. *Publication:* The Macroeconomy of Quasi-Fiscal Operations in Chile (with Osvaldo Larrañaga) 1990. *Address:* Ministry of Finance, Teatinos 120, 12° Santiago, Chile (Office). *Telephone:* (2) 675-5800 (Office). *Fax:* (2) 671-6479 (Office).

EZRA, Baron (Life Peer), cr. 1983, of Horsham in the County of West Sussex; **Derek Ezra,** Kt, MBE; British business executive; b. 23 Feb. 1919, Australia; s. of David and Lillie Ezra; m. Julia Elizabeth Wilkins 1950; ed Monmouth School and Magdalen Coll., Cambridge; mil. service 1939–47; rep. of Nat. Coal Bd at Cttees of OEEC and ECE 1948–52; mem. UK Del. to High Authority of European Coal and Steel Community 1952–56; Regional Sales Man. Nat. Bd 1958–60, Dir-Gen. of Marketing 1960–65; mem. Nat. Coal Bd 1965, Deputy Chair. 1965–71, Chair. 1971–82; Pres. British Inst. of Man. 1976–78, Vice-Chair. 1978; Chair. British Coal Int.; Chair. British Nationalised Industries Chairmen's Group 1980–81, Pres. Nat. Materials Handling Centre 1978; Pres. Coal Industry Soc. 1981–86, British Standards Inst. 1983–86, Econ. Research Council 1985–2000, Inst. of Trading Standards Admin. 1987–92; Dir Redland PLC 1982–89; Chair. Associated Heat Services PLC 1966–2000, British Iron and Steel Consumers Council 1983–86, Petrolex PLC 1982–85, Sheffield Heat and Power Ltd 1985–2000, Associated Gas Supplies Ltd 1987–95, Energy and Tech. Services Group 1990–2000, Micropower Ltd 2000–; Industrial Adviser to Morgan Grenfell 1982–88; Chair. Throgmorton Trust 1984–90; mem. British Overseas Trade Bd 1972–82, Bd, Solvay, Belgium; Hon. Fellow Inst. of Civil Engineers 1986; Hon. LLD (Leeds) 1982; Order of Merit, Italy, Commdr Order of Merit, Luxembourg, Officier, Légion d'honneur. *Publications:* Coal and Energy 1978, The Energy Debate 1983. *Address:* House of Lords, Westminster, London, SW1A 0PW, England. *Telephone:* (20) 7219-3180.

F

FABBRI, Fabio; Italian politician, lawyer and journalist; b. 15 Oct. 1933, Ciano d'Enza, Reggio Emilia; s. of Nello Fabbri and Gisella Brechi; m. Minnie Manzini 1959; one s. one d.; ed Univ. of Parma; fmr journalist with Il Mondo and contrib. to Nord e Sud, Itinerari, Mondo Operario; now contrib. to L'Avanti and other political and cultural magazines; Chair. Parma Provincial Transport Authority 1968–70; Socialist Senator for Borgotaro Salsomaggiore, Emilia Romagna 1976; fmr Under-Sec., Ministry of Agric. and Forestry; Minister for Regional Affairs 1982–83, for EEC Affairs 1986–87, of Defence 1993–94; Chair. of Socialist Parl. Group; Pres. Istituto per il dialogo e la cooperazione internazionale. *Leisure interests:* reading, trekking, skiing. *Address:* Piazza Garibaldi 17, 431000 Parma, Italy.

FABÉNYI, Júlia Borbala, PhD; Hungarian art historian and archaeologist; b. 27 Sept. 1953, Budapest; d. of Ede Fabényi and Ilona Tokay; m.; one s.; ed Univ. of Leipzig; Asst Prof., Univ. of Social Sciences, Faculty of Art History of Leipzig 1977–82; curator Budapest Art Gallery 1990–94, Head of Exhbn Dept 1994–95, Man. Dir 2000–; Dir of Picture Gallery of Szombathely 1996–2000; Fine Arts Curator Int. Book Fair, Frankfurt 1999–. *Publications:* Bloomsday Katalogs, Szombathely. *Leisure interest:* gardening. *Address:* Mücsarnok, 1146 Budapest, Dózsa György út 37 (Office); 1023 Budapest, Zsigmond tér 8, Hungary (Home). *Telephone:* (1) 363-6545 (Office); *Fax:* (1) 363-7205 (Office), (1) 335-0489 (Home). *E-mail:* jfabenyi@mucsarnok.hu (Office). *Website:* www.mucsarnok.hu (Office).

FABIANI, Simonetta (see Simonetta).

FABIUS, Laurent; French politician; b. 20 Aug. 1946, Paris; s. of André Fabius and Louise Mortimer; m. Françoise Castro 1981; two s.; ed Lycées Janson-de-Sailly and Louis-le-Grand, Paris, Ecole normale supérieure, Ecole Nat. d'Admin; Auditor, Council of State 1973; First Deputy Mayor of Grand-Quevilly 1977–, Mayor 1995–; Deputy (Seine-Maritime) to Nat. Ass. 1978–81, 1986–, Pres. 1988–92, 1997–2000; Nat. Sec. Parti Socialiste, in charge of press 1979–81, 1991–92, First Sec. 1992–93, Pres. Groupe Socialiste in Nat. Ass. 1995–97; Minister-Del. for the Budget, attached to Minister of Econ. and Finance 1981–83; Minister of Industry and Research 1983–84, Minister of Econs, Finance and Industry 2000–02; Prime Minister 1984–86; Pres. Regional Council, Haute Normandie 1981–82; Pres. Syndicat intercommunal à vocations multiples (Sivom) 1989–2000; mem. Gen. Council, Seine-Maritime 2000–; Grand Croix de l'Ordre nat. du Mérite. *Publications:* La France inégale 1975, Le coeur du futur 1985, C'est en allant vers la mer 1990, Les blessures de la vérité 1995 (Prize for Best Political Book 1996). *Address:* Assemblée Nationale, 75355 Paris, France.

FÁBREGA, Jorge, M.L.; Panamanian professor of law and attorney; b. Jorge Fábrega Ponce, 19 April 1922, Santiago; s. of Luis Ramon Fábrega and Maria Fábrega; m. Gloria de Fábrega 1960; two s. two d.; ed Univ. of Southern California, Univ. of Pennsylvania, Univ. of Panama; Alt. Justice Court of Appeals 1960–68, Supreme Court of Panama 1970–80, 1989, 1999–(2005); Prof. of Law, Univ. of Panama 1967; Pres. Govt Comm. drafting Labour Code 1969–71, Constitutional Comm. 1983, Panamanian Bar Asscn 1983–85; mem. Govt Comm. drafting new Judicial Code 1970–74; Hon. mem. Spanish Bar, Brazilian Labour Judicial Order. *Publications:* Enriquecimiento sin causa 1960, Institutes of Civil Procedure 1972, Casación 1978, Estudios Procesales 1984, Código de Trabajo Anotado 1970, 1971, 1986, Estudios Procesales 1988, Instituciones de Derecho Procesal 1998, Procesos Civiles 1999, Medios de Prueba, Casación Civil, Teoría General de la Prueba 2000. *Leisure interests:* reading, travel. *Address:* Torre Swiss Bank, Primer Piso, Calle 53 Este, Urbanización Marbella, Panamá (Office); Las Cumbres, Vía El Peñón, Panamá, Republic of Panama (Home). *Telephone:* 269-6412 (Office); 269-6621 (Home). *Fax:* 264-3933 (Office).

FABRICIUS, Fritz, DJur; German professor of law; b. 18 May 1919, Fedderwardergroden; s. of Martin Fabricius and Helene Fabricius (née Ehmen); m. Gisela Nagel 1948; one s.; ed Münster Univ.; naval officer 1940–45; Asst Münster Univ. 1956–61, lecturer 1961–64; Full Prof. of Commercial, Company and Labour Law Bochum Univ. 1964–84, Prof. Emer. 1984–; Man. Dir Verwaltungs- und Wirtschaftsakademie Industriebezirk 1967–84; mem. Cttee of Ind. Experts for the European Social Charter with the European Council, Strasbourg 1976–82, 1982–88, 1988–94; Grosses Verdienstkreuz des Verdienstordens der BRD. *Publications:* Relativität der Rechtsfähigkeit 1963, Mitbestimmung in der Wirtschaft 1970, Marktwirtschaft und Mitbestimmung 1978, Unternehmensrechtsreform und Mitbestimmung in einer sozialen Marktwirtschaft 1982, Rechtsprobleme gespaltener Arbeitsverhältnisse im Konzern 1982, Streik und Aussperrung im Internationalen Recht 1988, Human Rights and European Politics 1992, Kommentar zum Betriebsverfassungsgesetz (6th Edn) 1998. *Leisure interest:* music. *Address:* Dahlhauserstrasse 71, 45529 Hattingen, Germany. *Telephone:* (2324) 82983.

FABRIZI, Pier Luigi, BEcons; Italian banker and professor of finance; b. 23 April 1948, Siena; s. of Francesco Fabrizi and Bianca Corradeschi; m. Patrizia Vaselli; two c.; ed Siena Univ.; Asst Prof. of Banking Parma Univ. 1974–82, Assoc. Prof. 1982–87, Prof. of Financial Insts. 1987–93, Dean Faculty of Econs 1990–97; Prof. of Financial Markets Bocconi Univ., Milan 1993–; Chair. Banca Monte dei Paschi di Siena SpA 1998–; mem. Bd Dirs. S. Paolo IMI, Turin 1998–99, Ing. C Olivetti SpA Ivrea 1999, Banca Agricola Mantovana, Mantova 1999, Banco Nazionale del Lavoro SpA, Rome 2001, Unipol Assirazioni SpA Bologna 2001; Grande Ufficiale, Ordine al Merito. *Publications:* L'attività in titoli con clientela nelle banche di deposito 1986, La gestione dei flussi finanziari nelle aziende di credito 1990, La gestione integrata dell'attivo e del passivo nelle aziende di credito 1991, Nuovi modelli di gestione dei flussi finanziari nelle banche 1995, Le banche nell' intermediazione mobiliare e nell'asset management 1996, La formazione nelle banche e nelle assicurazioni-bancaria (ed.) 1998, Il futuro del sistema bancario italiano: Strategie e modelli organizzativi 2000; La gestione del risparmio privato (ed.) 2000. *Address:* c/o Banca Monte Paschi Siena SpA, P.za Salimbeni 3, 53100 Siena (Office); c/o Università Bocconi, Via Sarfatti 25, 20136 Milan (Office); Via Adelaide Coari 11, 20141 Milan, Italy. *Telephone:* (0577) 294211 (Siena) (Office); (02) 58365910 (Milan) (Office); (02) 55210884 (Milan). *Fax:* (0577) 294017 (Siena) (Office); (02) 58365909 (Milan) (Office). *E-mail:* pierluigi .fabrizi@banca.mps.it (Siena) (Office); pierluigi.fabrizi@uni.bocconi .it (Milan) (Office).

FADDEYEV, Ludvig Dmitriyevich; Russian mathematician and physicist; b. 23 March 1934, Leningrad; m.; two d.; ed Leningrad Univ.; Sr Research Fellow, Leningrad Branch, Inst. of Math., USSR (now Russian) Acad. of Sciences 1965–, Deputy Dir 1976–; mem. staff, Leningrad State Univ. 1967–, Prof. at Mathematical-Mechanical Faculty 1969–; Pres. Int. Mathematical Union 1986–; specialist in quantum mechanics; mem. USSR (now Russian) Acad. of Sciences 1976, Acad.-Sec. Dept of Mathematics; mem. American Acad. of Arts and Sciences, Boston 1979; D. Heinemann Prize, American Physical Soc. 1975, USSR State Prize 1971, Max Planck Gold Medal 1995. *Address:* St Petersburg Branch of V.A. Steklov Mathematical Institute, Nab. Fontanki 27, D-11, St Petersburg, Russia. *Telephone:* (812) 312-40-58 (Office); (812) 553-58-53 (Home).

FADEYETCHEV, Alexei Nikolayevich; Russian ballet dancer; b. 16 Aug. 1960, Moscow; s. of Nikolay Fadeyetchev (q.v.) and Nina Fetisova; m. Rastozguyeva Tatyana; ed Bolshoi Choreographic School; prin. dancer Bolshoi Ballet 1978, Artistic Dir 1998–2000; f. (with Nina Ananiashvili) ballet co. Moscow Theatre of Dance 2000; has performed with Mariinsky (fmrly Kirov) Ballet, Royal Danish Ballet, Royal Swedish Ballet, Nat. Ballet of Netherlands, Nat. Ballet of Finland, Nat. Ballet of Portugal, Birmingham Royal Ballet, Boston Ballet, Tokyo Ballet and numerous others; People's Artist of Russia. *Performances as a dancer include:* Frantz in Coppelia, Prince Siegfried in Swan Lake, Prince Desire in The Sleeping Beauty, Prince in The Nutcracker, Jean de Brienne in Raimonda, Basil in Don Quixote, Albrecht in Giselle, title roles in Spartacus, Ivan the Terrible, Macbeth, Romeo and Juliet, Cyrano de Bergerac, Prince of the Pagodas, leading roles in Les Sylphides, Paquita. *Address:* Karetny Ryad Str. 5/10 Apt. 20 Moscow 103006, Russia (Office). *Telephone:* (095) 419-35-31 (Home).

FADEYETCHEV, Nikolay Borisovich; Russian ballet dancer; b. 27 Jan. 1933; m. 1st Nina Kholina; m. 2nd Irina Kholina; two s.; ed Bolshoi Theatre Ballet School; Bolshoi Theatre Ballet Co., 1952–76, coach Bolshoi Theatre 1971–; People's Artist of USSR 1976. *Chief roles:* Siegfried (Swan Lake), Albert (Giselle), Jean de Brienne (Raimonde), Harmodius (Spartacus), Frondoso (Laurensia), Danila (Stone Flower), Romeo (Romeo and Juliet), Prince Desire (Sleeping Beauty), José (Carmen Suite), Karenin (Anna Karenina), Prince (Nutcracker), Illiys (Giselle), Vatslav. *Address:* Viktorenko str., 2/1 apt. 19, 125167 Moscow, Russia (Home). *Telephone:* (095) 157-33-22 (Home).

FADUL, Francisco; Guinea-Bissau politician; fmr adviser to Gen. Ansumane Mane; Prime Minister of Guinea-Bissau 1998–99. *Address:* c/o Office of the Prime Minister, Avenida Unidad Africana, CP 137, Bissau, Guinea-Bissau (Office).

FAECKE, Peter; German journalist and author; b. 3 Nov. 1940, Grunwald; awards include stipend of Villa Massimo, Rome and literature prizes of Lower Saxony, North-Rhine-Westphalia and City of Cologne. *Publications:* Die Brandstifter (novel) 1962, Der Rote Milan (novel) 1965, Postversand (novel) (with Wolf Vostell) 1970, Gemeinsam gegen Abriss: Ein Lesebuch aus Arbeitersiedlungen 1974, Das Unaufhaltsame Glück der Kowalskis 1982, Flug ins Leben 1988, Der Mann mit den besonderen Eigenschaften (novel) 1993, Grabstein für Fritz (documentary film) 1993, Als Elizabeth Arden Neunzehn war (novel) 1994, Eine Liebe zum Land (film script) 1994, Ankunft eines Schüchternen in Himmel (novel) 2000, Das Kreuz des Südens (reports) 2001, Von Überfliessen der Anden, Reportagen aus Peru 2001. *Address:* Mevissenstrasse 16, 50668 Cologne, Germany. *Telephone:* (221) 726207. *Fax:* (221) 723259. *E-mail:* edition@peterfaecke.de (Office); peterfaecke@t-online .de (Home). *Website:* www.peterfaecke.de.

FAGIN, Claire Mintzer, PhD; American professor of nursing; b. 25 Nov. 1926, New York; d. of Harry Fagin and Mae (Slatin) Mintzer; m. Samuel Fagin 1952; two s.; ed Wagner Coll., Teachers' Coll., Columbia Univ. and New York Univ.; Staff Nurse, Sea View Hosp., Staten Island, New York 1947, Clinical Instructor 1947–48; Bellevue Hosp., New York 1948–50; Psychiatric Mental Health Nursing Consultant, Nat. League for Nursing 1951–52; Asst Chief, Psychiatric Nursing Service Clinical Center, NIH 1953–54, Supt 1955; Research Project Co-ordinator, Children's Hosp., Dept of Psychiatry, Washington, DC 1956; Instructor in Psychiatric-Mental Health Nursing, New York

Univ. 1956–58, Asst Prof. 1964–67, Dir Grad. Programs in Psychiatric-Mental Health Nursing 1965–69, Assoc. Prof. 1967–69; Prof. and Chair. Nursing Dept, Herbert H. Lehman Coll. 1969–77; Dir Health Professions Inst., Montefiore Hosp. and Medical Center 1975–77; Dean, School of Nursing, Univ. of Pa, Philadelphia 1977–92, Prof. 1992–96, interim Pres. 1993–94, Dean Emer., Prof. Emer. 1996–; mem. Task Force Jt Cttee on Mental Health of Children 1966–69, Gov.'s Cttee on Children, New York 1971–75, Inst. of Medicine, NAS (Governing Council 1981–83), Comm. on Human Rights 1991–94, American Acad. of Nursing (Governing Council 1976–78), Expert Advisory Panel on Nursing, WHO 1974, Nat. Advisory Mental Health Council, Nat. Inst. of Mental Health 1983–87, Bd of Health Promotion and Disease Prevention 1990–94; Pres. American Orthopsychiatric Asscn 1985; Dir Salomon Inc. 1994–97; mem. Bd. of Dirs. Radian 1994–; Pres. Nat. League for Nursing 1991–93; consultant to many foundations, public and pvt. univs., health care agencies; speaker on radio and TV; Hon. DSc (Lycoming Coll., Cedar Crest Coll., Univ. of Rochester, Medical Coll. of Pa, Univ. of Md, Loyola Univ., Wagner Coll.); Hon. LLD (Pa); Hon. DHumLitt (Hunter Coll., Rush Univ.); numerous awards and distinctions including American Nursing Foundation Nightingale Lamp award 2002. *Publications:* numerous books including Nursing Leadership: Global Strategies (Ed.) 1990 and over 75 articles on nursing and health policy. *Address:* School of Nursing, University of Pennsylvania, 354 Nursing Education Building, Philadelphia, PA 19104-6096; 200 Central Park South, Apartment 12E, New York, NY 10019-1415, USA (Home).

FAGIOLO, Silvio, LLB; Italian diplomatist; b. 15 July 1938, Rome; m. Margret Klauth; two c.; ed Univ. La Sapienza, Rome; joined diplomatic service 1969; foreign missions to Moscow, USSR 1972–76, Detroit, USA 1976–79, Bonn, W Germany 1982–86; Deputy Chief Italian Embassy, Washington, DC 1991–95; Amb. to Germany 2001–; Adviser for European and Security Affairs, Ministry of Foreign Affairs, Head of Cabinet 1997–2000; mem. EU Group that organized Intergovernmental Conf. that led to the Maastricht Treaty; Personal Rep. of Italian Foreign Minister at Intergovernmental Confs. that led to Treaty of Amsterdam 1996, Treaty of Nice 2002; Perm. Rep. to EU 2001–. *Publications:* I gruppi di pressione in URSS 1977, L'operaio americano 1980, La Russia di Gorbaciov 1987, La pace fredda 1998. *Leisure interests:* sports, music. *Address:* Embassy of Italy, Hiroshimastr. 1, 10785 Berlin, Germany (Office). *Telephone:* (30) 254400 (Office). *Fax:* (30) 25440116 (Office). *E-mail:* ambitalia.segr@t-online.de (Office). *Website:* www.Botschaft-Italien.de (Office).

FAHD IBN ABD AL-AZIZ AS SA'UD, King of Saudi Arabia; b. 1921, Riyadh; s. of King Abdul Aziz ibn Saud; Minister of Educ. 1953, of the Interior 1962–75; Second Deputy Prime Minister 1967–75, First Deputy Prime Minister 1975–82, Prime Minister June 1982–; became Crown Prince 1975; succeeded to the throne on the death of his brother 13 June 1982; assumed title 'Servant of the Two Shrines' 1986. *Address:* Royal Diwan, Riyadh, Saudi Arabia.

FAHEY, Hon. John Joseph, AC; Australian politician and lawyer; b. 10 Jan. 1945, New Zealand; s. of Stephen Fahey and Annie Fahey; m. Colleen McGurran 1968; two s. two d.; ed St Anthony's Convent, Picton and Chevalier Coll. Bowral, Sydney Univ. Law Extension; mem. Parl. of NSW 1984–95; Minister for Industrial Relations and Employment and Minister Assisting Premier of NSW 1988–90; Minister for Industrial Relations, Further Educ., Training and Employment, NSW 1990–92; Premier and Treas. of NSW 1992; Premier and Minister for Econ. Devt of NSW 1993–95; Fed. mem. for Macarthur and Minister for Finance 1996–2001, for Admin. 1997–2001; consultant, adviser, dir 2002–; Chair. Sydney 2000 Olympic Bid Co. 1992–93. *Leisure interest:* keen sports follower. *Address:* c/o J P Morgan Australia Ltd, Level 26, Grosvenor Place, 225 George Street, Sydney, NSW (Office); Ashford, 39 Hurlingham Avenue, Burradoo, NSW 2576, Australia (Home). *Telephone:* (2) 9220-1649 (Office). *Fax:* (2) 4861-4113 (Office). *E-mail:* faheyj@bigpond .com (Home).

FAHIM KHAN, Gen. Mohammad; Afghanistan politician and guerrilla leader; ed Kabul Univ.; qualified doctor; joined troops fighting USSR occupation forces 1979–89; joined Northern Alliance (NA), led NA forces into Kabul 1992, Head of Intelligence, Chief of Staff, Leader Sept. 2001–; Vice-Chair. and Minister of Defence Afghan Interim Authority Dec. 2001–June 2002, Afghan Transitional Authority June 2002–. *Address:* Ministry of Defence, Daralaman Wat, Kabul, Afghanistan (Office).

FAHMY, Nabil, BSc, MA; Egyptian diplomatist; m.; two d. one s.; ed American Univ., Cairo; mem. Cabinet of Sec. of Pres. for External Communications 1974; Political Officer Cabinet of Vice-Pres. 1975–76; mem. Cabinet, Ministry of Foreign Affairs 1976–78; Second Sec. Mission to UN for Conf. on Disarmament 1978–82, First Sec. then Counsellor to UN 1986–91; Sr Disarmament Official, Dept for Int. Orgs., Ministry of Foreign Affairs 1991, Counsellor –1995; Amb. to Japan 1997–99, to USA 1999–; mem. UN Sec.-Gen.'s Advisory Bd on Disarmament Matters 1999–. *Publications include:* numerous publs on nuclear proliferation. *Address:* Embassy of Egypt, 3521 International Court, NW, Washington, DC 20008, USA (Office). *Telephone:* (202) 895-5400 (Office). *Fax:* (202) 244-4319 (Office). *E-mail:* embassy@egyptembdc.org (Office). *Website:* www.embassyofegyptwashingtondc.org (Office).

FAHRHOLZ, Bernd, LLB; German banking executive; joined Dresdner Bank as legal adviser 1977, with Domestic Corp. Customer Div. 1985–89, Man. Corp. Finance Div. 1989, later Co-Head, Int. Activities, Sr Gen. Man. 1996, Head of Global Finance, Investment Banking Div. 1997, mem. Bd of Man. Dirs 1998–2003, Chair. 2000–01, also Man. Dir Corp. Centre, Corp. Communications, Econs, Gen. Secr., Group Devt, Group Strategy, Human Resources and Legal Services, CEO 2000–03 (after acquisition of Dresdner Bank by Allianz A.G. forming Allianz-Dresdner A.G.). *Address:* c/o Allianz-Dresdner AG, Königinstrasse 28, 80802 Munich, Germany (Office).

FAHRNI, Fritz, PhD; Swiss business executive and professor of technology management and entrepreneurship; b. 7 Sept. 1942; two d.; ed Swiss Fed. Inst. of Tech. (ETH), Zürich, Ill. Inst. of Tech. Chicago and Harvard Business School; research worker, Ill. Inst. of Tech., NASA 1967–70; research and devt eng production, CIBA-GEIGY 1971–76; Head, Research and Devt Gas Turbine Dept Sulzer Bros. 1976–80, Head, Gas Turbine Dept 1980–82, Head, Weaving Machine Group 1982–88; Pres. and CEO Sulzer Corpn 1988–99; Prof. ETH & HSG for Tech. Man. and Entrepreneurship 2000–; Int. Entrepreneurial Leadership Award, Illinois Inst. of Tech. 2000. *Leisure interests:* sport, reading, music, garden. *Address:* Universität St Gallen, Institut für Technologiemanagement, Unterstrasse 22, 9000 St Gallen (Office); ETH – Swiss Federal Institute of Technology, D-BEPR, 8032 Zurich (Office); Guggerveg 17, 8702 Zollikon, Switzerland (Home). *Telephone:* (71) 2282431 (Office); (1) 3902595 (Home). *Fax:* (71) 2282455 (Office). *E-mail:* fritz.fahrni@ unisg.ch (Office).

FAILLARD, Hans, DR.PHIL., DIP.CHEM.; German professor of biochemistry; b. 2 April 1924, Cologne; s. of Hermann Faillard and Elisabeth Faillard (née Kühn); m. 1st Maria Scholl 1952 (died 1989); one s.; m. 2nd Gisela Gaertner 1993; ed Univ. of Cologne; Ordinary Prof. of Physiological Chem., Ruhr Univ., Bochum 1964–73, Rector 1969–72; Vice-Pres. West German Rectors' Conf. 1970–76; Ordinary Prof. of Biochem., Univ. of the Saarland, Saarbrücken 1973, Prof. Emer. 1992–, Pres. of Univ. 1973–79; Chair. Cttee for Int. Contacts of the Alexander von Humboldt Foundation 1973–92; mem. Cen. Cttee German Conf. of Ministers for Cultural Affairs 1978–92; mem. Cttee for Research, German Rectors' Conf. 1980–92, Chair. Advisory Body 1994–96; Hochhaus Award, Univ. of Cologne; medals from Hebrew Univ., Israel and Seoul Nat. Univ., Korea. *Publications:* more than 80 publs in the field of glycoproteins and more than 30 papers on educational topics. *Address:* Universität des Saarlandes, 66123 Saarbrücken (Office); Richard-Wagner Strasse 87, 66125 Saarbrücken; 35 An der Wallburg, 51427 Bensberg-Refrath, Germany (Home). *Telephone:* (681) 3022440 (Office); (6897) 761660; (2204) 63437. *Fax:* (681) 3022476 (Office); (2204) 63437 (Home). *E-mail:* pb13hb@r.z.uni-sb.de (Office).

FAINI, Riccardo, PhD; Italian economist and international organization official; b. 12 April 1951, Lausanne, Switzerland; m. Lauri Faini; three s.; ed Laurea Università Bocconi, M.I.T.; fmr. teacher Univ. of Essex, U.K., Univ. of Venezia, Bologna Center of Johns Hopkins University, U.S.A.; Prof. of Econs Univ. of Brescia; Researcher, World Bank 1985–88; Exec. Dir IMF 1998–2000; Dir.-Gen. Ministry of the Economy and Finance 2000–; Research Fellow Human Resources and Int. Trade Programs, Centre for Econ. and Policy Research; Research Dir Centro Studi Luca d'Agliano. *Publications:* Non-Traded Inputs and Increasing Returns 1999, Migration: The Controversy of the Evidence 1999. *Leisure interests:* Latin American literature, tennis. *Address:* Ministry of the Economy and Finance, Viale Europa 242, 00144 Rome, Italy. *Telephone:* (06) 59971 (Office). *Fax:* (06) 5910993 (Office). *E-mail:* riccardo.faini@tesoro.it (Office).

FAINSILBER, Adrien, D.P.L.G.; French architect and urban designer; b. 15 June 1932, Le Nouvion, France; s. of Fanny Moscovici and Sigismond Fainsilber; m. Julia Berg 1961; two s. one d.; ed Ecole Nationale Supérieure des Beaux Arts; architect Univ. of Villetaneuse 1969–70, Univ. of Tech. of Compiègne 1973, Evry Hosp. 1980, La Géode, Parc de la Villette, Paris 1984, Cité of Science and Industry, Paris 1985, Water Treatment Plant, Valenton 1987, Museum of Beaux Arts, Clermont-Ferrand 1992, Town Hall, La Flèche 1994, HQ Unedic, Paris 1994, master plan and housing for Zac Richter, Port Marianne, Montpellier 1995, Montsouris Mutual Inst. Psychiatric Centre for Adolescents, Paris 1996, Museum of Modern and Contemporary Art, Strasbourg 1997, Children's Hosp., Purpan, Toulouse 1998, Courthouse Avignon 2000, Municipal Library, Marseille 2003; mem. Int. Acad. of Architecture; Bronze Medal Soc. d'Encouragement à l'Art et à l'Industrie 1973, Silver Medal Acad. of Architecture 1986, Chevalier, Légion d'honneur 1987, U.I.A. Prix Auguste Perret 1990, Officier des Arts et des Lettres 1997. *Publications:* La Virtualité de l'Espace: Projets et Architecture 1962–1988, Adrien Fainsilber & Associés 1986–2002. *Leisure interests:* swimming, windsurfing, travel. *Address:* 7 rue Salvador Allende, 92000 Nanterre (Office); 9 cité de l'Alma, 75007 Paris, France (Home). *Telephone:* 1-55-69-36-20 (Office); 1-45-51-34-33 (Home). *Fax:* 1-55-69-36-21 (Office). *E-mail:* agence@fainsilber.com (Office). *Website:* www.fainsilber.com (Office).

FAIRCLOUGH, Anthony John, CMG, MA, FRSA; British environmental consultant; b. 30 Aug. 1924, Birmingham; s. of Wilfrid Fairclough and Lillian Anne Fairclough (née Townshend); m. Patricia Monks 1957; two s.; ed St Philip's Grammar School, Birmingham and St Catharine's Coll., Cambridge; Ministry of Aircraft Production and Ministry of Supply 1944–48; Colonial Office 1948–64; Sec. Nyasaland Comm. of Inquiry 1959; Private Sec. to Minister of State for Commonwealth Relations and for the Colonies 1963–64; Head, Pacific and Indian Ocean Dept Commonwealth Office 1964–68; Head, W Indian Dept FCO 1968–70; Head, New Towns 1 Div. Dept of Environment 1970–72, Under-Sec., Head of Planning, Minerals and Countryside Directorate 1973–74; Dir Cen. Unit on Environmental Pollution 1974–78; Dir Int. Transport, Dept of Transport 1978–81; Dir for the Environment, Comm. of the EC 1981–85; Acting Dir-Gen. for the Environment, Consumer Protection and Nuclear Safety, Comm. of the European Communities 1985–86, Deputy Dir-Gen. for Devt, 1986–89, Special Adviser 1989–94, Hon. Dir-Gen. European Comm. 1989–; Dir (later Sr Adviser) Environmental Resources Man. 1989–97; Capacity 21 Adviser UNDP 1992–. *Leisure interests:* travel, gardening, reading, photography. *Address:* 6 Cumberland Road, Kew, Richmond, Surrey, TW9 3HQ, England (Home); Apt. 12, Résidence Balderic, 32 Quai aux Briques, 1000 Brussels, Belgium. *Telephone:* (20) 8940-6999 (England). *Fax:* (20) 8940-3758 (England).

FAIRCLOUGH, Sir John (Whitaker), Kt, BSc, FIEE, FREng, FRSA; British engineer; b. 23 Aug. 1930, Thirsk; s. of Harold Whitaker and Elsinora Fairclough; m.1st Margaret A. Harvey 1954 (died 1996); two s. one d.; m. 2nd Karen Jefferson 2000; ed Thirsk Grammar School and Manchester Univ.; Ferranti Ltd, UK and Ferranti Electric, USA 1954–57; Project Eng IBM Poughkeepsie 1957–59; Project Man. IBM UK Labs. Ltd 1959–64, Lab. Dir 1964–68; Dir of Data Processing for Marketing and Service, IBM UK 1968–70, Lucas Industries; Lab. Dir IBM Lab. Raleigh, NC 1970–72; Vice-Pres. Communications Systems, IBM Corpn 1972–74; Chair. IBM UK Labs. Ltd 1974–82; Dir Mfg & Devt and Chair. IBM UK Labs. Ltd 1982–86; Chief Scientific Adviser, Cabinet Office 1986–90; Deputy Chair. Council Southampton Univ. 1996–2001; Dir (non-exec.) Oxford Instruments Group PLC 1990–98, N. M. Rothschild & Sons Ltd 1990–98, Infolink 1991–93, DSC (Europe) 1992–98, Lucas Industries 1992–96, Psion PLC 1995–2000, Southampton Innovation Ltd 1996–; Chair. Centre for the Exploration of Science and Tech. 1990–95, Rothschild Ventures Ltd 1990–99, Eng Council 1990–96, Smart Chemical Co. PLC 1998–, Opsys PLC 1998–; mem. Advisory Council on Science and Tech.; 1989–; Fellow, British Computer Soc., Nat. Acad. of Eng; Hon. FIMechE 1996; Hon. FIEE 1996; Hon. FICE; Hon. Fellow Portsmouth Polytechnic; Hon. DSc (Southampton) 1983, (Cranfield) 1987, (Manchester) 1988, (Aston) 1990, (Cen. London Polytechnic) 1991, (City Univ.) 1992; Hon. DTech (Loughborough) 1990; Gold Medal, Inst. of Production Engineers 1989, Gold Medal Award of Merit, Co. of Carmen 1995, Pres.'s Award, Eng Council 1996. *Leisure interests:* woodwork, gardening. *Address:* 3 Clockhouse Close, London, SW19 5NT, England (Home). *Telephone:* (20) 8947-5652. *E-mail:* john.fairclough@btinternet.com (Home).

FAIREY, Michael Edward, A.C.I.B.; British banker; b. 17 June 1948, Louth, Lincs.; s. of Douglas Fairey and Marjorie Fairey; m. Patricia Ann Dolby 1973; two s.; ed King Edward VI Grammar School; Asst Dir, Watford Group, Barclays Bank 1967–86, Operations Dir Barclaycard 1986–88, Exec. Dir Barclays Card Services 1988–92; Dir Retail Credit and Group Credit Dir, TSB Group 1992, Group Dir Credit Operations 1993–96, Information Tech. and Operations Dir 1996–97, Group Dir, Cen. Services, Lloyds TSB Group 1997–98, Deputy Group Chief Exec. 1998–. *Leisure interests:* tennis, opera, football. *Address:* Lloyds TSB Group PLC, 25 Gresham Street, London, EC2V 7HN (Office); Churchfields House, Hitchin Road, Codicote, Herts., SG4 8TH, England (Home). *Telephone:* (20) 7356-1410 (Office); (1438) 821710 (Home). *Fax:* (20) 7356-2080 (Office); (1438) 821079 (Home). *E-mail:* mike.fairey@lloydstsb.co.uk (Office).

FAIRWEATHER, Sir Patrick (Stanislaus), KCMG; British diplomatist; b. 17 June 1936; s. of John George Fairweather and Dorothy Jane Fairweather (née Boanus); m. Maria Merica 1962; two d.; ed Ottershaw School, Surrey and Trinity Coll. Cambridge; entered FCO 1965; served Rome 1966–69, Paris 1970–73, Vientiane 1975–76, First Sec., UK Representation to EEC, Brussels 1976–78; Amb. to Angola 1985–87; Asst Under-Sec. of State, FCO 1987–90, Deputy Under-Sec. of State 1990–92; Amb. to Italy and (non-resident) to Albania 1992–96; retd from HM Diplomatic Service 1996; Sr Adviser, Schroders 1996–; Dir The Butrint Foundation 1997–. *Leisure interests:* travel, gardening, photography, sailing. *Address:* c/o The Butrint Foundation, 14 St James's Place, London, SW1A 1NP, England.

FAITHFULL, Marianne; British popular singer; b. 29 Dec. 1947, Ormskirk, Lancs.; d. of Glynn Faithfull and Eva Faithfull; m. 1st John Dunbar; one s.; m. 2nd Ben Brierley; m. 3rd Giorgio della Terza; made first recording (As Tears Go By) aged 17; performed in The Threepenny Opera, Gate Theatre, Dublin 1992. *Albums include:* Broken English 1979, Strange Weather 1987, 20th Century Blues (Kurt Weill songs) 1996. *Publication:* Faithfull (autobiog.) 1994, Marian Faithfull Diaries 2002. *Address:* c/o The Coalition Group Ltd, 12 Barley Mow Passage, London, W4 4PH, England. *Telephone:* (20) 8987-0123. *Fax:* (20) 8987-0345. *Website:* pithuit.free.fr/FAITHFULL (Office).

FAIVRE d'ARCIER, Bernard, LèsL; French civil servant; b. 12 July 1944, Albertville; s. of Guy Faivre d'Arcier and Geneviève Teilhard de Chazelles; m. 1st Sylvie Dumont 1966; one s.; m. 2nd Madeleine Lévy 1991; ed Hautes études commerciales, Inst. d'études politiques and Ecole nationale d'administration; Civil Admin. Ministry of Culture 1972–79; Dir Festival d'Avignon 1979–84, Artistic Dir 1992–2003; Tech. Adviser to the Prime Minister's Cabinet 1984–86; Pres. la SEPT (TV Channel) 1986; Consultant, UNESCO 1987–88; Adviser to the Pres. of the Nat. Ass. 1988; Head of Dept of Theatre, Ministry of Educ. and Culture 1992–; Dir Nat. Centre for Theatre 1992–; Commdr des Arts et des Lettres, Officier, Ordre du Mérite, Chevalier, Légion d'honneur. *Leisure interests:* art, theatre. *Address:* 6 rue Saint-Bon, 75004 Paris, France. *Telephone:* 1-44-61-84-84 (Paris) (Office); 1-42-72-84-38 (Paris).

FAIZULLAEV, Alisher Omonullaevich, PhD; Uzbekistan diplomatist and social scientist; b. 10 Jan. 1957, Tashkent; s. of Omonulla Faizulaev and Nasiba Ashrapkhanova; m. Shakhnoz Faizullaeva; two s. two d.; ed Tashkent State Univ. and Inst. of Psychology, USSR Acad. of Sciences, Moscow; lecturer, Uzbekistan Acad. of Sciences, Tashkent 1979–80, Sr Lecturer 1983–86; Visiting Fellow Inst. of Psychology, USSR Acad. of Sciences 1986–87; Sr Lecturer, Tashkent State Univ. 1987–88; Head of Dept, Exec. Training Inst., Tashkent 1988–91; Intern, City Council of San Diego, CA 1989; Head of Dept, Inst. of Political Sciences and Man., Tashkent 1991–92; Distinguished Visiting Scholar, Western Washington Univ., Bellingham, USA 1992; Dir Inst. of Man., Univ. of World Econ. and Diplomacy, Tashkent 1992–93; Consultant on Political Affairs, then Chief Consultant on Int. Affairs and Foreign Econ. Relations, Office of the Pres. of Uzbekistan 1993–94; Deputy Minister of Foreign Affairs 1994–95; Amb. to Belgium and Head of Missions to EU and Euro-Atlantic Partnership Council/NATO 1995–98, concurrently Amb. to the Netherlands and Luxembourg with residence in Brussels 1997–98; State Adviser to the Pres. of Uzbekistan on Int. Affairs and Foreign Econ. Relations 1998–99; First Deputy Minister of Foreign Affairs Feb.–Dec. 1999; Amb. to UK 1999–; USSR Young Social Scientists Prize 1987. *Publications:* Motivational Self-Regulation of Personality (in Russian) 1987, Human Being, Politics, Management (in Russian and Uzbek) 1995; several papers on behavioural, social and political sciences in learned journals. *Leisure interests:* tennis, fencing. *Address:* Embassy of Uzbekistan, 41 Holland Park, London, W11 3RP, England (Office). *Telephone:* (20) 7229-7679 (Office). *Fax:* (20) 7229-7029 (Office). *E-mail:* info@uzbekistanembassy.uk.net (Office). *Website:* www.uzbekistanembassy.uk.net (Office).

FAKHFAKH, Mokhtar, BS; Tunisian banker; b. 10 Aug. 1930, Sfax; s. of Ahmed B. Abdessalem Fakhfakh and Fatouma Hamouda; m. Samira Fakhfakh; one s. one d.; ed law studies; Pres. and Gen. Man. Soc. Hotelière et Touristique de Tunisie 1961–67; Dir of Commerce, Ministry of Finance and Commerce 1967–69; Pres. and Gen. Man. Banque du Sud 1969–71; Gen. Man. Banque de Développement Economique de Tunisie 1971–78; Pres. and Gen. Man. Cie Financière Immobilière et Touristique de Tunisie 1978–80, Banque Int. Arabe de Tunisie 1980, now Pres.; African Banker of Year 1994; Commdr Ordre de la République. *Address:* Banque International Arabe de Tunisie, 70–72 Avenue Habib Bourguiba, B.P. 520, 1080 Tunis, Tunisia. *Telephone:* (1) 340-733. *Fax:* (1) 340-680. *E-mail:* abderrazak.lahiani@biat.com.tn (Office). *Website:* www.biat.com.tn (Office).

FAKHR, Maj.-Gen. Ahmed Ismail, MA, MBA; Egyptian national security expert and strategic analyst; b. 5 April 1931, Cairo; m. Bahiga Bahgat Helmy 1956; two s.; ed Nat. Defence Coll. Cairo, air defence studies in Moscow, Royal Coll. of Defence Studies, London and Nat. Defence Univ. Washington, DC; Dir Nat. Defence Coll. Cairo 1980–82, Nasser Higher Mil. Acad. Cairo 1982–84; Ed.-in-Chief, Defence Magazine, Al-Ahram Assen Cairo 1985; Adviser on Foreign Aid to Prime Minister 1986–89; Rep. of UNIMEG (pvt. business consortium), Moscow 1990; now Dir Nat. Center for Middle East Studies and elected Chair. of local people's council, Cairo Governate; mem. Egyptian del. to Madrid Peace Conf. 1992; other government appts.; Mil. Medal and other decorations. *Publications:* Defence of Egypt (classified) 1981, Arms Control Series 1992, Egypt and the 21st Century 1994, Conflict: Prevention and Resolution 1994, The Future of the Military in Egypt 1995, U.S.-Egyptian Relations 1995, The Middle East: Technological Edge 1995. *Leisure interests:* reading on int. affairs and nat. security, classical music, ballet. *Address:* National Center for Middle East Studies, 1 Kasr El Nil Street, 2nd Floor, Cairo; 27 Dr. Khalil Abdel Khalek Street, Heliopolis, Cairo, Egypt. *Telephone:* 771125; 770041; 770042 (Office); 2454551 (Home). *Fax:* 770063.

FALCAM, Leo A.; Micronesian politician; fmr Vice-Pres. of Micronesia, Pres. May 1999–. *Address:* Office of the President, P.O. Box PS-53, Palikir, Pohnpei, Eastern Caroline Islands, FM 96941, Micronesia (Office). *Telephone:* 320-2228 (Office). *Fax:* 320-2785 (Office).

FALCONER OF THOROTON, Baron (Life Peer), cr. 1997, of Thoroton in the County of Nottinghamshire; **Charles Leslie Falconer,** QC; British lawyer and politician; b. 19 Nov. 1951; s. of the late John Falconer and Anne Falconer; m. Marianna Hildyard 1985; three s. one d.; ed Trinity Coll., Glenalmond, Queen's Coll., Cambridge; called to the Bar 1974, took silk 1991; Solicitor-Gen. 1997–98; Minister of State Cabinet Office 1998–2001; Minister with responsibility for Millennium Dome 1998–2001; Minister of State for Housing and Planning 2001, for the Criminal Justice System 2002–; Labour. *Address:* Home Office, 50 Queen Anne's Gate, London, SW1H 9AT, England (Office). *Telephone:* (20) 7273-4608 (Office). *Fax:* (20) 7273-3094 (Office).

FALDO, Nick, MBE; British golfer; b. 18 July 1957, Welwyn Garden City; m. 1st Melanie Faldo (divorced); m. 2nd Gill Faldo 1986 (divorced); one s. two d.; m. 3rd Valerie Bercher; won England Boys' Int. 1974, England Youth Int. 1975, Herts. Co. Championship, Berkshire Trophy, Scrutton Jug, S. African Golf Union Special Stroke Championship, was Co. Champion of Champions, mem. GB Commonwealth team, Sr England Int. 1975–; became professional 1976; won Skol Lager Int., Rookie of the Year (best British newcomer) 1977, Colgate PGA Championship 1978, 1980, 1981, five titles on PGA European tour, Golf Writers' Asscn Trophy and Harry Vardon Trophy 1983, Open Championship, Muirfield 1987, French Open and Volvo Masters, Valderrama 1988, Masters, Augusta, Ga, USA 1989, French Open 1989, U.S. Masters 1989, 1990, 1996, Open Championship, St Andrew's 1990, Irish Open 1991,

1992, 1993, Open Championship, Muirfield 1992, Toyota World Match Play Championship 1992, Scandinavian Masters 1992, European Open 1992, Johnnie Walker World Championship 1992, (7 tournament victories 1992), Alfred Dunhill Belgian Open 1994, Doral Ryder Open, USA 1995; World No. 1 (Sony Ranking) 1992–94, Johnnie Walker Asian Classic 1993, Los Angeles Open, USA 1997, World Cup 1998; best finish 2002 PGA Tour, 5th in US Open. *Publications:* In Search of Perfection (with Bruce Critchley) 1995, Faldo – A Swing for Life 1995. *Leisure interests:* fly fishing, helicopter flying, golf course design. *E-mail:* nfdo@faldodesign.com.

FALIK, Yuri Aleksandrovich; Russian composer and conductor; b. 30 July 1936, Odessa; s. of Aleksander Yefimovich Falik and Yevgeniya Mikhailovna Bochko; m. Valentina Alexandrovna Papkova; one s. one d.; ed Odessa Specialized School, Leningrad State Conservatory as cellist (teachers A. Shtrimer and M. Rostropovich), as composer (B. Arapov); teacher Leningrad (now St Petersburg) Conservatory 1965–88, Prof. of Composition and Instrumentation 1988–; toured as conductor with orchestras in Russia and USA; First Prize Int. Cellists Competition Helsinki 1962; Merited Worker of Arts of Russia 1981. *Compositions:* for musical theatre Orestea (choreographic tragedy) 1968, Scapin Antics (opera) 1981; for symphony orchestra: Symphony No. 1 1963, No. 2 (Kaddish) 1993, Light Symphony 1971, Concertos 1967, 1977, Mass over Igor Stravinsky 1975, Symphonietta for strings 1984; for instruments with orchestra: Concertino for oboe 1961, Violin Concerto 1971, Chamber Concerto for three flutes 1983, Concertino for bassoon 1987, Concerto della Passione for cello 1988; vocal-symphony works: Five Poems by Anna Akhmatova for soprano and chamber orchestra 1978, Ringaday for mezzo-soprano and orchestra 1986, Polly and Dinosaurs (musical fairy-tale over Geraldine Freund) 1989, Mass 1996; works for choir a cappella, including Liturgy Chants 1992; chamber ensembles, including 8 Quartets 1955–2001; romances, instrumental pieces; 4 Concertos for chorus a capella 1979–98, Elegies: Concerto for soprano solo and chorus a capella 2001, Lyrical Concertino for cello and orchestra 2002. *Address:* Finlyandsky prospekt 1, Apt. 54, 194044 St Petersburg, Russia. *Telephone:* (812) 542-63-06 (Home). *Fax:* (812) 311-58-11 (Home). *E-mail:* afalik2000@mail.ru (Home).

FALISE, Michel, DenD, DèsScEcon; French economist and university professor; b. 11 March 1931, Marcinelle; s. of A. Falise and L. Falise; m. Marie-Françoise de Gheldere 1957; three s. three d.; ed Facultés Universitaires de Namur, Univ. Catholique de Louvain, Harvard Univ., USA; Econ. Adviser, Banque de Bruxelles 1958–60; Prof., Univ. Catholique de Lille 1960, Dean., Faculty of Social Sciences 1965–79, Pres.-Rector 1979–91, Pres. Conseil Supérieur 1991–95; Deputy Mayor of Lille 1995–2002, Pres. délégué du Conseil Communal de Concertation de la Ville de Lille 1996–; Consultant to OECD, WHO, EC and French Govt offices; Pres. Int. Fed. of Catholic Univs 1980–91, Féd. des Universités Catholiques Européennes 1991–97, Habitat et Humanisme 1994–2001; mem. Asscn Int. des Universités 1990–2000, Nat. Observatory of Poverty and Exclusion 1999–2001; Dr hc (Leuven, Belgium), (Sacred Heart, USA), (Catholique de Rio de Janeiro); Prix Asscn Française des Sciences Econs, Grand Prix de la Société Industrielle (Lille); Officier, Légion d'honneur, Chevalier des Palmes académiques, Commdr Ordre de la Couronne (Belgium), Officier de l'Ordre de Léopold (Belgium). *Publications:* La demande de monnaie 1960, L'équilibre macro-économique 1976, Une pratique chrétienne de l'économie 1985, Repères pour une éthique d'entreprise 1992, Economie et foi 1993. *Address:* Mairie de Lille, P.O.B. 667, 59033 Lille Cédex (Office); 9 allée Raoul Dufy, 59510 Hem, France. *Telephone:* (3) 20-75-65-17.

FALL, Sir Brian (James Proetel), GCVO, KCMG, MA, LLM; British diplomatist (retd); b. 13 Dec. 1937; s. of John William Fall and Edith Juliette Fall (née Proetel); m. Delmar Alexandra Roos 1962; three d.; ed St Paul's School, Magdalen Coll. Oxford, Univ. of Michigan Law School, USA; joined HM Foreign (now Diplomatic) Service 1962, UN Dept, Foreign Office 1963, Moscow 1965, Geneva 1968, Civil Service Coll. 1970, Eastern European and Soviet Dept and Western Orgs Dept, Foreign Office 1971, New York 1975, Harvard Univ. Center for Int. Affairs 1976, Counsellor Moscow 1977–79, Head of Energy, Science and Space Dept, FCO 1979–80, Head of Eastern European and Soviet Dept, FCO 1980–81, Prin. Pvt. Sec. to Sec. of State for Foreign and Commonwealth Affairs 1981–84, Dir Cabinet Sec.-Gen. of NATO 1984–86, Asst Under-Sec. of State (Defence), FCO 1986–88, Minister, Washington 1988–89, High Commr in Canada 1989–92; Amb. to Russia (also accred to several mems of CIS) 1992–95; Prin. Lady Margaret Hall, Oxford 1995–2002; Chair. MC Russian Market Fund 1996–2002; Adviser, Rio Tinto 1996–; Gov. St Mary's School, Calne 1996–; British Govt Special Rep. for Georgia 2002–; Hon. LLD (York Univ., Toronto) 2002. *Leisure interests:* reading, walking, travel. *Address:* 2 St Helena Terrace, Richmond, Surrey, TW9 1NR, England (Home).

FALL, Cheikh Ibrahima, M.SC.(ECON.), MBA; Senegalese international civil servant and banker; b. 1 Oct. 1947, Louga; m. Marième Diouma Faye 1972; two s. one d.; financial analyst, Operations Dept Banque Ouest-Africaine de Développement (BOAD) 1978–79, Rural Devt and Infrastructural Operations Dept 1979–81, Officer-in-Charge of Dept 1981. Dir of Dept 1981–85, Dir Loans and Equity Dept 1985–86; Dir Office of Pres. of African Devt Bank (ADB) 1986–92, Dir Co. Programmes, S. Region Dept 1992–95, Officer-in-Charge of Admin. and Gen. Services and ADB restructuring exercise 1995–96, Sec.-Gen. ADB 1996–99; Vice-Pres. and Corp. Sec. World Bank (IBRD) 1999–. *Leisure interests:* music, golf, reading. *Address:* World Bank, 1818 H Street, NW, Room MC 12-205, Washington, DC 20433, USA. *Telephone:* (202) 473-9212 (Office). *Fax:* (202) 522-1640 (Office). *E-mail:* cfall@worldbank.org (Office).

FALL, Ibrahima, LLM, PhD; Senegalese politician and educator; b. 1942, Tivaouane, Thies; s. of Momar Khoudia Fall and Seynabou (Diakhate) Fall; m. Déguène Fall; five c.; ed Univ. of Dakar, Inst. of Political Science, Paris, Faculty of Law, Univ. of Paris, Acad. of Int. Law, The Hague, Netherlands; Prof. of Int. Law and Int. Relations, Dean of Faculty of Law, Cheikh Anta Diop Univ., Dakar 1975–81; Minister of Higher Educ. 1983–84, of Foreign Affairs 1984–90; Adviser, Supreme Court of Senegal; Asst Sec.-Gen. for Human Rights and Dir UN Centre for Human Rights, Geneva 1992–97; Sec.-Gen. UN World Conf. on Human Rights, Vienna 1993; Asst Gen. Sec. UN Dept of Political Affairs 1997–2000; Special Envoy of UN Sec.-Gen. to Côte d'Ivoire 2000–02; Special Rep. and Head of West Africa Office March 2002–; Consultant, UNESCO; Founding-mem. and Hon. Pres. Senegalese Asscn for African Unity; mem. African Council for Higher Educ. *Publications:* articles in professional journals. *Address:* West African Office, United Nations, United Nations Plaza, New York, NY 10017, USA; Sicap Fenêtre Mermoz, Dakar, Senegal (Home).

FALLACI, Oriana; Italian writer and journalist; b. 29 June 1930, Florence; d. of Edoardo and Tosca (Cantini) Fallaci; ed Liceo Classico 'Galileo Galilei', Florence, Univ. of Medicine, Florence; entered journalism 1946, special corresp. 1950, war corresp. 1967– (Viet Nam, Indo-Pakistan war, Middle East, insurrections in S America and in Asia, Gulf War); political interviews with numerous heads of state and world leaders; Hon. DLitt (Columbia Coll., Chicago); St Vincent Prize for Journalism (twice), Bancarella Prize for Best Seller 1991, Hemingway Prize for Literature, Grand Prix Littéraire de la ville d'Antibes, numerous other prizes. *Publications:* The Useless Sex 1961, The Egotists 1963, If the Sun Dies 1965, Nothing and So Be It 1969, Interview with History 1974; novels: Penelope at War 1962, Letter to a Child Never Born 1975, A Man 1979 (Premio Viareggio 1979), Inshallah (Hemingway Prize, Grand Prix de la ville d'Antibes) 1990; The Rage and the Pride (pamphlet) 2001; numerous articles in Life, Look, New York Times magazines, Washington Post, New Republic, The Times, etc. and in Europe, Asia and South America. *Address:* c/o Rizzoli Corporation, 31 West 57th Street, New York, NY 10019, USA; RCS Rizzoli Libri, Via Mecenate 91, 20138 Milan, Italy (Office). *Telephone:* (212) 308-2000 (USA). *Fax:* (212) 308-4308 (USA) (Office).

FÄLLDIN, (Nils Olof) Thorbjörn; Swedish politician and farmer; b. 24 April 1926, Högsjö; s. of Nils Johan Fälldin and Hulda Katarina Fälldin (née Olsson); m. Rut Oberg 1956; two s. one d.; ed secondary school; mem., Second Chamber of Parl. 1958–64, First Chamber 1967–70; mem. Riksdag (Parl.) 1971–85; Chair. Centre Party 1971–85; Prime Minister 1976–78, 1979–82; Chair. Bd Nordic Museum 1986–96, Swedish Telecom/Telia 1988–95, Föreningen Norden 1988–2000, Föreningsbanken AB 1992–97; Hon. PhD (Mitthogskrlan) 2001; The King's Medal (12th Class with Chain) 1986, Grand Cross, Order of the White Rose (Finland) 1990, Grand Officer, Royal Norwegian Order of Merit 1999. *Leisure interests:* fishing, athletics. *Address:* Ås, 870 16 Ramvik, Sweden (Home). *Telephone:* (612) 43-097 (Home).

FALLON, Ivan Gregory, FRSA; Irish journalist; b. 26 June 1944; s. of Padraic Fallon and Dorothea Maher; m. 1st Susan Mary Lurring 1967 (divorced 1997); one s. two d.; m. 2nd Elizabeth Rees-Jones 1997; ed St Peter's Coll., Wexford, Trinity Coll. Dublin; on staff of Irish Times 1964–66, Thomson Prov. Newspapers 1966–67, Daily Mirror 1967–68, Sunday Telegraph 1968–70; Deputy City Ed., Sunday Express 1970–71, Sunday Telegraph 1971–84, City Ed. 1979–84; Deputy Ed. Sunday Times 1984–94; Group Editorial Dir, Argus Group, SA 1994–; Chief Exec. Ind. Newspapers Holdings Ltd, South Africa 1997–; Exec. Chair. iTouch PLC 2000–; mem. Council, Univ. of Buckingham 1982–, Council of Govs, United Medical and Dental Schools of Guy's and St Thomas' Hosps 1985–94; Trustee Project Trust 1984–94, Generation Trust, Guy's Hosp. 1985–; Dir N. Brown Holdings 1994–. *Publications:* DeLorean: The Rise and Fall of a Dream-maker (with James L. Srodes) 1983, Takeovers 1987, The Brothers: The Rise of Saatchi and Saatchi 1988, Billionaire: The Life and Times of Sir James Goldsmith 1991, The Player: The Life of Tony O'Reilly 1994. *Leisure interests:* tennis, walking. *Address:* Prospect House, Klein Constantia Road, Constantia, Cape Town, South Africa. *Telephone:* (11) 6332115. *Fax:* (11) 8342881.

FALOTTI, Pier Carlo; business executive; fmrly head of European, Middle East and African operations, Digital Equipment; fmrly head of non-USA operations A.T.&T.; Sr Vice-Pres. Oracle 1996–.

FÄLTHAMMAR, Carl-Gunne, PhD; Swedish professor of physics; b. 4 Dec. 1931, Markaryd; s. of Oskar Fälthammar and Ingeborg Fälthammar; m. Ann-Marie Sjunnesson 1957; one s. one d.; ed Royal Inst. of Tech. (KTH), Stockholm; Asst Prof. KTH 1966–69, Assoc. Prof. 1969–75, Chair. Dept of Plasma Physics 1967–97, Prof. of Plasma Physics 1975–; mem. Swedish Nat. Cttee for Radio Science 1970–96, Swedish Nat. Cttee for Geodesy and Geophysics 1973–96; Chair. Swedish Geophysical Soc. 1978–80; mem. Royal Swedish Acad. of Sciences, Int. Acad. of Astronautics, Acad. Europaea; other professional affiliations; Hon. Ph.D. (Oulu) 1989; Basic Sciences Award, Int. Acad. of Astronautics 1996, Golden Badge Award, European Geophysical Union 1996, Hannes Alfvén Medal, European Geophysical Soc. 1998. *Publications:* Cosmical Electrodynamics (with H. Alfvén) 1963, Magnetospheric Physics (with B. Hultqvist) 1990; papers in plasma physics and space physics. *Address:* Division of Plasma Physics, Alfvén Laboratory, The Royal Institute of Technology, 10044 Stockholm, Sweden. *Telephone:* (8) 790-76-85. *Fax:* (8) 24-54-31.

FALTLHAUSER, Kurt, BEcons, Dr rer. pol; German politician; b. 13 Sept. 1940, Munich; m.; two c.; ed Univ. of Munich; leader, Gen. Student Council, Univ. of Munich 1964–65; mem. Bavarian Landtag 1974–80, 1998–; Minister of State and Head, Bavarian State Chancellery 1995–98, State Minister of Finance Oct. 1998–; mem. Bundestag 1980–95; Chair. Finance and Budget Working Party, Christian Socialist Union (CSU); Financial Spokesman CDU/CSU Parl. Group., also Deputy Chair.; Parl. State Sec. to the Fed. Minister of Finance; lecturer and Hon. Prof. Faculty of Econs Univ. of Munich. *Address:* P.O. Box 22 00 03, 80535 Munich, Germany (Office). *Telephone:* (89) 230622 (Office). *Fax:* (89) 283096 (Office). *E-mail:* poststelle@stmf.bayern.de.

FALWELL, Jerry L., BA; American ecclesiastic; b. 11 Aug. 1933, Lynchburg, Va; s. of Cary H. Falwell and Helen V. Beasley; m. Macel Pate 1958; two s. and one d.; ed Baptist Bible Coll., Springfield, Missouri; ordained American Baptist minister; Founder and Pastor Thomas Road Baptist Church, Lynchburg 1956–, now Sr Pastor; Founder and Pres. Moral Majority Inc. (now Liberty Fed.) 1979–89, Liberty Broadcasting Network 1985–; host TV show Old Time Gospel Hour (nat. syndication); public lecturer; Founder Liberty Univ., Lynchburg 1971; Hon. DD (Tennessee Temple Theological Seminary); Hon. DLitt (California Grad. School of Theology); Hon. LLD (Central Univ., Seoul, Korea); Clergyman of the Year Award (Religious Heritage) 1979, Jabotinsky Centennial Medal, Israel 1980 and numerous other awards. *Publications:* Church Aflame (co-author) 1971, Capturing a Town for Christ (co-author) 1973, Listen, America! 1980, The Fundamentalist Phenomenon 1981, Finding Inner Peace and Strength 1982, When It Hurts Too Much to Cry 1984, Wisdom for Living 1984, Stepping Out on Faith 1984, If I Should Die Before I Wake 1986, Strength For the Journey (autobiog.) 1987, The New American Family 1992. *Address:* Liberty University, 1971 University Boulevard, Lynchburg, VA 24502-2269; P.O. Box 368, Madison Heights, VA 24572, USA.

FALZON, Michael, BArch; Maltese politician and architect; b. 17 Aug. 1945, Gzira; m. Mary Anne Aquilina; one s.; ed the Lyceum and Univ. of Malta; fmrly in practice as architect; mem. Nat. Exec. Nationalist Party 1975; Sec. of Information of the Party; Ed. The Democrat (weekly paper) 1975; MP 1976–96; Shadow Minister for Information and Broadcasting 1976–81; for Industry 1981–87; Minister for Devt of Infrastructure 1987–92, for Environment 1992–94, for Educ. and Human Resources 1994–96; Ed. The People and People on Sunday newspapers 1997–98; Chair. Water Services Corpn 1998–. *Address:* Water Services Corporation, Qormi Road, Luqa, LQA 05, Malta. *Telephone:* 234478. *Fax:* 251799.

FAN HSU LAI-TAI, Rita, JP, BA, M.SC.S.; Hong Kong politician; ed St Stephen's Girls' Coll., Univ. of Hong Kong; Chair. Bd of Educ. 1986–89, Educ. Comm. 1990–92; mem. Preparatory Cttee Hong Kong Special Admin. Region (HKSAR) 1995–97; Pres. Provisional Legis. Council 1997–98, Pres. Legis. Council of HKSAR 1998–. *Address:* Office of the President of the Legislative Council, Legislative Council Building, 8 Jackson Road, Central, Hong Kong Special Administrative Region, People's Republic of China (Office). *Telephone:* (852) 28699399 (Office). *Fax:* (852) 28452444 (Office).

FAN JINGYI; Chinese journalist; fmr Dir Foreign Languages Publ and Distribution Bureau; Ed.-in-Chief Econ. Daily 1986–94, People's Daily 1994–98; Vice-Chair. Economy Cttee of 8th CPPCC Nat. Cttee, Educ, Science, Culture and Public Health Cttee of 9th NPC 1998–; Hon. Pres. Photo-Journalism Soc. 1994–. *Address:* c/o Standing Committee of the National People's Congress, Beijing, People's Republic of China.

FAN ZHILUN, Maj.-Gen.; Chinese army official; b. 1935, Fushun Co., Sichuan Prov.; s. of Fan Ximing and Fan Zhougshi; m. Ding Xin 1966; one s. one d.; Deputy Commdr and Chief of Staff Chinese People's Armed Police Force 1985–; Deputy Pres. Mil. Educ. Coll. and Mil. Staff Coll. 1991–; Deputy Chief of Staff, Beijing Mil. Region of PLA 1993–. *Leisure interests:* climbing, swimming, calligraphy. *Address:* Headquarters of the Beijing Military Region, No. Jia 1, Badachu, Western Hill, Beijing, People's Republic of China.

FANG LIZHI; Chinese astrophysicist; b. 12 Feb. 1936, Beijing; s. of Cheng Pu and Peiji (née Shi) Fang; m. Li Shuxian 1961; two s.; ed Univ. of Peking; Asst Teacher Univ. of Science and Tech. of China 1958–63, Lecturer 1963–78, Prof. of Physics 1978–87, Vice-Pres. of Univ. 1984–87; Prof. and Head Theoretical Astrophysics Group, Beijing Astronomical Observatory, Chinese Acad. of Sciences 1987–; Sr Visiting Fellow Inst. of Astronomy, Cambridge Univ. 1979–80; Visiting Prof. Research Inst. of Fundamental Physics, Kyoto Univ. 1981–82, Physics Dept Univ. of Rome 1983; mem. Inst. for Advanced Study, Princeton 1986; Assoc. mem. Int. Centre for Theoretical Physics, Trieste 1984–89; lived in asylum in U.S. Embassy, Beijing 1989–90, to London, then to USA 1990–; Prof. of Physics and Astronomy, Univ. of Ariz., Tucson 1991–; mem. Chinese Acad. of Sciences 1981–89, New York Acad. of Sciences 1986–; mem. of Council Chinese Soc. of Physics 1982–87, Chinese Soc. of Astronomy 1982–85, Asscn pro Centro Int. de Fisica 1983–87, Int. Centre for Theoretical Physics 1984–89, Int. Centre for Relativistic Astrophysics 1985–89, Chinese Soc. of History of Science and Tech. 1987–89; Pres. Chinese Soc. of Gravitation and Relativistic Astrophysics 1983–89; Vice-Pres. Chinese Soc. of Astronomy 1985–89; mem. various IAU and IUPAP comms., etc.; Ed. Scientia Sinica 1978–89, Acta Physica Sinica 1979–89, Acta Astronomica Sinica 1980–83, Acta Astrophysica Sinica 1982–83, Journal of Modern Physics, etc.; Dr. hc (Rome Univ.) 1990; Nat. Award for Science and Tech. 1978, Chinese Acad. of Sciences Award 1982, New York Acad. of Sciences Award 1988, Robert F. Kennedy Human Rights Award 1989 etc. *Publications:*

Modern Cosmology Review (ed.) 1978, Astrophysics Today (ed.) 1980, Basic Concepts in Relativistic Astrophysics (with R. Ruffini) 1981, English ed. 1987, Cosmology of the Early Universe (ed. with R. Ruffini) 1984, Galaxies, Quasars and Cosmology (ed. with R. Ruffini) 1985, Advances in Science of China: Physics (ed. with others) 1986, Introduction to Mechanics (with S. X. Li) 1986, Observational Cosmology (co-ed.) 1987, Creation of the Universe (with S. X. Li) 1987, Quantum Cosmology (ed. with R. Ruffini) 1987, Collection of History of Sciences (ed.) 1987, Philosophy as a Tool of Physics 1988, Origin, Structure and Evolution of Galaxies (ed.) 1988. *Leisure interest:* swimming. *Address:* Department of Physics, University of Arizona, Tucson, AZ 85721, USA; Beijing Observatory, Zhongguancun, Beijing 100080, People's Republic of China (Office). *Website:* www.arizona.edu.

FANG SHOUXIAN; Chinese nuclear physicist; b. 27 Oct. 1932, Shanghai City; m. 1st Run Moyin (died 1965); m. 2nd Yao Mayli 1968, two d.; ed Shanghai Fudan Univ.; Prof. Research, Nuclear Physics Inst., Academia Sinica 1982–; Project Dir, Beijing Electron Positron Collider (BEPC) 1986; Dir Inst. of High Energy Physics 1988; Dir BEPC Nat. Lab. 1992–; mem. Chinese Acad. of Sciences 1992; Hon. Nat. Natural Science Award 1990. *Address:* c/o P.O. Box 918, Beijing 100039, People's Republic of China. *Telephone:* 8219574. *Fax:* 8213374.

FANG WEIZHONG; Chinese state official; b. 11 March 1928, Dongfeng Co., Jilin Prov.; three s.; ed Dongbei Univ., Northeast China Univ., Northeast China Teachers' Univ.; joined CCP 1950; Vice-Chair, State Planning Comm. 1977, Chair. Econ. Cttee CPPCC 1995; alt. mem. 12th CCP Cen. Cttee 1982–87; mem. 13th CCP Cen Cttee 1987–92; alt. mem. 14th CCP Cen. Cttee 1992–; mem. CPPCC 8th Nat. Cttee 1995–98, 9th Nat. Cttee 1998–; Chair. Economy Cttee 1995–; Pres. Chinese Macroeconomics Soc. 1995–; mem. Council of People's Bank of China 1974–; Chief Ed. Chronicle of Major Economic Events. *Leisure interest:* calligraphy. *Address:* c/o National Committee of the Chinese People's Political Consultative Conference, 23 Taipingqiao Street, Beijing, People's Republic of China.

FANG ZUQI, Gen.; Chinese army officer; fmr Dir Political Dept, PLA Shenyang and Beijing Mil. Area Command; Political Commissar, Nanjing Mil. Region 1994–; rank of Lt-Gen., Gen. 1998; mem. 15th CCP Cen. Cttee 1997–. *Address:* Political Commissar's Office, Nanjing Military Region, Jiangsu Province, People's Republic of China.

FANJUL, Oscar, PhD; Spanish economist; b. 1949, Santiago, Chile; ed Univ. Complutense de Madrid; Visiting Scholar, Harvard Univ. and MIT, Prof. Univ. Autónoma de Madrid; served as Sec.-Gen. and Under-Sec. Dept of Industry and Energy 1983–84; mem. team which negotiated Spain's entry to EC; has also served in Instituto Nacional de Industria (INI) and at Confederación Española de Cajas de Ahorros; Chair. Instituto Nacional di Hidrocarburos (INH) 1985–, Repsol SA 1987–2002; mem. Bd Argentaria (Corporación Bancaria Española) 1991–, Teneo 1992–, London Stock Exchange, Unilever (non-exec.), Acerinox, Técnicas Reunidas; mem. Int. Bd The Chubb Corpn, European Advisory Bd Carlyle Group; Int. advisor to Goldman Sachs; mem. Trilateral Comm. 1991–; Orden de Isabel la Católica, Order of Belgian Crown. *Publications:* several articles and books on industrial and financial matters. *Address:* P° de la Castellana, 278–280, 28046 Madrid, Spain. *Telephone:* (91) 3488100. *Fax:* (91) 3142821.

FARAH, fmr. Empress of Iran (see Pahlavi).

FARAH, Col. Hassan Abshir; Somali politician and diplomatist; b. 20 June 1945; fmr Mayor of Mogadishu; fmr Gov. of Middle Shabelle and Bakol; fmr Amb. to Austria, Repub. of Korea, Japan, Germany; Minister of Internal Affairs and Security, Puntland State –2000; Minister of Mineral Resources and Water 2000–01; Chair. Somali Peace Conf. 2000; Prime Minister of Somalia 2001–. *Address:* Office of the Prime Minister, Mogadishu, Somalia (Office).

FARAH, Nuruddin; Somali novelist; b. 24 Nov. 1945, Baidoa; s. of Farah Hassan and Fatuma Aleli; m. Amina Mama 1992; one s. one d.; ed Panjab Univ., Chandigarh, India, Univs. of London and Essex; lecturer Nat. Univ. of Somalia, Mogadishu 1971–74; Assoc. Prof. Univ. of Jos, Nigeria 1981–83; Writer-in-Residence Univ. of Minn. 1989, Brown Univ. 1991; Prof. Makerere Univ., Kampala 1990; Rhodes Scholar St Antony's Coll., Oxford 1996; Visiting Prof. Univ. of Texas at Austin 1997; now full-time novelist; Hon. DLitt (Univ. of Kent at Canterbury) 2000; English-speaking Union Literary Prize 1980, Neustadt Int. Literary Prize 1998. *Plays include:* The Offering 1976, Yussuf and His Brothers 1982. *Publications:* From a Crooked Rib 1970, Sweet and Sour Milk 1979, Sardines 1981, Close Sesame 1983, Maps 1986, Gifts 1992, Secrets 1998, Yesterday, Tomorrow 2000. *Address:* c/o Deborah Rogers, Rogers, Coleridge & White, 20 Powis Mews, London, W11 1JN, England.

FAREED, Abdul Sabur; Afghanistan politician; Prime Minister in Interim Govt 1992–93; mem. Hizb-i Islami. *Address:* c/o Office of the Prime Minister, Kabul, Afghanistan.

FARELL CUBILLAS, Arsenio, PhD; Mexican politician; b. June 1921, Mexico City; ed Nat. Univ of Mexico; Lecturer in Civil Law and Gen. Theory of Process, Nat. Univ. of Mexico and in Civil Law, Iberoamerican Univ., Mexico City; Pres. Nat. Chamber of Sugar and Alcohol Industries 1973; Dir-Gen. Fed. Electricity Comm. 1973–76; Dir-Gen. Social Security Inst. 1976–82; Sec. of State for Employment 1982–85, for Labour and Social Welfare

1985–95; now Comptroller Gen. *Publications:* essays and articles on legal matters. *Address:* Office of Comptroller General, Avenida Insurgentes 1775, 10 Piso, Mexico City 01020, Mexico (Office).

FAREMO, Grete, LLB; Norwegian politician; b. 16 June 1955, Byglandsfjord, Setesdal; partner Magne Lindholm; one d.; ed Univ. of Oslo; with Ministry of Finance, Norwegian Agency for Devt Co-operation; Head of Div. Ministry of Devt Co-operation 1984, Minister 1990–92; Chief Negotiating Officer Aker Eiendom 1986; Dir (of Cultural Affairs) Aker Brygge (business and leisure complex), Norsk Arbeiderpresse; Minister of Justice and Police 1992–96; Minister of Oil and Energy 1996; Mem. Parl. (Stortinget) 1996–97; Dir Storebrand Insurance Co. 1997–98, Exec. Vice-Pres. 1998–; mem. Bd Labour Party Forum for Art and Culture 1989–90, Int. Analysis 1997–. *Address:* Postboks 1380 Vika, 0114 Oslo (Office); c/o Norwegian Labour Party, Youngstorget 2, P.O. Box 8743, Oslo, Norway; *Telephone:* 22-31-29-08 (Office). *Fax:* 22-31-17-71 (Office); 22-50-70-74 (Home). *E-mail:* grete.faremo@storebrand .no (Office). *Website:* www.storebrand.no (Office).

FARHADI, Ravan A. G.; Afghanistan diplomatist and academic; b. 23 Aug. 1929, Kabul; m.; three c.; ed Istiqlal Coll., Kabul, Inst. d'Etudes Politiques de Paris, Inst. des Hautes Etudes Int., Univ. of Paris, Ecole Pratique des Hautes Etudes, Univ. of Paris; Lecturer in History of Political Thought, School of Law and Political Science, Univ. of Kabul 1955–58; First Sec. Embassy, Karachi 1958–61, Dir of UN Affairs, Ministry of Foreign Affairs 1961–62, Counsellor and Deputy Chief of Mission, Embassy, Washington, DC 1962–64, Dir.-Gen. for Political Affairs, Ministry of Foreign Affairs 1964–70, Deputy Foreign Minister 1970–72, also Sec. Council of Ministers 1965–71; Amb. to France 1973–75; mem. Advisory Scientific Comm. of Ministry of Culture 1975–78; Assoc. Prof., Univ. of Paris (Panthéon-Sorbonne) 1981–85, Dept of Near Eastern Studies, Univ. of Calif. at Berkeley, USA 1985–92; Prof., Inst. of Islamic Thought and Civilisation, Kuala Lumpur, Malaysia 1992–93; Perm. Rep. to UN 1993–; Visiting Fellow ANU, Canberra 1985. *Address:* Permanent Mission of Afghanistan to the United Nations, 360 Lexington Avenue, 11th Floor, New York, NY 10017, U.S.A. (Office). *Telephone:* (212) 972-1212 (Office). *Fax:* (212) 972-1216 (Office). *E-mail:* afgwatan@aol.com (Office).

FARHI, Nicole; French fashion designer; b. 25 July 1946; d. of Ephraim Farhi and Marcelle Farhi (née Babani); m. David Hare (q.v.) 1992; one d. by Stephen Marks; ed Lycée Calmette, Nice, Cours Berçot Art School, Paris; designer for Pierre d'Albi 1968; f. French Connection with Stephen Marks 1973; fmr designer Stephen Marks; Founder and Designer Nicole Farhi 1983–, Nicole Farhi For Men 1989–; opened Nicole's Restaurant 1994; British Fashion Award for Best Contemporary Designer 1995, 1996, 1997, FHM Awards Menswear Designer of the Year 2000, Maxim Awards British Designer of the Year 2001. *Leisure interest:* sculpture. *Address:* 16 Foubert's Place, London, W1F 7PJ, England. *Telephone:* (20) 7399-7500.

FARISH, William; American diplomatist, business executive and race-horse owner; b. 1938, Houston, Tex.; m. Sarah Sharp; one s. three d.; ed Univ. of Virginia; f. investment firm W.S. Farish & Co.; f. thoroughbred farm, Ky 1978; Chair. Exec. Cttee Breeders Cup Ltd; Vice-Chair. U.S. Jockey Club; Dir Thoroughbred Breeders and Owners Asscn; Chair. Bd Churchill Downs Inc., Ky; Amb. to UK 2001–. *Leisure interests:* horse breeding, hunting quail, polo. *Address:* W. S. Farish & Co., Houston, Texas, USA (Office); Embassy of USA, 24–32 Grosvenor Square, London, W1A 1AE, England. *Telephone:* (20) 7499-9000. *Fax:* (20) 7629-9124. *Website:* www.usembassy.org.uk.

FARLEY, Carole, MUS.B.; American soprano opera singer; b. 29 Nov. 1946, Le Mars, Ia; d. of Melvin Farley and Irene (Reid) Farley; m. José Serebrier 1969; one d.; ed Indiana Univ. and Hochschule für Musik, Munich (Fulbright Scholar); operatic début in USA in title role of La Belle Hélène, New York City Opera 1969; début at Metropolitan Opera as Lulu 1977; now appears regularly in leading opera houses of the world and in concert performances with maj. orchestras in USA and Europe; Metropolitan Opera première of Shostakovich's Lady Macbeth of Mitzensk (Katerina Ismailova); Wozzeck (Marie), Toulouse Opera; numerous prizes and awards. *Recordings include:* Le Pré aux Clercs, Behold the Sun, French songs by Chausson, Duparc, Satie and Fauré, Prokofiev songs, Poulenc's The Human Voice, Menotti's The Telephone, Britten's Les Illuminations, Prokofiev's The Ugly Duckling, Kurt Weill songs, Milhaud songs (with John Constable), Tchaikovsky opera arias, Delius songs with orchestra, Les Soldats Morts 1995 (Grand Prix du Disque), Grieg Songs with Orchestra, Ned Rorem Songs with Ned Rorem, Piano, Der Wampyr by Marschner. *Roles include:* Monteverdi's Poppea, Massenet's Manon, Mozart's Idomeneo, Verdi's La Traviata, Offenbach's Tales of Hoffmann and Strauss's Salome, Shostakovich's Lady Macbeth of Mtsensk, Wagner's Parsifal; (videos) Poulenc's La Voix Humaine, Menotti's The Telephone, Strauss's Four Last Songs and Songs with orchestra; mem. American Guild of Musical Artists; several awards and prizes including Grand Prix du Disque 1995 for Les Soldats Morts (by A. Lemeland) and Diapason d'Or (France) 1997. *Leisure interests:* skiing, jogging, swimming, dancing, cooking, entertaining, reading. *Address:* 20 Queen's Gate Gardens, London, SW7 5LZ, England; 270 Riverside Drive, New York, NY 10025, USA (Home). *E-mail:* michael@rlombardo.com (Office); caspi123@aol.com (Home). *Website:* www .phoenixartists.co.uk (Office).

FARMER, Beverley Anne, BA; Australian writer; b. 1941, Melbourne; one s.; ed Univ. of Melbourne; NSW Premier's Prize for Fiction (for Milk) 1984. *Publications:* Alone, Milk, Home Time, A Body of Water, The Seal Woman,

The House in the Light, Place of Birth, Collected Stories. *Address:* c/o University of Queensland Press, P.O. Box 42, St. Lucia, Queensland 4067, Australia (Office).

FARMER, Richard Gilbert, MS, MD, M.A.C.P.; American physician and professor of medicine; b. 29 Sept. 1931, Kokomo, Ind.; s. of Oscar I. Farmer and Elizabeth J. Gilbert Farmer; m. Janice M. Schrank 1958; one s. one d.; ed Indiana Univ., Univ. of Maryland, Milwaukee Co. Hosp. (Marquette Univ.), Mayo Foundation, Rochester, Minn. and Univ. of Minnesota; mil. service 1960–62; staff, Cleveland Clinic Foundation and Cleveland Clinic Hosp. 1962–91, Chair. Dept of Gastroenterology 1972–82, Chair. Div. of Medicine 1975–91; Asst and Assoc. Clinical Prof., Case Western Reserve Univ. School of Medicine 1972–91; Sr Medical Adviser, Bureau for Europe, US Agency for Int. Devt 1992–94; consultant in health care, Eastern Europe and Soviet Union 1994–96; Clinical Prof. of Medicine, Georgetown Univ. Medical Center 1992–; Medical Dir Quality Health Int. 1997–98, Eurasian Medical Educ. Program 1997–; medical consultant Scandinavian Care Consultants, Stockholm 1998–; mem. Inst. of Medicine, Nat. Advisory Bd, Nat. Foundation for Ileitis and Colitis, Nat. Comm. on Digestive Diseases 1977–79; Gov. for Ohio, American Coll. of Physicians 1980–84, Regent 1985–91; Chair. Health and Public Policy Comm. 1986–88; Pres. American Coll. of Gastroenterology 1978–79, Asscn of Program Dirs. in Internal Medicine 1977–79; Interstate Postgrad. Medical Asscn 1983–84; mem. council to assess quality of care in the Medicare program, Gen. Accounting Office, US House of Reps. 1986–89; Special Citation, American Coll. of Physicians 1984, Mastership American Coll. of Gastroenterology 1991, American Coll. of Physicians 1993, mem. Int. Org. for Study of Inflammatory Bowel Disease (Deputy Chair. 1982–86); Founder's Award, Asscn of Program Dirs in Internal Medicine 1993; Jubilee Medal, Charles Univ. of Prague, Czech Republic 1998. *Publications:* author or co-author of 260 publs in the medical literature, primarily relating to digestive diseases with a specific interest in inflammatory bowel disease and health care in Eastern Europe and the fmr Soviet Union; of six books and contrib. to others. *Leisure interests:* squash, tennis, running and reading (history and current events). *Address:* Department of Medicine, Georgetown University Medical Center, Washington, DC 20007 (Office); Eurasian Medical Education Program, 1150 18th Street; NW, Suite 275, Washington, DC 20036 (Office); 9126 Town Gate Lane, Bethesda, MD 20817, USA (Home). *Telephone:* (202) 463-8206 (Office); (301) 365-5828 (Home). *Fax:* (202) 463-8203 (Office); (301) 365-6202 (Home). *E-mail:* rgfarmer@emep-online.org (Office); rg.jm.farmer@worldnet.att.net (Home).

FARNELL-WATSON, Peter; British business executive; b. 8 Feb. 1947, Royston, Herts.; m. Bunny Farnell-Watson; one s. one d.; ed schools in SA, UK and New Zealand, Colchester School of Art and Cen. School of Art, London; industrial designer, Unimark Int. 1970; Corp. Identity Man. Rennies Consolidated, SA 1972, Dir of Corp. Communications 1974; seconded to Jardine Matheson, Hong Kong 1977; Account Dir Corp. Identity, Landor Assocs. San Francisco 1984, Vice-Pres. responsible for Consulting and Account. Man., Corp. and Product Branding 1986, Group Dir responsible for Corp. and Retail Branding Operations in San Francisco 1988, Man. Dir San Francisco office and mem. Bd Dirs Landor Assocs 1990, Exec. Dir Worldwide Accounts 1991, Co-Man. Dir Landor Assocs Europe 1992–96, Man. Dir 1996–. *Address:* Landor Associates, 18 Clerkenwell Green, London, EC1R 0DP, England. *Telephone:* (20) 7880-8360.

FARNHAM, John Peter, AO; Australian (b. British) singer and entertainer; b. 1 July 1949, Essex, UK; m. Jillian Farnham 1973; two s.; ed Lyndale High School; settled in Australia 1959; apprenticed as plumber; lead singer for Strings Unlimited 1965; began recording 1967; television appearances including nature series Survival with Johnny Farnham for ABC; f. John Farnham Band 1978; lead singer for Little River Band 1982–85; 12 Gold Record awards; Australian of the Year, Bicentennial 1998. *Recordings include:* Sadie the Cleaning Lady 1967 (3 Gold Records), Friday Kind of Monday 1968, Rose Coloured Glasses 1968, One 1969, Raindrops Keep Falling on My Head 1969, Comic Conversation 1970, Rock Me Baby 1972, Don't You Know It's Magic 1973, Everything is Out of Season 1973, Uncovered 1980, The Net 1982, Playing to Win 1984, Whispering Jack 1986, Chain Reaction 1990, Full House 1991, Jesus Christ Superstar: The Album 1992, Then Again 1992, Romeo's Heart 1996, Anthology Series I, II and III 1997, 33⅓ 2001. *Address:* c/o TalentWORKS, Suite 1, 663 Victoria Street, Abbotsford, Vic. 3067, Australia. *Telephone:* (3) 94296933. *Fax:* (3) 94287433.

FARQUHAR, John William, AB, MD; American/Canadian physician and professor of medicine; b. 13 June 1927, Winnipeg, Canada; s. of John Giles Farquhar and Marjorie Victoria Roberts; m. Christine Louise Johnson 1968; one s. one d. (and two s. from previous m.); ed Univ. of California, Berkeley and San Francisco, London School of Hygiene and Tropical Medicine; Intern Univ. of Calif. Hosp., San Francisco 1952–53, Resident 1953–54, 1957–58; Postdoctoral Fellow 1955–57; Resident Univ. of Minn. 1954–55; Research Assoc. Rockefeller Univ., New York 1958–62; Asst Prof. of Medicine Stanford Univ. 1962–66, Assoc. Prof 1966–73, Prof. 1973–97, C. F. Rehnborg Prof. in Disease Prevention 1989–99; Dir Stanford Center for Research in Disease Prevention 1973–98, Stanford Wellness Center 1998–; Dir Collaborating Center for Chronic Disease Prevention WHO 1985–99; Assoc. Chief of Staff for Health Promotion, Stanford Univ. Hosp. 1994–97; Pres. Soc. of Behavioral Medicine 1990–92; mem. NAS Inst. of Medicine, American Soc. of Clinical Investigation, Acad. of Behavioral Medicine, American Soc. of Preventive Cardiology; James D. Bruce Award 1983, Myrdal Prize 1986, Charles A. Dana

Foundation Award for Pioneering Achievements in Health 1990, Nat. Cholesterol Award for Public Educ. 1991, Research Achievement Award American Heart Asscn 1992, Order of Saint George for Service to Autonomous Govt of Catalonia 1996, Joseph Stokes Preventative Cardiology Award, American Soc. Preventative Cardiology 1999, Awardee, American Heart Asscn Ancel Keys Lectureship 2000. *Publications:* The American Way of Life Need Not Be Hazardous to Your Health 1978, The Last Puff (with Gene Spiller) 1990, The Victoria Declaration for Heart Health 1992, The Catalonia Declaration: Investing in Heart Health 1996, Worldwide Efforts to Improve Heart Disease 1997, Diagnosis: Heart Disease (with Gene Spiller) 2000; contribs. to professional journals. *Leisure interests:* 20th century history, classical music, ornithology, Scottish history, Canadian history, languages. *Address:* 649 Cabrillo Avenue, Stanford, CA 94305 (Home); School of Medicine, Stanford University, Center for Research in Disease Prevention, 730 Welch Road, Stanford, CA 94305, USA. *Telephone:* (650) 723-6051 (Office); (650) 327-1177 (Home). *Fax:* (650) 723-7018 (Office). *E-mail:* jfarquhar@stanford.edu (Office).

FARQUHAR, Robin Hugh, PhD; Canadian professor of public policy and administration, former university president and vice-chancellor; b. 1 Dec. 1938, Victoria, BC; s. of Hugh E. Farquhar and Jean MacIntosh; m. Frances Caswell 1963; three d.; ed Victoria High School, Victoria Coll., Univ. of British Columbia, Univ. of Chicago; teacher, Counsellor and Coach, Edward Milne Secondary School, Sooke, BC 1962–64; Assoc. Dir and Deputy Dir Univ. Council for Educational Admin 1966–71; Chair. Dept of Educational Admin and Asst Dir Ont. Inst. for Studies in Educ. and Assoc. Prof., then Prof., School of Grad. Studies, Univ. of Toronto 1971–76; Dean of Educ. and Prof. Univ. of Sask., Saskatoon 1976–81; Pres., Vice-Chancellor and Prof., Univ. of Winnipeg 1981–89; Pres., Vice-Chancellor and Prof., Carleton Univ., Ottawa 1989–96; Prof. of Public Policy and Admin 1996–; Hon. Diploma in Adult Educ.; Fellow Commonwealth Council for Educational Admin; Hon. Citizen City of Winnipeg; Hon. Scout; Award of Merit, Canadian Bureau for Int. Education. *Publications:* numerous books and articles on educational admin. *Leisure interests:* jogging, golf, music. *Address:* School of Public Policy and Administration, Carleton University, 1125 Colonel By Drive, Ottawa, K1S 5B6, Canada (Office); 64 Queen Elizabeth Drive, Ottawa, K2P 1E3, Canada (Home). *Telephone:* (613) 230-4735 (Home); (613) 520-2600 ext. 2636 (Office). *Fax:* (613) 230-1094 (Home). *E-mail:* rfarquha@ccs.carleton.ca (Office).

FARR, Dennis Larry Ashwell, CBE, MA, FRSA, F.M.A.; British art historian and museum director; b. 3 April 1929, Luton, Beds.; s. of Arthur W. Farr and Helen E. Farr; m. Diana Pullein-Thompson 1959; one s. one d.; ed Luton Grammar School and Courtauld Inst. of Art, Univ. of London; Asst Witt Librarian, Courtauld Inst. 1952–54; Asst Keeper, Tate Gallery, London 1954–64; Curator, Paul Mellon Collection, Washington, DC 1965–66; Sr Lecturer and Deputy Keeper Univ. Art Collections, Univ. of Glasgow 1967–69; Dir City Museums and Art Gallery, Birmingham 1969–80; Dir Courtauld Inst. Galleries 1980–93; Gen. Ed. Clarendon Studies in the History of Art, Oxford Univ. Press 1985–2001; Pres. Museums Asscn 1979–80; Chair. Asscn of Art Historians 1983–86; mem. Comité Int. d'Histoire de l'Art 1983–94, Hon. mem. 1994–; mem. Registration Cttee, Museums and Galleries Comm. 1993–99; Hon. D. Litt. (Birmingham) 1981. *Publications:* William Etty 1958, Tate Gallery Modern British School Catalogue (co-author) 1964, English Art 1870–1940 1978, Lynn Chadwick: Sculptor. A Complete Catalogue 1947–88 (with Eva Chadwick) 1990, 1998, Thomas Gambier Parry (1816–1888) as Artist and Collector (Ed. and contrib.) 1993, Francis Bacon: A Retrospective Exhibition (co-author) 1999, Lynn Chadwick Retrospective Exhibition 2003. *Leisure interests:* avoiding academics, riding, music. *Address:* Orchard Hill, Swan Barn Road, Haslemere, Surrey, GU27 2HY, England. *Telephone:* (1428) 641880.

FARRAKHAN, Louis; American religious leader; b. (Louis Eugene Wolcott), 11 May 1933, New York City; m. Betsy Wolcott; nine c.; ed Winston-Salem Teachers Coll.; fmrly Leader and Nat. Spokesman Nation of Islam Mosque, Harlem; f. reorganized org. Nation of Islam 1977, Leader 1977–; organizer 'Million Man March' 1995, Washington DC, 'Million Family March' 2000; barred from entering UK on grounds that his opinions would provoke disorder April 2002; apptd. Envoy of U.S. Govt to Baghdad, responsible for negotiating directly with Iraqi leadership July 2002. *Address:* Nation of Islam, 7351 South Stony Island Avenue, Chicago, IL 60649, USA.

FARRELL, Patrick M.; Irish politician; b. 30 Aug. 1957, Leitrim; s. of Bill Farrell and Mamie Casey; m. Margaret Logan 1988; one s. one d.; ed Man. College, Carrick-on-Shannon, Inst. of Public Admin.; Hosp. Admin. Sligo 1981–86; CEO Galvia Hosp., Galway 1986–91; Gen. Sec. Fianna Fáil 1991–98; fmr Chair. Irish Council of the European Movt; mem. of Senate 1992; mem. Bd of Friends of Fianna Fáil Inc., USA. *Leisure interests:* current affairs, reading, writing. *Address:* c/o Aras De Valera, 13 Upper Mount Street, Dublin 2, Ireland. *Telephone:* (1) 6761551. *Fax:* (1) 6785960.

FARRELL, Suzanne; American ballerina; b. 1945; ed School of American Ballet; fmr principal dancer with New York City Ballet until 1989; also danced with Béjart Ballet, Brussels; appeared in numerous Balanchine ballets choreographed for her including Mozartiana, Chaconne, Meditation, Vienna Waltzes; staged seven Balanchine ballets at John F. Kennedy Center for Performing Arts, Washington, DC 1995 and many other stagings of Balanchine's works; repetiteur for Balanchine Trust, including Kirov Ballet, Royal Danish Ballet and Paris Opéra Ballet; mem. Advisory Panel Princess Grace Foundation, Sr Advisory Bd of Arthritis Foundation; EPPES Prof. of Dance Florida State Univ.; trains ballet dancers in camp The Adirondacks. *Television:* Suzanne Farrell: Elusive Muse (documentary). *Publication:* Holding On To The Air (autobiog.) 1990. *Address:* Kennedy Center for the Performing Arts, Washington, DC 20566, USA.

FARRELL, Sir Terence (Terry), Kt., CBE, MCP, MArch, MRTPI, RIBA, FCSD, FRSA; British architect; b. 12 May 1938; s. of Thomas Farrell and Molly Farrell (née Maguire); m. 1st Angela Rosemarie Mallam 1960; two d.; m. 2nd Susan Hilary Aplin 1973; two s. one d.; ed St Cuthbert's Grammar School, Newcastle-upon-Tyne, Newcastle Univ., Univ. of Pennsylvania, USA; Harkness Fellow, Commonwealth Fund, USA 1962–64; Partner, Farrell Grimshaw Partnership 1965–80; Terry Farrell Partnership 1980–87; Chair. Terry Farrell & Partners 1987–; Visiting Prof., Univ. of Westminster 1998–2001; Hon. FAIA; Hon. DCL (Newcastle) 2000. *Exhibitions include:* Terry Farrell in the context of London RIBA Heinz Gallery 1987, Terry Farrell; a retrospective and current projects, RIBA Centre 1995. *Major projects include:* Vauxhall Cross (MI6), London, The Peak, Hong Kong, Kowloon Station, Hong Kong, Charing Cross Station Redevt, Edinburgh Int. Conf. Centre, British Consulate and British Council Bldgs, Hong Kong, Dean Centre Art Gallery, Edin., Int. Centre for Life, Newcastle, Transportation Centre for Inchon Int. Airport, Seoul. *Publications:* Architectural Monograph 1985, Urban Design Monograph 1993; articles in numerous journals. *Leisure interests:* walking, swimming. *Address:* Terry Farrell & Partners, 7 Hatton Street, London, NW8 8PL, England. *Telephone:* (20) 7258-3433. *Fax:* (20) 7723-7059. *E-mail:* staff@terryfarrell.co.uk (Office). *Website:* www.terryfarrell.com (Office).

FARRINGTON, David Philip, MA, PhD, FBA, FMedSci; British professor of psychological criminology; b. 7 March 1944, Ormskirk, Lancs.; s. of William Farrington and Gladys Holden Farrington; m. Sally Chamberlain 1966; three d.; ed Univ. of Cambridge; mem. staff, Inst. of Criminology, Univ. of Cambridge 1969–, Prof. of Psychological Criminology 1992–; Pres. European Asscn of Psychology and Law 1997–99; Visiting Fellow, US Nat. Inst. of Justice 1981; Chair. Div. of Criminological and Legal Psychology, British Psychological Soc. 1983–85; mem. Parole Bd for England and Wales 1984–87; Vice-Chair. US Nat. Acad. of Sciences Panel on Violence 1989–92; Visiting Fellow US Bureau of Justice Statistics 1995–98; Co-Chair. US Office of Juvenile Justice and Delinquency Prevention Study Group on Serious and Violent Juvenile Offenders 1995–97; Pres. British Soc. of Criminology 1990–93, Pres. American Soc. of Criminology 1998–99; Co-Chair. US Office of Juvenile Justice and Delinquency Prevention Study Group on Very Young Offenders 1998–2000; Chair. UK Dept of Health Advisory Cttee for the Nat. Programme on Forensic Mental Health 2000–03; mem. Bd of Dirs Int. Soc. of Criminology 2000–; Pres. Acad. of Experimental Criminology 2001–03; Chair. Campbell Collaboration Crime and Justice Group 2000–03; Sellin-Glueck Award of American Soc. of Criminology 1984, Sutherland Award of American Soc. of Criminology 2002. *Publications:* 28 books and over 320 articles on criminology and psychology. *Address:* Institute of Criminology, University of Cambridge, 7 West Road, Cambridge, CB3 9DT (Office); 7 The Meadows, Haslingfield, Cambridge, CB3 7JD, England (Home). *Telephone:* (1223) 335384 (Office); (1223) 872555 (Home). *Fax:* (1223) 335356.

FARROW, Mia Villiers; American actress; b. 9 Feb. 1945, Calif.; d. of John Villiers Farrow and Maureen O'Sullivan; m. 1st Frank Sinatra 1966 (divorced 1968); m. 2nd André Previn (q.v.) 1970 (divorced 1979); fourteen c.; Stage début in The Importance of Being Earnest, New York 1963; French Acad. Award for Best Actress 1969, David Donatello Award (Italy) 1969, Rio de Janeiro Film Festival Award 1969, San Sebastian Award. *Stage appearances in London:* Mary Rose, The Three Sisters, House of Bernarda Alba 1972–73, The Marrying of Ann Leete (RSC) 1975, The Zykovs 1976, Ivanov (RSC) 1976; appeared in Romantic Comedy (Broadway) 1979. *Films include:* Guns at Batasi 1964, Rosemary's Baby 1968, Secret Ceremony 1969, John and Mary 1969, See No Evil 1970, The Great Gatsby 1973, Full Circle 1978, A Wedding 1978, Death on the Nile 1978, The Hurricane 1979, A Midsummer Night's Sex Comedy 1982, Zelig 1983, Broadway Danny Rose 1984, Purple Rose of Cairo 1985, Hannah and Her Sisters 1986, Radio Days 1987, September 1988, Another Woman 1988, Oedipus Wrecks 1989, Crimes and Misdemeanours, Alice 1990, Shadows and Fog 1992, Husbands and Wives 1992, Widow's Peak 1994, Miami Rhapsody 1995, Private Parts 1997, Reckless 1995, Coming Soon 2000. *Television appearances:* Peyton Place 1964–66; Johnny Belinda 1965, Peter Pan 1975, Goodbye Raggedy Ann (TV film), Miracle at Midnight. *Publication:* What Falls Away (autobiog.) 1996. *Leisure interests:* reading, mind wandering, listening to music and certain people. *Address:* International Creative Management, c/o Sam Cohn, 40 West 57th Street, New York, NY 10019, USA. *Website:* www.mia-farrow.com.

FARULLI, Piero; Italian professor of viola; b. 13 Jan. 1920, Florence; s. of Lioniero Farulli and Maria (née Innocenti) Farulli; m. Antonia Parisi 1945; ed Conservatorio Statale Luigi Cherubini, Florence (under Gioacchino Maglioni); Prof. of Viola 1957–77; for thirty years a mem. of Quartetto Italiano; has also collaborated with Amadeus and Berg Quartets; appeared with Trio di Trieste 1978; has lectured at Accad. Chigiana di Siena and at Salzburg Mozarteum; mem. of judging panel at several int. competitions and is active in many aspects of musical life and education in Italy, notably at the Scuola di Musica di Fiesole, which he founded in 1974; Medaglia della Cultura e dell'Arte; Grand 'Ufficiale della Repubblica 1994. *Address:* Via G. d'Annunzio 153, Florence, Italy. *Telephone:* (055) 608007.

FASE, Martin M. G., PhD; Netherlands banker and economist; b. 28 Dec. 1937, Boskoop; s. of A. P. Fase and J. G. M. de Groot; m. Lida E. M. Franse 1965; two s.; ed Univ. of Amsterdam; Research Assoc. Inst. of Actuarial Sciences and Econometrics, Amsterdam 1965–69; Ford Foundation Fellow, Dept of Econs, Univ. of Wis., Madison, USA 1969–71; with De Nederlandsche Bank 1971–2001, Deputy Dir 1985–2001; Extraordinary Prof. of Business Statistics, Erasmus Univ., Rotterdam 1978–86; Extraordinary Prof. of Monetary Econs, Univ. of Amsterdam 1986–; Fellow Royal Netherlands Acad. of Arts and Sciences, Hollandsche Maatschappij der Wetenschappen. *Publications:* An Econometric Model of Age-Income Profiles: a Statistical Analysis of Dutch Income Data 1970, The Monetary Sector of the Netherlands in 50 Equations: a Quarterly Monetary Model for the Netherlands 1970–79, in Analysing the Structure of Econometric Models (ed. J. P. Ancot) 1984, Seasonal Adjustment as a Practical Problem 1991; articles in European Econ. Review, Journal of Int. Econs and other journals; several monographs. *Leisure interests:* Dutch literature, hiking. *Address:* Ruysdaelweg 3B, 2051 EM Overveen, Netherlands (Home). *Fax:* (20) 524 2529. *E-mail:* m.m.g.fase@uva.nl.

FASQUELLE, Jean-Claude; French publisher; b. 29 Nov. 1930, Paris; s. of Charles Fasquelle and Odette Cyprien-Fabre; m. 1st Solange de la Rochefoucauld; one d.; m. 2nd Nicola Jegher 1966; ed Ecole des Roches, Verneuil-sur-Avre, Sorbonne and Faculté de Droit, Paris; Pres.-Dir-Gen. Société des Editions Fasquelle 1953–60, Editions du Sagittaire 1958–; Admin.-Dir-Gen. Editions Grasset et Fasquelle 1960, Pres.-Dir-Gen. 1980–2000, Chair. of Bd 2000–; Dir Le Magazine littéraire (monthly) 1970–. *Address:* Éditions Grasset et Fasquelle, 61 rue des Saintes-Pères, 75006 Paris (Office); 13 Square Vergennes, 75015 Paris, France (Home). *Telephone:* 1-44-39-22-00 (Office). *Fax:* 1-44-39-22-18 (Office).

FASSBAENDER, Brigitte; German mezzo-soprano; b. 3 July 1939, Berlin; d. of the late Willi Domgraf-Fassbaender and Sabine Peters; ed Nuremberg Conservatoire and studied with father; début Bavarian State Opera, Munich 1961; has appeared at La Scala Milan, Vienna State Opera, Covent Garden London, Metropolitan Opera, New York, San Francisco and Salzburg; Teacher of Solo Vocal Music Musikhochschule, Munich; soloist, Dir of Opera, Braunschweig 1995–97; Fellow Royal Northern Coll. of Music (UK) 1991–; Intendantin Tiroler Landestheater, Innsbruck 1999; Bundesverdienstkreuz am Bande, Bayerischer Verdienstorden. *Recordings:* over 100 recordings since 1964. *Address:* c/o Sekretariat, Haiming, 83119 Obing, Germany (Office).

FASSI-FIHRI, Ahmed, LenD; Moroccan civil servant and diplomatist; b. 6 Aug. 1936, Oujda; m. Touria El Ouazzani; two s. two d.; pvt. sec. of Minister of Interior 1956; Head of Office, Dept of Minerals and Geology 1958; Head, Office of Minister of Foreign Affairs 1959; Chargé d'affaires, Moroccan Embassy, Berne 1960; Pres. Melnes Municipality 1963; Founder and Dir Nat. Documentation Centre 1967–, Information Science School 1974, Multimedia Centre 1993; Order of Ridha. *Publications:* articles in field of information science in Arabic and French. *Leisure interests:* listening to Arabic and classical music; reading of the Arabic intellectual literary productions. *Address:* Centre National de Documentation, BP 826, Rabat, Morocco. *Telephone:* (3) 774944; (3) 773139. *Fax:* (3) 773134.

FASSINO, Piero Franco Rodolfo, BSc; Italian politician; b. 7 Oct. 1949, Avigliana; m.; local councillor Turin 1975–80, 1985–90, Prov. Councillor 1980–85; various posts within Turin Fed. of Partito Comunista Italiano (P.C.I.) 1971–83, Prov. Sec. 1983–87, elected to P.C.I. Exec. 1983, Coordinator Nat. Secr. 1987, then Head of party org. during transition to Partito Democratico della Sinistra (PDS), mem. Nat. Secr. and Int. Sec. PDS 1991–96, PDS Rep. to Socialist Int. 1992, PDS re-named Democratici di Sinistra (DS) 1998, currently Gen. Sec. DS; Pres. Cen. and W Europe Cttee Socialist Int. 1993; fmr Vice-Pres. Socialist Group, Council of Europe; mem. Chamber of Deputies from Liguria (P.D.S.) 1994–96, from Piedmont 1996–; Under-Sec. Ministry for Foreign Trade 1996–98; Minister for Foreign Trade 1998–2000, for Justice 2000–01; mem. Parl. Asscn for Cen. Europe Initiative; Vice-Pres. Italian–Israeli Parl. Friendship Asscn 1995. *Address:* Democratici di Sinistra, Via delle Botteghe Oscure 4, 00186 Rome, Italy. *Telephone:* (06) 67111. *Fax:* (06) 6711596. *E-mail:* ufficio.stampa@democraticidisinistra.it. *Website:* www.dsonline.it.

FATHIMA BEEVI, M. S., BSc, LLB; Indian politician and judge (retd); b. 30 April 1927, Pathananthitta, Kerala; d. of Meera Sahib and Khadeeja Beevi; ed Coll., Trivandrum, Kerala; enrolled as advocate 1950; practised in civil, criminal and revenue fields at Quilon and Ernakulam; Subordinate Judge 1968; Dist and Sessions Judge 1974; Judicial mem., Income Tax Appellate Tribunal 1980; Judge, Kerala High Court 1983–89, Supreme Court of India 1989–93 (first woman in India and Asia); Gov. of Tamil Nadu 1997–2001; Chair. Kerala State Comm. for Backward Classes 1993; mem. Nat. Human Rights Comm. 1993; Hon. DLitt; Mahila Shiromani Award 1990. *Address:* Anna Veedu, Petta, Pathananthitta, Kerala, India (Home). *Telephone:* (44) 2351800 (Home); (473) 322151.

FATIN, Wendy, BSc; Australian politician; b. 10 April 1941, Harvey, WA; one s. one d.; ed West Australian Inst. of Tech.; trained as registered nurse; Adviser to Minister for Repatriation and Compensation and Minister for Social Security 1974–75; Political Research Asst 1975–77, 1981–83; mem. House of Reps. for Canning, WA 1983, for Brand, WA 1984–96; Minister for Local Govt, Minister Assisting Prime Minister for Status of Women 1990–93, Minister for Arts and Territories 1991–93; mem. Govt Econ. Cttee 1983–87; mem. House of Reps. Standing Cttee on Community Affairs 1987–96, on Employment, Educ. and Training 1987–96; Fellow Coll. of Nursing, Australia; Founder mem. Women's Electoral Lobby; Labor Party. *Address:* Lot 46, Soldiers Road, Roleystone, WA 6111, Australia.

FAUCI, Anthony Stephen, MD; American medical researcher; b. 24 Dec. 1940, Brooklyn, New York; s. of Stephen Fauci and Eugenia Fauci; m. Christine Grady 1985; three d.; ed Coll. of the Holy Cross, Cornell Univ. Medical Coll.; Instructor in Medicine, Cornell Medical Coll. 1971–72; Medical Dir US Public Health Service 1968–70, 1972; Clinical Assoc. Lab. of Clinical Investigation, NIAID 1968–71; Sr Staff Fellow, Lab. of Clinical Investigation 1970–71, Sr Investigator 1972–74, Head Physiology Section 1974–80, Deputy Clinical Dir Nat. Inst. of Allergy and Infectious Diseases 1977–84, Dir 1984–; Chief Resident in Medicine, New York Hosp., Cornell Univ. Medical Center 1971–72; Chief Lab. of Immunoregulation 1980–; Dir Office of AIDS Research and Assoc. Dir NIH for AIDS Research 1988–94; Consultant Naval Medical Center, Bethesda 1972–; Bristol Award of the IDSA 1999, Int. Prize for Scientific Research, Fondazione PISO 1999, Frank Berry Prize in Fed. Medicine 1999, Timely Topics Award Lecture of the US and Canadian Acad. of Pathology 1999; ed. of numerous learned journals on immunlogy. *Leisure interests:* jogging, tennis. *Address:* NIAID/NIH, 31 Center Drive MSC 2520, Bethesda, MD 20892-0001 (Office); 3012 43rd Street, NW, Washington, DC 20016, USA (Home). *Telephone:* (301) 496-2263 (Office). *Fax:* (301) 496-4409 (Office). *E-mail:* aflor@nih.gov (Office). *Website:* www.niaid.nih.gov (Office).

FAUCON, Bernard; French photographer; b. 12 Sept. 1950, Apt; ed Lycée d'Apt, Université d'Aix en Provence, Sorbonne, Paris; Grand Prix Nat. de la Photographie 1989. *Exhibitions include:* Agathe Gaillard, Paris 1979, 1984, 1986, 1988, 1990; Castelli, New York 1979, 1981, 1983, 1986, 1989, 1991; Musée Georges Pompidou, Paris 1982; Musée de la Vieille Charité, Marseille 1986; Guggenheim Museum, New York, 1986; Walker Art Center, Minneapolis 1987; PARCO Gallery, Tokyo 1987, 1991; Espace photo de la ville de Paris 1988; Yvon Lambert, Paris 1991, 1993, 1995; Maison européenne de la photographie, Paris 2000, Manège, Moscow 2002. *Publications:* Les grandes vacances 1980, Summer Camp 1980, Les Papiers qui volent 1986, Les Chambres d'amour 1987, Tables d'amis 1991, Les Idoles et les sacrifices 1991, Les Ecritures 1993, Jours d'images 1995, La Fin de l'Image 1997, La peur du voyage 1999, Le plus beau jour de ma jeunesse 2000, La plus belle route du monde 2000. *Leisure interest:* cookery. *Address:* 6 rue Barbanègre, 75019 Paris, France. *Telephone:* 1-40-05-99-70.

FAUL, Mgr Denis O'Beirne, BA, STL; Irish ecclesiastic; b. 14 Aug. 1932, Dundalk, Co. Louth; s. of Dr. Joseph Faul and Anne F. O'Beirne; ed St Mary's Coll. Dundalk, St Patrick's Coll. Armagh, St Patrick's Coll., Maynooth and Gregorian Univ., Rome; ordained priest 1956; teacher, St Patrick's Acad. Dungannon, Co. Tyrone 1958–83, Prin. 1983–98; cr. Mgr 1995; Parish Priest Termonmaguire, Omagh, Co. Tyrone 1998–. *Publications:* 15 books and 20 leaflets on NI problems; papers on Patristics and history of Irish Catholic Church. *Leisure interests:* books, modern languages. *Address:* Termonmaguire, Omagh, Co. Tyrone, BT79 9BE, Northern Ireland. *Telephone:* (28) 8076-1207. *Fax:* (28) 8076-0938.

FAULKS, Sebastian, CBE, BA, FRSL; British author and journalist; b. 20 April 1953, Newbury, Berks.; s. of Peter Faulks and Pamela Lawless; m. Veronica Youlten 1989; two s. one d.; ed Wellington Coll. and Emmanuel Coll., Cambridge; reporter Daily Telegraph newspaper 1979–83, feature writer Sunday Telegraph 1983–86; Literary Ed. The Independent 1986–89, Deputy Ed. The Independent on Sunday 1989–90, Assoc. Ed. 1990–91; columnist The Guardian 1992–97, Evening Standard 1997–99, Mail on Sunday 1999–2000. *Television:* Churchill's Secret Army 2000. *Publications:* The Girl at the Lion d'Or 1989, A Fool's Alphabet 1992, Birdsong 1993, The Fatal Englishman 1996, Charlotte Gray 1998, On Green Dolphin Street 2001. *Leisure interests:* wine, sport. *Address:* c/o Aitken and Stone, 29 Fernshaw Road, London, SW10 0TG, England. *Telephone:* (20) 7351-7561. *Fax:* (20) 7376-3594.

FAURE, Maurice Henri, DenD; French politician; b. 2 Jan. 1922, Azerat (Dordogne); s. of René Faure and Irène Joudinaud; m. Andrée Guillemain 1945; two s.; ed Lycée de Périgueux, Faculty of Law and Letters, Bordeaux and Toulouse Univs; Deputy for Lot (Radical-Socialist) 1951 (re-elected to Nat. Ass. 1958, 1962, 1967, 1968, 1973, 1978, 1981); Sec. of State for Foreign Affairs (Mollet Cabinet) 1956–57, (Bourgès-Maunoury Cabinet) June–Nov. 1957, (Gaillard Cabinet) 1957–58; Minister for European Insts. May–June 1958, for Justice May–June 1981; Minister of State for Equipment and Housing 1988–89; mem. Conseil Constitutionnel 1989–98; Pres. French del. Common Market and Euratom Conf., Brussels 1956; mem. del. 11th Session UN Gen. Ass., New York 1956; Special Asst Minister for Foreign Affairs on Morocco and Tunisia 1956–57; fmr mem. European Coal and Steel Community Ass.; MEP 1959–67, 1973–81; Senator of Lot 1983–88; fmr Mayor of Prayssac (Lot), Mayor of Cahors 1965–90; Conseiller Général, Salviac canton (Lot) 1957–58, Montcuq canton 1963; Pres. Departmental Asscn of Mayors of Lot, Mouvement européen; Pres. Entente démocratique de la Nat. Ass. 1960–62; Pres., later Leader, Parti republicain radical et radical-socialiste 1961–65, 1969–71; fmr Pres. Rassemblement démocratique Group, Nat. Ass.; Pres. Econ. Devt Comm. for Midi-Pyrénées 1964–70; Pres. Conseil général du Lot 1970–94, Hon. Pres. 1994–; resigned from Rassemblement pour la République May 1977; Vice-Pres. Conseil de la région Midi-Pyrénées 1974–

Commdr Mérite civil and other awards. *Publications:* D'une république à l'autre, Entretiens sur l'histoire et la politique 1999. *Address:* 28 boulevard Raspail, 75007 Paris, France (Home).

FAURE, Roland; French journalist; b. 10 Oct. 1926, Montelimar; s. of Edmond Faure-Geors and Jeanne Gallet; m. Véra Hitzbleck 1956; three s.; ed Enclos Saint-François, Montpellier and Faculté de Droit, Aix-en-Provence; journalist, Méridional-la France, Marseilles 1947; del. in America, Asscn de la presse latine d'Europe et d'Amerique 1951, Sec.-Gen. 1954–; Founder and Ed.-in-Chief, Journal français du Brésil, Rio de Janeiro 1952–53; Diplomatic Ed. L'Aurore 1954, Head of Diplomatic Service 1959, Ed.-in-Chief 1962, Dir and Ed.-in-Chief 1968–78; attached to Cabinet of Minister of Public Works 1957–58; Dir Toutes les nouvelles de Versailles 1954–86; mem. Admin. Bd Antenne 2 1975–79; Dir of Information, Radio-France 1979–81; Founder and Dir Radio CVS 1982; Pres. Dir-Gen. Société Nat. de programme Radio France 1986–89, Société Nat. de Radiodifffusion; Pres. Université radiophonique et télévisuelle int. (URTI) 1987–97; Communauté des radios publiques de langue française (CRPLF) 1987; Pres. Admin. Council Fondations Marguerite Long-Jacques Thibaud 1991–; Pres. Club DAB 1991–; mem. Conseil Supérieur de l'Audiovisuel (CSA) 1989–97, mem. numerous professional asscns. etc.; Officier, Légion d'honneur; Officier, Ordre Nat. du Mérite, des Arts et des Lettres. *Publications:* Brésil dernière heure 1954; articles in newspapers and journals. *Address:* La Radio numérique, 40 rue Guynemer, 92130 Issy-les-Moulineaux (Office); 94 boulevard de la Tour Maubourg, Paris 7e, France (Home). *Telephone:* 1-49-55-01-15 (Office).

FAUROUX, Roger, LèsL; French business executive; b. 21 Nov. 1926, Montpellier (Hérault); s. of Théo and Rose (née Ségu) Fauroux; m. Marie Le Roy Ladurie 1953; three s. three d.; ed Lycée de Besançon, Lycée Henri IV, Paris, Ecole normale supérieure, Ecole nationale d'admin; Asst Insp. of Finance 1956, Insp. 1958; Office of Minister of Educ. May–Nov. 1960; Admin. Dir Cie Pont-à-Mousson 1961, Finance Dir 1964–69; Finance Dir Cie de Saint-Gobain-Pont-à-Mousson 1970, Asst Dir-Gen. 1972–75, Admin. Dir-Gen. 1978–80, Pres. Dir-Gen. 1980–86; Dir Ecole nat. d'administration 1986–88; Pres. Soc. des Investisseurs du Monde (newspaper) 1986–88; Minister of Industry, also of Territorial Devt, then of Regional Planning 1988–91; Mayor of Saint-Girons 1989–95; Pres. Cerf Editions 1987, 1992–97; Pres. Haut Conseil à l'Integration 1999–; Dir Certain Teed Products, Fabbrica Pisana (Italy), Cristalería Española (Spain), Cie Générale des Eaux, Banque Nationale de Paris, Institut Pasteur, Petrofina (Belgique); mem. Admin. Council Eurotunnel 1991–92, Commercial Union 1992–97, MK2 1993–99; mem. Supervisory Bd Vereinigte Glaswerke Siemens 1993–97, Commercial Union France 1994, Usinor 1995–, France Télécom 2000–, Orange SA 2000–; Pres. Mission of S.E. European Integration 1999–2000; Officier, Légion d'honneur, Officier, Ordre Nat. du Mérite. *Publication:* Etats de service 1998. *Address:* c/o Compagnie de Saint-Gobain, Les Miroirs, 92096 Paris-la-Défense Cedex, France.

FAVIER, Jean, DèsSc; French historian; b. 2 April 1932, Paris; m. Lucie Calisti 1956; four s.; ed Faculté des Lettres, Paris and Ecole nationale des chartes; mem. Ecole française de Rome 1956–58; Master of Confs., Faculté des lettres, Rennes 1964, Rouen 1966–69; Dir of Studies, Ecole pratique des hautes études 1965–; Prof. of Medieval Econ. History, Univ. of Paris-Sorbonne 1969–97; Dir Inst. of History, Sorbonne 1971–75; Dir Revue Historique 1973–97; Dir-Gen. Archives de France 1975–94; Head Bibliothèque Nationale de France 1996–97; Pres. Conseil d'admin., Ecole normale supérieure 1988–97; Pres. Nat. Library of France 1994–96, Asscn des lauréats du concours général 1990–2001, French Comm. for UNESCO 1997–; mem. Acads. of Lyon, Reims and Rouen; hon. mem. Luxembourg Acad.; mem. Cttee. for Nat. Celebrations 1998–; several prizes including Prix des Ambassadeurs 1978 and Grand Prix Gobert (Acad. française) 1981; Chevalier Légion d'honneur; Officier, Ordre Nat. du Mérite; Commdr des Arts et des Lettres; Chevalier des Palmes académiques and decorations from Belgium, Luxembourg and Poland. *Publications:* Un conseiller de Philippe-le-Bel: Enguerran de Marigny 1963, Les Finances pontificales à l'époque du grand schisme d'Occident 1966, De Marco Polo à Christophe Colomb 1968, Les contribuables parisiens à la fin de la guerre de cent ans 1970, Finance et fiscalité au bas moyen age 1971, Paris au XVe siècle 1974, Le trafic fluvial dans la région parisienne au XVe siècle 1975, Philippe-le-Bel 1978, La guerre de cent ans 1980, François Villon 1982, Le Temps des principautés 1984, Chronicle of the French Revolution 1788–1789 (co-ed.) 1988, L'univers de Chartres 1988, les Grandes découvertes, d'Alexandre à Magellan 1991, les Archives de la France (ed.) 1992, Dictionnaire de la France médiévale 1993, Paris, deux mille ans d'histoire 1997, Charlemagne 1999. *Leisure interests:* organ, photography. *Address:* Institut de France, 23 quai de Conti, 75006 Paris (Office); 9 rue Reiter, 94100 St-Maur-des-Fossés, France (Home).

FAVORSKY, Oleg Nikolayevich; Russian expert on thermal technology; b. 27 Jan. 1929; m.; two d.; ed Moscow Aviation Inst.; engineer, sr engineer, leading engineer, sr researcher, First Deputy Dir of Div. Cen. Inst. of Aviation Engine 1953–73, Deputy Dir 1987–95; Dir-Gen. and Chief Constructor "Sojuz" Scientific-Production Unit, USSR Ministry of Aviation Industry 1973–87; Corresp. mem. USSR (now Russian) Acad. of Sciences 1982, mem. 1990; Acad.-Sec. Dept of Physical-Tech. Problems of Energy Consumption 1995–2002; Lenin Prize. *Publications:* author of scientific works and practical devt in the field of aviation gas-turbine engines, on thermal exchange in space and in high temperature devices, problems of space ecology. *Leisure interests:*

tennis, stamp-collecting. *Address:* Russian Academy of Sciences, 32A Leninsky Prospekt, 117334 Moscow, Russia. *Telephone:* (095) 938-14-00 (Office). *Fax:* (095) 938-13-54 (Office).

FAVRHOLDT, David Cornaby, DPhil; Danish professor of philosophy; b. 24 April 1931, Oregon, USA; s. of Elias Favrholdt and Bertha Cornaby; m. 1st Nina Fønss 1961; m. 2nd Anne Birch 1968; ed Copenhagen Univ.; Asst Prof. in Philosophy, Copenhagen Univ. 1961–66; Prof. of Philosophy and Head of Dept, Odense Univ. 1966–; mem. Royal Danish Acad. of Science and Letters, Academia Europaea; mem. Danish Research Council for Humanities 1985–91; Aarhus Univ. Gold Medal 1958; Fyens Stiftstid. Research Prize 1972. *Publications:* An Interpretation and Critique of Wittgenstein's Tractatus 1964, Philosophy and Society 1968, Chinese Philosophy 1971, The List of Sins 1973, Lenin: His Philosophy and World View 1978, Niels Bohr's Philosophical Background 1992, Studies in Niels Bohr's Philosophy 1994, Philosophical Codex 1999; trans. of Wittgenstein and John Locke; Niels Bohr: Collected Works, Vol. 10 Complementarity Beyond Physics (Ed.) 1999, Aesthetics and Philosophy 2000; articles on Niels Bohr. *Leisure interests:* piano, classical music. *Address:* Department of Philosophy, Odense University, Campusvej 55, 5230 Odense M (Office); Oehlenschlaegersvej 57, 5230 Odense M, Denmark (Home). *Telephone:* 65-50-33-19. *Fax:* 65-93-23-75. *E-mail:* dafa@filos.sdu.dk (Office).

FAWCETT, Don Wayne, MD; American anatomist; b. 14 March 1917, Springdale, Iowa; s. of Carlos J. Fawcett and Mary Mable Kennedy; m. Dorothy Secrest 1941; two s. two d.; ed Harvard Coll., Harvard Medical School; Capt., Medical Corps, US Army 1943–46; Research Fellow in Anatomy, Harvard Medical School 1946, Instructor 1946–68, Assoc. 1948–51, Asst Prof. 1951–55, Hersey Prof. of Anatomy and Head of Dept 1959–85, Prof. Emer.; Curator, Warren Anatomical Museum 1961–70, James Stillman Prof. of Comparative Anatomy 1962–85, Sr Assoc. Dean for Preclinical Affairs 1975–77; scientist Int. Laboratory for Research on Animal Diseases, Kenya 1980–85; Prof. and Chair. Dept of Anatomy, Cornell Medical Coll. 1955–59; Pres. American Asscn of Anatomists 1965–66, American Soc. for Cell Biology 1961–62, Int. Fed. of Socs. for Electron Microscopy 1976–79; mem. NAS and numerous socs.; numerous hon. degrees. *Publications:* over 200 papers and three textbooks on histology, cell biology and reproductive biology. *Leisure interests:* photography of nature and wildlife, shell collecting. *Address:* 1224 Lincoln Road, Missoula, MT 59802, USA. *Telephone:* (406) 549-1415. *E-mail:* dfawc20586@aol.com.

FAYE, Jean Pierre; French writer; b. 19 July 1925, Paris; m. Marie-Odile Demenge 1952; one s. one d.; ed Univ. de Paris à la Sorbonne; teacher, Lycée de Reims 1951–54; Exchange Fellow Univ. of Chicago 1954–55; Asst Prof. Univ. de Lille 1955–56, Univ. de Paris (Sorbonne) 1956–60; Research, CNRS 1960 (Dir of Research 1983); Founder of the Collectif Change and Centre d'Analyse et de Sociologie des Langages (CASL); Founder and Pres. High Council, Coll. Int. de Philosophie; Founder and Pres. The European Philosophical Univ., now European Univ. of Research, Paris 1985–90, 1993–, Inst. for Foundation of the European City of Culture 1997; Ed. of the review Change 1968–85; Prix Renaudot 1964, Chevalier Légion d'honneur, Commdr des Arts et des Lettres. *Artistic achievements:* art exhbns: paintings, books and catalogues of Titus-Carmel, Erro, Fromanger, Velickovic, Vieira da Silva, Henri Maccheroni, Kienholz; plays: Le Centre, directed by Polieri, Hommes et Pierres, directed by Roger Blin, Vitrine, directed by Jacques Mauclair; radio: 15 lectures on Nietzsche 2000; television: debate on Nietzsche 2002. *Publications:* novels: Entre les rues 1958, La cassure 1961, Battement 1962, Analogues 1964, L'écluse 1964, Les troyens 1970, Inferno versions 1975, L'ovale 1975, Yumi, visage caméra 1983; poems: Fleuve renversé 1959, Théâtre 1964 (produced at Odéon, Théâtre de France by Roger Blin 1965); Couleurs pliées 1965, Verres 1977, Syeeda 1984; essays: Le récit hunique 1967, Langages totalitaires, Théorie du récit 1972, La critique du langage et son économie 1973, Migrations du récit sur le peuple juif 1974, Les Grandes Journées du Père Duchesne 1981, Dictionnaire Politique, essai de Philosophie Politique 1982, La raison narrative 1990, Le livre de Lioube 1992, La Grande Nap 1992, Ode Europe 1992, La déraison antisémite et son langage 1993, Le piège: La philosophie heideggerienne et le nationalsocialisme 1993, Didjla, le Tigre 1994, Le langage meurtrier 1995, le Siècle des idéologies 1996, Qu'est-ce que la philosophie? 1997, Guerre trouvée 1997, Le vrai Nietzsche 1998, Le livre du vrai 1998, Nietzsche et Salomé 2000, Court traité sur le transformat 2000, Introduction aux langages totalitaires 2003. *Address:* European University of Research, 1 rue Descartes, 75005 Paris (Office); 1B rue Vaneau, 75007 Paris, France (Home). *Telephone:* (1) 4705-1803 (Home).

FAYED, Mohamed al-; Egyptian business executive; b. 27 Jan. 1933, Alexandria; s. of Aly Aly Fayed; m. 1st Samira Khashoggi 1954 (divorced 1958); one s. (died 1997); m. 2nd Heini Wathen; four c.; f. co. in Alexandria 1956; involved in shipping, property, banking, oil and construction; Chair. and owner Ritz Hotel, Paris 1979–; Chair. Harrods Ltd 1985–, Harrods Holdings PLC 1994–; owner Fulham Football Club 1997–; Hon. mem. Emmanuel Coll., Cambridge; Officier, Légion d'honneur 1993, La Grande Médaille de la Ville de Paris 1985, Plaque de Paris 1989, Commdr Order of Merit (Italy) 1990. *Address:* Harrods Ltd, Brompton Road, London, SW1X 7XL, England.

FAYEZ, Mohamed Baha-Eldin, PhD; Egyptian professor of chemistry; b. 4 Feb. 1927, Cairo; ed Alexandria and Glasgow Univs; scientist Nat. Research Centre (NRC), Cairo, f. Dept of Chem. of Natural Products, Dir NRC 1984–87, now Research Prof. Emer.; six industrial inventions including a urinary tract medicine; Science and Tech. Exec., Egyptian Acad. of Scientific Research and Tech., later Vice-Pres.; Founder and Dir UNDP Knowledge Transfer Programme in Egypt 1980; active in promoting tech. as essential part of econ. devt 1976–, maj. contrib. to formulation of a nat. tech. policy for Egypt 1984; Chair. UN Intergovernmental Cttee on Science and Tech. for Devt, UNCTAD Cttees on Transfer of Tech. and Reverse Transfer of Tech.; consultant to UN on tech. policies and tech. devt, adviser on tech. devt to UNCTAD in Zimbabwe; Egyptian del. int. and UN groups on tech. transformation and tech. transfer for developing countries; Fellow Islamic Acad. of Sciences; State Prize for Chem. (Egypt) 1966, Prize for Islamic Medicine, Kuwait Foundation for the Advancement of Science 1982, Prize for Outstanding Invention of the Year, WIPO 1984, State Prize of Merit in Sciences (Egypt) 1990. *Address:* Islamic Academy of Sciences, P.O. Box 830036, Amman, Jordan (Office). *Telephone:* 5522104 (Office). *Fax:* 5511803 (Office).

FAYYAD, Salam, PhD; Palestinian politician and economist; b. 1952, Tulkarm, W. Bank; ed American Univ. of Beirut, Lebanon, Univ. of Texas, USA; fmr Lecturer of Econs, Yarmuk Univ., Jordan; fmr official US Fed. Reserve Bank, St Louis; joined IMF, Washington DC 1987, various sr positions including Resident Rep. to Palestinian Authority (PA) 1995–2001; Regional Man. of West Bank–Gaza, Arab Bank 2001–02; Minister of Finance, PA June 2002–. *Address:* Ministry of Finance, Sateh Marhaba, Al-Birah/Ramallah (Office); Ministry of Finance, POB 4007, Gaza, Palestinian Autonomous Areas (Office). *Telephone:* (2) 2400372 (Office); (8) 2826295 (Office). *Fax:* (2) 2405880 (Office); (8) 2820696 (Office). *E-mail:* mofdep@hally.edu (Office). *Website:* www.mof.gov.ps (Office).

FAZIO, Antonio; Italian central banker; b. 11 Oct. 1936, Alvito, Frosinone; s. of the late Eugenio Fazio and Maria Giuseppa Persichetti; m. Maria Cristina Rosati; one s. four d.; ed Univ. of Rome, Massachusetts Inst. of Tech., USA; Research Fellow, Research Dept, Banca d'Italia 1960, Consultant to Research Dept 1961–66, Deputy Head, then Head Econometric Research Office 1966, Deputy Dir Research Dept.'s Monetary Section 1972, Head Research Dept 1973–79, Cen. Man. for Econ. Research 1980, Deputy Dir-Gen. Banca d'Italia 1982–93, Gov. 1993–; Asst Prof. of Demography, Univ. of Rome 1961–66; Paul Harris Fellow (Rotary Int.); Hon. DEcon (Bari); Hon. DLitt (John Hopkins) 1995; Hon. Rer.Pol. (Macerata) 1996; Hon. LLB (Cassino) 1999; Hon. D. Computer Eng (Lecce) 2000; Int. Award in the Humanities, Accademia di Studi Mediterranei 1999; St Vincent Prize for Econs 1997, 'Pico della Mirandola' Prize for Econs, Finance and Business 1997–98; Kt, Grand Gross Order of Merit (Italy). *Publications:* texts dealing mainly with monetary theory, econ. policy and monetary policy issues. *Address:* Banca d'Italia, Via Nazionale 91, 00184 Rome, Italy. *Telephone:* (06) 47921. *Fax:* (06) 47923365. *Website:* www.bancaditalia.it.

FEARON, Douglas Thomas, BA, MD, FRCP, FAAS; American professor of immunology; b. 16 Oct. 1942, Brooklyn, New York; s. of the late Henry Dana Fearon and of Frances Fearon (née Eubanks); m. 2nd Clare M. Wheless 1977; one s. one d.; ed Williams Coll., Johns Hopkins Univ. School of Medicine; residency Johns Hopkins Hosp. 1968–70; U.S. Army Medical Corps 1970–72; Post-doctoral Fellowship Harvard Medical School 1972–75, instructor Harvard Medical School 1975–76, Asst Prof. of Medicine 1976–79, Assoc. Prof. 1979–84, Prof. of Medicine 1984–87; Prof. of Medicine, Johns Hopkins Univ. School of Medicine 1987–93; Wellcome Trust Prof. of Medicine, Cambridge Univ. 1993–; Hon. Consultant Addenbrooke's Hosp. Cambridge 1993–; mem. Scientific Bd, Ludwig Inst. for Cancer Research 1998–; Founding mem. Acad. of Medical Sciences; Lee C. Howley Prize, Arthritis Foundation; Bronze Star (U.S. Army). *Publications:* over 100 articles in scientific journals. *Leisure interest:* golf. *Address:* Wellcome Trust Immunology Unit, MRC Centre, Hills Road, Cambridge, CB2 2SP, England. *Telephone:* (1223) 330528. *Fax:* (1223) 336815. *E-mail:* dtf1000@cus.cam.ac.uk (Office).

FEAST, Michael William, PhD, DSc, FRAS, FRSSA, ARCS; South African astronomer; b. 29 Dec. 1926, Deal, England; s. of Frederick Feast and Dorothy Feast (née Knight); m. Elizabeth Constance Maskew 1962; two s. two d.; ed Imperial Coll., London; Postdoctoral Fellow, Nat. Research Council of Canada 1949–51, astronomer Radcliffe Observatory 1952–74, South African Astronomical Observatory 1974–92, Dir 1977–92; Royal Soc. Guest Fellow Inst. of Astronomy, Cambridge 1992–93; Pres. Int. Astronomical Union Comm. on Stellar Spectra 1967–70, on Variable Stars 1970–76; Vice-Pres. Int. Astronomical Union 1979–85; Pres. Astronomical Soc. of SA 1957–58, 1979–80; Founder mem. S. African Acad. of Science 1995–; Hon. Prof. of Astronomy, Univ. of Cape Town 1983–; Assoc. Royal Astronomical Soc.; Hon. DSc (Cape Town) 1993; Gill Medal, Astronomical Soc. of SA 1983, de Beers' Gold Medal (S. African Inst. of Physics) 1992. *Publications:* over 300 astronomical and physics papers, mainly in Royal Astronomical Soc. monthly notices. *Address:* Astronomy Department, University of Cape Town, Rondebosch 7701, South Africa. *Telephone:* (21) 6502396. *Fax:* (21) 6503342. *E-mail:* mwf@artemisia .ast.uct.ac.za (Office).

FEBRES CORDERO RIVADENEIRA, León; Ecuadorean businessman, engineer and politician; b. March 1931, Guayaquil; s. of Augustín Febres Cordero Tyler and María Rivadeneira Aguirre; m. María Eugenia Cordovéz Pontón (divorced 1988); four d.; ed Charlotte Hall Mil. Acad., Md and Stevens Inst. of Tech., NM, U.S.A.; Deputy 1967–68, 1970–84; Senator 1968–70; Pres. Nat. Congress's Comm. on Econs. and Finance 1968–70; mem. Partido Social

Cristiano (PSC) 1970–; PSC cand. in elections 1978, 1979; Pres. of Ecuador 1984–88; Mayor of Guayaquil 1992–2000. *Address:* c/o Partido Social Cristiano, Carnón 548 y Reina Victoria, Casilla 9454, Quito, Ecuador.

FEDDEN, (Adye) Mary, OBE, RA; British painter; b. 14 Aug. 1915, Bristol; d. of Harry Vincent Fedden and Ida Margaret Fedden (née Prichard); m. Julian Trevelyan 1951 (died 1988); ed Badminton School, Bristol, Slade School of Art, London; taught painting at Royal Coll. of Art 1956–64, Yehudi Menuhin School 1964–74; exhbns at Redfern, Beaux Arts, Christopher Hull and New Grafton Galleries, London and various provincial galleries 1948–; works purchased by HM The Queen, Tate Gallery, Crown Prince of Jordan; Pres. Royal W of England Acad. 1984–88; Hon. DLitt (Bath) 1996. *Publication:* (illustrator) The Green Man 1998. *Leisure interests:* cycling, reading. *Address:* Durham Wharf, Hammersmith Terrace, London, W6 9TS, England.

FEDERMAN, Raymond; American professor of literature and writer; b. 15 May 1928, Paris, France; m. Erica Hubscher 1960; one d.; ed Univ. Calif. at Los Angeles and Columbia Univ.; Asst Prof. Univ. of Calif. at Santa Barbara 1959–64; Assoc. Prof. State Univ. of NY, Buffalo 1964–68, Prof. 1968–90, Distinguished Prof. of Literature 1990–, Melodia E. Jones Distinguished Prof. 1992–; Guggenheim Fellow 1966–67, NEA Fellow 1986; American Book Award 1987. *Publications:* novels: Double or Nothing 1971, Take It or Leave It 1976, The Voice in the Closet 1979, The Twofold Vibration 1982, Smiles on Washington Square 1985, To Whom It May Concern 1990; essays: Journey to Chaos 1965, Surfiction 1976, Critifiction 1992, The Supreme Indecision of the Writer 1996, La Fourrure de Ma Tante Rachel 1996, Loose Shoes 1999, The Precipice and Other Catastrophes 1999. *Leisure interests:* golf, tennis. *Address:* State University of New York, Department of English, Clemens Hall, Buffalo, NY 14620, USA (Office).

FEDERSPIEL, Thomas Holger; Danish lawyer; b. 25 Oct. 1935, Hellerup; s. of Per Torben Federspiel and Elin Federspiel (née Zahle); m. 1st Benedicte Buhl 1965 (divorced 1984); two s.; m. 2nd Bettina Hage 1997; ed Krebs Skole, Rungsted Statsskole, Copenhagen Univ; Assoc. Jonas Bruun 1961–66, Slaughter and May, London, Davis Polk & Wardwell 1966–67; Partner Per Federspiel 1968, Gorrissen & Federspiel (now Gorrissen Federspiel Kierkegaard) 1989–; admitted to Court of Appeal 1964, Supreme Court 1969; F. Gorrissen & Federspiel 1989; Chair. Danish Bar Council Cttee on Pvt. Int. Law 1971–81; Pres. Int. Bar Asscn 1980–82; mem. Council Int. Bar Asscn 1971–84; mem. Bd Queen Margrethe's and Prince Henrik's Foundation; Chair. and mem. Bd various cos. and charitable foundations; Hon. mem. Int. Bar Asscn 1984; Hon. mem. American Bar Asscn 1981; Hon. Legal Adviser to the British Embassy; Kt of the Order of Dannebrog, Insignia of Honour of the Order of Dannebrog. *Leisure interests:* tennis, skiing, shooting, reading. *Address:* 12 H.C. Andersens Boulevard, 1553 Copenhagen (Office); Rungsted Strandvej 22, 2950 Vedbaek, Denmark (Home). *Telephone:* 33-41-41-41 (Office); 45-86-13-42 (Home). *Fax:* 33-41-41-33 (Office). *E-mail:* tf@gfklaw.dk (Office).

FEDORENKO, Nikolay Prokofiyevich; Russian economist; b. 28 April 1917, Preobrazhenskoe Village, Zaporozhye Region; m. Nina Fedorenko; one d.; ed Moscow M. V. Lomonosov Inst. of Fine Chemical Tech. and Higher Party School of CPSU Cen. Cttee; Soviet Army 1942–45; Instructor, Head of Dept, Moscow M. V. Lomonosov Inst. of Fine Chemical Tech. 1946–62; Deputy Academician-Sec. Dept of Econs, USSR Acad. of Sciences 1962–63; Dir Cen. Econ.-Mathematical Inst., USSR Acad. of Sciences 1963–85, Adviser 1985–; Corresp. mem. USSR (now Russian) Acad. of Sciences 1962–64; mem. 1964; Academician-Sec. Dept of Economy, 1972–85, mem. Presidium 1985–88, Adviser to Presidium 1988–; Hon. Dir USSR (now Russian) Acad. of Sciences 1987–; Hon. Dr. (Geneva); State Prize 1970, V.S. Nemchinov Prize 1984, G. M. Krzhizhanovsky Prize. *Publications:* numerous works on economics of chemical industry. *Leisure interests:* Russian and foreign painting. *Address:* Central Economics-Mathematical Institute, Krasikova str. 22, 117418 Moscow, Russia. *Telephone:* (095) 129-06-33 (Office).

FEDOROV, Boris Grigorievich, D.ECON.SC.; Russian politician and economist; b. 13 Feb. 1958, Moscow; s. of Grigory Fedorov and Nina Fedorov; m. 1983; one s. one d.; ed Moscow Inst. of Finance; worked as economist, Sr Economist, Head Currency and Econ. Dept USSR State Bank 1980–87; researcher Inst. of World Econ. and Int. Relations USSR (now Russian) Acad. of Sciences 1987–90; consultant to Social-Econ. Dept Cen. Cttee CPSU 1980–90; Minister of Finance Govt of Russian Fed. July–Dec. 1990, first minister who resigned in protest against denunciation of Radical Reform Programme 500 Days; Counsellor of Pres. Boris Yeltsin on financial problems 1991; Sr Banker, EBRD, London 1991–92; Exec. Dir IBRD, Washington, DC Oct.–Dec. 1992; Deputy Chair. Govt of Russia 1992–94; Minister of Finance 1993–94; mem. State Duma (Parl.) 1993–98; Leader Russia Forward! (political movt) 1993–; Founder and Pres. Liberal-Democratic Fund 1997; Head State Taxation Service May–Sept. 1998; Deputy Prime Minister Aug. 1998; mem. Bd of Dirs Unified Power Grids of Russia (representing small shareholders) 1999–. *Publications:* International Commercial Arbitration 1999, New English Russian Banking Dictionary 2000; numerous articles on econ. matters. *Leisure interests:* reading biographies, collecting coins. *Address:* Vpered Russiya!, Kommunisticheskaya 13, sfr. 3G, Building 4, 109004 Moscow, Russia. *Telephone:* (095) 911-90-50.

FEDOROV, Nikolai Vasilievich, C.LAW; Russian/Chuvash politician and lawyer; b. 9 May 1958, Chuvash Autonomous Repub.; m.; one s. one d.; ed Kazan State Univ., Inst. of State and Law, USSR Acad. of Sciences; worked in legal bodies since 1983; teacher Chuvash State Univ. 1980–82, 1985–89; USSR People's Deputy 1989–91; Deputy Chair. Legis. Comm. Supreme Soviet 1989–90; Minister of Justice of RSFSR (later Russia) 1990–93; Pres. Chuvash Repub. 1994–; mem. Council of Fed. 1996–2002; Order for Merits to Fatherland 1998, State Prize of Russia 1999. *Address:* Office of the President, Respubliki Sq. 1, 428904 Cheboksary, Chuvash Republic, Russia (Office). *Telephone:* (8352) 62-46-87 (Cheboksary) (Office). *Fax:* (8352) 62-17-99 (Office). *E-mail:* president@chuvashia.com (Office). *Website:* www.cap.ru (Office).

FEDOROV, Valentin Petrovich, D.ECON.SC.; Russian politician and manager; b. 6 Sept. 1939, Zhatai, Yakutia; m.; two d.; ed G. Plekhanov Moscow Inst. of Nat. Econ., Inst. of World Econ. and Int. Relations USSR Acad. of Sciences; worked in State Planning Cttee Yakutia 1964–78; jr researcher, Head of Div., Corresp. Journal of Inst. of World Econ. and Int. Relations in W Germany 1978–84; Prorector on Int. Relations, Prof. G. V. Plekhanov Moscow Inst. of Nat. Econ., 1987–90; Governor Sakhalin Region, opposed transfer of S Kuril Islands to Japan 1990–93; Deputy Minister of Econ. 1993–94; Prime Minister of Sakhá (Yakutia) Repub. 1997–98; mem. Political Council Movt for Democratic Reforms, Co-Chair. Duma of Russian Nat. Sobor; Vice-Pres. Russian Union of Industrialists and Entrepreneurs 1994–2001; Pres. Asscn. of Road-Builders 1996–; Deputy Dir Inst. of Europe 2000–; mem. Russian Acad. of Natural Sciences, Russian Eng Acad. *Publications:* FRG: Country and People; several plays, collections of poems, monographs on econs. *Address:* Institute of Europe, Mokhovaya str. 11, 3B, 1038730 Moscow, Russia (Office). *Telephone:* (095) 203-32-67 (Office). *Fax:* (095) 200-42-98 (Office). *E-mail:* vpfyodorov@mail.ru. *Website:* www.ieras.ru (Office).

FEDOSEYEV, Vladimir Ivanovich; Russian conductor; b. 5 Aug. 1932, Leningrad; s. of Ivan Fedoseyev and Elena Fedoseyeva; m. Olga Dobrokhotova; two c.; ed conductors' class of Moscow Musical Pedagogical Inst., Moscow Conservatoire; mem. CPSU 1963–91; Artistic Dir and Chief Conductor Moscow Radio Symphony Orchestra of USSR Radio Network (now Tchaikovsky Acad. Symphony Orchestra) 1974–; concurrently Music Dir Vienna Symphony Orchestra 1997–; first Perm. Guest Conductor Tokyo Philharmonic Orchestra 1996–; Perm. Guest Conductor Zürich Opera 1997–; works with Bolshoi and Mariinsky Theatres, opera productions and concerts abroad, including Italy, France, Austria, Germany, Japan, Switzerland, Spain, UK, USA; People's Artist of USSR 1980, RSFSR State Prize 1989, Crystal Award of Asahi Broadcasting Corpn, Osaka 1989, Golden Orpheus, for recording of opera May Night. *Address:* Moscow House of Recording and Broadcasting, Malaya Nikitskaya 24, 121069 Moscow, Russia. *Telephone:* (095) 222-00-24 (Office); (095) 229-57-68(Moscow) (Home); (1) 406-54-96 (Vienna) (Home). *Fax:* (095) 202-49-85.

FEDOSOV, Yevgeny Aleksandrovich, DTechSc; Russian automation and avionics specialist; b. 14 May 1929, Moscow; s. of Alexander Yefimovitch Fedosov and Nadezhda Anempodistovna Smirnova; m. Lydia Petrovna Vasilyeva; one d.; ed Bauman Tech. Inst.; post-grad. work at Inst. 1953–56; mem. CPSU 1959–91; Research Fellow, Head of Dept, Deputy Dir of Inst. of Aviation Systems 1956–70, Dir 1970–; simultaneously Head of Dept of Physico-Tech. Inst. 1970–; Prof. 1969; Corresp. mem. USSR Acad. of Sciences 1979, mem. 1984–; Lenin Prize 1976, Hero of Socialist Labour 1983, B. N. Petrov Gold Medal, Acad. of Sciences 1989, Honoured Scientist of Russian Fed. 1996. *Publications:* works on analysis and synthesis of complex multilevel operational systems. *Leisure interests:* tennis, gardening. *Address:* Institute of Aviation Systems, Viktorenko str. 7, 125319 Moscow, Russia. *Telephone:* (095) 157-70-47 (Office). *Fax:* (095) 943-86-05 (Office).

FEDOTOV, Aleksei Leonidovich; Russian diplomatist; b. 29 June 1949, Moscow; m. Yelena Fedotova; one d.; ed Moscow State Inst. of Int. Relations; Counsellor USSR Embassy, Sri-Lanka 1972–74, Singapore 1983–85; attaché Dept of S Asia, Ministry of Foreign Affairs 1974–78, adviser, 1986; Third, Second, First Sec., Secr. of Deputy Minister, Asst to Deputy Minister 1978–83; Counsellor, Deputy Head of Div., Sr Counsellor, Head of Div. 1986–92, Head of Dept, Deputy Exec. Sec., Deputy Dir of Dept, Deputy Exec. Sec. 1992–96, Dir, Dept of Personnel, mem. Bd of Dirs Ministry of Foreign Affairs 1996–2000; Deputy Minister of Foreign Affairs 2000–. *Address:* Ministry of Foreign Affairs, Smolenskaya Sennaya str. 32/34, 121120 Moscow, Russia (Office). *Telephone:* (095) 244-41-39 (Office). *Fax:* (095) 244-36-91 (Office). *E-mail:* afedotov@mid.ru (Office).

FEDOTOV, Maxim Viktorovich; Russian violinist; b. 24 July 1961, Moscow; s. of Viktor Andreyevich Fedotov and Galina Nikolayevna Fedotova; m. Galina Yevgenyevna Petrova, pianist; one d.; ed Specialized Music School for Gifted Children in Leningrad, Moscow State Conservatory (with D. Tsyganov and I. Bezrodny); concert tours since 1975; Prof. Moscow State Conservatory 1987–; as soloist plays with G. Petrova, regular recitals in Moscow and St Petersburg; performed in Madrid, Berlin, Leipzig, Frankfurt, Cologne, Milan, Chicago and other cities; debut in London 1993 (Barbican Hall); took part in music festivals in Salzburg, Oakland, Bergen, Dresden, Klagenfurt; toured Australia, New Zealand, Korea, Turkey; prize winner All-Union Music Competition Riga 1981, N. Paganini Competition Genoa 1982, Vercelli 1984, P. Tchaikovsky (Moscow 1986), Tokyo 1986 (First Prize); Merited Artist of Russia. *Address:* Tolbukhin str. 8, korp. 1, Apt. 6, 121596 Moscow, Russia. *Telephone:* (095) 447-25-60 (Home).

FEDOTOV, Mikhail Aleksandrovich, D.JUR; Russian politician and lawyer; b. 18 Sept. 1949, Moscow; m. 3rd Maria Fedotova; one s. one d; ed Moscow State Univ., All-Union Inst. of Law; teacher of law All-Union Inst. of Law 1973–90; Deputy Minister of Press and Mass Information of Russia 1991–92, Minister 1992–93; rep. Pres. Yeltsin in Constitutional Court trial against CPSU 1992; Dir-Gen. Russian Agency of Intellectual Property (RAIS) Feb.–Dec. 1992; Russian rep. at UNESCO, Paris 1993–97; Sec. Russian Union of Journalists 1998–. *Address:* Russian Union of Journalists, Zubovskiy blvd 4, 119021 Moscow, Russia. *Telephone:* (095) 201-44-47.

FEDOTOV, Yuri Victorovich; Russian diplomatist; b. 14 Dec. 1947, Moscow; Yelena Fedotova; ed Moscow State Inst. of Int. Relations; entered diplomatic service 1971, different posts in Ministry of Foreign Affairs and abroad (Algeria, India, USA) 1971–93; Deputy Head, Dept of Int. Relations, Ministry of Foreign Affairs 1991–93; Deputy Perm. Rep. to UN, New York 1993–99; Dir, Dept of Int. Orgs., Ministry of Foreign Affairs 1999–2002, mem. Bd of Dirs 2000–; Deputy Minister of Foreign Affairs June 2002–. *Address:* Ministry of Foreign Affairs, Smolenskaya Sennaya str. 32/34, 121120 Moscow, Russia (Office). *Telephone:* (095) 244-92-94 (Office). *Fax:* (095) 244-92-95 (Office). *E-mail:* yfedotov@mid.ru (Office).

FEFFER, Marc-André (Patrice), M. DE DROIT PUBLIC; French television executive and lawyer; b. 22 Dec. 1949, Neuilly-sur-Seine; s. of Jacques Feffer and Marie-Jeanne Thirlin; m. Hélène Cataix 1976; three d.; ed Lycée Condorcet and Faculté de Droit, Inst. d'Etudes Politiques and Ecole Nat. d'Admin., Paris; official Conseil d'Etat 1976, Counsel 1980, now mem.; Sec.-Gen. Comm. des Sondages 1980; Adviser Office of Pres. of EEC 1981–84; Dir Centre Mondial Informatique et Ressource Humaine 1984; Head of Information (Legal and Tech.), Prime Minister's Staff 1985–88, Sr Defence Counsel, Information 1986–87; Sec.-Gen. Canal+ 1988–94, Gen. Man. 1994–95, Dir Exec. Cttee 1994, Exec. Vice-Pres. 1995–, Deputy Chair. Exec. Bd and Gen. Council 2000–; Chevalier, Légion d'honneur, Commdr Ordre des Arts et des Lettres. *Leisure interests:* sailing, windsurfing. *Address:* Canal +, 85–89 quai André Citroën, 75015 Paris (Office); 3 rue Jules Lefebvre, 75009 Paris, France (Home). *Telephone:* 1-44-25-14-30 (Office). *E-mail:* mfeffer@canal-plus.com (Office).

FEHER, George, PhD; American professor of physics; b. 29 May 1924, Czechoslovakia; s. of Ferdinand Feher and Sylvia Feher (née Schwartz); m. Elsa Rosenvasser Feher 1961; three d.; ed Univ. of Calif., Berkeley; Research Physicist Bell Telephone Labs, NJ 1954–60; Visiting Assoc. Prof. Columbia Univ., New York 1956–60; Prof. of Physics Univ. of Calif., San Diego 1960–; Visiting Prof. MIT 1967–68; mem. American Physical Soc., Biophysical Soc. (Nat. Lecturer 1983), mem. Bd of Dirs Technion-Israel Inst. of Tech., Haifa, Israel 1968; mem. Bd Govs Weizmann Inst. of Science, Rehovot 1988; Fellow AAA, Int. EPR/ESR Soc. 1996; mem. NAS, American Acad. of Arts and Sciences; Fellow Biophysical Soc. 2000; Hon. DPhil (Hebrew Univ. of Jerusalem) 1994; awards include American Physical Soc. Prize for origination and devt of Electron Nuclear Double Resonance (ENDOR) technique and for applying it to solid state and nuclear research problems 1960, Oliver E. Buckley Solid State Physics Prize 1976, Biophysics Prize 1982, Inaugural Annual Award, Int. Electron Spin Resonance Soc. 1991, Bruker Lectureship, Oxford Univ., UK 1992, Rumford Medal, American Acad. of Arts and Sciences 1992, Zavoiski Award 1996. *Publications:* over 200 articles in numerous specialist scientific journals, reviews, symposia. *Leisure interests:* photography, sports. *Address:* Department of Physics 0319, University of California at San Diego, 9500 Gilman Drive, La Jolla, CA 92093-0319, USA. *Telephone:* (858) 534-4389.

FEHN, Sverre, DipArch; Norwegian architect; b. 14 Aug. 1924, Kongsberg; m. Ingrid Loberg 1952; one s.; ed Oslo School of Architecture; pvt architecture practice, Oslo 1948–; residence in Paris 1953–54; Prof., Oslo School. of Architecture 1971–93; Visiting Lecturer at numerous overseas insts including The Cooper Union, NY, Cranbrook Acad. of Arts, Mich., MIT, Cambridge, Mass., Harvard Univ., Cornell Univ., Yale Univ., Int. Lab. of Architecture and Design, Urbino, Italy 1979, Geoarchitectural Inst., Brest, France 1979, Architectural Asscn, London 1981, 1982; Pritzker Architecture Prize 1997, Grosch Medal 2001. *Major works include:* Norwegian Pavilion, World Exhbn, Brussels 1958, Nordic Pavilion, Venice Biennale 1958, North Cape Church 1965, Oslo School for the Blind 1976, Villa Busk, Bamble 1990, Norwegian Glacier Museum, Fjaerland 1992, Aukrust Museum, Alvdal 1996, Ivan Aasen Centre, Orsta 2000. *Exhibitions include:* São Paulo Biennale, Brazil 1957, Vasa Univ., Finland 1964, Museum of Modern Art, NY 1968, Architecture Asscn of Minneapolis 1983, Venice Biennale 1992, 1996, Basilica, Vicenza, Italy 1997. *Publications include:* The Thought of Construction (with Per Olaf Fjeld). *Address:* Oslo School of Architecture, St. Olavsgt. 4, Oslo, 0130,Norway (Office). *Telephone:* 22-99-70-00 (Office). *Fax:* 22-99-70-22 (Office). *Website:* www.aho.no (Office).

FEHRENBACH, Charles Max, DèsSc; French professor of astronomy; b. 29 April 1914, Strasbourg; s. of Charles Fehrenbach and Alma (née Holtkemper) Fehrenbach; m. Myriam Léonie Graff 1939 (deceased); two s. one d.; m. 2nd Reine Bonnaud 1989; ed Lycée Fustel-de-Coulanges and Univ. of Strasbourg; Asst Lecturer Univ. of Strasbourg 1934; Teacher Lycée Saint-Charles, Marseille 1939; Astronomer Strasbourg Observatory 1941; Asst Dir Haute Provence Observatory 1943, Dir 1948–83; Prof. of Astronomy, Univ. of Marseilles 1948–83, Prof. Emer. 1983–; Dir Marseille Observatory 1949–81; Pres. Comm. des instruments, Observatoire européen austral 1958–72, mem. Bd

1965–72; mem. Bd Canada France Hawaii Telescope 1975–79, Pres. 1979; mem. Int. Astronomical Union, Vice-Pres. 1973–79; mem. Bureau des Longitudes 1973, Pres. 1987; mem. Rotary Int.; mem. Acad. des Sciences Paris 1968, Int. Astronautical Acad. 1986, Acad. of New York 1991; Assoc. mem. Royal Astronomical Soc., London 1961, Acad. Royale des Sciences de Belgique 1973–, Acad. of Marseille 1979, Acad. of Athens 1980; Corresp. mem. Acad. of Coimbra 1953, Halle 1966, Vienna 1973, Royal Soc. Uppsala 1984; Hon. mem. SA Astronomical Soc. 1965; Dr. hc (Geneva) 1982; Croix de guerre, Commdr Légion d'honneur, Palmes académiques, de Léopold II, Chevalier du Mérite agricole, Officier Ordre de Léopold de Belgique; Lauréat, Inst. de France, Acad. Royale de Belgique, Astron. Gesellschaft, Grand prix des sciences de la Ville de Paris 1976, Médaille d'or du CNRS 1978. *Publications:* Des hommes, des télescopes, des étoiles 1990; 280 publs in int. reviews on astronomy and related topics. *Leisure interests:* gardening, fishing. *Address:* Institut de France, 23 quai Conti, 75006 Paris (Office); Les Magnanarelles, Lourmarin 84160, France. *Telephone:* (4) 90-68-00-28. *Fax:* (4) 90-68-18-52 (Home). *E-mail:* fehrenbach.charles@wanadoo.fr (Home).

FEI XIAOTONG; Chinese social anthropologist; b. 2 Nov. 1910, Wujiang Dist, Jiangsu Prov.; s. of Fei Po-an and Yang Renglan; m. Meng Yin 1939; one d.; ed Yanjing Univ., Beijing, Qinghua Univ., Beijing, London School of Econs; Prof. of Social Anthropology, Nat. Yunnan Univ. 1939; Visiting Prof., Harvard Univ. (invited by State Dept), later Inst. of Pacific Relations, New York 1943; Prof. of Anthropology, Qinghua Univ., Beijing 1945; Visiting Fellow, LSE 1946; Deputy Dean, Qinghua Univ., Beijing 1949; Vice-Pres. Cen. Inst. of Nat. Minorities 1952; Vice-Chair. Nationalities Affairs Comm. (under State Council) 1957; Prof. of Anthropology, Cen. Inst. of Nat. Minorities 1957–1982; Pres. Sociology Soc. of China 1979; Prof. of Sociology, Beijing Univ. 1979; Dir Inst. of Sociology, Chinese Acad. of Social Sciences 1980, Emer. 1983–; Hon. Pres. Western Returned Students' Asscn 1986–, Minority Literature Foundation 1986–, Soc. of Social Devt Science 1992–; Vice-Chair. Nat. Cttee 6th CPPCC 1983–89; Vice-Chair. China Democratic League 1980–87, Chair. 1987–, Hon. Chair. 1997–; Vice-Chair. Standing Cttee 7th NPC 1988–93, 8th NPC 1993–98; Vice-Pres. Asscn for Int. Understanding of China 1988–; Hon. Chair. China Vocational Educ. Service 1994–; Huxley Lecturer, Royal Anthropological Inst. 1981; Hon. Fellow, LSE 1982; Adviser Nationalities Affairs Comm. 1983; Malinowski Award 1980; Raymond Magsaysay Award 1994. *Publications:* Peasant Life in China 1939, Earthbound China 1945, Systems of Child Rearing, Rural China 1947, Rural Reconstruction, Gentry Power and Imperial Power 1948, China's Gentry 1953, Toward a People's Anthropology 1981, Chinese Village Close-up 1983, Collections of Essays on Sociology 1985, Small Town in China 1986. *Leisure interests:* chess, jogging. *Address:* Institute of Sociology, Beijing University, Beijing, People's Republic of China.

FEIFFER, Jules; American cartoonist and writer; b. 26 Jan. 1929, New York; s. of David Feiffer and Rhoda Davis; m. 1st Judith Sheftel (divorced 1983) 1961; one d.; m. 2nd Jennifer Allen 1983; two c.; ed Art Students League, Pratt Inst.; asst to syndicated cartoonist Will Eisner 1946–51; cartoonist, author, syndicated Sunday page, Clifford, engaged in various art jobs 1953–56; contributing cartoonist Village Voice, New York City 1956–97; cartoons published weekly in The Observer (London) 1958–66, 1972–82, regularly in Playboy (magazine) 1959–; cartoons nationally syndicated in US 1959–, New Yorker 1993–, New Statesman and Society 1994–; sponsor Sane; US Army 1951–53; mem. Dramatists Guild Council 1970–; Hon. Fellow Inst. for Policy Studies 1987; Acad. Award for Animated Cartoon, Munro 1961; Special George Polk Memorial Award 1962; Best Foreign Play, English Press (for Little Murders) 1967, Outer Critics Circle Award (Obie) 1969, (The White House Murder Case) 1970, Pulitzer Prize, Editorial Cartooning 1986. *Publications:* books: Sick, Sick, Sick 1959, Passionella and Other Stories 1960, The Explainers 1961, Boy, Girl, Boy, Girl, 1962, Hold Me! 1962, Harry, The Rat With Women (novel) 1963, Feiffer's Album 1963, The Unexpurgated Memoirs of Bernard Mergendeiler 1965, The Great Comic Book Heroes 1967, Feiffer's Marriage Manual 1967, Pictures at a Prosecution 1971, Ackroyd (novel) 1978, Tantrum 1980, Jules Feiffer's America: From Eisenhower to Reagan 1982, Marriage is an Invasion of Privacy 1984, Feiffer's Children 1986, Ronald Reagan in Movie America 1988, Elliott Loves 1990 (book and play); plays: Crawling Arnold 1961, Little Murders 1966, God Bless 1968, The White House Murder Case 1970, Feiffer on Nixon: The Cartoon Presidency 1974, Knock Knock 1975, Grown Ups 1981, A Think Piece 1982; Carnal Knowledge 1988, Anthony Rose 1989; Feiffer The Collected Works Vols 1, 2, 3 1990; children's stories: The Man in the Ceiling 1993, A Barrel of Laughs, A Vale of Tears 1995; screenplays: Little Murders 1971, Carnal Knowledge 1971, Popeye 1980, I Want to Go Home 1989, I Lost My Bear 1998, Bark, George 1999. *Address:* c/o Universal Press Syndicate, 4520 Main Street, Kansas City, MO 64111, USA.

FEILDEN, Sir Bernard Melchior, Kt, CBE, DUniv, DLitt, FRIBA, FSA, FRSA; British architect; b. 11 Sept. 1919, London; s. of Robert Humphrey Feilden, MC and Olive Feilden (née Binyon); m. 1st Ruth Mildred Bainbridge 1949 (died 1994); two s. two d.; m. 2nd Christina Matilda Beatrice Murdoch 1995; ed Bedford School, Univ. Coll., London, Architectural Asscn, London; qualified as architect 1949; Sr Partner, Feilden and Mawson 1954–77, now Consultant; Architect, Norwich Cathedral 1963; Surveyor, York Minster 1965, St Paul's Cathedral, London 1969; Consultant Architect Univ. of East Anglia 1969, Hyde Park Estate, London 1972; St Giles Cathedral Project 1975, Conservation Plan for Chesterfield Town Centre 1976–81, RIBA Rep. on Ancient Monuments Bd 1962–77, mem. RIBA Council 1975–77; Pres. Ecclesiastical Architects' and Surveyors' Asscn 1976; Dir Int. Centre for the Study and Preservation of Cultural Property, Rome (ICCROM) 1977–81, Dir Emer. 1983; Pres. The Guild of Surveyors 1976; Chair. UK Cttee of Int. Council on Monuments and Sites 1981–87; Architectural Conservation Consultant; mem. Cathedrals Advisory Comm. 1981–96, Churches Conservation Cttee 1981–87; Trustee Intach UK Trust 1985–, Helen Hamlyn Trust 2000–; Hon. mem. Icomos; Hon. FAIA 1987; Dr. hc (Göteborg) 1988; Hon. DLit (Univ. East Anglia) 1989; Outstanding Conservation Award 1975, Aga Khan Award for Architecture 1986, three Civic Trust Awards and four Commendations; Gazzola Prize 1993. *Publications:* The Wonder of York Minster 1976, An Introduction to Conservation (for UNESCO) 1980, The Conservation of Historic Buildings 1982, Between Two Earthquakes 1987, Guidelines for Conservation 1989; Ed. Management Manual for World Cultural Heritage Sites (UNESCO). *Leisure interests:* painting, sailing, fishing, chess. *Address:* The Old Barn, Hall Farm Place, Bawburgh, Norwich, NR9 3LW, England. *Telephone:* (1603) 747472 (Home). *Fax:* (1603) 747472 (Home). *E-mail:* stiffkey@lineone.net (Home).

FEILDEN, Richard John Robert, OBE, MA; British architect; b. 29 March 1950, Lincoln; s. of Robert Feilden and Elizabeth Feilden; m. Patricia Feilden 1975; two s. one d.; ed Rugby School, King's Coll., Cambridge, Architectural Asscn, London; fmrly in practice with Barnsley Hewitt and Mallinson and Leonard Manasseh and Partners; f. Feilden Clegg Design 1976 (renamed Feilden Clegg 1995, then Feilden Clegg Bradley 1999), Sr Partner 1995–; Chair. Community Architecture Group, RIBA 1990–93, mem. RIBA Council 1994–2000, Vice-Chair. 1998–2000; Special Adviser, Urban Task Force 1999; Chair. Higher Educ. Design Quality Forum 1995–2000; Visiting Prof. Univ. of Cen. England 2000–; mem. Comm. for Architecture and the Built Environment 2000–. *Achievements:* wide range of projects particulary in the higher educ. sector; int. recognition for expertise in environmentally appropriate design; projects include new headquarters for Greenpeace, new environmental office for the Bldg Research Establishment. *Leisure interests:* cycling, forestry, woodwork, sailing. *Address:* Feilden Clegg Bradley Architects, Bath Brewery, Toll Bridge Road, Bath, BA1 7DE (Office); Sheephouse Farm Barn, Bathford, Bath, BA1 8EE, England (Home). *Telephone:* (1225) 852545 (Office); (1225) 858301 (Home). *Fax:* (1225) 852528 (Office). *E-mail:* rf@feildenclegg.com (Office); feildens@sheephouse.demon.co.uk (Home). *Website:* www.feildenclegg.com (Office).

FEINENDEGEN, Ludwig E., DrMed; German professor of nuclear medicine; b. 1 Jan. 1927, Garzweiler; s. of Ludwig Feinendegen and Rosa Klauth; m. Jeannine Gemuseus 1960; two s.; ed Univ. of Cologne; Asst Physician and Scientist, Medical Dept Brookhaven Nat. Lab., Upton, USA 1958–63; Scientific Officer, Euratom, Brussels and Paris 1963–67; Dir Inst. of Medicine Research Center Jülich GmbH and Prof. for Nuclear Medicine, Univ. Hosp., Düsseldorf 1967–93, Prof. Emer. 1993–; Scientist, Brookhaven Nat. Lab., USA 1993–98, Research Collaborator 2000–; Assignee, OBER Dept of Energy, USA 1994–98; Fogarty Scholar NIH, Bethesda 1998–99; mem. Advisory Council, Fed. Ministries of Interior and Defence and other professional appts; mem. Cttee for meetings of Nobel Laureates 1978–; mem. Rhine Westfalian Acad. of Sciences (Vice-Pres. 1978–79); Dist Gov. Rotary Int. 1992–93; numerous awards; Bundesverdienstorden. *Publications:* more than 600 publs in nat. and int. scientific journals and books on nuclear medicine and radiation biology. *Address:* Committee for the Meetings of Nobel Laureates in Lindau, P.O. Box 1325, 88131 Lindau 1B (Office); Medical Department, Brookhaven National Laboratory, Upton, NY 11973, USA (Office); Wannental 45, 88131 Lindau, Germany (Home). *Telephone:* (8382) 260025 (Germany) (Office); (631) 344-2837 (USA) (Office); (8382) 75673 (Home). *Fax:* (8382) 262694 (Germany) (Office); (631) 344-2653 (USA) (Office); (8382) 947626 (Home). *E-mail:* feinendegen@gmx.net (Home).

FEINGOLD, Russell Dana, BA, JD; American politician and lawyer; b. 2 March 1953, Janesville, Wis.; s. of Leon Feingold and Sylvia Binstock; m. 1st Susan Levine 1977; two d.; m. 2nd Mary Speerschneider 1991; two step-c.; ed Univ. of Wisconsin, Madison, Magdalen Coll. Oxford, UK, Harvard Univ. Law School; practised as attorney 1979–85; Democrat State Senator 1983–92, US Senator from Wisconsin 1993–. *Address:* US Senate, 506 Hart Senate Office Bldg, Washington, DC 20510-0001 (Office); 8383 Greenway Boulevard, Middleton, WI 53562, USA.

FEINSTEIN, Charles Hilliard, BCom, MA, PhD, C.A.(S.A.), FBA; British professor of economic history; b. 18 March 1932, Johannesburg, S. Africa; s. of Louis Feinstein and Rose Feinstein; m. 1st Ruth Loshak 1958; m. 2nd Anne Digby 1980; one s. three d.; ed Parktown Boys' High School, Johannesburg, Univs. of Witwatersrand and Cambridge; Research Officer, Dept of Applied Econs Univ. of Cambridge 1958–63, Lecturer, Faculty of Econs 1963–78; Fellow, Clare Coll., Cambridge 1963–78, Sr Tutor 1969–78; Prof. of Econ. and Social History, Univ. of York 1978–87, Head, Dept of Econs and Related Studies 1981–86; Reader in Recent Social and Econ. History, Univ. of Oxford; Professorial Fellow, Nuffield Coll., Oxford 1987–89; Chichele Prof. of Econ. History, Univ. of Oxford 1989–99; Fellow All Souls Coll., Oxford 1989–99; Man. Ed. Economic Journal 1980–86; mem. Council and Exec. Cttee Royal Econ. Soc. 1980–90; mem. Council, Econ. History Soc. 1980–98; mem. Econ. Affairs Cttee, Econ. and Social Research Council 1982–86; mem. Council British Acad. 1990–93 (Vice-Pres. 1991–93); Visiting Scholar, Dept of Econs, Harvard Univ. 1986–87; Visiting Prof. Div. of the Humanities and Social Sciences, Calif. Inst. of Tech. 1997; Visiting Prof. Dept of Econs, Univ. of Cape Town 1998–2002, Dept of Econs Keio Univ. 2001; Hon. Fellow Clare Coll.

Cambridge 1994, Hon. Fellow Nuffield Coll. Oxford 2002. *Publications:* Domestic Capital Formation in the United Kingdom 1920–38 1965, Socialism, Capitalism and Economic Growth (essays, ed.) 1972, National Income, Expenditure and Output of the United Kingdom, 1855–1965, 1972, York 1831–1981 (ed.) 1981, British Economic Growth (with R. C. O. Matthews and J. Odling-Smee) 1982, The Managed Economy, Essays in British Economic Policy and Performance since 1929 (ed.) 1983, Studies in Capital Formation in the United Kingdom, 1750–1920 (with S. Pollard) 1988, Banking, Currency and Finance in Europe between the Wars (ed.) 1995, The European Economy Between the Wars (with P. Temin and G. Toniolo) 1997, Chinese Technology Transfer in the 1990s (ed., with C. Howe) 1997, The Economic Development of the United Kingdom since 1870 (ed.) 1997, Making History Count (with M. Thomas) 2002. *Leisure interests:* reading, theatre, collecting secondhand books. *Address:* Treetops, Harberton Mead, Headington, Oxford, OX3 0DB, England (Home). *Telephone:* (1865) 763993 (Home). *Fax:* (1865) 279299 (Office). *E-mail:* charles.feinstein@all-souls.ox.ac.uk (Office).

FEINSTEIN, Dianne; American politician; b. 22 June 1933, San Francisco, Calif.; d. of Leon and Betty (Rosenburg) Goldman; m. 1st Bertram Feinstein 1962 (deceased); one d.; m. 2nd Richard C. Blum 1980; ed Stanford Univ., Calif.; Intern in Public Affairs, Coro Foundation, San Francisco 1955–56; Asst to Calif. Industrial Welfare Comm., Los Angeles, also San Francisco 1956–57; Vice-Chair. Calif. Women's Bd Terms and Parole 1962–66; Chair. San Francisco City and County Advisory Comm. for Adult Detention 1967–69; Supervisor City and County of San Francisco 1970–78; Mayor of San Francisco 1978–88; Senator from California 1992–; mem. numerous other public bodies etc.; Democrat; numerous hon. degrees. *Address:* US Senate, 331 Senate Hart Office Building, Washington, DC 20510-0001, USA.

FELBER, René; Swiss politician; b. 14 March 1933, Biel; m.; three c.; teacher, Boudevilliers 1953–55, Le Locle 1955–64; joined Social Democratic Party 1958; Mayor of Gen. Council, Le Locle 1960; Mayor of Le Locle 1964–80; mem. of Parl., Neuchâtel 1965–76; Nat. Councillor 1967–81; mem. Govt of Repub. and Canton of Neuchâtel; Head of Cantonal Dept of Finances 1981–87; Pres. Govt of Neuchâtel 1984; mem. Fed. Council 1988–93; Head Fed. Dept of Foreign Affairs 1988; Vice-Pres. Jan.–Dec. 1991, Pres. of Switzerland Jan.–Dec. 1992. *Address:* c/o Social Democratic Party, Spitalgasse 34, 3001 Bern, Switzerland.

FELCH, William Campbell, MD; American physician; b. 14 Nov. 1920, Lakewood, Ohio; s. of Don H. W. Felch and Beth Campbell; m. Nancy Cook Dean 1945; two s. one d.; ed Phillips Exeter Acad., Princeton Univ. and Columbia Coll. of Physicians and Surgeons; served US Army 1942–48; in pvt. practice, internal medicine 1951–88; Chief of Staff, United Hosp., Port Chester, New York 1975–77; Ed. The Internist 1975–86; Medical Dir Osborn Home, Rye 1979–88; Exec. Vice-Pres. Alliance for Continuing Medical Educ. 1979–91 (Distinguished Service Award 1991); mem. Inst. of Medicine, NAS; Fellow American Coll. of Physicians; Ed. ACME Almanac 1978–90, Journal of Continuing Educ. in the Health Professions 1992–94; Award of Merit, New York State Soc. of Internal Medicine 1976; Internist of Distinction, Soc. of Internal Medicine of New York 1973. *Publications:* Aspiration and Achievement 1981, Primer, Continuing Medical Education (Co-Ed.) 1986, Decade of Decisions 1989, Vision of the Future 1991, The Secrets of Good Patient Care 1996, Alliance for Continuing Medical Education: The First 20 years 1996, A Chronical of Commitments: A Memoir 2001. *Leisure interest:* travel. *Address:* 8545 Carmel Valley Road, Carmel, CA 93923, USA. *Telephone:* (831) 625-6593. *Fax:* (831) 624-4032 (Home). *E-mail:* srfelch@aol.com (Home).

FELD, Eliot; American dancer and choreographer; b. 5 July 1942, Brooklyn, New York; s. of Benjamin Feld and Alice Posner; ed High School of Performing Arts, New York; debut as Child Prince in Nutcracker, New York City Ballet 1954; mem. cast, West Side Story, Broadway 1958 (also appeared in film), I Can Get It For You Wholesale, Broadway 1962 and Fiddler on the Roof, Broadway; dancer and choreographer, American Ballet Theater 1963–68; Founder, Prin. Dancer and Choreographer, American Ballet Co. 1968–71; freelance choreographer, N America and Europe 1971–73; Founder, Artistic Dir and Choreographer, Feld Ballets, NY; Founder, The New Ballet School 1977, The Joyce Theater 1982, Ballet Tech 1996; Co-founder, Lawrence A. Wien Center for Dance & Theater 1986; has choreographed over 100 ballets since 1967 including Nodrog Doggo 2000, Coup de Couperin 2000, Organon 2001, Pacific Dances 2001, Skandia 2002, Pianola 2002, Lincoln Portrait 2002, Behold the Man 2002; Guggenheim Fellow; Dance Magazine Award 1990; Dr. hc (Juilliard) 1991. *Address:* c/o Ballet Tech., 890 Broadway, 8th Floor, New York, NY 10003-1211, USA (Office). *Telephone:* (212) 777-7710 (Office). *Fax:* (212) 353-0936.

FELDBAEK, Ole, MA, DPhil; Danish professor of economic history; b. 22 July 1936, Copenhagen; s. of Commdr Henri Feldbaek and Kathy Feldbaek; m. Inge Kjaergaard 1976; one s. one d.; ed Univ. of Copenhagen; Lecturer in Econ. History, Univ. of Copenhagen 1968, Prof. 1981–; Fellow, Royal Danish and Royal Norwegian Acads., Acad. Europaea; The Amalienborg Prize 2001. *Publications:* books and articles on 18th century European and Asian history (econ., political and mil.). *Address:* 15 Efteraarsvej, 2920 Charlottenlund, Denmark.

FELDMAN, Jerome Myron, MD; American physician and medical scientist; b. 27 July 1935, Chicago, Ill.; s. of Louis Feldman and Marian (Swichkow) Feldman; m. Carol B. Feldman; one s. two d.; ed Northwestern Univ., Michael Reese, Chicago and Duke Univ.; Chief, Endocrinology and Metabolism,

Durham Veteran's Admin. Hosp. 1971–2000, Staff Internist 1971–; Assoc. Prof. of Medicine, Duke Univ. 1972–98, Prof. of Medicine 1998–, Dir Clinical Research Unit Core Lab. 1984–; mem. Duke Comprehensive Cancer Center 1982–; Ed. Journal of Clinical Endocrinology and Metabolism 1983–89. *Publications:* 218 research articles, book chapters and reviews dealing with hormone-secreting tumours, endocrinology and metabolism. *Leisure interests:* music, art. *Address:* Duke University Medical Center, Box 2963, Durham, NC 27710, USA. *Telephone:* (919) 286-0411.

FELDMAN, Michael, PhD; Israeli biologist; b. 21 Jan. 1926, Tel Aviv; m. Lea Noyfeld 1946; one s. one d.; ed Herzlia High School, Tel Aviv, Hebrew Univ., Jerusalem; British Council Scholar, Inst. of Animal Genetics, Edinburgh, Scotland 1953–55; joined Weizmann Inst. of Science, Rehovot 1955; Dept of Virology, Univ. of Calif., Berkeley, USA 1960–61; Visiting Scientist, Nat. Cancer Inst., NIH, Bethesda, Md, USA 1961; fmr Head, Dept of Cell Biology, Weizmann Inst. 1961–90, Chair. Scientific Council 1962–64, Dean, Feinberg Grad. School 1966–72, Dean, Faculty of Biology 1983–85; Visiting Prof., Stanford Medical School, Stanford, Calif., USA 1976–77; Scholar-in-Residence, John F. Fogarty Int. Center, NIH, Bethesda 1978–79; Visiting Prof., Memorial Sloan Kettering Cancer Inst., New York 1990–91; research activities include cancer research (in particular, control of tumour metastasis), cellular immunology and developmental biology; mem. Israel Acad. of Sciences and Humanities 1980–; Hon. Fellow Open Univ. of Israel 2000; Dr. hc (Ben-Gurion Univ.) 1988; Griffuel Prize, Paris 1984, Rothschild Prize, Jerusalem 1986, San Marino Prize for Medicine 2000. *Publications:* numerous publs on cancer research immunology and developmental biology, in Scientific American, Nature, Nature Medicine, Journal of Experimental Medicine and other int. journals. *Leisure interests:* the arts, art history. *Address:* Dept. of Immunology, The Weizman Institute of Science, P.O. Box 26, Rehovot 76100, Israel (Office); c/o The Weizmann Institute of Science, P.O. Box 26, Rehovot 76100, Israel. *Telephone:* 8-9344073 (Office); 8-9472763 (Home). *Fax:* 8-9344125 (Office).

FELDMAN, Myer, BS(Econ.), LLB; American politician and lawyer; b. 22 June 1917, Philadelphia, Pa; s. of Israel and Bella Kurland Feldman; m. 1st Silva Moskovitz 1941; m. 2nd Adrienne Arsht 1980; one s. one d.; ed Univ. of Pennsylvania; Gowen Fellow, Univ. of Pa 1938–39, Prof. of Law 1940–42; Served USAAF 1942–46; Special Counsel, SEC, Exec. Asst to Chair., SEC 1949–53; Counsel, Senate Banking and Currency Cttee 1955–57; Prof. of Law, American Univ. 1956–59; Legislative Asst, Senator John F. Kennedy 1958–61; Dir of Research, Democratic Nat. Cttee 1960; Deputy Special Counsel to Pres. of the US 1961–64, Counsel 1964–65; Gov. Weizmann Inst., Israel 1962–84; Overseer Coll. of the Virgin Islands 1963–; Trustee, Eleanor Roosevelt Foundation 1963–76, United Jewish Appeal 1965–, Jewish Publication Soc. 1965–78; Chair. Bd Speer Publs, Capital Gazette Press Ind., Bay Publs 1968–77; contrib. to The Saturday Review 1965–71; Partner Ginsburg, Feldman and Bress 1965–98; Dir Flying Tiger Line 1966–82, Flame of Hope, Inc. 1967–; Del. to Democratic Nat. Convention 1968; Chair. Bd of Dirs of WWBA Inc., WLLH Inc. and WADK Inc., Financial Satellite Corpn 1984–; Chair., Pres and CEO Totalbank Corpn of Fla 1987–; Pres. Ardman Broadcasting Corpn 1992–; Vice-Pres. Crystal Galleria LLC 2000–; Vice-Chair. Congressional Leadership for the Future 1970; Pres. New York Int. Art Festival 1973–77; Pres. McGovern for Pres. Cttee 1972; Chair. and Treas. Birch Bayh for Pres. Cttee 1975–76; Dir Special Olympics Inc. 1983–, Henry M. Jackson Foundation 1984–92; John F. Kennedy Library 1983–; Pres. Radio Assoc. Inc. 1959–81; Democrat. *Publications:* Standard Pennsylvania Practice (4 vols). *Leisure interests:* tennis, swimming. *Address:* 10608 Stapleford Hall Drive, Potomac, MD 20854-4447, USA (Office).

FELDSTEIN, Martin Stuart, MA, DPhil; American economist; b. 25 Nov. 1939, New York; s. of Meyer Feldstein and Esther (Gevarter) Feldstein; m. Kathleen Foley 1965; two d.; ed Harvard and Oxford Univs; Research Fellow, Nuffield Coll., Oxford 1964–65, Official Fellow 1965–67, Lecturer in Public Finance 1965–67; Asst Prof. of Econs, Harvard Univ. 1967–68, Assoc. Prof. 1968–69, Prof. 1969–; George F. Baker Prof. 1984–; Pres. Nat. Bureau of Econ. Research 1977–82, 1984–; Chair. Pres.'s Council of Econ. Advisers 1982–84; Dir American Econ. Group, Eli Lilly, TRW Inc., HCA—The Health Care Co.; Econ. Adviser, Prudential Securities; mem. Advisory Bd Congressional Budget Office, New York Fed. Reserve Bank, Boston Fed. Reserve Bank, Keil Inst., Daimler Chrysler Corpn, Robeco; mem. J. P. Morgan Int. Council; columnist, mem. Bd of Contribs, Wall Street Journal; Fellow, American Philosophical Soc., American Acad. of Arts and Sciences, Econometric Soc., Nat. Asscn of Business Economists; mem. American Econ. Asscn (John Bates Clark Medal 1977), Vice-Pres. 1988, Pres. 2003; mem. Inst. Medicine, NAS, Council on Foreign Relations (Dir 1998–, Trustee 1999–), Trilateral Comm. (Exec. Cttee 1994–); Foreign mem. Austrian Acad. of Sciences; Corresp. Fellow British Acad.; Hon. LLD (Univ. of Rochester) 1984, (Marquette) 1985; Hon. Fellow Nuffield Coll. Oxford 1998; Bernhard Harms Prize, Weltwirtschafts Institut; Distinguished Service Award, The Tax Foundation. *Address:* National Bureau of Economic Research, 1050 Massachusetts Avenue, Cambridge, MA 02138 (Office); 147 Clifton Street, Belmont, MA 02478, USA (Home).

FELDT, Kjell-Olof, PhD; Swedish politician; b. 18 Aug. 1931, Holmsund; m. Birgitta von Otter; three c.; ed Univs. of Uppsala and Lund; Budget Sec., Ministry of Finance 1962–64, Budget Dir 1965, Under-Sec. 1967–70; Minister of Trade 1970–75, of Finance 1983–90; Minister without Portfolio 1975–76; MP 1971–90; mem. Exec. Cttee Social Democratic Party 1978–90; Chair.

Bank of Sweden 1967–70, 1994–99, Swedish Road Fed. 1992–, Vin & Sprit AB 1991–93; mem. Bd Dirs. Nordbanken 1991–94, Sandrew Theatre Co. 1990–. *Publication:* Memoirs 1991. *Address:* c/o Sveriges Riksbank, 103 37 Stockholm, Sweden.

FELICI, HE Cardinal Angelo; Italian ecclesiastic; b. 26 July 1919, Segni; ordained Catholic priest 1942, elected Archbishop of Cesariana, Numidia 1967, consecrated Bishop 1967; cr. Cardinal 1988; Apostolic Nuncio in France; Prefect for the Congregation of the Causes of the Saints 1988; Pres. Pontifical Comm. Ecclesia Deo 1995–. *Address:* Piazza della Città Leonina 9, 00193 Rome, Italy.

FELL, Sir David, KCB, BSc, F.I.B., DUniv; British business executive, banker and government official; b. 20 Jan. 1943, Belfast; s. of Ernest Fell and Jessie McCreedy; m. Sandra J. Moore 1967; one s. one d.; ed Royal Belfast Academical Inst. and Queen's Univ. Belfast; Sales Man. Rank Hovis McDougall Ltd 1965–66; teacher 1966–67; Research Assoc. 1967–69; Dept of Agric. 1969–72, Asst Sec. 1971–81; Dept of Commerce 1972–82, Under-Sec. 1981–82; Deputy Chief Exec. Industrial Devt Bd 1982–84; Perm. Sec. Dept of Econ. Devt 1984–91; Second Perm. Under-Sec. N Ireland Office and Head, N Ireland Civil Service 1991–97; Chair. Northern Bank Ltd (subsidiary of Nat. Australia Bank) 1998–, Boxmore Int. PLC 1998–2000; Nat. Irish Bank Ltd 1999–; Dir Nat. Australia Group Europe Ltd 1998–, Dunloe Ewart PLC 1998–2002, Fred Olsen Energy ASA 1999–, Chesapeake Corpn. 2000–; Chair. Prince's Trust Volunteers, N Ireland 1998–, Prince's Trust, N Ireland 1999–, Harland & Wolff Group PLC 2001–02, Titanic Properties Ltd 2001–; Fellow Inst. of Bankers, Ireland. *Leisure interests:* music, reading, golf, rugby. *Address:* Northern Bank Ltd, Head Office, P.O. Box 183, Donegal Square, Belfast, BT1 6JS, Northern Ireland.

FELLAG, Mohamed Said; Algerian actor and comedian; b. 1950; began career as classical actor. *Shows include:* The Adventures of Tchop 1986, Khorotov Cocktail 1989, Djurdjurassic Bled 1998.

FELLGETT, Peter Berners, PhD, FRS, FRSE, FIEE, CEng; British professor of cybernetics; b. 11 April 1922, Ipswich; s. of Frank Ernest Fellgett and Rowena Fellgett (née Wagstaff); m. Janet Mary Briggs 1947 (died 1998); one s. two d.; ed The Leys School, Cambridge and Cambridge Univ.; Sr Observer, the Observatories, Cambridge Univ. 1952–59; Prin. Scientific Officer, Royal Observatories, Edinburgh 1959–65; Prof. of Cybernetics, Reading Univ. 1965–87, Prof. Emer. 1987–; R. W. Wood Prize (Optical Soc. of America) 1977. *Publications:* over 100 publs in learned journals. *Leisure interests:* beekeeping, natural dyestuffs, musical instruments, high-quality audio, classical literature, astronomy, completed London Marathon 1986. *Address:* Little Brighter, St Kew Highway, Bodmin, Cornwall PL30 3DU, England (Home). *Telephone:* (1208) 850337. *Fax:* (1208) 850416.

FELLNER, Eric; British film producer; b. 10 Oct. 1959; three s.; ed London Guildhall; Co-Chair. Working Title Films; four Academy Awards and 18 BAFTA Awards. *Films include:* Sid and Nancy 1986, Pascali's Island 1988, The Rachel Papers 1989, Hidden Agenda 1990, A Kiss Before Dying 1991, Liebstraum 1991, Wild West 1992, Posse 1993, Romeo is Bleeding 1993, Four Weddings and a Funeral 1994, The Hudsucker Proxy 1994, Loch Ness 1995, French Kiss 1995, Dead Man Walking 1995, Fargo 1996, Bean 1997, The Borrowers 1997, Elizabeth 1998, The Big Lebowski 1998, Notting Hill 1999, Plunkott & Macleane 1999, O Brother, Where Art Thou? 2000, Billy Elliot 2000, Bridget Jones's Diary 2001, Captain Corelli's Mandolin 2001, The Man Who Wasn't There 2001, About a Boy 2002, The Guru 2002, 40 Days and 40 Nights 2002, Ali G Indahouse 2002, Long Time Dead 2002, My Little Eye 2002, Love Actually 2003, Calcium Kid 2003, Ned Kelly 2003, Shape of Things 2003, Johnny English 2003. *Address:* Working Title Films, 76 Oxford Street, London, W1D 1BS, England (Office); Working Title Films, 4th Floor, 9770 Wilshire Blvd, Beverly Hills, CA 90212, USA (Office). *Telephone:* (20) 7307-3000 (London) (Office); (310) 777-3100 (USA) (Office). *Fax:* (20) 7307-3001 (London) (Office); (310) 777-5243 (U.S.A.) (Office).

FELLNER, Fritz, PhD; Austrian professor of modern history; b. 25 Dec. 1922, Vienna; s. of Peter Fellner and Marie Obenaus; m. Liselotte Lamberg 1950; two s.; ed Realgymnasium, Matura, Univ. of Vienna and Inst. für Österreichische Geschichtsforschung; Research Fellow, Österreichisches Kulturinstitut, Rome 1951–52; Asst Lecturer, Univ. of Vienna 1954–64, Dozent 1960; Prof. of Modern History, Univ. of Salzburg 1964–93, Prof. Emer. 1993–. *Publications:* Schicksalsjahre Österreichs. Das pol. Tagebuch Josef Redlichs 1908 bis 1919 1953/54, Der Dreibund 1960, St Germain im Sommer 1919 1977, Dichter und Gelehrter. Hermann Bahr und Josef Redlich in ihren Briefen 1896–1934 1980, Vom Dreibund zum Völkerbund 1994, "...Ein Wahrhaft patriotisches Werk". Die Kommission für neuere Geschichte Österreichs 1897–2000 2001, Geschichtsschreibung und Nationale Identität: Probleme und Leistungen der Österreichischen Geschichtswissenschaft 2002. *Address:* Neustiftgasse 47/5, 1070 Vienna, Austria. *Telephone:* (1) 5260827. *Fax:* (1) 5260827 (Office).

FELLNER, Peter John, PhD; British pharmaceuticals and biotechnology executive; b. 31 Dec. 1943; s. of the late Hans Julius Fellner and of Jessica Fellner (née Thompson); m. 1st Sandra Head (née Smith) 1969; one d. one step-s.; m. 2nd Jennifer Mary Zabel (née Butler) 1982; two step-s.; ed Univ. of Sheffield and Trinity Coll. Cambridge; Post-doctoral Research Fellow, Univ. of Strasbourg, France 1968–70, Assoc. Prof. 1970–73; Sr Research Investigator, Searle UK Research Labs 1973–77, Dir of Chem. 1977–80, Dir

of Research 1980–84; Dir of Research Roche UK Research Centre 1984–86, Man. Dir Roche UK 1986–90; CEO Celltech PLC 1990–99, CEO Celltech Group (fmrly Celltech Chiroscience) PLC 1999–2003; Chair. British Biotech 2003–; Chair. (non-exec.) Ionix Pharmaceuticals Ltd, Astex Technology 2002–; Dir Colborn Dawes Ltd 1986–90, British Biotechnology Group PLC 1988–90, Synaptica Ltd 1999–, Isis Innovation Ltd; mem. MRC. *Leisure interest:* country walking. *Address:* British Biotech PLC, Watlington Road, Oxford, OX4 6LY, England (Office). *Telephone:* (1865) 748747 (Office). *Fax:* (1865) 781047 (Office). *E-mail:* webadmin@britishbiotech.com (Office). *Website:* www.britishbiotech.com (Office).

FELLS, Ian, C.B.E., MA, PhD, FRSE, F.R.ENG., F.INST.E., FIChemE; British professor of energy conversion; b. 5 Sept. 1932, Sheffield; s. of Dr. H. Alexander Fells and Clarice Fells; m. Hazel Denton Scott 1957; four s.; ed King Edward VII School, Sheffield and Trinity Coll. Cambridge; lecturer and Dir of Studies, Dept of Fuel Tech. and Chemical Eng Univ. of Sheffield 1958–62; Reader in Fuel Science, King's Coll. Univ. of Durham 1962; Prof. of Energy Conversion, Univ. of Newcastle-upon-Tyne 1975–; mem. Science Consultative Group, BBC 1976–81, Electricity Supply Research Council 1979–90; Exec. David Davies Inst. of Int. Affairs 1975–; Pres. Inst. of Energy 1978–79; Scientific Adviser World Energy Council 1990–; Chair. New and Renewable Energy Centre, Northumberland 2002–; Adviser to House of Commons and House of Lords Select Cttees.; other professional appts.; Hatfield Memorial Prize 1974, Beilby Memorial Medal and Prize 1976, Royal Soc. Faraday Medal and Prize 1993, Melchett Medal 1999, John Collier Memorial Medal 1999, Kelvin Medal 2002. *Television series:* Young Scientist of the Year, The Great Egg Race, Men of Science, Earth Year 2050, Take Nobody's Word For It, etc. *Radio:* extensive radio contribs. *Publications:* UK Energy Policy Post-Privatization 1991, Energy for the Future 1995, World Energy, 1923–1998 and Beyond 1998, Turning Point, An Independent Review of UK Energy Policy 2001. *Leisure interests:* cross-country skiing, sailing, swimming. *Address:* Fells Associates, 29 Rectory Terrace, Newcastle upon Tyne, NE3 1YB (Office); 29 Rectory Terrace, Newcastle upon Tyne, NE3 1YB, England (Home). *Telephone:* (191) 285-5343 (Office); (191) 285-5343 (Home). *Fax:* (191) 285-5343 (Office); (191) 285-5343 (Home). *E-mail:* ian@fellsassociates.com (Office).

FELTS, William Robert Jr, MD; American professor of medicine; b. 24 April 1923, Judsonia, Ark.; s. of Wylie R. Felts and Willie E. Lewis; m. 1st Jeanne E. Kennedy 1954 (divorced 1971); m. 2nd Lila Mitchell Dudley 1987 (died 1993); three s. one d.; ed Univ. of Arkansas; Asst Chief, Arthritis Research Unit, Veteran's Admin. Hosp., Washington, DC 1953–54, Adjutant Asst Chief 1954–58, Chief 1958–62; Consultant in Rheumatology, US Naval Hosp., Bethesda, Md 1957–70; mem. staff of Medicine, George Washington Univ. 1958–, Prof. 1980–93, Prof. Emer. 1993–; Dir Div. of Rheumatology 1970–79; mem. numerous advisory bds., professional orgs. etc.; Pres. Nat. Acads. of Practice 1993–96; Master, American Coll. of Rheumatology 1992; American Medical Asscn.'s Distinguished Service Award 1996. *Publications:* over 100 articles on medical socioeconomics, rheumatology and internal medicine. *Leisure interests:* photography, fishing, travel. *Address:* 1492 Hampton Hill Circle, McLean, VA 22101-6016, USA (Home). *Telephone:* (703) 356-6233 (Home). *Fax:* (703) 442-8550. *E-mail:* wfelts@starpower.net (Home).

FELTUS, Alan Evan, MFA; American artist and educator; b. 1 May 1943, Washington, DC; s. of Randolph Feltus and Anne Winter; m. Lani H. Irwin 1974; two s.; ed Tyler School of Fine Arts, Pa, Cooper Union for Advancement of Science and Art, NY, Yale Univ., Conn.; instructor School of Dayton Art Inst., Ohio 1968–70; Asst Prof. American Univ., Washington, DC 1972–84; full-time artist 1984–, represented by Forum Gallery, New York 1973–; exhibits regularly in USA; occasional teaching workshops and lectures; resident in Italy since 1987; Rome Prize Fellowship, American Acad. in Rome 1970–72, Nat. Endowment for Arts Fellowship 1981; Louis Comfort Tiffany Foundation Grant in Painting 1980, Pollock-Krasner Foundation Grant in Painting 1992; Thomas B. Clarke Prize, Nat. Acad. of Design 1984, Benjamin Altman Prize 1990, Joseph S. Isidor Memorial Medal 1995, Raymond Neilson Prize 2001. *Address:* c/o Forum Gallery, 745 Fifth Avenue, New York, NY 10151, USA (Office); Porziano 68, 06081 Assisi, Perugia Italy (Home). *Telephone:* (075) 802436. *Fax:* (075) 802436. *E-mail:* feltusirwin@inwind.it (Home).

FENBY, Jonathan Theodore Starmer, CBE; British journalist; b. 11 Nov. 1942, London; s. of the late Charles Fenby and June Fenby (née Head); m. Renée Wartski 1967; one s. one d.; ed King Edward's School, Birmingham, Westminster School and New Coll. Oxford; corresp. and ed. Reuters World Service, Reuters Ltd 1963–77; corresp. France and Germany, The Economist 1982–86; Home Ed. and Asst Ed. The Independent 1986–88; Deputy Ed. The Guardian 1988–93; Ed. The Observer 1993–95; Dir Guardian Newspapers 1990–95; Ed. South China Morning Post 1995–99; Ed. Netmedia Group; Assoc. Ed. Sunday Business 2000–01; Ed. Business Europe 2000–01; mem. Bd Journalists in Europe; Counsellor, European Journalism Centre; Chevalier, Ordre du Mérite (France) 1992. *Publications:* The Fall of the House of Beaverbrook 1979, Piracy and the Public 1983, The International News Services 1986, On the Brink: The Trouble with France 1998, Comment peut-on être Français? 1999, Dealing With the Dragon: A Year in the New Hong Kong 2000. *Address:* 101 Ridgmount Gardens, Torrington Place, London, WC1E 7AZ, England (Home). *E-mail:* jtfenby@hotmail.com (Home).

FENCHEL, Tom Michael, DPhil; Danish professor of marine biology; b. 19 March 1940, Copenhagen; s. of W. Fenchel and Käte (née Sperling); m. 1st Anne Thane 1964; m. 2nd Hilary Adler 1978 (divorced 1989); one s. one d.; m. 3rd Ilse Duun 1995; ed Univ. of Copenhagen; Lecturer in Marine Biology, Univ. of Copenhagen 1964–70; Prof. of Ecology and Zoology, Univ. of Aarhus 1970–87; Prof. of Marine Biology, Univ. of Copenhagen 1987–; Gold Medal, Univ. of Copenhagen 1964, Ecology Prize 1987, Huntsmann Award for Oceanography 1987. *Publications:* Theories of Populations in Biological Communities (with F. B. Christiansen) 1977, Bacteria and Mineral Cycling (with T. H. Blackburn) 1979, Ecology of Protozoa 1987, Ecology and Evolution in Anoxic Worlds (with B. J. Finlay), Bacterial Biochemistry (jtly), Bacterial Biogeochemistry (with G. M. King and T. H. Blackburn) 1998, Origin and Early Evolution of Life 2002. *Address:* Marine Biological Laboratory, University of Copenhagen, Strandpromenaden 5, 3000 Helsingor, Denmark. *Telephone:* 49-21-33-44. *Fax:* 49-26-11-65. *E-mail:* mbltf@inet.uni2.dk (Office).

FENDER, Sir Brian Edward Frederick, Kt, CMG, PhD; British academic; b. 15 Sept. 1934, Barrow; s. of the late George Clements Fender and of Emily Goodwin; m. 1st 1956; one s. three d.; m. 2nd Ann Linscott 1986; ed Carlisle and Sale Grammar Schools, Imperial Coll., London; Research Instructor, Univ. of Washington, Seattle 1959–61; Sr Research Fellow, Nat. Chemical Lab. Teddington 1961–63; Fellow, St Catherine's Coll., Oxford 1963–84, Lecturer in Inorganic Chem. 1965–80; Asst Dir Inst. Laue-Langevin, Grenoble 1980–82, Dir 1982–85; Vice-Chancellor, Keele Univ. 1985–95; Chief Exec. Higher Educ. Funding Council for England 1995–2001; mem. Science and Eng Research Council 1985–90; Pres. Nat. Foundation for Educational Research 1999–; Hon. Fellow St Catherine's Coll. Oxford, Imperial Coll. London, Cardiff. *Publications:* scientific articles on neutron scattering and solid state chemistry. *Leisure interests:* modern art, cooking. *Address:* Bishops Ottley Manor, Bishops Ottley, Stafford, ST21 6ET, England. *E-mail:* fenderbrian@hotmail.com.

FENECH-ADAMI, Edward, BA, LLD; Maltese politician, lawyer and journalist; b. 7 Feb. 1934, Birkirkara; s. of Luigi Fenech Adami and Josephine Pace; m. Mary Sciberras 1965; four s. one d.; ed St Aloysius Coll., Univ. of Malta; entered legal practice 1959; Ed. Il-Poplu (weekly) 1962–69; mem. Nat. Exec. Nationalist Party 1961, Asst Gen. Sec. 1962–75, Pres. Gen. and Admin. Councils 1975–77, Leader 1977–; mem. Parl. 1969–; Leader of Opposition 1977–82, 1983–87, 1996–98; Prime Minister 1987–96, 1998–, also fmr Minister of Foreign Affairs; Vice-Pres. European Union of Christian Democrat Parties 1979–; Nat. Order of Merit. *Address:* Office of the Prime Minister, Auberge de Castille, Valletta CMR02, Malta (Office). *Telephone:* (21) 242560 (Office). *Fax:* (21) 249888 (Office).

FENEUILLE, Serge Jean Georges, PhD; French academic and company director; b. 16 Nov. 1940, Rheims; s. of Georges Feneuille and Marguerite Lemoine; m. Jeannine Large 1960; ed Coll. Moderne de Rheims, Ecoles Normales d'Instituteurs de Chalons-sur-Marne and Nancy, Ecole Normale Supérieure de St-Cloud; Maître-Asst Univ. of Paris 1964–69; Maître de Recherche CNRS 1969–74, Dir of Research 1974–; Prof. Univ. Paris-Sud 1979–98; Dir of Research Lafarge Coppée 1981–85, Scientific Dir and mem. Exec. Cttee 1985–86, Asst Dir-Gen. 1988–89, Dir-Gen. and Head of Research, Tech. and Strategy 1989–94, Special Adviser to Chair. and CEO 1995–2000; Man. Dir Centre Expérimental du Bâtiment et des Travaux Publiques 1998–2000; Dir-Gen. CNRS 1986–88; Pres. Admin. Council Ecole Normale Supérieure de Lyon 1986–94; Chair. Orsan (subsidiary of Lafarge Coppée) 1992–94, Innovation and Research Comm., Conseil Nat. du Patronat Français (CNPF) 1993–97; mem. French Acad. of Tech. 2000–; Prix Daniel Guinier de la Soc. Française de Physique, Bronze Medal CNRS, Prix Servant de l'Acad. des Sciences, Prix Jaffé de l'Institut de France; Officier Ordre nat. du Mérite, Chevalier Légion d'honneur, Officier Ordre des Palmes académiques. *Publications:* numerous articles in scientific journals. *Leisure interests:* egyptology, painting, literature. *Address:* 25 avenue du Maréchal Maunoury, 75016 Paris, France (Home). *Telephone:* 1-45-27-14-50 (Home). *Fax:* 1-45-27-14-50 (Home). *E-mail:* sfeneuille@wanadoo.fr (Home).

FENG DUAN; Chinese physicist; b. 27 April 1923, Suzhou City, Jiangsu Prov.; s. of Feng Zhou-bai and Yan Su-qing; m. Chen Lian-fang 1955; three d.; ed Nat. Cen. Univ.; Prof. of Physics, Nanjing Univ. 1978–; Dir of Grad. School of Nanjing Univ. 1984–88; Dir Nat. Lab. of Solid State Microstructures 1986–95; mem. Chinese Acad. of Sciences 1980–; Pres. Chinese Physical Soc. 1991–95; Fellow, the Third World Acad. of Sciences 1993–; State Prize for Natural Sciences 1982, 1995; State Prize for Progress of Science and Tech. 1997, 1998, Tan Kah Kee Prize in Mathematics and Physics 1999. *Publications:* Physics of Metals (Vols 1–4) 1987–99, New Perspective on Condensed Matter Physics 1992. *Leisure interest:* literature. *Address:* Institute of Solid State Physics, Nanjing University, Nanjing, 210008, Jiangsu Province, People's Republic of China. *Telephone:* (25) 3593705 (Office); (25) 3592906 (Home). *Fax:* (25) 3590535 (Office); (25) 3300535. *E-mail:* duanf@netra.nju.edu.cn (Home).

FENG GONG; Chinese actor; b. Dec. 1957, Tianjin; joined China Railway Art Work Troupe 1980; actor China Broadcasting Art Troupe 1984–; performs comic dialogues with Niu Qun; numerous prizes. *Address:* China Broadcasting Art Troupe, Beijing, People's Republic of China.

FENG HE; Chinese sculptor; b. 12 Nov. 1931, Peixian, Jiangsu Prov.; s. of Feng Zigu and Chen Jiechen; m. Zhou Ji 1965; one s.; ed Cen. Inst. of Fine

Arts; mem. Sculpture Research Studio Inst. of Fine Arts, Deputy Dir 1981–84, Vice-Dir 1988–; specialized in ceramics and animal sculpture; exhibited work China Art Gallery 1979, 1981, also in France and Burma. *Works include:* Woman's Head 1958, The Master of the Land 1964, Doe 1964, Bellicose Goat 1978, Buffalo 1979, You are Always in Our Hearts Dear Premier Zhou 1979, Ah Bing the Blind Man 1979, Buffalo and the Leopard 1985, Moonlight 1985, Winter 1986, Monument of Juvenile Heroes, The Song of the Young Pioneer 1990, Dream 1990, 12 Animals, Young Pioneer Park 1991. *Leisure interest:* drama. *Address:* Central Institute of Fine Arts, East Beijing 100730, People's Republic of China. *Telephone:* 55-4731 (ext. 391).

FENG JICAI; Chinese writer; b. 9 Feb. 1942, Tianjin, Zhejiang Prov.; s. of Feng Jifu and Ge Changfu; m. Gu Tongzhao; ed Tianjin Middle School; Vice-Chair. China Fed. of Literary and Art Circles 1988, 2001–; Chair. Fiction Soc. of China 2000–; Dir Feng Jicai Research Inst. of Arts and Literature and Hon. Dean School of Social Sciences and Foreign Languages, Tianjin Univ. 2001–; Ed. Free Forum on Literature; Ed. Artists; Vice-Chair. UNESCO Int. Folk Arts Org. *Publications:* Magic Whip 1984, Gratitude to Life 1991. *Address:* Tianjin Municipal Federation of Literary and Art Circles, Tianjin, People's Republic of China (Office).

FENG LANRUI; Chinese economist; b. 17 Sept. 1920, Guiyang, Guizhou Province; d. of Feng Shaotang and Xie Guangyu; m. Li Chang 1946; two s. two d.; ed Senior Party School of the CCP Central Cttee; Sr Research Fellow, Inst. of Marxism-Leninism and Mao Zedong Thought, Chinese Acad. of Social Sciences 1980–, Deputy Dir 1980–82, Adviser 1983–; mem. Editorial Cttee, Encyclopedia of People's Repub. of China, for vol. Scientific Socialism 1980–, A Comprehensive Dictionary of Economics, for vol. Population, Labour and Consumption 1983–; Senior Advisor, Economy in the Special Zone 1989–; mem. Cttee of Specialists, Social Security in China 2002–; Sec.-Gen. China Council of Econ. Asscns. 1981–; mem. Standing Cttee Chinese People's Friendship Asscn 1988–93; Sun Yefang Prize for econ. article of 1984; Xinhya Digests Prize for Most Impressive Article of the Year 1998. *Publications:* Labour: Payment and Employment (collected articles) 1982, Regarding the Principle– To Each According to his Work, Chinese Research on Employment Theory 1982, Urban Employment and Wages in China (co-author) 1982, On the Relationship between Employment and Economic Growth (co-author) 1983, The Worldwide New Industrialization and China's Socialist Modernization (co-author) 1984, On Letting Some People Get Rich Ahead of Others 1984, The Incomplete Form of Distribution According to Work at the Initial Stage of Socialism 1985, Overcome Egalitarianism and Let Some People Get Rich Ahead of Others 1985, More on Letting Some People Get Rich Ahead of Others 1986, The Double Hundred Policy Cannot be Separated from Democracy and Freedom 1986, The Double Hundred Policy and Science Associations 1986, Distribution According to Work, Wage and Employment 1988, Employment at the Initial Stage of Socialism (co-author) 1988, On the Ageing of the Chinese Population 1989, The Labour Market of China 1991, Social Security Must be Unified 1994, Actively Foster the Labour Market 1995, Can Inflation be Reduced under 10% for the Current Year?, Unemployment in China: 21% by the year 2000? 1996 (Impressive Article of the Year 1998), The Restructuring of China's Social Security System 1997, Selected Works on Economics of Feng Lanrui (2 vols) 1999, Forward in the Same Ship: A Suggestion for Amending the PRC Constitution 2002, and numerous articles on the market economy. *Address:* 34 Dongzongbu Hutong, Beijing 100005, People's Republic of China. *Telephone:* 65124654 (Home).

FENG MENGBO; Chinese pop artist; ed Print-Making Dept Cen. Acad. of Fine Arts, Beijing; work consists of computer animations and paintings which resemble video-game screens; has exhibited at galleries in London, Sydney, Taipei and Hong Kong and at 45th Venice Biennale. *Leisure interests:* collecting industrial antiques.

FENG XIAOGANG; Chinese screenplay writer and director; b. 1958, Beijing; ed Beijing Broadcasting Acad.; art designer Beijing TV Art Centre 1985; began writing film and TV screenplays 1989; TV 'Gold Eagle Award' for A Beijing Man in New York, 'Hundred-Flower Award' for Party A, Party B. *Films:* After Separation 1992, Lost My Love 1994, The Funeral of a Famous Star, Living in Dire Strait, The Dream Factory 1997, Be There or Be Square 1998, Sorry, Baby 1999, A Sigh 2000. *Television:* Lend Me a Little Love, A Beijing Man in New York. *Publications:* After Separation 1992, A Born Coward 1994, Stories in the Editorial Office. *Address:* Beijing Television Art Centre, Beijing, People's Republic of China (Office).

FENG YING; Chinese ballet dancer; b. 28 Feb. 1963, Harbin; m. James Y. Ho 1989; one d.; ed Beijing Dance Acad.; Paris Opera Ballet School 1982–83; Prin. Dancer, Cen. Ballet of China 1980–; leading role in many classical and Chinese ballets; Guest Artist, 2nd Paris Int. Ballet Competition 1986; toured USA, UK, Russia, Japan, Singapore, Hong Kong, Taiwan; mem. Chinese Dancers' Asscn 1982, China Ballet Art Soc. 1992; First Prize Pas de Deux, Nat. Ballet Competition 1987; award at 5th Japan World Ballet Competition 1987; First Class Dancer of the State 1987. *Address:* Central Ballet of China, 3 Taiping Street, Beijing 100050, People's Republic of China.

FENIC, František (Fero); Slovak producer, writer and media executive; b. 20 March 1951, Nižná Šebastová; ed Comenius Univ., Bratislava, FAMU/Acad. of Musical Arts, Prague, Czech Repub.; mil. service 1978–79; Dir Studio of Short Films, Slovak Film Production, Bratislava 1979–83, 1985–86, Barrandov Film Studio Prague 1984; film-making interrupted for political reasons March 1984; freelance tourist guide Youth Travel Agency 1986–92;

f. FEBIO s.r.o. 1991, Dir 1992–; "1 June 1953" Journalism Award. *Films:* over twenty documentary films and full-length films including Vlak dospelosti, Praha slzám neverí, Noc, kdy se rospadl stát. *Television includes:* GEN, GENUS, OKO, VIP – Influential People, Czech Soda, The Way We Live. *Publication:* Encyclopedia of Slovak Dramatic Arts 1989. *Leisure interest:* travel. *Address:* FEBIO s.r.o., Ruzová 13, 11000 Prague 1, (Office); Vejvodova 4, 11000 Prague 1, Czech Republic (Home).

FENN, John B., AB, PhD; American professor of analytical chemistry; b. 1917, New York; ed Berea Coll., Yale Univ.; researcher in process devt Monsanto Co., then Sharples Chemical, Michigan 1940–52, co. specializing in combustion engines, Richmond 1952–59; apptd Dir of Project SQUID (USN program of basic and applied research in jet propulsion), Princeton Univ., Prof. of Aerospace and Mechanical Sciences; Prof. of Chemical Eng, Yale Univ. 1967–87, Prof. Emer. 1987–; Prof. of Analytical Chem., Va Commonwealth Univ. (VCU), Richmond 1994–, Affiliate Prof. of Chemical Eng, School of Eng, VCU; Visiting Prof. Trento Univ., Italy, Univ. of Tokyo, Japan, Indian Inst. of Science, Bangalore, Chinese Acad. of Science, Beijing; sole or co-inventor on 19 patents; Nobel Prize in Chem. for work in the field of mass spectrometry (jt recipient) 2002. *Address:* Department of Chemistry, Virginia Commonwealth University, 1001 W. Main Street, POB 842006, Richmond, VA 23284-2006, USA (Office). *E-mail:* jbfenn@vcu.edu (Office). *Website:* www.has.vcu.edu (Office).

FENN, Sir Nicholas M., GCMG, MA; British diplomatist; b. 19 Feb. 1936, London; s. of the late Rev. Prof. J. E. Fenn and Kathleen Fenn (née Harrison); m. Susan Clare Russell 1959; two s. one d.; ed Kingswood School, Bath and Peterhouse, Cambridge; Flying Officer, RAF 1954–56; Third Sec. Mandalay, then Rangoon 1959–63, Asst Pvt. Sec. to Sec. of State for Foreign Affairs 1963–67, First Sec. British Interests Section, Swiss Embassy, Algiers 1967–69, First Sec. and Spokesman, UK Mission to the UN, New York 1969–72, Deputy Head Energy Dept FCO 1972–75, Counsellor British Embassy, Beijing 1975–77, Royal Coll. of Defence Studies 1978, Head of News Dept and Foreign Office Spokesman 1979–82; Amb. to Burma 1982–86, to Ireland 1986–91; High Commr in India 1991–96; Chief Exec. Marie Curie Cancer Care 1996–2000, Chair. 2000–; Jt Chair. Encounter 1998–; Trustee Sight Savers Int., Guide Dogs for the Blind; Hon. Fellow, Peterhouse, Cambridge. *Leisure interest:* sailing. *Address:* Marie Curie Cancer Care, 89 Albert Embankment, London, SE1 7TP, England (Office). *Telephone:* (20) 7599-7130 (Office). *Fax:* (20) 7599-7131 (Office).

FENNER, Frank John, AC, CMG, MBE, MD, FAA, FRS, FRACP, FRCP; Australian research biologist; b. 21 Dec. 1914, Ballarat, Vic.; s. of Dr. and Mrs. Charles Fenner; m. E. M. Roberts 1944 (deceased); one d.; ed Thebarton Tech. High School, Adelaide High School, Adelaide Univ.; Medical Officer, Hosp. Pathologist, Australian Forces 1940–43, Malariologist 1943–46; Francis Haley Research Fellow, Walter and Eliza Hall Inst. for Medical Research, Melbourne 1946–48; Travelling Fellow, Rockefeller Inst. for Medical Research 1948–49; Prof. of Microbiology, ANU 1949–73, now Emer., Dir John Curtin School of Medical Research 1967–73, Dir Centre for Resource and Environmental Studies 1973–79; Foreign Assoc., U.S. Nat. Acad. of Sciences 1977; Chair. Global Comm. for the Certification of Smallpox Eradication, WHO 1977–80; Univ. Fellow, ANU 1980–82; Visiting Fellow, John Curtin School of Medical Research 1982–; Harvey Lecturer, Harvey Soc. of New York 1958; Overseas (Foundation) Fellow, Churchill Coll., Cambridge 1961–62; David Syme Prize, Melbourne Univ. 1949; Mueller Medal 1964; ANZAAS Medal 1980; Britannica Australia Award 1967; ANZAC Peace Prize 1980; Leeuwenhoek Lecture 1961; Flinders Lecture 1967, David Lecture 1973, Florey Lecture 1983, Burnet Lecture 1985; Stuart Mudd Award 1986, Japan Prize 1988, Advance Australia Award 1989, Copley Medal 1995, Albert Einstein World Award for Science 2000, Clunies Ross Nat. Science and Tech. Award for Lifetime Contrib. 2002, Prime Minister's Award for Science 2002, ACT Australian of the Year 2003. *Publications:* about 290 scientific papers, mainly on acidfast bacili, pox viruses, viral classification, environmental problems and the history of science; The Production of Antibodies (with F. M. Burnet) 1949, Myxomatosis (with F. N Ratcliffe) 1965, The Biology of Animal Viruses 1968, Medical Virology (with D. O. White) 1970, Classification and Nomenclature of Viruses, Second Report 1976, The Australian Academy of Science: The First Twenty-five Years (ed. with A. L. G. Rees) 1980, Veterinary Virology (with others) 1987, Smallpox and its Eradication (with others) 1988, Human Monkeypox (with Z. Jezek) 1988, The Orthopoxviruses (with others) 1988, Portraits of Viruses (ed. with A. Gibbs) 1988, History of Microbiology in Australia (Ed.) 1990, The Australian Academy of Science: The First Forty Years (ed.) 1995, Biological Control of Vertebrate Pests (with B. Fantini) 1999, The John Curtin School of Medical Research: The First Fifty Years, 1948 to 1998 (with D. R. Curtis) 2001. *Leisure interests:* gardening, tennis. *Address:* John Curtin School of Medical Research, GPO Box 334, Canberra, ACT (Office); 8 Monaro Crescent, Red Hill, Canberra, ACT 2603, Australia (Home). *Telephone:* (2) 6125 2526 (Office); (2) 6295-9176 (Home). *Fax:* (2) 6125-4712 (Office). *E-mail:* Frank.Fenner@anu.edu.au (Office).

FENTIE, Dennis G.; Canadian politician and business executive; b. 8 Nov. 1950, Edmonton, Alberta; Owner and Man. Francis River Construction Ltd; elected MLA (New Democratic Party) for Watson Lake, Yukon Territory 1996–; joined Yukon Party May 2002–, Leader June 2002–; Premier of Yukon Territory 2002–; fmr Dir Watson Lake Chamber of Commerce; fmr Commr Yukon Forest Comm.; fmr Dir Asscn of Yukon Forests; convicted of drug trafficking, Alberta 1976, spent 17 months in jail, received full pardon 1996.

Leisure interests: baseball, hockey, history, current affairs. *Address:* Government of Yukon, Box 2703, Whitehorse, Yukon Y1A 2C6, Canada (Office). *Telephone:* (867) 667-8288 (Office). *E-mail:* dennis.fentie@gov.yk.ca (Office). *Website:* www.gov.yk.ca (Office).

FENTON, Alexander, CBE, MA, DLitt; British professor of Scottish ethnology; b. 26 June 1929, Shotts, Lanarkshire; s. of Alexander Fenton and Annie S. Stronach; m. Evelyn E. Hunter 1956; two d.; ed Univs of Aberdeen, Cambridge and Edinburgh; Sr Asst Ed. Scottish Nat. Dictionary 1955–59; Dir Nat. Museum of Antiquities of Scotland 1978–85; Research Dir Nat. Museums of Scotland 1985–89; Dir European Ethnological Research Centre 1989–; Prof. of Scottish Ethnology and Dir School of Scottish Studies, Univ. of Edinburgh 1990–94, now Emer.; Ed. Review of Scottish Culture; Hon. Prof. of Antiquities, Royal Scottish Acad.; Hon. DLitt (Aberdeen) 1989. *Publications:* Scottish Country Life, The Northern Isles: Orkney & Shetland, Rural Architecture of Scotland, The Shape of the Past (two vols), Country Life in Scotland, Wirds An' Wark 'E Seasons Roon', The Turra Coo, The Island Blackhouse, Craiters—or Twenty Buchan Tales. *Leisure interest:* languages. *Address:* European Ethnological Research Centre, c/o National Museums of Scotland, Chambers Street, Edinburgh, EH1 1JF (Office); 132 Blackford Avenue, Edinburgh, EH9 3HH, Scotland (Home). *Telephone:* (131) 247-4086 (Office); (131) 667-5456 (Home). *E-mail:* afenton@nms.ac.uk (Office).

FENTON, James (Martin), MA, FRSL; British poet, author and journalist; b. 25 April 1949, Lincoln; s. of Rev. Canon J. C. Fenton and Mary Hamilton Ingoldby; ed Durham Choristers School, Repton School, Magdalen Coll. Oxford; Asst Literary Ed., New Statesman 1971, Editorial Asst 1972, Political Columnist 1976–78; freelance corresp. in Indo-China 1973–75; German Corresp., The Guardian 1978–79; Theatre Critic, Sunday Times 1979–84; Chief Book Reviewer, The Times 1984–86; Far East Corresp. The Independent 1986–88, columnist 1993–95; Prof. of Poetry, Oxford Univ. 1994–99, Trustee Nat. Gallery London 2002, Visitor Ashmolean Museum 2003; Hon. Fellow, Magdalen Coll., Oxford 1999; Antiquary to the RA 2002. *Publications include:* Our Western Furniture 1968, Terminal Moraine 1972, A Vacant Possession 1978, A German Requiem 1980, Dead Soldiers 1981, The Memory of War 1982, You Were Marvellous 1983, Children in Exile 1984, Poems 1968–83 1985, The Fall of Saigon (in Granta 15) 1985, The Snap Revolution (in Granta 18) 1986, Cambodian Witness: The Autobiography of Someth May (Ed.) 1986, Partingtime Hall (poems; with John Fuller) 1987, All the Wrong Places: Adrift in the Politics of Asia 1989, Underground in Japan, by Rey Ventura (Ed.) 1992, Out of Danger (poems) 1993, Collected Stories by Ernest Hemingway (Ed.), Leonardo's Nephew: Essays on Art and Artists 1998, The Strength of Poetry, Oxford Lectures, An Introduction to English Poetry 2002, A Garden from a Hundred Packets of Seed, The Love Bomb & Other Musical Pieces 2003. *Address:* c/o Peters, Fraser & Dunlop, Drury House, 34–43 Russell Street, London, WC2B 5HA, England (Office).

FERGUS-THOMPSON, Gordon; British pianist; b. 9 March 1952, Leeds; s. of the late George Thompson and Constance Webb; ed Temple Moor Grammar School, Leeds and Royal Northern Coll. of Music; debut, Wigmore Hall 1976; has appeared as soloist with orchestras including Orchestra of the Hague, Gotenburg Symphony Orchestra, Royal Liverpool Philharmonic, The Philharmonia, City of Birmingham Symphony, Hallé, BBC Symphony; extensive tours in Europe, N America, Australia, Far East and S. Africa; Prof. of Piano, Royal Coll. of Music 1996–; recordings include Complete Works of Debussy, Bach transcriptions 1990, Complete Works of Scriabin 1990, Complete Works of Ravel 1992; Gulbenkian Foundation Fellowship 1978; MRA Prize for Best Instrumental Recording of the Year 1991, 1992. *Leisure interests:* art, chess, cooking, tennis, humour. *Address:* 12 Audley Road, Hendon, London, NW4 3EY, England (Home). *Telephone:* (20) 8202-5861 (Home).

FERGUSON, Sir Alexander (Alex) Chapman, Kt, CBE; British professional football manager; b. 31 Dec. 1941, Glasgow; s. of the late Alexander Beaton Ferguson and Elizabeth Hardy; m. Catherine Ferguson 1966; three s.; ed Govan High School; player with Queen's Park 1958–60, St Johnstone 1960–64, Dunfermline Athletic 1964–67, Glasgow Rangers 1967–69, Falkirk 1969–73, Ayr United 1973–74 (two Scottish League caps); managed the following clubs: East Stirling 1974, St Mirren 1974–78 (First Div. Champions 1976–77), Aberdeen 1978–86 (winners European Cup Winners' Cup, Super Cup 1983, Premier Div. Champions 1980, 1982, 1984, winners Scottish FA Cup on four occasions, League Cup 1985), Scottish Nat. Team (Asst Man.) 1985–86, Manchester United 1986– (winners FA Cup 1990, 1994, 1996, 1999, European Cup Winners' Cup, Super Cup 1991, FA Premier League Championship 1992/93, 1993/94, 1995/96, 1996/97, 1998/99, 1999/2000, 2000/01, 2002/03, League and FA Cup double 1994 and 1996 (new record), Champions League European Cup 1999; Hon. MA (Salford) 1996; Hon. LLD (Robert Gordon) 1997; Hon. MSc (Manchester Metropolitan and UMIST) 1998; Hon. DLitt. (Glasgow Caledonian) 2001; Hon. DUniv. (Glasgow) 2001; Man. of the Year Scotland 1983–85, Man. of the Year England 1993–94, 1996, voted Best Coach in Europe, UEFA Football Gala 1999, Freeman, Cities of Aberdeen, Glasgow and Manchester. *Publications:* A Light in the North 1985, Alex Ferguson: Six Years at United 1992, Just Champion 1994, A Year in the Life 1995, A Will to Win (jtly) 1997, Managing My Life: My Autobiography (jtly) 1999, The Unique Treble 2000. *Leisure interests:* golf, snooker, horse racing, learning to play the piano, fine wine. *Address:* Manchester United FC, Old Trafford, Manchester, M16 0RA, England. *Telephone:* (161) 868-8700. *Fax:* (161) 868-8807.

FERGUSON, C. David; American business executive; ed Marietta Coll.; joined Engine Parts Div. Gould Inc. 1963, Foil Div. 1967; subsequently Group Vice-Pres. (Materials and Components); Exec. Vice-Pres. (Materials and Components); Chair., Pres. and CEO Gould Inc. 1988–; Pres. and Gen. Man. Foil Div., Gould Inc., Eastlake, O; mem. Bd Gould Foils Ltd, Nikko Gould Foil Co., Ltd, Gould Electronics (Canada) Ltd.

FERGUSON, Glenn Walker, BA, MBA, JD; American diplomatist and educator; b. 28 Jan. 1929, Syracuse, NY; s. of Forrest E. and Mabel W. Ferguson; m. Patricia Lou Head 1950; two s. one d.; ed Cornell Univ., Univ. of Santo Tomas (Manila), Univ. of Chicago and Univ. of Pittsburgh; USAF 1951–53; Staff Assoc. Governmental Affairs Inst., Washington, DC 1954–55; Asst Ed. and Asst Sec.-Treas., American Judicature Soc., Chicago 1955–56; successively Admin. Asst to Chancellor, Asst Dean and Asst Prof. Graduate School of Public and Int. Affairs, Assoc. Dir, Co-ordinated Educ. Center, Univ. of Pittsburgh 1956–60; Man. Consultant, McKinsey and Co., Washington, DC 1960–61; Special Asst to Dir, US Peace Corps 1961, Peace Corps Dir in Thailand 1961–63, Assoc. Dir Peace Corps, Washington, DC 1963–64; Dir Vista Volunteers, Office of Econ. Opportunity, Washington, DC 1964–66; Amb. to Kenya 1966–69; Chancellor Long Island Univ. 1969–70; Pres. Clark Univ. 1970–73, Univ. of Connecticut 1973–78, Radio Free Europe and Radio Liberty 1978–82, Lincoln Center 1983–84, Equity for Africa, Inc. 1985–92, American Univ. of Paris 1992–95; Visiting Prof. (Foreign Policy), Conn. Coll. and Univ. of RI 1990–91; Lecturer on Foreign Affairs and Higher Educ. 1995–; Assoc. Fellow Yale Univ.; mem. Fed. Bar Assoc., Council on Foreign Relations, American Bar Assoc., Bd of Trustees, Cornell Univ. 1972–76, Nat. Press Club, French-American Comm. for Educ. Exchange 1992–94, Dir Council of American Ambs.; USIS Lecturer (India, Sudan, Uruguay, Argentina) 1984–92; Consultant, Int. Exec. Service Corps (Uruguay) 1992; fmr Dir Foreign Policy Assoc and Pvt. Export Funding Corpn, Conn. Nat. Bank, Equator Bank; several hon. degrees; Arthur Flemming Award 1968. *Publications:* Unconventional Wisdom 1999, Americana Against the Grain 1999. *Address:* 1060 Governor Dempsey Drive, Santa Fe, NM 87501-1078, USA. *Telephone:* (505) 954-4910. *Fax:* (505) 954-4228 (Home).

FERGUSON, Marnie H., BA; Canadian business executive; b. 10 April 1949, Lindsay, Ont.; d. of Noble William Eberts and Gladys Eileen (née Smith-Emsley) Eberts; m. Garry S. Ferguson 1969; three s.; ed Ryerson Polytechnic Inst., Waterloo Lutheran Univ., Univ. of Waterloo; various human resources man. posts in consumer packaged-goods industries; Dir Human Resources, Monsanto Canada Inc. 1989–91, Vice-Pres., People, Quality and EH&S 1991–95, People-Canada and Transformation and Change, Monsanto Worldwide 1995–, Gen. Man. Monsanto Incite Consulting Div. 1991–94, Dir Continuous Improvement Monsanto Canada, Sr Consultant Incite Div. of Monsanto; Chair. Council on Total Quality Man. Conf. Bd of Canada; mem. Personnel Assoc of Ont., American Man. Assoc. *Leisure interests:* gardening, music, travel. *Address:* Monsanto Canada Inc., 2330 Argentia Road, P.O. Box 787, Streetsville, Mississauga, Ont., L5M 2G4, Canada. *Telephone:* (905) 826-9222 (Office). *Fax:* (905) 826-8961.

FERGUSON, Niall, MA, DPhil; British economic historian; b. 18 April 1964, British; m. Susan M. Douglas 1994; two s. one d.; ed Univ. of Oxford, Univ. of Hamburg; Fellow Christ's Coll., Cambridge 1989–90, Peterhouse, Cambridge 1990–92, Jesus Coll., Oxford, 1992–; Prof. of Political and Financial History Univ. of Oxford 2000–; Wadsworth Prize for Business History 1998. *Television:* Empire 2003. *Publications:* Paper and Iron: Hamburg Business and German Politics in the Era of Inflation 1897–1927 1995, (ed) Virtual History: Alternatives and Counterfactuals 1997, The World's Banker: A History of the House of Rothschild, The Pity of War 1998, The Cash Nexus: Money and Power in the Modern World 1700–2000 2001, Empire: How Britain Made the Modern World 2003. *Address:* Jesus College, Oxford, OX1 3DW, England (Office). *Telephone:* (1865) 279758 (Office). *E-mail:* niall.ferguson@jesus.ox.ac.uk.

FERGUSON, Paul; South African stockbroker; b. 23 Aug. 1943, Johannesburg; s. of Ray and Joy Ferguson; trained as chartered accountant; Dir Fergusson Bros., Hall Stewart & Co. Inc. 1973–, Chair. 1983–; Pres. Johannesburg Stock Exchange 1982–84, Cttee mem. 1979–, Chair. 1988–89, Vice-Chair. 1993–; Dir of various cos. *Leisure interest:* squash. *Address:* P.O. Box 691, Johannesburg 2000 (Office); 60 Kent Road, Dunkeld, Johannesburg 2196, South Africa (Home). *Telephone:* (11) 8335740 (Office); (11) 7882227.

FERGUSON-SMITH, Malcolm Andrew, MA, MB, ChB, FRCPath, FRCP(Glas), FRCOG, FRS, FRSE; British professor of pathology; b. 5 Sept. 1931, Glasgow, Scotland; s. of John Ferguson-Smith and Ethel May Ferguson-Smith (née Thorne); m. Marie Eva Gzowska 1960; one s. three d.; ed Stowe School, Univ. of Glasgow; Registrar in Lab. Medicine, Dept of Pathology, Western Infirmary, Glasgow 1958–59; Fellow in Medicine and Instructor, Johns Hopkins Univ. School of Medicine 1959–61; Lecturer, Sr Lecturer, then Reader in Medical Genetics, Univ. of Glasgow 1961–73, Prof. 1973–87; Prof. of Pathology, Univ. of Cambridge 1987–98, now Emer., Research Prof., Dept of Clinical Veterinary Medicine 1998–; Fellow Peterhouse Coll., Cambridge 1987–98; Dir W of Scotland Medical Genetics Service 1973–87, East Anglian Regional Clinical Genetics Service 1987–95; Pres. Clinical Genetics Soc. 1979–81, European Soc. of Human Genetics 1997–98, Int. Soc. for Prenatal Diagnosis 1998–2002; Ed. Prenatal Diagnosis 1980–; mem. Johns Hopkins Univ. Soc. of Scholars; Foreign mem. Polish Acad. of Science 1988, Nat. Acad. of Medicine Buenos Aires 2002; Pres. Assoc of Clinical Cytogeneticists 2003–;

Hon. Consultant in Medical Paediatrics, Royal Hosp. for Sick Children, Glasgow 1966–73, in Clinical Genetics, Yorkhill and Assoc. Hosps 1973–87, in Medical Genetics, Addenbrooke's Hosp., Cambridge 1987–98; Hon. Assoc. Royal Coll. Veterinary Surgeons 2002; Hon. DSc (Strathclyde Univ.) 1992, (Glasgow); Bronze Medal, Univ. of Helsinki 1968, Makdougall-Brisbane Prize of Royal Soc. of Edinburgh 1984–86, San Remo Int. Prize for Research in Genetics 1990, Mauro Baschirotto Award for achievements in human genetics 1996, Sir James Y. Simpson Award 1998, J. B. S. Haldane Medal 2000. *Publications:* Early Prenatal Diagnosis (ed.) 1983, Essential Medical Genetics (co-author) 1984, Prenatal Diagnosis and Screening (co-ed.) 1992; papers on cytogenetics, gene mapping, human genetics, comparative genomics and prenatal diagnosis in medical and scientific journals. *Leisure interests:* swimming, sailing, fishing. *Address:* Department of Clinical Veterinary Medicine, Cambridge University, Madingley Road, Cambridge, CB3 0ES, England. *Telephone:* (1223) 766496. *Fax:* (1223) 766496 (Office). *E-mail:* maf12@mole.bio.cam.ac.uk

FERGUSSON, Sir Ewen Alastair John, GCMG, GCVO, MA; British diplomatist (retd); b. 28 Oct. 1932, Singapore; s. of the late Sir Ewen MacGregor Field Fergusson and Lady (Winifred Evelyn) Fergusson; m. Sara Carolyn Montgomery Cuninghame (née Gordon Lennox) 1959; one s. two d.; ed Rugby and Oriel Coll., Oxford; 2nd Lt 60th Rifles (KRRC) 1954–56; Foreign (Diplomatic) Service 1956–92; Asst Pvt. Sec. to Minister of Defence 1957–59; British Embassy, Addis Ababa 1960; FCO 1963; British Trade Devt Office, New York 1967; Counsellor and Head of Chancery, Office of UK Perm. Rep. to EC 1972–75; Pvt. Sec. to Foreign and Commonwealth Sec. 1975–78, Asst Under-Sec. of State 1978–82; Amb. to SA 1982–84, to France 1987–92; Deputy Under-Sec. of State 1984–87; Chair. (non-exec.) Coutts & Co. 1993–99, Savoy Hotel Group 1995–98 (Dir 1993–98); Dir (non-exec.) BT 1993–99, Sun Alliance 1993–96; Chair. Rugby School 1995–2002 (Gov. 1985–2002); Trustee Nat. Gallery 1995–2002, Henry Moore Foundation 1998– (Chair. 2001–); Hon. Fellow Oriel Coll. Oxford 1988; King at Arms, Most Distinguished Order of St Michael and St George 1996–; Hon. LLD (Aberdeen) 1995; Grand Officier Légion d'honneur. *Achievements:* played rugby for Scotland (5 caps) 1954. *Address:* 111 Iverna Court, London, W8 6TX (Office); 22 Iverna Gardens, London, W8 6TN, England (Home). *Telephone:* (20) 7937-2240 (Office); (20) 7937-5545 (Home). *Fax:* (20) 7938-1136 (Office); (20) 7376-0418 (Home). *E-mail:* Sir.ewenfergusson@btinternet.com (Office).

FERIANTO, Djaduk; Indonesian composer and musician. *Compositions include:* Kompi Susu (Milk Brigade), Brigade Mailing (Thieves' Brigade).

FERLINGHETTI, Lawrence, MA, DR.UNIV.; American writer and painter; b. 24 March 1920, Yonkers, New York; s. of Charles Ferlinghetti and Clemence Mendes-Monsanto; m. 1951; one s. one d.; ed Columbia Univ., Univ. of Paris; served as Lieut. Commdr. USNR in World War II; f. (with Peter D. Martin) one of the first all-paperback bookshops in USA 1953; f. City Lights publishing co. 1955; arrested on obscenity charges following publ. of Allan Ginsberg's "Howl" 1956 (later acquitted); participant One World Poetry Festival, Amsterdam 1980, World Congress of Poets, Florence 1986; First Poet Laureate of San Francisco 1998–99; Poetry Prize, City of Rome 1993, Premio Internazionale Flaiano, Italy 1999, Premio Internazionale di Camaiore, Italy 1999, Premio Cavour, Italy 2000, LA Times Book Festival Lifetime Achievement award 2001. *One-man exhibitions:* Ethel Guttman Gallery, San Francisco 1985, Peter Lembcke Gallery, San Francisco 1991, Butler Inst., Youngstown OH 1993, Retrospective Exhbn., Palazzo delle Esposizioni, Rome 1996. *Publications include:* Pictures of the Gone World (poems), Selections from Paroles by Jacques Prévert, A Coney Island of the Mind (poems), Her (novel), Starting from San Francisco (poems), Unfair Arguments with Existence (7 plays), Routines (plays), The Secret Meaning of Things (poems), Tyrannus Nix? (poem), Back Roads to Far Places (poems), Open Eye, Open Heart (poems), The Mexican Night (travel journal), Who Are We Now? 1976, Landscapes of Living and Dying (poems) 1979, Endless Life: Selected Poems 1981; Literary San Francisco: A Pictorial History from the Beginnings to the Present (with Nancy J. Peters) 1980, Leaves of Life: Drawings from the Model 1983, Over All the Obscene Boundaries (poems) 1984, Seven Days in Nicaragua Libre 1984, Love in the Days of Rage (novel) 1988, When I Look at Pictures (poems and paintings) 1990, These Are My Rivers; New and Selected Poems 1993, A Far Rockaway of the Heart 1997, How to Paint Sunlight: New Poems 2001; Ed. City Lights Books; also translations, film-scripts and phonograph records. *Address:* c/o City Lights Bookstore, 261 Columbus Avenue, San Francisco, CA 94133-4519, USA (Office). *Telephone:* (415) 362-1901. *Fax:* (415) 362-4921. *E-mail:* ferlinghetti@citylights.com (Office).

FERM, Anders; Swedish diplomatist; b. 1938, Ockelbo; m.; one c.; ed Stockholm School of Econs; Special Political Asst to Minister of Transport 1965–69, Prime Minister's Chef de Cabinet 1969–73; Exec. Sec. of Ind. Comm. of Disarmament and Security Issues, Vienna 1980–83; Perm. Rep. to UN, New York 1983–88; Amb. to Denmark 1988–90; Ed.-in-Chief Arbetet 1990; exec. man. publishing 1973–80, fmr mem. numerous cttees. and bds. including PEN Club, Publrs. Assoc., Swedish Television Corpn. *Address:* c/o Arbetet, P.O. Box 125, 201 21 Malmö, Sweden.

FERMOR, Patrick Michael Leigh, DSO, OBE, CLit; British author; b. 11 Feb. 1915, London; s. of the late Sir Lewis Leigh Fermor and Muriel Eileen Fermor (née Ambler); m. Hon. Joan Eyres-Monsell 1968; ed King's School, Canterbury; travelled for four years in Cen. Europe, Balkans and Greece in 1930s;

enlisted in Irish Guards 1939; "I" Corps 1940; Lt British Mil. Mission, Greece 1940; Liaison Officer, Greek GHQ, Albania; with Cretan Resistance for two years in German-occupied Crete; Team-Commdr Special Allied Airborne Reconnaissance Force, N Germany 1945; Deputy Dir British Inst. Athens 1945–46; travelled in Caribbean and Cen. America 1947–48; Corresp. mem. Athens Acad. 1980; Hon. Citizen of Heraklion, Crete 1947, Gytheion, Laconia 1966, Kardamyli, Messenia 1967; Hon. DLitt (Kent) 1991, (American School of Greece) 1993, (Warwick) 1996; Int. PEN/Time Life Silver Pen Award 1986, Municipality of Athens Gold Medal of Honour 1988; Prix Jacques Audiberti, Ville d'Antibes 1992; Chevalier, Ordre des Arts et des Lettres (France) 1995. *Publications:* The Traveller's Tree (Heinemann Foundation Prize for Literature 1950, Kemsley Prize 1951), Colette's Chance Acquaintances (trans.) 1952, A Time to Keep Silence 1953, The Violins of Saint Jacques 1953, The Cretan Runner (trans.) 1955, Mani 1958 (Duff Cooper Prize), Roumeli 1966, A Time of Gifts 1977 (W.H. Smith Award 1978), Between the Woods and the Water 1986 (Thomas Cook Award 1986), Three Letters from the Andes 1991. *Leisure interests:* travel, reading. *Address:* c/o John Murray, 50 Albemarle Street, London, W1X 4BD, England.

FERNANDES, George; Indian trade unionist and politician; b. 3 June 1930, Bangalore, Karnataka; s. of John Fernandes and Alice Fernandes; m. Leila Kabir 1971; one s.; ed St Peter's Seminary, Bangalore; joined Socialist Party of India 1949; Ed. Konkani Yuvak (Konkani Youth) monthly in Konkani language 1949, Raithavani weekly in Kannada language 1949, Dockman weekly in English 1952–53, also New Society; fmr Chief Ed. Pratipaksha weekly in Hindi; trade union work in South Kanara 1949, 1950, in Bombay and Maharashtra 1950–58; Founding Pres. All-India Radio Broadcasters and Telecasters Guild, Khadi Comm. Karmachari Union, All-India Univ. Employees' Confed.; Pres. All-India Railwaymen's Fed. 1973–77; organized nat. railways strike 1974; Treas. All-India Hind Mazdoor Sabha 1958; formed Hind Mazdoor Panchayat 1958, Gen. Sec. for over 10 years; Convenor, United Council of Trade Unions; fmr mem. Gen. Council of Public Services Int. (PSI), Int. Transport Workers' Fed. (ITF); Founder Chair. New India Co-operative Bank Ltd (fmrly Bombay Labour Co-operative Bank Ltd); mem. Nat. Cttee of Socialist Party of India 1955–77, Treas. 1964, Chair. 1971–77; Gen. Sec. Samyukta Socialist Party of India 1969–70; mem. Bombay Municipal Corpn 1961–68; mem. for Bombay City, Lok Sabha 1967–77; went underground on declaration of emergency 1975; mem. Janata Party 1977, Gen. Sec. 1985–86; mem. for Muzzafarpur, Bihar, Lok Sabha 1977–79, also elected to Lok Sabha 1980, 1989, 1991, 1996, 1998; Minister for Communications March–July 1977, for Industry 1977–79 (resgnd from Govt 1979), for Railways 1989–90, for Kashmir Affairs 1990–91, for Defence 1998–2001, Oct. 2001–; Deputy Leader Lok Dal 1980–; mem. Standing Parl. Cttee on Finance 1993–96, also Consultative Cttee on Home Affairs; Pres. Samata Party 1994–; mem. Standing Parl. Cttee on External Affairs 1996–, also Consultative Cttee on Human Resources Devt; Chair. Ed. Bd Pratipaksh (Hindi monthly); Ed. The Other Side (English-language monthly); Pres. Hind Mazdoor Kisan Panchayat; Chair. India Devt Group, London 1979, Schumacher Foundation 1979; fmr mem. Press Council of India; mem. Amnesty Int., People's Union for Civil Liberties; involved in anti-nuclear and environmental campaigns. *Publications:* What Ails the Socialists: The Kashmir Problem, The Railway Strike of 1974, George Fernandes Speaks. *Leisure interests:* music, reading. *Address:* Ministry of Defence, South Block, New Delhi 110011 (Office); 3 Krishna Menon Marg, New Delhi, 110011 (Home); 30 Leonard Road, Richmond Town, Bangalore, Karnataka 560025, India. *Telephone:* (11) 3012380 (Office); (80) 221-4143 (Bangalore); (11) 3015403; (11) 3793397 (New Delhi). *Website:* www.mod.nic.in.

FERNANDEZ, Dominique, DèsSc; French author; b. 25 Aug. 1929, Neuilly-sur-Seine; s. of Ramon Fernandez and Liliane Chomette; m. Diane Jacquin de Margerie (divorced); one s. one d.; ed Lycée Buffon, Paris and Ecole Normale Supérieure; Prof. Inst. Français, Naples 1957–58; Prof. of Italian, Univ. de Haute-Bretagne 1966–89; literary critic, L'Express 1959–84, Le Nouvel Observateur 1985–; music critic, Diapason 1977–85, Opera International 1978; mem. reading Cttee Edns. Bernard Grasset 1959–; Chevalier, Légion d'honneur, Commdr, Ordre Nat. du Mérite; Commdr Cruzeiro do Sul (Brazil); Prix Médicis 1974; Prix Goncourt 1982, Grand Prix Charles Oulmont 1986, Prix Prince Pierre de Monaco 1986, Prix Méditerranée 1988, Prix Oscar Wilde 1988. *Publications:* Le roman italien et la crise de la conscience moderne 1958, L'écorce des pierres 1959, L'aube 1962, Mère Méditerranée 1965, Les Evénements de Palerme 1966, L'échec de Pavèse 1968, Lettre à Dora 1969, Les enfants de Gogol 1971, Il Mito dell'America 1969, L'arbre jusqu'aux racines 1972, Porporino 1974, Eisenstein 1975, La rose des Tudors 1976, Les Siciliens 1977, Amsterdam 1977, L'étoile rose 1978, Une fleur de jasmin à l'oreille 1980, Le promeneur amoureux 1980, Signor Giovanni 1981, Dans la main de l'ange 1982, Le volcan sous la ville 1983, Le banquet des anges 1984, L'amour 1986, La gloire du paria 1987, Le rapt de Perséphone (opera libretto) 1987, Le radeau de la Gorgone 1988, Le rapt de Ganymède 1989, L'Ecole du Sud 1991, Porfirio et Constance 1992, Séville 1992, L'Or des Tropiques 1993, Le Dernier des Médicis 1993, La Magie Blanche de Saint-Pétersbourg 1994, Prague et la Bohème (jtly.) 1995, la Perle et le croissant 1995, le Musée idéal de Stendhal 1995, Saint-Pétersbourg 1996, Tribunal d'honneur 1997, Le musée de Zola 1997, Le voyage d'Italie 1998, Rhapsodie roumaine 1998, Palerme et la Sicile 1998, Le loup et le chien 1999, Les douze muses d'Alexandre Dumas 1999, Bolivie 1999, Nicolas 2000, Errances solaires 2000, L'amour qui ose dire son nom 2001, Syrie 2002, La Course à

l'abîme 2002. *Leisure interest:* operatic music. *Address:* Editions Bernard Grasset, 61 rue des Saints-Pères, 75006 Paris (Office); 14 rue de Douai, 75009 Paris, France (Home).

FERNANDEZ, Mary Joe; American tennis player; b. 19 Aug. 1971, Dominican Republic; d. of José Fernandez and Sylvia Fernandez; m. Tony Godsick 2000; ed Carrollton School of the Sacred Heart; turned professional 1986; reached quarter-finals French Open 1986, quarter-finals Geneva 1987, semi-finals Eastbourne 1988, semi-finals French Open 1989; runner-up to Graf in singles and runner-up with Fendick in doubles, Australian Open 1990; reached semi-finals Wimbledon, Australian Open and Italian Open, 1991; with Fendick won Australian Open Doubles Title 1991; runner-up Australian Open 1992; won Bronze Medal in singles and Gold in doubles with G. Fernandez, Olympic Games 1992; reached semi-finals U.S. Open 1992; reached semi-finals Italian Open, quarter-finals Australian Open 1993; won singles title Strasbourg 1994, winner (with Davenport) French Open Doubles 1996; winner doubles Hilton Head, Carolina 1997, Madrid 1997, won singles title German Open 1997; mem. U.S. Fed. Cup Team 1991, 1994–99; Spokesperson for Will to Win Scholarship Programme 1998; retd 2000. *Publication:* Mary Joe Fernandez (biog. with Melanie Cole). *Leisure interests:* golf, wave running, water-skiing.

FERNÁNDEZ MALDONADO SOLARI, Gen. Jorge; Peruvian politician and army officer; b. 29 May 1922, Ilo, Moquegua; s. of Arturo Fernández Maldonado Soto and Amelia Solari de Fernández Maldonado; m. Estela Castro Faucheux; two s. two d.; ed Chorillos Mil. School; Head of Army Intelligence Service; Dir of Army Intelligence School, also of Mariscal Ramon Castilla Mil. School, Trujillo; Mil. Attaché, Argentina; mem. Pres. Advisory Cttee (COAP); Minister of Energy and Mines 1968–75; Army Chief of Staff 1975–76; Prime Minister, Minister of War, Commdr-Gen. of Army Feb.–July 1976; Senator 1985–; Sec.-Gen. Intergovernmental Council of Copper Exporting Countries 1990–.

FERNÁNDEZ-MURO, José Antonio; Argentine painter; b. 1 March 1920; Dir Nat. School of Fine Arts, Buenos Aires 1957–58; travelled and studied in Europe and America on UNESCO Fellowship of Museology 1957–58; lives in New York 1962–; represented in numerous Group Shows including 50 ans de Peinture Abstraite, Paris and The Emergent Decade, Guggenheim Museum 1965; prizes include Gold Medal, Brussels World Fair 1958, Guggenheim Int. and Di Tella Int. Awards. *Solo exhibitions include:* Buenos Aires, Madrid, Washington, New York, Rome and Detroit. *Major works:* Superimposed Circles 1958, In Reds, Di Tella Foundation, Buenos Aires 1959, Horizonte terroso, Museum of Modern Art, Caracas 1961, Círculo azogado, Museum of Modern Art, New York 1962, Lacerated Tablet, Rockefeller, New York 1963, Elemental Forms, MIT 1964, Silver Field, Guggenheim Museum 1965, Summit, Bonino Gallery, New York.

FERNÁNDEZ RETAMAR, Roberto, DR. EN FIL.; Cuban writer; b. 9 June 1930, Havana; s. of José M. Fernández Roig and Obdulia Retamar; m. Adelaida de Juan 1952; two d.; ed Univ. de la Habana, Univ. de Paris à la Sorbonne and Univ. of London; Prof. Univ. de la Habana 1955–; Visiting Prof. Yale Univ. 1957–58; Dir Nueva Revista Cubana 1959–60; Cultural Counsellor of Cuba in France 1960; Sec. Union of Writers and Artists of Cuba 1961–65; Ed. Casa de las Américas 1965–, now Pres.; Visiting Lecturer Columbia Univ. 1957, Univ. of Prague 1965; Nat. Prize for Poetry, Cuba 1952; Nat. Literary Award Cuban Book Inst. 1989. *Publications:* Poetry: Elegía como un Himno 1950, Patrias 1952, Alabanzas, Conversaciones 1955, Vuelta de la Antigua Esperanza 1959, Con las Mismas Manos 1962, Poesía Reunida 1948–1965 1966, Buena Suerte Viviendo 1967, Que veremos arder 1970, A quien pueda interesar 1970, Cuaderno paralelo 1973; studies: La Poesía contemporánea en Cuba 1954, Idea de la Estilística 1958, Papelería 1962, Ensayo de otro mundo 1967, Introducción a Cuba: la historia 1968, Caliban 1971, Lectura de Martí 1972, El son de Vuelo popular 1972. *Leisure interests:* reading, swimming. *Address:* 508 H Street, Vedado, Havana, Cuba.

FERNÁNDEZ REYNA, Leonel; Dominican Republic politician; currently Leader Partido de la Liberación Dominicana; Pres. of Dominican Republic 1996–2000. *Address:* Partido de la Liberación Dominicana, Avda Independencia 401, Santo Domingo, DN, Dominican Republic. *Telephone:* 685-3540.

FERNANDO, Most Rev. Nicholas Marcus, BA, PhL, STD; Sri Lankan ecclesiastic; b. 6 Dec. 1932; s. of W. Severinus Fernando and M. M. Lily Fernando; ordained priest 1959; Rector, St Aloysius Minor Seminary 1965–73; Archbishop of Colombo 1977–; mem. Sacred Congregation for the Evangelization of Peoples 1989; Pres. Catholic Bishops' Conf. of Sri Lanka 1989–95. *Address:* Archbishop's House, 976 Gnanartha Pradeepaya Mawatha, Colombo 8, Sri Lanka. *Telephone:* 695471-2-3. *Fax:* (1) 692009. *E-mail:* cyrilsp@sltnet.lk (Office). *Website:* www.ceylon.net/catholicchurchcolombo (Office).

FERNEYHOUGH, Brian John Peter, ARAM; British composer and professor of composition; b. 16 Jan. 1943, Coventry; s. of Frederick George Ferneyhough and Emily May Ferneyhough (née Hopwood); m. 1st Barbara J. Pearson 1967; m. 2nd Elke Schaaf 1980; m. 3rd Carolyn Steinberg 1984; m. 4th Stephanie Jan Hurtik 1990; ed Birmingham School of Music, RAM, Sweelinck Conservatory, Amsterdam, Music Acad., Basle; Composition teacher, Musikhochschule, Freiburg, Germany 1973–78, Prof. of Composition 1978–86; Prin. Composition Teacher, Royal Conservatory of The Hague 1986;

Prof. of Music, Univ. of Calif. at San Diego 1987–99; leader of Master Class in Composition, Civica Scuola di Musica, Milan 1985–87; Visiting Artist, Berlin 1976–77; Guest Prof. Musikhögskolan, Stockholm 1980, 1981, 1982, 1985; Visiting Prof. Univ. of Chicago 1986; Lecturer in Composition, Darmstadt Int. Courses 1976–96; Guest Prof. of Poetics, Mozarteum, Salzburg 1995; mem. Akad. der Künste, Berlin 1996; Fellow Birmingham Conservatoire 1996; William H. Bonsall Prof. of Music, Stanford Univ. 2000–; Koussevitsky Prize 1979, Grand Prix du Disque 1978, 1984, Chevalier des Arts et des Lettres 1984 and other awards and prizes. *Works include:* Sonatas for String Quartet 1967, Firecycle Beta 1969–71, Transit 1972–74, Time and Motion Study III 1974, La Terre Est Un Homme 1976–79, Second String Quartet 1979–80, Lemma-Icon-Epigram 1981, Carceri d' Invenzione 1981–86, 3rd String Quartet 1987, Kurze Schatten II 1988, La Chute d'Icare 1988, Fourth String Quartet 1989–90, Allgebrah 1991, Bone Alphabet 1991, Terrain 1992, Maisons Noires 1993, On Stellar Magnitudes 1994, String Trio 1995, Incipit 1995–96, Kranichtänze II 1996, Allgebrah 1996, Flurries 1997, Unsichtbare Farben 1999, The Doctrine of Similarity 2000, Opus Contra Naturam 2000, Stele for Failed Time 2001. *Publications:* Complete Writings on Music 1994, Collected Writings 1996; various articles published separately. *Leisure interests:* reading, cats, wife, wine (not in that order). *Address:* Office 225, Department of Music, Braun Music Center, Stanford University, 541 Lasuen Mall, Stanford, CA 94305-3076 (Office); 848 Allardice Way, Stanford, CA 94305, USA. *Telephone:* (650) 725-3102 (Office); (650) 565-8842. *Fax:* (650).725-2686 (Office); (650) 565-8842. *E-mail:* brian.ferneyhough@stanford.edu (Office). *Website:* www.stanford.edu/group/Music (Office).

FERNIOT, Jean; French journalist; b. 10 Oct. 1918, Paris; s. of Paul Ferniot and Jeanne Ferniot (née Rabu); m. 1st Jeanne Martinod 1942 (divorced); one s. two d.; m. 2nd Christiane Servan-Schreiber 1959 (divorced); two s.; m. 3rd Béatrice Lemaître 1984; ed Lycée Louis-le-Grand; Head, Political Dept, France-Tireur 1945–57; Political Columnist, L'Express 1957–58; Chief Political Correspondent France-Soir 1959–63; Ed. L'Express 1963–66; with Radio Luxembourg 1967–83; Political Commentator France-Soir 1967–70, Asst Chief Ed. 1969–70; Dir at Éditions Grasset, in charge of Collection Humeurs 1978–83; Dir then Adviser Cuisine et Vins de France 1981; Pres. Fondation Communication Demain 1980–89, Terminology Comm., Nat. Council for Tourism 1991–97; Pres. (Supervisory Council) Evénement du Jeudi 1992; mem. jury, Prix Interallié 1970–; Prix Interallié 1961; Commdr des Arts et des Lettres; Croix de Guerre, Chevalier du Mérite Agricole, Commdr du Mérite (Italy). *Publications:* Les ides de mai 1958, L'ombre porté 1961, Pour le pire 1962, Derrière la fenêtre 1964, De Gaulle et le 13 mai 1965, Mort d'une révolution 1968, Paris dans mon assiette 1969, Complainte contre X 1973, De de Gaulle à Pompidou 1972, Ça suffit! 1973, Pierrot et Aline 1973, La petite légume 1974, Les vaches maigres (with Michel Albert) 1975, Les honnêtes gens 1976, C'est ça la France 1977, Vous en avez vraiment assez d'être français 1979, Carnet de croûte 1980, Le Pouvoir et la sainteté 1982, Le Chien-loup 1983, Saint Judas 1984, Un mois de juin comme on les aimait 1986, Soleil orange 1988, Miracle au village 1989, Je recommencerais bien 1991, L'Europe à Table 1993, La France des Terroirs Gourmands 1993, Jérusalem, nombril du monde 1994, La Mouffe 1995, Morte saison 1996, Un temps pour aimer, un temps pour haïr 1999, Le soir ou jamais 2002. *Leisure interest:* history. *Address:* 11 bis rue d'Orléans, 92200 Neuilly-sur-Seine, France. *Telephone:* 1-46-24-25-30 (Home).

FERRAGAMO, Ferruccio; Italian business executive; b. 9 Sept. 1945, Fiesole, Florence; m. Amanda Collingwood; five c.; began career working on production side of family business Salvatore Ferragamo Italia SpA, later involved in worldwide management of Ferragamo stores; finance and admin. from 1983; now CEO Salvatore Ferragamo SpA; Vice-Pres. Polimoda, Florence; mem. Bd Società Gaetano Marzotto & Fratelli, La Fondaria Assicurazioni, Banca Mercantile, Florence, Centro di Firenze per la Moda Italiana. *Leisure interests:* golf, shooting, sailing, tennis. *Address:* c/o Salvatore Ferragamo Italia, SpA, Via di Tornabuoni 2, 50123 Florence, Italy. *Telephone:* (055) 33601.

FERRANTI, Marie; French writer; b. 1964, Corsica; fmr teacher in literature before becoming full-time novelist. *Publications include:* Les Femmes de San Stefano (Prix François Mauriac) 1995 , La Chambre des Défunts 1996, La Fuite aux Agriates 2000, Le Paradoxe de l'Ordre 2002, La Princess de Mantoue (Grand Prix du Roman, Acad. Française) 2002. *Address:* c/o Editions Gallimard, 5 rue Sébastian-Bottin, 75328 Paris Cedex 7, France (Office).

FERRARA, Abel; American film director and actor; b. 12 May 1951, Bronx, NY; m. Nancy Ferrara; two d.; began making short films while at school; has used pseudonym Jimmy Laine; television work includes episodes of Miami Vice and pilot for NBC's Crime Story. *Films include:* Driller Killer (also acted) 1979, Ms.45 (also acted) 1981, Fear City 1984, China Girl, Cat Chaser, The King of New York, Bad Lieutenant 1993, Body Snatchers, Dangerous Game 1994, The Addiction 1995, The Funeral 1996, California 1996, The Blackout 1997, New Rose Motel 1998. *Address:* c/o William Morris Agency, 151 El Camino Drive, Beverly Hills, CA 90212, USA.

FERRARI BRAVO, Luigi; Italian professor of law; b. 5 Aug. 1933; ed Univ. of Naples; Asst Prof. Univ. of Naples 1956–61; Prof. of Int. Org. Univ. of Bari 1961–65, of Int. Law 1965–68, Full Prof. of Int. Law and Dir Inst. of Int. Law 1968–74; Prof. of Int. Law, Istituto Universitario Orientale, Naples 1962–68, Full Prof. of Int. Org. 1974–79, Dean, Dept of Political Science 1975–76; Prof. of EC Law, High School of Public Admin. Rome 1965–79, Full Prof. 1975; Full Prof. of EC Law, Faculty of Political Science, Univ. of Rome 1979–82, Full Prof. of Public Int. Law 1982–91; Full Prof. of EC Law, Faculty of Law, Univ. of Rome 1991–; lecturer, Hague Acad. of Int. Law 1975, 1982 and many other univs. and scientific insts.; numerous professional appts.; mem. Italian Bar, Int. Law Asscn, American Soc. of Int. Law, Soc. Française de Droit Int. etc. *Publications:* articles in professional journals. *Address:* Faculty of Law, University of Rome, Piazzale Aldo Moro 5, 00185 Rome, Italy.

FERRARO, Geraldine Anne, JD; American politician and lawyer; b. 26 Aug. 1935, Newburgh, NY; d. of Dominick Ferraro and Antonetta L. (Corrieri) Ferraro; m. John Zaccaro 1960; one s. two d.; ed Marymount Manhattan Coll., Fordham Univ. School of Law; lawyer in New York Bar 1961, US Supreme Court 1978; practised law in New York 1961–74, Asst Dist Attorney, Queens County, New York 1974–78; mem. House of Reps. 1979–84; first woman from a maj. party to be a cand. for US Vice-Pres. in 1984 presidential election; man. partner Keck Mahin Cate & Koether, New York 1993–94; apptd. by Pres. Clinton as US Amb. to UN Human Rights Comm. 1994–96, World Conf., Vienna 1993, 4th World Conf. on Women 1995; Prof. Georgetown Univ. School of Public Policy; Pres. G & L Strategies; Fellow Harvard Univ., Kennedy School of Govt, 1988; Pres. Int. Inst. of Women Political Leaders; consultant Golin Harris Int.1999–; mem. Nat. Democratic Inst. for Int. Affairs; Democrat; hon. degrees from 14 colls. and univs.; numerous awards. *Television:* Co-host Crossfire, CNN 1996–98; currently political analyst for FOX News. *Publications:* My Story (with Linda Bird Francke) 1985, Changing History: Women, Power and Politics 1993, Framing a Life 1998. *Address:* 218 Lafayette Street, New York, NY 10012, USA (Office).

FERRÉ, Gianfranco; Italian couturier; b. 15 Aug. 1944, Legnano, Milan; ed Politecnico di Milano; started designing jewelry and belts 1969; designed first collection of clothes for women, under Baila label 1974; first collection under own name 1978; first collection for men 1982; introduced own perfume 1984; Artistic Dir at Christian Dior, Paris 1989–96; designer Oaks by Ferré, Milan 1978–, Studio 0.001 by Ferré, Milan 1987–, Ferré Jeans 1989–; Prof. Domus Acad. 1983–89; designs included in exhbns. at MIT, Boston, USA 1982, La Jolla Museum of Contemporary Art, Calif., USA and Daimaru Museum, Osaka and Museum of Fashion and Costume Acad., Tokyo; Modepreis, Munich 1958, Cutty Sark Men's Fashion Award, New York 1985, Gold Medal of Civic Merit, Milan 1985, De d'Or Prize, Paris (Best Couturier of the Season) 1989, L'Occhio d'Oro Award (Best Collection at Milan women's ready-to-wear shows) 1983, 1983/84, 1985, 1986/87 and 1987/88; Commendatore of Italian Order of Merit, Lorenzo il Magnifico Award 1990, Il Fiorino d'Oro 1991, Diva-Wollsiegel 1992, Pitti Immagine Uomo 1993. *Leisure interests:* reading, classical and folk music, cinema, collecting modern art. *Address:* Via della Spiga 19/A, 20121 Milan, Italy.

FERRER, Ibrahim; Cuban musician and singer; b. 20 Feb. 1927, Santiago; s. of Hermino Ferrer and Aurelia Planas; m. Caridad Ferrer; seven c.; started singing at age of 13 with first band Los Jóvenes del Son; debut hit record 'El platanar de Bartolo' with group Orquesta Chepín-Chóven 1955; worked with Orquesta Ritmo Oriental and Beny Moré 1957; sang with group 'Los Bocucos' until 1991; recorded with Afro Cuban All Stars, Rubén Gonzalez (q.v.) and recorded Buena Vista Social Club 1996; released own album 'Buena Vista Social Club Presents...' 1999 (achieved gold status in Austria, Netherlands, Denmark, Sweden, France, USA, Germany, Canada and platinum status in Switzerland); Latin Grammy for Best Newcomer 2000. *Film:* participated in award-winning documentary 'Buena Vista Social Club'. *Music:* Buena Vista Social Club 1999, Afro Cuban All Stars 'A toda Cuba le gusta', guest singer on 'Introducing Rubén Gonzalez', 'Buena Vista Social Club Presents...'. *Leisure interest:* relaxing at home with his family. *Address:* c/o World Circuit Records, 138 Kingsland Road, London, E2 8DY, England (Office). *Telephone:* (20) 7749-3222 (Office). *Fax:* (20) 7749-3232 (Office). *E-mail:* post@worldcircuit.co.uk (Office). *Website:* www.worldcircuit.co.uk (Office).

FERRER SALAT, Carlos; Spanish banker and business executive; Chair. Banco de Europa, Ferrer Int. (pharmaceutical co.); Founder and first Chair. Spanish Employers' Fed. (CEOE); Pres. European Employers' Union (UNICE), Brussels 1991–; mem. Bds. Volkswagen, IBM Europe and others.

FERRERO-WALDNER, Benita Maria, DIur; Austrian diplomatist and government minister; b. 5 Sept. 1948, Oberndorf, Salzburg; ed Univ. of Salzburg; export and sales managerial roles in German and US cos., Germany 1978–83; joined Diplomatic Service 1984, several posts Ministry of Foreign Affairs, Vienna 1984–86, First Sec., Dakar, Devt Aid Dept, Vienna; Counsellor for Econ. Affairs, Deputy Head of Mission, Chargé d'affaires, Paris 1986–93; Deputy Chief of Protocol, Ministry of Foreign Affairs 1993; UN Chief of Protocol, Exec. Office of Sec.-Gen., New York 1994–95; State Sec., Ministry of Foreign Affairs 1995–2000, Minister of Foreign Affairs 2000–; Mérite Européen Gold Medal. *Publication:* The Future of Development Co-operation, Setting Course in a Changing World. *Leisure interests:* reading, yoga, cycling. *Address:* Ministry of Foreign Affairs, Ballhausplatz 2, 1014 Vienna, Austria (Office). *Telephone:* (1) 53115-3350 (Office). *Fax:* (1) 535-50-91 (Office). *E-mail:* Benita.Ferrero-WALDNER@bmaa.gv.at (Office). *Website:* www.bmaa.gv.at (Office).

FERRES, Veronica Maria; German actress; b. 10 June, Cologne; m. Martin Krug 2001; one d.; ed Ludwig-Maximilian-Univ., Munich; several awards including: Golden Camera Award, Germany 1998 2002, Bavarian TV Award 2002, Romy Award (Austria) 2002. *Films:* The Mask of Desire, Bambi (Best Actress Award 1992) 1992, Lateshow, The Ladies Room, Schtonk 1992,

Superwoman 1996, Rossini 1997, Honeymoon, The Parrot, The Second Homeland, The Bride (Best Actress Award 9th Int. Film Festival, Pescara 1999) 1999. *Plays:* Gold 1998, The Casket 2000, The Geierwally, Talking With, The Bernauerin, Ghostride, Everyman 2002. *Television:* Jack's Baby, The Chaos Queen, The Naughty Woman, Dr Knock, Catherine the Great, Tatort Fatal Motherlove, The Mountain Doctor, Bobby 2002, Sans Famille 2002, The Manns, Les Misérables 2002, The Manns 2002 (Golden Grimme Award, Emmy Award), Forever Lost 2003, The Return of Anna 2003. *Leisure interests:* horseriding, skiing, fencing, golf, scuba diving, dancing. *Address:* Ferrres Management, Kurfürstenstr. 18, 80801 Munich (Office); c/o Management Etna Baumbauer, Keplerstr. 2, 81679 Munich, Germany. *Telephone:* (89) 478577 (Office); (89) 399733 (Home). *Fax:* (89) 4702198 (Office); (89) 399744 (Home).

FERRETTI, Alberta; Italian fashion designer and retailer; b. 1951; m. 1968 (separated); two s.; made clothes and opened first boutique The Jolly Shop, Cattolica 1968, launched first collection under the name Alberta Ferretti 1974; began mfg clothes for other designers in 1970s; launched Alberta Ferretti line 1981, Philosophy line 1984, lingerie, accessories and beachwear lines 2001; owner and Vice-Pres. Aeffe fashion design and mfg co.; Cavaliere del Lavoro 1998; Hon. degree (Bologna). *Leisure interests:* swimming, reading, sailing. *Address:* Via Donizetti 48, 20122 Milan, Italy (Office). *Telephone:* (2) 760591 (Office). *Fax:* (2) 782373 (Office). *E-mail:* info@aeffe.com (Office). *Website:* www.aeffe.com (Office).

FERRIER, Johan Henri Eliza, PH.D.; Suriname politician; b. 12 May 1910, Paramaribo; mem. Suriname Parl. 1946–48; Dir Dept of Educ., Paramaribo 1951–55; Prime Minister, Minister of Gen. Affairs, of Home Affairs 1955–58; Counsellor, Ministry of Educ., Arts and Science, Netherlands 1959–65; Man. Dir Billiton Mining Co., Suriname 1966–67; Gov. of Suriname 1968–75; Pres. Repub. of Suriname 1975–80.

FERRY, Bryan; British singer and songwriter; b. 26 Sept. 1945, Washington, Co. Durham; s. of the late Frederick Charles Ferry and Mary Ann Ferry (née Armstrong); m. Lucy Margaret Mary Helmore 1982 (divorced 2003); three s. one d.; ed Univ. of Newcastle-upon-Tyne; formed Roxy Music 1971; official debut, Lincoln Festival 1972; first U.S. concerts 1972; first British and European tours 1973. *Albums include:* (with Roxy Music): Roxy Music 1972, For Your Pleasure 1973 (Grand Prix du Disque, Golden Rose Festival, Montreux 1973), Stranded 1973, Country Life 1974, Siren 1975, Viva Roxy Music 1976, Manifesto 1979, Flesh & Blood 1980, Avalon 1982, The Atlantic Years 1983, Street Life 1987; (solo): These Foolish Things 1973, Another Time Another Place 1974, Let's Stick Together 1976, In Your Mind 1977, The Bride Stripped Bare 1978, Boys And Girls 1985, Bete Noire 1987, The Ultimate Collection 1988, Taxi 1993, Mamouna 1995, Bryan Ferry and Roxy Music Video Collection 1996, Frantic 2002. *Singles include:* Virginia Plain 1972, Pyjamarama 1973, All I Want Is You 1974, Dance Away 1979, Angel Eyes 1979, Over You 1980, Oh Yeah 1980, Same Old Scene 1980, Jealous Guy (tribute to John Lennon) 1981, Slave To Love 1985, I Put A Spell On You 1993. *Address:* c/o Barry Dickins, ITB, 3rd Floor, 27A Floral Street, London, WC2E 9DQ, England (Office). *Telephone:* (20) 7379-1313 (Office).

FERRY, John Douglass, PhD; American professor of chemistry; b. 4 May 1912, Dawson, Canada (of U.S. parents); s. of Douglass Hewitt Ferry and Eudora Beaufort Bundy; m. Barbara Norton Mott 1944; one s. one d.; ed Stanford Univ. and Univ. of London; Instructor, Harvard Univ. 1936–38, Soc. of Fellows, Harvard 1938–41, Research Assoc. 1942–45; Assoc. Chemist, Woods Hole Oceanographic Inst. 1941–45; Asst Prof., Univ. of Wisconsin 1946, Assoc. Prof. 1946–47, Prof. 1947–82, Farrington Daniels Research Prof. 1973–82, Prof. Emer. 1982–, Chair. Dept of Chem. 1959–67; Pres. Soc. of Rheology 1961–63; Chair. Int. Cttee on Rheology 1963–68; mem. NAS, Nat. Acad. of Eng; Fellow American Acad. of Arts and Sciences; Hon. mem. Groupe Français de Rhéologie, Soc. of Rheology, Japan; Special Lecturer, Kyoto Univ., Japan 1968, Univ. de Grenoble (Ecole d'Eté) 1973; Eli Lilly Award, ACS 1946, Bingham Medal, Soc. of Rheology 1953, Kendall Award, ACS 1960, High Polymer Physics Prize, American Physical Soc. 1966, Colwyn Medal, Inst. of the Rubber Industry (London) 1971, Witco Award, ACS 1974, Tech. Award, Int. Inst. of Synthetic Rubber Producers 1977, Goodyear Medal, Rubber Div. ACS 1981, Div. of Polymer Chem. Award, ACS 1984. *Publication:* Viscoelastic Properties of Polymers 1961, 1970, 1980. *Leisure interest:* travel. *Address:* 6175 Mineral Point Road, Madison, WI 53705, USA (Home).

FERRY, Luc; French philosopher and politician; b. 3 Jan. 1951, Colombes; s. of Pierre Ferry and Monique Faucher; m. Marie-Caroline Becq de Fouquières 1999; three c.; ed Lycée Saint-Exupéry, Centre nat. de télé-enseignement, Sorbonne, Univ. of Heidelberg; lecturer Teacher Training Coll., Arras; Asst Lecturer Univ. of Reims 1977–79; Asst Lecturer univ. teacher training college, rue d'Ulm, Paris 1977–79, 1980–82; Research Attaché Nat. CNRS; Asst Lecturer Univ. of Paris I-Panthéon Sorbonne and Paris X-Nanterre 1980–88; Prof. of Philosophy Univ. of Caen 1989–97; Asst Lecturer Paris I 1989; Prof. of Philosophy Univ. of Paris VII-Jussieu 1996–; Founder-mem., Sec. Gen. College of Philosophy 1974–; responsible for Ideas section then Editorial Adviser, l'Express 1987–94; Pres. Nat. Curriculum Council (C.N.P.) 1994–; Minister of Youth, Nat. Educ. and Research May 2002–; Dir Grasset edns. collection of Coll. of Philosophy; mem. Saint-Simon Foundation; columnist for Point 1995–; Chevalier Légion d'honneur, Ordre des Arts et des Lettres; awarded Prix des Nouveaux Droits de l'Homme. *Publications:* Philosophie politique (3 Vols 1984–85), la Pensée 68, le Nouvel ordre écologique:

l'arbre, l'animal et l'homme (Prix Médicis, Prix Jean-Jacques Rousseau) 1992, l'Homme Dieu ou le sens de la vie 1996, La Sagesse des Modernes 1998, Le Sens du Beau 1998, Philosopher à dix-huit ans (jtly) 1999, Qu'est-ce que l'homme? (jtly) 2000, Qu'est-ce qu'une vie réussie 2002, numerous articles on philosophy. *Address:* Ministry of Youth, National Education and Research, 110 rue de Grenelle, 75357 Paris (Office); 158 bis avenue de Suffren, 15015 Paris 07, France (Home). *Telephone:* 01-55-55-10-10. *E-mail:* luc.ferry@free.fr. *Website:* www.education.gouv.fr.

FERSHT, Sir Alan Roy, Kt, MA, PhD, FRS; British professor of organic chemistry; b. 21 April 1943, London; s. of Philip Fersht and Betty Fersht; m. Marilyn Persell 1966; one s. one d.; ed Sir George Monoux Grammar School, Walthamstow and Gonville and Caius Coll., Cambridge; Research Fellow, Brandeis Univ. Waltham, Mass. 1968–69; Fellow, Jesus Coll., Cambridge 1969–72; mem. scientific staff, MRC Lab. of Molecular Biology, Cambridge 1969–77; Eleanor Roosevelt Fellow, Stanford Univ., Calif. 1978–79; Wolfson Research Prof. of Royal Soc. 1978–89; Prof. of Biological Chem., Imperial Coll., London 1978–88; Herchel Smith Prof. of Organic Chem., Cambridge Univ. 1988–; Dir Cambridge Interdisciplinary Research Centre for Protein Eng 1989–; Dir MRC Unit for Protein Function and Design 1989–; Fellow Gonville and Caius Coll., Cambridge 1988–; Foreign Assoc. NAS (USA) 1993; Hon. mem. Japanese Biochemical Soc. 2002; Hon. PhD (Uppsala) 1999, (Free Univ. of Brussels) 1999; Fed. of European Biochemical Socs Anniversary Prize 1980, Novo Biotech. Award 1986, Charmian Medal, for Enzyme Chem., RSC 1986, Gabor Medal, Royal Soc. 1991, Max Tishler Prize (Harvard Univ.) 1992, Harden Medal (Biochem. Soc.) 1993, Feldberg Foundation Prize 1996, Davy Medal (Royal Soc.) 1998, Anfinse Award of the Protein Soc. 1999, Laureate of the 'Chaire Bruylants', Lourain 1999, Royal Soc. of Chem. Natural Products Award 1999, Stein and Moore Award of the Potein Soc. 2001. *Publications:* Enzyme Structure and Mechanism 1977, Structure and Mechanism in Protein Science 1999: A Guide to Enzyme Catalysis and Protein Folding; papers in scientific journals. *Leisure interests:* chess, horology. *Address:* Cambridge Centre for Protein Engineering, Department of Chemistry, University of Cambridge, Lensfield Road, Cambridge CB2 1EW (Office); 2 Barrow Close, Cambridge, CB2 2AT, England (Home). *Telephone:* (1223) 336341 (Office); (1223) 352963 (Home). *Fax:* (1223) 336445.

FERY, John Bruce, MBA; American business executive; b. 16 Feb. 1930, Bellingham, Wash.; s. of Carl S. and Margaret Fery; m. Delores L. Carlo 1953; three s.; ed Univ. of Washington and Stanford Univ. Graduate School of Business; Asst to Pres., Western Kraft Corpn 1955–56, Production Man. 1956–57; Asst to Pres., Boise Cascade Corpn 1957–58, Gen. Man. Paper Div. 1958–60, Vice-Pres. 1960–67, Exec. Vice-Pres. and Dir 1967–72, Pres. 1972–78, Chair, CEO 1978–94, Chair. 1995–; numerous directorships; Hon. Dr. of Natural Resources (Idaho) 1983; Hon. LLD (Gonzaga) 1982; Stanford Univ. School of Business Ernest Arbuckle Award 1980. *Address:* Boise Cascade Corporation, One Jefferson Square, Boise, ID 83728 (Office); 609 Wyndemere Drive, Boise, ID 83702, USA (Home). *Telephone:* (208) 384-7560 (Office).

FETISOV, Vyacheslav Aleksandrovich; Russian hockey player; b. 20 April 1958, Moscow; m. Lada Fetisova; one d.; played with Cen. Army Sports Club 1975–89; USSR champion 1975, 1979–89; seven times world champion with USSR teams 1977–91; Olympic champion 1984, 1988; Pres. Cup 1996, Stanley Cup 1997; played with New Jersey Devils 1983, later Detroit Red Wings 1995–98; Asst Coach New Jersey Devils 1998–; Gen. Man. and Coach of Russian hockey team 2002; Chair. State Cttee on Physical Culture and Sports 2002–; Soviet Honoured Masters of Sport Award 1984, 1986, 1990; inducted Hockey Hall of Fame 2001. *Address:* Goscomsport, Kazakovba str.18, 103064 Moscow, Russia (Office). *Telephone:* (095) 261-93-97 (Office).

FETSCHER, Iring, DPhil; German political scientist; b. 4 March 1922, Marbach; s. of Prof. Rainer Fetscher; m. Elisabeth Götte 1957; two s. two d.; ed König-George-Gymnasium, Dresden, Eberhard-Karls-Universität, Tübingen, Université de Paris and Johann Wolfgang Goethe-Univ., Frankfurt; Ed. Marxismusstudien 1956–; radio commentator on political, philosophical and sociological questions; Prof. of Political Science, Johann Wolfgang Goethe-Univ., Frankfurt 1963–88, Prof. Emer. 1988–; Theodor-Heuss Prof. New School for Social Research, New York 1968–69; Guest Prof. Tel Aviv Univ. 1972; Fellow, Netherlands Inst. for Advanced Study in the Humanities and Social Sciences 1972–73; Inst. for Advanced Studies, ANU, Canberra; Extraordinary Prof. for Social and Political Philosophy, Catholic Univ. of Nijmegen 1974–75; Goethe Plakette (Frankfurt) 1992; Bundesverdienstkreuz (First Class) 1993; Chevalier Ordre des Palmes Académiques 1993. *Publications include:* Von Marx zur Sowjetideologie 1956, Über dialektischen und historischen Materialismus (Commentary of Stalin) 1956, 1962, Rousseaus politische Philosophie 1960, 1968, 1975, Der Marxismus, seine Geschichte in Dokumenten Vol. I 1962, Vol. II 1964, Vol. III 1965, 4th edn in one vol. 1983, Marx-Engels Studienausgabe (4 vols) 1966, Introduction to Hobbes' Leviathan 1966, Karl Marx und der Marxismus 1967, Der Rechtsradikalismus 1967, Der Sozialismus 1968, Der Kommunismus 1969, Hegel: Grösse und Grenzen 1971, Modelle der Friedenssicherung 1972, Wer hat Dornröschen wachgeküsst?—das Märchenverwirrbuch 1972, 1974, Marxistische Porträts Vol. I 1975, Herrschaft und Emanzipation 1976, Terrorismus und Reaktion 1981, Analysen zum Terrorismus, Ideologien und Strategien 1981, Vom Wohlfahrtsstaat zur neuen Lebensqualität, die Herausforderungen des demokratischen Sozialismus 1982, Der Nulltarif der Wichtelmänner, Märchen- und andere Verwirrspiele 1982, Arbeit und Spiel (essays)

1983, Handbuch der politischen Ideen (Co-ed. with H. Münkler), Vols 1, 3, 4, 5 1985–93, Überlebensbedingungen der Menschheit zur Dialektik des Fortschritts 1986 (enlarged edn) 1991, Die Wirksamkeit der Träume, literarische Skizzen eines Sozialwissenschaftlers 1987, Utopien, Illusionen, Hoffnungen-Plädoyer für eine politische Kultur in Deutschland 1990, Toleranz—von der Unentbehrlichkeit einer kleinen Tugend für die Demokratie 1990, Neugier und Furcht: Versuch, mein Leben (autobiog.) 1995, Joseph Goebbels im Berliner Sportpalast: "Wollt ihr den totalen Krieg?" 1988, Marx 1999. *Leisure interests:* collecting autographed letters and manuscripts and first edns of philosophers and writers. *Address:* J. W Goethe Universität, P.O. Box 111932, 60054 Frankfurt am Main (Office); Ganghoferstrasse 20, 60320 Frankfurt am Main, Germany (Home). *Telephone:* (69) 79822300 (Office); (69) 521542 (Home). *Fax:* (69) 7988383 (Office); (69) 510034 (Home); (69) 510034. *E-mail:* iefetscher@jahoo.de (Home).

FETTING, Rainer; German painter and sculptor; b. 31 Dec. 1949, Wilhelmshaven; ed Hochschule der Künste; Co-founder, Galerie am Moritzplatz ("vehement painting") 1977; DAAD scholarship, Columbia Univ. New York 1978; one-man shows include: Mary Boone, New York, Bruno Bischoff Berger, Zürich 1981, Museum Folkwang, Essen, Kunsthalle, Basle and Marlborough Gallery, New York 1986, Museo di Barcelona 1989, Boukamel Gallery, London 1989, Nationalgalerie, Berlin 1990, Harenberg City Centre, Dortmund 1994; group shows include: A New Spirit in Painting, Royal Acad. London 1981, Zeitgeist, Martin Gropius Bau, Berlin 1982, Berlin Art, Museum of Modern Art, New York 1987, Refigured Painting, Guggenheim Museum, New York 1988; created statue of Willy Brandt for headquarters of German SDP, Berlin 1996. *Address:* Hasenheide 61, 1067 Berlin, Germany.

FETTWEIS, Alfred Leo Maria, D. ÈS SC.APPL., FIEEE; German professor of communications engineering; b. 27 Nov. 1926, Eupen, Belgium; s. of Paul Fettweis and Helene (née Hermanns) Fettweis; m. Lois J. Piaskowski 1957; two s. three d.; ed Catholic Univ. of Louvain, Columbia Univ., Polytechnic Inst. of Brooklyn; Devt Engineer with Int. Telephone and Telegraph Corpn (ITT), Belgium 1951–54, 1956–63 and USA 1954–56; Prof. of Theoretical Electricity, Eindhoven Univ. of Tech. 1963–67; Prof. of Communications Eng Ruhr-Univ. Bochum 1967–92, Prof. Emer. 1992–; Visiting Distinguished Prof., Univ. of Notre Dame 1994–96; mem. Rheinisch-Westfälische Akad. der Wissenschaften, Academia Europaea, Academia Scientiarum et Artium Europaea; invention and comprehensive theory of the wave-digital method for filtering and numerical integration; Dr hc (Linköping) 1986, (Mons) 1988, (Leuven) 1988, (Budapest) 1995; Prix Acta Technica Belgica 1963, Darlington Prize Paper Award 1980, Prix George Montefiore 1981, VDE-Ehrenring 1984, IEEE Centennial Medal 1984, Tech. Achievement Award of IEEE Circuits and Systems Soc. 1988, Karl-Küpfmüller-Preis of Informationstechnische Gesellschaft 1988, Basic Research Award of Eduard Rhein Foundation 1993, CASS Golden Jubilee Medal, IEEE Circuits and Systems Soc. 1999, Millennium Medal, IEEE 2000, Van Valkenburg Award, IEEE Circuits and Systems Soc. 2001. *Publications:* two books, many tech. papers on circuits, systems, telecommunications, digital signal processing, numerical integration and related areas; about 30 patents. *Leisure interests:* hiking, music. *Address:* Lehrstuhl für Nachrichtentechnik, Ruhr-Universität Bochum, Universitätsstrasse 150, D-44780 Bochum (Office); Im Königsbusch 18, D-44797 Bochum, Germany (Home). *Telephone:* (234) 322-2497/3063 (Office); (234) 797922 (Home). *Fax:* (234) 321-4100. *E-mail:* fettweis@nt.ruhr-uni-bochum.de (Office).

FETTWEIS, Günter Bernhard Leo, DrIng; Austrian/German mining engineer and university professor emeritus; b. 17 Nov. 1924, Düsseldorf, Germany; s. of Ewald I. Fettweis and Aninhas M. (née Leuschner-Fernandes) Fettweis; m. Alice Y. Fettweis 1949; one s. three d.; ed Univ. of Freiburg and Tech. Univ. of Aachen; Scientific Asst Tech. Univ. of Aachen 1950–52; Jr Mining Inspector Nordrhein-Westfalen 1953–54; Ruhr coal-mining industry, then Production Man. of the Osterfeld, Sterkrade and Hugo Haniel coal mines, B.A.G. Neue Hoffnung, Oberhausen/Ruhr 1955–59; Prof. and Head Dept of Mining Eng and Mineral Econs, Montan Univ. Leoben 1959–93, Rector (Vice-Chair.) 1968–70; Vice-Pres., later Pres. Mining Soc. of Austria 1963–93; Vice-Pres. Austrian Soc., of Rock Mechanics 1968–81, Int. Organizing Cttee World Mining Congress 1976–2001; mem. Supervising Bd ÖBAG (Austrian State Mining Industry) 1988–95; Chair. Bd Inst. for Research about Mineral Resources 1983–87; Corresp. mem. Austrian Acad. of Sciences 1977, mem. 1983; Foreign mem. Polish Acad. of Sciences 1991, European Acad. of Sciences, Salzburg 1990, Paris 1996, Russian Acad. of Natural Sciences 1997, Mining Sciences 1998; Hon. mem. Hungarian Acad. of Sciences 1990; Dr hc (Aachen), (Miskolc, Hungary), (Petrosani, Romania), (Moscow); Dr hc mit Laureate Assessor des Bergfachs; Austrian State Award of Energy Research; nat. and int. medals (Austria, Germany, Poland, The Vatican). *Publications:* World Coal Resources, Methods of Assessment and Results 1976–79, Atlas of Mining Methods (three vols, co-author) 1963–66, Mining in the Process of Change (Ed.) 1988, Bergwirtschaft (mineral econs; co-author) 1990, Deponietechnik und Entsorgungsbergbau (waste disposal) (Ed.) and about 250 other publs. *Leisure interests:* history, philosophy, cosmology, Africa, sailing. *Address:* Institut für Bergbaukunde, Borgtechnik und Bergwirtschaft der Montanuniversität Leoben, Franz-Josef-Strasse 18, A-8700 Leoben (Office); Gasteigergasse 5, A-8700 Leoben, Austria (Home). *Telephone:* (3842) 402/538 (Office); (3842) 21190 (Home). *Fax:* (3842) 402/530 (Office); (3842) 21190 (Home). *E-mail:* fettweis@unileoben.ac.at (Office).

FEYDER, Jean, DJur; Luxembourg diplomatist; b. 24 Nov. 1947; m.; two c.; joined Ministry of Foreign Affairs 1974, Head, UN Dept 1974–76, Deputy Perm. Rep. to UN, New York July–Dec. 1975, currently Dir. Co-operation and Humanitarian Action (with title of Amb.); assigned to Luxembourg mission to EC, Brussels (with responsibility for accession negotiations) 1977; Deputy Perm. Rep. to EEC 1983; Perm. Rep. to UN, New York 1987–93. *Address:* Direction de la Coopération et de l'Aide Humanitaire, 6, rue de la Congregation, 1352 Luxembourg, Luxembourg.

FEYIDE, Chief Meshach Otokiti, A.C.S.M., DIC, CEng, F.I.M.M., FInstPet; Nigerian chartered engineer; b. 31 March 1926, Ipele, Ondo State; s. of Chief Samuel and Juliana Elebe (née Adeola) Otokiti; m. Christiana Oluremi 1954; one s. two d.; ed Govt Coll., Ibadan, Camborne School of Mines, UK, Imperial Coll. of Science and Tech., London; Insp. of Mines 1954–59; Petroleum Engineer, Ministry of Mines and Power 1960, Chief Petroleum Engineer 1964, Dir Petroleum Resources 1970; Sec.-Gen. OPEC 1975–76; Chief Exec. Petroleum Inspectorate, Nigerian Nat. Petroleum Corpn 1977–78; Petroleum Consultant 1979–; Publr and Man. Ed. Nigerian Petroleum News 1984–; Nigerian American Chamber of Commerce Award to Leading Businessmen 1983; Austrian Grand Decoration of Honour 1978; Officer Order of the Fed. Repub. (OFR) 1982. *Leisure interests:* music, reading. *Address:* P.O. Box 1790, Lagos, Nigeria. *Telephone:* (1) 2636999.

FEYZIOĞLU, Turhan, LLD; Turkish university professor and government official; b. 19 Jan. 1922, Kayseri; s. of Sait Azmi and Neyyire Feyzioğlu; m. Leyla Firdevs 1949; one s.; ed Galatasaray Lycée, Istanbul Univ. and Ecole nationale d'Administration, Paris; Asst Prof. Ankara Political Science School 1945–47, Assoc. Prof. 1947–54; Research, Nuffield Coll., Oxford; Co-ed. Forum 1954–58; Prof. Ankara Univ. 1955; Dean, Political Science School, Ankara 1956; Participant Harvard Int. Seminar 1956; MP 1957, 1961, 1965–80; mem. Nat. Exec. Cttee Republican People's Party 1957–61, Vice-Pres. 1965, 1966; Pres. Middle East Tech. Univ. 1960; mem. Constituent Ass. 1960; Minister of Educ. 1960; Minister of State 1961; Deputy Prime Minister 1962–63; mem. Turkish High Planning Council 1961–63, 1975–78; Turkish Rep. Consultative Ass. Council of Europe 1964–66, 1972; Leader Republican Reliance Party 1967; Deputy Prime Minister 1975–77, Deputy Prime Minister and Minister of State Jan.–Sept. 1978, mem. Ataturk Research Centre 1983; Dr. hc (Kayseri Univ.) 1985. *Publications:* Administrative Law 1947, Judicial Review of Unconstitutional Laws 1951, Les partis politiques en Turquie 1953, The Reforms of the French Higher Civil Service 1955, Democracy and Dictatorship 1957, Communist Threat 1969, In the Service of the Nation 1975, Kemal Ataturk, Leader de la Libération Nationale 1981, Ataturk's Way 1982, Chypre, Mythes et Réalités 1984, Ataturk and Nationalism 1986, The Crux of the Cyprus Problem 1987. *Leisure interest:* gardening. *Address:* Ataturk Research Center, Ataturk Bulvarı, 217 Ankara (Office); Çevre sokak, 54/9, Cankaya, Turkey (Home). *Telephone:* 1270619 (Home).

FFOWCS WILLIAMS, John Eirwyn, MA, PhD, ScD (Cantab.), CEng, FREng, FRAeS, FInstP, FIMA, FRSA; British professor of engineering; b. 25 May 1935; m. Anne Beatrice Mason 1959; two s. one d.; ed Derby Tech. Coll., Univ. of Southampton; eng apprentice, Rolls-Royce Ltd 1951–55; Spitfire Mitchell Memorial Scholar to Southampton Univ. 1955–60 (Pres. Students' Union 1957–58); joined Aerodynamics Div., NPL 1960–62; with Bolt, Beranek & Newman, Inc. 1962–64; Reader in Applied Mathematics, Imperial Coll. of Science and Tech. 1964–69, Rolls-Royce Prof. of Theoretical Acoustics 1969–72; Rank Prof. of Eng, Cambridge Univ. 1972–2002; Master Emmanuel Coll., Cambridge 1996–2002 (Professorial Fellow 1972–96, Life Fellow 2002); Chair. Concorde Noise Panel 1965–75, Noise Research Cttee ARC 1969–76, Topexpress Ltd 1979–89; Dir VSEL Consortium PLC 1987–95; Foreign Assoc. NAE (USA) 1995; Fellow AIAA, Inst. of Acoustics, Acoustical Soc. of America; Hon. Prof. Beijing Inst. of Aeronautics and Astronautics 1992–, Foreign Hon. mem. American Acad. of Arts and Sciences 1989; Aero-Acoustics Medal, AIAA 1977, Rayleigh Medal, Inst. of Acoustics 1984, Silver Medal, Soc. Française d'Acoustique 1989, Gold Medal, RAeS 1990, Per Bruel Gold Medal, ASME 1997, Sir Frank Whittle Medal, Royal Acad. Eng. 2002. *Publications:* Sound and Sources of Sound 1983 (with A. P. Dowling), numerous articles in professional journals; film on Aerodynamic Sound (jtly). *Leisure interests:* friends and cigars. *Address:* c/o Emmanuel College, Cambridge, CB2 3AP, England.

FFRENCH-DAVIS MUÑOZ, Ricardo, PhD; Chilean economist; b. 27 June 1936, Santiago; m. Marcela Yampaglia 1966; ed Catholic Univ. of Chile, Univ. of Chicago; Researcher and Prof. of Econs, Econ Research Cen., Catholic Univ. 1962–64; Prof. of Econs, Univ. of Chile 1962–73, 1984–; Deputy Man. Research Dept, Cen. Bank of Chile 1964–70; Research Dir Cen. on Planning Studies, Catholic Univ. 1970–75; Vice-Pres. and Dir Centre for Latin American Econ. Research (CIEPLAN), Santiago 1976–90; Research Dir Cen. Bank of Chile 1990; mem. Acad. Council, Latin American Program, The Woodrow Wilson Center, Washington, DC 1977–80; mem. UN Cttee on Econ. Planning 1990–92; mem. Exec. Cttee Latin American Studies Asscn 1992–94; Visiting Fellow, Univ. of Oxford 1974, 1979; Visiting Prof., Boston Univ. 1976; Pres. Acad. Circle, Acad. de Humanismo Cristiano, Chile 1978–81; Co-ordinator Working Group on Econ. Issues of Inter-American Dialogue 1985–86; Prin. Regional Adviser, Econ. Comm. for Latin America and the Caribbean (ECLAC) 2000–; mem. Editorial Bds Latin American Research Review, El Trimestre Economico and Colección Estudios Cieplan; Ford Foundation Grants 1971, 1975, 2001, SSRC Grant 1976, Inter-American Dialogue Grant

1985–86. *Publications:* Políticas Económicas en Chile: 1952–70 1973, El cobre en el desarrollo nacional (co-ed.) 1974, Economía internacional: teorías y políticas para el desarrollo 1979, 1985, Latin America and a New International Economic Order (co-ed.) 1981, 1985, The Monetarist Experiment in Chile 1982, Relaciones financieras externas y la economía latinoamericana (ed.) 1983, Development and External Debt in Latin America (co-ed.) 1988, Debt-equity swaps in Chile 1990, Latin America and the Caribbean: Policies to Improve Linkages with the World Economy (ed.) 1998, Macroeconomics, Trade and Finance 2000, Financial Crisis in 'Successful' Emerging Economies (ed.) 2001, Economic Reforms in Chile: From Dictatorship to Democracy 2002; over 100 articles on int. econs, Latin-American econ. devt and Chilean econ. policies in 8 languages. *Address:* Economic Commission for Latin America and the Caribbean, Santiago, Chile (Office); Casilla 179-D, Santiago, Chile (Home). *Telephone:* (562) 210-2555 (Office). *Fax:* (562) 208-1801 (Office). *E-mail:* rffrenchdavis@eclac.cl (Office). *Website:* www.eclac.cl (Office).

FICHTENAU, Heinrich, PhD; Austrian professor of medieval history; b. 10 Dec. 1912, Linz; s. of Heinrich von Fichtenau and Maria von Fichtenau (née Schachermeyr); m. Anna Widl 1954; two d.; ed Univ. of Vienna, Austrian Inst. for Historical Research; Research Asst Univ. of Vienna 1936–50, Assoc. Prof. 1950–62, Prof. of Medieval History and Auxiliary Sciences 1962–83, Prof. Emer. 1983–; Dir Austrian Inst. for Historical Research 1962–83; Corresp. Fellow British Acad. Medieval Acad. of America; Fellow Austrian Acad. of Sciences. *Publications:* Mensch u. Schrift im Mittelalter 1946, Babenberger-Urkundenbuch (with E. Zoellnor), (Vol. 1) 1950, (Vol. 2) 1955, (Vols 3 and 4) 1968, Arenga 1957, Carolingian Empire 1957, Urkundenwesen in Österreich 1971, Beiträge zur Mediaevistik, (Vol. 1) 1975, (Vol. 2) 1977, (Vol. 3) 1986, Lebensordnungen des 10. Jahrhunderts (2 vols) 1984, Living in the Tenth Century 1991, Ketzer und Professoren 1992, Heretics and Scholars in the High Middle Ages, 1000–1200 1998. *Leisure interest:* bookworm.

FICO, ROBERT, DIur; Slovak politician and lawyer; b. 15 Sept. 1964, Topolcany; m.; one c.; ed Comenius Univ., Bratislava; mem. staff Inst. of Laws, Ministry of Justice 1986–91; mem. Parl. 1992–; Head of Slovak del. to Parl. Meeting of European Council, Rep. to European Cttee for Human Rights and European Court for Human Rights 1994–2000; mem. Party of Democratic Left—SDL –1999, Vice-Chair. 1998–99; Founder and Chair. Direction party—Smēr 1999–. *Publication:* Trest smrti (Punishment of Death). *Leisure interest:* sport. *Address:* Smēr, Sumračna 27, 821 02 Bratislava, Slovakia (Office). *Telephone:* (2) 43426297 (Office). *E-mail:* robert-fico@nrsr.sk (Office). *Website:* www.strana-smer.sk (Office).

FIDALGO, José María; Spanish trade union official and orthopaedic surgeon; b. 18 Feb. 1948, León; orthopaedic surgeon, Hosp. La Paz, Madrid; mem. trade union movt 1974–; mem. Confederación Sindical de Comisiones Obreras (CCOO) 1977–, Sec. of Institutional Policy 1987–2000, Gen. Sec. 2000–; Gen. Sec. Fed. of Health Workers 1981–87. *Address:* Confederación Sindical de Comisiones Obreras (CCOO), Fernández de la Hoz 12, 28010 Madrid, Spain (Office). *Telephone:* (91) 7028011 (Office). *Fax:* (91) 3104804 (Office). *E-mail:* aida@ccoo.es (Office). *Website:* www.ccoo.es (Office).

FIELD, Helen; British singer; b. 14 May 1951, Wrexham, Clwyd, Wales; ed Royal Northern Coll. of Music, Manchester and Royal Coll. of Music, London; studied FRG; won triennial Young Welsh Singers' Competition 1976; roles with Welsh Nat. Opera include Musetta, Poppea, Kristina, Gilda, Marzelline, Mimi, Tatyana, Jenůfa, the Vixen, Marenka and Desdemona; has also appeared with Opera North and Scottish Opera; début at Royal Opera House, Covent Garden as Emma in Khovanschina 1982; début with ENO, as Gilda 1982, at Metropolitan Opera, New York, as Gilda; has also appeared with Netherlands, Cologne and Brussels opera cos.; concert performances with several leading orchestras and regular radio and TV appearances; recordings include Rigoletto, A Village Romeo and Juliet and Osud. *Address:* c/o Athole Still International Management Ltd., Foresters Hall, 25–27 Weston Street, London, SE19 3RV (Office); c/o Askonas Holt Ltd, 27 Chancery Lane, London, WC2A 1PF, England.

FIELD, Sir Malcolm David, Kt.; British company director; b. 25 Aug. 1937, London; m. (divorced 1982); one d.; m. 2nd Rosemary Anne Charlton 2001; ed Highgate School and London Business School; joined W.H. Smith 1963, Wholesale Dir 1970–78, Man. Dir Retail Group 1978–82, Man. Dir 1982–93; Group Chief Exec. 1994–96; Chair. C.A.A. 1996–2001; Policy Adviser to Dept of Transport, London and the Regions 2000–; mem. Bd of Man. NAAFI 1973–93, Chair. 1986–93; Dir (non-exec.) MEPC 1989–99, Scottish & Newcastle PLC 1993–98, Phoenix Group 1994–97, The Stationery Office 1996–2001, Walker Greenbank PLC 1997–2001, Sofa Workshop Ltd 1998–2002, Beeson Gregory 2000–, Odgers 2002–; Chair. Tubelines Ltd 2003–. *Leisure interests:* cricket, tennis, ballet, modern art, reading biographies, recreating garden in Devon. *Address:* 21 Embankment Gardens, London, SW3 4LW, England (Office). *Telephone:* (20) 7351-7455 (Office). *Fax:* (20) 7351-7452 (Office). *E-mail:* mdfield@netcomuk.co.uk (Office).

FIELDHOUSE, David Kenneth, MA, DLitt, FBA; British academic; b. 7 June 1925, India; s. of Rev E. Fieldhouse and C. H. B. Fieldhouse (née Corke); m. Sheila Elizabeth Lyon 1952; one s. two d.; ed Dean Close School, Cheltenham, Queen's Coll. Oxford; war service as Sub. Lieut., RDVR 1943–47; Sr History Master, Haileybury Coll. 1950–52; Lecturer in History, Canterbury Univ., NZ 1953–57; Beit Lecturer in Commonwealth History, Oxford Univ. 1958–81; Vere Harmsworth Prof. of Imperial and Naval History, Cambridge Univ. 1981–92; Fellow Nuffield Coll. Oxford 1966–81, Jesus Coll. Cambridge

1981–92, Emer. 1992–. *Publications:* The Colonial Empires 1966, The Theory of Capitalist Imperialism 1967, Economics and Empire 1830–1914 1973, Unilever Overseas 1978, Black Africa 1945–1980 1986, Merchant Capital and Economic Decolonization 1994, The West and the Third World 1999, Kurds, Arabs and Britons 2001. *Leisure interests:* golf, sailing, music. *Address:* Jesus College, Cambridge, CB5 8BL, England. *Telephone:* (1223) 339339.

FIELDING, Sir Leslie, KCMG, LLD, FRSA, FRGS; British former diplomatist and university vice-chancellor; b. 29 July 1932, London; s. of Percy Archer Fielding and Margaret Calder Horry; m. Sally Harvey 1978; one s. one d.; ed Emmanuel Coll., Cambridge, School of Oriental and African Studies, London, St Antony's Coll., Oxford; with HM Diplomatic Service (served Tehran, Singapore, Phnom Penh, Paris and London) 1956–73; Dir External Relations Directorate-Gen., European Comm., Brussels 1973–77; Visiting Fellow, St Antony's Coll., Oxford 1977–78; Head European Community Del., Tokyo 1978–82; Dir-Gen. for External Relations, Brussels 1982–87; Vice-Chancellor Univ. of Sussex 1987–92; mem. Japan–EC Asscn 1988–98, UK–Japan 2000 Group 1993–2000; mem. House of Laity of Gen. Synod of Church of England 1990–92; Hon. Pres. Univ. Asscn for Contemporary European Studies 1990–2000, Hon. Fellow, Emmanuel Coll. Cambridge 1990–, Hon. Fellow Sussex European Inst. 1993; Grand Officer's Star of Order of St Agatha of San Marino 1987, White Rose of Finland 1988, Silver Order of Merit (Austria) 1989. *Leisure interests:* country life, theology. *Address:* Wild Cherry Farm, Elton, nr Ludlow, Shropshire, SY8 2HQ, England. *E-mail:* FieldingLeslie@aol.com (Home).

FIELDSEND, Sir John Charles Rowell, KBE, BA, LLB; British judge; b. 13 Sept. 1921, Lincoln; s. of Charles Fieldsend and Phyllis Fieldsend; m. Muriel Gedling 1945; one s. one d.; ed Michaelhouse, Natal, Rhodes Univ. Coll., Grahamstown, SA; served Royal Artillery 1943–45; called to the Bar, S. Rhodesia 1947, QC 1959; Advocate in pvt. practice 1947–63; Pres. Special Income Tax Court for Fed. of Rhodesia and Nyasaland 1958–63; High Court Judge, S. Rhodesia 1963–68 (resgnd); Asst Solicitor, Law Comm. for England and Wales 1968–78; Sec. Law Comm. 1978–80; Chief Justice of Zimbabwe 1980–83; Chief Justice, Turks and Caicos Islands 1985–87; Pres., Court of Appeal, St. Helena 1985–93; Judge, Court of Appeal, Falkland Islands and British Antarctic Territory 1985–96, Court of Appeal, Gibraltar 1985–97 (Pres. 1990); Prin. Legal Adviser, British Indian Ocean Territory 1984–87, Chief Justice 1987–98. *Leisure interest:* travel. *Address:* Great Dewes, Ardingly, Sussex, RH17 6UP, England.

FIENNES, Joseph Alberic; British actor; b. 27 May 1970, Salisbury; s. of Mark Fiennes and the late Jini Lash; brother of Ralph Fiennes (q.v.); ed Guildhall School of Music and Drama. *Theatre includes:* The Woman in Black, A Month in the Country, A View from the Bridge, Real Classy Affair, Edward II, Love's Labours Lost. *RSC performances include:* Son of Man, Les Enfants Du Paradis, As You Like It, Troilus and Cressida, The Herbal Bed. *Television includes:* The Vacillations of Poppy Carew 1995, Animated Epics: Beowulf (voice) 1998. *Films include:* Stealing Beauty 1996, Shakespeare in Love 1998, Martha – Meet Frank, Daniel and Laurence 1998, Elizabeth 1998, Forever Mine 1999, Rancid Aluminium 2000, Enemy at the Gates 2001, Killing Me Softly 2001, Dust 2001, Leo 2002, Sinbad: Legend of the Seven Seas 2003, Luther 2003, The Great Raid 2003. *Address:* c/o Ken McReddie, 91 Regent Street, London, W1R 7TB, England (Office). *Telephone:* (20) 7439-1456 (Office).

FIENNES, Ralph Nathanial; British actor; b. 22 Dec. 1962; s. of Mark Fiennes and the late Jini Lash; brother of Joseph Fiennes (q.v.); ed St Kieran's Coll., Kilkenny, Ireland, Bishop Wordsworth's School, Salisbury, Chelsea School of Art, Royal Acad. of Dramatic Art, London. *Plays include:* Open Air Theatre, Regent's Park: Twelfth Night, Ring Round the Moon 1985, A Midsummer's Night Dream 1985, 1986, Romeo and Juliet 1986; Royal Nat. Theatre: Six Characters in Search of an Author, Fathers and Sons, Ting Tang Mine 1987; RSC: King John, Much Ado About Nothing, title role of Henry VI in The Plantagenets 1988, Playing with Trains 1989, Troilus and Cressida, King Lear 1990, The Man Who Came to Dinner, Love's Labours Lost 1991; Almeida Theatre: Hamlet 1995, Ivanov 1997, Richard II 2000, Coriolanus 2000, Brand 2003. *TV appearances include:* A Dangerous Man: Lawrence after Arabia (TV) 1990, Prime Suspect 1991, The Cormorant 1993, The Great War and the Shaping of the 20th Century (voice) 1996, How Proust Can Change Your Life 2000, The Miracle Maker (voice) 2000. *Films include:* Wuthering Heights 1992, The Baby of Macon 1993, Schindler's List 1993, Quiz Show 1994, Strange Days 1995, The English Patient 1996, Oscar and Lucinda 1997, The Avengers 1998, The Prince of Egypt (voice) 1998, Onegin (also exec. producer) 1999, Sunshine 1999, The End of the Affair 1999, Spider 2002, The Good Thief 2002, Red Dragon 2002, Maid in Manhattan 2002. *Leisure interests:* swimming, reading, music. *Address:* c/o Larry Dalzell Associates, 91 Regent Street, London, W1R 7TB, England. *Telephone:* (20) 7287-5131. *Fax:* (20) 7287-5161.

FIENNES, Sir Ranulph Twisleton-Wykeham-, 3rd Bt, cr. 1916, OBE, DLitt; British travel writer, lecturer and explorer; b. 7 March 1944, Windsor; s. of Lt-Col Sir Ranulph Twisleton-Wykeham-Fiennes, DSO, 2nd Bt and Audrey Newson; m. Virginia Pepper 1970; ed Eton; Lt Royal Scots Greys 1966, Capt. 1968, retd 1970; attached 22 SAS Regt 1966, Sultan of Muscat's Armed Forces 1968; Leader, British Expdns to White Nile 1969, Jostedalsbre Glacier 1970, Headless Valley, BC 1971, (Towards) North Pole 1977; Leader, Transglobe Expdn. (1st polar circumnavigation of world on its polar axis) 1979–82;

led first unsupported crossing of Antarctic continent and longest unsupported polar journey in history Nov. 1992–Feb. 1993; Exec. Consultant to Chair. of Occidental Petroleum Corpn 1984–90; Hon. DSc (Loughborough Coll.) 1986; Hon. DUniv (Univ. of Cen. England in Birmingham) 1995, (Univ. of Portsmouth) 2000; Hon. DLitt (Glasgow Caledonian); Dhofar Campaign Medal 1969, Sultan's Bravery Medal 1970, Livingstone Medal, Royal Scottish Geographical Soc., Gold Medal of Explorers Club of NY 1983, Founders Medal Royal Geographical Soc. 1984, Polar Medal for Arctic and Antarctic, with Bars 1985, with clasp 1995, ITN Award for Int. Exploit of the Decade 1989, Explorers Club Millennium Award for Polar Exploration 2000. *Publications:* A Talent for Trouble 1970, Ice Fall in Norway 1972, The Headless Valley 1973, Where Soldiers Fear to Tread 1975, Hell on Ice 1979, To the Ends of the Earth 1983, Bothie—The Polar Dog (with Virginia Twisleton-Wykeham-Fiennes) 1984, Living Dangerously 1987, The Feather Men 1991, Atlantis of the Sands 1992, Mind over Matter 1993, The Sett 1996, Fit for Life 1998, Beyond the Limits 2000, The Secret Hunters 2001, Captain Scott 2003. *Leisure interests:* langlauf, photography. *Address:* Greenlands, Exford, Minehead, West Somerset, TA24 7NU, England. *Telephone:* (1643) 831350.

FIERSTEIN, Harvey Forbes; American actor and screenwriter; b. 6 June 1954, Brooklyn, New York; s. of Irving Fierstein and Jacqueline Harriet Gilbert; ed Pratt Univ.; began acting career as founding mem. The Gallery Players, Brooklyn; professional acting debut in Pork 1971; over sixty stage roles; wrote and acted in Torch Song Trilogy 1981 (Tony Award, Theater World Award, Drama Desk Award for Best Actor; Tony and Drama Desk Awards for Best Playwright); wrote and acted in Safe Sex 1987; acted in Hairspray (Broadway) 2002; Fund for Human Dignity Award 1983. *Films include:* Annie Hall, Dog Day Afternoon, Mrs Doubtfire, White Lies, Bullets Over Broadway, Dr Jekyll & Ms Hyde, The Celluloid Closet 1995, Independence Day 1996, Everything Relative 1996, Krull the Conqueror 1997, Safe Men 1998, Legend of Mulan 1998, Playing Mona Lisa, Death to Smochy 2002. *TV appearances include:* The Demon Murder Case, Apology, Cheers 1992, Murder She Wrote 1992, Swellegant Elegance 1993; narrated The Life and Times of Harvey Milk, La Cage Aux Folles, Legs Diamond; The Sissy Duckling (also writer) 1999, Common Ground 2000. *Leisure interests:* gay rights activist, painting, gardening, cooking. *Address:* c/o AGF Inc., 30 W 21st Street, Floor 7, New York, NY 10010-6905, USA.

FIGES, Eva, BA; British writer; b. 15 April 1932, Berlin; d. of Emil Unger and Irma Unger; m. John Figes 1954 (divorced 1963); one s. one d.; ed Kingsbury Co. School, Queen Mary Coll., Univ. of London; awarded Guardian Fiction Prize. *Publications include:* Patriarchal Attitudes 1970, Waking 1981, Light 1983, The Knot 1996. *Leisure interests:* music, films, theatre, visual arts. *Address:* Rogers, Coleridge & White Ltd., 20 Powis Mews, London, W11 1JN, England (Office). *Telephone:* (20) 7221-3717 (Office). *Fax:* (20) 7229-9084 (Office).

FIGES, Orlando, BA, PhD; British professor of history and author; b. 20 Nov. 1959; s. of John Figes and Eva Figes (née Unger); m. Stephanie Palmer 1990; two d.; ed Gonville and Caius Coll. Cambridge, Trinity Coll. Cambridge; Fellow Trinity Coll., Cambridge 1984–89, Dir of Studies in History 1988–98, Lecturer in History, Univ. of Cambridge 1987–99; Prof. of History, Birkbeck Coll., London Univ. 1999–. *Publications include:* Peasant Russia, Civil War: the Volga Countryside in Revolution 1917–21 1989, A People's Tragedy: the Russian Revolution 1891–1924 (Wolfson History Prize, WHSmith Literary Award, NCR Book Award, Los Angeles Times Book Prize) 1996, Interpreting the Russian Revolution (jt author) 1999, Natasha's Dance: a Cultural History of Russia 2002; numerous review articles and contribs to other published books. *Leisure interests:* football, wine, gardening. *Address:* School of History, Classics and Archaeology, Birkbeck College, Malet Street, London, WC1E 7HX, England (Office). *Telephone:* (20) 7631-6299 (Office). *Fax:* (20) 7631-6552 (Office). *E-mail:* orlando.figes@ntlworld.com (Office). *Website:* www.bbk.ac.uk (Office).

FIGGIS, Brian Norman, PhD, DSc, FAA; Australian professor emeritus of inorganic chemistry; b. 27 March 1930, Sydney; s. of John N. E. Figgis and Dorice B. M. (née Hughes) Figgis; m. Jane S. Frank 1968; one s. one d.; ed Univ. of Sydney, Univ. of New South Wales; Research Fellow, then Lecturer, Univ. Coll. London 1957–62, Visiting Prof. Univ. of Texas 1961, Reader Univ. of Western Australia 1963–69, Prof. 1969–, Visiting Prof. Univ. of Ariz. 1968, Univs of Florence and Sussex 1975, Visiting Scientist Institut Laue-Langevin, Brookhaven Nat. Lab. and Argonne Nat. Lab. 1984, 1991; Burrows Award Royal Australian Chemical Inst. 1985, Walter Burfitt Prize, Royal Soc. of NSW 1986; H. G. Smith Medal, Royal Australian Chemical Inst. 1989. *Publications:* Introduction to Ligand Fields 1966, Ligand Field Theory and Its Applications 2000; Ed. Transition Metal Chemistry, Vols 8 and 9, 1984–85; 220 articles. *Leisure interest:* DIY. *Address:* 9 Hamersley Street, Cottesloe, WA 6011, Australia (Home). *Telephone:* 9384-3032 (Home). *E-mail:* bnf@theochem.uwa.edu.au (Home).

FIGGIS, Mike; British film director, writer and musician; b. 28 Feb. 1949, Carlisle; came to England 1957; studied music, performing in band Gas Board; musician in experimental theatre group The People Show in early 1970s; made ind. films including Redheugh, Slow Fade, Animals of the City; made film The House for Channel 4; IFP Ind. Spirit Award 1996, Nat. Soc. of Film Critics Award. *Films include:* Stormy Monday (debut, also screenplay and music) 1988, Internal Affairs (also music) 1990, Liebestraum (also screenplay and music) 1991, Mr. Jones 1993, The Browning Version 1994,

Leaving Las Vegas (also screenplay and music) 1995, One Night Stand 1997, Flamenco Women 1997, Miss Julie 1999, The Loss of Sexual Innocence 1999, Time Code 1999. *Address:* c/o ICM, 8942 Wilshire Boulevard, Beverly Hills, CA 90211, USA.

FIGO, Luis Filipe Madeira Caeiro; Portuguese footballer; b. 4 Nov. 1972, Lisbon; m. Helene Svedin; one d.; played for Sporting Lisbon 1990–96, Barcelona 1996–2000, Portugal nat. team 1991– (82 caps and 27 int. goals as of May 2002), signed by Real Madrid for then world record transfer fee 2000; Golden Ball for Best Player of the Year 2000, FIFA European Footballer of the Year 2000, FIFA World Player of the Year 2001. *Leisure interests:* the beach, rock music, spending time with friends. *Address:* Real Madrid Club de Fútbol, Estadio Santiago Bemaeu, Concha Espinal, 28036 Madrid, Spain (Office). *Telephone:* (902) 271708 (Office). *Website:* www.realmadrid.com (Office).

FIGUERES OLSEN, José María; Costa Rican politician; s. of José Figueres Ferrer (fmr Pres. of Costa Rica); ed US Mil Acad., West Point NY, Harvard Univ.; mem. Partido de Liberación Nacional (PLN); Minister of Agric. 1986–90; Pres. of Costa Rica 1994–98; Pres. Leadership for Environment and Devt (LEAD); mem. Bd Worldwide Fund for Nature, World Resources Inst., Stockholm Environmental Inst. *Address:* c/o Partido de Liberación Nacional, Sabana Oeste, San José, Costa Rica.

FIGUEROA, Adolfo, PhD; Peruvian economist, university professor and international consultant; b. 14 April 1941, Carhuaz; s. of José Manuel Figueroa and Modesta Figueroa; m. Yolanda Vásquez 1965; one s. one d.; ed Colegio Guadalupe (High School), Lima, San Marcos Univ., Lima, Vanderbilt Univ., Nashville, Tenn., U.S.A; Prof. of Econs, Catholic Univ. of Lima 1970–, Head Dept of Econs 1976–79, 1987–90, 1996–98; Dir Research Project on Productivity and Educ. in Agric. in Latin America, ECIEL Program 1983-85; Consultant to ILO, FAO, Inter-American Foundation, Ford Foundation, IFAD, Inter-American Devt Bank, World Bank; Visiting Prof. Univ. of Pernambuco, Brazil 1973, St Antony's Coll., Oxford 1976, Univ. of Ill., USA 1980, Econs Dept, Univ. of Nicaragua 1985, Univ. of Notre Dame, USA 1992, Univ. of Tex., Austin 1997; mem. Exec. Council Latin American Studies Asscn (LASA) 1988–91, Editorial Advisory Bd, Journal of Int. Devt 1988–92, World Devt 1997–; Int. Network for Econ. Method, European Econ. Asscn, New York Acad. of Sciences; Winner, Collaborative Research Grant Competition, MacArthur Foundation 1999, Winner, Tinker Professorship Competition, Univ. of Wisconsin 2001. *Publications:* Estructura del Consumo y Distribución de Ingresos en Lima 1968–1969 1974, Distribución del Ingreso en el Perú 1975, La Economía Campesina de la Sierra del Perú 1981, Capitalist Development and the Peasant Economy in Peru 1984, Educación y Productividad en la Agricultura Campesina de América Latina 1986, Teorías Económicas del Capitalismo 1992, Crisis Distributiva en el Perú 1993, Social Exclusion and Inequality in Peru 1996, Reforms en sociedades desigules 2001; articles in econ. journals. *Leisure interests:* music, classical guitar. *Address:* Departamento de Economía, Universidad Católica del Perú, Apartado 1761, Lima 1 (Office); Robert Kennedy 129, Lima 21, Peru (Home). *Telephone:* (1) 4602870 (Office); (1) 2616241 (Home). *Fax:* (1) 4601126. *E-mail:* afiguer@pucp.edu.pe (Office).

FIGUEROA SERRANO, Carlos; Chilean politician and lawyer; b. 28 Nov. 1930, Angol; s. of Carlos Figueroa and Isabel Serrano; m. Sara Guzmán 1953; seven c.; ed Colegio de los Sagrados Corazones, School of Law, Universidad de Chile; practising lawyer 1957–, served at Appeals Court, Santiago 1971–72; Prof. of Procedural Law, Catholic Univ. of Chile 1960–76; joined Partido Demócrata Cristiano (PDC) 1957; Under-Sec. for Agric. 1967–69; Minister of Economy 1969–70; Acting Minister of Foreign Relations and of Finance, various occasions 1967–70; Pres. PDC Political Cttee 1980; Del. for Providencia to Prov. Bd of Eastern Santiago 1984–87; Head Communications and Publicity, Patricio Aylwin's Presidential Campaign 1989; Amb. to Argentina 1990–93; Dir Communications and Publicity, Eduardo Frei's Presidential Campaign 1993; Minister for Foreign Affairs March–Sept. 1994, for Interior 1994–99; Dir CIC SA 1971–, Financiera Condell 1986–90, Pesquera Guafo SA 1987–89; Gen. Man. VEEP SA (Bldg contractors) 1980–86; Pres. Asociación Radiodifusoras de Chile 1977–78; Counsellor Asociación Iberamericana de Radiodifusión 1973–79, Sec. Bd of Dirs. 1975–77. *Address:* c/o Ministro del Interior, Palacio de la Moneda, Santiago, Chile.

FIIL, Niels Peter, PhD; Danish business executive; b. 8 Feb. 1941; s. of Svend Rasmussen and Gerda Fiil Rasmussen; m. Berthe M. Willumsen 1978; one d.; ed Univ. of Copenhagen; Assoc. and Asst Prof. Univ. of Copenhagen 1970–81; Visiting Prof. Harvard Medical School 1978–79; Man. Molecular Biology R&D, Novo Industri A/S 1980–86, Vice-Pres. 1987–, Vice-Pres., Pharmaceutical Biotechnology, Novo Nordisk A/S 1989–; mem. European Molecular Biology Org. 1979, Royal Danish Acad. of Science and Letters 1982, Royal Swedish Acad. of Eng Science 1988. *Publications:* scientific papers in the field of microbial genetics and biotechnology. *Address:* Novo Nordisk A/S, Healthcare Chemistry, Novo Nordisk Park, 2760 Maalov (Office); Fuglebakkevej 5, 2000 Frederiksberg, Denmark (Home). *Telephone:* (45) 44-44-88-88 (Office).

FIKENTSCHER, Wolfgang, LLM, DJur; German professor emeritus of law; b. 17 May 1928, Nuremberg; s. of Erich Fikentscher and Elfriede (née Albers) Fikentscher; m. Irmgard van den Berge 1956; three s. one d.; ed Univs. of Erlangen, Munich and Ann Arbor, Mich.; teacher of Labour Law, Trade Union Schools 1952–56; Prof. of Law, Univ. of Münster 1958–65, Univ. of Tübingen 1965–71, Univ. of Munich 1971–; Visiting Prof. Univ. of Calif. Law School, Berkeley Fellow Netherlands Inst. for Advanced Study in the Social Sciences

1971–72, Santa Fe Inst. 1991–92, 1995–96, Gruter Inst. for Law and Behavioural Research 1992–; Hon. Dr.Jur. (Zurich); Bundesverdienstkreuz, Bayerischer Verdienstorden; Max-Planck Prize 1995. *Publications:* Methoden des Rechts in vergleichender Darstellung, (5 Vols) 1975–77, Wirtschaftsrecht (2 Vols) 1983, Modes of Thought 1995, Schuldrecht 1997, Die Freiheit und ihr Paradox 1997, numerous books and articles on civil and commercial law, antitrust law, int. law, anthropology and ethology of law. *Address:* Institut für internationales Recht der Universität Munich, Ludwigstr. 29/II, 80539 Munich (Office); Mathildenstr. 8A, 82319 Starnberg, Germany (Home). *Telephone:* (89) 2180-5823 (Office); (8151) 13454 (Home). *Fax:* (89) 2180-5823 (Office); (8151) 13454 (Home). *E-mail:* fikentscher@jura.uni-muenchen.de (Office).

FIKRE-SELASSIE, Wogderess; Ethiopian politician; mem. Shengo; fmr Deputy Chair. Provisional Mil. Admin. Council, now mem.; Prime Minister of Ethiopia 1987–89.

FILALI, Abdellatif; Moroccan politician and diplomatist; b. 26 Jan. 1928, Fez; m.; ed Univ. of Paris; joined Ministry of Foreign Affairs, rank of Amb. 1957; Perm. Rep. to the UN 1958–59; Chief of Royal Cabinet 1959–61; Chargé d'affaires, Embassy to France 1961–62; Amb. to Belgium, the Netherlands and Luxembourg 1962–63, to People's Repub. of China 1965–67, to Algeria 1967–68, to Spain 1970–71 and 1972–78; Minister of Higher Educ. 1968–70, of Foreign Affairs 1971–72; Perm. Rep. to the UN 1978–80; Amb. to UK 1980–81; Minister of Foreign Affairs, Co-operation and Information 1985–86, of Foreign Affairs and Co-operation 1986–98, Prime Minister of Morocco 1994–98; Perm. Sec. Acad. of Kingdom of Morocco 1981. *Address:* c/o Office of the Prime Minister, Rabat, Morocco.

FILARDO, Leonor, MS; Venezuelan banker and finance official; b. 1944; d. of Jesus Filardo and Carmen Vargas de Filardo; m. (divorced); three d.; ed Caracas Catholic Univ., Surrey Univ.; worked for Cen. Bank of Venezuela 1970–75, Sr Vice-Pres. Int. Operations 1979–84; Sr Vice-Pres. of Int. Finance, Venezuelan Investment Fund 1975–79; Exec. Dir, World Bank Exec. Bd 1984–86; Alt. Exec. Dir IMF 1986–88, Exec. Dir 1988–90; Rep. Office, Washington DC 1990; Vice-Pres. Cen. Bank of Venezuela 1993–94; Minister Counsellor Embassy USA 1994; fmr Adviser to Cen. American and Venezuelan govts. on stabilization and structural adjustment programmes, participant in negotiations with IMF for External Fund Facility for Venezuela; mem. Exec. Cttee. Youth Orchestra of the Americas; Francisco de Miranda Medal, (1st Class) Venezuela 1990. *Leisure interests:* art, music, opera, travel, workout.

FILARET (see Philaret).

FILATOV, Leonid Alexeyevich; Russian actor and writer; b. 24 Dec. 1946, Kazan, Tatarstan; s. of Alexei Yeremeyevich Filatov and Clavdia Nikolayevna Filatova; m. Nina Shatskaya; ed Shchukin Higher School of Theatre Art; actor Taganka Theatre, Moscow 1969–85; Sovremennik Theatre 1985–87; Taganka Theatre 1987–93; Sec. Union of Cinematographers 1989–93; Founder Creative Union Concord of Taganka Actors 1993–; Triumph Prize, Prize of Int. Film Festival in Karlovy Vary for Chicherin, People's Artist of Russia 1996. *Film roles include:* Elite, Rooks, Forgotten Tune for the Flute, Town Zero, Crew, Chicherin, Success, Step, Contender, European Story, Confession of His Wife; (dir) Bitch's Kids 1991. *Stage appearances include:* What to Do?, Hamlet, Perished and Alive, Ten Days That Shook the World, Rush Hour, A House on the Embankment, Fasten the Belts, Pugachev, Antiworlds, Master and Marguerite. *Television:* To Be Remembered (author and narrator) 1998–. *Publications:* author of poetry, songs, plays, parodies. *Plays include:* Great Love of Robin Hood, Watch with a Cuckoo, Love for Three Oranges, Lisistrata, The Perturber, Dangerous, Dangerous and Very Dangerous. *Leisure interests:* poetry, serious music, theatre. *Address:* Rogozhsky val 12, Apt. 106, 109147 Moscow, Russia (Home). *Telephone:* (095) 278-42-32 (Home).

FILATOV, Sergey Alexandrovich, C.TECH.SC.; Russian politician; b. 10 July 1936, Moscow; s. of Alexander Filatov and Maria Filatova; m.; two d.; ed Moscow Energy Inst.; constructor, head of project Dept "Serp i Molot" metallurgical plant 1957–66, engineer in Cuba 1966–68, chief engineer of project, leading constructor, Head of Lab., Head of Dept Tselikov All-Union Research Inst. of Metallurgic Machine Construction 1969–90; People's Deputy of Russia 1990–93; mem. Supreme Soviet 1990–91, Sec. Presidium of Supreme Soviet 1991, First Vice-Chair. Supreme Soviet of Russia 1991–93; Head of Staff of Russian Pres. 1993–96; Chair. Comm. of Pres. of Russian Fed. for State Prizes in Literature and Art 1993–; f. Union of Progressive Forces 1997, Chair. Co-ordination Bd in support of Russian Pres. 1996–, Organizing Cttee, Congress of Russian Intelligentsia 1997–; State Prize of USSR, State Prize Laureate, Order of Friendship, Medal for the Defender of Independent Russia 1987. *Publications:* On the Way to Democracy 1995, Full Non-secret 2000. *Leisure interests:* cycling, swimming. *Address:* Mira prospekt 49A, 129110 Moscow (Office); 33-102 Garibaldi Street, Moscow, Russia (Home). *Telephone:* (095) 208-26-65 (Office); (095) 561-66-23 (Home). *Fax:* (095) 971-15-00 (Office). *E-mail:* jah@mail.cnt.ru (Office).

FILATOVA, Ludmila Pavlovna; Russian opera singer (mezzo-soprano); b. 6 Oct. 1935, Orenburg; d. of Pavel Filatov and Valentina Semoylova; m. Rudakov Igor 1971; ed Faculty of Mathematics, Leningrad Univ.; mem. CPSU 1969–91; began singing in choir; mem. of Kirov Opera choir 1958–60; soloist with Kirov (now Mariinsky) Opera 1962–; teacher of singing, Leningrad Conservatoire 1973–; gives chamber concerts: Shostakovich, Tchaikovsky,

Rachmaninov, Glinka etc.; Glinka Prize 1960; People's Artist of USSR 1983. *Major roles include:* Lyubasha in A Bride for the Tsar, Marfa in Khovanshchina, Carmen, Marta-Ekaterina in Petrov's Peter I, Countess in The Queen of Spades. *Address:* Mariinsky Theatre, Teatralnaya pl. 1, St Petersburg, Russia.

FILBINGER, Hans, DR.JUR.; German politician and lawyer; b. 15 Sept. 1913, Mannheim; s. of Johann Filbinger and Luise Filbinger; m. Ingeborg Breuer 1950; one s. four d.; ed Albert-Ludwigs-Univ., Freiburg im Breisgau, Ludwig-Maximilians-Univ., Munich and Univ. de Paris; teacher, Univ. of Freiburg 1937–40; war service and POW 1940–46; lawyer, Freiburg 1946–60; mem. Staatsrat 1958; mem. Landtag of Baden-Württemberg 1960; Minister of Interior, Baden-Württemberg 1960–66; Minister-Pres. of Baden-Württemberg 1966–78; Pres. Bundesrat (Upper House) 1973–74; mem. Comm. on Decartelization Questions 1947; Founder mem. German-French Soc., Freiburg, Soc. for Supra-national Co-operation; mem. NATO Parl. Conf.; Chair. Baden-Württemberg Democrat (CDU) Fed.; Pres. Studienzentrum Weikersheim e.V.; Hon. Dr rer. nat 1969; Hon. Dr.Jur. 1977; Grosskreuz des Bundesverdienstkreuzes, Grand Officier Légion d'honneur; Dr. hc and other awards. *Publications:* Die Schranken der Mehrheitsherrschaft im Aktienrecht und Konzernrecht 1942, Entscheidung zur Freiheit 1972, Hans Filbinger—der Fall und die Fakten 1980, Hans Filbinger—ein Mann in unserer Zeit 1983, Hans Filbinger-die geschmähte Generation 1987, Festschrift für Hans Filbinger. Deutschland als Kulturstaat 1993, Filbinger: Die Wahrheit aus den Stasi-Akten 1994, Mitherausgeber der Schriftenreihe des Studienzentrum Weikersheim, seit 1979–2001. *Leisure interests:* mountain climbing, skiing, literature. *Address:* Riedbergstrasse 29, 79100 Freiburg, Germany. *Telephone:* (761) 290661. *Fax:* (761) 290663.

FILIMON, Valeria; Romanian journalist; b. 29 May 1949, Butimanu; d. of Ion Dumitrescu and Maria Dumitrescu; m. Vasile Filimon 1984; ed Univ. of Bucharest; freelance journalist for various Romanian dailies and literary magazines 1967–90; Assoc. Prof. 1970–90; journalist 1990–93; Ed.-in-Chief, The Modern Woman (magazine) 1993–98; Ed.-in-Chief Regala 1998–, Olimp 1999–; Project Co-ordinator in Romania, Int. Fed. of Journalists 1996–; Vice-Pres. Journalists' Soc. of Romania; Romanian Writers' Union Prize. *Publications:* co-author of critical edition of Romanian novelist Liviu Rebreanu 1968–75; Lyceum (collection of literary criticism in two Vols) 1974. *Address:* Bd Pache Protopopescu No. 11, Sector 2, 70311 Bucharest, Romania. *Telephone:* 3152482. *Fax:* 3130675.

FILIPACCHI, Daniel; French journalist; b. 12 Jan. 1928, Paris; s. of Henri Filipacchi and Edith Besnard; typographer, Paris-Match 1944, photographer 1948, head of information and dir of photographic service 1953; fashion photographer, Marie-Claire 1957; producer of radio transmissions, Europe no 1, 1955, 1960; Owner and Dir Jazz Magazine 1955, Cahiers du cinéma 1961–70; Founder and Dir Salut les copains (became Salut 1976) 1961, Lui, Mlle Age tendre (became OK Age tendre 1976), Pariscope 1965, Photo 1967, Le Monde des Grands Musées 1968, Ski 1969, Union 1972, Playboy France 1973–84, Girls 1982; editorial adviser to Newlook 1980, Penthouse 1984; Pres.-Dir-Gen. WEA Filipacchi Music SA 1971–84, Cogedipresse; Owner and fmr Dir Paris-Match 1976; mem. editorial Cttee Elle 1981; Vice-Pres. Hachette 1981–93, Pres.-Dir-Gen. Hachette Magazines Inc. (USA) 1990–; Pres.-Dir-Gen. Filipacchi Médias SA 1993–97; Jt Man. Cogédipresse 1994–97; Admin. and Hon. Pres. Hachette Filipacchi Médias 1997–. *Address:* Hachette Filipacchi Médias, Immeuble Europa, 149–151 rue Anatole-France, 92534 Levallois-Perret cedex, France.

FILIPOV, Grisha; Bulgarian politician (retd); b. 13 July 1919, Kadiyevka, Ukraine; ed Moscow Univ., USSR; returned to Bulgaria 1936; joined Bulgarian CP 1940; arrested for political activities and sentenced to 15 years' imprisonment 1941; released after coup 1944; various posts in party, including Head of Inspectorate in Ministry of Industry 1947; Counsellor, Deputy Head and Deputy Chair. of Cttee on Planning 1951–58; Deputy Head of a Dept, Cen. Cttee of Bulgarian CP 1958; cand. mem. Cen. Cttee of Bulgarian CP 1962–66, mem. 1966–89, Sec. Cen. Cttee 1971–82, 1986–89; Deputy Chair. State Planning Comm. 1962–66; mem. Politburo 1974–89; mem. State Council 1986–89; Chair. Council of Ministers 1981–86; fmr mem. Nat. Ass.

FILIPOVIĆ, Karlo; Bosnia and Herzegovina politician; b. 1954, Solakovicima, Bosnia and Herzegovina; m.; one c.; ed ed. Univ. of Sarajevo; Pres. Council of Municipalities, Sarajevo City Ass. 1987–89; mem. Cen. Cttee. Communist League of Bosnia and Herzegovina 1988–91, elected mem. of presidency 1989; Sec. Social Democratic Party of Bosnia and Herzegovina (SDP) 1995–97, Sec.-Gen. 1997–2001, Pres. Exec. Bd 2001–; mem. House of Reps (Parl.) 1998–; Pres. Fed. of Bosnia and Herzegovina Feb. 2001–02, Vice-Pres. 2002–. *Address:* Office of the Vice-President, 71000 Sarajevo, Bosnia and Herzegovina (Office). *Telephone:* (33) 472618 (Office). *Fax:* (33) 472618 (Office).

FILIPPENKO, Aleksander Georgyevich; Russian actor; b. 2 Sept. 1944, Moscow; m. 2nd Marina Ishimbayeva; one d.; ed Moscow Inst. of Physics and Tech., Moscow, Shchukin Higher School of Theatre; Sr Engineer Inst. of Geochemistry, USSR Acad. of Sciences 1967–69; actor Amateur Theatre Nash Dom 1967–69, Taganka Theatre 1969–75, Vakhtangov Theatre 1975–94; Founder and actor Experimental One-Man Theatre 1995–; staged Train to Chatanooga, Dead Souls, Fanbala; Merited Artist of Russia. *Films include:*

Star and Death of Joakin Murietta, My Friend Ivan Lapshin, Master and Marguerita; lead TV programme If 1997–98. *Address:* Spiridonyevsky per. 8, Apt. 17, 103104 Moscow, Russia (Home). *Telephone:* (095) 202-77-15 (Home).

FILIPPOV, Vladimir Mikhailovich, DR. PHYSICS-MATH.; Russian politician and mathematician; b. 1951; m.; one s. one d.; ed Patrice Lumumba Univ. of Friendship of Peoples, Steklov Math. Inst. USSR Acad of Sciences; Asst, Chair of Higher Math., Chair. Council of Young Scientists, Head Dept of Science, Lumumba Univ. of Friendship of Peoples 1973–85; Prof., Head, Chair of Math. Analysis, Dean, Faculty of Physics, Math. and Natural Sciences, Lumumba Univ. 1985–93, Rector 1993–98; Minister of Gen. and Professional Educ. of Russian Fed. 1998–2000; Minister of Educ. 2000–; Vice-Pres. Euro-Asian Asscn of Univs.; mem. Russian Acad. of Natural Sciences, Int. Acad. of Informatization. *Publications:* over 120 scientific works on problems of differential equations and functional analysis. *Address:* Ministry of Education, Lyusinovskaya str. 51, 113833 Moscow, Russia. *Telephone:* (095) 237-76-75 (Office).

FILLIOUD, Georges, LenD; French politician and journalist; b. 7 July 1929, Lyon; s. of Marius Fillioud and Camille Metifiot; m. 1st Aimée Dieunet 1949; one s. one d.; m. 2nd Danielle Evennou 1996; ed Ecole nationale professionnelle de Lyon, Univs. of Paris and Lyon; Journalist, Chief Reporter, then Sr Ed., Europe No.1 radio station 1956–66; Deputy (Drôme) to Nat. Ass. 1967–68, 1973–81; Asst Sec.-Gen. Convention des institutions républicaines 1970; Councillor, Romans 1970–77, Mayor 1977–81; Press Sec. Parti Socialiste 1971–; Sec.-Gen. Féd. des élus socialistes et républicains 1972–; mem. Parl. Del. for French broadcasting 1974; Vice-Pres. Nat. Ass. Socialist Group 1978–79; Minister of Communication 1981–83, Sec. of State 1983–86; Conseiller d'État 1986; Admin., Pres. Institut nat. de l'audiovisuel (Ina) 1990–94; Pres. Gen. Ass. of Art 1999–. *Publications:* Le dossier du Vercors 1965, L'affaire Lindemans 1966, la Mort d'un chien 1988, Homo Politicus 1996. *Address:* 30 passage Thiére, 75011 Paris, France (Home).

FILLON, François-Charles Amand; French politician; b. 4 March 1954, Mans; s. of Michel Fillon and Annie Soulet; m. Penelope Clarke 1980; three s. one d.; ed Univ. of Maine, Univ. René-Descartes, Paris and Fondation Nationale des Sciences Politiques; Parl. Asst to Joël Le Theule 1976–77; served in Office of Minister of Transport 1978–80, Office of Minister of Defence 1980–81; Head of Legis. and Parl. Work, Ministry of Industry 1981; Town Councillor, Sable-sur-Sarthe, Mayor 1983–2001; Pres. Conseil Général, Sarthe 1992–98, of Sablé-sur-Sarthe Dist 2001–; RPR Deputy to Nat. Ass. 1981–93; Pres. Comm. for Nat. Defence and Armed Forces 1986–88; Minister for Higher Educ. and Research 1993–95; Minister of Information Tech. and Posts May–Nov. 1995, Minister del. Nov. 1995–97; spokesman Exec. Comm. RPR 1998–, Political Adviser 1999–; Chair. Conseil Régional des Pays de la Loire 1998–; Municipal Councillor, Solesmes 2001–; Minister of Social Affairs, Labour and Solidarity May 2002–. *Address:* Ministry of Social Affairs, Labour and Solidarity, 127 rue de Grenelle, 75007 Paris (Office); Beaucé, 72300 Solesmes, France (Home). *Telephone:* 1-44-38-38-38. *Fax:* 1-44-38-20-10.

FILMON, Gary Albert, MSc; Canadian politician; b. 24 Aug. 1942, Winnipeg, Man.; s. of Albert Filmon and Anastasia (Dosckocz) Filmon; m. Janice Wainwright 1963; two s. two d.; ed Sisler High School, Univ. of Manitoba; consulting engineer, Underwood McLellan Ltd 1964–69; Pres. Success/Angus Commercial Coll. 1969–80; Winnipeg City Councillor 1975–79; mem. Legis. Ass. for River Heights 1979–81, for Tuxedo 1981–; Minister of Consumer and Corp. Affairs and Environment and Minister Reponsible for Man. Housing and Renewal Corpn 1981; Leader Man. Progressive Conservative Party 1983–88; Premier of Man., Pres. Exec. Council, Minister of Fed. Prov. Relations 1988–99; Leader of the Opposition 1999–2002. *Address:* Manitoba Legis. Assembly, Legislature Building, Room 204, Winnipeg, MB, R3C 0V8, Canada (Office).

FILO, David, MS; American computer executive; b. Moss Bluff, La.; ed Tulane Univ. and Stanford Univ. Calif.; Co-Founder, Chief Exec. Yahoo! Inc. 1994–. *Address:* Yahoo! Incorporated, 3420 Central Expressway, Suite 201, Santa Clara, CA 95051, USA.

FINCH, Jon Nicholas; British actor, writer and director; b. 2 March 1943, Caterham, Surrey; s. of Arthur Leonard Finch and Nancy Karen Houghton; m. Catriona MacColl 1981 (divorced 1989); one d. by Helen Elizabeth Drake; ed Caterham School; served 21 Special Air Service (SAS) Regt (Artists) Reserve 1960–63; theatre technician and Dir etc. 1963–67, actor in TV 1967–70; Hon. Dr. of Metaphysics; Most Promising Artiste, Variety Club of GB 1972. *Films include:* lead role in Roman Polanski's Macbeth, Alfred Hitchcock's Frenzy, Lady Caroline Lamb, The Final Programme, El hombre de la cruz verde, Die estandarte, La sabina, Gary Cooper que estas en los cielos, La amenaza, La più bella del reame, Une femme fidèle, Death on the Nile, Breaking Glass, Girocity, Doktor Faustus, Riviera, Paradiso, Plaza Real, Streets of Yesterday, The Voice, Beautiful in the Kingdom, Mirror, Mirror, Lurking Fear (USA), Darklands (UK), Lucan, Anazapta. *Television films:* The Rainbow, Unexplained Laughter, A Love Renewed, Beautiful Lies, Maigret, Sherlock Holmes: The Mazarin Stone, Merlin's Crystal Cave, Dangerous Curves (USA), The Acts of Peter and Paul (USA), White Men are Cracking Up, New Tricks. *Television includes:* Counterstrike (series), Steve, Ben Hall (series), Richard II, Henry IV Parts I and II, Much Ado About Nothing, Make or Break, The Odd Job Man (series), Mary Queen of Scots, Casualty. *Theatre:* Les Liaisons Dangereuses, King Lear, The Importance of

Being Earnest, Music to Murder By, The Invisible Man. *Leisure interests:* reading, collecting hip flasks. *Address:* 3 Cornwallis Gardens, Garden Flat, Hastings, E Sussex TN34 1LP, England. *Telephone:* (7905) 215030.

FINCHAM, John Robert Stanley, PhD, FRS; British professor emeritus of genetics; b. 11 Aug. 1926, Southgate, Middx; s. of Robert Fincham and Winifred Emily Fincham (née Western); m. Ann Katherine Emerson 1950; one s. three d.; ed Peterhouse and Botany School, Univ. of Cambridge; Lecturer in Botany, Univ. Coll. Leicester 1950–54, Reader in Genetics, Univ. of Leicester 1954–60; Head, Dept of Genetics, John Innes Inst. 1960–66; Prof. and Head, Dept of Genetics, Univ. of Leeds 1966–76, Univ. of Edinburgh 1976–84; Arthur Balfour Prof. of Genetics, Univ. of Cambridge 1984–91, now Emer.; Professorial Fellow, Peterhouse, Cambridge 1984–91, now Emer. Fellow; Emil Christian Hansen Medal (Copenhagen) 1977; Hon. Fellow Div. of Biology, Univ. of Edinburgh 1992–. *Publications:* Fungal Genetics (with P. R. Day, later edns. also with A. Radford) 1963, Microbial and Molecular Genetics 1965, Genetic Complementation 1966, Genetics 1983, Genetically Engineered Organisms 1991, Genetic Analysis 1994, numerous articles in professional journals. *Leisure interest:* books, walking, music. *Address:* 20 Greenbank Road, Edinburgh, EH10 5RY, Scotland (Home). *Telephone:* (31) 447-3313 (Home).

FINCK, August von; German business executive; b. 11 March 1930; owner, Bankhaus Merck, Finck & Co., Munich, Deutsche Spar- & Kreditbank AG, Munich, Carlton Holdings (controller of Mövenpick restaurant chain); majority shareholder, Löwenbräu AG, Munich, Würzburger Hofbräu AG. *Address:* Pacellistrasse 4, 80333 Munich, Germany.

FINDLAY, Paul Hudson Douglas, BA; British opera director; b. 26 Sept. 1943, New Zealand; s. of the late John Niemeyer Findlay and Aileen May (née Davidson) Findlay; m. Françoise Christiane 1966; one s. one d.; ed Univ. Coll. School, London, Balliol Coll., Oxford, London Opera Centre; Production and Technical Man. New Opera Co. 1967; Dir London Sinfonietta 1967–; Stage Man. Glyndebourne Touring Opera and English Opera Group 1968; Asst Press Officer Royal Opera House, Covent Garden 1968–72, Personal Asst to Gen. Dir 1972–76, Asst Dir 1976–87, Opera Dir 1987–93; Man. Dir Royal Philharmonic Orchestra 1993–95; Planning Dir European Opera Centre 1997–; Arts Man. Kirov Ballet; Chair. Opera 80 1987; currently Gen. Man. Mariinsky Theater, St Petersburg, Dir English Touring Opera, Arts Educational Trust; Vice-Pres. GMN Europe 1998–2001; Dir Youth and Mind 2000–; Cavaliere Ufficiale del Ordine al Merito della Repubblica Italiana; Chevalier des Arts et des Lettres 1991. *Leisure interests:* tennis, gardening.

FINE, Anne, BA; British writer; b. 7 Dec. 1947, Leicester; d. of Brian Laker and Mary Baker; m. Kit Fine 1968 (divorced 1991); two d.; ed Northampton High School for Girls and Univ. of Warwick; Children's Author of the Year, Publishing News 1990, 1993; Children's Laureate 2001–03; numerous awards and prizes. *Publications:* for older children: The Summer House Loon 1978, The Other Darker Ned 1978, The Stone Menagerie 1980, Round Behind the Icehouse 1981, The Granny Project 1983, Madame Doubtfire 1987, Goggle-Eyes (Guardian Children's Fiction Prize, Carnegie Medal 1990) 1989, The Book of the Banshee 1991, Flour Babies (Whitbread Children's Book of the Year, Carnegie Medal 1993) 1992, Step by Wicked Step 1995, The Tulip Touch 1996 (Whitbread Award), Very Different (short stories) 2001, Up on Cloud Nine 2002; for younger children: Scaredy-Cat 1985, Anneli the Art Hater 1986, Crummy Mummy and Me 1988, A Pack of Liars 1988, Stranger Danger 1989, Bill's New Frock 1989 (Smarties Prize), The Country Pancake 1989, A Sudden Puff of Glittering Smoke 1989, A Sudden Swirl of Icy Wind 1990, Only a Show 1990, Design-a-Pram 1991, A Sudden Glow of Gold 1991, The Worst Child I Ever Had 1991, The Angel of Nitshill Road 1991, Same Old Story Every Year 1992, The Chicken Gave It to Me 1992, The Haunting of Pip Parker 1992, The Diary of a Killer Cat 1994, Press Play 1994, How to Write Really Badly 1996, Countdown 1996, Jennifer's Diary 1996, Care of Henry 1996, Loudmouth Louis 1998, Charm School 1999, Roll Over Roly 1999, Telling Tales (interview/autobiog.), Bad Dreams 2000, Notso Hotso 2001, The Jamie and Angus Stories 2002; picture books: Poor Monty 1991, Ruggles 2001; novels: The Killjoy 1986, Taking the Devil's Advice 1990, In Cold Domain 1994, Telling Liddy 1998, All Bones and Lies 2001. *Leisure interests:* reading, walking. *Address:* c/o David Higham Associates, 5–8 Lower John Street, London, W1R 4HA, England (Office). *Website:* www.annefine.co.uk (Office).

FINE, Kit, PhD; British professor of philosophy; b. 26 March 1946, Farnborough; s. of Maurice Fine and Joyce Cicely Woolf; two d.; ed Cheltenham Grammar School for Boys, Balliol Coll. Oxford; Prof., Univ. of Mich., Ann Arbor, USA 1978–88, Univ. of Calif., LA 1988–97, New York Univ. 1997–; Ed. Journal of Symbolic Logic 1978–87, Notre Dame Journal of Formal Logic 1984–87, Studies in Logic 1989–93; Guggenheim Fellow 1978–79; Fellow American Council of Learned Socs. 1981–82. *Publications:* Worlds, Times and Selves (with A. N. Prior) 1977, Reasoning with Arbitrary Objects 1985, Limits of Abstraction 2002. *Leisure interests:* music, gardening, cooking. *Address:* Philosophy Department, 503 Main Building, New York University, New York, NY 10003, USA.

FINE, Leon Gerald, MB, ChB, FRCP, FACP, FRCP(Glas), FMedSci; American professor of medicine; b. 17 July 1943, Cape Town, South Africa; s. of Matthew Fine and Jeanette Lipshitz; m. Brenda Sakinovsky 1966; two d.; ed Univ. of Cape Town; mem. staff Albert Einstein Coll. of Medicine 1972–76, Univ. of Miami 1976–78, Univ. of Calif. at LA 1978–91; Head Dept of Medicine, Univ. Coll. London 1991–; numerous invited lectureships; Founding Fellow Acad.

of Medical Sciences, UK. *Publications:* over 100 articles in the area of kidney disease and renal biology. *Leisure interest:* book collecting. *Address:* Department of Medicine, 5 University Street, London, WC1E 6JJ (Office); Royal Free and University College Medical School, University College London, London, WC1, England (Home). *Telephone:* (20) 7679-6186 (Office); (20) 8342-9680 (Home). *Fax:* (20) 7679-6211 (Office); (20) 8342-9680 (Home). *E-mail:* l.fine@ucl.ac.uk (Office).

FINEBERG, Harvey Vernon, PhD; American physician and professor of public health; b. 15 Sept. 1945; s. of Saul Fineberg and Miriam Fineberg (née Pearl); m. Mary Elizabeth Wilson 1975; ed Harvard Univ.; Intern, Beth Israel Hosp., Boston 1972–73; Asst Prof. School of Public Health, Harvard Univ., Boston 1973–78, Assoc. Prof. 1978–81, Prof. 1981–2002, Dean 1984–97; Provost, Harvard Univ. 1997–2001; physician at E Boston Health Center 1974–76; Harvard St Health Center 1976–84; Trustee, Newton Wellesley Hosp., Mass. 1981–86; Chair. Nat. Center for Health Services Research 1982–85; mem. Public Health Council, Mass. 1976–79; mem. Bd Dirs American Foundation for AIDS Research 1986–97; mem. Inst. of Medicine, Pres. 2002–; mem. Nat. Acad. of Sciences; Jr Fellow, Harvard Univ. 1974–75, Mellon Fellow 1976. *Address:* Institute of Medicine, 500 5th Street NW, Washington, DC 20001-2721 (Office); 1812 Kalorama Square NW, Washington, DC 20008-4022, USA (Home).

FINETTE, Jean Regis, LèsL; Mauritian politician; b. 8 July 1934; m.; three c.; ed Coll. Royal Curepipe and Port Louis, Univ. of Mauritius; Lecturer in Co-operative Studies, Univ. of Mauritius for 17 years; Deputy to Legis. Ass. 1982–; Minister for Local Govt 1988–93, of Health 1993–96; Officier des Palmes Académiques. *Address:* Lothar Koenig Street, Cité Rosray, Beau Bassin, Mauritius.

FINI, Gianfranco; Italian politician; b. Bologna; mem. Movimento Sociale Italiano-Destra Nazionale (MSI) (now Alleanza Nazionale), Sec.-Gen. 1987–; Vice-Pres. Council of Ministers (Deputy Prime Minister) 2001–; Rep. to EU Special Convention on a Pan-European Constitution 2002–; fmr journalist. *Address:* Alleanza Nazionale, Via della Scrofa 39, 00186 Rome, Italy (Office); Office of the Prime Minister, Palazzo Chigi, Piazza Colonna 370, 00186 Rome. *Telephone:* (06) 68803014 (Office); (06) 67791. *Fax:* (06) 6548256 (Office); (06) 6783998. *Website:* www.alleanza-nazionale.it (Office); www.palazzochigi.it (Office).

FINK, Gerald R., PhD; American professor of genetics; b. 1 July 1940, Brooklyn, New York; s. of Rebecca Fink and Benjamin Fink; m. Rosalie Lewis 1961; two d.; ed Amherst Coll., Yale Univ.; Postdoctoral Fellow, NIH 1965–66, 1966–67; Instructor, NIH Grad. Program 1966; Instructor, Cold Spring Harbor Summer Program 1970–; Asst Prof. of Genetics Cornell Univ. 1967–71, Assoc. Prof. 1971–76, Prof. 1976–79, Prof. of Biochem. 1979–82; Prof. of Molecular Genetics, MIT 1982–; American Cancer Soc. Prof. of Genetics 1979–; mem. Whitehead Inst. for Biomedical Research 1982–, Dir 1990–; Sec. Genetics Soc. of America 1977–80, Vice-Pres. 1986–87, Pres. 1988–89; mem. NAS, American Acad. of Arts and Sciences; Hon. DSc (Amherst Coll.) 1982; NAS-US Steel Prize in Molecular Biology 1981, Genetics Soc. of America Medal 1982, Yale Science and Eng Award 1984, Emil Christian Hansen Foundation Award for Microbiological Research 1986. *Publications:* numerous scientific publs. *Address:* Whitehead Institute for Biomedical Research, 9 Cambridge Center, Cambridge, MA 02142, USA.

FINLAY, Frank, CBE; British actor; b. 6 Aug. 1926, Lancs.; s. of Josiah Finlay and Margaret Finlay; m. Doreen Joan Shepherd 1954; two s. one d.; ed St Gregory the Great, Farnworth, Royal Acad. of Dramatic Art, London; repertory 1950–52, 1954–57; Hon. Fellow (Bolton Inst.) 1992; Clarence Derwent Best Actor Award (for Chips with Everything) 1962, Best Actor Award, San Sebastian (for Othello) 1966, Soc. of Film and TV Arts Awards (for The Lie and Don Quixote), Best Actor Award (for Bouquet of Barbed Wire). *Stage appearances include:* Belgrade, Epitaph for George Dillon 1958, Sugar in the Morning, Sergeant Musgrave's Dance, Chicken Soup with Barley, Roots, I'm Talking About Jerusalem, The Happy Haven, Platonov, Chips with Everything 1958–62 (all at Royal Court), St Joan, The Workhouse Donkey, Hobson's Choice 1963, Othello, The Dutch Courtesan 1964, The Crucible, Much Ado About Nothing, Mother Courage 1965, Juno and the Paycock, The Storm 1966 (all at Nat. Theatre), After Haggerty (Aldwych, Criterion), Son of Man (Leicester Theatre, Round House) 1970, Saturday Sunday Monday, The Party 1973, Plunder, Watch It Come Down, Weapons of Happiness 1976, Amadeus 1982 (all at Nat. Theatre), Kings and Clowns (Phoenix), Filumena (Lyric) 1978, The Girl in Melanie Klein 1980, The Cherry Orchard 1983, Mutiny (Piccadilly) 1985, Beyond Reasonable Doubt 1987, Black Angel 1990, A Slight Hangover 1991, The Heiress 1992, The Woman in Black 1993–94, Capt. Hook/Mr Darling in Peter Pan 1994, Gaslight 1995, The Handyman 1996. *Film appearances include:* The Longest Day, Private Potter, The Informers, A Life for Ruth, Loneliness of the Long Distance Runner, Hot Enough for June, The Comedy Man, The Sandwich Man, A Study in Terror, Othello, The Jokers, I'll Never Forget What's 'Is Name, The Shoes of the Fisherman, Deadly Bees, Robbery, Inspector Clouseau, Twisted Nerve, Cromwell, The Molly Maguires, Assault, Victory for Danny Jones, Gumshoe, Shaft in Africa, Van Der Walk and the Girl, Van Der Walk and the Rich, Van Der Walk and the Dead, The Three Musketeers, The Ring of Darkness, The Wild Geese, The Four Musketeers, The Thief of Baghdad, Sherlock Holmes—Murder by Decree, Enigma, Return of the Soldier, The Ploughman's Lunch 1982, A Christmas Carol, The Key 1983, Sakharov 1983, Life Force 1985, The Return of the Musketeers

1988, King of the Wind, Cthulhu Mansion 1992, Charlemagne 1993, The Sparrow 1993, Limited Edition 1995, Gospa 1995, Romance and Rejection 1996, Stiff Upper Lips 1998, Dreaming of Joseph Lees 1999, Ghosthunter 2000, The Pianist 2001. *TV appearances include:* Julius Caesar, Les Misérables, This Happy Breed, The Lie, Casanova, The Death of Adolf Hitler, Don Quixote, Candide, Voltaire, Merchant of Venice, Bouquet of Barbed Wire, 84 Charing Cross Road, Saturday Sunday Monday, Count Dracula, The Last Campaign, Napoleon in Betzi, Dear Brutus, Tales of the Unexpected, Tales from 1001 Nights, Aspects of Love—Mona, Arc de Triomphe, In the Secret State, Verdict on Erebus, Mountain of Diamonds, Encounters, The Other Side, Stalin, Charlemagne, Exchange of Fire, Heartbeat, Dalgliesh, Sherlock Holmes. *Leisure interests:* reading, walking, the countryside. *Address:* c/o Ken McReddie Ltd, Paurelle House, 91 Regent Street, London, W1R 7TB, England.

FINLAY, Ian Hamilton, CBE; Scottish artist and poet; b. 28 Oct. 1925, Nassau, Bahamas; s. of James Hamilton Finlay and Annie Whitelaw Finlay; one s. one d.; ed Larchfield School, Helensborough, Dollar Acad.; served in army 1944–47; fmrly shepherd, road labourer, author, gardener; Dr hc (Aberdeen) 1987, (Heriot-Watt. Univ. of Edin.) 1993; Hon. Prof. (Dundee) 1999. *Solo exhibitions:* 'Inter Artes et Naturam', Musée d'Art Moderne, Paris 1987, 'Ideologische Ausserungen', Frankfurter Kunstverein 1991, Philadelphia Museum of Art 1991, 'Wildwachsende Blumen', Lenbachhaus, Munich 1993, 'Works, Pure and Political', Deichtorhallen, Hamburg 1995, 'Modern Antiquities', Landesmuseum Mainz, 'Variations on Several Themes', Joan Miró Foundation, Barcelona 1999, 'Maritime Works', St Ives, Tate 2002; also represented in various group exhbns. *Achievements (miscellaneous):* perm. installations in gardens and parks including garden of Max Planck Inst., Stuttgart 1975, Kröller-Müller Sculpture Garden, Otterlo 1982, campus of Univ. of Calif., San Diego 1991, Serpentine Gallery, London 1999, Wallraff-Richartz Museum, Cologne 2000. *Publications include:* Ian Hamilton Finlay—A Visual Primer 1992, Werke in Europa 1995, IHF, Prints 1963–97 1997, 100 Postcards by Ian Hamilton Finlay. *Leisure interests:* model boats, model aeroplanes, fishing, philosophy, French Revolution. *Address:* Stonypath, Little Sparta, Dunsyre, Lanark, ML11 8NG, Scotland. *Telephone:* (189) 981-0252. *Fax:* (189) 981-0252.

FINLAY, Thomas Aloysius, BA; Irish lawyer; b. 17 Sept. 1922; s. of Thomas A. Finlay and Eva Finlay; m. Alice Blayney 1948; two s. three d.; ed Xavier School, Dublin, Clongowes Wood Coll., University Coll., Dublin; called to the Bar, Dublin, King's Inn 1944; mem. Dail Eireann 1954–57; Sr Counsel 1961; Bencher 1972; Judge of the High Court 1972, Pres. 1974; Chief Justice 1985–94; Hon. Bencher (Inn of Court, NI) 1985, (Middle Temple) 1986; Hon. LLD (Dublin, Nat. Univ. of Ireland) 1992. *Leisure interests:* fishing, shooting, conversation. *Address:* 22 Ailesbury Drive, Dublin 4, Ireland. *Telephone:* 2693395.

FINLEY, Gerald Hunter, MA, ARCM; Canadian baritone; b. 30 Jan. 1960, Montreal; s. of Eric Gault Finley and Catherine Rae Hunter; m. Louise Winter 1990; two s.; ed Glebe Collegiate Inst., Ottawa, Univ. of Ottawa, Royal Coll. of Music, London, UK, Nat. Opera Studio, London, King's Coll. Cambridge; chorister St Matthew's Church, Ottawa 1969–78; mem. Ottawa Choral Soc., Cantata Singers, Ont. Youth Choir 1977–78, Glyndebourne Festival Chorus, UK 1986–89; debut as opera soloist, Papageno in The Magic Flute, London 1989; roles at Glyndebourne: Sid (Albert Herring) 1989, Papageno, Guglielmo, Count Dominik (Arabella), Kuligin (Katya Kabanova) 1990–93, Figaro (Marriage of Figaro) at opening of new opera house 1994; Owen Wingrave, Olivier (Capriccio), Nick Shadow; Agamemnon (Iphigénie en Avlide), debut Canadian Opera Co., Sid (Albert Herring) 1991; has sung Figaro at Covent Garden London and many other opera houses worldwide 1992–; other roles at Covent Garden include Pilgrim (Pilgrim's Progress), Achilla (Giulio Cesare), Creonte (L'Anima del Filosofo), Forester (Cunning Little Vixen), Don Giovanni; roles at Opéra de Paris include Valentin, Sharpless, Papageno, Figaro, Don Giovanni 2001; debut Metropolitan Opera, New York, Papageno (Magic Flute) 1998; role of Mr. Fox in Fantastic Mr. Fox, LA Opera 1998; debut ENO, Harry Heegan (The Silver Tassie) 2000; concert soloist and lieder singer; Visiting Prof. R.C.M. 2000; John Christie Award, Glyndebourne 1989; Juno Award for Best Vocal Peformance (Canada) 1998; Singer Award Royal Philharmonic Soc. 2001. *Film:* Owen Wingrave 2001. *Recordings:* Papageno, Guglielmo, Sid, Masetto, Haydn's Creation, Brahms' Requiem, Silver Tassie, Pilgrim's Progress, Dido and Aeneas; Songs of Travel 1998, Schubert Complete Songs 1817–1821, Complete Songs of Henri Duparc 2002. *Radio:* numerous recordings with BBC and CBC. *Leisure interests:* wine, reading, ice skating. *Address:* c/o IMG Artists Europe, 616 Chiswick High Road, London, W4 5RX, England; c/o IMG Artists, 825 Seventh Avenue, New York, NY 10019, USA. *Telephone:* (20) 8233-5800 (London); (212) 489-8300 (USA). *Fax:* (20) 8233-5801 (London); (212) 246-1596 (New York).

FINN, Pavel Konstantinovich; Russian scriptwriter; b. Pavel Finn-Halfin, 28 June 1940, Moscow; m. Irina Chernova-Finn; one s.; ed All-Union State Inst. of Cinematography; fmr journalist, documentary maker; freelance script writer 1968–; Head of Higher Workshop Course of Scriptwriters; Chair. Cinema Dramaturgy Council, Moscow Union of Cinematographers 2001; First Deputy Chair. Russian Union of Cinematographers 2001–. *Films include:* Headless Horse Rider 1973, Armed and Very Dangerous 1977, 26 Days of Dostoyevsky's Life 1980, Icicle in a Warm Sea 1983, Witness 1985, Lady Macbeth of Mtsensk Region 1989, Accidental Waltz 1989, Sunset 1990, Myth about Leonid 1991, A Big Concert of Peoples 1991, Shylock 1993,

Jester's Revenge 1994, For What 1995, Career of Arthur Whui 1996, Break Point, We Are Your Kids, Moscow, Eve's Gates, Death of Tairov or Princess Brambilla, Secrets of Court Coups. *Leisure interests:* buying books, reading. *Address:* Union of Cinematographers, Vassil'yevskaya str. 13, 123825 Moscow (Office); 4th Rostovsky per. 2/1, apt. 9, 119121 Moscow, Russia (Home). *Telephone:* (095) 248-53-28 (Home); (095) 334-59-34 (Home). *Fax:* (095) 251-51-06 (Office). *E-mail:* pavelfinn@mtu-net.ru (Home).

FINN, Victor Konstantinovich, DrSc; Russian philosopher, logician and computer scientist; b. 15 July 1933, Moscow; m. Irina Yevgenyevna Yavchunovskaya-Belova; one d.; ed Moscow State Univ.; researcher, Head of Sector, Lab. of Electromodelling, USSR Acad. of Sciences 1957–59; Head of Lab. All-Union Inst. for Scientific and Tech. Information (VINITI) 1959–; lecturer Moscow State Univ. 1967–68; Prof., Head Dept of Artificial Intelligence Moscow State Inst. of History and Archives (now Russian Humanitarian Univ.) 1979–; mem. Acad. of Natural Sciences; mem. Bd int. journals Studia Logica, Foundation of Science; mem. Council Russian Asscn of Artificial Intelligence. *Publications:* over 100 scientific papers and books including Logical Problems of Information Search 1976, Epistemological and Logical Problems of History (with K. Khvostova) 1995, Intellectual Systems and Society 2001. *Address:* 1st Miusskaya str. 20, Apt. 19, 125047 Moscow, Russia (Home). *Telephone:* (095) 251-08-99 (Home).

FINNBOGADÓTTIR, Vigdís; Icelandic politician and teacher; b. 15 April 1930, Reykjavík; d. of Finnbogi Rutur Thorvaldsson and Sigridur Eiríksdóttir; m. (divorced); one adopted d.; ed Junior Coll., Menntaskólinn i Reykjavík, Univs. of Grenoble and Sorbonne, France, Univ. of Iceland; taught French, Jr Colls., Menntaskólinn i Reykjavík, Menntaskólinn vid Hamrahlid; Iceland Tourist Bureau, Head Guide Training; Dir Reykjavik Theatre Co. 1972–80; taught French drama, Univ. of Iceland; worked for Icelandic State TV; fmr Chair. Alliance Française; mem. Advisory Cttee on Cultural Affairs in Nordic Countries 1976–80, Chair. 1978–80; Pres. of Iceland 1980–96; Hon. GCMG 1982; Dr. hc (Grenoble) 1985, (Bordeaux) 1987, (Smith Coll., USA) 1988, (Luther Coll., USA) 1989, (Manitoba) 1989; Hon. LLD (Nottingham) 1990. *Leisure interest:* theatre. *Address:* c/o Office of the President, Stornarráðshúsið, v/Lækjarötu, 150 Reykjavík, Iceland (Office).

FINNEY, Albert; British actor; b. 9 May 1936; m. 1st Jane Wenham (divorced); one s.; m. 2nd Anouk Aimée 1970 (divorced 1978); ed Salford Grammar School and Royal Acad. of Dramatic Art; Birmingham Repertory Co. 1956–58; Shakespeare Memorial Theatre Co. 1959; Nat. Theatre 1965, 1975; formed Memorial Enterprises 1966; Assoc. Artistic Dir English Stage Co. 1972–75; Dir United British Artists 1983–86; Hon. LittD (Sussex) 1966; Lawrence Olivier Award 1986; London Standard Drama Award for Best Actor 1986, Dilys Powell Award, London Film Critics Circle 1999; BAFTA Fellowship 2001. *Plays include:* Julius Caesar, Macbeth, Henry V, The Beaux' Stratagem, The Alchemist, The Lizard on the Rock, The Party 1958, King Lear, Othello 1959, A Midsummer Night's Dream, The Lily-White Boys 1960, Billy Liar 1960, Luther 1961, 1963, Much Ado About Nothing, Armstrong's Last Goodnight 1965, Miss Julie 1965, Black Comedy 1965, Love for Love 1965, A Flea in Her Ear 1966, A Day in the Death of Joe Egg 1968, Alpha Beta 1972, Krapp's Last Tape 1973, Cromwell 1973, Chez Nous 1974, Loot (Dir) 1975, Hamlet 1976, Tamburlaine the Great 1976, Uncle Vanya 1977, Present Laughter 1977, The Country Wife 1977–78, The Cherry Orchard 1978, Macbeth 1978, Has "Washington" Legs? 1978, The Biko Inquest (Dir) 1984, Sergeant Musgrave's Dance (Dir) 1984, Orphans 1986, J. J. Farr 1987, Another Time 1989, Reflected Glory 1992, Art 1996. *Films acted in include:* The Entertainer 1959, Saturday Night and Sunday Morning 1960, Tom Jones 1963, Night Must Fall 1963, Two for the Road 1967, Scrooge 1970, Gumshoe 1971, Murder on the Orient Express 1974, Wolfen 1979, Loophole 1980, Looker 1980, Shoot the Moon 1981, Annie 1982, Life of John Paul II 1983, The Dresser 1983, Under the Volcano 1983, Miller's Crossing 1989, The Image 1989; directed and acted in Charlie Bubbles 1968, Orphans 1987, The Playboys 1992, Rich in Love 1992, The Browning Version 1993, The Run of the Country 1995, Washington Square, Breakfast of Champions 1999, Simpatico 1999, Delivering Milo 1999, Erin Brockovich 2000. *TV appearances include:* The Endless Game 1989, The Green Man (mini-series) 1990, Karaoke 1995, Nostromo 1997, My Uncle Silas 2001, 2003, The Lonely War 2002, The Gathering Storm (Emmy Award 2002, Golden Globe for Best Actor in a mini-series or TV movie 2003, BAFTA Award for Best Actor 2003) 2002. *Address:* c/o Michael Simkins, 45/51 Whitfield Street, London, W1P 6AA, England. *Telephone:* (20) 7631-1050.

FINNEY, David John, CBE, MA, ScD, FRS, FRSE; British professor of statistics (retd) and consultant biometrician; b. 3 Jan. 1917, Latchford, Warrington; s. of Robert George Stringer Finney and Bessie Evelyn Finney (née Whitlow); m. Mary Elizabeth Connolly 1950; one s. two d.; ed Univs of Cambridge and London; statistician, Rothamsted Experimental Station 1939–45; Lecturer in the Design and Analysis of Scientific Experiment, Univ. of Oxford 1945–54; Reader in Statistics, Univ. of Aberdeen 1954–64, Prof. of Statistics 1964–66; Prof. of Statistics, Univ. of Edin. 1966–84; Dir Agricultural Research Council's Unit of Statistics 1954–84; Dir Research Centre, Int. Statistical Inst., Netherlands 1987–88; Pres. Biometric Soc. 1964–65; Chair. Computer Bd for Univs 1970–74; Pres. Royal Statistical Soc. 1973–74; Visiting Scientist Int. Rice Research Inst. 1984–85; FAO "Key Consultant" to Indian Agricultural Statistics Research Inst. 1983–91; mem. Adverse Relations Sub-Cttee of Cttee on Safety of Medicines 1963–80; Weldon Memorial Prize 1956; Paul Martini Prize 1971; Hon. DèsSc Agronomiques (Gembloux); Hon. DSc (City Univ., Heriot-Watt Univ.); Hon. DrMath. (Waterloo, Ont.) 1989. *Publications:* Probit Analysis 1947, 1952, 1971, Biological Standardization (with J. H. Burn and L. G. Goodwin) 1950, Statistical Method in Biological Assay 1952, 1964, 1978, Introduction to Statistical Science in Agriculture 1953, 1962, 1964, 1972, Experimental Design and its Statistical Basis 1955, Técnica y Teoría en el Diseño de Experimentos 1957, Introduction to the Theory of Experimental Design 1960, Statistics for Mathematicians 1968, Statistics for Biologists 1980; more than 290 papers. *Leisure interests:* music, travel, statistics. *Address:* 13 Oswald Court, South Oswald Road, Edinburgh, EH9 2HY, Scotland. *Telephone:* (131) 667-0135 (Home). *Fax:* (131) 667-0135 (Home). *E-mail:* david.finney@freeuk.com (Home).

FINNEY, Sir Tom, Kt, CBE; British football official; b. 5 April 1922, Preston; s. of the late Alf Finney and Margaret Finney; m.; one s. one d.; ed ed. Deepdale Modern School; joined Preston North End Football Club 1940, retd 1960, now Pres.; played 433 league games for Preston, scored 187 goals; 76 England caps, scored 30 goals; Hon. Freeman of Preston 1979; Hon. LLD (Lancaster) 1998; Football Writers' Asscn Footballer of the Year 1954, 1957; Professional Football Asscn Merit Award 1979. *Publications:* Football Around the World 1953, Finney on Football 1958, Finney: A Football Legend 1990. *Leisure interests:* walking, golf, reading autobiographies. *Address:* 4 Newgate, Fulwood, Preston, PR2 8LR (Home); Preston North End Football Club, Deepdale, Sir Tom Finney Way, Preston, PR1 6RU, England. *Telephone:* (1772) 902020.

FINNIE, Linda Agnes; British singer; b. 9 May 1952, Paisley; d. of William Finnie and Agnes Finnie; ed John Neilson Institution, Paisley, Carrick Acad., Maybole, Royal Scottish Acad. of Music and Drama; concert performances in many European countries, Australasia, the Far East and USA and regular radio broadcasts; has sung with all the maj. British orchestras and with Chicago, Boston, Pittsburgh and San Francisco Symphony orchestras, Hong Kong Philharmonic, Orchestre de Paris, Orchestre Philharmonique de Radio France, RAI Orchestra (Turin) and Danish Radio Orchestra, under many leading conductors, including Claudio Abbado, Lorin Maazel, Daniel Barenboim, André Previn, Michael Tilson-Thomas, Jeffrey Tate, Sir John Pritchard, Sir Colin Davis, Simon Rattle, Andrew Davis, Esa Pekka Salonen, Neemi Jarvi and Richard Hickox; opera roles with ENO include Amneris, Eboli, Brangäne and Ulrica, with Royal Opera House, Waltraute, Mme. Larina, Second Norn; has also sung at Geneva, Nice, Bayreuth and Frankfurt; Hertogenbosch Concours, John Noble Bursary, Countess of Munster Scholarship; Kathleen Ferrier Memorial Award; Kathleen Ferrier Prize. *Recordings include:* Alexander Nevsky, Elijah, Beethoven's 9th Symphony, Songs of the British Isles, Armide, La Rondine and l'Enfant et les Sortilèges. *Leisure interests:* reading, driving, sewing, going to concerts and opera. *Address:* c/o Christopher Tennant, Unit 2, 39 Tadema Road, London, SW10 0PY, England (Office); 16 Golf Course, Girvan, Ayrshire, KA26 9HW, Scotland.

FINNIS, John Mitchell, LLB, DPhil, FBA; Australian university teacher and barrister; b. 28 July 1940, Adelaide; s. of the late Maurice M. S. Finnis and of Margaret McKellar Stewart; m. Marie Carmel McNally 1964; three s. three d.; ed St Peter's Coll., Adelaide, Univ. of Adelaide, Oxford Univ.; Fellow and Praelector in Jurisprudence, Univ. Coll., Oxford 1966–; Stowell Civil Law Fellow 1973–, Vice-Master 2001–; Lecturer in Law, Oxford Univ. 1966–72, Rhodes Reader in the Laws of the British Commonwealth and the United States 1972–89, Prof. of Law and Legal Philosophy 1989–, mem. Philosophy Sub-Faculty 1984–, Chair. Bd of Faculty of Law 1987–89; Prof. and Head of Dept of Law, Univ. of Malawi 1976–78; Biolchini Family Prof. of Law, Univ. of Notre Dame, Ind., USA 1995–, Adjunct Prof. of Philosophy 1999–; Barrister, Gray's Inn 1970–; Gov., Plater Coll., Oxford 1972–92; Consultor, Pontificia Commissio Iustitia et Pax 1977–89, mem. 1990–95; Special Adviser, Foreign Affairs Cttee, House of Commons, on role of UK Parl. in Canadian Constitution 1980–82; mem. Catholic Bishops' Jt Cttee on Bioethical Issues 1981–89, Int. Theological Comm. (Vatican) 1986–92; Gov., Linacre Centre for Medical Ethics 1981–96, 1998– (Vice-Chair. 1987–96); Distinguished Visiting Prof., Boston Coll. Law School 1993–94; mem. Pontifical Acad. for Life 2001–. *Publications:* Halsbury's Laws of England, 4th Edn, Vol. 6 (Commonwealth and Dependencies) 1974, Natural Law and Natural Rights 1980, Fundamentals of Ethics 1983, Nuclear Deterrence, Morality and Realism (with Joseph Boyle and Germain Grisez) 1987, Moral Absolutes 1991, Aquinas: Moral, Political and Legal Theory 1998; articles on constitutional law, legal philosophy, ethics and moral theology. *Address:* University College, Oxford, OX1 4BH; 12 Staverton Road, Oxford, OX2 6XJ, England (Home); Notre Dame Law School, Notre Dame, IN 46556, USA. *Telephone:* (1865) 276641 (UK); (1865) 558660 (UK) (Home); (219) 631-5989 (USA).

FINO, Bashkim Muhamet; Albanian politician and economist; b. 12 Oct. 1962, Gjirokaster; m.; two c.; ed Tirana Univ.; economist Economic Data Inst., Gjirokaster Dist 1986–89, Dir 1989–92; Mayor of Gjirokaster (Socialist Party of Albania) 1992–96; Prime Minister of Albania March–July 1997; Deputy Prime Minister 1997–98. *Address:* c/o Council of Ministers, Këshilli i Ministrave, Tirana, Albania.

FIONDA, Andrew, MA, M.Design; British fashion designer; b. 8 February 1967, Middlesbrough, Cleveland; s. of Frederick Fionda and of Sarah Park; ed Nottingham Trent Univ., Royal Coll. of Art; designer for fashion houses in UK and for John McIntyre (q.v.), Hong Kong; launched Pearce Fionda collection with Reynold Pearce (q.v.) 1994; exhbns. include Design of the Times, RCA 1996, The Cutting Edge of British Fashion 1997; Man. Dir Pearce Fionda (London) Ltd; with Reynold Pearce received British Apparel Export

Award for Best New Designer 1994, New Generation Award Lloyds Bank British Fashion Award 1995, Int. Apparel Fed. World Young Designers Award 1996; Lloyds Bank British Fashion Award (Glamour Category) 1997. *Leisure interests:* cinema, gym, music, reading. *Address:* Pearce Fionda, 27 Horsell Road, Highbury, London, N5 1XL, England (Office). *Telephone:* (20) 7609-6470 (Office). *E-mail:* pearcef@dircon.co.uk (Office).

FIORENTINO, Linda; American actress; b. 9 March 1960, Philadelphia, Pa; ed Rosemont Coll., Circle in the Square Theatre School; mem. Circle in the Square Performing Workshops. *Films:* Vision Quest 1985, Gotcha! 1985, After Hours 1985, The Moderns 1988, Queens Logic 1991, Shout 1991, Wildfire 1992, Chain of Desire 1993, The Desperate Trail 1994, The Last Seduction 1994, Bodily Harm 1995, Jade 1995, Unforgettable 1997, The Split 1997, Men in Black 1997, Kicked in the Head 1997, Dogma 1998, Ordinary Decent Criminal 1999, Where the Money Is 1999, What Planet Are You From? 2000, Liberty Stands Still 2002. *Television films:* The Neon Empire 1989, The Last Game 1992, Acting on Impulse 1993, Beyond the Law 1994, The Desperate Trail. *Address:* c/o United Talent Agency, 9560 Wilshire Boulevard, Floor 5, Beverly Hills, CA 90212, USA.

FIORI, Publio; Italian politician and lawyer; b. 1938; elected Christian Democrat mem. Rome City Council 1971, Lazio Regional Council 1975; Christian Democrat Deputy 1979–94, Alleanza Nazionale Deputy March 1994–; fmr mem. Parl. Comm. on Finance, Under-Sec. for Posts and Tele-communications, for Health; Minister of Transport 1994–95. *Address:* c/o Alleanza Nazionale,Via della Scrofa 39, 00186 Rome, Italy.

FIORINA, Carly (Carleton), MS; American computer executive; m.; two step-d.; ed Stanford Univ., Sloan School of Man., MIT; began career with entry-level job, Hewlett-Packard Shipping Dept; fmr English teacher and seller of telephone services to fed. agencies; fmr Pres. of a core division of Lucent Technologies Inc.; Pres., CEO Hewlett-Packard Co. 1999–, Chair. 2000–. *Leisure interests:* piano, gardening. *Address:* Hewlett-Packard Co., 3000 Hanover Street, Palo Alto, CA 94304-1181, USA (Office). *Telephone:* (415) 857 1501 (Office).

FIRTH, Colin; British actor; b. 10 Sept. 1960; s. of David Firth and Shirley Firth; one s. by Meg Tilly; ed Montgomery of Alamein School, Winchester and Drama Centre, London; Radio Times Best Actor Award for Tumbledown, 1996 Best Actor Award of Broadcasting Press Guild for Pride and Prejudice. *Theatre includes:* Another Country 1983, Doctor's Dilemma 1984, The Lonely Road 1985, Desire Under the Elms 1987, The Caretaker 1991, Chatsky 1993, Three Days of Rain 1999. *Television appearances:* Dutch Girls 1984, Lost Empires (series) 1985–86, Robert Lawrence in Tumbledown 1987, Out of the Blue 1990, Hostages 1992, Master of the Moor 1993, The Deep Blue Sea 1994, Mr Darcy in Pride and Prejudice 1994, Nostromo 1997, The Turn of the Screw 1999, Donovan Quick 1999. *Radio:* Richard II in Two Planks and a Passion 1986, Rupert Brooke in The One Before The Last 1987. *Films:* Another Country 1983, Camille 1984, A Month in the Country 1986, Apartment Zero 1988, Valmont (title role) 1988, Wings of Fame 1989, Femme Fatale 1990, The Hour of the Pig 1993, Good Girls 1994, Circle of Friends 1995, The English Patient 1996, Fever Pitch 1996, Shakespeare in Love 1998. The Secret Laughter of Women 1999, My Life So Far 1999, Relative Values 1999, Londinium 2000, Bridget Jones's Diary 2000, The Importance of Being Earnest 2002, Hope Springs 2003. *Address:* c/o ICM Ltd, Oxford House, 76 Oxford Street, London, W1N 0AX, England. *Telephone:* (20) 7636-6565. *Fax:* (20) 7323-0101.

FIRTH, Peter; British actor; b. 27 Oct. 1953, Bradford; s. of Eric Firth and Mavis Firth; m. Lindsey Readman 1990; two s. one d.; has appeared with Nat. Theatre in Equus, Romeo and Juliet, Spring Awakening; Broadway appear-ances include role of Mozart in Amadeus; has appeared in several TV films, plays and series; Acad. Award for Best Supporting Actor, Tony Award, Golden Globe for Best Supporting Actor (all for Equus) and numerous other awards. *Films include:* Brother Sun and Sister Moon, Daniel and Maria, Diamonds on Wheels, Aces High, Joseph Andrews, Equus, When You Coming Back Red Ryder?, Tess, Lifeforce, Letter to Brezhnev, A Tree of Hands, Prisoner of Rio, Burndown, The Pleasure Principle, The Perfect Husband, White Angel, Shadowlands, Brighton Boy, An Awfully Big Adventure, Brother Sun and Sister Moon, Amistad, Mighty Joe Young. *Plays:* Equus, Romeo and Juliet, Spring Awakening. *TV appearances include:* The Flaxon Boys, Home and Away, Black Beauty, The Picture of Dorian Gray, Northanger Abbey, A Murder in Eden, The Laughter of God, Children Crossing, Anna Lee, The Man at the Top, The Broker's Man, Holding On. *Leisure interests:* cookery, sailing. *Address:* Susan Smith Associates, 121 North San Vicente Boulevard, Beverly Hills, CA 90211, USA. *Telephone:* (213) 852-4777. *Fax:* (213) 658-7170.

FISCHEL VOLIO, Astrid, PhD; Costa Rican politician and university professor; b. 26 Mar. 1954, San José; ed Univ. of Costa Rica, Cen. American Inst. of Business Admin., Southampton Univ., UK; Prof., History and Geog-raphy School, Univ. of Costa Rica 1984–98, Dir Doctorate Programme in Educ. 1994–95; researcher Inst. of Research for the Improvement of Costa Rican Educ. 1986–98; Pres. Fischel Corpn 1991–97; Vice-Pres. Bd of Dirs. Chamber of Commerce of Costa Rica 1994–95; Co-ordinator Govt Platform, Unidad Social Cristiana political party 1995–97; Minister of Culture, Youth and Sports 1998–99; First Vice-Pres. of Costa Rica and Minister of Culture 1998–2002; Minister of Public Educ. 2002–; Aquileo J. Echeverría Nat. Award for History 1987, 1992, Enterprising Woman of the Year 1992. *Publications:* The National Theatre of Costa Rica: Its History 1992, The Magic Box. A

Hundred Years of History of the National Theatre 1997, Consensus and Repression, a Socio-Political Interpretation of Costa Rican Education 1987. *Address:* Ministry of Public Education, Apdo 10.087, 1000 San José, Costa Rica (Office). *Telephone:* 233-9050 (Office). *Fax:* 233-0390 (Office). *E-mail:* afischel@gobnet.go.cr (Office).

FISCHER, Adam; Austrian conductor; b. 9 Sept. 1949, Budapest, Hungary; m. Doris Fischer 1979; one s. one d.; ed Budapest School of Music; conducting and composition studies in Budapest and Vienna with Swarowsky; held posts at Graz Opera, Karlsruhe; Gen. Music Dir Freiburg; work with Bavarian State Opera; regular conductor with Vienna State Opera 1973–, recently with Zurich Opera; maj. debuts Paris Opera 1984, La Scala 1986, Royal Opera House 1989, ENO 1991, San Francisco Opera 1991, Chicago Lyric Opera 1991, Metropolitan Opera, New York 1994; has conducted many world-class orchestras, particularly Helsinki Philharmonic, Boston and Chicago Sym-phony and LA Philharmonic and Vienna Chamber Orchestra; concert tours to Japan and USA; Music Dir Kassel Opera 1987–92, Founder and Artistic Dir first Gustav Mahler Festival, Kassel 1989; f. Austro-Hungarian Haydn Festival and Orchestra, Eisenstadt, Austria 1987, later Music Dir AHHO; Music Dir Mannheim Opera 2000–; Conductor Bayreuth Festival (Ring Cycle) 2001–; Chief Conductor Danish Radio Sinfonietta; won Jt first prize Milan Cantelli Competition 1973. *Film:* BBC TV film of Bartok's Bluebird's Castle with LPO (Italia Prize 1989 and Charles Heidsieck Prize). *Music:* numerous recordings including complete Haydn symphonies, and Lucio Silla and Des Knabaen Wunderhorn with Danish Radio Sinfonietta. *Address:* c/o Askonas Holt Ltd, Lonsdale Chambers, 27 Chancery Lane, London, WC2A 1PF, England. *Telephone:* (20) 7400-1700. *Fax:* (20) 7400-1799.

FISCHER, Andrea; German politician; b. 14 Jan. 1960, Arnsberg; ed Freie Univ. Berlin 1985–90; trained as offset printer 1978–81; printer and corrector in Hamburg and Berlin 1981–85, also mem. Print and Paper TU, German TU Fed.; joined Green Party 1985; worked as journalist 1985–90; research Asst for labour market and social affairs European Parl. 1990–91; researcher Berlin Science Centre 1991–94; mem. Bundestag 1994–; spokesperson of Alliance 90/Greens Parl. Group 1994–; Fed. Minister of Health 1998–2001. *Address:* Platz der Republik 1, 11011 Berlin Germany (Office). *E-mail:* andrea .fischer@bundestag.de. *Website:* www.andrea-fischer.de.

FISCHER, August A.; Swiss newspaper executive; b. 7 Feb. 1939, Zürich; m. Gillian Ann Fischer 1961; one s. one d.; various positions E.I. Du Pont De Nemours & Co. 1962–78; Man. Dir European subsidiary of Napp Systems Inc. 1978–81, Exec. Vice-Pres., then Pres. and COO Napp Systems Inc., San Diego, Calif. 1981–89; Gen. Man. Devt, News Int. PLC 1989–90, Man. Dir 1990–95, mem. Bd and COO News Corpn Ltd 1991–95, Chief Exec. News Int. PLC (UK subsidiary of News Corpn) 1993–95; mem. Supervisory Bd Ringier AG, Zürich, consultant 1995–97; Chair. Bd and CEO Axel Springer Verlag AG 1998–; mem. American Man. Asscn, The Pres.'s Asscn; Trustee St Katharine and Shadwell Trust. *Address:* Axel Springer Verlag AG, Axel-Springer-str. 65, 10117 Berlin, Germany (Office).

FISCHER, Birgit; German canoeist; b. 25 Feb. 1962, Brandenburg; m. Jorg Schmidt (divorced); one c.; became youngest-ever Olympic canoeing winner 1980; became fifth athlete in history to win gold medals at five Olympic Games; retd after Olympic Games 2000 with a record tally of 7 Olympic gold medals and 3 silver medals, making her the most successful Olympian canoeist ever; holds record for most world championships in canoeing (29) 1979–98; now works in the youth programme for the German Canoe-Kayak Fed.

FISCHER, Edmond H., DèsSc; American professor of biochemistry; b. April 1920, Shanghai, China; s. of Oscar Fischer and Renee C. (née Tapernoux) Fischer; m. Beverley B. Bullock; two s.; ed Faculty of Sciences, Univ. of Geneva, Asst Labs of Organic Chem. Univ. of Geneva 1946–47; Fellow, Swiss Nat. Foundation 1948–50; Research Fellow, Rockefeller Foundation 1950–53; Privat-dozent, Univ. of Geneva 1950; Research Assoc. Div. of Biology, Calif. Inst. of Tech. 1953; Asst Prof. Univ. of Washington 1953–56, Assoc. Prof. 1956–61, Prof. of Biochem. 1961–90, Prof. Emer. 1990–; mem. numerous cttees, professional orgs etc.; Gov. Basel Inst. for Immunology 1996–, Weiz-mann Inst. of Science, Rehovot, Israel 1997–; mem. NAS, AAAS, American Acad. of Arts and Sciences, Swiss Chem. Soc., British Biochem. Soc.; Dr hc (Montpellier) 1985, (Basel) 1988; shared Nobel Prize for Medicine 1992, several other awards and honours. *Leisure interests:* classical piano, flying (pvt. pilot). *Address:* University of Washington Medical School, P.O. Box 357350, Seattle, WA 98195 (Office); 5540 NE Windermere Road, Seattle, WA, USA (Home). *Telephone:* (206) 523-7372 (Home). *E-mail:* efischer@u .washington.edu (Office).

FISCHER, Erik, MA; Danish art historian; b. 8 Oct. 1920, Copenhagen; s. of Adolf Fischer and Ellen Henius; ed Univ. of Copenhagen; Asst Keeper of Prints and Drawings, Royal Museum of Fine Arts, Copenhagen 1948–57, Keeper of Prints and Drawings 1957–90; Asst Prof. of Art History, Univ. of Copenhagen 1964–90; Chair. Danish State Art Foundation 1965–67, Bd, Queen Margrethe and Prince Henrik Foundation 1970–2002; Pres. Int. Advisory Cttee of Keepers of Public Collections of Graphic Art 1971–76; Hon. mem. Germanisches Nationalmuseum, Nuremberg 1977; mem. Bd Politiken Foundation 1990–2001; Fellow, Royal Danish Acad.; Assoc. Ateneo Veneto; Hon. mem. Royal Danish Acad. of Fine Arts 2000; Hon. DPhil (Copenhagen) 1991; Klein Prize 1973; Amalienborg Medal 1983, 2002, N.L. Høyen Medal, Royal Danish Acad. of Fine Arts 1989, Danish Literary Acad. Prize 1989,

Ingenio et Arti Medal 1990; Kt, Order of Dannebrog, Order of Nordstjernen. *Publications:* Moderne dansk Grafik 1957, Melchior Lorck Drawings 1962, Tegninger af C. W. Eckersberg 1983, Von Abildgaard bis Marstrand 1985, Billedtekster (anthology) 1988, C. W Eckersberg—His Mind and Times 1993. *Address:* Agergårdsvej 5, Ammendrup, 3200 Helsinge, Denmark. *Telephone:* 48-79-44-04. *Fax:* 48-79-44-04. *E-mail:* erikfischer@mail.tele.dk (Home).

FISCHER, Ernst Otto, Dr rer. nat, DiplChem; German professor of chemistry; b. 10 Nov. 1918, Munich-Solln; s. of the late Prof. Dr. Karl Tobias Fischer and Valentine Danzer; ed Theresiengymnasium and Tech. High School, Munich; Lecturer in Chem. 1954–57, Prof. of Inorganic Chem. 1964; Prof. of Inorganic Chem., Munich Univ. 1957–64, Univ. of Marburg 1960, 1964; Firestone Lecturer, Univ. of Wis. 1969; Visiting Prof., Univ. of Fla 1971; Inorganic Chem. Pacific West Coast Lecturer, USA, Canada 1971; Arthur D. Little Visiting Prof., MIT 1973; Visiting Distinguished Lecturer, Univ. of Rochester 1973; mem. Bayerische Akad. der Wissenschaften 1964, Deutsche Akad. der Naturforscher Leopoldina 1969; Corresp. mem. Austrian Acad. of Sciences 1976, Acad. of Sciences Göttingen 1977; Foreign mem. Accad. Naz. dei Lincei 1976; Foreign Hon. mem. American Acad. of Arts and Sciences 1977; Hon. Dr rer. nat (Univs of Munich 1972, Erlangen, Nuremberg 1977, Veszprém 1983); Hon. DSc (Strathclyde) 1975; ACS Centennial Fellow 1976; Göttinger Acad. Prize for Chem. 1957, Alfred-Stock-Gedächtnis Prize 1959, Nobel Prize for Chem. 1973. *Publications:* 500 scientific publs, $Fe(C_5H_5)_2$ Structure 1952, $Cr(C_6H_6)_2$ 1955, Übergangsmetall-Carben-Komplexe 1964, Übergangsmetall-Carbin-Komplexe 1973, Metal-Complexes Vol. I (with H. Werner) 1966. *Leisure interests:* history, arts, mountaineering. *Address:* Sohnckestrasse 16, 81479 Munich 71, Germany. *Telephone:* 794623.

FISCHER, Heinz, DIur; Austrian politician; b. 9 Oct. 1938, Graz; ed Univ. of Vienna; Sec. Socialist Parl. Party 1963–75, Exec., Floor Leader 1975–83, 1987–90, Deputy Chair. Socialist Party 1979–; mem. Nationalrat (Parl.) for Vienna 1971–, Pres. Nationalrat 1990–; Fed. Minister for Science and Research 1983–87; Deputy Chair. European Socialist Party 1992–; Co-Ed. Europäische Rundschau. *Publications:* Reflexionen 1999; numerous books and articles on law and political science. *Address:* Nationalrat, Dr. Karl-Renner Ring 3, 1017 Vienna, Austria (Office). *Telephone:* (1) 401102201 (Office). *Fax:* (1) 401102345 (Office). *E-mail:* heinz.fischer@parlinkom.gv.at (Office). *Website:* www.parliament.at (Office).

FISCHER, Ivan; Hungarian/Dutch conductor; b. 20 Jan. 1951, Budapest; s. of Sándor Fischer and Éva Boschán; two d.; ed B. Bartók Music Conservatory, Budapest and Wiener Hochschule für Musik under Hans Swarowsky, Mozarteum, Salzburg under Nikolaus Harnoncourt; Jt Music Dir Northern Sinfonia of England, Newcastle 1979–82; Music Dir Kent Opera 1984–; Prin. Guest Conductor Cincinnati Symphony Orchestra 1989–96; Music Dir. Lyon Opera House 1999–; Founder and Music Dir Budapest Festival Orchestra 1983; debut in London with Royal Philharmonic Orchestra 1976; concert tours with London Symphony Orchestra to Spain 1981, USA 1982, world tour 1983; concerts with Berlin Philharmonic Orchestra, Concertgebouw Orchestra etc.; main performances in U.S.A.: Los Angeles Philharmonic, Cleveland, Philadelphia, San Francisco Symphony and Chicago Symphony Orchestras; operas: Idomeneo, Don Giovanni, Julius Caesar, La Bohème, La Clemenza di Tito, Marriage of Figaro, Magic Flute, in London, Paris, Vienna; Premio Firenze 1974, Rupert Foundation Award, BBC, London 1976, Gramophone Award for Best Orchestral Recording of the Year (for The Miraculous Mandarin), Philips 1998. *Address:* 1061 Budapest, 1 Andrássy út 27, Hungary. *Telephone:* (1) 342-6061.

FISCHER, Joseph (Joschka); German politician; b. 12 April 1948, Gerabronn; mem. Green Party 1982–, currently Leader; mem. German Bundestag 1983–85; Minister of the Environment and Energy, Hesse 1985–87, of the Environment, Energy and Fed. Affairs 1991–94; Deputy mem. Bundesrat (Federal Council) 1985–87; Chair. Green Parl. Group, Hesse Parl. 1987–91; Deputy Minister-Pres. of Hesse 1991–98; Vice-Chancellor and Minister of Foreign Affairs, Fed. Govt 1998–; Speaker Parl. Group Alliance 90/Greens, Bundestag 1994–98. *Address:* Ministry of Foreign Affairs, Werderscher Markt 1, 10117 Berlin, Germany (Office). *Telephone:* (1888) 170 (Office). *Fax:* (1888) 173402 (Office). *E-mail:* poststelle@auswaertiges-amt.de (Office). *Website:* www.auswaertiges-amt.de (Office).

FISCHER, Paul Henning, DIur; Danish diplomatist; b. 24 March 1919, Copenhagen; s. of Ernst Fischer and Ellen Dahl; m. Jytte Kalckar 1945; one s.; ed Lyceum Alpinum, Zuoz, Switzerland and Univ. of Copenhagen; Foreign Service 1944–89, Stockholm, The Hague, Ministry of Foreign Affairs 1944–60; Asst Prof. Univ. of Copenhagen 1948–52; Del. Gen. Ass., UN 1959, 1961; Amb. to Poland 1960–61; Perm. Under-Sec. of State for Foreign Affairs 1961–71; Amb. to France 1971–80, to FRG 1980–89; mem. UN register for fact-finding experts in internal disputes; mem. Perm. Court of Arbitration, The Hague 1982; Judge ad hoc Int. Court of Justice, The Hague 1988; mem. CSCE Dispute Settlement Mechanism; Treasurer of the Royal Orders; Chamberlain of HM Queen Margrethe; Grand Cross Order of Dannebrog and foreign decorations. *Publications:* European Coal and Steel Community, International Law Studies on International Co-operation; numerous articles. *Leisure interests:* literature, music. *Address:* Straedet 8, Borsholm, DK-3100 Hornbaek, Denmark. *Telephone:* 49-75-01-51 (Home).

FISCHER, Robert James (Bobby); American chess player; b. 9 March 1943, Chicago, Ill.; s. of Gerard Fischer and Regina (Wender) Fischer; started to play chess aged 6; mem. Manhattan Chess Club 1955; US Junior Chess Champion 1956, 1957; winner, US Open Championship 1957, 1959, 1960, 1962, 1963; participated in Interzonal Tournament, Portoroz, Yugoslavia 1958; named Int. Grand Master (the youngest ever) 1958; has participated in numerous int. chess tournaments 1958–; defeated Boris Spassky (q.v.) to become World Chess Champion 1972–75, thereafter refused to compete, forfeiting his title, but briefly returned to public competition in 1992 to defeat Spassky in Yugoslavia; City of New York Gold Medal 1972. *Publications:* Games of Chess 1959, My Sixty Memorable Games 1969, Bobby Fischer Teaches Chess 1972. *Address:* c/o United States Chess Federation, 186 Route 9W, New Windsor, NY 12550, USA.

FISCHER, Stanley, MSc, PhD; American economist; b. 15 Oct. 1943, Lusaka, Zambia; s. of Philip Fischer and Ann Kopelowitz; m. Rhoda Keet 1965; three s.; ed Univ. of London and MIT; Postdoctoral Fellow Univ. of Chicago 1969–70, Asst Prof. of Econs 1970–73; Assoc. Prof. MIT 1973–77, Prof. 1977–88, 1990, Killian Prof. 1992–94, Head of Dept 1993; Vice-Pres. and Chief Economist World Bank, Washington, DC 1988–90; Visiting Sr Lecturer Hebrew Univ., Jerusalem 1972, Fellow Inst. for Advanced Studies 1976–77, Visiting Prof. 1984; Visiting Scholar Hoover Inst. Stanford Univ. 1981–82; Consultant on Israeli Economy Dept of State 1984–87, 1991–94; First Deputy Man. Dir IMF 1994–2001; Vice-Chair. Citigroup 2002–; Pres. Citigroup Int. 2002–; Fellow Econometric Soc., American Acad. of Arts and Sciences. *Publications:* Rational Expectations and Economic Policy (Ed.) 1980, Indexing, Inflation and Economic Policy 1986, Macroeconomics and Finance: Essays in Honor of Franco Modigliani (Ed.) 1987, Economics (with Dornbusch and Schmalensee) 1988, Lectures in Macroeconomics (jtly) 1989, Macroeconomics (with Dornbusch) 1994, Ed. NBER Macroeconomics Annual and work on int. econ. and macroecon. issues. *Address:* Citibank NA, 399 Park Avenue, New York, NY 10022; 15 Gralynn Road, Newton, MA 02159, USA (Home). *Telephone:* (617) 964-2494 (Home). *E-mail:* fischers@citi.com. *Website:* www.citigroup.com.

FISCHER, Timothy Andrew; Australian politician; b. 3 May 1946, Lockhart, NSW; s. of J. R. Fischer and Barbara Mary Fischer; m. Judy Brewer 1992; two s.; ed Boree Creek School, Xavier Coll., Melbourne; joined Army 1966, officer with First Bn, Royal Australian Regt, Australia and Vietnam 1966–69; farmer, Boree Creek, NSW; mem. NSW Legis. Ass. 1970–84; MP for Farrer, NSW 1984–2002; Shadow Minister for Veterans' Affairs 1985–89 and Deputy Man. of Opposition Business 1989–90; Leader Nat. Party of Australia 1990–99; Shadow Minister for Energy and Resources 1990–93, for Trade 1993–96; Deputy Prime Minister and Minister for Trade 1996–99; Royal Decoration for Service to the Kingdom of Thailand 1997. *Leisure interests:* chess, tennis, skiing, water skiing, bush-walking, mountaineering. *Address:* 520 Swift Street, Albury, NSW 2640; P.O. Box 10, Boree Creek, NSW 2652, Australia.

FISCHER, Václav; Czech business executive; b. 22 June 1954; m. (divorced); ed School of Econs, Prague; fmr tourist guide, Prague; emigrated to Germany 1978, f. Fischer Reisen (travel agents) 1980; returned to Czechoslovakia 1989, f. Czech br. Fischer Reisen; f. Fischer a.s. 1996; mem. Senate 1999–2002; Matěj Hrebenda Prize for contribution to prosperous relations between Czech Repub. and Slovakia 2001. *Publications:* I am Writing to You. *Leisure interests:* cycling, theatre, travel. *Address:* Fischer a.s., Provaznická 13, 110 00 Prague 1, Czech Republic (Office). *Telephone:* (2) 21636501 (Office). *Fax:* (2) 21636517 (Office). *E-mail:* info@fischer.cz (Office).

FISCHER-APPELT, Peter, DTheol; German university administrator; b. 28 Oct. 1932, Berlin; s. of Hans Fischer-Appelt and Margret Fischer-Appelt (née Appelt); m. Hildegard Zeller 1959; two s. one d.; ed Schubart-Oberschule, Aalen and Univs. of Tübingen, Heidelberg and Bonn; Scientific Asst, Protestant Theology Faculty, Univ. of Bonn 1961–70; Pastor, Cologne-Mülheim 1964–65; Co-founder and Chair. Bundesassistentenkonferenz, Bonn 1968–69; Pres. Univ. of Hamburg 1970–91, Pres. Emer. 1991–, teaching assignment in Systematic Theology 1972–; Pres. 'Cyril and Methodius' Int. Foundation, Sofia 1992–98; mem. Exec. Cttee Inter-Univ. Centre for Postgrad. Studies, Dubrovnik 1974–81, Chair. of Council 1981–98; mem. Standing Conf. on Univ. Problems, Council of Europe 1987–94, Deputy Chair. 1987–88, Chair. 1989–90; Chair. Steering Group, Higher Educ. Legislation Reform Programme for Cen. and Eastern Europe 1992–98; mem. and Chair. Bd of Trustees UNESCO Inst. for Educ., Hamburg 1992–96; mem. German Comm. UNESCO 1991–; mem. Bd of Trustees, Deutscher Akad. Austauschdienst 1973– and various other comms., etc.; numerous hon. degrees; Gold Medal, Bulgarian Acad. of Sciences, Pro Cultura Hungarica Medal, Horseman of Madara (First Class), Order of Cyril and Methodius, Bulgaria (First Class), Medal of the Comm. of Nat. Educ., Poland 2001, Medal PRO MERITO of the Council of Europe. *Publications:* Metaphysik im Horizont der Theologie Wilhelm Herrmanns 1965, Albrecht Ritschl und Wilhelm Herrmann 1968, Rechtfertigung 1968, Wissenschaft und Politik 1971, Zum Verständnis des Glaubens in der liberalen und dialektischen Theologie 1973, Zum Gedenken an Ernst Cassirer 1975, Integration of Young Scientists into the University 1975, Wilhelm Herrmann 1978, Hiob oder die Unveräusserlichkeit der Erde 1981, The Future of the University as a Research Institution 1982, Was darf ich hoffen? Erwartungen an das Musiktheater 1982, Die Oper als Denk- und Spielmodell 1983, Die Kunst der Fuge: Ein deutsches Forschungsnetz im Aufbau 1984, Dialogue and Co-operation for World Peace Today 1985, Die Universität zwischen Staatseinfluss und Autonomie 1986, The University in the 21st Century 1988, Die Ostpolitik der Universitäten 1992, Die Universität im Prozess der Humanisierung der Gesellschaft 1994, Wer hat Angst vor den Wandlungen der Universität 1994, Die Erhellung des Mythos durch die

Sprache der Musik 1995, The University: Past, Present and Future 1996, Concepts of the University 1997, Die Buchstaben und Europa 1997, One Europe to Tend 2000, Gottes Sein im Werden des Wissens 2000, Hochschulpolitik als Sozialpolitik 2001, Wissenschaft in der Kaufmannsrepublik 2002, Felix Mendelssohn Bartholdy und Arnold Schönberg 2003. *Leisure interests:* chess, skiing, music, opera, theatre. *Address:* Waldweg 22, 25451 Quickborn-Heide, Germany. *Telephone:* (4106) 71212 (Home). *Fax:* (4106) 78637.

FISCHER-DIESKAU, Dietrich; German baritone; b. 28 May 1925, Berlin; s. of Dr. Albert Fischer-Dieskau and Dora Klinghöffer; m. 1st Irmgard Poppen 1949 (died 1963); three s.; m. 2nd Ruth Leuwerik 1965 (divorced 1967); m. 3rd Kristina Pugell 1968; m. 4th Julia Varady 1978; ed high school in Berlin, singing studies with Prof. Georg Walter and Prof. Hermann Weissenborn; mil. service 1943–45; POW in Italy until 1947; First Lyric and Character Baritone, Berlin State Opera 1948–; mem. Vienna State Opera Co. 1957–; Prof. of Singing Musikhochschule Berlin 1981–; numerous concert tours in Europe, USA and Asia; has appeared at a number of festivals: Bayreuth, Salzburg, Lucerne, Montreux, Edin., Vienna, Holland, Munich, Berlin, Coventry, etc.; best-known roles in Falstaff, Don Giovanni, The Marriage of Figaro, etc.; first performances of contemporary composers Britten, Henze, Tippett, etc.; mem. Akad. der Künste, Bayerische Akademie der Schönen Künste, Munich, Int. Mahler-Gesellschaft (Vienna) and German Section, Int. Music Council, High School for Music and Theatre, Munich 1999; Hon. mem. Wiener Konzerthausgesellschaft 1963, RAM (London), Royal Acad. (Stockholm), Deutschen Oper, Berlin 1978, Royal Philharmonic Soc.; Hon. DUniv (Oxford) 1978; Hon. DMus (Paris-Sorbonne) 1980, (Yale) 1980; Int. Recording Prizes almost every year since 1955; Berlin Kunstpreis 1950, Mantua Golden Orpheus Prize 1955; Bundesverdienstkreuz, 1st Class 1958; Edison Prize 1960, 1962, 1964, 1965, 1967, 1970; President's Prize, Charles Gros Acad., Paris 1980; Förderungspreis der Ernst-von-Siemens-Stiftung 1980; Mozart Medal 1962, Golden Orpheus 1967; Grosses Verdienstkreuz des Verdienstordens der Bundesrepublik Deutschland 1974; Grammy Award (more than once); Prix Mondial Montreux (more than once), etc.; Chevalier Légion d'honneur 1990; Ernst-Reuter-Plak 1993. *Publications:* Texte deutscher Lieder 1968, Auf den Spuren der Schubert-Lieder 1971, Wagner und Nietzsche, der Mystagoge und sein Abtrünniger 1974, Franz Schubert, ein Portrait 1976, Robert Schumann-Wort und Musik 1981, Töne sprechen, Worte klingen-Zur Geschichte und Interpretation des Gesanges 1985, Nachklang 1987, Wenn Musik der Liebe Nahrung ist: Künstlerschicksale im 19. Jahrhundert 1990, Johann Friedrich Reichardt: Kapellmeister dreier Preussenkönige 1992. *Leisure interest:* painting. *Address:* c/o Deutsche Verlanganstalt, Stüttgart, Germany (Office).

FISCHL, Eric, BFA; American artist; b. 9 March 1948; ed Phoenix Junior Coll., Ariz., Arizona State Univ., Tempe; California Inst. of the Arts; taught painting Nova Scotia Coll. of Art and Design, Halifax 1974–78, works in Museum of Contemporary Art, LA, Whitney Museum etc. and in pvt. collections, including Saatchi Collection, London, UK. *Solo exhibitions include:* Dalhousie Art Gallery, Halifax 1976, subsequent exhbns. at Mary Boone Gallery, New York, Whitney, Museum, Mendel Art Gallery, Saskatoon, Sask., Edward Thorp Gallery, New York, Mario Diacono Gallery, Rome, Italy, Museum of Contemporary Art, Chicago, Sidney Janis Gallery, New York, 1984 Venice Biennale, 13th Biennale de Paris, 1985 Carnegie Int., Pittsburgh.

FISCHLER, Franz; Austrian politician; b. 23 Sept. 1946, Absam, Tyrol; m.; two s. two d.; ed Franciscan secondary school, Tyrol and Agricultural Univ., Vienna; Asst Univ. of Vienna Dept of Agricultural Econs. 1973–79; Dept Head Tyrolean Provincial Chamber of Agric. 1979, Sec. 1982, Dir 1985–89; Minister of Agric. and Forestry 1989–94; EU Commr for Agric. and Rural Devt 1995–99, for Agric., Rural Devt and Fisheries 1999–. *Address:* European Commission, L 130 08/188, 1049 Brussels, Belgium (Office). *Telephone:* (2) 299-11-11 (Office). *E-mail:* kabinett-fischler@cec.eu.int (Office). *Website:* europa.eu.int/comm/commissioners/fischler/index_en.htm (Office).

FISHBURNE, Laurence; American actor; b. 30 July 1961, Augusta, Georgia; s. of Laurence John Jr and Hattie Bell Crawford Fishburne; m. Hanja Moss 1985 (divorced); one s. one d. *Stage appearances include:* Short Eyes, Two Trains Running, Riff Raff (also writer and Dir). *Television appearances include:* One Life to Live (series, debut aged 11), Pee-wee's Playhouse, Tribeca (Emmy Award 1993), A Rumour of War, I Take These Men, Father Clements Story, Decoration Day, The Tuskegee Airmen, Miss Ever's Boys, Always Outnumbered. *Film appearances include:* Cornbread Earl and Me 1975, Fast Break, Apocalypse Now, Willie and Phil, Death Wish II, Rumble Fish, The Cotton Club, The Color Purple, Quicksilver, Band of the Hand, A Nightmare on Elm Street 3: Dream Warriors, Gardens of Stone, School Daze, Red Heat, King of New York, Cadence, Class Action, Boyz 'N the Hood, Deep Cover, What's Love Got to Do With It? Searching for Bobby Fischer, Higher Learning, Bad Company, Just Cause, Othello, Fled, Hoodlums (also exec. producer), Event Horizon, Welcome to Hollywood, Once in the Life (also Writer), The Matrix 1999, Michael Jordan to the Max 2000, Once in the Life 2000, Osmosis Jones 2001, The Matrix Reloaded 2003, The Matrix Revolutions 2003. *Address:* c/o Paradigm, 10100 Santa Monica Boulevard, 25th Floor, Los Angeles, CA 90067, USA.

FISHER, Carrie; American actress and author; b. 21 Oct. 1956, Beverly Hills; d. of Eddie Fisher and Debbie Reynolds; m. Paul Simon 1983 (divorced 1984); one d.; ed Beverly Hills High School and Cen. School of Speech and Drama, London; appeared with her mother in nightclub act aged 13; appeared in chorus of Broadway production of Irene, starring Debbie Reynolds, aged 15; Broadway stage appearances in Censored Scenes from King Kong, Agnes of God; several TV credits; film debut in Shampoo (Photoplay Award as Best Newcomer of the Year) 1974; PEN Award for first novel Postcards From the Edge (also wrote screenplay). *Films include:* Star Wars, The Empire Strikes Back, Return of the Jedi, The Blues Brothers, Under the Rainbow, Garbo Talks, The Man With One Red Shoe, When Harry Met Sally . . ., Hannah and Her Sisters, The 'Burbs, Loverboy, Sibling Rivalry, Drop Dead Fred, Soapdish, This is My Life, Austin Powers: International Man of Mystery, Scream 3, Famous, Heartbreakers 2001, Jay and Silent Bob Strike Back 2001, A Midsummer Night's Rave 2002. *Publications:* Postcards From the Edge 1987, Surrender the Pink 1990, Delusions of Grandma 1994 (novels); short stories. *Address:* Creative Artists Agency, 9830 Wilshire Boulevard, Beverly Hills, CA 90212, USA.

FISHER, Donald G., BS; American business executive; b. 1928; m.; ed Univ. of Calif.; with M. Fisher & Son 1950–57; fmr partner, Fisher Property Investment Co.; Co-founder, Pres. The Gap Stores Inc., San Bruno, Calif., Chair. 1996–. *Address:* The Gap Stores, 1 Harrison Street, San Francisco, CA 94105, USA (Office).

FISHER, Hon. Sir Henry (Arthur Pears), Kt, MA; British business executive, lawyer and college principal; b. 20 Jan. 1918, Repton, Derbyshire; s. of the late Lord Fisher of Lambeth (Archbishop of Canterbury, 1945–61) and of Lady Fisher of Lambeth; m. Felicity Sutton 1948; one s. three d.; ed Marlborough Coll., Christ Church, Oxford; served in Leics. Regt (rank of Hon. Lt-Col) 1940–46; Barrister-at-law 1947–68, QC 1960, Judge of the High Court 1968–70; Dir J. Henry Schroder Wagg and Co. Ltd 1970–75, Thomas Tilling Ltd 1970–83, Equity and Law Life Assurance Soc. Ltd 1975–88; conducted inquiry into the Confait Case 1976–77; Chair. Bd of Govs Imperial Coll. 1975–88, of Council, Marlborough Coll. 1977–82, Cttee of Inquiry into Self-regulation at Lloyd's 1979–80, Appeal Cttee of City Takeover Panel 1981–87, Investment Man. Regulatory Org. 1986–89; Pres. Wolfson Coll., Oxford 1975–85, Hon. Fellow 1985; Trustee, Pilgrim Trust 1965–92, Chair. 1979–83, 1989–92; Fellow, All Souls Coll., Oxford 1946–73, 1991–, Emer. 1976–91, Estates Bursar 1961–66, Sub-Warden 1965–67; Hon. mem. Lloyds 1983; Hon. Fellow, Darwin Coll., Cambridge 1984; Hon. LLD (Hull) 1979. *Leisure interest:* music. *Address:* Garden End, Cross Lane, Marlborough, Wilts., SN8 1LA, England. *Telephone:* (1672) 515420.

FISHER, Joel, BA; American sculptor; b. 6 June 1947, Salem, Ohio; s. of James R. and Marye (née Giffin) Fisher; m. Pamela Robertson-Pearce 1977 (divorced); one s.; ed Kenyon Coll. Ohio; lecturer numerous schools; Artist in Residence, Univ. of Auckland 2000; Kress Foundation Art History Award 1967, 1968, Gast der Berliner Kunstler Program des DAAD 1973–74, 1994, George A. and Eliza Gardner Howard Foundation Fellow 1987, Guggenheim Fellow 1993, Pollock-Krassner Foundation Award 1993, Henry Moore Fellowship (Newcastle upon Tyne) 2001–03. *Art exhibitions:* over 30 one-person exhbns and many group exhbns in USA and Europe 1961–; works in many public collections. *Address:* 99 Commercial Street, Brooklyn, NY 11222 (Studio); P.O. Box 349, River Road, North Troy, VT 05859, USA (Home); c/o Dept of Fine Arts, Univ. of Newcastle, The Quadrangle, Newcastle upon Tyne, NE1 7RU, England (Office). *Telephone:* (718) 383-3704 (Studio); (191) 222-6036 (Office); (802) 988-2870 (Home). *Fax:* (802) 988-2870. *E-mail:* j.a.fisher@ncl.ac.uk (Office).

FISHER, Kenneth L., BA; American business executive and writer; b. 1950, San Francisco ; s. of Philip A. Fischer; m.; one s.; ed Humboldt State Univ.; began career in his father's investment firm; Founder, Chair. and CEO Fisher Investments 1978–, f. Fisher Investments Europe 2000; columnist, Forbes Magazine 1984–. *Publications include:* Super Stocks 1984, The Wall Street Waltz, 100 Minds that Made the Market; various research papers on investment and stocks. *Address:* Fisher Investments Inc., 13100 Skyline Boulevard, Woodside, CA 94062, USA (Office). *Telephone:* (800) 851-8845 (Office). *Fax:* (650) 851-3514 (Office). *E-mail:* info@fi.com (Office). *Website:* www.fi.com (Office).

FISHER, Michael Ellis, PhD, FRS, FAAS; British professor of chemistry, physics and mathematics; b. 3 Sept. 1931, Trinidad, West Indies; s. of Harold Wolf Fisher and Jeanne Marie Fisher (née Halter); m. Sorrel Castillejo 1954; three s. one d.; ed King's Coll., London; London Univ. Postgraduate Studentship 1953–56; DSIR Sr Research Fellow 1956–58; Lecturer in Theoretical Physics, King's Coll., London 1958–62, Reader in Physics 1962–64, Prof. 1965–66; Prof. of Chem. and Math., Cornell Univ., USA 1966–73, Horace White Prof. of Chem., Physics and Math. 1973–89, Chair. Dept of Chem. 1975–78; Wilson H. Elkins Prof., Inst. for Science and Tech., Univ. of Md 1987–93, Distinguished Univ. Prof. and Regent's Prof. 1993–; Guest Investigator, Rockefeller Inst., New York 1963–64; Visiting Prof. of Applied Physics, Stanford Univ., USA 1970–71; Walter Ames Prof., Univ. of Wash. 1977; Visiting Prof. of Physics, MIT 1979; Visiting Prof. of Theoretical Physics, Oxford 1985; Lorentz Prof., Univ. of Leiden 1993; Visiting Prof., Nat. Inst. of Standards and Tech., Gaithersburg, Md 1993; George Fisher Baker Lecturer, Cornell Univ. 1997; John Simon Guggenheim Memorial Fellow 1970–71, 1978–79; mem. American Philosophical Soc.; Fellow American Acad. of Arts and Sciences; Foreign Assoc., NAS; Foreign mem. Brazilian Acad. of Sciences; Festschrift and Conf. in honour of 60th Birthday: Current Problems in Statistical Mechanics 1991; Hon. FRSE; Hon. DSc (Yale) 1987; Hon. DPhil (Tel Aviv) 1992; Jr Collectors Silver Cup, British Philatelic Exhbn

1946, Irving Langmuir Prize in Chemical Physics, American Physical Soc. 1970, Award in Physical and Math. Sciences, New York Acad. of Sciences 1978, Guthrie Medal, Inst. of Physics 1980, Wolf Prize in Physics, Israel 1980, Michelson-Morely Award, Case-Western Reserve Univ. 1982, James Murray Luck Award, NAS 1983, Boltzmann Medal, IUPAP 1983, Lars Onsager Medal, Norwegian Inst. of Tech. 1993, Joel H. Hildebrand Award for Chem. of Liquids 1995, Hirschfelder Prize in Theoretical Chem., Univ. of Wis. 1995, First Lars Onsager Memorial Prize, American Physical Soc. 1995, G. N. Lewis Memorial Lecture Award, Univ. of Calif. 1995, American Physical Soc. Centennial Speaker 1998. *Publications:* Analogue Computing at Ultra-High Speed (with D. M. MacKay) 1962, The Nature of Critical Points 1964; contribs to scientific journals. *Leisure interests:* Flamenco guitar, travel. *Address:* Institute for Physical Science and Technology, University of Maryland, College Park, MD 20742, USA. *Telephone:* (301) 405-4819 (Office). *Fax:* (301) 314-9404.

FISHLOW, Albert, PhD; American professor of economics; b. 21 Nov. 1935, Philadelphia; m. Harriet Fishlow 1957; one s. two d.; ed Univ. of Pennsylvania, Harvard Univ.; Acting Asst Prof., Assoc. Prof., then Prof., Univ. of Calif. at Berkeley 1961–77, Prof. of Econs 1983–, Chair. Dept of Econs 1973–75, 1985–89, Dean Int. and Area Studies 1990, Dir Int. House 1990–, mem. Berkeley Foundation Trustees Int. Cttee 1990–; Prof. of Econs, Yale Univ. 1978–83; Visiting Fellow, All Souls Coll. Oxford 1972–73 (Guggenheim Fellow); Co-Ed. Journal of Devt Econs 1986–; Dir-at-large, Bd of Social Science Research Council 1990–; Deputy Asst Sec. of State for Inter-American Affairs 1975–76; mem. Council on Foreign Relations 1975–; Consultant to Rockefeller, Ford and other foundations, fmr Consultant to World Bank, Inter-American Devt Bank, UNDP; David Wells Prize, Harvard 1963, Arthur H. Cole Prize, Econ. History Asscn 1966, Joseph Schumpeter Prize, Harvard 1971, Outstanding Service Award, Dept of State 1976. *Publications include:* American Railroads and the Transformation of the Ante Bellum Economy 1965, International Trade, Investment, Macro Policies and History: Essays in Memory of Carlos F. Diaz-Alejandro (Co-Ed.) 1987; numerous articles. *Address:* Department of Economics, University of California, Berkeley, CA 94720, USA. *Telephone:* (510) 642-4827. *Fax:* (510) 642-6615.

FISIAK, Jacek, OBE, PhD, DLitt; Polish philologist and linguist; b. 10 May 1936, Konstantynów Łódzki; s. of Czesław Fisiak and Jadwiga Fisiak; m. Liliana Sikorska; ed Warsaw Univ.; staff mem. Łódź Univ. 1959–67, Asst Prof. 1962–67; staff mem. Adam Mickiewicz Univ., Poznań 1965–, Head English Philology Dept 1965–69, Dir English Philology Inst. 1969–, Extraordinary Prof. 1971–77, Prof. 1977–, Rector 1985–88; Chair. Comm. on Modern Languages and Literature, Ministry of Higher Educ. 1974–88; Minister of Educ. 1988–89; participant Round Table debates 1989; Visiting Prof. Univ. of Calif., LA 1963–64, Univ. of Kan. 1970, Univ. of Fla 1974, State Univ. of New York 1975, American Univ., Washington, DC 1979–80, 1991–92, Univ. of Kiel 1979–80, Vienna Univ. 1983, 1988–89, 1990–91, Univ of Zürich 1984, 1994, Univ. of Tromsø 1986, Univ. of Jyväskylä 1987, Univ. of Saarbrücken 1990, 1993, Univ. of Bamberg 1994; Ed. Studia Anglica Posnaniensia 1967–99, Papers and Studies in Contrastive Linguistics 1972–, Ed.-in-Chief Folia Linguistic Historica 1978–; Pres. Int. Asscn of Univ. Profs of English 1974–77, Societas Linguistica Europaea 1982–83, Int. Soc. for Historical Linguistics 1981–83; Chair. Neophilological Cttee, Polish Acad. of Sciences 1981–93; mem. Finnish Acad. of Sciences and Humanities 1990, Academia Europaea 1990, Norwegian Acad. of Sciences 1996, New York Acad. of Sciences 1996, Medieval Acad. of America 2001; Pres. Polish-British Friendship Soc. 1989–; mem. editorial bds of numerous foreign and int. philological journals, numerous scientific socs; consultant Ford Foundation, IREX, Swedish Govt, Austrian Ministry of Higher Educ., Encyclopaedia Britannica (Chicago); Dr. hc (Jyväskylä) 1982; Commdr.'s Cross of Polonia Restituta Order with Star, Officer's Cross of Polonia Restituta, Nat. Educ. Comm. Medal, Commdr's Cross of Lion of Finland Order, Officier, Ordre des Palmes académiques and numerous other decorations. *Publications:* 153 publs, 37 books including Morphemic Structure of Chaucer's English 1965, A Short Grammar of Middle English 1968, 1996, Recent Developments in Historical Phonology (ed.) 1978, Historical Syntax (ed.) 1983, A Bibliography of Writings for the History of English 1987, Historical Dialectology (ed.) 1990, An Outline History of English 1993, 2000, Medieval Dialectology 1995, Linguistic Change Under Contact Conditions 1995, Studies in Middle English Linguistics 1997, Typology and Linguistics Reconstruction 1997, East Anglia (co-author with P. Trudgill) 2001, The New Kościuszko Foundation Dictionary (English–Polish, Polish–English) 2003. *Leisure interests:* history, sport. *Address:* ul. Śniadeckich 30 m. 8, 60-774 Poznań, Poland (Home). *Telephone:* (61) 8659764 (Home).

FISICHELLA, Domenico; Italian politician and university professor; b. 15 Sept. 1935, Messina, Sicily; Prof. of Political Science, Università La Sapienza and Libera Università Internazionale degli Studi Sociali (LUISS), Rome; co-f. Alleanza Nazionale Party 1992, elected Senator 1994; Minister of Culture 1994–95. *Publications:* numerous books on political subjects; articles in nat. dailies. *Address:* c/o Ministero per i beni culturali e Ambientali, Via del Collegio Romano 27, 00186 Rome, Italy.

FISK, David John, CB, ScD, CEng, FREng, FInstP; British government scientist; b. 9 Jan. 1947; s. of the late John Howard Fisk and of Rebecca Elizabeth Fisk (née Haynes); m. Anne Thoday 1972; one s. one d.; ed Stationers' Co. School, Hornsey, St John's Coll. Cambridge and Univ. of Manchester; joined Bldg Research Establishment, Sr Prin. Scientific Officer, Head, Mechanical and Electrical Eng Div. 1978–84; with Dept of Environment (then Dept of the Environment, Transport and the Regions, then Dept for Transport, Local Govt and the Regions, now Office of the Deputy Prime Minister—ODPM) 1984–, Asst Sec. Cen. Directorate of Environmental Protection 1984–87, Under-Sec. 1987, Deputy Chief Scientist 1987–88, Chief Scientific Adviser 1988– (Dir Air Climate and Toxic Substances Directorate 1990–95, Environment and Int. Directorate 1995–98, Cen. Strategy Directorate 1999–2002); Visiting Prof. Univ. of Liverpool 1988–2002; Dir Watford Palace Theatre 2000–; Royal Acad. of Eng Prof. of Eng for Sustainable Devt, Imperial Coll. of Science, London 2002–; Hon. Fellow Chartered Inst. of Bldg Service Engineers. *Publications:* Thermal Control of Buildings 1981; numerous papers on bldg science, systems theory and econs. *Leisure interests:* theatre, music. *Address:* c/o Office of the Deputy Prime Minister, Eland House, Bressenden Place, London, SW1E 5DU (Office); Department of Civil and Environmental Engineering, Imperial College, London, SW7 2BU, England (Office). *Telephone:* (20) 7944-6980 (ODPM) (Office). *Fax:* (20) 7944-6589 (ODPM) (Office). *E-mail:* david.fisk@odpm.gsi.gov.uk (Office); d.fisk@imperial.ac.uk (Office). *Website:* www.odpm.gov.uk (Office).

FISMER, Christiaan Loedolff; South African politician; b. 1956, Pretoria; s. of William Fismer and Elizabeth Fismer; m. Linda Mills; twin d.; ed Univ. of Pretoria; mil. service; admitted to Pretoria Bar 1986; practised as advocate 1986–87; fmr Chair. Student Rep. Council, Univ. of Pretoria, Pres. Afrikaanse Studentebond (ASB – umbrella org. for univ. governing bodies); mem. Nat. Party; co-f. Nat. Party Youth Action; MP for Rissik 1987, Sr Transvaal Whip of Nat. Party 1989; apptd. party rep. to Conf. for a Democratic S. Africa (CODESA) working group on implementation of decisions 1991; Prov. Leader Nat. Party in Eastern Transvaal 1994; fmr Deputy Minister in Office of State Pres. F. W. de Klerk; Deputy Minister of Justice 1994–95; Minister of Gen. Services 1995–96, of Provincial and Constitutional Affairs March–May 1996; pvt. law practice 1996–; Univ. of Pretoria Gold Medal. *Address:* c/o National Party, Private Bag X402, Pretoria 0001, South Africa. *Telephone:* (12) 348-3100. *Fax:* (12) 348-5645.

FISZEL, Roland Henri Léon; French engineer; b. 16 July 1948, Paris; s. of Jean Fiszel and Marie Eber; m. Nadine Kohn 1974; one s. two d.; ed Lycée Pasteur, Neuilly-sur-Seine, Ecole polytechnique, Massachusetts Inst. of Tech., USA; Head of Housing Dept, Ministry of Construction 1974–77; Head of Studies and Planning Group, Infrastructure Div., Hauts-de-Seine 1977–81; Deputy Sec.-Gen. Codis-Cidise, in charge of Treasury 1981–82; Tech. Adviser, Office of Minister of Social Affairs and Nat. Solidarity 1983–84, then of Minister of the Economy and Finance 1984–86; Dir Nat. Printing Office 1986–92; Adviser to Chair. of Euris 1996; Pres. Dir-Gen. Société francaise de production 1997–; Ingénieur en chef des ponts et chaussées; Dir representing State, Agence Havas 1986–87; Dir Antenne 2 1988–92; fmr Sec.-Gen. Caisse nationale du Crédit agricole. *Leisure interests:* skiing, tennis. *Address:* Société francaise de production, 2 avenue de l'Europe, 94360 Bry-sur-Marne (Office); 4 rue Jobbé Duval, 75015 Paris, France (Home).

FITCH, Val Logsdon, BEng, PhD; American physicist; b. 10 March 1923, USA; s. of Fred B. Fitch and Frances M. Fitch (née Logsdon); m. 1st Elise Cunningham 1949 (died 1972); two s. (one deceased); m. 2nd Daisy Harper Sharp 1976; ed McGill and Columbia Univs; US Army 1943–46; Instructor, Columbia Univ. 1953–54, Princeton Univ. 1954, Prof., Princeton Univ. 1960–, Chair. Dept of Physics 1976, Cyrus Fogg Brackett Prof. of Physics 1976–84; James S. McDonnel Distinguished Univ. Prof. of Physics 1984–; Pres. American Physical Soc. 1987–88; Sloan Fellow 1960–64; mem. NAS, American Acad. of Arts and Sciences, President's Science Advisory Cttee 1970–73; American Philosophical Soc.; Research Corpn Award 1968; Ernest Orlando Laurence Award 1968, John Witherill Medal, Franklin Inst. 1976; Nobel Prize for Physics jtly with J. W. Cronin for work on elementary particles 1980; Nat. Medal of Science 1993. *Publications:* major publs in area of elementary particles. *Leisure interest:* conservation. *Address:* P.O. Box 708, Princeton University, Department of Physics, Princeton, NJ 08544, USA. *Telephone:* (609) 452-4374.

FITERMAN, Charles; French politician; b. 28 Dec. 1933, St-Etienne; s. of Moszek Fiterman and Laja Rozenblum; m. Jeannine Poinas 1953; Departmental Sec. Jeunesse Communiste 1952; Sec. CGT, St-Etienne S.F.A.C. 1958–62; Dir Cen. School, Parti Communiste Français (PCF) 1963–65; elected to PCF Cen. Cttee 1972, to Political Bureau and Cen. Cttee Sec. 1976; Gen. Councillor, Head, Econ. Section and PCF Rep. to Liaison Cttee of Signatory Parties to Common Programme of the Left 1977; Deputy (Val-de-Marne) to Nat. Ass. 1978–81; Minister of State, Minister of Transport 1981–84; Deputy for Rhône 1986–88; Mayor of Tavernes 1989–; f. Refondations Movt 1990, Convention pour une alternative progressiste 1994; Pres. Forum Alternatives Européennes 1994–99; mem. Socialist Party 1998–, Conseil Economique et Socral de France; Chevalier Légion d'honneur. *Address:* CES, 9 Place d'Iéna, 75016 Paris, France (Office). *Telephone:* 1-40-29-48-40. *Fax:* 1-40-29-48-39 (Office). *E-mail:* charles.fiterman@wanadoo.fr (Office).

FITOUSSI, Jean-Paul Samuel, DèsScEcon; French economist; b. 19 Aug. 1942, La Goulette; s. of Joseph Fitoussi and Mathilde Cohen; m. Anne Krief 1964; one s. one d.; ed Acad. Commerciale, Paris and Univs of Paris and Strasbourg; Asst Lecturer 1968–71; Dir of Studies 1971–73; Maître de Conférence Agrégé 1974–75; Prof. 1975–78; Titular Prof. 1978–82; Dean. Faculty of Econ. Science and Dir Dept of Econ. Science, Strasbourg 1980–81; Prof. in charge of research prog. on foundation of macroeconomic policy, Inst.

Universitaire Européen, Florence 1979–83; Prof. Inst. d'Etudes Politiques, Paris 1982–; Dir Dept of Studies Observatoire Français des Conjonctures Economiques (OFCE) 1982–89, Pres. 1990–; Chair. Scientific Council of Inst. d'Etudes Politiques, Paris 1997–; Sec.-Gen. Int. Econ. Asscn 1984–; consultant to EC Comm. 1978–; mem. Bd Ecole Normale Supérieure, Paris 1998–; External Prof. Univ. Européenne, Florence 1984–93; mem. Econ. Comm. of the Nation 1996–, Council of Econ. Analysis of the Prime Minister 1997–; Expert, Comm. of the European Parl. 2000–; mem. UN Research Inst. for Social Devt 2001–; Dr hc (Buenos Aires); Prize of Asscn Française de Sciences Economiques, Prize of Acad. des Sciences Morales et Politiques; Chevalier Ordre nat. du Mérite, Chevalier Légion d'honneur. *Publications:* Inflation, équilibre et chômage 1973, Le fondement macroéconomique de la théorie Keynesienne 1974, Modern Macroeconomic Theory 1983, Monetary Theory and Economic Institutions (with N. de Cecco) 1985, The Slump in Europe (with E. Phelps) 1988, Competitive Disinflation (with others) 1993, Pour l'emploi et la cohésion sociale 1994, Le débat interdit: monnaie, Europe, pauvreté 1995, Economic Growth, Capital and Labour Markets 1995, Le nouvel âge des inégalités (with Pierre Rosanvallon) 1996, Rapport sur l'état de l'Union européenne 1999, 2000, 2002, Réformes structurelles et politiques macroéconomique: les enseignements des modèles de pays (with O. Posset) 2000, contrib. to collected publs, L'enseignement supérieur de l'économie en question, Rapport au ministre de l'éducation nationale 2001, Rapport sur l'état de l'union européenne 2002; La Règle et le choix 2002, How to Reform the European Central Bank (with J. Creel) 2002. *Leisure interests:* travel, cinema, guitar, scuba-diving. *Address:* Observatoire Français des Conjonctures Economiques, 69 quai d'Orsay, 75340 Paris Cedex 07 (Office); 47 rue de boulainvilliers, 75016 Paris, France (Home). *Telephone:* 1-44-18-54-01. *Fax:* 1-44-18-54-71. *E-mail:* presidence@ofce.sciences-po.fr (Office). *Website:* www .ofce.sciences-po.fr (Office).

FITT, Baron (Life Peer), cr. 1983, of Bell's Hill in the County of Down; **Gerard Fitt;** British politician; b. 9 April 1926, Belfast; s. of George Patrick Fitt and Mary Ann Fitt; m. Susan Doherty 1947 (died 1996); five d. (and one d. deceased); entered local politics in Belfast 1955; mem. NI Parl., Stormont, for Dock Constituency 1962–72; mem. UK Parl., Westminster, for Belfast West 1966–83 (Republican Labour 1966–70, SDLP 1970–79, Socialist 1979–83); Deputy Chief Exec., NI Ass. 1974–1975; Leader, Social Democratic and Labour Party (SDLP), resgnd Nov. 1979. *Leisure interests:* full-time politics. *Address:* House of Lords, London, SW1A 0PW, England.

FITTIPALDI, Emerson; Brazilian racing driver; b. 12 Dec. 1946, São Paulo; s. of Wilson Fittipaldi and Juze Fittipaldi; m. 1st Maria Helena Dowding 1970; one s. two d.; m. 2nd Teresa Hotte 1995; ed scientific studies; Brazilian champion Formula V and Go-Kart 1967; Formula 3 Lombard Championship 1969; Formula 1 world champion 1972 (youngest ever), 1974; second in World Championship 1973, 1975; won Indianapolis 500 1989, 1993; retd (following injury) 1996 with 17 Indy Car victories; owns Fittipaldi Motoring Accessories, 500,000-acre orange plantation and exports orange concentrate; has Mercedes Benz partnership in Brazil; partner Hugo Boss fashion retailer; set up the Fittipaldi Foundation to help impoverished children in Brazil; mem. Bd of the Laureus World Sports Acad. *Leisure interests:* sport, music, water skiing, flying. *Website:* www.emersonfittipaldi.com.

FITZGERALD, Edmund Bacon, B.S.E.; American business executive; b. 5 Feb. 1926, Milwaukee; s. of Edmund Fitzgerald and Elizabeth Bacon Fitzgerald; m. Elisabeth McKee Christensen 1947; two s. two d.; ed Univ. of Michigan; fmr Chair. and CEO Cutler-Hammer Inc., Milwaukee; then Vice-Chair. and COO, Industrial Products, Eaton Corpn (following merger with Cutler-Hammer); Pres. Northern Telecom Inc., USA (subsidiary of Northern Telecom Ltd) 1980–82; CEO Northern Telecom Ltd 1984–89, Chair. 1985–90; Adjunct Prof. of Man. Vanderbilt Univ., Nashville 1990–; Man. Dir Woodmont Assocs., Nashville 1990–; Dir Ashland Oil Inc., Becton Dickinson and Co., GTI; mem. Pres. Reagan's Nat. Telecommunications Security Advisory Council; Trustee, Cttee for Econ. Devt, Washington, DC; fmr Pres. Nat. Electrical Mfrs Asscn; fmr Vice-Chair. Industry Advisory Council, Dept of Defense. *Address:* Woodmont Associates, 3434 Woodmont Blvd., Nashville, TN 37215-1422, USA.

FITZGERALD, Frances; American author; b. 1940; d. of Desmond Fitzgerald and Marietta Peabody Fitzgerald Tree; ed Radcliffe Coll.; author of series of profiles for Herald Tribune magazine; freelance author of series of profiles, Vietnam 1966; Overseas Press Club Award 1967; Nat. Inst. of Arts and Letters Award 1973; Pulitzer Prize 1973; Nat. Book Award 1973; Sydney Hillman Award 1973; George Polk Award 1973; Bancroft Award for History 1973. *Publications:* Fire in the Lake: The Vietnamese and the Americans in Vietnam 1972, America Revised 1979; articles in magazines. *Address:* c/o Simon and Schuster Inc., 1230 Avenue of the Americas, New York, NY 10020, USA.

FITZGERALD, Garret; Irish politician and economist; b. 9 Feb. 1926, Dublin; s. of the late Desmond Fitzgerald and Mabel McConnell; m. Joan O'Farrell 1947; two s. one d.; ed Belvedere Coll., Univ. Coll. and King's Inns, Dublin; called to the Bar 1946; Research and Schedules Man. Aer Lingus 1947–58; Rockefeller Research Asst, Trinity Coll., Dublin 1958–59; Lecturer in Political Econ. Univ. Coll., Dublin 1959–73; fmr Chair. and Hon. Sec. Irish Br., Inst. of Transport; mem. Seanad Éireann 1965–69; mem. Dáil Éireann for Dublin South-East 1969–92; Leader and Pres. Fine Gael 1977–87; Minister for Foreign Affairs 1973–77; Taoiseach (Prime Minister) of Repub. of Ireland 1981–82, 1982–87; Pres. Council of Ministers of EEC Jan.–June 1975, European Council July–Dec. 1984, fmr Pres. Irish Council of European Movt; fmr Vice-Pres. European People's Party, European Parl.; mem. Senate Nat. Univ. of Ireland 1973–, Chancellor 1997–; fmr Man. Dir Economist Intelligence Unit of Ireland; mem. Trilateral Comm. 1987–; Dir GPA Group 1987–93, Int. Inst. for Econ. Devt, London 1987–95, Trade Devt Inst. 1987–, Comer Int. 1989–94, Point Systems Int. 1996–, Election Commr 1999–; mem. Radio Telefís Éireann Authority; fmr Irish Corresp. BBC, Financial Times, Economist, Columnist Irish Times; Hon. LLD (New York, St Louis, Keele, Boston Coll., Westfield Coll., Mass., Nat. Univ. of Ireland, Univ. of Dublin); Hon. DCL (St Mary's Univ., Halifax, Nova Scotia) 1985, (Oxford) 1987; Dr. h.c. (Queen's Belfast) 2000; Order of Christ (Portugal) 1986, Order of Merit (Germany) 1987, Grand Cordon, Order of the Rising Sun (Japan) 1989, Commdr Légion d'honneur 1995. *Publications:* State-sponsored Bodies 1959, Planning in Ireland 1968, Towards a New Ireland 1972, Unequal Partners (UNCTAD) 1979, Estimates for Baronies of Minimum Level of Irish Speaking Amongst Successive Decennial Cohorts 1771–1781 to 1861–1871 1984, The Israeli/Palestinian Issue 1990, All in a Life (autobiog.) 1991. *Address:* 37 Annavilla, Dublin 6, Ireland. *Telephone:* (1) 496-2600. *Fax:* (1) 496-2126. *E-mail:* Garretfg@iol.ie (Home).

FITZGERALD, Mgr Michael Louis, BA, DTheol; British ecclesiastic; b. 1937, Walsall; ed Pontifical Gregorian Univ., School of Oriental and African Studies, London Univ.; ordained priest, Soc. of Missionaries of Africa (White Fathers) 1961; teacher, Makarere Univ., Kampala, Uganda and later Pontifical Inst. of Arabic and Islamic Studies, Rome; two years pastoral work, Sudan; mem. Gen. Council of Missionaries of Africa 1980–86; Sec. Secr. for Non Christians (now renamed Pontifical Council for Inter-Religious Dialogue) 1987–2002, Pres. Oct. 2002–; Titular Bishop of Nepte 1991–; presented von Hügel Lecture on Christian-Muslim Relations, Cambridge 2002. *Publications include:* Signs of Dialogue: Christian Encounter with Muslims (jt author) 1992; numerous specialist articles and lectures. *Address:* Pontifical Council for Inter-Religious Dialogue, Via dell'Erba 1, Rome, 00193, Italy (Office). *Telephone:* (06) 69884321 (Office). *Fax:* (06) 69884494 (Office). *E-mail:* pcid-office@interelg.va (Office).

FITZGERALD, Peter Gosselin, AB, JD; American politician; b. 20 Oct. 1960, Elgin, Ill.; s. of Gerald Francis Fitzgerald and Marjorie (née Gosselin) Fitzgerald; m. C. Nina Kerstiens 1987; one s.; ed Dartmouth Coll., Univ. of Michigan; called to Bar Ill. 1986; with US Dist Court Ill. 1986; Assoc. Isham, Lincoln & Beale 1986–88; Partner Riordan, Larson, Bruckert & Moore 1988–92; Counsel Harris Bankmont Inc. 1992–96; mem. Ill. Senate 1993–99, Chair. State Govt Operations Cttee 1997–99, Senator from Illinois Jan. 1999–; mem. various bds. and asscns.; Republican. *Address:* US Senate, 555 Dirksen Building, Washington, DC 20510 (Office); John C. Kluczynski Federal Bldg, 230 S Dearborn Street #3900, Chicago, IL 60604, USA. *E-mail:* fitzgerald@fitzgerald.senate.gov (Office).

FITZGERALD, Peter Hanley, PhD, DSc, FRCPath, FRSNZ; New Zealand director of cancer research (retd); b. 10 Oct. 1929, Gore; s. of John J. Fitzgerald and Nora Eileen (née Hanley) Fitzgerald; m. Kathleen O'Connell 1955 (divorced 1988); three s. two d.; ed St Bede's Coll., Christchurch, Univ. of Canterbury, Univ. of New Zealand and Univ. of Adelaide; Dir Cancer Soc. of NZ Cytogenetic and Molecular Oncology Unit, Christchurch School of Medicine 1967–95; Pres. NZ Genetics Soc. 1978, NZ Soc. for Oncology 1973–74; mem. Nat. Scientific Cttee Cancer Soc. of NZ 1981–85, Int. Scientific Advisory Bd Cancer Congress, Seattle 1982, Canterbury Museum Trust Bd 1985–2001, Royal Soc. of NZ Council 1986–89; Hon. Cytogeneticist Canterbury Area Health Bd 1967–95; Prof. (Research Fellow), Christchurch School of Medicine, Univ. of Otago 1990–95; Sir George Grey Scholarship 1952; NZ Nat. Research Fellowship 1955–57; Human Genetics Soc. of Australasia Orator 1994 (Pres. NZ Branch 1990); Hon. Lecturer in Botany and Zoology Univ. of Canterbury 1971–95, in Pathology, Univ. of Otago 1979–90; Hon. Life mem. Cancer Soc. NZ 1995, NZ Soc. for Oncology 1995, Emer. mem. Human Genetics Soc. Australasia 2002. *Publications:* over 140 publs on cancer-related topics. *Leisure interests:* gardening, walking, music, literature, horology. *Address:* Cytogenetic and Molecular Oncology Unit, Christchurch Hospital, Christchurch (Office); 115 Gardiners Road, Christchurch 5, New Zealand (Home). *Telephone:* (3) 359-4244 (Home). *Fax:* (3) 359-4104 (Home).

FITZGERALD, Stephen Arthur, AO, BA, PhD; Australian scholar and diplomatist; b. 18 Sept. 1938, Hobart, Tasmania; s. of F. G. FitzGerald; m. Helen Overton; one s. two d.; ed Tasmania Univ., Australian Nat. Univ.; Dept of Foreign Affairs 1961–66; Research Scholar, ANU 1966–69, Research Fellow 1969–71, Fellow 1972–73, Professorial Fellow 1977–, Head Dept of Far Eastern History 1977–79, Head Contemporary China Centre, Research School of Pacific Studies 1977–79; Amb. to People's Repub. of China (also accred to Democratic People's Repub. of Korea) 1973–76; Ed. Australian Journal of Chinese Affairs; Deputy Chair. Australia–China Council 1979–86; mem. Australian Acad. of Science Sub-Cttee on Relations with China; Trustee, Australian Cancer Foundation 1985–99; Chair. Asian Studies Council 1986–91; Chair. and Man. Dir Stephen Fitzgerald and Co. Ltd; Chair. Asia-Australia Inst., also Prof. Univ. of NSW 1990–; Co-Chair. Jt Policy Cttee on Relations between Northern Territory and Indonesia; mem. council Musica Viva Australia; Dunlop Asia Medal 1999, Australia–China Council Award 1999. *Publications:* China and the Overseas Chinese 1972, Talking with China 1972, China and the World 1977, Immigration: A Commitment to Australia (jtly) 1988, A National Strategy for the Study of Asia in Australia (jtly) 1988, Asia in Australian Education (jtly) 1989, Australia's China (jtly) 1989, Ethical Dimension to Australia's Engagement with Asia 1993, Is Australia an Asian Country? 1997, East View-West View: Divining the Chinese Business Environment 1999. *Address:* Stephen Fitzgerald & Co., P.O. Box 620, Woollahra, NSW 2025, Australia. *Telephone:* (2) 9385-9111. *Fax:* (2) 9385-9221. *E-mail:* aai@unsw.edu.au (Office). *Website:* www.aai@ unsw.edu.au (Office).

FITZGERALD, Tara; British actress; b. 18 Sept. 1969; d. of the late Michael Callaby and of Sarah Geraldine Fitzgerald; stage debut in Our Song, London; appeared in London as Ophelia in Hamlet 1995, Antigone 1999; Reims TV Festival Best Actress 1999. *Theatre:* Our Song (London), Hamlet (New York). *Films:* Sirens 1994, The Englishman Who Went up a Hill but Came Down a Mountain 1995, Brassed Off 1996, Childhood 1997, Conquest 1998, New World Disorder 1998, The Cherry Orchard 1999, Rancid Aluminium 1999, Dark Blue World 2000. *Television includes:* The Black Candle, The Camomile Lawn, Anglo-Saxon Attitudes, Six Characters in Search of an Author, Fall from Grace, The Tenant of Wildfell Hall, The Woman in White, Frenchman's Creek, In the Name of Love, The Student Prince. *Address:* c/o Caroline Dawson Associates, 19 Sydney Mews, London, SW3 6HL, England. *Telephone:* (20) 7581-8111. *Fax:* (20) 7589-4800.

FITZGERALD, William Henry Gerald, BS; American diplomatist and banker; b. 23 Dec. 1909, Boston; s. of William FitzGerald and Mary Smith; m. Annelise Petschek 1943; one s. one d.; ed U.S. Naval Acad. and Harvard Law School; with Borden Co., New York 1936–41; personal business interests in Mexico 1946–47; with Metallurgical Research and Devt Co. Washington, DC 1947, Vice-Pres. and Treas. 1947–56, Pres. 1956–58, Chair. 1960–82; with FitzGerald Corpn 1959, Pres. 1980–; Chair. and Dir numerous business and public appts.; Amb. to Ireland 1992–93; mem. Bretton Woods Comm. 1992–, Council of American Ambs. 1992–; Hon. Chair. Int. Tennis Hall of Fame 2000–; Hon. DSc (Adelphi Univ.) 1962; Hon. LLD (Catholic Univ. of America) 1990; Hon. DPS (Regis Univ., Denver); Grand Cross Honour & Devotion, Sovereign Military Order of Malta; decoration from Peru. *Leisure interests:* tennis, skiing, golf. *Address:* Suite 1105, 1730 Rhode Island Avenue, NW, Washington, DC 20036 (Office); 2305 Bancroft Place, NW, Washington, DC 20008, USA (Home). *Telephone:* (202) 659-8850 (Office); (202) 659-8850. *Fax:* (202) 659-4301 (Office).

FITZPATRICK, Sean; New Zealand rugby union player (retd); b. 4 June 1963, Auckland; s. of Brian Fitzpatrick; ed Sacred Heart Coll., Auckland; hooker New Zealand All Blacks 1986–97, capt. 1992–97; int. debut 28 June 1986; final appearance before retirement 29 Nov. 1997; rugby consultant to New Zealand Rugby Football Union 1999–; Man. Blues Super 12 Franchise 2001–; records: second-most capped New Zealand player of all time (92 caps), most consecutive int. rugby union appearances (63 in 1986–95), missed only two test matches during his career; totals: 128 All Black games; 92 All Black tests; 90 points; 55 test points (including 12 tries). *Publication:* Turning Point—The Making of a Captain. *Address:* c/o International Rugby Academy, PO Box 12420, Wellington, New Zealand (Office).

FITZWATER, Marlin, BA; American government official; b. 24 Nov. 1942, Salina, Kan.; s. of Max Fitzwater and Phyllis Seaton; m.; two c.; ed Univ. of Kansas; Sec. and speechwriter Dept of Transport, Washington 1970–72; with press relations dept, Environmental Protection Agency 1972–74, Dir Press Office 1974–81; Deputy Asst Sec. for Public Affairs, Dept of Treasury 1981–83; Deputy Press Sec. to Pres. 1983–85, Press Sec. to Vice-Pres. 1985–87; Prin. Deputy Press Sec. to Pres. 1987–89; Press Sec. to Pres. 1989–93; Advertising Pres. Fitzwater & Tutweiler, Inc. 1993–; served with USAF 1968–70; Presidential Merit Award 1982. *Publication:* Call the Briefing 1995.

FIVE, Kaci Kullmann; Norwegian politician; b. 13 April 1951, Oslo; m.; two c.; Deputy mem. Storting 1977–81, mem. 1981–; Deputy Chair. Conservative Party 1982–88; Vice-Chair. Conservative Party Parly. Group 1985–89; mem. Baerum Municipal Council 1975–81; Deputy mem. Nat. Council on Youth Affairs 1979–81; Exec. Officer, Norwegian Employers' Fed. 1980–81; Minister of Trade and Shipping 1989–90; mem. Storting 1981–; Leader Conservative Party 1991–94; Conservative Party Spokesperson for Foreign Affairs and EU 1994; Sr Adviser European Public Policy Advisers (EPPA) 1997–98; Sr Vice-Pres. Aker RGI 1998–. *Address:* c/o Aker RGI AS, Fjordalléen 16, P.O. Box 1423 Vika, N-0115 Oslo, Norway (Office). *Telephone:* 24-13-00-00 (Office). *Fax:* 24-13-01-01 (Office). *E-mail:* kaci@aker-rgi.com (Office). *Website:* www .aker-rgi.com/eng/1_html/1_five.html (Office).

FIXMAN, Marshall, PhD; American chemist and teacher; b. 21 Sept. 1930, St Louis, Mo.; s. of Benjamin Fixman and Dorothy Finkel; m. 1st Marian Beatman 1959 (died 1969); one s. two d.; m. 2nd Branka Ladanyi 1974; ed Univ. City High School, Mo., Washington Univ., Mo. and MIT; Postdoctoral Fellow, Yale Univ. 1953–54; served US Army 1954–56; Instructor in Chem., Harvard Univ. 1956–59; Sr Fellow, Mellon Inst., Pa 1959–61; Dir Inst. of Theoretical Science, Univ. of Ore. 1961–64, Prof. of Chem. 1961–65; Sloan Visiting Prof. of Chem., Harvard Univ. 1965; Prof. of Chem., Yale Univ. 1965–79; Prof. of Chem. and Physics, Colo State Univ. 1979–2000, Distinguished Prof. 1986–2000, Prof. Emer. 2000–; Fellow American Acad. of Arts and Sciences, American Physical Soc.; mem. NAS; Alfred P. Sloan Fellowship 1962–64; Assoc. Ed. Journal of Chemical Physics 1994–; mem. Editorial Bd Macromolecules, Journal of Physical Chem., Accounts of Chemical Research, Journal of Polymer Science; ACS Award in Pure Chem. 1964,

American Physical Soc. High Polymer Physics Prize 1980, ACS Polymer Chem. Award 1991. *Leisure interests:* hiking and photography. *Address:* Department of Chemistry, Colorado State University, Fort Collins, CO 80523-0001, USA (Office). *Telephone:* (970) 491-6037. *Fax:* (970) 491-3361.

FJÆRVOLL, Dag Jostein; Norwegian politician; b. 20 Jan. 1947, Hadsel; s. of Edmund Fjærvoll; m.; two c.; fmr teacher; Head Teacher Melbu School 1984; mem. Hadsel Municipal Council 1975, mem. Exec. Bd 1980–, Mayor 1980–85; mem. Storting Nordland Co. 1985–87; mem. Standing Cttee on Local Govt and the Environment 1985–89, on Shipping and Fisheries 1989–93, on Scrutiny and the Constitution 1993–97; Vice-Pres. Lagting 1989–93, Odelsting 1993–97; Minister of Defence 1997–99; Christian Democratic Party. *Address:* c/o Ministry of Defence, Myntgt. 1, P.O. Box 8126 Dep., 0030 Oslo, Norway.

FLAHAUT, André, MA; Belgian politician; b. 18 Aug. 1955, Walhain; ed Université Libre de Bruxelles; Asst to Emile Vandervelde Inst. 1979, Man. 1989; Councillor of Walhain 1982–94; Chair. Parti Socialiste (P.S.) Fed. of Wallon Brabant 1983–95; Provincial Councillor of Brabant 1987–91; Chair. Office de la Naissance et de l'Enfance 1989–95; Vice-Chair. of Intercommunale des Oeuvres Sociales du Brabant Wallon 1993–95; Chair. Mutualité Socialiste du Brabant Wallon 1993; Parl. Rep. 1994; Minister for Civil Service 1995–99, for Defence July 1999–. *Address:* Ministry of Defence, Lambermontstraat 8, 1000 Brussels, Belgium (Office). *Telephone:* (2) 550-28-11 (Office). *Fax:* (2) 550-29-19 (Office). *Website:* mod.fgov.be (Office).

FLAMMARION, Charles-Henri, LèsL, L. ÈS LET., MBA; French publishing executive; b. 27 July 1946, Boulogne-Billancourt; s. of the late Henri Flammarion and of Pierrette Chenelot; m. Marie-Françoise Mariani 1968; one s. two d.; ed Lycée de Sèvres, Sorbonne, Paris, Institut d'Etudes Politiques, Paris and Columbia Univ., USA; Asst Man. Edns. Flammarion 1972–81, Gen. Man. 1981–85, Pres. Flammarion SA 1985–; Pres. Edns. J'ai Lu 1982–, Audie-Fluide Glacial 1990–; mem. Bureau du Syndicat Nat. de l'Édition 1979–88, 1996–; Vice-Pres. Cercle de la Librairie 1988–94, Pres. 1994–2003; Pres. Casterman 1999–. *Leisure interests:* cooking, travel, skiing, walking. *Address:* Flammarion SA, 26 rue Racine, 75006 Paris (Office); 5 avenue Franco-Russe, 75007 Paris, France (Home).

FLANAGAN, Andrew Henry, CA; Scottish business executive; b. 15 March 1956, Glasgow; s. of Francis Desmond Flanagan and Martha Donaldson Flanagan; m. Virginia Walker 1972; one s. one d.; ed Glasgow Univ.; C.A. with Touche Ross 1976–79, Price Waterhouse 1979–81; Financial Control Man. ITT 1981–86; Finance Dir PA Consulting Group 1986–91; Group Finance Dir and Chief Financial Officer BIS Ltd 1991–94; Finance Dir Scottish TV PLC 1994–96, Man. Dir 1996–97; Chief Exec. Scottish Media Group 1997–; Dir ITV Network Ltd, Heart of Midlothian PLC, Scottish Rugby Union 2000–. *Leisure interests:* golf, cinema, reading, skiing. *Address:* Scottish Media Group PLC, Cowcaddens, Glasgow, G2 3PR, Scotland. *Telephone:* (141) 300-3000. *Fax:* (141) 300-3600.

FLANAGAN, Barry, OBE, RA; British sculptor; b. 11 Jan. 1941, Prestatyn, N Wales; ed Mayfield Coll., Sussex, Birmingham Coll. of Arts and Crafts and St Martin's School of Art, London; works in public collections including Art Inst., Chicago, Kunsthaus, Zurich, Museum of Modern Art, New York, Nagaoka Museum, Tokyo, Nat. Gallery of Canada, Ottawa, Stedelijk Museum, Amsterdam, Tate Gallery and Victoria and Albert Museum, London and Walker Art Gallery, Liverpool; outdoor sculpture commissioned by City of Ghent and by Camden Borough Council, London for Lincoln's Inn Fields, London, Equitable Life Tower West, NY, Stockley Park, Uxbridge, Kawakyo Co., Osaka; mem. Zoological Soc. of London. *Solo exhibitions include:* Rowan Gallery, London (several, 1966–74), Waddington Galleries, London (several, 1980–85, 1990–94), Serpentine and Whitechapel Art Galleries, London, Centre Georges Pompidou, Paris, Museum of Modern Art, New York and many others in Europe, USA, Argentina and Japan. *Address:* c/o Waddington Galleries, 11 Cork Street, London, W1S 3LT, England.

FLANAGAN, Richard; Australian writer and film director; b. 1961, Tasmania; ed Univ. of Oxford, UK; fmrly river guide; scriptwriter, author of history books, novelist; directed feature film based on novel The Sound of One Hand Clapping; Rhodes Scholar. *Publications include:* Non-Fiction: A Terrible Beauty: A History of the Gordon River County, Codename Iago: The Story of John Friedrich, Parish-Fed Bastards: A History of the Politics of the Unemployed in Britain 1884–1939 1994; Novels: Death of a River Guide (Victorian Premier's Award for Fiction) 1995, The Sound of One Hand Clapping (reprinted in hardback three times), Gould's Book of Fish (Commonwealth Writer's Prize) 2002. *Address:* c/o Pan Macmillan Australia Pty Ltd, Level 18/St. Martin's Tower, 31 Market Street, Sydney, NSW 2000, Australia (Office).

FLANNERY, Joseph Patrick, BS, MBA; American business executive; b. 20 March 1932, Lowell, Mass.; s. of Joseph Patrick Flannery and Mary Agnes Egan Flannery; m. Margaret Barrows 1957; three s. three d.; ed Lowell Tech. Inst., Harvard Grad. School of Business Admin.; Pres. Uniroyal Chemical Co. 1975–77; Exec. Vice-Pres. Uniroyal Inc., Middlebury, Conn. 1977; Pres. of parent co. and mem. Bd of Dirs. and Exec. Cttee 1977–, CEO 1980–; Chair. Uniroyal Inc. 1982–; Chair., Pres. and CEO Uniroyal Holding, Inc. 1986–; fmr Partner Clayton & Dubilier, Inc.; Dir Newmont Mining Corpn, K Mart Corpn,

Ingersoll-Rand Co., OM Scott & Sons, The Kendall Co., APS Inc., Newmont Gold Co., Arvin Industries. *Address:* Uniroyal Holding Inc., 70 Great Hill Road, Naugatuck, CT 06770-2224, USA.

FLAVELL, Richard Anthony, PhD, FRS; British professor of immunobiology; b. 23 Aug. 1945, Chelmsford; s. of John Trevor Flavell and Iris Flavell (née Hancock); m. Madlyn Nathanson 1987; one d.; two s. from fmr m.; ed Univ. of Hull, Univ. of Amsterdam and Univ. of Zurich, Wetenschappelijk Medewerker, Univ. of Amsterdam, The Netherlands; Head Lab. of Gene Structure and Expression, Nat. Inst. for Medical Research, Mill Hill, London 1979–82; Pres. and Chief Scientific Officer Biogen N.V. 1982–88; Prof. and Chair. of Immunobiology, Yale Univ. School of Medicine and Investigator, Howard Hughes Medical Inst., Conn., USA 1988–; Fed. of European Biochemical Socs. Anniversary Prize 1980, Colworth Medal 1980. *Publications:* approx. 388 scientific articles. *Leisure interests include:* music, tennis, horticulture. *Address:* Section of Immunobiology, Yale University School of Medicine, 310 Cedar Street, 412 FMB, New Haven, CT 06520, USA (Office). *E-mail:* richard.flavell@yale.edu (Office). *Website:* www.info.med.yale.edu (Office).

FLECKENSTEIN, Günther; German theatre director; b. 13 Jan. 1924, Mainz; m. Heike Kaase 1965; two d.; ed Realgymnasium, Mainz and Univ. Mainz; producer of plays and operas; Dir Deutsches Theater, Göttingen 1966–86, Hon. mem. 1990–; freelance producer 1986–; Guest Dir for theatres in Berlin, Hamburg, Stuttgart and Moscow; Guest Dir TV in Munich, Stuttgart and Berlin; Dir Hersfelde Festspiele 1976–81; has dramatized for stage and TV Der Grosstyrann und das Gericht (Bergengruen); stage production in German of Les jeux sont faits (Sartre), Im Räderwerk (Sartre); productions for children's and young people's theatre; Zückmayer Medal for services to the German language 1979, Hon. Plaque, Bad Hersfeld 1982, Hon. Plaque, Göttingen 1984, Polish Medal for Cultural Service 1986, Niedersachsen Verdienstkreuz 1990, Kolbenhoff Kulturpreis 1997. *Publications:* Norwegische Novelle, Gedichtband, Biographie: Lebensspüren, Ceterum censeo, Aphorismen und Commentare. *Address:* Sandstrasse 14, 82110 Germering, Germany.

FLEISCHER, Ari; American government official; b. 1962; ed Middlebury Univ. *Address:* c/o The White House, 1600 Pennsylvania Avenue, NW, Washington, DC 20500, USA (Office).

FLEISCHER, Ezra; Israeli poet and professor; b. 7 Aug. 1928, Romania; m. Anat Rappaport 1955; one s. one d.; ed Univ. of Bucharest and Hebrew Univ., Jerusalem; political prisoner in Romania 1952–55; emigrated to Israel 1960; Dir Geniza Research Inst. for Hebrew Poetry, Israel Nat. Acad. of Sciences and Humanities 1967–; Prof. of Medieval Hebrew Poetry, Hebrew Univ., Jerusalem 1973–; mem. Israel Acad. of Sciences and Humanities 1984–; Corresp. Fellow, American Acad. for Jewish Studies; Pres. World Union of Jewish Studies 1989–93; Hon. DHL (H.U.C., Jerusalem, J.T.S., New York); Israel Prize for Poetry 1959, Bialik Prize for Judaic Studies 1986, Rothschild Prize for Jewish Studies 1992. *Publications:* poetry: Fables 1957, The Burden of Gog 1959, At Midnight 1961; research: The Poems of Shelomo Ha-Bavli 1973, The Pizmonim of Anonymus 1974, Hebrew Liturgical Poetry in the Middle Ages 1975, The Yozer, its Emergence and Development 1984, Eretz Israel Prayer and Prayer Rituals as Portrayed in the Geniza Documents 1988, The Proverbs of Sa'id Ben Bâbshâd 1990, The History of Hebrew Poetry in Muslim Spain (jtly.) 1995, The History of Hebrew Poetry in Christian Spain and Southern France (jtly.) 1997, Yehuda ha-Levi and his Circle (jtly.) 2001; numerous articles in periodicals. *Address:* Hebrew University of Jerusalem, Mount Scopus, 91905 Jerusalem; 14/8 Gelber Street, Jerusalem 96755, Israel.

FLEISCHER, Richard O., MFA; American film director; b. 8 Dec. 1916, Brooklyn, New York; ed Brown Univ., Yale Univ.; joined RKO Pathe 1942; Acad. Award for Best Documentary Feature Film, American Cinematheque Major Film Retrospective 1999. *Films:* Flicker Flashbacks (writer, producer), This is America (Dir, writer), Design for Death (co-producer), Child of Divorce, Banjo, So This is New York, Bodyguard, Follow Me Quietly, The Clay Pigeon, Narrow Margin, The Happy Time, Arena, 20,000 Leagues Under the Sea, Violent Saturday, Girl in the Red Velvet Swing, Bandido, Between Heaven and Hell, The Vikings, These Thousand Hills, Compulsion, Crack in the Mirror, The Big Gamble, Barabbas, Fantastic Voyage, Doctor Dolittle, Boston Strangler, Tora! Tora! Tora!, Ten Rillington Place, The Last Run, See No Evil, The New Centurions, Soylent Green, The Don is Dead, The Spikes Gang, Mister Majestyk, Mandingo, The Incredible Sarah, Crossed Swords, Ashanti, The Jazz Singer, Tough Enough, Amityville 3-D, Conan the Destroyer, Red Sonja, Million Dollar Mystery, Call From Space. *Publication:* Just Tell Me When To Cry. *Address:* The Gersh Agency, 232 N Canon Drive, Beverly Hills, CA 90210, USA.

FLEISCHHAUER, Carl-August, DJur; German international lawyer; b. 9 Dec. 1930, Düsseldorf; s. of Kurt and Leonie (née Schneider-Neuenburg) Fleischhauer; m. Liliane Sarolea 1957; two d.; ed Univs. of Heidelberg, Grenoble, Paris and Chicago; Research Fellow, Max-Planck Inst. for Comparative Foreign Public Law and Int. Law, Heidelberg 1960–62; with Foreign Service of FRG 1962–83, Legal Adviser to Fed. Foreign Office 1975, Legal Adviser and Dir-Gen. Legal Dept 1976; Under-Sec.-Gen. for Legal Affairs, Legal Counsel, UN 1983–94; Judge, Int. Court of Justice 1994–2003; Bundesverdienstkreuz and foreign decorations. *Publications:* various legal publications. *Leisure interests:* modern history, literature. *Address:* Freier Weg 3, 53177 Bonn, Germany (Home). *Telephone:* (228) 317780 (Home).

FLEISCHMANN, Peter; German film director and producer; b. 26 July 1937, Zweibrücken; s. of Alexander Fleischmann and Pascal Fleischmann; two c.; ed IDHEC Film School, Paris; fmrly Asst to Dir of short feature films, documentaries and animations; Co-founder Hallelujah Film with Volker Schlondorff; now produces and directs feature and documentary films; Consultant to Studio Babelsberg; Pres. Fédération Européene des Réalisateurs Audiovisuels; Chair. European Audiovisual Centre, Babelsberg; mem. EC Expert Council for reform of audiovisual politics. *Films include:* Alexander und das Auto ohne linken Scheinwerfer 1965 (animation), Herbst der Gammler 1967 (documentary), Jagdszenen aus Niederbayern (feature) 1968, Der Dritte Grad 1971 (feature), Hamburger Krankheit 1979 (feature), Frevel 1983 (feature), Al Capone von der Pfalz 1984 (documentary), Es ist nicht leicht ein Gott zu sein 1988 (feature), Deutschland, Deutschland 1991 (documentary), Mein Onkel, der Winzer 1993 (documentary). *Address:* Europäisches Filmzentrum Babelsberg, August-Bebel-Strasse 26-53, 14482 Potsdam, Germany. *Telephone:* (331) 7062700 (Office). *Fax:* (331) 7062710 (Office).

FLEMING, Graham Richard, PhD, FRS; British professor of chemistry; b. 3 Dec. 1949, Barrow; s. of Maurice N. H. Fleming and Lovima E. Winter; m. Jean McKenzie 1977; one s.; ed Univs of London and Bristol; Research Fellow Calif. Inst. of Tech., USA 1974–75; Univ. Research Fellow Univ. of Melbourne, Australia 1975, ARGC Research Asst 1976; Leverhulme Fellow, Royal Inst. 1977–79; Asst Prof., Univ. of Chicago, USA 1979–83, Assoc. Prof. 1983–85, Prof. 1985–87, Arthur Holly Compton Distinguished Service Prof. 1987–97; Prof. of Chem. Univ. of Calif. Berkeley 1997–, Melvin Calvin Distinguished Prof. of Chem. 2002–, Dir Physical Biosciences Div., Lawrence Berkeley Nat. Lab. 1997–, Assoc. Lab. Dir for Physical Sciences; Co-Dir Calif. Inst. for Biotechnology, Bioengineering and Quantitative Biomedicine 2001; Fellow American Acad. of Arts and Sciences; A. P. Sloan Foundation Fellow, Guggenheim Fellowship; Marlow Medal, Royal Soc. of Chem., Coblentz Award, Tilden Medal, Nobel Laureate Signature Award for Grad. Educ. in Chemistry (ACS), Peter Debye Award in Physical Chem., ACS, Harrison Howe Award, ACS, Earle K. Pyler Prize, American Physical Soc. *Leisure interest:* climbing mountains. *Address:* Department of Chemistry, 884 Hildebrand #1460, University of California at Berkeley, Berkeley, CA 94720, USA. *Telephone:* (510) 643-2735. *Fax:* (510) 642-6340. *E-mail:* fleming@cchem.berkeley.edu (Office).

FLEMING, Osbourne Berlington; Anguillan politician and business executive; b. 18 Feb. 1940, East End; ed Valley Secondary School; Customs Officer, St Kitts 1959–64; lived St Thomas, U.S. Virgin Islands 1964–68, St Kitts 1968–81; f. Fleming's Transport shipping and transport co., St Croix 1974; People's Progressive Party (PPP) MP, Minister of Tourism, Agric. and Fisheries 1981–85; Anguilla Nat. Alliance (ANA) MP, Minister of Finance 1985–89; Ind. MP, Minister of Finance and Econ. Devt 1989–94; rejoined ANA, apptd. Leader Opposition in House of Ass. 1994–2000; mem. ANA/Anguilla Democratic Party United Front; Chief Minister and Minister of Home Affairs, Tourism, Agric., Fisheries and Environment 2000–. *Leisure interests:* playing draughts, dominoes and cards. *Address:* Office of the Chief Minister, The Secretariat, The Valley, Anguilla, West Indies.

FLEMING, Renée, M.MUS.; American opera singer and vocalist; b. 14 Feb. 1959, Indiana, Pa; d. of Edwin Davis Fleming and Patricia (Seymour) Alexander; m. Richard Lee Ross 1989 (divorced 2000); two d.; ed Potsdam State Univ., Eastman School of Music of Univ. of Rochester, Juilliard School American Opera Center; debuts Houston Grand Opera (Marriage of Figaro) 1988, Spoleto Festival, Charleston and Italy 1986–90, New York City Opera (La Bohème) 1989, San Francisco Opera, Metropolitan Opera, Paris Opera at Bastille, Teatro Colon, Buenos Aires (all Marriage of Figaro) 1991, Glyndebourne (Così fan tutte) 1992, La Scala Milan (Don Giovanni) 1993, Vienna State Opera (Marriage of Figaro) 1993, Lyric Opera of Chicago (Susannah) 1993, San Diego Opera (Eugene Onegin) 1994, Paris Opera 1996; Fulbright Scholar to Germany 1984–85; George London Prize 1988, Richard Tucker Award 1990, Solti Prize, Acad. du Disque Lyrique 1996, Vocalist of the Year, (Musical America) 1997, Prize Acad. du Disque Lyrique 1998, Grammy Award 1999, creation of the dessert "La Diva Renée" by Master Chef Daniel Boulud 1999. *Address:* c/o M. L. Falcone Public Relations, 155 West 68th Street, Apt. 1114, New York, NY 10023-5817, USA. *Telephone:* (212) 580-4302. *Fax:* (212) 787-9638.

FLEMMING, John Stanton, CBE, MA, FBA; British economist; b. 6 Feb. 1941, Reading, Berks.; s. of Sir Gilbert Nicolson Flemming and Virginia Flemming (née Coit); m. Jean Briggs 1963; one d. three s.; ed Rugby School and Trinity and Nuffield Colls., Oxford; Lecturer and Fellow in Econs Oriel Coll., Oxford 1963–65; Official Fellow in Econs Nuffield Coll., Oxford 1965–80, Bursar 1970–80, Fellow Emer. 1980–; Ed. Economic Journal 1976–80; Chair. Econ. Affairs Cttee Social Science Research Council 1980–84; Chief Adviser and Head of Econs Div. Bank of England 1980–84, Econ. Adviser to Gov. 1984–88, Exec. Dir 1988–91; Chief Economist EBRD London 1991–93; Warden Wadham Coll., Oxford 1993–(2003); mem. Royal Comm. on Environmental Pollution 1995–; mem. Council, Royal Econs Soc. 1976–98, Vice-Pres. 1998–, Inst. for Fiscal Studies, Advisory Bd on Research Councils (UK) 1986–91, Council European Econ. Asscn 1985–88; Chair. Man. Cttee Nat. Inst. for Econ. and Social Research 1996–2002; Harkness Fellow, Harvard Univ. 1968–69; Fellow British Acad. 1993–(Hon. Treas. 1995–2002).

Publications: Inflation 1976; articles in academic journals etc. *Address:* The Lodgings, Wadham College, Oxford, OX1 3PN, England. *Telephone:* (1865) 277903. *Fax:* (1865) 277937. *E-mail:* john.flemming@wadh.ox.ac.uk (Office).

FLETCHER, Hugh Alasdair, BSc, MCom, MBA; New Zealand business executive; b. 28 Nov. 1947, Auckland; s. of Sir James Muir Cameron Fletcher (q.v.) and Margery V. Fletcher (née Gunthorp); m. Rt. Hon. Dame Sian Seerpoohi Elias (Chief Justice of New Zealand) 1970; two s.; ed Auckland Univ. and Stanford Univ.; CEO Fletcher Holdings Ltd 1980, Man. Dir Fletcher Challenge Ltd 1981, CEO 1987–97; Chair. Air New Zealand 1985–89; mem. Prime Minister's Enterprise Council 1992–98, Asia-Pacific Advisory Cttee NY Stock Exchange 1995–; Harkness Fellowship 1970–72; Chair. Ministerial Inquiry into Telecommunications 2000–, CGU Insurance Australia, NZ Insurance. *Leisure interest:* horse riding/hunting. *Address:* P.O. Box 11468, Ellerslie, Auckland (Office); 79 Penrose Road, Auckland, New Zealand (Home). *Telephone:* (9) 307-2264 (Office). *Fax:* (9) 579-8408 (Office). *E-mail:* hughfletcher@hotmail.com (Office).

FLETCHER, Sir James Muir Cameron, Kt, ONZ, FCA; New Zealand business executive; b. 25 Dec. 1914, Dunedin; s. of Sir James Fletcher; m. Margery V. Gunthorp MBE 1942; two s.; ed Waitaki Boys' High School and Auckland Grammar School; South British Insurance Co. 1931–37; Fletcher Construction Co. and Fletcher Holdings; Pres. Fletcher Challenge Ltd, Auckland 1981–90; Chair. Fletcher Challenge Trust 1990–. *Leisure interests:* horse racing, deer farming. *Address:* Fletcher Building Ltd, Private Bag, 92114 Auckland (Office); 3/119 St Stephens Avenue, Parnell, Auckland, New Zealand (Home). *Telephone:* (9) 525-9000 (Office); (9) 379-7677 (Home). *Fax:* (9) 525-9021 (Office).

FLETCHER, Neville Horner, AM, PhD, DSc, FAA; Australian physicist; b. 14 July 1930, Armidale, NSW; s. of Alleine Horner Fletcher and Florence Mabel Glass; m. Eunice M. Sciffer 1953; one s. two d.; ed Armidale High School, New England Univ. Coll., Univ. of Sydney, Harvard Univ.; Research Engineer, Clevite Transistor Products, USA 1953–55; Researcher, CSIRO Radiophysics Lab. 1956–59, Dir Inst. of Physical Sciences 1983–88; Chief Research Scientist 1988–95; at Univ. of New England 1960–83, Sr Lecturer in Physics 1960–63, Prof. of Physics 1963–83, Dean, Faculty of Science 1963–65, mem. Univ. Council 1968–72, Chair. Professorial Bd 1970–72, Pro Vice-Chancellor 1969–72, Prof. Emer. 1983–; Adjunct Prof., Australian Nat. Univ. 1990–95, Visiting Fellow 1995–; Visiting Prof., Univ. of NSW 1997–2000; Chair. Antarctic Science Advisory Cttee 1990–96; mem. Australian Research Grants Cttee 1974–78, 1995–98; Sec. for Physical Sciences, Australian Acad. of Science 1980–84; Pres. Inst. of Physics 1981–83; mem. Govt Meteorology Policy Cttee 1981–84, Int. Comm. on Acoustics 1985–90; Fellow Australian Acad. of Science 1976, Fellow Australian Acad. of Technological Sciences and Eng 1987; Univ. Medal (Sydney) 1951, Frank Knox Fellowship (Harvard) 1952, Edgeworth David Medal (Royal Soc. of NSW) 1963, Lyle Medal (Australian Acad. of Science) 1993, Distinguished Alumni Award (Univ. of New England) 1994, Silver Medal in Musical Acoustics (Acoustical Soc. of America) 1998. *Publications:* The Physics of Rainclouds 1962, The Chemical Physics of Ice 1970, Physics and Music 1976, The Physics of Musical Instruments 1990, Acoustic Systems in Biology 1992, Principles of Vibration and Sound 1995; over 170 papers in scientific journals. *Leisure interests:* music (flute, bassoon and organ). *Address:* Department of Electronic Materials Engineering, Research School of Physical Sciences and Engineering, Australian National University, Canberra, ACT 0200 (Office); 30 Rosebery Street, Fisher, ACT 2611, Australia (Home). *Telephone:* (2) 6125-4406 (Office); (2) 6288-8988 (Home). *Fax:* (2) 6215-0511. *E-mail:* neville.fletcher@anu.edu.au (Office).

FLETCHER, Philip, MA; British public servant; b. 2 May 1946, London; s. of Alan Philip Fletcher and Annette Grace Fletcher (née Wright); m. Margaret Anne Boys; two d. (one deceased); ed Marlborough Coll., Trinity Coll., Oxford; joined Civil Service 1968, Under-Sec. of Housing, Water and Cen. Finance, Dept of the Environment 1986–90; Planning and Devt Control 1990–93; Chief Exec. PSA Services 1993–94; Deputy Sec. Cities and Countryside Group 1994–95; Receiver for the Metropolitan Police Dist 1996–2000; Dir.-Gen. of Water Services Aug. 2000–; Reader, Church of England. *Leisure interest:* walking. *Address:* Office of Water Services, Centre City Tower, 7 Hill Street, Birmingham, B5 4UA, England (Office). *Telephone:* (121) 625-1350 (Office). *Fax:* (121) 625-1348 (Office). *E-mail:* philip.fletcher@ofwat.gsi.gov.uk (Office).

FLETT, Kathryn Alexandra; British journalist; b. 1 April 1964, Herts.; d. of Douglas J. Flett and Patricia Jenkins; ed Notting Hill and Ealing High School and Hammersmith and West London Coll.; staff writer, I-D magazine 1985–87; Fashion Ed., Features Ed. The Face magazine 1987–89; freelance contrib. to many int. publs including The Times, The Sunday Times, The Observer, The Guardian, The Face, Arena, Elle, Harpers Bazaar, etc. 1989–92; Contributing Ed. Arena Magazine 1991–92, Ed. 1992–95; Ed. Arena Homme Plus 1993–95; columnist, The Observer 1994–, Assoc. Ed. Observer Life 1995–98. *Publication:* The Heart-Shaped Bullet 1999. *Address:* c/o The Observer, 119 Farringdon Road, London, EC1R 3ER, England (Office).

FLEURY, Gen. Jean André; French air force officer and aeronautical executive; b. 1 Dec. 1934, Brest; s. of René Fleury and Blanche-Marie Marsille; Commdt Saint Dizier Air Base 1977–78; Head, Office of Supply, Air Force Gen. Staff 1978–81; Deputy Chief of Planning, Armed Forces Gen. Staff 1983–85; Commdt Strategic Air Forces 1985–87; Chief of Staff to Pres. of

Repub. 1987–89; Chief of Staff of Air Force 1989–91; mem. Supreme Council of Army and Air Forces 1989; Pres. Aéroports de Paris 1992–99; Chair. Airports Council Int. 1998–99; aeronautics consultant 2000–; mem. Econ. and Social Regional Council of Britanny 2001–; Grand Croix, Légion d'honneur, Commdr Ordre nat. du Mérite, Croix de la Valeur militaire. *Publication:* Faire face—Memoires d'un chef d'état major. *Address:* Les Mirages, La Combe de Haut, 56140 Pleucadeuc, France (Office). *Telephone:* (2) 97-26-96-85 (Office). *Fax:* (2) 97-26-98-22 (Office). *E-mail:* fleurygeneral@aol.com (Office).

FLIMM, Jürgen; German theatre director; b. 17 July 1941, Giessen; s. of Werner Flimm and Ellen Flimm; m. Susanne Ottersbach 1990; early work at the Munich Kammerspiele; Dir Nationaltheater, Mannheim 1972–73; Prin. Dir Thalia Theater, Hamburg 1973–74; directed plays in Munich, Hamburg, Bochum, Frankfurt 1974–79 and in Zürich, Amsterdam, Salzburg, Vienna, Milan; Dir Cologne Theatre 1979–85, Thalia Theatre, Hamburg 1985–2000; Pres. German Bühnenvereins 1999–; Acting Dir Salzburg Festspiele 2001–; Bundesverdienstkreuz. *Address:* c/o Salzburger Festspiele, Mönchsberg 1, 5020 Salzburg, Austria (Office).

FLINDT, Flemming Ole; Danish ballet dancer and choreographer; b. 30 Sept. 1936; m. Vivi Gelker 1967; three d.; ed Royal Danish Ballet School; ballet dancer 1955–; solo dancer Royal Theatre, Copenhagen 1957–60; Danseur Etoile Théâtre Nat. de l'Opéra, Paris 1960–65; Artist Dir Royal Danish Ballet 1966–78, Dallas Ballet 1981–; Guest Artist Royal Ballet Covent Garden 1963; Guest Choreographer Metropolitan Opera House, New York and La Scala, Milan 1965; Grand Prix Italia (La Leçon) 1963. *Choreography:* La leçon, (Ionesco) 1963, Jeune homme à marier, (Ionesco) 1964, The Three Musketeers 1966, The Miraculous Mandarin 1966, The Triumph of Death, Dreamland 1974, Caroline Mathilde 1990; choreography and libretto: Felix Luna 1973.

FLOCKHART, Calista; American actress; b. 11 Nov. 1964, Freeport, Ill.; d. of Ronald Flockhart and Kay Flockhart; one adopted s. *Films:* Quiz Show 1994, Naked in New York 1994, Getting In 1994, The Birdcage 1996, Pictures of Baby Jane Doe 1996, Drunks 1997, Telling Lies in America 1997, Milk and Money 1997, A Midsummer Night's Dream 1999, Like a Hole in the Head 1999, Things You Can Tell Just By Looking At Her 2000. *Plays on Broadway include:* The Glass Menagerie, The Three Sisters. *Television work includes:* The Guiding Light 1978, Darrow 1991, An American Story 1991, Life Stories: Families in Crisis 1992, Ally McBeal (Best Actress Award Golden Globes 1998) 1997–. *Address:* c/o David E. Kelly Productions, Twentieth Century Fox, 10201 W Pico Boulevard, Building 80, Los Angeles, CA 90064, USA (Office).

FLOOD, Philip James, AO, BEcons; Australian diplomatist; b. 2 July 1935, Sydney; s. of Thomas C. Flood and Maxine S. Flood; m. 2nd Carole Henderson 1990; two s. one d. from previous m.; ed North Sydney High School, Univ. of Sydney; mem. staff Mission to EEC and Embassy, Brussels 1959–62, Rep. to OECD Devt Assistance Cttee, Paris 1966–69, Asst Sec. Dept of Foreign Affairs 1971–73, High Commr in Bangladesh 1974–76, Minister, Embassy, Washington, DC 1976–77, CEO Dept Special Trade Representations 1977–80; First Asst Sec. Dept of Trade 1980–84, Deputy Sec. Dept of Foreign Affairs 1985–89, Amb. to Indonesia 1989–93, Dir-Gen. Australian Int. Devt Assistance Bureau (AUSAID) 1993–95, Dir-Gen. Office of Nat. Assessments 1995–96, Sec. Dept of Foreign Affairs and Trade 1996–98; High Commr in London 1998–2000; Chair. Australia-Indonesia Inst. 2001–; Fellow Royal Australian Inst. Public Admin.; Bintang Jasa Utama (Indonesia) 1993. *Leisure interests:* reading, music, art, skiing, swimming. *Address:* 96 Jervois Street, Deakin, ACT 2600, Australia (Home).

FLOR, Claus Peter; German conductor; b. 16 March 1953, Leipzig; adopted s. of Richard Flor and Sigrid Langer; m. Sabine Winni 1985; one s.; ed Music School, Weimar and High School of Music, Weimar/Leipzig; studied under Rolf Reuter, Rafael Kubelik and Kurt Sanderling; learnt violin and clarinet before commencing conducting studies; Chief Conductor, Suhl Philharmonic 1981–84; Chief Conductor, Music Dir Berliner Sinfonie Orchester 1984–92; Prin. Conductor, Artistic Adviser, Zürich Tonhalle Orchestra 1991–; Prin. Guest Conductor, Philharmonia Orchestra, London 1991–; U.S. debut with Los Angeles Philharmonic 1985; debut with Berlin Philharmonic 1988; Prin. Guest Conductor Dallas Symphony Orchestra; regular appearances with Vienna Symphony, Orchestre de Paris, Royal Concertgebouw, Rotterdam Philharmonic and maj. German orchestras; frequent guest engagements with leading orchestras in UK, USA, Canada etc.; conductor of opera at many German opera houses including Berlin Staatsoper and Deutsche Oper, Berlin. *Recordings include:* Mendelssohn, Cherubini, Dvořák, Mozart, Shostakovich. *Leisure interests:* collecting red wines, history and genealogy of European nobility. *Address:* c/o Intermusica Artists' Management Ltd, 16 Duncan Terrace, London, N1 8BZ, England. *Telephone:* (20) 7278-5455. *Fax:* (20) 7278-8434.

FLORAKIS, Charilaos Ioannou; Greek politician; b. 20 July 1914, Rahoula; ed Coll. of Telegraph, Telephone, Post Office and Public Utility, law school; fmr Sec. Exec. Cttee, Fed. of Telegraphists; joined CP of Greece (KKE) during war; partisan during occupation; Commdr unit of First Div. of Democratic Army of Greece during civil war; mem. Cen. Cttee KKE 1949, First Sec. 1973, Gen. Sec. 1978–89, Pres. 1989; MP for Athens 1974, 1977, 1981; Friendship of the People Award (USSR), Karl Marx Decoration (GDR), Dimitrov Decoration (Bulgaria), Elas Decoration, Decoration of Military Valour, (Democratic Army of Greece), Order of Lenin 1984. *Address:* 6 Pythias Street, 152 33 Halandri, Greece. *Telephone:* (1) 2592111. *Fax:* (1) 2592 286.

FLORENTZ, Jean-Louis; French composer; b. 19 Dec. 1947, Asnières; s. of Jean-Paul Florentz and Reine Mathieu; m. 2nd Anne Le Forestier; ed Collège Mariste, St Chamond (Loire), Conservatoire de Paris, Ecole Pratique des Hautes Etudes; studied ethno-musicology, Arab and Ethiopian literature, natural science and music with Olivier Messiaen and Pierre Schaeffer; student at Acad. de France, Rome (Villa Médicis) 1979–81, Casa de Velázquez, Madrid and Palma de Mallorca 1983–85; numerous study trips to North Africa and the Sahara, Niger, Côte d'Ivoire, Egypt, Kenya, Antilles, Polynesia, Madagascar and Israel 1971–; Visiting Prof., Kenyatta Univ. Coll., Nairobi; teaches ethno-musicology and comparative musical analysis, CNSM, Lyon; mem. Acad. des Beaux-Arts, Inst. de France; Chevalier Ordre Nat. du Mérite, Chevalier des Palmes académiques, Officier des Arts et Lettres; Prix de Rome, Prix de Madrid, Prix de la Fondation Prince Pierre de Monaco, Prix de la Ville de Paris, Prix de l'Institut de France, Prix de la SACEM, Grand Prix de la Musique Symphonique, SACEM 1991, Prix R. Dumesnil, Acad. des Beaux Arts 1993 and several other prizes. *Compositions:* Magnificat: Antiphone pour la visitation, for tenor, mixed choir and orchestra 1980, Les Laudes, for organ 1985, Chant de Nyandarua, for four cellos 1986, Asún, for soprano, tenor, baritone, children's choir, mixed choir and orchestra 1988, Debout sur le Soleil, for organ 1991, Asmarâ, for mixed choir 1992, Le Songe de Lluc Alcari, for cello and orchestra 1994, L'Ange du Tamaris, for cello 1995, Second Chant de Nyandarua, for 12 cellos 1996, Les Jardins d'Amënta, for orchestra 1997, L'Anneau de Salomon, for orchestra 1999, La Croix du Sud, for organ 2000, L'enfant des îles, for orchestra 2002, L'enfant noir, for organ 2002, Qsar Ghilâne, for orchestra 2003. *Publications:* contribs to L'Orgue, Journal de Psychologie and other publs. *Leisure interests:* flying, ornithology. *Address:* c/o Ed. Alphonse Leduc, 175 rue St Honoré, 75040 Paris Cedex 01, France. *Telephone:* 1-42-96-89-11. *Fax:* 1-42-86-02-83. *E-mail:* AlphonseLeduc@wanadoo.fr (Office). *Website:* www.AlphonseLeduc.com (Office).

FLORES FACUSSÉ, Carlos Roberto, BEng, M.INT.ECON., PhD; Honduran politician; b. 1 March 1950, Tegucigalpa; s. of Oscar A. Flores and Margarita Facussé de Flores; m. Mary Carol Flake; one s. one d.; ed American School, Tegucigalpa and Louisiana State Univ.; Rep. for Francisco Morazan to Liberal Convention, Pres. Departmental Liberal Council, Francisco Morazan; Finance Sec. Nat. Directorate Movimiento Liberal Rodista; Congressman Nat. Ass. for Francisco Morazan 1980–97; Presidential Sec. 1982–83; Gen. Co-ordinator Movimiento Liberal Florista; Pres. Cen. Exec. Council Partido Liberal de Honduras; Pres. of Honduras 1998–2002; co-owner, Man. and mem. editorial Bd La Tribuna, co-owner and Man. Lithopress Industrial; fmr Man. CONPACASA; fmr Prof. School of Business Admin., Nat. Univ. of Honduras (UNAH), Cen. American Higher School of Banking; fmr mem. Bd of Dirs Honduran Inst. of Social Security, Cen. Bank of Honduras, Inst. Nacional de Formación Profesional (INFOP); mem. Industrial Eng Asscn of Honduras, Nat. Asscn of Industries (ANDI), Consejo Hondureño de la Empresa Privada (COHEP), Honduran Inst. of Inter-American Culture. *Publication:* Forjemos Unidos el Destino de Honduras. *Address:* Partido Liberal, Col. Miramonte, No. 1, Tegucigalpa, Honduras.

FLORES PEREZ, Francisco; Salvadorean politician; b. 17 Oct. 1959; m. Lourdes Rodríguez de Flores; one s. one d.; ed Amherst Coll.; fmr lecturer; fmr Deputy and Pres. Legislative Ass.; fmr Vice-Minister of Planning, then Vice-Pres. and Adviser to Pres. Cristiani; Information Sec. to Pres. Armando Calderón Sol; Pres. of El Salvador 1999–; mem. Nat. Republican Alliance (ARENA). *Address:* Ministry for the Presidency, Avda Cuba, Calle Darió González 806, Barrio San Jacinto, San Salvador, El Salvador (Office). *Telephone:* 221-8483 (Office). *Fax:* 771-0950 (Office). *Website:* www.casapres.gob.sv (Office).

FLOSSE, Gaston; French Polynesian politician; b. 24 June 1931, Rikitea (Gambier archipelago); m. Marie-Jeanne Mao 1994; Pres. City Council Pirae 1963–65, Mayor 1965–; Govt Councillor in charge of Agric. 1965–67; mem. French Polynesian Territorial Ass. for Windward Islands 1967–, Pres. 1972–77; Pres. Tahoeraa Huiraatira Party 1971–; Vice-Pres. Govt Council 1982, Pres. Council of Ministers of French Polynesia and Minister for Foreign Affairs, the Pearl Culture Industry and Urban Devt 1984–; mem. Cen. Cttee Union des Democrates pour la République (UDR), France, then Founding mem. Rassemblement pour la République (RPR); Deputy for French Polynesia, Nat. Ass., France 1978–97; Sec. of State in charge of S. Pacific Affairs, France 1986–88; Senator of French Repub. 1998–; Dr. h.c. (Kyung Hee Univ., Korea) 1985; Chevalier, Légion d'honneur, Ordre nat. du Mérite, First 'Grand Maître', Order of Tahiti Nui. *Address:* The President's Office, P.O. Box 2551, 98713 Papeete, French Polynesia (Office). *Telephone:* 472000 (Office). *Fax:* 419781 (Office). *E-mail:* presid@mail.pf (Office). *Website:* www.presidence.pf (Office).

FLOWERS, Baron (Life Peer), cr. 1979, of Queen's Gate in the City of Westminster; **Brian Hilton Flowers,** Kt, MA, DSc, FInstP, FRS, MRIA; British physicist; b. 13 Sept. 1924, Blackburn, Lancs.; s. of the late Rev. Harold J. Flowers and Marion V. Flowers (née Hilton); m. Mary Frances Behrens 1951; two step s.; ed Bishop Gore Grammar School, Swansea, Gonville and Caius Coll., Cambridge and Univ. of Birmingham; Anglo-Canadian Atomic Energy Mission (Tube Alloys) at Montreal and Chalk River, Canada 1944; joined staff AERE, Harwell 1946, Head of Theoretical Physics Div. 1952–58; Prof. of Theoretical Physics, Manchester Univ. 1958–61, Langworthy Prof. of Physics 1961–72, Chancellor 1994–2001; Chair. Science Research Council 1967–73; Rector Imperial Coll. of Science and Tech., London 1973–85; Vice-Chancellor Univ. of London 1985–90; Chair. Computer Bd for Univs and Research Councils 1966–70; Pres. Inst. of Physics 1972–74, European Science Foundation 1974–80, Nat. Soc. for Clean Air 1977–79; Chair. Royal Comm. on Environmental Pollution 1973–76, Standing Comm. on Energy and the Environment 1978–81, Univ. of London Working Party on Future of Medicine and Dentistry Teaching Resources 1979–80, Cttee of Vice-Chancellors and Prins of the Univs of the UK 1983–85; Founder-mem. Academia Europaea 1988; Vice-Chair. Asscn of Commonwealth Univs 1987–90; Chair. House of Lords Select Cttee on Science and Tech. 1989–93, Nuffield Foundation 1987–98, Cttee on Org. of the Academic Year 1992–93; Pres. Asscn for Colleges 1993–95; Fellow Physical Soc. 1956; Corresp. mem. Swiss Acad. of Eng Sciences 1986; Sr Fellow, Royal Coll. of Art 1983; Gov. Middx Univ. 1992–2001; Hon. Fellow (Imperial Coll.) 1972, (Gonville and Caius Coll., Cambridge) 1974, (Univ. of Manchester Inst. of Science and Tech.) 1985; Hon. FIEE 1975; Hon. FRCP 1992; Hon. DSc (Sussex) 1968, (Wales) 1972, (Leicester) 1973, (Manchester) 1973, (Liverpool) 1974, (Bristol) 1982, (Oxford) 1985, (Nat. Univ. of Ireland) 1990, (Reading) 1996, (London) 1997; Hon. ScD (Dublin) 1984; Hon. LLD (Dundee) 1985, (Glasgow) 1987, (Manchester) 1994; Hon. DEng (Nova Scotia) 1983; Chevalier Légion d'honneur 1975, Officier 1981; Rutherford Medal and Prize (Inst. of Physics and the Physical Soc.) 1968, Chalmers Medal (Sweden) 1980, Glazebrook Medal (Inst. of Physics) 1987. *Publications:* Properties of Matter (with E. Mendoza) 1970, An Introduction to Numerical Methods in C++ 1995; numerous scientific papers in the journals of learned societies on nuclear reactions and the structure of atomic nuclei, on science policy and on energy and the environment. *Leisure interests:* music, walking, computing, gardening. *Address:* 53 Athenaeum Road, London, N20 9AL, England. *Telephone:* (20) 8446-5993. *E-mail:* FOFQG@clumsies.demon.co.uk (Home).

FLOWERS, Matthew Dominic; British art dealer, musician and composer; b. 8 Oct. 1956, London; s. of Adrian John Flowers and Angela Mary Flowers (née Holland); m. Huei Chjuin Hong 1992; two s.; ed William Ellis School; worked with various bands including Sore Throat and Blue Zoo, appeared on TV programmes Top of the Pops and Old Grey Whistle Test 1974–83; joined Angela Flowers Gallery (now Angela Flowers Gallery PLC) as art gallery Asst 1975, Man. Dir 1988–. *Leisure interests:* soccer, chess, music. *Address:* Flowers East, 82 Kingsland Road, London, E8 8DP (Office); 41 Queen Elizabeth's Walk, London, N16 5UG, England (Home). *Telephone:* (20) 8985-3333 (Office). *Fax:* (20) 8985-0067 (Office); (20) 8802-6107 (Home). *E-mail:* matt@flowerseast.com (Office). *Website:* www.flowerseast.com (Office).

FLYNN, Padraig; Irish politician; b. 9 May 1939, Castlebar; m. Dorothy Tynan; one s. three d.; ed St Patrick's Teacher Training Coll., Dublin; fmr school teacher and publican; mem. Mayo County Council 1967–86; mem. Dáil. 1977–92; Minister of State, Dept of Transport and Power 1980–81; Minister for the Gaeltacht March–Oct. 1982, for Trade, Commerce and Tourism Oct.–Dec. 1982, for Environment 1987–91, for Justice Feb.–Dec. 1992, for Industry and Commerce Nov.–Dec. 1992; EU Commr for Employment and Social Affairs and for Relations with the Econ. and Social Cttee 1993–99; Fianna Fáil. *Leisure interests:* golf, reading, world affairs. *Address:* c/o Fianna Fáil, 65–66 Lower Mount Street, Dublin 2, Ireland.

FO, Dario; Italian playwright, clown and actor; b. 24 March 1926, San Giano; m. Franca Rame 1954; one c.; Comedian Teatro di Rivista; Jt Founder theatre group La Comune; Hon. D. Litt. (Westminster) 1997; Nobel Prize for Literature 1997. *Films:* Lo Svitato 1956, Musica per vecchi animali 1989. *Plays include:* Accidental Death of an Anarchist, Can't Pay? Won't Pay!, Manuale et minimo dell attore 1987, Mistero Buffo 1977, Coming Home, History of Masks, Archangels Don't Play Pinball, Hooters, Trumpets and Raspberries, The Tricks of the Trade 1991, The Pope and the Witch 1989, L'Eroina-Grassa e'Bello 1991, Johan Padan a la Descoverta de le Americhe 1991, Dario Fo Recita Ruzzante 1993, Il Diavolo con le Zinne 1997, Lu Santo Jullare Francesco 1999. *Radio:* Poer Nano 1950, Chicchirichì, Cocoricò, Ragazzi in Gamba, Non si vive di solo pane 1951. *Television:* Canzonissima 1962. *Address:* C. So di Porta Romana 132, 20122 Milan, Italy (Office). *Telephone:* (02) 58430506 (Office). *Fax:* (02) 58326719 (Office). *E-mail:* ctfr@iol.it (Office). *Website:* www.francarame.it (Office).

FOALE, Marion Ann; British designer; b. 13 March 1939, London; d. of S. D. Foale; one s. one d.; ed SW Essex Tech and School of Art, RCA; career fashion designer; designed Queen's mantle for OBE dedication ceremony 1960; founding partner (with Sally Tuffin) Foale and Tuffin Ltd 1961–72; signed with Puritan Fashion Corps, NY 1965–70; designed clothes for films; Susannah York (q.v.) in Kaleidoscope 1966, Audrey Hepburn in Two for the Road 1966; f. own label Marion Foale–Knitwear Designer 1982. *Publication:* Marion Foale's Classic Knitwear 1987. *Leisure interest:* studying fine art. *Address:* Foale Ltd, 133A Long Street, Atherstone, Warwicks., CV9 1AD, England. *Telephone:* (1827) 720333. *Fax:* (1827) 720444. *E-mail:* foale@talk21.com (Office).

FOBES, John Edwin; American diplomatist and international official; b. 16 March 1918, Chicago, Ill.; s. of Wilfred Franklin Fobes and Mabel Skogsberg; m. Hazel Ward Weaver 1941; one s. one d.; ed Northwestern Univ., Fletcher School of Law and Diplomacy and School for Advanced Int. Studies, Johns Hopkins Univ.; USAAF 1942–45; UN Secr., London and New York 1945–46; Admin. Analyst, US Bureau of the Budget 1947–48; Asst Dir Tech. Assistance, US Marshall Plan, Washington 1948–51; Deputy Dir Org. and Planning, Mutual Security Agency, Washington 1951–52; Adviser, US Del. to NATO and European Regional Orgs, Paris 1952–55; Dir Office of Int. Admin.,

Dept of State 1955–59; (elected) mem. UN Advisory Cttee on Admin. and Budgetary Questions 1955–60; Sr Adviser, US Del. to the 10th–14th sessions of UN Gen. Ass.; Special Adviser to Asst Sec. of State, Washington 1959–60; Program Officer and Deputy Dir US Agency for Int. Devt Mission to India 1960–64; Asst Dir-Gen. (Admin.), UNESCO, Paris 1964–70, Deputy Dir-Gen. 1971–77, Chair. US Nat. Comm. for UNESCO 1980–81, Vice-Chair. 1982–83; Pres. Americans for Universality of UNESCO 1984–; Chair. US Asscn for the Club of Rome 1982–87; mem. Club of Rome 1983–; Pres. American Library in Paris 1968–70, Western N Carolina UNA 1991–93, NC Div. UNA 1993–96; Visiting Scholar Indiana and Harvard Univs. 1970, D. H. Bucknell Univ. 1973; Visiting Scholar and Adviser on Int. Studies Duke Univ. 1978–82, Univ. of N Carolina, Adjunct Prof. of Political Science Western Carolina Univ. 1982–95; Nehru Gold Medal for Distinguished Int. Service (UNESCO) 1992. *Leisure interests:* community service, walking, reading, writing. *Address:* 28 Beaverbrook Road, Asheville, NC 28804, USA. *Telephone:* (828) 253-5383. *Fax:* (828) 252-9728 (Home). *E-mail:* jfobes@mountainx.com (Home).

FODOR, Gábor, D. JUR.; Hungarian politician and lawyer; b. 27 Sept. 1962, Gyöngyös; s. of Arpád Fodor and Klára Révfalvi; m. Barbara Czeizel; one s. one d.; ed János Nagy Berze Secondary School and Loránd Eötvös Univ. of Sciences, Budapest; teacher, István Bibó Special Coll. 1988–89; Research Fellow, Cen. European Research Group 1989–90; Asst Lecturer, Faculty of Philosophy, Eötvös Loránd Univ. of Sciences; Co-founder, Alliance of Young Democrats (FIDESZ), Vice-Pres. April–Nov. 1993; mem. Nat. Security Cttee 1990–92; mem. Parl. 1993–; Minister of Culture and Educ. 1994–95; Pres. Standing Cttee on Human Rights, Ethnic Minorities and Religious Affairs of Parl. 1993; mem. Council of Europe Cttee on Human Rights 1992, Constitutional and Legis. Cttee 1996–, Human Rights Minorities and Religious Affairs Cttee 1998, Environmental Cttee 1998; Leadership of Alliance of Free Democrats (SZDSZ) 1996–. *Leisure interest:* reading. *Address:* Képviselöi Irodaház, 1358 Budapest, Széchenyi rkp. 19, Hungary. *Telephone:* (1) 441-5830. *Fax:* (1) 441-5952. *E-mail:* gabor.fodor@szdsz.parlament.hu (Office).

FODOR, Gen. Lajos; Hungarian army officer; b. 29 July 1947, Debrecen; m. Éva Kovács; one s. one d.; ed Lajos Kossuth Land Forces Military Acad., Szentendre, Frunze Military Acad., Moscow, Defence Language Inst., San Antonio, American Nat. Defence Univ.; infantry officer 1970; platoon leader 14th Mechanized infantry Regt Nagykaniza 1971; Bn Commdr 63rd Mechanized Infantry Regt Nagyatád 1971–79, Deputy Commdr 1981–83, Regt Commdr 1983–85; Brig. 26th Mechanized Infantry Regt Lenti 1985–87; Deputy Chief and Chief of Mechanized Infantry and Armored Service, Gen. Dir of Training 1989; Deputy Commdr 5th Army, Székesfehérvár; Deputy Commdr and Major-Gen. of Hungarian Army 1992; Dir of Mil. Intelligence Office 1993; Deputy Chief of Defence Staff 1996–99, Chief 1999–; Under-Sec. for Policy, Ministry of Defence 1999–; apptd. Gen. and Commdr of Defence Forces 1999. *Address:* Honvédelmi Minisztérium, Balaton u. 7/11, 1055 Budapest, Hungary (Office). *Telephone:* 474-1109 (Office). *Fax:* 447-1110 (Office).

FOGEL, Robert William, PhD, FAAS; American historian, university professor and economist; b. 1 July 1926, New York; s. of Harry Gregory and Elizabeth (Mitnik) Fogel; m. Enid Cassandra Morgan 1949; two s.; ed Cornell, Columbia, Cambridge, Harvard and Johns Hopkins Univs; Instructor, Johns Hopkins Univ. 1958–59; Asst Prof., Univ. of Rochester 1960–64; Assoc. Prof., Univ. of Chicago 1964–65, Prof. 1965–75; Prof., Harvard Univ. 1975–81; Charles R. Walgreen Distinguished Service Prof. of American Insts., Univ. of Chicago 1981–, Dir Center for Population Econs 1981–; Chair. History Advisory Cttee of the Math. Social Science Bd 1965–72; Pres. Econ. History Asscn 1977–78; Social Science History Asscn 1980–81; Nat. Bureau of Econ. Research Assoc.; Fellow Econ. Soc., American Acad. of Arts and Sciences, NAS, Royal Historical Soc.; Arthur H. Cole Prize 1968, Schumpeter Prize 1971, Bancroft Prize in American History 1975, shared Nobel Prize in Econs 1993. *Publications:* The Union Pacific Railroad 1960, Railroads and American Economic Growth 1972, Time on the Cross 1974, Ten Lectures on the New Economic History 1977, Which Road to the Past?: Two Views of History 1983, Without Consent or Contract: The Rise and Fall of American Slavery (Vol. I) 1989, (Vols II–IV) 1992, The Fourth Great Awakening and the Future of Egalitarianism 2000. *Leisure interests:* carpentry, photography. *Address:* Center for Population Economics, University of Chicago, Graduate School of Business, 1101 East 58th Street, RO 118, Chicago, IL 60637-1511 (Office); 5321 S University Avenue, Chicago, IL 60615, USA (Home). *Telephone:* (312) 702-7709 (Office). *Fax:* (312) 702-2901.

FOGELBERG, Graeme, MCom, MBA, PhD; New Zealand university administrator; b. 10 Dec. 1939, Wellington; s. of the late Frederick Edward Fogelberg and Evelyn Fogelberg (née Greenwell); m. (divorced); three s. two d.; ed Wellington Coll., Victoria Univ. of Wellington and Univ. of Western Ontario; Prof. of Business Admin. Victoria Univ. of Wellington 1970, Dean Faculty of Commerce Admin. 1977–82, Deputy Vice-Chancellor 1986–92; professorial appts at Univ. of Western Ont. 1975–76, 1986–87 and Pa State Univ. 1992–93; Vice-Chancellor Univ. of Otago, Dunedin 1994–; Chair. NZ Vice-Chancellors Cttee 1999–2000; fmr Chair. Asscn of Commonwealth Univs; Fellow NZ Inst. of Dirs; Pres. Rotary Club of Wellington 1988–89. *Publications:* several business study books and articles in accounting, business, man. and econs journals. *Leisure interests:* tennis, skiing and fine New Zealand wines. *Address:* University of Otago, Union Street, P.O. Box 56, Dunedin, New Zealand. *Telephone:* (3) 479-8253. *Fax:* (3) 479-8544.

FOGELHOLM, Markus, MA; Finnish banker; b. 11 March 1946, Helsinki; s. of Eila Fogelholm and Georg Fogelholm; m. Saara RI Suokas 1969; one s. one d.; ed Univ. of Helsinki; joined Bank of Finland 1972, Head Foreign Financing Dept 1984–87, Market Operations Dept 1992–; Special Asst to Exec. Dir of UN Centre on Transnat. Corpns 1978–81; Alt. Exec. Dir IMF 1987–89, Exec. Dir 1989–91; Vice-Chair. Forex Finland. *Leisure interests:* wine, music, tennis, swimming. *Address:* Bank of Finland, Snellmanninaukio, P.O. Box 160, SF-00101 Helsinki, Finland. *Fax:* (9) 626038. *E-mail:* markus.foge.lholm@bof.fi (Office).

FOGLIETTA, Thomas M., BLL; American diplomatist, lawyer and politician; b. 3 Dec. 1929, Philadelphia, PA; ed St Joseph's Univ., Pa, Temple Univ., Pa; attorney 1953–80; served as Minority Leader on Philadelphia City Council 1955–75; District Dir and Rep., Sec. of Labor in Philadelphia 1976–77; elected to U.S. House of Reps. as Ind. 1980, Democrat 1981; Founding Chair. Urban Caucus 1991; served on Armed Services Cttee, Merchant Marine and Fisheries Cttee, Foreign Affairs Cttee and Select Cttee on Hunger; Amb. to Italy 1997–2002; Consultant Cassidy and Assocs. 2002–; numerous awards in recognition of his contribs. to health care. *Address:* Cassidy and Associates, Suite 400, 700 Thirteenth Street, N.W. Washington, DC 20005, U.S.A. *Telephone:* (202) 347-0773. *Fax:* (202) 347-0785. *E-mail:* info@cassidy.com. *Website:* www.cassidy.com.

FOKIN, Valery Vladimirovich; Russian theatre and film director; b. 28 Feb. 1946, Moscow; m. Tatiana Krivenko; two s.; ed Moscow Shchukin Theatre School; Stage Dir Moscow Sovremennik Theatre 1971–85; Chief Stage Dir Yermolova Theatre 1985–90; Artistic Dir M. Yermolova Theatre Centre 1990–2000; Founder, Artistic Dir and Dir-Gen. Meyerhold Artistic Centre 1990–; Theatre Prize, BITEFF Prize, State's Prize, Honoured Art Worker of Poland, three Crystal Turandot awards including for Last Night of the Tsar. *Film:* The Metamorphosis. *Theatre includes:* (Stage Dir) Valentin and Valentina, I'll Go and Go, Inspector, Provincial Anecdotes, Lorenzacchio, Who's Afraid of Virginia Woolf, In Spring I Shall Come Back to You, Transformation, (Chief Stage Dir) Speak Up, Second Year of Freedom, Sports Scenes of 1980, Invitation to Punishment (Artistic Dir), Hotel Room in Town N (Best Dir), (Dir) Artand and His Double. *Television:* over 25 films and performances. *Publications:* Hotel Room in Town N, The Metamorphosis; numerous articles and speeches. *Address:* Vsevolod Meyerhold Centre, Novoslobodskaya str. 23, Moscow (Office); Triohprudniy pereulok 13/11, 5, Moscow, Russia (Home). *Telephone:* (095) 363-10-46 (Office); (095) 299-16-76 (Home). *Fax:* (095) 363 1041 (Office). *E-mail:* meyerhold@meyerhold.ru (Office). *Website:* www.theatre.ru/meyerholdcentre/ (Office).

FOKIN, Vitold Pavlovych; Ukrainian politician; b. 25 Oct. 1932, Novomikolaivka, Zaporozhye region; m.; one s. one d.; ed m. Dnepropetrovsk Mining Inst.; fmr mem. C.P.; engineer 1954–71; Deputy Chair. Council of Ministers of Ukraine 1987–90; Chair. State Cttee for Econs Aug.–Nov. 1990; Chair. Council of Ministers (Prime Minister) of Ukraine 1990–92; Sr Researcher Inst. of World Econ. and Int. Relations 1993–, Pres. Int. Fund for Humanitarian and Econ. Relations with Russian Fed. 1993–; mem. Higher Econ. Council of Pres. of Ukraine 1997–; People's Deputy 1998–. *Address:* Verkhovna Rada, M. Hrushevskoho rul 5, 252019 Kiev, Ukraine.

FOKIN, Yuri Yevgenyevich; Russian diplomatist (retd.); b. 2 Sept. 1936, Gorky (now Nizhny Novgorod); m.; one s.; one d.; ed Moscow Inst. of Int. Relations; on staff USSR Ministry of Foreign Affairs 1960–; with USSR Mission in UN 1960–65, Secr. of Minister of Foreign Affairs 1966–73, Sr Adviser Dept of Planning of Int. Events 1973–76; Deputy Perm. Rep. of USSR to UN 1976–79; Deputy Dir-Gen. Ministry of Foreign Affairs 1979–80, Dir-Gen. 1980–86; Amb. to Cyprus 1986–90, to Norway 1995–97, to UK 1997–2000; Head Second European Dept Russian Ministry of Foreign Affairs 1990–92, Dir Second European Dept 1991–95; on staff Ministry of Foreign Affairs 1995–, Rector, Diplomatic Acad.; Decorations from Russia, Austria, Norway. *Publications:* Diplomatic Yearbook 2000, 2001, 2002, State & Diaspora: A Record of Interaction. *Leisure interests:* reading, ballet, theatre, tennis. *Address:* Ministry of Foreign Affairs, Smolenskaya-Sennaya 32/34, Moscow, Russia (Office).

FOLEY, Lieut.-Gen. Sir John Paul, KCB, OBE, MC; British civil servant, fmr army officer and business executive; b. 22 April 1939, London; s. of Henry Thomas Hamilton Foley and Helen Constance Margaret Foley (née Pearson); m. Ann Rosamond Humphries 1972; two d.; ed Bradfield Coll., Berks., Army Staff Coll., Camberley, Royal Coll. of Defence Studies, London; nat. service with Royal Green Jackets (RGJ) 1959–61, then Regimental Service 1962–70, attached Staff Coll. 1971; Brig.-Maj. 1974–75; instructor Staff Coll. 1976–78; CO 3 RGJ 1978–80, Commdt Jr Div. Staff Coll. 1981–82, Dir SAS 1983–85, Royal Coll. of Defence Studies 1986; Chief British Mission to Soviet Forces E Germany 1987–89; Deputy Chief Defence Intelligence 1989–91, Chief 1994–97; Commdr British Forces Hong Kong 1992–94, retd 1997; mem. Security Comm.; Chair. British Greyhound Racing Bd, Defence Appts., Defence Consultant Alpha Business Ventures Ltd 1998–2000; Lieut.-Gov. of Guernsey 2000–; KStJ. *Leisure interests:* gardening, reading, walking, tennis, bird watching, golf. *Address:* Government House, Guernsey, GY1 1GH, Channel Islands (Office). *Telephone:* (1481) 726666 (Office). *Fax:* (1481) 715919 (Office).

FOLEY, Thomas Stephen, BA, LLB; American politician; b. 6 March 1929, Spokane, Wash.; s. of Ralph E. Foley and Helen Marie Higgins; m. Heather Strachan 1968; ed Washington Univ.; Partner Higgins and Foley 1957–58;

Deputy Prosecuting Attorney, Spokane Co. 1958–60; Instructor of Law, Gonzaga Univ. 1958–60; Asst Attorney Gen., Wash. State 1960–61; Interior and Insular Affairs Cttee, US Senate, Washington, DC 1961–64; mem. 89th–100th Congresses from 5th Dist Wash. 1965–94, Chair. Agric. Cttee 1975–81, Vice-Chair. 1981–86; Chair. House Democratic Caucus 1976–80, House Majority Whip 1981–87, Majority Leader 1987–89, Speaker House of Reps. 1989–95; Partner Akin, Gump, Strauss, Hauer & Feld, Washington, DC 1995–98; Amb. to Japan 1997–2001; Democrat. *Publication:* Measuring Lives (novel) 1996. *Address:* c/o Department of State, 2201 C Street, NW, Washington, DC 20520, USA (Office).

FØLLESDAL, Dagfinn, PhD; Norwegian professor of philosophy; b. 22 June 1932, Askim; s. of Trygve Føllesdal and Margit Teigen; m. Vera Heyerdahl 1957; five s. one d.; ed Univs of Oslo and Göttingen and Harvard Univ.; Research Asst in Ionospheric Physics, Norwegian Research Council 1955–57; Instructor and Asst Prof. of Philosophy, Harvard Univ. 1961–64; Prof. of Philosophy, Univ. of Oslo 1967–; Prof. of Philosophy, Stanford Univ. 1968–76, C. I. Lewis Prof. of Philosophy 1976–; Visiting Prof. Coll. de France 1977; Guggenheim Fellow 1978–79; Fellow, Center for Advanced Study in Behavioral Sciences 1981–82, American Council of Learned Socs 1983–84, Inst. for Advanced Study, Princeton 1985–86, Wissenschaftskolleg, Berlin 1989–90, Centre for Advanced Study, Oslo 1995–96; mem. American Acad. of Arts and Sciences, Academia Europaea and scientific acads in Norway, Denmark, Sweden and Finland; Pres. Norwegian Acad. of Science 1993, 1995, 1997; Univ. of Oslo Research Prize 1995, Alexander von Humboldt Research Award 1997. *Publications:* Husserl und Frege 1958, Referential Opacity and Modal Logic 1966, Argumentasjonsteori språk og vitenskapsfilosofi (with L. Walløe and J. Elster) 1977; Ed. Journal of Symbolic Logic 1970–82, Philosophy of Quire, 5 vols 2000; numerous articles on philosophy of language, phenomenology, existentialism, action theory, educational and ethical issues. *Address:* Department of Philosophy, Stanford University, Stanford, CA 94305, USA (Office); Staverhagan 7, 1312 Slependen, Norway (Home). *Telephone:* (650) 723-2547 (Office); (47) 67-55-00-01 (Home). *Fax:* (47) 67-55-00-02 (Home). *E-mail:* dagfinn@csli.stanford.edu (Home).

FOLLETT, Ken, BA; British author; b. 5 June 1949, Cardiff, Wales; s. of Martin D. Follett and Veenie Evans; m. 1st Mary Elson 1968 (divorced 1985); one s. one d.; m. 2nd Barbara Broer 1985; one step-s. two step-d.; ed Univ. Coll. London; trainee reporter, South Wales Echo, Cardiff 1970–73; reporter, London Evening News 1973–74; Editorial Dir Everest Books, London 1974–76, Deputy Man. Dir 1976–77; full-time writer 1977–; Fellow Univ. Coll. London 1994; mem. Council, Nat. Literary Trust 1996–; Chair. Nat. Year of Reading 1998–99; Pres. Dyslexia Inst. 1998–; Vice-Pres. Stevenage Borough Football Club 2000–, Stevenage Community Trust 2002–; Patron, Stevenage Home-Start 2000–; Chair. Govs, Roebuck Primary School and Nursery 2001–. *Publications:* Eye of the Needle (Edgar Award, Mystery Writers of America 1979) 1978, Triple 1979, The Key to Rebecca 1980, The Man from St Petersburg 1982, On Wings of Eagles 1983, Lie Down with Lions 1986, The Pillars of the Earth 1989, Night Over Water 1991, A Dangerous Fortune 1993, A Place Called Freedom 1995, The Third Twin 1996, The Hammer of Eden 1998, Code to Zero 2000, Jackdaws 2001, Hornet Flight 2003. *Leisure interests:* left-wing politics, bass guitarist in blues band Damn Right I Got The Blues. *Address:* The Old Rectory, Old Knebworth Lane, Stevenage, Herts. SG3 6PT (Home); PO Box 4, Knebworth, SG3 6UT, England. *Website:* www.ken-follett.com (Office).

FOLZ, Jean-Martin; French motor executive; b. 11 Jan. 1947, Strasbourg; s. of Robert Folz and Marianne Bock; m. Marie-Claire Picardet 1968; two d.; ed Lycée Carnot, Dijon, Ecole Sainte-Geneviève à Versailles and Ecole Polytechnique; Training postgraduate Maison Franco-Japonaise, Tokyo 1970–71; mining engineer DRIRE Rouen 1972–74; Adviser, Office of Minister of Commerce and Crafts 1974–76; Asst Dir Office of Minister for Quality of Life 1976–77; Dir Office of Sec. of State at Ministry of Industry, Commerce and Crafts 1977–78; Factory Man. Rhône-Poulenc Polymères, Saint Fons 1979–80; Group Gen. Man. Rhône-Poulenc Special Chemicals 1981–84; Chair. and CEO Jeumont-Schneider 1984–87; CEO Péchiney 1987–91; Chair. Carbone Lorraine 1987–91; CEO Eridania Béghin-Say 1991–95; Man. Automobile Div. PSA Peugeot-Citroën 1996–97, Chair. Man. Bd PSA 1997–; Dir Ecole polytechnique 1999–; mem. Bd of Dirs. French Asscn of Pvt. Enterprise 2001–. *Address:* Peugeot SA, 75 avenue de la Grande Armée, B.P. 01 75116 Paris (Office); 3 allée des Drocourtes, 78290 Croissy-sur-Seine, France (Home). *Telephone:* (1) 40-66-55-11 (Office); (1) 40-66-54-14. *Website:* www.psa.fr (Office).

FOMENKO, Anatoly Timofeevich; Russian mathematician; b. 13 March 1945; m.; ed Moscow State Univ.; Asst, Sr Researcher, Prof. Moscow State Univ.; Corresp. mem. USSR (now Russian) Acad. of Sciences 1990, mem. 1994; research in theory of minimal surfaces, topology of multidimensional manifolds, simplectic geometry and theory of topological classifications of integrable differential equations; Chair. Moscow Math. Soc.; Award of Moscow Mathematical Soc. 1974, Award of Presidium of Russian Acad. of Sciences 1987, State Award of Russian Fed. 1996. *Publications include:* Simplectic Geometry: Methods and Applications 1988, The Plateau Problem 1990. *Leisure interests:* statistical analysis of historical texts, painting. *Address:* Dept of Mathematics and Mechanics, Moscow State University, Vorobyevy gory, 119992 Moscow, Russia. *Telephone:* (095) 939-39-40 (Office).

FOMENKO, Piotr Naumovich; Russian stage director; b. 13 July 1932, Moscow; m. Maya Andreyevna Tushkova; one s.; ed Ippolitov-Ivanov Higher School of Music, V. Lenin Pedagogical Inst., State Inst. of Theatre Art; stage dir in amateur clubs and studios of Moscow 1953–61; guest dir in Moscow theatres including Taganka, Na Maloy Bronnoy, Cen. Children's, Mayakovsky, Cen. Theatre of Soviet Army, Satire and others 1961–84; among productions Death of Tarelkin (M. Saltykov-Shchedrin), Fruit of Education (L. Tolstoy), New Mysteria-Buff (after V. Mayakovsky), Interrogation (P. Weiss), As You Like It (William Shakespeare); Stage Dir Theatre of Comedy in Leningrad 1972–78, Chief Stage Dir 1978–82; staged over 20 productions, some of which were banned; Dir Vakhtangov Theatre in Moscow 1985–; among productions Guilty Without Guilt (A. Ostrovsky) and The Queen of Spades (A. Pushkin); f. Little Stage (Under the Roof) Mossoviet Theatre, produced Caligula by A. Camus; f. Theatre-Workshop of P. Fomenko 1991, toured in Europe; directed films and TV productions 1965–; TV productions: Childhood, Boyhood and Youth (trilogy by L. Tolstoy), Belkin's Stories by A. Pushkin, To the Rest of the Lifetime (4 series); films: Almost Funny Story, About a Ride by Old Car; lecturer State Inst. of Theatre Art 1982, Prof. 1989; master classes in Paris Conservatory, Cen. Reimschad (Germany); People's Artist of Russia; Crystal Turandot Prize, K. Stanislavsky Prize and others. *Address:* Theatre Workshop of Piotr Fomenko, Kutuzovskiy Prosp. 30/32, 121165 Moscow (Office); Pobedy pl. 1, korp. A, Apt. 75, 121293 Moscow, Russia (Home). *Telephone:* (095) 249-17-03 (Office); (095) 148-07-73 (Home).

FONCHA, John Ngu; Cameroonian politician; b. 21 June 1916, Nkwen, NW Prov.; s. of Foncha Ngebi and Magdalene Ngebi; m. Anna Atang 1945; four s. three d.; ed Bamenda Govt School, St Michael's School, Delta Pastoral Church, Buguma, St Charles' Coll. Onitsha, Agric. Coll., Moore Plantation, Ibadan; Probationary teacher and teacher 1934–56; Co-founder Kamerun United Nat. Congress (KUNC) 1952; mem. Eastern Regional Ass., Nigeria 1951–53; mem. S. Cameroons Quasi-Regional Ass. 1954-65; Founder-Pres. Kamerun Nat. Democratic Party (KNDP) 1955–66; Prime Minister and Minister of Local Govt, Southern Cameroons 1959–61, Prime Minister W Cameroon 1961–65; Vice-Pres. Fed. Repub. of Cameroon 1961–70; Co-founder and Vice-Pres. Cameroon Nat. Union (CNU) 1966; Vice-Pres. Political Bureau 1970–75, Cen. Cttee 1975; Grand Chancellor of Cameroon Nat. Orders 1979. *Publication:* Farewell to Prime Minister and People of West Cameroon. *Leisure interest:* gardening. *Address:* P.O. Box 157, Bamenda, NW Province, Cameroon.

FONDA, Bridget; American actress; b. 27 Jan. 1964, Los Angeles, Calif.; d. of Peter Fonda (q.v.) and Susan Fonda; ed New York Univ. theater programme; studied acting at Lee Strasberg Inst. and with Harold Guskin; workshop stage performances include Confession and Pastels. *Films:* Aria (Tristan and Isolde sequence) (debut) 1987, You Can't Hurry Love 1988, Shag 1988, Scandal 1989, Strapless 1989, Frankenstein Unbound 1990, The Godfather: Part III 1990, Doc Hollywood 1991, Out of the Rain 1991, Single White Female 1992, Singles 1992, Bodies Rest and Motion 1993, Point of No Return 1993, Little Buddha 1994, It Could Happen To You 1994, Camilla 1994, The Road to Welville 1994, Rough Magic 1995, Balto (voice) 1995, Grace of My Heart 1996, City Hall 1996, Drop Dead Fred, Light Years (voice), Iron Maze, Army of Darkness, Touch, Jackie Brown, Finding Graceland, The Break Up, South of Heaven West of Hell, Monkey Bone, Lake Placid, Delivering Milo. TV: (series) 21 Jump Street, Jacob Have I Loved, Wonder-Works (episode) 1989, The Edge (The Professional Man); (film) Leather Jackets 1991, In the Gloaming 1997. *Address:* c/o IFA, 8730 West Sunset Boulevard, Suite 490, Los Angeles, CA 90069, USA.

FONDA, Jane; American actress; b. 21 Dec. 1937; d. of the late Henry Fonda and of Frances Seymour; m. 1st Roger Vadim 1967 (divorced 1973, died 2000); one d.; m. 2nd Tom Hayden 1973 (divorced 1989); one s.; m. 3rd Ted Turner 1991 (separated); ed Vassar Coll.; Acad. Award for Best Actress 1972, 1979; Golden Globe Award 1978. *Films include:* Tall Story 1960, A Walk on the Wild Side 1962, Period of Adjustment 1962, Sunday in New York 1963, The Love Cage 1963, La Ronde 1964, Histoires extraordinaires 1967, Barbarella 1968, They Shoot Horses Don't They? 1969, Klute 1970, Steelyard Blues 1972, Tout va bien 1972, A Doll's House 1973, The Blue Bird 1975, Fun with Dick and Jane 1976, Julia 1977, Coming Home 1978, California Suite 1978, The Electric Horseman 1979, The China Syndrome 1979, Nine to Five 1980, On Golden Pond 1981, Roll-Over 1981, Agnes of God 1985, The Morning After 1986, The Old Gringo 1988, Stanley and Iris 1990; producer Lakota Woman 1994. *Plays include:* There Was a Little Girl, Invitation to a March, The Fun Couple, Strange Interlude. *Television:* The Dollmaker (ABC-TV) 1984 (Emmy Award). *Publications:* Jane Fonda's Workout Book 1982, Women Coming of Age 1984, Jane Fonda's new Workout and Weight Loss Program 1986, Jane Fonda's New Pregnancy Workout and Total Birth Program 1989, Jane Fonda Workout Video, Jane Fonda Cooking for Healthy Living 1996. *Address:* c/o Kim Hodgert, CAA, 9830 Wilshire Boulevard, Beverly Hills, CA 90212, USA.

FONDA, Peter; American film actor, director and producer; b. 23 Feb. 1940, New York; s. of the late Henry Fonda and of Frances Seymour; m. Susan Brewer (divorced 1974); two c.; ed Univ. of Omaha. *Films include:* Tammy and the Doctor 1963, The Victors 1963, Lilith 1964, The Young Lovers 1964, The Wild Angels 1966, The Trip 1967, Easy Rider (also co-screenplay writer, co-producer) 1969, The Last Movie 1971, The Hired Hand (also Dir) 1971, Two People (also Dir) 1973, Dirty Mary, Crazy Harry 1974, Race with the Devil 1975, 92 in the Shade 1975, Killer Force 1975, Fighting Mad 1976, Futureworld 1976, Outlaw Blues 1977, High Ballin' 1978, Wanda Nevada (also Dir)

1979, Open Season, Smokey and the Bandit II 1980, Split Image 1982, Certain Fury 1985, Dead Fall 1993, Nadja 1994, Love and a 45 1994, Painted Hero 1996, Escape from LA 1996, Idaho Transfer (also Dir), Ulee's Gold 1997, Spasm, Fatal Mission, Reckless, Cannonball Run (cameo), Dance of the Dwarfs, Mercenary Fighters, Jungle Heat, Diajobu My Friend, Peppermint Frieden, The Rose Garden, Family Spirit, South Beach, Bodies Rest and Motion, Deadfall, Molly and Gina, South of Heaven West of Hell, The Limey, Keeping Time. *Television films:* The Hostage Tower 1980, Don't Look Back 1996, A Reason to Live, A Time of Indifference, Sound, Certain Honorable Men, Montana. *Address:* IFA Talent Agency, 8730 West Sunset Boulevard, Suite 490, Los Angeles, CA 90069, USA.

FONG WONG KUT MAN, Nellie; Hong Kong government official and accountant; b. 7 Feb. 1949, Hong Kong; m. Eddy C. Fong; one c.; practises as chartered accountant; mem. Hong Kong Urban Council 1983–89, Legis. Council 1988–91, People's Repub. of China Hong Kong Special Admin. Region Preliminary and Preparatory Cttees. 1993–97 (Leader Econ. Sub-Group), Exec. Council of Hong Kong Special Admin. Region 1997–98; Chair. Exec. Cttee The Better Hong Kong Foundation 1995, China Operations, Arthur Andersen, Exec. Cttee Lifeline Express 1997–; mem. Standing Comm. on Civil Service Salaries and Conditions of Service 1989–93, Hong Kong Baptist Univ. Council 1990–92, numerous other cttees and bds; Gold Bauhenia Star 1999. *Address:* c/o Executive Council Secretariat, 1st Floor, Main Wing, Central Government Offices, Central, Hong Kong Special Administrative Region, People's Republic of China. *Telephone:* 28520294 (Office). *Fax:* 28504092 (Office). *E-mail:* nellie.k.fong@hk.arthurandersen.com (Office).

FONSECA, Ralph H.; Belizean politician; b. 9 Aug. 1949; m.; three c.; ed St John's Coll.; fmr Asst Gen. Man. Texaco, Belize; fmr Area Gen. Man. Cardinal Distributors, Canada; fmr Research Engineer, Control Data; fmr Systems Analyst, Prescribe Data System; fmr gen. man. brewing co.; fmr Man. Dir. Hillbank Agroindustry; fmr Chair. Belize Electricity Co.; fmr Chair. Belize Telecommunications Authority Ltd; fmr Pres. Consolidated Electricity Services; mem. Parl. 1993–; Minister of Budget Man., Investment and Home Affairs 1999–. *Address:* Ministry of Budget Management, Investment and Home Affairs, New Administration Building, Cayo District, Belmopan, Belize (Office). *Telephone:* (8) 22218 (Office); (8) 22231 (Office). *Fax:* (8) 22195 (Office). *Website:* www.belize.gov.bz (Office).

FONSECA PIMENTEL, A(ntônio); Brazilian author and fmr government official; b. 3 July 1916, Ouro Fino, Minas Gerais; s. of Antônio Pimentel Jr and Maria Ignacia Pimentel; m. Irma de Mello (née Machado) 1945; three s. three d.; ed Ginasio Culto à Ciência, Campinas, São Paulo, Colegio Brasil, Ouro Fino and American Univ. Washington, DC; Adviser, Brazilian School of Public Admin. 1953–55; joined Dept of Civil Service 1955, Dir-Gen. 1961–63; Regional Adviser UN Cen. America Tech. Assistance Bd 1963–65; Asst Dir Personnel and Man., FAO 1966–69; Asst Head, Civil Staff of Presidency of Repub. 1969–71; Special Adviser Getúlio Vargas Foundation, Brasília 1971–94; mem. UN Int. Civil Service Comm. 1975–98; mem. Academia Brasiliense de Letras and other acads. *Publications:* A Apuração do Merecimento 1945, O Teatro de Nelson Rodrigues 1951, Alguns Aspectos do Treinamento 1954, Machado de Assis e Outros Estudos 1962, A Paz e o Pão (Desafio às Nações Unidas) 1970, A Presença Alemã na Obra de Machado de Assis 1974, Introdução à Administração Internacional de Recursos Humanos 1975, Democratic World Government and the United Nations 1979, Can a Third World War (Nuclear) be Avoided? 1983, Padre Germano e o Terceiro Milênio (Uma Visão do Apocalipse) 1998; memoirs: Memorial dos Setenta 1989, Retoques e Acréscimos ao Memorial dos Setenta 1990, Reflexões 1992. *Leisure interests:* classical music, farming. *Address:* SQS 208, Bloco F, Apt. 101, 70254-060 Brasília DF, Brazil. *Telephone:* (61) 242-2523. *Fax:* (61) 224-6314.

FONTAINE, André; French journalist; b. 30 March 1921, Paris; s. of Georges Fontaine and Blanche Rochon-Duvigneaud; m. Isabelle Cavaillé 1943; two s. one d.; ed Coll. Ste. Marie de Monceau, Paris, Sorbonne and Faculty of Law, Paris Univ.; journalist 1946–, joined Le Monde 1947, Foreign Ed. 1951–69, Chief Ed. 1969–85, Ed.-in-Chief and Dir 1985–91, Consultant to Dir 1991–; mem. Bd French Inst. of Int. Relations –1992, Bank Indosuez 1983–85; Chair. Group on Int. Strategy for the Ninth French Plan 1982; Vice-Chair. Franco-British Council (French section) 1999–2002; Atlas Int. Ed. of the Year 1976. *Publications:* L'alliance atlantique à l'heure du dégel 1960, History of the Cold War (two Vols) 1965, 1967, La guerre civile froide 1969, Le dernier quart du siècle 1976, La France au bois dormant 1978, Un seul lit pour deux rêves 1981, Sortir de l'hexagonie (with others) 1984, L'un sans l'autre 1991, Après eux le déluge 1995. *Address:* Le Monde, 21 bis rue Claude-Bernard, 75262 Paris Cédex 05, France. *Telephone:* 1-42-17-25-21.

FONTAINE, Maurice Alfred, DèsSc; French physiologist; b. 28 Oct. 1904, Savigny-sur-Orge; s. of Emile Fontaine and Lea Vadier; m. Yvonne Broca 1928; one s.; ed Lycée Henri IV, Paris and Faculty of Sciences and Faculty of Pharmacy, Univ. of Paris; various posts at Faculty of Sciences, Paris and Faculty of Pharmacy, Paris; Dir Lab. at Ecole pratique des hautes études 1946; Dir Inst. Océanographique, Paris 1957–68, 1975; Pres. Soc. Européenne d'Endocrinologie Comparée 1969; Dir of Musée Nat. d'Histoire Naturelle, Paris 1966–71; lectures on comparative and ecological physiology, particularly of marine animals; specializes in comparative endocrinology and fish migration; Dir of Research in these fields and also the study of ectocrine substances in sea water and marine pollution; fmr Pres. Acad. des Sciences;

mem. Acad. Nat. de Médecine, Acad. d'Agric., New York Acad. of Sciences; Hon. mem. Romanian Acad. 1991; Commdr Légion d'honneur, Commdr Ordre de Sahametrei (Cambodia), Commdr Ordre de St Charles (Monaco). *Publication:* Physiologie (collection La Pléïade) 1969, Rencontres insolites d'un biologiste autour du monde 1999. *Leisure interests:* the sea, especially migrations of fish, thalasso-éthique. *Address:* 25 rue Pierre Nicole, 75005 Paris, France (Home).

FONTAINE, Nicole; French politician and lawyer; b. 1942, Normandy; ed Inst. d'Etudes Politiques, Paris; admitted to Bar, Hauts-de-Seine; Legal Adviser Secrétariat général de l'Enseignement catholique, Deputy Sec.-Gen. 1972–81, Chief Rep. 1981–84; mem. Conseil supérieur de l'Educ. nationale 1975–81; mem. Standing Cttee 1978–81; mem. Conseil économique et social 1980–84; mem. European People's Party; mem. European Parl. 1984–, Vice-Pres. 1989–94, First Vice-Pres. 1994–99, Pres. 1999–2002, mem. Parl. Cttee on Legal Affairs and Citizens' Rights, on Culture, Youth, Educ. and the Media, on Women's Rights 1984–89, apptd. by European People's Party as perm. mem. Conciliation Cttee 1994–2002; Vice-Pres. Union pour la Démocratie Française (UDF). *Publications:* Les députés européens: Qui sont-ils? Que font-ils? 1994, l'Europe de vos initiatives 1997, Le traité d'Amsterdam 1998, My Battles at the Presidency of the European Parliament 2002. *Address:* European Parliament, Centre Européen, Plateau du Kirchberg, 2929 Luxembourg, Luxembourg (Office). *Telephone:* 4300-1 (Office). *Fax:* 4300-7009 (Office). *Website:* www.europarl.eu.int (Office).

FONTANA, Carlo; Italian opera house director and journalist; b. 15 March 1947, Milan; s. of Ciro Fontana; m. Roberta Cavallini; ed Univ. Statale di Milano; journalist 1968–77; responsible for youth activities, Piccolo Teatro di Milano 1968–71; Asst to Gen. Man. Teatro all Scala, Milan 1977–79, mem. Admin. Council 1980–84; Deputy Admin. Fonit Cetra 1979–84; Pres. AS.LI.CO. 1980–83; Dir Music Section, Venice Biennale 1983–86; Dir Ente Autonomo Teatro Comunale di Bologna 1984–90; Pres. Associazione Nazionale Enti Lirici e Sinfonici 1986–; mem. Commissione Centrale Musica, Consiglio Nazionale dello Spettacolo; Gen. Man. Teatro alla Scala, Milan 1990–; Prof. Univ. of Pavia; Grand 'Ufficialle della Repubblica Italiana; Ambrogino d'Oro, Milan 1999. *Leisure interests:* sport, music. *Address:* Teatro alla Scala, Via Filodrammatici 2, 20121 Milan, Italy. *Telephone:* (02) 88791 (Office). *Fax:* (02) 8879388 (Office).

FOOT, Michael David Kenneth Willoughby, CBE, MA, FCIB; British financial regulator; b. 16 Dec. 1946; s. of Kenneth Willoughby Foot and Ruth Joan Foot (née Cornah); m. Michele Annette Cynthia Macdonald 1972; one s. two d.; ed Pembroke Coll., Cambridge and Yale Univ.; joined Bank of England 1969, Man. 1978, Sr Man. 1985; seconded to IMF, Washington, DC as UK Alt. Exec. Dir 1985–87; Head Foreign Exchange Div., Bank of England 1988–90, European Div. 1990–93, Banking Supervision Div. 1993–94, Deputy Dir Supervision and Surveillance 1994–96, Exec. Dir 1996–98; Man. Dir Financial Services Authority 1998–. *Publications:* essays on monetary econs in various books and professional journals. *Leisure interests:* choral singing, tennis. *Address:* Financial Services Authority, 25 North Colonnade, Canary Wharf, London, E14 5HS, England. *Telephone:* (20) 7676-5000. *Fax:* (20) 7676-1013.

FOOT, Rt Hon Michael Mackintosh, PC, MP; British politician and journalist; b. 23 July 1913; s. of the late Isaac Foot; (brother of the late Lord Caradon); m. Jill Craigie 1949 (died 1999); ed Forres School, Swanage, Leighton Park School, Reading and Wadham Coll., Oxford; Pres. Oxford Union 1933; contested Monmouth 1935; Asst Ed. Tribune 1937–38, Jt Ed. 1948–52, Ed. 1952–59, Man. Dir 1952–74; mem. staff Evening Standard 1938, Acting Ed. 1942–44; political columnist Daily Herald 1944–64; MP for Plymouth, Devonport 1945–55, for Ebbw Vale 1960–83, for Blaenau Gwent 1983–92; fmr Opposition Spokesman on European Policy; Sec. of State for Employment 1974–76; Lord Pres. of Council, Leader of House of Commons 1976–79, Shadow Leader 1979–80; Deputy Leader of Labour Party 1976–80, Leader 1980–83; Hon. Fellow, Wadham Coll., Oxford 1969; Hon. mem. N.U.J. 1985; Hon. DLitt (Univ. of Wales) 1985, (Nottingham) 1990, (Plymouth) 1993; Hon. LLD (Exeter) 1990; Spanish Republican Order of Liberation 1973; Labour. *Publications:* Armistice 1918–1939 1940, Trial of Mussolini 1943, Brendan and Beverley 1944, part author Guilty Men 1940 and Who Are the Patriots? 1949, Still At Large 1950, Full Speed Ahead 1950, The Pen and the Sword 1957, Parliament in Danger 1959, Aneurin Bevan Vol. I 1962, Vol. II 1973, Harold Wilson: A Pictorial Biography 1964, Debts of Honour 1980, Another Heart and Other Pulses 1984, Loyalists and Loners 1986, The Politics of Paradise 1988, H.G.: The History of Mr. Wells 1995, Aneurin Bevan 1897–1960 1997, Dr. Strangelove I Presume 1999. *Address:* c/o Tribune, 9 Arkwright Road, London, NW3 6AN, England.

FOOT, Paul Mackintosh; British writer and journalist; b. 8 Nov. 1937; three s. one d.; Pres. Oxford Union 1961; Ed. Isis 1961; TUC del. from Nat. Union of Journalists 1967, 1971; Ed. Socialist Worker 1974–75; with The Daily Mirror 1979–93, Private Eye 1993–; Socialist Workers' Party parl. cand. Birmingham, Stechford 1977; Journalist of the Year, What The Papers Say Awards 1972, 1989, Campaigning Journalist of the Year, British Press Awards 1980, George Orwell Prize for Journalism (jtly. with Tim Laxton) 1994, Journalist of the Decade (1990s), What The Papers Say Awards 2000. *Publications:* Immigration and Race in British Politics 1965, The Politics of Harold Wilson 1968, The Rise of Enoch Powell 1969, Who Killed Hanratty? 1971, Why You Should Be a Socialist 1977, Red Shelley 1981, The Helen

Smith Story 1983, Murder at the Farm: Who Killed Carl Bridgewater? 1986, Who Framed Colin Wallace? 1989, Words as Weapons 1990, Articles of Resistance 2000. *Address:* Private Eye, 6 Carlisle Street, London W1D 3BN, England. *Telephone:* (20) 7437-4017 (Office). *Fax:* (20) 7437-0705 (Office). *E-mail:* strobes@private-eye.co.uk (Office). *Website:* www.private-eye.co.uk.

FOOT, Philippa Ruth, MA, FBA; British university professor; b. 3 Oct. 1920, Owston Ferry, Lincs.; d. of W. S. B. Bosanquet and Esther Cleveland Bosanquet; m. M. R. D. Foot 1945 (divorced 1960); ed Somerville Coll. Oxford; Lecturer in Philosophy, Somerville Coll. Oxford 1947–50, Fellow and Tutor 1950–69, Vice-Prin. 1967–69, Sr Research Fellow 1970–88, Hon. Fellow 1988–; Prof. of Philosophy, Univ. of Calif. Los Angeles 1974–91, Griffin Prof. 1988–91, Prof. Emer. 1991–; fmr Visiting Prof. Cornell Univ., MIT, Univ. of Calif. Berkeley, Princeton Univ., City Univ. of New York; Pres. Pacific Div. American Philosophical Asscn 1983–84; mem. American Acad. of Arts and Sciences; Dr. hc (Sofia, Bulgaria) 2000. *Publications:* Theories of Ethics (ed.) 1967, Virtues and Vices 1978, Natural Goodness 2001, Moral Dilemmas 2002; articles and reviews in professional journals. *Leisure interests:* reading, walking, gardening. *Address:* 15 Walton Street, Oxford, OX1 2HG, England. *Telephone:* (1865) 557130.

FOOTE, Huger, BA; American photographer; b. 13 Nov. 1961, Memphis, Tennessee; s. of Shelby Foote and Gwyn Foote; ed Sarah Lawrence Coll., NY; began photography at age of 12; photo assistant, Paris 1983–87; freelance photographer, New York 1987–93; began working as professional artist, Memphis 1993–98; moved to London 1998; has held exhbns. across Europe and the USA. *Solo exhibitions include:* Ledbetter Lusk Gallery, Memphis 1996, Gallery of Contemporary Photography, Santa Monica 1997, Dorothy de Pauw Gallery, Brussels 2000, Patrick de Brock Gallery, Knokke. *Group exhibitions include:* Ledbetter Lusk Gallery 1995, Memphis Coll. of Art 1996, Artfair Seattle 1997, Memphis Arts Council 1997, The Armory, NY 1998, River Gallery, Chatanooga 1999, Belgian Art Fair 1999, Hamiltons Gallery, Brussels 2000, Sotheby's, London 2000, Contemporary Art Center of Virginia 2000, Houldsworth Fine Art, London 2000. *Publications:* Seasons 1997, Sleep (photo essay) 2000, My Friend From Memphis (monograph) 2001; contribs. to Wall Street Journal, Vanity Fair, Vogue etc. *Leisure interests:* cycling, travelling in Africa and Pakistan. *Address:* Hamiltons Gallery, 3 Carlos Place, London W1 2TU (Office); 46 Cleveland Square, London, W2 6DA, Eng-land (Home). *Telephone:* (20) 7499-9493 (Office). *E-mail:* filippo@hamiltonsgallery .com (Office). *Website:* www.hamiltonsgallery.com (Office).

FORAY, Cyril; Sierra Leonean historian, diplomatist and fmr politician; b. March 1934, Baiama, Bo Dist.; s. of Michael Keman Foray and Mary Bridget Foray; m. Arabella Williams 1958, two s. two d.; ed St Edward's Catholic Secondary School, Freetown, Fourah Bay Coll., Durham Univ., UK; teacher, St Edward's School; Sales Man. BP 1962–64; lecturer, Faculty of Educ., Univ., of Njala; lecturer Univ. of Calif. at LA; entered politics as APC candidate in gen. elections 1967; following mil. coup, imprisoned briefly 1967; temporary lecturer, Fourah Bay Coll. 1968; elected MP for Bo 1969, Minister for Foreign Affairs 1969–71, for Health 1971; withdrew from Parl. 1973; imprisoned briefly 1974; Sr Lecturer and Head Dept of History, Fourah Bay Coll. 1977–81, Assoc. Prof. 1981–85, Prof. and Prin. 1985–93; Public Orator, Univ., of Sierra Leone 1976–85, Dean Faculty of Arts 1978–82; High Commr in UK 1993–95, 1996–2000. *Publications:* numerous books including Historical Dictionary of Sierra Leone 1977, The Road to the One Party—the Sierra Leone Experience 1988. *Leisure interests:* cricket, lawn tennis. *Address:* 2 Leicester Road, Freetown, Sierra Leone.

FORBES, Bryan; British film executive, director, screenwriter and novelist; b. 22 July 1926, Stratford, London; m. Nanette Newman (q.v.) 1955; two d.; ed West Ham Secondary School; studied at Royal Acad. Dramatic Art, first stage appearance 1942; served in Intelligence Corps 1944–48; entered films as actor 1948; wrote and co-produced The Angry Silence 1959; dir Whistle Down the Wind 1961; writer and dir The L-Shaped Room 1962, Seance on a Wet Afternoon 1963, King Rat 1964; writer Only Two Can Play 1964; producer and dir The Wrong Box 1965; writer, producer and dir The Whisperers 1966, Deadfall 1967, The Madwoman of Chaillot 1968, The Raging Moon (Long Ago Tomorrow in USA) 1970; dir Macbeth 1980, Killing Jessica 1986, Star Quality 1986, The Living Room 1987, One Helluva Life 2002; writer, producer and Dir filmed biography of Dame Edith Evans for Yorkshire TV 1973; filmed documentary on life style of Elton John for ATV 1974; wrote and dir The Slipper and the Rose 1975, Jessie (BBC) 1977, Ménage à trois (Better Late than Never in USA) 1981, The Endless Game 1989 (for Channel 4 TV); dir British segment of The Sunday Lovers 1980; dir The King in Yellow (for LWT Television) 1982, The Naked Face 1983; produced, wrote and dir International Velvet 1977; Head of Production, Assoc. British Picture Corpn 1969–71, subsequently became EMI Film Productions Ltd; mem. Gen. Advisory Council of BBC 1966–69, Experimental Film Bd of British Film Acad.; Govt Nominee BBC Schools Broadcasting Council 1972; Pres. Beatrix Potter Soc. 1982–96, Nat. Youth Theatre 1984–, Writers Guild of GB 1988–91; Founder and fmr Dir Capital Radio Ltd; Hon. DLitt (Council for Nat. Academic Awards) 1987, (Sussex) 1999; British Film Acad. Award for The Angry Silence; Best Screenplay Awards for Only Two Can Play, Seance on a Wet Afternoon; UN Award for The L-Shaped Room; many Film Festival prizes. *Publications:* Truth Lies Sleeping (short stories) 1951, The Distant Laughter (novel) 1972, Notes for a Life (autobiog.) 1974, The Slipper and the Rose 1976, Ned's Girl (biog. of Dame Edith Evans) 1977, International Velvet (novel) 1978, Familiar Strangers (novel, U.S. title Stranger) 1979, That Despicable

Race—a History of the British Acting Tradition 1980, The Rewrite Man (novel) 1983, The Endless Game (novel) 1986, A Song at Twilight (novel) 1989, A Divided Life (autobiog.) 1992, The Twisted Playground (novel) 1993, Partly Cloudy (novel) 1995, Quicksand (novel) 1996, The Memory of All That 1999. *Leisure interests:* collecting books, landscape gardening, collecting Napoleonic relics, avoiding bores. *Address:* The Gallery, Station Approach, Virginia Water, Surrey, GU25 4DP, England. *Fax:* (1344) 845174.

FORBES, Malcolm Stevenson, Jr., LHD; American publishing executive; b. 18 July 1947, Morristown, NJ; s. of Malcolm Forbes and Roberta Laidlaw; m. Sabina Beekman 1971; ed Princeton Univ. and Lycoming Coll. Jacksonville Univ.; with Forbes Inc., New York 1970–, Pres. and COO 1980–90, Deputy Ed.-in-Chief 1982–90, Ed.-in-Chief, Pres. and CEO 1990–; Chair. Forbes Newspapers 1989–; mem. Bd for Int. Broadcasting 1983–93, Chair. 1985–93; mem. Advisory Council, Dept of Econs Princeton Univ. 1985–; several hon. degrees. *Wrote:* Some Call It Greed (film script) 1977. *Publication:* Fact and Comment (ed.) 1974. *Address:* Forbes Inc., 60 Fifth Avenue, New York, NY 10011, USA.

FORD, Anna, BA, FRGS; British broadcaster; b. 2 Oct. 1943; d. of John Ford and Jean Beattie Winstanley; m. 1st Alan Holland Bittles (divorced 1976); m. 2nd Charles Mark Edward Boxer (died 1988); two d.; ed Minehead Grammar School, White House Grammar School, Brampton and Manchester Univ.; work for students' interests, Manchester Univ. 1966–69; lecturer Rupert Stanley Coll. of Further Educ., Belfast 1970–72; staff tutor, Social Sciences, NI Region, Open Univ. 1972–74, 1974–78; presenter and reporter Granada TV Man Alive, BBC Tomorrow's World; newscaster ITN 1978–80; with TV AM 1980–82; freelance broadcasting and writing 1982–86; BBC News and Current Affairs 1989–; Trustee Royal Botanic Gardens, Kew 1995–; Chancellor Univ. of Manchester 2001–; Hon. Fellow Open Univ. 1998; Hon. BA (Cen. Lancs.) 1998; Hon. LLD (Manchester) 1998; Hon. Bencher Middle Temple 2002. *Publication:* Men: A Documentary 1985. *Leisure interests:* talking, walking, drawing. *Address:* BBC Television Centre, Wood Lane, London, W12 7RJ, England. *Telephone:* (20) 7624-9991.

FORD, Hon. Anthony David, LLB; New Zealand judge; b. 8 May 1942, Hokitika; s. of Tom Ford and Cath Ford; five d. two s.; ed Auckland Univ.; currently Chief Justice of Tonga. *Address:* POB 1309, Nuku'alofa, Tonga (Home). *Telephone:* (676) 25-906 (Home); (676) 24-771 (Office). *Fax:* (676) 25-906 (Office). *E-mail:* valda@kalianet.to (Office).

FORD, Bruce; American tenor; m. H. Ypma 1982; one s.; ed Texas Tech. Univ., Houston Opera Studio; sings in maj. opera houses in N America and Europe, specializing in Mozart and bel canto composers; Rossini's Otello (Covent Garden), Ermione (Glyndebourne), Zelmira, Ricciardo e Zoraide (Pesaro) revived for him; concert appearances include La Scala, Edin. Festival, Covent Garden, San Francisco Opera, Düsseldorf Symphonic, Chicago Lyric Opera and Amsterdam Concertgebouw; extensive recording career including many rare 19th C operas; Seal of Tex. Tech. Univ. 1997. *Leisure interests:* scuba diving, sailing. *Address:* c/o Athole Still International Management Ltd, 25–27 Westow Street, London, SE19 3RY, England (Office). *Telephone:* (20) 8771-5271 (Office). *Fax:* (20) 8771-8172 (Office). *E-mail:* lucy@atholestillopera.co.uk (Office); TenorBruceFord@compuserve.com (Home). *Website:* www.bruce-ford.com (Office).

FORD, David Frank, MA, PhD, STM; Irish professor of divinity; b. 23 Jan. 1948, Dublin; s. of George Ford and Phyllis Woodman; m. Deborah Hardy 1982; one s. two d. (one d. deceased); ed High School, Dublin, Trinity Coll., Dublin, St John's Coll., Cambridge and Yale Univ.; Lecturer in Theology, Univ. of Birmingham 1976–90, Sr Lecturer 1990–91; Regius Prof. of Divinity, Univ. of Cambridge 1991–, Chair. Faculty Bd of Divinity 1993–95; Fellow, Selwyn Coll. Cambridge 1991–; Foundation mem. Trinity Coll. Cambridge 1991–; Chair. Council, Westcott House Theological Coll. 1991–97; mem. Archbishop of Canterbury's Urban Theology Working Group 1991–96; Fellow, Center of Theological Inquiry, Princeton Univ. 1993–; mem. Syndicate Cambridge Univ. Press 1993–; Chair. Man. Cttee of Centre for Advanced Religious and Theological Studies, Univ. of Cambridge 1995–; Pres. Soc. for the Study of Theology 1997–99; Founding mem. and mem. Mgt Cttee, Soc. for Scriptural Reasoning 1995–; mem. Church of England Doctrine Comm. 1997–2003; Hon. DD (Birmingham) 2000. *Publications:* Barth and God's Story 1981, Jubilate: Theology in Praise (with D. W. Hardy) 1984, Meaning and Truth in 2 Corinthians (with F. M. Young) 1987, The Modern Theologians, The Shape of Living 1997, Self and Salvation: Being Transformed 1999, Theology: A Very Short Introduction 1999, Jesus (ed with M. Higton) 2002. *Leisure interests:* literature, walking, ball games, kayaking, family and friends. *Address:* Faculty of Divinity, West Road, Cambridge, CB3 9BS, England. *Telephone:* (1223) 763031 (Office). *Fax:* (1223) 763003 (Office).

FORD, Sir David Robert, KBE, LVO; British government official (retd); b. 22 Feb. 1935; s. of William Ewart Ford and Edna Ford; m. 1st Elspeth Anne Muckart 1958 (divorced 1987); two s. two d.; m. 2nd Gillian Petersen (née Monsarrat) 1987; ed Tauntons School; officer, RA 1955–72, retd from army, rank of Maj.; seconded to Hong Kong Govt 1967; Deputy Dir Hong Kong Govt Information Service 1972–74, Dir 1974–76; Deputy Sec. Hong Kong Govt Secr. 1976; Under-Sec. NI Office 1977–79; Sec. for Information, Hong Kong Govt 1979–80; Hong Kong Commr in London 1980–81, 1994–96; Royal Coll. of Defence Studies 1982; Dir of Housing, Hong Kong Govt 1983–84, Sec. for Housing 1985, for the Civil Service 1985–86; Chief Sec., Hong Kong 1986–93, Hong Kong Commr in London 1994–97; retd from public service June 1997;

Chair. Council for the Protection of Rural England 1998–. *Leisure interests:* rare breeds of cattle and sheep, fishing, tennis. *Address:* c/o Council for the Protection of Rural England, 128 Southwark Street, London, SE1 0SW (Office); Culverwell Farm, Branscombe, Devon, EX12 3DA, England (Home). *Telephone:* (20) 7981-2800 (Office). *Fax:* (20) 7981-2899 (Office). *E-mail:* nfo@cpre.org.uk (Office). *Website:* www.cpre.org.uk (Office).

FORD, Gerald Rudolph, Jr.; American politician and lawyer; b. 14 July 1913, Omaha, Neb.; s. of Gerald R. Ford, Sr and Dorothy Gardner Ford; m. Elizabeth (Betty) Bloomer 1948; three s. one d.; ed Univ. of Michigan and Yale Univ. Law School; partner, law firm Ford and Buchen 1941–42; USN service 1942–46; mem. law firm Butterfield, Keeney and Amberg 1947–49; mem. U.S. House of Reps. 1949–73; House Minority Leader 1965–73; Vice-Pres. of USA 1973–74; Pres. of USA 1974–77; Visiting Prof. in Govt, Univ. of Mich.; Chair. Bd of Acad. for Educational Devt 1977; mem. Interparl. Union, Warsaw 1959, Brussels 1961, Belgrade 1963; mem. U.S.-Canadian Interparl. Group, Chair. House of Repub. Conf. 1963; Advisor American Express Co. 1981, Texas Commerce Bancshares, Inc.; mem. Warren Comm., American Enterprise Inst.; Bd mem. The Traveler's Inc., Alexander & Alexander; numerous hon. degrees and awards including Congressional Gold Medal 1999, Medal of Freedom 1999, Profile in Courage Award 2001; Republican. *Publications:* Portrait of the Assassin (with John R. Stiles), A Time to Heal (memoirs) 1979, The Humor and the Presidency 1987. *Address:* P.O. Box 927, Rancho Mirage, CA 92270, USA. *Telephone:* (714) 324-1763.

FORD, Harrison; American actor; b. 13 July 1942, Chicago; m. 1st Mary Ford; two s.; m. 2nd Melissa Ford; one s. one d.; ed Ripon Coll.; numerous TV appearances; Cecil B. DeMille Award, Golden Globes 2002. *Films include:* Dead Heat on a Merry-Go-Round 1966, Luv 1967, A Time for Killing 1967, Journey to Shiloh 1968, The Long Ride Home 1967, Getting Straight 1970, Zabriskie Point 1970, The Conversation 1974, American Graffiti 1974, Star Wars 1977, Heroes 1977, Force 10 from Navarone 1978, Apocalypse Now 1979, Hanover Street 1979, Frisco Kid 1979, The Empire Strikes Back 1980, Raiders of the Lost Ark 1981, Blade Runner 1982, Return of the Jedi 1983, Indiana Jones and the Temple of Doom 1984, Witness 1985, The Mosquito Coast 1986, Working Girl 1988, Frantic 1988, Indiana Jones and the Last Crusade 1989, Presumed Innocent 1990, Regarding Henry 1991, The Fugitive 1992, Patriot Games 1992, Clear and Present Danger 1994, Sabrina 1995, The Devil's Own 1996, Air Force One 1996, Six Days and Seven Nights 1998, Random Hearts 1999, What Lies Beneath 2000, K-19: The Widowmaker (also exec. producer) 2002. *Address:* 10279 Century Woods Drive, Los Angeles, CA 90067, USA.

FORD, Sir Hugh, Kt, PhD, DSc, FRS, F.R.ENG.; British professor and engineering consultant; b. 16 July 1913, Thornby, Northants.; s. of Arthur Ford and Constance Mary Ford; m. 1st Wynyard Scholfield 1942 (died 1991); two d.; m. 2nd Thelma Alys Jensen (née Morgan) 1993; ed Northampton School and Imperial Coll., Univ. of London; served apprenticeship Great Western Railway 1931–36; Research Engineer Imperial Coll. 1936–39, Imperial Chemical Industries 1939–42; Chief Tech. Officer British Iron and Steel Fed. 1942–47; Tech. Dir Paterson Eng 1947–48; Reader, then Prof. Imperial Coll. 1948–65, Prof. of Mechanical Eng and Head of Dept 1969–80, Pro-Rector 1978–80, Prof. Emer. 1980–; Dir Davy Ashmore, Alfred Herbert Ltd, etc. 1965–78; Chair. Ford and Dain Partners 1972–82 (Dir 1972–93), Sir Hugh Ford and Assocs. 1982–; Pres. Inst. of Mechanical Engineers 1976–77, The Welding Inst. 1983–85, Inst. of Metals 1985–87; Dr. hc (Belfast, Sheffield, Aston, etc.); Hawkesley Gold Medal 1948, Sir James Ewing Medal, James Watt Int. Gold Medal 1985. *Publications:* Advanced Mechanics of Materials 1962; 100 scientific papers. *Leisure interests:* music, gardening, model engineering. *Address:* 18 Shrewsbury House, Cheyne Walk, London, SW3 5LN; Shamley Cottage, Stroud Lane, Shamley Green, Surrey, GU5 0ST, England (Home). *Telephone:* (20) 7352-4948 (London); (1483) 898012 (Surrey). *Fax:* (20) 7352-5320.

FORD, Richard; American writer; b. 16 Feb. 1944, Jackson, Miss.; m. Kristina Hensley Ford 1968; ed Michigan State Univ., Univ. of California, Irvine; lecturer, William Coll. 1979–80, Princeton Univ. 1980–81, Harvard Univ. 1994–; Dr hc (Rennes, France, Michigan); American Acad. and Inst. of Arts and Letters Award for Literature 1989, Pulitzer Prize for Fiction 1996, PEN Faulkner Award for Fiction 1996; Officier, Ordre des Arts et des Lettres. *Publications:* (novels) A Piece of my Heart 1976, The Ultimate Good Luck 1981, The Sportswriter 1986, Wildlife 1990, Independence Day 1995; (stories) Rocksprings 1987, Women With Men: Three Stories 1996, A Multitude of Sins: Stories 2002; screenplays: American Tropical 1983, Bright Angel 1991; Ed.: The Granta Book of the American Short Story 1992, The Granta Book of the American Long Story 1999; My Mother in Memory 1988. *Address:* c/o Amanda Urban, ICM, 40 West 57th Street, New York, NY 10019, USA. *Telephone:* (212) 556-5764.

FORD, Richard John, BA, DipArch; British business executive; b. 10 April 1949; s. of the late Arthur Ford and of Violet Banbury; m. Janet K. Ford; one s.; ed Portsmouth Polytechnic and Polytechnic of London; Exec. Creative Dir Landor 1984–, with Landor Europe, currently with Landor New York; comms include identity and environmental design for British Airways 1984, Chase Manhattan Bank Europe 1985, Royal Jordanian Airlines and Alfred Dunhill 1986, BAe and Abbey National 1987, Cespa Petroleum Spain, Depasco Convenience Stores Spain and Ballantyne Cashmere 1988, Emlak Bank, Turkey 1989, Deutsche Shell 1990, Egnatia Bank Greece 1991, Seville Expo

and Neste Petroleum Finland 1992, Lincoln Mercury USA, Telia (Swedish Telecom) and Cathay Pacific Airline 1993, Royal Mail and Delta Air Lines USA 1994, Montell (Worldwide) and KF (Swedish Co-op) 1995, RIBA 1993, Adtranz (Worldwide) and Air 2000 (UK) 1996, Credit Lyonnais 1997, Shell Int. Petroleum and Compaq Computers (USA) 1998, Hyperion Software and Textron (USA) 1999. *Address:* Landor Associates, Klamath House, 230 Park Avenue South, New York, NY 10003, USA (Office). *Telephone:* (212) 614-4449 (Office). *Fax:* (212) 614-3966. *Website:* www.landor.com.

FORD, Tom; American fashion designer; b. 1962, Texas; ed New York Univ., Parsons School of Design; fmrly acted in TV commercials, Asst to designer Cathy Hardwick, with Perry Ellis Co.; joined Gucci 1990, Head of Advertising 1994, Creative Dir 1995–2000, Yves St Laurent 2000–; involved in fund-raising in U.S. and Europe. *Address:* c/o Yves Saint Laurent, 5 avenue Marceau, 75116 Paris, France. *Telephone:* 1-44-31-64-00 (Office). *Fax:* 1-47-20-62-13 (Office). *Website:* www.ysl-hautecouture.com (Office).

FORD, Wendell Hampton; American politician; b. 8 Sept. 1924, Owensboro, Ky; s. of E. M. Ford and Irene (Schenk) Ford; m. Jean Neel 1943; one s. one d.; ed Daviess County High School, Univ. of Kentucky, Maryland School of Insurance; served U.S. Army, Ky 1944–46, Nat. Guard 1949–62; Chief Asst to Gov. of Kentucky 1959–61; mem. Ky Senate 1966–67; Lt-Gov. Kentucky 1967–71, Gov. 1971–74; U.S. Senator from Kentucky 1974–97; Asst Minority Leader 1995–97; fmr mem. Senate Energy and Natural Resources Cttee, Commerce, Science, Transportation Cttee (Chair. Consumer Sub-Cttee); mem. Democratic Steering Cttee, Chair. Democratic Nat. Campaign Cttee 1976, Head of Democratic Senatorial Campaign Cttee; Majority Whip 1991–97; Chair. Senate Rules Cttee, Jt Cttee on Printing; Chair. Nat. Democratic Govs. 1973–74; Chair. Jt Congressional Cttee on Inaugural Ceremonies; fmr mem. Nat. Democratic Party Advisory Council; fmr Chair. Common Law Enforcement, Justice and Public Safety, Southern Govs.' Conf.; mem. U.S. Chamber of Commerce, Pres. 1956–57; Int. Vice-Pres. Jaycees, Distinguished Fellow Martin School of Public Policy and Admin., Univ. of Ky 1999–. *Leisure interests:* fishing, hunting. *Address:* 2017 Fieldcrest Drive, Owensboro, KY 42301, USA (Home).

FORD, William Clay, BS(Econ); American businessman; b. 14 March 1925, Detroit; s. of Edsel Ford and Eleanor Clay Ford; brother of Henry Ford II; m. Martha Firestone 1947; one s. three d.; ed Yale Univ.; Dir Ford Motor Co. 1948–; mem. of Sales and Advertising Staff 1948 and of the Industrial Relations Staff 1949; quality control Man. Lincoln-Mercury Div. Jet Engine Defence Project 1951; Man. Special Product Operations 1952; Vice-Pres. Ford Motor Co. and Gen. Man. Continental Div. 1953, Group Dir Continental Div. 1955, Vice-Pres. Product Design 1956–80, Chair. Exec. Cttee 1978–, mem. Company Finance Cttee 1987–; Pres./Owner Detroit Lions Professional Football Team 1964–; Chair. Emer. Edison Inst.; Trustee Eisenhower Medical Center, Thomas A. Edison Foundation; mem. Bd of Dirs Nat. Tennis Hall of Fame, Boys Club of America. *Address:* Ford Motor Company World Headquarters, 1 American Road, Dearborn, MI 48126-2798, USA. *Website:* www.ford.com.

FORD, William Clay, Jr., MBA; American motor company executive; b. 3 May 1957; s. of William Clay Ford (q.v.) and Martha Firestone; m.; ed Princeton Univ., Massachussetts Inst. of Tech.; with Ford Motor Co. 1979–, joined as product-planning analyst, then various positions in mfg, sales, marketing, product devt and finance; served on Ford's Nat. Bargaining Team in Ford–United Auto Workers talks 1982; Vice-Pres. Comm. for Vehicle Marketing, Ford of Europe 1986–87; Chair., Man. Dir Ford of Switzerland 1987–89; elected to Bd of Dirs, Ford Motor Co. 1988, Chair. Bd's Finance Cttee 1995–99, Chair. Bd's Environmental and Public Policy Cttee 1997, Chair. Bd's Nominating and Governance Cttee 1999, Chair. of Bd 1999–; Exec. Dir Business Strategy, Ford Automotive Group 1991–92; Gen. Man. Climate Control Div. 1992–94; Head of Commercial Truck Vehicle Centre 1994–95; Vice-Pres., Ford Motor Co. 1994, CEO 2001–; mem. World Econ. Forum's Global Leaders for Tomorrow; Vice-Chair. Bd of Dirs Greater Downtown Partnership, Detroit; Trustee Henry Ford Health System, Detroit Renaissance, Conservation Int.; Vice-Chair. Detroit Lions Football Team. *Leisure interests:* fly-fishing, Tae Kwon Do, hockey, tennis, cars. *Address:* Ford Motor Company Ltd, World Headquarters, 1 American Road, Dearborn, MI 48126-2798, USA. *Website:* www.ford.com.

FORDE, Sir Henry deBoulay, Kt, PC, QC, LLM; Barbadian politician and lawyer; b. 20 March 1933, Christ Church, Barbados; adopted s. of the late Courtley Ifill and of Elise Ifill; m. Cheryl Wendy Roach; four s.; ed Harrison Coll., Barbados, Christ's Coll., Cambridge, Middle Temple, London; Research Asst, Dept of Criminology, Univ. of Cambridge 1958, Research Student, Int. Law, worked on British Digest of Int. Law, Univ. of Cambridge 1958–59, Supervisor and Tutor in Int. Law, Emmanuel Coll., Cambridge 1958–59; called to English Bar 1959, to Barbadian Bar 1959; Lecturer, Extra-Mural Programme, Univ. of West Indies 1961–68, Part-time Lecturer, Caribbean Studies, 1964–69; mem. House of Ass. for Christ Church West 1971–; Minister of External Affairs and Attorney-Gen. 1976–81; Minister of State 1993; Leader of the Opposition 1986–89, 1991–93; mem. Privy Council 1976–92, 1996–; Chair. and Political Leader, Barbados Labour Party 1986–93; Chair. Commonwealth Observer Group to the Seychelles 1991, to Fiji Islands 2001; mem. Commonwealth Cttee on Vulnerability of Small States 1985, Commonwealth Parl. Assocn, Editorial Bds. of The Round Table, Int. Comm. of Jurists 1987–92, Barbados Bar Assocn, Hon. Soc. of Middle Temple, Int. Tax

Planning Asscn, Interparl. Human Rights Network, Barbados Nat. Trust, Int. Acad. of Estate and Trust Law, Int. Inst. for Democracy and Electoral Assistance, Inter-American Comm. on Human Rights. *Leisure interests:* reading, walking, gardening. *Address:* Juris Chambers, Fidelity House, Wildey Business Park, Wildey Road, St. Michael, Barbados (Office); Codrington Court, Society, St John, Barbados, West Indies (Home). *Telephone:* (246) 429-5320, 429-2208 (Office); (246) 423-3881 (Home). *Fax:* (246) 429-2206. *E-mail:* shf@jurischambers.com (Office). *Website:* www .jurischambers.com (Office).

FORDICE, Kirk, Jr (Daniel Kirkwood Fordice), MSc; American politician and business executive; b. 10 Feb. 1934, Memphis, Tenn.; s. of Daniel Kirkwood Fordice and Clara Augustine; m. Patricia Louise Owens 1955; three s. one d.; ed Purdue Univ.; worked as engineer in Miss. and La.; with Exxon, Baton Rouge 1956–62; partner Fordice Construction Co., Vicksburg, Mo. 1962–76, Pres. and CEO 1976–; Gov. of Mississippi 1992–2000; Sec. Mo. Repub. Party 1981–88; Vice-Chair. Southern Govs' Asscn 1992–2000, Chair. 1994–2000; mem. American Construction Industry Forum (Pres. 1991), Confed. Int. Contractors' Asscns (Vice-Pres. 1990–); Fellow ASCE; Republican; numerous awards for contribs in construction eng field.

FOREMAN, George; American boxer; b. 10 Jan. 1949, Marshall, Tex.; s.of J.D. Foreman and Nancy Foreman; m. five times; five s. five d.; Olympic heavyweight champion Mexico 1968; World heavyweight champion 1973–74, 1994–95; lost title to Muhammad Ali (knockout in 8th) in 1974; recaptured it on 5 Nov. 1994 at age 45 with a 10-round knockout of WBC/IBF champion Michael Moorer, becoming oldest man to win heavyweight crown; successfully defended title at age 46 against Axel Schulz; gave up IBF title after refusing rematch with Schulz; now an evangelical minister; f. a youth and community centre; has diverse business interests, has endorsed or sold numerous products such as hamburgers, hot dogs and grilling machines and rotisseries; AP Male Athlete of the Year 1994. *Publication:* By George (autobiog.). *Leisure interests:* raising livestock, breeding horses. *Address:* c/o The Church of Lord Jesus Christ, 2501 Lone Oak, Houston, TX 77093, USA. *E-mail:* george@ biggeorge.com. *Website:* www.biggeorge.com (Office).

FORERO DE SAADE, María Teresa, D. MED.; Colombian politician and doctor; b. 28 Feb. 1939, Vergara, Cundinamarca; m. Rafael Saade Abdala; three s.; ed Instituto Pedagógico Nacional, Colegio Departamental de la Merced, Bogotá and Pontificia Universidad Javeriana; qualified as doctor 1966; specialist in pediatrics; Prof. of Pediatrics at Univ. of Rosario 1968–69; Prof. of Pediatrics at Faculty of Nursing, Nat. Red Cross 1971–72; Gen.-Dir of Colsubsidio Clinic for Children 1974–82; Deputy Senator 1978–82; Vice-Minister of Health 1982; Minister at the Ministry of Health 1982; Minister of Labour and Social Security 1989–90; Minister of Health 1996–98. *Address:* FEPAFEM, calle 123, No. 8–20, Bogotá, Colombia. *Telephone:* (571) 620-36-30 (Office). *Fax:* (571) 213-6809 (Office).

FORGEARD, Noël, LN ÈS. SC.ECON.; French business executive and mining engineer; b. 8 Dec. 1946, Ferté-Gaucher; s. of Henri Forgeard and Laurence Duprat; m. Marie-Cécile de Place 1972; one s. three d.; ed Lycée Louis-le-Grand, Ecole Polytechnique, Paris; qualified as mining engineer; entered mining industry in Clermont-Ferrand, industry rep. to Auvergne prefecture 1972–73; Asst Sec.-Gen. Dept of Mining, Ministry for Industry 1973–76, Sec.-Gen. 1976–78; Tech. Adviser to Minister of Transport 1978–80, of Defence 1980; Head of Industrial Affairs and Armaments, Ministry of Defence 1980–81; Deputy Pres., Asst Gen. Man. Compagnie française des aciers spéciaux (CFAS) 1982–84, Prés., Dir-Gen. 1984–86; Man. Dir then Prés., Dir-Gen. Ascometal 1985–86; Chair. Asfor Steel Products 1986–87; Tech Adviser and Head of Industrial Affairs, Office of the Prime Minister 1986–87; Man. Defence and Space Divs. Matra 1987, Prés., Dir-Gen. Matra-défense espace finance co. (Sofimades), Matra Hautes technologies, Matra Bac Dynamics, mem. Exec. and Strategy Cttee and Gen. Man. Lagardère SCA 1993–98; Man. Dir Airbus Industrie 1998–, CEO 2000–; Dir Matra systèmes et information, Snecma, Matra-Marconi Space NV; Vice-Pres. Groupement des industries de l'aéronautique et de l'espace (Gifas); Public Enterprise Foundation Award 1971; Chevalier, Légion d'honneur, Ordre nat. du Mérite. *Leisure interests:* modern art, swimming. *Address:* Airbus Industrie, rond-point Maurice Bellonte 1, 31700 Blagnac (Office); 85 av. de Wagram, 75017 Paris (Home); Le Roc, 35800 St-Briac-sur-Mer, France (Home).

FORLANI, Arnaldo; Italian politician; b. 8 Dec. 1925, Pesaro; s. of Luigi and Caterina Forlani; m. Alma Ioni 1956; three s.; ed Univ. of Urbino; mem. Chamber of Deputies 1958; Deputy Sec. of Christian Democrat Party 1962–69, Political Sec. (Leader) 1969–73, 1989; Minister of State Enterprises 1969–70, of Defence 1974–76, of Foreign Affairs 1976–79; Prime Minister 1980–81, Deputy Prime Minister 1983–87; Pres. Christian Democratic Party 1986–89, Sec. Gen. 1989–92. *Leisure interest:* journalism. *Address:* Piazzale Schumann 15, Rome, Italy. *Telephone:* 6784109.

FORMAN, Sir Denis, Kt, OBE; British business executive; b. 13 Oct. 1917, Beattock, Scotland; s. of the late Rev. Adam Forman and of Flora (née Smith) Forman; m. 1st Helen de Mouilpied 1948 (died 1987); two s.; m. 2nd Moni Cameron 1990; one step-s. one step-d.; ed Loretto and Pembroke Coll., Cambridge; war service with Argyll and Sutherland Highlanders 1940–45 (Commdt Orkney and Shetland Defences Battle School 1942, wounded, Cassino 1944); Chief Production Officer, Cen. Office of Information Films 1947; Dir British Film Inst. 1948–55, Chair. Bd of Govs 1971–73; Jt Man. Dir, Granada TV Ltd 1965–81, Chair. 1974–87; Dir Granada Group 1964–90;

Deputy Chair. 1984–90, Consultant 1990–96; Chair. Novello & Co. 1971–78, Chair. Scottish Film Production Dept 1990–93; Dir Royal Opera House, Covent Garden 1981–91; Deputy Chair. 1983–92, Fellow BFI 1993; Dir Harold Holt Ltd 1992–; mem. Council Royal Northern Coll. of Music 1975–84, Hon. mem. 1981; Fellow BAFTA 1977; Hon. DUniv (Stirling) 1982, (Keele) 1990; Hon. DU (Essex) 1986; Hon. LLD (Manchester) 1983, (Lancaster) 1989; Ufficiale dell' ordine al Merito della Repubblica Italiana. *Publications:* Mozart's Piano Concertos 1971, Son of Adam (autobiog.) 1990 (filmed under the title My Life So Far 1999), To Reason Why (autobiog.) 1991, Persona Granada: Some Memories of Sidney Bernstein and the Early Days of Independent Television (autobiog.) 1997, The Good Wagner Opera Guide 2000. *Leisure interests:* music, shooting. *Address:* Flat 2, 15 Lyndhurst Gardens, London, NW3 5NT, England.

FORMAN, Miloš; American film director; b. 18 Feb. 1932, Čáslav; m. Martina Forman; four s.; ed Film Faculty, Acad. of Music and Dramatic Art, Prague; Dir Film Presentations, Czechoslovak TV 1954–56; of Laterna Magika, Prague 1958–62; mem. Artistic Cttee, Šebor-Bor Film Producing Group; Klement Gottwald State Prize 1967. *Films include:* Talent Competition, Peter and Pavla 1963 (Czechoslovak Film Critics' Award 1963, Grand Prix 17th Int. Film Festival, Locarno 1964), The Knave of Spades, A Blonde in Love (Cidalc Prize, Venice Festival 1965, Grand Prize French Film Acad. 1966) 1965, Episode in Zruč, Like a House on Fire (A Fireman's Ball) 1968, Taking Off 1971; Co-Dir Visions of Eight 1973, One Flew Over the Cuckoo's Nest 1975 (Acad. Award for Best Dir 1976), Hair 1979, Ragtime 1980, Amadeus 1983 (Acad. Award, César Award 1985), Valmont 1988, The People vs. Larry Flynt (Golden Globe for Best Dir 1996) 1965, Man on the Moon (Silver Bear for Best Dir, Berlin Film Festival 2000) 1999; appeared in New Year's Day 1989, Keeping the Faith 2000. *Publication:* Turnaround: A Memoir (with Jan Novak) 1993.

FORMICA, Salvatore; Italian politician; b. 1 March 1927, Bari; Senator, Milan VI 1979–83; Socialist (P.S.I.) MP for Bari 1983; Minister of Transport in second Cossiga Govt and Forlani Govt; fmr Minister of Finance; Minister for Foreign Trade 1986–87, for Labour 1987–88, 1988–89, of Finance 1989–90; mem. Parl. Comm. of Inquiry into Masonic Lodge P2.

FORMIGONI, Roberto, MA; Italian politician; b. 30 March 1947, Lecco; s. of the late Emilio Formigoni and Doralice Formigoni; ed Catholic Univ. of Milan; co-f. Movimento Popolare (political arm of Catholic Movt Comunione e Liberazione), Nat. Pres. 1976–87; MEP (Christian Democratic Party) 1984–94, Vice-Chair. Presidential Office 1989–91; elected Deputy 1989, 1992, 1994 (Italian Popular Party); Under-Sec. Ministry of Employment and Urban Areas 1993–94; Pres. Lombardy Region 1995–1999, 2000–04; mem. Forza Italia. *Leisure interests:* yachting, jogging. *Address:* Giunta Regionale della Lombardia, Via Fabio Filzi 22, 20124 Milan, Italy. *Telephone:* (02) 67654001 (Office). *Fax:* (02) 67655653 (Office). *E-mail:* roberto_formigoni@regione .lombardia.it (Office). *Website:* www.regione.lombardia.it (Office).

FORNÉ MOLNÉ, Marc; Andorran politician and lawyer; b. 1946; ed Univ. of Barcelona; lawyer; fmr Ed. Andorra 7 magazine; Leader Partit Liberal; Head of Govt of Andorra 1994–. *Address:* Office of the Head of Government, Govern d'Andorra, Carrer Prat de la Creu 62–64, Andorra la Vella, Andorra (Office). *Telephone:* 875700 (Office). *Fax:* 822882 (Office). *Website:* www .andorra.ad/govern/ (Office).

FORNI, Raymond, LenD; French politician and barrister; b. b. 20 May 1941, Belfort; s. of Alexis Forni and Antoinette Forni (née Borgatta); m. 2nd Dominique Girardeau; five c.; ed Strasbourg Univ.; Barrister, barre de Belfort 1968; Municipal Council Montreux-Château 1971–76, General Council Beaucourt 1976–87, Delle 1988–, Mayor of Delle 1991–; Deputy Assemblée Nationale 1973–86, 1988–93, 1997–2002, Vice-Pres. 1998–2000, Pres. 2000–02, Rep. Council of Europe 1973–78; MEP 1978–85; Vice-Pres. Nat. Comm. for Information Technology and Liberty 1978–85, 1988–91, 1998–2000; Pres. France-Cuba, France-Oman friendship groups; Chevalier Ordre national du Mérite. *Publications:* Un Enfant de la République Stock 2001. *Address:* c/o Assemblée Nationale, 126 rue de l'Université, 75355 Paris (Office); 4 rue Dumont d'Urville, 75016 Paris (Office); 37 rue au Filleul, 90150 Fontaine, France (Home). *Telephone:* 1-40-63-60-00 (Office); 1-53-57-72-72 (Office).

FORREST, Sir (Andrew) Patrick (McEwen), Kt, MD, ChM, FRCS, FRCPE, FRSE; British surgeon; b. 25 March 1923, Mount Vernon, Scotland; s. of Andrew J. Forrest and Isabella Pearson; m. 1st Margaret B. Hall 1955 (died 1961); m. 2nd Margaret A. Steward 1964; one s. two d.; ed Dundee High School and St Andrew's Univ.; Mayo Foundation Fellow, Rochester, Minn. 1952–53; lecturer and Sr lecturer, Univ. of Glasgow 1954–62; Prof. of Surgery, Welsh Nat. School of Medicine 1962–71; Regius Prof. of Clinical Surgery, Univ. of Edinburgh 1970–88, Prof. Emer. 1989–, Hon. Fellow, Faculty of Medicine 1989–95; Visiting Scientist, NIH 1989–90; Assoc. Dean (Clinical Studies) Int. Medical Coll., Kuala Lumpur 1993–96; mem. Medical Research Council 1975–79; Chief Scientist, Scottish Home and Health Dept (part-time) 1981–87; mem. Advisory Bd for Research Councils 1982–85; Hon. DSc (Wales, Chinese Univ. of Hong Kong); Hon. LLD (Dundee); Hon. FACS; Hon. FRACS; Hon. FRCS (Canada); Hon. FRCR; Hon. FFPHM; Gimbernat Prize, Catalonian Surgical Asscn 1996; European Inst. of Oncology Breast Cancer Award 2000; Lister Medal 1987, Gold Medal, Netherlands Surgical Asscn 1988. *Publications:* Prognostic Factors in Breast Cancer (jtly) 1968, Principles and Practice of Surgery (jtly) 1985, Breast Cancer: The Decision to Screen 1990;

over 250 publs in scientific and medical journals. *Leisure interests:* golf, sailing. *Address:* 19 St Thomas Road, Edinburgh, EH9 2LR, Scotland (Home). *Telephone:* (131) 667 3203 (Home). *Fax:* (131) 662 1193 (Home). *E-mail:* patforresthome@aol.com (Home).

FORSÉN, K. Sture, MSc, DTech; Swedish professor of physical chemistry; b. 12 July 1932, Piteå; s. of Helmer Forsén and Signe Forsén; m. Dr. Gunilla Isaksson 1973 (divorced 1986); ed Royal Inst. of Tech. Stockholm; Assoc. Prof. of Chemical Physics, Royal Inst. of Tech. 1963–67, Prof. of Physical Chem., Univ. of Lund 1966; mem. Bd of Dirs. Swedish Natural Science Research Council 1983–86, Perstorp AB 1986–, Swedish Nat. Chemicals Inspectorate 1989–; Fairchild Scholar, CalTech. 1986–87, Fogarty Scholar, NIH, USA 1987–94, Visiting Investigator Scripps Research Inst., La Jolla 1990–; mem. Scientific Advisory Council of Volvo Research Foundation 1987–; mem. Royal Swedish Acad. of Sciences 1973–, Nobel Cttee for Chem. 1982–; mem. Royal Swedish Acad. of Eng Sciences 1986–; Celsius Gold Medal, Royal Soc. of Uppsala 1979. *Publications:* co-author of two books on NMR spectroscopy 1972, 1976; over 300 scientific articles, at present mainly concerning biophysical studies of calcium-binding proteins, in int. journals. *Leisure interests:* music from Frescobaldi to Keith Jarrett, renovating old farmhouses. *Address:* St Laurentiigatan 8 IV, S-222 21 Lund, Sweden (Home). *Telephone:* 46-14-48-03 (Home). *Fax:* 41-45-14-57.

FORSTER, Carl-Peter, BSc; German automobile executive; b. 9 May 1954, London, UK; m.; three c.; ed Bonn Univ. and Munich Tech. Univ.; consultant McKinsey and Co., Munich 1982–86; Head of Planning and Logistics Tech. Devt Dept, BMW AG 1986–88, Systems and Project Man. 5-series 1988–90, Head of Dept for Test and Pilot Car Mfr, Tech. Devt Centre 1990–93, Head of 5-series 1993–96, Man. Dir BMW (SA) Pty Ltd 1996–99, mem. Man. Bd BMW AG 1999–2000; Chair. and Man. Dir Opel AG 2001–; mem. Bd Dirs Fiat–General Motors Powertrain 2001–; currently Vice-Pres. General Motors Europe. *Leisure interests:* skiing, regatta-sailing. *Address:* Adam Opel AG, Adam Opel Haus, 65423 Rüsselsheim, Germany (Office). *Website:* www .media.opel.de (Office).

FORSTER, Margaret, BA; British writer; b. 25 May 1938, Carlisle; d. of Arthur Gordon Forster and Lilian Forster (née Hind); m. Edward Hunter Davies 1960; one s. two d.; ed Carlisle Co. High School and Somerville Coll., Oxford. *Publications:* non-fiction: The Rash Adventurer: The Rise and Fall of Charles Edward Stuart 1973, William Makepeace Thackeray: Memoirs of a Victorian Gentleman 1978, Significant Sisters: Grassroots of Active Feminism 1839–1939 1984, Elizabeth Barrett Browning: A Biography 1988, Elizabeth Barrett Browning: Selected Poems (ed.) 1988, Daphne du Maurier: The Authorised Biography 1993, Hidden Lives: A Family Memoir 1995, Rich Desserts and Captains Thin: A Family and Their Times 1831–1931 1997, Precious Lives 1998, Good Wives?: Mary, Fanny, Jennie and Me 1845–2001 2001; novels: Dame's Delight 1964, Georgy Girl 1965 (filmscript with Peter Nichols 1966), The Bogeyman 1965, The Travels of Maudie Tipstaff 1967, The Park 1968, Miss Owen-Owen is At Home 1969, Fenella Phizackerley 1970, Mr Bone's Retreat 1971, The Seduction of Mrs Pendlebury 1974, Mother, Can You Hear Me? 1979, The Bride of Lowther Fell 1980, Marital Rites 1981, Private Papers 1986, Have the Men Had Enough? 1989, Lady's Maid 1990, The Battle for Christabel 1991, Mothers' Boys 1994, Shadow Baby 1996, The Memory Box 1999, Diary of an Ordinary Woman 2003. *Leisure interests:* walking, reading contemporary fiction. *Address:* 11 Boscastle Road, London, NW5 1EE; Grasmoor House, Loweswater, nr Cockermouth, Cumbria, CA13 0RU, England. *Telephone:* (20) 7485-3785 (London); (1900) 85303 (Cumbria).

FORSTMOSER, Peter, LLM, PhD; Swiss lawyer and insurance executive; b. 22 Jan. 1943, Zürich; s. of Alois Forstmoser-Locher and Ida Forstmoser-Locher; two s.; ed Zürich Univ. Law School, Harvard Law School, USA; attorney 1971–, partner Niederer, Kraft und Frey 1975–; lecturer Faculty of Law and Political Science, Univ. of Zürich 1971–74; Assoc. Prof. Univ. of Zürich Law School 1974–78, Full Prof. of Civil, Corp. and Capital Market Law 1978–; mem. Bd of Dirs. Swiss Reinsurance Co. (Swiss Re) 1990–, Chair. 2000–; Hon. Prof. (Beijing Normal Univ.) 2001. *Publications:* Schweizer Aktienrecht 1996, Schweizer Gesellschaftsrecht 1998, Einführung in das Recht 2003 and numerous other publs. on Swiss co. and capital market law. *Leisure interests:* sports, modern art. *Address:* Swiss Reinsurance Company, Mythenquai 50/60, 8022 Zürich, Switzerland (Office). *Telephone:* (1) 2859615 (Office). *Fax:* (1) 2855800 (Office). *E-mail:* peter_forstmoser@swissre.com (Office).

FORSYTH, Bill; British film-maker; b. 1947, Glasgow; one s. one d.; ed Nat. Film School, Beaconsfield; Hon. DLitt (Glasgow) 1984; Hon. DUniv (Stirling) 1989; BAFTA Award for Best Screenplay 1982, for Best Dir 1983. *Films:* That Sinking Feeling 1979, Gregory's Girl 1980, Andrina (TV film) 1981, Local Hero 1982, Comfort and Joy 1984, Housekeeping 1987, Breaking In 1988, Being Human 1994, Gregory's Two Girls 1999. *Address:* c/o A.D. Peters, The Chambers, Chelsea Harbour, Lots Road, London, SW10 0XF, England.

FORSYTH, Elliott Christopher, BA, DipEd, DUniv; Australian professor of French; b. 1 Feb. 1924, Mount Gambier; s. of Samuel Forsyth and Ida Muriel Forsyth (née Brummitt); m. Rona Lynette Williams 1967; two d.; ed Prince Alfred Coll., Adelaide, Univ. of Adelaide and Univ. of Paris; teacher Friends' School, Hobart, Tasmania 1947–49; Lecturer, Sr Lecturer in French Univ. of Adelaide 1955–66; Visiting Lecturer Univ. of Wisconsin, Madison 1963–65; Foundation Prof. of French La Trobe Univ., Melbourne 1966–87, Prof. Emer. 1988–; Visiting Prof., Univ. of Melbourne 1992, Sr Assoc. 1993–98, Professo-

rial Fellow 1999–; Fellow Australian Acad. of Humanities 1973, Australian Coll. of Educ. 1977; Commdr Ordre des Palmes Académiques 1983. *Publications:* La Tragédie française de Jodelle à Corneille (1553–1640): le thème de la vengeance 1962, 1994, Saül le furieux/La Famine (tragédies de Jean de la Taille) (ed.) 1968, Concordance des 'Tragiques' d'Agrippa d'Aubigné 1984, Baudin in Australian Waters (ed. with J. Bonnemains and B. Smith) 1988. *Leisure interests:* music, photography, bushwalking and church activities. *Address:* 25 Jacka Street, North Balwyn, Vic. 3104, Australia. *Telephone:* (3) 9857-4050. *E-mail:* linecf2@tpg.com.au (Home).

FORSYTH, Frederick, CBE; British author; b. 25 Aug. 1938, Ashford, Kent; m. 1st Carole Cunningham 1973; two s.; m. 2nd Sandy Molloy; ed Tonbridge School; with RAF 1956–58; Reporter, Eastern Daily Press, Norfolk 1958–61; joined Reuters 1961, Reporter, Paris 1962–63, Chief of Bureau, E Berlin 1963–64; joined BBC 1965; radio and TV reporter 1965–66; Asst Diplomatic Corresp., BBC TV 1967–68; freelance journalist, Nigeria and Biafra 1968–69; narrated Soldiers (TV) 1985; other TV appearances include Frederick Forsyth Presents 1989; Edgar Allen Poe Award, Mystery Writers of America 1971. *Publications:* The Biafra Story 1969, The Day of the Jackal 1971, The Odessa File 1972, The Dogs of War 1974, The Shepherd 1975, The Devil's Alternative 1979, No Comebacks 1982, The Fourth Protocol 1984, The Negotiator 1988, The Deceiver 1991, Great Flying Stories (ed.) 1991, The Fist of God 1993, Icon 1996, The Phantom of Manhattan 1999, Quintet 2000, The Veteran and Other Stories 2001. *Leisure interests:* sea angling, reading. *Address:* c/o Bantam Books, 62–63 Uxbridge Road, London, W5 5SA, England.

FORSYTH OF DRUMLEAN, Baron (Life Peer), cr. 1999, of Drumlean in Stirling; **Rt. Hon. Michael Bruce Forsyth,** Kt, MA; British politician and banker; b. 16 Oct. 1954, Montrose, Scotland; s. of John Forsyth and Mary Watson; m. Susan Jane Clough 1977; one s. two d.; ed Arbroath High School, St. Andrews Univ.; Minister of State for Health/Educ. (Scotland) 1981–92, Minister of State, Dept of Employment 1992–94, Home Office 1994–95, Sec. of State for Scotland and Lord Keeper of the Great Seal of Scotland 1995–97; Dir Flemings 1997–2000; Vice Chair. Investment Banking (Europe), JP Morgan 2000–02, Deputy Chair. JP Morgan (UK) 2002–; Parliamentarian of the Year 1996, mem. Privy Council. *Leisure interests:* mountaineering, astronomy, gardening, art, fly fishing, photography. *Address:* JP Morgan, 10 Aldermanbury, London, EC2V 7RF, England (Office); c/o House of Lords, London, SW1A 0PN. *Telephone:* (20) 7325-6366 (Office). *E-mail:* Michael .Forsyth@jpmorgan.com (Office).

FORSYTHE, William; American choreographer; b. 1949, New York; ed Jacksonville Univ., Fla, Joffrey Ballet School, NY; joined Stuttgart Ballet 1973, dancer, then choreographer; choreographed works commissioned by cos. including NY City Ballet, San Francisco Ballet, Nat. Ballet of Canada, Royal Ballet, Covent Garden and Nederlands Dans Theater; Dir Ballett Frankfurt 1984–, Ballett Frankfurt and TAT 1999–; Chevalier des Arts et Métiers 1991, Commdr. des Arts et Lettres 1999; Harlekin Preis, Frankfurt 1986, Bessie Award, NY 1988, Deutscher Kritikerpreis 1988, Olivier Award 1992, Evening Standard Award 1999 and numerous other awards. *Ballets include:* Urlicht 1976, Gänge 1983, Artifact 1984, Impressing the Czar 1988, Limb's Theorem 1991, The Loss of Small Detail 1991, Eidos: Telos 1995, Endless House 1999, Kammar/Kammer 2000 (Paris 2002). *Films include:* Berg Ab 1984, Solo 1995, From a Classic Position 1997. *Address:* Ballett Frankfurt, Untermainanlage 11, 60311 Frankfurt, Germany.

FORT, Dame Maeve Geraldine, MA DCMG, DCVO; British diplomatist (retd); b. 19 Nov. 1940, Liverpool; d. of the late Frank Fort and Ruby Fort; ed Trinity Coll., Dublin, Sorbonne, Paris; joined Foreign Service 1963; Perm. Mission to UN, New York 1964–65, Alt. Perm. Rep. Security Council, mem. Contact Group on Namibia 1978–82; Commonwealth Relations Office 1965–66; seconded to SEATO, Bangkok 1966–68; Embassy, Bonn 1968–71; Second Sec., Chancery, High Comm., Lagos 1971–73; Second Sec., First Sec., FCO 1973–78, Counsellor with special responsibility for Namibia 1982–83, Head of W African Dept 1986–89; with Royal Coll. of Defence Studies 1983; Counsellor, Head of Chancery, Consul-Gen., Santiago 1984–86; Amb. to Chad 1987–89, to Mozambique 1989–92, to Lebanon 1992–96; High Commr in S Africa 1996–2000; Trustee, Beit Trust 2000–, British Red Cross 2001–.

FORT-BRESCIA, Bernardo, BA, MArch, FAIA; American architect; b. 19 Nov. 1951, Lima, Peru; s. of Paul Fort and Rosa Brescia; m. Laurinda Spear 1976; five s. one d.; ed Princeton Univ., Harvard Univ.; co-f. (with Laurinda Spear, q.v.) Arquitectonica Int. Corpn 1977–; projects in USA, Europe, S America, Cen. America, Asia and Caribbean; designs include: corp. HQs, office blocks, banks, hotels, condominium apartments, symphony halls, public bldgs, retail complexes; Prof. Univ. of Miami 1975–77; numerous AIA Awards and Honors for Design Excellence, Architectural Digest AD100. *Publications:* Arquitectonica 1991, numerous articles in specialist and non-specialist journals. *Address:* Arquitectonica, 550 Brickell Avenue, Miami, FL 33131, USA. *Telephone:* (305) 372-1812. *Fax:* (305) 372-1175.

FORTE, Baron (Life Peer), cr. 1982, of Ripley in the County of Surrey; **Charles Forte,** Kt; British hotelier and caterer; b. 26 Nov. 1908, Monforte Casalattico, Frosinone, Italy; s. of Rocco and Maria Luigia Forte; m. Irene Mary Chierico 1943; one s. five d.; ed Alloa Acad., Dumfries Coll. and Mamiani, Rome; came to London and opened first milk bar 1935; acquired Criterion Restaurant 1953, Monico Restaurant, Café Royal, Slater and Bodega chain 1954, Hungaria Restaurant 1956, Waldorf Hotel 1958, Fuller's Ltd 1959; Chair. Forte's (Holdings) Ltd, Les Grands Hôtels Associés Ltd,

Paris, Hôtel George V, Paris; Deputy Chair. Trust House Forte Ltd (now Forte PLC) 1970–78, CEO 1971–75, Jt Chief Exec. 1975–78, Chair. 1982–92, Pres. 1992–96; Chair. Snamprogetti 1978–80; Dir TraveLodge Int. Inc., TraveLodge Australia; Dir Forte's and Co. Ltd, Nat. Sporting Club, Theatre Restaurants Ltd; Hon. Consul-Gen. of San Marino in London; Pres. Italian Chamber of Commerce for GB 1952–78, Pres. Westminster Chamber of Commerce 1983–86; mem. British Inst. of Florence, Italy; Bd mem. British Travel Asscn; Hon. PhD (Stirling) 1983; Free Enterprise Award from Aims of Industry 1981; Grand Officer of the Order of the Italian Repub., Cavaliere di Gran Croce della Repubblica Italiana; Cavaliere di Lavoro (Italy); Knight of Magistral Grace of Sovereign and Mil. Order of Malta; Grande Médaille de Vermeil de la Ville de Paris 1979. *Publications:* Forte (autobiog.) 1986, articles for catering trade journals. *Leisure interests:* literature, music, fishing, golf. *Address:* c/o House of Lords, London, SW1A 0PW; Lowndes House, Lowndes Place, London, SW1X 8DB, England (Home). *Telephone:* (20) 7235-6244 (Home).

FORTE, Hon. Sir Rocco (John Vincent), Kt, MA, FCA; British business executive; b. 18 Jan. 1945; s. of Lord Forte; m. Aliai Ricci 1986; one s. two d.; ed Downside and Pembroke Coll., Oxford; Dir of Personnel, Trusthouse Forte 1973–78, Deputy Chief Exec. 1978–82, Jt Chief Exec. 1982–83; Chief Exec. Trusthouse Forte PLC 1983–92; Chair. Forte PLC 1992–96; Chair. and Chief Exec. Rocco Forte Hotels 1996–; mem. Chairs' Cttee Savoy Group 1994–96; fmr Vice-Pres. Commonwealth Games Council for England. *Address:* Savannah House, 11 Charles II Street, London, SW1Y 4QU, England (Office). *Telephone:* (20) 7321-2626 (Office). *Fax:* (20) 7321-2424 (Office). *E-mail:* enquiries@rfhotels.com (Office). *Website:* www.roccofortehotels.com (Office).

FORTEY, Richard Alan, PhD, ScD, FRS; British palaeontologist and writer; b. 15 Feb. 1946, London; s. of Frank Allen Fortey and Margaret Fortey (née Wilshin); m. 1st Bridget Elizabeth Thomas (divorced); one s.; m. 2nd Jacqueline Francis 1977; one. s. two d.; ed Ealing Grammar School for Boys, King's Coll. Cambridge; Research Fellow, then Sr Scientific Officer, Natural History Museum, London 1970–77, Prin. Scientific Officer 1978–86, Sr Prin. Scientific Officer 1986–98, Merit Researcher 1998–; Howley Visiting Prof. Memorial Univ. of Newfoundland 1977–78; Visiting Prof. Palaeobiology, Oxford Univ. 2000–; Collier Chair in Public Understanding of Science and Tech., Univ. of Bristol 2002–03; mem. Geological Soc. of London 1972–, British Mycological Soc. 1980–; Natural World Book of the Year Award 1994; Lyell Medal, Geological Soc. of London 1996; Frink Medal Zoological Soc. of London 2001. *Publications:* The Roderick Masters Book of Money Making Schemes (as Roderick Masters) 1981, Fossels: The Key to the Past 1982, The Hidden Landscape 1993, Life: An Unauthorised Biography 1997, Trilobite! 2000. *Leisure interests:* mycology, humorous writing, cacti. *Address:* Department of Palaeontology, Natural History Museum, Cromwell Road, London, SW7 5BD, England (Office). *Telephone:* (20) 7942-5493 (Office). *Fax:* (20) 7942-5546 (Office). *E-mail:* r.fortey@nhm.ac.uk (Office). *Website:* www.nhm.ac.uk/palaeontology (Office).

FORTIER, L. Yves, CC, QC, BCL, BLitt; Canadian diplomatist and lawyer; b. 11 Sept. 1935, Québec City; s. of François and Louise (Turgeon) Fortier; m. Cynthia Carol Eaton 1959; one s. two d.; ed Univ. of Montreal, McGill Univ. and Univ. of Oxford; called to Bar of Québec 1960; Chair. and Sr Partner, Ogilvy, Renault (law firm), Montreal; Pres. Jr Bar Asscn Montreal 1965–66, Jr Bar Section, Canadian Bar Asscn 1966–67; mem. Gen. Council, Bar of Québec 1966–67; Councillor, Bar of Montreal 1966–67; Pres. London Court of Int. Arbitration; mem. Council, Canadian Section, 1st Comm. of Jurists 1967–87; mem. Canadian Bar Asscn (Pres. Québec br. 1975–76, Nat. Pres. 1982–83); Founding Dir Canadian Bar Asscn Law for the Future Fund; mem. Perm. Court of Arbitration, The Hague, American Arbitration Asscn Panel of Arbitrators and other arbitration insts.; Fellow American Coll. of Trial Lawyers (Regent 1992–96); Hon. mem. American Bar Asscn; Dir Canadian Inst. of Advanced Legal Studies, Canadian Law Inst. of the Pacific Rim 1986–88; mem. Int. Trade Advisory Council (ITAC) Canada; Amb. and Perm. Rep. to UN, New York 1988, Pres. UN Security Council 1989, Vice-Pres. UN Gen. Ass. 1990; Dir Dupont Canada Inc., Hudson's Bay Co. (also Gov.), Nortte Networks Corpn, Royal Bank of Canada, Nova Chemicals Corpn, Southam Inc. and other cos.; Gov. McGill Univ. 1970–85; Rhodes Scholar, Oxford Univ. 1958–60, Dir Canadian Asscn of Rhodes Scholars (Pres. 1975–77), Pres. LCIA (fmrly London Court of Int. Arbitration) 1998–. *Leisure interests:* skiing, tennis, golf, reading. *Address:* Suite 1100, 1981 McGill College Avenue, Montreal, Québec, H3A 3C1 (Office); 19 Rosemount Avenue, Westmount, Québec, H3Y 3G6, Canada (Home). *Telephone:* (514) 847-4747 (Office). *Fax:* (514) 286-5474 (Office).

FORTOV, Vladimir Yevgenyevich; Russian physicist; b. 23 Jan. 1946, Noginsk, Moscow Region; m.; one d.; ed Moscow Inst. of Physics and Tech.; researcher, head of lab. Inst. of Chemical Physics USSR (now Russian) Acad. of Sciences 1971–86; head div. Inst. of High Temperature Physics USSR Acad. of Sciences 1986–92; Dir Inst. for High Energy Densities, Russian Acad. of Sciences 1992–; Chair. Russian Foundation for Basic Research 1993–97; Deputy Chair., then Chair. State Cttee on (now Ministry of) Science and Tech. of Russian Fed. 1996–98; Corresp. mem. USSR (now Russian) Acad. of Sciences 1987, mem. 1992, Vice-Pres. 1996–2001, head Div. for Energetics, Machinery, Mechanics and Control Systems Russian Acad. of Sciences 2002–; Corresp. mem. Int. Asscn on Physics and Tech. of High-Pressures, US Nat. Acad. of Eng; mem. American Physics Soc., European Acad. of Arts and Sciences, Int. Acad. of Astronautics, Max Plank Soc.; State Award of Russian Fed., P. Bridgeman Prize for High Pressure Technology, Max Plank Award. *Publications:* numerous works on thermophysics of extremely high temperatures and pressures, physics of gas dynamics and physics of strong shock waves. *Address:* Presidium of the Russian Academy of Sciences, Leninski prospekt 32A, 119991 Moscow; Institute for High Energy Densities, Izhorskaya str. 13/19, 127412 Moscow, Russia. *Telephone:* (095) 938-12-04 (Acad.); (095) 485-79-88, 975-70-29 (Inst.) (Office). *Fax:* (095) 938-52-34 (Office).

FOSS, Lukas; American composer, conductor, pianist and professor of music; b. 15 Aug. 1922, Berlin, Germany; s. of Martin Foss and Hilda Schindler; m. Cornelia B. Brendel 1950; one s. one d.; ed Lycée Pasteur, Paris, Curtis Inst. of Music, Yale Univ. Music School; Prof. of Conducting and Composition, Univ. of Calif. at Los Angeles 1951–62; Founder Dir Center for Creative and Performing Arts, Buffalo Univ. 1963–; Musical Dir Conductor Buffalo Philharmonic Orchestra 1962–70; Musical Dir Conductor Brooklyn Philharmonic Orchestra 1971–90 (Conductor Laureate 1990–), Jerusalem Symphony Orchestra 1972–76, Milwaukee Symphony Orchestra 1981–87; Dir, Conductor Ojai Festival, Calif. 1955, 1956, 1957, Festival of the Arts Today, Buffalo 1960–67, Franco-U.S. Festival (New York Philharmonic Orchestra) 1964, Stravinsky Festival (New York Philharmonic Orchestra) 1965; Visiting Prof. Harvard Univ. 1969–70, Manhattan School of Music 1972–73, Carnegie Mellon Univ. 1987–90; Prof. of Composition, Boston Univ. 1991–; Visiting Prof. of Composition, Tanglewood 1989, 1990, Yale Univ. 1991; mem. Nat. Acad. of Arts and Letters; 19 hon. degrees; New York Music Critics' Circle Awards; Prix de Rome; Guggenheim Fellowship; Ditson Award 1973, Gold Medal, American Acad. of Arts and Letters 2001. *Compositions include:* Time Cycle, Echoi, Baroque Variations, Paradigm, Geod, three operas, Orpheus, Map, Percussion Concerto, String Quartets, American Cantata, Night Music for John Lennon, Thirteen Ways of Looking at a Blackbird, Solo Observed, Flute concerto, Clarinet concerto, Guitar concerto, Symphony No. 3 (Symphony of Sorrows), Griffelkin (opera). *Leisure interest:* literature. *Address:* 1140 Fifth Avenue, New York, NY 10128, USA. *Telephone:* (212) 722-8003.

FOSS, Per-Kristian; Norwegian politician; b. 19 July 1950, Oslo; ed Univ. of Oslo; journalist 1971–73; mem. Høyre (Conservative Party), Chair. Høyre Municipal Council 1973–77, Chair. Unge Høyre (Young Conservatives) 1973–77, Chair. Høyre Cttee on Party Program 1981–85, Chair. Høyre Cttee on Cultural Objectives and Strategies 1983–85, Deputy Chair. Høyre Party Parl. Mem. Group 1993–2001, Leader of Høyre 2002–; mem. Storting (Parl.) for Oslo 1977–, mem. Cttee on Energy and Industry 1981–89 (Second Vice-Chair. 1985–89), mem. Standing Cttee on Finance 1989–2001 (Chair. 1989–93, Vice-Chair. 1993–97), mem. Enlarged Foreign Affairs Cttee 1997–2001; Minister of Finance 2001–; Ed of Kontur (periodical) 1979–80; Consultant Norges Rederforbund (Norwegian Shipowners' Asscn) 1980–81; mem. Lillehammer Olympic Org. Cttee (LCOC) 1994. *Address:* Ministry of Finance, Akersgt. 42, POB 8001 Dep., Oslo, 0030, Norway (Office). *Telephone:* 22-24-41-00 (Office). *Fax:* 22-24-95-14 (Office). *E-mail:* postmottak@finans.dep.no (Office).

FOSSETT, Steve; American financier and adventure sportsman; b. 1944, Calif.; f. Lakota Trading Inc. and Marathon Securities Inc.; enthusiast for endurance sports; ballooning records include transatlantic flight 1994, first solo flight across the Pacific 1995 and Roziere balloon altitude flight 1996; achieved first solo circumnavigation of the globe in a hot-air balloon 2002; sailing achievements include Pacific Ocean record 1995, Pacific Ocean E to W record 1996 and Pacific Ocean single-handed record 1996; set five further world speed sailing records during 2000–01; record for highest air speed by a glider 2002; other activities: mountaineering (250 ascents), cross-country skiing, English Channel swim 1985 and Daytona 24-hour Endurance Sports Car Race 1993, 1994 and 1995; Fellow Royal Explorers Club, Royal Geographical Soc.; Hon. Mem. Adventurers' Club; Victor Award (special) (Victor Sports Awards) 1995, 1997, Diplôme de Montgolfier 1996, Balloon and Airship Hall of Fame Award 1997, US Sailing Rolex Yachtsman Award 2001.

FOSSIER, Robert, DèsSc; French professor of history; b. 4 Sept. 1927, Le Vésinet; s. of the late René Fossier and Marcelle Brillot; m. Lucie Dupont 1949; three s. two d.; ed Ecole des Chartes; Librarian of City of Paris 1949–53; Prof. Lycée de Fontainebleau and Lycée Carnot, Paris 1953–57; Asst Sorbonne 1957–62; Dir of Studies, then Prof. Univ. of Nancy 1962–71; Prof. of Medieval History, Sorbonne, Paris 1971–93, Prof. Emer. 1993–; Officier des Palmes Académiques. *Publications:* La terre et les hommes en Picardie jusqu'à la fin du XIIIe siècle 1968, Histoire sociale de l'occident médiéval 1971, Chartes de coutume en Picardie 1975, Polyptyques et censiers 1978, Le village et la maison au moyen âge 1980, La Picardie au moyen âge 1981, Enfance de l'Europe (Xe-XIIe) 1982, Le moyen âge 1984, Cartulaire: Chronique de S. Georges d'Hesdin, Paysans d'occident (Xe-XIVe) 1984, La Société mediévale 1992, Villages et villageois au moyen âge 1995, The Family 2000, Rural Economy 900–1024 (Vol. 3) 2000, Sources d'histoire économique du Moyen-âge 2000, Islam–Chrétienté occidentale 2000, Le Travail au Moyen-âge 2001. *Leisure interests:* gardening, mountain-walking. *Address:* Université de Paris 1, 17 rue de la Sorbonne, 75005 Paris (Office); 2 rue du Bel Air, 92190 Meudon (Home); Le Serre, 84240 La Tour-d'Aigues, France (Home).

FOSTER, Brendan, MBE, BSc; British athlete, sports commentator and business executive; b. 12 Jan. 1948, Hebburn, Co. Durham; s. of Francis Foster and Margaret Foster; m. Susan Margaret Foster 1972; one s. one d.; ed Sussex Univ., Carnegie Coll., Leeds; competed Olympic Games, Munich 1972, 5th in 1,500m; Montreal 1976, won bronze medal in 10,000m, 5th in

5,000m, Moscow 1980, 11th in 10,000m; competed Commonwealth Games, Edinburgh 1970, won bronze medal at 1,500m; Christchurch 1974, won silver medal at 5,000m; Edmonton 1978, won gold medal at 10,000m and bronze medal 5,000m; European Champion at 5,000m 1974 and bronze medallist at 1,500m 1971; has held world record at 3,000m and 2 miles, European record at 10,000m, Olympic record at 5,000m; Dir Recreation, Gateshead 1982; Man. Dir Nike Int. 1982–86, Vice-Pres. Marketing (Worldwide) and Vice-Pres. (Europe) 1986–87; Chair. and Man. Dir Nova Int.; BBC TV Commentator 1980–; Hon. Master of Educ. (Newcastle Univ.); Hon. Fellow (Sunderland Polytechnic); Hon. DLitt (Sussex Univ.) 1982; BBC Sports Personality of the Year 1974. *Publications:* Brendan Foster (with Cliff Temple) 1978, Olympic Heroes 1896–1984 1984. *Leisure interests:* sport and running every day. *Address:* Nova International, Newcastle House, Albany Court, Monarch Road, Newcastle upon Tyne, NE4 7YB, England. *Telephone:* (191) 402-0016 (Office). *Website:* www.onrunning.com (Office).

FOSTER, Sir Christopher David, Kt, MA; British economist; b. 30 Oct. 1930, London; s. of George Cecil Foster and Phyllis Joan Foster (née Mappin); m. Kay Sheridan Bullock 1958; two s. three d.; ed Merchant Taylors School and King's Coll., Cambridge; Fellow and Tutor, Jesus Coll., Cambridge 1964–66; Dir-Gen. of Econ. Planning, Ministry of Transport 1966–70; Head, Unit for Research in Urban Econs, LSE 1970–76, Prof. of Urban Studies and Econs 1976–78, Visiting Prof. 1978–86; Gov. Centre for Environmental Studies 1967–70, Dir 1976–78; Visiting Prof. of Econs MIT 1970; Head of Econ. and Public Policy Div. Coopers & Lybrand (fmrly Coopers & Lybrand Assocs., then Coopers & Lybrand Deloitte) 1978–84, Public Sector Practice Leader and Econ. Adviser 1984–86, Dir and Head Econs Practice Div. 1988–, Partner 1988–94, mem. Man. Cttee 1988–90, Adviser to Chair. 1990–92, 1994–99; Special Adviser to Sec. of Transport on Privatization of British Rail 1992–94; mem. Bd Railtrack 1994–2000; Commercial Adviser to Bd of British Telecommunications PLC 1986–88; Chair. RAC (Royal Automobile Club) Foundation 1999–; Hon. Fellow Jesus Coll., Cambridge 1992. *Publications:* The Transport Problem 1963, Politics, Finance and the Role of Economics: The Control of Public Enterprise (jtly.) 1972, Local Government Finance 1980, Privatization, Public Ownership and the Regulation of Natural Monopoly 1992, The State Under Stress 1996; papers in various econ. and other journals. *Leisure interests:* theatre, reading. *Address:* RAC Foundation for Motoring, 89–91 Pall Mall, London, SW1Y 5HS (Office); 6 Holland Park Avenue, London, W11 3QU, England. *Telephone:* (20) 7747-3445 (Office); (20) 7727-4757. *Fax:* (20) 7229-6581 (Home). *E-mail:* cd@foster46.fsnet.co.uk (Home). *Website:* www.racfoundation.org (Office).

FOSTER, David Manning, PhD; Australian writer; b. 15 May 1944, Katoomba; m. 1st Robin Bowers 1964; one s. two d.; m. 2nd Gerda Busch 1975; one s. two d.; ed Univ. of Sydney, Australian Nat. Univ., Univ. of Pennsylvania; professional fiction writer 1973–; numerous awards including Miles Franklin Award 1997. *Publications include:* Moonlite 1981, Plumbum 1983, Mates of Mars 1991, The Glade within the Grove 1996, In the New Country 1999, The Land Where Stories End 2001. *Leisure interests:* gardening, bushwalking. *Address:* P.O. Box 57, Bundanoon, NSW 2578, Australia.

FOSTER, Joanna Katharine; British administrator; b. 5 May 1939, Canterbury, Kent; d. of the late Michael Mead and of Lesley Mead; m. Jerome Foster 1961; one s. one d.; ed Benenden School, Kent, Grenoble Univ., France; fmr mem. staff Vogue magazine London, New York and San Francisco Chronicle; Man. Adviser The Industrial Soc. 1967–71, Head Pepperell Unit. 1981–88; Press. Attaché, Ed. INSEAD Business School, Fontainebleau, France 1971–79; Dir of Corp. Educ. Pittsburgh Univ., USA 1979–81; Chair. Equal Opportunities Comm. 1988–93; Pres. European Comm.'s Advisory Cttee on Equal Opportunities Jan.–Dec. 1992, Vice-Pres. Jan.–April 1993; Chair. UK Council of UN Int. Year of the Family 1994; Pres. Relate 1993–96; Trustee Lloyds TSB Foundation for England and Wales 1991–, Chair. 1998–; Deputy Chair. of Govs. Oxford Brookes Univ. 1993–; Gov. Birkbeck Coll., Univ. of London 1996–98; Dir The BT Forum 1995–97, Chair. 1997–; Trustee Employment Policy Inst.; mem. advisory group ERA; mem. Industrial Soc., European Women's Foundation; Chair. Nat. Work–Life Forum 1998–; mem. Govt Advisory Group on Work–Life Balance 2000–; also currently Chair. Nuffield Orthopaedic Trust Bd, Oxford; Hon. Fellow (St Hilda's Coll. Oxford) 1988; Hon. DLitt (Kingston) 1993, (Salford) 1994; Hon. DUniv (Essex) 1993; Hon. LLD (Oxford Brookes) 1993, (Univ. of West of England) 1993, (Strathclyde) 1994, (Bristol) 1996. *Leisure interests:* family, friends, food. *Address:* c/o Lloyds TSB Foundation for England and Wales, 3rd Floor, 4 St Dunstan's Hill, London, EC3R 8UL (Office); Confessor's Gate, Islip, Oxford, OX5 2SN, England.

FOSTER, Jodie (Alicia Christian), BA; American actress, film director and producer; b. 19 Nov. 1962, Los Angeles; d. of Lucius Foster and Evelyn (née Almond) Foster; two s.; ed Yale Univ.; acting début in TV programme Mayberry 1969; Hon. DFA (Yale) 1997. *Films include:* Napoleon and Samantha 1972, Kansas City Bomber 1972, Menace of the Mountain, One Little Indian 1973, Tom Sawyer 1973, Alice Doesn't Live Here Any More 1975, Taxi Driver 1976, Echoes of a Summer 1976, Bugsy Malone 1976, Freaky Friday 1976, The Little Girl Who Lives Down the Lane 1977, Candleshoe 1977, Foxes 1980, Carny 1980, Hotel New Hampshire 1984, The Blood of Others 1984, Siesta 1986, Five Corners 1986, The Accused 1988 (Acad. Award for Best Actress 1989), Stealing Home 1988, Catchfire 1990, The Silence of the Lambs (Acad. Award for Best Actress 1992) 1990, Little Man Tate (also Dir) 1991, Shadows and Fog 1992, Sommersby 1993, Maverick 1994, Nell 1994,

Home for the Holidays (Dir, co-producer only) 1996, Contact 1997, The Baby Dance (exec. producer only) 1997, Waking the Dead (exec. producer only) 1998, Anna and the King 1999, Panic Room 2001, The Dangerous Lives of Altar Boys (also producer) 2002. *Address:* EGG Pictures Production Co., Jerry Lewis Annex, 5555 Melrose Avenue, Los Angeles, CA 90038-3112, USA.

FOSTER, Lawrence; American conductor; b. 23 Oct. 1941, Los Angeles; m. Angela Foster 1972; one d.; studied with Fritz Zweig and Karl Böhm and at Bayreuth Festival Master Classes; Music Dir Young Musicians Foundation, Los Angeles 1960–64; Conductor San Francisco Ballet 1960–64; Asst Conductor LA Philharmonic Orchestra 1965–68; Chief Guest Conductor Royal Philharmonic Orchestra, London 1969–74; Music Dir Houston Symphony Orchestra 1971–78; Music Dir Orchestre Philharmonique, Monte Carlo 1978–96; Music Dir Duisburg Orchestra, FRG 1982–86; Music Dir Chamber Orchestra of Lausanne 1985; conductor Jerusalem Symphony Orchestra 1990; music Dir Aspen Music Festival and School 1990–96; Music Dir Orquestra Ciutat de Barcelona 1995–2002, Prin. Guest Conductor 2002–; Music Dir Gulbentrian Symphony Orchestra 2003–; Koussevitsky Memorial Conducting Prize, Tanglewood 1966. *Leisure interests:* reading history and biographies, films. *Address:* c/o ICM Artists Ltd, 8942 Wilshire Boulevard, Beverly Hills, CA 90211-1934, USA; c/o Harrison Parrott Ltd, 12 Penzance Place, London, W11, England.

FOSTER, Murphy J., Jr. (Mike Foster), BSc; American business executive and politician; b. Shreveport, La.; m.; ed Louisiana State Univ.; sugar cane farmer, La.; Founder Bayou Sale, La.; Pres. Sterling Sugars Inc.; Senator St Mary/Assumption Parish Dist, La. State Senate 1987, Chair. Commerce Cttee 1991; now Gov. of Louisiana. *Leisure interests:* hunting, fishing, tennis. *Address:* Office of the Governor, P.O. Box 94004, Baton Rouge, LA 70804, USA.

FOSTER, Roy F.; Irish historian; Carroll Professor of Irish History, Hertford Coll., Oxford. *Publications:* Modern Ireland 1600–1972, The Oxford Illustrated History of Ireland, biogs. of Charles Stewart Parnell and Lord Randolph Churchill, W. B. Yeats: A Life, Vol. I: The Apprentice Mage 1865–1914 2001, The Irish Story: Telling Tales and Making it Up in Ireland 2001. *Address:* Hertford College, Catte Street, Oxford, OX1 3BW, England (Office). *Telephone:* (1865) 279400 (Office). *Website:* www.hertford.ox.ac.uk (Office).

FOSTER OF THAMES BANK, Baron (Life Peer), cr. 1999 of Reddish in the County of Greater Manchester; **Norman Robert Foster,** Kt, OM, DipArch, MArch, RA, RWA, RIBA; British architect; b. 1 June 1935, Manchester; s. of Robert Foster and the late Lilian Foster; m. 3rd Elena Ochoa 1996; ed Manchester Univ. School of Architecture and Dept of Town and Country Planning, Yale Univ. School of Architecture; Urban Renewal and City Planning Consultants work 1962–63; pvt. practice, as "Team 4 Architects" (with Wendy Cheesman, Georgie Wolton, Lord Rogers of Riverside) London 1963–67, Foster Associates (now Foster and Partners), offices Berlin, Singapore 1967–; Chair. Foster and Partners 1967; collaboration with Buckminster Fuller 1968–83; Consultant Architect to Univ. of E Anglia 1978–87; fmr External Examiner RIBA Visiting Bd of Educ.; fmr mem. Architectural Asscn Council (Vice-Pres. 1974); fmr teacher Univ. of Pa, Architectural Asscn, London, London Polytechnic, Bath Acad. of Arts; FCSD 1975; IBM Fellow, Aspen Design Conf. 1980; Council mem. RCA 1981–; mem. I.A.A., European Acad. of Sciences and Arts, American Acad. of Arts and Sciences; mem. Order of French Architects, Akad. der Kunst, Royal Acad. of Fine Arts, Sweden; Hon. FAIA 1980; Royal West of England Academician; Hon. Fellow Royal Acad., Inst. of Structural Engineers, Royal Coll. of Eng, Kent Inst. of Art and Design; Hon. mem. BDA, RDI; Assoc. Acad. Royale de Belgique; Hon. LittD (Univ. of E Anglia) 1980; Hon. DSc (Bath) 1986, (Humberside) 1992, (Valencia) 1992, (Manchester) 1993; Dr hc (Royal Coll. of Art) 1991, (Tech. Univ. Eindhoven) 1996; Hon. DLitt. (Oxford) 1996, (London) 1997; Architectural Design Projects Awards 1964, 1965, 1966, 1969, Financial Times Industrial Architecture Awards 1967, 1974, 1984, citations 1970, 1971, 1981, 1993, RIBA Awards 1969, 1972, 1977, 1978, 1992, 1993, 1997, 1998, 1999; RSA Business and Industry Award 1976, 1991, Int. Design Awards (Brussels) 1976, 1980, R. S. Reynolds Int. Memorial Awards (USA) 1976, 1979, 1986, Structural Steel Awards 1972, 1978, 1984, 1986, 1992, 1999, 2000, citation 1980, Ambrose Congreve Award 1980, Royal Gold Medal for Architecture 1983, Civic Trust Award 1984, 1992, 1995, 1999, 2000, Constructa-European Award Program for Industrial Architecture 1986, Premio Compasso d'Oro Award 1987, Japan Design Foundation Award 1987, PA Innovations Award 1988, Annual Interiors Award (USA) 1988, 1992, 1993, 1994, Kunstpreis Award, Berlin 1989, BCI Award 1989, 1991, 1992, 1993, 1997, 1998; Pritzker Prize for Architecture 1999; Mies van der Rohe Award, Barcelona 1991, Gold Medal, French Acad. 1991, Concrete Soc. Award 1992, 1993, 1999, American Inst. of Architects Gold Medal 1994, Queen's Award for Export Achievement 1995, AIA Award 1995, 1997, "Mipim" Man of the Year 1996, "Building" Construction Personality of the Year 1996, Silver Medal of Chartered Soc. of Designers 1997, Pritzker Prize for Architecture 1999, Visual Arts Award 2000, Praemium Imperiale 2002; Officier Ordre des Arts et des Lettres (France), Order of N Rhine-Westphalia. *Major works include:* Pilot Head Office for IBM, Hampshire 1970, Tech. Park for IBM, Greenford 1975, Willis, Faber and Dumas, Ipswich 1975, Sainsbury Centre for Visual Arts, Norwich 1977, Renault Centre UK 1983, Hong Kong Bank HQ 1986, Third London Airport Terminal Stansted 1991, Century Tower Tokyo 1991, Barcelona Telecommunications Tower 1992, Sackler Galleries, Royal Acad. 1991, Cranfield Univ. Library 1992, Arts Centre, Nîmes 1993, Lycée, Fréjus 1993,

Microelectronics Park, Duisburg 1993, Bilbao Metro System 1995, Univ. of Cambridge Faculty of Law 1996, American Air Museum, Duxford 1997, Commerzbank HQ Frankfurt 1997, Chek Lap Kok Airport, Hong Kong 1998, new German Parl. Reichstag, Berlin 1999, Great Court, British Museum 2000, Al Faisaliah Complex, Riyadh 2000, Research Facility, Stanford Univ. Calif. 2000, Greater London Authority Bldg, London, Millennium Bridge, London, Swiss Re Tower 2002–03; work exhibited in France, Germany, Spain, Japan, The Netherlands, London, USA and Switzerland; work in perm. collection of Museum of Modern Art, New York and Centre Georges Pompidou, Paris. *Publications:* Norman Foster: Buildings and Projects Vols 1, 2, 3, 4, On Foster … Foster On 2000 and numerous contribs to the architectural and tech. press. *Leisure interests:* flying, skiing, running. *Address:* Foster and Partners, Riverside Three, 22 Hester Road, London, SW11 4AN, England. *Telephone:* (20) 7738-0455 (London). *Fax:* (20) 7738-1107 (London). *E-mail:* enquiries@fosterandpartners.com (Office). *Website:* www.fosterandpartners.com (Office).

FOTTRELL, Patrick, DSc, MRIA; Irish university administrator; b. 26 Sept. 1933, Youghal, Co. Cork; s. of Matthew Fottrell and Mary (née O'Sullivan) Fottrell; m. Esther Kennedy 1963; two s. two d.; ed CBS Youghal and North Mon schools, Univ. Coll., Cork, Univ. of Glasgow, Scotland, Univ. Coll., Galway; Sr Research Officer, Agric. Inst., Johnstown Castle, Wexford 1963–65; lecturer, later Assoc. Prof., Prof. of Biochem., Univ. Coll., Galway 1965–; Visiting Prof., Harvard Univ., USA 1972, 1982; Beit Memorial Fellow; EEC Science Writers Award. *Publications:* Perspectives on Coeliac Disease (jt author); over 100 scientific publs in int. journals on biochem. *Leisure interests:* walking, music, soccer. *Address:* University College, Galway (Office); Bunowen, Taylorshill, Galway, Ireland (Home). *Telephone:* (91) 24411 (Office); (91) 21022 (Home).

FOU TS'ONG, (FU CONG); Chinese pianist; b. 10 March 1934; s. of the late Fu Lei; m. 1st Zamira Menuhin 1960 (divorced 1970); one s.; m. 2nd Hijong Hyun 1973 (divorced 1978); m. 3rd Patsy Toh 1987; one s.; ed Shanghai and Warsaw; first performance, Shanghai 1953, concerts in Eastern Europe and USSR 1953–58; London debut 1959, concerts in Europe, N and S. America, Australia and Far East. *Leisure interests:* bridge, sport, oriental art. *Address:* 62 Aberdeen Park, London, N5 2BL, England. *Telephone:* (20) 7226-9589. *Fax:* (20) 7704-8896. *E-mail:* patsytoh@foutoh.demon.co.uk (Home).

FOUDA, Yosri; Egyptian journalist; b. 1964; ed American Univ. in Cairo; producer Arabic-language TV Service, BBC, London, UK –1996; reporter Al Jazeera London Bureau, UK 1996–, presenter 'Top Secret' TV programme (interviewed April 2002 Khalid Shaikh Mohammed, Chief of Al-Qaeda Mil. Cttee, believed to have masterminded 9/11 US attacks).

FOURCADE, Jean-Pierre; French politician; b. 18 Oct. 1929, Marmande; s. of Raymond and Germaine (née Raynal) Fourcade; m. Odile Mion 1958; one s. two d.; ed Coll. de Sorèze, Bordeaux Univ. Faculté de Droit, Inst. des Etudes politiques; student, Ecole Nat. d'Admin. 1952–54; Insp. des Finances 1954–73; Chargé de Mission to Sec. of State for Finance (later Minister of Finance) 1959–61, Conseiller technique 1962, Dir Adjoint du Cabinet 1964–66; Asst Head of Service, Inspection gén. des Finances 1962; Head of Trade Div., Directorate-Gen. of Internal Trade and Prices 1965, Dir-Gen. 1968–70; Asst Dir-Gen. Crédit industriel et commercial 1970, Dir-Gen. 1972–74, Admin. 1973–74; Admin., later Pres. and Dir-Gen. Soc. d'Epargne mobilière 1972–74; Admin. Banque transatlantique 1971–74, Soc. commerciale d'Affrètement et de Combustibles 1972–74; Minister of Econ. and Finance 1974–76, of Supply 1976–77, of Supply and Regional Devt 1977; Mayor of St-Cloud 1971–92, of Boulogne-billancourt 1995–; Conseiller-Gén., canton of St-Cloud 1973–89; Conseiller Régional, Ile de France 1976, Vice-Pres. 1982–86, First Vice-Pres. 1986–95; Senator, Hauts de Seine 1977; Pres. Comité des Finances Locales 1980–, Comm. des Affaires Sociales du Sénat 1983–99; Pres. Clubs Perspectives et Réalités 1975–82; Vice-Pres. Union pour la Démocratie française (U.D.F.) 1978–86, mem. 1978–; mem. UMP Parl. group 2002–; mem. Admin. Council of RATP 1984–93, Epad 1985–95, SNCF 1993–98; Pres. Conseil de Surveillance de la Caisse Nat. des Allocations Familiales 2002–; Vice-Pres. Asscn des Maires des Grandes Villes de France 2002–; Officier, Ordre nat. du Mérite. *Publications:* Et si nous parlions de demain 1979, la Tentation social-démocrate 1985, Remèdes pour l'assurance maladie 1989. *Address:* Mairie, 26 Ave. André Morizet, 92100 Boulogne-Billancourt; Sénat, Palais du Luxembourg, 75291 Paris, cedex 06; 8 Parc de Béarn, 92210 St-Cloud, France (Home).

FOURNIER, Jacques, LenD; French lawyer; b. 5 May 1929, Épinal; s. of Léon Fournier and Ida Rudmann; m. 1st Jacqueline Tazerout (deceased); three s.; m. 2nd Michèle Dubez 1980 (divorced); m. 3rd Noëlle Fréaud-Lenoir 1989 (divorced); ed Inst. for Political Studies, Paris and Nat. School of Admin.; Civil Servant, French State Council 1953, Master of Petitions 1960, State Councillor 1978; Legal Adviser, Embassy in Morocco 1961–64; Head of Dept of Social Affairs, Gen. Planning Office 1969–72; Asst Sec.-Gen. to Pres. of France 1981–82; Sec.-Gen. of the Govt 1982–86; Pres. of Admin. Council of Gaz de France 1986–88; Pres. S.N.C.F. 1988–94, Centre européen des entreprises publiques 1988–94, Sceta 1989–94, Ciriec-France 1994–; Chair. Carrefour 1992–98; fmr mem. Council of State, renewed mem. 1994–98; mem. Conseil supérieur de la magistrature 1998–; Chevalier, Ordre Nat. du Mérite; Commdr., Légion d'honneur. *Publications:* Politique de l'Education 1971, Traité du social, situations, luttes politiques, institutions 1976, Le Pouvoir du social 1979, Le travail gouvernemental 1987, le Train, l'Europe et le service public 1993. *Address:* Conseil supérieur de la magistrature, 15 quai Branly, 75007 Paris (Office); 19 rue Montorgueil, 75001 Paris, France (Home). *Telephone:* 1-47-54-22-24 (Office). *E-mail:* jfrnier@easynet.fr (Home).

FOURTOU, Jean-René; French business executive; b. 20 June 1939, Libourne; ed Ecole Polytechnique, Paris; Eng Consultant, Bossard & Michel 1963, mem. Bd of Dirs Bossard Consultants 1972, Chair. and CEO 1977; apptd Chair. and CEO Rhone-Poulenc 1986; Vice-Chair. Aventis 1999–2002, Hon. Chair. and Vice-Chair. Supervisory Bd May 2002–; Chair. and CEO Vivendi Universal March 2002–; Vice-Pres. ICC, Pres. Jan. 2003–; Dir of several cos including AXA, Schneider, Pernod-Ricard, EADS, La Poste; mem. European Round Table of Industrialists (ERT); Co-Founder Entreprise & Cité; Officier, Légion d'Honneur, Commdr, Ordre nat. du Mérite. *Publications include:* La Passion d'Entreprendre 1985. *Address:* Vivendi Universal, 42 avenue de Friedland, 75380 Paris Cedex 08, France (Office). *Telephone:* 1-71-71-10-00 (Office). *Fax:* 1-71-71-11-79 (Office). *Website:* www.vivendiuniversal.com (Office).

FOWKE, Philip Francis, FRAM; British concert pianist; b. 28 June 1950, Gerrards Cross, Bucks.; s. of Francis H. V. Fowke and Florence L. (née Clutton) Fowke; ed Downside Abbey School; began piano studies with Marjorie Withers 1957; awarded RAM Scholarship to study with Gordon Green 1967; Wigmore Hall début 1974; UK concerto début with Royal Liverpool Philharmonic 1975; Royal Festival Hall début 1977; BBC Promenade Concert début 1979; U.S. début 1982; débuts in Denmark, Bulgaria, France, Switzerland, Hong Kong, Belgium and Italy 1983; Austrian début at Salzburg Mozart week 1984; German début 1985; New Zealand début 1994; now appears regularly with all the leading orchestras in UK and gives regular recitals and concerto performances for BBC Radio; Prof. RAM 1984–91, Welsh Coll. of Music and Drama 1994; Head of Keyboard Dept, Trinity Coll. of Music, London 1995–98, Sr Fellow 1998; recordings of Bliss, Chopin, Delius, Finzi, Rachmaninoff and Tchaikovsky piano concertos; Recitalist and Piano Tutor, Dartington Int. Summer School 1996, 1997, 2000; Concerto appearances with the Hallé Orchestra and in U.S.A. 1997; 50th Birthday Recital, Wigmore Hall, London 2000; Soloist, BBC Proms 2001; mem. London Piano Quartet; Vice-Chair. European Piano Teachers' Asscn (UK) presenter and contrib. to music programmes on BBC Radio and to nat. press; Countess of Munster Musical Trust Award 1972, Nat. Fed. of Music Socs. Award 1973, BBC Piano Competition 1974, Winston Churchill Fellowship 1976 and numerous other awards and prizes. *Recordings include:* Hoddinott Piano Concerto, CD album of film scores 1998. *Publications:* reviews and obituaries in nat. press. *Leisure interests:* architecture, monasticism. *Address:* c/o Patrick Garvey Management, 59 Lansdowne Place, Hove, E Sussex, BN3 1FL, England. *Telephone:* (20) 8980-2680. *Fax:* (20) 8980-3679. *Website:* philipfowke@aol.com (Office).

FOWLER, Sir (Edward) Michael (Coulson), Kt, MArch, FNZIA, ARIBA; New Zealand architect; b. 19 Dec. 1929, Marton; s. of William Coulson Fowler and Faith Agnes Fowler (née Netherclift); m. Barbara Hamilton Hall 1953; two s. one d.; ed Christ's Coll., Christchurch, Auckland Univ.; with Ove Arup & Partners, London 1954–55; Partner, Gray Young, Morton Calder & Fowler, Wellington 1959; Sr Partner, Calder, Fowler & Styles 1960–89; travelled abroad to study cen. banking systems security methods; work includes Overseas Terminal, Wellington, Reserve Bank, Wellington, Dalmuir House, Wellington Club, office bldgs., factories, houses, churches; mem. Wellington City Council 1968–74; Chair. NZIA Educ. Cttee 1967–73; Mayor of Wellington 1974–83; Chair. Queen Elizabeth II Arts Council of NZ 1983–86; Pres. NZ Youth Hostel Asscn 1983–86; architectural consultant 1983–; Award of Honour, New Zealand Inst. of Architects 1983, Alfred O. Glasse Award, New Zealand Planning Inst. 1984. *Publications:* Country Houses of New Zealand 1972, Wellington Sketches: Folios I, II 1973, The Architecture and Planning of Moscow 1980, Eating Houses in Wellington 1980, Wellington-Wellington 1981, Eating Houses of Canterbury 1982, Wellington Celebration 1983, The New Zealand House 1983, Buildings of New Zealanders 1984, Michael Fowler's University of Auckland 1993. *Leisure interests:* sketching, writing, history, politics. *Address:* 31 George Street, Blenheim (Office); Branches, Giffords Road, R.D.3, Blenheim, New Zealand (Home). *Telephone:* (3) 578-7399 (Office); (3) 572-8987 (Home). *Fax:* (3) 577-7485 (Office). *E-mail:* michael.fowler@xtra.co.nz (Office).

FOWLER, Rt Hon (Peter) Norman, Baron (Life Peer), cr. 2001, of Sutton Coldfield in the Co. of West Midlands, PC, MA; British politician; b. 2 Feb. 1938; s. of the late N. F. Fowler and Katherine Fowler; m. 1st Linda Christmas 1968; m. 2nd Fiona Poole 1979; two d.; ed King Edward VI School, Chelmsford, Trinity Hall, Cambridge; Nat. Service Comm., Essex Regt 1956–58; joined The Times 1961, Special Corresp. 1962–66, Home Affairs Corresp. 1966–70; mem. Council, Bow Group 1967–69, Editorial Bd, Crossbow 1962–69; Vice-Chair. N Kensington Conservative Asscn 1967–68; Chair. E Midlands Area, Conservative Political Centre 1970–73; MP for Nottingham S 1970–74, for Sutton Coldfield 1974–2001, mem. Parl. Select Cttee on Race Relations and Immigration 1970–74; Jt Sec. Conservative Parl. Home Affairs Cttee 1971–72, Vice-Chair. 1974; Parl. Pvt. Sec. NI Office 1972–74; Opposition Spokesman on Home Affairs 1974–75; Chief Opposition Spokesman on Social Services 1975–76, on Transport 1976–79; Minister of Transport 1979–81, Sec. of State for Transport 1981, for Social Services 1981–87, for Employment 1987–90; Chair. Conservative Party 1992–94; Opposition Front Bench Spokesman on Environment, Transport and the Regions 1997–98, on Home Affairs 1998–99; mem. Lloyds 1989–98; Chair. Nat. House Bldg Council 1992–98, Midland Ind. Newspapers 1992–98, Regional Ind. Media (the

Yorkshire Post Group) 1998–2002; Numark Ltd 1998–; Chair. Aggregate Industries 2000–; mem. Bd Group 4 Security 1990–93; Dir NFC 1990–97. *Publications:* The Cost of Crime 1973, The Right Track 1977, After the Riots: The Police in Europe, Ministers Decide: A Memoir of the Thatcher Years 1991. *Address:* c/o The House of Lords, London, SW1A 0PN, England.

FOWLES, John; British author; b. 31 March 1926, Essex; s. of Robert J. Fowles and Gladys M. Richards; m. 1st Elizabeth Whitton 1954 (died 1990); m. 2nd Sarah Smith 1998; ed Bedford School and Univ. of Oxford; Fellow New Coll. Oxford 1997; Hon. DLitt (Exeter) 1983; Hon. LittD (E Anglia) 1997; PEN Silver Pen Award 1969, W.H. Smith Literary Award (for The French Lieutenant's Woman) 1969. *Publications:* The Collector 1963, The Aristos 1964, The Magus 1965, The French Lieutenant's Woman 1969, Poems 1973, Shipwreck 1974, The Ebony Tower 1974, Daniel Martin 1977, Islands (with Fay Godwin) 1978, The Tree 1979, The Enigma of Stonehenge 1980, Mantissa 1982, Thomas Hardy's England 1984, Land 1985, A Maggot 1985, The Tree 1991, Wormholes 1998, Lyme Worthies 2000. *Leisure interests:* local and natural history. *Address:* c/o Anthony Sheil, Gillon Aitken Associates Ltd, 29 Fernshaw Road, London, SW10 0TG, England (Office).

FOX, Edward, OBE; British actor; b. 13 April 1937; s. of Robin Fox and Angela Fox; brother of James Fox (q.v.); m. 1st Tracy Pelissier 1958 (divorced 1961); one d.; one s. one d. by Joanna David; ed Ashfold School, Harrow School and Royal Acad. of Dramatic Art; actor since 1957; started in provincial repertory theatre 1958 and has since worked widely in films, stage plays and TV; recipient of several awards for TV performance as Edward VIII in Edward and Mrs Simpson 1978. *Stage appearances include:* Knuckle 1973, The Family Reunion 1979, Anyone for Denis 1981, Quartermaine's Terms 1981, Hamlet 1982, The Dance of Death 1983, Interpreters 1986, The Admirable Crichton 1988, Another Love Story 1990, The Philanthropist 1991, My Fair Lady, Father 1995, A Letter of Resignation 1997, The Chiltern Hundreds 1999, The Browning Version 2000, The Twelve Pound Look 2000. *Films include:* The Go-Between 1971, The Day of the Jackal, A Doll's House 1973, Galileo 1976, A Bridge Too Far, The Duellists, The Cat and the Canary 1977, Force Ten from Navarone 1978, The Mirror Crack'd 1980, Gandhi 1982, Never Say Never Again 1983, Wild Geese, The Bounty 1984, The Shooting Party, Return from the River Kwai 1989, Circles of Deceit (TV) 1989, Prince of Thieves 1990, They Never Slept 1991, A Month by the Lake 1996, Prince Valiant 1997. *Television includes:* Daniel Deronda 2002. *Leisure interest:* playing the piano.

FOX, Frederick Donald, LVO; milliner; b. 2 April 1931; s. of the late Lesley James Fox and Ruby Mansfield (née Elliott); ed St Joseph's Convent School, Jerilderie, New South Wales, Australia; started millinery business 1962; designer for the Royal Family, granted Royal Warrant to HM The Queen 1974; now consultant to Philip Treacey, London 2002–; private clients; Pres. Millinery Trades Benevolent Asscn; Freeman City of London 1989, Liveryman Worshipful Co. of Feltmakers 1989. *Leisure interests:* gardening, photography. *Address:* Model Hats, 17 Avery Row, London, W1X 9HA, England (Office). *Telephone:* (20) 7629-5705 (Office). *Fax:* (20) 7629-3048 (Office). *E-mail:* frederick@frederick_fox.freeserve.uk (Office).

FOX, James; British actor; b. 19 May 1939, London; s. of Robin Fox and Angela Fox (née Worthington); brother of Edward Fox (q.v.); m. Mary Elizabeth Fox 1973; four s. one d.; ed Ashfold Prep. School and Harrow School. *Films include:* Mrs Miniver 1952, The Servant 1963, King Rat 1965, Those Magnificent Men in Their Flying Machines 1965, Thoroughly Modern Millie 1966, Isadora 1967, Performance 1969, A Passage to India 1984, Runners 1984, Farewell to the King 1987, Finding Mawbee (video film as the Mighty Quinn) 1988, She's Been Away 1989, The Russia House 1990, Afraid of the Dark 1991, Patriot Games 1991, As You Like It 1992, The Remains of the Day 1993, Elgar's Tenth Muse 1995, Anna Karenina 1997, Mickey Blue Eyes 1998, Jinnah 1998, Up at the Villa 1998, The Golden Bowl 1999, Sexy Beast 2000. *Plays:* Uncle Vanya 1995. *Television:* A Question of Attribution 1991, Gulliver's Travels 1995, The Lost World 2001. *Publication:* Comeback: An Actor's Direction 1983. *Leisure interests:* Russian language and culture. *Address:* c/o ICM Oxford House, 76 Oxford Street, London, W1D 1BS, England. *Telephone:* (20) 7636-6565 (Office). *Fax:* (20) 7323-0101 (Office).

FOX, Kerry; New Zealand actress; m. Jaime Robertson; ed New Zealand Drama School; fmr lighting designer. *Television appearances include:* Mr Wroe's Virgins, A Village Affair, Saigon Baby, The Affair. *Films include:* Country Life, An Angel at My Table (Elvira Notari Best Performance award), The Last Days of Chez Nous, Friends, Shallow Grave, Intimacy.

FOX, Liam, MB, CH.B.; British politician and physician; b. 22 Sept. 1961; s. of William Fox and Catherine Young; ed St Bride's High School, E Kilbride, Univ. of Glasgow; civilian army medical officer Royal Army Educ. Corps 1981–91; gen. practitioner, Beaconsfield 1987–91; Div. Surgeon St John's Ambulance 1987–91; contested Roxburgh and Berwickshire 1987; MP for Woodspring 1992–; Parl. Pvt. Sec. to Home Sec. Michael Howard 1993–94, Asst Govt Whip 1994–95, Lord Commr HM Treasury (Sr Govt Whip) 1995–96, Parl. Under-Sec. of State FCO 1996–97, Opposition Front Bench Spokesman on Constitutional Affairs 1997–98, Shadow Sec. for Constitutional Affairs 1998–99, Shadow Sec. of State for Health 1999–; mem. Scottish Select Cttee 1992–93; Sec. Conservative Backbench Health Cttee 1992–93; Pres. Glasgow Univ. Conservative Club 1982–83; Nat. Vice-Chair. Scottish Young Conservatives 1983–84; mem. Conservative Political Centre; Sec. Conservative West Country Mems. Group. 1992–93. *Publications include:* Making Unionism Positive 1988, Bearing the Standard (contrib.) 1991, contrib. to

House of Commons Magazine. *Leisure interests:* tennis, swimming, cinema, theatre. *Address:* House of Commons, London, SW1A 0AA, England. *Telephone:* (20) 7219-3000.

FOX, Maurice Sanford, PhD, FAAS; American professor of molecular biology; b. 11 Oct. 1924; s. of Albert Fox and Ray Fox; m. Sally Cherniavsky 1955; three s.; ed Stuyvesant High School, Queen's Coll.Univ. of Chicago; Instructor, Univ. of Chicago 1951–53; Asst, Rockefeller Univ. 1953–55, Asst Prof. 1955–58, Assoc. Prof. 1958–62; Assoc. Prof., MIT 1962–66, Prof. 1966–79, Lester Wolfe Prof. of Molecular Biology 1979–96, Head, Dept of Biology 1985–89; mem. Bd Council for a Liveable World 1962; Breast Cancer Task Force 1977–80; mem. Inst. of Medicine, NAS, American Acad. of Arts and Sciences, Radiation Effects Research Foundation, Hiroshima 1994–99, Int. Bioethics Cttee, UNESCO; Nuffield Research Fellow 1957. *Publications:* numerous learned papers. *Leisure interest:* ancient history. *Address:* Department of Biology, Massachussets Institute of Technology, 77 Massachussets Avenue, Cambridge, MA 02139 (Office); 983 Memorial Drive, Cambridge, MA 02138, USA (Home). *Telephone:* (617) 253-4728 (Office). *E-mail:* msfox@mit.edu (Office).

FOX, Michael J.; American actor; b. 9 June 1961, Edmonton, Alberta, Canada; s. of Bill Fox and Phyllis Fox; m. Tracy Pollan 1988; one s. two d.; ed Burnbay Cen. High School, Vancouver, BC, Canada. *TV appearances include:* Leo and Me 1976, Palmerstown USA 1980, Family Ties 1982–89 (Emmy Awards 1987, 1988), Spin City 1996–2000. *TV films include:* Letters from Frank 1979, Poison Ivy 1985, High School USA 1985. *Film appearances include:* Midnight Madness 1980, Class of '84 1981, Back to the Future 1985, Teen Wolf 1985, Light of Day 1986, The Secret of My Success 1987, Bright Lights, Big City 1988, Back to the Future II 1989, Back to the Future III 1989, The Hard Way 1991, Doc Hollywood 1991, The Concierge 1993, Give Me a Break 1994, Greedy 1994, The American President 1995, Mars Attacks! 1996, The Frighteners 1996, Stuart Little (voice) 1999, Atlantis: The Lost Empire (voice) 2001, Interstate 60 2002, Stuart Little 2 (voice) 2002. *Address:* c/o Kevin Huvane, CAA, 9830 Wilshire Blvd., Beverly Hills, CA 90212, USA.

FOX, Sir Paul Leonard, Kt, CBE; British business executive; b. 27 Oct. 1925; m. Betty R. Nathan 1948; two s.; ed Bournemouth Grammar School; Parachute Regt 1943; reporter, Kentish Times 1946, The People 1947; scriptwriter, Pathe News 1947; BBC TV scriptwriter 1950; Ed. Sportsview 1953, Panorama 1961; Head, BBC TV Public Affairs Dept 1963, Current Affairs Group 1965; Controller, BBC 1 1967–73; Dir of Programmes, Yorkshire TV 1973–74, Man. Dir Yorkshire TV 1977–89, Dir of Programmes 1973–84; Dir Independent Television News 1977–86, Chair. 1986–89; Man. Dir BBC TV 1988–91; Chair. BBC Enterprises 1988–91, Stepgrades Consultants 1991–; Chair. ITV Network Programme Cttee 1978–80, Council, Independent Television Cos. Asscn Ltd 1982–84; mem. Royal Comm. on Criminal Procedure 1978–80; Pres. Royal TV Soc. 1985–92; Dir Channel Four 1985–88, World TV News 1986–88, Thames TV Ltd 1991–95; Chair. Racecourse Asscn Ltd 1993–97, Racecourse Tech. Services 1994–, Disasters Emergency Cttee 1996–99; Dir British Horse Racing Bd 1993–97, Horserace Betting Levy Bd 1993–97, Barnes TV Trust Ltd 1997–; consultant Oflot 1994–; mem. Cttee Nat. Museum of Photography, Film and TV 1985–95, Cinema and TV Benevolent Fund 1986–92, Pres. 1992–95; Hon. LLD (Leeds) 1984; Hon. DLitt (Bradford) 1991. *Leisure interests:* television, attending race meetings. *Address:* c/o Stepgrades Consultants, 10 Charterhouse Square, London, EC1M 6LQ, England.

FOX, Peter Kendrew, MA; British university librarian; b. 23 March 1949, Beverley, Yorks.; s. of Thomas Kendrew Fox and Dorothy Wildbore; m. Isobel McConnell 1983; two d.; ed Baines Grammar School, Poulton-le-Fylde, Lancs., King's Coll. London and Univ. of Sheffield; Asst Library Officer, Cambridge Univ. Library 1973–77, Asst Under-Librarian 1977–78, Under-Librarian 1978–79; Deputy Librarian, Trinity Coll. Dublin 1979–84, Librarian 1984–94; Univ. Librarian, Univ. of Cambridge 1994–; Fellow, Selwyn Coll., Univ. of Cambridge 1994–; mem. British Library Project on Teaching and Learning Skills for Librarians 1978–79, SCONUL Advisory Cttee on Information Services 1979–91 (Chair. 1987–91), An Chomhairle Leabharlanna 1982–94, Cttee on Library Co-operation in Ireland 1983–94 (Chair. 1990–91), Nat. Preservation Advisory Cttee (British Library) 1984–95, Wellcome Trust Library Advisory Cttee 1996–, Chair. 2000–, Consortium of Univ. Research Libraries (Chair. of Bd 1997–2000), Lord Chancellor's Advisory Council on Public Records 2001–; Jt Ed. An Leabharlann: The Irish Library 1982–87; Assoc. King's College, Library Asscn. *Publications:* Reader Instruction Methods in Academic Libraries 1974, User Education in the Humanities in US Academic Libraries 1979, Trinity College Library Dublin 1982; Ed.: Library User Education—Are New Approaches Needed? 1980, Second (and Third) Int. Conf. on Library User Educ. Proc. 1982 (and 1984), Treasures of the Library—Trinity College Dublin 1986, Commentary Volume: Book of Kells Facsimile 1990, Cambridge University Library: The Great Collections 1998; contribs. to books and journals. *Address:* University Library, West Road, Cambridge, CB3 9DR, England. *Telephone:* (1223) 333045. *Fax:* (1223) 339973. *Website:* www.lib.cam.ac.uk (Office).

FOX BASSETT, Nigel; British lawyer; b. 1 Nov. 1929; m. Patricia Anne Lambourne 1961; one s. one d.; ed Trinity Coll. Cambridge; joined Coward Chance (solicitors) after graduation; firm merged with Clifford Turner to form Clifford Chance (world's largest law firm) 1987; Sr Partner, Clifford Chance 1990–93; Commr Building Socs Comm. 1993–2000; Dir London First Centre 1993–98, mem. Council London First 1998–; mem. Council 1977–, Chair.

Exec. Cttee British Inst. of Int. and Comparative Law 1986–95; Council mem. London Chamber of Commerce and Industry 1993–99; mem. numerous legal councils, cttees and socs. *Leisure interests:* art, opera, theatre, shooting, sailing cricket (MCC). *Address:* c/o Clifford Chance, 200 Aldersgate, London, EC1A 4JJ, England (Office). *Telephone:* (20) 7600-1000 (Office). *Fax:* (20) 7600-5555 (Office).

FOX QUESADA, Vicente; Mexican politician and business executive; b. 2 July 1942, Mexico City; s. of the late José Luis Fox and of Mercedes Quesada; m.1st (divorced); two s. two d.; m. 2nd Martha Sahagun 2001; ed Universidad Iberoamericana, Mexico City, Harvard Univ.; worked for Coca Cola Group, first as route supervisor, becoming Regional Pres. for Mexico and Latin America; also worked as farmer and shoemaker; joined Nat. Action Party (PAN); Fed. Deputy 1988–; Gov. of Guanajuato 1995–; Pres. of Mexico Dec. 2000–. *Address:* Office of the President, Los Pinos, Puerta 1, Col. San Miguel Chapultepec, 11850 México, DF, Mexico (Office). *Telephone:* (5) 515-3717 (Office). *Fax:* (5) 510-8713 (Office). *Website:* www.presidencia.gob.mx (Office).

FOXLEY RIOSECO, Alejandro, MSc, PhD; Chilean politician and economist; b. 26 May 1939, Viña del Mar; s. of Harold Foxley (Chapman) and Carmen Rioseco; m. Gisela Tapia 1963; two c.; ed Univ. of Wisconsin, Harvard Univ. and Catholic Univ., Valparaíso; Dir Global Planning Div., Nat. Planning Office, Govt of Chile 1967–70; Dir Center for Nat. Planning Studies, Catholic Univ. of Chile 1970–76; mem. Exec. Council, Latin-American Social Science Council (CLACSO) 1975–81; mem. Jt Cttee Latin-American Studies, Social Science Research Council, New York 1975–78; Pres. Corpn for Latin-American Econ. Research (CIEPLAN), Santiago 1976–90; Minister of Finance 1990–94; Pres. Christian Democratic Party (PDC) 1994; Helen Kellogg Prof. of Econs (part-time) and Int. Devt, Univ. of Notre Dame 1982–; Assoc. Ed. Journal of Development Economics 1977–; Visiting Fellow, Univ. of Sussex 1973, Oxford 1975, MIT 1978; Ford Int. Fellow 1963–64, Daugherty Foundation Fellow 1965–66; Ford Foundation Fellow 1970; mem. Exec. Cttee Interamerican Dialogue, Wash., Int. Advisory Bd Journal Latin American Studies. *Publications:* Income Distribution in Latin-America 1976, Redistributive Effects of Government Programmes 1979, Estrategia de Desarrollo y Modelos de Planificación, Legados del Monetarismo: Argentina y Chile, Para una Democracia Estable 1985, Chile y su futuro: Un país posible 1989, Chile puede más 1989, numerous articles and working papers. *Address:* c/o Partido Demócrata Cristiano (PDC), Carmen 8, 6°, Santiago; Golfo de Darién 10236, Santiago (Las Condes), Chile (Home). *Telephone:* 20-7924 (Home). *E-mail:* afoxley@congreso.cl (Office).

FRACKOWIAK, Richard, MA, MB, DSc, FRCP, FMedSci; British professor of neurology; b. 26 March 1950, London; m. Christine Frackowiak; two s. one d.; ed Latymer Upper School, Peterhouse Coll., Cambridge, Middx. Hosp. Medical School; MRC Clinical Scientist 1989–94; Asst Dir MRC Cyclotron Unit; Prof. of Neurology 1990–94; Dean, Inst. of Neurology, Univ. Coll., London 1998–2002; Dir of Leopold Muller Functional Imaging Laboratory 1994–2002; Chair. Wellcome Dept of Cognitive Neurology 1994–2002; Prin. Clinical Research Fellow Wellcome Trust 1994–; Vice Provost Univ. Coll. London 2002–; Adjunct Prof. Cornell Univ. Medical School 1992–; Visiting Prof. Univ. Catholique de Louvain, Beth Israel Boston, La Sapienza; Hon. mem. American Neurological Asscn, Foreign Assoc. Acad. Nat. de Médicine; Dr hc (NEGE); Ibsen Prize, Feldberg Prize. *Publications include:* Human Brain Function 1997, Brain Mapping: The Disorders 2000, numerous papers in scientific journals. *Leisure interests:* reading, travel, motorcycling. *Address:* Wellcome Department of Cognitive Neurology, 12 Queen Square, London, WC1N 3AR (Office); 3 North Court, Great Peter Street, London SW1P 3LL, England (Home). *Telephone:* (20) 7833-7458 (Office); (20) 7222-3973 (Home). *Fax:* (20) 7813-1445 (Office). *E-mail:* r.frackowiak@fil.ion.ucl.ac.uk (Office). *Website:* www.fil.ion.ucl.ac.uk (Office).

FRADKOV, Mikhail Yefimovich; Russian politician; b. 1 Sept. 1950, Kuybyshev region; m.; two c.; ed Moscow Inst. of Machines and Tools, USSR Acad. of Foreign Trade; on staff office of Counsellor on econ. problems USSR Embassy to India 1973–75; on staff Foreign Trade Agency Tyazhpromexport, USSR State Cttee on Econ. Relations 1975–84; Deputy, First Deputy Dir of Dept USSR State Cttee on Econ. Relations 1985–91; Sr Adviser Perm. Mission of Russian Fed. to UN; Deputy, First Deputy Minister of External Econ. Relations Russian Fed. 1992; Interim Acting Minister of External Econ. Relations 1997; Minister of External Econ. Relations and Trade Russian Fed. 1997–98; Chair. Bd of Dirs. Ingosstrakh 1998–99, Dir.-Gen. 1999–; Minister of Trade 1999–2000; First Deputy Sec. Security Council of Russia 2000–01; Head Fed. Service of Tax Police 2001–. *Address:* F.S.N.P., Maroseyka str. 12, 101968, Moscow, Russia. *Telephone:* (095) 206-94-38.

FRAGA IRIBARNE, Manuel; Spanish politician, writer and diplomatist; b. 23 Nov. 1922, Villalba, Lugo; m. María del Carmen Estévez 1948 (died 1996); two s. three d.; ed Santiago and Madrid Univs.; Attorney of the Spanish Parliament 1945; Diplomatic Service 1947–; Prof. of Political Law, Valencia Univ. 1948; Prof. Theory of State and Constitutional Law, Madrid Univ. 1953; Gen. Sec. Inst. of Hispanic Culture 1951; Gen. Sec. Nat. Educ. Ministry 1955; Dir Inst. of Political Studies 1961; Minister of Information and Tourism 1962–69; also Sec.-Gen. of Cabinet 1967–69; Amb. to UK 1973–75; Minister of the Interior and Deputy Premier for Internal Affairs 1975–76; f. Alianza Popular (now Partido Popular) 1976, Leader 1979–86, 1989–90; mem. European Parl. 1987–89; Pres. Govt of Galicia 1997–; mem. Cttee for Defence of Christian Civilization, Union of Family Orgs.; Pres. Delegación Expañola de Comité de las Regiones 1998, Comisión Arco Atlántico, Grupo Intercomisiones 'America Latina' de la CRFM 1998; Gran Cruz Orden de Isabel La Católica, Gran Cruz del Mérito Civil, Gran Cruz Orden de San Raimundo de Peñafort, Gran Cruz Orden del Mérito Militar, del Mérito Naval. *Publications:* 90 books on political, constitutional and social subjects. *Leisure interests:* hunting, fishing. *Address:* Xunta de Galicia, Edificio San Caetano, No. 1 Santiago de Compostela; Palacio de Rajoy, Plaza del Obradeiro, Santiago de Compostela, Spain. *Telephone:* (81) 541215 (San Caetano); (81) 544915 (Palacio de Rajoy). *Fax:* (81) 541219. *E-mail:* presid@xunta.es.

FRAGA NETO, Armínio, PhD; Brazilian banker; b. 20 July 1957, Rio de Janeiro; ed Pontificia Univ. Católica do Rio de Janeiro, Princeton Univ.; trainee, Atlantica-Companhia de Seguros Boavista 1976–77, Banco do Estado do Rio de Janeiro 1979–80, Int. Finance Div., Fed. Reserve Bd, Washington DC 1984; Chief Economist and Operations Man. Banco de Investimentos Garantia 1985–88; Vice-Pres. Salomon Brothers, New York 1988–91; consultant IBRD 1988–89; Dir responsible for Int. Affairs, Banco Cen. do Brasil 1991–92, Gov. 1999–2002; Man. Dir Soros Fund Man., New York 1993–99; Prof. Grad. School in Econs, Fundação Getúlio Vargas 1985–88, 1999–; Visiting Asst Prof. Finance Dept, Wharton School, Pa Univ. 1988–89; Adjunct Prof. of Int. Affairs, Columbia Univ., New York 1993–99; mem. Bd Pro-Natura USA 1993–99; mem. Council on Foreign Relations, Princeton Univ. Center for Econ. Policy Studies (CEPS) 1993–; Banco Boavista Award. *Publications:* numerous articles on banking and econs. *Address:* Fundação Getulio Vargas, Praia de Botafogo 190, 10º andar, 22253-900, Rio de Janeiro, RJ, Brazil (Office). *Telephone:* (21) 255-95860 (Office). *Fax:* (21) 255-24898 (Office). *E-mail:* arminio@fgv.br (Office). *Website:* www.fgv.br (Office).

FRAHM, Sheila, BS; American politician; b. 22 March 1945, Colby, Kan.; m. Kenneth Frahm; three d.; ed Fort Hays State Univ.; mem. Kan. Senate, Topeka 1988–94, Senate Majority Leader 1993–94, Lt-Gov. Kan. 1995–96; Republican Senator from Kansas 1996–; Exec. Dir Kansas Asscn Community Coll. Trustees 1996–; mem. Shakespeare Fed., Kan. Corn Growers, Kan. Livestock Asscn; Republican. *Address:* Suite 401, 700 South West Jackson Street, Topeka, KS 66603-3757 (Office); 410 N Grant, Colby, KS 67701-2036, USA (Home). *E-mail:* sfrahm@colbyweb.com (Home).

FRAME, Janet, CBE; New Zealand writer; b. 1924, Dunedin; ed Oamaru North School, Waitaki Girls' High School, Dunedin Training Coll. and Otago Univ.; Hubert Church Award for NZ Prose; NZ Scholarship in Letters 1964, Burns Fellow, Otago Univ., Dunedin. *Publications:* Lagoon 1951, Owls Do Cry 1957, Faces in the Water 1961, The Edge of the Alphabet 1962, Scented Gardens for the Blind 1963, The Reservoir (stories), Snowman, Snowman (fables), The Adaptable Man 1965, A State of Siege 1967, The Pocket Mirror (poetry), Yellow Flowers in the Antipodean Room 1968, Mona Minim and the Smell of the Sun (children's book) 1969, Intensive Care (novel) 1971, Daughter Buffalo (novel) 1972, Living in the Maniototo (novel) 1979, The Carpathians 1988, An Autobiography 1990.

FRAME, Ronald William Sutherland, MA, M.LITT.; British author; b. 23 May 1953, Glasgow, Scotland; s. of Alexander D. Frame and Isobel D. Frame (née Sutherland); ed The High School of Glasgow, Univ. of Glasgow, Jesus Coll. Oxford; full-time author 1981–; Betty Trask Prize (jtly.) (first recipient) 1984, Samuel Beckett Prize 1986; TV Industries' Panel's "Most Promising Writer New to Television" Award 1986, Saltire "Scottish Book of the Year" 2000. *Publications: books:* Winter Journey 1984, Watching Mrs. Gordon 1985, A Long Weekend with Marcel Proust 1986, Sandmouth People 1987, Paris (TV play) 1987, A Woman of Judah 1987, Penelope's Hat 1989, Bluette 1990, Underwood and After 1991, Walking My Mistress in Deauville 1992, The Sun on the Wall 1994, The Lantern Bearers 1999, Permanent Violet 2002, Carnbeg 2003. *TV screenplays:* Paris 1985, Out of Time 1987, Ghost City 1994, A Modern Man 1996, Four Ghost Stories for Christmas (adaptation) 2000, The Darien Venture 2003. *Radio scripts include:* Winter Journey 1985, Cara 1989, The Lantern Bearers 1997, The Hydro (serial) 1997–99, Havisham 1998, Maestro 1999, Pharos 2000, Don't Look Now (adaptation) 2001, Sunday at Sant' Agata 2001, Greyfriars 2002. *Leisure interests:* swimming, walking, classical music. *Address:* c/o Curtis Brown Ltd, 28/29 Haymarket, London, SW1Y 4SP, England. *Telephone:* (20) 7396-6600. *Fax:* (20) 7396-0110/1.

FRAMPTON, Kenneth; British professor of architecture; ed Architectural Asscn, London; Tech. Ed. Architectural Design (magazine) 1962–65; emigrated to USA 1964; Faculty Mem. School of Architecture, Princeton Univ. 1964–72; Faculty Mem. Dept of Architecture, Columbia Univ. 1972–, Chair. Div. of Architecture 1986–89, Dir Post-Grad. Program in History and Theory of Architecture 1993–, also Ware Prof. of Architecture; Faculty Mem. RCA, London 1974–77; Visiting Prof. numerous schools of architecture including Berlage Inst., Amsterdam, Eidgenossische Technische Hochschule, Switzerland, Chinese Univ. of Hong Kong, Univ. della Svizzera Italiana, Mendrisio, Switzerland; mem. jury Alvar Aalto Medal Cttee 1988; Pres. EEC Jury, Mies van der Rohe Foundation, Barcelona; presented Raoul Wallenberg Lecture 1999; Fellow Graham Foundation 1969–72; Loeb Fellow Harvard Univ. Grad. School of Design 1972; Guggenheim Fellow 1975; Fellow, Inst. for Architecture and Urban Studies, New York; Fellow, Wissenschaftskolleg, Berlin 1986, American Acad. of Arts and Sciences 1993; Dr hc (Royal Inst. of Tech., Stockholm) 1991, (Univ. of Waterloo) 1995, (Calif. Coll. of Arts and Crafts) 1999; AIA Nat. Honors Award 1985, Acad. d'Architecture Gold Medal 1987, AIA New York Chapter Award of Merit 1988, ASCA Topaz Award 1990. *Design work includes:* work in field of housing design in London and New

York. *Publications include:* Modern Architecture: A Critical History 1980, Modern Architecture and the Critical Present 1993, American Masterworks 1995, Studies in Tectonic Culture 1995, Latin American Architecture: Six Voices (jtly) 2002. *Address:* Barnard and Columbia Architecture, 310 Barnard Hall, Barnard College, 3009 Broadway, New York, NY 10027, USA (Office). *Telephone:* (212) 854-8430 (Office). *Fax:* (212) 8554-8442 (Office). *E-mail:* architecture@barnard.edu (Office). *Website:* www.columbia.edu (Office).

FRANÇA, José-Augusto, DèsSc, DHist; Portuguese writer and art historian; b. 16 Nov. 1922, Thomar; s. of José M. França and Carmen R. França; m. 2nd Marie-Thérèse Mandroux; one d. (by previous m.); ed Lisbon Univ., Ecole des Hautes Etudes and Univ. of Paris; travels in Africa, Europe, Americas and Asia1945–; Ed. Lisbon literary review Unicornio 1951–56, Co-Ed. Cadernos de Poesia 1951–53; Founder-Dir Galeria de Marco, Lisbon 1952–54; art critic 1946–; film critic 1948–; lexicographical publr 1948–58; lived in Paris 1959–63; Ed. Pintura & Não 1969–70; Ed. Colóquio Artes 1970–96; Prof. Cultural History and History of Art, Dir Dept of Art History, New Univ. of Lisbon 1974–92, Prof. Emer. 1992–; Dir elect Faculty of Social Sciences 1982; Dir Fondation C. Gulbenkian, Centre Culturel Portugais, Paris 1983–89; Visiting Prof. Univ. of Paris III 1985–89; Vice-Pres. Int. Asscn of Art Critics 1970–73, Pres. 1985–87, Hon. Pres. 1987–; Vice-Pres. Acad. Européenne de Sciences, Arts et Lettres Paris 1985–2000, Hon. Pres. 2000–; City Councillor, Lisbon 1974–75; mem. of City Ass. Lisbon 1990–93; Pres. Inst. Cultura Portuguesa 1976–80, World Heritage Cttee, UNESCO 1999–; mem. Int. Asscn of Art Critics, Int. Cttee of Art History, PEN Club, Soc. Européenne de Culture, Soc. de l'Histoire de l'Art français, Acad. Nacional de Belas Artes (Pres. 1977–80), Acad. das Ciencias de Lisboa, Acad. Européenne de Sciences, Arts et Lettres, World Acad. of Arts and Science, Acad. Nat. Sciences, Arts et Lettres de Bordeaux, Ateneo Veneto, Real Acad. Bellas Artes San Fernando (Spain); Officier Ordre nat. du Mérite; Chevalier Ordre des Arts et Lettres (France); Commdr Ordem Rio Branco (Brazil); Grand Cross Order of Public Instruction; Grand Officer Ordem Infante Dom Henrique; Officier Ordem Santiago; Medal of Honour (Lisbon). *Publications:* Natureza Morta (novel) 1949, Azazel (play) 1957, Despedida Breve (short stories) 1958; essays: Charles Chaplin—the Self-Made Myth 1952, Amadeo de Souza-Cardoso 1957, Situação da Pintura Ocidental 1959, Da Pintura Portuguesa 1960, Dez Anos de Cinema 1960, Une ville des lumières: La Lisbonne de Pombal 1963, A Arte em Portugal no Século XIX 1967, Oito Ensaios sobre Arte Contemporânea 1967, Le romantisme au Portugal 1972, Almada, o Português sem Mestre 1972, A Arte na Sociedade Portuguesa no Século XX 1972, Antonio Carneiro 1973, A Arte em Portugal no século XX 1974, Zé Povinho 1975, Manolo Millares 1977, Lisboa: Urbanismo e Arquitectura, O Retrato na Arte Portuguesa, Rafael Bordalo Pinheiro, o Português tal e qual 1980, Malhoa & Columbano, Historia da Arte Occidental 1780–1980 1987, Os Anos 20 em Portugal 1992, Bosch ou le visionnaire intégral, Thomar revisited 1994, Lisboa 1898, (In) definições de Cultura 1997, Memorias para o Ano 2000 2000, Monte Olivete, minha aldeia 2001, Buridan (novel) 2002, Regra de Três (novel) 2003, Historia da Arte em Portugal 1750–2000 2003. *Leisure interests:* travel and detective stories. *Address:* Mailing address: Rua Escola Politécnica 49/4 1250-069 Lisbon, Portugal; 9 Villa Virginie, 75014 Paris; 8 route de Beauvau, 49140 Jarzé, France. *Telephone:* (21) 3462028 (Lisbon); 1-45-40-49-19 (Paris); (2) 41-95-40-04 (Jarzé).

FRANCHET, Yves Georges; French international public servant; b. 4 March 1939, Paris; m. Marie Bernard Robillard; two s.; ed Ecole polytechnique, Paris, Université Paris I; Dir Statistics Office, UDEAC, Brazzaville, Congo 1964–68; mem. Govt econ. planning staff 1968–69; economist, World Bank, Washington, DC 1969–74; Head of Planning, Co-operation Div., INSEE 1974–77; Dir ENSAE 1977–80; Deputy Dir European Office of World Bank, Paris 1980–83; Vice-Pres. IDB, Washington, DC 1983–87; Dir-Gen. Statistical Office of the European Communities (Eurostat) 1987–; Chevalier Légion d'honneur, Commdr Order of Merit (Niger); Dr hc (Bucharest). *Address:* Statistical Office of the European Communities (Eurostat), Bâtiment Jean Monnet, rue Alcide de Gasperi, 2920 Luxembourg, Luxembourg (Office); 7 rue J. P. Brasseur, 1258 Luxembourg, Luxembourg (Home). *Telephone:* 43-01-33-10-7 (Office). *Fax:* 43-01–33-01-5 (Office).

FRANCIS, Dick (see Francis, Richard Stanley).

FRANCIS, Freddie; British film director, producer and cinematographer; b. 1917, London; joined Gaumont British Studios as apprentice to stills photographer; fmr clapper boy B.I.P. Studios, Elstree; fmr camera Asst British Dominion; fmr cameraman Shepperton Studios. *Films:* Dir: Two and Two Make Six (A Change of Heart/The Girl Swappers 1962), Paranoiac, Vengeance, The Evil of Frankenstein, Nightmare, Traitor's Gate, Hysteria, Dr. Terror's House of Horrors, The Skull, The Psychopath, The Deadly Bees, They Came from Beyond Space, Torture Garden, Dracula Has Risen from the Grave, Mumsy Nanny Sonny and Girly, Trog, Tales from the Crypt, The Creeping Flesh, Tales That Witness Madness, Son of Dracula, Craze, The Ghoul, Legend of the Werewolf, The Doctor and the Devils, Dark Tower; cinematographer: Moby Dick, A Hill in Korea (Hell in Korea), Time Without Pity, Room at the Top, The Battle of the Sexes, Saturday Night and Sunday Morning, Sons and Lovers (Acad. Award 1960), The Innocents, Night Must Fall, The Elephant Man, The French Lieutenant's Woman, Dune, Memed My Hawk, Clara's Heart, Her Alibi, Brenda Starr, Glory (Acad. Award 1989), Man in the Moon, Cape Fear, School Ties, Princess Caraboo, A Life in the Theatre (TV movie), Rainbow. *Address:* 12 Ashley Drive, Twickenham, Middx TW7 5QA, England (Home).

FRANCIS, Julian W., BSc, MBA; Bahamian central banker; m.; two s.; ed New York Univ., USA; Accounting Officer and Credit Officer SFE Banking Corpn, Nassau 1969–72, Asst Vice-Pres. Credit Dept 1976–79; worked for Barclays Bank, Nassau and Eleuthera; with Banque de la Société Financière Européenne, Paris, France 1980–92, positions include Asst Man. for Business Devt in Latin America, Deputy Man. for Assets Man., Man. of Assets Trading Dept, Cen. Man. for Corp. Finance, Jt Gen. Man. and mem. Man. Cttee; Deputy Gov. and mem. Bd Dirs Cen. Bank of the Bahamas 1993–97, Gov. 1997–; Vice-Chair. Securities Bd; Chair. The Bridge Authority; Bahamian jt negotiator on Competition Policy, Free Trade of the Americas negotiations 1997–; fmr Vice-Chair. Securities Market Task Force. *Leisure interests:* reading, fishing, tennis. *Address:* Governor's Office, Central Bank of the Bahamas, POB N-4868, Nassau, N.P., The Bahamas (Office). *Telephone:* 302-2700 (Office). *Fax:* 356-4307 (Office). *E-mail:* governor@centralbankbahamas.com (Office). *Website:* www.centralbankbahamas.com (Office).

FRANCIS, Richard (Dick) Stanley, CBE; British author; b. 31 Oct. 1920, Tenby, S. Wales; s. of George V. Francis and Catherine M. Francis; m. Mary M. Brenchley 1947 (died 2000); two s.; fighter and bomber pilot, RAF 1940–46; amateur steeplechase jockey (Nat. Hunt racing) 1946–48; professional steeplechase jockey 1948–57; champion steeplechase jockey 1953–54; racing columnist, Sunday Express 1957–73; author and novelist 1957–; Hon. D.Hum.Litt. (Tufts Univ., Mass., USA) 1991; Edgar Allan Poe Awards (for Forfeit, Whip Hand, Come to Grief), Crime Writers' Asscn Silver Dagger Award (for For Kicks), Gold Dagger Award (for Whip Hand), Cartier Diamond Dagger Award for life's work 1990, named Grand Master by Mystery Writers of America 1996. *Publications include:* The Sport of Queens (autobiog.) 1957, Dead Cert (novel) 1962, For Kicks 1965, Forfeit 1968, Whip Hand 1979, Lester (biog. of Lester Piggott) 1986, The Edge 1988, Straight 1989, Longshot 1990, Comeback 1991, Driving Force 1992, Decider 1993, Wild Horses 1994, Come to Grief 1995, To The Hilt 1996, 10lb Penalty 1997, Field of 13 1998, Second Wind 1999, Shattered 2000 and many novels of adventure and risk. *Leisure interests:* attending race meetings world-wide, travel, boating, living in the W Indies. *Address:* c/o John Johnson (Author's Agent) Ltd, 45/47 Clerkenwell Green, London, EC1R 0HT, England.

FRANCISCI DI BASCHI, Marco, DIur; Italian diplomatist; b. 3 Feb. 1920, Angleur, Belgium; s. of Francesco Francisci and Berthe Berlemont; m. Franca Angelini 1974; three c.; ed Rome Univ.; entered diplomatic service 1948; Sec., Washington Embassy 1950–51; mem. Perm. Del. to UN, New York 1951–55; Consul, Klagenfurt, Austria 1955–58; Dir Int. Orgs. Branch, Gen. Econ. Affairs Directorate, Foreign Ministry 1958–75; Amb. to People's Repub. of China 1975–80; Amb. and Perm. Rep. to OECD, Paris 1980–83, Amb. and Perm. Rep. to FAO, Rome 1983–85; Pres. Italy-China Asscn. 1985; mem. and Counsellor ISMEO (Inst. for the Middle and Far East) 1985–. *Address:* Via Cesalpino 10, 00161 Rome, Italy. *Telephone:* (06) 44231857.

FRANCK, Edouard; Central African Republic politician; fmrly Minister in charge of Cabinet Secr.; Prime Minister of the Cen. African Repub. 1991–93; Pres. Supreme Court 1995–. *Address:* Cour Suprême, BP 926, Bangui, Central African Republic. *Telephone:* 61-41-33.

FRANCO, Itamar Augusto Cantiero; Brazilian politician; b. 28 June 1931, Juiz de Fora, Minas Gerais; s. of Augusto Cesar Stiebler Franco and Itália Cautiero Franco; two d.; ed univ. studies in civil and electronic Eng, Minas Gerais; Mayor of Juiz de Fora, Minas Gerais 1967–71, 1973–74; Senator of the Repub. 1974, 1982; Pres. Parl. Tech. Cttees. on Econ. and Finance 1983–84; Vice-Pres. of Brazil 1989–92; Acting Pres. of Brazil Oct.–Dec. 1992, Pres. Dec. 1992–94; Amb. to Portugal 1995. *Publications:* books on anthropology, history, nuclear energy and political issues. *Address:* c/o Ministry of Foreign Affairs, Palácio do Hamaraty, Esplanada dos Ministérios, 70170 Brasília, Brazil.

FRANCO ESTADELLA, Antonio; Spanish journalist; b. 21 Jan. 1947, Barcelona; s. of Alfonso Franco and Lolita Estadella; m. Marie-Hélène Bigatá; one s. one d.; Ed. Sports Section Diario Barcelona 1970, Ed.-in-Chief 1973, Asst Dir 1975; Dir Siete Días (TV programme) 1977; f. El Periódico de Catalunya 1977, Ed. 1987–, Ed.-in-Chief; Jt Ed. El País 1982; Premio Ortega y Gasset (for journalism), Premio Godó (for journalism), Premio Luca de Tena (for journalism). *Leisure interests:* literature, music, sports. *Address:* El Periódico de Catalunya, Consell de Cent 425–427, 08009 Barcelona, Spain. *Telephone:* (93) 2655353. *Fax:* (93) 4846517. *E-mail:* afranco@elperiodico.com (Office). *Website:* www.elperiodico.es (Office).

FRANCO GOMEZ, Julio César, PhD; Paraguayan politician and doctor; b. 1952; ed Nat. Univ. of Cordoba, Argentina, Asunción Univ.; Senator 1998; Pres. of the Comm. for Public Health, Social Security and Drug Control 1999; Vice-Pres. of Paraguay 2000–. *Address:* Congreso Nacional, Asunción, Paraguay (Office).

FRANÇOIS-PONCET, Jean André, PhD; French diplomatist; b. 8 Dec. 1928, Paris; s. of André François-Poncet and Jacqueline Dilais; m. Marie-Thérèse de Mitry 1959; two s. one d.; ed Wesleyan Univ., Fletcher School of Law and Diplomacy at Tufts Univ., Paris Law School, Nat. School of Public Admin., Paris and Stanford Univ. Graduate School of Business; joined Ministry of Foreign Affairs 1955; worked in office of Sec. of State 1956–58; Sec.-Gen. of Del. to Negotiations for Treaties for EEC and EURATOM 1956–57; Head of European Insts. section in Ministry 1958–61; Prof., Institut d'études politiques de Paris 1960–; Head of Assistance and Co-operation

Mission in Morocco 1961–63; in charge of African Affairs in Ministry 1963–68; Counsellor, Embassy in Iran 1968–70; Chair. of Bd, Pres. and CEO, Etablissements J. J. Carnaud & Forges 1971–75; Sec. of State for Foreign Affairs Jan.–July 1976; Sec.-Gen. to Presidency of French Repub. 1976–78; Minister of Foreign Affairs 1978–81; mem. Conseil Général, Lot-et-Garonne 1967–, Pres. 1978–94, 1998–; Senator for Lot-et-Garonne 1983–; Dir FMC Corpn 1982–; Reporter, Figaro 1984–; Chair. Cttee Senate; Chevalier Légion d'honneur, Ordre nat. du Mérite. *Publication:* The Economic Policy of Western Germany 1970. *Address:* Senate, Palais du Luxembourg, 75291 Paris cedex 06 (Office); Conseil Général du Lot-et-Garonne, cité Saint-Jacques, 47922 Agen cedex 09 (Office); 53 rue de Varenne, 75007 Paris, France (Home). *Telephone:* 1-42-34-20-37 (Office). *E-mail:* j.francois-poncet@senat.fr (Office).

FRANÇOIS-PONCET, Michel, MBA; French business executive; b. 1 Jan. 1935; ed Paris Inst. d'Etudes Politiques, Harvard Business School; with Banque Paribas 1961, various positions in France and USA; Chair. Campagnie Financière de Paribas 1986, Chair. Supervisory Bd 1990, Chair. Supervisory Bd of Banque Paribas subsidiary 1991–; Chair. Banque Paribas (Suisse) SA, Vice-Pres. BNP Paribas 2000–; Vice-Chair. Pargesa Holding SA, mem. Bd of numerous French and int. cos. including Axa, LVMH, Schneider SA, Total Fina, Banca Commerciale Italiana (Comit), Erbé/Fibelpar, Power Corpn of Canada. *Address:* BNP Paribas, 5 rue d'Antin, 75078 Paris, France (Office). *Telephone:* 1-42-98-12-34. *E-mail:* michel.francois-poncet@bnpparibas.com (Office).

FRÄNGSMYR, Tore, DPhil; Swedish professor of history of science; b. 8 July 1938, Skelleftea; s. of Johan Frängsmyr and Linnea (née Lindberg) Frängsmyr; m. Birgitta Thunholm 1970; two s. two d.; ed Uppsala Univ.; Assoc. Prof., Uppsala Univ. 1969, Prof. of History of Science 1982–; Prof. of Tech. and Social Change, Linköping Univ. 1981–82; Dir Center for History of Science, Royal Swedish Acad. of Sciences, Stockholm 1988–; Ed. Les Prix Nobel 1988–; Sec.-Gen. Int. Union of History of Science 1989–93; Fellow Royal Swedish Acad. of Sciences, Royal Acad. of Eng Sciences, Academia Europaea, American Philosophical Soc. *Publications include:* Linnaeus, the Man and His Work 1984, Science in Sweden; The Royal Swedish Acad. of Sciences 1739–1989 1989, The Quantifying Spirit in the Eighteenth Century (co-ed.) 1990, Solomon's House Revisited: The Organization and Institutionalization of Science 1990, Enlightenment Science in the Romantic Era: The Chemistry of Berzelius and its Cultural Setting (co-ed.) 1992, A la recherche des lumières 1999. *Address:* Faculty of Arts, Uppsala University, Box 256, 751 05, Uppsala, Sweden. *Telephone:* (18) 471-00-00. *Fax:* (18) 471-20-00. *E-mail:* info@uadm.uu.se (Office). *Website:* www.uu.se (Office).

FRANK, Charles Raphael, Jr, PhD; American banker and economist; b. 15 May 1937, Pittsburgh., Pa; s. of Charles Raphael Frank and Lucille Frank (née Briscoe); m. 1st Susan Patricia Buckman (divorced 1976); one s. one d.; m. 2nd Eleanor Sebastian 1976; two s.; one step s. one step d.; ed Rensselaer Polytechnic Inst. and Princeton Univ.; Sr Research Fellow East African Inst. for Social Research, Makerere Univ. Coll., Kampala 1963–65; Asst Prof. Econs Yale Univ. 1965–67; Assoc. Prof. Econs and Int. Affairs Princeton Univ. 1967–70, Prof. 1970–74; Assoc Dir Research Programme on Econ. Devt, Woodrow Wilson School 1967–70, Dir 1970–74; Sr Fellow Brookings Inst. 1972–74; mem. Policy Planning staff and Chief Economist, US Dept of State 1974–77, Deputy Asst Sec. of State for Econ. and Social Affairs 1977–78; Vice-Pres. Salomon Bros., Inc. 1978–87; Pres. Frank & Co., Inc. 1987–88; Vice-Pres. and Man. Dir for Structured Finance GE Capital Corpn, Stamford, Conn. 1988–97; First Vice-Pres. EBRD 1997–2001; Consultant to various American and foreign insts including IBRD 1964–75; mem. Council on Foreign Relations. *Publications:* The Sugar Industry in East Africa 1965, Production Theory and Indivisible Commodities 1969, Economic Accounting and Development Planning (with Brian Van Arkadie) 1969, Debt and the Terms of Aid 1970, Statistics and Econometrics 1971, American Jobs and Trade with the Developing Countries 1973, Foreign Exchange Regimes and Economic Development: The Case of South Korea 1975, Foreign Trade and Domestic Adjustment 1976, Income Distribution and Economic Growth in the Less Developed Countries (jtly) 1977. *Address:* Flat 5, 70–72 Cadogan Square, London, SW1X 0EA, England (Home).

FRANK, Sergey Ottovich; Russian politician; b. 13 Aug. 1960, Novosibirsk; m.; one s.; ed Far E Higher Marine School of Eng, Far E State Univ., Higher School of Commerce, Ministry of Foreign Econ. Relations of Russian Fed.; Sec., Comsomol Cttee, later Deputy Head, Far E Higher Marine School; on staff Far E Marine Navigation Agency 1989–93, Deputy Dir-Gen. 1993–95; Deputy Head, Dept of Marine Transport, Ministry of Transport of Russian Fed. 1995–96; First Deputy Minister of Transport of Russian Fed. 1997–98, Minister 1998–; Chair. Bd of Dirs. Aeroflot 1999–. *Address:* Ministry of Transport, Sadovaya-Samotechnaya str. 10, GSP-4 101433 Moscow, Russia. *Telephone:* (095) 200-08-03 (Office).

FRANKEL, Max, MA; American journalist; b. 3 April 1930, Gera, Germany; s. of Jacob A. Frankel and Mary (Katz) Frankel; m. 1st. Tobia Brown 1956 (deceased 1987); two s. one d.; m. 2nd Joyce Purnick 1988; ed Columbia Univ., New York; mem. staff, The New York Times 1952, Chief Washington Corresp. 1968–72, Sunday Ed. 1973–76, Editorial Pages Ed. 1977–86, Exec. Ed. 1986–94, 1994–95, also columnist New York Times magazine 1995–2000; Pulitzer Prize for Int. Reporting 1973. *Publication:* The Time of My Life and My Life with the Times 1999. *Address:* c/o The New York Times Co., 15 West 67th Street, New York, NY 10023-6226, USA.

FRANKEN, Hendrik, PhD; Netherlands professor of jurisprudence and information law; b. 17 Sept. 1936, Haarlem; s. of Albert J. Franken and Catherine G. Weijland; m. 1st Boudewine D. M. Bonebakker 1966 (divorced 1993); two s. one d.; m. 2nd Ingrid L. E. Sanders 1995; ed Univ. of Leiden, Sorbonne, Paris, Univ. of Amsterdam; Sec., Mil. Tribunal 1960; Asst Prosecutor, Dist Court, Rotterdam 1964; mem. Rotterdam Bar 1967; Judge 1969; Prof. of Jurisprudence, Erasmus Univ., Rotterdam 1974, of Jurisprudence, Univ. of Leiden 1977–, of Information Law 1987–; Prof. of Information Law, Univ. of Groningen 1989–95; mem. State Council 1982–87, Court of Appeal, The Hague 1977–; Chair. Nat. Cttee of Information Tech. and Law; mem. Social Econ. Council, Sec.-Gen. Royal Acad. of Arts and Sciences; Modderman Prijs 1973, Wolffert van Borselenpenning 1982; Kt of Netherlands Lion 1995. *Publications:* Vervolgingsbeleid: the Policy of Public Prosecutors 1973, Maat en Regel 1975, Jurimetrics and the Rule of Law 1975, The New Law and Economics 1982, Models of Contracts in Information Law 1992, Introduction to the Law (8th Edn) 1999, Trusted Third Parties 1996, Law and Computer (2nd Edn) 1997, Independence and Responsibility of the Judge 1997. *Address:* Universiteit Leiden, Stationsweg 46, P.O. Box 9500, 2399 RA Leiden (Office); Weipoortseweg 95A, 2381 NJ Zoeterwoude, Netherlands (Home). *Telephone:* (71) 5272727 (Office); (71) 5804764 (Home). *Fax:* (71) 5273118 (Office); (71) 5804764 (Home). *E-mail:* h.franken@law.leidenuniv.nl (Office); hnsfrnk@cs.com (Home).

FRANKENHAEUSER, Marianne, PhD; Swedish professor of psychology; b. von Wright, 30 Sept. 1925, Helsinki, Finland; d. of Tor von Wright and Ragni Alfthan; m. Bernhard Frankenhaeuser 1946 (died 1994); one d.; ed Oxford Univ., UK, Univs. of Helsinki and Stockholm and Uppsala, Sweden; Asst Prof. of Psychology, Univ. of Stockholm 1960–63; Research Fellow, Swedish Council for Social Science Research 1963–65; Assoc. Prof. of Experimental Psychology, Swedish Medical Research Council 1965–69, Prof. 1969–80; Visiting Prof., Dept of Psychiatry and Behavioral Science Stanford Univ. 1976; Prof. of Psychology, Karolinska Institutet 1980–92, Chair. Dept of Psychology 1980–82, Head Psychology Div., Dept of Psychiatry and Psychology 1980–92; Research Fellow Swedish Inst. for Research on Man and Work 1990–95; Resident Scholar, Rockefeller Foundation Study and Conf. Centre, Bellagio, Como, Italy 1980; Gildersleeve Prof., Barnard Coll., Columbia Univ., USA 1981; Fellow Centre for Advanced Study in the Behavioural Sciences, Stanford, USA 1995–96; Visiting Scholar Inst. for Research on Women and Gender, Stanford Univ. 1997–98; Chair. Scientific Council of Swedish Psychological Asscn 1970–73; Pres. European Brain and Behaviour Soc. 1974–76; Foreign mem. NAS 1989, Finnish Soc. of Sciences and Letters 1994; Corresp. mem. Académie Internationale de Philosophie des Sciences 1983; mem. Academia Europaea 1989; Hon. D. Pol.Sc. (Turku, Finland) 1990; Royal Award: The King of Sweden's Medal 1985, Swedish Nat. Award for Zealous and Devoted Service 1986 and other awards; Prin. Investigator, John D. and Catherine T. MacArthur Foundation Mental Health Network on Health and Behavior 1983–89. *Publications:* Estimation of Time 1959, Stress (with Maj Ödman) 1983, Women, Work and Health (with Ulf Lundberg and Margaret Chesney) 1991, Stress and Gender 1993; and articles on psychology in scientific journals. *Leisure interests:* reading, writing and outdoor life in clean nature. *Address:* Department of Psychology, University of Stockholm, S-106 91 Stockholm (Office); Skeppargatan 32, S-114 52 Stockholm, Sweden. *Telephone:* (8) 163-684 (Office); (8) 663-94-68 (Home). *Fax:* (8) 153-587 (Office); (8) 667-02-61 (Home). *E-mail:* mf@psychology.su.se (Office); mf@psychology.su.se (Home).

FRANKENTHALER, Helen, BA; American artist; b. 1928, New York; m. 1st Robert Motherwell 1958 (divorced 1971); m. 2nd Stephen M. DuBrul, Jr 1994; ed Bennington Coll., Vt; Trustee Bennington Coll. 1967; Fellow Calhoun Coll., Yale Univ. 1968; solo exhbns throughout USA and Europe, particularly at André Emmerich Gallery 1959–, Whitney Museum of American Art and Metropolitan Museum of Art, New York 1951–73, Guggenheim Museum, New York 1975, retrospective 1985 (exhbn travelled USA, Canada 1986), Corcoran Gallery, Washington, DC 1975, Museum of Fine Arts, Houston 1976, Modern Art Museum, Fort Worth, 1989 (painting retrospective, travelled USA), Nat. Gallery of Art, Washington, DC 1993 (graphic retrospective, travelled USA, Japan), USIA (United States Information Agency) Exhbn, Janie C. Lee Gallery, Dallas 1973, 1975, 1976, 1978, 1980, Knoedler Gallery, London 1978, 1981, 1983, 1985, Sterling & Francine Clark Art Inst., Williamstown, Mass. 1980, Knoedler and Co., New York 1992, 1994; mem. American Acad. and Inst. of Arts and Letters 1974, NEA Council on the Arts 1985–92, Corpn of Yaddo 1973–78; Trustee Bennington Coll. 1967–82; Fellow, Calhoun Coll., Yale Univ. 1968–; mem. American Acad. of Arts and Sciences 1991; travelled to Far East, Australia, Latin America 1978–79; numerous hon. degrees; First Prize, Paris Biennale 1959; Joseph E. Temple Gold Medal Award, Pennsylvania Acad. of Fine Arts 1968, Spirit of Achievement Award, Albert Einstein Coll. of Medicine 1970, Gold Medal of the Commune of Catania, Florence 1972, Garrett Award, Art Inst. of Chicago 1972, Creative Arts Award, American Jewish Congress 1974, Art and Humanities Award, Yale Women's Forum 1976, Extraordinary Woman of Achievement Award, Nat. Conf. of Christians and Jews 1978; Mayor's Award of Honor for Art and Culture, New York City 1986, Conn. Arts Award 1989, Lifetime Achievement Award, Coll. Art Asscn 1994, Artist of the Year Award 1995, Jerusalem Prize 1999. *Address:* c/o M. Knoedler and Co. Inc., 19 East 70th Street, New York, NY 10021, USA.

FRANKEVICH, Yevgeniy Leonidovich, DR.PHYS.-MATH.SC.; Russian physicist; b. 19 Feb. 1930, Samara; s. of V. Eseleva and L. V. Frankevich; m.

Irene Lenchenko 1957; one s. one d.; ed Polytechnic Inst., Leningrad (now St Petersburg); postgrad., Jr then Sr researcher 1957–71; mem. CPSU 1961–91; Head of Lab. USSR Acad. of Sciences Inst. of Chemical Physics 1971–88; Prof. Moscow Inst. of Physics and Tech. 1972–; Head of Lab., USSR (now Russian) Acad. of Sciences Inst. of Energy Problems of Chemical Physics 1988–; Inst. for Molecular Science, Okazaki, Japan 1992–93, 1994; mem. Russian Acad. of Natural Science 1990–; Lenin Prize for Science 1986; two diplomas for scientific discoveries. *Publications include:* Chemical Generation and Reception of Radio- and Microwaves 1994; 280 papers in the field of radiation and photo physics, organic semiconductors and magnetic spin effects. *Leisure interests:* gardening, jogging. *Address:* Institute of Energy Problems of Chemical Physics, Leninsky Prosp. 38–2, 117829, Moscow, Russia. *Telephone:* (095) 939-79-93 (Office); (095) 336-11-84 (Home). *Fax:* (095) 137-82-75 (Office); (095) 137-34-79. *E-mail:* frankevich@chph.ras.ru (Office).

FRANKL, Peter; British concert pianist; b. 2 Oct. 1935, Budapest, Hungary; s. of Tibor and Laura Frankl; m. Annie Feiner 1958; one s. one d.; ed High School, Franz Liszt Music Acad., Budapest; began career in late 1950s, London début 1962, New York début 1967; has performed with world's major orchestras, including Berlin Philharmonic, Amsteram Concertgebouw, Israel Philharmonic, Leipzig Gewandhaus and all the London and the major American orchestras, under conductors including Abbado, Boulez, Colin Davis, Haitink, Maazel, Masur, Muti, Solti; Visiting Prof. Yale Univ., USA 1987; won first prize in several int. competitions; Officer's Cross Order of Merit (Hungary). *Recordings include:* complete works for piano by Schumann and Debussy, a solo Bartók and Chopin album, a Hungarian Anthology, Mozart concertos with mems. of English Chamber Orchestra, the complete 4-hand works by Mozart with Tamás Vásáry, Brahms, Schumann, Dvořák and Martinů quintets with the Lindsay Quartet, Brahms trios and violin sonatas with Kyung Wha Chung, Brahms Piano Concerti Nos. 1 and 2 (live). *Leisure interests:* football, opera, theatre, tennis. *Address:* 5 Gresham Gardens, London, NW11 8NX, England. *Telephone:* (20) 8455-5228. *Fax:* (20) 8455-2176.

FRANKLIN, Aretha; American singer; b. 25 March 1942, Memphis; d. of Rev. C. L. Franklin; m. 1st Ted White (divorced); m. 2nd Glynn Turman 1978; made first recordings at father's Baptist church, Detroit; toured as gospel singer; moved to New York, signed contract with Columbia Records 1960, with Atlantic 1966, with Arista 1980; recipient numerous Grammy Awards 1967–87; American Music Award 1984, John F. Kennedy Center Award 1994. *Recordings include:* Aretha 1961, The Electrifying Aretha Franklin 1962, Laughing on the Outside, The Tender, the Moving, the Swinging Aretha Franklin 1963, Running out of Fools, The Gospel Sound of Aretha Franklin 1964, Soul Sister 1966, I Never Loved a Man the Way I Love You 1967, Lady Soul, Aretha Now, Aretha in Paris 1968, Aretha's Gold 1969, This Girl's in Love with You, Spirit in the Dark 1970, Live at Fillmore West 1971, Young, Gifted and Black, Amazing Grace 1972, Hey Now Hey, The Best of Aretha Franklin, The First Twelve Sides 1973, Let Me in Your Life, With Everything I Feel in Me 1974, You 1975, Sparkle, Ten Years of Gold 1976, Sweet Passion 1977, Almighty Fire 1978, La Diva 1979, Aretha 1980, Love All the Hurt Away 1981, Jump to It 1982, Get It Right 1983, One Lord, One Faith 1988, Through the Storm 1989, What You See Is What You Sweat 1991, Jazz to Soul 1992, Aretha After Hours, Chain of Fools 1993, Unforgettable: A Tribute to Dinah Washington 1995, Love Songs 1997, The Delta Meets Detroit 1998, A Rose is Still a Rose 1998, Amazing Grace 1999. *Publication:* Aretha: From these Roots (with David Rib). *Address:* Arista Records, c/o Gwen Quinn, 6 West 57th Street, New York, NY 10019; 8450 Linwood Street, Detroit, MI 48206, USA.

FRANKLIN, Barbara Hackman, BA, MBA; American business executive and fmr government official; b. 19 March 1940, Lancaster, Pa; d. of Arthur A. Hackman and Mayme M. Hackman (née Haller); m. Wallace Barnes 1986; ed Pennsylvania State Univ., Harvard Business School; with Singer Co., New York 1964–68; Asst Vice-Pres. Citibank, New York 1969–71; White House Staff Asst to the Pres. for Recruiting Women to Govt, Washington, DC 1971–73; Commr and Vice-Chair. US Consumer Product Safety Comm., Washington, DC 1973–79; Sr Fellow and Dir Govt and Business Program, Wharton School, Univ. of Pa 1980–88; Pres. and CEO Franklin Assocs., Washington, DC 1984–92, Pres., CEO Barbara Franklin Enterprises 1995–; US Sec. of Commerce, Dept of Commerce, Washington, DC 1992–93; mem. Pres.'s Advisory Cttee for Trade Policy and Negotiations 1982–86, 1991–92, Chair. Task Force on Tax Reform 1985–86, mem. NAFTA Task Force 1991–92; mem. Services Policy Advisory Cttee US Trade Rep. 1986; mem. Investment Policy Advisory Cttee US Trade Rep. 1989; Alt. Rep. and Public Del. to 44th Session of UN Gen. Ass. 1989–90; mem. US Comptroller Gen.'s Consultant Panel 1984–92, 1994–; mem. Bd of Dirs Aetna Inc. 1979–92, 1993–, Dow Chemical Co. 1980–92, 1993–, AMP Inc. 1993–99, NASDAQ Stock Market 1995–98, MedImmune Inc. 1995–, Milacron Inc. 1996–, GenVec Inc. 2002–; Guest Services Inc. 1998–, Harvard Business School 1998–; fmr Dir Black & Decker Corpn, Nordstrom, Westinghouse Electric Corpn, Watson, Wyatt Worldwide and other cos; mem. Council on Foreign Relations 1991–, Vice-Chair. Atlantic Council 1995–; mem., Bd of Dirs Econ. Club of NY, Nat. Asscn of Corp. Dirs, Financial Accounting Foundation, US-China Business Council; Distinguished Visiting Fellow and Chair. Asian Studies Advisory Council, Heritage Foundation; mem. Bretton Woods Cttee, Council on Foreign Relations, Int. Women's Forum (founding mem.), Nat. Cttee for US-China Relations; several hon. degrees and numerous awards for business and social achievement, including the John J. McCloy Award and the 2000 NACD Dir of the Year Award. *Television:* Monthly Commentator, "Nighthly Business Report", Public Broadcasting Service 1997–. *Leisure interests:* exercise, hiking, reading, painting. *Address:* 2700 Virginia Avenue, NW, Apt 112, Washington, DC 20037, USA (Office). *Telephone:* (202) 337-9100 (Office). *Fax:* (202) 337-9104 (Office). *E-mail:* bhfranklin@aol.com (Office).

FRANKLIN, H Allen, BEE, MEng; American business executive; b. Corner, Alabama; ed Univ. of Alabama, Stanford Univ.; joined Southern Co. Services 1970, Sr Vice-Pres. Alabama Power 1981, Exec. Vice-Pres. Southern Co. Services 1983–88, Pres. and CEO 1988, Pres. and CEO Southern Co. 2001–, mem. Bd Dirs; Sr Mem. IEEE; Dir United Way of Metropolitan Atlanta, Georgia Chamber of Commerce, Atlanta Chamber of Commerce; Pres. Atlanta Area Council of the Boy Scouts of America; Chair. Nat. Wild Turkey Fed.; mem. Georgia Dept of Industry, Trade and Tourism. *Address:* Office of the President, 270 Peachtree Street, NW, Atlanta, GA 30303, USA (Office). *Telephone:* (404) 506-5000 (Office). *Fax:* (404) 506-0598 (Office). *Website:* www.southernco.com (Office).

FRANKLIN, John Hope, AM, PhD; American author, scholar and university professor; b. 2 Jan. 1915, Rentiesville, Okla; s. of Buck Colbert and Mollie (née Parker) Franklin; m. Aurelia E Whittington 1940 (died 1999); one s.; ed Fisk Univ., Harvard Univ.; Instructor in History Fisk Univ. 1936–38; Prof. of History St Augustine's Coll. 1939–43, NC Coll., Durham 1943–47, Howard Univ. 1947–56; Chair. Dept of History Brooklyn Coll. 1956–64; Prof. of American History Univ. of Chicago 1964–82, Chair. Dept of History 1967–70, John Matthews Manly Distinguished Service Prof. 1969–82; James B. Duke Prof. of History Duke Univ. 1982–85, Prof. Emer. 1985–; Prof. of Legal History, Duke Law School 1985–92; Pitt Prof. of American History and Institutions Cambridge Univ. 1962–63; Visiting Prof. Harvard, Wis., Cornell, Hawaii, Calif. and Cambridge Univs. and Salzburg Seminar; Chair. Bd of Foreign Scholarships 1966–69, Nat. Council on Humanities 1976–79; Chair. Pres.'s Initiative on Race 1997, Advisory Bd Nat. Park System 2000; Dir Ill. Bell Telephone Co. 1972–80; Edward Austin Fellow 1937–38, Rosenwald Fellow 1937–39, Guggenheim Fellow 1950–51, 1973–74; Pres.'s Fellow, Brown Univ. 1952–53, Center for Advanced Study in Behavioral Science 1973–74; Sr Mellon Fellow, Nat. Humanities Center 1980–82; Fulbright Prof., Australia 1960; Jefferson Lecturer in Humanities 1976; mem. Bd of Dirs. Salzburg Seminar, Museum of Science and Industry 1968–80; mem. American Historical Asscn (Pres. 1978–79), Southern Historical Asscn (Pres. 1970–71), Org. of American Historians (Pres. 1970–75), Asscn for Study of Negro Life and History, American Studies Asscn, American Philosophical Soc., American Asscn of Univ. Profs.; mem. Bd, Duke Endowment 1994; numerous hon. degrees; Jefferson Medal (American Philosophical Soc.) 1993, Presidential Medal of Freedom 1995, Spingarn Medal 1995; Skirball Award 2000, Harold Washington 2000, Lincoln Prize 2000. *Television:* First Person Singular (P.B.S.) 1997, Tutu and Franklin: Journey Towards Peace (P.B.S.) 1999, Biographical Conversations (P.B.S.) 2001. *Publications:* Free Negro in North Carolina 1943, From Slavery to Freedom: A History of Negro Americans 1947 (with A. A. Moss, Jr), 8th Edn 2000, Militant South 1956, Reconstruction After the Civil War 1961, The Emancipation Proclamation 1963, Land of the Free (with others) 1966, Illustrated History of Black Americans 1970, A Southern Odyssey 1976, Racial Equality in America 1976, George Washington Williams: A Biography 1985, Race and History: Selected Essays 1938–88 1990, The Color Line: Legacy for the 21st Century 1993; Ed. Civil War Diary of James T. Ayers 1947, A Fool's Errand (by Albion Tourgee) 1961, Army Life in a Black Regiment (by Thomas Higginson) 1962, Color and Race 1968, Reminiscences of an Active Life (by John R. Lynch) 1970, African Americans and the Living Constitution (ed. with Gemma R. McNeil) 1995, Runaway Slaves: Rebels on the Plantation (with Loren Schwenirager) 1999. *Leisure interests:* cultivating orchids, fly-fishing, classical music. *Address:* 208 Pineview Road, Durham, NC 27707, USA (Home). *Telephone:* (919) 489-7513 (Office). *Fax:* (919) 490-9789.

FRANKLIN, Kirk; American singer, songwriter and record company executive; b. Kirk Smith, 26 Jan. 1970, Fort Worth, Tex.; m.; one s.; Choir Dir Greater Strangers Rest Baptist Church, Fort Worth 1988; worked with Dallas-Fort Worth Mass Choir on albums I Will Not Let Nothing Separate Me 1991, Another Chance 1993; f. choir group the Family; f. record company Fo Yo Soul; Grammy Awards: Best Contemporary Soul Gospel Album (for Watcha Lookin' 4) 1997, Best Gospel Album by a choir or chorus (for God's Property from Kirk Franklin's Nu Nation) 1998, Best Contemporary Soul Gospel Album (for The Nu Nation Project) 1999. *Films:* film soundtrack contribution includes My Life is in Your Hands (for Get on the Bus 1996) and Joy (for The Preacher' Wife 1996). *Albums:* Albums with the Family include Kirk Franklin and the Family 1992, Christmas 1995, Watcha Lookin' 4 1996; album collaboration with God's Property from Kirk Franklin's Nu Nation (includes No. 1 single Stomp) 1997, The Nu Nation Project 1998 (includes Lean On Me with participation from Bono, Mary J. Blige and R. Kelly). *Publication:* Church Boy: My Music and My Life 1998 (autobiog.). *Address:* c/o Gerald Wright, Wright Group, 5609 S. Archbridge Court, Arlington, TX 76017, USA (Office).

FRANKLIN, Raoul Norman, CBE, DSc, F.R.ENG.; British scientist and university administrator; b. 3 June 1935, Hamilton, NZ; s. of N. G. Franklin and T. B. (née Davis) Franklin; m. Faith Ivens 1961; two s.; ed Auckland Grammar School, Auckland Univ., Oxford Univ.; Sr Research Fellow, Royal Mil. Coll. of Science 1961–63; Tutorial Fellow, Keble Coll., Oxford 1963–78, Univ. Lecturer, Eng Science, Oxford Univ. 1967–78; Consultant, UKAEA

Culham Lab. 1968–; Vice-Chancellor, City Univ. 1978–98, Prof. Plasma Physics and Tech. 1986–98; Visiting Prof. Open Univ. 1998, Oxford Research Unit; Chair. City Tech. Ltd 1978–93; Chair. Assoc. Examining Bd 1994–98, Assessment and Qualifications Alliance (AQA) 1998–2003; Vice-Chair. Gen. Bd of the Faculties, Oxford Univ. 1971–74; mem. of Hebdomadal Council, Oxford Univ. 1971–74, 1976–78, of Science Bd, Science and Eng Research Council 1982–85, of London Pensions Fund Authority 1989–95, of Bd Arab-British Chamber of Commerce 1995–2002; mem. Council Gresham Coll. 1980–98; mem. Int. Cttee of ESCAMPIG 1993–96; Freeman, City of London; Hon. Fellow, Keble Coll., Coll. of Preceptors; Gov. Ashridge Man. Coll. 1986–99, Council City & Guilds 1996–2000, Council Univ. of Buckingham 2001–; Foundation Master Guild of Educators 2001–02; Master Worshipful Co. of Curriers 2002–03; Hon. Fellow, Keble Coll., Coll. of Preceptors; Freeman, City of London. *Publications:* Plasma Phenomena in Gas Discharges 1976, Physical Kinetics, Vol. XII 1981, Interaction of Intense Electromagnetic Fields with Plasmas (ed.) 1981. *Leisure interests:* walking, tennis, gardening. *Address:* Open University Oxford Research Unit, Foxcombe Hall, Boars Hill, Oxford, OX1 5HR (Office); 12 Moreton Road, Oxford, OX2 7AX, England (Home). *Telephone:* (1865) 558311 (Home). *Fax:* (1865) 326322 (Office). *E-mail:* r.n.franklin@open.ac.uk (Office); randffranklin3@tiscali.co.uk (Home).

FRANKS, Lynne; British public relations executive; b. 16 April 1948; d. of Leslie Samuel Franks and Angela Franks (née Herman); m. Paul Howie (separated 1992); one s. one d.; ed Minchenden Grammar School, London; Sec. Petticoat Magazine 1965–67; est. Lynne Franks Ltd public relations consultants 1971, left full-time employment 1992; clients have included Katherine Hamnett, Ruby Wax, Lenny Henry, Gerald Ratner, Jasper Conran, Neil Kinnock, Brylcreem, Swatch, Harvey Nichols, Next, Littlewoods, Comic Relief, Greenpeace, Amnesty Int. *Publication:* Absolutely Now!: A Futurist's Journey to Her Inner Truth 1997. *Leisure interests:* New Age spirituality, healing, the environment.

FRANKS, Gen. Tommy Ray, MS; American army officer; b. 17 June 1945, Wynnewood, Okla; m. Cathryn Carley 1969; one d.; ed Univ. of Texas, Shippensburg Univ., Pa, Armed Forces Staff Coll., US Army War Coll.; commissioned 2nd Lt 1967; served with 9th Infantry Div., Vietnam, 2nd Armored Cavalry Regt, FRG; Commdr 2nd Bn 78th Field Artillery, FRG 1981–84; Deputy Asst G3, III Corps, Fort Hood, Tex. 1985–87; Commdr Div. Artillery, 1st Cavalry Div. 1987–88; Chief of Staff 1st Cavalry Div. 1988–89; Asst Div. Commdr (Maneuver), 1st Cavalry Div., Operation Desert Shield/Desert Storm, Saudi Arabia, Iraq 1990–91; Asst Commdt Field Artillery School, Fort Sill, Okla 1991–92; Dir La. Maneuvers Task Force, Office Chief of Staff US Army, Fort Monroe, Va 1992–94; Asst Chief of Staff Combined Forces Command and US Forces Korea 1994; Commdr 2nd Infantry Div., Korea 1995–97, Commdr 3rd US Army, Fort McPherson, Ga 1997–2000; promoted Gen., C-in-C US Cen. Command, MacDill Air Force Base, Fla 2000–; Defense Distinguished Service Medal, Distinguished Service Medal (with oak leaf cluster), Legion of Merit (with 3 oak leaf clusters), Bronze Star Medal (with 'V' device and 3 oak leaf clusters), Purple Heart (with 2 oak leaf clusters), Air Medal (with 'V' device) and other awards. *Leisure interests:* country music, Mexican food, antiques, golf. *Address:* c/o The Pentagon, Washington, DC 20301, USA (Office). *Telephone:* (813) 827-6200 (Office). *Fax:* (813) 827-5473 (Office). *E-mail:* frankstr@centcom.mil (Office).

FRANTZ, Justus; German pianist; b. 18 May 2944, Hohensalza; ed under Prof. Eliza Hansen in Hamburg and Wilhelm Kempff in Positano; prizewinner, Int. Music Competition, Munich 1967; since 1969 has appeared at all maj. European concert venues and toured USA, Far East and Japan; has made many tours and recordings in piano duo with Christoph Eschenbach and received Edison Int. Award for their recording of Schubert marches 1983; Co-founder and Dir Schleswig-Holstein Music Festival; Prof. Hamburg Musikhochschule 1985–; Founder Schleswig-Holstein Music Festival 1986, Dir 1986–94; performed complete cycle of Mozart concertos in several European cities 1987–88. *Recordings include:* works by Scarlatti, Beethoven, Mozart and concertos for two, three and four pianos by J. S. Bach. *Address:* c/o Anglo-Swiss Artists' Management, 72 Fairhazel Gardens, Suite 6, London, NW6 3SR, England (Office).

FRANZEN, Jonathan, BA; American author; b. 1959, Western Springs, Ill.; m. (divorced); ed Swarthmore Coll., Freie Univ. Berlin; fmrly worked in seismology lab., Harvard Univ. Dept of Earth and Planetary Sciences; currently full-time writer; columnist, The New Yorker, Harper's; American Acad. Berlin Prize 2000, Granta Best Young American Novelist. *Publications include:* The Twenty-Seventh City (Whiting Award) 1988, Strong Motion 1992, The Corrections (Nat. Book Award, New York Times Ed.'s Choice) 2001, How to be Alone (essays) 2002. *Address:* c/o Farrar, Straus and Giroux, 19 Union Square West, New York, NY 10003, USA (Office).

FRANZEN, Ulrich J., BFA, MArch, LHD, FAIA; American architect; b. 15 Jan. 1921, Rhineland, Germany; s. of Erik Franzen and Elizabeth (Hellersberg) Franzen; m. 1st Joan Cummings 1942 (divorced 1962); two s. one d.; m. 2nd Josephine Laura Hughes 1980; ed Williams Coll. and Harvard Univ.; Designer, I. M. Pei & Partners, New York 1950–55; Head of Ulrich Franzen and Assocs., New York 1955–; Visiting Critic, Prof., Washington, St Louis, Yale, Harvard and Columbia Univs., various occasions 1960–84; Chair. Architectural Bd of Review, Rye, NY 1960–62; mem. Cincinnati Architectural Bd Review Bd 1964–65; mem. Architectural League New York (Pres.

1968–70, mem. Bd of Dirs. 1962–); Commr New York City Landmarks Preservation Comm., Century Asscn 1992–96; numerous awards including Bruner Memorial Prize, Nat. Inst. of Arts and Letters 1962, Thomas Jefferson Award, AIA 1970, Gold Medal, AIA; decorated Bronze Star, Croix de Guerre avec Palme (Belgium). *Principal works include:* Alley Theatre 1968 (AIA Honor 1970), Agronomy Bldg 1970 (AIA Honor 1971), Christensen Hall 1970 (AIA Honor 1972), Harlem School of Arts 1982, Hunter Coll. New York 1984, Philip Morris World HQ 1984, Whitney Museum Br. 1984, Champion Int. World HQ with Whitney Museum Br. 1985. *Address:* Ulrich Franzen Architect, 530 East 76th Street, Unit 29D, New York, NY 10021-3561; 27 Lamy Drive, Santa Fe, NM 87506-6907, USA.

FRASER, Lady Antonia, CBE, MA, FRSL; British author; b. 27 Aug. 1932, London; d. of the late Earl and Countess of Longford; m. 1st Hugh Fraser 1956 (divorced 1977, died 1984); three s. three d.; m. 2nd Harold Pinter (q.v.) 1980; ed Dragon School, Oxford, St Mary's Convent, Ascot and Lady Margaret Hall, Oxford; mem. Cttee English PEN 1979–88 (Pres. 1988–89, Vice-Pres. 1990–), Crimewriters Asscn 1980–86; Hon. DLitt (Hull) 1986, (Sussex) 1990, (St Andrew's) 1994; Norten Medlicott Medal, Historical Asscn 2000. *TV plays:* Charades 1977, Mister Clay 1985. *Publications:* King Arthur 1954, Robin Hood 1955, Dolls 1963, History of Toys 1966, Mary, Queen of Scots 1969 (James Tait Black Memorial Prize), Cromwell: Our Chief of Men 1973, King James VI and I 1974, Scottish Love Poems, A Personal Anthology 1974, Kings and Queens of England (Ed.) 1975, Love Letters (anthology) 1976, Quiet as a Nun 1977, The Wild Island 1978, King Charles II 1979, Heroes and Heroines (Ed.) 1980, A Splash of Red 1981, Cool Repentance 1982, Oxford In Verse (Ed.) 1982, The Weaker Vessel 1984 (Wolfson History Prize), Oxford Blood 1985, Your Royal Hostage 1987, Boadicea's Chariot: The Warrior Queens 1988, The Cavalier Case 1990, Jemima Shore at the Sunny Grove 1991, The Wives of Henry VIII 1992, Charles II: His Life and Times 1993, Political Death: A Jemima Shore Mystery 1994, The Gunpowder Plot (St Louis Literary Award 1996, CWA Non Fiction Gold Dagger 1996) 1996, The Lives of the Kings and Queens of England 1998, Marie Antoinette: the Journey 2001; ed. The Pleasure of Reading 1992; television adaptations of Quiet as a Nun 1978, Jemima Shore Investigates 1983. *Leisure interests:* cats, grandchildren. *Address:* c/o Curtis Brown Group Ltd., Haymarket House, 28/29 Haymarket, London SW1Y 4SP, England. *Telephone:* (20) 7396-6600. *Fax:* (20) 7396-0110.

FRASER, Bernard William, BA; Australian bank governor; b. 26 Feb. 1941, Junee, NSW; s. of K. Fraser; m. Edna Gallogly 1965 (divorced); one s. two d.; ed Junee High School, NSW, Univ. of New England, Armidale, NSW, Australian Nat. Univ., ACT; joined Dept of Nat. Devt 1961; joined Dept of Treasury 1963, Treasury Rep., London, UK 1969–72, First Asst Sec. 1979, Sec. Dept 1984–89; with Dept of Finance 1976; Dir Nat. Energy Office 1981–83; Chair. and Gov. Reserve Bank of Australia 1989–96; Trustee Construction and Bldg Unions Superannuation Trust (C+BUS) 1996–, Superannuation Trust of Australia 1996–, Australian Retirement Fund 1996–. *Leisure interest:* farming. *Address:* Construction and Building Unions Superannuation Trust, Level 12, 313 La Trobe Street, Melbourne, Vic. 3000, Australia.

FRASER, Sir Campbell, Kt, BCom, FRSE, CBIM; British business executive; b. 2 May 1923, Dunblane, Scotland; s. of Alexander Ross and Annie McGregor Fraser; m. Maria Harvey (née McLaren) 1950 (died 1975); two d.; ed Glasgow Univ., Dundee School of Econs, McMaster Univ. Canada; served in RAF 1941–45; Raw Cotton Comm. 1950–52; Economist Intelligence Unit 1952–57; with Dunlop Rubber Co. Ltd 1957–83; Exec. Dir Dunlop Holdings Ltd 1969, Man. Dir 1972–78, Chair. 1978–83, Pres. 1983–84; Chair. Scottish TV 1975–91; founder, fmr Chair., Pres. Soc. of Business Economists; Dir Tandem Computers Inc., Chair. Tandem Computers Ltd. –1997; Dir British Petroleum PLC 1978–91, BAT Industries PLC 1980–93, Bridgewater Paper Co. 1984–99, Proudfoot PLC 1987–95; Chair. Advisory Bd Wells Fargo 1989–95; Chair. Riversoft Technologies Ltd; Deputy Pres. CBI 1981–82, Pres. 1982–84; mem. Council Confed. of British Industry, Council of SMMT; Dir (non-exec.) Arlen PLC 1991–95 (Chair. 1993–95), Barkers Communications Scotland Ltd 1992–95 (Chair. 1994–95); fmrly Visiting Prof. Univ. of Stirling and Univ. of Strathclyde; Trustee, The Economist 1978–; Hon. DUniv (Stirling); Hon. LLD (Strathclyde) 1979; Hon. DCL (Bishops Univ.) 1990. *Leisure interests:* athletics, reading, cinema, walking, soccer. *Address:* Silver Birches, 4 Silver Lane, Purley, Surrey, CR8 3HG, England.

FRASER, Dawn, MBE; Australian swimmer; b. 4 Sept. 1937, Balmain, near Sydney; m. Gary Ware (divorced); one c.; first female swimmer to win gold medals in three consecutive Olympic Games 1956, 1960, 1964; broke women's 100m freestyle world record nine times 1956–64; first female to break 60 seconds in 100m freestyle; shares record for most Olympic medals won by a woman swimmer (4 gold, 4 silver); set 39 world records; banned for 10 years after Tokyo Games for allegedly stealing an Olympic Flag from Japanese Imperial Palace, forcing retirement; became involved in coaching, business ventures, politics; attaché to Australian Olympic Team 2000; mem. Int. Swimming Hall of Fame Selection Cttee; retd from public life in 2001 to devote more time to farming interests in NSW; Int. Swimming Hall of Fame 1965, Olympic Order Award 1981, honoured as one of the greatest Olympians of all time at Atlanta Olympics 1996, named Nat. Living Treasure by Australian Govt. *Publication:* Below the Surface: Australian Title Gold Medal Girl (autobiog. with Harry Gordon) 1965; Dawn – One Hell of a Life (autobiog.) 2001. *Address:* 87 Birchgrove Road, Balmain, NSW 2041, Australia (Office).

FRASER, Donald Hamilton, RA; British artist; b. 30 July 1929, London; s. of Donald Fraser and Dorothy Lang; m. Judith Wentworth Sheilds 1954; one d.; ed Maidenhead Grammar School, St Martin's School of Art, London and in Paris (French Govt Scholarship); has held more than 70 one-man exhbns. in Europe, N America and Japan; work represented in public, corp. and pvt. collections throughout the world; taught at Royal Coll. of Art 1958–83, Fellow 1970; Vice-Pres. Artists' Gen. Benevolent Inst. 1981–, Chair. 1981–86; Vice-Pres. Royal Overseas League 1986–; mem. Royal Fine Art Comm. 1986–99; Hon. Curator, Royal Acad. 1992–99, Trustee 1993–99. *Publications:* Gauguin's 'Vision After the Sermon' 1969, Dancers 1989. *Address:* c/o Royal Academy of Arts, Burlington House, Piccadilly, London, W1V 0DS (Office); Bramham Cottage, Remenham Lane, Henley-on-Thames, Oxon., RG9 2LR, England.

FRASER, George MacDonald, OBE, FRSL; British author; b. 2 April 1925, Carlisle; s. of the late William Fraser and Anne Struth Donaldson; m. Kathleen Margarette Hetherington 1949; two s. one d.; ed Carlisle Grammar School, Glasgow Acad.; joined Army 1943, served as infantryman XIVth Army, Burma, later Lt Gordon Highlanders; journalist in England, Canada, Scotland 1947–65; Deputy Ed. Glasgow Herald 1965–69; author 1969–. *Publications include:* Flashman series of historical novels, The Pyrates, Mr American, Black Ajax, The General Danced at Dawn, The Steel Bonnets, The Candlemass Road 1993, Black Ajax 1997, The Light's On at Signpost 2002; screenplays: The Three Musketeers 1973, The Four Musketeers 1974, The Prince and the Pauper 1977, Octopussy 1981, Red Sonja 1985, Casanova 1987, The Return of the Musketeers 1989. *Leisure interests:* reading, writing. *Address:* c/o Curtis Brown, 28/29 Haymarket, London, SW1Y 4SP, England; Baldrine, Isle of Man.

FRASER, Honor; British model; b. 18 Dec. 1974, Beaufort Castle, Inverness; d. of the late Hon. Simon Augustine Fraser, Master of Lovat and of Virginia Fraser (née Grose); granddaughter of the late 17th Lord Lovat; first catwalk appearance in Milan at 19; with Storm Model Man., then with Select Model Man. 1997–; campaign for Givenchy 1997; appeared in campaigns for Ungaro and Nina Ricci; columnist Scotland on Sunday 1998–. *Film:* The Cookie Thief. *Address:* Select Model Management, Thomas Archer House, 43 King Street, London, WC2E 8RJ, England. *Telephone:* (20) 7470-5200. *Fax:* (20) 7470-5233.

FRASER, Hon. John Allen, PC, OC, O.B.C., CD, QC; Canadian politician; b. 15 Dec. 1931, Yokohoma, Japan; m. Catherine Findlay; three d.; ed Univ. of British Columbia; law practice, Vic., Powell River, Vancouver 1955–72; mem. House of Commons 1972–94; Minister of the Environment and Postmaster Gen. 1979–80; Minister of Fisheries and Oceans 1984–85 (resgnd), Speaker of the House of Commons 1986–94; Amb. for the Environment 1994–98; Chair. Pacific Fisheries Resource Conservation Council 1998–; Chair. Nat. Defence Minister's Monitoring Cttee on Change 1998–; Hon. Lt.-Col. Seaforth Highlanders of Canada 1994–, now Hon. Col; Hon. LLD (St Lawrence Univ.) 1999, (Simon Fraser Univ.) 1999. *Address:* Suite 701, 222 Queen Street, Ottawa, Ont., K1A 0K2; Suite 590, 800 Burrard Street, Vancouver, BC, V6Z 2G7, Canada. *Telephone:* (613) 992-6064 (Ottawa); (604) 775-5621 (Vancouver). *Fax:* (613) 992-6119 (Ottawa); (604) 775-5622 (Vancouver). *E-mail:* fraser@fish.bc.ca (Office). *Website:* www.fish.bc.ca (Office).

FRASER, Rt Hon (John) Malcolm, AC, CH, PC, MA; Australian politician; b. 21 May 1930, Melbourne; s. of the late J. Neville Fraser and of Una Fraser; m. Tamara Beggs 1956; two s. two d.; ed Melbourne Grammar School and Oxford Univ.; mem. Parl. for Wannon 1955–83; mem. Jt Parl. Cttee of Foreign Affairs 1962–66; Chair. Govt Mems.' Defence Cttee; Sec. Wool Cttee; mem. Council of Australian Nat. Univ., Canberra 1964–66; Minister for the Army 1966–68, for Educ. and Science 1968–69, for Defence 1969–71, for Educ. and Science 1971–72; Parl. Leader of Liberal Party 1975–83; Prime Minister 1975–83; Co-Chair. Commonwealth Eminent Persons Group (EPG) 1985–86; Hon. Fellow Magdalen Coll., Oxford 1982; Hon. Vice-Pres. Oxford Soc. 1983; Sr Adjunct Fellow, Center for Strategic and Int. Studies 1983; Fellow for Int. Council of Assocs. at Claremont Univ. 1985; Chair. UN Cttee on African Commodity Problems 1989–90; mem. InterAction Council for Fmr. Heads of Govt 1983– (Chair. 1997–), ANZ Int. Bd of Advice 1987–93; Chair. CARE Australia 1987–2001; Pres. CARE Int. 1990–95, Vice-Pres. 1995–99; Bd mem. Int.-Crisis Group 1995–2000; Hon. LLD (S. Carolina) 1981, (Univ. of NSW) 2002; Hon. DLitt (Deakin Univ.) 1989; B'nai B'rith Gold Medal 1980, Australian Human Rights Medal 2000. *Publications:* Common Ground: Issues That Should Bind and Not Divide Us 2002. *Leisure interests:* fishing, photography, vintage cars, motorcycles. *Address:* Level 32, 101 Collins Street, Melbourne, Vic. 3000, Australia. *Telephone:* (3) 9654-1822 (Office). *Fax:* (3) 9654-1301 (Office). *E-mail:* Malcolm.Fraser@aph.gov.au (Office).

FRASER, Peter Marshall, MC, MA, FBA; British classical scholar; b. 6 April 1918; s. of the late Archibald Fraser; m. 1st Catharine Heaton-Renshaw 1940 (divorced); one s. three d.; m. 2nd Ruth Elsbeth Renfer 1955; two s.; m. 3rd Barbara Ann Norbury 1973; ed City of London School and Brasenose Coll. Oxford; served Seaforth Highlanders 1941–45, Mil. Mission to Greece 1943–45; Sr Scholar, Christ Church Oxford 1946–47; Lecturer in Hellenistic History, Oxford Univ. 1948–64, Reader 1964–85; Fellow of All Souls Coll. Oxford 1954–87, Domestic Bursar 1962–65, Sub-Warden 1980–82, Acting Warden 1985–87, Fellow Emer. 1987–; Jr Proctor, Oxford Univ. 1960–61; Dir British School at Athens 1968–71; Chair. Man. Cttee, Soc. of Afghan Studies 1972–82; Ordinary mem. German Archaeological Inst.; Gen. Ed., British

Acad. Cttee, Lexicon of Greek Personal Names 1973– (Chair. 1973–95); Chair. Man. Cttee of Afghan Studies 1972–82; Hon. Vice-Pres. Archaeological Soc. of Athens; Hon. DPhil (Trier) 1984; Hon. DLitt (La Trobe) 1996, (Athens) 2002. *Publications:* The Rhodian Peraea and Islands (with G. E. Bean) 1954, Boeotian and West Greek Tombstones (with T. Rönne) 1957, Samothrace, The Inscriptions (Vol. I, Excavations of Samothrace) 1960, The Wares of Autolycus: Selected Literary Essays of Alice Meynell (Ed.) 1965, Ptolemaic Alexandria 1972, Rhodian Funerary Monuments 1977, A Lexicon of Greek Personal Names (Vol. I, with E Matthews) 1987, (Vol. IIIA, with E. Matthews) 1997, (Vol. IIIB, with E. Matthews) 2000, Memorial Addresses of All Souls College (Ed.) 1989, Cities of Alexander 1996. *Address:* All Souls College, Oxford, OX1 4AL, England.

FRASER, Sir William Kerr, GCB, MA, LLD, FRSE; British civil servant and administrator; b. 18 March 1929, Glasgow; s. of the late Alexander M. Fraser and Rachel Fraser; m. Marion Anne Forbes (Lady Marion Fraser) 1956; three s. one d.; ed Eastwood School, Clarkston and Univ. of Glasgow; Flying Officer RAF 1952–55; joined Scottish Office, Edinburgh 1955, Perm. Under-Sec. of State 1978–88; Prin. and Vice-Chancellor Univ. of Glasgow 1988–95, Chancellor 1996–; Chair. Royal Comm. on the Ancient and Historical Monuments of Scotland 1995–2000, Scottish Mutual Assurance PLC 1999; Hon. FRCP (Glas.) 1992; Hon. FRSAMD 1985; Hon. LLD (Glasgow) 1982, (Strathclyde) 1991, (Aberdeen) 1993; Dr. hc (Edinburgh) 1995. *Leisure interests:* reading, meditating on democracy. *Address:* Broadwood, Edinburgh Road, Gifford, East Lothian, EH41 4JE, Scotland. *Telephone:* (1620) 810319. *Fax:* (1620) 810319.

FRASER-MOLEKETI, Geraldine J.; South African politician; b. 24 Aug. 1960, Cape Town; m. Jabulani Moleketi; three c.; fmrly worked in Admin. and Communications, World Lutheran Fed.; fmr Personal Asst to Gen. Sec. of SA CP; fmr Office Man. and Nat. Admin. Union of Democratic Univ. Staff; exiled from SA 1980–90; fmr mem. Man. Cttee and Convention for a Democratic SA; Nat. Deputy Elections Coordinator, ANC 1993–94; MP 1994; Deputy Minister of Welfare and Population Devt 1995–96, Minister 1996–99, of Agric. and Land Affairs 1999, of Public Service and Admin. 2000–; fmr mem. Patriotic Health Forum, Nat. Health Forum; Co-founder and fmr Trustee Jabulile Ndlovu Educare Trust; observer of nat. elections, Pakistan 1993; mem. Nelson Mandela Children's Fund. *Address:* c/o Ministry of Public Service and Administration, Transvaal House, corner Vermeulen and van der Walts Streets, Pretoria 0002, South Africa (Office). *Telephone:* (12) 3147911 (Office). *Fax:* (12) 3232386 (Office). *E-mail:* info@dpsa.pwv.gov.za. *Website:* www.dpsa .gov.za.

FRASER OF CARMYLLIE, Baron (Life Peer), cr. 1989 in the District of Angus; **Peter Lovat Fraser,** BA, LLB, QC, MP; British politician and lawyer; b. 29 May 1945; s. of Rev. George Robson Fraser and Helen Jean Meiklejohn; m. Fiona Macdonald Mair 1969; one s. two d.; ed St Andrew's Prep. School, Grahamstown, SA, Loretto School, Musselburgh, Gonville and Caius Coll., Cambridge, Edinburgh Univ.; called to Scottish Bar 1969; Lecturer in Constitutional Law, Heriot-Watt Univ. 1972–74; Standing Jr Counsel in Scotland to FCO 1979; Chair. Scottish Conservative Lawyers Law Reform Group 1976; Conservative MP for S. Angus 1979–83, for Angus East 1983–87; Parl. Pvt. Sec. to Sec. of State for Scotland 1981–82; Solicitor Gen. for Scotland 1982–89, Lord Advocate 1989–92; Minister of State, Scottish Office 1992–95, Dept of Trade and Industry 1995–97; Deputy Leader of Opposition, House of Lords 1997–98; Chair. JFX Oil and Gas PLC 1997–; Dir Int. Petroleum Exchange 1997–, (Chair. 1999–), London Metal Exchange 1997–, Total Fine Elf Exploration UK 2000–; Chair. Ram Energy 2002–; Patron Queen Margaret Univ. Coll. 1999–, Statutory Cttee Royal Pharmaceutical Soc. 2000. *Leisure interests:* skiing, golf, wind-surfing. *Address:* Slade House, Carmyllie, by Arbroath, Angus, DD11 2RE, Scotland. *Telephone:* (1241) 860215.

FRASYNIUK, Władysław; Polish politician and union leader; b. 25 Nov. 1954, Wrocław; s. of Stanisław Frasyniuk and Zofia Frasyniuk; m. 1978; one s. three d.; driver, mechanic Municipal Transport, Wrocław, organizer of strike in bus depot, Wrocław Aug. 1980; press spokesman Founding Cttee of Ind. Self-Governing Trade Union; Chair. Solidarity Trade Union, Lower Silesia 1981–90 (resgnd); mem. Nat. Consultative Comm. of Solidarity; active underground under martial law, Jt Founder Provisional Exec. Cttee of Solidarity; arrested 1982, amnestied 1984; arrested again Feb. 1985, sentenced to over 4 years, amnestied 1986; mem. Provisional Council of Solidarity 1986–87, Nat. Exec. Comm. of Solidarity 1987–90; mem. Citizens' Cttee of Solidarity, Chair. 1988–90; took part in Round Table talks, Comm. for Trade Union Pluralism Feb.–April 1989; one of founders and leaders Citizens' Movt for Democratic Action (ROAD) 1990–91; mem. Social-Liberal faction of Democratic Union 1991–94; Vice-Chair. Democratic Union 1991–94; mem. Freedom Union 1994–, Chair. Silesia Region 1999–, Chair. 2001–; Deputy to Sejm (Parl.) 1991–2001. *Leisure interests:* dogs, individual sports, history of Russia. *Address:* Biuro Krajowe Unii Wolności, ul. Marszałkowska 77–79, 00-683 Warsaw; Biuro Dolnośląskiej Unii Wolności, ul. Zelwerowicza 16, 53-676 Wrocław, Poland (Office). *Telephone:* (22) 827-50-47; (71) 3548390 (Office). *Fax:* (71) 3548399 (Office). *E-mail:* frasyniuk@unia-wolnosci.pl (Office). *Website:* www.uw.org.pl (Office).

FRATTINI, Franco, LLB; Italian politician and attorney; b. 14 March 1957, Rome; ed La Sapienza Univ., Rome; State Attorney 1981, Attorney, State Attorney-Gen.'s Office 1984; Magistrate, Regional Admin. Tribunal, Piedmont 1984–86, State Councillor 1986–; Legal Adviser to Minister of the

Treasury 1986–90, to Deputy Prime Minister 1990–91; Deputy Sec. Office of the Prime Minister 1993–94, Sec.-Gen. 1994–95; Minister for Public Admin and Regional Affairs 1995–96; elected Deputy for Bolzano Laives (Forza Italia) 1996, elected Deputy for Div. VIII (Veneto 2) 2001–; Minister of Foreign Affairs 2003–; Chair. Parl. Cttee on Intelligence, Security Services and State Secrecy 1996; City Councillor, Rome 1997–2000; mem. Exec. Cttee Forza Italia 1998–; Sec.-Gen. Giulio Onesti Foundation 1995–; mem. Italian Nat. Olympic Cttee 1999–. *Publications include:* numerous specialist articles on law and public works. *Address:* Ministry of Foreign Affairs, Piazzale della Farnesina 1, 00194 Rome, Italy (Office). *Telephone:* (06) 36911 (Office). *Fax:* (06) 3236210 (Office). *E-mail:* info@mincomes.it (Office). *Website:* www.esteri .it (Office).

FRAYN, Michael; British playwright and author; b. 8 Sept. 1933; s. of the late Thomas A. Frayn and Violet A. Lawson; m. 1st Gillian Palmer 1960 (divorced 1989); three d.; m. 2nd Claire Tomalin (q.v.) 1993; ed Kingston Grammar School and Emmanuel Coll., Cambridge; reporter, The Guardian 1957–59, columnist 1959–62; columnist, The Observer 1962–68; Hon. DLitt (Cambridge) 2001; recipient of numerous drama awards. *Stage plays:* The Two of Us 1970, The Sandboy 1971, Alphabetical Order 1975, Donkeys' Years 1976, Clouds 1976, Balmoral 1978, Liberty Hall (new version of Balmoral) 1980, Make and Break 1980, Noises Off 1982, 2000, Benefactors 1984, Look Look 1990, Here 1993, Now You Know 1995, Copenhagen 1998, Alarms and Excursions 1998. *Plays and documentaries for TV include:* Jamie, on a Flying Visit (BBC) 1968, Birthday (BBC) 1969 (plays); Second City Reports (with John Bird—Granada) 1964, Beyond a Joke (with John Bird and Eleanor Bron—BBC) 1972, Making Faces (BBC) 1975 (series); One Pair of Eyes 1968, Laurence Sterne Lived Here 1973, Imagine a City Called Berlin 1975, Vienna: The Mask of Gold 1977, Three Streets in the Country 1979, The Long Straight (Great Railway Journeys of the World) 1980, Jerusalem 1984, Magic Lantern, Prague 1993, Budapest: Written in Water 1996 (all BBC documentaries). *Cinema:* Clockwise 1986, Remember Me? 1997. *Translated plays, including:* The Cherry Orchard, Three Sisters, The Seagull, Uncle Vanya, Wild Honey, The Sneeze (Chekhov), The Fruits of Enlightenment (Tolstoy), Exchange (Trifonov), Number One (Anouilh). *Film:* First and Last 1989. *Publications:* novels: The Tin Men 1965, The Russian Interpreter 1966, Towards the End of the Morning 1967, A Very Private Life 1968, Sweet Dreams 1973, The Trick of It 1989, A Landing on the Sun 1991 (Sunday Express Book of the Year), Now You Know 1992, Headlong 1999, Spies (Whitbread Award for Best Novel) 2002; non-fiction: Constructions (philosophy) 1974, Speak after the Beep 1995, Celia's Secret (with David Burke) 2000; several vols of collections of columns, plays and translations. *Address:* c/o Greene & Heaton Ltd, 37A Goldhawk Road, London, W12 8QQ, England.

FRCKOVSKY, Lubomir; Macedonian politician; b. 2 Dec. 1957; ed Skopje Univ., Ljubljana Univ.; mem. Inst. Francais des Relations Int., Paris; mem. Int. Law Asscn Skopje, Forum for Human Rights Macedonia; Prof. of Int. Law and Theory of Int. Relations Skopje Univ.; co-author of new Constitution of Repub. of Macedonia 1991; Minister without Portfolio 1990; Minister of Interior 1994; Minister of Foreign Affairs 1996–97; Prof., Skopje Univ. 1996–98, currently Prof. of Int. Law; Fellow Schloss Leopoldskron, Salzburg; Fellow 21st Century Trust, London. *Address:* SS Cyril and Methodius University of Skopje, P.O. Box 576, Krste Misirkov bb, 91000 Skopje, Macedonia. *Telephone:* (91) 116323 (Office).

FREARS, Stephen Arthur; British film director; b. 20 June 1941, Leicester; s. of Dr. Russell E. Frears and Ruth M. Frears; m. Mary K. Wilmers 1968 (divorced 1974); two s.; partner Anne Rothenstein; one s. one d.; ed Gresham's School, Holt, Trinity Coll., Cambridge; Asst Dir Morgan, a Suitable Case for Treatment 1966, Charlie Bubbles 1967, If . . . 1968; worked for TV for 13 years, including several TV films and plays in collaboration with Alan Bennett; Officier Ordre des Arts et des Lettres. *Films include:* Gumshoe 1971, Bloody Kids 1980, Going Gently 1981, Walter 1982, Saigon 1983, The Hit 1984, My Beautiful Laundrette 1985, Prick Up Your Ears 1986, Sammy and Rosie Get Laid 1987, Dangerous Liaisons 1989, The Grifters 1990, Hero 1992, The Snapper 1992, Mary Reilly 1996, The Van 1996, The Hi-Lo Country 1999, High Fidelity 2000, Liam 2001, Dirty Pretty Things 2003, Monkeyface 2003. *Television includes:* Fail Safe 2000. *Address:* c/o Casarotto Co. Ltd, National House, 60-66 Wardour Street, London, W1V 4ND, England. *Telephone:* (20) 7287-4450. *Fax:* (20) 7287-9128.

FRECCIA, Massimo; American conductor; b. 19 Sept. 1906, Florence; ed Cherubini Royal Conservatoire, Florence; guest conductor New York Philharmonic Orchestra 1938, 1939, 1940; Musical Dir and Conductor, Havana Philharmonic Orchestra 1939–43, New Orleans Symphony Orchestra 1944–52, Baltimore Symphony Orchestra 1952–59; Chief Conductor Rome (R.A.I.) Orchestra 1959–; frequent appearances as guest conductor of famous orchestras in Europe and U.S.; tours in Australia 1963, Japan 1967, S. Africa 1969; appeared at various int. festivals, including Vienna, Prague, Berlin, Lisbon, Montreux; Hon. DMus (Tulane Univ., New Orleans); Order of the Star of Italian Solidarity. *Recordings include:* Haydn, Mozart and Mendelssohn with Santa Cecilia Orchestra, Shostakovich with Royal Philharmonic.

FRÉCHETTE, Louise; Canadian international official and politician; with Dept of External Affairs, Govt of Canada early 1970s–, envoy to Argentina 1985; Asst Deputy Minister for Latin America and the Caribbean, Ministry of Foreign Affairs, for Int. Econ. and Trade Policy 1990–92; Amb. to UN 1992–94; Assoc. Deputy Minister, Dept of Finance 1994–95, Dept of Defence 1995–98; Deputy Sec.-Gen. UN 1998–. *Address:* Office of the Deputy Secretary-General, S-3862A, United Nations, New York, NY 10017, USA (Office). *Telephone:* (212) 963-8010 (Office).

FREEDBERG, Hugh; British business executive; b. 18 June 1945, Cape Town, South Africa; ed Univ. of Witwatersrand, Univ. of South Africa, Harvard Univ., Amos Tuck School of Business Admin., Dartmouth Coll., USA; Book Club Assocs., UK 1973–75; Marketing and Sales Dir for UK Card Div. American Express 1975–78, Gen. Man. 1978–86, Head of Divs. in the Benelux countries, S. Europe, the Middle East and Africa, the UK, Ireland, SE Asia; joined Salomon Inc. 1986, CEO The Mortgage Corpn –1990; joined TSB Group 1990, Exec. Dir, CEO Insurance and Investment Services Div., Deputy CEO 1992–96; CEO Hill Samuel Group (bought by TSB Group) 1991–96, now CEO Hill Samuel Bank Ltd (div. of Lloyds TSB Group PLC); Dir Macquarie Bank, Australia; Man. Partner Financial Services Practice, Korn Ferry Int.; CEO London Int. Financial Futures and Options Exchange (LIFFE) 1998–. *Address:* London International Financial Futures and Options Exchange, Cannon Bridge House, 1 Cousin Lane, London, EC4R 3XX, England (Office); Hill Samuel Bank Ltd, 100 Wood Green, London, EC2P 2AJ. *Telephone:* (20) 7623-0444 (LIFFE) (Office); (20) 7600-6000. *Fax:* (20) 7588-3624 (LIFFE); (20) 7920-3900. *Website:* www.liffe.com (Office).

FREEDMAN, Amelia, MBE, FRAM; British music administrator; b. 21 Nov. 1940; d. of Henry Freedman and Miriam Freedman (née Claret); m. Michael Miller 1970; two s. one d.; ed St George's School, Harpenden, Henrietta Barnet School, London; music teacher, King's School, Cambridge, Perse School for Girls, Cambridge, Chorleywood Coll. for the Blind, Sir Philip Magnus School, London 1961–72; Founder and Artistic Dir Nash Ensemble 1964–; Artistic Dir Bath Int. Festival 1984–93, Bath Mozartfest 1995–; Musical Adviser Israel Festival 1989–; Programme Advisor Philharmonia Orchestra 1992–95; Head of Classical Music, South Bank Centre 1995–; chamber music consultant for numerous projects at the Barbican and South Bank Centre, London; Hon. DMus (Bath) 1993; Chevalier, des Arts et des Lettres, Chevalier, Ordre Nat. du Mérite. *Leisure interests:* ballet, opera, theatre, cinema, sport. *Address:* 14 Cedars Close, Hendon, London, NW4 1TR, England (Home). *Telephone:* (20) 8203-3025 (Home). *Fax:* (20) 8203-9540 (Home).

FREEDMAN, Lawrence David, KCMG, CBE, DPhil, FRSA, FBA; British university professor; b. 7 Dec. 1948, Tynemouth; s. of the late Lt-Commdr Julius Freedman and Myra Robinson; m. Judith Hill 1974; one s. one d.; ed Whitley Bay Grammar School and Univs of Manchester, Oxford and York; Research Assoc. IISS 1975–76; Research Fellow, Royal Inst. of Int. Affairs 1976–78, Head of Policy Studies 1978–82; Fellow, Head Dept of War Studies, King's Coll. London 1978–, Prof. 1982–, Head School of Social Science and Public Policy 2001–; mem. Council, IISS 1984–92, 1993–, School of Slavonic and E European Studies 1993–97; Chair. Cttee on Int. Peace and Security, Social Science Research Council (USA) 1993–98; occasional newspaper columnist; Trustee Imperial War Museum 2001–; Hon. Dir Centre for Defence Studies 1990–; Silver Medallist, Arthur Ross Prize, Council on Foreign Relations (USA) 2002. *Publications:* U.S. Intelligence and Soviet Strategic Threat 1978, Britain and Nuclear Weapons 1980, The Evolution of Nuclear Strategy 1981, 1989, The Atlas of Global Strategy 1985, The Price of Peace 1986, Britain and the Falklands War 1988, Signals of War (with V. Gamba) 1989, The Gulf Conflict 1990–91 (with E. Karsh) 1993, War: A Reader 1994; (ed.) Military Intervention in Europe 1994, (ed.) Strategic Coercion 1998, The Politics of British Defence Policy 1979–1998 1999, Kennedy's Wars 2000; Superterrorism (ed.) 2002; articles etc. *Leisure interests:* tennis, political cartoons. *Address:* Department of War Studies, King's College, Strand, London, WC2R 2LS, England. *Telephone:* (20) 7848-2750/1238. *Fax:* (20) 7873-2026. *E-mail:* lawrence.freedman@kcl.ac.uk (Office); LFREED0712@aol.com (Home).

FREEH, Louis, LLM; American legal official, judge and lawyer; b. 6 Jan. 1950; ed Rutgers Coll., Rutgers Law School and New York Univ. Law School; agent F.B.I. 1974–80, Dir 1993–2001; Asst attorney New York 1980–90, Fed. Judge 1990–92; Adjunct. Assoc. Prof. of Law Fordham Law School 1988–92; Presidential Award for Distinguished Service 1987, Law Enforcement Officers Award 1989, John Marshall Award. *Address:* c/o U.S. Department of Justice, Federal Bureau of Investigation, J. Edgar Hoover Building, 935 Pennsylvania Avenue, NW, Washington, DC 20535, USA.

FREELING, Nicolas; British writer; b. 1927, London; m. Cornelia Termes 1954; four s. one d.; primary and secondary educ.; worked as cook in hotel restaurants all over Europe 1945–60; novelist 1960–; Gold Dagger, Crime Writers' Asscn, Grand Prix Polar, Paris, Edgar Allan Poe Prize. *Publications:* Love in Amsterdam 1961, Because of the Cats 1962, Gun before Butter 1962, Valparaiso 1963, Double Barrel 1963, Criminal Conversation 1964, King of the Rainy Country 1965, Dresden Green 1966, Strike Out Where Not Applicable 1967, This is the Castle 1968, Tsing-Boum 1969, Kitchen Book 1970, Over the High Side 1971, Cook Book 1971, A Long Silence 1972, Dressing of Diamond 1974, What Are the Bugles Blowing For? 1975, Lake Isle 1976, Gadget 1977, The Night Lords 1978, The Widow 1979, Castang's City 1980, One Damn Thing After Another 1981, Wolfnight 1982, Back of the North Wind 1983, No Part in Your Death 1984, A City Solitary 1985, Cold Iron 1986, Lady Macbeth 1987, Not as Far as Velma 1989, Sandcastles 1989, Those in Peril 1990, The Pretty How Town 1992, You Who Know 1993, Criminal Convictions 1994, The Seacoast of Bohemia 1994, A Dwarf Kingdom 1996,

One More River 1997, Some Day Tomorrow 2000, Village Book 2002, The Janeites 2002. *Leisure interest:* tree planting. *Address:* Grandfontaine, 67130 Schirmeck, France.

FREEMAN, Cathy (Catherine Astrid); Australian athlete; b. 16 Feb. 1973, Mackay; d. of Norman Freeman and Cecilia Barber; m. (Sandy) Alexander Bodecker; works as public relations adviser; winner Australian 200m. 1990–91, 1994, 1996, Australian 100m. 1996, Amateur Athletics Fed. 400m. 1992, 200m. 1993; Gold Medallist 4x100m. Commonwealth Games 1990; Gold Medallist 200m., 400m., Silver Medallist 4x100m. Commonwealth Games 1994; Silver Medallist 400m., Olympic Games, Atlanta 1996; winner World Championships 400m., Athens 1997 (first Aboriginal winner at World Championships); Gold Medallist 400m., Olympic Games, Sydney 2000; set 2 Australian 200m. records, 5 Australian 400m. records 1994–96; took break from athletics in 2001; returned to int. competition Commonwealth Games Manchester 2002, winning a gold medal in the 4x400m relay; Media and Communications Officer, Australia Post; numerous nat. awards including Young Australian of the Year 1990, Australian of the Year 1998 (only person to have been awarded both honours). *Leisure interests:* family, pets, children, movies. *Address:* c/o Michelle Tozer, IMG, 68 Drummond Street, Carlton, Vic. 3053; Catherine Freedman Enterprises Ltd, P.O. Box 700, South Melbourne, Vic. 3205 (Office); c/o Melbourne International Track Club, 43 Fletcher Street, Essendon, Vic. 3040, Australia. *Telephone:* (3) 9639-2333. *Fax:* (3) 9639-1022. *E-mail:* mtozer@imgworld.com.

FREEMAN, Charles (Chas.) Wellman, Jr, BA, JD; American diplomatist; b. 2 March 1943, Washington, DC; s. of Charles W. Freeman and Carla Park; m. 1st Patricia Trenery 1962 (divorced 1993); three s. (one deceased) one d.; m. 2nd Margaret Van Wagenen Carpenter 1993; ed Milton Acad., Milton, Mass., Nat. Autonomous Univ. of Mexico, México, Yale Univ., Harvard Law School, Harvard Univ., Foreign Service Inst. School of Chinese Language and Area Studies; entered U.S. Foreign Service 1965, Vice-Consul, Madras, India 1966–68, Taiwan 1969–71, State Dept, China Desk 1971–74, Visiting Fellow, E Asian Legal Research, Harvard Univ. 1974–75, Deputy Dir, Taiwan Affairs, Dept of State 1975–76, Dir Public Programs, Dept of State 1976–77, Plans and Man. 1977–78, Dir U.S. Information Agency programs 1978–79, Acting U.S. Co-ordinator for Refugee Programs 1979, Dir, Chinese Affairs, Dept of State 1979–81, Minister, U.S. Embassy, Beijing 1981–84, U.S. Embassy, Bangkok 1984–86, Prin. Deputy Asst Sec. of State for African Affairs 1986–89, Amb. to Saudi Arabia 1989–92; Asst Sec. of Defense (Int. Security Affairs) 1993–94; Chair. Bd Projects Int. Inc. 1995–; Vice-Chair. Atlantic Council of USA 1996; Co-Chair. U.S.-China Policy Foundation 1996; Pres. Middle East Policy Council 1997; Distinguished Fellow, Inst. for Nat. Strategic Studies, Nat. Defense Univ. 1992–93; U.S. Inst. of Peace, Wash. 1994–95; mem. American Acad. of Diplomacy 1995, mem. Bd 2001; mem. Bd Wash. World Affairs Council 1998–, Pacific Pension Inst. 2001–, Asscn for Diplomatic Studies and Training 2001–; Trustee of Inst. for Defense Analyses 1996–; Forrest Prize, Yale Univ., Superior Honor Awards 1978, 1982, Presidential Meritorious Service Awards 1984, 1987, 1989, Group Distinguished Honor Award 1988, Sec. of Defense Award for Meritorious Civilian Service 1991, Distinguished Honor Award 1991, Order of King Abd Al-Aziz (First Class) 1992, Sec. of Defense Awards for Distinguished Public Service 1994. *Publications:* Cooking Western in China 1987, The Diplomat's Dictionary 1994, Arts of Power: Statecraft and Diplomacy 1997. *Leisure interests:* swimming, sailing, tennis, reading, computers, cookery. *Address:* Projects International Inc., 1800 K. Street, NW, Suite 1018, Washington, DC 20006 (Office); 2500 Massachusetts Avenue, NW, Washington, DC 20008, USA (Home). *Telephone:* (202) 333-1277 (Office). *Fax:* (202) 333-3128 (Office).

FREEMAN, Rt Hon John, PC, MBE; British diplomatist, journalist and businessman (retd); b. 19 Feb. 1915; s. of Horace Freeman; m. 1st Elizabeth Johnston 1938 (divorced 1948); m. 2nd Margaret Kerr 1948 (died 1957); m. 3rd Catherine Dove 1962 (divorced 1976); m. 4th Judith Mitchell 1976; two s. three d. and one adopted d.; ed Westminster School and Brasenose Coll., Oxford; Advertising Consultant 1937–40; active service in North Africa, Italy and North-West Europe 1940–45; MP (Lab.) Watford 1945–55; Financial Sec. to the War Office 1946–47; Under-Sec. of State for War 1947–48; Parl. Sec. to the Ministry of Supply 1948–51 (resgnd); retd from politics 1955; Deputy Ed. New Statesman 1958–61, Ed. 1961–65; British High Commr in India 1965–68; Amb. to USA 1969–71; Chair. London Weekend TV 1971–84, CEO 1971–76; Chair. and CEO LWT (Holdings) 1977–84; Visiting Prof. of Int. Relations, Univ. of Calif. (Davis) 1985–90; mem. Bd, ITN (Ind. Television News) 1971–76, Chair. 1976–81; mem. Bd, Ind. Television Publs 1971–76; Chair. Bd of Govs., British Film Inst. 1976–77; Vice-Pres. Royal TV Soc. 1975–84; Chair. Communications and Marketing Foundation 1977–79; Chair. Page and Moy (Holdings) Ltd 1979–84, Thomson-CSF Racal PLC; mem. (fmr Chair.) Hutchinson Ltd 1978–84; Trustee Reuters 1984–88; Hon. Fellow Brasenose Coll., Oxford; Hon. LLD (Univ. of S. Carolina); Gold Medal (Royal TV Soc.) 1981. *Address:* c/o Racal PLC, Phoenix House, Station Hill, Reading, England.

FREEMAN, Michael Alexander Reykers, BA, MB, B.CH., MD, FRCS; British orthopaedic surgeon; b. 17 Nov. 1931, Surrey; s. of Donald G. Freeman and Florence J. Elms; m. 1st Elisabeth Jean Freeman 1951; one s. one d.; m. 2nd Janet Edith Freeman 1959; one s. one d.; m. 3rd Patricia Gill 1968; (one s. deceased) one d.; ed Corpus Christi Coll. Cambridge and London Hosp. Medical Coll.; Intern, London Hosp.; Resident in Orthopaedic Surgery, Westminster Hosp. and Middx Hosp. 1962–68; Consultant, London Hosp.

1968–96; Hon. Consultant Royal Hosps. NHS Trust 1996–; European Ed.-in-Chief Journal of Arthroplasty 1997–; Co-founder/Dir. Biomechanics Unit, Imperial Coll. London 1956–75; fmr mem. Bd MRC; inventor prostheses and surgical procedures for replacement of hip, knee, ankle and joints of the foot; Past-Pres. British Hip Soc.; British Orthopaedic Soc.; European Fed. of Nat. Asscns. of Orthopaedics and Traumatology (EFORT) 1994–95; mem. numerous professional socs. etc.; awards include Robert Jones Medal (British Orthopaedic Asscn) 1964. *Publications:* The Scientific Basis of Joint Replacement 1977, Arthritis of the Knee 1980; Ed. Adult Articular Cartilage 1973–79; and 200 papers on hip and knee surgery. *Leisure interests:* gardening, reading. *Address:* 79 Albert Street, London, NW1 7LX, England (Home). *Telephone:* (20) 7387-0817 (Home). *Fax:* (20) 7388-5731 (Home).

FREEMAN, Morgan; American actor and director; b. 1937, Memphis, Tenn.; s. of Grafton Freeman and Mayme Revere; m. 1st Jeanette Bradshaw 1967 (divorced 1979); m. 2nd Myrna Colley-Lee 1984; four c.; ed Los Angeles City Coll.; stage debut in Niggerlover 1967; other stage appearances include: Hello Dolly, Broadway 1967, Jungle of Cities 1969, The Recruiting Officer 1969, Purlie, ANTA Theatre, New York 1970, Black Visions 1972, Mighty Gents 1978 (Clarence Derwent Award, Drama Desk Award) 1978, White Pelicans 1978, Coriolanus, New York Shakespeare Festival 1979, Mother Courage and Her Children 1980, Othello Dallas Shakespeare Festival, 1982, Medea and the Doll 1984, The Gospel at Colonus (Obie Award), Driving Miss Daisy 1987, The Taming of the Shrew; appearances in TV shows and films. *Films include:* Who Says I Can't Ride a Rainbow? 1971, Brubaker 1980, Eyewitness 1980, Harry and Son 1983, Teachers 1984, Street Smart 1987, Clean and Sober 1988, Lean On Me 1989, Johnny Handsome 1989, Driving Miss Daisy (Golden Globe Award) 1989, Glory 1989, Robin Hood 1991, Unforgiven 1992, The Power of Ore 1992, Chain Reaction 1993, The Shawshank Redemption 1994, Outbreak 1995, Se7en 1996, Moll Flanders, Amistad (NAACP Image Award) 1997, Kiss the Girls 1998, Hard Rain 1998, Water Damage 1999, Mutiny 1999, Under Suspicion 2000, Nurse Betty 2000, Along Came a Spider 2000; Dir: Bopha! 1993, Long Walk to Freedom 1999. *Address:* c/o William Morris Agency, 151 El Camino Drive, Beverly Hills, CA 90212; 2472 Broadway, #227, New York, NY 10025, USA.

FREEMAN, Raymond, MA, DPhil, DSc, FRS; British research scientist; b. Raymond Freeman, 6 Jan. 1932, Long Eaton; s. of the late Albert Freeman and Hilda F. Freeman; m. Anne-Marie Périnet-Marquet 1958; two s. three d.; ed Nottingham High School and Lincoln Coll., Oxford; Engineer, French Atomic Energy Comm., Centre d'Etudes Nucléaires de Saclay 1957–59; Sr Scientific Officer, Nat. Physical Lab. 1959–63; Man. NMR Research, Instrument Div., Varian Assocs., Palo Alto, Calif. 1963–73; Univ. Lecturer in Physical Chem. and Fellow, Magdalen Coll., Oxford 1973–87, Aldrichian Praelector in Chem. 1982–87; John Humphrey Plummer Prof. of Magnetic Resonance, Univ. of Cambridge 1987–99, Prof. Emer. 1999–, Fellow Jesus Coll., Cambridge 1987–99, Emeritus Fellow 1999–; Hon. DSc (Durham) 1998; Leverhulme Medal, Royal Soc. 1990, Longstaff Medal, RSC 1999, Queen's Medal, Royal Soc. 2002. *Publications:* A Handbook of Nuclear Magnetic Resonance 1987, Spin Choreography: Basic Steps in High Resolution NMR 1997, Magnetic Resonance in Chemistry and Medicine 2003; several scientific papers on nuclear magnetic resonance spectroscopy in various journals. *Leisure interests:* swimming, traditional jazz. *Address:* Department of Chemistry, Lensfield Road, Cambridge, CB2 1EW (Office); Jesus College, Cambridge, CB5 8BL; 29 Bentley Road, Cambridge, CB2 2AW, England (Home). *Telephone:* (1223) 336458 (Office); (1223) 323958 (Home); (1223) 339418 (Coll.). *Fax:* (1223) 336362 (Office). *E-mail:* rf110@cus.cam.ac.uk (Office).

FREEMAN, Richard, PhD; American professor of economics; b. 29 June 1953, Newburgh, NY; m. Alida Castillo; one s. one d.; ed Dartmouth and Harvard Univs.; Asherman Prof. of Econs., Harvard Univ., Program Dir, Labour Studies, NBER; Co-Dir Centre for Econ. Performance, LSE, London; Clarendon Lecturer, Oxford Univ. 1994; Lionel Robins Lecturer, LSE 1999; Pres. Soc. of Labour Economists 1997; Vice-Pres. American Econs Asscn 1997; mem. American Acad. of Arts and Sciences. *Publications:* The Over-Educated American 1976, What Do Unions Do? 1984, Labor Markets in Action 1989, Working Under Different Rules 1994, What Workers Want 1999. *Leisure interest:* professional wrestling. *Address:* National Bureau of Economic Research, 1050 Massachusetts Avenue, Cambridge, MA 02138, USA (Office); Centre for Economic Performance, London School of Economics, Houghton Street, London, WC2A 2AE, England (Office). *Telephone:* (617) 588-0301 (USA) (Office); (20) 7955-7041 (UK) (Office). *Fax:* (617) 868-2742 (USA) (Office); (20) 7955-7595 (UK) (Office). *E-mail:* freeman@nber.org (USA) (Office); a.freeman@lse.ac.uk (UK) (Office). *Website:* users.nber.org/freeman (Office).

FREETH, Peter, RA, R.E.; British artist; b. 15 April 1938, Birmingham; s. of Alfred William Freeth and Olive Freeth (née Walker); m. Mariolina Meliadó 1967; two s.; ed King Edward's Grammar School, Aston, Birmingham, Slade School, London, British School, Rome; tutor, Etching Royal Acad. Schools 1966–; works in British Museum, Victoria & Albert Museum, Arts Council of England, Fitzwilliam Museum, Cambridge, Ashmolean Museum, Oxford, Nat. Gallery, Washington, DC, USA, Metropolitan Museum, New York; Prix de Rome (engraving) 1960, Best Print, Royal Acad. 1986, Drawing/Print Prize 2002, Hunting Art Prizes, Royal Coll. of Art. *Exhibitions include:* Christopher Mendez Gallery 1987–89, Wakayama 3rd Print Biennale, Japan 1989, The Infernal Method, Royal Acad. 1990, City Lights, Royal Acad. 1991, Indian Exchange, New Delhi 2001, Print Noir, Bankside Gallery, London 2001, Word

Play (one-man exhib.), Royal Acad. 2001, Solitary City, Beardsmore Gallery, London 2002. *Leisure interests:* books, music, his grandchildren. *Address:* 83 Muswell Hill Road, London, N10 3MT, England (Home).

FREI RUIZ-TAGLE, Eduardo; Chilean politician; b. 24 June 1942, Santiago; s. of the late Eduardo Frei Montalva (fmr Pres. of Chile) and María Ruiz-Tagle; m. María Larraechea; ed Univ. of Chile; joined Christian Democrat (CD) Party 1958, fmr Pres.; CD presidential cand. Dec. 1993, Pres. of Chile March 1994–2000; C-in-C of Armed Forces 1998–2000; elected to Senate 1989; Pres. Fundación Eduardo Frei Montalva 1982–93. *Address:* c/o Partido Demócrata Cristiano, Almeda B. O'Higgins 1460, 2°, Santiago, Chile.

FREIVALDS, Laila, LLB; Swedish lawyer; b. 22 June 1942, Riga, Latvia; m. Johan Hedström; one d.; ed Uppsala Univ.; service in Dist court 1970–72, Svea Court of Appeal 1973–74; Reporting Clerk, Court of Appeal 1974; Counsel, Västerås rent tribunal 1974–75; served in Riksdag Information Office 1975–76; Sr Admin. Officer, Head. of Div. Nat. Bd for Consumer Policies 1976–79, Dir-Gen. and Consumer Ombudsman 1983–88; Minister for Justice 1988–91, 1994–2001; Legal consultant, Baltic states 1991–94. *Address:* Riksdagen, 10012 Stockholm, Sweden.

FRÉMAUX, Louis Joseph Félix; French orchestral conductor; b. 13 Aug. 1921, Aire-sur-la-Lys; m. 1st Nicole Petitbon 11948; four s. one d.; 2nd Cecily Hake 1999; ed Conservatoire Nat. Supérieur de Musique, Paris; Musical Dir and Perm. Conductor of Orchestre Nat. de l'Opéra de Monte-Carlo, Monaco 1955–66; Prin. Conductor, Rhône-Alpes Philharmonic Orchestra, Lyons 1968–71; Prin. Conductor and Musical Dir, City of Birmingham Symphony Orchestra 1969–78; Chief Conductor, Sydney Symphony Orchestra 1979–81, Prin. Guest Conductor 1982–85; guest appearances in Austria, Belgium, Holland, France, Italy, New Zealand, Norway, Switzerland, South America and Germany; Hon. DMus (Birmingham Univ.) 1978; Hon. mem. RAM 1978; 8 Grand Prix du Disque Awards; Koussevitzky Award; Chevalier Légion d'honneur; Croix de Guerre (twice). *Address:* 25 Edencroft, Wheeley's Road, Birmingham, B15 2LW, England (Home).

FRENCH, Dawn; British actress and comedienne; b. 11 Oct. 1957, Holyhead, Wales; m. Lenny Henry (q.v.) 1984; one d. (adopted); ed Manchester Univ., London Con. School of Speech and Drama; stage shows and TV series with Jennifer Saunders (q.v.); Founder and Man. Sixteen47 (fashion business); Hon. Rose, Montreux 2002. *Stage appearances include:* Silly Cow, When We are Married 1996, My Brilliant Divorce 2003. *Radio:* guest appearances on numerous talk shows. *TV appearances include:* The Comic Strip (Strike, Consuela, Five Go Mad in Dorset, Supergrass, Ken, The Yob, Suzy), French and Saunders, The Vicar of Dibley, Tender Loving Care 1993, Sex and Chocolate 1997; presenter: Swank 1987, Scoff 1988 (Channel 4). *Address:* c/o BBC, Broadcasting House, London, W1A 1AA, England.

FRENCH, Marilyn, MA, PhD; American author and critic; b. 21 Nov. 1929, New York; d. of E. C. Edwards and Isabel Hazz; m. Robert M. French, Jr 1950 (divorced 1967); one s. one d.; ed Hofstra Coll. and Harvard Univ.; secretarial and clerical work 1946–53; Lecturer, Hofstra Coll. 1964–68; professional writer 1967–; Asst Prof. Holy Cross Coll. Worcester, Mass. 1972–76; Mellon Fellow, Harvard Univ. 1976–77; New Options' Political Book Award 1986. *Television:* The Women's Room 1979. *Publications:* The Book as World—James Joyce's Ulysses 1976, The Women's Room (novel) 1977, The Bleeding Heart (novel) 1981, Shakespeare's Division of Experience 1981, Beyond Power: On Women, Men and Morals 1985, Her Mother's Daughter 1987, The War Against Women 1992, Our Father (novel) 1994, My Summer with George (novel) 1996, A Season in Hell (memoir) 1998, From Eve to Dawn (2 vols) 2002. *Address:* c/o Charlotte Sheedy Literary Agency, 65 Bleecker Street, New York, NY 10012, USA.

FREND, Rev. William Hugh Clifford, TD, BD, MA, DPhil, DD, FRSE, FBA, FSA; British professor of ecclesiastical history (retd) and clergyman; b. 11 Jan. 1916, Shotterhill, Surrey; s. of Edwin George Clifford Frend and Edith Frend (née Bacon); m. Mary Grace Crook 1951 (died 2002); one s. one d.; ed Haileybury Coll., Keble Coll. Oxford, Sorbonne, Paris and Berlin Univs; served in War Office and War Cabinet Offices and as Intelligence Officer, Political Warfare Exec. 1940–47; full-time mem. Editorial Bd, German Foreign Ministry Documents 1947–51; Research Fellow, Nottingham Univ. 1951–52; S. A. Cook Bye-Fellow, Gonville and Caius Coll. Cambridge 1952–54, 1997–; Asst Lecturer, then Lecturer in Church History and Doctrine, Cambridge Univ. 1953–69, Fellow of Gonville and Caius Coll. 1956–69, Dir of Studies in Archaeology and Anthropology 1961–69, elected Bye-Fellow Gonville and Caius Coll. 1997; Prof. of Ecclesiastical History, Glasgow Univ. 1969–84, Prof. Emer. 1984–; Priest in Charge of Barnwell and Thurning with Luddington 1984–90; Pres. Asscn of Univ. Teachers (Scotland) 1976–78; TA, rank of Capt. 1947–67; ordained Church of England 1982; Pres. Comité Int. d'Histoire Ecclésiastique Comparée 1980–83; Vice-Pres. Asscn Int. d'Etudes Patristiques 1983–87; Hon. DD (Edinburgh) 1974; TD and Clasp. *Publications:* The Donatist Church 1952, Martyrdom and Persecution in the Early Church 1965, The Early Church 1965, Religion Popular and Unpopular in the Early Christian Centuries 1976, The Rise of the Monophysite Movement (2nd Edn) 1979, The Rise of Christianity 1984, Saints and Sinners in the Early Church 1985, History and Archaeology in the Study of Early Christianity 1988, The Archaeology of Early Christianity: A History 1996, Orthodoxy, Paganism and Dissent in the Early Christian Centuries 2002, From Dogma

to History 2003. *Leisure interests:* Romano-British archaeology, collecting old stamps and coins, gardening. *Address:* The Clerks Cottage, Little Wilbraham, Cambridge, CB1 5LB, England. *Telephone:* (1223) 811731.

FRENDO, Michael, LLD; Maltese politician and lawyer; b. 29 July 1955; s. of the late Joseph Frendo and of Josephine Frendo (née Felice); m. Irene Brincat 1984; one s. two d.; ed Univs of Malta and Exeter; admitted to the Bar 1977; lecturer, Faculty of Law, Univ. of Malta 1987–; Nat. Chair. for Malta, World Jurist Ass. 1975–; Dir Press and Media Relations and Editorial Dir (newspapers) of Nationalist Party (Christian Democrat) 1982–85; MP 1987–; mem. of Parl. Ass., Council of Europe 1987–92; mem. Malta Parl. Del. to European Parl. 1987–90, 1996– (Chair. 1990–92); Parl. Sec. for Youth, Culture and Consumer Protection 1990–92; Minister for Youth and the Arts 1992–94, for Transport, Communications and Tech. 1994–96; lawyer in pvt. practice 1996–; First Vice-Chair. Jt Parl. Cttee, European Parl. and Malta Parl. 1999–; Nationalist Party (Christian Democrat); mem. European Convention (EU) 2002–. *Publications:* books and articles in local and int. magazines and journals. *Leisure interests:* reading, 'talking books'. *Address:* Mrammiti, Lourdes Lane, St Julian's, STJ 02, Malta. *Telephone:* 242713 (Office); 341835. *Fax:* 245397 (Office); 341835. *E-mail:* mfrendo@gftlex.com (Office). *Website:* www.gftlex.com (Office).

FRENI, Mirella; Italian opera singer; b. 27 Feb. 1935, Modena; d. of Ennio Freni and Gianna (née Arcelli) Freni; m. 1st Leone Magiera 1955; one d.; m. 2nd Nicola Ghiarouv; debut 1955, debut at La Scala, Milan 1962, Glyndebourne Festival 1961, Royal Opera House, Covent Garden 1961, Metropolitan Opera, NY 1965; has sung at Vienna State Opera, Rome Opera, Barcelona Gran Teatro del Liceo, Boston Opera, La Scala and at Salzburg Festival and leading opera houses throughout the world. *Recordings include:* Carmen, Falstaff, La Bohème, Madame Butterfly, Tosca, Verdi Requiem, Aïda, Don Giovanni. *Major roles include:* Nanetta in Falstaff, Mimi in La Bohème, Zerlina in Don Giovanni, Susanna, Adina in L'Elisir d'amore, Violetta in La Traviata, Desdemona in Otello. *Address:* c/o Askonas Holt Ltd, Lonsdale Chambers, 27 Chancery Lane, London, WC2A 1PF (Office); c/o John Coast Opera Management, 31 Sinclair Road, London, W14 0NS, England.

FRENKEL, Jacob A., PhD; Israeli economist; b. 8 Feb. 1943, Tel-Aviv; m. Niza Frenkel 1968; two d.; ed Univ. of Chicago, Hebrew Univ.; on staff Chicago Univ. 1973–87, various positions including Ed. Journal of Political Economy, David Rockefeller Prof. of Int. Econs; Econ. Counsellor, Dir of Research IMF 1987–91; joined Tel-Aviv Univ. 1991, Weisfeld Prof. of Econs of Peace and Int. Relations 1994–; Gov. Bank of Israel 1991–2000; Co-Chair. of Israeli del. to multilateral peace talks on Regional Econ. Devts. 1991; Chair. Bd Govs Inter-American Devt Bank 1995–96; Research Assoc. Nat. Bureau of Econ. Research; distinguished mem. Advisory Cttee Inst. for Global Econs, Korea; mem. G-7 Council, Advisory Cttee for Int. Econs, G-30, Exec. Cttee Int. Econs Asscn; Fellow Econometric Soc.; Foreign Hon. mem. American Acad. of Arts and Science, Japan Soc. of Monetary Econs; Karel Englis Prize in Econs (Czech Repub.); Gran Cruz, Orden de Mayo al Mérito (Argentina). *Publications:* numerous books and articles on int. econs and macro-econs. *Address:* Tel-Aviv University, Ramat-Aviv, 69 978 Tel-Aviv (Office). *Telephone:* (3) 6408111 (Office). *Fax:* (3) 6408601 (Office). *E-mail:* jfrenkel@exchange.ml.com.

FRENZEL, Michael; German business executive; b. 2 March 1947, Leipzig; mem. Supervisory Bd Continental AG, Deutsche Hypothekenbank AG, Hannover, Hapag-Lloyd AG, Hamburg, Thomas Cook Holding Ltd, London, Expo 2000 Hannover, Norddeutsche Landesbank, Hannover, Kreditanstalt für Wiederaufbau, Frankfurt am Main, Preussag North America, Inc., Greenwich, USA; Chair. Supervisory Bd TUI-Group GmbH, Hannover, PreussenElektra AG, Hannover; Chair. Bd. of Dirs Creditanstalt AG, Vienna; mem. Bd Preussag AG 1988–92, Vice-Chair. 1992–93, Chair. 1994–. *Address:* Preussag AG, Karl-Wiechert-Allee 4, 30625 Hannover; Postfach 610209, 30602 Hannover, Germany. *Telephone:* (511) 56600. *Fax:* (511) 5661901.

FRERE, Albert; Belgian business executive; b. 4 Feb. 1926, Fontaine-L'Evêque; s. of Oscar Frere and Madeleine Bourgeois; m. Christine Hennuy; three c.; ed Athénée Provincial du Centre, Morlanwelz; responsible for sale of Petrofina SA to Total SA, English China Clays PLC to Imetal SA and merger of CLT with TV operations of Bertelsmann AG to create CLT-Ufa; controls Total, Imetal, CLT-Ufa; Chair. Bd Frère-Bourgeois 1970, ERBE SA 1975; Electrafina SA 1982, Bruxelles Lambert SA 1987–, PetroFina SA 1990; Vice-Chair., Man. Dir Pargesa Holdings SA, Geneva 1981; Vice-Pres. TotalFina Elf 1999; Dir TFI 1996–2000, Louis Vuitton Moët Hennessy 1997; Vice-Chair. Supervisory Bd MG 2000, Bd Suez 2001; mem. Advisory Bd Power Corpn of Canada 1985, Int. Cttee of Assicurazioni Generali SpA, Trieste 1992, Suez Lyonnaise des eaux 1997, Metropole TV 2000; Grand Officier Légion d'honneur, Commdr Ordre de Léopold; Dr hc (Univ. of Laval). *Leisure interests:* golf, skiing, hunting. *Address:* Groupe Bruxelles Lambert, avenue Marnix 24, 1000 Brussels, Belgium (Office); 33 avenue Foch, 75008 Paris, France (Home); La Peupleraie, allée des Peupliers 17, 6280 Gerpinnes, Belgium. *Telephone:* (2) 547-21-67 (Office). *Fax:* (2) 547-29-98 (Office). *E-mail:* fdromelet@gbl.be (Office). *Website:* www.gbl.be (Office).

FRÈRE, Jean; Belgian diplomatist and banker (retd); b. 15 Nov. 1919, Chatou, Seine-et-Oise, France; s. of Maurice Frère and Germaine Schimp; m. Marie-Rose Vanlangenhove 1949; one s. three d.; ed Germany, Austria, Brussels Univs; with Solvay & Cie (Chemical Industries), Brussels 1941–46; entered diplomatic service 1946, Attaché (Commercial and Econ.), Belgian

Legation, Prague 1948–51; Political Div., Ministry of Foreign Affairs 1951–52; First Sec. (Econ.), Belgian Embassy, Rome 1952–58; Gen. Sec. EIB 1958–; Conseiller Banque Lambert 1962–, Man. Partner 1967–; Conseiller Général Banque Bruxelles Lambert SA 1975–81, Conseiller Général Honoraire 1981–; fmr Chair. BBL-Australia; fmr mem. of Bd and Exec. Cttee Banco di Roma Belgio; many Belgian and foreign decorations. *Leisure interests:* violin, painting, photography, electronics. *Address:* 3315 San Marco, 30124 Venice, Italy. *Telephone:* (041) 5222647. *Fax:* (041) 5222647.

FRESCO, Paolo; Italian business executive; b. 12 July 1933, Milan; m. Marlene Fresco; ed Istituto Andrea Doria, Genoa, Univ. of Genoa; law graduate, pupillage at Studio Lefebre, Genoa; practised law in Rome; set up legal dept, CGE (Compagnia Generale Elettricità, a Gen. Electric investee co.) 1962, apptd CEO CGE 1972; responsible for Italy, the Middle East and Africa, Int. Activities, Gen. Electric 1976, Head of Int. Activities 1987; restructured Nuovo Pignone (following takeover by CGE) 1992; Exec. Vice-Pres. and Gen. Man. Gen. Electric, Fairfield, Conn., USA 1992–98; mem. Bd Fiat Group 1996–2003, Chair. 1998–2003; mem. Bd Istituto Finanziario Industriale SpA 1999–2003, Giovanni Agnelli & C. SpA 2001–03; fmr Vice-Chair. Assonime (Associazione Italiana fra le Società per Azioni). *Leisure interests:* art, chess, deep-sea fishing, mountain-climbing. *Address:* c/o Fiat SpA, Palazzina Fiat, Via Nizza 250, 10126 Turin, Italy.

FRESNO LARRAÍN, HE Cardinal Juan Francisco; Chilean ecclesiastic; b. 26 July 1914, Santiago; ed Pontifical Gregorian Univ. Rome; ordained 1937; consecrated Bishop of Copiapó 1958; Archbishop of La Serena 1971–83, of Santiago de Chile 1983–90; Chancellor Univ. Católica de Chile 1983; cr. Cardinal 1985. *Address:* Erasmo Escala 1822, Santiago 30-D, Chile.

FRESTON, Thomas E., BA, MBA; American media executive; b. 22 Nov. 1945, New York; s. of Thomas E. Freston and Winifred Geng; m. Margaret Badali 1980; one s.; Dir of Marketing MTV, MTV Networks, New York 1980–81; Dir of Marketing, The Movie Channel 1982–83; Vice-Pres. Marketing MTV, MTV Networks 1983–84, Vice-Pres. Marketing 1984–85, Sr Vice-Pres. and Gen. Man. Affiliate Sales, Marketing 1985, Sr Vice-Pres. and Gen. Man. MTV, VH-1 1985–86, Pres. Entertainment 1986–87, Pres. and CEO 1987–89; Chair. and CEO MTV Networks 1989–; mem. Bd Dirs Cable Advertising Bureau 1987–, MTV Europe, London 1986–, Rock and Roll Hall of Fame 1986–; mem. Smithsonian Comm. Music in America 1987–, Cable TV Admin. and Marketing Asscn, Nat. Acad. of Cable Programming. *Leisure interests:* photography, travel, antique rugs.

FRETTON, Tony (Anthony); British architect; b. 17 Jan. 1945, London; s. of Thomas C. Fretton and May Frances Diamond; m. Susan Pearce 1963 (divorced 1988); one s. one d.; ed Architectural Asscn School of Architecture; architect, Arup Assocs, then Neylan and Ungless 1972–81; f. own architectural practice Tony Fretton Architects 1982; Unit Master AA School of Architecture 1989–91; Visiting Prof. Berlage Inst., Amsterdam, Netherlands, Ecole Polytechnique de Lausanne, Switzerland 1994–96; Prof. of Architectural and Interior Design, Tech. Univ. of Delft, Netherlands 1999–; Corp. mem. RIBA. *Major projects include:* Lisson Gallery, London 1992, Artsway Centre for Visual Arts, Sway, Hampshire 1996, Quay Arts Centre, Newport, Isle of Wight 1998, house for an art collector, Tite Street, Chelsea, London 2001, apartment bldg in Lutkenieuwstraat, Groningen, Netherlands 2001, Camden Arts Centre, London 2003, Arts Council Sculpture Gallery, Yorkshire Sculpture Park 2003. *Exhibitions include:* Building and Project Four, British Architects, 9H Gallery, London 1990, The Art of the Process, RIBA, London 1993, In Search of Public Space, de Singel, Antwerp, Belgium 1997, Architecture, Experience and Thought, Architectural Asscn, London 1998, Tony Fretton Architects – Retrospective, RIBA, London 2001. *Publications:* Tony Fretton 1995, Tony Fretton Architects: Abstraction and Familiarity 2001. *Leisure interests:* travel, film, visual arts, poetry. *Address:* 49–59 Old Street, London, EC1V 9XH, England (Office). *Telephone:* (20) 7253-1800 (Office). *Fax:* (20) 7253-1801 (Office). *E-mail:* mail@tonyfretton.co.uk (Office). *Website:* www.tonyfretton.co.uk (Office).

FRETWELL, Sir John Emsley, GCMG, MA; British diplomatist (retd); b. 15 June 1930, Chesterfield; s. of F. T. Fretwell; m. Mary Ellen Eugenie Dubois 1959; one s. one d.; ed Chesterfield Grammar School, Lausanne Univ., King's Coll., Cambridge; HM Forces 1948–50; entered diplomatic service 1953, Third Sec., Hong Kong 1954–55, Second Sec., Embassy in Beijing 1955–57, Foreign Office 1957–59, 1962–67, First Sec., Moscow 1959–62, First Sec. (Commercial), Washington, DC 1967–70, Commercial Counsellor, Warsaw 1971–73, Head of European Integration Dept (Internal), FCO 1973–76, Asst Under-Sec. of State 1976–79, Minister, Washington, DC 1980–81; Amb. to France 1982–87; Political Dir and Deputy to Perm. Under-Sec. of State, FCO 1987–90; mem. Council of Lloyd's 1991–92; Specialist Adviser, House of Lords 1992–93; Chair. Franco-British Soc. 1995–. *Leisure interests:* skiing, walking. *Address:* c/o Brooks's, St James's Street, London, SW1A 1LN, England.

FREUD, Anthony, LLB; British opera administrator and barrister; b. 30 Oct. 1957, London; s. of the late Joseph Freud and Katalin Freud (née Löwi); ed King's Coll. School, Wimbledon and King's Coll., Univ. of London; trained as barrister before joining Sadlers Wells Theatre Co. 1980–84; Co. Sec., Welsh Nat. Opera 1984, Head of Planning 1989–92, Gen. Dir 1994–; Exec. Producer, Opera, Philips Classics 1992–94. *Leisure interests:* music, theatre, cinema, visual arts, travel, cookery. *Address:* Welsh National Opera, John Street, Cardiff, CF10 5SP, Wales (Office). *Telephone:* (29) 2046-4666 (Office). *Fax:* (29) 2048-3050 (Office). *E-mail:* anthony.freud@wno.org.uk (Office). *Website:* www.wno.org.uk (Office).

FREUD, Bella Lucia; British fashion designer; b. 17 April 1961, London; d. of Lucian Freud (q.v.) and Bernardine Coverley; ed Accademia di Costuma e di Moda, Rome and Institutto Mariotti, Rome; Asst to Vivienne Westwood (q.v.) on her designer collections 1986–89; Designer and Dir Bella Freud 1989–; exhibited at London Designer Show 1991, London Fashion Week 1993; Innovative Design—The New Generation Category (British Fashion Awards) 1991. *Leisure interests:* eating, reading, looking at paintings, watching ice-skating. *Address:* 21 St Charles Square, London, W10 6EF, England. *Telephone:* (20) 8968-7579. *Fax:* (20) 8969-3602.

FREUD, Lucian, OM, CH; British painter; b. 8 Dec. 1922, Berlin; s. of the late Ernst Freud and Lucie Freud; grands. of Sigmund Freud; m. 1st Kathleen Epstein 1948 (divorced 1952); two d.; m. 2nd Lady Caroline Maureen Blackwood 1953 (divorced 1957, died 1996); ed Cen. School of Art, E Anglian School of Painting and Drawing; Teacher at Slade School of Art, London 1948–58; first one-man exhbn 1944, subsequently 1946, 1950, 1952, 1958, 1963, 1968, 1972, 1978, 1979, 1982, 1983, 1988, 1990–96; retrospectives: Hayward Gallery 1974, 1988, 1989, Tate Gallery, Liverpool 1992; works included in public collections: Tate Gallery, Nat. Portrait Gallery, Victoria and Albert Museum, Arts Council of Great Britain, British Council, British Museum, Fitzwilliam Museum, Cambridge, Nat. Museum of Wales, Cardiff, Scottish Nat. Gallery of Modern Art, Edinburgh, Walker Art Gallery, Liverpool, Ashmolean Museum of Art, Oxford, etc.; in Australia at Brisbane, Adelaide, Perth; in France at Musée Nat. d'Art Moderne, Centre Georges Pompidou, Paris; in USA at The Art Inst. of Chicago, Museum of Modern Art, New York, Cleveland Museum of Art, Ohio, Museum of Art, Carnegie Inst., Pittsburgh, Achenbaach Foundation for Graphic Arts and Fine Arts, San Francisco, The St Louis Art Museum, Hirshhorn Museum and Sculpture Garden, Smithsonian Inst., Washington, DC; Rubenspreis, City of Siegen 1997. *Address:* c/o Diana Rawstron, Goodman Derrick, 90 Fetter Lane, London, EC4A 1EQ, England.

FREUDENTHAL, Dave; American state official and lawyer; b. 1950, Thermpolis; m. Nancy Freudenthal; four c.; ed Amhurst Coll., MA, Univ. of Wyoming; economist Dept of Econ. Planning, Wyo. 1973–, State Planning Co-ordinator 1975–80; f. law office, Cheyenne 1980; U.S. Attorney, Wyo. 1994–2001; Gov. of Wyo. 2003–; fmr. Chair. Greater Cheyenne Chamber of Commerce; Founder-Dir Wyo. Student Loans Corpn; mem. Bd Wyo. Community Foundation, Wyo. State Econ. and Devt Stabilization Dept, Laramie Co. Community Action. *Leisure interest:* layreader and vestryperson in local church. *Address:* Office of the Governor, Capitol Building, 200 West 24th Street, Cheyenne, WY 82002, USA (Office).

FREY, Bruno S.; Swiss professor of economics; b. 4 May 1941, Basel; s. of Leo Frey and Julie Frey (née Bach); ed Univs. of Basel and Cambridge; Assoc. Prof. Univ. of Basel 1969–; Prof. of Econs Univ. of Konstanz 1970–77, Univ. of Zurich 1977–; Visiting Fellow All Souls Coll., Oxford 1983; Fellow Coll. of Science, Berlin 1984–85; Visiting Research Prof. Univ. of Chicago, Ill. 1990; Visiting Prof. Univ. of Rome 1996–97, Antwerp Univ. 1999; Hon. DUniv (St Gallen) 1998, (Gothenburg) 1998. *Publications include:* Economics as a Science of Human Behaviour 1992, Not Just for the Money 1997, A New Federalism for Europe 1999, Arts and Economics 2000, Happiness and Economics 2001, Inspiring Economics 2001. *Leisure interest:* travel. *Address:* Institute for Empirical Economic Research, University of Zurich, Bluemlisalpstrasse 10, CH-8006 Zurich (Office); Niederdorfstr. 29, CH-8001 Zurich, Switzerland (Home). *Telephone:* (1) 6343730. *Fax:* (1) 6344907. *E-mail:* bsfrey@iew.unizh.ch (Office). *Website:* www.iew.unizh.ch/grp/frey (Office); www.bsfrey.ch (Home).

FREYNDLIKH, Alisa Brunovna; Russian actress; b. 8 Dec. 1934; d. of Bruno Arturovich Freyndlikh; ed Leningrad Theatre Inst.; worked with Komissarzhevskaya Theatre, Leningrad 1957–61; then with Lensoviet-Theatre, Leningrad 1961–83, Gorky Theatre 1983–; worked in films 1958–; RSFSR State Prize 1976, USSR People's Artist 1981, State Prize 1995. *Films include:* Family Happiness 1970, My Life 1973, The Princess and the Pea 1977, An Everyday Novel 1977, Always With Me 1977, The Business Love Affair 1977, Stalker 1980, An Old-Fashioned Comedy 1980, Agony 1981, The Canary Cage 1984, Success 1985, The Nights Near Moscow, The Hunt. *Stage roles include:* Lady Milford in Schiller's Perfidy and Love 1990, Autumn Violins 1997 and many others. *Address:* Rubinstein str. 11, Apt. 7, 191002 St Petersburg, Russia. *Telephone:* (812) 314-88-40.

FRICK, Mario, DrIur; Liechtenstein politician and civil servant; b. 8 May 1965, Balzers; s. of Kuno and Melita Frick-Kaufmann; m. Andrea Haberlander 1992; one s. one d.; ed St Gall University, Switzerland; State Admin. Legal Service 1991–93; mem. Municipal Council of Balzers 1991–93; Deputy Head of Govt May–Dec. 1993, Head of Govt 1993–99, also Minister of Finance and Construction. *Leisure interests:* football, tennis, biking. *Address:* c/o Office of Prime Minister, Government Building, 9490 Vaduz, Liechtenstein.

FRICKE, Manfred; German professor and university administrator; b. 24 June 1936, Hainichen; m. Edith (née Feldhahn) Fricke; two s.; ed Tech. Univ. Berlin; Univ. Lecturer, Tech. Univ. Berlin 1970, Dean Faculty of Transport and Communications 1970–75, Prof. 1978–, Vice-Pres. 1978–82, Pres. 1985–93; Bundesverdienstkrenz (1st Class) 1994. *Leisure interests:* surfing, tennis, cycling. *Address:* Temmeweg 6A, 14089 Berlin, Germany.

FRIDAY, William Clyde, BS, LLB, LLD, DCL; American educator; b. 13 July 1920, Raphine, Va; s. of David Latham and Mary Elizabeth Rowan Friday; m. Ida Willa Howell 1942; three d.; ed Wake Forest Coll., N Carolina State Coll. and Univ. of N Carolina Law School; Asst Dean of Students, Univ. of N Carolina at Chapel Hill 1948–51, Acting Dean of Students 1950–51, Admin. Asst to Pres. 1951–54, Sec. of Univ. 1954–55, Acting Pres. 1956, Pres. 1956–86; Pres. The William R. Kenan, Jr Fund 1986–99; Chair. Center for Creative Leadership 1981–96, Regional Literacy Center Comm. 1989–90, Southern Growth Policies Bd 1989–, LEAF Foundation 1999–; Hon. LLD (Wake Forest Coll., Belmont Abbey, Duke Univ., Princeton Univ., Elon Coll., Davidson Coll. Kentucky and Mercer Univs.); Hon. DCL (Univ. of the South) 1976, (St Augustine's Coll.) 1986; Hon. D.P.S. (Univ. of NC at Charlotte) 1986; Hon. DFA (N Carolina School of Arts) 1987; Hon. LHD (Univ. of North Carolina at Greensboro) 1988; Nat. Humanities Medal 1997. *Leisure interests:* gardening, golf, reading. *Address:* The William R. Kenan, Jr Fund, University of North Carolina, P.O. Box 3858, Bowles Drive, Chapel Hill, NC 27515, USA.

FRIDERICHS, Hans, Dr rer. pol; German politician and banker; b. 16 Oct. 1931, Wittlich; s. of Dr. Paul Friderichs and Klara Neuwinger; m. Erika Wilhelm; two d.; Man., Rhineland-Hesse Chamber of Industry and Trade 1959–63; Deputy Business Man. FDP 1963–64, Business Man. 1964–69; mem. Bundestag 1965–69, 1976–77; Sec. of State, Ministry of Agric., Viniculture and Protection of the Environment for Rhineland Palatinate 1969–72; Fed. Minister of Econs 1972–77; Dir Dresdner Bank 1977–85, Chair. Bd Man. Dirs 1978–85; Deputy Chair. FDP 1974–77; mem. Supervisory Bd AEG Telefunken 1979, Chair. 1980–84, now Pres., Int. adviser Goldman Sachs Int., London. *Leisure interests:* art, sport. *Address:* Kappelhofgasse 2, 55116 Mainz, Germany.

FRIDJONSSON, Thordur, MA(ECON.); Icelandic economist; b. 2 Jan. 1952, Reykjavík; s. of Fridjon Thordarson and Kristin Sigurdardottir; m. Thrudur Haraldsdottir 1971; two s. two d.; ed Univ. of Iceland and Queen's Univ., Ont., Canada; Chief Economist, Fed. of Icelandic Industries 1978–80; Econ. Adviser to Prime Ministe r of Iceland 1980–86; part-time lecturer Dept of Econs, Univ. of Iceland 1979–87; Man. Dir Nat. Econ. Inst. 1987–2002; Sec.-Gen. Ministry of Industry and Commerce 1998–99; Pres. and CEO Iceland Stock Exchange 2002–; mem. Bd Dirs. Nordic Project Fund 1982–; Chair. Asscn of Icelandic Economists 1982–85, Icelandic Man. Asscn 1986–87, Econ. Research. Inst. for Agric. 1991–, Co-ordinating Cttee Iceland-Norsk Hydro 1998; Alt. Gov. EBRD 1998–99, IMF 1998–; Rep. for Iceland EDRC and OECD 1987–; mem. Econ. Policy Cttee OECD 1987–; John Hicks Fellowship (Queen's Univ.). *Publications:* Icelandic Economy 1984; numerous articles in journals and books. *Leisure interests:* outdoor activities and sport. *Address:* Iceland Stock Exchange, Tryggvagata 11, 101 Reykjavík (Office); Engjasel 9, 109 Reykjavík, Iceland. *Telephone:* 5252800 (Office); 5676233 (Home). *Fax:* 5252888. *Website:* www.icex.is (Office).

FRIDMAN, Mikhail Maratovich; Russian business executive; b. 21 April 1964, Lvov, Ukraine; m.; two c.; ed Moscow Inst. of Steel and Alloys; with Electrostal, Moscow region 1986–88; Founder Alfa-Foto, Alfa-Eco, Alfa-Capital 1988, Chair. Bd of Dirs Alfa-Bank (later Alfa-Group) 1991–, Alfa-Consortium 1996–, Alfa Commercial Bank 1998–; mem. Bd of Dirs Russian Public TV (ORTV) 1995–98, Oil Co. SIDANKO 1996–2000, Perekrestok Trade House 1998–; Founder, Vice-Pres. Russian Jewish Congress 1996–, Head Cttee on Culture 1996–; mem. Council on Banking Activity, Fed. Govt. 1996–, Council on Business, Council of Ministers 2001–. *Address:* Commercial Innovation Bank Alfa-Bank, Mashy Poryvayevoy str. 9, 107078 Moscow, Russia (Office). *Telephone:* (095) 755-58-55 (Office). *Fax:* (095) 974-64-74 (Office). *E-mail:* skrasnova@alfabank.ru (Office).

FRIDRIKSSON, Fridrik Thor; Icelandic film director; b. 12 May 1954; s. of Fridrik Gudmundson and Gudridur Hjaltested; m. (divorced); one s. one d.; founder Reykjavik Film Festival; est. Icelandic Film Corp. 1984. *Films:* Eldsmiðurinn (The Blacksmith) 1981, Rokk í Reykjavik (Rock in Reykjavik) 1982, Kúreakr norðursins (Icelandic Cowboys) 1984, Hringurinn (The Circle) 1985, Skytturnar (White Whales) 1987, Flugprá (Sky Without Limit) 1989, Englakroppar (Pretty Angels) 1990, Börn náttúrunnar (Children of Nature) 1991, Bíódagar (Movie Days) 1994, Á köldum klaka (Cold Fever) 1995, Djöflaeyjan (Devil's Island) 1996, Englar alheimsins (Angels of the Universe) 2000. *Address:* Icelandic Film Corporation, Hverfisgata 46, 101 Reykjavik (Office); Bjarkargata 8, 101 Reykjavik, Iceland (Home). *Telephone:* 5512260 (Office); 5528566 (Home). *Fax:* 5525154 (Office). *E-mail:* icecorp@vortex.is (Office); f.thor@vortex.is (Home).

FRIED, Charles, MA, LLB; American lawyer; b. 15 April 1935, Prague, Czechoslovakia; s. of Anthony Fried and Marta (Wintersteinova) Fried; m. Anne Sumerscale 1959; one s. one d.; ed Princeton, Oxford and Columbia Univs; law clerk to Assoc. Justice John M. Harlan, U.S. Supreme Court 1960; mem. Faculty, Harvard Law School 1961–, Prof. of Law 1965–85, Carter Prof. of Gen. Jurisprudence 1981–85, 1989–95, Prof. Emer., Distinguished Lecturer 1995–, Beneficial Prof. of Law 1999–; Deputy Solicitor-Gen. and Counsellor to Solicitor-Gen. 1985, Solicitor-Gen. of USA 1985–89; Assoc. Justice Supreme Judiciary Court of Mass., Boston 1995–99. *Publications:* An Anatomy of Values 1970, Medical Experimentation: Personal Integrity and Social Policy 1974, Right and Wrong 1978, Contract as Promise: A Theory of

Contractual Obligation 1981, Order and Law: Arguing the Reagan Revolution 1991; contributions to legal and philosophical journals. *Address:* Harvard Law School, 1545 Massachusetts Avenue, Cambridge, MA 02138 (Office); 110 Irving Street, Cambridge, MA 02138, USA (Home). *Telephone:* (617) 495-4636 (Office); (617) 864-4172 (Home). *Fax:* (617) 496-4865 (Office). *E-mail:* fried@ law.harvard.edu (Office).

FRIEDAN, Betty; American feminist leader; b. 4 Feb. 1921, Peoria, Illinois; d. of Harry and Miriam (née Horwitz) Goldstein; m. Carl Friedan 1947 (divorced 1969); two s. one d.; ed Smith Coll.; f. Nat. Org. for Women 1966, first Pres. 1966–70, Chair. 1970–72; Organizer Nat. Women's Political Caucus 1971, Int. Feminist Congress 1973, First Women's Bank & Trust Co. 1973; Visiting Prof. of Sociology, Temple Univ. 1972, Yale Univ. 1974, Queen's Coll. 1975; Contributing Ed., McCalls Magazine 1971–74; Jt Chair. Nat. Comm. for Women's Equality; numerous lectures in USA and Europe; Distinguished Visiting Prof. George Mason Univ. 1995, Mount Vernon Coll. 1996; Visiting Prof., School of Journalism and Social Work, Cornell Univ. 1998–; mem. PEN; Dr hc (Columbia) 1994; American Humanist Award 1975. *Publications:* The Feminine Mystique 1963, It Changed My Life: Writings on the Women's Movement 1976, The Second Stage 1982, The Fountain of Age 1993, Through the Prison of Gender 1998, Life So Far: A Memoir 2000; articles in McCall's, Harper's, etc. *Address:* 2022 Columbia Road, NW, Washington, DC 20009, USA.

FRIEDEL, Jacques, PhD, D.ÈS SC.; French physicist; b. 11 Feb. 1921, Paris; s. of Edmond Friedel and Jeanne Friedel (née Bersier); m. Mary Winifred Horder 1952; two s.; ed Ecole Polytechnique, Ecole des Mines de Paris, Bristol Univ., Paris Univ.; Mining engineer, Ecole des Mines de Paris 1948–56; Maître de Conférences, Univ. de Paris 1956–59; Prof. of Solid State Physics, Univ. de Paris (later Paris Sud) 1959–89, Dir Third Cycle: Exact and Nat. Sciences 1974–77; Pres. Section 21, Consultative Cttee on Univs. 1975–80; Pres. Consultative Comm. of Scientific and Tech. Research 1978–80; mem. Acad. of Sciences 1977–, Vice-Pres. 1991–92, Pres. 1992–94; Pres. Observatoire nat. de la lecture 1994–2001; Hon. mem. Royal Soc., London, NAS, American Acad. of Sciences and Letters, Swedish Acad. of Sciences, Leopoldina, Belgian Royal Acad. of Sciences, Brazilian Acad. of Sciences, American Physical Soc., Inst. of Physics, Max Planck Gesellschaft; Hon. DSc (Bristol) 1977, (Lausanne) 1979, (Geneva) 1992, (Cambridge) 1995, (Zagreb) 1995; Grand Officier, Légion d'honneur, Commdr Ordre Nat. du Mérite, Commdr Order of Scientific Merit (Brazil); Gold Medal Conseil Nat. de la Recherche Scientifique, Soc. Francaise de Metallurgie, Acta Metallurgica (USA); several international scientific awards and prizes. *Publications:* Dislocations 1956, Graine de Mandarin 1994. *Leisure interest:* gardening. *Address:* 2 rue Jean-François Gerbillon, 75006 Paris, France (Home). *Telephone:* 1-42-22-25-85.

FRIEDKIN, William; American film director; b. 29 Aug. 1939, Chicago; s. of Louis Friedkin and Rae Green; m. 1st Lesley-Anne Down (divorced); one s.; m. 2nd Sherry Lansing (q.v.). *Films directed include:* Good Times 1967, The Night They Raided Minsky's 1968, The Birthday Party 1968, The Boys in the Band 1970, The French Connection 1971 (Acad. Award for Best Picture, 1971), The Exorcist 1973, Sorcerer 1977, The Brinks Job 1979, Cruising 1980, Deal of the Century 1983, To Live and Die in LA 1985, C.A.T. Squad 1986, The Guardian 1990, Rampage 1992, Blue Chip 1993, Jade 1995, Twelve Angry Men 1997, Rules of Engagement 1999, Night Train 2000; several TV films. *Address:* c/o ICM, 8942 Wilshire Blvd., Los Angeles, CA 90211, USA.

FRIEDMAN, Jane; American publishing executive; joined Random House 1968; fmr Pres. Random House Audio; fmr Exec. Vice-Pres. Knopf Publishing Group, Random House Inc.; fmr Publr Vintage Books; fmr mem. Random House Exec. Cttee; Pres., CEO HarperCollins 1997–. *Address:* c/o Harper-Collins, 10 East 53rd Street, New York, NY 10022-5299, USA (Office). *Telephone:* (212) 207-7000 (Office). *Fax:* (212) 207-7759 (Office). *Website:* www .harpercollins.com (Office).

FRIEDMAN, Jerome Isaac, PhD; American professor of physics; b. 28 March 1930, Chicago; s. of Selig Friedman and Lillian Warsaw; m. 1st 1956; two s. two d.; m. 2nd Tania Baranovsky 1972; ed Univ. of Chicago; Research Assoc. Univ. of Chicago 1956–57, Stanford Univ. 1957–60; Asst Prof., Assoc. Prof. Mass. Inst. of Tech. 1960–67, Prof. of Physics 1967–, Dir Lab. of Nuclear Science 1980–83, Head, Dept of Physics 1983–88, William A. Coolidge Prof. 1988–90, Inst. Prof. 1990–; mem. NAS; Fellow, American Acad. of Arts and Sciences, American Physical Soc.; Hon. DSc (Trinity Coll.); co-recipient, W. K. H. Panofsky Prize (American Physical Soc.) 1989, Nobel Prize in Physics (Jt-recipient) 1990. *Leisure interests:* painting, Asian ceramics, African Art. *Address:* Department of Physics, Room 24-512, Massachusetts Institute of Technology, Cambridge, MA 02139-4307 (Office); 75 Greenough Street, Brookline, MA 02146, USA (Home). *Telephone:* (617) 253-7585 (Office). *Fax:* (617) 253-1755 (Office).

FRIEDMAN, Milton, PhD; American economist; b. 31 July 1912, New York; s. of Jeno Saul Friedman and Sarah Esther Friedman; m. Rose Director 1938; one s. one d.; ed Rutgers Univ., Chicago and Columbia Univs; Assoc. Economist, Nat. Resources Cttee 1935–37, Nat. Bureau of Econ. Research 1937–45 (on leave 1940–45), 1948–81; Prin. Economist, Div. of Tax Research, US Treasury Dept 1941–43; Assoc. Dir Statistical Research Group, Div. of War Research, Columbia Univ., New York 1943–45; Prof. of Econs, Univ. of Chicago 1948–83, Prof. Emer. 1983–; Sr Research Fellow, Hoover Inst. of Stanford Univ., Calif. 1976–; Bd of Eds Econometrica; mem. Advisory Bd,

Journal of Money, Credit and Banking 1968–94; Pres. American Econ. Asscn 1967; mem. President's Comm. on All-Volunteer Armed Force 1969–70, on White House Fellows 1971–73, President's Econ. Policy Advisory Bd 1981–88; Pres. Mont Pelerin Soc. 1970–72, Western Econ. Asscn 1984–85; mem. NAS 1973–; numerous hon. degrees; Nobel Prize for Econ. Science 1976; Inst. for World Capitalism Prize on Moral-Cultural Affairs 1993; Grand Cordon First Class Order of the Sacred Treasure (Japan) 1986; Nat. Medal of Science (USA) 1988; Presidential Medal of Freedom (USA) 1988; Templeton Hon. Rolls Lifetime Achievement Award 1997, Goldwater Award 1997, James U. Blanchard III Freedom Award 2001. *Television:* presenter and host of Free to Choose 1980, Tyranny of the Status Quo 1984. *Publications:* Income from Independent Professional Practice (with Simon Kuznets) 1946, Sampling Inspection (with others) 1948, Essays in Positive Economics 1953, A Theory of the Consumption Function 1957, A Program for Monetary Stability 1960, Capitalism and Freedom 1962, Price Theory: a Provisional Text 1962, A Monetary History of the United States 1867–1960 (with Anna J. Schwartz) 1963, Inflation: Causes and Consequences 1963, The Balance of Payments: Free Versus Flexible Exchange Rates (with Robert V. Roosa) 1967, Dollars and Deficits 1968, Optimum Quantity of Money and Other Essays 1969, Monetary Statistics of the United States (with Anna J. Schwartz) 1970, A Theoretical Framework for Monetary Analysis 1972, Social Security: Universal or Selective (with Wilbur J. Cohen) 1972, An Economist's Protest 1972, Money and Economic Development 1973, Milton Friedman's Monetary Framework (with others) 1974, Price Theory 1976, Tax Limitation, Inflation and the Role of Government 1978, Free to Choose (with Rose D. Friedman) 1980, Monetary Trends in the United States and the United Kingdom (with Anna J. Schwartz) 1982, Bright Promises, Dismal Performance: An Economist's Protest (with William R. Allen) 1983, Tyranny of the Status Quo (with Rose D. Friedman) 1984, The Essence of Friedman 1987, Money Mischief 1992, Friedman and Szasz on Liberty and Drugs (with Thomas S. Szasz) 1992, Two Lucky People: Memoirs (with Rose D. Friedman) 1998. *Leisure interests:* carpentry, talk. *Address:* Hoover Institution, Stanford University, Stanford, CA 94305-6010, USA (Office). *Telephone:* (650) 723-0580 (Office). *Fax:* (650) 723-1687 (Office).

FRIEDMAN, Stephen, BA, LLB; American government official and lawyer; b. 1938; m. Barbara Benioff Friedman; ed Cornell Univ., Columbia Univ. Law School, NY; fmr law clerk to Fed. Dist Court Judge; attorney, New York City 1963–66; joined Goldman Sachs & Co. 1966, Pnr 1973, Man. Cttee 1982, Vice-Chair. and Co-COO 1987–90, Co-Chair. 1990–92, Chair. and Sr Pnr 1992–94; Sr Prin. Marsh & McLennan Capital Inc. –2002; Asst to Pres. for Econ. Policy and Dir Nat. Econ. Council, White House Dec. 2002–; Dir Goldman Sachs & Co. 2002–, Fannie Mae, Wal-Mart Stores Inc., Nat. Bureau of Econ. Research, In-Q-Tel; mem. Pres.'s Foreign Advisory Council; fmr mem. Council on Foreign Relations; Chair. Emer. Bd of Trustees, Columbia Univ.; Chair. Finance Cttee, Memorial Sloan-Kettering Cancer Center; Chair. Emer. Exec. Cttee, The Brookings Inst.; Eastern Collegiate Wrestling Champion 1959, AAU Nat. Wrestling Champion 1961, Maccabiah Games Gold Medal 1961, NCAA Silver Anniversary Medal for outstanding athletic and career achievements 1984. *Address:* National Economic Council, The White House, 1600 Pennsylvania Avenue NW, Washington, DC 20502, USA (Office). *Telephone:* (202) 456-1413 (Office). *Website:* www.whitehouse.gov/nec (Office).

FRIEDMAN, Thomas L., MPhil; American journalist; b. 20 July 1953, Minneapolis; m. Ann Friedman; two d.; ed Brandeis Univ., St Antony's Coll. Oxford, UK; joined The New York Times 1981, Beirut Bureau Chief 1982–84, Israel Bureau Chief 1984–88, Washington Chief Diplomatic Corresp., Chief White House Corresp., Chief Econs Corresp., Foreign Affairs Columnist 1995–; Pulitzer Prize for Int. Reporting 1983, 1988, for Distinguished Commentary 2002. *Publications include:* From Beirut to Jerusalem (Nat. Book Award for Non-Fiction, Overseas Press Club Award) 1989, The Lexus and the Olive Tree (Overseas Press Club Award for Best Non-Fiction Book on Foreign Policy) 2000, Longitudes and Latitudes: America in the Age of Terrorism 2002. *Address:* The New York Times, 229 West 43rd Street, New York, NY 10036, USA (Office). *Telephone:* (212) 556-1234 (Office). *Website:* www .nytimes.com (Office).

FRIEL, Brian, FRSL; Irish writer; b. 9 Jan. 1929, Omagh, Co. Tyrone; s. of Patrick Friel and Christina MacLoone; m. Anne Morrison 1954; one s. four d.; ed St Columb's Coll., Derry, St Patrick's Coll., Maynooth, St Joseph's Training Coll., Belfast; taught in various schools 1950–60; full-time writer 1960–; mem. Irish Acad. of Letters, Aosdana 1983–, American Acad. of Arts and Letters; Hon. Fellow Univ. Coll. Dublin; Hon. DLitt (Nat. Univ. of Ireland) 1983, (Queen's Univ., Belfast) 1992, (Georgetown Univ., Washington, DC, Dominican Coll., Chicago). *Plays:* Philadelphia, Here I Come! 1965, The Loves of Cass McGuire 1967, Lovers 1968, The Mundy Scheme 1969, Crystal and Fox 1970, The Gentle Island 1971, The Freedom of the City 1973, Volunteers 1975, Living Quarters 1976, Aristocrats 1979, Faith Healer 1979, Translations 1981 (Ewart-Biggs Memorial Prize, British Theatre Asscn Award), Three Sisters (trans.) 1981, The Communication Cord 1983, Fathers and Sons 1987, Making History (Best Foreign Play, New York Drama Critics Circle 1989) 1988, A Month in the Country 1990, Dancing at Lughnasa 1990, The London Vertigo 1991, Wonderful Tennessee 1993, Selected Stones 1994, Molly Sweeney 1995, Give Me Your Answer, Do! 1997, Uncle Vanya (after Chekov) 1998, The Yalta Game 2001, The Bear (trans.) 2002, Afterplay 2002. *Publications:* The Last of the Name (ed.) 1988; collected stories: The Saucer of

Larks 1962, The Gold in the Sea 1966. *Leisure interests:* reading, trout-fishing, slow tennis. *Address:* Drumaweir House, Greencastle, County Donegal, Ireland.

FRIEND, Lionel; British orchestral conductor; b. 13 March 1945, London; s. of Norman A. C. Friend and Moya L. Dicks; m. Jane Hyland 1969; one s. two d.; ed Royal Grammar School, High Wycombe, R.C.M., London, London Opera Centre; with Welsh Nat. Opera 1969–72, Glyndebourne Festival/Touring Opera 1969–72; 2nd Kapellmeister, Staatstheater, Kassel, FRG 1972–75; Conductor ENO 1976–89; Musical Dir New Sussex Opera 1989–96; Guest Conductor BBC Symphony, Philharmonia, Nash Ensemble, Scottish Chamber, Royal Ballet and in Australia, Brazil, Denmark, France, Hungary, Norway, Spain, Germany, Netherlands, Belgium, Sweden, USA. *Leisure interests:* reading, theatre, cooking. *Address:* 136 Rosendale Road, London, SE21 8LG, England. *Telephone:* (20) 8761-7845. *E-mail:* lionelfriend@hotmail .com (Home).

FRIGGEBO, Birgit; Swedish politician; b. 25 Dec. 1941, Falköping; m. 1st Lennart Rydberg 1968, one s.; m. 2nd Bo Södersten 1997; accountant in estate agency 1960; chief negotiator Swedish Asscn of Municipal Housing Cos. (SABO) 1969–76, rep. at Rents and Tenancies Court of Appeal 1975–76; Chair. Liberal Youth Stockholm 1963–64, mem. Exec. Cttee Liberal Party Nat. Youth League 1964–69; mem. Nat. Bd Liberal Party 1972–93, First Vice-Chair. and mem. Exec. Cttee 1983–93, Sec. 1983–85, Leader Parl. Liberal Party Group Council 1990–91; mem. Stockholm Social Welfare Bd 1967–70, Comm. on Housing for Young Persons 1968–70, Stockholm County Council 1971–76; MP 1979–82, 1985–97; Minister of Housing and Physical Planning 1976–82, of Cultural Affairs and Immigration 1991–94; Chair. Fourth Nat. Swedish Pension Fund 2000–; mem. Parl. Standing Cttee on the Constitution 1985–91, 1994–97 (Chair. 1994–97), mem. Bd Parl.'s Cen. Services Office 1986–91, Cttee on Child Pornography 1995–97, Cttee on Local Pvt. Radio 1996–97; mem. Nat. Debt Office, Data and Access to Information Comm., Cttee on Swedish Security 1985–88; Co-Gov. Jönköping 1998–; mem. Bd Nat. Agency for Govt Employers 1999–, Nat. Courts Admin. 2000–; mem. Bd Salusansvar Sakförsäkringar AB, Salus Bank AB 1998–2001; Chair. Swedish Univ. Coll. of Opera 2003–. *Address:* County Administrative Board, 551 86 Jönköping (Office); Skolgatan 5, 55316 Jönköping, Sweden (Home). *Telephone:* (36) 395001 (Office). *Fax:* (36) 150164 (Office). *E-mail:* birgit.friggebo@ f.lst.se (Office).

FRIGGIERI, Oliver, PhD; Maltese academic, poet, novelist and literary critic; b. 27 March 1947, Floriana; s. of Charles Friggieri and Mary Galea; m. Eileen Cassar; one d.; ed Univ. of Malta, Catholic Univ. of Milan; Prof. and Head of Dept of Maltese, Univ. of Malta 1987–; Founder mem. Academia Internationale Mihai Eminescu, Craiova 1995; mem. Asscn Int. des Critiques Litteraires, Paris; participant and guest speaker at 70 int. congresses throughout Europe; guest poet at numerous poetry recitals in maj. European cities; Co-founder of Saghtar nat. student magazine 1971; Literary Ed. of In-Nazzjon 1971–82; First Prize for Literary Criticism XIV Concorso Silarus 1982, Premio Internazionale Mediterraneo, Palermo 1988, Malta Govt Literary Award 1988, 1996, 1997, 1999, Premio Sampieri per la Poesia 1995; mem. Nat. Order of Merit 1999. *Achievements:* author of first oratorio in Maltese: Pawlu ta' Matta 1985. *Publications include:* poetry: Ribelle gentile 1988, A Distraught Pilgrim, Le rituel du crépuscule 1991, Nous sommes un désir, Poeziji 1998, Noi siamo un desiderio 1999. novels: Il-Gidba 1977, L-Istramb 1980, Fil-Parlament ma Jikbrux Fjuri 1986, A Turn of the Wheel 1987, La Menzogna 1997, Gizimin li qatt ma jiftah 1998, It-tfal jigu bil-vapuri 2000. short stories: Stejjer ghal Qabel Jidlam 1986, Fil-Gzira Taparsi jikbru I-fjuri 1991, Koranta and Other Short Stories from Malta 1994. literary criticism: La cultura italiana a Malta 1978, Storia della letteratura maltese 1986, Dizzjunarju ta' Termini Letterarji 1986, Il-Kuxjenza Nazzjonali Maltija 1995; numerous works translated into various languages and articles in academic journals and newspapers. *Leisure interest:* gardening. *Address:* Faculty of Arts, University of Malta, Msida, Malta (Office).

FRIMPONG-ANSAH, Jonathan Herbert, PhD; Ghanaian banker; b. 22 Oct. 1930, Mampong, Ashanti; s. of Hammond Owusu-Ansah and Elizabeth Achiaa; m. Selina Agyemang 1954; three s. one d.; ed Univ. of Ghana, London School of Economics and Univ. of Salford, UK; Statistician, Ghana Govt 1954–59; Bank of Ghana, Dir of Research 1961–65, Deputy Gov. 1965–68, Gov. 1968–73; Chair. Ghana Diamond Marketing Bd 1969–72; Dir Volta River Authority 1972–; Chair. Ashanti Goldfields Corpn Ltd 1973–96; Vice-Chair. Deputies of the Cttee of the Bd of Govs. on Reform of the Int. Monetary System and Related Issues, IMF, Wash. 1973–74; Consultant World Bank 1975; Chair. Standard Bank Ghana, Ltd, Accra 1975–81, Akosombo Textiles Ltd 1975–; Chair. UN Experts Group on Establishment of African-Caribbean-Pacific Investment and Trade Bank 1978–79 Dir SIFIDA, Geneva 1981; Fellow Center for Int. Affairs, Harvard 1978–, Ghana Acad. of Arts and Sciences 1979–; Hon. Prof. of Finance, Univ. of Ghana 1979–. *Publications:* Trade and Development in Africa, 1991, Saving for Africa's Economic Recovery 1991, The Vampire State in Africa—Political Economy of Decline in Ghana 1991; articles in Economic Bulletin (Ghana), Bulletin of the Inter Credit Bank (Geneva), Univ. of Ghana journals; contribs. in International Monetary Reform—Documents of the Committee of Twenty 1974. *Leisure interest:* art. *Address:* 3 Eleventh Road, Ridge, P.O. Box C1582, Accra, Ghana. *Telephone:* (21) 227711.

FRISELL, Bill; American jazz musician and composer; b. 18 March 1951, Baltimore; one d.; ed Univ. of Northern Colorado, Berklee Coll. of Music, Boston; has written compositions for TV series Tales From the Far Side; numerous recordings include Gone, Just Like a Train and works by Aaron Copland, Charles Ives, John Philip Sousa. *Albums include:* In Line, Rambler, Lookout for Hope, Before We Were Born, Is That You?, Where in the World?, Have a Little Faith and guest appearances on numerous other albums.

FRISINGER, Haakan H. J., MEng; Swedish business executive; b. 8 Dec. 1928, Skoevde; s. of Anders Johansson and Anna Johansson; m. Annakarin Lindholm 1953; two s. one d.; ed Chalmers Univ. of Tech., Gothenburg and Harvard Business School; Head, Man. Unit Product and Production Co-ordination, AB Volvo 1966; Head, Volvo Köping Plant 1971; Head of Volvo Car Production and mem. Corporate Exec. AB Volvo 1975; Head, Volvo Car Industry Div. and Exec. Vice-Pres. AB Volvo 1977; Pres. Volvo Car Corpn 1978; Pres. and COO, AB Volvo 1983–87, Dir 1994–, Chair. 1997–. *Leisure interests:* music, art, golf, sport, hunting. *Address:* AB Volvo, 405 08 Gothenburg, Sweden. *Telephone:* 31-59-00-90.

FRIST, Bill, MD; American politician and transplant surgeon; b. 22 Feb. 1952, Nashville, Tenn.; m. Karyn McLaughlin; three s.; Founder, transplant surgeon, Vanderbilt Transplant Medical Center 1986–; Senator from Tennessee 1995–, Senate Majority Leader 2002–; Chair. Nat. Representative Senatorial Cttee 2001–; Republican. *Address:* c/o United States Senate, 416 Russell Senate Office Bldg, Washington, DC 20510-4205, USA. *E-mail:* senator_frist@frist.senate.gov (Office).

FRITSCHE, Claudia; Liechtenstein diplomatist; b. 26 July 1952; m. Manfred Fritsche 1980; ed business and language schools in Schaan and St Gall; personal secretary to Head of Govt 1970–74; joined Office for Foreign Affairs 1978; Diplomatic Collaborator 1980–87; Sec. to Liechtenstein Parl. del. to Council of Europe and EFTA; First Sec., Liechtenstein Embassy, Berne 1987–90, Vienna (concurrently) 1989–90; Perm. Rep. of Liechtenstein to UN 1990–2002; Pres. Int. Asscn of Perm. Reps to the UN (IAPR) 1999–2002; Amb. of Liechtenstein to the USA 2002–; Certificate and Medal of Recognition Foreign Policy Asscn 2002. *Address:* 1300 Eye Street, NW, Suite 550W, Washington, DC 10017, USA (Office). *Telephone:* (202) 216-0460 (Office). *Fax:* (202) 216-0459 (Office). *E-mail:* Bettina.Marxer@was.rep.llv.li (Office).

FRITZ, Johann P.; Austrian press and broadcasting executive; b. 15 April 1940, Ober-Eggendorf; s. of Johann Fritz and Amalia Piringer; m. Brigitte Weick 1964; one d.; ed Univ. of Vienna, Western Reserve Univ., Cleveland, Ohio and Hochschule für Welthandel, Vienna; Sec.-Gen. Österreichische Jungarbeiterbewegung 1964–67, Exec. Vice-Pres. 1967–70; Ed. Der Jungarbeiter 1964–70, MC Report 1970–75; Deputy Sec.-Gen. Österreichischer Wirtschaftsbund 1970–75; Man. Dir Die Presse 1975–91; Man. Dir Kabel TV Wien 1975–83; Founder and Co-Man. Radio Adria 1977–84, Consultant 1984–90; Co-founder, Sec. Gen. and Report Ed.Man.-Club 1970–75; Founder and Chair., Cable TV Asscn, Austrian Chamber of Commerce 1980–90; mem. Supervisory Bd Telekabel Wien GmbH 1983–98, Bd Austrian Press Agency (APA) 1982–91; Dir Int. Press Inst. (IPI) 1992–; Publr Jazz Information (monthly) 1967–70, Cable TV: Project Study for Austria 1975, iPi Report 1992–97; mem. numerous professional asscns. etc.; life-time title "Senator" conferred by Int. Asscn for Newspaper and Media Tech. 1980; life-time Kommerzialrat Award 1991; life-time title "Professor" conferred 2000. *Television:* scripts for jazz productions 1968–73. *Publications:* Little Jazzbook of Vienna. *Leisure interests:* skiing, ice-skating, jazz, art deco, jugendstil. *Address:* c/o Int. Press Inst., Speigelgasse 2, A-1010 Vienna (Office); Hasenauerstrasse 37, 1180 Vienna, Austria. *Telephone:* (1) 5129011. *Fax:* (1) 5129014. *E-mail:* ipi@freemedia.at. *Website:* www.freemedia.at.

FRITZ, Walter Helmut; German writer; b. 26 Aug. 1929, Karlsruhe; s. of Karl T. Fritz and Hedwig Fritz; ed Univ. of Heidelberg; poetry teacher, Univ. of Mainz; has lectured in Europe, America and Africa; mem. Akad. der Wissenschaften und der Literatur, Mainz, Bayerische Akad. der Schönen Künste, Munich, Deutschen Akad. für Sprache und Dichtung, Darmstadt, PEN; Stuttgarter Literaturpreis, Villa Massimo-Stipendium, Georg-Trakl-Preis. *Publications:* poetry and prose, including: Gesammelte Gedichte 1979, Wunschtraum Alptraum (poems) 1981, Werkzeuge der Freiheit (poems) 1983, Cornelias Traum, Aufzeichnungen 1985, Immer einfacher immer schwieriger (poems) 1987, Zeit des Sehens (prose) 1989, Mit einer Feder aus den Flügen des Ikarus, Ausgewählte Gedichte, Mit einem Nachwort von Harald Hartung 1989, Die Schlüssel sind vertauscht (poems) 1992, Gesammelte Gedichte 1979–1994 1994, Das offene Fenster 1997, Zugelassen im Leben (poems) 1999. *Address:* Kolbergerstrasse 2A, 76139 Karlsruhe, Germany. *Telephone:* (721) 683346.

FRODSHAM, John David, MA, PhD, FAHA; British/Australian university professor and consultant; b. 5 Jan. 1930, Cheshire, UK; s. of J. K. Frodsham and W. E. Frodsham; m. Tan Beng-choo 1964; three s. two d.; ed Emmanuel Coll., Cambridge, Australian Nat. Univ.; Lecturer in English Univ. of Baghdad 1956–58, in Oriental Studies, Univ. of Sydney 1960–61, in Far Eastern History, Univ. of Malaya 1961–65, Sr Lecturer in Far Eastern History, Univ. of Adelaide 1965–67, Reader in Chinese, ANU 1967–71; Prof. of Comparative Literature, Univ. of Dar es Salaam 1971–73, Foundation Prof. English and Comparative Literature, Murdoch Univ. 1972–; Visiting Prof. Cornell 1965, Hawaii 1968, American Coll. of Greece 1985, Tamkang Univ. of Taiwan 1985; Visiting Fellow, Inst. of E Asian Philosophies, Univ. of Singapore 1989; Sr Teaching Fellow, NTU, Singapore 1990–92; Consultant

Ausean Int. Ltd 1987–89; Fellow and Pres. Professors' World Peace Acad. 1983; Pres. Australasian Soc. of Physical Research 1979–; mem. Australia–China Council 1979–83; Current Affairs Commentator for ABC 1958–. *Publications:* An Anthology of Chinese Verse, Vol. 1 1967, The Murmuring Stream (2 vols) 1967, The Poems of Li Ho 1970, New Perspectives in Chinese Literature 1971, The First Chinese Embassy to the West 1973, Foundations of Modernism: Modern Poetry 1980, Goddesses, Ghosts and Demons: The Collected Poems of Li He 1983, Classicism and Romanticism: A Comparative Period Study (4 vols) 1986, Turning Point 1988, Education for What? 1990, The Crisis of the Modern World and Traditional Wisdom 1990, The Decline of Sensate Culture 1990, Structure, Thought and Reality: A Reader (2 vols) 2000. *Leisure interests:* psychical research, sailing, swimming. *Address:* School of Arts, Murdoch University, Murdoch, Western Australia 6150 (Office); 24 Riversea View, Buckland Hill, Mosman Park, Western Australia 6107, Australia (Home). *Telephone:* (8) 9360-6203 (Office); (8) 9284-3451 (Home). *Fax:* (8) 9284-3451 (Home). *E-mail:* Frodsham@central.murdoch.edu.au.

FROGGATT, Sir Leslie (Trevor), Kt; Australian business executive; b. 8 April 1920; s. of Leslie Froggatt and Mary H. Brassey; m. Elizabeth Grant 1945; three s.; ed Birkenhead Park School, Cheshire; joined Asiatic Petroleum Co., Ltd 1937; Shell Singapore, Shell Thailand, Shell Malaya 1947–54, Shell Egypt 1955–56; Dir of Finance, Gen. Man. Kalimantan, Borneo and Deputy Chief Rep. PT Shell Indonesia 1958–62; Area Co-ordinator, S. Asia and Australasia, Shell Int. Petroleum Co., Ltd 1962–63, various assignments in Europe 1964–66; Shell Oil Co. Atlanta, Ga 1967–69; Chair. and CEO Shell Group Australia 1969–80, Dir 1980–87; Chair. Ashton Mining Ltd 1981–94, BRL Hardy Ltd 1992–95, Tandem Computers Pty Ltd 1992–98, Cooperative Research Centre for Cochlear Implant, Speech and Hearing Inst. 1993–2001; Dir Pacific Dunlop Ltd 1978–90, Chair. 1986–90; Dir Australian Industry Devt Corpn 1978–90; Dir Australian Inst. of Petroleum Ltd 1976–80, 1982–84, Chair. 1977–79; mem. Australian Nat. Airlines Comm. 1981–87, Vice-Chair. 1984–87. *Leisure interests:* reading, music, racing, golf. *Address:* 20 Albany Road, Toorak, Vic. 3142, Australia. *Telephone:* (3) 9666-5200 (Office); (3) 9822-1357 (Home). *Fax:* (3) 9666-5449 (Office); (3) 9822-1357.

FROGIER, Pierre Edouard Nahéa; New Caledonian politician; b. 16 Nov. 1950, Nouméa; m. Annick Morault; three c.; ed Lycée Lapérouse, Nouméa and Faculty of Law, Dijon, France; elected mem. Ass. Territoriale 1977–, Congress 1977–; Mayor of Mont-Dore 1987–2001; Sec.-Gen. Rassemblement pour la Calédonie dans la République (RPCR) 1989–; Territorial Sec. Rassemblement pour la République (RPR) 1995–; Deputy for New Caledonia in French Nat. Ass. 1996–; Pres. of New Caledonia 2001–; Chevalier, Ordre nat. du Mérite. *Address:* Présidence du Gouvernement, 19 avenue Maréchal Foch, B.P. M2, 98849 Nouméa Cédex, New Caledonia (Office). *Telephone:* 246565 (Office). *Fax:* 246550 (Office).

FROHNMAYER, John Edward, MA, JD; American civil servant, lawyer and author; b. 1 June 1942, Medford, Ore.; s. of Otto Frohnmayer and Marabel Frohnmayer; m. Leah Thorpe 1967; two s.; ed Stanford Univ., Univs. of Chicago and Oregon; partner Tonkon, Torp, Galen, Marmaduke & Booth 1975–89; Chair. Ore. Arts Comm. 1980–84; mem. Art Selection Cttee Ore. State Capitol Bldg; Chair. Nat. Endowment for the Arts 1989–92; Visiting Professional Scholar, The Freedom Forum, 1st Amendment Center, Vanderbilt Univ. 1993; trial lawyer in pvt. practice, Bozeman, Mont. 1995–; Republican; People for the American Way, 1st Amendment Award 1992, Oregon Gov.'s Award for the Arts 1993; Intellectual Freedom Award, Montana Library Asscn 1998. *Publication:* Leaving Town Alive 1993, Out of Tune: Listening to the First Amendment 1994. *Leisure interests:* skiing, rowing, reading, music. *Address:* 14080 Lone Bear Road, Bozeman, MT 59715, USA. *Telephone:* (406) 585-5918. *Fax:* (406) 582-4997. *E-mail:* frohn@wtp.net (Office).

FROLOV, Konstantin Vasilyevich, D.TECH.SCI.; Russian machine construction specialist; b. 22 July 1932; m.; one s.; ed Bryansk Inst. of Transport and Machine Construction; (Prof. 1971–); engineer at Leningrad Metal-lurgical Plant 1956–58; research work USSR (now Russian) Acad. of Sciences Inst. of Machine Construction 1961–63, Head of Lab. 1963–75, Dir 1975–; Vice-Pres. USSR (now Russian) Acad. of Sciences, Acad. Sec. of Mechanics Section 1985–; mem. USSR (now Russian) Acad. of Sciences 1984–, Vice-Pres. 1985–; mem. CPSU 1965–91, cand. mem. CPSU Cen. Cttee 1986–89, mem. 1990–91; USSR People's Deputy 1989–91; mem. Supreme Soviet 1989–91; concurrently Prof. at Moscow Univ. 1960–62, Moscow Inst. of Technology 1962–75, Moscow Bauman Tech. College 1975–; Dir Inst. of Eng Science 1991–; Chair. Bd Int. Soc. "Znanie" 1991–; Scientific Dir Russian-American Centre for Devt of Tech. 1992–; mem. Agricultural Acad. 1985–; Foreign mem. Swedish Royal Eng Acad. 1989, Nat. Acad. of Eng, USA 1990; Hon. mem. Slovak Scientific Soc. of Eng 1982–, Madrid Polytechnical Univ. 1990–; Silver Medal, Czechoslovak Acad. of Science 1982, USSR State Prize 1986, Lenin Prize 1988. *Address:* Institut Mashinovedeniya, Malyi Kharitonyevski per. str. 4, Moscow, Russia. *Telephone:* (095) 928-87-30.

FROMENT-MEURICE, Henri, LèsL; French diplomatist; b. 5 June 1923, Paris; m. Gabrielle Drouilh 1948 (deceased); three s. one d.; ed Ecole libre des Sciences Politiques, Ecole Nat. d'Admin; Sec., Ministry of Foreign Affairs 1950–52, Sec. for Far East, Tokyo 1952–53, Chief of Diplomatic Staff, Commissariat Gén. de France en Indochine 1953–54, Asst Pvt. Sec. to Sec. of State for Foreign Affairs 1954–56, First Sec. Embassy, Moscow 1956–59, with

Cen. Admin. (Europe) 1959–63, Chargé d'Affaires, Embassy, United Arab Repub. (now Egypt) 1963–64, First Counsellor, Cairo Embassy, 1964–65, Chief of Cultural Exchange Service, Cen. Admin. 1965–68, Minister Plenipotentiary 1968, Advisory Minister, Moscow 1968–69, Dir Cen. Admin., Asia and Pacific Ocean 1969–75, Econ. Affairs 1975–79, Amb. to USSR 1979–81, to FRG 1982–83; Ambassadeur de France 1984; Adviser to Chair. Banque Paribas 1985–91; Adviser Jeantet et Associés 1991–98; Dir Phillips France 1984–96, Robert Bosch (France) 1984–97; Pres. du Beirat, Inst. Berlin-Brandebourg; Commdr Légion d'honneur, Officier Ordre nat. du Mérite. *Publications:* Une puissance nommée Europe 1984 (Adolphe Bentinck Prize), Une éducation politique 1987, Europe 1992 1988, Vu du quai: Mémories 1945–83 1998; several articles in Preuves, Commentaire and Revue des Deux Mondes, Le Monde, Le Figaro. *Leisure interests:* music, piano. *Address:* 23 rue de Civry, 75016 Paris, France (Home). *Telephone:* 1-43-47-96-41. *Fax:* 1-43-47-96-41.

FROMM, Hans Walther Herbert, DPhil; Finnish/German professor of philology; b. 26 May 1919, Berlin; s. of Rudolf Fromm and Luise (née Hennig) Fromm; m. 1st Lore Sprenger 1950 (divorced 1974); one d.; m. 2nd Beatrice Müller-Hansen 1974; ed Berlin Univ.; Lecturer and Prof. of Germanic Philology, Univ. of Turku 1952–58; Prof. of German Philology and Finno-Ugric Languages, Univ. of Munich 1960–87, Prof. Emer. 1987–; mem. Bayerische Akad. der Wissenschaften 1971, Finnish Acad. of Sciences 1979, Acad. of Finland 1990–, Akad. der Wissenschaften, Göttingen 1992; Chair. Scientific Reviewers' Cttee, Deutsche Forschungsgemeinschaft, Bonn 1972–76, Comm. for Medieval German Literature, Bayerische Akad., Munich 1978–; Hon. DPhil (Turku) 1969, Bundesverdienstkreuz (1st Class), Commdr Order of Kts. of the Finnish Lion (1st Class) 1985, Brüder-Grimm-Preis 1987. *Publications:* Bibliographie deutscher Übersetzungen aus dem Französischen (6 Vols) 1950–53, Germanistische Bibliographie seit 1945, Theorie u. Kritik 1960, Der deutsche Minnesang (2 Vols) 1961, 1985, Kalevala (2 Vols) 1967, Konrad von Fussesbrunnen (Ed.) 1973, Finnische Grammatik (1982), Esseitä Kalevalasta 1987, Arbeiten z. deutschen Literatur d. Mittelalters 1989, Heinrich von Veldeke 1992. *Address:* Roseggerstrasse 35A, 85521 Ottobrunn, Germany. *Telephone:* (89) 605882.

FROMME, Friedrich Karl, DPhil; German journalist; b. 10 June 1930, Dresden; s. of Prof. Dr. Albert Fromme and Dr. Lenka Fromme; m. 1st Traute Kirsten 1961 (died 1992); m. 2nd Brigitte Burkert 1997; ed studies in science, politics and public law; teaching Asst, Univ. of Tübingen 1957–62; Ed. Süddeutscher Rundfunk 1962–64, Frankfurter Allgemeine Zeitung (FAZ) 1964–68; Bonn corresp. FAZ 1968–73; Ed. responsible for internal politics and co-ordination, FAZ 1974–97; freelance writer; Grosses Bundesverdienstkreuz 1995, Theodor Wolff Prize 1997. *Publications:* Von der Weimarer Verfassung zum Bonner Grundgesetz 1962, Der Parlamentarier–ein Freier Beruf? 1978, Gesetzgebung im Widerstreit 1980. *Address:* Welt am Sonntag, D 20350, Hamburg (Office); Mohrengarten 60, 40822 Mettmann, Germany. *Telephone:* (2104) 958768.

FROMSTEIN, Mitchell S.; American business executive; b. 1928; ed Univ. of Wis.; Krueger Homes Inc. 1948–49; Account Exec. Maultner Advertising Agency 1949–53; former Pres. TV Parts Inc.; Partner, Fromstein Assocs.; Pres., CEO and Dir The Parker Pen Co., Janesville, Wis. 1985–86; Chair., Pres. and CEO Manpower Inc., Milwaukee 1976–99; CEO Blue Arrow PLC 1989–, also Dir. *Address:* c/o Manpower Inc., P.O. Box 2053, 5301 North Ironwood Road, Milwaukee, WI 53217, USA.

FROST, Sir David Paradine, Kt, OBE, MA; British television personality and writer; b. 7 April 1939, Tenterden, Kent; s. of Rev. W. J. Paradine Frost; m. 1st Lynne Frederick 1981 (divorced 1982); m. 2nd Lady Carina Fitzalan Howard 1983; three s.; ed Gillingham and Wellingborough Grammar Schools, Gonville and Caius Coll., Cambridge; appeared in BBC TV satire series That Was The Week That Was 1962; other programmes with BBC included A Degree of Frost 1963, 1973, Not So Much A Programme More A Way of Life 1964–65, The Frost Report 1966–67, Frost Over England 1967; appeared in The Frost Programme, ITA 1966–67, 1967–68, 1972; Chair. and CEO David Paradine Ltd 1966–; Jt Founder London Weekend Television 1967; Jt Deputy Chair. Equity Enterprises 1973–76 (Chair. 1972–73); Jt Founder and Dir TV-AM 1981–93, host of numerous programmes including Frost On Friday, Frost On Saturday, Frost On Sunday etc., David Frost Show (USA) 1969–72, David Frost Revue (USA) 1971–73, Frost over Australia 1972–77, Frost over New Zealand 1973–74, That Was The Year That Was (USA) 1973, The Frost Interview 1974, We British 1975, The Sir Harold Wilson Interviews 1967–77, The Nixon Interviews 1976–77, The Crossroads of Civilisation 1977–78; David Frost Presents the Int. Guinness Book of World Records 1981–86, Frost over Canada 1982–83, The Spectacular World of Guinness Records 1987–88, Talking with David Frost 1991–; Presenter Sunday Breakfast with Frost 1993–; The Frost Programme 1993–; Pres. Lord's Taverners 1985, 1986; Companion TV and Radio Industries Club 1992; Hon. Prof. Thames Valley Univ. 1994; Golden Rose, Montreux (for Frost over England) 1967, Royal TV Soc.'s Award 1967, Richard Dimbleby Award 1967, Emmy Award 1970, 1971, Religious Heritage of America Award 1970, Albert Einstein Award (Communication Arts) 1971. *Films produced:* The Rise and Rise of Michael Rimmer 1970, Charley One-Eye 1972, Leadbelly 1974, The Slipper and the Rose 1975, Dynasty 1975, The Ordeal of Patty Hearst 1978, The Remarkable Mrs Sanger 1979. *Publications:* That Was The Week That Was 1963, How to Live under Labour 1964, Talking With Frost 1967, To England With Love (with Antony Jay) 1967, The Americans 1970, Whitlam and Frost 1974, I Gave Them a

Sword 1978, I Could Have Kicked Myself 1982, Who Wants to Be a Millionaire? 1983, The Mid-Atlantic Companion (jtly) 1986, The Rich Tide (jtly) 1986, The World's Shortest Books 1987, David Frost An Autobiography: Part One 1993. *Address:* David Paradine Ltd, 5 St Mary Abbots Place, Kensington, London, W8 6LS, England. *Telephone:* (20) 7371-1111. *Fax:* (20) 7602-0411.

FROST, Sir Terence Ernest Manitou, Kt; British artist; b. 13 Oct. 1915, Leamington; five s. one d.; ed Campion Central School, Camberwell Coll. of Arts and Crafts; Prof. of Painting Univ. of Reading 1977–81, Prof. Emer. 1981; numerous exhbns. including Waddington Galleries 1958–, Adelson Gallery, New York 1992–94, Belgrave Gallery, London 1997; represented in public collections in UK, Canada, USA, Germany, Australia; Hon. LLD (Council for Nat. Academic Awards). *Address:* Gernick Field Studio, Tredavoe Lane, Newlyn, Penzance, Cornwall, TR18 5DL, England. *Telephone:* (1736) 365902. *Fax:* (1736) 363005. *E-mail:* temfrost@aol.com (Home).

FROWEIN, Jochen Abraham, DJur, MCL; German professor of law; b. 8 June 1934, Berlin; s. of Dr Abraham Frowein and Hilde Frowein (née Matthis); m. Lore Flume 1962; one s. two d.; ed Univs of Kiel, Berlin, Bonn and Univ. of Michigan Law School, Ann Arbor; Research Fellow, Max-Planck-Inst. for Comparative Public and Int. Law 1962–66; Prof. Univ. of Bochum 1967–69, Univ. of Bielefeld 1969–81; Dir Max-Planck-Inst. and Prof. Univ. of Heidelberg 1981; mem. European Comm. of Human Rights 1973–93, Vice-Pres. 1981–93; Vice-Pres. German Research Foundation 1977–80, Max Planck Soc. 1999–2002; Hon. DrIur (Seville) 1984, (Louvain) 1997, (Paris) 2000; Grosses Bundesverdienstkreuz 1994. *Publications:* Das de facto-Regime im Völkerrecht 1968, EMRK-Kommentar (with W. Peukert) 1985; and many articles and contributions. *Address:* Max-Planck-Institut für ausländisches öffentliches Recht und Völkerrecht, Im Neuenheimer Feld 535, 69120 Heidelberg, Germany. *Telephone:* (6221) 482258.

FRÜH, Eugen; Swiss painter and illustrator; b. 22 Jan. 1914, St Gallen; s. of Huldreich and Teresa Früh; m. Erna Yoshida Blenk (artist) 1934; ed Zürich School of Art and in Paris and Rome; C. F. Meyer Foundation Fine Arts Prize 1943, Fine Arts Prize, Kanton Zürich 1967. *Works include:* Die kleine Stadt 1941, Pastorale d'été 1946, La comédie et la musique 1947, Capricci 1948, Spanisches Gespräch 1951, Notturno 1957, Château d'artiste 1962, Gartenfest 1964, Bambuswald 1972, Lotus 1973–74; also murals and book illustrations. *Leisure interests:* literature, music, travel. *Address:* Römergasse 9, 8001 Zürich, Switzerland. *Telephone:* (1) 478863.

FRÜHBECK DE BURGOS, Rafael; Spanish conductor; b. 15 Sept. 1933, Burgos; s. of Wilhelm Frühbeck and Stephanie Frühbeck (née Ochs); m. María Carmen Martínez 1959; one s. one d.; ed music acads. in Bilbao, Madrid and Munich and Univ. of Madrid; Chief Conductor, Municipal Orchestra, Bilbao 1958–62; Music Dir and Chief Conductor, Spanish Nat. Orchestra, Madrid 1962–78, Hon. Conductor 1998; Music Dir of Düsseldorf and Chief Conductor Düsseldorf Symphoniker 1966–71; Music Dir Montreal Symphony Orchestra 1974–76; Prin. Conductor Yomiuri Nippon Symphony Orchestra 1980–90, Hon. Conductor 1991–; Prin. Guest Conductor Nat. Symphony Orchestra, Washington, DC 1980–90; Music Dir Vienna Symphony Orchestra 1991–96; Gen. Music Dir Deutsche Oper Berlin 1992–97; Gen. Musik Dir Rundfunk Symphony Orchestra, Berlin 1994–2000; Chief Conductor RAI Symphony Orchestra, Turin 2001; mem. Real Academia de Bellas Artes, Madrid 1975; Gran Cruz al Mérito Civil Orden de Alfonso X 1966, Orden de Isabel la Católica 1966, Grand Cross of Civil Merit (Germany) 2001; Dr. hc (Univ. of Navarra) 1994, (Univ. of Burgos) 1998; Prize for Musical Interpretation, Larios Foundation CEOE, Madrid 1992, Fundación Guerrero Prize for Spanish Music, Madrid 1996, Gold Medal City of Vienna 1995, Medal of Civil Merit (Austria) 1996, Gold Medal Int. Gustav Mahler Soc., Vienna 1996, Gold Medal, State of Vienna 2000. *Orchestrations:* Suite Española (Albéniz), Tema y Variaciones (Turina). *Address:* 28007 Madrid, Avenida del Mediterráneo 21, Spain (Home). *Telephone:* (341) 5016933 (Home).

FRUTON, Joseph Stewart, PhD; American biochemist; b. 14 May 1912, Czestochowa, Poland; s. of Charles Fruton and Ella Eisenstadt; m. Sofia Simmonds 1936; ed Columbia Univ.; Assoc., Rockefeller Inst. for Medical Research 1934–45; Assoc. Prof. of Physiological Chem., Yale Univ. 1945–50, Prof. of Biochem. 1950–57, Chair. Dept of Biochem. 1951–67, Eugene Higgins Prof. of Biochem. 1957–82, Emer. 1982–, Dir Div. of Science 1959–62, Prof. History of Medicine 1980–82, Emer. 1982–; Exec. Sec. Yale Corpn Presidential Search Cttee 1985–86; Assoc. Ed. Journal of Biological Chem. and Journal of Biochem.; Harvey Lecturer 1955, Dakin Lecturer 1962; Visiting Prof. Rockefeller Univ. 1968–69; Sarton Lecturer 1976; Xerox Lecturer 1977; Benjamin Franklin Fellow, Royal Soc. of Arts; mem. American Philosophical Soc., NAS, American Acad. of Arts and Sciences, Harvey Soc., ACS, American Soc. of Biological Chemists, Biochemical Soc., History of Science Soc.; Fellow, Guggenheim Foundation 1983–84; Hon. ScD (Rockefeller Univ.) 1976; Eli Lilly Award in Biological Chem. 1944, Pfizer Award in History of Science 1973, John Frederick Lewis Award (American Philosophical Soc.) 1990, Dexter Award in History of Chem. 1993. *Publications:* General Biochemistry (with S. Simmonds) 1953, Molecules and Life 1972, Selected Bibliography of Biographical Data for the History of Biochemistry since 1800 1974, a Biobibliography for the History of the Biochemical Sciences Since 1800 1982, Contrasts in Scientific Style 1990, A Skeptical Biochemist 1992, Eighty Years 1994, Proteins, Enzymes, Genes 1999, Methods and Styles in the Development of Chemistry 2002; numerous scientific articles in Journal of Biological Chemistry, Biochemistry, Journal of American Chemical Soc., Proceedings of

NAS and other journals. *Leisure interests:* history of science, music. *Address:* 123 York Street, New Haven, CT 06511, USA. *Telephone:* (203) 624-3735. *Fax:* (203) 737-4130.

FRY, Christopher, FRSL; British dramatist; b. 18 Dec. 1907, Bristol; s. of Charles John Harris and Emma Marguerite Hammond; m. Phyllis Marjorie Hart 1936; one s.; ed Bedford Modern School; Actor, Citizen House, Bath 1927; teacher, Hazelwood Preparatory School 1928–31; Dir Tunbridge Wells Repertory Players 1932–35; Dir Oxford Repertory Players 1940 and 1944–46; at Arts Theatre, London 1945; Hon. Fellow, Manchester Polytechnic (now Manchester Metropolitan Univ.) 1988; Hon. Dip. Arts (Manchester) 1962; Hon. DLitt (Lambeth) 1988; Hon. DLitt (Sussex, De Montfort) 1994; Queen's Gold Medal for Poetry 1962, R. S. L. Benson Medal 2001. *Film Scripts:* The Beggar's Opera, The Queen is Crowned, Ben Hur, Barabbas, The Bible. *Publications:* The Boy with the Cart 1939, The Firstborn 1946, A Phoenix Too Frequent 1946, The Lady's Not for Burning 1949, Thor, with Angels 1949, Venus Observed 1950, A Sleep of Prisoners 1951, The Dark is Light Enough 1954, Curtmantle (R. S. L. Heinemann Award) 1962, A Yard of Sun 1970, The Brontës of Haworth (four plays for television) 1973, Can You Find Me 1978; trans. Ring Round the Moon 1950, The Lark (Anouilh) 1954, Tiger at the Gates 1955, Duel of Angels 1958, Judith (Giraudoux) 1962, Peer Gynt 1970, Cyrano de Bergerac 1975, The Best of Enemies (play for television) 1976, Sister Dora (three-part play for television) 1977, introduction and text Charlie Hammond's Sketchbook 1980, Selected Plays 1985, One Thing More, or Caedmon Construed 1986, Genius, Talent and Failure 1987, Looking for a Language 1992, foreword and ed. A Sprinkle of Nutmeg 1994, A Ringing of Bells 2000. *Leisure interest:* gardening. *Address:* The Toft, East Dean, nr Chichester, Sussex, England.

FRY, Hedy; Canadian politician and physician; b. 1941, Trinidad; three s.; ed Coll. of Physicians and Surgeons, Dublin, Ireland; fmr family physician, Vancouver Centre, BC; MP for Vancouver Centre 1993–; Parl. Sec. to Minister of Health 1993–96; Sec. of State (Multiculturalism, Status of Women) 1996–2002; Vice-Chair. Task Force on Canada-U.S. relations 2002; Chair. BC Caucus 2002–, Standing Cttee on Health 2002–03, Special Cttee on non-medical use of drugs 2002; fmr Pres. BC Medical Asscn; Liberal. *Leisure interests:* drama, racquetball, reading, swimming. *Address:* Confed. Building, Room 583, Ottawa Ont. K1A 0A6 (Office); House of Commons, Ottawa, Ont., Canada. *Telephone:* (613) 992-3213 (Office). *Fax:* (613) 995-0056 (Office). *E-mail:* fryh@parl.gc.ca (Office). *Website:* www.hedyfry.com (Office).

FRY, Jonathan Michael, MA; British business executive; b. 9 Aug. 1937, Jerusalem; s. of the late Stephen Fry and of Gladys Yvonne Blunt; m. Caroline Mary Dunkerly 1970 (divorced 1997); four d.; m. 2nd Marilyn Russell 1999; ed Repton School, Trinity College, Oxford; Account Exec., Pritchard Wood Ltd 1961–65; Account Supervisor, Norman Craig & Kummel Inc. 1965–66; Consultant, McKinsey & Co. 1966–73; Devt./Marketing Dir Unigate Foods Div. 1973, Man. Dir 1973, Chair. 1976–78; Group Planning Dir Burmah Oil Trading Ltd 1978–81, Chief Exec. Burmah Speciality Chemicals Ltd 1981–87; Chair. Burmah Castrol PLC 1998–2000 (Man. Dir 1990–93, Chief Exec. 1993–98); Chief Exec. Burmah Castrol Trading Ltd 1993–98, Chair. 1998–2000 (Man. Dir 1990–93); Chair. Castrol Int. (fmrly Castrol Ltd) 1993–96 (Chief Exec. 1987–93); Deputy Chair. Northern Foods PLC 1996–2002 (non-exec. Dir 1991–2002); Chair. Christian Salvesen PLC 1997– (non-exec. Dir 1995–); Chair. Elementis PLC (fmrly Harrisons & Crosfield PLC) 1997–; Chair. Control Risks Group Holdings Ltd 2000–. *Leisure interests:* cricket, skiing, archaeology. *Address:* Beechingstoke Manor, Pewsey, Wilts., SN9 6HQ, England (Home). *Telephone:* (167285) 1669 (Home).

FRY, Stephen John, MA; British actor and writer; b. 24 Aug. 1957; s. of Alan John Fry and Marianne Eve Fry (née Newman); ed Uppingham School, Queens' Coll. Cambridge; Columnist The Listener 1988–89, Daily Telegraph 1990–; wrote first play Latin, performed at Edin. Festival 1980; and at Lyric Theatre, Hammersmith 1983; appeared with Cambridge Footlights in revue The Cellar Tapes, Edinburgh Festival 1981; re-wrote script Me and My Girl, London, Broadway, Sydney 1984; mem. Amnesty Int., Comic Relief; Pres. Friends for Life Terrence Higgins Trust; Hon. LLD (Dundee) 1995, (East Anglia) 1999; Hon. DLit. *Plays:* Forty Years On, Chichester Festival and London 1984, The Common Pursuit, London 1988 (TV 1992). *Radio:* Loose Ends 1986–87, Whose Line Is It Anyway? 1987, Saturday Night Fry 1987, 1998. *TV series:* Alfresco 1982–84, The Young Ones 1983, Happy Families 1984, Saturday Night Live 1986–87, A Bit of Fry and Laurie 1989–95, Blackadder's Christmas Carol 1988, Blackadder Goes Forth 1989, Jeeves and Wooster 1990–92, Stalag Luft 1993, Laughter and Loathing 1995, Gormenghast 2000. *Films:* The Good Father, A Fish Called Wanda, A Handful of Dust, Peter's Friends 1992, IQ 1995, Wind in the Willows, Wilde 1997, Cold Comfort Farm 1997, A Civil Action 1997, Whatever Happened to Harold Smith? 2000, Relatives Values 2000, Discovery of Heaven 2001, Gosford Park 2002. *Publications:* Paperweight (collected essays) 1992, The Liar (novel), The Hippopotamus 1994, Fry and Laurie 4 (with Hugh Laurie) 1994, Paperweight 1995, Making History 1996, Moab is my Washpot 1997 (autobiog.), The Star's Tennis Balls (novel) 2000. *Leisure interests:* smoking, drinking, swearing, pressing wild flowers. *Address:* c/o Hamilton Asper Management, Ground Floor, 24 Hanway Street, London, W1P 9DD, England. *Telephone:* (20) 7636-1221. *Fax:* (20) 7636-1226.

FRYE, Richard Nelson, PhD; American orientalist; b. 10 Jan. 1920, Birmingham, Ala; s. of Nels Frye and Lillie Hagman; m. 1st Barbara York 1948 (divorced 1973); two s. one d.; m. 2nd Eden Naby 1975; one s.; ed Univ. of Illinois, Harvard Univ. and School of Oriental and African Studies, London; Jr Fellow, Harvard Univ. 1946–49, Founder Middle East Centre 1949; Visiting Scholar, Univ. of Tehran 1951–52; Co-founder Nat. Asscn of Armenian Studies 1955; Aga Khan Prof. of Iranian Studies, Harvard Univ. 1957–99, now Emer.; Visiting Prof., Oriental Seminary, Frankfurt Univ. 1958–59; Visiting Prof., Hamburg Univ. 1968–69; Dir Asia Inst., Pahlavi Univ., Shiraz 1969–75; Assoc. Ed. Cen. Asian Journal, Bulletin of the Asia Inst.; Corresp. Fellow, German Archaeological Inst. 1966–; Hon. DLitt (Oxford Univ.) 1987; Hon. PhD (Univ. of Tajikistan) 1991. *Publications:* Notes on the Early Coinage of Transoxiana 1949, History of the Nation of the Archers 1952, Narshakhi, The History of Bukhara 1954, Iran 1956, Heritage of Persia 1962, Bukhara, The Medieval Achievement 1965, The Histories of Nishapur 1965, Persia 1968, Inscriptions from Dura Europos 1969, Excavations at Qasr-i-Abu-Nasr 1973, The Golden Age of Persia 1975; Ed. Vol. 4 Cambridge History of Iran 1975, The Ancient History of Iran 1983, The Heritage of Central Asia 1996. *Address:* Harvard University, 6 Divinity Avenue, Cambridge, MA 02138 (Office); Tower Hill Road, Brimfield, MA 01010, USA (Home).

FRYER, Geoffrey, PhD, DSc, FRS; British biologist; b. 6 Aug. 1927; s. of W. Fryer and M. Fryer; m. Vivien G. Hodgson 1953; one s. one d.; ed Huddersfield Coll. and Univ. of London; colonial research student 1952–53; HM Overseas Research Service, Malawi 1953–55, Zambia 1955–57, Uganda 1957–60; Sr, then Prin., then Sr Prin. Scientific Officer, Freshwater Biological Asscn 1960–81; Deputy Chief Scientific Officer, Windermere Lab., Freshwater Biological Asscn 1981–88; Hon. Prof., Univ. of Lancaster 1988–; H. R. Macmillan Lecturer, Univ. of BC 1963; Distinguished Visiting Scholar, Univ. of Adelaide 1985; Distinguished Lecturer Dept of Fisheries and Oceans, Canada 1987; Frink Medal, Zoological Soc. of London 1983, Linnean Medal for Zoology, Linnean Soc. of London 1987, Elsdon-Dew Medal, Parasitological Soc. of Southern Africa 1998. *Publications:* The Cichlid Fishes of the Great Lakes of Africa: Their Biology and Evolution (with T. D. Iles) 1972, A Natural History of the Lakes, Tarns and Streams of the English Lake District 1991, The Freshwater Crustacea of Yorkshire: A Faunistic and Ecological Survey 1993; numerous articles in scientific journals. *Leisure interests:* natural history, walking, church architecture, photography. *Address:* Elleray Cottage, Windermere, Cumbria, LA23 1AW, England.

FU HAO; Chinese diplomatist; b. April 1916, Li Quan County, Xian Yang City, Shanxi Prov.; m. Jiao Ling 1945; two s., one d.; ed NW China Teachers Coll.; served in PLA during the civil war; CPC rep. (Col) Group of Beiping Exec. HQ of CPC, Kuomintang and USA in Dezhou, Shandong Prov. 1946; Counsellor, Embassy in Mongolia 1950–53; Attaché, Deputy Dir-Gen. Asian Affairs Dept, Ministry of Foreign Affairs 1952–55; Counsellor, frequently Chargé d'affaires, Embassy in India 1955–62; Deputy Dir-Gen., Personnel Dept, Ministry of Foreign Affairs 1963–69, Head Gen. Office, 1970–72; Rep. to 26th Session UN Gen. Ass. 1971; Vice-Minister of Foreign Affairs 1972–74; Amb. to Democratic Repub. of Viet Nam 1974–77, to Japan 1977–82; Vice Minister, Adviser Ministry of Foreign Affairs 1982–94; Deputy 6th NPC, mem. Standing Cttee, Vice-Chair. Foreign Affairs Cttee 1983–88; Chinese mem. 21st Century Cttee for Sino-Japanese Friendship 1984–95, Chinese Chair. 1996–98; Chair. NPC China-Japan Friendship Group 1985–93; Deputy 7th NPC, mem. Standing Cttee, Vice-Chair. Foreign Affairs Cttee 1988–93; mem. Exec. Cttee IPU 1989–91; Chair. China-Vietnamese Friendship Asscn 1992–96; Pres. Asscn of fmr Diplomats of China 1994–99, Hon. Pres. 2000; Chair. Inst. for Diplomatic History of People's Repub. of China 1994, Ed.'s Cttee of China Classical Stratagems 1995–; Grand Cordon of the Sacred Treasure (Japan). *Publications:* Tian Nan Di Bei (poems) 1992, My Life: Stormy but Memorable 2001, Feng Yu Cang Sang (essay) 2001. *Leisure interests:* poems and literature. *Address:* 69 Bao Fang Lane, East District, Beijing 100010, People's Republic of China. *Telephone:* 65252010.

FU KUIQING, Lt-Gen.; Chinese army officer; b. 1920, Yingshan Co., Anhui Prov.; Sec. CCP Prov. Cttee, Heilongjiang 1971–74; Vice-Gov., Heilongjiang 1972–74; Deputy Political Commissar, Shenyang Mil. Region, PLA 1977; Political Commissar, Fuzhou Mil. Region, PLA 1981–85; mem. 12th CCP Cen. Cttee 1982–87; Political Commissar Nanjing Mil. Region, PLA 1985–90, rank of Lt-Gen. PLA 1988; mem. Standing Cttee of 7th NPC; (3rd Class) Order of Independence and Freedom, 2nd Class Order of Liberation. *Address:* Nanjing Military Region Headquarters, Nanjing, Jiangsu, People's Republic of China.

FU MINGXIA; Chinese diver; b. 16 Aug. 1978, Wuhan, Hubei Prov.; m. Antony Leung 2002; ed Qinghua Univ., Beijing; youngest ever ten-metre platform diving world champion at the age of 12; first woman to win five Olympic diving medals; ten-metre platform diving gold medallist at 25th Olympics, Barcelona, 26th Olympics, Atlanta (also won three-metre platform gold medal), three-metre springboard gold medallist at Sydney Olympics; Nation's Best Ten Athletes Award. *Address:* c/o State General Bureau for Physical Culture and Sports, 9 Tiyuguan Road, Chongwen District, Beijing, People's Republic of China.

FU QIFENG; Chinese historian of magic and acrobatics; b. 15 March 1941, Chengdu, Sichuan; d. of Fu Tianzheng and Ceng Qingpu; m. Xu Zhuang 1961; one s. one d.; performer, acrobatics troupe, Beijing 1960–70; Founder and Deputy Chief Ed. Acrobatics and Magic (journal); mem. Research Dept, Asscn of Chinese Acrobats 1987–; Council mem. 1991–; mem. Editorial Cttee Acrobatics, in series Contemporary China 1991–; mem. China Magic Cttee

1993–. *Publications:* Chinese Acrobatics Through the Ages 1986, The Art of Chinese Acrobatics 1988; (with brother) Acrobatics in China 1983, History of Chinese Acrobatics 1989, History of Chinese Artistic Skills (in Japanese) 1993; (co-author) Literature and Art volume of China Concise Encyclopedia 1994, Secret of Spiritualist Activities 1995, Illusions and Superstitions 1997. *Address:* 5-2-501 Hongmiao Beili, Jintai Road, Beijing 100025, People's Republic of China. *Telephone:* 65002547.

FU QUANYOU, Gen.; Chinese army officer; b. 1930, Yuanping Co., Shanxi Prov.; joined Red Army 1946, CCP 1947; Army Chief of Staff 1981–83; Army Commdr 1983–85; Commdr Chengdu Mil. Region, PLA 1985–90; mem. 12th CCP Cen. Cttee 1985, 13th CCP Cen. Cttee 1987–92; 14th CCP Cen. Cttee 1992–97, 15th CCP Cen. Cttee 1997–2002; mem. Cen. Mil. Comm. of CCP 1992–, Gen. 1993–; Deputy Sec. CCP Cttee, Commdr Lanzhou Mil. Region 1990–92; Dir Gen. Logistics Dept 1992–95; Chief of Gen. Staff 1995–2003. *Address:* c/o Chinese Communist Party Central Committee, Zhongnanhai, Beijing, People's Republic of China.

FU TIANLIN; Chinese poet; b. 24 Jan. 1946, Zizhong Co., Sichuan Prov.; ed Chongqing Middle School, Electronic Tech. School; worked in orchard Chongqing 1962–79; clerk, Beibei Cultural Centre 1980–82; Ed. Chongqing Publishing House 1982–; First Prize of Chinese Poetry 1983. *Publications:* Green Musical Notes 1981, Between Children and the World 1983, Island of Music 1985, Red Strawberry 1986, Selected Poems of Seven Chinese Poets 1993. *Address:* Chongqing Publishing House, 205 Changjiang 2 Road, 630050, Chongqing City, Sichuan, People's Republic of China.

FU XISHOU; Chinese government official and engineer; b. 1931, Beijing; ed Dept of Civil Engineering, Qinghua Univ.; joined CCP 1959; Deputy Sec. Anhui Prov. CP Cttee 1987–; Deputy Gov. of Anhui Prov. 1988–90, Gov. 1991–95; mem. 14th CCP Cen. Cttee 1992–; NPC Deputy to Anhui Prov.; Deputy Sec. CPC 5th Anhui Provincial Cttee 1988–; Gov. Anhui Provincial People's Govt 1989–94; Chair. People's Armament Cttee 1991–. *Address:* c/o Office of Provincial Governor, Hefei City, Anhui Province, People's Republic of China.

FU ZHIHUAN; Chinese politician; b. March 1938, Haicheng Co., Liaoning Prov.; ed Moscow Railways Inst., USSR; joined CCP 1966; Chief Engineer, Science and Tech. Bureau, Ministry of Railways 1984; Dir Science and Tech. Bureau, Ministry of Railways 1985; Dir Harbin Railway Bureau 1989; Vice-Minister of Railways 1991–98, Minister 1998–2003; mem. CCP Cen. Comm. for Inspecting Discipline 1992–; mem. 15th CCP Cen. Cttee 1997–2002, 16th CCP Cen. Cttee 2002–. *Address:* c/o Zhongguo Gongchan Dang (Chinese Communist Party—CCP), Beijing, People's Republic of China (Office).

FUCHS, Anke, LLM; German politician and lawyer; b. Nevermann, 5 July 1937, Hamburg; d. of Paul Nevermann; m.; two c.; ed Hamburg, Innsbruck and School of Public Admin., Speyer; mem. Regional Exec., Young Socialist Org. 1954; joined Social Democratic Party (SPD) 1956; trainee, regional org. of German Fed. of Trade Unions, Nordmark (Hamburg) 1964–68; Regional Sec. Metal Workers' Union (IG Metall), mem. Reform Comm. on Training for Legal Profession, mem. SPD Regional Exec., mem. Hamburg Judge Selection Cttee 1968–70; mem. SPD Party Council 1970–, fmr Deputy Chair., Party Man. 1987–91; mem. Bundestag 1980–; mem. Hamburg Citizens' Ass. 1970–77; Exec. Sec. IG Metall 1971–77; State Sec. Fed. Ministry of Labour and Social Affairs 1977–80, Parl. State Sec. 1980–82; Chair. SPD Party Council 1993–; Pres. des Deutschen Mieterbundes 1995–; Fed. Minister for Youth, Family Affairs and Health April–Oct. 1982; Vice-Pres. Bundestag 1998–; Vice-Chair. Friedrich Ebert-Stiftung; Dr. hc 2000. *Address:* Deutscher Bundestag, Platz der Republik, 11011 Berlin, Germany. *Telephone:* (30) 22772577 (Office). *Fax:* (30) 22776175 (Office).

FUCHS, Victor Robert, MA, PhD; American professor of economics; b. 31 Jan. 1924, New York; s. of Alfred Fuchs and Frances S. (Scheiber) Fuchs; m. Beverly Beck 1948; two s. two d.; ed New York and Columbia Univs; Assoc. Prof. of Econs New York Univ. 1959–60; Program Assoc. Econs Ford Foundation 1960–62; Research Assoc. Nat. Bureau of Econ. Research 1962–; Prof. of Community Medicine, Mount Sinai School of Medicine 1968–74; Prof. of Econs City Univ. of New York Grad. Center 1968–74; Prof. of Econs (in Depts. of Econs and Health Research and Policy) Stanford Univ. 1974–95, Henry J. Kaiser Jr Prof. 1988–95, Prof. Emer. 1995–; Pres. American Econ. Assen 1995; mem. Inst. of Medicine, American Philosophical Soc.; Fellow, American Acad. of Arts and Sciences; Distinguished Fellow, American Econ. Assen 1990; Madden Memorial Award 1982, John R. Commons Award 2002 and other awards. *Publications:* The Economics of the Fur Industry 1957, Changes in the Location of Manufacturing in the US since 1929 1962, The Service Economy 1968, Production and Productivity in the Service Industries 1969, Who Shall Live? Health, Economics and Social Choice 1974 (expanded edn 1998), Economic Aspects of Health (ed.) 1982, How We Live 1983, The Health Economy 1986, Women's Quest for Economic Equality 1988, The Future of Health Policy 1993, Individual and Social Responsibility: Child Care, Education, Medical Care and Long Term Care in America (ed.) 1996. *Address:* National Bureau of Economic Research, 30 Alta Road, Stanford, CA 94305 (Office); 796 Cedro Way, Stanford, CA 94305, USA (Home). *Telephone:* (650) 326-7639 (Office). *Fax:* (650) 328-4163. *E-mail:* fuchs@newage3.stanford.edu (Office).

FUENTES, Carlos; Mexican author and diplomatist; b. 11 Nov. 1928, Mexico City; s. of Rafael Fuentes Boettiger and Berta Macías Rivas; m. 1st Rita

Macedo 1957; one d.; m. 2nd Sylvia Lemus 1973; one s. one d.; ed Univ. of Mexico, Inst. des Hautes Etudes Internationales, Geneva; mem. Mexican Del. to ILO, Geneva 1950–51; Asst Head, Press Section, Ministry of Foreign Affairs, Mexico 1954; Asst Dir Cultural Dissemination, Univ. de Mexico 1955–56; Head Dept of Cultural Relations, Ministry of Foreign Affairs 1957–59; Ed. Revista Mexicana de Literatura 1954–58, Co-Ed. El Espectador 1959–61, Ed. Siempre and Politica 1960–; Amb. to France 1974–77; fmr Prof. of Spanish and Comparative Literature, Columbia Univ., New York; Prof. of Comparative Literature, Harvard Univ. 1984–86, Robert F. Kennedy Prof. of Latin American Studies 1987–89; Prof.-at-Large Brown Univ. 1995–; Pres. Modern Humanities Research Asscn 1989–; fmr Adjunct Prof. of English and Romance Languages, Univ. of Pennsylvania, Pa; Fellow, Woodrow Wilson Int. Center for Scholars, Washington, DC 1974; Fellow of the Humanities, Princeton Univ.; Virginia Gildersleeve Visiting Prof., Barnard Coll., New York; Edward Leroc Visiting Prof., School of Int. Affairs, Columbia Univ., New York; Simon Bolívar Lecturer, Univ. of Cambridge, England; Mexican Nat. Award for Literature 1984, Ruben Dario Prize 1988, Prince of Asturias Prize 1992 and numerous other awards (see publications); Dr hc (Harvard, Wesleyan, Essex, Cambridge, Salamanca); Order of Merit, Chile 1992, Légion d'honneur 1992; Hon. Citizen of Santiago de Chile 1993, Buenos Aires 1993, Veracruz 1993, Picasso Medal, UNESCO 1994, Order of the South Cross, Brazil 1997, French Order of Merit 1998, Latin Civilization Prize, French and Brazilian Acads 1999, Mexican Senate Medal 2000, Los Angeles Public Library Award 2001, Commonwealth Award Delaware 2002. *Publications:* Los días enmascarados 1954, La región más transparente 1958, Las buenas conciencias 1959, Aura 1962, La muerte de Artemio Cruz 1962, Cantar de ciegos 1965, Zona sagrada 1967, Cambio de piel (Biblioteca Breve Prize 1967), Paris, La Revolución de Mayo 1968, La Nueva Novela Hispanoamericana 1969, Cumpleaños 1969, Le Borgne est Roi 1970, Casa con Dos Puertas 1970, Todos los gatos son pardos 1970, Tiempo Mexicano 1971, Don Quixote or the Critique of Reading 1974, Terra Nostra (Javier Villaurrutia Prize 1975, Rómulo Gallegos Prize 1977) 1975, La Cabeza de la Hidra 1978, Orchids in the Moonlight (play) 1982, The Old Gringo (IUA Prize 1989) 1985, The Good Conscience 1987, Cristóbal Nonato (novel, Miguel de Cervantes Prize) 1987, Myself With Others (essays) 1988, Christopher Unborn 1989, Constancia and Stories for Virgins 1991, The Campaign (novel) 1991, The Buried Mirror (essays, also TV series) 1992, Geography of the Novel (essays) 1993, El Naranjo (novelas) 1993, Diana: The Goddess Who Hunts Alone 1995, The Crystal Frontier 1995, A New Time for Mexico 1997, Por un Progreso Incluyente 1997, Retratos en el Tiempo 1998, Los Años con Laura Diaz 1999, Los Cinco Soles de México 2000, Inez 2000, Ce que je crois 2002, La Silla de Aguila 2003. *Address:* c/o Brandt & Brandt, 1501 Broadway, New York, NY 10036, USA; c/o Balcells, Diagonal 580, Barcelona 08021, Spain. *Telephone:* (212) 840-5760 (USA); (93) 200 8933 (Spain). *Fax:* (212) 840-5776 (USA; (93) 200 7041 (Spain).

FUGARD, Athol; South African actor and playwright; b. 11 June 1932; s. of Harold David Fugard and Elizabeth Magdelene Potgiefer; m. Sheila Fugard 1956; one d.; leading role in Meetings with Remarkable Men (film) 1977, The Guest (BBC production) 1977; acted in and wrote script for Marigolds in August (film); Hon. DLit (Natal and Rhodes Univs); Dr hc (Univ. of Cape Town, Georgetown Univ., Washington, DC, New York, Pennsylvania, City Univ. of New York); Hon. DFA (Yale Univ.) 1973; winner Silver Bear Award, Berlin Film Festival 1980, New York Critics Award for A Lesson From Aloes 1981, London Evening Standard Award for Master Harold and the Boys 1983, Commonwealth Award for Contrib. to American Theatre 1984. *Plays:* The Blood Knot, Hello and Goodbye, People are Living Here, Boesman and Lena 1970, Sizwe Banzi is Dead 1973, The Island 1973, Statements After an Arrest Under the Immorality Act 1974, No Good Friday 1974, Nongogo 1974, Dimetos 1976, The Road to Mecca 1984, My Children, My Africa, The Guest (film script) 1977, A Lesson from Aloes 1979 (author and dir Broadway production 1980), Master Harold and the Boys 1981, A Place with the Pigs (actor and dir) 1988, Playland 1992, Sign of Hope 1992, Valley Song (actor and dir) 1996, The Captain's Tiger 1999, Sorrows and Rejoicings 2001. *Films include:* Marigolds in August 1981, The Guest 1984; acted in films Gandhi 1982, Road to Mecca 1991 (also co-dir). *Publications:* Notebooks 1960–77, Playland 1992; novel: Tsotsi 1980; plays: Road to Mecca 1985, A Place with the Pigs 1988, Cousins: A Memoir 1994. *Address:* P.O. Box 5090, Walmer, Port Elizabeth 6065, South Africa.

FUHRMAN, Robert Alexander, M.S.E., FRAeS; American business executive and aerospace engineer; b. 23 Feb. 1925, Detroit, Mich.; s. of Alexander A. Fuhrman and Elva Brown Fuhrman; m. 1st Nan E. McCormick 1949 (died 1988); two s. one d.; m. 2nd Nancy Ferguson Richards 1989; ed Univs of Michigan and Maryland, Stanford Univ. Grad. School of Business; Vice-Pres. and Gen. Man. Missiles Systems Div., Lockheed Corpn 1966–70, Pres. Georgia Co. 1970–71, Pres. California Co. 1971–74, Pres. Missiles & Space Co. 1976–83, Group Pres. Missiles Space & Electronics 1983–85, Pres. and COO Lockheed Corpn 1985–88, Vice-Chair. and COO 1988–90, Sr Adviser 1990–; Chair. Bd Bank of the West 1990–, USAF Science and Tech. Bd 1996–; mem. Bd Charles Stark Draper Lab. 1986–, Burdeshaw Assoc. Ltd 1994–; mem. Defense Science Bd; mem. Nat. Acad. of Eng; Hon. Fellow AIAA, Pres. 1992–93; Mich. Aviation Hall of Fame 1991. *Publications:* The Fleet Ballistic Weapon System: Polaris to Trident (AIAA Von Karman Lecture) 1976, Defense Science Bd Task Force Report: The Defense Industrial Base (Chair.) 1988, The C-17 Review (Chair.) 1993. *Leisure interest:* golf. *Address:* Bank of the West, 180 Montgomery Street, San Francisco, CA 94104 (Office); P.O. Box

9, 1543 Riata Road, Pebble Beach, CA 93953, USA. *Telephone:* (408) 765-4800 (Office); (408) 625-2125. *Fax:* (408) 434-3470 (Office); (408) 625-2393. *Website:* www.bankofthewest.com (Office).

FUHRMANN, Horst, DPhil; German historian; b. 22 June 1926, Kreuzburg; s. of Karl and Susanna Fuhrmann; m. Dr. Ingrid Winkler-Lippoldt 1954; one s. one d.; collaborator, Monumenta Germaniae Historica 1954–56; Asst, Rome 1957; Asst and Lecturer 1957–62; Prof. Univ. of Tübingen 1962–71; Pres. Monumenta Germaniae Historica, Munich and Prof. Univ. of Regensburg 1971–94; Pres. Bavarian Acad. of Humanities and Science 1992–97; Hon. DrIur (Tübingen); Hon. DPhil (Bologna, Columbia, New York); Premio Spoleto 1962, Cultore di Roma 1981, Upper Silesian Culture Prize 1989, Premio Ascoli Piceno 1990; Orden Pour le Mérite; Grosses Bundesverdienstkreuz mit Stern, Bayerischer Verdienstorden, Maximiliansorden 1998. *Publications:* The Donation of Constantine 1968, Influence and Circulation of the Pseudoisidorian Forgeries (3 Vols) 1972–74, Germany in the High Middle Ages 1978, From Petrus to John Paul II: The Papacy 1980, Invitation to the Middle Ages 1987, Far from Cultured People: An Upper Silesian Town Around 1870 1989, Pour le Mérite: On Making Merit Visible 1992, Scholarly Lives 1996, Überall ist Mittelalter 1996. *Address:* Sonnenwinkel 10, 82237 Wörthsee, Germany (Home). *Telephone:* (89) 23031135 (Office). *Fax:* (89) 23031100.

FUJIMORI, Alberto Kenyo; Peruvian politician and academic; b. 28 July 1939, Lima; s. of the late Nagochi Minami and Matsue Inomoto; m. Susana Higushi (divorced 1996); two s. two d.; ed Nat. School of Agric., Univ. of Wisconsin; fmr Rector, Nat. Agrarian Univ.; Pres. Nat. Ass. of Rectors 1984–89; Founder-mem. Cambio '90 (political party); Pres. of Peru 1990–2000; in exile in Japan Nov. 2000–; arrested and charged in connection with state-sponsored murders Sept. 2001; allegedly planning return from exile 2002; Dr. hc (Glebloux, Belgium, San Martín de Porres, Lima).

FUJIMORI, Masamichi; Japanese executive; b. 22 Dec. 1921, Osaka; s. of Tatsumaro Fujimori and Kimiko Ono; m. Yoko Sato 1951; two d.; ed Tokyo Imperial Univ.; lecturer, First Faculty of Tech., Tokyo Univ. 1948; joined Sumitomo Metal Mining Co. Ltd 1950, Gen. Man. Metallurgy Dept 1971, Dir 1972, Man. Dir 1977, Sr Man. Dir 1979, Exec. Vice-Pres. 1981, Pres. 1983–88, Chair. 1988–92, Adviser 1992–; Pres. Japan Mining Industry Asscn 1987–88; Exec. Dir Fed. of Econ. Orgs. 1988–92; Hon. Fellow Inst. of Mining and Metallurgy 1985; Blue Ribbon Medal 1982; Order of the Sacred Treasure (First Class) 1995. *Leisure interest:* bonsai. *Address:* Sumitomo Metal Mining Co. Ltd, 5-11-3, Shimbashi, Minato-ku, Tokyo, Japan (Office). *Telephone:* (3) 3436-7744 (Office).

FUJIMOTO, Takao; Japanese politician; b. 1931, Kagawa Pref.; m.; one s.; ed Tokyo Univ.; joined Nomura Securities Co. Ltd 1944; joined Nippon Telegraph and Telephone Public Corpn 1957; elected House of Reps. for 1st constituency Kagawa Pref. 1963; Parl. Vice-Minister of Science and Tech. Agency 1970; Chair. Liberal Democratic Party (LDP) Science and Tech. Sub-Cttee of the Policy Research Cttee 1972; Parl. Vice-Minister of the Environment Agency 1973; Chair. Standing Cttee on Foreign Affairs 1976, LDP Standing Cttee on Public Information 1983; Minister of State, Dir-Gen. Okinawa Devt Agency 1985; Deputy Sec.-Gen. LDP 1985–86; Minister of Health and Welfare 1987–88, of Agric., Forestry and Fisheries 1996–98. *Leisure interests:* sports (baseball), reading, golf, karaoke singing. *Address:* c/o Liberal-Democratic Party, 1-11-23 Nagata-cho, Chiyoda-ku, Tokyo 100, Japan.

FUJITA, Akira; Japanese financial executive; b. 9 Dec. 1929; ed Tokyo Univ.; fmr Man. Dir The Daiwa Bank Ltd, fmr Pres.; fmr Counsellor, Advisor 1998–. *Leisure interests:* reading, sport. *Address:* Daiwa Bank Ltd, 21 Bingomachi 2-chome, Higashi-ku, Osaka 541, Japan.

FUJITA, Hiroyuki, PhD; Japanese university professor; b. 13 Dec. 1952, Tokyo; s. of Shigeru Fujita and Tokiko Fujita; m. Yumiko Kato 1982; ed Univ. of Tokyo; lecturer, Inst. of Industrial Science, Univ. of Tokyo 1980–81, Assoc. Prof. 1981–93, Prof. 1993–; Visiting Scientist, Francis Bitter Nat. Magnet Lab. Mass. Inst. of Tech. (MIT) 1983–85; M. Hetényi Award for Experimental Mechanics 1987. *Publications:* contribs. to books and numerous scientific papers in professional journals. *Leisure interests:* reading, skiing, tennis. *Address:* Institute of Industrial Science, 7-22-1 Roppongi, Minato-ku, Tokyo 106; 1-9-14 Senkawa, Toshima-ku, Tokyo 171, Japan (Home). *Telephone:* (3) 3402-6231 ext. 2353 (Office).

FUJITA, Yoshio, DrSc; Japanese astronomer; b. 28 Sept. 1908, Fukui City; s. of Teizo Fujita; m. Kazuko Nezu 1941; two s. one d.; ed Tokyo Univ.; Asst Prof. Univ. of Tokyo 1931, Prof. 1951–69, Prof. Emer. 1969–; Visiting Prof. Pa State Univ. 1971; Guest Investigator Dominion Astrophysical Observatory 1960, Mount Wilson and Palomar Observatories 1972, 1974; mem. Japan Acad. 1965–, Pres. 1994–2000; Foreign mem. Royal Soc. of Sciences, Liège 1969–; Imperial Prize, Japan Acad. 1955, Cultural Merit Award, Fukui City 1971, Hon. Citizen, Fukui City 1979, Cultural Merit Award 1996, Fukui Prefecture Award 2002. *Publications:* Interpretation of Spectra and Atmospheric Structure in Cool Stars 1970, Spectrocopic Study of Cool Stars 1977, Collected Papers on the Spectroscopic Behaviour of Cool Stars 1997. *Address:* 6-21-7 Renkoji, Tama-shi 206-0021, Japan. *Telephone:* (42) 374-4186.

FUKAYA, Takashi; Japanese politician; fmr Minister of Posts and Telecommunications; fmr Parl. Vice-Minister of Labour; mem. House of Reps., fmr Chair. Cttee on Communications; Minister of Home Affairs 1995–96.

FUKUDA, Yasuo; Japanese politician; b. 16 July 1936, Tokyo; s. of the late Takeo Fukuda (fmr Prime Minister of Japan); m. Kiyoko Fukuda; two s. one d.; ed Waseda Univ.; with petroleum refining and marketing co. 1959–76; Chief Sec. to Prime Minister Takeo Fukuda (father) 1977–78, Pvt. Sec. 1979–89; Liberal and Democratic Party (LDP) mem. House of Reps. for Gunma 4th Dist 1990–; Parl. Vice-Minister of Foreign Affairs 1995–96; Minister of State, Chief Cabinet Sec., Dir.-Gen. Okinawa Devt Agency 2000–01; Chief Cabinet Sec. (Gender Equality) and Minister of State April 2001–; Deputy Sec.-Gen. LDP 1997–98, Chair. Finance Cttee 1998, Dir.-Gen. Treasury Bureau 1999–2000, Deputy Chair. Policy Research Council 2000–. *Address:* Prime Minister's Office, 1-6-1, Nagata-cho, Chiyoda-ku, Tokyo 100-8914 (Office); 4-20-7, Nazawa, Setagaya-ku, Tokyo 154-0003, Japan (Home). *Telephone:* (3) 3508-7181 (Office); (3) 3410-2555 (Home). *Fax:* (3) 3508-3611 (Office); (3) 3410-3535 (Home).

FUKUI, Toshihiko; Japanese bank governor; b. 7 Nov. 1935; ed Univ. of Tokyo; joined Bank of Japan 1958, Exec. Dir 1989–94, Deputy Gov. 1994–98, Gov. 2003–; Chair. Fujitso Research Inst. 1998–; Vice-Chair. Japan Asscn of Corp. Execs 2001. *Address:* Nippon Ginko (Bank of Japan), 2-1-1, Hongoku-cho, Nihonbashi, Chuo-ku, Tokyo 100-8630, Japan (Office). *Telephone:* (3) 3279-1111 (Office). *Fax:* (3) 5200-2256 (Office). *Website:* www.boj.or.jp (Office).

FUKUKAWA, Shinji; Japanese business executive; b. 8 March 1932, Tokyo; s. of Tokushiro Fukukawa and Maki Fukukawa; m. Yoriko Kawada 1961; two d.; ed Univ. of Tokyo; served at Ministry of Int. Trade and Industry (MITI) 1955–88, Deputy Vice-Minister 1983–84, Dir-Gen. Industrial Policy Bureau 1984–86, Vice-Minister 1986–88; Pvt. Sec. to fmr Prime Minister Ohira 1978–80; Sr Adviser to MITI 1988–90, to Japan Industrial Policy Research Inst. 1988–90, to Global Industrial and Social Progress Research Inst. 1988–, to Nomura Research Inst. 1989–90; Exec. Vice-Pres. Kobe Steel Ltd 1990–94; CEO, Dentsu Inst. for Human Studies 1994–2002, Exec. Adviser Dentsu Inc. 2002–. *Publications:* Japan's Role in the 21st Century: Three Newisms 1990, Industrial Policy 1998, The Thinking of Successful Businessmen in the IT Age 2000. *Leisure interests:* tennis, golf, classical music, reading. *Address:* Dentsu Inc, Shiodome Annex Building, 1-8-3 Higashi-Shimbashi, Minato-ku, Tokyo 105-0021 (Office); 7-11, Okusawa 8-chome, Setagaya-ku, Tokyo 158-0083, Japan (Home). *Telephone:* (3) 6216-0101 (Office); (3) 3701-4956 (Home). *Fax:* (3) 6217-5611 (Office); (3) 3701-4956 (Home). *E-mail:* s.fukukawa@dentsu.co.jp (Office). *Website:* www.dihs.dentsu.co.jp (Office).

FUKUYAMA, Francis, PhD; American writer and social scientist; b. New York; ed Cornell and Harvard Univs; fmrly a sr social scientist, RAND Corpn, Washington, DC and Deputy Dir State Dept.'s Policy Planning Staff; Hirst Prof. of Public Policy, George Mason Univ., Fairfax, Va. *Publications:* The End of History and the Last Man 1992, Trust: The Social Virtues And the Creation of Prosperity 1996, The Great Disruption: Human Nature and the Reconstitution of the Social Order 1999. *Address:* George Mason University, Fairfax, VA 22030, USA.

FULCI, Francesco Paolo, LLD, MCL; Italian diplomatist; b. 19 March 1931, Messina; s. of Sebastiano Fulci and Enza Sciascia; m. Claris Glathar 1965; three c.; ed Messina Univ., Columbia Univ., New York, Coll. of Europe, Bruges and Acad. Int. Law, The Hague; entered Italian Foreign Service 1956; First Vice-Consul of Italy, New York 1958–61; Second Sec. Italian Embassy, Moscow 1961–63; Foreign Ministry, Rome 1963–68; Counsellor Italian Embassy, Paris 1968–74; Minister Italian Embassy, Tokyo 1974–76; Chief of Cabinet Pres. of Senate, Rome 1976–80; Amb. to Canada 1980–85; Amb. and Perm. Rep. to NATO, Brussels 1985–91; Sec.-Gen. Exec. Comm. of Information and Security Services, Rome 1991–93; Amb. and Perm. Rep. to UN, New York 1993–99; Vice-Pres. Ferrero Int., Rome 2000–; First Vice-Pres. ECOSOC 1998–99, Pres. 1999–2000; Ed. La Stampa, Turin 2000–; Hon. LLD (Windsor Univ., Ont.); Cross of Merit (FRG); Officier, Légion d'honneur (France); Commdr Imperial Order of the Sun (Japan), Great Cross, Order of Merit (Italy), Kt Order of Malta. *Leisure interest:* swimming. *Address:* La Stampa, Via Marenco 32, 10126 Turin, Italy (Office). *Telephone:* (011) 656811 (Office). *Fax:* (011) 655306 (Office). *E-mail:* lettere@lastampa.it (Office). *Website:* www.lastampa.it (Office).

FULLER, H. Larry; American business executive; Dir Amoco 1981–2000, Co-Chair., CEO 1991–2000; Dir (non-exec.) Chase Manhattan Corpn, Chase Manhattan Bank, Motorola, Security Capital Group, Abbott Labs; mem. Bd Catalyst, American Petroleum Inst., Rehabilitation Inst. of Chicago; Trustee Orchestral Asscn. *Address:* Primacy Business Centre, 1/11 E Wainville Road, Suite 257, Naferville, IL 60563, USA (Office).

FULLER, Kathryn, MS, JD; American international organization executive, environmentalist and attorney; b. 8 July 1946, New York; m. Stephen Paul Doyle 1977; two s. one d.; ed Brown Univ., Providence, RI, Univs of Maryland and Texas; law clerk New York, Houston and Austin, TX 1974–76; to Chief Justice John V. Singleton, Jr, US Dist Court, Southern Dist of TX 1976–77; called to Bar, DC and TX; Attorney and adviser, Office of Legal Counsel, Dept of Justice, Washington, DC 1977–79, Attorney Wildlife and Marine Resources Section 1979–80, Chief Wildlife and Marine Resources Section 1981–82; Exec. Vice-Pres., Dir TRAFFIC USA 1982–89; Pres. and CEO World Wildlife Fund (WWF) USA 1989–; mem. council on Foreign Relations, Int. Council of Environmental Law, Overseas Devt Council; Hon DSc (Wheaton Coll.) 1990; Hon LLD (Knox Coll.) 1992; Hon DHumLitt (Brown Univ.) 1992; William Rogers Outstanding Grad. Award, Brown Univ. 1990, UNEP Global 500

FULLER, Lawrence Robert, B.J.; American newspaper publisher; b. 9 Sept. 1941, Toledo; s. of Kenneth Fuller and Marjory Rairdon; m. Suzanne Hovik 1967; one s. one d.; ed Univ. of Missouri; reporter, Globe Gazette, Mason City, Ia 1963–67; reporter, later city ed. Minneapolis Star 1967–75; Exec. Ed. Messenger-Inquirer, Owensborough, Ky 1975–77; Exec. Ed. Argus Leader, Sioux Falls, S.D. 1977–78, Pres., Publr 1974–84, 1986–99; Pres. Gannett News Media, Washington 1984–85; Dir Corp. Communications, Gannett Co. Inc. Washington 1985–86; Vice-Pres. Gannett/West Regional Newspaper Group 1986–, The Honolulu Advertisers 1986–; several directorships; mem. American Newspaper Publishers' Asscn, American Soc. of Newspaper Eds. etc. *Address:* 605 Kapiolani Boulevard, Honolulu, HI 96813, USA.

FULLER, Simon; British music promoter, business executive and artiste manager; currently Artiste Man. of numerous artsists including Annie Lennox (q.v.), Emma Bunton, Will Young, Gareth Gates and Kelly Clarkson; fmr Man. of Paul Hardcastle 1985, Madonna (q.v.), Cathy Dennis, Spice Girls –1997, 21st Century Girls and S Club 7 (later S Club, including TV series and S Club Juniors); Creator of Popstars (ITV1), Pop Idol (ITV1), American Idol – The Search for a Superstar (Fox TV), Popstars – The Rivals (ITV1); Founder and Dir "19 Group" 1985 (comprising 19 Brands, 19 Entertainment, 19 Int. Sports Man., 19 Man., 19 Merchandising, 19 Productions, 19 Recordings, 19 Songs, 19 Touring, 19 TV, Brilliant 19); dir numerous other cos. *Address:* c/o 19 Management, Unit 32, Ransomes Dock, 35–37 Parkgate Road, London, SW11 4NP, England (Office). *Website:* www.19.co.uk (Office).

FULLERTON, R. Donald, BA; Canadian banker; b. 7 June 1931, Vancouver, BC; s. of the late C. G. Fullerton and Muriel E. Fullerton; m.; ed Univ. of Toronto; joined Canadian Bank of Commerce (now CIBC), Vancouver 1953, Agent, New York 1964, Exec. Vice-Pres. 1973, Dir 1974–, Pres. and Chief Operating Officer 1976–84, Chair. and CEO 1984–92, Chair. Exec. Cttee 1992–99; Dir Asia Satellite Telecommunications Holdings Ltd., George Weston Ltd., Hollinger Inc.; mem. a number of other medical, cultural and educational insts. *Address:* c/o CIBC, Head Office, Commerce Court W, Toronto, Ont., M5L 1A2, Canada.

FUMAROLI, Marc, DèsL; French professor of rhetoric; b. 10 June 1932, Marseille; ed Lycée Thiers Marseille, Univ. Aix-en-Provence, Univ. Sorbonne; Prof. Sorbonne, Paris 1976; Titular Prof. Chair. of Rhetoric and European Soc. of 16th and 17th Centuries, Collège de France 1986–; Prof. Univ. of Chicago 1996–; Dir XVIIe siècle (journal) 1981–88; mem. Advisory Council, Bibliothèque Nationale 1988–92; fmr Pres. Soc. Int. d'Histoire de la Rhétorique; Pres. Soc. of Friends of the Louvre 1996–; mem. Acad. Française 1995–, High Cttee of Nat. Celebrations 1998–; Corresp. mem. British Acad., mem. US Acad. of Sciences, Letters and Arts, Accad. dei Lincei; other appointments; Officier, Légion d'honneur, Commdr, Ordre des Palmes académiques, Officier Ordre nat. du Mérite, Cmmdr des Arts et des Lettres; Dr hc (Naples 1996, Bologna 1999); numerous academic prizes. *Publications include:* L'Age de l'éloquence 1980, La Diplomatie de l'esprit 1994, l'école du silence 1994, Trois institutions littéraires 1994, la Période 1600–1630 1994, Fables de Jean de la Fontaine (Ed., Vol. I 1985, Vol. II 1995), Le Poète et le roi, Jean de La Fontaine et son siècle 1997, Poussin: Sainte Françoise Romaine 2001, Quand l'Europe parlait français 2001; numerous articles in professional journals; numerous pamphlets, essays and articles. *Leisure interest:* photography. *Address:* Collège de France, 11 place Marcelin Berthelot, 75231 Paris cedex 05 (Office); 11 rue de l'Université, 75007 Paris, France (Home). *Telephone:* 1-44-27-10-17 (Office). *Fax:* 1-44-27-17-91 (Office).

FUNADA, Hajime; Japanese politician; b. 22 Nov. 1953, Utsunomiya City, Tochigi Pref.; s. of Yuzuru Funada and Masako Funada; m. Rumi Funada 1978; one s. two d.; ed Keio Univ.; mem. House of Reps. from Tochigi 1979–; Head, Youth Section of Nat. Organizing Cttee, LDP 1985–86; State Sec. for Man. and Co-ordination Agency 1986–87, for Ministry of Educ. 1987–88; Dir Educ. Div. of Policy Research Council, LDP 1988–89; Dir Foreign Affairs Div. 1990–92; Chair. Sub-Cttee of Counselling Japan Overseas Co-operation Volunteers 1989–90; Minister of State for Econ. Planning 1992–93; Co-founder of Japan Renewal Party (Shinseito) 1993, Deputy Sec. Gen. for Organizational Affairs 1993–94, Deputy Sec. Gen. for Political Affairs 1994; Vice-Chair. Diet Man. Cttee, 'Reform' In-House Grouping (Kaikaku) 1994; Co-founder New Frontier Party (Shinshinto) 1994, Vice-Chair. Org. Cttee 1994–95, Deputy Sec. Gen. 1995–96, Assoc. Chair. Gen. Council 1995–96, resgnd from Party 1996; Head of '21st Century' In-House Grouping (21seiki) 1996; rejoined Liberal Democratic Party 1997, Chair. Sub-Cttee on Asia and the Pacific, mem. Policy Deliberation Comm., mem. Gen. Council 1997–; mem. Ruling Parties Consultative Cttee on Guidelines for Japan–U.S. Defence Co-operation 1997–; Dir Cttee on Health and Welfare, House of Reps. 1998–. *Leisure interests:* astronomy, driving. *Address:* Shugiin Daini Giinkaikan, Room 412, 2-1-2 Nagata-cho, Chiyoda-ku, Tokyo 100, Japan. *Telephone:* (3) 3508-7412. *Fax:* (3) 3500-5612.

FUNCKE, Liselotte; German politician; b. 20 July 1918, Hagen; d. of Oscar Funcke and Bertha Funcke (née Osthaus); ed commercial studies in Berlin; fmrly in industry and commerce, Hagen and Wuppertal; mem. Diet of North Rhine-Westphalia 1950–61; mem. Bundestag 1961–79, Vice-Pres. Bundestag 1969–79; Chair. Bundestag Finance Cttee 1972–79; mem. Presidium, FDP 1968–82, Deputy Chair. FDP 1977–82; Minister of Economy and Transport,

North Rhine-Westphalia 1979–80; Govt Rep. responsible for integration of overseas workers and their families 1981–91; Dr. hc; Bundesverdienstkreuz 1973 and other medals. *Publication:* Hagener Strassen Erzählen Geschichte. *Address:* Ruhr-Str. 15, 58097 Hagen, Germany (Home). *Telephone:* (2331) 182034.

FUNG, Victor K., CBE; Chinese businessman; joined Li Fung 1973, Man. Dir 1981–89, Chair. 1989–; Chair. Prudential Asia Investments Ltd; Chair. Hong Kong Trade Devt Council 1991–2000, Hong Kong Airport Authority 1999–; mem. Hong Kong Judicial Officers Recommendation Cttee, Asian Business Advisory Council. *Address:* Li Fung Tower, 888 Cheung Sha Wan Road, Kowloon, Hong Kong Special Administrative Region, People's Republic of China (Office).

FUNKE, Karl-Heinz; German politician; b. 29 April 1946, Dangast; m. Petra Timm 1982; three c.; ed Hamburg Univ.; apprenticeship in admin. 1960–63; joined Social Democratic Party of Germany (SPD) 1966; mil. service 1966–68; Dist councillor Friesland 1972–, also city councillor at Varel vocational school and on family farm 1974, took over family farm 1983; mem. Lower Saxony Landtag 1978–; Mayor of Varel 1981–96; Minister of Food, Agric. and Forestry Lower Saxony 1990–98; Fed. Minister of Food, Agric. and Forestry 1998–2001. *Leisure interests:* literature, history, hunting. *Address:* c/o Ministry of Food, Agriculture and Forestry, Rochusstrasse 1, 53123 Bonn (Office); Calenberger Strasse 2, 30169 Hannover, Germany.

FURCHGOTT, Robert Francis, PhD; American professor of pharmacology; b. 4 June 1916, Charleston, SC; m. 1941; three c.; ed Univ. of N Carolina, Northwestern Univ.; Research Fellow in Medicine, Medical Coll., Cornell Univ. 1940–43, Research Assoc. 1943–47, Instructor in Physiology 1943–48, Asst Prof. of Medical Biochemistry 1947–49; Asst Prof., later Assoc. Prof. of Pharmacology, Medical School, Wash. Univ. 1949–56; Chair. of Dept, S.U.N.Y. Health Sciences Center, Brooklyn 1956–83; Prof. of Health Sciences Center, Brooklyn State Univ. 1956–88, Univ. Distinguished Prof. 1988–; Prof. Emer. of Pharmacology 1990–; Visiting Prof. Univ. of Geneva 1962–63, Univ of Calif., San Diego 1971–72, Medical Univ. of SC 1980, Univ. of Calif. 1980; Adjunct Prof. of Pharmacology, School of Medicine, Univ. of Miami 1989–2001; Distinguished Visiting Prof. Medical Univ. of SC 2001–; mem. AAAS, NAS, ACS, American Soc. Biochem., American Soc. of Pharmacology and Experimental Therapeutics (Pres. 1971–72); Hon. DM (Madrid) 1984, (Lund) 1984; Hon. DSc (NC) 1989, (Ghent) 1995; Goodman and Gilman Award 1984, Research Achievement Award, American Heart Asscn 1990, Bristol-Myers Squibb Award for achievement in cardiovascular research 1991, Gairdner Fund Int. Award 1991, Medal of NY Acad. of Medicine 1992, Roussel Uclaf Prize for research in cell communication and signalling 1994, Wellcome Gold Medal, British Pharmacology Soc. 1995, ASPET Award for Experimental Therapeutics 1996, jt winner Nobel Prize for Medicine 1998. *Address:* State University of New York Health Sciences Center, Department of Pharmacology, 450 Clarkson Avenue, #29, Brooklyn, NY 11203-2056, USA.

FURCHTGOTT-ROTH, Harold W., PhD; American economist; b. b. 13 Dec. 1956, Knoxville, Tenn.; s. of Ernest Furchtgott and Mary A. Wilkes Furchtgott; m. Diana E. Roth; five s. one d.; ed Massachusetts Inst. of Tech., Stanford Univ.; Research Analyst, Center for Naval Analyses, Alexandria, Va 1984–88; Sr Economist, Economists Inc., Washington, D.C. 1988–95; Chief Economist U.S. House Cttee on Commerce 1995–97; Commr Fed. Communications Comm. 1997–. *Publications:* (co-author): International Trade in Computer Software (jtly.) 1993, Economics of a Disaster: The Exxon Valdez Oil Spill (with others) 1995, Cable TV: Regulations or Competition (jtly.) 1996. *Address:* Federal Communications Commission, 445 12th Street S.W., Washington, DC 20554 (Office); 5207 Westwood Drive, Bethesda, MD 20816, USA (Home). *Telephone:* (202) 418-2000 (Office); (301) 229-3593 (Home). *E-mail:* hfurchtg@fcc.gov (Office); furchtgottroth@aol.com (Home). *Website:* www.fcc .gov (Office).

FURGLER, Kurt, DrIur; Swiss politician and lawyer; b. 24 June 1924, St-Gall; m. Ursula Stauffenegger; two s. four d.; ed Univs. of Fribourg, Zürich, Geneva, Grad. Inst. for Int. Studies, Geneva; Lawyer, St-Gall 1950–71; mem. Nat. Council 1955–71; Leader of Christian Dem. Party Group in Fed. Council; mem. Fed. Council 1972–, Vice-Pres. Jan.–Dec. 1976, Jan.–Dec. 1980, Jan.–Dec. 1984, Pres. of the Swiss Fed. Jan.–Dec. 1977, Jan.–Dec. 1981, Jan.–Dec. 1985; Head of Fed. Dept of Justice and Police 1972–83, of Dept of Public Economy 1983–86; Hon. DJur (Boston Univ.) 1985. *Leisure interests:* sport, music, literature. *Address:* Dufourstr. 34, 9000 St-Gall, Switzerland.

FURNO, HE Cardinal Carlo, PhD; Italian ecclesiastic; b. 2 Dec. 1921, Bairo Canavese; Sec. to Nunciature to Colombia 1953–57, to Ecuador 1957–60; Sec. Apostolic Del. to Jerusalem 1960–62; Sec. of State 1962–73; Apostolic Nuncio to Peru 1973–78, to Lebanon 1978–82, to Brazil 1982–92, to Italy 1992–94; cr. Cardinal 1994; mem. Pontifical Comm. for Vatican City State; Grand Master Equestrian Order of the Holy Sepulchre of Jerusalem 1995–; Pres. Admin. Council, Lumsa Univ.; Archpriest St Mary Major Basilica 1997. *Address:* Piazza Città Leonina, 00193 Rome, Italy. *Telephone:* (06) 9882053. *Fax:* (06) 9802298.

FURSE, Clara Hedwig Frances, BSc; British/Canadian business executive; b. 16 Sept. 1957; m. Richard Furse 1981; two s. one d.; ed St. James's School, West Malvern, London School of Econs; Man. Dir UBS 1983–98; Deputy Chair. LIFFE 1997–99; Group Chief Exec. Crédit Lyonnais Rouse 1998–2000; Chief Exec. London Stock Exchange PLC 2001–; mem. Financial Services

Practitioner Forum 2001–. *Address:* London Stock Exchange, London, EC2N 1HP, England (Office). *Telephone:* (20) 7797-1000 (Office). *Website:* www .londonstockexchange.com (Office).

FURSENKO, Aleksander Aleksandrovich; Russian historian; b. 11 Nov. 1927; s. of Alexander Vasilievich Fursenko and Vanda Vladislavovna Fursenko (née Rokitskaya); m. Natalia Lvovna Fursenko (Gol'dina) 1948; two s.; ed Leningrad State Univ.; researcher Leningrad br. of Inst. of History USSR (now Russian) Acad. of Sciences; fmr First Deputy Chair. Presidium Scientific Cen. Acad. of Sciences; Corresp. mem. USSR Acad. of Sciences 1987, mem. 1990, Acad.-Sec. Dept of History 1996–2002; with St Petersburg Inst. of History; research in history of USA, econ. history, int. relations. *Publications include:* Struggle for the Partition of China and the American Open Doors Doctrine 1956, Oil Trusts and World Politics 1880–1918 1965, Rockefellers' Dynasty 1970, American Revolution and Formation of USA 1978, The Battle for Oil: The Economics and Politics of International Corporate Conflict over Petroleum 1990, One Hell of a Gamble: Khrushchev, Kennedy and Castro 1958–64 (with Timothy Naftali) 1997. *Leisure interest:* mountain skiing. *Address:* 32A Leninskiy prospekt, Presidium of Academy of Sciences, Department of History, 117993 Moscow; 7 Petrozavodskaya ul., Institute of History, 197110 St Petersburg, Russia. *Telephone:* (095) 938-17-63 (Moscow); (812) 230-68-50, (812) 235-41-98 (St Petersburg). *Fax:* (095) 938-18-44 (Moscow); (812) 235-64-85 (St Petersburg). *E-mail:* fursenko@leontief.ru.

FÜRST, Janos Kalman; British orchestral conductor; b. 8 Aug. 1935, Budapest, Hungary; s. of Lajos Fürst and Borbala Spitz; m. 1st Antoinette Reynolds 1962 (divorced 1977); two s.; m. 2nd Ingeborg Nordenfelt; ed Franz Liszt Acad. of Music, Budapest and Brussels Conservatory; Dir Irish Chamber Orchestra 1963–66; Resident Conductor Ulster Orchestra 1967–71; Chief Conductor Malmö Symphony Orchestra 1974–78; Music Dir Marseilles Opera 1981–; Music Dir Aalborg Symphony Orchestra 1980–83; Dir Marseilles Philharmonic Orchestra 1985–; fmr Chief Conductor Irish Radio and TV Symphony Orchestra 1987; Swedish Gramophone Prize 1980. *Leisure interests:* reading and history. *Address:* c/o EMI Classics, 30 Gloucester Place, London, W1A 1ES, England (Office).

FURTH, Warren Wolfgang, AB, JD; American fmr international official, consultant and lawyer; b. 1 Aug. 1928, Vienna, Austria; s. of John W. Furth and Hedwig von Ferstel; m. Margaretha F. de la Court 1959; one s. one d.; ed Harvard Coll., Harvard Law School and Sloan School of Management of Mass. Inst. of Tech.; Law Clerk, Palmer, Dodge, Gardner, Bickford & Bradford, Boston, Mass. 1951; admitted to New York Bar 1952; Law Clerk to Hon. H. M. Stephens, Chief Judge, US Court of Appeals, Dist of Columbia Circuit 1952–53; US Army 1953–57; Assoc. Cravath, Swaine & Moore (law firm) 1957–58; with ILO, Geneva 1959–70, Exec. Asst to Dir-Gen. 1964–66, Chief of Tech. Co-operation Branch and Deputy Chief, Field Dept 1966–68, Deputy Chief, later Chief, Personnel and Admin. Services Dept 1968–70; Asst Dir-Gen. WHO (Admin. Services; Co-ordinator, Special Programme for Research & Training in Tropical Diseases and responsibility for Special Programme for Research, Devt and Research Training in Human Reproduction) 1971–89; int.

health consultant to US Govt, World Bank and pharmaceutical industry 1989–94; Assoc. Exec. Dir American Citizens Abroad 1994–2000; Chair. American Democrats Abroad, Switzerland 2001–. *Address:* 13 route de Presinge, 1241 Puplinge (Geneva), Switzerland (Home). *Telephone:* (22) 3497267. *Fax:* (22) 3493826 (Home). *E-mail:* wfurth@infomaniak.ch (Home).

FUSSELL, Paul, MA, PhD; American author and university professor; b. 22 March 1924, Pasadena, Calif.; s. of Paul Fussell and Wilhma Wilson Sill; m. 1st Betty Harper 1949 (divorced 1987); one s. one d.; m. 2nd Harriette Behringer 1987; ed Pomona Coll., Harvard Univ.; Instructor in English, Conn. Coll. 1951–54; Asst Prof. then Prof. of English, Rutgers Univ. 1955–76, John DeWitt Prof. of English Literature 1976–83; Donald T. Regan Prof. of English Literature, Univ. of Pa 1983–94, Emer. Prof. 1994–; Hon. LittD (Pomona Coll.) 1980, (Monmouth Coll., NJ) 1985; Nat. Book Award; Nat. Book Critics Circle Award; Emerson Award. *Publications:* Theory of Prosody in 18th Century England 1954, Poetic Meter and Poetic Form 1965, The Rhetorical World of Augustan Humanism 1965, Samuel Johnson and the Life of Writing 1971, The Great War and Modern Memory 1975, Abroad: British Literary Travelling between the Wars 1980, The Boy Scout Handbook and Other Observations 1982, Class: A Guide through the American Status System 1983, Sassoon's Long Journey (ed.) 1983, The Norton Book of Travel (ed.) 1987, Thank God for the Atom Bomb and Other Essays 1988, Wartime: Understanding and Behaviour in the Second World War 1989, Killing in Verse and Prose and other essays 1990, The Norton Book of Modern War (ed.) 1991, BAD: or, The Dumbing of America 1991, The Bloody Game: An Anthology of Modern War 1992, The Anti-Egotist: Kingsley Amis, Man of Letters 1994, Doing Battle: The Making of a Skeptic 1996, Uniforms 2002. *Leisure interest:* reading. *Address:* Apt. 4-H, 2020 Walnut Street, Philadelphia, PA 19103, USA. *Telephone:* (215) 557-0144.

FYFE, William Sefton, CC, PhD, FRS, FRSC, FRSNZ; Canadian professor of geochemistry; b. 4 June 1927, New Zealand; s. of Colin and Isabella Fyfe; m. Patricia Walker 1981; two s. one d.; ed Univ. of Otago, New Zealand; Lecturer in Chemistry, Otago Univ. 1955–58; Prof. of Geology, Univ. of Calif., Berkeley 1958–66; Royal Soc. Prof. Manchester Univ. 1966–72; Chair. Dept of Geology, Univ. of Western Ont. 1972–84, Prof. of Geology 1984–92, Prof. Emer. 1992–, Dean Faculty of Science 1986–90; Pres. Int. Union of Geological Sciences 1992–96; Hon. mem. Brazilian, Russian and Indian Acad. of Sciences; Hon. DSc (Memorial Univ.) 1989, (Lisbon) 1990, (Lakehead) 1990, (Guelph) 1992, (St Mary's) 1994, (Otago) 1995, (Univ. of Western Ont.) 1995; awards include Guggenheim Fellowships, Logan Medal, Holmes Medal, European Union of Geosciences 1989, Day Medal, Geological Soc. of America 1990, NZ Commemorative Medal 1991, Canada Gold Medal 1992, Roebling Medal 1995, Nat. Order of Scientific Merit, Brazil 1996, Wollaston Medal, Geological Soc., London 2000. *Publications:* 5 books, 800 scientific papers. *Leisure interests:* wildlife, swimming, travel. *Address:* Department of Earth Sciences, B and G Building, University of Western Ontario, London, Ont., N6A 5B7 (Office); 1197 Richmond Street, London, Ont., N6A 3L3, Canada (Home). *Telephone:* (519) 661-3180 (Office). *Fax:* (519) 661-2179 (Office). *E-mail:* pjfyfe@uwo.ca (Office).

GABAGLIO, Emilio, BA(Econs); Italian international trade union official; b. 1 July 1937, Como; m.; two d.; ed Catholic Univ., Milan; fmr high school teacher; mem. Italian Workers Christian Asscn, Nat. Pres. 1969–72; Officer, Italian Workers Unions Confed. (CISL) 1974–, elected to Nat. Secr. 1983–, represented CISL in ILO and in Exec. Cttees of European Trade Union Confed. (ETUC) and ICFTU; Gen. Sec. ETUC 1991–; mem. Exec. Cttee, European Movement Int., Bd Trustees, Acad. of European Law, Trier, Advisory Bd, European Policy Centre, Brussels. *Address:* European Trade Union Confederation, 5 blvd du Roi Albert II, 1210 Brussels, Belgium (Office). *Telephone:* (2) 224-04-39 (Office). *Fax:* (2) 224-05-46 (Office). *E-mail:* egabaglio@etuc.org (Office). *Website:* www.etuc.org (Office).

GABALLA, Ali Gaballa, PhD; Egyptian archaeologist and Egyptologist; b. El Menoufiah; m.; three c.; ed Cairo Univ., Liverpool Univ.; Asst lecturer Cairo Univ. 1962–63, lecturer –1974, Assoc. Prof. of Egyptology –1979, Chair. of Dept then Vice-Dean of Faculty of Archaeology, then Dean; f. archaeology section, Faculty of Arts, Kuwait Univ.; now Sec.-Gen. Supreme Council of Antiquities; State Award for History and Archaeology 1979, Order of Merit for Sciences and Arts. *Publications:* Glimpses of Ancient Egypt 1979, The Third Intermediate Period in Egypt 1996, The History and Culture of Nubia 1997, Encyclopaedia of the Egyptian Civilization (co-ed.) and numerous other books.

GABBANA, Stefano; Italian fashion designer; b. 14 Nov. 1962, Milan; studied graphic design; Asst in a Milan atelier; with Domenico Dolce (q.v.) opened fashion consulting studio 1982, selected to take part in New Talents show, Milano Collezioni 1985; f. Dolce & Gabbana 1985, first maj. women's collection 1985, knitwear 1987, beachwear 1989, men's wear 1990, women's fragrance, D&G line 1992, men's fragrance, home collection 1994, jeans line, eyewear 1996; opened boutiques Milan, Hong Kong, Singapore, Taipei, Seoul, London; Woolmark Award 1991, Perfume Acad. Int. Prize for Best Feminine Fragrance of Year 1993, Best Masculine Fragrance of Year 1995. *Address:* Dolce & Gabbana, Via Santa Cecilia 7, 20122 Milan, Italy (Office). *Telephone:* (02) 54108152 (Office). *Fax:* (02) 76020600 (Office).

GABLENTZ, Otto von der; German diplomatist; b. 9 Oct. 1930, Berlin; s. of Prof. Otto Heinrich von der Gablentz and Hilda von der Gablentz (née Zietlow); m. Christa Gerke 1965; one s. four d.; ed Univs. of Berlin and Freiburg, Coll. of Europe, Bruges, St Anthony's Coll. Oxford and Harvard Univ.; joined foreign service of Fed. Repub. of Germany 1959; served in Australia 1961–64, worked in Bonn on Berlin and Germany 1964–67, German Embassy, London 1967–72, Dept of European Political Co-operation 1973–78, seconded to Chancellor's Office 1978, Head of Section, Foreign and Defence Policy 1981; Amb. to Netherlands 1983–90; Amb. to Israel 1990–93; Amb. to Russia 1993–95; Rector Coll. of Europe, Bruges 1996–; Hon. Fellow Jerusalem Univ. 1993–; Hon. degree (Amsterdam) 1997. *Address:* Hoornstraat 4, 8000 Bruges (Office); Konstantinstrasse 22, 53179 Bonn, Germany; College of Europe, Dijver II, 8000 Bruges, Belgium. *Telephone:* (228) 355654 (Germany); (50) 44-99-11 (Belgium). *Fax:* (228) 357234 (Germany); (50) 44-99-00 (Belgium).

GABRE-SELLASSIE, Zewde, PhD; Ethiopian diplomatist; b. 12 Oct. 1926, Metcha, Shoa; ed Haile Sellassie I Secondary School, Coll. des Frères and St George School, Jerusalem, Coll. des Frères and American Mission, Cairo, Univ. of Exeter, Oxford Univ. and Lincoln's Inn, London; Econ. Attaché, later Head of Press, Information and Admin. Div., Ministry of Foreign Affairs 1951–53; Dir-Gen. Maritime Affairs 1953–55; Deputy Minister, Ministry of Public Works, Transport and Civil Aviation 1955–57; Mayor and Gov. of Addis Ababa 1957–59; Amb. to Somalia 1959–60; Minister of Justice 1961–63; Sr mem. St Antony's Coll., Oxford 1963–71; Perm. Rep. to the UN 1972–74; Minister of Interior March–May 1974, of Foreign Affairs May–Dec. 1974; Deputy Prime Minister July–Sept. 1974; Visiting lecturer, Univ. of Calif. 1965; Vice-Pres. ECOSOC 1974; Officer of Menelik II, Grand Cross of Phoenix (Greece), of Istiqlal (Jordan), Grand Officer Flag of Yugoslavia, Order of Merit (Fed. Repub. of Germany).

GABRIADZE, Revaz (Rezo) Levanovich; Georgian scriptwriter, film director, sculptor and artist; b. 29 June 1936, Kutaisi; m. 2nd Yelena Zakharyevna Dzhaparidze; one s. one d.; ed Tbilisi State Univ., Higher Courses of Scriptwriters and Film Directors in Moscow; worked as corresp. Molodezh Gruzii; works for Gruzia Film Studio 1970–; wrote scripts for over 35 films including Do not Grieve 1969, Serenade (after M. Zoshchenko) 1969, Jug (after L. Pirandello) 1970, Unusual Show 1970, White Stone 1973, Cranks 1974, Road, Mimino 1978, Kin-dza-dza; Founder and Artistic Dir Tbilisi Puppet Theatre 1981, wrote and produced plays Traviata, Diamond of Marshal Fantier, Fall of Our Spring (USSR State Prize), Daughter of the Emperor of Trapezund; puppet productions in Switzerland and France 1991–94 including Ree Triste la Fin de l'Allee (Lausanne), Kutaisi (Rennes); Artistic Dir Cen. Puppet Theatre, Moscow 1994–95; Dir St Petersburg Satire Theatre 1996; productions include Song of the Volga 1996; numerous monumental and miniature sculptures including Chizhik-Pyzhik, Nose (after N. Gogol) ceramics exhibited in St Petersburg, Rabinovich (Odessa); graphic and painting shows in Moscow, St Petersburg, Paris, Rennes, Berlin, Lausanne; in Dijon and St Petersburg; illustrated works of A. Pushkin. *Address:* Pyryeva str. 26. korp. 1, Apt. 14, 119285 Moscow, Russia. *Telephone:* (095) 147-45-94 (Home).

GABRIEL, Edward M., BS; American diplomatist and business executive; ed Gannon Univ., Pa; Pres. and owner Gabriel Group; Sr Vice-Pres. in charge of Corp. Public Affairs, CONCORD Corpn; Pres. and CEO Madison Public Affairs Group; Amb. to Morocco 1997–2001; Sr Counsellor, Middle Eastern and Russian Issues, Center for Democracy; Founding mem. Exec. Cttee and Bd of Dirs., American Task Force on Lebanon; Dir Keystone Center. *Address:* c/o Department of State, 2201 C Street, NW, Washington, DC 20520, USA (Office).

GABRIEL, Michal; Czech sculptor; b. 25 Feb. 1960, Prague; s. of František Gabriel and Jarmila Gabrielová; m. Milada Dočekalová 1987; two s. one d.; ed Secondary School of Applied Arts, Acad. of Fine Arts, Prague; apprenticed in timber industry; worked as skilled joiner 1975–78; graduated as woodcarver 1984, as sculptor 1987; Founding mem. creative group Tvrdohlaví ('The Stubborn' group) 1987; First Prize for statue Pegasus, Prague 1988 (work subsequently completed), for gates for Nat. Gallery Bldg 1989 (completed 1992); Angel Sculpture (bronze), Bank in Opava 1995, 'The Winged Leopard', gilded bronze sculpture, entrance Pres.'s Office, Prague Castle 1996; City Hall windows, České Budějovice 2000; Fountain (metal), Hradec Králové 2001; 'Trunk' sculpture, Philosophy Faculty Brno 2002; Lecturer Faculty of Performing Arts, Czech Univ. of Tech., Brno 1999–; co-f. new Exhbnhall, Palace Lucerne, Prague 2000; Jindřich Chalupecký Prize 1994. *Group exhibitions:* Graz, Austria 1989, Hořice v Podkrkonoší 1990, Prague 1999, 2000, 2001, 2002, Slovenia 1995, Germany 1996, Hungary 1997, Russia 1999, Estonia 2000, Netherlands 2000, New York 2001, Slovakia 2001, Brno 2002. *Publication:* Tvrdohlaví 2000. *Address:* Dlouhá 32, 110 00 Prague 1, Czech Republic (Home). *Telephone:* (2) 22314644 (Home). *Fax:* (2) 22314644 (Home). *E-mail:* michalgabriel@hotmail.com (Office). *Website:* www.ffa.vutbr.cz/gabriel (Office).

GABRIEL, Peter; British rock singer and songwriter; b. 13 Feb. 1950, Woking; m. Jill Gabriel; two d.; ed Charterhouse school; co-f. Genesis rock band 1966; left group to start career as soloist 1975; numerous solo albums; f. World of Music, Arts and Dance (WOMAD) featuring music from around the world 1982; f. Real World Group to develop interactive projects in arts and tech. 1985, Real World Studios 1986, Real World Records (world music record label) 1989, Real World Multimedia 1994; launched 'Witness' Human Rights Programme 1992; Dr hc (City Univ.) 1991; Hon. MA (Univ. Coll., Salford) 1994; Hon. DMus (Bath) 1996. *Singles include:* Solsbury Hill, Games Without Frontiers, Shock the Monkey, Big Time, Sledgehammer, Don't Give Up, Biko, In Your Eyes. *Solo albums:* PG I–IV, PG Plays Live 1983, So 1986, Shaking the Tree (compilation) 1990, Us 1992, Ovo 2000, Up 2002. *Soundtrack albums:* Birdy, Passion (Last Temptation of Christ). *Address:* c/o Martin Hopewell, Primary Talent, 2–12 Pentonville Road, London, N1 9PL (Office); Real World, Box Mill, Box, Wilts., SN14 9PL, England. *Telephone:* (20) 7833-8998 (Office).

GABRIEL, Sigmar; German politician; b. 12 Sept. 1959, Goslar; m.; one d.; ed Gottingen Univ.; joined Social Democratic Party (SPD) 1977; adult educ. lecturer 1983–88; teacher, Saxony Adult Educ. Inst. 1989–90; Dist Councillor for Goslar 1987–98, City Councillor 1991–, Chair. Environmental Cttee 1991–96, Econ. Affairs and Tourism Cttee 1996; mem. Lower Saxony Parl. 1990–; SPD Speaker for Home Affairs 1994–97; Deputy Chair. SPD 1997–98, Chair. 1998–99; Prime Minister of Lower Saxony Dec. 1999–. *Leisure interests:* cycling, travel (Middle East), sailing. *Address:* Office of the Prime Minister, Hanover, Lower Saxony, Germany (Office).

GABRIELSE, Gerald, MS, PhD; American professor of physics; ed Calvin Coll., Grand Rapids, Mich., Univ. of Chicago; teaching asst Calvin Coll., Grand Rapids, Mich. 1971–72, research asst 1972–73; grad. student, Univ. of Chicago 1973–78; Research Assoc., Univ. of Washington, Seattle 1978–82, Research Asst Prof. 1985–86, Assoc. Prof. 1986–87; Prof. of Physics, Harvard Univ. 1987– (Chair. Physics Dept 2000–03); Physicist, CERN, leader of ATRAP antimatter physics research project, Geneva, Switzerland; Consultant, Intermagnetics Gen. Corpn 1995, PolyChip Inc. 1999; Scientist in Residence, Lexington Christian Acad. 1995–96; mem. numerous cttees; Levenson Prize, Harvard Univ. 2000, Davisson-Germer Prize, American Physical Soc. 2002. *Lectures include:* around 200 lectures at scientific confs and univs. *Publications include:* more than 100 scientific publs. *Address:* Department of Physics, Harvard University, 17 Oxford Street, Cambridge, MA 02138, USA (Office). *Telephone:* (617) 495-4381 (Office). *E-mail:* gabrielse@hussle.harvard.edu (Office). *Website:* www.hussle.harvard.edu (Office).

GADDAFI, Col Mu'ammar Muhammad al-; Libyan political leader and army officer; b. 1942, Serte; s. of Mohamed Abdulsalam Abuminiar and Aisha Ben Niran; m. 1970; four s. one d.; ed Univ. of Libya, Benghazi; served with Libyan Army 1965–; Chair. Revolutionary Command Council 1969– (Head of State); C-in-C of Armed Forces Sept. 1969; Prime Minister 1970–72; Minister of Defence 1970–72; Sec.-Gen. of Gen. Secr. of Gen. People's Congress 1977–79; Chair. OAU 1982–83; mem. Presidential Council, Fed. of Arab Republics 1972; rank of Maj.-Gen. Jan. 1976, retaining title of Col. *Publications:* The Green Book (3 Vols), Military Strategy and Mobilization, The Story of the Revolution. *Address:* Office of the President, Tripoli, Libya.

GADDAFI, Wanis; Libyan politician; Head of Exec. Council in Cyrenaican Prov. Govt 1952–62; Fed. Minister of Foreign Affairs 1962–63, of Interior 1963–64, of Labour 1964; Amb. to Fed. Repub. of Germany 1964–65; Minister of Planning and Devt 1966–68, of Foreign Affairs 1968; Prime Minister 1968–69; imprisoned for two years 1971–73.

GADDAM, Encik Kasitah bin, BA; Malaysian politician; b. 18 Oct. 1947, Ranau, Sabah; m. Puan Rosnie bte Ambuting; four c.; ed Sabah Coll., Kota Kinabalu and Univ. of Malaya; Admin. Officer, Chief Minister's Dept Kota Kinabalu, Sabah 1971; Asst Dir of Immigration, Sabah 1971–76; Regional Man. K.P.D. for Kundasang, Ranau and Tambunan, Admin. Officer/ Purchasing Man. K.P.D. Headquarters, Kota Kinabalu 1977–80; Dir of Personnel for East Malaysia and Brunei, Inchcape Malaysia Holding Bhd. 1980–83; Chair. Sabah Devt Bank, Sabah Finance Bd, Soilogen (Sabah) Sdn. Bhd. 1985; mem. Parl. 1986–; Minister, Prime Minister's Dept 1986–89, Minister of Land and Regional Devt 1989–90; Vice-Pres. Parti Bersatu Sabah 1984.

GADJIYEV, Gadis Abdullayevich, DJur; Russian/Dagestani lawyer and judge; b. 27 Aug. 1957, Shovkra; m.; four s.; ed Moscow State Univ. 1975; teacher Dagestan State Univ. 1975–79; legal consultant Supreme Soviet Dagestan ASSR 1979–80, Head Legal Dept Admin. 1980–90, Chair. Comm. on Law and Local Self-Man. 1990–91; Justice Constitutional Court of Russian Fed. 1991–. *Publications:* over 80 scientific publs including 4 monographs on constitutional law. *Leisure interest:* pigeon raising. *Address:* Constitutional Court of Russian Federation, Ilyinka 21, 103132 Moscow, Russia (Office). *Telephone:* (095) 206-17-62 (Office). *Fax:* (095) 206-19-78 (Office).

GADSDEN, Sir Peter Drury Haggerston, GBE, MA, DSc, FREng, FIMM, FInstM, FRSH, FRCA; British business executive; b. 28 June 1929, Mannville, Canada; s. of late Rev. Basil C. Gadsen and Mabel F. Gadsden (née Drury); m. Belinda Ann de Marie Haggerston 1955; four d.; ed Rockport, Belfast, The Elms, Colwall, Wrekin Coll., Wellington and Jesus Coll., Cambridge; Dir of cos since 1952; marketing economist (mineral sands), UNIDO 1969; Dir City of London (Arizona) Corpn 1970–88 (Chair. 1985–88), Clothworkers' Foundation 1978–; Chair. Pvt. Patients Plan 1984–96, Pres. 1996–98; Chair. Inst. of Dirs City of London Br. 1993–99, PPP Healthcare Medical Trust Ltd 1996–99; Chair. PPP Healthcare Foundation 1996–; Deputy Chair. W. Canning PLC 1990–99 (Dir 1989–99); Dir William Jacks PLC 1984–; Sheriff of London 1970–71; Alderman of the City of London 1971–99; Lord Mayor of London 1979–80; Royal Commr for 1851 Exhbn 1986–99; Pres. Metropolitan Soc. for the Blind 1979–, Ironbridge Gorge Museum Devt Trust 1981–; Australia and NZ Chamber of Commerce 1997–2001; Hon. Pres. Australian Heritage Soc. 1986–; Vice-Pres. Sir Robert Menzies Memorial Trust, Blackwood Little Theatre 1986–; Chancellor, The City Univ. 1979–80; Chair. Britain-Australia Bicentennial Cttee 1984–89, Britain-Australia Bicentennial Trust 1984–; Vice-Pres. Britain-Australia Soc. 1992–; Chair. Royal Commonwealth Soc. 1984–88, City of London (Arizona) Corpn 1985–88; Hon. mem. London Metal Exchange, Inst. of Royal Engineers 1986; mem. Crown Agents 1981–87; Hon. Gov. The Irish Soc. 1984–87; Chair. The Cook Soc. 1999; Pres. City Pickwick Club 2000–; Patron Guild of Rahere, Museum of Empire and Commonwealth Trust 1986–, numerous other orgs; Trustee Chichester Festival Theatre 1986–; Chair. Govs The Elms School 1993–; Fellow Royal Acad. of Eng 1980–, Royal Soc. of Health 1993–, Royal Coll. of Anaesthetists 1994–; Liveryman, Clothworkers' Co. (Master 1989–90), World Traders' Co.; Founder Master Worshipful Co. of Engineers 1983–85; Hon. Freeman Borough of Islwyn, S Wales 1983; Hon. Liveryman, Plaisterers' Co., Marketers' Co., Actuaries' Co., Fruiterers' Co.; HM's Commr of Lieutenancy for the City of London 1979–90; Officier Etoile Equatoriale (Gabon) 1970; Hon. AC; KStJ; Christ Church-Midnite Award, Perth, WA 1997. *Publications:* articles on minerals and the minerals industry in professional journals. *Leisure interests:* walking, photography. *Address:* Cheriton, Middleton Scriven, Bridgnorth, Shropshire, WV16 6AG, England (Home). *Telephone:* (1746) 789650 (Home).

GAEHTGENS, Thomas Wolfgang, DPhil; German art historian; b. 24 June 1940, Leipzig; m. Barbara Feiler 1969; two s.; ed Univs. of Bonn, Freiburg and Paris; teacher Univ. of Göttingen 1973, Prof. of Art History 1974–79, Technische Hochschule, Aachen 1979, Freie Univ. Berlin 1979–; awarded bursary for the J. Paul Getty Center for the History of Art and the Humanities, Santa Monica, Calif. 1985–86; Dir Centre allemand d'histoire de l'art, Paris; mem. Akademie der Wissenschaften, Göttingen; Chevalier Légion d'honneur. *Publications:* Napoleon's Arc de Triomphe 1974, Versailles als Nationaldenkmal 1984, Joseph-Marie Vien 1988, Anton von Werner 1990, Die Berliner Museumsinsel im Deutschen Kaiserreich 1992. *Leisure interests:* art, history. *Address:* Kunsthistorisches Institut der Freien Universität Berlin, Koserstr. 20, 14195 Berlin (Office); Peter-Lenne-Strasse 28, 14195 Berlin, Germany. *Telephone:* (30) 83853843 (Office); (30) 8311439 (Home). *Fax:* (30) 83853842 (Office); (30) 8325519 (Home). *E-mail:* thogae@zedat.furberlin.de (Office).

GAFT, Valentin Iosifovich; Russian actor; b. 2 Sept. 1935, Moscow; m.; ed Studio-School of Moscow Art Theatre; worked in Mossoviet Theatre, Na Maloy Bronnoy, Lenkom, Satire Theatre 1959–69; leading actor Sovremennik Theatre 1969–; dozens of roles in classical and contemporary plays; in cinema since 1956; regularly acts on TV; People's Artist of Russia 1984. *Theatre roles include:* Glumov (Balalaikin and Co.), Lopatin (From the Notes of Lopatin), George (Who's Afraid of Virginia Woolf?), Governor (Inspector), Vershinin (Three Sisters), Bridegroom (Something Like a Comedy). *Film roles include:* Murder on Dante Street 1956, First Courier 1968, Crazy Gold 1977, Centaurs

1979, Parade 1980, Fuette 1986, Thieves by Law 1988, Blessed Heavens 1991, roles in TV productions and TV films including Buddenbrooks, The Mystery of Edwin Drood, Archipelago Lenoire, Kings and Cabbage. *Leisure interests:* writing verses and epigrams. *Address:* T. Shchevchenko nab. 1/2, Apt. 62, 121059 Moscow, Russia. *Telephone:* (095) 243-76-67 (Home).

GAGE, Peter William, MB, ChB, PhD, DSc; Australian professor of physiology; b. 21 Oct. 1937, Auckland, New Zealand; s. of John and Kathleen (née Burke) Gage; m. Jillian Shewan 1960 (divorced 1991); two s. two d.; ed Univ. of Otago; house surgeon, Auckland Hosp. 1961; research asst Green Lane Hosp., Auckland 1962; research scholar, ANU, Canberra 1963–65; NIH Int. Post-doctoral Fellow, Dept of Physiology and Pharmacology, Duke Univ., Durham, NC 1965–67, Asst Prof. 1967–68; Sr Lecturer, School of Physiology and Pharmacology, Univ. of NSW 1968, Assoc. Prof. 1971–76, Prof. 1976–84, Dir Nerve-Muscle Research Centre 1982–84; Prof. of Physiology, John Curtin School of Medical Research, ANU 1984–; Fellow, Australian Acad. of Science. *Leisure interests:* horse-riding, agriculture. *Address:* c/o JCSMR, Australia National University, G.P.O. Box 334, Canberra, ACT 2601; RMB 22, Powell Drive, Greenacres Estate, Queanbeyan, NSW 2620, Australia.

GAGNON, HE Cardinal Edouard, P.S.S.; Canadian ecclesiastic; b. 15 Jan. 1918, Port-Daniel, Gaspé; ordained 1940; consecrated Bishop of St Paul in Alberta 1969, renounced position 1972; Archbishop (Titular See of Iustiniana prima) 1983; cr. Cardinal 1985; Pres. Pontifical Council for the Family 1985–90, Pontifical Cttee for Int. Eucharistic Congresses 1991–. *Address:* Piazza San Calisto 16, 00153 Rome, Italy (Office). *Telephone:* (06) 69887366 (Office). *Fax:* (06) 69887366 (Office). *E-mail:* eucharistcongress@org.va (Office).

GAGNON, Jean-Marie, PhD, MBA, FRSC; Canadian professor of finance; b. 7 July 1933, Fabre; s. of Pierre Gagnon and Yvette Langlois; m. Rachel Bonin 1959; three s.; ed Univ. of Chicago and Univ. Laval; chartered accountant, Clarkson, Gordon, Cie 1957–59; Prof. of Finance, Univ. Laval 1959–; Visiting Prof. Faculté Universitaire Catholique à Mons, Belgium 1972–74, Univ. of Nankai, People's Repub. of China 1985; mem. Bd of Dirs SSQ-Vie; Commr Comm. des Valeurs Mobilières du Québec. *Publications:* Income Smoothing Hypothesis 1970, Belgian Experience with Mergers 1982, Taux de rendement et risque 1982, Traité de gestion financière (with N. Khoury) 1987, Taxes and Financial Decisions 1988, Taxes and Dividends 1991, Corporate Governance Mechanisms and Board Composition 1995, Distribution of Voting Rights and Takeover Resistance 1995. *Address:* 1340 Corrigan, Ste-Foy, G1W 3E9, Canada. *Telephone:* (418) 656-5535. *Fax:* (418) 656-2782 (Office). *E-mail:* jean-marie.gagnon@fas.ulaval.ca (Office).

GAHMBERG, Carl G., MD, DMedSc; Finnish professor of biochemistry; b. 1 Dec. 1942, Helsinki; s. of Gustaf-Adolf Gahmberg and Marie-Louise Gahmberg; m. Marianne Gripenberg-Gahmberg; one s. one d.; ed Univ. of Helsinki; Post-doctoral Fellow, Univ. of Washington 1972–74, Docent of cell biology, Univ. of Helsinki 1974; Prof. of Biochem. Åbo Akad. 1979–81, Univ. of Helsinki 1981–; Research Prof. Acad. of Finland 1986–91; Visiting Prof. La Jolla Cancer Research Foundation 1988–89; Vice-Chair. Finnish Medical Asscn 1998–99, Chair. 2000–01; Exec. Ed. Biochimica et Biophysica Acta 2000–; mem. Finnish Acad. of Science, Finnish Soc. of Sciences and Letters (Perm. Sec.), European Molecular Biology Org., Academia Europaea, World Cultural Council; Komppa Prize 1971, Scandinavian Jahre Prize 1981, 150th anniversary Prize, Finnish Medical Asscn 1985, Prof. of the Year in Finland 1995, The Finnish Äyräpää Prize for Medicine 1997; Kt of the Finnish White Rose (First Class). *Publications:* 240 int. publs on cell membrane, glyco-proteins, cell adhesion, cancer research. *Leisure interests:* nature, classical music, gardening. *Address:* Department of Biosciences, Division of Biochemistry, P.O. Box 56, Viikinkaari 5, 00014 University of Helsinki, Finland. *Telephone:* (9) 1915-9028. *Fax:* (9) 1915-9068. *E-mail:* carl.gahmberg@helsinki.fi (Office).

GAIDAR, Yegor (see Gaydar, Yegor).

GAILIS, Maris; Latvian politician and business executive; b. 1951, Riga; ed Riga Polytech. Inst., Latvian State Univ.; started work in furniture factory; worked in trade unions, co-operatives; author of book Furniture for Young People; f. Riga Videocentre and Cinema Forum Arsenal; responsible for foreign econ. relations in various state insts 1990–; State Sec. Ministry of Foreign Affairs 1992–93; elected to Saeima (Parl.) 1993; Minister for State Reforms, Deputy Prime Minister 1993–94; Prime Minister 1994–95; business exec. 1995–; Dir Linstow Varner Co. 1997–.

GAINUTDIN, Ravil Ibn Ismail; Tatar religious leader; b. 25 Aug. 1959, Tatarstan; m.; two d.; ed Islam Medrese Mir-Arab Bukhara; First Imam-Khatyb Kazan Mosque Nur Islam; Exec. Sec. Ecclesiastical Dept of Moslems European Section of U.S.S.R and Siberia, Ufa 1985–87; Imam-Khatyb Moscow Mosque 1987–88; Chief Imam-Khatyb 1988–; Pres. Islam Cen. of Moscow and Moscow Region 1991–; Chair. Council of Muftis of Russia; Prof. Moscow Higher Islam Coll.; mem. Int. Acad. of Sciences of Eurasia, Int. Slavic Acad., Int. Acad. of Information; mem. Council on Co-operation with Religious Unions, Russian Presidency. *Publications include:* books on Moslem dogma and rituals. *Address:* Moslem Centre of European Region of Russia, Vypolzov per. 7, 129090 Moscow, Russia (Office). *Telephone:* (095) 281-49-04 (Office).

GAJDUSEK, Daniel Carleton, MD; American medical research scientist; b. 9 Sept. 1923, Yonkers, NY; s. of Karl Gajdusek and Ottilia Dobroczki; 65 adopted s. and d. from Melanesia and Micronesia; ed Boyce Thompson Inst.

of Plant Research, Yonkers, NY, Marine Biological Laboratory, Woods Hole, Mass., Univ. of Rochester, Harvard Medical School, California Inst. of Tech.; served in Medical Corps; Babies Hosp. of Columbia Presbyterian Medical Center, NY 1946–47; Cincinnati Children's Hosp. 1947–48; Medical Mission in Germany 1948; Sr Fellow, Nat. Research Council, Calif. Inst. of Tech. 1948–49; Children's Hosp., Boston, Mass. 1949–51; Research Fellow, Harvard Univ. and Senior Fellow, Nat. Foundation for Infantile Paralysis 1949–52; mem. staff Walter Reed Army Medical Center 1952–53; with Institut Pasteur, Tehran, Iran and Univ. of Md 1954–55; Visiting Investigator at Walter and Eliza Hall Inst., Australia 1955–57; Lab. Chief Nat. Inst. of Neurological Disorders and Stroke, NIH, Bethesda, Md 1958–97, Chief of Study of Child Growth and Devt and Disease Patterns in Primitive Cultures and of Laboratory of Slow, Latent and Temperate Virus Infections 1958–97; Chief of Cen. Nervous System Studies Lab. 1970–97; Prof., Inst. of Human Virology, Univ. of Md 1996–; Silliman Prof., Yale Univ. 1981; Hitchcock Prof., Univ. of Calif. Berkeley 1982; Merrian Prof., Univ. of NC 1984; mem. Soc. for Paediatric Research, American Paediatric Soc., NAS, American Acad. of Arts and Sciences, American Philosophical Soc., Deutsche Akademie der Naturforscher Leopoldina, Third World Acad. of Science, American Acad. of Neurology, Russian Acad. of Medicine, Sakha (Iakut) Siberian Acad. of Science br. Russian Acad. of Science; Hon. Curator Melanesian Ethnology, Peabody Museum, Salem, Mass.; Hon. Prof. in 10 Chinese univs 1993–2002; Hon. Adviser to 3 Chinese acads 1999–2002; Hon. mem. Australian Acad. of Science, Czechoslovak Acad. of Science and Mexican, Colombian and Belgian Acads of Medicine; several hon. degrees; Meade Johnson Award, American Acad. of Pediatrics 1961, Dautrebande Prize 1976, shared Nobel Prize in Physiology or Medicine for discoveries concerning new mechanisms for the origin and dissemination of infectious diseases 1976, Cotzias Prize 1978, Huxley Medal, Royal Anthropological Inst. of GB and Ireland 1988, Stuart Mudd Prize 1989, award of 3rd Int. Congress on Alzheimer's Disease 1992, award of 3rd Pacific Rim Biotech. Conf. 1992, Gold Medal, Slovak Acad. of Science 1996. *Publications:* Hemorrhagic Fevers and Mycotoxicoses 1959, Slow, Latent and Temperate Virus Infections 1965, Correspondence on the Discovery of Kuru 1976, Kuru (with Judith Farquhar) 1980, Research, Travel and Field Expedition Journals (71 vols) 1937–99, Vilinisk Encephalomyelitis 1996; and over 1,000 papers on microbiology, immunology, paediatrics, neurology, cognitive and psychosexual devt and genetics. *Leisure interests:* linguistics, anthropology. *Address:* Institut Neurobiologie Alfred Fessard, C.N.R.S., Avenue de la Terrasse, 91198 Gif-sur-Yvette, Cedex, France. *Telephone:* 1-69-82-34-28 (Office). *Fax:* 1-69-07-05-38 (Office).

GÁL, Zoltán, D. JUR.; Hungarian politician and lawyer; m. Krisztina Pölz; one s.; ed Eötvös Loránd Univ.; with Trade Union HQ 1964–74; worked at Exec. and Admin. Dept of Cen. Cttee of Hungarian Socialist Workers Party (HSWP) 1974–86; lecturer, Political Coll. 1987–89; Deputy Minister of Interior, then State Sec. and Minister of Interior 1987–90; mem. Parl. 1990–94; leader faction of Hungarian Socialist Party 1990–94; mem. Cttee on Constitution, Legislation and Justice 1990–94; Chair. Cttee for Constitutional Reform 1994–; Speaker of Nat. Ass. 1994–98; Vice-Chair. Cttee on Constitution, Legislation and Justice 1998–. *Leisure interests:* tennis, swimming and reading. *Address:* 1357 Budapest, Kossuth Lajos tér 1–3, Hungary.

GALA, Antonio, LicenDer, LicenFilyLetras, LicenCienciasPoliticasyEcon; Spanish author; b. 2 Oct. 1936, Córdoba; s. of Luis Gala and Adoración Velasco; ed Univs. of Seville and Madrid; Dr hc (Córdoba); Nat. Prize for Literature, Hidalgo Prize, Planeta Prize; many other literary and theatre awards. *Publications include:* plays: Los Verdes Campos del Edén, Los Buenos Días Perdidos, Anillos Para Una Dama, La Vieja Señorita del Paraíso, El Cementerio de los Pájaros, Petra Regalada, El Hotelito, Carmen Carmen, Los Bellos Durmientes; novels: El Manuscrito Carmesí, La Pasión Turca, Más Allá del Jardín 1995, La Regla de Tres 1996, El Corazón Tardío 1998, Las Afuneras de Dios 1999; poetry: Enemigo Intimo, Sonetos de la Zubia, Testamento Andaluz; essays: Charlas con Troylo, La Soledad Sonora. *Address:* Calle Macarena No. 16, 28016 Madrid, Spain. *Telephone:* (91) 3592037.

GALADARI, Abdel-Wahab; United Arab Emirates business executive; b. 1938, Dubai; ed American Univ., Beirut; Clerk with British Bank of the Middle East, then admin. post with Dubai Electrical Co.; f. re-export business with brothers Abdel-Rahim and Abdel-Latif 1960, real estate co. c. 1962; Dir Nat. Bank of Dubai 1965–69; left family business 1976; formed Union Bank of the Middle East 1977, Chair. –1983; Chair. A. W. Galadari Holdings and over 20 associated cos; Propr Hyatt Regency and Galadari Galleria hotels; sponsored 1980 Dubai Grand Prix motor race. *Address:* A. W. Galadari Group of Companies, P.O. Box 22, Dubai, United Arab Emirates.

GALAL, Mohamed Noman, PhD; Egyptian diplomatist; b. 10 April 1943, Assiut; m. Kawther Elsherif 1969; two s.; ed Univ. of Cairo; joined Ministry of Foreign Affairs 1965; Third Sec. Jordan 1969–72; Vice-Consul, Kuwait 1972; Consul, Abu Dhabi 1972–73; Second Sec. Oslo 1975–79; Lecturer, Diplomatic Inst. 1979–80; First Sec. New Delhi 1980, Counsellor 1981–85; Counsellor, Cabinet of Deputy Prime Minister and Minister of Foreign Affairs 1985–87; Counsellor, Egyptian Mission at UN 1987–90, Minister and Deputy Perm. Rep. 1990–92; Perm. Rep. to League of Arab States, Cairo 1992–95; Amb. to Pakistan 1995–99, to People's Repub. of China 1999–2002; Visiting Lecturer, Farleigh Dickinson Univ. 1989–91, Univ. of Cairo 1994–95; St Olav Medal (Norway) 1972, Nat. Medal for Merit (Egypt) 1982. *Publications:* more

than 40 publs in Arabic and English on Arab and int. affairs, foreign policy, human rights, Egypt, Middle East, Pakistan, China, non-alignment, etc. *Address:* c/o Ministry of Foreign Affairs, Corniche en-Nil, Cairo, Egypt.

GALANOS, James; American fashion designer; b. 20 Sept. 1924, Philadelphia, Pa; s. of Gregory Galanos and Helen Galanos (née Gorgoliatos); ed Traphagen School of Fashion, New York 1943; began career selling sketches to New York clothing mfrs; worked for Hattie Carnegie 1944; asst to Jean Louis, head designer, Columbia Studios, Hollywood 1946–47; apprentice, Robert Piguet, Paris 1947–48; designer, Davidow, New York 1949–50; est. own business, Galanos Originals, Beverly Hills, Calif. 1951–63, LA 1963–; produced collection of couture-quality furs in collaboration with Neustadter Furs 1968; designed costumes for Rosalind Russell in films Never Wave at a WAC, 1952 and Oh Dad, Poor Dad, Mama's Hung You in the Closet and I'm Feeling So Sad 1967; retrospective exhbns LA Co. Museum of Art 1974, 1997, Inst. of Tech., New York 1976, Western Reserve Historical Soc. 1996, LA Co. Museum of Art 1997; designed Inaugural Gown worn by Nancy Reagan 1981; work represented in perm. collections including Metropolitan Museum of Art, New York, Smithsonian Inst. Washington and Art Inst. of Chicago; Council of Fashion Designers of America Lifetime Achievement Award 1985 and numerous fashion awards. *Leisure interests:* collecting art books, music, reading, architecture. *Address:* 1316 Sunset Plaza Drive, Los Angeles, CA 90069-1235 (Office); 2254 South Sepulveda Blvd., Los Angeles, CA 90064, USA. *Telephone:* (213) 272-1445. *Fax:* (310) 473-6725.

GALASSI, Jonathan White, MA; American publishing executive; b. 4 Nov. 1949, Seattle, Wash.; s. of Gerard Goodwin Galassi and Dorothea Johnston Galassi (née White); m. Susan Grace Galassi 1975; two d.; ed Harvard and Cambridge Univs; Ed. Houghton Mifflin Co., Boston, New York 1973–81; Sr Ed. Random House, Inc., New York 1981–86; Exec. Ed. and Vice-Pres. Farrar, Strauss & Giroux Inc., New York 1986–87, Ed.-in-Chief and Sr Vice-Pres. 1988–93, Exec. Vice-Pres. 1993–99, Publr 1999–, Pres. 2002–; Poetry Ed. Paris Review 1978–88; Guggenheim Fellow 1989; mem. Acad. of American Poets (Dir 1990–2002, Pres. 1994–99, Chair. 1999–2002, Hon. Chair. 2002–); Fellow American Acad. of Arts and Sciences 2002; Roger Klein Award for Editing, PEN 1984, Award in Literature, American Acad. of Arts and Letters 2000. *Publications:* Morning Run (poetry) 1988, The Second Life of Art: Selected Essays of Eugenio Montale (ed., trans.) 1982, Otherwise: Last and First Poems of Eugenio Montale (ed., trans.) 1986, Eugenio Montale, Collected Poems 1916–56 (ed., trans.) 1998, North Street (poetry) 2000, Eugenio Montale, Postumous Diary 2001. *Address:* Farrar, Strauss & Giroux Inc., 19 Union Square W, New York, NY 10003 (Office); 239 Sackett Street, Brooklyn, NY 11231, USA (Home). *Telephone:* (212) 741-6900 (Office).

GALATERI DI GENOLA, Count Gabriele, DIur, MBA; Italian business executive; b. 11 Jan. 1947, Rome; s. of Gen. Angelo Galateri di Genola and Carla Fontana; m. Evelina Christillin; one d.; ed Liceo Ennio Quirino Visconti, Rome, Univ. of Rome, Columbia Univ., New York; Asst Lecturer in Econ. Science, Univ. of Rome 1969–70; Head Financial Analysis Dept, later Int. Financing Dept, Banco di Roma 1971–74; Financial Dir Saint Gobain, Italy, then Asst to Financial Group Dir, Paris 1974–77; Head Foreign Finance Div., Fiat SpA 1977–83, Financial Dir 1983–86, CEO 2002, Dir 2002–, fmr Man. Dir and Gen. Man. IFI SpA, Man. Dir IFIL SpA; Gen. Partner Giovanni Agnelli e C., C. Sapaz; mem. Bd Fiat, Accor, Arjo Wiggins Appleton, SanpaoloIMI, SanpaoloIMI Investments, La Rinascente, Toro Assicurazioni, Birra Peroni, Alpitour, Galbani, Worms & Cie, Eurofind, Exor Group, Emittentic Titoli, CiaoHolding, CiaoWeb, Atlanet. *Leisure interests:* arts, music, tennis, skiing, gym. *Address:* IFI S.p.A., Corso Matteotti 26, 10121 Turin, Italy. *Telephone:* (011) 5090266. *Fax:* (011) 5090270.

GALAYR, Ali Khalif; Somali politician and business executive; fmr business exec.; Prime Minister of Somalia 2000–01. *Address:* c/o Office of the Prime Minister, c/o People's Palace, Mogadishu, Somalia (Office).

GALBRAITH, John Kenneth, PhD; American economist, diplomatist and writer; b. 15 Oct. 1908, Iona Station, Ont., Canada; m. Catherine Merriam Atwater 1937; three s.; ed Toronto, California and Cambridge (England) Univs.; Research Fellow, Calif. Univ. 1931–34; Instructor, Harvard Univ. 1934–39, Lecturer 1948–49, Prof. of Econs 1949–75; Asst Prof. Princeton Univ. 1939–42; Asst then Deputy Admin. Office of Price Admin. 1941–43; mem. Bd of Editors Fortune Magazine 1943–48; Amb. to India 1961–63; Dir Office of Econ. Security Policy, State Dept 1946; BBC Reith Lecturer 1966; American Econ. Asscn (Pres. 1971), American Farm Econs Asscn, Americans for Dem. Action (Chair. 1967–68); Fellow American Acad. of Arts and Sciences (Pres. Bd Dirs 1984–87); mem. American Acad., Inst. of Arts and Letters 1984–; numerous hon. degrees; Commdr Légion d'honneur; Medal of Freedom 2000. *Television series:* The Age of Uncertainty (BBC) 1977. *Publications include:* Theory of Price Control, American Capitalism 1952, The Great Crash, Economics and the Art of Controversy 1955, The Affluent Society 1958, Journey to Poland and Yugoslavia 1959, The Liberal Hour 1960, Made to Last 1964, The New Industrial State 1967, The Triumph (novel) 1968, Ambassador's Journal 1969, Indian Painting (co-author) 1969, A Contemporary Guide to Economics, Peace and Laughter 1971, A China Passage 1973, Economics and the Public Purpose 1974, Money: Whence It Came, Where It Went 1975, The Age of Uncertainty 1976, The Galbraith Reader 1978, Almost Everyone's Guide to Economics 1979, The Nature of Mass Poverty 1979, Annals of an Abiding Liberal 1980, A Life in Our Times (autobiog.) 1981, The Anatomy of Power 1984, A View from the Stands: Of People, Military Power and the Arts

1986, Economics in Perspective: A Critical History 1987, History of Economics: The Past as the Present 1987, Capitalism, Communism and Coexistence (with S. Menshikov, novel) 1988, A Tenured Professor (novel) 1990, A Short History of Financial Euphoria 1990, The Culture of Contentment 1992, A Journey through Economic Time 1994, The World Economy Since the War: A Personal View, The Good Society: The Humane Agenda 1996, Name Dropping From FDR On 1999. *Address:* Harvard University, 206 Littauer Centre, Cambridge, MA 02138 (Office); 30 Francis Avenue, Cambridge, MA 02138-2010, USA (Home). *Fax:* (617) 496 1200.

GALE, Ernest Frederick, PhD, ScD, FRS; British professor of chemical microbiology; b. 15 July 1914, Luton, Beds.; s. of Ernest Francis Edward Gale and Nellie Annie Gale; m. Eiry Mair Jones 1937; one s.; ed Weston-super-Mare Grammar School and St John's Coll., Cambridge; research in chemical microbiology, Cambridge 1937–38; Sr Student, Royal Comm. for Exhbn of 1851 1939–41; Beit Memorial Fellow 1941–43; mem. Staff, Medical Research Council 1943–60, Dir MRC Unit for Chemical Microbiology 1948–60; Prof. of Chemical Microbiology, Univ. of Cambridge 1960–81, Prof. Emer. 1981–; Fellow, St John's Coll., Cambridge 1949–88; Meetings Sec. Soc. for Gen. Microbiology 1952–58, Int. Rep. 1963–67, Pres. 1967–69, Hon. mem. 1978; Herter Lecturer, Baltimore 1948; Hanna Lecturer, Western Reserve Univ. 1951; Harvey Lecturer, NY 1955; Leeuwenhoek Lecturer, Royal Soc. 1956; Malcolm Lecturer, Syracuse Univ. 1967; Linacre Lecturer, St John's Coll., Cambridge Univ. 1973; Squibb Lecturer, Nottingham Univ. 1986. *Publications:* Chemical Activities of Bacteria 1947, Organisation and Synthesis in Bacteria 1959, Promotion and Prevention of Synthesis in Bacteria 1968, The Molecular Basis of Antibiotic Action 1972, 1981; scientific papers and reviews in journals of biochemistry and microbiology. *Leisure interests:* photography, wood carving. *Address:* 59 Blake Court, Winchmore Hill, London, N21 1SQ, England (Home); 7 Hazeldene, Sandhills Road, Salcombe, Devon TQ8 8JP. *Telephone:* (20) 7263-0228 (Home); (1548) 843426.

GALE, Gwendoline Fay, AO, PhD, DUniv; Australian university vice-chancellor and geographer; b. Gwendoline Fay Gilding, 13 June 1932, Balaklava, S Australia; d. of George Jasper Gilding and Kathleen Gertrude Pengelley; one s. one d.; ed Methodist Ladies' Coll., Univ. of Adelaide, S Australia; Lecturer, then Sr Lecturer, Univ. of Adelaide 1966–74, Reader 1975–77, Prof. of Geography 1978–89, Pro-Vice-Chancellor 1988–89, Prof. Emer. 1989–; Australian Heritage Commr 1989–95; Vice-Chancellor Univ. of Western Australia 1990–97; Pres. Inst. of Australian Geographers 1989–90; Chair. Social Justice Advisory Cttee 1989; Chair. Festival of Perth 1992–97; Chair. West Australian Symphony Orchestra 1995–97; Pres. Australian Vice-Chancellors Cttee 1996–97; Pres. Acad. of Social Sciences in Australia 1998–2000; Pres. Asscn Asian Social Science Councils 2001–; mem. Humanities and Social Science Panel, Australian Research Council 1987–89, Chair. 1989; Exec. mem. Acad. of the Social Sciences in Australia 1980–82, 1988–89; Elin Wagner Fellowship 1971, Catherine Helen Spence Fellowship 1972, Fellow Acad. of Social Sciences of Australia 1978, Hon. Fellow Acad. of Social Sciences of Australia 2001–; mem. Nat. Comm. of UNESCO, Australia 1999–, Australian Research Council 1999–2001; Hon. DLitt (Western Australia) 1998; British Council Award 1972, Officer of Order of Australia 1989, John Lewis Gold Medal 2000, Griffith Taylor Medal 2001. *Publications:* Women's Role in Aboriginal Society (ed.) 1970, Urban Aborigines 1972, Race Relations in Australia: the Aboriginal situation 1975, Poverty Among Aboriginal Families in Adelaide 1975, We are Bosses Ourselves: the Status and Role of Aboriginal Women Today (ed.) 1983, Tourists and the National Estate: Procedures to protect Australia's Heritage 1987, Aboriginal Youth and the Criminal Justice System: the Injustice of Justice 1990, Inventing Places: Studies in Cultural Geography 1991, Changing Australia 1991, Boyer Lectures 1991, Juvenile Justice: Debating the Issues 1993, Tourism and the Protection of Aboriginal Sites 1994, Cultural Geographies 1999, Making Space: Women and Education at St Aloysius College Adelaide 1880–2000. *Leisure interests:* music, theatre, reading. *Address:* c/o Office of the Vice-Chancellor, The University of Adelaide, Adelaide, S. Australia 5005, Australia. *Telephone:* (8) 8379-7476 (Office). *Fax:* (8) 8379-7378 (Office).

GALE, Michael Denis, PhD, FRS; British plant research scientist; b. 25 Aug. 1943, Wolverhampton; s. of Sydney Ralph Gale and Helen Mary Gale (née Johnston); m. Susan Heathcote Rosbotham 1979; two d.; ed West Buckland School, Barnstaple, Birmingham Univ., Univ. Coll. Wales, Aberystwyth; Researcher, Plant Breeding Inst. (subsequently Agric. and Ford Research Council Inst. of Plant Science Research), Cambridge 1968–86, Head Cereals Research Dept and Individual Merit Sr Prin. Scientific Officer, Cambridge Lab. 1986–92, Head Cambridge Lab., Norwich 1992–94; Research Dir John Innes Centre, Norwich 1994–98, Acting Dir Sept.–Dec. 1998, Dir 1999, Assoc. Research Dir 1999–; John Innes Prof., Univ. of E Anglia 1999–; Farrer Memorial Bicentennial Fellow, NSW Dept of Agric. 1989; Hon. Research Prof. Inst. of Crop Germplasm Resources, Academia Sinica 1992; Adviser Inst. of Genetics, Beijing 1992; Fellow Royal Soc. 1996, Foreign Fellow Chinese Acad. of Eng 1998; Research Medal, Royal Agric. Soc. of England 1994, Rank Prize for Nutrition 1997, Darwin Medal 1998. *Publications:* 200 scientific papers and articles on plant genetics and cytogenetics, especially dwarfism, quality and genome research in wheat. *Leisure interests:* golf, tennis. *Address:* John Innes Centre, Norwich Research Park, Colney, Norwich, NR4 7UH (Office); 9 Mount Pleasant, Norwich, NR2 2DG, England (Home). *Telephone:* (1603) 450599 (Office). *Fax:* (1603) 450024 (Office). *E-mail:* mike.gale@bbsrc.ac.uk (Office).

GALEA, Censu; Maltese politician and architect; b. 28 Aug. 1956; s. of Joseph Galea; m. Grace Sammut; two s. two d.; ed Univ. of Malta; practising architect 1982; Sec.-Gen. then Pres. of Nationalist Party Youth Section 1978–81; MP Nationalist Party 1987–; Parl. Sec. Ministry for Social Security 1992–94; Minister for Food, Agric. and Fisheries 1994–96, for Transport and Communications 1998–; Shadow Minister and Opposition Spokesman for Transport and Ports 1996–98, Sec. and Whip Nationalist Party Parl. Group 1997–98. *Address:* Ministry for Transport and Communications, House of Four Winds, Hastings Gardens, Valletta, CMR 02, Malta. *Telephone:* 225200. *Fax:* 248937. *E-mail:* vincent.galea@magnet.mt (Office); cgalea@waldonet.mt (Home).

GALEA, Louis, LLD; Maltese politician and lawyer; b. 2 Jan. 1948, Mqabba; s. of Joseph Galea and Joan Galea (née Farrugia); m. Vincienne Zammit 1977; one s. three d.; mem. Gen. Council and Exec. Cttee Nationalist Party 1972–, Gen. Sec. 1977–87; mem. Parl. 1976–; Minister for Social Policy including Health 1987–92, for Home Affairs and Social Development including Health 1992–95, Minister for Social Devt 1995–96; Shadow Minister for Educ. 1996–98; Minister of Educ. 1998–. *Leisure interests:* reading, music, tennis. *Address:* Ministry of Education, Floriana CMR02, Malta. *Telephone:* 231374. *Fax:* 221634.

GALEYEV, Albert Abubakirovich, DR.PHYS.MATH.SC.; Russian/Bashkir physicist; b. 19 Oct. 1940, Ufa; m.; two c.; ed Univ. of Novosibirsk; worked at USSR Acad. of Sciences Inst. of Nuclear Physics 1961–70; Sr researcher at Acad. of Sciences Inst. of High Temperatures 1970–73; mem. CPSU 1976–91; Corresp. mem. USSR (now Russian) Acad. of Sciences 1987–92, mem. 1992; Head of Section at Acad. of Sciences Inst. of Space Research 1973–88, Dir 1988–; Ed.-in-Chief Earth Research from Space; Lenin Prize 1984. *Publications:* works on physics of plasma and cosmic physics. *Address:* Institute of Space Research, Profsoyuznaya 84/32, 117810 Moscow, Russia. *Telephone:* (095) 333-25-88 (Office); (095) 135-10-94 (Home). *Fax:* (095) 333-33-11 (Office). *E-mail:* agaleyev@iki.rssi.ru (Office).

GALIBIN, Aleksander Vladimirovich; Russian actor and stage director; b. 28 Sept. 1955, Leningrad; m.; three d.; ed Leningrad State Inst. of Theatre, Music and Cinematography, A. Vasilyev Drama School, Moscow; actor Komissarzhevskaya Drama Theatre 1977–79; Stage Dir Aleksandrinsky Theatre 1995–; worked as stage dir in various St Petersburg theatres 1990–. *Films include:* acted in more than 20 films 1976–, including Pyatnitskaya Street, Courage, Silver Strings, Letters from the Front, Red Crown. *Theatre includes:* (stage dir) Three Sisters, Harp of Greeting, City Romance, Pupil, Tsar Piotr and His Dead Son Aleksey. *Address:* Griboyedova Canal 115, Apt. 9, 190088 St Petersburg, Russia. *Telephone:* (812) 114-16-80.

GALIMOV, Erik Mikhailovich, PhD, DSc; Russian geochemist; b. 29 July 1936, Vladivostok; s. of Zeya Galimova and Mikhail Piskunov; m. 1st; one d.; m. 2nd Galina Andriukhina; two d.; ed Moscow Inst. of Oil and Gas; operational engineer 1959–60; head of geophysics expeditions 1960–63; sr researcher 1965–73; Dir V. I. Vernadsky Inst. of Geochem. and Analytical Chem. 1992– (head of lab. 1973–92); Prof. Moscow State Univ.; Chair. Geochem. Council of Russian Acad. of Sciences, Int. Lunar Exploration Working Group; Vice-Pres. Int. Asscn of Geochem. Cosmochemistry; mem. Editorial Bd Geochem., Chemical Geology; Corresp. mem. USSR (now Russian) Acad. of Sciences 1991, mem. 1994; foreign mem. German Acad. of Sciences and Literature 1998; Geochemical Fellow 1998; research in geochem. of stable isotopes, organic geochem. and geochem. of oil and gas; Vernadsky Prize 1984. *Publications include:* Geochemistry of Stable Carbon Isotopes 1968, Carbon Isotopes in Oil and Gas Geology 1973, Biological Isotope Fractionation 1985, Sources and Mechanism Formation of Natural Gases 1988, Kimberlite Magmatism and Diamond Formation 1991, Evolution of the Biosphere 1995, Origin of the Moon 1996. *Address:* V. I. Vernadsky Institute of Geochemistry and Analytical Chemistry, Kosygin Street 19, Moscow 117975 (Office); Nikitski Blvd. 5–5, Moscow 121019, Russia (Home). *Telephone:* (095) 137-41-27 (Office); (095) 291-48-60 (Home). *Fax:* (095) 938-20-54.

GALIN, Aleksandr (pseudonym of Aleksandr Mikhailovich Pourer); Russian playwright, actor and film and theatre director; b. 10 Sept. 1947, Rosvovskya oblast (USSR); s. of Mikhail Pourer and Lubov Pourer; m. Galina Alekseyevna Pourer 1970; one s.; ed Inst. of Culture, Leningrad; factory worker, later actor in puppet theatre; freelance writer 1978–; Amb. of the Arts, Fla. *Plays include:* The Wall 1971, Here Fly the Birds 1974, The Hole 1975, The Roof 1976, Retro 1979, The Eastern Tribute 1980, Stars in the Morning Sky 1982, The Toastmaster 1983, Jeanne 1986, Sorry 1990, The Title 1991, The Czech Photo 1993, The Clown and the Bandit 1996, The Anomaly 1996, Sirena and Victoria 1997, The Competition 1998; plays translated into several languages include Stars in the Morning Sky (selected plays translated into English) 1989, The Group 1991, Rendezvous 2002. *Film:* (scriptwriter and dir) Casanova's Coat (The Delegation), (scriptwriter, actor and dir) Photo 2003. *Publication:* Selected Plays 1989. *Address:* Gorohowsky pereulok 15, Apt. 11, 103064 Moscow, Russia. *Telephone:* (095) 267-70-21. *Fax:* (095) 267-70-21. *E-mail:* agalin@online.ru. *Website:* www.webcenter.ru/~agalin.

GALJAARD, Hans, MD, PhD; Netherlands professor of cell biology; b. 8 April 1935, Leiden; m. Henriette H. van Boven 1960; two s. one d.; ed State Univ. Leiden; radiobiology training at Medical Biology Lab. Nat. Defence Org. Rijswijk 1962–65 and Atomic Energy Research Establishment, Harwell, England 1965; Prof. of Cell Biology, Erasmus Univ. Rotterdam 1966–; Chair. Dept of Clinical Genetics, Univ. Hosp. 1980–; Dir Rotterdam Foundation of

Clinical Genetics 1980–; mem. Nat. Health Council, Nat. Council for Science Policy, Advisory Council on Tech.; consultant for WHO and UNFPA; mem. Royal Dutch Acad. of Sciences 1984–, Acad. Europaea; Hon. mem. Dutch Soc. for Human Genetics, Indian Soc. for Prenatal Diagnosis and Therapy; Carter Memorial Medal, British Clincial Genetics Soc. *Publications:* The Life of the Dutchman 1981; some 400 articles in scientific journals, book chapters and monographs. *Leisure interests:* writing, filming, sailing. *Address:* Department of Cell Biology and Genetics, Erasmus University, P.O. Box 1738, 3000 DR Rotterdam, Netherlands. *Telephone:* (0) 10408732.

GALL, Hugues R.; French opera house director; b. 18 March 1940, Honfleur; s. of Max Gall and Geneviève Carel; ed Inst. des Sciences Politiques; fmr official, Ministries of Agric., Educ. and Culture; Sec.-Gen. Réunion des Théâtres Lyriques 1969–73; Deputy Dir-Gen. Paris Opéra 1973–80; Dir-Gen. Grand Theatre, Geneva 1980–95; Dir-Gen. Paris Opéra July 1995–; elected mem. Acad. des Beaux-Arts, Inst. de France 2002; Prix Montaigne 1996, Prix Grand Siècle-Laurent Perrier 1999; Officier Légion d'honneur, Ordre nat. du Mérite, des Palmes académiques, Chevalier du Mérite agricole, Commdr des Arts et des Lettres. *Address:* Opéra National de Paris, 120 rue de Lyon, 75012 Paris, France (Office). *Telephone:* 1-40-01-18-30. *Fax:* 1-40-01-18-51.

GALL, Joseph Grafton, PhD; American professor of biology; b. 14 April 1928, Washington, DC; s. of late John C. and Elsie (Rosenberger) Gall; m. 1st Dolores M. Hogge 1955; one s. one d.; m. 2nd Diane M. Dwyer 1982; ed Yale Univ.; Instructor, Asst Prof., Assoc. Prof., Prof., Dept of Zoology, Univ. of Minn. 1952–64; Prof. of Biology and Molecular Biophysics and Biochem., Yale Univ. 1964–83; mem. staff Dept of Embryology, Carnegie Inst. 1983–, American Cancer Soc. Prof. of Developmental Genetics 1984 (lifetime appointment); mem. Cell Biology Study Section, NIH 1963–67, Chair. 1972–74; Pres. American Soc. for Cell Biology 1968, Soc. for Developmental Biology 1984–85; mem. Bd of Scientific Counsellors, Nat. Inst. of Child Health and Human Devt, NIH 1986–90; mem. Bd of Scientific Advisers, Jane Coffin Childs Memorial Fund for Medical Research 1986–94; Visiting Prof. St Andrews Univ. 1960, 1968, Univ. of Leicester 1971; Visiting Scientist Max Planck Inst., Tübingen 1960; mem. NAS, AAAS, American Acad. of Arts and Sciences, American Philosophical Soc., Acad. Naz. dei Lincei (Rome) 1988; Fellow, Yale Corpn 1989–95; Hon. DrMed Charles Univ., Prague 2002; E. B. Wilson Medal, American Soc. for Cell Biology 1983, Wilbur Cross Medal of Yale Univ. 1988, AAAS Mentor Award for Lifetime Achievement 1996, Jan E. Purkyne Medal, Czech Acad. of Science 1999. *Publications:* scientific articles on chromosome structure, nucleic acid biochemistry, cell fine structure, organelles of the cell. *Leisure interest:* collecting books on the history of biology. *Address:* c/o Department of Embryology, Carnegie Institution, 115 West University Parkway, Baltimore, MD 21210 (Office); 107 Bellemore Road, Baltimore, MD 21210, USA (Home). *Telephone:* (410) 554-1217 (Office). *Fax:* (410) 243-6311. *E-mail:* gall@ciwemb.edu (Office).

GALLAGHER, Conrad; Irish chef and restaurateur; b. Letterkenny, Donegal; m. Domini Kemp; one c.; began career working in Great Northern Hotel, Bundoran and Renvale House, Connemara; moved to New York aged 17, chef Queen's Restaurant, Blue Street, then the Plaza Hotel, then Waldorf Astoria Hotel; chef at Hotel de Paris, Monte Carlo; founder and owner Peacock Alley restaurant and Lloyd's Brasserie, Dublin; Best Irish Chef 1994, Michelin Star 1998.

GALLAGHER, Liam (William John Paul); British singer, musician and producer; b. 21 Sept. 1972, Burnage, Manchester; s. of Peggy Gallagher; brother of Noel Gallagher (q.v.); m. Patsy Kensit (q.v.) 1997 (divorced 2000); one s.; partner Nicole Appleton; one s.; Founder mem. and singer with Oasis 1991–; recorded for Creation Records 1993–2000; f. and recorded for Big Brother records 2000–; major concerts included Earls Court (largest UK indoor concert) 1995, Glastonbury Festival 1995, Knebworth (largest UK outdoor concert) 1996, Finsbury Park 2002; regular tours UK, Europe and USA; four platinum discs for Definitely Maybe in UK, eight platinum discs for (What's The Story) Morning Glory? in UK (May 1996), three Brit Awards 1996. *Singles include:* Supersonic (debut) 1994, Shakermaker, Live Forever, Cigarettes and Alcohol, Some Might Say, Wonderwall, Cast No Shadow, Don't Look Back in Anger, D'You Know What I Mean, All Around the World, Go Let It Out, The Hindu Times. *Albums:* Definitely Maybe 1994, (What's The Story) Morning Glory? 1995, Be Here Now 1997, The Masterplan 1998, Standing on the Shoulder of Giants 2000, Familiar to Millions (live) 2001, Heathen Chemistry 2002. *Address:* c/o Ignition Management, 54 Linhope Street, London, NW1 6HL, England. *Website:* www.oasisnet.com.

GALLAGHER, Noel; British songwriter, musician and singer; b. 29 May 1967; s. of Peggy Gallagher; brother of Liam Gallagher (q.v.); m. Meg Matthews 1997 (divorced 1997); one d.; fmrly worked with Inspiral Carpets; Founder mem., songwriter, guitarist and singer with Oasis 1991–; recorded for Creation Records 1993–2000; f. and recorded for Big Brother records 2000–; major concerts included Earls Court (largest UK indoor concert) 1995, Glastonbury Festival 1995, Knebworth (largest UK outdoor concert) 1996, Finsbury Park 2002; regular tours UK, Europe and USA; Founder Sour Mash records 2001; mem. Tailgunner; contributed vocals Chemical Brothers' singles Setting Sun 1996, Let Forever Be 1999; four platinum discs for Definitely Maybe in UK, eight platinum discs for (What's The Story) Morning Glory? in UK (May 1996), three Brit Awards 1996, Best song Grammy Awards (Wonderwall) 1997. *Singles include:* Supersonic (debut) 1994, Shakermaker, Live Forever, Cigarettes and Alcohol, Some Might Say, Wonderwall, Cast No

Shadow, Don't Look Back in Anger, D'You Know What I Mean, All Around the World, Go Let It Out, The Hindu Times. *Albums:* Definitely Maybe (debut) 1994, (What's The Story) Morning Glory? 1995, Be Here Now 1997, The Masterplan 1998, Standing on the Shoulder of Giants 2000, Familiar to Millions (live) 2001, Heathen Chemistry 2002. *Leisure interest:* supporting Manchester City. *Address:* c/o Ignition Management, 54 Linhope Street, London, NW1 6HL, England. *Website:* www.oasisnet.com.

GALLAND, Yves; French politician; b. 8 March 1941; s. of Jean Galland and Suzanne Vershave; m. Anne Marie Chauvin 1967; one s. two d.; Pres. of publishing and publicity cos. 1969; mem. European Parl. 1979–, Vice-Pres. 1989–91; Deputy Mayor of Paris in charge of housing 1983–95, of architecture 1995–1998; Minister of Local Affairs and Decentralization 1986–88, of Industry 1995, of Finance and Foreign Trade 1995–97; Pres. Valoise Radical Party 1988–94; mem. nat. council Union pour la démocratie française (UDF), delegate to Paris 1979, mem. nat. political bureau 1990–, Pres. Liberal Group, European Parl. 1991–94; Pres. UDF Group 1998–; Chair. European Assistance Group 2000–. *Address:* Hôtel de Ville, 75196 Paris RP; 6 rue des Haudriettes, 75003 Paris; European Assistance, 1 Promenade de la Bonnette, 92230 Gennevilliers, France (Office).

GALLEY, Carol; British business executive; ed Univ. of Leicester; fmr Librarian; joined Mercury Asset Man. (now Merrill Lynch Investment Man. 2000) 1971, Dir 1982, Vice-Chair. 1995–2001, mem. Exec. Man. Cttee, joined Merrill Lynch 1997. *Address:* c/o Merrill Lynch Investment Management PLC, 33 King William Street, London, EC4, England (Office).

GALLEY, Robert; French politician and engineer; b. 11 Jan. 1921, Paris; s. of Léon and André (neé Habrial) Galley; m. Jeanne Leclerc de Hauteclocque 1960; two s.; ed Lycée Louis-le-Grand, Paris, Lycée Hoche, Versailles, Ecole centrale des arts et manufactures and Ecole Nat. Supérieure du pétrole et des moteurs; Engineer, Société chérifienne des pétroles 1950–54; in Commissariat à l'Energie atomique 1955–66; Adviser on information tech. to Prime Minister 1966–68; Pres. Institut de recherche d'informatique (IRIA) 1967; mem. Nat. Ass. (representing L'Aube) 1968–78, 1981, RPR Deputy to Nat. Ass. for L'Aube 1981–; Treasurer RPR 1984–90; fmr Minister holding various portfolios, including Infrastructure and Housing, Scientific Research, Posts and Telecommunications, Transport, the Armed Forces and Devt Co-operation; Mayor of Troyes 1972–95; Chair. Comité de bassin Seine-Normandie 1987–; Pres. Parl. Office for Scientific and Tech. Evaluation 1996–; Bd Dir Caisse Nationale de l'Industrie 1988–; mem. Comm. de la production et des échanges; mem. French del. to Council of Europe Consultative Ass. 1988; Commdr, Légion d'honneur, Compagnon de la Libération, Croix de guerre (1939–45). *Address:* Assemblée nationale, 75355 Paris; 18 boulevard Victor Hugo, 10000 Troyes, France.

GALLIANO, John Charles, CBE; British fashion designer; b. 28 Nov. 1960, London; s. of John J. Galliano and Anita Guillen; ed Wilsons Grammar School and St Martin's School of Art; presenter of designer collections 1985–; worked on Courtelle project 1985; first British designer ever to show collection in Paris at the Louvre during Paris Fashion Week 1990; introduced Galliano's Girl 1991; designer of costumes for Ballet Rambert 1990, Kylie Minogue's UK tour 1991; Chief Designer Givenchy 1995–96, Christian Dior 1996–; Designer of Year Award (British Council) 1987, 1994, 1995, 1997 (jt winner), Int. Womenswear Designer of the Year, CFDA 1997, VH1 Womenswear Designer of the Year 1997, Int. Designer Award, Council of Fashion Designers of America 1998 and other awards. *Address:* 60 rue d'Avron, 75020 Paris; Christian Dior, 90 Avenue Montaigne, 75008 Paris, France (Office). *Telephone:* 1-55-25-11-11. *Fax:* 1-55-25-11-12.

GALLINER, Peter; British publisher; b. 19 Sept. 1920, Berlin, Germany; s. of Dr. Moritz Galliner and Hedwig Isaac; m. 1st Edith Marguerite Goldschmidt 1948; one d.; m. 2nd Helga Stenschke 1990; ed in Berlin and London; worked for Reuters, London 1942–45; Foreign Man. Financial Times, London 1945–61; Chair. of Bd and Man. Dir Ullstein Publishing Group, Berlin 1961–64; Vice-Chair. and Man. Dir British Printing Corpn Publishing Group, London 1967–70; Int. Publishing Consultant 1965–67, 1970–75; Chair. Peter Galliner Assocs. 1970–; Dir Int. Press. Inst. 1975–93; Dir Emer., Int. Press Inst., Zürich 1993–; Chair. Int. Encounters London/Zürich 1995–; Fed. Cross of Merit, First Class (FRG) 1961, Encomienda, Orden de Isabel la Católica (Spain) 1982, Kt Commdr's Cross (Badge and Star) of Order of Merit (FRG) 1990, Press Freedom Award (Turkey) 1995, Europäischer Media and Communications Award (Poland) 1998. *Leisure interests:* international affairs, literature, arts, reading, music. *Address:* Bregenzerstrasse 3, D-10707 Berlin, Germany; Untere Zäune 9, 8001 Zürich, Switzerland. *Telephone:* (30) 887–1166 (Berlin); (1) 2518664 (Zürich). *Fax:* (30) 887–11677 (Berlin).

GALLINGER, Yuri Yiosifovich, DrMed; Russian surgeon; b. 3 Sept. 1939, Moldova; s. of Joseph Gallinger and Yekaterina Roor; m.; one s.; ed Kishinev Inst. of Medicine; gen. practitioner in polyclinics, then in 59th Clinic Hosp., Moscow 1962–67; researcher Moscow Medical Univ., Head Dept of Endoscopic Surgery, Russian Scientific Centre of Surgery, Acad. of Medical Sciences 1986–; Pres. Russian Scientific Soc. of Endoscopic Surgery; mem. European Asscn of Endoscopic Surgery, Pirogov Asscn of Surgeons, NY Acad. of Sciences; State Prize of Russian Fed. 1990. *Publications:* over 200 scientific publs. *Leisure interests:* detective films and literature. *Address:* Russian Academy of Medical Sciences, Abrikosovski per. 2, 119874 Moscow, Russia (Office). *Telephone:* (095) 248-13-75 (Office).

GALLO, Max Louis, DenH, DèsSc; French politician, writer and university teacher; b. 7 Jan. 1932, Nice; s. of Joseph Gallo and Mafalda Galeotti; ed Univ. de Paris and Inst. d'Etudes Politiques; teacher Lycée de Nice 1960–65; Sr Lecturer Univ. of Nice 1965–70; Gen. Ed. book series Ce Jour-là, l'Histoire que nous vivons, la Vie selon..., le Temps des révélations; contrib. to various newspapers; devised TV programme Destins du Siècle 1973; Deputy (Socialist) for Alpes-Maritimes 1981–83; jr minister and Govt spokesman 1983–84; Ed. Matin de Paris newspaper 1985–86; MEP 1984–94; Nat. Sec. (Culture) Parti Socialiste 1988–90. *Publications:* L'Italie de Mussolini 1964, La Grande Peur de 1989 (as Max Laugham) 1966, L'Affaire d'Ethiopie 1967, Maximilien Robespierre, Histoire d'une solitude 1968, Gauchisme, réformisme et révolution 1968, Histoire de l'Espagne franquiste 1969, Cinquième Colonne 1930–1940 1970, la Nuit des longs couteaux 1970, Tombeau pour la Commune, Histoire de l'Espagne franquiste 1971, Le Cortège des vainqueurs 1972, La Mafia, un pas vers la mer 1973, L'Affiche, miroir de l'Histoire (illustrated) 1973, L'Oiseau des origines 1974: La Baie des anges (Vol. I) 1975, Le Palais des fêtes (Vol. II) 1976, La Promenade des Anglais (Vol. III) 1976, Le Pouvoir à vif, Despotisme, démocratie et révolution, Que sont les siècles pour la mer 1977, Les hommes naissent tous le même jour: Aurore (Vol. I) 1978, Crépuscule (Vol. II) 1979, Une affaire intime 1979, L'Homme Robespierre: histoire d'une solitude 1978, Un crime très ordinaire 1982, Garibaldi 1982, La Demeure des puissants 1983, La Troisième alliance, pour un nouvel individualisme, Le Grand Jaurès 1984, Le Beau Rivage 1985, Lettre ouverte à Maximilien Robespierre sur les nouveaux Muscadins, Belle Epoque 1986, Que passe la justice du roi, la Route Napoléon 1987, Jules Vallès 1988, Une Affaire publique 1989, Les Clés de l'histoire contemporaine 1989, Manifeste pour une fin de siècle obscure 1989, La Gauche est morte, vive la gauche! 1990, Le Regard des femmes 1991, La Fontaine des innocents (Prix Carlton 1992), Une femme rebelle: Vie et mort de Rosa Luxembourg 1992, L'Amour au temps des solitudes 1993, Les Rois sans visage 1994, Le Condottiere 1994, Le Fils de Klara H. 1995, L'Ambitieuse 1995, La Part de Dieu 1996, Le Faiseur d'or 1996, La Femme derrière le miroir, Napoléon, Le chant du départ (biog., Vol. I) 1997, L'Immortel de Saint-Hélène (Vol. IV) 1997, De Gaulle: L'Appel du destin (Vol. I) 1998, La Solitude du combattant (Vol. II) 1998, Le Premier des Français (Vol. III) 1998, La Statue du Commandeur (Vol. IV) 1998, L'Amour de la France expliqué a mon fils, le Jardin des oliviers 1999, Bleu, blanc, rouge (Vol. I: Mariella) 2000, Les Patriotes (four vols) 2000–01. *Address:* Editions Robert Laffont, 24 avenue Marceau, 75008 Paris, France.

GALLO, Robert C., MD; American biomedical scientist; b. 23 March 1937, Waterbury, Conn.; m. Mary J. Hayes 1961; two s. one d.; ed Providence Coll., Jefferson Medical Univ., Philadelphia and Yale Univ.; Intern and Resident in Medicine, Univ. of Chicago 1963–65; Clinical Assoc. Nat. Cancer Inst. Bethesda, Md 1965–68, Sr Investigator 1968–69, Head, Section on Cellular Control Mechanisms 1969–72, Chief, Lab. of Tumor Cell Biology, Div. of Cancer Etiology 1972–93; Prof. and Dir Inst. of Human Virology, Univ. of Md, Baltimore 1993–; Rep. World Conf. Int. Comparative Leukemia and Lymphoma Asscn 1981–; Hon. Prof. Johns Hopkins Univ. 1985–, Karolinska Inst., Stockholm 1998–; mem. Bd of Govs Franco American AIDS Foundation, World AIDS Foundation 1987; jt discoverer of AIDS virus and first human retroviruses; 15 hon. degrees; numerous honours and awards including Lasker Award for Basic Medical Research 1982, Gen. Motors Cancer Research Award 1984, Armand Hammer Cancer Research Award 1985, Lasker Award for Clinical Medical Research 1986, Gairdner Foundation Int. Award 1987 and other awards for cancer research; 1st Dale McFarlin Award for Research, Int. Retrovirology Asscn. 1994, Promesa Award 1997, Nomura Prize for AIDS and Cancer Research (Japan) 1998, Warren Alpert Prize, Harvard Univ. 1998, Paul Erlich Award (Germany) 1999, Príncipe de Asturias Award (Spain) 2000, Frank Annunzio Award in Science 2000, World Health Award 2001. *Publications:* over 1,100 scientific publs. *Leisure interests:* swimming, reading historical novels, tennis, theatre. *Address:* University of Maryland, Baltimore, Institute of Human Virology, 725 West Lombard Street, Suite S307, Baltimore, MD 2120, USA. *Telephone:* (410) 706-8614 (Office). *Fax:* (410) 706-1952 (Office). *E-mail:* coleman@umbi.umd.edu (Office). *Website:* ihv.org (Office).

GALLOIS, Louis; French business executive; b. 26 Jan. 1944, Montauban, Tarn-et-Garonne; s. of Jean Gallois and Marie Prax; m. Marie-Edmée Amaudric du Chaffaut 1974; one s. two d.; ed Ecole Nat. d'Admin; Head of Bureau, Treasury 1972; Dir of Cabinet of M. Chevènement, Ministry of Research and Tech. 1981–82, Ministry of Research and Industry 1982; Dir-Gen. for Industry, Ministry of Research and Industry 1983; Civil Admin. Ministry of Econ. and Finance 1986; Dir of Civil and Mil. Cabinet, Minister of Defence 1988–89; Pres.-Dir-Gen. Soc. Nationale d'Etude et de Construction de Moteurs d'Aviation (SNECMA) 1989–92; Pres. (Econ. Interest Group) Avion de Combat européen-Rafale 1989; Pres., Dir-Gen. of Aérospatiale 1992–96; Pres. SNCF 1996–; Pres. Société Gestion de Participations Aéronautiques (SOGEPA) 1993–96; Vice-Pres. Supervisory Council Airbus-Industrie 1992–96; Pres. Communauté des chemins de fer européens 1999–; mem. Dassault aviation 1992–, European Aeronautic Defence and Space Co.(EADS) 1999–; Chevalier, Ordre nat. du Mérite, Légion d'honneur. *Address:* SNCF, 34 rue du Commandant René Mouchotte, 75699 Paris cedex 14, France. *E-mail:* louis.gallois@sncf.fr (Office).

GALMOT, Yves; French judge; b. 5 Jan. 1931, Paris; s. of Jean-Jacques Galmot and Marie Germaine Lengauer; m. Katrine-Marie Nicholson 1958; two s.; ed Lycée Louis le Grand, Paris, Inst. d'Etudes Politiques de Paris, Faculté de Droit de Paris, Ecole Nat. d'Administration; auditor, Council of State 1956; Tech. Adviser, Office of High Commr for Youth and Sport 1958; Maître des Requêtes, Council of State 1962–; Govt Commr Legal Section, Council of State 1964–68; Sec.-Gen. Entreprise Minière et Chimique 1970–74; Councillor of State 1981–94; Judge, Court of Justice of European Communities 1982–88; Chair. Financial Section, Council of State 1994–96; mem. Court of Budget and Finance 1996–99; Chair. Comm. Interministérielle des Installations Nucléaires de Base 1996–, Comm. of Appeal, Agence Intergouvernmentale de la Francophonie 1999–. *Leisure interest:* golf. *Address:* Conseil d'Etat, 75100 Paris RP (Office); 95 rue de la Santé, 75013 Paris, France (Home).

GALSWORTHY, Sir Anthony Charles, KCMG, MA; British diplomatist; b. 20 Dec. 1944, London; s. of Sir Arthur Galsworthy and Lady Galsworthy; m. Jan Dawson-Grove 1970; one s. one d.; ed St Paul's School, Corpus Christi Coll. Cambridge; Foreign Office, London 1966, Third Sec., Hong Kong 1967, Third, later Second Sec., Beijing 1970, Second, later First Sec., FCO, London 1972, First Sec., Rome 1977, First Sec., later Counsellor, Beijing 1981, Counsellor and Head Hong Kong Dept, FCO 1984, Prin. Pvt. Sec. to Sec. of State for Foreign and Commonwealth Affairs 1986, with Royal Inst. of Int. Affairs, London 1988, British Sr Rep., Jt Liaison Group, Hong Kong 1989, Cabinet Office 1993, Deputy Under-Sec. of State, FCO 1995, Amb. to People's Repub. of China 1997–2002; Scientific Assoc. Nat. History Museum, London 2001–; Hon. Fellow Royal Botanic Gardens, Edin. 2002. *Leisure interests:* wildlife, entomology. *Address:* c/o Foreign and Commonwealth Office, King Charles Street, London, SW1A 2AH, England.

GALTUNG, Johan, PhD; Norwegian professor of peace studies; b. 24 Oct. 1930, Oslo; s. of August Galtung and Helga Holmboe; m. 1st Ingrid Eide 1956 (divorced 1968); two s.; m. 2nd Fumiko Nishimura 1969; one s. one d.; ed Univ. of Oslo; Prof. of Sociology, Columbia Univ., NY 1957–60; Founder and Dir Int. Peace Research Inst., Oslo 1959–69; Prof. of Peace Research, Univ. of Oslo 1969–77; Prof., Princeton Univ. 1985–89; Prof. of Peace Studies, Univ. of Hawaii 1985–; Prof. of Peace and Co-operation Studies, Univ. Witten-Herdecke, Germany; Olof Palme Prof. of Peace, Stockholm, Sweden 1990–91; f. and Dir Transcend (peace and devt network); Rector Transcend Peace Univ.; Hon. Prof. Berlin, Alicante, Sichuan, Witten/Herdecke; Dr hc (Finland, Romania, Uppsala, Tokyo, Hagen, Alicante, Osnabrück, Turin); Alternative Nobel Peace Prize (Right Livelihood Award), Bajaj Int. Gandhi Prize. *Publications:* Theory and Methods of Social Research (4 Vols) 1967, 1977, 1980, 1988, There are Alternatives 1983, Hitlerism, Stalinism, Reaganism 1984; Essays in Peace Research Vols I–VI 1974–88, Human Rights in Another Key, Peace by Peaceful Means: Peace, Conflict, Development, Civilization, Conflict Transformation by Peaceful Means. *Leisure interests:* travel, writing. *Address:* Casa 227, Urb. Escandinavia, ALFAZ Del Pi, Alicante, Spain; 11009 Kinship Court, Apt. 302, Manassas, VA 20109, USA; 51 Bois Chatton, 01210 Versonnex, France; APA, Garden Court, Apt. 912, Kawaramachi/Shomen, Kyoto 600, Japan. *Telephone:* (4) 50-42-73-06 (France); (96) 5889919 (Spain). *Fax:* (4) 50-42-75-06 (France); (96) 5889919 (Spain). *E-mail:* galtung@transcend.org (Office). *Website:* www.transcend.org (Office).

GALUN, Esra, PhD; Israeli university professor; b. Amiel Esra Galun, 7 April 1927, Leipzig, Germany; s. of David Mendel Galun and Erna Esther Markus; m. Margalith Katz 1953; two s.; ed Hebrew Univ. Jerusalem, California Inst. of Tech., USA; Sr Scientist, Plant Genetics, Weizmann Inst. of Science 1963–67, Assoc. Prof. of Plant Genetics 1968–72, Head Dept of Plant Genetics 1970–88, Prof. of Biology 1972–, Dean Feinberg Grad. School 1974–75, Dean Faculty of Biology 1988–91; Maria Moors Cabot Research Fellow Biological Labs, Harvard Univ., USA 1967–68; Chair. Israeli Nat. Council for Research and Devt 1982–84; Distinguished Visiting Scientist The Roche Inst. of Molecular Biology, Nutley, NY 1985; Armando Kaminitz Award for Achievements in Agric. Research. *Publications:* Pollination Mechanisms, Reproduction and Plant Breeding (jtly) 1977, Transgenic Plants (with Adina Breiman) 1997, Manufacture of Medical and Health Products by Transgenic Plants (with Eithan Galun) 2001, Transposable Elements 2003; over 180 publs in learned journals. *Leisure interests:* music, archaeology, philosophy. *Address:* Department of Plant Sciences, The Weizmann Institute of Science, Rehovot 76100 (Office); 54 Hanassi, Harishon Street, Rehovot 76302, Israel (Home). *Telephone:* (8) 9342637 (Office); (8) 9468103 (Home). *Fax:* (8) 9344181 (Office); (8) 9464016 (Home). *E-mail:* esra.galun@weizmann.ac.il (Office); esra.galun@weizmann.ac.il (Home).

GALUŠKA, Vladimír, JD; Czech diplomatist and lawyer; b. 2 Oct. 1952, Prague; s. of Miroslav Galuška and Milena Galušková (née Králová); m. Marcela Wintrová 1975; two s.; ed Charles Univ., Prague; corp. lawyer Škoda Co., Prague 1975–90; Consul, Deputy Chief of Mission, Czech Embassy, Washington, DC 1990–94; Dir Personnel Dept, Ministry of Foreign Affairs 1994–97, Head of Int. Relations 2002–; Perm. Rep. of Czech Repub. to UN 1997–2001; Pres. ECOSOC 1997, Exec. Bd UNDP/UNFPA 2000; Chair. 3rd Cttee 54th UNGA 1999. *Address:* Ministry of Foreign Affairs, Loretánské nám. 5, 118 000 Prague 1, Czech Republic. *Telephone:* (2) 2418-2555. *Fax:* (2) 2418-2041. *E-mail:* www.mzv.cz (Office).

GALVÊAS, Ernane; Brazilian politician, economist and banker; b. 1 Oct. 1922, Cachoeiro do Itapemirim; s. of José Galvêas and Maria de Oliveira; m. Odaléa dos Santos 1948; one s. one d.; ed Coll. of Economics and Finance, Rio de Janeiro Univ., Centro de Estudios Monetarios Latino-Americanos, Mexico and Yale Univ.; fmrly Prof. of Banking and Finance, Coll. of Econs and

Finance, Rio de Janeiro, subsequently Prof. of Int. Trade, of Monetary Policy and of Int. Monetary Policy; Assoc. Chief, Econs Dept, Supervisory Council for Finance and Credit (SUMOC) 1953–61; Econ. Consultant to Minister of Finance 1961–63; Financial Dir Merchant Marine Comm. 1963–65; Dir Foreign Trade Dept, Banco do Brasil 1966–68; Pres. Banco Central do Brasil 1968–74, 1979; Minister of Finance 1980–84; Exec. Vice-Pres. Aracruz Celulose SA 1974–79, Gen. Man. GB-Repres. Negócios Ltda 1987–; Econ. Consultant Nat. Conf. on Commerce 1987–; Pres. Asscn to Promote Econ. Studies (APEC) 1985–; Dir Lorentzen Empreendimentos, Cia Paraibuna de Metais, Quimio Ind. Farmacêutica, Banco Santista, SANBRA SA; mem. Acad. of Int. Law and Econs (São Paulo). *Publications:* Brazil – Frontier of Development 1974, Development and Inflation 1976, Brazil – Open or Closed Economy? 1978, Apprentice of Entrepreneur 1983, Financial System and Capital Market 1985, The Saga of the Crisis 1985, The Oil Crisis 1985, The Two Faces of Cruzado 1987, Inflation, Deficit and Monetary Policy 1995; numerous articles on economic and financial topics. *Address:* Avenida Atlântica, 2492 Apt. 301, Rio de Janeiro, RJ, Brazil. *Fax:* (21) 2406920.

GALVIN, Gen. John Rogers; American army officer and educationalist; b. 13 May 1929, Wakefield, Mass.; s. of John James Galvin and Mary Josephine Logan; m. Virginia Lee Brennan 1961; four d.; ed U.S. Military Acad., Columbia Univ., Univ. of Pennsylvania, Command and Gen. Staff Coll. and Fletcher School of Law and Diplomacy; commissioned 2nd Lt U.S. Army 1954; Military Asst and ADC to Sec. of U.S. Army 1968–69; Commdr 1st Bn 8th Cavalry 1970; Mil. Asst to Supreme Allied Commdr, Europe (SACEUR) 1974–75; Commdr Div. Support Command 3rd Infantry Div. 1975–77, Chief of Staff 1977–78; Commanding Gen. 24th Infantry Div. 1981–83; VII (U.S.) Corps 1983–85; C-in-C U.S. Southern Command 1985–87; Supreme Allied Commdr Europe and C-in-C U.S. European Command 1987–92; Olin Distinguished Prof. of Nat. Security, U.S. Military Acad., West Point 1992–93; Distinguished Visiting Policy Analyst Mershon Center, Ohio State Univ. 1994–95; Dean Fletcher School of Law and Diplomacy, Tufts Univ., Boston 1995–2000, now Dean Emer.; Dir Raytheon; Defense Distinguished Service Medal, Army, Navy and Air Force Distinguished Service Medal, Silver Star, Legion of Merit (with 2 oak leaf clusters), Soldier's Medal, Bronze Star with 2 oak leaf clusters, Combat Infantryman Badge, Ranger Tab and 20 foreign decorations. *Publications:* The Minute Men 1967, Air Assault 1969, Three Men of Boston 1974 and 80 articles on leadership, tactics and training. *Leisure interests:* reading, writing and walking. *Address:* 2714 Lake Jodeco Drive, Jonesboro, GA 30236, USA (Home). *Telephone:* (770) 210-4110 (Home). *Fax:* (770) 210-9488 (Home). *E-mail:* johngalvin@atl.mediaone.net (Home).

GALVIN, Robert W.; American executive; b. 9 Oct. 1922, Marshfield, Wis.; m. Mary Barnes 1944; two s. two d.; ed Univs of Notre Dame and Chicago; Motorola Inc. Chicago 1940–, Pres. 1956, Chair. of Bd 1964–90, CEO 1984–86, Chair. Exec. Cttee 1990–; Dir Harris Trust and Savings Bank, Chicago; Trustee Illinois Inst. of Tech.; Fellow, Univ. of Notre Dame; Dir Jr Achievement of Chicago; mem. Pres.'s Comm. on Int. Trade and Investment; Electronic Industries Asscn Medal of Honour 1970, Golden Omega Award 1981. *Leisure interests:* skiing, water-skiing, tennis, horse-riding. *Address:* c/o Motorola Inc., 1303 East Algonquin Road, Schaumburg, IL 60196, USA (Office).

GALWAY, Sir James, Kt, OBE, FRCM; British flautist; b. 8 Dec. 1939, Belfast; s. of James and Ethel Stewart Galway (née Clarke); m. 1st 1965; one s.; m. 2nd 1972; one s. two d. (twins); m. 3rd Jeanne Cinnante 1984; ed Mountcollyer Secondary School, Royal Coll. of Music, Guildhall School of Music, Conservatoire National Supérieur de Musique, Paris; first post in Wind Band of Royal Shakespeare Theatre, Stratford-on-Avon; later worked with Sadler's Wells Orchestra, Royal Opera House Orchestra, BBC Symphony Orchestra; Prin. Flute, London Symphony Orchestra and Royal Philharmonic Orchestra; Prin. Solo Flute, Berlin Philharmonic Orchestra 1969–75; int. soloist 1975–; soloist/conductor 1984–; Prin. Guest Conductor, London Mozart Players 1999–; has made numerous recordings; Hon. MA (Open Univ.) 1979; Hon. DMus (Queen's Univ., Belfast) 1979, (New England Conservatory of Music) 1980; Grand Prix du Disque 1976, 1989; Officier des Arts et des Lettres 1987. *Publications:* James Galway: An Autobiography 1978, Flute (Menuhin Music Guide) 1982, James Galway's Music in Time 1983. *Leisure interests:* music, walking, swimming, films, theatre, TV, computing, chess, backgammon, talking to people. *Address:* c/o Vicky Corley-Smith, IMG Artists (Europe), First Floor, Lovell House, 616 Chiswick High Road, London, W4 5RX, England.

GAMA, Jaime José Matos Da; Portuguese politician; b. 1947, Azores; Minister of Home Affairs 1978, Minister of Foreign Affairs 1983–85, 1995–2002; unsuccessful cand. in contest for leadership of Socialist Party 1986, 1988. *Address:* c/o Ministry of Foreign Affairs, Placáio das Necessidades, Largo do Rilvas, 1399-030 Lisbon, Portugal.

GAMASSI, Gen. Mohamed Abdul Ghani al-; Egyptian government official and army officer; b. 9 Sept 1921, el-Batanoun, Menoufia Governorate; ed Mil. Acad., Staff Coll., Nasser Higher Mil. Acad.; Asst Dir of Mobilization Dept 1954–55; Commdr 5th Reconnaissance Regt 1955–57; Staff Officer, Armoured Corps 1957–59; Commdr 2nd Armoured Brigade 1959–61; Commdr Armour School 1961–66; Chief, Army Operational Branch 1966–67; Chief of Staff, Eastern Mil. Zone 1967–68; Deputy Dir Reconnaissance and Intelligence Dept 1968–70; Commdr Operational Group, Syrian Front 1970–71; Chief, Armed Forces Training Dept 1971–72; Chief of Operations Dept and Deputy

Chief of Staff of Armed Forces 1972–73; Chief of Staff of Armed Forces 1973–74; Minister of War and C-in-C of Armed Forces 1974–78, also a Deputy Prime Minister 1975–78; Mil. Adviser to Pres. 1978; Order of Liberation 1952, Memorial Order of Founding of UAR 1958, Star of Honour 1973, Star of Honour (PLO) 1974, Kt Order of Mil. Honour (Syria) 1974, Order of Courage (Libya) 1974, Order of the Two Niles, First Class (Sudan) 1974, Order of King Abdel Aziz, First Class (Saudi Arabia) 1974, Order of Homayoun, First Class (Iran) 1975; numerous ribbons and medals. *Address:* Office of the President, Abdeen, Cairo, Egypt.

GAMBARI, Ibrahim Agboola; Nigerian diplomatist and academic; b. 24 Nov. 1944, Ilorin, Kwara State; m. Fatima Oniyangi 1969; one s. one d.; ed Kings Coll., Lagos, London School of Econs, Columbia Univ.; lecturer, Queen's Coll. 1969–74; Asst Prof., State Univ. of New York (Albany) 1974–77; Sr Lecturer, Ahmadu Bello Univ., Zaria 1977–80, Assoc. Prof. 1980–83, Prof. 1983–89; Dir-Gen. Nigerian Inst. of Int. Affairs 1983–84; Minister for Foreign Affairs 1984–85; Visiting Prof., Johns Hopkins Univ. School of Advanced Int. Studies, Howard Univ., Georgetown Univ. and Brookings Inst. 1986–89; Resident Scholar, Rockefeller Foundation Bellagio Study and Conf. Centre, Italy Nov.–Dec. 1989; Perm. Rep. to UN 1990–2001; Hon. Prof. Chugsan Univ., Guangzhou, People's Repub. of China 1985; fmr Guest Scholar, Wilson Center for Int. Scholars, Smithsonian Inst., USA; Chair. Nat. Seminar to Commemorate 25th Anniversary of OAU, Lagos 1988. *Publications:* Party Politics and Foreign Policy in Nigeria During the First Republic 1981, Theory and Reality in Foreign Policy Making: Nigeria After the Second Republic 1989, Political and Comparative Dimensions of Regional Integration: the Case of ECOWAS 1991. *Address:* c/o Ministry of Foreign Affairs, Zone 3, Wuse District, Abuja, Nigeria (Office).

GAMBAROV, Isa Yunis ogly; Russian-Azerbaijani politician and historian; b. Feb. 1957, Baku, Azerbaijan; s. of Yunis Gambarov and Tahira Gambarov; m. two s.; ed Baku State Univ.; researcher Inst. of Oriental Studies Azerbaijan Acad. of Sciences; active participant in democratic movt in late 1980s, Head of organizational div. of Popular Front 1990–, Deputy Chair. 1991–; mem. then Chair. Azerbaijan Supreme Soviet 1990–95, mem. Milli-Medzhlis and Chair. Comm. on Foreign Affairs; Chair. Musavat (Muslim Democratic Party) 1992–, re-elected 2001. *Address:* Azerbaijan Prospekti 37, Baku 370000, Azerbaijan. *Telephone:* (12) 611500, 980061. *Fax:* (12) 983166.

GAMBIER, Dominique, D. ÈS SC.ECON.; French university teacher; b. 14 Aug. 1947, Rouen; s. of Michel Morel and Yvette Morel; two d.; ed Lycée Corneille, Rouen and Ecole Centrale de Paris; Asst Univ. of Rouen 1972–81; Prof. Ecole Centrale de Paris 1981–83; special assignment, Commissariat Général au Plan 1983–84; Maître de conférences and Dir Inst. of Research and Documentation in Social Sciences (I.R.E.D.), Univ. of Rouen 1984–87; expert adviser, EEC, Brussels 1980–81; scientific adviser, Observatoire français des conjonctures économiques (OFCE) 1981–83; Regional Councillor, Haute-Normandie 1986–, Vice-Pres. of Regional Council 1998–; Pres. Univ. of Rouen 1987–88; Deputy for Seine Maritime 1988–93; Mayor of Déville-les-Rouen 1995–; Officier des Palmes Académiques. *Publications:* Analyse conjoncturelle du chômage, Théorie de la politique économique en situation d'incertitude 1980, Le marché du travail 1991, L'emploi en France 1997; numerous articles on economy of work and labour etc. *Leisure interests:* football, tennis, skiing. *Address:* Mairie de Déville, 1 Place François Mitterrand, 76250 Déville; 5 allée du Houssel, 76130 Mont-St-Aignan, France (Home). *Telephone:* 35-76-88-18. *Fax:* 35-74-30-73.

GAMBLE, Christine Elizabeth, PhD; British cultural administrator; b. 1 March 1950, Rotherham; d. of the late Albert Edward Gamble and of Kathleen Laura Wallis; m. Edward Barry Antony Craxton; ed Royal Holloway Coll., Univ. of London; worked in Anglo-French cultural org. 1974–75; Office of the Cultural Attaché, British Embassy, Moscow 1975–76; joined British Council, New Delhi 1977, returned to UK (Stratford-upon-Avon) 1979, posted to Harare 1981–82, Regional Officer for the Soviet Union and Mongolia 1982–85, Deputy Dir Athens 1985–87, with Corp. Planning Dept 1988–90, Head Project Pursuit Dept and Dir Chancellor's Financial Sector Scheme 1990–92, Dir Visitor's Dept 1992–93, Gen. Man. Country Services Group and Head European Services 1993–96; Cultural Councillor, British Embassy, Paris and Dir British Council, France 1996–98; Dir Royal Inst. of Int. Affairs, London 1998–2002; Order of Rio Branco, Brazil 2000. *Leisure interests:* literature, art, music, theatre. *Address:* c/o The Royal Institute of International Affairs, Chatham House, 10 St James's Square, London, SW1Y 4LE, England.

GAMBLING, William Alexander, PhD, DSc, FR.ENG., FRS; British electrical engineer and industrial consultant; b. 11 Oct. 1926, Port Talbot, Glamorgan; s. of George Alexander Gambling and Muriel Clara Gambling; m. 1st Margaret Pooley 1952 (separated 1987); one s. two d.; m. 2nd Barbara Colleen O'Neil 1994; ed Univs of Bristol and Liverpool; Lecturer in Electric Power Eng, Univ. of Liverpool 1950–55; Fellow, Nat. Research Council, Univ. of BC 1955–57; Lecturer, Sr Lecturer and Reader, Univ. of Southampton 1957–64, Prof. of Electronics 1964–80, Dean of Eng and Applied Science 1972–75, Head of Dept 1974–79, British Telecom Prof. of Optical Communication 1980–95, Dir UK Nat. Optoelectronics Research Centre 1989–95; Royal Soc. Visiting Prof. and Dir, Optoelectronics Research Centre, City Univ. of Hong Kong 1996–2001; Dir of Optoelectronics Research and Devt, LTK Industries Ltd 2002–; Visiting Prof., Univ. of Colo 1966–67, Bhabha Atomic Research Centre, India 1970, Osaka Univ., Japan 1977; Hon. Prof. Huazhong Univ. of Science and Tech., Wuhan, 1986–, Beijing Univ. of Posts and Telecommunications,

Shanghai Univ. 1991–, Shandong Univ. 1999–; Hon. Dir Beijing Optical Fibres Lab., People's Repub. of China 1987–; Pres. I.E.R.E. 1977–78; Chair. Comm.D, Int. Union of Radio Science 1981–84, Eng Council 1983–88; mem. Bd, Council of Eng Insts 1974–79, Electronics Research Council 1977–80, Nat. Electronics Council 1977–78 and 1984–89; Dir York Ltd 1980–97; mem. British Nat. Cttee for Radio Science 1978–87, Educational Advisory Council, IBA 1980–82, Eng Industries Training Bd 1985–88; mem. Council, Royal Acad. of Eng 1989–92; Selby Fellow, Australian Acad. of Science 1982; Foreign mem. Polish Acad. of Sciences 1985; Liveryman, Worshipful Co. of Engineers 1988; Fellow and Council mem. Hong Kong Acad. of Eng Sciences; Hon. Fellow IEE; Freeman, City of London 1988; Dr hc (Madrid) 1994, (Aston) 1995, (Bristol) 1999; Academic Enterprise Award 1982, J. J. Thomson Medal, IEE 1982, Faraday Medal, IEE 1983, Churchill Medal, Soc. of Engineers 1985, Simms Medal, Soc. of Engineers 1988, Micro-optics Award (Japan) 1989, Dennis Gabor Award (USA) 1990, Rank Prize for Optoelectronics 1991, C & C Medal (Japan) 1993, Mountbatten Medal 1993, Royal Soc. of Int. Civil Engineers James Alfred Ewing Medal 2002. *Publications:* some 300 research papers on electrical discharges, microwave devices, quantum electronics, optical fibre communication and education. *Leisure interests:* reading, music. *Address:* LTK Industries, 13/F Vanta Industrial Centre, 21 Tai Lin Pai Road, Kwai Chung, Hong Kong Special Administrative Region (Office); c/o Shanghai Electric Wire Ltd, 12 Lane 5, Loupu Road, Anting, Shanghai 201805, People's Republic of China (Home). *Telephone:* 2425-4399 (Office); (21) 6465-6587 (Home). *Fax:* 2418-1627 (Office); (21) 6465-6587 (Home). *E-mail:* wag@ltkcable.com.

GAMBON, Sir Michael John, Kt, CBE; British actor; b. 19 Oct. 1940, Dublin; s. of Edward Gambon and Mary Gambon; m. Anne Miller 1962; one s.; ed St Aloysius School for Boys, London; fmr mechanical engineer; Trustee Royal Armouries 1995–98; Hon. DLitt 2003. *TV:* numerous appearances including: Ghosts, Oscar Wilde, The Holy Experiment, Absurd Person Singular, The Borderers, The Singing Detective (BAFTA for Best Actor 1987), The Heat of the Day, Maigret 1992, The Entertainer, Truth, Wives and Daughters (BAFTA for Best Actor 2000), Longitude 2000 (BAFTA for Best Actor 2001), Perfect Strangers (BAFTA Best Actor 2002). *Films:* The Beast Must Die 1975, Turtle Diary 1985, Paris by Night 1988, The Cook, The Thief, His Wife and Her Lover 1989, A Dry White Season 1989, The Rachel Papers 1989, State of Grace 1989, The Heat of the Day 1989, Mobsters 1992, Toys 1992, Clean Slate 1993, Indian Warrior 1993, The Browning Version 1993, Mary Reilly 1994, Midnight in Moscow 1994, A Man of No Importance 1995, The Innocent Sleep 1995, All Our Fault 1995, Two Deaths 1996, Nothing Personal 1996, The Gambler 1996, Dancing at Lughnasa 1997, Plunket and McClean 1997, The Last September 1998, Sleepy Hollow 1998, The Insider, End Game 1999, Charlotte Gray 2001, Gosford Park 2001, Ali G Indahouse 2001, Path to War 2001, The Actors 2002, Open Range 2002. *Theatre:* first stage appearance with Edwards/Mácliammoir Co., Dublin 1962; Nat. Theatre, Old Vic 1963–67; Birmingham Repertory and other provincial theatres 1967–69, title roles including Othello, Macbeth, Coriolanus; RSC Aldwych 1970–71; The Norman Conquests 1974, Otherwise Engaged 1976, Just Between Ourselves 1977, Alice's Boys 1978, The Caretaker 2000; with Nat. Theatre 1980, appearing in Galileo (London Theatre Critics' Award for Best Actor), Betrayal, Tales from Hollywood; with RSC, Stratford and London 1982–83, title roles in King Lear, Antony and Cleopatra, Old Times 1985, A Chorus of Disapproval, Nat. Theatre 1985 (Olivier Award for Best Comedy Performance), A Small Family Business 1987, Uncle Vanya 1988, Mountain Language 1988, Othello 1990, Taking Steps 1990, Skylight (play) 1995, Volpone (Evening Standard Drama Award) 1995, Tom and Clem 1997, The Unexpected Man 1998, Cressida 2000 (Variety Club Award for Best Actor), A Number, Jerwood Theatre, Royal Court, London 2002. *Leisure interests:* flying, gun collecting, clock making. *Address:* c/o ICM, Oxford House, 76 Oxford Street, London, W1N 0AX, England (Office).

GAMES, David Edgar, PhD, D.Sc, CChem, FRSC; British university professor; b. 7 April 1938, Ynysddu; s. of Alfred William Games and Frances Elizabeth Bell Games (née Evans); m. Marguerite Patricia Lee 1961; two s.; ed Lewis School, Pengam, King's Coll., Univ. of London; Lecturer, Sr Lecturer, Reader and Personal Chair. Univ. Coll., Cardiff 1965–89; Prof. of Mass Spectrometry and Dir of Mass Spectrometry Research Unit, Univ. of Wales at Swansea 1989–, Head Dept of Chem. 1996–; Royal Soc. of Chem. Award in Analytical Separation Methods 1987, The Chromatographic Soc. Martin Medal 1991, Royal Soc. of Chem. SAC Gold Medal 1993, J. J. Thomson Gold Medal, Int. Mass Spectrometry Cttee 1997, Aston Medal, British Mass Spectrometry Soc. 1999. *Leisure interests:* swimming, walking. *Address:* Mass Spectrometry Research Unit, University of Wales Swansea, Singleton Park, Swansea, SA2 8PP (Office); 9 Heneage Drive, West Cross, Swansea, SA3 5BR, Wales (Home). *Telephone:* (1792) 295297 (Office); (1792) 405192 (Home). *Fax:* (1792) 295747 (Office).

GAMKRELIDZE, Thomas V.; Georgian linguist and cultural historian; b. 23 Oct. 1929, Kutaisi, Georgia; s. of Valerian Gamkrelidze and Olimpiada Gamkrelidze; m. Nino Djavakhishvili 1968; one s. one d.; ed Tbilisi Univ.; post-grad. work 1952–55; Lecturer, Georgian Acad. of Sciences Inst. of Linguistics 1956–60; Head of Dept 1960–73, Dir, The Oriental Inst. 1973–; Head of Dept Tbilisi State Univ. 1966–72; main work in area of theoretical linguistics, Kartvelian, Semitic and Indo-European linguistics and semiology; People's Deputy of the USSR 1989–91; mem. Parl. Repub. of Georgia 1992–; Ed.-in-Chief Voprosy Jazykoznanija (Russian Acad. of Sciences) 1988–94;

mem. Georgian Acad. of Sciences 1974; mem. USSR (now Russian) Acad. of Sciences 1984; Corresp. FBA; mem. Austrian Acad. of Sciences; Foreign mem. Sächsische Akad. der Wissenschaften; Foreign Hon. mem. American Acad. of Arts and Sciences; Hon. mem. Indogermanische Gesellschaft, Linguistic Soc. of America, Societas Linguistica Europaea (Pres. 1986); Dr. hc (Bonn, Chicago); Lenin Prize 1988, Humboldt Prize (Fed. Repub. of Germany) 1989, Djavakhishvili Prize (Tbilisi Univ.) 1992. *Publications:* Indo-European and the Indo-Europeans (2 Vols) (with V. V. Ivanov) 1984, Alphabetic Writing and the Old Georgian Script. Typology and Provenance of Alphabetic Writing Systems 1989. *Leisure interests:* music, tennis. *Address:* The Oriental Institute, Georgian Academy of Sciences, Acad. Tsereteli Street 3, 380062 Tbilisi; Jac. Nikoladze Street 6, 380009 Tbilisi, Georgia (Home). *Telephone:* (32) 23-38-85 (Office); (32) 22-64-92 (Home). *Fax:* (32) 23-38-85 (Office). *E-mail:* orientge@hotmail.com.

GAMZATOV, Rasul Gamzatovich; Russian/Avar poet; b. 8 Sept. 1923, Tsadasa, Daghestan Autonomous Republic; s. of G. Tsadasa (nat. poet); ed Moscow A. M. Gorky Literary Inst.; mem. CPSU 1944–91; worked on newspaper Bolshevik Gor 1941–51; radio ed. of programmes in Avar language, Daghestan; mem. staff, Maxim Gorky Inst., Moscow 1945–50; Chair. Bd Union of Daghestan Writers 1951–; Deputy of Supreme Soviet of USSR 1962–66; People's Deputy of USSR 1989–91; mem. Presidium; mem. Soviet Cttee of solidarity with countries of Asia and Africa –1991; Hero of Socialist Labour; Lenin Prize, State Prizes of Russia and Daghestan. *Publications:* Hot Love and Burning Hate 1943, My Country 1947, Our Mountains 1947, The Homeland of a Miner 1950, Verse 1950, Tales of my Elder Brother 1952, Poems 1954, Spring in Daghestan 1955, My Heart is in the Mountains 1959, Stars on High 1962, Mountains and Valleys 1963, Zarema 1963, And Star Speaks with Star 1964, Selected Lyrics 1965, Mutlaka 1966, Sick Teeth (poetry) 1967, My Daghestan 1968, The Last Price 1978 (Firdausi Prize), Look After Mothers 1978, Collected Works (5 Vols) 1980–82, Island of Women 1983, The Wheel of Life 1987, The Dawn of Hope 1988, The Moment and the Eternity 1989, The Bowl of Life 1992, Collected Works (3 Vols) 1993. *Address:* M. Gorky str. 15, 367000 Makhachkala, Russia. *Telephone:* (872) 007-72-82.

GAN ZIYU; Chinese government official and senior engineer; b. 15 Oct. 1929, Canton; two s.; ed Zhongshan Univ.; joined CCP 1953; Vice-Chair. of State Planning Comm. 1978–, of Admin. Comm. on Import and Export Affairs 1981–82, of State Foreign Investment Comm. 1981–82; Vice-Chair. Drafting Cttee for Nat. Defence Law of PRC 1994–; Deputy Chair. Nat. Leading Group for Work Concerning Foreign Capital 1994–; mem. Preliminary Working Cttee of the Preparatory Cttee of the Hong Kong Special Admin. Region 1993–97; Chair. Overseas Chinese Affairs Cttee, 9th NPC 1998–. *Address:* c/o Standing Committee of the National People's Congress, Beijing, People's Republic of China.

GANBAATAR, Adiya; Mongolian politician and academic; b. 8 Feb. 1959, Ulan Bator; s. of Adiya Ganbaatar and Ichinkhorlo Ganbaatar; m.; three d.; ed Łódź Univ., Poland; lecturer, Mongolian State Univ. 1983–90; Chair. Democratic Socialist Movt 1990; mem. State Great Hural (Parl.) 1992–2000, Chair. Standing Cttee on the Budget 1997–; Vice-Chair. Cen. Asia Devt Foundation 1992–; Pres. Mongolian Tennis Assen 1997–; Distinguished Officer, Banking and Finance 1999, Distinguished Officer, Educ. 2000. *Publications:* three books on mathematics. *Leisure interests:* chess, tennis. *Address:* Parliament, State House, Ulan Bator 12, Mongolia. *Telephone:* (1) 372980 (Office); (1) 321648 (Home). *Fax:* (1) 372980. *E-mail:* ganbaatar@mail.parl.gov.mn (Office).

GANBOLD, Davaadorjiin, M.SC.(ECON.), PhD; Mongolian politician; b. 26 June 1957, Ulan Bator; s. of Tsedevsuren Davaadorj and Lodongiin Oyun; m. M. Tserengyn Oyun; two d.; ed Moscow State Univ., USSR; Asst to Prof. of Political Econ., Mongolian State Univ. 1979–84; Prof. of Political Econ., State and Social Studies Acad. 1988–90; Founder-mem. Nat. Progress Party, Chair. Party Council; First Deputy Prime Minister 1990; mem. Great Hural (legislature) July 1992–; Chair. Standing Cttee on Budget, Finance and Econs; Chair. Mongolian Nat. Democratic Party (merger of four opposition parties) 1992–96, Deputy Leader 1998. *Leisure interests:* fishing, cycling, collecting stamps and model cars. *Address:* Room 221, Government House, Ulan Bator, Mongolia. *Telephone:* 320879 (Office); 322669 (Home). *Fax:* 328172.

GANDHI, Maneka Anand; Indian politician; b. 26 Aug. 1956, New Delhi; d. of the late Col T. S. Anand and of Amteshwar Anand; m. Sanjay Gandhi 1974 (died 1980); one s.; ed Jawaharlal Univ., New Delhi; Ed. Surya (Sun) magazine 1977–80; Founder and Leader of political party Rashtriya Sanjay Manch (merged with Janata Party 1988) 1983; Minister of State for the Environment and Forests 1989–91; MP 1996–; Minister for Social Justice and Empowerment 1999–2001; Minister of State for Statistics and Programme Implementation 2002–; Chair. People for Animals Trust, Cttee on Control and Supervision of Experiments on Animals, Soc. for Prevention of Cruelty to Animals; Founder Greenline Trees; Special Adviser to Voice (consumer action forum); cr. environmental film series New Horizons; writer and anchorwoman nat. TV programmes on animals, Heads and Tails, Maneka's Ark; Pres. Ruth Cowell Trust, Sanjay Gandhi Animal Care Centre; Lord Erskine Award (Royal Soc. for the Prevention of Cruelty to Animals) 1991, Vegetarian of the Year (Vegetarian Soc.) 1995, Prani Mitra Award (Nat. Animal Welfare Bd) 1997, Marchig Prize (Marchig Animal Welfare Trust, GB) 1997, Venu Menon Lifetime Achievement Award 1999, Bhagwan Mahavir Award 1999, Diwaliben Award 1999, Aadishakti Puruskar 2001, Woman of the Year 2001.

Publications: Sanjay Gandhi 1980, Mythology of Indian Plants, Animal Quiz, Penguin Book of Hindu Names, The Complete Book of Muslim and Parsi Names, First Aid for Animals, Animal Laws of India, Rainbow and Other Stories, Natural Health for Your Dog, Heads and Tails, Wise and Wonderful Animal Alphabet Quiz Book. *Leisure interests:* reading, working with animals. *Address:* Ministry of Statistics and Programme Implementation, Sardar Patel Bhavan, Patel Chowk, New Delhi 110 001 (Office); A-4 Maharani Bagh, New Delhi 110065, India (Home). *Telephone:* (11) 3732150 (Office); (11) 6840402 (Home). *Fax:* (11) 3732067 (Office); (11) 6823144 (Home). *Website:* www.pmindia.nic.in.

GANDHI, Sonia; Indian (b. Italian) politician; b. 9 Dec. 1946, Italy; d. of Stefano Maino and Paola Maino; m. Rajiv Gandhi 1968 (fmr Prime Minister of India) (died 1991); ed Univ. of Cambridge, Nat. Gallery of Modern Art, Delhi; Pres. Rajiv Gandhi Foundation; mem. All India Congress Cttee (I), Pres. March 1998–; Leader of Opposition in Parl. (Lok Sabha). *Publications:* Rajiv 1992, Rajiv's World 1994. *Address:* 10 Janpath, New Delhi 110011 (Home); Rajiv Gandhi Foundation, Jawahar Bhawan, Dr. Rajendra Prasad Road, New Delhi 110001; All India Congress Committee (I), 24 Akbar Road, New Delhi 110011, India. *Telephone:* (11) 3017470 (Office); (11) 3014161 (Home); (11) 3755117 (Rajiv Gandhi Foundation); (11) 3019080 (All India Congress Cttee (I)). *Fax:* (11) 3017047 (All India Congress Cttee).

GANDOIS, Jean Guy Alphonse; French company executive; b. 7 May 1930, Nieul; s. of Eugène and Marguerite Gandois (née Teillet); m. Monique Testard 1953; two s.; ed École Polytechnique, Paris; Civil Engineer, Ministry of Public Works, French Guinea 1954–58; mem. of tech. co-operation missions to Brazil and Peru 1959–60; Asst to Commercial Dir Wendel & Cie 1961, Econ. Dir 1966; Econ. and Commercial Dir Wendel-Sidelor 1968; Gen. Man. Sacilor 1973; Pres., Dir-Gen. Sollac 1975; Dir-Gen. Rhône-Poulenc SA 1976, Vice-Pres. 1977–79, Chair. and CEO 1979–82 (resgnd); Chair. and CEO Pechiney 1986–94; Chair. Cockerill-Sambre (Belgium) 1987–99; Pres. CNPF (Nat. Council of French Employers) 1994, now Hon. Pres.; Chair Supervisory Council and Strategy Cttee, Suez Lyonnaise des Eaux 2000-01, Vice-Pres. 2001-; mem. Bd of Dirs Danone (fmrly BSN), Eurazeo (fmrly Eurafrance), Air Liquide España (Spain), Air Liquide Italia (Italy), Société Générale de Belgique (Belgium); mem. Supervisory Bd Suez Lyonnaise des Eaux; Hon. mem. Order of Australia; Dr. hc (Liège, Louvain); Commdr, Légion d'honneur; Grand Cordon, Ordre de Léopold, Grand Croix, Ordre de la Couronne (Belgium); Grand Officier, Couronne du Chêne (Luxembourg). *Address:* Suez, 16 Rue de la Ville- l'Eveque, 75383 Paris cedex 08 (Office); 23 Quai Voltaire, 75007 Paris, France (Home).

GANDOLFINI, James; American actor; b. 18 Sept. 1961, Westwood, N.J.; m. Marcy Wudarski 1999 (divorced 2002); ed Rutgers Univ., Actors Studio; began acting career in NY Theatre; Broadway debut in A Streetcar Named Desire 1982; Golden Globe Best Actor in a Drama Series 1999 (for The Sopranos), Emmy Outstanding Lead Actor in a Drama Series 2000, 2001 (for The Sopranos). *Films:* A Stranger Among Us 1992, True Romance 1993, Mr Wonderful 1993, Money for Nothing 1993, Italian Movie 1993, Angie 1994, Terminal Velocity 1994, The New World 1995, Crimson Tide 1995, Get Shorty 1995, The Juror 1996, She's So Lovely 1997, Night Falls on Manhattan 1997, Perdita Durango 1997, Gun 1997, Dance with the Devil 1997, The Mighty 1998, A Civil Action 1998, Fallen 1998, 8MM 1999, A Whole New Day 1999, The Mexican 2001, The Man Who Wasn't There 2001, The Last Castle 2001. *Television:* Gun (series) 1997, 12 Angry Men 1997, The Sopranos (series) 1999–. *Address:* c/o Creative Artists Agency, 9830 Wilshire Boulevard, Beverly Hills, CA 90212, USA (Office).

GANELIUS, Tord Hjalmar, D.PHIL; Swedish mathematician; b. 23 May 1925, Stockholm; s. of Hjalmar Ganelius and Ebba Bejbom; m. Aggie Hemberg 1951; three s. one d.; ed Stockholm Univ.; Asst Prof. Lund Univ. 1953–57; Prof. of Math., Univ. of Göteborg 1957–80, Dean, Faculty of Science 1963–65, 1977–80; Scientific Sec.-Gen. Swedish Royal Acad. of Sciences 1981–91; mem. Bd of Dirs., Nobel Foundation 1981–89, V. and E. Hasselblad Foundation 1983–95; Guest Prof. Univ. of Washington, Seattle 1962, Cornell Univ. 1967–68, Madras Inst. of Math. Sciences 1969, Univ. of Calif., San Diego 1972–73; Fellow, Swedish Royal Acad., Finnish Acad., Royal Soc. of Göteborg, European Acad. of Arts and Sciences; King's Medal 1987. *Publications:* Tauberian Remainder Theorems 1971, Lectures on Approximation, etc. 1982. *Address:* Bergianska trådgården, 104 05 Stockholm, Sweden (Home). *Telephone:* (8) 158548. *E-mail:* tord.ganelius@telia.com (Home).

GANELLIN, Charon Robin, PhD, DSc, FRS, FRSC; British professor in medicinal chemistry; b. 25 Jan. 1934, London; s. of Leon Ganellin and Beila Cluer; m. Tamara Greene 1956; one s. one d.; ed Harrow County Grammar School for Boys and Queen Mary Coll., Univ. of London; Research Assoc. MIT 1960; Research Chemist in Medicinal Chem., Smith Kline and French Labs. Ltd (UK) 1958–59, Head of Dept 1961–75, Dir of Histamine Research, Smith Kline and French Research Ltd 1975–80, Vice-Pres. Research 1980–84, Vice-Pres. Chemical Research 1984–86; Hon. Lecturer, Dept of Pharmacology, Univ. Coll., London 1975–86, Smith Kline and French Prof. of Medicinal Chem. 1986–; Fellow Queen Mary and Westfield Coll., Univ. of London 1992; co-inventor of Cimetidine (Tagamet™) 1970s; Hon. Prof. of Medicinal Chem., Univ. of Kent 1979–; Hon. mem. Sociedad Española de Química Terapéutica 1982–; Hon. DSc (Aston) 1990; UK Chemical Soc. Medallion in Medicinal Chemistry 1977, Prix Charles Mentzer, Soc. de Chimie Thérapeutique (France) 1978, American Chemical Soc., Div. of Medicinal Chem. Award 1980,

Royal Soc. of Chem. Tilden Medal 1982, Soc. for Chemical Industry Messel Medal 1988, Soc. for Drug Research Award 1989, Nat. Inventors Hall of Fame (USA) 1990, Royal Soc. of Chemistry Adrien Albert Medal 1999. *Publications:* Pharmacology of Histamine Receptors 1982, Frontiers in Histamine Research 1985, Dictionary of Drugs 1990, Medicinal Chemistry 1993, Dictionary of Pharmacological Agents 1997; research papers and reviews in various journals. *Address:* Department of Chemistry, University College London, 20 Gordon Street, London, WC1H 0AJ, England. *Telephone:* (20) 7679-7459.

GANEV, Stoyan; Bulgarian politician and lawyer; b. 1955; specialises in constitutional law; Minister of Foreign Affairs 1991–92; a Deputy Prime Minister of Bulgaria 1991–92; mem. Union of Democratic Forces (UDF). *Address:* c/o Union of Democratic Forces, Boulevard Rakovski 134, 1000 Sofia, Bulgaria.

GANIĆ, Ejup, DSc; Bosnia and Herzegovina politician and scientist; b. 3 March 1946, Novi Pazar; ed Belgrade Univ., Massachusetts Inst. of Tech.; researcher, consultant, Prof. of Mechanical Eng, Univ. of Ill. Chicago 1975–82; returned to Bosnia and Herzegovina 1982; worked as Exec. Dir UNIS Co.; mem. Presidency of Bosnia and Herzegovina 1990–96, Vice-Pres. 1992–96; Vice-Pres. Fed. of Bosnia and Herzegovina 1994–96, Co-Pres. 1996–2002; currently Prof. Univ. of Sarajevo, Pres. MET Foundation. *Publications:* Handbook of Heat Transfer Applications 1985, Handbook of Heat Transfer Fundamentals 1985, Handbook of Essential Engineering Information and Data 1991, Engineering Companion 2003. *Address:* University of Sarajevo, Vilsonovo Setaliste 9, 71000 Sarajevo, Bosnia and Herzegovina.

GANIEV, Rivner Fazilovich; Russian mechanical engineer; b. 1 April 1937, Bashkiriya; m. Galina Mikhailovna Antonovskaya; two s.; ed Ufa Aviation Inst.; engineer constructor, jr, sr researcher, Head of Dept, Inst. of Mechanics Ukrainian Acad. of Sciences 1959–78; head of lab. Research Inst. of Machine Devt 1978–89, Deputy Dir 1989–95; Dir of Non-linear Wave Mechanics and Tech. Centre, Russian Acad. of Sciences 1995–; corresp. mem. USSR (now Russian) Acad. of Sciences 1987, mem. 1994; research in theory of resonance phenomena at nonlinear spatial oscillations of solid and deformable matter, theory of nonlinear oscillations of multiphase systems, vibration and wave processes and tech.; mem. Scientific Council on Problem Reliability of Machines. *Publications include:* Dynamics of Particles under Influence of Vibrations 1975, Solid Matter Oscillations 1976, Oscillatory Phenomena in Multiphase Media and their Applications to Technology 1980; numerous articles in scientific journals. *Leisure interests:* sport, skiing. *Address:* Wave Mechanics and Technology Centre, Russian Academy of Sciences, 4 Bardin Street, 117334 Moscow, Russia. *Telephone:* (095) 135-55-93 (Office). *Fax:* (095) 135-61-26.

GANSER, Gérard Robert Gaston; French civil servant; b. 6 Jan. 1949, Montreuil-Sous-Bois; s. of Pierre Ganser and Simone Braillon; m. Aimée Fontaine (divorced); one s.; ed Lycées Paul Valéry and Louis le Grand, Nat. School of Admin.; auditor Court of Revenue 1976–80, public auditor 1980, chief adviser 1993–98, Sec.-Gen. 1998–; with Interministerial Mission of the Sea 1979–80; commercial adviser Mexico 1981–82; with Ministry of Agric. 1983, Jt Dir Ministry of Trade and Tourism 1983–84, with Ministry of Industrial Redeployment and Trade 1984, Ministry for Communications 1988, Dir 1989–91; Jt Dir-Gen. Commercial Affairs Télédiffusion de France 1984–86; reporter to Constitutional Council 1987–88; Pres., Dir-Gen. Soc. financière de radiodiffusion (Sofirad) 1991–94; Vice-Pres. Radio Monte Carlo 1991–94; auditor European Examinations Office 1995; auditor Inst. des hautes études de la défense nat. 1996; Sec.-Gen. Cour des comptes 1998–99 (Chief Adviser 1993–); Chevalier Ordre nat. du Mérite. *Address:* Cour des Comptes, 13 rue Cambon, 75001 Paris (Office); 11 rue de Verneuil, 75007 Paris, France (Home).

GANTIN, HE Cardinal Bernardin; Benin ecclesiastic (retd); b. 8 May 1922, Toffo; ordained priest 1951; elected to titular Church of Tipasa, Mauritania 1956, consecrated 1957; apptd to Cotonou, Benin 1960; cr. Cardinal 1977; Prefect, Sacred Congregation of Bishops 1984–99, Prefect Emer. 1999–; Dean, Coll. of Cardinals 1993–; Titular Bishop of Suburbicarian Church, Ostia Antica 1993–; fmrly Pres. Pontifical Cttee for Justice and Peace, Pres. Pontifical Comm. for Latin America; Deacon of the Sacred Heart of Christ the King; Pres. Papal Council 'Cor unum'; Cardinalizia di Vigilanza, Inst. per le Opere di Religione. *Address:* Palazzo dell' Arciprete, 00120 Citta del Vaticano, Rome, Italy.

GANTNER, Carrillo Baillieu, MFA; Australian theatre manager, director and actor; b. 17 June 1944, San Francisco, Calif.; s. of Vallejo Gantner and Neilma Gantner; m. 1st Nancy Black 1971 (divorced 1982); two s. one d. (deceased); m. 2nd Dr. Jennifer Webb; two s.; ed Melbourne Grammar School and Melbourne, Stanford and Harvard Univs; Fellow, Stanford Univ. 1968–69; Asst. Admin. Adelaide Festival of Arts 1969–70; Drama Officer, Australian Council for the Arts 1970–73; Gen. Man. Melbourne Theatre Co. 1973–75; Exec. Dir Playbox Theatre Co. Ltd 1976–84, The CUB Malthouse; Cultural Counsellor, Australian Embassy, Beijing 1985–87; Artistic Dir Playbox Theatre Centre 1988–93, Chair. Playbox Malthouse Ltd 1994–96; Councillor, City of Melbourne 1996–99 (Chair. Planning and Devt Cttee 1996–98, Docklands Cttee 1998–99, Deputy Chair. Finance and Service Cttee and Audit Cttee 1998–99); Chair. Performing Arts Bd Australia Council 1990–93, Nat. Circus Summit 1990, Nat. Dance Summit 1991, Nat. Advisory Council, Musica Viva 1993–; Melbourne Int. Comedy Festival 1995–; Pres. Melbourne Chapter of URASENKE 1995–; Dir Myer Foundation 1984–92

(Vice-Pres. 1992–), Asialink 1990–92 (Chair. 1992–), Mayfair Hanoi Ltd (Hong Kong) 1996–98, Deputy Chair. 1999–; mem. Australia–China Council 1989–94, Australia Abroad Council 1991–95, Exec. Cttee Asia Pacific Philanthropy Consortium 1994–, Nat. Advisory Council, Adelaide Festival 1996–; Corresp. mem. The Hague Club 1994–; Trustee Sidney Myer Fund 1991–; Gov. Fed. for Asian Cultural Promotion 1994–; Japan Foundation Visitors Program 1991; mem. Working Group to establish an Asian Business Council for the Arts 1997–98; Chair. Arts Man. Course Advisory Cttee, Victorian Coll. of the Arts 1996–98; other professional appts.; Chair. Barclay Investment Pty Ltd, Myer Investment Pty Ltd 1998–. *Publications:* articles in professional journals. *Leisure interests:* viticulture, tennis. *Address:* Level 45, 55 Collins Street, Melbourne, Vic. 3000, Australia. *Telephone:* (3) 9207-3050. *Fax:* (3) 9207-3061.

GANZURI, Kamal Ahmad Al-, MA, PhD; Egyptian politician; b. 1933; ed Cairo Univ. and Michigan Univ.; Gov. of Beni Suef and Under-Sec. Ministry of Planning 1975; fmr consultant for planning and devt at UN; fmr Head, Nat. Planning Inst., Minister of Planning 1982–85; Deputy Prime Minister and Minister of Planning 1985–96, Int. Co-operation 1985–87; Prime Minister of Egypt 1996–99; Minister of Planning and Int. Co-operation 1997–99. *Address:* c/o Office of the Prime Minister, Cairo, Egypt.

GAO CHANGLI; Chinese politician; b. July 1937, Yutai, Shandong Prov.; ed Chinese People's Univ.; joined CCP 1956; cadre Yutai Co. People's Govt, cadre Office of CCP Jining Pref. Cttee; Vice-Sec. CCP Yishui Co. Cttee, Sec. CCP Rizhao Co. Cttee, Vice-Chief Sec. then Chief Sec. CCP Shandong Prov. Cttee; Vice-Gov. of Shandong Prov. and Sec. Political and Legal Cttee of CCP Shandong Prov. Cttee; mem. Trial Cttee of Supreme People's Court; Vice-Chair. Supreme People's Court 1993–98; Minister of Justice 1998–2000; alt. mem. CCP 15th Cen. Cttee 1997. *Address:* Ministry of Justice, 11 Xiaguangli, Sanyuanqiao, Chao Yang Qu, Beijing 100016, People's Republic of China.

GAO DEZHAN; Chinese state official and senior engineer; b. 6 Aug. 1932; joined CCP 1950; worked in chemical, petrochemical and light industries; alt. mem. 12th CCP Cen. Cttee; Dir Jilin Prov. Econ. Comm., Vice-Gov. Jilin 1983–85, Gov. 1985–87; Deputy Sec. CCP Prov. Cttee, Jilin 1985; Minister of Forestry 1987–93; Vice-Chair. All-China Greening Cttee 1988–93; a Deputy Head State Leading Group for Comprehensive Agricultural Devt 1990–; Deputy Head Cen. Forest Fire Prevention 1988–93; alt. mem. 13th CCP Cen. Cttee 1987–92; mem. 14th CCP Cen. Cttee 1992–97; Sec. Tianjin City CCP Cttee 1993–; Chair. Agric. and Rural Affairs Cttee 9th NPC 1998–. *Address:* c/o Standing Committee of the National People's Congress, Beijing, People's Republic of China.

GAO HONGBO (Xiang Chuan); Chinese poet; b. 1951, Kailu, Nei Monggol; ed Peking Univ.; joined the PLA 1969; Vice-Chief News Section, Literature and Art Gazette; Vice-Dir Gen. Office of Chinese Writers Asscn; Assoc. Ed. Chinese Writers; Ed. Journal of Poetry; Sec. Secr. of Chinese Writers Asscn; Nat. Award for Best Children's Literature for I Wonder, Whisper. *Publications:* Elephant Judge, Geese, Geese, Geese, The Crocodile that Eats Stones, The Secret of the Shouting Spring, I Love You, Fox, The Fox that Grows Grapes, The Maid and the Bubble Gum, Flying Dragon and Magic Pigeon, I Wonder, Whisper. *Address:* Chinese Writers Association, Beijing, People's Republic of China (Office).

GAO SHANGQUAN; Chinese government official and professor of economics; b. 1929, Jia Ding County, Shanghai; s. of Gao Ruyu and Xiang Shi; m. Cha Peijun 1958; one s.; ed St John's Univ., Shanghai; worked as researcher, Deputy Div. Chief, Div. Chief, Bureau for Machine-Bldg Industry of Ministry of Industry of local North-Eastern People's Govt; Policy Research Dept, First Ministry of Machine-Bldg Industry; Research Dept, Ministry of Agricultural Machine-Bldg Industry; Office of Agricultural Mechanization, State Council; Policy Research Dept, State Comm. of Machine-Bldg Industry; Research Fellow, Research Centre for Agricultural Devt and Sr Economist, State Comm. of Machine-Bldg Industry; State Comm. for Restructuring Econ. System 1982, then Deputy Dir and Head, Research Inst. of Restructuring the Econ. System; Vice-Minister in charge of State Comm. for Restructuring the Econ. System 1985–93; mem. Nat. Cttee of CPPCC, preliminary working Cttee of preparatory Cttee of the Hong Kong S.A.R. and Head of Econ. Panel 1993–97; mem. Sino-Japanese Econ. Exchange Comm.; Vice-Group-Leader, Leading Group for Restructuring Housing System, under State Council; Pres. China Research Soc. for Restructuring the Econ. Systems, China Soc. of Enterprise Reform and Devt, China Reform & Devt Inst., China Reform Foundation, China Soc. of Urban Housing System Reform, Asscn of Future Market of China; Vice-Pres. Asscn of China's Urban Economy, Asscn of China's Industrial Economy, Asscn for Study of China's Specific Condition, Asscn of Social and Economics Publs; Chair. Research Group for Rural and Urban Housing Reform 1995–; mem. UN Cttee for Devt Policy; Doctorate Supervisor, Prof., Beijing Univ. and Shanghai Jiaotong Univ.; Dean Man. School, Zhejiang Univ.; Prof. Nankai Univ., Chinese People's Univ., Shanghai Univ. of Finance and Econs; MBA programme adviser of Nat. Univ. of Australia; Outstanding Scholar Award Hong Kong Polytechnic. *Publications:* Enterprises Should Enjoy Certain Autonomy 1956, Follow A Road of Our Own In Agricultural Modernization 1982, Nine Years of Reform in China's Economic System 1987, A Road To Success 1987, Selected Works of Gao Shangquan 1989, China: A Decade of Economic Reform 1989, The Reform of China's Economic System 1991, Lead to a Powerful Country 1991, On Planning and Market in China 1992, From Planned Economy to the Socialist

Market Economy 1993, An Introduction to Socialist Market Economy 1994, China: The Second Revolution 1995, China's Economic Reform 1996, Extensive Talk About China's Market Economy 1998, The Second Revolution 1998, Market Economy and China's Reform 1999, Two Decades of Reform in China 1999; also ed. of numerous publications. *Address:* State Commission for Restructuring the Economic System, 22 Xianmen Street, Beijing 100017, People's Republic of China. *Telephone:* (10) 63096649. *Fax:* (10) 66014562. *E-mail:* sqgao@bj.col.com.cn (Office).

GAO XINGJIAN; Chinese writer and dramatist; b. 4 Jan. 1940, Ganzhou, Jiangxi Prov.; translator China Reconstructs (magazine), later for Chinese Writers Asscn.; writer for People's Art Troupe; spent five years in "re-education" during Cultural Revolution; left China 1987 after work banned in 1985, living in Paris 1988–; Chevalier des Arts et des Lettres; Nobel Prize for Literature 2000. *Publications:* Bus Stop (play), The Other Shore (plays), Fugitives (play), Soul Mountain, Return to Painting 2001, One Man's Bible (novel) 2002, Snow in August (opera) 2002. *Address:* c/o Swedish Academy, PO Box 5232, Sturegatan 14, 10245 Stockholm, Sweden.

GAO YAN; Chinese government official and engineer; b. 1942, Yushu Co., Jilin Prov.; joined CCP 1965; Vice-Gov. of Jilin Prov. 1988–92; Gov. 1992–95; Sec. CCP Cttee, Yunan Prov. 1995–97; Dir Political Dept, Chinese People's Armed Police Force; Sec. CCP 6th Yunnan Prov. Cttee; mem. 14th CCP Cen. Cttee 1992–97, 15th CCP Cen. Cttee 1997–; Gen. Man. State Electrical Power Corpn 1998–. *Address:* c/o State Council, Beijing, People's Republic of China.

GAO YING; Chinese author; b. 25 Dec. 1929, Jiaozuo, Henan; s. of Gao Weiya and Sha Peifen; m. Duan Chuanchen 1954; one s. two d.; Vice-Chair. Sichuan Br. and mem. Council, Chinese Writers' Asscn; Deputy Dir Ed. Bd, Sichuan Prov. Broadcasting Station 1983–; mem. Sichuan Political Consultative Conf. *Publications:* The Song of Ding Youjun, Lamplights around the Three Gorges, High Mountains and Distant Rivers, Cloudy Cliff (long novel), Da Ji and her Fathers (novel and film script), The Orchid (novel), Loving-Kindness of the Bamboo Storey (collection of prose), Mother in my Heart (autobiographical novel), Songs of Da Liang Mountains (collection of poems), Frozen Snowflakes (collection of poems), Reminiscences, Xue Ma (novel), Gao Ying short novel collection. *Leisure interests:* painting, music. *Address:* Sichuan Branch of Chinese Association of Literary and Art Workers, Bu-hou-jie Street, Chengdu, Sichuan, People's Republic of China. *Telephone:* 66782836.

GAO YISHENG, PhD; Chinese scientist; ed Oxford Univ.; fmr Dir Shanghai Inst. of Materia Medica; won Nat. Prize of Science 1990. *Address:* Shanghai Institute of Materia Medica, 294 Tai-Yuan Road, Shanghai 20031, People's Republic of China.

GAO YOUXI; Chinese physicist; b. 1920; Dir Plateau Atmospheric Physics Inst. 1981–; mem. Dept of Earth Sciences, Academia Sinica, 1985–; Nat. Science Award 1989. *Address:* Plateau Atmospheric Physics Institute, Lanzhou, People's Republic of China.

GAO ZHANXIANG; Chinese party official; b. 1935, Tongxian Co., Hebei Prov.; joined CCP 1953; mem. Communist Youth League Cen. Cttee 1964, Sec. 1978–82; alt. mem. 12th CCP Cen. Cttee 1982–87; mem. 8th CCP Nat. Cttee 1993–; Sec. CCP Cttee, Hebei Prov. 1983–86; Vice-Minister of Culture 1986–96; Pres. Soc. of Mass Culture 1990–93; Vice-Pres. 1993–, Chinese Asscn for Promotion of Population Culture; Pres. China Children's Culture and Art Promotion Soc. 1993–; Chair. Soc. of Photographic Arts 1994; Sec. Party Group China Fed. of Literary and Art Circles, Vice-Chair. 1996; Dir, Ed.-in-Chief Chinese Arts. *Address:* c/o Ministry of Culture, A83 Beiheyan, Dongamen, Beijing 100722, People's Republic of China.

GAPONOV-GREKHOV, Andrey Viktorovich; Russian physicist; b. 7 June 1926, Moscow; m.; one d.; ed Gorky State Univ.; Instructor, Gorky Polytech. Inst. 1952–55; Sr Scientific Assoc., Head of Dept of Radio Physics, Applied Physics Inst., Gorky (now Nizhni Novgorod) State Univ. 1955–, Dir 1984–; Corresp. mem. USSR (now Russian) Acad. of Sciences 1964–68, mem. 1968–; USSR People's Deputy 1989–91; Hero of Socialist Labour 1986; State Prize 1967, 1983. *Publications:* numerous theoretical and experimental works in field of inducted cyclotronic radiation, which led to development of a new class of electronic instruments – masers with cyclotronic resonance. *Address:* Institute of Applied Physics, Ulyanova str. 46, Nizhni Novgorod GSP-120, Russia. *Telephone:* (8312) 36-66-69 (Office); (8312) 36-36-67 (Home).

GAPRINDASHVILI, Nona; Georgian chess player; b. 3 May 1941, Zugdidi, Georgia; one s.; ed Tbilisi State Univ.; 5 times World Champion 1962–78; 11 times Olympic Champion, Gold Medals bearer; twice won European Cup of Champions, First Chess Oscar Prize for the best achievements of the year 1980; first woman to win men's Int. Grandmaster Title; winner of numerous int. chess tournaments; First Chair. Nat. Olympic Cttee of Georgia 1985–96. *Leisure interests:* snooker, football. *Address:* Georgian Chess Federation, Tbilisi, Georgia.

GARABEDIAN, Paul R., PhD; American professor of mathematics; b. 2 Aug. 1927, Cincinnati, Ohio; s. of Carl A. Garabedian and Margaret R. Garabedian; m. 1st Gladys Rappaport 1949 (divorced 1963); m. 2nd Lynnel Marg 1966; two d.; ed Brown and Harvard Univs; Nat. Research Council Fellow 1948–49; Asst Prof. of Math., Univ. of Calif. 1949–50; Asst Prof. of Math., Stanford Univ. 1950–52, Assoc. Prof. 1952–56, Prof. 1956–59; Scientific Liaison Officer, ONR-London 1957–58; Prof., Courant Inst. of Math. Sciences, New York Univ. 1959–, Dir Courant Math. and Computing Lab. of U.S. Dept of Energy.

1972–73, Dir Div. of Computational Fluid Dynamics 1978–; Sloan Foundation Fellowship 1961–63; Guggenheim Fellowship 1966, 1981–82; Fairchild Distinguished Scholar, Calif. Inst. of Tech. 1975; mem. NAS, American Acad. of Arts & Sciences, American Math. Soc., American Physical Soc., Soc. Industrial and Applied Math., Editorial Bd Applicable Analysis, Complex Variables and Applications; NASA Public Service Group Achievement Award 1976; NASA Certificate of Recognition 1980; Boris Pregal Award, New York Acad. of Sciences 1980; Birkhoff Prize in Applied Math. 1983; von Karman Prize, S.I.A.M. 1989; Applied Mathematics and Numerical Analysis Prize, NAS 1998. *Publications:* numerous books and papers in learned journals. *Leisure interest:* piano. *Address:* Courant Institute of Mathematical Sciences, New York University, 251 Mercer Street, New York, NY 10012; 110 Bleecker Street, New York, NY 10012, USA (Home). *Telephone:* (212) 998-3237 (Office).

GARAIKOETXEA URRIZA, Carlos; Spanish (Basque) politician, lawyer and economist; b. 2 June 1939, Pamplona; s. of Juan Garaikoetxea and Dolores Urriza; m. Sagrario Mina Apat 1966; three s.; mem. Inst. Príncipe de Viana, org. to protect and promote Basque culture, Navarra Dist Council 1971; Dist Councillor, Navarra 1971; Chair. Navarra Chamber of Commerce and Industry 1971; mem. Regional Council of Partido Nacionalista Vasco (Basque Nationalist Party—PNV) 1974, Chair. Nat. Council PNV 1977, re-elected 1978; mem. Navarra Dist Parl. 1979; Pres. Gen. Council of the Basque Country 1979; elected to Basque Parl. as PNV cand. for Guipúzcoa March 1980; Pres. of Basque Govt 1980–86; Hon. Pres. and gold medals from many orgs and asscns. *Leisure interests:* music (especially classical), skiing, Basque pelota, reading (especially political essays and history). *Address:* Palacio de Ajuria-Enea, Vitoria-Gasteiz, Spain. *Telephone:* (945) 23-16-16.

GARANG, Col John, PhD; Sudanese guerrilla leader; b. 1943, Jonglei; ed Cornell Univ., Iowa State Univ.; Sudanese Army 1969–70; trained as Co. Commdr, Fort Benning, USA, later Lt-Col Mil. Research Center, Khartoum; Founder and fmr Leader Sudan People's Liberation Movt, Founder and Leader Sudan People's Liberation Army (SPLA) 1983–.

GARAS, Klára, PhD; Hungarian art historian; b. 19 June 1919, Rákosszentmihály; d. of Pál Garas and Irén Strasser; ed Budapest Univ. of Sciences; joined staff Budapest Museum of Fine Arts 1945, subsequent posts to Gen. Dir 1964–84; Ordinary mem. Hungarian Acad. of Sciences 1972, mem. 1985–; Labour Order of Merit (golden degree) 1974, 1979. *Publications:* Magyarországi festészet a XVII. században (Hungarian Painting in the 17th century) 1953, Magyarországi festészet a XVIII. században (Hungarian Painting in the 18th century) 1955, Franz Anton Maulbertsch 1724–1796, with preface by Oskar Kokoschka 1960, Olasz reneszánsz portrék a Szépmüvészeti Muzeumban (Italian Renaissance Portraits in the Museum of Fine Arts) 1965, 1973, Carlo Innocenzo Carloni (co-author) Milano 1966, Franz Anton Maulbertsch. Leben und Werk 1974, A velencei settecento festészete (Venetian Paintings of the 18th Century) 1977, A 17. század német és osztrák rajzművészete (Deutsche und Österreichische Zeichnungen des 18. Jahrhunderts) 1980; several publs on the Budapest Museum of Fine Arts. *Leisure interests:* 15th- to 18th-century European and Hungarian painting. *Address:* 1126 Budapest, Kiss János altábornagy utca 48/c, Hungary.

GARAUDY, Roger Jean Charles, DèsSc; French author and university professor; b. 17 July 1913, Marseilles; s. of Charles Garaudy and Marie Garaudy; m. 1st Henriette Vialatte 1937 (divorced 1937); m. 2nd Paulette Gayraud; two s. one d.; ed Sorbonne, Paris; prisoner-of-war 1940–43; Deputy to Nat. Ass. 1945–58, Vice-Pres. 1956–58; Senator 1959–62; Dir Inst. Int. pour le Dialogue des Cultures, Geneva 1974–; Prof. of Philosophy, Univ. of Paris (Sorbonne); f. Univ. des Mutants, Dakar, Senegal; f. Fondation Roger Garaudy, Cordoba, Spain; f. of only museum in Spain devoted to Islamic art; Dr hc (Konya, Turkey); Croix de Guerre; Prix Méditerranée; Prix Faycal; Prix Brennam (Barcelona). *Publications:* 53 books translated into 29 languages including: Hegel 1962, Karl Marx 1965, De l'anathème au dialogue 1965, Appel aux vivants 1979, A contre-Nuit (poem) 1987, Mon Tour du siècle en solitaire (memoirs) 1989, Vers une guerre de religion 1995, Les Etats-Unis, avant-garde de la décadence 1996, L'Avenir, Mode d'emploi 1997, The Founding Myths of Israeli Politics 1998, Le Procès du sionisme israélien 1998. *Address:* 69 rue de Sucy, 94430 Chennevières-sur-Marne, France. *Telephone:* (331)45769038. *Fax:* (331)49627794.

GARAYEV, Tamerlan; Azerbaijani politician; b. 1952, Gasimly, Agdam Region; s. of Yelmar Garayev and Khalida Garayeva; m. Farida Garayeva 1976; two s.; ed Azerbaijan Univ.; public prosecutor 1973–78; lecturer, Azerbaijan Univ. 1978–91; became involved in opposition politics late 1980s; leader moderate wing Popular Front, elected Deputy to Supreme Soviet 1990, Deputy Chair., First Deputy Chair. 1991–93; Amb. to China 1993–2000; mem. Org. for the Liberation of Karabakh. *Leisure interest:* golf. *E-mail:* safirprc@public.fhnet.cn.net.

GARBERS, Christoph Friedrich, DPhil; South African scientist; b. 21 Aug. 1929, Piet Retief, Transvaal; s. of Andris Wilhelm Friedrich and Lucy Sophia Carolina (née Wolhuter) Garbers; m. Barbara Z. G. Viljoen 1957; three s. one d.; ed Pretoria Univ., Zürich Univ.; Research Officer Klipfontein Organic Products 1951; Research Officer Council for Scientific and Industrial Research (CSIR) 1954–58; Sr Lecturer, Stellenbosch Univ. 1958–65, Prof. Organic Chem. 1966–78; Vice-Pres. CSIR 1979, Deputy Pres. 1980, Pres. 1980–90; Chair. S African Acad. for Science and Arts 1983–85; Chair. S African Inventions Devt Corpn 1980–90; Dir Tech. Finance Corpn (Pty) Ltd 1988–90; Chair. Certification Bd for Technikons 1989–95; Chancellor Univ. of SA 1990–; Chair. Foundation for Research Devt 1990–91; mem. Scientific Advisory Council 1980–87 (Chair. 1991–94), Water Research Comm. 1980–89, Advisory Council for Tech. 1987–89; Council mem. Univ. of SA 1980–90; Trustee Hans Merensky Foundation 1980–97 (Vice-Pres. 1992–97), Trust for Health Systems Planning and Devt 1992–95; Dir (non-exec.) Allied Technologies Ltd 1991–96, Power Technologies Ltd 1992–96; mem. Nat. Comm. for Higher Educ. 1995–96, IUPAC/UNESCO Int. Council for Chemistry; Rep. at ICSU 1980–90; Hon. DSc (UNISA) 1989, (Cape Town) 1990, (Stellenbosch) 1991, (Pretoria) 1994; Havenga Prize for Chem. 1977, Gold Medal, SA Chem. Inst. 1980, State Pres. Order for Meritorious Service (Gold) 1989, M.T. Steyn Gold Medal 1990, SA Medal (Gold) 1990, H. J. van Eck Medal 1991. *Address:* POB 36716, Menlo Park 0102; 5 Domein, 443 Sussex Street, Lynnwood, Pretoria; Chancellors Office, University of South Africa, POB 392, Unisa 003, South Africa (Office). *Telephone:* 429-3111 (Office). *Fax:* 475114; 429-3221 (Office). *E-mail:* artes@alpha.unisa.ac.za (Office). *Website:* www.unisa.ac.uk (Office).

GARCÍA, Amalia; Mexican politician; b. Zacatecas; d. of Francisco García and Conceptión Medina; one d.; ed Universidad Autónoma de Puebla; Fed. Deputy 1988–91; mem. Rep. Ass. for Fed. Dist 1991–94; Senator 1997–2002; Nat. Pres. Partido de la Revolución Democrática; mem. Consultative Council of Women, Human Rights Comm. *Leisure interests:* reading, films. *Address:* Office of the President, Partido de la Revolución Democrática, Monterrey 50, Col Roma, C.P. 06700, México, DF, Mexico (Office). *Telephone:* 207-1212 (Office). *Website:* www.cen-prd.org.mx (Office).

GARCIA, Andy; Cuban film actor, producer and director; b. Andres Arturo Garcia Menendez, 12 April 1956, Havana; s. of Rene Garcia and Amelie Garcia; m. Marivi Lorido Garcia; one s., three d.; ed Florida Int. Univ.; moved to USA 1961; several years acting with regional theatres Fla; Hon. DFA (St John's Univ. NY) 2000; numerous awards including Harvard Univ. Foundation Award 1994, Lifetime Achievement Award, American Cancer Soc. 1996, Spirit of Hope Award 2001, Desert Palm Award, Palm Springs Film Festival 2002, Imagen Foundation Creative Achievement Award 2002. *Films (as actor) include:* The Mean Season 1985, 8 Million Ways to Die 1986, The Untouchables 1987, Stand and Deliver 1987, American Roulette 1988, Black Rain 1989, Internal Affairs 1990, The Godfather III 1990, Dead Again 1991, When A Man Loves A Woman 1994, Steal Big Steal Little (also producer) 1995, Things to Do in Denver When You're Dead 1995, Night Falls on Manhattan 1997, The Disappearance of García Lorca 1997, Hoodlum 1997, Desperate Measures 1998, Just the Ticket (also producer) 1999, The Unsaid (also producer) 2000, The Man from Elysian Fields (also producer) 2000, Oceans Eleven 2001, Confidence 2003, Blackout 2003; Dir: Cachao, Like His Rhythm There Is No Other 1993. *Albums produced include:* Cachao Master Sessions, Vol. I 1993 (Grammy Award 1994), Vol. II 1994 (Down Beat Critics Poll Winner 1996), Just the Ticket (soundtrack) 1999, Cachao-Cuba Linda 2000, For Love Or Country: The Arturo Sandoval Story (soundtrack) 2000, Score (Emmy Award) 2001. *Television appearances include:* Hill Street Blues, Brothers, Foley Square, Clinton and Nadine, Swing Vote (also producer) 1999, For Love Or Country: The Arturo Sandoval Story (also producer) 2000. *Leisure interests:* golf, fishing. *Address:* Paradigm, attn. Clifford Stevens, 200 West 57th Street, New York, NY 10019, USA. *Telephone:* (212) 246-1030 (Office). *Fax:* (212) 246-1521 (Office). *E-mail:* cineson@cineson.com (Office). *Website:* www.cineson.com (Office).

GARCÍA MÁRQUEZ, Gabriel (Gabo); Colombian writer; b. 1928, Aracataca; s. of Gabriel Eligio García and Luisa Santiaga Márquez ; m. Mercedes García Márquez; two s.; ed secondary school and Univ. of Bogotá, Univ. of Cartagena; began writing books 1946; lived in Baranquilla; Corresp. Espectador in Rome, Paris; first novel published while living in Caracas, Venezuela 1957; est. bureau of Prensa Latina (Cuban press agency) in Bogotá; worked for Prensa Latina in Havana, Cuba, then as Deputy Head of New York Office 1961; lived in Spain, contributing to magazines Mundo Nuevo, Casa de las Américas; went to Mexico; invited back to Colombia by Pres. July 1982; Rómulo Gallegos Prize 1972, Nobel Prize for Literature 1982, Prince of Asturias Prize 1999. *Publications:* La hojarasca (Leaf Storm) 1955, El colonel no tiene quien le escriba (No One Writes to the Colonel) 1961, La mala hora (In Evil Hour) 1962, Los funerales de la Mamá Grande (Big Mama's Funeral) 1962, Cien años de soledad (One Hundred Years of Solitude) 1967, La increíble y triste historia de la cándida Eréndira (Innocent Erendira and Other Stories) 1972, El otoño del patriarca (The Autumn of the Patriarch) 1975, Crónica de una muerte anunciada (Chronicle of a Death Foretold) 1981, El Olor de la Guayaba (Fragrance of Guava) 1982, El amor en los tiempos del cólera (Love in the Time of Cholera) 1984, Relato de un náufrago (The Story of a Shipwrecked Sailor) 1986, Miguel Littín's Adventure: Undercover in Chile 1986, The General in His Labyrinth (translated from Spanish edn of 1989) 1991, Amores Difíciles 1989, I Rent Myself Out to Dream 1989, Collected Stories 1991, Strange Pilgrims: Twelve Stories 1993, Of Love and Other Demons 1995, News of a Kidnapping 1997, La bendita manía de contar 1998, Vivir para contarla (memoirs) 2002. *Address:* c/o Agencia Literaria Carmen Balcelos, Diagonal 580, Barcelona, Spain.

GARCÍA PELÁEZ, Raúl, LLD; Cuban politician, diplomatist and lawyer; b. 15 Jan. 1922; ed Univ. of Havana; fmr mem. July 26th Revolutionary Cttee; later Prosecutor at Camagüey Court of Appeal, then Chair. Camagüey Municipal Council for Co-ordination and Inspection; then Gen. Treas. Revolutionary Forces in Camagüey Prov., Rep. of Nat. Inst. of Agrarian Reform in Nuevitas and Gen. Sec. Matanzas Prov. Cttee of United Party of Cuban

Socialist Revolution; mem. Cen. Cttee of Cuban CP 1965–80, Head of Revolutionary Orientation Comm. of Cent. Cttee of Cuban CP until 1967; Amb. to USSR 1967–74. *Address:* c/o Partido Comunista, Plaza de la Revolución, Havana, Cuba.

GARCÍA PÉREZ, Alan; Peruvian politician; b. 23 May 1949, Lima; s. of Carlos García Ronceros and Nyta Pérez de García; m. Pilar Nores; four d.; ed José María Eguren Nat. Coll., Universidad Católica, Lima, Universidad Nacional Mayor de San Marcos (graduated as lawyer), Universidad Complutense, Madrid, Spain, Sorbonne and Inst. of Higher Latin American Studies, Paris, France; mem. of Partido Aprista Peruano since his teens; returned to Peru and elected mem. of Constituent Ass. 1978; subsequently apptd Org. Sec. and Chair. Ideology of Aprista Party (now Alianza Popular Revolucionaria Americana), Parl. Deputy 1980–85, Sec.-Gen. of Party 1982, later Pres.; Senator for Life 1990–; nominated Presidential Candidate 1984; obtained largest number of votes, Nat. Presidential Elections April 1985; on withdrawal of Izquierda Unida candidate, Alfonso Barrantes Lingán, proclaimed Pres.-elect June 1985, assuming powers 1985–89; granted political asylum in Colombia June 1992; returned from exile Jan. 2001. *Address:* Alianza Popular Revolucionaria Americana, Avda Alfonso Ugarte 1012, Lima 5, Peru.

GARCÍA RAMÍREZ, Sergio, PhD; Mexican politician and lawyer; b. 1938, Guadalajara; ed Nat. Univ. of Mexico; Research Fellow and teacher of penal law, Inst. of Juridical Research, Nat. Univ. of Mexico 1966–76; Dir Correction Centre, State of Mexico and Judge, Juvenile Courts; Asst Dir of Govt Ministry of Interior; Attorney-Gen. of Fed. Dist; Under-Sec. Ministries of Nat. Resources, Interior, Educ., Industrial Devt; Dir Prevention Centre of Mexico City; fmr Minister of Labour; Attorney-Gen. 1982–88; mem. Mexican Acad. of Penal Sciences, Mexican Inst. of Penal Law, Nat. Inst. of Public Admin., Ibero-American Inst. of Penal Law etc. *Publications:* Teseo Alucinado 1966, Asistencia a Reos Liberados 1966, El Artículo 18 Constitucional 1967, La Imputabilidad en el Derecho Penal Mexicano, El Código Tutelar para Menores del Estado Michoacán 1969, La Ciudadanía de la Juventud 1970, La Prisión 1975, Los Derechos Humanos y el Derecho Penal 1976, Legislación Penitenciaria y Correccional Comentada 1978, Otros Minotauros 1979, Cuestiones Criminológicas y Penales Contemporáneas 1981, Justicia Penal 1982. *Address:* c/o Oficina del Procurador General, México, DF, Mexico.

GARCÍA SAYAN LARABURRE, Diego, LLB; Peruvian politician and lawyer; b. 1950; ed Univ. of Lima, Univ. of Texas, USA; constitutional lawyer; Head Andean Comm. of Jurists; Rep. of Peru Inter-American Comm. on Human Rights; fmr Minister of Justice; Minister of Foreign Affairs 2001–02; Chair. UN Working Group on Enforced or Involuntary Disappearances 2002. *Address:* c/o Ministry of Foreign Affairs, Palacio de Torre Tagle, Jirón Ucayali 363, Lima 1, Peru (Office).

GARCÍA-VALDECASAS Y FERNÁNDEZ, Rafael, DJur; Spanish judge; b. 9 Jan. 1946, Granada; m. Rosario Castaño Parraga 1975; ed Univ. of Granada; lawyer, Office of Attorney-Gen. 1976; mem. Office of Attorney-Gen. Tax and Judicial Affairs Office, Jaén 1976–85; mem. Office of Attorney-Gen. Econ. and Admin. Court of Jaén 1979–85; mem. Jaén Bar 1979–89, Granada Bar 1981–89; mem. Office of Attorney-Gen. Econ. and Admin. Court of Córdoba 1983–85, Tax and Judicial Affairs Office of Granada 1986–87; Head, Spanish State Legal Service for cases before EC Court of Justice (Ministry of Foreign Affairs) 1987–89; Judge, Court of First Instance of European Communities 1989–; Encomienda de la Orden Civil del Mérito Agrícola 1982, Encomienda de la Orden de Isabel la Católica 1990, Gran Cruz de la Orden del Mérito Civil 1999. *Publications:* Comentarios al Tratado de Adhesión de España a la C.E.: La Agricultura 1985, El 'acquis' comunitario 1986, El medio ambiente: conservación de espacios protegidos en la legislación de la CE 1992, La Jurisprudencia del Tribunal de Justicia CE sobre la libertad de establecimiento y libre prestación de servicios por los abogados 1993, El Tribunal de Primera Instancia de las Comunidades Europeas 1993, El respeto al derecho de defensa en materia de competencia 1997, El desarollo normativo de los reglamentos comunitarios 1999; also papers in books and learned journals. *Leisure interests:* swimming, cycling, fishing. *Address:* European Court of First Instance of the European Communities, Erasmus 2036, Rue du Fort Niedergrünewald, 2925 Luxembourg (Office); 11 boulevard Gustave Jacquemart, 1833 Luxembourg, Luxembourg (Home).

GARDAM, Jane Mary, BA, FRSL; British novelist; b. 11 July 1928, Coatham; d. of William Pearson and Kathleen Pearson (née Helm); m. David Hill Gardam 1954; two s. one d.; ed Saltburn High School for Girls, Bedford Coll. for Women, London Univ.; Co-ordinator UK Hosp. Libraries British Red Cross 1951–53; Literary Ed. Time and Tide 1952–54; Hon.DLitt; Prix Baudelaire (for God on the Rocks), Whitbread Literary Award (for The Hollow Land), Whitbread Novel Award (for The Queen of the Tambourine), David Higham Award, Winifred Holtby Award (for Black Faces, White Faces), Katherine Mansfield Award (for The Pangs of Love) 1984. *Publications:* novels: A Long Way From Verona 1971, The Summer After the Funeral 1973, Bilgewater 1977, God on the Rocks 1978, The Hollow Land 1981, Bridget and William 1981, Horse 1982, Kit 1983, Crusoe's Daughter 1985, Kit in Boots 1986, Swan 1987, Through the Doll's House Door 1987, The Queen of the Tambourine 1991, Faith Fox 1996, Tufty Bear 1996, The Green Man 1998, The Flight of the Maidens 2001; short stories: A Few Fair Days 1971, Black Faces, White Faces 1975, The Sidmouth Letters 1980, The Pangs of Love 1983, Going into a Dark House 1994, Missing the Midnight 1997; radio play: The Tribute; non-

fiction: The Iron Coast 1994. *Leisure interests:* agriculture. *Address:* Haven House, Sandwich, Kent CT13 9ES; Throstlenest Farm, Crackpot, N Yorks; 34 Denmark Road, London, SW19, England. *Telephone:* (14304) 612680.

GARDEL, Louis; French publishing editor, novelist and screenplay-writer; b. 8 Sept. 1939, Algiers, Algeria; s. of Jacques Gardel and Janine Blasselle; m. 1st Béatrice Herr (deceased) 1963; m. 2nd Hélène Millerand 1990; two s. two d.; ed Lycée Bugeaud, Algiers, Lycée Louis-le-Grand, Paris and Institut d'Etudes Politiques, Paris; Head of Dept Inst. des Hautes Etudes d'Outre-Mer 1962–64; Man. Soc. Rhône-Progil 1964–74; Head of Dept Conseil Nat. du Patronat 1974–80; Literary Consultant Editions du Seuil 1980, Literary Ed. 1980–; mem. juries Prix Renaudot, Conseil Supérieur de la Langue Française. *Film screenplays:* Fort Saganne, Nocturne Indien, Indochine, La Marche de Radetzky 1996, Est.Ouest, Himalaya 1999. *Publications:* L'Eté Fracassé 1973, Couteau de chaleur 1976, Fort Saganne 1980 (Grand Prix du Roman de l'Académie Française), Notre Homme 1986, Le Beau Rôle 1989, Darbaroud 1993. L'Aurore des Bien-Aimés 1997, Grand-Seigneur 1999. *Leisure interest:* horses. *Address:* Editions du Seuil, 27 rue Jacob, 75004 Paris (Office); 25 rue de la Cerisaie, 75004, Paris, France (Home). *Telephone:* 1-40-46-50-50.

GARDEN, Sir Timothy, KCB, MA, M.PHIL., FRAeS, FRUSI, FCGI; British academic, writer and broadcaster; b. 23 April 1944, Worcester; s. of Joseph Garden and Winifred Mayes; m. Susan Button 1965; two d.; ed King's School, Worcester, St Catherine's Coll. Oxford, Magdalen Coll. Cambridge and Army Staff Coll. Camberley; RAF pilot and flying instr. 1965–75; Staff Officer to Air Mem. for Personnel, Ministry of Defence 1977–79; Squadron Commdr No. 50 Squadron (Vulcan bombers) 1979–81; Dir of Defence Studies for RAF 1982–85; Station Commdr RAF Odiham (Support Helicopters) 1985–87; Dir of Air Force Staff Duties, Ministry of Defence 1988–90; Asst Chief of Air Staff 1991–92; Asst Chief of Defence Staff (programmes) 1992–94; Commdt Royal Coll. of Defence Studies (Air Marshal) 1994–95; retd from RAF 1996; Dir Royal Inst. of Int. Affairs, Chatham House 1997–98; mem. advisory Bd NATO Defense Coll., Rome 1996–2001, Int. Studies Centre, Cambridge Univ. 1996–, Centre for Strategic Studies, Univ. of Hull 1996–, Rippon Group 1999–, Visiting Professor Kings Coll. London 2000–; Ed.The Source 1998–2002; Council for Arms Control 1999–2001; Dir UK-Japan 2000 Group 1997–99; Commr Commission on Globalisation 2002; Trustee World Humanity Action Trust 1996–2000; Pres. Combined Cadet Force 2000–; Fellow, Royal United Services Inst. 1996, City and Guilds Inst.; Hon. Fellow, St Catherine's Coll. Oxford 1994, Distinguished Citizen Fellow, Indiana Univ. 2001. *Publications:* Can Deterrence Last? 1984, The Technology Trap 1989. *Leisure interests:* computing, writing, dining-out, bridge. *Address:* Centre for Defence Studies, Kings College, London, WC2R 2LS England (Office). *Telephone:* (20) 7848-2338 (Office). *Fax:* (20) 7209-0859 (Home); (20) 7209-0859 (Office). *E-mail:* timothy.garden@kcl.ac.uk (Office); tg@tgarden.demon.co.uk (Home).

GÄRDENFORS, Peter, PhD; Swedish professor of cognitive science; b. 21 Sept. 1949, Degeberga; s. of Torsten Gärdenfors and Ingemor Gärdenfors (née Jonsson); m. Annette Wald 1975; three s. one d.; ed Lund Univ., Princeton Univ., USA; Lecturer in Philosophy, Lund Univ. 1974–80, Reader in Philosophy of Science 1975–77, Reader in Philosophy 1980–88, Prof. of Cognitive Science, 1988–; Visiting Fellow, Princeton Univ., USA 1973–74, ANU 1986–87; Visiting Scholar, Stanford Univ., USA 1983–84; Visiting Prof., Univ. of Buenos Aires 1990; Ed. Theoria 1978–86, Journal of Logic, Language and Information 1991–96; mem. Royal Swedish Acad. of Letters, Academia Europaea; Rausing Prize 1986. *Publications:* Generalized Quantifiers (ed.) 1986, Knowledge in Flux 1988, Decision, Probability and Utility (with N.-E. Sahlin) 1988, Belief Revision (ed.) 1992, Blotta Tanken 1992, Fangslande Information 1996, Cognitive Semantics (with J. Allwood) 1998, Conceptual Spaces 2000. *Leisure interests:* botany, walking, judo, climbing. *Address:* Department of Philosophy, Kungshuset, Lundagard, 222 22 Lund, Sweden (Office). *Telephone:* (46) 2224817 (Office). *Fax:* (46) 2224424 (Office). *E-mail:* peter.gardenfors@lucs.lu.se (Office). *Website:* www.lucs.lu.se/people/Peter .Gardenfors.

GARDENT, Paul; French mining executive; b. 10 July 1921, Grenoble; s. of Louis Gardent and Edith Gardent (née Rocher); m. Janine Robert 1958; one s.; ed Ecole Polytechnique, Ecole Nat. des Mines; Mining Engineer, Valenciennes 1944–48; Asst Chief Mining Engineer, Lille 1948–49, Chief Mining Engineer 1950; Tech. Adviser to J. M. Louvel (Minister of Industry and Commerce) 1950–52; Dir of Gen. Studies, Charbonnages de France 1952–58; Dir of Gen. Studies and Financial Services, Houillères du bassin de Lorraine 1958–63; Asst Dir, then Dir-Gen. Houillères du bassin du Nord et du Pas-de-Calais 1963–68; Dir-Gen. Charbonnages de France 1968–80; Conseiller d'Etat 1980–86; Pres. Coll. de la Prévention des Risques Technologiques 1989–91; Pres. Comm. Interministérielle des Radioéléments artificiels 1981–2002, Comm. d'Aide aux Riverains des Aéroports 1985–97; Hon. Conseiller d'Etat; Commdr Légion d'honneur, Commdr Ordre national du Mérite. *Publications:* Le Charbon, Panorama Economique. *Address:* 5 rue de la Chaise, Paris 75007, France (Home). *Telephone:* 1-45-44-03-43. *Fax:* 1-45-48-64-21.

GARDINER, Sir John Eliot, Kt, CBE, MA, FRSA; British conductor; b. 20 April 1943; s. of late Rolf Gardiner and of Marabel Gardiner (née Hodgkin); m. 1st Elizabeth S. Wilcock 1981 (divorced 1997); three d.; m. 2nd Isabella de Sabata 2001; ed Bryanston School, King's Coll., Cambridge, King's Coll., London and in Paris and Fontainebleau with Nadia Boulanger; f. Monteverdi Choir, 1964, Monteverdi Orchestra 1968, English Baroque Soloists 1978,

Orchestre Révolutionnaire et Romantique 1990; concert début Wigmore Hall, London 1966; operatic début Sadler's Wells, London 1969; Prin. Conductor CBC Vancouver Orchestra 1980–83; Musical Dir Lyon Opera 1982–88, Chef fondateur 1988–; Artistic Dir Göttingen Handel Festival 1981–90, Veneto Music Festival 1986; Prin. Conductor NDR Symphony Orchestra 1991–94; residency at the Châtelet, Paris Oct. 1999–; regular guest conductor with maj. orchestras in Europe; over 200 recordings; Hon. Fellow King's Coll., London 1992, Royal Acad. of Music 1992; Dr. hc (Univ. Lumière de Lyon) 1987; Commdr Ordre des Arts et des Lettres 1997 (Officier 1988); 15 Gramophone awards including Record of the Year 1991, Artist of the Year 1994; many other awards including 7 Edison awards, 2 Arturo Toscanini Music Critics awards, 3 Deutscher Schallplattenpreis. *Publications:* Claude le Jeune Hélas, Mon Dieu (ed.) 1971, contrib. Gluck's Orfeo 1980. *Leisure interests:* forestry, organic farming. *Address:* IMG Artists Europe, Lovell House, 616 Chiswick High Road, London, WA 5RY; Gore Farm, Ashmore, Salisbury, Wilts., SP5 5AR, England (Home). *Telephone:* (20) 8233-5800 (Agent). *Fax:* (20) 8233-5801 (Agent).

GARDNER, David Pierpont, BSc, MA, PhD; American university president, professor of education and foundation executive; b. 24 March 1933, Berkeley, Calif.; s. of Reed S. Gardner and Margaret Pierpont Gardner; m. 1st Elizabeth Fuhriman 1958 (died 1991); four d.; m. 2nd Sheila Sprague Gardner 1995; ed Brigham Young Univ. and Univ. of California Berkeley; Admin. Asst, Personnel Man. and Prin. Asst to Chief Admin. Officer, Calif. Farm Bureau Fed. Berkeley 1958–60; Field and Scholarship Dir Calif. Alumni Asscn, Univ. of Calif. Berkeley 1960–62, Dir Calif. Alumni Foundation 1962–64; Asst to Chancellor and Asst Prof. of Higher Educ., Univ. of Calif. Santa Barbara 1964–67, Asst Chancellor and Asst Prof. of Higher Educ. 1967–69, Vice-Chancellor, Exec. Asst and Assoc. Prof. of Higher Educ. 1969–70; Vice-Pres. Univ. of Calif. and Prof. of Higher Educ. (on leave from Univ. of Calif. Santa Barbara) 1971–73; Pres. Univ. of Utah and Prof. of Higher Educ. 1973–83, Pres. Emer. 1985; Pres. Univ. of Calif. 1983–92 (Pres. Emer. 1992), Prof. of Higher Educ., Univ. of Calif. Berkeley 1983–92, Chair. Nat. Comm. on Excellence in Educ. 1981–83; Chair. J. Paul Getty Trust, LA 2000; Pres. William and Flora Hewlett Foundation, Menlo Park Calif. 1993–99; Visiting Fellow, Clare Hall, Cambridge Univ. 1979, Assoc. 1979–; numerous professional appts., directorships, trusteeships etc.; Fellow, American Acad. of Arts and Sciences, Nat. Acad. of Public Admin.; mem. Nat. Acad. of Educ., American Philosophical Soc.; Fulbright Fellow, Japan 1987; 12 hon. degrees; numerous awards and distinctions including Chevalier Légion d'honneur 1985, James Bryant Conant Award, Educ. Comm. of USA 1991, Kt Commdr's Cross Order of Merit (Germany) 1992. *Publications:* The California Oath Controversy 1967; numerous articles in professional journals. *Leisure interests:* fly fishing, travel. *Address:* Center for Studies in Higher Education, University of California, Berkeley, CA 94720 (Office); 2441 Iron Canyon Drive, Park City, UT 84060, USA (Home). *Telephone:* (510) 642-5040 (Office); (435) 647-3889 (Home). *Fax:* (510) 643-6845 (Office); (435) 647-3890 (Home). *E-mail:* gardner1@qwest.net (Home).

GARDNER, Richard Lavenham, PhD, FRS; British scientist; b. 10 June 1943, Dorking; s. of the late Allan Constant and Eileen May Gardner; m. Wendy Joy Cresswell 1968; one s.; ed St John's School, Leatherhead, NE Surrey Coll. of Tech., St Catharine's Coll. Cambridge; Research Asst Physiological Lab., Cambridge 1970–73; lecturer in Devt and Reproductive Biology Dept of Zoology, Oxford 1973–77, Research Student Christ Church 1974–77, Ordinary Students 1978–, Royal Soc. Henry Dale Research Prof. 1978–; Hon. Dir Imperial Cancer Research Fund Developmental Biology Unit 1986–96; independent mem. Advisory Bd for the Research Councils 1990–93; Scientific Medal, Zoological Soc. 1977, March of Dimes Prize in Developmental Biology 1999, Royal Medal, Royal Soc. 2001. *Publications:* various scientific papers. *Leisure interests:* ornithology, music, sailing, gardening, painting. *Address:* Christ Church, Oxford, OX1 1DP, England. *Telephone:* (1865) 281319 (Office). *Fax:* (1865) 281310 (Office). *E-mail:* richard.gardner@zoo.ox.ac.uk.

GARDNER, Richard Newton, DPhil; American diplomatist and lawyer; b. 9 July 1927, New York; s. of Samuel I. Gardner and Ethel E. Gardner; m. Danielle Almeida Luzzatto 1956; one s. one d.; ed Harvard Univ., Yale Law School, Oxford Univ.; Rhodes Scholar to Oxford Univ. 1951–54; Prof. of Law and Int. Org., Columbia Univ. 1957–61, 1965–76, 1981–; Deputy Asst Sec. of State for Int. Org. Affairs, US State Dept 1961–65; US Amb. to Italy 1977–81; Lawyer, Coudert Bros 1981–93; Consultant to Sec.-Gen., UN Conf. on Environment and Devt 1992; Amb. to Spain 1993–97; counsel Morgan, Lewis and Bockius 1997–; mem. US Advisory Cttee on Law of the Sea 1971–76, Pres.'s Advisory Cttee for Foreign Trade Policy and Negotiations 1998–; Del. to UN Gen. Ass. 2000; Arthur S. Flemming Award 1963, Thomas Jefferson Award 1998. *Publications:* Sterling-Dollar Diplomacy 1956, In Pursuit of World Order 1964, Blueprint for Peace 1966, The Global Partnership: International Agencies and Economic Development 1968, Negotiating Survival: Four Priorities after Rio 1992. *Leisure interests:* tennis, classical music, reading. *Address:* Columbia University School of Law, 435 West 116th Street, New York, NY 10027, USA.

GARDNER, Roy Alan, FCCA; British business executive; b. 20 Aug. 1945, Chiswick, London; s. of Thomas Gardner and Iris Gardner; m. Carol Gardner 1969; one s. two d.; ed Strodes School, Egham; Finance Dir, The Marconi Co. Ltd 1984–85; Finance Dir STC PLC, Man. Dir STC Communications Ltd 1986–91, mem. Bd Dirs STC PLC 1986–91; COO Northern Telecom Europe Ltd 1991–92; Man. Dir GEC-Marconi Ltd 1992–94; Dir GEC PLC 1994;

Finance Dir British Gas PLC 1994–95, Exec. Dir 1995–96; Chief Exec. Centrica PLC 1997–; Dir (non-exec.) Manchester United PLC, Chair. (non-exec.) 2002. *Leisure interests:* golf, running family. *Address:* Centrica PLC, Millstream, Maidenhead Road, Windsor, Berks., SL4 5GD, England. *Telephone:* (1753) 494000. *Fax:* (1753) 494001.

GARDNER, W. Booth, MBA; American state governor; b. 21 Aug. 1936, Tacoma; m. Jean Gardner; one s. one d.; ed Univ. of Washington and Harvard Univ.; Asst to Dean, School of Business Admin. Harvard Univ. 1966; Dir School of Business & Econs Univ. of Puget Sound, Tacoma 1967–72; Pres. Laird Norton Co. 1972–80; mem. Washington Senate 1970–73; County Exec. Pierce Co., Tacoma 1981–84; Gov. State of Washington 1985–93; Democrat. *Address:* c/o Legislative Building, AS-13, Olympia, WA 98504, USA.

GARDOCKI, Lech; Polish judge and professor of law; b. 13 April 1944, Rydzewo; s. of Józef Gardocki and Filomena Gardocki; one s. two d.; ed Univ. of Warsaw; Prof. of Law, Univ. of Warsaw 1991–; Judge of the Supreme Court 1996–, First Pres. 1998–. *Publications:* An Outline of International Criminal Law 1986, Problems of Theory of Criminalization 1990, Criminal Law 1994. *Leisure interest:* film. *Address:* Office of the First President, Supreme Court, pl. Krasińskich 2/4/6, 00-951 Warsaw 41, Poland (Office). *Telephone:* (22) 530-82-03 (Office). *Fax:* (22) 530-91-00 (Office). *E-mail:* pp@sn.pl (Office). *Website:* www.sn.pl (Office).

GAREYEV, Gen. Makhmud Akhmedovich; Russian army officer and historian; b. 23 July 1923; m.; two c.; ed Tashkent Infantry School, M. Frunze Mil. Acad., Gen. Staff Acad.; involved in mil. operations on Western Front, officer Operative Div., Gen. Staff of Far E Army at end of Second World War; Commdr of Regt, Tank Div. Belarus Mil. Command, Head of Gen. Staff Urals Mil. Command, then officer Gen. Staff; Head Mil. Scientific Dept, then Deputy Head Chief Operative Dept, Deputy Head Gen. Staff 1974–; Chief Mil. Counsellor, Afghanistan, then Commdr 1989–; mem. Russian Acad. of Mil. Sciences, Council on Interaction with Orgs. of War Veterans; Order of Lenin and numerous other decorations and medals. *Publications:* Frunze – Military Theoretician, General Army Exercises, Marshal G. Zhukov and over 60 scientific works. *Leisure interest:* athletics. *Address:* Academy of Military Sciences, Myasnitskaya str. 37, 103175 Moscow, Russia (Office). *Telephone:* (095) 293-33-55 (Office).

GARFUNKEL, Art, MA; American singer and actor; b. 13 Oct. 1941, Forest Hills, New York; m. Kim Cermak 1988; one s.; ed Columbia Univ.; fmrly mem. singing duo Simon (Paul Simon and Garfunkel 1964–71, now solo performer; mem. Rock and Roll Hall of Fame 1990; recipient two Grammy Awards for song Mrs Robinson 1969, six Grammy Awards for album Bridge Over Troubled Water 1970, Grammy Award for film soundtrack of The Graduate. *Singles include:* (with Simon) The Sounds of Silence, Dangling Conversation, Homeward Bound, I Am a Rock, At the Zoo, 7 O'Clock News, Silent Night, 59th Street Bridge Song, Scarborough Fair, Parsley, Sage, Rosemary and Thyme, Mrs Robinson, The Boxer, Bridge Over Troubled Water. *Albums include:* (with Simon) Wednesday Morning 3 a.m. 1964, Sounds of Silence 1966, Parsley, Sage, Rosemary and Thyme 1966, The Graduate 1968, Bookends 1968, Bridge Over Troubled Water 1970. *Solo albums include:* Angel Clare 1973, Breakaway 1975, Watermark 1978, Fate for Breakfast (Doubt for Dessert) 1979, Art Garfunkel 1979, Scissors Cut 1981, Simon & Garfunkel: The Concert in Central Park 1982, The Animals' Christmas 1986, Garfunkel 1989, Up Till Now 1993. *Films include:* Catch-22 1970, Carnal Knowledge 1971, Bad Timing . . . A Sensual Obsession 1980, Good to Go 1986, Lefty 1988, Boxing Helena. *Address:* c/o Mary Ellen Kirby, 12182 Daugherty Drive, Zionsville, IN 46077, USA (Office).

GARLAND, George David, PhD, FRSC; Canadian geophysicist; b. 29 June 1926, Toronto, Ont.; s. of N. L. Garland and Jean McPherson; m. Elizabeth MacMillan 1949; two s. one d.; ed Univ. of Toronto and St Louis Univ.; Geophysicist, Dominion Observatory, Ottawa 1950–54; Prof. of Geophysics, Univ. of Alberta, Edmonton 1954–63; Prof. of Geophysics, Univ. of Toronto 1963; Deputy Gen. Sec. Int. Union of Geodesy and Geophysics 1960–63, Gen. Sec. 1963–73, Pres. 1979–; Vice-Pres. Acad. of Science, Royal Soc. of Canada 1980–. *Publications:* The Earth's Shape and Gravity 1965 and papers in scientific journals dealing with gravity, terrestrial magnetism, structure of the earth's crust, electrical conductivity of the crust, heat flow from the earth. *Leisure interests:* canoeing, history of Canadian exploration, early maps. *Address:* 5 Mawhiney Court, Huntsville, Ont., P0A 1K0, Canada.

GARLAND, Patrick, MA; British theatre and television director and writer; b. 10 April 1935, London; s. of the late Ewart Garland and Rosalind Fell; m. Alexandra Bastedo 1980; ed St Mary's Coll., Southampton, St Edmund Hall, Oxford; actor, Bristol Old Vic 1959, Age of Kings, BBC TV 1961; lived Paris 1961–62; wrote two plays for ITV 1962; Research Asst, Monitor, BBC TV 1963; Dir and Producer, BBC Arts Dept 1962–74; Hon. Fellow St Edmund Hall, Oxford 1997; Hon. DLitt (Southampton) 1994. *Plays directed:* Forty Years On 1968, 1984, Brief Lives 1968, Getting On 1970, Cyrano 1971, Hair (Israel) 1972, The Doll's House (New York and London) 1975, Under the Greenwood Tree 1978, Look After Lulu 1978, Beecham 1980, York Mystery Plays 1980, My Fair Lady (USA) 1980, Kipling (London and New York) 1984, Canaries Sometimes Sing 1987, The Secret of Sherlock Holmes 1988, Victory 1989, A Room of One's Own 1989, 2001, Song in the Night 1989, The Dressmaker 1990, Tovarich 1991, Pickwick! 1993–96, The Tempest 1996, The Importance of Being Oscar 1997, Talking Heads 1998, Chimes at Midnight (Chichester Festival) 1998, The Mystery of Charles Dickens 2000, (NY) 2002, Woman in

Black 2001; wrote and directed Brief Lives (on tour and West End) 1998; Co-Author of Underneath the Arches 1982–83; Artistic Dir Chichester Festival Theatre (The Cherry Orchard, The Mitford Girls, On the Rocks, Cavell, Goodbye, Mr Chips, As You Like It, Forty Years On, Merchant of Venice) 1980–84, 1991–94, Mystery of Charles Dickens 2002. *Films:* The Snow Goose 1974, The Doll's House 1976; produced: Fanfare for Elizabeth (Queen's 60th birthday gala) 1986, Celebration of a Broadcaster (for Richard Dimbleby Cancer Fund) 1986. *TV work includes:* writer and creative consultant Christmas Glory from St Paul's Cathedral 1997, St George's Chapel, Windsor 1998, Westminster Abbey 1998; Talking Heads – Miss Fozzard Finds Her Feet 1998, Telling Tales – Alan Bennett monologues 2001. *Publications:* Brief Lives 1967, The Wings of the Morning 1989, Oswald the Owl 1990, Angels in the Sussex Air: an Anthology of Sussex Poets 1995, Sussex Seams (Vol. I) 1995, (Vol. II) 1999, The Incomparable Rex 1996; poetry in London Magazine, New Poems, Poetry West, Encounter; short stories in Transatlantic Review; England Erzählt, Gemini, Light Blue, Dark Blue. *Leisure interests:* Victorian novels, walking in Corsica. *Address:* Poplars Farm House, Almodington, Chichester, W Sussex, PO20 7LD, England. *Fax:* (1243) 513933 (Home).

GARN, Edwin Jacob (Jake), BS; American politician; b. 12 Oct. 1932, Richfield, Utah; s. of Jacob E. Garn and Fern Christensen; m. 1st Hazel R. Thompson 1957 (died 1976); two s. two d.; m. 2nd Kathleen Brewerton 1977; two s. one d.; ed Univ. of Utah; Special Agent, John Hancock Mutual Life Insurance Co., Salt Lake City 1960–61; Asst Man. Home Life Insurance Co. New York, Salt Lake City 1961–66; Gen. Agent, Mutual Trust Life Insurance Co., Salt Lake City 1966–68; City Commr Salt Lake City 1968–72, Mayor 1972–74; Dir Metropolitan Water Dist 1968–72; Senator from Utah 1974–93; Vice-Chair. Huntsman Chemical Corpn, Salt Lake City 1993–99; Man. Dir Summit Ventures LLC, Salt Lake City 1999–; Republican. *Publication:* Night Launch 1989. *Address:* Summit Ventures LLC, 1 Utah Center, #600, 201 S. Main Street, Salt Lake City, UT 84111, USA (Office).

GARN, Stanley Marion, PhD; American physical anthropologist and educator; b. 27 Oct. 1922, New London, Conn.; s. of Harry Garn and Sadie Edith Garn (née Cohen); m. Priscilla Crozier 1950; one s. one d.; ed Harvard Coll. and Harvard Univ.; Research Assoc., Chemical Eng, Chemical Warfare Service Devt Lab., MIT 1942–44; Tech. Ed., Polaroid Co. 1944–46, Consultant in Applied Anthropology 1946–47; Research Fellow, Cardiology, Mass. Gen. Hosp., Boston 1946–52; Instructor in Anthropology, Harvard Univ. 1948–52; Anthropologist, Forsyth Dental Infirmary, Boston 1947–52; Dir Forsyth Face Size Project, Army Chemical Corps 1950–52; Chair. Dept of Growth and Genetics, Fels Research Inst., Yellow Springs, Ohio 1952–68; Fellow Center for Human Growth and Devt, Univ. of Mich., Ann Arbor 1968–1992, Prof. of Nutrition 1968–92, Prof. of Anthropology 1972–92, Prof. Emer. 1993–; Harvey White Lecturer, Children's Hosp., Chicago; Walker-Ames Visiting Prof., Univ. of Washington; Raymond Pearl Memorial Lecturer, Human Biology Council; 1992– Neuhauser Lecturer, Soc. for Pediatric Radiology; Fellow, American Acad. of Arts and Sciences, American Inst. of Nutrition; mem. NAS; Hon. Fellow American Acad. of Pediatrics; Distinguished Faculty Award, Univ. of Mich., Charles Darwin Lifetime Achievement Award, American Asscn of Physical Anthropologists 1994, Franz Boas Award, Human Biology Council 2001. *Publications:* Races 1950, Readings on Race 1960, Human Races 1961, Culture and the Direction of Human Evolution 1964, The Earlier Gain and Later Loss of Cortical Bone 1970, Writing the Biomedical Research Paper 1970. *Leisure interests:* photomicrography and culture of succulents. *Address:* Center for Human Growth and Development, 300 North Ingalls Street, Ann Arbor, MI 48109-2007; 827 Asa Gray Drive, Suite 258, Ann Arbor, MI 48105-2566, USA (Home). *Telephone:* (734) 764-2443 (Office); (734) 665-5235 (Home).

GARNAUT, Ross Gregory, AO, BA, PhD; Australian economist and diplomatist; b. 28 July 1946, Perth, WA; s. of the late L. Garnaut and P. W. Garnaut; m. Jayne Potter 1974; two s.; ed Perth Modern School, WA and Australian Nat. Univ., Canberra; Research Fellow, Sr Research Fellow and Sr Fellow Econs Dept Research School of Pacific Studies ANU 1972–75, 1977–83; First Asst Sec.-Gen. Financial and Econ. Policy, Papua New Guinea Dept of Finance 1975, 1976; Research Dir ASEAN-Australia Econ. Relations Research Project 1980–83; Sr Econ. Adviser to Prime Minister Bob Hawke 1983–85; Amb. to People's Repub. of China 1985–88; Prof. of Econs, Head of Dept, Research School of Pacific Studies, ANU 1989–, Dir Asia Pacific School of Econs and Man. 1998–; Chair. Bd of Dirs Aluminium Smelters of Victoria 1988–89, Rural and Industries Bank of Western Australia 1988–95, Primary Industry Bank of Australia 1988–94, Lihir Gold 1995–, Australian Centre for Int. Agric. Research 1994–. *Publications:* Irian Jaya: The Transformation of a Melanesian Economy 1974, ASEAN in a Changing Pacific and World Economy 1980, Indonesia: Australian Perspectives 1980, Taxation and Mineral Rents 1983, Exchange Range and Macro-Economic Policy in Independent Papua New Guinea 1984, The Political Economy of Manufacturing Protection: Experiences of ASEAN and Australia 1986, Australian Protectionism: Extent, Causes and Effects 1987, Australia and the Northeast Asian Ascendancy (report to Prime Minister) 1989, Economic Reform and Internationalization 1992, Grain in China 1992, Structuring for Global Realities (report on Wool Industry to Commonwealth Governments) 1993, The Third Revolution in the Chinese Countryside 1996, Open Regionalism: An Asian Pacific Contribution to the World Trading System 1996, East Asia in Crisis 1998. *Leisure interests:* cricket, tennis, watching Australian football and the history

of humanity. *Address:* Department of Economics, Research School of Pacific and Asian Studies, Australian National University, Canberra ACT 0200, Australia. *Telephone:* (2) 6249-3100. *Fax:* (2) 6249-8057.

GARNER, Alan, OBE; British author; b. 17 Oct. 1934; s. of Colin Garner and Marjorie Garner (née Greenwood Stuart); m. 1st Ann Cook 1956; one s. two d.; m. 2nd Griselda Greaves 1972; one s. one d.; ed Manchester Grammar School, Magdalen Coll. Oxford; mil. service with rank of Lt, RA; mem. Ed. Bd Detskaya Literatura Publrs, Moscow. *Publications: books:* The Weirdstone of Brisingamen 1960, The Moon of Gomrath 1963, Elidor 1965, Holly from the Bongs 1966, The Old Man of Mow 1967, The Owl Service 1967 (Library Asscn Carnegie Medal 1967, Guardian Award 1968), The Hamish Hamilton Book of Goblins 1969, Red Shift 1973, The Breadhorse 1975, The Guizer 1975, The Stone Book 1976, (Phoenix Award, Children's Book Asscn of US 1996), Tom Fobble's Day 1977, Granny Reardun 1977, The Aimer Gate 1978, Fairy Tales of Gold 1979, The Lad of the Gad 1980, A Book of British Fairy Tales 1984, A Bag of Moonshine 1986, Jack and the Beanstalk 1992, Once Upon a Time 1993, Strandloper 1996, The Little Red Hen 1997, The Voice That Thunders 1997, The Well of the Wind 1998, Thursbitch 2003. *Plays:* Holly from the Bongs 1965, Lamaload 1978, Lurga Lom 1980, To Kill a King 1980, Sally Water 1982, The Keeper 1983, Pentecost 1997, The Echoing Waters 2000. *Dance drama:* The Green Mist 1970. *Libretti:* The Bellybag 1971, Potter Thompson 1972, Lord Flame 1996. *Screenplays:* The Owl Service 1969, Red Shift 1978, Places and Things 1978, Images 1981 (First Prize, Chicago Int. Film Festival), Strandloper 1992. *Leisure interest:* work. *Address:* Blackden, Holmes Chapel, Cheshire, CW4 8BY, England.

GARNER, James (James Baumgardner); American actor; b. 7 April 1928, Norman, Okla; m. Lois Clarke 1956; one s. two d.; ed New York Berghof School; worked as travelling salesman, oil field worker, carpet layer, bathing suit model; toured with road cos; Emmy Award; Purple Heart. *Television appearances include:* Cheyenne, Maverick 1957–62, Nichols 1971–72, The Rockford Files 1974–79, Space 1985, The New Maverick, The Long Summer of George Adams, The Glitter Dome, Heartsounds, Promise (also exec. producer), Obsessive Love, My Name is Bill (also exec. producer), Decoration Day, Barbarians at the Gate, The Rockford Files: A Blessing in Disguise, Dead Silence, First Monday (series) 2002. *Films include:* Toward the Unknown, Shoot-out at Medicine Bend 1957, Darby's Rangers 1958, Sayonara, Up Periscope 1959, The Americanization of Emily 1964, 36 Hours 1964, The Art of Love 1965, A Man Could Get Killed 1966, Duel at Diablo 1966, Mister Buddwing 1966, Grand Prix 1966, Hour of the Gun 1967, Marlowe 1969, Support Your Local Sheriff 1971, Support Your Local Gunfighter 1971, Skin Game 1971, They Only Kill Their Masters 1972, One Little Indian 1973, Health 1979, The Fan 1980, Victor/Victoria 1982, Murphy's Romance 1985, Promise (TV) 1986, Sunset 1987, Decoration Day (TV) 1990, Fire in the Sky 1993, Maverick (TV) 1994, My Fellow Americans 1996, Twilight 1998, Space Cowboys 2000, Atlantis: The Lost Empire 2001, Roughing It (TV) 2002, Divine Secrets of the Ya-Ya Sisterhood 2002.

GARNER, Lt-Gen. Jay, BA, MPA; American government official and fmr army general; b. 15 April 1938; m. Connie Garner; one d.; ed Fla State Univ., Shippensburg Univ., Penn.; joined US Army 1960, served in Viet Nam; commanded Patriot missile batteries in first Gulf War, supervised resettlement of Kurdish refugees in immediate post-war period; later Commdr of Space and Strategic Defense Command; Asst Chief of Staff –1997; rank of Lt-Gen.; retd from service 1997; Pres. SY Coleman (defence contractor specializing in missile systems) 1997–2003; mem. Presidential Panel on Space and Missile Threats; Dir Office of Reconstruction and Humanitarian Assistance for Iraq (interim Gov. of Iraq) March–April 2003. *Address:* c/o The Pentagon, Washington, DC 20301, USA (Office).

GARNER, Wendell Richard, PhD; American psychologist and university professor (retd); b. 21 Jan. 1921, Buffalo, NY; s. of Richard Charles and Lena Cole Garner; m. Barbara Chipman Ward 1944; one s. two d.; ed Franklin and Marshall Coll. and Harvard Univ.; Instructor, rising to Prof., Johns Hopkins Univ. 1946–67, Chair. Dept of Psychology 1954–64; James Rowland Angell Prof. of Psychology, Yale Univ. 1967–89, Prof. Emer. 1989–, Dir of Social Sciences 1972–73, 1981–88, Chair. Dept of Psychology 1974–77, Dean of the Graduate School 1978–79; mem. Nat. Acad. of Sciences; Hon. DSc (Franklin and Marshall Coll.) 1979; Hon. DHumLitt (Johns Hopkins Univ.) 1983; Distinguished Scientific Contribution Award, American Psychological Asscn 1964, Warren Medal, Soc. of Experimental Psychologists 1976, Gold Medal, American Psychological Foundation 1999. *Publications:* Applied Experimental Psychology (with A. Chapanis and C. T. Morgan) 1949, Uncertainty and Structure as Psychological Concepts 1962, The Processing of Information and Structure 1974, Ability Testing (ed. with A. Wigdor) 1982. *Leisure interests:* gardening, hiking. *Address:* 1122 Meadow Ridge, Reddings, CT 06896, USA (Home). *Telephone:* (203) 544-7133 (Home).

GARNETT, Tony; British television producer; b. 3 April 1936, Birmingham; ed Cen. Grammar School, Univ. Coll., London; began career as television actor; producer of numerous TV programmes and films; worked in USA 1980–90; Co-Founder World Productions 1990; Visiting Prof. of Media Arts, Royal Holloway Coll., Univ. of London 2000–. *TV appearances include:* Dixon of Dock Green 1960s. *TV productions include:* Up the Junction 1965, Cathy Come Home 1966, The Resistable Rise of Arturo Ui 1972, Hard Labour 1973, The Enemy Within 1974, Days of Hope 1975, Law and Order 1978, Between the Lines 1992, Cardiac Arrest 1994, Ballykissangel 1996, This Life 1996, The

Cops 1998, Attachments 2000. *Films produced include:* Kes 1969, Handgun 1983, Earth Girls are Easy 1989, Shadow Makers 1989. *Address:* c/o World Productions, Eagle House, 50 Marshall Street, London, W1F 9BQ, England (Office). *Telephone:* (20) 7734-3536 (Office). *Fax:* (20) 7758-7000 (Office). *Website:* www.world-productions.com (Office).

GARNIER, Jean-Pierre, PhD, MBA; French business executive; b. 31 Oct. 1947; m.; three d.; ed Univ. of Louis Pasteur, Stanford Univ.; joined Schering-Plough 1975, numerous man. positions including Gen. Man. of numerous overseas subsidiaries, then Vice-Pres. of Marketing, U.S. Pharmaceutical Products Div. 1983, then Sr Vice-Pres. and Gen. Man. with responsibility for sales and marketing for U.S. prescription business, then Pres. U.S. business; Pres. pharmaceutical business in N America, SmithKline Beecham 1990, mem. Bd Dirs. 1992–, Chair. Pharmaceuticals 1994–95, COO 1995–2000, CEO GlaxoSmithKline April 2000–; mem. Bd dirs. United Technologies Corpn, Biotech. Industry Org., Eisenhower Exchange Fellowships Inc.; Oliver R. Grace Award for distinguished service in advancing cancer research 1997, named a Star of Europe, Business Week 2001, Marco Polo Award 2001, Corporate Citizenship Award, Henry H. Kessler Foundation; Chevalier, Légion d'honneur. *Address:* GlaxoSmithKline, 1 Franklin Plaza, P.O. Box 7929, Philadelphia, PA 19101 (Office). *E-mail:* jean-pierre.garnier@sb.com (Office).

GAROFANO, Giuseppe; Italian engineer; b. 25 Jan. 1944, Nereto, Teramo; ed Milan Polytechnic Inst., Bocconi Univ. Business School; Man. Dir Cotonificio Cantoni 1981–84; Vice-Chair. and Man. Dir Iniziativa META SpA 1984–88, Chair. and CEO 1988; Man. Dir Ferruzzi Finanziaria SpA 1988–92, Vice-Chair. 1989–; Vice-Chair. Milano Assicurazioni SpA 1987–, Fondiaria SpA 1989–, La Previdente Assicurazioni SpA 1991–; Vice-Chair. Montedison SpA 1989–90, Chair. 1990–92.

GAROUSTE, Gérard; French painter and sculptor; b. 10 March 1946, Paris; s. of Henri Garouste and Edmée Sauvagnac; m. Elizabeth Rochline 1970; two s.; ed Académie Charpentier, Beaux-Arts de Paris; first exhbn Galérie Zunini, Paris 1969; other exhbns include Paris 1978, 1980, 1988 (Centre Pompidou), Milan 1980, Noto 1981, New York 1982, 1983, 1985, 1988, Venice Biennale 1982, Düsseldorf 1982 (Kunsthalle), 1984, 1989 (Kunsthalle), Rome 1984, Charleroi 1984, Dublin 1986, Munich 1986, Budapest 1986, Tokyo 1986 (Museum of Modern Art), 1990, Montreal 1986 (Musée d'art contemporain), Seoul 1987, Bordeaux 1987, Bienale de São Paulo 1987, Yugoslavia 1988, 1990, Amsterdam 1989 (Stedelikmuseum); created Le classique et l'Indien show 1977; sets, Théâtre de la Ville 1978, Palace et Privilège, Théâtre du Chatelet, Paris 1990; fresco, Elysée Palace 1983, Town Hall, Mons (Belgium); ceiling, Théâtre Royal, Namur; subject of several monographs and catalogues; Chevalier des Arts et des Lettres, Chevalier Légion d'honneur. *Address:* La Mésangère, 27810 Marcilly-sur-Eure, France. *Telephone:* 37-48-47-18. *Fax:* 37-48-45-39 (Office).

GARRARD, Rose, DipAD; British sculptor and mixed media artist; b. 21 Sept. 1946, Bewdley, Worcs.; d. of Col W. V. Garrard and Germaine Garrard; m. (divorced); no c.; ed Stourbridge, Birmingham and Chelsea Colls of Art and Acad. des Beaux Arts, Paris; freelance designer, model and prop-maker to magazines, theatres, advertisers and TV 1969–83; arts consultant to architects advising on public works projects including Liverpool Shopping Precinct and Elephant & Castle Shopping Centre 1971–74; Artist in Schools Residency, Cen. Foundation School for Girls, Bow, E London 1982; Artist-in-Residence, Birmingham City Art Gallery 1983; Sr Lecturer, half full-time, Art and Social Context, Dartington Coll. of Arts; has held various other part-time teaching and lecturing appointments throughout UK; has participated in numerous group exhbns in UK, Europe, USA, Canada and Australia since 1967; works in many public and pvt. collections including Victoria & Albert Museum, Contemporary Art Soc. and Arts Council of GB; mem. numerous selection panels etc.; Int. Multiples Prize Award by Paolozzi 1969; Prix d'honneur de Paris for Sculpture 1971; Arts Council of GB Purchase Award 1979; Greater London Arts Asscn Major Award 1980. *Solo exhibitions include:* Worcester 1967, London 1977, 1983, Cambridge 1983, Birmingham, Liverpool, Bristol, Nottingham and Rochdale 1984, Inst. of Contemporary Art (ICA), London 1984.

GARRATT, Sheryl, BA; British journalist; b. 29 March 1961, Birmingham; d. of Frank Garratt and June Garratt (née Fray); m. Mark McGuire 1994; one s.; ed Barr Beacon Comprehensive, Univ. Coll., London; various freelance and staff positions including contribs. to New Musical Express, Honey, Looks, News on Sunday, The Observer, The Sunday Telegraph; Music Ed. City Limits; joined The Face 1988, Ed. 1990–95; freelance journalist 1995–98, for The Observer, Guardian 2002–; ed. The Observer Magazine 1998–2001. *Publications:* Signed, Sealed and Delivered 1984, Adventures in Wonderland – a Decade of Club Culture 1998. *Leisure interests:* clubbing, drinking, talking, cooking for friends. *Address:* 52 Milton Grove, London, N16 8QY, England (Home). *Telephone:* (20) 7503-6748 (Home). *E-mail:* sherylg@blueyonder.co.uk (Home).

GARRETT, Lesley, CBE, FRAM; British opera singer; b. 10 April 1955; d. of Derek Arthur Garrett and Margaret Wall; m. 1991; one s. one d.; ed Thorne Grammar School, Royal Acad. of Music, Nat. Opera Studio; winner Kathleen Ferrier Memorial Competition 1979; performed with Welsh Nat. Opera, Opera North, at Wexford and Buxton Festivals and at Glyndebourne; joined ENO (Prin. Soprano) 1984; Hon. D.Arts (Plymouth) 1995; Best Selling Classical Artist, Gramophone Award 1996. *Television:* appeared in BBC TV series Lesley Garrett . . . Tonight. *Major roles include:* Susanna in The Marriage of Figaro, Despina in Così Fan Tutte, Musetta in La Bohème, Jenny in The Rise and Fall of The City of Mahaggony, Atalanta in Xerxes, Zerlinda in Don Giovanni, Yum-Yum in The Mikado, Adèle in Die Fledermaus, Oscar in A Masked Ball, Dalinda in Ariodante, Rose in Street Scene, Bella in A Midsummer Marriage, Eurydice in Orpheus and Eurydice and title roles in The Cunning Little Vixen and La Belle Vivette; numerous concert hall performances in UK and abroad (including Last Night of the Proms); TV and radio appearances. *Leisure interest:* watching cricket. *Address:* The Music Partnership Ltd, 41 Aldebert Terrace, London, SW8 1BH, England. *Telephone:* (20) 7787-0361. *Fax:* (20) 7735-7595.

GARRETT, Malcolm, BA (Hons); British graphic designer; b. 2 June 1956, Northwich, Cheshire; ed Reading Univ., Manchester Polytechnic; f. Assorted Images Design Co., Design Dir 1978; formed Assorted Images Ltd 1983; f. AMX Digital Ltd 1994, joined Havas Advertising (re-named AMX Studios, then AMX) 1998, Chair. 1999-2001. Visiting Prof. The London Inst. and Royal Coll. of Art 2000; MA hc 1999, RDI 2000. *Exhibitions:* Malcolm Garrett: Ulterior Motifs, Design Museum, London, Parco Gallery, Tokyo, SVA Gallery, New York, Savannah Coll. of Art and Design, USA, Univ. of Salford; has work included in perm. collection of 20th Century Graphic Design at the Victoria and Albert Museum, London. *Publications:* Duran Duran: Their Story 1982, When Cameras go Crazy: Culture Club 1983 (both co-written with Kasper de Graaf). *Address:* AMX, 14 Welbeck Street, London, W1G 9XU (Office); 59 Knighthead Point, West Ferry Road, London, E14 8SS England (Home). *Telephone:* (20) 7908-2700 (Office); (20) 7908-2701 (Home). *E-mail:* malcolm.garrett@amxnetworks.com (Office). *Website:* www.amxnetworks.com (Office).

GARRETT, Peter Robert, BA, LLB; Australian environmentalist and musician; b. 16 April 1953, Wahroonga, NSW; s. of the late Peter Maxwell Garrett and Betty Garrett; m.; three d.; ed Barker Coll., Hornsby, Australian Nat. Univ., Univ. of New South Wales; lead singer, Midnight Oil –2002; Pres. Australian Conservation Foundation 1989–91, 1998–; mem. Bd Greenpeace Int. 1991–93; Hon. DLitt (Univ. of NSW); Australia's Living Treasures Award, Nat. Trust of Australia 1999. *Albums:* (with Midnight Oil) Midnight Oil, Head Injuries, Place Without a Postcard, 10-1, Red Sails, Diesel and Dust, Blue Sky Mining, 20,000 Watt RSL, Breathe, Redneck Wonderland, Capricornia. *Publication:* Political Blues 1987. *Leisure interests:* surfing, Australian literature. *Address:* Locked Bag 18/172, Newtown, NSW 2042, Australia (Office). *Telephone:* (2) 9517-9776 (Office). *Fax:* (2) 9517-1072 (Office). *E-mail:* oils@ozemail.com.au (Office). *Website:* www.petergarrett.com.au (Office).

GARRISON-JACKSON, Zina; American tennis player; b. 16 Nov. 1963, Houston, Tex.; m. Willard Jackson Jr 1989; winner WTA Championships 1985; singles semi-finalist, Wimbledon Championships 1985, finalist 1990 (lost to Martina Navratilova, q.v.); semi-finalist US Open 1988, 1989; gold medal winner, ladies doubles (with P. Shriver), Seoul Olympic Games 1988; winner mixed doubles (with S. Stewart), Australian Open 1987, Wimbledon Championships 1988, (with Leach) 1990; mem. US Fed. Cup Team 1984–87, 1989–91, 1994, Whiteman Cup Team 1987–88; retd 1992; f. Zina Garrison Foundation to support various charities 1988; Head Coach US Nat. team 1999; Asst Coach US Fed. Cup team 1999–; Int. Hall of Fame Educ. Merit Award, Texas Tennis Hall of Fame 1998. *Leisure interests:* jogging, softball, artwork – designs own printed T-shirts. *Address:* c/o USTA, 70 W Red Oak Lane, White Plains, NY 10604; c/o Advantage International, 1751 Pinnacle Drive, Suite 1500, McLean, VA 22102, USA.

GARWIN, Richard L., MS, PhD; American physicist; b. 19 April 1928, Cleveland, Ohio; s. of Robert and Leona S. Garwin; m. Lois E. Levy 1947; two s. one d.; ed public schools in Cleveland, Case Western Reserve Univ. and Univ. of Chicago; Instructor and Asst Prof. of Physics, Univ. of Chicago 1949–52; mem. staff, IBM Watson Lab., Columbia Univ. 1952–65, 1966–70; Adjunct Prof. of Physics, Columbia Univ. 1957–; Dir of Applied Research, IBM T. J. Watson Research Center 1965–66, IBM Fellow 1965–93, Fellow Emer. 1993–; mem. Defense Science Bd 1966–69; mem. President's Science Advisory Cttee 1962–66, 1969–72; mem. IBM Corporate Tech. Cttee 1970–71; Adjunct Prof. Col Univ. 1957; Prof. of Public Policy, Kennedy School of Govt, Harvard 1979–81, Adjunct Research Fellow 1982–; Andrew D. White Prof.-at-Large, Cornell Univ. 1982–87; mem. Council on Foreign Relations; mem. NAS 1966–, Inst. of Medicine 1975–81, Nat. Acad. of Eng 1978–, American Philosophical Soc. 1979–; Consultant to Los Alamos 1950–93, to Sandia Nat. Lab. 1994–; Fellow, American Physical Soc. American Acad. of Arts and Sciences; Ford Foundation Fellow, CERN, Geneva 1959–60; Dr hc (Case Western Reserve Univ.) 1966, (Rensselaer Polytechnic Inst.), (State Univ. of New York); R. V. Jones Intelligence Award (Nat. Foreign Intelligence Community) 1996, Enrico Fermi Award 1997. *Publications:* Nuclear Power Issues and Choices (co-author) 1977, Nuclear Weapons and World Politics 1977, Energy, the Next Twenty Years (co-author) 1979, The Dangers of Nuclear Wars 1979, Unresolved Issues in Arms Control 1988, A Nuclear-Weapon-Free World: Desirable? Feasible? 1993, Managing the Plutonium Surplus: Applications and Technical Options 1994, U.S. Intervention Policy for the Post-Cold War World: New Challenges and New Responses 1994, Feux Follets et Champignons Nucléaires (with G. Charpak) 1997; about 200 published papers and 42 US patents. *Leisure interests:* skiing, military technology, arms control, social use of technology. *Address:* c/o T. J. Watson Research Center, P.O. Box 218, Yorktown Heights, New York, NY 10598, USA.

GARZÓN, Baltasar; Spanish judge; b. 1955, Villa de Torres (Jaen); m.; provincial judge 1978–87, Nat. Court 1987–; MP 1993–94; has investigated numerous high profile cases involving drug trafficking, Basque terrorism, Govt corruption, Spain's security forces and human rights abuses and Islamic fundamentalism; issued arrest warrant for Gen. Augusto Pinochet Ugarte to face charges of genocide, terrorism and torture 1998; banned Basque politicial party Batasuna Aug. 2002. *Address:* Audiencia Nacional, García Gutiérrez 1, 28004 Madrid, Spain (Office).

GASCOIGNE, Paul John; British footballer; b. 27 May 1967, Gateshead; s. of John Gascoigne and Carol Gascoigne (née Harold); m. Sheryl Failes 1996 (divorced 1998); one s.; ed Heathfield Sr School; joined Newcastle United as apprentice 1983; played for Newcastle United 1985–88, for Tottenham Hotspur 1988–92 (FA Cup winners' medal 1991), for Lazio, Italy 1992–95, for Rangers 1995–98, for Middlesbrough 1998–2000, for Everton 2000–02, for Burnley 2002; signed as player-coach for Gansu Tianma (Gansu Sky Horses), Chinese B-League 2003; played for England, 13 Under-21 caps, 57 full caps. *Publication:* Paul Gascoigne (autobiog. with Paul Simpson) 2001. *Leisure interests:* football, fishing, tennis, swimming. *Address:* c/o Robertson Craig & Co., Clairmont Gardens, Glasgow, G3 7LW Scotland. *Telephone:* (141) 332-1205. *Fax:* (141) 332-8035.

GASKILL, William; British theatre and opera director; b. 24 June 1930; s. of Joseph Linnaeus Gaskill and Maggie Simpson; ed Salt High School, Shipley and Hertford Coll., Oxford; Dir, Granada Television 1956–57; Asst Artistic Dir Royal Court Theatre, London 1958–60; Dir Royal Shakespeare Co. 1961–62; Assoc. Dir Nat. Theatre, London 1963–65, 1979; Artistic Dir English Stage Co., Royal Court Theatre 1965–72; Dir Jt Stock Theatre Group 1974–83. *Stage productions include:* (Royal Court Theatre) Epitaph for George Dillon, One Way Pendulum, Saved, Early Morning, Man is Man, Lear, Big Wolf, The Sea, The Gorky Brigade; (Nat. Theatre) The Recruiting Officer, Mother Courage, Philoctetes, Armstrong's Last Goodnight, The Beaux Stratagem, The Madras House, A Fair Quarrel, Man, Beast and Virtue, Black Snow; (Royal Shakespeare Co.) The Caucasian Chalk Circle, Richard III, Cymbeline; (Joint Stock) The Speakers, Fanshen, Yesterday's News, A Mad World, My Masters, The Ragged Trousered Philanthropists; other productions include The Way of the World; opera productions include: The Barber of Seville, La Bohème and Lucia di Lammermoor (Welsh Nat. Opera). *Publication:* A Sense of Direction: life at the Royal Court (autobiog.) 1988. *Address:* 124A Leighton Road, London, NW5 2RG, England.

GASKÓ, István; Hungarian trade union official; b. 21 July 1951, Sajòszent-pèter; m.; one s.; ed Econ. Univ., Budapest; mem. Democratic Trade Union of Scientific Workers 1988; f. Social Democratic Party 1989; f. Free Trade Union of Railway Workers 1989, Pres. 1991–; Pres. Democratic Confed. of Free Trade Unions (LIGA) 1996–. *Leisure interests:* reading, music, film, theatre. *Address:* Democratic Confederation of Free Trade Unions, FSzDL, Benczúr u. 41, 1068 Budapest, Hungary (Office). *Telephone:* (1) 321-5262 (Office). *Fax:* (1) 321-5405 (Office). *E-mail:* info@liganet.hu (Office). *Website:* www.liganet.hu (Office).

GASPAROV, Mikhail Leonovich, DLitt; Russian literary scholar; b. 13 April 1935, Moscow; m.; two c.; ed Moscow State Univ.; jr, sr researcher, head of div., chief researcher Inst. of World Literature 1957–90; Chief Researcher Inst. of Russian Language USSR Acad. of Sciences 1990–99; Corresp. mem. USSR (now Russian) Acad. of Sciences 1990, mem. 1992; research in Latin poetics, Russian poetry, study of versification; State Prize 1994. *Publications include:* Classical Literary Fable 1971, Contemporary Russian Verse 1974, Survey of History of Russian Verse 1984, History of European Versification 1989, Selected Works I–III 1997, Essays on Russian Poetry 1998, Meter and Meaning 1999. *Leisure interests:* reading, translation of classics and poetry. *Address:* Institute of Russian Language, Russian Academy of Sciences, Volkhonka str. 18/2, 121019 Moscow, Russia. *Telephone:* (095) 202-65-10.

GAŠPAROVIČ, Ivan, LLD; Slovak politician and lawyer; b. 27 March 1941, Poltár Lučenec Dist; s. of Vladimír Gašparovič and Elena Gašparovič; m. Silvia Gašparovičová 1964; one s. one d.; ed Komenský Univ., Bratislava; clerk, Prosecutor's Office, Martin Trenčín 1965–66; Mun. Public Prosecutor, Bratislava 1966–68; teacher, Faculty of Law, Komenský Univ., Bratislava 1968–90, Vice-Rector 1990–; Gen. Prosecutor of C.S.F.R. 1990–92; mem. Movt for Democratic Slovakia 1992–2002 (Movt became a political party 2000); deputy to Slovak Nat. Council, mem. of Presidium; Chair. of Slovak Nat. Council 1992–98; Chair. Special Body of Nat. Council of Slovakia for Control of Slovak Intelligence Services 1993–98; Founder and Leader Movement for Democracy 2002–. *Publications:* author and co-author of many univ. textbooks, numerous articles and reviews on criminal law. *Leisure interests:* tennis, hockey, motoring. *Address:* Mudroňova 1, 812 80 Bratislava, Slovakia. *Telephone:* (2) 5934-1111 (Office).

GASSIYEV, Nikolai Tengizovich; Russian tenor; b. 2 Feb. 1952, Tskhin-vali, Georgia; ed Leningrad State Conservatory; soloist Mariinsky Opera and Ballet Theatre 1990–; debut in Metropolitan Opera as Yurodivy (Boris Godunov) and Agrippina (Fairy Angel) 1992, Dresdner Staatsoper 1993, Brooklyn School of Music 1995, Edinburgh Festival 1995, Albert Hall 1995, La Scala 1996; Prize of Union of Theatre Workers Best Actor of the Year 1994. *Address:* Mariinsky Theatre, Teatralnaya pl. 1, St Petersburg, Russia (Office). *Telephone:* (812) 315-57-24 (Office).

GAT, Joel R., MSc, PhD; Israeli professor of isotope research; b. Joel R. Gutmann, 17 Feb. 1926, Munich, Germany; m.; two c.; ed Hebrew Univ., Jerusalem; Asst Dept of Physical Chem., Hebrew Univ. 1949–50; Research Officer Ministry of Defence Labs., Jerusalem 1950–52; Israel Atomic Energy Comm., Rehovot 1952–59; at Isotope Dept (renamed Dept of Environmental Sciences and Energy Research 1990), Weizmann Inst. of Science, Rehovot 1959–, Acting Prof. 1967–71, Prof. 1971–92, Prof. Emer. 1992–, Head of Dept 1975–86, Dean, Faculty of Chem., Weizmann Inst. 1986–89; Dir Centre for Water Science and Tech., Ben Gurion Univ. of the Negev 1997–; Visiting Scientist Enrico Fermi Inst. for Nuclear Science, Univ. of Chicago 1955–56, Scripps Inst. of Oceanography, Univ. of Calif. 1964–65, Nat. Centre for Atmospheric Research, Boulder, Colo 1972–73, Univ. of Wis. 1988–89; mem. Editorial Bd Isotope Geosciences, Earth and Planetary Science Letters; undertook IAEA-sponsored projects in Brazil, Iran, Mexico and Turkey. *Publications:* Environmental Isotopes in The Hydrological Cycle: Vol. II, Physics and Chemistry of Lakes (co-ed.) 1995, Oxford Monograph on Geology and Geophysics 1997, Atmospheric Waters 2001, The Dead Sea: The Lake and its Setting (co-ed.). *Address:* Department of Environmental Sciences and Energy Research, The Weizmann Institute of Science, P.O. Box 26, Rehovot, Israel.

GATES, Henry Louis, Jr., MA, PhD; American professor of Afro-American studies, author and editor; b. 16 Sept. 1950, Piedmont, W Va; s. of Henry-Louis Gates and Pauline Augusta Gates (née Coleman); m. Sharon Lynn Adams 1979; two d.; ed Yale Univ. and Clare Coll. Cambridge; fmr European corresp. for Time magazine; lecturer in English, Yale Univ. 1976–79, Asst Prof. English and Afro-American Studies 1979–84, Assoc. Prof. 1984–85; Prof. of English, Comparative Literature and Africana Studies, Cornell Univ. 1985–90; John Spencer Bassett Prof. of English, Duke Univ. 1990–91; Prof., Chair. Dept of Afro-American Studies, Harvard Univ. 1991–; also Dir W. E. B. DuBois Inst. for Afro-American Research (Prof. of Literature 1988–90, of Humanities 1991), Harvard Univ. 1991–; Pres. Afro-American Acad. 1984–; ed. African American Women's Writings (Macmillan reprint series), Encyclopedia Africana; columnist, New Yorker, New York Times; numerous hon. degrees; American Book Award for The Signifying Monkey; McArthur Foundation Award, Nat. Humanities Medal 1998, Hon. Citizenship of Benin 2001. *Publications include:* Figures in Black (literary criticism) 1987, The Signifying Monkey 1988, Loose Canons (literary criticism) 1992, Colored People (short stories) 1994, The Future of the Race (with Cornel West) 1996, Thirteen Ways of Looking at a Black Man., Africana (jtly) (TV documentary), Wonders of the African World 1999, The Curitas Enthology of African–American Slave Narratives, The African-American Century 2000; Co-Ed. Encarta Africana Encyclopaedia 1999; Ed. The Bondswoman's Narrative 2002. *Address:* Department of Afro-American Studies, Barker Center, 12 Quincy Street, Cambridge, MA 02138, USA. *Telephone:* (617) 496-5468. *Fax:* (617) 495-9490.

GATES, Marshall De Motte, Jr.; American professor of chemistry; b. 25 Sept. 1915, Boyne City, Mich.; s. of Marshall D. Gates and Virginia Orton Gates; m. Martha L. Meyer 1941; two s. two d.; ed Rice and Harvard Univs; Asst Prof. of Chem., Bryn Mawr Coll. 1941–46, Assoc. Prof. 1947–49; Tech. Aide, Nat. Defense Research Council 1943–46; Lecturer in Chem., Univ. of Rochester 1949–52, part-time Prof. 1952–60, Prof. 1960–68, Charles Houghton Prof. of Chem. 1968–81, Prof. Emer. 1981–; first synthesis of morphine 1952; Visiting Prof. Dartmouth 1982, 1984, 1985; mem. Cttee on Drugs Addiction and Narcotics, Div. of Medical Sciences, Nat. Research Council 1956–69; Charter Fellow Coll. of Problems of Drug Dependence 1992–; mem. NAS, American Chem. Soc.; Fellow, American Acad. of Arts and Sciences, New York Acad. of Sciences; Asst Ed. Journal of American Chemical Society 1949–62, Ed. 1963–69; Max Tishler Lecturer, Harvard 1953, Welch Foundation Lecturer 1960; mem. President's Cttee on Nat. Medal of Science 1968–70, Advisory Bd, Chem. Abstract Services 1974–76; E. P. Curtis Award 1967, Distinguished Alumnus Award, Rice Univ. 1987. *Leisure interests:* skiing, sailing. *Address:* Department of Chemistry, Rochester University, Rochester, NY 14627 (Office); 41 West Brook Road, Pittsford, NY, USA (Home).

GATES, Robert M., PhD; American intelligence officer; b. 25 Sept. 1943, Wichita, Kansas; m. Becky Gates; two c.; ed Coll. of William and Mary, Indiana Univ., Georgetown Univ.; service with USAF 1966–68; career training program CIA 1968, intelligence analyst 1969–72, staff of Special Asst to the Dir of Central Intelligence for Strategic Arms Limitations 1972–73, Asst Nat. Intelligence Officer for Strategic Programs 1973–74, staff Nat. Security Council The White House 1974–76, staff Center for Policy Support 1976–77, Special Asst to Asst to the Pres. for Nat. Security Affairs 1977–79, Dir Strategic Evaluation Center 1979–80, Exec. Asst to Dir of Cen. Intelligence and Dir of the Exec. Staff, Dir of Office of Policy and Planning and Nat. Intelligence Officer for the Soviet Union and Eastern Europe 1980, Deputy Dir for Intelligence 1981–82, Chair. Nat. Intelligence Council 1982–86, Acting Dir of Central Intelligence 1986–87, Deputy Dir of Central Intelligence 1986–89, Asst to the Pres. and Deputy for Nat. Security Affairs The White House 1989–91, Dir CIA 1991–93; Nat. Intelligence Distinguished Service Medal, Distinguished Intelligence Medal (twice), Intelligence Medal of Merit, Arthur S. Fleming Award. *Publication:* From the Shadows 1996. *Address:* c/o Central Intelligence Agency, Washington, DC 20505, USA.

GATES, William Henry (Bill) III; American computer software executive; b. 28 Oct. 1955, Seattle; s. of William H. Gates and Mary M. Maxwell; m. Melinda French 1994; two d. one s.; ed Lakeside School, Harvard Univ.; joined

MITS 1975; Programmer for Honeywell 1975; Founder, Chair. Bd Microsoft Corpn (disk operating system, windows system) 1976–, CEO 1976–99, Chief Software Architect 1999–; Bd Dirs ICOS; Howard Vollum Award, Reed Coll. Portland, Ore. 1984; named CEO of the Year, Chief Executive Magazine. *Publications:* The Future 1994, The Road Ahead 1996, Business at the Speed of Thought 1999. *Leisure interest:* tennis. *Address:* Microsoft Corporation, 1 Microsoft Way, Redmond, WA 98052-8300, USA (Office).

GATT, Austin, LLD; Maltese politician and lawyer; b. 29 July 1953; m. Marisa Zammit Maempel; two c.; ed Lyceum and Univ. of Malta; practised law 1975–82; Nationalist Party org. 1980; Chair. Man. Bd Independence Print Co. Ltd 1982–87; Head Legal Office of Nationalist Party 1982–87, Sec. Gen. 1988–98; Chair. Euro Tours Co. Ltd; MP 1996–, Opposition Spokesman for Justice, Local Councils and Housing 1996–98; Parl. Sec. Office of Prime Minister 1998–99; Minister of Justice and Local Govt 1999–. *Address:* Auberge De Castille, Valletta, CMR 02, Malta (Home). *Telephone:* 226808 (Home). *Fax:* 250700 (Home). *E-mail:* info.justice@magnet.mt (Office). *Website:* justice.magnet.mt (Office).

GATTAZ, Yvon; French business executive; b. 17 June 1925, Bourgoin; s. of Marceau Gattaz and Gabrielle Brotel; m. Geneviève Beurley 1954; two s. one d.; ed Coll. of Bourgoin, Lycée du Parc, Lyon, Ecole Centrale des Arts et Manufactures, Paris; with Aciéries du Nord 1948–50; Automobiles Citroën 1950–54; Founder Soc. Radiall 1952, Chair. 1952–93, Pres. Supervisory Council 1994–; Chair. group of commercial and industrial cos, Rosny-sous-Bois 1967–81; Admin. Centre for External Trade 1979–82, Nat. Council for Scientific Research 1979–81; Founder Mouvement des entreprises à taille humaine industrielles et commerciales (ETHIC) 1976, Pres. 1976–81, Hon. Pres. 1981–; Founder Les Quatre Vérités 1974, Co-Ed. 1974–81; mem. Conseil économique et social 1979–89; Pres. Conseil National du Patronat Français 1981–86, Hon. Pres. 1986; Pres. Admin. Council, Fondation jeunesse et entreprise 1986–; Pres. Comité d'expansion de Seine-Saint-Denis 1987 (Hon. Pres. 1998–), asscn Entreprises Télévision Educ. Formation (ETEF) 1994, ASMEP (Asscn des moyennes entreprises patrimoniales) 1994–; Pres. Acad. of Moral and Political Sciences 1999–; mem. Institut de France (Acad. des Sciences morales et politiques) 1989; Commdr, Légion d'honneur; Commdr, Ordre nat. du Mérite, Prix Mondial Cino del Duca 2001. *Publications:* Les hommes en gris 1970, La fin des patrons 1980, Les patrons reviennent 1988, Le modèle français 1993 (prix du Livre de l'entreprise 1995), Mitterrand et les patrons 1981–86 (jtly.) 1999. *Address:* 4 rue Léo-Delibes, 75116 Paris, France (Office).

GATTI, Daniele; Italian conductor; b. 6 Nov. 1961, Milan; m. Silvia Chiesa 1990; ed Milan Conservatory; founded Stradivari Chamber Orchestra 1986; début at La Scala, Milan with Rossini's L'occasione fa il Ladro 1987–88 season; US début with American Symphony Orchestra, Carnegie Hall, New York 1990; Covent Garden début with I Puritani 1992; Music Dir Accad. di Santa Cecilia, Rome 1992–; Prin. Guest Conductor, Royal Opera House, Covent Garden 1994–96; début at Metropolitan Opera, New York with Madam Butterfly 1994–95 season; début with Royal Philharmonic 1994, Music Dir 1996–; Music Dir Teatro Communale, Bologna 1997–; début with New York Philharmonic 1995; has conducted many leading orchestras in Europe and USA and at many of the world's leading opera houses. *Address:* Via Scaglia Est 134, 41100 Modena, Italy (Office); c/o Royal Philharmonic Orchestra, 16 Clerkenwell Green, London, EC1R 0DP, England.

GATTING, Michael William (Mike), OBE; British cricketer; b. 6 June 1957, Kingsbury, Middx; m. Elaine Mabbott 1980; two s.; ed John Kelly High School; right-hand batsman and right-arm medium bowler; played for Middx 1975–99 (Capt. 1983–97); 79 Tests for England 1977–95 (23 as Capt.), scoring 4,409 runs (average 35.5) including 10 hundreds; scored 36,549 first-class runs (94 hundreds); toured Australia 1986–87 (Capt.), 1987–95; Capt. rebel cricket tour to SA 1989–90; 92 limited-overs ints, 37 as Capt.; mem. England Selection Cttee 1997–99; Dir of Coaching, Middx Cricket Club 1999–2000; Dir Ashwell Leisure 2001–; Wisden Cricketer of The Year 1984. *Radio:* analyst on Test Match Special. *Publications:* Limited Overs 1986, Triumph in Australia 1987, Leading from the Front (autobiog.) 1988. *Leisure interests:* golf, soccer and sport in general. *Address:* c/o Middlesex County Cricket Club, Lord's Cricket Ground, St John's Wood Road, London, NW8 8QN (Office); 8A Villlage Road, Enfield, Middlesex, EN1 2DH, England (Home). *Telephone:* (20) 7289-1300 (Office); 07768 541693 (Home).

GAULTIER, Jean-Paul; French fashion designer; b. 24 April 1952, Arcueil, Paris; s. of Paul Gaultier; launched first collection with his Japanese partner 1978; since then known on int. scale for his men's and women's collections; first jr collection 1988; costume designs for film The Cook, The Thief, His Wife and Her Lover 1989; for ballet Le Défilé de Régine Chopinot 1985, Madonna's World Tour 1990; released record How to Do That (in collaboration with Tony Mansfield) 1989; launched own perfume 1993; designed costumes for Victoria Abril in Pedro Almodóvar's film Kika 1994, film La Cité des Enfants Perdus 1995, The Fifth Element 1996, Absolutely Fabulous 2001; launched perfume brands Jean-Paul Gaultier (1993), Le Mâle (1995), Fragile (1999); Fashion Oscar 1987, Progetto Leonardo Award for How to Do That 1989; Chevalier des Arts et des Lettres. *Leisure interest:* television. *Address:* Jean-Paul Gaultier SA, 30 rue du Faubourg-Saint-Antoine, 75012 Paris, France.

GAUS, Günter; German journalist, diplomatist and politician; b. 23 Nov. 1929, Braunschweig (Brunswick); s. of Willi and Hedwig Gaus; m. Erika Butzengeiger 1955; one d.; ed Oberrealschule Braunschweig and Munich

Univ.; journalist with various daily and weekly newspapers and Second German TV 1953–65; Programme Dir Südwestfunk 1965–69; Chief Ed. Der Spiegel 1969–73; State Sec., Chancellery of Fed. Repub. of Germany, Bonn 1973; Head of Perm. Representation of Fed. Repub. of Germany, Berlin (GDR) 1974–81; Senator (Minister) for Science and Research, West Berlin Jan.–June 1981; Adolf Grimme Prize, Bronze 1964, Silver 1965; Fr.-Ebert-Stiftung Das Politische Buch des Jahres 1987; Adolf Grimme Prize: Besondere Ehrung 1988, Kritikerpreis 1990, Hans-Joachim-Friedrichs TV Prize 2001. *Publications:* Zur Person (two Vols), Bonn ohne Regierung 1965, Gespräche mit Herbert Wehner 1966, Zur Wahl gestellt 1969, Wo Deutschland liegt 1983, Deutschland und die NATO 1984, Die Welt der Westdeutschen 1986, Deutschland im Juni 1988, Wendewut 1990, Zur Person 1990, Porträts in Frage und Antwort (4 Vols) 1991–93, Zur Person (3 Vols) 1997–98, Kein einig Vaterland 1998, Was Bleibt, sind Fragen – Die klassichen Interviews 2001. *Address:* Bahnsenallee 74, 21465 Reinbek, Germany.

GAVAHI, Abdulrahim, MBA, PhD; Iranian diplomatist and international organization official; ed Abadan Inst. of Tech., Iran Center for Man. Studies; with Ministry of Oil, Govt of Iran 1979; Amb. to Sweden (also accred to Denmark, Finland, Iceland and Norway) 1980–82, to Japan 1982–84; with Ministry of Foreign Affairs 1987–89, 2000, Ministry of Int. and Econ. Affairs 1989–; Amb. to Norway 1994; Sec.-Gen. Iran Chamber of Commerce, Industries and Mines 1998; Sec.-Gen. Econ. Co-operation Org. (ECO) 2000–02. *Address:* c/o Economic Co-operation Organization, 1 Golbou Alley, Kamranieh Street, P.O. Box 14155-6176, Tehran, Iran (Office).

GAVASKAR, Sunil ('Sunny') Manohar, BA; Indian cricketer and business executive; b. 10 July 1949, Bombay (now Mumbai); s. of Manohar Keshav Gavaskar and Meenal Manohar Gavaskar; m. Marshniel Mehrotra 1974; one s.; ed St Xavier's High School, Bombay and St Xavier's College, Bombay Univ.; right-hand opening batsman; played for Mumbai 1967–87, Somerset 1980; 125 Tests for India 1970–97 (47 as Capt.), scoring 10,122 runs (average 51.1) with 34 hundreds (world record) and holding 108 catches; toured England 1971, 1974, 1975 (World Cup), 1979, 1982, 1983 (World Cup); scored 25,834 first-class runs with 81 hundreds; highest score (236 v. Australia Dec. 1983) by Indian in Test match; first player to score more than 10,000 Test runs 1987; first player to score over 2,000 runs against three countries 1987; only man to play in a hundred successive Tests; nominated to Rajya Sabha 1992; Match Referee Int. Cricket Council 1993-94; f. Sunil Gavaskar Foundation for Cricket in Bengal 1996; Chair. Int. Cricket Council Cttee, Indian Nat. Cricket Acad. 2001–; Arjuna Award 1975, Padma Bhushan 1980, both Govt of India, Wisden Cricketer of The Year 1980. *Publications:* Sunny Days – An Autobiography 1976, Idols (autobiog.) 1982, Runs 'n' Ruins 1984, One-day Wonders. *Address:* Nirlon Synthetic Fibres and Chemicals Ltd, Nirlon House, 254-B, Dr Annie Besant Road, Worli, Mumbai-18, India (Office).

GAVIN, John, BA; American actor and diplomatist; b. 8 April 1932, Los Angeles; s. of Herald Ray Gavin and Delia Diana Pablos; m. Constance Mary Towers; one s. three d.; ed Stanford Univ.; actor in feature films 1956–80; Special Adviser to Sec.-Gen. OAS 1961–74; Vice-Pres. Atlantic Richfield Co. (to head Fed. & Int. Relations Unit) 1986–87; Pres. Univisa Satellite Communications 1987–90; Pres. Gamma Services Corpn 1968–; spokesman Bank of America 1973–80; Amb. to Mexico 1981–86; Chair. the Century Council 1990–; partner Gavin, Dailey & Co. LA 1990–; consultant to Dept of State; mem. Screen Actors' Guild (Pres. 1971–73). *Films include:* A Time to Live, A Time to Die, Psycho, Midnight Lace, Backstreet, Spartacus, Thoroughly Modern Millie, Mad Woman of Chaillot, Jennifer, History of the World Part I, Seesaw (musical), Pussycat Pussycat I Love You.

GAVIRIA TRUJILLO, César; Colombian politician; b. Pereira; m. Milena Gaviria; ed Univ. of the Andes; mem. town council of Pereira; mem. Chamber of Deputies and Dir Comm. for Econ. Affairs 1972; Vice-Minister for Devt; Minister of Finance and Public Credit 1986, of the Interior 1988; Pres. of Colombia 1990–94; Sec.-Gen. OAS 1994–. *Address:* Organization of American States, 17th Street and Constitution Avenue, NW, Washington, DC 20006, USA (Office). *E-mail:* pi@oas.org (Office). *Website:* www.oas.org (Office).

GAVRIISKI, Svetoslav; Bulgarian politician and bank governor; b. 18 Dec. 1948, Svishtov; ed Univ. of Nat. and World Economy, Sofia; joined Ministry of Finance 1972, Deputy Minister of Finance 1992–97, Minister 1997; Gov. of Bulgaria to IMF 1992–96, 1997–, to IBRD, EBRD and European Investment Bank 1997–, to Black Sea Trade and Devt Bank 1998–; Leader Group Negotiations on Bulgaria's External Debt 1991–94; mem. Man. Bd Bulbank 1991–97; Gov. Bulgarian Nat. Bank 1997–; Man. mem. Int. Bank for Econ. Co-operation, Moscow 1992–, Int. Investment Bank, Moscow 1992–; mem. Bd Dirs Bank Consolidation Co. 2001–. *Address:* Bulgarska Narodna Banka, Aleksandur Battenberg Sq 1, 1000 Sofia, Bulgaria (Office). *Telephone:* (92) 91459 (Office). *Fax:* (92) 9802425 (Office). *E-mail:* press_office@bnbank.org (Office). *Website:* www.bnb.bg (Office).

GAVRILOV, Andrei Vladimirovich; Russian pianist; b. 21 Sept. 1955, Moscow; ed Moscow Conservatory; winner of the Tchaikovsky Competition in Moscow 1974; performs regularly throughout Europe, America and Japan, including recitals at Salzburg, Roque d'Antheron, Schleswig-Holstein, Istanbul and Chichester Festivals; has performed in England with the Philharmonia, London Philharmonic, Royal Philharmonic, BBC Symphony and London Symphony Orchestras, in America with the Baltimore Symphony, Detroit Symphony, New York Philharmonic and Philadelphia Orchestras; lives in Germany; disc awards include the French suites of J. S. Bach and the Etudes of Chopin; several int. prizes. *Address:* c/o Konzertdirektion Schlote, Danreitergasse 4, 5020 Salzburg, Austria.

GAVRIN, Alexander Sergeyevich; Russian politician and engineer; b. 22 July 1953, Orlovo, Zaporozhye Region, Ukraine; ed Tumen Industrial Inst., Tumen State Inst. of Oil and Gas; army service 1972–74; controller, master Zaporozhye plant Radiopribor 1974–79; controlling master Manuylsky Research Inst., Kiev 1979–80; engineer constructor Kiev plant generator 1980–81; technician Kiev production co. 1981–83; electrician Povkhneft Kogalym, Tumen Region 1983–88; engineer head of group Kogalymneftegas Co., Tumen Region 1988–89; Chair. Trade Union LUKOil-Kogalymneftegas 1989–93; Head of Admin. Kogalym. Tumen Region 1993–96; Mayor of Kogalym 1996–2000; Minister of Energy of Russian Fed. 2000–01; fmr Rep. of Tumen Region to Council of Fed., Russian Fed. Ass. *Address:* c/o Council of Federation, B. Dmitrovka Str. 26, 103426 Moscow, Russia (Office).

GAY, Peter, PhD; American professor of history; b. 20 June 1923, Berlin, Germany; s. of Morris Fröhlich and Helga Fröhlich; m. Ruth Slotkin 1959; three step-d.; ed Univ. of Denver and Columbia Univ.; left Germany 1939; Dept of Public Law and Govt, Columbia Univ. 1947–56, Dept of History 1956–69, Prof. of History 1962–69, William R. Shepherd Prof. 1967–69; Prof. of Comparative European Intellectual History, Yale Univ. 1969–, Durfee Prof. of History 1970–84, Sterling Prof. of History 1984–93, Sterling Prof. Emer. 1993–; Guggenheim Fellow 1967–68; Overseas Fellow, Churchill Coll., Cambridge, England 1970–71; Visiting Fellow, Inst. for Advanced Study, Berlin 1984; Dir Center for Scholars and Writers, New York Public Library 1997–; mem. American Historical Asscn, French Historical Soc.; Hon. DHumLitt (Denver) 1970, (Md) 1979, (Hebrew Univ. Coll., Cincinnati) 1983, (Clark Univ., Worcester) 1985; Nat. Book Award 1967, Melcher Book Award 1967, Gold Medal for Historical Science, Amsterdam 1990, Geschwister Scholl Prize 1999. *Publications:* The Dilemma of Democratic Socialism: Eduard Bernstein's Challenge to Marx 1951, Voltaire's Politics: The Poet as Realist 1959, Philosophical Dictionary 1962, The Party of Humanity: Essays in the French Enlightenment 1964, The Loss of Mastery: Puritan Historians in Colonial America 1966, The Enlightenment: An Interpretation, Vols I, II 1966, 1969, Weimar Culture: The Outsider as Insider 1969, The Bridge of Criticism: Dialogues on the Enlightenment 1970, The Question of Jean-Jacques Rousseau 1974, Modern Europe (with R. K. Webb) 1973, Style in History 1974, Art and Act: On Causes in History – Manet, Gropius, Mondrian 1976, Freud, Jews and Other Germans: Masters and Victims in Modernist Culture 1978, The Bourgeois Experience: Victoria to Freud, Vols I, II, III 1984, 1986, 1993, Freud for Historians 1985, Freud: A Life for Our Time 1988, A Freud Reader 1989, Reading Freud: Explorations and Entertainments 1990, The Cultivation of Hatred 1993, The Naked Heart 1995, Pleasure Wars 1998, My German Question: Growing Up in Nazi Berlin 1998, Mozart 1999, Schnitzler's Century 2001, Savage Reprisals 2002; also translations and anthologies. *Leisure interests:* reading, listening to music. *Address:* 760 West End Avenue, Apt 15A, New York, NY 10025, USA (Home). *Telephone:* (212) 930-9257 (Office); (212) 865-0577 (Home). *Fax:* (212) 930-0040 (Office). *E-mail:* pgay@nypl.org.

GAYAN, Anil Kumarsingh, LLB, LLM; Mauritius politician and lawyer; b. 22 Oct. 1948; m. Sooryakanti Nirsimloo; three c.; ed Royal Coll., Port Louis, London School of Econs; called to the Bar, Inner Temple, London 1972; mem. Mauritius Bar and Seychelles Bar 1972–73, pvt. practice 1973–74, 1982, 1986–90, 1995–2000; Chair. Bar Council 1989–90; joined Chambers of Mauritius Attorney Gen. as Crown Counsel 1974, Sr Counsel 1995; Del. to UN Conf. on the Law of the Sea 1974–82; mem. Parl. 1982–86, Minister of External Affairs, Tourism and Emigration 1983–86, Foreign Affairs and Regional Co-operation Sept. 2000–; Chair. Council of Univ. of Mauritius 1983; Consultant for Geneva-based Centre for Human Rights, consultancy work in Bhutan, Mongolia, Armenia and Togo 1991. *Address:* Ministry of Foreign Affairs and Regional Co-operation, New Government Centre, Level 5, Port Louis, Mauritius (Office). *Telephone:* 201-1648 (Office). *Fax:* 208-8087. *E-mail:* mfa@mail.gov.mu. *Website:* foreign.gov.mu (Office).

GAYDAR, Yegor Timurovich, DSc(Econs); Russian politician; b. 19 March 1956, Moscow; s. of Timur Gaydar and Ariadna (Bajova) Gaydar; m. 2nd Maria Strugatskaya 1986; three s.; ed Moscow State Univ.; journalist Kommunist and Pravda 1987–90; Dir Inst. of Econ. Policy of USSR (now Russian) Acad. of Sciences 1990–91; Deputy Chair. Russian Govt (and co-ordinator of the 13 ministries responsible for econ. affairs) 1991–92; Acting Chair. Russian Govt June–Dec. 1992; Dir Inst. for the Economy in Transition 1992–93, 1994–; Adviser to Pres. Yeltsin on Econ. Reform 1992–93; First Deputy Chair. Russian Govt 1993–94, Minister of Econ. 1993–94; Head Political Bloc, Russian Choice (Vibor Rossii) 1993–94; Founder and Leader Democratic Choice of Russia Party 1994–; mem. State Duma (Parl.) 1993–95, 1999–; joined right-wing coalition Pravoye Delo 1999; mem. faction Union of Right-Wing Forces. *Publications:* State and Evolution 1994, Anomalies of Economic Growth 1995, Days of Defeats and Victories 1996; articles in scientific journals and newspapers. *Address:* Institute for the Economy in Transition, Gazetny per. 5, 111024 Moscow, Russia. *Telephone:* (095) 229-64-13. *Fax:* (095) 229-64-48.

GAYDON, Alfred Gordon, DSc, FRS; British physicist; b. 26 Sept. 1911, Hampton Wick; s. of Alfred Bert Gaydon and Rosetta Juliet Gordon; m. Phyllis Maude Gaze 1940 (died 1981); one s. one d.; ed Kingston Grammar School, Kingston-upon-Thames, Imperial Coll., London; Warren Research Fellow of Royal Soc. 1945–74; Prof. of Molecular Spectroscopy, Imperial Coll. of Science and Tech., London 1961–73, Prof. Emer. 1973–, Fellow 1980; worked on molecular spectra and on measurement of high temperatures, on spectra and structure of flames and shock waves; Dr hc (Dijon) 1957; Rumford Medal, Royal Soc. 1960, Bernard Lewis Gold Medal, Combustion Inst. 1960. *Publications:* Identification of Molecular Spectra (with R. W. B. Pearse) 1941, Spectroscopy and Combustion Theory 1942, Dissociation Energies and Spectra of Diatomic Molecules 1947, Flames, their Structure, Radiation and Temperature (with H. G. Wolfhard) 1953, The Spectroscopy of Flames 1957, The Shock Tube in High-temperature Chemical Physics (with I. Hurle) 1963. *Leisure interests:* wildlife photography and fmrly rowing. *Address:* Dale Cottage, Shellbridge Road, Slindon Common, Near Arundel, West Sussex, BN18 0LT, England. *Telephone:* (1243) 814277.

GAYER, Yevdokiya Alexandrovna, CAND.HIST.SC.; Russian/Nanai ethnographer and politician; b. 8 March 1934, Podali, Khabarovsk Territory; m. (husband deceased); two s.; ed in Vladivostok; researcher Inst. of History, Archaeology and Ethnography Far E br. of USSR Acad. of Sciences in Vladivostok 1969–89; USSR People's Deputy, mem. Soviet of Nationalities, mem. Comm. on Problems of Int. Relations and Nat. Policy 1989–92; adviser to Pres. 1992–; Deputy Chair. State Cttee on Social-Econ. Devt of the North 1993–; mem. Council of Fed. of Russia 1993–96; Deputy Chair. Comm. of the North and Indigenous Peoples 1996–2000; Sec.-Gen. Int. League of Small Nations and Ethnic Groups 1996–; Chief Adviser State Cttee on Problems of Devt of North Territories (later Cttee on Northern, Siberian and Far Eastern Affairs, Council of Fed.) 1997–98; Prof. Int. Acad. of Marketing and Man. (Mamarmen); mem. Presidium Russian Acad. of Natural Sciences; mem. Acad. of Information Science, Acad. of Polar Medicine. *Address:* Rublyovskoye Sh. 3, korp. 2, Apt. 388, 121609 Moscow, Russia. *Telephone:* (095) 413-76-95.

GAYOOM, Maumoon Abdul, MA; Maldivian politician; b. 29 Dec. 1937, Malé; m. Nasreena Ibrahim 1969; two s. two d.; ed Al-Azhar Univ., Cairo; Research Asst in Islamic History, American Univ. of Cairo 1967–69; Lecturer in Islamic Studies and Philosophy, Abdullahi Bayero Coll., Ahmadu Bello Univ., Nigeria 1969–71; Teacher, Aminiya School 1971–72; Man. Govt Shipping Dept 1972–73; Writer and Trans. Press Office 1972–73, 1974; Under-Sec. Telecommunications Dept 1974; Dir Telephone Dept 1974; Special Under-Sec. Office of the Prime Minister 1974–75; Deputy Amb. to Sri Lanka 1975–76; Under-Sec. Dept of External Affairs 1976; Perm. Rep. to UN 1976–77; Deputy Minister of Transport 1976, Minister 1977–78; Pres. of Repub. of Maldives and C-in-C of the Armed Forces 1978–; Gov. Maldives Monetary Authority 1981–; Minister of Defence and Nat. Security 1982–; Minister of Finance 1989–93; Minister of Finance and Treasury 1993–; mem. Constituent Council of Rabitat Al-Alam Al-Islami; Hon. DLitt (Aligarh Muslim Univ. of India) 1983; Hon. DrLit (Jamia Millia Islamia Univ., India) 1990; Hon. DLit (Pondicherry Univ.) 1994; Global 500 Honour Roll (UN Environment Progamme) 1988; Grand Order of Mugunghawa 1984; Man of the Sea Award (Lega Navale Italiana) 1991; Hon. GCMG 1997; WHO Health-for-All Gold Medal 1998; DRV Int. Environment Award 1998; Al-Azhar Univ. Shield 2002. *Publication:* The Maldives: A Nation in Peril. *Leisure interests:* astronomy, calligraphy, photography, badminton, cricket. *Address:* The President's Office, Boduthakurufaanu Magu, Malé (Office); Ma. Ki'nbigasdhoshuge, Malé, 20-02 (Home); The Presidential Palace (Theemuge), Orchid Magu, Malé, 20-02, Maldives (Official Residence). *Telephone:* 323701. *Fax:* 325500. *E-mail:* horizen@dhivehinet.net.mv (Office). *Website:* presidencymaldives.gov.mv (Office).

GAYSSOT, Jean-Claude; French politician and trade unionist; b. 6 Sept. 1944, Béziers (Hérault); m. Jacqueline Guiter 1963; three c.; ed Lycée Technique, Béziers; worked as technician, SNCF (French state railways); official in Railworkers' Union, then in Conféd. générale du travail (CGT) 1976–79; mem. Parti Communiste Français 1963–, mem. Nat. Secr. 1985–, head dept for relations with other political parties and trade union and community movt 1994–; elected municipal councillor, Bobigny (Seine-Saint-Denis) 1977; Nat. Ass. Deputy for 5th Seine-Saint-Denis Constituency 1986–97; Minister for Public Works, Transport and Housing 1997–2002; Mayor of Drancy 1997–2002; Trombinoscope Prize for Minister of the Year 2000. *Publications:* Le Parti communiste française 1989, Sur ma route 2000. *Address:* Parti Communiste Français, 2 place du Colonel Fabien, 75940 Paris, France.

GAZENKO, Lt-Gen. Oleg Georgievich, PhD, MD; Russian physiologist; b. 12 Dec. 1918, Nikolayevka, Stavropol territory; m.; one s. one d.; ed Moscow Medical Inst; service in the Army 1941–46; Research Assoc. Kirov Mil. Medical Acad. 1946–47; USSR Acad. of Sciences Inst. of Experimental Medicine 1947–69, Dir Inst. of Medical and Biological Problems 1969–88; Consultant 1988–; mem. CPSU 1953–91; Corresp. mem. USSR (now Russian) Acad. of Sciences 1966, mem. 1976–; mem. Int. Acad. of Astronautics, Aerospace Medical Asscn; Corresp. mem. American Physiological Soc. 1979–; Pres. USSR (now Russian) Nat. Physiological Soc. 1983–91; People's Deputy of the USSR 1989; Ed.-in-Chief Space Biology and Medicine; mem. New York Acad. of Sciences; Order of Lenin, Daniel and Florence Guggenheim Int. Astronautics Award 1975. *Publications:* works on experimental physiology and space medicine; co-author Mankind and Outer Space 1990; Co-Ed. Foundations of Space Biology and Medicine (USA–USSR jt publ). *Leisure interests:* mountaineering, canoeing. *Address:* Institute of Medical and Biological Problems, Khroshevskoye sh. 76A, 123007 Moscow, Russia. *Telephone:* (095) 195-02-33.

GAZIT, Maj.-Gen. Shlomo; Israeli army officer and administrator; b. 1926, Turkey; s. of Efrayim and Zippora Gazit; m. Avigayil-Gala Gazit; one s. two d.; ed Tel Aviv Univ.; joined Palmach 1944, Co. Commdr Harel Brigade 1948; Dir Office of Chief of Staff 1953; Liaison Officer with French Army Del., Sinai Campaign 1956; Instructor Israel Defence Forces (IDF) Staff and Command Coll. 1958–59; Gen. Staff 1960–61; Deputy Commdr Golani Brigade 1961–62; Instructor Nat. Defence Coll. 1962–64; Head IDF Intelligence assessment div. 1964–67; Co-ordinator of Govt Activities in Administered Territories, Ministry of Defence 1967–74; rank of Maj.-Gen. 1973; Head of Mil. Intelligence 1974–79; Fellow at Center for Int. Affairs, Harvard Univ. 1979–80; Pres. Ben Gurion Univ. of the Negev 1981–85; Dir-Gen. Jewish Agency, Jerusalem 1985–88; Sr Research Fellow Jaffee Centre for Strategic Studies, Tel Aviv Univ. 1988–94; Fellow Woodrow Wilson Center, Washington, DC 1989–90; Distinguished Fellow U.S. Inst. of Peace, Washington, DC 1994–95; Adviser to Israeli Prime Minister on Palestinian Peace Process 1995–96; Chair. Galili Centre for Defence-Hagana Studies 1996–. *Publications:* Estimates and Fortune-Telling in Intelligence Work 1980, Early Attempts at Establishing West Bank Autonomy 1980, Insurgency, Terrorism and Intelligence 1980, On Hostages' Rescue Operations 1981, The Carrot and the Stick – Israel's Military Govt in Judea and Samaria 1985, The Third Way – The Way of No Solution 1987, Policies in the Administered Territories 1988, Intelligence Estimates and the Decision Maker 1988, (ed.) The Middle East Military Balance 1988–89, 1990–91, 1993–94, Trapped: 30 Years of Israeli Policy in Judea, Samaria and Gaza Strip 1999. *Address:* 20 Tarpad Street, Ramat Hasharon 47250 (Home); The Galili Centre for Defence-Hagana Studies, 1 Hayasmin Street, Ramal Ef'al 52960, Israel (Office). *Telephone:* (3) 6407719 (Office); (3) 5492077 (Home). *Fax:* (3) 6422404 (Office); (3) 5440764 (Home). *E-mail:* jcsssg@post.tau.ac.il (Office).

GAZIZULLIN, Farit Rafikovich, C.PHIL.SC., DSc; Russian/Tatar politician; b. 20 Sept. 1946, Zelenodolsk, Tatar ASSR; m.; one s.; ed Gorky (now Nizhny Novgorod) Inst. of Water Transport Eng; engineer Zelenodolsk 1965–67; Comsomol and CP work 1967–87; Head of Dept, First Deputy Chair., State Planning Cttee Tatar Autonomous Repub. 1987–95; Vice-Prime Minister of Tatarstan, Chair. State Cttee on Property 1995–96; First Deputy Chair., Cttee on State Property of Russian Fed. 1996–97; Deputy Chair., Govt of Russian Fed. 1997–98; Minister of State Property (temporarily Ministry of Property Relations) 1997–; Chair. Bd of Dirs Gazprom 1998–99, Adviser 1999–. *Address:* Ministry of State Property, Nikolsky per. 9, 102132 Moscow, Russia. *Telephone:* (095) 298-77-11; 206-15-73 (Office).

GAZZAR, Abdel Hadi el; Egyptian artist; b. 1925; ed Cairo and Rome Acad. of Fine Arts; Prof. of Painting, Cairo Faculty of Fine Arts; rep. at numerous exhbns, including the 28th and 30th Venice Biennale, Brussels Int. Exhbn 1958 and São Paulo Bienale 1961; exhbns in Cairo, Alexandria and Rome; First Prize '10 Years of the Revolution' Exhbn 1962. *Address:* Faculty of Fine Arts, Cairo University, Cairo, Egypt.

GBAGBO, Laurent, MA, PhD; Côte d'Ivoire politician; b. 31 May 1945, Central-Western Prov.; m.; four c.; ed Univ. of Lyon, Sorbonne, Paris VII Univ.; taught history and geography at Lycée Classique d'Abidjan 1970–71; imprisoned for unauthorised political activities 1971–73; worked in Dept of Educ. 1973–79; exile in France 1982–88; f. Front populaire Ivoirien (FPI) in secret 1982, FPI Sec.-Gen. 1988; mem. Parl. 1990; arrested Feb. 1992, sentenced to three years' imprisonment under anti-riot law, granted presidential pardon Aug. 1992; Pres. of Côte d'Ivoire Oct. 2000–. *Address:* Office of the President, 01 B.P. 1354 Abidjan, Côte d'Ivoire (Office). *Telephone:* 20-22-02-22 (Office). *Fax:* 20-21-14-25. *Website:* www.pr.ci (Office).

GBEZERA-BRIA, Michel, BL; Central African Republic politician and diplomatist; b. 1946, Bossongoa; m.; five c.; ed Brazzaville School of Law, Caen School of Econs and Int. Inst. of Public Admin.; with civil service 1973–, Vice-Minister Sec.-in-charge of diplomatic missions 1975; Deputy Minister of Foreign Affairs 1976; Minister of Public Works, Labour and Social Security 1976–77, of Foreign Affairs 1977–78, of Public Works and Social Security 1978–79; State Comptroller 1979–80, Perm. Rep. to UN, Geneva 1980–83, New York 1983–89; Minister of Justice 1987–88, of Foreign Affairs 1988–90; Prime Minister of Cen. African Repub. 1997–99; Dir Econ. Man. Project 1991–. *Address:* c/o Office of the Prime Minister, Bangui, Central African Republic.

GDLYAN, Telman Khorenovich; Russian/Armenian prosecutor and politician; b. 20 Dec. 1940, Samsar, Georgia; m. Susanna Aramovna Gdlyan; one s. one d.; ed Saratov Inst. of Law; mem. CPSU 1962–90, when expelled; investigator Ulyanovsk Dist 1968–83, investigator for important cases of corruption in Uzbekistan, Office of Public Prosecutor of USSR 1983–90; successfully prosecuted mems. of political establishment of Uzbekistan for corruption; USSR People's Deputy 1989–91; mem. Armenian Supreme Soviet 1990–; f. and Chair. People's Party of Russia 1990; expelled from Prosecutor's Office 1990, reinstated 1991; founder and Pres. All-Russian Fund of Progress, Defence of Human Rights and Charity; mem. State Duma (Parl.) 1995–99. *Publications:* Piramide, Mafia in Times of Lawlessness, Kremlin Case. *Address:* People's Party, Novy Arbat 15, 121012, Moscow, Russia. *Telephone:* (095) 202-01-09.

GE WUJUE; Chinese writer; b. 12 Sept. 1937, Wenzhou, Zhejiang; s. of Ge Luyan and Zhang Wencang; m. Zhao Baoqing 1962 (divorced); one s.; ed Beijing Univ.; worked as journalist for over 20 years; published first book 1961; in political disgrace 1963–77; some works translated into English,

French and Japanese; Vice-Chair. Fed. of Art and Literature, Ningxia and Ningxia Branch of Union of Chinese Writers. *Publications:* The Wedding, A Journalist and Her Story, An Experience in the Summer, She and her Girl Friend, The Golden Deer, A View of an Ancient Ferry (short stories), Meditate on the Past (novel), Years and Man (novel), Going to the Ancient Ferry on Today (TV Drama), Four Days in All of Life 1988 (short stories), The Earth. The Moon (novel), The Passport on the Earth, Zhang Daqian in Dunhuan (TV drama) 1991, Quality of Life (reportage) 1995, Tango Rumba (screenplay) 1996. *Leisure interests:* sports, music, drawing, calligraphy. *Address:* 268-9 Bailidong Road, Wenzhou, Zhejiang, People's Republic of China. *Telephone:* (577) 8282374 (Office); (577) 8525866 (Home).

GE YOU; Chinese actor; b. 1957; Beijing; joined All-China Fed. of Trade Unions Art Troupe 1979; Best Actor Award for To Live (Cannes). *Films include:* Farewell My Concubine. *Address:* All-China Federation of Trade Unions Art Troupe, Beijing, People's Republic of China.

GEACH, Peter (Thomas), MA, FBA; British professor of logic; b. 29 March 1916, London; s. of George Hender Geach and Eleonora Frederyka Adolfina Sgonina; m. Gertrude Elizabeth Margaret Anscombe 1941 (died 2001); three s. four d.; ed Balliol Coll. Oxford; Gladstone Research Student, St Deiniol's Library 1938–39; postgrad. studies Cambridge Univ. with Profs Wittgenstein and Von Wright; Asst Lecturer, Lecturer, Sr Lecturer, then Reader in Logic, Univ. of Birmingham 1951–65; Prof. of Logic, Univ. of Leeds 1965–81, Prof. Emer. 1981–; Foreign mem. American Acad. of Arts and Sciences 1987; Alexander von Humboldt Prize 1984, Papal Medal, Pro Ecclesia et Pontifice 1999. *Publications:* Mental Acts 1957, Reference and Generality 1962, God and the Soul 1969, Providence and Evil 1977, The Virtues 1977, Truth, Love and Immortality 1979, Logic Matters 1980, Truth and Hope 2001. *Leisure interests:* reading thrillers, reading and marginally annotating bad old logic books. *Address:* 3 Richmond Road, Cambridge, CB4 3PP, England. *Telephone:* (1223) 353950.

GEBRSELASSIE, Haile; Ethiopian athlete; b. 18 April 1973, Arssi; m. 1996; two c.; set 14 world records or best times indoors and outdoors 1994–98, including world 5,000m and 10,000m records 1997, 1998; silver medal World Jr Cross Country Championships 1992; gold medals World Jr Championships 5,000m and 10,000m 1992; silver medal World Championships 5,000m 1993; gold medal World Championships 10,000m 1995, 1997; gold medal World Indoor Championships 3,000m 1995; gold medal Olympic Games 10,000m 1996, 2000; winner IAAF World Half-Marathon Championship, England 2001; 5,000m (indoor and outdoor), 10,000m, 10km road race world record holder (as at end 2002); indoor record holder for two miles Feb. 2003; IAAF Athlete of the Year 1998. *Leisure interests:* boxing, soccer. *Address:* Waterdelweg 14, 5427 LS Boehel 98007, Monaco.

GEDDA, Nicolai; Swedish operatic tenor; b. 11 July 1925, Stockholm; s. of Michael Ustinov and Olga Ustinov (née Gedda); m. Anastasia Caraviotis 1965; one s. one d.; ed Musical Acad., Stockholm; debut, Stockholm 1952; concert appearances Rome 1952, Paris 1953, 1955, Vienna 1955, Aix-en-Provence 1954, 1955; first operatic performances in Munich, Lucerne, Milan and Rome 1953, Paris, London and Vienna 1954; Salzburg Festival 1957–59, Edin. Festival 1958–59; with Metropolitan Opera, NY 1957–, Tokyo Opera 1975–; worldwide appearances in opera, concerts and recitals; numerous recordings. *Address:* Valhallavagen 110, 114 41 Stockholm, Sweden.

GEE, Maggie, PhD, BLitt, FRSL; British author, journalist and lecturer; b. 2 Nov. 1948, Poole; d. of V. V. Gee and Aileen Gee (née Church); m. Nicholas Rankin 1983; one d.; ed Horsham High School, Somerville Coll., Oxford; Writing Fellow Univ. of E Anglia 1982; Visiting Fellow Sussex Univ. 1986–, Teaching Fellow 1996–; Writer-in-Residence Northern Arts 1996; regular reviews in Daily Telegraph, Times Literary Supplement, Sunday Times; judge Booker Prize 1989; mem. Man. Cttee Soc. of Authors 1991–94, mem. Council 1999–; Hawthornden Fellow 1989; Best of Young British Novelists 1982. *Publications:* (novels) Dying in Other Words 1981, The Burning Book 1983, Light Years 1985, Grace 1988, Where are the Snows 1991, Lost Children 1994, The Ice People 1998, The White Family 2002. *Leisure interests:* visual arts, swimming, walking, film, theatre. *Address:* c/o David Godwin Associates, 55 Monmouth Street, London, WC2H 9DG, England (Office); c/o Society of Authors, 84 Drayton Gardens, London SW10 9SB. *Telephone:* (20) 7240-9992 (Office). *Fax:* (20) 7395-6110 (Office).

GEE, Maurice Gough, MA; New Zealand novelist; b. 22 Aug. 1931, Whakatane; m. Margaretha Garden 1970; one s. two d.; ed Avondale Coll., Auckland, Auckland Univ.; school teacher, librarian, other casual employment 1954–75; Robert Burns Fellow Univ. of Otago 1964; Writing Fellow Vic. Univ. of Wellington 1989; Katherine Mansfield Memorial Fellow, Menton, France 1992; Hon. DLitt (Vic.) 1987; NZ Fiction Award 1976, 1979, 1982, 1991; NZ Book of the Year Award (Wattie Award) 1979, 1993; James Tait Black Memorial Prize 1979; NZ Children's Book of the Year Award 1986, 1995. *Publications include:* The Plumb Trilogy 1978–84, Prowlers 1987, The Burning Boy 1990, Going West 1992, Crime Story 1994, Loving Ways 1996, Live Bodies 1998, Collected Stories 1986; for children: Under the Mountain 1979, The O Trilogy 1982–85, The Fat Man 1994; also scripts for film and TV. *Address:* 41 Chelmsford Street, Ngaio, Wellington, New Zealand.

GEERTZ, Clifford, PhD; American anthropologist; b. 23 Aug. 1926, San Francisco; s. of Clifford James Geertz and Lois Geertz (née Brieger); m. 1st Hildred Storey 1948 (divorced 1981); m. 2nd Karen Blu; one s. one d.; ed

Antioch Coll., Harvard Univ.; Asst Prof. of Anthropology, Univ. of Calif. 1958–60; Asst Prof., then Prof. Dept of Anthropology, Univ. of Chicago 1960–70, mem. Cttee for Comparative Study of New Nations 1962–70; Prof. of Social Science, Inst. for Advanced Study 1970–, Harold F. Linder Prof. of Social Science 1982–2000, Prof. Emer. 2000–); field work in Java 1952–54, 1986, Bali 1957–58, Morocco 1965–66, 1985–86; Fellow NAS, American Philosophical Soc., American Acad. of Arts and Sciences; Corresp. FBA. *Publications:* The Religion of Java 1960, Person, Time and Conduct in Bali 1966, Local Knowledge 1983, Works and Lives 1988 (Nat. Book Critics Circle Award for Criticism), After the Fact 1995, Available Light 2000 and others. *Address:* Institute for Advanced Study, Princeton, NJ 08540, USA. *Telephone:* (609) 734-8000.

GEFFEN, David; American film, recording and theatre executive; b. 21 Feb. 1943, Brooklyn, New York; s. of Abraham Geffen and Batya (Volovskaya) Geffen; ed New Utrecht High School, Brooklyn; joined William Morris talent agency as mail clerk 1964, promoted to jr agent; launched new film studio with Steven Spielberg (q.v.) and Jeffrey Katzenberg (q.v.); f. music publishing co. Tunafish Music, with Laura Nyro; joined Ashley Famous Agency, then apptd Exec. Vice-Pres. Creative Man. (now Int. Creative Man.) 1968; f. Asylum Records and Geffen-Roberts Man. Co. with Elliot Roberts 1970; sold Asylum to Warner Communications, but remained Pres. 1971, merged it with Elektra, signed up Bob Dylan and Joni Mitchell, Vice-Chair. Warner Brothers Pictures 1975–76; f. Geffen Records, Pres. 1980–, signed up Elton John, John Lennon and Yoko Ono and many others, sold label to Music Corpn of America Inc. 1990; f. Geffen Film Co., produced Little Shop of Horrors, Beetlejuice 1988, Men Don't Leave, Defending Your Life; Co-Producer musical Dreamgirls 1981–85, Little Shop of Horrors, Cats 1982, M. Butterfly 1986, Social Security, Chess 1990, Miss Saigon; f. DGC record label, co-f. Dreamworks SKG 1995–. *Address:* Dreamworks SKG, 100 Universal City Plaza, Building 477, Universal City, CA 91608, USA.

GEGHMAN, Yahya Hamoud; Yemeni diplomatist; b. 24 Sept. 1934, Jahanah; s. of Hamoud Geghman and Ezziya Geghman; m. Cathya Geghman 1971; one s. one d.; ed Law Schools, Cairo, Paris, Damascus and Boston and Columbia Univs; Teacher of Arabic Language and Literature, Kuwait 1957–59; Dir-Gen. Yemen Broadcasting System 1962–63; Gov. Yemen Bank for Reconstruction and Devt 1962–63; Sec.-Gen. Supreme Council for Tribal Affairs 1962–63; Special Adviser, Ministry of Foreign Affairs 1962–63; Deputy Perm. Rep. to UN 1963–66, 1967–68; Minister Plenipotentiary, Yemen Arab Repub. Embassy to USA 1963–67; Minister of Foreign Affairs 1968–69; Minister of State, Personal Rep. of the Pres. 1969; Deputy Prime Minister, Pres. Supreme Council for Youth Welfare and Sport 1969–71; Perm. Rep. to UN 1971–73; Amb. to USA 1972–74; Minister for Foreign Affairs 1974–75; Deputy Prime Minister for Econ. and Foreign Affairs 1975–76; Personal Rep. of Pres. of the Repub. 1977–85; Chief, Bureau of South Yemen Affairs and Chair. Yemen Reunification Comms 1980–83; Amb. to Switzerland and Perm. Rep. to UN in Vienna and UNIDO 1985–90; Perm. Rep. to UN European HQ and Int. Orgs, Geneva, 1985–; Gov. and Exec. Dir UN Common Fund for Commodities, Amsterdam 1989–; mem. Governing Council, UN Compensation Comm. 1991; Pres. Diplomatic Cttee on Host Country Relations 1991. *Publications:* articles on politics, economics and literature, poems. *Leisure interests:* reading, horseback riding, swimming, writing, chess, music. *Address:* Permanent Mission of the Republic of Yemen, 19 chemin du Jonc, 1216 Cointrin, Geneva, Switzerland. *Telephone:* 798-53-33.

GEHRING, Gillian Anne, DPhil, MA, FInstP; British professor of physics; b. 19 May 1941, Nottingham; d. of H.L. (Max) Murray and F. Joan Murray; m. Karl A. Gehring 1968; two d.; ed Univs. of Manchester and Oxford; Leverhulme Postdoctoral Research Fellowship, St Hugh's Coll. Oxford 1965–67; NATO Fellowship, Univ. of Calif. (Berkeley) 1967–68; Fellow and Tutor in Physics, St Hugh's Coll. Oxford 1968–70; CUF lecturer in Theoretical Physics, Univ. of Oxford 1970–89; Prof. of Solid State Physics, Univ. of Sheffield 1989–. *Publications:* research papers on theoretical condensed matter physics. *Leisure interests:* family activities. *Address:* Department of Physics, University of Sheffield, Sheffield, S10 2TN (Office); 27 Lawson Road, Broomhill, Sheffield, S10 5BU, England (Home). *Telephone:* (114) 2768555 (Office); (114) 2682238 (Home). *E-mail:* cics@shef.ac.uk (Office). *Website:* www.shef.ac.uk (Office).

GEHRING, Walter Jakob, PhD; Swiss professor of genetics and developmental biology; b. 20 March 1939, Zurich; s. of late Jakob Gehring and of Marcelle Gehring-Rebmann; m. Elisabeth Lott 1964; two s.; ed Realgymnasium, Zürich, Univ. of Zürich and Yale Univ., USA; Assoc. Prof., Depts. of Anatomy and Molecular Biophysics, Yale Univ. 1969–72; Prof. of Genetics and Developmental Biology, Dept of Cell Biology, Univ. of Basel 1972–; Foreign mem. Royal Soc. 1997; Otto Naegeli Prize, Prix Charles-Leopold, Warren Triennial Prize, Prix Louis Jeantet de médecine, Gairdner Int. Award, Kyoto Prize 2000. *Publications:* Zoologie (with R. Wehner) 1990, Master Control Genes in Development and Evolution: The Homeobox Story; over 160 publs. *Leisure interests:* bird watching, photography. *Address:* Biozentrum, University of Basel, Department of Cell Biology, Klingelbergstrasse 70, 4056 Basel (Office); Hochfeldstrasse 32, 4106 Therwil, Switzerland (Home). *Telephone:* (61) 2672051 (Office); (61) 7213593 (Home). *Fax:* (61) 2672078.

GEHRY, Frank Owen; American architect; b. 29 Feb. 1929, Toronto, Canada; s. of Irving Gehry and Thelma Caplan; m. Berta Aguilera 1975; two s.; two d. (from previous m.); ed Univ. of Southern California and Harvard Univ.; designer, Victor Gruen Asscn Los Angeles 1953–54, planning, design and project Dir 1958–61; project designer, planner, Pereira & Luckman, LA 1957–58; Prin. Frank O Gehry & Assocs., Santa Monica, Calif. 1962–; architect for Temporary Contemporary Museum 1983, Calif. Aerospace Museum 1984, Loyola Law School 1981–84, Frances Howard Goldwyn Regional Br. Library 1986, Information and Computer Science Eng Research Facility, Univ. of Calif. Irvine 1986, Vitra Furniture Mfg Facility and Design Museum, Germany 1989, Chiat/Day HQ, Venice, Calif. 1991, American Center, Paris 1992–94, Weisman Art Museum, Minneapolis 1993, Disney Ice, Anaheim 1995, EMR Communication & Tech. Centre, Bad Oeynhausen, Germany 1995, Team Disneyland Admin., Anaheim 1996, ING Office Bldg, Prague 1996, Guggenheim Museum, Bilbao 1997, Experience Music Project, Seattle 2000; Fellow, American Inst. of Architects; Charlotte Davenport Chair. Yale Univ. 1982, 1985; Eliot Noyes Design Chair. Harvard 1984; Arnold W. Brunner Memorial Architecture Prize 1983, Pritzker Architecture Prize 1989, shared Wolf Prize 1992, Imperial Prize (Japan) 1992; Lillian Gish Award 1994, Gold Medal of Inst. of Architects 1999. *Publications:* Individual Imagination and Cultural Conservatism 1995. *Address:* Frank O. Gehry & Associates, 1520-B Cloverfield Boulevard, Santa Monica, CA 90404, USA. *Telephone:* (310) 828-6088.

GEIDUSCHEK, E(rnest) Peter, PhD; American scientist and professor of biology; b. 11 April 1928, Vienna, Austria; s. of Sigmund Geiduschek and Frieda Tauber; m. Joyce B. Brous 1955; two s.; ed Columbia and Harvard Univs.; Instructor in Chem. Yale Univ. 1952–53, 1955–57; Asst Prof. of Chem., Univ. of Mich. 1957–59; Asst Prof. of Biophysics and Research Assoc. in Biochemistry, Univ. of Chicago 1959–62, Assoc. Prof. of Biophysics and Research Assoc. in Biochemistry 1962–64, Prof. of Biophysics and Research Assoc. in Biochemistry 1964–70; Prof. of Biology, Univ. of Calif., San Diego 1970–94, Chair. 1981–83, (acting) 1994, Research Prof. of Biology 1994–; mem. Bd of Scientific Counselors, Nat. Cancer Inst., NIH 1998–; EMBO Lecturer 1977, Hilleman Lecturer, Univ. of Chicago 1978, Paul Doty Lecturer, Harvard Univ. 1993, Adriano Buzzati-Traverso Lecture, Rome 1996; Jean Weigle Lecture, Geneva 2001; Lalor Foundation Faculty Fellow, Yale 1957, Guggenheim Fellow, Inst. de Biologie Moléculaire, Geneva 1964–65; Fellow AAAS, Acad. of Microbiology (USA); mem. NAS, American Acad. of Arts and Sciences; Grande Ufficiale, Ordine al Merito della Repubblica Italiana. *Publications:* numerous articles on molecular biology, biochemistry and virology. *Address:* University of California, San Diego, Division of Biological Sciences, Center for Molecular Genetics (0634), 9500 Gilman Drive, La Jolla, CA 92093-0634, USA. *Telephone:* (858) 534-3029. *Fax:* (858) 534-7073.

GEIGER, Helmut; German banker and lawyer; b. 12 June 1928, Nuremberg; m.; one s. one d.; ed Univs. of Erlangen and Berlin; legal asst Deutsche Bundestag and asst lawyer, Bonn 1957–59; lawyer in Bonn and man. of office of Öffentliche Bausparkassen 1959–66; Man. Dir Deutsche Sparkassen-und Giroverband 1966–72, Pres. 1972–93; Pres. Int. Inst. der Sparkassen (Int. Savings Bank Inst.), Geneva 1978–84; Pres. EEC Savings Banks Group, Brussels 1985–88; Chair. Sparkassenstiftung für Int. Kooperation 1992–98; mem. Bundestag 1965; mem. Admin. Bd Deutsche Girozentrale Int., Luxembourg, Kreditanstalt für Wiederaufbau, Frankfurt, Landwirtschaftliche Rentenbank, Frankfurt, Rhineland-Westphalian Inst. of Econ. Research, Essen; mem. Cen. Cttee, German Group, ICC; mem. Presidium, German Red Cross; Chair. and mem. of various charitable and professional bodies; Dr hc (Cologne); Grand Fed. Cross of Merit. *Publications:* Herausforderungen für Stabilität und Fortschritt 1974, Bankpolitik 1975, Gespräche über Geld 1986, Die deutsche Sparkassenorganisation 1992 and numerous publs on banking matters. *Address:* Buschstrasse 32, 53113 Bonn, Germany. *Telephone:* (228) 9703610.

GEIMAN, Leonid Mikhailovich, DrTechSci; Russian scientific publisher; b. 12 Aug. 1934, Moscow; ed Moscow Ore Inst.; researcher ore industry research Orgs; Head of Div. Publishers' Sovietskaya Encyclopaedia 1963–88; Prof. Moscow Ore Inst.; researcher All-Union Inst. of Foreign Geology; f. Ind. Encyclopaedic Ed. House (ETA); Pres. Encyclopaedic Creative Asscn; mem. Russian Acad. of Natural Sciences 1992, Academician-Sec. Dept of Encyclopaedia. *Publications:* Russian Encyclopaedia of Banks 1995, Russian Nat. Electronic Encyclopaedia 1995, Encyclopaedia of Moscow Streets 1996, Encyclopaedia America 1997. *Address:* Russian Academy of Natural Sciences, Varshavskoye shosse 8, 113105 Moscow, Russia (Office). *Telephone:* (095) 954-26-11 (Office).

GEINGOB, Hage Gottfried, MA; Namibian politician; b. 3 Aug. 1941, Grootfontein Dist; m. Loine Kandume 1993; one s. three d. from previous marriage; ed Augustineum Coll. Okahandja and studies in int. relations in USA; joined South-West Africa People's Org. (SWAPO) 1962; teacher, Tsumeb 1962; exiled for political activities Dec. 1962; became SWAPO Asst Rep. Botswana 1963–64; subsequently moved to USA, studied at Fordham Univ. and New School for Social Research, New York and became SWAPO Rep. at UN –1971; mem. SWAPO Politburo 1975; Dir UN Inst. for Namibia, Lusaka, Zambia 1975–89; returned to Namibia as Election Dir 1989; Chair. Constituent Ass. and Namibia Independence Celebrations Cttee 1989; Prime Minister of Namibia 1990–; Hon. LLD (Col Coll., Chicago) 1994; Officier Palmes Académiques 1980, Ongulumbashe Medal for bravery and long service 1987. *Leisure interests:* playing tennis, reading, watching soccer and rugby. *Address:* Office of the Prime Minister, Robert Mugabe Avenue, Private Bag 13338, Windhoek, Namibia. *Telephone:* (61) 2879111. *Fax:* (61) 230648. *Website:* www.opm.gov.na (Office).

GEISS, Johannes, Dr rer. nat; Swiss professor of physics; b. 4 Sept. 1926, Stolp, Pomerania (Poland); s. of Hans Geiss and Irene Wilke; m. Carmen Bach 1955; one d.; ed Univ. of Göttingen; Research Assoc., Enrico Fermi Inst., Univ. of Chicago 1955–56; Assoc. Prof., Marine Lab., Univ. of Miami 1958–59; Assoc. Prof., Univ. of Berne 1960, Prof. of Physics 1964–91, Dir Inst. of Physics 1966–90; Visiting Scientist, NASA Goddard Inst. for Space Studies, New York 1965, NASA Manned Spacecraft Center, Houston 1968–69; Chair. Launching Programme Advisory Cttee, European Space Agency, Paris 1970–72; Visiting Prof. Univ. of Toulouse 1975; Chair. Space Science Cttee, European Science Foundation 1979–86; Exec. Dir Int. Space Science Inst. 1995–; Adjunct Prof. Univ. of Michigan; Rector, Univ. of Berne 1982–83; Fellow of the American Geophysical Union; Foreign mem. American Acad. of Arts and Sciences, NAS, Max-Planck-Inst. für Aeronomie, Int. Acad. of Astronautics, Max-Planck-Inst. für Kernphysik, Austrian Acad. of Sciences; mem. Academia Europaea; Hon. Dr. (Univ. of Chicago); NASA Medal for Exceptional Scientific Achievement. *Publications:* over 300 publs on nucleosynthesis, cosmology, the origin of the solar system, geochronology, climatic history of the earth, the age of meteorites and lunar rocks, comets, solar wind, solar terrestrial relations. *Address:* International Space Science Institute, Hallestr. 6, 3012 Berne, Switzerland. *Telephone:* (31) 6314896 (Office); (31) 6314897.

GEISSLER, Heiner, DJur; German politician; b. 3 March 1930, Oberndorff; s. of Heinrich Geissler and Maria Buck; m. Susanne Thunack 1962; three s.; ed Univs of Tübingen and Munich; Dir Office of Minister of Labour and Social Welfare, Baden-Wurttemberg; mem. Bundestag 1965–67, 1980–; Minister for Social Welfare, Health and Sport, Rheinland-Pfalz 1967–77; mem. Parl. of Rheinland-Pfalz 1971–79; Gen. Sec. CDU 1977–89, Deputy Chair. 1989–90, mem. Presiding Bd 1990–; Deputy Chair. CDU/CSU Parl. group 1991–98; mem. CDU Parl. Cttee 1994–; mem. TV Council, Second German TV 1970–82, 1987–92; Fed. Minister for Youth, Family and Health 1982–85; Bundesverdienstkreuz 1970, Bergverlagspreis Deutsches Alpenverein 1983. *Publications:* Die neue soziale Frage 1976, Der Weg in die Gewalt 1978, Sicherheit für unsere Freiheit 1978, Verwaltete Bürger-Gesellschaft in Fesseln 1978, Grundwerte in der Politik 1979, Zukunftschancen der Jugend 1979, Sport – Geschäft ohne Illusionen? 1980, Mut zur Alternative 1981, Zugluft-Politik in stürmischer Zeit 1990, Heiner Geissler im Gespräch mit Gunter Hofmann und Werner A. Perger 1993, Gefährlicher Sieg 1995, Der Irrweg der Nationalismus 1995, Bergsteigen 1997, Das nicht gehaltene Versprechen 1997, Zeit, das Visier zu öffnen 1998. *Leisure interest:* mountaineering. *Address:* Bundeshaus, 53113 Bonn; Platz der Republik, 11011 Berlin, Germany. *Telephone:* (228) 161.

GEITONAS, Costas I.; Greek politician; b. Lagadia, Arcadia; ed Nat. Tech. Univ. of Athens; Gen. Sec. Ministry of Public Works 1981–85; Deputy Minister of Environment, Land Use and Public Works 1985–86, Alt. Gen. Dir Pvt. Political Office of Prime Minister 1986–89; an MP for Athens 1989–; Deputy Minister of Public Order 1993–94; Alt. Minister of Environment, Land Use and Public Works 1994–96, Minister of Public Order 1996, Minister of Health and Welfare 1996–99; mem. Cen. Cttee PASOK (Panhellenic Socialist Movt). *Address:* c/o Ministry of Health and Welfare, Odos Aristotelous 17, 104 33 Athens, Greece. *Telephone:* (1) 5232820. *Fax:* (1) 5231707.

GELB, Peter; American business executive; b. 1959; Pres. Sony Classical USA 1993–, in charge of Sony Classical Int. Operations March 1995–. *Address:* Sony Classical USA, 550 Madison Avenue, New York, NY 10022, USA (Office). *Telephone:* (212) 833-8000 (Office). *Website:* www.sonyclassical.com (Office).

GELBARD, Robert Sidney, MPA; American diplomatist; b. 6 March 1944, New York; s. of Charles Gelbard and Ruth Fisher Gelbard; m. Alene Marie Hanola 1968; one d.; ed Colby Coll., Harvard Univ.; volunteer Peace Corps, Bolivia 1964–66, Assoc. Dir, Philippines 1968–70; joined Foreign Service 1967, Staff Asst Sr Seminar in Foreign Policy 1967–68; Vice-Consul Porto Alegre, Brazil 1970–71, Prin. Officer 1971–72; int. economist Office of Devt Finance 1973–75, Office of Regional Political and Econ. Affairs 1976–78; First Sec. Embassy, Paris 1978–82; Deputy Dir Office of Western European Affairs, Washington, DC 1982–84; Dir Office of S African Affairs, Washington, DC 1984–85; Deputy Asst Sec. Bureau of Inter-American Affairs, Washington, DC 1985–88; Amb. to Bolivia 1988–91; Prin. Deputy Asst Sec. of State for Bureau of Inter-American Affairs 1991–93, Asst Sec. of State for Int. Narcotics and Law Enforcement Affairs 1993–97; Special Rep. for Implementation of the Dayton Peace Accords 1997–99; Amb. to Indonesia 1999–2001; Sr Vice-Pres. for Int. Affairs and Govt Relations ICN Pharmaceuticals 2002–; mem. Museum of American Folk Art int. advisory council, NY, American Foreign Service Assen. *Address:* Department of State, Washington, DC 20520-0001 (Office); 371 Huntington Street NW, Washington, DC 20015, USA. *Telephone:* (21) 344-2211. *Fax:* (21) 380-5583 (Office).

GELBART, Larry; American playwright and scriptwriter; b. 25 Feb. 1928, Chicago, Ill.; s. of Harry Gelbart and Frieda Gelbart; m. Pat Marshall 1956; three s. one d.; prin. writer, sometime dir and co-producer (first four seasons) M*A*S*H*; other television shows including Caesar's Hour, United States, The Bob Hope Show, The Danny Kaye Show; scriptwriter for various radio shows; Dir A Funny Thing Happened on the Way to the Forum, Chichester Festival Theatre, UK 1986; mem. Writers Guild of America, Authors League, Motion Picture Acad. of Arts and Sciences, Directors Guild of America, PEN Int. etc.; Hon. DLitt (Union Coll.) 1986, Hon. LHD (Hofstra) 1999; other awards and distinctions; Tony Award for co-authoring A Funny Thing Happened on the Way to the Forum; Writers Guild of America Awards for Oh, God, Movie Movie, Tootsie, 3 M*A*S*H* episodes; Peabody Awards for M*A*S*H*, The Danny Kaye Show; Emmy Awards for M*A*S*H* and V.I.P.; Edgar Allan Poe Award for Oh, God; Los Angeles Film Critics, New York Film Critics and Nat. Soc. of Film Critics Awards for Best Screenplay for Tootsie; Golden Rose, Montreux for writing/producing The Marty Feldman Comedy Machine; AMA citation for distinguished services 2001. *Plays:* My LA (revue), The Conquering Hero (musical), A Funny Thing Happened on the Way to the Forum (musical), Jump, Mastergate, Sly Fox, City of Angels (musical), Power Failure. *Films:* Notorious Landlady 1962, The Thrill of It All 1963, The Wrong Box 1966, Oh, God 1977, Movie Movie 1978, Neighbors 1981, Tootsie 1982, Blame it on Rio 1984, Barbarians at the Gate 1994, Weapons of Mass Distraction 1997, Bedazzled 2000. *Publication:* Laughing Matters 1998. *Leisure interest:* travel. *Address:* 807 North Alpine Drive, Beverly Hills, CA 90210-2901, USA.

GELDOF, Bob; Irish rock singer and charity promoter; b. 5 Oct. 1954, Dublin; m. Paula Yates 1986 (divorced 1996, died 2000); three d.; ed Black Rock Coll.; many casual jobs, lorry-driving, busking, teaching English, working in factory, etc., then journalist on pop music paper, Georgia Strait, Vancouver, Canada; returned Dublin and f. rock group, Boomtown Rats; brought group to London 1977, recorded for Ensign Records, then Phonogram; organized recording of Do They Know It's Christmas? by Band Aid, raising £8 million for African famine relief Nov. 1984, f. Band-Aid Trust to distribute proceeds 1985, Chair.; organized Live Aid concerts Wembley, London and Philadelphia, USA with int. TV link-up by satellite, raising £48 million July 1985; f. Live Aid Foundation, USA; organized publ. of Live Aid book The Greatest Show on Earth 1985; Dir (non-exec.) Ten Alps Communications 2001–; Freeman of Ypres 1986; Hon. KBE 1986; Elder of the Repub. of Tanzania; Dr hc (Ghent) 1986; Hon. DLit (London) 1987; Third World Prize 1986. *Films include:* Number One, Pink Floyd – The Wall. *Publication:* Is That It? (autobiog.) 1986. *Address:* Davington Priory, Kent, England.

GELFAND, Israel Moiseyevich, DSc; Russian mathematician and biologist; b. 2 Sept. 1913, Krasnye Okny, Ukraine; s. of Moshe Gelfand and Perl Gelfand; m. 1st Zorya Yakovlevna Shapiro 1942 (divorced); m. 2nd Tanya Alekseevskaya 1979; two s. one d.; ed Moscow State Univ.; Asst Professor, Dept of Mathematics, Moscow State Univ. 1935–40, Prof. 1940–91; Corresp. mem. USSR (now Russian) Acad. of Sciences 1953, mem. 1984, Head of Dept Inst. of Applied Mathematics 1953–91; Head of Laboratory of Mathematical Methods in Biology, Moscow State Univ.; f. and ed. Funktsionalny analiz i yego prilozheniya 1967–91; Prof. Rutgers Univ. 1991–; f. and Head Gelfand Outreach Programme in Mathematics 1995–; Prof. Foreign mem. Royal Soc., NAS, Acad. des Sciences (France), Royal Swedish Acad. of Sciences, Royal Irish Soc., American Acad. of Arts and Sciences; Dr hc (Univs of Oxford, Harvard, Uppsala, Milan, Pisa, Paris); State Prize 1951, 1953, Lenin Prize 1961, Wolf Prize in Mathematics 1978, Kyoto Prize 1989; McArthur Fellowship 1994. *Publications:* numerous works including Unitary Representations of Classical Groups 1950, Generalized Functions Vols I–VI 1958–66, Normed Rings 1960, Automorphic Functions and the Theory of Representations 1962, Cohomology of Infinite Dimensional Lie Algebras and Some Questions of Integral Homology 1970, Representations of the Group SL 2R, Where R is a Ring of Functions 1973, Mechanisms of Morphogenesis in Cell Structures 1977, Collected Papers (Vols 1–3) 1986–89, Discriminants, Resultants and Multidimensional Determinants 1994; Hon. mem. Moscow Mathematical Soc., London Mathematical Soc. *Leisure interest:* classical music. *Address:* GOPM Centre for Mathematics, Science and Computer Education, SERC Building, Room 239, Busch Campus, Piscataway, NJ 08855-1179, USA (Office). *Telephone:* (732) 445-3491 (Office); (732) 445-3477 (Home). *E-mail:* gopm@math.rutgers.edm.

GELL-MANN, Murray, PhD; American physicist; b. 15 Sept. 1929, New York City; s. of the late Arthur Gell-Mann and Pauline (Reichstein) Gell-Mann; m. 1st J. Margaret Dow 1955 (died 1981); one s. one d.; m. 2nd Marcia Southwick 1992; one step-s.; ed Yale Univ., Massachusetts Inst. of Tech.; mem. Inst. for Advanced Study, Princeton 1951, 1955, 1967–68; Instructor, Asst Prof. and Assoc. Prof., Univ. of Chicago 1952–55; Assoc. Prof., Calif. Inst. of Tech. 1955–56, Prof. 1956–66, R. A. Millikan Prof. of Theoretical Physics 1967–93, R. A. Millikan Prof. Emer. 1993–; Research Assoc. Univ. of Illinois 1951, 1953; Visiting Assoc. Prof. Columbia Univ. 1954; Visiting Prof. Collège de France and Univ. of Paris 1959–60, Mass. Inst. of Tech. 1963, European Council for Nuclear Research 1971–72, 1979–80, Univ. of NM 1995–; Consultant, Inst. for Defense Analyses, Arlington, Va 1961–70, RAND Corpn, Santa Monica, Calif. 1956; Overseas Fellow Churchill Col, Cambridge, England 1966; mem. NASA Physics Panel 1964, President's Science Advisory Cttee 1969–72, Council on Foreign Relations 1975–, President's Council of Advisors on Science and Tech. 1994–2001; Consultant to Los Alamos Scientific Laboratory, Los Alamos, NM 1956–, Laboratory Fellow 1982–; Citizen Regent, Smithsonian Inst. 1974–88; Chair. Western Center, American Acad. of Arts and Sciences 1970–76; Chair. of Bd Aspen Center for Physics 1973–79; Founding Trustee Santa Fe Inst. 1982, Chair. Bd of Trustees 1982–85, Co-Chair. Science Bd 1985–2000; Prof. and Distinguished Fellow 1993–; mem. Bd Calif. Nature Conservancy 1984–93, J. D. and C. T. MacArthur Foundation 1979– (Chair. World Environment and Resource Cttee 1982–97), Lovelace Insts 1993–95; mem. Science and Grants Cttee, Leakey Foundation 1977–88, NAS, American Physical Soc. 1960–, American Acad. of Arts and Sciences 1964–, American Philosophical Soc. 1993–, Science Advisory Cttee, Conservation Inst. 1993,

AAAS 1994–, Advisory Bd Network Physics 1999–; Hon. mem. French Physical Soc. 1970; Foreign mem. Royal Soc. 1978–, Pakistan Acad. of Sciences 1985–, Indian Acad. of Sciences 1985–, Russian Acad. of Sciences 1993–; Hon. ScD (Yale) 1959, (Chicago) 1967, (Illinois) 1968, (Wesleyan) 1968, (Utah) 1970, (Columbia) 1977, (Cambridge Univ.) 1980, (Oxford Univ.) 1992, (Southern Illinois Univ.) 1993, (Southern Methodist Univ.) 1999; Dr hc (Turin, Italy) 1969; Dannie Heineman Prize, American Physical Soc. 1959; Ernest O. Lawrence Award 1966, Franklin Medal 1967, John J. Carty Medal (NAS) 1968, Nobel Prize in Physics 1969, Research Corpn Award 1969, UNEP Roll of Honor for Environmental Achievement 1988, Erice Prize 1990. *Major works:* Developed strangeness theory, theory of neutral K mesons, eightfold way theory of approximate symmetry; current algebra, quark scheme; contributed to theory of dispersion relations, theory of weak interaction and formulation of quantum chromodynamics. *Publications:* (with Yuval Ne'eman, q.v.) The Eightfold Way 1964, The Quark and the Jaguar 1994. *Leisure interests:* historical linguistics, wilderness trips, ornithology, numismatics. *Address:* c/o Santa Fe Institute, 1399 Hyde Park Road, Santa Fe, NM 87501, USA. *Telephone:* (505) 984-8800. *Fax:* (505) 982-0565. *E-mail:* mgm@ santafe.edu (Office). *Website:* www.santafe.edu/sfi/people/mgm (Office).

GELLEH, Ismael Omar; Djibouti politician; b. 1947, Dire Dawa, Ethiopia; joined gen. security dept, French police force 1968, rank of Police Insp. 1970; fmr Chief of Staff of Pres. Hassan Gouled Aptidon (q.v.); mem. Rassemblement populaire pour le progrès (RPP), currently Pres.; Pres. of Djibouti and Commdr-in-Chief of the Armed Forces May 1999–. *Address:* Office of the President, Djibouti, Republic of Djibouti.

GELMAN, Aleksandr Isaakovich; Russian playwright and scriptwriter; b. 25 Oct. 1933, Moldavia; m. Tatyana Pavlovna Kaletskaya; two s.; ed Kishinev Univ; mem. CPSU 1956–90; worked in factories 1956–67; coresp. for daily papers 1967–71; wrote scripts for series of documentary films 1971–74; work with Moscow Art Theatre 1975–; People's Deputy of the USSR 1989–91; USSR State Prize 1976. *Film scripts include:* Night Shift 1971, Consider me Grown Up 1974, Xenia, Fyodor's Favourite Wife 1974 (all with T. Kaletskaya), Prize 1975, Clumsy Man 1979, We, The Undersigned 1981, Zinulya 1984. *Theatre work includes:* A Man with Connections, The Bonus, The Bench, We, the Undersigned, Misha's Party (jtly.), Pretender 1999, Zinulya, Back, Connection. *Television documentary:* Gorbachev: After Empire 2001. *Publication:* Book of Plays 1985. *Address:* Tverskoy blvd 3, Apt. 12, 103104 Moscow, Russia. *Telephone:* (095) 202-68-59. *E-mail:* idcg@cityline.ru (Home).

GEMAYEL, Amin; Lebanese politician; b. 1942, Bikfayya; s. of Pierre Gemayel; ed St Joseph Univ., Beirut; MP 1970–; Pres. of Lebanon 1982–88; f. The House of the Future, The Amin Gemayel Educational Foundation, Le Reveil newspaper; mem. Al-Katae'b Party (Phalanges Libanaises).

GEMS, Iris Pamela (Pam); British playwright; b. Bransgore, Dorset; d. of the late Jim Price and Elsie Mabel Annetts; m. Keith Leopold Gems 1949; two s. two d.; ed Brockenhurst Grammar School, Univ. of Manchester; career playwright; mem. Dramatists' Guild (USA), Writers' Guild. *Plays:* Betty's Wonderful Christmas 1974, Dusa, Fish, Stas and Vi 1976, Queen Christina 1977, Piaf 1978, Franz into April 1978, The Treat 1979, Pasionaria 1981, Aunt Mary 1983, Camille 1985, The Danton Affair 1986, The Blue Angel 1991, Deborah's Daughter 1994, Stanley 1995 (Best Play, Evening Standard Awards 1996, Best Play, Olivier Awards 1997), Marlene 1996, The Snow Palace 1998. *Adaptations:* Uncle Vanya 1981, A Doll's House 1983, The Cherry Orchard 1984, Ghosts 1992, The Seagull 1995, Yerma 2003, The Lady from the Sea 2003. *Novels:* Mrs Frampton 1989, Bon Voyage, Mrs Frampton 1990. *Leisure interest:* gardening. *Address:* c/o Jenny Casarotto, National House, 60–66 Wardour Street, London W1V 4ND, England. *Telephone:* (20) 7287-4450. *Fax:* (20) 7287-9128.

GENDREAU-MASSALOUX, Michèle; French public servant; b. 28 July 1944, Limoges; d. of François Massaloux and Marie-Adrienne Delalais; m. Pascal Gendreau 1970; ed Ecole Normale Supérieure de Jeunes Filles, Sèvres, Inst. d'Etudes Politiques, Paris; univ. teacher, Sorbonne, Villetaneuse (Paris XIII), then Univ. of Limoges (fmr Vice-Pres.); Rector Acad. d'Orléans-Tours 1981–84; Tech. Adviser to Secr.-Gen. for Nat. Educ. and Univs., Presidency of the Repub., then to Secr.-Gen. for Admin. Reform and Improvement of Relations between Public Services and their Users, Deputy Sec.-Gen. 1985–88, Spokesperson 1986–88, Head of Mission May 1988; Rector, Acad. de Paris 1989–98; Conseiller d'Etat 1998; mem. Comm. Nat. de la Communication et des Libertés 1988–89, French Comm. for UNESCO 1991, Conseil orientation Ecole du Louvre 1991, Council, Coll. Univ. Français de Moscou 1991, Council, Coll. Univ. Français de Saint-Petersbourg 1992, Conseil Scientifique de la Cinquième 1996; mem. Comm. de contrôle des sondages 1999; Dir Gen. Agence Universitaire de la francophonie (AUF) 1999–; Prof. Univ. Paris VIII–Vincennes St-Denis 1999–; Chevalier, Légion d'honneur, Officier, Ordre Nat. du Mérite, Chevalier, Ordre des Palmes Académiques. *Publication:* Recherche sur l'Humanisme de Francisco de Quevedo 1977, works and translations concerning the Spanish Golden Age. *Leisure interest:* music. *Address:* Conseil d'Etat, 75100 Paris 01 SP (Office); 34 rue de Penthièvre, 75008 Paris, France (Home).

GENERALOV, Sergey Vladimirovich; Russian politician; b. 7 Sept. 1963, Simferopol; ed Moscow Inst. of Energy, Higher School of Man. at State Acad. of Man.; Commercial Dir TET 1991–92; Deputy Chair. NIPEBANK 1992–93; Head of Div., Head of Dept, Promradtechbank 1993; Vice-Pres. YUKOS Oil Co., 1993–97, ROSPROM-YUKOS 1997; Deputy Chair. MENATEP 1997–98;

Minister of Fuel and Power Eng of Russian Fed. 1998–99; Dir Fuel and Energy Complex Investments Agency 1999–2000; mem. State Duma 1999–, faction Right-Wing Forces, Chair. Comm. for Defence of Investor Rights; Chair. Investor Protection Asscn. *Address:* State Duma, Okhotny Ryad 1, 103265 Moscow, Russia. *Telephone:* (095) 292-18-42 (Duma), (095) 292-55-78 (Centre of Strategic Studies) (Office). *Fax:* (095) 937-49-56 (Office). *E-mail:* office@ generalov.ru.

GENIEVA, Yekaterina Yuryevna, DLitt; Russian librarian and literary scholar; b. 1 April 1946, Moscow; m. Yuri S. Belenky; one d.; ed Moscow State Univ.; nurse Moscow hosp.; Sr, Deputy Dir State Library for Foreign Literature 1971–92, Dir Gen. 1992–; Pres. Inst. Open Soc. (Soros Foundation) 1995–; Vice Pres. Russian Library Asscn 1994–; mem. Council on Culture, Russian Presidency 1996–2000; mem. Bd First Vice-pres. Int. Fed. of Library Asscns. 1990-99; mem. Ed. Bds. journals Biblioteka, Libri, Inostrannaya Literatura, Znamya; Hon. DLitt (Univ. of Ill. at Urbana-Champaign) 2001; Order of Friendship 1999. *Publications include:* monographs, trans. of English authors, numerous articles. *Leisure interests:* books, travelling, Irish culture. *Address:* VGBIL, Nikoloyamskaya str. 1, 109189 Moscow, Russia (Office). *Telephone:* (095) 915-36-21 (Office). *Fax:* (095) 915 3637 (Office). *E-mail:* genieva@libfl.ru (Office).

GENILLARD, Robert Louis, MA (ECON.); Swiss financier; b. 15 June 1929, Lausanne; Gen. Partner White, Weld & Co. New York 1958; Chair. and Chief Exec. Credit Suisse White Weld 1960–77; Chief Exec. Thyssen-Bornemisza Group and TBG Holdings NV 1977–83, Deputy Chair. 1971–99; Ind. Corp. Dir 1983–, for American Express, Cabot Int., Clariden Bank (also Chair., now Hon. Chair.), Cie des Machines Bull, Credit Suisse Group (Vice-Chair.), Honeywell Int., Novartis, Said Holdings (Vice-Chair.), Soc. des Bains de Mer, Swiss Aluminium. *Publications:* numerous articles in professional journals. *Address:* 1 quai du Mont-Blanc, 1211 Geneva 1, Switzerland (Office).

GENISARETSKY, Oleg Igorevich; Russian sociologist; b. 28 Feb. 1942, Kovrov, Vladimir region; ed Moscow Inst. of Physics and Eng, Moscow State Univ.; researcher All-Union Inst. of Tech. Aesthetics 1965–93; Deputy Dir Inst. of Man, Russian Acad. of Sciences 1993–97; freelance writer 1997–; Triumph Prize. *Publications:* numerous publs, on theory and methods of system and artistic design, ecology of culture, aesthetic educ., theoretical sociology of culture and psychology of creativity. *Address:* Institute of Man, Russian Academy of Sciences, Volkhonka str. 14, 119842 Moscow, Russia (Office). *Telephone:* (095) 203-01-09 (Office). *Fax:* (095) 203-91-69 (Office). *E-mail:* olegen@msses.ru.

GENNES, Pierre-Gilles de, PhD; French physicist; b. 24 Oct. 1932, Paris; ed Ecole Normale Supérieure; Research Scientist, Centre d'Etudes Nucléaires de Saclay 1955–59; Prof. of Solid State Physics, Univ. of Paris, Orsay 1961–71; Prof. Coll. de France 1971–, also Dir Ecole de Physique et Chimie, Paris 1976–2002; mem. Académie des Sciences 1979–, Dutch Acad. of Sciences, Royal Soc., American Acad. of Arts and Sciences, NAS; Hollweck Prize 1968, Prix Cognac-Jay 1970, Prix Ampère 1977, Gold Medal (CNRS) 1981, Matteuci Medal 1987, Harvey Prize 1988, Wolf Prize 1990, Nobel Prize 1991, Heyrovsky Medal 1993, Onsager Medal 1996. *Publications:* Superconductivity of Metals and Alloys 1965, The Physics of Liquid Crystals 1973, Scaling Concepts in Polymer Physics 1979, Simple views on condensed matter 1992, Les Objets Fragiles (jtly.) 1994, Gouttes, Bulles, Perles et Ondes 2002, Petit Point 2002. *Leisure interests:* drawing. *Address:* 11 place Marcelin-Berthelot, 75005 Paris (Office); 10 rue Vauquelin, 75005 Paris, France (Home). *E-mail:* pgg@curie.fr (Office).

GENOVÉS, Juan; Spanish artist; b. 31 May 1930, Valencia; ed Escuela Superior de Bellas Artes, Valencia; has taken part in numerous group exhbns; one-man exhbns in Spain, Portugal, USA, Italy, Germany, Netherlands, Japan, UK, Cuba, Puerto Rico, Canada, Switzerland, France and S America 1957–; took part in Paris Biennale 1961, Venice Biennale 1962, 1966, São Paulo Biennale 1965, etc.; works in collections and museums in Germany, SA, Guinea, Australia, Austria, Belgium, Brazil, Canada, Colombia, Cuba, Spain, Finland, France, Netherlands, England, Israel, Italy, Japan, Mexico, Nicaragua, Poland, Switzerland, USA and Venezuela; Gold Medal, San Marino Biennale 1967, Premio Marzotto Internazionale 1968, Premio Nacional de Artes Plásticas 1984. *Address:* Arandilla 17, 28023 Aravaca (Madrid), Spain (Home); c/o Marlborough Fine Art, 6 Albemarle Street, London, W1, England.

GENSCHER, Hans-Dietrich; German politician; b. 21 March 1927, Reideburg, Saale; s. of Kurt Genscher and the late Hilda Kreime; m. 1st Luise Schweitzer 1958; m. 2nd Barbara Schmidt 1969; one d.; ed Leipzig and Hamburg Univs; Scientific Asst, Parl. Free Democratic Party (FDP) 1956, later Sec., Hon. Chair. 1992–; Fed. Party Man. 1962–64, Vice-Chair. 1968–74, Chair. 1974–85; Deputy in Bundestag 1965–98; Fed. Minister of the Interior 1969–74; Vice-Chancellor, Minister of Foreign Affairs 1974–92; Chair. Bd of Dirs WMP Eurocom AG, Berlin 1998–; Counsel Büsing, Müffelmann & Theye, Berlin 1999–; Man. Partner Hans-Dietrich Genscher Consult GmbH 2000–; Pres. German Council on Foreign Relations 2001–; Asscn Friends and Patrons State Opera, Berlin; Hon. Prof. FU Berlin 1994, Peking 1999; Hon. Citizen of Costa Rica 1988; numerous Dr hc 1977–2002; Onassis Foundation Award 1991; Bundesverdienstkreuz 1973 and other medals; Freeman of Halle 1993, of Berlin 1997. *Publications:* Bundestagsreden 1972, Deutsche Aussenpolitik, Reden und Aufsätze aus 10 Jahren, 1974–84, Nach vorn gedacht. . . Perspektiven deutscher Aussenpolitik 1986, Erinnerungen (memoirs)

1995. *Leisure interest:* reading. *Address:* Hans-Dietrich Genscher Consult GmbH, Postfach 20 06 55, 53136 Bonn, Germany. *Fax:* (228) 264652. *E-mail:* consult@genscher.de.

GENT, Sir Christopher Charles, Kt; British business executive; b. 10 May 1948; s. of the late Charles Arthur Gent and of Kathleen Dorothy Gent; m. 1st Lynda Marion Tobin (divorced); two d.; m. 2nd Kate Elizabeth Lock 1999; two s.; ed Archbishop Tenison's Grammar School; Man. Trainee, NatWest Bank 1967–71; with Schroder Computer Services 1971–79; Market Devt Man. Baric Computing Services, then Man. Dir 1979–84; Dir Network Services Div. ICL 1983–84; joined Vodafone as Man. Dir (when part of Racal PLC) 1985, Dir Racal Telecom PLC 1988–91, Man. Dir Vodafone Ltd and Dir Vodafone Group PLC (after demerger from Racal) 1991–97, CEO Vodafone Group PLC 1997–2003; GSMA (Global System for Mobile Communications Asscn) Chair. Award 2003. *Leisure interests:* cricket, family, horse racing. *Address:* c/o Vodafone Group PLC, The Courtyard, 2–4 London Road, Newbury, Berks., RG14 1JX, England (Office).

GEOANĂ, Mircea Dan, LLB; Romanian politician and international organization official; b. 14 July 1958; m. Mihaela Geoană; one s. one d.; ed Bucharest Polytechnic Inst., Univ. of Bucharest, Acad. for Econ. Studies, Bucharest, Ecole Nat. d'Admin., Paris, France, Harvard Univ., USA; joined Ministry of Foreign Affairs 1990, Dir European Affairs Dept, Head Romanian Del. to CSCE Cttee of Sr Officials 1991, Ministry Spokesperson 1993–95, Dir-Gen. for Asia, Latin America, Middle East and Africa 1994, Dir-Gen. for Europe, N America, Asia, Latin America, Middle East and Africa 1995, Minister of Foreign Affairs 2000–; Amb. to USA 1996–2000; Chair.-in-Office OSCE 2001–; Prof. Nat. School for Political and Admin. Sciences, Nicolae Titulescu Univ., Bucharest; Commdr of the Nat. Order Star of Romania 2000. *Address:* Ministry of Foreign Affairs, Aleea Modrogan 14, Sector 1, 71274 Bucharest, Romania (Office). *Telephone:* (1) 2122160 (Office). *Fax:* (1) 2307489 (Office). *E-mail:* maero@mae.kappa.ro (Office). *Website:* www.mae.ro (Office).

GEOGHEGAN-QUINN, Máire; Irish fmr business consultant and fmr politician; b. 5 Sept. 1950, Carna, Co. Galway; d. of the late John Geoghegan and of Barbara Folan; m. John V. Quinn 1973; two s.; ed Carysfort Teacher Training Coll. Blackrock, Co. Dublin; fmr primary school teacher; mem. Galway City Council 1985–92; mem. Dáil (Parl.) 1975–97; Parl. Sec. to Minister of Industry, Commerce and Energy 1977–78; Minister of State with responsibility for Consumer Affairs, Ministry of Industry, Commerce and Energy 1977–78; Minister for the Gaeltacht 1979–81; Minister of State with responsibility for Youth and Sport, Dept of Educ. March–Dec. 1982; Minister of State for European Affairs 1987, 1991; Minister for Tourism, Transport and Communications 1992, of Justice 1993; columnist Irish Times 1997–2000; consultant to several cos.; mem. Audit Devt and Reports Group, Court of Auditors of the EC 2000–; fmr Chair. The Saffron Initiative; fmr Chair. Fianna Fáil; fmr Dir (non-exec.) The Ryan Hotel Group, Aer Lingus; fmr TV broadcaster. *Publication:* The Green Diamond (novel) 1996. *Leisure interests:* reading, writing and travel. *Address:* European Court of Auditors, 12 Rue Alcide de Gasperi, 1615 Luxembourg, Luxembourg (Office). *Telephone:* 4398-45303 (Office). *Fax:* 4398-46493 (Office). *Website:* www.eca.eu.int (Office).

GEORGE; British artist; b. George Passmore, 1942, Devon; ed Dartington Hall Coll. of Art, Oxford School of Art, St Martin's School of Art; began collaboration with Gilbert Proesch in 1967 as Gilbert and George; est. reputation as performance artists, presenting themselves, identically dressed, as living sculptures; later work includes large composite drawings and vividly coloured photo-pieces often featuring likenesses of the artists. *Exhibitions include:* Museum of Contemporary Art, Chicago 2000–01. *Publication:* Manifesto – What Our Art Means (jtly). *Address:* c/o White Cube 2 Gallery, 48 Hoxton Square, London, N1, England (Office). *E-mail:* g-and-g@dircon.co.uk (Office). *Website:* www.gilbertandgeorge.co.uk/e/start.html (Office).

GEORGE, Rt Hon Sir Edward Alan John, GBE, PC, MA; British banker; b. 11 Sept. 1938; s. of Alan George and Olive Elizabeth George; m. Clarice Vanessa Williams 1962; one s. two d.; ed Dulwich Coll., Emmanuel Coll., Cambridge; joined Bank of England 1962, seconded to BIS 1966–69, to IMF as Asst to Chair. of Deputies of Cttee of Twenty on Int. Monetary Reform 1972–74, Adviser on Int. Monetary Questions 1974–77, Deputy Chief Cashier 1977–80, Asst Dir Gilt-Edged Div. 1980–82, Exec. Dir 1982–90, Deputy Gov. 1990–93, Gov. 1993–2003; Chair. G10 Govs 1999–2003; Hon. DSc(Econs) (Hull) 1993, (City) 1995, (Cranfield) 1997, (Manchester) 1998, (Buckingham) 2000; Hon. DLitt (Loughborough) 1994, (Sheffield) 1999; Hon. LLD (Guildhall, London) 1996; Hon. LLD (Exeter) 1997, (Bristol) 1999, (Hertfordshire) 1999, (Cambridge) 2000. *Leisure interests:* family, sailing, bridge. *Address:* c/o Bank of England, Threadneedle Street, London, EC2R 8AH, England.

GEORGE, HE Cardinal Francis Eugene, O.M.I., PhD; American ecclesiastic; b. 16 Jan. 1937, Chicago, Ill.; ordained priest 1963; Bishop of Yakima 1990, of Portland in Oregon 1996–97; Archbishop of Chicago 1997–; cr. Cardinal Feb. 1998; Knight of Malta. *Publications:* Inculturation and Ecclesiastical Communion 1990. *Address:* Archdiocese of Chicago Pastoral Center, PO Box 1979, Chicago, IL 60690, USA. *Telephone:* (312) 751-8230.

GEORGE, Jennie, BA; Australian trade unionist; b. 20 Aug. 1947, Italy; ed Sydney Univ.; Gen. Sec. NSW Teachers Fed. 1980–82, Pres. 1986–89; mem. Exec. Australian Council of Trade Unions (ACTU) 1983, Vice-Pres. 1987, Asst Sec. 1991–95, Pres. 1996–2000; Fed. MP for Throsby 2001–; Asst Nat. Dir

Trade Union Training Authority 1989–91. *Address:* c/o Australian Labour Party, Centenary House, 19 National Circuit, Barton, ACT 2600, Australia (Office). *Telephone:* (2) 6273-3133 (Office). *Fax:* (2) 6273-2031. *E-mail:* jennie .george.MP@aph.gov.au (Office).

GEORGE, Kenneth Montague, LLM; Guyanese judge; b. 12 March 1930; s. of Stephen N. George and Etheline George; m. Hazel Ester McLean 1965; two s. two d.; ed London and Harvard Univs and Gray's Inn, London; Registrar of Supreme Court 1964–66, Judge 1967–76; Justice of Appeal 1976–81; Chief Justice 1981–88; Chancellor of the Judiciary and Pres. Court of Appeal 1988; Cacique's Crown of Honour, Order of Roraima. *Leisure interest:* reading. *Address:* c/o Court of Appeal, 60 High Street, Kingston, Georgetown (Office); 43 Arakaka Place, Bel Air Park, Georgetown, Guyana (Home). *Telephone:* (2) 65906 (Home).

GEORGE, Richard Lee, BS, JD; Canadian businessman; b. 16 May 1950, Colorado; s. of Albert H. George and Betty Lou McDill; m. Julie G. White 1972; two s. one d.; ed Harvard Business School, Univ. of Houston, Colorado State Univ.; Deputy Man. Dir Sun Oil Britain, London 1982–86, District Man., Aberdeen 1986–87; Vice-Pres. Sun Exploration and Production, Dallas 1987–88; Man. Dir Sun Int. Exploration and Production, London, UK 1988–91, Pres. and COO Suncor Inc. Ontario, Canada Feb.–Oct. 1991, Pres. and CEO 1991–93, Pres., CEO 1993–94 (fmr Chair.); Dir IPL Energy Inc., Dofasco Inc.; Canada's Outstanding CEO for 1999. *Leisure interests:* skiing, golf, fitness. *Address:* Suncor Energy Inc., 112 4th Ave, SW, P.O. Box 38, Calgary, Alberta, T2P 2V5, Canada. *Telephone:* (403) 269-8100. *Fax:* (403) 269-6221. *Website:* www.suncor.com (Office).

GEORGE, Susan; British actress; b. 26 July 1950; d. of Norman Alfred George and Eileen Percival; m. Simon MacCorkindale 1984; began acting career 1954; partner Amy Int. Productions, London; Dir 5G Naturally Ltd. *Films include:* Cup Fever, Davey Jones' Locker, Billion Dollar Brain, Twinky 1969, Spring and Port Wine 1970, Eyewitness 1970, Straw Dogs 1971, Dirty Mary and Crazy Larry 1974, Mandingo 1975, Out of Season 1975, A Small Town in Texas 1977, Tomorrow Never Comes 1978, Venom 1980, A Texas Legend 1981, The House Where Evil Dwells 1982, The Jigsaw Man 1984, Czechmate 1985, Lightning, The White Stallion 1986, Stealing Heaven (producer) 1987, That Summer of White Roses (producer) 1988, The House That Mary Bought (also producer) 1994. *Television appearances include:* Swallows and Amazons, Human Jungle, The Right Attitude 1968, Dr Jekyll and Mr Hyde 1973, Lamb to the Slaughter 1979, Royal Jelly 1979, The Bob Hope Special 1979, Pajama Tops 1982, Masquerade 1983, Hotel 1985, Blacke's Magic 1986, Jack the Ripper 1988, Castle of Adventure 1990, Cluedo 1992, Stay Lucky 1992, Eastenders 2001. *Theatre:* The Sound of Music 1962, The Country Girl 1984, Rough Crossing 1987. *Publication:* illustrated book of poetry 1987. *Leisure interests:* Arab horse breeding, singing. *Address:* c/o MacCorkindale & Holton, P.O. Box 2398, 1–2 Langham Place, London, W1A 3DD, England. *Telephone:* (20) 7636-1888.

GEORGEL, Pierre, D. EN LETT.; French museum director; b. 14 Jan. 1943, Safi, Morocco; s. of Lucien Georgel and Santia Maria Georgel (née Santini); m. Chantal Martinet 1985; ed Univs of Montpellier, Paris and Lille, Ecole du Louvre, Paris; Asst, Musée du Louvre 1966–70; seconded to CNRS, Paris 1970–74; Curator of Graphic Art, Musée Nat. d'Art Moderne 1974–79; Dir Musée des Beaux-Arts, Dijon 1980–86; Dir Musée Picasso, Paris 1986–89; Chief Curator of French Museums (based at Musée Picasso) 1989–93; Dir Musée nat. de l'Orangerie des Tuileries 1993; Prof. Ecole du Louvre 1980–85, 1995–96; Conservateur-général du Patrimoine 2000. *Publications:* Dessins de Victor Hugo 1971, La Gloire de Victor Hugo 1985, La Peinture dans la peinture 1987, Courbet: le Poème de la nature 1995, Monet: le Cycle Nymphéas 1999. *Address:* Musée de l'Orangerie, Jardin des Tuileries, 75041 Paris, Cedex 01 (Office); 41 Boulevard Saint-Germain, 75005 Paris, France (Home). *Telephone:* 1-40-20-67-71 (Office). *Fax:* 1-42-61-30-82 (Office).

GEORGES, Rt Hon Philip Telford, BA; Trinidad and Tobago judge; b. 5 Jan. 1923, Dominica; s. of John H. D. Georges and Milutine C. Cox; m. 1st Grace E. Georges 1954; m. 2nd Joyce L. Georges 1981; two s. two d.; ed Univ. of Toronto and Middle Temple, London; pvt. practice as barrister-at-law 1949–62; Judge, High Court of Trinidad & Tobago 1962–65, 1971–74; Chief Justice of Tanzania 1965–71; Prof. of Law, Univ. of W Indies 1974–81; Judge, Supreme Court of Zimbabwe 1981–84, Chief Justice June–Dec. 1984, of The Bahamas 1984–89; Judge, Court of Appeal, Cayman Islands 1984–, Bermuda 1990–94; Judge Court of Appeal, Belize 1992–97, mem. 1993–; mem. Juridical Cttee, OAS 1992–95; Law Reform Commr, The Bahamas 1989–95; Judge, Admin. Tribunal, IADB 1993; Hon. LLD (Toronto, Dar es Salaam, West Indies, Dalhousie); Order of the Caribbean Community, Award of Dominica. *Leisure interests:* walking, swimming. *Address:* Kilimani, 5A The Mount, St. George, Barbados. *Telephone:* 435-1185. *Fax:* 429-0223.

GEORGESCU, Florin, PhD; Romanian politician and economist; b. 25 Nov. 1953, Bucharest; ed Acad. of Econ. Studies, Bucharest; Fulbright Scholar 1991–92; author of more than 200 studies and papers; worked at Finance Ministry, Prof. at Acad. of Econ. Studies; State Sec. of the Economy and Finance Ministry 1992, Minister of Finance and Deputy Prime Minister 1992–96; mem. Parl. (Social Democratic Party) Dec. 1996–. *Address:* Chamber of Deputies, 76 117 Bucharest, Parliament Buildings, September 13 Avenue 1, Sector 5, Romania.

GEORGESCU, Peter Andrew, MBA; American advertising executive; b. 9 March 1939, Bucharest, Romania; s. of V. C. Georgescu and Lygia Bocu; m. Barbara A. Armstrong 1965; one s.; ed Princeton and Stanford Univs; joined Young & Rubicam Inc., New York 1963–, Dir of Marketing 1977–79; Exec. Vice-Pres. and Dir Cen. Region, Young & Rubicam Inc., Chicago 1979–82; Pres. Young & Rubicam Int., New York 1982–86, Young & Rubicam Advertising, New York 1986–99, Young & Rubicam Inc. 1990–99 (CEO 1994–99), Chair. Emer. 2000–; mem. Bd of Dirs Briggs & Stratton Inc.; mem. Council on Foreign Relations. *Address:* c/o Young & Rubicam Inc., 285 Madison Avenue, New York, NY 10017, USA.

GEORGIEV, Georgii Pavlovich; Russian biologist; b. 4 Feb. 1933, Leningrad (now St Petersburg); s. of Pavel K. Georgiev and Anastasia Georgieva; m. Nekrasova Anastasia Georgieva; one s. one d.; ed First Moscow Medical Inst.; researcher A. Severtsev Inst. of Morphology of Animals USSR (now Russian) Acad. of Sciences 1956-63; head of lab., V. Engelhart Inst. of Molecular Biology USSR (now Russian) Acad. of Sciences 1963–88; Founder and Dir Inst. of Gene Biology USSR (now Russian) Acad. of Sciences 1990–; Corresp. mem. USSR (now Russian) Acad. of Sciences 1970, mem. 1987; research in molecular biology and genetics; author of discoveries of pro-m RNA and study of nuclear RNP particles containing pro-m RNA and investigation of a new type of nucleoprotein complex structure; first description of nuclear skeleton components; discovery of mobile elements in animals; studies of chromosome structure and transcription-active chromatin, tumour metastasis genes and cancer gene therapy; mem. European Acad., Royal Acad. of Spain, German Acad. Leopoldina, Scientific Acad. of Norway, European Molecular Biology Org.; Lenin Prize 1976, USSR State Prize 1983, Russian State Prize 1996. *Publications include:* Genes of Higher Organisms and their Expression 1989; over 400 scientific articles. *Leisure interest:* mountain climbing. *Address:* Institute of Gene Biology, Russian Academy of Sciences, Vavilov str. 34/5, 117334 Moscow, Russia. *Telephone:* (095) 135-60-89 (Office); (095) 125-74-54 (Home). *Fax:* (095) 135-41-25 (Office). *E-mail:* georg@biogen.msk.su.

GEORGIEVSKI, Ljubiša (Ljubčo); Macedonian politician and philologist; b. 1966, Stip; ed Skopje Univ.; active in movt for autonomous and independent Macedonia 1990–; Vice-Pres. Repub. of Macedonia 1991–92; Founder and Pres. Democratic Party for Macedonian Nat. Unity VMRO-DPMNE 1993–; Prime Minister of Macedonia 1998–99, 2000–02. *Publications:* books of poetry Apocalypse 1988, City 1991, Direct Investments and Short Stories (essays) 1994, numerous articles. *Address:* VMRO-DPMNE, 1000 Skopje, Petar Drapshin br. 36, Macedonia (Office). *Telephone:* (2) 111441 (Office). *Fax:* (2) 211586 (Office).

GEPHARDT, Richard Andrew, BS, JD; American politician; b. 31 Jan. 1941, St Louis; s. of Louis Andrew Gephardt and Loreen Estelle Cassell; m. Jane Ann Byrnes 1966; one s. two d.; ed Northwestern Univ. and Univ. of Michigan; mem. Mo. Bar 1965; Partner firm Thompson and Mitchell, St Louis 1965–76; Alderman 14th Ward, St Louis 1971–76, Democratic Committeeman 1968–71; mem. 95th to 105th Congress from Third Mo. Dist 1979–; Cand. for Democratic nomination to US Presidency 1988; Majority Leader 1989–94; Democratic Leader 1995–2002; Minority Leader 2000–; Pres. Children's Hematology Research Asscn, St Louis Children's Hosp. 1973–76; mem. Bar Assscn, St Louis, Mo., American Legion, Young Lawyers' Soc. (Chair. 1972–73). *Address:* US House of Representatives, 1226 Longworth House Office Building, Washington, DC 20515, USA (Office).

GERASHCHENKO, Victor Vladimirovich; Russian banker; b. 21 Dec. 1937, Leningrad; s. of Vladimir Gerashchenko and Anastasia Klinova; m. Nina Drozdkova 1960; one s. one d.; ed Moscow Financial Inst.; Man. Div. of Foreign Exchange Dept, USSR Bank for Foreign Trade (BFT) 1960–65, Man. Dir of Dept 1972–74, Man. Dir Foreign Exchange Dept 1982–83, Deputy Chair. 1983–89; Dir Moscow Narodny Bank Ltd, London 1965–67, Deputy Gen. Man., then Gen. Man. Beirut 1967–71, Gen. Man. Singapore 1977–82; Chair. Bd Ost-West Handelsbank, Frankfurt am Main 1974–77; Chair. Bd State Bank of USSR 1989–91, Head of Dept Fund Reforma 1991–92; Chair. Cen. Bank of Russian Fed. 1992–94, 1998–2001, Adviser 1994–96; Chair. Bd Moscow Int. Bank (MIB) 1996–98; Chair. Supervisory Bd Vneshtorgbank 1998–; Order of Banner of Labour (twice). *Leisure interest:* literature. *Address:* c/o Central Bank of Russian Federation, Neglinnaya str. 12, 103016 Moscow, Russia.

GERE, Richard; American actor; b. 31 Aug. 1949, Phila; m. 1st Cindy Crawford 1991 (divorced); m. 2nd Carey Lowell 2002; one s. one step-d.; ed Univ. of Massachusetts; fmrly played trumpet, piano, guitar and bass and composed music with various groups; stage performances with Provincetown Playhouse and off-Broadway; appeared in London and Broadway productions of The Taming of the Shrew, A Midsummer Night's Dream and Broadway productions of Habeas Corpus and Bent; film debut 1975; Founding Chair. and Pres. Tibet House, New York; Hon. DLit (Leicester) 1992. *Films include:* Report to the Commissioner 1975, Baby Blue Marine 1976, Looking for Mr Goodbar 1977, Days of Heaven 1978, Blood Brothers 1978, Yanks 1979, American Gigolo 1980, An Officer and a Gentleman 1982, Breathless 1983, Beyond the Limit 1983, The Cotton Club 1984, King David 1985, Power 1986, No Mercy 1986, Miles From Home 1989, 3000 1989, Internal Affairs 1990, Pretty Woman 1990, Rhapsody in August 1991, Final Analysis 1991, Sommersby (co-exec. producer) 1993, Mr Jones (co-exec. producer) 1994, Intersection 1994, First Knight 1995, Primal Fear 1996, Red Corner 1997, Burn

Hollywood Burn 1998, Runaway Bride 1999, Dr T. and the Women 2000, Autumn in New York 2000, The Mothman Prophecies 2002, Unfaithful 2002, Chicago (Golden Globe for Best Actor in a Musical 2003) 2002. *Publication:* Pilgrim Photo Collection 1998.

GEREMEK, Bronisław, PROF.HIST.; Polish politician and historian; b. 6 March 1932, Warsaw; s. of Stefan Geremek and Alicja Geremek; m. Hanna Geremek 1952; two s.; ed Warsaw Univ., Ecole Pratique des Hautes Etudes, Paris; scientific worker History Inst., Polish Acad. of Sciences, Warsaw 1954–60; lecturer, Sorbonne, Paris 1962–65; History Inst. of Polish Acad. of Sciences, Warsaw 1965–85, Asst Prof. 1972, Head Research Unit of History of Medieval Culture 1965–80, Prof. 1989–; mem. Polish United Workers' Party (PZPR) 1950–68; Co-Founder and Lecturer Scientific Courses Soc. 1978–81; adviser to Interfactory Strike Cttee, Gdańsk Shipyard Aug. 1980, subsequently to Interfactory Founding Cttee of Solidarity Ind. Self-governing Trade Union, Gdańsk and to Nat. Understanding Comm. of Solidarity Trade Union 1980; Chair. Programme Council of Social and Labour Study Centre attached to Nat. Comm. of Solidarity 1980–81; Chair. Programme Comm., First Nat. Congress of Solidarity Trade Union, Gdańsk 1981; interned 1981–82; adviser to Provisional Co-ordinating Comm. of Solidarity Trade Union and to Lech Wałęsa (q.v.) 1983–87; arrested May 1983, released under amnesty July 1983; adviser to Nat. Exec. Comm. of Solidarity Trade Union 1987–90; mem. Civic Cttee attached to Lech Wałęsa, Chair. of Solidarity Trade Union 1988–91; participant Round Table debates, mem. and Co-Chair. group for political reforms Feb.–April 1989; Deputy to Sejm (Parl.) 1989–97; Chair. Civic Parliamentary Caucus 1989–90; Chair. Constitutional Comm., Chair. Sejm Cttee of Foreign Affairs 1991–97; Chair. Democratic Union Parl. Caucus 1991–94; Prof. Collège de France 1992–; Chair. Parl. Club 'Freedom Union' 1994–97; Chair. Freedom Union Party 2001; Minister of Foreign Affairs 1997–2000; mem. Polish Historical Soc., PEN Club, Royal Historical Soc., Soc. Européenne de Culture, Asscn of Authors of Scientific Works, Academia Europaea, European Medieval Acad., Académie Universelle des Cultures; Dr hc (Tours) 1982, (Utrecht) 1986, (Columbia Univ.) 1989, (Bologna) 1989, (Oberlin Coll., USA, Univ. of Paris-Sorbonne) 1990, (Univ. Libre, Brussels) 1991, (Leicester) 1992, (Brown Univ., Providence) 1994, (Bucharest) 1995, (Università degli Studi, Turin) 1997, (Sofia, Faculté Catholique de Mons) 1998, (Freie Universität, Berlin, Brandeis Univ., New York) 1999, (Waseda Univ., Tokyo) 2000, (Univ Marc Bloch, Strasbourg) 2001, Alfred Jurzykowski Foundation Award, New York 1986; Prix Louise Weiss 1989, Herder Foundation Award, Vienna 1990, Société Européenne de Culture Prize 1993, Karl Preis, Aachen 1998, Distinguished Leaders Award, Univ. of Calif., Los Angeles 1999, F. D. Roosevelt Award, Middelburg 2000, Open Soc. Prize, Budapest 2000, Premi Speciali per la Cultura 2002, Grand Prix de la Francophonie 2002; Officier, Légion d'honneur, Grande Oficial, Ordem da Liberdade (Portugal), Grosses Verdienstkreuz mit Stern (Germany), Commdr, Ordre nat. du Mérite, Lietuvos Didžiojo Kuningaikščio Gedimino III laipsnio ordinas (Lithuania), Grand Croix, Ordre de Léopold II (Belgium), Cruz Grande, Orden del Mérito (Chile), White Eagle Order. *Publications:* numerous works on medieval history of Europe (mainly France) and medieval history of Polish culture, including Najemna siła robocza w rzemiośle Paryża XIII–XV w., Ludzie, towary, pieniądze (co-author) 1968, Ludzie marginesu w średniowiecznym Paryżu XIV-XVw. 1971 (Acad. française award 1976), Życie codzienne w Paryżu Franciszka Villona 1972, Inutiles au monde. Vagabonds et marginaux en Europe aux XIV–XVI siècles 1980, Dzieje kultury średniowiecznej Polski (co-author) 1985, Litość i szubienica 1989, Świat Opery żebraczej. Obraz włóczęgów i nędzarzy w literaturach europejskich XV–XVII wieku 1989, La Democrazia in Europa (co-author) 1993, Passions communes (co-author) 1993, The Common Roots of Europe 1996. *Address:* College of Europe, Natolin Campus, ul. Nowoursynowska 84, 02-797 Warsaw (Office); ul. Stonimskiego 19/144, 00-195 Warsaw, Poland (Home). *Telephone:* (22) 545-9407 (Office). *Fax:* (22) 648-9823 (Office). *E-mail:* bgeremek@natolin.edu.pl.

GERGEN, David Richmond, JD; American government official; b. 9 May 1942, Durham, NC; ed Yale and Harvard Univs; Staff Asst Nixon Admin. Washington, DC 1971–72; special Asst to Pres. and Chief, White House writing/research team 1973–74; special counsel to Pres. Ford and Dir White House Office Communications 1975–77; Research Fellow, American Enterprise Inst.; Man. Ed. American Enterprise Inst. Public Opinion magazine 1977–81; Asst to Pres. Reagan, Staff Dir White House 1981; Asst to Pres. Reagan for Communications 1981–83; Research Fellow, Inst. of Politics, John F. Kennedy School of Govt Cambridge, Mass. 1983–85; Man. Ed. U.S. News & World Report, Washington, DC 1985–86, Ed. 1986, later Ed.-at-Large 1996–; Adviser to Pres. Clinton 1993–2001, for Foreign Policy 1994–95, to Sec. of State 1994; Visiting Prof. Duke Univ. N Carolina 1995–; Sr Fellow Aspen Inst. *Address:* 1779 Massachusetts Avenue, Suite 515, Washington, DC 20036, USA.

GERGIEV, Valery Abesalovich; Russian conductor; b. 2 May 1953, Moscow; m. Natalia Gergieva; one s. one d.; ed Leningrad Conservatory; prize winner at All-Union Conductors' Competition, Moscow (while still a student) and at Karajan Competition, Berlin; Chief Conductor of Armenian State Orchestra 1981–84; Asst Conductor (to Yuriy Temirkanov, q.v.) of Kirov Opera, Leningrad; Music Dir Kirov (now Mariinsky) Opera Theatre 1988– (Artistic Man. 1996–); Prin. Guest Conductor of Rotterdam Philharmonic 1989–92, Prin. Conductor 1992–; Prin. Guest Conductor New York Metropolitan Opera 1998–; tours extensively in Europe and the USA; has guest-conducted Berlin Philharmonic, Dresden Philharmonic, Bayerischer Rundfunk, Royal Concertgebouw, London Philharmonic, City of Birmingham Symphony, Royal Philharmonic, London Symphony, Orchestra of Santa Cecilia, Japan Philharmonic; orchestras of Boston, Chicago, Cleveland, New York, San Francisco and Toronto; operas at Covent Garden, Metropolitan and San Francisco; State Prize of Russia 1993, Musician of the Year (Musical Life Magazine) 1992, 1993, Classical Music Awards 1994, Conductor of the Year (Musical America Yearbook) 1996, Triumph Prize 1999. *Address:* c/o Columbia Artists, 165 West 57th Street, New York, NY 10019, USA; Mariinsky Theatre, Teatralnaya pl. 1, St Petersburg, Russia. *Telephone:* (212) 841-9506 (New York); (812) 114-44-41 (St Petersburg). *Fax:* (212) 841-9599 (New York); (812) 314-17-44 (St Petersburg).

GERHARDT, Wolfgang; German politician; b. 31 Dec. 1943, Ulrichstein-Helpershain; two c.; Hessian Minister for Science and Art 1970; Party Whip Freie Demokratische Partei (FDP) (Free Democratic Party), State Parl., Hesse 1983–87, 1991–94, Rep. and Deputy Prime Minister 1987–91; Chair. FDP 1994–2001; Leader FDP Group in Bundestag (Parl.) 1998–. *Publication:* Es geht – wir haben alle Chancen 1997. *Address:* Liebenaustrasse 8B, 75191 Wiesbaden, Germany (Office). *E-mail:* wolfgang.gerhardt@bundestag.de (Office). *Website:* www.fdp.de (Office); www.wolfgang-gerhardt.de (Home).

GERINGER, James E. (Jim), BS; American politician; b. 24 April 1944, Wheatland, Wyo.; m. Sherri Geringer; five c.; ed Kansas State Univ.; farmer and substitute teacher; officer USAF, Space Devt Programs; fmr Wyo. State Rep. Platte Co.; mem. Wyo. State Senate for Platte Co., Dist 3 until 1995; Gov. of Wyoming 1994–2003; Chair. Western Govs.' Asscn, Educ. Comm. of States; Republican. *Address:* c/o Office of the Governor, Capitol Building, 200 West 24th Street, Cheyenne, WY 82002-0001, USA.

GERKAN, Meinhard von; German architect; b. 3 Jan. 1935, Riga, USSR (now Latvia); freelance architect in collaboration with Volkwin Marg 1965– (seven other partners 1974–); with Freie Akad. der Künste Hamburg 1972–74; Prof. Inst. für Baugestaltung A, Technische Univ. Brunswick 1974–; with Kuratorium Jürgen-Ponto-Stiftung Frankfurt 1982; Guest Prof. Nihon Univ. Tokyo 1988, Univ. of Pretoria 1993; mem. Akad. der Künste; Hon. Fellow AIA 1995, Inst. of Mexican Architects 1995; work includes airport bldgs, cultural insts, railway stations, hotels, offices, public bldgs and housing throughout Germany and in Saudi Arabia, Italy, Latvia, China and Algeria; recipient of more than 350 prizes at nat. and int. competitions, Fritz Schumacher Award 2000, Romanian National Award 2002. *Publications:* Architektur 1966–1978 1978, Die Verantwortung des Architekten 1982, Architektur 1978–1983 1983, Alltagsarchitektur, Gestalt und Ungestalt 1987, Architektur 1983–1988 1988, Architektur 1988–1991 1992, von Gerkan, Marg and Partners 1993, Idea and Model: 30 years of architectural models 1994, Architektur im Dialog 1994, Culture Bridge 1995, Architecture 1991–1995 1995, Architecture for Transportation 1997, Architecture 1995–97 1998, Möbel Furniture 1998, Architecture 1997–1999: Vol. 1 Selected Projects 2000, Modell Virtuell 2000, Architecture 1999–2000 2002. *Address:* Elbchaussee 139, 22763 Hamburg, Germany (Office). *Telephone:* (40) 881510 (Office). *Fax:* (40) 88151177 (Office). *E-mail:* hamburg-e@gmp-architekten.de (Office). *Website:* www.gmp-architekten.de (Office).

GERMAIN, Paul, D. ÈS SC.; French professor of theoretical mechanics; b. 28 Aug. 1920, Saint-Malo; s. of Paul Germain and Elisabeth Frangeul; m. Marie-Antoinette Gardent 1942; one s. one d.; ed Ecole Normale Supérieure de Paris and Univ. of Paris; Research Engineer, Office Nat. d'Etudes et de Recherches Aérospatiales (O.N.E.R.A.) 1946–49, Dir 1962–68; Assoc. Prof. Univ. of Poitiers 1949–54; Prof. Univ. of Lille 1954–58; Prof. of Theoretical Mechanics Univ. of Paris 1958–77, Ecole Polytechnique 1977–85, Univ. Pierre and Marie Curie 1985–87; Visiting Prof., Brown Univ. 1953–54, Stanford Univ. 1969–70; mem. Acad. des Sciences 1970–, Perm. Sec. 1975–96, Hon. Perm. Sec. 1996–; mem. Int. Acad. of Astronautics, Pontifical Acad. of Sciences; Foreign mem. Accad. Nazionale dei Lincei, Rome 1976, Polish Acad. of Sciences 1978; Foreign Assoc. Nat. Acad. of Eng, Washington 1979; Hon. Fellow, AIAA 1981; Foreign Assoc. Acad.-Royale Belgique des Lettres, des Sciences et des Arts 1984, Acad. of Sciences (USSR) 1988; Dr. hc (Louvain) 1961, (Strathclyde) 1975, (Madrid Univ.) 1980, (Brussels) 1984; Commdr Légion d'honneur, Grand-Croix Ordre nat. du Mérite, Medaille de l'aéronautique, Commdr des Palmes académiques. *Publications:* Mécanique des milieux continus 1962, Cours de mécanique des milieux continus 1973, Mécanique 1986 and more than 100 papers on theoretical aerodynamics, magnetohydrodynamics, shock wave theory and mechanics of continua. *Leisure interests:* hiking, swimming, skiing. *Address:* Institut de France, 23 quai de Conti 75006, Paris (Office); 3 Avenue de Champaubert, 75015 Paris, France (Home). *Telephone:* 1-44-41-43-52 (Office); 1-43-06-35-53 (Home).

GERMAN, Aleksey Georgievich; Russian film director; b. 20 July 1938, Leningrad; s. of Yuri Pavlovich German and Tatyana Rittenberg; m. Svetlana Karmalina; one s.; ed Leningrad State Inst. of Theatre, Music and Cinema; dir theatres in Leningrad and Smolensk; works with Lenfilm Studios 1964–; Head, St Petersburg experimental film studio; USSR State Prize 1988, State Prize of Russia, Triumph Prize 1998. *Films include:* The Seventh Traveller 1968, Twenty Days Without War 1977, My Friend Ivan Lapshin 1984, Trial on the Road 1986, Khrustalev, My Car! 1997. *Address:* Marsovo Pole 7, Apt. 37, 191041 St Petersburg, Russia. *Telephone:* (812) 315-17-06.

GERMANI, Fernando; Italian musician; b. 5 April 1906; ed Rome Conservatoire and Pontifical Inst. of Sacred Music; Prof. of Organ Music at the Rome Conservatoire, Chigiana Music Acad. (Siena), Curtis Inst. (Philadelphia); recitals in the Americas, Australasia, South Africa, Europe; Commdr Order of St Gregory the Great, Commdr Order of St Sylvester, Kt Crown of Italy. *Publications:* Revision of works of Girolamo Frescobaldi 1936, A Method of Organ Playing 1942. *Address:* Via delle Terme Deciane 11, Rome, Italy.

GERMANOVA, Yevdokiya Alekseyevna; Russian actress; b. 8 Nov. 1959, Moscow; ed State Inst. of Theatre Art; with Oleg Tabakov Theatre Studio 1983–; roles in productions including Mystery by J. B. Priestley (production in Austria), Trust, Love, Hope by O. Horvat (Dir M. Schell); Stanislavski Prize of Russia and numerous prizes for best women's roles at int. and nat. festivals in Kiev, Karlovy Vary, Nizhny Novgorod, Ange, Moscow. *Numerous film appearances:* Moslem (Dir V. Khotinenko), Close Circle (A. Konchalovsky), Kix (S. Livnev), Crazy (S. Garazov), Here is Freedom (A. Waida), Niagara (A. Vizir), We Cannot Guess (O. Narutskaya). *Address:* Chaplygina Str., 1A, Oleg Tabakov Theatre Studio, Moscow, Russia. *Telephone:* (095) 916-21-21 (Theatre) (Office).

GERSON, Mark; British photographer; b. 3 Oct. 1921, London; s. of Bernard Gerson and Esther Gerson; m. Renée Cohen 1949; two d.; ed Cen. Foundation School for Boys, London and Regent Polytechnic, London; served in RAF 1941–46; taught photography under EVT scheme while serving in RAF in Paris 1946; specialist portrait photographer concentrating on literary personalities and industrialists; ran photographic studio 1947–87; now freelance photographer; major exhbns Fox Talbot Museum, Lacock, Wilts. 1981, Shaw Theatre, London 1983, Writers Observed, Nat. Theatre, London 1984, The Poetry Library, Royal Festival Hall 1991, Literati, Nat. Portrait Gallery, London 1996; Fellow Inst. British of Professional Photography. *Leisure interests:* cinema, theatre. *Address:* 3 Regal Lane, Regent's Park, London, NW1 7TH, England. *Telephone:* (20) 7286-5894; (20) 7267-9246. *Fax:* (20) 7267-9246. *E-mail:* mark.gerson@virgin.com (Office); mark.gerson@virgin.com (Home).

GERSTNER, Louis Vincent, Jr, BA, MBA; American business executive; b. 1 March 1942, New York; s. of Louis Vincent Gerstner and Marjorie Rutan Gerstner; m. Elizabeth Robins Link 1968; one s. one d.; ed Dartmouth Coll. and Harvard Univ.; Dir McKinsey & Co., New York 1965–78; Exec. Vice-Pres. American Express Co., New York 1978–81, Vice-Chair. 1981–83, Chair. Exec. Cttee 1983–85, Pres. 1985–89, Chair., CEO RJR Nabisco 1989–93; Chair., CEO IBM 1993–2002; Vice-Chair. New American Schools Devt Corpn Bd 1991–98; Dir The New York Times Co. 1986–97, Bristol-Myers Squibb Co., Japan Soc.1992–97; mem. Exec. Cttee, Bd of Trustees Jt Council on Econ. Educ. 1975–87, Chair. 1983–85; mem. Bd of Dirs Memorial Sloan Kettering Hosp. 1978–89, 1998–, Vice-Chair. 2000–; Chair. Computer Systems Policy Project 1999–2001; Advisory Bd DaimlerChrysler 2001–, Sony Corpn 2002–; Chair. Carlyle 2002–; mem. Policy Cttee, Business Roundtable 1991–98; mem. Bd of Overseers Annenberg Inst. for School Reform, Brown Univ.; mem. Business Council, American China Soc., Council on Foreign Relations, Nat. Security Telecommunications Advisory Cttee 1994–97, Advisory Cttee for Trade Policy and Negotiations 1995–, Nat. Acad. of Eng; Trustee NY Public Library 1991–96; Hon. KBE 2001; Hon. DBA (Boston Coll.) 1994; Hon. LLD (Wake Forest, Brown) 1997; Hon. DEng (Rensselaer Polytechnic Inst.) 1999; Washington Univ. Acad. for Excellence in Business, Eng and Technology 1999; numerous awards for work in educ. *Publication:* Reinventing Education (co-author) 1994. *Address:* c/o IBM Corporation, New Orchard Road, Armonk, NY 10504-1709, USA.

GERTH, Donald R., PhD; American university president; b. 4 Dec. 1928, Chicago, Ill.; s. of late George C. Gerth and Madeleine A. Canavan; m. Beverly J. Hollman 1955; two d.; ed Univ. of Chicago; USAF 1952–56; lecturer in History, Univ. of Philippines 1953–54; Admissions Counsellor, Univ. of Chicago 1956–58; Assoc. Dean of Students, Admissions and Records and mem. Dept of Govt, San Francisco State Univ. 1958–63; Assoc. Dean of Institutional Relations and Student Affairs, Calif. State Univ., Chico 1963–64, Dean of Students 1964–68, Prof. of Political Science 1964–76, Co-Dir Danforth Foundation Research Project 1968–69, Coordinator, Inst. for Local Govt and Public Service and of Public Admin. 1968–70, Assoc. Vice-Pres. for Acad. Affairs and Dir Int. Programs (Dir of Center at Univ. of Skopje, Yugoslavia) 1969–70, Vice-Pres. for Acad. Affairs 1970–76; Pres. and Prof. of Political Science and Public Admin., Calif. State Univ., Dominguez Hills 1976–84; Pres. and Prof. of Govt and Public Admin. Calif. State Univ., Sacramento 1984–; Pres. Int. Asscn of Univ. Presidents 1996–99; numerous other appts. *Leisure interest:* international affairs. *Address:* California State University, 6000 J Street, # 206, Sacramento, CA 95819; 417 Webster's Court, Roseville, CA 95747, USA (Home). *Telephone:* (916) 278-7737 (Office); (916) 771-3412 (Home). *Fax:* (916) 278-6959 (Office.).

GERWEL, Gert Johannes (Jakes), DLitt, DPhil; South African university vice-chancellor; b. 18 Jan. 1947, Somerset East; s. of John Gerwel and Sarah Becket; m. Phoebe Abrahams 1970; one s. one d.; ed Paterson High School, Port Elizabeth and Univs of Western Cape and Brussels; Educ. Adviser, SA Students' Org. Durban 1972–73; Lecturer, Sr Lecturer, Prof., Dean, Univ. of Western Cape, Rector and Vice-Chancellor 1987–94; Dir-Gen. Office of Pres. and Sec. to Parl. 1994–; Chair. Careers Research and Information Centre, Cape Town, Equal Opportunity Foundation, Johannesburg, Community

Agency for Social Enquiry, Johannesburg. *Publication:* Literatuur en Apartheid 1983. *Leisure interest:* cricket. *Address:* Private Bag X1000, Cape Town 8000, South Africa.

GESANG DOJE; Chinese party official; b. Feb. 1936, Qinghai Prov.; s. of Giamucuo and Sangdang Shiji; m. Zenen Namu 1956; one s. three d.; ed Nat. Middle School, Sining, Qinghai and in Beijing; returned to Sining as a corresp. 1955; Vice-Chair. Qinghai Provincial People's Congress Standing Cttee 1991–; started writing poetry 1956. *Publications:* Legend of Hot Spring, The Childbirth of a New Town at Daybreak, The Name of Maji Snow Mountain, You are an Infant of Daylight, Raindrops from the Clouds 1992. *Leisure interests:* riding, hunting, painting.

GESCHKE, Charles M., MS, PhD; American computer executive; ed Carnegie-Mellon Univ., Xavier Univ.; fmr Prin. Scientist and Researcher, Xerox Palo Alto Research Center (PARC), f. PARC Imaging Sciences Lab. 1980; co-Founder and Jt Chair. Adobe Systems Inc. 1982–, Pres. 1987–2000, co-Chair. 2000–; Dir Rambus, Inc.; mem. Nat. Acad. of Eng, Govt-Univ. Industry Research Roundtable, Nat. Acad. of Sciences; mem. Bd of Govs. San Francisco Symphony; mem. Advisory Bd Carnegie-Mellon Univ., Princeton Univ.; mem. Bd of Trustees Univ. of San Francisco; honoured by several orgs. including Asscn for Computing Machinery (ACM), Nat. Computer Graphics Asscn, Rochester Inst. of Tech. *Address:* Adobe Systems Inc., 375 Park Avenue, San José, CA 95110-2704, USA (Office). *Website:* www.adobe.com (Office).

GESTSSON, Svavar; Icelandic diplomatist and politician; b. 26 June 1944; m. Gudrun Agustsdottir; MP 1978–99; Minister of Trade 1978–79, of Social Affairs and Minister of Health 1980–83, of Culture and Educ. 1988–91; Parl. Leader Althydubandalag (People's Alliance); Amb., Consul-Gen. of Iceland and Special Envoy for Millennium Affairs in Canada 1999–2001; Amb. to Sweden 2001–, Albania 2002–, Bulgaria 2002–, Yugoslavia 2002–, Bangladesh 2003–; Order of the Icelandic Falcon 2001. *Publication:* The Horizon – A Book of Political Affairs 1995. *Address:* Embassy of Iceland, Kommendorsgt. 35, 114 58 Stockholm (Office); Strandvaegen 15, 114 56 Stockholm, Sweden (Home). *Telephone:* (8) 442-83-00 (Home). *Fax:* (8) 660-74-23 (Home). *E-mail:* icemb.stock@utn.stjr.is.

GETTY, Donald; Canadian politician; b. 30 Aug. 1933, Westmount, Québec; s. of Charles Ross Getty and Beatrice Lillian Getty; m. Margaret Mitchell 1955; four s.; ed Univ. of Western Ont.; joined Imperial Oil Ltd Edmonton 1955; Lands and Contracts Man. Midwestern Industrial Gas Ltd 1961; Pres. and Man. Dir Baldonnel Oil and Gas Ltd 1964–67; Partner, Doherty, Roadhouse & McCuaig Ltd (investment firm) 1967; mem. Alberta Legis. 1967–79, 1985–; Minister of Fed. and Intergovernmental Affairs, Prov. of Alberta 1971–75, of Energy and Natural Resources 1975–79; Pres. D. Getty Investments Ltd 1979; Chair. of Bd Ipsco 1981–85; Pres., CEO Sunnybank Investments Ltd 1993–94; served as dir of numerous cos; Leader Progressive Conservative Party, Alberta 1985–93; Premier of Alberta 1985–92. *Leisure interests:* golf, horse-racing, hunting. *Address:* 3145 Manulife Place, 10180-101 Street, Edmonton, Alberta, T5J 3S4; Box 300, Erskine, Alberta T0C 1G0, Canada.

GETTY, Mark; American business executive; fmr investment banker; co-Founder Getty Images Inc. 1995–. *Address:* c/o Getty Images, 701 North 34th Street, Suite 4001, Seattle, WA 98103, USA (Office).

GHAFFARI, Abolghassem, DSc, PhD; Iranian mathematician; b. 1909, Tehran; s. of Hossein Ghaffari and Massoumeh Shahpouri; m. Mitra Meshkati 1966; two d.; ed Darolfonoun School, Tehran and Univs. of Nancy, Paris, London and Oxford; Assoc. Prof. Tehran Univ. 1937–42, Prof. of Math. 1942–72; Temp. Sr Lecturer in Math. King's Coll. London 1946–48; Sr Research Fellow and Research Assoc. in Mathematics, Harvard 1950–51; Visiting Fellow Princeton Univ. 1951–52; mem. Inst. for Advanced Study, Princeton 1951–52; Senior mathematician, Nat. Bureau of Standards, Washington, DC 1956–57; Aeronautical research scientist 1957–64; Aerospace scientist NASA, Goddard Space Flight Center, Greenbelt, Md 1964–72; Professorial Lecturer in Mathematics and Statistics, American Univ. Washington, DC 1958–60 and other American Univs.; Prof. Emer. of Mathematics (Tehran Univ.) 1972; mem. American, French (1935–70) and London Mathematical Socs., UNESCO Nat. Cttee 1948-50, Higher Council of Educ., American Astronomical Soc., Philosophical Soc. of Washington (1958–80); Fellow, New York Acad. of Sciences 1961, Washington Acad. of Sciences 1963, AAAS 1965; Chair. Washington Acad. of Science Awards Cttee for Math., Statistics and Computer Science 1975–90; Orders of Homayoun, Danesh (1st class) and Sepass (1st class), U.S. Special Apollo Achievement Award, Apollo 11 Commemorative Certificate. *Publications:* Sur l'équation fonctionnelle de Chapman-Kolmogoroff 1936, The Hodograph Method in Gas Dynamics 1950; about 60 research articles on Differential Equations in the Large, Brownian Motion, Transonic and Supersonic Flow, Lunar Flight Optimization and Orbit Determination, Astrodynamics, General Relativity and Relativistic Cosmology in Persian, French and English in nat. and int. journals. *Leisure interests:* reading, walking. *Address:* 7532 Royal Dominion Drive, Bethesda, MD 20817-4659, USA. *Telephone:* (301) 469-7372. *Fax:* (301) 469-7372. *E-mail:* ghaffari@erols.com (Home).

GHAI, Dharam Pal, PhD; Kenyan international civil servant and economist; b. 29 June 1936, Nairobi; s. of Basti Ghai and Widya Wati; m. Neela Korde 1963; one s. two d.; ed Queen's Coll. Oxford, Yale Univ.; Lecturer in Econs, Makerere Univ., Uganda 1961–65; Visiting Fellow Econ. Growth Centre, Yale Univ. 1966–67; Research Prof. and Dir of Econs Research, Inst. of Devt Studies, Univ. of Nairobi 1967–71, Dir Inst. of Devt Studies 1971–74; Sr Economist, Comm. on Int. Devt (Pearson Comm.), Washington, DC 1968–69; Chief, World Employment Programme Research Br., Employment and Devt Dept, ILO, Geneva 1973–74, Chief, Tech. Secr., World Employment Conf. 1975–76, Chief, Rural Employment Policies Br., Employment and Devt Dept 1977–87; Dir UNRISD 1987–99; Coordinator ILO Transition Team 1998–99; Adviser Int. Inst. of Labour Studies; Fellow African Acad. of Sciences. *Publications:* Collective Agriculture and Rural Development in Soviet Central Asia (with A.R. Khan) 1979, Planning for Basic Needs in Kenya (co-author) 1979, Agricultural Prices, Policy and Equity in Sub-Saharan Africa (with Lawrence Smith) 1987, Labour and Development in Rural Cuba (co-author) 1987, Social Development and Public Policy (ed.), Renewing Social and Economic Progress in Africa (ed.);, co-ed. and contrib. several other books. *Leisure interests:* photography, gardening, swimming. *Address:* 32 chemin des Voirons, 1296 Coppet, Vaud, Switzerland (Home). *Telephone:* (22) 7765281 (Home). *Fax:* (22) 7765282 (Home). *E-mail:* ghai@ilo.org (Office); ghai@bluewin.ch (Home).

GHAI, Yash, BA, LLM, DCL; Kenyan constitutional lawyer and professor of law; b. 1938; ed Univ. of Oxford, UK, Harvard Univ., USA; barrister Middle Temple, London, UK 1962; Lecturer Univ. of Dar–es–Salaam 1963–66, Sr Lecturer 1966–69, Prof. and Dean 1969–70; Sr Fellow and Lecturer Yale Univ., USA 1971–73; Prof. Warwick Univ., UK 1974–89; Prof. of Law (Sir Y. K. Pau Chair in Public Law) Univ. of Hong Kong 1989–; involved in drafting constitutions for Papua New Guinea, Fiji, Solomon Islands and others; Chair. Constitution of Kenya Review Comm. 2000–03; Distinguished Researcher Award, Univ. of Hong Kong 2001. *Publications include:* Hong Kong's New Constitutional Order: The Resumption of Chinese Sovereignty and Basic Law 1997, Hong Kong's Constitutional Debate: Conflict over Interpretation (co-author) 1999, Autonomy and Ethnicity: Negotiating Competing Claims in Multi-Ethnic States (ed. and contrib.) 2000, Public Participation and Minorities 2001. *Address:* Department of Law, University of Hong Kong, Pokfulam Road, Hong Kong Special Administrative Region, People's Republic of China (Office). *Telephone:* (852) 28592111 (Office). *Fax:* (852) 28582549 (Office). *Website:* www.hku.hk (Office).

GHANEM, Mohamed Hafez, PhD; Egyptian government official and lawyer; b. 28 Sept. 1925; m. Jouman M. Gaafar 1956; two s. one d.; ed Cairo Univ. and Univ. de Paris; Lecturer, Faculty of Law, Alexandria Univ. 1949; Prof. of Public Int. Law and Vice-Dean, Faculty of Law, Ain Shams Univ. 1960–68; Minister of Tourism 1968–69, of Educ. 1969–71; Sec.-Gen. Arab Socialist Union 1973–75; Deputy Prime Minister 1975–78, Minister of Higher Educ. 1975–76, for Social Devt and Services, Presidency Affairs and the Sudan 1976–78; Head of Ministerial Cttee for Local Govt 1976; Attorney, Legal and Econ. Consultant 1978–; Prof. of Public Int. Law, Ain Shams Univ. 1978–; fmr Pres. Egyptian Soc. of Int. Law; mem. Arbitration, Conciliation and Mediation Comm. of O.A.U. 1966–71; mem. Legal Consultative Comm. for Afro-Asian Countries 1958–65; State Prize for Pest Publ. in field of Int. Law and Political Science 1960. *Publications:* Public International Law (Arabic) 1964, International Organization 1967, International Responsibility 1972. *Leisure interests:* fishing, reading. *Address:* 3 Sharia El Bergass, Garden City, Cairo, Egypt (Home). *Telephone:* 970431 (Office); 980987 (Home).

GHANIM, Faraj Said bin; Yemeni politician; Prime Minister of Yemen 1997–98; independent. *Address:* c/o Office of the Prime Minister, San'a, Yemen.

GHANNOUCHI, Muhammad; Tunisian politician; b. 1941; fmr Minister of Finance and the Economy, of Int. Co-operation and Foreign Investment; Prime Minister of Tunisia 1999–. *Address:* Bureau du Premier Ministre, Tunis, Tunisia (Office).

GHARBI, El Mostafa, LLB; Moroccan international postal official; b. 9 Feb. 1935, El Jadida; m. Lalla Hafida Regragui 1962; three d.; ed Ecole Nat. Supérieure des Postes, Télégraphes et Téléphones, Paris; various positions, Ministry of Posts, Telegraphs and Telephones, Rabat 1956–65, Dir of Postal and Financial Services 1965–71; Counsellor, Universal Postal Union (UPU), Berne 1971–78, Sr Counsellor 1978–81, Asst Dir-Gen. in charge of postal services and studies 1981–90, in charge of legal and admin. questions 1990–; Médaille de Chevalier. *Publications include:* The UPU: Present Situation – Main Policies 1990; other books on postal services and strategies. *Leisure interests:* reading, sport. *Address:* Merzenacker 29, 3006 Berne, Switzerland. *Telephone:* (31) 9410046. *Fax:* (31) 3503110.

GHATTAS, HE Cardinal Stephanos II (Andreas Ghattas); Egyptian ecclesiastic; b. 16 Jan. 1920, Shaikh Zein-el-Din, Sohag; ordained priest 1944; Bishop of Luxor 1967; Patriarch of Alexandria 1986–; cr. Cardinal 2001. *Address:* Patriarcat Copte Catholique, P.O. Box 69, 34 Sharia Ibn Sandar, Pont de Koubbeh, 11712 Cairo, Egypt (Office). *Telephone:* (2) 2571740 (Office); (2) 2599494 (Home). *Fax:* (2) 4545766 (Office).

GHAZALA, Lt-Gen. Mohamed Abdel Halim Abu- (see Abdel Halim Abu-Ghazala, Marshal Mohamed).

GHEORGHIU, Angela; Romanian soprano; b. 1965, Adjud; m. 1st Andrei Gheorghiu 1988; m. 2nd Roberto Alagna; ed Bucharest Acad.; début Nat. Opera, Cluj 1990; first appearance at Royal Opera House Covent Garden, London 1992, Vienna State Opera 1992, New York Metropolitan Opera 1993, Monte Carlo 1999, Berlin 2001; Belvedere Prize, Vienna, Schatzgraber-Preis,

Hamburg State Opera, Gulbenkian Prize. *Operas:* Don Giovanni, La Bohème, Turandot, Carmen, Cherubin, La Traviata, L'Elisir d'Amore, Falstaff, Roméo et Juliette, La Rondine, Verdi's Requiem. *Recordings include:* La Traviata (as Violetta) 1995, selection of arias. *Address:* c/o Stafford Law Associates, 6 Barham Cose, Weybridge, Surrey, KT13 9PR (Office); c/o Royal Opera House, Covent Garden, London, WC2, England; c/o M. Levon Sayan, 76–78 avenue des Champs-Elysées, 75008 Paris, France.

GHEORGHIU, Ion (Alin); Romanian painter and sculptor; b. 29 Sept. 1929, Bucharest; s. of Emil Gheorghiu and Chiriachiţa Gheorghiu; m. Anamaria Smigelschi 1970; ed N. Grigorescu Fine Arts Coll.; mem. Fine Arts Union, Sec. 1978–; creator of extensive cycles: Suspended Gardens (paintings), Around Archimboldo (drawings, paintings, sculpture), Chimeras (sculpture); Corresp. mem. Romanian Acad. 1993–; Hon. mem. Fine Arts Union of Bulgaria; Romanian Acad. Award 1966, Yomiuri Shimbun Award, Tokyo 1971, Great Award of the Fine Arts Union 1972, Italian Acad. Award and Gold Medal 1980, Trionfo '81 Prize 1981, Homage to Picasso Prize 1981, Homage to Raphael Prize 1993, Sofia Biennial Great Prize 1985, Ministry of Culture Prize (Chişinău, Moldova) 1996, Bucharest Municipality First Prize for Painting 1996. *Exhibitions include:* Romania, Helsinki, Moscow, London, Paris, Warsaw, Rome, Philadelphia, Washington, Glasgow, Tokyo, Venice, Szczecin, Mannheim, Lisbon, Geneva, Prague, Tel Aviv, Tunis, Athens, Madrid, Mexico, Oslo, New York, etc. *Leisure interests:* hunting and fishing. *Address:* 27–29 Emil Pangratti Street, Bucharest (Studio); 6 Aviator Petre Creţu Street, Bucharest, Romania (Home). *Telephone:* (1) 6335560 (Studio).

GHEORGHIU, Mihnea, PhD, DLitt; Romanian university professor and writer; b. 5 May 1919, Bucharest; m. Anda Boldur 1953; one d.; ed Univ. of Bucharest and studies in France, Italy and UK; Chief Ed. Scînteia Tineretului (newspaper) 1944–45; Ed. and Founder, Secolul 20 (monthly int. literary review) 1960–64; Ed.-in-Chief Romanian–American Review; Chair. of Bd Social Future (sociology and political sciences bi-monthly), Studies in the History of Art 1975–; Univ. Prof. 1946–72; Pres. Council of Cinematography 1962–65; Deputy Minister of Culture and Arts 1965–67; Pres. Inst. for Cultural Rels. 1967–72, Acad. of Social and Political Sciences 1972–88, Romanian Filmmakers' Union 1990–; Corresp. mem. Romanian Acad. 1974, mem. 1993; Adviser UNESCO European Centre for Higher Educ.; mem. Club of Rome, Société Européenne de Culture, Acad. Mondiale de Prospective Sociale (Geneva), New York Acad. of Sciences, Int. Shakespeare Asscn 1964–2000; Nat. State Prize; Special Prize, Int. Film Festivals 1964, 1966; Ordre des Arts et des Lettres (France), Italian Order of Merit, Grosse Verdienstkreuz mit Stern (FRG), Order of Orange-Nassau (Netherlands); Acad. Award 1972. *Film screenplays and scripts:* Porto Franco 1962, Tudor 1963–64, Zodia Feciorei 1967, Pădurea pierdută 1992, Cantemir & Muşchetarul român 1974, Hyperion 1975, Tănase Scatin 1976, Burebista 1980. *Plays acted in:* Tudor din Vladimiri, Istorii dramatice, Capul, Zodia Taurului, Patetica '77, Fierul şi aurul. *Radio:* has written more than 20 plays. *Publications:* Orientations in World Literature 1957, Scenes of Shakespeare's Life 1958, Dionysos 1969, Letters from the Neighbourhood 1971, Scenes of Public Life 1972, The Last Landscape (poems) 1974, Five Worlds as Spectacle (collection of plays) 1980, Tobacco Flowers (essays) 1984, Enigma in Fleet Street (novel) 1988, The Two Roses (collection of tales) 1991; translations from Shakespeare, Walt Whitman, Burns, Gabriel García Márquez, etc. *Leisure interest:* swimming. *Address:* Mendeleev Street 28-30, Sector 1, 70169 Bucharest (Office); Dionisie Lupu 74, Bucharest, Romania (Home). *Telephone:* 6504969 (Home); 6505741 (Office). *Fax:* 3111246 (Office).

GHIAUROV, Nicolai; Bulgarian singer; b. 13 Sept. 1929, Velingrad; m. Zlatina Ghiaurov; two c.; ed Sofia Music Acad., Moscow Conservatoire; played violin, piano and clarinet from an early age; debut at Sofia Opera House as Don Basilio in Barber of Seville 1955, debut in Bologna 1958, debut at La Scala, Milan as Varlaam in Boris Godunov 1959, Gremin in Eugene, Barcelona 1990, Colline in La Bohème 1992, Gremin, Turin 1998; regular appearances at La Scala, Metropolitan Opera, New York, Vienna State Opera; maj. roles include title role in Boris Godunov, Mephistopheles in Faust. *Address:* c/o Askonas Holt Ltd, Lonsdale Chambers, 27 Chancery Lane, London, WC2A 1PF, England (Office).

GHIGO, Enzo; Italian politician; b. 1953, Turin; m. Anna Casale; one s.; fmr Scientific Ed., UTET (publishing co.), Turin; self employed in tech. components industry –1982; joined Pubblitalia '80 (advertising co.) 1982, Man. 1986–90, Area Man. for Veneto and Marche 1990–; Regional Co-ordinator, Forza Italia 1993–; elected as MP for Piedmont 2 1994–, Pres. Piedmont 1995–, Vice-Pres. Regional Pres. Congress 1997–; Pres. Conf. of Presidents of Italian Regions 2000–; Vice-Pres. Foundation Italia in Japan 2001; Grand'Ufficiale al merito della Repubblica Italiana 1999, Cavaliere di Gran Croce 2002. *Leisure interests:* cinema, reading, cycling. *Address:* c/o Giunta Regionale del Piemonte, Piazza Castello 165, 10122 Turin, Italy (Office). *Telephone:* (011) 4321600 (Office).

GHIUSELEV, Nicola; Bulgarian bass opera singer; b. 17 Aug. 1936, Pavlikeni; s. of Nicolai Ghiuselev and Elisaveta Ghiuseleva; m. 1st Roumiana Ghiuseleva 1960; m. 2nd Annamaria Petrova-Ghiuseleva 1984; two s. one d.; ed Acad. of Art, Sofia and singing studies under Christo Brumbarov; joined State Opera Co., Sofia; debut as Timur in Puccini's Turandot, State Opera, Sofia 1961; has since appeared at most of the maj. opera houses of the world and is noted for Russian roles such as Boris Godunov, Dositheus, Prince Igor, Ivan the Terrible and the bass repertoire of Verdi, Rossini, Bellini, Donizetti,

Mozart, Berlioz, Cherubini, Ponchielli, etc. *Address:* Villa Elpida, 1616 Sofia, Bulgaria; Via della Pisana 370/B2, 00163 Rome, Italy. *Telephone:* (2) 562929 (Sofia); (06) 66162834 (Rome). *Fax:* (2) 562929 (Sofia); (06) 66162834 (Rome).

GHIZIKIS, Gen. Phaidon; Greek army officer; b. 16 June 1917, Volos; m. (wife deceased); one s.; ed Mil. Acad., War Coll. and Nat. Defence Coll.; Lt-Col 1957, Col 1966, Brig.-Gen. 1968, Maj.-Gen. 1969, Lt-Gen. 1971, Gen. 1973, Commdr of Raiding Force, Dept of Hellenic Army Command 1970; Deputy Commdr of Hellenic Army Command 1971; Commdr C Corps 1972; Commdr of First Army 1973; Pres. of Repub. of Greece 1973–74; Kt Commdr Royal Order of George I, Grand Cross of the Redeemer. *Address:* 25 Kountouriotou, 151 21 Pefki, Greece. *Telephone:* (1) 8021530.

GHOSH, Gautam; Indian film director; b. 24 July 1950, Calcutta; s. of Prof. Himangshu Ghosh and Santana Ghosh; m. Neelanjana Ghosh 1978; one s. one d.; ed Cathedral Mission School, Calcutta, City Coll., Calcutta and Calcutta Univ.; mem. Int. Jury (Oberhausen) 1979; official del., Cannes and London Film Festivals 1982, Venice and Tokyo Film Festivals 1984; mem. Nat. Jury 1985; Exec. Dir Nat. Film Inst. 1987; Dir Nat. Film Devt Corpn, West Bengal Film Devt Corpn; Pres. Award (five times), Human Rights Award (France), Silver Medal and UNESCO Award, Grand Prix Award (USSR). *Films include:* Hungry Autumn 1974, Ma Bhoomi 1980, Dakhal 1982, Paar 1984, Antarjali Yatra 1988, Padma Nadir Majhi 1992, Patang 1994, Gudiya. *Publications:* numerous articles on the cinema. *Leisure interests:* music, reading, travel. *Address:* Block 5, Flat 50, 28/1A Gariahat Road, Kolkata 700029, India. *Telephone:* (33) 4405630 (Home). *Fax:* (33) 4640315 (Home).

GHOSN, Carlos; French business executive; b. 1954; ed Ecole Polytechnique, Ecole des Mines, Paris; trained as mining eng; Man. Dir Michelin Le Puy factory 1981; CEO Michelin Brazil 1985; Michelin North America 1989; Asst. Dir-Gen. Renault Group 1996, Dir (non-exec.) 2001–; COO and Pres. Nissan Motor Co. Ltd 1999–. *Publication:* Renaissance 2001. *Address:* Nissan Motor Co. Ltd, 17-1 Ginza 6-chome, Chuo-ku, Tokyo 104-23, Japan (Office).

GHOZALI, Sid Ahmed; Algerian politician and petroleum executive; b. 31 March 1937, Marnia; ed Ecole des Ponts et Chaussées, Paris; fmr Dir of Energy, Ministry of Industry and Energy; Adviser, Ministry of the Economy 1964; Under-Sec., Ministry of Public Works 1964–65; Pres., Dir-Gen. Société nationale pour la recherche, la production, le transport, la transformation et la commercialisation des hydrocarbures (SONATRACH) 1966–84, Chair., Man. Dir; Minister of Hydraulics March–Oct. 1979, of Foreign Affairs 1989–91; Prime Minister of Algeria 1991–92; Amb. to Belgium 1987–89, to France 1992–93; mem. Cen. Cttee Front de Libération Nat.; Chair. Front Démocratique (FD) May 2000–; mem. Org. technique de mise en valeur des richesses du sous-sol saharien 1962. *Address:* Front Démocratique, Algiers, Algeria (Office).

GIACCONI, Riccardo, PhD; American astrophysicist; b. 6 Oct. 1931, Genoa, Italy; s. of Antonio Giacconi and Elsa Giacconi Canni; m. Mirella Manaira 1957; one s. two d.; ed Univ. of Milan; Asst Prof. of Physics, Univ. of Milan 1954–56; Research Assoc. Indiana Univ. 1956–58, Princeton Univ., 1958–59; joined American Science & Eng Inc. 1959–73, mem. Bd of Dirs. 1966, Exec. Vice-Pres. 1969–73; Assoc. Harvard Coll. Observatory 1970–72; Assoc. Dir Center for Astrophysics 1973–81; Prof. of Astrophysics, Harvard Univ. 1973–81; Prof. of Astrophysics, Johns Hopkins Univ. 1981–99, Research Prof. 1999–; Dir Space Telescope Science Inst., Baltimore 1981–92; Prof. of Astrophysics, Milan Univ., Italy 1991–99; Dir-Gen. European Southern Observatory, Garching, Germany 1993–99; Pres. Associated Univesities, Inc. 1999–; Chair. Task Group on Directions in Space Science 1995–; mem. NASA Space Science Advisory Cttee 1978–79, NASA Advisory Council's Informal Ad Hoc Advisory Subcommittee for the Innovation Study 1979–; mem. NAS (mem. Space Science Bd and High Energy Astrophysics Panel of the Astronomy Survey Cttee 1979–), American Acad. of Arts and Sciences, AAAS, American Astronomical Soc., American Physical Soc. (Fellow 1976), Italian Physical Soc., Int. Astronomical Union; Vice-Chair. COSPAR, I.S.C.E.-1 1980; Astronomy Rep. to Int. Astronomical Union 1979–81; mem. High Energy Astrophysics Division, American Astronomical Soc., Chair. 1976–77, mem. Fachbeirat, Max-Planck Institut für Physik und Astrophysik, Comitato Scientifico del Centro Internazionale di Storia dello Spazio e del Tempo; Foreign mem. Accademia Nazionale dei Lincei; External mem. Max-Planck Soc.; Fulbright Fellow 1956–58; Laurea hc in Astronomy, Univ. of Padua, 1984; Hon. DSc (Chicago) 1983, (Warsaw) 1996; Laurea hc in Physics (Rome) 1998; Hon. DTech and Science (Uppsala) 2000; Space Science Award, AIAA 1976, NASA Medal for Exceptional Scientific Achievement 1980, Gold Medal, Royal Astronomical Soc. 1982, A. Cressy Morrison Award in Natural Sciences, New York Acad. of Sciences 1982, Wolf Prize 1987, Nobel Prize in Physics 2002 and numerous other awards. *Publications:* X-ray Astronomy (co-editor) 1974, Physics and Astrophysics of Neutron Stars and Black Holes (co-editor) 1978, A Face of Extremes: The X-ray Universe (co-ed.) 1985, also numerous articles in professional journals. *Leisure interest:* painting. *Address:* Associated Universities, Inc., 1400 16th Street, NW, Suite 730, Washington, DC 20036-2252 (Office); 6530 Wisconsin Avenue, Apt. 604, Chevy Chase, MD 20815, USA (Home). *Telephone:* (202) 462-1676 (Office); (301) 941-0464 (Home). *Fax:* (202) 232-7161 (Office). *E-mail:* giacconi@aui.edu (Office). *Website:* www.aui.edu (Office).

GIACOMELLI, Giorgio, MA; Italian international civil servant and diplomatist; b. 25 Jan. 1930, Milan; s. of Gino Giacomelli and Maria Van der Kellen; one s. one d.; ed Padua Univ., Cambridge Univ., England and Geneva Inst.

of Higher Int. Studies, Switzerland; joined diplomatic service 1956, Second Sec., Madrid 1958, Second Sec., NATO Del. 1961, First Sec. 1962, Chargé d'affaires, Léopoldville (now Kinshasa) 1964, Counsellor, New Delhi 1966, Ministry of Foreign Affairs, Rome: Personnel 1969, Cultural Dept 1971, Head of Service for Tech. Co-operation 1972, Amb. to Somalia 1973, to Syria 1976; Deputy Dir-Gen., Emigration Dept, with Ministry of Foreign Affairs, Rome 1980, Dir-Gen. 1981, Dir-Gen. Devt Co-operation Dept 1981; Commr-Gen. UNRWA 1985–90; Under-Sec. Gen. UN Vienna Office 1992–97; Exec. Dir UN Int. Drug Control Program; Dir Gen. UN Office, Vienna; Silver Medal for Civil Bravery (Italy), Légion d'honneur (France), Kt Order of Merit (Italy). *Leisure interests:* music, literature, mountaineering, hunting and riding. *Address:* c/o United Nations, Vienna International Centre, P.O. Box 500, 1400 Vienna, Austria.

GIAEVER, Ivar, PhD; American physicist; b. 5 April 1929, Bergen, Norway; s. of John A. Giaever and Gudrun M. Skaarud; m. Inger Skramstad 1952; one s. three d.; ed Norwegian Inst. of Tech., Rensselaer Polytechnical Inst., NY; Norwegian Army 1952–53; Patent Examiner, Norwegian Patent Office 1953–54; Mechanical Engineer, Canadian Gen. Electric Co. 1954–56; Applied Mathematician, Gen. Electric Co. 1956–58; Physicist, Gen. Electric Research and Devt Center 1958–88; Inst. Prof., Physics Dept, Rensselaer Polytechnic, NY 1988–; Prof. Univ. of Oslo 1988–; mem. NAS 1974–; eight hon. PhD degrees; Oliver E. Buckley Prize 1965, Nobel Prize for Physics 1973; Zworkin Award 1974. *Publications in Physics Review Letters:* Energy Gap in Superconductors Measured by Electron Tunneling 1960, Study of Superconductors by Electron Tunneling 1961, Detection of the AC Josephson Effect 1965, Magnetic Coupling Between Two Adjacent Superconductors 1965, The Antibody-Antigen Reaction: A Visual Observation 1973, A Morphological Biosensor for Mammalian Cells 1993, Cell Adhesion Force Microscopy 1999. *Leisure interests:* skiing, sailing, tennis, hiking, camping, playing go. *Address:* Physics Department, Rensselaer Polytechnic Institute, 110 8th Street, Troy, NY 12180-3522 (Office); 2080 Van Antwerp Road, Schenectady, NY 12309, USA (Home). *Telephone:* (518) 276-6429 (Office). *Fax:* (518) 276-2825 (Office). *E-mail:* giaevi@rpi.edu (Office). *Website:* www.rpi.edu/~giaevi (Office).

GIANVITI, François Paul Frédéric, DenD; French professor of law and legal official; b. 2 Aug. 1938, Paris; s. of Dominique Gianviti and Suzanne Fournier; m. Barbara Zawadsky 1965; one s. two d.; ed Lycées Henri IV and Louis-le-Grand, Paris, Facultés des Lettres et de Droit, Paris and New York Univ. School of Law; Asst Faculté de Droit, Paris 1963–67; Lecturer, Faculté de Droit, Nancy 1967–68, Caen 1968–69; Maître de conférences, Faculté de Droit, Besançon, on secondment to IMF 1970–74; Maître de conférences, Univ. of Paris XII 1974–75, Prof. of Law 1975–, Dean 1979–85; Dir of Legal Dept, IMF 1986–, Gen. Counsel 1987–; Chevalier, Ordre Nat. du Mérite, Chevalier des Palmes académiques. *Publication:* Les Biens 1984. *Address:* International Monetary Fund, Legal Department, 700 19th Street, NW, Washington, DC 20431, USA (Office); Faculté de Droit, Université de Paris XII, 38 Avenue Didier, 94210 La Varenne-Saint-Hilaire, France (Office); 11402 Dorchester Lane, Rockville, MD 20852, USA (Home).

GIAP, Gen. Vo Nguyen (see Vo Nguyen Giap, Gen.).

GIBARA, Samir G., MBA; French business executive; b. 23 April 1939, Cairo, Egypt; s. of late Selim Gibara and Renée Bokhazi; m. Salma Tagher 1968; ed Harvard Business School; Adviser, Inst. for Int. Trade, Paris 1967–70; Pres. and Man. Dir Goodyear France 1983; Pres. and CEO Goodyear Canada 1989; Vice-Pres. and Gen. Man. Goodyear Europe 1990; Vice-Pres. Strategic Planning and Acting Chief Financial Officer, Goodyear Tire & Rubber Co. 1992, Exec. Vice-Pres. N American Operations 1994, Pres. and COO 1995–96, Chair., Pres. and CEO Jan. 1996–, Chair. and CEO July 1996–; mem. Admin. Council Int. Paper Co. 1999; Chevalier, Ordre Nat. du Mérite; Chevalier du Tastevin. *Publications:* articles in Le Monde and business journals. *Leisure interests:* theatre, music, reading, tennis, swimming. *Address:* The Goodyear Tire & Rubber Co., 1144 East Market Street, Akron, OH 44316, USA; Goodyear France, 101 avenue de la Chataigneraie, B.P. 310, 92506 Reuil-Malmaison, France. *Telephone:* (216) 796-3840 (Office). *Fax:* (216) 796-2108 (Office).

GIBB, Barry, CBE; British singer and songwriter; b. 1 Sept. 1946, Isle of Man; s. of the late Hughie Gibb and of Barbara Gibb; m. Linda Gray; five c.; emigrated to Australia 1958, returned to UK 1967; formed Bee Gees with brothers Robin Gibb (q.v.) and the late Andy Gibb and Maurice Gibb; started singing in nightclubs, Australia; first single Spikes and Specks 1966 (no.1, Australia); numerous best-selling singles and albums; writer or co-writer of numerous songs for other artists including: Elvis Presley (Words), Sarah Vaughan (Run to Me), Al Green, Janis Joplin, Barbra Streisand (Guilty album), Diana Ross (Chain Reaction), Dionne Warwick (Heartbreaker), Dolly Parton and Kenny Rogers (Islands in the Stream), Ntrance (Staying Alive), Take That (How Deep is Your Love), Boyzone (Words), Yvonne Elliman (If I Can't Have You); the Bee Gees are 5th most successful recording artists ever, have sold over 100 million records world-wide; 7 Grammy awards; elected to Rock and Roll Hall of Fame 1996 (inducted 1997), Int. Achievement Award American Music Awards 1997, Brit Award for Outstanding Contribution to Music 1997, World Music Award for Lifetime Achievement 1997. *Albums include:* Bee Gees 1st, Odessa, Main Course, Children of the World, Saturday Night Fever (has sold over 40 million copies, more than any other soundtrack), Spirits Having Flown, High Civilisation, Size Isn't Everything, Still Waters, One Night Only, This Is Where I Came In, Their Greatest Hits – The Record.

Singles include: NY Mining Disaster 1941, Massachusetts, To Love Somebody, Holiday, I've Gotta Get a Message to You, I Started a Joke, Lonely Days, How Can You Mend a Broken Heart, Jive Talkin', Staying Alive, Night Fever, How Deep Is Your Love, Too Much Heaven, Tragedy, Love You Inside Out, One, You Win Again, First of May. *Address:* c/o Middle Ear, Studio, 1801 Bay Road, Miami Beach, FL 33139, USA.

GIBB, Sir Frank (Francis Ross), Kt, CBE, FREng, FICE; British engineer; b. 29 June 1927, London; s. of Robert Gibb and Violet M. Gibb; m. 1st Wendy M. Fowler 1950 (died 1997); one s. two d.; m. 2nd Kirsten Harwood (née Møller) 2000; ed Loughborough Coll.; Joint Man. Dir Taylor Woodrow PLC 1979–85, Jt Deputy Chair. 1983–85, Chair. and Chief Exec. 1985–89; Man. Dir Taylor Woodrow Construction Ltd 1970–78, Chair. 1978–85, Pres. 1985–; Dir Taylor Woodrow Int. Ltd 1969–85; Chair. Taywood Santa Fe Ltd 1975–85; Jt Deputy Chair. Seaforth Maritime Ltd 1986–89; Dir Seaforth Maritime Holdings 1978–89, Eurotunnel PLC 1986–87, Babcock Int. Group PLC 1989–97, Nuclear Electric PLC 1990–94, Steetley PLC 1990–92, Energy Saving Trust Ltd 1992–99 (Chair. 1995–99), H. R. Wallingford 1995–; Chair. Nat. Nuclear Corpn Ltd 1981–88; mem. Group of Eight 1979–81; mem. Bd British Nuclear Associates 1980–88; Chair. Agrément Bd 1980–82; Chair. Fed. of Civil Eng Contractors 1979–80, Pres. 1984–87; Vice-Pres. Inst. of Civil Engineers 1988–90; Dir (non-exec.) A.M.C.O. Ltd 1995–99, F.B.E. 1998–2002; Hon. FCGI; Hon. FINucE; Dr. hc (Loughborough) 1989; Hon. DTech. *Leisure interests:* ornithology, gardening, walking, music. *Address:* Ross Gibb Consultants, 11 Latchmoor Avenue, Gerrards Cross, Bucks., SL9 8LJ, England.

GIBB, Robin, CBE; British singer and songwriter; b. 22 Dec. 1949, Isle of Man; s. of the late Hughie Gibb; m. Dwina Murphy; one s.; emigrated to Australia 1958, returned to UK 1967; formed Bee Gees with brothers Barry Gibb (q.v.) and the late Maurice Gibb and Andy Gibb; started singing in nightclubs, Australia; first single Spikes and Specks 1966 (no. 1, Australia); numerous performances at major venues around the world; the Bee Gees are 5th most successful recording artists ever, have sold over 100 million records world-wide; 7 Grammy awards; elected to Rock and Roll Hall of Fame 1996, Int. Achievement Award American Music Awards 1997, Brit Award for Outstanding Contribution to Music 1997, World Music Award for Lifetime Achievement 1998; mem. Songwriters' Hall of Fame 1994, Rock 'n' Roll Hall of Fame 1997. *Albums include:* Bee Gees 1st, Odessa, Main Course, Children of the World, Saturday Night Fever (has sold over 40 million copies, more than any other soundtrack), Spirits Having Flown, High Civilisation, Size Isn't Everything, Still Waters, One Night Only; Solo album: Magnet 2003. *Singles include:* NY Mining Disaster 1941, Massachusetts, To Love Somebody, Holiday, I've Gotta Get a Message to You, I Started a Joke, Lonely Days, How Can You Mend a Broken Heart, Jive Talkin', Staying Alive, Night Fever, How Deep Is Your Love, Too Much Heaven, Tragedy, Love You Inside Out, One, You Win Again, First of May. *Writer or co-writer of numerous songs for other artists including:* Elvis Presley (Words), Sarah Vaughan (Run to Me), Al Green, Janis Joplin, Rod Stewart (To Love Somebody), Tina Turner (I Will Be There), Ntrance (Staying Alive), Take That (How Deep is Your Love), Boyzone (Words), Yvonne Elliman (If I Can't Have You). *Address:* Middle Ear, 1801 Bay Road, Miami, FL 33139, USA.

GIBBARD, Allan Fletcher, PhD; American professor of philosophy; b. 7 April 1942, Providence, RI; s. of Harold A. Gibbard and Eleanor Reid Gibbard; m. 1st Mary Craig 1972 (died 1990); m. 2nd Beth Genné 1991; two s.; ed Swarthmore Coll., Harvard Univ.; teacher of math. and physics with U.S. Peace Corps, Achimota School, Ghana 1963–65; Asst Prof. then Assoc. Prof. of Philosophy, Univ. of Chicago 1969–74; Assoc. Prof. of Philosophy, Univ. of Pittsburgh 1974–77; Prof. of Philosophy, Univ. of Mich., Ann Arbor 1977–, Richard B. Brandt Prof. 1992–; Fellow Econometric Soc. 1984, American Acad. of Arts and Sciences 1990. *Publications:* Wise Choices, Apt Feelings: A Theory of Normative Judgement 1990; articles in journals. *Address:* Department of Philosophy, University of Michigan, Ann Arbor, MI 48109, USA. *Telephone:* (313) 764-6285 (Office); (313) 769-2628 (Home). *Fax:* (313) 763-8071.

GIBBONS, Hon. Sir John David, KBE, BA, JP, CBIM; British politician; s. of the late Edmund G. Gibbons and Winifred G. Gibbons; m. Lully Lorentzen 1958; three s.; one d. by fmr marriage; ed Saltus Grammar School, Bermuda, Hotchkiss School, Lakeville, Conn., USA, Harvard Univ., USA; Government service in Bermuda with Social Welfare Bd 1948–58, Bd of Civil Aviation 1958–60, Bd of Educ. 1956–59, Chair. 1973–74; mem. Governing Body and later Chair. Bermuda Tech. Inst. 1956–70; Trade Devt Bd 1960–74; MP 1972–84; Minister of Health and Welfare 1974–75, of Finance 1975–84; Prime Minister 1977–82; Chair. Bermuda Monetary Authority 1984–86, Bank of N. T. Butterfield & Son Ltd 1986–97, Econ. Council 1984–87, Global Asset Man. Ltd 1986–, Colonial Insurance Co. 1986–; mem. Law Reform Cttee 1966–72. *Leisure interests:* tennis, golf, skiing, swimming. *Address:* Edmund Gibbons Ltd, 21 Reid Street, Hamilton, HM 11 (Office); Leeward, 5 Leeside Drive, Pembroke, HM 05, Bermuda (Home). *Telephone:* (441) 295-2396 (Home).

GIBBONS, John H., PhD; American physicist; b. 15 Jan. 1929, Harrisonburg, Va; s. of Howard Gibbons and Jesse Conrad; m. Mary Hobart 1955; three c.; ed Randolph-Macon Coll. Va and Duke Univ. NC; Group leader (nuclear geophysics), Oak Ridge Nat. Lab. 1954–69, Environmental Programme Dir 1969–73; Dir of Energy, Environmental and Resources Center and Prof. of Physics, Univ. of Tennessee 1973–79; Dir Office of Energy Conservation, Fed.

Energy Admin. 1974; Dir Office of Tech. Assessment 1979–92; Asst to Pres. Clinton for Science and Tech. and Dir Office of Science and Tech. Policy 1993–98; Pres. Resource Strategies Inc. 1998–; Sr Adviser US Dept of State 1999–2001; Sr Fellow Nat. Acad. of Eng 1999–2000; Fellow, AAAS, American Physical Soc., American Philosophical Soc., Nat. Acad. of Eng; numerous professional appointments and affiliations; Hon. PhD (Mount Sinai Medical School) 1995; Hon. ScD (Duke) 1997, (Maryland) 1997; Commdr Ordre des Palmes Académiques (France); Bundesverdienstkreuz (Germany); NASA Distinguished Service Medal 1998; Art Beuche Prize, Nat. Acad. of Eng 1998, Abelson Prize, AAAS 1998; Seymour Cray Award 1998; many other awards and distinctions. *Publications:* This Gifted Age: Science and Technology at the Millennium 1997; numerous books and articles in areas of energy and environmental policy, etc. *Leisure interests:* farming, hiking. *Address:* P.O. Box 397, The Plains, VA 20198, USA. *Telephone:* (540) 253-9843 (Office); (540) 253-5409 (Home). *Fax:* (540) 253-5076 (Office); (540) 253-5076 (Home). *E-mail:* jackgibbons@erols.com (Office). *Website:* www.johnhgibbons.org.

GIBBONS, Michael Gordon, MBE, BEng, MSc, PhD; Canadian academic; b. 15 April 1939, Montreal; s. of Albert Gordon Gibbons and Dorothy Mildred Gibbons; m. Gillian Monks 1968; one s. one d.; ed Concordia Univ., Montreal, McGill Univ., Montreal, Queens Univ., Ont., Univ. of Manchester, UK; lecturer Univ. of Manchester 1967–72, Sr Lecturer 1972–75, Prof. 1975–92, Head Dept 1975–92; Dir Univ. UMIST Pollution Research Unit 1979–86, Chair. and Founding Dir Policy Research in Eng, Science and Tech. 1979–92, Dir Research Exploitation and Devt, Vice-Chancellor's Office 1984–92; Dean Grad. School and Dir Science Policy Research Unit, Univ. of Sussex 1992–96, mem. Senate, Man. Cttee, Court and Council; Sec.-Gen. Asscn of Common-wealth Univs. 1996–; Visiting Prof., Univ. of Montreal 1976–81, Univ. of Calif. at Berkeley 1992; Special Adviser House of Commons Science and Tech. Cttee 1993; mem. Council, ESRC 1997; mem. Research Priorities Bd 1994, Chair. 1997; Consultant Cttee of Science and Tech. Policy, OECD, Paris; Fellow Royal Swedish Acad. of Eng Sciences 2000; Hon. LLD (Univ. of Ghana, Legon) 1999; Lt-Gov.'s Silver Medal 1959, Government of Canada Commemorative Medal 2002. *Publications:* Wealth from Knowledge (jtly.) 1972, Science as a Commodity 1984, Post-Innovation Performance: Technical Development and Competition 1986, The Evaluation of Research: A Synthesis of Current Practice 1987, The New Production of Knowledge 1994, Re-thinking Science 2000. *Leisure interests:* classical music, American football. *Address:* Association of Commonwealth Universities, 36 Gordon Square, London, WC1H 0PF (Office); 22 Kensington Court Gardens, London, W8 5QF, England (Home). *Telephone:* (20) 7380-6731 (Office); (20) 7937-4626 (Home). *Fax:* (20) 7387-2655 (Office). *E-mail:* secgen@acu.ac.uk (Office).

GIBBS, Anthony Matthews, MA, BLitt, FAHA; Australian professor of English; b. 21 Jan. 1933, Victoria; s. of J. F. L. Gibbs and S. T. Gibbs; m. 1st Jillian Irving Holden 1960; m. 2nd Donna Patricia Lucy 1983; two s. one step d.; ed Ballarat Church of England Grammar School, Univ. of Melbourne and Oxford Univ.; lecturer in English, Univ. of Adelaide 1960–66, Univ. of Leeds 1966–69; Prof. of English, Univ. of Newcastle, NSW 1969–75; Prof. of English, Macquarie Univ. 1975–98, Emer. Prof. 1999–; mem. Exec. Cttee Int. Asscn for the Study of Anglo-Irish Literature 1973–78, Exec. Cttee English Asscn (Sydney Br.) 1975–91; Rhodes Scholarship 1956; Vice-Pres. Australian Acad. of Humanities 1988–89; Ed. 1989–93. *Publications:* Shaw 1969, Sir William Davenant 1972, The Art and Mind of Shaw 1983, Shaw: Interviews and Recollections 1990, Bernard Shaw: Man and Superman and Saint Joan 1992, Heartbreak House: Preludes of Apocalypse 1994, A Bernard Shaw Chronology 2001. *Leisure interests:* theatre, cooking. *Address:* Department of English, Macquarie University, Sydney, NSW 2109 (Univ.); 4 Acacia Close, Turramurra, NSW 2074, Australia (Home). *Telephone:* (2) 9850-8739 (Office). *Fax:* (2) 9850-6593 (Office). *E-mail:* tony.gibbs@mq.edu.au (Office).

GIBBS, Rt Hon Sir Harry (Talbot), PC, GCMG, AC, KBE, BA, LLM; Australian lawyer; b. 7 Feb. 1917, Sydney; s. of Harry Victor Gibbs and Flora MacDonald Gibbs; m. Muriel Ruth Dunn 1944; one s. three d.; ed Ipswich Grammar School, Queensland and Univ. of Queensland; admitted to Queensland Bar 1939; war service 1939–45 (despatches); Judge, Supreme Court, Queensland 1961, Fed. Court of Bankruptcy and Supreme Court of Australian Capital Territory 1967–70; Justice, High Court, Australia 1970–81; Chief Justice of Australia 1981–87; Chair. Court of Appeal of Kiribati 1988–99, Australian Tax Research Foundation 1990–2002; Hon. LLD; Hon. DUniv; Hon. Bencher, Lincoln's Inn. *Leisure interests:* reading, tennis, swimming. *Address:* 30 Lodge Road, Cremorne, NSW 2090, Australia (Home).

GIBBS, Lancelot ("Lance") Richard; Guyanese cricketer and sports organizer; b. 29 Sept. 1934, Georgetown, British Guiana (now Guyana); s. of Ebenezer and Marjorie Gretna (Archer) Gibbs; cousin of cricketer Clive Lloyd; m. Joy Roslyn Margarete Rogers 1963; one s. one d.; ed St Ambrose Anglican Primary School and Day Commercial Standard High School; right-arm off-spin bowler; played for British Guiana/Guyana 1953–54 to 1974–75, Warwickshire 1967 to 1973, S Australia 1969–70; played in 79 Tests for West Indies 1957–58 to 1975–76, taking then world record 309 wickets (average 29); only bowler to take 100 or more wickets against both England and Australia; toured England 1963, 1966, 1969, 1973, 1975 (World Cup); took 1,024 first-class wickets; Man. 1991 West Indies tour of England; now a sports organizer based in USA, which he represented against Canada 1983; man. posts in transportation business including Booker Shipping, Guyana and Kent Line, Canada; Wisden Cricketer of The Year 1972. *Leisure interests:* reading, all sport. *Address:* 276 Republic Park, Peter's Hall, E.B.D., Guyana.

GIBBS, Sir Roger Geoffrey, Kt; British business executive and administrator; b. 13 Oct. 1934, Herts.; s. of Sir Geoffrey Gibbs, KCMG and Lady Gibbs; ed Eton Coll. and Millfield School; with Jessel Toynbee & Co. Ltd 1954–64, Dir 1960, de Zoete & Gorton (later de Zoete & Bevan) stockbrokers 1964–71; Gov. The Wellcome Trust 1983–99 (Chair. 1989–99); Chair. London Discount Market Asscn 1984–86; Dir Arsenal Football Club 1980–, Gerrard & Nat. Holdings PLC 1989–94 (Chair. 1975–89), Howard De Walden Estates Ltd 1989–2001 (Chair. 1993–98), The Colville Estate Ltd 1989–; Chair. Arundel Castle Cricket Foundation 1986–95, Council for Royal Nat. Pension Fund for Nurses 1975–2000, Court of Advisers, St Paul's Cathedral 1989–2000, Fleming Family & Partners 2000–; mem. Cttee Marylebone Cricket Club 1991–94, St Paul's Cathedral Foundation (Chair. 2000–); Trustee Winston Churchill Memorial Trust 2001–; Liveryman, Merchant Taylor's Co.; Freeman, City of London. *Leisure interests:* sport, travel. *Address:* 23 Tregunter Road, London, SW10 9LS, England. *Telephone:* (20) 7370-3465 (Home). *Fax:* (20) 7373-5263.

GIBBS, Field Marshal Sir Roland Christopher, GCB, CBE, DSO, MC, JP; British army officer; b. 22 June 1921, Barrow Gurney; s. of Guy Melvil Gibbs and Margaret Olivia St John; m. Davina Jean Merry 1955; two s. one d.; ed Eton Coll. and Royal Mil. Coll., Sandhurst; commissioned into 60th Rifles 1940; served in N Africa, Italy, NW Europe 1939–45; commanded Parachute Bn 1960–62; British Army Staff, Washington, DC 1962–63; commanded Parachute Brigade 1963–66; Chief of Staff, HQ Middle East 1966–67; Commdr British Forces, Gulf 1969–71, British First Corps 1972–74; C-in-C UK Land Forces 1974–76; Chief of Gen. Staff 1976–79; Regional Dir Lloyds Bank 1979–91; Constable of HM Tower of London 1985–90; Lord-Lt for Wilts. 1989–96. *Leisure interests:* pictures, country pursuits. *Address:* Patney Rectory, Devizes, Wilts., SN10 3QZ, England. *Telephone:* (1380) 840733.

GIBSON, Frank William Ernest, DPhil, DSc, FAA, FRS; Australian professor of biochemistry; b. 22 July 1923, Melbourne; s. of John William and Alice Ruby (née Hancock) Gibson; m. 1st Margaret Burvill 1949 (divorced 1979); two d.; m. 2nd Robin Barker (née Rollason) Gibson 1980; one s.; ed Collingwood Tech. Coll., Univs. of Queensland, Melbourne and Oxford; Research Asst Melbourne and Queensland Univs. 1938–47, Sr Demonstrator Melbourne Univ. 1948–49, Sr Lecturer 1953–58, Reader in Chemical Microbiology 1959–65, Prof. 1965–66; Australian Nat. Univ. Scholar, Oxford 1950–52; Research Assoc. Stanford Univ. 1959; Dir of John Curtin School and Howard Florey Prof. of Medical Research Australian Nat. Univ. 1977–80, Prof. of Biochemistry 1967–88, Prof. Emer. 1989–; Visiting Prof. and Fellow Lincoln Coll., Oxford 1982–83; Fellow ANU 1989–; Pres. Australian Biochemical Soc. 1978–79; Gowland Hopkins Medallist, Leeuwenhoek Lecturer Royal Soc. 1981, Biochemical Soc. 1982, Burnet Medallist, Australian Acad. of Sciences 1991. *Publications:* many scientific papers and reviews on biochemistry and microbial metabolism. *Leisure interests:* tennis, skiing, music. *Address:* 7 Waller Crescent, Campbell, ACT, 2601, Australia (Home). *Telephone:* (2) 6249-5056 (Office); (2) 6247-0760 (Home).

GIBSON, Mel, AO; Australian actor and producer; b. 3 Jan. 1956, Peekskill, NY, USA; s. of Hutton Gibson and Anne Gibson; m. Robyn Moore; five s. one d.; ed Nat. Inst. for Dramatic Art, Sydney; f. ICONS productions; Commdr Ordre des Arts et des Lettres. *Films include:* Summer City, Mad Max 1979, Tim 1979, Attack Force Z, Gallipoli 1981, The Road Warrior (Mad Max II) 1982, The Year of Living Dangerously 1983, The Bounty 1984, The River 1984, Mrs. Soffel 1984, Mad Max Beyond Thunderdome 1985, Lethal Weapon, Tequila Sunrise, Lethal Weapon II, Bird on a Wire 1989, Hamlet 1990, Air America 1990, Lethal Weapon III 1991, Man Without a Face (also dir) 1992, Maverick 1994, Braveheart (also Dir, co-producer, Acad. Award for Best Picture 1996) 1995, Ransom 1996, Conspiracy Theory 1997, Lethal Weapon IV 1998, Payback 1997, The Million Dollar Hotel 1999, The Patriot 2000, What Women Want 2000, We Were Soldiers 2002, Signs 2002. *Plays include:* Romeo and Juliet, Waiting for Godot, No Names No Pack Drill, Death of a Salesman. *Address:* c/o ICONS Productions, 4000 Warner Boulevard, Room 17, Burbank, CA 91522, USA; c/o Shanahan Management, P.O. Box 478, King's Cross, NSW 2011, Australia.

GIBSON, Rt Hon Sir Peter (Leslie), Rt Hon Lord Justice Peter Gibson, Kt; British judge; b. 10 June 1934; s. of Harold Leslie Gibson and Martha Lucy (née Diercking) Gibson; m. Dr. Katharine Mary Beatrice Hadow 1968; two s. one d.; ed Malvern Coll., Worcester Coll., Oxford; nat. service 2nd Lt RA 1953–55; called to Bar, Inner Temple 1960; Bencher, Lincoln's Inn 1975; Second Jr Counsel to Inland Revenue (Chancery) 1970–72; Jr Counsel to the Treasury (Chancery) 1972–81; Judge of the High Court of Justice, Chancery Div. 1981–93; Chair. Law Comm. for England and Wales 1990–92; a Judge of the Employment Appeal Tribunal 1984–86; Lord Justice of Appeal 1993–; Hon. Fellow Worcester Coll., Oxford 1993; Treasurer Lincoln's Inn 1996. *Address:* Royal Courts of Justice, Strand, London, WC2A 2LL, England.

GIBSON, Rex; South African journalist; b. 11 Aug. 1931, Salisbury; s. of Arthur David Gibson and Mildred Joyce Adam; three d.; ed King Edward VII School, Johannesburg; articled clerk 1948–52; entered journalism 1952, joined Rand Daily Mail 1959, Chief Sub-Ed. 1962, Arts Ed. 1969, Asst Ed. then Chief Asst Ed. 1969–72, Deputy Ed. 1973–76, Ed. 1982–85; Founding Ed. Mining News 1967; Ed. The Northern Reporter (first local suburban newspaper) 1968–69; Ed. The Sunday Express 1976–82; Deputy Ed. The Star, Johannesburg 1985–93; Deputy Man. Dir Sussens Mann Communications 1993–; Bursar Imperial Relations Trust 1960; Atlas World Review Joint Int.

Ed. of the Year Award 1979, Pringle Award for Journalism 1979. *Leisure interests:* reading, tennis, golf. *Address:* P.O. Box 1014, Johannesburg 2000, South Africa.

GIBSON, Robert Dennis, PhD, FTS, FAIM; Australian university vice-chancellor; b. 13 April 1942, Newcastle, England; s. of Edward Gibson and Euphemia Gibson; m. 1st. Eileen Hancox 1964; one s. two d.; m. 2nd Catherine Bull 1994; ed Hull and Newcastle Univs; Prof. and Head, School of Math. and Computing, Newcastle Polytechnic 1977–82; Deputy Dir Queensland Inst. of Tech. 1982–83, Dir 1983–88; Vice-Chancellor Queensland Univ. of Tech. 1989–; mem. Australian Research Council; Hon. DSc (CNAA) 1984. *Publications:* over 80 publs in mathematical modelling. *Leisure interests:* cricket, running. *Address:* Queensland University of Technology, 2 George Street, Brisbane, Queensland 4000, Australia.

GIBSON, Robin Warwick, OBE, BA; British art historian and museum curator; b. 3 May 1944, Hereford; s. of the late Walter Edward Gibson and Freda Mary Yates (née Partridge); ed Royal Masonic School, Bushey, Magdalene Coll., Cambridge; Asst Keeper, City Art Gallery, Manchester 1967–68; Asst Keeper, Nat. Portrait Gallery, London 1968–83, Curator, Twentieth Century Collection 1983–94, Chief Curator 1994–2001; mem. Cttee Nat. Trust Foundation for Art 1997–2001. *Publications:* The McDonald Collection 1970, British Portrait Painters (jtly.) 1971, Flower Painting 1976, The Clarendon Collection 1977, 20th Century Portraits 1978, Glyn Philpot 1984, John Bellany: New Portraits 1986, John Bratby Portraits 1991, The Portrait Now 1993, The Sitwells (jtly.) 1994, Glenys Barton (jtly.) 1997, The Face in the Corner 1998, Painting the Century (jtly.) 2000. *Leisure interests:* music, gardening. *Address:* Brookside, Hempstead, Nr. Saffron Walden, Essex, CB10 2PE, England (Home). *E-mail:* robline@btinternet.com (Home).

GIBSON, Roy; British scientific consultant; b. 4 July 1924, Manchester; s. of Fred Gibson and Jessie Gibson; m. Inga Elgerus 1971; one s. one d. (by previous marriage); ed Chorlton Grammar School, Wadham Coll., Oxford, London School of Econs with Colonial Admin. Service, Malaya 1948–58; UK Atomic Energy Authority, London 1959–67; Deputy Dir Technical Centre, European Space Research Org. (ESRO) 1967–71, Dir of Admin. ESRO 1971–74, Acting Dir-Gen. 1974–75; Dir-Gen., European Space Agency 1975–81, Aerospace Consultant 1980–; Dir-Gen. British Nat. Space Centre 1985–87; Adviser to Dir-Gen., Int. Maritime Satellite Org. and EUMETSAT 1987–. *Publications:* Space 1992; numerous articles in aerospace technical journals. *Leisure interests:* music, languages, bridge, walking. *Address:* Résidence Les Hespérides, 51 Allée J. de Beins, 34000 Montpellier, France. *Telephone:* (4) 67-64-81-81. *Fax:* (4) 67-22-34-02. *E-mail:* roy.gibson@wanadoo.fr (Office).

GIBSON-SMITH, Chris, BSc, MS, PhD; British business executive; m.; two c.; ed Durham Univ., Newcastle Univ., Stanford Business School; with British Petroleum (BP) 1970–2001, positions include COO BP Chemicals, CEO BP Exploration Europe, Group Man. Dir 1997–2001; Chair. Nat. Air Traffic Services 2001–03; Chair. London Stock Exchange July 2003–; Dir (non-exec.) Lloyds TSB Group PLC 1999–, Powergen UK PLC 2001–02, British Land Co. PLC 2003–; Trustee Public Policy Research, Arts and Business. *Leisure interests:* skiing, golf, music, the arts. *Address:* London Stock Exchange, Old Broad Street, London, EC2N 1HP, England (Office). *Telephone:* (20) 7797-1000 (Office). *E-mail:* enquiries@londonstockexchange.com (Office). *Website:* www.londonstockexchange.com (Office).

GIDADA, Negaso, PhD; Ethiopian politician; fmr Minister of Health; Pres. of Ethiopia 1995–2001. *Address:* c/o Office of the President, Addis Ababa, Ethiopia.

GIDASPOV, Boris Veniaminovich, DSc; Russian scientist; b. 16 April 1933, Kuibyshev; s. of Veniamin Aleksandrovich Gidaspov and Maria Aleksandrovna Smirnova; m. Zinaida Ivanovna Kuznetsova 1961; one s.; ed Kuibyshev Industrial Inst.; mem. CPSU 1962–91; research, Kuibyshev Chemical Inst. 1955–59 and Leningrad Tech. Inst. 1959–77; Dir State Inst. of Applied Chem. 1977–89; Consultant Russian Scientific Center 'Applied Chemistry' 1989–; Dir Technoferm Eng (representation in St Petersburg) 1993–; founder mem. of Tekhnokhim (a commercial asscn for research), Leningrad 1985–88, Chair. Tekhnokhim Corpn 1991–; corresp. mem. USSR (now Russian) Acad. of Sciences 1981–; USSR People's Deputy 1989–91; First Sec. Leningrad CPSU City Cttee 1989–91; mem. and Sec. CPSU Cen. Cttee 1990–91; mem. Russian Eng Acad. 1994–; Lenin Prize 1976; USSR State Prize 1981. *Leisure interests:* Russian history, sport. *Address:* Tekhnokhim, Angliyskaya nab. 10, St Petersburg 190000, Russia. *Telephone:* (812) 314-91-18 (Office); (812) 316-72-31 (Home). *Fax:* (812) 311-47-69.

GIDDENS, Anthony, PhD; British professor of sociology; b. 18 Jan. 1938; m. Jane Ellwood 1963; ed Univ. of Hull, London School of Econs, Univ. of Cambridge; Lecturer in Sociology, Univ. of Leicester 1961–70; Visiting Asst Prof., Simon Fraser Univ., Vancouver 1967–69, Univ. of Calif., LA 1968–69; Lecturer in Sociology and Fellow King's Coll., Cambridge 1970–84, Reader in Sociology 1984–86, Prof. of Sociology 1986–96, Dir LSE 1997–2003; Chair. and Dir Polity Press Ltd 1985–; Dir Blackwell-Polity Ltd 1985–; Chair. and Dir Centre for Social Research 1989–; BBC Reith Lecturer 1999; numerous visiting professorships; Founder of 'The Third Way'; mem. Russian Acad. of Sciences; Nat. Order of the Southern Cross (Brazil), Grand Cross, Order of the Infante Dom Henrique (Portugal); Hon. DLitt (Salford), (Hull), (Open Univ.), (South Bank); Dr hc (Vesalius Coll., Vrije Univ. Brussels); Prince of Asturias

Award (Spain) 2002. *Publications:* Capitalism and Modern Social Theory 1971, Power, Property and State 1981, Constitution of Society 1984, Sociology 1989, The Transformation of Intimacy 1992, Beyond Left and Right 1994, Third Way 1998. *Leisure interests:* theatre, tennis, cinema, Tottenham Hotspur. *Address:* London School of Economics, Houghton Street, London, WC2A 2AE, England (Office). *Telephone:* (20) 7405-7686 (Office). *Fax:* (20) 7242-0392 (Office).

GIELEN, Michael Andreas; Austrian conductor and composer; b. 20 July 1927, Dresden, Germany; m. Helga Augsten 1957; one s. one d.; ed Univ. of Buenos Aires; studied composition under E. Leuchter and J. Polnauer; pianist in Buenos Aires; on music staff of Teatro Colón 1947–50; with Vienna State Opera 1951–60, Perm. Conductor 1954–60; First Conductor, Royal Swedish Opera, Stockholm 1960–65; conductor and composer in Cologne 1965–69; Musical Dir Nat. Orchestra of Belgium 1969–73; Chief Conductor Netherlands Opera 1973–75; Music Dir and Gen. Man. Frankfurt Opera House Sept. 1977–87; Music Dir Cincinnati Symphony 1980–86; Prin. Conductor SWF Radio Orchestra, Baden-Baden 1986–99; Prof. of Conducting, Mozarteum, Salzburg 1987–95, Emer. 1995–; Chief Guest Conductor, BBC Symphony Orchestra 1979–82; Perm. Guest Conductor, Berlin State Opera 1998–, Berlin Symphony Orchestra 1998–; Dr hc (Berlin Hochschule der Künste) 2000; State Prize, Hessen 1985, Adorno Prize, Frankfurt 1986, Vienna Music Prize 1997, Frankfurt Music Prize 1999. *Address:* AU 57, 5311 Loibichl, Austria. *Telephone:* (6232) 2082 (Home).

GIELGUD, Maina Julia Goroon; British ballet director and teacher; b. 14 Jan. 1945, London; d. of the late Lewis Gielgud and of Elisabeth Grussner; with Cuevas Co. and Roland Petit Co. until 1963; Grande Ballet Classique de France 1963–67; Béjart Co. 1967–71; Berlin 1971; London Festival Ballet 1972–76; ballerina, Sadler's Wells Royal Ballet 1976–78; freelance ballerina and guest artist 1978–82; Rehearsal Dir London City Ballet 1982; Artistic Dir The Australian Ballet 1983–96; Ballet Dir Royal Danish Ballet 1997–99; freelance dir, coach and teacher 1999–; Artistic Assoc. Houston Ballet 2000–; Hon. AO 1991. *Ballets produced:* (for The Australian Ballet) The Sleeping Beauty 1985, Giselle 1987; (for Boston Ballet) Giselle 2002; (for Ballet du Rhin) Giselle 2003. *Ballets performed:* L'Heure Exquisite. *Address:* 1/9 Stirling Court, 3 Marshall Street, London, W1F 9BD, England (Home). *Telephone:* (20) 7734-6612 (Home). *E-mail:* gielgud@attglobal.net (Home).

GIENOW, Herbert Hans Walter, DIur; German business executive; b. 13 March 1926, Hamburg; s. of Günther and Margarethe Gienow; m. Imina Brons 1954; one s. one d.; ed Hamburg Univ.; Head Clerk Deutsche Warentreuhand AG, mem. Bd of Man. 1959; mem. Hamburg Bar; chartered accountant 1961; mem. Bd of Man. Klöckner-Werke AG 1962, Chair. Exec. Bd 1974–91; Pres. ALSTOM Germany 1991–98; Chair. Supervisory Bd ALSTOM GmbH 1994–99, Maschinenfabrik Niehoff GmbH, SteelDex AG; Pres. Academia Baltica; fmr Chair. Consultative Cttee Deutsche Bank AG, Essen; mem. Supervisory Bd ASL Aircraft Services Lemwerder; Chevalier, Légion d'honneur; Hon. mem. Iron and Steel Inst. Brussels. *Leisure interests:* books, sailing, model soldiers. *Address:* An der Pont 51, 40885 Ratingen (Office); Am Adels 7, 40883 Ratingen (Germany (Home). *Telephone:* (2102) 131688 (Office); (2102) 60692 (Home). *Fax:* (2102) 126903 (Office). *E-mail:* woneig@aol.com (Home).

GIEROWSKI, Stefan; Polish painter; b. 21 May 1925, Częstochowa; s. of Józef Gierowski and Stefania (Wasilewska) Gierowska; m. Anna Golka 1951; one s. one d.; ed Acad. of Fine Arts, Cracow; Docent, Acad. of Fine Arts, Warsaw, Dean of Painting Dept 1975–80, Extraordinary Prof. 1976–; mem. Union of Polish Artists and Designers, Sec.-Gen. 1957–59, Pres. of Painting Section 1959–61, 1963–66; Kt's and Officer's Cross of Order of Polonia Restituta; Silver Medal, Third Festival of Fine Arts, Warsaw 1978, Prize of Chair. Council of Ministers (1st class) 1979, Jan Cybis Prize 1980. *Solo exhibitions include:* Warsaw 1955, 1957, 1960, 1967, 1972, 1974, 1978, 1986, 1992, Galerie la Cloche, Paris 1961, 1965, Auverrier Galerie Numaga, Neuchâtel 1967, 1976, 1987, K. Pułaski Museum, Warka 1973, Galerie Simone Von Dormoel, Brussels 1977, Teatr Studio, Warsaw 1983, Cracow 1991. *Group exhibitions include:* Contemporary Art Exhbn, Warsaw 1957, Carnegie Inst., Pittsburgh 1964, 1967, Biennale Int. d'arte, San Marino 1965, 34th Biennale, Venice 1968, Triennale of India, New Delhi 1968, Mexico 1975, Lisbon 1976, Madrid 1977, Naples 1986, Kleinjassen 1987, Apeldoorn 1989, Vienna 1992, Berlin 1992. *Address:* ul. Gagarina 15 m. 97, 00-753 Warsaw, Poland. *Telephone:* (22) 8411633.

GIERSCH, Herbert, Dr rer. pol; German economist; b. 11 May 1921, Reichenbach; s. of Hermann and Helene (née Kleinert) Giersch; m. Dr. Friederike Koppelmann 1949; two s. one d.; ed Univs of Breslau, Kiel and Münster; Asst to Prof. Walther Hoffmann, Univ. of Münster 1947–48; British Council Fellow, London School of Econs 1948–49; Admin., Econs Directorate, OEEC 1950–51; Lecturer Univ. of Münster 1951–55; Counsellor and Head of Div., Trade and Finance Directorate, OEEC 1953–54; Prof. of Econs Saar Univ., Saarbrücken 1955–69; Visiting Prof. of Econs, Yale Univ. 1962–63, Dean Acheson Visiting Prof. at Yale Univ. 1977–78; Prof. of Econs, Univ. of Kiel and Pres. Inst. of World Econs, Kiel 1969–89, Prof. Emer. 1989–; Chair. Asscn of German Econ. Research Insts. 1970–82; Pres. Assoc. of European Business Cycle Research Insts. 1974–78; f. Herbert Giersch Stiftung, Frankfurt am Main 1998; mem. Advisory Council, Fed. Ministry of Econs 1960–; founding mem. German Council of Econ. Advisers 1964–70, Council and Exec. Comm. Int. Econ. Asscn 1970–82, Treas. 1974–83, Hon. Pres. 1983–; Corresp. Fellow,

British Acad. 1983; Foreign mem. Royal Swedish Acad. of Eng Sciences, Stockholm 1987; Hon. mem. American Econ. Asscn; Hon. Fellow, LSE; Dr. hc (Erlangen-Nürnberg) 1977, (Basle) 1984, (Saarbrücken) 1993; Grosses Bundesverdienstkreuz, mit Stern und Schulterband 1995; Ludwig Erhard Award; Paolo Baffi Int. Prize for Econs 1989; Orden pour le Mérite für Wissenschaften und Künste; Prognos Preis (Basle) 1993, Joachim Jungius Medal 1998, August-Lösch-Ehrenring 2000. *Publications:* Allgemeine Wirtschaftspolitik, Vol. I Grundlagen 1960, Vol. II Konjunktur- und Wachstumspolitik 1977, Kontroverse Fragen der Wirtschaftspolitik 1977, Economic Policy for the European Community (co-author) 1974, Im Brennpunkt: Wirtschaftspolitik. Kritische Beiträge von 1967–77, 1978, Perspectives on the World Economy 1986, Gegen Europessimismus. Kritische Beiträge von 1977–85 1986, Offener Rat. Kolumnen aus der Wirtschaftswoche 1986, The World Economy in Perspective: Essays on International Trade and European Integration 1991, The Fading Miracle: Four Decades of Market Economy in Germany (co-author) 1992, Openness for Prosperity, Essays in World Economics 1993, Marktwirtschaftliche Perspektiven für Europa. Das Licht im Tunnel 1993, Kontrovers im Kontext: Wirtschaftspolitische Anstösse 1996, Abschied von der Nationalökonomie 2002. *Address:* Preusserstrasse 17–19, 24105 Kiel, Germany (Home). *Telephone:* (431) 561872 (Home). *Fax:* (431) 8814500. *E-mail:* giersch@ifw.uni-kiel.de (Office).

GIERTYCH, Roman, Polish politician and lawyer; b. 27 Feb. 1971, Srem; s. of Maciej Giertych and Antonina Giertych; m. Barbara Giertych; one d.; ed Adam Mickiewicz Univ., Poznan; owner of a legal practice; Vice-Pres. Bd, Nat. Party 1994–; Deputy to Sejm (Parl.) 2001–; co-f. League of Polish Families 2001, Pres. Congress of League of Polish Families 2001–; mem. Polish Academic Union 1988–; Hon. Pres. Mlodziez Wszechpolska;. *Publications include:* Kontrrewolucja mlodych (Counter-Revolution of the Young) 1994, Pod walcem historii. Polityka zagraniczna ruchu narodowego 1938–1945 (Under History's Roller. Foreign Policy of the National Movement 1938–1945) 1995, Lot orla (Flight of the Eagle) 2000, Mozemy wygrac Polske (We Can Win Poland) 2001; numerous articles, including Nasz Dziennik, Mysl Polska, Rodzina Radia Maryja, Wszechpolak. *Leisure interests:* historical books, chess (Vice-Champion of Poznan Voivodship), tennis. *Address:* Biuro Posla Ligi Polskich Rodzin Romana Giertycha, ul. Hoza 9, 00-528 Warsaw, Poland (Office). *Telephone:* (22) 6223648 (Office). *Fax:* (22) 6223138 (Office). *E-mail:* roman.giertych@sejm.pl (Office). *Website:* www.sejm.gov.pl (Office).

GIESBERT, Franz-Olivier; French journalist and author; b. 18 Jan. 1949, Wilmington, Del., USA; s. of Frederick Giesbert and Marie Allain; m. Christine Fontaine 1974; two s. one d.; journalist at Le Nouvel Observateur 1971, Sr Corresp. in Washington 1980, Political Ed. 1981, Ed.-in-Chief 1985–88; Ed.-in-Chief Le Figaro 1988–2000, Figaro Magazine 1997–2000, mem. Editorial Bd Le Figaro 1993–2000, Figaro Magazine 1997–2000; Ed. Le Point 2000–; presenter 'le Gai savoir' TV programme, Paris Première cable channel 1997–; mem. jury Prix Théophraste Renaudot 1998–; Aujourd'hui Best Essay Prize 1975, Prix Gutenberg 1987, Prix Pierre de Monaco 1997, Prix Richelieu 1999. *Publications:* François Mitterrand ou la tentation de l'Histoire (essay) 1977, Monsieur Adrien (novel) 1982, Jacques Chirac (biog.) 1987, Le Président 1990, L'Affreux 1992 (Grand Prix du Roman de l'Acad. Française 1992), La Fin d'une Époque 1993, La Souille (William the Conqueror and Interallie Prize), Le Vieil homme et la Mort 1996, François Mitterrand, une vie 1996, Le Sieur Dieu 1998. *Address:* Le Point, 74 avenue du Maine, 75682 Paris Cedex; Paris Première, 14 place des Vins de France, 75012 Paris, France.

GIESKE, Friedhelm, DJur; German business executive; b. 12 Jan. 1928, Schwege/Osnabrück; began career with RWE AG 1953, Deputy mem. Man. Bd 1968, mem. Man. Bd (Finance) 1972, Bd Spokesman 1988, Chair. Man. Bd 1989–94; mem. Supervisory Bd ALLIANZ AG, Munich, Dresdner Bank AG, Frankfurt, Karstadt AG, Essen, MAN AG, Munich, National-bank, Essen, RWEAG, Essen, Thyssen AG, Duisburg; Grosses Bundesverdienstkreuz 1995. *Address:* Opernplatz 1, 45128 Essen, Germany. *Telephone:* (201) 1200.

GIFFEN, John A., MBA; Canadian business executive; b. 17 Dec. 1938, Ingersoll, Ont.; s. of John Giffen and Kathleen Marion Giffen (née McQuinn); m. Joan E Rothwell 1962; one s. two d.; ed Univ. of Windsor; plant foreman, Hiram Walker 1962, Project Engineer 1965, Div. Supt 1972, Inventory Man. 1973, N American Distribution Man. 1977, Asst to Pres. 1979, Vice Pres. Worldwide Production 1980; Chair. Corby Distilleries Ltd 1992– (Dir 1980–); Regional Chair. The Americas, Allied-Lyons 1992–93; Chair., CEO The Hiram Walker Group 1991–92; Man. Dir Hiram Walker-Allied Vintners 1989–91; Pres. HW-G & W Ltd 1989–92; Deputy Chair. 1992–93; Chair., CEO Hiram Walker-Allied Vintners (Canada) Ltd 1988–89; Pres. Hiram Walker & Sons Ltd 1988–89, Allied-Lyons PLC 1988–93, HW-G & W Ltd 1982–86, 1988–93; Dir Hallmark Technologies Inc. 1995–; mem. of Windsor Advisory Bd Royal Trustco, of Canadian-UK Cttee, Canadian Chamber of Commerce 1983–91; Dir and Vice-Pres., Windsor Chamber of Commerce 1979–83; Gov. Metropolitan Gen. Hosp., Windsor 1979–85; Dir Inst. of Canadian-American Studies 1983–86. *Leisure interests:* golf, curling. *Address:* Walkerville, P.O. Box 2518, Ont., Canada.

GIFFIN, Gordon D., BA, JD; American diplomatist and lawyer; b. Springfield, Mass.; m. Patti Alfred Giffin; one d.; ed Duke and Emory Univs; with law firm Hansell and Post 1979–84; Dir of Legis. Affairs and Chief Counsel to Senator Sam Nunn; Treas. Campaign Cttee of Sam Nunn 1974–94; f. Democratic Leadership Council with Senator Nunn and Gov. Clinton 1984,

mem. Bd 1984–96; Gen. Counsel Democratic Nat. Convention 1992, 1996; Chair. Clinton Primary Campaign and Clinton–Gore Gen. Election Campaign 1992; Deputy Dir of Personnel, White House Transition Team 1992; Sr Adviser on the South, Clinton Re-election Campaign and Chair. Democratic Campaign in Ga 1996; Sr Partner Long, Aldridge and Norman law firm, specializing in energy regulatory and govt procurement cases –1997, re-joined firm as Vice-Chair. 2001; Amb. to Canada 1997–2001; fmr Prof. of Law, Emory Univ.; mem. Atlanta Olympic Games Cttee; mem. Bd Dirs Overseas Pvt. Investment Corpn 2001–, Ga Chamber of Commerce, Trees Atlanta Foundation, Atlanta Ballet. *Address:* Long, Aldridge and Norman, 701 Pennsylvania Avenue, Suite 600, Washington, DC 20004, USA (Office). *Telephone:* (202) 624-1200 (Office).

GIFFORD, Michael Brian, BSc (ECON.); British business executive; b. 9 Jan. 1936; s. of Kenneth Gifford and Maude Palmer; m. Nancy Baytos; (two s. two d. by previous m.); ed London School of Econs; joined Leo Computers (later part of ICL) 1960; Man. Dir ICL (Pacific) 1973–75; Chief Exec. Cadbury Schweppes Australia 1975–78; Finance Dir Cadbury Schweppes PLC 1978–83; Man. Dir and Chief Exec. Rank Org. 1983–96; Dir Fuji Xerox 1984–96, English China Clays PLC 1992–99, The Gillette Co. 1993–, Danka Business Systems PLC 2001–. *Address:* 568 9th Street South, Suite 354, Naples, FL 34102, USA.

GIL, Gilberto; Brazilian politician and musician; b. Gilberto Passos Gil Moreira, 3 March 1942, Salvador; ed Fed. Univ., Bahia; began playing accordion aged eight; composed songs for TV advertisements in early 1960s; appeared in Nós Por Exemplo (show directed by Caetano Veloso) 1964; moved to São Paulo 1965; had first hit when Elis Regina recorded Louvação; participated in Tropicalia movt, sang protest songs that proved controversial with mil. dictatorship; imprisoned 1968; forced to leave Brazil on release and moved to UK; worked with groups such as Pink Floyd, Yes, Incredible String Band and Rod Stewart's band in London clubs; returned to Brazil in 1972; toured with Caetano Veloso, Gal Costa and Maria Bethania; recorded album Nightingale in USA 1978; appearances at Montreux Jazz Festival; Pres. Fundação Gregorio de Matos, Salvador 1987; mem. Council of City Hall of Salvador 1988–92, Pres. Environmental Defence Cttee 1989; mem. Advisory Council Fundação Mata Virgem and Fundação Alerta Brasil Pantanal; Pres. Negro-Mestizo Reference Centre (CERNE); mem. Green Party 1989, later mem. Nat. Exec. Cttee; mem. Parl. for Salvador; Minister of Culture 2003–; Pres. Fundação Onda Azul (Blue Wave Foundation); Chevalier des Arts et des Lettres (France); Shell and Sharp Prize 1990, Cruz da Ordem de Rio Branco. *Recordings include:* singles: Sua Música, Sua Interpretação 1963, Procissão/Roda 1965, Oriente 1972, No Woman, No Cry (with Jimmy Cliff) (No. 1 in Brazil) 1980; albums: Louvação 1967, Gilberto Gil 1968, Gilberto Gil (recorded in London) 1971, Expresso 2222 1972, Temporada de Verão (live with Caetano Veloso and Gal Costa) 1974, Refazenda 1975, Refavela 1977, Nightingale 1978, Realce 1979, Gente Precisa Ver O Luar 1981, Quilombo 1984, Vamos Fugir (with The Wailers) 1984, Dia Dorim Noite Neon 1985, Ao Vivo Em Tóquio – Live in Tokyo 1987, O Eterno Deus Mu Dança 1989, Parabolicamará 1991, Tropicália 2 1993, Acoustic – Gilberto Gil Unplugged 1994, Luar 1996, Indigo Blue 1997, Quanta Ao Vivo (Grammy Award for Best World Music Record 1998) 1997, Copacabana Mon Amour 1998, Eu Tu Eles – Me You Them (film soundtrack) 2001, São João Vivo 2001. *Address:* Ministry of Culture, Esplanada dos Ministérios, Bloco B, 3° andar, 70068-900 Brasília, DF, Brazil (Office). *Telephone:* (61) 316-2172 (Office). *Fax:* (61) 225-9162 (Office). *E-mail:* info@minc.gov.br (Office). *Website:* www.minc.gov.br (Office); www.gilbertogil.com.br (Office).

GILBERT; British artist; b. Gilbert Proesch, 1943, Dolomites, Italy; ed Wolkenstein School of Art, Hallein School of Art, Munich Acad. of Art, St Martin's School of Art; began collaboration with George (Passmore) in 1967 as Gilbert and George; est. reputation as performance artists, presenting themselves, identically dressed, as living sculptures; later work includes large composite drawings and vividly coloured photo-pieces often featuring likenesses of the artists. *Exhibitions include:* Museum of Contemporary Art, Chicago 2000–01. *Publication:* What Our Art Means (jtly). *E-mail:* g-and-g@dircon.co.uk (Office). *Website:* www.gilbertandgeorge.co.uk/e/start.html (Office).

GILBERT, Kenneth Albert, OC, DMus, FRCM; Canadian harpsichordist; b. 16 Dec. 1931, Montreal; s. of Albert George Gilbert and Reta Mabel (Welch); ed Conservatoire de Musique, Montreal and Conservatoire de Paris; Prof. Conservatoire de Musique, Montreal 1965–72; Assoc. Prof. Laval Univ. 1970–76; Guest Prof. Royal Antwerp Conservatory 1971–73; Dir Early Music Dept Conservatoire de Strasbourg 1981–85; Prof. Staatliche Hochschule für Musik, Stuttgart 1981–89, Hochschule Mozarteum, Salzburg 1984–, Paris Conservatoire 1988–96; Instructor at other music acads, summer schools etc.; Fellow, Canada Council 1968, 1974, Calouste Gulbenkian Foundation 1971; has recorded complete harpsichord works of Couperin, Scarlatti and Rameau, suites and partitas of J. S. Bach, Well-tempered Clavier of Bach and concertos for 2, 3, 4 harpsichords by Bach; Fellow Royal Coll. of Music; Hon. mem. RAM; Officier Ordre des Arts et des Lettres, Cross of Honour 1st Class (Austria). *Publications:* editions of complete harpsichord works of Couperin, Scarlatti and Rameau and Bach's Goldberg Variations, Frescobaldi Toccatas. *Address:* 11 rue Ernest-Psichari, 75007 Paris, France (Office). *Telephone:* 1-45-56-04-93 (Office). *Fax:* 1-45-56-04-93 (Office). *E-mail:* kengil@online.fr.

GILBERT, Lewis, CBE; British film director; b. 6 March 1920, London; m. Hylda Henrietta Tafler; two s.; entered films as child actor; joined RAF and became Asst Dir to William Keighley on Target for Today, etc. 1939; joined GB Instructional (GBI) 1944, for whom he wrote and directed The Ten Year Plan, Sailors Do Care, Arctic Harvest, etc. 1946–47; wrote and directed The Little Ballerina 1947–48, worked on series of documentaries for GBI; Producer/Dir Int. Realist 1948; numerous awards including Special Evening Standard Film Award 1996. *Films include:* The Little Ballerina 1947, Once a Sinner 1950, Scarlet Thread 1951, There is Another Sun 1951, Time Gentlemen Please 1952, Emergency Call 1952, Cosh Boy, Johnny on the Run 1953, Albert RN 1953, The Good Die Young 1954, The Sea Shall Not Have Them 1954, Cast a Dark Shadow 1955, Reach for the Sky 1956, The Admirable Crichton 1957, Carve Her Name With Pride 1957, A Cry From the Streets 1958, Ferry to Hong Kong 1959, Sink the Bismarck 1960, Light Up The Sky 1960, The Greengage Summer 1961, HMS Defiant 1962, The Seventh Dawn 1964, Alfie 1966, You Only Live Twice 1967, Paul and Michelle (also producer) 1973, Seven Men at Daybreak 1975, Seven Nights in Japan 1976, The Spy Who Loved Me 1977, Moonraker 1978, Dubai (also producer), Educating Rita 1982, Shirley Valentine (also producer) 1989, Stepping Out 1991, Haunted; co-produced Spare The Rod 1959–60. *Address:* 19 blvd de Suisse, Monaco.

GILBERT, Sir Martin (John), Kt, CBE, MA, DLitt, FRSL; British historian; b. 25 Oct. 1936; s. of Peter and Miriam Gilbert; m. 1st Helen Robinson 1963; one d.; m. 2nd Susan Sacher; two s.; ed Highgate School and Magdalen Coll., Oxford; Sr Research Fellow, St Antony's Coll., Oxford 1960–62, Fellow, Merton Coll., Oxford 1962–; Visiting Prof. Univ. of S Carolina 1965, Tel Aviv 1979, Hebrew Univ. of Jerusalem 1980–; official biographer of Sir Winston Churchill 1968–; Gov., Hebrew Univ. of Jerusalem 1978–; Non-Governmental Rep. UN Commn. on Human Rights, Geneva 1987, 1988; mem. Prime Minister's del. to Israel, Gaza and Jordan 1995, to USA 1995; has lectured on historical subjects throughout Europe and USA; adviser to BBC and ITV for various documentaries; script designer and co-author, Genocide (Acad. Award for best documentary feature film) 1981; presenter History Channel 1996–; Recent History Corresp. Sunday Times 1967; Hon. Fellow Univ. of Wales, Lampeter 1997; Hon. DLitt (Westminster Coll., Fulton, Mo.) 1981. *Publications:* The Appeasers (with R. Gott) 1963, Britain and Germany between the Wars 1964, The European Powers 1900–1945 1965, Plough My Own Furrow: The Life of Lord Allen of Hurtwood 1965, Servant of India: A Study of Imperial Rule 1905–1910 1966, The Roots of Appeasement 1966, Recent History Atlas 1860–1960 1966, Winston Churchill 1966, British History Atlas 1968, American History Atlas 1968, Jewish History Atlas 1969, First World War Atlas 1970, Winston S. Churchill, Vol. III, 1914–16 1971, companion vol. 1973, Russian History Atlas 1972, Sir Horace Rumbold: Portrait of a Diplomat 1973, Churchill: a photographic portrait 1974, The Arab-Israeli Conflict: its history in maps 1974, Winston S. Churchill, Vol. IV, 1917–22 1975, companion vol. 1977, The Jews in Arab Lands: their history in maps 1975, Winston S. Churchill, Vol. V, 1922–39, 1976, companion Vols 1980, 1981, 1982, The Jews of Russia: Illustrated History Atlas 1976, Jerusalem Illustrated History Atlas 1977, Exile and Return: The Emergence of Jewish Statehood 1978, Children's Illustrated Bible Atlas 1979, Final Journey, the Fate of the Jews of Nazi Europe 1979, Auschwitz and the Allies 1981, Atlas of the Holocaust 1982, Winston S. Churchill, Vol. VI, 1939–41 1983, The Jews of Hope: A Study of the Crisis of Soviet Jewry 1984, Jerusalem: Rebirth of a City 1985, Shcharansky: Hero of our Time 1986, Winston S. Churchill, Vol. VII, 1941–45 1986, The Holocaust, The Jewish Tragedy 1986, Winston Churchill, Vol. VIII 1945–65 1988, Second World War 1989, Churchill, A Life 1991, The Churchill War Papers: At the Admiralty (ed.), Atlas of British Charities 1993, In Search of Churchill: A Historian's Journey 1994, The First World War: A Complete History 1994, The Churchill War Papers: 'Never Surrender' (ed.) 1995, The Day the War Ended 1995, Jerusalem in the 20th Century 1996, The Boys, Triumph over Adversity 1996, A History of the World in the Twentieth Century (Vol. I 1900–1933) 1997, (Vol. II 1933–1951) 1998, (Vol. III 1952–1999) 1999, Holocaust Journey: Travelling in Search of the Past 1997, Israel, A History 1998, Winston Churchill and Emery Reeves; Correspondence 1998, Never Again: A History of the Holocaust 1999, The Jewish Century 2001, History of the Twentieth Century 2001, The Churchill War Papers: '1941, the Ever-Widening War' (ed.) 2001, Letters to Auntie Fori: 5,000 Years of Jewish History and Faith 2002, The Righteous: the Unsung Heroes of the Holocaust 2002, Churchill at War: His "Finest Hour" in Photographs. *Leisure interest:* travel. *Address:* Merton College, Oxford, England.

GILBERT, Michael Francis, CBE, LLB, FRSL; British writer and fmr solicitor; b. 17 July 1912, Billinghay, Lincs.; s. of Bernard Gilbert and Berwyn Mina Cuthbert; m. Roberta Mary Marsden 1947; two s. five d.; ed Blundells School, Univ. Coll., London; Asst Master Salisbury Cathedral School 1931–38; with Royal Horse Artillery 1938–46; partner Trowers & Hamlins 1950–82; legal adviser to Govt of Bahrain 1960; f. mem. Crime Writers' Asscn; mem. Arts Council Cttee on Public Lending Right 1968, Royal Literary Fund 1969, Council of Soc. of Authors 1975; Grand Master Mystery Writers of America 1987; Crime Writers' Asscn Diamond Dagger 1994. *Publications:* novels: Close Quarters 1947, They Never Looked Inside 1948, The Doors Open 1949, Smallbone Deceased 1950, Death has Deep Roots 1951, Death in Captivity 1952, Fear to Tread 1953, Sky High 1955, Be Shot for Sixpence 1956, The Tichborne Claimant 1957, Blood and Judgement 1958, After the Fine Weather 1963, The Crack in the Tea Cup 1965, The Dust and the Heat 1967, The Etruscan Net 1969, The Body of a Girl 1972, The Ninety Second Tiger 1973, Flash Point 1974, The Night of the Twelfth 1976, The Empty House 1978, Death of a Favourite Girl 1980, The Final Throw 1983, The Black Seraphim 1983, The Long Journey Home 1985, Trouble 1987, Paint Gold and Blood 1989, The Queen against Karl Mullen 1991, Roller Coaster 1993, Ring of Terror 1995, Into Battle 1997, Over and Out 1999; plays: A Clean Kill, The Bargain, Windfall, The Shot in Question; short stories: Game Without Rules 1967, Stay of Execution 1971, Petrella at Q 1977, Mr Calder and Mr Behrens 1982, Young Petrella 1988, Anything for a Quiet Life 1990; Crime in Good Company 1959 (ed.), The Oxford Book of Legal Anecdotes 1986 (ed.), The Fraudsters 1988 (ed.), Prep School 1991; also radio and TV plays. *Leisure interests:* bridge, walking. *Address:* The Old Rectory, Luddesdown, Gravesend, Kent, DA13 0XE, England.

GILBERT, Stephen; British painter and sculptor; b. 15 Jan. 1910, Fife, Scotland; s. of F. G. W. and Cicely Gilbert (née Kellett); m. Jocelyn Chewett 1935 (died 1979); one s. one d.; ed Univ. Coll. School and Slade School of Art, London; Group Cobra 1948–51; one-man exhbns in London, Dublin, Paris, Amsterdam, Copenhagen, Sheffield, Hull, Cardiff and The Hague 1938–92; has participated in many group exhbns in Paris and elsewhere; work exhibited in Tate Gallery, British Museum and Arts Council (all in London), art galleries and univs. in UK and museums in Denmark, Netherlands, USA, Venezuela; public works for London Co. Council 1965, Chappell of Bond St 1966, British Steel, London 1971; Gulbenkian Foundation Award 1962; Tokyo Biennale First Award 1962; Welsh Arts Council Award for Sculpture 1966. *Address:* 13 rue Rambuteau, 75004 Paris; 7 Impasse du Rouet, 75014 Paris, France. *Telephone:* 1-48-87-99-39; 1-45-42-69-42.

GILBERT, Walter, PhD; American molecular biologist; b. 21 March 1932, Boston, Mass.; s. of Richard V. Gilbert and Emma Gilbert (née Cohen); m. Celia Stone 1953; one s. one d.; ed Harvard and Cambridge Univs; NSF Postdoctoral Fellow, Harvard 1957–58, Lecturer in Physics 1958–59, Asst Prof. of Physics 1959–64, Assoc. Prof. of Biophysics 1964–68, Prof. of Biochemistry 1968–72; American Cancer Soc. Prof. of Molecular Biology 1972–81, Prof. of Biology 1985–86; H. H. Timken Prof. of Science 1986–87; Carl M. Loeb Univ. Prof. 1987–, Chair. Dept of Cellular and Developmental Biology 1987–93; Chair. Scientific Bd, Biogen NV 1978–83, Co-Chair. Supervisory Bd 1979–81, Chair. Supervisory Bd and CEO 1981–84; Vice-Chair. Bd of Dirs., Myriad Genetics, Inc. 1992–; Chair. Bd of Dirs, NetGenics Inc. 1996–, Paratek Pharmaceuticals, Inc. 1996; Foreign mem. Royal Soc.; mem. NAS, American Physical Soc., American Soc. of Biological Chemists, American Acad. of Arts and Sciences; Hon. Fellow Trinity Coll. Cambridge, England 1991; Guggenheim Fellowship, Paris 1968–69; V. D. Mattia Lectureship, Roche Inst. of Molecular Biology 1976; Smith, Kline and French Lecturer, Univ. of Calif. at Berkeley 1977; Hon. DSc (Univ. of Chicago, Columbia Univ.) 1978, (Univ. of Rochester) 1979, (Yeshiva Univ.) 1981; US Steel Foundation Award in Molecular Biology (NAS) 1968, Ledlie Prize, Harvard Univ. (with M. Ptashne) 1969, Warren Triennial Prize, Mass. Gen. Hosp. (with S. Benzer) 1977, Louis and Bert Freedman Award, New York Acad. of Sciences 1977, Prix Charles-Léopold Mayer, Acad. des Sciences, Inst. de France (with M. Ptashne and E. Witkin) 1977, Harrison Howe Award of the Rochester br. of the American Chem. Soc. 1978, Louisa Gross Horwitz Prize, Columbia Univ. (with F. Sanger) 1979, Gairdner Foundation Annual Award 1979, Albert Lasker Basic Medical Research Award (with F. Sanger 1979), Prize for Biochemical Analysis, German Soc. for Clinical Chem. (with A. M. Maxam, F. Sanger and A. R. Coulsen) 1980, Sober Award, American Soc. of Biological Chemists 1980, Nobel Prize for Chem. 1980 with F. Sanger and P. Berg for work on deoxyribonucleic acid (DNA), New England Entrepreneur of the Year Award 1991, Ninth Nat. Biotech. Ventures Award 1997. *Address:* Biological Laboratories, 16 Divinity Avenue, Cambridge, MA 02138, USA. *Telephone:* (617) 495-0760 (Office). *Fax:* (617) 496-4313. *E-mail:* gilbert@nucleus.harvard.edu (Office). *Website:* mcb.harvard.edu/gilbert (Office).

GILDRED, Theodore Edmonds, BA; American diplomatist; b. 18 Oct. 1935, Mexico City; s. of Theodore Gildred and Maxine Edmonds; m. 1st Suzanne Gail Green (divorced 1975); three s. one d.; m. 2nd Stephanie Ann Moscini 1978 (divorced 1992); one s. one d.; ed Stanford Univ., Univ. of Paris (Sorbonne), France and Univ. of Heidelberg, Fed. Repub. of Germany; served with US Army 1955–57, US Air Force 1957–69; Project Supervisor, Investors Marine, Inc., Newport Beach, Calif. 1961; owner, Pres. and CEO Costa Pacifica, Inc., Newport Beach, Calif. 1961–65; Admin. Grupo Lindavista, SA, Mexico City 1965–68; owner, Pres. and CEO The Lomas Santa Fe Group, Solana Beach, Calif. 1968–86, Chair. 1989–; Chair. Bd of Dirs., Torrey Pines Bank, Solana Beach 1979–86, Inst. of Americas, La Jolla, Calif. 1984–86; Amb. to Argentina 1986–89; mem. Univ. of Calif. at San Diego Center for US–Mexican Studies; Founder-Chair. Bd of Govs, Inst. of Americas; Trustee and Pres. Gildred Foundation; mem. Bd Dirs Security Pacific Nat. Bank, Int. Advisory Bd, N American Airlines, numerous other orgs; numerous awards. *Address:* The Lomas Santa Fe Group, 265 Santa Helena, Suite 200, Solana Beach, CA 92075 (Office); 16056 El Camino Real Rancho, Santa Fe, CA 92067, USA (Home). *E-mail:* tgildred@lsfg.com (Home).

GILES, Alan James, MA, MS; British business executive; b. 4 June 1954, Dorchester, Dorset; m. Gillian Rosser 1978; two d.; ed Blandford School, Dorset, Merton Coll. Oxford, Stanford Univ., USA; buyer, Boots the Chemists 1975–78, Promotions Man. 1978–80, Asst Merchandise Controller 1980–82; Retail Devt Man., W.H. Smith 1982–85, Merchandise Controller (Books) 1985–88, Operations & Devt Dir, Do It All 1988–92; Man. Dir Waterstone's

Booksellers 1992–99; CEO HMV Group PLC 1998–. *Address:* HMV Group PLC, Shelley House, 2–4 York Road, Maidenhead, Berks., SL6 1SR, England. *Telephone:* (1628) 818300 (Office). *Fax:* (1628) 818305 (Office).

GILIOMEE, Hermann Buhr, MA, DPhil; South African university professor; b. 4 April 1938, Sterkstroom; s. of Gerhardus Adriaan Giliomee and Catherine Geza Giliomee; m. Annette van Coller 1965; two d.; ed Porterville High School and Univ. of Stellenbosch; Lecturer in History, Univ. of Stellenbosch 1967–83; Prof. of Political Studies Univ. of Cape Town 1983–98; recipient of Fellowships to Yale Univ. 1977–78, Cambridge Univ. 1982–83, Woodrow Wilson Center for Int. Scholars, Washington, DC 1992–93; Pres. South African Inst. of Race Relations 1995–97; political columnist. *Publications:* The Shaping of South African Society 1652–1820 1979, Ethnic Power Mobilized: Can South Africa Change? 1979, Afrikaner Political Thought 1750–1850 1983, Up Against the Fences: Poverty, Passes and Privilege 1985, From Apartheid to Nation-building 1990, The Bold Experiment: South Africa's New Democracy, The Awkward Embrace: Dominant-Party Rule and Democracy in Semi-Industrialized Countries 1998. *Leisure interest:* tennis. *Address:* 5 Dennerand, Stellenbosch 7600, South Africa. *Telephone:* (21) 8832964. *Fax:* (21) 8878026. *E-mail:* hgiliome@mweb.co.za (Home).

GILL, Sir Anthony (Keith), Kt, FREng, BSc(Eng), FCGI, FIMechE; British business executive; b. 1 April 1930, Colchester; s. of Frederick W. Gill and Ellen Gill; m. Phyllis Cook 1953; one s. two d.; ed Colchester High School and Imperial Coll. London; Nat. Service REME 1954–56; Production Engineer, Bryce Berger Ltd 1956, Dir 1960, Gen. Man. 1965; Dir Lucas CAV Ltd 1967; Gen. Man. Fuel Injection Equipment 1972–74; Dir Joseph Lucas Ltd 1974, Div. Man. Dir 1978; Dir Lucas Industries PLC 1978, Jt Group Man. Dir 1980, Group Man. Dir 1984–87, Deputy Chair. 1986–87, Chair. 1987–94 and CEO 1987–94; Pres. Inst. of Production Eng 1985–86; Chair. London Docklands Light Railway 1994–99; mem. Council IMechE 1986–91, Advisory Council on Science and Tech. 1985–91; Chair. Educ. and Training Comm. 1988–91, Tarmac PLC 1992–2000; Dir (non-exec.) Post Office 1989–91, Nat. Power PLC 1990–98; mem. Eng Council (Deputy Chair. 1994–96); Chair. Teaching Co. Scheme 1990–96; Pro-Chancellor Cranfield Univ. 1991–2001; mem. Nat. Training Task Force 1991–94; Vice-Pres. Inst. of Man. 1992 (Chair. Council 1996–99), Pres. 1998–99; Hon. FIEE; Hon. DEng (Univ. of Birmingham) 1990; Hon. DSc (Cranfield Univ.) 1991, (Southampton Univ.) 1992, (Warwick Univ.) 1992, Hon. DTech (Coventry Univ.) 1992; Dr hc (Sheffield Hallam Univ.) 1993. *Leisure interests:* music, boating. *Address:* The Point House, Astra Court, Hythe Marina Village, Hythe, Hants., SO45 6DZ, England. *Telephone:* (23) 8084-0165. *Fax:* (23) 8084-0175. *E-mail:* anthony.gill@btinternet.com.

GILLAM, Sir Patrick, Kt, BA; British business executive; b. 15 April 1933, London; s. of the late Cyril B. Gillam and Mary J. Gillam; m. Diana Echlin 1963; one s. one d.; ed LSE; Foreign Office 1956–57; joined British Petroleum (BP) 1957; Vice-Pres. BP North America Inc. 1971–74; Gen. Man. Supply Dept 1974–78; Dir BP Int. Ltd 1978–82; Chair. BP Shipping Ltd 1981–88, BP Minerals Int. Ltd 1981–88; Man. Dir BP Co. 1981–91, Chair. BP Africa Ltd 1982–88, BP Coal Inc. 1988–90, BP Nutrition 1989–91, BP America 1989–91, BP Oil 1990–91; Chair. Booker Tate Ltd 1991–93, Asda Group PLC 1991–96, Royal and Sun Alliance 1997–2003; Deputy Chair. Standard Chartered Bank Africa PLC 1988–89, Standard Chartered Overseas Holdings Ltd 1988–89, Standard Chartered Bank Aug.–Nov. 1988, Chair. 1993–2003, Standard Chartered PLC 1991–92, Chair. 1993–2003 (Dir 1988–2002); Dir (non-exec.) Commercial Union PLC 1991–96; Chair. ICC (UK) 1989–98; mem. of Court of Govs., LSE 1989–, Hon. Fellow 2000. *Leisure interest:* gardening. *Address:* Asia House, 105 Piccadilly, London, W1V, England. *Telephone:* (20) 7499-1287 (Office).

GILLÈS, Daniel; Belgian writer; b. 1917, Bruges; m. Simone Lambinon 1948; one d.; ed law studies; Prix Rossel (Belgium), Grand Prix de la critique littéraire (France) 1967, Prix Triennal du Roman. *Publications:* Jetons de présence, Le coupon 1944, Les brouillards de Bruges, L'état de grâce, La termitière, Mort-la-douce, La rouille (stories), Le festival de Salzbourg, Nés pour mourir, La tache de sang, Le spectateur Brandebourgeois; biographies: Tolstoi, D. H. Lawrence ou le puritain scandaleux, Tchékhov. *Leisure interests:* travel, tennis, painting.

GILLES, Herbert Michael Joseph, D.MED.SC., DSc, MD, FRCP, FFPHM, DTM&H; British professor of tropical medicine; b. 10 Sept. 1921, Port Said, Egypt; s. of Joseph Gilles; m. 1st Wilhelmina Caruana 1955 (died 1972); three s. one d.; m. 2nd Mejra Kacic-Dimitri 1979; ed St Edward's Coll., Malta, Royal Univ. of Malta, Univ. of Oxford; mem. Scientific Staff MRC 1954–58; Sr lecturer in Tropical Medicine Univ. of Ibadan, Nigeria 1959–61, Prof. 1962–65; Sr lecturer in Tropical Medicine Univ. of Liverpool, England 1965–70, Prof. 1970–86, Emer. Prof. 1986–; Dean Liverpool School of Tropical Medicine 1978–83, Vice-Pres. 1991–; Visiting Prof. of Public Health, Univ. of Malta 1989–; Visiting Prof. of Int. Health, Royal Coll. of Surgeons in Ireland 1994–, of Tropical Medicine, Mahidol Univ. Bangkok 1994–; Pres. Royal Soc. of Tropical Medicine and Hygiene 1985–87; Hon. Pres. Malta Asscn of Public Health; Consultant in Malariology, British Army 1972–86, in Tropical Medicine, RAF and DHSS 1972–86; Hon. mem. Swedish Soc. of Tropical Medicine 1999; Rhodes Scholar (Malta) 1943; KStJ 1971; WHO Darling Foundation Medal and Prize 1989, Mary Kingsley Medal 1995. *Publications:* Management and Treatment of Tropical Diseases 1971, Pathology in the Tropics 1976, Tropical Medicine for Nurses 1979, Recent Advances in Tropical Medicine 1984, Human Antiparasitic Drugs 1985, Epidemiology and Control of Tro-

pical Diseases 1986, Preventive Medicine for the Tropics 1990, Hookworm Infections 1991, Management of Severe and Complicated Malaria 1991, Essential Malariology 1993, Atlas of Tropical Medicine and Parasitology 1994, Protozoal Diseases 1999, Tropical Medicine: A Clinical Text 2001. *Leisure interests:* swimming, music. *Address:* 3 Conyers Avenue, Birkdale, Southport, PR8 4SZ, Merseyside, England.

GILLESPIE, Charles Anthony, Jr., BA; American diplomatist and consultant; b. 22 March 1935, Long Beach, Calif.; s. of Charles A. Gillespie and Ann H. Gillespie; m. Vivian Havens 1958; one s. one d.; ed Univ. of Calif. at Los Angeles, Maxwell School of Public Affairs (Syracuse Univ.) and Nat. War Coll. Washington, DC; entered foreign service 1965; served at embassies in Manila, Djakarta, Brussels, Mexico City and Managua, at US Mission to NATO and at State Dept; Amb. and Chief of Mission in Grenada, concurrently serving as Deputy Asst Sec. of State for the Caribbean and Deputy for Operations, Bureau of Inter-American Affairs, State Dept 1983–85; Amb. to Colombia 1985–88, to Chile 1988–91; Special Asst to the Pres. and Sr Dir, Latin America and the Caribbean, Nat. Security Council 1992–93; Dir N American Free Trade Agreement Task Force, State Dept 1993–94; Sr Coordinator, Summit of the Americas 1994, State Dept; Sr Fellow The Forum for Int. Policy 1995–; mem. The Scowcroft Group 1995–. *Address:* 900 17th Street, NW, Suite 500, Washington, DC 20006, USA. *Telephone:* (202) 296-9312. *Fax:* (202) 296-9395.

GILLESPIE, Norman, PhD; British arts administrator and business executive; b. 1957, Lurgan, NI; m. Nicole Gillespie; one d.; ed Queen's Univ. Belfast, Univ. of London, Harvard Business School, USA, Chinghua Univ., Beijing, China; grad. trainee UK civil service; joined BP (British Petroleum) 1987, various positions including Tax Controller for North Sea Operations, Glasgow, mem. Group Strategy Team, London, Head of Pvt. Office of CEO and Chair., US Man. of Planning and Reporting, Houston, TX; Dir of Group Planning and Financial Control, Cable & Wireless, London 1994–97, Head of Group Strategy 1995–97; Chief Financial Officer Cable & Wireless Optus (following merger of Cable & Wireless and Optus 1997), Sydney, Australia 1997–2002, Deputy CEO –2002; Deputy Chair. Australian Brandenburg Orchestra 1998–; Deputy Chair. NSW Div., Australian Business Arts Foundation 2001–; CEO Sydney Opera House Sept. 2002–. *Leisure interests:* music, resistance training. *Address:* Sydney Opera House, GPO Box R239, Royal Exchange, Sydney, NSW 1225, Australia (Office). *Telephone:* (2) 9250-7111 (Office). *Fax:* (2) 9251-3843 (Office). *E-mail:* infodesk@sydneyoperahouse.com (Office). *Website:* www.sydneyoperahouse.com (Office).

GILLESPIE, Rhondda, BMus; British concert pianist; b. 3 Aug. 1941, Sydney, Australia; d. of David Gillespie and Marie Gillespie; m. Denby Richards 1972; ed NSW Conservatorium with Alexander Sverjensky and in London with Louis Kentner and Denis Matthews; debut on Australian radio aged 8 1949; first public recital 1953; winner NSW Concerto Competition, Sydney 1959; European debut in London with Tchaikovsky Piano Concerto 2 1960; since then has played with major orchestras throughout UK, Netherlands, Germany, Scandinavia, Far East and USA and made many festival appearances. *Leisure interests:* golf, languages, exotic cooking. *Address:* 2 Princes Road, St Leonards-on-Sea, East Sussex, TN37 6EL, England. *Telephone:* (1424) 715167. *Fax:* (1424) 712214.

GILLESPIE, Ronald James, PhD, FRS, FRSC, FRSC (UK), FCIC; Canadian/British professor of chemistry; b. 21 Aug. 1924, London; s. of James A. Gillespie and Miriam Gillespie (née Kirk); m. Madge Ena Garner 1950; two d.; ed London Univ.; Asst Lecturer, Dept of Chem., Univ. Coll. London 1948–50, Lecturer 1950–58; Commonwealth Fund Fellow, Brown Univ., RI, USA 1953–54; Assoc. Prof., Dept of Chem., McMaster Univ., Hamilton, Ont., Canada 1958–60, Prof. 1960–88, Chair. Dept of Chem. 1962–65; Professeur Associé, Univ. des Sciences et Techniques de Languedoc, Montpellier, France 1972–73; Visiting Prof. Univ. of Geneva, Switzerland 1976, of Göttingen, FRG 1978; mem. Chem. Soc., ACS; Hon. LLD (Concordia) 1988, (Dalhousie) 1988, Dr hc (Montpellier) 1991; Hon. DSc (McMaster Univ.) 1993; numerous medals and awards. *Publications:* Molecular Geometry 1972, Chemistry (jtly) 1986, 1989, The VSEPR Model of Molecular Geometry (with I. Hargittai) 1991, Atoms, Molecules and Reactions: An Introduction to Chemistry (jtly) 1994, Chemical Bonding and Molecular Geometry: From Lewis to Electron Densities (jtly) 2001; papers in scientific journals. *Leisure interests:* skiing, sailing. *Address:* Department of Chemistry, McMaster University, Hamilton, Ont., L8S 4M1; 150 Wilson Street West, Ancaster, Ont. L9G 4E7, Canada (Home). *Telephone:* (905) 525-9140 (Office); (905) 648-8895 (Home). *Fax:* (905) 522-2509. *E-mail:* gillespi@mcmaster.ca (Office). *Website:* www.mcmaster.ca/faculty/gillespie (Office).

GILLETT, Sir Robin Danvers Penrose, Bt, GBE, RD; British company executive (retd); b. 9 Nov. 1925, London; s. of Sir (Sydney) Harold Gillett, Bt, MC (Lord Mayor of London 1958–59) and Audrey Isobel Penrose Gillett (née Wardlaw); m. 1st Elizabeth Marion Grace Findlay 1950 (died 1997); two s.; m. 2nd Alwyne Winifred Cox 2000; ed Nautical Coll., Pangbourne; served Canadian Pacific Steamships 1943–60, Master Mariner 1951, Staff Commdr 1957; Consultant, Sedgwick Ltd –1986; Underwriting Mem. of Lloyd's; Common Councilman for Ward of Bassishaw, City of London 1965–69, Alderman 1969–96, Sheriff 1973–74, Lord Mayor of London 1976–77; Chancellor of The City Univ. 1976–77; Liveryman and past Master of the Hon. Co. of Master Mariners; Chair. of local Civil Defence Cttee 1967–68; Pres. Nat. Waterways Transport Asscn 1978–83; UK Pres. Royal Life Saving Soc.

1978–82, Deputy Commonwealth Pres. 1982–96 (Vice-Pres. 1996–); Vice Pres. City of London Centre, St John Ambulance Asscn; Vice-Chair. Port of London Authority 1979–84; Vice-Pres. City of London District Red Cross; Chair of Govs Pangbourne Coll. 1979–92; Chair. St Katharine Haven 1990–93; Chair. Council Maritime Volunteer Service 1998–2001, Gov. 2001–; Founder mem. and Fellow, Nautical Inst.; Fellow, Inst. of Admin. Man., Pres. 1980–84 (Inst.'s Medal 1982); RNR Decoration (RD) 1965, Hon. Commdr RNR 1971; HM Lt for City of London 1975; Elder Brother of Trinity House; Trustee, Nat. Maritime Museum 1982–92; Gentleman Usher of the Purple Rod 1985–2000; Fellow Royal Coll. of Music 1991; KStJ 1977; Hon. DSc (City Univ.) 1976; Officer, Order of the Leopard (Zaire), Commdr, Royal Order of Dannebrog (Denmark), Order of Johan Sedia Makhota (Malaysia), Grand Cross of Municipal Merit (Lima, Peru) 1977, Admin. Management Soc. Gold Medal (USA) 1983. *Publication:* A Fish Out of Water 2001. *Leisure interest:* sailing. *Address:* 4 Fairholt Street, Knightsbridge, London, SW7 1EQ, England. *Telephone:* (20) 7589-9860 (Home); (07802) 174734 (mobile). *Fax:* (20) 7589-9860 (Home).

GILLIAM, Terry Vance, BA; American film director, animator, actor, illustrator and writer; b. 22 Nov. 1940, Minn.; s. of James Hall and Beatrice (Vance) Gilliam; m. Margaret Weston 1973; one s. two d.; ed Occidental Coll.; Assoc. Ed. HELP! magazine 1962–64; freelance illustrator 1964–65, advertising copywriter/art dir 1966–67; with Monty Python's Flying Circus (UK) 1969–76; animator, And Now For Something Completely Different (film); co-dir and actor, Monty Python and the Holy Grail; dir Jabberwocky; designer, actor, animator, Monty Python's Life of Brian; co-author, producer, dir Time Bandits; actor and dir Monty Python Live at the Hollywood Bowl 1982; co-writer Monty Python's Meaning of Life (film) 1983; co-writer and dir Brazil 1985, The Adventures of Baron Munchhausen 1988; dir The Fisher King (film) 1991, Twelve Monkeys 1996; Presenter (TV Series) The Last Machine 1995; exec. producer Monty Python's Complete Waste of Time 1995; dir and co-writer Fear and Loathing in Las Vegas 1998; exec. producer Monty Python's Complete Waste of Time (CD-ROM) 1995; appeared in Lost in La Mancha, documentary about failed film project The Man Who Killed Don Quixote 2002; dir Good Omens 2003; Hon. Dr of Arts (Occidental Coll.); Hon. DFA (Royal Coll. of Art, London) 1989. *Publications:* Monty Python's Big Red Book, Monty Python's Papperbok 1977, Monty Python's Scrapbook 1979, Animations of Mortality 1979, Monty Python's The Meaning of Life, Monty Python's Flying Circus – Just the Words (co-ed.) 1989, The Adventures of Baron Munchhausen 1989, Not the Screenplay of Fear and Loathing in Las Vegas 1998, Gilliam on Gilliam 1999, Dark Nights and Holly Fools 1999. *Address:* c/o Jenne Casarotto, National House, 60–66 Wardour Street, London, W1V 4ND, England. *Telephone:* (20) 7287-4450 (Office). *Fax:* (20) 7287-9128 (Office).

GILMAN, Alfred Goodman, MD, PhD, FAAS; American professor of pharmacology; b. 1 July 1941, New Haven, Conn.; s. of Alfred Gilman and Mabel Schmidt; m. Kathryn Hedlund 1963; one s. two d.; ed Yale and Case Western Reserve Univs; Research Assoc. NIH, Bethesda, Md 1969–71; Asst Prof., Assoc. Prof. of Pharmacology, Univ. of Va, Charlottesville 1971–77, Prof. 1977–81; Prof. of Pharmacology and Chair. Dept of Pharmacology Univ. of Texas Southwestern Medical Center, Dallas 1981–, Raymond and Ellen Willie Distinguished Chair. of Molecular Neuropharmacology 1987–, Regental Prof. 1994–; Dir Regeneron Pharmaceutics 1989–, Eli Lilly and Co. 1995–; mem. numerous scientific, advisory and editorial bds; mem. NAS, Inst. of Medicine of NAS, American Soc. of Biological Chemists etc.; Fellow American Acad. of Arts and Sciences; Gairdner Foundation Int. Award 1984; Albert Lasker Basic Medical Research Award 1989, Nobel Prize for Medicine (with Martin Rodbell) 1994, many other awards and distinctions. *Address:* Department of Pharmacology, University of Texas Southwestern Medical Center, 5323 Harry Hines Boulevard, Dallas, TX 75390-9041, USA. *E-mail:* alfred.gilman@utsouthwestern.edu (Office).

GILMARTIN, Raymond V., MBA; American business executive; b. 6 March 1941, Washington, DC; m. Gladys Higham 1965; one s. two d.; ed Union Coll. and Harvard Univ.; Devt Engineer Eastman Kodak 1963–67; various exec. positions, Becton Dickinson & Co. 1976–92, Chair., Pres. and CEO 1992–94; Chair., Pres. and CEO Merck & Co., Inc. 1994–; Dir (non-exec.) Microsoft 2001–. *Address:* Merck and Co., 1 Merck Drive, Whitehouse Station, NJ 08889-0100, USA.

GILMORE, James Stuart, III, JD; American politician and lawyer; b. 6 Nov. 1949, Richmond, Va; s. of James Stuart Gilmore, Jr and Margaret Kandle Gilmore; m. Roxane Gatling Gilmore; two s.; ed Univ. of Virginia; US Army 1971–74; practising attorney 1977–80, 1984–87; fmrly Commonwealth's Attorney, Henrico Co.; fmr Attorney Gen. State of Va; Gov. of Virginia 1997–2001; Alt. Del. Repub. Nat. Convention 1976; Chair. Henrico Co. Repub. Cttee 1982–85, now Vice-Chair.; Chair. Repub. Nat. Cttee; Republican. *Address:* Executive Mansion, Capitol Square, Richmond, VA 23219, USA (Home). *Telephone:* (804) 371-2642 (Home). *Website:* www.thedigitaldominion.com (Office).

GILMORE, Rosalind E. J., CB, MA, FRSA, CIM GT.; British business executive; b. 23 March 1937, London; d. of Sir Robert Fraser and Lady (Betty) Fraser; m. Brian Terence Gilmore 1962; ed King Alfred School, N London, Univ. Coll. London and Newnham Coll. Cambridge; entered HM Treasury 1960; Exec. Asst to Econs Dir IBRD 1966–67; Cabinet Office 1974; Asst Sec. HM Treasury 1975, Head Financial Insts. Div. 1977–80; Press Sec. to

Chancellor of Exchequer 1980–82; Gen. Man. Corp. Planning, Dunlop Ltd 1982–83; Dir of Marketing, Nat. Girobank 1983–86; Directing Fellow, St George's House, Windsor Castle 1986–89; Dir Mercantile Group PLC 1986–89, Mercantile Credit Co. Ltd 1986–89, London and Manchester Group PLC 1986–89; Marketing Consultant, FI Group PLC (Software) 1986–89; mem. Financial Services Act Tribunal 1986–89; Deputy Chair. and Commr Bldg Socs Comm. 1989–91, Chair. 1991–94; Chief Registrar of Friendly Socs and Industrial Insurance Commr 1991–94; Chair. Homeowners Friendly Society Ltd 1996–98, Arrow Broadcasting 1996–98; Dir Moorfields Eye Hosp. Trust 1994–2000, BAT Industries PLC 1996–98, Zurich Financial Services AG (Zurich) 1998–2002; mem. Securities and Investment Bd 1993–96; Dir Leadership Foundation 1997–, Trades Union Fund Mans 2000–; mem. Court, Cranfield Univ. 1992–; mem. Bd Opera North 1993–96; mem. Lloyd's Regulatory Bd 1994–98 (Dir Regulatory Services, Lloyds 1994–95); mem. Council Royal Coll. of Music 1997–; Fellow, Univ. Coll. London 1988; Hon. Fellow, Newnham Coll. Cambridge 1986; . *Achievements:* Cambridge Univ. Swimming Team (blue 1960), Cambridge Univ. Squash Team. *Publication:* Mutuality for the Twenty-first Century 1998. *Leisure interests:* music, reading, house in Greece, languages (Greek, French and Spanish). *Address:* Zurich Financial Services AG, 22 Arlington Street, London, SW1A 1RW (Office); 3 Clarendon Mews, London, W2 2NR, England. *Telephone:* (20) 7317-3957 (Office); (20) 7402-8554. *Fax:* (20) 7402-8554 (Home).

GILMOUR OF CRAIGMILLAR, Baron (Life Peer), cr. 1992, of Cragmillar in the District of the City of Edinburgh; **Ian (Hedworth John Little) Gilmour,** Bt, PC, MP; British politician; b. 8 July 1926; s. of Lt-Col Sir John Little Gilmour and Hon. Victoria Laura Gilmour; m. Lady Caroline Margaret Montagu-Douglas-Scott 1951; four s. one d.; ed Eton Coll., Balliol Coll., Oxford; served with Grenadier Guards 1944–47, rank of Lt 1946; called to the Bar, Inner Temple 1952; Ed. The Spectator 1954–59; MP for Norfolk Central 1962–74, for Chesham and Amersham 1974–92; Parl. Under-Sec., Ministry of Defence 1970–71, Minister of State for Defence Procurement 1971–72, for Defence 1972–74, Sec. of State for Defence 1974; Lord Privy Seal 1979–81; Chair. Conservative Research Dept 1974–75; Pres. Medical Aid for Palestinians 1992–96, Al Quds Medical Foundation 1999–, Hacan Clear Skies 1999–. *Publications:* The Body Politic 1969, Inside Right, A Study of Conservatism 1977, Britain Can Work 1983, Riot, Risings and Revolution 1992, Dancing with Dogma 1992, Whatever Happened to the Tories? (with M. Garnett) 1997, The Making of the Poets 2002. *Address:* The Ferry House, Old Isleworth, Middx, TW7 6BD, England. *Telephone:* (20) 8560-6769.

GIMFERRER, Pere; Spanish writer and literary manager; b. 22 June 1945, Barcelona; s. of Pere Gimferrer and Carmen Torrens; m. María Rosa Caminals 1971; ed Univ. of Barcelona; Head Literary Dept Editorial Seix Barral 1970, Literary Consultant 1973, Literary Man. 1981–; Academician Real Acad. Española 1985–, Acad. Européenne de Poésie, Luxembourg, World Acad. of Poetry, Verona; Nat. Prize for Poetry 1966, 1989, Critic's Prize 1983, 1989, Premio Nacional de las Letras Españolas 1998, Queen Sofía Prize for Iberoamerican Poetry 2000. *Publications:* Arde el Mar 1966, L'Espai Desert 1977, Dietari 1981, Fortuny 1983, El Vendaval 1988, La Llum 1991, The Roots of Miró 1993, Complete Catalan Work, Vol. I 1995, Vol. II 1995, Vol. III 1996, Vol. IV 1996, Vol. V 1997, Masquerade (poem) 1996, L'Agent Provocador 1998, Marea Solar, Marea Lunar 2000, El Diamant dins l'Aigua 2001. *Leisure interests:* cinema, travel. *Address:* Editorial Seix Barral, Provenza 260, Barcelona 08008 (Office); Rambla de Catalunya 113, Barcelona 08008, Spain (Home). *Telephone:* (93) 4967003 (Office). *Fax:* (93) 4967004 (Office).

GINER, Salvador, PhD; Spanish sociologist and university professor; b. 10 Feb. 1934, Barcelona; m. Montserrat Sariola 1966; one s. one d.; ed Int. School Barcelona, Univs of Barcelona, Cologne, Germany and Chicago, USA; Visiting Prof., Univ. of Puerto Rico 1962–63; lecturer, Univ. of Reading, UK 1965–70; Sr Lecturer, Univ. of Lancaster, UK 1970–76; Reader, then Prof. and Head Dept of Sociology and Social Anthropology, Brunel Univ., West London, UK 1976–87; Prof. and Head Dept of Sociology, Univ. of Barcelona 1987–90; Dir Inst. of Advanced Social Studies, Higher Council for Scientific Research 1988–97, Barcelona Metropolitan Region Sociological Survey 2001–02; Pres. Spanish Sociological Asscn 1986–91; Ed. Revista Internacional de Sociología 1992–; Asst Ed. European Journal of Social Theory 1988–; mem. Scientific Cttee European Prize for Social Science (Amalfi Prize) 1989–; Order of Civil Merit 1987, St George's Cross, Catalonia 1998. *Publications:* Contemporary Europe (Vol. I) 1971, (Vol. II) 1978, Mass Society 1976, Ensayos Civiles 1985, El Destino de la Libertad 1988, España: Sociedad y Política 1990, La Gobernabilidad 1992, Religión y Sociedad en España 1994, Carta sobre la Democracia 1996, Buen Gobierno y Política Social 1997, La Societat Catalana 1998 (Coll. of Economists' Prize 1999), Diccionario de Sociología (ed.) 1998, Sociology (revised edn) 2001, Historia del Pensamiento Social (revised edn) 2002, Teoria Sociológica Clasica 2001. *Address:* Department of Sociology, University of Barcelona, Diagonal 690, 08034 Barcelona, Spain. *Telephone:* (93) 2110686 (Home); (93) 4035553. *Fax:* (93) 4021894. *E-mail:* salva@eco.ub.es (Office); sginer@terra.es (Home).

GINGRICH, Newt (Newton Leroy), PhD; American politician; b. 17 June 1943, Harrisburg, Pa; s. of Robert Bruce Gingrich and Kathleen (née Daugherty) Gingrich; m. 2nd Marianne Ginther 1981; two d. by previous marriage; ed Emory and Tulane Univs; mem. faculty, W Ga Coll., Carrollton 1970–78, Prof. of History –1978; mem. 96–103rd Congresses from 6th Dist of Ga 1979–92; Chair. GOPAC, now Chair. Emer.; House Republican Whip 1989; Speaker House of Reps 1994–98; Adjunct Prof. Reinhardt Coll., Waleska, Ga

1994–95; co-f. Congressional Mil. Reform Caucus, Congressional Space Caucus; mem. AAAS. *Publications:* Window of Opportunity, 1945 1995, To Renew America 1995. *Address:* The Committee for New American Leadership, 1800 K. Street #714, Washington, DC 20006, USA (Office).

GINKAS, Kama Mironovich; Russian stage director; b. 7 May 1941, Kaunas, Lithuania; m. Yanovskaya Henrietta Yanovna; one s.; ed Leningrad Inst. of Theatre, Music and Cinema; worked in Krasnoyarsk Theatre of Young Spectators 1971–73; accused of aestheticism and barred from working in theatres; now Prof. Swedish Theatre Acad. *Theatre includes:* Little Car, Moscow Art Theatre 1981, Hedda Gabler, Moscow Mossoviet Theatre 1984, Performing Crime, Moscow Theatre of Young Spectators 1991, Love is Wonderful, Finland, K.I. from Crime, Moscow Theatre of Young Spectators, Idiot (opera), Germany. *Address:* Tishinsky per. 24, Apt. 7, Moscow, Russia. *Telephone:* (095) 299-53-60 (Office); (095) 253-43-15 (Home).

GINOLA, David; French professional footballer and sportsman; b. 25 Jan. 1967, Gassin, Var; s. of René Ginola and Mireille Collet; m. Coraline Delphin 1990; two d.; ed Lycée du Parc Impérial, Nice; with the following clubs: first div. Toulon clubs 1986–87, Matraracing, Paris 1987–88, Racing Paris 1 1988–89, Brest-Armorique 1989–90, Paris-Saint-Germain 1991–95 (French nat. champions 1993–94, winners Coupe de France 1993, 1995, winners Coupe de la ligue 1995); with Newcastle United, England, 1995–97, Tottenham Hotspur 1997–2000, Aston Villa 2000–02; 17 int. caps; anti-landmine campaigner for Red Cross 1998–; Professional Football Asscn Player of the Year 1999, Football Writers' Asscn Player of the Year 1999. *Publication:* David Ginola: The Autobiography (with Niel Silver) 2000. *Leisure interests:* golf, tennis, skiing, car racing. *Website:* www.ginola14.com (Office).

GINSBURG, Ruth Bader, LLB; American judge; b. 15 March 1933, Brooklyn; d. of Nathan Bader and Celia Amster; m. Martin Ginsburg 1954; one s. one d.; ed Cornell Univ. and Harvard and Columbia Law Schools; admitted New York Bar 1959, DC Bar 1975, US Supreme Court Bar 1967; Law Sec. to Judge, US Dist Court (southern Dist) New York 1959–61; Research Assoc. Columbia Law School, New York 1961–62, Assoc. Dir project on int. procedure 1962–63; Asst Prof. Rutgers Univ. Law School, Newark 1963–66, Assoc. Prof. 1966–69, Prof. 1969–72; Prof. Columbia Univ. School of Law, New York 1972–80; Fellow, Center for Advanced Study in Behavioral Sciences, Stanford, Calif. 1977–78; US Circuit Judge, US Court of Appeals, DC Circuit, Washington, DC 1980–93; Judge, US Supreme Court 1993–; mem. American Bar Asscn, AAAS, American Law Inst., Council on Foreign Relations; numerous hon. degrees. *Publications:* Civil Procedure in Sweden (with A. Bruzelius) 1965, Swedish Code of Judicial Procedure 1968, Sex-Based Discrimination (with others); articles in legal journals. *Address:* United States Supreme Court, 1 First Street, NE, Washington, DC 20543, USA.

GINWALA, Frene Noshir, DPhil, LLB; South African politician; b. 25 April 1932, Johannesburg; ed Oxford Univ. and London Univ., UK; left SA in 1960 to est. external mission of the ANC, fmr ANC Spokeswoman, UK; contrib. to The Guardian, The Economist and the BBC, UK; Ed. Tanzania Standard and Sunday News, Tanzania; lectured at various univs; returned to SA 1991; mem. Secr., Office of the Pres. of the ANC, Head ANC Research Dept 1991–94; Speaker of Nat. Ass. 1994–; Pres. S African Speakers' Forum; Co-Chair. Global Coalition for Africa (GCA); Chair. Presidential Award for Youth Empowerment; Hon. Fellow Linacre Coll. Oxford, UK; Grand Officier de l'Ordre nat. (Côte d'Ivoire) 1998; Hon. LLD (Rhodes) 1996, (Natal) 1996, (Cape Town) 1997; Global Award for Outstanding Contrib. to the Promotion of Human Rights and Democracy, Priyadarshni Acad., India 2000, Black Man. Forum Leadership Award 2000, Woman of the Year Award (Univ. of Pretoria Law Faculty) 2000. *Publications include:* Sanctions in South Africa in Question, Gender and Economic Policy in a Democratic South Africa, Women and the Elephant: Putting Women on the Agenda. *Leisure interest:* reading. *Address:* Office of the Speaker, National Assembly, Parliament Buildings, Pretoria, South Africa (Office). *Telephone:* (21) 4032595 (Office). *Fax:* (21) 4619462 (Office). *E-mail:* amaduna@parliament.gov.sa (Office). *Website:* www.parliament.gov.sa (Office).

GINZBURG, Vitaly Lazarevich, DrSc; Russian physicist; b. 4 Oct. 1916, Moscow; s. of Lazar and Augusta Ginzburg; m. Nina Ginzburg 1946; one d.; ed Moscow Univ.; at P. N. Lebedev Physical Inst., USSR (now Russian) Acad. of Sciences 1940–; Prof. Gorky Univ. 1945–68, Moscow Inst. of Physics 1968–, Adviser to Dir 1987–; Corresp. mem. USSR (now Russian) Acad. of Sciences 1953–66, mem. 1966–; USSR People's Deputy 1989–91; mem. Int. Acad. of Astronautics 1969; Assoc. Royal Astronomical Soc., London 1970; Foreign mem. Royal Danish Acad. of Sciences and Letters 1977; Foreign Hon. mem. American Acad. of Art and Science 1971; Hon. Fellow, Indian Acad. of Science 1977; Foreign Fellow, Indian Nat. Science Acad. 1981; Foreign Assoc., NAS, USA 1981; Foreign mem. Royal Soc., London 1987; mem. Academia Europaea 1990; Hon. DSc (Sussex) 1970; Mandelstam Prize 1947, Lomonosov Prize 1962, USSR State Prize 1953, Lenin Prize 1966, Gold Medal, Royal Astronomical Soc. 1991, Bardeen Prize 1991, Wolf Prize 1994, 1995, Vavilov Gold Medal (Russian Acad. of Sciences) 1995, Lomonosov Great Gold Medal (Russian Acad. of Sciences) 1995, UNESCO-Nils Bohr Gold Medal 1998, APS Nicholson Medal 1998, IUPAP O'Ceallaigh Medal 2001, Order of Lenin, etc. *Publications:* The Physics of a Lifetime 2001, works on theoretical physics (superconductivity, etc.), astrophysics and radiophysics. *Address:* P. N. Lebedev Physical Inst., Russian Academy of Sciences, Leninsky Prospect 53,

119991 GSP, Moscow B-333, Russia. *Telephone:* (095) 135-85-70 (Office); (095) 135-10-96 (Home). *Fax:* (095) 938-22-51; (095) 135-85-33. *E-mail:* ginzburg@lpi.ru (Office).

GIOIA, (Michael) Dana, MA, MBA; American writer and poet; b. 24 Dec. 1950, Los Angeles; m. Mary Hiecke 1980; three s. (one deceased); ed Stanford Univ., Harvard Univ.; fmr Visiting Writer Colo Coll., Johns Hopkins Univ., Wesleyan Univ.; Chair. Nat. Endowment for the Arts 2003–; mem. Bd and Vice-Pres. Poetry Soc. of America; mem. Wesleyan Univ. Writers' Conf.; regular contrib. to various journals, reviews and periodicals including San Francisco magazine (classical music critic); Esquire Best of New Generation Award 1984, Frederick Bock Prize for Poetry 1985. *Publications include:* The Ceremony and Other Stories 1984, Daily Horoscope 1986, Mottetti: Poems of Love (trans.) 1990, The Gods of Winter 1991, Can Poetry Matter? 1992, An Introduction to Poetry 1994, The Madness of Hercules (trans.) 1995, Interrogations at Noon 2001, Nosferatu (opera libretto with Alva Henderson) 2001, The Barrier of a Common Language (essays) 2002; also ed. of several works of literary criticism. *Address:* National Endowment for the Arts, 1100 Pennsylvania Avenue, NW, Washington, DC 20506 (Office); 7190 Faught Road, Santa Rosa, CA 95403, USA (Office). *Telephone:* (202) 682-5400 (Office). *Website:* www.nea.gov (Office).

GIOJA, José Luis; Argentine politician and lawyer; b. 4 Dec. 1949, San Juan Prov.; m.; ed Escuela Normal de Jáchal, San Juan and Nat. Univ. of Cuyo; Pres. Agrupación Nacional de Estudiantes Universitarios 1972–73; Pvt Sec. to Gov. Eloy Camus 1973; Sec.-Gen. Juventud Peronista, Partido Justicialista de San Juan 1975, Congresal Provincial 1975–76; Interventor Instituto Provincial de la Vivienda 1974–75; Pres. Unidad Básica del Barrio Edilco 1983; Cand., Departamento de Rawson 1983; Pres. Junta Departamental de Rawson 1984–85; mem. Consejo Nacional Justicialista 1987–93, Consejo Provincial Justicialista 1987–93; Provincial Deputy and Vice-Pres. Justicialista Bloc, Chamber of Deputies, San Juan Prov. 1987–91, Pres. Comisión de Minería, Obras Públicas y Recursos Hídricos; Deputy in Nat. Ass. 1991–99, Pres. Jt Party Comm. Argentina–Chile 1993; Senator 1995–, Pres. Comisión Bicameral de Minería y de Coparticipación Fed. de Impuestos, Pres. Senate Justicialistas Bloc 2000–02, Pres. (provisional) of Senate Dec. 2002–. *Address:* Senado, Hipólito Yrigoyen 1849, 3° Piso, Oficina 6 "D", 1310 Buenos Aires, Argentina (Office). *Telephone:* (11) 4959-3000 (Office). *E-mail:* gioga@senado.gov.ar (Office). *Website:* www.senado.gov.ar/web/presidencia (Office).

GIORDANO, HE Cardinal Michele; Italian ecclesiastic; b. 26 Sept. 1930, S. Arcangelo (Pz); ordained 1953, elected to the titular Church of Lari Castello 1971, consecrated bishop 1972, prefect at Matera e Irsina 1974, transferred to Naples 1987; cr. HE Cardinal 1988. *Address:* Arcivescovado di Napoli, Largo Donnaregina 23, 80138 Naples, Italy. *Telephone:* (081) 449118. *Fax:* (081) 292487.

GIORDANO, Richard Vincent, BA, LLB, PhD; American business executive; b. 24 March 1934, New York; s. of Vincent and Cynthia (née Cardetta) Giordano; m. Barbara Claire Beckett 1956 (divorced); one s. two d.; ed Stuyvesant School, New York, Harvard Univ. and Columbia Univ. Law School; admitted New York Bar 1961; Assoc. Shearman and Sterling (law firm), New York 1959–63; Asst Sec. Air Reduction Co. Inc., New York 1963–64, Vice-Pres. Distribution of Products Div. 1964–65, Exec. Vice-Pres. 1965–67, Group Vice-Pres. 1967–71, Pres. and COO 1971–74, CEO 1977–79; Dir BOCI 1974; Man. Dir and CEO BOC Group 1979–84, Chair. 1985–92, CEO 1985–91, Chair. (non-exec.) 1994–96; Dir (non-exec.) Reuters 1991–94; Chair. (non-exec.) British Gas PLC (renamed BG PLC 1997, BG Group PLC 1999) 1994–; Dir (non-exec.) Cen. Electricity Generating Bd 1982–89, Georgia Pacific Corpn 1984–, Grand Metropolitan 1985–97 (Deputy Chair. (non-exec.) 1991–97), RTZ (renamed Rio Tinto PLC) Deputy Chair. (non-exec.) 1992–, Lucas Industries (non-exec.) 1993–94; Hon. Fellow Royal Coll. of Anaesthetists, London Business School; Hon. KBE; Hon. DCS (St John's Univ.); Hon. LLB (Bath) 1998. *Leisure interests:* sailing, opera. *Address:* c/o BG Group PLC, Eagle House, 108–110 Jermyn Street, London, SW1Y 6RP, England. *Telephone:* (20) 7707-4878 (Office). *Fax:* (20) 7707-4858 (Office). *E-mail:* richard.giordano@bg-group.com (Office).

GIOVANNI, Nikki, BA; American poet; b. 7 June 1943, Knoxville, Tenn.; d. of Jones Giovanni and Yolande Watson; one s.; ed Fisk Univ. and Univ. of Pennsylvania; Asst Prof. of Black Studies, City Coll. of New York 1968; Assoc. Prof. of English, Rutgers Univ. 1968–72; Prof. of Creative Writing, Coll. Mt. St Joseph on the Ohio 1985; Prof. Va Polytechnic Inst. and State Univ. Blacksburg 1987–; founder, Nixtom Ltd 1970; Visiting Prof. Ohio State Univ. 1984; recordings and TV appearances; recipient of numerous awards and hon. degrees. *Publications:* Black Feeling, Black Talk 1968, Black Judgement 1968, Re: Creation 1970, Poem of Angela Yvonne Davis 1970, Spin A Soft Black Song 1971, Gemini 1971, My House 1972, A Dialogue: James Baldwin and Nikki Giovanni 1973, Ego Tripping and Other Poems for Young Readers 1973, A Poetic Equation: Conversations Between Nikki Giovanni and Margaret Walker 1974, The Women and the Men 1975, Cotton Candy on a Rainy Day 1978, Vacationtime 1980, Those Who Ride the Night Winds 1983, Sacred Cows . . . and other Edibles 1988, Conversations with Nikki Giovanni 1992, Racism 101 1994, Grand Mothers 1994, Blues: For All the Changes 1999. *Address:* Department of English, PO Box 0112, Virginia Polytechnic Institute and State University, Blacksburg, VA 24063, USA.

GIRARD, Jean-François, MD, MSc; French civil servant and professor of medicine; b. 20 Nov. 1944, Luçon (Vendée); two d. one s.; ed Univ. of Paris;

Prof. of Medicine 1979–97; Dir-Gen. Ministry of Health 1986–97; Chair. Exec. Council WHO 1992, 1993; Conseiller d'Etat 1997–; Pres. Inst. de recherche pour le développement 2001–; Chevalier, Légion d'honneur, Officier, Ordre Nat. du Mérite. *Publications:* Quand la Santé devient publique 1998, La maladie d'Alzheimer 2000. *Leisure interest:* sailing. *Address:* Institut de recherche pour le développement, 213 rue La Fayette, 75010 Paris (Office); 10 avenue René Coty, 75014 Paris, France (Home). *Telephone:* 1-48-03-77-48 (Office); 1-43-27-58-32 (Home). *Fax:* 1-48-03-77-42 (Office). *E-mail:* president@ird.fr (Office).

GIRARD, René Noël, PhD; French/American professor and author; b. 25 Dec. 1923, Avignon; s. of Joseph Girard and Thérèse Fabre; m. Martha Virginia McCullough 1951; two s. one d.; ed Lycée d'Avignon, Ecole des Chartes and Indiana Univ.; Instructor of French, Indiana Univ. 1947–51, Duke Univ. 1952–53; Asst Prof. Bryn Mawr Coll. 1953–57; Assoc. Prof. The Johns Hopkins Univ. 1957–61, Prof. 1961–68, Chair. Romance Languages 1965–68, James M. Beall Prof. of French and Humanities 1976–80; Prof. Inst. d'études françaises Bryn Mawr, Avignon 1961–68, Dir 1969; Distinguished Faculty Prof. of Arts and Letters, State Univ. of New York at Buffalo 1971–76; Andrew B. Hammond Prof. of French Language, Literature and Civilization, Stanford Univ. 1981–95, Courtesy Prof. of Religious Studies and Comparative Literature 1986–95, Dir Program of Interdisciplinary Research, Dept of French and Italian 1987–95, Prof. Emer. 1995–; mem. Center for Int. Security and Arms Control, 1990–95; mem. Emer. 1995–; Fellow American Acad. of Arts and Sciences 1979–, Guggenheim Fellow 1960, 1967; Hon. DLit (Vrije Univ.) 1985, Hon. DTheol (Innsbruck) 1988, Hon. DLit (Padua) 2001; Acad. Française Prize 1973, Grand Prix de Philosophie 1996; Prix Médicis-Essai 1990, Premio Nonino (Percoto, Udine, Italy) 1998; Chevalier, Ordre Nat. de la Légion d'honneur 1984, Officier, Ordre des Arts et Lettres 1984. *Publications include:* Mensonge romantique et vérité romanesque 1961, Dostoïevski: du double à l'unité 1963, La violence et le sacré 1972, Des choses cachées depuis la fondation du monde 1978, Le bouc émissaire 1982, La route antique des hommes pervers 1985, The Girard Reader 1996, Shakespeare: Les feux de l'envie 1990, A Theatre of Envy. William Shakespeare 1991, Quand ces choses commenceront 1994, Je vois Satan tomber comme l'éclair 1999, (in English) 2001, Celui par qui le scandale arrive 2001, La voix méconnue du réel 2002. *Address:* 705 Frenchman's Road, Stanford, CA 94305, USA; 17 avenue la Bourdonnais, 75007 Paris, France.

GIRARDET, Herbert, BSc(Econs); German ecologist, consultant, writer and television producer; b. 25 May 1943, Essen; s. of Herbert Girardet and Ingrid Girardet; m. Barbara Hallifax 1967; two s.; ed Tübingen and Berlin Univs, London School of Econs, UK; consultant to Town and Country Planning Asscn, London 1976–86, Channel 4 TV, London 1987–89, Habitat II Conf., Istanbul 1995–96, Sustainable London study for Bridge House Estate Fund 1998–99, GLA 2001–, Corpn of London (on tall bldgs and sustainable devt) 2001–; Visiting Prof. of Environmental Planning, Middx Univ. 1995–; Dir Footprint Productions (documentary production co.) 1997–, Urban Futures consultancy 1998–; mem. Balaton Group of int. environment experts 1993–, Urban Advisory Bd, World Bank, Washington, DC 1999–; Chair. The Schumacher Soc., UK 1994–; Trustee The Sustainable London Trust 1996–; Patron The Soil Asscn, UK 1990–; Hon. FRIBA 2000; UN Global Award for Outstanding Environmental Achievements, prizes for TV documentaries. *Television:* initiator and researcher: Far from Paradise (series) 1983–86; producer: Jungle Pharmacy 1988, Metropolis 1994, Urban Best Practices 1996, Deadline 2000 (28 three-minute films) 1997–99; writer and producer: Halting the Fires 1990; series consultant: The People's Planet 1999–2000. *Publications:* Far From Paradise: The Story of Human Impact on the Environment (co-author) 1986, Earthrise 1992, The Gaia Atlas of Cities 1992, Getting London in Shape for 2000 1995, Making Cities Work (co-author) 1996, Creating a Sustainable London (co-author) 1996, Creating Sustainable Cities 1999. *Address:* 93 Cambridge Gardens, London, W10 6JE, England (Office); Forest Cottage, Trelleck Road, Tintern, Chepstow, Monmouthshire, NP6 16SN, Wales (Home). *Telephone:* (20) 8969-6375 (Office); (1291) 689392 (Home). *Fax:* (20) 8960-2202 (Office); (1291) 689392 (Home). *E-mail:* herbie@easynet.co.uk (Office).

GIRARDOT, Annie Suzanne; French film actress; b. 25 Oct. 1931, Paris; m. Renato Salvatori 1962 (deceased); one d.; ed Centre d'art dramatique, Paris, Conservatoire nat. d'art dramatique; with Comédie-Française 1954–57; Suzanne-Bianchetti Prize 1956, Prize for Best Actress, Venice Film Festival (for Trois chambres à Manhattan) 1965, Courteline Prize (for Déclics et des claques) 1965, Prize for Best Actress, Mar del Plata Festival (for Vivre pour vivre) 1968, Best Actress of the Year (for Docteur Françoise Gailland) 1976; Commdr des Arts et des Lettres. *Plays include:* la Tour Eiffel qui tue, la Paix chez soi, le Jeu de l'amour et du hasard, la Machine à écrire, les Amants magnifiques, Aux innocents les mains pleines, Une femme trop honnête, Deux sur une balançoire, l'Idiote, Après la chute 1965, le Jour de la tortue 1965, Seule dans le noir 1966, Persephone (speaking part, La Scala, Milan) 1966, Madame Marguerite (1974–75), Marguerite et les autres 1983, l'Avare 1986, Première Jeunesse 1987, le Roi se meurt 1988, Helden platz 1991, les Chutes du Zambèze 1995, Le Sixième ciel 1998. *Films include:* Treize à table 1955, l'Homme aux clefs d'or 1956, le Rouge est mis, Maigret tend un piège, le Désert de Pigalle 1957, la Corde raide, Recours en grâce 1959, la Française et l'amour, la Proie pour l'ombre, Rocco et ses frères 1960, le Rendez-vous, les Amours célèbres, le Bateau d'Emile 1961, le Vice et la vertu 1962, l'Autre femme 1963, Déclics et des claques, Trois chambres à Manhattan, l'Or du duc 1965, Vivre pour vivre 1967, les Gauloises bleues, la Bande à Bonnot 1968, Il pleut dans mon village, Erotissimo, Un homme qui me plaît 1969, Dillinger est mort, l'Histoire d'une femme, Elle boit pas, elle fume pas, elle drague pas, mais ... elle cause, Disons un soir à dîner, les Novices, le Clair de terre 1970, Mourir d'aimer, la Vieille fille, la Mandarine 1971, les Feux de la chandeleur, Elle cause plus ... elle flingue 1972, Traitement de choc, Jessua 1973, Il n'y a pas de fumée sans feu 1972, Ursule et Grelu 1973, Juliette et Juliette, la Gifle 1974, Il faut vivre dangereusement, le Gitan, Il pleut sur Santiago 1975, Docteur Françoise Gailland, le Soupçon, D'amour et d'eau fraîche, Cours après moi ... que je t'attrape 1976, A chacun son enfer 1977, le Dernier baiser, Jambon d'Ardenne, le Point de mire 1977, la Zizanie, la Clé sur la porte, l'Amour en question 1978, Vas-y maman 1978, Cause toujours ... tu m'intéresses 1979, Bobo, Jacco, le Grand embouteillage 1979, la Vie continue, une Robe noire pour un tueur, la Revanche 1981, Partir, revenir 1985, Adieu Blaireau 1985, Prisonnières 1988, Cinq jours en juin 1989, Comédie d'amour 1989, Il y a des jours ... et des lunes 1990, Merci la vie 1991, les Misérables 1995 (César award for Best Supporting Actress), Préférence et l'age de braise 1998, T'aime 2000, la Pianiste 2001. *Television appearances:* le Pain de ménage 1966, Bobo, Jaco, Florence ou la vie de château 1987, le Vent des moissons 1989, Un pull par-dessus l'autre 1993, Jeanne 1994, le Dernier voyage 1995, la Façon de le dire 1999. *Publication:* Vivre d'aimer 1989. *Address:* c/o Artmédia, 20 avenue Rapp, 75007 Paris, France.

GIRAUD, Michel Jean Lucien; French politician and business executive; b. 14 July 1929, Pontoise, Seine-et-Oise; s. of Jean Giraud and Suzanne Le Goaziou; m. Simonne Wietzel 1952; two s. (one deceased) one d.; ed secondary school at Saint-Martin de France-Pontoise, Lycée Louis le Grand and Univ. de Paris; Deputy Dir Société Centrale des Bois 1951–57; Dir Société A. Charles & Fils 1960–72; Pres. Dir-Gen. SONIBAT 1972–93, Société d'Economie Mixte d'Aménagement et de Gestion du Marché d'Intérêt Nat. de Paris-Rungis 1975–77; Senator for Val-de-Marne 1977–88; Conseiller-Gén. Val de Marne 1967–85; Admin., Conseil d'Admin. Parisian Regional Dist 1968–, Sec. 1969–72, Pres. 1972–73; Pres. Conseil Régional, Ile-de-France 1976–88, 1992–98; RPR Deputy for Val-de-Marne 1988–93, 1995–; Mayor of Perreux-sur-Marne 1971–92 (Municipal Councillor 1971–); Pres. Nat. Fed. of Local Councillors 1977–83, Asscn of Mayors of France 1983–92; Founder, Pres. World Asscn of Major Metropolises–Metropolis 1985–98; Minister of Labour, Employment and Professional Training 1993–95; Chevalier, Légion d'honneur, Ordre Nat. du Mérite, des Palmes Académiques, Médaille d'Argent de la Jeunesse et des Sports. *Publications:* Nous tous la France 1983, Raconte-moi Marianne 1984, Notre Ile-de-France région capitale 1985, le Perreux, 100 ans d'histoire 1987, le Temps des Métropoles 1987, Histoire de l'Ile de France 1996, Histoires de communes 1996, Citadins de l'an 2000 1997. *Leisure interests:* sport, history, music, skiing. *Address:* Assemblée nationale, 75355 Paris (Office); 4 Grande rue, 91250 Morsang-sur-Seine, France (Home).

GIRAY, I. Safa; Turkish politician; b. 5 March 1931, Izmir; s. of Nuri Giray and Nimet Giray; m. 1st Sema Babaç 1955; m. 2nd Misler Ünlüyol 1972; two s. one d.; ed Istanbul Tech. Univ.; planning engineer at Gen. Directorate of Electricity Works Study Dept 1968; worked on project studies of Keban and Oymapinar Dams; adviser at Gen. Directorate of Electrical Works; Man. Black Sea Copper Enterprises 1969–74; Gen. Man. Akkardan Co. 1974–80; Gen. Man. Anadolu Machine Co. 1980–83; Deputy for Istanbul 1983–; Minister of Public Works and Housing 1983–89, of Defence 1989–90, of Foreign Affairs 1991, MP 1991–95, Deputy for Balikesir 1995–. *Leisure interests:* music, games. *Address:* Abidin Daver Sk. No. 20/7, Cankaya-Ankara, Turkey. *Telephone:* (312) 4423496.

GIRI, Tulsi; Nepalese politician; b. Sept. 1926; Deputy Minister of Foreign Affairs 1959; Minister of Village Devt 1960; Minister without Portfolio 1960; Minister of Foreign Affairs, the Interior, Public Works and Communications 1961; Vice-Chair. Council of Ministers and Minister of Palace Affairs 1962; Chair. Council of Ministers and Minister of Foreign Affairs 1962–65; mem. Royal Advisory Cttee 1969–74; Adviser to the King 1974–; Prime Minister, Minister of Palace Affairs and Defence 1975–77. *Address:* Jawakpurdham, District Dhanuka, Nepal.

GIROLAMI, Sir Paul, Kt, BCom, FCA; British business executive and chartered accountant; b. 25 Jan. 1926, Fanna, Italy; m. Christabel Mary Gwynne Lewis 1952; two s. one d.; ed London School of Economics; with Chantrey and Button (Chartered Accountants) 1950–54, Coopers and Lybrand, 1954–65; joined Glaxo as Financial Controller 1965, mem. of Bd and Finance Dir 1968, Chief Exec. 1980–86, Deputy Chair. April-Dec. 1985; Chair. Glaxo Holdings 1985–94; Pres. Glaxo Finanziaria SpA Italy; Dir Nippon Glaxo Ltd, Japan 1975–94, Glaxo-Sankyo Ltd 1984–94, Credito Italiano Int. 1990–93, Forte PLC 1992–96, UIS France 1994–; mem. CBI Council 1986–93; Chair. Senate for Chartered Accountants in Business 1990–; Chair. Council Goldsmith's Coll., Univ. of London 1994–2000; Dir American Chamber of Commerce (UK) 1983; mem. Appeal Cttee of Inst. of Chartered Accountants 1987, Stock Exchange Listed Cos Advisory Cttee 1987–92, Open Univ. Visiting Cttee 1987–89, Court of Assts of The Worshipful Company of Goldsmiths 1986; Chair. Senate of the Bd for Chartered Accountants in Business 1989; Freeman, City of London Liveryman 1980; Hon. Fellow, LSE 1989; Hon. mem. Emmanuel Coll., Cambridge 1994; Grande Ufficiale, Ordine al Merito della Repubblica Italiana 1987; Insignia of the Order of the Rising Sun; Cavaliere del Lavoro 1991; Dr hc (Aston) 1991, (Trieste) 1991; Hon. DSc (Sunderland) 1991, (Bradford) 1993; Hon. LLD (Singapore) 1993, (Warwick)

1996; City and Guilds Insignia Award in Tech. (hc) 1988, Public Service Star, Singapore 2000. *Leisure interests:* reading, music. *E-mail:* pgirol@aol.com (Home).

GISCARD D'ESTAING, Valéry, KCB; French politician and civil servant; b. 2 Feb. 1926, Koblenz, Germany; s. of the late Edmond Giscard d'Estaing and May Bardoux; m. Anne-Aymone de Brantes 1952; two s. two d.; ed Ecole Polytechnique, Ecole Nat. d'Admin; Official, Inspection des Finances 1952, Insp. 1954; Deputy Dir du Cabinet of Prés. du Conseil June-Dec. 1954; Deputy for Puy de Dôme 1956–58, re-elected for Clermont 1958, for Puy de Dôme 1962, 1967, 1984, 1986, 1988, resgnd 1989; Sec. of State for Finance 1959, Minister for Finance and Econ. Affairs 1962–66, 1969–74; Pres. Comm. des Finances, de l'Economie général et du plan 1967–68; Pres. Cttee des Affaires Etrangères 1987–89; Pres. of the French Repub. 1974–81; Founder-Pres. Fed. Nat. des Républicains Indépendants (from May 1977 Parti Républicain) 1965; Del. to UN Gen. Ass. 1956, 1957, 1958; Chair. OECD Ministerial Council 1960; mem. Conseil Constitutionnel 1981–; Conseiller gen., Puy-de-Dôme 1982–88; Pres. Regional Council of Auvergne 1986–; Pres. Union pour la democratie française (UDF) 1988–96; Deputy to European Parl. 1989–93; Pres. European Movt Int. 1989–97; Pres. Council of European Municipalities and Regions 1997–; Deputy for Puy-de-Dôme 1993–2002; Pres. Comm. of Foreign Affairs, Nat. Ass. 1993–97; Chair. EU Convention on the Future of Europe 2001–; mem. Royal Acad. of Econ. Science and Finance, Spain 1995–; Grand Croix, Ordre de la Légion d'honneur, Grand Croix, Ordre national du Mérite, Croix de guerre, Chevalier, Ordre de Malte, Grand Cross, Order of Isabel la Católica, Nansen Medal 1979, Onassis Foundation Prize 2000, Trombinoscope Prize for Political Personality of the Year 2000, Jean Monnet Foundation Medal 2001, Trombinoscope European of the Year 2002, Charlemagne Prize 2002. *Publications:* Démocratie française 1976, Deux français sur trois 1984, Le pouvoir et la vie, (Vol. I) 1988, (Vol. II, L'affrontement) 1991, Le passage 1994, Dans cinq ans, l'an 2000 (essay) 1995, Les français 2000. *Leisure interests:* shooting, skiing. *Address:* Conseil régional d'Auvergne, 13–15 Avenue de Fontmaure, PO Box 60, 63402 Chamalières cedex; 199 blvd Saint-Germain, 75007 Paris, France. *Telephone:* 1-45-44-30-30. *Fax:* 1-45-49-11-16.

GITARI, Most Rev. David Mukuba, BA, BD; Kenyan ecclesiastic; b. 16 Sept. 1937; s. of Samuel Mukuba Gituku and Jessie Wanjiku; m. Grace Wanjiro Gajembo 1966; three c.; ed Kangaru School, Embu, Royal Coll., Nairobi, Tyndale Coll., Bristol; Gen. Sec. Pan-African Evangelical Fellowship 1966–68, Bible Soc. of Kenya 1971–75; Anglican Bishop of Diocese of Mt. Kenya E 1975–90, of Diocese of Kirinyaga 1990–96; Archbishop of Anglican Church of Kenya and Bishop of Diocese of Nairobi 1976–; Dir Oxford Centre for Mission Studies 1983–; Chair. Kenya Students Christian Fellowship (KSCF) 1971–74, Kenya Peace 1978–, World Evangelical Fellowship Theological Comm. 1978–88, Nat. Council of Churches of Kenya (NCCK) 1978–80, 1981–83; Deputy Chair. WCC Comm. on Evangelism 1983–91; First Chair. Int. Fellowship of Mission Theologians 1981–94; Hon. DD (Ashland Seminars, Ohio, USA) 1983, (Univ. of Canterbury) 1993. *Publications:* Let the Bishop Speak, In Season and Out of Season. *Leisure interests:* driving, farming (keeping pigs and cows and growing mangoes). *Address:* Anglican Church of Kenya, Provincial Office, P.O. Box 40502, Nairobi, Kenya (Office). *Telephone:* (2) 714755 (Office); (161) 30832 (Home). *Fax:* (2) 718442 (Office); (161) 30824 (Home). *E-mail:* ackenya@insightkenya.com (Office).

GITELSON, Yosif Isayevich; Russian biophysicist; b. 6 July 1928; m.; four d.; ed Krasnoyarsk Inst. of Medicine; worked as practitioner Krasnoyarsk Blood Transfusion Station 1952–53; docent Krasnoyarsk Inst. of Agric. 1953–57; Sr Researcher, Head of Lab., Inst. of Physics, Siberian br. of USSR (now Russian) Acad. of Sciences 1957–82; Head of Lab., Inst. of Biophysics Siberian br. of USSR Acad. of Sciences 1982–86, Dir 1986–96, Adviser 1996–; Corresp. mem. USSR Acad. of Sciences 1979, mem. 1990–; adviser to Russian Acad. of Sciences 1996–. *Publications:* Experimental Ecological Systems Including Man, Problems of Space Biology 1975, Light from the Sea 1986, Distant Studies of Siberia 1988; numerous articles in scientific journals. *Address:* Institute of Biophysics, Akademgorodok, 660036 Krasnoyarsk, Russia (Office). *Telephone:* (3912) 43-46-23 (Office); (095) 433-63-57 (Home).

GIULIANI, Rudolph W., KBE, BA, JD; American politician and lawyer; b. 28 May 1944, New York City; s. of the late Harold Giuliani and Helen Giuliani; m. Donna Hanover (divorced 2002); one s. one d.; ed Manhattan Coll., New York Univ.; law clerk; Judge US Dist Court, New York City 1968–70; Asst US Attorney Southern Dist, New York; US Attorney 1983–89; with Patterson, Belknap, Webb and Tyler 1977–81; with White & Case 1989–90; with Anderson Kill Olick & Oshinsky 1990–93; Mayor of New York 1994–2001; f. Giuliani Partners LLC (with Ernst & Young) 2002, Chair. and CEO; Time Magazine Person of the Year 2001. *Publications:* Leadership 2002. *Address:* Giuliani Partners LLC, 5 Times Square, New York, NY 10036, USA. *Telephone:* (212) 931-7300. *Fax:* (212) 931-7310. *Website:* www.giulianipartners .com.

GIULINI, Carlo Maria; Italian conductor; b. 9 May 1914, Barletta; m.; three s.; ed Accad. S. Cecilia, Rome; debut as conductor, Rome 1944; f. Orchestra of Milan Radio 1950; Prin. Conductor La Scala, Milan 1953–55; debut in UK, Verdi's Falstaff, Edinburgh Festival 1955; closely associated with Philharmonia Orchestra 1955–; debut Covent Garden, Verdi's Don Carlos 1958; Prin. Guest Conductor Chicago Symphony Orchestra 1969–78; Music Dir Vienna Symphony Orchestra 1973–76, Los Angeles Philharmonic Orchestra

1978–84; conducted Schumann and Brahms Rhineland Festival 1996; Hon. mem. Gesellschaft der Musikfreunde, Vienna 1978; Hon. DHumLitt (DePaul Univ., Chicago) 1979; Gold Medal, Bruckner Soc. 1978, Gold Medal of Honour, Vienna, Légion d'honneur. *Music:* numerous recordings. *Publication:* Una vita nella musica. *Leisure interest:* sailing. *Address:* c/o Robert Leslie, 53 Bedford Road, London, SW4, England (Office); c/o Francesco Giulini, Via Bonnet 7, 20121 Milan, Italy. *Telephone:* (02) 6575021. *Fax:* (02) 6575021.

GIURANNA, Bruno; Italian viola player and conductor; b. 6 April 1933, Milan; ed Coll. S. Giuseppe and Conservatorio di Musica Santa Cecilia, Rome and Conservatorio di Musica S. Pietro a Maiella, Naples; Founder mem. I Musici 1951–61; Prof. Conservatorio G. Verdi, Milan 1961–65, Conservatorio S. Cecilia, Rome 1965–78, Prof. Acad. Chigiana, Siena 1966–83; Prof. Nordwest-deutsche Musikakademie, Detmold, Germany 1969–83; Prof. Hochschule der Künste, Berlin 1981–98; Prof. W. Stauffer Foundation 1985–; Prof. Royal Music Acad., London 1994–96; Prof. Acad. S. Cecilia, Rome 1995–97; mem. Int. Music Competition jury, Munich 1961–62, 1967, 1969, Geneva 1968, Budapest 1975; soloist at concerts in festivals including Edinburgh Festival, Holland Festival and with orchestras including Berlin Philharmonic, Amsterdam Concertgebouw and Teatro alla Scala, Milan; Artistic Dir of Orchestra da Camera di Padova 1983–92; Academician of Santa Cecilia 1974; DLit hc (Univ. of Limerick) 2003. *Address:* Via Bembo 96, 31011 Asolo, TV, Italy. *Telephone:* (423) 55734. *Fax:* (423) 520115. *E-mail:* bg@giuranna.it (Home). *Website:* www.giuranna.com (Home).

GIURESCU, Dinu C., PhD; American historian; b. 15 Feb. 1927, Bucharest, Romania; s. of Constantin C. Giurescu and Maria S. Giurescu; m. Anca Elena Dinu 1960; two d.; ed Univ. Bucharest; curator Bucharest Art Museum 1956–64; with Ministry of Foreign Affairs 1964–68; Prof. of European Civilization, Acad. of Fine Arts, Bucharest 1968–87; lecturer in Switzerland, France, Bulgaria, Hungary, FRG, Dallas (USA) 1977, Washington 1980, Univs of Columbia, Ind., Ill., Ariz., Calif. (Berkeley), Kan., Colo, Ore., Neb., Ohio, Rochester and Huntington Coll. 1982–85; Prof. Faculty of History, Univ. of Bucharest 1990–; Pres. Nat. Comm. of Museums and Collections (Romania) 1991–92, 1996–2000; Gen. Dir Romanian Peasants' Museum 2001–; Visiting Prof., William Paterson Coll., NJ, USA 1988–89, Texas A. & M. Univ., USA 1989–90, Cen. European Univ., Hungary 1993; mem. Romanian Acad. 1990; Prize of the Romanian Acad. 1973. *Publications:* Ion Vodă cel Viteaz 1966, History of the Romanians from Ancient Times Until Today (in Romanian) 1971 (with C. C. Giurescu), Wallachia in the 14th–15th Centuries (in Romanian) 1971, Istoria Românilor I-II, Din cele mai vechi timpuri pînă la finele sec. XVI (History of the Romanians I–II. From Ancient Times to the end of the XVI century) 1974–76 (with C. C. Giurescu), Illustrated History of the Romanian People (in Romanian, English, French, German, Russian, Spanish) 1981–82, The Razing of Romania's Past 1989, The Communist Takeover in Romania, I 1994, The Radescu Government (in Romanian) 1996, The Fall of the Iron Curtain: Romania (in Romanian) 1997, Romania in World War II (in Romanian) 1999 (in English) 2000, The Impossible Attempt. The Royal Strike (1945) (in Romanian) 1999, The "Elections" of November 1946 (in Romanian) 2001. *Leisure interests:* walking, visiting sites and museums, jazz music. *Address:* Museum of the Romanian Peasant, Soseana Kiseleff 3, Bucharest, 71268, Romania (Office); 30–33 32nd Street, apt. 3i, Astoria, NY 11102, USA (Office). *Telephone:* (21) 2129661 (Bucharest); (718) 545-7269 (New York) (Office). *Fax:* (21) 3129875 (Bucharest). *E-mail:* mtr@digicom.ro (Office).

GIVENCHY, Hubert de; French fashion designer; b. 21 Feb. 1927, Beauvais; s. of Lucien Taffin de Givenchy and Béatrice Badin; ed Coll. Félix-Faure, Beauvais, Ecole Nat. Supérieure des Beaux-Arts, Paris and Faculté de Droit, Univ. de Paris; apprentice, Paris fashion houses of Lucien Lelong 1945–46, Robert Piguet 1946–48, Jacques Fath 1948–49, Elsa Schiaparelli 1949–51; est. own fashion house in Parc Monceau, Paris 1952–56, in Avenue George V 1956; Pres.-Dir-Gen. Soc. Givenchy-Couture and Soc. des Parfums Givenchy, Paris 1954; Hon. Pres. Admin. Council Givenchy SA 1988–; Pres. Christie's France 1997–; work included in Fashion: An Anthology, Victoria and Albert Museum, London 1971; costume designer for films Breakfast at Tiffany's 1961, Charade 1963, The VIPs 1963, Paris When It Sizzles 1964, How to Steal a Million 1966; Chevalier, Légion d'honneur. *Leisure interests:* tennis, riding, skiing. *Address:* 3 Avenue George V, 75008 Paris, France.

GJEDREM, Svein, MA; Norwegian banker; b. 25 Jan. 1950; ed Univ. of Oslo; Exec. Officer, Norges Bank (Cen. Bank of Norway) 1975–79, Gov. 1999–; Head, Div. for Banking and Monetary Affairs, Ministry of Finance and Customs 1979–82, Deputy Dir 1982–86, Dir.-Gen. Head of Econ. Policy Dept 1986–95, Sec.-Gen. 1996–98; visiting engagement, EU Comm., Brussels 1994–95. *Address:* Office of the Governor, Norges Bank, Bankplassen 2, P.O. Box 1179, Sentrum, 0107 Oslo, Norway (Office). *E-mail:* svein.gjedrem@ norges-bank.no (Office). *Website:* www.norges-bank.no (Office).

GJERDE, Bjartmar; Norwegian politician; b. 6 Nov. 1931, Sande Sunnmøre; s. of Astrid Gjerde and Hjalmar Gjerde; m. Anna Karin Hoel 1954; three s.; journalist Sunnmøre Arbeideravis 1948–53; Ed. Fritt Slag 1953–58; Chair. Labour League of Youth 1958–61; mem. State Youth Council; Sec. Labour Parl. Group 1961–62; Chief. Sec. Workers' Educ. League 1962–71; mem. Council on Broadcasting 1963–74, UNESCO Comm. 1964–66, Norwegian Cultural Council 1965–85, Council on Adult Educ. 1966–71; Minister of Church and Educ. 1971–72, 1973–76, for Industries 1976–78, for Petroleum and Energy 1978–80; mem. Labour Party Nat. Exec. 1973–81; Dir-Gen. Norwegian Broadcasting Corpn (NRK) 1981–89, Dir Gen. Directorate of Labour 1989–94.

GJINUSHI, Skender; Albanian politician; fmr univ. lecturer in science; mem. Kuvendi Popullor (People's Ass.) 1992–; fmr Minister of Educ., Speaker of Parl.; Deputy Prime Minister, Minister of Labour and Social Affairs 2002–; Leader Social Democratic Party of Albania. *Address:* Council of Ministers, Këshilli i Ministrave, Tirana, Albania (Office). *Telephone:* (42) 28210 (Office). *Fax:* (42) 27888 (Office).

GLADILIN, Anatoliy Tikhonovich; Russian writer; b. 21 Aug. 1935, Moscow; s. of Tikhon Illarionovich Gladilin and Polina Moïseevna Dreizer; m. Maria Gladilina 1955; two d.; ed Gorky Literary Inst., Moscow; literary activity started 1956; one of main contributors (with V. Aksyonov, to Katayev's journal Youth 1956–65; one of founders of "Youth Prose" movement in early 1960s; signed letter of 80 writers in support of Solzhenitsyn's letter on abolition of censorship 1967; left USSR, expelled from Union of Writers 1976 (readmitted 1998); settled in France. *Publications include:* Chronicle of the Times of Viktor Podgursky 1956, The Gospel from Robespierre 1970, Prognosis for Tomorrow 1972, The Dreams of Shlisselburg Fortress 1974, The Making and Unmaking of a Soviet Writer 1979, The Paris Fair 1980, A Big Race Day 1983, F.S.S.R. The French Soviet Socialist Republic Story 1985, As I Was Then: Tales 1986, The Beast Pell Killed Me 1991, A Rider's Shadow 2000. *Address:* 11 Château Gaillard, Maisons Alfort, 94700 Paris, France. *Telephone:* 1-43-96-21-99.

GLAMANN, Kristof, OBE; Danish business executive, professor of history and author; b. 26 Aug. 1926, Kerteminde; s. of Kai Kristof Glamann and Ebba H. K. Glamann (née Madsen); m. Kirsten Jantzen 1954; two s.; ed Univ. of Copenhagen; Assoc. Prof. of History, Univ. of Copenhagen 1948–60, Prof. of Econ. History 1961–80; Visiting Prof., Univ. of Pa 1960, Univ. of Wisconsin 1961, Visiting Northern Scholar, London School of Econs 1966, Visiting Overseas Fellow, Churchill Coll., Cambridge Univ. 1971–72, 1994, Visiting Fellow, Toho Gakkai, Tokyo 1977; Master, 4th May and Hassager Coll., Copenhagen; mem. and Chair. Danish Research Council on Humanities 1968–70; mem. Bd of Dirs., Carlsberg Foundation 1969–93, Pres. 1976–93; mem. Bd of Dirs., Carlsberg Ltd 1970–94, Deputy Chair. 1975–77, Chair. 1977–93; mem. Bd of Dirs., Carlsberg Brewery Ltd 1978–94, Royal Copenhagen Ltd 1978–93, Fredericia Brewery 1979–94, Politiken Foundation 1990; Chair. Council, Investor and Reinvest Ltd; Deputy Chair. The Scandinavia-Japan Sasakawa Foundation 1985–; mem. Royal Danish Acad. of Science and Letters 1969, Royal Danish History Soc. 1961, Swedish Acad., Lund 1963, History Soc. of Calcutta 1962; Corresp. mem. French History Soc. 1972; Hon. Pres. Int. Econ. History Asscn 1974; Hon. FBA 1985; Corresp. Fellow Royal Belgian Acad. 1989; Hon. DScS (Univ. of Gothenburg) 1974; Commdr Order of Dannebrog (First Class); Commdr Falcon of Iceland 1987, Das Grosse Verdienstkreuz (Germany) 1989, Order of Gorkha Dakshina Bahu (3rd Class) 1989, Erasmus Medal, Academia Europaea 2000. *Publications:* History of Tobacco Industry in Denmark 1875–1950 1950, Prices and Wages 1500–1800 1958, Dutch-Asiatic Trade 1620–1740 1958, Brewing 1962, European Trade 1500–1750 1971, Carlsberg Foundation (in Danish) 1976, contributed to the Cambridge Economic History of Europe (Vol. V) 1977, Mercantilism 1982, Festschrift 1983, 1993, J. C. Jacobsen of Carlsberg: A biography 1990, Beer and Marble: A biography of Carl Jacobsen 1995, The Carlsberg Group Since 1970 1997, Time-Out 1998, Memoirs 2002, The Carlsberg Foundation 1876–1976 2003; Ed.-in-Chief Scandinavian Econ. History Review 1961–80. *Leisure interests:* walking and drawing. *Address:* Hoeghsmindeparken 10, 2900 Hellerup, Denmark. *Telephone:* 39-40-39-77. *Fax:* 39-40-39-76.

GLANVILLE, Brian Lester; British author and journalist; b. 24 Sept. 1931, London; s. of James A. Glanville and Florence Manches; m. Elizabeth De Boer 1959; two s. two d.; ed Charterhouse; first sports columnist and football corresp. Sunday Times 1958–92; sports columnist, The People 1992–96, The Times 1996–98, Sunday Times 1998–; literary adviser, Bodley Head 1958–62; Silver Bear Award, Berlin Film Festival, for European Centre Forward (BBC TV documentary) 1963. *Plays for radio:* The Rise of Gerry Logan, The Diary, I Could Have Been King, A Visit to the Villa. *Television:* original writer of That Was The Week That Was 1962; wrote BBC documentary European Centre Forward (winner Berlin Prize) 1963. *Publications:* novels: Along the Arno 1956, The Bankrupts 1958, Diamond 1962, A Roman Marriage 1966, The Olympian 1969, A Cry of Crickets 1970, The Comic 1974, The Catacomb 1988, Dictators 2001; Sport: Champions of Europe 1991, Story of the World Cup 1993; short stories: A Bad Streak 1961, The Thing He Loves 1973; plays: A Visit to the Villa 1981, Underneath the Arches (musical) (co-author) 1981, The Diary (radio play) 1986, Football Memories (autobiography) 1999. *Leisure interest:* playing football. *Address:* 160 Holland Park Avenue, London, W11 4UH, England. *Telephone:* (20) 7603-6908 (Home). *Fax:* (20) 7603-6908 (Home).

GLASER, Donald Arthur, PhD; American physicist; b. 21 Sept. 1926, Cleveland, Ohio; s. of William Joseph and Lena Glaser; one s. one d.; ed Case Inst. of Technology, California Inst. of Technology; Univ. of Mich. 1949–59; Univ. of Calif. 1959–; Nat. Science Foundation Fellow 1961; Guggenheim Fellow 1961–62; Biophysicist, Univ. of Calif., Berkeley 1962–64; Prof. of Physics, Neurobiology and Molecular and Cell Biology, Univ. of Calif. 1964–; mem. NAS; Hon. ScD; Henry Russell Award 1955, Charles Vernon Boys Prize (The Physical Soc.) 1958, Nobel Prize 1960; several awards. *Publications:*

Some Effects of Ionizing Radiation on the Formation of Bubbles in Liquids 1952, A Possible Bubble Chamber for the Study of Ionizing Events 1953, Bubble Chamber Tracks of Penetrating Cosmic-Ray Particles 1953, Progress Report on the Development of Bubble Chambers 1955, Strange Particle Production by Fast Pions in Propane Bubble Chamber 1957, Weak Interactions: Other Modes, Experimental Results 1958, The Bubble Chamber 1958, Development of Bubble Chamber and Some Recent Bubble Chamber Results in Elementary Particle Physics 1958, Decays of Strange Particles 1959, Computer Identification of Bacteria by Colony Morphology 1972, Effect of Nalidixic Acid on DNA Replication by Toluene-treated E.coli 1973, The Isolation and Partial Characterization of Mutants of E.coli and Cold-sensitive Synthesis of DNA 1974, Rates of Chain Elongation of Ribosomal RNA Molecules in E.coli 1974, Chromosomal Sites of DNA-membrane Attachment in E.coli 1974, Effect of Growth Conditions in DNA-membrane Attachment in E.coli 1975, Characteristics of Cold-sensitive Mutants of E.coli K12 Defective in Deoxyribonucleic Acid Replication 1975, A New Anisotrophy in Apparent Motion 1986, Differences betweeen Vertical and Horizontal Apparent Motion 1987, Speed Discrimination using Simple Sampled-Motion Stimuli 1987, Motion Interference in Speed Discrimination 1989, Influence of Remote Objects on Local Depth Perception 1991, Shape Analysis and Stereopsis for Human Depth Perception 1992, Depth Discrimination of a Line is Improved by Adding Other Nearby Lines 1992, Temporal Aspects of Depth Contrast 1993, Comparison of Human Performance with Algorithms for Estimating Fractal Dimension of Fractional Brownian Statistics 1993, Depth Discrimination of a Crowded Line Is Better When It Is More Luminant than the Lines Crowding It 1995, Stereopsis Due to Luminance Difference in the Two Eyes 1995, Multiple Matching of Features in Simple Stereograms 1996; many papers written jointly with other physicists. *Leisure interests:* skiing, sailing, skin diving, music. *Address:* 41 Hill Road, Berkeley, CA 94708-2131 (Home); Department of Molecular and Cell Biology, 337 Stanley Hall, University of California at Berkeley, CA 94720-0001, USA. *Telephone:* (510) 642-7231.

GLASER, Robert Joy, SB, MD, FRCP(UK), MACP; American foundation executive, physician and medical consultant; b. 11 Sept. 1918, St Louis, Mo.; s. of Joseph and Regina Glaser; m. Helen H. Hofsommer 1949 (died 1999); two s. one d.; ed Harvard Coll. and Medical School; appointments include instructor to Assoc. Prof., Washington Univ. School of Medicine 1949–57, Assoc. Dean 1955–57; Dean and Prof. of Medicine, Univ. of Colo School of Medicine 1957–63, Vice-Pres. for Medical Affairs 1959–63; Prof. of Social Medicine, Harvard Univ. 1963–65; Vice-Pres. for Medical Affairs, Dean of the School of Medicine, Prof. of Medicine, Stanford Univ. 1965–70, Acting Pres. 1968, Visiting Prof. of Medicine 1972–73, Consulting Prof. 1972–99, Prof. Emer. 1999–; Clinical Prof. of Medicine, Columbia Univ. Coll. of Physicians and Surgeons 1971–72; Consultant 1997–; Vice-Pres. The Commonwealth Fund 1970–72; Pres. and CEO The Henry J. Kaiser Family Foundation 1972–83; Dir First Boston Inc. 1982–88; Dir Hewlett-Packard Co. 1971–91, Calif. Water Service Co. 1973–93, The Equitable Life Assurance Soc. of the US 1979–86, Maxygen 1998–; mem. Bd of Dirs Alza Corpn 1993–2001, DCI, Hanger Orthopedic Group 1993–2003; charter mem., Inst. of Medicine, Nat. Acad. of Science; mem., Bd of Trustees, Washington Univ., St Louis, Mo.; Lucille P. Markey Charitable Trust Dir for Medical Science 1984–97, Trustee 1989–97; mem. American Philosophical Soc. 2000–; Fellow, American Acad. of Arts and Sciences 1964–; Trustee, David and Lucile Packard Foundation 1985–97, Packard Humanities Inst. 1987–, Albert and Mary Lasker Foundation 1997–; ten hon. degrees; Centennial Award for Distinguished Service, Univ. of Colo 1983; Medal for Distinguished Service, Univ. of Calif., San Francisco 1983; Abraham Flexner Award, Asscn of American Medical Colls 1984; Hubert H. Humphrey Cancer Research Center Award 1985, Special Recognition Award, Asscn of American Medical Colls. 1999, John Stearns Award for Lifetime Achievement in Medicine, NY Acad. of Medicine 2000, Dean's Medal Harvard Medical School 2003. *Publications:* 126 papers on experimental streptococcal infections, antibiotics and other topics concerning medicine and medical educ.; numerous chapters in medical books. *Leisure interests:* travel, reading and music. *Address:* 555 Byron Street, #305, Palo Alto, CA 94301, USA. *Telephone:* (650) 328-5869. *Fax:* (650) 473-9775. *E-mail:* robert.glaser@stanford.edu (Office).

GLASHOW, Sheldon Lee, PhD, FAAS; American physicist; b. 5 Dec. 1932, New York; s. of Lewis Glashow and Bella Rubin; m. Joan Shirley Alexander 1972; three s. one d.; ed Bronx High School of Science, Cornell and Harvard Univs; Nat. Science Foundation Post-Doctoral Fellow, Univ. of Copenhagen 1958–60; Research Fellow, Calif. Inst. of Tech. 1960–61; Asst Prof., Stanford Univ. 1961–62; Assoc. Prof., Univ. of Calif. (Berkeley) 1962–66; Prof. of Physics, Harvard 1967–84, Higgins Prof. 1979–2000, Prof. Emer. 2000–; Mellon Prof. of Sciences 1988–93; Arthur G. B. Metcalf Prof., Boston Univ. 2000–; Alfred P. Sloan Foundation Fellowship 1962–66; Visiting Scientist, CERN 1968; Visiting Prof., Univ. of Marseille 1970, MIT 1974, 1980–81, Boston Univ. 1983–84; Consultant, Brookhaven Lab. 1966–73, 1975–; Affiliated Sr Scientist, Univ. of Houston 1983–96; Univ. Scholar, Texas A & M Univ. 1983–86, Distinguished Visiting Scientist, Boston Univ. 1984–2000; Fellow American Physical Soc.; Pres. Int. Sakharov Cttee 1980–85; mem. American Acad. of Arts and Sciences, NAS; Sponsor, Fed. of American Scientists (FAS) and Bulletin of the Atomic Scientists; mem. Advisory Council American Acad. of Achievement 1979–, Science Policy Cttee, CERN 1979–84; Founding Ed. Quantum (magazine) 1989–2000; Hon. Prof. Univ. of Nanjing 1998–; Dr hc (Univ. of Aix-Marseille) 1982; Hon. DSc (Yeshiva Univ.) 1978, (Bar Ilan Univ., Gustavus Adolphus Coll., Adelphi Univ.) 1989; Oppenheimer

Memorial Medal 1977, George Ledlie Award 1978; shared Nobel Prize for Physics with Abdus Salam and Steven Weinberg (q.v.) for work on elementary particles 1979. *Publications:* Interactions (with Ben Bova) 1989, Charm of Physics 1990, From Alchemy to Quarks 1994; over 200 articles on elementary particle physics. *Address:* Department of Physics, Boston University, 121 Bay State Road, Boston, MA 02215 (Office); 30 Prescott Street, Brookline, MA 02146, USA (Home). *Telephone:* (617) 495-2904.

GLASS, David D.; American business executive; b. 1935, Liberty, Mo.; m.; Gen. Man. Crank Drug Co. 1957–67; Vice-Pres. Consumers Markets Inc. 1967–76; Exec. Vice-Pres. Wal-Mart Stores Inc. –1976, Chief Financial Officer 1976–84, Pres. 1984–2000, COO 1984–88, CEO 1988–2000, Chair. Exec. Comm. 2000–, also Dir; CEO and Chair. Bd Dirs. Kansas City Royals 1993–. *Address:* Wal-Mart Stores Inc., 702 SW 8th Street, Bentonville, AR 72716; Kansas City Royals, P.O. Box 419969, Kansas City, MO 64141, USA.

GLASS, Philip; American composer; b. 31 Jan. 1937, Baltimore; s. of Benjamin Glass and Ida Glass (née Gouline); m. 1st JoAnne Akalaitis (divorced); m. 2nd Luba Burtyk (divorced); one s. one d.; m. 3rd Candy Jernigan (died 1991); m. 4th Holly Critchlow 2001; two s. one d.; ed Univ. of Chicago and Juilliard School of Music; Composer-in-Residence, Pittsburgh Public Schools 1962–64; studied with Nadia Boulanger, Paris 1964–66; f. Philip Glass Ensemble 1968, concert tours USA and Europe 1968–; f. record co. Chatham Square Productions, New York 1972, Dunvagen Music Publrs, Orange Mountain Music record co. 2002; Broadcast Music Industry Award 1960, Lado Prize 1961, Benjamin Award 1961, 1962, Young Composer's Award, Ford Foundation 1964–66, Fulbright Award 1966–67, New York Dance and Performance Award 1995 and other awards. *Compositions include:* (operas, theatre) Orphée, The Voyage, The Juniper Tree, The Palace of the Arabian Nights, The Fall of the House of Usher, Einstein on the Beach 1976, Satyagraha 1980, The Photographer 1982, The Civil Wars 1982–84, Akhnaten 1984, The Making of the Representative for Planet 8 1988, Mattogrosso 1989, 1,000 Airplanes on the Roof (with David Henry Hwang) 1989, Hydrogen Jukebox (with Allen Ginsberg) 1990; (film scores) North Star 1977, Koyaanisqatsi 1983, Mishima 1985, Powaqqatsi 1987, The Thin Blue Line 1988, Hamburger Hill 1989, Mindwalk 1990, A Brief History of Time 1991, Anima Mundi 1991, Candyman 1992, The Voyage 1992, Orphee 1993, Candyman II: Farewell to the Flesh 1994, Monsters of Grace 1998, Bent 1998, Kundun 1998; (instrumental works) String Quartets (1–4), Violin Concerto, Low Symphony; recent works include Symphony No. 5 1999, Symphony No. 6 (Plutonian Ode) 2000, In the Penal Colony 2000, Tirol Concerto 2000, Voices for Organ, Didgeridoo and Narrator 2001, Concerto for Cello and Orchestra 2001, Concerto Fantasy 2001, Danassimo 2001, The Man in the Bath 2001, Passage 2001, Diaspora 2001, Notes 2001, The Hours 2002. *Publications:* Music by Philip Glass 1987, Opera on the Beach 1988. *Address:* Dunvagen Music, 632 Broadway, Suite 902, New York, NY 10012, USA (Office). *Telephone:* (212) 979-2080 (Office). *Fax:* (212) 473-2842 (Office). *E-mail:* info@dunvagen.com (Office). *Website:* www.philipglass.com.

GLATZ, Ferenc, PhD; Hungarian historian; b. 2 April 1941; Research Fellow Inst. of History of Hungarian Acad. of Sciences 1968–, Scientific Deputy Dir 1986–88, Dir of Inst. 1988–; Corresp. mem. Hungarian Acad. of Sciences 1993–, Pres. 1996–; Prof. Eötvös Loránd Univ., Budapest 1974–; Minister for Culture and Educ. 1989–90; organizer and Dir Europa Inst., Budapest 1990–. *Publications:* numerous studies and books on 19th- and 20th-century history of Hungarian and European culture and historiography. *Address:* Magyar Tudományos Akadémia, 1051 Budapest, Roosevelt tér. 9, Hungary. *Telephone:* (1) 332-7176. *Fax:* (1) 332-8943.

GLAUBER, Robert, DEcon; American economist; b. 1939; ed Harvard Univ.; lecturer, Dept of Econs, Harvard Univ. 1964–73, Prof. 1973–87, lecturer John F. Kennedy School of Govt, Harvard; fmr Visiting Prof. Stanford Univ., Calif.; Consultant to Reagan Admin. 1987, to Bush Admin. 1989; Under-Sec. to Treasury 1989; mem. Bd Nat. Asscn of Securities Dealers (NASD) 1996–, CEO and Pres. Nov. 2000–, Chair. and CEO Sept. 2001–; CEO Bond Market Asscn. *Address:* c/o National Association of Securities Dealers, 33 Whitehall Street, New York, NY 10004-2193, USA (Office).

GLAVIN, William F., MBA; American business executive; b. 29 March 1932, Albany, New York; s. of John Glavin; m. Cecily McClatchy 1955; three s. four d.; ed Coll. of the Holy Cross, Worcester and Wharton Graduate School of the Univ. of Pennsylvania; fmr Exec. Int. Business Machines and Vice-Pres. Operations, Service Bureau Corpn (an IBM subsidiary); Exec. Vice-Pres. Xerox Data Systems 1970, Group Vice-Pres. 1972, Man. Dir and COO 1974, Exec. Vice-Pres. Xerox 1980, Exec. Vice-Pres. for Reprographics and Operations 1982, Pres. Business Equipment Group 1983–89, Vice-Chair. Xerox Corpn 1985–89; mem. Bd of Dirs Xerox, Fuji Xerox and Rank Xerox, also the Xerox Foundation; Pres. Babson Coll., Wellesley, Mass. 1989–99; mem. Bd of Dirs Gould Inc., State Street Boston Corpn, Norton Co.; mem. Bd of Trustees and Pres.'s Council Coll. of the Holy Cross. *Leisure interests:* golf, reading, art, music. *Address:* c/o Office of the President, Babson College, Babson Park, MA 02157, USA.

GLAZER, Nathan, PhD; American educationist; b. 25 Feb. 1923, New York; s. of Louis Glazer and Tillie Glazer (née Zacharevich); m. 1st Ruth Slotkin 1943 (divorced 1958); three d.; m. 2nd Sulochana Raghavan 1962; ed City Coll. of New York, Univ. of Pennsylvania and Columbia Univ; mem. of staff, Commentary Magazine 1944–53; Ed. and Editorial Adviser, Doubleday Anchor Books 1954–57; Visiting Lecturer, Univ. of Calif., Berkeley 1957–58;

Instructor, Bennington Coll., Vermont 1958–59; Visiting Lecturer, Smith Coll. 1959–60; Prof. of Sociology, Univ. of Calif., Berkeley 1963–69; Prof. of Educ. and Social Structure, Harvard Univ. 1969–93; Fellow, Center for Advanced Study in the Behavioural Sciences, Stanford, Calif. 1971–72; Co-Ed. The Public Interest Magazine 1973–; mem. American Acad. of Arts and Sciences, Library of Congress Council of Scholars; Guggenheim Fellow 1954, 1966; Hon. LLD (Franklin and Marshall Coll.) 1971, (Colby Coll.) 1972; Hon. DHL (Long Island Univ.) 1978, (Hebrew Union Coll.) 1986. *Publications:* American Judaism 1957, 1972, The Social Basis of American Communism 1961, Remembering the Answers 1970, Affirmative Discrimination 1976, Ethnic Dilemmas 1964–1982 1983, The Limits of Social Policy 1989; co-author: The Lonely Crowd 1950, Faces in the Crowd 1952, Studies in Housing and Minority Groups 1960, Beyond the Melting Pot 1963, Conflicting Images, India and the United States 1990, We Are All Multiculturalists Now 1997; co-ed.: The Public Interest 1973–. *Address:* 12 Scott Street, Cambridge, MA 02138, USA. *Telephone:* (617) 868-5459. *Fax:* (617) 496-3095.

GLAZ'IEV, Sergey Yurievich, DR.EC.SC.; Russian economist; b. 1 Jan. 1961, Zaporozhye; m.; three c.; ed Moscow State Univ.; Head of Lab., Cen. Econ. Math. Inst. 1986–91; First Deputy Chair. Cttee on External Econ. Relations Ministry of Foreign Affairs 1991–92; First Deputy Minister of External Econ. Relations of Russia 1992, Minister 1992–93; mem. State Duma (Parl.) 1993–95 (CP of Russian Fed. faction) 1999–; Chair. Cttee for Econ. Policy of State Duma 1994–95, 2000–; Chair. Nat. Cttee of Democratic Party of Russia 1994–97; Head of Econ. Dept, Security Council 1996; Head, Information-Analytical Bd, Council of Fed. (Parl.) 1996–; author of econ. programme for CP of Russian Fed. for Parl. Elections 1999; Corresp. mem. Russian Acad. of Sciences 2000. *Publications:* Economic Theory of Technical Development 1993, Economy and Politics 1994, One and a Half Years in the Duma 1995, Under the Critical Level 1996, Genocide 1997 1998. *Address:* State Duma, Okhotny Ryad 1, 103265 Moscow, Russia. *Telephone:* (095) 292-42-60. *Fax:* (095) 292-43-22.

GLAZUNOV, Ilya Sergeyevich; Russian painter; b. 10 June 1930, Leningrad; s. of S. F. Glazunov and O. K. Glazunova (née Flug); m. M. Vinogradova-Benua (deceased); one s. one d.; ed Repin Arts Inst. (pupil of B. Ioganson); first one-man show, Moscow 1957; teacher of drawing in Izhevsk, then Ivanovo; moved to Moscow 1960; Prof., Surikov Inst., Moscow 1978–; exhibited in art exhbns in Moscow 1959–99, Warsaw, Rome, Copenhagen, Vietnam, Laos, Paris, Leningrad, Santiago, Stockholm, Berlin (East and West), Leipzig, FRG 1960–77, London (Barbican) 1987; Founder and Pres. All-Russian Acad. of Painting, Sculpture and Architecture 1991–; projects include designs for the decoration of the interior of the Kremlin, Moscow and the Russian Embassy, Madrid; Corresp. mem. Russian Acad. of Arts 1997; Hon. mem. Royal Acads of Art Madrid, Barcelona 1979; Order (First Class) for Services to the Motherland 1996; Order of Sergei Radonezsky 1998; First Prize Int. Art Exhbn, Prague 1956, People's Artist of the USSR 1980; Russian State Prize 1997; Pablo Picasso Gold Medal, UNESCO 1999. *Exhibitions:* one-man exhbns in Moscow and St Petersburg 2000. *Publications:* The Road to You 1965, Russia Crucified 1996. *Leisure interests:* philosophy, history, classical music. *Address:* Russian Academy of Painting, Sculpture and Architecture, Myasnitskaya str. 21, 101000, Moscow (Office); Kamergerski pr. 2, 103009, Moscow, Russia. *Telephone:* (095) 292-33-74 (Office).

GLEESON, Hon. (Murray) Anthony Murray, AC; Australian chief justice and lawyer; b. 30 Aug. 1938, Wingham, NSW; s. of L. J. Gleeson; m. Robyn Gleeson 1965; one s. three d.; ed Univ. of Sydney; barrister 1963; tutor in law, St Paul's Coll., Univ. of Sydney 1963–65, Lecturer in Co. Law 1965–74; appointed QC 1974; mem. Council NSW Bar Asscn 1979–86, Pres. 1984–86; Chief Justice Supreme Court NSW 1988–98; Pres. Judicial Comm. NSW 1988–98; Lt-Gov. NSW 1989–98; Chief Justice High Court of Australia 1998–; Hon. Bencher Middle Temple 1989. *Leisure interests:* tennis, skiing. *Address:* High Court of Australia, P.O. Box E435, Kingston, A.C.T. 2604, Australia (Office). *Telephone:* (2) 6270-6811 (Office). *Fax:* (2) 6270-6868 (Office). *Website:* www.hcourt.gov.au (Office).

GLEMP, HE Cardinal Józef, DrIurUtr; Polish ecclesiastic; b. 18 Dec. 1929, Inowrocław; s. of Kazimierz Glemp and Salomea (née Kośmicka) Glemp; ed Primatial Spiritual Seminary, Gniezno and Poznań and Pontifical Lateran Univ., Rome; ordained priest, Gniezno 1956; educational and catechistic work 1956–58; studied in Rome 1958–64; various posts, Curia, Tribunal and Lecturer, Primatial Spiritual Seminary, Gniezno 1964–67; with Secr., Primate of Poland 1967–79; Roman Law Lecturer, Acad. of Catholic Theology, Warsaw 1967–79; mem. Episcopal Comm. for Revision of Canon Law and Sec. Comm. for Polish Insts Rome 1975–79; Hon. Chaplain to His Holiness the Pope 1972; Gremial Canon of the Primatial Capitular, Gniezno 1976; Bishop and Ordinary, Diocese of Warmia, Olsztyn 1979–81; Archbishop-Metropolitan of Gniezno and Warsaw and Primate of Poland 1981–92, Archbishop-Metropolitan of Warsaw and Primate of Poland 1992–; cr. Cardinal 1983; Co-Chair. Working Group for Legis. Affairs, Joint Comm. of Govt and Episcopate Jan.–July 1981; Chair. Chief Council of Polish Episcopate, Chair. Conf. of Polish Episcopate 1981; Pres. Bishop's Cttee for Pastoral Care of Poles Abroad; Pres. Bishop's Cttee for Catholic Univ. of Lublin 1981; Ordinary for the Armenian-rite Communities in Poland 1981–92, for the Greek-Catholic Communities in Poland 1981–89, for believers of Oriental rites 1992; mem. Congregation for the Oriental Churches 1983, Pontifical Council of Culture 1993, Supreme Tribunal of the Apostolic Signatura 2002; High Chancellor Stefan Card. Wyszyński Univ. and Pontifical Dept of Theology, Warsaw; Dr hc (Acad. of Catholic Theology, Warsaw) 1982, (Villanova Univ., USA) 1985, (Lublin Catholic Univ.) 1985, (St Thomas Univ., Manila) 1988, (Univ. of Bari) 1990, (Seton Hall Univ., NJ) 1991, (Pontifical Dept of Theology, Warsaw, and Warsaw Agricultural Univ.) 1992, (Loyola Univ. of Chicago) 1998, Stefan Card. Wyszyński Univ. Warsaw 2001. *Publications:* De conceptu fictionis iuris apud Romanos 1974, Lexiculum iuris romani 1974, Przez sprawiedliwośċ ku miłości 1982, Człowiek wielkiej miary 1983, Kościół na drogach Ojczyzny 1985, Chcemy z tego sprawdzianu wyjśċ prawdomówni i wiarygodni 1985, Kościół i Polonia 1986, Umocnieni nadzieją 1987, W tęczy Franków orzeł i krzyż 1987, O Eucharystii 1987, Nauczanie pasterskie (5 Vols) 1981–95, Let My Call Come to You 1988, A wołanie moje niech do Ciebie przyjdzie 1988, Boże, coś Polskę posłał nad Tamizę 1988, Nauczanie społeczne 1981–1986, 1989, Na dwóch wybrzeżach 1990, U przyjaciół Belgów 1990, I uwierzyli uczniowie 1990, Zamyślenia Maryjne 1990, Solidarietà. La Polonia che sogniamo 1991, Słowo Boże nad Łyną 1991, Tysiąclecie wiary Świętego Włodzimierza 1991, Gniezno ciągła odnowa 1991, Służyć Ewangelii słowem 1991, Na Skałce – na opoce 1991, Niebo ściągają na ziemię 1991, Między Ewangelią a konstytucją 1992, Na wyspie Świętego Patryka 1992, Idźmy do Betlejem 1992, Wartości chrześcijańskie nabywane pod Kalwarią 1993, W blaskach Zmartwychwstania 1994, Byċ znakiem miłości 1994, Rodzina drogą Kościoła 1995, Boskie i cesarskie 1995, Idzie, idzie Bóg prawdziwy 1995, Les chemins des pèlerins 1996, Od Kalwarii na drogi Europy 1997, PietnasŚcie lat posługi pryma sowskiej 1997, Święci idą przez Warszawę 1997, Poles – Now We Enter the Twenty-First Century 1998, Maintenance of National Identity and Solidarity Between People 1998, Z krzyżem przez dzieje wierzącej Stolicy 1998, Modlimy się w kraju Helwetów 1998, Odkrywaċ drogi Opatrzności Bożej 1999, Listy pasterskie 1999, La speranza a Varsavia si stringe alla Croce 1999, Sławny w męczenników gronie 1999, Chrystus wciaż żyje 2001, Ścisle duszpasterskie 2002, Caritati in institia 2002. *Address:* Rezydencja Prymasa Polski, ul. Miodowa 17/19, 00-246 Warsaw, Poland. *Telephone:* (22) 531 71 00. *Fax:* (22) 635 87 45. *Website:* www.spp.perytnet.pl.

GLEN, Sir Alexander Richard, KBE, DSC; British polar explorer and shipowner; b. 18 April 1912, Glasgow; s. of the late R. Bartlett Glen; m. 1st Nina Nixon (divorced 1945); one s.; m. 2nd Baroness Zora de Collaert 1947; ed Fettes Coll. and Balliol Coll., Oxford; Organizer and Leader, Oxford Univ. Arctic Expedition 1933, 1935–36; in banking, New York and London 1936–39; RDVR 1939–58, rank of Capt. 1952; Chair. H. Clarkson & Co. Ltd 1962–72; Deputy Chair. Export Council for Europe 1960–64, Chair. 1964–66; mem. Council Royal Geographical Soc. 1945–47, 1954–57, 1961–62; mem. Council, Mount Everest Foundation 1955–57; Chair. British Tourist Authority 1969–77; Group Chair. Anglo World Travel 1978–81; Deputy Chair. British Transport Hotels 1978–83; Dir Gleneagles Hotels 1980–83; mem. Historic Bldgs Council for England 1976–80, Horse-race Totalisator Bd 1976–84, Advisory Council, Victoria and Albert Museum 1978–83, Chair. 1978–84; Pres. British Airline Pilots' Asscn 1982–94; Vice-Pres. British Hospitality Asscn 1980–; numerous medals and decorations including Patron's Gold Medal, Royal Geographical Soc. 1939, Andre Silver Plaque, Royal Swedish Soc. 1940, Bruce Medal, Royal Soc. of Edin., Norwegian War Cross, Czechoslovak Military Cross. *Publications:* Young Men in the Arctic 1935, Under the Pole Star 1937, Footholds Against a Whirlwind (autobiog.) 1975, Target Danube: A River Not Quite Too Far 2002. *Leisure interests:* the visual arts, Balkan history and current problems, the Arctic. *Address:* The Dower House, Stanton, Broadway, Worcs., WR12 7NE, England.

GLENAMARA, Baron (Life Peer), cr. 1977, of Glenridding, Cumbria; **Edward Watson Short,** PC, CH; British politician; b. 17 Dec. 1912; s. of Charles Short and Mary Short; m. Jennie Sewell 1941; one s. one d.; ed Bede Coll., Durham; served Second World War and became Capt. in Durham Light Infantry; Headmaster, Princess Louise County Secondary School, Blyth, Northumberland 1947; Leader Labour Group, Newcastle City Council 1950; MP for Newcastle-upon-Tyne Central 1951–76; Opposition Whip (N Area) 1955–62; Deputy Chief Opposition Whip 1962–64; Parl. Sec. to Treasury and Govt Chief Whip 1964–66; Postmaster-Gen. 1966–68; Sec. of State for Educ. and Science 1968–70; Deputy Leader of Labour Party 1972–76; Lord Pres. of Council, Leader of House of Commons 1974–76; Chair. Cable and Wireless Co. 1976–80; Pres. Finchdale Abbey Training Coll. for the Disabled, Durham; Chancellor Univ. of Northumbria (fmrly Polytechnic of Newcastle-upon-Tyne) 1984–; Hon. DCL (Durham), (Newcastle) 1998; Hon. DUniv (Open Univ.) 1989; Hon. DLitt (CNAA) 1990. *Publications:* The Story of the Durham Light Infantry 1944, The Infantry Instructor 1946, Education in a Changing World 1971, Birth to Five 1974, I Knew My Place 1983, Whip to Wilson 1989. *Leisure interests:* painting. *Address:* House of Lords, London, SW1A 0PW; 21 Priory Gardens, Corbridge, Northumberland, NE45 5HZ, England. *Telephone:* (143) 463-2880 (Corbridge).

GLENCROSS, David, CBE, BA; British broadcasting executive; b. 3 March 1936, Salford; s. of John William Glencross and Elsie May Glencross; m. Elizabeth Louise Richardson 1965; one d.; ed Salford Grammar School, Trinity Coll., Cambridge; BBC Gen. Trainee 1958–59, Producer 1959–68, Exec. (North Region) 1968–70; Sr Programme Officer, Independent TV Authority 1970–76, Head of Programme Services 1976–77, Deputy Dir of TV 1977–83, Dir of TV 1983–90; Chief Exec. Ind. TV Comm. 1990–96; Chair. British Screen Advisory Council 1996–97; Dir Ind. Media Support Ltd 1996–99; Chair. Disasters Emergency Cttee 1999–; Trustee Sandford St Martin Trust 1998–; Fellow Royal TV Soc. 1981–, Vice-Pres. 1993–99; Hon. MA (Salford) 1993. *Publications:* various articles in European newspapers

and magazines. *Leisure interests:* music, walking, travel, theatre, cinema. *Address:* Disasters Emergency Committee, 52 Great Portland Street, London, W1N 5AH, England. *Telephone:* (20) 7580-6550 (Office); (20) 7580-2854. *E-mail:* info@dec.org.uk (Office).

GLENDENING, Parris Nelson, MA, PhD; American state governor; b. 11 June 1942, Bronx, NY; m. Frances A. Hughes 1976; one s.; ed Florida State Univ. Fort Lauderdale and Tallahassee; Asst Prof. Univ. of Md, College Park 1967–72, Assoc. Prof. 1972–95; Co. Exec. Prince George's Co. Council, Upper Marlboro, Md 1982–95; various public appointments at co. level; Dir World Trade Center 1990–97; Gov. of Maryland 1995–2003; Chair. Nat. Govs' Assen 2001–03; mem. AAAS, American Political Science Asscn, etc.; Democrat; American Soc. of Landscape Architects' Olmstead Award, Harward Innovations in American Govt Award. *Publications:* Controversies of State and Local Political Systems (with M. M. Reeves) 1972, Pragmatic Federalism 1977; articles in professional publs. *Address:* c/o Office of the Governor, State House, Annapolis, MD 21401, USA (Office). *Telephone:* (410) 974-3901. *Fax:* (410) 974-3278.

GLENDINNING, Hon. Victoria, CBE, MA, FRSL; British author and journalist; b. 23 April 1937, Sheffield; d. of Baron Seebohm of Hertford and Lady Seebohm (née Hurst); m. 1st O. N. V. Glendinning 1959 (divorced 1981); four s.; m. 2nd Terence de Vere White 1981 (died 1994); m. 3rd Kevin O'Sullivan 1996; ed St Mary's School, Wantage, Millfield School, Somerville Coll., Oxford and Univ. of Southampton; part-time teaching 1960–69; part-time psychiatric social work 1970–73; Editorial Asst Times Literary Supplement 1974–78; Pres. English Centre of PEN 2001; Vice-Pres. Royal Soc. of Literature 2000; Hon. DLitt (Southampton Univ.) 1994; Dr hc (Ulster) 1995; Hon. LittD (Dublin Univ.) 1995; Hon. DLitt (York) 2000. *Publications:* A Suppressed Cry 1969, Elizabeth Bowen: Portrait of a Writer 1977, Edith Sitwell: A Unicorn Among Lions 1981, Vita: A Biography of V. Sackville-West 1983, Rebecca West: A Life 1987, The Grown-Ups (novel) 1989, Hertfordshire 1989, Trollope 1992, Electricity (novel) 1995, Sons and Mothers (co-ed.) 1996, Jonathan Swift 1998; articles in newspapers and journals.

GLENN, Sir Archibald (see Glenn, Sir Joseph Robert Archibald).

GLENN, Lt-Col John Herschel, Jr; American astronaut, politician and aviator; b. 18 July 1921, Cambridge, Ohio; s. of John H. Glenn and Clare Sproat; m. Anna Margaret Castor 1943; one s. one d.; ed Muskingum Coll., Univ. of Maryland; naval aviation cadet 1942; commissioned Marine Corps 1943; Marine Fighter Squadron 155 in Marshall Islands 1944 (59 combat missions); mem. Fighter Squadron 218 North China Patrol; Instructor Corpus Christi, Texas 1948–50; Marine Fighter Squadron Korea (63 missions); Fighter Design Branch, Navy Bureau of Aeronautics, Washington 1956; speed record Los Angeles–New York (3 hr 23 min) 1957; training for space flight 1960–61; completed 3 orbits of the Earth in Spaceship Friendship VII, 20 Feb. 1962; resigned from US Marine Corps 1965; Dir Royal Crown Cola Co. 1965–74; Consultant to NASA; US Senator from Ohio 1975–99; announced return as astronaut Oct. 1997, on board Discovery shuttle 1998; mem.-at-large Ohio State Democratic Cttee 1999–; DFC (8 times) and Air Medal with 18 clusters; NASA Distinguished Service Medal 1962; US Nat. Space Hall of Fame Award 1969, Centennial Award, Nat. Geographic Soc. 1988. *Publications:* (co-author) We Seven 1962, P.S., I Listened to Your Heart Beat. *Address:* Ohio State University, John Glenn Institute, 100 Bricker Hall, 190 North Oval Mall, Columbus, OH 43210, USA (Office).

GLENNIE, Evelyn Elizabeth Ann, OBE, GRSM, FRAM, FRCM, FRNCM; British musician; b. 19 July 1965, Aberdeen; d. of Isobel Glennie and Herbert Arthur Glennie; m. Gregorio Malcangi 1993; ed Ellon Acad., Aberdeenshire, Royal Acad. of Music, London; solo debut at Wigmore Hall, London, 1986; concerto, chamber and solo percussion performances worldwide; gave Promenade concerts' first-ever percussion recital 1989; numerous TV appearances, including three documentaries on her life; composer of music for TV and radio; many works written for her by composers, including Bennett, Rouse, Heath, Macmillan, McLeod, Muldowney, Daugherty, Turnage and Musgrave; f. Evelyn Glennie Percussion Composition Award, Evelyn Glennie Nat. Music Scholarship; Munster Trust Scholarship 1986; Hon. Fellow Welsh Coll. of Music and Drama; Hon. DMus (Aberdeen) 1991, (Bristol, Portsmouth) 1995, (Leicester, Surrey) 1997, (Queen's, Belfast) 1998, (Exeter, Southampton) 2000; Hon. DLitt (Warwick) 1993, (Loughborough) 1995, (Salford) 1999; Hon. LLD (Dundee) 1996; Hon. DUniv (Essex, Durham) 1998; many prizes and awards, including Shell/LSO Music Gold Medal 1984, Queen's Commendation Prize at RAM 1985, Grammy Award 1988, Scotswoman of the Decade 1990, Charles Heidsieck Soloist of the Year, Royal Philharmonic Soc. 1991, Personality of the Year, Int. Classical Music Awards 1993, Young Deaf Achievers Special Award 1993, Best Studio Percussionist, Rhythm Magazine 1998, 2000, Best Live Percussionist, Rhythm Magazine 2000, Classic FM Outstanding Contribution to Classical Music 2002, Walpole Medal of Excellence 2002, Musical America 2003, two Grammy Awards. *Films:* wrote and played music for The Trench. *Plays:* Playing from the Heart. *Recordings include:* Rhythm Song, Dancin', Light in Darkness, Rebounds, Veni Veni Emmanuel, Wind in the Bamboo Grove, Drumming, Her Greatest Hits, The Music of Joseph Schwantner, Sonata for Two Pianos and Percussion (Bartók), Last Night of the Proms – 100th Season, Street Songs, Reflected in Brass, Shadow Behind the Iron Sun, African Sunrise, Manhattan Rave, UFO, Bela Fleck-Perpetual Motion, Oriental Landscapes, Fractured Lines. *Television includes:* music for Trial and Retribution 1–5 (Yorkshire TV), music for Mazda commercial Blind Ambition, Survival Special (Anglia) and others. *Publications:* Good Vibrations (autobiog.) 1990, Great Journeys of the World, Beat It! *Leisure interests:* reading, walking, cycling, martial arts, antiques, collecting musical instruments. *Address:* PO Box 6, Sawtry, Huntingdon, Cambs., PE17 5YF, England (Office). *Telephone:* (1480) 891772. *Fax:* (1480) 891779 (Office). *E-mail:* carla@evelyn.co.uk; chris@evelyn.co.uk (Office). *Website:* www.evelyn.co.uk (Office).

GLESKE, Leonhard, Dr rer. pol; German banker; b. 18 Sept. 1921, Bydgoszcz (Poland); s. of Gustav Gleske and Lydia Gohl; m. Christa Reimann 1956; one s. three d.; fmr mem. of the Bd and mem. Central Bank Council, Deutsche Bundesbank; Deputy Chair. Bd of Dirs Bank of Tokyo-Mitsubishi (Deutschland) AG, BDO-Deutsche Warentreuhand Aktiengesellschaft, STU Hestia Insurance SA (Sopot, Poland); mem. Advisory Bd J. P. Morgan GmbH; Hon. Prof. (Mannheim) 1986; Dr hc (Univ. of Münster) 1985. *Address:* Kaiser-Friedrich Promenade 151, 61352 Bad Homburg, Germany. *Telephone:* (6172) 42951 (Home). *Fax:* (6172) 923993 (Home).

GLICKMAN, Daniel Robert, JD; American politician; b. 24 Nov. 1944, Wichita, Kan.; s. of Milton Glickman and Gladys A. Kopelman; m. Rhoda J. Yura 1966; one s. one d.; ed Univ. of Michigan, Ann Arbor and George Washington Univ.; mem. Kan. Bar 1969, Mich. Bar 1970; trial attorney, Securities & Exchange Comm. 1969–70; Assoc. then Partner, Sargent, Klenda & Glickman, Wichita 1971–76; mem. 95th–103rd Congresses from 4th Kansas Dist 1977–95; Sec. of Agric. 1995–2001; Partner Akin, Gump, Strauss, Hauer & Feld LLP 2001–; Dir Inst. of Politics, John F. Kennedy School of Govt, Harvard Univ. 2002–; Democrat. *Address:* Akin, Gump, Strauss, Hauer & Feld, Robert S. Strauss Building, 1333 New Hampshire Avenue, NW, Washington, DC 20036, USA (Office).

GLIDEWELL, Rt Hon Sir Iain (Derek Laing), Kt, PC; British judge; b. 8 June 1924; s. of Charles Norman Glidewell and Nora Glidewell; m. Hilary Winant 1950; one s. two d.; ed Bromsgrove School, Worcester Coll., Oxford; served RAFVR 1942–46; called to Bar, Gray's Inn 1949, Bencher 1977, Treas. 1995; QC 1969; a Recorder of the Crown Court 1976–80; a Judge of Appeal, Isle of Man 1979–80; a Judge of the High Court of Justice, Queen's Bench Div. 1980–85; Presiding Judge, NE Circuit 1982–85; a Lord Justice of Appeal 1985–95; conducted review of Crown Prosecution Service 1997–98; a Judge of Court of Appeal, Gibraltar 1998–; mem. Senate of Inns of Court and the Bar 1976–79, Supreme Court Rule Cttee 1980–84; Chair. Judicial Studies Bd 1989–92, Panels for Examination of Structure Plans: Worcs. 1974, W Midlands 1975; conducted Heathrow Fourth Terminal Inquiry 1978; Hon. Fellow Worcester Coll. Oxford 1986. *Leisure interests:* walking, theatre. *Address:* Rough Heys Farm, Macclesfield, Cheshire, SK11 9PF, England.

GLIGOROV, Kiro; Macedonian politician (retd); b. 3 May 1917, Štip; s. of Blagoje and Katarina Gligorov; m. Nada Gligorov; one s. two d.; ed Faculty of Law, Univ. of Belgrade; mem. Presidium of Antifascist Assembly of People's Liberation of Macedonia and Antifascist Council People's Liberation of Yugoslavia during Second World War; Deputy Sec.-Gen. to Govt of Yugoslavia 1946–47; Asst Minister of Finance 1947–52; Prof. of Econs Belgrade Univ. 1948–49; Deputy Dir Exec. Council for Gen. Econ. Affairs 1955–62; Fed. Sec. for Finance 1962–67; Vice-Pres. Fed. Exec. Council 1967–69; mem. League of Communists of Yugoslavia (mem. Exec. Bureau 1969–74); mem. Presidency, Socialist Fed. Repub. of Yugoslavia 1971–72; Pres. Parl. 1974–78; Pres. of Macedonia 1991–99; holder of many Yugoslav and foreign honours. *Publications:* many articles and studies in finance and economics. *Leisure interests:* tennis, hunting. *Address:* c/o Office of the President, 91000 Skopje, Dame Grueva 6, Macedonia.

GLISTRUP, Mogens; Danish politician and lawyer; b. 28 May 1926, Rønne; s. of Lektor Lars Glistrup; m. Lene Borup Svendsen 1950; one s. three d.; ed Rønne, Copenhagen Univ.; training in American law Univ. of Calif., Berkeley 1951–52; teacher in income tax law Univ. of Copenhagen 1956–63; law practice 1950–81, own firm 1956–82; f. Progress Party 1972, expelled Nov. 1990, Leader 2000–01; mem. Parl. 1973–83, re-elected 1984; on trial for alleged tax evasion and fraud from 1974, convicted June 1983, sentenced to three years' imprisonment for infringing tax laws Feb. 1984, released March 1985; mem. Parl. 1987–90. *Publications:* Skatteret 1957, Income Tax – Enemy Number One of Society 1979, Glistrup on the Glistrup Case 1983, Tax Reform 1986, Salvation of Denmark 1989. *Leisure interests:* chess, bicycling, bridge, football. *Address:* c/o Fremskridtspartiet, P.O. Box 180, 2630 Taastrap, Denmark (Office).

GLITMAN, Maynard Wayne, MA; American diplomatist; b. 8 Dec. 1933, Chicago; s. of Ben and Reada (née Kutok Klass) Glitman; m. G. Christine Amundsen 1956; three s. two d.; ed Univ. of Illinois, Fletcher School of Law and Diplomacy, Univ. of California; with US army 1957; with Foreign Service Dept of State 1956, 1966–67, Dir Office of Int. Trade 1973–74, Deputy Asst Sec. of State for Internal Trade policy 1974–76; economist 1956–59; Vice-Consul Bahamas 1959–61; Econ. Officer Embassy, Ottawa 1961–65; mem. Del. to UN Gen. Ass. 1967, Nat. Security Council Staff 1968; Political Officer, First Sec. Embassy in Paris 1968–73; Deputy Asst Sec. of Defense for Europe and NATO 1976–77, Deputy Perm. Rep. to NATO 1977–81; Amb. and Deputy Chief US Del. to Intermediate Nuclear Forces Negotiations, Arms Control and Disarmament Agency, Switzerland 1981–84; Amb. and US Rep. Mutual and Balanced Forces Negotiation, Vienna 1985; Amb. and Chief US Negotiator Intermediate Nuclear Forces Negotiation, Geneva 1985–88; Amb. to Belgium 1988–91; Diplomat in Residence, Univ. of Vt 1991–94; Adjunct Prof., now

Lecturer in Political Science, Univ. of Vt 1994–; Public Service Medal (USA Dept of Defense) 1977, 1981, Presidential Distinguished Service Award 1984, 1987. *Address:* Department of Political Science, PO Box 54110, Burlington, VT 05405-0001 (Office); PO Box 438, Jeffersonville, VT 05464-0438, USA (Home).

GLOAG, Ann Heron; British business executive; b. 10 Dec. 1942; d. of Iain Souter and Catherine Souter; m. 1st Robin N. Gloag 1965; one s. (deceased) one d.; m. 2nd David McCleary 1990; ed Perth High School; trainee nurse Bridge of Earn Hosp., Perth 1960–65, Theatre Sister 1969–80; ward sister Devonshire Royal Hosp., Buxton 1965–69; founding partner Gloagtrotter (renamed Stagecoach Express Services) 1980–83, Co-Dir Stagecoach Ltd 1983–86, Exec. Dir Stagecoach Holdings PLC 1986–2000 (Man. Dir 1986–94); Scottish Marketing Woman of the Year, Scottish Univs 1989; UK Businesswoman of the Year, Veuve Clicquot and Inst. of Dirs 1989–90. *Leisure interests:* family, travel, charity support. *Address:* c/o Stagecoach Group, 10 Dunkeld Road, Perth PH1 5TW, Scotland (Office).

GLOBUS, Yoram; Israeli film producer; b. 7 Sept. 1943; f. Noah Films with Menahem Golan (q.v.) 1963; bought Cannon Films (USA) with Menahem Golan 1979 and has since produced over 100 motion pictures; Chair., CEO Cannon Entertainments 1989; Officer Cannon Group Inc. 1989; Co-Pres. Pathé Communications Corpn, Chair., CEO Pathé Int. until 1991. *Films produced include:* Over the Top, Barfly, Dancers, Missing in Action I, II & III, Death Wish IV, The Assault (winner of 1986 Acad. Award for Best Foreign Language Film), Surrender, Runaway Train, Hanna's War, Masters of the Universe, King Lear, Tough Guys Don't Dance, Shy People, A Cry In The Dark.

GLOCER, Thomas Henry, BA, JD; American lawyer and business executive; b. 8 Oct. 1959, New York; s. of Walter Glocer and Ursula Glocer (née Goodman); m. Maarit Leso 1988; one s. one d.; ed Columbia Coll., Yale Univ. Law School; mergers and acquisitions lawyer, Davis Polk and Wardwell, New York, Paris and Tokyo 1985–93; joined Reuters 1993, mem. Legal Dept, Gen. Counsel, Reuters America Inc., New York 1993–96, Exec. Vice-Pres., Reuters America Inc. and CEO Reuters Latin America 1996–98, CEO Reuters business in the Americas 1998–2001, Reuters Inc. 2000–01, CEO Reuters Group PLC 2001–; Dir New York City Investment Fund 1999–, Instinet Corpn 2000–; mem. Advisory Bd Singapore Monetary Authority 2001–; mem. Corporate Council, Whitney Museum of American Art 2000–; New York Hall of Science Award 2000, John Jay Alumni Award 2001. *Publications include:* author of computer software, including Coney Island: A Game of Discovery (jt author) 1983. *Address:* c/o Reuters Group plc, 85 Fleet Street, London, EC4P 4AJ, England (Office). *Website:* www.reuters.com (Office).

GLOSSOP, Peter; British opera singer (baritone) (retd); b. 6 July 1928, Sheffield; s. of Cyril Glossop and Violet Elizabeth Wright; m. 1st Joyce Blackham 1955 (divorced 1977); m. 2nd Michele Yvonne Amos 1977 (divorced 1987); two d.; ed High Storrs Grammar School, Sheffield; joined Sadler's Wells Opera 1952; with Covent Garden Opera Co. 1962–66; freelance singer 1966–86; debut at La Scala, Milan as Rigoletto 1965; sang at all major opera houses during career; First Prize Bulgarian First Competition for Young Opera Singers 1961; Hon. DMus (Sheffield) 1971; 'Amici di Verdi' Gold Medal 1995, Silver Cross of St George 1996. *Films:* Pagliacci, Otello. *Television includes:* Billy Budd, BBC 1971, Rigoletto, BBC 1972, Otello, BBC 1973. *Leisure interest:* golf. *Address:* End Cottage, 7 Gate Close, Hawkchurch, near Axminster, Devon, England. *Telephone:* (1297) 678266.

GLOUCESTER, HRH Richard Alexander Walter George, The Duke of, Earl of Ulster and the Baron Culloden, KG, GCVO; b. 26 Aug. 1944, Northampton; s. of the late Duke of Gloucester (third s. of HM King George V) and the Lady Alice Montagu-Douglas-Scott (d. of the 7th Duke of Buccleuch); m. Birgitte van Deurs 1972; one s. (Alexander, Earl of Ulster) two d. (the Lady Davina Windsor and the Lady Rose Windsor); ed Wellesley House, Broadstairs, Eton Coll. and Magdalene Coll., Cambridge; Corporate mem. RIBA 1972; Commdr-in-Chief St John Ambulance Brigade 1972–74; Col-in-Chief Gloucestershire Regt 1974–94, Deputy Col-in-Chief Royal Gloucestershire, Berks. and Wilts. Regt 1994–; Deputy Col-in-Chief The Royal Logistic Corps 1993–; Hon. Col Royal Monmouthshire Royal Engineers (Militia) 1977–; Hon. Air Cdre RAF Odiham 1993–; Grand Prior Order of St John 1975–; Royal Trustee, British Museum 1973–; Pres. Inst. of Advanced Motorists 1971, Cancer Research Campaign 1973, Nat. Asscn of Clubs for Young People 1974, Christ's Hosp. 1975, St Bartholomew's Hosp. 1975, Royal Smithfield 1975, British Consultants and Construction Bureau 1978; Patron of Heritage of London Trust 1982; Commr Historic Buildings and Monuments Comm. for England 1983-2001; Pres. The London Soc.; Sr Fellow Royal Coll. of Art 1984; as Rep. of HM The Queen visited Australia 1963, wedding of Crown Prince of Nepal 1963, seventieth birthday celebrations of King Olav V of Norway 1973, Mexico 1973, Nepal 1975, Saudi Arabia and the Philippines 1975, independence celebrations of Seychelles 1976 and of Solomon Islands 1978, Australia and Hawaii 1979, independence celebrations of Vanuatu 1980, Philippines, Indonesia and Burma 1981, India, Cyprus and Belgium 1982, France, Repub. of Korea, Canada, Jordan and UAE 1983, USA, Thailand, Brunei, Bahrain, Kuwait and Qatar 1984, New Zealand, Canary Islands, Egypt, Algeria and Tunis 1985, USSR, FRG, Berlin and Italy 1986, Spain, Sweden, Saudi Arabia, Indonesia, Bangladesh and Hong Kong 1987, USA, Gibraltar, Turkey, Pakistan, Kenya, Bahrain and Qatar 1988, Netherlands, Denmark and Portugal 1989, Canada, USA, France, Laos, Malaysia and

Singapore 1990, Poland, Dubai, France, Luxembourg, Germany, Hungary and Czechoslavakia 1991, Egypt, Spain, Belgium and USA 1992, Ukraine 1993, USA, Singapore, Japan and Portugal 1994, France, India, Malaysia and Mexico 1995, USA, Vietnam, Philippines, Indonesia and South Africa 1996, Repub. of Korea, Luxembourg, Yemen, Bahrain, Qatar and UAE 1997, Tunisia, China, Hong Kong, Tokyo, Angola, South Africa 1998, Poland, Barbados, Jamaica, Trinidad 1999, Kazakhstan, Kyryzstan, Nigeria 2000, Argentina, Armenia 2001, Kuala Lumpur and Singapore 2002. *Publication:* On Public View, The Face of London, Oxford and Cambridge. *Address:* Kensington Palace, London, W8 4PU, England. *Telephone:* (20) 7937-6374 (Office). *Fax:* (20) 7376-0859 (Office).

GLOVER, Danny; American actor; b. 22 July 1947, Georgia; m. Asake Bomani; one d.; ed San Francisco State Univ.; researcher, Office of Mayor, San Francisco 1971–75; Head TransAfrica (African-American Lobby) 2002–; mem. American Conservatory Theater's Black Actor Workshop; Broadway debut, Master Harold . . . and the Boys 1982; other stage appearances include: The Blood Knot 1982, The Island, Sizwe Banzi is Dead, Macbeth, Suicide in B Flat, Nevis Mountain Dew, Jukebox; appearances in TV movies and series; with his wife f. Bomani Gallery, San Francisco; Chair.'s Award, Nat. Asscn for the Advancement of Colored People (NAACP) 2003. *Films:* Escape from Alcatraz 1979, Chu Chu and the Philly Flash 1981, Out 1982, Iceman 1984, Places in the Heart 1984, Birdy 1984, The Color Purple 1984, Silverado 1985, Witness 1985, Lethal Weapon 1987, Bat 21 1988, Lethal Weapon II 1989, To Sleep with Anger 1990, Predator 2 1990, Flight of the Intruder 1991, A Rage in Harlem 1991, Pure Luck 1991, Grand Canyon 1992, Lethal Weapon III 1992, The Saint of Fort Washington 1993, Bopha 1993, Angels in the Outfield 1994, Operation Dumbo Drop 1995, America's Dream 1996, The Rainmaker 1997, Wings Against the Wind 1998, Beloved 1998, Lethal Weapon IV 1998, Prince of Egypt (voice) 1998, Antz (voice) 1998, The Monster 1999, Bàttu 2000, Boseman and Lena 2000, Wings Against the Wind 2000, Freedom Song 2000, 3 A.M. 2001, The Royal Tenenbaums 2001. *Address:* Cary Productions Inc., PMB 352, 6114 LaSalle Avenue, Oakland, CA 94611, USA.

GLOVER, Jane Alison, CBE, MA, DPhil, FRCM; British conductor; b. 13 May 1949; d. of Robert Finlay Glover and Jean Muir; ed Monmouth School for Girls and St Hugh's Coll., Oxford; Jr Research Fellow St Hugh's Coll. 1973–75, Lecturer in Music 1976–84, Sr Research Fellow 1982–84; Lecturer St Anne's Coll., Oxford 1976–80, Pembroke Coll. 1979–84; mem. Oxford Univ. Faculty of Music 1979–; professional conducting debut at Wexford Festival 1975; operas and concerts for BBC, Glyndebourne 1982–, Royal Opera House 1988–, Covent Garden, English Nat. Opera 1989–, London Symphony Orchestra, London Philharmonic Orchestra, Royal Philharmonic Orchestra, Philharmonia, Royal Scottish Orchestra, English Chamber Orchestra, Royal Danish Opera, Glimmerglass Opera, New York 1994–, Australian Opera 1996– and many orchestras in Europe and USA; Prin. Conductor London Choral Soc. 1983–2000; Artistic Dir London Mozart Players 1984–91; Prin. Conductor Huddersfield Choral Soc. 1989–96; mem. BBC Cen. Music Advisory Cttee 1981–85, Music Advisory Cttee Arts Council 1986–88; Gov. RAM 1985–90, BBC 1990–95; Hon. DMus (Exeter) 1986, (CNAA) 1991, (London) 1992, (City Univ.) 1995, (Glasgow) 1996; Hon. DLitt (Loughborough) 1988, (Bradford) 1992; Dr. hc (Open Univ.) 1988, (Brunel) 1997. *Television:* documentaries and series and presentation, especially Orchestra 1983, Mozart 1985. *Radio:* talks and series including Opera House 1995, Musical Dynasties 2000. *Publications:* Cavalli 1978; contribs. to The New Monteverdi Companion 1986, Monteverdi 'Orfeo' Handbook 1986; articles in numerous journals. *Leisure interests:* The Times crossword puzzle and theatre. *Address:* c/o Askonas Holt Ltd., Lonsdale Chambers, 27 Chancery Lane, London, WC2A 1PF, England. *Telephone:* (20) 7400-1700.

GŁOWACKI, Janusz; Polish writer and playwright; b. 13 Sept. 1938, Poznań; m.; one d.; ed Warsaw Univ.; columnist in Kultura weekly 1964–81; lecturer in many colls and univs in USA including Bennington, Yale, Cornell, Columbia; playwright in residence New York Shakespeare Festival 1984 and Mark Taper Forum, LA 1989; Fellow in Writing Univ. of Iowa 1977, 1982; Hon. mem. Univ. of Iowa 1977, 1982; Nat. Endowment for the Arts Fellowship 1988, Master of Arts Atlantic Center for the Arts 1991; mem. American and Polish PEN Club 1984–, Polish Film Union; Joseph Kesserling Award 1987, Drama League of New York Playwrighting Award 1987, Guggenheim Award 1988, Alfred Jurzykowski Foundation Award 1997, Tony Cox Award, Nantucket, USA 1999. *Publications:* (short stories) Nowy taniec la-ba-da 1970, Paradis 1973, Polowanie na muchy 1974, My Sweet Raskolnikov 1977, Opowiadania wybrane 1978, Skrzek. Coraz trudniej kochać 1980, Rose Café 1997; (novels) Moc truchleje 1981, Ostani cieć 2001; (film scripts) Rejs 1970, Psychodrama (with Marek Piwowski) 1971, Polowanie na muchy 1971, Trzeba zabić te miłość 1974, No Smoking Section (co-author) 1987, Hairdo 1999; (plays) Cudzołóstwo ukarane 1971, Mecz 1977, Obciach 1977, Kopciuch 1981 (Premio Molière, Argentina 1986), Fortinbras Gets Drunk 1986, Hunting Cockroaches 1986 (1st Prize, American Theatre Critics Asscn), Antigone in New York 1993, Czwarta siostra 1999, Ścieki, Skrzeki, karaluchy (selected works) 1996. *Address:* ul. Bednarska 7 m. 4, 00-310 Warsaw, Poland; 845 West End Avenue Apt. 4B, New York, NY 10025, USA.

GLUSHCHENKO, Fedor Ivanovich; Russian conductor; b. 29 March 1944, Rostov Region; m. 1st; one s. one d.; m. 2nd Galina Baryshnikova; one d.; ed Moscow and Leningrad State Conservatories, Vienna Acad. of Music; studied under Herbert von Karajan; Chief Conductor, Karelian Radio and TV Symphony Orchestra, Petrozavodsk 1971–73; Chief Conductor and Artistic Dir,

Ukrainian State Symphony Orchestra, Kiev 1973–87; British debut in 1989 with BBC Scottish Symphony, also appeared with Royal Liverpool Philharmonic and Scottish Chamber Orchestra; Conductor, Istanbul Opera 1990–91; Chief Conductor and Artistic Dir, J. S. Bach Chamber Orchestra, Yekaterinburg 1996–; Guest Conductor, Moscow Philharmonic Orchestra, Russian State Symphony Orchestra, Moscow Symphony, Ministry of Culture Orchestra and orchestras in Riga, Vilnius, Sverdlovsky, Tbilisi and Tashkent; tours in UK, Sweden, Italy, Denmark, People's Repub. of China, Germany, France and Spain. *Address:* 1st Pryadilnaya str. 11, apt. 5, 105037 Moscow, Russia. *Telephone:* (095) 165-49-46 (Home).

GLUSHENKO, Yevgeniya Konstatinovna; Russian actress; b. 4 Sept. 1952; m. Aleksandr Kalyagin; ed Shchepkin Theatre School; worked with Maly Theatre 1974–. *Films include:* Unfinished Play for Mechanical Piano 1977, Profile and Front-View 1979, Oblomov 1980, First-Time Married 1980, In Love of One's Own Accord (Moscow and West Berlin Film Festival Prizes 1983) 1982, Zina-Zinulya 1985. *Stage roles:* Liza in Misfortune from Sense 1975, Cordelia in King Lear 1979, Masha in The Savage 1990, Yefrosinya in Infanticide 1991, Matrena in The Hot Heart 1992, Susanna in A Criminal Mother or the Second Tartuffe 1993, Glafira in The Feast of Victors 1995, Madeleine in Queen Margo 1996. *Address:* 1905 Goda str. 3, Apt. 91, 123100 Moscow, Russia. *Telephone:* (095) 205-26-54.

GLYNN, Ian Michael, MD, PhD, FRCP, FRS; British professor of physiology; b. 3 June 1928, London; s. of Hyman and Charlotte Glynn; m. Jenifer Muriel Franklin 1958; one s. two d.; ed City of London School, Trinity Coll. Cambridge, Univ. Coll. Hosp. London; House Physician Cen. Middlesex Hosp. 1952–53; Nat. Service RAF Medical Branch 1956–57; MRC Scholar Physiological Lab. Cambridge 1956, Fellow Trinity Coll. 1955–, demonstrator in Physiology 1958–63, Lecturer 1963–70, Reader 1970–75, Prof. of Membrane Physiology 1975–86, Prof. of Physiology 1986–95, Prof. Emer. 1995–, Vice-Master Trinity Coll. 1980–86; Visiting Prof. Yale Univ. 1969; mem. British MRC 1976–80, Council of Royal Soc. 1979–81, 1991–92, Agric. Research Council 1981–86; Chair. Editorial Bd Journal of Physiology 1968–70; Hon. foreign mem. American Acad. of Arts and Sciences 1984, American Physiological Soc.; Hon. MD (Univ. of Aarhus) 1988. *Publications:* The Sodium Pump (with J. C. Ellory) 1985, An Anatomy of Thought: the Origin and Machinery of the Mind 1999; papers in scientific journals. *Address:* Trinity College, Cambridge, CB2 1TQ; Daylesford, Conduit Head Road, Cambridge, CB3 0EY, England. *Telephone:* (1223) 353079.

GNAEDINGER, Angelo; Swiss international organization official; b. 1951; trained as lawyer; examining magistrate, Schaffhausen –1984; joined Int. Cttee of the Red Cross (ICRC) 1984, followed field assignments in Middle East and Africa, held various positions in Dept of Operations, Geneva, Head of Detention Div. 1992–94, Del.-Gen. for W Cen. Europe and the Balkans 1994–98, Del.-Gen. for Europe, the Middle East and N. Africa 1998–, Dir-Gen. ICRC 2002–. *Address:* International Committee of the Red Cross, 19 avenue de la Paix, 1202 Geneva, Switzerland (Office). *Telephone:* (22) 7346001 (Office). *Fax:* (22) 7332057 (Office). *E-mail:* press.gva@icrc.org (Office). *Website:* www.icrc.org (Office).

GNANAM, Arumugham, PhD; Indian scientist; b. 5 Oct. 1932, Veeracholagan, Tamil Nadu; s. of Arumugham Pillai; m. Saratham Gnanam 1953; one s. three d.; ed Cornell Univ., USA; Asst Prof. of Plant Sciences, Cornell Univ. 1967–68; Lecturer, Annamalai Univ. 1968–69; reader, Madurai Kamaraj Univ. 1969–73, Prof. 1973–85, Dir Centre for Plant Molecular Biology 1990–91; Vice-Chancellor Pondicherry Univ. 1991–99; Vice-Chancellor, Bharathidasan Univ., Trichy 1985–88, Univ. of Madras 1988–90; elected Founder Fellow Tamil Nadu Acad. of Sciences 1976; Nat. Fellow Univ. Grants Comm. 1978, Nat. Lecturer in Botany 1980; Fellow Indian Nat. Science Acad., New Delhi 1984, Nat. Acad. of Sciences, Allahabad 1985; Rafi Ahmed Kidwai Award for best contrib. in plant genetics; Best Teacher Award, Govt of Tamil Nadu. *Publications:* numerous scientific papers. *Leisure interests:* photography, music, pets. *Address:* Office of the Vice-Chancellor, University of Pondicherry, R. Venkataraman Nagar, Kalapet, Pondicherry 605014, India. *Telephone:* 65175.

GNEDOVSKY, Yuri Petrovich, PhD; Russian architect; b. 3 July 1930, Sverdlovsk; m. Elena Andreyevna Borisova; one s. one d.; ed Moscow Inst. of Architecture, Acad. of Architecture; Sr Researcher Research Inst. of Public Bldgs Acad. of Architecture 1957–63; Head of div., Deputy Dir Cen. Research Inst. of Public Bldg Design 1964–82; Sec. Bd USSR Union of Architects 1982–91; Pres. Russian Union of Architects 1992–, Theatre Architects Partnership 1995–; mem. Council of Int. Union of Architects 1996–2002, currently Vice-Pres.; mem. Presidium Russian Acad. of Architecture and Construction Sciences; author of projects of numerous bldgs. including Taganka Theatre, Meyerhold Cen., Russian Cultural Cen. Red Hills in Moscow; Pres.'s Prize for Arts and Literature 1999, People's Architect of Russia 2002. *Publications include:* Architecture of Soviet Theatre, Architecture of Public Buildings, World Architecture: A Critical Mosaic 1900–2000 (Vol. 7) 2000, over 60 articles. *Address:* Union of Architects of Russia, Granatny per. 22, 123001 Moscow, Russia (Office). *Telephone:* (095) 291-55-78 (Office). *E-mail:* uarus@cityline.ru (Office). *Website:* www.uar.ru (Office).

GNEHM, Edward William, Jr, MA; American diplomatist; b. 10 Nov. 1944, Ga; s. of Edward W. Gnehm, Sr and Beverly Thomasson; m. Margaret Scott 1970; one s. one d.; ed George Washington Univ. and American Univ. Cairo; Head, Liaison Office, Riyadh 1976–78; Deputy Chief of Mission, Embassy,

Sanaa 1978–81; Dir Jr Officer Div. Personnel, Washington, DC 1982–83, Dir Secr. Staff 1983–84; Deputy Chief of Mission, Amman 1984–87; Deputy Asst Sec. of Defense for Near East and S Asia 1987–89; Deputy Asst Sec. of State, Bureau of Near East and S Asian Affairs 1989–90; Amb. to Kuwait 1990–94, to Australia 2000–01, to Jordan 2001–; Deputy Perm. Rep. to UN 1994–97; Dir-Gen. of Foreign Service, Dir of Personnel US Dept of State, Washington DC 1997–2000. *Leisure interests:* history, foreign policy, stamps. *Address:* American Embassy, PO Box 354, Amman 11118, Jordan (Office). *Telephone:* (6) 5920101 (Office). *Fax:* (6) 5920121 (Office). *E-mail:* gnehmew@state.gov (Office); administration@usembassy-amman.org.jo (Office).

GNEUSS, Helmut Walter Georg, DPhil; German professor of English; b. 29 Oct. 1927, Berlin; s. of Kurt Gneuss and Margarete Gneuss (née Grimm); m. Mechthild Gretsch 1974; ed Freie Universität Berlin, St John's Coll., Cambridge; lecturer German Dept, Durham Univ. 1955–56, Dept of English, Freie Univ. Berlin 1956–62, Heidelberg Univ. 1962–65; Prof., English Univ. of Munich 1965–; Visiting Professorial Fellow Emmanuel Coll., Cambridge 1970, Visiting Prof. Univ. of NC, Chapel Hill 1974; mem. Bayerische Akad. der Wissenschaften, British Acad., Österreichische Akad. der Wissenschaften, Medieval Acad. of America; Vice-Pres. Henry Bradshaw Soc. *Publications:* Lehnbildungen und Lehnbedeutungen im Altenglischen 1955, Hymnar und Hymnen im englischen Mittelalter 1968, English Language Scholarship 1996, Language and History in Early England 1996, Books and Libraries in Early England 1996; Handlist of Anglo-Saxon Manuscripts 2001. *Address:* Institut für Englische Philologie, Universität Munich, Schellingstrasse 3, 80799 Munich, Germany. *Telephone:* (89) 21802369. *Fax:* (89) 2180 3399.

GNUTTI, Vito; Italian politician, chemical engineer and industrialist; b. 14 Sept. 1939, Lumezzane, Brescia; s. of Basilio Gnutti and Leoni Cenzina; m. Nerina Codini 1965; two d.; Chair. Lombardy Regional Group, Young Industrialists 1975–78, mem. Nat. Council, Confindustria (nat. employers' org.) –1993; mem. Chamber of Deputies 1992–, re-elected as Lega Nord Deputy 1994, elected as Lega Nord Senator April 1996; Minister of Industry 1994–95. *Address:* Via Leno 4, 25010 Isorella, Italy. *Telephone:* (030) 9958130. *Fax:* (030) 9958244. *E-mail:* silexpor@tin.it (Office).

GOBURDHUN, Jagdishwar; Mauritian politician; b. 1 Jan. 1946; m. 1981; one s. one d.; ed diplomas in cooperative and industrial man.; f. and Sec. Mauritius Planters' Asscn; Sec. Mauritius Planters' and By-Products Cooperative Credit Soc.; mem. Legislative Ass. 1976–; Minister of Health 1983–90, Minister of Co-operatives and Handicraft 1990–96. *Address:* c/o Ministry of Co-operatives, Life Insurance Corporation of India Building, 3rd Floor, John Kennedy Street, Port Louis, Mauritius.

GOCKLEY, (Richard) David, BA, MBA; American opera director; b. 13 July 1943, Phila; s. of Warren Gockley and Elizabeth Gockley; m. Adair Lewis; two s. one d.; ed Brown Univ., Columbia Univ.; Dir of Music, Newark Acad. 1965–67; Dir of Drama, Buckley School, New York 1967–69; Box Office Man., Santa Fe Opera 1969–70; Business Man., Houston Grand Opera 1970–71, Assoc. Dir 1971–72, Gen. Dir 1972–; co-founder Houston Opera Studio 1977; mem. Bd of Dirs. Texas Inst. of Arts in Educ.; mem. Opera America, Pres. 1985–; fmr Chair. Houston Theater Dist; Hon. DHL Univ. of Houston 1992, Hon. DFA (Brown Univ.) 1993; Tony Award, League of New York Theaters and Producers 1977, Grammy Award 1977 (for Porgy and Bess), Dean's Award, Columbia Business School 1982, Music Theater Award, Nat. Inst. of Music Theater 1985, Emmy Award 1988 (for Nixon in China), William Rogers Award (Brown Univ.) 1995. *Operas produced:* Nixon in China, Harvey Milk, Florencia en el Amazonas, Porgy and Bess, Treemonisha, A Quiet Place, Willie Stark, Resurrection, Carmen. *Leisure interest:* tennis. *Address:* Houston Grand Opera, Suite 500, 510 Preston Street, Houston, Texas, TX 77002, USA (Office). *Telephone:* (713) 546-0260 (Office). *Fax:* (713) 247-0906 (Office). *E-mail:* gockley@houstongrandopera.org (Office).

GODAL, Bjørn Tore; Norwegian politician; b. 20 Jan. 1945, Skien; s. of Kari Godal and Aksel Godal; m. Gro Balas 1988; one c.; ed Oslo Univ.; office clerk, Skien 1964–65; Pres. Labour League of Youth 1971–73 (sec. for org. 1970–71), Fritt Forum (Labour Party's Student Org.) 1967–68; research officer Labour Party 1973–80, Sec.-Gen. Oslo Labour Party 1980–82, Leader 1982–90 (mem. Cen. Cttee Labour Party 1983–90); Pres. Council of European Nat. Youth Cttees. (CENYC) 1973–75; Head of Secr. Labour Party Group of the Oslo Municipal Council 1986; Deputy Rep. Storting (Parl.), then elected Rep.; Minister of Trade and Shipping 1991–94, of Foreign Affairs 1994–97, of Defence 2000–01; mem. council for the study of power distribution in Norway 1972–80, Standing Cttee on Finance 1986–89, on Foreign and Constitutional Affairs 1989–91, on Defence 1997–2000, Storting; Chair. Middle East Cttee, Socialist Int.; mem. North Atlantic Ass. 1997–. *Address:* c/o Norwegian Parliament, 0026 Oslo, Norway.

GODANA, Bonaya Adhi, LLM, PhD; Kenyan politician and lawyer; b. 2 Sept. 1952, Marsabit; s. of Adhi Godana and Yatane Adi Godana; m. 1986; two s. two d.; ed Univ. of Nairobi, Univ. of London, Univ. of Geneva; lecturer, Dept of Public Law, Univ. of Nairobi 1977–86, Sr Lecturer and Chair. of Dept 1986–88; Advocate of the High Court of Kenya 1985; mem. of Parl. for N Horr, Marsabit Dist 1988–; Asst Minister, Ministry of Health 1988–91, Office of the Pres. 1991–92, Ministry of Foreign Affairs 1992–93; Deputy Speaker, Nat. Ass. of Kenya 1993–97; Minister of Foreign Affairs 1998–2001, of Agric. 2002–. *Publication:* Africa's Shared Water Resources – Legal and Institutional Aspects of the Nile, Niger and Senegal River Systems 1985. *Address:*

Ministry of Agriculture, Kilimo House, Cathedral Road, P.O. Box 30028, Nairobi, Kenya (Office). *Telephone:* (20) 718870 (Office). *Fax:* (20) 720586 (Office).

GODARD, Jean-Luc; French film director; b. 3 Dec. 1930, Paris; s. of Paul Godard and Odile Monad; m. 1st Anna Karina 1961 (divorced); m. 2nd Anne Wiazemsky 1967; ed Lycée Buffon and Faculté des Lettres, Paris; journalist and film critic; film director 1958–; mem. Conseil supérieur de la langue française 1989–; Prix Jean Vigo for A bout de souffle 1960, Jury's Special Prize and Prix Pasinetti, Venice Festival 1962, Diploma of Merit, Edin. Film Festival 1968 for Weekend, Grand Prix Nat. 1982, Grand Prix Nat. de la culture 1999; Chevalier, Ordre nat. du Mérite. *Films:* Opération Béton 1954, Une femme coquette 1955, Tous les garçons s'appellent Patrick 1957, Charlotte et son Jules 1958, Une histoire d'eau 1958, A bout de souffle 1959, Le petit soldat 1960, Une femme est une femme 1961, Les sept péchés capitaux 1961, Vivre sa vie 1962, RoGoPaG 1962, Les carabiniers 1963, Le mépris 1963, Les plus belles escroqueries du monde 1963, Paris vu par … 1963, Bande à part 1964, Une femme mariée 1964, Alphaville 1965, Pierrot le fou 1965, Masculin-féminin 1966, Made in USA 1966, Deux ou trois choses que je sais d'elle 1966, La chinoise 1967, Loin du Vietnam 1967, Weekend 1967, Le plus vieux métier du monde 1967, Vangelo '70 1967, Le gai savoir (TV) 1968, Un film comme les autres 1968, One Plus One 1968, One American Movie – 1 a.m. 1969, British Sounds 1969, Le vent d'est 1969, Lotte in Italia 1970, Vladimir et Rosa 1971, Tout va bien 1972, Numéro deux 1975, Ici et ailleurs 1976, Bugsy 1979, Sauve qui peut 1980, Passion 1982, Prénom Carmen 1983, Detective 1984, Je vous salue, Marie 1985, Soigne ta droite 1987, Aria (segment) 1987, Nouvelle Vague 1989, Allemagne neuf zero 1991, Hélas pour moi 1993, JLG/JLG 1995, Forever Mozart 1996, De l'origine du XXIe siècle 2000, Eloge de l'amour 2001, King Lear 2001. *Publication:* Introduction à une véritable histoire du cinéma 1980. *Address:* 15 rue du Nord, 1180 Roulle, Switzerland (Home); 26 ave Pierre 1er de Serbie, 75116 Paris, France.

GODBER, John Harry, BEd, MA, PhD, DLitt; British playwright, drama teacher and film and theatre director; b. 18 May 1956, Hemsworth, W Yorks.; s. of Harry Godber and Dorothy Godber; m. Jane Thornton; two d.; ed Bretton Hall Coll., Wakefield, Leeds Univ.; Hon. DLitt (Hull) 1988, (Humberside) 1997; Laurence Olivier Award 1984, LA Critics' Awards (six) 1986, Joseph Jefferson Award, Chicago 1988. *Plays:* 32 stage plays, including Bouncers, Teechers, Up'N'Under, Happy Families, Salt of the Earth, Thick as a Brick, April in Paris; also radio plays and TV programmes. *Film:* Up'N'Under 1998. *Address:* c/o Alan Brodie, A.B.R., 211 Piccadilly, London, W1 (Office); 64 Riverview Avenue, North Ferriby, HU14 3DT, England (Home). *Telephone:* (20) 7917-2871 (Office); (1482) 633854 (Home). *Fax:* (20) 7917-2872 (Office). *E-mail:* johngodber@compuserve (Home).

GODDARD, Leonard, MA, BPhil, FAHA; British professor of philosophy; b. 13 Feb. 1925, Nottingham; s. of Bertram Goddard and Frances Goddard; m. 1st Phyllis Dunsdon 1945 (divorced 1981); m. 2nd Patricia Johnson 1988 (divorced 1997); m. 3rd Dorothy Spencer 2001; two d.; ed Univ. of St Andrews, Univ. of Cambridge; RAF 1943–47; Asst Lecturer, Univ. of St Andrews 1952–55; lecturer and then Sr Lecturer Univ. of New England, Australia 1956–61, Prof. of Philosophy, Univ. of New England 1961–66, Dean of Arts 1964–66; Prof. of Logic and Metaphysics, Univ. of St Andrews 1966–77, Dean of Arts 1972–74; Boyce Gibson Prof. of Philosophy, Univ. of Melbourne 1977–90, Prof. Emer. 1990–; Visiting Fellow Australian Nat. Univ. 1974–76. *Publications:* (with R. Routley) The Logic of Significance and Context, Vol. 1 1973, Philosophical Problems 1977, (with B. Judge) The Metaphysics of Wittgenstein's Tractatus 1982. *Leisure interests:* golf, boating. *Address:* Department of Philosophy, University of Melbourne, Parkville, Victoria, Australia 3052. *Telephone:* (3) 9755-1471.

GODDIO, Franck, BSc; American archaeologist; b. 1947; ed Ecole Nat. de la Statistique Admin. Economique, Paris; adviser to various int. orgs.; gained experience in marine archaeology in late 1970s; Founder and Chair. Franck Goddio Soc.; excavated historically important sunken ships and discovered submerged ruins of Alexandria. *Address:* The Franck Goddio Society, 100 West Fifth Street, Tulsa, OK 74103, USA (Office). *Fax:* (509) 479-3653 (Office). *E-mail:* info@franckgoddio.org (Office). *Website:* www.franckgoddio .org (Office).

GODEAUX, Jean, Baron, DenD, LicEcon; Belgian banker; b. 3 July 1922, Jemeppe sur Meuse; s. of Léon Godeaux and Claire de Barsy; m. Thérèse Ceron 1950; two s. three d.; ed Univ. Catholique de Louvain; Bar of Namur 1944–47; Asst, Inst. for Econ. and Social Research 1947; Nat. Bank of Belgium 1947–49; Technical Asst, IMF 1949–50, Alt. Exec. Dir 1950–54, Exec. Dir 1954, Adviser 1992–98; Man. Banque Lambert 1955–59, Man. Partner 1960–72, Pres. 1973–74; Pres. Banking Comm. 1974–82; Gov. Nat. Bank of Belgium 1982–89; Pres. and Chair. BIS 1985–87; Hon. Dir Société Générale de Belgique 1990–; Grand officier de l'Ordre de Léopold, Officier, Légion d'honneur, Commdr, Ordre de St Grégoire le grand, Grand Croix, Ordre du Mérite (Luxembourg), (Austria), Grand Croix, Order of Orange-Nassau (Netherlands), Grand Cordon, Order of Sacred Treasure (Japan), Grand Cordon, Order of Infante Enrique (Portugal). *Leisure interests:* swimming, reading. *Address:* rue du Piroy 2, 5340 Strud-Haltinne, Belgium (Home). *Telephone:* (81) 58-82-45. *Fax:* (81) 58-98-43.

GODFREY, Malcolm Paul Weston, CBE, MB, BS, FRCP; British medical practitioner; b. 11 Aug. 1926, London; s. of Harry Godfrey and Rose Godfrey; m. Barbara Goldstein 1955; one s. two d. (one deceased); ed Hertford

Grammar School, King's Coll. London and King's Coll. Hosp. Medical School; various appointments in Nat. Health Service 1950–60; Fellow in Medicine and Asst Physician, Johns Hopkins Hosp. Baltimore, Md 1957–58; HQ staff, MRC 1960–74; Dean, Royal Postgrad. Medical School, Hammersmith Hosp. 1974–83; Second Sec. MRC 1983–88; Queen's Hon. Physician 1987–90; Chair. Public Health Lab. Service Bd 1989–96, United Medical and Dental Schools of Guys and St Thomas' Hosps. 1996–98; mem. Soc. of Scholars, Johns Hopkins Univ. (USA) 2000; Fellow Royal Postgraduate Medical School 1985, Imperial Coll. School of Medicine 1999, King's Coll. London 2000. *Publications:* articles on cardio-respiratory disorders in medical and scientific journals. *Leisure interests:* theatre, reading, current affairs, walking. *Address:* 17 Clifton Hill, St John's Wood, London, NW8 0QE, England. *Telephone:* (20) 7624-6335. *Fax:* (20) 7328-9474.

GODINE, David R., MA, EdM; American publisher; b. 4 Sept. 1944, Cambridge, Mass.; s. of Morton R. Godine and Bernice Beckwith; m. Sara Sangree Eisenman 1988; one s. one d.; ed Dartmouth Coll., Harvard Univ.; f. David R. Godine, Publisher and Pres. 1969–; mem. Bds. Massachusetts Historical Soc., Massachusetts Horticultural Soc.; Fellow Pierpoint Morgan Library; Dwiggins Award 1984. *Publications:* Renaissance Books of Science 1970. *Leisure interests:* sailing, skiing. *Address:* David R. Godine Publishers Inc., 9 Hamilton Place, Boston, MA 02108 (Office); 196 School Street, Milton, MA 02186, USA (Home). *Telephone:* (617) 451-9600 (Office). *Fax:* (617) 350-0250 (Office). *E-mail:* info@godine.com (Office). *Website:* www.godine.com (Office).

GODLEY, Georgina, MA; British fashion and product designer and art director; b. 11 April 1955, London; d. of Michael Godley and Heather Godley; m. Sebastian Conran 1988 (divorced 2000); two s.; ed Putney High School, Thames Valley Grammar School, London, Wimbledon School of Art, Brighton Polytechnic and Chelsea School of Art; designer, Browns, London and Paris 1979–80; partner and designer, Crolla, London 1980–85; Dir and sole designer Georgina Godley Ltd (produces own label collections) 1986–; designer/co-ordinator Tabletop Habitat 1999, head of design Home Accessories, Habitat 2000, Group Style Dir 2002–; fmr Sr Lecturer St Martin's School of Art and School of Fashion and Textiles, Royal Coll. of Art; mem. British Fashion Council Designer Cttee; Visiting lecturer at various fashion and art colls. in London and elsewhere in UK; work included in perm. exhbn at Victoria & Albert Museum, London and Bath Costume Museum; ICA Young Contemporaries Award 1978. *Address:* Habitat, 42–46 Princelet Street, London, N6 6JR (Office); 42 Bassett Road, London, W10 6UL, England (Home). *Telephone:* (20) 7614-5500 (Office); (20) 7813-4412 (Home). *E-mail:* georgina.godley@habitat.co.uk.

GODLEY, Wynne Alexander Hugh; British economist; b. 2 Sept. 1926; s. of Hugh John, 2nd Baron Kilbracken and Elizabeth Helen Monteith; m. Kathleen Eleonora Epstein 1955; one d.; ed Rugby School, New Coll., Oxford, Conservatoire de Musique, Paris; professional oboist 1950; joined econ. section, HM Treasury 1956, Deputy Dir 1967–70, Econ. Consultant 1975; Dir Investing in Success Ltd 1970–85, Royal Opera House, Covent Garden 1976–87; Dir Applied Econs Dept, Cambridge Univ. 1970–85, Prof. 1980–93, Dir (a.i.) 1985–87; Official Adviser Select Cttee on Public Expenditure 1971–73; Visiting Prof., Aalborg Univ. 1987–88; Distinguished Scholar, Jerome Levy Econs Inst., Annandale-on-Hudson, New York 1991–92, 1993–95, 1996–2001; Fellow of King's Coll., Cambridge 1970–98, Emer. Fellow 2001–; Dir Kent Opera 1993–; mem. Panel of Economists to advise the Chancellor of the Exchequer 1992–95; Visitor Judge Inst. of Man., Cambridge Univ. 2001. *Publications:* Pricing in the Trade Cycle (jtly.) 1978, Macroeconomics (jtly.) 1983; numerous articles in magazines and journals. *Address:* Jasmine House, The Green, Cavendish, Suffolk, CO10 8BB, England. *Telephone:* (1787) 281166.

GODMANIS, Ivars; Latvian politician and scientist; b. 27 Nov. 1951, Riga; s. of Teodors Godmanis and Ingride Godmanis; m. Ramora Godmanė 1978; two s. one d.; ed Latvian State Univ.; scientific work since 1973, staff-mem. of the Physical Inst. of Latvian Acad. of Sciences 1973–86; teacher in Latvian Univ. 1986–90; active involvement in the Movt for Independence of Latvia, Deputy Chair. of the People's Front; Chair. Council of Ministers of the Latvian Republic 1990–93; with commercial co. SWH (Software House) 1994–95; Vice-Chair. Asscn of Commercial Banks of Latvia 1995–96; Pres. Latvia Savings Bank (Jt stock co.) 1996–; mem. Saeima (Parl.) 1998–. *Leisure interest:* tennis. *Address:* Palasta Street 1, 1954 Riga, Latvia. *Telephone:* (2) 722-2871. *Fax:* (2) 721-0807.

GODREJ, Adi Burjor, MS; Indian business executive; b. 3 April 1942, Bombay; s. of Dr. Burjori Pirojsha Godrej and Jai Burjor Godrej; m. Parmeshwar Mader 1966; one s. two d.; ed St Xavier's High School & Coll., Bombay and Massachusetts Inst. of Technology; Chair. Godrej Foods Ltd, Godrej Agrovet Ltd, Godrej & Kis Ltd, Godrej Hl Care Ltd, Godrej Properties & Investments Ltd, Godrej Pillsbury Ltd, Godrej Oil Palm Konkan Pvt. Ltd; Man. Dir Godrej Soaps Ltd; Dir Godrej & Boyce Mfg Co. Ltd, Swadeshi Detergents Ltd, Vora Soaps Ltd, Godrej Investments Ltd, Godrej-GE Appliances Ltd, Godrej Capital Ltd, Godrej Pacific Technology Ltd, Godrej Telecom Ltd, Ensemble Holdings & Finance Pvt. Ltd, Godrej Int. Ltd; Chair. Bd of Trustees of Dadabhai Naoroji; mem. Nat. Council, Confed. of Indian Industries; fmr Chair. Pres. Indian Soap & Toiletries Makers' Asscn, Cen. Org. for Oil Industry and Trade, Solvent Extractors' Asscn of India, Indo-American Soc., Compound Livestock Feeds, Mfrs Asscn. *Leisure interests:* sailing and motor boating, water-skiing, horse riding, squash, bridge, reading. *Address:*

Godrej Industries Ltd, Pirojshanagar, Eastern Express Highway, Vikhroli, Mumbai 400079 (Office); Aashraye Godrej House, 67 H Walkeshwar Road, Mumbai 400006, India (Home). *Telephone:* (22) 5188060, (22) 5188010 (Office); (22) 3642955 (Home). *Website:* www.godrejindia.com (Office).

GODSELL, Robert Michael, MA; South African business executive; b. 14 Sept. 1952, Johannesburg; s. of Cyril H. Godsell and Winnefred (née Stephens) Godsell; m. Gillian Hall 1975; three d.; Deputy Provincial Leader Progressive Party, Natal 1969–70, Nat. Youth Chair. 1975–76; Dir Industrial Relations and Public Affairs Anglo-American Corpn 1974–95, CEO Gold Div. 1995–, Deputy Chair. 1995–96, Chair. 1996–; Chair. CEO AngloGold Ltd 2000–; Pres. Chamber of Mines 1992, 1997–98; mem. Nat. Econ. Forum 1994–; Chair. World Gold Council. *Publications:* A Future South Africa: Visions, Strategies and Relations 1988 (co-ed.); of econ. report. *Leisure interest:* squash. *Address:* P.O. Box 62117, Marshalltown 2107, South Africa. *Telephone:* (11) 637-6150.

GODSOE, Peter C., BSc, MBA, FCA; Canadian banker; b. 2 May 1938, Toronto; s. of Joseph Gerald Godsoe and Margaret Graham Cowperthwaite; m. Shelagh Cathleen Reburn 1963; three c.; ed Univ. of Toronto, Harvard Univ.; fmr Deputy Chair. Bd, Pres., CEO and Dir Bank of Nova Scotia, Chair. CEO 1995–, also Chair. Bd Dirs. Bank of Nova Scotia Int. 1995–; Chair. and Dir Scotia Centre Ltd, Scotia Futures Ltd, Scotia Mortgage Corpn; Vice-Chair. and Dir Bank of Nova Scotia Properties Inc., Scotia Properties Québec Inc., Scotia Realty Ltd; Dir various Bank of Nova Scotia subsidiary cos., Alexander & Alexander Services Inc., Reed Stenhouse Cos. Ltd, Nova Scotia Corpn, Scotiabank Jamaica Trust and Merchant Bank Ltd, West India Co. of Merchant Bankers Ltd, etc.; fmr Chair. Canadian Bankers' Asscn. *Address:* Bank of Nova Scotia, Scotia Plaza, 44 King Street W, Toronto, Ont., M5H 1H1, Canada (Office). *Telephone:* (416) 866-6161 (Office). *Fax:* (416) 866-3750 (Office). *E-mail:* email@scotiabank.com (Office). *Website:* www.scotiabank .com (Office).

GODUNOV, Sergey Konstantinovich; Russian mathematician; b. 17 July 1929; m.; two c.; ed Moscow State Univ.; jr, sr researcher, head of div., Inst. of Math. USSR Acad. of Sciences 1951–66; head of div. Inst. of Applied Math. USSR Acad. of Sciences 1966–69; head of div. Computer's Cen. Siberian br. USSR Acad. of Sciences 1969–80; head of lab., Deputy Dir, Exec. Dir Inst. of Math. Siberian br. USSR Acad. of Sciences 1980–86; head of dept, S. Sobolev Inst. of Math. Siberian br. Acad. of Sciences 1986–; Corresp. mem. USSR (now Russian) Acad. of Sciences 1976, mem. 1994; research in computational math., differential equations, mathematical physics, mem. Scientific Council Math. Modelling; mem. Ed. Board Siberian Math. Journal; Lenin Prize, A. Krylov Prize. *Publications:* On the Minkowsky Problem 1948, On the Idea of a Generalized Solution 1960, Numerical Solution of Multidimensional Problems of Gas Dynamics 1976 and others. *Address:* Institute of Mathematics, Siberian Branch of Russian Academy of Sciences, Universitetskyi pr. 4, 630090 Novosibirsk, Russia. *Telephone:* (3832) 35-06-53 (Office); 35-60-84 (Home).

GODWIN, Fay S.; British photographer; b. 17 Feb. 1931, Berlin, Germany; d. of Sidney Simmonds and Stella MacLean; m. Tony Godwin; two s.; ed many schools all over the world; had no photographic training; started photographing her young children 1966; touring exhbns relating to publ. of The Oldest Road 1975; commissioned by Nat. Trust to photograph the Trust's historic properties and sites in Wessex 1982; British Council's overseas tour of Fay Godwin's Landscape Photographs started 1984; joined Network Photographers Picture Agency 1991; teaches at photographic schools and workshops; Pres. Ramblers Asscn 1987–90, Life Vice-Pres. 1990–; major award from Arts Council of GB to continue landscape work in British Isles 1978; Bradford Fellowship 1986/87; Fellow Nat. Museum of Photography, Bradford 1987; Hon. Fellow Royal Photographic Soc. 1991, Royal Inst. of Scottish Architects 1992. *Exhibitions include:* maj. retrospective landscape Exhbn, Serpentine Gallery, London 1985; Land Exhbn at Yale Center for British Art, USA; Our Forbidden Land Exhbn, Royal Photographic Soc. Gallery and nat. tour; retrospective, Barbican, London 2001 and nat. tour. *Publications:* The Oldest Road: An Exploration of the Ridgeway (with J. R. L. Anderson) 1975, The Oil Rush (with Mervyn Jones) 1976, The Drovers' Roads of Wales (with Shirley Toulson) 1977, Islands (with John Fowles) 1978, Remains of Elmet: A Pennine Sequence (with poems by Ted Hughes) 1979, Romney Marsh and the Royal Military Canal (with Richard Ingrams) 1980, Tess: The Story of a Guide Dog (with Peter Purves) 1981, The Whisky Roads of Scotland (with Derek Cooper) 1982, Bison at Chalk Farm 1982, The Saxon Shore Way from Gravesend to Rye (with Alan Sillitoe) 1983, The National Trust Book of Wessex 1985, Land (with an essay by John Fowles) 1985, The Secret Forest of Dean 1986, Our Forbidden Land 1990, Elmet (with Ted Hughes) 1994, The Edge of the Land 1995, Glassworks & Secret Lives 1999, Landmarks 2001. *Leisure interests:* walking, photography and reading. *Address:* Fay Godwin, c/o Network, 4 Nile Street, London, N1 7ZZ, England. *Telephone:* (20) 7490-3633.

GODWIN, Gail Kathleen, PhD; American author; b. 18 June 1937, Birmingham, Ala; d. of Mose Godwin and Kathleen Krahenbuhl; m. 1st Douglas Kennedy 1960 (divorced 1961); m. 2nd Ian Marshall 1965 (divorced 1966); ed Peace Jr Coll. Raleigh, NC and Univs. of NC and Iowa; news reporter, Miami Herald 1959–60; reporter, consultant, US Travel Service, London 1961–65; Editorial Asst Saturday Evening Post 1966; Fellow, Center for Advanced Study, Univ. of Ill. Urbana 1971–72; lecturer, Iowa Writers' Workshop

1972–73, Vassar Coll. 1977, Columbia Univ. Writing Program 1978, 1981; American specialist, USIS 1976; Guggenheim Fellow 1975–76; librettist for various productions; mem. PEN, Authors' Guild, Authors' League, Nat. Book Critics' Circle; American Acad. and Inst. of Arts and Letters Literature Award 1981; other awards and distinctions. *Publications:* novels including: The Perfectionists 1970, Glass People 1972, The Odd Woman 1974, Violet Clay 1978, A Mother and Two Daughters 1982, The Finishing School 1985, A Southern Family 1987, Father Melancholy's Daughter 1991, The Good Husband 1994, Evensong 1998; short stories including Heart 2001 and librettos. *Address:* PO Box 946, Woodstock, NY 12498-0946, USA.

GOEHR, Alexander, MA; British composer; b. 10 Aug. 1932, Berlin; s. of Walter Goehr and Laelia Goehr; m. 1st Audrey Baker 1954; m. 2nd Anthea Felicity Staunton 1972; m. 3rd Amira Katz; one s. three d.; ed Berkhamstead School, Royal Manchester Coll. of Music, Paris Conservatoire (with Olivier Messiaen) and privately with Yvonne Loriod; composer, teacher, conductor 1956–; held classes at Morley Coll., London; part-time post with BBC, being responsible for production of orchestral concerts 1960–; works performed and broadcast world-wide; awarded Churchill Fellowship 1968; Composer-in-Residence, New England Conservatory, Boston, Mass. 1968–69; Assoc. Prof. of Music, Yale Univ. 1969–70; Prof. West Riding Chair of Music Univ. of Leeds 1971–76; Prof. of Music, Univ. of Cambridge 1976–99, Prof. Emer. 1999–, Fellow of Trinity Hall, Cambridge 1976–; Reith Lecturer 1987; Hon. Prof. Beijing Univ. 2001; Hon. mem. American Acad. and Inst. of Arts and Letters; Hon. ARCM 1976; Hon. FRNCM 1980; Hon. FRCM 1981; Hon. DMus (Southampton) 1973, (Manchester), (Nottingham) 1994, (Siena) 1999; Dr hc (Cambridge) 2000. *Works include:* Songs of Babel 1951, Sonata 1952, Fantasias 1954, String Quartet 1956–57, Capriccio 1957, The Deluge 1957–58, La belle dame sans merci 1958, Variations 1959, Four Songs from the Japanese 1959, Sutter's Gold 1959–60, Suite 1961, Hecuba's Lament 1959–61, A Little Cantata of Proverbs 1962, Concerto for Violin and Orchestra 1961–62, Two Choruses 1962, Virtutes 1963, Little Symphony 1963, Little Music for Strings 1963, Five Poems and an Epigram of William Blake 1964, Three Pieces for Piano 1964, Pastorals 1965, Piano Trio 1966, Arden muss sterben (Arden Must Die, opera) 1966, Warngedichte 1967, String Quartet 1967, Romanza 1968, Naboth's Vineyard 1968, Konzertstück 1969, Nonomiya 1969, Paraphrase 1969, Symphony in One Movement 1970, Shadowplay 1970, Sonata about Jerusalem 1970, Concerto for Eleven Instruments 1970, Piano Concerto 1972, Chaconne for Wind 1974, Lyric Pieces 1974, Metamorphosis/Dance 1974, String Quartet No. 3 1976, Psalm IV 1976, Fugue on the Notes of the Fourth Psalm 1976, Romanza on the Notes of the Fourth Psalm 1977, Prelude and Fugue for Three Clarinets 1978, Chaconne for Organ 1979, Das Gesetz der Quadrille 1979, Babylon the Great is Fallen 1979, Sinfonia 1980, Cello Sonata 1984, Behold the Sun 1984, Two Imitations of Baudelaire 1985, Symphony with Chaconne 1986, Eve Dreams in Paradise 1987, Carol for St Steven 1989, ...in real time 1989, Sing, Ariel 1989, String Quartet No. 4 1990, Still Lands 1990, Bach Variations 1990, The Death of Moses 1991, The Mouse Metamorphosed into a Maid 1991, Colossus or Panic 1992, I Said, I Will Take Heed 1993, Cambridge Hocket 1993, Arianna (opera) 1995, Schlussgesang 1997, Kantan (opera) 2000, Piano Quintet 2001, Second Musical Offering (GFH) 2001. *Address:* Trinity Hall, Cambridge, CB3 9DP; University Music School, 11 West Road, Cambridge CB3 9DP; c/o Schott and Co. Ltd, 48 Great Marlborough Street, London, W1V 2BN, England.

GOENKA, Harsh Vardhan, MBA; Indian industrialist; b. 10 Dec. 1957, Calcutta; s. of Rama Prasad Goenka and Sushila Goenka; m. Mala Sanghi 1977; one s. one d.; ed St Xavier's Coll., Calcutta, Int. Man. Inst., Geneva; joined family business RPG Enterprises, became Dir-in-Charge Aryodaya Ginning Mills, Agarpara Jute Mills; Vice-Chair. Ceat Ltd; Chair. RPG Enterprises 1988–, RPG Life Science, KEC Int. Ltd, RPG Cables, etc.; Dir numerous cos. *Leisure interests:* sports, theatre. *Address:* RPG Enterprises Ltd, CEAT Mahal, 463 Dr. Annie Besant Road, Mumbai 400 025, India. *Telephone:* (22) 4930621 (Office); (22) 3630873 (Home). *Fax:* (22) 4938933 (Office). *E-mail:* hgoenka@rpgnet.com (Office).

GOERENS, Charles; Luxembourg politician; b. 6 Feb. 1952, Ettelbruck; m.; three c.; ed Lycée Technique Agricole; mem. Parl. for Parti Démocratique 1979; mem. European Parl. 1982–84; Pres. Ass. of EU 1987–90, 1999–; Parti Démocratique 1989–94; Minister for Co-operation, Humanitarian Action and Defence and for the Environment 1999–. *Address:* Ministry of Co-operation, Humanitarian Action and Defence, 5 rue Notre Dame, 2240 Luxembourg, Luxembourg (Office). *Telephone:* 478-1 (Office). *Fax:* 22-31-44 (Office).

GOETZ, Hannes, PhD; Swiss airline executive; b. 27 March 1934, Schaffhausen; m.; one s.; ed Fed. Inst. of Tech. Zürich; Sika AG, Zürich 1961–62; Sika USA 1962–66; Sika Int. 1966–71; CEO Sika Finance AG 1971–79; mem. Bd and Pres. Sika Finanz AG 1979–83, Georg Fischer AG, Schaffhausen 1981–83; mem. Bd and CEO Georg Fischer AG 1983–92; Chair. Bd SAirGroup 1992–. *Address:* SAirGroup, P.O. Box, CH-8058 Zürich-Airport, Zurich, Switzerland. *Telephone:* (1) 8121212. *Fax:* (1) 8128046.

GOFF, Philip Bruce, MA, MP; New Zealand politician; b. 22 June 1953, Auckland; s. of Bruce Charles Goff and Elaine Loyola Goff; m. Mary Ellen Moriarty 1979; two s. one d.; ed Papatoetoe High School; Lecturer in Political Science at Auckland Univ.; field officer in Insurance Workers' Union; fmr Chair. Labour Youth Council; MP for Roskill 1981–90, 1993–96; MP for New Lynn 1996–99, for Mt. Roskill 1999–; Minister of Housing, for the Environment, responsible for Government Life Insurance Corpn, in charge of the Public Trust Office 1986–87, of Employment, of Youth Affairs and Assoc. Minister of Educ. 1987–89, Minister of Tourism 1987–88, of Educ. 1989–90, of Foreign Affairs and Trade and of Justice 1999–; British Council Scholarship to Nuffield Coll. 1992; Labour. *Leisure interests:* sports, gardening, squash. *Address:* Ministry of Foreign Affairs and Trade, Private Bag 18901, Wellington (Office); Creightons Road RD 2, Papakura, Auckland, New Zealand (Home). *Telephone:* (4) 494-8500 (Office); (9) 292-8377 (Home). *Fax:* (4) 472-9596 (Office). *E-mail:* enquiries@mfat.govt.nz (Office). *Website:* www.mfat.govt.nz (Office).

GOFF OF CHIEVELEY, Baron (Life Peer), cr. 1986, of Chieveley in the Royal County of Berkshire; Rt Hon Lord Goff of Chieveley; **Robert (Lionel Archibald) Goff,** Kt, PC, DCL, FBA; British lawyer; b. 12 Nov. 1926; s. of L. T. Goff; m. Sarah Cousins 1953; two s. (one deceased) two d.; ed Eton Coll., New Coll., Oxford; served in Scots Guards 1945–48 (commissioned 1945); called to the Bar, Inner Temple 1951; Bencher 1975; QC 1967; Fellow and Tutor, Lincoln Coll., Oxford 1951–55; in practice at the Bar 1956–75; a Recorder 1974–75; Judge of the High Court, Queen's Bench Div. 1975–82; Judge in charge of Commercial List and Chair. Commercial Court Cttee 1979–81; Chair. Council of Legal Educ. 1976–82, Vice-Chair. 1972–76, Chair. Bd of Studies 1970–76; Chair. Common Professional Examination Bd 1976–78; Chair. British Inst. of Int. and Comparative Law 1986–2001, Court of Univ. of London 1986–91, Sub-Cttee E (Law) of House of Lords Select Cttee on European Communities 1986–88; Chair. Pegasus Scholarship Trust 1987–2001; Pres. Bentham Club 1986, Chartered Inst. of Arbitrators 1986–91, Holdsworth Club 1988, British Inst. of Int. and Comparative Law 2001–; Hon. Prof. of Legal Ethics, Univ. of Birmingham 1980–81; Maccabean Lecturer 1983; Lionel Cohen Lecturer (Jerusalem) 1987; Cassel Lecturer (Stockholm) 1993; mem. Gen. Council of the Bar 1971–74; mem. Senate of Inns of Court and Bar 1974–82; Chair. Law Reform and Procedure Cttee 1974–76; Lord Justice of Appeal 1982–86; Lord of Appeal in Ordinary 1986–98; Sr Law Lord 1996–98; High Steward Oxford Univ. 1990–2001; Hon. Fellow, Lincoln Coll., Oxford, New Coll., Oxford, Wolfson Coll., Oxford; Hon. Fellow, American Coll. of Trial Lawyers 1997; Hon. DLitt (City) 1977, (Buckingham) 1989; Hon. LLD (Reading, London) 1990, (Bristol) 1996; Grand Cross, Order of Merit (Germany) 1999. *Publication:* The Law of Restitution (with Prof. Gareth Jones) 1966. *Address:* House of Lords, Westminster, London, SW1A 0PW, England.

GOGOBERIDZE, Lana, DLitt; Georgian politician, film director and translator; b. 13 Oct. 1928, Tbilisi; d. of Levan Gogoberidze and Ninio Gogoberidze; m. Lado Aleksi-Meskhishvili 1958 (died 1978); two d.; ed Tbilisi State Univ., State Univ. of Cinematography (VGIK), Moscow; mem. CPSU 1965–89; Dir of studio at Rustaveli Theatre School 1975–; Dir Kartuli Filmi (Georgian Film) 1988–; Chair. Liberal Democratic Faction 1992–95; mem. Georgian Parl. 1994–, Leader of Majority 1995–, Head, Georgia–France Friendship Group 1997–; mem. Citizens' Union party 1997–; Head, Perm. Nat. Del. to Council of Europe 1997–; Pres. Int. Asscn of Women Film-Makers; mem. Bd of Union of Georgian Film-Makers; San Remo Film Festival Prize (Grand Prix) 1979, USSR State Prize 1980, Tokyo Film Festival Prize (Best Dir) 1986, Venice Film Festival Prize 1992, Berlin Film Festival Prize 1993; People's Artist of Georgian SSR 1979, Culture Diploma of Honor, American Biographical Inst. 1995, Ordre Nat. du Mérite (France) 1997. *Films include:* documentary: Gelathi 1957, Tbilisi – 1500 1958, Letters to the Children 1981; fiction: Under the Same Sky 1961, I See the Sun 1965, Boundaries 1970, When the Almond Blossomed 1973, Turmoil 1974, Interviews on Personal Problems 1979, A Day Longer than Night 1985, Turnover 1986, Waltz on the Pechora River 1986 (five prizes). *Publications:* Walt Whitman 1955, Walt Whitman: Leaves of Grass (trans.) 1956, Rabindranath Tagore (trans.) 1957, Foreign Poetry in Georgian (trans.) 1995. *Leisure interests:* tennis, skiing, painting. *Address:* Parliament of Georgia, Rustaveli Avenue 8, Tbilisi (Office); Kazbegi Str. 17, Apt. 26, Tbilisi, Georgia (Home). *Telephone:* (32) 93-19-92 (Office); (32) 22-76-79 (Home). *Fax:* (32) 99-58-53 (Office).

GOH, Kun, MS; South Korean politician; b. 2 Jan. 1938, Seoul; m.; three s.; ed Kyung Ki High School, Seoul Nat. Univ.; Pres. Gen. Students' Council, Seoul Nat. Univ. 1959; Asst Jr Official Ministry of Home Affairs 1962–65, Asst Dir Planning Office 1965–68; Dir Interior Dept Jeonbuk Prov. 1968–71; Commr New Village Movt 1971–73; Vice-Gov. Gangwon Prov. 1973; Gov. of S Jeolla Prov. 1975–79; Chief Sec. of Political Affairs to the Pres., Chong Wa Dae (The Blue House) 1979–80; Chief Adviser Korea Research Inst. for Human Settlement 1980; Minister of Transportation 1980–81, of Agric. and Marine Affairs 1981–82; Visiting Fellow, Harvard Univ. 1983; Visiting Prof. MIT 1984; mem. 12th Nat. Ass. 1985–88; Minister of Home Affairs 1987; Dir Local Admin. Bureau 1973–75; Mayor Seoul Metropolitan Govt 1988–90; Pres. Myong Ji Univ. 1994–97; Co-Pres. Korea Fed. for Environment Movt 1996–97; Prime Minister of the Republic of Korea 1997–98, 2003–; Mayor of Seoul 1998–2002; Pres. Transparency Int. Korea 2002–; Hon. LLD (Won Kwang Univ.) 1992, (Syracuse Univ.) 2001; Order of Service Merit (Blue Stripes) 1972, (Red Stripes) 1982; Outstanding Policy-Maker Award, Korea Univ. 2000, Transparency Int. Global Integrity Medal 2001, Polestar Order from the Mongolian Pres. 2002. *Address:* Office of the Prime Minister, 77 Sejong-no, Jongno-gu, Seoul, Republic of Korea. *Telephone:* (2) 737-0094. *Fax:* (2) 739-5830. *E-mail:* m_opm@opm.go.kr. *Website:* www.opm.go.kr.

GOH CHOK TONG, MA; Singaporean politician; b. 20 May 1941, Singapore; s. of Goh Kah Khoon (deceased) and Quah Kwee Hwa; m. Tan Choo Leng 1965; one s. one d. (twins); ed Raffles Inst., Univ. of Singapore and Williams Coll.,

USA; with Singapore Admin. Service 1964–69, Neptune Orient Lines Ltd 1969–77; MP 1976–; First Org. Sec. Peoples' Action Party 1979, Second Asst Sec.-Gen. 1979–84, Asst Sec.-Gen. 1984–89, First Asst Sec.-Gen. 1989–92, Sec.-Gen. 1992; Sr Minister of State, Ministry of Finance 1977–79, Minister for Trade and Industry 1979–81, Minister for Health and Second Minister for Defence 1981–82, Minister for Defence and Deputy Minister for Health 1982–85; First Deputy Prime Minister and Minister for Defence 1985–90; Prime Minister of Singapore 1990–; Chair. Singapore Labour Foundation, Bd of Dirs. Nat. Trades Union Congress (NTUC) Fairprice and NTUC Income; mem. Econs Soc., Singapore; Medal of Honour, NTUC Congress 1987. *Leisure interests:* tennis, golf. *Address:* Prime Minister's Office, Orchard Road, Istana Annexe, Istana, Singapore 238823 (Office). *Telephone:* 2358577 (Office). *Fax:* 7324627 (Office). *E-mail:* goh-chok-tong@pmo.gov.sg (Office). *Website:* www .pmo.gov.sg (Office).

GOH KENG SWEE, PhD; Singaporean politician; b. 6 Oct. 1918, Malacca; s. of Goh Leng Inn and Tan Swee; m. Alice Woon 1942; one s.; ed Anglo-Chinese School, Singapore and Raffles Coll., London Univ; fmrly Vice-Chair. People's Action Party; fmr mem. Legis. Assembly from Kreta Ayer Div. and Minister for Finance 1959–65; initiated Singapore's industrialization plan, the establishment of Econ. Devt Board; Minister of Defence 1965–67, of Finance 1967–70, of Educ. 1979–81, 1981–84, of Defence 1970–79, concurrently Deputy Prime Minister 1973–80, First Deputy Prime Minister 1980–84 and with responsibility for the Monetary Authority of Singapore 1980–81 (Deputy Chair. –1992); Econ. Adviser to Chinese Govt July 1985–; mem. Governing Council, Asian Inst. for Econ. Devt and Planning, Bangkok 1963–66; Ramon Magsaysay Award for Govt Service 1972. *Publications:* Urban Incomes and Housing; a Report on the Social Survey of Singapore, 1953–54 1958, Economics of Modernization and Other Essays 1972, The Practice of Economic Growth 1977. *Address:* Parliament House, 1 Parliament Place, Singapore 178880 (Office). *E-mail:* www.gov.sg/parliament (Office).

GOHEEN, Robert Francis, PhD; American diplomat, educator and public servant; b. 15 Aug. 1919, Vengurla, India; s. of Robert H. H. and Anne (Ewing) Goheen; m. Margaret M. Skelly 1941; two s. four d.; ed Lawrenceville School and Princeton Univ.; service in US Army 1941–45, rank of Lt. Col 1945; Instructor, Princeton Univ. 1948–50, Asst Prof. 1950–57, Prof. 1957–72, Pres. 1957–72, Pres. Emer. 1972–; Senior Fellow in Classics, American Acad. in Rome 1952–53; Dir Nat. Woodrow Wilson Fellowship Programme 1953–56; Sr Fellow Woodrow Wilson School of Public and Int. Affairs 1981–; Amb. to India 1977–80; Dir Mellon Fellowships in the Humanities 1982–92; mem. Bd Bharatiya Vidya Bhavan (USA), Village Charter School, Advisory Bd Center for Advanced Study of India, Univ. of Pa, American Acad. of Diplomacy, American Acad. of Arts and Sciences, Asscn of Asian Studies, Council of American Ambs., Council on Foreign Affairs, Council on Foundations; Emer. Trustee Nat. Humanities Center, Advisory Bd Nat. Foreign Language Center, NJ Scholars Program, Woodrow Wilson Nat. Fellowship Foundation; Hon. LLD, LittD, L.C.D., LHD, degrees from 26 univs. and colls. including Harvard, Yale, Madras, North Carolina, Notre Dame; Combat Infantry Badge, Bronze Star, Legion of Merit. *Publications:* The Imagery of Sophocles' Antigone 1951, The Human Nature of a University 1969; various articles on educational and diplomatic subjects. *Leisure interests:* golf, reading, fishing, gardening. *Address:* 1 Orchard Circle, Princeton, NJ 08540, USA. *Telephone:* (609) 924-2751.

GOIRIGOLZARRI, José Ignacio; Spanish banker and business executive; b. 1955; fmrly with the BBC; Dir-Gen. for Retail Banking in Spain and Latin America, Banco Bilbao Vizcaya Argentaria (BBVA) SA –2001, CEO 2001–. *Address:* Banco Bilbao Vizcaya Argentaria (BBVA) SA, Paseo de la Castellana 81, 28046 Madrid, Spain (Office). *Telephone:* (91) 3746000 (Office). *Fax:* (91) 3746202 (Office). *Website:* www.bbva.es (Office).

GOLAN, Menahem; Israeli film director and producer; b. 31 May 1929, Tiberius; ed Old Victoria, London; f. Noah Films with Yoram Globus (q.v.) 1963; Sr Vice-Pres. Cannon Group Inc. 1979–89; f. and Chair., CEO 21st Century Production Corpn Feb. 1989–. *Films include:* Over the Top, Delta Force, Over the Brooklyn Bridge, Enter the Ninja, The Magician of Lublin, Barfly, Surrender, Death Wish IV, Superman IV, Street Smart, Dancers, 52 Pickup, Otello, The Assault, Hanoi Hilton, Cannon Movie Tales, Masters of the Universe, Duet for One, Tough Guys Don't Dance, Shy People, Hanna's War, The Rose Garden, Rope Dancing, The Phantom of the Opera, Armstrong; all have Golan and Globus as exec. producers.

GOLANI, Rivka; Canadian viola soloist and painter; b. 22 March 1946, Israel; d. of Jacob and Lisa Gulnik; m. Jeremy Fox 1993; one s.; ed Univ. of Tel-Aviv; studied with Oedon Partos; concerts as soloist worldwide; has inspired many new works including viola concerti by Holloway, Hummel, Fontajn, Colgrass, Holmboe, Yuasa and Turner, solo works by Holliger, Holmboe and others; has collaborated with composers as a visual artist in presenting multimedia performances; art exhbns. in Israel, Britain, Germany and N America; Grand Prix du Disque 1985. *Recordings include:* 3 CD set of solo works by J. S. Bach (CBC Rcords). *Publication:* Birds of Another Feather (book of drawings). *Address:* c/o Margaret Barkman, 54 Long Point Drive, Richmond Hill, Ont., L4E 3W8, Canada. *Telephone:* (416) 722-6977. *Fax:* (905) 773-6261. *E-mail:* mbarkman@compuserve.com. *Website:* members.rogers .com/aaionline.

GOLANT, Victor Yevgenyevich, DR. PHYS.-MATH. SC.; Russian physicist; b. 14 Jan. 1928; m.; one s. two d.; ed Leningrad Polytech Inst.; engineer, head of lab. factories in Leningrad; Sr Researcher, Head of Lab, Head of Div. Inst. of Physics and Eng; Prof., Head of Chair Leningrad Tech. Univ.; Dir Ioffe Inst. of Physics and Tech.; Corresp. mem. USSR (now Russian) Acad of Sciences 1984, mem. 1990–; research in physics of plasma and thermonuclear synthesis; USSR State Prize 1991. *Publications include:* Fundamentals of Plasma Physics 1977, Super High-Frequency Method of Plasma Diagnostics 1985. *Address:* Ioffe Institute of Physics and Technology, Polytekhnicheskaya 26, St Petersburg 194021, Russia (Office). *Telephone:* (812) 247-41-50, ext. 52 (Office); 552-59-08 (Home).

GÖLCÜKLÜ, Ahmet Feyyaz; Turkish judge and academic; b. 4 Oct. 1926, Ula; s. of Zeki and Ruhiye Gölcüklü; m. (divorced 1977); two s.; ed Univs of Istanbul and Neuchâtel; Asst Prof. Faculty of Political Sciences, Univ. of Ankara 1954–, Assoc. Prof. 1958–, Prof. 1965–, Dir School of Journalism and Broadcasting 1969–72, Dean, Faculty of Political Sciences 1973–76, now Prof. Emer.; Judge, European Court of Human Rights 1977–98; mem. Turkish Consultative Ass. (Constituent Ass.) 1981–82; Dir of Human Rights Research and Implementation Centre, Ankara Univ. 1988–. *Publications:* Examination of the Accused Person in Penal Matters 1952, Personal Liberty of the Accused in Criminal Procedure 1958, Research on Juvenile Delinquency in Turkey 1963, The Turkish Penal System 1965, Mass Communication Law 1973, The European Convention on Human Rights and its Implementation 1994. *Address:* University of Ankara, Tandoğan, 06100 Ankara, Turkey.

GOLD, Jack, B.SC.(Econs), LLB; British film director; b. 28 June 1930; m. Denyse Macpherson 1957; two s. one d.; ed London Univ.; Asst Studio Man., BBC radio 1954–55; Ed. Film Dept, BBC 1955–60; Dir TV and film documentaries and fiction 1960–. *TV films include:* Tonight, Death in the Morning (British Acad. of Film and TV Arts Award) 1964, Modern Millionairess, Famine, Dowager in Hot Pants, World of Coppard (BAFTA Award 1967), Mad Jack (Grand Prix, Monte Carlo) 1971, The Resistible Rise of Arturo Ui, Stockers Copper (BAFTA Award 1972), Catholics (Peabody Award) 1974, The Naked Civil Servant (Italia Prize, Int. Emmy, Critics Award, Desmond Davies Award 1976), 1976, Thank You Comrades, A Walk in the Forest, Merchant of Venice, Praying Mantis, Macbeth, L'Elégance 1982, The Red Monarch 1983, The Tenth Man 1988, The Rose and the Jackal 1989, Ball Trap on Côte Sauvage 1989, The Shlemiel, The Shlemazi and The Doppess 1990, The War that Never Ends 1991, She Stood Alone 1991, The Last Romantics 1992, Spring Awakening 1995, Kavanagh QC 1995, Heavy Weather 1996, Mute of Malice 1997, Blood Money 1997, Into the Blue 1997, Care in the Community 1998, Goodnight Mr. Tom 1998 (Silver Hugo Award, Chicago 1998, BAFTA Award 1999), The Remorseful Day 2001 (BAFTA Award 2001), Kavanagh QC 2001, The John Thaw Story 2002. *Theatre:* Council of Love, The Devil's Disciple, Danger Memory, This Story of Yours, Three Hotels. *Films include:* The Bofors Gun 1968, The National Health (Evening News Best Comedy Film 1973) 1973, Who? 1974, Aces High (Evening News Best Film Award) 1976, The Medusa Touch 1977, The Sailor's Return (Monte Carlo Catholic Award, Monte Carlo Critics Award) 1978, Little Lord Fauntleroy (Christopher Award) 1981, A Lot of Happiness (Int. Emmy Award) 1983, Sakharov (Ace Award) 1984, Me and the Girls 1985, Murrow (Ace Award) 1986, Escape from Sobibor, (Golden Globe Award) 1987, Stones for Ibarra 1988, The Lucona Affair 1993, Return of the Native 1994, Spring Awakening 1994. *Leisure interests:* music, reading. *Address:* 24 Wood Vale, London, N10 3DP, England. *Telephone:* (20) 8883-3491. *Fax:* (20) 8444-3406.

GOLD, Phil, CC, OQ, M.D.C.M., PhD, F.R.C.P.(C), M.A.C.P.; Canadian professor of medicine; b. 17 Sept. 1936, Montreal; m. Evelyn Katz; three c.; ed McGill Univ.; postgraduate training and research, The McGill Univ. Medical Clinic of The Montreal Gen. Hosp.; Medical Research Council of Canada Centennial Fellow 1967–68, Assoc. and Career Scientist 1969–80; Lecturer, Teaching Fellow, Asst and Assoc. Prof., Dept of Physiology and Dept of Medicine, McGill Univ. 1965–73, Prof. of Medicine and Clinical Medicine, 1973–, of Physiology 1974–, of Oncology 1989–; Chair. Dept of Medicine 1985–90, Douglas G. Cameron Prof. of Medicine 1987–; Dir McGill Cancer Centre 1978–80; Dir McGill Univ. Medical Clinic (now Centre), The Montreal Gen. Hosp. 1980–, Exec. Dir Clinical Research Centre 1995–; Sr Physician, The Montreal Gen. Hosp. 1973–, Physician-in-Chief 1980–95, Sr Investigator Hosp. Research Inst.; Hon. Consultant, Royal Victoria Hosp., Montreal 1981–; mem. numerous professional socs., scientific research bds. and orgs. etc.; numerous honours and awards including Sir Arthur Sims Commonwealth Travelling Professorship 1998, Carl Govesky Memorial Award 1999, 20th Anniversary of L'Actualité Medicale Award for Outstanding Contrib. to Medicine 2000, Montreal General Hospital Corpn Merit Award 2002, Queen Elizabeth II Golden Jubilee Medal 2002. *Publications:* 146 articles in professional journals (1988). *Leisure interests:* photography, sailing, cinema, music, literature. *Address:* Clinical Research Center, Montreal General Hospital, 1650 Cedar Avenue, Montreal, Que. H3G 1A4, Canada (Office). *E-mail:* phil.gold@mcgill .ca (Office).

GOLD, Thomas, FRS, ScD; American astronomer; b. 22 May 1920, Vienna, Austria; s. of Max Gold and Josefine Gold; m. 1st Merle Eleanor Tuberg 1947; m. 2nd Carvel Lee Beyer 1972; four d.; ed Zuoz Coll., Switzerland and Trinity Coll., Cambridge; Experimental Officer, British Admiralty (radar research) 1943–46; Fellow, Trinity Coll., Cambridge 1947; Chief Asst to Astronomer Royal, Royal Greenwich Observatory 1952–56; Prof. of Astronomy, Harvard Univ. 1957–59; Prof. of Astronomy, Cornell Univ. 1960–86, Prof. Emer. 1987–; Dir Cornell Univ. Center for Radiophysics and Space Research 1959–81; Fellow, Royal Soc., London; mem. NAS, American Philosophical Soc.; Fellow

American Acad. of Arts and Sciences; Hon. Fellow, Trinity Coll. Cambridge 1986–; Gold Medal, Royal Astronomical Soc. 1985. *Publications:* Hearing II: the Physical Basis of the Action of the Cochlea 1948, The Steady State Theory of the Expanding Universe 1948, The Alignment of Galactic Dust 1952, The Field of a Uniformly Accelerated Charge 1954, Instability of the Earth's Axis of Rotation 1955, The Lunar Surface 1956, Cosmic Rays from the Sun 1957, Plasma and Magnetic Fields in the Solar System 1959, The Origin of Solar Flares 1960, The Nature of Time 1967, Rotating Neutron Stars as the Origin of the Pulsating Radio Source 1968, Rotating Neutron Stars and the Nature of Pulsars 1969, Apollo 12 Seismic Signal: Indication of a Deep Layer of Powder 1970, Terrestrial Sources of Carbon and Earthquake Outgassing 1978, Power from the Earth 1987, The Deep, Hot Biosphere 1992, The Origin of Methane in the Crust of the Earth 1993, The Deep, Hot Biosphere 1999. *Leisure interests:* skiing, water skiing. *Address:* 7 Pleasant Grove Lane, Ithaca, NY 14850, USA. *Telephone:* (607) 257-6696. *E-mail:* tg21@cornell.edu (Home). *Website:* www.people.cornell.edu/pages/tg21 (Home).

GOLDBERG, Sir Abraham, Kt, MD, DSc, FRCP, FRSE, FFPHM; British professor of medicine (retd); b. 7 Dec. 1923, Edinburgh; s. of the late Julius Goldberg and Rachel Goldberg; m. Clarice Cussin 1957; two s. one d.; ed George Heriots School, Edinburgh and Univs of Edinburgh and Glasgow; Nuffield Research Fellow, Univ. Coll. Hosp., London 1952–54; Eli Lilly Travelling Fellow in Medicine, Univ. of Utah 1954–56; Regius Prof. of Materia Medica, Univ. of Glasgow 1970–78, Regius Prof. of Practice of Medicine 1978–89; Chair. Cttee on Safety of Medicines 1980–86; mem. other medical research cttees. etc.; Founder Pres. of Faculty of Pharmaceutical Medicine of Royal Colls. of Physicians (UK) 1989–91; Hon. Professorial Research Fellow Dept of Modern History, Univ. of Glasgow; Sydney Watson Smith Lectureship, Royal Coll. of Physicians (Edinburgh) 1964; Henry Cohen Lectureship, Hebrew Univ. 1973; Fitzpatrick Lecture, Royal Coll. of Physicians (London) 1988, Archbishop Goodall Lecturer, Royal Coll. of Physicians and Surgeons (Glasgow) 1989; Alex Fleck Award (Univ. of Glasgow) 1967; City of Glasgow Lord Provost's Award for Public Service 1988; Fellow, Faculty of Pharmaceutical Medicine. *Publications:* Diseases of Porphyrin Metabolism (jtly) 1962, Recent Advances in Haematology (jt ed.) 1971, Clinics in Haematology 'The Porphyrias' (jtly) 1980, Disorders of Porphyrin Metabolism (jtly) 1987, Pharmaceutical Medicine and the Law (jt ed.) 1991. *Leisure interests:* medical history, literature, writing, walking, swimming. *Address:* 16 Birnam Crescent, Bearsden, Glasgow, G61 2AU, Scotland (Home).

GOLDBERG, Whoopi; American actress; b. Caryn Johnson, 13 Nov. 1955; d. of Robert Johnson and Emma Harris; m. 2nd Dave Claessen 1986 (divorced 1988); one d.; m. 3rd Lyle Trachtenberg 1994 (divorced 1995); first stage appearance, aged 8, Hudson Guild Theater, New York; worked with Helena Rubinstein Children's Theater; moved to San Diego 1974; co-f. San Diego Repertory Theater, appeared in Mother Courage (Brecht) and Getting Out (Marsha Norman); moved to San Francisco, became mem. Blake St Hawkeyes Theater; toured USA in The Spook Show; co-wrote and appeared in Moms (one-woman show); Broadway debut, Lyceum Theater 1984; TV appearances in comedy series Moonlighting 1985–86, own TV show 1992–93; Grammy Award for Best Comedy Album 1985, Hans Christian Andersen Award for Outstanding Achievement by a Dyslexic, Mark Twain Prize for Humor, Kennedy Centre of Arts 2001. *Films:* The Color Purple (Acad. Award nomination as Best Actress, Image Award from NAACP, Golden Globe Award, Hollywood Foreign Press Asscn), Sarah's Heart, Jumpin' Jack Flash, Burglar, The Telephone, Fatal Beauty, Ghost 1990, Sarafina 1992, Sister Act, Made in America 1992, Alice 1993, Sister Act II 1993, Corrina Corrina 1993, Boys on the Side 1994, Star Trek Generation 5, Moonlight and Valentino, Bogus, Eddie, The Associate 1996, The Ghost of Mississippi 1996, How Stella Got Her Groove Back 1998, Deep End of the Ocean 1999, Jackie's Back! 1999, Girl Interrupted 1999, Rat Race 2001, Call Me Claus 2001, Kingdom Come 2001, Monkeybone 2001, Golden Dreams 2001, Star Trek: Nemesis 2002, Blizzard (voice) 2002.

GOLDBERGER, Marvin Leonard, PhD; American professor of physics; b. 22 Oct. 1922, Chicago, Ill.; s. of Joseph and Mildred Sedwitz Goldberger; m. Mildred C. Ginsburg 1945; two s.; ed Carnegie Inst. of Technology and Univ. of Chicago; Research Assoc. Radiation Lab., Univ. of Calif. (Berkeley) 1948–49; MIT 1949–50; Asst Prof., Prof., Univ. of Chicago 1950–57; Eugene Higgins Prof. of Physics, Princeton Univ. 1957–77, Chair. Physics Dept 1970–76, Joseph Henry Prof. of Physics 1977–78; Pres. Calif. Inst. of Tech. 1978–87; Dir Inst. for Advanced Study 1987–91; Prof. of Physics, Univ. of Calif., LA 1991–93, Univ. of Calif., San Diego 1993–2000, Prof. Emer. 2000– (Dean Div. of Natural Sciences 1994–2000); Chair. Fed. of American Scientists 1971–72; mem. NAS, American Acad. of Arts and Sciences; Hon. ScD (Carnegie-Mellon Univ. 1979, Univ. of Notre Dame 1979, Brandeis Univ. 1991); Hon. LLD (Occidental Coll. 1980); Hon. DHL (Hebrew Union Coll. 1980, Univ. of Judaism 1982); Dannie Heineman Prize for Mathematical Physics 1961. *Publication:* Collision Theory (with K. M. Watson) 1964. *Leisure interests:* running, tennis, cooking. *E-mail:* mgoldberger@ucsd.edu (Office).

GOLDBLUM, Jeff; American actor; b. 22 Oct. 1952, Pittsburgh; m. 1st Patricia Gaul (divorced); m. 2nd Geena Davis (q.v.) (divorced); studied at New York Neighborhood Playhouse. *Films include:* California Split 1974, Death Wish 1974, Nashville 1975, Next Stop Greenwich Village 1976, Annie Hall 1977, Between the Lines 1977, The Sentinel 1977, Invasion of the Bodysnatchers 1978, Remember My Name 1978, Thank God it's Friday 1978, Escape from Athena 1979, The Big Chill 1983, The Right Stuff 1983,

Threshold 1983, The Adventures of Buckaroo Banzai 1984, Silverado 1985, Into the Night 1985, Transylvania 6-5000 1985, The Fly 1986, Beyond Therapy 1987, The Tall Guy 1989, Earth Girls are Easy 1989, First Born (TV) 1989, The Mad Monkey 1990, Mister Frost 1991, Deep Cover 1992, The Favour, the Watch and the Very Big Fish 1992, Father and Sons 1993, Jurassic Park 1993, Lushlife (TV) 1994, Future Quest (TV) 1994, Hideaway 1995, Nine Months 1995, Independence Day 1996, The Lost World 1997, Holy Man 1998, Popcorn 1999, Chain of Fools 2000, Angie Rose 2000, Cats and Dogs 2001; producer Little Surprises 1995, Holy Man 1999. *Address:* c/o Peter Lemie, William Morris Agency, 151 El Camino Drive, Beverly Hills, CA 90212, USA.

GOLDENBERG SCHREIBER, Efrain; Peruvian politician, businessman and lawyer; b. 28 Dec. 1929, Lima; s. of Aron Goldenberg and Charna Schreiber; m. Irene Pravatiner 1952; one s. four d.; ed San Andrés (fmrly Anglo-Peruvian) School, Universidad Nacional Mayor de San Marcos; pvt. entrepreneur 1951–; fmr Dir FOPEX, Sociedad Nacional de Pesquería and other cos.; Minister of Foreign Affairs 1993–94, Pres. Council of Ministers (Prime Minister) and Minister of Foreign Affairs 1994–95; work in pvt. sector 1995–99; Minister of Econ. and Finance 1999–2000. *Address:* Av. Javier Prado Oeste 1661, Lima 27, Peru. *Telephone:* (1) 421-2264. *Fax:* (1) 221-6458.

GOLDHABER, Maurice, PhD, FAAS; American physicist; b. 18 April 1911, Lemberg, Austria; s. of Charles Goldhaber and Ethel Frisch Goldhaber; m. Gertrude Scharff 1939 (died 1998); two s.; ed Berlin Univ. and Cambridge Univ., UK; Prof. of Physics, Univ. of Ill. 1938–50; Sr Scientist, Brookhaven Nat. Lab. 1950–60, Chair. Dept of Physics 1960–61, Dir 1961–73, Distinguished Scientist Emer. 1973–; Adjunct Prof. of Physics, State Univ. New York 1965–; mem. NAS, American Philosophical Soc.; Fellow American Acad. of Arts and Sciences; Rabi Scholar Lecturer 1995; Hon. PhD (Tel-Aviv) 1974; Dr hc (Univ. of Louvain-La-Neuve) 1982; Tom W. Bonner Prize in Nuclear Physics of American Physical Soc. 1971, US Atomic Energy Comm. Citation for Meritorious Contribs 1973, J. Robert Oppenheimer Memorial Prize 1982, Wolf Foundation Prize 1991. *Publications:* numerous articles in professional scientific journals on neutron physics, radioactivity, nuclear isomers, nuclear photo-electric effect, nuclear models, fundamental particles. *Leisure interests:* tennis, hiking. *Address:* Brookhaven National Laboratory Building, 510 Upton, NY 11973, USA.

GOLDIN, Daniel S., BSc; American space research administrative official; b. 23 July 1940, New York; m. Judith Kramer; two d.; ed City Coll. of New York; research scientist, NASA Lewis Research Center, Cleveland 1962–67; joined TRW Space & Tech. Group, Redondo, Calif. 1967, Vice-Pres. and Gen. Man. until 1992; Admin., NASA 1992–2001; Sr. Fellow Council on Competitiveness 2001–; numerous awards. *Address:* Council on Competitiveness, 1500 K Street, N.W., Suite 850, Washington, DC 20005, USA. *Website:* www.compete .org.

GOLDMAN, John Michael, DM, FRCP, F.R.C.PATH.; British physician; b. 30 Nov. 1938, London; s. of Carl Heinz Goldman and Bertha (née Brandt) Goldman; m. Jeannine Fuller 1967; one s. two d.; ed Westminster School, Magdalen Coll., Oxford, St Bartholomew's Hosp., London; MRC perm. mem. of staff Leukaemia Unit, Hammersmith Hosp., 1976–93, Dir Leukaemia Research Fund Unit 1988–; Prof. of Leukaemia Biology Royal Postgrad. Medical School (later Imperial Coll. Medical School), London 1987–, Chair. Dept of Haematology 1994–; Pres. European Haematology Asscn 1996–98, British Soc. for Blood and Marrow Transplantation 1996–98; fmr Pres. Int. Soc. for Experimental Hematology 1983, European Group for Bone Marrow Transplantation 1990–94; Sec. World Marrow Donor Asscn; Medical Dir Anthony Nolan Bone Marrow Trust 1988–; Hon. MD (Louvain, Poitiers). *Publications:* books, chapters and papers on leukaemia, oncogenes, bone marrow transplantation. *Leisure interests:* reading, riding, skiing. *Address:* Department of Haematology, Hammersmith Hospital/Imperial College Faculty of Medicine, Du Cane Road, London, W12 0NN; 33 Northumberland Place, London, W2 5AS, England. *Telephone:* (20) 8383-3238. *Fax:* (20) 8749-2748. *E-mail:* jgoldman@imperial.ac.uk (Office).

GOLDMAN, Sir Samuel, KCB; British civil servant and fmr banker; b. 10 March 1912, London; s. of late Philip and Sarah Goldman; m. Patricia Rosemary Hodges 1943 (died 1990); one s.; ed Davenant Foundation School, Raines Foundation School and London School of Econs; Moody's Economist Services 1934–38; Sebag and Co. 1938–39; Bank of England 1940–47; joined Civil Service as statistician, Central Statistical Office 1947, transferred to Treasury 1947, Chief Statistician 1948, Asst Sec. 1952, Under-Sec. 1960, Third Sec. 1962; Second Perm. Sec., Treasury 1968–72; fmr Man. Dir Orion Bank Ltd; fmr Chair. Henry Ansbacher Holdings Ltd; fmr Chair. Covent Garden Market Authority. *Leisure interests:* gardening, music. *Address:* 3 Little Tangley, Wonersh, Guildford, Surrey, GU5 0PW, England. *Telephone:* (1483) 568913.

GOLDMAN, William, MA; American author; b. 12 Aug. 1931, Chicago, Ill.; s. of M. Clarence Goldman and Marion Weil; m. Ilene Jones 1961; two d.; ed Oberlin Coll. and Columbia Univ.; Acad. Award for best original screenplay for Butch Cassidy and the Sundance Kid 1970, Acad. Award for best screenplay adaptation 1977, Laurel Award for Lifetime Achievement in Screenwriting 1983. *Publications:* novels: The Temple of Gold 1957, Your Turn to Curtsy, My Turn to Bow 1958, Soldier in the Rain 1960, Boys and Girls Together 1964, The Thing of It Is 1967, No Way to Treat a Lady (under pseudonym Harry Longbaugh), Father's Day 1971, The Princess Bride 1973,

Marathon Man 1974, Wigger 1974, Magic 1976, Tinsel 1979, Control 1982, The Silent Gondoliers 1983, The Color of Light 1984; play: Blood, Sweat and Stanley Poole 1961 (with James Goldman); musical comedy: A Family Affair (with James Goldman and John Kander) 1962; non-fiction: Adventures in the Screen Trade 1983, Hype and Glory 1990; Four Screenplays 1995, Five Screenplays 1997, Which Lie Did I Tell? 2000; screenplays: Harper 1966, Butch Cassidy and the Sundance Kid 1969, The Princess Bride 1973, Marathon Man 1976, All the President's Men 1976, A Bridge Too Far 1977, Magic 1978, Heat 1985, Brothers 1987, Year of the Comet 1992, Memoirs of an Invisible Man 1992, Chaplin 1992, Indecent Proposal 1993, Maverick 1994, The Ghost and the Darkness 1996, Absolute Power 1997, Hearts in Atlantis 2001. *Address:* c/o William Morris, 151 El Camino Drive, Beverly Hills, CA 90212-1804, USA (Office).

GOLDMARK, Peter Carl, Jr, BA; American newspaper executive; b. 2 Dec. 1940, New York; s. of Peter Carl Goldmark and Frances Charlotte Trainer; m. Aliette Marie Misson 1964; three d.; ed Harvard Univ.; worked for US Office of Econ. Opportunity, Washington; fmr teacher of history Putney School, Vt; employed in Budget Office, City of New York for four years, later Asst Budget Dir Program Planning and Analysis then Exec. Asst to the Mayor 1971; Sec. Human Services, Commonwealth of Mass. 1972–75; Dir of Budget, NY State 1975–77; Exec. Dir Port Authority of NY and NJ 1977–85; joined Times Mirror Co., Los Angeles 1985, fmr Sr Vice-Pres. Eastern Newspapers Div.; Pres. Rockefeller Foundation 1988–97; Chair. and CEO Int. Herald Tribune 1998–2003; mem. Bd Dirs Financial Accounting Foundation, Lend Lease Corpn, Whitehead Inst. for Biomedical Research. *Address:* c/o International Herald Tribune, 6 bis rue des Graviers, 92521 Neuilly Cédex, France (Office).

GOLDREICH, Peter, PhD; American professor of planetary science and astronomy; b. 14 July 1939, New York; s. of Paul Goldreich and Edith Rosenfield Goldreich; m. Susan Kroll 1960; two s.; ed Cornell Univ; Post-Doctoral Fellow Cambridge Univ. 1963–64; Asst Prof. Astronomy and Physics, Univ. of Calif. (Los Angeles Campus) 1964–66, Assoc. Prof. 1966; Assoc. Prof. Planetary Science and Astronomy Calif. Inst. Tech. 1966–69, Prof. 1969–, Lee Du Bridge Prof. of Astrophysics and Planetary Physics 1981–; mem. NAS 1972–; Chapman Medal, Royal Astronomical Soc. 1985, Dirk Brouwer Award, American Astronomical Soc. 1986, Nat. Medal of Science 1995. *Publications:* on planetary dynamics, pulsar theory, radio emission from Jupiter, galactic stability and interstellar masers. *Leisure interest:* competitive athletics. *Address:* California Institute of Technology, 1200 East California Boulevard, Pasadena, CA 91125 (Office); 471 S. Catalina Avenue, Pasadena, CA 91106, USA (Home).

GOLDSCHMIDT, Neil Edward, AB, LLB; American politician and lawyer; b. 16 June 1940, Eugene, Ore.; s. of Lester H. and Annette G. Goldschmidt (née Levin); m. Margaret Wood 1965; one s. one d.; ed Univs of Oregon and California; Civil Rights Worker, Miss. 1964; Attorney with Legal Aid Service, Portland, Ore. 1967–70; City Commr, Portland 1971–72; Mayor of Portland 1973–79; US Sec. of Transportation 1979–81; Vice-Pres. Int. Marketing NIKE/BRS Inc., Beaverton, Ore. 1981–; Chair. Standing Cttee on Housing and Community Devt 1976–79, Ad Hoc Housing Task Force 1977–79, Energy Task Force of the Nat. League of Cities 1977–79; Trustee, US Conf. of Mayors 1978–79; Gov. of Oregon 1987–91; fmrly mem. Advisory Cttee on State and Local Govt Affairs, Harvard's John F. Kennedy School of Govt; mem. Bd of Kaiser Health and Hosp. Plan, Oakland, Calif. 1981–, Bd of Nat. Semi-conductor, Santa Clara, Calif., Bd of Gelco Corpn, Eden Prairie, Minn. *Leisure interests:* reading, swimming, all spectator sports.

GOLDSMITH, Harvey, CBE; British impresario; b. 4 March 1946, London; s. of Sydney Goldsmith and Minnie Goldsmith; m. Diana Goldsmith 1971; one s.; ed Christ's College and Brighton Coll. of Tech.; joined Big O Posters, Kensington Market 1966; organized open-air free concerts, Parl. Hill Fields 1968; in partnership with Michael Alfandary opened Round House, London 1968; organized 13 Garden Party concerts at Crystal Palace, London 1969; merged with John Smith Entertainment 1970–75; formed Harvey Goldsmith Entertainment promoting rock tours by Elton John, Rolling Stones etc.; in partnership with Ed Simons, rescued Hotel Television Network 1983; formed Allied Entertainment Group as public co. 1984–86, returned to pvt. ownership 1986; subsidiary Harvey Goldsmith Entertainment promotes some 250 concerts per year; formed Classical Productions with Mark McCormack, promoting shows at Earls Court including Pavarotti concert and lavish productions of Aida 1988, Carmen 1989, Tosca 1991; produced Bob Dylan Celebration, New York 1992, Mastercard Masters of Music (Hyde Park), The Eagles (Wembley), Three Tenors (Wembley), Lord of the Dance (world tour) 1996, Music for Montserrat (Royal Albert Hall), Boyzone (tour), Paul Weller (tour), Pavarotti (Manchester), Cirque du Soleil (Royal Albert Hall) 1997, Alegria (Royal Albert Hall), The Bee Gees (Wembley), Ozzfest (Milton Keynes Bowl), Paul Weller (Victoria Park) 1998; Chair. Nat. Music Day; Vice-Chair. Prince's Trust Bd; Vice-Pres. React 1989–; Trustee Gret, Band Aid 1985–, Live Aid Foundation 1985–; Dir Pres.'s Club, London First, London Tourist Bd; Amb. for London Judges Award 1997; mem. Advisory Group Red Cross. *Leisure interest:* golf. *Address:* Harvey Goldsmith Entertainments Ltd, Greenland Place, 115–123 Bayham Street, London, NW1 0AG, England. *Telephone:* (20) 7482-5522. *Fax:* (20) 7428-9252.

GOLDSMITH, Jerry, MUS.D.; American film music composer and conductor; b. 10 Feb. 1929, Los Angeles; m. Carol Sheinkopf; ed Los Angeles City Coll.,

Berklee Coll. of Music; studied with Jakob Gimpel, Mario Castelnuovo-Tedesco; guest conductor with many American and European symphony orchestras; Max Steiner Award, Nat. Film Soc. 1982, first annual Richard Kirk Award, BMI 1987, Golden Score Award, American Soc. of Music Arrangers 1990, Career Achievement Award, Soc. for Preservation of Film Music 1993, first American Music Legend Award, Variety 1995. *Radio scores:* Romance, Suspense, CBS Radio. *TV scores:* Twilight Zone, General Electric Theatre, Doctor Kildare, Gunsmoke, Climax, Playhouse 90, Studio One, Star Trek: Voyager (Emmy Award 1995). *Film scores include:* Black Patch 1956, Lonely Are The Brave 1961, Freud 1962, The Stripper 1962, Lilies of the Field 1963, The Prize 1963, Seven Days in May 1963, In Harm's Way 1964, The Man from UNCLE 1965, Von Ryan's Express 1965, A Patch of Blue 1965, The Blue Max 1965, Our Man Flint 1965, Seconds 1965, Stagecoach 1965, The Sand Pebbles 1966, In Like Flint 1967, Planet of the Apes 1968, The Ballad of Cable Hogue 1969, Tora! Tora! Tora! 1970, Patton 1970, Wild Rovers 1971, The Other 1972, The Red Pony (Emmy Award) 1972, Papillon 1973, QB VII (Emmy Award) 1974, Chinatown 1974, The Reincarnation of Peter Proud 1974, Logan's Run 1975, The Wind and the Lion 1976, The Omen (Acad. Award) 1976, Islands in the Stream 1976, MacArthur 1977, Coma 1977, The Boys from Brazil 1978, Damien – Omen II 1978, Alien 1979, Babe (Emmy Award), Masada (Emmy Award) 1981, Star Trek: The Motion Picture 1979, The Final Conflict 1981, Outland 1981, Raggedy Man 1981, Mrs Brisby: The Secret of NIMH 1982, Poltergeist (Edgar Allan Poe Award) 1982, First Blood 1982, Twilight Zone: The Movie 1983, Psycho II 1983, Under Fire 1983, Gremlins (Saturn Award) 1984, Legend (European version) 1985, Explorers 1985, Rambo: First Blood II 1985, Poltergeist II: The Other Side 1986, Hoosiers 1986, Innerspace 1987, Extreme Prejudice 1987, Rambo III 1988, Criminal Law 1989, The 'Burbs 1989, Leviathan 1989, Star Trek V: The Final Frontier 1989, Total Recall 1990, Gremlins 2: The New Batch 1990, The Russia House 1990, Not Without My Daughter 1991, Sleeping With the Enemy 1991, Medicine Man 1991, Love Field 1992, Mom and Dad Save the World 1992, Basic Instinct 1992, Mr. Baseball 1992, Forever Young 1992, Matinee 1992, The Vanishing 1993, Dennis the Menace 1993, Malice 1993, Rudy 1993, Six Degrees of Separation 1993, Angie 1994, Bad Girls 1994, The Shadow 1994, I.Q. 1994, The River Wild 1994, First Knight 1995, Congo 1995, Powder 1995, City Hall 1995, Executive Decision 1996, Chain Reaction 1996, The Ghost and the Darkness 1996, Star Trek: First Contact 1996, Fierce Creatures 1996, LA Confidential 1997, Air Force One 1997, The Edge 1997, Deep Rising 1997, U.S. Marshals 1998, Small Soldiers 1998, Mulan 1998, Star Trek: Insurrection 1998, The Mummy 1999, The 13th Warrior 1999, The Haunting 1999, Hollow Man 2000, Along Came a Spider, The Last Castle 2001, The Sum of All Fears 2002, Star Trek: Nemesis 2002. *Ballet scores include:* A Patch of Blue 1970, Othello 1971, Capricorn One 1989. *Address:* c/o Savitsky & Co., Suite 1450, 1901 Avenue of Stars, Los Angeles, CA 90067-6087, USA.

GOLDSMITH, Baron (Life Peer), cr. 1999, of Allerton in the County of Merseyside; **Peter Henry Goldsmith,** MA, LLM, QC, PC; British barrister; b. 5 Jan. 1950, Liverpool; ed Quarry Bank High School, Caius Coll. Cambridge, Univ. Coll. London; called to Bar, Gray's Inn, began practising as barrister 1972; a Jr Counsel to Crown (Common Law) 1985–87, QC 1987, Chair. Bar of England and Wales 1995, Financial Reporting Review Panel 1997–2000; called to Paris Bar 1997; Personal Rep. of Prime Minister to EU Charter of Fundamental Rights 1999–2000; Attorney-Gen. 2001–; Privy Councillor 2002–; Fellow American Law Inst. 1997–, Univ.Coll. London 2002–. *Address:* Office of the Attorney-General, 9 Buckingham Gate, London, SW1E 6JP, England (Office). *Telephone:* (20) 7271-2460 (Office). *Fax:* (20) 7271-2432 (Office).

GOLDSTEIN, Abraham S., MA; American professor of law; b. 27 July 1925, New York; s. of Isidore and Yetta (Kutcher) Goldstein; m. 1st Ruth Tessler 1947 (died 1989); one s. one d.; m. 2nd Sarah Feidelson 1995; ed City Coll. NY and Yale Law School; Assoc., Cook and Berger, Washington, DC 1949; Law Clerk to Circuit Judge David Bazelon, US Court of Appeals 1949–51; Partner, Donohue and Kaufman 1951–56; Assoc. Prof., Yale Law School 1956–61, Prof. 1961–, Dean 1970–75, Sterling Prof. of Law 1975–; Visiting Prof. of Law, Stanford Law School; Visiting Fellow, Inst. of Criminology, Cambridge Univ. 1964–65; mem. Faculty, Salzburg Seminar in American Studies 1969; Visiting Prof. Hebrew Univ. Jerusalem 1976, UN Asia and Far East Inst. for Prevention of Crime, Tokyo 1983, Tel-Aviv Univ. 1986; mem. Comm. to Revise Criminal Statutes of Conn. 1966–70; Consultant, President's Comm. on the Admin. of Criminal Justice 1966–67; mem. Gov.'s Planning Comm. of Criminal Admin. 1967–71, Conn. Bd of Parole 1967–69; Vice-Pres. Conn. Bar Foundation 1976–79; Sr Vice-Pres. American Jewish Congress 1977–84, mem. Gov. Council 1977–94; mem. American Acad. of Arts and Sciences 1975–; Hon. MA (Cambridge, Yale), Hon. LLD (New York Law School, Depaul Univ.). *Publications:* The Insanity Defence 1967, Crime, Law and Society (with J. Goldstein) 1971, Criminal Procedure (with L. Orland) 1974, The Passive Judiciary 1981; articles and book reviews in professional journals. *Address:* Yale Law School, New Haven, CT 06520, USA (Office).

GOLDSTEIN, Avram, MD; American professor of pharmacology and neuro-biologist; b. 3 July 1919, New York; s. of Israel Goldstein and Bertha Markowitz; m. Dora Benedict 1947; three s. one d.; ed Harvard Coll. and Harvard Medical School; Instructor, then Asst Prof. in Pharmacology, Harvard 1948–55; Prof. and Chair., Pharmacology, Stanford Univ. 1955–70, Prof. 1970–89, Prof. Emer. 1989–; Dir Addiction Research Foundation, Palo Alto,

Calif. 1974–87; mem. NAS; Franklin Medal, Sollmann Award, Nathan Eddy Award. *Publications:* Biostatistics 1964, Principles of Drug Action 1968, Addiction: From Biology to Drug Policy 2001; over 300 articles in the primary scientific journals. *Leisure interests:* aviation and aviation writing. *Address:* Edwards Building, School of Medicine, Stanford University, 300 Pasteur Drive, Stanford, CA 94305 (Office); 735 Dolores Street, Palo Alto, CA 94305, USA (Home).

GOLDSTEIN, Jeffrey Alan, MA PhD; American international civil servant and economist; b. 2 Dec. 1955, Pennsylvania; m. Nancy Coles; ed Yale Univ., Vassar Coll., London School of Econs; Research Asst, Brookings Inst., Washington, DC 1977–78; Int. Economist, Office of Int. Monetary Affairs, US Dept of Treasury, Washington, DC 1979; Consultant, Securities Group, New York 1980–81; Vice-Chair. Wolfensohn & Co. Inc., New York, then Co-Chair. BT Wolfensohn, New York 1984–99; Man. Dir World Bank, Washington, DC 1999–; Virginia Swinburn Brownell Prize in Political Econ. Studies. *Address:* World Bank, 1818 H Street, NW, Washington, DC 20433, USA (Office). *Telephone:* (202) 458-4001 (Office); (202) 237-9249 (Home). *Fax:* (202) 522-1853 (Office); (202) 249-9258 (Home). *E-mail:* jgoldstein@worldbank.org (Office).

GOLDSTEIN, Joseph Leonard, MD; American genetics educator and physician; b. 18 April 1940, Sumter, SC; s. of Isadore E. Goldstein and Fannie A. Goldstein; ed Washington and Lee Univ., Lexington, Va, Univ. of Texas Southwestern Medical Center; Intern, then Resident in Medicine, Mass. Gen. Hosp., Boston 1966–68; Clinical Assoc., Nat. Insts. of Health 1968–70; Postdoctoral Fellow, Univ. of Washington, Seattle 1970–72; mem. Faculty, Univ. of Texas Southwestern Medical Center, Dallas 1972–, Paul J. Thomas Prof. of Medicine, Chair. Dept of Molecular Genetics 1977–, Harvey Soc. Lecturer 1977, Regental Prof. 1985–; Chair. Albert Lasker Medical Research Awards Jury 1996–; mem. Advisory Bd Howard Hughes Medical Inst. 1985–90, Chair. 1995–2002, Trustee 2002–; non-resident Fellow, The Salk Inst. 1983–93; mem. Scientific Advisory Bd Welch Foundation 1986–, Bd Dirs. Passano Foundation 1985–, Rockefeller Foundation 1994–, Bd of Scientific Govs, Scripps Research Inst. 1996–; mem. Editorial Bd Cell, Arteriosclerosis and Science; mem. NAS (mem. Council 1991–94), American Acad. of Arts and Sciences, American Philosophical Soc., Inst. of Medicine, Asscn of American Physicians, American Soc. of Clinical Investigation (Pres. 1985–86), American Soc. of Human Genetics, American Soc. of Biological Chemists, American Fed. of Clinical Research; Foreign mem. Royal Soc., London; Hon. DSc (Univ. of Chicago, Rensselaer Polytech. Inst., Washington and Lee Univ., Univ. of Paris-Sud, Univ. of Buenos Aires, Southern Methodist Univ., Univ. of Miami); Heinrich-Wieland Prize 1974, Pfizer Award in Enzyme Chem., American Chemical Soc. 1976, Passano Award, Johns Hopkins Univ. 1978, Gairdner Foundation Award 1981, Award in Biological and Medical Sciences, New York Acad. of Sciences 1981, Lita Annenberg Hazen Award 1982, Research Achievement Award, American Heart Asscn 1984, Louisa Gross Horwitz Award 1984, 3M Life Sciences Award 1984, Albert Lasker Award in Basic Medical Research 1985, Nobel Prize in Physiology or Medicine 1985, Trustees' Medal, Mass. Gen. Hosp. 1986, US Nat. Medal of Science 1988. *Publication:* The Metabolic Basis of Inherited Disease (co-author) 1983. *Address:* Department of Molecular Genetics, University of Texas Southwestern Medical Center at Dallas, 5323 Harry Hines Boulevard, Dallas, TX 75390; 3831 Turtle Creek Boulevard, Apt. 22-B, Dallas, TX 75219, USA (Home).

GOLDSTONE, David Joseph, LLB; British property executive; b. 21 Feb. 1929; s. of Solomon Goldstone and Rebecca Goldstone (née Degotts); one s. two d.; ed Dynevor Secondary School, Swansea and London School of Econs; admitted Solicitor 1955; legal practice 1955–66; Chief Exec. Regalian Properties PLC 1970–2001 Chair. 1990–2001; Dir Swansea Sound Commercial Radio 1974–95, London Welsh Rugby Football Club 1997–2001, Wales Millennium Centre 1998–; Chair. Coram Family 2001–; mem. Court of Govs. LSE 1985–; Council mem. Football Asscn of Wales 1970–72, Welsh Nat. Opera 1984–89, London Univ. 1994–, Royal Albert Hall 1999–; Hon. Fellow, LSE 1995. *Leisure interests:* reading, sport. *Address:* 18 Grosvenor Hill Court, 15 Bourdon Street, London, W1K 3PX (Home); 15 Stratton Street, London, W1J 8LQ, England (Office). *Telephone:* (20) 7659-0413 (Office); (20) 7499-4525 (Home). *Fax:* (20) 7659-0414 (Office); (20) 7491-2388 (Home). *E-mail:* djg@davstone.co.uk (Office).

GOLDSTONE, Jeffrey, MA, PhD, FRS; British physicist; b. 3 Sept. 1933, Manchester; s. of Hyman and Sophia Goldstone; m. Roberta Gordon 1980; one s.; ed Manchester Grammar School and Trinity Coll., Cambridge; Research Fellow, Trinity Coll., Cambridge 1956–60, Staff Fellow 1962–82; Univ. lecturer, Applied Math. and Theoretical Physics, Cambridge 1961–76, Reader in Mathematical Physics 1976; Prof. of Physics, MIT 1977–83, Dir Center for Theoretical Physics 1983–89, Cecil and Ida Green Prof. of Physics 1983–; Fellow, American Acad. of Arts and Sciences, American Physical Soc.; Hon. Fellow Trinity Coll., Cambridge 2000; Heineman Prize, American Physical Soc. 1981; Guthrie Medal, Inst. of Physics 1983, Dirac Medal, Int. Centre for Theoretical Physics 1991. *Publications:* articles in scientific journals. *Address:* Department of Physics, 6–313, Massachusetts Institute of Technology, Cambridge, MA 02139, USA (Office). *Telephone:* (617) 253-6263 (Office); (617) 876-6027 (Home). *Fax:* (617) 253-8674 (Office). *E-mail:* goldston@mit.edu (Office).

GOLDSTONE, Richard J., LLB; South African judge; b. 26 Oct. 1938, Boksburg; m. Noleen Behrman 1962; two d.; ed King Edward VII School,

Johannesburg and Univ. of Witwatersrand; admitted to Johannesburg Bar 1963, Sr Counsel 1976; Judge, Transvaal Supreme Court 1980–89; Judge, Appellate Div. Supreme Court of SA 1989–94; Justice, S African Constitutional Court 1994–; Chair. Comm. of Inquiry regarding Public Violence and Intimidation 1991–94; Prosecutor, Int. Criminal Tribunal for the Fmr Yugoslavia and Int. Criminal Tribunal for Rwanda 1994–96; Nat. Pres. Nat. Inst. for Crime Prevention and Rehabilitation of Offenders 1982–99; Chair. Cttee which drafted Valencia Declaration of Human Duties and Responsibilities 1998; Ind. Int. Comm. on Kosovo 1999–2001, Int. Bar Asscn Task Force on Int. Terrorism 2001–; mem. Council, Univ. of Witwatersrand 1988–94, Chancellor 1996–; Chair. Standing Advisory Cttee on Co. Law (Chair. 1991–), Exec. Cttee World ORT (Pres. 1997–); Chair. Bd Human Rights Inst. of SA; Gov. Hebrew Univ. of Jerusalem 1982–; Chair. Bradlow Foundation 1989–; other professional appts.; Faculty mem. Salzburg Seminar 1996, 1998, 2001; Foreign mem. American Acad. of Arts and Sciences; Fellow Centre for Int. Affairs, Harvard Univ. 1989; Hon. mem. Bar Asscn of New York; Hon. Bencher Inner Temple, London; Hon. Fellow, St John's Coll. Cambridge; Hon. LLD (Cape Town) 1993, (Natal, Hebrew Univ. of Jerusalem, Witwatersrand) 1994, (Wilfred Laurier Univ., Waterloo, Canada) 1995, (Maryland Univ. Coll.) 1995, (Tilbury Univ.) 1996, (Univ. of Glasgow, Notre Dame Univ.) 1997, (Univ. of Calgary) 1998, (Emory Univ.) 2001; several awards including Toastmasters Int. Communication and Leadership Award 1994, Int. Human Rights Award (American Bar Asscn) 1994. *Publication:* For Humanity – Reflections of a War Crimes Investigator. *Leisure interests:* reading, walking, wine. *Address:* Constitutional Court, Private Bag X32, Braamfontein Johannesburg 2017 (Office); 22 West Road South, Morningside, South Africa (Home). *Telephone:* (11) 3597408. *Fax:* (11) 4039131 (Office); (11) 4039131. *E-mail:* goldstone@concourt.org.za (Office).

GOLDSWORTHY, Andrew Charles, OBE, BA; British sculptor; b. 25 July 1956, Cheshire; s. of Fredrick Alan Goldsworthy and Muriel Goldsworthy (née Stanger); m. Judith Elizabeth Gregson 1982; two s. two d.; ed Bradford and Lancaster Art Colls; has exhibited internationally in USA, France, Australia, Germany and Japan; numerous public and pvt. comms since 1984 including pieces for Grizedale Forest, Cumbria 1984, 1985, 1991, 'Enclosure', Royal Botanic Gardens, Edinburgh 1990, 'Seven Holes', Greenpeace, London 1991, 'Steel Cone', Gateshead 1991, 'Black Spring', Botanical Gardens, Adelaide 1992, 'Fieldgate', Poundridge, NY 1993, Laumeier Sculpture Park 1994, two pieces for Nat. Museum of Scotland, Edin. 1998; works represented in collections at Michael Hue-Williams Fine Arts Ltd, London, Galerie Lelong, New York and Paris, Haines Gallery, San Francisco, Galerij S65, Belgium, Springer and Winckler Galerie, Berlin; residency Yorks. Sculpture Park 1988; featured on Royal Mail Spring issue stamps 1995; Sr lecturer in Fine Art and Craft Univ. of Herts. 1996; Prof.-at-Large Cornell Univ., USA 2000–; Visiting Prof. Crichton Coll., Univ. of Glasgow 2000–; collaborated with Cirque du Soleil, Montreal 1998; Hon. Fellow Univ. of Cen. Lancs. 1995; Hon. BA (Bradford) 1993; North West Arts Award 1979, Yorks. Arts Award 1980, Northern Arts Award 1981, 1995, Scottish Arts Council Award 1988. *Dance:* Vegetal, with Regine Chopinot 1995, La danse du Temps, with Regine Chopinot and Ballet Atlantique 2000. *Art exhibitions:* Barbican Centre, London 2000, Abbot Hall Art Gallery 2001. *Film:* Two Autumns (for Channel 4) 1991, Rivers and Tides 2000. *Publications:* A Collaboration With Nature 1989, Hand to Earth 1991, Touching North 1994, Stone 1994, Wood 1996, Time 2000. *Leisure interests:* fishing, reading, listening to music. *Address:* c/o Michael Hue-Williams Fine Arts Ltd, 21 Cork Street, London, W1X 1HB, England. *Telephone:* (20) 7434-1318. *Fax:* (20) 7434-1321.

GOLDTHORPE, John Harry, MA, FBA; British sociologist and academic; b. 27 May 1935, Barnsley; s. of Harry and Lilian Eliza Goldthorpe; m. Rhiannon Esyllt Harry 1963; one s. one d.; ed Wath-upon-Dearne Grammar School, Univ. Coll. London, London School of Econs; Asst Lecturer Dept of Sociology, Univ. of Leicester 1957–60; Fellow, King's Coll. Cambridge 1960–69; Asst Lecturer, then Lecturer in Faculty of Econs and Politics, Univ. of Cambridge 1962–69; Official Fellow, Nuffield Coll., Oxford 1969–2002, Emer. Fellow 2002–; mem. British Econ. and Social Research Council 1988–91; mem. Academia Europaea 1989; Foreign mem. Royal Swedish Acad. of Sciences 2001; Hon. DPhil (Stockholm Univ.) 1990; Helsinki Univ. Medal 1990. *Publications:* The Affluent Worker series (3 Vols) (with David Lockwood et al.) 1968–69, The Social Grading of Occupations (with Keith Hope) 1974, The Political Economy of Inflation (with Fred Hirsch, eds.) 1978, Social Mobility and Class Structure 1980, Order and Conflict in Contemporary Capitalism (ed. and contrib.) 1984, Die Analyse sozialer Ungleichheit: Kontinuität, Erneuerung, Innovation (with Hermann Strasser; ed. and contrib.) 1985, The Constant Flux: a Study of Class Mobility in Industrial Societies (with Robert Erikson) 1992, The Development of Industrial Society in Ireland (with Christopher T. Whelan; ed. and contrib.) 1992, On Sociology: Numbers, Narratives and the Integration of Research and Class Theory 2000. *Leisure interests:* lawn tennis, bird watching, computer chess. *Address:* Nuffield College, Oxford, OX1 1NF; 32 Leckford Road, Oxford, OX2 6HX, England. *Telephone:* (1865) 278516 (Office); (1865) 556602 (Home). *Fax:* (1865) 278621. *E-mail:* john.goldthorpe@nuf.ox.ac.uk (Office).

GOLEMBIOVSKY, Igor Nestorovich; Russian journalist; b. 7 Sept. 1935, Samtredia, Georgia; m.; one s.; ed Tbilisi State Univ.; journalist activities since 1958; with Izvestia 1966–, deputy-editor of div., special corresp., deputy-exec. sec., exec. sec., First Deputy-Ed.-in-Chief 1988–91, Ed.-in-Chief 1991–97; Founder and Ed. Noviye Izvestiya 1997–. *Publications:* author of articles on key problems of social and political life. *Leisure interests:* tennis, football. *Address:* Noviye Izvestia, Dolgorukovskaya str. 19/8, 103006 Moscow, Russia. *Telephone:* (095) 795-31-57. *Fax:* (095) 795-31-38.

GÖLHAN, Mehmet; Turkish politician and engineer; b. 1929, Adapazari; m.; two c.; ed Istanbul Tech. Univ.; Chief Industrial Dept, Ministry of Industry 1974; Dir-Gen. Road, Water and Electricity Authority (YSE), Turkish Petroleum Corpn (TPA); Under-Sec. Ministry of Industry and Tech. –1980; a founding mem. Grand Turkey Party and Doğru Yol Partisi (DYP), fmr Acting Chair.; parl. deputy (DYP) 1987; Minister of Nat. Defence 1993–96. *Address:* c/o Doğru Yol Partisi, Selanik Cad. 40, Kızılay, Ankara, Turkey.

GOLITSYN, Georgy Sergeyevich; Russian physicist; b. 23 Jan. 1935, Moscow; s. of Sergei Golitsyn and Claudia Golitsyna; m. Ludmila Lisitskaya; two d.; ed Moscow State Univ.; Head of Lab., Head of Div., Dir Inst. of Physics of Atmosphere, USSR (now Russian) Acad. of Sciences 1958–; Corresp. mem. USSR (now Russian) Acad. of Sciences 1979, mem. 1987, mem. Presidium 1988–2000; Chair. Council, Int. Inst. of Applied Systems Analysis 1992–97; main research on geophysical fluid dynamics, climate theory; Demidov Prize, A. Friedmann Prize. *Publications include:* Introduction to Dynamics of Planet Atmospheres 1973, Study of Convection with Geophysical Applications and Analogies 1980, Global Climate Catastrophes 1986, Convection of Rotating Fluids 1995. *Leisure interests:* history, art, literature. *Address:* A. M. Obukhov Institute of Atmospheric Physics, Russian Academy of Sciences, Pyzh'yevsky per. 3, 109017 Moscow, Russia (Office). *Telephone:* (095) 951-55-65 (Office); 331-32-69 (Home). *Fax:* (095) 953-16-52.

GOLL, Gerhard; German business executive and lawyer; b. 18 June 1942; Chair. Energie Baden-Württemberg (EnBW) AG 1998–. *Address:* Energie Baden-Württemberg AG, Durlacher Allee 93, 76131 Karlsruhe, Germany (Office). *Telephone:* (800) 9999966 (Office). *Fax:* (800) 9999977 (Office). *E-mail:* info@enbw.com (Office). *Website:* www.enbw.com (Office).

GÖLLNER, Theodor, PhD; German professor of musicology; b. 25 Nov. 1929, Bielefeld; s. of Friedrich Göllner and Paula Brinkmann; m. Marie Louise Martinez 1959; one s. one d.; ed Univs of Heidelberg and Munich; lecturer, Univ. of Munich 1958–62, Asst Prof., Assoc. Prof. 1962–67; Assoc. Prof., then Prof. Univ. of Calif. Santa Barbara 1967–73; Prof., Chair. Inst. of Musicology, Univ. of Munich 1973–97; mem., Dir Comm. of Music History, Bavarian Acad. of Sciences 1982–. *Publications:* Formen früher Mehrstimmigkeit 1961, Die mehrstimmigen liturgischen Lesungen 1969, Die Sieben Worte am Kreuz 1986, Et incarnatus est in Bachs h-moll-Messe und Beethovens Missa solemnis 1996; (ed.) Münchner Veröffentlichungen zur Musikgeschichte 1977–, Münchner Editionen zur Musikgeschichte 1979–. *Address:* Institute of Musicology, University of Munich, Geschwister-Scholl-Platz 1, 80539 Munich (Office); Bahnweg 9, 82229 Seefeld, Germany (Home). *Telephone:* (1089) 21802364 (Office).

GOLU, Mihai, MA, PhD; Romanian politician and scientist; b. 4 March 1934, Bumbești-Pitic, Gorj County; s. of Ion Golu and Gheorghita Golu; m. Elena Filip 1957; two s.; ed Psychology Coll., Bucharest and Lomonosov Univs; worked as psychologist, Prof., Bucharest Univ.; research at Carnegie-Mellon Univ. (USA) 1973–74; deputy (independent cand.) 1990–92, Party of Social Democracy 1992–96; Minister of Educ. and Science 1991–92, of Culture 1992–93; Deputy, Parl. Ass. of Council of Europe 1993–96; Pres. Romanian Asscn of Psychologists 1990–; Nat. Soc. for Educ. 1993–; Nat. Comm. for UNESCO 1990–95; mem. Acad. of Scientists 1998–; mem. NY Acad. of Science; Romanian Acad. Prize 1981, Pablo Picasso Medal, UNESCO 1991, Jan Amos Komenius Medal, Czech Acad. 1992. *Publications:* Sensibility 1970, Principles of Cybernetic Psychology 1975, Dynamics of Personality 1993, Neuropsychology 2000, Fundamentals of Psychology 2000; scientific papers and articles. *Leisure interests:* reading biographies of famous people, classical music. *Address:* Bulevardul Libertatii 22, Bloc 102, Scara 5, Apt. 89, Bucharest, Romania. *Telephone:* 336-66-62.

GOLUB, Harvey, BS; American finance executive; b. 16 April 1939, New York; s. of Irving Golub and Pearl Fader; m. Roberta Glunts 1980; one s. and two s. one d. by previous m.; Jr partner, McKinsey & Co. Inc. New York 1967–74, Sr partner 1977–83; Pres. Shulman Air Freight, New York 1974–77; Sr officer, American Express Co. New York 1983–84, Vice-Chair. 1990–93, CEO, Chair. 1993–2001; Chair., Pres. IDS Financial Services (now American Express Financial Advisors) Minn. 1984–90, Chair., CEO 1990–2001; Chair. AirClic, Blue Bell 2001–. *Address:* AirClic, 512 Township Line Road, F12 #5, Blue Bell, PA 19422, USA (Office).

GOLUB, Leon, MFA; American artist; b. 23 Jan. 1922, Chicago, Ill.; m. Nancy Spero 1951; three s.; ed School of the Art Inst. of Chicago, Univ. of Chicago; John C. Van Dyck Prof. of Visual Arts, Rutgers Univ. 1984–; Ford Foundation Grant 1960, Cassandra Foundation Grant 1967, Guggenheim Grant 1968; mem. American Acad. of Arts and Sciences 1996; Hon. DFA (Swarthmore Coll.) 1985, School of the Art Inst. of Chicago 1982. *Exhibitions:* solo exhibitions include: Pasadena Museum of Art, Calif. 1956, ICA, London 1957, 1982, Hayden Gallery, MA 1970, Nat. Gallery of Victoria, Australia 1971, Musée de L'Abbaye Saint Croix, France 1973, Honolulu Acad. of Arts, Hawaii 1983, Kunstmuseum, Luzern, Switzerland 1987, The Saatchi Collection, London 1988, The Brooklyn Museum, NY (Worldwide) 1991, Inst. Contemporary Art, Philadelphia 1992, Musée d'Art Contemporain de Montreal, Québec 1992, Kunstverein, Munich 1993, List Visual Arts Center, Cambridge, Mass. 1994, Vancouver Art Gallery 1995, Ronald Feldman Fine Art, NY 1996, 1998,

Darthea Speyer Gallery, Paris 1996, Hiroshima City Museum of Contemporary Art 1996, Crown Gallery, Brussels 1997, Anthony Reynolds Gallery, London 1998, Stefania Miscetti Arte Contemporanea, Rome 1998, Galerie Christine Konig, Vienna 2000, Irish Museum of Modern Art, Dublin (retrospective exhbn) 2000; group exhibitions; work in public and pvt. collections includes: Art Inst. of Chicago, Eli Broad Family Foundation, LA, Whitney Museum of American Art, Musée des Beaux Arts, Montreal, Nat. Museum of American Art, Smithsonian Inst. Washington, DC, Australia, Museum of Modern Art, New York. *Publications:* Leon Golub: Do Paintings Bite. Selected Texts 1948–96 1997. *Address:* 530 La Guardia Place, New York, NY 10012, USA (Studio). *Telephone:* (212) 477-5396. *Fax:* (212) 533-0506.

GOLUTVA, Alexander Alekseyevich; Russian cinematographer; b. 18 March 1948, Liepaia, Latvia; m.; one d.; ed Moscow State Univ.; fmr teacher; fmr lecturer Div. of Propaganda and Agitation, Petrograd Exec. CP Cttee 1974–80, then instructor, then Head; consultant House of Political Educ. 1980–83; Head of Sector, Div. of Culture Leningrad Regional CP Cttee 1983–85; Ed.-in-Chief Lenfilm Film Studio 1985–87, Dir 1987–96; First Deputy Chair. State Cttee on Cinematography 1996–97, State Sec. then First Deputy Chair. 1997–99, Chair. 1999–2000; First Deputy Minister of Culture, Head of Cinema Dept 2000–; mem. Presidential Council for Culture and Art; Badge of Honour of Russian Fed. 1998, Nika Prize of Russian Fed. *Address:* Cinema Departments, Ministry of Culture of Russian Federation, Gnezdnikovsky per. 7, 103877 Moscow, Russia. *Telephone:* (095) 229-70-55. *E-mail:* mincult.mgivc@g23relcom.ru (Office).

GOMA, Col Louis Sylvain; Republic of Congo politician and army officer; b. 1941; ed Versailles and Saint-Cyr; Asst Dir of Mil. Engineers until 1968; Chief of Staff of Congolese People's Nat. Army 1968, promoted Capt. 1968; mem. Parti Congolais du Travail (PCT) 1969, Cen. Cttee 1970, Special Gen. Staff of Revolution 1974, Political Bureau; Sec. of State for Defence 1969–70; Minister of Public Works and Transport 1970–74; promoted Maj. 1973; Chief of Gen. Staff of Armed Forces 1974; Prime Minister 1975–84, 1991, responsible for Plan 1975–79; mem. Council of State 1975–77; mem. PCT Mil. Cttee (Second Vice-Pres.) 1977–79. *Address:* c/o Office du Premier Ministre, Brazzaville, Republic of the Congo.

GOMAN, Vladimir Vladimirovich; Russian politician; b. 29 Jan. 1952, Baku, Azerbaijan; ed Troitsk Higher School of Civil Aviation, Tumen Industrial Inst., Tumen State Univ.; technician first civil aviation team 1972–74; fmr mechanic Severgazstroi, Nadym, then head of sector, head of dept 1974–89; Chair. Nadym Municipal Exec. Cttee 1989; Head of Admin., Nadym and Autonomous Territory of Yamal 1991–93; mem. State Duma, Chair. State Duma Cttee on Peoples of the N 1993–98, Cttee on Devt of the N 1998–, Cttee on Problems of the N 1999–; Deputy Minister of Regional Policy State Sec. 1999–2000, Deputy Rep. of the Pres. in Siberian Fed. Dist, Novosibirsk 2000–. *Address:* Office of the Plenipotentiary Representative of the President, Derzhavina str. 18, 630091 Novosibirsk, Russia (Office). *Telephone:* (3832) 21-56-22 (Office).

GOMARD, Bernhard, DJur; Danish professor of law; b. 9 Jan. 1926, Karise; s. of C. J. Gomard and Karen (née Magle) Gomard; m. 1st 1974; one s.; m. 2nd Marianne Rosen 1994 (died 2000); ed Univ. of Copenhagen; Legal Adviser Danish Dept of Justice 1950–58, Danish Atomic Comm. 1956–76, Danish Insurance Cos. 1958–2002; Prof. of Law, Univ. of Copenhagen 1958–96; Prof. of Law, Copenhagen Business School 1996–; mem. Bd of Dirs. Danske Bank 1974–96; mem. and Chair. numerous Govt cttees.; Hon. Prof. Univ. of Freiburg; mem. Danish Acad. of Sciences 1975, Academia Europae 1989, Inst. of Int. Business Law and Practice; DrIur hc (Univ. of Lund); Nordic Jurists Prize 1987; Oersted Medal 1995; Kt of Order of the Dannebrog. *Publications:* articles and treatises on contract co. law, civil procedure, with particular emphasis on Danish law. *Leisure interests:* opera, French art and literature. *Address:* Law Dept, Copenhagen Business School, Jul Thomsens Plads 10, 1925 Frederiksberg C (Office); 3 Hammerensgade, 1267 Copenhagen K, Denmark (Home). *Telephone:* 38-15-26-42 (Office); 33-22-80-20 (Home). *Fax:* 38-15-26-10 (Office). *E-mail:* bg.jur@cbs.dk.

GOMBOSUREN, Tserenpiliin; Mongolian politician; b. 5 Jan. 1943, Hujirt Dist, Oborkhangai Prov.; s. of T. Tserenpil and O. Handjav; m. Dembereliin Surenhorlo 1970; three s.; ed Printing Inst. of USSR, Higher Party School of CPSU Cen. Cttee, USSR; engineer, State Printing Factory 1967–74; Head of Dept, Deputy Minister of Foreign Affairs 1976–84; Minister-Counsellor, Embassy in Moscow 1984–87; Deputy Head External Relations, Mongolian People's Revolutionary Party (MPRP) Cen. Cttee 1987–88; Minister of Foreign Affairs 1988–90, of External Relations 1990–96; mem. Political Bureau of MPRP Cen. Cttee March–April 1990, mem. Presidium April–Nov. 1990; mem. State Great Hural 1992–96; Chair. Mongolian Nat. Security Printing Co. 1997–. *Leisure interest:* translating from Russian. *Address:* Mongolian National Security Printing Company, Khudaldaany Gudamj 6, Chingeltey Duure 6, Ulan Bator 13, Mongolia.

GOMER, Robert, PhD; American professor of chemistry; b. 24 March 1924, Vienna, Austria; s. of Richard Gomer and Mary Gomer; m. Anne Olah 1955; one s. one d.; ed Pomona Coll. and Univ. of Rochester; Instructor, then Assoc. Prof., James Franck Inst. and Dept of Chem., Univ. of Chicago 1950–58, Prof. 1958–96, Dir James Franck Inst. 1977–83, Carl William Eisendrath Distinguished Service Prof. of Chem. 1984–96, Prof. Emer. 1996–; Assoc. Ed. Journal of Chemical Physics 1957–59, Review of Scientific Instruments 1963–65; mem. Editorial Bd Surface Science 1964–70; Consultant, Pres.'s

Science Advisory Bd 1961–65; Chair. Editorial Bd Bulletin of the Atomic Scientists 1965–70, mem. Bd of Dirs. 1960–84; Assoc. Ed. Applied Physics 1974–89; Co-Ed. Springer Series in Chemical Physics 1978–; mem. NAS, American Acad. of Arts and Sciences and Leopoldina Akademie der Naturforscher; Bourke Lecturer, Faraday Soc. 1959; Kendall Award in Colloid or Surface Science, American Chemical Soc. 1975; Davisson-Germer Prize, American Physical Soc. 1981, M. W. Welch Award, American Vacuum Soc. 1989, ACS A. Adamson Award 1996. *Publications:* over 240 scientific articles; Field Emission and Field Ionization 1961. *Leisure interests:* skiing, music and literature. *Address:* The University of Chicago, The James Franck Institute, 5640 South Ellis Avenue, Chicago, IL 60637-1433 (Office); 4824 South Kimbark Avenue, Chicago, IL 60615-1916, USA (Home). *Telephone:* (773) 702-7191 (Univ.). *Fax:* (773) 702-5863.

GOMERSALL, Sir Stephen John, Kt, KCMG, MA; British diplomatist; b. 17 Jan. 1948, Doncaster; s. of Harry Raymond Gomersall and Helen Gomersall; m. Lydia Veronica Parry 1975; two s. one d.; ed Queens' Coll., Cambridge, Stanford Univ., Calif.; entered diplomatic service 1970; in Tokyo 1972–77; Rhodesia Dept, FCO 1977–79; Pvt. Sec. to Lord Privy Seal 1979–82; Washington 1982–85; Econ. Counsellor, Tokyo 1986–90; Head of Security Policy Dept, FCO 1990–94, Dir Int. Security 1998–99; Deputy Perm. Rep., Perm. Mission to the UN 1994–98; Amb. to Japan 1999–. *Leisure interests:* music, golf. *Address:* Embassy of the United Kingdom, 1, Ichiban-cho, Chiyoda-ku, Tokyo 102-8381, Japan (Office); c/o Foreign and Commonwealth Office Tokyo, King Charles Street, London, SW1A 2AH, England (Office). *Telephone:* (3) 5211-1100 (Japan) (Office). *Fax:* (3) 5211-1111 (Japan) (Office). *E-mail:* stephen.gomersall@fco.gov.uk (Office). *Website:* www.uknow.or.jp.

GOMEZ, Alain Michel, LenD; French businessman; b. 18 Oct. 1938, Paris; s. of Francis Gomez and Simone Blet; m. 1st Francine le Foyer 1967 (divorced); m. 2nd Clémentine Gustin 1986; two d.; ed Univ. of Paris, Ecole nat. d'administration; Inspecteur des Finances 1965–69; Asst Dir of Finance, Saint-Gobain SA 1970–71, Financial Dir 1971–72, Pres. and Dir-Gen. 1977–; joined Société Générale pour l'Emballage 1972, Dir-Gen. 1972, Pres. 1977–; Pres. and Dir-Gen. Saint-Gobain Desjonquères 1973–, Saint-Gobain Emballage 1974–, Dir Duralex br., Saint-Gobain 1978–, Dir Saint-Gobain Pont à Mousson 1977–; Pres. Thomson SA and Thomson-CSF 1982–96, now Hon. Pres.; Chair. and CEO Thomson CSF 1982–96; Vice-Pres., Dir-Gen. Sefimeg 1996–; Counsellor to Bank Wasserstein Perella 1997–99; mem. Exec. Cttee Fimalac 1996–; Pres. Strafor Facom 1999–; Chevalier, Légion d'honneur. *Publications:* (co-author under name Jacques Mandrin) L'Enarchie 1967, Socialisme ou Social-médiocratie 1968. *Address:* Fimalac, 97 rue de Lille, 75007 Paris; Facom, 6-8 rue Gustave Eiffel, 91420 Morangis, France.

GOMEZ, Jill, FRAM; British opera and concert singer; b. 21 Sept. 1942, New Amsterdam, British Guiana; ed Royal Acad. of Music, Guildhall School of Music; operatic début as Adina in L'Elisir d'Amore with Glyndebourne Touring Opera 1968 and has since sung leading roles with Glyndebourne Festival Opera incl. Mélisande, Calisto and Ann Truelove in The Rake's Progress; has appeared with The Royal Opera, English Nat. Opera and Scottish Opera in roles including Pamina, Ilia, Fiordiligi, the Countess in Figaro, Elizabeth in Elegy for Young Lovers, Tytania, Lauretta in Gianni Schicchi and the Governess in The Turn of the Screw; cr. the role of Flora in Tippett's The Knot Garden, at Covent Garden 1970 and of the Countess in Thea Musgrave's Voice of Ariadne, Aldeburgh 1974; sang title role in Massenet's Thaïs, Wexford 1974 and Jenifer in The Midsummer Marriage with Welsh Nat. Opera 1976; cr. title role in William Alwyn's Miss Julie for radio 1977; performed Tatiana in Eugene Onegin with Kent Opera 1977; Donna Elvira in Don Giovanni, Ludwigsburg Festival 1978; cr. title role in BBC world premiere of Prokofiev's Maddalena 1979; Fiordiligi in Così fan tutte, Bordeaux 1979; sang in première of the Eighth Book of Madrigals in Zürich Monteverdi Festival 1979; Violetta in Kent Opera's production of La Traviata, Edin. Festival 1979; Cinna in Lucio Silla, Zurich 1981; The Governess in The Turn of the Screw, Geneva 1981; Cleopatra in Giulio Cesare, Frankfurt 1981; Teresa in Benvenuto Cellini, Berlioz Festival, Lyon 1982, Leila in Les Pêcheurs de Perles, Scottish Opera 1982–83; Governess in The Turn of the Screw, English Nat. Opera 1984; Helena in Glyndebourne's production of Britten's A Midsummer Night's Dream; Donna Anna in Don Giovanni, Frankfurt Opera 1985 and with Kent Opera 1988; Rosario in Goyescas by Granados 1988, Helena in Midsummer Night's Dream, London Opera 1990; cr. role of Duchess of Argyll in Thomas Adès's Powder Her Face, Cheltenham Int. Music Festival and London 1995; regular engagements including recitals in France, Austria, Belgium, Netherlands, Germany, Scandinavia, Switzerland, Italy, Spain and the USA; Festival appearances include Aix-en-Provence, Spoleto, Bergen, Versailles, Flanders, Netherlands, Prague, Edin. and BBC Promenade concerts; masterclasses Pears-Britten School, Aldeburgh, Trinity Coll. of Music, London, Dartington Summer Festival, Meridian TV. *Recordings include:* Vespro della Beata Vergine 1610 (Monteverdi), Acis and Galatea (Handel), The Knot Garden (Tippett), three recital discs of French, Spanish and Mozart songs, Quatre Chansons Françaises (Britten), Trois Poèmes de Mallarmé (Ravel), Chants d'Auvergne (Canteloube), Les Illuminations (Britten), Bachianas Brasileiras No. 5 (Villa Lobos), Cabaret Classics with John Constable, Knoxville-Summer of 1915 (Barber), South of the Border (Down Mexico Way...) arranged by Christopher Palmer for Jill Gomez, Britten's Blues (songs by Britten and Cole Porter); première recordings of Cantiga – The Song of Inês de Castro commissioned by her from

David Matthews, Seven Early Songs (Mahler), A Spanish Songbook (with John Constable), Powder Her Face, The Knot Garden, Miss Julie. *Address:* 16 Milton Park, London, N6 5QA, England.

GOMEZ-PIMIENTA, Bernardo, MArch; Mexican architect and lecturer; b. 18 Aug. 1961, Brussels, Belgium; s. of Jose Luis Gomez-Pimienta and Danielle Magar; m. Loredana Dall'Amico; one d. one s.; ed Universidad Anáhuac, Mexico City, Columbia Univ., NY, USA; draftsman George Wimpey Contractors Ltd, London, UK 1980–81; Co-Dir Ten Arquitectos 1987–; Dir Furniture Design, Visual Int. 1995–; Prof. of Architecture Universidad Iberoamericana 1987–89, Universidad Anáhuac 1989, Universidad Nacional Autónoma de México 1992–96, 1998–, Federico E. Marcial Chair. of Architecture 2002; Visiting Prof. Southern Calif. Inst. of Architecture 1994, Univ. of Ill. at Urbana-Champaign 1996–97; mem. Mexican Coll. of Architects 1990; mem. Editorial Bd and Founding mem. Arquine Review 1997–; mem. Bd Architecture Cttee, Colegio de Arquitectos de la Ciudad de Mexico AC 1998–; mem. Editorial Bd. Periódico Reforma 2002; mem. Jury AIA Design Honour Awards (New Mexico) 1997, (Iowa) 1999, (San Juan) 1999, Premios Alfher 2000, Fere Ambiente, Frankfurt 2002, Il Bienal Nacional de Diseño 2003; mem. Academia Nacional de Arquitectura 2003; over 40 architectural awards from Mexico, USA, Ecuador, UK and Argentina. *Architectural works include:* House 'O' 1992, Televisa Services Bldg 1994, Museum of Natural History, Mexico City 1996, Nat. Centre of the Arts, Mexico City 1996, Casa IA 2001, Hotel Habita 2002, Educare 2002, Arquine 2002, Mesa Lupa 2002, Perchero Ti 2002, Mesa Lobe 2002, Silla IA 2002. *Publications include:* numerous books, monographs, periodicals, catalogues and reviews. *Address:* Ten Arquitectos, Cuernacava 114-PB, Col. Condesa, Mexico City 06 140, Mexico (Office). *Telephone:* (55) 5211-8004 (Office). *Fax:* (55) 5286-1735 (Office). *E-mail:* b.gomezpimienta@ten-arquitectos.com (Office). *Website:* www .ten-arquitectos.com (Office).

GOMORY, Ralph Edward, PhD; American foundation executive, mathematician and business executive; b. 7 May 1929, Brooklyn Heights, NY; s. of Andrew L. Gomory and Marian Schellenberg; m. 1st Laura Secretan Dumper 1954 (divorced 1968); two s. one d.; m. 2nd Lilian Wu; ed Williams Coll., King's Coll., Cambridge and Princeton Univ.; Lt, USN 1954–57; Higgins Lecturer and Asst Prof., Princeton Univ. 1957–59; joined IBM 1959, Fellow 1964, filled various managerial positions including Dir Mathematical Science Dept, Dir of Research 1970–86, Vice-Pres. 1973–84, Sr Vice-Pres. 1985–89, mem. Corporate Man. Bd 1983–89, Sr Vice-Pres. for Science and Tech. 1986–89; Andrew D. White Prof.-at-Large, Cornell Univ. 1970–76; Pres. Alfred P. Sloan Foundation, New York 1989–; Dir Bank of New York 1986–88, Industrial Research Inst. 1986–91; mem. NAS, Nat. Acad. of Eng, American Acad. of Arts and Sciences, Council on Foreign Relations, White House Science Council (1986–89), Visiting Cttee Harvard Univ. Grad. School of Business 1995–; Fellow, Econometric Soc., American Acad. of Arts and Sciences 1973; Trustee, Hampshire Coll. 1977–86, Princeton Univ. 1985–89; Hon. DSc (Williams Coll.) 1973, (Polytechnic Univ.) 1987, (Syracuse Univ.) 1989, (Carnegie Mellon Univ.) 1989; Hon. LHD (Pace Univ.) 1986; Lanchester Prize, Operations Research Soc. of America 1964, John von Neumann Theory Prize 1984, Harry Goode Memorial Award 1984, IRI Medal 1985, IEEE Eng Leadership Recognition Award 1988, Nat. Medal of Science 1988, Presidential Award (New York Acad. of Sciences) 1992, Arthur M. Bueche Award, Nat. Acad. of Eng 1993. *Address:* Alfred P. Sloan Foundation, 630 Fifth Avenue, New York, NY 10111 (Office); 260 Douglas Road, Chappaqua, NY 10514, USA (Home).

GOMRINGER, Eugen; Swiss professor of aesthetics; b. 20 Jan. 1925, Cachuela Esperanza, Bolivia; s. of Eugen Gomringer and Delicia Rodriguez; m. 1st Klara Stöckli 1950; m. 2nd Nortrud Ottenhausen; five s. one d.; ed Kantonsschule, Zürich and Univ. of Berne; Sec. and Docent, Hochschule für Gestaltung, Ulm 1954–58; Art Dir Swiss Industrial Abrasives 1959–67; Man. Dir Schweizer Werkbund, Zürich 1961–67; Man. of Cultural Relations, Rosenthal AG, Germany 1967–85; Prof. of Aesthetics, Düsseldorf Art School 1976–90; Man. Int. Forum for Design, Ulm 1988–; f. Inst. für Konstruktive Kunst und Poesie IKKP Rehau 1999; Hon. Prof. Univ. of Zwickau; mem. Akad. der Künste, Berlin, PEN. *Publications:* several books of poetry and monographs in the art field. *Leisure interests:* mountaineering, art collecting, farming, dogs. *Address:* Wurlitz 22, 95111 Rehau, Germany (Home).

GOMUŁKA, Stanisław, DEcon; Polish economist and academic; b. 11 Sept. 1940, Krężoły; m.; one s.; ed Warsaw Univ.; researcher Dept of Econs Warsaw Univ. 1962–65, LSE 1970–, Netherlands Inst. for Advanced Studies 1980–81, Pennsylvania Univ. 1985–86, Stanford Univ. 1986, Columbia Univ. 1987, Harvard Univ. 1989–90; econ. adviser to Polish govts. 1989–, to Chair. Nat. Bank of Poland 1996–97; consultant IMF, OECD, EU. *Publications:* Inventive Activity, Diffusion and the Stages of Economic Growth 1971, Growth, Innovation and Reform in Eastern Europe 1986, The Theory of Technological Change and Economic Growth 1990. *Address:* 4 Woodfield Way, London, N11 2PH, England (Office). *E-mail:* gomulka@chrzan.demon.co.uk (Office).

GONÇALVES, Gen. Vasco dos Santos; Portuguese army officer; b. 3 May 1921, Lisbon; s. of Victor Candido Gonçalves and Alda Romana dos Santos; m. Aida Rocha Afonso 1950; one s. one d.; ed Army School; joined Portuguese Army 1942; mem. teaching staff, Bridges and Roads Section, Army School; promoted to rank of Lt 1946, Capt. 1954, Maj. 1963, Lt-Col 1967, Brig. 1974, Gen. 1975; various commissions in Eng Br. of Army, later mem. Directorate, Eng Branch; mem. Armed Forces Movt 1974–75, Supreme Revolutionary Council March-Sept. 1975; Prime Minister 1974–75; several awards and decorations. *Leisure interests:* political economy, philosophy, history, natural history. *Address:* Avenida Estados Unidos da América, 86, 5° esq., 1700 Lisbon, Portugal.

GONCHAR, Andrei Aleksandrovich; Russian mathematician; b. 21 Nov. 1931, Moscow; m.; two c.; ed Moscow State Univ.; lecturer, docent Moscow State Univ. 1957–63, Scientific Sec. Dept of Math. 1964–65; Sr Researcher, Head of Div., then Deputy Dir V. A.Steklov Math. Inst. 1966–68; main scientific research carried out in complex analysis and approximations theory; Ed.-in-Chief Matematicheskiye Sborniki; corresp. mem. USSR (now Russian) Acad. of Sciences 1974, mem. 1987, Vice-Pres. 1991–98; mem. Nat. Acad. of Math. *Publications:* numerous scientific publs on complex analysis and approximation theory, theory of analytical functions. *Address:* Russian Academy of Sciences, Department of Mathematics, Leninsky pr. 14, Moscow, Russia (Office). *Telephone:* (095) 938-18-12 (Office).

GONCHAR, Nikolai Nikolayevich, CEconSc; Russian politician; b. 16 Oct. 1946, Murmansk; m.; one d.; ed Moscow Energy Inst.; engineer, then head of div. Moscow City Council on research activities of students 1972–75; Head of Div. Research Inst. of Complex Devt of Nat. Econs of Moscow 1976–82; Deputy, then First Deputy Chair. Exec. Cttee of Deputies, Soviet of Bauman Region of Moscow 1987–89, Chair. 1990–91; Sec. Regional CPSU Cttee 1989–90; Deputy Chair. Moscow City Soviet of People's Deputies 1990–91, Chair. 1991–93; mem. Council of Fed. 1993–95, Deputy Chair. Cttee on Budget and Financial Regulations 1994–95; mem. State Duma 1995–. *Address:* State Duma, Okhotny Ryad 1, 103265 Moscow, Russia (Office). *Telephone:* (095) 292-75-08 (Office).

GONCHIGDORJ, Radnaasümberelyn, PhD, DSc; Mongolian politician and mathematician; b. 1954, Tsakhir Dist, Arkhangai Prov.; s. of Radnaasumberel Gonchigdorj and Namjaa Gonchigdorj; m. Damdinsurengiin Hishigt 1977; two s. two d.; ed Mongolian State Univ.; Lecturer in Math., Mongolian State Univ. 1975–88; Dir Inst. of Math., Mongolian Acad. of Sciences 1988–90; Chair. Exec. Cttee Mongolian Social-Democratic Movt 1990; Chair. Mongolian Social-Democratic Party 1994–; Deputy to Great People's Hural 1990–92; Vice-Pres. of Mongolia and Chair. State Little Hural 1990–92; mem. State Great Hural 1992–96, Chair. 1996–2000; Presidential Cand. 2001. *Address:* c/o State Great Hural, Government House, Ulan Bator 12, Mongolian People's Republic. *Telephone:* (1) 326877. *Fax:* (1) 322866.

GÖNCZ, Árpád, LLD; Hungarian politician and writer; b. 10 Feb. 1922, Budapest; s. of Lajos Göncz and Ilona Heimann; m. Mária Zsuzsanna Göntér 1946; two s. two d.; ed Pázmány Péter University of Budapest; employed as banking clerk with Land Credit Inst.; joined Ind. Smallholders, Landworkers and Bourgeois Party; leading positions in Ind. Youth Org.; Ed.-in-Chief Generation (weekly); sentenced in 1957 to life imprisonment as defendant in political Bibó trial; released under amnesty 1963; then freelance writer and literary translator, especially of English works; Wheatland Prize, Attila József Prize; Pres. Hungarian Writers Federation 1989–90; Founding mem. Free Initiatives Network, Free Democratic Fed., Historic Justice Cttee; mem. of Parl. 1990; Acting Pres. of Hungary May–Aug. 1990, Pres. of Hungary 1990–2000; Hon. KCMG 1991; Dr hc (Butler) 1990, (Connecticut) 1991, (Oxford) 1995, (Sorbonne) 1996, (Bologna) 1997; George Washington Prize 2000, Pro Humanitate Award 2001, Polish Business Oscar Award 2002. *Publications include:* Men of God (novel), Homecoming (and other stories), Hungarian Medea (and other plays), political essays. *Leisure interests:* reading, walking. *Address:* Office of the Former President, 1055 Budapest, Kossuth tér 4, Hungary. *Telephone:* (1) 441-3550. *Fax:* (1) 441-3552.

GONG LI; Chinese actress; m. Ooi Hoe-Seong 1996. *Films include:* Red Sorghum 1987, Raise the Red Lantern, Farewell My Concubine, To Live, Shanghai Triad.

GONG PUSHENG; Chinese diplomatist (retd); b. 6 Sept. 1913, Shanghai; m. Chang Hanfu (deceased); two d.; Deputy Dir Int. Orgs. and Confs. Dept, Ministry of Foreign Affairs 1949–58, Dir 1958–67; mem. 1st-4th Exec. Cttee, All-China Democratic Women's Fed. 1949–84; Vice-Pres. Red Cross Soc. of China 1979–85; Amb. to Ireland 1980–83; mem. of Nat. Cttee, Chinese People's Political Consultative Conf. 1983–93, Council, Chinese People's Inst. of Foreign Affairs 1985–; Vice-Pres. China UN Asscn 1985–; Vice-Chair. Yenching Grad. Inst. 1993–; Prof. Foreign Affairs Coll., Beijing 1985–; mem. Foreign Affairs Cttee of Nat. Cttee CPPCC 1988–93; Hon. Pres. Beijing Society for Comparative Int. Studies 1991–. *Address:* c/o Ministry of Foreign Affairs, Chaoyangmennei Street, Dongsi, Beijing, People's Republic of China.

GONG YUZHI; Chinese politician; b. 1929, Xiangtan, Hunan Prov.; ed Qinghua Univ.; researcher, CCP Cen. Cttee Propaganda Dept 1952–66; Deputy Office Dir Cttee for Editing and Publishing Works of Mao Zedong 1977–80; Deputy Dir CCP Cen. Cttee Party Documents Research Office 1982; Deputy Dir CCP Cen. Cttee Propaganda Dept 1988; mem. 5th to 8th CPPCC Nat. Cttee; Vice-Pres. CCP Cen. Cttee Party School 1994–96, Soc. of Research on History of CCP; Dir Research Centre for Theory of Building Socialism with Chinese Characteristics; Exec. Deputy Dir Cen. Party History Research Centre; fmr mem. Academic Council, Inst. of Philosophy, Chinese Acad. of Social Sciences; fmr part-time Prof. Beijing and Qinghua Univs. *Publications:* Some Questions on the Law of Development for Natural Sciences, On Science, Philosophy and Society, From New Democracy to Primary Stage of Socialism. *Address:* c/o Central Committee of the Chinese Communist Party, Beijing, People's Republic of China.

GONSALVES, Ralph, PhD; Saint Vincent and the Grenadines politician and lawyer; b. 1946; ed Univ. of West Indies, Victoria Univ. of Manchester, UK; called to Bar, Gray's Inn, London; practised law at Eastern Caribbean Supreme Court; fmr lecturer Depts of Govt, Political Science and Sociology, Univ. of W Indies; Leader United People's Movt (UPM) 1979–82, Movt for Nat. Unity (MNU) 1994–98; Leader United Labour Party (ULP); Prime Minister of Saint Vincent and the Grenadines and Minister of Finance, Planning, Economic Development, Labour and Information March 2001–. *Address:* Office of the Prime Minister, Administrative Centre, Kingstown, Saint Vincent and the Grenadines (Office).

GONZALES POSADA, Luis; Peruvian politician and lawyer; b. 30 July 1945, Pisco; fmr Legal Adviser, Banco Industrial, Corporación Financiera de Desarrollo, Electricidad del Perú and of Social Security Dept; mem. of Bd of Dirs., Seguro Social Obrero, Seguro Social del Empleado, Empresa Nacional de Turismo del Perú, La Crónica, Futura and Visión Peruana publishing cos.; Dir and Founder of the daily Hoy and the weekly Visión; has been on staff of La Tribuna, La Prensa, Correo and La Crónica; mem. Colegio de Abogados de Lima (Pres. Foreign Affairs Comm. 1999) and of Colegio de Periodistas de Lima; Minister of Justice 1985–86. *Address:* c/o Ministry of Justice, Palacio de Gobierno, Pescadería, Lima, Peru.

GONZÁLEZ, Ángel; Spanish poet; b. 1925, Oviedo; Prof. Univ. of New Mexico, Albuquerque 1972–90; mem. Spanish Royal Acad. 1996–; winner of several literary prizes including Premio Príncipe de Asturias 1985. *Publications include:* Áspero mundo (Harsh World), Prosemas y menos, Palabra sobre palabra (Word upon Word). *Address:* c/o Spanish Royal Academy, Calle Felipe IV 4, 28014 Madrid, Spain.

GONZALEZ, Antonio Erman; Argentine politician; b. 16 May 1935, La Rioja Prov.; ed Nat. Univ. of Córdoba; fmr Prof. of Accountancy, La Rioja Univ.; econ., accountancy and taxation adviser to various firms in La Rioja; accountant, Inst. for Social Security and Welfare (IPSAS), La Rioja Prov. 1961–64; Sec. for Finance, Buenos Aires Municipality 1963–64, Econ. Adviser ad honorem 1964–66; Gen. Man. IPSAS 1964–65; auditor, Bank of La Rioja Prov. 1966; Under-Sec. of Finance, Prov. of La Rioja 1967; mem. Bd IPSAS 1967–69; mem. State Exchequer of La Rioja 1971–72, 1974–75; Pres. Bank of La Rioja 1972–74, 1985, econ. consultant 1981–82, Dir 1984, adviser 1987; Minister of Finance and Public Works 1985–87, 1988–89, of Health and Social Welfare 1989, of Economy 1989–92; Dist deputation 1987–88; elected Deputy 1989–; Vice-Pres. Argentine Cen. Bank 1989; charged with illegal arms sales to Ecuador and Croatia July 2001. *Publications:* numerous tech. papers.

GONZÁLEZ, Rubén; Cuban pianist; b. April 1917, Santa Clara; m. Eneida González; one s.; full-time musician from 1941 until retirement mid-1980s; made first recording in 1943; came out of retirement 1998; regular tours with Buena Vista Social Club; recent tours include Europe May 1999, Japan Aug.–Sept. 2000, S America, USA and Australia 2000–01. *Solo recordings include:* Introducing... Rubén González; joint recordings include A Toda Cuba Le Gusta (with the Afro-Cuban All Stars), Buena Vista Social Club (with Ry Cooder). *Address:* 2 Main Street, 4th Floor, Gloucester, MA 01930, USA (Office).

GONZÁLEZ CASANOVA, Pablo; Mexican researcher and professor; b. 11 Feb. 1922, Toluca; s. of Pablo González Casanova and Concepción del Valle; m. Natalia Henríquez Ureña 1947; three s.; ed El Colegio de México, Escuela Nacional de Antropología, Univ. Nacional Autónoma de México and Univ. de Paris; Asst Researcher, Inst. de Investigaciones Sociales, Univ. Nacional Autónoma de México (UNAM) 1944–50, Researcher 1950–52, Full-time Researcher 1973–78; Researcher, El Colegio de México 1950–54; Sec. Gen. Asscn of Univs. 1953–54; Titular Prof. of Mexican Sociology, Escuela Nacional de Ciencias Políticas y Sociales, UNAM 1952–66, of Gen. Sociology 1954–58; Dir Escuela Nacional de Ciencias Políticas y Sociales 1957–65, Full-time Titular Prof. 1964–65, Titular Prof. of Research Planning 1967–; Dir Inst. Investigaciones Sociales, UNAM 1966–70; Rector, UNAM 1970–72; Visiting Prof. Cambridge Univ. 1981–82; Pres. Admin. Cttee Facultad Latinoamericana de Ciencias Sociales, Santiago and Centro Latinoamericano de Investigaciones Sociales, Rio de Janeiro, UNESCO 1959–65; Consultant UN Univ. 1983–87; Dir Centro de Investigaciones Interdisciplinarias en Humanidades Univ. Nacional Autónoma de Mexico 1986–; mem. Asscn Int. de Sociologues de Langue Française, Comité Int. pour la Documentation des Sciences Sociales, Acad. de la Investigación Científica; Pres. Asociación Latinoamericana de Sociología 1969–72. *Publications:* El Poder al Pueblo 1985, El misoneísmo y la modernidad cristiana 1948, Satira del Siglo XVIII (with José Miranda) 1953, Una utopia de América 1953, La literatura perseguida en la crisis de la Colonia 1958, La ideología norteamericana sobre inversiones extranjeras 1955, Estudio de la técnica social 1958, La Democracia en México 1965, Las categorías del desarrollo económico y la investigación en ciencias sociales 1967, Sociología de la explotación 1969, América Latina: Historia de Medio Siglo 1925–1975 (2 Vols, Ed.) 1977, Historia del Movimiento Obrero en América Latina, Siglo XX 1981, El Estado y los Partidos Políticos en México 1981, América Latina, Hoy 1990, El Estado y la Política en el Sur del Mundo 1994. *Address:* Peña Pobre 28, Tlalpan, México, DF 14050, Mexico. *Telephone:* 5506702.

GONZÁLEZ DEL VALLE, Jorge; Guatemalan international official and economist; b. 24 Jan. 1929; ed Univ. of San Carlos, Guatemala, Columbia Univ., New York, Yale Univ., New Haven, Conn.; worked in Bank of Guatemala and Cen. American Bank for Econ. Integration; Prof. of Econs

1956–; Exec. Dir IMF for four years; Exec. Sec. Cen. American Monetary Council for nine years; Head Centre for Latin American Monetary Studies (CEMLA) 1978–90.

GONZÁLEZ MACCHI, Luis Angel; Paraguayan politician and lawyer; b. 13 Dec. 1947, Asunción; s. of Dr. Saúl González and the late Julia Macchi; m. Susana Galli; two d.; ed Univ. Nacional de Asunción; fmr Pres. Nat. Congress; Dir.-Gen. and Pres. of Exec. Council, Servicio Nacional de Promoción Profesional (SNPP) 1993–98; Pres. of Paraguay March 1999–; mem. Asociación Nacional Republicana (Partido Colorado). *Address:* Office of the President, Palacio de López, Asunción, Paraguay (Office). *Telephone:* (21) 44-1889 (Office). *Fax:* (21) 49-3154 (Office).

GONZÁLEZ MÁRQUEZ, Felipe; Spanish politician and lawyer; b. 5 March 1942, Seville; m. Carmen Romero; two s. one d.; ed lower and high school, school of law, continued studies at Catholic Univ. of Louvain, Belgium; on graduating from law school, opened first labour law office to deal with workers' problems in Seville 1966; mem. Spanish Socialist Youth 1962; mem. Spanish Socialist Party (Partido Socialista Obrero Español, PSOE) 1964–; mem. Seville Provincial Cttee 1965–69, Nat. Cttee 1969–70, mem. Exec. Bd 1970, First Sec. 1974–79, resigned; re-elected Sept. 1979, then Sec.-Gen. –1997; mem. for Madrid, Congress of Deputies 1977–; Prime Minister of Spain and Pres. Council of Ministers 1982–96; Chair. Socialist Parl. Group; mem. Japanese Bonsai Asscn; Grand Cross of the Order of Mil. Merit 1984; Order of Isabel the Catholic 1996; Golden Cross of Merit (Austria) 1997; Dr hc (Louvain) 1995, Charlemagne Prize 1993, Carlos V Prize, Academia Europaea 2000. *Publications:* What is Socialism? 1976, P.S.O.E. 1977, El futuro no es lo que era (with J. Cebrián) 2001. *Leisure interests:* reading, bonsai plants. *Address:* Fundación Progreso Global, Gobelas 31, 28023 Madrid, Spain. *Telephone:* (91) 5820282 (Office). *Fax:* (91) 5820283 (Office). *E-mail:* fpglobal@psoe.es (Office).

GONZÁLEZ MARTÍN, HE Cardinal Marcelo; Spanish ecclesiastic; b. 16 Jan. 1918, Villanubla, Valladolid; ordained 1941; consecrated Bishop of Astorga 1961; titular Archbishop of Case Mediane 1966; auxiliary Archbishop of Barcelona 1967; Archbishop of Toledo and Primate of Spain 1971–95; created Cardinal by Pope Paul VI 1973. *Address:* Residencia Madre Genoveva, Avda. de Francia 6, 45005 Toledo, Spain (Office). *Telephone:* 220284 (Office).

GONZALEZ PANTALEON, Rafael; Dominican diplomatist and doctor; b. 1937, Yayabo; m.; seven c.; ed Faculty of Medicine, St Thomas Aquinas Univ. (now Autonomous Univ. of San Domingo), Massillon State Hosp. and Mount Vernon Hosp., NY; Resident Physician, St Vincent de Paul Hosp.; Medical Dir Social Security Clinic, Yayabo 1964; Gen. Practitioner Salvador B. Gautier Hosp. and Prof. of Anatomy, Autonomous Univ. 1965–68; Medical Dir, Pocahontas Memorial Hosp., W Va 1974; Gen. Dir Dominican Social Security Inst., 1986; Medical and Social Security Adviser to Exec. Br. of Govt of Dominican Repub.; Perm. Rep. to the UN 1989–91; sentenced to 78 months prison and a US$3.5 million fine in Jan. 1998 for Medicare fraud; f. Enriquillo Cultural Soc. 1977; Doctor of the Year, Mount Vernon Hosp. 1971.

GONZÁLEZ ZUMÁRRAGA, HE Cardinal Antonio José; Ecuadorean ecclesiastic; b. 18 March 1925, Pujilí, Latacunga; ordained priest 1951; consecrated Bishop of Tagarata 1969; Bishop of Machala 1978–80; Coadjutor 1980; Archbishop of Quito 1985; cr. Cardinal 2001. *Address:* Arzobispado, Apartado 17-01-00106, Calle Chile 1140, Quito, Ecuador (Office). *Telephone:* (2) 524002 (Office). *Fax:* (2) 580973.

GONZI, Lawrence, LLD; Maltese politician and lawyer; b. 1 July 1953; s. of Louis Gonzi and Inez Gonzi (née Galea); m. Catherine Gonzi (née Callus); two s. one d.; ed Malta Univ.; practised law 1975–88; Speaker House of Reps. 1988–96; MP Nationalist Party 1996–; Shadow Minister and Opposition Spokesman for Social Policy 1996–98, Sec. and Whip Nationalist Party Parl. Group 1996–97; Leader of the House, Minister for Social Policy 1998–, Deputy Prime Minister 1999–; Sec. Gen. of Nationalist Party 1997–; Gen. Pres. Malta Catholic Action 1976–86; Chair. Pharmacy Bd 1987–88, Nat. Comm. for Persons with Disabilities 1987–94 (Pres. 1994–96), Nat. Comm. for Mental Health Reform, Electoral System (Revision) Comm. 1994–95, Mizzi Org. Bd of Dirs 1989–97; mem. Prisons Bd 1987–88. *Address:* Ministry for Social Policy, Palazzo Ferreria, Republic Street, Valletta, CMR 02, Malta. *Telephone:* 21243166; 21225709. *Fax:* 21243017. *E-mail:* lawrence.gonzi@gov.mt (Office). *Website:* www.msp.gov.mt (Office).

GOOCH, Graham Alan, OBE; British cricketer; b. 23 July 1953, Leytonstone; s. of late Alfred and of Rose Gooch; m. Brenda Daniels 1976; three d.; ed Norlington Junior High School, Leytonstone; right-hand opening batsman, right-arm medium bowler; played for Essex 1973–97 (Capt. 1986–87 and 1989–94), Western Province 1982–83 and 1983–84; played in 118 Tests for England 1975 to 1994–95, 34 as Capt., scoring 8,900 runs (England record) (average 42.5) including 20 hundreds (highest score 333 and record Test match aggregate of 456 v. India, Lord's 1990, becoming only batsman to score a triple century and a century in a first-class match) and holding 103 catches; scored 44,841 runs (128 hundreds) and held 555 catches in first-class cricket; toured Australia 1978–79, 1979–80, 1990–91 (Capt.) and 1994–95; 125 limited-overs internationals, including 50 as Capt. (both England records); mem. England Selection Cttee 1996–99; Man. England Tour to Australia 1998–99; Head Coach Essex 2001–; Wisden Cricketer of the Year 1980, mem. Fed. of Int. Cricketers Asscn Hall of Fame 2000. *Publications:* Testing Times

1991, Gooch: My Autobiography 1995. *Leisure interests:* squash, golf, football. *Address:* c/o Essex County Cricket Club, The County Ground, New Writtle Street, Chelmsford, Essex, CM2 0PG, England.

GOOD, Anthony Bruton Meyrick, FID; British public relations consultant and marketing consultant; b. 18 April 1933, Sutton, Surrey; s. of Meyrick G. B. Good and Amy M. Trussell; m. (divorced); two d.; ed Felsted School, Essex; man. trainee, Distillers Group; Editorial Asst Temple Press 1952–55; Public Relations Officer, Silver City Airways; Public Relations and Marketing Man., Air Holdings Group 1955–60; f. and Chair. Good Relations Ltd (later Good Relations Group PLC) 1961–89; Dir Cox and Kings Travel Ltd 1971–, Chair. 1975–; Chair. Good Relations (India) Ltd 1988–, Cox and Kings (India) Ltd 1988–, Good Consultancy Ltd 1989–, Flagship Group 1999–, Tranquil Moment 2000–, Sage Nutritionals 2000–; (non-exec.) Dir IM Group Ltd, Miller Insurance Group Ltd 2000–; Fellow Inst. of Public Relations. *Leisure interest:* travel. *Address:* Clench Lodge, Wootton Rivers, Marlborough, Wilts., SN8 4NT (Office); Clench House, Wootton Rivers, Marlborough, Wilts., SN8 4NT, England (Home). *Telephone:* (1672) 810126 (Office); (1672) 810670 (Home). *Fax:* (1672) 810869 (Office); (1672) 810149 (Home). *E-mail:* anthony.good@btinternet.com.

GOODALL, Sir (Arthur) David (Saunder), GCMG, MA; British diplomatist (retd); b. 9 Oct. 1931, Blackpool; s. of Arthur William Goodall and Maisie Josephine Byers; m. Morwenna Peecock 1962; two s. one d.; ed Ampleforth Coll., Trinity Coll., Oxford; army service in Kenya, Aden, Cyprus 1954–56; joined Foreign (now Diplomatic) Service 1956, served at Nicosia, Jakarta, Bonn, Nairobi, Vienna 1956–75, Head Western European Dept, FCO 1975–79, Minister, Bonn 1979–82, Deputy Sec., Cabinet Office 1982–84, Deputy Under-Sec. of State, FCO 1984–87, High Commr in India 1987–92; Joint Chair. Anglo-Irish Encounter 1992–97; Pres. Irish Genealogical Research Soc. 1992–; Chair. Leonard Cheshire Foundation 1995–2000 (Chair. Int. Cttee 1992–95); Vice-Chair. British-Irish Asscn 1994–97, Chair. 1997–2002; Chair. Governing Body, Heythrop Coll., Univ. of London 2000–; Visiting Prof. in Irish Studies, Univ. of Liverpool 1996–; mem. Council Univ. of Durham 1992–2000 (Vice-Chair. 1997–2000); Hon. Fellow Trinity Coll. Oxford; Distinguished Friend of the Univ. of Oxford 2001; Hon. LLD (Hull) 1994. *One-man exhibitions:* (watercolours): Berlin 1979, Bonn 1982, London 1987, 1994, New Delhi 1991, Durham 1996, Hull 1998, Helmsley (York). *Publications:* Remembering India 1997, Ryedale Pilgrimage 2000; contribs. to The Tablet, The Ampleforth Journal, The Past, The Irish Genealogist. *Leisure interests:* painting in watercolours, reading, walking. *Address:* Greystones, Ampleforth, N Yorks., YO62 4DU, England.

GOODALL, Jane, CBE, PhD; British ethologist; b. 3 April 1934, London; d. of Mortimer Herbert Morris-Goodall and Vanne Morris-Goodall (née Joseph); m. 1st Hugo Van Lawick 1964 (divorced 1974); one s.; m. 2nd M. Derek Bryceson 1975 (died 1980); ed Uplands School, Univ. of Cambridge; Sec. Oxford Univ.; Asst Ed. Documentary Film Studio; waitress; Asst Sec. to Louis Leakey, worked in Olduvai Gorge, then moved to Gombe Stream Game Reserve (now Gombe Nat. Park), camp became Gombe Stream Research Centre 1964; Scientific Dir Gombe Wildlife Research Inst. 1967–; Founder Jane Goodall Inst. for Wildlife Research 1977–; Founder Cttee for Conservation and Care of Chimpanzees 1986; Hon. Visiting Prof. in Zoology Dar es Salaam Univ. 1973–; A. D. White Prof.-at-Large Cornell Univ. 1996–; mem. advisory panel World Summit on Sustainable Devt 2002; UN(O) Messenger of Peace 2002; visiting lecturer numerous univs including Yale Univ., USA; speaker on conservation issues, appearing on numerous TV shows including: 20/20, Nightline, Good Morning America; contrib. to New York Times; Hon. Foreign mem. American Acad. for Advancement of Sciences; Conservation Award (New York Zoological Soc.), Franklin Burr Award (twice, Nat. Geographic Soc.), Nat. Geographic Soc. Centennial Award, Hubbard Medal 1995, Medal of Mt Kilimanjaro 1996, Public Service Award, Nat. Scientific Bd 1998, John Hay Award, Orion Soc. 1998, Int. Peace Award, Reorganized Church of the Latter Day Saints, Gandhi/King Peace Award 2001. *Publications:* Shadow of Man, Chimpanzees of Gombe 1986, The Chimpanzee Family Book 1989, Through a Window 1990, The Chimpanzee: The Living Link Between "Man" and "Beast" 1992, Visions of Caliban 1993, Jane Goodall: With Love 1994, Dr White 1999, 40 Years at Gombe 1999, Brutal Kinship 1999, Reason for Hope 1999, Africa in My Blood: An Autobiography in Letters 2000, Beyond Innocence: An Autobiography in Letters, the Later Years 2001, Chimpanzees I Love: Saving Their World and Ours 2001. *Address:* The Jane Goodall Institute for Wildlife Research, Education and Conservation, PO Box 14890, Silver Spring, MD 20911-4890, USA. *Telephone:* (301) 565-0086. *Fax:* (301) 565-3188. *Website:* www.janegoodall.org.

GOODE, Anthony William, MD, FRCS FACS; British surgeon; b. 3 Aug. 1945, Newcastle-upon-Tyne; s. of William Henry Goode and Eileen Veronica Goode; m. Patricia Josephine Flynn 1987; ed Corby School and Univ. of Newcastle-upon-Tyne; clinical surgical posts in Newcastle Hosps. Group 1968–76; Univ. of London Teaching Hosps. 1976–; Prof. of Endocrine and Metabolic Surgery, Univ. of London, Consultant Surgeon Royal London Hosp., Whitechapel and St Bartholomew's Hosp., Hon. Prof. Centre for Biological and Medical Systems, Imperial Coll. 1982–; Clinical Dir Helicopter Emergency Medical Service, London 1998–2000; Ed.-in-Chief Medicine, Science and the Law 1996–; Asst Sec. Gen. British Acad. of Forensic Science 1982–87, Pres. 1999–; Hon. Sec. British Asscn of Endocrine Surgeons 1983–96; Fellow Royal Soc. of Medicine 1971–; mem. Int. Soc. of Surgery 1984–, Int. Soc. of Endocrine Surgeons 1984–, New York Acad. of Sciences 1986–, MCC 1982–, Hunterian

Soc. 1998 (Orator 1998); Trustee Smith and Nephew Foundation 1990–; Liveryman, Worshipful Soc. of Apothecaries of London; Freeman City of London 1992. *Publications:* numerous papers and articles on nutrition in surgical patients, endocrine diseases, metabolic changes in manned space-flight and related topics. *Leisure interests:* cricket, music (especially opera). *Address:* The Surgical Unit, The Royal London Hospital, Whitechapel, London, E1 1BB, England. *Telephone:* (20) 7601-7032 (Office).

GOODE, Richard; American pianist; b. 1 June 1943, New York; m. Marcia Weinfeld; ed Mannes Coll. of Music, Curtis Inst.; studied with Nadia Reisenberg and Rudolf Serkin; has played with Baltimore, Boston, Chicago, Cleveland, New York, Philadelphia, Berlin Radio, Finnish Radio and Bamberg Symphony Orchestras; mem. Piano Faculty, Mannes Coll. of Music 1969–; concerts and recitals in USA, Europe, Japan; Carnegie Hall recital début 1990; prizes include Young Concert Artists Award, 1st Prize Clara Haskil Competition, Avery Fischer Prize, Grammy Award (with clarinettist Richard Stoltzman). *Leisure interests:* book collecting, museums. *Address:* 12 East 87th Street, Apt. 5A, New York, NY 10128 (Office); c/o Frank Salomon Associates, 201 W 54th Street, Apt. 1C, New York, NY 10019, USA.

GOODE, Sir Royston (Roy) Miles, Kt, CBE, QC, LLD, FBA, FRSA; British professor of law; b. 6 April 1933, London; s. of Samuel Goode and Bloom Goode; m. Catherine A. Rueff 1964; one d.; ed Highgate School and Univ. of London; admitted solicitor 1955; partner, Victor Mishcon & Co. (solicitors) 1966–67; called to Bar, Inner Temple 1988, Hon. Bencher 1992–; Prof. of Law, Queen Mary Coll. London 1971–73, Crowther Prof. of Credit and Commercial Law 1973–89, Head of Dept and Dean of Faculty of Laws 1976–80, Dir and founder, Centre for Commercial Law Studies 1980–89; Norton Rose Prof. of English Law, Univ. of Oxford 1990–98, Prof. Emer. 1998–; Hon. Fellow, Queen Mary & Westfield Coll. London 1991–, Fellow St John's Coll. Oxford 1990–98 (Emer. Fellow 1998–); mem. Monopolies and Mergers Comm. 1981–86, Council of the Banking Ombudsman 1989–92; Chair. Pension Law Review Cttee 1992–93; mem. Council and Chair. Exec. Cttee JUSTICE 1994–96; Hon. Pres. Centre for Commercial Law Studies 1990–, Oxford Inst. of Legal Practice 1994–; Hon. DSc (London) 1997. *Publications include:* Consumer Credit 1978, Commercial Law 1982, Legal Problems of Credit and Security 1982, Payment Obligations in Commercial and Financial Transactions 1983, Proprietary Rights and Insolvency in Sales Transactions 1985, Principles of Corporate Insolvency Law 1990, Consumer Credit Legislation (looseleaf); books on hire purchase; contribs. to Halsbury's Laws of England (4th Edn). *Leisure interests:* chess, reading, walking, browsing in bookshops. *Address:* 42 St John Street, Oxford, OX1 2LH (Home); St John's College, Oxford, OX1 3JP, England. *Telephone:* (1865) 277348 (Office); (1865) 515494 (Home). *Fax:* (1865) 277383 (Office). *E-mail:* roy.goode@sjc.ox.ac.uk (Office).

GOODFELLOW, Julia Mary, CBE, PhD, FInstP, FRSA, FMedSci, FIBiol; British scientist; b. Julia Mary Lansdall, 1 July 1951, Liverpool; d. of Gerald Landsall and the late Brenda Landsall; m. Peter Neville Goodfellow 1972; one s. one d.; ed Woking Co. School for Girls, Reigate Co. School for Girls, Univ. of Bristol, Open Univ.; NATO Research Fellow Stanford Univ. 1976–78; Research Fellow Birkbeck Coll., Univ. of London 1979–83, Lecturer, then Sr Lecturer and Reader 1983–95, Prof. of Biomolecular Sciences 1995–, Chair. Dept of Crystallography 1996–, Vice-Master 1998–, Chair. Wellcome Trust Molecular and Cell Panel 1995–98; mem. Biotechnology and Biological Sciences Research Council (BBSRC) 1997–, Chief Exec. 2002–; Fellow Inst. of Physics, Fellow Royal Soc. of Arts, Fellow of Medical Science, Fellow Inst. of Biologists. *Publications:* Molecular Dynamics Applications in Molecular Biology (ed.) 1990, Computer Modelling in Molecular Biology (ed.) 1992, Computer Simulation in Molecular Biology (ed.) 1995; contribs. to learned journals. *Leisure interests:* reading, tapestry, opera. *Address:* BBSRC, Polaris House, North Star Avenue, Swindon, SN2 1UH, England (Office). *Telephone:* (1793) 413208 (Office). *Fax:* (1793) 413201 (Office). *Website:* www.bbsrc.ac.uk.

GOODFELLOW, Peter Neville, BSc, DPhil, FRS, FMedSci; British geneticist; b. 4 Aug. 1951; s. of Bernard Clifford Roy Goodfellow and Doreen Olga (née Berry); m. Julia Mary Lansdall 1972; one s. one d.; ed Bristol Univ., Oxford Univ.; MRC Postdoctoral Fellow, Oxford Univ. 1975–76; Jane Coffin Childs Postdoctoral Fellow, Stanford Univ. 1976–78; Sr Fellow American Cancer Soc. 1978–79; Staff Scientist, Imperial Cancer Research Foundation 1979–83, Sr Scientist 1983–86, Prin. Scientist 1986–92; Arthur Balfour Prof. of Genetics, Univ. of Cambridge 1992–96; Sr Vice-Pres. of Biopharmaceuticals and Neuroscience, later Discovery, Smithkline Beecham Pharmaceuticals 1996–2001, Sr Vice-Pres. Discovery Research, GlaxoSmithKline 2001–. *Publications include:* The Mammalian Y Chromosone: Molecular Search for the Sex Determining Gene (Jt Ed.) 1987, Cystic Fibrosis (Ed.) 1989, Molecular Genetics of Muscular Disease (Jt Ed.) 1989, Sex Determination and the Y Chromosone (Jt Ed.) 1991, Mammalian Genetics (Jt Ed.) 1992; numerous reviews and specialist articles in learned journals. *Leisure interests:* science, football. *Address:* GlaxoSmithKline, Gunnels Wood Road, Stevenage, Herts, SG1 2NY, England (Office). *Website:* www.gsk.com (Office).

GOODHART, Charles Albert Eric, CBE, PhD, FBA; British economist; b. 1936, London; s. of Sir A. L. Goodhart; m. Margaret (Miffy) Smith 1960; one s. three d.; ed Eton Coll., Trinity Coll., Cambridge, Harvard Univ.; Asst Lecturer Dept of Econs Cambridge Univ. and Prize Fellow, Trinity Coll., economist Dept of Econ. Affairs, London 1965–66; lecturer LSE 1966–68, Norman Sosnow Prof. of Banking and Finance 1985–2002, Deputy Dir Financial Markets Group and Emer. Prof. 2002–; Adviser on Monetary Affairs

Bank of England 1968–85, external mem. Monetary Policy Cttee 1997–2000; Adviser to Gov. of Bank of England on Financial Regulation 2002–; mem. Exchange Fund Advisory Council, Hong Kong 1988–97. *Publications:* Money, Information and Uncertainty 1989, The Evolution of Central Banks 1985, The Central Bank and the Financial System 1995, The Emerging Framework of Financial Regulation (ed.) 1998, The Foreign Exchange Market (with R. Payne) 2000, Financial Crises, Contagion and the Lender of Last Resort (ed with G. Illing) 2002. *Leisure interest:* sheep farming. *Address:* Financial Markets Group, London School of Economics, Houghton Street, London, WC2A 2AE (Office); 27 Abbotsbury Road, London, W14 8EL, England (Home). *Telephone:* (20) 7955-7555 (Office); (20) 7603-5817 (Home). *Fax:* (20) 7371-3664 (Home).

GOODING, Cuba, Jr.; American actor; b. 2 Jan. 1968, Bronx, NY; s. of Cuba Gooding Sr and Shirley Gooding; two Nat. Asscn for the Advancement of Colored People (NAACP) Awards; Acad. Award, Best Supporting Actor (for Jerry Maguire) 1997; Chicago Film Critics Award; Screen Actor Guild Award. *Television appearances include:* Kill or Be Killed 1990, Murder with Motive: The Edmund Perry Story 1992, Daybreak 1993, The Tuskegee Airmen. *Films include:* Coming to America 1988, Sing 1989, Boyz N the Hood 1991, Gladiator 1992, A Few Good Men 1992, Hitz 1992, Judgement Night 1993, Lightning Jack 1994, Losing Isaiah 1995, Outbreak 1995, Jerry Maguire 1996, The Audition 1996, Old Friends 1997, As Good As It Gets 1997, What Dreams May Come 1998, A Murder of Crows 1999, Instinct 1999, Men of Honor 2000, Pearl Harbor 2001, Rat Race 2001, In the Shadows 2001, Snow Dogs 2002, Boat Trip 2002.

GOODISON, Sir Nicholas Proctor, Kt, PhD, FSA, FRSA; British banker; b. 16 May 1934, Radlett; s. of Edmund Harold Goodison and Eileen Mary Carrington Proctor; m. Judith Abel Smith 1960; one s. two d.; ed Marlborough Coll. and King's Coll., Cambridge; joined H. E. Goodison & Co. (now Quilter & Co. Ltd) 1958–88, partner 1962, Chair. 1975–88; mem. Council of The Stock Exchange 1968–88, Chair. 1976–88; Pres. British Bankers Asscn 1991–96; Pres. Int. Fed. of Stock Exchanges 1985–86; Chair. TSB Group plc 1989–95; Chair. TSB Bank PLC 1989–2000; Deputy Chair. Lloyds TSB Group PLC 1995–2000; Dir (non-exec.) Corus Group PLC (fmrly British Steel PLC) 1989–2001 (Deputy Chair. 1993–99); Dir Gen. Accident 1987–95; Trustee, Nat. Heritage Memorial Fund 1988–97; Vice-Chair. Bd of English Nat. Opera 1980–98 (Dir 1977–98); Chair. Nat. Art-Collections Fund 1986–, Courtauld Inst. 1982–, Crafts Council 1997–, Burlington Magazine Publs 2001–; Hon. Keeper of Furniture, Fitzwilliam Museum, Cambridge; Pres. Furniture History Soc.; Gov. Marlborough Coll. 1981–97; Sr Fellow Royal Coll. of Art 1991; Hon. Fellow King's Coll. Cambridge 2001, Hon. FRIBA 1992; Hon. DLitt (City Univ.) 1985; Hon. LLD (Exeter) 1989; Hon. DSc (Aston Univ.) 1994; Hon. D.Art (De Montfort Univ.) 1998; Hon. DCL (Univ. of Northumbria) 1999; Légion d'honneur 1990. *Publications:* English Barometers 1680–1860 1968, Ormolu: the Work of Matthew Boulton 1974; many papers and articles on the history of furniture, clocks and barometers. *Leisure interests:* visual arts, history of furniture and decorative arts, opera, walking. *Address:* P.O. Box 2512, London, W1A 5ZP, England.

GOODLAD, John I., PhD; American educator; b. 19 Aug. 1920, N Vancouver, BC, Canada; s. of William Goodlad and Mary Inkster; m. Evalene M. Pearson 1945; one s. one d.; ed Univs of British Columbia and Chicago; fmr school teacher, school prin. and Dir of Educ. in BC; consultant in curriculum, Atlanta (Ga) Area Teacher Educ. Service 1947–49; Assoc. Prof. Emory Univ. and Agnes Scott Coll. 1949–50; Prof. and Dir Div. of Teacher Educ., Emory Univ. and Dir Agnes Scott Coll.–Emory Univ. Teacher Educ. Program 1950–56; Prof. and Dir Center for Teacher Educ. Univ. of Chicago 1956–60; Dir Corinne A. Seeds Univ. Elementary School, Univ. of Calif., Los Angeles 1960–84; Prof. Graduate School of Educ., Univ. of Calif. (LA) 1960–85, Dean 1967–83; Dir of Research, Inst. for Devt of Educ. Activities Inc. 1966–82; Prof., Coll. of Educ. Univ. of Washington 1985–; Pres. Inst. for Educ. Inquiry 1992–; 20 hon. degrees and other awards; Harold W. McGraw Prize in Educ. 1999, ECS James Bryant Conant Award 2000, Brock Int. Prize in Educ. 2002. *Publications:* numerous books and articles in educational journals. *Leisure interests:* boating, fishing, walking. *Address:* Institute for Educational Inquiry, 124 E Edgar Street, Seattle, WA 98102, USA. *Telephone:* (206) 325-3010.

GOODMAN, Elinor Mary; British political broadcaster and journalist; b. 11 Oct. 1946; d. of Edward Weston Goodman and Pamela Longbottom; m. Derek John Scott 1985; ed pvt. schools and secretarial coll.; Consumer Affairs Corresp. Financial Times newspaper 1971–78, Political Corresp. 1978–82; Political Corresp. Channel Four News (TV) 1982–88, Political Ed. 1988–. *Leisure interests:* riding, walking. *Address:* Martinscote, Oare, Marlborough, Wilts., SN8 4JA, England.

GOODMAN, John, BFA; American film actor; b. 20 June 1952, St Louis; m. Annabeth Hartzog 1989; one d.; ed Meramac Community Coll. and SW Missouri State Univ.; Broadway appearances in Loose Ends 1979, Big River 1985. *Films include:* The Survivors 1983, Eddie Macon's Run 1983, Revenge of the Nerds 1984, C.H.U.D. 1984, Maria's Lovers 1985, Sweet Dreams 1985, True Stories 1986, The Big Easy 1987, Burglar 1987, Raising Arizona 1987, The Wrong Guys 1988, Everybody's All-American 1988, Punchline 1988, Sea of Love 1989, Always 1989, Stella 1990, Arachnophobia 1990, King Ralph 1990, Barton Fink 1991, The Babe 1992, Born Yesterday 1993, The Flintstones 1994, Kingfish: A Story of Huey P. Long 1995, Pie in the Sky, Mother

Night 1996, Fallen 1997, Combat! 1997, The Borrowers 1997, The Big Lebowski 1998, Blues Brothers 2000 1998, Dirty Work 1998, The Runner 1999, Bringing Out the Dead 1999, Coyote Ugly 2000, O Brother Where Art Thou 2000, The Adventures of Rocky and Bullwinkle 2000, One Night at McCool's 2000, Emperor's New Groove (voice) 2000, Happy Birthday 2001, My First Mister 2001, Storytelling 2001, Monsters Inc. (voice) 2001, Mike's New Car (voice) 2002, Dirty Deeds 2002. *Television includes:* The Mystery of Moro Castle, The Face of Rage, Heart of Steel, Moonlighting, Chiefs (mini-series), The Paper Chase, Murder Ordained, The Equalizer, Roseanne (series), Normal, Ohio 2000, Pigs Next Door 2000. *Address:* c/o Fred Spektor, CAA, 9830 Wilshire Boulevard, Beverly Hills, CA 90212, USA.

GOODPASTER, Gen. Andrew Jackson, M.S.E., PhD; American army officer (retd); b. 12 Feb. 1915, Granite City, Ill.; s. of Andrew Jackson Goodpaster and Teresa Mary Goodpaster (née Mrovka) ; m. Dorothy Anderson 1939; two d.; ed McKendree Coll., Lebanon, Ill., US Mil. Acad., Command and Gen. Staff School, Fort Leavenworth, Kan. and Princeton Univ.; CO 48th Engineer Battalion, Italy 1943; Staff Officer, War Dept 1944–47; Graduate study, Princeton Univ. 1947–50; Special Asst to Chief of Staff, Supreme HQ Allied Powers Europe (SHAPE) 1950–54; District Engineer, San Francisco 1954; Staff Sec. to Pres. of USA 1954–61; Asst Div. Commdr 3rd Infantry Div. 1961; Commdg Gen. 8th Infantry Div., Europe 1961–62; Asst to Chair. Joint Chiefs of Staff 1962–66; Dir Joint Staff, Org. of Joint Chiefs of Staff 1966–67; Commandant, Nat. War Coll., Washington, DC, with added duty as US Army Rep., UN Mil. Staff Cttee 1967–68; mem. US Del. to Paris talks on Viet Nam April–June 1968; Deputy Commdr US Mil. Assistance Command, Viet Nam 1968–69; C-in-C US European Command 1969–74; Supreme Allied Commdr Europe (NATO) 1969–74; Fellow, Woodrow Wilson Int. Center for Scholars, Washington, DC 1975–76; Prof., Govt and Int. Studies, The Citadel, Charleston, SC 1976–77; Supt US Mil. Acad., West Point 1977–81; Chair. American Battle Monuments Comm. 1985–90, Atlantic Council of the US 1985–97; Chair. George C. Marshall Foundation 1992–2000; US Medal of Freedom 1984; Distinguished Service Cross, Defense DSM with Oak Leaf Cluster, Army DSM with Three Oak Leaf Clusters, Navy DSM, Air Force DSM, Silver Star, Legion of Merit with Oak Leaf Cluster, Purple Heart with Oak Leaf Cluster; numerous other US and foreign decorations from Italy, Repub. of Korea, Netherlands, Belgium, Luxembourg, Fed. Repub. of Germany, Turkey and Portugal. *Publication:* For the Common Defense 1977. *Address:* c/o Eisenhower Institute, 915 15th Street, NW, 8th Floor, Washington, DC 20005 (Office); 6200 Oregon Avenue NW, Apt 345, Washington, DC 20015-1542, USA. *Telephone:* (202) 223-6710 (Office). *Fax:* (202) 452-1837 (Office).

GOODWIN, Frederick (Fred) Anderson, BL, FCIB; British banker; b. 17 Aug. 1958, Paisley; ed Paisley Grammar School, Glasgow Univ.; with Touche Ross & Co. 1979–96, partner 1988–96; CEO Clydesdale Bank 1996–98, Yorkshire Bank 1997–98; Deputy CEO The Royal Bank of Scotland Group PLC 1998–2000, Group CEO 2000–; Fellow Chartered Inst. of Bankers in Scotland 1996–. *Leisure interests:* cars, golf. *Address:* Royal Bank of Scotland, 42 St Andrew Square, Edinburgh, EH2 2YE, Scotland (Office). *Telephone:* (131) 523-2033 (Office). *Fax:* (131) 556-7468 (Office). *Website:* www.rbs.co.uk (Office).

GOODWIN, Leonard George, CMG, BSc, MB, BS, B.PHARM., FRCP, FRS, FIBiol; British medical scientist; b. 11 July 1915; s. of Harry George Goodwin and Lois Goodwin; m. Marie Evelyn Coates 1940; ed William Ellis School, London, Univ. Coll. London, Univ. Coll. Hosp.; Demonstrator, School of Pharmacy, London 1935–39; Protozoologist, Wellcome Labs of Tropical Medicine 1939–63, Head of Labs 1958–63; Dir Nuffield Labs of Comparative Medicine, Inst. of Zoology, The Zoological Soc. of London 1964–80, Dir of Science, Zoological Soc. of London 1966–80; Consultant, Wellcome Trust 1984–; Jt Hon. Sec. Royal Soc. of Tropical Medicine and Hygiene 1968–74, Pres. 1979–81; Chair. Trypanosomiasis Panel, Overseas Devt Ministry 1974–77; Filariasis Steering Cttee, WHO Special Programme 1978–82; Chair. Editorial Bd Parasitology 1980–2000, Royal Soc./Univs Fed. for Animal Welfare Steering Group on Guidelines on Care of Lab. Animals 1985; Hon. Dir Wellcome Museum for Medical Science 1984–85, Wellcome Trust Film Unit 1986; Fellow Univ. Coll. London 1981; Hon. Fellow Royal Pharmaceutical Soc. of GB; Hon. DSc (Brunel) 1986; Soc. of Apothecaries Gold Medal 1974, Harrison Memorial Medal 1978, Schofield Medal, Guelph Univ. 1979, Silver Medal, Zoological Soc. 1980, Manson Medal (Royal Soc. of Tropical Medicine and Hygiene) 1992. *Films include:* William Harvey and the Circulation of the Blood (Royal Coll. of Physicians, 1956), Silas Mainville Burroughs: the Missing Story (Wellcome Trust, 1999). *Publications:* Biological Standardization (co-author) 1950, Biochemistry and Physiology of Protozoa (contrib.) 1955, A New Tropical Hygiene (co-author) 1960, Recent Advances in Pharmacology (contrib.) 1962, Oxford Textbook of Medicine (contrib.) 1982, Manson's Tropical Diseases (contrib.) 1996; many contribs. to scientific journals, mainly on pharmacology and chemotherapy of tropical diseases, especially malaria, trypansomiasis and helminth infections. *Leisure interests:* dabbling in arts and crafts, especially pottery (slipware), gardening and passive participation in music and opera. *Address:* Shepperlands Farm, Park Lane, Finchampstead, Berks., RG40 4QF, England. *Telephone:* (118) 973-2153.

GOODY, Joan Edelman, MA, MArch; American architect; b. 1 Dec. 1935, New York; d. of Sylvia Feldman Edelman and Beril Edelman; m. 1st Marvin E. Goody 1960 (died 1980); m. 2nd Peter H. Davison 1984; ed Harvard Univ. Grad. School of Design, Cornell Univ.; Prin. Goody, Clancy & Assocs. Inc., Architects 1961–; Design Critic and Asst Prof. Harvard Univ. Grad. School of Design 1973–80, Eliot Noyes Visiting Critic 1985; Faculty for Mayors Inst. for City Design 1989–; Chair. Boston Civic Design Comm. 1992–; Dir Historic Boston; Honor Award for Design (AIA) 1980, Citation for Excellence in Urban Design (AIA) 1988, FAIA 1991. *Address:* Goody, Clancy & Associates, Inc., 334 Boylston Street, Boston, MA 02116, USA. *Telephone:* (617) 262-2760. *Website:* www.gcassoc.com.

GOONETILLEKE, Albert, MD, F.R.C.P.A., F.R.C. PATH.; pathologist; b. 4 Feb. 1936, Colombo; s. of late Arlis Goonetilleke; m. Sunanaseele Wijesinghe 1958; one s. one d.; medical officer Sri Lanka Health Dept 1962–68; lecturer Univ. of Edin. 1968–70, Univ. of Leeds 1970–71; with Charing Cross Medical School, London 1972–80; Consultant Pathologist, Charing Cross & Westminster Medical School 1980–88; Chief Pathologist, King Faisal Hosp., Saudi Arabia 1988–94; Chief Pathologist, Royal Comm. Hosp., Saudi Arabia 1994–96; Consultant Pathologist, Princess Margaret Hosp., Swindon 1996–, Harold Wood Hosp. Romford 1998-; mem. British Asscn for Forensic Medicine; Ananda Coll. Gold Medal Sri Lanka 1954, C. H. Milburn Award, BMA 1982. *Publications:* Injuries Caused By Falls from Heights, Safety at Work, Safety in the Home; various articles on forensic medicine and pathology. *Leisure interests:* still and video filming, water colour painting. *Address:* Department of Pathology, Harold Wood Hospital, Romford, Essex (Office); Morningside, Long Park, Chesham Bois, Amersham, Bucks. HP6 5LF, England. *Telephone:* (1494) 721524.

GOPALAKRISHNAN, Adoor; Indian film maker; b. 3 July 1941, Adoor, Kerala; s. of late Madhavan Unnithan and Gouri Kunjamma; m. R. Sunanda 1972; one d.; mem. Working Group on Nat. Film Policy 1979–80; Dir Nat. Film Devt Corpn 1980–83; mem. Faculties of Fine Arts, Univ. of Kerala, Calicut and Mahatma Gandhi Univs. 1985–89; Chair. Film & Television Inst. of India 1987–89, 1993–96; Chair. 7th Int. Children's Film Festival of India 1991; mem. Advisory Cttee Nat. Film Archive of India 1988–90; Chair. Jury Singapore Int. Film Festival; mem. Jury, Int. Film Festival of India 1983, Venice Int. Film Festival 1988, Bombay Int. Festival 1990, Hawaii Int. Film Festival, Sochi Int. Film Festival, Alexandria Int. Film Festival; numerous int. film awards; awarded title of Padmashri 1984. *Films include:* Swayamvaran 1972, Kodiyettam 1977, Elippathayam 1981 (British Film Inst. Award), Mukhamukham 1984 (Int. Film Critics' Prize, New Delhi), Anantaram 1987, Mathilukal 1989, Vidheyan 1993, Kathapurushan 1995, Nizhalkkuthu 2002, Elippattiam and more than 24 short and documentary films. *Publications include:* plays: Vaiki vanna velicham 1961, Ninte rajyam varunnu 1963, The World of Cinema 1983; collections of essays. *Address:* Darsanam, Thiruvananthapuram, 695 017, Kerala, India. *Telephone:* (471) 551144. *Fax:* (471) 446567.

GOPALAKRISHNAN, S. Kris, MSc, MTech; Indian business executive; ed IIT, Chennai; Co-Founder and Dir Infosys Technologies, Bangalore 1981–, Tech. Dir –1987, Tech. Vice-Pres. KSA/Infosys, USA 1987–94, Head of Tech. Support Services 1994–, Head of Client Delivery and Technology 1996–98, now COO and Deputy Man. Dir. *Address:* Infosys Technologies, Plot No. 44 & 97A, Electronics City, Hosur Road, Bangalore 561 229, India (Office). *Telephone:* (80) 8520261 (Office). *Fax:* (80) 8520362 (Office). *Website:* www .infy.com (Office).

GORAI, Rt Rev Dinesh Chandra, BA, BD, DD; Indian ecclesiastic; b. 15 Jan. 1934, West Bengal; s. of Joyram and Sushila Gorai; m. Binapani Gorai 1962; two s.; ed Calcutta Univ. and Serampore Coll.; ordained priest as Methodist 1962; consecrated as Church of N India Bishop 1970; Bishop of Barrackpore 1970–82, of Kolkata 1982–; Moderator Church of North India 1983–86; social worker and rural devt expert, ecumenical leader. *Publications:* Society at the Cross Roads 1968, New Horizons in Christian Ministry 1993. *Address:* Binapani Villa, 28 M. G. Road, Keorapukur Mission, Kolkata, 700 082, India. *Telephone:* (33) 4028867. *Fax:* (33) 4028867.

GÖRANSSON, Bengt; Swedish politician; b. 25 July 1932, Stockholm; ed Univ. of Stockholm; Reso Ltd (travel org.) 1960–71; Chair. Manilla School for the Deaf 1970–78; Head, Community Centre Asscn 1971; Chair. of Bd Nat. Theatre Centre 1974–82; mem. various official cttees.; Chair. of Bd Fed. of Workers' Educational Asscns. 1980–82; Minister for Cultural Affairs 1982–89, Minister of Educ. and Cultural Affairs 1989–91; Chair. Ansvar Insurance Co. 1991–97, Int. Inst. of Alcohol Policy 1996–99, Center for Biotechnology 1996–98, Parl. Cttee on Democracy 1997–2000; Chair. Dalhalla Festival Stage 1994–2002, Norden Asscn 2001–. *Address:* ABF, PO Box 1305, 11183 Stockholm, Sweden.

GORBACHEV, Mikhail Sergeyevich; Russian politician; b. 2 March 1931, Privolnoye, Krasnogvardeisky Dist, Stavropol Territory; s. of Sergei Andreevich Gorbachev and Maria Panteleimonovna Gorbachev (née Gopcalo); m. Raisa Titarenko 1953 (died 1999); one d.; ed Faculty of Law, Moscow State Univ. and Stavropol Agricultural Inst.; began work as machine operator 1946; joined CPSU 1952; Deputy Head, Dept of Propaganda, Stavropol Komsomol Territorial Cttee 1955–56, Second, then First Sec. 1958–62; First Sec. Stavropol Komsomol City Cttee 1956–58; Del. to CPSU Congress 1961, 1971, 1976, 1981, 1986, 1990; Party Organizer, Stavropol Territorial Production Bd of Collective and State farms 1962; Head, Dept of party bodies of CPSU Territorial Cttee 1963–66; First Sec. Stavropol City Party Cttee 1966–68; Second Sec. Stavropol Territorial CPSU Cttee 1968–70, First Sec. 1970–78; mem. CPSU Cen. Cttee 1971–91, Sec. for Agric. 1978–85, alt. mem. Political Bureau CPSU, Cen. Cttee 1979–80, mem. 1980–91, Gen. Sec. CPSU Cen. Cttee 1985–91; Deputy Supreme Soviet of USSR 1970–89 (Chair. Foreign

Affairs Comm. of the Soviet Union 1984–85), mem. Presidium 1985–88, Chair. 1988–89, Supreme Soviet of RSFSR 1980–90, elected to Congress of People's Deputies of USSR 1989, Chair. 1989–90; Pres. of USSR 1990–91; Head Int. Foundation for Socio-Economic and Political Studies (Gorbachev Fund) 1992–; Head Int. Green Cross/Green Crescent 1993–; Co-Founder Social Democratic Party of Russia 2000; syndicated columnist for numerous leading newspapers worldwide 1992–; Nobel Peace Prize 1990; jt recipient Albert Schweitzer Leadership Award, Ronald Reagan Freedom Award 1992, Hon. Citizen of Berlin 1992; Freeman of Aberdeen 1993; Urania-Medaille (Berlin) 1996; Order of Lenin (three times), Orders of Red Banner of Labour, Badge of Honour and other medals. *Publications:* A Time for Peace 1985, The Coming Century of Peace 1986, Speeches and Writings 1986–90, Peace Has No Alternative 1986, Moratorium 1986, Perestroika: New Thinking for Our Country and the World 1987, The August Coup (Its Cause and Results) 1991, December 1991: My Stand 1992, The Years of Hard Decisions 1993, Life and Reforms 1995. *Leisure interests:* literature, theatre, music, walking. *Address:* International Foundation for Socio-Economic and Political Studies, Leningradsky prosp. 49, 125468 Moscow, Russia. *Telephone:* (095) 943-99-90. *Fax:* (095) 943-95-94.

GORBULIN, Volodomir Pavlovich, DTech; Ukrainian politician and space scientist; b. 17 Jan. 1939, Zaporozhya; ed Dnieprotrovsk State Univ.; fmr engineer and mechanic Pivdenne construction co., then jr researcher 1962–76; took part in devt of Cosmos space rockets; mem. Cen. Cttee CP 1977–; Head Rocket, Space and Aviation Tech. Sector 1980–; Head of Defence Complex Section, Cabinet of Ministers 1990–92; Dir.-Gen. Ukrainian Nat. Space Agency 1992–94; Sec. Council on Nat. Security 1994–96, Council on Nat. Security and Defence 1996–; Head Supreme Econ. Council 1997–; Deputy Chair. Council on Problems of Science and Tech. Policy 1999–; Chair. State Cttee of Defence-Industrial Complex 1999–; Pres. Ukrainian Basketball Fed.; mem. Ukrainian Nat. Acad. of Sciences 1997–; USSR State Prize 1990, Ukrainian Nat. Acad. of Sciences Prize. *Leisure interests:* music, playing cards. *Address:* Office of the President, Bankovskaya str. 11, 252011 Kiev, Ukraine (Office). *Telephone:* (44) 291-5152 (Office).

GORBUNOVS, Anatolijs; Latvian politician; b. 10 Feb. 1942, Ludza Dist; s. of Valerians Gorbunovs and Aleksandra Gorbunova (née Mekša); m. Lidija Klavina; one s.; ed Riga Polytech. Inst., Moscow Acad. of Social Sciences; constructor on a state farm; Sr Mechanic Riga Polytech. Inst. 1959–62; served Red Army 1962–65; various posts in the structure of the Latvian CP 1974–88; Chair. Supreme Council of Latvia 1988–93; Chair. of Saeima (Parl.) 1993–95; mem. Parl. for Latvia's Way party; Chair. Saeima Cttee on European Affairs Feb.–Aug. 1996; Minister of Environmental Protection and Regional Devt, Deputy Prime Minister 1996–98, Minister of Communications 1998, Minister of Transport 1999–; Chair. Latvian-Russian Intergovernmental Comm. 1996–. *Leisure interests:* hunting, gardening. *Address:* Ministry of Transport, 3 Gogola Street, 1743 Riga, Latvia (Office). *Telephone:* 722-69-22 (Office). *E-mail:* satmin@sam.gov.lv. *Website:* www.sam.gov.lv.

GORCHAKOVA, Galina Vladimirovna; Russian opera singer (soprano); b. 1962, Novokuznetsk; m. Nikolai Petrovich Mikhalsky (divorced); one s.; ed Novosibirsk State Conservatory; soloist Sverdlovsk (now Yekaterinburg) Theatre of Opera and Ballet 1987–91, Kirov (now Mariinsky) Theatre 1990–96; leading roles in opera productions Madam Butterfly, Prince Igor, The Invisible City of Kitezh, Queen of Spades, Aida, Don Carlos, Tosca, Cavalleria Rusticana; regularly performs in European and American opera theatre including Covent Garden (debut Renata, The Fiery Angel by Prokofiev 1991), La Scala, Metropolitan Opera, Opera Bastille, also in Tokyo; Merited Artist of Russia. *Leisure interest:* travelling by car. *Address:* c/o Askonas Holt, Lonsdale Chambers, 27 Chancery Lane, London, WC2A 1PF, England. *Telephone:* (20) 7400-1700.

GORCHAKOVSKY, Pavel Leonidovich; Russian biologist; b. 3 Jan. 1920; m.; one s.; ed Siberian Inst. of Wood Tech.; Latvian Inst. of Wood Tech. 1945–58; head of Lab. Inst. of Ecology of Plants and Animals Urals br., USSR Acad. of Sciences 1958–88; chief researcher 1988–; corresp. mem. USSR (now Russian) Acad. of Sciences 1990, mem. 1994; research in ecology and geography of plants, genesis of flora, protection of environment; Merited Worker of Science. *Publications include:* Main problems of Historical Phytogeography of Urals 1969, Flora of High-mountain Urals 1975; numerous articles in scientific journals. *Leisure interests:* reading fiction, travel. *Address:* Institute of Ecology of Plants and Animals, Urals Branch of Russian Academy of Sciences, 8 March str. 202, 620219 Yekaterinburg, Russia. *Telephone:* (3432) 29-40-92 (Office); 55-23-85 (Home).

GORDEYEV, Aleksey Vassilyevich, CAND.ECON.SCI; Russian politician and economist; b. 28 Feb. 1955, Frankfurt an der Oder, Germany; ed Acad. of Nat. Econs, USSR Council of Ministers; Sr Supervisor SU-4 Govt Glavmosstroi 1980–81, Chief Expert, Head of Div., then Deputy Head Dept. of Glavagrostroi 1981–86; Deputy Dir-Gen. Moskva. (agro-industrial co.), Moscow region 1986–92; Deputy Head Admin. Lyubertsy Dist, Moscow region 1992–97; Head Dept of Econ., mem. Exec. Bd Ministry of Agric. and Food 1997–98, First Deputy Minister of Agric. and Food 1998–99, Minister 1999–; concurrently Deputy Chair. Govt of Russian Fed. 2000–; Merited Econ. of Russian Fed. *Address:* Council of Ministers, House of Government, Krasnopresnenskaya nab. 2, 103274 Moscow; Ministry of Agriculture, Orlikov per. 1/11, 107139 Moscow, Russia (Office). *Telephone:* (095) 205-40-16 (Govt) (Office); (095) 207-42-43 (Ministry) (Office).

GORDEYEV, Vyacheslav Mikhailovich; Russian ballet dancer and choreographer; b. 3 Aug. 1948, Moscow; s. of Mikhail Gordeyev and Lyubov Gordeyeva; m. 2nd Maya Saidova 1987; one s. one d.; ed Moscow State Univ., State Inst. of Theatrical Arts; leading dancer of Bolshoi Theatre 1968–87; mem. CPSU 1977–90; Artistic Dir Russian State Ballet; Founder and Dir Russian State Ballet Theatre of Moscow 1990–95; Head, Ballet co. of Bolshoi Theatre 1995–97; First Prize Moscow Int. Ballet Competition 1973, USSR People's Artist 1984, Best Choreographer of the Year 1992–93 (Germany), Maurice Béjart Special Prize for Best Choreography 1992. *Roles include:* Prince, Désiré (Tchaikovsky's Nutcracker, Sleeping Beauty), Romeo (Prokofiev's Romeo and Juliet), Spartacus, Ferhat (Melnikov's Legend of Love), Albert (Giselle), Basile (Minkus's Don Quixote), Prince (Tchaikovsky's Swan Lake). *Choreographic works:* Revived Pictures, Memory, Surprise Manoeuvres, or Wedding with the General and more than 30 choreographic compositions; own versions of classical ballets Paquita, Don Quixote and Walpurgisnacht, Nutcracker 1993, Last Tango (Bolshoi Theatre) 1996, Sleeping Beauty (Russian State Ballet) 1999, Cinderella (Russian State Ballet) 2001. *Leisure interests:* classical music, athletics, tennis. *Address:* Volgogradsky Praspekt 121, Moscow 109443 (Office); Tverskaya str. 9, Apt. 78, Moscow 103009, Russia. *Telephone:* (095) 3799482 (Office); (095) 3794324 (Office); (095) 229-13-36, (095) 2013172. *Fax:* (095) 3799482 (Office). *E-mail:* russian_ballet_@mail.ru (Office). *Website:* www.russianstateballet.de (Office).

GORDIMER, Nadine, FRSL; South African writer; b. 20 Nov. 1923, South Africa; d. of Isidore Gordimer and Nan Myers; m. 2nd Reinhold Cassirer 1954 (died); one s. one d.; ed convent school; mem. ANC 1990–; Vice-Pres. Int. PEN; Fellow American Acad. of Arts and Letters, American Acad. of Arts and Science; Goodwill Amb. CINDP; Hon. mem. American Acad. and Inst. of Arts and Letters, American Acad. of Arts and Sciences; Commdr, Ordre des Arts et des Lettres 1986, Officier Ordre des Arts et des Lettres 1987; Charles Eliot Norton Lecturer in Literature, Harvard Univ. 1994; Dr hc (Cambridge) 1992, (Oxford) 1994; W. H. Smith Literary Award 1961, Thomas Pringle Award (English Acad. of SA) 1969, James Tait Black Memorial Prize 1971, Booker Prize (co-winner) 1974, Grand Aigle d'Or Prize (France) 1975, CNA Literary Award (S Africa) 1974, 1979, 1981, 1991, Scottish Arts Council Neil M. Gunn Fellowship 1981, Modern Language Asscn Award (USA) 1981, Premio Malaparte (Italy) 1985, Nelly Sachs Prize (Germany) 1985, Bennett Award (USA) 1987, Benson Medal (Royal Soc. of Literature) 1990, Nobel Prize for Literature 1991, Primo Levi Award. *Publications:* The Soft Voice of the Serpent (stories), The Lying Days (novel) 1953, Six Feet of the Country (stories) 1956, A World of Strangers (novel) 1958, Friday's Footprint (stories) 1960, Occasion for Loving (novel) 1963, Not For Publication (stories) 1965, The Late Bourgeois World (novel) 1966, A Guest of Honour (novel) 1970, Livingstone's Companions (stories) 1972, The Black Interpreters (literary criticism) 1973, The Conservationist (novel) 1974, Selected Stories 1975, Some Monday for Sure (stories) 1976, Burger's Daughter 1979, A Soldier's Embrace (stories) 1980, July's People (novel) 1981, Something Out There (novella) 1984, A Sport of Nature (novel) 1987, The Essential Gesture (essays) 1988, My Son's Story (novel) 1990, Jump (short stories) 1991, Crimes of Conscience (short stories) 1991, None to Accompany Me (novel) 1994, Writing and Being (lectures) 1995, The House Gun 1997, Living in Hope and History: Notes on our Century (essays) 1999, The Pickup 2001, Loot and Other Stories 2003; co-ed. South African Writing Today 1967. *Address:* c/o A. P. Watt, 20 John Street, London, WC1N 2DR, England.

GORDIN, Yakov Arkadyevich; Russian writer and historian; b. 23 Dec. 1935, Leningrad; m.; one s.; ed Moscow Ore Inst.; freelancer specializing in ind. historical research of crisis situations in Russian political history of 18th–20th centuries; Dir and Co-Ed. Zvezda (literary journal), St. Petersburg. *Publications:* numerous articles and books including The Death of Pushkin, Between Slavery and Freedom, Duels and Duelists, Coup of the Reformers, etc. *Address:* Mokhovaya str. 36, apt. 24, 191028 St Petersburg, Russia (Home). *Telephone:* (812) 273-05-27 (Home). *E-mail:* ariev@cityline.spb.ru.

GORDON, Donald; South African business executive; b. 24 June 1930, Johannesburg; s. of Nathan Gordon and Sheila Gordon; m. Peggy Cowan 1958; two s. one d.; ed King Edward VII School, Johannesburg; Partner Kessel Feinstein accountants 1955–57; founder Liberty Life Asscn of Africa Ltd, Chair. 1957–99; Chair. Liberty Holdings Ltd 1968–99, Liberty Investors Ltd 1971–, Guardian Nat. Insurance Co. Ltd 1980–99, Capital & Counties PLC (UK) 1982–; Deputy Chair. Standard Bank Investment Corpn Ltd 1979–99, Premier Group Holdings Ltd 1983–96; Dir Guardbank Man. Corpn Ltd 1969–99, Guardian Royal Exchange Assurance PLC (UK) 1971–94, Charter Life Insurance Co. Ltd 1985–99, The South African Breweries Ltd 1982–99, Beverage & Consumer Industry Holdings Ltd 1989–99, GFSA Holdings Ltd 1990–94, Sun Life Corpn PLC (UK) 1992–95, Chair. Liberty Int. PLC (fmrly Transatlantic Holdings PLC) 1981–, Capital Stopping Centres PLC 1994–; Hon. Life Pres. Liberty Life; Hon. D.Econ.Sc. (Witwatersrand) 1991; Financial Mail Businessman of the Year 1965; Sunday Times Man of the Year 1969; Business Statesman Award (Harvard Business School); London Entrepreneur of the Year Award 2000, Special Award for Lifetime Achievement 2001. *Leisure interest:* tennis, reading, opera, hiking. *Address:* Liberty International PLC, 40 Broadway, London W1H 0BJ England. *Telephone:* (20) 7960-1200. *Fax:* (20) 7960-1333.

GORDON, Douglas Lamont, MA; British artist; b. 20 Sept. 1966, Glasgow; s. of James Gordon and Mary Clements Gordon (née McDougall); ed Glasgow

School of Art, Slade School of Art; works in painting, installation and film; works include List of Names, Something Between My Mouth and Your Ear, 24 Hour Psycho, Hysterical, The Confessions of a Justified Sinner; contrib. to The British Art Show and Spellbound 1996; solo exhibition What Have I Done, Hayward Gallery, London Dec. 2002–Jan. 2003; Visiting Prof. Fine Art, Glasgow School of Art, Glasgow Univ. 1999–; Turner Prize 1996; Hugo Bass Prize 1998. *Leisure interests:* eating, sleeping, drinking. *Address:* c/o Lisson Gallery, 67 Lisson Street, London, NW1 5DA, England.

GORDON, Pamela, MBA; Bermudan politician; b. 4 Sept. 1955; d. of E F. Gordon; ed Queen's Univ.; fmr Minister of the Environment; Leader United Bermuda Party; Prime Minister of Bermuda 1997–98; Hon. LLD (New Brunswick). *Address:* c/o United Bermuda Party, Central Office, 87 John F. Burrows Building, Chancery Lane, P.O. Box HM 715, Hamilton, HM CX, Bermuda (Office). *Telephone:* 295-0729 (Office). *E-mail:* info@ubp.bm (Office). *Website:* www.ubp.bm (Office).

GORDON, Robert James, PhD; American professor of economics; b. 3 Sept. 1940, Boston, Mass.; s. of Robert A. Gordon and Margaret S. Gordon; m. Julie S. Peyton 1963; ed Harvard Univ., Oxford Univ., MIT; Assoc. Prof. of Econs, Harvard Univ. 1967–68, Univ. of Chicago 1968–73; Prof. of Econs, North-western Univ. 1973–, Chair. Dept of Econs 1992–96, Stanley G. Harris Prof. of Econs 1987–; Fellow, Econometric Soc. 1977, American Acad. of Arts and Sciences 1997; John Simon Guggenheim Memorial Fellowship 1980–81, Lustrum Award, Erasmus Univ., Rotterdam 1999. *Publications:* The American Business Cycle: Continuity and Change 1986, The Measurement of Durable Goods Prices 1990, The Economics of New Goods 1997, Macroeconomics (9th Edn) 2003. *Leisure interests:* photography, gardening, mil. history, airline man. *Address:* Department of Economics, Northwestern University, Evanston, IL 60208-0001 (Office); 202 Greenwood Street, Evanston, IL 60201, USA (Home). *Telephone:* (847) 491-3616 (Office); (847) 869-3544 (Home). *Fax:* (847) 491-5427 (Office); (847) 328-7863 (Home). *E-mail:* rjg@northwestern.edu (Office and Home).

GORDON, William Edwin, PhD; American radio physicist; b. 8 Jan. 1918, Paterson, NJ; s. of William and Mary Scott Gordon; m. Elva Freile 1941; one s. one d.; ed Montclair State Coll., NJ and New York and Cornell Univs; Assoc. Prof. Cornell Univ. 1953–59, Prof. 1959–65, Walter R. Read Prof. of Eng 1965–66; Dir Arecibo Ionospheric Observatory, Puerto Rico 1960–66 (conceived and directed construction of world's largest antenna reflector); Prof. of Electrical Eng and Space Physics and Astronomy, Rice Univ. 1966–86, Dean of Eng and Science 1966–75, Vice-Pres. 1969–72, Dean, School of Natural Sciences 1975–80, Provost and Vice-Pres. 1980–86, Distinguished Prof. Emer. 1986–; Foreign Sec., NAS 1986–90; Chair. Bd of Trustees, Upper Atmosphere Research Corpn 1971–72, 1973–78; Pres. Taping for the Blind, Houston 1993–97; Vice-Pres. Int. Union of Radio Science 1975–78, Senior Vice-Pres. 1978–81, Pres. 1981–85, Hon. Pres. 1990–; Bd of Trustees and Exec. Cttee Univ. Corpn for Atmospheric Research 1975–81, Vice-Chair. Bd of Trustees 1977–78, Chair. 1978–81, Trustee 1975–81, 1986–89, 1991–92; Bd of Trustees, Cornell Univ. 1976–80; mem. Arecibo Observatory Advisory Bd 1977–80, 1990–93; mem. NAS, AAAS, Nat. Acad. of Eng, Foreign Assoc. Acad. of Eng Japan; mem. Int. Council of Scientific Unions 1981, Vice-Pres. 1988–93; Councillor American Meteorological Soc.; Fellow, American Geophysical Union, Inst. of Electrical and Electronic Engineers, Guggenheim Fellow 1972–73; Hon. DS (Austin Coll.) 1978; Balth Van der Pol Gold Medal for distinguished research in radio sciences 1966, 50th Anniversary Medal of American Meteorological Soc. 1970, Arktowski Medal 1984, USSR Medal Geophysics 1985, Milestone in Electrical and Mechanical Engineering 2001. *Publications:* numerous articles in learned journals. *Leisure interests:* sailing, swimming, music. *Address:* Department of Space Physics, Rice University, PO Box 1892, Houston, TX 77251, USA. *Telephone:* (713) 348-4939. *E-mail:* bgordon@spacsun.rice.edu (Office).

GORE, Albert, Jr., American politician and financial executive; b. 31 March 1948; s. of the late Albert Gore and Pauline (LaFon) Gore; m. Mary E. Aitcheson 1970; one s. three d.; ed Harvard and Vanderbilt Univs; investigative reporter, editorial writer, The Tennessean 1971–76; home-builder and land developer, Tanglewood Home Builders Co. 1971–76; livestock and tobacco farmer 1973–; Head Community Enterprise Bd 1993–; mem. House of Reps. 1977–79; Senator from Tennessee 1985–93; Vice-Pres. of USA 1993–2001; Democrat cand. in Presidential Elections 2000; lecturer Middle Tennessee State, Fisk, Columbia Univs 2001–; Vice-Chair. Metropolitan West Financial 2001–; Democrat; Dr hc (Harvard) 1994, (New York) 1998. *Publication:* Earth in the Balance 1992. *Address:* Metwest Financial, 11440 San Vicente Boulevard, 3rd Floor, Los Angeles, CA 90049, USA (Office). *Telephone:* (310) 979-6300 (Office). *Fax:* (310) 979-6399 (Office). *E-mail:* information@mwfin.com (Office). *Website:* www.mwfin.com (Office).

GORE, Frederick John Pym, CBE, RA; British painter; b. 8 Nov. 1913; s. of Spencer Frederick Gore and Mary Joanna Gore (née Kerr); ed Lancing Coll. and Trinity Coll., Oxford, Ruskin, Westminster and Slade Schools of Art; war service 1939–45; taught at Westminster School of Art 1937, Chelsea and Epsom 1947, St Martin's 1946–79, Head of Painting Dept 1951–79, Vice-Prin. 1961–79; Chair. RA Exhbns. Cttee 1976–87; Trustee Imperial War Museum 1967–84. *Solo exhibitions include:* Galerie Borghèse, Paris 1938, Redfern Gallery 1937, 1949, 1950, 1953, 1956, 1962, Mayor Gallery 1958, 1960, Juster Gallery, New York 1963, Royal Acad., Retrospective 1989. *Publications:* Abstract Art 1956, Painting, Some Principles 1965, Piero della Francesca's

'The Baptism' 1969. *Leisure interests:* Russian folk dancing, tap-dancing. *Address:* Flat 3, 35 Elm Park Gardens, London, SW10 9QF, England. *Telephone:* (20) 7352-4940.

GÓRECKI, Henryk Mikołaj; Polish composer; b. 6 Dec. 1933, Czernica, nr Rybnik; s. of Otylia Górecka and Roman Górecki; m. Jadwiga Górecka 1959; one s. one d.; studied composition at State Higher School of Music, Katowice, under B. Szabelski; Docent, Faculty of Composition, State Higher School of Music, Katowice, Rector 1975–79, Extraordinary Prof. 1977–79; Dr hc (Acad. of Catholic Theology, Warsaw) 1993, (Warsaw Univ.) 1994, (American Catholic Univ., Washington, DC) 1995, (Ann Arbor Univ., Mich.) 1996, (Concordia Univ., Montreal) 1998; First Prize, Young Composers' Competition, Warsaw, for Monologhi 1960, Paris Youth Biennale, for 1st Symphony 1961; Prize, UNESCO Int. Tribune for Composers for Refrain 1967, for Ad Matrem 1973; First Prize, Composers' Competition, Szczecin, for Kantata 1968; Prize of Minister of Culture and Arts 1965, 1969, 1973, Prize of Union of Polish Composers 1970, of Cttee for Polish Radio and TV 1974, of Minister of Culture and Arts 1965, 1969, 1973; State Prize 1st class for Ad Matrem and Nicolaus Copernicus Symphony 1976. *Compositions include:* Symphony No. 3 (Threnodies for soprano and orchestra) 1976 (more than 700,000 records sold), Valentine Piece for flute and little bell 1996, Three Fragments to Words of Stanisław Wyspianski for voice and piano 1996, Little Fantasy for violin and piano 1997, Salve Sidus Polonorum, Cantata of St Adalbert, Opus 72, for large mixed choir, two pianos, organ and percussion ensemble 1997–2000, String Quartet No. 3 1999, Niech nam żyją i śpiewają for vocal ensemble 2000. *Address:* ul. H. A. Górnika 4 m.1, 40-133 Katowice, Poland. *Telephone:* (32) 258-17-58.

GOREGLYAD, Valery Pavlovich; Russian economist; b. 18 June 1958, Gluzk, Mogilev Region, Belarus; m. Yaketarina Goreglyad; two s.; ed Moscow Inst. of Aviation; fmrly with mil. space industry; Head Tourism Co. –1990; Peoples' Deputy, Russian Fed. 1990–93; mem. Council of Feds, Fed. Ass. 1994; Exec. Dir Cttee on Budget, Revenue and Banking Activity 1994–2000, Deputy Head 2001–; elected mem. (for Sakhalin region) Council of Feds 2001–02, Leader Parl. Grouping Fed. 2002–. *Address:* State Duma, Bolshaya Dmitrovka str. 26, Moscow, Russia (Office). *Telephone:* (095) 292-30-13 (Office). *E-mail:* pvgoreglad@council.gov.ru (Office). *Website:* www.council.gov.ru (Office).

GORENSTEIN, Mark Borisovich; Russian conductor; b. 16 Sept. 1946, Odessa, Ukraine; m. 2nd; one s.; ed Chişinău State Conservatory as violinist, Novosibirsk State Conservatory as conductor; violinist with Bolshoi Theatre Orchestra 1973–75; State Academic Symphony Orchestra 1975–84; Chief Conductor and Artistic Dir, MAV Orchestra, Budapest, Hungary 1985–88; Chief Conductor, Pusan City Symphony Orchestra, South Korea 1989–91; f., Chief Conductor and Artistic Dir New Russia State Symphony Orchestra 1992–2002, Russian Academic State Symphony Orchestra 2002–; Honoured Art Worker of Russia. *Address:* Rublevskoye shosse 28, Apt. 25, 121609 Moscow (Home); Bolshaya Nikitskaya 13, 103871 Moscow, Russia. *Telephone:* (095) 229-74-69 (Office); (095) 414-52-03 (Home). *Fax:* (095) 290-58-13 (Office); (095) 414-52-03 (Home). *E-mail:* gasorus@cityline.ru.

GORETTA, Claude; Swiss film director; b. 23 June 1929, Geneva. *Films include:* Le fou 1970, Le jour des noces 1971, L'invitation 1973, The Wonderful Crook 1976, The Lacemaker 1977, Bonheur toi-même 1980, The Girl from Lorraine 1981, The Death of Mario Ricci 1983, Orpheus 1985, Si le soleil ne revenait pas 1987. *Address:* 10 Tour de Boël, 1204 Geneva, Switzerland.

GOR'KOV, Lev Petrovich, PhD, DPhysSc; Russian physicist; b. 14 June 1929, Moscow; s. of Petr Ivanovich Gorkov and Antonina Grigor'evna Gorkova; m. Donara Chernikova 1965; two s. (one d. from 1st marriage); ed Moscow Inst. of Mechanics; jr then sr researcher, Inst. of Physical Problems 1953–64; Head of Sector Inst. of Chemical Physics 1964–65; Head of Sector L. D. Landau Inst. of Theoretical Physics 1965–88, Deputy Dir 1988–91; Prof. and Dept Head, Inst. for Physics and Tech. 1965–92; Theory Program Dir and Prof., Nat. High Magnetic Field Lab., Fla State Univ. 1992–; Foreign Hon. mem. American Acad. of Art and Science; Fellow Russian Acad. of Sciences, American Physical Soc.; main research on concept of order parameter in microscopic theory of superconductivity, phenomenon of gapless superconductivity, microscopic derivation of Ginzburg-Landau equations for superconductors and superconducting alloys, thermodynamic diagrammatic technique, electron localization by disorder in one and two dimensions, theory of organic conductors; Dr hc (NY City Univ., Univ. of Illinois); Lenin Prize, L. D. Landau Prize, Bardeen Prize in Superconductivity. *Publications:* Methods of Quantum Field Theory in Statistical Physics 1962, Superconducting Properties and Structural Transitions in Compounds with A-15 Lattice 1976, Physical Phenomena in New Organic Superconductors 1984, Phase Stratification of Liquid in New Superconductors 1987, Superconductivity in Heavy Fermion Systems 1987; articles in scientific journals. *Address:* National High-Magnetic Field Laboratory, Florida State University, 1800 E Paul Dirac Drive, Tallahassee, FL 32310, USA. *Telephone:* (850) 644-41-87 (Office); (095) 137-32-44 (Moscow). *Fax:* (850) 644-50-38.

GORMAN, Joseph Tolle, BA, LLB; American business executive; b. 1937, Rising Sun, Ind.; m. Bettyann Gorman; ed Kent State Univ. and Yale Univ.; Assoc. Baker, Hostetler & Patterson, Cleveland 1962–67; Legal Dept TRW Inc., Cleveland 1968–69, Asst Sec. 1969–70, Sec. 1970–72, Vice-Pres. Gen Counsel, Automotive Worldwide Operations 1972–73, Vice-Pres. Asst Gen. Counsel 1973–76, Vice-Pres. Gen. Counsel 1976–80, Exec. Vice-Pres. Industrial and Energy Sector 1980–84, Exec. Vice-Pres., Asst Pres. 1984–85, Chair., Pres. and COO 1985–91, Chair., CEO 1988–; mem. Bd of Dirs. Soc. Corpn, Soc. Nat. Bank, Cleveland, Standard Oil Co.; mem. Council on Foreign Relations and other public appts.; Japan Prime Minister's Trade Award 1994. *Address:* TRW Inc., 1900 Richmond Road, Cleveland, OH 44124, USA. *Fax:* (212) 334-2463. *E-mail:* nhgall@mindspring.com (Office).

GORMLEY, Antony, OBE, MA, DFA; British sculptor; b. 30 Aug. 1950, London; s. of Arthur J. C. Gormley and Elspeth Brauninger; m. Vicken Parsons 1980; two s. one d.; ed Ampleforth Coll., Trinity Coll., Cambridge, Cen. School of Arts and Crafts, London, Goldsmiths' Coll., Univ. of London and Slade School of Fine Arts, London; has participated in numerous group exhbns in Europe, N America, Japan, Brazil, Russia, Australia and NZ; works in collections of Tate Gallery, London, Scottish Nat. Gallery of Modern Art, Moderna Museet, Stockholm, Neue Galerie, Kassel, Victoria and Albert Museum, London, British Council, Arts Council of GB, Art Gallery of NSW, Sydney, Leeds City Art Galleries, Modern Art Museum of Fort Worth, Louisiana Museum of Modern Art, Humblebaek, Denmark, Irish Museum of Modern Art, Dublin, Sapporo Sculpture Park, Japan; sculpture in public places: Out of the Dark, Martinsplatz, Kassel 1987, Open Space, Place Jean Monnet, Rennes 1993, Iron:Man, Vic. Square, Birmingham 1994, Havmann, Mo I Rana, Norway 1995, Angel of the North, Gateshead 1998, Quantum Cloud, The Thames, Greenwich, London 1999, Site of Remembrance, Oslo 2000, Mind-Body Column, Osaka, Japan 2000, Dorotheenblocke Haus 6, Berlin 2001, Planets, British Library 2002; Hon. Fellow Goldsmith's Coll., Univ. of London 1998; Dr hc (Univ. of Cen. England, Birmingham) 1998; Turner Prize 1994; South Bank Art Award for Visual Art 1999. *Solo exhibitions include:* Whitechapel Art Gallery, London 1981, Coracle Press Gallery, London 1983, Salvatore Ala, New York, Riverside Studios, London, Salvatore Ala Gallery, Milan, Chapter Gallery, Cardiff 1984, Salvatore Ala, New York, Frankfurt Kunstverein, Regensburg Städtisches Museum, Salvatore Ala, Milan 1985, Victoria Miro, London 1986, Serpentine Gallery, London, Salvatore Ala, New York, Seibu Contemporary Arts, Tokyo, Le Criée, Rennes 1987, Burnett Miller, LA, Contemporary Sculpture Centre, Tokyo, Leeds City Art Gallery 1988, Louisiana Museum, Denmark, Salvatore Ala, NY, Scottish Nat. Gallery of Modern Art, Edin., Art Gallery of NSW, Australia 1989, Galerie Isy et Christine Brachot, Brussels, Galerie Nordenhake, Stockholm, Modern Art Museum, Fort Worth, Tex. 1991, Centro Cultural Arte Contemporáneo, Mexico City, San Diego Museum of Contemporary Art, La Jolla, Calif., Burnett Miller, LA, Contemporary Sculpture Centre, Tokyo, Learning to Think, British School, Rome 1992, Field, Corcoran Gallery, Washington and Montreal Museum of Fine Arts, Oktagon, Stuttgart, Galerie Thaddaeus Ropac, Paris and Salzburg, Konsthall Malmö, Tate Gallery, Liverpool, Galerie Nordenhake, Stockholm 1993, Irish Museum of Modern Art, Moderna Galerija, Ljubljana, White Cube, London, Muzej Suvremene Umjetnosti, Zagreb, Ludwig Museum, Budapest, Oriel Mostyn, Llandudno, Galeria Pedro Oliveira, Porto 1994, Prague Castle, Sala Ronda, Bucharest, Orchard Gallery, Derry, Ikon Gallery, Birmingham, Nat. Gallery of Wales, Cardiff, Kohji Ogura Gallery, Nagoya, Pace Roberts Foundation for Contemporary Art, San Antonio, StadtRaum Remise, Vienna 1995, Obala Art Centar, Sarajevo, Galerie Xavier Hufkens, Brussels, Arts 04, St Rémy de Provence, Hayward Gallery, London, Museum of Modern Art, Kamakura 1996 (then touring Japan 1996–97), Koelnischer Kunstverein, Cologne, Kunsthalle, Kiel, Galerie Nordenhake, Stockholm, Cuxhaven, Germany, Herning Museum, Denmark 1997, Jablonka Galerie, Cologne, Royal Acad., London, Stavanger, Norway, Rupertinum, Salzburg 1998, Jablonka Galerie, Cologne 1999, Galerie Thaddaeus Ropac, Paris, fig-1, London, White Cube², London 2000, New Art Centre and Sculpture Park, Roche Court, East Winterslow, Contemporary Sculpture Centre, Tokyo, Tate St Ives, Cornwall, Orchard Gallery, Derry 2001, Centro Galego de Arte Contemporanea, Santiago de Compostela 2002, Galleria Mimmo Scognamiglio, Naples 2002, Galerie Xavier Hufkens, Brussels 2002, British Museum, London 2002. *Leisure interests:* walking, talking. *Address:* 153A Bellenden Road, London, SE15 4DH (Studio); 13 South Villas, London, NW1 9BS, England (Home). *Telephone:* (20) 7639-1303 (Studio); (20) 7482-7383 (Home). *Fax:* (20) 7639-2674 (Studio); (20) 7267-8336 (Home). *Website:* www.antonygormley.com (Office).

GORMLY, Allan Graham, CBE; British business executive and chartered accountant; b. 18 Dec. 1937, Paisley, Scotland; s. of William Gormly and Christina Swinton Flockhart; m. Vera Margaret Grant 1962; one s. one d.; ed Paisley Grammar School; with Peat Marwick Mitchell & Co. 1956–61, Rootes Group 1961–65; joined John Brown PLC, apptd. Chief Exec. 1983, Dir Trafalgar House PLC (when it acquired John Brown PLC) 1986–95, CEO 1992–94; Deputy Chair. Royal Insurance Holdings PLC 1992–93, Chair. 1994–96 (mem. Bd 1990–96), Deputy Chair. Royal and Sun Alliance Insurance Group PLC 1996–98; Chair. BPB PLC 1997– (Dir 1995–); Chair. Overseas Projects Bd 1989–91; Deputy Chair. Export Guarantees Advisory Council 1990–92; Dir Brixton PLC 1994– (Chair. 2000–), European Capital Co. 1996–99, Bank of Scotland 1997–2001; Dir (non-exec.) Nat. Grid. Co. 1994–95; Chair. Q-One Group Ltd 1999–; mem. British Overseas Trade Bd 1989–91, Top Salaries Review Body 1990–92, Bd of Man., FCO 2000–. *Leisure interests:* golf, music. *Address:* 56 North Park, Gerrards Cross, Bucks., SL9 8JR, England (Home). *Telephone:* (1753) 885079 (Home).

GÖRNE, Matthias; German baritone; b. 1966, Chemnitz; ed in Leipzig from 1985, then with Dietrich Fischer-Dieskau (q.v.) and Elisabeth Schwarzkopf (q.v.); performed with the children's choir at Chemnitz Opera; sang in Bach's St Matthew Passion under Kurt Masur (q.v.), Leipzig 1990; appearances with Hanns Martin Schneidt and Munich Bach Choir and with NDR Symphony Orchestra Hamburg; further engagements under Horst Stein, with Bamberg Symphony Orchestra and in Hindemith's Requiem under Wolfgang Sawallisch (q.v.); concerts at Leipzig Gewandhaus under Helmuth Rilling (q.v.) and in Amsterdam and Paris; Lieder recitals with pianist Eric Schneider; sang title role in Henze's Prinz von Homburg, Cologne 1992, Marcello in La Bohème at Komische Oper, Berlin 1993, Wolfram in Tannhäuser, Cologne 1996, Die Schöne Müllerin, Bath 1997; engaged for Die Zauberflöte, Salzburg Festival 1997. *Recordings include:* Winterreise 1997, Entarte Musik. *Address:* c/o IMG Artists, Lovell House, 616 Chiswick High Road, London W4 5RX, England (Office).

GORTON, Slade; American politician and lawyer; b. 8 Jan. 1928, Chicago, Ill.; s. of Thomas Slade Gorton and Ruth Israel; m. Sally Clark 1958; one s. two d.; ed Evanston High School, Ill., Dartmouth Columbia Univ. Law School; US Army 1945–46, USAF 1953–56, presently Col USAF Reserve; admitted to Bar, Wash. State 1953; mem. Wash. State House of Reps. 1958–68, Majority Leader 1967–68; Wash. State Attorney-Gen. 1968–80; Senator from Washington State 1981–87, 1989–2001; Partner Davis, Wright and Jones, Seattle 1987–89; with Preston, Gates & Ellis 2001–; mem. Wash. State Law and Justice Comm. 1969–80 (Chair. 1969–70), State Criminal Justice Training Comm. 1969–80 (Chair. 1969–76), Pres.'s Consumer Advisory Council 1975–77, Nat. Asscn of Attorneys-Gen. 1969–80 (Pres. 1976–77), Nat. Comm. on Terrorist Attacks 2002–; Republican; Wyman Award 1980. *Address:* Preston, Gates & Ellis LLP, 701 5th Avenue, Suite 5000, Seattle, WA 98104-7011, USA (Office).

GOSDEN, Roger Gordon, PhD, DSC; British professor of medical sciences; b. 23 Sept. 1948, Ryde, Isle of Wight; s. of the late Gordon Conrad Jason Gosden and Peggy Gosden (née Butcher); m. Carole Ann Walsh 1971 (divorced 2003); two s.; ed Chislehurst and Sidcup Grammar School, Bristol Univ., Cambridge Univ.; MRC Research Fellow, Cambridge Univ. 1973–76; Population Council Fellow, Duke Univ., USA 1974–75; lecturer in Physiology, Edin. Univ. 1976–84, Sr Lecturer 1984–94; Prof. of Reproductive Biology, Univ. of Leeds 1994–99, Visiting Prof. 1999–; Research Dir and Prof., McGill Univ. 1999–2001, Adjunct Prof. 2001–; Howard and Georgeanna Jones Prof. of Reproductive Medicine and Scientific Dir, Eastern Va Medical School 2001–, Adjunct Prof. Old Dominion Univ. Va 2002–; pioneer in fertility conservation; scientific adviser to Govt bodies (UK, The Netherlands, Canada); numerous radio and TV broadcasts; Distinguished Scientist Lecture, American Soc. of Reproductive Medicine 2001, British Fertility Soc. Steptoe Lecture 2003 and many other awards and lectureships. *Publications:* Biology of Menopause 1985, Cheating Time 1996, Designer Babies 1999, Biology and Pathology of the Oocyte (with A. O. Trounson) 2003 and numerous articles in academic journals, magazines and newspapers. *Leisure interests:* reading, natural history, walking. *Address:* The Jones Institute for Reproductive Medicine, Eastern Virginia Medical School, 601 Colley Avenue, Norfolk, VA 23507, USA (Office). *Telephone:* (757) 446-5775 (Office). *Fax:* (757) 446-5905 (Office). *E-mail:* gosdenrg@evms.edu (Office). *Website:* www.jonesinstitute.org.

GOSEV, Petar, MA; Macedonian politician; b. 5 Sept. 1948, Pirava; m.; two s.; ed Univ. of Skopje; with 11 Oktomvri Bus Co. 1971–73; mem. council Macedonian Trade Union Fed. 1973–87 (econ. adviser 1973–84, Chief, Office of the Union Pres. 1977, mem Presidency 1982–87); mem. Presidency, Cen. Cttee Union of Communists of Macedonia (renamed SKM–PDP 1990, Social Democratic Alliance of Macedonia 1991) 1986–89, Pres. 1989–91; Chief of the Del. of the Nat. Ass. in the Ass. of the former SFRY 1990; mem. Parl. 1990–2002; f. Democratic Party 1993, Pres. 1993–97; Pres. Liberal-Democratic Party–LDP (f. with merger of Liberal Party and Democratic Party) 1997–99; Vice-Pres. Parl. Group of the Nat. Ass. to the Inter-Parl. Union 1998–2002; Vice-Pres. of Macedonia and Minister of Finance Nov. 2002–. *Address:* Ministry of Finance, Dame Gruev 14, Skopje, 1000 Macedonia (Office). *Telephone:* (2) 116-012 (Office). *Fax:* (2) 117-280 (Office). *E-mail:* ljupka.mindesova@finance.gov.mk (Office). *Website:* www.finance.gov.mk (Office).

GOSLING, Sir Donald, Kt; British business executive; b. 2 March 1929; m. Elizabeth Shauna Ingram 1959 (divorced 1988); three s.; joined RN 1944, served on HMS Leander; Jt Chair. Nat. Car Parks Ltd 1950–98; Chair. Palmer & Harvey 1967–; Chair. Council of Man. White Ensign Assen Ltd 1978–83, Vice-Pres. 1983–93, Pres. 1993– (mem. 1970–); mem. Exec. Cttee Imperial Soc. of Kts. Bachelor 1977–; Chair. Berkeley Square Ball Trust 1982–, Mountbatten Memorial Hall Appeals Cttee 1980; Vice-Pres. King George's Fund for Sailors 1993–; Hon. Capt. RNR 1993–; Trustee Fleet Air Arm Museum, Yeovilton 1974–, Royal Yachting Assen Seamanship Foundation 1981–; Patron Submarine Memorial Appeal 1978–, HMS Ark Royal Welfare Trust 1986–. *Leisure interests:* swimming, sailing, shooting. *Address:* CPI Ltd, 21 Bryanston Street, Marble Arch, London, W1H 8PR, England (Office). *Telephone:* (20) 7495-5599 (Office).

GOSS, Richard John; South African chartered accountant; b. 8 July 1928, Cape Town; s. of John Archer Goss; m. Myrtle Atherstone 1955; one s. two d.; ed Rondebosch Boys' High School; joined SA Breweries as Man. Accountant, Head Office, Johannesburg 1952, Chief Accountant 1954–57, Asst Admin. Man. 1957–60, Group Commercial Man. 1960–64; attended Harvard Business School, USA 1964; Gen. Man., Beer Div., SA Breweries 1965–67, Group

Man. Dir 1967–83; Chair. Kersaf Investments Ltd 1983–89; Deputy Chair. Nedcor 1996–, Old Mutual 1997–; Dir Safren. *Leisure interests:* game conservation, tennis. *Address:* P.O. Box 163, Constantia 7848, South Africa. *Telephone:* (21) 7942225.

GOTCHEV, Dimitar; Bulgarian judge; b. 27 Feb. 1936, Sofia; s. of Maj.-Gen. Boncho Gotchev and Zdravka Gotchev; m. Jova Gotcheva-Cholakova 1976; one d.; ed Univ. of Sofia St Kliment Ochridsky; legal adviser 1959–66; Arbiter, State Court of Arbitration 1966–89; Judge, Supreme Court 1990, Judge, Head of Commercial Div. 1990–, Deputy Chief Justice, Supreme Court 1993–; Judge, Constitutional Court 1994–; Judge, European Court of Human Rights, Strasbourg 1992–98. *Leisure interests:* music, mountaineering, skiing. *Address:* Constitutional Court of Republic of Bulgaria, Bul. Dondoukov 1, 1202 Sofia (Office); Koslodui Str. N34, 1202 Sofia, Bulgaria (Home). *Telephone:* (2) 940-23-31 (Office); (2) 31-54-25 (Home). *Fax:* (2) 87-19-86. *E-mail:* dgotchev@constcourtgovrn.bg (Office).

GÖTHE, (Lars) Staffan; Swedish playwright, actor and director; b. 20 Dec. 1944, Luleå, s. of late Thorsten Göthe and of Margit Grape-Göthe; m. Kristin Byström 1969; one s.; ed Acad. of Performing Arts, Gothenburg; actor and playwright, regional theatre of Växjö 1971, Folkteatern, Gothenburg 1974; Headmaster Acad. of Performing Arts, Malmö 1976; actor, Folkteatern, Gävleborg 1983; Dir The RTC Co. 1986–95; actor and playwright, Royal Dramatic Theatre, Stockholm 1995–. *Publications:* En natt i februari 1972, Den gråtande polisen 1980, La strada dell'amore 1986, En uppstoppad hund 1986, Den perfekta Kyssen 1990, Arma Irma 1991, Boogie Woogie 1992, Blått Hus Med Röda Kinder 1995, Ruben Pottas Eländiga Salonger 1996, Ett Lysande Elände 1999, Temperance 2000. *Address:* Vindragarvägen 8, 117 50 Stockholm, Sweden.

GOTODA, Masaharu; Japanese politician; b. 9 Aug. 1914; ed Tokyo Univ.; mem. House of Reps. 1976–; with Ministry of Home Affairs 1939; Chief Sec., Home Affairs Ministry, 1959, Dir, Local Tax Bureau 1959–62; Sec.-Gen. Nat. Police Agency 1962–63, Dir of Security Bureau 1963–65, Dir-Gen. 1969–72; Deputy Chief Cabinet Sec. 1972–73; Minister of Home Affairs 1979–80; Chief Cabinet Sec. 1982–83, 1985–87; Dir-Gen. Nat. Public Safety Comm. 1979–80, Hokkaido Devt Agency 1979–80, Admin. Man. Agency 1983–84, Man. Co-ordination Agency 1984–85; Minister of Justice 1992–93; Deputy Prime Minister Aug.–April 1993.

GOTT, Karel; Czech singer; b. 14 July 1939, Plzeň; two d.; ed Prague Conservatory (studied under Prof. Karenin); mem. Semafor Theatre, Prague 1963–65; mem. Apollo Theatre, Prague, 1965–67; freelance artist 1967–; numerous foreign tours; charity concerts with Eva Urbanová 1998; CD Rocky mého mládí ("Rocks of my Youth") 1999; exhbn of paintings, Bratislava 1999; f. and Chair. Interpo Foundation 1993–96; concerts in Carnegie Hall, New York, Expo, Hanover, Kremlin Palace, Moscow 2000; charity concerts in Czech Repub. after 2002 floods; Golden Nightingale trophy (annual pop singer poll 1963–66, 1968–81, 1983, 1989–90, 1997–2001), MIDEM Prize, Cannes 1967, MIDEM Gold Record 1969, Polydor Gold Record 1970, Supraphon Gold Record 1972, 1973, 1979, 1980, 1996, Music Week Star of the Year 1974 (UK) 1975, Artist of Merit 1982, Gold Aerial 1983, radio station BRT (Belgium) 1984, Nat. Artist 1985, Polydor Golden Pin (Germany) 1986, Czech Nightingale Trophy 1996, 1997, 1999, 2001, 2002 (28 times in total), Czech TV Prize 1997, 1999, Platinum Record (for duets with Lucia Bílá) 1998 and many other awards. *Radio:* presenter monthly show Radio Impuls 2002–. *Film appearance:* Luck from Hell. *Publication:* Why Painting is Important for Me 2001. *Address:* Nad Bertramkou 18, 150 00 Prague 5, Czech Republic (Home).

GÖTTE, Klaus, DJur; German business executive; b. 22 April 1932, Diepholz; s. of Heinrich and Anneliese (née Engel) Götte; m. Grazia Michaela Elsaesser 1958; one s. two d.; ed Göttingen; Man. Bankhaus C.G. Trinkhaus, Düsseldorf 1955–68, Fried. Krupp GmbH, Essen 1968–72; mem. Bd of Man., Allianz Versicherungs-AG, Munich and Allianz Lebensversicherungs-AG, Stuttgart 1972–80; Man. Partner, Friedrich Flick Industrieverwaltung KGaA, Düsseldorf 1980–82; Chair. Bd Man. Dirs. MAN Aktiengesellschaft (fmrly Gutehoffnungshütte Aktienverein), Munich 1983–96, Chair. Supervisory Bd 1996–; Dr rer. pol (hc). *Address:* Ungererstrasse 69, 80805 Munich, Germany. *Telephone:* (89) 360980.

GOTTI, Irv (Irv Lorenzo); American music company executive and producer; b. Hollis, Queens, New York City; m. Debbie Gotti; began music career as DJ Irv; fmr producer Island Def Jam Records, artistes produced include Ashanti, Charli Baltimore, Toni Braxton, DMX, Ja Rule, Jay-Z; currently CEO Murder Inc. Records. *Recordings include:* Irv Gotti Presents...series of albums. *Address:* c/o Murder Inc. Records, 2220 Colorado Avenue, Santa Monica, CA 90404, USA (Office). *Website:* www.murderincrecords.com (Office).

GOTTLIEB, Robert Adams, BA; American editor and critic; b. 29 April 1931, New York; s. of Charles Gottlieb and Martha (née Kean) Gottlieb; m. 1st Muriel Higgins 1952; m. 2nd Maria Tucci 1969; two s. one d.; ed Columbia Coll. and Cambridge Univ.; employee Simon and Schuster 1955–65, Ed.-in-Chief 1965–68; Ed.-in-Chief Alfred A. Knopf 1968–87, Pres. 1973–87; Ed.-in-Chief The New Yorker 1987–92; now dance and book critic for New York Observer, New York Times and New York Review of Books. *Publications:* Reading Jazz 1996, Reading Lyrics (co-author) 2000. *Leisure interests:* ballet, movies, reading. *Address:* 237 East 48th Street, New York, NY 10017, USA.

GOTTSCHALK, Gerhard, PhD; German professor of microbiology; b. 27 March 1935, Schwedt/Oder; s. of Gerhard Gottschalk and Irmgard Gottschalk (née Ploetz); m. Ellen-Marie Hrabowski 1960; two s. one d.; ed Univs. of Berlin and Göttingen; Research Assoc. Dept of Biochem., Univ. of Calif. Berkeley 1964–66; Docent, Univ. of Göttingen 1967–70, Prof. of Microbiology 1970–, Rector 1975–76, Vice-Pres. 1979–81; Vice-Pres. Acad. of Science, Göttingen 1996, Pres. 1998–2000; Pres. ALLEA (All European Acads.) 1998–2000; Philip Morris Prize 1992. *Publications:* Bacterial Metabolism 1986, Biotechnologie 1986, Göttinger Gelehrte (Co.-Ed. with K. Arndt, R. Smend) 2001. *Address:* Institute of Microbiology and Genetics, University of Göttingen, Grisebachstrasse 8, 37077 Göttingen, Germany. *Telephone:* (551) 393781. *Fax:* (551) 393801. *E-mail:* ggottsc@gwdg.de. *Website:* www.img.bio.uni-goettingen.de.

GOUGH, Barry Morton, MA, PhD, DLit; Canadian professor of history and consultant; b. Barry Morton Gough, 17 Sept. 1938, Victoria, BC; s. of John Gough and Dorothy Mouncy Morton Gough; m. 1st B. Louise Kerr 1964 (divorced 1977); one s. one d.; m. 2nd Marilyn J. Morris 1981; two s.; ed Vic. public schools, Univs of BC and Montana and King's Coll., London; Prof. of History, Western Washington Univ. and Wilfrid Laurier Univ. 1972–; Adjunct Prof. of War Studies, Royal Mil. Coll. of Canada 1994–; Asst Dean of Arts and Sciences, Wilfrid Laurier Univ. 1999–2001; founding mem. Asscn for Canadian Studies in US and Co-Dir and archivist, Center for Pacific Northwest Studies, Western Washington Univ. Bellingham, Wash. 1968–72; founding mem. Asscn of Canadian Studies; mem. Canadian Historical Asscn, Canadian Nautical Research Soc.; Visiting Prof., Duke Univ., Univ. of BC, Otago Univ., Natal Univ., ANU etc.; Fellow, King's Coll. London; Archives Fellow, Churchill Coll. Cambridge; Pres. North American Soc. for Oceanic History, Canadian Nautical Research Soc.; Vice-Pres. Social Sciences Fed. of Canada; Ed. American Neptune: Maritime History and Arts 1995–2001; Roderick Haig-Brown and other book prizes; Lt Gov. of BC Medal for Historical Writing 1985; Queen's Jubilee Medal 2002. *Publications:* Royal Navy and the Northwest Coast 1971, Distant Dominion 1980, Gunboat Frontier 1984, Journal of Alexander Henry the Younger 1988, 1992, The Northwest Coast 1992, Falkland Islands/Malvinas 1992, First Across The Continent: Sir Alexander Mackenzie 1997, Historical Dictionary of Canada 1999, HMCS Haida: Battle Ensign Flying 2001, Fighting Sail on Lake Huron and Georgian Bay 1812 2002; numerous reviews and articles. *Leisure interests:* golfing, jazz clarinet, collecting benefactions. *Address:* 37 Ahrens Street, W, Kitchener, Ont. N2H 4B6, Canada; 107 Pall Mall, London, SW1Y 5ER, England. *Telephone:* (519) 884-1970 (Office); (519) 578-9164 (Home). *Fax:* (519) 884-8854 (Office). *E-mail:* bgough@wlu.ca (Office). *Website:* www.wlu.ca (Office).

GOUGH, Douglas Owen, MA, PhD, FRS, F. INST. P.; British astrophysicist; b. 8 Feb. 1941, Stourport; s. of Owen Albert John Gough and Doris May (Camera) Gough; m. Rosanne Penelope Shaw 1965; two s. two d.; ed Hackney Downs School, London, St John's Coll. Cambridge; Research Assoc., JILA, Univ. of Colo, USA 1966–67; Nat. Acad. of Sciences Sr Postdoctoral Research Assoc., New York 1967–69; mem. Grad. Staff, Inst. of Theoretical Astronomy, Cambridge 1969–73, lecturer in Astronomy and Applied Math., Inst. of Astronomy and Dept of Applied Math. and Theoretical Physics, Cambridge Univ. 1973–85, Reader in Astrophysics, Inst. of Astronomy 1985–93, Prof. of Theoretical Astrophysics, Cambridge Univ. 1993–, Deputy Dir Inst. of Astronomy 1993–99, Dir 1999–; Fellow Churchill Coll. Cambridge 1972–; Foreign mem. Royal Danish Acad. of Sciences and Letters 1998; James Arthur Prize, Harvard Univ., USA 1982, William Hopkins Prize, Cambridge Philosophical Soc. 1984, George Ellery Hale Prize, American Astronomical Soc. 1994, Mousquetaire d'Armagnac 2001. *Publications:* Problems in Solar and Stellar Oscillations (Ed.) 1983, Seismology of the Sun and the Distant Stars (Ed.) 1986, Challenges to Theories of the Structure of Moderate-Mass Stars (Ed. with J. Toomre) 1991. *Leisure interest:* cooking. *Address:* Institute of Astronomy, Madingley Road, Cambridge, CB3 0HA, England. *Telephone:* (1223) 337518. *Fax:* (1223) 337523.

GOUGH, Michael; British actor; b. 23 Nov. 1917, Malaya; numerous film and TV appearances. *Films include:* Women in Love, Velvet House, Julius Caesar, Trog, The Go Between, Henry VIII and his Six Wives, Horror Hospital, Boys from Brazil, Memed, Out of Africa, Wittgenstein, Caravaggio, Machenka, Batman, Blackeyes, Batman Returns, The Age of Innocence, The Life of Galileo, Uncovered, Batman Forever 1995, Young Indiana Jones 1996, Batman and Robin 1997, What Rats Won't Do 1998.

GOUGH, Piers William, CBE, RIBA, FRSA; British architect; b. 24 April 1946; s. of Peter Gough and Daphne Mary Unwin Banks; m. Rosemary Elaine Fosbrooke Bates 1991; ed Architectural Asscn School of Architecture; partner, CZWG Architects 1975–; mem. London Advisory Cttee English Heritage 1995, Commr 2000; Pres. Architectural Asscn 1995–97 (mem. Council 1970–72, 1991); mem. Cultural Strategy Group, Greater London Authority 2000–; Commr English Heritage 2000; RIBA Gold Medal Panel 2000, Tunnel Wharf, Rotherhithe 2000, Office at Edinburgh Park 2000; Hon. DUniv (Middlesex) 1999. *Television:* presenter, Shock of the Old (6-part series), Channel 4 2000. *Principal works include:* Phillips West 2, Bayswater 1976, Cochrane Square (Phase I), Glasgow 1987, China Wharf, Bermondsey 1988, Craft, Design and Tech. Bldg, Bryanston School 1988, Street-Porter House 1988, The Circle, Bermondsey 1990, Westbourne Grove Public Lavatories 1993, 1–10 Summers Street, Clerkenwell 1994, Leonardo Centre, Uppingham School 1995, Cochrane Square (Phase II), Glasgow 1995, 90 Wardour Street,

Soho 1995, 19th and 20th Century Galleries, Nat. Portrait Gallery 1996, Suffolk Wharf, Camden Lock 1996–, Brindleyplace Café, Birmingham 1997, Bankside Lofts, London 1997, The Glass Building, Camden 1999, The Green Bridge, Mile End Park 2000. *Publication:* English Extremists 1988. *Leisure interest:* throwing parties. *Address:* CZWG Architects, 17 Bowling Green Lane, London, EC1R 0QB, England (Office). *Telephone:* (20) 7253-2523 (Office). *Fax:* (20) 7250-0594 (Office). *E-mail:* mail@czwgarchitects.co.uk (Office).

GOULD, Bryan Charles, LLM (NZ), MA, BCL (OXON); British politician; b. 11 Feb. 1939, Hawera, NZ; s. of Charles T. and Elsie M. (née Driller) Gould; m. Gillian A. Harrigan 1967; one s. one d.; ed Victoria and Auckland Univs., NZ and Balliol Coll., Oxford; in diplomatic service, British Embassy Brussels 1964–68; Fellow and Tutor in Law, Worcester Coll., Oxford 1968–74; MP for Southampton Test 1974–79, Dagenham 1983–94; presenter and reporter Thames TV 1977–83; Opposition Spokesman on Trade 1983–86, on Trade and Industry 1987–89, on the Environment 1989–92; mem. of Shadow Cabinet, Labour's Campaign Co-ordinator 1986–89; Shadow Heritage Secretary 1992, resgnd 1992; Vice-Chancellor Waikato Univ. 1994–. *Publications:* Monetarism or Prosperity? 1981, Socialism and Freedom 1985, A Future for Socialism 1989, Goodbye to All That (memoirs) 1995. *Leisure interests:* food, wine, gardening. *Address:* University of Waikato, Private Bag 3105, Hamilton, New Zealand.

GOULD, Elliott; American actor; b. 29 Aug. 1938, Brooklyn, New York; s. of Bernard and Lucille (née Gross) Goldstein; m. 1st Barbra Streisand (q.v.) 1963 (divorced 1971); one s.; m. 2nd Jenny Bogart 1973 (divorced 1975, remarried 1978); one s. one d.; made Broadway début in Rumple 1957; other appearances include Say Darling 1958, Irma La Douce 1960, I Can Get It For You Wholesale 1962, Drat! The Cat 1965, Alfred in Little Murders 1967; toured in The Fantastiks with Liza Minnelli; nat. tour Deathtrap, Luv with Shelley Winters; Hon. LLD (Univ. of West Los Angeles). *Films include:* The Confession 1966, The Night They Raided Minsky's 1968, Bob and Carol and Ted and Alice 1969, Getting Straight 1970, M*A*S*H 1970, The Touch 1971, Little Murders 1971, The Long Good-Bye 1972, Nashville 1974, I Will . . . I Will . . . For Now 1976, Harry and Walter Go to New York 1976, A Bridge Too Far 1977, The Silent Partner 1979, The Lady Vanishes 1979, Escape to Athens 1979, The Muppet Movie 1979, Falling in Love Again 1980, The Devil and Max Devlin 1981, Over the Brooklyn Bridge 1984, The Naked Face 1984, Act of Betrayal 1988, Dead Men Don't Die 1989, Secret Scandal 1990, Strawanser, The Player, Exchange Lifeguards, Wet and Wild Summer, Naked Gun 33$^1/_3$: The Final Insult (cameo), White Man's Burden, The Glass Shield, Kicking and Screaming, A Boy Called Hate, Johns, The Big Hit, American History, X, Bugsy, Hoffman's Hunger, Capricorn One, Boys Life 3 2000, Ocean's Eleven 2001. *TV appearances include:* Doggin' Around (BBC TV), Once Upon a Mattress (CBC), Friends. *Website:* www.elliottgould.net (Office).

GOULD, Philip; British political adviser; b. 30 March 1950; m. Gail Rebuck (q.v.) 1985; two d.; fmrly worked in advertising; f. Philip Gould Assocs. 1985; adviser to Labour Party 1985–, f. Shadow Communications Agency 1995; co-owner and partner Gould Greenberg Carville Ltd, political strategy and polling 1997–; Visiting Prof. LSE 2002–03; Trustee Policy Network; mem. Labour Party. *Publication:* The Unfinished Revolution: How the Modernisers Saved the Labour Party 1998. *Address:* Philip Gould Associates, Ludgate House, 245 Blackfriars Road, London, SE1 9UL, England (Office). *Telephone:* (20) 7890-9003 (Office).

GOULDEN, Sir (Peter) John, Kt, GCMG, BA; British diplomatist (retd.) and civil servant; b. 21 Feb. 1941; s. of George H. Goulden and Doris Goulden; m. Diana Waite 1962; one s. one d.; ed Queen's Coll., Oxford; joined FCO 1962, Ankara 1963–67, Manila 1969–70, Dublin 1976–79, Head Personnel Services Dept 1980–82, News Dept 1982–84, Asst Under-Sec. of State 1988–92; Counsellor, Head Chancery Office of UK Perm. Rep. to EC 1984–87; Amb. to Turkey 1992–95; Amb., Perm. Rep. to North Atlantic Council and WEU 1995–2001; Consultant Home Office 2001–. *Leisure interests:* music, travel, family. *Address:* c/o Home Office, 50 Queen Anne's Gate, London, SW1H 9AT, England (Office).

GOULDING, Sir Marrack Irvine, KCMG; British diplomatist, international civil servant and university college warden; b. 2 Sept. 1936, Plymouth; s. of Sir Irvine Goulding and Gladys Goulding; m. 1st Susan Rhoda D'Albiac 1961 (divorced 1996); two s. one d.; m. 2nd Catherine Pawlow 1996; ed St Paul's School and Magdalen Coll. Oxford; joined HM Foreign (later Diplomatic) Service 1959; with Middle East Centre for Arab Studies 1959–61; Kuwait 1961–64; Foreign Office 1964–68; Tripoli, Libya 1968–70; Cairo 1970–72; Private Sec. Minister of State for Foreign and Commonwealth Affairs 1972–75; seconded to Cabinet Office 1975–77; Counsellor, Lisbon 1977–79; Counsellor and Head of Chancery, UK Mission to UN, New York 1979–83; Amb. to Angola and concurrently to São Tomé e Príncipe 1983–85; UN Under-Sec.-Gen. for Special Political Affairs, 1986–91, for Peace-keeping Operations 1992–93, for Political Affairs 1993–97; Warden St Antony's Coll., Oxford 1997–. *Publications:* Peacemonger 2002. *Leisure interests:* travel and bird-watching. *Address:* St Antony's Coll., Oxford, OX2 6JF, England. *Telephone:* (1865) 284717.

GOULED APTIDON, Hassan; Djibouti politician; b. 1916, Djibouti; Rep. of French Somaliland (now Repub. of Djibouti) to French Govt 1952–58; Vice-Pres. Territorial Ass. 1958–59; Deputy to French Nat. Ass. 1959–62; Minister

of Educ. 1963–67; mem. (later Pres.) Ligue Populaire Africaine pour l'Indépendance—LPAI (fmrly Ligue Populaire Africaine) 1967–79; Pres. Council of Govt, responsible for Co-operation May–June 1977; Chair. Rassemblement Populaire pour le Progrès (RPP) 1979–99; Pres. Repub. of Djibouti, C-in-C of the Armed Forces 1977–99. *Address:* c/o Rassemblement Populaire pour le Progrès, Djibouti (Office); c/o Présidence de la République, Djibouti, Republic of Djibouti.

GOULIAN, Mehran, AB, MD; American physician; b. 31 Dec. 1929, Weehawken, NJ; s. of Dicran Goulian and Shamiram Mzrakjian; m. Susan Hook 1961; three s.; ed Columbia Coll. and Columbia Coll. of Physicians and Surgeons; Medical Internship, Barnes Hosp. 1954–55; Medical Residency, Mass. Gen. Hosp. 1958–59, 1960; Fellow in Medicine (Hematology), Yale Univ. School of Medicine 1959–60; Research Fellow in Medicine (Hematology), Harvard Univ. July–Dec. 1960, 1962–63, Instructor in Medicine 1963–65; Clinical and Research Fellow in Medicine (Hematology), Mass. Gen. Hosp. July–Dec. 1960, 1962–63, Asst in Medicine, 1963–65; Fellow in Biochem., Stanford Univ. School of Medicine 1965–67; Research Assoc. in Biochem., Univ. of Chicago and Argonne Cancer Research Hospital 1967–69, Assoc. Prof. of Medicine 1967–70, Assoc. Prof. of Biochem. 1969–70; Prof. of Medicine, Univ. of Calif., San Diego 1970–1994. *Leisure interest:* music. *Address:* 8433 Prestwick Drive, La Jolla, CA 92037, USA. *Telephone:* (858) 459-0088. *E-mail:* mgoulian'ussd.edu (Home).

GOULLI, Salah Eddine el, DIur; Tunisian fmr diplomatist and business executive; b. 22 June 1919, Sousse; m. M. J. Zeineb Larre 1958; one d.; ed Univ. of Paris (Sorbonne); Consul Gen., Marseilles 1956–57; Minister, Embassy, Washington, DC 1958–61; Alt. Exec. Dir Int. Bank for Reconstruction and Devt 1961; Amb. to Belgium (also accred to Netherlands, Luxembourg, EEC) 1962–69, to UN 1969, to USA (also accred to Venezuela and Mexico) 1970–73, to Netherlands 1976–78; Adviser to Minister of Foreign Affairs 1973–75, 1979–81; Pres. Philips Electronics Tunisia 1981–90, World Trade Centre, Tunis 1990–; Grand Cordon of the Repub., Gold Cross of Leopold and Grand Cross Crown of Belgium; Grand Cross Chêne and Grand Cross Nassau, Luxembourg. *Publications:* lectures on political and econ. matters in USA, Europe and Middle East; numerous articles in European press. *Leisure interests:* golf, reading, swimming. *Address:* World Trade Centre Tunis, 34–36 Avenue de la Foire, 2035 Lacharguia, Tunis (Office); 2 rue des Roses, 2070 Lamarsa, Tunisia. *Telephone:* (1) 809377 (Office); (1) 774307 (Home). *Fax:* (1) 807955 (Office). *E-mail:* wtct@planet.tn (Office).

GOULONGANA, Jean-Robert; Gabonese politician and diplomatist; b. 30 April 1953, Lambarene; m.; three c.; ed Dakar Univ., Senegal, Aix-Marseille III Univ., France; Minister of Waters, Forests and the Environment 1990–91; Amb. to Italy 1992, to Belgium 1996; Head, Gabonese Mission to EU; Sec.-Gen. African, Caribbean and Pacific States 2000–; Officier, Ordre du Mérite Maritime Gabonais. *Address:* African, Caribbean and Pacific States Secretariat, ACP House, 451 avenue Georges Henri, Brussels, Belgium. *Telephone:* (2) 743-06-00. *Fax:* (2) 735-55-73. *E-mail:* info@acpsec.org.

GOUMBA, Abel, DenM; Central African Republic politician and professor of medicine; b. 18 Sept. 1926, Grimari; m.; 15 children; ed Univ. of Bordeaux; doctor in People's Repub. of Congo 1950–56; Vice-Pres. Gov. Council of Oubangui-Chari, Minister of Finance and Planning and Deputy to Regional Ass. 1957–58, Pres. Gov. Council July–Nov. 1958; Minister of Finance and Econ. Affairs, Central African Repub. 1958–59; Minister of State April–Oct. 1959; Deputy to Nat. Ass. 1959; Senator 1960; under house arrest 1960; political prisoner 1960–64; in exile abroad 1964–81; lecturer, Ecole Nat. de Santé Publique, Rennes 1971–73; Prof. of Public Health, Faculty of Medicine, Butaré, Rwanda 1973–77; Prof. of Public Health, Centre Régional de Développement Sanitaire, Cotonou, Benin 1977–81; Prof. of Public Health, Univ. of Bangui 1981–82, 1988–, Rector Feb.–Aug. 1982; political prisoner 1982–84; unemployed 1985–88; fmr leader of Consultative Group of Democratic Forces (CFD), alliance of 14 opposition groups; presidential cand. 1993; Deputy for Kouango, Nat. Ass. 1988–; presidential cand. 1999; now Leader Front Patriotique pour le Progrès (FPP); Prime MinisterCen. African Repub. 2003–. *Address:* Front Patriotique pour le Progrès, B.P. 259, Bangui, Central African Republic (Office). *Telephone:* 61-52-23. *Fax:* 61-10-93.

GOUNARIS, Elias, LLM; Greek diplomatist; b. 7 Sept. 1941, Athens; s. of Panayotis Gounaris and Christine Gounaris; one s.; ed Univ. of Athens; Consul, New York 1969; Ministry of Foreign Affairs 1973; Sec. Perm. Mission of Greece to int. orgs. Geneva 1975; Counsellor 1976; Embassy, Belgrade 1979; Ministry of Foreign Affairs 1983; Minister-Counsellor, then Minister, Embassy, Bonn 1987, Minister Plenipotentiary 1988; Amb. to USSR (also accred to Mongolia) 1989; Amb. to UK 1993–96; Dir Gen. for Political Affairs, Ministry of Foreign Affairs 1997–99; Perm. Rep. to the UN 1999–2002; decorations from Austria, Finland, Germany, Greece, Italy, Spain, Ukraine and the Russian Orthodox Church. *Address:* c/o Ministry of Foreign Affairs, Odos Zalokosta 2, 106 71 Athens (Office); Akadimias Street 1, 106 71 Athens, Greece.

GOUNELLE DE PONTANEL, Hugues; French professor of medicine; b. 27 Feb. 1903, Chateauroux; m. Jeanne Gamas 1940; one s. two d.; ed Lycée de Chateauroux; Intern and Chef de Clinic, Faculté de Médecine, Strasbourg 1925–32; Prof. Agrégé, Val de Grâce, Paris 1938; founder, Foch Research Centre for Human Nutrition 1940; Pres. Acad. Nat. de Médecine 1983;

Commdr Légion d'honneur; Commdr Ordre nat. du Mérite, du Mérite agricole, Croix de Guerre, etc. *Publications:* 400 scientific publs. *Address:* 5 rue Auguste Maquet, 75016 Paris, France (Home).

GOURAD HAMADOU, Barkad; Djibouti politician; fmr mem. of French Senate; fmr Minister of Health; Prime Minister of Djibouti Sept. 1978–, Minister of Ports 1978–87, Minister of Planning and Land Devt 1987, Prime Minister, Minister of Nat. and Regional Devt –2001; mem. Rassemblement Populaire pour le Progrès (RPP). *Address:* c/o Office du Premier Ministre, P.O. Box 2086, Djibouti, Republic of Djibouti (Office).

GOURISSE, Daniel, DèsSc; French administrator and professor of chemical engineering; b. 13 March 1939, Charleville; s. of Robert Gourisse and Marie-Marguerite Lalle; m. Michèle Maës 1961; three s.; ed Ecole Centrale Paris; Laboratory head, Commissariat à l'Energie Atomique (Atomic Energy Comm.) 1964–73, Tech. adviser to the Gen. Admin. 1973–76, Head, Chem. Eng Dept 1976–84; Prof. of Chem. Eng, Ecole Centrale Paris 1969–78, Dir Ecole Centrale 1978–; Pres. Conf. des Grandes Ecoles 1985–93 (now Hon. Pres.), Office de robotique et de productique du Commissariat à l'énergie atomique 1985–89; Scientific Adviser to Dir du Cycle du Combustible 1990–; Pres. Asscn TIME of European Tech. Univs. 1998–2001, Hon. Pres. 2001–; Officier, Ordre nat. du Mérite, Commdr, Palmes académiques, Chevalier, Légion d'honneur. *Publications:* many articles in int. journals. *Address:* Ecole Centrale des Arts et Manufactures, Grande Voie des Vignes, 92295 Chatenay-Malabry Cedex; 12 avenue de la Cure d'Air, 91400 Orsay, France (Home). *Telephone:* 1-41-13-12-54 (Ecole Centrale).

GOURNAY, Patrick P.; British business executive; fmrly with Groupe Danone; CEO The Body Shop 1998–. *Address:* The Body Shop Int. PLC, Watersmead, Littlehampton, England (Office). *Telephone:* (1903) 731500 (Office). *Fax:* (1903) 726250 (Office). *Website:* www.the-body-shop.com (Office).

GOUTARD, Noël; French business executive; b. 22 Dec. 1931, Casablanca, Morocco; s. of F. Antoine Goutard and M. Edmée (née Lespinasse) Goutard; m. Dominique Jung 1964; one s. one d.; ed Lycée Louis le Grand, Paris, Univ. of Bordeaux and Pace Coll., New York; Vice-Pres. Frenville Co., New York 1954–60; Finance Exec. Warner Lambert Int., Morris Plains, NJ 1960–62; African Area Man. Pfizer Inc., New York 1962–66; Exec. Vice-Pres. Gevelot SA Paris 1966–71; Pres. and COO Compteurs Schlumberger SA, Paris 1971–76; Exec. Vice-Pres. and mem. Bd of Dirs. Chargeurs SA, Paris 1976–83; Exec. Vice-Pres. and COO Thomson SA, Paris 1983–84, Dir-Gen. 1983–86; Pres.-Dir Gen. Valéo SA 1987–2000, Hon. Pres. 2000–01; Pres. NG Investments 2000–; mem. Bd Thomson CSF, Banque Thomson, Thomson-Brandt Armements, Imétal 1996–, Alcatel-Alsthom 1997–, etc.; Officier, Légion d'honneur. *Leisure interests:* tennis, travel, golf. *Address:* NG Investments, 90 avenue des Champs-Elysées, 75008, Paris, France (Office); Valeo, 43 rue Bayen, 75017 Paris. *E-mail:* ng.investments@wanado.fr (Office); noel .goutard@valeo.com (Office).

GOUYOU BEAUCHAMPS, Xavier; French television executive; b. 25 April 1937, Paris; s. of Charles Gouyou Beauchamps and Anne-Marie Coulombeix; m. 2nd Geneviève Decugis 1986; two s. (from previous marriage); ed Ecole St Joseph à Sarlat, Inst. d'études politiques and Ecole nat. d'admin; Dir of Staff Loiret Pref. 1964–66; Asst Head of Staff, Minister of Agric. 1966–68, Minister of Educ. 1968–69; Official Staff Rep., Minister of Econ. and Finance 1969–74; Press Sec. to the Pres. 1974–76; Prefect of Ardèche 1976–77; Pres. and Dir-Gen. SOFIRAD 1977–81; Pres. Télédiffusion de France 1986–92, Pres. Asscn des organismes français de radiodiffusion et de télévision (OFRT) 1990–92; Pres. French broadcasters' group (GRF) of European Union of Radio and TV (UER) 1990–, Vice-Pres. UER 1990–; Pres. Admin. Council Nat. Park of Port Cros, Sofipost 1992–94; Dir-Gen. France 3 1994–96, Chair. Bd of Dirs. 1998–; Pres., Dir-Gen. France 2 and France 3 cos. 1996–99; Pres. Asscn des employeurs du service public de l'audiovisuel 1998–; Founder GBX Conseil 1900–; Chevalier, Légion d'honneur, Officier, Ordre nat. du Mérite, Chevalier du Mérite agricole, Croix de la Valeur militaire. *Publication:* Le ministère de l'économie et des Finances, un Etat dans l'Etat? 1976. *Address:* 73 avenue Franklin D. Roosevelt, 75008 Paris, France (Home).

GOVORUKHIN, Stanislav Sergeyevich; Russian politician, film director and actor; b. 29 March 1936, Berezniki, Sverdlovsk Region; m.; one s.; ed All-Union Inst. of Cinematography; with Odessa Film Studio 1967–89; Mosfilm Studio 1989–; active participant opposition movt since early 1990s; mem. State Duma (Homeland faction) 1993–, mem. Cttee on Security 1994–95, Chair. Cttee on Culture 1996–99; one of leaders Democratic Party of Russia, Chair. Deputies of Democratic Party of Russia in State Duma 1995; leader Bloc of Stanislav Govorukhin in elections to Duma 1995. *Films include:* Vertical 1967, The Day of the Angel 1969, White Explosion 1970, The Life and Wonderful Adventures of Robinson Crusoe 1973, Smuggle 1975, A Wind of Hope 1978, The Place of Meeting Cannot Be Changed (TV) 1979, Adventures of Tom Sawyer 1981, In Search of Captain Grant, Drops of Champagne; Act in Assa, On First Breath; documentaries: It Is Impossible To Live So 1990 (Nica Prize), The Russia We Have Lost 1992, Aleksander Solzhenitsyn 1992, Great Criminal Revolution 1994, The Voroshilov's Sniper 2000. *Publications:* Pirates of the 20th Century, Secrets of Madame Vong, Great Criminal Revolution; articles in periodicals. *Address:* State Duma, Okhotny Ryad 1, 103265 Moscow, Russia. *Telephone:* (095) 292-84-01 (Office).

GOW, Gen. Sir (James) Michael, GCB, ; British army officer (retd); b. 3 June 1924, Sheffield, Yorks.; s. of late J. C. Gow and Mrs. Alastair Sanderson; m. Jane Emily Scott 1946; one s. four d.; ed Winchester Coll.; commissioned Scots Guards 1943; served NW Europe 1944–45; Malayan Emergency 1949; Equerry to HRH Duke of Gloucester 1952–53; graduated Staff Coll. 1954; Brigade Maj. 1955–57; Regimental Adjt. Scots Guards 1957–60; Instructor Army Staff Coll. 1962–64; commanded 2nd Bn Scots Guards, Kenya and England 1964–66; GSO1 HQ, London Dist 1966–67; Commdr 4th Guards Brigade 1968–70; at Imperial Defence Coll. 1970; Brig.-Gen. Staff (Int.) HQ, British Army of the Rhine (BAOR) and Asst Chief of Staff G2 HQ, Northag 1971–73; GOC 4th Armoured Div., BAOR 1973–75; Col Commandant Intelligence Corps 1973–86; Dir Army Training 1975–78; GOC Scotland 1979–80; Gov. Edin. Castle 1979–80; Commdr Northern Army Group and C-in-C BAOR, 1980–83; Commandant, Royal Coll. of Defence Studies 1984–86; ADC Gen. to HM The Queen 1981–83; Commr British Scouts W Europe 1980–83; Lt, Queen's Bodyguard for Scotland (Royal Co. of Archers); Vice-Pres. Royal Caledonian Schools, Bushey 1980–96, Royal Patriotic Fund Corpn 1983–88; Pres. Royal British Legion Scotland and Earl Haig Fund Scotland 1986–96; Sec.-Gen. The Prince's Youth Business Trust 1986; Chair. Scottish Ex-Service Charitable Orgs (SESCO) 1989–96, Scots at War Trust 1994–; Ludus Baroque 1999–; Pres. Nat. Asscn of Supported Employment 1993–2000; Vice-Pres. Scottish Nat. Inst. for War Blinded 1995–; Freeman City of London, Freeman and Liveryman Painters and Stainers Co.; Patron Disablement Income Group Scotland 1993–. *Publications:* Trooping The Colour – A History of the Sovereign's Birthday Parade 1980, Jottings in a General's Notebook 1989, General Reflections: A Military Man at Large 1991; articles in military and historical journals. *Leisure interests:* sailing, music, travel, reading. *Address:* 18 Ann Street, Edinburgh, EH4 1PJ, Scotland. *Telephone:* (131) 332-4752 (Home). *Fax:* (131) 332-4752 (Home).

GOWAN, James, FRCA; British architect; b. 18 Oct. 1925, Glasgow; s. of James Gowan and Isabella G. MacKenzie; m. Marguerite A. Barry 1947; two d.; ed Hyndland School, Glasgow, Glasgow School of Art and Kingston School of Art; pvt. practice 1956–, in partnership with James Stirling 1956–63, design of new hosp., Milan 1991, Techint Int. co. HQ offices, Milan 1999; tutor, Architectural Asscn London 1958–60, 1970–72; Visiting Prof. Princeton Univ. 1965, Simón Bolívar Univ. Venezuela 1982, Heriot Watt Univ. Edin. 1990; Banister Fletcher Prof. Univ. Coll. London 1975; Sr tutor, Royal Coll. of Art 1983–86; exhbn of drawings at RIBA Heinz Gallery 1994, at Scottish Nat. Gallery of Modern Art 1994; Hon. Dr of Design (Kingston Univ.) 1996; Reynolds Memorial Award (with James Stirling) 1965. *Publications:* Projects: Architectural Association 1946–71, 1972, A Continuing Experiment 1975, James Gowan (monograph) 1978, Style and Configuration 1994. *Leisure interests:* drawing, reading. *Address:* 2 Linden Gardens, London, W2 4ES, England. *Telephone:* (20) 7229-0642. *Fax:* (20) 7792-9771.

GOWANS, Sir James Learmonth, Kt, CBE, MD, DPhil, FRCP, FRS, FRSA; British medical scientist and administrator; b. 7 May 1924, Sheffield; s. of John Gowans and Selma Josefina Ljung; m. Moyra Leatham 1956; one s. two d.; ed Trinity School, Croydon, King's Coll. Hospital Medical School, Oxford Univ.; Fellow, St Catherine's Coll., Oxford Univ. 1961–; Sec. Gen. Human Frontiers Science Programme, Strasbourg 1989–93; Consultant, WHO Global Programme on AIDS 1987–88; Henry Dale Research Prof. of Royal Soc. 1962–77; Dir MRC Cellular Immunology Unit 1963–77, mem. MRC 1965–69, Sec. (Chief Exec.) 1977–87, Chair. MRC Biological Research Bd 1967–69; mem. Advisory Bd for the Research Councils 1977–87; mem. Council and a Vice-Pres. Royal Soc. 1973–75; Dir Celltech PLC 1980–87; Chair. European Medical Research Councils 1985–87; mem. Acad. Europaea 1991; Foreign Assoc. NAS (USA); Hon. ScD (Yale) 1966, Hon. DSc (Chicago) 1971, (Birmingham) 1978, (Rochester, NY) 1987, Hon. MD (Edinburgh) 1979, (Sheffield) 2000, Hon. LLD (Glasgow) 1988, Hon. DM (Southampton) 1987; Gairdner Award, Ehrlich Prize, Feldberg Award, Royal Medal of Royal Soc., Wolf Prize, Medawar Prize, Galen Medal. *Publications:* articles in scientific journals. *Leisure interest:* old books. *Address:* 75 Cumnor Hill, Oxford, OX2 9HX, England. *Telephone:* (1865) 862304. *Fax:* (1865) 865548.

GOWEILI, Ahmed, PhD; Egyptian politician; fmrly Minister of Trade and Supply in Egyptian Govt; Gen. Sec. Council of Arab Econ. Unity June 2000–. *Address:* Council of Arab Economic Unity, 1191 Corniche en-Nil, 12th Floor, P.O. Box 1, Mohammed Fareed, Cairo, Egypt (Office). *Telephone:* (2) 5755321 (Office). *Fax:* (2) 5754090 (Office).

GOWER, David Ivon, OBE; British journalist, cricketer and broadcaster; b. 1 April 1957, Tunbridge Wells, Kent; s. of Richard Hallam Gower and Sylvia Mary Gower (née Ford); m. Thorunn Ruth Nash 1992; two d.; ed King's School, Canterbury and Univ. Coll. London; left-hand batsman; played for Leicestershire 1975 to 1989 (Capt. 1984–86), Hampshire 1990 to 1993; played in 117 Tests for England 1978 to 1992, 32 as Capt., scoring then England record 8,231 runs (average 44.2) with 18 hundreds; toured Australia 1978–79, 1979–80, 1982–83, 1986–87 and 1990–91; scored 26,339 first-class runs with 53 hundreds; 114 limited-overs internationals; Sunday Express Cricket Correspondent 1993–95; Public Relations Consultant for cricket sponsorship NatWest Bank 1993–2000; commentator, Sky TV 1993–; commentator and presenter, BBC TV 1994–99; columnist, Sunday Telegraph 1995–98, Sun 2000–; presenter Sky TV cricket 1999–; Trustee David Shepherd Conservation Foundation; Hon. MA (Southampton Inst., Nottingham Trent Univ., Loughborough Univ.); Wisden Cricketer of the Year 1979, Int. Cricketer of the Year 1982/83. *Television:* They Think It's All Over. *Publications:*

With Time to Spare 1979, Heroes and Contemporaries 1983, A Right Ambition 1986, On the Rack 1990, The Autobiography 1992. *Leisure interests:* Cresta run, skiing, tennis, photography, wildlife conservation. *Address:* c/o SFX Sports Group, 35/36 Grosvenor Street, London W1K 4QX England. *Telephone:* (20) 7529-4300 (Office). *Fax:* (20) 7529-4347 (Office).

GOWERS, Andrew, MA; British journalist; b. 19 Oct. 1957, Reading, Berks; s. of Michael Gowers and Anne Gowers; m. Finola Gowers (née Clarke); one s. one d.; ed Trinity School, Croydon and Univ. of Cambridge; grad. trainee, Reuters 1980, Brussels Corresp. 1981, Zurich Corresp. 1982, joined Foreign Desk, Financial Times (FT), London 1983, Agric. Corresp. 1984, Commodities Ed. 1985, Middle East Ed. 1987, Foreign Ed. 1992, Deputy Ed. 1994, Acting Ed. 1997, Ed. FT Deutschland (German Language Business Paper) 1999, Ed. FT 2001–. *Publication:* Arafat, The Biography (jtly.) 1991. *Leisure interests:* film, opera, music, theatre, gastronomy. *Address:* Financial Times, 1 Southwark Bridge, London, SE1 9HL (Office); 17 Gilkes Crescent, Dulwich, London, SE21 7BP, England (Home). *Telephone:* (20) 7873-3000 (Office). *Fax:* (20) 7873-3924 (Office). *E-mail:* andrew.gowers@FT.com (Office). *Website:* www .FT.com (Office).

GOWERS, (William) Timothy, PhD, FRS; British mathematician; b. 20 Nov. 1963, Marlborough; s. of (William) Patrick Gowers and Caroline (Molesworth) Maurice; m. Emily Joanna Thomas 1988; two s. one d.; ed Eton Coll., Trinity Coll., Cambridge; lecturer Univ. Coll. London 1991–94, Reader 1994–95; Fellow Trinity Coll., Cambridge 1989–93; lecturer Univ. of Cambridge 1995–98, Rouse Ball Prof. of Mathematics 1998–; Hon. Fellow Univ. Coll. London 1999; Jr Whitehead Prize, London Mathematical Soc. 1995, European Mathematical Soc. Prize 1996; Fields Medal 1998. *Publications:* Mathematics: A Very Short Introduction 2002; mathematical papers in various journals. *Leisure interest:* playing jazz piano. *Address:* Department of Pure Mathematics and Mathematical Statistics, Centre for Mathematical Sciences, Wilberforce Road, Cambridge, CB3 0WB, England. *Telephone:* (1223) 337973. *Fax:* (1223) 337920 (Department). *E-mail:* wtg10@dpmms.cam.ac.uk (Office).

GOWON, Gen. Yakubu, BA, PH.D; Nigerian army officer; b. 19 Oct. 1934, Garam, Pankshin Div., Plateau State; s. of Yohanna and Saraya Gowon; m. Victoria Hansatu Zakari 1969; one s. two d.; ed St Bartholomew's School, Wusasa, Zaria, Govt Coll. (Barewa), Zaria, Royal Military Acad., Sandhurst, Staff Coll., Camberley and Jt Services Staff Coll., Latimer, England; Adjutant, Nigerian Army March 1960; with UN peacekeeping force, Congo 1960–61, Jan.–June 1963; promoted Lt-Col and apptd. Adjutant-Gen. Nigerian Army June 1963; Chief of Staff 1966; Maj.-Gen. June 1967; promoted Gen. Oct. 1971; Head of Fed. Mil. Govt and C-in-C of Armed Forces of Fed. Repub. of Nigeria 1966–75 (deposed in coup); studying at Warwick Univ. 1975–83, Postgrad. 1978–82; Chair. Ass. of Heads of State, OAU 1973–74; Chair. Nigerian Nat. Oil and Chemical Marketing Co. 1996–; Chair. Trustees, Commonwealth Human Ecology Foundation 1986–; Hon. LLD, Hon. DSc, Hon. DLitt. *Publication:* Faith in Unity 1970. *Leisure interests:* squash, tennis, photography, pen-drawings. *Address:* National Oil and Chemical Marketing Co., 38–39 Marina, P.M.B. 2052, Lagos, Nigeria.

GOWRIE, Rt Hon Alexander Patrick Greysteil Hore-Ruthven, The Earl of Gowrie, PC, BA, AM; British/Irish politician and company director; b. Alexander Hore-Ruthven, 26 Nov. 1939; s. of late Hon. A. H. P. Hore-Ruthven and Pamela Margaret Fletcher; m. 1st Xandra Bingley 1962 (divorced 1973); one s.; m. 2nd Adelheid Gräfin von der Schulenburg 1974; ed Eton Coll., Balliol Coll. Oxford and Harvard Univ., USA; Fellow and Tutor, Lowell House, Harvard Univ. 1965–68; Asst Prof., Emerson Coll., Boston 1967–68; Lecturer in English and American Literature, Univ. Coll. London 1969–72; a UK del. to UN 1971; a Lord-in-Waiting to HM the Queen 1972–74; Govt Whip, House of Lords 1972–74; Consultant, Thomas Gibson Fine Art 1974–79; Opposition Spokesman on Econ. Affairs and Adviser to Margaret Thatcher 1977–79; Minister of State, Dept of Employment 1979–81; Minister of State and Deputy to the Sec. of State, Northern Ireland Office 1981–83; Minister of State, Privy Council Office and Minister for the Arts 1983–84; mem. of Cabinet as Chancellor of the Duchy of Lancaster (retaining portfolio as Minister for the Arts) 1984–85; Chair. The Really Useful Group 1985–90, Sotheby's Europe 1985–94, Arts Council 1994–98 (Chair. Literature Panel 1995–), Harefield Research Foundation, Fine Art Fund; Dir Sotheby's Holdings Inc. 1985–98; Provost RCA 1986–95; Chair. Devt Securities 1995–99, Dir (non-exec.) 1995–2001; Dir (non-exec.) NXT PLC, ITG PLC 1998–2002, Yeoman Investment Trust; Privy Counsellor 1984. *Publications:* A Postcard from Don Giovanni (poems) 1972, The Genius of British Painting: The Twentieth Century 1975, Derek Hill: An Appreciation 1987. *Leisure interests:* the arts. *Address:* Harefield Research Foundation, Science Centre, Harefield, Middlesex, England. *Telephone:* (20) 7828-4777.

GOYTISOLO, Juan; Spanish author; b. 5 Jan. 1931, Barcelona; ed Univs. of Barcelona and Madrid; emigrated to France 1957; reporter, Cuba 1965; assoc. with Gallimard Publishing Co.; Visiting Prof. at various univs. in USA; Premio Europalia 1985; numerous awards for novel Juegos de manos; Octavio-Paz Essay and Poetry Prize 2002. *Publications:* novels: Juegos de manos 1954, Duelo en el paraíso 1955, El circo 1957, Fiestas 1958, La resaca 1958, La isla 1961, Señas de identidad 1966, Reivindicación del Conde don Julián 1970, Juan sin tierra 1975, Makbara 1980, Paisajes después de la

batalla 1982, The Marx Family Saga 1996, The Garden of Secrets 2001; autobiog.: Coto vedado 1985, En los reinos de taifa 1986; short stories, travel narratives, literary criticism, essays etc.

GRABER, Pierre; Swiss politician; b. 6 Dec. 1908, La Chaux-de-Fonds; s. of Paul and Blanche Graber (née Vuilleumier); m. Renée Graber (née Alivon); one s., one d.; ed Gymnasiums in Neuchâtel and Berne and Univs. of Neuchâtel and Vienna; Lawyer, Lausanne 1933–46; mem. Lausanne Legis. Council 1933–46; mem. Great Council of Vaud 1937–46; Mayor of Lausanne 1946–49; mem. Lausanne City Council and Dir Dept of Finance, Lausanne 1949–62; mem. Council Canton Vaud, Dir Dept of Finance 1962–70, Pres. 1968; mem. Nat. Council 1942–69, Pres. 1966; Leader of Socialist Group in Fed. Ass. 1967–69; mem. Fed. Council 1970–77, Head of Fed. Political (Foreign Affairs) Dept 1970–77; Vice-Pres. Fed. Council Jan.–Dec. 1974; Pres. of Swiss Confed. Jan.–Dec. 1975; Social Democrat; Citoyen d'honneur de la Ville de Lausanne; Gold Medal of the Int. Olympic Cttee. *Publication:* Mémoires et Reflexions 1992. *Leisure interests:* gymnastics, athletics, shooting, football, tennis. *Address:* CH 1003, Lausanne, avenue de Montbenon 2, Switzerland. *Telephone:* (21) 3202434.

GRABINER, Baron (Life Peer), cr. 1999, of Aldwych in the City of Westminster; **Anthony Stephen Grabiner,** QC, LLM; British barrister; b. 21 March 1945, London; s. of late Ralph Grabiner and Freda Grabiner (née Cohen); m. Jane Aviva Portnoy 1983; three s. one d.; ed Cen. Foundation Boys' Grammar School, LSE; called to the Bar (Lincoln's Inn) 1968; Droop Scholar, Lincoln's Inn 1968; Jr Counsel to Dept of Trade 1976–81; QC 1981; Bencher 1989–; Recorder 1990–; Deputy High Court Judge 1998–; Vice-Chair. Court of Govs. LSE 1993–98, Chair. 1998–; Head of Chambers One Essex Court 1994–; Leader Inquiry into Black Economy 1999–2000. *Publication:* Sutton and Shannon on Contracts 1970, The Informal Economy 2000. *Leisure interests:* golf, theatre, swimming. *Address:* 1 Essex Court, Temple, London, EC4Y 9AR, England. *Telephone:* (20) 7583-2000. *Fax:* (20) 7583-0118. *E-mail:* clerks@oneessexcourt.co.uk (Office).

GRACH, Eduard Davidovich; Russian violinist; b. 19 Dec. 1930, Odessa; s. of David Grach and Evelina Grach; m. 2nd Valentina Vasilenko 1990; one s. one d.; ed P. Stolyarsky Odessa School of Music, Moscow State Conservatory (pupil of A. Yampolsky); winner of int. competitions in Budapest 1949 (1st prize), J. Thibaud in Paris 1955, P. Tchaikovsky in Moscow 1962; solo performances since 1953 in most countries of Europe; performer of classical and contemporary concertos and sonatas for violin; participant in the Trio with pianist Y. Malinin and cellist N Shakhovskaya 1960–70; first performer of a number of works by Russian composers dedicated to him, including concertos by A. Eshpai; Head Violin Dept, Moscow State Conservatory; Founder and Artistic Dir Moskovia Chamber Orchestra 1994–; gives master classes in several countries; People's Artist of USSR 1987, 1990. *Leisure interest:* football. *Address:* Moscow State Conservatory, Bolshaya Nikitskaya str. 13, 103871 Moscow (Office); 1st Smolensky per. 9, kv. 98, 121099 Moscow, Russia (Home). *Telephone:* (095) 241-21-57 (Home). *Fax:* (095) 241-21-57 (Home).

GRACHEV, Army Gen. Pavel Sergeevich; Russian army officer; b. 1 Jan. 1948, Revy, Tula Region; m.; two s.; ed Ryazan Air Landing Force School, Military Acad., Gen. Staff Acad.; mem. CPSU 1968–91; Commdr parachute landing platoon, Kaunas, Co. Commdr, Ryazan, Commdr of Bn, Lithuania 1969–81; Deputy Commdr, Commdr 354 Parachute landing Regt, Afghanistan 1981–83, Head of Staff 7th Army, Lithuania 1983–85, Div. Commdr, Afghanistan 1985–88; First Deputy Commdr USSR Air Landing Forces 1990–91, Commdr Jan.–Aug. 1991; First Deputy Minister of Defence of USSR (later CIS) 1991–92, Minister of Defence of Russia 1992–96; took part in neutralization of revolt Oct. 1993; Chief Mil. Expert Rosvooruzheniye co. 1997–; Hero of Soviet Union and other decorations. *Address:* Rosvooruzheniye, Ovchinnikovskaya nab. 18/1, 113324 Moscow, Russia. *Telephone:* (095) 220-17-52.

GRACHEVA, Nadezhda Aleksandrovna; Russian ballet dancer; b. 21 Dec. 1969, Semipalatinsk; d. of Aleksander Aleksandrovich Grachev and Vera Petrovna Gracheva; m. 1st Aleksei Yuryevich Seregin (divorced); m. Yevgeny Kern; ed Moscow School of Choreography; with Bolshoi Theatre 1987–; leading parts in Bayadera, Swan Lake, Nutcracker, Sleeping Beauty, Les Sylphides, Stone Flower, Romeo and Juliet and others; toured in many European and American countries, Japan, Israel, New Zealand; Benoît Prize 1991; prizes at int. competitions Varna 1984, 1986, Moscow 1987, Osaka 1995; State Prize of Russia 1996; People's Artist of Russia 1996. *Leisure interests:* cooking. *Address:* Bolshoi Theatre, Teatralnaya pl. 1, 103009 Moscow; 1st Truzhennikov per. 17, Apt. 49, 119121 Moscow, Russia (Home). *Telephone:* (095) 248-27-53 (Home).

GRADE, Michael Ian, CBE, FRTS; British broadcasting executive; b. 8 March 1943, London; s. of the late Leslie Grade; m. 1st Penelope Jane Levinson 1967 (divorced 1981); one s. one d.; m. 2nd Hon. Sarah Lawson 1982 (divorced 1991); m. 3rd Francesca Mary Leahy 1998; one s.; ed St Dunstan's Coll., London; trainee journalist Daily Mirror 1960, Sports Columnist 1964–66; Theatrical Agent Grade Org. 1966; Jt Man. Dir London Man. and Representation 1969–73; Deputy Controller of Programmes (Entertainment) London Weekend TV 1973–77, Dir of Programmes and mem. Bd 1977–81; Pres. Embassy TV 1981–84; Controller BBC 1 1984–86, Dir of Programmes BBC TV 1986–87; CEO Channel Four 1988–97; Chair. VCI PLC 1995–98; Chair., CEO First Leisure Corpn 1997–98 (Dir 1991–2000, non-exec. Chair.

1995–97); Chair. Ind. Inquiry into Fear of Crime 1989, Devt Council, Royal Nat. Theatre 1997–; Deputy Chair. Soc. of Stars 1995–; Pres. TV and Radio Industries Club 1987–88, Newspaper Press Fund 1988–89, Entertainment Charities Fund 1994–, Royal TV Soc. 1995–97; Vice-Pres. Children's Film Unit 1993–; Dir ITN 1989–93, Open Coll. 1989–97, Delfont Macintosh Theatres Ltd 1994–99, Charlton Athletic Football Club 1997–, Jewish Film Foundation 1997–, New Millennium Experience Co. 1997–, Camelot Group 2000–, Digitaloctopus 2000–; Chair. Octopus 2000–, Pinewood Studio Ltd 2000–, Hemscott.NET 2000–; mem. Int. Council. Nat. Acad. of TV Arts and Sciences 1991–97; mem. Council, London Acad. of Music and Dramatic Art 1981–93, BAFTA 1981–82, 1986–88 (Fellow 1994), Gate Theatre, Dublin 1990–, Cities in Schools 1991–95, Cinema and TV Benevolent Fund 1993–, Royal Acad. of Dramatic Art 1996–, Royal Albert Hall 1997–; mem. 300 Group, Milton Cttee, British Screen Advisory Council 1986–97, Nat. Comm. of Inquiry into Prevention of Child Abuse 1994–96; mem. Bd of Govs. BANFF TV Festival 1997–; Hon. Prof. Thames Valley Univ. 1994; Hon. Treas. Stars Org. for Spastics 1986–92; Trustee Band Aid, Nat. Film and TV School, Virgin Health Care Foundation; Hon. LLD (Nottingham) 1997, Royal TV Soc. Gold Medal 1997. *Publication:* It Seemed Like a Good Idea at the Time (autobiog.) 1999. *Leisure interest:* entertainment. *Address:* First Leisure Corporation, 7 Soho Street, London, W1V 5FA, England (Office).

GRADIN, Anita; Swedish politician; b. 12 Aug. 1933, Hörnefors, Väster-botten Co.; m. Lt-Col Bertil Kersfelt; one d.; ed Coll. of Social Work and Public Admin., Stockholm and in USA; journalist 1950, 1956–58, 1960–63; with Swedish Union of Forest Workers and Log Drivers 1952; with Social Welfare Planning Cttee and Municipal Exec. Bd Cttee on Women's Issues, Stockholm 1963–67; mem. Exec. Cttee, Nat. Fed. of Social Democratic Women 1964–93, Vice-Chair. 1975–93; mem. Stockholm City Council 1966–68; First Sec. Cabinet Office 1967–82; mem. SDP Exec. Cttee of Stockholm 1968–82; mem. Parl. 1968–92; Chair. Dist Br., Fed. of Social Democratic Women, Stockholm 1968–82; Chair. Swedish Union of Social Workers and Public Admin. 1970–81; Chair. Nat. Bd for Intercountry Adoptions 1973–80; del. Council of Europe 1973–82, Chair. Cttee on Migration, Refugees and Democracy 1978–82; Minister with responsibility for Migration and Equality Affairs 1982–86; Vice-Chair. Socialist Int. Women's Council 1983–86, Chair. Socialist Int. Women 1986–92, Vice-Chair. Socialist Int. 1986–92; Minister with responsibility for Foreign Trade and European Affairs 1986–91; Amb. to Austria, Slovenia and to UN insts. including IAEA, UNIDO and UNRWA 1992–94; EC Commr for Migration, Home and Judicial Affairs 1995–99; Chair. Research Council of Social Science and Working Life 2001; Chair. of Stockholm Conf. on Vietnam 1974–76, of Swedish Cttee for Vietnam, Laos and Cambodia 1977–82; mem. Exec. Cttee of RFSU (Nat. Asscn for Sexual Enlightenment) and Otterfonden 1969–92; mem. EFTA del. 1991–92; mem. Bd Stockholm School of Econs; Marisa Bellizario European Prize (Italy) 1998; Pro Merito Medal, Council of Europe 1982, Wizo Woman of the Year 1986, Cavalieri di Gran Croce (Italy) 1991, Das Grossen Goldene Ehrenzeichen am Bande (Austria) 1994, The King's Medal in the 12th Dimension with ribbon of the Royal Order of the Seraphim 1998. *Address:* Fleminggatan 85, 11245 Stockholm, Sweden. *Telephone:* (8) 269872. *Fax:* (8) 269872. *E-mail:* gradin .kersfelt@telia.com (Home).

GRAF, Hans; Austrian conductor and administrator; b. 15 Feb. 1949, Linz; ed Bruckner Conservatory, Linz, Academy of Music, Graz; Music Dir Iraqi Nat. Symphony Orchestra 1975, Mozarteum Orchestra, Salzburg 1984–94, Calgary Philharmonic Orchestra 1995–, Nat. Orchestre de Bordeaux-Aqui-taine 1998–, Opéra de Bordeaux 1998–, Houston Symphony Orchestra 2001–; guest conductor with several orchestras including Vienna Symphony, Vienna Philharmonic, Orchestre Nat. de France, Leningrad Philharmonic, Pitts-burgh Symphony, Boston Symphony; First Prize, Karl Böhm Conductors Competition, Salzburg 1979. *Address:* Calgary Philharmonic Orchestra, 205 8th Avenue SE, Calgary, AB, T2G 0K9, Canada (Office); Unit 2, 39 Tadema Road, London, SW10 0PX, England.

GRAF, Steffi; German tennis player; b. 14 June 1969, Mannheim; d. of Peter and Heidi Graf; m. Andre Agassi; one s.; coached by her father; won Orange Bowl 12s 1981, European 14-and-under and European Circuit Masters 1982, Olympic demonstration event, LA; winner German Open 1986, French Open 1987, 1988, 1993, 1995, 1996, 1999; Australian Open 1988, 1989, 1990, 1994; Wimbledon 1988, 1989, 1991, 1992, 1993, 1995, 1996, US Open 1988 1989, 1993, 1995, 1996, won ATP Tour World Championship 1996, German Open 1989, numerous women's doubles championships with Gabriela Sabatini, Federation Cup 1992; Olympic Champion 1988; ranked No. 1 Aug. 1987; named Official World Champion 1988; Grand Slam winner 1988, 1989; youngest player to win 500 singles victories as a professional Oct. 1991; 118 tournament wins, 23 Grand Slam titles; announced retirement Aug. 1999; Amb. World Wildlife Fund 1984–; Founder and Chair. Children for Tomorrow; Amb. of EXPO 2000; Olympic Order 1999, German Medal of Honour 2002. *Publication:* Wege Zum Erfolg 1999. *Leisure interests:* music, dogs, photog-raphy, art, reading. *Address:* Stefanie Graf Marketing GmbH, Mallaustrasse 75, 68219 Mannheim, Germany (Office). *E-mail:* kontakt@stefanie-graf.com (Office). *Website:* www.stefanie-graf.com (Office).

GRAFFMAN, Gary; American pianist; b. 14 Oct. 1928; s. of Vladimir and Nadia (Margdin) Graffman; m. Naomi Helfman 1952; ed Curtis Inst. of Music, Philadelphia under Mme. Isabelle Vengerova; professional début with Phil-adelphia Orchestra 1947; concert tours all over the world; appears annually in America with major orchestras; Dir Curtis Inst. 1986–, Pres. 1995–; year

offstage to correct finger injury 1980–81; gramophone recordings for Columbia Masterworks and RCA Victor including concertos of Tchaikovsky, Rachmaninoff, Brahms, Beethoven, Chopin and Prokofiev; Leventritt Award 1949; several hon. degrees. *Publication:* I Really Should be Practising (autobiog.) 1981. *Leisure interest:* Asian art. *Address:* Office of the Director, Curtis Institute of Music, 1726 Locust Street, Philadelphia, PA 19103-6187, USA (Office). *Telephone:* (215) 893-5252 (Office). *Fax:* (215) 893-0897 (Office).

GRAFTON, Sue, BA; American writer; b. April 24 1940, Louisville, Ky; d. of C.W. Grafton and Vivian Harnsberger; m. 3rd Steven F. Humphrey; one s. two d. from previous marriages; ed Univ. of Louisville, Ky; worked as admissions clerk, cashier and clinic sec., St John's Hosp., Santa Monica, CA; receptionist, later medical educ. sec., Cottage Hosp., Santa Barbara, CA. *Television:* has written numerous films for TV, including Walking Through the Fire (Chris-topher Award) 1979, Sex and the Single Parent, Mark, I Love You, Nurse; also adaptations of Caribbean Mystery and Sparkling Cyanide by Agatha Christie. *Publications:* Keziah Dane 1967, The Lolly-Madonna War 1969, A is for Alibi 1982, B is for Burglar 1985, C is for Corpse 1986, D is for Deadbeat 1987, E is for Evidence 1988, F is for Fugitive 1989, G is for Gumshoe 1990, H is for Homicide 1991, I is for Innocent 1992, J is for Judgement 1993, K is for Killer 1994, L is for Lawless 1995, M is for Malice 1996, N is for Noose 1998, O is for Outlaw 1999, P is for Peril 2001, Q is for Quarry 2003; Killer in the Family (Jt author with S. Humphrey), Love on the Run (Jt author with S. Humphrey). *Leisure interests:* cats, gardening, good food. *Address:* PO Box 41447, Santa Barbara, CA 93140, USA (Office). *Website:* www.suegrafton.com (Office).

GRAHAM, Sir Alexander Michael, GBE, JP, DCL, CBIM, FCII, FCIS, FRSA; British chartered insurance broker; b. 27 Sept. 1938, London; s. of Dr Walter Graham and Suzanne Simon; m. Carolyn Stansfeld 1964; three d.; ed St Paul's School; nat. service with Gordon Highlanders 1957–59; broker, Frizzell Group Ltd 1957–67, Dir 1967–73, Man. Dir 1973–90, Deputy Chair. 1990–92; Alderman, City of London 1979–, Sheriff 1986–87, Lord Mayor 1990–91; Chair. Nat. Employers Liaison Cttee for TA and Reserve Forces 1992–97; Chair. First City Insurance Brokers Ltd 1993–98; Chair. Council, Order of St John, Herts. 1993–; Chair. Bd of Trustees, Morden Coll. 1995–; Chair. Folgate Insurance Co. Ltd1995–2002, Employment Conditions Abroad Ltd 1993–, Euclidian PLC 1994–2001, United Response 1994–2002; Pres. British Insur-ance Law Asscn 1994–96; Underwriting mem. of Lloyd's; Fellow Chartered Insurance Inst.; Liveryman Mercers' Co. 1971–, Master 1983–84; Vice-Pres. Royal Soc. of St George 1999–; KStJ; Grand Cross Order of Merit (Chile); Order of Wissam Alouite Class 3 (Morocco). *Leisure interests:* golf, shooting, tennis, swimming, wine, music, calligraphy. *Address:* 13–15 Folgate Street, London, E1 6BX (Office); Walden Abbotts, Whitwell, Hitchin, Herts., SG4 8AJ, England (Home). *Telephone:* (1438) 871997 (Home). *Fax:* (1438) 871997 (Home).

GRAHAM, Andrew Winston Mawdsley, MA; British economist; b. 20 June 1942; s. of Winston Mawdsley Graham; m. Peggotty Fawssett 1970; ed Charterhouse, St Edmund Hall, Oxford; Econ. Asst Nat. Econ. Devt Office 1964, with Dept of Econ. Affairs 1964–66, Asst to Econ. Adviser to Cabinet 1966–68, Econ. Adviser to Prime Minister 1968–69; Fellow and Tutor in Econs Balliol Coll. Oxford 1969–97, Estates Bursar 1978, Investment Bursar 1979–83, Vice Master 1988, 1992–94, Acting Master 1997–2001, Master 2001–; Policy Adviser to Prime Minister (leave of absence from Balliol) 1974–75; Econ. Adviser to Shadow Chancellor of Exchequer 1988–92, to Leader of Opposition 1992–94; Tutor Oxford Univ. Business Summer School 1971, 1972, 1973, 1976; Visiting Scholar MIT, Visiting Fellow Center for European Studies, Harvard Univ., USA 1994; Chair. St James Group (Econ. Forecasting) 1982–84, 1985–92; Consultant BBC 1989–92; Bd mem. Channel 4 TV 1998–; Acting Dir Oxford Internet Inst. 2001; mem. Media Advisory Cttee, Inst. for Public Policy Research 1994–97, Council of Man. Templeton Coll. Oxford 1990–96; Founder mem. Editorial Bd Library of Political Economy 1982–94; Sr Fellow Gorbachev Foundation of N America 1999; Trustee Foundation for Information Policy Research 1998–2001. *Publica-tions:* Government and Economies in the Postwar Period (ed.) 1990, Broad-casting, Society and Policy in the Multimedia Age (jtly) 1997; contribs. to books on econs and philosophy. *Leisure interest:* windsurfing. *Address:* Balliol College, Oxford, OX1 3BJ, England. *Telephone:* (1865) 277777.

GRAHAM, Billy (see Graham, William Franklin).

GRAHAM, Christopher Forbes, DPhil, FRS; British biologist; b. 23 Sept. 1940; ed Oxford Univ.; fmrly Jr Beit Memorial Fellow in Medical Research, Sir William Dunn School of Pathology; Lecturer, Dept of Zoology, Univ. of Oxford 1970–85, Prof. of Animal Devt 1985–; Professorial Fellow St Cather-ine's Coll., Oxford 1985–; mem. British Soc. for Cell Biology, British Society for Developmental Biology, Soc. for Experimental Biology, Genetical Soc. *Publication:* Developmental Control in Plants and Animals 1984. *Address:* Department of Zoology, University of Oxford, South Parks Road, Oxford, OX1 3PS, England.

GRAHAM, Daniel Robert (Bob), BA, LLD; American politician and farmer; b. 9 Nov. 1936, Coral Gables, Fla; s. of Ernest R. Graham and Hilda Simmons; m. Adele Khoury 1959; four d.; ed Univ. of Florida and Harvard Univ.; Vice-Pres. Sengra Devt Corpn 1963–79; Florida State Rep. from Coral Gables 1966–70; Florida State Senator from Coral Gables 1970–78; Gov. of Florida 1979–87, Senator 1986–; mem. of numerous govt and public cttees; Democrat;

Audubon Soc. Conservation Award 1974. *Leisure interests:* golf, tennis and reading. *Address:* US Senate, 524 Hart Senate Building, Washington, DC 20510-0001, USA.

GRAHAM, Donald Edward, BA; American newspaper publisher; b. 22 April 1945, Baltimore, Md; s. of late Philip L. Graham and of Katharine Meyer Graham; m. Mary L. Wissler 1967; one s. three d.; ed Harvard Univ.; joined the Washington Post 1971, Asst Man. Ed./Sports 1974–75, Asst Gen. Man. 1975–76, Exec. Vice-Pres. and Gen. Man. 1976–79, Publr 1979–; Pres., CEO Washington Post Co. 1991–93, Chair., CEO 1993–; fmrly reporter and writer for Newsweek. *Address:* The Washington Post, 1150 15th Street, NW, Washington, DC 20071, USA. *Telephone:* (202) 334-7138.

GRAHAM, Rt Hon Sir Douglas Arthur Montrose, KNZM, PC, LLB; New Zealand lawyer and fmr politician; b. 12 Jan. 1942, Auckland; m. Beverley V. Graham 1966; two s. one d.; ed Southwell School, Auckland Grammar School and Univ. of Auckland; practising lawyer since 1965; est. own practice 1968; barrister and solicitor of High Court of NZ; Lecturer in Legal Ethics, Univ. of Auckland 1973–83; mem. Parl. 1984–99; Minister of Justice and of Courts, also in charge of Treaty of Waitangi Negotiations 1990–99; Attorney Gen. 1997–99; co. dir and consultant 1999–; fmr Minister of Disarmament and Arms Control and Cultural Affairs; Dr hc (Waikato) 1999. *Publication:* Trick or Treaty? 1997. *Leisure interests:* golf, music, rugby football, gardening. *Address:* Elderslie, Manuwai Lane, RD2 Drury, South Auckland, New Zealand. *Telephone:* (9) 294-8608. *Fax:* (9) 294-8672. *E-mail:* douglas.graham@ xtra.co.nz (Home).

GRAHAM, Lindsay O.; American politician; served in armed forces, assignments including Operation Desert Shield and Desert Storm; legal career in USAF; Base Staff Judge Advocate, McEntire Air Nat. Guard Base, Eastover 1989–94; est. pvt. law practice 1988; asst attorney in Oconee Co.; mem. S. Carolina House of Reps from 2nd Dist Oconee Co. 1992–94; mem. US Congress from 3rd Dist S. Carolina 1994–2003, mem. Cttee on Educ. and the Workforce, on Judiciary, on Armed Services; Senator from S Carolina 2003–; currently Lt-Col. Air Force Reserves; mem. Republican Party. *Address:* Office of the Senator from South Carolina, US Senate, Senate Buildings, Washington, DC 20510, USA (Office).

GRAHAM, Patricia Albjerg, PhD; American educator; b. 9 Feb. 1935, Lafayette, Ind.; d. of Victor L. Albjerg and Marguerite Hall Albjerg; m. Loren R. Graham 1955; one d.; ed Purdue and Columbia Univs; teacher Deep Creek and Maury High Schools, Norfolk, Va 1955–58; Chair. History Dept, St Hilda's and St Hugh's School, New York 1958–60, part-time Coll. Adviser 1961–63, 1965–67; Lecturer, Ind. Univ., School of Educ., Bloomington 1964–65; Asst Prof., Barnard Coll. and Columbia Teacher's Coll., New York 1965–68, Assoc. Prof. 1968–72, Prof. 1972–74; Prof., Harvard Univ. Graduate School of Educ., Cambridge, Mass. 1974–79, Warren Prof. 1979–, Dean Graduate School of Educ. 1982–91; Dean Radcliffe Inst. and Vice-Pres. for Institutional Planning, Radcliffe Coll., Cambridge, Mass. 1974–76, Dean Radcliffe Inst. and Vice-Pres. Radcliffe Coll. 1976–77; Dir Nat. Inst. of Educ. 1977–79; Vice-Pres. for Teaching, American Historical Asscn 1985–89; Pres. Nat. Acad. of Educ. 1985–89; Dir Spencer Foundation 1983–2000, Pres. 1991–2000; Dir Johnson Foundation 1983–2001; mem. AAAS (mem. Council 1993–96, Vice-Pres. 1998–2001); mem. Center for Advanced Study in the Behavioral Sciences (Bd Dirs 2001–); several hon. degrees. *Publications:* Progressive Education: From Arcady to Academe, A History of the Progressive Education Association 1967, Community and Class in American Education, 1865–1918 1974, Women in Higher Education (co-ed. with Todd Furniss) 1974, S.O.S. Sustain Our Schools 1992, Acceptability (with Richard Lyman and Martin Trow) 1995. *Address:* Harvard University Graduate School of Education, Longfellow Hall, Appian Way, Cambridge, MA 02135, USA (Office). *Telephone:* (617) 496-4839 (Office). *Fax:* (617) 496-3095 (Office). *E-mail:* patricia_graham@harvard.edu (Office).

GRAHAM, William, BA, LLB, DJur; Canadian politician, lawyer and academic; b. 1939; m. Catherine Graham; one d. one s.; ed Upper Canada Coll., Trinity Coll., Univ. of Toronto, Univ. of Paris, France; Prof. of Law, Univ. of Toronto, Univ. de Montréal, McGill Univ.; Dir Centre of Int. Studies, Univ. of Toronto; Pres. Alliance Française, Toronto; Partner Fasken and Calvin law firm; MP 1993–; Chair. Standing Cttee on Foreign Affairs and Int. Trade 1995–; Minister of Foreign Affairs 2002–; Vice-Pres. Parl. Assen of OSCE; Chair. Inter-Parl. Forum of the Americas; mem. Inter-Parl. Council Against Anti-Semitism, PD Burma; Chevalier, Légion d'honneur. *Address:* Foreign Affairs and International Trade Canada, Lester B. Pearson Building, 125 Sussex Drive, Ottawa, Ont., K1A 0G2, Canada (Office). *Telephone:* (613) 996-9134 (Office). *Fax:* (613) 952-3904 (Office). *E-mail:* infotech@dfait-maeci.gc.ca (Office). *Website:* www.dfait-maeci.gc.ca (Office).

GRAHAM, William B., BS, JD; American business executive and lawyer; b. 14 July 1911, Chicago Ill.;; s. of William Graham and Elizabeth Burden Graham; m. 1st Edna Kanaley 1940 (died 1981); two s. two d.; m. 2nd Catherine Van Duzer Gaubin 1984; ed Univ. of Chicago; patent lawyer 1936–39; Partner Dawson and Oooms 1940–45; Vice-Pres. and Gen. Man. Baxter Int. Inc., Deerfield 1945–53, Pres., CEO 1953–71, Chair., CEO 1971–80, Chair. 1980–85, Sr Chair. 1985–95, Chair. Emer., Hon. Dir 1995–; Dir First Nat. Bank of Chicago, Northwest Industries, Deere and Co.; Pres., Dir Lyric Opera of Chicago; Dir Nat. Park Foundation, Washington, DC, Botanic Garden Skokie, Ill.; Trustee Univ. of Chicago, Evanston Hosp. and Orchestral Assen Ill.; Weizman Inst. Professional Chair. 1978; several hon.

degrees including Hon. DHumLitt 1998; St Andrew Award 1974, HIMA Pioneering Award, Nat. Kidney Foundation First Award, Achievement Award, Medical Technical Services 1983, Chicago Civil Award, Depaul Univ. 1986, Making History Award, Chicago Historical Soc. 1996, Depaul Univ., Art Alliance Legend Award 2000. *Address:* Baxter International Inc., 1 Baxter Parkway, Deerfield, IL 60015-4625 (Office); 40 Devonshire Lane, Kenilworth, IL 60043-1205, USA (Home).

GRAHAM, William Franklin (Billy), BA, BTh; American evangelist; b. 7 Nov. 1918, Charlotte, NC; s. of William Franklin and Morrow Graham; m. Ruth M. Bell 1943; two s. three d.; ed Florida Bible Inst., Tampa and Wheaton Coll.; ordained to Baptist Ministry 1939; Minister First Baptist Church, Western Springs, Ill. 1943–45; First Vice-Pres. Youth for Christ Int. 1945–50; Pres. Northwestern Schools, Minneapolis 1947–52; founder World Wide Pictures, Burbank, Calif.; worldwide evangelistic campaigns 1947–; speaker weekly Hour of Decision radio programme 1950–; also periodic crusade telecasts; Founder, Billy Graham Evangelistic Assen 1950; Hon. Chair. Lausanne Congress on World Evangelization 1974; Hon. KBE 2001; Dr hc (Hungarian Calvinist Church) (Christian Acad. of Theol.) 1981; numerous awards including Bernard Baruch Award 1955, Humane Order of African Redemption 1960, Gold Award, George Washington Carver Memorial Inst. 1964, Horatio Alger Award 1965, Int. Brotherhood Award Nat. Conf. of Christians and Jews 1971, Sylvanus Thayer Award, Assen of Graduates of US Mil. Acad. 1972, Franciscan Int. Award 1972, Man of South Award 1974, Liberty Bell Award 1975, Templeton Prize 1982, Presidential Medal of Freedom 1983, William Booth Award 1989, Congressional Gold Medal 1996, Ronald Reagan Presidential Foundation Award 2000. *Publications:* Peace with God 1953 (revised edn 1984), The Secret of Happiness 1955, My Answer 1960, World Aflame 1965, The Challenge 1969, The Jesus Generation 1971, Angels – God's Secret Agents 1975, How to be Born Again 1977, The Holy Spirit 1978, Till Armageddon 1981, Approaching Hoofbeats: The Four Horsemen of the Apocalypse 1983, A Biblical Standard for Evangelists 1984, Unto The Hills 1986, Facing Death and the Life After 1987, Answers to Life's Problems 1988, Hope for the Troubled Heart 1991, Storm Warning 1992, Just As I Am (autobiog.) 1997. *Address:* PO Box 9313, Minneapolis, MN 55440-9313, USA (Office). *Telephone:* (612) 338-0500 (Office). *Fax:* (612) 335-1317.

GRAHAM-DIXON, Andrew, MA; British critic, writer and broadcaster; b. 26 Dec. 1960, London; s. of Antony Philip Graham-Dixon and Suzanne Graham-Dixon (née Villar); m. Sabine Marie-Pascale Tilly 1986; one s. two d.; ed Westminster School, Christ Church Coll. Oxford, Courtauld Inst., London; chief arts critic The Ind. 1986–98; arts writer and presenter BBC TV 1992–; curator Broken English, Serpentine Gallery, London 1992; chief arts writer Sunday Telegraph Magazine 1999–; BP Arts Writer of the Year 1988, 1989, 1990; First Prize Reportage, Montreal Film & TV Festival 1992; Hawthornden Prize 1992. *Television:* Gericault 1992; TV documentary series: A History of British Art 1994, Renaissance 1999, 1,000 Ways of Getting Drunk in England 2001, Secret Lives of the Artists 2003. *Publications:* A History of British Art, Paier Museum, Howard Hodgkin – A Monograph 1994, Renaissance 1999. *Leisure interests:* walking, snooker, football, existentialism. *Address:* 21 Croftdown Road, London, NW5 1EL, England (Home).

GRAHAM-SMITH, Sir Francis, Kt, PhD, FRS, FRAS; British professor of radio astronomy; b. 25 April 1923, Roehampton, Surrey; m. Elizabeth Palmer 1946; three s. one d.; ed Rossall School, Epsom Coll., Downing Coll., Cambridge; with Telecommunications Research Establishment 1943–46; Cavendish Lab. 1947–64; 1851 Exhbn 1951–52; Warren Research Fellow, Royal Soc. 1959–64; Prof. of Radio Astronomy, Univ. of Manchester 1964–74, 1981–87, Pro-Vice-Chancellor 1987, Dir Nuffield Radio Astronomy Labs. 1981–88, Langworthy Prof. of Physics 1987–90, Prof. Emer.; Deputy Dir Royal Greenwich Observatory 1974–75, Dir 1976–81; Astronomer Royal 1982–90; Visiting Prof. of Astronomy, Univ. of Sussex 1975–81; Sec. Royal Astronomical Soc. 1964–71, Pres. 1975–77; Sec., Vice-Pres. Royal Soc. 1988–94; Fellow Downing Coll. 1953–64, Hon. Fellow 1970; Chair. of Govs., Manchester Grammar School 1987–98; Hon. DSc (Queens Univ., Belfast) 1986, (Keele) 1987, (Birmingham) 1989, (Nottingham) 1990, (Trinity Coll. Dublin) 1990, (Manchester) 1993; Royal Medal, Royal Soc. 1987, Glazebrook Medal, Inst. of Physics 1991. *Publications:* Radio Astronomy 1960, Optics (with J. H. Thomson) 1971, Pulsars 1977, Pathways to the Universe (with Sir Bernard Lovell) 1988, Introduction to Radioastronomy (with B. F. Burke) 1997, Pulsar Astronomy (with A. G. Lyne) 1990, Optics and Photonics (with T. A. King) 2000. *Leisure interests:* gardening, beekeeping. *Address:* Old School House, Henbury, Macclesfield, Cheshire, SK11 9PH, England. *Telephone:* (1625) 612657. *E-mail:* fgs@jb.man.ac.uk (Office); fgsegs@ukonline-co .uk (Home).

GRAINVILLE, Patrick; French novelist; b. 1 June 1947, Villers-sur-mer; s. of Jacques and Suzanne (née Laquerre) Grainville; m. Françoise Lutgen 1971; ed Lycée Deauville, Sorbonne; teacher, Lycée de Sartrouville 1975–96; mem. CNRS literature section 1975; Prix Goncourt for Les flamboyants 1976; Officier, Ordre nat. du Mérite, Ordre des Arts et des lettres. *Publications:* La toison 1972, La lisière 1973, L'abîme 1974, Les flamboyants 1976, La Diane rousse 1978, Le dernier viking 1980, Les fortresses noires 1982, La caverne céleste 1984, Le paradis des orages 1986, L'atelier du peintre 1988, L'orgie, La neige 1990, Colère 1992, Mathieu (jtly.) 1993, Les anges et les faucons 1994, Le lien 1996, Le tyran éternel 1998, Le tour de la fin du monde, Une femme me cache 2000. *Leisure interests:* travelling, making collages, sculpture. *Address:* c/o Editions du Seuil, 27 rue Jacob, 75261 Paris cedex 06, France.

GRAMM, (William) Philip, PhD; American politician; b. 8 July 1942, Fort Benning, Ga; s. of Kenneth M. and Florence (Scroggins) Gramm; m. Wendy Lee 1970; two s.; ed Univ. of Georgia; mem. Faculty, Dept of Econs Tex. A. and M. Univ. Coll. Station 1967–78, Prof. 1973–78; Partner, Gramm & Assocs 1971–78; mem. House of Reps. 1979–85; Senator from Texas 1985–2002; fmr Chair. Senate Steering Cttee, Banking, Housing and Urban Affairs Cttee; fmr Democrat; Republican; Vice-Chair. UBS Warburg 2003–. *Publications:* articles in professional journals. *Address:* UBS Warburg LLC, UBS Warburg Center, 677 Washington Boulevard, Stamford, CT 06901 (Office); 2323 Bryan Street, Suite 2150, Dallas, TX 75201, USA (Home). *Telephone:* (203) 719-3000 (Office). *Fax:* (212) 719-1410 (Office). *Website:* www.ubswarburg.com (Office).

GRAMS, Rod; American politician, construction executive and television producer; b. 1948; m. Laurel Grams; one s. three d.; ed Univ. of Minnesota, Brown Inst. Minneapolis and Carroll Coll. Helena, Mont.; eng consultant, Orr-Schelen Mayeron & Assoc. Minneapolis; anchor, producer KFBB-TV, Great Falls, Mont., WSAU-TV, Wausau, Wis., WIFR-TV, Rockford, Ill., KMSP-TV, Minneapolis; Pres. and CEO Sun Ridge Builders; mem. 103rd Congress from 3rd Minn. Dist 1993–95; Senator from Minnesota 1995–2001; Republican. *Address:* c/o United States Senate, 257 Dirksen Senate Office Bldg, Washington, DC 20510, USA.

GRANBERG, Aleksander Grigorevich, DEconSc; Russian economist; b. 25 June 1936, Moscow; m. Tatyana Baranova 1962; one s.; ed Moscow Econ. Inst.; Prof. Univ. of Novosibirsk 1965–91; Dir Inst. of Econ. and Org. of Production, Siberian Dept, USSR (now Russian) Acad. of Sciences (IEOPP) 1985–91; Corresp. mem. of Acad. of Sciences 1984, mem. 1990; People's Deputy of Russia 1990–93; Chair. Cttee of the Supreme Soviet for Interrepublican Relations and Regional Policy 1990–92; Counsellor to Russian Pres. 1991–93; Chair. Council for the Study of Productive Forces 1992–; Chair. Nat. Cttee on Pacific Econ. Co-operation 1992–99; Prof. Acad. of Nat. Econ. 1993–; Pres. Int. Acad. of Regional Devt and Co-operation 1996–; mem. New York Acad. of Sciences 1993; Order 'The Honour Symbol' 1986, V. S. Nemchinov Prize 1990, Medal 'To Free Russia Defender' 1994, State Prize of Russian Federation 1997, Order 'Friendship' 1999, Russian Govt Prize 1999. *Publications:* Economic-mathematical Analysis of Interbranches Balance of USSR (co-ed.) 1968, The Optimization of Territorial Proportions of National Economy 1973, Dynamic Models of National Economy 1985, The Modeling of Social Economy 1988, Regional Development in Russia: Past Policies and Future Prospects (co-ed.) 2000, Regional Development: The Experience of Russia and European Union 2000, The Foundations of Regional Economics 2000; more than 550 monographs and articles. *Leisure interests:* theatre, skiing. *Address:* Council for the Study of Productive Forces, Vavilova Street 7, Moscow 117997 (Office); Koroleva str. 8–2, 491, Moscow 129515, Russia (Home). *Telephone:* (095) 135-61-08 (Office); (095) 216-41-71 (Home). *Fax:* (095) 135-63-39 (Office). *E-mail:* council@sops.ru (Office); granberg@online.ru (Home). *Website:* www.sops.ru (Office); www.A-granberg.narod.ru (Home).

GRANDAGE, Michael; British theatre director; b. 2 May 1962; ed Humphry Davy Grammar School Cornwall, Cen. School of Speech and Drama; began theatre career as actor 1981–96; full-time dir 1996–, Assoc. Dir Sheffield Theatres (including Sheffield Crucible) 2000–; Assoc. Dir Donmar Warehouse, London 2000–02, Artistic Dir Dec.2002–; also Visiting Prof., Sheffield Univ.; Dr hc (Sheffield Hallam Univ.); Best Dir (for As You Like It and Passion Play), Evening Standard Theatre Awards 2000; Best Dir (for As You Like It, Passion Play and Merrily We Roll Along), Critics Circle Awards; Theatre Award (for As You Like It), South Bank Show Awards. *Plays directed include:* Mercury Theatre: As You Like It, Passion Play; Almeida Theatre: The Jew of Malta (also nat. tour), The Doctor's Dilemma (also nat. tour); Sheffield Theatres: The Tempest (also Old Vic, London), Richard III, Don Juan, Edward II, The Country Wife, As You Like It (also Lyric Hammersmith), Twelfth Night, What the Butler Saw; Donmar Warehouse: Caligula, The Vortex, Privates on Parade, Merrily We Roll Along (Olivier Award for Best Musical), Passion Play, Good. *Address:* Donmar Warehouse, 41 Earlham Street, London, WC2H 9LX, England (Office). *Telephone:* (20) 7240-4882 (Office). *Fax:* (20) 7240-4878. *Website:* www.donmar-warehouse.com (Office).

GRANDMONT, Jean-Michel, LèsL, PhD; French economist and researcher; b. 22 Dec. 1939, Toulouse; s. of Jancu Wladimir Grunberg and Paule Cassou; m. 1st Annick Duriez 1967 (divorced 1978); m. 2nd Josselyne Bitan 1979; two d.; ed Ecole Polytechnique, Paris, Ecole Nationale des Ponts et Chaussées, Paris, Université de Paris, Univ. of California at Berkeley, USA; Research Assoc., CNRS, Centre d'Etudes Prospectives d'Economie Mathématique Appliquées à la Planification (CEPREMAP) 1970–75, then Dir various research units, Dir of Research, CNRS and CEPREMAP 1987–96, Dir Research Unit CNRS 928, 'Recherches Fondamentales en Economie Mathématiques' 1991–96, Dir of Research, CNRS and Centre de Recherche en Economie et Statistique (CREST) 1996–; Assoc. Prof., Ecole Polytechnique, Palaiseau 1977–92, Prof. 1992–, Chair. Dept of Econs 1997–2000; Prof. (part-time), Yale Univ., USA 1987, 1989–91, 1994; Pres. Econometric Soc. 1990; Hon. mem. American Econ. Asscn; mem. Academia Europaea 1989–; Foreign Hon. mem. American Acad. of Arts and Sciences 1992–; Dr hc (Lausanne) 1990; Alexander von Humboldt Award 1992. *Publications:* Money and Value 1983, Nonlinear Economic Dynamics (ed.) 1987, Temporary Equilibrium (ed.)

1988; articles in scientific econ. journals. *Leisure interests:* skiing, swimming. *Address:* CREST-CNRS, 15 blvd Gabriel Péri, 92245 Malakoff Cedex (Office); 55 boulevard de Charonne, Les Doukas 23, 75011 Paris, France (Home). *Telephone:* 1-41-17-78-04 (Office); 1-43-70-37-28 (Home). *Fax:* 1-41-17-60-46. *E-mail:* grandmont@ensae.fr (Office).

GRANDY, Marshal of the RAF Sir John, GCB, GCVO, KBE, DSO; British air force officer; b. 8 Feb. 1913, Northwood, Middx; s. of late Francis Grandy and Nell Grandy (née Lines); m. Cecile Elizabeth Florence Rankin 1937 (died 1993); two s.; ed Univ. Coll. School, London; Pilot Officer 1931; served Second World War; Deputy Dir Operational Training, Air Ministry 1946–49; Air Attaché, Brussels 1949–50; Commdr Northern Sector Fighter Command 1950; Air Staff HQ Fighter Command 1952–54; Commdt Cen. Fighter Establishment 1954–57; Imperial Defence Coll. 1957; Commdr Task Force Grapple 1957–58; Asst Chief of Air Staff 1958–61; C-in-C RAF Germany, Commdr 2nd Allied Tactical Air Force 1961–63; Air Officer Commanding-in-Chief Bomber Command 1963–65; C-in-C British Forces Far East and UK Mil. Rep. to SEATO 1965–67; Air Commodore 1956; Air Vice-Marshal 1958; Air Marshal 1961; Air Chief Marshal 1965; Marshal of the RAF 1971; Chief of Air Staff 1967–71; Gov. and Commdr-in-Chief of Gibraltar 1973–78; Constable and Gov. Windsor Castle 1978–88; Dir Brixton Estate Ltd 1971–73, 1978–83; Sr Pres. The Officers Asscn 1980–82, Disablement in the City, Berkshire Branch BLESMA; Deputy Chair. Council RAF Benevolent Fund 1980–95; Patron Polish Air Force Asscn, GB 1979–2000; Chair. Trustees Imperial War Museum 1978–89; Trustee RAF Church St Clement Danes 1971–97, Shuttleworth Remembrance Trust 1978–88, RAF Trustee, Burma Star Asscn, 1979–96, The Prince Philip Trust Fund 1982–92; Pres. The Air League 1984–87; a Vice-Pres. Nat. Asscn of Boys Clubs; mem. Cttee Royal Humane Soc. 1978–95, Life Vice-Pres. Royal Nat. Lifeboat Asscn 1988–; Hon. Liveryman of the Haberdashers' Co.; Freeman of City of London; KStJ; Hon. Panglima Mangku Negara. *Address:* c/o White's, St James's Street, London SW1, England.

GRANGE, Kenneth Henry, CBE, FCSD; British industrial designer; b. 17 July 1929; s. of Harry Alfred Grange and Hilda Gladys Grange (née Long); ed London; Tech. Illustrator Royal Engineers 1948–50; Design Asst Arcon Chartered Architects 1948; Bronek Katz & Vaughn 1950–51; Gordon Bowyer & Partners 1951–54; Jack Howe & Partners 1954–58; industrial designer in pvt. practice 1958–; f. partner Pentagram Design 1972–2000; one-man shows Victoria and Albert Museum 1974, Tokyo 1985, 'Those That Got Away' London 2003; Pres. Chartered Soc. of Designers 1987–88; Master of Faculty R.D.I. 1985–87; mem. Bd of Dirs Shakespeare Globe Centre 1997–2002; Royal Designer for Industry (Royal Soc. of Arts) 1969; Hon. Prof. Heriot-Watt Univ. 1987; Dr hc (RCA) 1985, (De Montfort Univ.) 1998, (Staffordshire Univ.) 1998; Hon. DUniv (Heriot-Watt) 1986; ten Design Council Awards, Duke of Edinburgh Award for Elegant Design 1963, Chartered Soc. of Designers Gold Medal 1996, Prince Philip Designers' Prize 2001. *Leisure interests:* building. *Address:* 53 Christchurch Hill, London, NW3 1LG, England (Home).

GRANHOLM, Jennifer Mulhern, BA, JD; American state official and lawyer; b. 5 Feb. 1959, Vancouver, BC; d. of Civtor Ivar Alfreda and Shirley Alfreda (née Dowden); m. Daniel Granholm Mulhern 1986; one s. two d.; ed Univ. of Calif. at Berkeley, Harvard Univ.; law clerk Court of Appeal, Detroit 1987–88; Exec. Asst Wayne Co. Exec., Detroit 1988–89; Asst U.S. Attorney, Dept of Justice, Detroit 1990–94; Corp. Counsel, Wayne Co. 1994–99; Attorney-Gen. of Mich.1999–2002; Gov. of Mich. 2003–; Vice-Pres. YWCA Inkster, Mich. 1995–; mem. Detroit Bar Asscn, Leadership Detroit, Womens' Law Asscn, Inc. Soc. of Irish Lawyers; Public Servant of the Year, Mich. Asscn of Chiefs of Police, Michigander of the Year, Michigan Jaycees. *Leisure interests:* running, family, laughing. *Address:* Office of the Governor, State Capitol Building, POB 30013, Lansing, MI 48909, USA (Office).

GRANIC, Mate, DrSc; Croatian politician and physician; b. 19 Sept. 1947, Baska Voda; m. Jadranka Granic; one s. two d.; ed Zagreb Univ.; physician, Vuk Vrhovac Inst. for Diabetes Endocrinology and Metabolic Diseases, School of Medicine, Zagreb Univ. 1975–79; Head of Clinical Dept Vuk Vrhovac Inst. 1979–85; Prof., Deputy Dir 1985–89; Vice-Dean, Faculty of Medicine, Zagreb Univ. 1989, Dean 1990; mem., Vice-Pres. Croatian Democratic Union; Deputy Prime Minister 1991–99; concurrently Minister of Foreign Affairs 1993–99; presidential cand. Jan. 2000; Founder and Pres. Croatian Democratic Centre Party March 2000–. *Publications:* papers and articles on diabetes. *Address:* Demokratski Centar, 10000 Zagreb, Croatia. *Website:* www .demokratski-centar.hr.

GRANIN, Daniil Aleksandrovich; Russian writer; b. German Daniil, 1 Jan. 1919, Volya, Kursk; m. R. Mayorova; ed Leningrad Polytechnic Inst.; mem. CPSU 1942–90; engineer 1940–50; first publs 1949; USSR People's Deputy 1989–91; Hero of Socialist Labour 1989, Order of Merits for Homeland 1999, Cross of Merit (First Class), Germany 2000, Hon. mem. German Acad. of Arts. *Publications:* Second Variant 1949, Those Who Seek 1955, The House on Fontanka 1958, After the Wedding 1958, I Challenge the Storm 1962, Selected Works 1978, The Picture 1980, The Blockade Book (with A. Adamovich), 1981, The Leningrad Catalogue 1984, Buffalo 1987, The Clemency 1988, Collected Works (5 Vols) 1989, Our Dear Roman Avdeyevich 1991, The Destroyed Clemency 1993, The Escape to Russia 1995, Fear 1997, Evenings with Peter the Great 2000. *Address:* Brat'yev Vasilyevich Str. 8, Apt. 14, 197046 St Petersburg, Russia (Home). *Telephone:* (812) 232-85-53.

GRANN, Phyllis, BA; American publisher and editor; b. 2 Sept. 1937, London, UK; d. of Solomon Grann and Louisa (Bois-Smith) Eitingon; m. Victor Grann 1962; two s. one d.; ed Barnard Coll.; Sec., Doubleday Publrs., New York 1958–60; Ed., William Morrow Inc., New York 1960–62, David McKay Co., New York 1962–70, Simon & Schuster Inc., New York 1970; Vice-Pres. Simon & Schuster Inc. 1976; Pres., Publr G. P. Putnam's & Sons, New York 1976–86; Pres. Putnam Publishing Group Inc. (now Penguin Putnam Inc.), New York 1986–96, CEO 1987–96, Chair. 1997–2001; Vice-Chair. Random House, Inc. 2001–02. *Address:* c/o Random House, Inc., 201 East 50th Street, New York, NY 10014, USA (Office).

GRANÖ, Olavi Johannes, PhD; Finnish professor of geography; b. 27 May 1925, Helsinki; s. of Prof. Dr J. Gabriel Granö and Hilma Ekholm; m. Eeva Kaleva 1953; two d.; ed Turku, Helsinki and Copenhagen Univs; Asst Prof. of Geography, Helsinki Univ. and Helsinki School of Econs 1948–57; Assoc. Prof. of Geography, Turku Univ. 1958–61, Prof. 1962–88, Chancellor 1984–94; Pres. Archipelago Research Inst. 1965–84; Pres. Finnish Nat. Research Council for Sciences 1964–69; Pres. Cen. Bd of Research Councils (Acad. of Finland) 1970–73; mem. Science Policy Council 1964–74; Pres. Advisory Cttee for Research of Nordic Council of Ministers 1976–82; Fellow Acad. of Finland 1980–; mem. Finnish Acad. of Science and Letters 1970; (Chair. 1993–95); mem. Royal Swedish Acad. of Sciences 1985, Academia Europaea 1989; Visiting Fellow, Clare Hall, Cambridge Univ. 1982; Hon. Corresp. mem. Royal Geographical Soc. (London) 1980; Hon. mem. Geographical Soc. of S. Sweden 1981, Geographical Soc. of Turku 1991, Students' Union of Turku Univ. 1992, Geographical Soc. of Finland 2001; Hon. Pres. Finnish Inst. of Migration 1999; Dr hc (Toruń, Poland) 1980, (Tartu, Estonia) 1989, (Åbo Academy, Turku) 1993; Finnish Geographical Soc. Fennia Medal 1988, Hon. award Finnish Acad. of Science and Letters 1993. *Publications:* scientific publications on geography, geology, history of science and science policy. *Address:* Department of Geography, Turku University, 20014 Turku (Office); Sirppitie 1A, 20540 Turku, Finland (Home). *Telephone:* (2) 3335595 (Office); (2) 2370640 (Home); (2) 2370640. *Fax:* (2) 3335896 (Office). *E-mail:* olavi.grano@utu.fi (Office); olavi.grano@nic.fi (Home).

GRANT, Bruce Alexander, BA; Australian writer and diplomatist; b. 4 April 1925, Perth; s. of Leslie John Grant and Myrtle Rapson Williams; ed Perth Modern School, Univ. of Melbourne, Harvard Univ.; served Royal Australian Navy 1943–45; with The Age 1950–65, Film, Theatre Critic and Literary Ed. 1950–53, Foreign Corresp., Europe 1954–57, Asia 1959–63, Wash. 1964–65; Fellow in Political Science Univ. of Melbourne 1965–68, Visiting Fellow 1976; columnist 1968–72; High Comm. to India (also accred to Nepal) 1973–76; Research Assoc. Int. Inst. for Strategic Studies., London 1977; Dir Inst. Political Science 1979–; Dir, then Chair. Australian Dance Theatre 1979–82; Writer-in-Residence Monash Univ. 1981; Adviser on Arts Policy State Govt of Victoria 1982–86; Visiting Fellow, ANU, Canberra 1983; Pres. Melbourne Spoleto Festival of Three Worlds 1984–87; Chair. Victorian Premier's Literary Awards 1984–86, Victorian Australian Bicentennial Authority 1985–86; Consultant to Minister for Foreign Affairs and Trade 1988–91; Chair. Australia-Indonesia Inst. 1989–92; Prof. of Diplomacy and Statecraft, Dept of Man., Monash Univ. 1994–2001. *Publications:* Indonesia 1964, The Crisis of Loyalty 1972, Arthur and Eric 1977, The Boat People 1979, Cherry Bloom 1980, Gods and Politicians 1982, The Australian Dilemma 1983, What Kind of Country? 1988, Australia's Foreign Relations (with Gareth Evans) 1991, The Budd Family 1995, A Furious Hunger: America in the 21st Century 1999, What Kind of World? 2001; numerous short stories, articles and chapters in books on int. affairs. *Leisure interests:* films, theatre, Asian literature, swimming. *Address:* c/o Curtis Brown (Australia) Pty Ltd, 19 Union Street, Sydney, NSW 2021, Australia (Office).

GRANT, Hugh John Mungo, BA; British actor; b. 9 Sept. 1960, London; s. of James Murray Grant and the late Fynvola Susan Grant (née Maclean); ed Latymer Upper School, Hammersmith, New College, Oxford; acting in theatre, TV and films and producer for Simian Films; began career in theatre performing Jockeys of Norfolk (written with Chris Lang and Andy Taylor); Best Actor, Venice Film Festival (jtly with James Wilby, q.v.) 1987; Golden Globe Award and BAFTA Award for Best Actor in Four Weddings and a Funeral 1995; Peter Sellers Award for Comedy, Evening Standard British Film Awards 2002. *Principal films:* White Mischief 1987, Maurice 1987, Lair of the White Worm 1988, La Nuit Bengali 1988, Impromptu 1989, Bitter Moon 1992, Remains of the Day 1993, Four Weddings and a Funeral 1994, Sirens 1994, The Englishman Who Went up a Hill But Came down a Mountain 1995, Nine Months 1995, An Awfully Big Adventure 1995, Sense and Sensibility 1995, Restoration 1996, Extreme Measures (for Simian Films) 1996, Mickey Blue Eyes (for Simian Films) 1998, Notting Hill 1999, Small Time Crooks 2000, Bridget Jones' Diary 2001, About a Boy 2002, Two Weeks' Notice 2002. *Leisure interests:* soccer, singing. *Address:* c/o Simian Films, 3 Cromwell Place, London, SW7 2JE, England. *Telephone:* (20) 7589-6822. *Fax:* (20) 7589-9405.

GRANT, Keith Frederick, NDD, ARCA; British landscape painter, muralist and lecturer; b. Frederick Nall, 10 Aug. 1930, Liverpool; adopted s. of Charles Grant and Gladys Emma Grant; m. 1st Gisèle Barka Djouadi 1964 (divorced 1999); one s. (deceased) one d.; m. 2nd Hilde Ellingsen 2000; one d.; ed Bootle Grammar School, Willesden School of Art and RCA, London; State Scholarship to Norway 1960; Head of Fine Art Dept, Maidstone Coll. of Art, Kent 1968–71; Gulbenkian Award Artist-in-Residence, Bosworth Coll., Leics. 1973–75; mem. Fine Art Bd Council for Nat. Academic Awards 1978–81; Head

of Painting Dept, Newcastle Polytechnic 1979–81; Head of Dept of Art, The Roehampton Inst., London 1981–90, Artist-in-Residence 1990–95; Expedition Artist to Guyana 1991; Art Dir Operation Raleigh 1991–95; one-man shows in London 1960– and shows in Iceland, Norway, France, Italy and Luxembourg; recorded volcanic eruption, Iceland 1973; painted launch of Ariane Rocket 1982; visited Soviet Union for Anglo-Soviet cultural exchange programme of the British Council 1979; other British Council tours to Cyprus 1976, Hungary, Cuba 1985 and Norway 1987; visited Sarawak 1984 and 1985; designed prints for use in Earthlife Foundation's Rainforest Campaign; designed book covers for 6 Peter Mattheissen works 1988–89; visited Greenland to study icebergs at Ilulissat (Jakobshavn); Guest Artist, Ben Gurion Univ. of the Negev and British Israel Art Foundation 1988; elected mem. Telemark Artists' Asscn, Norway 1996; mem. Royal Cambrian Acad. 2001; selected to inaugurate Artists' and Writers' Programme Antarctica 2001/2002 of the British Antarctic Survey; Silver Medal for Mural Painting, RCA 1958. *Exhibitions include:* Ice and Fire (retrospective), Fitzwilliam Museum, Cambridge 1994, one-man exhbn Haugesund City Art Gallery, Norway 1998, Explorations Out of This World, A.T. Kearney, London 2000, Antarctic Works, Univ. of Surrey 2002, Cadogan Gallery, London 2003. *Works:* works in many public collections including Arts Council of GB, Nat. Gallery of NZ, Nat. Gallery of S Australia, Hamilton Art Gallery, Ontario, Trondheim Art Gallery, Norway, Contemporary Art Soc., Fitzwilliam Museum, Cambridge, Abbot Hall Gallery, Kendal, British Council, All Souls Coll. Oxford, Univ. of Bradford, Imperial Coll. London, Victoria and Albert Museum, Richmond College, London, Univ. of E Anglia, Haugesund Art Gallery, Norway, Nat. Gallery of Iceland; mural/mosaics, stained glass window, Charing Cross Hosp., London, Gateshead Metro Station; painting, Guildhall School of Music and Drama, London, Avaldsnes triptych, Karmøy Kommune, Norway; sculpture, Shaw Theatre, London. *Leisure interests:* walking, music, travel and writing. *Address:* Gamlegata, P.O. Box 7, 3834 Gvarv, Telemark, Norway (Home and Studio). *Telephone:* 35959795 (Studio).

GRANT, Peter James, CBE; British business executive; b. 5 Dec. 1929; s. of late Lieut-Col P. C. H. Grant and Mrs. Grant (née Gooch); m. 1st Ann Pleydell-Bouverie; one s. one d.; m. 2nd Paula Eugster; one s. two d.; ed Winchester Coll. and Magdalen Coll. Oxford; Lt Queens Own Cameron Highlanders; joined Edward de Stein & Co. 1952, merged with Lazard Brothers & Co., Ltd 1960; Dir Standard Industrial Group 1966–72, Charrington, Gardner, Lockett & Co., Ltd 1970–74, Walter Runciman PLC 1973–90; Dir Sun Life Assurance Soc. PLC 1973–, Vice-Chair. 1976, Chair. 1983–95; Chair. Paine-Webber Int. (UK) Ltd 1988–90, Highlands & Islands Airports Ltd 1993–; Deputy Chair. LEP Group PLC 1988; Dir London Merchant Securities 1985– (Deputy Chair. 1994–), Scottish Hydro-Electric PLC 1990–94; mem. Industrial Devt Bd 1985–92, Council and Policy Exec. Cttee, Inst. of Dirs. 1989–99, Civil Aviation Authority 1993–95, Cromarty Firth Port Authority 1994–, Chair. 2000. *Leisure interests:* shooting, golf, gardening. *Address:* 33 Robert Adam Street, London, W1M 5AH, England (Office); Mountgerald, nr Dingwall, Ross-shire, IV15 9TT, Scotland. *Telephone:* (1349) 62244 .

GRANT, Peter Raymond, BA, PhD, FRS; British professor of biology; b. 26 Oct. 1936, London; s. of Frederick Thomas Charles Grant and Mavis Irene Grant; m. Barbara Rosemary Matchett 1962; two d.; ed Cambridge Univ. and Univ. of British Columbia; Postdoctoral Fellowship Yale Univ. 1964–65; Asst Prof. of Biology McGill Univ., Canada 1965–68, Assoc. Prof. 1968–73, Prof. 1973–78; Prof. Univ. of Michigan 1978–85; Prof. of Biology Princeton Univ. 1985–89, Class of 1877 Prof. of Zoology 1989–; FLS; Fellow American Asscn for Advancement of Science, American Acad. of Arts and Science; mem. American Philosophical Soc. 1991; Hon. PhD (Uppsala) 1986; Hon. DSc (McGill) 2000. *Publications:* Ecology and Evolution of Darwin's Finches 1986, Evolutionary Dynamics of a Natural Population: The Large Cactus Finch of the Galápagos (with B. Rosemary Grant) 1989, Evolution on Islands (ed.) 1998. *Leisure interests:* camping, hiking, music and reading. *Address:* Department of Ecology and Evolutionary Biology, Princeton University, Princeton, NJ 08544-1003, USA. *Telephone:* (609) 258-5156.

GRANT, Richard E.; actor; b. 1957; s. of late Hendrick Grant and of Leonie Grant; m. Joan Washington; one d.; ed S Africa; grew up in Swaziland. *Television appearances include:* Honest, Decent, Legal and True 1986, Here is the News 1989, Suddenly Last Summer 1992, Hard Times 1993, Karaoke 1996, A Royal Scandal 1996, The Scarlet Pimpernel 1998, Hound of the Baskervilles 2002, Posh Nosh 2003. *Stage appearances include:* Man of Mode 1988, The Importance of Being Earnest 1993, A Midsummer Night's Dream 1994. *Films:* Withnail and I 1986, How to Get Ahead in Advertising 1989, Warlock 1989, Henry and June 1990, Mountains of the Moon 1990, LA Story 1991, Hudson Hawk 1991, Bram Stoker's Dracula 1992, The Player 1993, The Age of Innocence 1993, Prêt à Porter 1995, Jack and Sarah 1995, Portrait of a Lady 1995, Twelfth Night 1995, The Serpent's Kiss 1996, Food of Love 1996, All For Love 1997, Spice World – The Movie 1997, The Match 1998, A Christmas Carol 1999, Trial and Retribution 1999, Little Vampires 1999, Hildegarde 2000, Gosford Park 2001, Monsieur 'N' 2002, Bright Young Things 2003. *Publications:* With Nails: The Film Diaries of Richard E. Grant 1995, Twelfth Night 1996, By Design – A Hollywood Novel 1998. *Leisure interests:* scuba diving, building dolls houses, photography. *Address:* c/o ICM, Oxford House, 76 Oxford Street, London, W1N 0AX, England. *Telephone:* (20) 7636-6565. *Fax:* (20) 7323-0101. *Website:* www.richard-e-grant.com (Office).

GRANT, Verne E., PhD; American biologist; b. 17 Oct. 1917, San Francisco, Calif.; s. of Edwin E. and Bessie C. (Swallow) Grant; m. 1st Alva Day 1946 (divorced 1959); one s. two d.; m. 2nd Karen S. Alt 1960; ed Univ. of California (Berkeley); Visiting Investigator, Carnegie Inst. of Washington, Stanford, Calif. 1949–50; geneticist and experimental taxonomist, Rancho Santa Ana Botanic Garden, Claremont, Calif. 1950–67; Prof. of Biology, Inst. of Life Science, Texas A. & M. Univ. 1967–68; Prof. of Biological Sciences, Univ. of Ariz. 1968–70; Dir Boyce Thompson Arboretum, Ariz. 1968–70; Prof. of Botany, Univ. of Tex. 1970–87, Prof. Emer. 1987–; Nat. Research Council Fellowship 1949–50; Phi Beta Kappa Award in Science 1964; Certificate of Merit, Botanical Soc. of America 1971; mem. NAS; Fellow American Acad. of Arts and Sciences. *Publications:* Natural History of the Phlox Family 1959, The Origin of Adaptations 1963, The Architecture of the Germplasm 1964, Flower Pollination in the Phlox Family (with Karen Grant) 1965, Hummingbirds and Their Flowers (with Karen Grant) 1968, Plant Speciation 1971, 1981, Genetics of Flowering Plants 1975, Organismic Evolution 1977, The Evolutionary Process 1985, 1991, The Edward Grant Family and Related Families in Massachusetts, Rhode Island, Pennsylvania and California 1997; numerous papers on plant genetics, plant evolution and gen. evolution. *Leisure interests:* railroading, classical music. *Address:* Section of Integrative Biology, University of Texas at Austin, Austin, TX 78712 (Office); 2811 W Fresco Drive, Austin, TX 78731, USA (Home). *Fax:* (512) 232-3402 (Office).

GRASS, Günter; German writer and artist; b. 16 Oct. 1927, Danzig (now Gdańsk, Poland); m. 1st Anna Schwarz 1954; three s. one d.; m. 2nd Utte Grunert 1979; ed art school; mem. Akad. der Künste, Berlin (Pres. 1983–86), American Acad. of Arts and Sciences; mem. Social Democratic Party (resgnd Dec. 1992); Dr hc (Kenyon Coll.) 1965, (Harvard) 1976; Lyric Prize, Süddeutscher Rundfunk 1955, Group 47 Prize 1959, Literary Prize, Asscn of German Critics 1960, Georg-Büchner Prize 1965, Theodor-Heuss Prize 1969, Int. Feltrinelli Prize 1982, Karel Čapek Prize 1994, Sonning Arts Prize (Denmark) 1996, Thomas Mann Prize 1996, Hermann Kestan Medal 1995, Nobel Prize for Literature 1999. *Publications:* Die Vorzüge der Windhühner (poems and drawings) 1955, Die Blechtrommel 1959 (film The Tin Drum 1979), Gleisdreieck (poems and drawings) 1960, Katz und Maus 1961 (film 1967), Hundejahre 1963, Ausgefragt (poems) 1967, Über das Selbstverständliche 1968, Örtlich betäubt 1969, Aus dem Tagebuch einer Schnecke 1972, Dokumente zur politischen Wirkung 1972, Die Bürger und seine Stimme 1974, Der Butt 1976, Denkzettel 1978, Das Treffen in Telgte 1979, Kopfgeburten 1980, Aufsätze zur Literatur 1980, Zeichnen und Schreiben Band I 1982, Widerstand lernen-Politische Gegenreden 1980–83 1984, Band II 1984, On Writing and Politics 1967–83 1985, Die Ratte 1987, Zünge Zeigen 1988, Werkansgabe, 10 Vols 1988, Two States—One Nation? 1990, Vier Jahrzehnte 1992, Der Ruf der Kröte (novel) 1992, Ein Weites Feld 1995, Fundsachen für Nichtleser (poems) 1997, Auf eine anderen Blatt 1999, My Century 1999, Vom Abenteuer der Aufklärung (jtly.) 1999, Nie wieder schweigen 2000, Fünf Jahrzehnte 2001, Im Krebsgang 2002 (Crabwalk 2003); plays: Hochwasser 1956, Noch 10 Minuten bis Buffalo 1958, Onkel, Onkel 1958, Die bösen Köche 1961, Die Plebejer proben den Aufstand 1965, Davor 1968. *Leisure interest:* cooking. *Address:* Glockengiesserstrasse 21, 23552 Lübeck, Germany.

GRASSER, Karl-Heinz, MBA; Austrian politician; b. 2 Jan. 1969, Klagenfurt; ed Univ. of Klagenfurt; mem. Freedom Party (FPÖ), Spokesperson for Tourism and European Integration 1992, FPÖ Sec.-Gen. and Man. Dir party educational centre 1993; Second Deputy Gov. Prov. of Carinthia 1994–98; Vice Pres. for Human Resources and Public Relations, Magna Europe 1998; Man. Dir Sport Man. Int. (SMI) 1999; Fed. Minister of Finance 2000–02; mem. Karl Popper Foundation (mem. Man. Bd –1999). *Address:* Freedom Party, 1015 Vienna, Austria (Office).

GRASSLEY, Charles Ernest, MA; American politician, farmer and teacher; b. 17 Sept. 1933, New Hartford, Ia; s. of Louis Arthur Grassley and Ruth Corwin; m. Barbara Ann Speicher; five c.; ed Univs of Northern Iowa and Iowa; farmer; Instructor Political Science, Drake Community Coll. 1962, Charles City Coll. 1967–68; mem. Ia House of Reps. 1959–75; mem. House of Reps 1975–81 from 3rd Dist, Ia; Senator from Iowa 1981–; Chair. Senate Finance Cttee 2001–; Republican; mem. Nat. Farm Bureau. *Address:* US Senate, 135 Hart Senate Office Building, Washington, DC 20510-0001, USA.

GRASSO, Richard A., BS; American stock exchange executive; ed Pace and Harvard Univs; New York Stock Exchange 1968–, Dir Listing and Marketing 1973–77, Vice-Pres. Corp. Services 1977–81, Sr Vice-Pres. Corp. Services 1981–83, Exec. Vice-Pres. Marketing Group 1983–86, Exec. Vice-Pres. Capital Markets 1986–88, Pres., COO 1988–93, Exec. Vice-Chair., Pres. 1993–95, Chair. CEO 1994–; Dir. Nat. Italian American Foundation, Police Foundation, Washington; numerous awards. *Address:* New York Stock Exchange, 11 Wall Street, 6th Floor, New York, NY 10005, USA.

GRATTAN, Michelle, BA; Australian journalist; b. 30 June 1944, Melbourne; ed Melbourne Univ.; Chief Political Corresp. The Age 1976–93, Political Ed. 1995–96; Ed. Canberra Times 1993–95; sr writer and columnist Australian Financial Review 1996–98; Chief Political Corresp. Sydney Morning Herald 1999–2002, Political Commentator The Age 2002–. *Publications:* Australian Prime Ministers (ed.) 2000, Reconciliation (ed.) 2000. *Address:* Press Gallery, Parliament House, Canberra ACT, 2600 (Office); 147 Mugga Way, Red Hill, Canberra, Australia (Home). *Telephone:* 6273-7687 (Office); 6295-6554 (Home). *Fax:* 6240-4022 (Office).

GRATZ, Leopold; Austrian politician; b. 4 Nov. 1929, Vienna; m.; ed Univ. of Vienna; served in Fed. Ministry for Social Admin. 1952–53; mem. Secr. Socialist Parl. Party 1953, Sec. 1957; Sec. Socialist Party Exec. 1963; mem.

Bundesrat 1963–66, Nationalrat 1966–; Chair. Educational Policy Comm. of Exec. of Socialist Party 1968; Minister of Educ. 1970–71; Mayor of Vienna 1973–84; Minister of Foreign Affairs 1984–86; Pres. Nat. Council 1986–89. *Address:* c/o Social Democratic Party of Austria, Löwelstrasse 18, 1014 Vienna, Austria.

GRAUBNER, Most Rev. Jan; Czech ecclesiastic; b. 29 Aug. 1948, Brno; s. of Oldrich Graubner and Ludmila Graubner; ed Univ. of Olomouc; ordained priest 1973; ordained Bishop 1990; Auxiliary Bishop of Olomouc 1990–92, Archbishop of Olomouc 1992–; Vice-Chair. Czech Bishops' Conf. 1991–2000, Chair. 2000–. *Address:* Archdiocese of Olomouc, Biskupské náměstí 2, p. schr. 193, 77101 Olomouc, Czech Republic (Office). *Telephone:* (68) 5500211 (Office). *Fax:* (68) 5222244 (Office). *E-mail:* graubner@mbox.vol.cz (Office).

GRAUERT, Johannes (Hans), Dr rer. nat; German professor of mathematics; b. 8 Feb. 1930, Haren/Ems; s. of Clemens Grauert; m. Marie-Luise Meyer 1956; one s. one d.; ed Univs of Mainz and Münster and ETH, Zürich; Inst. for Advanced Study, Princeton 1957–59; Inst. des Hautes Etudes, Paris 1959 (mem. Supervisory Bd 1976–82); Prof. Univ. of Göttingen 1959–; mem. Acad. of Science, Göttingen (Pres. 1994–96, mem. Acad. of Science and of Literature Mainz, mem. Acad. Mediterranea Catania, Academia Europaea, Acad. of Bayern (von Staudt Prize 1991); Hon. Dr rer. nat (Bayreuth, Bochum, Bonn). *Publications:* ten books and numerous papers in leading journals. *Leisure interests:* pure mathematics, philosophy. *Address:* Ewaldstrasse 67, 37075 Göttingen, Germany. *Telephone:* 41580.

GRAVEL, Mike; American politician; b. 13 May 1930, Springfield, Mass.; s. of Alphonse and Maria Gravel; m. Rita Martin 1959; one s. one d.; ed Columbia Univ.; real estate developer; mem. Alaska House of Reps. 1962–66; Speaker, Alaska House of Reps. 1965; US Senator from Alaska 1969–81; f. Mike Gravel Resource Analysts, Anchorage, Alaska 1981–; Democrat. *Publications:* Jobs and More Jobs, Citizen Power, The Pentagon Papers (ed.). *Address:* 512 1/2 G Street, SE, Washington, DC 20022, USA.

GRAVES, Rupert; British actor; b. 30 June 1963, Weston-Super-Mare. *Theatre includes:* Killing Mr Toad, Sufficient Carbohydrates, Torch Song Trilogy, The Importance of Being Earnest, A Midsummer Night's Dream, Madhouse in Goa, The Elephant Man 2002. *Films include:* A Room With A View 1986, Maurice 1987, A Handful of Dust 1988, The Children 1990, The Plot To Kill Hitler 1990, Where Angels Fear To Tread 1991, Damage 1992, Royal Celebration 1993, The Madness of King George 1994, Sheltering Desert 1994, The Innocent Sleep 1995, Intimate Relations (Best Actor, Montreal Film Festival 1996) 1996, Different for Girls 1996, The Revengers' Comedies 1997, Mrs. Dalloway 1997, Dreaming of Joseph Lees 1998, Room to Rent 2000, The Extremists 2001, Snake 2001. *TV includes:* Fortunes of War 1987, Open Fire 1994, Doomsday Gun 1994, The Tenant of Wildfell Hall 1996, Blonde Bombshell 1999, Cleopatra 1999, The Forsyte Saga 2002. *Website:* www .rupert-graves.com (Office).

GRAVES, William Preston; American politician; b. 9 Jan. 1953, Salina, Kan.; s. of William Graves and Helen Mayo; m. Linda Richey 1990; one d.; ed Kansas Wesleyan Univ. Salina and Univ. of Kansas; Deputy Asst Sec. of State, Kan. 1980–85, Asst Sec. of State 1985–87, Sec. of State 1987–95; Gov. of Kansas 1995–2003; Trustee Kansas Wesleyan Univ. 1987–; Republican. *Leisure interests:* running, reading, travel. *Address:* c/o Office of the Governor, State Capitol, 2nd Floor, Topeka, KS 66612, USA (Office).

GRAY, Alasdair James; British writer and painter; b. 28 Dec. 1934, Glasgow; s. of Alexander Gray and Amy Fleming; m. 1st Inge Sørensen (divorced); one s.; m. 2nd Morag McAlpine 1991; ed Glasgow School of Art; art teacher, Glasgow and Lanarkshire 1958–62; scene painter, Pavilion and Citizens' theatres 1962–63; freelance writer and painter 1963–76; artist recorder, People's Palace Local History Museum, Glasgow 1976–77; Writer-in-Residence, Glasgow Univ. 1977–79; freelance writer and painter 1979–2001; Prof. of Creative Writing, Univ. of Glasgow 2001–; works in collections of People's Palace Local History Museum, Glasgow, Collin's Gallery, Strathclyde Univ.; mural paintings in Palace Rigg Nature Reserve Exhibition Centre, New Cumbernauld, Abbot's House Local History Museum, Dunfermline, The Ubiquitous Chip Restaurant, Glasgow; Saltire Soc. Award 1981, Times Literary Supplement Award 1982, Whitbread and Guardian Awards 1992. *Exhibitions include:* Retrospective, Collins Gallery Glasgow 1974; Retrospective, Glasgow, Edinburgh and Aberdeen Art Galleries 1987–88. *Plays include:* Quiet People 1968, The Trial of Thomas Muir 1970, Dialogue 1971, Homeward Bound 1973, The Loss of the Golden Silence 1973, McGrothy and Ludmilla 1993, Working Legs 1998. *Television plays include:* The Fall of Kelvin Walker 1967, The Man Who Knew about Electricity 1973, The Story of a Recluse 1987. *Works include:* has designed and illustrated several books including Shoestring Gourmet 1986, Songs of Scotland 1997. *Publications include:* The Comedy of the White Dog (short story) 1979, Lanark: A Life in Four Books (novel) 1981, Unlikely Stories Mostly 1982, Janine (novel) 1984, The Fall of Kelvin Walker (novel) 1985, Lean Tales (co-writer) 1985, Five Scottish Artists (catalogue) 1986, Saltire Self-Portrait 4 (autobiographical sketch) 1988, Old Negatives (four verse sequences) 1989, Something Leather (novel) 1990, McGrotty and Ludmilla (novel) 1990, Poor Things (novel) 1992, Why Scots Should Rule Scotland (polemic) 1992, Ten Tales Tall and True (Short Stories) 1993, A History Maker (novel) 1994, Mavis Belfrage (novel) 1996, Working Legs (play) 1997, The Book of Prefaces 2000, Sixteen Occasional Poems 2000, A Study in Classic Scottish Writing 2001,

The End of Their Tethers (short stories) 2003. *Leisure interests:* reading, walking. *Address:* 2 Marchmont Terrace, Glasgow, G12 9LT, Scotland. *Telephone:* (141) 339-0093.

GRAY, Cleve; American artist; b. 22 Sept. 1918, New York; m. Francine du Plessix 1957; two s.; ed Phillips Acad., Andover, Princeton Univ.; mem. American Acad. of Arts and Letters 1998; Hon. DFA (Hartford) 1992; Gov. of Connecticut Art Award 1987, Lifetime Achievement Award, Neuberber Museum of Art 1999. *Exhibitions:* nation-wide 1947–; wall paintings 'Threnody', Neuberger Museum, New York 1974–. *Address:* 102 Melius Road, Warren, CT 06754, USA. *Fax:* (860) 868-7492.

GRAY, Douglas, MA, FBA; British/New Zealand professor of English literature and language; b. 17 Feb. 1930, Melbourne; s. of Emmerson Gray and Daisy Gray; m. Judith Claire Campbell, 1959; one s.; ed Wellington Coll. NZ, Victoria Univ. of Wellington, Merton Coll., Oxford; Asst lecturer Vic. Univ. of Wellington 1952–54, lecturer in English, Pembroke and Lincoln Colls. Oxford 1956–61, Fellow in English, Pembroke Coll. 1961–80, J. R. R. Tolkien Prof. of English Literature and Language and Fellow of Lady Margaret Hall, Oxford 1980–97, Emer. Prof. 1997–; Hon. Fellow, Lady Margaret Hall 1997–; Hon. LittD (Victoria Univ. of Wellington) 1995. *Publications:* Themes and Images in the Medieval English Lyric 1972, A Selection of Religious Lyrics 1974, Robert Henryson 1979, Oxford Book of Late Medieval Verse and Prose 1985 (ed.), J. A. W. Bennett, Middle English Literature 1986 (ed.); From Anglo-Saxon to Early Middle English 1994 (jt ed.); Selected Poems of Robert Henryson and William Dunbar (ed.) 1998. *Leisure interests:* travel, walking. *Address:* 31 Nethercote Road, Tackley, Oxford, OX5 3AW, England (Home). *Telephone:* (1869) 331319 (Home).

GRAY, Dulcie Winifred Catherine, CBE, FRSA, FLS; British actress, playwright and author; b. Dulcie Savage-Bailey, 20 Nov. 1920, Kuala Lumpur, Federated Malay States (now Malaysia); d. of the late Arnold Savage-Bailey and Kate Edith Clulow Gray; m. Michael Denison (deceased) 1939; ed England and Malaya; has worked in theatre since 1939; repertory includes Aberdeen, Edin., Glasgow, Harrogate; debut as Sorrel in Hay Fever 1939; Queen's Silver Jubilee Medal 1977. *Theatre includes:* The Little Foxes, Midsummer Night's Dream 1942, Brighton Rock, Landslide 1943, Lady from Edinburgh 1945, Dear Ruth, Wind is 90 1946, Queen Elizabeth Slept Here 1949, Sweet Peril 1952, We Must Kill Toni, The Diary of a Nobody 1954, Love Affair (also writer) 1956, Double Cross 1959, Let Them Eat Cake 1959, Candida 1960, Heartbreak House 1961, Where Angels Fear to Tread 1963, An Ideal Husband 1965, Happy Family 1967, Number 10 1967, Out of the Question 1968, Three 1970, The Wild Duck 1970, Ghosts 1972, At the End of the Day 1973, Time and the Conways (tour) 1977, A Murder is Announced 1977, Lloyd George Knew my Father (tour) 1980, A Coat of Varnish 1982, School for Scandal (British Council 50th Anniversary European Tour) 1983, The Living Room 1987, The Best of Friends (tour) 1990, 1991, The Importance of Being Earnest (tour) 1991, Tartuffe 1991–92, Two of a Kind (tour) 1995, The Ladykillers (tour) 1999, Les Liaisons Dangereuses (tour) 2000, The Lady Vanishes (tour) 2001. *Films include:* They Were Sisters 1944, Wanted for Murder 1945, A Man about the House 1946, Mine Own Executioner 1947, The Glass Mountain 1948, There Was a Young Lady 1953, A Man Could Get Killed 1965, The Black Crow 1994. *Radio includes:* Front Line Family (BBC serial) 1941; numerous plays. *Television includes:* Howards' Way (series) 1985–90, several plays. *Publications:* Murder on the Stairs, Murder in Melbourne, Baby Face, Epitaph for a Dead Actor, Murder on a Saturday, Murder in Mind, The Devil Wore Scarlet, No Quarter for a Star, The Murder of Love, Died in the Red, The Actor and His World (with Michael Denison), Death in Denims, Butterflies on my Mind (Times Educational Supplement Sr Information Book Prize 1978), Dark Calypso, The Glanville Women, Anna Starr, Mirror Image, Looking Forward, Looking Back (autobiog.), J. B. Priestly (biog.). *Leisure interests:* swimming, butterflies. *Address:* Shardeloes, Missenden Road, Amersham, Bucks., HP7 0RL, England (Home). *Telephone:* (1494) 725555 (Home).

GRAY, George William, CBE, PhD, CChem, FRSC, FRSE, FRS, MRIA; British professor of chemistry; b. 4 Sept. 1926, Edinburgh; s. of John William Gray and Jessie Colville (née Hunter); m. Marjorie Mary Canavan; three d.; ed Univs of Glasgow and London; mem. staff, Dept of Chem., Univ. of Hull 1946–, Sr Lecturer 1960, Reader 1964, Prof. of Organic Chem. 1978–84, G. F. Grant Prof. of Chem. 1984–90; Research Co-ordinator E. Merck Ltd 1990–93, Consultant 1993–; Emer. Prof. Univ. of Hull, Visiting Prof. Univ. of Southampton 1990–; Ed. Liquid Crystals 1992–2002; Foreign mem. Japanese Acad. of Eng 1996; Hon. MRIA; Hon. DSc (Hull) 1991, (Nottingham Trent) 1994, (Southampton) 1996, (E Anglia) 1997, (Aberdeen) 2001, (Exeter) 2002; Queen's Award for Technological Achievement 1979, 1992; Rank Prize for Optoelectronics 1980; Leverhulme Medal of Royal Soc. 1987; Royal Soc. of Chemistry Fine Chemicals Award 1992; Kyoto Prize Laureate in Advanced Tech. 1995; Karl Ferdinand Braun Medal of Soc. for Information Display 1996; Freedericksz Medal of Russian Liquid Crystal Soc. 1997. *Publications:* Molecular Structure and the Properties of Liquid Crystals 1962, Liquid Crystals and Plastic Crystals (ed. and jtly with P. A. Winsor) 1974, The Molecular Physics of Liquid Crystals (ed. and jtly with G. R. Luckhurst) 1979, Smectic Liquid Crystals – Textures and Structures (with J. W. Goodby) 1984, Thermotropic Liquid Crystals (ed.) 1987, Handbook of Liquid Crystals (four vols) (jt ed.) 1998; 350 papers on liquid crystals in scientific journals. *Leisure interests:* gardening, philately. *Address:* PO Box 3307, Wimborne, Dorset,

BH21 4YD (Office); Juniper House, Furzehill, Wimborne, Dorset, BH21 4HD, England (Home). *Telephone:* (1202) 880164 (Office and Home). *Fax:* (1202) 840702 (Home). *E-mail:* ggray83828@aol.com (Office).

GRAY, Harry Barkus, PH.D; American chemist; b. 14 Nov. 1935, Kentucky; m. Shirley Barnes 1957; two s. one d.; ed Northwestern Univ. and Univ. of Copenhagen; Asst Prof. of Chem., Columbia Univ. 1961–63, Assoc. Prof. 1963–65, Prof. 1965–66; Prof. of Chem. Calif. Inst. of Tech. 1966–, now Arnold O. Beckman Prof. and Dir Beckman Inst.; mem. NAS, American Acad. of Arts and Sciences; Foreign mem. Royal Danish Soc. of Science and Letters, Royal Soc.; Franklin Award 1967, Fresenius Award 1970, American Chem. Soc. Award in Pure Chem. 1970, Harrison Howe Award 1972, MCA Award 1972, Guggenheim Fellow 1972–73, American Chem. Soc. Award in Inorganic Chem. 1978, Remsen Award 1979, Tolman Award 1979, Centenary Medal 1985, Nat. Medal of Science 1986, Pauling Medal 1986, Calif. Scientist of the Year 1988, Alfred Bader Award 1990, Gold Medal American Inst. of Chemists 1990, Waterford Prize 1991, Priestley Medal 1991, Gibbs Medal 1992, Linderstrøm-Lang Prize 1992, Chandler Medal, Columbia Univ. 1999, Harvey Prize, Technion Israel Inst. of Tech. 2000. *Publications:* Electrons and Chemical Bonding 1965, Molecular Orbital Theory 1965, Ligand Substitution Processes 1966, Basic Principles of Chemistry 1967, Chemical Dynamics 1968, Chemical Principles 1970, Models in Chemical Science 1971, Chemical Bonds 1973, Electronic Structure and Bonding 1981, Molecular Electronic Structures 1980, Braving the Elements 1995. *Leisure interests:* tennis, music. *Address:* Noyes Laboratory of Chemical Physics, California Institute of Technology, 139–74 1200 East California Blvd, Pasadena, CA 91125-0001 (Office); 1415 East California Boulevard, Pasadena, CA 91106-4101, USA (Home). *Telephone:* (626) 395-6500 (Office); (626) 793-1978 (Home).

GRAY, Herb E., PC, QC, BComm, LLD; Canadian politician; b. 25 May 1931, Windsor, Ont.; s. of the late Harry Gray and of Fannie Gray; m. Sharon Sholzberg 1967; one s. one d.; ed Victoria Public School, Kennedy Coll. Inst. Windsor, McGill Univ., Montreal and Osgoode Hall Law School, Toronto; MP 1962–2002; Chair. of House of Commons Standing Cttee on Finance, Trade and Econ. Affairs 1966–68; Parl. Sec. to Minister of Finance 1968–69; Minister without Portfolio (Finance) 1969–70, Minister of Nat. Revenue 1970–72, of Consumer and Corporate Affairs 1972–74, of Industry, Trade and Commerce 1980–82, of Regional Economic Expansion Jan.–Oct. 1982; Pres. of Treasury Bd 1982–84; Opposition House Leader 1984–90, Deputy Opposition Leader 1989–90, Leader of the Opposition 1990, Opposition Finance Critic 1991–93; Solicitor Gen. and Leader of the Govt in House of Commons 1993–97; Deputy Prime Minister 1997–2002; given responsibility for co-ordinating Govt of Canada's activities to mark new Millennium 1998–2000; Chair. Canadian section Int. Joint Comm. 2002–; Govt Observer Inter-American Conf. of Ministers of Labour, Bogotá 1963; Vice-Chair. Del. to NATO Parl. Conf., Paris 1963; mem. Del. to Canada–France Interparl. Conf. 1966; mem. Canadian Del. to IMF and IBRD meeting 1967, Canada–U.S. Interparl. Conf. 1967–68. *Address:* International Joint Commission, 234 Laurier Avenue W., 22nd Floor, Ottawa, Ont., K1P 6K6 (Office); 1504–75 Riverside Drive East, Windsor, Ont., N9A 7C4, Canada (Home). *Telephone:* (613) 995-2984 (Office). *Fax:* (613) 993-5583 (Office). *Website:* www.ijc.org (Office).

GRAY, Sir John Archibald Browne (Kt), MA, MB, BChir, ScD, FRCP, FRS; British administrator (retd) and physiologist; b. 30 March 1918, London; s. of Sir Archibald Gray, KCVO, CBE; and Elsie Cooper; m. Vera K. Mares 1946; one s. and d.; ed Cheltenham Coll., Clare Coll., Cambridge and Univ. Coll. Hospital, London; Service Research for MRC 1943–45; Surgeon Lt, RDVR 1945–46; MRC Scientific Staff, Nat. Inst. for Medical Research 1946–52; Reader in Physiology, Univ. Coll. London 1952–58, Prof. of Physiology 1958–66; Dean, Faculty of Science, Univ. of London 1960–65; Second Sec. MRC 1966–68, Sec. 1968–77; Chair. of Council, Int. Agency for Cancer Research 1972–74, of EU Cttee for Medical Research 1973–75; mem. Scientific Staff MRC 1977–83; Pres. Freshwater Biological Asscn 1983–88, Vice-Pres. 1988–; mem. Council, Marine Biological Asscn 1969–88, Vice-Pres. 1989–; Hon. Fellow Clare Coll., Cambridge 1976; Hon. DSc (Exeter) 1985. *Publications:* numerous papers on sensory receptors and sensory nervous system. *Leisure interest:* painting. *Address:* Seaways, Kingsway, Kingsand, Nr. Torpoint, Cornwall, PL10 1NG, England. *Telephone:* (1752) 822745.

GRAY, John Malcolm, CBE; British banker; b. 28 July 1934, Hong Kong; s. of Samuel Gray and Christina Mackay-Sim; m. Ursula Siong Koon 1984; three d.; ed Sydney, Australia and Strathallan School, Scotland; served RAF; joined Hong Kong Bank 1952, Chief Accountant 1979, Asst Gen. Man. Finance 1981, Gen. Man. Group Finances 1985, Exec. Dir Finance 1986–90; Deputy Chair. The Hongkong and Shanghai Banking Corpn Ltd 1990–93, Chair. 1993–96, CEO 1993–96; Deputy Chair. HSBC Holdings PLC 1991–93, Exec. Dir 1993–96; Chair. Hong Kong Port Devt Bd; Dir World Maritime Ltd 1985–; mem. Council, Univ. of Hong Kong; mem. Hong Kong Exec. Council 1993–96; Deputy Chair. Harvey Nichols Group 1996–; Dir N & T Argonaut AB, Stockholm 1997–. *Leisure interests:* golf, reading. *Address:* c/o The Hongkong and Shanghai Banking Corporation Ltd., Level 34, 1 Queen's Road, Central, Hong Kong, Special Administrative Region, People's Republic of China (Office); Harvey Nichols Group, 67 Brompton Road, London, SW3, England (Office).

GRAY, Sir John (Walton David), KBE, CMG, MA; British diplomatist (retd) and business consultant; b. 1 Oct. 1936, Burry Port; s. of Myrddin Gray and

Elsie Gray (née Jones); m. Anthoula Yerasimou 1957; one s. two d.; ed Queen Elizabeth's Grammar School, Crediton, Blundell's School, Devon, Christ's Coll. Cambridge, Middle East Centre, Oxford Univ. and American Univ. Cairo; nat. service, Royal Army Service Corps 1954–56; joined Foreign Office 1962; served Beirut, Bahrain, FCO, Geneva, Sofia 1962–77; Counsellor, Jeddah 1978–81; Head of Dept FCO 1982–85; Amb. to Lebanon 1985–88; Perm. Rep. to OECD, Paris 1988–92; Amb. to Belgium 1992–96; Rapporteur, OECD Group on Eastern Europe 1993; Chair. Financial Bd, Spadel UK 1997–, Deffrainc Ltd 1998–; Chair. Vandemoorteel UK Ltd 2000–02; Adviser to Hyder plc 1996–99, IMC Group 1997–98, Fortis Bank 1998–, MEM Group 1999–2000, Springpoint Ltd 1999–2000, mem. Bd Cardiff Bay Devt Corpn 1998–2000; Chair. Welsh Centre for Int. Affairs 1997–; Pres. Wales Council, European Movt 1997–; Trustee Nat. Botanic Garden of Wales 1998–; mem. Commonwealth War Graves Comm. 1998–; Pres. IoD Wales 1999–; Hon. Consul of Belgium at Cardiff 1999–; Chair. Anglo-Belgian Club 1998–; Gov. Univ. of Glamorgan 2000–; Hon. Fellow Cardiff Univ. 1998, Univ. of Wales Inst. Cardiff 1999; Hon. Freeman Gardeners' Co. 1995; Freeman City of London 1997; Murr Prize, Beirut 1988; Int. Guild of Toastmasters After Dinner Speaker of the Year 1993. *Publications:* Europe and Wales (with John Osmond) 1997, An Agenda for the Assembly (contrib.) 1998. *Leisure interests:* rugby football, history, things Welsh, historic buildings and gardens, travel. *Address:* 10 Marine Parade, Penarth, Vale of Glamorgan, CF64 3BG, Wales. *Fax:* (29) 2070-3354 (Home).

GRAY, Paul Edward, MS; American academic; b. 7 Feb. 1932, Newark, NJ; s. of Kenneth F. Gray and Florence Gilleo; m. Priscilla W. King 1955; one s. three d.; ed Grover Cleveland High School, Caldwell, NJ and Mass. Inst. of Tech.; Faculty mem. in Electrical Eng MIT 1960–71, 1990–, Dean, School of Eng 1970–71; Chancellor, MIT 1971–80, Pres. 1980–90, mem. of Corpn 1990–, Chair., Dir 1990–97, Pres. Emer. 1997–; Dir The Boeing Co., Seattle; Fellow, American Acad. of Arts and Sciences, AAAS, IEEE, Nat. Acad. of Eng (Treasurer 1994–2001); Corresp. mem. Nat. Acad. of Eng in Mexico; various trusteeships and other professional appointments. *Publications:* The Dynamic Behavior of Thermoelectric Devices 1960, Introduction to Electronics 1967; co-author of six other books. *Address:* Massachusetts Institute of Technology, 77 Massachusetts Avenue, Cambridge, MA 02139; 100 Memorial Drive, Apartment 11-4A, Cambridge, MA 02142, USA. *Telephone:* (617) 253-4665 (Office).

GRAY, Robert Keith, MBA; American business executive; b. 2 Sept. 1928, Hastings, Neb.; s. of Garold Gray and Marie Burchess; ed Carleton Coll. and Harvard Univ.; service in U.S. Navy 1943–48; Assoc. Prof. of Finance, Hastings Coll. Neb. 1950–51; Prof. Univ. of S. Calif. Los Angeles 1952; Special Asst to Sec. of Navy 1954; Special Asst to Pres. Eisenhower, White House, Washington, DC 1955–57, Appts. Sec. 1958; Sec. Eisenhower Cabinet, Washington, DC 1959–60; Co-Chair. Reagan-Bush Presidential Inaugural Cttee 1980; Vice-Pres. Hill & Knowlton Inc., Washington, DC 1961–64, Sr Vice-Pres. 1965–70, Exec. Vice-Pres. 1971–76, Vice-Chair. 1977–81, CEO, Chair. 1991–; Founder, Chair. Gray & Co. Public Communications Int. (merger Hill & Knowlton Inc.), Washington 1981–86; Chair. and CEO Hill & Knowlton Public Affairs Worldwide 1986–91; Chair. and Pres. Gray & Co. II 1988–; Chair. Gray Investment Properties Inc., 1988–; Chair. and CEO Powerhouse Leasing Corpn 1988–; Dir Forward Air Corpn, Official Kiosk Group, Store 2.com, Credit Cars.com, Advanced Multimedia Group; Chair. Hill & Knowlton, USA; mem. numerous bds., advisory cttees. etc; Hon. D. Business (Marymount Univ.) 1982, Hon. DLitt (Hastings Coll.) 1984, Hon. DH (Creighton Univ.) 1989, Hon. DL (Barry Univ.) 1998; Légion d'honneur, Grande Ufficiale decoration (Italy). *Publications:* Casebook on Organization and Operation of a Small Business Enterprise 1950, Eighteen Acres Under Glass 1962, Right Time, Right Place 2000, January River 2000. *Leisure interests:* tennis, skiing, philanthropy. *Address:* Gray & Co.II, 4731 Pine Tree Drive, Miami Beach, FL 33140 (Office); Gray & Co., 1497 Chain Bridge Road, McLean, VA 22101 (Office); 4731 Pine Tree Drive, Miami Beach, FL 33140, USA (Home). *Telephone:* (305) 538-1050 (Office); (305) 970-8158 (Home). *Fax:* (305) 538-7338 (Office). *E-mail:* grayandco2@aol.com (Office); bob@robertkeithgray.com (Home). *Website:* grayprops.com (Office).

GRAY, Robin Trevor, BAgrSc, DDA; Australian politician; b. 1 March 1940, Victoria; s. of Rev. W. J. Gray; m. Judith F. Boyd 1965; two s. one d.; ed Box Hill High School, Dookie Agric. Coll. and Univ. of Melbourne; teacher, Victoria Educ. Dept 1961, Middx County Council, UK 1964; agric. consultant Colac, Victoria 1965, Launceston, Tasmania 1965–76; part-time lecturer in Agric. Econs Univ. of Tasmania 1970–76; Deputy Leader of Opposition, Tasmania 1979–81, Leader of Opposition 1981–82, 1989–91, Premier 1982–89, Minister for Racing and Gaming 1982–84, for Energy 1982–88, for Forests 1984–86, for State Devt 1984–89, for Primary Industry and Sea Fisheries 1992–95, for Energy 1992–95, for TT-Line 1993–95; Chair. R. T. Gray and Assocs. Pty Ltd 1995–; partner Evers Gray 1996–; Dir Gunns Ltd 1996–; Chair. Botanical Resources Australia Pty Ltd 1996–; Dir AMC Search Ltd 1996–. *Leisure interests:* cricket, golf, reading. *Address:* 11 Beech Road, Launceston, Tasmania 7250, Australia.

GRAY, Simon James Holliday, MA; British writer and teacher; b. 21 Oct. 1936; s. of Dr. James Davidson Gray and Barbara Cecelia Mary Holliday; m. 1st Beryl Mary Kevern 1965 (divorced); one s. one d.; m. 2nd Victoria Katherine Rothschild 1997; ed Westminster School, Dalhousie Univ., Halifax, NS, Univ. of Cambridge; Supervisor in English, Univ. of BC 1960–63, Sr Instructor in English, Queen Mary Coll., Univ. of London

1965–84; Hon. Fellow, Q.M.C., Univ. of London. *Radio plays:* Suffer the Little Children 1993, With a Nod and a Bow 1993, The Rector's Daughter (adaptation) 1992. *Television:* After Pilkington 1987, Old Flames 1990, They Never Slept 1991, Running Late 1992, Unnatural Pursuits 1992 (Emmy Award, New York 1993), Femme Fatale 1993. *Film:* A Month in the Country 1997. *Publications:* Novels: Colmain 1963, Simple People 1965, Little Portia 1967, A Comeback for Stark 1968, Breaking Hearts 1997; Non-fiction: An Unnatural Pursuit and Other Pieces 1985, How's That for Telling 'Em, Fat Lady (memoirs) 1988, Fat Chance 1995; Plays: Wise Child 1968, Sleeping Dog 1968, Dutch Uncle 1969, The Idiot 1971, Spoiled 1971, Butley 1971 (Evening Standard Award), Otherwise Engaged 1975 (Best Play, New York Drama Critics' Circle, Evening Standard Award), Plaintiffs and Defendants 1975, Two Sundays 1975, Dog Days 1976, Molly 1977, The Rear Column 1978, Close of Play 1979, Quartermaine's Terms 1981, Tartuffe 1982, Chapter 17 1982, Common Pursuit 1984, Melon 1987, The Holy Terror and Tartuffe 1990, Hidden Laughter 1990, Cell Mates 1994, Simply Disconnected 1996, Life Support 1997, Just the Three of Us 1997, The Late Middle Classes 1999, Japes 2001, Enter a Fox (memoirs) 2001. *Leisure interests:* squash, watching cricket and football, tennis, swimming. *Address:* c/o Judy Daish Associates, 2 St Charles Place, London, W10 6EG, England. *Telephone:* (20) 8964-8811. *Fax:* (20) 8964-8966.

GRAYDON, Air Chief Marshal Sir Michael (James), GCB, CBE, FRAeS, FRSA; British air force officer; b. 24 Oct. 1938, Kew, London; s. of James Graydon and Rita Alkan; m. Margaret Clark 1963; ed Wycliffe Coll. and RAF Coll. Cranwell; qualified flying instr. No. 1, Flight Training School, Linton-on-Ouse 1960–62; No. 56 Squadron 1962–64; No. 226 Operational Conversion Unit (Queen's Commendation) 1965–67; Flight Command, No. 56 Squadron 1967–69; RAF Staff Coll. Bracknell 1970; Personal Staff Officer to Deputy C-in-C Allied Forces Cen. Europe, Brunssum 1971–73; Operations, Jt Warfare, Ministry of Defence 1973–75; Nat. Defence Coll. Latimer 1976; Officer Commdg No. 11 Squadron, Binbrook 1977–79; Mil. Asst to Chief of Defence Staff 1979–81; Officer Commdg RAF Leuchars 1981–83, RAF Stanley, Falkland Islands 1983; Royal Coll. of Defence Studies 1984; Sr Air Staff Officer, 11 Group, Bentley Priory 1985–86; Asst Chief of Staff, Policy, SHAPE 1986–89; Air Officer Commdg-in-Chief, RAF Support Command 1989–91, H.Q. Strike Command 1991–92; Chief of Air Staff 1992–97; Air A.D.C. to HM The Queen 1992–97; Consultant and Adviser Celebrand PLC 1997–; Dir Thomson-CSF (UK) 1999–; Pres. Battle of Britain Memorial Trust 1999–, The Officers' Asscn 2000; Gov. Wycliffe Coll. 1986–; Vice-Patron Air Cadet Council 1999–; Freeman City of London 1995. *Publications:* contribs. to professional journals. *Leisure interests:* golf, birdwatching, reading, photography. *Address:* c/o Lloyds TSB Bank PLC, Cox & King's Branch, P.O. Box 1190, 7 Pall Mall, London, SW1Y 5NA, England.

GRAZER, Brian; American film company executive; Co-Chair. Imagine Films Entertainment. *Films produced include:* Night Shift 1982, Splash 1984, Real Genius 1985, Spies Like Us (jtly.) 1985, Armed and Dangerous (jtly.) 1986, Like Father, Like Son (jtly.) 1987, Parenthood 1989, Cry Baby (jtly.) 1990, Kindergarten Cop 1990, Closet Land (jtly.) 1991, The Doors (jtly.) 1991, Backdraft (jtly.) 1991, My Girl 1991, Far and Away (jtly.) 1992, Housesitter 1992, Boomerang 1992, CB4 (jtly.) 1993, For Love Or Money 1993, The Paper (jtly.) 1994, My Girl 2 1994, Greedy 1994, The Cowboy Way 1994, Apollo 13 (jtly.) 1995, Sergeant Bilko 1996, Ransom 1996, Bowfinger 1999, Curious George 2000, Nutty Professor II: The Klumps 2000, How the Grinch Stole Christmas 2000. *Television:* Wonderland (series) 2000. *Address:* Imagine Films Entertainment, 9465 Wilshire Boulevard, Floor 7, Beverly Hills, CA 90212, USA (Office).

GREAVES, Derrick, ARCA; British artist; b. 5 June 1927, Sheffield; s. of Harry Greaves and Mabel Greaves; m. Mary Margaret Johnson 1951; two s. one d.; ed RCA, London and British School at Rome; part-time teacher St Martins School of Art 1954–64, Maidstone Coll. of Art and Royal Acad. Schools 1960; Head of Printmaking, Norwich Coll. of Art 1983–; first one-man exhbn, Beaux Arts Gallery 1953; subsequent one-man exhbns at Zwemmer Gallery 1958, 1960, 1962, 1963, Inst. of Contemporary Arts (ICA), London 1969, 1971, Bear Lane Gallery, Oxford 1970, 1973, Belfast 1972, Dublin 1972, Whitechapel Gallery 1973, Monika Kinley 1973–, City Gallery, Milton Keynes 1975–, Cranfield Inst. of Tech. 1978, Exposición Int. de la Plástica, Chile 1978; group exhbns include Contemporary Arts Soc. 1956, Venice Biennale 1956, Pushkin Museum, Moscow 1957, Whitechapel Gallery 1963, Carnegie Int. Exhbn, Pa 1964, Haymarket Gallery 1974, Royal Acad. 1977, Graves Art Gallery, Sheffield 1980, Fischer Fine Art 1980, Mall Galleries, London 1981, Mappin Art Gallery 1986, Leeds Art Gallery 1986, Philadelphia Museum of Art 1986, Walker Art Gallery; Prize John Moore's Exhbn 1957, Belfast Open Painting Exhbn purchase prize 1962. *Publications:* Derrick Greaves. Paintings 1958–80; numerous catalogues.

GREBENÍČEK, Miroslav, PhD; Czech politician; b. 21 March 1947, Staré Město, Uherské Hradiště Dist; m.; one s. two d.; ed Masaryk Univ., Brno; worked as teacher at several schools; specialist with Regional Museum, Mikulov 1973–75; mem. CP of Czechoslovakia 1975; lecturer 1975–86, Reader 1986–89, Teaching-Training Coll., Masaryk Univ., Brno; Deputy to House of Nations, Fed. Ass. of Č.S.F.R. 1990–92; First Vice-Pres. Aug.–Nov. 1991, Pres. 1991–92, Council of the Fed. of CP of Czechlands and Moravia and Party of the Democratic Left; mem. Presidium, Fed. Ass. of Č.S.F.R. 1992; Chair. CP of Czechlands and Moravia 1992–; mem. Parl. 1996–, of Organizational Cttee of Parl. 1996–98, of Parl. Cttee for Petitions 1996–98, for Culture, Youth and

Physical Training 1998–. *Publications:* monographs, articles and reviews focusing on the history of 19th and 20th centuries. *Address:* Komunistická strana Čech a Moravy, Politických vězňů 9, Prague 1, (Office); Zlámalova 9, 692 01 Mikulov, Czech Republic. (Home). *Telephone:* (2) 2289 7111 (Office). *Fax:* (2) 2289 7422 (Office). *E-mail:* leftnews@kscm.cz (Office). *Website:* www .kscm.cz (Office).

GREBENNIKOV, Valery Vassil'yevich; Russian lawyer and politician; b. 14 Oct. 1946; ed Lumumba Univ. of Peoples' Friendship; elected Deputy Chief State Arbiter, Russian Fed. 1990–91, Chief State Arbiter; mem. State Duma 1995–, mem. Our Home Russia Faction (Motherland – All Russia) 1999–, Vice-Chair., then Chair. Cttee on State Construction; Vice-Pres. OLBI co.; mem. Bd of Dirs Bank Nat. Credit. *Address:* State Duma, Okhotny Ryad 1, 103265 Moscow, Russia (Office). *Telephone:* (095) 292-32-65 (Office). *Fax:* (095) 292-05-99 (Office).

GREBENSHCHIKOV, Boris Borisovich; Russian rock musician and popular singer; b. 27 Nov. 1953, Leningrad; s. of Boris A. Grebenshchikov and Ludmila Grebenshchikova; m.; one s. one d.; ed Leningrad Univ.; worked as a computer programmer 1977–80; lead singer and guitarist of rock group Akvarium 1975–; recordings include Akvarium (USSR) 1987, Radio Africa 1987, Equinox 1988, Radio Silence 1989, Lilith 1997, Hyperborea 1997, Psi 1999; music for films and sound track albums includes Assa 1988, Black Rose 1990, St Petersburg Sands 1993, The Snow Lion 1996; tours and recordings in USA, Canada, Great Britain, all-Russia tour 1991 (110 concerts in 68 cities); as a painter has taken part in various art exhbns throughout fmr USSR; Triumph Prize (for outstanding achievements in Russian culture) 1998. *Publications:* Ivan and Danilo 1989, poetry and song lyrics. *Leisure interests:* music, painting, writing, religions, travelling. *Address:* 2 Marata Street, Apt. 3, 191025 St Petersburg, Russia. *Telephone:* 311-04-58. *Fax:* (812) 272-05-41 (Home). *E-mail:* bg@aquarium.ru (Office). *Website:* www.aquarium .ru (Office).

GRECH, Joe Debono; Maltese politician; b. 17 Sept. 1941, B'Kara; s. of Carmelo Debono and Giovanna Grech; m. Edith Vella; two c.; ed St Aloysius Coll.; mem. Gen. Workers, Union Rep. for Gozo 1971; Sec. Petrol and Chemicals Section 1973–76; fmr Pres. Nat. Exec. Socialist Youth Movt, Gen. Sec. 1967–76; fmr mem. Nat. Exec. Labour Party, Propaganda Sec. 1971–88; Man. Nat. Cargo Handling Co., Interprint; MP 1976–; Minister of Parastatal and People's Investments May–Sept. 1983, of Agric. and Fisheries 1983–87, for Transport and Ports 1996–98; Deputy Leader Labour Party 1988. *Leisure interests:* reading, farming. *Address:* c/o Pamit Laburista, National Labour Centre, Mile End Road, Hamrun, HMR 02 (Office); 105 Fleur de Lys Road, B'kara, Malta. *Telephone:* 443712. *Website:* www.mlp.org.mt (Office).

GREEN, Anthony Eric Sandall, RA; British artist; b. 30 Sept. 1939, Luton; s. of Frederick Sandall and Marie Madeleine (née Dupont) Green; m. Mary Louise Cozens-Walker 1961; two d.; ed Highgate School, Slade School of Fine Art, Univ. Coll. London; Asst Art Master, Highgate School 1961–67; Harkness Fellowship USA 1967–69; Fellow, Univ. Coll. London 1991; Trustee Royal Acad. of Art; held over 80 one-man exhbns.; works in public and private collections worldwide; French Govt Scholarship, Paris 1960; Exhibit of the Year RA Summer Exhbn 1977. *Publication:* A Green Part of the World (with Martin Bailey) 1984. *Leisure interests:* family, travel. *Address:* Mole End, 40 High Street, Little Eversden, Cambridge, CB3 7HE, England. *Telephone:* (1223) 262292. *Fax:* (1223) 265656.

GREEN, Dan, BA; American book publishing executive; b. 28 Sept. 1935, Passaic, NJ; s. of Harold Green and Bessie Roslow; m. Jane Oliphant 1959; two s.; ed Syracuse Univ., NY; Publicity Dir Dover Press 1957–58; Station WNAC-TV 1958–59; Bobbs-Merrill Co. 1959–62; Simon & Schuster Inc. 1962–85, Assoc. Publr 1976–80, Vice-Pres., Publr 1980–84; Pres. Trade Publishing Group 1984–85; Founder, Publr, Kenan Press 1979–80; CEO Grove Press and Weidenfeld & Nicolson, New York 1985–89; Pres. Kenan Books, New York 1989–, Pom Literary Agency 1989. *Address:* Pom Inc., 611 Broadway, New York, NY 10012; Kenan Books, 611 Broadway, New York, NY 10012, USA. *Telephone:* (212) 673-3835. *Fax:* (212) 673-4653 (Office). *E-mail:* pom-inc@att.net (Office).

GREEN, Hon. Sir Guy Stephen Montague, AC, KBE, CVO, LLB; Australian administrator and judge; b. 26 July 1937, Launceston, Tasmania; s. of the late Clement Francis Montague and Beryl Margaret Jenour (née Williams) Green; m. Rosslyn Marshall 1963; two s. two d.; ed Launceston Church Grammar School and Univ. of Tasmania; admitted to Bar 1960; Partner Ritchie & Parker Alfred Green & Co. 1963–71; Pres. Tasmanian Bar Asscn 1968–70; Magistrate 1971–73; Chief Justice of Tasmania 1973–95; Lt-Gov. of Tasmania 1982–95; Gov. of Tasmania 1995–; mem. Faculty of Law Univ. of Tasmania 1974–85; Chair. Council of Law Reporting 1978–85; Chair. Tasmanian Cttee, Duke of Edinburgh's Award in Australia 1975–80; Dir Winston Churchill Memorial Trust 1975–85, Deputy Nat. Chair. 1980–85; Chancellor, Univ. of Tasmania 1985–95; Deputy Chair. Australian Inst. of Judicial Admin. 1986–88; Pres. St John Council 1984–92; Priory Exec. Officer, Order of St John in Australia 1984–91, Chancellor 1991–95; Deputy Prior St John Ambulance Australia 1995–; Hon. LLD (Univ. of Tasmania) 1996; Kt of Grace, Most Venerable Order of the Hosp. of St John of Jerusalem 1985. *Address:* Government House, Domain Road, Hobart, Tasmania 7000, Australia. *Telephone:* (3) 6234-2611. *Fax:* (3) 6234-2556.

GREEN, Hamilton; Guyanese politician; b. 9 Nov. 1934, Georgetown; s. of Wilfred Amelius Green and Edith Ophelia Dorothy Green; m. 1st Shirley Field-Ridley 1970 (died 1982); five s. three d.; m. 2nd Dr. Jennifer Veronica Basdeo 1990; two d.; ed Queen's Coll.; fmrly Gen. Sec., People's Nat. Congress, Minister of Works, Hydraulics and Supply, of Public Affairs, of Co-operatives and Nat. Mobilization, of Health, Housing and Labour; fmrly Vice-Pres. with responsibility for Public Welfare, Vice-Pres. with responsibility for Production; Vice-Pres. and Prime Minister of Guyana 1985–92; expelled from People's Nat. Congress 1992; f. political and environmental group Good And Green Guyana; Mayor of Georgetown 1994; presidential cand. 1997. *Publication:* From Pain to Peace – Guyana 1953–1964 (series of lectures at Cyril Potter Coll. of Educ. 1986). *Leisure interest:* reading (history and philosophy), table tennis, boxing and fitness training. *Address:* c/o City Hall, Regent Street, Georgetown (Office); Plot 'D' Lodge, Georgetown, Guyana (Home). *Telephone:* (2) 57870 (Office). *Fax:* (2) 57871.

GREEN, Howard, MD, MSc; American medical school professor and scientist; b. 10 Sept. 1925, Toronto, Canada; s. of Benjamin Green and Rose M. Green; m. Rosine Kauffmann; ed Univ. of Toronto and Northwestern Univ., USA; Research Asst, Dept of Physiology, Northwestern Univ. 1948–50; Research Assoc. (Instructor), Dept of Biochemistry, Univ. of Chicago 1951–53; Instructor, Dept of Pharmacology, New York Univ. School of Medicine 1954; Capt., MC, U.S. Army Reserve, Immunology Div., Walter Reed Army Inst. of Research 1955–56; Dept of Pathology, New York Univ. School of Medicine 1956–68, Prof. and Chair., Dept of Cell Biology 1968–70; Prof. of Cell Biology, MIT 1970–80; Higgins Prof. of Cellular Physiology and Chair. Dept of Physiology and Biophysics, Harvard Medical School 1980–86, George Higginson Prof. of Physiology 1986–, Chair. Dept of Cellular and Molecular Physiology 1988–93, Higgins Prof. of Cell Biology 1993–; Mr and Mrs J. N Taub Int. Memorial Award for Psoriasis Research 1977; Selman A. Waksman Award in Microbiology 1978; Lewis S. Rosenstiel Award in Basic Medical Research 1980, Lila Gruber Research Award, American Acad. of Dermatology 1980, The Passano Award 1985. *Publications:* numerous articles on cell biology, genetics, growth and differentiation. *Address:* Department of Cell Biology, Harvard Medical School, 240 Longwood Avenue, Boston, MA 02115 (Office); 82 Williston Road, Brookline, MA 02146, USA (Home).

GREEN, Michael Boris, PhD, FRS; British professor of physics; b. 22 May 1946, London; s. of Genia Green and Absalom Green; ed William Ellis School, London, Cambridge Univ.; Post-doctoral Fellowship Inst. for Advanced Study, Princeton, NJ, USA 1970–72; Cambridge Univ. 1972–77; SERC Advanced Fellowship, Oxford Univ. 1977–79; lecturer, Queen Mary and Westfield Coll., London 1979–85; Prof. of Physics 1985–93; John Humphrey Plummer Prof. of Theoretical Physics, Cambridge Univ. July 1993–; SERC Sr Fellowship 1986–91; numerous fellowships at US and European Insts including Distinguished Fairchild Fellowship, Calif. Inst. of Tech. 1990; Maxwell Medal, Inst. of Physics 1987, William Hopkins Prize, Cambridge Philosophical Soc. 1987, Dirac Medal, Int. Center for Theoretical Physics 1989. *Publications:* Superstring Theory (2 vols; with J. H. Schwarz and E. Witten) 1987; numerous publs in scientific journals. *Leisure interests:* pottery, music. *Address:* Department of Applied Mathematics and Theoretical Physics, University of Cambridge, Cambridge, CB3 0WA, England. *Telephone:* (1223) 330884. *E-mail:* mbg15@damtp.cam.ac.uk (Office).

GREEN, Michael Philip; British business executive; b. 2 Dec. 1947; s. of Cyril Green and Irene Green; m. 1st Hon. Janet F. Wolfson 1972 (divorced 1989); two d.; m. 2nd Theresa Buckmaster 1990; three s.; ed Haberdashers' Aske's School; Dir and co-founder, Tangent Industries 1968; Chief Exec. Carlton Communications PLC 1983–91, Chair. 1983–; Chair. Carlton TV Ltd 1991–94; Chair. ITN 1993–; Chair. ONdigital PLC 1997–; Chair. The Open Coll. 1986–; founder Tangent Charitable Trust 1984; Dir GMTV Ltd 1992–, Reuters Holdings PLC 1992–99, Getty Communications PLC 1997–98; Chair. The Media Trust 1997–; Hon. D. Litt. (City) 1999. *Leisure interests:* reading, bridge, television. *Address:* Carlton Communications PLC, 25 Knightsbridge, London, SW1X 7RZ, England. *Telephone:* (20) 7663-6363. *Fax:* (20) 7663-6300.

GREEN, Norman Michael, PhD, FRS; British biochemist; b. 6 April 1926; s. of Ernest Green and Hilda Margaret Carter; m. Iro Paulina Moschouti 1953; two s. one d.; ed Dragon School, Oxford, Clifton Coll., Bristol, Magdalen Coll., Oxford and Univ. Coll. Hosp. Medical School, London; Research Student, Univ. of Wash., Seattle 1951–53; Lecturer in Biochem., Univ. of Sheffield 1953–55; Research Fellow and Lecturer in Chem. Pathology, St Mary's Hosp. Medical School, London 1956–62; Visiting Scientist, NIH, Md 1962–64; Research Staff, Div. of Biochem., Nat. Inst. for Medical Research 1964–91, affiliated to Dept of Mathematical Biology 1992–. *Publications:* research papers in scientific journals on the structure of proteins and of membranes. *Leisure interests:* mountain climbing, pyrotechnics. *Address:* 57 Hale Lane, Mill Hill, London, NW7 3PS, England.

GREEN, Dame Pauline, DBE, MSc; British politician and business executive; b. 8 Dec. 1948, Gzira, Malta; d. of the late Bertram Wiltshire and Lucy Wiltshire; m. Paul Adam Green 1971; one s. one d.; ed John Kelly Secondary Modern School for Girls, Brent, London, Kilburn Polytechnic, Open Univ., London School of Econs; fmr policewoman with Metropolitan Police; Sec. Chipping Barnet Labour Party 1981, Chair. 1983; Parl. adviser on European Affairs to Co-operative Movt 1986–89; MEP for London N 1989–99, Leader European Parl. Labour Party 1993–94; Leader Parl. Group of Party of

European Socialists, European Parl. 1994–99; Chief Exec. Co-operative Union Ltd. 2000–; mem. Nat. Exec. Cttee Labour Party 1993–99; Vice-Pres. Socialist Int. Women 1994–99; Hon. DUniv (Middx) 1988, (N London), (Open Univ.) 2003; Medal of Honour, Greece 1994, Grand Golden Cross with Star, Austria 1995, Grand Commdr Order of Merit, Cyprus. *Publication:* Embracing Cyprus: the Path to Unity in the New Europe 2003. *Leisure interests:* music, swimming, walking. *Address:* The Co-operative Union Ltd., Holyoake House, Hanover Street, Manchester, M60 0AS (Office); 55 Slaithwaite Road, Meltham, Holmfirth, West Yorks., HD9 5PG, England (Home). *Telephone:* (161) 246-2900 (Office). *E-mail:* pgreen.coopunion@co-op.co.uk (Office).

GREEN, Philip; British retail executive; b. 1952, Croydon; m. Tina Green; took over family property co. 1973; bought Jean Jeanie 1985 (sold to Lee Cooper), Owen Owen 1994, Sports Division (sold to JJB Sports), Mark One 1996, Shoe Express 1997, Sears 1999, British Home Stores (Bhs) 2000, Arcadia (including Top Shop, Top Man, Miss Selfridge, Dorothy Perkins, Wallis, Evans and Burtons clothing chains) 2002; Chair. and CEO Amber Day 1988–92; lives in Monaco. *Address:* Bhs Ltd, Marylebone House, 129–137 Marylebone Road, London, NW1 5DQ, England (Office). *Website:* www.bhs.co.uk (Office).

GREEN, Roger Curtis, PhD, FRSNZ, FSA; American/New Zealand professor of prehistory; b. 15 March 1932, Ridgewood, NJ; s. of Robert J. Green and Eleanor Richards; m. 1st Kaye Chandler Smith 1959; m. 2nd Valerie J. Sallen 1984; two c.; ed Univ. of New Mexico and Harvard Univ.; Research Assoc. American Museum of Natural History 1959; Sr Lecturer in Prehistory, Univ. of Auckland 1961–66, Assoc. Prof. 1966–67, Prof. in Prehistory 1973–92, Prof. Emer. 1992–, Head, Dept of Anthropology 1980–84; Anthropologist, B.P. Bishop Museum 1967–73, Research Assoc. 1973–; R.S.N.Z. Capt. James Cook Fellowship 1970–73; Assoc. Prof. in Anthropology, Univ. of Hawaii 1967–70, James Cook Visiting Prof. 1981–82; Visiting Prof. Miller Inst. for Research in Basic Science, Univ. of Calif., Berkeley; Visiting Summer Scholar, School of American Research Santa Fe 1999; Visiting Research Fellow Univ. of Otago 2002; mem. Bd Foundation for Research Science and Tech. 1993–95; mem. NAS (USA) 1984– and numerous other learned socs.; Hon. Fellow Soc. of Antiquaries, London 2000; Fulbright Scholar 1958–59; Elsdon Best Medal, Polynesian Soc. 1973; Maharaia Winiata Memorial Prize 1974; Hector Memorial Medal, Royal Soc. of NZ 1992. *Publications:* Hawaiki: Ancestral Polynesia (with P.V. Kirch); numerous articles in historical, anthropological, archaeological journals etc. *Leisure interests:* music, travel, walking. *Address:* Department of Anthropology, University of Auckland, Private Bag 92019, Auckland (Office); PO Box 60-054 Titirangi, Auckland 1230, New Zealand (Home). *Telephone:* (9) 373-7599; (9) 817-7608 (Home). *Fax:* (9) 373-7441 (Office); (9) 817-2015 (Home). *E-mail:* r.green@auckland.ac.nz (Office); pounamu@ihug.co.nz (Home).

GREENAWAY, Peter; British film director, writer and painter; b. April 1942, Wales; m.; two d.; ed Forest School and Walthamstow Coll. of Art; trained as painter and first exhibited pictures at Lord's Gallery 1964; film ed. Cen. Office of Information 1965–76; began making own films in 1966, numerous curatorial exhbns., one-man shows and group shows in Europe, USA, Australia and Japan 1988–; Officier Ordre des Arts et des Lettres. *Films include:* Train, Tree 1966, Revolution, Five Postcards from Capital Cities 1967, Intervals 1969, Erosion 1971, H is for House 1973, Windows, Water, Water Wrackets 1975, Goole by Numbers 1976, Dear Phone 1977, 1–100, A Walk Through H (Hugo Award, Chicago), Vertical Features Remake 1978, Zandra Rhodes (Hugo Award, Chicago 1981) 1979, The Falls (BFI Award, L'Age d'Or Brussels) 1980, Act of God (Melbourne Short Film Prize, Sydney Short Film Prize) 1981, The Draughtsman's Contract 1982, Four American Composers 1983, Making a Splash 1984, Inside Rooms: 26 Bathrooms 1985, A Zed & Two Noughts 1986, The Belly of An Architect (Best Actor Prize, Chicago) 1987, Drowning by Numbers (Best Artistic Contribution Prize), Fear of Drowning, Death in the Seine 1988, A TV Dante Cantos 1–8, Hubert Bals Handshake 1989, The Cook, The Thief, His Wife and Her Lover 1989, Prospero's Books, M is for Man, Music, Mozart 1991, Rosa (Dance Screen Prize), Darwin 1992, The Baby of Macon 1993, The Stairs, Geneva 1994, The Pillow Book (La Distinction Gervais, Cannes, Best Film and Best Cinematographer, Sitges, Spain) 1995, Flying over Water 1997, 8½ Women 2000. *Opera:* Rosa, a Horse Drama 1994, Writing to Vermeer 1999. *Publications:* A Zed and Two Noughts 1986, Belly of an Architect 1987, Drowning By Numbers, Fear of Drowning 1988, The Cook, The Thief, His Wife and Her Lover 1989, Papers 1990, Prospero's Books 1991, Prospero's Subjects (picture book) 1992, Rosa, The Falls, The Baby of Macon 1993, The Draughtsman's Contract 1994, The Pillow Book 1996. *Address:* c/o The Vue, 387b King Street, London, W6 9NJ, England. *Fax:* (20) 8748-3597. *Website:* www.petergreenaway.org (Office).

GREENBERG, Jack, BSc, JD, CPA; American business executive; b. 1942; s. of Edith S. Scher; m. Donna Greenberg; one s. two d.; ed Depaul Univ., Chicago; with Arthur Young & Co. 1964–82; Chief Finance Officer and Exec. Vice-Pres. McDonald's Corpn 1982–, Vice-Chair. 1992, Pres., CEO 1997–99, Chair., CEO 1999–2002, also Dir; Dir Abbott Labs., Harcourt Gen.; mem. American Inst. of Certified Public Accountants, ABA, Illinois CPA Soc., Council of the World Econ. Forum; Trustee Field Museum, Chicago Symphony Orchestra, DePaul Univ.; Hon. DHumLitt (DePaul) 1999. *Address:* c/o McDonald's Corporation, 1 McDonald's Plaza, Oak Brook, IL 60523-1911, USA (Office).

GREENBERG, Jeffrey; American business executive; b. 1952; fmrly with Marsh & McLennan; fmr head property/casualty American Int. Group; joined Marsh & McLennan Risk Capital 1996; Pres., CEO Marsh and McLennan Cos 1999–, Chair. 2000–, also Dir. *Address:* Marsh & McLennan Companies Inc., 1166 Avenue of the Americas, New York, NY 10036-2774, USA.

GREENBERG, Maurice Raymond, LLB; American lawyer and insurance executive; b. 4 May 1925; s. of Jacob Greenberg and Ada (Rheingold) Greenberg; m. Corinne Phyllis Zuckerman 1950; four c.; ed Univ. of Miami, New York Law School; service with US army in Second World War and Korean War, rising to rank of capt.; admitted to NY Bar 1953; employee Continental Casualty Co. 1952–60; joined American Int. Group (AIG), Inc. 1960, Pres. American Home Assurance Co. 1962–67, CEO AIG, Inc. 1967–, Chair. 1989–; mem. The Business Roundtable, Pres.'s Advisory Cttee for Trade Policy and Negotiations; Chair. US–China Business Council, US–ASEAN Council on Business and Tech., US–Philippine Business Cttee, The Starr Foundation; Vice Chair. Center for Strategic and Int. Studies, Council on Foreign Relations; Chair. Emer. and Gov. Soc. of the NY Hosp.; hon. degrees from New England School of Law, NY Law School, Bryant Coll., Middlebury Coll., Brown Univ., Pace Univ. *Address:* American International Group Inc., 70 Pine Street, New York, NY 10270-0002, USA (Office). *Website:* www.aig.com (Office).

GREENBLATT, Stephen J., PhD; American academic; b. 7 Nov. 1943, Cambridge, Mass.; s. of Harry Greenblatt and Mollie Brown; three s.; m. Ramie Targoff 1998; ed Yale Univ., Univ. of Cambridge (Fulbright Scholar); Prof. of English Univ. of Calif., Berkeley 1969–97; Prof. of English Harvard Univ. 1997–, Cogan Univ. Prof. of the Humanities 2000–; numerous visiting professorships; Fellow American Acad. of Arts and Sciences; Porter Prize 1969, British Council Prize 1982; Guggenheim Fellow 1975, 1983; James Russell Lowell Prize 1989; Distinguished Teaching Award, Erasmus Inst. Prize 2001; Mellon Distinguished Humanist award 2002. *Publications:* Three Modern Satirists: Waugh, Orwell and Huxley 1965, Sir Walter Raleigh 1970, Renaissance Self-Fashioning 1980, Shakespearean Negotiations 1988, Learning to Curse 1990, Marvelous Possessions 1991; Ed. Allegory and Representation 1981, Power of Forms 1982, Representing the English Renaissance 1988, Redrawing the Boundaries of Literary Study in English 1992, New World Encounters 1992, The Norton Shakespeare 1997, Norton Anthology of English Literature 2000, Practising New Historicism 2000, Hamlet in Purgatory 2001. *Address:* Department of English, Harvard University, Cambridge, MA 02138, USA (Office). *Telephone:* (617) 495-2101 (Office). *E-mail:* greenbl@fas.harvard.edu (Office).

GREENBURY, Sir Richard, Kt; British business executive; b. July 1936; m. 1st Sian Eames Hughes (dissolved); two s. two d.; m. 2nd Gabrielle Mary McManus 1985 (divorced 1996); remarried Sian Eames Hughes 1996; ed Ealing Co. Grammar School; Jr man. trainee, Marks and Spencer 1953, Alt. Dir 1970, Dir 1972, Jt Man. Dir 1978–85, 1985–86; COO Marks and Spencer PLC 1986, CEO 1988–99, Chair. 1991–99; part-time mem. British Gas Corpn 1976–87; Dir (non-exec.) Metal Box PLC 1985–89, ICI 1992–96, Lloyds Bank (now Lloyds TSB Group) 1992–97, Zeneca 1993–99; mem. Supervisory Bd, Philips Electronics NV 1998–; Dir (non-exec.) UNIFI Inc. 1999–, Electronic Boutique 2000–; Dr. hc (Ulster) 1993, (Greenwich) 1993, (Nottingham Trent) 1994, (City and Guilds of London Inst.) 1994, (UMIST) 1994, (London Business School) 1996, (Bradford) 1999. *Leisure interests:* tennis, music, reading, watching football. *Address:* Ambarrow Wood, Ambarrow Lane, Sandhurst, Berks., GU47 8JE, England. *Telephone:* (1344) 779305 (Home). *Fax:* (1344) 776913 (Home).

GREENE, Brian; American physicist; ed Harvard Univ., Oxford Univ.; postdoctoral fellow, Harvard Univ. 1987–90; Asst Prof. Cornell Univ. 1990, Assoc. Prof. 1995, later Prof.; now Prof. of Physics and Maths, Columbia Univ.; Dir Theoretical Advanced Study Inst. 1996; has lectured in more than 20 countries; mem. Editorial Bd Physical Review D, Advance in Theoretical and Mathematical Physics (Aventis Prize for Science Books 2000). *Publications:* Duality in Calabi-Yau Moduli Space (co-author); Black Hole Condensation and the Unification of String (co-author); The Elegant Universe. *Address:* Faculty of Science, Columbia University, New York, NY 10032, USA (Office). *Telephone:* (212) 854-3349 (Office).

GREENE, Graham Carleton, CBE, MA; British publisher; b. 10 June 1936, Berlin, Germany; s. of Sir Hugh Carleton Greene and Helga Mary Connolly; m. 1st Judith Margaret Gordon Walker 1957 (divorced); m. 2nd Sally Georgina Horton 1976; one s.; also one step-s. one step-d.; ed Eton and Univ. Coll., Oxford; Dir Jonathan Cape Ltd 1962–90, Man. Dir 1966–88; Dir Chatto, Virago, Bodley Head and Cape Ltd 1969–88, Chair. 1970–88; Dir Book Reps (NZ) Ltd 1971–88, CVBC Services 1972–88, Australasian Publishing Co. Ltd (Chair. 1978–88) 1969–88, Guinness Peat Group 1973–87, Triad Paperbacks 1975–88, Greene King PLC 1979–, Statesman and Nation Publishing Co. (Chair. 1981–85) 1980–85, Statesman Publishing Co. Ltd (Chair. 1981–85) 1980–85, Random House Inc. 1987–88, Jupiter Int. Investment Trust PLC 1989–, Henry Sotheran Ltd 1990–, Ed Victor Ltd 1991–, Rosemary Sandberg Ltd 1991–, Libra KFT (Budapest) 1991–, London Merchant Securities PLC 1996– (Chair. 2000–); Chair. Random House UK Ltd 1988–90, British Museum Devt Trust 1986–93 (Vice-Chair. 1993–), British Museum Publications (now British Museum Company) Ltd (Chair. 1988–96), Museums and Galleries Comm. 1991–96, Bd of Trustees, British Museum 1996–; Chair. Nation Pty Co. Ltd 1981–87, New Society 1984–86, Great Britain–China

Centre (Chair. 1986–); Dir Garsington Opera Ltd 1996–; mem. Bd of British Council 1977–88, mem. Council of Publishers Asscn (Pres. 1977–79) 1969–88; Trustee, British Museum 1978– (Chair. 1996), Open Coll. of the Arts 1990–97; Int. Cttee of Int. Publishers Asscn 1977–88, Groupe des Editeurs de Livres de la CEE (Pres. 1984–86) 1977–86; Chevalier, Ordre des Arts et des Lettres. *Address:* 6 Bayley Street, Bedford Square, London WC1B 3HB, England. *Telephone:* (20) 7304-4101. *Fax:* (20) 7304-4102 (Office).

GREENE, Jack Phillip, PhD; American professor of history; b. 12 Aug. 1931, Lafayette, Ind.; s. of Ralph B. Greene and Nellie A. (Miller) Greene; m. 1st Sue L. Neuenswander 1953 (divorced 1990); one s. one d.; m. 2nd Amy Turner Bushnell 1990; ed Univ. of North Carolina, Indiana Univ. and Duke Univ., Durham, NC; History Instructor Mich. State Univ., E Lansing 1956–59; Asst Prof. of History Western Reserve Univ., Cleveland, Ohio 1959–62, Assoc. Prof. 1962–65; Visiting Assoc. Prof. and Visiting Ed. William and Mary Quarterly Coll. of William and Mary in Va, Williamsburg 1961–62; Assoc. Prof. of History Univ. of Mich., Ann Arbor 1965–66; Visiting Assoc. Prof. of History Johns Hopkins Univ., Baltimore, Md 1964–65, Prof. 1966–75, Chair. Dept of History 1970–72, Andrew W. Mellon Prof. in Humanities 1975–, Distinguished Prof., Univ. of Calif., Irvine 1990–92; Harmsworth Prof. of American History Oxford Univ. 1975–76; Visiting Prof. Hebrew Univ. of Jerusalem 1979, Ecole des Hautes Etudes en Science Sociale 1986–87; Freeman Prof., Univ. of Richmond, Va, 1996; Sweet Prof., Mich. State Univ. 1997; mem. Inst. for Advanced Study 1970–71, 1985–86; mem. American Philosophical Soc.; Corresp. mem. British Acad.; Fellow, Woodrow Wilson Int. Center for Scholars 1974–75, Center for Advanced Study in Behavioral Sciences 1979–80, Churchill Coll., Cambridge 1986–, Nat. Humanities Center 1987–88, Guggenheim Fellow 1964–65; Sweet Prof. Michigan State Univ. 1997; John Carter Brown Library Fellow 1999–2000. *Publications:* twenty-nine books, including Quest for Power 1963, Diary of Colonel Landon Carter of Sabine Hall (2 vols) 1965, Settlements to Society 1966, Colonies to Nation 1967, Reinterpretation of American Revolution 1968, All Men are Created Equal 1976, Colonial British America 1983, Encyclopedia of American Political History 1984, Peripheries and Center 1986, Political Life in Eighteenth Century Virginia 1986, Intellectual Heritage of the Constitutional Era 1986, Magna Carta for America 1986, American Revolution 1987, Pursuits of Happiness 1988, Selling the New World 1988, Encyclopedia of the American Revolution (co-ed.) 1991, Imperatives, Behaviors and Identities 1992, Intellectual Construction of America 1993, Negotiated Authorities 1994, Understanding the American Revolution 1995, Interpreting Early America 1996, Companion to the American Revolution 2000. *Leisure interests:* travel, cinema. *Address:* Department of History, The Johns Hopkins University, Baltimore, MD 21218 (Office); 1974 Division Road, East Greenwich, RI 02898, USA (Home). *Telephone:* (410) 516-7596 (Office); (410) 884-5883 (Home). *Fax:* (410) 516-7586 (Office); (401) 886-4633 (Home). *E-mail:* jpgreene@jhunix.hcf .jhv.edu (Office); jack_greene@brown.edu (Home).

GREENE, Maurice; American athlete; b. 23 July 1974, Kansas City, Mo.; s. of Ernest Greene and Jackie Greene; ed Schlage High School and Park Coll., Kansas City; world record-holder indoor 50m (shared with Donovan Bailey) and 60m (as at end 2002); coached by John Smith 1996–; silver medal US Championships 60m 1995; gold medal US Indoor Championships 60 m 1997; gold medal US Championships 100m 1997; gold medal World Championships 100m 1997, 100m, 200m and 4×100m relay 1999, 100m 2001; Olympic gold medallist 100m and 4×100m 2000; set world record for 100m in Athens 1999 (9.79 seconds), since beaten by Tim Montgomery; f. Finish the Race Foundation. *Address:* HS International, 2600 Michelson Drive, Suite 680, Irvine, CA 92612, USA. *Website:* www.hsi.net.

GREENE, Sally, MBA; British impresario and producer; b. 27 May 1954; d. of Basil Greene and Clare Tully; m. Robert Bourne; one s. one d.; ed St Maur's Convent, Weybridge and Guildhall School of Music and Drama; bought Richmond Theatre, Surrey 1986, programmed it, then restored theatre 1991; took over Criterion Theatre, Piccadilly 1992, restored theatre, re-opening it 1993; f. Criterion Productions PLC 1994; bought The Old Vic Theatre 1998, formed a charitable trust to run it; launched Old Vic Productions PLC with Kevin Spacey (q.v.) 2000. *Productions include:* Taking Sides, Criterion Theatre 1994, Hot House, Comedy Theatre 1994, Jack 1993, Cyrano de Bergerac, RSC 1995, Car Man, Old Vic 2000, Medea 2001, Life x 3, Old Vic 2001, Vagina Monologues, Ambassador's Theatre 2001–02. *Leisure interests:* piano, skiing, singing. *Address:* Old Vic Productions, Park House, 26 North End Road, London, NW11 7PT (Office); Lindsay House, 100 Cheyne Walk, London, SW10 0DQ, England (Home). *Telephone:* (20) 7928-2651 (Office). *E-mail:* s.greene@dial.pipex.com (Home).

GREENER, Sir Anthony Armitage, Kt, FCMA; British business executive; b. 26 May 1940, Bowden; s. of William Greener and Diana Greener; m. Min Ogilvie 1974; one s. one d.; ed Marlborough Coll.; Marketing Man. Thames Board Mills 1969; Retail Controller, Alfred Dunhill Ltd (later Dunhill Holdings PLC) 1972, Dir 1974, Man. Dir 1975; Man. Dir United Distillers 1987–92; Dir Guinness PLC 1986–97, Jt Man. Dir 1989–91, Chief Exec. 1992–97, Chair. 1993–97; Co-Chair. Diageo (after merger with Grand Metropolitan PLC) PLC 1997–98, Chair. 1998–2000; Chair. University for Industry Ltd 2000–; Deputy Chair. BT 2001–; Dir Louis Vuitton Moet Hennessy 1989–97, Reed Int. 1990–93, Reed Elsevier 1993–98, Robert Mondavi 2000–. *Leisure interests:* skiing, sailing, gardening. *Address:* University for Industry Ltd., 88 Kingsway, London, WC2B 6AA, England (Office). *Telephone:* (20) 7681-6103 (Office). *Fax:* (20) 7681-6602 (Office).

GREENFIELD OF OTMOOR, Baroness (Life Peer), cr. 2001, of Otmoor in the County of Oxfordshire; **Susan Adele Greenfield,** CBE, DPhil; British pharmacologist; b. 1 Oct. 1950; d. of Reginald Myer Greenfield and Doris Margaret Winifred Greenfield; m. Peter William Atkins 1991; ed Godolphin and Latymer School for Girls, St Hilda's Coll., Oxford; MRC Training Fellow Univ. Lab. of Physiology, Oxford 1977–81; fmrly with Coll. de France, Paris; MRC-INSERM French Exchange Fellow 1979–80; Jr Research Fellow Green Coll., Oxford 1981–84, lecturer in Synaptic Pharmacology 1985–96, Prof. in Synaptic Pharmacology 1996–, Gresham Prof. of Physic Gresham Coll. 1995–; Dir Royal Inst. 1998–; Visiting Fellow Inst. of Neuroscience La Jolla, USA 1995; Sr Research Fellow Lincoln Coll. Oxford; Hon. Fellow St Hilda's Coll. Oxford, Royal Coll. of Physicians 2000; Visiting Distinguished Scholar Queen's Univ., Belfast 1996; Trustee Science Museum; awarded 21 Hon. DSc degrees 1997–2002; Woman of Distinction, Jewish Care 1998, Michael Faraday Medal, Royal Soc. 1998. *Radio appearances include:* Start the Week, Any Questions and other discussion programmes; presenter of Turn On, Turn Off series on drugs and the brain. *Television appearances include:* Dimbleby Lecture 1999, author and presenter of Brain Story 'Landmark' (series of programmes on the brain) 2000. *Publications include:* numerous articles in learned journals; Mindwaves (co-ed. with C. B. Blakemore) 1987, Journey to the Centres of the Brain (with G. Ferry) 1994, Journey to the Centres of the Mind 1995, The Human Mind Explained (ed.) 1996, The Human Brain: A Guided Tour 1997; Brainpower (ed.) 2000, Brain Story 2000, Private Life of the Brain 2000. *Leisure interests:* aerobics, travel. *Address:* Department of Pharmacology, Mansfield Road, Oxford, OX1 3QT (Office). *Telephone:* (1865) 271628 (Office). *Fax:* (1865) 271853 (Office). *E-mail:* susan.greenfield@pharm .ox.ac.uk (Office).

GREENGARD, Paul, PhD; American biochemist; b. 11 Dec. 1925, New York; ed Johns Hopkins Univ., Baltimore; post-doctoral studies in biochemistry, Univ. of London, Cambridge Univ. and NIH, England and Bethesda, MD 1953–59; Dir Dept of Biochemistry, Geigy Research Lab., Ardsley, NY 1959–67; Visiting Assoc. Prof. and Prof. of Pharmacology, Albert Einstein Coll. of Medicine, NY 1961–70; Prof. of Pharmacology and Psychiatry, Yale Univ. School of Medicine 1968–83; Vincent Astor Prof. and Head, Lab. of Molecular and Cellular Neuroscience, Rockefeller Univ., NY 1983–; mem. NAS, NARSAD Scientific Council; numerous awards and prizes including Dickson Prize and Medal in Medicine, Univ. of Pittsburgh 1977, NY Acad. of Sciences Award in Biological and Medicinal Sciences 1980, 1993, 3M Life Sciences Award, Fed. of American Societies for Experimental Biology 1987, NAS Award in the Neurosciences 1991, Lieber Prize for Outstanding Achievement in Schizophrenia Research 1996, Metropolitan Life Foundation Award for Medical Research 1998, Bristol-Myers Squibb Award for Distinguished Achievement in Neuroscience Research 1989, Nobel Prize for Medicine (jt recipient) 2000. *Publications:* numerous publs and articles in journals. *Address:* Laboratory of Molecular and Cellular Neuroscience, The Rockefeller University, 1230 York Avenue, New York, NY 10021, USA (Office). *Telephone:* (212) 327-8780 (Office). *Fax:* (212) 327-7746 (Office). *E-mail:* greengd@mail .rockefeller.edu (Office).

GREENGRASS, Paul; British film and television director; b. 13 Aug. 1955, Cheam; began career as an investigative journalist and award-winning documentary filmmaker. *Films include:* Resurrected (Interfilm and OCIC Jury Awards, Berlin Film Festival), Sophie's World, The One That Got Away, The Fix, The Theory of Flight 1998, Bloody Sunday 2002 (Golden Bear, Berlin Int. Film Festival). *Television work includes:* World In Action, Food and Trucks and Rock and Roll, U2 – Anthem for the Eighties, Moscow Week, Coppers, What Ever Happened to Woodward and Bernstein, When The Lies Run Out (Chicago Film Festival Silver Medal), Kavanagh QC, The Murder of Stephen Lawrence. *Publications include:* Spycatcher (with Peter Wright). *Address:* c/o Granada plc, The London Television Centre, London, SE1 9LT, England (Office). *Telephone:* (20) 7620-1620 (Office). *Website:* www .granadamedia.com (Office).

GREENLAND, Dennis James, DPhil, FRS, FIBiol; British university professor; b. 13 June 1930, Portsmouth; s. of James John Greenland and Lily Gardener; m. Edith Mary Johnston 1955; one s. two d.; ed Portsmouth Grammar School, Christ Church, Oxford; lecturer Univ. of Ghana 1955–59; lecturer Waite Inst., Univ. of Adelaide, Australia 1960–63, Reader and Head of Soil Science 1963–70, Hanniford Lecturer 1978; Prof. and Head of Dept of Soil Science, Univ. of Reading 1970–79, Visiting Prof. 1988–; Chair. Scientific Advisory Panel, Commonwealth Devt Corpn 1991–96; Research Dir Int. Inst. of Tropical Agric. (seconded from Univ. of Reading) 1974–76; Deputy Dir Gen. (Research) Int. Rice Research Inst., Philippines 1979–87; Dir Scientific Services, CAB Int., UK 1987–92, Fellow World Acad. of Arts and Science 1988; Hon. mem. American Soc. of Agronomy, American Soc. of Soil Science 1993; Blackman Lecturer, Univ. of Oxford 1988; DrAgr hc (Univ. of Ghent) 1982. *Publications:* The Soil Under Shifting Cultivation (jtly.) 1960, The Sustainability of Rice Farming 1997; numerous scientific articles in learned journals. *Leisure interests:* golf, walking, watching cricket. *Address:* Low Wood, The Street, South Stoke, Oxon., RG8 0JS, England. *Telephone:* (1491) 873259 (Home). *Fax:* (1491) 872572 (Home). *E-mail:* greenland.dennis@virgin.net (Home).

GREENSPAN, Alan, KBE, MA, PhD; American economist; b. 6 March 1926, NY; s. of Herbert Greenspan and Rose Goldsmith; m. Andrea Mitchell 1997; ed New York and Columbia Univs; Pres., CEO Townsend-Greenspan & Co. Inc. 1954–74, 1977–87; mem. Nixon for Pres. Cttee 1968–69; mem. Task Force for Econ. Growth 1969, Comm. on an All-Volunteer Armed Force 1969–70, Comm. on Financial Structure and Regulation 1970–71; Consultant to Council of Econ. Advisers 1970–74, to US Treasury 1971–74, to Fed. Reserve Bd 1971–74; Chair. Council of Econ. Advisers 1974–77, Nat. Comm. on Social Security Reform 1981–83; Chair. Bd of Govs Fed. Reserve System 1987–; Dir Council on Foreign Relations; mem. Sec. of Commerce's Econ. Comm.'s Cen. Market System Cttee 1972, GNP Review Cttee of Office of Man. and Budget, Time Magazine's Bd of Economists 1971–74, 1977–87, President's Econ. Policy Advisory Bd 1981–87, President's Foreign Intelligence Advisory Bd 1983–85, Exec. Cttee Trilateral Comm.; Sr Adviser Brookings Inst. Panel on Econ. Activity 1970–74, 1977–87; Adjunct Prof. Graduate School of Business Man., New York 1977–87; Past Pres., Fellow, Nat. Asscn of Business Economists; Dir Trans World Financial Co. 1962–74, Dreyfus Fund 1970–74, Gen. Cable Corpn 1973–74, 1977–78, Sun Chemical Corpn 1973–74, Gen. Foods Corpn 1977–86, J. P. Morgan & Co. 1977–87, Mobil Corpn 1977–87, Aluminum Co. of America (ALCOA) 1978–87; Jefferson Award 1976; William Butler Memorial Award 1977. *Leisure interest:* golf. *Address:* Office of the Chairman, Federal Reserve System, 20th and C Streets, NW, Washington, DC 20551-0001, USA.

GREENSTOCK, Sir Jeremy (Quentin), GCMG, MA; British diplomatist; b. 27 July 1943, Harrow; s. of the late John Wilfrid Greenstock and Ruth Margaret Logan; m. Anne Derryn Ashford Hodges 1969; one s. two d.; ed Harrow School and Worcester Coll., Oxford; Asst master Eton Coll. 1966–69; entered diplomatic service 1969, studied Arabic at MECAS 1970–72, served in Dubai 1972–74, Pvt. Sec. to Amb., Washington 1974–78, with FCO (Planning, Personnel Operations Dept, N East and N African Dept) 1978–83; Commercial Counsellor, Jeddah 1983–85, Riyadh 1985–86; Head of Chancery, British Embassy, Paris 1987–90; Asst Under-Sec. of State, FCO 1990–93; Minister, British Embassy, Washington 1994–95; Deputy Under-Sec. of State FCO 1995; Political Dir FCO 1996–98; Perm. Rep. to UN 1998–2003, Chair. UN Security Council Counter-Terrorism Cttee 2001–03. *Leisure interests:* travel, golf, skiing, listening to music. *Address:* c/o Foreign and Commonwealth Office, Whitehall, London, SW1A 2AH, England. *E-mail:* jeremy.greenstock2@fco.gov.uk (Office).

GREENWOOD, Duncan Joseph, CBE, DSc, FRS, FRSC; British agronomist; b. 16 Oct. 1932, New Barnet, Herts; s. of Herbert James Greenwood and Alison Fairgrieve Greenwood; ed Hutton Grammar School, Liverpool Univ. and Aberdeen Univ.; Research Fellow, Aberdeen Univ. 1957–59; Research Leader, Nat. Vegetable Research Station 1959–66; Head of Soil Science, Horticulture Research Int. (fmrly Nat. Vegetable Research Station) 1966–92, Emer. Fellow 1992–; Visiting Prof. of Plant Sciences, Leeds Univ. 1985–93; Hon. Prof. of Agricultural Chem., Birmingham Univ. 1986–93; Chair. Agricultural Group, Soc. of Chemical Industry 1975–77; Pres. Int. Cttee Plant Nutrition 1978–82, British Soc. of Soil Science 1990–92; Emer. Fellow Horticulture Research Int. 1992–; Sir Gilbert Morgan Medal, Soc. of Chemical Industry 1962, Research Medal of the Royal Agricultural Soc. of England 1979, Grower of the Year Lifetime Achievement Award 2000. *Publications:* over 170 publs in scientific journals, mostly on soils and plant nutrition. *Address:* 23 Shelley Road, Stratford upon Avon, CV37 7JR (Home); Horticulture Research International, Wellesbourne, Warwick, CV35 9EF, England. *Telephone:* (1789) 470382 (Office); (1789) 204735 (Home). *Fax:* (1789) 470552 (Office). *E-mail:* duncan.greenwood@hri.ac.uk (Office); duncangreenwood@compuserve.com (Home).

GREENWOOD, Norman Neill, PhD, DSc, ScD, CChem, FRIC, FRS, MRI; British professor of inorganic and structural chemistry; b. 19 Jan. 1925, Melbourne, Australia; s. of the late Prof. J. Neill Greenwood and Gladys Uhland; m. Kirsten M. Rydland 1951; three d.; ed Univs of Melbourne and Cambridge; Resident Tutor and Lecturer, Trinity Coll., Univ. of Melbourne 1946–48; Sr Harwell Research Fellow, AERE 1951–53; Lecturer, then Sr Lecturer in Inorganic Chem. Univ. of Nottingham 1953–61; Prof. and Head, Dept of Inorganic Chem. Univ. of Newcastle-upon-Tyne 1961–71; Prof. and Head, Dept of Inorganic and Structural Chem. Univ. of Leeds 1971–90, Dean of Faculty of Science 1968–88, Emer. Prof. 1990–; Visiting Prof. at univs in Australia, USA, Canada, China, Japan and Denmark since 1966; Pres. Inorganic Chem. Div. (IUPAC) 1977–81; Pres. Dalton Div. Royal Soc. of Chemistry 1979–81; Pres. British Asscn for the Advancement of Science, Section B (Chemistry) 1990–91; Foreign Assoc. Académie des Sciences, Institut de France 1992; Humphry Davy Lecture, Royal Soc. 2000; Hon. DUniv (Nancy) 1977; Hon. DSc (Toho Univ., Tokyo) 2000; Tilden Lectureship and Medal (Chem. Soc.) 1966; RSC Medal for Main Group. Element Chem. 1974; Gold Medal of City of Nancy (France) 1977; A. W. von Hofmann Lectureship (Gesellschaft Deutscher Chemiker) 1983; Liversidge Lectureship and Medal (RSC) 1984; Egon Wiberg Lectureship (Univ. of Munich) 1989; Ludwig Mond Lectureship and Medal 1991; Medal for Tertiary Educ. 1993; and other awards and distinctions. *Publications:* over 460 original research papers in refereed journals and monographs; books include, Ionic Crystals, Lattice Defects and Nonstoichiometry 1968, Mössbauer Spectroscopy (with T. C. Gibb) 1971, Chemistry of the Elements (with A. Earnshaw) 1984. *Leisure interests:* music, skiing, travel. *Address:* Department of Chemistry, University of Leeds, Leeds, LS2 9JT, England. *Telephone:* (113) 3436406. *Fax:* (113) 3436565. *E-mail:* n.n.greenwood@chem.leeds.ac.uk (Office).

GREER, David Steven, MD; American medical specialist; b. 12 Oct. 1925, Brooklyn, New York; s. of Jacob Greer and Mary (née Zaslawsky) Greer; m. Marion Clarich 1950; one s. one d.; ed Univs of Notre Dame and Chicago;

Intern, Yale-New Haven Medical Center 1953–54; Resident in Medicine, Univ. of Chicago Clinics 1954–57; specialist in internal medicine, Fall River, Mass. 1957–74; Chief of Staff, Dept of Medicine, Fall River Gen. Hosp. 1959–62; Medical Dir Earle E. Hussey Hosp., Fall River 1962–72; Chief of Staff, Dept of Medicine, Truesdale Clinic and Truesdale Hosp., Fall River 1971–74; Faculty mem. Tufts Univ. Coll. of Medicine, Boston, Mass. 1969–78; Faculty mem. Brown Univ. Program in Medicine 1973–75, Prof. of Community Health 1975–93, Prof. Emer. 1993–, Assoc. Dean 1974–81, Dean 1981–92, Dean Emer. 1992–; Acting Dir Generalist Physician Programs, AAMC 1993–94; mem. NAS Inst. of Medicine; academic medical consultant 1993–; various public appts.; Cutting Foundation Medal for Service to Religion and Medicine 1976 and other awards. *Publications:* numerous articles on chronic disease, geriatrics, long-term care and health-care evaluation. *Leisure interest:* squash. *Address:* Brown University, Box G, Providence, RI 02912, USA. *Telephone:* (401) 863-1274. *E-mail:* Greer@brown.edu.

GREER, Germaine, PhD; Australian feminist and author; b. 29 Jan. 1939, Melbourne; d. of Eric Reginald Greer and Margaret May (Lafrank) Greer; ed Star of the Sea Convent, Vic., Melbourne and Cambridge Univ., England; Sr Tutor in English, Sydney Univ. 1963–64; Asst Lecturer then Lecturer in English, Warwick Univ. 1967–72, Prof. of English and Comparative Studies, 1998–; lecturer throughout N America with American Program Bureau 1973–78, to raise funds for Tulsa Bursary and Fellowship Scheme 1980–83; Visiting Prof., Grad. Faculty of Modern Letters, Univ. of Tulsa 1979, Prof. of Modern Letters 1980–83, Founder-Dir of Tulsa Centre for the Study of Women's Literature, Founder-Ed. Tulsa Studies in Women's Literature 1981; Dir Stump Cross Books 1988–; Special Lecturer and Unofficial Fellow, Newnham Coll., Cambridge 1989–98; broadcaster/journalist/columnist/reviewer 1972–; Jr Govt Scholarship 1952, Diocesan Scholarship 1956, Sr Govt Scholarship 1956, Teacher's Coll. Studentship 1956, Commonwealth Scholarship 1964; numerous television appearances and public talks including discussion with Norman Mailer (q.v.) in The Theatre of Ideas, New York; Dr hc (Univ. of Griffith, Australia) 1996, (Univ. of York, Toronto) 1999, (UMIST) 2000. *Publications:* The Female Eunuch 1969, The Obstacle Race: The Fortunes of Women Painters and Their Work 1979, Sex and Destiny: The Politics of Human Fertility 1984, Shakespeare (co-ed.) 1986, The Madwoman's Underclothes (selected journalism 1964–85) 1986, Kissing the Rod: An Anthology of 17th Century Women's Verse (co-ed.) 1988, Daddy, We Hardly Knew You 1989 (J. R. Ackerly Prize and Premio Internazionale Mondello), The Uncollected Verse of Aphra Behn (ed.) 1989, The Change: Women, Ageing and the Menopause 1991, The Collected Works of Katherine Philips, the Matchless Orinda, Vol. III: The Translations (co-ed.) 1993, Slip-Shod Sibyls: Recognition, Rejection and The Woman Poet 1995, The Surviving Works of Anne Wharton (co-ed.) 1997, The Whole Woman 1999, John Wilmot, Earl of Rochester 1999, 101 Poems by 191 Women (ed.) 2001; articles for Listener, Spectator, Esquire, Harper's Magazine, Playboy, Private Eye and other journals. *Leisure interest:* gardening. *Address:* c/o Gillon Aitken Associates, 29 Fernshaw Road, London, SW10 0TG, England.

GREET, Rev. Kenneth Gerald; British minister of religion; b. 17 Nov. 1918, Bristol; s. of Walter and Renée Greet; m. Mary Eileen Edbrooke 1947; one s. two d.; ed Cotham Grammar School, Bristol, Handsworth Coll., Birmingham; Cwm and Kingstone Methodist Church 1940–42; Ogmore Vale Methodist Church 1942–45; Tonypandy Cen. Hall 1947–54; Sec. Dept of Christian Citizenship of Methodist Church and Social Responsibility Div. 1954–71; Sec., Methodist Conf. 1971–84, Pres. 1980–81; mem. British Council of Churches 1955–84 (Chair. Exec. 1977–80), World Methodist Council 1957– (Chair. Exec. Cttee 1976–81); Chair. Exec. Temperance Council of Christian Churches 1961–71; Moderator, Free Church Fed. Council 1982–83; Co-Chair. World Disarmament Campaign 1982–86, Pres. 1989–94, Vice-Pres. 1994–; Rep. to Cen. Cttee, WCC, Addis Ababa 1971, Nairobi 1975; Beckly Lecturer 1962, Willson Lecturer, Kansas City 1966, Cato Lecturer, Sydney 1975; Chair. of Govs., Southlands Coll. 1986–98; Hon. DD (Ohio) 1967; Hon. D. Univ. (Surrey) 1998. *Publications:* The Mutual Society 1962, Man and Wife Together 1962, Large Petitions 1962, Guide to Loving 1965, The Debate About Drink 1969, The Sunday Question 1969, The Art of Moral Judgement 1970, When the Spirit Moves 1975, A Lion from a Thicket 1978, The Big Sin: Christianity and the Arms Race 1982, Under the Rainbow Arch 1984, What Shall I Cry 1986, Jabez Bunting: a biography 1995, Fully Connected 1997. *Leisure interest:* photography. *Address:* 89 Broadmark Lane, Rustington, Sussex, BN16 2JA, England. *Telephone:* (1903) 773326. *E-mail:* greet@skynow.net (Home).

GREEVY, Bernadette; Irish mezzo-soprano concert singer; b. 3 July 1940, Dublin; d. of Patrick J. Greevy and Josephine F. Miller; m. Peter A. Tattan 1965 (died 1983); one s.; ed Convent of the Holy Faith, Clontarf, Dublin; London début, Wigmore Hall 1964; has since appeared on maj. concert platforms in Europe, USA, Canada and Far East; recordings of works by Brahms, Handel, Haydn, Bach, Berlioz, Britten, Elgar and Mahler; mem. Bd Nat. Concert Hall 1981–86, 1991–; Hon. DMus (Univ. Coll., Dublin), (Trinity Coll., Dublin); Harriet Cohen Int. Music Award; Order of Merit (Order of Malta); Dame of the Holy Sepulchre; Pro Ecclesia et Pontifice (Vatican). *Leisure interests:* gardening, cooking, painting. *Address:* c/o Trinity College, Dublin (Office); Melrose, 672 Howth Road, Dublin 5, Ireland.

GREF, German Oskarovich; German politician and jurist; b. 8 Feb. 1964, Panfilovo, Pavlodar Region, Kazakhstan; m.; one s.; ed Omsk State Univ.; legal adviser Pavlodar regional agric. co. 1981–82; army service 1982–84;

Lecturer in law Omsk State Univ. 1990; legal adviser Cttee on Econ. Devt and Property, Petrodvorets Dist Admin, St Petersburg 1991–92; Chair. Cttee on Property Man., concurrently Deputy Head Petrodvorets Dist Admin. 1992–94; Deputy Chair., Dir Dept of Real Estate, First Deputy Chair. Cttee on Man. of Municipal Property St Petersburg Admin. 1994–97; Vice-Gov., Chair. Cttee on Man. of Municipal Property St Petersburg Admin. 1997–98; mem. Exec. Bd Ministry of State Property Russian Fed. 1998; First Deputy Minister 1998–2000; mem. Exec. Bd Fed. Comm. on Market of Securities 1999–; head of team working on econ. reform plan for Pres. Putin 1999–2000; Minister of Econ. Devt and Trade of Russian Fed. 2000–. *Address:* Ministry of Economic Development and Trade, 1st Tverskaya-Yamskaya str. 1–3, Moscow A-47, Russia (Office). *Telephone:* (095) 200-52-98; 200-07-45 (Office). *E-mail:* presscenter@economy.gov.ru (Office). *Website:* www.economy.gov.ru (Office).

GREGER, Janet L., MS, PhD; American professor of nutritional sciences; b. 18 Feb. 1948, Illinois; d. of Harold Greger and Marjorie Greger; ed Univ. of Illinois at Urbana-Champaign and Cornell Univ. ; Asst Prof. Purdue Univ. 1973–78; Asst Prof., Assoc. Prof. Univ. of Wis.-Madison 1978–83, Prof. of Nutritional Sciences 1983–, Assoc. Dean, Grad. School 1990–96, Assoc. Dean, Medical School 1996–98; Vice-Provost of Research and Grad. Educ. and Dean of Grad. School, Univ. of Connecticut 2002–; AAAS Congressional Sciences Eng Fellow 1984–85; mem. Bd of Man. COGR 1993–99; mem. Bd of Dirs AAALAC 1992–2002, NIH Panel on Regulatory Burden 1999–2002; AAAS Congressional Science and Eng Fellowship 1984–85; mem. Council Soc. of Experimental Biology and Medicine 2002–(05). *Publications:* Nutrition for Living 1985, 1988, 1991, 1994; over 159 papers in scientific journals and books. *Leisure interests:* travel, reading. *Address:* Whetten Graduate Center, University of Connecticut, 438 Whitney Road Extension, Unit 1006, Storrs, CT 06269-1006 (Office); 21 Fort Griswold Lane, Mansfield Center, CT 06250, USA (Home). *Telephone:* (860) 486-5381 (Office). *Fax:* (860) 486-5381 (Office). *E-mail:* jl.greger@uconn..edu (Office).

GREGG, Judd, JD, LLM; American politician; b. 14 Feb. 1947, Nashua, NH; m. Kathleen McLellan 1973; one s. two d.; ed Columbia and Boston Univs; admitted NH Bar 1972; law practice, Nashua, NH; mem. 97th–100th Congresses from 2nd NH Dist 1981–89; mem. NH Gov.'s Exec. Council 1978–80; Gov. of New Hampshire 1989–93; Senator from New Hampshire Jan. 1993–; Republican. *Address:* US Senate, 393 Russell Senate Building, Washington, DC 20510-0001, USA.

GREGORIAN, Vartan, MA, PhD; American professor of history; b. 8 April 1934, Tabriz, Iran; s. of Samuel B. Gregorian and Shushanik G. (née Mirzaian) Gregorian; m. Clare Russell 1960; three c.; ed Coll. Arménien, Stanford Univ.; Instructor, Asst Prof., Assoc. Prof. of History San Francisco State Coll. 1962–68; Assoc. Prof. of History Univ. of Calif., LA 1968, Univ. of Texas, Austin 1968–72, Dir Special Programs 1970–72; Tarzian Prof. Armenian and Caucasian History Univ. of Pa 1972–80, Dean 1974–79, Provost 1978–80; Prof. of History and Near Eastern Studies, New York City 1984–89; Prof. New School for Social Research, New York 1984–89; Pres. New York Public Library 1981–89; Pres. Brown Univ. 1989–97, mem. Nat. Humanities Faculty 1970–; Pres. Carnegie Corpn of New York 1997–; mem. Acad. of Arts and Letters 1989–, Historical Assocn, Asscn for Advancement of Slavic Studies, American Philosophical Soc.; John Simon Guggenheim Fellow 1971–72; Silver Cultural Medal Italian Ministry of Foreign Affairs 1977, Gold Medal of Honour City and Province of Vienna 1976, Ellis Island Medal of Honor 1986. *Publications:* The Emergence of Modern Afghanistan 1880–1946 1969; numerous articles for professional journals. *Address:* Office of the President, Carnegie Corporation of New York, 437 Madison Avenue, New York, NY 10022, USA. *Telephone:* (212) 371-3200. *Fax:* (212) 223-8831 (Office).

GREGSON, Sir Peter Lewis, GCB, MA, FRSA, CIMgt; British civil servant; b. 28 June 1936, Yorkshire; s. of late Walter Henry Gregson and the late Lillian Margaret Gregson; ed Nottingham High School, Balliol Coll., Oxford and London Business School; Nat. Service 1959–61; official Bd of Trade 1961–68; Pvt. Sec. to the Prime Minister 1968–72; Asst Sec., Dept of Trade and Industry, also Sec. Industry, Industrial Devt Bd 1972–74; Under Sec., Dept of Industry, also Sec., Nat. Enterprise Bd 1975–77; Under Sec., Dept of Trade 1977–80, Deputy Sec. 1980–81; Deputy Sec., Cabinet Office 1981–85; Perm. Under-Sec. of State, Dept of Energy 1985–89; Perm. Sec., Dept of Trade and Industry 1989–96; Dir Scottish Power PLC 1996–, Woolwich PLC 1998–2000 (Chair. Woolwich Pension Fund Trust Co. Ltd 1999–2000). *Leisure interests:* gardening, listening to music. *Address:* Scottish Power PLC, 1 Atlantic Quay, Glasgow, G2 8SP, Scotland. *Telephone:* (141) 248-8200.

GREGURIĆ, Franjo, DSc; Croatian politician; b. 12 Oct. 1939, Lobor, Zlata Bistrica; m. Jozefina Greguric (née Abramović); one s. one d.; ed Univ. of Zagreb; worked in chemical factories; tech. Dir Radonia at Sisak; Dir-Gen. Chromos factory, Zagreb; rep. of Foreign Trade Co. Astra in Moscow, Gen. Dir Astra-Int. Trade, Zagreb –1990; Vice-Dir, then Dir Chamber of Econs, Zagreb; mem. Christian Democratic Union (CDU); Deputy Premier of Croatia 1990; Prime Minister 1991–92; mem. of Croatian Parl. for Sabor 1990–; Adviser to Pres. of Croatia 1992–, apptd. Special Del. (with rank of Amb.) to Croat-Bosnian Fed. and Bosnia and Herzegovina 1997; Dir INA Co., Zagreb 1992–; numerous nat. and int. awards for econs. *Leisure interests:* oenology, pomology. *Address:* Ilica 49, 41000 Zagreb, Croatia. *Telephone:* (41) 517-230 (Office). *Fax:* (41) 650-110.

GREČIUS, Vytautas, LLM; Lithuanian judge; b. 9 May 1949, Tauragė; m. Teresė Greičuis; one d. two s.; ed Faculty of Law, Vilnius Univ.; Judge Ukmergė Dist People's Court 1976–90; Judge Supreme Court of Lithuania 1990–94, Chair. Div. of Criminal Cases 1995–99, Pres. of Supreme Court 1999–. *Address:* Supreme Court, Gyneju 6, 2600 Vilnius (Office); Fabijoniškiu 43-42, 2000 Vilnius, Lithuania (Home). *Telephone:* (5) 2610560 (Office). *Fax:* (5) 2627950 (Office). *E-mail:* lat@tic.lt (Office). *Website:* www.lat.litlex.lt (Office).

GREIG, Geordie Carron, MA; British journalist; b. 16 Dec. 1960, London; s. of Sir Carron Greig and Monica Greig (née Stourton); m. Kathryn Elizabeth Terry 1995; one s. two d.; ed Eton, St Peter's Coll., Oxford; reporter South East London and Kentish Mercury 1981–83, Daily Mail 1984–85, Today 1985–87; reporter The Sunday Times 1987–89, Arts Corresp. 1989–91, New York Corresp. 1991–95, Literary Ed. 1995–99; Ed. of Tatler 1999–. *Publications:* Louis and the Prine 1999. *Address:* Tatler, Condé Nast Publications Ltd, Vogue House, Hanover Square, London, W1S 1JU, England (Office). *Telephone:* (20) 7499-9080 (Office). *Fax:* (20) 7409-0451 (Office).

GREIG, Sir (Henry Louis) Carron, KCVO, CBE, DL; British businessman; b. 21 Feb. 1925, London; s. of Sir Louis and Lady Greig; m. Monica Stourton 1955; three s. one d.; ed Eton Coll. and Royal Military Coll., Sandhurst; Scots Guards 1943–47, attained rank of Capt.; joined Horace Clarkson and Co. Ltd 1948, Dir 1954, Man. Dir 1962, Chair. 1973–85; Chair. Horace Clarkson Holdings PLC 1976–93; Dir James Purdey and Sons Ltd 1972–2000; Baltic Exchange Ltd 1978–82, Vice-Chair. 1982, Chair. 1983–85; Dir Williams and Glyn's Bank 1983–85, Royal Bank of Scotland 1985–95; Gentleman Usher to HM the Queen 1961–95. *Address:* Brook House, Fleet, Hants., England; Binsness, Forres, Moray, Scotland. *Telephone:* (1252) 617596; (1309) 672334.

GREILSAMER, Laurent, LèsL; French journalist; b. 2 Feb. 1953, Neuilly; s. of Marcel Greilsamer and Francine Alice Greilsamer; m. Claire Méheut 1979; three s.; ed Ecole Supérieure de Journalisme, Lille; Le Figaro 1974–76, Quotidien de Paris 1976; ed. Le Monde 1977–84, sr reporter 1984–94, 1994–; Prix des lectrices de Elle 1999. *Publications:* Interpol, le siège de soupçon 1986, Un certain Monsieur Paul, L'affaire Touvier 1989, Hubert Beuve-Méry 1990, Enquête sur l'affaire du sang contaminé 1990, Les juges parlent 1992, Interpol, Policiers sans frontières 1997, Le Prince foudroyé, la vie de Nicholas de Staël 1998, Où vont les juges? 2002. *Leisure interests:* painting, reading. *Address:* c/o Le Monde, 21 bis, rue Claude Bernard, 75005 Paris, France. *Telephone:* 1-42-17-26-05 (Office). *Fax:* 1-42-17-21-22 (Office). *E-mail:* greilsamer@lemonde.fr (Office).

GREINER, Walter Albin Erhard, PhD, FRSA; German physicist; b. 29 Oct. 1935, Neuenbau/Thür; s. of Albin and Elsa (Fischer) Greiner; m. Bärbel Chun 1960; two s.; ed Univs. of Darmstadt and Freiburg; Research Asst, Univ. of Freiburg 1961–62; Asst Prof., Univ. of Md, USA 1962–64; Prof. and Dir Inst. of Theoretical Physics, Univ. of Frankfurt am Main 1965–; Guest Prof., numerous univs. worldwide; Adjunct Prof., Vanderbilt Univ., Nashville, Tenn., USA and Oak Ridge Nat. Lab., Tenn. 1978, 1979, 1981; Perm. Consultant, Gesellschaft für Schwerionenforschung, Darmstadt 1976–97; European Ed. Int. Journal of Modern Physics 1991–; Ed. Foundations of Physics, Heavy Ion Physics; Hon. Prof. (Beijing Univ.) 1988; Hon. DSc (Witwatersrand) 1982; Max Born Prize, Inst. of Physics, UK 1974; Otto Hahn Prize, Frankfurt 1982; Hon. mem. Lorand Eötvös Soc. (Budapest) 1989, Romanian Acad. of Science 1992; Dr. hc (Tel Aviv) 1991, (Louis Pasteur Univ., Strasbourg) 1991, (Bucharest) 1992, (Lajos Kossuth Univ., Hungary) 1997; Alex von Humboldt Medal 1998. *Publications:* Nuclear Theory (with Eisenberg) (3 Vols) 1972, Lectures on Theoretical Physics (12 Vols), Dynamics of Heavy-Ion Collisions (with Cindro and Ricci), Quantum Electrodynamics of Strong Fields (jtly.) 1985; Experimental Techniques in Nuclear Physics (with D. N. Poenarů), Handbook of Nuclear Properties (with D. N. Poenarů), Heavy Elements and Related Phenomena (with R. K. Guph); over 500 papers in nat. and int. journals. *Leisure interests:* music, mycology, fishing, walking, swimming. *Address:* Institut für Theoretische Physik, Johann Wolfgang Goethe Universität, Robert Mayer Strasse 8–10, 60054 Frankfurt am Main, Germany.

GRENFELL, 3rd Baron, cr. 1902, of Kilvey; **Julian Pascoe Francis St Leger Grenfell;** British politician; b. 23 May 1935, London; s. of the late 2nd Baron Grenfell of Kilvey; m. 1st Loretta Reali 1961 (divorced 1970); one d.; m. 2nd Gabrielle Raab 1970 (divorced 1987); two d.; m. 3rd Elizabeth Porter Scott 1987 (divorced 1992); m. 4th Dagmar Langbehn Debreil 1993; ed Eton Coll., King's Coll., Cambridge; Second Lt, Kings Royal Rifle Corps 1954–56; Pres. Cambridge Union 1959; Capt. Queen's Royal Rifles (Territorial Army) 1963; television journalist 1960–64; with World Bank 1965–95, Chief of Information and Public Affairs in Europe 1969–72, Deputy Dir European Office 1973–74, Special Rep. to the UN Orgs 1974–81, Adviser HQ 1983–90, Head External Affairs, European Office 1990–95, Sr Adviser European Affairs 1995–; mem. UK del. to Council of Europe 1997–99; sits in the House of Lords as Lord Grenfell of Kilvey 1999–; Chair. House of Lords Sub-Cttee on Econ. and Financial Affairs 1998–, mem. Select Cttee on EU 1999; Labour. *Publication:* Margot (novel) 1984. *Leisure interest:* writing fiction. *Address:* 24 rue Chaptal, 75009 Paris, France (Home); c/o House of Lords, London, SW1A 0PW, England. *Telephone:* (20) 7219-3210. *Fax:* (20) 7219-4931.

GRENIER, Jean-Marie René, LIC. EN DROIT; French business executive; b. 27 June 1926, Paris; s. of Henri Grenier and Germaine Pissavy; m. Marie-Alix Bonnet de Paillerets 1958; three s. one d.; ed Lycée Fustel-de-Coulanges,

Strasbourg, Ecole Bossuet, Lycée Louis-le-Grand, Faculté de Droit, Paris and Ecoles des Hautes Etudes Commerciales, Paris; Deputy Dir Soc. des Usines Chimiques Rhône-Poulenc 1962, Dir 1970, Commercial Dir 1971; Dir Rhône-Poulenc SA 1977–82; Pres. Syndicat de l'industrie chimique organique de synthèse et biochimie 1975–84, Hon. Pres. 1984–; Chevalier Ordre nat. du Mérite, Croix de la valeur militaire. *Leisure interest:* tennis. *Address:* Le Moulin Pocancy (Marne), 51130 Vertus; 74 rue Claude Bernard, 75005 Paris, France (Home). *Telephone:* (3) 26-70-93-15; 1-47-07-79-82 (Home).

GRENS, Elmars; Latvian molecular biologist; b. 9 Oct. 1935, Riga; s. of Janis Grens and Melita Grené; m. Eva Stankevich 1957; one s. one d.; ed Latvian State Univ.; researcher, Head of Lab., Research Dir Inst. of Organic Synthesis Latvian Acad. of Sciences 1958–90, Dir Inst. of Molecular Biology, Latvian Acad. of Sciences 1991–93; Dir Biomedical Research and Study Centre, Univ. of Latvia 1993–; mem. Latvian Acad. of Sciences, Academia Europaea; main research in molecular biology of viruses, fine biotech., genetic eng. *Publications include:* RNA Bacteriophages 1957; more than 180 scientific articles. *Leisure interest:* downhill skiing. *Address:* Biomedical Research and Study Centre, University of Latvia, Ratsupites 1, Riga 1067, Latvia. *Telephone:* 780-8003. *Fax:* 744-2407. *E-mail:* grens@biomed.lu.lv (Office).

GRETZKY, Wayne; American ice hockey player; b. 26 Jan. 1961, Brantford, Canada; s. of Walter Gretzky and Phyllis Gretzky; m. Janet Jones 1988; two s. one d.; fmr player with Edmonton; played with Los Angeles Kings 1988–96, with St Louis Blues 1996, with NY Rangers 1996–99; retd 1999; most prolific scorer in Nat. Hockey League history; Most Valuable Player (nine times); winner Stanley Cup with Edmonton (four times); record points scored 2,857, 894 goals, 1,963 assists; investor Los Acros Sports LLC/Phoenix Coyotes, 1999–; owns restaurant in Toronto, Canada; Hockey Hall of Fame 1999. *Publication:* Gretzky: An Autobiography (with Rick Reilly). *Address:* c/o Phoenix Coyotes, Cellular One Ice Den, 9375 E Bell Road, Scottsdale, AZ 85260, USA.

GREVISSE, Fernand; French judge and public servant; b. 28 July 1924, Boulogne-Billancourt; m. Suzanne Seux 1958; two d.; ed Ecole Nationale d'Administration; apptd. Auditeur, Conseil d'Etat 1949, Maître des Requêtes 1956; apptd. Head of Office of Minister of Justice 1959; Dir-Gen., Water Resources and Forests, Ministry of Agric. 1964–65, Rural Areas 1965–66; Head of Office of Minister of State in charge of civil service April–July 1967; Dir-Gen., Admin. and Civil Service Dept, Govt Secr.-Gen. 1967–71; mem. Conseil d'Etat 1973–, Chair. Public Works Section 1984–88, Hon. Chair. 1988, mem. Consultative Comm.; Prof., Institut d'études politiques de Paris 1977–80; Chair. Centre d'études supérieures du management public 1977–79; Judge, EC Court of Justice 1981–82, 1988–89, 1989–94; Commdr Légion d'honneur, Médaille militaire, Commdr Ordre nat. du Mérite, Croix de guerre. *Address:* 28 rue Desaix, 75015 Paris, France (Home).

GREY, Dame Beryl Elizabeth, DBE; British prima ballerina; b. 11 June 1927, London; d. of Arthur Ernest and Annie Elizabeth Groom; m. Sven Gustav Svenson 1950; one s.; ed Dame Alice Owens School, London, Madeline Sharp School, Royal Ballet School and de Vos School of Dance; début Sadler's Wells Co. 1941; Prima Ballerina with Royal Ballet until 1957; freelance int. prima ballerina since 1957; first full-length ballet Swan Lake on 15th birthday; has appeared since in leading roles of classical and numerous modern ballets including Giselle, Sleeping Beauty, Sylvia, Casse Noisette, Les Sylphides, Checkmate, Donald of the Burthens, Dante Sonata, Three Cornered Hat, Ballet Imperial, Lady and the Fool, Les Rendezvous; American, Continental, African, Far Eastern tours with Royal Ballet since 1945; guest artist European Opera Houses in Norway, Finland, Sweden, Denmark, Belgium, Romania, Germany, Italy, etc.; guest artist South and Central America, Middle East, Union of South Africa, Rhodesia, Australasia; first foreign guest artist ever to dance with the Bolshoi Ballet in Russia 1957–58 (Moscow, Leningrad, Kiev, Tiflis) and first to dance with Peking Ballet and Shanghai Ballet 1964; Dir-Gen. of Arts Educational Trust, London 1966–68; Artistic Dir of London Festival Ballet 1968–79; produced and staged Giselle, Perth, Australia 1984, 1986, Sleeping Beauty, Royal Swedish Ballet, Stockholm 1985, 2002; Pres. Dance Council for Wales 1982–, E Grinstead Operatic Soc. 1986–, Keep-fit Soc. 1992–93; Vice-Pres. Fed. of Music Festivals, The Music Therapy Charity 1980–, Royal Acad. of Dancing 1981–, E Grinstead Music Arts Festival 1991–; Chair. Imperial Soc. Teachers of Dancing 1982–91, Pres. 1991–2001, Life Pres. 2002–, Fellow; Gov. Royal Ballet 1993, Vice-Chair. 1995–2002; a Dir Birmingham Royal Ballet 1995–99; a Dir Royal Opera House, Covent Garden 1999–; Trustee of Royal Ballet Benevolent Fund (Chair. 1992–), Dance Teachers' Benevolent Fund (Vice-Chair. 1987–), Discs 1994–; Patron Dancers Resettlement Trust, Benesh Inst., Language of Dance Centre, Lisa Ullman Travelling Scholarship Fund 1986–, Friends of Sadler's Wells 1991–, Furlong Hip Replacement 1993–, Osteopathic Centre for Children 1994–, Sussex Opera and Ballet Soc. 2001–; Theatre Design Trust for Dance 1995–; Hon. DMus (Leicester) 1970, (London) 1996; Hon. DLit (City of London) 1974, (Buckingham) 1993; Hon. DEd (CNAA) 1989; Queen Elizabeth II Coronation Award, Royal Acad. of Dancing 1996, Critics Circle Service to Dance Award 2002. *Publications:* Red Curtain Up 1958, Through the Bamboo Curtain 1965; My Favourite Ballet Stories (ed.) 1981. *Leisure interests:* piano playing, painting, swimming, opera. *Address:* Fernhill, Priory Road, Forest Row, East Sussex, RH18 5JE, England. *Telephone:* (1342) 822539. *Fax:* (1342) 822539 (Home).

GREY-THOMPSON, Tanni (Carys Davina), OBE; British athlete; b. Tanni Carys Davina Grey, 26 July 1969, Cardiff; d. of Peter Grey and Sulwen Grey (née Jones); m. Ian Thompson 1999; one d.; ed Loughborough Univ.; represented GB in Paralympics 1988, 1992, 1996, 2000, in Olympics 1992, 1996, 2000; winner gold medals for 100m, 200m, 400m and 800m wheelchair races, Sydney Paralympics 2000; winner women's wheelchair race, London Marathon 1992, 1994, 1996, 1998, 2001, 2002; has broken over 20 world records 2001; Devt Officer UK Athletics 1996–2001; mem. Sports Council for Wales 1996–, for UK Sport 1998–2003; TV presenter and motivational speaker; Vice-Pres. Women's Sports Foundation; Deputy Chair. UK Lottery Sports Fund; Patron Youth Sport Trust, British Sport Trust, Nat. Blood Service; mem. Nat. Disability Council 1997–2000, organizing council Manchester Commonwealth Games 2002; Hon. Fellow Univ. of Swansea 2001; numerous hon. degrees; BBC Wales Sports Personality of the Year (twice), Welsh Hall of Fame 1992, Sunday Times Sportswoman of the Year 1992, 2000, Sportswriters Award 2000, mem. elect World Sports Acad. 2001. *Radio:* numerous appearances including as presenter The Rush Hour, BBC Radio Wales 1995–96, Sportfirst, BBC Radio 5 1995–96. *Television:* numerous appearances including as presenter From the Edge, BBC2 1998–2000, X-Ray, BBC Wales 2002. *Publication:* Seize the Day: My Autobiography 2001. *Address:* Creating Excellence, Equity House, 1st Floor, Knight Street, South Woodham Ferrers, Chelmsford, Essex, CM3 5ZL, England (Office). *Telephone:* (1245) 328303 (Office). *Fax:* (1245) 323512 (Office). *E-mail:* enquiries@creatingexcellence.co.uk (Office).

GRIER, Pam; American actress, writer and singer; b. 26 May 1949, Winston-Salem, NC; d. of Clarence Ransom Grier and Gwendolyn (Sylvia) Samuels; mem. Acad. of Motion Picture Arts and Sciences. *Films:* The Big Doll House 1971, Women in Cages 1971, Big Bird Cage 1972, Black Mama, White Mama 1972, Cool Breeze 1972, Hit Man 1972, Twilight People 1972, Coffy 1973, Scream, Blacula, Scream! 1973, The Arena 1973, Foxy Brown 1974, Bucktown 1975, Friday Foster 1975, Sheba Baby 1975, Drum 1976, Greased Lightning 1977, Fort Apache: The Bronx 1981, Something Wicked This Way Comes 1983, Stand Alone 1985, The Vindicator 1986, On the Edge 1986, The Allnighter 1987, Above The Law 1988, The Package 1989, Class of 1999 1991, Bill and Ted's Bogus Journey 1991, Tough Enough, Posse 1993, Serial Killer 1995, Original Gangstas 1996, Escape from LA 1996, Mars Attacks! 1996, Strip Search 1997, Fakin' Da Funk 1997, Jackie Brown 1997, No Tomorrow 1998, Jawbreaker 1999, Holy Smoke 1999, In Too Deep 1999, Fortress 2 1999, Snow Day 2000, Wilder 2000, 3 A.M. 2001, Love the Hard Way 2001, Bones 2001, John Carpenter's Ghosts of Mars 2001, Undercover Brother 2002, The Adventures of Pluto Nash 2002, Baby of the Family 2002. *Television includes:* (mini-series) Roots: The Next Generations 1979; (films) Badge of the Assassin 1985, A Mother's Right: The Elizabeth Morgan Story 1992, Family Blessings. *Stage appearances:* Fool for Love, Frankie and Johnnie, In the Claire De Lune; Best Actress NAACP 1986. *Leisure interests:* skiing, scuba diving, western and English horseback riding, tennis.

GRIERSON, Philip, MA, LittD, FBA, FSA; British historian; b. 15 Nov. 1910, Dublin; s. of Philip Henry Grierson and Roberta Ellen Jane Pope; ed Marlborough Coll., Gonville and Caius Coll., Cambridge; Univ. Lecturer in History, Cambridge 1945–59; Reader in Medieval Numismatics, Cambridge 1959–71; Prof. of Numismatics, Univ. of Cambridge 1971–78, Emer. Prof. 1978–; Prof. of Numismatics and History of Coinage, Univ. of Brussels 1948–81; Ford's Lecturer in History, Univ. of Oxford 1956–57; Fellow, Gonville and Caius Coll., Cambridge 1935–, Librarian 1944–69, Pres. 1966–76; Literary Dir Royal Historical Soc. 1945–55; Hon. Keeper of the Coins, Fitzwilliam Museum, Cambridge 1949–; Adviser in Byzantine Numismatics to Dumbarton Oaks Library and Collection, Harvard Univ., Washington, DC, USA 1955–98; Pres. Royal Numismatic Soc. 1961–66; Corresp. mem. Koninklijke Vlaamse Acad. 1955; Assoc. mem. Acad. Royale de Belgique 1968; Corresp. Fellow, Medieval Acad. of America 1972; Hon. LittD (Ghent) 1958, (Leeds) 1978; Hon. LLD (Cambridge) 1993. *Publications:* Les Annales de Saint-Pierre de Gand 1937, Books on Soviet Russia 1917–42 1943, Sylloge of Coins of the British Isles, Vol. I (Fitzwilliam Museum: Early British and Anglo-Saxon Coins) 1958, Bibliographie numismatique 1966, English Linear Measures: a study in origins 1973, Catalogue of the Byzantine Coins in the Dumbarton Oaks Collection and in the Whittemore Collection, Vols I, II and III (with A. R. Bellinger) 1966–73, Vol. V 1999, Numismatics 1975, Monnaies du Moyen Age 1976, The Origins of Money 1977, Les monnaies 1977, Dark Age Numismatics 1979, Later Medieval Numismatics 1979, Byzantine Coins 1982, Medieval European Coinage, 1: The Early Middle Ages (5th–10th Centuries) (with M. Blackburn) 1986, 14: Italy (III) (with Lucia Travaini) 1998, Coins of Medieval Europe 1991, Catalogue of the Late Roman Coins in the Dumbarton Oaks Collection and in the Whittemore Collection (with M. Mays) 1992, Scritti storici e numismatici 2001; Ed.: C. W. Previté-Orton, The Shorter Cambridge Medieval History 1952, H. E. Ives, The Venetian Gold Ducat and its Imitations 1954, Studies in Italian History presented to Miss E. M. Jamison 1956, O. Mørkholm, Early Hellenistic Coinage (with U. Westermark) 1991; trans. Feudalism (F. L. Ganshof) 1952. *Leisure interest:* science fiction. *Address:* Gonville and Caius College, Cambridge, CB2 1TA, England. *Telephone:* (1223) 332450. *Fax:* (1223) 332456.

GRIERSON, Sir Ronald Hugh, Kt, MA; British/German banker; b. 6 Aug. 1921, Nuremberg, Germany; s. of Ernest Grierson and Gerda Grierson; m. Elizabeth Heather, Viscountess Bearsted 1966 (died 1993); one s. one step-d.; ed Realgymnasium, Nuremberg, Lycée Pasteur, Paris, Highgate School,

London and Balliol Coll. Oxford; Dir S.G. Warburg & Co. Ltd 1948–86; Deputy Chair. and Chief Exec. Industrial Reorganization Corpn 1966–68; Chair. Orion Bank 1970–73; Dir-Gen. for Industry and Tech., Comm. of the European Communities 1973–74; Dir Chrysler Corpn, W. R. Grace, Inc. 1987; Dir General Electric Co. PLC 1968–91, Vice-Chair. 1983–91; Chair. GEC Inc. 1984–, Bain & Co. Int. 1988–, Advisory Bd Blackstone Group 1989–, GEC Int. 1992–, Daily Mail & Gen. Trust 1993–; Exec. Chair. South Bank Centre 1985–90; Dir W. R. Grace & Co. 1987–94; Hon. DCL (Grove City Coll., Pa) 1986; Commdr's Cross, Order of Merit (Germany) 1993; Officier, Légion d'honneur 1994. *Address:* 5-7 Carlton Gardens, Stirling Square, London, SW1Y 5AD, England.

GRIFFEY, George Kenneth (Ken), Jr; American baseball player; b. 21 Nov. 1969, Donora, Pa; s. of Ken Griffey Sr (fmr professional baseball player); m. Melissa Griffey; one s.; one d.; ed Moeller High School, Cincinnati; outfielder Seattle Mariners 1987–99, Cincinnati Reds 1999–; on numerous All Star teams 1990–96; numerous records including eight for home runs in consecutive games; supports actively various charities including Make-a-Wish Foundation; many TV and media appearances including The Simpsons; Baseball Player of the Year 1986, 1987, Most Valuable Player 1990, 10 Golden Glove Awards. *Address:* Cincinnati Reds, 100 Cinergy Field, Cincinnati, OH 45202, USA.

GRIFFIN, Jasper, MA, FBA; British classical scholar; b. 29 May 1937, London; s. of Frederick William Griffin and Constance Irene Cordwell; m. Miriam Tamara Dressler 1960; three d.; ed Balliol Coll., Oxford; Jackson Fellow, Harvard Univ. 1960–61; Dyson Research Fellow, Balliol Coll., Oxford 1961–63, Fellow and Tutor in Classics 1963–, Univ. Reader 1989–, Prof. of Classical Literature 1992–, Public Orator 1992–; T. S. Eliot Memorial Lectures, Univ. of Kent 1984. *Publications:* Homer on Life and Death 1980, Snobs 1982, Latin Poets and Roman Life 1985, The Mirror of Myth 1985, Virgil 1986; Ed. The Oxford History of the Classical World 1986, Homer: The Odyssey 1987, The Iliad: Book Nine 1995; articles and reviews. *Leisure interests:* music, wine. *Address:* Balliol College, Oxford, England. *Telephone:* (1865) 277782.

GRIFFITH, Alan Richard, MBA; American banker; b. 17 Dec. 1941, Mineola, NY; s. of Charles E. Griffith and Amalie Guenther; m. Elizabeth Ferguson 1964; one s. one d.; ed Lafayette Coll. and City Univ. of New York; Asst credit officer, The Bank of New York 1968–72, Asst Vice-Pres. 1972–74, Vice-Pres. 1974–82, Sr Vice-Pres. 1982–85, Exec. Vice-Pres. 1985–88, Sr Exec. Vice-Pres. 1988–90, Pres. 1990–94, Vice-Chair. 1994–. *Address:* The Bank of New York, 1 Wall Street, New York, NY 10286, USA. *Telephone:* (212) 635-1030 (Office). *Fax:* (212) 635-1200 (Office).

GRIFFITH, Gavan, AO, QC, LLM, DPhil; Australian lawyer; b. 11 Oct. 1941, Melbourne; s. of F. E. Griffith; m. Vanessa Fitts 1968; one s. three d.; ed Melbourne Univ. and Magdalen Coll. Oxford; barrister 1963; QC 1981; Solicitor-Gen. of Australia 1984–97; del. to UN Int. Trade Law Comm. (UNCITRAL) 1984–, Vice-Chair. 1987–88, 1994–95; Agent and Counsel for Australia at Int. Court of Justice 1989–95; mem. Perm. Court of Arbitration, The Hague 1987–99; mem. Intelsat Panel of Legal Experts 1988–97, Chair. 1993–94; del. Hague Conf. of Pvt. Int. Law 1992–97; Arbitrator, Int. Comm. for Settlement of Int. Disputes (ISCID) 1994–; Consultant, Office of Legal Counsel, UN, New York 1994–95; Dir Australian Centre for Int. Commercial Arbitration 1997–; mem. Council, Nat. Gallery of Australia 1986–92; Visiting Fellow, Magdalen Coll. Oxford 1973–74, 1976, 1980, 1995; Order of the Repub. of Austria. *Publications:* contribs. to various legal journals and books. *Address:* Owen Dixon Chambers, 205 William Street, Melbourne, Vic. 3000, Australia (Office). *Telephone:* (613) 9225-7658 (Office); (614) 1925-0666. *Fax:* (613) 9225-8974 (Office). *E-mail:* griffithqc@aol.com (Office); griffithqc@aol.com (Home).

GRIFFITH, Kenneth; Welsh actor, director and writer; b. 12 Oct. 1921, Tenby; grandson of Ernest Griffiths and Emily Griffiths; m. three times, divorced three times; three s. two d.; ed Tenby Council School and Tenby Grammar School; began acting at Festival Theatre, Cambridge 1938; Old Vic (under Tyrone Guthrie) 1942 and 1944; Royal Air Force 1942–44; has acted in approx. 100 films; researched, wrote and made over 25 factual films and films for TV, including lives of Cecil Rhodes, Michael Collins, Clive of India, Edmund Kean, Thomas Paine, David Ben Gurion, Roger Casement, Napoleon, Dr. Ambedkar, Alfred Dreyfus; made three films for centenary of Anglo-Boer War (Broadcasting Press Guild Award) 1999. *Publications:* Thank God We Kept the Flag Flying 1974, Curious Journey 1982, The Discovery of Nehru 1989, The Fool's Pardon (autobiog.) 1994. *Leisure interest:* postal history of the second British/Boer war (1899–1902). *Address:* Michael Collins House, 110 Englefield Road, Islington, London, N1 3LQ, England. *Telephone:* (20) 7226-9013.

GRIFFITH, Melanie; American actress; b. 9 Aug. 1957, New York; d. of Tippi Hedren and Peter Griffith; m. 1st Don Johnson 1975 (divorced 1976, remarried 1989, divorced 1993); one d.; m. 2nd Steven Bauer (divorced); m. 3rd Antonio Banderas 1996; one d.; ed Hollywood Professional School; moved to LA aged four. *Films:* Night Moves 1975, Smile 1975, The Drowning Pool 1975, One on One 1977, Underground Aces 1979, Roar, Fear City, Body Double 1984, Something Wild 1986, Stormy Monday 1987, The Milagro Beaufield War 1988, Working Girl 1988, Pacific Heights, Bonfire of the Vanities, Shining Through, Paradise 1991, A Stranger Amongst Us 1992, Close to Eden 1993, Born Yesterday 1993, Milk Money 1994, Nobody's Fool 1994, Now and

Then, Two Much, Mulholland Falls 1996, Lolita 1996, Shadow of Doubt 1998, Celebrity 1998, Another Day in Paradise 1998, Crazy in Alabama 1999, Cecil B. Demented 2000, Forever Lulu 2000, Life with Big Cats 2000, Tart 2001, Stuart Little 2 (voice) 2002. *Television:* Once an Eagle (mini-series), Carter Country (series), Coast to Coast, Steel Cowboy, Golden Gate, She's in the Army Now, Starmaker. *Address:* c/o Creative Artists Agency, 9830 Wilshire Boulevard, Beverly Hills, CA 90212, USA; 201 South Rockingham Avenue, Los Angeles, CA 90049. *Website:* www.melaniegriffith.com (Office).

GRIFFITH, Nanci; American singer, songwriter and guitarist; b. 6 July 1953, Seguin, Tex.; d. of Griff Griffith and Ruelene Griffith; fmr schoolteacher; appeared in Nanci Griffith on Broadway 1994. *Albums include:* There's A Light Beyond These Woods 1977, Once In A Very Blue Moon 1984, The Last Of The True Believers 1985, Poet In My Window 1986, Lone Star State of Mind 1987, Little Love Affairs 1988, One Fair Summer Evening 1988, Storms 1989, Late Night Grand Hotel 1991, The MCA Years – A Retrospective 1993, Other Voices, Other Rooms 1993 (Grammy Award for Best Folk Album), Flyer 1994. *Publications:* novels and short stories including Two Of A Kind Heart 1988, Love Wore A Halo Back Before The War.

GRIFFITHS, Alan Gordon, BEcons, LLB; Australian trade unionist, politician, entrepeneur and investment banker; b. 4 Sept. 1952, Melbourne; s. of Alan and Joy Griffiths; m. Sandra Griffiths 1970; one s.; three d.; ed Traralgon High School, Victoria, Monash Univ.; with Maurice Blackburn and Co. solicitors 1979–82; trade union industrial officer, Federated Rubber and Allied Workers' Union of Australia 1982–83; Labor mem. House of Reps for Maribyrnong, Vic. 1983–96; Jt Parl. Cttee Nat. Crime Authority 1984–87; Chair. House Reps Standing Cttee, Legal and Constitutional Affairs 1987–90; Minister for Resources and Energy 1990–93, for Tourism 1991–93, for Industry, Tech. and Regional Devt 1993–94; Chair. Griffiths Group Int. Pty Ltd 1996–; f., Exec. Chair. and Principal Quantm Ltd 1999–. *Leisure interests:* the arts, sport, politics, travel, sailing. *Address:* Level 4, 333 Flinders Lane, Melbourne, Vic. 3000, Australia (Office). *Telephone:* (613) 9620-3445 (Office). *Fax:* (613) 9620-3446 (Office). *E-mail:* alan.griffiths@quantm.net (Office). *Website:* www.quantm.net (Office).

GRIFFITHS, Phillip A., PhD; American professor of mathematics; b. 18 Oct. 1938, Raleigh, NC; s. of Phillip Griffiths and Jeanette Griffiths (née Field); m. 1st Anne Lane Crittenden 1958 (divorced 1967); one s. one d.; m. 2nd Marian Jones; two d.; ed Wake Forest and Princeton Univs.; Univ. of Calif. (Berkeley) Miller Fellow 1962–64, 1975–76, Faculty mem. 1964–67; Princeton Univ. Visiting Prof. 1967–68, Prof. 1968–72; Harvard Univ. Prof. 1972–83, Dwight Parker Robinson Prof. of Math. 1983; Provost and James B. Duke Prof. of Math. Duke Univ. 1983–91; Guest Prof. Univ. of Beijing 1983; Dir Inst. for Advanced Study, Princeton 1991–; Chair. Science Insts Group 1999–; mem. NAS 1979–, N.S.B. 1991–96, Bd of Dirs Bankers Trust NY Corpn 1994–99, Bd of Dirs Oppenheimer Funds 1999–, Bd of Dirs GSI Lumonics 2001–; Sec. Int. Math. Union 1999–; Foreign Assoc. Third World Acad. of Sciences 2001–; hon. degrees from Wake Forest, Angers, Oslo and Beijing Univs; Guggenheim Fellow 1980–82; other awards and distinctions. *Publications:* some 90 articles in professional journals. *Leisure interest:* sailing. *Address:* Office of the Director, Institute for Advanced Study, Einstein Drive, Princeton, NJ 08540, USA. *Telephone:* (609) 734-8200 (Office). *Fax:* (609) 683-7605 (Office). *E-mail:* pg@ias.edu (Office). *Website:* www.ias.edu (Office).

GRIFFITHS, Terry; British snooker player; b. 16 Oct. 1947, Llanelli, Wales; s. of Martin Griffiths and the late Ivy Griffiths; m. Annette Jones 1968; two s.; turned professional snooker player 1978; Embassy World Champion 1979, Coral UIT Champion 1982, Benson & Hedges Masters Champion 1980, Benson & Hedges Irish Masters Champion 1981 (twice), 1982, Welsh Champion three times; Dir World Snooker 1999–2000; Coach The Sportsmasters Network 2000–. *Publications:* Championship Snooker, Complete Snooker, Griff. *Leisure interests:* golf, music, playing snooker. *Address:* 110sport Ltd, Spencers Leisure, Kerse Road, Stirling, FK7 7SG, Scotland. *Telephone:* (1786) 462634. *Fax:* (1786) 450068. *Website:* www.tsnsnooker.com.

GRIFFITHS, Trevor, BA; British playwright; b. 4 April 1935, Manchester; s. of Ernest Griffiths and Anne Connor; m. 1st Janice Elaine Stansfield 1961 (died 1977); one s. two d.; m. 2nd Gillian Cliff 1992; ed Manchester Univ.; taught English language and literature 1957–65; Educ. Officer, BBC 1965–72; Dir Saint Oscar 1990, The Gulf Between Us 1992, Who Shall be Happy...? 1995, Food for Ravens 1997; Writer's Award, British Acad. of Film and TV Artists 1981. *Film scripts:* Reds (with Warren Beatty, WGA Award 1981) 1981, Fatherland 1986. *Plays include:* Occupations 1972, The Party 1974, Comedians 1976, Oi for England 1981, Real Dreams 1984, The Gulf Between Us 1992, Thatcher's Children 1993, Who Shall Be Happy 1994. *TV includes:* All Good Men 1974, Through the Night 1976, Country 1981, Sons and Lovers 1982, The Last Place on Earth 1985, Hope in the Year, Two 1994, Food for Ravens 1997 (Royal TV Soc. Best Regional Programme 1998, Gwyn A. Williams Special Award, BAFTA Wales 1998). *Publications:* Occupations, Sam Sam 1972, The Party 1974, Comedians 1976, All Good Men, Absolute Beginners, Through the Night, Such Impossibilities, Thermidor and Apricots 1977, Deeds (co-author), The Cherry Orchard (trans.) 1978, Country 1981, Oi for England, Sons and Lovers (TV version) 1982, Judgement Over the Dead 1986, Fatherland, Real Dreams 1987, Collected Plays for TV 1988, Piano 1990, The Gulf Between Us 1992, Hope in the Year Two, Thatcher's Children

1994, Plays One (Collected Stage Plays) 1996, Food for Ravens 1998. *Address:* c/o Peters Fraser & Dunlop, Drury House, 34-43 Russell Street, London, WC2B 5HA, England. *Telephone:* (20) 7344-1000. *Fax:* (20) 7836-9539.

GRIFFITHS, Baron (Life Peer), cr. 1985, of Govilon in the county of Gwent; **William Hugh Griffiths,** Kt, MC, PC; British judge; b. 26 Sept. 1923; s. of late Sir Hugh Griffiths; m. 1st Evelyn Krefting 1949; one s. three d.; m. 2nd Baroness Brigstocke 2000; ed Charterhouse and St John's Coll. Cambridge; called to Bar, Inner Temple 1949, QC 1964; Treas. Bar Council 1968–69; Recorder of Margate 1962–64, Cambridge 1964–70; Judge, Queen's Bench Div., High Court of Justice 1971–80; Pres. Senate of Inns of Court and the Bar 1982–; a Lord Justice of Appeal 1980–85; a Lord of Appeal in Ordinary 1985–93; Chair. Security Comm. 1985–92; Chair. Advisory Cttee on Legal Educ. and Conduct 1991–93; Judge, Nat. Industrial Relations Court 1973–74; mem. Advisory Council on Penal Reform 1967–70; Vice-Chair. Parole Bd 1976–77; Capt. Royal and Ancient Golf Club, St Andrew's; mem. Chancellor's Law Reform Cttee 1976–93; Hon. mem. Canadian Bar Asscn 1981; Hon. Fellow American Inst. of Judicial Admin. 1985, American Coll. of Trial Lawyers 1988; Hon. LLD (Wales) 1987, (De Montfort) 1993. *Leisure interests:* golf, fishing. *Address:* c/o House of Lords, London, SW1A 0PW, England.

GRIFFITHS OF FFORESTFACH, Baron (Life Peer), cr. 1991, of Fforestfach in the County of West Glamorgan; **Brian Griffiths,** MSc; British professor of banking and international finance; b. 27 Dec. 1941; s. of Ivor Winston Griffiths and Phyllis Mary Griffiths (née Morgan); m. Rachel Jane Jones 1965; one s. two d.; ed Dynevor Grammar School and London School of Econs; Asst Lecturer in Econs, LSE 1965–68, Lecturer 1968–76; Dir Centre for Banking and Int. Finance, City Univ., London 1977–82, Prof. of Banking and Int. Finance 1977–85, Dean, City Univ. Business School 1982–85; Dir Bank of England 1984–86, mem. Panel of Acad. Consultants 1977–86; Head of Prime Minister's Policy Unit 1985–90; Chair. Centre for Policy Studies 1991–2000; Head School Examinations and Assessment Council 1991–93; Vice-Chair. Goldman Sachs (Europe) 1991–; Dir Thorn-EMI 1991–96, Hermann Miller 1991–, HTV 1991–93, Times Newspapers Ltd 1991–, Servicemaster 1992–, Telewest 1994–98, English, Welsh and Scottish Railway 1996–; Chair. Trillium 1998–, Westminster Health Care 1999–; Hon. Fellow Trinity Coll., Carmarthen 1997; Hon. DSc (City) 1999. *Publications:* Is Revolution Change? (ed. and contrib.) 1972, Mexican Monetary Policy and Economic Development 1972, Invisible Barriers to Invisible Trade 1975, Inflation: The Price of Prosperity 1976, Monetary Targets (co-ed. with G. E. Wood) 1980, The Creation of Wealth 1984, Monetarism in the United Kingdom (co-ed. with G. E. Wood) 1984, Morality and the Market Place 1989. *Leisure interests:* the family and reading. *Address:* c/o House of Lords, London, SW1A 0PW, England.

GRIGORESCU, Dan, MA, PhD; Romanian historian of culture and critic; b. 13 May 1931, Bucharest; s. of Vasile Grigorescu and Ecaterina Grigorescu (née Tomescu); m. Petrovan Valentina; one s. one d.; ed Bucharest Univ.; State Publishing House for Art and Literature 1954–58; museographer Nat. Museum of Art, Bucharest 1958–63; chief ed. Meridiane Publishing House 1963–68; Dir Fine Arts Dept, State Cttee for Culture and Arts 1968; Dir Romanian Library New York 1971–74; Prof. in Comparative Literature Bucharest Univ. 1963–; Dir G. Călinescu 1995; Inst. of Literary History and Theory, Romanian Acad.; Visiting Prof. Univ. of Wash., Seattle 1970–71, UCLA 1970; Vice-Pres. Int. Soc. for the History of Culture 1973–85; mem. Romanian Acad., Romanian Fine Arts Union, Romanian Writers' Union, Int. Asscn of Art Criticism, Int. Asscn of Comparative Literature, Int. Asscn for the History of Culture; R. W. Emerson Award 1973; Prize of the Romanian Acad. 1978. *Works include:* Shelley, a monograph 1962; Three Romanian Painters in the 1848 Revolution 1965, Expressionism 1969, Cubism 1971, Pop Art 1972, American Art – A History 1974, Tendencies in 20th Century Poetry 1975, Shakespeare and Romanian Modern Culture 1975, A Chronological Dictionary of American Literature 1977, The Buffalo's Song, an anthology of Indian American verse and prose 1978, The Adventures of the Image 1979, History of a Lost Generation—The Expressionists 1980, Brancusi 1982, Reality, Myth, Symbol: A Portrait of James Joyce 1984, North of Rio Grande 1986, Primitive and Modern Art 1988, A History of English Art 1989, Sentiment and Idea: Trends in Contemporary Romanian Art 1991, History of Culture and its Anxieties, The Twilight of Postmodernism 1992, Mr Rubens and His Voyages 1994, Columbus and the Flying Islands 1996, Introduction to Comparative Literature 1997, A History of American Art 1998, Brancusi and the World Art of the 20th Century 1999, The American Novel in the 20th Century 1999. *Address:* 7 Edgar Quinet, Bucharest 70118 (Office); 3-5 Vasile Conta, Bucharest 70138, Romania (Home). *Telephone:* (1) 4103200 (Office); (1) 3148334 (Home). *Fax:* (1) 4103200 (Office). *E-mail:* grigorescudan@hotmail.com (Home).

GRIGOROVICH, Yuriy Nikolayevich; Russian ballet-master; b. 2 Jan. 1927, Leningrad; s. of K. A. Grigorovich-Rozay and N. E. Grigorovich; m. Natalya Igorevna Bessmertnova; ed Leningrad Choreographic School and Lunarcharski Inst. of Theatrical Art, Moscow; soloist, Kirov (now Mariinsky) Theatre 1946–64, Ballet-Master 1962–64; Chief Ballet Master, Bolshoi Theatre, Moscow 1964–95; Chief Choreographer, Artistic Dir Kremlin Palace of Congresses Ballet 1998–; now works in various theatres in Russia and abroad; Ed.-in-Chief Soviet Ballet Encyclopaedia 1981; f. Bolshoi Ballet Grigorovich Co. (now Grigorovich-Ballet) 1990–; Lenin Prize 1970; People's Artist of USSR 1973, USSR State Prize 1985; Hero of Socialist Labour 1986. *Ballets include:* Stone Flower (Kirov-Mariinsky) 1957, Legend of Love (Kirov-Mariinsky) 1960, Sleeping Beauty (Bolshoi) 1963, Nutcracker (Bolshoi) 1966, Spartacus 1968, Swan Lake 1969, Ivan the Terrible 1975, Angara 1976, Romeo and Juliet (Paris) 1978, Giselle 1979, Golden Age (Bolshoi) 1982, Raymonda 1984, Bayaderka 1991, Elektra (Grigorovich Ballet co-produced with Melanin and Bobrov) 1992, La Fille Mal Gardée (Grigorovich Ballet) 1993, Le Corsaire (Bolshoi) 1994. *Address:* Sretenskii blvd 6/1, Apt. 9, Moscow, Russia. *Telephone:* (095) 925-6431 (Home).

GRIGORYANTS, Sergey Ivanovich; Russian human rights activist and journalist; b. 12 May 1941, Kiev; s. of Ivan Arkadievich Grigoryants and Vera Sergeevna Shenberg; m. Tamara Vsevolodovna Grigoryants; one s. (died 1995) one d.; studied Moscow Univ., was expelled by KGB 1968; f. and ed. Information Bulletin on violation of human rights in USSR 1982–83; imprisonment for political activities 1975–80, 1983–87; Founder, Ed. and Publr Glasnost magazine 1987–91, Glasnost Information Agency 1991–; Founder, Chair. Public Fund Glasnost 1990–; organized regular conf. KGB Yesterday, Today, Tomorrow; Head Centre on Information and Analysis, Russian Special Service 1993, Initiator of Int. Non-Governmental Tribunal on the War Crimes and Crimes Against Humanity in Chechnya; Co-Chair. Coalition for Support for Int. Criminal Court; Head Glasnost-Caucasus Information Agency 2000–; Gold Pen of Freedom Award, Medal of Bayern Lantague. *Publications:* contribs to New York Times and Washington Post. *Leisure interests:* collecting paintings, antiques, early medieval artefacts. *Address:* Tsvetnoi Boulevard, Building 2215, Apt. 40, 103051 Moscow (Office); 1st Naprudnaya Str. 3, Apt. 121, 129346 Moscow, Russia. *Telephone:* (095) 208-28-53 (Office); (095) 474-45-90 (Home). *Fax:* (095) 299-85-38 (Office); (530) 326-88-17. *E-mail:* fondglas@online.ru. *Website:* www.glasnostonline.org (Office).

GRIGORYEV, Anatoly Ivanovich, DrMed; Russian biologist and space scientist; b. 23 March 1943, Zhitomir region, Ukraine; s. of Ivan Grigoryevych Grigoryev and Olga Isakovna Grigoryeva; m. Dorokhova Bella Radikovna; two s.; ed Moscow 2nd Inst. of Med.; researcher, sr researcher, Head of Lab., Head of Div., Deputy Dir, Dir Inst. of Medical-Biological Problems, Ministry of Public Health 1966–; Chief Medical Commr Russian Cosmic Agency 1988–, Chief Medical Expert 1996–; Co-Chair., Jt Soviet-American Workgroup on Cosmic Biology and Med. 1989–92; Chair. Section on Sciences of Life, Int. Acad. of Astronautics 1989–93, Section of Space Medicine, Russian Acad. of Sciences 1991–, Scientific Council on Space Medicine, Russian Acad. of Med. 1993–; mem. Co-ordination Council Russian Fed., Ministry of Science and Tech. 1998–; mem. Aviacosmic Medical Asscn, USA 1991–, Int. Union of Physiological Sciences 1992–, Russian Acad. of Medicine 1993, New York Acad. of Sciences 1994, Int. Acad. of Sciences 1995–, Russian Acad. of Natural Sciences 1996, Russian Acad. of Sciences 1997, Russian R. Tsyolkovsky Acad. of Cosmonautics 1997–; Vice-Pres. Int. Acad. of Astronautics 1993–; Order, Sign of Hon. 1976, Labour Red Banner 1982, Banner of Labour (DDR) 1985; Dr hc (Lyon Univ.) 1989; USSR State Prize 1989, Russian Acad. of Medicine Prize 1996, Bointon Prize, American Astronautics Asscn 1995, 1999, Struckhold Prize, American Aviacosmic Asscn 1996, Françoise Xavier Banier Prize, Michigan Univ., USA 1999; S. Korolev and Yu. Gagarin Medals, USSR Fed. of Cosmonautics, Merited Worker of Science of Russia 1996. *Publications:* over 400 scientific Publs including 7 monographs and 22 patents. *Leisure interests:* music, theatre, historical literature. *Address:* Institute of Medical-Biological Problems, Khoroshovskoye shosse 76a, 123007 Moscow, Russia (Office). *Telephone:* (095) 195-15-73 (Office). *E-mail:* grigoriev@mmcc.ibmp.rssi.ru.

GRILLI, Enzo, PhD; Italian banker and economist; b. 7 Oct. 1943, Casarza Ligure; s. of Agostino Grilli and Dominica Giambruno Grilli; m. Mary A. Jacobs; two d.; ed Univ. of Genoa and Johns Hopkins Univ. USA; Dir Econ. Research, Confed. of Italian Industries, Rome 1978–80; Dir-Gen. Ministry of Budget and Planning 1982–84; Dir Econ. Advisory Staff, IBRD, Washington, DC 1989–92; Exec. Dir for Italy, Greece, Portugal, Albania and Malta, IBRD 1993–95; Exec. Dir for Italy, Greece, Portugal, Albania, Malta and San Marino, IMF, Washington, DC 1995–98; Prof. of Int. Econs. Johns Hopkins Univ. 1998–; Fulbright Fellow; Editorialist of Corriere della Sera; TV Commentator; St Vincent Prize for Econs 1995; Grand Officer of Italian Repub. 1981. *Publications:* The European Community and the Developing Countries 1993, Interdipendenze Macroeconomiche Nord–Sud 1995, Regionalism and Multilateralism after the Uruguay Round (ed.) 1997, Prospettive sullo Sviluppo dei Paesi Emergenti 1999. *Leisure interests:* reading, book collection, tennis. *Address:* 3917 Oliver Street, Chevy Chase, MD 20815, USA (Home).

GRIMLEY EVANS, Sir John, Kt, MA, MD, FRCP, FFPHM, FMedSci; British physician and academic; b. 17 Sept. 1936, Birmingham; s. of Harry Walter Grimley Evans and Violet Prenter Walker; m. Corinne Jane Cavender 1966; two s. one d.; ed King Edward's School, Birmingham, St John's Coll., Cambridge, Balliol Coll., Oxford; Visiting Scientist Univ. of Mich. 1966–67; Research Fellow, Wellington, New Zealand 1967–70; lecturer Univ. of London 1970–71; Prof. of Medicine Univ. of Newcastle-upon-Tyne 1973–84; Prof. of Clinical Geratology, Univ. of Oxford 1985–, Fellow Green Coll., Oxford 1985–; Consultant Physician, Oxford Hospitals 1985–; mem. MRC 1993–95, Chair. Health Services Research Bd 1990–95; Vice-Pres. Royal Coll. of Physicians 1993–95; Ed. Age and Ageing 1988–95, Oxford Textbook of Geriatric Medicine; Hon. Fellow Royal Soc. of Medicine 2000; Harveian Orator Royal Coll. of Physicians 1997. *Publications:* papers on epidemiology and gerontology. *Leisure interests:* literature, fly-fishing. *Address:* Green College, Oxford, OX2 6HG, England. *Telephone:* (1865) 224863. *Fax:* (1865) 224108.

GRIMMEISS, Hermann Georg, Dr rer. nat; Swedish physicist; b. 19 Aug. 1930, Hamburg, Germany; s. of Georg Grimmeiss and Franziska März; m. Hildegard Weizmann 1956; one s. one d.; ed Oberschule Nördlingen and Univ. of Munich; Prof. of Solid State Physics, Head of Dept Univ. of Lund 1965–96, Prof. Emer. 1996–, Dean for Research 1993–96; Chair. I.C.P.S. 1986; Chair. Nobel Symposium, Sweden 1996; mem. Programme Cttee for Physics-Math. Swedish Natural Science Research Council 1971–80; mem. Bd Swedish Nat. Cttee for Physics 1971–72, 1981–97; Prof. of Physics, Dir, Univ. of Frankfurt am Main 1973–74; mem. Cttee for Electronics, Swedish Bd for Tech. Devt 1978–80; mem. Bd Swedish-German Research Asscn 1980–; mem. f. Cttee Univ. Frankfurt/Oder (Germany) 1991–93; mem. Cttee for Science and Research, Brandenburg (Germany) 1993–95; Vice-Pres. RIFA (mem. Ericsson Group) 1981–83; Visiting Prof. Univ. of Calif. Berkeley 1990; Dir Inst. of Semiconductor Physics, Frankfurt (Oder), Germany 1991–93; mem. Bd Einstein Forum, Potsdam, Germany 1993–; mem. Exec. Cttee European Materials Research Soc. 2001–; mem. Int. Prize Cttee Global Energy, Moscow 2002–; mem. several other bds.; ed. and co-ed. several int. journals; mem. Royal Physiographic Soc. Lund, Royal Swedish Acad. of Eng Sciences, Royal Swedish Acad. of Sciences, Societas Scéntarium Sennica; Fellow, American Physical Soc.; Hon. mem. Roland Eötvös Physical Soc. 1983, Ioffe Inst., St Petersburg, Russia 1998; Order of North Star 1969, Bundesverdienstkreuz 1 Klasse 1993; King's Medal of 8th Dimension with Blue Ribbon, Stockholm 1998. *Publications:* more than 250 scientific publs in int. journals and books. *Leisure interests:* tennis, classical music. *Address:* Department of Solid State Physics, University of Lund, Box 118, 221 00 Lund (Office); Målsmansvägen 5, 224670 Lund, Sweden (Home). *Telephone:* (46) 2227675 (Office); (46) 140980 (Home). *Fax:* (46) 140980 (Home); (46) 2223403 (Office). *E-mail:* hermann .grimmeiss@ftf.lth.se (Office).

GRIMSHAW, Sir Nicholas Thomas, Kt, CBE, RA, FCSD, RIBA; British architect; b. 9 Oct. 1939, Hove; s. of Thomas Cecil Grimshaw and Hannah Joan Dearsley; m. Lavinia Russell 1972; two d.; ed Wellington Coll., Edinburgh Coll. of Art, Architectural Asscn School, London; Chair. Nicholas Grimshaw & Partners Ltd 1980–; Pres., Architectural Asscn, Council of Royal Acad.; Assessor for British Construction Industry Awards, RIBA, Dept of Environment; Hon. FAIA; Hon. DLitt; Hon. BDA; awards and commendations include: 15 RIBA awards 1975–2001; 7 Financial Times Awards for Industrial Architecture 1977–95; 12 Structural Steel Design Awards 1969–2001; 8 Civic Trust Awards 1978–96; 8 British Construction Industry Awards 1988–2001; 3 Royal Fine Art Comm./Sunday Times Bldg of the Year Awards 1989–94; 5 Concrete Soc. Awards 1995–2001; Constructa Preis for Industrial Architecture in Europe 1990; European Award for Steel Structures 1981; Quaternario Foundation Int. Awards for Innovative Tech. in Architecture; Gold Award 1993; Mies Van der Rohe Pavilion Award for European Architecture 1994; RIBA Bldg of the Year Award 1994; Design Innovation Award 1996; British Council for Offices Award 1996; Int. Brunel Award 1996; AIA (UK) Excellence in Design Award 2001; Leisure Property Award for Best Regeneration Scheme 2001; European Award for Aluminium in Architecture 2001. *Major projects include:* Channel Tunnel Terminal, Waterloo, London; British Pavilion for Expo '92, Seville; Berlin Stock Exchange and Communications Centre; British Airways Combined Operations Centre, Heathrow Airport, London; Financial Times Printing Plant; HQ for Igus GmbH, Cologne, Germany; head office and printing press for Western Morning News, Plymouth; BMW HQ, Bracknell; new satellite and piers, Heathrow Airport; Western Region HQ for RAC; Herman Miller Factory, Bath; Oxford Ice Rink; Gillingham Business Park; Research Centre for Rank Xerox; J. Sainsbury Superstore, Camden, London; redevt of Terminal One, Manchester Airport; New Teaching and Research Bldg, Univ. of Surrey; Regional HQ for Orange Telecommunications, Darlington; Railway Terminus, Pusan, Korea; redevt of Zürich Airport, Restoration of Paddington Station 1996; Restoration of Spa, new Bldg, Bath & E Somerset Council 1997; Caixa Galicia Foundation, La Coruña, Spain; Restoration of Battersea Power Station; Exhbn Hall for Frankfurt Fair; Eden Project, Cornwall; Nat. Space Science Centre, Leicester; Experimental Media and Performing Arts Center for Rensselaer Polytechnic Inst., Troy, NY, USA. *Publications:* Process 1988, Product 1988, Structure, Space and Skin 1993, Architecture, Industry and Innovation 1995, Equilibium 2000; articles for RSA Journal and RIBA Journal. *Leisure interests:* sailing, tennis. *Address:* 1 Conway Street, Fitzroy Square, London, W1T 6LR, England. *Telephone:* (20) 7291-4141. *Fax:* (20) 7291-4194 (Office). *E-mail:* ngp@ngrimshaw.co.uk (Office). *Website:* www.ngrimshaw.co.uk (Office).

GRÍMSSON, Ólafur Ragnar, PhD; Icelandic politician; b. 14 May 1943, Isafjörður; s. of Grimur Kristgeirsson and Svanhildur Ólafsdóttir; m. Guðrún Katrín Thorbergsdóttir 1974 (died 1999); two d. (twins); ed Reykjavik Higher Secondary Grammar School, Univ. of Manchester; fmr Lecturer in Political Science Univ. of Iceland, Prof. 1973; involved in production of political TV and radio programmes 1966–70; mem. Bd Progressive Party Youth Fed. 1966–73, Exec. Bd Progressive Party 1971-73, alt. mem. Althing representing East Iceland (Liberal and Left Alliance) 1974–75; Chair. Exec. Bd Liberal and Left Alliance 1974–75; mem. Althing for Reykjavik 1978–83, for Reykjanes 1991– (People's Alliance); Leader People's Alliance 1987–95; Minister of Finance 1988–91; Pres. of Iceland 1996–; Chair. Cttee on Relocation of Public Insts. 1972–75, Icelandic Social Sciences Asscn 1975, Organizing Cttee Parl. Conf. of Council of Europe 'North-South: Europe's Role' 1982-84, Parliamentarians for Global Action 1984–90 (also fmr Pres., mem. Bd 1990–); Vice-Chair. Icelandic Security Comm. 1979–90; mem. Bd Icelandic Broadcasting Service 1971–75, Nat. Power Co. 1983–88; mem. Parl. Ass. Council of Europe

1980–84, 1995–; fmr adviser to several Icelandic cos. *Address:* Office of the President, Staðastaður, Sóleyjargata 1, 150 Reykjavik, Iceland (Office). *Telephone:* 540-4400 (Office). *Fax:* 562-4802 (Office). *E-mail:* forseti@forseti .is (Office).

GRIMWADE, Sir Andrew (Sheppard), Kt, CBE, MA, FAIM; Australian industrialist; b. 26 Nov. 1930, Melbourne; s. of late Frederick Grimwade and Gwendolen Grimwade; m. Barbara Gaerloch Kater 1959 (died 1990); one s.; ed Melbourne Grammar School, Trinity Coll., Melbourne Univ., Oriel Coll. Oxford, England; Dir Commonwealth Industrial Gases Ltd 1960–90, Nat. Australia Bank Ltd 1965–85, IBM Australia 1975–82, Sony (Australia) 1975–82, Turoa Holdings Ltd 1975–82; Chair. Australian Consolidated Industries Ltd 1977–82; Vice-Chair. Nat. Mutual Life 1988– (Dir 1970–); mem. Australian Govt Remuneration Tribunal 1976–82; mem. First Australian Govt Trade Mission to China 1973; Pres. Walter and Eliza Hall Inst. of Medical Research 1978– (Bd mem. 1963–); Deputy Pres. Australiana Fund 1978–82; Trustee Nat. Gallery of Victoria, Trustee Emer. 1990–, Pres. 1976–90, mem. Felton Bequests Cttee 1973–; Trustee Victorian Arts Centre 1980–90; mem. Council for Order of Australia 1975–82. *Publication:* Involvement: The Portraits of Clifton Pugh and Mark Strizic 1969. *Leisure interests:* skiing, Santa Gertrudis cattle breeding, Australian art. *Address:* P.O. Box 134, East Melbourne, Victoria 3002, Australia. *Telephone:* (3) 9822-5990.

GRINDENKO, Tatyana Tikhonovna; Russian violinist; b. 29 March 1946, Kharkov, Ukraine; m. 1st Gidon Kremer (q.v.); m. 2nd Vladimir Martynov; ed Moscow State Conservatory; Prize, World Int. Youth Competition in Bulgaria 1968, Wieniawski Competition in Poland 1972; repertoire includes baroque, avant-garde, jazz, rock, experimental music; co-f. (with A. Lyubimov) and Artistic Dir. Moscow Acad. of Ancient Music. *Leisure interest:* driving sports cars. *Address:* Moscow State Philharmonia, Tverskaya str. 31, 103050 Moscow, Russia. *Telephone:* (095) 253 7425 (Home).

GRINDROD, Most Rev. John Basil Rowland, KBE, MA; Australian ecclesiastic; b. 14 Dec. 1919, Aughton; s. of Edward B. Grindrod and Dorothy G. (née Hunt) Grindrod; m. 1st Ailsa W. Newman 1949 (died 1981); two d.; m. 2nd Dell Judith Cornish 1983; ed Repton School, Univ. of Oxford and Lincoln Theological Coll.; ordained priest, Manchester; Rector All Souls, Ancoats 1956–60; Archdeacon of Rockhampton, Queensland 1960–65; Vicar of Christ Church, S Yarra, Melbourne 1965–66; Bishop of Riverina, NSW 1966–71; Bishop of Rockhampton 1971–80; Archbishop of Brisbane 1980–89, Primate of Anglican Church of Australia 1982–89. *Address:* 14B Thomas Street, Murwillumbah, NSW 2484, Australia. *Telephone:* (2) 6672-6640.

GRININ, Vladimir Mikhailovich; Russian diplomatist; b. 15 Nov. 1947; m.; one d.; ed Moscow State Inst. of Int. Relations, Diplomatic Acad., USSR Ministry of Foreign Affairs; mem. staff Ministry of Foreign Affairs 1970–, Dir 4th European Dept 1994–96, Dir Gen. Secr. 2000–; Amb. to Austria 1996–2000; mem. of Collegium. *Address:* Ministry of Foreign Affairs, Smolenskaya Sennaya 32/34, 121200 Moscow, Russia (Office). *Telephone:* (095) 244-92-47 (Office). *Fax:* (095) 244-92-48 (Office).

GRINSTEIN, Gerald, LLB; American business executive; b. 1932; m.; ed Yale and Harvard Univs; Counsel to merchant marine and transport subcttees., Chief Counsel, US Senate Commerce Cttee 1958–67; Admin. Asst to US Senator Warren Magnuson 1967–69; partner, Preston, Thorgrimson, Ellis & Holman 1969–73; Chair. Bd Western Air Lines Inc. LA 1983–84, Pres. and COO 1984–85, CEO 1985–86, Chair. and CEO 1986–87; Vice-Chair. Burlington Northern Inc. Fort Worth 1987–88, Pres., CEO 1989–90, Chair. 1990–96, CEO 1990–95; Pres., CEO Burlington Northern R.R. Co. 1989–90, Chair. 1990–96, CEO 1990–95; Chair. Delta Airlines Inc. 1997–99, Agilent Techs. 1999–; mem. Bd Dirs. Burlington Northern Inc., Seattle First Nat. Bank, Browning Ferris Industries Inc., Sundstrand Corpn, Expedia.com, Imperial Sugar Corpn. *Address:* 1000 2nd Avenue, Suite 3700, Seattle, WA 98104-1053, USA.

GRISEZ, Germain, MA, PhL, PhD; American professor of Christian ethics; b. 30 Sept. 1929, University Heights, Ohio; m. Jeannette Selby 1951; four c.; ed John Carroll Univ., Univ. Heights, Ohio, Dominican Coll. of St Thomas Aquinas, River Forest, Ill. and Univ. of Chicago; Asst Prof. to Prof. Georgetown Univ. Washington, DC 1957–72; part-time Lecturer in Medieval Philosophy, Univ. of Va, Charlottesville 1961–62; Special Asst to HE Cardinal O'Boyle, Archbishop of Washington 1968–69; consultant (part-time) Archdiocese of Washington 1969–72; Prof. of Philosophy, Campion Coll. Univ. of Regina, Canada 1972–79; Most Rev. Harry J. Flynn Prof. of Christian Ethics, Mount Saint Mary's Coll. Emmitsburg, Md 1979–; mem. Catholic Theol. Soc. of America, American Catholic Philosophical Asscn; Pro ecclesia et pontifice medal 1972; HE Cardinal Wright Award for service to the Church 1983 and other awards. *Publications:* The Way of the Lord Jesus, Vol. I, Christian Moral Principles (with others) 1983, Vol. II, Living a Christian Life (with others) 1993, Vol. III, Difficult Moral Questions (with others) 1997, Nuclear Deterrence, Morality and Realism (with J. Finnis and Joseph M. Boyle) 1987, Beyond the New Morality: The Responsibilities of Freedom (with R. Shaw) 3rd Edn 1988; numerous articles in learned journals. *Address:* Mount Saint Mary's College, 16300 Old Emmitsburg Road, Emmitsburg, MD 21727 (Office); Mount Saint Mary's College, Emmitsburg, MD 21727-7799, USA (Home). *Telephone:* (301) 447-5771. *Fax:* (301) 447-5755. *E-mail:* grisez@ msmary.edu (Office).

GRISHAM, John, BS, JD; American author and lawyer; b. 8 Feb. 1955, Jonesboro, Ark.; m. Renée Grisham; one s. one d.; ed Mississippi State Univ., Univ. of Mississippi, law school ; ran one-man criminal defence practice in Southhaven, Miss. 1981–90. *Publications:* A Time to Kill 1989, The Firm 1991, The Pelican Brief 1992, The Client 1993, The Chamber 1994, The Rainmaker 1995, The Runaway Jury 1996, The Partner 1997, The Street Lawyer 1998, The Testament 1999, The Brethren 2000, A Painted House 2001, Skipping Christmas 2001, The Summons 2002, The King of Torts 2003. *Address:* Doubleday & Co. Inc., 1540 Broadway, New York, NY 10036, USA. *Website:* www.jgrisham.com.

GROCHOLEWSKI, HE Cardinal Zenon; Polish ecclesiastic; b. 11 Oct. 1939, Bródki; s. of Stanisław Grocholewski and Józefa Grocholewski (née Stawińska); ed Archbishop's Seminary, Poznań, Pontifical Gregorian Univ., Rome, Studio Rotale, Rome; ordained priest 1963, parish work in Poznań 1963–66; studies in Rome 1966–72; Official of Supreme Tribunal of Apostolic Signatura 1972–82, Sec. 1982–98, Prefect 1998–99; consecrated Bishop 1983; mem. Pontifical Cttee for Int. Eucharistic Congresses 1989–2001; promoted to Archbishop 1991; Prefect Congregation for Catholic Educ. 1999–; mem. Congregation for Bishops 1999–, Pontifical Council for Interpretation of Legis. Texts 2000–; Congregation for the Doctrine of the Faith 2001–; cr. Cardinal 2001; Lecturer (later Prof.) in Canon Law, Pontifical Gregorian Univ. 1975–99, Pontifical Lateran Univ. 1980–89 and Studio Rotale 1986–98; Dr. hc (Acad. of Catholic Theology, Warsaw) 1998, (Catholic Univ. of Lublin) 1999, (Passau) 2001, (Glasgow) 2001, (Bratislava) 2002, (Catholic Univ. of Buenos Aires) 2002; Polonia Semper Fidelis Medal 1998, Grand Medal of St. Gorazd, Slovakia 2000; Hon. Citizen Trenton, NJ 1988, Princeton, NJ 1992, Agropoli, Italy 1992, Levoča, Slovakia 1997; Hon. mem. Pontifical Acad. of St Thomas Aquinas, Rome 2001. *Publications:* De exclusione indissolubilitatis ex consensu matrimoniali eiusque probatione 1973, Documenta recentoria circa rem matrimonialem et processualem, Vol. 1 (with I. Gordon) 1977, Vol. II 1980; La filosofía del derecho en las enseñanzas de Juan Pablo II y otros escritos 2001; four books in Slovakian, Hungarian and Polish and co-author of many other books. *Leisure interest:* tourism. *Address:* Congregazione per l'Educazione Cattolica, 00120 Cittädel Vaticano (Office); Palazzo della Cancelleria 1, 00186 Rome, Italy (Home). *Telephone:* (06) 69884156 (Office); (06) 69887546 (Home). *Fax:* (06) 69884156 (Office).

GROENING, Matthew, BA; American writer and cartoonist; b. 15 Feb. 1954, Portland, Ore.; s. of Homer Philip Groening and Margaret Ruth Wiggum; m. Deborah Lee Caplan; two c.; ed Evergreen State Coll.; cartoonist Life in Hell syndicated weekly comic strip, Sheridan, Ore. 1980–; Pres. Matt Groening Productions, Inc., LA 1988–, Bongo Entertainment, Inc., LA 1993–; creator The Simpsons interludes, The Tracey Ullman Show 1987–89; creator and Exec. Producer The Simpsons TV show 1989–; Founder and Publr Bongo Comics Group; Founder and Publr Zongo Comics (including Jimbo 1995, Fleener 1996); cartoonist for TV cartoon Futurama 1999. *Publications:* Love Is Hell 1985, Work Is Hell 1986, School Is Hell 1987, Childhood Is Hell 1988, Akbar and Jeff's Guide to Life 1989, Greetings from Hell 1989, The Postcards That Ate My Brain 1990, The Big Book of Hell 1990, The Simpsons Xmas Book 1990, Greetings from The Simpsons 1990, With Love from Hell 1991, The Simpsons Rainy Day Fun Book 1991, The Simpsons Uncensored Family Album 1991, The Simpsons Student Diary 1991, How to Go to Hell 1991, Maggie Simpson's Alphabet Book 1991, Maggie Simpson's Counting Book 1991, Maggie Simpson's Book of Colors and Shapes 1991, Maggie Simpson's Book of Animals 1991, The Road to Hell 1992, The Simpsons Fun in the Sun Book 1992, Making Faces with the Simpsons 1992, Bart Simpson's Guide to Life 1993, The Simpsons Ultra-Jumbo Rain-Or-Shine Fun Book 1993, Cartooning with the Simpsons 1993, Bongo Comics Group Spectacular 1993, Binky's Guide to Love 1994, Love Is Hell 10th Anniversary Edition 1994, Simpsons Comics Extravaganza 1994, Simpsons Comics Spectacular 1994, Bartman: The Best of the Best 1994, Simpsons Comics Simps-O-Rama 1995, Simpsons Comics Strike Back 1995, Simpsons Comics Wing Ding 1997, The Huge Book of Hell 1997; Bongo Comics.

GROENINK, Rijkman, LLB, MBA; Dutch banking executive; b. 25 Aug. 1949; ed Utrecht Univ., Manchester Univ.; joined Amro Bank 1974, apptd. Head of Syndicated Loans 1978, Head. of Int. Corp. Accounts, Int. Div. 1980–82, Man. Dutch Special Credit Dept 1982–86, Exec. Sr Pres. of Corp. Business 1986–90, mem. Man. Bd 1988–90, mem. Man. Bd ABN AMRO (following merger with ABN) 1990–, Chair. and CEO May 2000–; Dir Mondriaan Foundation, Rembrandt Soc., Dutch Bankers' Asscn. *Address:* ABN AMRO, Corporate Communications/Press Relations (HQ 1190), P.O. Box 283, 1000 EA, Amsterdam, Netherlands (Office). *Website:* www.abnamro.com (Office).

GROMOV, Aleksey Alekseyevich; Russian politician; b. 1960; m.; two c.; ed Moscow State Univ.; joined staff USSR Ministry of Foreign Affairs 1982, Attaché Prague embassy, Czech Repub. 1985–88, Sec. Office of the Deputy Minister 1988–91, First Sec. Gen. Office 1991–92, mem. Council Bratislava consulate of Russian Fed., Slovakia 1992–93, Counsellor 1993–96; Head Press Service of Russian President 1996–2000, Press Sec. 2000–. *Address:* The Kremlin, korp. 14A, Moscow, Russia (Office). *Telephone:* (095) 910-07-38 (Office). *Fax:* (095) 206-51-73 (Office). *E-mail:* agromov@prpress.gov.ru (Office).

GROMOV, Col-Gen. Boris Vsevolodovich; Russian army officer and politician; b. 7 Nov. 1943, Saratov; m. 2nd Faina Gromov; two s. two adopted d.; ed Leningrad Gen. Troops School, Frunze Mil. Acad., Gen. Staff Acad.;

mem. CPSU 1966–91; Commdr of platoon, co., Bn, Regt, div. 1965–87, Commdr 40 Army in Afghanistan 1987–89, Commdr of troops Kiev Command 1989–90, First Deputy Minister of Internal Affairs of USSR 1990–91, First Deputy Commdr of Armed Forces of CIS 1991–92, First Deputy Minister of Defence of Russia 1992–95; Chief Mil. Expert and Deputy Minister of Foreign Affairs 1995–97; mem. State Duma 1996–99, Chair. Sub-Cttee on Arms Control and Int. Security; Gov. of Moscow Region Jan. 2000–; f. war veterans' movt, Fighting Fraternity (later Honour and Homeland) 1997–; Hero of Soviet Union and other decorations. *Publication:* Memoirs of the Afghan War 1994. *Leisure interests:* tennis, bicycling. *Address:* Administration of Moscow Region, Staraya Pl. 6, 103070 Moscow, Russia. *Telephone:* (095) 206-68-62; (095) 206-60-42. *Fax:* (095) 928-98-12.

GROMOV, Mikhael, PhD; Soviet-born (now stateless) mathematician; b. 23 Dec. 1943, Boksitogorsk, USSR; s. of Lea Rabinovitz and Leonid Gromov; m. Margarita Gromov 1967; ed Univ. of Leningrad; Asst Prof., Univ. of Leningrad 1967–74; Prof., Univ. of New York, Stony Brook, USA 1974–81; Prof., Univ. of Paris VI, France 1981–82; Perm. Fellow, Dept of Math., Institut des Hautes Etudes Scientifiques 1982–; Foreign Assoc. mem. NAS (USA); Foreign mem. American Acad. of Arts and Sciences; Foreign Assoc., Académie des Sciences, Institut de France, mem. 1997–; Moscow Math. Soc. Prize 1971, Oswald Veblen Prize for Geometry, American Math. Soc. 1981, Prix Elie Cartan, Académie des Sciences, Paris 1984, Prix Union des Assurances de Paris 1989. *Publications:* Structures métriques pour les variétés riemanniennes 1981, Partial Differential Equations 1986. *Address:* Institut des Hautes Etudes Scientifiques, 35 route de Chartres, 91440 Bures-sur-Yvette (Office); 91 rue de la Santé, 75013 Paris, France (Home). *Telephone:* 1-69-07-48-53 (Office); 1-45-88-14-42 (Home).

GROMOV, Vassily Petrovich; Russian diplomatist; b. 10 Jan. 1936, Navesnoye, Orel Region; m.; two d.; ed Timiryazev Acad. of Agric., All-Union Acad. of External Trade; economist on Cuba 1961–68; on staff USSR Embassies in Chile, Mexico, Ecuador, Nicaragua; Div. of Latin America USSR Ministry of Foreign Affairs 1971–92; Amb. to Chile 1992–96; Dir Latin American Dept Ministry of Foreign Affairs 1996–98; Amb. to Brazil (also accred to Surinam) 1999–. *Address:* SES, Av. das Nações, Lote A, Quadra 801, CEP 70476-900, Brasília, DF Brazil (Office). *Telephone:* (61) 223-30-94 (Office); (61) 223-40-94 (Office). *Fax:* (61) 226-73-19 (Office). *E-mail:* embrus@linkexpress.com.br.

GROMYKO, Anatoly Andreyevich, D.HIST.SC.; Russian political scientist; b. 15 April 1932, Borisov; s. of Andrey Gromyko and Lidia Dmitrievna Gromyko; m.; two s. one d.; ed Moscow Inst. of Int. Relations; mem. CPSU 1956–91; First Sec., USSR Embassy in London 1961–65; Head of Int. Relations section, Africa Inst. of USSR Acad. of Sciences 1966–68; Head of Section for US Foreign Policy, Inst. of the United States and Canada (USSR Acad. of Sciences) 1968–73; Minister Plenipotentiary Wash. Embassy 1973–74, Berlin 1974–76; Dir Africa Inst. (USSR, now Russian, Acad. of Sciences) 1976–92; Pres. of Centre for Global and Strategic Studies (RAS), Africa Inst. 1992–94; living in Cyprus 1994–; Corresp. mem. of Acad. of Sciences 1981–; mem. Royal Acad. of Morocco 1992–, Russian Acad. of Political Science 1997; USSR State Prize 1980. *Exhibitions:* oil and acrylic paintings, Nicosia, Cyprus 1997; oil, acrylic and watercolours, Nicosia 1999. *Publications:* US Congress: Elections, Organization, Powers 1957, The 1,036 Days of President Kennedy 1968, The Foreign Policy of the USA: Lessons and Reality the 60's and 70's 1978, The Conflict in the South of Africa: international aspects 1979, Africa: Progress, Problems, Prospects 1981, Masks and Sculpture of Sub-Saharan Africa 1984, New Thinking in the Nuclear Age 1984, Kennedy Brothers 1985, Breakthrough (ed.) 1986, Will We Survive? (with others) 1989, Andrei Gromyko – In the Kremlin's Labyrinth 1997. *Leisure interest:* lawn tennis, painting. *Address:* c/o Africa Institute, Russian Academy of Sciences, 30/1 Alexey Tolstoy Str., Moscow 103001, Russia. *Telephone:* (095) 202-69-41 (Office); (5) 323255 (Cyprus). *Fax:* (095) 436-85-24 (Office). *E-mail:* alexey@gromyko.ru (Office). *Website:* www.gromyko.ru (Office).

GRONCHI, Divo, PhD; Italian banker; b. 21 Jan. 1939, Pisa; m. Anna Maria Alocchi; two c.; ed Univ. of Florence; employed at Banca Toscana 1958; joined Monte dei Paschi di Siena as Deputy Cen. Man. (Balance Sheets and Planning) 1988, Deputy Man. Dir 1993–96, Man. Dir and CEO 1996–2001; Chair. Credito Commerziale SpA 1990–91; mem. Bd Dirs. and CEO Monte Paschi Finanza Sim SpA 1988–95, Monte Paschi Mercato Sim SpA 1989–93, Mediocredito Toscano SpA 1992–93; Chair. Monte Paschi Vita SpA, Ticino Assicurazioni SpA, Ticino Vita SpA 1993; mem. Bd Dirs. and Exec. Cttee ABI (Italian Banking Asscn) 1995–, Istituto Bancario S. Paolo di Torino–IMI SpA (following merger with Istituto Mobiliare Italiano) 1998–; mem. Bd Cassa di Risparmio di Trento e Rovereto SpA 1995–96; Grand Officer, Order of Merit of Italian Repub. *Leisure interest:* reading. *Address:* c/o Banca Monte dei Paschi di Siena SpA, Piazza Salimbeni 3, 53100 Siena, Italy (Office).

GRØNDAHL, Kirsti Kolle; Norwegian politician; b. 1 Sept. 1943, Røyken; m. Svein Erik Groendahl 1967; two c.; mem. Røyken Municipal Council and Municipal Exec. Bd 1972–77, Chair. Røyken Labour Party 1980–82, Spikkestad Labour Party 1990–, mem. Labour Party's Cttee for Environment 1983–; mem Storting 1977–; mem. Standing Cttee on Church and Educ. 1977–85, on Foreign and Constitutional Affairs 1989–, Minister of Church and Educ. 1986–88, of Devt Co-operation 1988–89, Vice-Pres. 1990–93, Pres. 1993–; mem. Norwegian del. to Parl. Ass. of Council of Europe 1989–90; Leader del. to CSCE Parl. Ass. 1991–; mem. Nordic Council and of

Council's Presidium 1990–93, Leader Norwegian del. to Nordic Council 1992–93. *Address:* Stortinget, Karl Johansgt. 22, 0026 Oslo, Norway (Office). *Telephone:* 22-31-30-50 (Office). *Fax:* 22-31-38-50 (Office). *E-mail:* stortinget .postmottak@st.dep.telemax.no (Office). *Website:* www.stortinget.no (Office).

GRÖNEMEYER, Herbert; German actor, singer and composer; b. 12 April 1956, Goettingen; wrote first compositions for Bochum Schauspielhaus Theatre 1974; Musical Dir, actor Schauspielhaus 1975. *Film appearances include:* The Hostage 1975, Daheim unter Fremden 1979, Springtime Symphony 1983, Father and Sons 1986. *Albums:* 16 albums. *Theatre appearances include:* John, Paul, George, Ringo and Bert 1974, Spring Awakening 1976, The Winter's Tale 1978, The Merchant of Venice 1979, Big and Little 1982. *Address:* c/o ZBF Agentur, 80802 Munich, Germany (Office). *Telephone:* (30) 89355081 (Office). *E-mail:* groenland@groenemeyer.de (Office). *Website:* groenemeyer.de (Office).

GRONKIEWICZ-WALTZ, Hanna, LLD; Polish banker and lawyer; b. 4 Nov. 1952, Warsaw; m.; one d.; ed Warsaw Univ.; mem. of academic staff, Warsaw Univ. 1975–; expert on public and econ. law. Polish Parl. 1989; mem. of academic staff, Univ. of Cardinal Wyszy 1990–; Pres. Nat. Bank of Poland 1992–2000; mem. Solidarity Trade Union 1980; Chair. faculty Solidarity branch 1989–92; ind. cand. in presidential election 1995; Vice-Pres. EBRD 2001–; Dr. hc (Marie Curie-Skłodowska Univ., Lublin) 1999; Global Finance magazine award for Best Chair. of a Cen. Bank 1994, 1997, 1998, 1999, The Central European Award 1995, 1998, Życie Gospodarne Award 1995, The Warsaw Voice Award 1995. *Publications:* Central Bank from Centrally Controlled Economy to Market Oriented Economy: Legal Aspects 1993, Economic Law (co-author) 1996; over 50 works and articles in econ. and financial journals. *Leisure interests* American literature, classical music. *Address:* European Bank for Reconstruction and Development, 1 Exchange Square, London, EC2A 2EA, England (Office). *Telephone:* (20) 7338-6341 (Office). *E-mail:* gronkieh@ebrd.com (Office). *Website:* www.ebrd.com (Office).

GROS, André; French judge; b. 19 May 1908, Douai; s. of Maurice Gros and Adèle Berr; m. Dulce Simões-Corrêa 1940; two s.; ed Univs. of Lyon and Paris; Asst, Law Faculty Paris 1931, Asst Prof. Univ. Nancy 1935, Toulouse 1937, Univ. Prof. Public Law 1938–63; seconded to Ministry of Foreign Affairs 1939; Prof. Political Science Rio de Janeiro Univ. 1939, 1941–42; served France 1940; legal Counsellor to French Embassy in London; French Rep. on War Crimes Comm., London 1943; legal adviser to French Del. Council of Foreign Ministers and Peace Conf. Paris 1946; Legal Adviser Ministry of Foreign Affairs 1947; mem. Perm. Court of Arbitration, The Hague 1950; del. to Comm. for the Rhine 1950; Agent to Int. Court of Justice 1950–60; Conseiller d'Etat 1954; Judge, Int. Court of Justice, The Hague 1964; mem. Chamber of Court for delimitation maritime boundary Canada–U.S.A. 1982; mem. Inst. of Int. Law 1959, Vice-Pres. 1977–79; mem. UN Int. Law Comm. 1961; mem. Court of Arbitration in Beagle Channel case between Argentina and Chile 1977; mem. Court of Arbitration between France and UK (continental shelf delimitation) 1977; mem. Court of Arbitration between Senegal and Guinea-Bissau (delimitation of maritime boundary) 1986, Hon. Master of the Bench (Inner Temple) 1972; Commdr, Légion d'honneur, Croix de guerre (1939–45). *Publications:* Survivance de la raison d'état 1932, Problèmes politiques de l'Europe 1942–44 (Spanish trans. 1943), La Convention de Genève sur les pêcheries 1959, Traités et documents diplomatiques (with Paul Reuter) 1960, La protection diplomatique (in Encyclopédie française) 1964. *Leisure interests:* reading, golf. *Address:* Hôtel Beau-Rivage, Lausanne, 6 Ouchy, CH-1000, Switzerland (Home).

GROS, Francisco Roberto André, BA; Brazilian/French banker and economist; b. 21 April 1942, Rio de Janeiro; s. of André Paul Adolphe Gros (q.v.) and Dulce Simões Corrêa Gros; m. 1st Sandra Mattmann 1968; m. 2nd Isabel Teixeira Mendes; two s. one d.; ed Woodrow Wilson School of Public and Int. Affairs, Princeton Univ., USA; Founding mem. Brazilian Securities and Exchange Comm. 1977–81; Exec. Dir in charge of investment banking activities, Unibanco–Banco de Investimento do Brasil 1981–85; Exec. Dir Nat. Devt Bank (BNDES) 1985–87; Pres. Cen. Bank of Brazil Feb.–May 1987, 1991–92; Pres. and CEO Aracruz SA (eucalyptus pulp exporter) 1987–89; Founding Partner and CEO BFC Banco SA, Rio de Janeiro 1989–91, 1993; Man. Dir Morgan, Stanley and Co., New York 1994–2000; Pres. and CEO Nat. Devt Bank (BNDES) 2000–01; Pres. and CEO Petrobras 2002–; several Brazilian decorations; Officier Légion d'honneur. *Leisure interests:* travel, tennis, fishing. *Address:* Rua Paulo Cezar de Andrade 200, apt. 902, Rio de Janeiro, 22221-090 Brazil. *Telephone:* (21) 2556-3511. *Fax:* (21) 2556-3368 (Home). *E-mail:* fgros@uol.com.br (Home).

GROS, François; French biochemist; b. 24 April 1925, Paris; s. of Alexandre Gros and Yvonne Haguenauer; m. 1st Françoise Chasseigne (divorced 1963); m. 2nd Danièle Charpentier 1964; three s.; ed Lycée Pasteur, Neuilly, Univs of Toulouse and Paris, Rockefeller Inst., Univ. of Illinois, USA; joined CNRS 1947, Researcher, Lab. Prof. J. Monod 1955, Head of Research 1959–62, Scientific Dir 1962–; Head of Dept Inst. de Biologie Physico-chimique 1963–69; Prof., Faculté des Sciences de Paris 1968, Inst. Pasteur 1972, Collège de France (Chair in Cellular Biochemistry) 1973–; Dir Inst. Pasteur 1976–81, Dir of Biochemistry Unit 1981; Adviser to Prime Minister 1981–85; mem. EC's CODEST 1984–90; Pres. Asscn Franco-Israélienne pour la recherche scientifique et tech. 1983, Scientific Council of Asscn Française de lutte contre la myopathie 1987–; Scientific Council of Nat. Agency for Research into AIDS 1989–; Chief Ed. Bulletin de la Société de chimie

biologique 1964; Perm. Sec. Science Acad. (France) 1991–; mem. Nat. Consultative Cttee on the Ethics of Life and Health Sciences 1990–94; mem. EU Ass. on Science and Tech. 1994–97; mem. Inst. de France 1979–, Perm. Sec. 1991–2000, Hon. Perm. Sec. 2001–; mem. Institut Français, Acad. des Sciences, NAS, Acad. of Athens, Indian Nat. Acad. Sciences 1990; Assoc. mem. Acad. Royale de Belgique; Officier Légion d'honneur; Commdr Ordre nat. du Mérite; several foreign decorations; Dr hc (Weizmann Inst., Israel); Gold Medal, Pontifical Acad. of Sciences 1964, Fondation Lacassagne Prize 1968, Charles Léopold Mayer Prize, Acad. des Sciences 1969, Alexander von Humboldt Prize 1990. *Publications:* Initiation à la biochimie (with others); Sciences de la vie et société (with others) 1979, Les secrets du gène 1986, La civilisation du gène 1989, L'ingénierie du vivant 1990, Regard sur la biologie contemporaine 1992. *Leisure interests:* music, drawing. *Address:* Institut de France, 23 quai Conti, 75006 Paris (Office); 102 rue de la Tour, 75116 Paris, France. *Telephone:* 1-45-04-80-63. *E-mail:* gros-zajdman@academie-sciences .fr (Office).

GROSS, John Jacob, MA; British author, editor and publisher; b. 12 March 1935, London; s. of late Abraham and Muriel Gross; m. Miriam May 1965 (divorced 1988); one s. one d.; ed City of London School, Wadham Coll., Oxford; Ed. with Victor Gollancz Ltd 1956–58; lecturer, Queen Mary Coll., Univ. of London 1959–62, Hon. Fellow 1988; Fellow of King's Coll., Cambridge 1962–65; Asst Ed. Encounter 1963–65; Literary Ed. New Statesman 1972–73; Ed. Times Literary Supplement 1974–81; Literary Ed. Spectator 1983; journalist, New York Times 1983–88; theatre critic Sunday Telegraph 1989–; Dir Times Newspapers Holdings Ltd (fmrly Times Newspapers Ltd) 1982; editorial consultant The Weidenfeld Publishing Group 1982; a Trustee Nat. Portrait Gallery 1977–84; Fellow Queen Mary Coll. 1987; Duff Cooper Memorial Prize 1969. *Publications:* The Rise and Fall of the Man of Letters 1969, James Joyce 1971, Shylock, The Oxford Book of Aphorisms (ed.) 1983, The Oxford Book of Essays (ed.) 1991, The Modern Movement (ed.) 1992, The Oxford Book of Comic Verse (ed.) 1994, The New Oxford Book of English Prose (ed.) 1998, A Double Thread 2001. *Address:* Sunday Telegraph, 1 Canada Square, Canary Wharf, London, E14 5DT (Office); 74 Princess Court, Queensway, London, W2 4RE, England.

GROSS, Mgr Stanislav, LLM; Czech politician; b. 30 Oct. 1969, Prague; m. 2nd Šárka Gross; two d.; ed Charles Univ., Prague; mem. Czechoslovakia Democratic Party, Vice-Chair. 2000–; mem. Parl. 1992–; Minister of the Interior 2000–; Deputy Prime Minister 2002–; Vice-Chair. Cttee for Defence and Security 1994–; Vice-Chair. of Parl. 1998–2000; Cross of Honour First Class 2002. *Leisure interests:* country music, football, hockey. *Address:* Úřad vlády České republiky, Nábřeží E. Beneše 4, Prague 1, 1100 Czech Republic (Office). *Telephone:* (2) 4002111 (Office). *Website:* www.vlada.cz (Office).

GROSSART, Sir Angus McFarlane McLeod, Kt, CBE, LL.D., D.L., FRSE; British merchant banker and company director; b. 6 April 1937; s. of William John White Grossart and Mary Hay Gardiner; m. Gay Thomson 1978; one d.; ed Glasgow Acad. and Gasgow Univ.; mem. Faculty of Advocates 1963; practised at Scottish Bar 1963–69; Man. Dir Noble Grossart Ltd Merchant Bankers, Edin. 1969–, Chair. 1990–; Chair. Scottish Investment Trust PLC 1975–2003; Dir of numerous cos. including Royal Bank of Scotland PLC 1982– (Vice-Chair. 1996–), Scottish and Newcastle 1998–, Trinity Mirror PLC 1998–; Chair. Bd of Trustees Nat. Galleries of Scotland 1988–97; Trustee Nat. Heritage Memorial Fund 1999– and other public and charitable appointments; Hon. LLD (Glasgow) 1985, Hon. DBA (Strathclyde) 1998; Livingstone Captain of Industry Award 1990, Lord Provost of Glasgow Award for public service 1994. *Leisure interests:* golf, the applied and decorative arts, Scottish castle restoration. *Address:* c/o 48 Queen Street, Edinburgh, EH2 3NR, Scotland.

GROSSER, Alfred, DèsSc; French professor, author and journalist; b. 1 Feb. 1925, Frankfurt; s. of the late Paul Grosser and Lily (née Rosenthal) Grosser; m. Anne-Marie Jourcin 1959; four s.; ed Univs of Aix en Provence and Paris; Asst Dir UNESCO Office in Germany 1950–51; Asst Prof. Univ. of Paris 1951–55; lecturer, later Prof. Inst. d'études politiques 1954, Prof. Emer. 1992; Dir Studies and Research, Fondation nat. des Sciences politiques 1956–92; with Ecole des hautes études commerciales 1961–66, 1986–88, with Ecole Polytechnique 1974–95; Political Columnist La Croix 1955–65, 1984–, Le Monde 1965–94, Ouest-France 1973–, L'Expansion 1979–89; Pres. Centre d'information et de recherche sur l'Allemagne contemporaine 1982–, Eurocréation 1986–92 (Hon. Pres. 1992–); mem. Bd L'Express 1998–; Grosses Verdienst Kreuz mit Stern 1995; Grand Ofiicer Légion d'Honneur 2001; Dr hc (Aston, Birmingham, UK) 2001, (European Univ. of Humanities, Minsk, Belarus) 2001; Peace Prize, Union of German Publrs 1975; Grand Prix, Acad. des Sciences Morales et Politiques 1998. *Publications:* L'Allemagne de l'Occident 1953, La démocratie de Bonn 1958, Hitler, la presse et la naissance d'une dictature 1959, La Quatrième Republique et sa politique extérieure 1961, La politique extérieure de la Ve République 1965, Au nom de quoi? Fondements d'une morale politique 1969, L'Allemagne de notre temps 1970, L'explication politique 1972, les Occidentaux: Les pays d'Europe et les Etats Unis depuis la guerre 1978, Le sel de la terre. Pour l'engagement moral 1981, Affaires extérieures: la politique de la France 1944–84, 1984 (updated 1989), L'Allemagne en Occident 1985, Mit Deutschen streiten 1987, Vernunft und Gewalt. Die französische Revolution und das deutsche Grundgesetz heute 1989, Le crime et la mémoire 1989 (revised 1991), Mein Deutschland 1993, Allemagne (jtly.) 1994, Was ich denke 1995, Les identités difficiles 1996, Une Vie de français (memoirs) 1997, Deutschland in Europa 1998, Les fruits de leur arbre: regard athée sur les Chrétiens 2001, L'Allemagne de Berlin 2002. *Leisure interest:* music. *Address:* 8 rue Dupleix, 75015 Paris, France (Home). *Telephone:* 1-43-06-41-82 (Home). *Fax:* 1-40-65-00-76 (Home). *E-mail:* grosser .alfred@wanadoo.fr.

GROTENFELT, Georg Erik Jan; Finnish architect; b. 7 June 1951, Helsinki; s. of Nils Grotenfelt and Antonia Marsman; m. Hannele Grönlund 1992; one d.; ed Helsinki Polytechnic Univ.; Sr Tutor and Lecturer, Dept of Architecture, Helsinki Univ. of Tech. 1984–96, Prof. of Wood Architecture 2001–;Sr Tutor and Lecturer, Helsinki Univ. of Art and Design 1990–95; Visiting Prof. Technische Universität Graz 1997–98; projects include wooden saunas, leisure bldgs and family homes. *Has directed documentary films including:* Pinega-Bjarmaland återfunnet 1994, Herrgårdarna 1996, The Last Karelians 1998, Silent Rhapsody 2000. *Leisure interests:* photography, tennis, books, yoga. *Address:* Kapteeninkatu 8F, 00140 Helsinki (Office); Kapteeninkatu 20D, 00140 Helsinki (Home); Teknillinen Korkeakoulu, P.O. Box 1000, 02015 Helsinki, Finland. *Telephone:* 2609621 (Office); 625184 (Home); (9) 4511. *Fax:* (9) 4512017. *Website:* www.hut.fi (Office).

GROTTANELLI DE' SANTI, Giovanni, LLD; Italian lawyer; b. 1928, Livorno; m. Felicity Bennett 1962; three c.; ed Ginnasio Liceo E.S. Piccolomini, Siena, Univ. of Siena, Yale Law School and Coll. of Europe, Bruges; admitted to bar 1952; Univ. Asst 1955; law clerk, Constitutional Court, Rome 1956–62; Asst in Constitutional Law, Univ. of Rome 1956–62; libero docente (constitutional law), Univ. of Siena 1962; also taught at Univ. of Florence; Visiting Fellow, Wolfson Coll. Cambridge 1981–82; Visiting Fellow Commoner, Trinity Coll. Cambridge 1985; Visiting lecturer, Tulane Law School, Univ. of Ga Law School, Dean Rusk Center of Int. and Comparative Law, Athens, Ga 1991; Chair. Monte dei Paschi di Siena 1992–98, Italian Int. Bank 1993–, Accad. Chigiana di Siena 1993–; Deputy Chair. Monte Paschi Banque 1993–; mem. Bd British Inst. of Florence 1993–, Fondo Interbancario Tutela dei Depositi 1993–, Associazione Bancaria Italiana 1993–, Consorzio Siena Ricerche 1993–, IMI SpA 1995–, IMI Int. 1996–. *Publications:* books, articles and reviews on constitutional and comparative law.

GROUÈS, Henri (called Abbé Pierre); French ecclesiastic and philanthropist; b. 5 Aug. 1912, Lyons; s. of Antoine Groués and Eulalie Perra; ed Collège des Jésuites and Univ. of Lyons; entered Capuchin Order 1930; left for health reasons 1938; ordained priest 1938; almoner at the hosp. of La Mure and in charge of the Groupements de Jeunesse and the Orphanage of the Côte Ste. André 1940, vicar of Grenoble Cathedral 1941; f. an escape org. through the Alps and the Pyrenees, f. the Cttee against forced labour; joined Free French Forces in Algiers as Almoner to the Fleet 1944; Deputy for Meurthe-et-Moselle 1946–51; organized help for the destitute and the homeless in France and abroad and cr. the Centre d'Emmaüs through an appeal to public opinion; f. the revue Faims et Soifs 1954; Grand Officier, Légion d'honneur 1981, Croix de guerre (2 citations avec palmes), Médaille de la Résistance, Médaille des Evadés, Médaille des Combattants Volontaires, Médaille des Maquisards Belges, Médaille Albert Schweitzer 1975. *Publications:* 23 mois de vie clandestine, Vers l'homme, Feuilles éparses (poems), L'Abbé Pierre vous parle, Emmaüs 1959, Pleine vie, Le scandale de la faim interpelle l'église, Abbé Pierre Emmaüs ou Venger l'homme 1979, Revue 'Faims et Soifs' des hommes, Le Mystère de la joie 1985, Dieu et les hommes 1993, Testament 1994, Mémoire d'un croyant 1997. *Address:* La Halte d'Emmaüs, 76690 Esteville, France.

GROVE, Andrew S., PhD; American business executive; b. 1936, Budapest, Hungary; m.; two c.; ed City Coll. of New York and Univ. of California Berkeley; Fairchild Instrument & Camera Co. 1963–67; Pres. and COO Intel Corpn, Santa Clara, Calif. 1967–87, Pres. 1987–98, CEO 1987–98, Chair. 1998–; also mem. Bd Dirs.; mem. Nat. Acad. of Eng; Hon. DSc (City Coll. of NY) 1985; Hon. D. Eng (Worcester Polytechnic Inst.) 1989; 1997 "Time" Man of the Year; Heinz Family Foundation Award for Tech. and Economy 1995; other awards and distinctions. *Publication:* Only the Paranoid Survive 1996. *Address:* Intel Corporation, P.O. Box 58119, 2200 Mission College Boulevard, Santa Clara, CA 95052, USA. *Telephone:* (408) 765-1904 (Office). *Fax:* (408) 765-1739 (Office).

GRUDZINSKI, Przemyslaw, PhD; Polish diplomatist and academic; b. 30 Oct. 1950, Torun; m.; two c.; ed Univ. of Nicolaus Copernicus, Torun, Inst. of History, Polish Acad. of Sciences, Warsaw; Prof., Inst. of History, Polish Acad. of Sciences 1976–96; Adviser to Deputy Minister of Nat. Defence 1990; Dir Bureau of Research and Dir.-Gen. of the Sejm (Parl.) 1991; Deputy Minister of Nat. Defence 1992–93; Prof. Marshall European Centre for Security Studies, Germany 1994–97; Under-Sec. of State, Ministry of Foreign Affairs 1997–2000; Amb. to USA 2000–; mem. Solidarity Movt 1980s; Founder-mem. Euro–Atlantic Asscn 1994, Council on Foreign Policy, Warsaw 1996; Fellow, American Council of Learned Socs. 1978–80, Fulbright Fellow, Princeton Univ. 1988, Visiting Fellow, Princeton Univ. 1978–80, 1988, Univ. of Southern Calif., UCLA 1989. *Publications include:* The Future of Europe in the Ideas of Franklin D. Roosevelt 1933–1945 1987, Scientists and Barbarians: The Nuclear Policy of the United States 1939–45 1987, Theology of the Bomb: The Origins of Nuclear Deterrence Vols 1–3 1988, A Critical Approach to European Security: Identity and Institutions 1999; numerous articles in professional journals. *Leisure interests:* walking, mountains. *Address:* Embassy of Poland, 2640 16th Street, NW, Washington, DC 20009, USA (Office). *Telephone:* (202) 234-3800 (Office). *Fax:* (202) 328-6271 (Office). *E-mail:* information@ioip.com. *Website:* www.polandembassy.org.

GRUENBERG, Erich, OBE, FRCM, FGSM; British violinist and music teacher; b. 12 Oct. 1924, Vienna, Austria; s. of Herman and Kathrine Gruenberg; m. Korshed Madan 1956; two d.; ed in Vienna, Jerusalem and London; Leader, Philomusica of London 1954–56, Stockholm Philharmonic Orchestra 1956–58, London Symphony Orchestra 1962–65, Royal Philharmonic Orchestra 1972–76; leader of London String Quartet and mem. Rubbra-Gruenberg-Pleeth Piano Trio in 'fifties; now appears as soloist with leading orchestras in Britain and abroad; taught at Royal Coll. of Music 1960–65; fmr Prof. Guildhall School of Music and Drama 1981; Prof. Royal Acad. of Music; winner, Carl Flesch Int. Violin Competition. *Leisure interests:* family, garden, sport. *Address:* c/o Intermusica Artists' Management, 16 Duncan Terrace, London, N1 8BZ; 80 Northway, Hampstead Garden Suburb, London, NW11 6PA, England. *Telephone:* (20) 7278-5455; (20) 8455-4360. *Fax:* (20) 7278-8434.

GRUEVSKI, Nikola; Macedonian economist and politician; b. 31 Aug. 1970, Skopje; ed Univ. Kliment Ohridski, Bitola; with Credit Dept, Foreign Dept, then Currency Dealing, Balkanska Banka ad Skopje 1993–95, Liquidity, Plan, Analyses and Securities Dept 1995–96; with Metal Bank, Frankfurt 1996–97, MG Finance PLC, London 1997, Flemings Private Asset Man. Ltd, London 1997–98; Minister without Portfolio, then Minister of Trade 1998–99; Minister of Finance 1999–, Pres. Security and Exchange Comm. 2000–; Pres. Broker's Asscn of Macedonia 1998–; financial affairs commentator, MTM TV, Skopje 1998–. *Publications:* The Macedonian Economy at a Crossroads – On the Way to a Healthier Economy 1998; numerous articles on econ. matters. *Address:* Ministry of Finance, Dame Gruev 14, 1000 Skopje (Office); Vasil Gjorgov 29-2/56, 1000 Skopje, Former Yugoslav Republic of Macedonia (Home). *Telephone:* (2) 116012 (Office). *Fax:* (2) 117280 (Office). *E-mail:* gruevski@finance.gov.mk (Office); gruevski@mol.com.mk (Home). *Website:* www.finance.gov.mk (Office).

GRUMBACH, Melvin Malcolm, MD, FAAS; American physician and university professor; b. 21 Dec. 1925, New York; s. of Emanuel Grumbach and Adele (Weil) Grumbach; m. Madeleine F. Butt 1951; three s.; ed Columbia Coll. and Columbia Univ. Coll. of Physicians and Surgeons; Resident in Pediatrics, Babies' Hosp., Presbyterian Hosp., New York, 1949–51; Visiting Fellow, Oak Ridge Inst. of Nuclear Studies 1952; Post-doctoral Fellow, Asst in Pediatrics, Johns Hopkins School of Medicine 1953–55; mem. Faculty, Columbia Univ. Coll. of Physicians and Surgeons 1955–65; Asst Attending Pediatrician, subsequently Assoc. Prof. of Pediatrics, Head of Pediatric Endocrine Div. and Postdoctoral Training Programme in Pediatric Endocrinology, Babies' Hosp. and Vanderbilt Clinic, Columbia-Presbyterian Medical Center 1955–65; Prof. of Pediatrics, Chair. Dept, Univ. of Calif. School of Medicine, San Francisco 1966–86, first Edward B. Shaw Prof. of Pediatrics 1983–, Acting Dir Lab. of Molecular Endocrinology 1987–89; Dir Pediatric Service Univ. of Calif. Hosps. 1966–86; Pres. Asscn of Pediatric Dept Chairmen 1973–75, Lawson Wilkins Pediatric Endocrine Soc. 1975–76, Western Soc. for Pediatric Research 1978–79, Endocrine Soc. 1981–82, American Pediatric Soc. 1989–90; Exec. Cttee Int. Soc. of Endocrinology 1984–92 (Hon. Pres. 2000–04); mem. NAS Inst. of Medicine; Fellow American Acad. of Arts and Sciences; Hon. mem. Royal Soc. of Medicine, London, etc.; Dr hc (Geneva) 1991, (Paris V) 2000; Joseph M. Smith Prize, Columbia Univ. 1962, Career Scientist Award, Health Research Council, New York 1961–66, Silver Medal, Bicentenary Columbia Coll. of Physicians and Surgeons 1967, Borden Award, American Acad. of Pediatrics 1971, Robert H. Williams Distinguished Leadership Award, Endocrine Soc. 1980, Alumni Gold Medal, Columbia Coll. of Physicians and Surgeons 1988, Fred Conrad Koch Award, Endocrine Soc. 1992, Lifetime Achievement Award: Medical Educ., American Acad. of Pediatrics 1996, John Howland Award, American Pediatric Soc. 1997 and many others. *Television:* NOVA: Sex Unknown (WBQH Boston, MA) 2001. *Publications:* numerous scientific and clinical papers and monographs. *Leisure interests:* tennis, gardening, literature. *Address:* Dept of Pediatrics, University of California San Francisco School of Medicine, San Francisco, CA 94143-0434, USA. *Telephone:* (415) 476-2244. *Fax:* (415) 476-4009. *E-mail:* grumbac@itsa.ucsf.edu.

GRUNBERG-MANAGO, Marianne, PhD; French biochemist; b. 6 Jan. 1921, Leningrad, USSR (now St Petersburg, Russia); d. of Vladimir Grunberg and Catherine Riasanoff; m. Armand Manago 1948 (deceased); one s. one d.; ed Univ. of Paris; Research Asst, subsequently Researcher then Sr Researcher, Nat. Centre for Scientific Research (CNRS) 1946–61, Head Dept of Biochem., Inst. of Physico-Chemical Biology 1959, Dir of Research, CNRS 1961, Head Biochem. Div. 1967–; Assoc. Prof., Univ. of Paris VII 1972–; Ed.-in-Chief Biochimie; Pres.-elect Int. Union of Biochemistry 1983, Pres. 1985–88; Vice-Pres. Comm. for Sciences and Tech., UNESCO 1985; Pres. Acad. des Sciences 1995– (Vice-Pres. 1994, mem. 1982–); mem. Soc. de Chimie Biologique, American Soc. of Biological Chemists, Int. Council of Scientific Unions Gen. Cttee, Acad. des Sciences; Foreign mem. American Acad. of Arts and Sciences, New York Acad. of Sciences, Acad. of Sciences of Russia (Ukraine), American Philosophical Soc.; Fogarty Fellow 1977–82; Foreign Hon. mem. NAS (USA); Charles-Léopold Mayer Prize 1955, 1966; Officier Légion d'honneur, Commdr, Ordre nat. du Mérite. *Publications:* Polynucleotide phosphorylase, in Journal of American Chemical Soc. (with S. Ochoa) 1955, Biosynthèse des acides nucléiques (with F. Gros) 1974, :threonine tRNA ligase gene in *Escherichia coli*, in PNAS (with others) 1986, Escherichia coli and Salmonella typhimurium 1987; more than 300 scientific articles. *Leisure* *interest:* paintings. *Address:* Institut de Biologie Physico-chimique, 13 rue Pierre-et-Marie Curie, 75005 Paris; 80 Boulevard Pasteur, 75015 Paris, France. *Telephone:* 1-43-25-26-09.

GRUNWALD, Henry Anatole, LHD, FRSA; American editor, diplomatist and author; b. 3 Dec. 1922, Vienna; s. of Alfred Grunwald and Mila Loewenstein; m. 1st Beverly Suser 1953 (died 1981); one s. two d.; m. 2nd Louise Melhado 1987; ed New York Univ.; mem. editorial staff, Time Magazine 1945–87, Asst Man. Ed. 1966–68, Man. Ed. 1968–77; Corp. Ed., Time Inc. 1977–79, Ed.-in-Chief 1979–87; Amb. to Austria 1988–90; Trustee New American-Austrian Foundation; Dir Metropolitan Opera Guild, Center for Communication, Int. Media Fund; mem. Advisory Bd World Press Freedom Cttee, Nat. Press Inst. of Russia; mem. Council on Foreign Relations; mem. Bd of Dirs Int. Rescue Cttee 1997–, Metropolitan Opera Guild; mem. Bd of Overseers Faculty of Arts and Sciences, New York Univ.; Sr Fellow, Salzburg Seminar; mem. Century Asscn, Int. Press Inst., Bd Dirs Lighthouse Int.; Hon. LLD (Iona Coll.) 1981, (Webster Univ., Vienna) 1989; Hon. LHD (Bennett Coll.) 1983; Hall of Fame Award, American Soc. of Magazine Eds. 1997, Distinguished Alumni Award, New York Univ. 1997, Medallion, Int. Rescue Cttee 1997. *Publications:* Salinger, a Critical and Personal Portrait 1962, Churchill, The Life Triumphant 1965, The Age of Elegance 1966, One Man's America: A Journalist's Search for the Heart of His Country 1997 (memoirs), Twilight: Losing Sight, Gaining Insight 1999; contrib. to various journals, newspapers and magazines. *Address:* 654 Madison Avenue, Suite 1605, New York, NY 10021-8404, USA.

GRYAZNOVA, Alla Georgiyevna, DEcon; Russian professor of economics; b. 27 Nov. 1937, Moscow; m.; one c.; ed Moscow Inst. of Finance; asst, Lecturer, Sr Lecturer, Docent, Prof., Moscow Inst. of Finance (now Acad. of Finance of Russian Govt) 1964–74, Pro-rector on int. relations and research 1976–85, Rector 1985–; organizer various int. symposia and confs on banking problems; Ed.-in-Chief Banking System in Russia; Merited Worker of Science of Russian Fed.; mem. New Way Movt 1995; First Vice-Pres., Guild of Financiers; Vice-Pres., Acad. of Man. and Market; mem. Acad. of Econ. Sciences, Int. Acad. of Informatics, Int. Acad. of Eurasia; Pres., Moscow Int. School of Finance and Banking. *Publications:* over 200 articles on econ. problems 1994. *Leisure interests:* tennis, ballet, volleyball, poetry. *Address:* Academy of Finance, Leningradsky prosp. 49, 125468 Moscow, Russia. *Telephone:* (095) 157-56-61 (Office).

GRYZLOV, Boris Vyacheslavovich; Russian politician and engineer; b. 15 Dec. 1950, Vladivostok; s. of Vyacheslav Gryzlov; m.; two c.; ed Leningrad Inst. of Electro-Tech. Communications; radio engineer Research Inst. of Heavy Radio Construction, took part in devt of space systems of communications –1977; leading constructor, Dir Dept Production Co. Electronpribor 1977–96; worked in Inst. of Accelerated Mans Training 1996, Cen. Inst. of Mun. Econ. 1997; Head Cen. of New Technologies of Training, Baltic State Univ. 1996–99; Head Interregional Foundation of Business Co-operation Devt of Business 1999–; Founder mem. Yedinstvo Movt 1999–, Leader Yedinstvo-Otechestvo Party 2002–03; mem. State Duma 1999–2001, leader Yedinstvo faction 2000–01; Minister of Internal Affairs March 2001–. *Leisure interests:* chess, tennis, shooting, other sports. *Address:* Ministry of Internal Affairs, 117049 Moscow, ul. Zhitnaya 16, Russia. *Telephone:* (095) 239-65-00; 239-74-26. *Fax:* (095) 293-59-98.

GRYZUNOV, Sergey Petrovich; Russian journalist; b. 23 July 1949, Kuybyshev; m.; one s.; ed Moscow State Univ., Acad. of Public Sciences, Cen. Communist Party Cttee; fmr ed Novosti, then reviewer, then Deputy Head of Bureau, Yugoslavia; Deputy Chair. Cttee on Press April–Sept. 1994, Chair. 1994–95; mem. Pres. Yeltsin's Election Campaign March 1996; Vice-Pres. ICN Pharmaceutical Corpn 1998–2000; Vice-Pres. Moscow News Publrs 2000–. *Leisure interests:* cooking, fishing, underwater swimming. *Address:* Moscow News, Tverskaya str. 16/2, 103829 Moscow, Russia (Office). *Telephone:* (095) 200-20-10 (Office).

GRZEŚKOWIAK, Alicja, PhD; Polish politician and professor of criminal law; b. 10 June 1941, Świrz, Lvov Prov., Ukraine; m. (husband deceased); one d.; ed Nicolaus Copernicus Univ., Toruń; research worker Faculty of Law and Admin. of Nicolaus Copernicus Univ., Toruń 1966–96, Prof. 1990; Catholic Univ. of Lublin (KUL) 1990, Prof. 1991, mem. Scientific Council of John Paul II Inst.; Lecturer in Religious Law Higher Ecclesiastic Seminary, Toruń 1994; mem. Solidarity Trade Union 1980; Senator 1989–2001, Vice-Marshal of Senate 1991–93, Marshal 1997–2001, del. Parl. Ass. of the Council of Europe 1989–97, mem. 1991–97, Chair. Group of Christian Democrats 1992–97; mem. Social Movt of Solidarity Election Action (RSAWS) 1998–; mem. Admin. Council of John Paul II Foundation, Vatican 1992; consultant of Pontifical Council for the Family 1993; Founder Foundation of Assistance to Single Mothers, Toruń; Dame of the Holy Sepulchre Friars of Jerusalem; Hon. mem. Ass. of Catholic Families; Dr hc (Acad. of Catholic Theology, Warsaw) 1995, (Holy Family Coll., Phila.) 1998, (Int. Indl. Univ. of Moldova) 1999; Pro Ecclesia et Pontifice medal 1991; Medal of 13th Jan. of Lithuanian Rep.; Great Cross, Order of Crown (Belgium) 1999. *Publications:* numerous scientific publs on penal law, human rights and family rights. *Leisure interests:* reading, listening to music. *Address:* Katolicki Uniwersytet Lubelski, al. Racławickie 14, 20–950 Lublin, Poland.

GU CHAOHAO; Chinese mathematician; b. 15 May 1926; ed Fudan Univ. and USSR; Prof. Dept of Math. at Fudan Univ., Shanghai 1960; Deputy, 3rd NPC 1964–66; mem. Scientific Council of Academia Sinica 1981; Deputy, 6th NPC 1983–88; Vice-Pres. Fudan Univ. 1984–88; mem. Dept of Math. and Physics, Academia Sinica 1985; Vice-Chair. China–Brazil Friendship Group of NPC 1986; Pres. Science and Tech. Univ. Hefei Feb. 1988; Dir Mathematical Research Centre, Shanghai Communications Univ. 1988; Standing Cttee mem. CPPCC 8th Nat. Cttee 1993–. *Address:* c/o Science and Technology University, 59 Tunxi Road, Hefei, Anhui Province 230009, People's Republic of China. *Telephone:* 74711.

GU JINCHI; Chinese party and government official; b. 1932, Xiong Co., Hebei Prov.; joined CCP 1949; Vice-Gov. Sichuan Prov. 1982–86; mem. 13th CCP Cen. Cttee 1987–92; mem. 14th CCP Cen. Cttee 1992–97; Deputy Sec. Sichuan Provincial Cttee 1988–90; Sec. Gansu Provincial Cttee 1990–93, Sec. CCP Liaoning Prov. Cttee 1993–97; Vice-Chair Internal Affairs and Judicial Cttee of 9th NPC 1998–. *Address:* c/o Standing Committee of National People's Congress, Beijing, People's Republic of China.

GU MU; Chinese politician (retd); b. 1914, Roncheng City, Shandong Prov.; joined CP 1932; Mayor of Jinan 1950–52; Deputy Sec. CCP Shanghai 1953–54; Vice-Chair. State Construction Comm. 1954–56, State Econ. Comm. 1956–65; Chair. State Capital Construction Comm. 1965–67; criticized and removed from office during Cultural Revolution 1967; Minister of State Capital Construction Comm. 1973–81, of Foreign Investment Comm. 1979–82, of Import-Export Comm. 1979–82; Political Commissar, PLA Capital Construction Engineering Corps 1979–; Vice-Premier, State Council 1975–82; mem. 11th Cen. Cttee CCP 1977, Deputy for Shandong, 5th NPC 1978, mem. Secr. 1980–82, 1982–85, State Councillor, State Council 1982–88; mem. 12th Cen. Cttee CCP 1982–87, Exec. Chair. 1988–92; Head Co-ordination Group for Tourist Industry 1986–, for Econ. Devt of Ningbo 1985–; Most Hon. Pres. Asscn of Enterprises with Foreign Investment; Hon. Pres. Soc. for Study of Econs of Capital Construction 1980–, Confucius Foundation 1986–, China Asscn for Promotion of Int. Science and Tech. 1988–, China Asscn for Advancement of Int. Friendship; Pres. China Econ. Law Research Soc. 1984–92, China Strategy and Admin. Research Soc.; Hon. Chair. China Tourism Asscn 1986–; Vice Chair. of the Nat. Cttee of 7th CPPCC 1988–92; Chair. Econ. Cttee 7th CPPCC 1988–92; Pres. China Population Welfare Foundation 1994–; Hon. Adviser "Happiness Project" Organization Cttee; mem. Presidium of 14th CCP Nat. Congress Oct. 1992. *Address:* Chinese People's Political Consultative Conference, Taiping Qiao Road, Beijing, People's Republic of China.

GU SONGFEN; Chinese engineer; b. 1930, Suzhou, Jiangsu Prov.; ed Shanghai Jiaotong Univ.; engineer Aeronautical Industry Admin. of Ministry of Heavy Industry; group leader Aerodynamic Group of Design Dept, Shenyang Aeroplane Mfg Factory; Vice-Chief Designer, Chief Designer, Vice-Pres. then Pres. Aviation Science and Tech. Research Inst.; Fellow Chinese Acad. of Sciences; mem. 4th Presidium of Depts. 2000–; responsible for jet fighter design; Chief Designer Shenyang Aeroplane Mfg Co.; Vice-Chair. Science and Tech. Cttee, Ministry of Aviation Industry. *Address:* Shenyang Aeroplane Manufacturing Company, Shenyang, Liaoning Province, People's Republic of China (Office).

GU XIULIAN; Chinese party and government official; b. 1935, Jiangsu Prov.; cadre, State Council 1970; Vice-Minister State Planning Comm., State Council 1973–83; alt. mem., Cen. Cttee, CCP 1977; Vice-Chair. Cen. Patriotic Sanitation Campaign Cttee, Cen. Cttee 1981–89; mem. 12th Cen. Cttee, CCP 1982–87; mem. 13th Cen. Cttee CCP 1987–92; mem. 14th Cen. Cttee CCP 1992–97; Deputy Sec. CCP Prov. Cttee, Jiangsu 1982–89; Gov. of Jiangsu 1983–89; Minister of Chemical Industry 1989–93, 1993–98 (also Party Cttee Sec. at the Ministry); mem. 15th Cen. Cttee CCP 1997–; fmr standing mem. Nat. Fed. of Women. *Address:* c/o Ministry of Chemical Industry, Hepingli Street, Anding Menwai, Beijing 100723, People's Republic of China.

GU YINGQI; Chinese politician; b. 1930, Xinmin, Liaoning; m.; two s. one d.; joined PLA 1948, CCP 1950; Vice-Minister of Public Health 1984–95; Chief Physician; mem. Standing 8th Nat. Cttee 1993–; Co-ordinator State Co-ordination of Control of Narcotics and Against Drugs 1987–90; Head of del. to UN Int. Conf. on Drug Abuse and Illicit Trafficking 1987, to Signing of Sino-U.S. Memorandum of Understanding on Co-operation and Control of Narcotic Drugs, Washington 1987, to UN Conf. for Adoption of a Convention Against Illicit Traffic in Narcotic Drugs and Psychotropic Substances 1988, to 17th Special Session of UN Gen. Ass. on Int. Co-operation against Drugs 1990, to 44th Gen. Ass. of WHO 1991, to Int. Conf. for Protection of War Victims, Geneva 1993, to 9th Session of Gen. Ass. of Int. Fed. of Red Cross and Red Crescent Socs., Birmingham, UK 1993; Conf. Chair. 15th Meeting of Nat. Drug Law Enforcement Agencies for Asia and Pacific 1990, 4th Asia and Pacific Red Cross and Red Crescent Conf., Beijing 1993; Head of Chinese Red Cross del. to 26th Int. Conf. of Red Cross and Red Crescent, Geneva 1995; Pres. China Rural Hygiene Asscn 1986–, Chinese Asscn of Rehabilitation Medicine 1985–, Chinese Asscn of Hosp. Man.; Exec. Vice-Pres. Red Cross Soc. of China 1990–; Vice-Pres. Int. Fed. of Red Cross and Red Crescent Socs. 1991–93. *Address:* c/o Red Cross Society of China, 53 Ganmian Hutong, Beijing 100010, People's Republic of China. *Telephone:* (10) 513-5838. *Fax:* (10) 512-4169.

GUAN GUANGFU; Chinese politician and banker; b. 1931, Muling Co., Heilongjiang Prov.; joined CCP 1948; Vice-Pres. Hubei Br. People's Bank of China 1971–78, Pres., Hubei Br. 1978–82; Sec. Hubei Prov. CCP Cttee 1983–94; First Political Commissar, First Party Sec. Hubei Prov. Mil. Dist 1983–; Chair. Hubei Prov. 8th People's Congress 1993–; mem. 12th Cen. Cttee

1985, 13th Cen. Cttee 1987, 14th Cen. Cttee 1992; mem. Presidium, 13th and 14th Nat. Congresses CCP. *Address:* Shui Guo Hu, Wuhan, Hubei Province, People's Republic of China.

GUAN QIAO; Chinese engineer; b. 2 July 1935, Taiyuan, Shanxi Prov.; ed Moscow Bauman Eng Inst.; Fellow Chinese Acad. of Eng 1994–; invented low-stress no-distortion welding method; mem. Council Chinese Acad. of Eng; Research Fellow and Vice-Chair. Science and Tech. Cttee, Beijing Aeronautical Manufacturing Tech. Research Inst.; Nat. Invention Prize (2nd Class), Int. Inst. of Welding Lifetime Achievement Award 1999. *Address:* Beijing Aeronautical Manufacturing Technology Research Institute, PO Box 863, 100024 Beijing, People's Republic of China (Office). *Telephone:* (10) 8570-1243.

GUAN WEIYAN; Chinese physicist; b. 18 Aug. 1928, Rudong Co., Jiangsu Prov.; s. of Guan Deyi and Han Quanzheng; m. Zheng Zongshuang 1960; one s. one d.; ed Harbin Polytechnical Inst., Tsinghua, Beijing, Leningrad, Tbilisi and Moscow Univs; researcher, Inst. of Physics, USSR Acad. of Sciences 1957–60; researcher, Inst. of Physics, Chinese Acad. of Sciences, Beijing 1960–, Deputy Dir 1978–81, Dir 1981–85, mem. Dept of Math. and Physics; Visiting Scholar, Low-temperature Research Centre, Grenoble, France 1980; Pres. Univ. of Science and Tech. of China, Hefei 1984–87, Asscn of Science and Tech., Anhui Prov. 1986; Vice-Pres. Chinese Physics Soc. 1987–; Visiting Prof. Univ. Giesson 1987, KFK Karlsruhe, Germany 1988, Univ. of Notre Dame (USA) 1989, Univ. of Houston 1989–90, KFA, Julich, Germany 1990–91, Nat. Tsing Hua Univ. (Taiwan) 1991–, Dan Jiang Univ. (Taiwan) 1995–; mem. bd of various Chinese and int. journals; mem. Int. Cttee, Int. Conf. on Low Temperature Physics 1981–. *Address:* Room 1201, Bldg 812, Zhong Guan Cun, Beijing 100080, People's Republic of China. *Telephone:* 6255-4965.

GUARD, Mark Perrott, MA, RIBA, MRIAI, MCSD; Irish architect; b. 22 May 1952, Dublin; s. of Wilson Perrott Guard and Ethena Joy Wallace; ed Avoca School, Dublin, Univ. of Toronto, Royal Coll. of Art, London; worked for architectural, film and textile design cos in Ireland and UK 1969–73; emigrated to Canada 1973; architect, Toronto and Vancouver 1973–76; worked for Richard Rogers Partnership, Rick Mather Architects, Eva Jiricna Architects, London 1982–86; started pvt. practice in modernist residential design and devt of transformable spaces 1986; Prin. Mark Guard Design 1986–88, Mark Guard Assocs 1988–93, Mark Guard Architects 1993–; Dir Mark Guard Ltd 1998–; Dir Guard Tillman Pollock Ltd 2002–; RIBA Regional Award for New House, London, W2 1992, for house refurbishment, London, NW6 1995, CSD Commendation for transformable flat, London, EC2 1993, for house refurbishment, London, NW6 1995, RIAI Commendation for new house, Galway 1993, RIBA Award for Houses and Housing for penthouse apartment, Paris 1997. *Address:* 161 Whitfield Street, London, W1T 5ET, England (Office). *Telephone:* (20) 7380-1199 (Office). *Fax:* (20) 7387-5441 (Office). *E-mail:* mga@markguard.com (Office). *Website:* www.markguard .com (Office).

GUARDADO, Facundo; Salvadorean politician; b. 27 Nov. 1954, Arcatao, Dept of Chalatenengo; s. of Sixto Guardado and Herlinda Guardado; m. Carmen Cristina Alvarez Basso 1993; one s. three d.; ed fellowship to econ. seminars at Cen. American Business Admin. Inst. and Heredia Nat. Univ. of Costa Rica; co-operative movt leader 1972–; Sec.-Gen. Revolutionary Popular Bloc 1977; mem. Cen. Cttee Nat. Liberation Front (FMLN) in 1980s, mem. Political Comm. 1993, Campaign Man. 1997, Gen. Co-ordinator 1997–; Counselor at San Salvador Majorship 1997–; presidential cand. 1999; mem. peace negotiations del. La Palma 1984, Ayagualo 1984, La Nunciatura 1987, Mexico 1991; Vice-Pres. Perm. Conf. of Political Parties of Latin America and the Caribbean; mem. Initiatives Group for Latin America; Pres. El Salvador XXI Century Foundation. *Publications:* Political and Social Struggles in El Salvador, Participation and Social Change, Evolution of the Democratic Process in El Salvador. *Leisure interests:* agriculture, football. *Address:* Frente Farabundo Martí para la Liberación Nacional, 27 Calle Poniente 1316 y 9A Avda Norte 229, San Salvador (Office); Paseo Miralvalle 155, Colonia Miralvalle, San Salvador (Home); c/o Motocross #49, Colonia Monteverde, San Salvador, El Salvador (Home). *Telephone:* 224-5572 (Office); 274-2104 (Home). *Fax:* 224-1066 (Office); 224-1066 (Home); 224-1066. *E-mail:* fagualbasso@ejje.com (Office).

GUBAIDULINA, Sofia Asgatovna; Russian (b. Tatar) composer; b. 24 Oct. 1931, Chistopol; d. of Asgat Gubaidulin and Fedossia Gubaidulina; m. Peter Meschaninov; one d.; ed Kazan and Moscow Conservatories, composition class Nikolai Peiko and Vissarian Shebalin, piano Grigori Kogan; first noticed abroad Paris 1979; British debut 1987 (Symphony in 12 Movements); lives in Germany 1991–; Polar Prize, Royal Swedish Acad. of Music 2002. *Compositions include:* (orchestral pieces) The Steps 1971, The Hour of Soul 1976, Offertorium 1980, Stimmen. . . verstummen (symphony) 1986, Zeitgestalten (symphony) 1994; 2nd cello concerto 1994, Viola concerto 1998; concertos for solo instruments with chamber orchestra; (cantatas) The Night in Memphis 1968, Rubaiyat 1969, Perception 1983, Dedication to Marina Tsvetayeva 1984, Johannes Passion 2000; instrumental music for non-traditional groups. *Address:* 2d Pugachevskaya 8, Korp. 5, Apt. 130, 107061 Moscow, Russia; Ziegeleiweg 12, 25482 Appen, Germany. *Telephone:* (095) 161-80-61 (Moscow).

GUBBAY, Hon. Mr Justice Anthony Roy, MA, LLM; Zimbabwean judge; b. 26 April 1932, Manchester, England; m. Wilma Sanger 1962 (died 2002); two s.; ed Univ. of Witwatersrand, S Africa, Univ. of Cambridge; admitted to practice 1957; advocate Bulawayo, S Rhodesia 1958, Sr Counsel 1974; Pres. Matabeleland and Midlands Valuations Boards; Nat. Pres. Special Court for Income Tax Appeals, Fiscal Court and Patents Tribunal; Vice-Chair. Bar Asscn; Judge of the High Court, Bulawayo 1977–83, Judge of the Supreme Court 1983; Chair. Legal Practitioners' Disciplinary Tribunal 1981–87, Law Devt Comm., Judicial Service Comm.; Chief Justice of Zimbabwe 1990–2001, retd 2001; mem. Perm. Court of Arbitration; Pres. Oxford and Cambridge Soc. of Zimbabwe; Patron Commonwealth Magistrates and Judges Asscn; mem. Advisory Bd of Commonwealth Judicial Educ. Inst., Commonwealth Reference Group on the Promotion of the Human Rights of Women and the Girl Child through the Judiciary; Hon. Fellow Jesus Coll. Cambridge; Hon. Bencher of Lincoln's Inn (UK); Great Cross, Rio Branco Order (Brazil) 1999; Dr hc (Univ. of Essex) 1994; Peter Gruber Foundation Justice Award 2001. *Leisure interests:* classical music, philately, watching all forms of sport, travel. *Address:* 26 Dacomb Drive, Chisipite, Harare, Zimbabwe (Home). *Telephone:* (4) 496882 (Home). *E-mail:* supreme-court@gta.gov.zw (Office); gubbay@zol .co.zw (Home).

GUBBAY, Raymond, CBE; British music promoter; b. 2 April 1946, London; s. of David Gubbay and the late Ida Gubbay; m. Johanna Quirke 1972 (divorced 1988); two d.; ed Univ. Coll. School, Hampstead; concert promoter 1966–; f. and Man. Dir Raymond Gubbay Ltd 1966–; presents regular series of concerts at maj. London and regional concert halls including Royal Albert Hall, Royal Festival Hall, Barbican Centre, Symphony Hall Birmingham, Bridgewater Hall Manchester, Royal Concert Hall Glasgow and in Ireland, Belgium and Scandinavia; has presented productions of: (operas and operettas) The Ratepayer's Iolanthe 1984, Turandot 1991–92, La Bohème (centenary production) 1996, Carmen 1997, Madame Butterfly 1998, 2000, The Pirates of Penzance 1998–99, 2000, Tosca 1999, Aida 2001; (ballets) Swan Lake 1997, 1999, Romeo and Juliet 1998, The Sleeping Beauty 2000; Hon. FRAM 1988. *Leisure interests:* living in Paris, gardening. *Address:* Oliver House, 27–31 East Barnet Road, New Barnet, Herts., EN4 8RN, England (Office); 51 rue Monsieur le Prince, Paris, France. *Telephone:* (20) 8216-3000. *Fax:* (20) 8216-3001.

GUBBINS, David, BA, PhD, FRS, FInstP; British professor of geophysics; b. 31 May 1947, Southampton; s. of late Albert Edmund Gubbins and of Joyce Lucy Gubbins (née Rayner); m. Margaret Stella McCloy 1972; one s. two d.; ed King Edward VI Grammar School, Trinity Coll., Cambridge; Visiting Research Fellow Univ. of Colorado 1972–73; instructor MIT 1973–74; Asst Prof. Univ. of Calif. at LA 1974–76; Asst Dir of Research Dept of Geodesy & Geophysics, Univ. of Cambridge 1976–89; Fellow Churchill Coll., Cambridge 1978–90; Ed. Geophysical Journal of the Royal Astronomical Soc. 1982–90, Physics of the Earth and Planetary Interior 1990–; Head of Geophysics Univ. of Leeds 1989–2001, Research Prof. 2001–; Fellow American Geophysical Union 1985; Murchison Medal of Geological Soc. of London 1998. *Publications:* Seismology and Plate Tectonics 1990; over 100 articles in scientific journals. *Leisure interests:* sailing, walking. *Address:* School of Earth Sciences, University of Leeds, Leeds, LS2 9JT, England. *Telephone:* (113) 343-5255. *Fax:* (113) 343-5259. *E-mail:* gubbins@earth.leeds.ac.uk (Office).

GUBENKO, Nikolai Nikolayevich; Russian actor and theatrical director; b. 17 Aug. 1941, Odessa; m. Jeanna Bolotova; ed All-Union Inst. of Cinema; mem. CPSU 1987–91, Cen. Cttee 1990–91, CP of Russian Fed. 1992–2002, expelled from party 2002, Ind. 2002–; actor at Taganka Theatre, Moscow 1964–, Artistic Dir 1987–89; Founder and Head of Concord of Taganka actors 1993–; dir several films including The Orphans (Soviet entry Cannes Film Festival 1977), The Life of Holidaymakers (based on story by Ivan Bunin), Life ... Tears ... Love, Restricted Area 1988; stage appearances include Boris Godunov; USSR Minister of Culture 1989–91; mem. State Duma (Parl.) 1995–; Deputy Chair. Cttee for Culture 1997–, Chair.; Pres. Int. Asscn of Help for Culture 1992–; RSFSR People's Artist 1985. *Address:* Franzenskaya nab. 46, Apt. 65, 110270 Moscow, Russia. *Telephone:* (095) 292-90-36 (Duma); (095) 242-65-58 (Home).

GUCCIONE, Robert Charles Joseph Edward Sabatini; American publisher; b. 17 Dec. 1930, Brooklyn; s. of Anthony Guccione and Nina Guccione; m. Kathy Keeton 1988; five c. from previous m.; artist 1948–55, 1992–; fmr cartoonist and greetings card designer; Man. London American; f./publr Penthouse Magazine, UK 1965–; also Publr Forum, Variations, Penthouse Letters, Omni, Saturday Review, Four Wheeler, Longevity, Girls of Penthouse, Compute, Open Wheel, Stock Car Racing, Superstock and Drag, Hot Talk; Chair. Gen. Media Int. Inc. 1988–; producer of film Caligula 1979; exec. producer, TV show Omni: The New Frontier, Omni: Visions of Tomorrow. *Address:* General Media International, 1100 Penn Plaza, New York, NY 10001, USA (Office).

GUDANOV, Dmitry Konstantinovich; Russian ballet dancer; b. Moscow; ed Moscow Academic School of Choreography; ballet dancer Bolshoi Theatre 1994–98, leading dancer 1998–; 1st Prize and Gold Medal 7th Int. Moscow Ballet Competition 1997, 1st Prize Int. Ballet Competition Paris 1998. *Ballet:* leading roles in Sleeping Beauty, Nutcracker, Le Mégère Apprivoisée, La Sylphide, Fantasia on the Theme of Casanova, Giselle, Romeo and Juliet, Symphony C-major (production of G. Balanchine), Heir in Hamlet (production of B. Eifman). *Achievements:* Tours in European countries. *Address:* Bolshoi Theatre, Teatralnaya pl. 1, Moscow, Russia (Office). *Website:* www.ballet .classical.ru/b_gudanov.

GUDEV, Vladimir Victorovich; Russian diplomatist; b. 17 Sept. 1940, Moscow; s. of Victor Gudev; m. Valentina Goudeva 1960; one d.; ed Moscow Inst. of Int. Relations; sr posts in Ministry of Foreign Affairs at home and abroad 1963–75; Embassy First Sec. in Iraq 1975–79; Chief of Section, Deputy Chief of Near East Dept of Ministry of Foreign Affairs 1979–86; Deputy Dir, Chief of Dept in Directorate of Near East and North Africa 1986–87; Amb. to Iran 1987–93; Head of Africa and Near East Dept, Russian Ministry of Foreign Affairs 1993–95; Amb. to Egypt 1995–2000, to Georgia 2001–02. *Address:* Ministry of Foreign Affairs, Smolenskaya-Sennaya 32/34, 121200 Moscow, Russia.

GUEBUZA, Armando Emílio; Mozambican politician; b. 20 Jan. 1943, Murrupula, Nampula Prov.; joined Frente de Libertação de Moçambique (Frelimo) 1963; elected to Politburo 1968; guerilla commdr during war with Portugal, rising to rank of Gen.; has served in every govt 1975–; fmr Resident Minister in Sofala 1980s; fmr Minister of the Interior; fmr Political Commissar of the Army; Sec.-Gen. Frente de Libertação de Moçambique (Frelimo) June 2002–; Cand. (desig.) in Presidential Elections 2004. *Address:* Frente de Libertação de Moçambique (Frelimo), Rua Pereira do Lago 229, Maputo, Mozambique (Office). *E-mail:* sg@frelimo.org.mz (Office). *Website:* www .frelimo.org.mz (Office).

GUÉDIGUIAN, Robert; French film maker; b. 3 Dec. 1953, L'Estaque, Marseille; m. Ariane Ascaride; producer associated with AGAT Films & Cie. *Films:* Fernand (writer) 1979, Le souffleur (writer, producer) 1985; writer, dir, producer: Dernier été (Prix Georges Sadoul) 1980, Rouge midi 1983, Ki lo sa? 1985, Dieu vomit les tièdes (TV) 1989; writer, dir: L'argent fait le bonheur (Prix Michel Kuhn, Rencontres européennes de Reims) 1992; producer: Un tour de manège, Montalvo et l'enfant, Variétés 1989, Le cri du cochon 1990, Suzanne Linke, Bali, les couleurs du divin 1992, Marseille, la vieille ville indigne 1993, Baudelaire modernité 1986, Vittel Design 1987 (Grand Prix, Vidéo Festival de Biarritz), Le coupeur d'eau 1989, En direct de l'être humain 1991, C'est trop con (Prix du Jury, Festival européen d'Angers) 1992, Ça se passe en Equateur, Que la vie est belle 1993, A la vie à la mort, Marius et Jeannette, La ville est tranquille 2001. *Address:* c/o AGAT Films & Cie., 52 rue Jean-Pierre Timbaud, 75011 Paris, France (Office).

GUÉGUINOU, Jean, GCVO; French diplomatist; b. 17 Oct. 1941; s. of Louis-Bernard Guéguinon and Jeanne-Rose Le Fur; ed Ecole Nat. d'Admin; Press and Information Dept Ministry of Foreign Affairs 1967–69; Second Sec. London 1969–71; Head of Mission, Ministry of State/Ministry of Defence 1971–73; Head of Cabinet and Counsellor 1973–76; Dir of Cabinet of Sec. of State reporting to Prime Minister 1976–77; Asst Dir for Southern Africa and Indian Ocean 1977–82; Consul-Gen. Jerusalem 1982–86; Dir Press and Information Service 1986–90; Amb. to Czechoslovakia 1990–92, to Czech Repub. 1993, to UK 1993–98, to the Holy See 1998–2000, Ambassadeur de France 2000; Chair., Cttee de patronage, Franco-Scottish Asscn 2001–; mem. Admin Council, Agence France-Presse 1986–90, Soc. of Friends of the Louvre 2000–, Arts florissants 2001–; Chevalier, Légion d'honneur, Ordre Nat. du Mérite; Commdr Order of St Gregory the Great. *Address:* c/o Ministry of Foreign Affairs, 37 quai d'Orsay, 75007 Paris (Office); 5 avenue Montespan, 75116 Paris, France (Home).

GUÉHENNO, Jean-Marie; French international organization official; b. 30 Oct. 1949, Boulogne sur Seine; s. of the late Jean Guéhenno; m. 1981; one d.; ed Ecole Normale Supérieure, Inst. d'Etudes Politiques, Ecole Nat. d'Admin., Paris; mem. Court of Auditors 1976–2000, Sr Auditor 1993–2000; Dir Cultural Affairs, French Embassy in Washington, DC 1982–86; Dir Policy Planning Staff, Ministry of Foreign Affairs 1989–93; Amb. to WEU 1993–95; Under-Sec.-Gen. for Peace-keeping Operations, UN, New York 2000–; Chair. Bd, Inst. for Higher Defence Studies, Paris 1998–2000; Chevalier, Légion d'honneur, Commdr, Order of Merit (Germany). *Publications:* La fin de la démocratie (English trans. The End of the Nation-State) 1993, L'avenir de la liberté – la démocratie dans la mondialisation 1999. *Leisure interests:* sailing, walking, reading, museums. *Address:* Office of the Under-Secretary-General for Peace-keeping Operations, Room S-3727, United Nations, United Nations Plaza, New York, NY 10017, USA (Office). *Telephone:* (212) 963-8079 (Office). *Fax:* (212) 963-9222 (Office). *E-mail:* guehenno@un.org (Office).

GUEILER TEJADA, Lydia; Bolivian politician and diplomatist; b. 1926, Cochabamba; active role in revolution of 1952; became Pvt. Sec. to Pres. Paz Estenssoro 1952; mem. Chamber of Deputies 1956; left Movimiento Nacional Revolucionario and joined Partido Revolucionario de la Izquierda Nacional (PRIN) 1964; f. PRIN-Gueiler as part of Alianza Democrática de la Revolución Nacional 1979; Pres. Chamber of Deputies July–Nov. 1979; Pres. Congress Aug.–Nov. 1979; interim Pres. of Bolivia 1979–80 (overthrown in coup); in exile in Paris, France 1980–82; Amb. to Colombia 1983–86, to Venezuela 1992–2001. *Publications:* La Mujer y la Revolución 1956, Mi Pasión de Lidereza 2000. *Address:* Casilla de Correo 12345, San Miguel, La Paz, Bolivia. *Telephone:* (2) 2784806 (Home). *Fax:* (2) 777777 (Home).

GUELAR, Diego Ramiro; Argentine diplomatist and lawyer; b. 24 Feb. 1950; m. Magdalena D. Custodio; three c.; Prof. Sociology of Law, Univ. of Buenos Aires 1971; outlawed by military for political activities (nat. leader, Peronist Youth) 1972–73; attorney, Justicialist Party of Buenos Aires Province 1973–76; Prof. Faculties of Architecture and Law, Univ. of Buenos Aires 1973–76; outlawed for political activities 1976–78; nat. adviser of coordinator for Justicialist activities 1978–83; Vice-Pres. Comm. for Budget and Finance, Nat. Chamber of Deputies 1984; Sec.-Gen. bloc of Nat. Justicialist Deputies

1985; Ed. and Dir La Razón (newspaper) 1987; Head, Foundation for Growth Arrangement (FUNCRE); Amb. to EC (now EU) 1989–96, to USA 1997–. *Publications include:* Chronicles of Transition (collection), political and econ. works etc. *Address:* Embassy of Argentina, 1600 New Hampshire Avenue, NW, Washington, DC 20009, USA. *Website:* www.embassyofargentina-usa .org.

GUÉNA, Yves René Henri; French politician; b. 6 July 1922, Brest; m. Oriane de la Bourdonnaye 1945; five s. two d.; ed Ecole Nat. d'Administration; mem. Free French Forces 1940–45; Official in Morocco 1947, Maître des Requêtes, Conseil d'Etat 1957, Dir de Cabinet to M. Debré (Minister of Justice) 1958–59, Deputy Dir de Cabinet to M. Debré (Prime Minister) Jan.–July 1959; High Commr Ivory Coast 1959–60, Envoy Extraordinary (Dean of Diplomatic Corps) 1960–61; elected Deputy for Dordogne, Nat. Ass. 1962, 1967, 1968, 1973, 1974, 1978, lost seat 1981, re-elected 1986, lost seat 1988; elected Senator for Dordogne 1989; Vice-Pres. of Senate 1992–95, 1995–97; mem. Constitutional Council 1997–, Pres. 1999; Minister of Posts and Telecommunications 1967–68, 1968–69, of Information May–July 1968, of Transport 1973–74, of Industrial and Scientific Devt, March–May 1974; Deputy Sec.-Gen. UDR 1974, Sec.-Gen. 1976; Political Adviser and Nat. Treasurer, Rassemblement pour la République 1977–79; Mayor of Périgueux (Dordogne) 1971, re-elected 1977, 1983, 1989, 1995–97 (resgnd); Conseiller d'Etat 1972; Grand Officier Légion d'honneur, Croix de guerre, Médaille de la Résistance. *Publications:* Historique de la communauté 1962, Maintenir l'état 1970, L'enjeu (in collaboration) 1975, Le temps des certitudes 1940–69 1982, Catilina ou la gloire dérobée 1984, Les cent premiers jours (co-author) 1985, Ecrits et discours (25 années de vie publique) 1987, Moi duc de Lauzun, citoyen Biron 1997, Ecrits et discours (II) 1999, Le Baron Louis 1999, Phèdre 2000 (play) 2000. *Address:* Conseil constitutionnel, 2 rue Montpensier, 75001 Paris; 13 rue René Bazin, 75016 Paris, France (Home).

GUENÉE, Bernard Marie Albert, DèsSc; French university teacher; b. 6 Feb. 1927, Rennes; s. of Ernest Guenée and Antoinette (née Caisso) Guenée; m. Simonne Lucas 1955; ed Ecole Normale Supérieure, Paris, Fondation Thiers; Prof. Univ. de Strasbourg 1958–65, Sorbonne 1965–95 (Prof. Emer. 1995–); Dir of Studies Ecole Pratique des Hautes Etudes 1980–; mem. of Institut de France (Académie des Inscriptions et Belles-Lettres) 1981; Chevalier, Légion d'honneur, Commdr, Ordre nat. du Mérite, Commdr des Palmes académiques; Grand Prix nat. d'Histoire 1995. *Publications:* Tribunaux et gens de justice dans le bailliage de Senlis à la fin du Moyen Age (vers 1380–vers 1550) 1963, Les entrées royales françaises de 1328 à 1515, 1968, L'occident aux XIVe et XVe siècles: Les etats 1971, Histoire et culture historique dans l'Occident médiéval 1980, Politique et histoire au Moyen Age: recueil d'articles sur l'histoire politique et l'historiographie médiévales (1956–81) 1981, Entre l'Eglise et l'Etat: quatre vies de prélats français à la fin du Moyen Age 1987, Un meurtre, une société: l'assassinat du duc d'Orléans, 23 novembre 1407 1992, Un roi et son historien: Vingt études sur le règne de Charles VI et la "Chronique du Religieux de Saint-Denis" 1999, L'opinion publique à la fin du Moyen Age 2002. *Address:* 8 rue Huysmans, 75006 Paris, France. *Telephone:* 1-45-48-44-40.

GUENIN, Marcel André, PhD; Swiss university professor and company director; b. 17 July 1937, Geneva; s. of Léandré André and Isabelle Guenin-Bontempo; m. Ingrid Marina Selbach 1962; three s.; ed Eidgenössische Technische Hochschule Zürich, Univ. of Geneva and Harvard Univ., USA; Asst and Master Asst, Univ. of Geneva 1960–64; Research Assoc., Princeton Univ. 1964–66; Lecturer, Grad. Programme, Univs. of Lausanne, Neuchâtel and Geneva 1966–68; Asst Prof., Univ. of Geneva 1968–70, Professeur extraordinaire 1970–73, Professeur ordinaire 1973–2000, Hon. Prof. 2000–, Dir Dept of Theoretical Physics 1974–77, Dir Group of Applied Physics (GAP) 1993–2000, Vice-Rector Univ. of Geneva 1980–83, Rector 1983–87; Pres. PBG Pvt. Bank, Geneva 1987–89; Chair. Bd COGITAS 1988–94; mem. Bd BBC Brown Boveri Ltd 1987–96, Brunet 1990–93, Lasarray 1990–93, Soc. d'Instruments de physique (SIP) 1998–; Sec.-Gen. European Physical Soc. 1974–79, Fellow 1980; Sec. Swiss Physical Soc. 1975–79; mem. Bd Soc. Financière de Genève 1988–89; Founding mem. Int. Asscn of Math. Physicists; mem. American Physical Soc. *Publications:* three books and about 40 scientific publs. *Leisure interests:* skiing, sailing, music. *Address:* Applied Physics Group, University of Geneva, 20 Ecole de Medicine, 1211 Geneva 4 (Office); 2B chemin des Manons, 1218 Grand-Saconnex (GE), Switzerland (Home).

GUÉRARD, Michel Etienne; French chef, restaurateur and hotelier; b. 27 March 1933, Vetheuil; s. of Maurice Guérard and Georgine Guérard; m. Christine Barthelemy 1974; two d.; ed Lycée Corneille, Rouen; apprentice patissier, Mantes la Jolie; head patissier, Hotel Crillon, Paris; chef to brothers Clérico, Lido, Paris; created restaurant le Pot au Feu, Asnières (two Michelin stars); undertook complex renovation of hotel and thermal treatment centre Les Prés d'Eugénie, Eugénie les Bains; consultant to Nestlé; opened first Comptoir Gourmand Michel Guérard; restored Chai de Bachen and produced a white Tursan, Baron de Bachen; Chevalier, Légion d'honneur 1990, Officier, Ordre nat. du Mérite, Chevalier, Ordre nat. du Mérite agricole, Officier des Arts et des Lettres, Meilleur Ouvrier de France (MOF Patisserie) 1958. *Publications:* La Grande Cuisine Minceur 1976, La Cuisine Gourmande 1978, Mes Recettes à la TV 1982, Minceur Exquise 1989, Le Sud-Ouest Gourmand de Relais en Châteaux 1993, La Cuisine Gourmande des Juniors 1997, Le Jeu de l'Oie et du Canard 1998, La Cuisine à Vivre 2000. *Leisure interests:*

antiques, painting, sketchbooks, food and wine. *Address:* Les Prés d'Eugénie, 40320 Eugénie les Bains, Geaune, France. *Telephone:* (5) 58-05-06-07. *Fax:* (5) 58-51-10-10. *Website:* www.michelguerard.com.

GUERRAOUI, Abdellatif; Moroccan government minister; b. 10 July 1939, Safi; s. of Abdeslam Guerraoui and Oumhani Benazzouz; m. Laila Laoufir 1968; one s. two d.; ed ENSEEIHT, Toulouse, France; Chief of Staff, Computer Systems, Cherifien Office of Phosphates (OCP) 1964–70, Chief of Personnel Admin. Div. 1970–71, Sec.-Gen. of OCP 1971–90, mem. Bd of Dirs; Man. Dir Moroccan-Saudi Investment Soc. (ASMA-INVEST) 1991–96; Minister of Energy and Mines 1993–97, of Social Affairs, Health, Youth and Sports, Nat. Mutual Aid 1997–98; Admin. Del., Sud Actif Groupe Finance (SAGFI) 1998–; mem. bd of dirs many pvt. cos. 1998–; consultant (econ. adviser); Chair. bd of dirs of many public insts 1993–97; Throne Award from King of Morocco 1985. *Leisure interests:* classical literature, history, management, economy, futurology. *Address:* 45 rue Ksar El Badii, Hay El Hana, Préfecture Ain Chock–Hay Hassani, Casablanca 20200, Morocco. *Telephone:* (2) 2396009; (2) 2945252. *Fax:* (2) 2353897.

GUERROUJ, Hicham el-; Moroccan athlete; b. 14 Sept. 1974, Berkane; set 6 world records indoors and outdoors 1997–99 (including 1,500m, 3:26.00, Rome, July 1998, mile, 3:43.12, Rieti, July 1999, 2,000m, 4:44.79, Berlin, Sept. 1999); bronze medal, World Jr Championships 5,000m 1992; World Champion 1,500m 1997, 1999, 2001; Indoor World Champion 1500m 2001; silver medallist in 2000 Olympics; holder of outdoor world record for 1,500m, 2,000m and 1 mile, of indoor record for 1,500m and 1 mile (as at end 2002); winner of 72 races from 75 starts 1996–2002; IAAF Male Athlete of the Year 2001, 2002, US Track and Field Male Athlete of the Year 2002.

GUESNERIE, Roger Sylvain Maxime Auguste, DèsSc(Econs); French economist; b. 17 Feb. 1943, Ste Gemmes Le Rt.; s. of Sylvain Guesnerie and Marie Chapelière; ed Lycée de Rennes, Ecole Polytechnique and Ecole Nat. des Ponts et Chaussées; Research Assoc. CNRS 1976, Research Dir 1978–; Dir of Studies, Ecole des Hautes Etudes en Sciences Sociales (EHESS) 1978; Dir Asscn pour le Développement de la Recherche en Economie et Statistique (ADRES) 1989–94; Dir Delta (mixed research unit. of CNRS-EHESS-ENS) 1988–2000; Prof. at Coll. de France 2000–; various part-time appts.; Vice-Pres. European Econ. Asscn 1992, Pres. 1994; Fellow, Econometric Soc., Pres. 1996; Foreign mem. American Acad. of Arts and Sciences 2000–; Hon. Foreign mem. American Econ. Asscn 1997, American Acad. of Arts and Sciences 2000; Silver Medal, CNRS 1994; Chevalier, Ordre du Mérite. *Publications:* La documentation Française, 2 vols (co-author), Modèles de l'economie publique 1980, A Contribution to the Pure Theory of Taxation 1995, L'Economie de marché 1996, Assessing Rational Expectations 1 2001; about 100 articles in econ. journals. *Leisure interests:* cycling, jogging, walking. *Address:* DELTA, 48 boulevard Jourdan, ENS, 75014 Paris, France (Office). *Telephone:* 1-43-13-63-15 (Office). *Fax:* 1-43-13-63-10 (Office). *E-mail:* guesnerie@delta.ens.fr (Office).

GUEST, John Rodney, DPhil, FRS; British professor of microbiology; b. 27 Dec. 1935, Leeds; s. of Sidney R. Guest and Kathleen (Walker) Guest; m. Barbara Dearsley 1962; one s. two d.; ed Campbell Coll., Leeds Univ. and Trinity Coll. Oxford; Guinness Research Fellow, Oxford Univ. 1960–65; Research Assoc. and Fulbright Scholar, Stanford Univ. 1963, 1964; Lecturer in Microbiology, Univ. of Sheffield 1965–68, Sr Lecturer and Reader 1968–81, Prof. of Microbiology 1981–; Science and Eng Research Council Sr Fellowship 1981–86; Royal Soc. Leeuwenhoek Lecturer 1995. *Publications:* research papers in scientific journals. *Leisure interests:* hill walking, beekeeping. *Address:* Department of Molecular Biology and Biotechnology, University of Sheffield, Western Bank, Sheffield, S10 2TN, England. *Telephone:* (114) 222-4406.

GUI, Luigi; Italian politician; b. 26 Sept. 1914, Padua; s. of Corinto Gui and Angelina Pinzan; m. Alessandra Volpi 1947; three s.; war service, Italy and Russia 1941–43; Christian Democrat underground movement 1943–45; elected to Constituent Ass. 1946, re-elected 1948, 1953, 1958, 1963, 1968, 1972, 1976, 1979; fmr Sec. of the Parl. Comm. on Agric. and Under-Sec. Ministry of Agric. and Forestry; Minister of Labour 1957–58, of Educ. 1962–68, of Defence 1968–70, of Health 1973–74, of Civil Service Reform March–Nov. 1974, of Interior 1974–76; Pres. Christian Democrat Deputies Parl. Group 1958–62; Senate 1976–79, Chamber of Deputies 1979–83, Pres. 1st Comm. on Constitutional Affairs; mem. European People's Party, Paduan Acad. of Sciences, Letters and Arts, Council of European Soc. of Culture; Pres. Nat. Petrarch Soc., Casa di Dante, Rome; Hon. Pres. Associazione Nazionale Combattenti Reduci; Cavaliere di Gran Goce dell'Ordine al Merito. *Publications:* works on history of philosophy, political history, education and travel. *Address:* Via S. Rosa 38, 35141 Padua, Italy. *Telephone:* (049) 656607.

GUI SHIYONG; Chinese politician; b. Feb. 1935, Huzhou City, Zhejiang Prov.; ed Chinese People's Univ.; joined CCP 1956; Dir Econs Inst. of Chinese Acad. of Sciences; Deputy Ed.-in-Chief Renmin Ribao (People's Daily); alt. mem. 13th CCP Cen. Cttee 1987; mem. State Planning Comm. and Vice-Dir Research Office of the State Council 1988; Vice-Chair. State Planning Comm. and Dir Econs Research Centre 1989; alt. mem. 14th CCP Cen. Cttee 1992; Vice-Pres. State Admin. Inst. 1994–; mem. 15th CCP Cen. Cttee 1997–. *Address:* Office of the President, State Administrative Institute, Beijing, People's Republic of China.

GUICHARD, Baron Olivier Marie Maurice; French politician; b. 27 July 1920, Néac; s. of Baron Louis Guichard and Madeleine Brisson; m. 1st Suzanne Vincent 1944 (deceased); three d.; m. 2nd Daisy de Galard 1990; ed Univ. de Paris and Ecole libre des sciences politiques; mem. Rassemblement du peuple français and Prin. Sec. to Gen. de Gaulle 1947–54; Press Officer Atomic Energy Commissariat 1955–58; Asst Dir Office of Gen. de Gaulle 1958, Tech. Adviser to the Pres. 1959–60; Del. Gen. of Org. des régions sahariennes 1960–62; Gen. Asst Office of the Prime Minister 1962–67; Del. for Regional and Territorial Affairs 1963–67; elected Deputy for Loire-Atlantique, Nat. Ass. 1967–97; Minister of Industry 1967–68, of Econ. Planning 1968–69, of Educ. 1969–72, of Supply 1972–73, of Supply, Housing, Tourism and Territorial Devt 1973–74, of Transport March–May 1974; Minister of State, Keeper of the Seals and Minister of Justice 1976–77; Mayor of La Baule 1971–95; Pres. Conseil régional des Pays de la Loire 1974–98; Conseiller d'Etat 1978–87; Dir Cie nat. du Rhône 1966–67; mem. Council of Admin. Radio-diffusion-Télévision française 1964–67; Pres. Mouvement pour l'indépendance de l'Europe 1975; Pres. Admin. Council Conservatoire de l'espace littoral et des rivages lacustres 1986–89; Pres. Syndicat de conception et d'animation de la métropole de Nantes 1987–; Pres. Centre culturel de l'Ouest, Fontevraud 1998–; Médaille militaire, Officier, Légion d'honneur, Croix de guerre. *Publications:* Aménager la France 1965, Education nouvelle 1971, Un chemin tranquille 1975, Mon Général 1980 (Prix des Ambassadeurs), Vingt ans en 40 1999. *Leisure interest:* cars. *Address:* SCE, Baronne Guichard, Château Siourac, 33500 Néac (Office); 30 rue Washington, 75008 Paris, France (Home).

GUIG, Mohamed Lemine Ould; Mauritanian politician; fmr Dir of Higher Educ.; Prime Minister of Mauritania 1997–98. *Address:* c/o Office of the Prime Minister, Nouackchott, Mauritania.

GUIGNABODET, Liliane, LèsL; French author; b. 26 March 1939, Paris; d. of Moïse and Olympia M. Graciani; m. Jean Guignabodet 1961; one s. two d.; ed primary school in Sofia (Bulgaria), Lycée Jules Ferry, Paris, Sorbonne and Univ. of London; Prof. of French, San José, USA 1961–62; Prof. of Arts and Culture, Ecole Technique d'IBM France 1966–69; author 1977–; mem. PEN Club Français, Asscn des Ecrivains Croyants, Société des Gens de Lettres, Acad. Européenne des Sciences, des Arts et des Lettres, Acad. Valentin, Jury du Prix de Journalisme de l' Asscn Franco-Bulgare; Prix George Sand 1977, Grand Prix du Roman, Acad. Française 1983, Grand prix du Roman, Ville de Cannes 1991. *Publications:* L'écume du silence 1977, Le bracelet indien 1980, Natalia 1983, Le livre du vent 1984, Dessislava 1986, Car les hommes sont meilleurs que leur vie 1991, Un sentiment inconnu 1998. *Leisure interests:* piano, travel, decorating, skiing. *Address:* 55 rue Caulaincourt, 75018 Paris; 16 chemin du Clos d'Agasse, 06650 Le Rouret, France. *Telephone:* 1-46-06-09-86. *Fax:* 1-46-06-09-86.

GUIGOU, Elisabeth Alexandrine Marie, LèsL; French politician; b. 6 Aug. 1946, Marrakesh, Morocco; d. of Georges Vallier and Jeanne Flecchia; m. Jean-Louis Guigou 1966; one s.; ed Lycée Victor Hugo, Marrakesh, Lycée Descartes, Rabat, Facultés des Lettres, Rabat and Montpellier, Faculté des Sciences Economiques, Montpellier and Ecole Nat. d'Admin; civil servant, Ministry of Finance 1974, Office of the Treasury 1974–75, Office of Banks 1976–78, Office of Financial Markets 1978–79; Deputy Chair. Finance Cttee VIIth Plan 1975–78; Maître de Conférences, Inst. d'Etudes Politiques, Paris 1976; Financial Attaché, Embassy, London 1979–81; Head, Office for Europe, America and Asia, Treasury 1981; Tech. Counsellor, Office of Minister of Economy and Finance 1982; Tech. Counsellor 1982–88; Office of Pres. of Repub. 1988–90; Sec.-Gen. Interministerial Cttee on European Econ. Cooperation 1985–90; Minister Delegate for European Affairs 1990–93; mem. Regional Council of Provence Alpes Côte-d'Azur 1992–2002, European Parl. 1994–97; elected Deputy to Nat. Ass. for Vaucluse (Socialist Party) 1997; Minister of Justice 1997–2000, of Employment and Solidarity 2000–02. *Publications:* Pour les Européens 1994, Etre femme en politique 1997. *Address:* c/o Conseil Régional de Provence Alpes Côte d'Azur, 27 place Jules Guesde, 13481 Marseille cedex, France.

GUILFOYLE, Dame Margaret Georgina Constance, DBE, LLB; Australian politician and accountant; b. 15 May 1926, Belfast, Northern Ireland; d. of William McCartney and Elizabeth Jane Ellis; m. Stanley Martin Leslie Guilfoyle 1952; one s. two d.; chartered sec. and accountant 1947–; Liberal mem. Senate for Victoria 1971–87; Minister for Educ. Nov.–Dec. 1975, for Social Security 1975–80, for Finance 1980–83; Deputy Chair. Mental Health Research Inst. 1988–2000, Infertility Treatment Authority 1996–2002; Chair. Judicial Remuneration Tribunal 1995–2001, Ministerial Advisory Cttee on Women's Health 1996–99, Australian Political Exchange Council 1996–; Dir Australian Children's TV Foundation 1989–; mem. Nat. Inquiry Concerning Human Rights of People with Mental Illness 1990–93; Fellow, Australian Soc. of Accountants; Fellow, Chartered Inst. of Secs. and Administrators; mem. Review of the Australian Blood Banking and Plasma Product Sector 1999. *Leisure interests:* reading, opera. *Address:* 21 Howard Street, Kew, Victoria 3101, Australia (Home).

GUILLAUD, Jean Louis; French news agency executive; b. 5 March 1929, Caen; s. of Marcel Guillaud and Suzanne Le Brun; m. 2nd Catherine Chichet 1978; one d.; one s. one d. from previous relationships; ed Inst. d'Etudes Politiques, Paris; political journalist, Soc. Générale de Presse 1953–58, Paris-Jour 1958–60, France-Soir and Nouveau Candide 1961–63; Ed.-in-Chief, ORTF 1963, Dir of TV News 1968–69; special assignment at Secr.-Gen. of

Presidency of Repub. 1970–72; Dir of Regional Stations and Third Channel, ORTF 1972–74; Dir-Gen. TFI 1975–78, Pres., Dir-Gen. 1978–81; later TV Dir Hachette Group; Pres., Dir-Gen. Agence France Presse (AFP) 1987–90; Pres. Polycom SA 1988–90; Pres., Dir-Gen. HDSA 1990–95, Media Campus 1990–95; Pres. TV France Int. 1994–; mem. (Admin. Council) Revue de Défense Nationale 1991–; Officier, Légion d'honneur, Officier, Ordre nat. du Mérite, Chevalier des Arts et des Lettres. *Address:* Office of the President, TV France International, 5 rue Cernuschi, 75017 Paris (Office); 13 rue de la Mairie, 27140 Bazincourt-sur-Epte, France (Home).

GUILLAUME, Gilbert, LenD; French judge; b. 4 Dec. 1930, Bois-Colombes; s. of Pierre Guillaume and Berthe Guillaume; m. Marie-Anne Hidden 1961; one s. two d.; ed Univ. of Paris, Paris Inst. of Political Studies and Ecole Nat. d'Administration; mem. Council of State 1957; Legal Adviser, State Secr. for Civil Aviation 1968–79; French Rep. Legal Cttee of ICAO 1968–69, Chair. of Cttee 1971–75; Chair. Conciliation Comm. OECD 1973–78; Dir of Legal Affairs, OECD 1979; mem. European Space Agency Appeals Bd 1975–78; French Rep. Central Comm. for Navigation of the Rhine 1979–87, Chair. 1981–82; Dir of Legal Affairs, Ministry of Foreign Affairs 1979–87; Conseiller d'Etat 1981–96; Prof. Inst. d'études politiques de Paris 1983–95; Counsel/ agent for France in int. arbitration proceedings, numerous cases before European Courts etc.; mem. Perm. Court of Arbitration 1980–; del. to numerous int. legal and diplomatic confs.; Prof. Inst. of Political Studies, Univ. of Paris and other lecturing appts.; mem. various legal asscns., insts. etc.; Judge, Int. Court of Justice 1987–, Pres. 2000–; Commdr., Légion d'honneur, Chevalier, Ordre nat. du Mérite, du Mérite agricole, du Mérite maritime, Commdr des Arts et des Lettres. *Publications:* numerous books and articles on administrative and international law; Terrorisme et droit international 1989, Le grandes crises internationales et le droit 1994. *Address:* International Court of Justice, Peace Palace, Carnegieplein 2, 2517 KJ, The Hague, The Netherlands (Office); 36 rue Perronet, 92200 Neuilly-sur-Seine, France (Home). *Telephone:* (70) 3022323 (Office); 1-46-24-25-67 (Home). *Fax:* (70) 3022409 (Office); 1-47-45-67-84 (Home). *E-mail:* g.guillaume@icj-cij.org (Office).

GUILLEM, Sylvie; French ballet dancer; b. 23 Feb. 1965, Le Blanc Mesnil; joined Ecole de Danse, Paris Opera 1976; Ballet de l'Opéra as Quadrille 1981, promoted to Coryphée 1982, to Sujet 1983, Première Danseuse, later Etoile 1984; with Royal Ballet, London 1989–; choreographer Giselle, Nat. Ballet of Finland 1999; Chevalier, Légion d'honneur, Commdr des Arts et Lettres 1988. *Leading roles in:* Romeo and Juliet, Don Quixote, Raymonda, Swan Lake, Giselle, Notre Dame de Paris, Manon, Marguerite and Armand. *Created roles include:* Cendrillon, In the Middle, Somewhat Elevated, Magnificat, Le Martyre de Saint-Sébastien. *Created and produced:* Evidentia (TV) 1995; Prize for Excellence and Gold Medal, Varna Int. Dance Competition 1983, Prix Carpeau 1984, Hans Christian Andersen Award 1988, Arpège Prize (Lanvin perfumes) 1989. *Address:* c/o Royal Ballet, Royal Opera House, London, WC2E 9DD, England.

GUILLEMIN, Roger Charles Louis, MD, PhD; American professor of medicine; b. 11 Jan. 1924, Dijon, France; s. of Raymond and Blanche Guillemin; m. Lucienne Jeanne Billard 1951; one s. five d.; ed Univs. of Dijon, Lyons, Montreal; Prosector of Anatomy, Univ. of Dijon Medical School 1946–47; Research Asst, Inst. of Experimental Medicine and Surgery, Univ. of Montreal 1949–51, Assoc. Dir and Asst Prof. of Experimental Medicine 1951–53; Asst Prof. of Physiology, Coll. of Medicine, Baylor Univ., Houston, Tex. 1953, Assoc. Prof. 1957, Prof. of Physiology and Dir Laboratories for Neuroendocrinology 1963–70, Adjunct Prof. of Physiology 1970–; Consultant in Physiology, Veterans' Admin. Hosp., Houston 1954–60, 1967–70; Lecturer in Experimental Endocrinology, Dept of Biology, W. M. Rice Univ., Houston 1958–60; Assoc. Dir, Dept of Experimental Endocrinology, Coll. de France, Paris, as jt appointment with Coll. of Medicine, Baylor Univ. 1960–63; Resident Fellow and Research Prof., The Salk Inst. for Biological Studies, San Diego, Calif. 1970–89, Dean 1972–73, 1976–77, Distinguished Prof. 1997–; Distinguished Scientist, Whittier Inst. for Diabetes and Endocrinology, La Jolla 1989–93, Medical and Scientific Dir, Dir 1993–94, 1995–97; Adjunct Prof. of Medicine Univ. of Calif., San Diego 1995–97; mem. NAS 1974–, American Acad. of Arts and Sciences, American Physiological Soc., Soc. for Experimental Biology and Medicine, Int. Brain Research Org., Int. Soc. for Research in Biology and Reproduction, Swedish Soc. of Medical Sciences, Acad. Nat. de Médecine, France, Acad. des Sciences, France, Acad. Royale de Médecine de Belgique, Belgium; Pres. The Endocrine Soc. 1986; hon. degrees (Univ. of Rochester, NY) 1976, (Univ. of Chicago, Ill.) 1977, (Baylor Coll. of Medicine, Houston, Tex.) 1978, (Univ. of Ulm) 1978, (Univ. of Dijon) 1978, (Univ. Libre de Bruxelles) 1979, (Univ. de Montreal) 1979, (Univ. of Manitoba) 1984, (Univ. of Turin) 1985, (Kung Hee Univ., Seoul) 1986, (Univ. Paris VII) 1986, (Autónoma, Madrid) 1988, (McGill Univ.) 1988, (Sherbrook Univ. Quebec) 1997, (Univ. Franche-Conté) 1999; Bonneau and La Caze Awards in Physiology (Acad. des Sciences) 1957, 1960, Gairdner Award (Toronto) 1974, Officier, Légion d'honneur, Lasker Foundation Award 1975, co-recipient of Nobel Prize in Physiology or Medicine with Andrew V. Schally (q.v.) for discoveries relating to peptide hormones 1977, Nat. Medal of Science 1977, Barren Gold Medal 1979, Dale Medallist, UK Soc. for Endocrinology 1980; numerous int. awards and lectureships. *Address:* The Salk Institute, 10010 North Torrey Pines Road, La Jolla, CA 92037, USA.

GUILLEN, Fernando; Peruvian diplomatist; b. 24 July 1939, Arequipa; m.; one c.; ed Catholic Univ. of Peru, Universidad Nacional Mayor de San Marcos,

Lima, Diplomatic Acad. of Peru; joined diplomatic service 1966, fmrly mem. staff Mission to UN, Geneva, Head Dept of Int. Econ. Policy, Head Div. of Econ. Integration, Ministry for Foreign Affairs; Minister, Embassy, France 1981, Colombia 1982–84; Amb. to India 1986–91; Under-Sec.-Gen. for Multilateral Affairs, Ministry for Foreign Affairs and Co-ordinator for Peru, Rio Group 1991; Sec. Consultative Cttee to Minister for Foreign Affairs 1991–92; Perm. Rep. to UN 1992–2001; mem. Peruvian Soc. of Int. Law. *Address:* c/o Ministry of Foreign Affairs, Palacio de Torre Tagle, Jirón Ucayali 363, Lima 1, Peru.

GUILLERMIN, John; British film director; b. 11 Nov. 1925, London. *Films include:* Torment 1949, Smart Alec 1951, Two on the Tiles 1951, Four Days 1951, Bachelor in Paris 1952, Miss Robin Hood 1952, Operation Diplomat 1953, Adventure in the Hopfields 1954, The Crowded Day 1954, Dust and Gold 1955, Thunderstorm 1955, Town on Trial 1957, The Whole Truth 1958, I Was Monty's Double 1958, Tarzan's Greatest Adventure 1959, The Day They Robbed the Bank of England 1960, Never Let Go 1960, Waltz of the Toreadors 1962, Tarzan Goes to India 1962, Guns at Batasi 1964, Rapture 1965, The Blue Max 1966, P.J. 1968, House of Cards 1969, The Bridge at Remagen 1969, El Condor 1970, Skyjacked 1972, Shaft in Africa 1973, The Towering Inferno 1974, King Kong 1976, Death on the Nile 1978, Mr Patman 1980, Sheena 1984, King Kong Lives 1986, The Favourite, The Tracker 1988.

GUILLERY, Rainer W., PhD, FRS; British university teacher, anatomist and neurobiologist; b. 28 Aug. 1929, Greifswald, Germany; s. of Eva Hackel and Hermann Guillery; m. Margot Cunningham Pepper 1954 (divorced 2000); three s. one d.; ed Univ. Coll. London; Asst Lecturer, Anatomy Dept, Univ. Coll. London 1953–56, Lecturer 1956–63, Reader 1963–64; Assoc. Prof., Dept of Anatomy, Univ. of Wis., Madison, USA 1964–68, Prof. 1968–77, Visiting Prof. 1996–2002, Emer. Prof. 2002–; Prof., Dept of Pharmacological and Physiological Sciences and Chair. Cttee on Neurobiology, Univ. of Chicago, USA 1977–84; Dr. Lee's Prof. of Anatomy, Oxford Univ., England 1984–96; Pres. Anatomical Soc. of Great Britain and Ireland 1994–96; Ed.-in-Chief European Journal of Neuroscience 1988–92; Fellow, Hertford Coll., Oxford 1984–96, Emer. 1996–; Hon. Fellow Univ. Coll. London 1987, Fellow Royal Soc. *Publications:* Exploring the Thalamus (with M. S. Sherman) 2001–; contribs. to Journal of Comparative Neurology, Journal of Neuroscience, Neuroscience, Brain Research, etc. *Leisure interests:* working with wood, growing fruit and vegetables, needle point embroidery. *Address:* c/o Department of Anatomy, University of Wisconsin, 1300 University Avenue, Madison, WI 53706, USA (Office). *Telephone:* (608) 263-4763 (Office). *Fax:* (608) 262-7306 (Office). *E-mail:* rguiller@facstaff.wisc.edu (Office).

GUINGONA, Teofisto; Philippine politician; Vice-Pres. of the Philippines 2001–; Sec. of Foreign Affairs 2001–02; Pres. Lakas party. *Address:* Office of the Vice-President, PICC, 2nd Floor, CCP Complex, Roxas Boulevard, Pasay City, Metro Manila, The Philippines (Office). *Telephone:* (2) 8312658 (Office). *Fax:* (2) 8312614 (Office). *E-mail:* gma@easy.net.ph (Office).

GUINHUT, Jean-Pierre; French diplomatist; b. 1946; joined French foreign service 1975, posted to French Embassy, Qatar 1975–76, Iran 1980–82, 1988–93, First Counsellor, Libya 1982–85, Middle East Desk, French Mission to UN, New York 1985–88, Head of Middle East Div., Foreign Service, Paris 1993–96; Amb. to Azerbaijan 1996–2002, to Afghanistan March 2002–. *Publication:* The Man Who Loved Too Much: The Legend of Leyli and Majnun 1998. *Address:* Embassy of France, POB 62, Avenue de Cherpou, Shar-i-Nau, Kabul, Afghanistan (Office). *Telephone:* (763) 0198678 (Office). *Fax:* (682) 084817 (Office).

GUINN, Kenny C., EdD; American state official; b. 24 Aug. 1936, Garland, Ark.; m.; ed Calif. State Univ., Utah State Univ.; Supt Clark Co. School Dist; Vice-Pres. of Admin., Nevada Savings and Loan Asscn (PriMerit Bank) 1978–80, Pres., COO 1980–85, CEO 1985–92, currently Chair.; Pres. South West Gas Corpn 1987–88, Chair., CEO 1988–93, currently Chair.; Gov. of Nevada 1999–. *Address:* Office of the Governor, 101 Carson Street, Carson City, NV 89701, USA (Office).

GUJRAL, Inder Kumar, MA; Indian politician; b. 4 Dec. 1919, Jhelum (now in Pakistan); s. of the late Avtar Narain Gujral and Pushpa Gujral; m. Sheila Gujral 1944; two s.; ed Forman Christian Coll. and Hailey Coll. of Commerce in Lahore, Punjab Univ.; jailed for participation in freedom movt 1930–31 (and again during Quit India movt 1942); Pres. Lahore Students' Union; Gen.-Sec. Punjab Students' Fed.; migrated to India 1947; helped nat. effort for rehabilitation of displaced persons; Vice-Pres. New Delhi Municipal Cttee 1959–64; MP 1964–76, 1989–91, 1992–98, mem. Lok Sabha Punjab 1998–; Leader Rajya Sabha June–Nov. 1996, 1997–98; mem. Council of Ministers, Govt of India 1967–76 holding portfolios for Communications and Parl. Affairs, Information, Broadcasting and Communications, Works, Housing and Urban Devt, Information and Broadcasting and Planning 1975–76; Minister of External Affairs 1989–90, 1996–97; Prime Minister of India 1997–98; Chair. Parl. Cttee on External Affairs 1998–; Amb. to USSR (with ministerial rank) 1976–80; Vice-Pres. New Delhi Municipal Cttee 1959–64; helped organize Citizens Cttee, for Civil Defence; leader several Indian dels to UNESCO 1970–77, to UN Special Session on Econ. Devt 1990, to UN Gen. Ass. 1990, 1996, to UN Session on Human Rights, Geneva 1995 and leader or mem. numerous Indian dels to other int. orgs; mem. UN Panel of Eminent Persons to study and report on situation in Algeria 1998; Pres. Inst. of Defence Studies and Analysis; Chair. Indian Council of S Asian Co-operation; Founder-Pres. Delhi Arts Theatre; Treas. Fed. of Film Socs of India; fmr

Chancellor Vishva Bharati Univ., Shanti Niketan. *Leisure interests:* theatre, poetry, painting, ecological problems. *Address:* G-13, Maharani Bagh, New Delhi 110065, India.

GUL, Abdullah, PhD; Turkish politician; b. 1949, Qaisari Prov.; m.; three c.; ed Istanbul Univ., Univ. of London, UK; teacher in several Turkish univs; economist with Islamic Devt Bank, Jeddah 1983–91; MP representing Al-Rafah Party (now outlawed) 1991, later Al-Rafah Deputy Head of Foreign Affairs; held numerous ministerial posts including Minister of State for Foreign Affairs, Spokesman for Al-Rafah Govt, also mem. European Council; sought leadership of Al-Fadila Party following dissolution of Al-Rafah Party; Founder-mem. AK Partisi (Justice and Devt Party) 2001–; Prime Minister of Turkey Nov. 2002–March 2003; Minister of Foreign Affairs 2003–. *Address:* Ministry of Foreign Affairs, Dışişleri Bakanlığı, Yeni Hizmet Binası, 06520 Balgat, Ankara (Office); AK Partisi, Genel Merkezi Ceyhun Atif Kansu Cad., No. 202 Balgat, Ankara, Turkey. *Telephone:* (312) 2873556 (Office); (312) 2868989. *Fax:* (312) 2873869 (Office); (312) 2863084. *E-mail:* akparti@akparti.org.tr. *Website:* www.mfa.gov.tr (Office); www.akparti.org.tr.

GULAMOV, Kadir G., PhD; Uzbekistan professor of nuclear physics; b. 17 Feb. 1945, Tashkent; m. two c.; Sr Scientific Researcher, Physical Tech. Inst., Tashkent, later Head of Lab. 1983–88; Prof. of Physics 1980; Prof., Faculty of Physics, Tashkent State Univ.; Dir Gen. and Sec. Gen. Physics Uzbekistan Acad. of Sciences; Fellow Islamic Acad. of Sciences; Corresp. mem. Uzbekistan Acad. of Sciences; Beruni State Prize (Uzbekistan) 1983, Independence Memorial Medal (Uzbekistan) 1992. *Publications:* over 250 publs in fields of high energy and nuclear physics. *Address:* Tashkent State University, 700095 Tashkent, Vuzgorodok, Universitetskaya ul. 95, Uzbekistan (Office). *Telephone:* (712) 46-02-24 (Office).

GULBINOWICZ, HE Cardinal Henryk Roman, DTheol; Polish ecclesiastic; b. 17 Oct. 1928, Szukiszki (now in Lithuania); s. of Antoni Gulbinowicz and Waleria Gajewska; ed Metropolitan Higher Ecclesiastic Seminary, Vilnius and Białystok, Catholic Univ. of Lublin (KUL); ordained priest 1950; Titular Bishop, Apostolic Admin. Archdiocese of Białystok 1970–76, Archbishop Metropolitan of Wrocław 1976–; mem. Congregation for the Evangelization of Nations, Congregation for Eastern Churches, Congregation Clergy Affairs; mem. Main Council Polish Episcopate and several episcopate cttees.; High Chancellor Pontifical Faculty Theology, Wrocław; cr. HE Cardinal 1985; Dr. hc (Pontifical Faculty of Theology, Wrocław) 1995, (Agricultural Acad., Wrocław) 2000; Commdr.'s Cross with Star, Order of Polonia Restituta; hon. citizen Wrocław 1996. *Publications:* more than 240 works on moral theology, ethics, ecumenism and history of the Polish Eastern Territories. *Address:* Kuria Metropolitakna, ul. Katedralna 11, 50-328 Wrocław, Poland. *Telephone:* (71) 322-42-14.

GULEGHINA, Maria; Belarus/Armenian soprano; b. 1959, Odessa; m. Mark Gulegin; ed Odessa Conservatory (studied with Yevgeni Ivanov); soloist Minsk Opera Theatre 1983–90; taught in Minsk Conservatory 1986–90; regular appearances at La Scala (since 1986), Wiener Staatsoper, Metropolitan Opera 1990, other major European theatres; First Prize All-Union Glinka Competition 1984, Zanatello Award, Verona 1997. *Music:* video-audio: Tosca, Manon Lescaut, Macbeth (all at La Scala, Milan); Andrea Chenier, Nabucco (both at Metropolitan Opera, New York); audio Tabarro, Oberto, Francesca di Rimini, Picovcia Dama. *Radio:* many live broadcasts from the Met, La Scala, Vienna etc. *Television:* Nabucco (Vienna Met), Andrea Chenier, Tosca, Manon Lescaut, Macbeth (all at La Scala), Verdi Arias, Italian Arias (both for NHK). *Opera roles include:* parts in Tosca, Manon Lescaut (Puccini), Due Foscari, Il Trovatore, Un Ballo in Maschera, Ernani, Aida, Otello, Nabucco (Verdi), Cavalleria Rusticana (Mascagni), Andrea Chenier, Fedora (Giordano), Yolanta, Eugene Onegin, Queen of Spades (Tchaikovsky); concert performances of Verdi's Requiem; solo recitals in Germany, Italy, Switzerland, Austria, France, Hungary, USA, Japan. *Address:* c/o Askonas Holt, Lonsdale Chambers, 27 Chancery Lane, London, WC2A 1PF, England. *Telephone:* (20) 7400-1700. *Fax:* (20) 7400-1799.

GULIYEV, Fuat Khalil-ogly; Azerbaijani politician; b. 6 July 1941, Baku; m.; two c.; ed Azerbaijani Inst. of Oil Chem.; worked in Belorussia in oil chemical industry; Chief Engineer, later Dir Air Conditioners Factory, Baku; First Deputy Prime Minister of Azerbaijan 1994–95; Prime Minister of Azerbaijan 1995–96; mem. Milli Majlis (Nat. Ass.) 1991–; mem. New Azerbaijan Party. *Address:* House of Parliament, Azizbekova Prospeci 1, 370001 Baku, Azerbaijan.

GULLICHSEN, Johan Erik, MSc; Finnish professor of pulping technology and engineer; b. 28 June 1936, Pihlava; s. of Harry Gullichsen and Maire Ahlström; m. Anna Ramsay 1958; one s. one d.; ed Abo Akademi, Helsinki Univ. of Tech.; Research Asst, FPPRI 1962–64; Project Engineer, EKONO 1964–70; Pres. and Partner, Arhippainen, Gullichsen & Co. 1970–; Prof. of Pulping Tech., Helsinki Univ. of Tech. 1989–2000; Chair. Bd A. Ahlstrom Corpn 1999–; fmr Chair. Bd A. Ahlstrom Oy, Dir Kymmene Oy; Hon. DTech (Abo Akademi) 1988; Engineer of the Year in Finland 1984, The Marcus Wallenberg Prize 1986. *Publications:* tech. and scientific papers on pulping tech., econs and environmental control. *Leisure interest:* yachting. *Address:* Arhippainen, Gullichsen & Co., Tekniikantie 12, 02150 Espoo, Finland. *Telephone:* (9) 2517-2505.

GULYAEV, Yury Vasilievich, DPhys-MathSc; Russian physicist; b. 18 Sept. 1935; m.; two c.; ed Moscow Inst. of Physics and Tech.; jr researcher, sr researcher, Head of Lab., Vice-Dir Inst. of Radioelectronics and Electrotech., USSR (now Russian) Acad. of Sciences 1960–87, Dir 1988–; Corresp. mem. USSR (now Russian) Acad. of Sciences 1979, mem. 1984–, mem. Presidium 1992–; Chair. Saratov br., Russian Acad. of Sciences 1987–; mem. Russian Acad. of Natural Sciences; USSR People's Deputy 1989–91; USSR State Prize, Prize of European Hewlett-Packard Physical Soc.; mem. Polish Acad. of Sciences; Vice-Pres. World Fed. of Eng Orgs (WFEO). *Publications:* more than a hundred articles, mainly on acoustic electronics, acoustic optics and spin-wave electronics. *Address:* Institute of Radiotechnology and Electronics, Mokhovaya ul. 11, 103907 Moscow, Russia. *Telephone:* (095) 200-52-58. *Fax:* (095) 203-84-14.

GULYÁS, Dénes; Hungarian opera singer; b. 31 March 1954; s. of Dénes Gulyás and Mária Szitár; m. Judit Szekeres; two s. one d.; ed Liszt Ferenc Acad. of Music, Budapest; joined State Opera, Budapest 1978; debut as Rinuccio in Gianni Schicchi; debut in USA, Carnegie Hall and Avery Fisher Hall, New York: concert performances; numerous tours in the USA; 1st prize Parma 1979, won Luciano Pavarotti singing competition, Philadelphia 1981; Holder of Liszt Prize, titled Merited Artist. *Repertoire includes:* Faust, des Grieux (Manon), Werther, Hoffman, Titus (La Clemenza di Tito), Percy (Anne Boleyn), Ernesto (Don Pasquale), Duke of Mantua (Rigoletto), Fenton (Falstaff), Ferrando (Così fan tutte), Don Ottavio, Tamino, Alfredo (La Traviata), Edgardo (Lucia di Lammermoor), Nemorino, Rodolfo (La Bohème), Tom Rakewell (The Rake's Progress). *Leisure interests:* riding, sailing, viticulture. *Address:* Hungarian State Opera, Budapest 1062, Andrássy ut 22, Hungary. *Telephone:* (1) 131-2550.

GUMBEL, Bryant Charles; American broadcaster; b. 29 Sept. 1948, New Orleans; s. of Richard Gumbel and Rhea LeCesne; m. June C. Baranco 1973; one s. one d.; ed Bates Coll.; writer, Black Sports (magazine), New York 1971, Ed. 1972; sportscaster, KNBC-TV, Burbank, Calif. 1972–76, Sports Dir 1976–81; sports host, NBC Sports 1975–82; co-host, Today Show, NBC 1982–97; host Public Eye, CBS 1997–, The Early Show 1999–; recipient of two Emmy Awards and two Golden Mike Awards (LA Press Club); Edward R. Murrow Award (Overseas Press Club) 1988. *Address:* c/o CBS, 51 West 52nd Street, New York, NY 10019, USA (Office).

GUMBS, Walford Vincent, JP; Saint Christopher and Nevis politician; b. 21 Dec. 1946; m.; three c.; ed Basseterre Sr School, Ruppin Inst. of Agric., Israel, ILO Int. Training Centre, Turin, Italy; customs clerk St Kitts Sugar Factory Ltd, Basseterre 1965–70; Accounts Officer and Acting Man. Sun Island Clothes Ltd 1973–77; Field Officer St Kitts–Nevis Trades and Labour Union 1970–73, Exec. Officer 1978–, Second Vice-Pres. 1979–89, First Vice-Pres. 1989–2000, Pres. 2000–; Pres. Young Labour 1969–71, Vice-Chair. St Kitts–Nevis Labour Party 1992–96; apptd Senator (Labour Party) Nat. Ass. 1989, Speaker Nat. Ass. 1995–. *Leisure interests:* sports, jogging, int. affairs. *Address:* Office of the Speaker, National Assembly, Basseterre (Office); Suncrest Housing #43, Basseterre, Saint Christopher and Nevis (Home). *Telephone:* 465-2229 (Office); 465-8320 (Home). *Fax:* 466-9866 (Office). *E-mail:* sknunion@caribsurf.com (Office).

GUMMER, Rt Hon John Selwyn, PC, MA; British politician; b. 26 Nov. 1939, Stockport; s. of the late Canon Selwyn Gummer and Sybille Gummer (née Mason); brother of Peter Selwyn Gummer, now Lord Chadlington; m. Penelope J. Gardner 1977; two s. two d.; ed King's School, Rochester and Selwyn Coll., Cambridge; Ed., Business Publs 1962–64; Ed.-in-Chief, Max Parrish and Oldbourne Press 1964–66; Special Asst to Chair. BPC Publishing 1967; Dir Shandwick Publishing Co. 1966–81; Dir Siemssen Hunter Ltd 1973–80, Chair. 1979–80; Man. Dir EP Group of Cos 1975–81; Chair. Selwyn Sancroft Int. 1976–81; MP for Lewisham W 1970–74, Eye, Suffolk (now Suffolk Coastal) 1979–; Parl. Pvt. Sec. to Minister of Agric. 1972; Vice-Chair. Conservative Party 1972–74, Chair. 1983–85; Asst Govt Whip 1981, Lord Commr Treasury (Whip) 1982; Under-Sec. of State for Employment Jan.–Oct. 1983, Minister of State for Employment 1983–84, Paymaster-Gen. 1984–85; Minister of State at Ministry of Agric., Fisheries and Food 1985–88; Minister for Local Govt, Dept of Environment 1988–89; Minister of Agric. 1989–93; Sec. of State for the Environment 1993–97; Chair. Conservative Group for Europe 1997–, Marine Stewardship Council 1998–, Sancroft Int. Ltd 1997–, Valpak Ltd 1998–; mem. Gen. Synod of Church of England 1979–92 (resgnd); joined Roman Catholic Church 1994. *Publications:* When the Coloured People Come 1966, To Church with Enthusiasm 1969, The Permissive Society 1970, The Christian Calendar (with L. W. Cowie) 1971, Faith in Politics (with Alan Beith and Eric Heffer) 1987, Christianity and Conservatism 1990. *Leisure interests:* gardening, Victorian buildings. *Address:* House of Commons, London, SW1A 0AA, England (Office).

GUNA-KASEM, Pracha, PhD; Thai diplomatist; b. 29 Dec. 1934, Bangkok; s. of Jote Guna-Kasem and Rabieb Guna-Kasem; m. Sumanee Chongcharoen 1962; one s.; ed Dhebsirinda School, Bangkok, Marlborough Coll., Hertford Coll., Oxford and Yale Univ.; joined Ministry of Foreign Affairs 1959, Chief of Section, Political Div. of Dept of Int. Org. 1960–61, Second Sec. SEATO Div. 1962–63, Alt. Mem. for Thailand, SEATO Perm. Working Group 1962–63, Embassy in Egypt 1964–65, Chief of Foreign News Analysis Div. of Information Dept and concurrently in charge of Press Affairs 1966–69, Chief of Press Div. 1970–71, Consul-Gen. in Hong Kong 1971–73, Dir-Gen. of Information Dept 1973–75; Perm. Rep. to UN 1975–80, UN (Geneva) 1980–82; Dir-Gen. ASEAN-Thailand 1982; Dir-Gen. Dept of Econ. Affairs, Foreign Ministry 1984–85; Amb. to France and Algeria 1985–87; Perm. Del. to UNESCO 1985;

Dir-Gen. Dept of Econ. Affairs, Bangkok 1988; Perm. Sec. Ministry of Foreign Affairs 1992–2001, Adviser to the Minister 2001–; Special Lecturer, Thammasat Univ., Thai Nat. Defence Coll.; mem. del. to UN Gen. Ass. 1962, 1968, 1970, 1974, to 2nd Afro-Asian Conf., Algeria 1965, to SEATO Council 1966; Kt Grand Cordon of Order of White Elephant, Grand Cordon (Highest Class) of the Order of the Crown of Thailand, Commdr Order of Chula Chomklao. *Leisure interests:* golf, bridge, tennis, swimming. *Address:* Ministry of Foreign Affairs, Thanon Sri Ayudhya, Bangkok, Thailand. *Telephone:* (2) 6435000. *Website:* www.mfa.go.th.

GUNDAREVA, Natalya Georgiyevna; Russian actress; b. 28 Aug. 1948, Moscow; m. Mikhail Filippov; ed B. Shchukin Theatre School; with Mayakovsky Theatre since 1971; cinema debut in 1973; mem. State Duma (Parl.) (rep. of Political Movt Women of Russia) 1993–96; USSR People's Actress, USSR State Prize 1984, State Prize of Russia 1981. *Films include:* Hello and Goodbye 1973, Autumn 1975, Sweet Woman 1977, Autumn Marathon 1979, Once Twenty Years Later 1981, The Term of Prescription 1983, Dogs' Feast 1990, The Promised Heaven 1991, Chicken 1991, The Petersburg Secrets 1997 and many others. *Address:* Mayakovsky Theatre, Bolshaya Nikitskaya str. 19, Moscow, Russia (Office); Tverskaya 42, Apt. 14, 125047 Moscow, Russia (Home). *Telephone:* (095) 250-43-55 (Home).

GUNGAADORJ, Sharavyn; Mongolian politician; b. 2 May 1935, Ikh Khet soum, Dornogobi Aimak (Prov.); ed Acad. of Agriculture, USSR; Chief Agronomist, Amgalan State farm; agronomist, Dept of State Farms 1959–67; Instructor at the Mongolian People's Revolutionary Party (MPRP) Cen. Cttee 1967–68; Deputy Minister for Agric.; head of fodder farm in Zabhan Aimak Prov.; Head of group, Ministry of Agric. 1968–80; First Deputy Minister for State Farms 1980–81; First Sec. Party Cttee of Selenge Aimak Prov. 1981–86; Minister for Agric. 1986–90; Deputy Chair. Council of Ministers 1987–90; Alt. mem. MPRP Cen. Cttee 1981–86, mem. 1986–; Deputy to Great People's Hural (Ass.) 1981–89, Chair. Council of Ministers April–Sept. 1990, Counsellor to the Pres., Chair. of the Civic Council attached to the Pres. 1990–91; Amb. to Democratic People's Repub. of Korea and Kazakhstan 1991–96; Pres. Co-operatives Asscn 1997–. *Address:* c/o Ministry of External Relations, Ulan Bator, Mongolia. *Telephone:* 321870. *Telex:* 245.

GUNN, John Charles, CBE, MD, F.R.C.PSYCH., FMedSci; British psychiatrist; b. 6 June 1937, Hove; s. of Albert Gunn and Lily Hilda Gunn (née Edwards); m. Celia Willis 1959 (divorced 1986, died 1989); one s. one d.; m. 2nd Pamela Taylor 1989; ed Brighton, Hove and Sussex Grammar School, Reigate Grammar School, Birmingham Univ. Medical School; Consultant Psychiatrist, Bethlem Maudsley Hosp. 1971–; Dir Special Hosps. Research Unit 1975–78; Prof. of Forensic Psychiatry, Inst. of Psychiatry, Univ. of London 1978–2002, Emer.Prof. 2002–; Chair. Research Cttee, Royal Coll. of Psychiatrists 1976–80, Chair. Faculty of Forensic Psychiatry 2000–; Chair. Academic Bd, Inst. of Psychiatry 1980–85; Chair. Forensic Specialist Cttee, Jt Cttee on Higher Psychiatric Training 1982–85; Consultant European Cttee for Prevention of Torture 1991–; Ed. Criminal Behaviour and Mental Health 1991–; mem. Ont. Govt Enquiry in Oakridge, Ont., Canada 1984–85, Home Sec.'s Advisory Bd on Restricted Patients 1982–91, Bethlem Maudsley Special Health Authority 1986–90, Royal Comm. on Criminal Justice 1991–93; Council, Royal Coll. of Psychiatrists 1997–; foundation mem. Acad. of Medical Sciences 1998; RMPA Bronze Medal 1970, H. B. Williams Travelling Professorship to Australasia 1985. *Publications:* Violence 1973, Epileptics in Prison 1977, Psychiatric Aspects of Imprisonment 1978, Current Research in Forensic Psychiatry and Psychology (Vols 1–3) 1982–85, Forensic Psychiatry: Clinical, Legal and Ethical Issues 1993. *Leisure interests:* theatre, cinema, opera, walking, photography. *Address:* Department of Forensic Mental Health Sciences, Institute of Psychiatry, De Crespigny Park, Denmark Hill, London, SE5 8AF, England (Office). *Telephone:* (20) 7848-0123 (Office). *Fax:* (20) 7848-0754 (Office). *E-mail:* j.gunn@iop.kcl.ac.uk (Office). *Website:* www .iop.kcl.ac.uk/i.o.p./departments/forensic/index-stm (Office).

GUNN, Thomson William (Thom Gunn); British poet and teacher; b. 29 Aug. 1929, Gravesend; s. of Herbert Gunn and Ann Thomson; ed Univ. Coll. School, Hampstead and Trinity Coll. Cambridge; moved to Calif. 1954; lecturer, later Assoc. Prof. Dept of English, Univ. of Calif. (Berkeley) 1958–66; Visiting Lecturer 1975–90; Sr Lecturer 1990–99; Forward Prize 1992, MacArthur Fellowship 1993, David Cohen Prize, Art Council of England 2003. *Publications:* Poetry from Cambridge 1953, Fighting Terms 1954, The Sense of Movement 1957, My Sad Captains 1961, Selected Poems (with Ted Hughes) 1962, Five American Poets (ed. with Ted Hughes) 1962, Positives (with Ander Gunn) 1966, Touch 1967, Poems 1950–66: a selection 1969, Moly 1971, Jack Straw's Castle and Other Poems 1976, Selected Poems 1979, The Passages of Joy 1982, The Occasions of Poetry (ed. Clive Wilmer) 1982, The Man with Night Sweats 1992, Collected Poems 1993, Shelf Life 1994, Boss Cupid 2000. *Leisure interests:* cheap thrills. *Address:* 1216 Cole Street, San Francisco, CA 94117, USA.

GUNNARSSON, Birgir Ísleifur; Icelandic politician, lawyer and banker; b. 19 July 1936, Reykjavík; s. of Gunnar Espólín Benediktsson and Jorunn Ísleifsdóttir; m. Sonja Backman 1956; one s. three d.; ed Univ. of Iceland; advocate to lower courts 1962, Supreme Court 1967; law practice 1963–72; Leader Heimdallur Youth Soc. 1959–62; Sec.-Gen. Youth Fed. of Independence Party 1959–62; mem. Reykjavík City Council 1962–82; Mayor of Reykjavík 1972–78; mem. Parl. for Reykjavík 1979–91; Second Deputy Speaker of Althing 1983–87; Minister for Culture and Educ. 1987–88; Chair. Cttee on

Heavy Industry 1983–87; mem. Bd Nat. Power Co. 1965–91, Civil Aviation Bd 1984–87; Gov. Cen. Bank of Iceland 1991–, Chair. Bd of Govs 1994–; Commdr Order of the Falcon, Order of Dannebrog (Denmark), Order of St Olav (Norway), Order of the White Rose (Finland), Grosse Verdienstkreuz (Germany). *Leisure interests:* music, the outdoor life. *Address:* Central Bank of Iceland, Kalkoforsvegur 1, 150 Reykjavík (Office); Fjölnisvegur 15, 101 Reykjavík, Iceland (Home). *Telephone:* 569-9600 (Office); 552-0628 (Home). *Fax:* 569-9605 (Office). *E-mail:* sedlabanki@sedlabanki.is (Office). *Website:* www.sedlabanki.is (Office).

GUNNELL, Sally, OBE; British athlete (retd); b. 29 July 1966, Chigwell, Essex; m. Jon Bigg 1992; two s.; ed Chigwell High School; specialized in hurdles; coached by Bruce Longdon; fitness consultant Crown Sports 2001–; mem. Essex Ladies Athletic Club; competed 400 m hurdles Olympic Games, Seoul 1988; second 400m hurdles World Championship, Tokyo 1991; bronze medal 400m relay, Olympic Games, Barcelona 1992; women's team captain Olympic Games 1992–97; gold medal, 400m hurdles, Barcelona 1992; gold medal, 400m hurdles, World Championships 1993 (world record); gold medal 400m hurdles European Championships, Helsinki 1994; gold medal 400m hurdles Commonwealth Games, Canada 1994; only woman in history to have held concurrently four gold medals – Olympic, World, European and Commonwealth (as at end of 2002); retd 1997. *Publications:* Running Tall (with Christopher Priest) 1994, Be Your Best 2001. *Address:* Old School Cottage, School Lane, Pyecombe, W Sussex, England.

GUNSON, Ameral Blanche Tregurtha; British classical singer; b. 25 Oct. 1948, London; d. of Charles Cumbria and Auriol Cornwall; m. 1st Maurice Powell 1969 (divorced 1974); m. 2nd Philip Kay 1979; two s.; ed Convent of Jesus and Mary, London and Guildhall School of Music and Drama; freelance singing career 1972–74, with BBC Singers 1976–80; solo singing career in Britain and abroad, Proms Seasons 1979, 1985, 1988, 1989, 1990; Assoc. Guildhall School of Music and Drama; Gramophone Award for recording of Peter Grimes 1997; Lubslith Asscn (Finland) Award for vocal teaching 1997. *Leisure interests:* gardening, reading, walking, Russian music, relaxation. *Address:* 40 Brooklands Way, Redhill, Surrey, RH1 2BW, England. *Telephone:* (1737) 762726.

GUO BOXIONG, Lt-Gen.; Chinese army officer; b. 1942, Liquan Co., Shaanxi Prov.; joined PLA 1961; joined CCP 1963; Divisional Chief-of-Staff; Army Chief-of-Staff; Deputy Chief-of-Staff Lanzhou Mil. Area Command; Army Group Commdr 1990; fmr Vice-Commdr Beijing Mil. Area Command; Exec. Deputy Chief of Staff PLA 1999–; mem. 15th CCP Cen. Cttee 1997–. *Address:* Ministry of National Defence, Beijing, People's Republic of China.

GUO DONGPO; Chinese politician; b. Aug. 1937, Jiangdu Co., Jiangsu Prov.; ed Beijing Foreign Trade Inst.; joined CCP 1960; Vice-Chair. China Council for the Promotion of Int. Trade 1982; Dir Macau Br. of Xinhua News Agency 1990; Vice-Dir Drafting Cttee of the Basic Law of Macau Special Admin. Zone 1990; mem. CPPCC 1991; alt. mem. 14th CCP Cen. Cttee 1992; Dir Office of Overseas Chinese Affairs of the State Council 1997–; mem. 15th CCP Cen. Cttee 1997–. *Address:* Office of Overseas Chinese Affairs, State Council, Beijing, People's Republic of China.

GUO JINLONG; Chinese politician; b. July 1947, Nanjing, Jiangsu Prov.; ed Nanjing Univ.; joined CCP 1979; Vice-Dir then Dir Cultural Bureau of Zhongxian Co., Sichuan Prov. 1980–83; Vice-Sec. CCP Zhongxian Co. Cttee then Magistrate of Zhongxian 1983–85; Vice-Dir Rural Policy Research Office, CCP Sichuan Prov. Cttee, Vice-Dir Sichuan Provincial Rural Econ. Comm. 1985–87; Vice-Sec. then Sec. CCP Leshan City Cttee 1987–92; Vice-Sec. CCP Sichuan Prov. Cttee 1992–93; Vice-Sec. then Exec. Vice-Sec. CCP Tibetan Autonomous Region Cttee 1993–2000, Sec. 2000–; First Sec., Tibet Regional Military Command 2000–; alt. mem. CCP 15th Cen. Cttee. *Address:* Chinese Communist Party Tibetan Autonomous Region Committee, Lhasa, Tibet, People's Republic of China (Office).

GUO MUSUN, Mooson Kwauk; Chinese academic; b. 9 May 1920, Hangyang; s. of Zung-Ung Kwauk and Za-Nan Chow; m. Huichun Kwei Kwauk 1950; two s. one d.; ed Univ. of Shanghai, Princeton Univ., USA; Prof. Inst. of Chemical Metallurgy, Chinese Acad. of Sciences 1956, Dir 1982–86, Emer. Dir 1986–; Visiting Prof. Ohio State Univ. 1989; Vice-Pres. Chemical Industry and Eng Soc. of China 1978–; Davis-Swindin Memorial Lecturer, Loughborough Univ., England 1985; Visiting Prof. Virginia Polytechnic Inst. and State Univ. 1986–87; mem. Chinese Acad. of Sciences 1981–; Pres. Chinese Soc. of Particuology 1986–; Corresp. mem. Swiss Acad. of Eng Sciences 1997–; Distinguished Scholar, CSCPRC Program, US Nat. Acad. of Science 1984; Danckwerts Memorial Lecturer, Inst. of Dirs, London 1989; Int. Fluidization Award 1989. *Publications:* Fluidization: Idealized and Bubbleless, with Applications 1992, Fast Fluidization 1994, Geometric Mobiles 1998. *Leisure interests:* kites, mobiles. *Address:* Institute of Chemical Metallurgy, Chinese Academy of Sciences, Beijing, 100080, People's Republic of China. *Telephone:* (10) 6255-4241 (Office); (10) 6255-4050 (Home). *Fax:* (10) 6255-8065 (Office). *E-mail:* mooson@lcc.icm.ac.cn (Home).

GUO XIEXIAN; Chinese chemist; b. 9 Feb. 1925, Hangzhou City, Zhejiang Prov.; m. Liang Yuan 1950; two s. one d.; Deputy Dir, Chemical Physics Inst. 1982–; mem. Dept of Chemistry Academia Sinica 1985–; Hon. State Prize of Science of China 1986. *Address:* Chemical Physics Institute, Dalian City, Liaoning Province, People's Republic of China. *Telephone:* (411) 3631730. *Fax:* (411) 3632426.

GUO ZHENQIAN; Chinese party and government official; b. Feb. 1933, Loning Co., Henan Prov.; ed Trade Dept People's Univ. of China; joined CCP 1949; Vice-Gov. Hubei Prov. 1983–84, Acting Gov. Jan. 1986, Gov. May–Oct. 1986; Dir Hubei Branch People's Construction Bank of China 1983–84; Deputy Sec. Hubei Prov. CCP Cttee 1985–; Gov. Hubei Provincial People's Govt 1986–90; First Vice-Pres. People's Bank of China 1990–93; First Deputy Auditor-Gen. of People's Repub. of China 1993–94, Auditor-Gen. 1994–98; Sr Economist, concurrently Prof., People's Univ. of China; Pres. Securities Asscn of China 1991–; mem. 13th and 14th CCP Cen. Cttee 1985–98. *Leisure interests:* reading, swimming, tennis, table tennis. *Address:* Securities Association of China, Olympic Hotel, 52 Baishiqiao Lu, Beijing 100081, People's Republic of China (Office). *Telephone:* (10) 68316688 (Office). *Fax:* (10) 68318390 (Office).

GUPTE, Shridhar, PhD; Indian university vice-chancellor and professor of geography; b. 4 Feb. 1933, Bombay (now Mumbai); s. of Shri Chandrashekhar Trimbak Gupte; m. 1961; two s.; lecturer in Geography, Univ. of Poona, Maharashtra 1959–77, Reader 1977–79, Prof. 1979–, Vice-Chancellor 1989–95; Best Teacher's Award (Poona Municipal Corpn) 1982. *Leisure interests:* music and reading. *Address:* Department of Geography, University of Pune, Ganeshkhind, Pune-411 007 (Maharashtra), India. *Telephone:* (20) 5650765 (Home); (20) 56061/9.

GURBANMYRADOV, Yolly; Turkmenistan politician and economist; b. 1960, Ashgabat; ed Turkmen State Inst. of Nat. Econ.; worker in construction co. 1977–82; Sr Econ., Deputy Head Ashgabat br. USSR State Bank 1982–87; Head Div. of Banking Automation State Bank (Ashgabat) 1988; Deputy Head Regional Dept USSR Zhilsotsbank 1988–89; man. of div. Agroprombank 1989–90; Br.Man. USSR Vnesheconombank 1990–92; First Deputy Chair., then Chair. Bd of Dirs State Bank of Foreign Trade of Turkmenistan 1992–96; Dir Turkmenistan State Agency on Foreign Investments 1996–97; Deputy Chair. Turkmen Cabinet of Ministers, concurrently Chair. Interbanking Council 1997–99; Deputy Prime Minister of Turkmenistan 1999–. *Address:* Cabinet of Ministers, Ashgabat, Turkmenistan (Office).

GURCHENKO, Ludmila Markovna; Russian actress; b. 12 Nov. 1935, Kharkov; ed Moscow All-Union Inst. of Cinema; has worked in films since 1956; People's Artist of USSR 1983. *Major roles include:* Lena in Carnival Night, Sonya in Baltic Sky, Anna Georgevna in Old Walls, Tamara Vasilevna in Five Evenings, Rita in Mechanic Gavrilov's Favourite Woman (Best Actress Award, Manila Film Festival), Vera in Station for Two (Best Actress Award, 16th All-Union Cinema Festival Leningrad 1983), Mrs Chieveley in An Ideal Husband, Raisa in Love and Doves, Larisa in Dreams and Waking Flights, Marty in Secret of Her Youth. *Appeared in films:* Applause, Applause, Forgive Us, Stepmother Russia, White Clothes, The Sex Tale, The Pretender, The Burn, Listen, Fellini and others; concert appearances as a singer. *Publications:* My Grown-up Childhood 1980, Applause, Applause. *Address:* Trekhprudny per. 5/15, Apt. 22, 103001 Moscow, Russia. *Telephone:* (095) 209-68-37.

GURDON, Sir John Bertrand, Kt, DPhil, FRS; British cell biologist; b. 2 Oct. 1933, Hampshire; s. of the late W. N. and E. M. Gurdon (née Byass); m. Jean Elizabeth Margaret Curtis 1964; one s. one d.; ed Edgeborough School, Eton Coll., Univ. of Oxford; Beit Memorial Fellow 1958–61; Gosney Research Fellow, Calif. Inst. of Tech., USA 1961–62; Research Fellow, Christ Church, Oxford 1962–72, Departmental Demonstrator 1963–64, Lecturer, Dept of Zoology 1966–72; Visiting Research Fellow, Carnegie Inst., Baltimore, Md, USA 1965; mem. Scientific Staff, Medical Research Council, Molecular Biology Lab., Univ. of Cambridge 1973–83, Head of Cell Biology Div. 1979–83, John Humphrey Plummer Prof. of Cell Biology 1983–2001; Master, Magdalene Coll. Cambridge 1995–2002; Fellow of Churchill Coll., Cambridge 1973–95; Croonian Lecturer, Royal Soc. 1976; Dunham Lecturer, Harvard Medical School 1974; Carter-Wallace Lecturer, Princeton Univ. 1978; Fellow Eton Coll. 1978–93; Hon. Student, Christ Church, Oxford 1985; Fullerian Prof. of Physiology and Comparative Anatomy, Royal Inst. 1985–91; Pres. Int. Soc. for Developmental Biology 1990–94; Foreign Assoc., NAS, USA 1980, Belgian Royal Acad. of Science, Letters and Fine Arts 1984, French Acad. of Sciences 1990; Foreign mem. American Philosophical Soc. 1983; Chair. Wellcome Cancer Campaign Inst., Univ. of Cambridge 1990–2001; Gov. The Wellcome Trust 1995–2000; Chair. Co. of Biologists 2001–; Hon. Foreign mem. American Acad. of Arts and Sciences 1978; Hon. DSc (Chicago) 1978, (Oxford) 1988, (Hull) 1998, (Glasgow) 2000; Hon. Dr (Paris) 1982; Albert Brachet Prize (Belgian Royal Acad.) 1968, Scientific Medal of Zoological Soc. 1968, Feldberg Foundation Award 1975, Paul Ehrlich Award 1977, Nessim Habif Prize (Univ. of Geneva) 1979, CIBA Medal, Biochem. Soc. 1981, Comfort Crookshank Award for Cancer Research 1983, William Bate Hardy Triennial Prize (Cambridge Philosophy Soc.) 1983, Charles Léopold Mayer Prize (Acad. des Sciences, France) 1984, Ross Harrison Prize (Int. Soc. for Devt Biology) 1985, Royal Medal (Royal Soc.) 1985, Emperor Hirohito Int. Biology Prize 1987, Wolf Prize for Medicine (jtly. with Edward B. Lewis, q.v.), 1989, Distinguished Service Award, Miami 1992, Jean Brachet Memorial Prize, Int. Soc. Diffn. 2000, Conklin Medal, Soc. Developmental Biology 2001. *Publications:* Control of Gene Expression in Animal Development 1974. *Leisure interests:* skiing, horticulture, lepidoptera. *Address:* Whittlesford Grove, Whittlesford, Cambridge, CB2 4NZ, England. *Telephone:* (1223) 32100.

GURFINKEL, Viktor Semenovich; Russian physiologist; b. 2 April 1922; ed Kyrgyz State Medical Inst.; during World War II head. div. of blood

transfusion 19th Army 1941–45, chief dr hospital 1946–48; sr researcher, head of lab., Inst. of Orthopaedics 1949–58; head of lab. Inst. of Experimental Biology and Medical Siberian br. USSR Acad. of Sciences 1949–58; head of lab. Inst. of Biophysics USSR Acad. of Sciences 1960–67; head of lab. Inst. for Information Transmission Problems, Russian Acad. of Sciences; corresp. mem. USSR (now Russian) Acad. of Sciences 1987, mem. 1994; research in physiology of movements, space physiology and medicine; resident in USA 1999–; USSR State Prize, R. Dow Prize (USA), Humboldt Foundation Award. *Publications:* three books and numerous articles in scientific journals. *Leisure interest:* fishing. *Address:* Neurological Sciences Institute, 1120 NW 20th Avenue, Portland, OR, USA. *E-mail:* gurfinkv@ohsu.edu.

GURGULINO de SOUZA, Heitor, BSc, LIC.; Brazilian educator and scientist; b. 1 Aug. 1928, São Lourenço, Minas Gerais; s. of Arthur Gurgulino de Souza and Catarina Sachser de Souza; m. Lilian Maria Quilici; ed Univ. of Mackenzie, São Paulo, Aeronautics Inst. of Tech., Univ. of Kansas, USA, Univ. of São Paulo; Program Specialist, Interamerican Science Program, Pan American Union, Wash. DC 1962–64; Head, Unit of Educ. and Research, Dept of Scientific Affairs, OAS, Wash. DC 1964–69; Rector, Fed. Univ. of São Carlos, State of São Paulo 1970–74; Dir, Dept of Univ. Affairs (DAU), Ministry of Educ. and Culture, Brasília 1972–74; Chair. Interamerican Cttee on Science and Tech. (CICYT) of the Council for Educ., Culture, OAS, Wash. DC 1974–77; Dir CNPq (Nat. Council for Scientific and Tech. Devt), Brasília 1975–78, Special Adviser to Pres. 1979–80; Vice Pres., Int. Asscn Univ. Pres. (IAUP) 1985–87, 1999–2002; Pres., Grupo Universitario Latinoamericano (GULERPE), Caracas 1985–87; Rector, UN Univ., Tokyo 1987–97; Special Adviser to Dir-Gen. for Higher Education, UNESCO, Paris 1997–99; Vice-Pres. Fed. Council of Educ. of Brazil (CFE), mem. 1972–87; mem. Nat. Order of Educational Merit, MEC, Brasília 1973, Commdr Order of Rio Branco, MRE, Brasília 1974; Dr. hc (Guadalajara) 1984, (Espírito Santo) 1986; Hon. DJur (Calif. State Univ.) 1997. *Publications:* Gamma-rays from the proton bombardment of Natural Silicon 1957, Computers and Higher Education in Brazil 1984 (articles); (co-ed.) Science Policy 1974; author of chapter on Brazil in International Encyclopedia of Higher Education 1978. *Leisure interests:* sailing, swimming, music. *Address:* 1 bis, Rue Clément Marot, 75008 Paris, France (Office); S.Q.S. 116 Bloco B, Apto. 501, Edificio Cap Ferrat, Brasília, DF, CEP 70386-020, Brazil (Home). *Telephone:* 1-49-23-53-11 (Office); (61) 3461414 (Home). *Fax:* 1-47-23-54-62 (Office); (61) 3460938 (Home).

GURIRAB, Theo-Ben; Namibian politician; b. 1938; ed Augustineum Training Coll., Okahandja, Temple Univ.; in exile 1962; Chief Rep. in N America for South West Africa People's Org. (SWAPO) 1971; Head of SWAPO's Mission, UN 1972–86; mem. of Senate, UN Inst. for Namibia, Lusaka; Sr Adviser to SWAPO Pres. during Resolution 435 negotiations; Minister of Foreign Affairs, Information and Broadcasting 1990–. *Address:* Ministry of Foreign Affairs, Information and Broadcasting, Government Buildings, East Wing, 4th Floor, Robert Mugabe Avenue, Private Mail Bag 13347, Windhoek, Namibia (Office). *Telephone:* (61) 2829111 (Office). *Fax:* (61) 223937 (Office). *E-mail:* headquarters@mfa.gov.na (Office). *Website:* www.mfa.gov.na (Office).

GURLEY BROWN, Helen; American author and editor; b. 18 Feb. 1922, Green Forest, Ark.; d. of Ira M. and Cleo (Sisco) Gurley; m. David Brown 1959; ed Texas State Coll. for Women, Woodbury Coll.; Exec. Sec. Music Corpn of America 1942–45, William Morris Agency 1945–47; Copywriter Foote, Cone & Belding advertising agency, Los Angeles 1948–58; advertisement writer and account exec. Kenyon & Eckhard advertising agency, Hollywood 1958–62; Ed.-in-Chief Cosmopolitan magazine 1965–97, Editorial Dir Cosmopolitan Int. Edns. 1972–, Ed.-in-Chief 1997–; mem. Authors League of America, American Soc. of Magazine Eds., AFTRA; establishment of Helen Gurley Brown Research Professorship at Northwestern Univ. 1986; Hon. LLD (Woodbury) 1987; Hon. DLitt (Long Island) 1993; Francis Holm Achievement Award 1956–59, Univ. of S. Calif. School of Journalism 1971, Special Award for Editorial Leadership of American Newspaper Woman's Club 1972, Distinguished Achievement Award in Journalism, Stanford Univ. 1977, New York Women in Communications Inc. Award 1985, Publrs.' Hall of Fame 1988, Henry Johnson Fisher Award, Magazine Publrs. of America 1995. *Publications:* Sex and the Single Girl 1962, Sex and the Office 1965, Outrageous Opinions 1967, Helen Gurley Brown's Single Girl's Cook Book 1969, Sex and the New Single Girl 1970, Having It All 1982, The Late Show: A Semiwild but Practical Survival Guide for Women over 50 1993, The Writer's Rules: The Power of Positive Prose 1998, I'm Wild Again: Snippets from My Life and a Few Brazen Thoughts 2000. *Address:* Cosmopolitan, 959 8th Avenue, New York, NY 10019 (Office); 1 West 81st Street, New York, NY 10024, USA (Home). *Telephone:* (212) 649-2222 (Office). *Fax:* (212) 245-4518 (Office).

GURNEY, Albert Ramsdell, MFA; American playwright; b. 1 Nov. 1930, Buffalo, NY; s. of Albert R. Gurney and Marion Gurney (née Spaulding); m. Mary F. Goodyear 1957; two s. two d.; ed Williams Coll., Yale School of Drama; joined MIT, Faculty of Humanities 1960–96, Prof. 1970–96; Hon. DDL (Buffalo State Univ., Williams Coll.); Drama Desk Award 1971, American Acad. of Arts and Letters Award 1987, Lucille Lortel Award 1992, William Inge Award 2000. *Publications include:* plays: The Dining Room, The Cocktail Hour, Love Letters, Later Life, A Cheever Evening, Sylvia, Overtime; Let's Do It!, The Guest Lecturer, Labor Day, Far East, Ancestral Voices 1999, Human Events 2000, Buffalo Gal 2001; novels: The Gospel According to Joe, Entertaining Strangers, The Snow Ball; opera libretto: Stawberry Fields

1999. *Address:* 40 Wellers Bridge Road, Roxbury, CT 06783-1616, USA (Home). *Telephone:* (860) 354-3692 (Home). *Fax:* (860) 354-3692 (Home). *E-mail:* a.r.gurney@worldnet.att.net (Home).

GUROV, Maj.-Gen. Aleksander Ivanovich, DJur; Russian civil servant and politician; b. 17 Nov. 1945, Shushkan-Olshanka, Tambov Dist; m. Yelena Nikolayevna Gurova; one s.; ed Moscow State Univ.; inspector Div. of Criminal Investigation, Vnukovo Airport 1970–74; mem. of staff Dept of Criminal Investigation, USSR Ministry of Internal Affairs 1974–78, Head Dept for Struggle Against Organized Crime, Corruption and Drug Business; USSR People's Deputy 1990–93; First Deputy Head Centre of Public Relations, Ministry of Security; Vice-Pres. Inform-Service; Head Tepko-Bank (security service) 1994–98; Head All-Russian Inst., Ministry of Internal Affairs 1998–99; Co-Founder and Co.-Leader Yedinstvo 1999; mem. State Duma 1999–; Chair. Cttee on Security 2000–. *Publications:* Red Mafia; over 150 scientific articles on struggle against original crime. *Address:* State Duma, Okhotny Ryad 1, 103265 Moscow, Russia (Office). *Telephone:* (095) 292-89-32 (Office). *Fax:* (095) 292-95-75 (Office).

GURRÍA TREVIÑO, José Angel, BEcons, M.FIN.; Mexican politician; b. 8 May 1950, Tampico, Tamaulipas State; s. of Francisco José Lacroix Gurria and Carmen Humana Treviño; m. Lulu Ululani Quintana Pali 1973; one s. two d.; Dir Gen. for Public Credit, Ministry of Finance 1983–88, Under Sec. for Int. Financial Affairs 1989–92; Pres. and CEO Nat. Bank for Foreign Trade (Bancomext) 1993, Nac. Financiera 1993–94; Sec. for Foreign Affairs Nat. Exec. Cttee Institutional Revolutionary Party (PRI) April–Nov. 1994; Minister of Foreign Affairs 1994, Minister for Finance and Public Credit –2000; decorations from several countries. *Publications:* The Politics of External Debt 1994 and articles on Mexican economy. *Leisure interests:* tennis, reading, swimming. *Address:* c/o Partido Revolucionario Institucional, Insurgentes Norte 59, Edif. 2, subsōtano, Col. Buenavista, 06359 México, DF, Mexico. *Website:* www.pri.org.mx (Office).

GUSAROV, Yevgeny Petrovich; Russian diplomatist; b. 30 July 1950, Moscow; m.; one s.; ed Moscow State Inst. of Int. Relations; on staff Ministry of Foreign Affairs 1972–; reviewer USSR Gen. Consulate, Montreal 1972–77; attaché, Third, Second Sec. Second European Dept Ministry of Foreign Affairs 1977–81; Second, First Sec., Counsellor USSR Embassy to Canada 1981–86; Head of Sector, Deputy Head Second European Dept 1986–88; Deputy Head Div. (then Dept) of USA and Canada 1988–90, Deputy Head Dept of Security and Co-operation in Europe, USSR Ministry of Foreign Affairs 1990–92; Head Dept of Europe, Russian Ministry of Foreign Affairs 1992; Amb. to Repub. of S Africa (also accred to Lesotho) 1992–98; Dir Dept of All-European Co-operation, Ministry of Foreign Affairs 1998–99; Deputy Foreign Minister 1999–2002. *Address:* Ministry of Foreign Affairs, Smolenskaya-Sennaya 32/34, 12/200 Moscow, Russia (Office).

GUSEV, Pavel Nikolayevich; Russian journalist; b. 4 April 1949; s. of Nikolai Gusev and Alla Guseva; m. Eugenia Efimova; two d.; ed Moscow Inst. of Geological Survey, Maxim Gorky Inst. of Literature; Komsomol work 1975–; First Sec. Komsomol Cttee of Krasnaya Presnya Region of Moscow 1975–80; Exec. Cen. Komsomol Cttee 1980–83; Ed.-in-Chief. Moskovsky Komsomolets (newspaper) 1983–; Minister Govt of Moscow, Head Dept of Information and Mass Media Jan.–Oct. 1992; press adviser to Mayor of Moscow 1992–95. *Address:* Moskovsky Komsomolets, 1905 Goda Str. 7, 123995 Moscow, Russia. *Telephone:* (095) 259-50-36 (Office). *Fax:* (095) 259-46-39 (Office). *E-mail:* letters@mk.ru.

GUSINSKY, Vladimir Aleksandrovich; Russian banker; b. 6 Oct. 1952, Moscow; m. Yelena Gusinskaya; two s.; ed Gubkin Moscow Inst. of Oil and Chem., A. Lunacharsky State Inst. of Theatre Art; Dir cultural programme Moscow Festival of Youth and Students 1982–85; Dir cultural programme Goodwill Games in Moscow 1985–86; f. co-operative Infex, later transformed into Holding Most, now comprising over 40 enterprises in the field of construction, construction materials production, real estate and trade operations, also Most-Bank est. 1991; owner maj. non-state TV company NTV, Segodnya (newspaper) 1992, radio station Ekho Moskvy, Obshcheye Delo weekly, weekly TV programme 7 Days; Dir-Gen. Holding Group Most 1989–97, concurrently Pres. Most-Bank 1992–97, Pres. Media-Most co. 1997–2001; Vice Pres. Asscn of Russian Banks, Chair. Council of Authorized Banks of the Govt of Moscow; Pres. Jewish Congress of Russia 1995–2001; arrested in Spain on Russian prosecutor's request for extradition Jan. 2000–01, released after request rejected; now lives in Spain.

GUS'KOVA, Yelena Yuryevna, D.HIST; Russian historian and political scientist; b. 23 Sept. 1949, Moscow; m.; two d.; ed Moscow State Univ.; Head Centre of Contemporary Studies, Balkan Crisis Inst. of Slavic and Balkan Studies, Russian Acad. of Sciences; leading researcher INION, Russian Acad. of Sciences; mem. Presidium Russian Asscn of Co-operation with the UN; Political and Policy Analyst UN Headquarters of Peace-keeping Operations in fmr Yugoslavia; Outstanding Scientist of Russia. *Publications:* over 220 scientific works on the history of Yugoslavia and problems of today's crises in the Balkans. *Address:* Institute of Slavic and Balkan Studies, Russian Academy of Sciences, Leninsky prosp. 32A, Moscow, Russia (Office). *Telephone:* (095) 938-58-61 (Office). *Fax:* (095) 938-00-96 (Office). *E-mail:* eguskova@com2com.ru.

GUSMAN, Mikhail Solomonovich; Russian journalist; b. b. 23 Jan. 1950, Baku, Azerbaijan; m.; one s.; ed Baku Higher CPSU School, Azerbaijan Inst.

of Foreign Languages; Deputy Chair. Cttee of Youth Orgs., Azerbaijan 1973–86; Head of Information Dept, then Head of Press Centre, USSR Cttee of Youth Orgs. 1986–91; Head Gen. Admin. of Information Co-operation INFOMOL 1991–95; Vice-Pres. Int. Analytic Press Agency ANKOM-TASS 1995–98; Head Chief Dept of Int. Co-operation, Public Contacts and Special Projects ITAR-TASS 1998–99, Deputy Dir-Gen., First Deputy Dir-Gen. 1999–; Co-Founder World Congress of Russian Press 1999; Exec. Dir World Asscn of Russian Press; Diploma of the USSR Supreme Soviet, numerous medals. *Leisure interests:* travelling, reading newspapers. *Address:* ITAR-TASS Agency, Tverskoy blvd 10-12, 103009 Moscow, Russia (Office). *Telephone:* (095) 290-59-89 (Office).

GUSMÃO, José Alexandre (Xanana); Timor Leste resistance leader; b. José Alexandre Guzmao, 20 June 1946, Laleia, Manatuto; m. 1st Emilia Batista 1969; one s.; m. 2nd Kirsty Sword 2000; ed Nossa Senhora de Fatima seminary, Dare; fmr poet, teacher and chartered surveyor; joined pro-independence Fretilin/(Revolutionary Front of the Independence of Timor Leste) 1974, Commdr 1978, now retd; C-in-C FALINTIL (Nat. Liberation Armed Forces of Timor Leste) 1981; arrested by Indonesian troops and sentenced to life imprisonment (later commuted to 20 years) 1992; released August 1999; Pres. Nat. Council of Timorese Resistance 1999–2001; Chair. Timor Leste Nat. Council 2000–01; Pres. of Timor Leste May 2002–; Sakharov Prize for Freedom of Expression 1999. *Address:* Office of the President, Dili, Timor Leste.

GUSTAFSSON, Lars Erik Einar, DPhil; Swedish author, philosopher and educator; b. 17 May 1936, Västerås; s. of Einar Gustafsson and Margaretha Carlsson; m. 1st Madeleine Gustafson 1962; m. 2nd Dena Alexandra Chasnoff 1982; two s. two d.; ed Uppsala Univ.; Editor-in-Chief, Bonniers Litterära Magasin 1966–72; Research Fellow, Bielefeld Inst. of Advanced Studies 1980–81; Adjunct Prof. Univ. of Texas at Austin 1983–, Jamail Distinguished Prof. in the Plan II Program 1995–; Aby Warburg Foundation Prof., Hamburg 1997; mem. Akad. der Wissenschaften und der Literatur, Mainz, Akad. der Künste, Berlin, Royal Swedish Acad. of Eng, Bayerische Akad. der schönen Künste, Munich; Officier des Arts et des Lettres; Kommendör des Bundesverdienstzeichens; Prix Charles Veillon, Heinrich Steffen Preis, Övralidspriset, Bellman Prize of Swedish Acad.; John Simon Guggenheim Memorial Fellow of Poetry 1993. *Exhibitions include:* Galleri Händer, Stockholm 1989, 1991, Gallerie am Savignyplatz, Berlin 2001. *Television:* 18th Century Pessimism (Swedish TV2), The Philosopher (syndicated). *Plays:* Celebration at Night, Zürich, Frankfurt, Berlin 1979. *Publications:* The Death of a Beekeeper 1978, Language and Lies 1978, Stories of Happy People 1981, Bernard Foy's Third Castle 1986, The Silence of the World before Bach (poems) 1988, Fyra Poeter 1988, Problemformuleringsprivilegiet 1989, Det sällsamma djuret från norr 1989, The Afternoon of a Tiler 1991, Historien med Hunden 1993, The Tail of the Dog 1997, Windy 1999. *Leisure interests:* painting, boating, tennis. *Address:* University of Texas at Austin, Waggener Hall, Room 413, Department of Philosophy, Austin, TX 78712 (Office); 2312 Tower Drive, Austin, TX 78203, USA; (512) 471-5632 (Office). *Telephone:* (512) 477-6859. *Fax:* (512) 472-6722. *E-mail:* lars.gustafsson@mail.utexas .edu (Office).

GUSTAFSSON, Leif Axel, MSc; Swedish business executive; b. 2 Jan. 1940, Hofors; s. of Axel Gustafsson and Brita Brandström; m. Monica Stellan 1965; one s. one d.; ed Royal Inst. of Tech.; operation engineer rolling mill, Hagfors (Uddeholm) 1966–69; rolling and steel mill man. SKF Steel, Hofors 1969–77; Man. Dir Smedjebacken AB 1978–82; Man. Dir Smedjebacken-Boxholm Stål AB 1982–87; Pres. and CEO SSAB Swedish Steel AB 1987–98, Chair. of Bd 1998–. *Leisure interests:* hunting, sports. *Address:* SSAB, Box 7280, S-103 89 Stockholm, Sweden (Office). *Telephone:* (8) 54-50-10-96 (Office). *Fax:* (8) 54-50-10-99 (Office).

GUSTOV, Vadim Anatolyevich; Russian politician; b. 26 Dec. 1948, Kalinino, Vladimir Region; m.; two c.; ed Moscow State Inst. of Geological Prospecting, Leningrad Inst. of Politology; Head of uranium mines Navoi Metallurgy Factory, Uzbekistan 1971–77; Head of mine, Phosphorite Kingisepp, Leningrad Region 1977–78; instructor, Head of Div., Kingisepp City CP Cttee 1978–86; First Deputy Chair. Kingisepp City Exec. Cttee 1986–87; Second Sec. Kingisepp City CP Cttee 1987–90; Chair. Kingisepp City Soviet 1990–91; Chair. Soviet of People's Deputies Leningrad Region 1991–93; mem. Council of Feds. of Russia, Chair. Cttee on CIS Cos. 1993–98; Gov. Leningrad Region 1996–98; First Deputy Chair., Govt of Russian Fed. 1998–99; Rep. of Vladimir Region to Council of Federation 2001–. *Leisure interests:* hunting, fiction, sports. *Address:* Council of Federation, B. Dmitrovka str. 26, 103426 Moscow, Russia (Office). *Telephone:* (095) 292-11-50 (Office).

GUT, Rainer Emil; Swiss banker; b. 24 Sept. 1932, Baar; s. of Emil Anton and Rosa (Müller) Gut; m. Josephine Lorenz 1957; two s. two d.; ed Cantonal School of Zug; professional training in Switzerland, France and England; Gen. Partner Lazard Frères & Co., NY 1968–71; Chair. and CEO, Swiss American Corpn (Credit Suisse's US investment banking affiliate) 1971–73; mem. Exec. Bd Credit Suisse, Zürich 1973–77, Speaker of Exec. Bd 1977–82, Pres. Exec. Bd 1982–83, Chair. 1983–2000, Chair. Credit Suisse Group (fmrly CS Holding) 1986–2000, Chair. Credit Suisse First Boston, New York 1988–97, Chair. Credit Suisse First Boston Zürich 1997–2000, Hon. Chair. Credit Suisse Group 2000–; Chair. Nestlé SA 2000–; Chair. and Del. Uprona (Canada) Ltd, Toronto 2000–; Vice-Pres. Gesparal, Paris 2000–; mem. Bd of

Dirs L'Oréal, Paris, Pechiney SA, Paris, Sofina SA, Brussels. *Address:* Nestlé SA, Avenue Nestlé 55, 1800 Vevey, Switzerland (Office). *Telephone:* (21) 924-21-11 (Office). *Fax:* (21) 924-45-40 (Office).

GUTERRES, António Manuel de Oliveira; Portuguese politician; b. 30 April 1949, Lisbon; m. (wife deceased); one s. one d.; ed Inst. Superior Técnico; trained as electrical engineer; joined Socialist Party 1974; Chief of Staff to Sec. of State for Industry 1974–75; fmr asst to several cabinet ministers; Pres. Municipal Ass. of Fundão 1979–95; Deputy to Ass. of the Repub. 1976–83, 1985–, Pres. several parl.comms, Pres. Socialist Parl. Group 1988–91; Strategic Devt Dir IPE (State Investment and Participation Agency) 1984–85; mem. Council of State 1991–; Leader of Socialist Party 1992–; Vice-Pres. Socialist Int. 1992–99, Pres. 1999–; Prime Minister of Portugal 1995–2001; Co-ordinator Tech. Electoral Comm. 1980–87; Founder, Vice-Pres. Portuguese Asscn for the Defence of the Consumer 1973–74; mem. Asscn for Econ. and Social Devt 1970–96. *Publications:* various articles for newspapers and magazines. *Leisure interests:* travel, history (especially Middle Ages), cinema, opera. *Address:* Socialist International, Maritime House, Clapham, London, SW4 0JW, England. *Telephone:* (20) 7627-4449. *Fax:* (20) 7720-4448. *E-mail:* socint@gn.apc.org. *Website:* www.gn.apc.org/socint.

GUTERSON, David, BA, MFA; American author; b. 4 May 1956, Seattle; s. of Murray Guterson and Shirley (née Zak) Guterson; m. Robin Ann Radwick 1979; three s. one d.; ed Univ. of Washington, Brown Univ.; fmr high school English teacher; sometime Contributing Ed. Harper's; PEN/Faulkner Award, Barnes & Noble Discovery Award, Pacific NW Booksellers Award (all for Snow Falling on Cedars) 1995. *Publications:* The Country Ahead of Us, The Country Behind (short stories) 1989, Family Matters: Why Home Schooling Makes Sense 1992, Snow Falling on Cedars 1994, East of the Mountains 1998. *Address:* c/o Georges Borchardt Inc., 136 East 57th Street, New York, NY 10020, USA.

GUTFREUND, Herbert, PhD, FRS; British academic; b. 21 Oct. 1921, Vienna, Austria; s. of Paul and Clara (née Pisko) Gutfreund; m. Mary Kathleen Davies 1958; two s. one d.; ed Vienna and Cambridge Univs.; Research Fellow, Univ. of Cambridge 1947–57; with Agricultural Research Council, Univ. of Reading 1957–64; Visiting Prof., Univ. of Calif. 1965, Max Planck Inst., Germany 1966, Dir Molecular Enzymology Lab. and Prof. of Physical Biochem., Univ. of Bristol 1967–86, Prof. Emer. 1986–; part-time Scholar in Residence, Nat. Insts. of Health, Bethesda, USA 1986–89; Scientific mem. (external) Max Planck Inst. for Medical Research 1987–; Fogarty Scholar, Nat. Insts. of Health, Washington 1987–89. *Publications:* An Introduction to the Study of Enzymes 1966, Enzymes: Physical Principles 1972, Molecular Evolution 1981, Biothermodynamics 1983, Kinetics for the Life Sciences: Receptors, Transmitters and Catalysts 1995. *Leisure interests:* hill walking, reading. *Address:* University of Bristol Medical School, University Walk, Bristol, BS8 1TD (Office); 12A The Avenue, Bristol, BS9 1PA (Home); Somerset House, Upton, Oxon., OX11 9JL, England. *Telephone:* (117) 928-7435 (Office); (1235) 851468 (Home); (117) 968-4453. *E-mail:* h.gutfreund@bristol.ac.uk (Office).

GUTH, Alan Harvey, PhD; American physicist; b. 27 Feb. 1947, New Brunswick, NJ; s. of Hyman Guth and Elaine Cheiten; m. Susan Tisch 1971; one s. one d.; ed Mass. Inst. of Tech.; Instructor Princeton Univ. 1971–74; Research Assoc. Columbia Univ. New York 1974–77, Cornell Univ. 1977–79, Stanford Linear Accelerator Center, Calif. 1979–80; Assoc. Prof. of Physics, MIT 1980–86, Prof. 1986–89, Jerrold Zacharias Prof. of Physics 1989–91; Victor F. Weisskopf Prof. of Physics 1992–; Physicist, Harvard-Smithsonian Center for Astrophysics 1984–89, Visiting Scientist 1990–91; Alfred P. Sloan Fellow 1981; Fellow, American Physics Soc. (Chair. Astrophysics Div. 1989–90), AAAS, American Acad. of Arts and Sciences; mem. NAS, American Astronomical Soc.; Rennie Taylor Award of the American Tentative Soc. 1991, Julius E. Lilienfeld Prize of the American Physical Soc. 1992; Benjamin Franklin Medal for Physics, Franklin Institute 2001. *Address:* Center for Theoretical Physics, Massachusetts Institute of Technology, 77 Massachusetts Ave, Cambridge, MA 02139-4307, USA (Office). *Telephone:* (617) 253-6265 (Office).

GUTHRIE, Roy David (Gus), AM, DSc; Australian fmr vice-chancellor and consultant; b. 29 March 1934, England; s. of David Ephraim Guthrie and Ethel (née Kimmins) Guthrie; m. 2nd Lyn Fielding 1982; three s. from first m.; ed King's Coll., London Univ.; Research Officer, Shirley Inst. 1958–60; Asst Lecturer then Lecturer, Univ. of Leicester 1963–73; Lecturer then Reader, Univ. of Sussex 1963–73; Foundation Prof. Griffith Univ., Australia 1973–81, Pro-Vice-Chancellor 1980–81, Emer. Prof. 1981; Vice-Chancellor, Univ. of Tech., Sydney 1986–96; Provost Insearch Educ. 1996–97; Prin. Consultant, Gus Guthrie Consulting Pty Ltd 1996–; Sec.-Gen. Royal Soc. of Chem. 1982–85; Chair. Queensland Innovation Council 1999–2002; mem. Council Univ. of the Sunshine Coast 1999–. *Publications:* Introduction to Carbohydrate Chemistry (with J. Honeyman), over 130 research papers in learned chemical journals. *Leisure interests:* gardening, theatre, croquet, Tai Chi, clowning. *Address:* P.O. Box 369, Buderim, Queensland 4556, Australia. *E-mail:* guscon@powerup.com.au (Office).

GUTHRIE OF CRAIGIEBANK, Baron (Life Peer), cr. 2001, of Craigiebank in the City of Dundee; **Charles (Ronald Llewelyn) Guthrie,** GCB, LVO, OBE; British army officer and business executive; b. 17 Nov. 1938, London; s. of the late Ronald Guthrie and Nina Llewelyn; m. Catherine Worrall 1971; two s.; ed Harrow School and Royal Mil. Acad. Sandhurst; commissioned Welsh

Guards 1959; served BAOR, Aden; 22 SAS Regt 1965–69; Staff Coll. 1972; Mil. Asst (GSO2) to Chief of Gen. Staff, Ministry of Defence 1973–74; Brigade Maj. Household Div. 1976–77; Commdg Officer, 1st Bn Welsh Guards, Berlin and N Ireland 1977–80; Col, Gen. Staff, Mil. Operations, Ministry of Defence 1980–82; Commdr British Forces New Hebrides 1980; 4th Armoured Brigade 1982–84; Chief of Staff 1st (British) Corps 1984–86; Gen. Officer Commdg NE Dist and Commdr 2nd Infantry Div. 1986–87; Asst Chief of Gen. Staff, Ministry of Defence 1987–89; Commdr, 1st (British) Corps 1989–91; Commdr, Northern Army Group 1992–93 and C-in-C British Army of the Rhine 1992–94; Col Commdt Intelligence Corps 1986–96; ADC Gen. to HM the Queen 1993–, Gold Stick to HM the Queen 1999–; Chief of Gen. Staff 1994–97, of the Defence Staff 1997–2001; Special Envoy to Pakistan 2001; Dir (non-exec.) N. M. Rothschild & Sons 2001–; Col of the Life Guards 1999–; Col Commdt Special Air Service (SAS) 1999–2002; Pres. Army Benevolent Fund, Action Research, London Fed. of Youth Clubs, Freeman of City of London; Kt Sovereign Mil. Order of Malta 1999, Commdr Legion of Merit (USA) 2001. *Leisure interests:* tennis, opera, travel. *Address:* P.O. Box 25439, London, SW1P 1AG, England.

GUTIERREZ, Carl T. C.; American politician and computer executive; b. 15 Oct. 1941, Agana Heights, Guam; s. of the late Tomas Taitano Gutierrez and of Rita Benavente Cruz; m. Geraldine Chance Torres; one s. two d.; ed S. San Francisco High School; service with USAF; est. first data processing centre in Guam; f. Carltom Enterprises 1971; Propr Carltom Consulting; elected Senator 1972, Speaker of Legislature; Gov. of Guam 1994–98, 1998–; Pres. Asscn of Pacific Island Legislatures; Chair. Guam Tax Code Comm., Cttee on Ways and Means; Vice-Chair. Cttee on Rules, Cttee on Tourism and Transportation; f. People Helping People 1994; Hon. Dr.Hum.Litt. (World Acad. of Art and Sciences); Hon. Citizen (Belau). *Leisure interests:* tennis, fishing, hunting. *Address:* PO Box 2950, Agana, GU 96932-2950, USA. *E-mail:* governor@mail.gov.gu (Office).

GUTIÉRREZ, Gustavo, DTheol; Peruvian ecclesiastic; b. 8 June 1928, Lima; ed Univ. Nacional Mayor de San Marcos, Lima, Univ. Catholique de Louvain, Univ. de Lyon, Univ. Gregoriana and Inst. Catholique de Paris; ordained priest 1959; Adviser, Nat. Union of Catholic Students 1960–; Prof. Catholic Univ. of Lima 1960–; mem. Pastoral-Theological team, Latin American Conf. of Catholic Bishops (CELAM) 1967–68; Bd Dir Inst. Bartolomé Las Casas-Rímac 1974–; Assoc. Vicar, Rímac, Lima 1980–; Visiting Prof. and lecturer at univs, colls and seminaries in USA and elsewhere; mem. EATWOT (Ecumenical Asscn of Third World Theologians); Dr hc (Nijmegen) 1979, (Tübingen) 1985, (King's Coll., USA) 1989, (Haverford Coll., USA) 1990, (Fribourg, Germany) 1990, (San Marcos, Lima) 1991, (Montreal) 1993, (Universidad Nacional de Ingeniería, Peru) 1993, (State of NY) 1994, (Holy Cross, MA) 1994, (San Agustín Peru) 1995, (Catholic Theol. Union USA) 1995, (St Norbert Coll., USA) 1996, (St Michael, Canada) 1996, (Simón Bolívar, Peru) 1997, (Freiburg, Suiza) 1998, (Southern Methodist, USA) 2000, (Brown, USA) 2000. *Publications:* A Theology of Liberation 1971, The Power of the Poor in History 1980, We Drink from Our Own Wells: the Spiritual Journey of a People 1983, On Job, God-talk and the Suffering of the Innocent 1986, La Verdad los hará libres 1986, Dios o el Oro en las Indias 1989, El Dios de la Vida 1989, Entre las Calandrias 1990, En Busca de los Pobres de Jesucristo 1992, Compartir la Palabra 1995, Essential Writings (with Nikoloff) 1996, Densidad del Presente 1996. *Leisure interests:* swimming, literature. *Address:* Instituto Bartolomé Las Casas-Rímac, Apartado 3090, Lima 100, Peru. *Telephone:* 4820028; 4709088; 4723410. *Fax:* 4820028. *E-mail:* casaus@amauta.rcp.net.pe (Office).

GUTIERREZ, Lucio; Ecuadorean politician; b. 1957; m.; fmr pentathelete; fmr col in army; staged Indian uprising against Pres. Jamil Mahuad 2000, sentenced to six months in a mil. prison; Pres. of Ecuador Nov. 2002–. *Address:* Office of the President, Palacio Nacional, García Moreno 1043 Quito, Ecuador (Office). *Telephone:* (2) 221-6300 (Office).

GUTIÉRREZ GIRÓN, Edgar Armando; Guatemalan politician; b. 27 July 1960, Guatemala City; m. María Elena Aiza Meade de Gutiérrez; two s. three d.; Political and Econ. Analyst in Guatemala and Cen. America 1982–; consultant for various int. agencies in Europe and USA; Co-Founder Asscn for the Advancement of the Social Sciences 1987, Coordinadora de ONG y Cooperativas 1992, Myrna Mack Foundation 1993; Co-ordinator-Gen. Interdiocesan Project "Recuperación de la Memoria Histórica" 1995–98; Jt Ed. Periódico de Guatemala 1999; Sec. of Strategic Analysis 2000–02; Minister of Foreign Affairs Dec. 2002–. *Publications include:* Centroamérica en el vórtice de la crisis 1986, Modelos heterogéneos en Centroamérica 1987, Guatemala: política exterior y estabilidad del Estado 1988, ¿Quién quiso asaltar el cielo? 1998, Sociedad civil y derechos humanos en la difícil transición guatemalteca 1998, Hacia un paradigma democrático del sistema de inteligencia en Guatemala 1999; poetry: Para conjurar su hechizo 1990, Al final de esta luna 1992, Memoria de la Muerte 1997. *Address:* Ministry of Foreign Affairs, 2A Avenida "La Reforma" 4-47, zona 10, Guatemala City, 01010 Guatemala (Office). *Telephone:* (2) 332-1900 (Office). *Fax:* (2) 332-2000 (Office). *E-mail:* despacho@minex.gob.gt (Office). *Website:* www.minex.gob.gt (Office).

GUTIONTOV, Pavel Semenovich; Russian journalist; b. 23 Jan. 1953; ed Moscow State Univ.; mem. of staff Moskovski Komsomolets 1970–75; fmr corresp. Komsomolskaya Pravda, then Head of Div. 1975–85; special corresp. Sovetskaya Rossiya 1985–87; political observer Izvestia; Co-Chair. Liberal Journalists Club –1997; Chair. Cttee for Defence of Freedom of Speech and

Journalists' Rights; Sec. Russian Journalists' Union; winner of numerous professional prizes. *Publications:* Games in the Fresh Air of Stagnation 1990, Fate of Drummers 1997 and numerous articles. *Address:* Russian Journalists' Union, Zubovsky blvd 4, 119021 Moscow, Russia (Office). *Telephone:* (095) 201-23-95 (Office).

GUTMAN, Natalia Grigorievna; Russian cellist; b. 14 Nov. 1942; m. Oleg Kagan (deceased); three c.; ed Gnessin Music School, Moscow (under R. Shposhnikov), Moscow Conservatory (under Prof. Kozolupova and Mstislav Rostropovich); tours include: visits to Europe, USA and Japan, appearing with the Berlin Philharmonic Orchestra, Vienna Philharmonic Orchestra, London Symphony orchestra, Orchestre Nat. de France and Orchestre de Paris; played chamber music in USSR and Europe with Eliso Virsaladze and Oleg Kagan 1982–; played sonatas, trios and quartets with Sviatoslav Richter; plays sonata and concerto written for her by Alfred Schnittke; solo tours include: the USA with USSR State Symphony Orchestra and Yevgeny Svetlanov, Italy with BBC Symphony and Yuri Temirkanov, USSR with Sir John Pritchard; performed with Royal Philharmonic Orchestra under Yuri Temirkanov, Royal Festival Hall, London, the Concertgebouw, the London Philharmonic, the Munich Philharmonic, the Berlin Philharmonic, the Orchestre Nat. de France, the LA Philharmonic under André Previn, the Chicago Symphony under Claudio Abbado 1988–89; teacher at Moscow Conservatory 1967–77; Prof. Stuttgart Conservatory 1997–; f. Oleg Kagan Memorial Festival, Krems, Moscow; prizes at the Vienna Student Festival Competition, the Tchaikovsky Competition, the Munich Chamber Music Competition and the Dvořák Competition, Prague. *Address:* Askonas Holt, Lonsdale Chambers, 27 Chancery Lane, London, WC2A 1PF, England. *Telephone:* (20) 7400-1700 (London); (095) 203-33-91 (Moscow).

GUTMANN, Francis Louis Alphonse Myrtil; French diplomatist; b. 4 Oct. 1930, Paris; s. of Robert Gutmann and Denise (née Coulom) Gutmann; m. Chantal de Gaulle 1964; two s. one d.; ed Lycée Pasteur, Neuilly-sur-Seine; Head of Dept, Ministry of Foreign Affairs 1951–57; Asst Head Office of Sec. of State for Econ. Affairs 1955, mem. French Del. to Econ. and Social Council and to UN Gen. Ass. 1952–55, to Common Market Conf., Brussels 1956–57; Adviser Pechiney Co. 1957–59, Sec.-Gen. 1963, Dir 1970–71; Sec.-Gen. Fria 1960–62; mem. Governing Bd Pechiney-Ugine-Kuhlmann group 1962–78, Pres.-Dir-Gen. Ugine-Kuhlmann 1971–76, in charge of social affairs 1975–78; Pres. Alucam 1968–72; Pres. Frialco and Vice-Pres. Friguia 1977–81; Dir-Gen. French Red Cross 1980–81; Sec.-Gen. Ministry for External Relations 1981–85; Admin. representing the State, Paribas 1982–84, Gaz de France 1984–85, St Gobain 1982–85; Amb. to Spain 1985–88; Pres. Admin. Council Gaz de France 1988–93, Hon. Pres. 1993–; Pres. Fondation Méditerranéenne d'Etudes Stratégiques 1989–2000, Assoc. Eurogas-Union 1990–94, (Admin. Council) Institut Français du Pétrole (IFP) 1993–96; Vice-Pres. Mémoire et espoirs de la Résistance 1994–2000; attached to Ministry of Foreign Affairs 1996–; Pres. Scientific Council for Defence, Ministry of Defence 1998–; Dir French Red Cross 1992–2000; Officier, Légion d'honneur; Commdr, Ordre nat. du Mérite; Grand croix de l'ordre du Merité (Spain); numerous foreign awards. *Publications:* Les chemins de l'effort 1975, Le nouveau décor international 1994. *Address:* c/o Institut Français du Pétrole, 1–4 ave. de Bois-Préau, BP 311, 92506 Rueil-Malmaison cedex, France (Office). *Telephone:* 1-47-52-68-84 (Office). *Fax:* 1-47-52-67-54 (Office).

GUTTON, André Henry Georges; French architect and town planner; b. 8 Jan. 1904, Fontenay-sous-Bois; s. of Henry B. Gutton and Amelia Hoesli; m. Elisabeth Lafargue 1927; two s. one d.; ed Ecole nationale supérieure des beaux arts and Inst. d'Urbanisme de l'Univ. de Paris; architect for pvt. bldgs and nat. palaces 1936–; Prof. Inst. of Town Planning 1946–63; Prof. of Theory of Architecture, Nat. School of Fine Arts 1949–58, of Town Planning 1958–74; Tech. Counsellor, Govt of Syria 1951; mem. Exec. Cttee Int. Union of Architects 1949–57; Pres. Town Planning Comm. 1951–58; Consultant Town-Planner Canton of Geneva 1960–70, Bilbao 1962, Brasília 1967, Bratislava 1967, Belgrade 1986; mem. (rapporteur) Planning Cttee for the Parisian Region 1965–73; Hon. Pres. Order of Architects 1960–66; Vice-Pres. Congress of Architects 1965; mem. Acad. of Architecture, Royal Acad. of Belgium; Hon. Fellow AIA; Officier, Légion d'honneur, Polar Star (Sweden), Kt, Order of Orange-Nassau, of Dannebrog, Officier des Palmes académiques, Officier des Arts et des Lettres; Int. Prize for Antwerp (IMALSO) 1933; first Int. Prize for plan for Place des Nations, Geneva 1958. *Major works:* Chief Architect of Institut de France 1936–70, Post Office Buildings, Paris 1945, The Opera 1950–54, Post Office Buildings in Paris, Versailles, Nancy, Besançon, Chateauroux, Roanne, Neuilly-sur-Marne, Lyon, Chambéry and schools and offices in France, town planning: Plans for Nancy 1938, Dakar (Senegal), Boulogne, Issy 1945, Aleppo (Syria) 1952, Sihanoukville (Cambodia) 1960. *Publications:* Charte de l'urbanisme 1941, Conversations sur l'architecture: (L'édifice dans la cité, La maison des hommes, Les églises et les temples, Les écoles, lycées, universités, L'urbanisme au service de l'homme) 1952–62, De la nuit à l'aurore 1985, Urbanisme et urbanité 1993. *Leisure interests:* painting, writing. *Address:* 3 avenue Vavin, 75006 Paris, France (Home). *Telephone:* 1-46-33-72-76.

GUTZWILLER, Peter Max, DrIur, LLM; Swiss lawyer; b. 30 April 1941, Basle; s. of Max and Helly Gutzwiller; m. 1st Vreny Lüscher 1971 (divorced); one s.; m. 2nd Barbara Menzel; ed Univs. of Basle and Geneva and Harvard Law School; Assoc. Staehelin Hafter & Partners 1970–76, Partner 1977–; mem. Bd of Int. Law Asscn (Swiss Branch) 1975–; Sec. Swiss Assocn of Int. Law 1976; Maj., Swiss Army 1979. *Publications:* Swiss International Divorce Law

1968, Von Ziel und Methode des IPR 1968, Arbeitsbewilligungen für Ausländer 1975, 1976, Grundriss des schweizerischen Privat- und Steuerrechtes (co-author) 1976. *Leisure interests:* art collection (cartoons), music, travel. *Address:* Bleicherweg 58, 8027 Zurich (Office); Sonnenrain 15, 8700 Küsnacht, Switzerland (Home). *Telephone:* 2014540 (Office); 9109988 (Home).

GUZY, Carol; American photographer; b. 7 March 1956; m. Jonathan Utz; ed Northampton Co. Area Community Coll., Art Inst. of Fort Lauderdale; staff photographer Miami Herald 1980–88, The Washington Post 1988–; notable assignments include coverage of volcanic eruption in Colombia, famine in Ethiopia, civil war in Somalia and daily life in Haiti; Pulitzer Prize 1986, 1995, Photographer of the Year (Nat. Press Photographers Asscn) 1990, 1993, 1997, Robert F. Kennedy Memorial Prize 1997, Pulitzer Prize in feature photography 2000 and numerous other awards. *Address:* The Washington Post, 1150 15th Street, NW, Washington, DC 20071-0002, USA.

GVISHIANI, Jermen Mikhailovich, DPhil; Georgian politician and sociologist; b. 24 Dec. 1928, Akhaltsikhe; s. of Mikhail Maksimovich and Irma Khristophorovna Gvishiani; m. Lyudmila Alekseyevna Kosygina (d. of the late Aleksey Kosygin, Chair. of USSR Council of Ministers 1964–80) (died 1990); one s. one d.; ed Moscow State Univ. of Int. Relations, Moscow State Univ., Inst. of Philosophy, USSR Acad. of Science; navy service 1951–55; with State Cttee for Science and Tech., Int. Relations Dept 1955–65, Deputy Chair. 1965–85; Prof. of Philosophy, Moscow State Univ. 1960–71; Deputy Chair. State Planning Cttee 1985–86; Chair. Cttee for Systems Analysis, Presidium of Acad. of Sciences 1971–86, Chair. Council Int. Inst. for Applied Systems Analysis 1972–81, Int. Research Inst. for Man. Problems 1977–85, Int. Council for New Initiatives in East-West Co-operation (Int. Vienna Council) 1979–85, Deputy Chair. 1985–93, Hon. Chair. 1993–; mem. UN Advisory Cttee on Applications of Science and Tech. (ACAST), Bd of Trustees of UNITAR 1962–71; Co-Chair. USA-USSR Trade and Econ. Council, Sub-Cttee for Science and Tech. 1974–91; Dir Inst. for Systems Studies/Inst. for Systems Analysis 1976–92, Hon. Dir and Head of Dept 1992–; Vice-Chair. Jt Perm. USSR-France Comm. 1967, Soviet Div., USSR-Fed. Repub. of Germany Comm. for Econ. and Tech. Co-operation 1972; mem. Presidium, Soviet Sociologists' Asscn 1972–86; mem. USSR (now Russian) Acad. of Sciences 1979, Int. Man. Acad., Sweden Royal Acad. of Eng Sciences, American Man. Asscn, American Man. Acad., Foreign mem. Finnish Acad. Tech. Sciences; mem. The Club of Rome; Dr. hc (Prague High Econ. School); RSFSR State Prize 1979, Gold Mercury Int. Award and various medals; Grosse Goldene Ehrenzeichen mit Stern (Austria). *Publications:* Sociology of Business, Organization and Management, Social Function of Science and Science Policy, Scientific and Technological Revolution and Social Progress, etc. *Leisure interests:* music, sport. *Address:* Institute for Systems Studies, 60 Years of October prosp. 9, 117312 Moscow, Russia (Office). *Telephone:* (095) 135-75-75 (Office); (095) 137-25-44 (Home).

GWATHMEY, Charles, MArch; American architect; b. 19 June 1938, Charlotte, NC; s. of Robert Gwathmey and Rosalie Dean Hook; m. Bette A. Damson 1974; ed Music and Art High School, New York, Univ. of Pennsylvania School of Arch. and Yale Univ. School of Arch; William Wirt Winchester Travelling Fellowship 1962; Fulbright Fellow in France 1962–63; pvt. practice in New York 1964–66; partner, Gwathmey-Henderson, New York 1966–70, Gwathmey-Henderson-Siegel 1970–71; partner, with Robert Siegel, Gwathmey Siegel & Assocs New York 1971–; Prof. of Architectural Design, Pratt Inst. Brooklyn, New York 1964–66, Yale Univ. 1966, Princeton Univ. 1966–69, 1975–76, Harvard Univ. 1970–72, Cooper Union, New York 1971–72, Univ. of Calif. at LA 1973–74, Columbia Univ. 1976–77; Eliot Noyes Prof. of Architecture Harvard Univ. 1985; works include single houses, housing projects, school and coll. bldgs, libraries, offices, public bldgs, interiors etc. throughout USA and addition to Solomon Guggenheim Museum, New York 1995; mem. American Acad., American Inst. of Arts and Letters; Fellow, American Inst. of Architects; numerous awards and distinctions including Distinguished Architecture Award 1982, 1984, Medal of Honor 1983, Nat. Honor Award 1968, 1976, 1984 and Nat. Firm Award, American Inst. of Architects 1982. *Address:* Gwathmey, Siegel and Associates, Architects, 3rd Floor, 475 Tenth Avenue, New York, NY 10018-1198 (Office); 1115 5th Ave, New York, NY 10128, USA.

GWYNN-JONES, Peter Llewellyn, CVO, MA, FSA; British public official; b. 12 March 1940; s. of the late Maj. Jack Llewellyn Gwynn-Jones and Mary Muriel Daphne Harrison and step-s. of the late Lt-Col Gavin David Young; ed Wellington Coll., Trinity Coll. Cambridge; Asst to Garter King of Arms 1970; Bluemantle Pursuivant of Arms 1973; House Comptroller Coll. of Arms 1982; Lancaster Herald of Arms 1982–95; Garter Prin. King of Arms 1995–; Genealogist Order of the Bath, OStJ; Insp. of Regimental Colours of RAF Badges; Sec. Harleian Soc. 1981–94; KStJ; Hon. Genealogist Order of St Michael and St George. *Publications:* Heraldry 1993, The Art of Heraldry 1998. *Leisure interests:* tropical forests, wildlife conservation, fishing. *Address:* College of Arms, Queen Victoria Street, London, EC4V 4BT (Office); 79 Harcourt Terrace, London, SW10, England (Home).

GYANENDRA BIR BIKRAM SHAH DEV, BS; King of Nepal; b. b. 7 July 1947; brother of the late King Birendra Bir Bikram Shah Dev; m. Komal Rajya Laxmi Devi Shah; two c.; ed St Joseph's Coll., Darjeeling, India, Tribhuvan Univ.; owner of a tea estate in E Nepal, a cigarette factory and a hotel in Kathmandu; has made numerous diplomatic visits to India, Japan, China, USA, UK, Pakistan, Germany, France, Russia, etc.; crowned King June 2001;

fmr Pres. King Mahendra Nature Conservation Trust; mem. World Wildlife Fund. *Leisure interest:* nature conservation. *Address:* Narayanhity Royal Palace, Kathmandu, Nepal (Office).

GYIBUG PUNCOG CEDAIN; Chinese politician; b. 1930, Tibet; Vice-Chair. of People's Govt of Tibet Autonomous Region 1983–; deputy for Tibet to 7th NPC 1988. *Address:* People's Government of Tibet Autonomous Region Lhasa, People's Republic of China.

GYLL, John Sören; Swedish company executive; b. 26 Dec. 1940, Skorped; s. of Josef Gyll and Gertrud Gyll; m. Lilly Margareta Hellman 1974; two s. one d.; Marketing Dir and Vice-Pres. Rank Xerox 1963–77; Pres. Uddeholms Sweden AB 1977–79, Exec. Vice-Pres. Uddeholms AB 1979–81, Pres. and CEO 1981–84; Pres. and CEO Procordia AB 1984–92; Pres. and CEO AB Volvo 1992–97, also Dir; Chair. Bd Dirs. Pharmacia and Upjohn Inc.; mem. European Advisory Bd, Schroder Salomon Smith Barney 2001–; mem. Royal Swedish Acad. of Eng, Fed. of Swedish Industries (currently Chair.). *Leisure interests:* hunting, skiing. *Address:* c/o AB Volvo, S-405 08 Gothenburg, Sweden.

GYLLENHAMMAR, Pehr Gustaf, BLL; Swedish business executive; b. 28 April 1935, Gothenburg; s. of Pehr Gustaf Victor Gyllenhammar and Aina Dagny Kaplan; m. Eva Christina Engellau 1959; one s. three d.; ed Univ. of Lund, studied int. law in England, vocational studies in maritime law, USA, Cen. d'Etudes Industrielles, Geneva; employed by Mannheimer & Zetterlöf (solicitors), Gothenburg 1959, Haight, Gardner, Poor & Havens (Admiralty lawyers), New York 1960, Amphion Insurance Co., Gothenburg 1961–64; Asst Admin. Man. Skandia Insurance Co., Stockholm 1965–66, Vice-Pres. Corporate Planning 1966–68, Exec. Vice-Pres. 1968, Pres. and CEO 1970; joined AB Volvo, Gothenburg 1970, Man. Dir and CEO 1971–83, Chair. of Bd and CEO 1983–90, Exec. Chair. Bd of Dirs 1990–93; Chair. Bd MC European Capital SA 1994–96; Chair. Bd of Dirs Swedish Ships' Mortage Bank 1976–, Procordia AB 1990–92; Sr Adviser Lazard Frères & Co. 1996–99, Man. Dir 2000–; Chair. Cofinec NV 1996–, CGU PLC 1998– (Chair. CGNU 2000– after merger of CGU PLC and Norwich Union PLC, co. changed name to Aviva 2002); mem. Bd of Dirs, Skandinaviska Enskilda Banken 1979–94, United Technologies Corpn 1981–, Kissinger Assocs, Inc. 1982–, Pearson PLC 1983–97, Reuters Holdings PLC 1984–97, Philips Electronics NV 1990–96, Renault SA 1990–93 and numerous other cos and orgs; Trustee Reuters Founder Share Co. Ltd 1997–; mem. Royal Swedish Acad. of Eng Sciences 1974; Officer (1st Class) Royal Order of Vasa 1973, Commdr Order of the Lion of Finland 1977, Commdr Ordre nat. du Mérite 1980, King's Medal (12th Size) with ribbon of Order of the Seraphim 1981, Commdr St Olav's Order 1984, Commdr Order of the Lion of Finland (1st Class) 1986, Commdr Légion d'honneur 1987, Kt Grand Officer, Order of Merit (Italy) 1987, Commdr Order of Leopold 1989; Hon. DrMed (Gothenburg Univ.) 1981;Hon. DTech (Brunel) 1987; Hon. DEng (Nova Scotia) 1988, Hon. DScS (Helsinki) 1990, Hon. LLD (Vermont) 1993; Golden Award, City of Gothenburg 1981. *Publications:* Mot sekelskiftet på måfå (Towards the Turn of the Century at Random) 1970, Jag tror på Sverige (I Believe in Sweden) 1973, People at Work 1977, En industripolitik för människan (Industrial Policy for Human Beings) 1979. *Leisure interests:*

tennis, sailing, skiing, riding. *Address:* Aviva PLC, St Helen's, 1 Undershaft, London, EC3P 3DQ, England. *Telephone:* (20) 7283-2000. *Fax:* (20) 7283-0067.

GYLLENSTEN, Lars Johan Wictor, MD; Swedish writer and physician; b. 12 Nov. 1921, Stockholm; s. of Carl Gyllensten and Ingrid Gyllensten (née Rangström); m. Inga-Lisa Hultén 1946; one d.; Prof. of Histology Karolinska Inst. 1969–73; mem. Swedish Acad. 1966–89; mem. Nobel Cttee for Literature 1967–87, Chair. 1981–87, Bd mem. Nobel Foundation 1979–93; mem. Royal Swedish Acad. of Sciences 1975; Hon. mem. Royal Swedish Acad. of History, Arts and Antiquities 1979; Hon. DTech 1993; Hon. DTheol 1998; 20 literary prizes. *Publications:* Senilia 1956, Juvenilia 1965, Palatset i parken 1970, Grottan i öknen 1973, I skuggan av Don Juan 1975, Skuggans återkomst 1985, Det himmelska gästabudet 1991, Anteckningar från en vindskupa 1993, Ljuset ur skuggornas värld 1995, Kistbrev 1998. *Address:* c/o Albert Bonniers Forlag AB, Box 3159, S10363 Stockholm, Sweden.

GYLYS, Povilas, DSc (ECON.); Lithuanian politician; b. 14 Feb. 1948, Didziokai, Moletai Region; m. Nijole Rezaitė 1969; two s.; ed Vilnius Univ.; lecturer, Prof. of Econs 1969–92; Head of Dept of Int. Econ. Relations, Vilnius Univ. 1992; mem. Parl. (Seimas), Minister of Foreign Affairs 1992–96; mem. of Parl. (Seimas) 1996–. *Address:* Seimás of Lithuania, Gediminas prosp. 53, 2026 Vilnius, Lithuania. *Telephone:* (2) 621-632.

GYOHTEN, Toyoo; Japanese economist; b. 1931, Yokohama; m.; one s. one d.; ed Univ. of Tokyo, Princeton Univ., USA; joined Ministry of Finance 1955; Japan Desk, Asian Dept IMF 1964–66; Special Asst to Pres. of Asian Devt Bank, Manila, Philippines 1966–69; Dir-Gen. Int. Finance Bureau 1984–86, Vice-Minister of Finance for Int. Affairs 1986–89; Visiting Prof., Business School, Harvard Univ., USA 1990, Woodrow Wilson School, Princeton Univ. 1990–91, Univ. of St Gallen, Switzerland 1991; joined Bank of Tokyo Ltd (merged with Mitsubishi Bank Ltd 1996) 1991, Chair. Bd 1992–96, Sr Adviser The Bank of Tokyo-Mitsubishi Ltd1996–; Pres. Inst. for Int. Monetary Affairs 1995–; Chair. Working Party III, OECD, Paris 1988–90, Inst. of Int. Finance Inc., USA 1994–97; mem. Bd of Trustees, Princeton in Asia, USA 1989–, Advisory Panel, E African Devt Bank, Kampala, Uganda 1990–, Asia Pacific Advisory Cttee, New York Stock Exchange 1990–, Int. Council, The Asia Soc., New York 1991–, Exec. Cttee of Trilateral Comm., New York, Paris and Tokyo 1991–, Group of Thirty, Washington, DC 1992–, Council of Inst. Aspen France, The Aspen Inst. Japan Council, Banking Advisory Group of IFC, Washington, DC; Founding mem. Int. Advisory Bd of Council on Foreign Relations, New York; Fulbright Scholar 1956–58. *Publication:* Changing Fortunes (with Paul Volcker) 1992. *Address:* 3-2, Nihombashi Hongokucho 1-chome, Chuo-ku, Tokyo 103-0021, Japan.

GYSI, Gregor; German politician and lawyer; b. 16 Jan. 1948, Berlin; s. of the late Klaus Gysi; m. 1st (divorced); two s.; m. 2nd; one d.; defence lawyer; elected leader Communist Party (CP) Nov. 1989, name changed to Partei des Demokratischen Sozialismus (PDS) (Party of Democratic Socialism), now parl. leader; mem. Bundestag 1990–2002; Deputy Mayor of Berlin and Senator for Econs, Labour and Women's Issues 2002. *Publications:* Das Waris: Noch Lange Nicht (biog. notes) 1999, Ein Blick Züruck: Ein Schritt Nachvorn 2001. *Address:* c/o Senate Department for Economics, Labour and Women's Issues, 10820 Berlin, Germany (Office).

HAACKE, Hans Christoph Carl, MFA; German artist and professor of art; b. 12 Aug. 1936, Cologne; s. of Dr. Carl Haacke and Antonie Haacke; m. Linda Snyder 1965; two s.; ed State Art Acad., Kassel; Asst Prof. Cooper Union, New York 1971–75, Assoc. Prof. 1975–79, Prof. 1979–; Guest Prof. Hochschule für Bildende Künste, Hamburg 1973, 1994, Gesamthochschule, Essen 1979; numerous awards and honours including Hon. DFA (Oberlin Coll.) 1991; Dr. hc (Bauhaus-Universität, Weimar) 1998; Golden Lion, Venice Biennale 1993. *Solo exhibitions include:* Galerie Schmela, Düsseldorf 1965, Howard Wise Gallery, New York 1966, 1968, 1969, Galerie Paul Maenz, Cologne 1971, 1974, 1981, Museum Haus Lange, Krefeld 1972, John Weber Gallery, New York, 1973, 1975, 1977, 1979, 1981, 1983, 1985, 1988, 1990, 1992, 1994, Kunstverein, Frankfurt 1976, Lisson Gallery, London 1976, Galerie Durand-Dessert, Paris 1977, 1978, Museum of Modern Art, Oxford 1978, Stedelijk van Abbemuseum, Eindhoven 1979, Tate Gallery, London 1984, Neue Gesellschaft für Bildende Kunst, Berlin 1984, Kunsthalle, Berne 1985, Le Consortium, Dijon 1986, The New Museum of Contemporary Art, New York 1986, Victoria Miro Gallery, London 1987, Centre Georges Pompidou, Paris 1989, Venice Biennale, German Pavilion 1993, Fundació Tàpies, Barcelona 1995, Boijmans Van Beuningen Museum, Rotterdam 1996, Portikus, Frankfurt 2000, Serpentine Gallery, London 2001, Generali Foundation, Vienna 2001; designed stage set for Volksbühne, Berlin 1994; participant in numerous group exhbns. 1962–. *Publications:* Werkmonographie (with Edward F. Fry) 1972, Framing and Being Framed (jtly.) 1975, Nach allen Regeln der Kunst 1984, Unfinished Business (with others) 1987, Artfairismes 1989, Bodenlos (with others) 1993, Libre-Echange (with Pierre Bourdieu) 1994, Obra Social 1995, AnsichtsSachen/Viewing Matters 1999, Mia san mia 2001; numerous articles and interviews in int. art magazines. *Address:* c/o Cooper Union for the Advancement of Science and Art, Cooper Square, New York, NY 10003, USA.

HAAG, Rudolf, Dr rer. nat; German professor of theoretical physics; b. 17 Aug. 1922, Tubingen; s. of Albert Haag and Anna (née Schaich) Haag; m. 1st Kaethe Fues 1948 (died 1991); three s. one d.; m. 2nd Barbara Klie 1992; ed Tech. Univ., Stuttgart and Univ. of Munich; Prof. of Physics, Univ. of Ill., USA 1960–66; Prof. of Theoretical Physics, Hamburg Univ. 1966–87, Prof. Emer. 1987–; Dr. hc (Aix-Marseille) 1979; Henri Poincaré Prize 1997; Max-Planck-Medal 1970. *Publications:* Local Quantum Physics 1992 and over 100 articles on fundamental physical theory. *Address:* Waldschmidt Strasse 4b, 83727 Schliersee Neuhaus, Germany. *Telephone:* 80267444.

HAAK, Willem E. (Pim), LLM; Netherlands chief justice; b. 19 April 1934, Haarlem; s. of Willem Adriaan Haak and Elisabeth Willemina A. ten Hooven; m. Cornelia Jacoba van Heek 1968; two s.; ed Univ. of Amsterdam; worked as advocate in Amsterdam until 1972; Dist Court Judge 1972–76; Justice, Amsterdam Court of Appeal 1976–79; Advocate Gen. to the Supreme Court 1979–81, Justice, Supreme Court 1981–92, Deputy Pres. 1992–99, Chief Justice 1999–; fmr Sec. Asscn of Dutch Lawyers; fmr Deputy Chair. Int. Law Inst.; fmr Pres. Appeals Tribunal, Dutch Inst. of Psychologists; fmr mem. Insurance Cos. Supervisory Bd; currently sits on Court of Appeals for the Cen. Comm. for the Navigation of the Rhine, Strasbourg; Chair. Bd Frits Lugt art collection; Deputy Chair. Supervisory Bd, Institut Néerlandais, Paris; mem. Advisory Cttee on Endowed Chairs., Univ. of Amsterdam; mem. Perm. Appeals Tribunal of the Gen. Meeting of the Remonstrant Church; Kt, Order of the Dutch Lion. *Publications:* several articles and monographs on private int. law, transport law, comparative law and criminal law. *Leisure interest:* mountain hiking. *Address:* De Hoge Raad der Nederlanden, P.O. Box 20303, 2500 EH The Hague (Office); Joh. Vermeerstraat 75, 1071 DN Amsterdam, The Netherlands (Home). *Telephone:* (70) 3611237 (Office); (20) 6796935 (Home). *Fax:* (70) 3658700 (Office); (20) 6701821 (Home). *E-mail:* s.smits-kampf@hogeraad.nl (Office); pimhaak@xs4all.nl (Home). *Website:* www.hogeraad.nl (Office).

HAAKON, HRH Crown Prince, BSc; Norwegian crown prince and naval officer; b. 20 July 1973; s. of HM King Harald and HM Queen Sonja; m. Mette-Marit Tjessem Hoiby 2001; one step-s.; ed Kristelig Gymnasium, Officers' Cand. School/Navy, Horten, Royal Norwegian Naval Acad., Bergen, Univ. of California at Berkeley, USA; second-in-command, missile torpedo boat 1995–96; numerous official functions. *Leisure interests:* skiing, cycling, paragliding, sailing, theatre. *Address:* Royal Palace, Det Kgl. Slott, Drammensveien 1, 0010 Oslo, Norway. *Telephone:* (47) 2244-1920. *Fax:* (47) 2255-0880. *Website:* www.kongehuset.no (Office).

HAAKONSEN, Bent, LLB; Danish diplomatist; b. 10 Jan. 1936; m. Kirsten Haakonsen; one d.; joined Ministry of Foreign Affairs 1961; served Bonn 1964–67, Perm. Representation to EEC, Brussels 1972–74; Amb. to Czechoslovakia 1978–79; Head, Danish del. to CSCE, Madrid 1980–81; Under-Sec. for Trade Relations 1983–86; Perm. Under-Sec. of State 1986–91; Perm. Rep. to UN 1991–95; Amb. to Germany 1995–2001, to Sweden 2001–. *Address:* Royal Danish Embassy, Jakobs Torg 1, 111 86 Stockholm, Sweden.

HAAN, Pieter de, MA; Netherlands academic; b. 4 Nov. 1927, Augustinusga; s. of Aan de Haan and Klaaske de Beer; m. F. A. Zijlstra 1956; two c.; ed Univ. of Groningen; Asst Sec. Landbouwschap, The Hague 1956; Scientific Asst Univ. of Agriculture Wageningen 1956–61; Prof. of Land Law, Delft Univ. of Tech. 1961–88, Emer. Prof. 1988–; Prof. of Admin. Law and Land Law, Free Univ. Amsterdam 1974–88, Emer. Prof. 1988–; Pres. Inst. of Construction

Law 1972–97, Scientific Council Inst. of Agrarian Law 1993, Visiting Cttee Faculties of Law 1990–91; mem. Advisory Council for Physical Planning 1976–90, Royal Netherlands Acad. of Sciences 1979–; Dr. hc (Amsterdam) 1990. *Publications:* Land Law (9 Vols) 1969, 1973, 1983, 1984, 1988, 1992, 1996, 2000, 2001; Administrative Law (10 Vols) 1978, 1981, 1986, 1996, 1998, 2000, 2001, 2002. *Leisure interests:* travelling, gardening, fishing. *Address:* Fabriciuslaan 74, 9203 LH Drachten, Netherlands (Home). *Telephone:* (512) 510376 (Home).

HAARDE, Geir H., MA; Icelandic politician and economist; b. 8 April 1951; m. Inga Jona Thordardottir; five c.; ed Brandeis Univ., Johns Hopkins Univ., Univ. of Minnesota, USA; teaching Asst Univ. of Minn. 1976–77; economist Int. Dept, Cen. Bank of Iceland 1977–83; lecturer Econs Dept, Univ. of Iceland 1979–83; Special Asst to Minister of Finance 1983–87; mem. Althing (Parl.) 1987–; mem. Foreign Affairs Cttee 1991–98, Chair. 1995–98; Minister of Finance 1998–; Chair. Youth Org. of Independence Party 1981–85, Chair. Parl. Group 1991–98, Vice-Chair. 1999–; Pres. Icelandic Group Inter-Parl. Union 1988–98, mem. Exec. Cttee 1994–98, Vice-Pres. 1995–97; mem. Control Cttee Nordic Investment Bank 1991–95; mem. Presidium Nordic Council 1991–98, Pres. 1995, Chair. Conservative Party Group 1995–97; Chair. Standing Cttee of Parliamentarians of Arctic Region 1995–98. *Address:* Ministry of Finance, Arnarhváli, 150 Reykjavik, Iceland (Office). *Telephone:* 5459200 (Office). *Fax:* 5628280 (Office). *E-mail:* postur@fjr.stjr.is (Office). *Website:* www.stjr.is/fjr (Office).

HAAS, Peter E., MBA; American business executive; b. 20 Dec. 1918, San Francisco; s. of Walter A. Haas and Elise Stern; m. 1st Josephine Baum 1945; m. 2nd Mimi Lurie 1981; two s. one d.; ed Deerfield Acad., Univ. of Calif. and Harvard Univ.; joined Levi Strauss & Co., San Francisco 1945, Exec. Vice-Pres. 1958–70, Pres. 1970–81, CEO 1976–81, Chair. 1981–89, Chair. Exec. Cttee 1989–; Dir AT&T 1966, now Dir Emer.; fmr Pres. Jewish Welfare Fed.; various public and charitable appts. *Address:* Levi Strauss & Co., 1155 Battery Street, San Francisco, CA 94111, USA.

HAAS, Richard John, BS, MFA; American artist; b. 29 Aug. 1936, Spring Green, Wis.; s. of Joseph F. Haas and Marie N. Haas; m. 1st Cynthia Dickman 1963 (divorced 1970); m. 2nd Katherine Sokolnikoff 1980; one s.; ed Univ. of Wisconsin-Milwaukee and Univ. of Minnesota; Instructor of Art, Univ. of Minn. 1963–64; Asst Prof. of Art, Mich. State Univ. 1964–68; Instructor in Printmaking, Bennington Coll. 1968–80, Fine Arts Faculty, School of Visual Arts 1977–81; mem. New York City Art Comm. 1976–79; mem. Bd Public Art Fund 1980–84, NY State Preservation League 1983–90; Gov. Skowhegan School of Painting and Sculpture 1980–; mem. Bd of Trustees, Hudson River Museum 1989–; Vice-Pres., Dir Abbey Mural Fund, Nat. Acad. of Design, New York, NY; participant in numerous group exhbns since 1962; more than 120 commissioned outdoor and indoor murals, including New York Public Library Periodical Room, Nashville Public Library, Nashville, TN, Bank One Ballpark Stadium, Phoenix, AZ, US Courthouse and Federal Centers in Beckley, W Va and Kansas City, KS 1975–; Guggenheim Fellowship 1983; Fellowship, Macdowell Colony 2003; AIA Medal of Honor 1977; Municipal Art Soc. Award 1977; Nat. Endowment for the Arts Fellowship 1978; Doris C. Freedman Award 1989. *Solo exhibitions include:* San Francisco Museum of Modern Art 1980, Young-Hoffman Gallery, Chicago 1981, 1982, Rhone Hoffman Gallery, Chicago 1983, Univ. of Tennessee 1984, Aspen Art Museum, Colo 1985, Williams Coll. Museum of Art, Mass. 1987, Brooke Alexander, New York 1989, Richard Haas: Architectural Projects 1983–89 and Architectural Facades 1976–86, Rhona Hoffman, Chicago 1990, The Century Asscn, NY 1996, Huntington Museum of Art 1997, Southern Alleghenies Museum of Art 2000. *Publications:* Richard Haas: An Architecture of Illusion, Richard Haas: The City Is My Canvas. *Leisure interests:* tennis, film. *Address:* 361 West 36th Street, New York, NY 10018, USA. *Telephone:* (212) 947-9868. *Fax:* (212) 947-7785. *E-mail:* haasnyc@aol.com (Office). *Website:* www.richardhaas.com (Office).

HAAS, Robert Douglas, MBA; American business executive; b. 3 April 1942, San Francisco; s. of late Walter Haas and of Evelyn Danzig; m. Colleen Gershon 1974; one d.; ed Univ. of Calif. (Berkeley) and Harvard Univ.; with Peace Corps, Ivory Coast 1964–66; with Levi Strauss & Co., San Francisco 1973–, Sr Vice-Pres. (corp. planning and policy) 1978–80, Pres. New Business Group 1980, Pres. Operating Groups 1980–81, Exec. Vice-Pres. and COO 1981–84, Pres. and CEO 1984–89, CEO, Chair. Bd 1989–99, Chair. Bd Dirs. 2000; Hon. Dir San Francisco AIDS Foundation; Trustee Ford Foundation; mem. Bd of Dirs. Levi Strauss Foundation. *Address:* Levi Strauss & Co., 1155 Battery Street, San Francisco, CA 94111, USA.

HAASS, Richard N., BA, PhD; American politician and diplomatist; m.; two c.; ed Oberlin Coll., Ohio and Univ. of Oxford; fmr legis. aide, U.S. Senate; various posts in Dept of Defense 1979–80, Dept of State 1981–85, Special Asst to Pres. and Sr Dir for nr East and S. Asian Affairs, Nat. Security Council 1989–93; Vice-Pres. and Dir of Foreign Policy Studies, Sydney Stein Jr Chair in Int. Security, Brookings Inst. –2001; Dir of Policy Planning, Dept of State March 2001–, U.S. Co-ordinator for Afghanistan policy; leading U.S. Govt Official in support of N Ireland peace process, fmr Special Envoy of Pres.

George W. Bush to NI Peace Process; fmr Sr Fellow and Dir of Nat. Security Programs, Council on Foreign Relations; mem. Int. Inst. for Strategic Studies (fmr Research Assoc.), Trilateral Comm.; Senior Assoc. Carnegie Endowment for Int. Peace; fmr Sol. M. Linowitz Visiting Prof. of Int. Studies, Hamilton Coll.; fmr Lecturer in Public Policy, Harvard Univ. Kennedy School of Govt; fmr Consultant, NBC News; Presidential Citizen's Medal 1991. *Publications:* The Reluctant Sheriff: The United States after the Cold War, Economic Sanctions and American Diplomacy, Intervention: The Use of American Military Force in the Post-Cold War World, The Bureaucratic Entrepreneur: How to Be Effective in Any Unruly Organization; frequent contribs. to foreign affairs journals. *Address:* Department of State, 2201 C Street, NW, Washington, DC 20520, USA (Office). *Telephone:* (202) 647-6575 (Office). *Website:* www.state.gov (Office).

HAAVIKKO, Paavo Juhani; Finnish writer and publisher; b. 25 Jan. 1931, Helsinki; s. of Heikki Adrian Haavikko and Rauha Pyykönen; m. 1st Marja-Liisa Vartio (née Sairanen) 1955 (died 1966); one s. one d.; m. 2nd Ritva Rainio (née Hanhineva) 1971; worked in real estate concurrently with career as writer 1951–67; mem Bd, Finnish Writers' Asscn 1962–66; mem. State Cttee for Literature 1966–67; mem. Bd of Yhtyneet Kuvalehdet magazine co. and Suuri Suomalainen Kirjakerho (Great Finnish Book Club) 1969; Literary Dir Otava Publishing Co. 1967–83; Publr Arthouse Publishing Group 1983–; Academician hc; six state prizes for literature; Neustadt Int. Prize for Literature 1984, Nordic Prize of Swedish Acad.; Pro Finlandia Medal; Nossack-Akademiepreise, Akademie der Wissenschaften und der Literatur, Mainz. *Publications:* Tiet etäisyyksiin 1951, Tuuliöinä 1953, Synnyinmaa 1955, Lehdet lehtiä 1958, Talvipalatsi 1959, Runot 1962, Puut, kaikki heidän vihreytensä 1966, Neljätoista hallitsijaa 1970, Puhua vastata opettaa 1972, Runoja matkalta salmen ylitse 1973, Kaksikymmentä ja yksi 1974, Kaksiky m mentä ja yksi 1974, Runot 1949–1974 1975, Runoelmat 1975, Viiniä, Kirjoitusta 1976, Toukokuu, ikuinen 1988 (poems); Poésie 1965, Jahre 1967, Geschichte 1967, Selected Poems 1968, The Superintendent 1973, Le palais d'hiver 1976 (translations); Münchhausen, Nuket 1960, Ylilääkäri 1968, Sulka 1973, Harald Pitkäikäinen 1974 (plays); Ratsumies 1974 (libretto); Yksityisiä Asioita 1960, Toinen taivas ja maa 1961, Vuodet 1962, Lasi Claudius Civiliksen salaliittolaisten pöydällä 1964 (prose); Kansakuninan linja 1977, Yritys omaksikuvaksi 1987, Vuosien aurinkoiset varjot (memoirs), Prospero (memoirs) 1967–1995. *Address:* Art House Oy, Bulevardi 19C, 00120 Helsinki, Finland. *Telephone:* (9) 6932727. *Fax:* (9) 6949028.

HAAVISTO, Heikki Johannes, MSc, LLM; Finnish politician; b. 20 Aug. 1935, Turku; s. of Johan Haavisto and Alli Svensson; m. Maija Rihko 1964; three s.; Head of Dept Oy Vehnä Ab 1963–66; Sec.-Gen. Cen. Union of Agricultural Producers and Forest Owners in Finland (MTK) 1966–75, Pres. 1976–94; Vice-Pres. Int. Fed. of Agricultural Producers (IFAP) 1977–80, 1986–90, mem. Bd of Dirs. 1984–86; mem. Cen. Council of Nordic Farmer Orgs. (NBC), Pres. 1977, 1985–87; Chair. Del. of Finn Cooperative Pellervo (Confed. of Finnish Cooperatives) 1979–2000; mem. Admin. Council, Osuuskunta Metsäliitto, Vice-Chair. 1976–82, Pres. 1982–93; Vice-Chair. Admin. Council, OKO (Cen. Union of Cooperative Credit Banks) 1985–93; mem. Bd Dirs. Metsä-Serla Oy 1986–93; Pres. Admin. Council, Raisio Group 1987–96, Pres. Bd of Dirs. 1997–2000; mem. Int. Policy Council on Agric. and Trade 1988–2000; Minister for Foreign Affairs 1993–95, for Devt Co-operation 1994–95; three hon. doctorates. *Address:* Hintsantie 2, 21200 Raisio, Finland. *Telephone:* (2) 4383020. *Fax:* (2) 4383499.

HABASH, George, MD; Palestinian nationalist leader; b. 1925, Lydda, Palestine; m. Hilda Habash 1961; two d.; ed American Univ. of Beirut; founder Youth of Avengeance 1948 and Arab Nationalists' Movement early 1950s; practised as doctor 1950s; founder of Popular Front for the Liberation of Palestine Dec. 1967–, Sec. Gen. of Cen. Cttee 1967–2000 (introduced Marxist-Leninist thought to the Palestinian cause); leader Arab Nationalists' Movt. *Publications include:* Evaluation of New Era, The Past Experiences and Future Horizons, The Palestinian Uprising, The Palestinian Struggle in Practice. *Leisure interests:* reading, swimming, classical and oriental music, chess. *Address:* Popular Front for the Liberation of Palestine, Box 12144, Damascus, Syria. *Telephone:* (11) 3324987 (Office). *Fax:* (11) 3329326 (Office). *E-mail:* alnaji@cyberia.net.lb (Office).

HABBEL, Wolfgang R., DJur; German business executive and lawyer; b. 25 March 1924, Dillenburg; s. of Werner and Dorothea Habbel; m. Susan Roedter 1951; two s.; Asst to Bd of Man., Auto Union GmbH 1951–59; Personnel Man., European Labour Relations Co-ordinator, Ford of Europe 1960–69; mem. Man. Bd, Boehringer, Ingelheim 1970–71, Audi NSU 1971–78; Chair. Man. Bd, Audi NSU (Audi AG from Jan. 1985) 1979–87; now Sr Exec. Dir Russell Reynolds Asscn Inc.; mem. Man. Bd, Volkswagen 1979–, des Landesverbandes der Bayerischen Ind.; mem. Bd of Dirs., Gerresheimer Glas AG, Triumph Adler Werke AG, Digital Equipment GmbH, Maynard, Deutsche Sport-Marketing; Pres. Gesellschaft für Sicherheitswissenschaft; Manager Junge Industriemagazin 1984; Dir numerous cos. and other appointments; Bayerischer Verdienstorden, Bundesverdienstkreuz, Hon. Senator Univ. of Bayreuth 1987; State Medal for Services to the Bavarian Economy 1984. *Leisure interest:* golf. *Address:* Russell Reynolds Association Inc., Höhenstrasse 5, 85276 Pfaffenhofen, Germany. *Telephone:* (8441) 2233.

HABERER, Jean-Yves; French government official; b. 17 Dec. 1932, Mazagan, Morocco; m. Anne du Crest 1959; two c.; ed Inst. d'Etudes politiques, Ecole Nat. d'Admin.; Insp. des Finances 1959, Insp. Gen. 1980; Tech. Adviser to Finance Ministry 1966–68; an Asst Dir of Treasury 1967–69, in charge of Intervention Service, Treasury 1969, of Financial Activities 1970, of Int. Business 1973; Dir of Treasury 1978–82; Head of Office of Minister of Foreign Affairs 1968, of Minister of Defence 1969, of Minister of Econ. and Finance 1976; Prof. Inst. d'Etudes politiques 1970–82; Chair. Monetary Cttee of the EEC 1980–82; Pres. and Dir-Gen. Bank Paribas and Cie Financière de Paribas 1982–86, Chair. of Supervisory Bd Compagnie Bancaire 1982–88; Chair. Crédit Lyonnais 1988–93, Crédit Nat. 1993–94; Dir Cie Bancaire, Pallas Invest, Fondation Recherche Médicale, Institut Vaisseaux et Sang; Officier, Ordre nat. du Mérite 1981, Officier, Légion d'honneur 1989. *Publication:* Cinq ans de Crédit Lyonnais 1988–1993 1999. *Address:* 82 avenue Marceau, 75008 Paris (Office); 10 rue Rémusat, 75016 Paris, France (Home). *Telephone:* 1-53-57-93-12 (Office). *Fax:* 1-53-57-93-16.

HABERMAS, Jürgen, DPhil; German professor of philosophy; b. 18 June 1929, Düsseldorf; m. Ute Habermas-Wesselhoeft 1955; one s. two d.; ed Univs. of Bonn and Göttingen; Research Asst, Inst. für Soziale Forschung, Frankfurt 1956; Prof. of Philosophy, Univ. of Heidelberg 1961, of Philosophy and Sociology, Univ. of Frankfurt 1964; Dir Max Planck Inst., Starnberg, Munich 1971; Prof. of Philosophy, Univ. of Frankfurt 1983–94, Prof. Emer. 1994–; Foreign mem. American Acad. of Arts and Sciences 1984, British Acad. of Science 1994; Hon. DD (New School for Social Research) 1984, hon. degrees from Hebrew Univ. (Jerusalem), Univs. of Hamburg, Buenos Aires, Evanston (Northwestern), Utrecht, Athens, Bologna, Paris, Tel Aviv, Cambridge, Harvard Univ.; Hegel Prize 1972, Sigmund Freud Prize 1976, Adorno Prize 1980, Geschwister Scholl Prize 1985, Leibniz Prize 1986, Sonning Prize 1987, Jaspers Prize 1997, Culture Prize of the State of Hesse 1999, Friedenspreis des deutschen Buchhandels 2001. *Publications:* Strukturwandel der Öffentlichkeit 1962, Theorie und Praxis 1963, Erkenntnis und Interesse 1968, Legitimationsprobleme im Spätkapitalismus 1973, Theorie des kommunikativen Handelns 1981, Moralbewüsstsein und Kommunikatives Handeln 1983, Der Philosophische Diskurs ober Moderne 1985, Eine Art Schadensabwicklüng 1987, Nachmetaphysisches Denken 1988, Nachholende Revolution 1990, Texte und Kontexte 1991, Erläuterungen zur Diskursetnik 1991, Faktizität und Geltung 1992, Vergangenheit als Zukunft 1993, Die Normalität einer Berliner Republik 1995, Die Einbeziehung des Anderen 1996, Vom sinnlichen Eindruck zum symbolischen Ausdruck 1997, Die postnationale Konstellation 1998, Wahrheit und Rechtfertigung 1999, Zeit und Übergänge 2001, Kommunikatives Handeln und Detranszendentalisierte Vernuft 2001, Die Zukunft der Menschlichen Natur 2001. *Address:* Department of Philosophy, University of Frankfurt, Grüneburgplatz 1, 60629 Frankfurt am Main (Office); Ringstrasse 8B, 82319 Starnberg, Germany. *Telephone:* (8151) 13537 (Home). *Fax:* (8151) 13537 (Home).

HABGOOD, Baron (Life Peer), cr. 1995, of Calverton in the County of Buckinghamshire; **Rt Rev and Rt Hon. John Stapylton Habgood,** PC, DD, MA, PhD; British ecclesiastic (retd); b. 23 June 1927, Stony Stratford; s. of Arthur Henry Habgood and Vera Chetwynd-Stapylton; m. Rosalie Mary Anne Boston 1961; two s. two d.; ed Eton Coll., King's Coll. Cambridge Univ. and Cuddesdon Coll. Oxford; Demonstrator in Pharmacology, Cambridge Univ. 1950–53; Fellow, King's Coll. Cambridge Univ. 1952–55; Curate, St Mary Abbott's Church, Kensington 1954–56; Vice-Prin. Westcott House, Cambridge 1956–62; Rector, St John's Church, Jedburgh, Scotland 1962–67; Prin. Queen's Coll., Birmingham 1967–73; Bishop of Durham 1973–83; Archbishop of York 1983–95; Pres. (UK) Council on Christian Approaches to Defence and Disarmament 1976–95; Chair. World Council of Churches' Int. Hearing on Nuclear Weapons 1981; mem. Council for Science and Society 1975–90, Council for Arms Control 1981–95; Moderator of Church and Soc. Sub-Unit, World Council of Churches 1983–90; Chair. UK Xenotransplantation Interim Regulatory Authority 1997–2003; Hon. Fellow King's Coll., Cambridge 1984; Bampton Lecturer, Oxford Univ. 1999, Gifford Lecturer, Aberdeen Univ. 2000; Hon. DD (Durham) 1975, (Cambridge) 1984, (Aberdeen) 1988, (Huron) 1990, (Hull) 1991, (Oxford) 1996, (Manchester) 1996; Hon. DUniv (York) 1996; Hon. DHL (York, Pa) 1995. *Publications:* Religion and Science 1964, A Working Faith 1980, Church and Nation in a Secular Age 1983, Confessions of a Conservative Liberal 1988, Making Sense 1993, Faith and Uncertainty 1997, Being a Person 1998, Varieties of Unbelief 2000, The Concept of Nature 2002. *Leisure interests:* carpentry, painting. *Address:* 18 The Mount, Malton, North Yorks., YO17 7ND, England.

HABIB, Randa, MA; Jordanian/French journalist; b. 16 Jan. 1952, Beirut, Lebanon; d. of Farid Habib; m. Adnan Gharaybeh 1973; one s. one d.; ed French Lycée, Rio de Janeiro and Univ. of Beirut; corresp. Agence France Presse (AFP) 1980, Dir and Head AFP Office, Amman 1987–; corresp. Radio Monte Carlo 1988–, also for several int. publs and TV; Médaille du Travail (France) 2000; Chevalier Ordre nat. du Mérite 2001. *Publications:* articles in Politique Internationale. *Leisure interests:* reading, swimming, painting. *Address:* Agence France Presse, Jebel Amman, 2nd Circle, PO Box 3340, Amman 11181, Jordan. *Telephone:* (6) 4642976. *Fax:* (6) 4654680. *E-mail:* randa16@go.com.jo (Office).

HABIB-DELONCLE, Michel, LèsL, LenD; French politician, lawyer and international consultant; b. 26 Nov. 1921, Neuilly-sur-Seine; s. of Louis Habib and Jeanne Deloncle; m. Colette Sueur 1944; three s. (one deceased) two d.; ed Ecole libre des Sciences Politiques, Paris and Faculties of Law and Letters (Sorbonne), Univ. of Paris; Resistance Movt 1941–45; Journalist, France Catholique 1945–53; Sec.-Gen. Parl. Group Rassemblement du Peuple Français 1948–54; barrister, Cour d'Appel, Paris 1955–89, hon. barrister, 1990–;

Deputy, Nat. Ass. 1958–63, 1967–73; Sec. of State to the Ministry of Foreign Affairs 1962–66, to the Ministry of Educ. 1966–67; MEP 1967–73, Vice-Pres. 1972; mem. del. UN Gen. Ass. 1967–72; Int. Relations Del., Exec. Cttee Union des Démocrates pour la République (UDR) 1968–74; Deputy Sec.-Gen. UDR 1971; mem. Cen. Cttee RPR 1977–84, mem. Nat. Council 1990–2002; Political Ed. La Nation 1968–74; Pres. Chambre de Commerce Franco-arabe 1970–2002, Hon. Pres. 2002–; Vice-Pres. Union Paneuropéenne Int. 1989–; First Vice-Pres. French Cttee for Paneuropean Union 1993–99; int. consultant 1989–; Commdr Légion d'honneur; Croix de guerre. *Publication:* La Vᵉ République: un chef d'oeuvre en péril 1988. *Leisure interest:* music. *Address:* 124 rue de Tocqueville, 75017 Paris, France. *Telephone:* 1-47-54-03-25 (Office). *Fax:* 1-42-86-92-94. *E-mail:* habdelon@free.fr (Home).

HABIBI, Hassan Ibrahim; Iranian politician; ed in France; with the late Ayatollah Ruholla Khomeini, Paris 1978–79; apptd. mem. Revolutionary Council 1979, Minister of Justice 1984, First Vice-Pres. 1989–2001. *Address:* c/o Office of the President, Palestine Avenue, Azerbaijan Intersection, Tehran, Iran (Office).

HABIBIE, Bacharuddin Jusuf, DEng; Indonesian politician and aviation engineer; b. 25 June 1936, Pare-Pare, South Sulawesi; m. H. Hasri Ainun Besari 1962; two s.; ed Bandung Inst. of Tech., Technische Hochschule, Aachen; Head of Research at Messerschmitt-Boelkow-Blohm, Hamburg 1966; Govt Adviser 1976; Chair., CEO, Pres. Indonesian State Aircraft Industry 1976–98; Minister of State for Research and Tech. 1978–98; Head of Agency for Tech. Evaluation and Application 1978–98; Chair., CEO, Pres. Indonesian Shipbldg. Industry 1978–98; Chair. Batam Industrial Devt 1978–98; Chair. Team for Defence Security Industrial Devt 1980–99; mem. Indonesian Parl. 1982–99; Chair., CEO, Pres. Small Arms and Munitions Industry 1983–98; Chair. Nat. Research Council 1984–; Vice-Chair. Bd of Patrons, Indonesian Strategic Industries 1988–; Chair. Agency for Strategic Industries 1989–98; Head of Indonesian Muslim Intellectuals Asscn 1990–; Vice-Pres. of Indonesia March–May 1998, Pres. 1998–99; founder and Chair. Indonesian Aeronautics and Astronautics Inst.; mem. Royal Swedish Acad. of Eng Sciences, Acad. Nat. de l'Air et de l'Espace, France; Fellow Royal Aeronautical Soc.; Gran Cruz del Mérito Aeronáutico con Distintivo Blanco (Spain) 1980, Grosses Bundesverdienstkreuz 1980, Dwidya Sistha Medal 1982, Grand Cross of the Order of Orange Nassau 1983, Grand Officier Ordre nat. du Mérite and numerous other awards and decorations. *Publications:* numerous scientific and technical papers. *Address:* c/o House of Representatives, Jakarta, Indonesia (Office).

HABICHT, Werner, DPhil; German professor of English; b. 29 Jan. 1930, Schweinfurt; s. of Wilhelm Habicht and Magda (née Müller) Habicht; ed Univ. of Munich, Johns Hopkins Univ., Univ. of Paris; Asst Freie Universität, Berlin 1957–60, Univ. of Munich 1960–65; Prof. of English, Univ. of Heidelberg 1966–70, Univ. of Bonn 1970–78, Univ. of Würzburg 1978–95, Prof. Emer. 1995–; Visiting Prof. Univ. of Texas at Austin 1981, Univ. of Colorado, Boulder 1987, Ohio State Univ., Columbus 1988, Univ. of Cyprus 1995–96; mem. Akademie der Wissenschaften und der Literatur, Mainz, Bayerische Akademie der Wissenschaften; Pres. Deutsche Shakespeare-Gesellschaft West 1976–88, Vice-Pres. 1988–93; Hon. Vice-Pres. Int. Shakespeare Asscn 1996–. *Publications:* Die Gebärde in englischen Dichtungen des Mittelalters 1959, Studien zur Dramenform vor Shakespeare 1968, Shakespeare and the German Imagination 1994; Ed. English and American Studies in German 1968–82; Ed. Jahrbuch, Deutsche Shakespeare-Gesellschaft West 1982–95; Co-ed. Literatur Brockhaus, 3 Vols 1988; numerous articles on English literature and drama. *Address:* Institut für Englische Philologie, Universität Würzburg, Am Hubland, 97074 Würzburg (Office); Allerseeweg 14, 97204 Höchberg, Germany (Home). *Telephone:* (931) 8885658 (Office); (931) 49267 (Home). *Fax:* (931) 8885674 (Office). *E-mail:* WHabicht@t-online.de (Home).

HABILA, Helon; Nigerian writer; b. 1967, Kaltungo, Gombe State; ed Univ. of Jos; Lecturer in English and Literature, Fed. Polytechnic, Bauchi 1997–99; fmr contrib. to Hints magazine, Lagos; currently Arts Ed. Vanguard newspaper, Lagos; 1st Prize MUSON Festival Poetry Competition (for poem Another Age) 2000, Caine Prize for African Writing, U.K. (for short story Love Poems) 2001. *Publications:* Mai Kaltungo (biog.) 1997, Prison Stories (short stories) 2000, Waiting for an Angel 2002; short stories and poems in anthologies. *Address:* c/o Vanguard, Kirikiri Canal, PMB 1007, Apapa, Nigeria (Office). *Website:* vanguard@linkserve.com.ng (Office).

HABRAKEN, Nicolaas John; Netherlands architect; b. 29 Oct. 1928, Bandung, Indonesia; s. of late J. W. L. Habraken and J. L. S. Heyting; m. E. Marleen van Hall 1958; one s. one d.; ed Delft Tech. Univ.; architect, Lucas & Niemeyer (architects), Voorburg 1961–65; Dir Stichting Architecten Research (SAR), Voorburg 1965–66, Eindhoven 1966–75; Prof. and First Chair. Dept of Architecture, Eindhoven Tech. Univ. 1966–70, Prof. of Architecture 1966–75; Head, Dept of Architecture, MIT 1975–81, Prof. of Architecture 1975–89, Prof. Emer. 1989–; partner, Infill Systems BV, Delft 1986–99; Hon. mem. Architectural Inst. of Japan 1994; David Roell Prize 1979; ACSA Creative Achievement Award 1989, B.K.V.B. Nat. Architecture Award 1996. *Publications:* Supports: An Alternative to Mass Housing 1962, Transformations of the Site 1983, The Appearance of the Form 1985, The Structure of the Ordinary 1998; research reports and numerous articles. *Address:* 63 Wildernislaan, 7313 BD Apeldoorn, The Netherlands. *Telephone:* (55) 3556354. *Fax:* (55) 3554765. *E-mail:* habraken@xs4all.nl. *Website:* habraken.com (Home).

HABRÉ, Hissène; Chadian politician; formerly one of the leaders of the Front de Libération Nationale du Tchad (FROLINAT); head of Northern Armed Forces Command Council –1977; held the French archaeologists M. and Mme Claustre captive 1974–77; Leader of Forces Armées du Nord 1977; negotiated with Govt of Brig.-Gen. Félix Malloum 1978; Prime Minister 1978–79; resigned after Kano peace agreement with FROLINAT forces led by Goukouni Oueddei March 1979; Minister of State for Defence and War Veterans in Provisional Govt April–May 1979; Minister of Defence 1979 (in conflict with Goukouni Oueddei in civil war, reported in exile 1980); Minister of Nat. Defence, Veterans and War Victims 1986–90; Pres. of Chad June–Oct. 1982, Pres. 1982–90 (ousted in coup); living in Cameroon 1990, in Senegal 1999; indicted for complicity in torture by Senegalese Court, Feb. 2000, case later dismissed, then under investigation by a Belgian court Feb. 2002.

HABSBURG-LOTHRINGEN, Georg von; Hungarian business executive and diplomatist; b. 16 Dec. 1964, Starnberg, Bavaria, Germany; s. of Otto von Habsburg-Lothringen (q.v.) and Regina, Princess of Sachsen-Meiningen; m. Eilika Habsburg Lothringen, Duchess of Oldenburg 1997; ed Univs. of Munich and Madrid; settled in Hungary 1993; mem. Bd MTM-SBS Televisio R.T.; Dir TV2 1997–2002; Amb.-at-large of Hungary 1996–; Pres. Eutop Budapest 2002–. *Address:* Prime Minister's Office, 4 Kossuth Square, 1055 Budapest; Eutop Budapest, Romer Floris u.58, H-1024 Budapest; IV Károly Király utja 1, 2038 Sóskút, Hungary (Home). *Telephone:* (1) 4412357 (Prime Minister's Office); (1) 4383536 (Eutop). *Fax:* (1) 4412359 (Prime Minister's Office); (1) 3162649 (Eutop). *E-mail:* habsburg@axelero.hu (Office). *Website:* www.meh.hu (Office).

HABSBURG-LOTHRINGEN, Otto von, DrPolSc; Austrian/German/Hungarian politician and author; b. 20 Nov. 1912, Reichenau, Austria; s. of late Archduke Charles, later Emperor of Austria and King of Hungary and Zita, Princess of Bourbon-Parma; m. Regina, Princess of Sachsen-Meiningen 1951; two s. five d.; ed Univ. of Louvain, Belgium; mem. Pan-European Union 1936–, rep. in Washington 1940–46, Vice-Pres. 1957, Pres. 1973–; MEP for Bavaria (Christian Social Union) 1979–99; lectures throughout the world on int. affairs and is author of weekly column appearing in 21 daily papers in 5 languages since 1953; mem. Acad. des Sciences Morales et Politiques, Inst. de France, Paris, Real Acad. de Ciencias Morales y Políticas, Madrid, Acad. da Cultura Portuguesa, Acad. Mejicana de Derecho Internacional, Acad. of Morocco, etc.; Dr hc (Univs of Nancy, Tampa, Cincinnati, Ferrara, Pécs, Budapest, Turku, Veszprém); numerous awards and decorations including Bayerischer Verdienstorden, Order of Gregory the Great (Vatican), Robert Schuman Gold Medal 1977, Gold Medal of City of Paris, Konrad Adenauer Prize 1977, Medal of Europe of Free State of Bavaria 1991, Maarjaa Maa Order (Estonia), Grand Cross of Merit (Hungary). *Publications:* 38 books in seven languages on history, politics, world affairs and especially European politics. *Address:* Hindenburgstrasse 15, 82343 Pöcking, Germany. *Telephone:* (8157) 7015 (Office). *Fax:* (8157) 7087 (Office).

HACHETTE, Jean-Louis, LenD; French publisher; b. 30 June 1925, Paris; s. of Louis and Blanche (née Darbou) Hachette; m. Y. de Bouillé 1954; one s. two d.; ed Collège Stanislas, Paris and Faculté de Droit, Paris; joined Librairie Hachette (founded by great-grandfather in 1826) 1946 (now Hachette Livre); entire career spent with Librairie Hachette, Admin. Dir 1971–; Pres. Librairie Gén. Française 1954–. *Leisure interests:* polo, golf, skiing.

HACKING, Ian MacDougall, PhD, FRSC, FBA; Canadian professor of philosophy; b. 18 Feb. 1936, Vancouver; s. of Harold Eldridge Hacking and Margaret Elinore MacDougall; m. 1st Laura Anne Leach 1962; m. 2nd Judith Polsky Baker 1983; one s. two d.; ed Univ. of British Columbia, Cambridge Univ.; Asst then Assoc. Prof., Univ. of BC 1964–69; Univ. Lecturer in Philosophy, Cambridge and Fellow of Peterhouse 1969–74; Prof., then Henry Waldgrave Stuart Prof. of Philosophy, Stanford Univ. 1975–82; Prof., Univ. of Toronto 1983–, Univ. Prof. 1991–; Prof., Chair of Philosophy and History of Scientific Concepts Collège de France, Paris 2000–; Fellow American Acad. of Arts and Sciences 1991; Hon. Fellow Trinity Coll. Cambridge 2000; Hon. LLD (Univ. of BC) 2001; Molson Prize, Canada Council 2001, Killam Prize, Canada Council 2002. *Publications:* Logic of Statistical Inference 1965, Why Does Language Matter to Philosophy? 1975, The Emergence of Probability 1975, Representing and Intervening 1983, The Taming of Chance 1991, Le plus pur nominalisme 1993, Rewriting the Soul: Multiple Personality and the Sciences of Memory 1995, Mad Travelers 1998, The Social Construction of What? 1999, Historical Ontology 2002. *Leisure interests:* walking, canoeing. *Address:* Department of Philosophy, University of Toronto, 215 Huron Street, Toronto, Ont., M5S 1A1 (Office); Collège de France, 11 place Marcelin Berthelot, 75005 Paris, France (Office); 391 Markham Street, Toronto, Ont., M6G 2K8, Canada (Home); 2 chez d'harcourt, 22 rue Saint Louis en l'Île, 75004 Paris, France (Home). *Telephone:* (416) 978-4951 (Office); 1-44-27-16-06 (Office). *Fax:* (416) 978-8703 (Office). *E-mail:* ian.hacking@college-de-france.fr (Office).

HACKMAN, Gene; American actor; b. 30 Jan. 1930, San Bernardino, Calif.; s. of Eugene Ezra Hackman; m. Fay Maltese 1956 (divorced 1985); one s. two d.; studied acting at the Pasadena Playhouse; Acad. Award for Best Actor, New York Film Critics' Award, Golden Globe Award, British Acad. Award, The French Connection, British Acad. Award, The Poseidon Adventure, Cannes Film Festival Award, Scarecrow, Nat. Review Bd Award, Mississippi Burning 1988, Berlin Film Award 1989, Acad. Award, The Unforgiven 1993; Cecil B. DeMille Award, Golden Globes 2003. *Films include:* Lilith 1964,

Hawaii 1966, Banning 1967, Bonnie and Clyde 1967, The Split 1968, Downhill Racer 1969, I Never Sang For My Father 1969, The Gypsy Moths 1969, Marooned 1970, The Hunting Party 1971, The French Connection 1971, The Poseidon Adventure 1972, The Conversation 1973, Scarecrow 1973, Zandy's Bride 1974, Young Frankenstein 1974, The French Connection II 1975, Lucky Lady 1975, Night Moves 1976, Domino Principle 1977, Superman 1978, Superman II 1980, All Night Long 1980, Target 1985, Twice in a Lifetime 1985, Power 1985, Bat 21, Superman IV 1987, No Way Out 1987, Another Woman 1988, Mississippi Burning 1988, The Package 1989, The Von Metz Incident 1989, Loose Connections 1989, Full Moon in Blue Water 1989, Postcards from the Edge 1989, Class Action 1989, Loose Canons 1990, Narrow Margin 1990, Necessary Roughness 1991, Company Business 1991, The William Munny Killings 1991, The Unforgiven 1992, The Firm 1992, Geronimo, Wyatt Earp 1994, Crimson Tide, The Quick and the Dead 1995, Get Shorty, Birds of a Feather, Extreme Measures 1996, The Chamber 1996, Absolute Power 1996, Twilight 1998, Enemy of the State 1998, Under Suspicion 2000, Heist 2001, The Royal Tenenbaums (Golden Globe for Best Actor in a Musical or Comedy) 2001. *Stage plays include:* Children From Their Games 1963, Cass Henderson in Any Wednesday 1964, Poor Richard, 1964, Death and the Maiden 1992. *Television includes:* Many guest appearances on US series; also My Father, My Mother, CBS Playhouse 1968 and Shadow on the Land 1971, Under Suspicion 1999. *Publication:* Wake of the Perdido Star (with David Lenihan) 2000. *Address:* c/o Barry Haldeman, 1900 Avenue of the Stars, Suite 2000, Los Angeles, CA 90067; c/o Fred Spector, Creative Artists Agency, 9830 Wilshire Boulevard, Beverly Hills, CA 90212, USA.

HACKNEY, Francis Sheldon, PhD; American historian; b. 5 Dec. 1933, Birmingham, Ala; s. of Cecil Hackney and Elizabeth Morris; m. Lucy Durr 1957; one s. two d.; ed Vanderbilt and Yale Univs; mem. faculty, Princeton Univ. 1965–75; Assoc. Prof. of History 1969–72, Prof. and Provost 1972–75; Pres. Tulane Univ. New Orleans 1975–80; Prof of History Univ. of Pa 1981–93, 1997–, Pres. 1981–93; mem. Bd Dirs. Carnegie Foundation for Advancement of Teaching 1976–84, 1986–93; Chair. Nat. Endowment for the Humanities 1993–97; mem. American Philosophical Soc., American History Assen. *Publications:* Populism to Progressivism in Alabama 1969, Populism: The Critical Issues (ed.), Understanding the American Experience (with others) 1973, One America Indivisible 1997. *Address:* c/o Department of History, University of Pennsylvania, 3401 Walnut Street, Room A-328F, Philadelphia, PA 19104, USA. *E-mail:* shackney@history.upenn.edu (Office).

HACKNEY, Roderick Peter, PhD, PPRIBA; British architect; b. 3 March 1942, Liverpool; s. of William Hackney and Rose (Morris) Hackney; m. Christine Thornton 1964; one s.; ed John Bright's Grammar School, Llandudno, School of Architecture, Manchester Univ.; Job Architect, Expo '67, Montreal, for monorail stations 1967; Housing Architect for Libyan Govt, Tripoli 1967–68; Asst to Arne Jacobsen, working on Kuwait Cen. Bank, Copenhagen 1968–71; est. practice of Rod Hackney Architect, Macclesfield 1972, architectural practices in Birmingham, Leicester, Belfast, Cleator Moor, Workington, Carlisle, Millom, Clitheroe, Manchester, Stirling, Burnley, Chesterfield and Stoke on Trent 1975–88; Council mem. RIBA, including Vice-Pres. for Public Affairs and Vice-Pres. for Overseas Affairs 1978–84, Pres. 1987–89, mem. of Council 1991–, Vice-Pres. Int. Affairs 1992–94, Hon. Librarian 1998–; Council mem. Int. Union of Architects 1981–85, 1991–, Pres. 1987–90; Hon. Fellow American Inst. of Architects, Fed. de Colegios de Arquitectos de la Repúb. Mexicana, United Architects of the Philippines, Royal Arch. Inst. of Canada, Indian Inst. of Architects, Architectural Soc. of China; Patron Llandudno Museum and Art Gallery 1988–; Pres. Snowdonia Nat. Park Soc. 1987–; Pres. North Wales Centre of The Nat. Trust 1990–; mem. Editorial Bd, UIA Journal of Architectural Theory and Criticism; Jury mem. Cembureau Award for Low Rise Housing in France 1982, for Prix Int. d'Architecture de l'Institut Nat. du Logement 1983; Chair. Jury for Hérouville Town Centre Competition, France 1982–83; Pres. Young Architects Forum, Sofia 1985, Building Communities (Int. Community Architecture Conf.), London 1986; presentation of case for Int. Year of Shelter for the Homeless to all 4 party confs. 1986; Chair. Times/RIBA Community Enterprise Scheme 1985–89, Trustees of Inner City Trust 1986–97, British Architecture Library Trust 1999–; Special Prof. in Architecture, Univ. of Nottingham 1987–91; Int. Adviser Univ. of Manchester School of Architecture Centre for Int. Architectural Studies 1992–; Adviser on regeneration and inner city problems in Sweden, Italy and the USA 1990–; consultant, World Architecture Review Agency 1992–; Adviser, Centre for Human Settlements Int. 1994–, Habitat Centre News Journal, India 1996; mem. Chartered Inst. of Building 1987–, Assen of Planning Supervisors 1996–; attained registration for BSI ISO9001 1996; Adviser, World Habitat Awards, Social Housing Foundation, Coalville, UK 2003; Hon. DLitt (Keele) 1989; Dept of Environment Good Design in Housing Award 1975, 1980, First Prize, for St Ann's Hospice, Manchester 1976, Prix Int. d'Architecture de l'Institut Nat. du Logement 1979–80, RICS/Times Conservation Award 1980, Civic Trust Award of Commendation 1980, 1981, 1984, Sir Robert Matthews Award (Honourable Mention) 1981, Manchester Soc. of Architects Pres.'s Award 1982, Otis Award 1982, Gold Medal, Bulgarian Inst. of Architects 1983, Gold Medal, Young Architect of the Year, Sofia 1983, Grand Medal of Federación de Colegios de Arquitectos (Mexico) 1986, Commendation, Business Enterprise Award for Housing 1993, Millennium Expo Competition Greenwich (short-listed), Citation for World Habitat Awards 1996, Stone Award 1996. *Solo Exhbn:* Blanc de Berge. *Musical:* Good Golly Miss Molly. *TV:* Consultant to Chapman Clarke Films' Forever England, Central TV 1995; TV features: Build Yourself a House 1974, Community Architecture 1977, BBC Omnibus 1987. *Publications:* Highfield Hall, A Community Project 1982, The Good, the Bad and the Ugly 1990, Good Golly Miss Molly 1991 (musical play). *Leisure interests:* outdoor pursuits, walking, Butterfly Society, fossils, geology, travelling, ballooning, looking at buildings, talking at conferences. *Address:* St Peter's House, Windmill Street, Macclesfield, Cheshire, SK11 7HS, England. *Telephone:* (1625) 431792 (Office). *Fax:* (1625) 616929 (Office). *E-mail:* rod@stpeter.demon.co.uk (Office).

HADDADIN, Muwaffaq, PhD; Jordanian pharmacist and administrator; b. 1942, Ma'in; m.; two s.; ed American Univ. of Beirut, Lebanon, Univs. of Washington and Kansas, USA; Asst and Assoc. Prof. Coll. of Medicine, Univ. of Jordan 1972–80; Prof., Dean of Pharmacy School, Yarmouk Univ. 1980–83; Chair. Bd Société Arabe des Industries Pharmacéutiques (SAIPH), Tunis; mem. Bd Arab Co. for Antibiotics Industry in Baghdad, Iraq; Dir Arab Co. for Drug Industries and Medical Appliances (ACDIMA) 1983–; mem. Jordanian Pharmacist Soc.; two medals of honour, Yarmouk Univ. *Publications:* several articles in scientific journals. *Leisure interests:* swimming, chess and classical music. *Address:* Arab Company for Drug Industries and Medical Appliances, PO Box 925161, Amman (Office); University of Jordan Street, PO Box 1076, Jubaiha 11941, Jordan.

HADI, Lt-Gen. Abdrabuh Mansoor; Yemeni politician and army officer; b. 1944, Al-Wadhee'a Region, Governorate of Abyan; m.; three s. two d.; ed Supreme Acad. of Nasser, Egypt, Sandhurst Mil. Acad., UK, Frunze Acad., fmr USSR; mem. staff Armoured Brigades, Mil. Acad.; Dir of Combat Training, of Supply and Provisions; Deputy Chief of Staff, Supply and Provisions; Adviser to Presidential Council 1990–; Minister of Defence 1994; Vice-Pres. of Repub. of Yemen 1994–; rank of Gen. 1994, Lieut.-Gen. 1997; many decorations and awards including Medal of Honour of Mil. Service 1980, Order of the First Grade Badge 1995. *Leisure interests:* reading, current affairs, public folklore, local and classical music, swimming. *Address:* c/o Office of the President, San'a, Yemen (Office). *Telephone:* (1) 272283. *Fax:* (1) 252803.

HADI, Hashim el-; Sudanese vice-chancellor and academic; m.; four c.; Research Asst then lecturer, Dept of Physiology and Biochem., Univ. of Khartoum 1964–77, Assoc. Prof. 1977–91, Prof. of Animal Physiology 1991, Dean of Students 1990–92, Dean of Veterinary Science 1992–94, Vice-Chancellor 1994–98; Vice-Chancellor Sudan Int. Univ. 1998–; Assoc. Prof. King Faisal Univ., Saudi Arabia 1979–87, Vice-Dean of Veterinary Medicine 1982–84; Chair. Sudan Veterinary Assen 1997–; Chair. Assen of Arab Univs. 1995–97, Sudan Assen of Univs. 1995–98; mem. Bd Assen of Int. Univs. 1995–2000; fmr Chair. Sudan Nat. Cttee for Dry Land Husbandry; mem. Sudan Veterinary Council 1997–, World Poultry Science Assen, Euro-Arab Veterinary Assen 1997–; mem. Editorial Bd Sudan Journal of Animal Production; Fellow Islamic Acad. of Sciences. *Publications:* contribs. to int. scientific journals. *Address:* Islamic Academy of Sciences, PO Box 830036, Amman, Jordan (Office); International University of Africa, PO Box 2469 Khartoum, Sudan. *Telephone:* 5522104 (Office). *Fax:* 5511803 (Office). *E-mail:* africa@sudanet.net (Office).

HADID, Zaha; Iraqi architect; b. 31 Oct. 1950, Baghdad; ed American Univ. Beirut, Architectural Assen London; won competition for The Peak leisure complex, Hong Kong 1982 (project later cancelled); designed restaurant interior, Sapporo 1991 (first completed work), fire station, Vitra Furniture Co., Germany 1991, block of flats, Berlin; won competition for Cardiff Bay Opera House, Wales 1994 (design subsequently rejected by financing body, the Millennium Comm.); commissioned to design Contemporary Arts Center, Cinn. 1998, Mind Zone in Millennium Dome, London, 1999; Kenzo Tange Prof., Columbia Univ. 1994; Sullivan Prof., Univ. of Ill. 1997; guest Prof. Hochschüle für Bildende Kunst, Hamburg 1997, Knolton School of Architecture, Ohio; numerous exhbns worldwide; Hon. mem. American Acad. of Arts and Letters. *Address:* Studio 9, 10 Bowling Green Lane, London, EC1R 0BD, England. *Telephone:* (20) 7253-5147. *Fax:* (20) 7251-8322.

HADLEE, Sir Richard John, Kt, KBE; New Zealand cricketer; b. 3 July 1951, Christchurch; s. of W. A. Hadlee (New Zealand cricketer); m. Dianne Hadlee; ed Christchurch Boys High School; middle-order left-hand batsman, right-arm fast-medium bowler; played for Canterbury 1971–72 to 1988–89, Nottinghamshire 1978 to 1987, Tasmania 1979–80; played in 86 Tests 1972–73 to 1990, scoring 3,124 runs (average 27.1) and taking then world record 431 wickets (average 22.9); first to take 400 Test wickets (at Christchurch in Feb. 1990 in his 79th Test); took 5 or more wickets in an innings a record 36 times in Tests; highest test score 151 v Sri Lanka, Colombo 1987; best test bowling performance 9–52 v Australia, Brisbane 1985–86; toured England 1973, 1978, 1983, 1986, 1990; scored 12,052 first-class runs (14 hundreds) and took 1,490 wickets, including 5 or more in an innings 102 times; achieved Double (1,179 runs and 117 wickets) 1984; now Level III Coach, Christchurch; Public Relations Amb. for Bank of NZ 1990–; Chair. NZ's selectors 2001–; Wisden Cricketer of the Year 1982; NZ Sportsman of the Year 1980, 1986, NZ Sportsman of the Decade 1987, NZ Sportsman of the last 25 years 1987; Knighted for services to NZ cricket 1990. *Publication:* Rhythm and Swing (autobiog.) 1989, Cricket: the Essentials of the Game, Howzat: Tales from the Boundary, Caught Out, Soft Deliveries, Hard Knocks, Hadlee, Hadlee on Cricket. *Leisure interests:* movies, golf, gardening. *Address:* Box 29186, Christchurch, New Zealand. *E-mail:* hadleerj@ihug.co.nz (Office). *Website:* www.hadlee.co.nz (Office).

HAEBLER, Ingrid; Austrian pianist; b. 20 June 1929, Vienna; ed Vienna Acad., Salzburg Mozarteum and Geneva Conservatory; specializes in Haydn, Mozart, Schubert and Schumann; mem. Faculty, Salzburg Mozarteum 1969–; concerts with Concertgebouw Orchestra, London Symphony, Royal Philharmonic, Vienna and Berlin Philharmonics, Boston Symphony, Lamoureux Orchestra, Stockholm and Warsaw Philharmonics, London Mozart Players; has appeared in festivals worldwide; won 1st Prize, Int. Competition Munich 1954; Mozart Medal, Vienna 1971, Mozart Medal, Salzburg 1979, Gold Medal of Honour, Vienna 1986, Gold Medal 'Viotti d'oro', Vercelli, Italy 2000. *Address:* 5412 St Jakob am Thurn, Post Puch Bei Hallein, Land Salzburg, Austria.

HAEFLIGER, Andreas; Swiss pianist; b. Berlin, Germany; ed Juilliard School, New York ; studied with Herbert Stessin, twice won Gina Bachauer Memorial Scholarship; has appeared with many of world's leading orchestras in N. America, Europe and Japan; numerous recital appearances including Great Performers Series, Lincoln Center, New York, Wigmore Hall, London and in Germany, Austria, France and Italy; has performed twice at BBC Proms, London; tours USA with Takacs String Quartet; performs frequently with baritone Matthias Goerne; recordings include Mozart Sonatas, Schumann's Davidsbündlertanze and Fantasiestücke, Schubert's Impromptus, music by Sofia Gubaidulina and (with Matthias Goerne) Schubert's Goethe Lieder; Preis der Deutschen Schallplattenkritik (for recording of Schubert's Goethe Lieder). *Address:* c/o Intermusica Artists Management Ltd., 16 Duncan Terrace, London, N1 8BZ, England (Office). *Telephone:* (20) 7278-5455 (Office). *Fax:* (20) 7278-8434 (Office). *E-mail:* mail@intermusica.co.uk (Office). *Website:* www.intermusica.co.uk.

HAEFNER, Walter; Swiss computer executive; two c.; owner Amag Group, Careal Holding; investment in Computer Assocs. *Address:* AMAG Group, Utoquai 49, 8008 Zurich, Switzerland (Office). *Telephone:* (1) 2695353 (Office). *Fax:* (1) 2695363 (Office).

HAEKKERUP, Hans; Danish politician; b. 3 Dec. 1945, Copenhagen; m. Susanne Rumohr Haekkerup; five s.; ed Copenhagen Univ.; with Ministry of Social Affairs 1973–76, of Educ. 1976–77, of Labour 1977–79; Prof. Danish School of Admin. 1977–80; MP 1979–2000, served on several Cttees. including Cttee on Danish Security Policy, Cttee on Greenlandic Affairs, Cttee on Foreign Policy; economist with Civil Servants Org. 1981–85; Chair. Defence Cttee 1991–93; Minister of Defence 1993–2000; Special Rep. of UN Sec.-Gen. for Kosovo Jan.–Dec. 2001. *Address:* Groennegade 27, 1107 Copenhagen K, Denmark (Office).

HAENDEL, Ida, CBE; Polish-born British violinist; b. 15 Dec. 1928, Chelm, Poland; ed Warsaw Conservatoire, pvt. tuition in Paris and London; studied with Carl Flesch and Georges Enescu; first public appearance in GB, Queen's Hall, London 1938; performances throughout world with many noted conductors including tour with London Philharmonic Orchestra to first Hong Kong Festival of Arts and China and three tours of USSR; participated in centenary anniversary Festival of Bronislav Huberman, Tel Aviv 1982; celebrated 50th anniversary of debut at Promenade Concerts, London 1987; numerous recordings; Hon. mem. RAM 1982–; Sibelius Medal (Finland) 1982. *Publication:* Woman with Violin (autobiog.) 1970. *Leisure interests:* drawing, reading. *Address:* c/o Askonas Holt Ltd, 27 Chancery Lane, London, WC2A 1PF, England. *Telephone:* (20) 7400-1700. *Fax:* (20) 7400-1799. *E-mail:* melanie.evans@askonasholt.co.uk (Office).

HAFEZ, Maj.-Gen. Amin El; Syrian politician and army officer; b. 1911; fmr Mil. Attaché in Argentina; took part in the revolution of March 1963; Deputy Prime Minister, Mil. Gov. of Syria and Minister of Interior March–Aug. 1963; Minister of Defence and Army Chief of Staff July–Aug. 1963; Pres. of Revolutionary Council and C-in-C of Armed Forces 1963–64; Prime Minister Nov. 1963–64, 1964–65; Chair. of Presidency Council 1965–66; sentenced to death in absentia Aug. 1971; living in exile.

HAFEZ, Mahmoud, PhD; Egyptian professor of entomology; b. 10 Jan. 1912; ed Cairo Univ.; Research Fellow Cambridge Univ. 1946–48; Prof. and Head Dept of Entomology, Cairo Univ. 1953, Vice-Dean 1964, Prof. Emer. 1972–; Under-Sec. of State for Scientific Research 1966; Pres. Nat. Research Council for Basic Sciences, Acad. of Scientific Research and Tech. in Egypt, Entomological Soc. of Egypt, Egyptian Soc. of Parasitology, Egyptian Science Asscn, Egyptian Soc. for the History of Science; Chair. Nat. Cttee for Biological Sciences; mem. Higher Council for Educ. and Scientific Research and Tech. in Egypt; Fellow and fmr Pres. Egyptian Acad. of Sciences; Fellow Islamic Acad. of Sciences, African Acad. of Sciences, Royal Entomological Soc., London, Third World Acad. of Sciences; Emer. mem. Entomological Soc. of America; Founding Mem. African Asscn of Insect Sciences; mem. Network of African Scientific Orgs., Int. Union of Biological Sciences, Int. Org. for Biological Control; State Prize (Egypt) 1977, Gold Medal (Egypt) 1977, Order of Merit, First Class 1978, Order of Science and Art (First Class) 1981. *Publications:* 10 books on zoology and entomology; over 150 scientific papers on insect science. *Address:* Entomology Department, Faculty of Science, Cairo University, Giza, Cairo, Egypt (Office). *Telephone:* (2) 5729584 (Office). *Fax:* (2) 628884 (Office).

HAGEDORN, Jürgen, Dr rer. nat; German professor of geography; b. 10 March 1933, Hankensbüttel; s. of Ernst Hagedorn and Dorothea Schulze; m. Ingeborg A. Carl 1965; one d.; ed Hermann-Billung-Gymnasium, Celle, Tech. Hochschule Hanover and Univ. of Göttingen; Asst Lecturer Univ. of Göt-

tingen 1962–69, Dozent 1969–70, Prof. 1970–72, Prof. of Geography and Dir Inst. of Geography 1972–2001, now Prof. Emer.; mem. Göttingen Acad., Akad. Leopoldina. *Publications:* Geomorphologie des Uelzener Beckens 1964, Geomorphologie griechischer Hochgebirge 1969, Late Quaternary and Present-Day Fluvial Processes in Central Europe (Ed.) 1995. *Address:* Jupiterweg 1, 37077 Göttingen, Germany. *Telephone:* (551) 21323. *E-mail:* jhagedo@gwdg .de (Office); a.j.hagedorn@t-online.de (Home).

HAGEL, Charles; American politician; b. 4 Oct. 1946, North Platte, Neb.; m. Lilibet Ziller; two s.; ed Brown Inst. of Radio & Television, Minn., Univ. of Nebraska; with US Army 1967–68; Deputy Admin. Va 1981–82; Pres., CEO World U.S.O. 1987–90; Pres. McCarthy & Co. 1991–96; Senator from Nebraska 1996–; Founder Dir Vanguard Cellular Systems Inc.; mem. numerous US Senate cttees; mem. American Legion for Veterans of Foreign Wars; active in numerous charitable orgs.; Trustee Omaha Chamber of Commerce. *Address:* 248 Russell Senate Office Building, Washington, DC 20510-0001, USA.

HAGEN, Carl I.; Norwegian politician; b. 6 May 1944, Oslo; s. of Ragnar Hagen and Gerd Gamborg Hagen; m. 1st Nina Aamodt 1970; m. 2nd Eli Engum Hagen 1983; one s. one d.; ed Inst. of Marketing, London; MP 1974–77, 1981–; Leader of Progress Party and Parl. Group 1978–. *Publication:* Aerlighet Varer Lengst (biog.). *Leisure interests:* tennis, family, golf. *Address:* Fremskrittspartiet, PO Box 8903, Youngstorget, 0028 Oslo; Stortinget, Karl Johansgt. 22, 0026 Oslo, Norway. *Telephone:* 22-41-07-69. *Fax:* 22-42-32-55. *E-mail:* postmottak.frp@stortinget.no (Office). *Website:* www.frp.no (Office).

HAGEN, Uta Thyra; American actress; b. 12 June 1919, Göttingen, Germany; d. of Oskar F. L. Hagen and Thyra Leisner; m. 1st José V. Ferrer 1938; m. 2nd Herbert Berghof 1957 (died 1990); one d.; ed Univ. of Wisconsin High School, Royal Acad. of Dramatic Art, London and Univ. of Wisconsin; début as Ophelia in Hamlet, Dennis, Mass. 1937; Teacher (and Co-Founder) Herbert Berghof Studio (School of Acting) 1947–, now Chair.; Chair. Bd HB Playwrights Foundation 1991–; Hon. DFA (Smith Coll.) 1978, (Univ. of Wisconsin) 2000, (Pa State Univ.) 2000; Hon. Dr (De Paul Univ., Chicago) 1980; Hon. DHumLitt (Worcester Coll.) 1982; Critics Award 1951, 1963, Tony Award 1951, 1963, Donaldson Award 1951, London Critics Award 1964, New York City Mayor's Liberty Medal 1986, Lucille Lortell, Drama League, Boston Critics Lifetime Achievement Awards 1996, Antoinette Perry Special Tony Award for Lifetime Achievement in the Theatre 1999; Fellow American Acad. of Arts and Sciences 1999, Wisconsin Acad. of Arts, Sciences and Letters 1999; Dramatists' Guild Lifetime Achievement Award 2002; NEA Nat. Medal of Honor 2003. *Plays include:* The Seagull, Arms and the Man, The Latitude of Love, The Happiest Days, Key Largo, Othello, The Master Builder, Angel Street, A Streetcar Named Desire, The Country Girl, Saint Joan, Tovarich, In Any Language, The Lady's not for Burning, The Deep Blue Sea, Cyprienne, A Month in the Country, The Good Woman of Szechuan, The Affairs of Anatol, The Queen and the Rebels, Who's Afraid of Virginia Woolf?, The Cherry Orchard, Charlotte 1980, Mrs. Warren's Profession (with Roundabout Theatre, New York) 1985, You Never Can Tell, Circle in the Square (Broadway) 1986, Mrs. Klein (off Broadway) 1995–96, (nat. tour) 1996–97, Collected Stories 1998–2000, Six Dance Lessons in Six Weeks 2001. *Films:* The Other 1972, The Boys from Brazil 1978, Reversal of Fortune 1990. *Television appearances:* numerous guest star appearances 1950–. *Publications:* Respect for Acting 1973, Love for Cooking 1976, Sources (memoirs) 1983, A Challenge for the Actor 1991. *Leisure interests:* gardening, cooking, needlework. *Address:* HB Studio, 120 Bank Street, New York City, NY 10014, USA.

HÄGGLUND, Gen. Gustav; Finnish army officer; b. 6 Sept. 1938, Wyborg; m. Ritva Ekström; one s. two d.; ed Finnish Mil. Acad., Univ. of Helsinki, Finnish War Coll.; nat. mil. service 1957–58; commanded Finnish Bn UNEF II, Sinai 1978–79, Nyland Brigade, Finland 1984–85, UNDOF, Golan Heights 1985–86, UNIFIL, Lebanon 1986–88, South East Mil. Area Finland 1988–90; Chief of Defence Staff 1990–94, Chief of Defence 1994–2001; Chair. EU Mil. Cttee, Brussels 2001–; US Army Command and Gen. Staff Coll. 1972–73; Fellow Harvard Univ. Center for Int. Affairs 1981–82. *Publications:* Peacemaking in the Finnish Winter War 1969, Northern Europe in Strategic Perspective 1974, US Strategy for Europe 1974, Parliamentary Defence Committees in Finland 1981, Modern US Cruise Missiles, an Evaluation 1982, Peace-keeping in a Modern War Zone 1990, Defence of Finland 2001. *Leisure interests:* hunting, shooting, roaming in the wilderness. *Address:* rue de la Loi 175, 1048 Brussels, Belgium (Office). *Telephone:* (2) 285-59-86 (Office). *Fax:* (2) 285-59-28 (Office).

HAGLER, Marvelous Marvin; American boxer (retd) and actor; b. 23 May 1954, Newark; s. of Robert James Sims Hagler and Ida Mae Lang; m. Bertha Joann Dixon 1980; five c.; undisputed world middleweight champion 1980–87; won championship from Alan Minter and defended it successfully 11 times before losing WBC version to Sugar Ray Leonard (q.v.) April 1987; legally changed his name to incorporate "Marvelous" (his ring nickname) in 1982; stripped of other versions of title for agreeing to fight unranked Leonard March 1987; 63 professional fights, 62 wins, 3 draws, 2 defeats with 52 KOs; now lives in Milan, Italy, and acts in action films; Int. Boxing Hall of Fame 1993.

HAGUE, Rt Hon William Jefferson, PC, MA, MBA; British politician; b. 26 March 1961; s. of Timothy N. Hague and Stella Hague; m. Ffion Jenkins 1997; ed Wath-upon-Dearne Comprehensive School, Magdalen Coll. Oxford and INSEAD; Pres. Oxford Union 1981; man. consultant, McKinsey & Co.

1983–88; political adviser, HM Treasury 1983; mem. Parl. for Richmond, Yorks. 1989–; Parl. Pvt. Sec. to Chancellor of Exchequer 1990–93; Parl. Under-Sec. of State, Dept of Social Security 1993–94; Minister for Social Security and Disabled People, Dept of Social Security 1994–95; Sec. of State for Wales 1995–97; Leader of Conservative Party and Leader of the Opposition 1997–2001; Chair. Int. Democratic Union 1999–2001; Econ. and Political Adviser JCB PLC 2001–; Dir (non-exec.) AES Eng PLC 2001–; mem. Political Council of Terra Firma Capital Partners 2001–. *Leisure interests:* walking, judo, playing the piano. *Address:* House of Commons, London, SW1A 0AA, England. *Telephone:* (20) 7219-3000.

HAHN, Carl Horst, Dr rer. pol; Austrian business executive; b. 1 July 1926, Chemnitz; m. Marisa Traina 1960; three s. one d.; Chair. of Bd, Continental Gummi-Werke AG 1973–81; Chair. Man. Bd, Volkswagen AG 1981–92; Chair. Supervisory Bd, Gerling-Konzern Speziale Kreditversicherungs-AG, Cologne; mem. Supervisory Bd HAWESKO, Hamburg, Sachsenring AG, Zwickau, Perot Systems, Dallas, MainControl, Vienna, Va; mem. Int. Advisory Bd Merloni Eletrodomestici, Fabriano, Inst. de Empresa, Madrid; mem. Int. Advisory Cttee, Salk Inst., Calif.; Chair. Bd of Trustees, Kunstmuseum Wolfsburg; Adviser to Pres. of Repub. of Kyrgyzstan; mem. Bd Mayo Clinic, Stiftung, Frankfurt, Lauder-Inst., Wharton School, Pa. *Address:* Porsches-trasse 53, 38440 Wolfsburg, Germany.

HAHN, Erwin Louis, PhD; American professor of physics; b. 9 June 1921, Sharon, Pa; s. of Israel and Mary Hahn; m. 1st Marian Ethel Failing 1944 (deceased); one s. two d.; m. 2nd Natalie Woodford Hodgson 1980; ed Juniata Coll. and Univ. of Illinois; Asst, Purdue Univ. 1943–44; Research Asst, Univ. of Illinois 1950; Nat. Research Council Fellow, Stanford Univ. 1950–51, Instructor 1951–52; Research Physicist Watson IBM Lab., New York 1952–55; Assoc., Columbia Univ. 1952–55, Univ. of Calif., Berkeley 1955–; Asst Prof. 1955–56, Assoc. Prof. 1956–61, Assoc. Prof. Miller Inst. for Basic Research 1958–59, Prof. of Physics 1961–91, Prof. Emer. 1991–; Visiting Fellow, Brasenose Coll., Oxford 1960–61, 1981–82 (Hon. Fellow 1982–); Eastman (Visiting) Prof., Balliol Coll., Oxford 1988–89; mem. NAS; Fellow American Acad. of Arts and Sciences, American Physical Soc., Int. Soc. of Electron Paramagnetic Spin Resonance; Assoc. mem. Slovenian Acad. of Sciences; Foreign Assoc. mem. Acad. des Sciences (France); Miller Prof. Univ. of Calif. 1985–86; Foreign Fellow Royal Soc. (UK) 2001, Physical Soc. (UK) 2001; Guggenheim Fellow, 1961, 1970; discoverer of spin echoes; introduced pulsed nuclear magnetic resonance free precession spectroscopy; Hon. DSc (Juniata Coll.) 1966, (Purdue Univ., Indiana) 1975; Hon. Dr rer. nat (Stuttgart) 2001; Buckley Prize 1971, Int. Soc. of Magnetic Resonance Prize 1971, Alexander Humboldt Foundation Award (Fed. Repub. of Germany) 1976–77; co-winner Wolf Foundation Prize 1983/84, Calif. Inventors Hall of Fame 1984, The Berkeley Citation 1991, Comstock Prize (co-recipient), NAS (for research in radiation and electromagnetism) 1993 and other prizes and awards. *Publications:* Nuclear Quadruple Resonance Spectroscopy (with T. P. Das) 1958; articles in learned journals. *Leisure interests:* violin, chamber music. *Address:* Department of Physics, University of California, 367 Birge Hall, Berkeley, CA 94720-0001 (Office); 69 Stevenson Avenue, Berkeley, CA 94708-1732, USA (Home). *Telephone:* (510) 642-2305 (Office); (510) 845-0082 (Home). *Fax:* (510) 643-8497 (Office); (510) 841-4618 (Home). *E-mail:* hahn@physics.berkeley.edu (Office).

HAHN, Frank, PhD, FBA; British university professor; b. 26 April 1925, Berlin, Germany; s. of Arnold and Maria Hahn; m. Dorothy Salter 1946; ed Bournemouth Grammar School, London School of Econs; Lecturer, then Reader in Mathematical Econs, Univ. of Birmingham 1948–60; Lecturer in Econs, Univ. of Cambridge 1960–67, Prof. of Econs, 1972–92, Prof. Emer. 1992–; Prof. of Econs, LSE 1967–72; Professore Ordinario, Univ. of Siena, Italy 1989–; Frank W. Taussig Resident Prof., Harvard Univ. 1974; Visiting Prof., MIT 1956–57, 1971–72, 1982, Univ. of Calif., Berkeley 1959–60; Pres. Econometric Soc. 1968–69; Man.-Ed. Review of Economic Studies 1963–66; Pres. Royal Econ. Soc. 1986–89; Pres. Section F., British Asscn 1990; Fellow of Churchill Coll., Cambridge 1960–; Fellow of British Acad., American Acad. of Arts and Sciences; Foreign Assoc. NAS 1988; mem. Academia Europaea 1989; Hon. mem. American Econ. Asscn 1986; Hon. Fellow LSE 1989; Hon. DSocSc (Univ. of Birmingham) 1981; Hon. DLitt (Univ. of East Anglia) 1984, (Leicester) 1993; Dr hc (Univ. Louis Pasteur, Strasbourg) 1984, (York) 1991, (Paris X, Nanterre) 1999; Hon. DSc (Econ.) (London) 1985; Hon. PhD (Athens) 1993; Palacky Gold Medal of Czechoslovak Acad. of Sciences 1991. *Publications:* General Competitive Analysis (with K. J. Arrow) 1971, The Share of Wages in National Income 1972, Money and Inflation 1982, Equilibrium and Macroeconomics 1984, Money, Growth and Stability 1985, The Economics of Missing Markets, Information and Games 1989 (Ed.), Handbook of Monetary Economics 1990 (Jt Ed.), A Critical Essay on Modern Macroeconomic Theory (with Robert Solow) 1995, New Theories in Growth and Development (Jt Ed.) 1998; also more than 80 articles in learned journals. *Leisure interests:* reading, gardening. *Address:* 16 Adams Road, Cambridge, CB3 9AD, England. *Telephone:* (1223) 352560.

HAHN, Heinz W., DEng; German engineering executive; b. 13 Feb. 1929, Rüsselsheim; m. Lisel Hummel 1955; one d.; ed Tech. Univ. Darmstadt, Tech. Univ. Karlsruhe; diesel engine engineer Motoren-Werke, Mannheim 1958–61; Chief Eng Hanomag-Henschel, Hanover 1961–69; Dir and mem. Bd Klöckner-Humboldt-Deutz AG, Cologne 1970–74; Pres. and CEO Magirus-Deutz AG, Ulm 1975–81; Exec. Vice-Pres. and Deputy Chair. IVECO, Ulm

1981–85; Vice-Pres. IVECO, Turin 1985–89, Deputy Chair. 1989–, now Chair. Admin. Bd IVECO Motorenforschung AG, Switzerland. *Address:* Ginsterweg 31, 89233 Neu-Ulm, Germany (Home).

HAHN, James Kenneth (Jim), BA, JD; American lawyer and politician; b. 1951, Los Angeles; s. of Kenneth Hahn; m. Monica Teson 1984; one s. one d.; ed Lutheran High School, South LA, Pepperdine Univ.; City Prosecutor LA City Attorney's Office 1975–79; City Controller 1981–85, City Attorney 1985–2001; Mayor of LA 2001–; pvt. practice Marina del Rey 1979–81; Democrat. *Address:* City Hall, 200 N Spring Street, Room 303, Los Angeles, CA 90012, USA (Office). *E-mail:* info@JimHahn.org.

HAIDALLA, Lt-Col Mohamed Khouna Ould; Mauritanian politician and army officer; Chief of Staff of Mauritanian Army 1978–79; Minister of Defence April–May 1979, 1980, Prime Minister 1979–80, Pres. of Mauritania 1980–84 (overthrown in coup); Chair. Mil. Cttee for Nat. Recovery (now Cttee for Nat. Salvation) 1978–84.

HAIDER, Jörg; Austrian politician; b. 26 Jan. 1950, Carinthia; m.; two d.; ed Vienna Univ.; joined Liberal Youth Movt 1964, Freedom Party 1971; worked in pvt. industry 1976–77; mem. Parl. 1979–83, 1986–2002; Leader Freedom Party 1986–2000; fmr Gov. Carinthia (resgnd 1991), re-elected Gov. 1999. *Address:* Freedom Party of Austria, Esslingasse 14–16, 1010 Vienna, Austria. *Telephone:* (1) 512-35-35. *Fax:* (1) 513-35-35-9. *Website:* www.fpoe.at (Office).

HAIDER, Syed Zahir, PhD, FRSC, CChem; Bangladeshi professor of chemistry; b. 1 Sept. 1927, Dhaka; ed Imperial Coll., London Univ. and Stuttgart Univ.; lecturer in Chem. Dhaka Univ. 1950, Reader then Prof. 1970–98, Chair. Dept of Chem. 1982–85, Khundkar Chair. of Chem. 1985–92; Head Dept of Chem. Chittagong Univ. 1968–70; fmr Dir Bose Centre for Advanced Studies and Research; mem. Swedish Inst. research programme at Arrhenius Lab., Stockholm; Pres. Bangladesh Chem. Soc., Bangladesh Environmental Soc. 1998–2000; Fellow Islamic Acad. of Sciences, mem. Council 1994–99; Fellow and mem. Council Bangladesh Acad. of Sciences, Fellow Asiatic Soc. of Bangladesh; Founding Ed. Journal of Bangladesh Acad. of Sciences 1977; Chief Ed. Journal of Bangladesh Chem. Soc.; First H. P. Roy Gold Medal for original contributions in chemical research 1961, First Gold Medal in Physical Sciences, Bangladesh Acad. of Sciences 1983. *Publications include:* Science in Arts and Architectures, Enlightenment and Environment; over 250 papers on inorganic, analytical co-ordination, nuclear and bio-inorganic chem. *Leisure interests:* tourism, historical places. *Address:* Department of Chemistry, Dhaka University, Dhaka 1000 (Office); 5/12 Block A, Lalmatia, Dhaka 1207, Bangladesh (Home). *Telephone:* (2) 9115991 (Home). *Fax:* (2) 8615583 (Office). *E-mail:* hshabbir@bdmail.net (Home).

HAIG, Gen. Alexander Meigs, Jr, BS, MA; American army officer, politician and business executive; b. 2 Dec. 1924, Philadelphia, Pa; s. of Alexander M. and Regina Murphy Haig; m. Patricia Fox 1950; two s. one d.; ed US Mil. Acad., Naval War Coll., Georgetown Univ. and Columbia Univ.; joined US Army 1947, rising to Brig.-Gen. 1969, Maj.-Gen. 1972, Gen. 1973; Deputy Special Asst to Sec. and Deputy Sec. of Defence 1964–65; Battalion and Brigade Commdr 1st Infantry Div., Repub. of Viet Nam 1966–67; Regimental Commdr and Deputy Commdt US Mil. Acad. 1967–69; Sr Mil. Adviser to Asst to Pres. for Nat. Security Affairs, the White House 1969–70; Deputy Asst to Pres. for Nat. Security Affairs 1970–73; Vice-Chief of Staff, US Army Jan.–July 1973; special emissary to Viet Nam Jan. 1973; retd from US Army Aug. 1973; Asst to Pres. and White House Chief of Staff Aug. 1973–Oct. 1974; recalled to active duty, US Army Oct. 1974; C-in-C, US European Command 1974–79; Supreme Allied Commdr Europe, NATO 1974–79; Pres., COO and Dir United Technologies Corpn 1980–81; Sec. of State 1981–82; Chair. Atlantic and Pacific Advisory Councils of United Technologies 1982; Chair. and Pres. Worldwide Assocs, Inc. 1984–; Founding Dir America Online, Inc. 1989, Indevus Pharmaceuticals Inc. 1990, MGM Mirage Inc. 1990, Metro-Goldwyn-Mayer Inc. 1995, CompuServe, Inc. 2001–03; Dir Sointernational Inc. 2002–; Chair. & Dir DOR Biopharma Inc. 2003–; mem. Presidential Comm. on Strategic Forces 1983–84; Sr Fellow, Hudson Inst. for Policy Research 1982–84;; numerous hon. degrees including Hon. LLD (Utah and Niagara); Gold Medal Nat. Inst. of Social Sciences 1980, Distinguished Grad. Award of West Point 1997, James Doolittle Award of Hudson Inst. 1999; numerous medals, awards and citations, including DSC for heroism. *TV:* host of World Business Review. *Publications:* Caveat: Realism, Reagan and Foreign Policy 1984, Inner Circles: How America Changed the World, A Memoir 1992. *Leisure interests:* golf, tennis. *Address:* Suite 800, 1155 15th Street, NW, Washington, DC 20005, USA. *Telephone:* (202) 429-9788 (Office). *Fax:* (202) 833-5296 (Office). *E-mail:* AHaig@aol.com (Office).

HAILEY, Arthur; British/Canadian author; b. 5 April 1920, Luton, Beds., England; s. of George and Elsie Hailey (née Wright); m. 1st Joan Fishwick (divorced 1950); three s.; m. 2nd Sheila Dunlop 1951; served as pilot/Flight-Lt RAF 1939–47 (Air Efficiency award); Lifetime mem. Writers Guild of America; Life mem. Authors League of America; Hon. Life mem. Alliance of Canadian Cinema, TV and Radio Artists. *Films include:* Zero Hour 1956, Time Lock 1957, The Young Doctors 1961, Hotel 1966, Airport 1970, The Moneychangers 1976, Wheels 1978, Overload 1983, Strong Medicine 1986. *TV plays include:* Flight into Danger 1956, Time Lock 1957, Death Minus One 1958. *Poem:* A Last Request. *Publications:* Runway Zero Eight (with John Castle) 1958, The Final Diagnosis 1959, In High Places 1962, Hotel 1965, Airport 1968, Wheels 1971, The Moneychangers 1975, Overload 1979, Strong

Medicine 1984, The Evening News 1990, Detective 1997; novels published in 38 languages; collected plays: Close-Up 1960. *Leisure interests:* reading, music, wine, boating. *Address:* Lyford Cay, PO Box N-7776, Nassau, Bahamas (Home). *Fax:* (242) 362-4411 (Home). *E-mail:* ahailey@coralwave.com (Office); ahailey@coralwave.com (Home).

HAIRIKYAN, Paruir Arshavirovich; Armenian nationalist leader; b. 1949; ed Yerevan Univ.; leading role in Nat. United Party of Armenia 1968–; sentenced to imprisonment for various kinds of nationalist activity 1969–73, 1974–87; latest arrest after mass demonstrations in Yerevan in 1988; deprived of Soviet citizenship 1989, deported from USSR; citizenship restored 1990; elected to Parl. 1990; cand. for Presidency of Armenia Oct. 1991; currently Chair. Union for Nat. Self-Determination (UNS) (also 1991–96); Adviser to Pres. of Armenia 1998–99; Chair. Comm. on Human Rights in Presidential Admin. *Address:* Union for National Self-Determination, Demirchan str. 25, 375002 Yerevan, Armenia.

HAITHEM, Muhammad Ali; Yemeni politician; b. 1940, Dathina, Southern Arabia; fmr school teacher; Minister of Interior 1967; mem. Presidential Council of S. Yemen 1969–71; Chair. Council of Ministers 1969–70; mem. Nat. Front Gen. Command; living in Cairo, Egypt.

HAITINK, Bernard John Herman; Netherlands conductor; b. 4 March 1929, Amsterdam; Conductor Netherlands Radio Philharmonic Orchestra 1955–61; appeared regularly as Guest Conductor for Concertgebouw Orchestra, Amsterdam 1956–61, Joint Conductor 1961–64, Chief Conductor and Musical Dir 1964–88; Prin. Conductor London Philharmonic Orchestra 1967–79, Artistic Dir 1970–78, Pres. 1990–; Musical Dir Glyndebourne Festival Opera 1978–88, Royal Opera House, Covent Garden 1987–2002, European Union Youth Orchestra 1994–; Prin. Guest Conductor Boston Symphony Orchestra 1995–; Chief Conductor and Music Dir, Sächsische Staatskapelle, Dresden 2002–; tours with Concertgebouw in Europe, N and S America, Japan, with London Philharmonic in Europe, Japan, USA; Guest Conductor Los Angeles Philharmonic, Boston Symphony, Cleveland, Chicago Symphony, New York Philharmonic, Berlin Philharmonic, Vienna Philharmonic, Dresden Staatskapelle, Concertgebouw and other orchestras; Hon. mem. RAM, London 1973, Int. Gustav Mahler Soc.; records for Philips, Decca and EMI; Hon. DMus (Oxford) 1988, (Leeds) 1988; Medal of Honour, Bruckner Soc. of America 1970, Gold Medal of Int. Gustav Mahler Soc. 1971, Erasmus Prize 1991; Royal Order of Orange-Nassau, Chevalier des Arts et des Lettres, Officer, Order of the Crown (Belgium); Conductor Laureate, Concertgebouw 1999, CH 2002–. *Address:* c/o Askonas Holt Ltd., 27 Chancery Lane, London, WC2A 1PF, England. *Telephone:* (20) 7400-1700. *Fax:* (20) 7400-1799.

HAJI-IOANNOU, Stelios, MSc; Greek business executive; b. 14 Feb. 1967, Athens; s. of Loucas Haji-Ioannou; ed Doucas School, Athens, LSE and City of London Business School, UK; joined father's co. Troodos Maritime 1988, CEO –1991; est. Cyprus Marine Environment Protection Assoc (CYMEPA) 1992; Founding Chair. Stelmar Tankers, Athens and London 1992–; Founder easyJet 1995– (Chair. 1995–2002), easyGroup 1998, easyInternetCafe (operations in London, Edin., Amsterdam, Rotterdam, Barcelona, Munich, New York) 1999–, easyCar 2000–, easyValue 2000–, easyMoney 2001–, easyDorm 2002, easyCinema 2002. *Leisure interest:* yachting. *Address:* easyGroup Head Office, The Rotunda, 42/43 Gloucester Crescent, London, NW1 7DL, England (Office). *Telephone:* (20) 7241-9000 (Office). *Website:* www.stelios.com (Office).

HAJJRI, Abdulwahab Abdulla Al-, LLM; Yemeni diplomatist; b. 1958; m.; three c.; ed Sana'a Univ., American Univ., Washington DC, USA, Al Azhar Univ., Cairo, Egypt; joined Ministry of Foreign Affairs 1979; diplomatic attaché, Political Dept, Sana'a 1980–82; cultural attaché, Cairo 1982–87, Washington, DC 1987–92; Counsellor, Embassy in Cairo 1992–95; Minister Plenipotentiary, Embassy in Washington DC 1995–97; Amb. to USA (also accred (non-resident) to Mexico and Venezuela) and Perm. Observer of Yemen to OAS Sept. 1997–. *Address:* Embassy of Yemen, 2600 Virginia Avenue, NW, Suite 705, Washington, DC 20037, USA (Office). *Telephone:* (202) 337-8113 (Office). *Fax:* (202) 337-2017 (Office). *E-mail:* ambassador@yemenembassy.org (Office). *Website:* www.yemenembassy.org (Office).

HÄKKÄNEN, Matti Klaus Juhani, LLM; Finnish diplomatist; b. 21 July 1936, Helsinki; s. of Klaus Häkkänen and Kaiju Broms; m. Pirkko Hentola 1962; two s.; ed Univ. of Helsinki; served in Finnish Foreign Service Helsinki, Paris, New York, Moscow and Peking 1960–76; Amb. to Romania (concurrently to Albania) 1976–80; Under-Sec. of State 1980–83; Amb. to Netherlands (also accred to Ireland) 1983–87, to Argentina (also accred to Chile and Uruguay) 1987–88, to France 1988–93, to Italy (also accred to Malta and San Marino) 1993–97, to Portugal (also accred to Morocco) 1997–2001; First Lt Finnish Defence Forces; Kt Commdr, Order of Lion of Finland, Grand Cross, Orange Nassau of the Netherlands, Officer, Black Star of France, Grand Cross, Nat. Merit of Italy, Kt Commdr, Ordre nat. du mérite, France; Mil. Medal of Finland. *Leisure interests:* cycling, practical map studies, tennis. *Address:* c/o Ministry of Foreign Affairs, Merikasarmi, PO. Box 176, 00161 Helsinki, Finland.

HAKKINEN, Mika; Finnish racing driver; b. 28 Sept. 1968, Helsinki; m. Erja Honkanen; one s.; fmrly go-kart driver, Formula Ford 1600 driver, Finnish, Swedish and Nordic Champion 1987; Formula 3 driver, British Champion with West Surrey Racing 1990; Formula 1 driver Lotus 1991–93, McLaren 1993–2001; Grand Prix wins: European 1997, Australia 1998, Brazil 1998, 1999, Spain 1998, 1999, 2000, Monaco 1998, Austria 1998, 2000, Germany 1998, Luxembourg 1998, Japan 1998, 1999, Canada 1999, Malaysia 1999, Hungary 1999, 2000, Belgium 2000; Formula One Driver's Championship Winner 1998, 1999; took sabbatical at end of 2001, then announced retirement from Formula One; announced intention to take part in the first round of the FIA European Rally Championship in Finland in Jan. 2003. *Publications:* Mika Hakkinen: Doing What Comes Naturally (by Christopher Hilton). *Leisure interests:* playing golf.

HAKOPIAN, Vilen Paruirovich; Armenian university rector and neuropharmacologist; b. 1 May 1938, Garnahovit, Talin; s. of Paruir Hakopian and Inthizar Hakopian; m. Rosa Hovhannes Gasparian; one s. one d.; ed Yerevan Medical Inst.; Jr research worker, Biochem. Inst., Nat. Acad. of Sciences of Armenia 1961–65; Sr research worker and Asst, Dept of Pharmacology, Yerevan State Medical Univ. (YSMU) 1965–80, Prof. 1980–94, Dean of Foreign Students 1972–79, Dean of Medical Faculty 1979–83, Vice-Rector of Educational Affairs 1986–87, Rector of YSMU 1987–, Head Dept of Pharmacology 1994–; mem. Nat. Acad. of Sciences of Armenia, NAS (USA), Int. Union of Pharmacology (Belgium), Int. Pharmaceutical Fed. (Netherlands), Int. Information Acad., Moscow, Int. Higher Educ. Acad. of Sciences, Moscow, Int. Acad. of Ecology and Life Protection Sciences, St Petersburg, Fellow Scientific Council of Int. Coll. of Angiology, New York; Ed.-in-Chief Medical Science of Armenia; mem. Editorial Bd Experimental and Clinical Pharmacology (Moscow) 1993–, Int. Asscn of Pathophysiology (Moscow) 1991– and many other scientific bodies. *Publications:* nearly 200 works, including 9 monographs. *Leisure interests:* chess, reading, geology, apiculture. *Address:* Department of Pharmacology, Yerevan State Medical University, 2 Korjun Street, 375025 Yerevan (Office); Apt. 33, 28 Orbelli Street, Yerevan 375012, Armenia (Home). *Telephone:* (2) 521711 (Office); (2) 22575 (Home). *Fax:* (2) 151812.

HALBRON, Jean-Pierre; French business executive; ed Ecole Polytechnique, Paris, Corps des Mines, Inst. Français du Pétrole; various posts with Compagnie Financière 1968–74, including Gen. Man. 1968–74, CEO 1974–82; Finance Dir Rhône-Poulenc SA 1983, Deputy Man. Dir 1984–87; Gen. Man. CdF Chimie (later Orkem) 1987–90; Finance Dir Total SA 1990–92; Man. Dir Wasserstein Perella Corpn and Chair. Wasserstein Perella France 1992–95; Dir Strategy and Finance, Alcatel 1995–, mem. Exec. Cttee, currently Pres. and Chief Financial Officer. *Address:* Alcatel SA, 54 rue la Boétie, 75006 Paris, France (Office). *Website:* www.alcatel.com (Office).

HALEFOĞLU, Vahit M., KCVO, MA; Turkish diplomatist; b. 19 Nov. 1919, Antakya; s. of Mesrur and Samiye Halefoğlu; m. Zehra Bereket 1951; one s. one d.; ed Antakya Coll. and Univ. of Ankara; Turkish Foreign Service 1943–, served Vienna, Moscow, Ministry of Foreign Affairs, London 1946–59; Dir-Gen., First Political Dept, Ministry of Foreign Affairs 1959–62; Amb. to Lebanon 1962–65, concurrently accred to Kuwait 1964–65, Amb. to USSR 1965–66, to Netherlands 1966–70; Deputy Sec.-Gen. of Political Affairs, Ministry of Foreign Affairs 1970–72; Amb. to Fed. Repub. of Germany 1972–82, to USSR 1982–83; Minister of Foreign Affairs 1983–87; MP 1986; Dr hc; Légion d'honneur and other French, Finnish, British, Lebanese, Saudi and Italian decorations. *Leisure interests:* classical literature, history, international relations, music, walking, swimming. *Address:* c/o Ministry of Foreign Affairs, Dişişleri Bakanlığı, Yeni Hizmet Binası, 06520 Balgat, Ankara, Turkey.

HALES, Antony John (Tony), BSc; British business executive; b. 25 May 1948, Blackpool; s. of S. A. Hales and M. J. Hales; m. Linda Churchlow 1975; three s. one d.; ed Repton School and Bristol Univ.; Marketing Man. Cadbury Schweppes 1969–79; joined Allied Domecq 1979, Marketing Dir Joshua Tetley 1979–83, Man. Dir Hall's Oxford SW 1983–85, Man. Dir Taylor Walker 1985–87, Man. Dir Ansells 1987–89, Dir Allied Breweries, Chair. CEO Allied Domecq Spirits and Wine (fmrly Hiram Walker Group) 1995; CEO J. Lyons 1989–91, Dir Allied Domecq (fmrly Allied-Lyons) PLC 1989–99, CEO 1991–99; Dir Hyder PLC 1994–97, Midland Bank PLC (now HSBC Bank) 1994–2001, Aston Villa PLC 1997–, David Halsall Int. 2000–, Tempo Holdings Ltd 2000–01, Reliance Security Group 2001–; Chair. Naati 2001–; Chair. Workspace Group PLC 2002–; Dir Satellite Information Services Holdings 2002–. *Address:* Belvoir House, Edstone Court, Wooton Wawen, Solihull, West Midlands, B95 6DD, England. *E-mail:* thales_uk@yahoo.com (Office).

HALÍK, Tomáš, ThD, PhD; Czech philosopher, academic and priest; b. 1 June 1948, Prague; s. of Miroslav and Marie Halík; ed Charles Univ., Prague, Pontifical Lateran Univ., Rome; psychologist, Inst. of Ministry of Industry 1972–89; clandestinely ordained priest, Erfurt 1978; psychotherapist U Apolináře hospital, Prague 1984–90; involved in "underground" RC Church as close co-worker with HE Cardinal Tomášek; Gen. Sec. Czech Bishops' Conf. 1990–93; Prof., Head Dept of Philosophy of Religion, Faculty of Philosophy, Charles Univ., Rector Univ. church; lectures in univs. around the world; Pres. Czech Christian Acad.; mem. European Acad. of Sciences and Arts and various bds. and socs. in Czech Repub. and abroad; Konrad Adenauer Silver Medal 1995, Masaryk's Arts Acad. Prize 1997, American Prize of Tolerance 2002. *Publications:* I Asked the Ways: Talks by Jan Jandourek 2000, What is Without Vibration is Not Stable 2002; over 200 works (some distributed secretly in Czechoslovakia before 1989). *Address:* Czech Christian Academy, Vyšehradská 49, Prague 2 120 00; Naprstkova 2, Prague 1 110 00, Czech Republic (Home). *Telephone:* (2) 22220295. *E-mail:* haliktom@cesnet.cz (Home). *Website:* www.halik.cz (Home).

HALILOVIĆ, Safet; Bosnia and Herzegovina politician; Chair. Municipal Bd, Party of Democratic Action (Stranka Demokratske Akcije – SDA), Sarajevo 1994–; Pres. of Fed. of Bosnia and Herzegovina Feb. 2002–. *Address:* Office of the President, 71000 Sarajevo, Bosnia and Herzegovina (Office). *Telephone:* (33) 472618 (Office).

HALIMI, Gisèle Zeïza, LIC. EN DROIT ET PHIL.; French writer and lawyer; b. 27 July 1927, La Goulette, Tunisia; d. of the late Edouard Taïeb and Fortunée Metoudi; m. Claude Faux; three s.; ed Institut d'études politiques, Paris; Counsel, Paris Courts 1956–; Deputy to Nat. Ass. 1981–84; Amb. of France to UNESCO and Pres. Human Rights Cttee 1985–87; f. and Pres. feminist movt Choisir la Cause des Femmes 1971–; lecturer; Chevalier Légion d'honneur, Grand Officier Ordre de la République (Tunisia), Medal of Achievement of the Greek People. *Publications:* Djamila Boupacha 1962, Resistance Against Tyranny 1966, Le procès de Burgos 1971, La cause des femmes 1974, Le programme commun des femmes 1978, Le lait de l'oranger 1988, Femmes: moitié de la terre, moitié du pouvoir 1994; Une embellie perdue 1996, La nouvelle cause des femmes 1997, Fritna 1999; Choisir: Avortement: une loi en procès. L'affaire de Bobigny 1973, Viol: le procès d'Aix-en-Provence 1978, Choisir de donner la vie 1979, Quel Président pour les femmes? 1981, Fini le féminisme? 1984. *Leisure interests:* classical music, football. *Address:* 102 rue Saint Dominique, 75007 Paris, France (Office). *Telephone:* 1-47-05-21-48.

HALL, Aleksander, MA; Polish politician, historian and publicist; b. 20 May 1953, Gdańsk; ed Gdańsk Univ.; history teacher, Secondary School No 6, Gdańsk 1977; active in Acad. Pastoral Cure, Gdańsk in early 1970s; mem. Movt for Defence of Human and Civic Rights (ROPCIO) 1977–79; Ed. Bratniak 1977–81; co-f. and leader, Young Poland's Movt 1979; mem. Solidarity Trade Union 1980–; co-f. Cttee for Defence of Persons Imprisoned because of their Opinions, attached to Solidarity Trade Union 1980; mem. Regional Co-ordinative Comm. of Solidarity Trade Union, Gdańsk 1981–84; publicist, Przegląd Katolicki (Catholic Review) 1984–89, Polityka Polska (Polish Politics) 1982–89; mem. Primatial Social Council 1986–; mem. Civic Cttee attached to Lech Wałęsa (q.v.), Chair. Solidarity Trade Union 1988–90, Vice-Pres., Dziekania Political Thought Club 1988–89; participant Round Table debates, mem. group for political reforms Feb.–April 1989; Minister-mem. Council of Ministers (for co-operation with political orgs. and asscns.) 1989–90; Deputy to Sejm (Parl.) 1991–93, 1997–2001; Vice-Chair. Solidarity Election Action Parl. Caucus 1997–2000; leader Democratic Right Forum 1990–92; Co-f. and leader Conservative Party 1992–96; mem. Conservative Peasant Party (SKL) 1996–, mem. Bd and Political Council. *Publications:* Refleksje i polemiki, Wybór publicystyki politycznej 1989, Spór o Polskę 1993, Zanim będzie za późno 1994, Polskie patriotyzmy 1997, Pierwsza taka dekada 2000, Widziane z prawej strony 2000; numerous articles in Polish periodicals. *Leisure interests:* reading, history, politics, political thought and history of ideas, culture and history of France.

HALL, Alfred Rupert, MA, PhD, LittD, FBA; British science historian; b. 26 July 1920, Stoke-on-Trent; s. of Alfred Dawson Hall and Margaret Catherine Ritchie; m. 1st Annie Shore Hughes; m. 2nd Marie Boas; two d.; ed Alderman Newton's School, Leicester, Christ's Coll., Cambridge; served Royal Corps of Signals 1940–45; Fellow, Christ's Coll., Cambridge 1949–59, Univ. Lecturer, Cambridge 1950–59; posts at Univs. of Calif. and Indiana 1959–63; Prof. History of Science and Tech., Imperial Coll., London 1963–80, Prof. Emer. 1980–; Consultant, Wellcome Trust 1980–85; Pres. Int. Acad. of the History of Science 1977–81; Allen Scholar, Cambridge 1948, Royal Soc. Wilkins Lecturer 1973, Leeuwenhoek Lecturer 1988; Hon. PhD (Bologna) 1999; Sarton Medal, History of Science Soc. (jtly.) 1981. *Publications:* various books and articles on history of science and tech. including Philosophers at War 1980, The Revolution in Science 1500–1750 1983, Physic and Philanthropy: a history of the Wellcome Trust 1986, Henry More: Magic, Religion and Experiment 1990, Isaac Newton: Adventurer in Thought 1992, Newton, His Friends and His Foes 1993, All Was Light: an Introduction to Newton's Opticks 1993, Science and Society (essays) 1994, Isaac Newton: Eighteenth Century Perspectives 1998. *Leisure interests:* walking, gardening. *Address:* 14 Ball Lane, Tackley, Oxford, OX5 3AG, England. *Telephone:* (1869) 331257.

HALL, Anthony William (Tony), MA, FRSA; British broadcasting executive; b. 3 March 1951, Birkenhead; s. of Donald William Hall and Mary Joyce Hall; m. Cynthia Lesley Davis 1977; one s. one d.; ed King Edward's School, Birmingham, Birkenhead School, Merseyside, Keble Coll., Oxford; joined BBC 1973, News Ed. 1987–90, Dir News and Current Affairs 1990–93, Man. Dir News and Current Affairs 1993–96, Chief Exec. BBC News 1996–2001; Exec. Dir Royal Opera House 2001–; mem. Council Brunel Univ. 1999–; Fellow, Vice-Chair. Royal TV Soc. (Chair. 1998–2000); Dir (non-exec.) Customs and Excise 2002–; Hon. Visiting Fellow City Univ. 1999–2000; Patron Newsworld 1999–2000; Chair. Theatre Royal Stratford East. *Publications:* King Coal: A History of the Miners 1981, Nuclear Politics 1984, articles in various periodicals. *Leisure interests:* reading, writing, church architecture, opera, walking in Dorset. *Address:* Royal Opera House, Covent Garden, London, WC2E 9DD, England (Office). *Telephone:* (20) 7240-1200 (Office). *Fax:* (20) 7212-9502 (Office). *Website:* www.royaloperahouse.org (Office).

HALL, Sir David Michael Baldock, Kt., MB, BS, BSc, FRCP; British professor of paediatrics; b. 4 Aug. 1945; s. of Ronald Hall and Ethel Gwen Hall (née Baldock); m. Susan M. Luck 1966; two d.; ed Reigate Grammar School, St. George's Hosp., Univ. of London; Sr Medical Officer, Baragwanath Hosp., Johannesburg 1973–76; Sr Registrar Charing Cross Hosp. 1976–78; Consultant Paediatrician, St George's Hosp. 1978–93; Prof. of Community Paediatrics, Univ. of Sheffield 1993–; Fellow Royal Coll. of Paediatrics and Child Health 1996–, Pres. 2000–; Hon. FFPHM 1999; Univ. of London Gold Medal. *Publications include:* Health for All Children 1989, Child with a Disability 1996; numerous articles in scientific journals. *Leisure interests:* horses, plumbing. *Address:* Storrs House Farm, Storrs Lane, Stannington, Sheffield, S6 6GY, England (Home).

HALL, Donald, LHD, DLitt; American writer; b. 20 Sept. 1928, New Haven; s. of Donald A. Hall and Lucy (née Wells) Hall; m. 1st Kirby Thompson 1952 (divorced 1969); one s. one d.; m. 2nd Jane Kenyon 1972 (died 1995); ed Harvard Univ., Oxford Univ., Stanford Univ.; Jr Fellow Harvard Univ. 1954–57; Asst Prof. Univ. of Michigan 1957–61, Assoc. Prof. 1961–66, Prof. 1966–77; Poetry Ed. Paris Review 1953–61; Consultant Harper & Row 1964–81; Guggenheim Fellow 1963, 1972; mem. Authors Guild; Newdigate Prize for Poetry from Oxford Univ. 1952, Lamont Poetry Selection, Acad. of American Poets 1955, Leonore Marshal Award 1987, New England Booksellers Asscn Award 1993, Ruth Lilly Prize 1994 and other awards. *Publications: poems:* Exiles and Marriages 1955, The Dark Houses 1958, A Roof of Tiger Lilies 1963, The Alligator Bride 1969, The Yellow Room 1971, The Town of Hill 1975, A Blue Wing Tilts at the Edge of the Sea 1975, Kicking the Leaves 1978, The Toy Bone 1979, The One Day (Nat. Book Circle Critic's Award 1989) 1988, Old and New Poems 1990, The Museum of Clear Ideas 1993, Lucy's Christmas 1994, I Am the Dog, I Am the Cat 1994, Lucy's Summer 1995; numerous essays and plays; as Ed.: Harvard Advanced Anthology (with L. Simpson and R. Pack) 1950, The New Poets of England and America (with R. Pack) 1957, Second Selection 1962, A Poetry Sampler 1962, Contemporary American Poetry (with W Taylor) 1962, Poetry in English (with S. Spender) 1963, A Concise Encyclopaedia of English and American Poets and Poetry 1963, Faber Book of Modern Verse 1966, The Modern Stylists 1968, A Choice of Whitman's Verse 1968, Man and Boy 1968, Anthology of American Poetry 1969, Pleasures of Poetry (with D. Emblen) 1971, A Writer's Reader 1976, To Read Literature 1981, To Read Poetry 1982, Oxford Book of American Literary Anecdotes 1981, Claims for Poetry 1982, Oxford Book of Children's Verse in America 1985, To Read Fiction 1987, Anecdotes of Modern Art 1990, Their Ancient Glittering Eyes 1992.

HALL, Henry Edgar, PhD, FRS; British professor of physics; b. 1928; s. of John A. Hall; m. Patricia A. Broadbent 1962; two s. one d.; ed Latymer Upper School, Hammersmith and Emmanuel Coll. Cambridge; Royal Soc. Mond Lab. Cambridge 1952–58; Sr Student, Royal Comm. for Exhbn of 1851, 1955–57; Research Fellow, Emmanuel Coll. Cambridge 1955–58; Lecturer in Physics, Univ. of Manchester 1958–61, Prof. 1961–95, Emer. Prof. 1995–; has held visiting professorships in Australia, USA and Japan; Simon Memorial Prize (with W. F. Vinen) 1963. *Publications:* Solid State Physics 1974; papers in scientific journals. *Leisure interest:* mountain walking. *Address:* The Schuster Laboratory, The University, Manchester, M13 9PL, England.

HALL, Jerry; American model and actress; b. 2 July 1956, Texas; d. of the late John P. Hall and Marjorie Sheffield; m. Mick Jagger (q.v.) 1990 (divorced 1999); two s. two d.; began modelling career in Paris in 1970s; numerous television appearances including David Letterman Show, USA; stage debut in William Inge's Bus Stop, Lyric Theatre, London 1990; contributing ed. Tatler 1999–; contracts include Yves Saint Laurent, Revlon Cosmetics, L'Oriel Hair, Thierry Mugler. *Films:* Batman, Princess Caraboo 1994, Diana and Me 1996, RPM 1996. *Plays:* The Graduate, Gielgud Theatre, London 2000. *Publication:* Tell Tales 1985. *Address:* c/o Eclipse Management Production, 32 Tavistock Street, London, WC2E 7PB, England (Office); c/o Models One, Omega House, 471–473 Kings Road, London, SW10 0LU. *Telephone:* (20) 7257-8725 (Eclipse) (Office); (20) 7351-1195 (Models One). *Fax:* (20) 7240-9029 (Eclipse) (Office); (20) 7376-5821 (Models One).

HALL, Nigel John, MA (RCA); British sculptor; b. 30 Aug. 1943, Bristol; s. of Herbert John Hall and Gwendoline Mary Hall (née Olsen); m. Manijeh Yadegar 1986; ed Bristol Grammar School, West of England Coll. of Art, RCA, London; Harkness Fellowship to USA 1967–69; first one-man Exhbn, Galerie Givaudan, Paris 1967; represented in the following collections: Tate Gallery, London, Musée Nat. d'Art Moderne, Paris, Nat. Galerie, Berlin, Museum of Modern Art, New York, Australian Nat. Gallery, Canberra, Art Inst. of Chicago, Kunsthaus, Zurich, Tokyo Metropolitan Museum, Musée d'Art Moderne, Brussels, Louisiana Museum, Denmark, Nat. Museum of Art, Osaka, Museum of Contemporary Art, Sydney, Tel-Aviv Museum; sculpture commissioned for Thameslink Tunnel, London 1993; Jack Goldhill Prize for Sculpture (RA London) 2002. *Exhibitions:* solo exhbns. include: Robert Elkon Gallery, New York 1974, 1977, 1979, 1983, Annely Juda Gallery, London 1978, 1981, 1985, 1987, 1991, 1996, 2000, 2003, Galerie Maeght, Paris 1981, 1983, Staatliche Kunsthalle, Baden-Baden 1982, Nishimura Gallery, Tokyo 1980, 1984, 1988, Garry Anderson Gallery, Sydney 1987, 1990, Hans Mayer Gallery, Düsseldorf 1989, 1999, Fondation Veranneman, Kruisthoutem, Belgium 1987, 1995, 1997, Galerie Ziegler, Zürich 1986, 1988, 1995, Park Gallery, Seoul 1997, 2000, Galerie Konstruktiv Tendens, Stockholm 2000, Schoenthal Monastery, Langenbrucke, Switzerland 2001; group shows include: Documenta VI, Kassel 1977, British Sculpture in the Twentieth Century, Whitechapel Gallery, London 1981, Aspects of British Art Today, Tokyo Metropolitan Museum 1982, Britannica: Thirty Years of Sculpture, Le Havre Museum of Fine Art 1988, Drawings in Black and White, Museum of Modern Art, New York 1993, Prints of Darkness, Fogg Art Museum, Harvard Univ. 1994, British Sculpture, Schloss Ambras, Innsbruck 1998, The Shape of the Century, Salisbury Cathedral 1999, The Eye of the Storm, La Mandria Park, Turin 2000, Out of Line: Drawings from the Arts Council Collection, York City Art Gallery and tour 2001–02. *Address:* 11 Kensington Park Gardens, London, W11 3HD, England. *Telephone:* (20) 8675-5945; (20) 7727-3162. *Fax:* (20) 7229-1852.

HALL, Peter Gavin, DPhil, FAA, FRS, FRSE; Australian professor of statistics; b. 20 Nov. 1951, Sydney; s. of William Holmen Hall and Ruby Violet Hall; m. Jeannie Jean Chien; ed Sydney Univ., Australian Nat. Univ. (ANU), Oxford Univ.; lecturer in Statistics, Univ. of Melbourne 1976–78, ANU 1978–82, Sr Lecturer 1983–95, Reader 1986–88, Prof. 1988–; Centennial Professorship, LSE, UK 2000–02; S.S. Wilks Lecture, Princeton Univ. 1988; Fellow American Statistical Asscn 1996; Hon. Fellow Royal Statistical Soc. 1989; Kolmogorov Lecture, Vienna 1996; Invited Lecture, Int. Congress of Mathematicians, Berlin 1998; Pres. Bernoulli Soc. for Math. Statistics and Probability 1999–2003; mem. Editorial Bd Annals of Statistics and several other journals; Dr hc (Univ. Catholique de Louvain) 1997; Australian Math. Soc. Medal 1986, Rollo Davidson Prize, Univ. of Cambridge 1986, Lyle Medal, Australian Acad. of Science 1989, Pitman Medal, Statistical Soc. of Australia 1990, Hannan Medal 1995. *Publications:* Rates of Convergence in the Central Limit Theorem 1982, Introduction to the Theory of Coverage Processes 1988, The Bootstrap and Edgeworth Expansion 1992; over 400 papers in journals. *Address:* Centre for Mathematics and its Applications, Australian National University, Canberra, ACT 0200 (Office); 6 Ramsay Place, Wanniassa, ACT 2903, Australia (Home). *Telephone:* (2) 6125-3474 (Office). *Fax:* (2) 6125-5549 (Office). *E-mail:* peter.hall@anu.edu.au (Office).

HALL, Sir Peter Geoffrey, Kt, MA, PhD, FBA; British professor of geography and planning; b. 19 March 1932, London; s. of Arthur Vickers and Bertha (née Keefe) Hall; m. 1st Carla M. Wartenberg 1962 (dissolved 1967); m. 2nd Magdalena Mróz 1967; ed Blackpool Grammar School and St Catharine's Coll., Cambridge; Asst Lecturer, Birkbeck Coll., Univ. of London 1956–60, Lecturer 1960–65; Reader in Geography with special reference to planning, LSE 1966–67; Prof. of Geography, Univ. of Reading 1968–89, Prof. Emer. 1989–; Prof. of City and Regional Planning, Univ. of Calif. (Berkeley) 1980–92, Prof. Emer. 1993–, Dir Inst. of Urban and Regional Devt 1989–92; Special Adviser to Sec. of State for the Environment 1991–94; Prof. of Planning, Bartlett School of Planning, Univ. College, London 1992–; mem. South East Econ. Planning Council 1966–79, Social Science Research Council 1974–80; nine hon. degrees; Gill Memorial Prize, Royal Geographical Soc. 1968, Adolphe Bentinck Prize 1979, Founder's Medal, Royal Geographical Soc. 1988, Prix Vautrin Lud 2001. *Publications:* London 2000 1963, The World Cities 1966, The Containment of Urban England 1973, Urban and Regional Planning 1974, Europe 2000 1977, Growth Centres in the European System 1980, Great Planning Disasters 1980, The Inner City in Context 1981, Silicon Landscapes 1985, Can Rail Save the City? 1985, High-Tech America 1986, Western Sunrise 1987, Cities of Tomorrow 1988, The Carrier Wave 1988, London 2001 1989, The Rise of the Gunbelt 1992, Technopoles of the World 1993, Cities in Civilization 1998, Urban Future 21 2000, Working Capital 2002. *Leisure interests:* reading, talking. *Address:* University College, 22 Gordon Street, London, WC1H 0QB (Office); 12 Queens Road, London, W5 2SA, England (Home). *Telephone:* (20) 7697-7456 (Office); (20) 8997-3717 (Home). *Fax:* (20) 7697-7502 (Office).

HALL, Sir Peter Reginald Frederick, Kt, CBE, MA; British theatre, opera and film director; b. 22 Nov. 1930, Bury St Edmunds, Suffolk; s. of late Reginald Hall and Grace Hall; m. 1st Leslie Caron 1956 (divorced 1965); one s. one d.; m. 2nd Jacqueline Taylor 1965 (divorced 1981); one s. one d.; m. 3rd Maria Ewing (q.v.) 1982 (divorced 1989); one d.; m. 4th Nicola Frei 1990; one d.; ed Perse School and St Catharine's Coll., Cambridge; Produced and acted in over 20 plays at Cambridge; first professional production The Letter, Windsor 1953; produced in repertory at Windsor, Worthing and Oxford Playhouse; two Shakespearean productions for Arts Council; Artistic Dir Elizabethan Theatre Co. 1953; Asst Dir London Arts Theatre 1954, Dir 1955–57; formed own producing co., Int. Playwright's Theatre 1957; Man. Dir Royal Shakespeare Co., Stratford-upon-Avon and Aldwych Theatre, London 1960–68 (resgnd); Assoc. Dir –1973; mem. Arts Council 1969–73; Co-Dir, Nat. Theatre (now Royal Nat. Theatre) with Lord Olivier April-Nov. 1973, Dir 1973–88; f. Peter Hall Co. 1988; Artistic Dir Glyndebourne 1984–90; Artistic Dir The Old Vic 1997; Wortham Chair in Performing Arts, Houston Univ., Tex. 1999; Chancellor Kingston Univ. 2000–; Assoc. Prof. of Drama, Warwick Univ. 1964–67; mem. Bd Playhouse Theatre 1990–91; acted in The Pedestrian (film) 1973; Hon. Fellow St Catharine's Coll. Cambridge 1964; Dr hc (York) 1966, (Reading) 1973, (Liverpool) 1974, (Leicester) 1977; Hon. DSocSc (Birmingham) 1989; London Theatre Critics' Award for Best Dir for The Wars of the Roses 1963, The Homecoming and Hamlet 1965; Antoinette Perry Award for Best Dir for The Homecoming 1966, Tony Award for Best Dir for Amadeus 1981; Hamburg Univ. Shakespeare Prize 1967, Evening Standard Special Award 1979, Evening Standard Award for Outstanding Achievement in Opera 1981, Evening Standard Best Dir Award for The Oresteia 1981, Evening Standard Best Dir Award for Antony and Cleopatra 1987, South Bank Show Lifetime Achievement Award 1998, Olivier Special Award for Lifetime Achievement 1999; Chevalier, Ordre des Arts et des Lettres 1965. *Productions:* Blood Wedding, The Immoralist, The Lesson, South, Mourning Becomes Electra, Waiting for Godot, Burnt Flowerbed, Waltz of the Toreadors, Camino Real, Gigi, Wrong Side of the Park, Love's Labours Lost, Cymbeline, Twelfth Night, A Midsummer Night's Dream, Coriolanus, Two

Gentlemen of Verona, Troilus and Cressida, Ondine, Romeo and Juliet, Becket, The Collection, Cat on a Hot Tin Roof, The Rope Dancers (on Broadway), The Moon and Sixpence (opera, Sadler's Wells), Henry VI (parts 1, 2 and 3), Richard III, Richard II, Henry IV (parts 1 and 2), Henry V, Eh?, The Homecoming, Moses and Aaron (opera, Covent Garden), Hamlet, The Government Inspector, The Magic Flute (opera), Staircase, Work is a Four Letter Word (film) 1968, Macbeth, Midsummer Night's Dream (film) 1969, Three into Two Won't Go (film) 1969, A Delicate Balance, Dutch Uncle, Landscape and Silence, Perfect Friday (film) 1971, The Battle of Shrivings, La Calisto (opera, Glyndebourne Festival) 1970, The Knot Garden (opera, Covent Garden) 1970, Eugene Onegin (opera, Covent Garden) 1971, Old Times 1971, Tristan and Isolde (opera, Covent Garden) 1971, All Over 1972, Il Ritorno d'Ulisse (opera, Glyndebourne Festival) 1972, Alte Zeiten (Burgtheater, Vienna) 1972, Via Galactica (musical, Broadway) 1972, The Homecoming (film) 1973, Marriage of Figaro (opera, Glyndebourne) 1973, The Tempest 1973, Landscape (film) 1974, Akenfield (film) 1974, Happy Days 1974, John Gabriel Borkman 1974, No Man's Land 1975, Judgement 1975, Hamlet 1975, Tamburlaine the Great 1976, Don Giovanni (opera, Glyndebourne Festival) 1977, Volpone (Nat. Theatre) 1977, Bedroom Farce (Nat. Theatre) 1977, The Country Wife (Nat. Theatre) 1977, The Cherry Orchard (Nat. Theatre) 1978, Macbeth (Nat. Theatre) 1978, Betrayal (Nat. Theatre) 1978, Così Fan Tutte (opera, Glyndebourne) 1978, Fidelio (opera, Glyndebourne) 1979, Amadeus (Nat. Theatre) 1979, Betrayal (New York) 1980, Othello (Nat. Theatre) 1980, Amadeus (New York) 1980, Family Voices (Nat. Theatre) 1981, The Oresteia (Nat. Theatre) 1981, A Midsummer Night's Dream (opera, Glyndebourne) 1981, The Importance of Being Earnest (Nat. Theatre) 1982, Other Places (Nat. Theatre) 1982, The Ring (operas, Bayreuth Festival) 1983, Jean Seberg (musical, Nat. Theatre) 1983, L'Incoronazione di Poppea (opera, Glyndebourne) 1984, Animal Farm (Nat. Theatre) 1984, Coriolanus (Nat. Theatre) 1984, Yonadab (Nat. Theatre) 1985, Carmen (opera, Glyndebourne) 1985, (Metropolitan Opera) 1986, Albert Herring (opera, Glyndebourne) 1985, The Petition (New York and Nat. Theatre) 1986, Simon Boccanegra (opera, Glyndebourne) 1986, Salome (opera, Los Angeles) 1986, Coming in to Land (Nat. Theatre) 1986, Antony and Cleopatra (Nat. Theatre) 1987, Entertaining Strangers (Nat. Theatre) 1987, La Traviata (Glyndebourne) 1987, Falstaff (Glyndebourne) 1988, Salome (Covent Garden) 1988, Cymbeline (Nat. Theatre) 1988, The Winter's Tale (Nat. Theatre) 1988, The Tempest 1988, Orpheus Descending 1988, Salome (opera, Chicago) 1988, Albert Herring 1989, Merchant of Venice 1989, She's Been Away (TV) 1989, New Year (opera, Houston and Glyndebourne) 1989, The Wild Duck 1990, Born Again (musical) 1990, The Homecoming 1990, Orpheus Descending (film) 1990, Twelfth Night 1991, The Rose Tattoo 1991, Tartuffe 1991, The Camomile Lawn (TV) 1991, The Magic Flute 1992, Four Baboons Adoring the Sun (New York) 1992, Siena Red 1992, All's Well That Ends Well (RSC) 1992, The Gift of the Gorgon (RSC) 1992, The Magic Flute (LA) 1993, Separate Tables 1993, Lysistrata 1993, She Stoops to Conquer 1993, Piaf (musical) 1993, An Absolute Turkey (Le Dindon) 1994, On Approval 1994, Hamlet 1994, Jacob (TV) 1994, Never Talk to Strangers (film) 1995, Julius Caesar (RSC) 1995, The Master Builder 1995, The Final Passage (TV) 1996, Mind Millie for Me 1996, The Oedipus Plays (Nat. Theatre at Epidaurus and Nat. Theatre) 1996, A School for Wives 1995, A Streetcar Named Desire 1997, The Seagull 1997, Waste 1997, Waiting for Godot 1997, 1998, King Lear 1997, The Misanthrope 1998, Major Barbara 1998, Simon Boccanegra (Glyndebourne) 1998, Filumena 1998, Amadeus 1998, Kafka's Dick 1998, Measure for Measure (LA) 1999, A Midsummer Night's Dream (LA) 1999, Lenny (Queens Theatre) 1999, Amadeus (LA, NY) 1999, Cuckoos 2000, Tantalus (Denver, Colo) 2000, Japes 2000, Romeo and Juliet (LA) 2001, Japes 2001, Troilus and Cressida (NY) 2001, Tantalus 2001, A Midsummer Night's Dream (Glyndebourne) 2001, Otello (Glyndebourne) 2001, Japes (Theatre Royal) 2001, The Royal Family (Theatre Royal) 2001, Lady Windermere's Fan (Theatre Royal) 2002, The Bacchai (Olivier Theatre) 2002. *Publications:* The Wars of the Roses 1970, Shakespeare's three Henry VI plays and Richard III (adapted with John Barton), John Gabriel Borkman (English version with Inga-Stina Ewbank) 1975, Peter Hall's Diaries: The Story of a Dramatic Battle 1983, Animal Farm: a stage adaptation 1986, The Wild Duck 1990, Making an Exhibition of Myself (autobiog.) 1993, An Absolute Turkey (new trans. of Feydeau's Le Dindon, with Nicki Frei) 1994, The Master Builder (with Inga-Stina Ewbank) 1995, Mind Millie for Me (new trans. of Feydeau's Occupe-toi d'Amélie, with Nicki Frei), The Necessary Theatre 1999, Exposed by the Mask 2000. *Leisure interest:* music. *Address:* 48 Lamont Road, London, SW10 0HX, England. *Telephone:* (20) 8464-5309 (Office). *Fax:* (20) 8464-6409 (Office). *E-mail:* phpetard@aol.com (Office).

HALL, Philip David; British journalist; b. 8 Jan. 1955; s. of Norman Philip Hall and Olive Jean Hall; m. Marina Thomson 1997; two c.; ed Beal Grammar School, Ilford; reporter Dagenham Post 1974–77, Ilford Recorder 1977–80; Sub-Ed. Newham Recorder 1980–84, Weekend Magazine 1984–85; reporter The People 1985–86, Chief Reporter 1986–89, News Ed. 1989–92; News Ed. Sunday Express 1992–93; Asst Ed. (Features) News of the World 1993–94, Deputy Ed. 1994–95, Ed. 1995–2000; with Max Clifford Assocs 2000–; Ed.-in-Chief Hello! 2001–02; mem. Press Complaints Comm. 1998–2000, 2002–. *Leisure interests:* golf, cinema, theatre. *Address:* Max Clifford Associates, 109 New Bond Street, London, W1Y 9AA, England (Office). *Telephone:* (20) 7408-2350 (Office).

HALL, Rodney, AM; Australian writer, musician and actor; b. 18 Nov. 1935; s. of D.E. Hall; m. Maureen McPhail 1962; three d.; ed City of Bath School for

Boys, UK, Brisbane Boys' Coll., Univ. of Queensland; leader Baroque Music Group; published over 500 poems in Australia, UK, USA, USSR, Philippines, France, India, several published books of poetry and novels; Creative Arts Fellow ANU 1968, Literary Bd Fellow 1974–80, tutor New England Univ. Summer School of Music 1967–71, 1977–80; lecturer Dept of Foreign Affairs; Recorder Canberra School of Music 1979–83; Chair. Australia Council 1991–94; Miles Franklin Award 1994. *Publications:* Selected Poems 1975, Just Relations 1982, Kisses of the Enemy 1987, Captivity Captive 1988, The Second Bridegroom 1991, The Grisly Wife 1994, The Island in the Mind 1996. *Address:* c/o Dawn Devery, Australia Council, P.O. Box 788, Strawberry Hill, NSW 2012, Australia.

HALL, Rev. Wesley Winfield; Barbadian cricketer, politician and public relations consultant; b. 12 Sept. 1937, St Michael; m. (divorced); four c.; ed Combermere School and Industrial Soc. London (personnel man.); right-arm fast bowler and lower-order right-hand batsman; took 192 wickets (average 26.38) in 48 Tests; took 546 first-class wickets (average 26.14); played amateur and professional cricket in England, Australia, NZ, India, Sri Lanka and throughout W Indies including 48 Test matches in which he took 192 wickets and first hat-trick by a West Indian 1961–69; Man. W Indies Cricket Team throughout W Indies and abroad 1983–85; Pres. West Indies Cricket Bd 2001–; trainee telegraphist, Cable and Wireless, Barbados 1955–60; Public Relations Consultant, Esso, Queensland, Australia 1960–63; British American Tobacco Co. Ltd (Trinidad and Tobago) 1968–78; Personnel and Public Relations Man. Banks Barbados Breweries Ltd 1975–85; Independent Senator, Barbados Senate 1971–76, Opposition Senator 1981–86; Minister of Employment, Labour Relations and Community Devt 1986–88, of Tourism and Sports 1988–93, of Industrial Relations, Community Devt and Sports 1993–94; Life mem. MCC; Hon. Life mem. Barbados Football Asscn; Humming Bird Gold Medal 1987. *Publications:* Secrets of Cricket 1962, Pace Like Fire 1965. *Address:* c/o Ministry of Tourism and Sports, Harbour Road, St Michael, Barbados.

HALLBERG, Paul Thure, FilLic; Swedish library director; b. 10 Dec. 1931, Gothenburg; s. of late Severin Hallberg and Eva Hallberg (née Theorell); m. Elisabeth Löfgren 1958; one s.; ed Gothenburg Univ. and Yale Univ., USA; Asst Teacher, Dept of English Language and Literature, Gothenburg Univ. 1958–59; Librarian, Gothenburg Univ. Library 1960–68, Head of Dept 1968–77, Dir 1977–96; Sec. Main Cttee for Scandia Plan 1964–65; Sec. Scandinavian Fed. of Research Librarians 1966–69, mem. Bd 1979–84; mem. and Librarian, Royal Soc. of Arts and Sciences in Gothenburg 1977–99, Hon. mem. 1999–; mem. Nat. Bibliographic Council 1983–96; Chair. Swedish Cataloguing Cttee 1979–85; Chair. Steering Group of Swedish LIBRIS system 1992–96; mem. of Bd NORDINFO (Nordic Council for Scientific Information and Research Libraries) 1986–88; mem. Standing Cttee, Int. Fed. of Library Asscns and Insts, Section on Acquisition and Exchange 1977–85, mem. Standing Cttee, Section of Univ. Libraries and other Gen. Research Libraries 1985–93, Sec. 1985–89; Fil. Dr hc (Gothenburg Univ.) 1997. *Publications:* A Passage to China: Colin Campbell's Diary of the First Swedish East India Company Expedition to Canton 1732–33 (ed. with C. Koninckx) 1996; author and ed. of numerous books and articles on bibliography and librarianship. *Leisure interests:* music and country cottage. *Address:* Goteborg University Library, PO Box 222, SE-405 30 Gothenburg (Office); Orangerigatan 34, SE-412 66 Gothenburg, Sweden (Home). *Telephone:* (31) 40-23-18 (Home). *Fax:* (31) 16-37-97 (Office). *E-mail:* Paul.Hallberg@ub.gu.se (Office); Paul.Hallberg@ub.gu.se (Home).

HALLIDAY, Frederick, PhD; Irish professor of international relations and journalist; b. 1946, Dublin; ed Queen's Coll. Oxford, SOAS, LSE, UK; Prof. of Int. Relations, LSE 1983–; columnist for Prospect magazine, Middle East Research and Information Project (MERIP); broadcaster with ABC, BBC, CNN and CBC; Editorial Assoc. New Left Review; Fellow Transnational Inst. 1976–, also adviser on Middle Eastern and Cen. Asian matters; fmr Chair. Research Cttee, Royal Inst. of Int. Affairs; mem. Advisory Council, Foreign Policy Inst. *Publications include:* 14 books on int. politics including Dictatorship and Development 1978, Rethinking International Relations 1994, Islam and the Myth of Confrontation 1995, Revolution and World Politics 1999, Two Hours that Shook the World 2002. *Address:* Department of International Relations, London School of Economics, Houghton Street, London, WC2A 2AE, England (Office). *Telephone:* (20) 7955-7389 (Office). *Fax:* (20) 7242-0392 (Office). *E-mail:* f.halliday@lse.ac.uk. *Website:* www.lse.ac.uk (Office).

HALLIER, Hans-Joachim, DIur; German diplomatist; b. 25 April 1930, Offenbach; s. of Christian L. Hallier and Sophie Heberer; m. Almuth H. Frantz 1966; two s.; ed Lessing Gymnasium, Frankfurt and Univs. of Frankfurt and Heidelberg; attaché, German NATO Del. Paris 1960–61; Second Sec. Djakarta 1962–66; First Sec. Tokyo 1966–69; Dir Cabinet of Foreign Minister, Bonn 1970–74; Amb. to Malaysia 1974–76, to Indonesia 1980–83, to Japan 1986–90, to Holy See 1990–95; Dir-Gen. Foreign Office, Bonn 1983–86. *Publications:* Völkerrechtliche Schiedsinstanzen für Einzelpersonen und ihr Verhältnis zur innerstaatlichen Gerichtsbarkeib 1962, Zwischen Fernost und Vatikan (memoirs) 1999, Das Dorf – eine mecklenburgische Chronik 2001; books and research papers on int. law. *Address:* Eifelblick 11, 53619 Rheinbreitbach, Germany. *Telephone:* (2224) 5931 (Home). *Fax:* (2224) 70183 (Home). *E-mail:* poreta91@aol.com (Home).

HALLIWELL, Geri; British singer; mem. (with Victoria Adams, Melanie Brown, Emma Bunton and Melanie Chisholm) The Spice Girls 1993–98; UN Goodwill Amb. 1998–; signed to Chrysalis Records 1999–; Best Single (for Wannabe) Brit Awards 1997, Best Video for Say You'll Be There 1997; two Ivor Novello songwriting awards 1997; Best British Band Smash Hits Show 1997; three American Music Awards 1998; Special Award for Int. Sales Brit Awards 1998. *Albums include:* Spice Girls 1996, Spiceworld 1997, Schizophonic (solo), Scream if You Want to Go Faster 2001. *Singles include:* Wannabe 1996, Say You'll Be There 1996, 2 Become 1 1996, Mama/Who Do You Think You Are 1997, Spice Up Your Life 1997, Too Much 1997, Stop 1998, Viva Forever 1998, (solo) Look at Me 1999, Mi chico Latino 1999, Lift me Up 1999, Bag it Up 2000, It's Raining Men 2001, Scream if You Want to Go Faster 2001. *Film:* Spiceworld the Movie 1997. *Publication:* If Only (autobiog.) 1999. *Address:* c/o Freud Communications Ltd, 19–21 Mortimer Street, London, W1N 8DX (Office); c/o A&R Department, Chrysalis Records, 43 Brook Green, London, W6 7EF, England. *Telephone:* (20) 7580-2626 (Office); (20) 7605-5000 (Chrysalis). *Fax:* (20) 7637-2626 (Office).

HALLMAN, Viola; German business executive; b. 8 Dec. 1944, Hagen, North Rhine Westphalia; d. of Werner and Helga Flachmeier; m. Olof J. Hallman 1971; one d.; ed Univs. of Hamburg, Marburg and Padua; Chief Exec. Friedrich Gustav Theis Kaltwalzwerke GmbH 1972, Friedrich Gustav Theis GmbH & Co. Flachdraht- und Profilwerk Hagen-Hohenlimburg 1972, Theis Verpackungssysteme GmbH, Packbandwerk Gelsenkirchen 1975, Alte & Schröder GmbH & Co., Stahl- und NE-Veredlungswerke Halver und Hagen-Halden 1979; Chair. and CEO Theis Group, Chair. and CEO Theis Precision Steel Corpn, Bristol, Conn., Chair. Bd and Pres. Theis of America Inc., Wilmington, Del.; mem. Fed. Cttee of Business Econs (BBW) of the RKW, Eschborn, VvU Asscn of Women Entrepreneurs, Cologne, ASU Working Asscn of Independent Business Entrepreneurs, Bonn; Man. of the Year 1979. *Publication:* Entrepreneur—Profession Without Future? *Leisure interests:* riding, swimming, literature, history. *Address:* Bandstahlstrasse 14-18, 58093 Hagen-Halden, Germany. *Telephone:* (2331) 6930.

HALLSTRÖM, Lasse; Swedish film director; b. 1946, Stockholm; m. Lena Olin. *Films include:* A Lover and his Lass 1975, Abba—The Movie 1977, Father-to-be 1979, The Rooster 1981, Happy We 1983, My Life as a Dog 1985 (Film of the Year 1985), The Children of Bullerby Village 1986, More about the Children of Bullerby Village 1987, Once Around 1991, What's Eating Gilbert Grape (also co-exec. producer), Something to Talk About, The Golden Hour, Chocolat 2000, The Shipping News 2002.

HALLYDAY, Johnny; French singer and actor; b. Jean-Philippe Smet, 15 June 1943, Paris; s. of Léon Smet; m. 1st Sylvie Vartan; one s.; m. 2nd Elisabeth Etienne; m. 3rd Adeline Blondiau; m. 4th Laetitia Boudou 1996; one c. with Nathalie Baye; appeared on stage aged 5; music hall tours with his cousin and her husband, American dancer Lee Halliday; numerous concerts; Chevalier Légion d'honneur, Officier des Arts et des Lettres, Officier Ordre de la Couronne, Belgium; 60 gold discs. *Films include:* Detective 1985, Conseil de famille 1986, Terminus 1987, La Gamine 1992, Pourquoi pas moi 1999, Love Me 2000, L'Homme du Train 2003. *Albums include:* Hamlet-Halliday 1976, Destination Vegas 1996, Ce que je sais 1998, Sang pour sang 1999, À la Vie, À la Mort 2002. *Publications include:* Johnny raconte Hallyday 1980, Johnny la forme (jtly) 1990, Déraciné (1943-1964) 1996. *Address:* Camus and Camus Productions, 6 rue Daubigny, 75017 Paris, France.

HALONEN, Tarja, LLM; Finnish politician and lawyer; b. 24 Dec. 1943, Helsinki; m. Pentti Arajärvi 2000; one d. from a previous m.; ed Univ. of Helsinki; lawyer, Lainvalvonta Oy 1967–68; social welfare officer, organizing Sec. Nat. Union of Finnish Students 1969–70; lawyer, Cen. Org. of Finnish Trade Unions 1970–2000; Parl. Sec. to Prime Minister Sorsa 1974–75; mem. Helsinki City Council 1977–96; mem. Parl. 1979–; Chair. Parl. Social Affairs Cttee 1984–87; Second Minister, Ministry of Social Affairs and Health 1987–90, for Nordic Co-operation 1989–91, of Justice 1990–91, for Foreign Affairs 1995–2000; Pres. of Finland 2000–; Social Democratic Party. *Leisure interests:* swimming, sculpture, painting, gardening. *Address:* Office of the President, Mariankatu 2, 00170 Helsinki, Finland. *Telephone:* (9) 661133 (Office). *Fax:* (9) 630292 (Office). *E-mail:* presidentti@tpk.fi (Office).

HALPERIN, Bertrand Israel, PhD; American professor of physics; b. 6 Dec. 1941, Brooklyn, New York; s. of Morris Halperin and Eva Teplitsky Halperin; m. Helena Stacy French 1962; one s. one d.; ed George Wingate High School, Brooklyn, Harvard Coll. and Univ. of California (Berkeley); NSF Postdoctoral Fellow Ecole Normale Supérieure, Paris 1965–66; mem. tech. staff Bell Labs. 1966–76; Prof. of Physics Harvard Univ. 1976–, Chair. Dept of Physics 1988–91, Hollis Prof. of Math. and Natural Philosophy 1992–; Assoc. Ed. Reviews of Modern Physics 1974–80; mem. NAS, American Acad. of Arts and Sciences, American Philosophical Soc.; Fellow American Physical Soc.; Oliver Buckley Prize for Condensed Matter Physics 1982, Lars Onsager Prize 2001. *Publications:* about 200 articles in scientific journals. *Address:* Lyman Laboratory of Physics, Harvard University, Cambridge, MA 02138, USA. *Telephone:* (617) 495-4294. *Website:* www.physics.harvard.edu/fac_staff/halperin .html (Office).

HALPERIN, (Donghi) Tulio, DPhil; Argentine historian; b. 27 Oct. 1926, Buenos Aires; ed Univ. de Buenos Aires, Ecole Pratique des Hautes Etudes, Paris; Prof., Univ. Nac. del Litoral (Rosario, Argentina) 1955–61; Prof. Univ. de Buenos Aires 1959–66, Univ. of Oxford 1970–71, Univ. of Calif. (Berkeley) 1971–; Lecturer, History Dept, Harvard Univ. 1967–. *Publications:* El Pensamiento de Echeverría 1951, Un Conflicto Nacional: Moriscos y Cristianos Viejos en Valencia 1955, El Río de la Plata al Comenzar el Siglo XIX 1960,

Tradición Política Española e Ideología Revolucionaria de Mayo 1961, Historia de la Universidad de Buenos Aires 1962, Argentina en el Callejón 1964, Historia contemporánea de América Latina 1969, Hispanoamérica después de la Independencia 1972 (in English The Aftermath of Revolution in Latin America 1973), Revolución y guerra 1972 (in English Politics, Economics and Society in Argentina in the Revolutionary Period 1975). *Address:* History Department, University of California, Berkeley, CA 94720, USA. *Website:* www.berkeley.edu (Office).

HALPERN, Daniel, MFA; American editor and author; b. 11 Sept. 1945, Syracuse, NY; s. of Irving Halpern and Rosemary Halpern; m. Jeanne Carter 1982; ed California State Univ. and Columbia Univ.; Ed.-in-Chief, The Ecco Press (Antaeus) 1970–; Adjunct Prof. Columbia Univ. 1975–; Dir Nat. Poetry Series 1978–; Visiting Prof. Princeton Univ. 1975–76, 1987–88; Nat. Endowment for the Arts Fellowship 1974, 1975, 1987; Robert Frost Fellowship, CAPS; Guggenheim Fellow 1988; Carey Thomas Award for Creative Publishing, etc. *Publications:* poetry: Travelling on Credit 1972, Street Fire 1975, Life Among Others 1978, Seasonal Rights 1982, Tango 1987, Halpern's Guide to the Essential Restaurants of Italy 1990, Foreign Neon 1991, Selected Poems 1994, Antaeus 1970 1996, Something Shining 1998; ed. several anthologies. *Leisure interest:* cooking. *Telephone:* (609) 466-4748 (Office).

HALPERN, Jack, PhD, FRS; American university professor; b. 19 Jan. 1925, Poland; s. of Philip Halpern and Anna Sass; m. Helen Peritz 1949; two d.; ed McGill Univ., Montreal; NRC Postdoctoral Overseas Fellow, Univ. of Manchester 1949–50; Prof. of Chem., Univ. of BC, Canada 1950–62; Nuffield Fellow, Univ. of Cambridge 1959–60; Louis Block Distinguished Service Prof., Univ. of Chicago 1962–; External Scientific Mem. Max Planck Inst. für Kohlenforschung, Mulheim 1983–; Visiting Prof. at various univs. in USA, UK and Copenhagen; mem. Council NAS 1990– (Chair. Chemistry Section 1991–93, Vice-Pres. 1993–); Chair. German-American Council 1993–96, Chair. Bd of Trustees 1996–; numerous other lectureships, professional and editorial appointments; Fellow American Acad. of Arts and Sciences; Hon. Fellow Royal Soc. of Chem. 1987; Dir American Friends of the Royal Soc. 2000–; mem. Advisory Bd Humboldt Foundation Transatlantic Science and Humanities Program 2001–; Hon. DSc (Univ. of BC) 1986, (McGill) 1997; American Chemical Soc. Award in Inorganic Chem. 1968, Royal Soc. of Chem. Award in Catalysis 1977, Humboldt Award 1977, Richard Kokes Award 1978, American Chemical Soc. Award for Distinguished Service in the Advancement of Inorganic Chem. 1985, Willard Gibbs Award 1986, Bailar Medal 1986, German Chemical Soc. August Wilhelm von Hoffman Medal 1988, American Inst. of Chemists Chemical Pioneer Award 1991, Swiss Chemical Soc. Paracelsus Prize 1992, Basolo Medal 1993, Robert A. Welch Award 1994, American Chemical Soc. Award in Organo-metallic Chem. 1995, Int. Precious Metals Inst. Henry Alberts Award 1995; Cross of Merit (Germany) 1996. *Publications:* more than 250 scientific articles in various scientific journals. *Leisure interests:* art, music, theatre. *Address:* Department of Chemistry, University of Chicago, Chicago, IL 60637 (Office); 5630 S. Dorchester Avenue, Chicago, IL 60637, USA (Home). *Telephone:* (773) 702-7095 (Office); (773) 643-6837 (Home). *Fax:* (773) 702-8809 (Office). *E-mail:* jhjh@midway.uchicago.edu (Office).

HALPERN, Sir Ralph (Mark), Kt, CBIM, FID; British business executive; b. 1938, London; s. of Bernard Halpern and Olga Halpern; m. Joan Halpern (divorced); one s. one d.; ed St Christopher School, Letchworth; former trainee Selfridges; joined Burton Group PLC 1961, Chief Exec. and Man. Dir 1978–90, Chair. 1981–90; co-founder, Top Shop 1970; Chair. Halpern Assocs.; Chair. CBI Marketing and Common Affairs Cttee 1984; Chair. Police and Community Partnership Group, E Surrey; fmr Hon. Prof. Warwick Univ.; mem. CBI City-Industry Task Force 1986; mem. Pres.'s Cttee, Chair. British Fashion Council 1990–94; mem. advisory council Prince's Youth Business Trust 1991–92. *Leisure interest:* country pursuits. *Address:* c/o The Reform Club, Pall Mall, London, W.1, England.

HALSE, Bengt Gösta, DEng; Swedish business executive; b. 2 Feb. 1943, Gothenburg; ed Chalmers Inst. of Tech., Gothenburg; with Ericsson Group 1974–95; Pres., CEO Saab AB 1995–; Hon. Fellow Royal Aeronautical Soc., London 2001, mem. Royal Swedish Acad. of Engineering Sciences, Royal Swedish Acad. of War Sciences; Hon. DEng (Linköping Univ.) 1999; Hon. mem. Royal Swedish Soc. of Naval Sciences. *Address:* Saab AB, 581 88, Linköping, Sweden. *Telephone:* (8) 4630000. *Fax:* (13) 187111.

HALSEY, Albert Henry, MA, PhD; British university professor; b. 13 April 1923, London; s. of William T. Halsey and Ada Draper; m. Gertrude M. Littler 1949; three s. two d.; ed London School of Econs; research worker, Univ. of Liverpool 1952–54; Lecturer, Univ. of Birmingham 1954–62; Fellow, Centre for Advanced Study of Behavioral Sciences, Palo Alto, Calif. 1956–57; Prof. of Sociology, Univ. of Chicago 1959–60; Dir Barnett House and Fellow, Nuffield Coll., Oxford 1962–90; Prof. of Social and Admin. Studies, Univ. of Oxford 1978–90, Prof. Emer. 1990–; Sr Fellow British Acad. 1995; mem. Acad. Europaea 1992; Foreign mem. American Acad. of Arts and Sciences 1988; Hon. Fellow Goldsmiths Coll. London 1992, LSE 1993, Royal Statistical Soc. 1999; Hon. DSc (Birmingham) 1987; Dr hc (Open Univ.) 1989; Hon. DLit (Warwick, Leicester) 1994, (Glamorgan) 1995. *Radio:* Reith Lecturer, BBC 1978. *Publications:* Origins and Destinations 1980, Change in British Society 1986, English Ethical Socialism (with Norman Dennis) 1988, The Decline of Donnish Dominion 1992, No Discouragement: an Autobiography of A. H. Halsey 1996, Education, Culture, Economy and Society 1997, British Social

Trends: The Twentieth Century 2000, A History of Sociology in Britain: Science, Literature and Society 2004. *Leisure interest:* gardening. *Address:* Nuffield College, Oxford, OX1 1NF (Office); 28 Upland Park Road, Oxford, OX2 7RU, England (Home). *Telephone:* (1865) 278521 (Office); (1865) 558625 (Home). *E-mail:* Chelly.Halsey@nuf.ox.ac.uk (Office).

HALSTEAD, Sir Ronald, Kt, CBE, MA, CBIM, FRSC, FRSA; British business executive; b. 17 May 1927, Lancaster; s. of Richard and Bessie Harrison Halstead; m. Yvonne Cecile de Monchaux 1968 (deceased); two s.; ed Queens' Coll., Cambridge; Research Chemist H.P. Bulmer & Co. 1948–53; Mfg Man. Macleans Ltd 1954–55; Factory Man. Beecham Products Inc. (USA) 1955–60, Asst Man. Dir Beecham Research Lab. Ltd 1960–62, Pres. Beecham Research Labs., Inc. (USA) 1962–64, Vice-Pres. Marketing, Beecham Products, Inc. (USA) 1962–64, Chair. Food and Drink Div. Beecham Group 1964–67; Chair. Beecham Products 1967–84; Man. Dir (consumer products) Beecham Group 1973–84, Chair. and Chief Exec. Beecham Group 1984–85; Dir The Otis Elevator Co. Ltd 1978–83, Burmah Oil 1983–89; Dir (Non-exec.) American Cyanamid Co. 1986–94, Davy Corpn PLC 1986–91, Gestetner Holdings PLC 1986–95; Dir Laurentian Financial Group PLC 1991–95; Chair. CAB Int. 1995–98; Deputy Chair. Tech. Colls. Trust 1993–; Vice-Chair. Proprietary Asscn of GB 1968–77; Pres. Nat. Advertising Benevolent Soc. 1978–80; Vice-Pres. Inst. of Packaging 1979–81, Pres. 1981–83; Non-Exec. Dir British Steel Corpn 1979–86, Deputy Chair. 1986–94; Gov. Ashridge Man. Coll. 1970–, Vice-Chair. 1977–; Pres. Inc. Soc. of British Advertisers 1971–73; Chair. British Nutrition Foundation 1970–73, Council mem. 1967–79; Vice-Chair. Advertising Asscn 1973–81; Vice-Chair. Food & Drink Industries Council 1973–76; Pres. Food Mfrs Fed. 1974–76; Fellow, Inst. of Marketing 1975–, Vice-Pres. 1980–99; mem. Council, Food Mfrs Fed. Inc. 1966–85; mem. CBI 1970–86, BIM 1972–77, Cambridge Univ. Appointments Bd 1969–73, Agric. Research Council 1978–84; Dir Nat. Coll. of Food Tech. 1977–78, Chair. of Bd 1978–83; Chair. Knitting Sector Working Group, NEDO 1978–90, Textile and Garment Working Group, 1991–93; Fellow, Inst. of Grocery Distribution 1979–, Marketing Soc. 1981–99; Trustee, Inst. of Econ. Affairs 1980–93; mem. Monopolies and Mergers Comm. Newspaper Panel 1980–92; mem. Industrial Devt Advisory Bd Dept of Trade and Industry 1983–93, Chair. 1984–93; Hon. Treas. and Dir, Centre for Policy Studies 1984–93; mem. Priorities Bd for Research and Devt in Agric. and Food, Ministry of Agric. Fish and Food 1984–87; Chair. Bd of Food Studies Univ. of Reading 1983–86; Pres. Eng Industries Asscn 1991–; mem. Monopolies and Mergers Comm. 1993–99; Council mem. European Policy Forum 1993–; Council mem. Univ. of Buckingham 1973–95, Univ. of Reading 1978–98; Council and Exec. Cttee mem., Imperial Soc. of Kts. Bachelor 1985–; Chair. Conservative Foreign and Commonwealth Council 1995–; Hon. Fellow Inst. of Food Science and Tech., Inst. of Marketing; Hon. Fellow, Queens' Coll. Cambridge 1985; Gov. De Montfort Univ. (fmrly Leicester Polytechnic) 1989–97; Hon. DSc (Reading) 1982, (Univ. of Lancaster) 1987. *Leisure interests:* sailing, squash racquets, skiing. *Address:* 37 Edwardes Square, London, W8 6HH, England. *Telephone:* (20) 7603-9010.

HAMAD, Abdul-Latif Yousef al-, BA; Kuwaiti international official, banker and politician; b. 1936; m.; four c.; ed Claremont Coll., Calif., Harvard Univ.; mem. del. to UN 1962; Dir-Gen. Kuwait Fund for Arab Econ. Devt 1963–81; Dir, then Man. Dir Kuwait Investment Co. 1963–71; Man. Dir Kuwait Investment Co. 1965–74; Chair. Kuwait Prefabricated Bldg Co. 1965–78, United Bank of Kuwait Ltd, London 1966–84; Exec. Dir Arab Fund for Econ. and Social Devt 1972–81, Dir-Gen. and Chair. Bd of Dirs. 1985–; Chair. Compagnie Arabe et Internationale d'Investissements, Luxembourg 1973–81; mem. Bd of Trustees, Corporate Property Investors, New York 1975–; mem. Governing Body Inst. of Devt Studies, Sussex, UK 1975–87; mem. Ind. Comm. on Int. Devt Issues (Brandt Comm.) 1976–79; mem. Bd Int. Inst. for Environment and Devt, London 1976–80; Minister of Finance and Planning 1981–83; Gov. for Kuwait, World Bank and IMF 1981–83; mem. UN Cttee for Devt Planning 1982–91, Chair. 1987; mem. IFC Banking Advisory Bd Group 1987–, Advisory Group on Financial Flows for Africa (UN) 1987–88, South Comm. 1987–89, Group of Ten (African Devt Bank) 1987–, World Bank's Pvt. Sector Devt Review Group 1988–, UN Panel for Public Hearings on Activities of Transnat. Corpns. in S. Africa and Namibia 1989–92, Bd Trustees of Stockholm Environment Inst. 1989–92, Comm. on Global Governance 1992–. *Address:* Arab Fund for Economic and Social Development, P.O. Box 21923, Safat 13080, Kuwait.

HAMAD, Seif Sharif, BA; Tanzanian politician and political scientist; b. 22 Oct. 1943, Pemba; s. of the late Sharif Hamad Shehe and Time Seif Haji; m. 1st Furtunah Saleh Mbamba 1971; m. 2nd Aweinah Sanani Massoud 1977; one s. four d.; ed King George VI Secondary School, Zanzibar, Univ. of Dar es Salaam; teacher Lumumba Coll., Fidel Castro Coll. 1964–72; Asst to Pres. of Zanzibar 1975–77, Minister of Educ., Zanzibar 1977–80; mem. Tanzanian Parl. 1977–80; mem. Zanzibar House of Reps. 1980–99; mem. Cen. Cttee Chama Cha Mapinduzi (CCM) Party 1977–88, Head Econ. and Planning Dept of CCM 1982–88; Chief Minister of Zanzibar 1984–88; political prisoner in Zanzibar 1989–91; Nat. Vice-Chair. Civic United Front 1992–, now Sec.-Gen.; Presidential cand. Zanzibar elections 2000; Chair. Gen. Ass. Unrepresented Nations and Peoples' Org. (UNPO) 1997–. *Leisure interests:* reading, swimming. *Address:* Civic United Front, Mtendeni Street, Urban District, P.O. Box 3637, Zanzibar (Office); P.O. Box 10976, Dar es Salaam, Tanzania. *Telephone:*

(54) 237446 (Office); (51) 861009; (811) 324886; (812) 787790. *Fax:* (54) 237445 (Office); (51) 861010. *E-mail:* headquarters@cuftz.org (Office). *Website:* www.cuftz.org (Office).

HÄMÄLÄINEN, Sirkka Aune-Marjatta, DSc(Econs); Finnish banker; b. 8 May 1939, Riihimäki; m.; two c.; ed Helsinki School of Econs and Business Admin.; Economist, Econs Dept, Bank of Finland 1961–72, Head of Office, Econs Dept 1972–79, Acting Head of Dept 1979–81, Dir 1982–91, mem. Bd 1991–92, Gov. and Chair. Bd 1992–98; Dir Econs Dept, Ministry of Finance 1981–82; Chair. Bd of Dirs. Financial Supervision Authority 1996–97; mem. Exec. Bd European Cen. Bank, Frankfurt June 1998–2003; Docent, Adjunct Prof. of Econs Helsinki School of Econs and Business Admin. 1991–; mem. of numerous orgs. including Trilateral Comm. 1995–, Supervisory Bd Finnish Cultural Foundation 1996–, Cen. Bank Governance Steering Cttee, Bank of Int. Settlements 1996–, Finnish Public Research and Devt Financing Evaluation Group 1998–; Dr hc (Turku School of Econs and Business Admin.) 1995; Commdr First Class of Order of the White Rose, Merit Medal, First Class of Order of the White Star (Estonia). *Address:* 60066 Frankfurt am Main, Postfach 160319, Germany (Office). *Telephone:* (69) 13440 (Office). *Fax:* (69) 13446000 (Office). *E-mail:* info@ecb.int (Office). *Website:* www.ecb.int (Office).

HAMAMOTO, Manso; Japanese politician; Chair. Social Democratic Party of Japan (SDPJ) Diet Affairs Cttee for House of Councillors; Chair. of SDPJ mems. in House of Councillors; Minister of Labour 1994–96. *Address:* c/o Social Democratic Party of Japan, 1-8-1, Nagata-cho, Chiyoda-ku, Tokyo 100-0014, Japan.

HAMARI, Julia; Hungarian mezzo-soprano; b. 21 Nov. 1942, Budapest; d. of Sándor Hamari and Erzsébet Dokupil; m. Lajos Petö; ed Franz Liszt Music Acad. of Budapest; specializes in Rossini, Mozart, Bellini; lieder recitalist and oratorio performer; Prof. Staatliche Hochschule für Musik, Stuttgart 1989–; Kodály Prize 1987. *Participation in festivals:* performed in festivals of Edinburgh, Glyndebourne, Florence (Maggio Musicale). *Address:* Stuttgart 40, Max Brodweg 14, Germany.

HAMARNEH, Sami K., PhD; American medical historian and university professor (retd); b. 2 Feb. 1925, Madaba, Jordan; s. of Khalaf Odeh Hamarneh and Nora Zumot Hamarneh; m. Nazha T. Ajaj 1948; one s.; ed Syrian Univ., Damascus, Syria, North Dakota State Univ., Fargo and Wisconsin Univ., Madison, Wis.; Curator, Div. of Medical Sciences, Smithsonian Inst. 1977–, U.S. Nat. Museum, Washington, DC 1959–78; Curator Emer. Museum of History and Tech.; Prof. of History of Medical Sciences, Aleppo Univ., Syria 1978–79, King Abdulaziz Univ., Saudi Arabia 1982–83; Prof. and Researcher, Yarmouk Univ., Jordan 1984–87, Prof. and Researcher (History of Medicine, Nursing and Pharmacy), Univ. of Jordan 1987–90; Prof. of Islamic Medicine, Int. Inst. of Islamic Thought and Civilization (ISTAC), Kuala Lumpur, Malaysia 1993–99; mem. Advisory Bd Hamdard Medicus 1980–; Hon. DLitt (Hamdard Univ., Karachi) 1998; Ed. Kremers Award (USA) 1966, Citation of Merit, Univ. of Wis. 1997; Star of Jordan Medal 1965. *Publications:* Customs and Civilization in Bible Lands 1960, Bibliography on Medicine and Pharmacy in Medieval Islam 1964, Origins of Pharmacy and Therapy in the Near East 1973, The Physician, Therapist and Surgeon, Ibn al-Quff 1974, Catalogue on Medicine and Pharmacy at the British Library 1975, Directory of Historians of Arab-Islamic Science 1980, Health Sciences in Early Islam; collected papers 1983–85, Promises, Heritage and Peace 1986, History of Arabic Medicine and Allied Health Sciences 1986, Introduction to al-Biruni's Book on Precious Stones and Minerals 1988, Ibn al-Quff al-Karaki's Book on the Preservation of Health 1989, Ibn al-Quff al-Karaki's Book on Surgery 1994, Directory of Historians of Islamic Medicine and the Allied Sciences 1995, Arabic-Islamic Medicine and Pharmacy During the Golden Age 1997. *Leisure interests:* reading, jogging, travel. *Address:* 4631 Massachusetts Avenue, NW, Washington, DC 20016-2361, USA. *Telephone:* (202) 966-7196. *E-mail:* fham@erols.com (Office).

HAMBLING, Maggi, OBE; British artist; b. 23 Oct. 1945, Sudbury, Suffolk; d. of Harry Leonard Hambling and Marjorie Rose Hambling; ed Hadleigh Hall School and Amberfield School, Suffolk, Ipswich School of Art, Camberwell School of Art, London, Slade School of Fine Art, London; studied painting with Lett Haines and Cedric Morris 1960–; Oscar Wilde memorial Adelaide St, London 1998; First Artist in Residence, Nat. Gallery, London 1980–81; Boise Travel Award 1969, Arts Council Award 1977, Jerwood Prize (co–winner) 1995. *Exhibitions:* first solo exhbn at Hadleigh Gallery, Suffolk 1967; further solo exhbns in London 1973, 1977; at Nat. Gallery 1981, Nat. Portrait Gallery 1983, 1997, Serpentine Gallery 1987, Richard Demarco Gallery, Edinburgh 1988, Arnolfini Gallery, Bristol 1988, Bernard Jacobson Gallery 1990, Yale Center for British Art, USA 1991, Northern Centre for Contemporary Art, Sunderland, Cornerhouse, Manchester, Angel Row, Nottingham, Christchurch Mansions, Ipswich, Barbican, London, Harris Museum, Preston 1993–94, Marlborough Fine Art, London 1996, 2001, Yorkshire Sculpture Park 1997, Hugh Lane Gallery, Dublin 1997, Morley Coll. 2001, Henrietta Moraes – Paintings and Drawings by Maggi Hambling, Marlborough Fine Art and Marlborough Graphics 2001. *Public collections include:* Arts Council, Ashmolean Museum, Oxford, British Council, British Museum, Chelmsford and Essex Museum, Contemporary Art Soc., European Parl. Collection, Imperial War Museum, Ipswich Museum, Leicestershire Ed. Cttee, Minories Colchester, Nat. Gallery, Nat. Portrait Gallery, Royal Army Medical Coll., Rugby Museum, Southampton Art Gallery, Tate Gallery, William Morris School, Birmingham City Art Gallery, Morley Coll. London, Clare Coll. Cambridge, Whitworth Art Gallery, Gulbenkian Foundation, Preston Art Gallery, HTV Bristol, Scottish Nat. Gallery of Modern Art, Scottish Nat. Portrait Gallery, St Thomas' Hosp., London, Univ. Coll., London, Wakefield Art Gallery, Swindon Museum, Art Gallery, All Souls Coll., Oxford, Nat. Gallery of Australia, Yale Center for British Art, New Hall, Cambridge, Victoria & Albert Museum, London, Norwich Castle Museum, Templeton Coll., Oxford, Jesus Coll. Cambridge, The Prudential, Barclays Bank, Govt Art Collection, Usher Gallery, Lincoln, Fitzwilliam Museum, Cambridge. *Publication:* Maggi and Henrietta 2001. *Address:* Morley College, Westminster Bridge Road, London, SE1 7HT, England.

HAMBRO, Rupert Nicholas; British banker; b. 27 June 1943, London; s. of late Jocelyn Olaf Hambro and Ann Silvia Muir; m. Mary Robinson Boyer 1970; one s. one d.; ed Eton Coll., Aix-en-Provence; joined Hambros Bank 1964, Dir 1969, Chair. 1983–86; Chair. Rupert Hambro and Partners Ltd 1986–; Group Man. Dir J. O. Hambro & Co. 1986–94, Chair. 1994–99, Chair. J. O. Hambro Mansford Ltd 1998–, J. O. Hambro Ltd 1999–; Chair Wilton's (St James's) Ltd 1987–, Mayflower Corpn PLC 1988–, CTR Group 1990–97, Fenchurch PLC 1993–97, Longshot Ltd 1996–, Woburn Golf & Country Club Ltd, 1998–, Kapital Ventures PLC 2001–; Asscn of Int. Bond Dealers 1979–82, Third Space Group Ltd 1999–, Walpole 2000–, Jermyn Street Asscn 2000–, Roland Berger and Partners Ltd 2000–01; Dir Daily Telegraph Group Ltd 1983–2001 (Dir Advisory Bd 2002–), Anglo-American Corpn of SA Ltd 1981–97, Pioneer Concrete Holdings PLC 1982–99, Abel Hadden and Co. Ltd 1998–2001, KBC Peel Hunt Ltd 1997–2003, Bank Gutmann AG 2000–; mem. Int. Council US Information Agency 1988–; Chair. of Trustees, Silver Trust; Vice-Patron Royal Soc. of British Sculptors 1997; Treas. Nat. Art Collections Fund; Deputy Pres. Anglo-Danish Soc. 1987–; Chair. of Govs. Museum of London 1996–; Hon. Fellow, Univ. of Bath 1998; Liveryman Fishmongers' Co.; mem. Court of Worshipful Co. of Goldsmiths; Kt of the Falcon (Iceland). *Leisure interests:* shooting, golf. *Address:* 54 Jermyn Street, London, SW1Y 6LX, England (Office). *Telephone:* (20) 7292-3777 (Office); (20) 7259-0101 (Home). *Fax:* (20) 7292-3778 (Office); (20) 7823-4803 (Home). *E-mail:* rnhambro@joh.co.uk (Office).

HAMBURGER, Michael Peter Leopold, OBE, MA; British poet; b. 22 March 1924, Berlin, Germany; s. of late Richard Hamburger and L. Hamburger (née Hamburg); m. Anne Ellen File 1951; one s. two d.; ed Westminster School and Christ Church, Oxford; army service 1943–47; freelance writer 1948–52; Asst Lecturer in German Univ. Coll., London 1952–55; lecturer, then Reader Univ. of Reading 1955–64; Florence Purington Lecturer Mount Holyoke Coll., Mass. 1966–67; Visiting Prof. State Univ. of NY, Buffalo 1969, Stony Brook 1971; Visiting Fellow Center for Humanities Wesleyan Univ., Conn. 1970; Visiting Prof. Univ. of SC 1973; Regent's Lecturer Univ. of Calif., San Diego 1973; Visiting Prof. Boston Univ. 1975–77; Prof. (part-time) Univ. of Essex 1978; Bollingen Foundation Fellow 1959–61, 1965–66; FRSL 1972–86; Corresp. mem. Deutsche Akademie für Sprache und Dichtung, Darmstadt 1973; Hon. DLitt (Univ. of East Anglia) 1988; Hon. DPhil hc (Technische Universität, Berlin) 1995; prizes for translation: Deutsche Akademie für Sprache und Dichtung 1964, Arts Council 1969, Arts Prize, Inter Nationes, Bonn 1976, Medal, Inst. of Linguists 1977, Schlegel-Tieck Prize, London 1978, 1981, Wilhelm-Heinse Prize (medallion), Mainz 1978, Goethe Medal 1986, European Translation Prize 1990, Hölderlin Prize, Tübingen 1991, Petrarca Prize, Modena 1992; Cholmondeley Award for Poetry, London 2000, Horst-Bienek Prize, Munich 2001. *Publications: poetry:* Flowering Cactus 1950, Poems 1950–51 1952, The Dual Site 1958, Weather and Season 1963, Feeding the Chickadees 1968, Penguin Modern Poems (with A. Brownjohn and C. Tomlinson) 1969, Travelling 1969, Travelling I-V 1973, Ownerless Earth 1973, Travelling VI 1975, Real Estate 1977, Moralities 1977, Variations 1981, Collected Poems 1984, Trees 1988, Selected Poems 1988, Roots in the Air 1991, Collected Poems 1941–1994 1995, Late (Variations III) 1997, Intersections 2000; The Take-Over (short story) 2000, Philip Larkin: A Retrospect 2002; From a Diary of Non-events 2002. *translations:* Poems of Hölderlin 1943, C. Baudelaire, Twenty Prose Poems 1946, L. van Beethoven, Letters, Journals and Conversations 1951, J. C. F. Hölderlin, Selected Verse 1961, G. Trakl, Decline 1952, A. Goes, The Burnt Offering 1956, H. von Hofmannsthal, Poems and Verse Plays (with others) 1961, B. Brecht, Tales from the Calendar 1961, Modern German Poetry 1910–1960 (with C. Middleton) 1962, H. von Hofmannsthal, Selected Plays and Libretti (with others) 1964, G. Büchner, Lenz 1966, H. M. Enzensberger, Poems 1966, G. Grass, Selected Poems (with C. Middleton) 1966, J. C. F. Hölderlin, Poems and Fragments 1967, enlarged edns. 1980, 1994, H. M. Enzensberger, The Poems of Hans Magnus Enzensberger (with J. Rothenberg and the author) 1968, H. M. Enzensberger, Poems for People Who Don't Read Poems 1968, Selected Poems 1994, G. Grass, Poems (with C. Middleton) 1969, P. Bichsel, And Really Frau Blum Would Very Much Like to Meet the Milkman 1968, G. Eich, Journeys 1968, N Sachs, Selected Poems 1968, Peter Bichsel, Stories for Children 1971, Paul Celan, Selected Poems 1972, East German Poetry (Ed.) 1972, Peter Huchel, Selected Poems 1974, German Poetry 1910–1975 1977, Helmut Heissenbüttel, Texts 1977, Franco Fortini, Poems 1978, An Unofficial Rilke 1981, Peter Huchel, The Garden of Theophrastus 1983, Goethe, Poems and Epigrams 1983, Poems of Paul Celan 1988, Pigeons and Moles: Selected Writing of Günter Eich 1991, 1995, Hölderlin: Poems and Fragments 1994 Dingfest/Thingsure: Selected Poems by Ernst Jandl 1997, Paul Celan: Wolf's-Bean 1997, H. M. Enzensberger: Kiosk 1997, Hölderlin: Selected Poems and Fragments 1998, W. G. Sebald: After Nature 2002. *criticism:* Reason and Energy 1957, From

Prophecy to Exorcism 1965, The Truth of Poetry 1969, 1982, 1996, Hugo von Hofmannsthal 1973, Art as Second Nature 1975, A Proliferation of Prophets 1983, After the Second Flood: essays in modern German Literature 1986, Testimonies 1989, Michael Hamburger in Conversation with Peter Dale 1998. *autobiography:* A Mug's Game 1973, String of Beginnings 1991. *Leisure interest:* gardening. *Address:* c/o John Johnson Ltd, Clerkenwell House, 45/47 Clerkenwell Green, London, EC1R 0HT, England.

HAMDAN, Mohammed, PhD; Jordanian mathematician and politician; b. 3 Nov. 1934; m.; two c.; ed Cairo and Sydney Univs.; visiting Prof. Va Polytechnic Inst. and State Univ. 1969–71; Assoc. Prof. of Mathematics American Univ. of Beirut 1970–76, Prof. of Mathematics 1976–77, also at American Univ. of Cairo 1977–78; Prof. of Math., Dean Faculty of Sciences, Univ. of Jordan 1984–86; Pres. Yarmouk Univ. 1986–89; Minister of Educ. and Higher Educ. 1989–91, 1998; Pres. Hashemite Univ. 1991–98; Sec.-Gen. Higher Council for Science and Tech. 1998–; mem. Int. Statistical Inst., American Statistical Asscn, Third World Acad. of Sciences, Jordan Acad. of Arabic Language, Union of Arab Physicists and Mathematicians; mem. Bd Trustees Hitteen, Ibn Khaldoun and Al-Razi Community Coll.; mem. Editorial Bd Int. Statistical Review, Arab Journal of Mathematics, Mu'tah Journal of Research and Studies and Research Journal, Univ. of Jordan; mem. Islamic Acad. of Sciences, mem. Council 1994–99. *Publications:* over 60 tech. papers. *Address:* Islamic Academy of Sciences, P.O. Box 830036, Amman 11183, Jordan (Office). *Telephone:* 5523385 (Office). *Fax:* 5511803 (Office).

HAMDANI, Smail; Algerian politician; m.; one c.; fmrly Govt Sec.-Gen., adviser to Presidency, Amb. to Scandinavia, Spain, France, to UNESCO, Sec.-Gen. at Foreign Ministry; mem. Council of the Nation; Pres. of Algeria 1998–99; fmr lecturer École Nat. d'Admin.; consultant and mem. Nat. Inst. for Strategic Studies; Chair. Algerian Asscn for Int. Relations. *Address:* c/o Office of the President, el-Mouradia, Algiers, Algeria.

HAMDOON, Nizar, BArch; Iraqi diplomatist and architect; b. 18 May 1944, Baghdad; m. Sahar Hamdoon; two d.; ed Baghdad Coll. and Univ. of Baghdad; Iraqi Air Force 1968–70; worked at Arab Ba'ath Party Nat. Command 1970–81; Under-Sec. Ministry of Culture and Information 1981–83; joined Ministry of Foreign Affairs 1983; Head, Iraqi Interests Section, Washington, DC 1983; Amb. to USA 1984–87; Under-Sec. Ministry of Foreign Affairs 1987–92; Perm. Rep. to UN 1992–98; Special Adviser to Tariq Aziz (Deputy Prime Minister) –2001; Founder and Chair. Soc. of Iraqi Architects 1990. *Address:* c/o Ministry of Foreign Affairs, Opposite State Organisation for Roads and Bridges, Karradat Mariam, Baghdad, Iraq (Office).

HAMEED, A. C. S.; Sri Lankan politician; b. 10 April 1929; MP for Harispattuwa 1960–; Minister of Foreign Affairs 1977–89, of Educ., Science and Tech. 1989–90, of Justice 1990–93, of Foreign Affairs 1993–94; first to hold separate portfolio of foreign affairs; Chair. United Nat. Party (UNP) 1995. *Publications:* In Pursuit of Peace 1983, Owl and the Lotus 1986, Disarmament—a multi-lateral approach 1988, Foreign Policy Perspectives of Sri Lanka 1988. *Address:* c/o United National Party, 400 Kotte Road, Pitakotte, Sri Lanka.

HAMELIN, Louis-Edmond, OC, MA, PhD, DèsSc, FRSC; Canadian researcher and consultant in polar affairs; b. 21 March 1923, St Didace; m. Colette Lafay 1951; one s. one d.; ed Laval Univ., Canada and Univs. of Grenoble and Paris, France; Prof. Laval Univ. 1951–78, Dir Inst. of Geography 1955–61, Founding-Dir Centre of Northern Studies 1962–72; mem. Legis Ass., Yellowknife, Northwest Territories, Canada 1971–75; Rector Université de Québec, Trois-Rivières 1978–83; Gov. Int. Devt Research Centre, Ottawa 1984–88; Corresp., Inst. de France, Paris 1989; Dr. hc (McGill, Ottawa, Waterloo, Sherbrooke, Montreal, Trois-Rivières); Gov.-Gen. Award 1976, Grand Prix Geography (Paris) 1977, Molson Sciences Prize (Canada) 1982, Human Sciences Prize (Québec) 1987; Grand Officier Québec. *Publications:* Illustrated Glossary of Periglacial Phenomena 1967, Atlas du Monde 1967, Canada: A Geographical Perspective 1973, Canadian Nordicity 1979, The Canadian North 1988, Obiou 1990, Le rang d'habitat 1993, Écho des pays froids 1996, Le Québec par des mots 2000–03 (electronic and printed versions, 3 vols). *Leisure interests:* travel, mountaineering, photography. *Address:* 1244 Albert-Lozeau, Sillery, Québec, G1T 1H4, Canada. *Telephone:* (418) 683-0386. *E-mail:* louis-edmond.hamelin@sittel.ca (Home).

HAMER, Hon. Sir Rupert James, AC, KCMG, ED, LLM, FAIM; Australian politician and solicitor; b. 29 July 1916, Melbourne; s. of Hubert Ralph Hamer and Elizabeth Anne Hamer (née McLuckie); m. April Mackintosh 1944; three s. two d.; ed Melbourne and Geelong Grammar Schools, Univ. of Melbourne; joined Australian Imperial Forces 1940, served 5½ years N Africa, New Guinea, NW Europe; CO Vic. Scottish Regt, Citizen Mil. Forces 1954–58; mem. Vic. Legis. Council for E Yarra 1958–71; Minister for Immigration, Vic. 1962–64, for Local Govt, Vic. 1964–71; mem. Vic. Legis. Assembly for Kew 1971–81; Chief Sec., Deputy Premier, Vic. 1971–72, Premier 1972–81, Treas. and Minister of the Arts 1972–79, Minister of State Devt, Decentralization and Tourism 1979–81; Chair. Bd Advice Data Connection 1993–; Pres. Victorian Coll. of Arts 1982–; Nat. Pres. Save the Children Fund Australia, Friends of Royal Botanic Gardens Melbourne, Friends of Australian Broadcasting Comm.; Pres. Vic. State Opera 1981–95, Greenhouse Action Australia 1989–, Consultative Council on Cancer and Heart Disease 1994–, Nat. Heritage Foundation 1995–, Nat. Inst. of Circus Arts 1999–; Fellow Trinity Coll. Melbourne Univ.; Trustee Melbourne Cricket Ground, Yarra Bend Nat. Park 1975–; Hon. LLD (Melbourne) 1984; Hon. DUniv (Swinburne) 1994.

Leisure interests: tennis, sailing, football, reading, music. *Address:* 35 Heather Grove, Kew, Vic. 3101, Australia. *Telephone:* (3) 9817-2272. *Fax:* (3) 9817-2893.

HAMILTON, Linda; American actress; b. 26 Sept. 1956, Salisbury, Md; m. 1st Bruce Abbott (divorced); m. 2nd James Cameron 1996; one d. *Stage appearances:* Looice 1975, Richard III 1977. *Films include:* T.A.G.: The Assassination Game 1982, Children of the Corn 1984, The Stone Boy 1984, The Terminator 1984, Black Moon Rising 1986, King Kong Lives! 1986, Mr Destiny 1990, Terminator 2: Judgment Day 1991, Silent Fall 1994, The Shadow Conspiracy 1997, Dante's Peak 1997, Skeletons in the Closet 2001. *Television series include:* The Secrets of Midland Heights 1980–81, King's Crossing 1982, Beauty and the Beast 1987–90. *Television films:* Reunion 1980, Rape and Marriage—The Rideout Case 1980, Country Gold 1982, Secrets of a Mother and Daughter 1983, Secret Weapons 1985, Club Med 1986, Go Toward the Light 1988, On the Line 1998, Point Last Seen 1998, The Color of Courage 1999, The Secret Life of Girls 1999, Sex & Mrs X 2000, A Girl Thing 2001, Bailey's Mistake 2001. *Address:* United Talent Agency, 5th Floor, 9560 Wilshire Boulevard, Beverly Hills, CA 90212, USA.

HAMILTON, Richard, CH; British artist; b. 24 Feb. 1922; s. of Peter and Constance Hamilton; m. 1st Terry O'Reilly 1947 (died 1962); one s. one d.; m. 2nd Rita Donagh 1991; ed elementary school, evening classes, St Martin's School of Art, Royal Academy Schools and Slade School of Art; jig and tool draughtsman, Design Unit 1941–42, Electrical & Musical Industries (EMI) 1942–45; Exhbn of Reaper engravings, Gimpel Fils 1950; devised Growth and Form Exhbn, Inst. of Contemporary Arts (ICA) 1951; teacher of design, Cen. School of Arts and Crafts 1952–53; mem. Independent Group, ICA 1952–55; Lecturer, Fine Art Dept, King's Coll., Univ. of Durham (later Univ. of Newcastle-upon-Tyne) 1953–66; teacher of Interior Design RCA 1957–61; exhbns. of paintings 1951–55 and 1956–64, Hanover Gallery 1955 and 1964; organized Exhbn of works by Marcel Duchamp, Tate Gallery 1966; Exhbn of Guggenheim reliefs and studies, London 1966; exhbns. in Kassel 1967, New York 1967, Studio Marconi, Milan 1968, Hamburg 1969; Exhbn of Swinging London 1967 and beach scene paintings, London 1969; Exhbn of Cosmetic Studies, Milan 1969, Berlin 1970; other solo exhbns. Edin. 1988, Stockholm 1989, Hanover 1990, Valencia 1991, London 1991, 1995, San Francisco 1996; retrospective exhbns., Tate Gallery 1970, (seen in Switzerland, Netherlands Eindhoven and Bern), also 1992, Guggenheim Museum, New York 1973, Nationalgalerie, Berlin 1974, Paintings, Pastels, Prints, London 1975, Amsterdam 1976, Musée Grenoble 1977, Drawings retrospective, Bielefeld 1978, Prints retrospective, Vancouver 1978, Interfaces Exhbn, Denmark 1979, Interiors Exhbn, London, New York 1980, Paris 1981, Image and Process Exhbn, London 1983, Dublin 1992; Venice Biennale 1993 (awarded Golden Lion), Bremen 1998; William and Noma Copley Foundation Award for painting 1960, Jt First Prize, John Moores Liverpool Exhbn 1969, Talens Prize, Amsterdam 1970, World Print Award 1983, Nord/LB Prize 1996, Arnold Bode Prize 1997, Gold Medal, Ljubljana 1999. *Exhibition:* Imaging Ulysses, British Museum 2002. *Publications:* Polaroid Portraits (Vol. I) 1972, (Vol. II) 1977, (Vol. III) 1983, (Vol. IV) 2002, Collected Words 1982, Image and Process 1983, Prints 1939–83 1984. *Address:* c/o Tate Gallery, Millbank, London, SW1P 4RG, England.

HAMLISCH, Marvin, BA; American composer; b. 2 June 1944, New York; s. of Max and Lilly (née Schachter) Hamlisch; m. Terre Blair 1989; ed Queen's Coll., New York; on tour with Groucho Marx 1974–75; made his debut as pianist with Minn. Orchestra 1975; conductor of orchestras throughout USA; Musical Dir and Conductor Barbra Streisand Tour 1994 (Emmy Award 1995); Prin. Pops Conductor Pittsburgh Symphony Orchestra 1994–, Baltimore Symphony Orchestra 1994–; Outstanding Music Direction Emmy Award 1994, Outstanding Music and Lyrics Emmy Award 1994. *Compositions include:* film scores: The Swimmer 1968, Take the Money and Run 1969, Bananas 1971, The Way We Were 1974, The Sting 1974, Same Time Next Year 1979, Starting Over 1979, Ordinary People 1980, Seems Like Old Times 1980, Sophie's Choice 1982, D.A.R.Y.L. 1985, Frankie and Johnny 1991, Switched at Birth 1991; popular songs: Sunshine, Lollipops and Rainbows 1960, Good Morning America 1975, Nobody Does It Better 1977; theme songs for The January Man 1988, Three Men and a Baby, Little Nikita, The Experts; composed symphonic work in one movement Anatomy of Peace 1991, composed music for global anthem One Song (lyrics by Alan and Marilyn Bergman); int. debut at Barcelona Olympics 1992; Broadway musicals: A Chorus Line 1975, They're Playing Our Song 1979, The Goodbye Girl 1993. *Publication:* The Way I Was 1992. *Address:* c/o Nancy Shear Arts Services, 180 West End Avenue, # 28N, New York, NY 10023, USA.

HAMMADI, Sa'adoun; Iraqi politician and economist; b. 22 June 1930, Karbala; m. Lamia Hammadi 1961; five s.; ed in Beirut, Lebanon and USA; Prof. of Econs, Univ. of Baghdad 1957; Deputy Head of Econ. Research, Nat. Bank of Libya, Tripoli 1961–62; Minister of Agrarian Reform 1963; Econ. Adviser to Presidential Council, Govt of Syria 1964; Econ. Expert, UN Planning Inst., Syria 1965–68; Pres. Iraq Nat. Oil Co. (INOC) 1968; Minister of Oil and Minerals 1969–74, of Foreign Affairs 1974–83; Deputy Prime Minister 1991; Prime Minister of Iraq March–Sept. 1991; Speaker of Nat. Ass. 1984–88, 1996–2003; Adviser to Pres. –2003; mem. Revolutionary Command Council –2003; mem. Iraqi Acad. *Publications:* Towards a Socialist Agrarian Reform in Iraq 1964, Views about Arab Revolution 1969, Memoirs and Views on Oil Issues 1980, About Nationalism and Arab Unity 1993. *Leisure interests:* swimming, walking, coin collection, reading novels.

HAMMAMI, Hamma; Tunisian politician; b. 8 Jan. 1952, El Aroussa; m. Radhia Nasraoui 1981; three d.; Co-Founder and Leader Parti Communiste des Ouvriers de Tunisie (PCOT) (banned communist party); Dir El Badil (The Alternative—banned newspaper); imprisoned for participation in students' movt 1972–74, for membership of asscn El Aamel Ettounsi (The Tunisian Worker) 1974–80, exiled in France, sentenced in absentia May 1987, returned to Tunisia, numerous arrests 1989–91, went into hiding Oct. 1992, tried in absentia Dec. 1992, arrested Feb. 1994, imprisoned June 1994–Nov. 1995, went into hiding, sentenced in absentia July 1999, emerged from hiding and imprisoned Feb.–Sept. 2002.

HAMMARSKJÖLD, Knut Olof Hjalmar Akesson, PH.M.; Swedish diplomatist; b. 16 Jan. 1922, Geneva, Switzerland; s. of Åke Hammarskjöld and the late Britte Hammmarskjöld; nephew of the late Dag Hammarskjöld, Sec.-Gen. of the UN; four s.; ed Stockholm Univ.; entered Foreign Service 1946, served Paris, Vienna, Moscow, Bucharest, Kabul, Sofia 1947–55; First Sec. Foreign Office 1955–57; Head of Foreign Relations Dept, Royal Bd of Civil Aviation, Stockholm 1957–59; Deputy Head, Swedish Del. to OEEC, Paris 1959–60; Deputy Sec.-Gen. European Free Trade Asscn (EFTA) 1960–66; Minister Plenipotentiary 1966–; Dir-Gen. of Int. Air Transport Asscn (IATA), Montreal, Geneva 1966–84, Chair. Exec. Cttee 1981–84; Dir Inst. of Air Transport, Paris 1974–; Dir Gen. 1985–; Chair, CEO Atwater Inst., Montreal 1985–; Special Adviser to Dir-Gen. UNESCO; mem. Inst. of Transport, London; mem. Alexander S. Onassis Public Benefit Foundation Int. Cttee for Award of Athens and Olympia Prizes 1977–83; Gov. Atlantic Inst. for Int. Affairs 1983–87; Chair. Corp. Bd Sydvenska Dagbladet AB, Newspaper Conglomerate, Malmö 1987–94, (Dir 1948–), now Chair. Emer.; Hon. Fellow, Canadian Aeronautics and Space Inst.; Commdr Order of the Lion (Finland), Order of the Falcon (1st Class) (Iceland), Commdr Order of Orange-Nassau (Netherlands), Légion d'honneur and Order of the Black Star (France), Grand Officer, Order Al-Istiqlal (Jordan); Commdr (1st Class) Order of the North Star (Sweden), NOR (Sweden), Grand Cross of the Order of Civil Merit (Spain). *Publications:* articles on political, economic and aviation topics. *Address:* Rue St Germain 11, Geneva, Switzerland.

HAMMEL, Eugene Alfred, PhD; American professor of anthropology and demography; b. 18 March 1930, New York; s. of William Hammel and Violet Brookes; m. Joan Marie Swingle 1951; ed Univ. of Calif., Berkeley; field work in archaeology and linguistics, Calif. 1947–51, in ethnography, Peru 1957–58, in archaeology and ethnography in New Mexico 1959–61, in ethnography in Mexico 1963, in Yugoslavia and Greece 1963, 1965–66; Asst Prof. Univ. of New Mexico 1959–61; Asst Prof. Univ. of Calif. (Berkeley) 1961–63, Assoc. Prof. 1963–66, Prof. 1966–93, Prof. of Anthropology and Demography 1978–93, Prof. Emer. 1993–, Dir Quantitative Anthropology Lab. 1974–90, Chair. Demography 1978–88; archival research in Yugoslavia, Hungary, Austria 1983–; mem. NAS. *Publications:* Wealth, Authority and Prestige in the Ica Valley, Peru 1962, Ritual Relations and Alternative Social Structures in the Balkans 1968, The Pink Yoyo: Occupational Mobility in Belgrade c. 1915–65 1969, Statistical Studies of Historical Social Structure (with Wachter and Laslett) 1978; approximately 100 articles. *Leisure interests:* hiking, guitar, carpentry, photography. *Address:* Department of Demography, University of California, Berkeley, 2232 Piedmont Avenue, CA 94720, USA. *Telephone:* (415) 642-3391. *Website:* www.berkeley.edu (Office).

HAMMERSLEY, John Michael, DSc, FRS; British mathematician; b. 21 March 1920, Helensburgh, Scotland; s. of Guy Hugh and Marguerite Hammersley (née Whitehead); m. Shirley Gwendolene Bakewell 1951; two s.; ed Sedbergh School, Emmanuel Coll., Cambridge; Maj. RA 1940–46; Prin. Scientific Officer Theoretical Physics Div., AERE, Harwell 1955–59; Grad. Asst Design and Analysis of Scientific Experiments, Oxford 1948–55, Sr Research Fellow Trinity Coll. 1960–69, Sr Research Officer, Inst. of Econ. 1960–69, Reader in Math. Statistics 1969–87, Emer. Reader 1987–, Professorial Fellow 1969–87, Emer. Fellow 1987–; numerous short appointments in USA 1952–84; Rouse Ball Lecturer, Cambridge 1980; Fulbright Fellow 1955, Erskine Fellow 1978; Polya Prize 1997; Von Neumann Medal (Brussels) 1966, IMA Gold Medal 1984. *Publications:* Monte Carlo Methods (with D. C. Handscomb) 1964. *Address:* Trinity College, Oxford, OX1 3BH (Office); 11 Eynsham Road, Oxford, OX2 9BS, England (Home). *Telephone:* (1865) 862181 (Home).

HAMMES, Gordon G., PhD; American university vice-chancellor and professor of chemistry; b. 10 Aug. 1934, Fond du Lac, Wis.; s. of Jacob Hammes and Betty (Sadoff) Hammes; m. Judith Ellen Frank 1959; one s. two d.; ed Princeton Univ. and Univ. of Wisconsin; Postdoctoral Fellow Max Planck Inst. für physikalische Chemie Göttingen, Fed. Repub. of Germany 1959–60; instructor, subsequently Assoc. Prof. MIT, Cambridge, Mass. 1960–65; Prof., Cornell Univ. 1965–88, Chair. Dept of Chem. 1970–75, Horace White Prof. of Chem. and Biochemistry 1975–88, Dir Biotech. Program 1983–88; Prof., Univ. of Calif., Santa Barbara 1988–91, Vice-Chancellor for Academic Affairs 1988–91; Prof. Duke Univ., Durham, NC 1991–, Vice-Chancellor Duke Univ. Medical Center 1991–98, Univ. Distinguished Service Prof. of Biochem. 1996–; mem. Physiological Chem. Study Section, Physical Biochem. Study Section, Training Grant Cttee, Nat. Insts. of Health; mem. Bd of Counsellors, Nat. Cancer Inst. 1976–80, Advisory Council, Chem. Dept, Princeton 1970–75, Polytechnic Inst., New York 1977–78, Boston Univ. 1977–85; mem. Nat. Research Council, U.S. Nat. Comm. for Biochem. 1989–95; mem. American Chem. Soc., American Soc. of Biochem. and Molecular Biology (Pres. 1994–95), NAS, American Acad. of Arts and Sciences; ed. Biochemistry 1992–; Award in Biological Chem., American Chemical Soc. 1967, William C. Rose Award, American Soc. of Biochem. and Molecular Biology 2002. *Publications:* Principles of Chemical Kinetics, Enzyme Catalysis and Regulation, Chemical Kinetics: Principles and Selected Topics (with I. Amdur), Thermodynamics and Kinetics for the Biological Sciences; articles. *Address:* 11 Staley Place, Durham, NC 27705, USA. *Telephone:* (919) 684-8848 (Office). *E-mail:* hamme001@mc.duke.edu (Office).

HAMMES, Michael Noel, MBA; American business executive; b. 25 Dec. 1941, Evanston, Ill.; s. of Ferdinand Hammes and Winifred Hammes; m. Lenore Lynn Forbes 1964; three s. two d.; ed Georgetown Univ., New York Univ.; Asst Controller, Ford Motor Ass. Div. 1974, Plant Man., Ford Wixom Ass. Plant 1975, Man. Program Planning, Ford Automotive Ass. Div. 1976, Dir Int. Business Planning, Int. Operations, Ford 1977, Man. Dir and Pres., Ford Motor Co. of Mexico 1979, Vice-Pres. Truck Operations, Ford of Europe 1983–86; Vice-Pres., Int. Operations, Chrysler Motors Corpn 1986–90; Chair., CEO Coleman Co. 1993–97; CEO Guide Corpn, Anderson 1998–2000; Pres., CEO Sunrise Medical Inc., Carlsbad, Calif. 2000–, Chair. audit comm. 1998–. *Leisure interests:* skiing, tennis, golf, antique cars. *Address:* Sunrise Medical Inc., 2382 Faraday Avenue, Suite 200, Carlsbad, CA 92008, USA (Office).

HAMMOND, Norman David Curle, PhD, ScD, FSA, FBA; British archaeologist; b. 10 July 1944, Brighton; s. of William Hammond and Kathleen Jessie Howes; m. Jean Wilson 1972; one s. one d.; ed Varndean Grammar School, Peterhouse, Cambridge; Research Fellow, Centre of Latin American Studies, Cambridge 1967–71, Leverhulme Research Fellow 1972–75; Research Fellow, Fitzwilliam Coll., Cambridge 1973–75; Sr Lecturer, Univ. of Bradford 1975–77; Visiting Prof., Univ. of Calif. (Berkeley) 1977, Rutgers Univ., USA 1977–78, Assoc. Prof. 1978–84, Prof. of Archaeology 1984–88; Prof. of Archaeology, Boston Univ. and Assoc. in Maya Archaeology, Peabody Museum, Harvard Univ. 1988–; Archaeology Corresp. The Times 1967–; Ed. South Asian Archaeology 1970–73, Afghan Studies 1976–79; Consulting Ed. Library of Congress, USA 1977–89; Archaeological Consultant Scientific American 1979–95; Curl Lecturer, Royal Anthropological Inst. 1985; Bushnell Lecturer, Cambridge Univ. 1997, Stone Lecturer, Archaeological Inst. of America 1998; Acad. Trustee Archaeological Inst. of America 1990–93; mem. Council, Soc. of Antiquaries of London 1996–; excavations and surveys in Libya and Tunisia 1964, Afghanistan 1966, Belize 1970–98, Ecuador 1972–84; Fellow Dumbarton Oaks, Washington, DC; Visiting Fellow, Worcester Coll., Oxford, Peterhouse, Cambridge; Hon. DSc (Bradford) 1999; British Archaeological Press Award 1994, 1998, Soc. of Antiquaries Medal, London 2001. *Publications include:* South Asian Archaeology (Ed.) 1973, Mesoamerican Archaeology (Ed.) 1974, Lubaantun: a Classic Maya Realm 1975, Social Process in Maya Prehistory (Ed.) 1977, The Archaeology of Afghanistan (Ed. with F. R. Allchin) 1978, Ancient Maya Civilisation 1982, Nohmul: excavations 1973–83, 1985, Cuello: an early Maya community in Belize 1991, The Maya 2000; Archaeology Procs. 44th Congress of Americanists (Gen. Ed.) 1982–84; contribs. to learned and other journals. *Leisure interests:* heraldry, genealogy, wine. *Address:* Wholeway, Harlton, Cambridge, CB3 7ET, England; 83 Ivy Street, Apt. 32, Brookline, MA 02446, USA. *Telephone:* (617) 358-1651 (USA) (Office); (1223) 262376 (UK); (617) 739-9077 (USA).

HAMNETT, Katharine; British designer; b. 16 Aug. 1947; d. of Group Capt. James Appleton; two s.; ed Cheltenham Ladies' Coll. and St Martin's School of Art; co-f. Tuttabankem (with Anne Buck) 1969–74; designed freelance in New York, Paris, Rome and London 1974–76; f. Katharine Hamnett Ltd 1979; launched Choose Life T-Shirt collection 1983; involved in Fashion Aid 1985; opening of first Katharine Hamnett shop, London 1986, followed by two more shops in 1988; production moved to Italy 1989; Visiting Prof. London Inst. 1997–; Int. Inst. of Cotton Designer of the Year 1982, British Fashion Industry Designer of the Year 1984, Bath Costume Museum Menswear Designer of the Year Award 1984, British Knitting and Clothing Export Council Award for Export 1988. *Publications:* various publs in major fashion magazines and newspapers. *Leisure interests:* travel, photography, gardening, archaeology.

HAMPE, Michael, DPhil; German theatre, opera and television director and actor; b. 3 June 1935, Heidelberg; s. of Hermann and Annemarie Hampe; m. Sibylle Hauck 1971; one d.; ed Falckenberg Schule, Munich, Univs. of Vienna and Munich and Syracuse Univ., USA; Deputy Dir Schauspielhaus, Zürich 1965–70; Dir Nat. Theatre, Mannheim 1972–75, Cologne Opera 1975–95, Dresden Music Festival; directs opera at La Scala, Milan, Covent Garden, London, Paris Opera, Salzburg and Edin. Festivals, Munich, Stockholm, Cologne, Geneva, Brussels, Zürich, San Francisco, Sydney, Los Angeles, Tokyo; directs drama at Bavarian State Theatre, Munich Schauspielhaus, Zürich, etc.; directs and acts in film and TV; Prof. State Music Acad., Cologne and Cologne Univ.; mem. Bd European Acad. of Music, Bayern; theatre-bldg consultant; Bundesverdienstkreuz, Commendatore Ordine al Merito (Italy), Goldenes Ehrenabzeichen des Landes Salzburg, Olivier West End Award 1983. *Address:* Tiergartenstrasse 36, 01219 Dresden, Germany.

HAMPEL, Sir Ronald Claus, Kt, MA; British businessman; b. 31 May 1932, Shrewsbury; s. of Karl Victor Hugo Hampel and Rutgard Emil Klothilde Hauck; m. Jane Bristed Hewson 1957; three s. one d.; ed Canford School, Wimborne, Dorset, Corpus Christi Coll., Cambridge; nat. service 2nd Lt Royal Horse Artillery 1950–51; joined ICI 1955; Vice-Pres. ICI Agrochemicals USA 1973–75, ICI Latin America 1975–77; ICI Gen. Man. Commercial 1977–80; Chair. ICI Paints 1980–83, ICI Agrochemicals 1983–85; Dir ICI 1985–99,

COO ICI 1991–93, CEO ICI 1993–95, Chair. 1995–99; Chair. United News and Media (now United Business Media) 1999–2002; Dir (non-exec.) Powell Duffryn 1983–88, Commercial Union 1987–95, British Aerospace 1989–2002, ALCOA 1995–, Teijin 1999–; Dir American Chamber of Commerce 1985–90; mem. Exec. Cttee British North America Cttee 1989–96, Listed Companies Advisory Cttee, London Stock Exchange 1996–99, Nomination Cttee, NY Stock Exchange 1996–99; mem. European Round Table 1995–99, UK Advisory Bd INSEAD 1994–99, Advisory Cttee Karlpreis Aachen 1997–2001, Exec. Cttee All England Lawn Tennis Club 1994–; Chair. Cttee on Corp. Governance 1995–97; Chair. Bd of Trustees Eden Project 2000–; Hon. Fellow Corpus Christi Coll. Cambridge 1997. *Leisure interests:* tennis, golf, skiing. *Address:* c/o United Business Media PLC, Ludgate House, 245 Blackfriars Road, London, SE1 9GY, England. *Telephone:* (20) 7921-5000.

HAMPSHIRE, Sir Stuart, Kt, FBA; British university professor; b. 1 Oct. 1914, Healing, Lincs.; s. of George N. Hampshire and Marie West; m. 1st Renée Orde-Lees 1961 (died 1980); m. 2nd Nancy Cartwright 1985; two d.; ed Repton School and Balliol Coll., Oxford; Fellow, All Souls Coll., Oxford 1936–45; service in army and Foreign Office 1940–46; lecturer in Philosophy Univ. Coll., London 1947–50; Fellow, New Coll., Oxford 1950–55; Research Fellow, All Souls Coll., Oxford 1955–60; Prof. of Philosophy, Univ. Coll., London 1960–63; Prof. and Chair. Dept of Philosophy, Princeton Univ. 1963–70; Warden of Wadham Coll., Oxford 1970–84; Prof. Stanford Univ. 1984–91; Fellow, British Acad., American Acad. of Arts and Sciences; Hon. DLitt (Glasgow) 1973. *Publications:* Spinoza 1951, Thought and Action 1959, Freedom of the Individual 1965, Modern Writers and Other Essays 1969, Freedom of Mind and Other Essays 1971, Morality and Pessimism 1972, The Socialist Idea (joint ed.) 1975, Two Theories of Morality 1977, Public and Private Morality (ed.) 1978, Morality and Conflict 1983, Innocence and Experience 1989, Justice Is Conflict 1990. *Address:* 7 Beaumont Road, The Quarry, Headington, Oxford, England. *Telephone:* (1865) 761688.

HAMPSHIRE, Susan, OBE; British actress; b. 12 May 1942; d. of the late George Kenneth Hampshire and the late June Hampshire; m. 1st Pierre Granier-Deferre 1967 (dissolved 1974); one s. (one d. deceased); m. 2nd Sir Eddie Kulukundis (q.v.) 1981; ed Hampshire School, Knightsbridge; Hon. DLitt (City Univ., London) 1984, (St Andrews) 1986, (Exeter) 2001, Dr hc (Kingston) 1994, Hon. D.Arts (Pine Manor Coll., Boston, USA) 1994; Emmy Award, Best Actress for The Forsyte Saga 1970, for The First Churchills 1971, for Vanity Fair 1973, E. Poe Prize du Film Fantastique, Best Actress for Malpertius 1972. *Stage roles include:* Expresso Bongo 1958, Follow that Girl 1960, Fairy Tales of New York 1961, Marion Dangerfield in Ginger Man 1963, Kate Hardcastle in She Stoops to Conquer 1966, On Approval 1966, Mary in The Sleeping Prince 1968, Nora in A Doll's House 1972, Katharina in The Taming of the Shrew 1974, Peter in Peter Pan 1974, Jeannette in Romeo and Jeannette 1975, Rosalind in As You Like It 1975, Miss Julie 1975, Elizabeth in The Circle 1976, Ann Whitefield in Man and Superman 1977, Siri Von Essen in Tribades 1978, Victorine in An Audience Called Edouard 1978, Irene in The Crucifer of Blood 1979, Ruth Carson in Night and Day 1979, Elizabeth in The Revolt 1980, Stella Drury in House Guest 1981, Elvira in Blithe Spirit 1986, Marie Stopes in Married Love, The Countess in A Little Night Music 1989, Mrs Anna in The King and I 1990, Gertie in Noel and Gertie 1991, The Countess of Marshwood in Relative Values 1993, Suzanna Andler in Suzanna Andler, Alicia Christie in Black Chiffon 1995–96, Sheila Carter in Relatively Speaking 2000–01, Felicity Marshwood in Relative Values 2002. *TV roles:* Andromeda, Fleur Forsyte in The Forsyte Saga, Becky Sharp in Vanity Fair, Sarah Churchill, Duchess of Marlborough, in The First Churchills, Glencora Palliser in The Pallisers, Lady Melford in Dick Turpin 1980, Madeline Neroni in The Barchester Chronicles 1982, Martha in Leaving 1984, Martha in Leaving II 1985, Going to Pot 1985, Don't Tell Father, Esme Harkness in The Grand 1996–98, Miss Catto in Coming Home 1998–99, Miss Catto in Nancherrow, Molly in Monarch of the Glen 1999–2003, Lucilla Drake in Sparkling Cyanide. *Films include:* During One Night 1961, The Three Lives of Thomasina 1963, Night Must Fall 1964, Wonderful Life 1964, Paris in August, The Fighting Prince of Donegal 1966, Monte Carlo or Bust 1969, Rogan, David Copperfield, Living Free 1972, A Time for Loving 1970, Malpertius 1972, Neither the Sea Nor the Sand, Roses and Green Peppers, Bang. *Publications:* Susan's Story (autobiographical account of dyslexia) 1981, The Maternal Instinct, Lucy Jane at the Ballet 1985, Lucy Jane on Television 1989, Trouble Free Gardening 1989, Every Letter Counts 1990, Lucy Jane and the Dancing Competition 1991, Easy Gardening 1991, Lucy Jane and the Russian Ballet 1993, Rosie's First Ballet Lesson 1997. *Leisure interests:* gardening, music. *Address:* c/o Chatto & Linnit Ltd, 123A King's Road, London, SW3 4PL, England. *Telephone:* (20) 7352-7722. *Fax:* (20) 7352-3450.

HAMPSON, Christopher, CBE, BEng; Canadian/British business executive; b. 6 Sept. 1931, Montreal; s. of Harold Ralph Hampson and Geraldine Mary Hampson (née Smith); m. Joan Margaret Cassils Evans 1954; two s. three d.; ed Ashbury Coll. School, Ottawa, McGill Univ.; joined Canadian Industries Ltd (subsidiary of ICI) 1956, Vice-Pres., Dir 1973; seconded to ICI PLC as Gen. Man. Planning 1978, Sr Vice-Pres. Canadian Industries Ltd 1982, fmr CEO, Dir ICI Australia Ltd, Exec. Dir, mem. Bd ICI 1987–94; Chair. Yorks. Electricity Group 1995–97, RMC Group 1996–2002, British Biotech PLC 1998–2002; Dir TransAlta Corp. *Leisure interests:* gardening, tennis, skiing. *Address:* 77 Kensington Court, London, W8 5DT, England. *Telephone:* (20) 7937-0325. *Fax:* (20) 7376-1906.

HAMPSON, Norman, MA, DUniv; British professor of history; b. 8 April 1922, Leyland, Lancs.; s. of Frank Hampson and Elizabeth Jane Hampson (née Fazackerley); m. Jacqueline Gardin 1948; two d.; ed Manchester Grammar School and Univ. Coll. Oxford; war service in RN and Free French Navy 1941–45; Lecturer and Sr Lecturer in French History, Univ. of Manchester 1948–67; Prof. of Modern History, Univ. of Newcastle-upon-Tyne 1967–74; Prof. of History, Univ. of York 1974–89; Hon. DLitt (Edin.) 1989. *Publications:* La Marine de l'An II 1959, A Social History of the French Revolution 1963, The Enlightenment 1968, The Life and Opinions of Maximilien Robespierre 1974, Danton 1978, Will and Circumstance: Montesquieu, Rousseau and the French Revolution 1983, Prelude to Terror 1988, Saint-Just 1991, The Perfidy of Albion 1998, Not Really What You'd Call a War 2001. *Leisure interest:* gardening. *Address:* 305 Hull Road, York, YO10 3LU, England. *Telephone:* (1904) 412661.

HAMPSON, Sir Stuart, Kt, MA; British business executive; b. 7 Jan. 1947; s. of Kenneth Hampson and Mary Hampson; m. Angela McLaren 1973; one s. one d.; ed Royal Masonic School, Bushey, St John's Coll., Oxford; with Board of Trade 1969–72; FCO Mission to UN, Geneva 1972–74; Dept of Prices and Consumer Protection 1974–79; Dept of Trade 1979–82; with John Lewis Partnership 1982–, Dir of Research and Expansion 1986, Deputy Chair. 1989–93, Chair. 1993–. *Address:* John Lewis Partnership, 171 Victoria Street, London, SW1E 5NN, England. *Telephone:* (20) 7828-1000.

HAMPSON, (Walter) Thomas, BA; American baritone; b. 28 June 1955, Elkhart, Ind.; s. of Walter Hampson and Ruthye Hampson; one d.; ed Eastern Washington Univ., Fort Wright Coll., Music Acad. of West; with Düsseldorf Ensemble 1981–84; title role in Der Prinz von Homburg, Darmstadt 1982; debut in Cologne, Munich, Santa Fé 1982–84, Metropolitan Opera, NY, Vienna Staatsoper, Covent Garden 1986, La Scala, Milan, Deutsche Oper, Berlin 1989, Carnegie Hall, San Francisco Opera 1990; has performed with Wiener Philharmoniker, NY Philharmonic, London Philharmonic and Chicago Symphony orchestras; Hon. RAM 1996; Edison Prize, Netherlands 1990, 1992, Grand Prix du Disque 1990, 1996, Cannes Classical Award 1994, Echo Klassik 1995, EMI Artist of the Year 1997, Deutsche Schallplattenkritik Award 1999, Cecilia Award 2000, Diapason D'Or Award 2000; Citation of Merit, Vienna Kammersänger 1999. *Roles include:* Guglielmo in Così fan tutte, the Count in Le Nozze di Figaro, Billy Budd (title role), Hamlet (title role) 1976, Il Barbiere di Siviglia (title role), Posa in Don Carlos, Riccardo in I Puritani 1997. *Recordings include:* Schubert's Winterreise 1997, Das Lied von der Erde 1997, Belshazzar's Feast 1998, Operetta Album with London Philharmonic 1999, Verdi Arias with Orchestra of the Age of Enlightenment 2001. *Address:* c/o IMG Artists Europe, Media House, 616 Chiswick High Road, London W4 5RX, England (Office). *Website:* www.thomashampson.com (Office).

HAMPTON, Christopher James, CBE, MA, FRSL; British playwright; b. 26 Jan. 1946, Fayal, the Azores, Portugal; s. of Bernard Patrick and Dorothy Patience (née Herrington) Hampton; m. Laura Margaret de Holesch 1971; two d.; ed Lancing Coll., New Coll., Oxford; wrote first play When Did You Last See My Mother? 1964; Resident Dramatist, Royal Court Theatre 1968–70; freelance writer 1970–; Evening Standard Award for best comedy 1970, 1983 and for best play 1986; Plays and Players London Critics' Award for best play 1970, 1973, 1985; Los Angeles Drama Critics Circle Award 1974; Laurence Olivier Award for Best Play 1986; New York Drama Critics' Circle Award for Best Foreign Play 1987, Prix Italia 1988, Writers Guild of America Screenplay Award 1989, Oscar for Best Adapted Screenplay 1989; BAFTA for best screenplay 1990, Special Jury Award, Cannes Film Festival 1995, Tony Awards for Best Original Score (lyrics) and Best Book of a Musical 1995, Scott Moncrieff Prize 1997; Officier, Ordre des Arts et des Lettres 1998. *Plays:* When Did You Last See My Mother? 1967, Total Eclipse 1969, The Philanthropist 1970, Savages 1973, Treats 1976, Able's Will (TV) 1978, Tales from Hollywood 1983, Les Liaisons Dangereuses 1985, White Chameleon 1991, Alice's Adventures Underground 1994, The Talking Cure 2002. *Translations include:* Marya (Babel) 1967, Uncle Vanya, Hedda Gabler 1970, A Doll's House 1971 (film 1974), Don Juan 1972, Tales from the Vienna Woods 1977 (film 1979), Don Juan Comes Back from the War 1978, The Wild Duck 1980, Ghosts 1983, Tartuffe 1984, Faith, Hope and Charity 1989, Art 1996, An Enemy of the People 1997, The Unexpected Man 1998, Conversations After a Burial 2000, Life × Three 2001, Three Sisters 2003. *Directed:* (films) Carrington 1995, The Secret Agent 1996, Imagining Argentina 2003. *Publications:* When Did You Last See My Mother? 1967, Total Eclipse 1969 (film 1995), The Philanthropist 1970, Savages 1973, Treats 1976, Able's Will (TV) 1978, The History Man (TV adaptation of novel by Malcolm Bradbury,) 1981, The Portage to San Cristobal of A.H. (play adaptation of novel by George Steiner) 1983, Tales from Hollywood 1983, The Honorary Consul (film adaptation of a novel by Graham Greene) 1983, Les Liaisons Dangereuses (adaptation of a novel by Laclos) 1985, Hotel du Lac (TV adaptation of a novel by Anita Brookner,) 1986, The Good Father (film adaptation of a novel by Peter Prince) 1986, Wolf at the Door (film) 1986, Dangerous Liaisons (film) 1988, The Ginger Tree (adaptation of novel by Oswald Wynd, TV) 1989, White Chameleon 1991, Sunset Boulevard (book and lyrics with Don Black) 1993, Alice's Adventures Underground (with Martha Clarke) 1994, Carrington (film) 1995, Mary Reilly (film) 1996, The Secret Agent (film) 1996, Nostromo (screenplay) 1997, The Quiet American (screenplay) 2002, Collected Screenplays 2002, The Talking Cure 2002. *Leisure interests:* travel, cinema. *Address:* 2 Kensington Park Gardens, London, W11, England. *Telephone:* (20) 7229-2188. *Fax:* (20) 7229-7644 (Office).

HAMZA, Ahmed Amin, PhD; Egyptian professor of experimental physics; b. 8 March 1941, Giza; s. of late Amin Hamza and Hanim Abdel Meguid; m. Sahar Khalil 1968; three d.; ed Saaidiya Secondary School, Giza and Ain Shams Univ. Cairo; Head, Printing Dept Cairo Dyeing & Finishing Co. 1962–72; Lecturer in Physics, Univ. of Mansoura 1972–76, Asst Prof. 1976–81, Prof. of Experimental Physics 1981–, Head, Dept of Physics 1984–86, Vice-Dean, Faculty of Science 1986–92, Vice-Pres. Univ. for Community and Environmental Devt 1992–94; Pres. Univ. of Mansoura 1994–2001; mem. Cttee for Promoting Asst Profs. of Physics 1985–; mem. Cttee (affiliated to Egyptian Acad. of Science and Tech.) for Researches in Textile Industries 1989–; Fellow, Royal Microscopical Soc. (Oxford), Inst. of Physics (London); mem. Int. Soc. for Optical Eng; Dr hc (Tech. Univ. of Liberec, Czech Repub.) 2000; Egyptian Nat. Award in Physics 1987; Sr Academic Prize and Certificate Distinction of the Univ. of Mansoura in Basic Sciences 1992; First-Class Medal for Distinction 1995; State Prize of Merit in Basic Sciences 1997. *Publications:* Interferometry of Fibrous Materials (co-author) 1990; numerous publs in fields of interferometry, fibre optics, colour measurement and polymer physics. *Leisure interest:* playing football. *Address:* University of Mansoura, Faculty of Science, El-Gomhoria Street, 35516 (Office); 6 Korash Street, 6th District, Nasr City, Cairo, Egypt (Home). *Telephone:* (50) 2259427 (Office); (2) 22462549 (Home). *Fax:* (50) 247900. *E-mail:* hamzaaa@.mans.edu.eg (Office); hamzaaa@idsc.net.eg (Home). *Website:* www.mans.eun.eg (Office).

HAMZAH, Tengku Tan Sri Datuk Razaleigh (see Razaleigh).

HAMZAH HAZ, BA; Indonesian politician; b. 15 Feb. 1940, Ketapang, W Kalimantan; m. (two wives); twelve c.; ed Sr Econ. High School, Ketapang, Tanjungpura Univ.; newspaper journalist, Pontianak; teacher of Econs Tanjungpura Univ.; mem. W Kalimantan Prov. Legis. Council 1968–71; mem. Nahdlatul Ulama (NU; later amalgamated into United Devt Party – PPP), Leader PPP 1999–; mem. House of Reps. 1971–; fmr State Minister of Investment, Co-ordinating Minister for People's Welfare and Eradication of Poverty; Vice-Pres. of Indonesia 2001–. *Address:* Office of the Vice-President, Jalan Merdeka Selatan 6, Jakarta, Indonesia (Office). *Telephone:* (21) 363539 (Office).

HAMŽÍK, Pavol, JUDr; Slovak politician, diplomatist and university lecturer; b. 20 Aug. 1954, Trenčín; s. of Pavol Hamžík and Júlia Hamžíková; m. Dagmar Hamžíková (née Kiššová) 1976; two d.; ed Komensky Univ., Bratislava, Diplomatic Acad., Moscow; lawyer 1978–84; joined Czechoslovak Foreign Ministry 1984; Consul in Copenhagen 1985–89; studied at Diplomatic Acad., Moscow 1989–91; Vice-Chair. del. to int. disarmament negotiations, Vienna 1991; mem. del. to CSCE 1991–92, Pres. CSCE Steering Group on crisis in Yugoslavia 1992, head Slovak del. to CSCE 1993, head Slovak Perm. Mission to CSCE 1993–94; Slovak Amb. to Germany 1994–96; Foreign Minister 1996–98; f. Party of Civic Understanding (SOP) Feb. 1998, Chair. 1999–2002; MP 1998–2002, mem. Defence and Security Cttee 2001–02; Vice Prime Minister 1998–2001; Deputy of Slovakia in European Convention; lecturer, mem. of Scientific Bd Faculty of Political Sciences and Int. Relations, Matej Bell Univ. 1997–; Golden Biatec, Informal Economic Forum 2000. *Leisure interests:* history, skiing, literature, tennis. *Address:* Strmy Vrsok 10, 841 06 Bratislava (Home); Národná rada SR, nám Slobody 1, 813 70 Bratislava, Slovakia. *E-mail:* rk@sop.sk (Office). *Website:* www.sop.sk (Office).

HAN HUAIZHI, Lt-Gen.; Chinese army official; b. 1922, Pingshan Co., Hebei Prov.; Asst to the Chief of the PLA Gen. Staff 1980–85; Deputy, 6th NPC 1983–87, 7th NPC 1988–; Dir of the Mil. Training Dept under the PLA Gen. Staff 1984–85; Deputy Chief of the PLA Gen. Staff 1985; Lt-Gen. PLA 1985–; Chair. Sports Comm. 1990–; mem. Nat. Degrees Cttee Oct. 1988–. *Address:* Chinese People's Liberation Army General Staff, Beijing, People's Republic of China.

HAN SEUNG-SOO, PhD; South Korean politician, economist and United Nations official; b. 1936, Chunchon, Kangwon Prov.; m.; two c.; ed Yonsei Univ., Seoul Nat. Univ. and Univ. of York, UK; taught econs at Univ. of York, UK 1965–68, Univ. of Cambridge 1968–70; Prof. of Econs. Seoul Nat. Univ. 1970–88; Sr Fulbright Scholar, Dept of Econs, Harvard Univ. 1985–86; Visiting Prof. Univ. of Tokyo 1986–87; currently Distinguished Visiting Prof., Yonsei Univ.; served as adviser to Bank of Korea, Korea Export–Import Bank, Korea Industrial Bank, Korea Chamber of Comm. and Industry, Fed. of Korea Industries and Korea Int. Trade Asscn; consultant to World Bank and UN Econ. Comm. for Asia and the Pacific (ESCAP), seconded by World Bank as Financial Adviser to Govt of Jordan 1974–76; Pres. Korea Int. Econ. Asscn 1983–84; first Chair. Korea Trade Comm. 1987–88; elected mem. of Nat. Ass., Repub. of Korea 1988; Minister of Trade and Industry 1988–90; Amb. to USA 1993–94; Chair. Council of the Repub. of Korea Group of the Inter-Parl. Union (IPU); Chief of Staff to Pres. of Repub. of Korea 1994–95; Deputy Prime Minister and Minister of Finance and Economy 1996–97; Minister of Foreign Affairs and Trade 2001–02; Pres. 56th Session of UN Gen. Ass. 2001; f. Korean Acad. of Industrial Tech. (KAITEC) 1989; Pres. Korea–Britain Soc., Korea–UK Forum for the Future, Alumni Asscn of the Grad. School of Public Admin of Seoul Nat. Univ.; mem. Royal Econ. Soc., Korean Econ. Asscn, Int. Inst. of Public Finance, Seoul Forum for Int. Affairs, Korean Council on

Foreign Relations, Korean Soc. for Future Studies, Korean Asscn of Public Admin, Bretton Woods Club; Hon. Prof. Univ. of York, Hon. DUniv (York) 1997; Order of Public Service Merit (First Class, Blue Stripes), Order of Industrial Merit (Bronze Tower), Order of Nat. Security Merit (Cheonsu Medal); Sixth European Communities Prize 1971, Columbia Law School/ Parker School Award for Distinguished Int. Service 1997. *Publications include:* Taxes in Britain and the EEC: The Problem of Harmonization 1968 (jtly), Britain and the Common Market (jtly) 1971, The Growth and Function of the European Budget 1971, The Health of Nations 1985; numerous articles in learned journals and press commentaries in both Korean and English. *Address:* c/o General Assembly, United Nations, New York, NY 10017, USA (Office).

HAN SHAO GONG; Chinese writer; b. 1 Jan. 1953, Chang Sha; s. of Han Ke Xian and Zhang Jing Xing; m. Liang Yu Li 1980; one d.; ed Hunan Teacher's Univ.; Council mem. Chinese Writers' Asscn 1984; Vice-Chair. Hunan Youth Union 1985; Chief Ed. of Hainan Review 1988; Pres. Hainan Literature Correspondence Coll. 1988; Chair. Hainan Writers Asscn 1995; mem. Standing Cttee CPCC Hainan Prov. 1988; Chair. Hainan Artists' Asscn 2000; mem. Council Chinese Artists' Union 2001; Prize for Best Chinese Stories 1980, 1981. *Film:* The Deaf and Mute 1983. *Publications:* Biography of Ren Bi Shi 1979; (collections of short stories): Yue Nan 1981, Flying Across the Blue Sky 1983, New Stories 1986, Fondness for Shoes 1994, Red Apple is an Exception 1994; To Face the Mystical and Wide World (selection of articles) 1985, The Other Shore (selection of prose pieces) 1988, The Murder 1990, Pa Pa Pa and Seduction and Femme Femme Femme 1990–91, Homecoming 1992, The Play and Holy War 1993, Raving of a Pedestrian in the Night 1994, The Thought of the Sea 1994, Dictionary of Ma-Bridge (novel) 1995; trans: The Unbearable Lightness of Being (Kundera) 1987, The Book of Disquiet (F. Pessoa) 1999, Collected Works (10 Vols) 2001. *Leisure interest:* Chinese calligraphy. *Address:* Room 2-602, Hainan Teachers' University, Haikou 571100, Hainan (Home); 1st Building, Hainan Plaza, 69 Guoxing Road, Haikou, People's Republic of China (Office). *Telephone:* (898) 5882748 (Home); (898) 5336231 (Office). *Fax:* (898) 53328034 (Office). *E-mail:* hanshaog@ public.hk.hi.cn (Home).

HAN SUNG-JOO; South Korean politician; b. 1940; ed Seoul Nat. Univ. and Univ. of Calif. Berkeley; fmr Vice-Chair. Int. Political Science Asscn; fmr columnist, Newsweek; Adviser to Govt on foreign affairs, nat. defence and unification since late 1970s; Minister of Foreign Affairs 1993–95; Prof. of Political Science and Dir Ilmin Int. Relations Inst., Korea Univ., Seoul; Deputy Chair. for Asia Pacific, Trilateral Comm.; Chair. East Asia Vision Group; Co-Chair. Council for Security Co-operation in the Asia-Pacific. *Publication:* Changing Values in Asia: Their Impact on Governance and Development (ed.). *Address:* Korea University 1-5-ga, Anam-dong, Seongbuk-gu, Seoul, Republic of Korea.

HAN WAN-SANG; South Korean politician and professor of sociology; b. 18 March 1936; s. of Han Young-Jik; m. 1966; three d.; ed in USA; Prof. of Sociology, Seoul Nat. Univ. 1970–; adviser to Kim Young Sam; Deputy Prime Minister and National Unification Bd Minister 1993; Chair. Korea Cable Communication Comm. 1994–; Pres. Korea Nat. Open Univ. 1994–. *Leisure interest:* tennis. *Address:* 169 Dongseong-dong, Jongno-gu, Seoul 110-791, Republic of Korea. *Telephone:* (2) 7404-114. *Fax:* (2) 744-5882.

HAN ZHAOSHAN; Chinese business executive; b. 1949, Yingkou, Liaoning Prov.; Vice-Dir Shuiyuan Township Agric. Machinery Factory, Yingkou 1970–83; founded Yingkou Great Wall Metal Product Factory 1983–92; Chair. and Gen. Man. Panpan Group Ltd 1992–. *Address:* Panpan Group Ltd, Yingkou, Liaoning Province, People's Republic of China (Office).

HAN ZHUBIN; Chinese politician; b. Feb. 1932, Harbin, Heilongjiang Prov.; ed Beijing Econs Corresp. Univ.; joined CCP 1950; fmr railway worker; fmr Vice-Sec., then Sec. Communist Youth League, Liuzhou Railway Bureau Cttee, Dir 1975–83; Dir and Party Sec. Shanghai Railway Bureau 1983–90; Vice-Sec. CCP Group and Sec. CCP Cttee for Discipline Inspection, Ministry of Railways 1990–92; Minister of Railways 1993–98; Deputy Head Leading Group for Beijing-Kowloon Railway Construction 1993–; Deputy Sec. Cen. Comm. for Discipline Inspection 1997–; Chair. Supreme People's Procuratorate 1998; mem. 14th and 15th Cen. Cttee CCP 1992–. *Address:* Supreme People's Procuratorate, 27 Donjiaamin Xiang, Beijing 100745, People's Republic of China.

HANAFUSA, Hidesaburo, PhD; Japanese biochemist; b. 12 Jan. 1929, Nishinomiya; m. Teruko Inoue 1958; one d.; ed Univ. of Osaka; Research Assoc. Research Inst. for Microbial Diseases, Univ. of Osaka 1958–61; Postdoctoral Fellow, Virus Lab. Univ. of Calif. Berkeley 1961–64; Visiting Scientist, Coll. de France, Paris 1964–66; Assoc. mem., Chief, Dept of Viral Oncology, Public Health Research Inst. of NY 1966–68, mem. 1968–73; Prof. Rockefeller Univ. 1973, Leon Hess Prof. 1986; Foreign Assoc. NAS; mem. editorial Bd Journal of Virology 1975–, Molecular Cell Biology 1984–; Harvey Lecturer 1980; H. T. Ricketts Award 1981; Albert Lasker Basic Medical Research Award 1982; Clowes Memorial Award 1986; Japan Culture Merit Award 1991; Alfred Sloan Prize 1993, Order of Culture 1995. *Publications:* contribs. on retroviruses and oncogenes to professional journals. *Address:* 500 East 63rd Street, New York, NY 10021, USA (Home).

HANAWA, Yoshikazu, BA; Japanese business executive; b. 14 March 1934, Tokyo; ed Tokyo Univ.; joined Nissan 1957, Pres. Nissan N America 1989, various marketing and planning positions, Exec. Vice-Pres. 1991–96, Pres. 1996–2000, CEO and Chair. 2000–. *Address:* Nissan Motor Co., 6-17-1 Ginza chome, Chuo-ku, Tokyo 104-8023, Japan (Office). *Telephone:* (3) 3543-5523 (Office). *Fax:* (3) 3544-0109 (Office). *Website:* www.nissan.co.jp (Office).

HANCOCK, Herbert Jeffrey (Herbie Hancock); American jazz pianist and composer; b. 12 April 1940, Chicago, Ill.; s. of Wayman Edward Hancock and Winnie Griffin; m. Gudrun Meixner 1968; ed Roosevelt Univ., Chicago, Manhattan School of Music and New School for Social Research; owner and Publr Hancock Music Co. 1962–; founder Hancock and Joe Productions 1989–; Pres. Harlem Jazz Music Center, Inc.; performed with Chicago Symphony Orchestra 1952, Coleman Hawkins, Chicago 1960, Donald Byrd 1960–63, Miles Davis Quintet 1963–68; recorded with Chick Corea; composed film music for: Blow Up 1966, The Spook Who Sat by the Door 1973, Death Wish 1974, A Soldier's Story 1984, Jo Jo Dancer, Your Life is Calling 1986, Action Jackson 1988, Colors 1988, Harlem Nights 1989, Livin' Large 1991; wrote score and appeared in film Round Midnight 1986 (Acad. Award Best Original Score 1986); mem. Nat. Acad. of Recording Arts and Sciences, Jazz Musicians Asscn, Nat. Acad. of TV Arts and Sciences, Broadcast Music; numerous awards including Citation of Achievement, Broadcast Music, Inc. 1963, Jay Award, Jazz Magazine 1964, Grammy Award for Best Rhythm and Blues Instrumental Performance 1983, 1984, for Best Jazz Instrumental Composition (co-composer) 1987, Best Jazz Instrumental Performance 1995. *Albums include:* Takin' Off 1963, Succotash 1964, Speak Like a Child 1968, Fat Albert Rotunda 1969, Mwandishi 1971, Crossings 1972, Sextant 1972, Headhunters 1973, Thrust 1974, The Best of Herbie Hancock 1974, Man-Child 1975, The Quintet 1977, V.S.O.P. 1977, Sunlight 1978, An Evening with Herbie Hancock and Chick Corea In Concert 1979, Feets Don't Fail Me Now 1979, Monster 1980, Greatest Hits 1980, Lite Me Up 1982, Future Shock 1983, Perfect Machine 1988, Jamming 1992, Cantaloupe Island 1994, Tribute to Miles 1994, Dis Is Da Drum 1995, The New Standard 1996, Gershwin's World 1998 (Grammy Award). *Address:* Hancock Music, 1880 Century Park East, Suite 1600, Los Angeles, CA 90067, USA.

HANDLEY, Eric Walter, CBE, MA, FBA; British professor of Greek; b. 12 Nov. 1926, Birmingham; s. of Alfred Walter Handley and A. Doris Cox; m. Carol Margaret Taylor 1952; ed King Edward's School, Birmingham and Trinity Coll. Cambridge; Asst Lecturer in Greek and Latin, Univ. Coll., London 1946, Lecturer 1949, Reader 1961, Prof. 1967, Prof. of Greek and Head of Greek Dept 1968–84; Dir of Inst. of Classical Studies, Univ. of London 1967–84; Regius Prof. of Greek, Cambridge Univ. 1984–94, Fellow of Trinity Coll. 1984–; Prof. of Ancient Literature, Royal Acad. of Arts 1990–; Foreign Sec. British Acad. 1979–88; Pres. Classical Asscn 1984–85, Soc. for the Promotion of Hellenic Studies 1993–96; Hon. Fellow, Univ. Coll., London 1989; Hon. RA; Cromer Greek Prize (jtly) 1958. *Publications:* The Telephus of Euripides (with John Rea) 1958, The Dyskolos of Menander 1965, Relire Ménandre (with A. Hurst) 1990, Aristophane (with J.-M. Bremer) 1993, Images of the Greek Theatre (with Richard Green) 1995; edns. of Greek literary papyri, papers in classical journals. *Leisure interests:* walking and travel. *Address:* Trinity College, Cambridge, CB2 1TQ, England. *Telephone:* (1223) 338400. *Fax:* (1223) 338564.

HANDLEY, Vernon George, BA, FRCM; British conductor; b. 11 Nov. 1930, Enfield; s. of Vernon Douglas and Claudia Lillian Handley; m. 1st Barbara Black 1954 (divorced); one s. one d. (one s. deceased); m. 2nd Victoria Parry-Jones (divorced); one s. one d.; m. 3rd Catherine Newby 1987; one s.; ed Enfield School, Balliol Coll., Oxford, Guildhall School of Music; Conductor, Oxford Univ. Musical Club and Union 1953–54, Oxford Univ. Dramatic Soc. 1953–54, Tonbridge Philharmonic Soc. 1958–61, Hatfield School of Music and Drama 1959–61, Proteus Choir 1962–81; Musical Dir and Conductor, Guildford Corpn and Conductor, Guildford Philharmonic Orchestra and Choir 1962–83; Assoc. Conductor, London Philharmonic Orchestra 1983–86 (Guest Conductor 1961–83); Prof. for Orchestra and Conducting, Royal Coll. of Music 1966–72, for Choral Class 1969–72; Prin. Conductor, Ulster Orchestra 1985–89, Malmö Symphony Orchestra 1985–89; Prin. Guest Conductor Royal Liverpool Philharmonic Orchestra 1989–95 (Conductor Laureate 1995–), Melbourne Symphony Orchestra 1992–95; Chief Conductor W Australian Symphony Orchestra 1993–; Assoc. Conductor Royal Philharmonic Orchestra 1994– (Guest Conductor 1961–94); Bournemouth Symphony Orchestra, BBC Welsh Orchestra, BBC Northern Symphony (now BBC Philharmonic) Orchestra, Ulster Orchestra, BBC Scottish Symphony Orchestra, New Philharmonia (now Philharmonia) Orchestra; conducted London Symphony Orchestra in int. series, London 1971; Fellow Goldsmiths' Coll., London 1987; tours of Germany 1966, 1980, S Africa 1974, Holland 1980, Sweden 1980, 1981, Germany, Sweden, Holland and France 1982–83, Australia 1986, Japan 1988, Australia 1989, 1991, 1992; Hon. R.C.M. 1970; Hon. mem. Royal Philharmonic Soc. 1989; Hon. DUniv (Surrey) 1980; Hon. DMus (Liverpool) 1992; Hon. DLitt (Bradford) 1998; Arnold Bax Memorial Medal for Conducting 1962; Conductor of the Year, British Composer's Guild 1974; Hi-Fi News Audio Award 1982; Gramophone Record of the Year 1986, 1989; British Phonographic Industry Award 1988. *Leisure interests:* bird photography, building furniture. *Address:* Cwm Cottage, Bettws, Abergavenny, Monmouthshire, NP7 7LG, Wales; Hen Gerrig, Pen-y-Fan, nr Monmouth (Gwent). *Telephone:* (1873) 890135.

HANDS, Terence David (Terry), BA; British theatre director; b. 9 Jan. 1941, Aldershot; s. of Joseph Ronald and Luise Bertha (Köhler) Hands; m. 1st Josephine Barstow 1964 (divorced 1967); m. 2nd Ludmila Mikael (divorced 1980); one d.; partner Julia Lintott; two s.; ed Woking Grammar School, Birmingham Univ., RADA; Founder-Dir Everyman Theatre, Liverpool 1964–66; Artistic Dir Theatregoround, RSC 1966; Assoc. Dir RSC 1967–77, Jt Artistic Dir 1978–86, Artistic Dir and Chief Exec. 1986–91, Dir Emer. 1991; Dir Clwyd Theatr Cymru 1997–; Consultant Dir Comédie Française 1975–80; Hon. Fellow Shakespeare Inst. 1990, Welsh Coll. of Music and Drama; Hon. DLit (Birmingham) 1988; Hon. LLD (Middx) 1997; Meilleur Spectacle de l'Année for Richard III 1972, for Twelfth Night 1976; Plays and Players Award for Henry VI 1977, Society of West End Theatre Award 1978 and 1984; Pragnell Shakespeare Award 1991; Evening Standard Best Dir Award 1993; Chevalier, Ordre des Arts et des Lettres. *Productions:* over 50 plays with RSC, 5 with Comédie Française, 2 with Burgtheater, Vienna, one opera at Paris Opera House, one at Covent Garden, London, one at Bremen, 15 at Clwyd Theatr Cymru; Women Beware Women, Teatro Stabile di Genova, Italy; Arden of Faversham, Schauspielhaus, Zürich; Hamlet, Paris 1994, Merry Wives of Windsor, Oslo 1995, Kongsemnerne 1996, The Seagull 1998; recording: Murder in the Cathedral 1976; transl. (with Barbara Wright), The Balcony (Genet) 1971, Pleasure and Repentance 1976, Henry V (ed. Sally Beauman) 1976, Cyrano de Bergerac (TV). *Translation:* Hamlet, into French. *Address:* Clwyd Theatr Cymru, Mold, Flintshire, CH7 1YA, N Wales. *Telephone:* (1352) 756331.

HANEGBI, Tzachi, BA; Israeli politician; b. 1957, Jerusalem; m.; three c.; ed Hebrew Univ. of Jerusalem; served in an Israeli Defence Forces paratroopers unit 1974–77; Pres. Hebrew Univ. Student Union 1979–80, Nat. Union of Israeli Students 1980–82; Adviser to Minister of Foreign Affairs 1984–86; Bureau Dir, Prime Minister's Office 1986–88; mem. Knesset (Parl.) 1988–, mem. Knesset Foreign Affairs and Defence Cttee, Cttee on Constitution, Law and Justice, Knesset House Cttee, Cttee on Labour and Social Welfare, Cttee on Educ. and Culture 1988–92; Head (in rotation) Econ. Affairs Cttee; mem. Cttee on Constitution, Law and Justice 1992–96; Minister of Health 1996–97, Minister of Justice 1997–2001, of the Environment March 2001–; mem. Likud-Tzomet-Gesher political group. *Address:* Ministry of the Environment, PO Box 34033, 5 Kanfei Nesharim Street, Givat Shaul, Jerusalem 95464, Israel (Office). *Telephone:* 2-6553745 (Office). *Fax:* 2-6553752 (Office). *E-mail:* l_sar@environment.gov.il (Office). *Website:* www.sviva.gov.il (Office).

HANEKOM, Derek; South African politician; b. 1953; Chair. Man. Cttee Nat. Rural Devt Forum; mem. ANC; fmr ANC Co-ordinator of Land and Agricultural Devt; Minister of Land Affairs 1994–99, of Agric. 1996–99; arrested 1977 for protesting against detentions, imprisoned for ANC activities 1983–86; in exile in Zimbabwe 1987–90. *Address:* c/o Ministry of Agriculture and Land Affairs, Private Bag X844, Pretoria 0001, South Africa.

HANFT, Ruth, PhD; American health policy consultant; b. 12 July 1929; d. of Ethel Schechter and Max Samuels; m. Herbert Hanft 1951; one s. one d.; ed School of Industrial and Labor Relations, Cornell Univ., Hunter Coll. and George Washington Univ.; Social Science Analyst, Social Security Admin. 1964–66; Program Analyst, Office of Econ. Opportunity 1966–68, Dept of Health, Educ. and Welfare 1968–72; Sr Research Assoc., Inst. of Medicine, NAS 1972–76; Deputy Asst Sec., US Dept of Health and Human Services 1977–81; Health Policy Consultant 1981–88; Visiting Prof., Dartmouth Medical School 1976–; Consultant, Research Prof. Dept of Health Services and Admin., George Washington Univ. 1988–91, Prof. 1991–95, consultant 1995–; mem. Inst. of Medicine, NAS; Fellow Hastings Inst.; Walter Patenge Medal of Public Service. *Publications:* Hospital Cost Containment (with M. Zubkoff and I. Raskin) 1978, Improving Health Care Management in the Workplace (with J. Rossow and R. Zager) 1985, Physicians and Hospitals: Changing Dynamics in The Health Policy Agenda (Ed. M. Lewin) 1985; Human in Vitro Fertilization; Political, Legal and Ethical Issues, in Gynecology and Obstetrics Vol. 5 Chapter 98 1984, Technology in American Health Care (with Alan B. Cohen) 2003; articles in professional journals. *Leisure interests:* gardening, needlepoint, travel. *Address:* 3340 Brookside Drive, Charlottesville, VA 22901, USA (Home). *Telephone:* (434) 295-8674 (Home). *Fax:* (434) 295-8675 (Home). *E-mail:* hrhanft@aol.com (Home).

HANGST, Jeffrey Scott; Danish professor of physics; Assoc. Prof., later Prof. Dept of Physics and Astronomy, Univ. of Aarhus; Physics Co-ordinator Laser Spectroscopy Lab., Athena collaboration project, CERN, Geneva, Switzerland (co-ordinated research by 39 physicists in 10 insts); European Physical Soc. Accelerator Prize 1996. *Address:* Department of Physics and Astronomy, University of Aarhus, Ny Munkegade, Aarhus C 8000, Denmark (Office). *Telephone:* 89-42-37-51 (Office). *Fax:* 86-12-07-40 (Office). *E-mail:* hangst@phys.au.dk (Office). *Website:* www.phys.au.dk (Office).

HANIN, Roger (pseudonym of Roger Paul Lévy); French actor and director; b. 20 Oct. 1925, Algiers; s. of Joseph Lévy and Victorine Hanin; m. 2nd Christine Gouze-Renal 1959; one d.; ed Faculté Mixte de Médecine et de Pharmacie, Algiers; Dir Pau Festival; producer, Lucrèce Borgia 1979 (play); author and producer, Argent mon bel amour (play) 1983; numerous stage and TV appearances, including Shakespearean roles; Chevalier, Ordre nat. du Mérite, Dramatic Art Grand Prize, Enghiem 1972, Médaille Achir, Algeria 2000. *Films include:* Le Protecteur (also Dir) 1973, Big Guns 1974, L'Intrépide 1975, Le Faux Cul (also Dir) 1975, Le coup de Sirocco, Le Sucre 1978, Le Grand Pardon 1981, La Baraka 1982, L'Etincelle 1984, La Galette du Roi 1985, Train d'enfer (also Dir) 1985, Dernier été à Tanger 1986, La Rumba (also Dir) 1987, L'Orchestre Rouge 1989, Jean Galmot, aventurier 1990, Le Grand Pardon II 1992. *Publications:* plays: Ciel, où sont passées les dattes de tes oasis? 1968,

Virgule 1974; books: L'Ours en lambeaux 1981, Le Voyage d'Arsène 1985, Les Gants Blancs 1994, L'hotel de la vieille lune 1998, Dentelles 2000, Lettre à un ami mystérieux 2001. *Leisure interests:* basketball, table-tennis, waterpolo, boxing. *Address:* 9 rue du Boccador, 75008 Paris, France.

HANKEL, Wilhelm; German economist and professor; b. 10 Jan. 1929, Danzig; s. of Oskar and Jenny (née Schoffmann) Hankel; m. Uta Wömpner; three d.; ed Univs. of Mainz and Amsterdam; worked in Cen. Planning Bureau of Netherlands Govt 1951; subsequently joined Deutsche Bundesbank; served in Ministry of Econ. Co-operation and later in Foreign Ministry 1954–57; with Berliner Bank, Berlin and Kreditanstalt für Wiederaufbau, Frankfurt am Main 1957–68; Dir Money and Credit Dept, Fed. Ministry of the Economy and Finance 1968–72; Pres. Hessische Landesbank, Girozentrale, Frankfurt am Main 1972–74; lecturer, Univ. of Frankfurt 1966–70, Hon. Prof. 1971–; Monetary Adviser EEC, Brussels 1974–76; Visiting Prof., Harvard, Georgetown and Johns Hopkins Univs., USA and Wissenschaftszentrum, Berlin. *Publications:* Die zweite Kapitalverteilung 1961, Währungspolitik 1971, Heldensagen der Wirtschaft oder schöne heile Wirtschaftswelt 1975, Der Ausweg aus der Krise 1976, Weltwirtschaft 1977, Caesar 1978, Gegenkurs, von der Schuldenkrise zur Vollbeschaftigung 1984, Keynes, Die Entschlüsselung des Kapitalismus 1986, Vorsicht, unser Geld 1989, Eine Mark für Deutschland 1990, Dollar und Ecu, Leitwährungen im Wettstreit 1992, Die sieben Todsünden der deutschen Vereinigung 1993, Das grosse Geldtheater 1995, Die Euro-Klage. Warum die Währungsunion scheitern muss (jtly.) 1998; various articles, lectures, etc. *Leisure interests:* literature, music. *Address:* Berghausenerstrasse 190, 53639 Königswinter 21, Germany. *Telephone:* (2244) 7447.

HANKES-DRIELSMA, Claude Dunbar; British business strategist; b. 8 March 1949; with Robert Fleming & Co., Ltd 1972–74, Dir 1974–77; Chair. Man. Cttee Price Waterhouse and Partners 1983–89, Action Resource Centre 1986–91; Adviser to the Bd of Corange (Boehringer Mannheim) 1988–94; mem. Gov. Council, Business in the Community 1986–91, Pres.'s Cttee 1988–91; Deputy Chair. Leutwiler and Partners Ltd 1992–96; assisted Dr. Fritz Leutwiler in his role as ind. mediator between SA Govt and foreign banks 1985/86; Nobel Ind. Report 1991; Chair. Advisory Cttee to Jordan on Strategic Econ. Policy Matters 1993–94; Dir Shaw & Bradley 1993–; Trustee and Adviser St George's House, Windsor Castle 2000–; Trustee Windsor Leadership Trust 1998– (Chair. 2000–); Hon. Fellow Corpus Christi Coll. Oxford. *Publication:* The Dangers of the Banking System: Funding Country Deficits 1975. *Leisure interests:* gardening, walking, skiing, reading, ancient art. *Address:* Stanford Place, Faringdon, Oxon., SN7 8EX, England. *Telephone:* (1367) 240547. *Fax:* (1367) 242853. *E-mail:* office@stanfordplace.com (Office).

HANKS, Tom; American actor; b. 9 July 1956, Oakland, Calif.; m. 1st Samantha Lewes 1978 (divorced 1985); two c.; m. 2nd Rita Wilson 1988; two s.; ed California State University; began acting career with Great Lakes Shakespeare Festival; appeared in Bosom Buddies, ABC TV 1980; mem. Bd Govs. Acad. of Motion Picture Arts and Sciences 2001–; Acad. Award for Best Actor for Philadelphia 1994, for Forrest Gump 1995. *Films include:* Splash, Bachelor Party, The Man with One Red Shoe, Volunteers, The Money Pit, Dragnet, Big, Punch Line, The Burbs, Nothing in Common, Every Time We Say Goodbye, Joe Versus the Volcano 1990, The Bonfire of the Vanities 1990, A League of Their Own 1991, Sleepless in Seattle, Philadelphia 1993, Forrest Gump 1994, Apollo 13 1995, That Thing You Do (also Dir) 1996, Turner & Hooch 1997, Saving Private Ryan 1998, You've Got Mail 1998, Cast Away 1999, The Green Mile 1999, Toy Story 2 (voice) 1999, From the Earth to the Moon 1999, Road to Perdition 2002, Catch Me If You Can 2003. *Address:* c/o Richard Lovett, CAA, 9830 Wilshire Boulevard, Beverly Hills, CA 90212, USA.

HANLEY, Rt Hon. Sir Jeremy James, KCMG, PC, FCA, FCCA, FCIS; British politician and chartered accountant; b. 17 Nov. 1945, Amersham, Bucks.; s. of late Jimmy Hanley and Dinah Sheridan; m. 1st Helene Mason 1968 (dissolved 1973); one s.; m. 2nd Verna, Viscountess Villiers (née Stott) 1973; one s. one stepd.; ed Rugby School; with Peat Marwick Mitchell & Co. 1963–66; Dir Anderson Thomas Frankel (ATF) 1969, Man. Dir ATF (Jersey and Ireland) 1970–73; Deputy Chair. The Financial Training Co. Ltd 1973–90; Sec. Park Place PLC 1977–83; Chair. Fraser Green Ltd 1986–90; Parl. Adviser to ICA 1986–90; Conservative MP for Richmond and Barnes 1983–97; Parl. Under-Sec. of State, Northern Ireland Office 1990–93; Minister for Health, Social Security and Agric. 1990–92, for Political Devt, Community Relations and Educ. 1992–93; Minister of State for the Armed Forces, Ministry of Defence 1993–94; Cabinet Minister without Portfolio 1995; Chair. Conservative Party 1994–95; Foreign Office Minister of State for the Middle East and Hong Kong 1995–97; Chair. AdVal Group PLC, Int. Trade and Investment Ltd 1998–2002; Dir ITE Group PLC 1996–, GTECH Corpn (USA) 2001–; Dir Arab-British Chamber of Commerce 1998–; Chair. British Iran Chamber of Commerce 2000 (Vice-Pres. 2001), Brain Games Network PLC 2000–02; Dir European Advisory Bd, Credit Lyonnais 2000–; mem. British-American Parl. Group 1983–97, Anglo-French Parl. Group 1983–97, CPA 1983–97, IPU 1983–97, British-Irish Interparl. Body 1990; Vice-Chair. Nat. Anglo-West Indian Conservative Soc. 1982–83; Chair. Conservative Candidates Asscn 1982–83; mem. Bow Group 1974–, European Movt 1974–; Mensa 1968–; Freeman City of London 1989; mem. Court of Assts. Worshipful Co. of Chartered Accountants. *Leisure interests:* cookery,

chess, cricket, languages, theatre, cinema, music, golf. *Address:* 6 Butts Mead, Northwood, Middx, HA6 2TL, England. *Telephone:* (1923) 826675. *Fax:* (1923) 836447 (Home). *E-mail:* jeremy@hanley.com (Home).

HANNAH, Daryl; American actress; b. 3 Dec. 1960, Chicago, Ill.; ed Univ. of Calif. at Los Angeles; studied with Stella Adler; studied ballet with Marjorie Tallchief (q.v.); appeared on TV in Paper Dolls. *Films:* The Fury 1978, The Final Terror, Hard Country, Blade Runner, Summer Lovers, Splash, The Pope of Greenwich Village, Reckless, Clan of the Cave Bear, Legal Eagles, Roxanne, Wall Street, High Spirits, Steel Magnolias, Crazy People, At Play in the Fields of the Lord, Memoirs of an Invisible Man, Grumpy Old Men, Attack of the 50 ft Woman, The Tie That Binds, Grumpier Old Men 1995, Two Much 1996, The Last Days of Frankie the Fly 1996, Wild Flowers 1999, My Favorite Martian 1999, Dancing in the Blue Iquand 2000, Cord 2000, Speedway Junky 2001, Jackpot 2001, A Walk to Remember 2002; Dir The Last Supper 1994, A Hundred and One Nights 1995. *Play:* The Seven Year Itch 2000.

HANNAH, John; British actor; b. 23 April 1962, Glasgow; s. of John Hannah and Susan Hannah; m. Joanna Roth; ed Royal Scottish Acad. of Music and Drama; fmrly electrician; fmrly with Workers' Theatre Co. *Television appearances include:* McCallum (series), Joan, Faith. *Films include:* Four Weddings and a Funeral 1994, Sliding Doors 1998, The James Gang, The Mummy 1999, The Mummy Returns 2001, Pandaemonium 2001.

HANNAY OF CHISWICK, Baron (Life Peer), cr. 2001, of Chiswick, of Bedford Park in the London Borough of Ealing; **David Hugh Alexander Hannay,** GCMG, BA; British diplomatist; b. 28 Sept. 1935, London; s. of Julian Hannay and Eileen Hannay; m. Gillian Rosemary Rex 1961; four s.; ed Craigflower School, Torryburn, Fife, Scotland, Winchester Coll. and New Coll. Oxford; Second Lt, King's Royal Irish Hussars 1954–56; Persian language student, Foreign Office and British Embassy, Tehran 1959–61; Oriental Sec., British Embassy, Kabul 1961–63; Second Sec., Eastern Dept, Foreign Office, London 1963–65; Second, then First Sec., UK Del. to European Community, Brussels 1965–70, First Sec. UK Negotiating Team 1970–72; Chef de Cabinet to Sir Christopher Soames, Vice-Pres. of the European Community Comm. 1973–77; Counsellor, Head of Energy, Science and Space Dept, FCO, London 1977–79, Counsellor, Head of Middle East Dept 1979, Asst Under-Sec. of State (EC) 1979–84; Minister, British Embassy, Washington, DC 1984–85; UK Perm. Rep. to EC 1985–90, to UN 1990–95; British Govt Special Rep. for Cyprus 1996–; British Prime Minister's Personal Envoy to Turkey and EU Special Rep. for Cyprus 1998; Dir (non-exec.) Chime Communications 1996–, Aegis 2000–; mem. Court and Council, Univ. of Birmingham 1998–, Pro-Chancellor 2001–; mem. Council of Britain in Europe 1999–; Hon. Fellow, New Coll. Oxford. *Publication:* Britain's Entry into the European Community: Report on the Negotiations 1970–72 (Ed.). *Leisure interests:* gardening, travel, photography. *Address:* 3 The Orchard, London, W4 1JZ, England. *Telephone:* (20) 8987-9012. *Fax:* (20) 8987-9012.

HANNIBALSSON, Jón Baldvin, MA; Icelandic politician and diplomatist; b. Jón Baldvin, 21 Feb. 1939, Ísafjörður; s. of Hannibal Valdimarsson and Sólveig Ólafsdóttir; m. Bryndís Schram 1959; one s. three d.; ed Menntaskólinn í Reykjavik, Univ. of Edinburgh, Nationalökonomiska Inst., Stockholm, Univ. of Iceland and Harvard Univ.; teacher secondary school, Reykjavik 1964–70; journalist Frjáls thjóð, Reykjavik 1964–67; Founder and Rector Ísafjörður Coll. 1970–79; Chief Ed. Althýðublaðið, Reykjavik 1979–82; MP 1982–98; Chair. SDP 1984–96; Minister of Finance 1987–88, for Foreign Affairs and Foreign Trade 1988–95; Chair. Council of Ministers, EFTA 1989, 1992, 1994; Amb. to USA (also accred to Mexico, Brazil, Chile and Argentina) 1998–; Hon. Citizen of Vilnius, Lithuania 1995, Order of Terra Marina, Estonia 1996, Order of Grand Duke Gediminas, Lithuania 1996, Order of Pres. of Latvia 1996, Order of Prince Trpimir and Croatian Morning Star 2001. *Television:* Dialogue with Jón Baldvin (TV-2) 1997. *Publications:* Who Owns Iceland? 1985, Economic Strategy for Social Democrats (jtly.) 1986, The Icelandic Tax Reform 1987, Iceland and the Baltic Nations' Struggle for Independence 1998, The Age of Extremes 2000, Iceland in a New Century (jtly.) 2000, Expectations and Disappointments of the 20th Century 2001, Contemporary Issues (jtly.) 2002. *Leisure interests:* reading, swimming. *Address:* Embassy of Iceland, 1156 15th Street, Suite 1200, NW, Washington, DC 20005, USA (Office). *Telephone:* (202) 265-6653 (Office). *Fax:* (202) 265-6656 (Office). *E-mail:* icemb.wash@utn.stjr.is (Office). *Website:* www.iceland.org (Office).

HANS-ADAM II, HSH Prince of Liechtenstein; b. 14 Feb. 1945, Zurich, Switzerland; s. of the late Prince Franz Josef II and late Princess Gina; m. Countess Marie Aglaë Kinsky von Wchinitz und Tettau 1967; three s. one d.; ed Schottengymnasium, Vienna, School of Econs and Social Sciences, St Gallen, Switzerland; Chief Exec. of Prince of Liechtenstein Foundation 1970–84; took over exec. authority of Liechtenstein Aug. 1984. *Address:* Schloss Vaduz, 9490 Vaduz, Principality of Liechtenstein.

HANSEID, Einar; Norwegian journalist; b. 19 Nov. 1943, Sandefjord; m. Mari Onsrud 1977; two s.; reporter, Sandefjords Blad 1965; News Ed. Dagbladet 1974; Chief Ed. Hjem & Fritid 1982; Man. Ed. Verdens Gang 1984, Chief Ed. 1987–93; Chief Ed. Aftenposten 1994–. *Address:* Aftenposten, Biskop Gunnerus Gate 14, 0155 Oslo, Norway.

HANSEN, Barbara C., PhD; American scientist and university administrator; b. 24 Nov. 1941, Boston, Mass.; d. of Reynold Caleen and Dorothy

Richardson Caleen; m. Kenneth D. Hansen 1976; one s.; ed Univ. of Calif., Los Angeles, Univ. of Pa, Phila and Univ. of Washington, Seattle; Research Fellow, Univ. of Pa Inst. of Neurosciences 1966–68; Asst and Assoc. Prof. Univ. of Washington 1971–76; Prof. and Assoc. Dean Univ. of Michigan, Ann Arbor 1977–83; Assoc. Vice.-Pres. of Academic Affairs and Research and Dean of Grad. School, Southern Ill. Univ., Carbondale 1983–85; Vice-Pres. for Grad. Studies and Research, Univ. of Md, Baltimore 1986–90, Prof. of Physiology Univ. of Md 1990–, Dir Obesity and Diabetes Research Center 1990–; Pres. Int. Asscn for Study of Obesity 1987–90, N American Asscn for Study of Obesity 1984–85, American Soc. of Clinical Nutrition 1995–96; mem. several advisory cttees. etc.; mem. NAS Inst. of Medicine. *Publications:* Controversies in Obesity (Ed.) 1983, The Commonsense Guide to Weight Loss for People with Diabetes 1998, The Metabolic Syndrome X 1999; book chapters and articles in learned journals. *Leisure interests:* sailing, scuba diving, golf, reading. *Address:* Obesity and Diabetes Research Center, University of Maryland School of Medicine, MSTF600, 10 S. Pine Street, Baltimore, MD 21201, USA. *Telephone:* (410) 706-3168. *Fax:* (410) 706-7540.

HANSEN, Bent, FIL. DR.; Swedish economist; b. 1 Aug. 1920, Ildved, Denmark; s. of Henrik Poulsen and Anna Louise (Pedersen) Hansen; m. Soad Ibrahim Refaat 1962; two s. four d.; ed Univs. of Copenhagen and Uppsala; civil servant, State Dept, Copenhagen 1946; Lecturer Uppsala Univ. 1947–48 and 1950–51, Gothenburg 1948–50; Reader, Uppsala 1951–55; Prof. and Head of Konjunkturinst. (Nat. Inst. of Econ. Research), Stockholm 1955–64, Consultant, Inst. of Nat. Planning, Cairo 1962–65; Special Consultant for OECD, Paris 1965–67; Prof. of Political Economy, Stockholm Univ. 1967–68; Prof. of Econs Univ. of Calif., Berkeley 1967–87, Prof. Emer. 1987–, Chair. Dept of Econs 1977–85; Consultant ECAFE Bangkok 1970–73, IMF 1973, U.S. Treasury 1974, Morocco 1976–77, Bogadizi Univ., Istanbul 1978, World Bank 1985–89 (Consultant Emer. 1987–); Chief ILO Employment Mission to Egypt 1980–81. *Publications:* A Study in the Theory of Inflation 1951, The Economic Theory of Fiscal Policy 1958, Foreign Trade Credits and Exchange Reserves 1961, Development and Economic Policy in the UAR (Egypt) 1965, Lectures in Economic Theory, I and II 1967, Long and Short Term Planning 1967, Fiscal Policy in Seven Countries, OECD, 1969, A Survey of General Equilibrium Systems 1970, Exchange Controls and Development: Egypt 1975, Employment Opportunities and Equity: Egypt in the 1980s, 1982, Political Economy of Poverty, Equity and Growth, Egypt and Turkey 1990.

HANSEN, Kai Aaen, MSc; Danish central banker and international civil servant; b. 26 Nov. 1942, Hadsten; s. of Hans Helge Hansen and Kathrine Elisabeth Hansen; m. Ann Marie Skovløv 1970; ed Univ. of Aarhus; economist, Danmarks Nat. Bank 1972–77, Asst Head of Dept 1980–82, Head of Dept 1985–91, Dir 1992–97, 2000–; economist, OECD, Paris 1977–80; Econ. Adviser, IMF, Washington, DC 1983–85, Exec. Dir 1998–2000; Deputy Chair. Nordic Comm. on Money Transmission 1981–83; mem. UN Informal Group on Money Transmission 1981–83, Govt Comm. on Money Transmission 1982–83, Econ. Ministry Cttee on Econ. Policies 1987–91, on Econ. and Monetary Union Issues 1996–97; alt. mem. EU Comm. of Cen. Bank Govs. 1991–94, European Monetary Comm. 1987–93; alt. Council mem. European Monetary Inst. 1994–97; now Chair. Nordic-Baltic Monetary and Financial Alt. Cttee; part-time Asst Prof., Copenhagen School of Econs 1974–77, 1980–83; Kt Order of Dannebrog. *Publications:* The International Monetary System, an Essay to Interpretation (with Erik Hoffmeyer) 1991, Pengepolitiske Problemstillinger (with Erik Hoffmeyer) 1993. *Address:* Danmarks Nationalbank, Havnegade 5, 1093 Copenhagen, Denmark (Office). *Telephone:* 33-63-60-70 (Office). *Fax:* 33-63-71-12 (Office). *E-mail:* kah@nationalbanken .dk (Office).

HANSEN, Mogens Herman, DPhil; Danish reader in classical philology; b. 20 Aug. 1940, Copenhagen; s. of Herman Hansen and Gudrun Maria (née Heslet) Hansen; m. Birgitte Holt Larsen; one s.; ed Univ. of Copenhagen; Research Fellow, Inst. of Classics, Univ. of Copenhagen 1967–69, lecturer in Classical Philology 1969–88, Reader 1988–; Dir The Copenhagen Polis Centre 1993–; Visiting Fellow, Wolfson College, Cambridge 1974; Visiting Prof. Melbourne Univ. 1988, Univ. of BC, Vancouver 2001; mem. Inst. for Advanced Study, Princeton 1983; Fellow Royal Danish Acad. of Sciences and Letters; Corresp. mem. British Acad., Deutsches Archaeologisches Institut; Einar Hansen Stipendium 2000. *Publications include:* The Sovereignty of the People's Court in 4th Century Athens 1974, Eisangelia 1975, Aspects of Athenian Society 1975, Apagoge, Endeixis and Ephegesis 1976, The Athenian Ecclesia I 1983, II 1989, Demography and Democracy 1985, The Athenian Assembly 1987, The Athenian Democracy in the Age of Demosthenes 1991, Acts of the Copenhagen Polis Centre I 1993, II 1995, III 1996, IV 1997, V 1998, A Comparative Study of Thirty City-State Cultures 2000, A Comparative Study of Six City-State Cultures 2002 and over 100 articles in int. journals on Athenian democracy and ancient Greek constitutional history. *Leisure interests:* playing the flute, writing poetry, book binding. *Address:* Wilhelm Marstrandsgade 15, 2100 Copenhagen Ø, Denmark. *Telephone:* 35-32-91-03 (Univ.); 35-26-15-88 (Home). *Fax:* 32-54-89-54. *E-mail:* mhh@hum.ku.dk (Office).

HANSEN, P. Gregers, MSc, DPhil; Danish physicist; b. 11 Jan. 1933, Frederiksberg; m. Bitten Bisbjerg 1957; two s.; ed Tech. Univ. of Denmark, Copenhagen; Research Scientist, Group Leader, Atomic Energy Research Inst. 1956–66; Prof. of Physics at the Univ. of Aarhus 1966–95; John A. Hannah Prof. Mich. State Univ. 1995–; Sr Research Physicist and Group Leader, CERN Geneva 1969–79; mem. numerous scientific advisory bds., primarily in Germany, France and at CERN; mem. Danish Royal Acad. of Sciences and Letters. *Publications:* many research papers and review articles on subjects in nuclear and atomic physics. *Leisure interests:* skiing, mountaineering, hiking, literature. *Address:* NSCL-Cyclotron, Michigan State University, East Lansing, MI 48824, USA (Office). *Telephone:* (517) 333-6433 (Office).

HANSEN, Peter, BSc; Danish international organization official; b. 2 June 1941, Aahlborg; m.; one s. two d.; ed Aarhus Univ.; Assoc. Prof. Aarhus Univ. 1966–68, Chair. Dept of Political Science 1968–70, Sr Research Fellow 1970–74; Prof. of Int. Relations, Odense Univ.; Adviser, Ministry of Foreign Affairs; Chair. UN Consultative Cttee on Substantive Questions of the Admin. Cttee on Co-ordination and of the Appointment and Promotion Bd, mem. UN Programme Budgeting Bd, Asst Sec.-Gen. Programme Planning and Co-ordination 1978–85; Asst Sec.-Gen. and Exec. Dir UN Centre on Transnat. Corpns. 1985–92; Rep. of UN Sec.-Gen. to Food Aid and Policies Cttee, World Food Programme; Team Leader UN Operation in Somalia 1992; Exec. Dir Comm. on Global Governance, Geneva, Switzerland 1992–94; Special Rep. of Sec.-Gen. ad hoc Liaison Cttee in support of Middle East peace process 1993–; Under-Sec.-Gen. for Humanitarian Affairs and UN Emergency Relief Co-ordinator, New York, USA 1994–96; Commr-Gen. UNRWA Jan. 1996–; King Hussein Humanitarian Leadership Prize, King Hussein Foundation 2001. *Publications:* World Politics 1969, International Organization 1975. *Address:* Bayader Wasdi Seer, P.O. Box 140157, Amman 11814, Jordan (Office); Gamal Abdul Nasser Street, Gaza, via Israel (Office). *E-mail:* unrwapoio@unrwa.org (Office). *Website:* www.unrwa.org (Office).

HANSENNE, Michel, DenD; Belgian politician; b. 23 March 1940, Rotheux-Rimiere; MP 1974–89; Minister of French Culture 1979–81, of Employment and Labour 1981–88, for Civil Service 1988–89; Dir-Gen. Int. Labour Org., Geneva 1989–98; MEP 1999–. *Publication:* Emploi, les scénarios du possible. *Address:* European Parliament, Plateau du Kirchberg, B.P. 1601, 2929, Luxembourg.

HANSON, Curtis; American film director and screenplay writer; b. 24 March 1945, Los Angeles, Calif.; Ed. Cinema magazine; began film career as screenplay writer; mem. Bd Govs. Acad. of Motion Picture Arts and Sciences 2001–. *Films directed:* The Arousers 1970, Sweet Kill (also screenplay) 1972, Little Dragons (also co-producer) 1977, Losin' It 1983, The Bedroom Window (also screenplay) 1988, Bad Influence 1990, The Hand that Rocks the Cradle 1992, The River Wild 1994, LA Confidential 1998, The Children of Times Square (TV film), Wonder Boys 1999. *Screenplays:* The Dunwich Horror 1970, The Silent Partner 1978, White Dog 1982, Never Cry Wolf 1983. *Television:* Hitchcock: Shadow of a Genius (actor) 1999. *Address:* United Talent Agency, 9560 Wilshire Boulevard, Floor 5, Beverly Hills, CA 90212, USA.

HANSON, Baron (Life Peer), cr. 1983, of Edgerton in the County of West Yorkshire; **James Edward Hanson,** Kt, FRSA, CBIM; British business executive; b. 20 Jan. 1922; s. of late Robert Hanson and Louisa A. (Cis) Rodgers; m. Geraldine Kaelin 1959; two s. one step-d.; Chair. Hanson PLC 1965–97, Chair. Emer. 1998–; Chair. Hanson Transport Group, Ltd 1965–96; Fellow Cancer Research Campaign; mem. Court of Patrons, Royal Coll. of Surgeons of England 1991–; Hon. Fellow St Peter's Coll. Oxford 1996, Royal Coll. of Radiologists 1998; Trustee Hanson Fellowship of Surgery; Freeman of London; Hon. Liveryman, Worshipful Co. of Saddlers; Hon. LLD (Leeds) 1984, Hon. DBA (Huddersfield) 1991. *Address:* 28 Old Brompton Road (Box 164), London, SW7 3SS, England. *Telephone:* (20) 7245-6996. *Fax:* (20) 7245-9900 (Office).

HANSON, Sir John Gilbert, KCMG, CBE, MA; British university college warden and fmr government official; b. 16 Nov. 1938, Sheffield; s. of Gilbert F. Hanson and Gladys Kay; m. Margaret Clark 1962; three s.; ed Manchester Grammar School and Wadham Coll. Oxford; War Office 1961–63; British Council, Madras, India 1963–66; Middle East Centre for Arab Studies, Lebanon 1966–68; British Council, Bahrain 1968–72, London HQ 1972–75, Dir British Council, Iran and Cultural Counsellor, British Embassy, Tehran 1975–79, Controller (Finance), British Council, London 1979–82; Royal Coll. of Defence Studies 1983; Dir British Council, India and Minister (Cultural), British High Comm. New Delhi 1984–88; Deputy Dir-Gen. British Council 1988–92, Dir-Gen. 1992–98; Warden Green Coll., Oxford 1998–; Chair. Trustees, British Skin Foundation 1997–, Bahrain-British Foundation 1997–2002; mem. Gov. Council, SOAS 1991–99, London Univ. 1996–98; Hon. Fellow Wadham Coll., Oxford 1997, St Edmund's Coll., Cambridge 1998; Patron GAP 1989–98; Trustee Charles Wallace (India) Trust 1998–2000; Hon. DLitt (Oxford Brookes) 1995, (Lincolnshire & Humberside) 1996, (Greenwich) 1996; Great Gold Medal, Comenius Univ. (Slovakia) 1997. *Leisure interests:* books, music, sport, travel. *Address:* Warden's Lodgings, Green College, Woodstock Road, Oxford, OX2 6HG, England. *Telephone:* (1865) 274770. *Fax:* (1865) 274796. *E-mail:* john.hanson@green.ox.ac.uk (Office).

HANUSZKIEWICZ, Adam; Polish actor and theatre director; b. 16 June 1924, Lvov, Ukraine; s. of Włodzimierz Hanuszkiewicz and Stanisława Szydłowska; m. 1st Zofia Ryś; one s. two d.; m. 2nd Zofia Kucówna; m. 3rd Magdalena Cwenówna; ed State High School of Drama, Łódź and State Higher School of Drama, Warsaw; début as actor 1945, acted in Cracow, Poznań and Warsaw; début as Dir 1953, directed in Poznań and Warsaw; Artistic Dir Theatre of Polish TV 1956–63; Dir and Producer, Teatr Powszechny (Popular Theatre), Warsaw 1963–68, visited, with theatre company,

Prague 1964, 1966, Moscow 1965, London, Paris 1966, Helsinki 1967, Bucharest 1968, Stockholm, Oslo 1969; Gen. Man. and Artistic Dir Teatr Narodowy, Warsaw 1968–82, visited Helsinki, Leningrad, Moscow 1973, Berlin 1975, Bremen, Budapest, Moscow 1976; Gen. Man. and Artistic Dir Teatr Nowy, Warsaw 1989–; visited Wilno 1989; acted in 50 major roles in theatre; directed over 30 plays in theatre, 100 television plays; Dr. hc (Opole Univ.) 2001; State Prize (First Class) for TV work, City of Warsaw Award for theatre work, Theatre Critics' Prize 1964, Order of Banner of Labour, 1st Class 1974, Gold Screen TV Award 1978, Prize of Minister of Foreign Affairs 1979. *Principal roles include:* Hamlet (Hamlet) 1951–59, Tytus (Bérénice) 1962, Prospero (The Tempest) 1963, Raskolnikov (Crime and Punishment) 1964, Don Juan (Don Juan) 1965, Fantazy (Fantazy) 1967, Count Henryk (Un-divine Comedy) 1969, Duncan (Macbeth) 1972, Créon (Antigone) 1973. *Plays directed include:* Wesele (The Wedding, Wyspiański), Crime and Punishment, Coriolanus, Don Juan, The Columbus Boys (Bratny), Kordian (Słowacki), St Joan 1969, Hamlet 1970, Norwid 1970, Beniowski (Słowacki) 1971, Three Sisters 1971, 1983, 1988, Twelfth Night 1971, Macbeth 1973, Antigone 1973, The Inspector General 1973, Balladyna (Słowacki) 1974, A Month in the Country 1974, Wacława dzieje (Garczyński) 1974, The Card Index (Różewicz) 1974, Don Juan 1975, Wesele (Wyspiański) 1976, Mickiewicz 1976, Mąż i żona (Fredro) 1977, Phèdre 1977, Peace 1977, Sen srebrny Salomei (Słowacki) 1977, Wyszedł z domu (Różewicz) 1978, Dziady (Mickiewicz) 1978, Białe małżeństwo (Różewicz) 1978, Treny (Kochanowski) 1979, The Brothers Karamazov, The Decameron 1980, As You Like It, Platonov 1962, 1980, School of Wires, Leśmian 1982, Śpiewnik domowy 1982, 1984, 1989, Wilno, Cyd 1984, 1991, Komedia pasterska 1991, Gombrowicz 1992, Panna Isabela (Prus) 1993, Lilla Weneda (Słowacki) 1995, Dulska-musical (Zapolska), Balladyna 1996, Ballads and Romances 1998. *Opera:* Così fan tutte 1986, Marriage of Figaro 1987, La Traviata 1997, Romeo and Juliet 1997, Don Giovanni 1998, The Dance of Death 1998, Six Figures 1998. *Television:* Fuga 1994, Nim przyjdzie wiosna (Iwaszkiewicz) 1994, Panienka z poczty 1994, Chopin: His Life, His Loves, His Music (also wrote screenplay) 1999. *Publication:* Psy, hondy i drabina 1994. *Address:* Teatr Nowy, ul. Puławska 37/39, 02-508 Warsaw, Poland (Office). *Telephone:* (22) 8498491 (Office). *Fax:* (22) 8498491 (Office). *Website:* www.teatrnowy.waw.pl (Office).

HAO BAILIN; Chinese physicist; b. 26 June 1934, Beijing; s. of Hao Kingsheng and Zhao Weimei; m. Zhang Shuyu 1959; one s. one d.; ed Kharkov State Univ., Ukraine; mem. Chinese Acad. of Sciences 1980–; Research Prof. Inst. of Theoretical Physics 1978– (Dir 1990–94); mem. Third World Acad. of Science 1995–; Science and Tech. Progress Award 1987, Nat. Award in Natural Science 1993, Chinese Acad. of Sciences Award 1992, 1999. *Publications:* 10 books, including Applied Symbolic Dynamics and Chaos 1998; 130 scientific papers on theoretical physics, computational physics, nonlinear science and theoretical life science. *Leisure interest:* reading classical Chinese poems. *Address:* c/o Institute of Theoretical Physics, PO Box 2735, Beijing 100080 (Office); Apartment 1401, Building 811, Huangzhaung Complex, Academy of Sciences, Haidian District, Beijing 100080, People's Republic of China (Home). *Telephone:* (10) 62541807 (Office); (10) 62559478 (Home). *Fax:* (10) 62562587 (Office). *E-mail:* hao@itp.ac.cn (Office). *Website:* www.itp.ac.cn/~hao (Office).

HAO JIANXIU; Chinese politician; b. 1935, Qingdao; worker, State Operated Cotton Factory No. 6, Qingdao; originated Hao Jianxiu Work Method; mem. Exec. Council, Women's Fed. 1953; mem. Cen. Cttee, Communist Democratic Youth League 1953; joined CCP 1954; Deputy Dir Cotton Factory No. 6, Qingdao 1964; mem. Cen. Cttee Communist Youth League 1964–Cultural Revolution; mem. Qingdao Municipality Revolutionary Cttee 1967; mem. Standing Cttee, Cotton Factory No. 6 Revolutionary Cttee 1968; Vice-Chair. Qingdao Municipality Revolutionary Cttee 1971, Trade Union, Shandong 1975; Chair. Women's Fed., Shandong 1975; mem. Standing Cttee, Shandong Prov. CCP Cttee 1977; mem. 11th CCP Cen. Cttee 1977–82; Vice-Minister of Textile Industry 1978–81, Minister 1981–83; Vice-Minister State Planning Cttee 1987–; mem. Politburo 13th Cen. Cttee CCP 1985; Vice-Chair. Women's Fed. 1978; Vice-Chair. State Tourism Cttee 1988; mem. 12th Cen. Cttee CCP 1982–87, 13th Cen. Cttee CCP 1987–92; mem. 14th Cen. Cttee CCP 1992–97; mem. 15th Cen. Cttee CCP 1997–; Alt. Sec. Secr. 1982, Sec. 1985; mem. Financial and Econ. Leading Group, CCP Cen. Cttee 1986; Hon. Pres. Factory Dirs.' Study Soc., Acad. of Social Sciences 1985; Deputy Dir Leading Group for the Placement of Demobilized Army Officers 1993–; Vice-Chair. Cttee for Women and Children's Work 1987–; Nat. Model Worker in Industry 1951. *Address:* Zhonggong Zhongyang, A8, Taipingjie Street, Beijing 100050, People's Republic of China.

HARABÍN, Štefan, DJur; Slovak judge; b. 4 May 1957, Lubica; ed Univ. of Pavel Jozef Šafárik; Judge, Dist Court, Poprad 1983–90, Regional Court, Košice 1990–91; Judge of the Supreme Court 1991–98, Chair. 1998–; Head of Penal Dept, Section of Justice Admin., Ministry of Justice, Slovak Repub. 1991–92; Pres. of Senate and Penal Bd 1996–98. *Address:* Office of the Chairman, Supreme Court, Bratislava, Slovakia (Office). *Telephone:* (2) 5441-6157 (Office). *Fax:* (2) 5441-1535 (Office).

HARAD, George Jay, BA, MBA; American business executive; b. 24 April 1944, Newark, NJ; s. of Sidney Harad and Irma Harad; m. Beverly Marcia Harad 1966; one s. one d.; ed Franklin & Marshall Coll., Harvard Business School; Admin. Asst to Sr Vice-Pres. Housing Group, Boise Cascade Corpn 1971–72, Finance Man. Boise Cascade Realty Group 1972–76; Man. Corp. Devt, Boise Cascade Corpn 1976–80, Dir Retirement Funds 1980–82, Vice-Pres. Controller 1982–84, Sr Vice-Pres., Chief Financial Officer 1984–89, Exec. Vice-Pres., Chief Financial Officer 1989–90, Exec. Vice-Pres. Paper 1990–91, Pres., COO 1991–94, Pres., CEO 1994–95, Chair. Bd and CEO 1995–; George F. Baker Scholar. *Leisure interest:* golf. *Address:* Boise Cascade Corporation, 1111 West Jefferson Street, PO Box 50, Boise, ID 83728 (Office); 224 East Braemere Road, Boise, ID 83702, USA. *Telephone:* (208) 384-7557 (Office); (208) 345-0808 (Home).

HARALD V, HM; King of Norway; b. 21 Feb. 1937, Skaugum; s. of the late King Olav V and Crown Princess Märtha; m. Sonja Haraldsen 1968; one s. one d.; ed Oslo Katedralskole, Cavalry Officers' Cand. School, Mil. Acad. and Balliol Coll. Oxford; lived in Washington, DC 1940–45; has participated in many int. sailing competitions representing Norway at Olympic Games several times; undertook frequent official visits abroad while Crown Prince; succeeded his father, King Olav V, Jan. 1991. *Address:* Royal Palace, 0010 Oslo, Norway. *Telephone:* 22-04-87-00.

HARBERGER, Arnold C., PhD; American economist; b. 27 July 1924, Newark, NJ; s. of Martha L. Bucher and Ferdinand C. Harberger; m. 1958; two s.; ed Univ. of Chicago; Asst Prof. Johns Hopkins Univ. 1949–53; Assoc. Prof. Univ. of Chicago 1953–59, Prof. 1959–76, Gustavus F. and Ann M. Swift Distinguished Service Prof. 1976–91, Prof. Emer. 1991–; Prof. of Econs, Univ. of Calif. at LA 1984–; Pres. Western Econ. Asscn 1988–89, American Econ. Asscn 1997; Fellow Econometric Soc. 1967, American Acad. of Arts and Sciences 1969; mem. NAS 1989; consultant to numerous econ. Govt depts. and int. orgs. *Publications:* Project Evaluation 1972, Taxation and Welfare 1974, World Economic Growth 1984. *Address:* 8283 Bunche Hall, University of California at Los Angeles, 405 Hilgard Avenue, Los Angeles, CA 90095 (Office); 136 Buckskin Road, Bell Canyon, CA 91307, USA (Home). *Telephone:* (310) 825-1011 (Office). *Fax:* (310) 825-9528 (Office). *E-mail:* harberger@econ.ucla.edu (Office).

HARBISON, Peter, MA, DPhil, MRIA, FSA; Irish archaeologist, art historian and editor; b. 14 Jan. 1939, Dublin; s. of Dr. James Austin Harbison and Sheelagh Harbison (née McSherry); m. Edelgard Soergel 1969; three s.; ed St Gerard's School, Bray, Glenstal, Univ. Coll. Dublin and Univs. of Marburg, Kiel and Freiburg; awarded travelling scholarship by German Archaeological Inst. 1965; archaeological officer, Irish Tourist Bd 1966–84, editorial publicity officer 1984–86, Ed. Ireland of the Welcomes (magazine) 1986–95; Sec. Friends of the Nat. Collections of Ireland 1971–76; mem. Council, Royal Irish Acad. 1981–84, 1993–96, 1998–2001, Vice-Pres. 1992–93, Hon. Academic Ed. 1997–; Prof. of Archaeology, Royal Hibernian Acad. of Arts; Chair. Nat. Monuments Advisory Council 1986–90, Dublin Cemeteries Cttee 1986–89, 1996–2002; corresp. mem. German Archaeological Inst.; Hon. mem. Royal Hibernian Acad. of Arts 1998; Hon. Fellow Trinity Coll., Dublin 1999; Hon. mem. Royal Inst. of Architects of Ireland. *Publications:* Guide to National Monuments of Ireland 1970, The Archaeology of Ireland 1976, Irish Art and Architecture (co-author) 1978, Pre-Christian Ireland (Archaeological Book of the Year Award 1988) 1988, Pilgrimage in Ireland 1991, Beranger's Views of Ireland 1991, The High Crosses of Ireland 1992, Irish High Crosses 1994, Ancient Ireland (with Jacqueline O'Brien) 1996, Ancient Irish Monuments 1997, Beranger's Antique Buildings of Ireland, L'Art Médiéval en Irlande 1998, Spectacular Ireland 1999, The Golden Age of Irish Art 1999, The Crucifixion in Irish Art 2000, Cooper's Ireland 2000, Our Treasure of Antiquities 2002; articles in books and journals. *Leisure interests:* music, travel, wining, dining, cruising. *Address:* Royal Irish Academy, 19 Dawson Street, Dublin 2 (Office); 5 St Damian's, Loughshinny, Skerries, Co. Dublin, Republic of Ireland. *Telephone:* (1) 6762570 (Office); (1) 8490940. *Fax:* (1) 6762346 (Office). *Website:* www.ria.ie (Office).

HARCOURT, Geoffrey Colin, AO, PhD, DLitt, FASSA; Australian professor of economics; b. 27 June 1931, Melbourne; s. of Kenneth and Marjorie Harcourt (née Gans); m. Joan Bartrop 1955; two s. two d.; ed Univs. of Melbourne and Cambridge; lecturer in Econs, Univ. of Adelaide 1958–62, Sr lecturer 1963–65, Reader 1965–67, Prof. (Personal Chair) 1967–85, Prof. Emer. 1988; lecturer in econs and politics, Univ. of Cambridge 1964–66, 1982–90, Reader in the History of Econ. Theory 1990–98, Emer. Reader 1998–, Dir of Studies in Economics and Fellow of Trinity Hall, Cambridge 1964–66, Fellow and Lecturer in Econs, Jesus Coll., Cambridge 1982–98, Emer. Fellow 1998–, Pres. 1988–92; Visiting Fellow, Clare Hall, Cambridge 1972–73; Visiting Prof., Univ. of Toronto, Canada 1977, 1980, Univ. of Melbourne 2002; Hon. Prof., Univ. of NSW 1997, 1999; Visiting Fellow, Australian Nat. Univ. 1997; Fellow, Acad. of the Social Sciences in Australia 1971–; Pres. Economic Soc. of Australia and New Zealand 1974–77; mem. Council Royal Econ. Soc. 1990–95, Life mem. 1998–; Distinguished Fellow, Econ. Soc. of Australia 1996; Hon. Fellow Queen's Coll. Melbourne 1998, Sugden Fellow 2002; Wellington Burnham Lecturer, Tufts Univ., Medford, Mass. 1975, Edward Shann Memorial Lecturer, Univ. of Western Australia 1975, Newcastle Lecturer in Political Economy, Univ. of Newcastle 1977, Acad. Lecturer, Acad. of the Social Sciences in Australia 1978, G. L. Wood Memorial Lecturer, Univ. of Melbourne 1982, John Curtin Memorial Lecturer, ANU 1982, special lecturer in Econs, Univ. of Manchester 1984, Lecturer Nobel Conf. XXII, Gustavus Adolphus Coll., Minn. 1986, Laws Lecturer, Univ. of Tennessee at Knoxville 1991, Donald Horne Lecturer 1992, Sir Halford Cook Lecturer, Queen's Coll., Univ. of Melbourne, Kingsley Martin Memorial Lecturer, Cambridge 1996, Colin Clark Memorial Lecturer, Brisbane 1997; Hon. LittD (De Montfort Univ.) 1997, Hon. DComm (Melbourne) 2003. *Publications:* Economic Activity (with P. H. Karmel and R. H. Wallace) 1967, Readings in the Concept and Measurement of Income (ed., with R. H. Parker) 1969, 2nd Edn (with R. H. Parker and G. Whittington) 1986, Capital and Growth, Selected Readings (ed., with N. F. Laing) 1971, Some Cambridge Controversies in the Theory of Capital 1972, The Microeconomic Foundations of Macroeconomics (ed.) 1977, The Social Science Imperialists, Selected Essays (edited by Prue Kerr) 1982, Keynes and his Contemporaries (ed.) 1985, Controversies in Political Economy, Selected Essays of G. C. Harcourt (edited by Omar Hamouda) 1986, International Monetary Problems and Supply-Side Economics: Essays in Honour of Lorie Tarshis (edited with Jon S. Cohen) 1986, On Political Economists and Modern Political Economy, Selected Essays of G. C. Harcourt (ed. by Claudio Sardoni) 1992, Post-Keynesian Essays in Biography: Portraits of Twentieth Century Political Economists 1993, The Dynamics of the Wealth of Nations. Growth, Distribution and Structural Change: Essays in Honour of Luigi Pasinetti (edited with Mauro Baranzini) 1993, Income and Employment in Theory and Practice. Essays in Memory of Athanasios Asimakopulos (Ed. with Alessandro Roncaglia and Robin Rowley) 1994, Capitalism, Socialism and Post-Keynesianism. Selected Essays of G. C. Harcourt 1995, A 'Second Edition' of The General Theory, 2 vols (with P. A. Riach) 1997, 50 Years a Keynesian and Other Essays 2001, Selected Essays on Economic Policy 2001, L'Economie rebelle de Joan Robinson (Ed.) 2001, Joan Robinson: Critical Assessments of Leading Economists (5 vols, ed. with Prue Veu) 2002, Editing Economics: Essays in Honour of Mark Perlman (Co-Ed.) 2002. *Leisure interests:* running (not jogging), bike riding, cricket, reading, politics. *Address:* Jesus College, Cambridge, CB5 8BL; 43 New Square, Cambridge, CB1 1EZ, England (Home). *Telephone:* (1223) 339 436 (Jesus College); (1223) 360833 (Home).

HARDCASTLE, Jack Donald, CBE, MA, M.CHIR., FRCS, FRCP; British professor of surgery; b. 3 April 1933, Yorks.; s. of Albert Hardcastle and Bertha Hardcastle (née Ellison); m. Rosemary Hay-Shunker 1965; two c.; ed Emmanuel Coll. Cambridge; House Physician, London Hosp. 1959–60; House Surgeon, Hammersmith Hosp., London 1961–62; Research Asst London Hosp. 1962, lecturer in Surgery 1963, Senior in Surgery 1964, Registrar in Surgery, Thoracic Unit 1965, Sr Registrar 1965, Sr Lecturer 1968; Sr Registrar St Mark's Hosp., London 1968; Prof. of Surgery Univ. of Nottingham 1970–98; Sir Arthur Sims Commonwealth Travelling Prof., Royal Coll. of Surgeons 1985; Mayne Visiting Prof. Univ. of Brisbane, Australia 1987, Univ. of Melbourne 2001; Dir of Educ. Royal Coll. of Surgeons 1993–98, mem. Council 1987–99, Vice-Pres. 1995–97, Dir of Overseas Office 1996–99; Hon. Fellow Royal Coll. of Physicians and Surgeons (Glasgow), Asscn of Coloproctology; Pres. Surgical Section Royal Soc. Medicine 1981, Pres. Colproctology Section Royal Soc. 1983, Pres. Asscn of Surgical Oncology 1992–3; Pres. Surgical Research Soc. 1995–96; Royal Coll. of Surgeons (England) Gold Medal 1999; Huntarian Orator 1998. *Publications:* Isolated Organ Perfusion (with H.D. Ritchie) 1973; articles in professional journals. *Leisure interest:* golf, gardening. *Address:* Goverton Heights, Goverton, Bleasby, Notts., NG14 7FN, England (Home). *Telephone:* (1636) 830316 (Office). *Fax:* (1636) 830316.

HARDIE, (Charles) Jeremy (Mawdesley), CBE, B.PHIL.ECONS., ACA; British business executive; b. 9 June 1938; s. of Sir Charles Hardie; m. 1st Susan Chamberlain 1962 (divorced 1976); two s. two d.; m. 2nd Xandra, Countess of Gowrie 1978 (divorced 1994); one d.; m. 3rd Kirsteen Margaret Tait 1994; ed Winchester Coll. and New Coll. Oxford; Nuffield Coll. Oxford 1966–67; Jr Research Fellow, Trinity Coll. Oxford 1967–68; Fellow and Tutor in Econs Keble Coll. Oxford 1968–75; partner, Dixon Wilson & Co. 1975–82; Dir John Swire and Sons Ltd 1982–; Dir (non-exec.) W. H. Smith Group 1988– (Deputy Chair. 1992–94, Chair. 1994–99); Chair. Nat. Provident Inst. 1980–89, Alexander Syndicate Man. Ltd 1982–95, Radio Broadland Ltd 1983–85, David Mann Underwriting Agency Ltd 1983–, Dir Alexanders Discount Co. Ltd 1978–87, Alexanders Laing & Cruickshank Gilts Ltd 1986–87; Dir Northdor Holdings 1989–93; Chair. Centre for Econ. Policy Research 1984–89; other business and public appts.; parl. cand. (SDP), Norwich South 1983 (SDP/Alliance) 1987. *Leisure interests:* sailing, skiing. *Address:* 13 Ainger Road, London, NW3 3AR, England. *Telephone:* (20) 7722-6916.

HARDIE BOYS, Rt. Hon. Sir Michael, G.N.Z.M., GCMG, PC; New Zealand fmr Governor-General and fmr judge; b. 6 Oct. 1931, Wellington; s. of Justice Reginald Hardie Boys and Edith May (née Bennett) Hardie Boys; m. Edith Mary Zohrab 1957; two s. two d.; ed Wellington Coll., Victoria Univ. of Wellington; barrister, solicitor with pvt. practice 1950–80; Councillor then Pres. Wellington Dist Law Soc. 1974–79; Judge High Court 1980–89, Court of Appeal 1989–95; Gov.-Gen. of NZ 1996–2001; mem. Legal Aid Bd (Chair.); Hon. Bencher of Gray's Inn; Hon. Fellow Wolfson Coll., Cambridge; Hon. LLD (Victoria Univ., Wellington) 1997. *Leisure interest:* the outdoors. *Address:* 340A Ngarara Road, Waikanae, Kapiti Coast, Wellington, New Zealand (Home).

HARDING, David; British business executive; b. 1948; m.; two c.; fmr Group Finance Dir T&N PLC; fmr Deputy Group Finance Dir TI Group PLC; Finance Dir Rugby Group –2001; Finance Dir Railtrack Group PLC 2001–02, CEO March 2002–; Dir Coventry Building Society 1996–, Deputy Chair. 1999–. *Address:* Railtrack Group PLC, Regent's Place, 339 Euston Road, London, NW1 3BT, England (Office). *Website:* www.railtrack-group.co.uk (Office).

HARDING, Marshal of the RAF Sir Peter Robin, GCB, DSc, FRAeS, CCMI; British fmr air force officer (retd); b. 2 Dec. 1933, London; s. of Peter Harding

and Elizabeth Kezia Clear; m. Sheila Rosemary May 1955; three s. one d.; ed Chingford High School; joined RAF 1952; Pilot, numerous appts. in fighter, light bomber, strike/attack, reconnaissance and helicopters; Air Officer Commanding Number 11 Group 1981–82; Vice-Chief Air Staff 1982–84, of Defence Staff 1985; Air Officer Commanding-in-Chief, RAF Strike Command and C-in-C UK Air Forces (NATO) 1985–88; Chief of Air Staff 1988–92, Chief of Defence Staff 1993–94; ADC to HM the Queen 1975, Air ADC to HM the Queen 1988–92; Deputy Chair. GEC-Marconi Ltd 1995–98; Chair. Thorlock Int. Ltd 1998–2000, Merlyn Int. Assocs Ltd 1995–2002; Council mem. Winston Churchill Memorial Trust 1990–; Cttee mem. Leonard Cheshire Conflict Recovery Centre 1996–; Vice-Pres. The Guild of Aviation Artists 1994–; Liveryman Guild of Air Pilots and Navigators; Fellow and Hon. Companion Royal Aeronautical Soc. 1989; mem. Pilgrims Soc. of GB; Fellow RSA; Hon. DSc (Cranfield Inst. of Tech.) 1990; Commdr Legion of Merit (USA); CB 1980, KCB 1982, GCB 1988. *Leisure interests:* nine grandchildren, swimming, piano, bridge, birdwatching and shooting (normally separately); the Beefsteak and Garrick gentlemen's clubs. *Address:* Avalon House, Marnhull, Dorset DT10 1PT, England (Home); c/o Winston Churchill Memorial Trust, 15 Queen's Gate Terrace, London, SW7, England. *Telephone:* (1558) 820789 (Office). *E-mail:* alice_merlyn@btinternet.com (Home).

HARDWICK, Elizabeth, MA; American author; b. 27 July 1916, Lexington, Ky; d. of Eugene Allen Hardwick and Mary (née Ramsey) Hardwick; m. Robert Lowell 1949 (divorced 1972); one d.; ed Kentucky Univ., Columbia Univ.; Assoc. Prof. Barnard Coll.; Guggenheim Fellow 1947; mem. American Acad., Inst. of Arts and Letters (Gold Medal for Criticism 1993), American Acad. of Arts and Sciences; Founder, Advisory Ed. New York Review of Books; Dr. hc (Smith Coll., Kenyon Coll., Skidmore Coll., Bard Coll.); George Jean Nathan award 1966. *Publications:* (novels) The Ghostly Lover 1945, The Simple Truth 1955, Sleepless Nights 1979; (essays) A View of My Own 1962, Seduction and Betrayal 1974, Bartleby in Manhattan 1983, Sight Readings 1998; Herman Melville, A Life 2000; Ed. The Selected Letters of William James 1960; contribs to New Yorker. *Address:* 15 W 67th Street, New York, NY 10023, USA.

HARDY, Sir David William, Kt, CBIM; British business executive; b. 14 July 1930; s. of late Brig. John H. Hardy; m. Rosemary Collins 1957; one s. one d.; ed Wellington Coll. and Harvard Business School; chartered accountant; with Funch Edye Inc. and Imperial Tobacco, USA 1954–70; HM Govt Coordinator of Industrial Advisers 1970–72; Group Finance Dir Tate & Lyle Ltd 1972–77; Dir Ocean Transport & Trading PLC 1977–83; Dir Globe Investment Trust PLC 1976–90, Exec. Chair. 1983–90; Chair. Ocean Inchcape 1980–83, London Park Hotels 1983–87, Docklands Light Railway 1984–87, Swan Hunter 1986–88, MGM Assurance 1986–99, London Docklands Devt Corpn 1988–92, Europa Minerals 1991–94, Bankers Trust Investment Man. Ltd 1992–94, Burmine 1992–96, James Fisher 1992–93, Y. J. Lovell 1994–99; Dir (nonexec.) Imperial Tobacco Group 1996–2001, Milner Estates 1996–99, Sons of Gwalia 1996–98, Hanson 1991–2001, Ciba Geigy 1991–96, J. Devenish 1991–93; mem. Financial Services Practitioner Forum 2001–; numerous other directorships, professional appts. etc.; Chair. of Trustees Nat. Maritime Museum 1995–, Transport Research Lab. 1996–. *Address:* National Maritime Museum, Greenwich, London, SE10 9NF, England. *Telephone:* (20) 8312-6630. *Fax:* (20) 7584-0086 (Home); (20) 8312-6648. *E-mail:* seahardy@aol.com (Office).

HARDY, Françoise; French singer, author and astrologer; b. 17 Jan. 1944, Paris; m. Jacques Dutronc 1981; one s.; ed Institution La Bruyère, Faculté des Lettres de Paris; first record, Tous les garçons et les filles 1962; last record, Décalages 1988; now writes lyrics for musicians including Diane Tell, Julien Clerc, Khalil Chahine, Guesch Patti and composer-arranger Alain Lubrano; presents Horoscope RTL; several awards and prizes. *Publications:* Le grand livre de la Vierge (with B. Guenin), Entre les lignes, entre les signes (with Anne-Marie Simond) 1986, Notes Secrètes (with E. Dumont) 1991; contribs. to Françoise Hardy présente l'Astrologie Universelle 1986. *Leisure interest:* reading, especially books dealing with spirituality. *Address:* c/o VMA, 20 avenue Rapp, 75007 Paris (Office); 13 rue Hallé, Paris 75014, France.

HARDY, John Philips, MA, DPhil, FAHA; Australian professor of English; b. 1 Jan. 1933, Brisbane; s. of late E. A. Hardy and N. A. (née Philips) Hardy; m. 1st 1961 (divorced); three s. one d.; m. 2nd 1992; ed Church of England Grammar School, Brisbane, Univ. of Queensland and Univ. of Oxford; Fellow Magdalen Coll., Oxford 1962–65; Asst Prof. Univ. of Toronto, Canada 1965–66; Prof. of English Univ. of New England 1966–72, Australian Nat. Univ. 1972–87; Foundation Prof. of Humanities and Social Sciences, Bond Univ. 1988–94; Sec. Australian Acad. of the Humanities 1981–88; Harold White Hon. Fellow, Nat. Library of Australia 1992; Queensland Rhodes Scholar 1957. *Publications:* Reinterpretations: Essays on Poems by Milton, Pope and Johnson 1971, Samuel Johnson 1979, Jane Austen's Heroines 1984, Stories of Australian Migration (Ed.) 1988, Terra Australis to Australia (Ed. with Alan Frost) 1989, European Voyaging towards Australia (Ed. with Alan Frost) 1990. *Leisure interests:* swimming, fishing. *Address:* 26 Rawson Street, Deakin, Canberra, ACT 2600, Australia.

HARDY, Robert, CBE, FSA; British actor and author; b. 29 Oct. 1925; s. of late Major Henry Harrison Hardy and Edith Jocelyn Dugdale; m. 1st Elizabeth Fox 1952 (divorced); one s.; m. 2nd Sally Pearson 1961 (divorced 1986); two d.; Trustee, Royal Armouries 1984–95; Consultant, Mary Rose Trust 1979–, Trustee 1991–; Master of Worshipful Co. of Bowyers 1988–90; Hon. D.Litt

(Reading) 1990, (Durham) 1997. *Films include:* How I Won the War, Yellow Dog, Dark Places, Young Winston, Ten Rillington Place, Le Silencieux, Gawain and the Green Knight, The Spy Who Came In From The Cold, La Gifle, Robin Hood, The Shooting Party, Paris by Night, War and Remembrance, Mary Shelley's Frankenstein, Sense and Sensibility, Mrs. Dalloway, The Tichborne Claimant 1998, An Ideal Husband 1999, The Gathering 2001. *Theatre:* theatre appearances 1949– include four seasons of Shakespeare at Stratford-on-Avon, two at Old Vic; world tours include Henry V and Hamlet, USA; numerous appearances London and Broadway theatres 1952–; Winston Churchill in Celui Qui a Dit Non, Palais des Congrès, Paris 1999–2000. *Television:* writer and/or presenter of numerous programmes 1952– including The Picardy Affair, The History of the Longbow, Heritage, Horses in our Blood, Gordon of Khartoum etc.; other TV appearances have included Prince Hal and Henry V in Age of Kings, Prince Albert in Edward VII, Malcolm Campbell in Speed King, Winston Churchill in the Wilderness Years, Siegfried Farnon in All Creatures Great and Small, Twiggy Rathbone and Russell Spam in Hot Metal, the Commandant in The Far Pavilions, Sherlock Holmes, Inspector Morse, Middlemarch, Castle Ghosts, Gulliver's Travels, Midsomer Murders, Tenth Kingdom, Justice in Wonderland, Lucky Jim, Shackleton. *Publications:* Longbow 1976, The Great War Bow 2002. *Leisure interests:* making and shooting longbows, most country pursuits. *Address:* c/o Chatto and Linnit, 123A King's Road, London, SW3 4PL, England. *Telephone:* (20) 7352-7722.

HARE, Sir David, Kt, MA, FRSL; British playwright; b. 5 June 1947, Hastings, Sussex; s. of Clifford Theodore Rippon Hare and Agnes Cockburn Gilmour; m. 1st Margaret Matheson 1970 (dissolved 1980); two s. one d.; m. 2nd Nicole Farhi (q.v.) 1992; ed Lancing Coll., Jesus Coll., Cambridge; Literary Man. and Resident Dramatist, Royal Court 1969–71; Resident Dramatist, Nottingham Playhouse 1973; f. Joint Stock Theatre Group 1975, Greenpoint Films 1983; Assoc. Dir Nat. Theatre 1984–88, 1989–; UK/US Bicentennial Fellowship 1978; Hon. Fellow Jesus Coll. Cambridge 2001; Evening Standard Drama Award 1970, John Llewelyn Rhys Prize 1974, BAFTA Best Play of the Year 1978, New York Critics' Circle Award 1983, Golden Bear Award for Best Film 1985, Evening Standard Drama Award for Best Play 1985, Plays and Players Best Play 1985, City Limits Best Play 1985, Drama Magazine Awards Best Play 1988, Plays and Players Best Play Award 1988 and 1990, Critics' Circle Award for Best Play 1990, Laurence Olivier Best Play of the Year 1990, Time Out Award 1990, Dramalogue Award 1992, Laurence Olivier Best Play of the Year 1996, New York Critics' Circle Award 1997, Time Out Award for Outstanding Theatrical Achievement 1998, Outer Critics' Circle Award, Drama League Award, Drama Desk Award, New York Critics' Circle Award, Joan Cullman Award 1999; Officier, Ordre des Arts et des Lettres 1997. *Plays:* Slag, Hampstead 1970, Royal Court 1971, New York Shakespeare Festival (NYSF) 1971, The Great Exhibition, Hampstead 1972, Brassneck, Nottingham Playhouse 1973 (also Dir), Knuckle, Comedy Theatre 1974, Fanshen, Inst. of Contemporary Arts 1975, Hampstead 1975, Nat. Theatre 1992, Teeth 'n' Smiles, Royal Court 1975 (also Dir), Wyndhams 1976 (also Dir), Plenty, Nat. Theatre 1978 (also Dir), NYSF and Broadway 1982 (also Dir), Albery 1999, A Map of the World, Nat. Theatre 1983 (also Dir) NYSF 1985 (also Dir), Pravda (with Howard Brenton), Nat. Theatre 1985 (also Dir), The Bay at Nice, Nat. Theatre 1986 (also Dir), The Secret Rapture, Nat. Theatre 1988, NYSF and Broadway 1989 (also Dir), Racing Demon, Nat. Theatre 1990, 1993, Broadway 1995, Murmuring Judges, Nat. Theatre 1992, 1993, The Absence of War, Nat. Theatre 1993, Skylight, Nat. Theatre 1995, Wyndhams and Broadway 1996, Vaudeville 1997, Amy's View, Nat. Theatre 1997, Aldwych 1998, Broadway 1999, The Judas Kiss, Almeida and Broadway 1998 (Dir on radio only), Via Dolorosa, Royal Court 1998 (also acted), Almeida and Broadway 1999 (also acted), My Zinc Bed, Royal Court 2000 (also Dir), The Breath of Life, Theatre Royal, Haymarket 2002. *Plays adapted:* The Rules of the Game, Nat. Theatre 1971, Almeida 1992, The Life of Galileo, Almeida 1994, Mother Courage and Her Children, Nat. Theatre 1995, Ivanov, Almeida and Broadway 1997 (Dir on radio only), The Blue Room, Donmar and Broadway 1998, Theatre Royal 2000, Platonov, Almeida 2001. *Plays directed:* Christi in Love, Portable Theatre 1969, Fruit, Portable Theatre 1970, Blowjob, Portable Theatre 1971, England's Ireland, Portable Theatre 1972 (co-Dir), The Provoked Wife, Palace, Watford 1973, The Pleasure Principle, Theatre Upstairs 1973, The Party, Nat. Theatre 1974, Weapons of Happiness, Nat. Theatre 1976, Devil's Island, Joint Stock 1977, Total Eclipse, Lyric 1981, King Lear, Nat. Theatre 1986, The Designated Mourner, Nat. Theatre 1996, Heartbreak House, Almeida 1997. *Films for TV:* Licking Hitler, BBC 1978 (also Dir), Dreams of Leaving, BBC 1979 (also Dir), Saigon: Year of the Cat, Thames 1983 (also assoc. producer), Heading Home, BBC 1991 (also Dir), The Absence of War, BBC 1995. *Film screenplays:* Wetherby 1985 (also Dir), Plenty 1985, Paris by Night 1989 (also Dir), Strapless 1990 (also Dir), Damage 1992, The Secret Rapture 1993 (also assoc. producer), Via Dolorosa (also actor) 2000, The Hours 2001, Lee Miller 2002. *Film directed:* The Designated Mourner 1996 (also produced). *Opera libretto:* The Knife, New York Shakespeare Festival 1988 (also Dir). *Publications:* Writing Lefthanded 1991, Asking Around 1993, Acting Up 1999. *Address:* c/o Casarotto Ramsay Ltd, 60–66 Wardour Street, London, W1V 3HP, England.

HARE, (Frederick) Kenneth, CC, PhD, FRSC; Canadian professor of geography; b. 5 Feb. 1919, Wylye, Wilts., England; s. of Frederick E. Hare and Irene Smith; m. 1st Suzanne A. Bates 1941 (dissolved 1952); m. 2nd Helen N. Morrill 1953; two s. one d.; ed Univs. of London and Montreal; Asst, Assoc. and Full Prof. of Geography, McGill Univ. 1945–62, Chair. Geography Dept

1950–62, Dean of Arts and Science 1962–64; Prof. of Geography King's Coll., London 1964–66; Master of Birkbeck Coll., Univ. of London 1966–68; Pres. Univ. of British Columbia 1968–69; Prof. of Geography and Physics, Univ. of Toronto 1969–84, Univ. Prof. Emer. 1984–; Dir Inst. for Environmental Studies 1974–79, Provost of Trinity Coll. 1979–86; Chancellor Trent Univ. 1988–95; Chair. Royal Soc. of Canada Comm. on Lead in the Environment 1984–86; Commr Ont. Nuclear Safety Review 1986–88; Chair. Tech. Advisory Panel on Nuclear Safety, Ont. Hydro 1991–94; ten hon. degrees, numerous medals and awards including Order of Ont. *Publications:* author and co-author of books and articles on climate, environment, nuclear safety, etc. *Leisure interests:* music, gardening, walking the dog.

HARE DUKE, Rt Rev. Michael Geoffrey, MA; British ecclesiastic; b. 28 Nov. 1925, Calcutta, India; s. of late A. R. A. Hare Duke and Dorothy Holmes; m. Grace Lydia Frances McKean Dodd 1949; one s. three d.; ed Bradfield Coll., Berks., Trinity Coll., Oxford, Westcott House, Cambridge; Sub-Lt RDVR 1944–46; ordained Deacon 1952, Priest 1953; Curate St John's Wood, London 1952–56; Vicar St Mark's, Bury 1956–62; Pastoral Dir Clinical Theology Asscn 1962–64; Vicar St Paul's, Daybrook 1964–69; Bishop of St Andrew's, Dunkeld and Dunblane 1969–94; Chair. Age Concern Scotland 1994–2000, Nat. Forum on Older Volunteers 2000; Hon. DD (St Andrew's). *Publications:* Understanding the Adolescent 1969, The Break of Glory 1970, Freud 1972, Good News 1976, Stories, Signs and Sacraments in the Emerging Church 1982, Praying for Peace: Reflections on the Gulf Crisis 1991, Hearing the Stranger: Reflections, Poems and Hymns 1994, One Foot in Heaven 2001. *Leisure interests:* writing and broadcasting. *Address:* 2 Balhousie Avenue, Perth, PH1 5HN, Scotland. *Telephone:* (1738) 622642. *Fax:* (1738) 622642. *E-mail:* bishmick@aol.com (Home).

HAREWOOD, 7th Earl of, cr. 1812; **George Henry Hubert Lascelles,** KBE; British musical administrator; b. 7 Feb. 1923, London; s. of the late 6th Earl of Harewood and HRH Princess Mary, The Princess Royal (d. of HM King George V); m. 1st Maria Donata Stein 1949 (dissolved 1967); three s.; m. 2nd Patricia Tuckwell 1967; one s.; ed Eton Coll. and King's Coll., Cambridge; Capt. Grenadier Guards 1942–46; POW 1944–45; ADC to Earl of Athlone, Gov.-Gen. of Canada 1945–46; Counsellor of State during absence of the Sovereign 1947, 1954 and 1956; mem. Bd of Dirs. Royal Opera House, Covent Garden 1951–53, 1969–72, Admin. Exec. 1953–60; Dir-Gen. Leeds Musical Festival 1958–74; Artistic Dir Edinburgh Int. Festival 1961–65; Chair. British Council Music Advisory Cttee 1956–66, Arts Council Music Panel 1966–72; Artistic Adviser New Philharmonia Orchestra, London 1966–76; Pres. English Football Asscn 1964–71, Leeds United Football Club; Chancellor, York Univ. 1963–67; mem. Gen. Advisory Council of BBC 1969–77, Gov. of BBC 1985–87; Man. Dir English Nat. Opera 1972–85, Chair. 1986–95; Man. Dir Opera North 1978–81, Vice-Chair. 1981–; Pres. British Bd of Film Classification 1985–97; English Nat. Opera 1995–; Artistic Dir Adelaide Festival for 1988; Artistic Adviser Buxton Festival 1993–98; Ed. Opera 1950–53, Kobbé's Complete Opera Book 1954, 1976, 1987, 1997; Austrian Great Silver Medal of Honour 1959, Lebanese Order of the Cedar 1970, Janáček Medal 1978. *Publications:* The Tongs and the Bones (autobiog.) 1981, Kobbé's Illustrated Opera Book 1989, Pocket Kobbé 1994. *Leisure interests:* looking at painting, sculpture, football, cricket. *Address:* Harewood House, Leeds, Yorkshire, LS17 9LG, England.

HARGROVE, Basil (Buzz); Canadian business executive; b. 8 March 1944, Bath, New Brunswick; s. of Percy Hargrove and Eileen Doucet; mem. Cttee Chrysler Canada 1965–75; Nat. Rep. 1975–78; Asst to Pres. and Dir CAW-Canada 1978–92; Pres., CAW-Canada 1992–. *Publication:* Labour of Love 1998. *Address:* CAW-Canada, 205 Placer Court, North York, Willowdale, Ont., M2H 3H9, Canada (Office). *Telephone:* (416) 497-4110 (Office). *Fax:* (416) 495-6552 (Office). *E-mail:* cawpres@caw.ca (Office). *Website:* www.caw .ca (Office).

HARGROVE, Roy; American jazz trumpeter; b. 16 Oct. 1969; ed Berklee School of Music, Boston, New School Univ., New York; toured Europe and Japan, playing with established jazz artists; formed own quintet and made debut solo record 1989; f. Roy Hargrove's Big Band 1995; performed at jazz festivals in Japan, Cuba and Italy. *Albums include:* Tokyo Sessions 1991, With the Tenors of our Time 1993, Of Kindred Souls 1993, Habana 1997.

HARIRI, Rafik Bahaa Edinburghe; Lebanese politician and business executive; b. 1944, Sidon, Lebanon; emigrated to Saudi Arabia 1965; teacher, then auditor with Eng co.; prin. Civil Construction Establishment (CICONEST) 1970–78; f. Saudi Oger (with Oger Enterprises) 1978; prin. Oger Co. 1979, Oger Liban, Saudi Oger Services UK; Prime Minister of Lebanon 1992–98, 2000–; Minister of Finance 1992–98, also of Posts and Telecommunications; f. Hariri Foundation for Culture and Higher Educ. 1979; Chevalier, Légion d'honneur 1981, Kt of the Italian Repub. 1982, Nat. Cedars Medal (Lebanon) 1983, Saint Butros and Saint Boulos Medal 1983, Save the Children 50th Anniversary Award 1983, King Faisal Medal 1983, Médaille de Paris 1983, Beirut Golden Key 1983 and numerous other medals and awards. *Address:* Office of President of Council of Ministers, Grand Sérail, place Riad es-Solh, Beirut, Lebanon. *Telephone:* (1) 746800. *Fax:* (1) 865630.

HARISH, Michael, BA; Israeli politician and economist; b. 28 Nov. 1936, Romania; s. of Joseph Harish and Esther Harish; m. Edith Normand 1963; three s. one d.; ed studies in econs and political science; Sec.-Gen. Labour Party's Student Org. 1961–63; Dir and Chair. Int. Dept Israel Labour Party 1967–82, Sec.-Gen. Israel Labour Party 1989–92; Minister of Industry and

Trade 1992–96; mem. Knesset 1974–; Deputy Chair. Defence and Foreign Affairs Cttee 1984–88; Chair. Finance Cttee 1988–89; Co-Chair. Jt Science and Tech. Cttee (US-Israel); mem. several ministerial cttees including Econ. Affairs, Immigrants' Absorption, Devt Areas, Jerusalem Affairs; mem. Cttee for co-ordinating activities between Govt and the Jewish Agency and the Zionist Org.; Pres. Me Harish Enterprises Ltd 1997–. *Leisure interests:* sport, music. *Address:* 3 Achout Ha'avoda Street, Givatayim, 53204 (Office); 5 Mishmar Hayarden Street, Givatayim, 53582 Israel (Home). *Telephone:* (3) 752-8012 (Office); (3) 571-5233 (Home). *Fax:* (3) 752-8011 (Office); (3) 571-5233 (Home). *E-mail:* meharish@internet-zahav.net.il.

HARKIANAKIS, Stylianos, D.D; Australian ecclesiastic; b. 29 Dec. 1935, Rethymnon, Crete, Greece; ed Theological School of Halki, Univ. of Athens; Deacon Constantinople (Istanbul) 1957; priest Rethymnon 1958; abbot Holy Patriarchal Monastery of Vlatadon, Thessaloniki 1966; Pres. Patriarchal Inst. of Patristic Studies; lecturer Univ. of Thessaloniki 1969–75, Univ. of Sydney 1975–85; Titular Bishop of Miletoupolis 1970; Exarch of Mount Athos 1970–75; Visiting Prof. Univ. of Regensberg 1973; Archbishop Greek Orthodox Church of Australia 1975, Primate 1975–; Co.-Chair. official theological dialogue between Roman Catholic and Orthodox churches 1980–; Dean St Andrew's Greek Orthodox Theological Coll. 1986–; mem. Jt official comm. of theological dialogue between Orthodox and Anglicans 1970; Dr. hc (Univ. of Lublin) 1985; Gottfried von Herder Prize (Vienna) 1973, Award for Poetry (Acad. of Athens) 1980, Golden Cross of St Andrew (Constantinople), Golden Cross of Holy Sepulchre, Archdiocese of Thyateira); awarded Key to City of Adelaide 1995. *Publications include:* The Infallibility of the Church in Orthodox Theology 1965, The Constitution "De Ecclesia" of the Second Vatican Council 1969, Orthodoxy and Catholicism, Incarnations of Dogma 1996, For Present and Future 1999, 21 Vols of poetry (in Greek), over 65 theological essays in periodicals. *Leisure interests:* poetry, reading, swimming, walking. *Address:* 242 Cleveland Street, Redfern, Sydney 2016, Australia. *Telephone:* (612) 9698-5066. *Fax:* (612) 9698-5368.

HARKIN, Thomas R., JD; American politician; b. 19 Nov. 1939, Cumming, Ia; s. of Patrick and Frances Harkin; m. Ruth Raduenz 1968; two d.; ed Iowa State Univ. and Catholic Univ. of America; mem. House of Reps. 1975–85; Senator from Iowa 1984–; Chair. Agric. Cttee 2001–; mem. Small Business Cttee, various subcttees., Democratic Steering Cttee; Democrat. *Publication:* Five Minutes to Midnight 1990. *Address:* United States Senate, 731 Hart Senate Office Bldg, Washington, DC 20510, USA.

HARLAND, Bryce, MA; New Zealand diplomatist; b. 11 Dec. 1931, Wellington; s. of Edward Harland and Annie McDonald (Gordon) Harland; m. 1st 1957; m. 2nd 1979; four c. (one deceased); ed Victoria Univ., Wellington and Tufts Univ., USA; with Ministry of Foreign Affairs 1953–91, various missions in Singapore, Bangkok, New York 1956–62, Head S. Pacific and Antarctic Div. 1962–64, Counsellor, Washington, DC 1965–69, Head Research Div., then Head Asian Affairs Div. 1969–70; Amb. to China (also accred to Viet Nam) 1973-76; asst Sec. 1976–81, also Dir of External Aid Div. 1981–82; Perm. Rep. to UN 1982–85; High Commr in UK (also accred to Ireland) 1985–91; Dir NZ Inst. of Int. Affairs 1997–2001; Visiting Fellow All Souls Coll., Oxford 1991; Queen's Service Order 1992. *Publications:* On Our Own, Asia: What Next? 1992, Collision Course 1996. *Leisure interests:* walking, music. *Address:* 9 Tinakori Road, Wellington, New Zealand.

HARLEY, Ian; British finance executive; articled clerk Touche Ross & Co. 1972; later with Corp. Planning Dept, Morgan Crucible Ltd; joined Abbey Nat. Building Soc. (later Abbey Nat. PLC) 1977, Financial Analyst then various Sr Man. posts with Finance, Treasury and Retail Divs., Reg. Man. for the SE, Retail Operations Div. 1984–86, Commercial Man. for Business Devt 1986, Group Financial Controller 1986–88, Asst Gen. Man. of Finance 1988–91, Finance Dir of Retail Operations 1991–92, Operations Dir Jan.–Oct. 1992, Group Treas. and Chief Exec. Abbey Nat. Treasury Services PLC 1992–98, Finance Dir and mem. Bd 1993–2002, CEO 1998–2002. *Address:* c/o Abbey National PLC, Abbey House, 215–229 Baker Street, London, NW1 6XL, England.

HARLIN, Renny; Finnish film director; b. 1958, Helsinki; m. Geena Davis (q.v.) (divorced); ed Univ. of Helsinki Film School; f. The Forge production co. with Geena Davis. *Films:* Born American (debut) 1986, Prison, A Nightmare on Elm Street IV: The Dream Master, Die Hard 2, The Adventures of Ford Fairlane, Rambling Rose (producer only), Cliffhanger, Speechless (co-producer only), Cutthroat Island (also producer), The Long Kiss Goodnight (also producer) 1996, Deep Blue Sea 1999, Blast from the Past (producer) 1999. *Films for television include:* Freddy's Nightmares 1990, T.R.A.X. 2000. *Address:* c/o Jim Wiatt, William Morris Agency, 151 South El Camino Drive, Beverly Hills, CA 90212, USA.

HÄRMÄLÄ, Jukka, BSc; Finnish business executive; b. 1946; CEO Stora Enso; mem. Bd Finnish Forest Industries Fed.; Vice-Chair. Finnlines; mem. European Round Table of Industrialists. *Address:* Stora Enso, World Trade Center, Klarabergsviadukten 70, C6, POB 70395, Stockholm 107 24, Sweden (Office). *Telephone:* (8) 613-66-00 (Office). *Fax:* (8) 10-60-20 (Office). *Website:* www.storaenso.com (Office).

HARMAN, Gilbert Helms, PhD; American professor of philosophy; b. 26 May 1938, E Orange, NJ; s. of William H. Harman, Jr and Marguerite Page; m. Lucy Newman 1970; two d.; ed Swarthmore Coll. and Harvard Univ.; mem. Dept of Philosophy, Princeton Univ. 1963–, Prof. of Philosophy 1971–, Co-Dir

Cognitive Science Lab. 1986–, Chair. Cognitive Studies Programme 1992–97; Fellow Cognitive Science Soc. 2003. *Publications:* Thought 1973, The Nature of Morality: An Introduction to Ethics 1977, Change in View: Principles of Reasoning 1986, Moral Relativism and Moral Objectivity (with Judith Jarvis Thomson) 1996, Reasoning, Meaning and Mind 1999, Explaining Values and other Essays in Moral Philosophy 2000. *Address:* Department of Philosophy, Princeton University, Princeton, NJ 08544 (Office); 106 Broadmead Street, Princeton, NJ 08540, USA (Home). *Telephone:* (609) 258-4301. *Fax:* (609) 258-1502. *E-mail:* harman@princeton.edu (Office).

HARMAN, Rt Hon Harriet, PC; British politician and solicitor; b. 30 July 1950; d. of the late John Harman and of Anna Spicer; m. Jack Dromey 1982; two s. one d.; ed St Paul's Girls' School and Univ. of York; Brent Community Law Centre 1975–78; Legal Officer, Nat. Council for Civil Liberties 1978–82; MP for Peckham 1982–97, for Camberwell and Peckham 1997–; Shadow Chief Sec. to Treasury 1992–94; Shadow Spokesperson on Employment 1994–95, on Health 1995–96, on Social Security 1996–97; Sec. of State for Social Security 1997–98; Solicitor-Gen. 2001–; Labour. *Publications:* Sex Discrimination in Schools 1977, Justice Deserted: the subversion of the jury 1979, The Century Gap 1993. *Address:* House of Commons, London, SW1A 0AA, England.

HARMAN, Sir John, Kt, BSc, FRSA; British civil servant; b. 30 July 1950, Leeds; s. of John Edward Harman and Patricia Josephine Harman (née Mullins); m. Susan Harman; one s. three d.; ed St George's Coll., Weybridge, Univ. of Manchester and Huddersfield Coll. of Educ.; teacher and lecturer until 1997; elected to W Yorkshire Metropolitan Co. Council 1981–86; elected to Kirklees Metropolitan Co. Council 1986, Leader 1986–99; first Leader Regional Ass. for Yorkshire and Humberside 1999–2000; mem. Bd Environment Agency 1996, later Deputy Chair., currently Chair.; Vice-Chair. Asscn of Metropolitan Authorities 1992–97; Deputy Leader Labour Group and Chair. Local Govt Asscn Urban Comm. 1997–2000; mem. Energy Savings Trust; Local Govt Adviser to UK Del. to the Earth Summit, Rio de Janeiro 1992; Founder Chair. UK Local Agenda 21 Steering Group; mem. Mathematical Asscn, Child Poverty Action Group; Chair. Kirklees Stadium Devt Ltd; Hon. Fellow ICE, Chartered Inst. of Wastes Man.; Hon. DCL. *Leisure interests:* music, gardening, Huddersfield Town Football Club. *Address:* Environment Agency, 25th Floor, Millbank Tower, 21-24 Millbank, London, SW1P 4XL, England (Office). *Telephone:* (20) 7863-8720 (Office). *Fax:* (20) 7863-8722 (Office). *E-mail:* enquiries@environment-agency.gov.uk (Office).

HARMEL, (Count) Pierre Charles José Marie, DenD; Belgian politician and university professor; b. 16 March 1911, Uccle, Brussels; s. of Charles Harmel and Eusébie André; m. Marie-Claire van Gehuchten 1946; four s. two d.; Prof., Faculty of Law, Univ. of Liège 1947–81; Prof. Emer.; mem. Chamber of Reps. 1946–71; Minister of Public Instruction and Fine Arts 1950–54; Minister of Justice 1958; Minister of Cultural Affairs 1959–60; Minister of Admin. 1960–61; Prime Minister 1965–66; Minister of Foreign Affairs 1966–73; co-opted Senator 1971; Minister of State Feb. 1973; Pres. of Senate 1973–77; mem. Acad. Royale de Belgique 1977–; Croix de guerre avec palmes 1940. *Publications:* Principes non bis in idem et les droits d'enregistrement 1942, La famille et l'impôt en Belgique 1944, Culture et profession 1944, Les sources et la nature de la responsabilité civile des notaires, en droit Belge de 1830 à 1962 1964, Organisation et déontologie du notariat 1977, Droit commun de la Vente 1985, Grandes avenues du droit 1988. *Address:* 8 avenue de l'Horizon, 1150 Brussels, Belgium. *Telephone:* (2) 762-46-80.

HARMOKO, Haji; Indonesian politician and journalist; b. 7 Feb. 1939, Kertosono, E Java; ed Sr High School, Kediri, E Java and Inst. of Nat. Defence (LEMHANAS), Jakarta; journalist, Merdeka (magazine and daily) 1960–65; Ed. Api (daily); Man. Ed. Merdeka and Chief Ed. Merdiko 1966–68; Chief Ed. Mimbar Kita 1968–69; Gen. Man., Chief Ed. Pos Kota (daily); mem. Bd of Film Censors 1974; mem. Press Council 1975; Chief Ed. Warna Sari 1976–83; mem. House of Reps. and People's Consultative Ass. and Head of Information and Mass Media Div. of Functional Group (GOLKAR) 1978, Pres. and Chair., then Co-ordinator of Advisers Golkar Party Oct. 1993–; Head of Advisory Bd of Newspaper Publrs. Asscn 1979–84; mem. Exec. Bd Press and Graphics Asscn 1980–84; Minister of Information 1983–97; Speaker People's Consultative Ass. and House of Reps. 1997–2001. *Address:* c/o People's Consultative Assembly, Jalan Gatot Subroto 6, Jakarta, Indonesia.

HARNICK, Sheldon Mayer; American lyricist; b. 30 April 1924, Chicago; s. of Harry M. and Esther (née Kanter) Harnick; m. 1st Mary Boatner 1950 (annulled 1957); m. 2nd Elaine May 1962 (divorced 1963); m. 3rd Margery Gray 1965; one s. one d.; ed Northwestern Univ.; wrote songs for univ. musicals; contrib. to revues: New Faces of 1952, Two's Company 1953, John Murray Anderson's Almanac 1954, The Shoestring Revue 1955, The Littlest Revue 1956, Shoestring '57 1957; with composer Jerry Bock wrote shows Body Beautiful 1958, Fiorello 1959 (Pulitzer Prize), Tenderloin 1960, Smiling the Boy Fell Dead (with David Baker) 1961, She Loves Me 1963, Fiddler on the Roof (Tony Award) 1964, The Apple Tree 1966, The Rothschilds 1970, Captain Jinks of the Horse Marines (opera, with Jack Beeson) 1975, Rex (with Richard Rodgers) 1976, Dr. Heidegger's Fountain of Youth (opera, with Jack Beeson) 1978, Gold (cantata, with Joe Raposo) 1980, trans.: The Merry Widow 1977, The Umbrellas of Cherbourg 1979, Carmen 1981, A Christmas Carol 1981 (musical; book and lyrics), Songs of the Auvergne 1982, A Wonderful Life 1986, The Appeasement of Aeolus 1990, Cyrano 1994. *Address:* c/o Alvin Deutsch, Deutsch and Blasband, 800 3rd Avenue, New York, NY 10022, USA.

HARNONCOURT, Nikolaus; Austrian musician and conductor; b. 6 Dec. 1929, Berlin, Germany; s. of Eberhard and Ladislaja Harnoncourt (née Meran); m. Alice Hoffelner 1953; three s. one d.; ed Matura Gymnasium, Graz, Acad. of Music, Vienna; mem. of Vienna Symphony Orchestra 1952–69; Prof. Mozarteum and Inst. of Musicology, Univ. of Salzburg 1972–; founder mem. of Concentus Musicus, Ensemble for Ancient Music 1954; Conductor, Zürich Opera and Amsterdam Concertgebouw Orkest; conducted Schubert's Alfonso, Vienna Festival 1997, La Perichole, Zürich 1998, Die Fledermaus, Vienna 2001; has given numerous concerts in Europe, Australia and the USA; Hon. DMus (Univ. of Edin.) 1987; shared Erasmus Prize 1980; H.G. Nägeli Medal, Zürich 1983; numerous awards for recordings. *Publications:* Musik als Klangrede, Wege zu einem neuen Musikverständnis 1982, Der musikalische Dialog 1983. *Leisure interests:* cultural history, woodwork. *Address:* 38 Piaristengasse, 1080 Vienna, Austria.

HARNOY, Ofra, CM; Israeli/Canadian cellist; b. 31 Jan. 1965, Hadera, Israel; d. of Jacob Harnoy and Carmela Harnoy; m. Robert S. Cash; studied with her father in Israel, William Pleeth in London, Vladimir Orloff in Toronto and in master classes with Mstislav Rostropovich, Pierre Fournier and Jacqueline du Pré; professional début, aged 10, with Boyd Neel Orchestra, Toronto; solo appearances with many maj. orchestras in the USA, Canada, Japan, Europe, Israel and Venezuela; TV appearances in Canada, the UK and other European countries, Japan and Australia; played world premiere performance Offenbach cello concerto, N American premiere Bliss cello concerto, world premiere recording of several Vivaldi cello concertos; many solo recordings; prizes and awards include: JUNO Award for Best Classical Soloist (Canada) 1987/88, 1988/89, 1991, 1992, 1993; First Prize Montreal symphony competition 1978, Canadian Music Competition 1979, Concert Artists Guild, New York 1982; Young Musician of the Year, Musical America magazine, USA 1983; Grand Prix du Disque; Critics' Choice, Best Records of the Year, The Gramophone, UK 1986, 1988, 1990. *Address:* P.O. Box 23046, 437 Spadina Road, Toronto, Ont., M5P 2W0, Canada; Suite 1000, 121 Richmond Street West, Toronto, Ont., M5H 2KA (Office). *Telephone:* (416) 863-1060. *Fax:* (416) 861-0191.

HAROUTUNIAN, Gagik Garushevich, DL; Armenian politician and lawyer; b. 1948, Gekhashen; 3 c.; ed Yerevan Univ.; lecturer, Yerevan Inst. of Industry 1975–77; in Yugoslavia 1977–78; on staff Cen. Cttee Armenian CP 1982–88; Head of Dept 1988–90; Deputy Chair. Armenian Supreme Soviet 1990–91; Vice-Pres. of Armenia 1991–; Acting Chair. Council of Ministers (Prime Minister) 1991–92; Pres. Constitutional Court 1996–; Pres. Int. Conf. of Constitutional Justice Organs of Young Democratic States; Council Pres. Centre of Constitutional Law; mem. IACL Council, Comm. for Democracy through Law, Council of Europe. *Publications:* Constitutional Review (with A. Mavčič) 1999, 2002. *Address:* Marshal Baghramyan Avenue 10, Yerevan 375019 (Office); Avan, Quchak Quart. Apt 11, Yerevan, Armenia (Home). *Telephone:* (1) 52-96-55; (1) 52-47-61. *Fax:* (1) 52-67-64. *E-mail:* armlaw@ concourt.am.

HAROUTUNIAN, Martin; Armenian engineer, metallurgist and trade union official; b. 10 Feb. 1928, Sisian Region; one s. one d.; ed Yerevan Polytech. Inst., Leningrad (now St Petersburg) Polytech. Inst.; Chief Metallurgist and Head of Founding Workshop, Armenian Electromachine-Building Plant 1949–72; Head of Charentsavan Founding Plant 'Tzentrolit' 1972–76; Deputy Chief Industry, Transport and Communications Dept, Cen. Cttee of Communist Party of Armenia 1976–77, First Sec. Rasdan Dist Cttee 1977–83; currently Pres. Confed. of Trade Unions in Armenia; Hero of Socialist Labour 1981, Order of Lenin (twice), Badge of Honour; Honoured Engineer of Armenia, Honoured Inventor of Armenia. *Publications include:* 35 published works including Founding Industry in Armenia and Moulding Materials of Armenia. *Leisure interests:* reconstruction and production of the technological process of decorative moulding from cast iron, bronze and other materials. *Address:* Confederation of Trade Unions of Armenia, Nalbandian Street 26, 375010 Yerevan (Office); 10/1 Zarubyan Street, Apt. 17, Yerevan, Armenia (Home). *Telephone:* 58-36-82 (Office); 52-70-60 (Home). *Fax:* 3741-54-33-82 (Office).

HARPER, Charles Michel, MBA; American business executive; b. 26 Sept. 1927, Lansing, Mich.; s. of Charles F. Harper and Alma Michel; m. Joan F. Bruggema 1950; one s. three d.; ed Purdue Univ. and Univ. of Chicago; Gen. Motors Corpn, Detroit 1950–54; Pillsbury Co., Minneapolis 1954–74, Group Vice-Pres. Poultry, Food Service and Venture Businesses 1970–74; Exec. Vice-Pres., COO, Dir Conagra Inc., Omaha 1974–76, Chair., CEO 1976–81, Chair. 1981–92; CEO 1981–92, CEO RJR Nabisco Holdings Inc. 1993–95, Chair. Bd 1995–96; mem. Bd of Dirs. Norwest Corpn, Valmont Industries, Inc., Peter Kiewit Sons Inc. and numerous other cos; several hon. degrees. *Address:* 6625 State Street, Omaha, NE 68152, USA. *Telephone:* (402) 571-6612. *Fax:* (402) 571-2151. *E-mail:* 104041.2015@compuserve.com (Office).

HARPER, Edward James, BA, BMus, ARCM, LRAM; British composer; b. 17 March 1941, Taunton, Somerset; m. 1st Penelope Teece 1969 (divorced 1984); m. 2nd Dorothy C. Shanks 1984; one s. one d.; ed King Edward VI Grammar School, Guildford, Royal Coll. of Music and Christ Church, Oxford; Lecturer in Music, Univ. of Edin. 1964, Sr Lecturer 1972–90, Reader 1990–; Dir New Music Group of Scotland 1973–91. *Compositions include:* Bartok Games 1972, Fanny Robin (chamber opera) 1975, Ricercari 1975, 7 Poems by E. E. Cummings 1977, Symphony 1979, Clarinet Concerto 1981, Hedda Gabler (opera) 1985, Qui creavit coelum (mass) 1986, The Mellstock Quire (opera)

1987, Homage to Thomas Hardy (orchestra, song cycle) 1990, The Lamb (soprano, chorus and orchestra) 1990, Overture for chamber orchestra 1992, And Winds, Austere and Pure (three songs for choir and piano duet) 1993, Chanson Minimale (for chamber orchestra) 1994, chamber opera based on William Golding's The Spire 1996, Psalm 150 (for unaccompanied choir) 1996, Scena (for solo cello) 1996, Trio (for clarinet, cello and piano) 1997, Souvenir for Two Pianos and Percussion 1998, Etude for Orchestra 1999, Lochinvar Opera for Schools 2000. *Address:* 7 Morningside Park, Edinburgh, EH10 5HD, Scotland.

HARPER, Heather, CBE, FRCM; British soprano; b. 8 May 1930, Belfast; d. of Hugh and Mary Eliza Harper; m. 2nd Eduardo J. Benarroch 1973; ed Trinity Coll. of Music, London; created soprano role in Britten's War Requiem, Coventry Cathedral 1962; toured USA with BBC Symphony Orchestra 1965, USSR 1967, soloist opening concerts at the Maltings, Snape 1967, Queen Elizabeth Hall 1967; annual concert and opera tours USA 1967–91 (retd); prin. soloist BBC Symphony Orchestra on 1982 tour of Hong Kong and Australia; prin. soloist Royal Opera House US visit 1984; also concerts in Asia, Middle East, Australia, European Music Festivals, S. America; prin. roles at Covent Garden, Bayreuth Festival, La Scala (Milan), Teatro Colón (Buenos Aires), Edinburgh Festival, Glyndebourne, Sadler's Wells, Metropolitan Opera House (New York), San Francisco, Frankfurt, Deutsche Oper (Berlin), Japan (with Royal Opera House Covent Garden Co.), Netherlands Opera House, New York City Opera; renowned performances of Arabella, Ariadne, Chrysothemis, Kaiserin, Marschallin (Richard Strauss); TV roles include Ellen Orford (Peter Grimes), Mrs. Coyle (Owen Wingrave), Ilia (Idomeneo), Donna Elvira (Don Giovanni), La Traviata, La Bohème; 25 consecutive years as prin. soloist at the Promenade concerts; Dir Singing Studies at the Britten-Pears School for Advanced Musical Studies, Aldeburgh, Suffolk 1986–; Prof. of Singing and Consultant Royal Coll. of Music, London 1985–93; First Visiting Lecturer in Residence, Royal Scottish Acad. of Music 1987–; retd from operatic stage 1986 (operatic farewell, Teatro Colón, Buenos Aires 1986), from concert stage 1991; mem. BBC Music Panel 1989, Royal Soc. of Arts 1989–; Hon. Fellow Trinity Coll. of Music; Hon. mem. RAM, Hon. DMus (Queen's Univ.); Edison Award 1971, Grammy Award 1979, 1984, 1991. *Recordings include:* Les Illuminations (Britten), Symphony No. 8 (Mahler), Don Giovanni (Mozart), Requiem (Verdi) and Missa Solemnis (Beethoven), Seven Early Songs (Berg), Marriage of Figaro, Peter Grimes, Four Last Songs (Strauss), 14 Songs with Orchestra. *Leisure interests:* gardening, painting, cooking, swimming, tennis. *Address:* c/o Royal Scottish Academy of Music and Drama, 100 Renfrew Street, Glasgow, G2 3DB, Scotland.

HARPER, John Lander, CBE, MA, DPhil, FRS; British research biologist, consultant and author; b. 27 May 1925, Rugby, Warwicks.; s. of John H. and Harriet M. (née Archer) Harper; m. Borgny Lerø 1954; one s. two d.; ed Magdalen Coll., Oxford; Demonstrator, Dept of Agric., Univ. of Oxford 1951–52, lecturer 1953–59; Rockefeller Foundation Fellow, Univ. of Calif. (Davis) 1959–60; Prof., Dept of Agric. Botany, Univ. Coll. of N Wales, Bangor 1960–67, Prof. of Agric. Botany and Head, School of Plant Biology 1967–78, Prof. of Botany and Head, School of Plant Biology 1978–82, Prof. Emer. 1982–, Dir of Unit. of Plant Population Biology 1982–90; mem. Nat. Environmental Research Council 1971–81, Agricultural and Food Research Council 1980–90, Jt Nature Conservation Cttee 1991–94; Ed. Proc. of the Royal Soc., B. 1993–99; Foreign Assoc. NAS (1984) and other learned socs.; Trustee British Museum of Nat. History 1990–98; Hon. DSc (Sussex) 1984; Dr. hc (Nat. Autonomous Univ. of Mexico) 1996; Darwin Medal, Royal Soc. 1990. *Publications:* Population Biology of Plants 1977, Ecology: Individuals, Populations and Communities 1986, 1990, 1996, Fundamentals of Ecology 2000; numerous papers in scientific journals. *Leisure interest:* gardening. *Address:* The Lodge, Chapel Road, Brampford Speke, Exeter, EX5 5HG, England. *Telephone:* (1392) 841929.

HARPER, Judson Morse, BS, PhD; American professor, academic administrator and consultant; b. 25 Aug. 1936, Lincoln, Neb.; s. of Floyd Harper and Eda Harper; m. Patricia A. Kennedy 1958; three s.; ed Iowa State Univ.; with General Mills 1963–70, latterly Man. for New Business Ventures in Research Div.; Prof. of Chemical and Bioresource Eng Colo State Univ. 1970–82, Vice-Pres. for Research and Information Tech. 1982–2000, Interim Pres. 1989–90, Special Asst to Pres. 2000–; Fulbright Scholar, Dept of Food Eng and Biotech. Technion, Haifa, Israel 1978–79; holder of six US patents; Fellow Inst. of Food Technologists 1992, AAAS 1995; Int. Award, Inst. of Food Techs. 1990, Charles A. Lory Public Service Award, Colo State Univ. 1993. *Publications include:* Extrusion of Foods 1981, Extrusion Cooking 1989. *Leisure interests:* running, skiing, gardening. *Address:* Special Projects Office, Colorado State University, Fort Collins, CO 80523 (Office); 1818 Westview Road, Fort Collins, CO 80524, USA (Home). *Telephone:* (970) 491-7628 (Office); (970) 493-1191 (Home). *Fax:* (970) 491-2293 (Office). *E-mail:* judson.harper@colostate .edu (Office). *Website:* www.research.colostate.edu (Office).

HARPPRECHT, Klaus Christoph; German author and television producer; b. 11 April 1927, Stuttgart; s. of Christoph and Dorothea (née Bronisch) Harpprecht; m. Renate Lasker 1961; ed Evangelical Theological Seminary, Blaubeuren, Württemberg and Univs. of Tübingen, Munich and Stuttgart; junior and Bonn corresp. Christ und Welt 1948–53; commentator and corresp., RIAS Berlin (Rundfunk im amerikanischen Sektor), Sender Freies Berlin and Westdeutscher Rundfunk, Cologne 1953–61; America corresp., Zweites Deutsches Fernsehen 1962–65; Publr, S. Fischer Verlag and ed. Monat 1966–71; consultant and chief speech writer to Chancellor Willy

Brandt 1972–74; ed. GEO magazine, Hamburg 1978–79; now ind. writer; Theodore Wolff and Drexel awards. *Radio:* regular contribs. to political and cultural programmes. *TV:* c. 100 documentary films. *Publications:* The East German Rising 1954, Viele Grüsse an die Freiheit 1964, Beschädigte Paradiese 1966, Willy Brandt: Portrait 1970, Deutsche Themen 1973, L'Evolution Allemande 1978, Der Fremde Freund Amerika: Eine Innere Geschichte 1982, Amerikaner: Freunde, Freunde, Ferne Nachbarn 1984, (with Thomas Hoepker) Amerika die Geschichte seiner Eroberung 1986, Georg Forster—oder die Liebe zur Welt 1987, Das Ende der Gemuetlichkeit 1987, Die Lust der Freiheit. Deutsche Revolutionaere in Paris 1989, (with Hans Hillmann) Die Leute von Port Madeleine-Dorfge-schichten aus der Provence 1989, Welt-Anschauung Reisebilder 1991, Thomas Mann. Eine Biographie 1995, Schreibspiele: Bemerkungen zur Literatur 1996, Mein Frankreich—eine schwierige Liebe 1999, Dieu est-il encore français? 2000, Im Kanzleramt Tagebuch der Jahre mit Willy Brandt 2000. *Leisure interests:* music, literature, history. *Address:* 16 Cros des Palmeraie, 83420 La Croix-Valmer, France. *Telephone:* (4) 94-79-60-76. *Fax:* (4) 94-54-20-30. *E-mail:* klausharpprecht@aol.com (Office).

HARRELL, Lynn; American cellist; b. 30 Jan. 1944, New York; s. of Mack Harrell and Marjorie Fulton; m. Linda Blandford 1976; one s. one d.; ed Juilliard School of Music, New York and Curtis Inst. of Music, Philadelphia; principal 'cellist, Cleveland Orch. (under George Szell) 1963–71; now appears as soloist with the world's major orchestras; Piatigorsky Prof. of Cello at Univ. of Southern Calif. 1987–93; Prof. Int. Cello Studies Royal Acad. of Music, London 1988–93, 1993–95; Artistic Dir LA Philharmonic Inst. 1988; soloist Memorial Concert for Holocaust Victims, Vatican 1994; Music Adviser, San Diego Symphony Orchestra 1988–89. *Music:* Recordings include works by J.S. Bach, Beethoven, Bloch, Boccherini, Brahms, Bruch, Debussy, Dutilleux, Dvořák, Elgar, Fauré, Haydn, Herbert, Hindemith, Lalo, Mendelssohn, Prokofiev, Rachmaninov, Rosza, Saint-Saëns, Schoenberg, Schubert, Schumann, Shostakovich, Strauss, Tchaikovsky, Villa-Lobos, Vivaldi, Walton. *Leisure interests:* chess, fishing, golf, writing. *Address:* c/o IMG Artists, Lovell House, 616 Chiswick High Road, London, W4 5RX, England.

HARRELSON, Woody (Woodrow Tracy), BA; American actor; b. 23 July 1961, Midland, Tex.; m. Laura Louie 1997; one c.; ed Hanover Coll. *Theatre includes:* The Boys Next Door, Two on Two (author, producer, actor), The Zoo Story (author, actor), Brooklyn Laundry, Furthest from the Sun (also playwright), On An Average Day, Comedy Theatre, London 2002. *Television includes:* Cheers, Bay Coven, Killer Instinct. *Films include:* Wildcats, Cool Blue, LA Story, Doc Hollywood, Ted and Venus, White Men Can't Jump, Indecent Proposal, I'll Do Anything, The Cowboy Way, Natural Born Killers, Money Train, The Sunchaser, Kingpin, The People vs Larry Flynt, Kingpin, Wag the Dog 1997, The Thin Red Line 1998, EdTV 1999, Play It to the Bone 1999, American Saint 2000. *Leisure interests:* sports, juggling, writing, chess. *Address:* c/o Creative Artists Agency, 9830 Wilshire Boulevard, Beverly Hills, CA 90212, USA.

HARRIES, Rt Rev Richard Douglas, DD, FKC, FRSL; British ecclesiastic; b. 2 June 1936; s. of Brig. W. D. J. Harries and G. M. B. Harries; m. Josephine Bottomley 1963; one s. one d.; ed Wellington Coll., Royal Mil. Acad, Sandhurst, Selwyn Coll, Cambridge, Cuddesdon Coll., Oxford; Lt, Royal Corps of Signals 1955–58; Curate, Hampstead Parish Church 1963–69; Chaplain, Westfield Coll. 1966–69; Lecturer, Wells Theological Coll. 1969–72; Warden, Salisbury and Wells Theological Coll. 1971–72; Vicar, All Saints, Fulham, London 1972–81; Dean, King's Coll., London 1981–87; Bishop of Oxford 1987–; Vice-Chair. Council of Christian Action 1979–87, Council for Arms Control 1982–87; Chair. Southwark Ordination Course 1982–87, Shalom, End Loans to South Africa (ELSTA) 1982–87, Christian Evidence Soc.; Chair. Church of England Bd of Social Responsibility 1996–2001; Consultant to the Archbishops on Jewish-Christian Relations 1986–92; Chair. Council of Christians and Jews 1993–2001, House of Lords select Cttee on Stem Cell Research 2001–02; Visiting Prof. Liverpool Hope Univ. 2002; mem. Home Office Advisory Cttee for Reform of Law on Sexual Offences 1981–85; mem. Royal Comm. on Lords Reform 1999–; mem. Bd Christian Aid 1994–2001; Hon. Fellow Selwyn Coll., Cambridge; Hon. DD (London) 1996; D. Univ.(Oxford Brookes) 2001; Sir Sigmund Steinberg Award 1989; FRSL 1996. *Publications:* Prayers of Hope 1975, Turning to Prayer 1978, Prayers of Grief and Glory 1979, Being a Christian 1981, Should Christians Support Guerrillas? 1982, The Authority of Divine Love 1983, Praying Round the Clock 1983, Seasons of the Spirit (Co-Ed.) 1984, Prayer and the Pursuit of Happiness 1985, Reinhold Niebuhr and the Issues of Our Time (Ed.) 1986, Morning has Broken 1985, Christianity and War in a Nuclear Age 1986, C. S. Lewis: The Man and his God 1987, Christ is Risen 1988, Is There a Gospel for the Rich? 1992, Art and the Beauty of God 1993, The Value of Business and its Values (jtly.) 1993, The Real God 1994, Questioning Faith 1995, A Gallery of Reflections 1995, In the Gladness of Today 2000, Christianity: Two Thousand Years (Co-Ed.) 2000, God Outside the Box: Why Spiritual People Object to Christianity 2002, After the Evil: Judaism and Christianity in the Shadow of the Holocaust 2003; contrib. to several books; numerous articles. *Leisure interests:* theatre, literature, sport. *Address:* Diocesan Church House, North Hinksey Lane, Oxford, OX2 0NB, England. *Telephone:* (1865) 208222. *Fax:* (1865) 790470. *E-mail:* bishopoxon@dch.oxford.anglican.org (Office). *Website:* www.oxford.anglican.org (Office).

HARRINGTON, Anthony Stephen; American diplomatist, lawyer and government official; b. 9 March 1941, Taylorsville, NC; s. of Atwell Lee Harrington and Louise (Chapman) Harrington; m. Hope Reynolds 1971; two

s.; ed Univ. of North Carolina, Duke Univ.; Sr Partner Hogan & Hartson; Amb. to Brazil 2000–01; Pres. Stonebridge Int. LCC 2001–; Chair. Pres.'s Intelligence Oversight Bd; Vice-Chair. Pres.'s Foreign Intelligence Advisory Bd 1994–99; Co-Chair. Nat. Alliance to End Homelessness; Dir Center for Democracy; Founder Telecom USA; Founder and Dir Ovation. *Leisure interests:* politics, tennis, gardening, reading. *Address:* Stonebridge International, 555 13th Street, NW, Washington, DC 20004 (Office); 701 Pennsylvania Avenue, NW, Washington, DC 20004; Ratcliffe Manor, 7768 Ratcliffe Manor Lane, Easton, MD 21601, USA (Home).

HARRIS, Chauncy Dennison, PhD, DLitt; American geographer; b. 31 Jan. 1914, Logan, Utah; s. of Franklin S. and Estella S. Harris; m. Edith Young 1940; one d.; ed Brigham Young Univ., Oxford and Chicago Univs; Prof. of Geography, Univ. of Chicago 1947–84, Samuel N. Harper Distinguished Service Prof. 1969–84, Prof. Emer. 1984–, Dean, Grad. Div. of Social Sciences 1954–60; Dir Centre for Int. Studies 1966–84; Asst to the Pres. 1973–75, Vice-Pres. for Academic Resources 1975–78; mem. Bd of Dirs, Social Science Research Council 1959–70, Vice-Chair. 1963–65, mem. Cttee on Programs and Policy 1959–67, Exec. Cttee 1967–70; mem. Exec. Cttee, Nat. Research Council Div. of Behavioral Sciences 1967–70; mem. Int. Research and Exchanges Bd 1968–71; mem. Exec. Cttee ICSU 1969–72; Del. 17th Gen. Conf. UNESCO, Paris 1972; Vice-Pres. Int. Geographical Union 1956–64, Sec.-Gen. 1968–76; mem. Asscn of American Geographers (Pres. 1957), American Asscn for Advancement of Slavic Studies (AAASS) (Pres. 1962), American Geographical Soc. (Vice-Pres. 1969–74), Nat. Council for Soviet and East European Research (Bd of Dirs 1977–83); mem. Council of Scholars, Library of Congress 1980–83, Visiting Cttee Univ. of Chicago Library (Life mem.); Conseil de la Bibliographie Géographique Internationale 1986–94; del. to numerous Int. Geographic Congresses 1949–; Foreign mem. Polish Acad. of Sciences; Hon. mem. Royal Geographical Soc. and geographical socs. of Paris, Berlin, Frankfurt, Rome, Florence, Warsaw, Belgrade and Japan; DEcon hc (Catholic Univ., Chile); Hon. LLD (Indiana Univ.); Hon. DSc (Univ. of Bonn, Univ. of Wisconsin-Milwaukee); Honors Award, Asscn of American Geographers 1976, Lauréat d'honneur, Int. Geographical Union 1976, Alexander Csoma de Körösi Memorial Medal, Hungarian Geographical Soc. 1971, Alexander von Humboldt Gold Medal, Gesellschaft für Erdkunde zu Berlin 1978, Award for Distinguished Contributions to Slavic Studies, AAASS 1978, Cullom Geographical Medal, American Geographical Soc. 1985, Master Teacher Award, Nat. Council for Geographic Educ. 1986, Victoria Medal, Royal Geographical Soc. 1987. *Publications:* Economic Geography of the USSR 1949, International List of Geographical Serials 1980, Soviet Geography: Accomplishments and Tasks 1962, Cities of the Soviet Union 1970, Annotated World List of Selected Current Geographical Serials 1980, Guide to Geographical Bibliographies and Reference works in Russian or on the Soviet Union 1975, Bibliography of Geography Part I, Introduction to General Aids 1976, Part II, Regional (Vol. 1) United States of America 1984, A Geographical Bibliography for American Libraries 1985, Directory of Soviet Geographers 1946–1987 1988; contributor to Sources of Information in the Social Sciences 1973, 1986, Encyclopaedia Britannica 1989, Columbia Gazetteer of the World 1998; articles in professional journals. *Address:* Department of Geography, University of Chicago, 5828 University Avenue, Chicago, IL 60637, USA.

HARRIS, (David) Kenneth, CBE, MA; British author, journalist and broadcaster; b. 11 Nov. 1919, Aberaman, Wales; s. of David Harris and Kathleen Powell; m. Doris Young-Smith 1949 (died 1970); m. 2nd Jocelyn Rymer 1987; two step-d.; ed Trowbridge High School for Boys and Wadham Coll., Oxford; war service, RA 1940–45; Washington Corresp., The Observer 1950–53, Assoc. Ed. 1976–84, Dir 1978–93; Chair. George Outram Ltd 1981–92, Caledonian Newspapers 1992–93; radio and TV work (mainly for BBC) 1957–85. *Publications:* Travelling Tongues: Debating Across America 1949, About Britain 1967, Conversations 1968, Life of Attlee 1982, The Wildcatter 1987, David Owen Personally Speaking 1987, Thatcher 1988, The Queen 1994. *Leisure interests:* reading, walking, horse racing. *Address:* 45 Molyneux Street, London, W1H 5HW, England. *Telephone:* (20) 7262-6172. *Fax:* (20) 7224-9201 (Home); (1775) 820686 (Home). *E-mail:* kenneth@harris45.demon .co.uk (Home).

HARRIS, Edward Allen (Ed), BFA; American actor; b. 28 Nov. 1950, Englewood, NJ; s. of Bob L. Harris and Margaret Harris; m. Amy Madigan; ed Columbia Univ., Univ. of Oklahoma, Norman, Calif. Inst. of Arts. *Stage appearances include:* A Streetcar Named Desire, Sweet Bird of Youth, Julius Caesar, Hamlet, Camelot, Time of Your Life, Grapes of Wrath, Present Laughter, Fool for Love (Obie award 1983), Prairie Avenue (LA Drama Critics Circle award 1981), Scar 1985 (San Francisco Critics award), Precious Sons 1986 (Theater World award), Simpatico 1994, Taking Sides 1996. *Films include:* Come 1978, Borderline 1978, Knightriders 1980, Creepshow 1981, The Right Stuff 1982, Swing Shift 1982, Under Fire 1982, A Flash of Green 1983, Places in the Heart 1983, Alamo Bay 1984, Sweet Dreams 1985, Code Name: Emerald 1985, Walker 1987, To Kill a Priest 1988, Jacknife 1989, The Abyss 1989, State of Grace 1990, Paris Trout 1991, Glengarry Glen Ross 1992, Needful Things 1993, The Firm 1993, China Moon 1994, Milk Money 1994, Apollo 13 1995, Just Cause 1995, Eye for an Eye 1995, The Rock 1996, Riders of the Purple Sage 1996, Absolute Power 1997, Stepmom 1998, The Truman Show 1998, The Third Miracle 1999, Enemy at the Gates 2001, A Beautiful Mind 2001, The Hours 2002. *Television films include:* The Amazing Howard

Hughes 1977, The Seekers 1979, The Aliens are Coming 1980, The Last Innocent Man 1987, Running Mates 1992, The Stand 1994. *Address:* 22031 Carbon Mesa Road, Malibu, CA 90265, USA.

HARRIS, Sir Henry, Kt, FRCP, FRCPath, FRS; British cell biologist; b. 28 Jan. 1925; s. of Sam and Ann Harris; m. Alexandra Brodsky 1950; one s. two d.; ed Sydney Boys High School, Univ. of Sydney, Lincoln Coll., Oxford; Dir of Research, Cancer Research Campaign, Sir William Dunn School of Pathology, Oxford 1954–59; Visiting Scientist, Nat. Inst. of Health, USA 1959–60; Head Dept of Cell Biology, John Innes Inst. 1960–63; Prof. of Pathology, Univ. of Oxford 1963–79, Regius Prof. of Medicine 1979–92; Head of the Sir William Dunn School of Pathology, Oxford 1963–94; Corresp. mem. Australian Acad. of Science; Foreign mem. Max Planck Soc.; Foreign Prof. Coll. de France; Foreign Hon. mem. American Acad. of Arts and Sciences; Hon. mem. American Asscn of Pathologists, German Soc. of Cell Biology; Hon. Fellow, Cambridge Philosophical Soc.; Hon. FRCPath (Australia); Hon. DSc (Edinburgh); Hon. MD (Geneva, Sydney); Feldberg Foundation Award; Ivison Macadam Memorial Prize; Prix de la Fondation Isabelle Decazes de Nöue for cancer research, Madonnina Prize for Medical Research; Katherine Burkan Judd Award of the Memorial-Sloan Kettering Cancer Center; Medal of Honour, Univ. of Pavia, Royal Medal of the Royal Soc., Osler Medal of the Royal Coll. of Physicians. *Publications:* Nucleus and Cytoplasm 1968, Cell Fusion 1970, La fusion cellulaire 1974, The Balance of Improbabilities 1987, The Cells of the Body 1995, The Birth of the Cell 1999, Things Come to Life 2002; papers on cellular physiology and biochemistry in various scientific books and journals and some fiction. *Leisure interests:* history and literature. *Address:* Sir William Dunn School of Pathology, South Parks Road, Oxford, OX1 3RE, England. *Telephone:* (1865) 275500. *Fax:* (1865) 275501.

HARRIS, John Robert, FRIBA, FRSA; British architect; b. 5 June 1919; s. of late Maj. Alfred Harris, CBE, DSO and Rosa A. Alderson; m. Gillian Rowe 1950; one s. one d.; ed Harrow School and Architectural Asscn School of Architecture; Lt Royal Engineers, Hong Kong 1940–41, prisoner-of-war 1941–45; Founder and Sr Partner, John R. Harris Architects, London 1949–2001 (also assoc. firms in Oman, Qatar, Dubai and Hong Kong), now consultant; partner, Courbe Duboz et Harris, Paris 1978–; Silver Jubilee Medal 1997. *Projects won in int. competition:* State Hosp. Qatar 1953, New Dubai Hosp. 1976, Corniche Devt and Traffic Intersection, Dubai 1978, HQ for Ministry of Social Affairs and Labour, Oman 1979, Tuen Mun Hosp. Hong Kong 1981, Ruler's Office Devt Dubai 1984, architects and planners for Zhuhai New Town, Econ. Zone, People's Republic of China 1984, Q-Tel HQ Qatar 1991, Deira Sea Corniche masterplan Dubai 1993. *Major works in UK include:* Royal Northern Hosp., London 1973, Ealing Hosp. 1976, RAF Upper Heyford Hosp. 1982, Stoke Mandeville Hosp. 1983 and several dept stores, redevt. of Dorchester Hotel 1989, Gloucester Park devt, London, re-devt Sheraton Grand Hotel, Edinburgh 1993; major works abroad include Dubai Int. Trade Centre (third tallest bldg in Arab world), British Amb.'s Residence, Abu Dhabi, 3000-seat Conference Centre, Doha 1997 and numerous banks, hosps., shopping centres, particularly in Gulf States. *Publications:* John R. Harris Architects (jtly) 1984; contribs. to books and architectural and tech. journals. *Leisure interests:* architecture, sailing, travel. *Address:* 24 Devonshire Place, London, W1G 6BX, England. *Telephone:* (20) 7935-9353. *Fax:* (20) 7935-5709. *E-mail:* harris_architect@compuserve.com (Office).

HARRIS, Julie; American actress; b. 2 Dec. 1925, Mich.; d. of William Picket and Elsie (née Smith) Harris; m. 1st Jay I. Julien 1946 (divorced 1954); 2nd Manning Gurian 1954 (divorced 1967); one s.; 3rd Walter Erwin Carroll 1977 (divorced 1982); ed Yale Drama School; New York Drama Critics' Award for I Am a Camera, Nat. Medal of the Arts 1994; numerous other awards. *Theatre work includes:* Sundown Beach 1948, The Young and Fair 1948, Magnolia Alley 1949, Montserrat 1949, The Member of the Wedding 1950, Sally Bowles in I Am a Camera 1951, The Lark 1956, A Shot in the Dark 1961, Marathon 33 1964, Ready When You Are, C.B. 1964, And Miss Reardon Drinks a Little 1971, Voices 1972, The Last of Mrs. Lincoln 1973, In Praise of Love 1974, The Belle of Amherst, New York 1976, London 1977, Break a Leg, New York 1979, Mixed Couples, New York 1980, Driving Miss Daisy 1988, Lucifer's Child 1991, Lettice and Lovage, The Fiery Furnace (off-Broadway debut) 1993, The Glass Menagerie 1996, The Gin Game 1997, Ellen Foster 1997, Love is Strange 1999. *Films include:* East of Eden 1955 (Antoinette Perry Award), I Am a Camera 1956, Poacher's Daughter 1960, The Haunting, The Moving Target, Voyage of the Damned 1976, The Bell Jar 1979, Gorillas in the Mist, Housesitter, The Dark Half, Carried Away, Bad Manners 1997, The First of May 1998, Frank Lloyd Wright 1998. *Television:* Little Moon of Alban (TV film) 1960, Knots Landing 1982, Scarlett, The Christmas Tree, Ellen Foster. *Address:* c/o Gail Naehlis, William Morris Agency, 151 South El Camino Drive, Beverly Hills, CA 90212, USA.

HARRIS, Martin Best, Kt, CBE, PhD, DL; British university vice-chancellor; b. 28 June 1944, Ruabon, Wales; s. of William Best Harris and Betty Evelyn Harris (née Martin); m. Barbara Mary Daniels 1966; two s.; ed Devonport High School, Plymouth, Queens' Coll., Cambridge, School of Oriental and African Studies, London Univ.; lecturer in French Linguistics, Univ. of Leicester 1967–72; Sr Lecturer in French Linguistics, Univ. of Salford 1972–76, Prof. of Romance Linguistics 1976–87, Pro-Vice-Chancellor 1981–87; Vice-Chancellor Univ. of Essex 1987–92; Vice-Chancellor Univ. of Manchester 1992–; Chair. Cttee of Vice-Chancellors and Prins. 1997–99; mem. Univ. Grants Cttee 1984–87, Chair. Northern Ireland Sub-Cttee 1985–87; Chair. Northern Ireland Cttee, Univs. Funding Council 1987–91, Nat. Curriculum Working Group on Modern Languages 1989–90, HEFCE/CVCP review of postgraduate educ. 1995–96; Chair. Clinical Standards Advisory Group 1996–99; Chair. North West Univs. Asscn. 1999–2001, Higher Educ. Careers Advisory Services Review 2000–01; Deputy Chair. North West Devt Agency Bd 2002–, Comm. for Health Improvement 1999–2002; Chair. of Govs., Centre for Information on Language Teaching 1990–96; Crown Gov. SOAS 1990–93; Gov. Anglia Polytechnic Univ. 1989–93; mem. High Council, European Univ. Inst., Florence 1992–97; DL (Greater Manchester) 1997; Hon. mem. Royal Northern Coll. of Music 1996; Hon. Fellow Queens' Coll., Cambridge 1992, Bolton Inst. 1996, Univ. of Cen. Lancs. 1999; Hon. LLD (Queen's Univ., Belfast) 1992, Hon. DUniv (Essex) 1993, Hon. DLitt (Salford) 1995, (Manchester Metropolitan) 2000. *Publications:* The Evolution of French Syntax 1978, The Romance Languages (with N Vincent) 1988; numerous articles in anthologies and professional journals. *Leisure interests:* gardening, walking. *Address:* University of Manchester, Oxford Road, Manchester, M13 9PL, England (Office). *Telephone:* (161) 275-7399. *Fax:* (161) 272-6313. *E-mail:* martin.harris@man.ac.uk (Office).

HARRIS, Mike; Canadian business executive; b. 1945, Toronto; s. of Deane Harris and Hope Harris; m. Janet Harris; two s.; began career in tourism and recreation industry owning ventures including a tourist resort and a ski centre; first elected to Ont. Prov. Legis. as MPP for Nipissing 1981, Minister of Natural Resources and Energy 1985, Premier of Ont. Prov. 1995–2002; Leader of Conservative Party 1990–2002; Dir Magna Int. Inc. 2003–; Strategic Business Adviser Goodmans LLP; Sr Fellow, Fraser Inst., Vancouver. *Leisure interests:* golf, skiing, bridge. *Address:* Magna International Inc., 337 Magna Drive, Aurora, L4G 7K1, Canada (Office). *Telephone:* (905) 726-2462 (Office). *Fax:* (905) 726-7164 (Office). *Website:* www.magnaint.com (Office).

HARRIS, Rene; Nauruan politician; b. 11 Nov. 1947; m. Roslyn Harris; five c.; ed Geelong Coll., Australia; fmr Man. Nauru Pacific (shipping) Line; MP for Aiwo 1977; mem. of numerous parl. cttees. and select cttees.; Deputy Speaker of Parl. 1978, 1986; fmr Pres. Nauru Nat. Group, Asian Pacific Parliamentarians' Union; Speaker of Parl. 1986; labour officer Nauru Phosphate Corpn 1979, later Asst, Personnel Man. 1981, Chair. Bd of Dirs. 1992–95; Pres. of Nauru 1999–2000, ousted following vote of no confidence April 2000, re-elected March 2001, resgnd Jan. 2003 after no-confidence resolution approved by Parl.; also Minister of Foreign Affairs 2001–03. *Leisure interests:* Australian rules football, tennis. *Address:* c/o Office of the President, Yaren, Nauru (Office).

HARRIS, Robert Dennis, FRSL; British journalist and author; b. 7 March 1957, Nottingham; s. of late Dennis Harris and Audrey Harris; m. Gill Hornby 1988; two s. two d.; ed Univ. of Cambridge; Pres. Cambridge Union; Dir and reporter, BBC 1978–86; Political Ed. Observer 1987–89; columnist Sunday Times 1989–92, 1996–97. *Publications:* non-fiction: A Higher Form of Killing (with Jeremy Paxman, q.v.) 1982, Gotcha! 1983, The Making of Neil Kinnock 1984, Selling Hitler 1987, Good and Faithful Servant 1990; novels: Fatherland 1992, Enigma 1995 (film 2001), Archangel 1998. *Leisure interests:* collecting books, walking. *Address:* Old Vicarage, Kintbury, Berkshire, RG17 9TR, England.

HARRIS, Rolf, OBE, AM; Australian entertainer; b. 30 March 1930, Perth; s. of C. G. Harris and A. M. Harris (née Robbins); m. Alwen Hughes 1958; one d.; ed Perth Modern School, Univ. of Western Australia, Claremont Teachers' Coll.; appeared in "The Rolf Harris Show" (BBC TV) 1967–71; represented Australia at seven World Fairs 1969–85; host of BBC TV's "Animal Hospital" 1994–, "Rolf's Amazing Animals" 1997–; host and narrator of TV documentary series "Bligh of the Bounty—World Navigator" 1998–99; Hon. mem. Royal Soc. of British Artists. *Exhibition:* Rolf on Art, Nat. Gallery, London 2002. *Singles include:* Tie Me Kangaroo Down Sport 1960, Two Little Boys 1969. *Publications:* Rolf Harris Picture Book of Cats 1978, Your Cartoon Time 1986, Win or Die 1989, Your Animation Time 1991, Personality Cats 1992, Me and You and Poems Too 1993, Can You Tell What It Is Yet (autobiog.) 2001. *Leisure interests:* painting and portraiture, photography, wood carving, lapidary. *Address:* c/o Billy Marsh and Associates, 174–178 North Gower Street, London, NW1 2NB, England. *Telephone:* (20) 7388-6858. *Fax:* (20) 7388-6848. *Website:* www.rolfharris.com (Office).

HARRIS, Stephen E., MS, PhD; American professor of electrical engineering and applied physics; b. 29 Nov. 1936, Brooklyn, New York; s. of Henry Harris and Anne Alpern Harris; m. Frances J. Greene 1959; one s. one d.; ed Rensselaer Polytechnic, Troy, New York and Stanford Univ.; Prof. of Electrical Eng Stanford Univ. 1963–79, of Electrical Eng and Applied Physics 1979–, Dir Edward L. Ginzton Lab. 1983–88, Kenneth and Barbara Oshman Prof. 1988–, Chair. Dept of Applied Physics 1993–96; Guggenheim Fellowship 1976–77; mem., Nat. Acad. of Eng, Frederic Ives Medal 1999; A. Noble Prize 1965, McGraw Research Award 1973, Sarnoff Award 1978, Davies Medal 1984, C. H. Townes Award 1985, Einstein Prize 1991, Quantum Electronics Award 1994. *Publications:* articles in professional journals. *Leisure interests:* skiing, jogging, hiking. *Address:* Edward L. Ginzton Laboratory, Stanford University, 450 Via Palou, Stanford, CA 94305, USA (Office). *Telephone:* (650) 723-0224 (Office). *Fax:* (650) 725-4115 (Office). *E-mail:* seharris@ee.stanford.edu (Office). *Website:* www.-ee.stamford.edu/seharris/ (Office).

HARRIS, Thomas; American writer; b. 1940, Jackson, Tenn.; s. of William Thomas Harris, Jr and Polly Harris; m. (divorced); one d.; ed Baylor Univ., Tex.; worked on newsdesk Waco News-Tribune; mem. staff Associated Press,

New York. *Publications:* Black Sunday, Red Dragon (filmed as Manhunter), The Silence of the Lambs (filmed). *Address:* St Martin's Press, 175 Fifth Avenue, New York, NY 10010, USA.

HARRIS OF HIGH CROSS, Baron (Life Peer), cr. 1979, of Tottenham in Greater London; **Ralph Harris,** MA; British economist; b. 10 Dec. 1924, London; m. Jose Pauline Jeffery 1949; two s. (both deceased) one d.; ed Tottenham Grammar School, Queens' Coll. Cambridge; lecturer in Political Economy, St Andrew's Univ. 1949–56; Gen. Dir Inst. of Econ. Affairs 1957–87, Chair. 1987–89, Founder Pres. 1990–; Liberal-Unionist parl. cand., Kirkcaldy 1951, Edinburgh Cen. 1955; Vice-Pres. Ross McWhirter Foundation; Chair. Bruges Group 1989–91, FOREST 1989–; Jt Chair. Int. Centre for Research into Econ. Transformation, Moscow 1990–95; Dir (Ind. Nat.) Times Newspapers Holdings Ltd 1988–2001; Hon. DSc (Buckingham) 1984; Free Enterprise Award 1975. *Publications include:* Politics Without Prejudice (biography of R. A. Butler) 1956, Libraries: Free for All? (with A. P. Herbert) 1962, Challenge of a Radical Reactionary 1980, Welfare Without the State (with Arthur Seldon) 1987, Beyond the Welfare State 1988, No, Prime Minister! 1994 and numerous others. *Leisure interests:* word-processing and sea-swimming. *Address:* 5 Cattley Close, Wood Street, Barnet, Herts., EN5 4SN, England. *Telephone:* (20) 8449-6212.

HARRISON, Sir David, Kt, CBE, ScD, FREng, FRSC, FIChemE, CIMgt, FRSA; British academic; b. 3 May 1930, Clacton-on-Sea; s. of Harold David Harrison and Lavinia Wilson; m. Sheila Rachel Debes 1962; one s. one d. (one s. deceased); ed Bede School, Sunderland, Clacton County High School, Selwyn Coll., Cambridge Univ.; lecturer in Chemical Eng, Cambridge Univ. 1956–79, Sr Tutor, Selwyn Coll. 1967–79; Vice-Chancellor Univ. of Keele 1979–84, Univ. of Exeter 1984–94; Master Selwyn Coll., Cambridge 1994–2000, Chair. Faculty of Eng 1994–2001; mem. Council, Cambridge Univ. 1967–75, 1995–2000, Deputy Vice-Chancellor 1995–2000, Pro-Vice-Chancellor 1997; Visiting Prof. of Chemical Eng, Univ. of Delaware, USA 1967, Univ. of Sydney, Australia 1976; Chair. Faculty Bd of Educ., Cambridge Univ. 1976–78; Hon. Ed. Transactions, Inst. of Chemical Engineers 1972–78; Chair., Bd of Trustees, Homerton Coll., Cambridge 1979–, Univs Cen. Council for Admissions 1984–91, Church & Associated Colls Advisory Cttee of the Polytechnics and Colls Funding Council 1989–91, Cttee of Vice-Chancellors & Prins. of UK 1991–93, Shrewsbury School 1989–, Advisory Cttee on Safety of Nuclear Installations 1993–99, Eastern Arts Bd 1994–98, Arts Council of England 1996–98; Dir Salters' Inst. of Industrial Chem. 1993–; Vice-Pres. Inst. of Chemical Engineers 1989, Pres. 1991–92; Fellow Selwyn Coll., Cambridge 1957–; Liveryman Salters' Co. 1998; Hon. DUniv (Keele) 1992; Hon. DSc (Exeter) 1995; George E. Davis Medal, Inst. of Chemical Engineers 2001. *Publications:* Fluidized Particles (with J. F. Davidson) 1963, Fluidization (with J. F. Davidson) 1971, Fluidization (with J. F. Davidson and R. Clift) 1985. *Leisure interests:* music, tennis, hill walking, good food. *Address:* 7 Gough Way, Cambridge, CB3 9LN, England. *Telephone:* (1223) 359315. *Fax:* (1223) 319822. *E-mail:* sirdavidharrison@waitrose.com (Home).

HARRISON, Sir Terence, Kt, BSc, DL, FREng, FIMechE, FIMARE; British business executive; b. 7 April 1933; s. of late Roland Harrison and Doris Wardle; m. June Forster 1956; two s.; ed A. J. Dawson Grammar School, Co. Durham, West Hartlepool and Sunderland Tech. Colls. and Univ. of Durham; marine Eng apprenticeship, Richardson's Westgarth, Hartlepool 1949–53; mil. service, Nigeria 1955–57; Clarke Chapman Ltd, Gateshead 1957–77, Man. Dir 1976–77; Northern Eng Industries 1977, Chief Exec. 1983–86, Exec. Chair. 1986–89; Dir Rolls-Royce PLC 1989–96, Chief Exec. 1992–96; Dir (non-exec.) Alfred McAlpine PLC 1995–2002, Chair. 1996–2002; Hon. DEng (Newcastle) 1991; Hon. D. Tech. (Sunderland) 1995; Hon. DSc (Durham) 1996. *Publications:* technical papers. *Leisure interests:* golf, fell walking. *Address:* Alfred McAlpine, 8-10 Suffolk Street, London, SW1Y 4HG (Office); 2 The Garden Houses, Whalton, Northumberland, NE61 3HB, England. *Telephone:* (1670) 775400 (Home). *Fax:* (1670) 775291 (Home).

HARRISON, Tony; British poet; b. 30 April 1937, Leeds; s. of Harry Ashton Harrison and Florence (née Wilkinson) Horner; ed Leeds Grammar School and Univ. of Leeds; Cholmondeley Award for Poetry, Geoffrey Faber Memorial Award, European Poetry Translation Prize, Whitbread Poetry Prize 1993, Mental Health Award 1994, Prix Italia 1994. *Television and film work includes:* The Big H 1984, 'V' 1987, Loving Memory 1987, Yan Tan Tethera 1987, The Blasphemers' Banquet 1989, The Gaze of the Gorgon 1992, Black Daisies for the Bride 1993, A Maybe Day in Kazakhstan 1994, The Shadow of Hiroshima 1995, Prometheus 1999, Crassingo 2002. *Theatre includes:* Aikin Mata 1965, The Misanthrope 1973, Phaedra Britannica 1975, The Passion 1977, Bow Down 1977, The Bartered Bride 1978, The Oresteia 1981, Yan Tan Tethera 1983, The Mysteries 1985, The Trackers of Oxyrhynchus 1988–90, The Common Chorus 1992, Square Rounds 1992, Poetry or Bust 1993, The Kaisers of Carnuntum 1995, The Labourers of Herakles 1995, The Prince's Play 1996, Fire and Poetry 1999. *Publications include (poetry):* Earthworks 1964, The Loiners 1970, Palladas: Poems 1975, The School of Eloquence and Other Poems 1978, Continuous 1981, A Kumquat for John Keats 1981, US Martial 1981, Selected Poems 1984, The Mysteries 1985 (also known as Plays 1), 'V' 1985, 'V' and other poems 1990, A Cold Coming: Gulf War Poems 1991, The Gaze of the Gorgon and other poems 1992, The Shadow of Hiroshima and other film/poems 1995, Permanently Bard 1995, Plays 3 1996, The Prince's Play 1996, Prometheus 1999, Laureate's Block 2000, Plays 2 2002, Plays 4 2002. *Address:* c/o Gordon Dickerson, 2 Crescent Grove, London, SW4 7AH, England.

HARRISON, Wayne David, BA; Australian theatre director and producer; b. 7 March 1953, Melbourne; s. of Lindsay Graham Harrison and Florence Rosina Cannell; ed Christian Brothers' Coll., Melbourne, Univ. of Melbourne, Univ. of NSW; Dramaturge, Sydney Theatre Co. 1981–86; Asst Dir Northside Theatre Co., NSW 1987–89; Artistic Dir Sydney Theatre Co. 1990–99; Creative Dir Back Row Int., London 1999–2000. *Address:* Back Row Productions, Garrick Theatre, 2 Charing Cross Road, London, WC2H 0HH, England (Office).

HARRISON, William Burwell, Jr, BA; American banker; b. 12 Aug. 1943, Rocky Mount, NC; s. of William Burwell and Katherine Spruill; m. Anne MacDonald Stephens 1985; two d.; ed Univ. of N Carolina, Chapel Hill; trainee Chemical Bank, New York 1967–69, Mid-South Corpn and corresp. banking group 1969–74, West Coast corp. and corresp. banking group 1974–76, Dist Head and Western Regional Co-ordinator San Francisco 1976–78, Regional Co-ordinator and Sr Vice-Pres. London 1978–82, Sr Vice-Pres. and Divisional Head, Europe 1982–83, Exec. Vice-Pres. US corp. div. New York 1983–87, Group Exec., banking and corporate finance group 1987–90, Vice-Chair. institutional banking 1990–; Vice-Chair. Global Bank 1992–; Vice-Chair. Manhattan Corpn (now Chase Manhattan Corpn.) New York 1995–2000, Pres., CEO 1999–2000, Chair., CEO 2000–; Pres., CEO JP Morgan Chase (after merger) 2000, Chair. 2001–; Bd Dirs. Freeport-McMoRan Copper & Gold, Inc., New Orleans; Bd Trustees Carnegie Hall; Trustee Cen. Park Conservancy. *Leisure interests:* athletics, travel. *Address:* JP MorganChase, 270 Park Avenue, New York, NY 10017, USA (Office). *Telephone:* (212) 270-6000 (Office). *Fax:* (212) 682-3761 (Office). *Website:* www.jpmorganchase.com (Office).

HARRISS, Gerald Leslie, MA, DPhil, FBA; British historian and university teacher; b. 22 May 1925, London; s. of W. L. Harriss and M. J. O. Harriss; m. Margaret Anne Sidaway 1959; two s. three d.; ed Chigwell School, Essex, Magdalen Coll., Oxford; war service in RDVR 1944–46; Oxford Univ. 1946–53; Lecturer, Durham Univ. 1953–65, Reader 1965–67; Fellow and Tutor in History, Magdalen Coll., Oxford 1967–92, Emer. Fellow 1992–, Reader in Modern History, Univ. of Oxford 1990–92. *Publications:* King, Parliament and Public Finance in Medieval England 1975, Henry V: the Practice of Kingship (Ed.) 1985, Cardinal Beaufort 1988, (Ed.) K. B. McFarlane, Letters to Friends 1997. *Address:* Fairings, 2 Queen Street, Yetminster, Sherborne, Dorset, DT9 6LL, England.

HARRY, Deborah Ann; American singer; b. 11 July 1945, Miami, Fla; d. of Richard Smith and Catherine (Peters) Harry; ed Centenary Coll.; singer and songwriter, rock group Blondie 1975–83; awarded Gold, Silver and Platinum records. *Singles include:* Heart of Glass, Call Me, Tide is High, Rapture. *Albums include:* Blondie: The Hunter, Plastic Letters, Parallel Lines, Eat to the Beat, Autoamerican, Koo Koo (solo), Rockbird, Def, Dumb and Blond 1989, Blonde and Beyond 1993, Rapture 1994, Virtuosity 1995, Rockbird 1996, Der Einziger Weg 1999. *Film appearances:* Union City Blues, Videodrome, Roadie, Hairspray, Tales from the Darkside: The Movie 1990, Joe's Day 1999, 200 1999, Six Ways to Sunday 1999, Ghost Light 2000, Deuces Wild 2000, Red Lipstick 2000. *Television appearances:* Saturday Night Live, The Muppet Show, Tales from the Darkside, Wiseguys. *Theatre:* Teaneck Tanzi, The Venus Flytrap. *Address:* Innovative Artists, Suite 2850, 1999 Avenue of the Stars, Los Angeles, CA 90067, USA (Office).

HARRYHAUSEN, Ray; American film producer, writer and special effects creator; b. 29 June 1920, Los Angeles, Calif.; s. of Frederick W. Harryhausen and Martha Reske; m. Diana Livingstone 1962; one d.; ed Los Angeles City Coll.; model animator for George Pal's Puppetoons in early 1940s; served US. Signal Corps; made series of filmed fairy tales with animated puppets for schools and churches; Asst to Willis O'Brien working on Mighty Joe Young 1946; designed and created special effects for The Beast from 20,000 Fathoms; evolved own model animation system Dynarama used for first time in conjunction with producer Charles H. Schneer in film It Came from Beneath the Sea; subsequently made many films in Dynarama with Schneer; Gordon E. Sawyer Award 1992. *Films include:* Twenty Million Miles to Earth, The Three Worlds of Gulliver, Jason and the Argonauts, The First Men in the Moon, One Million Years BC, The Valley of the Gwangi, The Golden Voyage of Sinbad, Sinbad and the Eye of the Tiger, Clash of the Titans.

HART, Garry Richard Rushby, LLB; British solicitor; b. 29 June 1940, London; s. of Dennis George Hart and Evelyn Mary Hart; m. 1st Paula Lesley Shepherd 1966 (dissolved 1986); two s. one d.; m. 2nd Valerie Elen Mary Davies 1986; two d.; ed Northgate Grammar School, Ipswich, Univ. Coll. London; solicitor, Herbert Smith 1966–70, partner 1970–98, Head of Property Dept 1988–97; Special Expert Adviser to Lord Chancellor 1998–; Deputy Chair. Trustees Architecture Foundation 1997–; Trustee Almeida Theatre 1997–, Chair. 1997–2002; Trustee British Architectural Library Trust 2000–; Fellow Univ. Coll. London 2001; Hon. FRIBA 2000. *Leisure interests:* travel, conservation, talking. *Address:* Lord Chancellor's Department, Selborne House, 54–60 Victoria Street, London, SW1E 6QW, England. *Telephone:* (020) 7210-8500.

HART, Gary, LLB; American politician and lawyer; b. 28 Nov. 1936, Ottawa, Kan.; m. Lee Ludwig 1958; one s. one d.; ed Bethany Coll., Okla, Yale Univ.; called to bar 1964; Attorney, US Dept of Justice and Special Asst to Sec., US Dept of Interior 1964–67; legal practice, Denver, Colo 1967–70, 1972–74; Nat. Campaign Dir, George McGovern Democratic Presidential Campaign 1970–72; Senator for Colorado 1975–86; with Davis, Graham & Stubbs,

Denver 1985–; assisted in John F. Kennedy Presidential Campaign 1960; voluntary organizer, Robert F. Kennedy Presidential Campaign 1968; fmr mem. Bd of commrs., Denver Urban Renewal Authority; fmr mem., Park Hill Action Cttee. *Publications:* Right From the Start, A New Democracy 1983, The Double Man (with W. S. Cohen,) 1985, America Can Win 1986, The Strategies of Zeus 1987, Russia Shakes the World 1991.

HART, Michael, CBE, PhD, FInstP, CPhys, FRS; British professor of physics; b. 4 Nov. 1938, Bristol; s. of Reuben H.V. Hart and Phyllis M. Hart (née White); m. Susan M. Powell 1963; three d.; ed Cotham Grammar School, Bristol and Univ. of Bristol; Research Assoc. Dept of Materials Science and Eng Cornell Univ. 1963–65; Dept of Physics, Univ. of Bristol 1965–67, Lecturer in Physics 1967–72, Reader 1972–76; Sr Resident Research Assoc. Nat. Research Council, NASA Electronics Research Center, Boston, Mass. 1969–70; Special Adviser, Cen. Policy Review Staff 1975–77; Wheatstone Prof. of Physics, King's Coll. London 1976–84; Prof. of Physics, Univ. of Manchester 1984–93, Prof. Emer. of Physics 1993–; Visiting Prof. of Applied Physics, De Montfort Univ. 1993–1998, Hon. Prof. in Eng, Warwick Univ. 1993–1995; Science Programme Co-ordinator (part-time), Daresbury Lab. Science and Eng Research Council 1985–88; Chair. Nat. Synchrotron Light Source, Brookhaven Nat. Lab., USA 1995–2000; Visiting Prof. of Physics, Univ. of Bristol 2000–; Bertram Eugene Warren Award, American Crystallographic Asscn 1970, Charles Vernon Boys Award, Inst.of Physics 1971. *Publications:* contribs to learned journals. *Leisure interests:* flying kites, cookery. *Address:* Department of Physics, University of Bristol, Bristol, BS8 1TL (Office); 2 Challoner Court, Merchants Landing, Bristol, BS1 4RG, England (Home). *Telephone:* (0117) 921-5291 (Home). *E-mail:* M.Hart@Bristol.ac.uk (Office).

HART, Oliver D'Arcy, PhD; British professor of economics; b. 9 Oct. 1948, London; s. of Philip D'Arcy Hart and Ruth Meyer; m. Rita B. Goldberg 1974; two s.; ed Univs. of Cambridge and Warwick and Princeton Univ.; lecturer in Econs Univ. of Essex 1974–75; Asst lecturer, then lecturer in Econs Univ. of Cambridge 1975–81; Prof. of Econs LSE 1981–85, BP Centennial Visiting Prof. 1992–93, 1997–; Prof. of Econs MIT 1984–93, Harvard Univ. 1993–97, Andrew E. Furer Prof. of Econs 1997–; Fellow, American Acad. of Arts and Sciences; Corresp. Fellow British Acad. 2000; Dr hc (Free Univ. of Brussels) 1992; Hon. DPhil (Basle) 1994. *Publications:* Firms, Contracts and Financial Structure 1995; numerous articles in professional journals. *Address:* Department of Economics, Harvard University, Littauer 200, Cambridge, MA 02138, USA. *Telephone:* (617) 496-3461. *Fax:* (617) 495-7730.

HART, Stanley Robert, MS, PhD; American geochemist; b. 20 June 1935, Swampscott, Mass.; s. of Robert W. Hart and Ruth M. Hart; m. 1st Joanna Smith 1956 (divorced 1976); m. 2nd Pamela Shepherd 1980; one s. two d.; ed Mass. Inst. of Technology, Calif. Inst. of Technology; Fellow, Carnegie Inst. of Washington 1960–61, mem. staff 1961–75; Visiting Prof. Univ. of Calif. at San Diego 1967–68; Prof. of Geology and Geochem. MIT 1975–89; Sr Scientist, Woods Hole Oceanographic Inst.1989–; mem. NAS; Fellow, American Geophysical Union, Geological Soc. of America, European Asscn of Geochem., Geochemical Soc.; Goldschmidt Medal (Geochemical Soc.) 1992, Hess Medal (American Geophysical Union) 1997, Columbus O'Donnell Iselin Chair for Excellence in Oceanography. *Publications:* more than 195 articles in scientific journals. *Leisure interests:* woodworking, fishing, running. *Address:* Woods Hole Oceanographic Institution, Woods Hole, MA 02543 (Office); 53 Quonset Road, Falmouth, MA 02540, USA (Home). *Telephone:* (508) 289-2837 (Office); (508) 548-1656. *Fax:* (508) 457-2175 (Office). *E-mail:* shart@whoi.edu (Office).

HARTARTO SASTRO SUNARTO; Indonesian politician; b. 30 May 1932, Delanggu, Cen. Java; ed Inst. of Technology, Bandung and Univ. of New South Wales; mem. Man. Bd state-owned paper factories of Padalarang and Leces 1959; Tech. Dir Leces paper factory 1961; Man. Dir of Bd dealing with paper industries, Dept of Industry 1965; Dir Silicate Industry Div., Directorate-Gen. of Basic Chemical Industries, Dept of Industry 1974, Dir-Gen. for Basic Chemical Industries 1979; Minister of Industry 1983–93, Co-ordinating Minister for Industrial and Trade Affairs 1993–96; Co-ordinating Minister for Production and Distribution 1996–98, for Devt Supervision and State Admin. Reform 1998–99. *Address:* c/o Office of Co-ordinating Minister for Development Supervision and State Administrative Reform, Jalan Veteran III/2, Jakarta Pusat, Indonesia.

HARTFORD, Huntington, BA; American art patron and financier; b. 18 April 1911, New York; s. of Edward Hartford and Henrietta (Guerard) Hartford; m. 1st Mary Lee Epling (divorced 1939); m. 2nd Marjorie Steele 1949 (divorced 1961); one s. one d.; m. 3rd Diane Brown 1962 (divorced 1970); one d.; m. 4th Elaine Kay 1974 (divorced 1981); ed St Paul's School and Harvard Univ.; Co-Chair. Oil Shale Corpn (New York) 1949; Founder Huntington Hartford Foundation Calif. 1949, Huntington Hartford Theatre Hollywood 1954, Gallery of Modern Art (New York) 1964 (now called New York Cultural Center in Asscn with Fairleigh Dickinson Univ.); fmr Developer and owner Paradise Island (Nassau, Bahamas) 1959; Publr Show Magazine; Adviser Cultural Affairs to Pres. of Borough of Manhattan 1967; Patron Lincoln Center for the Performing Arts; mem. Advisory Council of Columbia Univ. Dept of Art History and Archaeology, Nat. Council of the Arts 1969, US People's Fund for UN Inc.; Hon. Fellow, Nat. Sculpture Soc., Broadway Asscn Man. of Year Award; OAS Award 1966. *Publications:* Jane Eyre (play) 1958, Art or Anarchy 1964, You Are What You Write 1973.

HARTINGTON, Marquess of; Peregrine Andrew Morny Cavendish, CBE; British horse racing executive; b. 27 April 1944; s. of 11th Duke of Devonshire; m. Amanda Carmen Heywood-Lonsdale 1967; one s. two d.; ed Eton, Exeter Coll., Oxford; Sr Steward Jockey Club 1989–94; Chair. British Horseracing Bd 1993–96; Dir Sotheby's Holdings Inc. 1994–, Deputy Chair. 1996–; HM's Rep. at Ascot 1997–; Trustee Yorkshire Dales Nat. Park Millennium Trust. *Address:* Beamsley Hall, Skipton, N Yorks., BD23 6HD, England. *Telephone:* (1756) 710424 (Home); (1756) 710419.

HARTLAND, Michael (see James, Michael Leonard).

HARTLEY, Frank Robinson, DSc, FRSC, FRAeS; British chemist; b. 29 Jan. 1942, Epsom; s. of Sir Frank Hartley and Lydia May England; m. Valerie Peel 1964; three d.; ed Kings Coll. School, Wimbledon, Magdalen Coll., Oxford; Post-doctoral Fellow, Commonwealth Scientific and Industrial Research Org., Div. of Protein Chem., Melbourne, Australia 1966–69; ICI Special Fellow and Tutor in Physical Chem., Univ. Coll., London 1969–70; Lecturer in Inorganic Chem., Univ. of Southampton 1970–75; Prof. of Chem. and Head of Dept of Chem. and Metallurgy, Royal Mil. Coll. of Science, Shrivenham 1975–82, Acting Dean 1982–84, Prin. and Dean 1984–89; Man. Dir CIT Holdings Ltd 1989–; Dir (non-exec.) T&N PLC 1989–98, Nat. Westminster Bank Eastern Region Advisory Bd 1990–92, Kalon PLC 1994–99, Kenwood PLC 1995–99; Asscn of Commonwealth Univs. Sr Travelling Fellow 1986; Special Adviser on Defence Systems to the Prime Minister 1988–90; Specialist Adviser to House of Lords Select Cttee on Science and Tech. 1993–94; Chair. AWE Academic Council 1998–2001; mem. Int. Advisory Bd Kanazawa Acad. of Science and Tech., Japan 1989–; Dir Shuttleworth Trust 1994–97; Trustee Lorch Foundation 1994–; AWE Corporate Advisory Panel 2002–; Companion of the Chartered Man. Inst. *Publications:* The Chemistry of Platinum and Palladium (Applied Science) 1973, Elements of Organometallic Chemistry (Chemical Soc.) 1974, Solution Equilibria (with C. Burgess and R. M. Alcock) 1980; The Chemistry of the Metal Carbon Bond (Vols 1–5) 1983–89, Supported Metal Complexes 1985, Brasseys New Battlefield Weapons Systems and Technology series 1988– (Ed.-in-Chief), The Chemistry of Organophosphorus Compounds Vols 1–4 1990–96, Chemistry of the Platinum Group Metals 1991, papers in inorganic, co-ordination and organometallic chemistry in maj. English, American and Australian journals. *Leisure interests:* cliff walking, golf, swimming, gardening. *Address:* Vice-Chancellor's Office, Cranfield University, Cranfield, Beds., MK43 0AL, England (Office). *Telephone:* (01234) 754013 (Office). *Fax:* (01234) 752583 (Office). *E-mail:* a.perkins@cranfield.ac.uk (Office). *Website:* www.cranfield.ac.uk (Office).

HARTLEY, Hal (also known as Ned Rifle), BA; American film director, producer and scriptwriter; b. 3 Nov 1959, Lindenhurst, NY; ed State Univ. of New York-Purchase Film School; film maker True Fiction Pictures 1984–. *Films:* Kid 1984, Home of The Brave 1986, The Cartographer's Girlfriend 1987, Dogs 1988, The Unbelievable Turn 1990, Trust 1991, Simple Men 1992, From a Motel 6 1993, Iris 1993, The Only Living Boy in New York 1993, Flirt 1993, Amateur 1994, Henry Fool 1997, The Book of Life 1998, Monster 2000, Kimono 2000. *Television films:* Surviving Desire 1989, Achievement 1991, Ambition 1991. *Address:* True Fiction Pictures, 39 W. 14th Street, Suite 406, New York, NY 10011, USA.

HÄRTLING, Peter; German writer and journalist; b. 13 Nov. 1933, Chemnitz; s. of Rudolf Härtling and Erika Härtling (née Häntzschel); m. Mechthild Maier 1959; two s. two d.; ed Gymnasium (Nürtingen/Neckar); childhood spent in Saxony, Czechoslovakia and Württemberg; journalist 1953–; Literary Ed. Deutsche Zeitung und Wirtschaftszeitung, Stuttgart and Cologne; Ed. of magazine Der Monat 1962–70, also Co-publisher; Ed. and Man. Dir S. Fischer Verlag, Frankfurt 1968–74, Ed. Die Väter; mem. PEN, Akad. der Wissenschaften und der Literatur Mainz, Akad. der Künste Berlin, Deutsche Akad. für Sprache und Dichtung Darmstadt; Prof. hc 1996; Hon. DPhil 2001; Dr. hc (Giessen) 2001; Literaturpreis des Deutschen Kritikerverbandes 1964, Literaturpreis des Kulturkreises der Deutschen Industrie 1965, Literarischer Förderungspreis des Landes Niedersachsen 1965, Prix du meilleur livre étranger, Paris 1966, Gerhart Hauptmann Preis 1971, Deutscher Jugendbuchpreis 1976, Stadtschreiber von Bergen-Enkheim 1978–79, Hölderlin-Preis 1987, Lion-Feuchtwanger-Preis 1992, Stadtschreiber von Mainz 1995, Leuschner-Medaille des Landes Hessen 1996, Grosses Bundesverdienstkreuz 1996, Eichendorff-Preis 1999, Deutscher Jugendbuchpreis 2001. *Publications:* Yamins Stationen (poetry) 1955, In Zeilen zuhaus (essays) 1957, Palmström grüsst Anna Blume (essays) 1961, Spielgeist-Spiegelgeist (poetry) 1962, Niembsch oder Der Stillstand (novel) 1964, Janek (novel) 1966, Das Familienfest (novel) 1969, Gilles (play) 1970, Ein Abend, Eine Nacht, Ein Morgen (novel) 1971, Zwettl—Nachprüfung einer Erinnerung (novel) 1973, Eine Frau (novel) 1974, Hölderlin (novel) 1976, Anreden (poetry) 1977, Hubert oder Die Rückkehr nach Casablanca (novel) 1978, Nachgetragene Liebe (novel) 1980, Die dreifache Maria 1982, Das Windrad (novel) 1983, Felix Guttmann (novel) 1985, Waiblingers Augen (novel) 1987, Der Wanderer (novel) 1988, Briefe von drinnen und draußen (poetry) 1989, Herzwand (novel) 1990, Schubert (novel) 1992, Božena (novel) 1994, Schumanns Schatten (novel) 1996, Grosses, Kleine Schwester (novel) 1998, Hoffmann oder Die vielfältige Liebe (novel) 2001. *Address:* Finkenweg 1, 64546 Mörfelden-Walldorf, Germany. *Telephone:* (6105) 6109. *Fax:* (6105) 74687.

HARTMAN, Arthur A., AB; American diplomatist (retd); b. 12 March 1926, New York; m. Donna Van Dyke Ford; three s. two d.; ed Harvard Univ., Harvard Law School; served in US Army Air Corps 1944–46; Econ. Officer, Econ. Co-operation Admin., Paris 1948–52; Econ. Officer of US del. to European Army Conf., Paris 1952–54; Politico-Mil. officer, US Mission to

NATO, Paris 1954–55; Econ. Officer, Jt US Embassy/Agency for Int. Devt Mission, Saigon, Repub. of Viet Nam 1956–58; Int. Affairs Officer, Bureau of European Affairs, Dept of State 1958–61; Staff Asst to Under-Sec. of State for Econ. Affairs 1961–62, Special Asst 1962–63; Head of Econ. Section, US Embassy, London 1963–67; Special Asst to Under-Sec. of State 1967–69; Staff Dir of Sr Interdepartmental Group 1967–69; Deputy Dir of Co-ordination to Under-Sec. of State 1969–72; Deputy Chief of Mission and Minister-Counsellor, US Mission to European Communities, Brussels 1972–74; Asst Sec. of State for European Affairs 1974–77; US Amb. to France 1977–81, to USSR 1981–87; Consultant APCO Consulting Group, Wash. 1989–; Chair. Barings' First NIS Regional Investment Fund; mem. Bd, ITT Hartford Insurance Group, Dreyfus Funds, Lawter Int. Ford Meter Box Co.; mem. Council on Foreign Relations; mem. Bd French-American Foundation Fund for Devt and Democracy; fmr Pres. Harvard Univ. Bd of Overseers; Hon. degrees (Wheaton Coll., American Coll. in Paris); Presidential Man. Improvement Award 1970, Distinguished Honor Award 1972, Veterans of Foreign Wars Medal of Honor 1981, Sec. of State's Distinguished Service Award 1987, Dept of State Wilbur J. Carr Award 1987, Annual Nat. Conf. on Soviet Jewry Award 1987; Officier Légion d'honneur. *Address:* APCO Worldwide, 1615 L Street NW, Washington, DC 20036 (Office); 2738 McKinley Street, NW, Washington, DC 20015, USA (Home).

HARTMAN, George Eitel, MFA; American architect; b. 7 May 1936, Fort Hancock, NJ; s. of George E. Hartman and Evelyn Ritchie; m. 1st Ann Burdick 1965 (divorced 2000); one s. one d.; m. 2nd Ian Cigliano 2001; ed Princeton Univ.; with Keyes Lethbridge & Condon Architects 1960–64; own pvt. practice George E. Hartman 1964–65, Hartman-Cox Architects 1965–; mem. US Comm. of Fine Arts 1990–93, Architectural Advisory Bd, Foreign Bldg Office, US Dept of State 1991–, American Inst. of Architects (AIA) Coll. of Fellows; Fellow American Acad. Rome; AIA Nat. Honor Awards 1970, 1971, 1981, 1988, 1989 and numerous other awards. *Buildings include:* US Embassy, Kuala Lumpur 1979, 1001 Pennsylvania Avenue, Washington, DC 1979, HEB HQ, San Antonio, Tex. 1982, Chrysler Museum, Norfolk, NJ 1984, Georgetown Univ. Law Library 1989, Market Square, Washington, DC 1990, 800 N Capital Street, Washington, DC 1990, 1200 K Street and 154 K Street, Washington, DC 1991. *Leisure interest:* sailing. *Address:* Hartman Cox Architects, 1074 Thomas Jefferson Street, NW, Washington, DC 20007 (Office); 1657 31st Street, Washington, DC 20007, USA (Home). *Telephone:* (202) 333-6446.

HARTMANN, Peter, DPhil; German diplomatist; b. 9 Oct. 1935, Aachen; s. of Leonhard Hartmann and Gertrud Hartmann; m. Lonny Freifrau von Blomberg 1968; two d.; ed Gymnasium, Aachen, Univs of Frankfurt, Rome, Cologne, Fribourg; joined Foreign Service 1965, Consulate, Karachi, Pakistan 1968–71, EC Del. Brussels 1971–74, Foreign Ministry Bonn 1974–77, Embassy, Buenos Aires, Argentina 1977–80, Head of Office for Foreign Relations CDU, Bonn 1981–84, Chancellor's Office, Bonn 1984–93, Head European Policy 1987–91, Foreign and Security Policy 1991–93; Amb. to UK 1993–95, to France 1998–2001 (retd); State Sec. of Foreign Affairs 1995–98; Hon. KBE. *Publication:* Interessenpluralismus und politische Entscheidung 1966. *Leisure interests:* tennis, literature. *Address:* Auf dem Reeg 19, 53343 Wachtberg-Pech, Germany (Home). *Telephone:* (228) 2894300 (Home).

HARTMANN, Peter C., DPhil; German professor of history; b. 28 March 1940, Munich; s. of Alfred Hartmann and Manfreda Knote; m. Beate Just 1972; two s. two d.; ed Univs of Munich and Paris; Research Assoc. Deutsches Historisches Institut, Paris 1970–81; Privatdozent, Munich 1979; Prof. Univ. of Passau 1982; Prof. of History, Univ. of Mainz 1988–; Chevalier des Palmes académiques 2001; Hon. DUniv (Paris); Strasbourg Int. Prize. *Publications:* Pariser Archive, Bibl. u. Dok.zentren 1976, Geld als Instrument europäischer Machtpolitik im Zeitalter des Merkantilismus 1978, Das Steuersystem der europäischen Staaten am Ende der Ancien Regime 1979, Karl Albrecht-Karl VII: Glücklicher Kurfürst, Unglücklicher Kaiser 1985, Französische Geschichte 1914–1945, Französische Verfgeschichte der Neuzeit (1450–1980), Ein Überblick 1985, Bayerns Weg in die Gegenwart: Vom Stammesherzogtum bis zur Freistaat heute 1989, Der Jesuitenstaat in Südamerika 1609–1768 1994, Franz. Könige u. Kaiser der Neuzeit 1994, Regionen in der Frühen Neuzeit 1994, Der Mainzer Kurfürst als Reichskanzler 1996, Der Bayerische Reichskreis (1500–1803) 1997, Kurmainz, das Reichskanzleramt und der Reich 1998, Geschichte Frankreichs 1999, Geschichte aktuell, hg. v.K. Amann 2000, Reichskirche, Kurmainz und Reichserzkanzleramt 2001, Die Jesuiten 2001, Kulturgeschichte des Heiligen Römischen Reiches 1648 bis 1806 Verfassung, Religion und Kultur 2001, Die Mainzer Kurfürsten d. Hauses Schönborn 2002. *Address:* Saarstrasse 21, 55099 Mainz, Germany.

HARTSHORN, Michael Philip, FRSNZ, DPhil; British/New Zealand professor of chemistry; b. 10 Sept. 1936, Coventry, England; m. Jacqueline Joll 1963; four s.; ed Imperial Coll. of Science and Tech., London, University Coll., Oxford; Lecturer in Chem., Univ. of Canterbury, NZ 1960–66, Sr Lecturer 1966–68, Reader 1968–72, Prof. 1972–97, Prof. Emer. 1996–; Fulbright Visiting Prof., Cornell Univ., New York 1966–67; Guest Prof., Lund Univ., Sweden 1991–92, 1995, 1997; Fürth Visiting Lecturer, Royal Soc. of Edinburgh 1991; Wilsmore Fellow Melbourne Univ. June–July 1996; Fellowship NZ Inst. of Chem. 1969; Hector Medal, Royal Soc. of NZ 1973. *Publications:* approx. 255 scientific papers; Steroid Reaction Mechanisms (with D. N. Kirk)

1968. *Leisure interests:* reading, music, gardening. *Address:* 1 Repton Street, Christchurch 8001, New Zealand. *Telephone:* (3) 3556-450. *Fax:* (3) 3558-357. *E-mail:* m.hartshorn@chem.canterbury.ac.nz (Home).

HARTUNG, Harald; German poet, professor and critic; b. 29 Oct. 1932, Herne; s. of Richard Hartung and Wanda Hartung; m. Freia Schnackenburg 1979; two s.; secondary school teacher 1960–66; Prof., Pädagogische Hochschule Berlin 1971–80, Tech. Univ. Berlin 1980–; mem. Akad. der Künste, Berlin, PEN; Kunstpreis Berlin, Drostepreis 1987, Premio Antico Fattore 1999. *Publications:* Experimentelle Literatur und Konkrete Poesie 1975, Das Gewöhnliche Licht 1976, Augenzeit 1978, Deutsche Lyrik seit 1965 1985, Traum im Deutschen Museum 1986, Luftfracht 1991, Jahre mit Windrad 1996, Masken und Stimmen 1996. *Address:* Rüdesheimer Platz 4, 14197 Berlin, Germany.

HARTWELL, Leland H., BS, PhD; American geneticist; b. 30 Oct. 1939; ed California Inst. of Technology, MIT; Assoc. Prof. Univ. of Calif. 1965–68; Assoc. Prof., then Prof. Univ. of Washington 1968–; Pres. and Dir Fred Hutchinson Cancer Research Center 1997–; mem. NAS 1987–; numerous awards including General Motors Sloan Award 1991, Gairdner Foundation Int. Award 1992, Genetics Soc. of America Medal 1994, Albert Lasker Basic Medical Research Award 1998, Nobel Prize in Medicine (Jt recipient) 2001. *Address:* Fred Hutchinson Cancer Research Center, 1100 Fairview Avenue North, D1-060 Seattle, WA 98109-1024, USA (Office). *Website:* www.fhcrc.org (Office).

HARTZENBERG, Ferdinand, DSc; South African politician; b. 8 Jan. 1936, Lichtenburg; s. of Ferdinand Hartzenberg; m. Magdalena Judith de Wet 1962; two s.; ed Sannieshof, Hoër Volkskool, Potchefstroom and Univ. of Pretoria; mem. Parl. for Lichtenburg; Leader Conservative Party of SA (CPSA) 1993–; Deputy Minister of Devt 1976; Minister of Educ. and Training 1979–82. *Address:* Conservative Party of South Africa, 203 Soutpansberg Road, Rietondale, Pretoria 0001, South Africa (Office). *Telephone:* (12) 3291220 (Office). *Fax:* (12) 3291229.

HARVEY, Anthony; British film director; b. 3 June 1931; s. of Geoffrey Harrison and Dorothy Leon; entered film industry, joining Crown Film Unit 1949; ed. numerous films including Private Progress, Brothers-in-Law, Carleton Brown of the Foreign Office, I'm Alright Jack, The Angry Silence, The Millionairess, Lolita, The L-Shaped Room, Dr. Strangelove, The Spy Who Came in from the Cold, The Whisperers; directed Dutchman 1968, The Lion in Winter 1969 (Directors' Guild Award, New York Film Critics' Award), They Might be Giants 1970, The Abdication 1973, The Glass Menagerie 1973, The Disappearance of Aimee (TV) 1978, Eagle's Wing, Players 1979, Richard's Things 1980, The Patricia Neal Story 1981 (Christopher Award), Svengali (TV) 1982, Grace Quigley, This Can't Be Love (TV) 1994. *Leisure interest:* gardening. *Address:* c/o Arthur Greene, 101 Park Avenue, 26th Floor, New York, NY 10178, USA (Office). *Telephone:* (212) 661-8200 (Office).

HARVEY, Barbara Fitzgerald, CBE, MA, BLitt, FRHistS, FSA, FBA; British academic; b. 21 Jan. 1928, Teignmouth, Devon; d. of Richard Henry Harvey and Anne Fitzgerald Harvey (née Julian); ed Teignmouth Grammar School, Bishop Blackall School, Exeter and Somerville Coll. Oxford; Asst, Univ. of Edinburgh, Scotland 1951–52; Lecturer, Queen Mary Coll., Univ. of London 1952–55; Tutor, Somerville Coll. Oxford 1955–93, Fellow 1956–93, Fellow Emer. 1993–, Vice-Prin. 1976–79 and 1981–83; Ford's Lecturer, Univ. of Oxford 1989; Reader in Medieval History 1990–93; Vice-Pres. Royal Historical Soc. 1986–90; Gen. Ed. Oxford Medieval Texts 1987–99; mem. Royal Comm. on Historical Manuscripts 1991–97; Jt Winner Wolfson Foundation Prize for History 1993. *Publications:* Westminster Abbey and its Estates in the Middle Ages 1977, The Westminster Chronicle, 1381–94 (Ed. with L.C. Hector) 1982, Living and Dying in England 1100–1540: The Monastic Experience 1993, The Twelfth and Thirteen Centuries (Oxford History of the British Isles) (Ed.) 2001, The Obedientiaries of Westminster Abbey and Their Financial Records c. 1275 to 1540 2002, articles in learned journals. *Address:* 66 Cranham Street, Oxford, OX2 6DD, England.

HARVEY, Cynthia Theresa; American ballet dancer and teacher; b. 17 May 1957, San Rafael, Calif.; d. of Gordon Harvey and Clara Harvey; m. Christopher D. Murphy 1990; ed High School of Professional Children's School, New York; joined American Ballet Theater 1974, Prin. ballerina 1982–86, 1988–; with Royal Ballet, London 1986–88; guest appearances touring with Mikhail Baryshnikov, Rudolf Nureyev and Alexander Godunov; has performed with Stuttgart Ballet, Birmingham Royal Ballet and Northern Ballet Theatre; teacher of ballet at many leading schools in USA. *Publication:* The Physics of Dance and the Pas de Deux (with Ken Laws) 1994. *Leisure interests:* motor racing, music, theatre, soccer, design. *Address:* c/o American Ballet Theater, 890 Broadway, 3rd Floor, New York, NY 10003, USA. *Telephone:* (212) 477-3030.

HARVEY, Jonathan Dean, MA, PhD, DMus, FRCM, FRSCM; British composer and professor of music; b. 3 May 1939, Sutton Coldfield; s. of Gerald Harvey and Noelle Harvey; m. Rosaleen Marie Barry 1960; one s. one d.; ed St Michael's Coll., Tenbury, Repton, St John's Coll., Cambridge, Glasgow Univ., Princeton Univ.; lecturer, Southampton Univ. 1964–77; Reader, Sussex Univ. 1977–80, Prof. of Music 1980–94; Prof. of Music, Stanford Univ. 1995–2000; Visiting Prof. Imperial Coll. 1999–2002; Hon. Research Fellow, R.C.M. 2001–; mem. Arts Council of England's Music Advisory Panel 1995–97, British Council's Music Advisory Panel 1993–95, Acad. Europaea 1989, Acad. Cttee of RCM 1990–94; Hon. DMus (Southampton, Bristol, Sussex), Hon. RAM, Hon. Fellow St John's Coll. Cambridge; The Britten Award 1993. *Compositions include:* Four Quartets 1977, 1989, 1995, 2003, Mortuos plango, vivos voco (for tape) 1980, Passion and Resurrection 1981, Bhakti 1982, Gong Ring 1984, Song Offerings 1985, Madonna of Winter and Spring 1986, Lightness and Weight 1986, Tendril 1987, Time Pieces 1987, From Silence 1988, Valley of Aosta 1989, Ritual Melodies 1990, Cello Concerto 1990, Inquest of Love (opera) 1991, Serenade in Homage to Mozart 1991, Scena 1992, One Evening 1993, The Riot 1993, Missa Brevis 1995, Percussion Concerto 1996, Ashes Dance Back 1997, Wheel of Emptiness 1997, Death of Light/Light of Death 1998, Calling Across Time 1998, Tranquil Abiding 1998, White as Jasmine 1999, Mothers Shall Not Cry 2000, Bird Concerto with Pianosong 2001, The Summer Cloud's Awakening 2001, Songs of Li Po 2002; about 20 works for choir. *Publications:* The Music of Stockhausen 1975, Music and Inspiration 1999, In Quest of Spirit 1999. *Leisure interests:* tennis, meditation. *Address:* c/o Faber Music, 3 Queen Square, London, WC1N 3AU, England. *Telephone:* (020) 7833-7911. *Fax:* (020) 7833-7939.

HARVEY-JONES, Sir John (Henry), Kt, MBE; British business executive; b. 16 April 1924, London; s. of Mervyn Harvey-Jones and Eileen Harvey-Jones; m. Mary Evelyn Bignell 1947; one d.; ed Tormore School, Deal, Royal Naval Coll., Dartmouth; served with RN 1937–56, specializing in submarines, later working with Naval Intelligence; resgnd with rank of Lt Commdr 1956; joined ICI as Work Study Officer 1956, then held various commercial posts at Wilton and with Heavy Organic Chemicals Div. until apptd. Techno-Commercial Dir 1967; Deputy Chair. HOC Div. 1968; Chair., ICI Petrochemicals Div. 1970–73; appointed to Main Bd ICI 1973, Deputy Chair 1978–82, Chair. 1982–87; Chancellor Bradford Univ. 1986–91; mem. Tees and Hartlepool Port Authority 1970–73; Chair. Phillips-Imperial Petroleum 1973–75; Non-Exec. Dir Burns Anderson 1987–91 (Chair. 1987–90); Chair. Parallax Enterprises Ltd 1987–97; Non-Exec. Chair. Business Int. Bd Cttee 1988–91; Dir (non-exec.) Reed Int. PLC 1975–84, Carrington Viyella Ltd 1974–79 (Dir 1981–82), Grand Metropolitan PLC 1983–94, (Deputy Chair. 1987–91), The Economist 1987–94 (Chair. 1989–94), G.P.A. Ltd 1987–93 (Deputy Chair. 1989–93), Trendroute Ltd 1988–91; Pres. Conseil Européen des Fédérations de l'Industrie Chimique 1982–84; Hon. Pres. Brecon Jazz 1996–; Vice-Pres. Hearing and Speech Trust 1985–, Heaton Woods Trust 1986, Book Trust Appeal Fund 1987–, Wider Share Ownership Council 1988–92; Chair. Council, Wildfowl Trust 1987–94; Vice-Chair. Policy Studies Inst. 1980–85, BIM 1980–85 (mem. 1978–); Hon. Vice-Pres. Inst. of Marketing 1982–89; mem. Court of British Shippers' Council 1982–87, Police Foundation 1983–91 (Chair. Trustees 1984–88), Advisory Editorial Bd of New European 1987–; mem. Council, Chemical Industries Asscn Ltd 1980–82, British-Malaysian Soc. 1983–87, Youth Enterprise Scheme 1984–86; mem. Foundation Bd, Int. Man. Inst., Geneva 1984–87; mem. Bd Welsh Devt Int. 1989–93; mem. Advisory Council, Prince's Youth Business Trust 1986–97; mem. Int. Council, European Inst. of Business Admin. 1984–87; Hon. mem. The City & Guilds of London Inst. 1988–; Hon. Consultant, Royal United Services Inst. for Defence Studies 1987–; Hon. Fellow, RSC 1985, The Inst. of Chemical Engineers 1985; Hon. Fellow Liverpool John Moores Univ. 1998; Trustee Science Museum 1983–87, Conf. Bd 1984–86, MSRT 1999–; Patron Cambridge Univ. Young Entrepreneurs Soc. 1987–91, Manpower Services Comm. Nat. Training Awards 1987, Nat. Canine Defence League 1990–, Steer Org., Centre for Tomorrows Co. 1997–, RN Submarine Centennial Appeal 1999–, Professional Contractors Group 2000–, Soc. of Turnaround Professionals 2001–; Vice-Patron British Polio Fellowship 1988–; Gov. English Speaking Union 1987–91; Fellow Smallpiece Trust 1988–; mem. RSA, Soc. of Chemical Industry; Hon. LLD (Manchester) 1985, (Liverpool) 1986, (London) 1987, Cambridge (1987); Hon. DUniv (Surrey) 1985; Hon. DSc (Bradford) 1986, (Leicester) 1986, (Keele, Exeter) 1989; Hon. DCL (Newcastle) 1988; Hon. DTech (Loughborough Univ. of Tech.) 1991; Jo Hambro British Businessman of the Year 1986; Int. Asscn of Business Communicators Award of Excellence in Communication 1987; Radar Man of the Year 1987; City & Guilds Insignia Award in Tech. (hc) 1987; Commdr.'s Cross of Order of Merit (FRG); BAFTA Special Award for Originality for Troubleshooter, BBC, 1990. *Television:* The Richard Dimbleby Lecture: Does Industry Matter? 1986, Troubleshooter (series) 1990, Troubleshooter Specials—Eastern Europe 1991, Troubleshooter 2 1992, Troubleshooter Returns 1995, Troubleshooter Back in Business 2000. *Publications:* Making it Happen, Reflections on Leadership 1987, Troubleshooter 1990, Getting it Together (memoirs) 1991, Troubleshooter 2 1992, Managing to Survive 1993, All Together Now 1994, Troubleshooter Returns 1995. *Leisure interests:* swimming, the countryside, cooking, contemporary literature. *Address:* P.O. Box 18, Ross-on-Wye, Herefordshire, HR9 7PH, England. *Telephone:* (01989) 567171.

HARWOOD, Ronald, CBE, FRSL; British author and playwright; b. (Ronald Horwitz), 9 Nov. 1934, Cape Town, South Africa; s. of the late Isaac Horwitz and Isobel Pepper; m. Natasha Riehle 1959; one s. two d.; ed Sea Point Boys' High School, Cape Town and Royal Acad. of Dramatic Art; actor 1953–60; author 1960–; Artistic Dir Cheltenham Festival of Literature 1975; presenter, Kaleidoscope, BBC Radio 1973, Read All About It, BBC TV 1978–79, All The World's A Stage, BBC TV; Chair. Writers' Guild of GB 1969; Visitor in Theatre, Balliol Coll. Oxford 1986; Pres. PEN (England) 1989–93, Int. PEN 1993–97; Gov. Cen. School of Speech and Drama; author of numerous TV plays and screenplays; mem. Council Royal Soc. of Literature 1998–2001, Chair. 2001–; Trustee Booker Foundation 2002; Chevalier des Arts et des Lettres; Hon. DLitt (Keele). *TV plays include:* The Guests, Breakthrough at Reykjavik. *Screenplays include:* The Dresser, One Day in the Life of Ivan Denisovich, The Browning Version, Taking Sides, The Pianist (Acad. Award for Best Adapted Screenplay 2003), The Statement, Being Julia. *Plays include:* Country Matters 1969, The Good Companions (musical libretto) 1974, The Ordeal of Gilbert Pinfold 1977, A Family 1978, The Dresser 1980, After the Lions 1982, Tramway Road 1984, The Deliberate Death of a Polish Priest 1985, Interpreters 1985, J. J. Farr 1987, Ivanov (from Chekhov) 1989, Another Time 1989, Reflected Glory 1992, Poison Pen 1994, Taking Sides 1995, The Handyman 1996, Equally Divided 1998, Quartet 1999, Mahler's Conversion 2002. *Publications include:* All the Same Shadows 1961, The Guilt Merchants 1963, The Girl in Melanie Klein 1969, Sir Donald Wolfit, CBE: His Life and Work in the Unfashionable Theatre (biog.) 1971, Articles of Faith 1973, The Genoa Ferry 1976, César and Augusta 1978, Home 1993, The Faber Book of the Theatre (Ed.) 1994; vols of essays and short stories. *Leisure interest:* cricket. *Address:* c/o Judy Daish Associates, 2 St Charles Place, London, W10 6EG, England. *Telephone:* (020) 8964-8811.

HASANI, Baqir Husain, BSc, LLB; Iraqi/Italian diplomatist; b. 12 Feb. 1915, Baghdad; ed Columbia Univ., New York and Law Coll. Baghdad Univ.; Dir of Commerce and Registrar of Patents, Trade Marks and Companies, Ministry of Econs Iraq 1947–51; Dir-Gen. of Contracts and Econ. Research, Devt Bd 1951–54; Dir-Gen. of Income Tax, Ministry of Finance 1954–55; Dir-Gen. and Chair. Bd of Dirs Tobacco Monopoly Admin. 1955–59; Envoy Extraordinary and later Amb. to Austria 1959–63; Chair. Bd of Govs IAEA 1961–62; Special Adviser to Dir-Gen. IAEA, Vienna 1963–66, 1970–76; Adviser to Saudi Arabian Mission in Vienna 1978–81; consultant on Middle Eastern Affairs 1985–; mem. numerous govt cttees and del. to the UN and to int. confs, etc.; lecturer Coll. of Business Admin., Coll. of Pharmacy, Mil. Staff Coll.; Rafidain Decoration; Austrian Grand Golden Decoration. *Leisure interests:* horse riding, swimming, collecting stamps and coins. *Address:* Via Civelli 9, 21100 Varese, Italy; 7 Ashenden Road, Guildford, Surrey, GU2 7UU, England. *Telephone:* (0332) 22-9633 (Italy); (01483) 838371 (England).

HASEEB, Khair El-Din, MSc, PhD; Iraqi economist and statistician; b. 1 Aug. 1929, Mosul; m. 1955; one s. two d.; ed Univ. of Baghdad, London School of Econs and Univ. of Cambridge; civil servant, Ministry of Interior 1947–54; Head of Research and Statistics Dept, Iraqi Oil Co. 1959–60; Full-time Lecturer, Univ. of Baghdad 1960–61, Part-time 1961–63; Dir-Gen. Iraqi Fed. of Industries 1960–63; Gov. and Chair. of Bd, Cen. Bank of Iraq 1963–65; Pres. Gen. Org. for Banks 1964–65; Acting Pres. Econ. Org., Iraq 1964–65; Assoc. Prof., Dept of Econs Univ. of Baghdad 1965–71, Prof. of Econs 1971–74; mem. Bd of Dirs Iraq Nat. Oil Co. 1967–68; Chief, Programme and Co-ordination Unit and Natural Resources, Science and Tech. Div. UN Econ. Comm. for Western Asia, then Lebanon and Iraq 1974–76 and 1976–83; Acting Dir-Gen. Centre for Arab Unity Studies, Lebanon 1978–83, Dir-Gen. 1983–; Chair. Bd of Trustees and Dirs Arab Cultural Foundation, London 1987; Chair. Bd of Trustees Arab Org. for Translation, Lebanon 1999–. *Publications:* The National Income of Iraq 1953–1961, 1964, Workers' Participation in Management in Arab Countries (in Arabic) 1971, Sources of Arab Economic Thought in Iraq 1900–71 (in Arabic) 1972, Arab Monetary Integration (Co-Ed.) 1982, Arabs and Africa (Ed.) 1985, The Future of the Arab Nation 1991, Arab-Iranian Relations (Ed.); numerous articles. *Leisure interests:* swimming, tennis. *Address:* Centre for Arab Unity Studies, Sadat Tower Bldg, 9th Floor, Lyon Street, PO Box 113-6001, Hamra, Beirut 1103 2090, Lebanon. *Telephone:* (1) 801582, (1) 801587, (1) 869164. *Fax:* (1) 865548. *E-mail:* info@caus.org.lb (Office). *Website:* www.caus.org.lb (Office).

HASEGAWA, Kaoru, BEcons; Japanese business executive; b. 15 April 1924, Hyogo; m. Shizue Hasegawa 1952; one s. one d.; ed Naval Acad. of Japan, Gakushuin Univ.; joined Rengo Co. Ltd 1952, Gen. Man. Corp. Planning Dept 1960, Man. Dir 1962, Sr Man. Dir 1970, Exec. Vice-Pres. 1973, Pres. and CEO 1984–; Pres. Japan Corrugated Case Asscn 1986; Vice-Chair. Japan Paper Asscn 1995; consultant on overseas Devt, China Packaging Tech. Asscn 1999. *Publications:* Two Lives: My Personal History, Cultural and Economic Dialogues: Learning from the History and Wisdom of Europe. *Address:* Rengo Co. Ltd., 5-25 Umeda, 2-chome, Kita-ku, Osaka 530 0001, Japan (Office). *Telephone:* (6) 6342-0266 (Office). *Fax:* (6) 6342-0379 (Office).

HASELTINE, William A., PhD; American scientist; ed Harvard Univ.; Prof. Dana-Farber Cancer Inst., Harvard Medical School and Harvard School of Public Health 1976–93; f. Human Genome Sciences Inc. (HGS) 1992, Chair. and Chief Exec. 1993–; Scientific Adviser HealthCare Ventures; fmr Ed.-in-Chief Journal of AIDS; Founder and Ed. on-line journal E-Biomed; holder of more than 50 patents for his discoveries; numerous awards and honours for his achievements in science, medicine and business. *Publications:* over 250 scientific publs. *Address:* Human Genome Sciences Inc., 9410 Key West Avenue, Rockville, MD 2085, USA (Office). *Telephone:* (301) 309-8504 (Office). *Fax:* (301) 309-8512 (Office). *Website:* www.hgsi.com (Office).

HASHAM PREMJI, Azim, BS; Indian business executive; b. 24 July 1945, Mumbai; s. of Mohamed Husain and G. M. H. Premji; m. Yasmeen Premji; two s.; ed Stanford Univ.; Chair. and Man. Dir Wipro Ltd 1983–; has expanded portfolio from processing of cooking oil and manufacture of several basic consumer product lines to include production of information tech. products; Businessman of the Year 2000, Business India magazine. *Leisure interests:* jogging, spending time at hillside resorts. *Address:* Bakhtawar, 229, Nariman

Point, Mumbai 400021, India (Home); Doddakannelli, Sarjapur Road, Bangalore, 560035. *Telephone:* (22) 2026436 (Office); (22) 2870353 (Office); (80) 5569991. *Website:* www.wiproindia.com (Office).

HASHIMOTO, Ryutaro; Japanese politician; b. 29 July 1937; s. of Ryogo Hashimoto; m. Kumiko Hashimoto; two s. three d.; ed Keio Univ.; previous posts include: Chair. Cttee on Social and Labour Problems, House of Reps.; Deputy Chair. Liberal Democratic Party (LDP) Policy Research Council; Chair. LDP Research Comm. on Public Admin. and Finances; Minister of Transport 1986–87, of Finance 1989–91, of Int. Trade and Industry 1994–96; Prime Minister of Japan 1996–98; Sec.-Gen. LDP July–Aug. 1989, Pres. 1995–98; Dir-Gen. Okinawa Devt Agency 2000–; Liberal Democratic Party. *Leisure interests:* Kendo (5th dan), mountaineering, photography. *Address:* c/o Liberal-Democratic Party, 1-11-23 Nagata-cho, Chiyoda-ku, Tokyo 100, Japan.

HASHMI, Moneeza, M.ED., MA; Pakistani television executive; b. 22 Aug. 1946, Simla; d. of Faiz Ahmad Faiz; m. Humair Hashmi; two s.; ed Univ. of Hawaii, USA, Punjab Univ., Lahore; producer Pakistan TV (PTV) 1976–98, Gen. Man. 1998–; Nat. UND – PTV Project Dir "Portrayal of Women in Media"; Grad. Award 2000, 2001, Commonwealth Broadcasting Award Citation 2002, Pres. of Pakistan's Pride of Performance 2002. *Television includes:* KHWATEEN TIME (exec. producer). *Leisure interests:* travelling, reading. *Address:* PTV Lahore Centre, 21 Mahmood Ghaznavi Road, Lahore (Office); 102-H Model Town, Lahore, Pakistan (Home). *Telephone:* (42) 9200611 (Office); (42) 5884320 (Home). *Fax:* (42) 9200612 (Office). *E-mail:* moneezahashmi@hotmail.com (Office).

HASHMI, Syed Haseen; Pakistani advertising executive; b. 1935, Gaya, India; s. of the late Syed Abdul Quddoos Hashmi; Chair. Pakistan Advertising Asscn 1978–87, 1992–93, 1996–99; Pres. Int. Advertising Asscn (IAA), Pakistan Chapter 1996–98; fmr Sec.-Gen. Seerat Cttee, Karachi; Presidential Award, APNS Millennium Award, FPCCI Gold Medal, Best Business Performance 1981–98. *Publications include:* Advertising Scene (Blue Book). *Leisure interests:* reading, social welfare. *Address:* 195-A, S.M.C.H.S., Karachi (Office); 73/11 Khavaban-e-Badar, Phase-VI, D.H.A., Karachi, Pakistan (Home). *Telephone:* (21) 4550184 (Office); (21) 5849841 (Home). *Fax:* (21) 4550187 (Office). *E-mail:* omek@orientmccann.com (Office).

HASINA WAJED, Sheikh; Bangladeshi politician; b. 28 Sept. 1947, Tungipara, Gopalganj Dist, E Pakistan (now Bangladesh); d. of the late Sheikh Mujibur Rahman (fmr Prime Minister of Bangladesh) and Begum Fazilatunnesa; m. M. A. Wazed Miah; one s. one d.; ed Univ. of Dhaka; active in politics as a student; arrested during civil war 1971; assumed leadership of opposition Awami League (AL) from her father, first elected Pres. 1981, fifth time in 2002; lived in exile 1975–81; arrested and placed under house arrest on several occasions during 1980s; Prime Minister of Bangladesh 1996–2001, also Minister of the Armed Forces Div., of the Cabinet Div., of Special Affairs, of Defence, of Power, Energy and Mineral Resources and of the Establishment; charged with corruption and alleged plundering of state funds while in office Dec. 2001; Leader of official parliamentary opposition 2001–; shared Houphouet-Boigny Peace Prize 1999. *Publications:* several books and numerous articles. *Address:* Central Awami League Office, Dhamondi Road 5, Dhaka, Bangladesh. *Telephone:* 8126288.

HASKELL, (Donald) Keith, CMG, CVO, MA; British diplomatist (retd); b. 9 May 1939, Southsea; s. of Donald Eric Haskell and Beatrice Mary Haskell (née Blair); m. Maria Luisa Soeiro Tito de Morais; two s. two d.; ed Portsmouth Grammar School, St Catharine's Coll., Cambridge; joined FCO 1961, served in Baghdad 1962–66, Libya 1969–72; Chargé d'affaires, Consul-Gen. Santiago, Chile 1975–78; Consul-Gen. Dubai, UAE 1978–81; Head Nuclear Energy Dept FCO 1981–83, Head Middle East Dept 1983–84, Counsellor Bonn, FRG 1985–88; Amb. to Peru 1990–95, to Brazil 1995–99, on secondment to industry 1988–89; Grand Cross, Order of Rio Branco (Brazil) 1997. *Leisure interests:* rifle and pistol shooting, skiing, squash, tennis, wine and food. *Address:* Barn Cottage, Brightstone Lane, Farringdon, Alton, Hants., GU34 3DP, England. *Telephone:* (1420) 588485. *Fax:* (1420) 588485. *E-mail:* maria.haskell@virgin.net.

HASKINS, Baron (Life Peer), cr. 1998; of Skidby in the County of the East Riding of Yorks.; **Christopher Robin Haskins,** BA; Irish business executive; b. 30 May 1937, Dublin; s. of Robin Brown Haskins and Margaret Elizabeth Haskins (née Mullen); m. Gilda Susan Horsley 1959; three s. two d.; ed St Columba's Coll., Dublin, Trinity Coll., Dublin; with Ford Motor Co. 1960–62; joined Northern Foods PLC 1962, Chair. 1986–2002 (retd); mem. Culliton Irish Industrial Policy Review Group 1991–92, Ind. Comm. Social Justice 1992–94, UK Round Table on Sustainable Devt 1995–98, CBI's Pres. Cttee 1996–99, Hampel Cttee on Corp. Governance 1996–97; Chair. Better Regulation Task Force 1997–2002, Express Dairies 1998–2002; mem. New Deal Task Force 1997–2001, Ed. Yorkshire and Humber Regional Devt Agency; Co-ordinator Rural Recovery 2001–; Trustee Legal Assistance Trust; Dir Lawes Agricultural Trust, Nat. Childrens Trust; Dir Yorkshire TV 2002–; Chair. DEFRA (Dept for Environment, Food and Rural Affairs) Review Group 2002–03. *Leisure interests:* farming, watching cricket, writing, politics. *Address:* Quarryside Farm, Main Street, Skidby, Nr Cottingham, East Yorks., HU15 6TG, England (Home). *Telephone:* (1482) 842692 (Home). *Fax:* (1482) 845249 (Home).

HASKINS, Sam (Samuel Joseph); British/South African photographer and designer; b. 11 Nov. 1926, Kroonstad; s. of Benjamin G. Haskins and Anna E. Oelofse; m. Alida Elzabé van Heerden 1952; two s.; ed Helpmekaar School and Witwatersrand Technical Coll., Johannesburg, Bolt Court School of Photography, London; freelance work, Johannesburg 1953–68, London 1968–; Prix Nadar (France) for Cowboy Kate and Other Stories 1964, Israel Museum Award, Int. Art Book Contest Award, Gold Medal Award for Haskins Posters, New York 1974, Kodak Book Prize 1980 (for Photo Graphics). *Solo exhibitions include:* Johannesburg 1953, 1960, Tokyo 1970, 1973, 1976, 1979, 1981, 1985, 1990, 1992, 1993, 1996, London 1972, 1976, 1978, 1980, 1997, Paris 1973, 1981, Amsterdam 1974, 1981, Geneva 1981, Zurich 1981, New York 1981, San Francisco 1982, Toronto 1982, 1986, Bologna 1984, Cologne 1990, Osaka 1990, 1992, 1993, 1997, 2000, Auckland 1991, Sydney 1991, Hong Kong 1991, Taipei 1991, Singapore 1991, Palermo 1993, Prague 1993, Glasgow 1997, Berlin 2000. *Publications:* Five Girls 1962, Cowboy Kate and Other Stories 1964, African Image 1966, November Girl 1967, Haskins Posters 1972, Photo Graphics 1980, Sam Haskins à Bologna 1984; and portfolios in most maj. int. photographic magazines. *Leisure interests:* vintage car rallying, books, music, horticulture. *Address:* 9A Calonne Road, London, SW19 5HH; PO Box 59, Wimbledon, London, SW19, England. *Telephone:* (20) 8946-9660. *E-mail:* sam@haskins.com (Office). *Website:* www.haskins.com (Office).

HASLER, Otmar; Liechtenstein politician; b. 28 Sept. 1953; s. of Lorenz Hasler and Maria Lydia Oehri; m. Traudi Hasler-Hilti; two s. two d.; ed secondary school-teaching diploma from Fribourg Univ.; teacher Realschule, Eschen 1979–; Pres. Progressive Citizens' Party of Liechtenstein (FBP) 1993–95, mem. Exec. Cttee 1993–; mem. Parliament, Liechtenstein, Vice-Pres. 1993–94, 1997–2001, Pres. 1995; Head of Govt of Liechtenstein, also responsible for Family and Equal Opportunities, Finance and Construction 2001–; Pres. newly founded Liechtenstein Senior Citizens' Org. 1999–. *Leisure interests:* reading, playing the piano and guitar, working in the garden, woodwork. *Address:* Office of the Head of Government, Regierungsgebäude, 9490 Vaduz, Liechtenstein (Office); Kirchgässle 2, 9487 Bendern. *Telephone:* (423) 752366111 (Office). *Fax:* 2366622.

HASMY, Agam, MA; Malaysian diplomatist; b. 3 Feb. 1944, Malacca; m.; two c.; joined Foreign Ministry as Asst Sec. 1968, various positions in Ministry and in missions in Saigon, Washington, DC, Hanoi and London; seconded to Nat. Inst. of Public Admin. as Head, Centre for Int. Relations and Diplomacy 1981; Amb. to Libya (also accred to Malta) 1986–88; to France (also accred to Portugal) 1990–92; Alt. Perm. Rep. to UN, Alt. Del. to Security Council 1988–90; Dir.-Gen. Relations with ASEAN, Foreign Ministry 1993, Deputy Sec.-Gen. for Int. Orgs. and Multilateral Econs 1994–96; Alt. Perm. Rep. to UN 1996–98, Perm. Rep. 1998–. *Address:* Permanent Mission of Malaysia to the United Nations, 313 East 43rd Street, New York, NY 10017, USA (Office). *Telephone:* (212) 986-6310 (Office). *Fax:* (212) 490-8576 (Office). *E-mail:* malaysia@un.int (Office). *Website:* www.un.int/malaysia (Office).

HASQUIN, Hervé, PhD; Belgian politician and professor of history; b. 31 Dec. 1942, Charleroi; s. of René-Pierre Hasquin and Andrée Jacquemart; m. Michèle Nahum 1986; one s.; Dean Faculty of Arts and Philosophy, Université Libre de Bruxelles 1979–82, Rector 1982–86, Chair. Bd of Dirs. 1986–95, Pres. Inst. for Religious and Secular Studies 1987–; Head French-speaking network Scientific Information and Technological Devt 1986–87; Vice-Pres. Parti Réformateur Libéral (PRL) 1986–89, Gen. Sec. 1990–92, Head PRL Group, Council of Brussels, Capital Region 1991–; Senator 1988–95; Regional Councillor, Brussels 1989–99; Minister of Environmental Planning, Town Planning and Transport, Brussels Capital Region 1995–99; Minister-Pres. of French-speaking Community of Belgium responsible for Int. Relations 1999–; Prés. de la Fédération MR du Hainaut 2000–; Royal Acad. of Belgium Prize 1990, Literary Prize of French-speaking Community Council 1981 and other prizes; Chevalier, Légion d'honneur 1989, Commdr, Order of Leopold II 1984, Order of the Lion (Senegal) 1987; Grand Officer, Order of Leopold 1999; sociétaire hc Acad. des Sciences et des Arts 2000, mem. Acad. Royale de Belgique 2002. *Publications:* La Wallonie: Le Pays et les Hommes, Histoire de la Laïcité principalement en Belgique et en France, La Wallonie, son histoire 1999, Dictionnaire d'histoire de Belgique: Vingt siècles d'institutions. Les hommes. Les faits 2000; about 150 articles and papers in Belgian and foreign learned journals. *Leisure interests:* writing, teaching, football, cycling, cinema. *Address:* Université Libre de Bruxelles, Ave. F. Roosevelt 50, 1050 Brussels; Cabinet du Ministre-Président de la Communauté Wallonie-Bruxelles, Place Surlet de Chokier 15-17, 1000 Brussels (Office); Ave du Prince Héritier 105, 1200 Brussels; Rue du Long Bois 1, 7830 Graty Silly, Belgium (Home). *Telephone:* (2) 227-32-11 (Office). *Fax:* (2) 227-33-53 (Office); (67) 41-02-08 (Home). *E-mail:* contact@hasquin.be (Office). *Website:* www.hasquin.be (Office).

HASSAN, Jean-Claude Gaston; French banker and public servant; b. 11 Nov. 1954, Tunis, Tunisia; s. of Charles Hassan and Yvonne Lellouche; m. Françoise Benhamou 1981; two s. one d.; ed Lycée de Mutuelleville, Tunis, Lycée Louis-le-Grand, Paris, Ecole normale supérieure, Ecole nat. d'admin.; mem. Conseil d'Etat, Auditeur 1981, Counsel 1985; Tech. Adviser to Office of Minister of Social Affairs and Nat. Solidarity 1984–85; Deputy Dir-Gen. Banque Stern 1986–89, Dir-Gen. 1989–92; Dir-Gen. Banque Worms 1992–94; rejoined Conseil d'Etat 1994–2000; Conseiller pour l'euro de Laurent Fabins, Ministry of the Econ., Finance and Industry 2000–. *Address:* c/o Ministry of the Economy, Finance and Industry, Hôtel des Ministres, Télédoc 146, 139 rue de Bercy, 75572 Paris Cedex 12 (Office); Conseil d'Etat, Palais-Royal, 75100 Paris 01 SP, France. *Website:* www.finances.gouv.fr (Office).

HASSAN, Mohamed Hag Ali, PhD; Sudanese professor of mathematics; b. 21 Nov. 1947; ed Oxford Univ.; Sr Lecturer Dept of Mathematical Sciences, Khartoum Univ. 1977, Assoc. Prof. 1979, Prof. 1986, Dean of Mathematical Sciences 1985; Fulbright Research Fellow 1984; Exec. Dir Third World Acad. of Sciences 1983–; Sec.-Gen. Third World Network of Scientific Orgs. 1988–; Fellow African Acad. of Sciences, Pres. 1999–; Fellow Islamic Acad. of Sciences, mem. Council 1999–; Hon. mem. Colombian Acad. of Exact Sciences. *Publications:* over 40 articles on applied mathematics. *Address:* c/o African Academy of Sciences, P.O. Box 24916, Nairobi, Kenya (Office). *Telephone:* (2) 884401 (Office). *Fax:* (2) 884406 (Office). *E-mail:* aas@africaonline.co.ke (Office).

HASSAN IBN TALAL, HRH, GCVO, MA; b. 20 March 1947, Amman; m. Sarrath Khujista Akhter Banu 1968; one s. three d.; ed Harrow School, England, Christ Church, Oxford Univ.; brother of the late Hussein ibn Talal, King of Jordan and heir to the throne until the changes in succession announced by the late King Hussein Jan. 1999; fmrly acted as Regent during absence of King Hussein; Ombudsman for Nat. Devt 1971–; Founder of Royal Scientific Soc. of Jordan 1970, Royal Acad. for Islamic Civilization Research (Al AlBait) 1980, Arab Thought Forum 1981, Forum Humanum (now Arab Youth Forum) 1982; Co-Chair. Independent Comm. on Int. Humanitarian Issues; Co-Patron Islamic Acad. of Sciences; Pres. Higher Council for Science and Tech.; Hon. Gen. of Jordan Armed Forces; Hon. PhD (Econ.) (Yarmouk) 1980; Hon. DSc (Bogazici, Turkey) 1982; Hon. Dr. Arts and Sciences (Jordan) 1987; Hon. DCL (Durham) 1990; Dr. hc (Ulster) 1996; Medal of Pres. of Italian Repub. 1982; Kt of Grand Cross of Order of Merit (Italy) 1983. *Publications:* A Study on Jerusalem 1979, Palestinian Self-Determination 1981, Search for Peace 1984, Christianity in the Arab World 1994. *Leisure interests:* polo, squash, scuba diving, mountaineering, archaeology, Karate, Taekwondo, helicopter piloting, skiing. *Address:* The Royal Palace, Amman, Jordan.

HASSAN SHARQ, Mohammad; Afghanistan politician; b. 1925, Farah; Deputy Prime Minister, 1974–77; Prime Minister of Afghanistan 1988–89. *Address:* c/o Office of the Prime Minister, Kabul, Afghanistan.

HASSANALI, Noor Mohamed; Trinidad and Tobago fmr Head of State and fmr judge; b. 13 Aug. 1918; m. Zalayhar Mohammed 1952; one s. one d.; ed Naparima Coll. San Fernando and Univ. of Toronto; called to Bar, Gray's Inn, London 1948; pvt. practice as barrister-at-law in Trinidad and Tobago 1948–53; magistrate, Vic. Trinidad 1953–60; Sr magistrate, Trinidad and Tobago 1960; Sr Crown Counsel, Attorney-Gen.'s Chambers 1960; Asst Solicitor-Gen. 1965; Judge, High Court 1966; Justice of Appeal, Supreme Court of Trinidad and Tobago 1978; retd 1985; mem. Judicial and Legal Service Comm. 1985–, Trinidad and Tobago Defence Force Comms. Bd 1985–; Pres. of Trinidad and Tobago 1987–97. *Address:* c/o President's House, St Ann's, Trinidad and Tobago.

HASSANOV, Hassan Aziz Oglou; Azerbaijani politician; b. 20 Oct. 1940, Tbilisi, Georgia; s. of Aziz Hassanov and Ruhsara Adjalova; m. 1964; one s. one d.; ed Azerbaijan Polytech. Inst., Higher Party School; mem. various student groups 1958–61; with Lenin Young Communists League (Komsomol) Orgs of Yasamal region of Baku 1961–66; with Komsomol Cen. Cttee, Moscow, 1967–; with Construction Section, Cent. Cttee, Azerbaijan CP 1971–; First Sec. CP, Sabail region, then of Komsomol of Sumgayit and Gandja cities 1975–81; mem.Azerbaijan Supreme Soviet 1977–95, USSR Supreme Soviet 1979–84; Sec.Cent. Cttee Komsomol 1–1, Azerbaijan (Ideology) 1981, (Construction and Transport) 1983–, (Econ.) 1989; first Prime Minister of the Repub. of Azerbaijan 1990–1992; Perm. Rep. to UN 1992–93; Minister of Foreign Affairs 1993–98; mem. of Mili Mejlis (Parl.) 1995–. *Play:* Letter from Brussels 2001. *Publications:* more than 100 articles on Azerbaijani economy, policies, diplomacy and history. *Leisure interests:* art, music, history, politics, chess. *Address:* Gendjler Meydani 3, Baku 370001; Apt. 36, 9 Istiglad Str., Baku 370001 Azerbaijan (Home). *Telephone:* (12) 927744 (Home); (12) 929114. *Fax:* (12) 651038; (12) 988480. *E-mail:* Ggassuhov@hotmail.com (Home).

HASSELL, Michael Patrick, MA, PhD, FRS; British professor of insect ecology; b. 2 Aug. 1942, Tel Aviv; s. of Albert Hassell and Ruth Hassell; m. 1st Glynis M. Everett 1966; m. 2nd Victoria A. Taylor 1982; three s. one d.; ed Whitgift School, Croydon, Clare Coll., Cambridge and Oriel Coll., Oxford; Visiting Lecturer, Univ. of Calif., Berkeley 1967–68; NERC Research Fellowship, Hope Dept of Entomology, Oxford 1968–70; Lecturer, Dept of Zoology and Applied Entomology, Imperial Coll., London 1970–75, Reader 1975–79, Prof. of Insect Ecology, Dept of Biology 1979–, Deputy Head, Dept of Biology 1984–92, Head 1993–2001; Prin. Faculty of Life Sciences 2001–; Dir Imperial Coll., Silwood Park 1988–; Storer Life Sciences Lecturer, Univ. of Calif., Davis 1985; Pres. British Ecological Soc. 1998–99; Fellow Acad. Europaea 1998; Trustee Natural History Museum 1999–; Scientific Medal (Zoological Soc.) 1981, Gold Medal (British Ecological Soc.) 1994, Weldon Prize (Univ. of Oxford) 1995. *Publications:* Insect Population Ecology (with G. C. Varley and G. R. Gradwell) 1973, The Dynamics of Competition and Predation 1975, The Dynamics of Arthropod Predator-Prey Systems 1978; The Spatial and Temporal Dynamics of Host-Parasitoia Interactions 2000, numerous Publs on

population ecology. *Leisure interests:* walking, natural history. *Address:* Silwood Lodge, Silwood Park, Ascot, Berks., SL5 7PZ, England. *Telephone:* (1344) 294207. *Fax:* (1344) 874957.

HASSELMO, Nils, PhD; American university president; b. 2 July 1931, Köla, Sweden; s. of Wilner Hasselmo and Anna Backlund; m. Patricia Tillberg 1958 (died 2000); two s. one d.; ed Uppsala Univ., Augustana Coll. Rock Island, Ill. and Harvard Univ.; Asst Prof. of Swedish, Augustana Coll. 1958–59, 1961–63; Visiting Asst Prof. in Scandinavian Studies, Univ. of Wis. 1964–65; Assoc. Prof. of Scandinavian Lang. and Literature, Univ. of Minn. 1965–70, Dir Center for NW European Lang. and Area Studies 1970–73, Prof. of Scandinavian Language and Literature 1970–73, Assoc. Dean and Exec. Officer, Coll. of Liberal Arts 1973–78, Vice-Pres. for Admin. and Planning 1980–83; Prof. of English and Linguistics and Sr Vice-Pres. for Academic Affairs and Provost, Univ. of Ariz. 1983–88; Pres. Univ. of Minn. 1988–97, Asscn of American Univs. 1998–; mem. Bd Dirs Swedish Council 1978–, Chair. 1999–; mem. numerous professional orgs. etc.; Dr. hc (Uppsala) 1979, (North Park Univ., Chicago) 1992, (Augustana Coll., Ill.) 1995; recipient of many honours and awards including Royal Order of North Star (Sweden), King Carl XVI Gustaf Bicentennial Gold Medal. *Publications:* books and articles and reviews in learned journals. *Leisure interests:* reading, music, hiking, tennis, golf. *Address:* AAU, 1200 New York Ave., NW, Suite 550, Washington, DC 20005, USA (Office). *Telephone:* (202) 408-7500. *Fax:* (202) 408-8184. *E-mail:* nils_hasselmo aau.@edu (Office).

HASSON, Maurice; French/Venezuelan violinist; b. 6 July 1934, Berck-Plage; m. Jane Hoogesteijn, 1969; one s. three d.; ed Conservatoire Nat. Supérieur de Musique, Paris, further studies with Henryk Szeryng; Prof. RAM, London 1986; concert artist in maj. concert halls throughout world, also in TV and radio performances; Hon. mem. RAM, London: First Prize Violin, Prix d'honneur and First Prize Chamber Music, Conservatoire Nat. Supérieure de Musique, Paris 1950, Int. Prize Long Thibaut 1951, Int. Prize Youth Festival, Warsaw 1955, Grand Prix Musique de Chambre 1957, Orden Andrés Bello, Orden Francisco de Miranda (Venezuela). *Recordings include:* Concerto No. 1 (Paganini), Concerto No. 2 (Prokofiev), Debussy Sonatas, Fauré Sonatas, Concerto No. 1, Scottish Fantasy (Bruch), Concerto for 2 and 4 violins (Vivaldi), Double Concerto (Bach), Concerto (Brahms), Brilliant Showpieces for the Violin, Tzigane (Ravel), Rondo Capriccioso (Saint Saëns), Poème (Chausson), Gypsy Airs (Sarasate), Violin Concerto (Castellanos-Yumar), Sonata (Franck), virtuoso pieces. *Leisure interests:* painting, sport, cars. *Address:* c/o Manygate Management, 13 Cotswold Mews, 30 Battersea Square, London, SW11 3RA; 18 West Heath Court, North End Road, London, NW11 7RE, England (Home). *Telephone:* (20) 7223-7265 (Agent); (20) 8458-3647 (Home). *Fax:* (20) 7585-2830 (Agent); (20) 8458-3647 (Home).

HASTE, Andy; British insurance executive; fmrly with National Westminster (NatWest) Bank, Head Consumer Loans Products Div., NatWest US operations 1992–95, Pres. US consumer credit business 1995–99; Pres. and CEO Global Consumer Finance Europe, GE Capital; CEO AXA Sun Life (also Exec. Dir AXA UK) 1999–2003; Group CEO Royal & Sun Alliance Group (also mem. Main Bd Dirs Royal & Sun Alliance) 2003–. *Address:* Royal & Sun Alliance, Worldwide Group Office, 30 Berkeley Square, London, W1J 6EW, England (Office). *Telephone:* (20) 7636-3450 (Office). *Fax:* (20) 7636-3451 (Office). *Website:* www.royalsunalliance.com (Office).

HASTERT, (J.) Dennis, BA, MS; American politician; b. 2 Jan. 1942, Aurora, Ill.; m. Jean Kahl 1973; two s.; ed Wheaton Coll., Ill., Northern Illinois Univ.; fmr teacher Yorkville High School, Ill., also wrestling coach; mem. Ill. House of Reps., Springfield 1980–86; mem. 100th–105th Congresses from 14th Dist Ill. 1987–, mem. Commerce Comm., Govt Reform and Oversight Comm.; Speaker of House of Reps. 1999–; Republican. *Address:* United States House of Representatives, 2369 Rayburn House Office Building, Washington, DC 20515, USA.

HASTINGS, Sir Max Macdonald, Kt, FRSL, FRHistS; British journalist; b. 28 Dec. 1945, London; s. of Macdonald Hastings and Anne Scott-James (Lady Lancaster); m. 1st Patricia Edmondson 1972 (divorced 1994); one s. (and one s. deceased) one d.; m. 2nd Penelope Grade 1999; ed Charterhouse and Univ. Coll., Oxford; reporter, London Evening Standard 1965–67, 1968–70; Fellow, US World Press Inst. 1967–68; reporter, current affairs, BBC Television 1970–73; freelance journalist, broadcaster and author 1973–; columnist, Evening Standard 1979–85, Daily Express 1981–83, Sunday Times 1985–86; Ed. Daily Telegraph 1986–95, Dir 1989–95, Ed.-in-Chief 1990–95; Ed. Evening Standard 1996–2002; Dir Associated Newspapers PLC 1996–, Evening Standard Ltd 1996–2002; columnist Daily Mail 2002–; mem. Press Complaints Comm. 1990–92; Trustee Liddell Hart Archive, King's Coll. London 1988–, Nat. Portrait Gallery 1995–; Pres. Council for the Protection of Rural England 2002–; Journalist of the Year 1982; Reporter of the Year 1982; Somerset Maugham Prize for Non-fiction 1979; Ed. of the Year 1988; Hon. DLitt (Leicester) 1992. *Television:* documentaries: Ping-Pong in Peking 1971, The War About Peace 1983, Alarums and Excursions 1984, Cold Comfort Farm 1985, The War in Korea (series) 1988, We Are All Green Now 1990, Spies (in series Cold War) 1998. *Publications:* America 1968: The Fire, The Time 1968, Ulster 1969 1970, Montrose: The King's Champion 1977, Yoni: Hero of Entebbe 1979, Bomber Command 1979, Das Reich 1981, Battle for the Falklands (with Simon Jenkins) 1983, Overlord 1984, Victory in Europe 1985, The Oxford Book of Military Anecdotes (Ed.) 1985, The Korean War 1987, Outside Days 1989, Scattered Shots 1999, Going to the Wars 2000, Editor

2002–. *Leisure interests:* shooting, fishing. *Address:* c/o Peters, Fraser and Dunlop, Drury House, 34–43 Russell Street, London, WC2B 5HA, England (Office).

HATA, Tsutomu; Japanese politician; b. 24 Aug 1935, Tokyo; ed Seijo Univ.; fmr bus tour operator; elected to House of Reps. 1969; fmr Parl. Vice-Minister of Posts and Telecommunications, Agric., Forestry and Fisheries; fmr Minister of Agric., Forestry and Fisheries; Chair. Liberal-Democratic Party (LDP) Research Comm. on the Election System; Minister of Finance 1991–92; left LDP to found Shinseito (New Life Party), Pres. 1993–94, Shinseito dissolved 1994 (merged with eight others to form New Frontier Party); leader Good Governance Party 1998 (merged with two others to form Democratic Party of Japan—DPJ); currently Special Rep. Standing Officers Council of DPJ; Deputy Prime Minister and Minister of Foreign Affairs 1993–94; Prime Minister of Japan May–June 1994. *Address:* House of Representatives, Tokyo, Japan.

HATANO, Yoshio, BA; Japanese diplomatist; b. 3 Jan. 1932, Tokyo; s. of Keizo Hatano and Tatsuko Hatano; m. Sumiko Shimazu 1961; one s. one d.; ed Tokyo Univ., Princeton Univ., USA; joined Foreign Ministry 1953, held various positions including Dir Econ. Affairs, Asian Affairs and Treaties Bureaux, Personnel Div., Gen. Co-ordination Div.; First Sec., Embassy, London 1970; Counsellor, Embassy, Jakarta 1971; Minister, Embassy, Washington, DC 1979, Envoy Extraordinary and Minister Plenipotentiary 1981; Dir-Gen. Middle Eastern and African Affairs Bureau, Dir-Gen. for Public Information and Cultural Affairs, Ministry of Foreign Affairs 1982–87; Perm. Rep. to int. orgs. in Geneva 1987–90; Perm. Rep. to UN, New York 1990–94; Pres. Foreign Press Center 1994–. *Television:* regular mem. of Wake Up panel, Yomiuri TV. *Leisure interests:* golf, opera. *Address:* 2-14-13 Hiroo, Shibuya-ku, Tokyo, Japan. *Telephone:* (3) 3501-3401 (Office); (3) 3407-0463 (Home). *Fax:* (3) 3407-0463 (Home); (3) 3501-3622. *E-mail:* cp@fpc.jpn (Office).

HATCH, Marshall Davidson, AM, PhD, FAA, FRS; Australian research scientist; b. 24 Dec. 1932, Perth; s. of Lloyd D. Hatch and Alice Dalziel; m. 2nd Lyndall Langman 1983; two s.; ed Newington Coll., Sydney, Sydney Univ. and Univ. of Calif.; research scientist, CSIRO 1955–59; Post-doctoral Fellow, Univ. of Calif. 1959–61; research scientist, Colonial Sugar Refining Co., Ltd 1961–70; Chief Research Scientist, Div. of Plant Industry, CSIRO, Canberra 1970–; Foreign Assoc. NAS 1990; Dr hc (Göttingen) 1993, (Queensland) 1997; Clark Medal (Royal Soc. of NSW) 1973, Lemberg Medal (Australian Biochem. Soc.) 1974, Charles Kettering Award for Photosynthesis (American Soc. of Plant Physiologists) 1980, Rank Award (Rank Foundation) 1981, Int. Prize for Biology (Japan Soc. for Promotion of Science) 1991. *Publications:* over 165 review articles, chapters in books and research papers in scientific journals relating to the mechanism and function of c-4 photosynthesis. *Leisure interests:* reading, skiing, cycling, hiking. *Address:* Division of Plant Industry, CSIRO, PO Box 1600, Canberra (Office); 34 Dugdale Street, Cook, ACT 2614, Australia (Home). *Telephone:* 6246-5264 (Office); 6251-5159 (Home).

HATCH, Orrin Grant, BS, JD; American politician and lawyer; b. 22 March 1934, Homestead Park Pa; s. of Jesse Hatch and Helen Kamm Hatch; m. Elaine Hansen 1957; three s. three d.; ed Brigham Young Univ., Univ. of Pittsburgh; journeyman metal lather; Partner, Thomson, Rhodes & Grigsby 1962–69; Senior Vice-Pres. and Gen. Counsel, American Minerals Man. and American Minerals Fund Inc., Salt Lake City, Utah 1969–71; Partner, Hatch & Plumb, Salt Lake City 1976; Senator from Utah 1977–; Chair. Senate Labor and Human Resources Cttee 1981, Senate Judiciary Cttee 1995–2001, Jt Cttee on Taxation, Cttee on Indian Affairs, Sub Cttee on Taxation; mem. Senate Cttee on Finance, Senate Cttee on Intelligence 1977–; Dir Holocaust Memorial Museum; Republican; numerous hon. degrees. *Publications:* ERA Myths and Realities 1983, Good Faith under the Uniform Commercial Code, articles in legal journals. *Address:* US Senate, 104 Hart Senate Building, Washington, DC 20510, USA. *Telephone:* (202) 224-5251 (Office). *Fax:* (202) 224-6331 (Office). *Website:* www.senate.gov/hatch (Office).

HATFIELD, Mark O.; American politician; b. 12 July 1922, Dallas, Oregon; s. Charles Dolen Hatfield and Dovie Odomy ; m. Antoinette Kuzmanich 1958; two s. two d.; ed Willamette Univ. and Stanford Univ.; US Navy Second World War; Instructor, Asst Prof., Assoc. Prof. in Political Science, Willamette Univ. 1949–56, Dean of Students 1950–56; State Rep., Marion County 1951–55, State Senator, Marion County 1955–57; Sec. of State, Oregon 1957–59; Gov. of Oregon 1959–67; US Senator from Oregon 1967–97; Chair. Senate Appropriations Cttee 1981–97; fmr mem. Energy and Natural Resources Cttee and Senate Rules and Admin. Cttee; Republican; numerous awards and over 100 hon. degrees. *Publications:* Not Quite So Simple (autobiog.), Conflict and Conscience (religious speeches), Between a Rock and a Hard Place 1976, The Causes of World Hunger (co-author) 1982, What About the Russians? 1984 (jtly), Vice-Presidents of the United States 1789-1993 (jtly) 1997. *Leisure interests:* gardening, reading. *Address:* 4380 SW Macadam, Suite 460, PO Box 8639, Portland, OR 97201 (Office); 6036 SW Riverpoint Lane, Portland, OR 97201, USA (Home).

HATOYAMA, Yukio, BSc, PhD; Japanese politician; b. 11 Feb. 1947, Tokyo; brother of Kunio Hatoyama; ed Tokyo Univ., Stanford Univ., USA; Asst Prof. Senshyu Univ. 1981; Pvt Sec. to Iichiro Hatoyama, House of Councillors 1983; elected to House of Reps as MP for Hokkaido 9th Dist 1986; Parl. Vice-Minister, Hokkaido Devt Agency 1990–; Vice Chief Sec. to Hosokawa Cabinet 1993; mem. New Party Sakigake 1993, Chief Sec. New Party Sakigake Perm.

Cttee 1994; Jt Leader Democratic Party of Japan (DPJ) 1996–97, DPJ Sec.-Gen. 1997, Deputy Sec.-Gen. 1998–99, Pres. of DPJ 1999–; Vice-Chair. Japan-Russia Soc.; mem. House of Reps Standing Cttee on Science and Tech.; Chair. Touch Football Asscn of Japan. *Leisure interests:* touch football, tennis, karaoke, computers. *Address:* Democratic Party of Japan, 1-11-1 Nagata-Cho, Chiyoda-ku, Tokyo 100-0014, Japan (Office). *Telephone:* (3) 3595-7312 (Office). *Fax:* (3) 3595-9922 (Office). *E-mail:* dpjnews@dpj.or.jp (Office). *Website:* www.dpj.or.jp (Office).

HATTERSLEY, Baron (Life Peer), cr. 1997, of Sparkbrook in the County of West Midlands; **Roy Sydney George Hattersley,** PC, BSc(Econ.); British politician; b. 28 Dec. 1932; s. of the late Frederick Roy Hattersley and Enid Hattersley (née Brackenbury); m. Molly Loughran 1956; ed Sheffield City Grammar School, Univ. of Hull; Journalist and Health Service exec. 1956–64; mem. Sheffield City Council 1957–65; MP for Sparkbrook Div. of Birmingham 1964–97; Parl. Pvt. Sec. to Minister of Pensions and Nat. Insurance 1964–67; Dir Campaign for European Political Community 1965; Jt Parl. Sec. Dept of Employment and Productivity 1967–69; Minister of Defence for Admin. 1969–70; Opposition Spokesman for Defence 1970–72, for Educ. 1972–74, for the Environment 1979–80, for Home Affairs 1980–83, on Treasury and Econ. Affairs 1983–87, on Home Affairs 1987–92; Minister of State for Foreign and Commonwealth Affairs 1974–76; Sec. of State for Prices and Consumer Protection 1976–79; Deputy Leader of the Labour Party 1983–92; Pres. Local Govt Group for Europe 1998–; Public Affairs Consultant IBM 1971, 1972; Columnist Punch, The Guardian, The Listener 1979–82; Visiting Fellow, Inst. of Politics, Univ. of Harvard 1971, 1972, Nuffield Coll., Oxford 1984–; Labour; Hon. LLD (Hull) 1985; Dr. hc (Aston) 1997. *Publications:* Nelson—A Biography 1974, Goodbye to Yorkshire—A Collection of Essays 1976, Politics Apart—A Collection of Essays 1982, Press Gang 1983, A Yorkshire Boyhood 1983, Choose Freedom: The Future for Democratic Socialism 1987, Economic Priorities for a Labour Government 1987, The Maker's Mark (novel) 1990, In That Quiet Earth 1991, Skylark's Song 1994, Between Ourselves 1994, Who Goes Home? 1995, Fifty Years On 1997, Buster's Diaries: As Told to Roy Hattersley 1998, Blood and Fire: The Story of William and Catherine Booth and their Salvation Army 1999, A Brand from the Burning: The Life of John Wesley 2002. *Leisure interests:* watching cricket and football, writing. *Address:* 59 St. Martin's Lane, London, WC2N 4JS (Office); House of Lords, Westminster, London, SW1A 0PW, England. *Telephone:* (20) 7836-3533 (Office). *Fax:* (20) 7836-3531 (Office). *E-mail:* roy.hattersley@ukgateway.net (Office).

HATTON, Stephen Paul, BComm; Australian politician; b. 28 Jan. 1948, Sydney; s. of Stanley J. and Pauline Hatton (née Taylor); m. 1st Deborah J. Humphreys 1969 (divorced 1993); three s. one d.; m. 2nd Cathy Huyer 1995; one d.; ed Univ. of New South Wales; Personnel Officer, James Hardie & Co. Pty Ltd 1965–70; Industrial Officer Nabalco Pty Ltd 1970–75; Exec. Dir NT Confed. of Industries and Commerce Inc. 1975–83; elected NT Legislative Ass. (Nightcliff) 1984, Minister for Lands, Conservation, Ports and Fisheries, Primary Production 1983–84, for Mines and Energy, Primary Production 1986, for Health and Community Services 1989, for Conservation 1989, for Industries and Devt and for Trade Devt Zone and Liquor Comm. 1990–91, for Lands, Housing and Local Govt and Minister for Aboriginal Devt 1992, for Constitutional Devt 1994, Attorney-Gen., Minister for Educ. for Constitutional Devt 1995–96, for Sport and Recreation 1995–97, for Correctional Services 1996–97, for Parks and Wildlife 1996–97, for Ethnic Affairs 1996–97; Chief Minister for NT 1986–88. *Leisure interest:* sport. *Address:* Shop 5, Nightcliff Shopping Centre, Pavonia Way, Nightcliff, NT 0810, Australia.

HAUER, Rutger; Netherlands actor; b. 23 Jan. 1944, Amsterdam; m. 2nd Ieneke Hauer 1985. *Films include:* Turkish Delight 1973, The Wilby Conspiracy 1975, Keetje Tippel 1975, Max Havelaar 1976, Mysteries 1978, Soldier of Orange 1978, Woman Between Dog and Wolf 1979, Spetters 1980, Nighthawks 1981, Chanel Solitaire 1981, Blade Runner 1982, Eureka 1982, Outsider in Amsterdam 1983, The Osterman Weekend 1983, A Breed Apart 1984, Ladyhawke 1984, Flesh and Blood 1985, The Hitcher 1986, Wanted Dead or Alive 1986, The Legend of the Holy Drinker 1989, Salute of the Juggler, Ocean Point, On a Moonlit Night, Split Second, Buffy the Vampire Slayer, Past Midnight, Nostradamus, Surviving the Game, The Beans of Egypt Maine, Angel of Death, New World Disorder 1999, Wilder 2000, Lying in Wait 2000, Partners in Crime 2000. *Television:* commercials for Guinness 1989. *TV Films include:* Angel of Death 1994, Menin 1998, The 10th Kingdom 2000. *Address:* c/o William Morris Agency, 151 El Camino Drive, Beverly Hills, CA 90212, USA.

HAUFF, Volker, Dr rer. pol; German politician and business consultant; b. 9 Aug. 1940, Backnang; s. of Richard and Ilse (Dieter) Hauff; m. Ursula Irion 1967; two s.; ed Free Univ. of Berlin; with IBM Deutschland, Stuttgart 1971–72; Sec. of State to Fed. Minister for Research and Tech. 1972–78; Fed. Minister for Research and Tech. 1978–80, of Transport 1980–82; mem. Bundestag 1969; mem. Social Democratic Party (SPD) 1959, Vice-Pres. of Parl. Group 1983; Mayor of Frankfurt 1989–91; Generalbevollmächtigte KPMG Germany 1995–2000, mem. Bd Bearing Point GmbH 2002–; Chair. German Council for Sustainable Devt 2001–; fmr. mem. UN World Comm. on Environment and Devt. *Publications:* Programmierfibes—Eine verständliche Einführung in das Programmieren digitaler Automaten 1969, Wörterbuch der Datenverarbeitung 1966, Für ein soziales Bodenrecht 1973, Modernisierung der Volkswirtschaft 1975, Politik als Zukunftsgestaltung 1976, Damit der Fortschritt nicht zum Risiko wird 1978, Sprachlose Politik 1979,

Global Denken – Lokal Handeln 1992. *Leisure interests:* modern art, cooking. *Address:* Fritschestrasse 24, 10585 Berlin, Germany (Home). *Telephone:* (30) 34703841 (Office); (172) 2902902. *E-mail:* vhauff@bearingpoint.biz. *Website:* www.bearingpoint.de.

HAUGHEY, Charles James, BCom; Irish politician and barrister-at-law; b. 16 Sept. 1925, Castlebar, Co. Mayo; s. of Commdt John Haughey and Sarah Ann McWilliams; m. Maureen Lemass 1951; three s. one d.; ed Scoil Mhuire, Marino, Dublin, St Joseph's Christian Brothers' School, Fairview, Dublin, Univ. Coll. Dublin and King's Inns, Dublin; commissioned Officer Reserve Defence Force 1947–57; Mem. Dublin City Council 1953–55; MP 1957–92; represented Dublin (North Central)); Parl. Sec. to Minister for Justice 1960–61, Minister for Justice 1961–64; Minister of Agric. 1964–66, Minister for Finance 1966–70, for Health and Social Welfare 1977–79; Taoiseach (Prime Minister) 1979–81, March–Dec. 1982, 1987–92, Minister for the Gaeltacht 1987–92; Leader of the Opposition 1981–82, 1982–87; Chair. Irish Parl. Jt Cttee on the Secondary Legislation of the European Communities 1973–77; Pres. Fianna Fáil 1979–92; Pres. European Council 1990; Hon. Bencher Hon. Soc. of King's Inns Dublin; Hon. Fellow Royal Irish Acad.; Hon. PhD (Dublin City Univ.); Hon. LLD (Univ. Blaise-Pascal, France), (Univ. Notre Dame, USA), (Nat. Univ. of Ireland). *Publication:* The Spirit of the Nation. *Leisure interests:* reading, music, riding, swimming, sailing. *Address:* Abbeville, Kinsealy, Co. Dublin, Ireland. *Telephone:* (1) 8450111.

HAUGHTON, Rosemary Elena Konradin; British/American writer, lecturer, social philosopher and theologian; b. 13 April 1927, London; d. of Peter Luling and Sylvia Luling (née Thompson); sister of Dr. Virginia Luling; m. Algernon Haughton 1948; seven s. three d.; ed Farnham Girls Grammar, Queen's Coll., London, Slade School of Art; had no formal educ. after age of 15; has lectured internationally; Assoc. Dir Wellspring House Inc., providing shelter for homeless families, educ., low-income housing and econ. Devt in Mass., USA 1981–; Dr hc (Notre Dame, Ind. Nazareth Coll., Rochester, NY, Georgian Court Coll., NJ, St Mary's Coll., Notre Dame, Ind.); Avila Award. *Publications:* 35 books including The Transformation of Man, The Drama of Salvation, Tales from Eternity, Elizabeth's Greeting, The Catholic Thing, The Passionate God, The Re-Creation of Eve, Song in a Strange Land, The Tower that Fell (illustrated), Images for Change: The Transformation of Society. *Leisure interests:* wood-carving, embroidery, gardening, reading, country cottage. *Address:* Wellspring House Inc., 302 Essex Avenue, Gloucester, MA 01930, USA; 5 Draper Corner, Heptonstall, Hebden Bridge, W Yorkshire, HX7 7EY, England. *Telephone:* (508) 281-3221 (USA).

HĂULICĂ, Dan; Romanian art critic; b. 7 Feb. 1932, Iaşi; s. of Neculai Hăulică and Lucreţia Hăulică; m. Cristina Isbăşescu 1971; one d.; ed Coll. of Philology, Iaşi, N. Grigorescu Fine Arts Inst., Bucharest; Reader Iaşi Coll. of Philology 1954–56; ed. Literary Magazine, Bucharest 1956–58; Researcher of the Inst. for Literary History and Theory of the Romanian Acad. 1958–63; Deputy Ed.-in-Chief Secolul 20 (journal) 1963–67, Ed.-in-Chief 1967; Prof. N. Grigorescu Coll. of Fine Arts, Bucharest 1965; Chair. Int. Asscn of Arts Critics 1981–84, Hon. Chair. 1984; Chair. Conseil audiovisuel mondial pour l'édition et la recherche sur l'art (CAMERA) 1986; UNESCO consultant; Amb. to UNESCO 1990–; mem. European Soc. of Culture 1988, European Acad. of Sciences, Letters and Arts 1987; Chair. Int. Confs. on Arts, TV and Problems of the Image: Paris, UNESCO 1981, Biennale di Venezia 1982, Sophia Antipolis, Moscow-Tashkent 1982, Helsinki 1983, Caracas 1983, Delphi 1984, Lisbon, Gulbenkian 1984, Paris 1986, Prague 1987, Alger-Tipasa 1987; Chair. Int. Jury of the Arts Film Festivals, Montreal 1984, Le Carnival et la Fête, Nice 1985, Politiques Culturelles et Télévision, Paris 1986; mem. leading bds. Romanian Writers' Union, Romanian Fine Arts Union; Prize of the Romanian Fine Arts Union 1967, Prizes of the Romanian Writers' Union 1974, 1984; Prize of the Romanian Film Studio Al. Sahia, Great Prize of the Romanian Fine Arts Union 1975; Grand Prix Int. de la meilleure revue d'art (Festival Int. d'Art de Beaubourg) Paris 1987. *Works include:* Peintres roumains (UNESCO, Vol. I 1963, Vol. II 1965), Brancusi ou l'anonymat du génie 1967, Critică şi cultură (Criticism and Culture) 1967, Calder, Variations sur le thème Homo Faber 1971, Geografii spirituale (Spiritual Geographies) 1973, Nostalgia sintezei (The Nostalgia for Synthesis) 1984. *Address:* Str. Docenţilor 26, Bucharest 71311, Romania (Home).

HÄUPL, Michael, DPhil; Austrian politician; b. 14 Sept. 1949, Altlengbach; m.; two c.; ed Bundesrealgymnasium, Krems a.d. Donau, Univ. of Vienna; Scientific worker, Natural History Museum, Vienna 1975–83; mem. SPÖ (Austrian Socialist Party), Chair. VSSTÖ (Asscn. of Austrian Socialist Students) 1975–77, mem. Ottakring Party Cttee 1978–, various appts in SPÖ youth div. (JG) 1978–84, elected Chair. Vienna JG and Vice-Chair. Nat. JG 1982–; mem. Vienna regional legis. 1983–88, City Councillor for Environment and Sport 1988–94, Chair. SPÖ Regional Cttee 1993–; Mayor of Vienna Nov. 1994–; Dir. Austria Vienna Football Club. *Leisure interest:* football. *Address:* Rathaus, Rathausplatz 1, Stiege 5, 1 Vienna 1010, Austria (Office). *Telephone:* (1) 4000-8111 (Office). *Fax:* (1) 4000-8111 (Office). *E-mail:* buergermeister@magwien.gv.at (Office). *Website:* www.wien.gv.at (Office).

HAUSER, Erich; German sculptor and professor; b. 15 Dec. 1930, Rietheim, Tuttlingen; s. of Ludwig Hauser and Berta Hauser; m. Gretl Kawaletz 1955; one s. one d.; ed Volksschule, Rietheim, Oberschule, Spaichingen and evening classes at Freie Kunstschule, Stuttgart; studied engraving in Tuttlingen and drawing and modelling under Pater Ansgar, Kloster Beuron; ind. sculptor, Schramberg 1952; Visiting Lecturer, Hochschule für Bildende Künste, Hamburg 1964–65, Visiting Prof. 1984; Visiting Prof., Hochschule der Künste, Berlin 1984–85; mem. Akad. der Künste, Berlin; Kunstpreis der Stadt Wolfsburg für Plastik 1965, Burdapreis für Plastik 1966, Premio Itamaraty 1969, Grand Prix, São Paulo Biennale 1969, Verdienstkreuz am Bande des Verdienstordens der Bundesrepublik 1972, Biennale Preis für Kleinplastik, Budapest 1975, Verdienstkreuz, 1st Class 1979, Helmut-Kraft-Stiftung First Prize 1988, Oberschwäbischer Kunstpreis, Rottweil 1995, Gründung der Erich Hauserstiftung 1996, Ehrenbürger der Stadt Rottweil 1995, Kulturpreis der Stadt Rottweil 2000, Verdienstmedaille des Landes Baden-Württemberg 2000. *Exhibitions:* many one-man exhbns. in galleries throughout Germany and in Austria and Switzerland since 1961; has participated in many group exhbns. in Europe, New Delhi, Cairo and the São Paulo Biennale 1969. *Sculpture:* has executed sculptures for many public bldgs in Germany including Säulenwand for Univ. of Konstanz, a relief for theatre foyer, Bonn and a sculpture for the Düsseldorf Stock Exchange. *Publication:* Erich Hauser Werkverzeichnis 1960–2000. *Address:* Saline 36, 78628 Rottweil, Germany. *Telephone:* (741) 2800180. *Fax:* (741) 28001821. *E-mail:* Prof.Erich.Hauser@web.de (Home).

HAUSSMANN, Helmut, DEcon, Dr rer. pol; German politician; b. 18 May 1943, Tübingen; s. of Emil Haussmann and Elisabeth Rau; m. Margot Scheu 1980; business exec. 1968–71; Research and Academic Asst, Univ. of Erlangen-Nuremberg 1971–75; joined Free Democratic Party (FDP) 1969; mem. Bad Urach Town Council, FDP Dist Chair., Reutlingen 1975–80; mem. Deutscher Bundestag 1976–; Econ. Cttee 1977–88; mem. FDP Fed. Exec. Cttee 1978–; Ombudsman FDP Econs Cttee 1980–; Econ. Spokesman, FDP Parl. Party 1980–84; Vice-Chair. FDP in Land Baden-Württemberg 1983–88, 1995–; Sec.-Gen. FDP 1984–88; Fed. Minister of Econ. Affairs 1988–91; mem. Foreign Affairs Cttee and Spokesman on EC Policy 1991–. *Leisure interests:* tennis and golf. *Address:* Deutscher Bundestag, Platz der Republik, 11011 Berlin, (Office); Am Forst 1, 72574 Bad Urech, Germany (Home). *Telephone:* (30) 227-73325 (Office). *Fax:* (30) 227-76223. *E-mail:* helmut.haussmann@bundestag.de (Office). *Website:* www.helmet-haussmann.de (Office).

HAVEL, Richard Joseph, MD, FAAS; American professor of medicine; b. 20 Feb. 1925, Seattle, Wash.; s. of Joseph Havel and Anna Fritz; m. Virginia J. Havel 1947; three s. one d.; ed Reed Coll., Portland, Ore., Univ. of Ore. Medical School and Cornell Univ. Medical Coll.; Asst in Biochem. Univ. of Ore. Medical School 1945–49; Asst Resident in Medicine, New York Hospital 1950–51, Chief Resident in Medicine 1952–53; Instructor Cornell Univ. Medical Coll. 1952–53; Clinical Assoc. Nat. Heart Inst. 1953–54, Research Assoc. 1954–56; Asst Prof. of Medicine, Univ. of Calif., San Francisco 1956–59, Assoc. Prof. 1959–64, Prof. of Medicine 1964–, Chief Metabolism Section 1967–97, Dir Cardiovascular Research Inst. 1973–92; Dir Arteriosclerosis Specialized Center of Research 1970–96; Ed. Journal of Lipid Research 1972–75; mem. Editorial Bd, Journal of Arteriosclerosis 1980–; mem. Food and Nutrition Bd, Nat. Research Council 1983, (Chair. 1987–90); mem. NAS, Inst. of Medicine, American Acad. of Arts and Sciences, American Soc. of Clinical Nutrition, Asscn of American Physicians, American Soc. for Clinical Investigation; Fellow American Inst. of Nutrition; Fellow AAAS; T. Smith Award, AAAS 1960, Bristol-Myers Award for nutrition research 1989, McCollum Award 1993, Gold Medal Charles Univ. (Czech Repub.) 1996, Mayo Soley Award 1997. *Publications:* over 300 scientific articles and book chapters. *Address:* University of California, Cardiovascular Research Institute, San Francisco, CA 94143 USA (Office). *E-mail:* havelr@itsa.ucsf.edu (Office).

HAVEL, Václav; Czech politician, playwright and writer; b. 5 Oct. 1936, Prague; s. of Václav M. Havel and Božena (Vavrečková) Havel; m. 1st Olga Šplíchalová 1964 (died 1996); m. 2nd Dagmar Veškrnová 1997; ed Acad. of Arts, Drama Dept, Prague; worked as freelance; fmr spokesman for Charter 77 human rights movement, received a sentence of 14 months in 1977, suspended for 3 years, for "subversive" and "antistate" activities, under house arrest 1978–79; mem. Cttee for the Defence of the Unjustly Prosecuted (VONS), convicted and sentenced to $4^1/_2$ years' imprisonment for sedition 1979, released March 1983, arrested Jan. 1989 and sentenced to 9 months imprisonment for incitement and obstruction Feb. 1989; sentence reduced to 8 months and charge changed to misdemeanour March 1989; released May 1989; f. Civic Forum 1989; Pres. of Czechoslovakia 1989–92, Pres. of Czech Repub. 1993–2003; C-in-C of Armed Forces 1989–92; Chair. Prague Heritage Fund 1993–; mem. jury Int. Prize Awarding Body for Human Rights 1994–; mem. Acad. des Sciences Morales et Politiques; Hon. mem. Acad. of Sciences and Arts, Salzburg; numerous hon. degrees including Dr hc (Bar Ilan Univ. Israel, Kiev Univ., Ukraine, Jordan Univ., Oxford) 1997, (Glasgow) 1998 (Manitoba, St. Thomas Univ., USA) 1999, (Bilkent Univ., Turkey) 2000; Austrian State Prize for European Literature 1968, Jan Palach Prize 1982, (JAMU, Brno) 2001, Erasmus Prize 1986, Olof Palme Prize 1989, German Book Trade Peace Prize 1989, Simón Bolívar Prize 1990, Malaparte Prize 1990, Sonning Cultural Prize 1991, Athinai Prize (Onassis Foundation) 1993, Indira Gandhi Prize 1994, European Cultural Soc. Award 1993, Philadelphia Liberty Medal 1994, Premi Internacional Catalunya 1995, TGM Prize (Canada) 1997, Medal of Danish Acad. 1997, European Statesman Prize (USA), 1997, Husajn bin Ali Distinction (Jordan) 1997, J. W. Fulbright Prize for Int. Understanding (USA) 1997, Le Prix Spécial Europe, European Theatre Council 1997, Cino del Duca Prize (France), Prince of Asturias Prize (Spain) 1997, Open Soc. Prize, Budapest Univ., Gazeta Wyborcza Prize (Poland), St Vojtěch Prize (Slovakia) 1999, Citizen Prize, Berlin 2000, Evelyn Burkey's Prize, Author's Guild of America 2000, Elie Wiesel Prize 2000, Hon.

Citizen Vrtislav 2001; Order of White Eagle, Poland 1993, Golden Hon. Order of Freedom, Slovenia 1993, Chain of Order of Isabel of Castille, Spain 1995, Charles Univ. Medal 1998, Grand Cross Order with Chain (Lithuania) 1999, Federal Cross for Merit, Berlin 2000; Hon. KCB, UK 1996. *Plays include:* Garden Party 1963, Memorandum 1965, The Increased Difficulty of Concentration 1968, The Conspirators 1971, The Beggar's Opera 1972, Audience 1975, Vernissage 1975, The Mountain Resort 1976, Protest 1978, The Mistake 1983, Largo Desolato 1984, Temptation 1985, Redevelopment 1987, Tomorrow! 1988. *Publications include:* Letters to Olga (in Czech, as Dopisy Olge) 1983, Disturbing the Peace (in Czech, as Dálkový výslech) 1986, (English) 1990, Václav Havel or Living in Truth (essays, in English) 1986, Open Letters: Selected Writings 1965–1990 (in English) 1991, Selected Plays by Václav Havel (in English) 1992, Summer Meditations (in Czech, as Ledric piemidánt) 1991, (English) 1992, Plays (in Czech, as Hry) 1991, Toward a Civil Society 1994, The Art of the Impossible (speeches) 1997, In Various Directions (in Czech, as Do různých stran) 1999, Spisy (7 Vols) 1999. *Address:* Dělostřelecká 1, 160 00 Prague 6, Czech Republic. *Telephone:* (2) 2437-1111. *Fax:* (2) 2437-3300. *E-mail:* vaclav.havel@volny.cz (Office).

HAVELANGE, Jean Marie Faustin Godefroid (João); Brazilian sports administrator; b. 8 May 1916, Rio de Janeiro; m.; practising lawyer 1936–; Head of Importation and Exportation, Cia Siderúrgica Belgo-Mineira 1937–41; Dir-Pres. Viação Cometa SA, EMBRADATA, Orwec Química e Metalúrgica Ltda; took part in Olympic Games as swimmer, Berlin 1936, as water polo player, Helsinki 1952, Head of Brazilian Del., Sydney 1956; Pres. Fed. Paulista de Natação, São Paulo 1949–51, Fed. Metropolitana de Natação (GB) 1952–56; mem. Brazilian Olympic Cttee 1955–73; Vice-Pres. Confed. Brasileira de Desportos 1956–58, Pres. 1958–73; Dir, mem. for South America Cttee of Int. Cyclists Union 1958; mem. Int. Olympic Cttee 1963; Pres. Indoor Football Int. Fed. (FIFUSA) 1971; Pres. Int. Fed. of Asscn Football (FIFA) 1974–98, Hon. Pres. 1998–; Portuguese and Brazilian decorations. *Leisure interests:* swimming and water polo. *Address:* Av. Rio Branco 89-B, conj. 602 Centro, 20040-004 Rio de Janeiro, RJ, Brazil.

HAVIARAS, Stratis, MFA; Greek author; b. 28 June 1935, Nea Kios, Argos; s. of Christos Haviaras and Georgia Hadzikyriakos; m. 1st Gail Flynn 1967 (divorced 1973); m. 2nd Heather Cole 1990; one d.; fmr construction worker; lived in USA 1959–61; went to USA following colonels' coup in Greece 1967, obtaining position at Harvard Univ. Library; Curator, Poetry Room, Harvard Univ. Library 1974–; Founder and Ed. Harvard Review 1992–. *Publications:* four Vols of Greek verse 1963, 1965, 1967, 1972; Crossing the River Twice (poems in English) 1976; novels: When the Tree Sings 1979, The Heroic Age 1984; ed. Seamus Heaney: a Celebration 1996. *Leisure interest:* wood sculpture. *Address:* Poetry Room, Harvard University, Cambridge, MA 02138, USA. *Telephone:* (617) 495-2454 (Office); (617) 354-4724 (Home). *Fax:* (617) 496-3692.

HAVIGHURST, Clark Canfield, JD; American professor of law; b. 25 May 1933, Evanston, Ill.; s. of Harold Canfield and Marion Clay (Perryman) Havighurst; m. Karen Waldron 1965; one s. one d.; ed Princeton and Northwestern Univs.; Research Assoc. Duke Univ. School of Law 1960–61; Private Practice, Debevoise, Plimpton, Lyons & Gates, New York 1958, 1961–64; Assoc. Prof. of Law, Duke Univ. 1964–68, Prof. 1968–86, William Neal Reynolds Prof. 1986–; Interim Dean Duke Univ. School of Law 1999; numerous other professional appts.; mem. Inst. of Medicine, NAS. *Publications:* Deregulating the Health Care Industry 1982, Health Care Law and Policy 1988, Health Care Choices: Private Contracts as Instruments of Health Reform 1995; articles on regulation in the health services industry, the role of competition in the financing and delivery of health care and anti-trust issues arising in the health care field. *Address:* Box 90360, Duke University School of Law, Durham, NC 27708 (Office); 3610 Dover Road, Durham, NC 27707, USA (Home). *Telephone:* (919) 613-7061 (Office); (919) 489-4970 (Home). *Fax:* (919) 613-7231. *E-mail:* hav@law.duke.edu (Office).

HAWASS, Zahi, PhD; Egyptian archaeologist and Egyptologist; b. 28 May 1947, Damietta; ed Cairo Univ., Univ. of Pennsylvania; Inspector of Antiquities of Middle Egypt, Tuna El-Gebel and Mallawi 1969, Italian Expedition, Sikh Abada, Minia 1969, Edfu-Esna, Egypt 1969, Pa Yale Expedition at Abydos 1969, Western Delta at Alexandria 1970, Embaba, Giza 1972–74, Abu Simbel 1973–74, Pa Expedition, Malkata, Luxor 1974, Giza Pyramids (for Boston Museum of Fine Arts) 1974–75; First Inspector of Antiquities, Embaba and Bahria Oasis 1974–79, Chief Inspector 1980, Gen. Dir 1987–98; Gen. Dir Saqqara and Bahria Oasis 1987–98; Archaeological Site Man. Memphis 1991–; Under-Sec. of State for Giza Monuments 1998; Dir of numerous excavations and conservation projects; numerous consultancy roles; mem. Bd Egyptian Nat. Museum 1996–; Trustee Egyptian Nat. Museum; Sound and Light Co. 1990; mem. German Archaeological Inst. 1991–; mem. of numerous cttees.; Presidential Medal 1998. *Publications:* numerous papers on Egyptology and archaeology. *Address:* Egyptian National Museum, Midan-el-Tahrir, Cairo, Egypt (Office).

HAWKE, Ethan; American actor; b. 6 Nov. 1970, Austin, Tex.; m. Uma Thurman (q.v.) 1998; one d.; ed New York University; co-f. Malaparte Theatre Co. *Theatre appearances include:* Casanova 1991, A Joke, The Seagull 1992, Sophistry. *Films include:* Explorers 1985, Dead Poets Society 1989, Dad 1989, White Fang 1991, Mystery Date 1991, A Midnight Clear 1992, Waterland 1992, Alive 1993, Rich in Love 1993, Straight to One 1993 (Dir), Reality Bites 1994, Quiz Show 1994, Floundering 1994, Before Sunrise 1995, Great Expectations, Gattaca, Joe the King 1999, Hamlet 2000, Tape 2001, Waking Life 2001, Training Day 2001. *Publication:* Ash Wednesday 2002.

HAWKE, Gary Richard, DPhil, FRSNZ; New Zealand economic historian; b. 1 Aug. 1942, Napier; s. of Vyvyan Nesbitt Hawke and Jean Avis Hawke (née Carver); m. Helena Joyce Powrie 1965; two s.; ed Victoria Univ. of Wellington, Balliol and Nuffield Colls., Oxford; lecturer Victoria Univ. of Wellington 1968–70, Reader 1971–73, Prof. of Econ. History 1974–; Dir Inst. of Policy Studies 1987–97; visiting appointments Stanford Univ. 1972–73, All Souls Coll., Oxford 1977–78, Japan Foundation 1993, Japan Soc. for Promoting Knowledge 1994; Chair. NZ Planning Council 1986–91; Head School of Govt, Victoria Univ. 2003. *Publications include:* Railways and Economic Growth 1970, Between Governments and Banks 1973, Economics for Historians 1980, The Making of New Zealand 1985, The Thoroughbred Among Banks 1997. *Leisure interests:* classical music, armchair criticism. *Address:* School of Government, Victoria University of Wellington, PO Box 600, Wellington (Office); 7 Voltaire Street, Karori, Wellington, New Zealand (Home). *Telephone:* (4) 463-5794 (Office); (4) 476-5454 (Home). *Fax:* (4) 463-5014 (Office). *E-mail:* gary.hawke@vuw.ac.nz (Office). *Website:* www.vuw.ac.nz (Office).

HAWKE, Robert James Lee, AC, BA, LLB, BLitt; Australian politician and fmr trade unionist; b. 9 Dec. 1929, Bordertown, S Australia; s. of A. C. Hawke; m. 1st Hazel Masterson 1956 (divorced 1995); one s. two d.; m. 2nd Blanche d'Apulget 1995; ed Univs of Western Australia and Oxford; Rhodes scholar 1953; Research Officer, Australian Council of Trade Unions 1958–70, Pres. 1970–80; Sr Vice-Pres. Australian Labor Party 1971–73, Pres. 1973–78, Leader 1983–91; MP for Wills, Melbourne 1980–92; Prime Minister 1983–91, mem. Nat. Exec. 1971–91; reporter 1992; Business Consultant 1992; Adjunct Prof. Research School of Pacific Studies and Social Sciences, ANU 1992–95; Hon. Visiting Prof. in Industrial Relations Sydney Univ.; mem. Advisory Council of Inst. for Int. Studies, Stanford Univ., Calif.; Chair. Cttee of Experts on mem. of Educ. Int. 1993–; Sydney City Mission Fundraising Task Force; Dir Quantum Resources Ltd 1996–; mem. Bd Reserve Bank of Australia 1973–83, Governing Body ILO 1972–80; mem. Australian Council for Union Training, Australian Population and Immigration Council; mem. Australian Manufacturing Council 1977, Nat. Labour Consultative Council 1977–92, Australian Refugee Advisory Council; Patron Australia-China Sports Friendship Cttee 2000; Hon. Fellow, Univ. Coll., Oxford 1984; Dr hc (Nanjing) 1986; Hon. DPhil (Hebrew Univ. of Jerusalem) 1987; Hon. LLD (Univ. of NSW) 1987; UN Media Peace Prize 1980. *Publication:* The Hawke Memoirs 1994. *Leisure interests:* tennis, golf, cricket, reading. *Address:* Suite 1, Level 13, 100 Williams Street, Sydney, NSW 2001, Australia.

HAWKER, Graham Alfred, CBE, CIMgt, FCCA, FRSA; British business executive; b. 12 May 1947; s. of Alfred Hawker and Sarah Rebecca Bowen; m. Sandra Ann Evans 1967; one s. one d.; ed Bedwelty Grammar School; trainee accountant Caerphilly Dist Council 1964–66; accountant Abercarn Dist Council 1966–67, Chief Accountant 1967–68, Deputy Treas. 1968–70; Chief Auditor Taf Fechan Water Bd 1970–74; Audit Man. Welsh Water Authority 1974–78, Div. Finance Man. 1978–84, Chief Accountant 1984–86, Dir Planning and Devt 1986–87, Finance 1987–89; Dir Finance Welsh Water PLC 1989–91, Group Man. Dir 1991–93, Chief Exec. Hyder (fmrly Welsh Water) PLC 1993–2000; Chair. Dwr Cymru Ltd 1993–2000, Hyder Consulting (fmrly Acer) 1993–2000, Swalec 1996–2000; Dir (non-exec.) Bank of England 1998–2000; Chair. BITC (Wales) 1994–2000; Dir Welsh Devt Agency 1995–, Deputy Chair. 1998–2000, CEO 2000–; Chair. New Deal Task Force Advisory Cttee (Wales) 1997–98; mem. New Deal Advisory Cttee (UK) 1997–98; mem. CBI Council, Wales 1994–97, Prince of Wales Review Cttee on Queen's Awards 1999; Fellow Inst. of Certified Accountants; Hon. DL (Gwent) 1998; Prince of Wales Ambassador's Award for Corporate Social Responsibility 1999. *Leisure interests:* family, walking, wine, career. *Address:* Welsh Development Agency, Principality House, The Friary, Cardiff, CF10 3FE, Wales (Office). *Telephone:* (29) 2082-8669 (Office). *Fax:* (1874) 624167 (Office).

HAWKING, Stephen William, CH, CBE, PhD, FRS; British professor of mathematics; b. 8 Jan. 1942, Oxford; s. of Dr F. Hawking and Mrs E. I. Hawking; m. 1st Jane Wilde 1965; two s. one d.; m. 2nd Elaine Mason 1995; ed St Albans School, Univ. Coll., Oxford, Trinity Hall, Cambridge; Research Fellow, Gonville and Caius Coll., Cambridge 1965–69, Fellow for Distinction in Science 1969–; Research Asst, Inst. of Astronomy, Cambridge 1972–73; Research Asst, Dept of Applied Math. and Theoretical Physics, Cambridge Univ. 1973–75, Reader in Gravitational Physics 1975–77, Prof. 1977–79, Lucasian Prof. of Math. 1979–; mem. Inst. of Theoretical Astronomy, Cambridge 1968–72; mem. Papal Acad. of Science 1986; Foreign mem. American Acad. Arts and Sciences 1984; several hon. degrees; William Hopkins Prize, Cambridge Philosophical Soc. 1976, Wolf Prize 1988, Maxwell Medal, Inst. of Physics 1976, Hughes Medal, Royal Soc. 1976, Albert Einstein Award 1978, Gold Medal Royal Astronomical Soc. 1985, Sunday Times Special Award for Literature 1989, Britannica Award 1989, Albert Medal (RSA) 1999. *Publications:* The Large Scale Structure of Space-Time (with G. F. R. Ellis) 1973, General Relativity: An Einstein Centenary Survey 1979, Superspace and Supergravity (Co.-Ed.) 1981, The Very Early Universe (Co.-Ed.) 1983, 300 Years of Gravitation 1987, A Brief History of Time 1988, Black Holes and Baby Universes 1993, The Nature of Space and Time (with Roger Penrose) 1996, The Universe in a Nutshell 2001, The Theory of Everything: The Origin and Fate of the Universe 2002, The Future of Space Time (Co.-Ed.) 2002, On the Shoulders of Giants 2002. *Address:* Department of Applied Mathematics and Theoretical Physics, Silver Street, Cambridge, CB3 9EW, England. *Telephone:* (1223) 337843.

HAWKINS, Jeff, BS; American computer scientist and inventor; b. 1 June 1957, Long Island, Huntingdon, New York; s. of Robert Hawkins; m.; two d.; ed Cornell Univ.; various key tech. positions with Intel Corpn 1979–82; Vice-Pres. of Research, GriD Systems Corpn 1982–92; f. Palm Computing 1994, invented PalmPilot (hand held computer) 1994; Co-Founder, Chair. and Chief Product Officer Handspring Inc. 1998–; mem. Bd Cold Spring Harbor Lab., New York; PC Magazine Lifetime Achievement Award for Tech. Excellence 2000, Cornell Univ. Entrepreneur of the Year 2000. *Leisure interests:* sailing, music, family. *Address:* Office of the Chairman, Handspring Inc., 189 Bernardo Avenue, Mountain View, CA 94043, USA (Office). *Telephone:* (650) 230-5000 (Office). *Website:* www.handspring.com (Office).

HAWKINS, Paula; American politician; b. Salt Lake City, Utah; d. of Paul B. and Leoan (née Staley) Fickes; m. Walter Eugene Hawkins 1947; one s. two d.; ed Utah State Univ.; mem. Republican Precinct Cttee, Orange Co., Fla 1965–74, Rep. Nat. Comm. for Fla 1968–87; Speakers Chair. Fla Republican Exec. Cttee 1967–69, mem. Fla Republican Nat. Convention 1972, S Regional Rep., Republican Nat. Cttee 1972–; Republican Senator, Fla 1981–87; Pres. Paula Hawkins and Assocs. 1988–; mem. Maitland Civic Cen. 1965–76; Charter mem. Bd of Dirs Fla Americans Constitutional Action Cttee of 100 1966–68, Sec.-Treas. 1966–68; mem. Gov. of Fla Comm. on Status of Women 1968–71; Public Service Commr Fla, Tallahassee 1972–80; mem. Perm. Sub-Cttee on Narcotics Control and Terrorism OAS 1981–; US Del. to UN Narcotics Convention, Vienna 1987, US Del. to UN Convention NY 1994; Chair. Nat. Cttee on Responsibilities for Financing Postsecondary Educ. 1990–92; mem. Bd Dirs Freedom Foundation 1981–; fmr Chair. Legis. Council. Orange Co. Drug Abuse Council, fmr Co-Chair. Orange Co. March of Dimes; fmr mem. Cen. Fla Museum Speakers Bureau; Dr hc (Nova Univ.), (St Thomas Villa Nova), (Rollino Coll.); Citation for Service, Fla Republican Party; Above and Beyond Award (Outstanding Woman in Fla Politics). *Address:* PO Box 193, Winter Park, FL 32790, USA.

HAWLEY, Sir Donald Frederick, KCMG, MBE, MA; British diplomatist (retd), company chairman and consultant; b. 22 May 1921, Essex; s. of the late F. G. and G. E. C. Hawley (née Hills); m. Ruth Morwenna Graham 1964; one s. three d.; ed Radley, New Coll., Oxford; Barrister-at-Law, Inner Temple; served with HM Forces 1941–44; Sudan Political Service 1944–47; Sudan Judiciary 1947–55; Foreign Office 1956–58; HM Political Agent, Trucial States 1958–61; Head of Chancery British Embassy, Cairo 1962–64; Counsellor, High Commission, Lagos 1965–67; Counsellor (Commercial), Baghdad 1968–71; Amb. to Sultanate of Oman 1971–75; Asst Under Sec. of State, Foreign and Commonwealth Office 1975–77; High Commr in Malaysia 1977–81; mem London Advisory Comm. Hongkong and Shanghai Banking Corpn 1981–91; Chair. Ewbank Preece Ltd 1982–86; Chair. The Centre for British Teachers 1987–91; Chair. Royal Soc. for Asian Affairs 1994–2002, Vice-Pres. 2002; Chair. Anglo-Omani Soc. 1975–77, Vice-Pres. 1981; Chair. British-Malaysian Soc. 1983 (Vice-Pres. 1993); Pres. of Council Reading Univ. 1987–94; Gov. ESU 1989–95; Chair. Sudan Pensioners Asscn 1992–; Hon. DLitt (Reading) 1994; Hon. DCL (Durham) 1997. *Publications:* Courtesies in the Trucial States 1965, The Trucial States 1970, Oman and its Renaissance 1977, 1995, Courtesies in the Gulf Area 1978, Manners and Correct Form in the Middle East 1996, Sandtracks in the Sudan 1995, Sudan Canterbury Tales 1998, Desert Wind and Tropical Storm 2000, Khartoum Perspectives 2001. *Leisure interests:* gardening, walking, tennis and travel. *Address:* Cheverell Place, Little Cheverell, Devizes, Wilts., SN10 4JJ, England. *Telephone:* (1380) 813322. *Fax:* (1380) 818418 (Office).

HAWLEY, Robert, CBE, PhD, DSc, C.ENG, CPhys, FRSE, FREng, FInstP, FIMechE, FIEE; British business executive and engineer; b. 23 July 1936, Wallasey; s. of William Hawley and Eva Hawley; m. 1st Valerie Clarke 1961 (divorced); one s. one d.; m. 2nd Pamela Swan; ed Wallasey Grammar School, Wallasey Tech. Coll., Birkenhead Tech. Coll. and King's Coll., Univ. of Durham; joined C. A. Parsons 1961, Electrical Designer, Generator Dept 1964, Chief Electrical Eng 1970, Dir of Production and Eng 1973–74; Dir of Production and Eng NEI Passons 1974, Man. Dir 1976; Man. Dir Power Eng Group, NEI PLC 1984–88, Man. Dir Operations 1989–92; Main Bd Dir Rolls Royce PLC 1989–92; Chief. Exec. Nuclear Electric PLC 1992–95, British Energy PLC 1995–97; Chair. Taylor Woodrow PLC 1999, Colt Telecom 1998, Eng Council 1999–2002, Particle Physics and Astronomy Research Council 1999–2002, Rocktron 2001; Pres. IEE 1996–97; Advisor HSBC Investment Bank PLC; Chair. Council Durham Univ.; Jr Warden Worshipful Co. of Engineers 2002–; Order of Diplomatic Service Gwanghwa Medal 1999. *Publications:* Dielectric Solids (co-author) 1970, Conduction and Breakdown in Mineral Oil 1973, Fundamentals of Electromagnetic Field Theory 1974, Vacuum as an Insulator. *Leisure interests:* philately, gardening. *Address:* Taylor Woodrow PLC, International House, 1 St Katharine's Way, London E1W 1UN (Office); Summerfield, Rendcomb, nr Cirencester, Glos., GL7 7HB (Home); 823 Whitehouse Apartments, 9 Belvedere Road, London, E1 9AT, England (Home). *Telephone:* (20) 7265-2340 (Office); (1285) 831610 (Glos) (Home); (20) 7620-3145 (London) (Home). *Fax:* (20) 7265-2341 (Office); (1285) 831801 (Home); (20) 7620-3144 (London) (Home). *E-mail:* robert.hawley@uk.taylorwoodrow.com (Office).

HAWN, Goldie; American actress; b. 21 Nov. 1945, Washington, DC; d. of Edward Rutledge Hawn and Laura Hawn; m. 1st Gus Trikonio 1969 (divorced); m. 2nd Bill Hudson (divorced); two s. one d.; ed American Univ., Washington, DC; began career as chorus-line dancer, World's Fair, New York 1964. *Stage appearances include:* Romeo and Juliet (Williamsburg), Kiss Me Kate, Guys and Dolls (New York). *Television series include:* Good Morning, World, Rowan and Martin's Laugh-In, Goldie and Kids—Listen to Us. *Films include:* Cactus Flower, There's a Girl in My Soup, Butterflies are Free, The Sugarland Express, $, The Girl from Petrovka, Shampoo, The Duchess and the Dirtwater Fox, Foul Play, Seems Like Old Times, Private Benjamin, Best Friends, Protocol, Swing Shift, Overboard, Bird On A Wire, Housesitter, Deceived, Death Becomes Her, Something to Talk About (exec. producer only), The First Wives Club 1996, Everybody Says I Love You 1996, The Out Of Towners 1999, Town and Country 2001, The Banger Sisters 2003. *Address:* c/o Ed Limato, ICM, 8942 Wilshire Boulevard, Beverly Hills, CA 90211, USA.

HAWTHORNE, James Burns, CBE; British management consultant; b. 27 March 1930, Belfast; s. of Thomas Hawthorne and Florence Burns; m. Patricia King 1958 (died 2002); one s. two d.; ed Methodist Coll., Strammillis Coll. Queen's Univ. Belfast; Asst Master, Sullivan Upper School 1951–60; radio and TV producer and Publr, BBC 1960–68; Chief Asst BBC NI 1969–70; Controller TV, Govt of Hong Kong 1970–72, Dir of Broadcasting 1972–78; Controller, BBC NI 1978–88; Chair. Health Promotion Agency for NI 1988–97, NI Community Relations Council 1990–96; Chair. Prison Arts Foundation 1996–; partner James Hawthorne Assocs 1993–; Chair. Down Co. Museum Trustees 1999–, Lecale Historical Soc. 2000–; Visiting Prof. Univ. of Ulster 1993–99; Fellow Royal TV Soc.; Winston Churchill Fellowship 1968; mem. Fair Employment Agency 1987–89; mem. Comm. for Racial Equality NI 1997–99; Hon. LLD (Queen's, Belfast) 1988; New Ireland Soc. Community Relations Award 1966, Royal TV Soc. Special Award 1986. *Publications:* Two Centuries of Irish History (ed.) 1966, Broadcasting to a Divided Community 1982; contribs to various Publs. *Leisure interests:* angling, local history, music, building restoration. *Address:* The Long Mill, Lissara, 67 Kilmore Road, Crossgar, Co. Down, BT30 9HJ, Northern Ireland. *Telephone:* (28) 4483-1830. *Fax:* (28) 4483-1840. *E-mail:* jameshawthorne@dnet.co.uk (Home). *Website:* www.jameshawthorne.co.uk (Office).

HAWTHORNE, Sir William (Rede), Kt, CBE, MA, ScD, FRS, FR.ENG., F.INST.MECH.E.; British professor of applied thermodynamics; b. 22 May 1913, Benton, Newcastle-on-Tyne; s. of William Hawthorne and Elizabeth Curle Hawthorne; m. Barbara Runkle 1939 (died 1992); one s. two d.; ed Westminster School, London, Trinity Coll., Cambridge and Mass. Inst. of Tech., USA; Devt Eng, Babcock & Wilcox Ltd 1937–39; Scientific Officer, Royal Aircraft Establishment 1940–44, seconded to Sir Frank Whittle 1940–41; British Air Comm., Washington, DC 1944–45; Deputy Dir of Engine Research, Ministry of Supply (UK) 1945–46; Assoc. Prof. of Mechanical Eng MIT 1946–48; George Westinghouse Prof. of Mechanical Eng, MIT 1948–51; Prof. of Applied Thermodynamics Univ. of Cambridge 1951–80, Head of Eng Dept 1968–73; Fellow Trinity Coll., Cambridge 1951–68; Master of Churchill Coll., Cambridge 1968–83; Hunsaker Prof. of Aeronautical Eng, MIT 1955–56; Visiting Inst. Prof., MIT 1962–68, 1973–78, Sr Lecturer 1978–; mem. of Corpn of MIT 1969–73; Chair. Home Office Scientific Advisory Council 1967–76, Advisory Council on Energy Conservation 1974–79; Dir Cummins Engine Co., Inc. 1974–86, Dracone Developments Ltd 1957–87; Foreign Assoc. NAS, U.S. Nat. Acad. of Eng; Vice-Pres. Royal Soc. 1969–70, 1979–81; mem. Electricity Supply Research Council 1953–83, Comm. on Energy and the Environment 1978–81; Fellow of the Fellowship of Eng 1976; Fellow Imperial Coll. London 1983; Hon. FRAeS AIAA, Royal Soc. of Edin. 1983; Hon. Mem. ASME 1982; Hon. Fellow Trinity Coll. Cambridge 1995; Hon. DEng (Sheffield) 1976, (Liverpool) 1982; Hon. DSc (Salford) 1980, (Strathclyde, Bath) 1981, (Oxford) 1982, (Sussex) 1984; Medal of Freedom (USA) 1947, Royal Medal (Royal Soc.) 1982, Dudley Wright Prize (Harvey Mudd Coll., Calif.) 1985, Tom Sawyer Award (ASME) 1992. *Publications:* (Ed.) Aerodynamics of Compressors and Turbines, Vol. X, (Co-Ed.) Design and Performance of Gas Turbine Power Plants, Vol. XI, High Speed Aerodynamics and Jet Propulsion; numerous papers in scientific and tech. journals. *Address:* Churchill College, Cambridge, CB3 0DS, England; 19 Chauncy Street, Cambridge, MA 02138, USA. *Telephone:* (1223) 362601 (England); (617) 253-2479 (USA).

HAYAISHI, Osamu, MD, PhD; Japanese institute director; b. 8 Jan. 1920, Stockton, Calif., USA; s. of Jitsuzo Hayaishi and Mitsu Hayaishi; m. Takiko Satani 1946; one d.; ed Osaka High School, Osaka Univ.; Asst Prof., Dept of Microbiology, Washington Univ. School of Medicine, St Louis, Mo., USA, 1952–54; Chief, Toxicology, Nat. Inst. of Arthritis and Metabolic Diseases, Nat. Insts. of Health, Bethesda, Md, USA 1954–58; Prof., Dept of Medical Chem. 1958–83, Prof., Dept of Molecular Biology, Inst. for Chemical Research, Kyoto Univ. 1959–76; Prof. Dept of Physiological Chem. and Nutrition, Univ. of Tokyo 1970–74; Prof. Inst. of Scientific and Industrial Research, Osaka Univ. 1975–76; Dean Faculty of Medicine, Kyoto Univ. 1979–81; Prof. Emer. Kyoto Univ. 1983–; Pres. Osaka Medical Coll. 1983–89; Dir Osaka Bioscience Inst. 1987–98, Dir Emer. 1998–; mem. Scientific Council Int. Inst. of Cellular and Molecular Pathology (Belgium) 1979–; Foreign Assoc. NAS 1972; Dunham Lecture (Harvard) 1980, Pfeizer Lecture, Albert Einstein School of Medicine 1980; mem. Japan Acad. 1974, New York Acad. of Sciences 1975; Foreign Hon. mem. of American Acad. of Arts and Sciences 1969; Hon. mem. American Soc. of Biological Chemists 1974, Int. Soc. on Clinical Entymology 1988, Soc. for Free Radical Research 1988; Hon. DSc (Michigan) 1980; Hon.

MD (Karolinska Institutet, Sweden) 1985; Dr hc (Padua) 1988; Award of Japan Soc. of Vitaminology 1964, Award of Matsunaga Science Foundation 1964, Asahi Award for Science and Culture 1965, Award of Japan Acad. 1967, Order of Culture 1972, Award of Fujiwara Science Foundation 1975, Médaille de Bronze de la Ville de Paris 1975, CIBA Foundation Gold Medal 1976, Louis and Bert Freedman Foundation Award for Research in Biochemistry 1976, Deutsche Akademie der Naturforscher Leopoldina (FRG) 1978, Jiménez Díaz Memorial Award (Spain) 1979, Wolf Foundation Prize in Medicine, Israel 1986, Jaroslav Heyrovský Gold Medal, Czechoslovak Acad. of Sciences 1988, Special Achievement Award, Miami Biotech. Winter Symposium 1989, Distinguished Lecturer in Neuroscience Awards, La. State Univ. Medical Center, USA 1990, Distinguished Visitor Awards, Univ. of New Orleans, USA 1990; 4th Vaajasalo Lecture, 5th Nordic Neuroscience Meeting, Finland 1991, Invited Lecture, Founding Congress of World Fed. of Sleep Research Socs., France 1991, Luigi Musajo Award, Italy 1995; Hon. Citizen of Kyoto 1984, Int. Hon. Citizen of New Orleans, USA 1990, 1st Order of Merit Grand Cordon of Sacred Treasure, Distinguished Scientist Award, World Fed. of Sleep Research Socs., 3rd Int. Congress, Germany 1999. *Publications:* Oxygenases 1962, Molecular Mechanisms of Oxygen Activation 1974, Molecular Oxygen in Biology 1974 and 510 scientific reviews and articles. *Leisure interest:* golf. *Address:* Osaka Bioscience Institute, 6-2-4 Furuedai Suita, Osaka 565-0874 (Office); 159-505 Kageyukoji-cho, Shimotachiuri-agaru, Muromachi-dori, Kamigyo-ku, Kyoto 602-8014, Japan (Home). *Telephone:* (6) 6872-4833 (Office); (75) 417-2751 (Home). *Fax:* (6) 6872-4818 (Office); (75) 417-2752 (Home). *E-mail:* hayaishi@obi.or.jp (Office).

HAYAMI, Masaru; Japanese banker and economist; joined Bank of Japan 1947, Man. Ooita Br. 1967, Chief Rep. Europe 1971, Dir Foreign Dept 1975, Man. Nagoya Br. 1976, Exec. Dir 1978, Gov. Bank of Japan 1998–2003; Sr Man. Dir Nissho Iwai Corpn 1981, Exec. Vice-Pres. 1982, Pres. 1984, Pres. and Chair. 1987, Chair. 1990–94; Chair. Keizai Doyukai (Japan Asscn of Corp. Execs) 1991–95; Chair. Bd of Trustees, Tokyo Woman's Christian Univ. 1992–98. *Publication:* The Day the Yen will be Respected, Integrity of Money, Navigation through Uncharted Water, Honesty (Calling). *Address:* c/o Bank of Japan, 2-1-1, Nihonbashi-Hongokucho, Chuo-ku, Tokyo 103-8660, Japan (Office).

HAYAMI, Yujiro, PhD; Japanese professor of economics; b. 26 Nov. 1932, Tokyo; s. of Kannosuke Hayami and Chiyoko Hayami; m. Takako Suzuki 1962; one s. two d.; ed Univ. of Tokyo and Iowa State Univ.; economist, Japan Nat. Research Inst. of Agricultural Econs 1956–66; Assoc. Prof. of Econs Tokyo Metropolitan Univ. 1966–72, Prof. 1972–86; economist, Int. Rice Research Inst. 1974–76; Prof. of Int. Econs Aoyama-Gakuin Univ. 1986–2000; Dir of Graduate Program, Foundation for Advanced Studies in Int. Devt 2000–; Purple Medal for Contribs. to Arts and Sciences (Japan). *Publications:* Development Economics: From the Poverty to the Wealth of Nations 1997, A Rice Village Saga: Three Decades of Green Revolution in the Philippines 2000. *Leisure interest:* tennis. *Address:* GRIPS/FASID Joint Graduate Programme, 2-2 Wakamatsu-Cjo, Shinjaku-Ku, Tokyo 162-8677 (Office); 6-8-14 Okusawa, Setagaya-ku, Tokyo 158, Japan. *Telephone:* (3) 3341-0324 (Office); (3) 3701-1345 (Home). *Fax:* (3) 3701-1345 (Home).

HAYASHIDA, Yukio; Japanese politician; b. 26 Nov. 1915, Kyoto Pref.; s. of Nobumaru and Yurie Hayashida; m. Yoko Takahata 1942; two s.; ed Tokyo Imperial Univ.; joined Ministry of Agric. and Forestry 1939, Chief, Fisheries Admin. Dept Fisheries Agency 1959, Chief Sec. to Minister of Agric. and Forestry 1962; Chief, Kinki Agric. Admin. Bureau 1963; Head, Horticulture Bureau 1964; mem. House of Councillors 1966–78; Parl. Vice-Minister for Int. Trade and Industry 1971; Gov. of Kyoto 1978–86; mem. House of Councillors 1986–; Minister of Justice 1987–88. *Publications:* The Countries of Oceania, Discovering the New History of Kyoto. *Leisure interests:* painting, calligraphy. *Address:* 1-9-18 Wakabayashi, Setagaya-ku, Tokyo, Japan. *Telephone:* (3) 3413-2200 (Home). *Fax:* (3) 3413-9690 (Home).

HAYCRAFT, Anna Margaret (pseudonym Alice Thomas Ellis), FRSL; British writer; b. 9 Sept. 1932, Liverpool; d. of John Lindholm and Alexandra Lindholm; m. Colin Haycraft 1956 (died 1994); four s. one d. (also one s. one d. deceased); ed Bangor Co. Grammar School for Girls and Liverpool School of Art; columnist The Spectator, The Universe, Catholic Herald, The Oldie; journalist all tabloids and broadsheets; Welsh Arts Council Award for The Sin Eater 1977, Yorkshire Post Novel of the Year for Unexplained Laughter 1985; Writers Guild Award for Best Fiction for Inn at the Edge of the World 1990. *Television adaptation:* Unexplained Laughter 1987. *Radio play:* The Cat's Whiskers 1990. *Screenplay for film:* The Summerhouse Trilogy 1993. *Publications include:* (as Alice Thomas Ellis) The Sin Eater 1977, The Birds of the Air 1980, The Twenty-Seventh Kingdom 1982, The Other Side of the Fire 1983, Unexplained Laughter 1985, Secrets of Strangers (with Tom Pitt-Aikens) 1986, Home Life 1986, More Home Life 1987, The Clothes in the Wardrobe 1987, The Skeleton in the Cupboard 1988, Home Life Three 1988, The Loss of the Good Authority (with Tom Pitt-Aikens) 1989, Wales: an anthology (ed.) 1989, Home Life Four 1989, The Fly in the Ointment 1989, A Welsh Childhood 1990, The Inn at the Edge of the World 1990, Pillars of Gold 1992, Serpent on the Rock 1994, The Evening of Adam (short stories) 1994, Cat Among the Pigeons 1994, Fairy Tale 1996; (as Anna Haycraft) Natural Baby Food 1977, Darling, You Shouldn't Have Gone to So Much Trouble (with Caroline Blackwood) 1980. *Address:* c/o Robert Kirby, Peters, Fraser and Dunlop, Drury House, 34–43 Russell Street, London, WC2B 5HA, England.

HAYDÉE PEREIRA DA SILVA, Marcia; Brazilian ballet dancer and choreographer; b. 18 April 1937, Niterói; d. of Dr. Alcides Pereira da Silva and Margarita Haydée Salaverry Pereira da Silva; m. Günther Schöberl 1996; ed Royal Ballet School, London and in Paris under Olga Preobrajendska and Lubov Egorova; mem. Grand Ballet du Marquis de Cuevas 1951–61; Prin. Dancer, Stuttgart Ballet 1961, Artistic Dir 1976–96; Artistic Dir Ballet de Santiago de Chile 1992–96; creator of roles in numerous ballets by John Cranko, John Neumeier and Maurice Béjart. *Address:* Stuttgart Ballet, Direktion, Oberer Schlossgarten 6, 70173 Stuttgart, Germany. *Telephone:* (711) 2032235. *Fax:* (711) 2032491.

HAYDEN, Hon. William George, AC, BEcons; Australian politician; b. 23 Jan. 1933, Brisbane, Queensland; m. Dallas Broadfoot 1960; one s. two d.; ed Brisbane State High School, Univ. of Queensland; mem. Queensland Police Force 1953–61; mem. Fed. Parl. for Oxley 1961–88; Parl. Spokesman on Health and Welfare 1969–72; Treasurer 1975; Minister for Social Security 1972–75, for Foreign Affairs 1983–88, for Foreign Affairs and Trade 1987–88; Gov.-Gen. 1989–96; Leader Parl. Labor Party (Opposition) 1977–83; Fellow hc RACP 1995; Adjunct Prof. Queensland Univ. of Tech. 1996; Resident Visiting Fellow, Jane Franklin Hall, Univ. of Tasmania 2000; Hon. Dr. Univ. (Griffith) 1990, (Central Queensland) 1992; Hon. LLD (Queensland) 1990; Hon. DLitt (S. Queensland) 1997; Gwanghwa Medal (Korean Order of Diplomatic Merit); KStJ; Commdr Order of the Three Stars, Latvia; Australian Humanist of the Year 1996. *Publication:* Hayden: An Autobiography 1996. *Leisure interests:* reading, music, golf, riding, fishing, skiing, bush walking. *Address:* Level 13, Waterfront Place, 1 Eagle Street, Brisbane, Queensland (Office); G.P.O. Box 7829, Waterfront Place, Brisbane, Queensland 4001, Australia. *Telephone:* (7) 3229-3500 (Office). *Fax:* (7) 3229-3499 (Office). *E-mail:* bdhayden@dpmc.gov.au (Office).

HAYEK, His Beatitude Ignace Antoine II, DPhil; Syrian ecclesiastic; b. 14 Sept. 1910; s. of Naum Hayek and Chafica Sciamsi; ed Séminaire Patriarcal, Charfé, Lebanon, Pontifical Coll., of Propaganda Fide, Rome and Oriental Pontifical Inst., Rome; ordained priest 1933, successively or concurrently Dir of School, Curate and Vicar-Gen., Aleppo; Archbishop of Aleppo 1959–68; Syrian Patriarch of Antioch 1968. *Address:* c/o Patriarcat Syrien Catholique d'Antioche, B.P. 116-5087, rue de Damas, Beirut, Lebanon.

HAYEK, Nicolas G.; Swiss business executive; b. 19 Feb. 1928, Beirut; m.; one s. one d.; of American-Lebanese parentage; f. consultancy firm Hayek Eng 1963; firm acts as adviser to govts. and business concerns in Europe, USA, China and notably to Swiss watch and high precision industry; Co-founder, Chair and CEO, SMH (high-tech. co.) 1986; alt. Chair. Bd of Dirs. MCC. Micro Compact Car Ltd (Biel), SMH/Swatch and Chair. Swatch-Telecom (Biel); Chair., CEO Swatch Group Ltd 1986–2002; Pres. French Govt Reflection Group on Econ. Strategy 1996–; mem. Council for Research, Tech. and Innovation (Germany) 1995–; Dr. hc Neuchâtel Univ. (Switzerland) 1996. *Leisure interests:* swimming, tennis. *Address:* c/o SMH, Seevorstadt 6, 2502 Biel, Switzerland.

HAYEK, Salma; Mexican actress; b. 2 Sept. 1966, Coatzacoalcos, Veracruz. *Films:* Mi vida loca 1993, Desperado 1995, Four Rooms 1995, Fair Game 1995, From Dusk Till Dawn 1996, Fled 1996, Fools Rush In 1997, Breaking Up 1997, Follow Me Home 1997, The Velocity of Gary 1998, 54 1998, Wild Wild West 1999, Dogma 1999, Frida 2003 (also producer). *Television:* appearances in TV serials including NYPD Blue, Dream On, Nurses, Action. *Address:* c/o William Morris Agency, 1325 Avenue of the Americas, New York, NY 10019-4701, USA (Office).

HAYES, Sir Brian David, GCB; British civil servant; b. 5 May 1929, Norwich; s. of the late Charles Hayes and Flora Hayes; m. Audrey Jenkins 1958; one s. one d.; ed Norwich School, Corpus Christi Coll., Cambridge; joined Ministry of Agric., Fisheries and Food 1956, Deputy Sec. for Agricultural Commodity Policy 1973–78, Perm. Sec. 1979–83; Jt Perm. Sec., Dept of Trade and Industry 1983–85, Perm. Sec. 1985–89; Advisory Dir Unilever 1990–99; Dir Tate and Lyle PLC 1989–98, Guardian Royal Exchange PLC 1989–99, SANE 1990–; Lloyd's Mems' Ombudsman 1994–. *Leisure interests:* reading, opera, ballet. *Address:* Office of the Lloyd's Members' Ombudsman, G5/86, 1 Lime Street, London, EC3M 7HA, England (Office).

HAYES, Colin Graham Frederick, MA, RA, FRCA; British artist; b. 17 Nov. 1919, London; s. of G. Hayes and Winifred Yule; m. 1st Jean Law 1949 (died 1988); m. 2nd Marjorie Berry 1992; three d.; ed Westminster School, Christ Church, Oxford and Ruskin School of Drawing, Oxford; R.E. Field Survey 1940, invalided out (Capt.) 1945; Tutor, Sr Tutor, Reader, RCA 1949–84, now Hon. Fellow; Pres. Royal Soc. of British Artists 1993–98; De Laszlo Medal. *Publications:* Renoir, Stanley Spencer, Landscape Painting in Oils, Robert Buhler. *Leisure interest:* travel. *Address:* Flat 1, 2 Annandale Road, London, W4 2HF, England. *Telephone:* (20) 8994-8762.

HAYES, Francis Mahon, BA, DPA, BL; Irish diplomatist; b. 2 March 1930, Cork; s. of Francis Mahon Hayes and Aileen Hayes (née Walsh); m. Kathleen O'Donoghue 1958; one s. three d.; ed Nat. Univ. of Ireland (Univ. Coll. Dublin), King's Inns, Dublin; Asst Legal Adviser, Dept of Justice 1957–65; Asst Legal Adviser, First Sec. Dept of Foreign Affairs 1965–70, Legal Adviser, Counsellor 1970–74, Legal Adviser, Asst Sec. 1974–77; Amb. to Denmark, Norway and Iceland 1977–81; Perm. Rep. to UN Office at Geneva 1981–87; Deputy Sec. Dept of Foreign Affairs 1987–89; Perm. Rep. to UN, New York 1989–95; mem. Int. Law Comm. 1986–91, The (Irish) Constitution Review Group 1995–96;

Prime Minister's Alt. Rep. on EU Charter of Human Rights Convention; mem. Advisory Task Force on Immigrants; freelance consultant. *Leisure interests:* reading, film watching, sport spectating, golf. *Address:* Tara, 28 Knocknashee, Goatstown, Dublin 14, Ireland. *Telephone:* (1) 2983787. *Fax:* (1) 2983787.

HAYES, John Trevor, CBE, MA, PhD, FSA; British art administrator and art historian; b. 21 Jan. 1929, London; s. of the late Leslie Thomas Hayes and Gwendoline (née Griffiths) Hayes; ed Ardingly, Keble Coll., Oxford, Courtauld Inst. of Art, London, Inst. of Fine Arts, NY; Asst Keeper, London Museum 1954–70, Dir 1970–74; Dir The Nat. Portrait Gallery 1974–94; Commonwealth Fund Fellow, NY Univ. 1958–59; Visiting Prof. in History of Art, Yale Univ. 1969; Chair. Walpole Soc. 1981–96; Hon. Fellow, Keble Coll., Oxford 1984. *Publications:* London, A Pictorial History 1969, The Drawings of Thomas Gainsborough 1970, Catalogue of Oil Paintings in the London Museum 1970, Gainsborough as Printmaker 1971, Rowlandson, Watercolours and Drawings 1972, Gainsborough, Paintings and Drawings 1975, The Art of Graham Sutherland 1980, Catalogues of Gainsborough exhbns. for the Tate Gallery and the Grand Palais 1980–81, Landscape Paintings of Thomas Gainsborough 1982, Gainsborough Drawings (with Lindsay Stainton) 1983, The Art of Thomas Rowlandson 1990, The Portrait in British Art 1991, Catalogue of the British Paintings in the National Gallery of Art, Washington 1992, London in Paint (with Mireille Galinou) 1996, Catalogue of Gainsborough Exhbn at Ferrara Arte 1998, Gainsborough and Rowlandson: A New York Private Collection 1998, The Letters of Thomas Gainsborough (Ed.) 2001. *Leisure interests:* music, walking, European travel. *Address:* 61 Grantham Road, Chiswick, London, W4 2RT, England. *Telephone:* (20) 8747-9768.

HAYES, Roger Peter, BSc(Econ), MA; British public relations executive and company director; b. 15 Feb. 1945, Hampton; s. of Peter Hall and Patricia Hall; m. Margaret Jean Eales 1974; one s.; ed Isleworth Grammar School, London Univ., Univ. of Southern Calif., USA; Reuters Corresp., Paris and London 1967–72; Vice-Pres. and Dir Buson-Marsteller 1972–79; Man. P.A. Consulting Group 1979–83; Dir Corp. Communications, Thorn-EMI PLC 1983–87; Chair. Hayes-MacLeod; Sec.-Gen. Int. Public Relations Asscns. (Bd mem. 1984–88); Dir (non-exec.) IT World 1985–; Chair. Int. Foundation for Public Affairs Studies 1986–89; Pres. Int. Public Relations Asscn 1997; Dir-Gen. British Nuclear Industry Forum 1993–97; Vice-Pres. (Public Affairs and Govt Relations) Ford of Europe 1991–93; Dir Int. Inst. of Communications 1997–; Dir (non-exec.) Echo Communications Research Group 1999–; Fellow Inst. of Public Relations (UK). *Publications:* (Co-author) Corporate Revolution 1986, Experts in Action 1988, Systematic Networking 1996. *Leisure interests:* books, music, cinema, int. politics, tennis, travel. *Address:* 11C Westcott House, 35 Portland Place, London, W1N 3AG (Office); 75 Ellerby Street, London, SW6 6EL, England (Home). *Telephone:* (20) 7323-9622 (Office); (20) 7731-1255 (Home). *Fax:* (20) 7323-9623 (Office). *E-mail:* roger@iic.org (Office); roger_p_hayes@yahoo.co.uk (Home).

HAYES, William, MA, PhD, DPhil; Irish physicist and university administrator (retd); b. 12 Nov. 1930, Killorglin; s. of Robert Hayes and Eileen Tobin; m. Joan Ferriss 1962 (died 1996); two s. one d.; ed Univ. Coll. Dublin and St John's Coll. Oxford; Official Fellow, St John's Coll. Oxford 1960–87, Prin. Bursar 1977–87, Pres. 1987–2001; Univ. Lecturer in Physics, Univ. of Oxford 1962–87; Dir Clarendon Lab. Oxford 1985–87; Pro-Vice-Chancellor, Univ. of Oxford 1990–2001; Chair. Curators of Oxford Univ. Chest 1992–2000; Sr Foreign Fellow, American Nat. Science Foundation, Purdue Univ. 1963–64; Visiting Prof. Univ. of Ill. 1971; mem. Tech. Staff, Bell Labs, NJ 1974; Hon. MRIA 1998; Hon. Fellow St John's Coll. Oxford 2001–; Hon. DSc (Nat. Univ. of Ireland) 1988, (Purdue Univ.) 1996. *Publications:* Scattering of Light by Crystals (with R. Loudon) 1978, Defects and Defect Processes in Non-Metallic Solids (with A. M. Stoneham) 1985; research papers in professional journals. *Leisure interests:* walking, reading, listening to music. *Address:* 91 Woodstock Road, Oxford, OX2 6HL, England (Home). *Telephone:* (1865) 559112. *Fax:* (1865) 277421. *E-mail:* w.hayes1@physics.ox.ac.uk (Office).

HAYMAN, Walter Kurt, MA, ScD, FRS; British mathematician; b. 6 Jan. 1926, Cologne, Germany; s. of Franz Samuel Haymann and Ruth Therese Hensel; m. 1st Margaret Riley Crann 1947 (died 1994); three d.; m. 2nd Waficka Katifi 1995 (died 2001); ed Gordonstoun School, Cambridge Univ.; Lecturer, Kings Coll., Newcastle and Fellow, St John's Coll., Cambridge 1947; Lecturer 1947–53 and Reader, Univ. of Exeter 1953–56; Visiting Lecturer, Brown Univ., US 1949–50, Stanford Univ. Summer 1950, 1955, American Math. Soc. 1961; Prof. of Pure Math., Imperial Coll. of Science and Technology, London 1956–85 (Prof. Emer. 1985–, Sr Research Fellow 1995–), Univ. of York 1985–93 (Prof. Emer. 1993–); mem. London Math. Soc.; mem. Cambridge Philosophical Soc.; Fellow Imperial Coll. 1989; Foreign mem. Finnish Acad. of Science and Letters, Accademia dei Lincei; Corresp. mem. Bavarian Acad. of Science; first organizer (1964–68) British Math. Olympiad; Hon. DSc (Exeter) 1981, (Birmingham) 1985, (Giessen) 1992, (Uppsala) 1992, (Nat. Univ. of Ireland) 1997; 1st Smiths Prize 1948, shared Adams Prize, Cambridge Univ. 1949, Junior Berwick Prize 1955, Senior Berwick Prize 1964, de Morgan Medal of the London Math. Soc. 1995. *Publications:* Multivalent Functions 1958, 1994, Meromorphic Functions 1964, Research Problems in Function Theory 1967, Subharmonic Functions I 1976, II 1989; and over 190 articles in various scientific journals. *Leisure interests:* music, travel, television. *Address:* Department of Mathematics, Imperial College, 180 Queen's Gate, London, SW7 2AZ (Office); 104, Cranford Lane, Harlington, Middlesex, UB3 5HB, England (Home). *Telephone:* (20) 7589-5111 (Ext. 58609) (Office); (20) 8476-1425 (Home).

HAYNES, Desmond Leo; Barbadian cricketer; b. 15 Feb. 1956, Holders Hill, Barbados; m. Dawn Haynes 1991; ed Fed. High School, Barbados; right-hand opening batsman; teams: Barbados 1976–95 (Capt. 1990–91), Scotland (Benson & Hedges Cup) 1983, Middx 1989–94, W Prov. 1994–97; 116 Tests for W Indies 1977–94 (4 as Capt.), scoring 7,487 runs (average 42.2) including 18 hundreds; scored 26,030 first-class runs (61 hundreds); toured England 1979 (World Cup), 1980, 1983 (World Cup), 1984, 1988, 1991; 238 limited-overs ints., scoring record 8,648 runs including record 17 hundreds; Chair. Barbados Cricket Asscn Sr Selection Panel 1999–2001; elected Senator in Parl. Sept. 2001–.

HAYS, Hon. Daniel, BA, LLB; Canadian senator; m. Kathy Hays; three d.; ed Univ. of Alberta and Univ. of Toronto; lawyer, farmer and rancher; Senator for Alberta, Parl. of Canada 1984–, Deputy Leader of the Govt in the Senate 1999–2001, Speaker of the Senate 2001–; mem. Liberal Party of Canada, Pres. 1994–98; Chair. Agric. and Forestry Cttee 1986–88, 1994–96, Energy, the Environment and Natural Resources Cttee 1989–93; Chair. Canada-Japan Inter-Parl. Group 1994–99, Asia-Pacific Parl. Forum 1994–99; mem. Law Soc. of Alberta, Bar Asscn, Canadian Tax Foundation, Canadian Hays Converter Asscn; Trustee Rotary Challenger Park Soc.; mem. Rotary Club; Grand Cordon, Order of the Sacred Treasure, Japan; Hon. Lt Col King's Own Calgary Regt. *Address:* The Senate, Parliament Buildings, Ottawa, Ont., K1A 0A4, Canada (Office). *E-mail:* haysd@sen.parl.gc.ca (Office).

HAYS, Adm. Ronald Jackson, BS; American naval officer; b. 19 Aug. 1928, Urania, La.; s. of George H. Hays and Fannie E. (née McCartney) Hays; m. Jane M. Hughes 1951; two s. one d.; ed Northwestern State Univ., US Naval Acad.; Commdt Ensign US Navy 1950, Destroyer Officer Atlantic Fleet 1950–51, Attack Pilot Pacific Fleet 1953–56; Test Pilot 1956–59, Squadron Leader 1961–63; Air Warfare Officer 7th Fleet Staff 1967–68; Tactical Aircraft Planning Officer, Office Chief Naval Operations 1969–71; C-in-C US Naval Force Europe, London 1980–83; Vice-Chief Naval Operations Dept, Washington 1983–85; C-in-C US Pacific Command 1985–88; rank of Adm. 1983; Pres. and CEO The Pacific Int-Center for High Tech. Research 1988–92, Tech. Consultant 1992–; DSM with three gold stars, Silver Star with two gold stars, DFC with gold and silver star; Legion of Merit and numerous other awards and medals. *Leisure interest:* golf. *Address:* 869 Kamoi Place, Honolulu, HI 96825, USA (Home). *E-mail:* rjhayshawaii@msn.com (Office).

HAYTHORNTHWAITE, Richard (Rick), SM, MA; British business executive; b. Dec. 1956; m.; one s. one d.; ed Colston's School, Bristol, Queen's Coll. Oxford; joined 1978, exploration geologist, then Man. Magnus Oilfield, Pres. Venezuela and other group posts until 1995; Corp. and Commercial Dir Premier Oil PLC 1995–97; joined Blue Circle Industries PLC 1997, CEO Heavy Bldg Materials Asia and Europe, CEO 1999–2001; CEO Invensys 2001–; Dir (non-exec.) Cookson Group PLC 1999–; Chair. British American Arts Asscn, Centre for Creative Communications, Almeida Theatre; Trustee Nat. Museum of Science & Industry; Sloan Fellow MIT. *Leisure interests:* travel, tennis, skiing, theatre, visual arts. *Address:* Invensys PLC, Carlisle Place, London, SW1P 1BX, England (Office). *Website:* www.invensys.com (Office).

HAYWARD, Sir Jack (Arnold), Kt, OBE, FRGS; British business executive; b. 14 June 1923, Wolverhampton; s. of the late Sir Charles Hayward and Hilda Arnold; m. Jean Mary Forder 1948; two s. one d.; ed Northaw Preparatory School, Stowe School, Buckingham; joined RAF 1941, active service as pilot officer in SE Asia Command, demobilized with rank of Flight-Lt 1946; joined Rotary Hoes Ltd 1947, with S Africa br. –1950; f. US arm Firth Cleveland Group of Cos. 1951; joined Grand Bahama Port Authority 1956, Chair. Grand Bahama Devt Co. Ltd and Freeport Commercial and Industrial Ltd 1976–; Pres. Lundy Field Soc., Wolverhampton Wanderers FC; Vice-Pres. SS Great Britain Project; Paul Harris Fellow (Rotary) 1983; Hon. Life Vice-Pres. Maritime Trust 1971; Hon. LLD (Exeter) 1971; Hon. DBA (Wolverhampton) 1994; William Booth Award, Salvation Army 1987. *Leisure interests:* sport, watching cricket, amateur dramatics. *Address:* Seashell Lane, PO Box F-40099, Freeport, Grand Bahama Island, Bahamas. *Telephone:* (242) 3525165.

HAZELHOFF, Robertus, LLM; Netherlands banker; b. 21 Oct. 1930, Delft; s. of Hendricus Hazelhoff and Rinske van Terwisga; m. G.M. van Huet 1960; ed Univ. of Leiden; Man. Banco Tornquist, Buenos Aires 1965; Man. Algemene Bank Nederland, New York Office 1968, mem. Man. Bd Algemene Bank Nederland NV 1971–, Chair. 1985–90, Vice-Chair. 1990; Vice-Chair. Man. ABN AMRO Holding NV 1991–92, Chair. 1992; Vice-Chair. Amsterdam-Rotterdam Bank NV 1990–; Vice-Chair. ABN AMRO Bank NV 1991–92, Chair. 1992–94; Chair. Supervisory Bd Heineken NV, NV Koninklijke Bijenkorf Beheer KBB, Stork NV, ABN, AMRO Bank NV; mem. Supervisory Bd Nedlloyd NV, Corus Group PLC. *Leisure interest:* playing golf. *Address:* Nw. Bussummerweg 208, 1272 CN Huizen, Netherlands (Home).

HAZELTINE, Richard Deimel, MS, PhD; American professor of physics; b. 12 June 1942, Jersey City, NJ; s. of the late Alan Hazeltine and of Elizabeth Barrett Hazeltine; m. Cheryl Pickett 1964; one s. one d.; ed Harvard Coll. and Univ. of Michigan; mem. Inst. for Advanced Study 1969–71; research scientist, Univ. of Texas, Austin 1971–82, Prof. of Physics 1986–; Asst Dir Inst. for Fusion Studies 1982–86, Acting Dir 1987–88, 1991, Dir 1991–2002; Assoc. Ed.

Reviews of Modern Physics 1990–; Fellow, American Physical Soc. *Publications:* Plasma Confinement (with J. D. Meiss) 1992, Framework of Plasma Physics (with F. Waelbroeck) 1998; over 120 articles in scientific journals. *Address:* University of Texas at Austin, Inst. for Fusion Studies, 1 Univ. Station, CI500, Austin, TX 78712-0262, USA. *Telephone:* (512) 471-4307 (Office). *Fax:* (512) 471-6715. *E-mail:* rdh@physics.utexas.edu (Office).

HAZEN, Paul Mandeville, MBA; American banker; b. 1941, Lansing, Mich.; m.; ed Univ. of Ariz. and Univ. of Calif. (Berkeley); Asst Man. Security Pacific Bank 1964–66; Vice-Pres. Union Bank 1966–70; Chair. Wells Fargo Realty Advisors 1970–76; with Wells Fargo Bank, San Francisco 1979–, Exec. Vice-Pres. and Man. Real Estate Industries Group 1979–80, mem. Exec. Office 1980, Vice-Chair. 1980–84, Pres. and COO 1984–94, Chair. 1995–, also Dir; Pres. and Treas. Wells Fargo Mortgage & Equity Trust 1977–84; with Wells Fargo & Co. (parent), San Francisco 1978–, Exec. Vice-Pres., then Vice-Chair., Pres., COO and Dir 1978–95, Chair., CEO 1995–2000; Trustee, Wells Fargo Mortgage and Equity Trust; mem. Bd of Dirs. Pacific Telesis Group. *Address:* c/o Wells Fargo Bank N.A., 420 Montgomery Street, San Francisco, CA 94163, USA.

HAZIM, Mgr Ignatius IV; Lebanese ecclesiastic; b. 1920, Mharde; ed Beirut Univ. and Institut Saint-Serge, Paris; Dir of a secondary Theological Inst., Beirut, Lebanon; Rector of Theological Inst. Balamand Monastery then elected Bishop of Lattakia, Syria 1966, took up post 1970; Greek Orthodox Patriarch of Antioch and All the East (with jurisdiction over Syria, Lebanon, Iran and Iraq) 1979–; several times Pres. Middle East Council of Churches, Geneva; Founder Univ. of Balamand, Lebanon 1987, Pres. Bd of Trustees; lectures in European and Middle-Eastern univs. *Publications:* La résurrection et l'homme d'aujourd'hui and in Arabic: I Believe, The Telling of Your Word Enlightens, Words on Pastoral Matters, The Church in the Middle East (trans. of the work by Père Corbon), God's Design (trans. of the work by Suzanne de Dietrich). *Address:* PO Box 9, Damascus, Syria. *Telephone:* (11) 5424400. *Fax:* (11) 5424404.

HAZZARD, Shirley, FRSL; author; b. 30 Jan. 1931, Sydney, Australia; d. of Reginald Hazzard and Catherine Hazzard; m. Francis Steegmuller 1963 (died 1994); ed Queenwood School, Sydney; Combined Services Intelligence, Hong Kong 1947–48; UK High Commr.'s Office, Wellington, NZ 1949–50; UN, New York (Gen. Service Category) 1952–61; novelist and writer of short stories and contrib. to The New Yorker 1960–; Guggenheim Fellow 1974; mem. Nat. Acad. of Arts and Letters, American Acad. of Arts and Sciences; Boyer Lecturer, Australia 1984, 1988; Hon. Citizen of Capri 2000; US Nat. Acad. of Arts and Letters Award in Literature 1966; First Prize, O. Henry Short Story Awards 1976; Nat. Critics Circle Award for Fiction 1981, Clifton Fadiman Medal for Literature 2001. *Publications:* short stories: Cliffs of Fall 1963; novels: The Evening of the Holiday 1966, People in Glass Houses 1967, The Bay of Noon 1970, The Transit of Venus 1980; history: Defeat of an Ideal: A Study of the Self-destruction of the United Nations 1973, Countenance of Truth: The United Nations and the Waldheim Case 1990, Greene on Capri (memoir) 2000. *Leisure interest:* Parthenophile. *Address:* Apt. c-1705, 200 East 66th Street, New York, NY 10021, USA.

HE CHUNLIN; Chinese politician; b. Aug. 1933, Wuxi City, Jiangsu Prov.; ed Northeast China Agricultural Coll.; joined CCP 1951; Dir Special Econ. Zones Office of State Council 1984–93; Deputy Sec.-Gen. State Council 1988–98, Sec.-Gen. Standing Cttee of Nat. People's-Congress 1998–; mem. 14th CCP Cen. Cttee 1992, 15th CCP Cen. Cttee 1997–. *Address:* State Council, Beijing, People's Republic of China.

HE GUANGWEI; Chinese civil servant; Deputy Dir China Nat. Tourism Admin. 1986–95, Dir 1995–. *Address:* China National Tourism Administration, 9A Jian Guo Men Nei Dajie, Beijing 100740, People's Republic of China. *Telephone:* (10) 65138866. *Fax:* (10) 65122096.

HE GUANGYUAN; Chinese state official; b. 1930, Anxin Co., Hebei Prov.; Vice-Minister of Machinery and Electronics Industry 1982–88, Minister 1988–93, of Machine-Bldg Industry 1993–96; alt. mem. 12th CCP Cen. Cttee 1982–87, 13th Cen. Cttee 1987–92; mem. 8th NPC 1993–, 14th CCP Cen. Cttee 1992–97; Chair. Motions Cttee, 9th Nat. Cttee of CPPCC. *Address:* c/o National Committee of Chinese People's Political Consultative Conference, 23 Taipingqiao Street, Beijing, People's Republic of China.

HE GUOQIANG; Chinese politician; b. Oct. 1943, Xiangxiang Co., Hunan Prov.; ed Beijing Chemical Eng Inst.; joined CCP 1966; Dir and CCP Sec. Shandong Petro-Chemical Dept 1984; alt. mem. 12th CCP Cen. Cttee 1985, 13th CCP Cen. Cttee 1987, 14th CCP Cen. Cttee 1992; mem. of the Standing Cttee of CCP Shandong Provincial Cttee, Vice-Sec., Sec. CCP Ji'nan City Cttee 1986; Vice-Minister of Chemical Industry 1991; Vice-Sec. CCP Fujian Provincial Cttee, Acting Gov. Fujian Prov. 1996, Gov. 1997–99; Sec. CCP Chongqing Municipal Cttee 1999; mem. 15th CCP Cen. Cttee 1997–. *Address:* c/o Office of the Governor, Chongqing Municipality, People's Republic of China.

HE KANG, BSc; Chinese politician; b. 26 Feb. 1923, Hebei Prov.; m. Miao Shixia 1945; two s.; m. 2nd Yu Junmin 1993; ed Agric. Coll. of Guangxi Univ.; Chief Dir of Agric. and Forestry under Shanghai Mil. Control Cttee 1949–50; Deputy Head Dept of Agric. and Forestry under E China Mil. and Political Cttee 1950–52; Dir Dept of Special Forestry of Ministry of Forestry 1952–54; Dir Dept of Tropical Plants, Ministry of Agric. 1955–57; Dir S China Tropical Crop Science Research Inst. and Tropical Crop Coll. 1957–72; Deputy to 3rd

NPC 1965–75; Deputy Dir Gen. Bureau of Land Reclamation, Guangdong Prov. 1972–77; Vice-Minister of Agric., Deputy Dir Nat. Planning Comm., Deputy Dir Nat. Comm. on Agric. 1978–82; mem. 12th Cen. Cttee CCP 1982–87, mem. 13th Cen. Cttee 1987–93; mem. Standing Cttee 8th NPC 1993–98; Minister of Agric. 1983–90; Vice-Chair. Nat. Cttee, China Asscn for Science and Tech. 1986–96; Vice-Chair. Nat. Agric. Regional Planning Cttee 1979–90; Pres. Chinese Village & Township Enterprises Asscn 1990–2000, Chair. China-Bangladesh Friendship Asscn 1993–; Vice-Chair. Bd of Dirs Zhongkai Inst. of Agric. Tech.; World Food Prize 1993; Hon. DUniv (Maryland, USA) 1986. *Publications:* Agricultural Reform and Development in China, Rubber Culture in Northern Tropical Area (Ed. and writer). *Leisure interests:* photography, listening to music, reading. *Address:* Ministry of Agriculture, 11 Nongzhanguan Nanli, Chaoyang Qu, Beijing 100026, People's Republic of China (Office). *Telephone:* (10) 64192406 (Office). *Fax:* (10) 64192468 (Office). *E-mail:* heyu@agri.gov.cn (Office).

HE LULI; Chinese administrator and paediatrician; b. 7 June 1934, Jinan, Shandong Prov.; d. of the late He Siyuan and He Yiwen; m. Rong Guohuang 1958 (died 1989); two s.; ed Beijing Coll. of Medicine; paediatrician, Beijing Children's Hospital 1957–; Vice-Mayor Beijing Municipality 1988–96; Vice-Chair. Women and Youth Cttee, Revolutionary Cttee of the Chinese Kuomintang 1988–96, Chair. 1997–; Pres. Cen. Acad. of Socialism 1999–; mem., Vice-Chair. CPPCC 8th Nat. Cttee 1993–98; Vice-Chair. Standing Cttee of 9th NPC 1998–; Vice-Pres. All China Women's Fed. 1993–; Pres. China Population Welfare Foundation 2000–. *Address:* Central Academy of Socialism, Beijing 100081, People's Republic of China.

HE QIZONG, Maj.-Gen.; Chinese army officer; b. 1943, Yingshan Co., Sichuan Prov.; joined PLA 1961; joined CCP 1965; Deputy Commdr Kunming Mil. Region 1979–85; Chief of Staff of Div. 1982–83, Div. Commdr 1983, Deputy Commdr of Army 1983–84, Commdr 1984–85, Deputy Chief of Gen. Staff, PLA 1985; alt. mem. 13th CCP Cen. Cttee 1987–92; alt. mem. 14th Cen. Cttee 1992–; Deputy Commdr Nanjing Mil. Region 1993–; rank Maj.-Gen. 1988. *Address:* People's Liberation Army General Staff Headquarters, Beijing, People's Republic of China.

HE YONG; Chinese politician; b. Oct. 1940, Qianxi Co., Hebei Prov.; ed Tianjin Univ.; joined CCP 1958; Vice-Dir Org. Dept of CCP Cen. Cttee; Vice-Minister of Supervision 1988–98, Minister 1998–2003; mem. Standing Cttee of CCP Cen. Comm. for Discipline Inspection 1992; mem. 15th CCP Cen. Cttee 1997–2002, 16th CCP Cen. Cttee 2002–; Vice-Sec. CCP Cen. Comm, for Discipline Inspection 1997–. *Address:* c/o Zhongguo Gongchan Dang (Chinese Communist Party), Beijing, People's Republic of China.

HE ZEHUI, EngD; Chinese physicist; b. 5 March 1914, Suzhou City, Jiangsu Prov.; m. Qian Sanqiang (deceased); three d.; ed Qinghua Univ., Berlin Univ.; researcher Curie Inst., France 1941–48; researcher Modern Physics Inst., Academia Sinica 1953–; Vice-Dir Inst. of Atomic Energy, Academia Sinica 1964–66; in disgrace during Cultural Revolution 1966–76; rehabilitated 1977; Deputy Dir Inst. of High Energy Physics, Academia Sinica 1978–; mem., Dept of Math. and Physics, Academia Sinica 1985–; won 3rd prize of Academia Sinica Science Awards for paper Research into the Process of Preparing Nuclear Emulsoid, 1957. *Address:* Room 203, Bldg 14, Zhong Guan Cun, Beijing 100080, People's Republic of China. *Telephone:* 284314 (Beijing).

HE ZHENLIANG; Chinese government official; b. 29 Dec. 1929, Zhejiang Prov.; m. 1953; one s. one d.; ed Aurora Univ., Shanghai; Sec.-Gen. Chinese Olympic Cttee 1982–86, Vice-Pres. 1986–89, Pres. 1989–94, Hon. Pres. 1994–; Dir Int. Liaison Dept, State Comm. of Physical Culture and Sports 1982–85, Vice Minister 1985–94; Vice-Pres. Int. Ass. for the Nat. Org. of Sports 1984; mem. IOC 1981–, Exec. Bd 1985–89, 1994–98, 1999–, Vice-Pres. 1989–93, Pres. Cultural Comm. 1995–99, Pres. Cultural and Olympic Education Comm. 2000–; Vice-Chair. All-China Sports Fed. 1986, Councillor 1997–; mem. CPPCC 1988–92, Standing Cttee of CPPCC 1993–98; Pres. Athletic Asscn of PRC 1992–96, Rowing Asscn of PRC 1986–, Rowing Fed. of Asia 1990–94. *Address:* 9 Tiyuguan Road, Beijing, People's Republic of China.

HE ZHIQIANG; Chinese government official and engineer; b. 1934, Lijiang Co., Yunnan Prov.; ed Chongqing Univ.; joined CCP 1956; Deputy Chief Engineer of Yunnan Prov. Geological Bureau 1979–83; Vice-Gov. of Yunnan Prov. 1983–85; Gov. 1985–98; Deputy Sec., CPC 6th Yunnan Prov. Cttee 1996–; NPC Deputy for Yunnan Prov.; mem. 14th CCP Cen. Cttee 1992–97. *Address:* Yunnan Provincial Government, 5 Wuchua Shan Road, Kunming City, Yunnan Province, People's Republic of China.

HE ZUOXIU; Chinese physicist; b. 27 July 1927, Shanghai; m. Qing Chengrui 1962; one s.; ed Shanghai Jiaotong Univ., Qinghua Univ.; researcher, Beijing Modern Physics Inst. and Atomic Energy Inst., Academia Sinica 1951–80; Deputy Dir of Theoretical Physics Inst. Academia Sinica 1980–; mem. Dept of Math. and Physics, Academia Sinica 1980–. *Publications:* A New Possible Quantum Field Theory of Composite Particles, (with Falung Gong), From Theory of Elementary Chi to Particle Physics. *Address:* Theoretical Physics Institute, PO Box 2735, Beijing 100080, People's Republic of China. *Telephone:* (10) 62555248. *Fax:* (10) 62562587 (Office); (10) 62571624 (Home). *E-mail:* qcr@itp.ac.cn (Office); qcr@itp.ac.cn (Home). *Website:* itp.ac .cn.

HEAD, Alan Kenneth, AO, DSc, FAA, FRS; Australian physicist and mathematician; b. 10 Aug. 1925, Melbourne; s. of Rowland H. J. and Elsie M. (née Burrell) Head; m. Gwenneth N Barlow 1951; ed Univ. of Melbourne and Univ.

of Bristol; Research Scientist CSIRO Div. of Aeronautics 1947–50, Aeronautical Research Labs. 1953–57, Div. of Tribophysics 1957–81, Div. of Chemical Physics 1981–86, Div. of Materials Science 1987–; Visiting Prof. Brown Univ. 1961–62, Univ. of Fla 1971; Christensen Fellow, St Catherine's Coll., Oxford 1986; Syme Research Medal 1965. *Publications:* Computed Electron Micrographs and Defect Identification 1973. *Address:* CSIRO, Division of Manufacturing Science, Private Bag 33, Clayton South MDC, Vic. 3169 (Office); 10 Ellesmore Court, Kew, Vic. 3101, Australia (Home). *Telephone:* (3) 9545-2861 (Office); (3) 9853-0673 (Home). *Fax:* (3) 9544-1128 (Office).

HEAD, Tim David, BA; British artist; b. 22 Oct. 1946, London; s. of Percy Head and Muriel Head; m. Vivian Katz 1973; two d.; ed Dept of Fine Art, Univ. of Newcastle-upon-Tyne, St Martin's School of Art, London; Lecturer, Goldsmith's Coll. School of Art, London 1971–79; Lecturer, Slade School of Fine Art, Univ. Coll. London 1976–; Fellowship at Clare Hall and Kettle's Yard, Cambridge 1977–78; Gulbenkian Foundation Visual Arts Award 1975, First Prize, John Moores Liverpool Exhbn 15, Walker Art Gallery, Liverpool 1987. *Commissions:* Sculpture, Nat. Museum of Photography, Film and TV, Bradford, Yorks. 1985, Floor Design, Science Museum, London 1995 Installation, Chatham Historic Dockyard, Rochester, Kent, Sculpture, Dance Performance with Laurie Booth Co. 1997–98, Light Rain, Artezium Arts and Media Centre, Luton 1998, A Hard Day's Night (CD ROM) 2000 www.eyestorm.com; Artistic Dir Eurythmics Peace Tour 1999. *Solo exhibitions:* Museum of Modern Art, Oxford 1972, Gallery House, London 1973, Whitechapel Art Gallery and Garage Gallery, London 1974, Rowan Gallery, London 1975, 1976, 1978, Arnolfini Gallery, Bristol 1975, Anthony Stokes Gallery, London 1977, Kettle's Yard, Cambridge, Henie-Onstad Kunstcenter, Oslo 1978, I.C.A., Brisbane, Paola Betti Gallery, Milan, Serpentine Gallery, London, Third Eye Centre, Glasgow 1979, Gallery Bama, Paris, British Pavilion, Venice Biennale 1980, Locus Solus, Genoa 1981, Prov. Museum, Hasselt 1983, I.C.A., London 1985, Anthony Reynolds Gallery, London 1986, Whitechapel Art Gallery, London 1992, Frith Street Gallery, London 1992, 1995, City Art Gallery, Manchester 1993, Kunstverein Freiburg 1995, Kunstverein Heilbronn 1995, Stadtgalerie Saarbrücken 1995, Kunstverein Braunschweig 1995, Osterwalder Art Office Hamburg 1995, 1997; numerous group exhbns in Milan, Kassel, Paris, Brussels, Sydney, New York, Vienna, London, Pa, Basle, Regensburg, Leeds, Montreal and Swansea. *Address:* 271 Eversholt Street, London, NW1 1BA, England.

HEAL, Barbara Jane, PhD, FBA; British professor of philosophy; b. 21 Oct. 1946, Oxford; d. of William Calvert Kneale and Martha Kneale (née Hurst); m. John Gauntlett Benedict Heal 1968 (divorced 1987); one s. one d.; ed Oxford High School for Girls, New Hall, Cambridge; Research Fellow Newnham Coll., Cambridge 1971–74; Harkness Fellow of the Commonwealth Fund, Visiting Fellow Princeton and Berkeley, USA 1974–76; Lecturer in Philosophy, Univ. of Newcastle upon Tyne 1976–86, Univ. of Cambridge 1986–96, Reader in Philosophy 1996–99, Prof. 1999–; Pres. St John's Coll. 1999–2003. *Publications:* Fact and Meaning 1989, Mind, Reason and Imagination 2003. *Address:* St. John's College, Cambridge, CB2 1TP, England (Office). *Telephone:* (1223) 338668 (Office); (1223) 314317 (Home). *E-mail:* bjh1000@cam.ac.uk (Office).

HEALEY, Baron (Life Peer), cr. 1992, of Riddlesden in the County of West Yorkshire; **Denis Winston Healey,** PC, CH, MBE, FRSL; British politician; b. 30 Aug. 1917, Mottingham; s. of William Healey; m. Edna May (née Edmunds) Healey 1945; one s. two d.; ed Bradford Grammar School and Balliol Coll., Oxford; Maj., Royal Engineers 1945; Sec. Labour Party Int. Dept 1945–52; MP 1952–92; Sec. of State for Defence 1964–70; Chancellor of the Exchequer 1974–79; Opposition Spokesman for Treasury and Econ. Affairs 1979–80, for Foreign and Commonwealth Affairs 1980–87; Chair. Interim Ministerial Cttee of IMF 1977–79; Deputy Leader of Labour Party 1980–83; Pres. Birkbeck Coll. London 1993–99; Hon. Fellow, Balliol Coll. Oxford 1980; Hon. DLitt (Bradford) 1983; Hon. LLD, (Sussex) 1989, (Leeds) 1991; Grand Cross of Order of Merit, FRG 1979; Freeman of Leeds 1991. *Publications:* The Curtain Falls 1951, New Fabian Essays 1952, Neutralism 1955, Fabian International Essays 1956, A Neutral Belt in Europe 1958, NATO and American Security 1959, The Race Against the H Bomb 1960, Labour Britain and the World 1963, Healey's Eye (photographs) 1980, Labour and a World Society 1985, Beyond Nuclear Deterrence 1986, The Time of My Life (autobiog.) 1989, When Shrimps Learn to Whistle (collection of essays) 1990, My Secret Planet 1992, Denis Healey's Yorkshire Dales 1995, Healey's Word (photographs) 2002. *Leisure interests:* music, painting, literature, photography. *Address:* House of Lords, London, SW1A 0PW; Pingles Place, Alfriston, East Sussex BN26 5TT, England. *Telephone:* (20) 7219-3546 (Office).

HEALY, Thomas William, PhD, F.R.A.C.I., FAA, F.T.S.E.; Australian professor of physical chemistry; b. 1 June 1937; s. of W. T. Healy and C. M. Healy; m. Beverley M. L. Fay 1960; four s.; ed St Kilda, Univ. of Melbourne and Columbia Univ., NY, USA; lecturer, Univ. of Calif. (Berkeley) 1963–65; Sr Lecturer in Physical Chem., Univ. of Melbourne 1967–75, Reader 1975–77, Prof. 1977–98, Prof. Emer. 1998–, Assoc. Dean Research and Grad. Studies 1983–84, Dean Faculty of Science 1985–90, Dir Advanced Mineral Products Special Research Centre 1991–99, Pres. Academic Bd and Pro-Vice-Chancellor 1997–98; Visiting Assoc. Prof., Univ. of Calif. (Berkeley) 1970; Visiting Sr Research Scientist, ICI Corp. Colloid Group. (UK) 1981; Chair. Australian Landscape Trust 1997–; Queen Elizabeth II Fellow, Univ. of Melbourne 1965–67, Sr Visiting Research Fellow, Univ. of Bristol, England 1975, Visiting Prof., Clarkson Univ., NY, USA 1981; Gov. Ian Potter Foundation

1990–; mem. Australasian Inst. of Mining and Metallurgy, Chemical Soc.; mem. and Founding Cttee mem. Int. Asscn of Colloid and Interface Scientists; Fellow Australian Acad. of Tech. Sciences; Hon. D. Sc. (Melbourne) 1999; ACS Certificate of Merit 1967, Rennie Medal RACI 1968, Grimwade Prize, Univ. of Melbourne 1974, Royal Soc. of Vic. Medallist 1992, Ian Wark Medal and Lecture, Australian Acad. of Science 1999. *Publications:* 200 research papers in physical chem., colloid and surface science, mineral processing, textbooks. *Leisure interests:* sailing, photography, reading. *Address:* Particulate Fluids Processing Centre, Department of Chemical Engineering, University of Melbourne, Parkville, Vic. 3010 (Office); 98 Barkly Street, Carlton, Vic. 3053, Australia (Home). *Telephone:* (3) 83446481 (Office); (3) 93474741 (Home). *Fax:* (3) 83446233 (Office). *E-mail:* thealy@chemistry.unimelb.edu.au (Office).

HEANEY, Seamus; Irish poet and author; b. 13 April 1939, Northern Ireland; s. of Patrick Heaney and Margaret (née McCann) Heaney; m. Marie Devlin 1965; two s. one d.; ed St Columb's Coll., Londonderry, Queen's Univ. of Belfast; Lecturer St Joseph's Coll. of Educ., Belfast 1963–66, Queen's Univ. of Belfast 1966–72; freelance writer 1972–75, Lecturer, Carysfort Coll. 1975–81, Sr Visiting Lecturer, Harvard Univ. 1982–84, Boylston Prof. of Rhetoric and Oratory 1985–97, Ralph Waldo Emerson Poet in Residence 1998–; Prof. of Poetry, Oxford Univ. 1989–94; Hon. DLitt (Oxford) 1997, (Birmingham) 2000; W. H. Smith Prize 1975, Bennet Award 1982, Sunday Times Award for Excellence in Writing 1988, Lannan Literary Award 1990, Nobel Prize for Literature 1995; Commdr des Arts et des Lettres. *Poems:* Death of a Naturalist 1966, Door into the Dark 1969, Wintering Out 1972, North 1975, Field Work 1979, Sweeney Astray 1984, Station Island 1984, The Haw Lantern 1987, New Selected Poems 1966–1987 1990, Seeing Things 1991, Sweeney's Flight 1992, The Spirit Level 1996 (Whitbread Book of the Year Award 1997), Opened Ground: Poems 1966–96 1998 (Irish Times Literary Award 1999), Beowulf: A New Translation 1999, Electric Light 2001. *Prose:* Preoccupations 1980, The Government of the Tongue 1988, The Place of Writing 1990, The Redress of Poetry (lectures) 1995. *Anthology:* The School Bag 1997 (co-ed. with Ted Hughes). *Play:* The Cure at Troy 1991. *Translations:* Laments, by Jan Kochanowski (with Stanislaw Baranczak); Beowulf: a New Verse Translation (Whitbread Book of the Year 1999) 1999. *Address:* c/o Faber and Faber, 3 Queen Square, London, WC1N 3AU, England. *Telephone:* (20) 7465-0045. *Fax:* (20) 7465-0034.

HEAP, Sir Robert Brian, Kt, CBE, MA, CChem, PhD, FRS, FRSC, FIBiol; British director of research; b. 27 Feb. 1935, Derbyshire; s. of the late Bertram Heap and Eva M. Melling; m. Marion P. Grant 1961; two s. one d.; ed New Mills Grammar School, Univ. of Nottingham and King's Coll. Cambridge; univ. demonstrator, Cambridge 1960; Lalor Research Fellow, ARC Babraham, Cambridge, staff mem. 1964, Head, Dept of Physiology 1976, Head Cambridge Research Station 1986; Dir of Research, AFRC (Agricultural and Food Research Council) Inst. of Animal Physiology and Genetics Research, Cambridge and Edinburgh 1989–93, Acting Dir of Science, AFRC 1991–94, Dir of Research, Babraham Inst. 1993–94; Visiting Prof. Univ. of Nairobi 1974; Visiting Research Fellow, Murdoch Univ. 1976; Visiting Sr Fellow School of Clinical Medicine, Cambridge Univ. 1994–, Babraham Inst. 1995–; Master St Edmund's Coll., Cambridge 1996–; Special Prof. Univ. of Nottingham 1988–; Pres. Inst. of Biology 1996–98; mem. Council Royal Soc. 1994–2001 (Foreign Sec. and Vice-Pres. 1996–2001); mem. Nuffield Council on Bioethics 1997–2001; other professional appts. and distinctions. *Publications:* papers on reproductive biology endocrinology, growth and lactation in biological and medical journals. *Leisure interests:* music, walking, travel. *Address:* St Edmund's College, Cambridge, CB3 0BN; Lincoln House, 8 Fendon Road, Cambridge, CB1 4RT, England (Home). *Telephone:* (1223) 248509 (Home). *Fax:* (1223) 415868 (Home).

HEARNE, Sir Graham James, Kt, CBE; British business executive and solicitor; b. 23 Nov. 1937, Birmingham; s. of Frank Hearne and Emily (née Shakespeare) Hearne; m. Carol Jean Brown 1961; one s. three d.; ed George Dixon Grammar School, Birmingham; admitted solicitor 1959; with Pinsent & Co. Solicitors 1959–63, Fried, Frank, Harris, Shriver & Jacobson Attorneys, New York 1963–66, Herbert Smith & Co., Solicitors 1966–67, Industrial Reorganization Corpn 1967–68, N. M. Rothschild & Sons Ltd 1968–77; Finance Dir Courtaulds Ltd 1977–81; Chief Exec. Tricentrol 1981–83; Group Man. Dir Carless, Capel & Leonard 1983–84; Dir (non-exec.) N. M. Rothschild & Sons Ltd 1977–, Courtaulds PLC 1991–98, Gallaher Group PLC 1997–, Invensys (fmrly BTR) PLC 1998–, Seascope PLC 1999–; Chief Exec. Enterprise Oil PLC 1984–91, Chair. 1991–; Chair. Novar (fmrly Caradon) PLC 1999–; High Sheriff of Greater London 1995–96. *Address:* Grand Buildings, Trafalgar Square, London, WC2N 5EJ, England (Office). *Telephone:* (20) 7925-4000.

HEARNS, Thomas; American boxer; b. 18 Oct. 1958, Grand Junction, Tenn.; professional boxer 1977–2000; 59 wins, 5 defeats, 1 draw (46 KOs); won WBA world welterweight championship 1980, lost it to Sugar Ray Leonard (q.v.) 1981, drew rematch June 1989; WBA world super-welterweight Champion 1982–86; unsuccessfully challenged Marvelous Marvin Hagler (q.v.) for world middleweight championship 1985; won world light-heavyweight championship from Dennis Andries 1987, 1993; boxed at cruiserweight 1992; won WBO super-middleweight championship 1988; won WBA light-heavyweight championship 1991, lost it to Ivan Barkley 1992; won World Boxing Union cruiserweight title 1995; Golden Gloves Champion 1977. *Address:* 19244 Bretton Drive, Detroit, MI 48223, USA.

HEARST, George Randolph, Jr; American newspaper executive; b. 13 July 1927, San Francisco; s. of George Randolph Hearst and Blanche Wilbur; m. 1st Mary Thompson 1951 (died 1969); two s. two d.; m. 2nd Patricia Ann Bell 1969 (divorced 1985); Staff Los Angeles Examiner 1948–50, San Francisco Examiner 1954–56, Los Angeles Evening Herald-Express 1956– (Business Man. 1957, Publr 1960–); Publr Los Angeles Herald-Examiner 1962–; Vice-Pres. The Hearst Corpn 1977–96, Chair. 1996–; Dir, Trustee The Hearst Foundation.

HEATH, Rt Hon. Sir Edward Richard George, KG, PC, MBE, MP; British politician and conductor; b. 9 July 1916, Thanet; s. of the late William George Heath and Edith Anne Pantony; ed Chatham House School, Ramsgate and Balliol Coll., Oxford; fmr Pres. Oxford Univ. Conservative Asscn; fmr Chair. Fed. of Univ. Conservative Asscns.; fmr Pres. Oxford Union; served in RA during Second World War, rising to rank of Lt-Col; Commdr 2nd Regt HAC 1947–51; Master Gunner within Tower of London 1951–54; Civil Service 1946–47; MP for Bexley 1950–74, for Bexley, Sidcup 1974–83, for Old Bexley and Sidcup 1983–2001; Asst Opposition Whip 1951; Lord Commr of the Treasury (Sr Govt Whip) 1951, Jt Deputy Chief Whip 1952–53, Deputy Chief Whip 1953–55, Parl. Sec. to Treasury and Govt Chief Whip 1955–59; Minister of Labour 1959–60; Lord Privy Seal with Foreign Office responsibilities 1960–63, Sec. of State for Industry, Trade and Regional Devt and Pres. Bd of Trade 1963–64; Leader British Del., Brussels Conf. for countries seeking entry into Common Market 1961–63; Leader British Del. to first UN Conf. on Trade Aid and Devt 1964; Leader of Conservative Party 1965–75; Leader of Opposition 1965–70, 1974–75; Prime Minister 1970–74; completed negotiations for Britain's entry into EEC 1971, signed Treaty 1972; mem. Independent Comm. on Int. Devt Issues (Advisory Cttee to Brandt Comm.) 1977–80; mem. Public Review Bd Arthur Andersen & Co. 1978–; Chair. IRIS 1981–83; Devt Adviser to China Investment and Devt Fund, Kleinwort Benson China Man.; Chair. London Symphony Orchestra (LSO) Trust 1963–70, mem. Trust 1974–, has conducted LSO in London, Cologne, Bonn; has conducted numerous orchestras worldwide, including Liverpool Philharmonic, English Chamber, Berlin Philharmonic, Chicago Symphony, Philadelphia Symphony, Jerusalem Symphony, Shanghai Philharmonic and Beijing Cen. Symphony Orchestras; Vice-Pres. Bach Choir 1970–; Co-Founder, Pres. European Community Youth Orchestra 1977–80; has conducted on several records; Visiting Chubb Fellow, Yale 1975, Montgomery Fellow, Dartmouth Coll. 1980; Conservative; Hon. Bencher, Gray's Inn, Scholar of Gray's Inn 1938; Hon. mem. LSO 1974–; Hon. FRCM; Hon. FRCO; Hon. Fellow Balliol Coll.; Oxford, Nuffield Coll.; Inst. of Devt Studies, Sussex; Royal Canadian Coll. of Organists, (Univ. of London) 1994; Goldsmiths' Coll., Univ. of London 1996; Hon. Fellow Queen Mary and Westfield Coll., London; Hon. DCL (Oxford, Kent); Hon. DTech (Bradford); Dr. hc (Sorbonne) (Univ. of London) 1990, (Open Univ.) 1997; Hon. LLD (Westminster Coll., Salt Lake City), (Wales) 1998; Hon. DL (Westminster Coll., Miss.); Hon. DPA (Wesleyan Coll., Ga); Charlemagne Prize 1963, Freiherr von Stein Foundation Award 1971, Estes J. Kefauver Foundation Award, Stresemann Medal 1971, Gold Medal (City of Paris) 1978, European Peace Cross 1979, World Humanity Award 1980, Gold Medal, European Parl. 1981, Schuman Medal 1996; Grand Cross of Merit with Star and Sash (Germany); Grand Cordon, Order of the Rising Sun; "Pro Arte" of the Förderergemeinschaft der Europäischen Wirtschaft 1997. *Publications:* One Nation: A Tory Approach to Social Problems (co-author) 1950, Old World, New Horizons 1970, Sailing—A Course of My Life 1975, Music—A Joy for Life 1976, revised Edn 1997, Travels—People and Places in My Life 1977, Carols—the Joy of Christmas 1977, Our Europe 1990, The Course of My Life (memoirs) 1998. *Leisure interests:* music, sailing (Capt. British Admiral's Cup Team 1971, 1979, Capt. British Sardinia Cup Team 1980). *Address:* c/o House of Commons, London, SW1A 0AA, England.

HEATH-STUBBS, John (Francis Alexander), OBE, FRSL; British poet; b. 9 July 1918; s. of Francis Heath Stubbs and Edith Louise Sara Marr; ed Bembridge School, Worcester Coll. for the Blind, The Queen's Coll., Oxford; English tutor 1944–45; Editorial Asst, Hutchinson's 1945–46; Gregory Fellow in Poetry, Univ. of Leeds 1952–55; Visiting Prof. of English, Univ. of Alexandria 1955–58, Univ. of Mich. 1960–61; Lecturer in English Literature, Coll. of St Mark and St John, Chelsea 1963–73; Pres. The Poetry Soc. 1991–94; Fellow, English Asscn 1999; Queen's Gold Medal for Poetry 1973, Oscar Williams—Jean Durwood Award 1977, Howard Sergeant Memorial Award 1989, Cross of St Augustine 1999. *Publications:* Poetry: Wounded Thammuz, Beauty and the Beast, The Divided Ways, The Swarming of the Bees, A Charm Against the Toothache, The Triumph of the Muse, The Blue Fly in his Head, Selected Poems, Satires and Epigrams, Artorius, A Parliament of Birds, The Watchman's Flute, Birds Reconvened, Buzz Buzz, Naming of the Beast, The Immolation of Adelph, Collected Poems, Cats' Parnassus, A Partridge in a Pear Tree, Time Pieces, The Game of Love and Death 1990, A Ninefold of Charms 1991, Selected Poems 1991, Selected Poems 1992, Sweet Apple Earth 1993, Chimeras 1994, Galileo's Salad 1996, Torriano Sequences 1997, The Colour of Sound 1999, The Sound of Light 2000; Ed. Selected Poems of Jonathan Swift, of Tennyson, of Alexander Pope, The Forsaken Garden, Faber Book of Twentieth Century Verse (both with David Wright), Images of Tomorrow, Homage to George Barker on his Sixtieth Birthday, Selected Poems of Thomas Gray, Poems of Science (with Philips Salman), In the Shadows, David Gray 1991; Autobiography: Hindsights 1993; Drama: Helen in Egypt, The Darkling Plain, Charles Williams, The Pastoral, The Ode, The Verse Satire; Translations: Hafiz of Shiraz, The Rubaiyyat of Omar Khayyam (both with Peter Avery), Leopardi: Selected Prose and Poetry (with Iris Origo),

The Poems of Anyte (with Carol A. Whiteside), The Poems of Sulpicia 2000. *Leisure interest:* taxonomy. *Address:* 22 Artesian Road, London, W2 5AR, England. *Telephone:* (20) 7229-6367.

HEATHER, Brenda, BL, BA; Samoan/New Zealand barrister and solicitor; b. 23 Dec. 1961, Wellington, New Zealand; d. of Cuthbert Stanley Heather and Winnie Anesi Heather; m. George Latu; one d.; ed Wellington Girls Coll., Vic. Coll. of Wellington; Crown Counsel, Crown Law Office, Wellington 1991–96; Prin. State Solicitor, Office of the Attorney-Gen., Apia, Samoa 1996–97; Attorney-Gen. of Samoa 1997–. *Leisure interests:* family, cuisine, genealogy. *Address:* Office of the Attorney General, POB 27, Apia, Samoa (Office). *Telephone:* 20295 (Office). *Fax:* 22118 (Office). *E-mail:* attorney.general@samoa.ws (Office).

HEATON, Brian Thomas, DSc, DPhil, CChem, FRSC; British professor of chemistry; b. 16 Feb. 1940, Broughton-in-Furness; s. of William Edwin Heaton and Mabel Heaton (née Benson); m. Wendy Janet Durrant 1964; three d.; ed Ulverston Grammar School, Hatfield Polytechnic, Univ. of Sussex; Lecturer in Chem. Univ. of Kent at Canterbury 1968–81, Sr Lecturer 1981–84, Reader 1984, Prof. 1984–85; Grant Prof. of Inorganic Chem. Univ. of Liverpool 1985–, Head of Dept of Chem. 1988–97; Nuffield Fellowship 1981; Chair. SERC Inorganic Cttee 1990–93; Sec. and Treas. Dalton Div. RSC 1990–93; Fellowship Japanese Soc. for Promotion of Science 1989; Leverhulme Foundation Research Fellowship 1997; Visiting Prof. Univ. Louis Pasteur, Strasbourg 2001; Tilden Lectureship and Prize RSC 1986, RSC (Royal Soc. Chem.) Award for research on platinum metals 2002. *Publications:* articles in journals. *Leisure interests:* rugby, walking, listening to and playing music, eating and drinking (especially wine). *Address:* 44 Graham Road, West Kirby, CH48 5DW (Office); Department of Chemistry, University of Liverpool, P.O. Box 147, Liverpool, L69 7ZD, England. *Telephone:* (151) 632-3206 (Home); (151) 794-3524. *Fax:* (151) 794-3540 (Office); (151) 794-3540. *E-mail:* bth@liverpool.ac.uk (Office). *Website:* www.liv.ac.uk (Office).

HEATON, Frances Anne, BA, LLB; British finance executive; b. 11 Aug. 1944, Winchester, Hants.; d. of John Ferris Whidborne and Marjorie Annie Maltby; m. Martin Heaton 1969; two s.; ed Trinity Coll., Dublin, Civil Service Coll., London Business School; with Dept of Econ. Affairs 1967–70; joined HM Treasury 1970, Asst Sec. 1979–80; seconded to S. G. Warburg & Co. Ltd 1977–79; with Corp. Finance Div., Lazard Bros. & Co. Ltd 1980, Dir 1986–; Dir (non-exec.) W. S. Atkins PLC 1990–, Deputy Chair. (non-exec.) 1996–; Dir (non-exec.) Bank of England 1993–2001; mem. Cttee on Standards in Public Life 1997–; Dir (non-exec.) BUPA 1998–2001, World Pay Group PLC 2000–, Fountain GB Ltd 2001–. *Leisure interests:* bridge, gardening, riding. *Address:* c/o Lazard Brothers & Co. Ltd, 21 Moorfields, London, EC2P 2HT, England (Office). *Telephone:* (20) 7588-2721. *Fax:* (20) 7588-7894 (Office).

HEBEISH, Ali Ali, PhD; Egyptian professor of chemistry; b. 21 Dec. 1936, Mehalla El-Kubra, Gharbia; m.; two c.; ed Cairo Univ., Gujarat Univ.; Research Fellow Nat. Research Centre, Cairo 1960–61, other research positions 1962–74, Assoc. Prof. 1974–79, Prof. 1979–84; Under-Sec. of State Office of the Pres., Acad. of Scientific Research and Tech. (ASRT), Cairo 1985–88, Vice-Pres. 1988–91, Pres. 1992–96; Pres. Egyptian Asscn for Scientific Culture 1993–, Egyptian Textile Soc. 1993–; mem. Council IFSTAD 1992–96; Fellow Alexander von Humboldt Foundation 1973–75; Prof. Emer. Nat. Research Centre 1996–; Fellow African Acad. of Sciences, Third World Acad. of Sciences, Islamic Acad. of Sciences; State Prize for Chemistry 1972, Order of Science and Art, First Class 1974, Order of the Repub. Second Class 1983, Production Prize 1985, 1990. *Publications:* over 360 publs. *Telephone:* 5522104 (Office). *Fax:* 5511803 (Office).

HECHE, Anne; American actress; b. 25 May 1969, Aurora, Ohio; d. of Donald Heche; m. Coleman Lafoon 2001; one s. *Films:* An Ambush of Ghosts 1993, The Adventures of Huck Finn 1993, A Simple Twist of Fate 1994, Milk Money 1994, I'll Do Anything 1994, The Wild Side 1995, Pie in the Sky 1995, The Juror 1996, Walking and Talking 1996, Donnie Brasco 1997, Volcano 1997, Subway Stories, Wag the Dog 1997, Six Days Seven Nights 1998, A Cool Dry Place 1998, Psycho 1998, The Third Miracle 1999, Auggie Rose 2000. *Television:* (series) Another World; (films) O Pioneers! 1992, Against the Wall 1994, Girls in Prison 1994, Kingfish: A Story of Huey P. Long 1995, If These Walls Could Talk 1996.

HECHT, Anthony Evan, MA; American poet and professor of English; b. 16 Jan. 1923, New York; s. of Melvyn Hahlo and Dorothea (née Holzman) Hecht; m. 1st Patricia Harris 1954 (divorced 1961); two s.; m. 2nd Helen d'Alessandro 1971; one s.; ed Bard Coll. and Columbia Univ.; Teacher, Kenyon Coll. 1947–48, State Univ., Iowa 1948–49, New York Univ. 1949–56, Smith Coll. 1956–59; Assoc. Prof. of English, Bard Coll. 1961–67; Faculty mem., Univ. of Rochester 1967, John H. Deane Prof. of Rhetoric and Poetry 1968; Hurst Prof., Washington Univ. 1971; Prof. Graduate School, Georgetown Univ., Washington DC 1985–93; Visiting Prof., Harvard Univ. 1973, Yale Univ. 1977; Consultant in Poetry, Library of Congress 1982–84; Trustee, American Acad., Rome; mem. American Acad. of Arts and Letters, American Acad. of Arts and Science; Guggenheim Fellow 1954, 1959, Ford Foundation Fellow 1967, Rockefeller Foundation Fellow 1967; Fellow Acad. of American Poets, Chancellor 1971; Prix de Rome 1950; Brandeis Univ. Creative Arts Award 1965; Pulitzer Prize, Miles Poetry Award, Wayne Univ., Russell Loines Awards, Nat. Inst. of Arts and Letters (all for The Hard Hours) 1968; Bollingen Prize 1983, Eugenio Montale Prize for Poetry 1985, Hariet Monroe Award 1987,

Ruth B. Lilly Award 1988, Aiken Taylor Award, Nat. Educ. Asscn 1989, Wallace Stevens Award 1999. *Publications:* (poetry) A Summoning of Stones 1954, The Seven Deadly Sins 1958, A Bestiary 1960, The Hard Hours 1968, Millions of Strange Shadows 1977, Collected Earlier Poems 1990, Jiggery Pokery (co-author and co-auditor) 1967, Seven Against Thebes (trans. with Helen Bacon) 1973, The Venetian Vespers 1979, Obbligati: Essays in Criticism 1986, The Transparent Man 1990, The Hidden Law: The Poetry of W. H. Auden 1993, On the Laws of the Poetic Art 1995, The Presumptions of Death 1995, Flight Among the Tombs 1996, The Darkness and the Light 2001. *Address:* 4256 Nebraska Avenue, NW, Washington, DC 20016, USA (Home).

HECHTER, Daniel; French couturier; b. 30 July 1938, Paris; s. of Raymond Hechter and Rosy Mendelsohn; m. 1st Marika Stengl Diez Deaux (deceased); one d.; m. 2nd Jennifer Chambon 1973; ed Lycées Voltaire and Chaptal, Paris; designer 1954–; designer at House of Pierre d'Alby 1959–62; Founder and Dir-Gen. Vêtements Hechter 1962–; Pres. Fed. Française du Pret-à-Porter Féminin 1984–87; Pres. Festival de la Mode 1987; Pres. Strasbourg Racing Club 1987. *Leisure interests:* football, tennis, swimming, skiing, curling, golf. *Address:* SMB SA, rue de Maurapans, BP 87504, 25075 Besançon, cedex 09, France.

HECKER, Zvi, BArch; Israeli architect; b. 31 May 1931, Cracow, Poland; m. Deborah Houchman 1957; one s. one d.; ed Cracow Polytechnic School of Architecture, Israel Inst. of Tech. Haifa and Avni Acad. Tel Aviv; worked in office of Arieh Sharon and Benjamin Idelson, Tel Aviv 1957–58; in partnership with Eldar Sharon, Tel Aviv 1959–65, with Alfred Neumann, Tel Aviv 1960–65; Visiting Prof. Laval Univ. Québec 1968–69, Adjunct Prof. 1969–72; Visiting lecturer, McGill Univ. Montreal and Univ. of Pa 1969–72; pvt. practice, Tel Aviv 1972–; work includes housing projects, synagogues, public bldgs. etc. *Publications:* Exhbn catalogues, articles in professional journals. *Address:* 19 Elzar Street, Tel Aviv 65157, Israel.

HECKMAN, James Joseph; American professor of economics; b. 19 April 1944, Chicago; s. of John Heckman and Bernice Heckman; m. Lynne Pettler Heckman; one s. one d.; ed Colorado Coll. and Princeton Univ.; on staff Columbia Univ. 1970–74; Prof. of Econs, Chicago Univ. 1973–, Henry Schultz Distinguished Service Professor 1973–; Yale Univ. 1988–90; Guggenheim Fellow 1977–78; mem. Center for Advanced Study in the Behavioral Sciences 1977–78; Fellow Econometric Soc. 1980; mem. American Acad. 1985; Hon. PhD (Colo Coll.) 2001, DUniv hc (Chile) 2002, (UAEM Mexico) 2003; Clerk Medal, AEA 1983, Benezet Medal Colo Coll. 1985, Nobel Prize in Econs 2000. *Publications:* numerous books and over 180 articles in journals. *Address:* Department of Economics, University of Chicago, 1126 East 59th Street, Chicago, IL 60637 (Office); 4807 S. Greenwood, Chicago, IL 60615, USA (Home). *Telephone:* (773) 702-0634 (Office); (773) 268-4547 (Home). *Fax:* (773) 702-8490 (Office); (773) 268-6844 (Home). *E-mail:* jjh@uchicago.edu (Office). *Website:* lily.src.uchicago.edu (Office).

HEDELIUS, Tom Christer, MBA; Swedish banker; b. 3 Oct. 1939, Lund; s. of Curt Hedelius and Brita (Påhlsson) Hedelius; m. Ulla Marianne Ericsson 1964; three s.; ed Univ. of Lund; industrial expert, Svenska Handelsbanken 1967–69, Credit Man. 1969–74, Head, Regional Unit (Stockholm City) 1974–76, Head, Cen. Credit Dept 1976–78, Pres. 1978–, Chair. of Bd 1991–2001; Chair. Bd AB Industrivärden, Bergman & Beving AB, Svenska AB Le Carbone, Anders Sandrews Stiftelse; Vice-Chair. Telefon AB LM Ericsson 1991–, Addtech. AB 2001–, Lagercrantz Group AB 2001–; mem. Bd Svenska Cellulosa AB, AB Volvo; Hon. Chair. Svenska Handelsbanken; Hon. DEcon (Umeå) 1989. *Address:* AB Industrivärden, Box 5403, 11484 Stockholm (Office); Sturegatan 38, 11436 Stockholm, Sweden (Home). *Telephone:* (8) 6666400. *Fax:* (8) 6616235.

HEEGER, Alan J., PhD; American physicist; b. 22 Jan. 1936, Sioux City; ed Univ. of California, Berkeley; Prof. of Physics, Univ. of Calif. at Santa Barbara 1982–, Dir Inst. for Polymers and Organic Solids 1982–2000, Prof. of Materials 1987–; Adjunct Prof. of Physics, Univ. of Utah 1988–; Chief Scientist 1999–; Pres. UNIAX Corpn 1990–94, Chair. Bd 1990–99, Chief Tech. Officer 1999–; Nobel Prize for Chemistry (Jt recipient) 2000 for pioneering work on conductive polymers. *Address:* Department of Physics, Univ. of California at Santa Barbara, Santa Barbara, CA 93106 (Office); UNIAX Corporation, 6780 Cortona Drive, Santa Barbara, CA 93117, USA. *Telephone:* (805) 893-3184 (Office). *Fax:* (805) 893-4755 (Office). *E-mail:* ajh@physics.ucsb.edu (Office).

HEEMSKERK, H. "Bert", BEcons; Netherlands banker; b. 13 April 1943, Noordwijkerhoud; ed Philosophy-Theology Hochschule, Frankfurt, Eberhard Karls Univ., Tübingen, Univ. Catholique, Paris, Nederlandse Economische Hogeschool, Rotterdam; with ABN/AMRO Bank, Tokyo, Dubai and London for 20 years, becoming Dir-Gen. for Domestic Markets; Chair. Man. Bd F. van Lanschot Bankiers –2002; Chair. Exec. Bd Rabobank Group. Dec. 2002–; Vice-Chair. Netherlands Bankers' Asscn (NVB). *Address:* Office of the Chairman, Rabobank Group, Postbus 17100, Croeselaan 18, Utrecht, 3500 HG, Netherlands (Office). *Telephone:* (30) 2160000 (Office). *Fax:* (30) 2162672 (Office). *Website:* www.rabobank.com (Office).

HEFFER, Simon James, MA; British journalist and author; b. 18 July 1960, Chelmsford, Essex; s. of the late James Heffer and of Joyce Mary Clements; m. Diana Caroline Clee 1987; two s.; ed King Edward VI School Chelmsford, Corpus Christi Coll. Cambridge; medical journalist 1983–85; freelance journalist 1985–86; Leader Writer Daily Telegraph 1986–91, Deputy Political Corresp. 1987–88, Political Sketch Writer 1988–91, Political Columnist

1990–91, Deputy Ed. 1994–96; Deputy Ed. The Spectator 1991–94; columnist Evening Standard 1991–93, Daily Mail 1993–94, 1995–; Charles Douglas-Home Prize, 1993. *Publications:* A Tory Seer (Jt Ed. with C. Moore) 1989, A Century of County Cricket (Ed.) 1990, Moral Desperado: A Life of Thomas Carlyle 1995, Power and Place: The Political Consequences of King Edward VII 1998, Like the Roman: The Life of Enoch Powell 1998, Nor Shall My Sword; the Reinvention of England 1999, Vaughan Williams 2000. *Leisure interests:* cricket, music, ecclesiology, bibliophily. *Address:* The Daily Mail, 2 Derry Street, London, W8 5TT, England. *Telephone:* (20) 7938-6000.

HEFNER, Hugh Marston, BS; American publisher; b. 9 April 1926, Chicago, Ill.; s. of Glenn L. Hefner and Grace Hefner (née Swanson); m. 1st Mildred Williams 1949 (divorced 1959); one s. one d.; m. 2nd Kimberley Conrad 1989; two s.; ed Univ. of Illinois; Ed.-in-Chief Playboy Magazine 1953–, Oui Magazine 1972–81; Chair. Emer. Playboy Enterprises 1988–; Pres. Playboy Club Int. Inc. 1959–86; Int. Press Directory Int. Publisher Award 1997. *Leisure interests:* cinema, jazz. *Address:* Playboy Enterprises Inc., 9242 Beverly Boulevard, Beverly Hills, CA 90210, USA.

HEGARTY, Anthony Francis, PhD, MRIA; Irish professor of chemistry; b. 5 Aug. 1942, Cork; s. of Daniel F. Hegarty and Patricia Doyle; m. Ann M. Fleming 1967; two s. two d.; ed Univ. Coll. Cork (Nat. Univ. of Ireland) and Univs. of Paris and Calif.; Lecturer in Chem., Univ. Coll. Cork 1970–79; Prof. of Organic Chem., Univ. Coll. Dublin (UCD) 1980–, Dean of Postgraduate Studies 1989–95, mem. Governing Body of UCD 1990–, Vice-Pres. for Research UCD 1997–; Visiting Prof. Brandeis Univ. 1975, Kuwait Univ. 1983, Univ. of Paris VII 1987; Chair. Nat. Trust for Ireland 1984–87; Chair. Royal Soc. of Chem. in Ireland 1987–90; mem. Senate, Nat. Univ. of Ireland 1992–; Council mem. Royal Irish Acad. 1982–96, Sec. for Science 1986–88, Treas. 1988–96. *Publications:* 175 papers in int. journals in area of organic reaction mechanisms and bioorganic chem. *Leisure interests:* sailing, walking, classical music. *Address:* Department of Chemistry, University College, Dublin, Belfield, Dublin 4, Republic of Ireland. *Telephone:* (1) 71162305. *Fax:* (1) 71162029.

HEGAZY, Abdel Aziz Muhammad, DPhil; Egyptian politician; b. 3 Jan. 1923; ed Fuad Univ., Cairo, Birmingham Univ.; Dean, Faculty of Commerce, Ain Shams Univ. 1966–68; mem. Nat. Ass. 1969–75; Minister of the Treasury 1968–73; Deputy Prime Minister, Minister of Finance, Econ. and Foreign Trade 1973–74; First Deputy Prime Minister April–Sept. 1974, Prime Minister 1974–75; Chair. Allied Arab Bank 1985; teaching and working as a management consultant and certified accountant in Cairo, Jeddah and Beirut.

HEGDE, Ramakrishna; Indian politician; b. 29 Aug. 1926, Doddamane, Siddapur Taluk, Uttara Kannada Dist; m. Saraswati Hegde; three c.; ed Kashi Vidyapeeta, Benares and Lucknow Univs; active in Quit India movement, imprisoned twice; organized Ryots' (Tenants') Movt, Uttara Kannada Dist; Pres. Dist Congress Cttee, Uttara Kannada Dist 1954–57; entered State Legis. as Deputy Minister for Planning and Devt 1957; Gen. Sec. Mysore Pradesh Congress 1958–62; Minister in charge of Rural Devt, Panchayatraj and Co-operation, Nijalingappa's Cabinet 1962–65, Minister for Finance, Excise, Prohibition, Information and Publicity 1965–67, for Finance, Excise and Planning 1967–68, for Finance, Planning and Youth Services 1968, 1971, of Commerce 1998–99; Leader of Opposition 1971–77; imprisoned during Emergency; elected Gen. Sec. All India Janata Party 1977; elected to Rajya Sabha from Karnataka Ass. 1978; Leader, Karnataka Janata Legislature Party 1983; first-ever non-Congress Chief Minister in the State; continued as head of caretaker ministry 1984; following State Legislature by-election, Chief Minister of Karnataka 1985–88; Deputy Chair. Planning Comm. 1989–90; Pres. World Fed. UN Asscns. *Address:* 229, Rajmahal Vilas Extension, Bangalore 560080, India (Home). *Telephone:* (11) 4604749.

HEGEDÜS, Lóránt, DTheol; Hungarian ecclesiastic; b. 1930, Hajdunánás; s. of Géza Hegedüs and Magdolna Szabó; m. Zsuzsa Illés; two s. two d.; ed Theological Acad., Budapest, Basel; Asst Minister Bicske, Budapest 1956, Komló Nagykörös, Alsónémedi 1954–63, Hidas 1963–65; Minister Hidas 1965–68, Szabadság tér, Budapest 1983–96, Kálvin tér, Budapest 1996–; Bishop 1990–; Prof. 1993–; Acting Chair. Hungarian Presbyterian Churches Ecumenical Council 1994; mem. Presidium of European Churches Conf. 1992–97, Council of Hundreds 1997–; Prof. hc (Budapest, Veszprém, Cluj (Kolozsvár), Romania); Bocskai Díj Award 1997. *Publications include:* Aspekte der Gottesfrage 1979, Nyitás a Végtelenre (Opening for Eternity) 1989, The Concept of Transcendence 1991, Testvérek, menjünk bátran! (Brethren, Let Us Go On) 1992, Kálvin teológiája (Calvin's Theology) 1996, Isten szuverenitása és az ember felelössége (The Sovereignty of God and the Responsibility of Man) 1996, Jézus és Europa (Jesus and Europe) 1998, Újkantiánus és értékteologia (Neo-Kantian and Value Theology in Hungary) 1998, Isten kezében a történelem (History in God's Hand) 1998, Házasság (Wedding) 1998, Magyar reformatus millénium (Hungarian Reformed Millennium) 2000, Mózes Huszonkettö 2001. *Leisure interests:* reading, listening to music. *Address:* 1054 Budapest, Szabadság tér 2, Hungary. *Telephone:* (1) 311-8695. *Fax:* (1) 311-8695.

HEGEL, Eduard, DPhil, DTheol; German theologian; b. 28 Feb. 1911, Wuppertal-Barmen; s. of Albert and Maria (née Ommer) Hegel; ed Univs. Bonn, Münster and Munich; Prof. for Middle and New Church History, Trier 1949, Münster 1953, Bonn 1966–76, Prof. Emer. 1976; mem. Historical Comm. for Westphalia 1958, Rheinisch-Westfälische Akad. der Wissenschaften 1973–;

Apostolic Protonotar, Prelate. *Publications include:* Die Kirchenpolitischen Beziehungen Hannovers 1934, Kirchliche Vergangenheit im Bistum Essen 1960, Geschichte der Katholisch-Theologischen Fakultät Münster (2 Vols) 1966, 1971, Geschichte des Erzbistums Cologne, Bd 4–5 1979, 1987, Ecclesiastica Rhenana 1986, St Kolumba in Cologne. Eine mittelalterliche Grossstadtpfarrei in ihrem Werden und Vergehen 1996. *Address:* Gregor-Mendel-Strasse 29, 53115 Bonn, Germany. *Telephone:* (228) 232273.

HEGGESSEY, Lorraine Sylvia, BA; British television executive; b. 16 Nov. 1956; d. of Sam Heggessey and Doris Heggessey; m. Ronald de Jong 1985; two d.; ed Durham Univ.; journalist Westminster Press Group; News Trainee and Sub Ed. BBC 1979–83, producer, Panorama 1983–86, This Week 1986–91, Ed. Biteback 1991–92, Series Producer, The Underworld 1992–94, Exec. Producer, BBC Science (QED, Animal Hospital, The Human Body, Minders) 1994–97; Head of Children's Programmes, BBC 1997–2000, Jt Dir Factual and Learning Programmes 2000, Controller BBC1 Sept. 2000–. *Leisure interests:* tennis, gym, skiing, her children. *Address:* Room 6239, BBC TV Centre, Wood Lane, London, W12 7RJ, England (Office). *Telephone:* (20) 8576-1622 (Office). *Fax:* (20) 8576-8248 (Office). *E-mail:* lorraine.heggessey@bbc.co.uk (Office). *Website:* www.bbc.co.uk.

HEIDE, Ola Mikal, MSc, DrAgr; Norwegian professor of botany; b. 26 April 1931, Trondenes; s. of Hans Kr. Heide and Marit Heide; m. Gerd Lillebakk 1955; three s. two d.; ed Agricultural Univ. of Norway and Univ. of Wisconsin; Research Fellow, Agric. Univ. of Norway 1961–70; Prof. of Plant Sciences, Makerere Univ. of Kampala, Uganda 1970–72; Prof. of Plant Physiology, Univ. of Tromsö 1972–76; Prof. of Botany, Agric. Univ. of Norway 1976–, Head, Dept of Biology and Nature Conservation 1990–95, Rector 1978–83; Vice-Chair. Agric. Research Council of Norway 1979–84; mem. Norwegian Acad. of Sciences, Royal Soc. of Sciences of Uppsala 1991, Finnish Acad. of Science and Letters 1994; Pres. Scandinavian Soc. of Plant Physiology 1976–82, 1988–94, Fed. of European Socs. of Plant Physiology 1988–90; Kellogg Foundation Fellowship 1965; Norsk Varekrigsforsikrings Fund Science Prize 1968. *Publications:* more than 100 primary scientific Publs in the fields of plant physiology and ecophysiology. *Leisure interests:* sport, especially cross country skiing and running. *Address:* Agricultural University of Norway, Dept of Biology and Nature Conservation, 1432 Ås-NLH (Office); Skogvegen 34, 1430 Ås, Norway (Home). *Telephone:* 64-94-84-86 (Office); 64-94-16-01 (Home). *Fax:* 64-94-85-02 (Office). *E-mail:* ola.heide.@ibn.nlh.no (Office).

HEIDEN, Eric A., MD; American speed skater (retd) and orthopaedic surgeon; b. 14 June 1958, Madison, Wis.; m. Karen Drews 1995; ed Univ. of Wisconsin, Stanford Medical School; competed in Winter Olympics, Innsbruck, Austria 1976, Lake Placid, New York 1980 (five gold medals for men's speed skating, became first athlete ever to win five gold medals in a single winter olympics); winner, three consecutive World Speed Skating Championships 1977–79 (set new world records for 3,000 metres 1978, 1,000 metres 1978); retd from speed skating 1980; professional cyclist Jan. 1981–, winner US Professional Cycling Championships 1985; took part in Tour de France 1986; Asst Prof. UC Davis Sports Medicine Clinic, Sacramento, Calif.; US speed skating team physician, Winter Olympics 2002; mem. American Acad. of Orthopedic Surgeons; Sullivan Award for Best US Amateur Athlete 1980, UPI Int. Athlete of the Year 1980, USOC Sportsman of the Year 1980. *Address:* UC Davis Medical Group-Sports Medicine, 2805 J Street, Suite 300, Sacramento, CA 95815, USA (Office). *Telephone:* (916) 734-6805 (Office). *E-mail:* eric.heiden@ucdmc.ucdavis.edu (Office). *Website:* www.ucdmc.ucdavis.edu (Office).

HEIGHTON, (John) Steven, MA; Canadian author; b. 14 Aug. 1961, Toronto, Ont.; s. of John Heighton and Lambie Stephanopoulos; m. Mary Huggard 1988; one d.; ed Silverthorn Coll. Inst., Queen's Univ.; Ed. Quarry magazine 1988–94; Writer-in-Residence Concordia Univ. 2002–03; Gerald Lampert Award for Best First Book of Poetry 1990, Air Canada Award 1990, Gold Medal for Fiction, Nat. Magazine Awards 1992, Petra Kenney Award 2002. *Publications include:* Stalin's Carnival (poetry) 1989, Foreign Ghosts (travelogue/poetry) 1989, Flight Paths of the Emperor (stories) 1992, Théâtre de revenants (French translation of Flight Paths of the Emperor) 1994, The Ecstasy of Skeptics (poetry) 1994, On Earth As It Is (stories) 1995, The Admen Move on Lhasa: Writing and Culture in a Virtual World (essays) 1997, La rose de l'érèbe (French translation of On Earth As It Is) 1998, The Shadow Boxer (novel) 2000; poetry, fiction and critical articles in nat. and int. periodicals and anthologies 1984–. *Address:* Box 382, Kingston, Ont., K7L 4W2, Canada. *Telephone:* (613) 546-9677. *E-mail:* sheighton@kos.net (Office).

HEIKAL, Mohamed Hassanein; Egyptian journalist; b. 1923; m.; three s.; Reporter The Egyptian Gazette 1943, Akher Sa'a magazine 1945; Ed. Al-Akhbar daily newspaper 1956–57; Ed. Al-Ahram 1957, Chair. Bd Dirs. 1961–74; mem. Central Cttee Socialist Union 1968; Minister of Information and Foreign Affairs 1970; arrested Sept. 1981, released Nov. 1981. *Publications:* Nahnou wa America 1967, Nasser: The Cairo Documents 1972, The Road to Ramadan 1975, Sphinx and Commissar 1979, The Return of the Ayatollah 1981, Autumn of Fury 1983, Cutting the Lion's Tail 1986, Suez Through Egyptian Eyes 1986, Boiling Point 1988, (The) Explosion 1990, Illusions of Triumph 1992, Arms and Politics 1993, Secret Channels 1996. *Address:* c/o HarperCollins Publishers, 77–85 Fulham Palace Road, Hammersmith, London, W6 8JB, England.

HEILBRONER, Robert L., PhD, LLD; American economist; b. 24 March 1919, New York; s. of Louis and Helen (née Weiller) Heilbroner; m. 1st Joan Knapp 1952 (divorced 1975); two s.; m. 2nd Shirley Davis 1975; ed Harvard Univ., New School for Social Research, New York; Norman Thomas Professor, Dept of Econs, Graduate Faculty, New School for Social Research 1966–72, Norman Thomas Prof. Emer. 1972–; hon. degrees from La Salle Coll., Philadelphia, Pa, Long Island Univ., Ripon Coll., Wis. and Wagner Coll., State Univ. of New York; Guggenheim Fellow 1983, Scholar of the Year, NY Council for the Humanities 1994. *Publications:* numerous articles and books, including The Worldly Philosophers 1953, The Future as History 1959, An Inquiry into the Human Prospect 1975, Beyond Boom and Crash 1978, Marxism: For and Against 1980, Five Economic Challenges (with Lester Thurrow) 1981, Economics Explained 1982, The Nature and Logic of Capitalism 1985, Behind the Veil of Economics 1988, Twenty-First Century Capitalism 1993, Visions of the Future 1995, Teachings from the Worldly Philosophy 1996. *Leisure interest:* piano. *Address:* 425 East 57th Street, New York, NY 10022, USA; c/o New School for Social Research, 66 West 12th Street, New York, NY 10011.

HEILBRONNER, François; French government official; b. 17 March 1936, Paris; s. of Paul Heilbronner and Elsie Schwob; m. Nathalie Ducas 1966; two s. two d.; ed Lycée Charlemagne, Paris, Inst. d'Etudes Politiques, Paris and Ecole Nat. d'Admin; Insp. des Finances 1964; apptd. to secr. of interministerial Cttee on questions of European econ. cooperation 1966, Deputy Sec.-Gen. 1969–72; Adviser to Minister of Foreign Affairs 1968–69; Deputy Dir Office of Minister of Agric. 1972–73, Dir 1973–74; Econ. and Financial Adviser to Prime Minister Jacques Chirac 1974, Deputy Dir of Office of Prime Minister Chirac 1975–76, 1986; Insp.-Gen. des Finances 1983; Pres. Groupe des assurances nationales (Gan) 1986, Banque pour l'industrie française, Phénix Soleil SpA (Italy) (now Gan Italia SpA) 1986–94; consultant FH Conseil 1995–; Pres. HL Gestion 1997–99; Dir Fondation Médecins sans Frontières, COJYP; Man. Dir REFCO HL Securities 1999–2000; Chair and CEO Arbel 2001; Chevalier, Légion d'honneur, du Mérite maritime; Officier, Ordre Nat. du Mérite; Commdr du Mérite agricole. *Address:* 12 rue Théodule Ribot, 75017 Paris, France.

HEILBRUN, Carolyn Gold, PhD; American author and professor of English literature; b. 13 Jan. 1926, East Orange, NJ; d. of Archibald Heilbrun and Estelle (Roemer) Gold; m. James Heilbrun 1945; one s. two d.; ed Wellesley Coll., Columbia Univ.; Instructor, Brooklyn Coll. 1959–60; Instructor, Columbia Univ., New York 1960–62, Asst Prof. 1962–67, Assoc. Prof. 1967–72, Prof. of English Literature 1972–; Avalon Foundation Prof. of Humanities, Columbia Univ. 1986–93, Prof. Emer. 1986–93; mem. Mystery Writers of America (mem. Exec. Bd 1982–84); Guggenheim Fellow 1966; Rockefeller Fellow 1976; several hon. degrees including Hon. DHL (Pace) 1996, (Brown) 1997; Nero Wolfe Award 1981, Life Achievement Award, Modern Language Asscn 1999. *Publications:* The Garnett Family 1961, Christopher Isherwood 1970, Towards Androgyny 1973, Reinventing Womanhood 1979, Writing A Woman's Life 1988, Hamlet's Mother and Other Women 1990, The Education of a Woman: The Life and Times of Gloria Steinem 1995, The Last Gift of Time 1997, Collected Stories 1997; (as Amanda Cross) eleven novels. *Address:* c/o Eilen Levine Literary Agency, Suite 1801, 15 East 26th Street, New York 10010, USA.

HEINDORFF, Michael, MA; German artist; b. 26 June 1949, Braunschweig; s. of Hans Heindorff and Sigrid Bootz (née Hampe); m. Monica Buferd 1983 (died 2002); one s. one d.; ed Art Coll. and Univ. of Braunschweig, Royal Coll. of Art; has been represented in numerous group exhbns. internationally 1976–, also numerous solo exhbns. 1977–; Sr Tutor in Painting, RCA 1980–99; various comms. 1986–, Hon. Fellow 2001; Life mem. Chelsea Arts Club 1988–; John Moore's Liverpool Award 10 1976; Schmidt-Rotluff Prize 1981, Villa Massimo Prize 1984. *Art exhibitions:* Drawn to Seeing, London 1995; Drawn to Seeing II, touring Germany 1999–2001, Guildhall Art Gallery, London 2002, Deutsche Bank, London 2003. *Leisure interest:* walking. *Address:* 33 Charlotte Road, Hoxton, London, EC2A 3PB England (Office). *Telephone:* (20) 7739-1096 (Office); (20) 7254-9241 (Home). *E-mail:* looplight@aol.com. (Home).

HEINE, Volker, PhD, FRS; British professor of theoretical physics (retd); b. 19 Sept. 1930, Germany; m. Daphne Hines 1955; one s. two d.; ed Wanganui Collegiate School, Otago Univ., New Zealand and Cambridge Univ.; Demonstrator, Lecturer and Reader, Cambridge 1958–76, Prof. in Theoretical Physics 1976–97; Visiting Prof. Univ. of Chicago 1965–66; Visiting Scientist Bell Labs., USA 1970–71; Fellow, Clare Coll., Cambridge 1960–; Fellow, American Physical Soc.; Foreign mem. Max Planck Gesellschaft; Maxwell Medal, Inst. of Physics, Royal Medal, Royal Soc., Dirac Medal, Inst. of Physics, Max Born Medal, Inst. of Physics and German Physical Soc. *Publications:* Group Theory in Quantum Mechanics 1960, Solid State Physics (Vol. 24) 1970, (Vol. 35) 1980; articles in Journal of Physics, Physical Review, etc. *Address:* Cavendish Laboratory, Madingley Road, Cambridge, CB3 0HE, England. *Telephone:* (1223) 337258.

HEINONEN, Olavi Ensio, LLD; Finnish judge; b. 12 Sept. 1938, Kuopio; s. of Eino Ensio Heinonen and Aili Vesa; m. Marjatta Rahikainen 1962; two s. two d.; ed Univ. of Helsinki; Asst Prof. of Law, Univ. of Helsinki 1969–70; Justice, Supreme Court of Finland 1970–86; Parl. Ombudsman 1986–89; Chief Justice, Supreme Court of Finland 1989–2001; Hon. LLD (Turku); Grand Cross, Order of White Rose of Finland. *Publications:* books and articles on criminal justice and criminal policy. *Leisure interests:* cycling, basketball. *Address:* c/o Supreme Court, Pohjoisesplanadi 3, P.O. Box 301, 00171 Helsinki, Finland.

HEINTEL, Erich, DPhil; Austrian professor of philosophy; b. 29 March 1912, Vienna; s. of Rudolf Heintel and Luise Kästner; m. 1st Margarete Weininger 1939 (died 1982); two s. two d.; m. 2nd Waltraud Sammet 1984; ed Univ. of Vienna; Dozent Univ. of Vienna 1940, Prof. of Philosophy 1952–82, Prof. Emer. 1982–; mem. Austrian Acad. of Sciences, Allgemeine Gesellschaft für Philosophie in Deutschland, Humboldt-Gesellschaft, Internationale Hegel-Vereinigung; Hon. Pres. Vienna Philosophical Soc.; Grosses Ehrenzeichen für Verdienste um die Republik Österreich; Ehrenmedaille der Bundeshaupstadt Wien in Gold; Bundesverdienstkreuz (FRG); Goldene František Palacky-Medaille (CSSR Acad. of Sciences) 1989; other awards and decorations; Hon. DTheol (Hamburg) 1986. *Publications include:* Hegel und die analogia entis 1958, Die beiden Labyrinthe der Philosophie 1968, Einführung in die Sprachphilosophie 1972, Grundriss der Dialektik (2 Vols) 1984, Was kann ich wissen? Was soll ich tun? Was darf ich hoffen? Versuch einer gemeinverständigen Einführung in das Philosophieren 1986, Gesammelte Abhandlungen (6 Vols) 1988–96, Die Stellung der Philosophie in der "universitas litterarum" 1990. *Leisure interests:* philosophy, collecting mushrooms, swimming. *Address:* 1190 Vienna, Bauernfeldgasse 7/1/6, Austria. *Telephone:* (1) 3681562.

HEISBOURG, François, FRSA; French academic and business executive; b. 24 June 1949, London, England; s. of Georges Heisbourg and Hélène Pinet; m. Elyette Levy 1989; two s.; ed Coll. Stanislas, Paris, Inst. d'Etudes Politiques, Cycle Supérieur d'Aménagement et d'Urbanisme, Ecole Nat. d'Admin; Asst to Dir of Econ. Affairs, Ministry of Foreign Affairs 1977–78; policy planning staff, Ministry of Foreign Affairs 1978–79; First Sec. Perm. Mission of France to UN 1979–81; Int. Security Adviser to Minister of Defence 1981–84; Vice-Pres. Thomson Int. 1984–87; Dir Int. Inst. for Strategic Studies (IISS), London 1987–92, later Chair. Council; Sr Vice-Pres. Matra Défense Espace 1992–98; Head French Interministerial Group on teaching of and research in, strategic and int. affairs; Chair. Geneva Centre for Security Policy 1998–2000; Dir Fondation pour la Recherche Stratégique, Paris 2001–; Chevalier, Légion d'honneur, Chevalier, Ordre nat. du Mérite; decorations from Spain, Germany, etc. *Publications:* La Puce, les Hommes et la Bombe (with P. Boniface) 1986, Les Volontaires de l'an 2000 1995, The Future of Warfare 1997, European Defence: Making it Work 2000, Hyperterrorisme: La Nouvelle Guerre 2001; numerous articles in int. media and scholarly journals. *Leisure interests:* hiking, chess, collecting atlases. *Address:* Fondation pour la Recherche Stratégique, 27 rue Damesme, 75013 Paris, France (Office). *Telephone:* 1-43-13-77-80 (Office). *Fax:* 1-43-13-77-52. *E-mail:* f.heisbourg@frstrategie.org (Office); heisbour@cybercable.fr (Home). *Website:* www.gcsp.ch,www.frstrategie.org (Office).

HEITSCH, Ernst, DPhil; German professor of classics; b. 17 June 1928, Celle; s. of Ernst Heitsch and Luise Meineke; m. Paula Sötemann 1961; two s. one d.; ed Univ. Göttingen; Univ. Lecturer in Classical Linguistics Univ. Göttingen 1960–66, Professor 1966–67; Prof. of Classical Linguistics Univ. of Regensburg 1967–; mem. Akad. der Wissenschaften und der Literatur zu Mainz, Akad. der Wissenschaften zu Göttingen, Deutsches Archäologisches Institut. *Publications:* Die griechischen Dichterfragmente der römischen Kaiserzeit 1963, Epische Kunstsprache und Homer 1968, Parmenides 1974, 1995, Parmenides und die Anfänge der Erkenntniskritik und Logik 1979, Xenophanes 1983, Antiphon aus Rhamnus 1984, Willkür und Problembewusstsein in Platons Kratylos 1984, Platon über die rechte Art zu reden und zu schreiben 1987, Überlegungen Platons im Theaetet 1988, Wollen und Verwirklichen 1989, Wege zu Platon 1992, Platon Phaidros 1993, Erkenntnis und Lebensführung 1994, Geschichte und Situationen bei Thukydides 1996, Grenzen philologischer Echtheitskritik 1997, Beweishäufung in Platons Phaidon 2000, Gesammelte Schriften I 2001, II 2002, III 2003, Platon Apologie 2002; numerous articles in periodicals. *Leisure interest:* sailing. *Address:* Mattinger Strasse 1, 93049 Regensburg, Germany. *Telephone:* (941) 31944.

HEKMATYAR, Gulbuddin; Afghanistan politician and fmr guerrilla leader; Leader Hezb-e-Islami Mujahideen Movt against Soviet-backed regime; Prime Minister of Afghanistan 1993–94, 1996–97; returned from exile in Iran 1998; currently Leader Hezb-e-Islami Gulbuddin (Gulbuddin Islamic Party). *E-mail:* info@hezb-e-islami.org. *Website:* www.hezb-e-islami.org.

HELD, Al; American artist; b. 12 Oct. 1928, New York; ed Art Students League, New York and Acad. de la Grande Chaumière, Paris; Prof. of Art, Yale Univ. 1962–78, Adjunct Prof. of Painting 1978–; has participated in numerous group shows and work appears in many permanent collections including Whitney Museum, Museum of Modern Art, New York, San Francisco Museum of Art, Nat. Gallery Berlin, Hirshhorn Museum and Sculpture Gardens, Washington; Co-founder Brata Gallery, New York 1965; Guggenheim Fellow 1966; Logan Medal, Art Inst. of Chicago 1964, Brandeis Univ. Creative Arts Award 1983. *Solo exhibitions include:* André Emmerich Gallery, New York, 1965, 1967, 1968, 1970, 1972, 1973, 1975, 1976, 1978, 1979, 1980, 1982, 1984–92, 1995, 1996, 1997, Inst. of Contemporary Art, Boston 1978, Robert Miller Gallery, New York 1980, 1982, 1987, 1990, 1994, Richard Gray Gallery, Chicago 1984, Pace Editions, New York 1984 and also in Zürich, Amsterdam, Stuttgart, London etc. *Publications:* articles in professional journals. *Address:* c/o Robert Miller, 524 West 26th Street, New York, NY 10001, USA.

HELD, Heinz Joachim, DrTheol; German theologian and clergyman; b. 16 May 1928, Wesseling/Rhein; s. of Heinrich Held and Hildegard Röhrig; m. Anneliese Novak 1959; one s. three d.; ed Wuppertal, Göttingen, Heidelberg, Bonn and Austin, Tex.; Research Asst Wuppertal Theological Seminary 1953–56; parish pastor, Friedrichsfeld/Niederrhein 1957-64; Prof. of Theology, Buenos Aires Lutheran Seminary 1964–68; Pres. River Plate Evangelical Church, Buenos Aires 1968–74; mem. Cen. Cttee World Council of Churches 1968–91, Moderator of Cen. Cttee and Exec. Cttee 1983–91; Pres. Dept of Ecumenical Relations and Ministries Abroad of the Evangelical Church in Germany 1975–93; Bishop 1991; Chair. Council of Christian Churches, FRG 1982–88, 1992–95; Hon. DrTheol (Lutheran Theological Acad. Budapest) 1985; Hon. DD (Acad. of Ecumenical Indian Theology and Church Admin., Chennai) 1988. *Publications:* Matthew as Interpreter of the Miracle Stories 1960, Von Nairobi nach Canberra.EKD und ÖRK im Dialog 1975–1991 1994/1996, Den Reichen wird das Evangelium gepredigt 1997, Ökumene im Kalten Krieg 2000, Der Ökumenische Rat der Kirchen im Visier der Kritik 2001. *Leisure interests:* stamp collecting, amateur music (piano), photography. *Address:* Bussilliatweg 32, 30419 Hanover, Germany. *Telephone:* (511) 2714308.

HELD, Richard M., MA, PhD; American professor of vision science; b. 10 Oct. 1922, New York; s. of Lawrence Walter Held and Tessie Klein Held; m. Doris Bernays 1951; three c.; ed Columbia and Harvard Univs and Swarthmore Coll.; Research Asst Dept of Psychology, Swarthmore Coll. 1946–48; Research Asst, Teaching Fellow and NIH Postdoctoral Fellow, Dept of Psychology, Harvard Univ. 1949–53; Instructor, Asst Prof., Assoc. Prof., Prof. and Chair. Dept of Psychology, Brandeis Univ. 1953–62; mem. Inst. for Advanced Study, Princeton 1955–56; Sr Research Fellow NSF and Visiting Prof. Dept of Psychology, MIT 1962–63, Prof., Dept of Brain and Cognitive Sciences 1963–93, Dept Chair. 1977–86, Prof. Emer. and Sr Lecturer 1994–; Research Prof. of Vision Science 1995– and Dir of Research 1996–, New England Coll. of Optometry; Fellow, American Acad. of Arts and Sciences; mem. NAS and many other learned socs; numerous other professional appointments; Glenn A. Fry Award 1979, H. C. Warren Medal 1983, Kenneth Craik Award 1985; Dr. hc (Free Univ. of Brussels) 1984, (New England Coll. of Optometry), Galileo Award 1996. *Leisure interests:* tennis, theatre, visual arts. *Address:* New England College of Optometry, 424 Beacon Street, Boston, MA 02115, USA (Office). *Telephone:* (617) 369-0180 (Office); (617) 491-7218 (Home). *Fax:* (617) 369-0188 (Office). *E-mail:* heldd@optometry.edu.

HELFT, Jorge Santiago; Argentine arts foundation director; b. 10 June 1934, France; s. of the late Jacques Helft and Marianne Loevi; m. Mariana Eppinger 1955; three s.; ed New York Univ. and Columbia Univ., USA; lived in Paris until 1940, New York 1940–47, Buenos Aires 1947–; business exec. with Continental Grain Co. 1956–74, Vesuvio SA 1974–82; Trustee and Dir Fundación Antorchas 1985–, Fundación Lampadia, Vaduz, Liechtenstein; Pres. Fundación San Telmo 1980–; Founding mem. and Dir Fundación Teatro Colón 1978–; Oficial, Ordem de Rio Branco (Brazil). *Leisure interests:* arts and music. *Address:* Fundación Antorchas, Chile 300 (1098), Buenos Aires (Office); Defensa 1364 (1143), Buenos Aires, Argentina (Home).

HELINSKI, Donald Raymond, PhD, FAAS; American professor of biology; b. 7 July 1933, Baltimore, Md; s. of George L. Helinski and Marie M. Helinski; m. Patricia M. Doherty 1962; one s. one d.; ed Univ. of Maryland, Case Western Reserve Univ., Cleveland, Ohio, Stanford Univ.; U.S. Public Health Service Postdoctoral Fellow Stanford Univ. 1960–62; Asst Prof., Princeton Univ. 1962–65; Assoc. Prof. Dept of Biology, Univ. of Calif., San Diego 1965–70, Prof. 1970–, Chair. Dept of Biology 1979–81, Dir Center for Molecular Genetics 1984–95, Assoc. Dean of Natural Sciences 1994–97; mem. NIH Advisory Cttee on DNA Recombinant Research 1975–78; mem. NAS, AAAS; Assoc. mem. EMBO; Fellow American Soc. of Microbiology; Guggenheim Fellow. *Publications:* over 180 publications and 50 review articles in the fields of biochemistry, molecular genetics and microbiology. *Address:* Division of Biology, University of California, San Diego, 9500 Gilman Drive, La Jolla, CA 92093 (Office); 8766 Dunaway Drive, La Jolla, CA 92037, USA (Home). *Telephone:* (858) 534-3638 (Office); (858) 453-2758 (Home). *Fax:* (858) 534-0559 (Office). *E-mail:* dhelsinki@ucsd.edu (Office).

HELLAWELL, Keith, QPM, MSc, LLD; English anti-drugs co-ordinator and police officer; b. 18 May 1942, Yorks.; s. of Douglas Hellawell and Ada Alice Hellawell; m. Brenda Hey 1963; one s. two d.; ed Kirkburton Secondary Modern School, Dewsbury Tech. Coll., Cranfield Inst. of Tech. and London Univ.; worked for five years as a miner before joining Huddersfield Borough Police; progressed through every rank within W Yorks. Police to Asst Chief Constable; Deputy Chief Constable of Humberside 1985–90, Chief Constable of Cleveland Police 1990–93, Chief Constable of W Yorks. Police 1993–98; first UK Anti-Drugs Co-ordinator 1998–2001; Adviser to Home Sec. on Int. Drug Issues 2001–; Asscn of Police Officers Spokesman on Drugs; mem. Advisory Council on the Misuse of Drugs, Bd Community Action Trust; Chair. Cataput Presentations Ltd; Dir (non-exec.) Universal Vehicles Group Ltd.; Trustee Nat. Soc. for the Prevention of Cruelty to Children; mem. Editorial Advisory Bd Journal of Forensic Medicine. *Publication:* The Outsider (autobiog.) 2002. *Leisure interests:* gardening, design. *Address:* 50 Queen Anne's Gate, London, SW1H 9AT, England. *Telephone:* (20) 7273-2891. *Fax:* (20) 7273-8262.

HELLER, Michał Kazimierz; Polish professor of philosophy of science and ecclesiastic; b. 12 March 1936, Tarnów; ed Inst. of Theology, Tarnów; Catholic Univ. of Lublin, Pontifical Acad. of Theology, Cracow; Extraordinary Prof.

1985; Ordinary Prof. 1990; ordained Priest 1959; Prof. of Cosmology and Philosophy of Science Pontifical Acad. of Theology, Cracow; Jt Mem. Vatican Astronomical Observatory; ordinary mem. Pontifical Acad. of Sciences, Rome 1991; mem. Petersburg Acad. of Sciences 1997; mem. Int. Astronomical Union, Int. Soc. for General Relativity and Gravitation, European Physical Soc., Int. Soc. of the Study of Time, Polish Physical Soc., Polish Astronomical Soc., Science Soc. of Catholic Univ. of Lublin; Dr hc (Acad. of Mining and Metallurgy, Cracow) 1996. *Publications:* The Singular Universe – An Introduction to the Classical Singularity Theory 1991, Theoretical Foundations of Cosmology – Introduction to the Global Structure of Space-Time 1992, Physics of Space-Time and Motion 1993, The New Physics and a New Theology 1996, To Catch Passing Away 1997, Quantum Cosmology 2001, The Beginning is Everywhere 2002; and over 600 publns on relativistic physics, cosmology, history and philosophy of science and relations between science and theology and articles in journals. *Address:* Papieska Akademia Teologiczna, Wydział Filozoficzny, ul. Franciszkańska 1, 30-004 Cracow, Poland (Office). *E-mail:* mheller@wsd.tarnow.pl (Home).

HELLMAN, Peter S., MBA, BEcons; American business executive; b. 16 Oct. 1949, Cleveland, Ohio; s. of Arthur Cerf Hellman and Joan Alburn; m. Alyson Dulin Ware 1976; one s. one d.; ed Hobart Coll. and Case Western Reserve Univ.; with The Irving Trust Co., New York 1972–79; Financial Planning Assoc., BP America 1979–82, Man. Financial Planning 1982–84, Dir, Operations Analysis 1984–85, Asst Treas. 1985–86, Corp. Treas. 1986–89; Vice-Pres. and Treas. TRW Inc. 1989–91, Exec. Vice-Pres. and Chief Financial Officer 1991–94, Exec. Vice-Pres. and Asst Pres. 1994–95, Pres. and COO 1995–2000; Exec. Vice-Pres., Chief Financial Officer Nordson Corpn, Ohio 2000– ; Dir Arkwright Mutual Insurance Co.; mem. Soc. of Automotive Engineers, Cttee on Foreign Relations of Cleveland Council of World Affairs; Trustee Cleveland Zoological Soc. *Address:* Nordson Corporation, 28601 Clemens Road, Westlake, OH 44145, USA.

HELLSTRÖM, Mats, MA; Swedish politician and diplomatist; b. 12 Jan. 1942, Stockholm; m. Elisabeth Hellström; two c.; ed Univ. of Stockholm; Lecturer in Econs Univ. of Stockholm 1965–69; MP 1968, 1969–96, mem. Exec. Cttee Social Democratic Party Youth League 1969–72; mem. Bd Social Democratic Party 1969–96; Special Adviser, Ministry of Labour 1973–76; Minister of Foreign Trade at Ministry of Foreign Affairs 1983–86; Minister of Agric. 1986–91, for Foreign Trade and European Union Affairs 1994–96; Amb. to Germany 1996–2001; Gov. Stockholm Co. 2002–. *Publications:* A Seamless Globe? A Personal Story of the Uruguay Round in GATT 1999. *Address:* Box 22067, Laensstyrelsen i Stockholms Laen, 104 22 Stockholm (Office); Slottsbacken 4, 111 30 Stockholm, Sweden (Home). *Telephone:* (8) 785-50-02 (Office); (8) 20-98-48 (Home). *Fax:* (8) 652-24-45 (Office); (8) 20-12-22 (Home). *E-mail:* mats.hellstrom@fab.lst.se (Office).

HELLSVIK, Gun, LLB; Swedish politician; b. (Gun Blongren), 27 Sept. 1942, Lund; m.; one s.; ed Lund Univ.; fmr Lecturer in Commercial Law, Lund Univ.; mem. Bd Lund Inst. of Tech., IDEON Research Park; Municipal Commr and Chair. Municipal Exec. Bd, Lund 1982; mem. Nat. Bd Moderate Party 1985–; leader municipal opposition group 1988; Minister of Justice 1991–94; MP 1994–2001, Chair. Standing Cttee of Legal Affairs 1994–2001; Dir.-Gen. Swedish Patent and Registration Office 2001–. *Leisure interest:* cooking. *Address:* Swedish Patent and Registration Office, Box 5055, 10242 Stockholm, Sweden (Office). *Telephone:* (8) 782-25-00 (Office). *E-mail:* gun .hellsvik@prv.se (Office).

HELLWIG, Fritz, D.PHIL.HABIL.; German politician and economist; b. 3 Aug. 1912, Saarbrücken; s. of Friedrich H. Hellwig and Albertine (Christmann) Hellwig; m. Dr Margarete Werners 1939; two s. one d.; ed Marburg, Vienna and Berlin Univs; Staff mem. of the Saarbrücken Chamber of Industry and Commerce 1933–39; Dir of the Saarwirtschaftsarchiv 1936–39; Man. of the Dist Orgs. of the Iron and Steel Industry at Düsseldorf and Saarbrücken, 1940–43; war service 1943–47; Econ. Adviser and Dir of Deutsches Industrieinstitut, Cologne 1951–59; Substitute del., Consultative Ass. of Council of Europe 1953–56; mem. of Bundestag 1953–59; Chair. of the Econ. Affairs Cttee of the Bundestag 1956–59; mem. of European Parl. 1959; mem. of High Authority of the European Coal and Steel Community, Luxembourg 1959–67; Vice-Pres. of the Comm. of the European Communities, Brussels 1967–70; Exec. mem. Bd of German Shipowners' Asscn 1971–73; Hon. Prof. Univ. of Trier (for History of Cartography 1990); Int. Charlemagne Prize, Aachen (with EEC Comm.) 1969, Grosses Bundesverdienstkreuz mit Stern und Schulterband 1971. *Publications:* Westeuropas Montanwirtschaft, Kohle und Stahl beim Start der Montan-Union 1953, Saar zwischen Ost und West, Die wirtschaftliche Verflechtung 1954, 10 Jahre Schumanplan 1960, Gemeinsamer Markt und Nationale Wirtschaftspolitik 1961, Montanunion zwischen Bewährung und Belastung 1963, Politische Tragweite der europäischen Wirtschaftsintegration 1966, Das schöne Buch und der Computer 1970, Die Forschungs- und Technologiepolitik der Europäischen Gemeinschaften 1970, Verkehr und Gemeinschaftsrecht: Seeschiffahrt und Europäische Wirtschaftsgemeinschaft 1971, Die deutsche Seeschiffahrt: Strukturwandel und künftige Aussichten 1973, Zur älteren Kartographie der Saargegend I 1977, II 1981, Alte Pläne von Stadt und Festung Saarlouis 1980, Die Hogenberg-Geschichtsblätter 1983, Landkarten der Pfalz am Rhein (with W. Reiniger and K. Stopp) 1984, Mittelrhein und Moselland im Bild alter Karten 1985, Überwindung der Grenzen. Robert Schuman zum Gedenken 1986, Caspar

Dauthendeys Karte des Herzogtums Braunschweig 1987. *Leisure interests:* collecting old maps, views and illustrated books. *Address:* Klosterbergstrasse 117C, 53177 Bonn, Germany. *Telephone:* (228) 322017.

HELLYER, Hon. Paul Theodore, PC, BA; Canadian politician; b. 6 Aug. 1923, Waterford, Ont.; s. of Audrey S. Hellyer and Lulla M. Anderson; m. Ellen Jean Ralph; two s. one d.; ed Waterford High School, Curtiss Wright Tech. Inst., California and Univ. of Toronto; Fleet Aircraft Manufacturing Co., Fort Erie 1942–44; RCAF 1944–45; Owner, Mari-Jane Fashions, Toronto 1945–56; Treas. Curran Hall Ltd 1950, Pres. 1951–62; Pres. Trepil Realty Ltd 1951–62; Pres. Hendon Estates Ltd 1959–62; mem. House of Commons 1949–57, 1958–74, Parl. Asst to Minister of Nat. Defence 1956–57, Assoc. Minister April–June 1957, Minister of Nat. Defence 1963–67, of Transport 1967–69, responsible for Central Mortgage and Housing Corpn 1968–69; Chair. Task Force on Housing and Urban Devt 1968; Acting Prime Minister 1968–69; joined Progressive Conservative Party July 1972; rejoined Liberal Party 1982; Leader Canadian Action Party 1997–; Opposition Spokesman on Industry, Trade and Commerce 1973; Distinguished Visitor, Faculty of Environmental Studies, York Univ. 1969–70; Founding Chair. Action Canada 1971; Syndicated Columnist, Toronto Sun 1974–84; Exec. Dir Canada UNI Asscn 1991–95; Fellow Royal Soc. for Encouragement of the Arts. *Publications:* Agenda: A Plan for Action 1971, Exit Inflation 1981, Jobs For All: Capitalism on Trial 1984, Canada at the Crossroads 1990, Damn the Torpedos 1990, Funny Money: A Common Sense Alternative to Mainline Economics 1994, Surviving the Global Financial Crisis: The Economics of Hope for Generation X 1996, Arundel Lodge; A Little Bit of Old Muskoka 1996, The Evil Empire: Globalization's Darker Side 1997, Stop: Think 1999, Goodbye Canada 2001. *Leisure interests:* swimming, skin and scuba diving, stamp collecting. *Address:* Suite 506, 65 Harbour Square, Toronto, Ont. M5J 2L4, Canada. *Telephone:* (416) 535-1008 (Office); (416) 366-4092 (Home). *Fax:* (416) 535-6325 (Office). *E-mail:* phellyer@canadianactionparty.ca (Office).

HELME, Mart; Estonian diplomatist; b. 31 Oct. 1949, Parnu; ed Tartu Univ.; Eesti Raamat Publishing House 1973–75; reporter Harju Elu (newspaper) 1975–77; Sr Ed. Literature section Pioneer magazine 1977–86; farmer 1986–89; publisher 1989–91; Acting Dir Union of Publishers of Estonia, political observer Paeveleht (daily) 1991–93; Head Fourth Bureau (Asia, Africa, S America) Political Dept, Ministry of Foreign Affairs Feb.–May 1994; Head Third Bureau (Russia, CIS, E and Cen. Europe) Political Dept, Ministry of Foreign Affairs 1994–95; Amb. to Russian Fed. 1995–99; Vice-Chancellor Ministry of Foreign Affairs 1999–. *Address:* Ministry of Foreign Affairs, Rävala pst 9, EE0100 Tallinn, Estonia.

HELMFRID, Staffan, PhD; Swedish professor of human geography; b. 13 Dec. 1927, Stockholm; s. of Hartwig E. W. Helmfrid and Greta Helmfrid (née Kristiansson); m. Antje Teichmann 1954; three d.; ed Stockholm Univ.; Asst, Dept of Geography, Stockholm Univ. 1951, Asst Prof. 1955, Assoc. Prof. 1962, Research Fellow 1967, Prof. of Human Geography 1969–92, Dean of Faculty of Social Sciences 1970, Pro-Rector (Vice-Pres.) Stockholm Univ. 1974, Rector 1978–88; Chair. Bank of Sweden Tercentenary Foundation 1980–86, Fulbright Comm. in Sweden 1984–85; CC-PU, Council of Europe 1983–88; Chair. Swedish Nat. Cttee of Geography 1988–94; mem. Royal Acad. of Letters, History and Antiquities (Sec.-Gen. 1993–98), Royal Acad. of Sciences (Vice-Pres. 1988–91), Academia Europaea; Hon. Corresp. mem. Royal Geographical Soc., London 1995; Dr hc (Helsinki) 1988; Kt, Royal Order of North Star; HM Gold Medal, 12th size; Lord in Waiting 1987; Great Gold Medal, Royal Acad. of Letters, History and Antiquities 1999, Höpken Gold Medal, Royal Acad. of Sciences 2000. *Publications:* Östergötland Västanstång. Studien über die ältere Agrarlandschaft und ihre Genese 1962; books and articles on agrarian and historical geography; textbooks on geography and social science, National Atlas of Sweden. *Leisure interests:* mountain hiking, local history. *Address:* Stockholm University, 10691 Stockholm; Björkhagsvägen 40, 18635 Vallentuna, Sweden (Home). *Telephone:* (8) 51-17-48-33 (Home). *E-mail:* staffan .helmfrid@swipnet.se (Home).

HELMS, Jesse; American politician; b. 18 Oct. 1921, Monroe, NC; s. of Jesse Alexander Helms and Ethel Mae Helms; m. Dorothy Jane Coble 1942; one s. two d.; ed Wingate Coll. and Wake Forest Coll. (now Wake Forest Univ. at Winston-Salem); served USN 1942–45; subsequently became city ed., The Raleigh Times and Dir of news and programmes for Tobacco Radio Network and Radio Station WRAL; Admin. Asst to Senators Willis Smith and Alton Lennon; Exec. Dir NC Bankers Asscn and Ed., The Tarheel Banker 1953–60; editorial writer and presenter, WRAL-TV and Tobacco Radio Network 1960; Exec. Vice-Pres., Vice-Chair. of Bd and Asst CEO, Capitol Broadcasting Co. (which operates WRAL-TV and Tobacco Radio Network) 1960–72; Senator from N Carolina 1973–2002, Chair. Senate Agric. Cttee 1981–87, mem. Foreign Relations Cttee 1981–2002 (Chair. 1995–2002), Ranking Repub. 1987–; Republican. *Leisure interests:* reading, community service, fishing. *Address:* US Senate, 403 Dirksen Senate Office Building, Washington, DC 20510, USA. *Telephone:* (202) 224-6342 (Office).

HELØE, Leif Arne; Norwegian politician and dentist; b. 8 Aug. 1932, Harstad; ed Univ. of Oslo; school and Dist dentist, Harstad region 1957; Prof. of Community Dentistry, Univ. of Oslo 1975; mem. Harstad City Council 1960–69, mem. Municipal Exec. Bd 1968–69, Mayor of Harstad 1968–69; proxy mem. Storting (Parl.) 1965–73; Minister of Health and Social Affairs 1981–86; Dir-Gen. Norwegian Research Council for Science and Humanities 1988–91; Co-Gov. of Troms 1991–2000; Prof. Norwegian Inst. for Urban and

Regional Research 2000–; Conservative; Hon. Dr of Dentistry (Kupio) 1982, (Lund) 1984; Commdr Order of the Finnish Lion 1996. *Address:* Rosenborggaten 5, 0356 Oslo, Norway.

HELSØ, Gen. Hans Jesper; Danish army officer; b. 9 July 1948, Copenhagen; m. Pernille Vibeke Helsø; four c.; enlisted in nat. service 1968; rank of Sergeant 1969, 2nd Lt 1970, 1st Lt 1974; Gun Position Officer, Fire Direction Officer, Battery Exec. Officer, Battery Commdr, Kings Artillery 1974–78; Co. Exec. Officer 1979; Capt. 1979; Staff Officer, Logistic Br. LANDZEALAND 1979–82, Procurement Br. CHODDEN 1983–87, NATO Office, Ministry of Defence 1987–90; rank of Maj. 1986, Lt-Col 1990; Bn Commdr, 1st and 2nd ARTY-Bn, Kings Artillery 1990–92; DCOS Plans and Policy, Army Operational Command 1992–94; rank of Col 1994; C.O. Kings Artillery 1994–96; Commdr Bihac Area, UNPROFOR 1995; C.O. 1st Zealand Brigade 1996–98; rank of Maj.-Gen. 1998; Commdr Army Operational Command 1998–2000; rank of Lt-Gen. 2000; Deputy Chief of Defence 2000–02, Chief of Defence May 2002–; rank of Gen. 2002; Commdr, Order of Dannebrog; Badge of Honour for Good Service in the Army; Badge of Honour, Danish Reserve Officers' Org.; Grand Officier, Ordre nat. du Mérite; UN Medals, UNFICYP and UNPROFOR. *Address:* Defence Command, POB 202, 2950 Vedbaek, Denmark (Office). *Telephone:* 45-67-30-00 (Office). *Fax:* 45-89-07-48 (Office). *E-mail:* fko@fko.dk (Office). *Website:* www.fko.dk (Office).

HELTAU, Michael; Austrian actor; b. 5 July 1938, Ingolstadt; s. of Georg Heltau and Jakobine Heltau; ed gymnasium and Reinhardt Seminar; appeared at Würzburg and Bayerische Staatstheater, Munich 1953, Schillertheater, Berlin and Hamburg Schauspielhaus 1964–68, Théâtre du Châtelet, Paris 1968, Theater in der Josefstadt, Vienna 1957–69, Volkstheater, Vienna 1970, Salzburg Festival 1965–75; Kammerschauspieler, Burgtheater, Vienna 1972–, Doyen of the Burgtheater; noted for appearances in Shakespearean roles including Hamlet, Romeo, Richard II, Henry VI, Schnitzler's Anatol, von Hofmannsthal's Der Schwierige, Schiller's Wallenstein, etc.; second career as singer, especially songs of Jacques Brel (in German) and Viennese songs; numerous one-man shows on stage and TV; Austrian Cross of Honour, 1st Class, for Science and Art; Karl Skraup Prize; Kainz Medal/Goldener Rathausmann; Gold Award of City of Vienna. *Leisure interests:* reading, swimming. *Address:* Sulzweg 11, 1190 Vienna, Austria.

HELY-HUTCHINSON, Timothy Mark, MA; British publisher; b. 26 Oct. 1953, London; s. of Earl of Donoughmore and Countess of Donoughmore (née Parsons); ed Eton Coll., Oxford Univ.; Man. Dir Macdonald & Co. (Publrs) Ltd 1982–86, Headline Book Publishing PLC 1986–93; Group Chief Exec. Hodder Headline PLC 1993–; Dir W. H. Smith PLC 1999–, Chair. W. H. Smith News Ltd; Dir (non-exec.) Inflexion PLC 2000–; Venturer of the Year (British Venture Capital Asscn) 1990, Publr of the Year (British Book Awards) 1992. *Leisure interests:* opera, racing, bridge. *Address:* Hodder Headline Limited, 338 Euston Road, London, NW1 3BH (Office). *Telephone:* (20) 7873-6011 (Office). *Fax:* (20) 7873-6012 (Office).

HEMINGFORD, (Dennis) Nicholas, MA; British journalist; b. Dennis Nicholas Herbert, 25 July 1934, Watford, Herts.; s. of Dennis George Ruddock Herbert, 2nd Baron Hemingford and Elizabeth McClare (née Clark); m. Jennifer Mary Toresen Bailey 1958; one s. three d.; ed Oundle School, Clare Coll., Cambridge; Sports Desk, Reuters 1956–57, Diplomatic Desk 1957–60, Washington Bureau 1960–61; Asst Washington Corresp., The Times 1961–65, Middle East Corresp. 1965–69, Deputy Features Ed. 1969–70; Ed. Cambridge Evening News 1970–74; Editorial Dir Westminster Press 1974–91, Deputy Chief Exec. 1991–95; Pres. Guild of British Newspaper Eds. 1980–81, Media Soc. 1982–84; Hon. Sec. Asscn of British Eds. 1985–95; mem. E Anglian Regional Cttee, Nat. Trust 1983–2000, Chair. 1990–2000; Gov. Bell Educational Trust 1985–90; mem. Council Europa Nostra 1999–, Culture Cttee, UK comm., UNESCO 1999–; Hon. mem. Soc. of Eds. 1999; Pres. Huntingdonshire Family History Soc.; Hon. Sr mem. Wolfson Coll., Cambridge; Fellow Royal Soc. for Encouragement of Arts, Manufacture and Commerce; Liveryman, Grocers' Co. *Publications:* Jews and Arabs in Conflict 1969, Press Freedom in Britain (with David Flintham) 1991. *Leisure interests:* Egyptian War 1882, family history, computers, sport. *Address:* The Old Rectory, Hemingford Abbots, Huntingdon, Cambs., PE28 9AN, England. *Telephone:* (1480) 466234. *Fax:* (1480) 380275.

HEMINGWAY, Gerardine; British designer and design consultant; b. 7 Dec. 1961, Padiham, Lancs; m. Wayne Hemingway (q.v.); two s. two d.; ed St Augustine's, Billington; together with husband started in business with market stall in Camden, London; cr. footwear, clothing and accessory label Red or Dead 1992; collection retailed through eight Red or Dead shops in UK and three Red or Dead shops in Japan and wholesaled to int. network of retailers; left Red or Dead 1999; f. hemingwaydesign 1999; designed new wing for Inst. of Dirs 2001; current design and consultancy projects include a 700-unit housing estate, carpet design and wall coverings; Street Designers of the Year, British Fashion Awards 1996, 1997, 1998. *Publication:* Red or Dead: The Good, the Bad and the Ugly (with Wayne Hemingway) 1998. *Address:* 15 Wembley Park Drive, Wembley, Middx, HA9 8HD, England. *Telephone:* (20) 8903-1074 (Office). *Fax:* (20) 8903-1076 (Office). *E-mail:* gerardine@ hemingwaydesign.co.uk (Office).

HEMINGWAY, Wayne, BSc; British designer; b. 19 Jan. 1961, Morecambe, Lancs; s. of Billy Two Rivers (Mohawk Indian chief); m. Gerardine Hemingway (q.v.); two s. two d.; ed Univ. Coll., London; together with wife started in business with market stall in Camden, London; cr. footwear, clothing and

accessory label Red or Dead 1992 (now non-exec. Chair.); collection retailed through eight Red or Dead shops in UK and three Red or Dead shops in Japan and wholesaled to int. network of retailers; jt venture with Pentland Group PLC 1996–; f. hemingwaydesign 1999; designed new wing for Inst. of Dirs 2001; current design and consultancy projects include a 700-unit housing estate, carpet design, wall coverings and menswear; Chair. Prince's Trust Fashion Initiative; Street Designers of the Year, British Fashion Awards 1996, 1997, 1998. *Television:* appeared The Big Breakfast 1996– and other contribs. *Publications:* Red or Dead: The Good, the Bad and the Ugly (with Gerardine Hemingway) 1998, Kitsch Icons 1999, Just Above the Mantelpiece 2000; articles in newspapers and journals. *Address:* 15 Wembley Park Drive, Wembley, Middx, HA9 8HD, England. *Telephone:* (20) 8903-1074 (Office). *Fax:* (20) 8903-1076 (Office). *E-mail:* hemingway@tesco.net (Office); wayne@ hemingwaydesign.co.uk (Office).

HEMMING, John Henry, CMG, MA, DLitt, FSA; Canadian author and publisher; b. 5 Jan. 1935, Vancouver, BC; s. of H. Harold Hemming, OBE, MC and Alice L. Hemming, OBE; m. Sukie Babington-Smith 1979; one s. one d.; ed Eton Coll. and McGill and Oxford Univs; Dir and Sec. Royal Geographical Soc. 1975–96; Jt Chair. Hemming Group Ltd 1976–; Chair. Brintex Ltd, Newman Books Ltd; explorations in Peru and Brazil 1960, 1961, 1971, 1972, 1986–88; Hon. DLitt (Warwick) 1989, (Stirling) 1991; Pitman Literary Prize 1970, Christopher Award (USA) 1971, Founder's Medal, Royal Geographical Soc. 1989, Bradford Washburn Medal, Boston Museum of Science 1989, Mungo Park Medal, Royal Scottish Geographical Soc. 1988; Orden al Mérito (Peru), Special Award, Instituto Nacional de Cultura (Peru) 1996, Citation of Merit, Explorers' Club (New York) 1997, Order of Southern Cross (Brazil) 1998. *Publications:* The Conquest of the Incas 1970, Tribes of the Amazon Basin in Brazil (with others) 1973, Red Gold: The Conquest of the Brazilian Indians 1978, The Search for El Dorado 1978, Machu Picchu 1982, Monuments of the Incas 1983, Change in the Amazon Basin, 2 Vols (Ed.) 1985, Amazon Frontier: The Defeat of the Brazilian Indians 1987, Maracá 1988, Roraima, Brazil's Northernmost Frontier 1990, The Rainforest Edge (Ed.) 1993, Royal Geographical Society Illustrated (Ed.) 1997, The Golden Age of Discovery 1998, Die If You Must 2003. *Leisure interests:* exploration, writing. *Address:* Hemming Group Ltd, 32 Vauxhall Bridge Road, London, SW1V 2SS (Office); 10 Edwardes Square, London, W8 6HE, England (Home). *Telephone:* (20) 7602-6697 (Home); (20) 7973-6634. *Fax:* (20) 7233-5049 (Office). *E-mail:* j .hemming@hemming-group.co.uk (Office).

HEMMINGS, David Leslie Edward; British actor and feature film director; b. 18 Nov. 1941; m. 1st Genista Ouvry 1960; one d.; m. 2nd Gayle Hunnicutt 1969 (divorced 1975); one s.; m. 3rd Prudence J. de Casembroot 1976; two s.; m. 4th; two c.; ed Glyn Coll., Epsom; in entertainment industry 1949–, Dir Int. Home Video FGH Pty Ltd, Melbourne, Film and General Holdings Inc., Calif.; appeared in The Turn of the Screw (English Opera Group) 1954. *Films include:* Five Clues to Fortune 1957, Saint Joan 1957, The Heart Within 1957, Men of Tomorrow 1958, In The Wake of a Stranger 1958, No Trees in the Street 1959, Some People 1962, Play it Cool 1962, Live it Up 1963, Two Left Feet 1963, The System 1964, Be My Guest 1965, Eye of the Devil 1966, Blow Up 1966, Camelot 1967, Barbarella 1968, Only When I Larf 1968, The Charge of the Light Brigade 1968, The Long Day's Dying 1968, The Best House in London 1968, Alfred the Great 1969, Fragment of Fear 1970, The Walking Stick 1970, Unman, Wittering & Zigo 1971, The Love Machine 1971, Voices 1973, Don't Worry Momma 1973, Juggernaut 1974, Quilp 1974, Profundo Rosso 1975, Islands in the Stream 1975, The Squeeze 1976, Power Play 1978, Harlequin 1980, Beyond Reasonable Doubt 1982, The Rainbow 1989, Last Orders, Gladiator (Cannes Award) 2000, Gangs of New York 2001, The Mean Machine 2001; Jeeves (musical), Her Majesty's Theatre, London 1975; Scott Fitzgerald, BBC TV 1975, The Rime of the Ancient Mariner 1978 and Charlie Muffin 1979, ITV; Dir feature films Running Scared 1972, The 14 1973 (Silver Bear Award, Berlin Film Festival 1973), Just a Gigolo 1978, David Bowie Stage 1979, Murder by Decree 1979, Survivor 1979, Race to the Yankee Zephyr 1980, Dark Horse; produced: Strange Behaviour 1981, Turkey Shoot 1981. *Leisure interest:* watercolour painting. *Address:* c/o Michael Whitehall Ltd, 125 Gloucester Road, London, SW7, England.

HEMPEL, Rt Rev. Johannes, CBE, DTheol; German ecclesiastic; b. 23 March 1929, Zittau; s. of Albert Hempel and Gertrud (née Buchwald) Hempel; m. Dorothea Schönbach 1956; two s. one d.; ed Univs of Tübingen, Heidelberg, Kirchliche Hochschule, Berlin; Rev. Evangelical Lutheran Church, Saxony 1952–57, Bishop 1972–94; Student Pastor and Teacher of Theology, Leipzig 1957–72; a Pres. of WCC; 3 hon. degrees. *Publications:* Kirche auch in Zukunft sein 1994, Annehmen und frei bleiben 1996. *Address:* Hutbergstr. 78, 01326 Dresden, Germany. *Telephone:* (351) 2632097. *Fax:* (351) 2683142. *E-mail:* johanneshempel@t-online.de (Home).

HEMPSTONE, Smith; American journalist, author and diplomatist; b. 1 Feb. 1929, Washington, DC; s. of Smith Hempstone and Elizabeth Noyes; m. Kathaleen Fishback 1954; one d.; ed St Albans School for Boys, Washington, DC, Culver Mil. Acad., Ind. and Univ. of the South, Sewanee, Tenn.; Fellow, Inst. of Current World Affairs (in Africa), New York 1956–60; African corresp. (Nairobi), Chicago Daily News 1960–64; Nieman Fellow, Harvard Univ. 1964–65; Latin American corresp. The Washington Star 1965–67, European corresp. (London) 1967–70, Assoc. Ed. 1970–75; Ed.-in-Chief, The Washington Times 1982–85; syndicated newspaper columnist 1970–75, 1975–82, 1982–89; Amb. to Kenya 1989–93; Amb.-in-Residence, Univ. of the South, Sewanee, Tenn. 1993, Virginia Mil. Inst., Lexington, Va 1994; Hon. PhD

(Univ. of the South); Hon. LLD (Westminster Coll.). *Publications:* Africa, Angry Young Giant 1961, Rebels, Mercenaries & Dividends 1962, A Tract of Time (novel) 1966, In the Midst of Lions (novel) 1968, Rogue Ambassador 1997; numerous magazine articles, newspaper columns etc. *Leisure interests:* hunting, fishing, reading, travel, boating. *Address:* 7611 Fairfax Road, Bethesda, MD 20814, USA. *Telephone:* (301) 907-3961 (winter); (207) 594-4176 (summer).

HEN, Józef; Polish author and playwright; b. 8 Nov. 1923, Warsaw; s. of Roman Cukier and Ewa Cukier; m. Irena Hen 1946; one s. one d.; self-educated; lecturer Sorbonne, France 1993 and Univ. of Warsaw 1995–96; mem. Académie des Sciences, Belles Lettres et des Beaux Arts, Bordeaux, France; mem. Polish PEN Club; ZAIKS Book of the Year Award for Błazen – wielki mąż (Jester – The Great Man) 1999. *Film screenplays include:* Krzyż walecznych (Cross of Valour) 1959, Kwiecień (April) 1961, Nikt nie woła (Nobody's Calling) 1961, Bokser i śmierć (The Boxer and Death), Prawo i pięść (Law and the Fist) and Don Gabriel. *Screenplays for TV serials:* Życie Kamila Kuranta (The Life of Kamil Kurant) 1983, Crimen and Królewskie Sny (Royal Dreams) 1987. *Theatre plays:* Ja, Michał z Montaigne (I, Michel de Montaigne) 1984, Justyn! Justyn!, Popołudnie kochanków (Lovers' Afternoon) 1994. *Publications include:* Skromny chłopiec w haremie (A Modest Boy in a Harem) 1957, Kwiecień (April) 1960 (Book of the Year 1961), Teatr Heroda (Herod's Theatre) 1966, Twarz pokerzysty (Pokerface) 1970, Oko Dajana (Dayan's Eye) 1972, Crimen 1975, Bokser i śmierć (The Boxer and Death) 1975, Ja, Michał z Montaigne (I, Michel de Montaigne) 1978, Milczące między nami (Silent between Us) 1985, Nie boję się bezsennych nocy (I'm Not Afraid of Sleepless Nights) 1987, Nikt nie woła (Nobody's Calling) 1990, Nowolipie 1991, Odejście Afrodyty (Aphrodite's Departure) 1995, Najpiękniejsze lata (The Most Beautiful Years) 1996, Niebo naszych ojcow (Sky of Our Fathers 1997, Błazen – wielki mąż (Jester – The Great Man) 1998. *Leisure interests:* historical and literary monographs, watching sports programmes on television, films. *Address:* Al. Ujazdowskie 8 m. 2, 00-478 Warsaw, Poland (Home). *Telephone:* (22) 629-19-03 (Home).

HENARE, Tau; New Zealand politician; m.; five c.; fmr Advisory Officer in Maori Devt, Waitakere City Council, Youth Educ. Co-ordinator, Race Relations Conciliator, Advisory Officer, Dept of Internal Affairs; MP for Northern Maori (now Te Tai Tokerau) 1993–; Minister of Maori Affairs 1997–99, for Racing, Assoc. Minister for Sport, Fitness and Leisure; Deputy Leader NZ First Party, Spokesperson on Cultural Affairs and Treaty of Waitangi Negotiations. *Address:* c/o Ministry of Maori Affairs, PO Box 3943, Wellington 6015, New Zealand. *Telephone:* (4) 494-7000. *Fax:* (4) 494-7010.

HENDERSON, Sir Denys (Hartley), Kt, MA, LLB, FRSA; British business executive and solicitor; b. 11 Oct. 1932, Colombo, Sri Lanka; s. of the late John Hartley Henderson and Nellie Henderson (née Gordon); m. Doreen Mathewson Glashan 1957; two d.; ed Aberdeen Grammar School and Univ. of Aberdeen; Commercial Asst ICI 1957–58, Chair. Paints Div. 1977–80, Main Bd Dir 1980, Deputy Chair. 1986–87, Chair. 1987–95; Chancellor Univ. of Bath 1993–98; Chair. Zeneca Group PLC 1993–95; Dir (non-exec.) Barclays Bank PLC 1983–97, Barclays PLC 1985–97, RTZ Corpn PLC 1990–96, Rank 1994–2001 (Chair. 1995–2001), MORI 1995–, Dalgety PLC 1996–98 (Chair. 1997–98); mem. Law Soc. of Scotland 1955–; Chair. Court of Govs. of Henley Man. Coll. 1989–96; mem. Pres.'s Cttee, CBI 1987–96; First Crown Estate Commr 1995–2002; Trustee, The Natural History Museum 1989–98; Chair. Univ. of Aberdeen Quincentenary Appeal Cttee 1993–96; Pres. and Chair. Bd British Quality Foundation 1993–97; Hon. Fellow City and Guilds of London Inst. 1990, Soc. of Chemical Industry Centenary Medal 1993; Hon. DUniv (Brunel) 1987, (Strathclyde) 1993; Hon. LLD (Aberdeen) 1987, (Nottingham) 1990, (Manchester) 1991, (Bath) 1993; Hon. DSc (Cranfield Inst. of Tech.) 1989, (Teesside) 1993. *Leisure interests:* family life, swimming, reading, travel, gardening and "unskilled but enjoyable" golf. *Address:* c/o The Crown Estate, 16 Carlton House Terrace, London SW1Y, 5AH, England (Office).

HENDERSON, Donald Ainslie, MD, MPH; American professor of epidemiology and international health; b. 7 Sept. 1928, Cleveland, Ohio; s. of David A. Henderson and Grace E. McMillan; m. Nana I. Bragg 1951; two s. one d.; ed Oberlin Coll., Univ. of Rochester and Johns Hopkins Univ.; Intern, Mary Imogene Bassett Hosp., Cooperstown, New York 1954–55, Resident 1957–59; various posts at Communicable Diseases Center, Dept of Health, Educ. and Welfare 1955–66, Chief Smallpox Eradication Program 1965–66; Chief Medical Officer, WHO Smallpox Eradication 1966–77; Dean and Prof. of Epidemiology and Int. Health, Johns Hopkins Univ. School of Hygiene and Public Health 1977–90; Assoc. Dir, Office of Science and Tech. Policy, Exec. Office of the Pres. 1991–93; Deputy Asst Sec. Dept of Health and Human Services, Wash. 1993–95, Sr Scientific Advisor 1993–95; Prof. Johns Hopkins Univ. School of Public Health, Baltimore 1977–, Dir Civilian Biodefense Studies Center 1998–2001; Dir Office of Public Health Preparedness, Dept of Health and Human Services 2001–02; mem. numerous professional socs, cttees and advisory panels and recipient of numerous scientific awards and recognitions from orgs. in USA, Canada, UK, Japan, Brazil, Uruguay, Switzerland, Repub. of China, Ethiopia, Afghanistan, Germany, Australia, India and Pakistan; thirteen hon. degrees; Nat. Medal of Science 1986, Japan Prize 1988; Presidential Medal of Freedom 2002. *Publications:* more than 200 dealing primarily with smallpox eradication, epidemiology and immunization. *Address:* Johns Hopkins University School of Public Health, Candler Building, Suite 830, 111 Market Place, Baltimore, MD 21202 (Office); 3802 Greenway, Baltimore, MD 21218, USA (Home). *Telephone:* (410) 223-1667 (Office); (410) 889-2880 (Home). *Fax:* (410) 223-1665 (Office); (410) 889-6514 (Home). *E-mail:* dahzero@aol.com (Office). *Website:* hopkins-biofense.org (Office).

HENDERSON, Horace Edward; American military historian, peace advocate and fmr public affairs consultant; b. 30 July 1917, Henderson, NC; s. of Thomas Brantley Henderson MD and Ethel Maude Duke; m. Vera Schubert 1966; two d.; ed Coll. of William and Mary and Yale Univ.; Army Capt., Second World War; Owner, Henderson Real Estate, Williamsburg, Va 1947–52; Vice-Pres. Jr Chamber Int. 1951–52; Nat. Pres. US Jr Chamber of Commerce 1952–53; Asscns Co-ordinator, Nat. Auto Dealers Asscn, Wash. 1954–55; Dir Chamber of Commerce of the USA 1954; Exec. Cttee US Cttee for the UN 1954; Trustee, Freedoms Foundation 1955; Vice-Chair. Operation Brotherhood 1954–56; Republican Party cand. for Congress 1956; Lt-Gov. of Va 1957; Independent cand. for US Senate 1972; Dir Office of Special Liaison and Special Asst, Deputy Under-Sec. of State 1958; US Del. to ILO 1959–60, WHO 1959–60, UNESCO 1960, FAO 1959, High Comm. for Refugees 1959, ECOSOC 1959, US Del. to UN 1960; Deputy Asst Sec. of State for Int. Orgs, Dept of State, Washington, DC 1959–60; Chair. Republican Party of Virginia 1962–64; mem. Republican Nat. Cttee 1962–64; Chair. of Bd, Henderson Real Estate Agency McLean, Va 1962–65; Dir-Gen. World Peace Through Law Center, Geneva 1965–69; Pres. and Chair. Community Methods Inc. 1969–75; Chair. World Peace Treaty Campaign 1997–2003; Pres. Int. Domestic Devt Corps 1975, Chair. Asscn for Devt of Educ. 1977–78; Exec. Dir World Asscn of Judges 1968; Chair. Congressional Reform Cttee 1976; Exec. Vice-Pres. American Lawmakers Asscn 1977; Real Estate and Man. Consultant 1978–83; Pres. Williamsburg Vacations Inc. 1983–84, Nat. Asscn for Free Trade 1986; mem. St Andrew's Soc.; Elder, Presbyterian Church; Citizenship Award, American Heritage Foundation 1953, Outstanding Jaycee of the World 1954. *Publications:* The Greatest Blunders of World War II 2001, The Scots of Virginia – America's Greatest Patriots 2001, The Final Word – Quotations on War and Peace 2003. *Address:* 1100 Gough Street 15F, San Francisco, CA 94109, USA (Home). *Telephone:* (415) 922-5861 (Home). *E-mail:* DukeHen@cs.com (Home).

HENDERSON, Sir (John) Nicholas, GCMG, KCVO, MA; British diplomatist (retd); b. 1 April 1919, London; s. of Prof. Sir Hubert Henderson; m. Mary Barber 1951; one d.; ed Stowe School and Hertford Coll., Oxford; Asst Pvt. Sec. to British Foreign Sec. 1944–47; served in British Embassies in Washington, Athens, Vienna, Santiago; Prin. Pvt. Sec. to Foreign Sec. 1963–65; Minister, Madrid 1965–69; Amb. to Poland 1969–72, to FRG 1972–75, to France 1975–79, to USA 1979–82; Dir Hambros PLC 1982–89, Foreign and Colonial Investment Trust 1982–89, Mercantile and Gen. Reinsurance Co. Ltd 1982–89, Tarmac 1983–89, F&C Eurotrust 1984–90 (Consultant 1990–), Eurotunnel PLC 1986–88, Sotheby's 1989–, Fuel Tech Europe 1990–; mem. supervisory Bd Fuel Tech NV 1987–90; Lord Warden of the Stanneries and Keeper of the Privy Seal of the Duke of Cornwall 1985–90; Chair. Channel Tunnel Group 1985–86; Trustee, Nat. Gallery 1985–89; mem. Council Duchy of Cornwall 1985–90; Hon. Fellow, Hertford Coll., Oxford Univ.; Hon. DCL (Oxford). *Publications:* Prince Eugen (biog.), The Birth of NATO, The Private Office 1984, Channels and Tunnels 1987, Mandarin: The Diary of an Ambassador 1994, Old Friends and Modern Instances, The Private Office Revisited; various articles and stories. *Leisure interest:* gardening. *Address:* 6 Fairholt Street, London, SW7 1EG, England. *Telephone:* (20) 7589-4291.

HENDERSON, Richard, PhD, FRS; British molecular biologist; b. 19 July 1945, Edinburgh; s. of John W. Henderson and Grace S. (Goldie) Henderson; m. 1st Penelope Fitzgerald 1969 (divorced 1988); one s. one d. (one d. deceased); m. 2nd Jade Li 1995; ed Hawick High School, Boroughmuir Secondary School, Univs. of Edinburgh and Cambridge; professional interest in structure and function of protein molecules, especially in biological membranes; Helen Hay Whitney Postdoctoral Fellow, Yale Univ., USA 1970–73; Fellow, Darwin Coll., Cambridge 1982–; mem. research staff, MRC Lab. of Molecular Biology 1973–, Dir 1996–; Foreign Assoc. NAS; Ernst Ruska Prize for Electron Microscopy 1981; Lewis S. Rosenstiel Award, Brandeis Univ. 1991, Louis Jeantet Award 1993, Gregori Aminoff Award 1999. *Publications:* many scientific articles in books and journals. *Leisure interests:* canoeing, wine. *Address:* Medical Research Council Laboratory of Molecular Biology, Hills Road, Cambridge, CB2 2QH, England. *Telephone:* (1223) 248011.

HENDRICKS, Barbara Ann, BSc, BMus; Swedish soprano; b. 20 Nov. 1948, Stephens, Ark.; d. of M. L. and Della Hendricks; m. Martin Engström 1978; one s. one d.; ed Univ. of Neb. and Juilliard School of Music, New York, studying with Jennie Tourel; operatic début, San Francisco Opera (L'Incoronazione di Poppea) 1976; has appeared with opera companies of Boston, Santa Fe, Glyndebourne, Hamburg, La Scala (Milan), Berlin, Paris, LA, Florence and Royal Opera, Covent Garden (London), Vienna; recitals in most maj. centres in Europe and America; has toured extensively in USSR and Japan; concert performances with all leading European and US orchestras; has appeared at many maj. music festivals including Edin., Osaka, Montreux, Salzburg, Dresden, Prague, Aix-en-Provence, Orange and Vienna; nearly 50 recordings; nominated Goodwill Amb. for Refugees at UN 1987; Founder of the Barbara Hendricks Foundation for Peace and Rerconciliation in 1988; Hon. mem. Inst. of Humanitarian Law, San Remo, Italy 1990; Hon. DMus (Nebraska Wesleyan Univ.) 1988; Dr hc (Univ. of Louvain, Belgium) 1990, (Juilliard, NY) 2000; Commdr des Arts et des Lettres; Prince of Asturias Foundation Award 2000, Lions Club International Award for the Defense of Human Rights 2001. *Film appearance:* La Bohème 1988. *Leisure interest:*

reading. *Address:* B H Office, CP 224, 1815 Clarens, Switzerland (Office). *E-mail:* bh.office@bluewin.ch (Office). *Website:* www.barbarahendricks.com (Office).

HENDRICKSE, Ralph George, MD, FRCP, FRCP(E); British consultant paediatrician (retd); b. 5 Nov. 1926, Cape Town, S Africa; s. of William G. Hendrickse and Johanna T. (Dennis) Hendrickse; m. Begum Johanahara Abdurahman 1948; one s. four d; ed Livingstone High School, Cape and Univ. of Cape Town Medical School; Sr Medical Officer, McCord Zulu Hosp. Durban 1949–54; Sr Registrar, Univ. Coll. Hosp. Ibadan, Nigeria 1956–57; Lecturer, Sr Lecturer, Univ. of Ibadan 1957–62, Prof. and Head, Dept of Paediatrics 1962–69, Dir Inst. of Child Health 1964–69; Sr Lecturer and Dir Diploma in Tropical Child Health Course, Univ. of Liverpool and Liverpool School of Tropical Medicine 1969–75, Prof. of Tropical Paediatrics 1975–91, Dean Liverpool School of Tropical Medicine 1988–91, Prof. and Head of newly created Dept of Tropical Paediatrics and Int. Child Health, Liverpool Univ. 1988–91, Prof. Emer. 1991–; Hon. Consultant Paediatrician, Liverpool Health Authority 1969–91; Founder and Ed.-in-Chief, Annals of Tropical Paediatrics 1981–; mem. Advisory Expert Panel on Tropical Pediatrics of Int. Pediatric Asscn; mem. Standing Panel of Experts in Public Health Medicine of London Univ. 1990–93, 1993–; Sr Heinz Fellow British Paediatric Asscn 1961; Rockefeller Foundation Fellow 1961–62; Hon. Foundation Fellow, Medical Council of Nigera in Paediatrics 1970, Royal Coll. of Paediatrics and Child Health 1996; Hon. DSc (Cape Town) 1998; Frederick Murgatroyd Memorial Prize, Royal Coll. of Physicians 1970. *Publications:* Tropical Paediatrics: Update and Current Review 1981, Paediatrics in the Tropics 1991, over 150 articles in scientific journals (1954–2001). *Leisure interests:* swimming, gardening, painting, travel. *Address:* Annals of Tropical Paediatrics, International Child Health School of Tropical Medicine, Pembroke Place, Liverpool, L3 5QA (Office); Beresford House, 25 Riverbank Road, Heswall, Wirral, Merseyside, CH60 4SQ, England (Home). *Telephone:* (151) 708-9393 (Office); (151) 342-5510 (Home). *Fax:* (151) 707-9115 (Office); (151) 342-1312 (Home). *E-mail:* vcoulter@liv.ac.uk (Office). *Website:* www.carfax.co.uk (Office).

HENDROPRIYONO, Lt-Gen. (retd) Abdullah Mahmud; Indonesian politician; b. 1945, Jakarta; ed AMN Military Acad.; mil. career with Kopassus Unit, including several tours of combat duty in Kalimantan 1960s and 1970s, in East Timor 1975; sr positions in Bais (Indonesian mil. intelligence agency) 1990s, Jakarta Area Commdr 1993–94; Minister of Transmigration and Resettlement 1998–99; Head of Nat. Intelligence Agency (BIN) Aug. 2001–; also owner of a law firm. *Address:* c/o Office of the Co-ordinating Minister for Political Affairs, Security and Social Welfare, Jalan Medan Merdeka Barat 15, Jakarta 10110, Indonesia (Office).

HENDRY, Stephen Gordon, MBE; British snooker player; b. 13 Jan. 1969, Edin.; s. of Gordon J. Hendry and Irene Anthony; m. Amanda Elizabeth Teresa Tart 1995; one s.; ed Inverkeithing High School; commenced professional career 1985; winner of more than 50 major competitions including Grand Prix 1987, 1990, 1991, 1995, British Open 1988, 1991, 1999, UK Championship 1989, 1990, 1994, 1995, 1996, Embassy World Championship 1990, 1992, 1993 1994, 1995, 1996, 1999; Dr hc (Stirling) 2000; MacRoberts Trophy 2001. *Publication:* Snooker Masterclass 1994. *Leisure interests:* golf, music, Formula 1. *Address:* Stephen Hendry Snooker Ltd, Kerse Road, Stirling, FK7 7SG, Scotland. *Telephone:* (1786) 462634. *Fax:* (1786) 450068.

HENG SAMRIN; Cambodian politician; b. 25 May 1934; Political Commissar and Commdr of Khmer Rouge 4th Infantry Div. 1976–78; led abortive coup against Pol Pot and fled to Viet Nam 1978; Pres. Nat. Front for Nat. Salvation of Kampuchea 1978; Pres. People's Revolutionary Council 1979 (took power after Vietnamese invasion of Kampuchea); Chair. Council of State of Cambodia 1991; Sec. Gen. People's Revolutionary Party of Kampuchea (KPRP) 1981–91; mem. Politburo of Cambodia 1991–. *Address:* Council of State, Phnom Penh, Cambodia.

HENKEL, Hans-Olaf; German business executive; b. 14 March 1940, Hamburg; European Head Int. Business Machines (IBM) –1995, Chair. IBM Germany; Pres. Bundesverband der Deutschen Industrie 1995–2000; mem. Supervisory Bd Audi AG, Ingolstadt. *Address:* c/o IBM Deutschland GmbH, Ernst-Reuter-Platz 2, 10587 Berlin, Germany.

HENKIN, Louis, LLD, LHD; American professor of law; b. 11 Nov. 1917, Russia; s. of Yoseph Henkin and Frieda Kreindel; m. Alice Hartman 1960; three s.; ed Yeshiva Coll. and Harvard Univ.; admitted New York Bar 1941, US Supreme Court Bar 1947; law clerk 1940–41, 1946–47; mil. service 1941–45; with State Dept 1945–46, 1948–57; UN Legal Dept 1947–48; Lecturer in Law, Columbia Univ. 1956–57; Visiting Prof. Univ. of Pa 1957–58, Prof. of Law 1958–62; Prof. Columbia Univ. 1962, mem. Inst. for War and Peace Studies 1962–, Hamilton Fish Prof. of Int. Law and Diplomacy 1963–78, Harlan Fiske Stone Prof. of Constitutional Law 1978–79, Univ. Prof. 1979–88, Univ. Prof. Emer. and Special Service Prof. 1988–; Chair. Directorate, Columbia Univ. Center for Study of Human Rights 1986–; Pres. US Inst. of Human Rights 1970–93; mem. Lawyers' Cttee on Human Rights, Immigration and Refugee Services 1994–; Chair. Human Rights Inst., Columbia Law School 1999–; mem. Human Rights Cttee (UN) under ICCPR 1999–; numerous professional and public appts., affiliations and distinctions etc. –2002; Fellow, American Acad. of Arts and Sciences; mem. American Philosophical Soc., Council on Foreign Relations, American Soc. of Int. Law, Int. Law Asscn, Inst. de Droit Int., US Asscn of Constitutional Law etc.; Guggenheim Fellow 1979–80. *Publications:* numerous books and articles on constitutional law, constitutionalism, int. law, Law of the Sea and human rights including: How Nations Behave (2nd Edn) 1979, Constitutionalism and Rights: The Influence of the United States Abroad 1989, Foreign Affairs and the US Constitution 1990, International Law: Politics and Values 1995, Foreign Affairs and the US Constitution (2nd Edn) 1996, Human Rights (with others) 1999, International Law (with others) (4th Edn) 2001. *Address:* 460 Riverside Drive, New York, NY 10027, USA (Home). *Fax:* (212) 854-7946.

HENLE, Christian-Peter; German business executive; b. 9 Nov. 1938, Duisburg; s. of the late Günter Henle and of Anne-Liese Henle (née Küpper); brother of Jörg Alexander Henle (q.v.); m. Dr Susanne Beitz 1967; two s.; ed High School, Duisburg, Institut d'Etudes Politiques, Paris; joined Klöckner Eisenhandel GmbH, Düsseldorf 1963–64; with Klöckner and Co., Duisburg 1964–65, Vice-Pres. Klöckner Inc., New York 1965–67; Pres. Klöckner Industrie-Anlagen GmbH, Duisburg 1967–70; mem. Bd of Dirs. responsible for depts. for liquid fuels, motor fuels and lubricants, gas, chemicals, industrial plants, Klöckner and Co., Duisburg 1971–, partner 1977–; Chair. Supervisory Bd Klöckner-Humboldt-Deutz AG (KHD), Cologne, Mietfinanz GmbH, Mülheim/Ruhr; mem. Supervisory Bd KHD Humboldt Wedag AG, Cologne, Deutsche Babcock AG, Oberhausen, Gerling-Konzern Welt-Versicherungs-Pool AG, Cologne, Gerling-Konzern Globale Rückversicherungs-AG, Cologne, Knipping-Dorn GmbH, Herne; Chair. Advisory Bd Fisser & v. Doornum, Hamburg, Montan Brennstoffhandel und Schiffahrt GmbH & Co. KG, Munich; mem. Advisory Bd Dresdner Bank AG, Frankfurt, Arnold Knipping GmbH, Gummersbach; mem. of Bd Mineralölwirtschaftsverband e.V., Hamburg; mem. Int. Advisory Bd The American Univ., Washington, DC, USA; Pres. Deutsche Gesellschaft für Auswärtige Politik e.V., Bonn; Verdienstkreuz am Bande des Verdienstordens (FRG); Chevalier de l'Ordre du Mérite (Senegal). *Publication:* Auf dem Weg in ein neues Zeitalter (Ed. and Co-Author) 1985. *Leisure interests:* music, sports (tennis, golf), collecting contemporary works of art. *Address:* Klöckner & Co. AG, Klöckner Haus, Neudorfer Strasse 3–5, 47057 Duisburg, Germany. *Telephone:* (203) 182253.

HENLE, Jörg Alexander; German business executive; b. 12 May 1934, Aachen; s. of Dr. Günter and Anne-Liese (née Küpper) Henle; brother of Christian-Peter Henle (q.v.); one s. three d.; ed Cologne, Munich, Princeton (NJ), Stanford, Geneva and Berlin Univs; joined Klöckner-Werke AG 1962; Man. Establecimientos Klöckner SA, Buenos Aires 1964–65; Deputy mem. Directorate of Klöckner Mannstaedt-Werke, Troisdorf 1965–67; mem. Directorate, Klöckner-Werke AG, Hütte Bremen 1967–68; mem. Man. Bd. Klöckner-Werke AG 1968–71, Chair. Supervisory Bd 1979–92; Chair. Bd of Man. Klöckner & Co. AG 1971–92; Chair. Bd Peter-Klöckner-Stiftung, Duisburg 1992–; mem. Bd Stichting Verenigt Bezit, The Hague, Stichting HORIZON, The Hague, Int. Yehudi Menuhin Foundation, Brussels; fmr mem. Supervisory Bd Allianz Lebensversicherungs-AG, Deutsche Banks AG, Mietfinanz GmbH, AG, Robert Bosch GmbH, Readymix AG; fmr mem. Advisory Bd HERMES Kreditversicherungs-Aktiengesellschaft; fmr Vice-Pres. Niederrheinische Industrie- und Handelskammer Duisburg-Wesel-Kleve zu Duisburg; Bundesverdienstkreuz. *Leisure interests:* plastic arts, theatre, music. *Address:* Karlsbader Strasse 1, 14193 Berlin, Germany. *Fax:* (30) 8265228.

HENLEY, Elizabeth Becker, BFA, PhD; American playwright and actress; b. 8 May 1952, Jackson, Miss.; d. of Charles and Lydy Henley; ed Univ. of Illinois; Pulitzer Prize for Drama 1981, NY Drama Critics Circle Best Play Award 1981, George Oppenheimer/Newsday Playwriting Award 1980–81. *Publications:* Crimes of the Heart 1981, The Wake of Jamey Foster 1982, Am I Blue 1982, The Miss Firecracker Contest, The Debutante Ball 1985, The Lucky Spot 1987, Abundance 1989, The Debutante Ball 1991, Beth Henley: Monologues for Women 1992; screenplays: Nobody's Fool 1986, Crimes of the Heart 1986, Miss Firecracker 1989, Signatures (stage, film) 1990, Control Freaks (stage) 1993, Revelers (stage, film) 1994. *Address:* The William Morris Agency, 151 S. El Camino Drive, Beverly Hills, CA 90212, USA.

HENN, Walter, BArch, DrIng; German architect; b. 20 Dec. 1912, Reichenberg/Bez. Dresden; m. Dr Hilde Leistner 1938 (died 1995); two s. three d.; ed Technische Hochschule Dresden and Akad. der Bildenden Künste, Dresden; Prof. of Bldg and Industrial Construction, Technische Hochschule, Dresden 1946–53, Technische Hochschule, Braunschweig 1953– (Prof. Emer. 1982–); founder and dir of first inst. for industrial construction in Germany 1957–82; mem. Deutsche Wissenschaftsrat 1969; Foreign mem. Acad. of Eng of the Russian Fed. 1992–; mem. numerous comms., working parties etc; has undertaken bldgs. in Germany and elsewhere including industrial, admin. and school bldgs, research centres, electricity and water works etc.; mem. Mainz Acad.of Science and Literature, Braunschweig Scientific Soc.; Hon. Drtech. (T. U. Vienna); Hon. Dr-Ing. (T. U. Dresden), (Cracow Univ. of Tech.); Peter-Joseph-Krahe Prize, Braunschweig 1965. *Publications:* several books (translated in 11 languages) and more than 200 articles in professional journals. *Address:* Ramsachleite 13, 82418 Murnau, Germany. *Telephone:* (8841) 9531. *Fax:* (8841) 628994.

HENNEKINNE, Loïc; French diplomatist; b. 20 Sept. 1940, Caudéran, Gironde; s. of Michel Hennekinne and Elisabeth Declemy; m. 2nd Marie Bozelle 1987; one d.; two s. (by first m.); ed Ecole Nat. d'Admin; First Sec. French embassies in Vietnam 1969–71, Chile 1971–73; Minister-Counsellor, Japan 1979–81; Del. for External Action, Ministry of Industry 1981–82; Dir of Cabinet of Minister of Research and Industry 1982; Dir of Personnel and Admin. Ministry of Foreign Affairs 1983–86; Amb. to Indonesia 1986–88; Gen.

Sec. summit conf. of Western industrialized nations, Paris 1989; Diplomatic Adviser to Pres. Mitterrand 1989–91; Amb. to Japan 1991–93; Inspector-Gen. of Foreign Affairs 1993–96; Amb. to Canada 1997–98; Sec.-Gen. Ministry of Foreign Affairs (with rank of Amb. of France) 1998–2002; Amb. to Italy Aug. 2002–; Chevalier, Ordre nat. du Mérite, Officier, Légion d'honneur. *Leisure interest:* tennis. *Address:* Embassy of France, Piazza Farnese 67, 00186 Rome, Italy; 15 avenue Frochot, 75009 Paris, France (Home). *Telephone:* (06) 686011. *Fax:* (06) 68601360. *Website:* www.france-italia.it.

HENNESSY, Edward L., Jr., BS; American business executive; b. 22 March 1928, Boston, Mass.; s. of Edward L. Hennessy and Celina Mary Doucette; m. Ruth F. Schilling 1951; one s. one d.; ed Fairleigh Dickinson Univ., Rutherford, NJ and New York Univ. Law School; Asst Controller, Textron 1950–55; Group Controller, Eastern Electronics Group, Lear Siegler Inc. 1956–60; Controller, Int. Electronic Corpn, Int. Telephone & Telegraph Corpn 1960–61, Controller, Corporate Staff 1961–62, Controller, ITT Europe 1962–64; Dir of Finance, Europe, Middle East and Africa, Colgate Palmolive Co. 1964–65; Vice-Pres. Finance, Heublein Inc. 1965–68, Sr Vice-Pres. Admin. and Finance 1969–72; Dir United Technologies Corpn 1972–79, Sr Vice-Pres. Finance and Admin. 1972–77, Exec. Vice-Pres., Group Vice-Pres. Systems & Equipment Group and Chief Financial Office 1977–79; Chair., CEO and Pres. Allied Corpn 1979–; Chair. and CEO Allied-Signal Inc. 1985–91; Dir Martin Marietta Corpn, Bank of New York, Coast Guard Foundation; Trustee, Fairleigh Dickinson Univ., Catholic Univ. of America. *Leisure interests:* sailing, tennis, reading. *Address:* P.O. Box 3000 R, Morristown, NJ 07960, USA.

HENNESSY, John Basil, AO, DPhil, DLitt, FSA, FAHA; Australian archaeologist; b. 10 Feb. 1925, Horsham, Vic.; s. of Thomas B. Hennessy and Nellie M. Poultney; m. Ruth M. R. Shannon 1954; one s. two d.; ed Villa Maria & St Patrick's Coll. Ballarat, Univ. of Sydney and Magdalen Coll. Oxford; lecturer, Near Eastern Archaeology, Univ. of Sydney 1955–61; Asst Dir British School of Archaeology, Jerusalem 1965–66, Dir 1966–70; Edwin Cuthbert Hall Visiting Prof. of Middle Eastern Archaeology, Univ. of Sydney 1970–72, Edwin Cuthbert Hall Prof. 1973–90, Prof. Emer. 1991–, also Hon. Assoc. School of Archaeology, Classics and Ancient History; Dir Australian Foundation for Near Eastern Archaeology 1973–91, Gov. 1992–; Gov. Cyprus Research Centre 1992–; Dir of Excavations Sphagion, Stephania (Cyprus) 1951, Damascus Gate, Jerusalem 1964–66, Amman 1966, Teleilat Ghassul (Jordan) 1967–77, Samaria 1968, Pella (Jordan) 1978–88. *Publications:* Stephania 1964, The Foreign Relations of Palestine During the Early Bronze Age 1967, World Ceramics, The Ancient Near East 1968, The Arab States in the Modern World 1977–79, Masterpieces of Western Ceramics 1978, Pella in Jordan 1982, Archaeology of Jordan I 1986, Ayia Paraskevi and Vasilia 1988, Archaeology of Jordan II 1989. *Address:* 497 Old Windsor Road, Kellyville, NSW, 2155, Australia. *Telephone:* 9629-1514 (Home).

HENRI, HRH Grand Duke of Luxembourg, Albert Félix Marie Guillaume, L. ES. SC.POL.; Luxembourg head of state; b. 16 April 1955, Château de Betzdorf; s. of Jean Benoît Guillaume Marie Robert Louis Antoine Adolphe Marc d'Aviano, HRH fmr Grand Duke of Luxembourg and Princess Josephine-Charlotte of Belgium; m. Maria Teresa Mestre 1981; four s. one d.; ed Royal Mil. Acad. Sandhurst, Univ. of Geneva; mem. State Council 1980–98; apptd. Lt Rep. of Grand Duke March 1988; succeeded father as Grand Duke of Luxembourg Oct. 2000; Chair. Bd of Econ. Devt, Galapagos Darwin Trust Luxembourg; Pres. Organizing Cttee, Int. Trade Fairs of Luxembourg; mem. Mentor Foundation, Int. Olympic Cttee; Hon. Maj. Parachute Regt; Hon. Dr rer. pol (Trier); Hon. DHumLitt (Sacred Heart); Hon. LLD (Miami), Hon. D. Econ. (Khon Kaen). *Leisure interests:* reading, listening to classical music, skiing, swimming, water skiing, tennis, hunting. *Address:* Grand Ducal Palace, 2013 Luxembourg, Luxembourg (Home).

HENRICH, Dieter, DPhil; German professor of philosophy; b. 5 Jan. 1927, Marburg; s. of Hans Harry Henrich and Frieda Henrich; m. Dr. Bettina von Eckardt 1975; two d.; ed Univ. of Heidelberg; Prof. Freie Univ. Berlin 1960–65, Univ. of Heidelberg 1965–81; now. Prof. of Philosophy, Univ. of Munich; Visiting Prof. Columbia Univ. 1968–72, Univ. of Mich. 1969, Harvard Univ. 1973–86, Tokyo Univ. 1979, Yale Univ. 1987; mem. Heidelberg and Bavarian Acads; Hon. Prof. Humboldt Univ., Berlin 1997; Hon. Foreign mem. American Acad. of Arts and Sciences; Hon. DTheol (Münster) 1999, (Marburg) 2002; Hoelderlin Prize 1995. *Publications:* Der ontologische Gottesbeweis 1960, Fichtes ursprüngliche Einsicht, 1967, Hegel im Kontext 1971, Identität und Objektivität 1976, Fluchtlinien 1982, Der Gang des Andenkens 1986, Konzepte 1987, Ethik zum nuklearen Frieden 1990, Konstellationen 1991, Der Grund im Bewusstsein 1992, The Moral Image of the World 1992, The Unity of Reason 1994, I. C. Diez 1997, Bewusstes Leben 1999, Versuch über Kunst und Leben 2001, Fixpunkte 2003. *Address:* Gerlichstrasse 7A, 81245 Munich, Germany. *Telephone:* (89) 8119131. *Fax:* (89) 81179878.

HENRY, André Armand; French teacher, trade union official and politician; b. 15 Oct. 1934, Fontenoy-le-Château; s. of Alice Henry; m. Odile Olivier 1956; one s. one d.; ed Cours Complémentaire de Bains-les-Bains, Ecole normale d'instituteurs, Mirecourt; teacher, Fontenoy-le-Château 1955–56, Thaon-les-Vosges 1956–69; began trade union career with Syndicat Nat. des Instituteurs (SNI), Training Coll. Rep. (Vosges) 1954, mem Exec. Comm. (Vosges) 1955–69, Asst Sec.-Gen. 1960–63, Sec.-Gen. 1963–69, mem. Nat. Council, SNI 1965–74, Perm. Sec. 1969–74; in charge of youth, then gen. admin. section of SNI; mem. Fed. Council, in charge of culture, youth and leisure sections, Fédération de l'éducation nationale (FEN) 1971, Perm. Sec. and Sec.-Gen.

1974–81; Minister for Free Time 1981–83; Délégué Général à l'économie sociale 1983–; Chair. and Man. Dir Caisse Nat. de l'Energie 1984–87; Inspecteur Général de l'administration de l'education nat. 1989-95; Nat. Vice-Pres. Association laïque pour l'éducation et la formation professionelle des adolescents (ALEFPA) 1995, then Pres.; Délégué départemental de l'education nationale; Vice-Pres. Mission Laïque française –2001; Commdr, Ordre du Mérite; Chevalier, Légion d'honneur, Chevalier des Palmes académiques. *Publications:* Dame l'école 1977, Serviteurs d'idéal (2 vols) 1988, Conquérir l'avenir 1992, Le Ministre qui voulait changer la vie 1996. *Leisure interests:* football, volleyball, photography, flying light aircraft. *Address:* 1 bis rue de l'Espérance, 94000 Créteil, France (Home). *Telephone:* 1-48-99-37-79. *Fax:* 1-48-99-37-79 (Office); 1-48-99-37-79.

HENRY, Brad; American state official and lawyer; b. Shawnee; m. Kimberley Henry (née Blain); three d.; ed Shawnee High School, Univ. of Okla; est. law firm Henry, Canavan & Hopkins PLLC; mem. Senate, Okla 1992–2002, Chair. Senate Judiciary Cttee; Gov. of Okla 2003–; mem. Pottawatomie Co. Bar Asscn, Okla Bar Asscn, Norman Chamber of Commerce; Dir Shawnee Chamber of Commerce; mem. Bd Trustees, St Gregories Coll.; Letzeiser Gold Medal Award, Outstanding Young Oklahoman 1997. *Address:* Office of the Governor, 212 State Capitol Building, Oklahoma City, OK 73105, USA (Office).

HENRY, Rev. Carl F. H., ThD, PhD; American theologian and author; b. 22 Jan. 1913, New York; s. of Karl F. Henry and Johanna (Vaethroeder) Henry; m. Helga I. Bender 1940; one s. (died 1993) one d.; ed Wheaton Coll., Ill., Northern Baptist Theological Seminary, Boston Univ., New Coll., Edinburgh and King's Coll., Cambridge; Prof. of Theology, Northern Baptist Theological Seminary, Chicago 1942–47; Prof. of Theology and Christian Philosophy, Fuller Theological Seminary 1947–56; Ed. Christianity Today 1956–68; Visiting Prof. of Theology, Eastern Baptist Theological Seminary 1968–70, Prof.-at-Large 1970–74; Lecturer-at-Large, World Vision Int. 1974–87; Visiting Prof. of Theology, Calvin Theological Seminary 1986, Trinity Evangelical Divinity School 1987–96, Tyndale Seminary, Netherlands 1990; Sr Research Prof., Southern Baptist Theological Seminary 1994–96; Corresp. World Magazine 1995–; Chair. World Congress on Evangelism, Berlin 1966; Program Chair. Jerusalem Conf. on Biblical Prophecy 1971; Pres. Evangelical Theological Soc. 1969–70, American Theological Soc. 1974–75, Inst. for Advanced Christian Studies 1971–74, 1976–79; Vice-Pres. Inst. for Religion and Democracy 1984–96; Sec. Carl F. H. Henry Study and Resource Centre; visiting lecturer Southern Baptist Theological Seminary 1998–; mem. Bd ME Foundation, Prison Fellowship Ministries 1991–98, Riverside Foundation; mem. Bd of Judges, Amy Foundation, writing awards 1989–; Fellow Christianity Today Inst. 1987–94; numerous hon. degrees; Religious Heritage of America Gold Award for 50 years of Spiritual and Moral Leadership 1993; Distinguished Alumnus Award for contrib. in Theology, Boston Univ. 1998. *Publications:* author of 45 books, including God, Revelation and Authority (6 Vols). *Leisure interests:* writing, browsing in antique shops. *Address:* 1141 Hus Drive (Apt. 206), Watertown, WI 53098, USA. *Telephone:* (920) 262-2251. *Fax:* (920) 262-2251.

HENRY, Sir Geoffrey Arama, KBE; Cook Islands politician; b. 16 Nov. 1940, Aitutaki; s. of Arama Henry and Mata Uritaua; m. Louisa Olga Hoff 1965; four s. two d.; ed Wanganui Collegiate School, Victoria Univ., Wellington, NZ; school teacher 1965–67; active in politics 1965–68; public service 1970–72; returned to politics, Cabinet Minister 1972–78; Leader of Opposition 1978–89; Prime Minister 1983, Deputy Prime Minister in Coalition Govt 1984, Prime Minister and Minister of Police, State-owned Enterprises, Tourism and Transport 1989–99; organizer Jt Commercial Comm., USA and Pacific Islands 1990; Chair. Econ. Summit of Small Island States 1992; Chancellor Univ. of S Pacific 1992; Leader of the Opposition 1999; Deputy Prime Minister 2002, Minister of Finance, Offshore Financial Services Police, PERCA (Audit Commission); Silver Jubilee Medal 1977, NZ Commemoration Medal 1990. *Leisure interests:* golf, rugby and other sports, reading, music. *Address:* Office of the Deputy Prime Minister, POB 138, Avarua, Rarotonga, Cook Islands (Office). *Telephone:* (682) 29033 (Office). *Fax:* (682) 29034 (Office). *E-mail:* henry@dpmoffice.gov.ck.

HENRY, Lenny, CBE; British comedian and actor; b. 29 Aug. 1958; m. Dawn French (q.v.); numerous tours including Loud! UK and Australia 1994 and 1995, Large! UK, Australia and NZ 1998; Monaco Red Cross Award, The Golden Nymph Award (for Alive and Kicking) 1992, BBC Personality of the Year, Radio and Television Industry Club 1993, Golden Rose of Montreux Award for Lenny in Pieces (Christmas Special) 2000. *Television includes:* New Faces (debut) 1975, Tiswas 1978, 1979, 1980, Three of a Kind 1981–83, Coast to Coast 1990, The Lenny Henry Show 1984, 1985, Alive and Kicking 1991, Bernard and the Genie 1991, In Dreams 1992, The Real McCoy 1992, Chef (title role) (three series), Lenny Hunts the Funk, New Soul Nation, White Goods 1994, Funky Black Shorts 1994, Comic Relief, Lenny Go Home 1996, British Acad. Awards (host) 1997, Lenny's Big Amazon Adventure 1997, Lenny Goes to Town 1998, The Delbert Wilkins Show 1987, 1988, The Man 1999, Hope and Glory 1999, 2000, Lenny's Atlantic Adventure 2000, Lenny in Pieces (Christmas Special) 2000, Lenny in Pieces (Christmas Special) 2001. *Films include:* True Identity 1991. *Videos:* Lenny Henry Live and Unleashed 1989, Lenny Henry Live and Loud 1994. *Publications:* The Quest for the Big Woof (autobiog.) 1991, Charlie and the Big Chill (children's book) 1995.

Address: c/o PBJ Management Ltd, 7 Soho Street, London, W1D 3DQ, England. *Telephone:* (20) 7287-1112. *Fax:* (20) 7287-1191. *E-mail:* general@pbjmgt.co.uk (Office). *Website:* www.pbjmgt.co.uk (Office).

HENRY, Pierre; French composer; b. 9 Dec. 1927, Paris; s. of Georges Henry and Germaine Mazet; m. Isabelle Warnier 1971; one d. and one s. by previous m.; ed Conservatoire Nat. Supérieur de Musique and studies with Nadia Boulanger, Olivier Messiaen and Félix Passerone; head of group researching concrete music, ORTF 1950–58; Founder and Dir Studio Apsome 1959–; Founder, Asscn for Electro-acoustic Composition and Research 1972; cr. Son et Recherche Asscn 1982; Commdr Légion d'honneur, Officier, Ordre Nat. du Mérite, Commdr des Arts et des Lettres; Grand Prix, Acad. du Disque 1966; Grand Prix, Acad. Charles Cros 1970; Grand Prix Nat. de la Musique 1985; Grand Prix de la Musique Symphonique (Sacem) 1987; Victoires de la Musique 1998, Grand Prix Karl Sczuka 1997, etc. *Works include:* Symphonie pour un homme seul 1950, Messe de Liverpool 1967, Messe pour le temps présent 1970, Deuxième Symphonie 1972, Nijinsky, clown de Dieu (ballet by Maurice Béjart) 1973, Dieu, action de voix, de sons et de gestes (spectacular, Lille 1977, Paris 1978), Hommage à Beethoven 1979, Les noces chymiques, rituel féerique en 12 journées (Opéra comique) 1980, Paradis perdus 1982, Berlin, symphonie d'une grande ville (film, concert) 1987, Livre des morts égyptien 1988, Une maison de sons 1990, Maldoror-Feuilleton 1992, L'homme à la caméra (film/concert) 1993, Une ample comédie à cent actes divers: Hommage à La Fontaine 1995, Intérieur/Extérieur 1996, Schubert 97 (1997), Histoire naturelle 1997, La Xème remix 1998, L'homme au microphone 1999, Tam tam du merveilleux 2000, Concerto sans orchestre 2000. *Address:* 32 rue Toul, 75012 Paris, France.

HENRY, Thierry Daniel; French footballer; b. 17 Aug. 1977, Paris; signed as schoolboy player, Versailles football club; striker, Ulis (Paris), Monaco 1990–98, Juventus (Italy) 1998–99, Arsenal (England) Aug. 1999–; mem. French nat. team; PFA Player of the Year 2003, Football Writers' Asscn Footballer of the Year 2003. *Address:* c/o Arsenal Football Club, Arsenal Stadium, Avenell Road, Highbury, London, N5 1BU, England (Office). *Telephone:* (20) 7704-4000 (Office). *Fax:* (20) 7704-4001 (Office). *Website:* www.arsenal.com (Office).

HENRY de VILLENEUVE, Xavier, LenD; French banker; b. 8 July 1932, Quintin; s. of Jacques Henry de Villeneuve and Yvonne de la Motte de la Motte Rouge; m. Simone de Vigneral 1963; two s. one d.; ed Ecole des Frères, Quintin, Coll. des Cordeliers, Dinan, Coll. St Charles, St Brieuc and Faculté de Droit, Rennes; joined Banque de Bretagne 1959, Asst Dir-Gen. 1971, Dir-Gen. 1979, Pres. and Man. Dir 1986; Pres. and Man. Dir, Banque de la Cité 1978–82, Pres. 1983–85, Hon. Pres., Admin. 1991; Pres. Comm. des Affaires Sociales of Asscn Française des Banques 1988, Pres. Compagnie Financière de Participation 1988, Ronceray 1991–93, ACLPME 1995–98, ACLPME Finances 1997–98; Vice-Pres. Asscn d'Eloge 1995–96, Résidences ACL 1997–98; Pres. Diocesan Cttee of Catholic Educ., Nanterre (Codiec 92) 1999–; Chevalier, Légion d'honneur, des Arts et des Lettres, Ordre du Saint-Sépulcre de Jérusalem. *Publication:* Contes et nouvelles des quatre vents. *Leisure interests:* the arts, reading, old wars, hunting. *Address:* 19 rue de la Convention, 75015 Paris (Home); Kerbic, 22200 Pommerit-le-Vicomte, France (Home).

HENRYSSON, Haraldur; Icelandic judge; b. 17 Feb. 1938, Reykjavik; m. Elisabet Kristinsdóttir 1972; one s.; ed Reykjavik High School, Univ. of Iceland; Asst Judge 1964–73; Judge Criminal Court, Reykjavik 1973–89, Supreme Court 1989–, Pres. 1996–97; Chair. Cttee Investigating Accidents at Sea 1973–83; Pres. Nat. Life Saving Asscn 1982–90; Vice-mem. Althing 1967–71; Kt Grand Cross of Icelandic Falcon. *Leisure interests:* outdoor sports. *Address:* Hæstirettur Islands, Domhus v. Arnarhol, 150 Reykjavik, Iceland. *Telephone:* 510-3030. *Fax:* 562-3995.

HENSCHEL, Jane Elizabeth, BA; American opera singer; b. 2 March 1952, Appleton, Wis.; d. of Lester Haentzschel and Betty Haentzschel (née Lau); ed Univ. of Southern California; debut with the Netherlands Opera as the Nurse in Die Frau ohne Schatten 1992; ensemble mem. Aachen Oper 1977–80; joined Wuppertal Opera, Germany 1980, later with Dortmund and Düsseldorf Operas; appearances at the Glyndebourne, Salzburg and Saito Kinen Festivals and at La Scala, Milan, Deutsche Oper, Berlin, Amsterdam Opera, Paris Opera, Bayerische Staatsoper, Munich, Staatsoper, Berlin, Royal Opera House, Covent Garden, London and the San Francisco Opera; has performed with numerous conductors including Seiji Ozawa, Sir Colin Davis, Daniel Barenboim, Bernard Haitink, Riccardo Muti, Christian Thielemann, Sir Andrew Davis, Lorin Maazel; Baroque repertoire includes Vivaldi's oratorio Juditha Triumphans (Radio France). *Operatic roles include:* Die Amme (the nurse) in Die Frau ohne Schatten (Netherlands Opera, Royal Opera House, London 1992, Los Angeles, Bavarian State Opera, Munich, Vienna, Paris, Deutsche Oper Berlin), Fricka in Das Rheingold and Die Walküre (Royal Opera House, London 1996), Ulrica in Un Ballo in Maschera (Royal Opera House, London), Klytemnestra in Elektra (Bavarian State Opera, Munich, Royal Opera House, London), Herodias in Salome (Bavarian State Opera, Munich, La Scala, Milan, San Francisco Opera), Brangäne in Tristan und Isolde (Orange Festival, Los Angeles Music Center Opera, Paris Opera), Queen of Sheba in Königin von Saba (Concertgebouw, Amsterdam), Genevieve in Pelléas et Mélisande (Japan), Cassandre in Les Troyens (La Scala, Milan), Waltraute in Götterdämmerung (Royal Opera House, London), Mrs Grose in The Turn of the Screw (Royal Opera House, London), Judy in

Birtwistle's Punch and Judy (Netherlands Opera 1993), Kostelnicka in Jenufa (Japan), Mistress Quickly in Falstaff (Vienna, Munich, with the London Symphony Orchestra), The Witch in Rusalka, Ottavia in L'Incoronazione di Poppea (Aachen Oper), Amneris, Eboli, Ortrud, Erda, Carmen, Azucena, Venus. *Recordings include:* Mahler's 8th Symphony, The Rake's Progress, Die Verlobung im Traum, Die Drei Groschen Oper. *Leisure interests:* reading, concerts. *Address:* c/o Music International, 13 Ardilaun Road, London, N5 2QR, England (Office).

HENSON, Lisa; American film company executive; b. 1961; d. of the late Jim Henson and of Jane Henson; ed Harvard Univ.; joined Warner Bros. as Exec. Asst to Head of Production 1983, apptd. Dir of Creative Affairs 1985, Exec. Vice-Pres. (Production) 1992; Pres. (Production) Columbia Pictures 1993, Studio Pres. 1994–. *Address:* Columbia Pictures, 3400 Riverside Drive, Burbank, CA 91505, USA.

HENZE, Hans Werner; German composer and conductor; b. 1 July 1926, Gütersloh; s. of Franz Henze and Margarete Geldmacher; ed Staatsmusikschule, Braunschweig, Kirchenmusikalisches Institut, Heidelberg; Musical collaborator Deutsches Theater in Konstanz 1948; Artistic Dir and Conductor Ballet of the Hessian State Theatre in Wiesbaden 1950; living in Italy as an ind. artist since 1953; Prof. of Composition, Mozarteum, Salzburg 1962–67; Prof. of Composition, Hochschule für Musik, Cologne 1980–91; Artistic Dir Accad. Filarmonica Romana 1982–91; Prof. of Composition RAM, London 1987–91; mem. Akad. der Künste, Berlin 1960–68, Bayerische Akad. der Schönen Künste, Munich, Akad. der Künste, Hamburg; Hon. FRNCM 1998; Hon. DrMus. (Edin.) 1971; Robert Schumann Prize 1951, North-Rhine-Westphalia Art Prize 1957, Prix d'Italia 1954, Sibelius Gold Medal, Harriet Cohen Awards, London 1956, Music Critics Prize, Buenos Aires 1958, Kunstpreis, Berlin, Niedersächsischer Kunstpreis 1962, Ludwig-Spohr-Preis 1976, Heidelberg-Bach-Preis 1983, Siemens-Preis 1990, Preis des Internationales Theaterinstituts 1991, Grosses Bundesverdienst-kreuz 1991, Kultureller Ehrenpreis, Munich 1996, Hans-von-Bülow Medal of the Berlin Philharmonic Orchestra 1997, Bayerischer Maximiliansorden für Wissenschaft und Kunst 1998, Praemium imperiale, Tokyo 2000, Best Living Composer, Cannes Classical Award 2001, German Dance Prize 2001. *Compositions include:* operas: Das Wundertheater 1948, Boulevard Solitude 1951, König Hirsch 1953, Der Prinz von Homburg 1958, Elegy for Young Lovers 1959, Der Junge Lord 1964, Die Bassariden 1964, Der langwierige Weg in die Wohnung des Natascha Ungeheuer 1971, La Cubana 1973, We Come to the River 1974, Don Chischiotte 1976, Pollicino 1979, The English Cat 1980, Il ritorno d'Ulisse in Patria 1981, Das verratene Meer 1986, Il re Teodoro in Venezia 1991, Venus and Adonis 1993; radio operas: Ein Landarzt 1964, Das Ende einer Welt 1964; ballets: Variationen 1949, Das Vokaltuch der Kammersängerin Rosa Silber 1950, The Idiot 1952, Maratona 1956, Undine 1956, Des Kaisers Nachtigall 1959, Tancredi 1964, Orpheus 1978, Le disperazioni del Signor Pulcinella 1992, Le fils de l'air 1995, Labyrinth 1996; oratorios: Novae de Infinito Laudes 1962, The Raft of the Medusa 1968; cantatas: Being Beauteous 1963, Ariosi 1963, Cantata della Fiaba Estrema 1963; vocal music: Nachtstücke and Arien 1957, Kammermusik 1958, Lieder von einer Insel 1964, Musen Siziliens 1966, Versuch über Schweine 1968, El Cimarrón 1969, Voices 1973, Jephte 1976, El Rey de Harlem 1979, Paraphrasen über Dostoiewsky 1990, Richard Wagnersche Klavierlieder 1998; nine Symphonies, Violin and Piano and Violoncello Concertos, Double Concerto for Oboe, Harp and Strings, five String Quartets, Quattro Fantaisie 1958, Heliogabalus Imperator 1971, Tristan 1974, Ragtimes and Habaneras 1975, Aria de la Folía española 1977, Barcarola 1979, Requiem 1990, Quintetto 1990, Fünf Nachtstücke 1990, Sieben Boleros 1998, Trio in drei Sätzen 1998, Fraternité 1999, L'Heure bleue 2001, Scornbanda 2001, 10th Symphony 2002. *Publications:* Das Ende einer Welt 1953, Undine, Tagebuch eines Balletts 1959, Essays 1964, El Cimarrón: ein Werkstattbericht 1971, Musik und Politik 1976, Die Englische Katze—Ein Arbeitsbuch 1978–82 1983, Reiselieder mit böhmischen Quinten 1996, Komponieren in der Schule 1998, Bohemian Fifths: An Autobiography (trans. by Stewart Spencer) 1998. *Leisure interests:* poetry, botany. *Address:* c/o Künstler Sekretariat Christa Pfeffer, Schongauer Str. 22, 81377 Munich, Germany (Office); c/o Chester Music, 8/9 Frith Street, London, W1D 3JB, England. *Telephone:* (6131) 246884 (Mainz), (20) 7342-4238 (London), (89) 718041 (Munich) (Office). *Fax:* (6131) 246250 (Mainz), (20) 7287-6329 (London) (Office). *E-mail:* com@schott-musik.de; wiebke.busch@musicsales.co.uk (Office). *Website:* www.hanswernerhenze.de (Home).

HEPBURN, Katharine; American actress; b. 12 May 1907, Hartford, Conn.; d. of the late Dr Thomas N. Hepburn and Katharine Houghton; m. Ludlow Ogden Smith (divorced); ed Bryn Mawr Coll., Pa; professional stage actress since 1928; film actress since 1932; also appears on TV; received Gold Medal for Best Film Actress, Venice 1934, Whistler Soc. Award 1957; Lifetime Achievement Award (Annual American Comedy Awards) 1989; four Acad. Awards (Oscars). *Stage plays include:* The Lake, The Philadelphia Story, Without Love 1942, As You Like It 1950, The Millionairess 1952, The Taming of the Shrew 1955, The Merchant of Venice 1955, Much Ado About Nothing 1955, Coco (musical) 1970 (on tour 1971), A Matter of Gravity 1976 (on tour 1977), The West Side Waltz 1981. *Films include:* A Bill of Divorcement 1932, Morning Glory 1933 (Acad. Award 1934), Little Women 1933, Alice Adams 1935, Sylvia Scarlett 1935, Mary of Scotland 1936, A Woman Rebels 1936, Quality Street 1937, Stage Doors 1937, Bringing Up Baby 1938, Holiday 1938, The Philadelphia Story (NY Critics' Award) 1940, Woman of the Year 1942, Keeper of the Flame 1942, Undercurrent 1946, Sea of Grass 1947, State of the

Union 1948, Adam's Rib 1949, The African Queen 1951, Pat and Mike 1952, Summer Madness 1955, The Rainmaker 1956, Desk Set 1957, Suddenly Last Summer 1959, Long Day's Journey Into Night 1962, Guess Who's Coming to Dinner? 1967 (Acad. Award 1968), The Lion in Winter 1968 (Acad. Award 1969), The Madwoman of Chaillot 1969, The Trojan Women 1971, A Delicate Balance 1973, The Glass Menagerie (TV) 1973, Love Among the Ruins (TV) 1975, Rooster Cogburn 1975, Olly Olly Oxen Free 1976, The Corn is Green (TV) 1979, Christopher Strong 1980, On Golden Pond 1981 (Acad. Award 1982), The Ultimate Solution of Grace Quigley 1984, Mrs. Delafield Wants to Marry (TV) 1986, Laura Lansing Slept Here (TV) 1988, The Man Upstairs (TV) 1992, Love Affair 1993, This Can't Be Love (TV) 1994, One Christmas 1994. *Publication:* The Making of The African Queen 1987, Me (autobiog.) 1991. *Address:* James D. Miller Ltd, 350 5th Avenue, Suite 5019, New York, NY 10118, USA.

HEPPELL, (Thomas) Strachan, C.B.; British public service official; b. 15 Aug. 1935, Teesside; s. of the late Leslie Heppell and Doris Potts; m. Felicity Rice 1963; two s.; ed Acklam Hall Grammar School, Middlesbrough and Queen's Coll. Oxford; Asst Prin. Nat. Assistance Bd (NAB) 1958; Prin. NAB, Cabinet Office, Dept of Health and Social Security (DHSS) 1963; Asst Dir of Social Welfare, Hong Kong 1971–73; Asst Sec. DHSS 1973, Under-Sec. 1979; Deputy Sec. DHSS, Dept of Health 1983–95; Chair. Man. Bd European Medicines Evaluation Agency (EMEA) 1994–2000; consultant, Dept of Health 1995–2000; mem. Broadcasting Standards Comm. 1996–; Chair. Family Fund Trust 1997–; Visiting Fellow LSE 1996–2000. *Publications:* contribs. to Publs on social security, social welfare, health and pharmaceuticals. *Address:* c/o Broadcasting Standards Commission, 7 The Sanctuary, London, SW1P 3JC, England. *Telephone:* (20) 7233-0544. *Fax:* (20) 7233-0397.

HEPTULLA, Najma, MSc, PhD; Indian politician and international organization executive; b. 13 April 1940; m.; three d.; Deputy Chair. Rajya Sabha (Upper House of Parl.) 1985–86, 1988–; Gen.-Sec. All India Congress Cttee (I) 1986–87, Spokesperson 1986–87, 1998; Special Envoy of the Prime Minister on numerous missions abroad; mem. Exec. Cttee Inter-Parliamentary Union (IPU) 1995–2002, Vice-Pres. 1999, Acting Pres. IPU Council July-Oct. 1999, Pres. 1999–2002, Hon. Pres. 2002–; Chair. Meeting of Women Parliamentarians 1993, mem. Co-ordinating Cttee 1993–; Founder-Pres. Parliamentarians' Forum for Human Devt 1993; Head. Indian Del. to UN Comm. on the Status of Women 1997; Pres. Indian Housewives Fed. 1985–, Azad Foundation for Research and Devt, Indo–Arab Soc.; mem. Nat. Integration Council, Exec. Cttee Indian Council for Cultural Relations (ICCR); Distinguished Human Devt Amb. for UNDP. *Publications include:* Indo–West Asian Relations: The Nehru Era 1992, Reforms for Women: Future Options 1992, Environmental Protection in Developing Countries 1993, Human Social Security and Sustainable Development 1995, AIDS: Approaches to Prevention 1996. *Address:* c/o Inter-Parliamentary Union, CP 438, 1211 Geneva 19, Switzerland (Office).

HERBEN, Mat; Netherlands politician; b. 1953; started career as spokesman Freemason's lodge; fmr spokesman Ministry of Defence, Ed. Ministry of Defence staff magazine; fmr journalist; joined Pim Fortuyn List party (LPF) 2002, Spokesman and Leader May 2002–. *Address:* Pim Fortuyn List (LPF), Vlaardingweg 62, Rotterdam, 3044 CK, Netherlands (Office). *Telephone:* (10) 7507050 (Office). *Fax:* (10) 7507057 (Office). *E-mail:* info@lijst-pimfortuyn.nl (Office). *Website:* www.lijst-pimfortuyn.nl (Office).

HERBERT, Rt Rev. Christopher William, FRSA, BA, MPhil; British ecclesiastic; b. 7 Jan. 1944, Lydney, Glos.; s. of Walter Herbert and the late Hilda Dibben; m. Janet Turner 1968; two s.; ed Monmouth School, Univ. of Wales, Lampeter, Univ. of Bristol and Wells Theological Coll., Univ. of Leicester; Curate, St Paul's, Tupsley, Hereford 1967–71; Adviser in Religious Educ. Diocese of Hereford 1971–76, Dir of Educ. 1976–81; Vicar, St Thomas on the Bourne, Diocese of Guildford 1981–90; Dir of Post-Ordination Training, Diocese of Guildford 1984–90; Archdeacon of Dorking 1990–95; Bishop of St Albans 1995–. *Publications include:* Be Thou My Vision 1985, This Most Amazing Day 1986, The Question of Jesus 1987, Alive to God 1987, Ways Into Prayer 1987, Help in Your Bereavement 1988, Prayers for Children 1993, Pocket Prayers 1993, The Prayer Garden 1994, Words of Comfort 1994, A Little Prayer Diary 1996, Pocket Prayers for Children 1999. *Leisure interests:* cycling, reading, writing, walking, art history. *Address:* Abbey Gate House, St Albans, Herts., AL3 4HD, England. *Telephone:* (1727) 853305. *Fax:* (1727) 846715.

HERBERT, Sir Walter William (Wally), Kt; British explorer, writer and painter; b. 24 Oct. 1934, York; s. of Capt. W. W. J. Herbert and Helen Manton; m. Marie McGaughey 1969; two d. (one deceased); trained as surveyor, Royal Engineers 1950–53, Egypt 1953–54; Surveyor with Falkland Islands Dependencies Survey based at Hope Bay, Antarctica 1955–58; travelled in S and N America 1958; expedition to Lapland and Spitsbergen 1960; Surveyor with NZ Antarctic Expedition mapping routes of Capt. Scott and Capt. Amundsen 1960–62; Leader Expedition to NW Greenland 1967–68; Leader of British Trans-Arctic Expedition 1968–69, which made first surface crossing of Arctic Ocean from Alaska to Spitsbergen via North Pole by dog sledges; Leader Expedition to NW Greenland 1971–73, to Lapland 1974, several expeditions to NW Greenland 1975–87; second visit to N Pole April 1987, third visit Aug. 1991; Lecturer on cruise ships to Arctic and Antarctic 1989–99; total of 15 years spent in Arctic and Antarctic wilderness regions, travelling 23,000 miles with dog teams; Jt Hon. Pres., World Expeditionary Asscn; Hon. Vice-

Patron British Schools Exporing Soc.; Polar Medal 1962 and Clasp 1969, Livingstone Gold Medal, Royal Scottish Geographical Soc. 1969, Founder's Gold Medal, Royal Geographical Soc. 1970, City of Paris Medal 1983, French Geographical Soc. Medal 1983, Explorer's Medal, Explorer's Club 1985, Finn Ronne Award for Antarctic Exploration 1985. *Films:* Across the Top of the World, 1969; The Noose of Laurels 1988; The Last Great Journey on Earth 2002. *Exhibitions:* one-man shows of paintings at the Royal Geographical Soc. 1994, 2000, Explorers Club, New York 1994, QE-2 1994, 1995, Australian Geographical Soc. 1995, Traveller's Club, London 1997, Atlas Studio Gallery, London 1999. *Radio:* Travellers Tales (several) 1959–60. *Publications:* A World of Men 1968, Across the Top of the World 1969, The Last Great Journey on Earth 1971, Polar Deserts 1971, Eskimos 1976, North Pole 1978, Hunters of the Polar North 1982, The Noose of Laurels 1989, The Third Pole 2002; and contribs to several other books. *Leisure interest:* painting. *Address:* c/o Royal Geographical Society, 1 Kensington Gore, London, SW7 2AR, England; Rowan Cottage, Catlodge, Laggan, Invernessshire, PH20 1AH, Scotland (Home). *Telephone:* (1582) 544396 (Home). *Fax:* (1582) 544396. *E-mail:* polarman@ndirect.co.uk (Home). *Website:* www.sirwallyherbert.com (Home).

HERBIG, George Howard, PhD; American astronomer; b. 2 Jan. 1920, Wheeling, W Va; s. of George A. Herbig and Glenna Howard; m. 1st Delia McMullin 1943 (divorced 1968); three s. one d.; m. 2nd Hannelore Tillmann 1968; ed Univ. of California (Los Angeles and Berkeley); Jr Astronomer, Lick Observatory, Mount Hamilton, Calif. 1948–50, Asst Astronomer 1950–55, Assoc. Astronomer 1955–60, Astronomer 1960–87; Asst Dir Lick Observatory 1960–63, Acting Dir 1970–71; Prof. of Astronomy, Univ. of Calif. (Santa Cruz) 1967–87; Astronomer, Inst. for Astronomy, Univ. of Hawaii 1987–2001, Astronomer Emer. 2001–; Visiting Prof. and Lecturer Chicago 1959, Mexico 1961, Observatoire de Paris 1965, Max-Planck-Institut für Astronomie, Heidelberg 1969, Stockholm 1973, Hawaii 1976–77; mem. NAS, astronomy del. to People's Repub. of China 1977; Henry Norris Russell Lecturer, American Astronomical Soc. 1975; lectured in USSR and Poland under exchange agreement, US-USSR Acads. of Science 1965, 1987; US NSF Sr Postdoctoral Fellow 1965; mem. NAS, American Acad. of Arts and Sciences; Corresp. mem. Société scientifique Royale de Liège; Foreign Scientific mem., Max-Planck-Inst. für Astronomie, Heidelberg; Warner Prize, American Astronomical Soc. 1955, Medaille, Univ. de Liège 1969, Gold Medal, Astronomical Soc. of Pacific 1980, Petrie Prize Canadian Astronomical Soc. 1995. *Publications:* Ed. of and contrib. to Non-Stable Stars 1957, Spectroscopic Astrophysics 1970; approx. 250 scientific papers, articles and reviews. *Leisure interests:* none. *Address:* Institute for Astronomy, University of Hawaii, 2680 Woodlawn Drive, Honolulu, HI 96822, USA (Office). *E-mail:* herbig@galileo .ifa.hawaii.edu (Office).

HERBST, John Edward; American diplomatist; ed School of Foreign Service, Georgetown Univ., Fletcher School of Law and Diplomacy; worked in embassies in Moscow and Saudi Arabia; Dir Office of Ind. States and Commonwealth Affairs; Dir Office of Regional Affairs, Near East Asia Bureau; Political Counsellor, Embassy, Tel-Aviv; Deputy Dir for Econs, Office of Soviet Union Affairs; Dir for Policy, Nat. Security Council; Prin. Deputy to Amb.-at-Large for the New Ind. States; Consul-Gen. Jerusalem 1997–2000; Amb. to Uzbekistan 2000–. *Address:* American Embassy, ul. Chilanzarskaya 82, 700115 Tashkent, Uzbekistan (Office); 8355 Thompson Road, Annandale, VA 22003, USA (Home). *Telephone:* (71) 120-54-50 (Office). *Fax:* (71) 120-63-35 (Office). *E-mail:* consul_tashkent@yahoo.com (Office). *Website:* www.usis .uz (Office).

HERCUS, Luise Anna, AM, PhD; Australian academic; b. 16 Jan. 1926, Munich, Germany; d. of Alfred Schwarzschild and Theodora Schwarzschild; m. Graham Robertson Hercus 1954; one s.; ed Oxford Univ., UK and Australian Nat. Univ., Canberra; tutor and lecturer St Anne's Coll., Oxford 1946–54; Research Fellow Univ. of Adelaide 1964–68; Sr Lecturer Asian Studies Australian Nat. Univ. 1969–71, Reader 1972–91, now Visiting Fellow in Linguistics; much work on recording nearly extinct Aboriginal languages 1963–. *Publications:* The Languages of Victoria: A Late Survey 1969, The Bagandji Language 1982, This is What Happened, Historical Narratives by Aborigines (Co-Ed.) 1986, Nukunu Dictionary 1992, Wembawemba Dictionary 1992, Paakanyi Dictionary 1993, The Wirangu Language of the West Coast of South Australia 1999; articles on Middle Indo-Aryan and on oral traditions of S Australian Aborigines, The Arabana – WangKanguru Language. *Leisure interest:* raising orphaned marsupials. *Address:* School of Language Studies, Australian National University, Canberra ACT 0200 (Office); Kintala via Gundaroo, Dick's Creek Road, NSW 2620, Australia. *Telephone:* 62 36-8145.

HERCUS, Dame Margaret Ann, DCMG, BA, LLB; New Zealand int. consultant; b. 24 Feb. 1942, Hamilton; d. of Horace Sayers and Mary Sayers (née Ryan); m. John Hercus; two s.; ed Victoria, Auckland and Canterbury Univs; Lawyer and Staff Training Officer, Beath & Co., Christchurch 1969–70; mem. Price Tribunal and Trade Practices Comm. 1973–75; Deputy Chair. Commerce Comm. 1975–78; Chair. Consumer Rights Campaign 1975; MP for Lyttelton 1978–87; Opposition Spokesperson on Social Welfare, Consumer Affairs and Women's Affairs 1978–84; Minister of Social Welfare, Police and Women's Affairs 1984–87; Perm. Rep. of NZ to the UN 1989–90; int. consultant 1991–98; Chief of Mission, UN Force in Cyprus 1998–99; Labour. *Leisure interests:* collecting original New Zealand prints, theatre, reading. *Address:* 82A Park Terrace, Christchurch 8001, New Zealand.

HERCZEGH, Géza Gábor, PhD; Hungarian judge; b. 17 Oct. 1928, Nagy-kapos; s. of the late Károly Herczegh and Jolán Olchváry; m. Melinda Petnehazy 1961; one s. one d.; ed French Grammar School, Gödöllö, Univ. of Szeged; Research Fellow in Public Int. Law Inst. of Political Science, Buda-pest 1951–67; Prof. of Law, Head Int. Law Dept, Univ. of Pécs 1967–90; Judge, Vice-Pres. Constitutional Court 1990–93; Judge Int. Court of Justice, The Hague 1993–; mem. Hungarian Acad. of Sciences 1985; Dr hc (Marburg) 1990, (Pécs) 2000. *Publications:* The Colonial Question and International Law 1962, General Principles of Law and the International Legal Order 1969, Develop-ment of International Humanitarian Law 1984, Foreign Policy of Hungary 896–1919 1987, From Sarajevo to the Potsdam Conference 1999. *Leisure interests:* history, archaeology. *Address:* 1133 Budapest, Pozonyi ut 54 iv 3, 4e étage, porte 3, Hungary.

HERINCX, Raimund (Raymond Frederick); British opera and concert singer and voice teacher and therapist; b. 23 Aug. 1927, London; s. of Florent Herincx and Marie Cheal; m. Margaret J. Waugh (known as Astra Blair) 1954; one s. two d.; ed Thames Valley Grammar School and Univ. of London; Educ. Officer, Household Cavalry 1946–48; studied singing in Antwerp, Brussels, Barcelona and London with Giovanni Valli, Samuel Worthington and Harold Williams 1949–53; mem. Royal Opera House chorus; joined Welsh Nat. Opera 1956; Prin. Baritone, Sadler's Wells Opera 1957–67; début Royal Opera House, Covent Garden 1968; joined Metropolitan Opera House, New York 1976, subsequently appearing in most major U.S. opera houses mainly in works of Wagner and Richard Strauss; Prof. of Voice RAM 1970–77; Sr Voice Teacher, North East of Scotland Music School 1979–; voice therapist 1979–; voice teacher Trinity Coll. of Music, London 1993–; lecturer, Univ. Coll., Cardiff 1984–87; Music Critic for Music and Musicians; Hon. RAM 1971; Opera Medal, Int. Music Awards 1968. *Leisure interests:* Artists' Asscn Against Aids, vineyard man., plant breeding (begonias and geraniums), wine and its history, wildfowl. *Address:* c/o English National Opera, St. Martin's Lane, London, WC2N 4ES, England (Office).

HERING, Jürgen; German librarian; b. 15 Sept. 1937, Chemnitz; s. of the late Karl Hering and Margot (Schubert) Hering; m. Inge Rich 1961; one s. two d.; ed Univs. of Stuttgart, Munich and Tübingen; Library Asst Stuttgart Univ. Library 1968, Library Adviser 1971, Sr Library Adviser 1972, Librarian 1974, Chief Librarian 1975–96; Dir Sächsische Landesbibliothek–Staats and Dresden Univ. Library 1997–; Chair. Verein Deutscher Bibliothekare 1979–83, First Deputy Chair. 1983–85; Dir Max-Kade-Stiftung Stuttgart 1982–, Wissenschaftlicher Beirat Bibliothek für Zeitgeschichte, Stuttgart 1986–99, Kuratorium Deutsches Biblioteksinstitut Berlin 1990–95; mem. Exec. Cttee German Libraries Assn 1992–95 (Chair. 1989–92); Adviser Stiftung für Preussischen Kulturbesitz 1999; Dr Josef Bick Ehrenmedaille, Austria 1992. *Leisure interests:* photography, travel. *Address:* Sächsische Landesbibliothek — Staats- und Universitätsbibliothek Dresden, 01054 Dresden (Office); Eichenparkstr. 34, 70619 Stuttgart, Germany (Home). *Telephone:* (351) 4677123. *Fax:* (351) 4677111 (Office). *E-mail:* jhering@ slub-dresden.de (Office). *Website:* www.slub-dresden.de (Office).

HERKSTRÖTER, Cornelius Antonius Johannes, BSc; Netherlands petroleum company executive; b. 21 Aug. 1937, Venlo; m. Regina Maria Haske 1959; two s. one d.; qualified as chartered accountant; joined Billiton as business economist 1967, following acquisition of Billiton by Shell Petroleum, apptd. Head Dept Financial and Econ. Affairs 1971, various Sr posts in Billiton cos., Switzerland and Netherlands 1972–80, Area Co-ordinator SE Asia, Shell Int. Petroleum Co. Ltd 1980, Vice-Pres. (Finance) Shell Française SA 1982, Chair. Bd of Man. Deutsche Shell A.G. 1985, Regional Co-ordinator Europe, Dir Shell Internationale Petroleum Mij. B.V. 1988, Man. Dir The Shell Petroleum Co. Ltd, Chair. Supervisory Bd Shell Nederland B.V., Group Man. Dir 1989, Chair. Supervisory Bd Deutsche Shell A.G. 1990, Dir Shell UK Ltd, Chair. Bd of Dirs. Billiton Int. Metals B.V. 1991, Pres. N.V. Koninklijke Nederlandsche Petroleum Maatschappij (Royal Dutch Petroleum Co.) 1992–98; Dir numerous cos. in group; retd; Verdienstkreuz (First Class) (Germany); Kt Order of Netherlands Lion.

HERMAN, Alexis M.; American politician and administrator; b. 16 July 1947, Mobile, Ala; ed Xavier Univ.; Founder, fmr CEO H. M. Herman & Assocs., Washington; Nat. Dir Minority Women's Employment Program until 1977; Dir Women's Bureau Dept of Labor 1977–81; Chief of Staff, Deputy Chair. Democratic Nat. Convention Cttee until 1991, CEO 1991–92; Deputy Dir Clinton-Gore Presidential Transition Office 1992–93; Asst to Pres. of USA, Public Liaison Dir White House 1993–96; Sec. of Labor 1997–2000; Chair. Coca Cola Co. Task Force on Diversity 2001–; mem. Nat. Council of Negro Women; Sara Lee Front Runner Award 1999. *Address:* Suite 1012, 1501 M Street, NW, Suite 1175, Washington, DC 20005 (Office); c/o Office of the Secretary, US Department of Labor, Washington, DC 20210, USA.

HERMANN, Jacques; Danish chief justice; b. 10 Nov. 1934; ed Univ. of Copenhagen; civil servant, Ministry of Justice 1959–77, section chief from 1972; Public Prosecutor 1977–80; High Court Judge 1981–83; Permanent Under-Sec. Ministry of Defence 1984–88; Justice, Supreme Court 1988–, Chief Justice and Pres. Supreme Court 2001–. *Address:* Supreme Court, Prins Jørgens Gård 13, 1218 Copenhagen K, Denmark (Office). *Telephone:* 33-63-27-50 (Office). *Fax:* 33-15-00-10 (Office). *Website:* www.hoejesteret.dk (Office).

HERMANNSSON, Steingrímur, MSc; Icelandic fmr central bank governor, engineer and politician; b. 22 June 1928, Reykjavik; s. of the late Hermann Jónasson and Vigdís Steingrímsdóttir; m. 1st Sara Jane Hermannsson 1951; m. 2nd Gudlaug Edda Gudmundsdóttir 1962; four s. two d.; ed Reykjavik Coll., Illinois and California Insts. of Tech.; engineer, City of Reykjavik Electrical Power Works 1952–53; electrical engineer, Fertilizer Plant Inc., Iceland 1953–54; engineer S Calif. Edison Co. 1954–56; Dir Nat. Research Council, Iceland 1957–78; MP 1971–94; Sec. Progressive Party 1971–79, Chair. 1979–94; Minister of Justice, Ecclesiastical Affairs and Agric. 1978–79; Minister of Fisheries and Communications 1980–83; Prime Minister of Iceland 1983–87, 1988–91, also Minister of Econ. Planning; Minister of Foreign Affairs and Foreign Trade 1987–88; Gov. Cen. Bank of Iceland 1994–98; Chair. Surtsey Research Soc., Millennium Inst., USA, Environment Protection Asscn of Iceland; Caltech's Alumni Distinguished Service Award 1986, IIT's Professional Achievement Award 1991, Icelandic Athletics Asscn Gold Medal, Paul Harris Rotary Fellow. *Leisure interests:* outdoor sports, skiing, golf, forestry, carpentry. *Address:* Mavanes 19, 210 Gardabae, Iceland (Home). *Telephone:* 5641509 (Home). *Fax:* 5542402 (Home). *E-mail:* steingrimur@vortex.is.

HERMANS, Christopher, MA; Botswana banker; b. 23 Dec. 1936, Cape Town, South Africa; s. of Henry Hodgson Hermans and Marjorie Stanhope Hermans; m. 1st Janet Gallagher 1960 (divorced 1987); one s. two d.; m. 2nd Vonna Deulen 1987; two d.; ed Diocesan Coll., Rondebosch, Cape Town, Trinity Coll., Oxford, Howard Univ., Wash., Vanderbilt Univ., Nashville, Tenn.; Asst Sec. for Devt, Bechuanaland Protectorate Admin. 1961–66; Perm. Sec., Ministry of Devt Planning, Botswana Govt 1966–70, Ministry of Finance and Devt Planning 1970–75; Gov. Bank of Botswana 1975–77, 1987–99; Sr Planning Adviser/Loan Officer, World Bank 1977–82, CEO Thailand and Indonesia Programs Div., 1982–84; CEO of World Bank Regional Mission, Bangkok 1984–87; Presidential Order of Meritorious Service. *Leisure interests:* tennis, wildlife, windsurfing, gardening. *Address:* c/o Bank of Botswana, P.O. Box 712, Gaborone, Botswana.

HERMASZEWSKI, Gen. Mirosław; Polish astronaut and air force officer; b. 15 Sept. 1941, Lipniki (now Ukraine); s. of Roman Hermaszewski and Kamila Hermaszewska; m. 1965; one s. one d.; ed Air Force Officers' School, Dęblin 1961–64, Gen. Staff Acad., Warsaw; served in Nat. Air Defence 1964–76; 1st class pilot 1966, supersonic MiG-21 pilot 1967, flight leader 1971–72, deputy squadron leader 1972–75, Regt Commdr 1975–76; master's class pilot; in Cosmonauts' Training Centre, Zvezdnoy Gorodok, nr Moscow 1976–78; space flight on board Soyuz-30 and space-station SALUT-6 June–July 1978; service in HQ of Nat. Air Defence 1978–80; student, Gen. Staff Acad., Moscow 1980–82; Second-in-Command, Air Forces and Air Defence of Polish Repub. 1990–91; Commdr Air Force Officers' School, Dęblin 1984–90; mem. Space Research Cttee of Polish Acad. of Sciences 1978–, Asscn of Space Explorers 1985–87; Pres. Gen. Bd Polish Astronautical Soc. 1983–87; Maj.-Gen. 1988; Gold Cross of Merit 1976, Cross of Grunwald Order (1st Class) 1978, Gold Star of Hero of USSR 1978, Order of Lenin 1978, Mil. Champion Pilot 1978, Cosmonaut of Polish People's Repub. 1978, Int. Order of Smile 1991. *Leisure interests:* literature, hunting, tourism, dogs. *Address:* ul. Czeczota 25, 02-607 Warsaw, Poland.

HERMON, Sir John (Charles), Kt, OBE, QPM; British police officer; b. 23 Nov. 1928, Belfast; s. of the late William Rowan Hermon and Agnes Hermon; m. 1st Jean Webb 1954 (died 1986); one s. one d.; m. 2nd Sylvia Paisley 1988; two s.; ed Larne Grammar School; accountancy training and business 1946–50; joined Royal Ulster Constabulary 1950, Chief Constable 1980–89; Pres. Int. Professional Security Asscn 1993–96; CStJ 1984–99. *Publication:* Holding the Line (autobiog.) 1997. *Leisure interests:* boating, reading and walking. *Address:* Warren Road, Donaghadee, Co. Down, Northern Ireland.

HERNÁNDEZ COLÓN, Rafael, AB, LLB; Puerto Rican politician and lawyer; b. 24 Oct. 1936, Ponce; s. of Rafael Hernández Matos and Dorinda Colón Clavell; m. Lila Mayoral 1959; three s. one d.; ed Valley Forge Mil. Acad., Wayne Pa, Johns Hopkins Univ., Univ. of Puerto Rico Law School; pvt. law practice 1959–69, 1977–84; Assoc. Commr of Public Service 1960–62; Lecturer in Law, Catholic Univ. of Puerto Rico 1961–65; Sec. of Justice 1965–67; Senator at Large, Popular Democratic Party 1968; Pres. of Senate 1969–73; Leader of Popular Democratic Party 1969; Gov. of Puerto Rico 1972–76, 1989–93; Trustee Carnegie Foundation for Int. Peace; mem. Inter-American Bar Asscn; Dr hc (Johns Hopkins Univ., Catholic Univ. of Puerto Rico); Harvard Foundation Award 1987, Great Cross of Isabel la Católica (Spain), Order of El Libertador (Venezuela). *Publications:* Text on Civil Procedure 1968 and many articles on topics of law. *Address:* c/o Popular Democratic Party, 403 Ponce de León Avenue, PO Box 5788, Puerta de Tierra, San Juan 00906, Puerto Rico.

HERRERA, Gérard; French diplomatist; b. 30 Oct. 1943; m. Virginie Herrera; three c.; ed Inst. d'Etudes Politiques, Ecole Nat. d'Admin.; entered Ministry of Foreign Affairs 1969; First Sec., Embassy in Washington 1971–75; Special Adviser to the Minister of Foreign Affairs 1975–77, 1980–81; Political Counsellor, Embassy in Madrid 1977–80; Consul Gen. in San Francisco 1982–85; Dir for Int. Relations, French Atomic Energy Comm. 1985–90; Gov. for France to the IAEA 1985–90; Amb. to Conf. on Disarmament, Geneva 1991–95; Amb. to NATO, Brussels 1995–98; Dir of Political Affairs, Ministry of Foreign Affairs 1992–2002; Amb. to London Aug. 2002–; Chevalier, Légion d'honneur, Officier, Ordre nat. du Mérite, Officier, Order of the White Rose of Finland, Officier, Order of Civil Merit (Spain). *Address:* Embassy of France,

58 Knightsbridge, London, SW1X 7JT, England (Office). *Telephone:* (20) 7201-1000 (Office). *Fax:* (20) 7201-1004 (Office). *E-mail:* press.londres-amba@diplomatie.gouv.fr. *Website:* www.ambafrance-uk.org.

HERRERA, Luis Felipe; Chilean banker, lawyer and economist; b. 17 June 1922, Valparaíso; s. of Joaquín Herrera and Inés Lane; m. Inés Olmo 1961; two s.; ed Colegio Alemán de Santiago, Escuela Militar, Univs. of Chile and London; Legal Dept, Central Bank of Chile 1943–47; Attorney for Cen. Bank of Chile and pvt. law practice 1947–52; Prof. of Econs, Schools of Law and Sociology, Univ. of Chile 1947–58; Under-Sec. for Economy and Commerce 1952; Minister of Finance April–Oct. 1953; Gen. Man. Cen. Bank of Chile 1953–58; Gov. Int. Bank for Reconstruction and Development, IMF 1953–58, Exec. Dir 1958–60; Pres. Inter-American Devt Bank 1960–71; Pres. Soc. for Int. Devt 1970–71; Co-ordinator-Gen. ECIEL Program (Jt Studies for Latin American Econ. Integration) 1974–, Perm. Consultant 1981–; Pres. Admin. Council, Int. Fund for Promotion of Culture (UNESCO) 1976–; Chair. Bd of Trustees, UN Inst. for Training and Research 1976–; Pres. World Soc. of Ekistics, Inst. for Int. Co-operation 1977–80, Corporación Investigaciones para el Desarrollo (CINDE) 1986, Chilean Chapter of S.I.D. 1986; mem. Bd of Govs. Int. Devt Research Centre (IDRC) 1980; mem. Bd of Trustees, Third World Foundation; mem. Hon. Bd, Raul Prebisch Foundation 1986; Perm. Consultant Emer. Int. American Devt Bank; Dr. hc (Santiago de Chile) 1993 and numerous other hon. degrees; Bronfman Award, American Public Health Asscn 1969, Condecoración al Mérito, Minas Gerais State, Brazil 1969, Premio "Diego Portales", Chile 1971, Premio Serfin de Integración Mexico 1987, Premio ONU: Medalla Plata a la Paz, Cepal, Santiago 1988, U.N. Personnel Peace Prize 1989, Universidad Austral de Chile: Condecoración al Mérito Universitario 1990; numerous other awards and prizes; Great Cross for Distinguished Service, FRG 1958, Kt Grand Cross, Order of Merit, Italy 1966, Medalla Cívica "Camilo Torres", Colombia 1968, Grand Cross for Educational Merit, Brazil 1969, Gran Cruz de la Orden del Sol, Peru 1971, Gran Cruz Placa de Plata, Dominican Repub. 1971, Gran Cruz Orden Rubén Darío, Nicaragua 1971, Orden Boyacá, Colombia 1971, do Cruzeiro do Sul, Brazil 1971, de la Orden Manuel Amador Guerrero, Panama 1971, Orden Abdón Calderón, Ecuador 1971, al Mérito Nacional, Paraguay 1971, Orden del Aguila Azteca, Mexico 1972, Antonio José de Irisarri, Guatemala 1975, Orden al Mérito Cultural "Andrés Bello", Venezuela 1978, Officier de l'Ordre Nat. du Mérite, France 1979, Gran Cruz de Isabel La Católica, Spain 1980. *Publications:* El Banco Central de Chile 1945, Política económica 1950, Fundamentos de la Política Fiscal 1951, Manual de Política Económica 1952, Elementos de Economía Monetaria 1955, ¿Desarrollo económico o Estabilidad Monetaria? 1958, América Latina Integrada 1964, El Desarrollo Latinoamericano y su Financiamiento 1967, Nacionalismo Latinoamericano 1968, Chile en América Latina 1969, Internacionalismo, Regionalismo, Nacionalismo 1970, América Latina: Experiencias y Desafíos 1974, América Latina: Viejas y Nuevas Fronteras 1978, El Escenario Latinoamericano y el Desafío Cultural 1981, Despertar de un Continente: América Latina 1960–1980 1983, Comunidad Latinoamericana de Naciones: Presencia de Chile 1983, Visión de América Latina: 1974–1984, 1985, América Latina: Desarrollo e Integración 1986. *Address:* Calle El Cerro 1991, Santiago 9, Chile (Home). *Telephone:* 232-8097 (Home).

HERRERA, Paloma; Argentine ballet dancer; b. 21 Dec. 1975, Buenos Aires; d. of Alberto Herrera and Marisa Herrera; ed Teatro Colón, Buenos Aires, Minsk Ballet School, School of American Ballet; joined American Ballet Theater (ABT) corps de ballet; roles in Sleeping Beauty, Don Quixote and La Bayadère; soloist, ABT 1992, prin. dancer 1995; leading role in How Near Heaven (created for her by Twyla Tharp, q.v., 1994; other notable roles include Clara in The Nutcracker, Medora in Le Corsaire, Kitri in Don Quixote, Juliet in Romeo and Juliet 1995. *Address:* American Ballet Theater, 890 Broadway, New York, NY 10003, USA (Office); One Lincoln Plaza, 20 W 64th Street, Apt. F, New York, NY 10023 (Home); Billinghurst 2553, 10 Piso Dto, CP 1425 Buenos Aires, Argentina.

HERRERA CAMPÍNS, Luis, DIur; Venezuelan politician; b. 4 May 1925, Acarigua, Portuguesa State; mem. Partido Social Cristiano (COPEI) 1946–; represented COPEI at first World Conf. of Christian Democrat Parties 1956; Deputy for Lara State 1958; Pres. COPEI 1961; elected Deputy for Lara 1963, 1968; elected Senator for Portuguesa 1968; Pres. of Venezuela 1979–83. *Address:* c/o Partido Social Cristiano, esq. San Miguel, Avda. Pantéon cruce con Fuerzas Armadas, San José, Caracas 1010, Venezuela.

HERRERO RODRIGUEZ DE MIÑON, Miguel, PhD, LPh; Spanish politician and barrister; b. 18 June 1940; s. of Miguel Herrero and Carmen Rodríguez de Miñon; m. Cristina de Jáuregui; one s. two d.; ed Univs. of Madrid, Oxford, Luxembourg, Geneva, Paris and Louvain; Lecturer in Int. Law, Univ. of Madrid 1963–65; Sr Legal Adviser to Spanish Admin. 1966; Gen. Sec. Ministry of Justice 1976; mem. Parl. 1977–93; Leader, Parl. Group of UCD in Govt 1980–81; Deputy Leader of Parl. Group of AP, major opposition group in Parl. 1982–87; Pres. Constitutional Court, Andorra 2001; mem. Real Academia de Ciencias Morales y Políticas, Trilateral Comm.; Dr hc (UNED); Gran Cruz de Isabel la Católica, Gran Cruz de San Raimundo de Peñafort, Orden Mérito Constitucional, Creu San Jordi. *Publications:* several books on constitutional law and int. relations. *Address:* Calle Mayor 70, bajo, 28013 Madrid, Spain (Office). *Telephone:* (1) 5595405. *Fax:* (1) 5417092.

HERRING, (William) Conyers, PhD; American physicist; b. 15 Nov. 1914, Scotia, NY; s. of Dr W. Conyers Herring and Mary Joy Herring; m. Louise C. Preusch 1946; three s. one d.; ed Univ. of Kansas and Princeton Univ.; Nat. Research Council Fellow, MIT 1937–39; Instructor in Math. and Research Assoc. in Math. Physics, Princeton Univ. 1939–40; Instructor in Physics, Univ. of Missouri 1940–41; mem. Scientific Staff, Columbia Univ. Div. of War Research 1941–45; Prof. of Applied Mathematics, Univ. of Texas 1946; Research Physicist, Bell Telephone Laboratories 1946–78; Prof. of Applied Physics, Stanford Univ. 1978–81, Prof. Emer. 1981–; mem. Inst. for Advanced Study, Princeton 1952–53; mem. NAS; Fellow, American Acad. of Arts and Sciences; Oliver E. Buckley Solid State Physics Prize, American Physical Soc. 1959, Distinguished Service Citation, Univ. of Kansas 1973, James Murray Luck Award for Excellence in Scientific Reviewing, NAS 1980, Von Hippel Award, Materials Research Soc. 1980, Wolf Prize in Physics 1985. *Publication:* Exchange Interactions among Itinerant Electrons (Vol. 4 of series Magnetism) 1966. *Leisure interests:* church and cultural activities. *Address:* Department of Applied Physics, Stanford University, Stanford, CA 94305 (Office); 3945 Nelson Drive, Palo Alto, CA 94306, USA (Home). *Telephone:* (650) 723-0686 (Office); (650) 856-9649 (Home). *Fax:* (650) 725-2189 (Office). *E-mail:* conyers@loki.stanford.edu (Office).

HERSCHBACH, Dudley Robert, BS, MS, AM, PhD, FRSC; American professor of chemistry; b. 18 June 1932, San José, Calif.; s. of Robert Dudley Herschbach and Dorothy Edith Beer; m. Georgene Lee Botyos 1964; two d.; ed Stanford and Harvard Univs; Asst Prof. Univ. of Calif., Berkeley 1959–61, Assoc. Prof. 1961–63; Prof. of Chem., Harvard Univ. 1963–76, Frank B. Baird, Jr, Prof. of Science 1976–, Chair. Chemical Pysics Program 1964–77, Chair. Dept of Chem. 1977–80, mem. Faculty Council 1980–83, Co-Master of Currier House 1981–86; Chair. Bd of Trustees Science Service; Assoc. Ed., Journal of Physical Chem. 1980–88; Fellow, American Acad. of Arts and Sciences, N.A.S., American Philosophical Soc.; Hon. DSc (Toronto) 1977, (Adelphi) 1990; shared Nobel Prize for Chem. 1986; Pure Chem. Prize, ACS 1965, Pauling Medal, ACS 1978, Polanyi Medal, RSC 1981, Langmuir Prize, American Physical Soc. 1983, Nat. Award of Science 1991, Sierra Nevada Distinguished Chemist Award 1993, Kosolapoff Medal 1994, William Walker Prize 1994. *Publications:* more than 350 research papers. *Leisure interests:* viola, running. *Address:* Department of Chemistry, Harvard University, 12 Oxford Street, Cambridge, MA 02138, USA.

HERSHEY, Barbara; American actress; b. 5 Feb. 1948, Hollywood, Calif.; d. of William H. Herzstein; one s.; m. Stephen Douglas 1992 (divorced 1995); ed Hollywood High School; début in TV series The Monroes. *Films include:* With Six you Get Eggroll, The Last Summer, The Baby Maker, Boxcar Bertha, The Stuntman, The Entity, The Right Stuff, The Liberation of Lord Byron Jones, Love Comes Quietly, The Pursuit of Happiness, Passion Flower, The Natural, Hannah and Her Sisters, Tin Men, Shy People 1987 (Best Actress, Cannes Film Festival), The Last Temptation of Christ 1988, A World Apart 1988 (Best Actress, Cannes Film Festival), Beaches 1989, Defenceless 1989, Aunt Julia and the Scriptwriter 1990, Paris Trout 1990, A Killing in a Small Town 1990 (Best Actress, Emmy and Golden Globe), The Public Eye 1991, Defenseless 1991, Swing Kids 1993, Splitting Heirs 1993, Falling Down 1993, A Dangerous Woman 1994, Last of the Dogmen, Portrait of a Lady, The Pallbearer 1996, A Soldier's Daughter Never Cries 1998. *TV films include:* Just a Little Inconvenience, A Killing in a Small Town (Emmy and Golden Globe Awards 1990), The Bible 1993, Portrait of a Lady 1996, A Soldier's Daughter Never Cries 1998, Frogs for Snakes 1998, The Staircase 1998, Breakfast of Champions 1999, Passion 1999. *Address:* c/o Suzan Bymel, Bymel O'Neill Management, N. Vista, Los Angeles, CA 90046 (Office); c/o Jenny Rawlings, CAA, 9830 Wilshire Boulevard, Beverly Hills, CA 90212, USA.

HERSHKO, Avram, MD, PhD; Israeli doctor and molecular biologist; b. 1937, Hungary; ed Hebrew Univ. of Jerusalem; prisoner in Nazi concentration camp; emigrated to Israel with parents 1950; mil. service as a doctor in Israeli army; studied molecular biology in San Francisco 1969–72; Prof. Faculty of Medicine, Technion–Israel Inst. of Tech.; studied protein degradation at biochemical level with Aaron Ciechanover 1976–81; Albert Lasker Basic Medical Research Award 2000, shared Wolf Prize with Alexander Varshavsky (q.v.) 2001. *Address:* Faculty of Medicine, Technion–Israel Institute of Technology, Haifa, Israel (Office).

HERSOM, Naomi Louisa, M.ED., PhD; Canadian academic; b. 4 Feb. 1927, Winnipeg; d. of Frederick Hersom and Anna Hersom; ed Univs. of Manitoba and Alta; teacher and prin., Winnipeg 1954–67; Prof. of Curriculum Studies, Univ. of Alta 1969–75; Dir of Undergrad. Programmes and Assoc. Dean (Academic), Univ. of BC 1975–79, Prof. of Educational Admin. 1979–81; Dean, Coll. of Educ. Univ. of Sask. 1981–86; Pres. Mt. St Vincent Univ. 1986–91; Visiting Scholar Univ. of Ottawa 1991–92; Vice-Pres. Int. Fellowship of Evangelical Students (IFES) 1991–96; Dir and Vice-Pres. Social Science Fed. of Canada 1979–82; Pres. Canadian Educ. Asscn 1989–90; mem. numerous comms., task forces etc.; Hon. LLD (McGill, York) 1988, (Manitoba) 1989, (Ottawa) 1990, (St Mary's Univ. and Univ. of Vic.) 1991, (Alberta) 1992, (Providence Coll.) 1998; George Croskery Memorial Award 1985; Grand Dame of Merit, Kts. of Malta. *Publications:* co-author: Curriculum Development for Classroom Teachers 1971, Locally Initiated School Evaluation 1973, Developing Evaluation Systems in Schools: Organizational Strategies 1975, A Study of Open Area Schools in the Edmonton Public School System 1978, Women and the Canadian Labour Force 1982, contrib. to Educational

Leadership 1992. *Leisure interest:* bird-watching. *Address:* 405 Québec Street, #311, Victoria, BC, V8V 4Z2, Canada. *Telephone:* (250) 360-1892. *Fax:* (250) 360-1892. *E-mail:* nhersom@islandnet.com (Home).

HERSOV, Basil Edward, DMS, MA, LLD, FRSA; South African business executive; b. 18 Aug. 1926, Johannesburg; s. of Abraham Sundel Hersov and Gertrude Hersov (née Aronson); m. Antoinette Herbert 1957; two s. two d.; ed Michaelhouse, Natal and Christ's Coll., Cambridge; pilot in SA Air Force (SAAF) 1944–46; joined Anglovaal Ltd as Learner Official on gold mine 1949, later holding a number of Sr positions with Anglovaal Group: Deputy Chair. 1970, Chair. and Man. Dir 1973–98; Chair. Hartebeestfontein Gold Mining Co. Ltd, Anglovaal Industries Ltd, The Associated Manganese Mines of SA Ltd; mem. Bd of many other cos within and outside Anglovaal Group; Dir Mutual and Fed. Insurance Co. Ltd; Pres. and Fellow Inst. of Dirs. (SA); Hon. Pres., mem. Council, SA Foundation; Gov. Rhodes Univ. Bd of Trustees, Business S. Africa, Nat. Business Initiative; Fellow, SA Inst. of Mining and Metallurgy, SA Inst. of Man.; Hon. LLD (Rhodes); Hon. Col 21 Squadron SAAF; Decoration for Meritorious Service; Witwaterstand Univ. Award for Business Excellence 1984, Brig. Stokes Memorial Award, SAInst. of Mining and Metallurgy 1996. *Leisure interests:* skiing, horse racing, tennis, flying and sailing. *Address:* Angloval Industries Ltd., Box 1897, Saxonwold 2132 (Office); "Springwaters", Box 65097, Benmore 2010, South Africa (Home). *Telephone:* (11) 7792898 (Office). *Fax:* (11) 8842356 (Office). *E-mail:* basilh@avi.co.za (Home).

HERTELEER, Vice-Adm. Willy Maurits; Belgian military officer; b. 1 Oct. 1941, Assenede; m. Jacqueline Liekens 1962; one s. three d.; ed Royal Cadet School, Brussels, Merchant Navy Acad., Belgian Staff Coll., Brussels, Ecole Supérieure de Guerre Navale, Paris; commissioned Belgian Navy 1962, as ensign served on minesweepers and a supply/command ship 1963-68, became mine warfare specialist 1969–70, Staff Officer Mine Countermeasures, Operational Command 1970–72; Commdr coastal minesweeper 1975, ocean minesweeper/hunter 1978, (instructor Belgian-Dutch School for Mine Warfare, Ostend between these postings); rank of Lt-Commdr 1979; apptd. to Planning section, Belgian Naval Staff, also mem. Naval Bd, NATO Mil. Standardization Agency 1979–82; Second-in-Command frigate Westdiep 1982–84, Commdg Officer 1984–85; Asst Chief of Staff Operations, Naval Operations Command 1986, Chief of Staff 1986–87; Head Belgian-Dutch School for Mine Warfare 1987–89; mem. Audit Team, Belgian Naval Staff, Brussels 1989, Staff Officer, Operations 1990, Commdr Naval Operations 1990–92; rank of Rear-Adm. 1992; joined Gen. Staff Headquarters, Brussels 1992, Chief of Naval Staff 1993–95; rank of Vice-Adm. 1995; Chief of the Gen. Staff 1995–; Aide to King Albert II; Grand Cross, Order of the Crown. *Address:* Rue d'Evère, 1140 Brussels, Belgium. *Telephone:* (2) 701-31-50. *Fax:* (2) 701-66-25.

HERTRICH, Rainer; German aerospace industry executive; b. 6 Dec. 1949, Ottengrün; ed Tech. Univ. of Berlin, Univ. of Nuremberg; apprenticeship and business training Siemens AG 1969–71; Information Processing Supervisor controlling Dept., Mil. Aircraft Div., Messerschmitt-Bölkow-Blohm (MBB) GmbH 1977, Head Controlling Dept MBB Service Div., Ottobrunn 1978–83, Chief Financial Officer 1983–84, Head Controlling and Finance Dept, MBB Dynamics Div. 1984–87, Chief Financial Officer and mem. Div. Man., MBB Marine and Special Products Div. 1987–90; Head Divisional Controlling, Cen. Controlling Section, Deutsche Aerospace AG, Dasa (now European Aeronautic Defence and Space Co., EADS) 1990–91, Sr Vice-Pres., Corp. Controlling, Dasa 1991–96, Head Aeroengines Business Unit, Dasa, Pres. and CEO Motoren- und Turbinen-Union München (MTU München) GmbH, mem. Exec. Cttee Dasa 1996–, Pres. and CEO DaimlerChrysler Aerospace (Dasa) AG 2000–, Co-CEO EADS 2000–. *Address:* EADS Deutschland GmbH, 81663 Munich, Germany (Office). *Telephone:* (89) 60734700 (Office). *Fax:* (89) 60734706 (Office). *Website:* www.eads. net (Office).

HERTZBERGER, Herman; Netherlands architect and professor of architectural design; b. 6 July 1932, Amsterdam; m. J.C. Van Seters 1959; one s. two d.; ed Delft Tech. Univ.; pvt. practice, Amsterdam 1958–; Co-Ed. (Dutch) Forum 1959–63; Teacher Acad. of Architecture, Amsterdam 1965–69; Prof. of Architectural Design, Tech. Univ. of Delft 1970–99; Prof., Univ. of Geneva 1986–93; Chair. Berlage Inst., Amsterdam 1990–95, teacher 1999–; Hon. mem. Acad. Royale de Belgique 1975, Bund Deutscher Architeckten 1983, Akad. der Künste 1993, Accad. delle Arti del Disegno, Florence 1995, Acad. d'Architecture de France 1997, Bond Nederlandse Architectes 2002; Hon. FRIBA 1991; Hon. Fellow Royal Incorporation of Architects in Scotland 1996; Hon. DUniv (Geneva) 2001; numerous prizes and awards including Architectural Award of the Town of Amsterdam 1968, Eternit Award 1974, Fritz Schumacher Award 1974, Architecture Award of the City of Amsterdam 1985, Kt Order of Oranje Nassau 1991, Premio Europa 1991, BNA Award 1991, Concrete Award 1991, Prix Rhénan 1993, Architecture Award, City of Breda 1998, Premios Vitruvio 98 Trayectoria Internacional 1998, Dutch School Bldg Award 2000, Leone d'oro (Venice) 2002. *Exhibitions:* four travelling exhbns 1985–90, 1986–89, 1995, 1998; has featured in numerous other exhbns in Europe, Japan and USA 1967–. *Major works include:* ten kindergartens/primary schools 1966–2000, office Bldg, "Centraal Beheer", Apeldoorn 1972, housing for old and disabled people "De Drie Hoven", Amsterdam 1974, music centre "Vredenburg", Utrecht 1978, urban renewal "Haarlemmer Houttinen", Amsterdam 1982, office Bldg Ministry of Social Welfare and Employment, The Hague 1990, Theatre Centre Spui, The Hague 1993, library and art and music centre, Breda 1993, Chassé Theater, Breda 1995, Theater Markant, Uden 1996, residential buildings, Haarlem 1996, Düren, Germany 1996, Berlin 1997, extension to Vanderveen Department Store, Assen 1997, YKK Dormitory Guesthouse, Kurobe City, Japan 1998, Bijlmer Monument (with Georges Descombes) 1998, residential area "Merwestein Noord", Dordrecht 1999, Montessori Coll. Oost. Amsterdam 1999, Waterhouse, Middelburg 2002, Il Fiore office bldg Maastricht 2002. *Publications:* Homework for More Hospitable Form (Dutch) Forum XXIV 1973, Herman Hertzberger 1959–86 Bauten und Projekte/Buildings and Projects/Bâtiments et Projets (jtly.) 1987, Lessons for Students in Architecture 1991, Herman Hertzberger Projekte/Projects 1990–1995 1995, Chassé Theater 1995, Herman Hertzberger: view of projects of 1960–1997 (jtly.) 1997, Space and the Architect: Lessons for Students in Architecture part II 2000, Articulations 2002. *Leisure interest:* music. *Address:* Architectuurstudio Herman Hertzberger, Gerard Doustraat 220, P.O. Box 74665, 1070 BR Amsterdam, Netherlands (Office). *Telephone:* (20) 6765888 (Office). *Fax:* (20) 6735510 (Office). *E-mail:* office@hertzberger.nl (Office); hrtzbrgr@euronet.nl (Office). *Website:* www.hertzberger.nl (Office).

HERVÉ, Edmond; French politician; b. 3 Dec. 1942, La Bouillie, Côtes du Nord; s. of Marcel Hervé; m. Jeannine Le Gall 1978; two s. one d.; Prof. of Constitutional Law, Rennes Univ.; Conseiller Général, Ille-et-Vilaine 1973–82; Deputy for Ille-et-Vilaine to Nat. Ass. 1986–93; Mayor of Rennes 1977–; fmr Minister of Health; Minister Del. to Minister of Industry for Energy 1981–83; Sec. of State for Health 1983–86; Regional Councillor, Brittany 1986–88; Pres. regional hosp. centre and univ. hosp. centre, both in Brittany 1977–; Pres., District Urbain de l'agglomeration rennaise (Audiar) 1989, Conf. permanente du tourisme urbain 1989–95, Hon. Pres. 1995–; Chair. Conf. de villes de l'arc atlantique 2000–; mem. Conseil de Surveillance du Crédit local de France 1990, City Scientific Cttee on Science and Industry of La Villette 1990, Nat. Council on Towns and Urban Social Devt 1991; charged with manslaughter arising from the use of HIV-contaminated blood in transfusions Feb. 1999, found guilty but court ruled he should not be punished; Parti Socialiste. *Address:* Permanence parlementaire, 5 rue Chateaurenault, 35000 Rennes; Assemblée nationale, 75355 Paris; Mairie, B.P. 3126, 35031 Rennes, France.

HERZOG, Jacques, DipArch; Swiss architect; b. 1950, Basel; ed Swiss Federal Technical Univ. (ETH), Zurich; Asst. to Prof. Dolf Schnebli, ETH, Zurich 1977; f. architectural practice Herzog & De Meuron (with Pierre de Meuron, q.v.) 1978; Prof. of Architecture and Design, ETH 1999–; Visiting Prof. Harvard Univ., Cambridge, Mass. 1989, Tulane Univ., New Orleans 1991; (all jtly with Pierre de Meuron) Architecture Prize, Berlin Acad. of Arts 1987, Andrea Palladio Int. Prize for Architecture, Vicenza, Italy 1988, Pritzker Architecture Prize 2001. *Principal works include:* Blue House, Oberwil 1979–80, Photostudio Frei, Weil am Rhein 1981–82, Sperrholz Haus, Bottmingen 1984–85, Apartment Bldg, Hebelstr. 11, Basel 1984–88, Wohn- und Geschäftshaus Schwitter, Basel 1985–98, Goetz Art Gallery, Munich 1989–92, Wohn- und Geschäftshaus Schützenmattstr., Basel 1992–93, Dominus Winery, Napa Valley, Yountville, Calif. 1995–97, Tate Gallery Extension (Tate Modern), Bankside, London 1995–99, Cultural Centre and Theatre, Zurich 1996, Ricola Marketing Bldg, Laufen 1998. *Works in progress include:* Prada Headquarters, New York, De Young Museum, San Francisco, Walker Art Center Extension, Minneapolis, as well as projects in UK, France, Germany, Italy, Spain and Japan. *Address:* Herzog & de Meuron Architekten, Rheinschanze 6, 4056 Basel, Switzerland (Office). *Telephone:* (61) 3855758 (Office). *Fax:* (61) 3855757 (Office). *E-mail:* hdemarch@access.ch (Office).

HERZOG, Maurice, LèsSc, LLL; French/Swiss former mountaineer, civil servant and businessman; b. 15 Jan. 1919, Lyons (Rhône); s. of the late Robert Herzog and Germaine Beaume; m. 1st Comtesse Marie Pierre de Cossé Brissac 1964 (divorced 1976); one s. one d.; m. 2nd Elisabeth Gamper 1976; two s.; ed Collège Chaptal, Paris, Faculty of Science, Lyon and Faculty of Law, Paris; Leader, French Himalayan Expedition 1950; fmr Dir Kléber-Colombes Soc.; High Commr for Youth and Sport 1958–63, Sec. of State 1963–66; mem. UN Econ. and Social Council 1966–67; mem. IOC 1970, Chief of Protocol 1975; fmr Deputy, Haute Savoie, Mayor of Chamonix; Pres. Financial Comm. Rhône-Alpes Regional Council; Pres. Spie-Batignolles Int., Spie-Loisirs; Dir Spie-Capag, Triton-Europe (London), Tractebel-Finance (Geneva), Tractebel (Belgium), Caixa Bank (Paris); Hon. Pres. Société du Tunnel du Mont-Blanc 1984–; Pres. Triton-France 1984–94; Pres. Int. Project Reseach 1995–2001; Commdr, Légion d'honneur; Croix de guerre and other French and foreign decorations; Prix du Littérature, Académie Française. *Publications:* Annapurna premier 8000, Regards sur L'Annapurna, L'Expédition de l'Annapurna, La Montagne, Les Grandes Aventures de l'Himalaya, L'Autre Annapurna (Prix Vérité 1999). *Leisure interests:* history, literature, science, adventure, sports. *Address:* 21 boulevard Richard Wallace, 92200 Neuilly-sur-Seine (Home); La Tournette, 84 chemin de la Tournette, 74400 Chamonix-Mont-Blanc, France (Home). *Telephone:* 1-47-47-96-11. *Fax:* 1-58-37-30-69.

HERZOG, Roman, DJur; German politician; b. 5 April 1934, Landshut; m. Christiane Krauss 1958; ed Univ. of Munich, Freie Univ. Berlin and Hochschule für Verwaltungswissenshaft, Speyer; mem. Bd Evangelische Kirche in Deutschland Chamber for Public Accountability 1971–80; Rep. of Rhineland-Palatinate in Bundestag 1973–78; Chair. Evangelical Working Party, CDU/CSU 1978–83; Minister for Culture and Sport, Baden-Württemberg 1978–80, for Interior 1980–83; mem. Fed. Cttee CDU 1979–83; Vice-Pres. Fed. Constitutional Court 1983–87, Pres. 1987–94; Pres. of Germany 1994–99; Hon. Prof. Hochschule für Verwaltungswissenschaft, Speyer, Univ. of Tübingen;

Chair. Bd of Trustees Stiftung Brandenburger Tor 1999–; Chair. Bd of Trustees Konrad Adenauer Foundation 2000–; Hon. DCL (Oxford) 1996; Hon. Citizen of Berlin 1999, of Bonn 1999; Karlspreis 1997, Ludger-Westrick-Preis 1999, Forum-Kiedrich-Preis 2000. *Publications include:* Kommentar zur Grundgesetz (co-author) 1968, Staaten der Frühzeit: Ursprünge und Herrschaftsformen 1988. *Address:* Postfach 860445, 81631 Munich (Office); Schloss Bellevue, Spreeweg 1, 10557 Berlin, Germany (Home). *Telephone:* (228) 2001 (Office).

HERZOG, Werner; German film director; b. 5 Sept. 1942, Munich. *Films include:* Signs of Life 1967, Even Dwarfs Started Small 1970, Fata Morgana 1971, The Land of Darkness and Silence 1971, Aguirre Wrath of God 1973, The Enigma of Kaspar Hauser 1974, The Great Ecstasy of Woodcutter Steiner 1974, How Much Wood Would Woodchuck Chuck 1976, Heart of Glass 1976, Stroszek 1976–77, Woyzeck 1979, Nosferatu 1979, Le pays du silence et de l'obscurité 1980, Fitzcarraldo 1982, Where the Green Ants Dream 1984, Cobra Verde 1987, Scream from Stone 1991, My Intimate Enemy 1999, Lessons in Darkness, Bride of the Orient (actor), Burning Heart (actor), Mexico, My Best Friend, Aguirre, Wrath of God 2001. *Opera directed:* Lohengrin (Bayreuth) 1987.

HESBURGH, Rev. Theodore M., STD; American ecclesiastic and fmr university president; b. 25 May 1917; s. of Theodore Hesburgh and Anna Hesburgh; ed Univ. of Notre Dame, Gregorian Univ., Rome and Catholic Univ. of America; ordained priest of Congregation of Holy Cross 1943; joined Univ. of Notre Dame 1945, Head of Theology Dept 1948–49, Exec. Vice-Pres. of Univ. 1949–52, Pres. 1952–87, Pres. Emer. 1987–; mem. U.S. Comm. on Civil Rights 1957–72 (Chair. 1969–72), President's Comm. on All-Volunteer Armed Force, Carnegie Comm. on the Future Structure and Financing of Higher Educ., Comm. on the Future of Pvt. and Ind. Higher Educ. in New York State, Presidential Clemency Bd 1974–75; Perm. Rep. of Holy See to Int. Atomic Energy Agency, Vienna 1957; Pres. Int. Fed. of Catholic Univs.; Trustee, Rockefeller Foundation, Chair. Bd of Trustees 1977–82, Carnegie Foundation for Advancement of Teaching (Pres. 1963–64); Chair. Acad. Council, Ecumenical Inst. for Advanced Theological Studies in Jerusalem; Chair. with rank of Amb. U.S. Del. to UN Conf. on Science and Tech. for Devt 1977–79; Chair. Select Comm. on Immigration and Refugee Policy 1979–81; Dir U.S. Inst. of Peace 1991; fmr Dir American Council on Educ.; Fellow, American Acad. of Arts and Sciences; 138 hon. degrees; Distinguished Service Medal, U.S. Navy; Presidential Medal of Freedom 1964, Jefferson Award 1976, Congregational Gold Medal 2000. *Publications:* God and the World of Man 1950, Patterns for Educational Growth 1958, Thoughts for Our Times 1962, More Thoughts for Our Times 1965, Still More Thoughts for Our Times 1966, Thoughts IV 1968, Thoughts V 1969, The Humane Imperative: A Challenge for the Year 2000 1974, The Hesburgh Papers: Higher Values in Higher Education 1979, God, Country, Notre Dame 1990, Travels with Ted and Ned 1992. *Address:* c/o 1315 Hesburgh Library, University of Notre Dame, Notre Dame, IN 46556, USA. *Telephone:* (219) 631-6882.

HESELTINE, Baron (Life Peer), cr. 2001, of Thenford in the County of Northamptonshire; **Rt Hon. Michael Ray Dibdin Heseltine,** PC, CH; British politician; b. 21 March 1933, Swansea, Wales; s. of the late Col Rupert and of Eileen Ray Heseltine; m. Anne Edna Harding Williams 1962; one s. two d.; ed Shrewsbury School, Pembroke Coll., Oxford (Hon. Fellow 1986); Pres. Oxford Union 1954; Chair. Haymarket Press 1965–70, 1999–; MP for Tavistock 1966–74, for Henley 1974–2001; Parl. Sec. Ministry of Transport 1970; Parl. Under-Sec. of State, Dept of the Environment 1970–72; Minister of Aerospace and Shipping 1972–74; Opposition Spokesman for Industry 1974–76, for the Environment 1976–79; Sec. of State for the Environment 1979–83, 1990–92, for Defence 1983–86, Sec. of State for Industry and Pres. of the Bd of Trade 1992–95; Deputy Prime Minister and First Sec. of State 1995–97; Dir Haymarket Publishing Group 1997–, Chair. 2001–; Pres. Assen of Conservative Clubs 1982–83, Chair. Conservative Mainstream 1998–; Pres. Quoted Companies Alliance Int. Advisory Council 2000–, Fed. of Korean Industries, Anglo-China Forum 1998–; Pres. Conservative Group for Europe 2001–; Devt Patron Trinity Coll. of Music, Inst. of Marketing; Hon. Fellow Chartered Inst. of Man. 1998, Univ. of Wales (Swansea), RIBA; Hon. LLD (Liverpool) 1990. *Publications:* Reviving the Inner Cities 1983, Where There's a Will 1987, The Challenge of Europe: Can Britain Win? 1988 (Bentinck Prize 1989), Life in the Jungle (memoirs) 2000. *Address:* House of Lords, London, SW1A 0PW (Office); Thenford House, nr Banbury, Oxon., England (Home).

HESS, Benno, MD; German medical research director; b. 22 Feb. 1922, Berlin; s. of Ludwig Hess and Herta Hess; m. Ulrike Hess 1955; one s. four d.; ed Heidelberg Univ.; Dir and Scientific mem. Max-Planck-Inst. Dortmund 1965–; Prof. Ruhr Univ. Bochum 1970–; Vice-Pres. Max-Planck-Gesellschaft zur Förderung der Wissenschaften, Munich 1980–90; mem. European Molecular Biology Org.; Special Adviser, Comm. for Science and Tech. of European Community; mem. Deutsche Akad. der Naturforscher Leopoldina, Düsseldorf and Heidelberg Acads.; mem. AAAS and other learned socs. etc; Hon. mem. American Soc. of Biological Chemists. *Publications:* articles in scientific journals. *Leisure interests:* nonlinear dynamics and organization of biology, structure and function of biomembranes, science as a historical process. *Address:* c/o Max-Planck-Institut für medizinische Forschung, Jahnstrasse 29, 69120 Heidelberg, Germany (Office). *Telephone:* (6221) 486341. *Fax:* (6221) 486340.

HESSEL, Stephane F.; French diplomatist; b. 20 Oct. 1917, Berlin; s. of Franz Hessel and Helen Hessel (née Grund); m. 1st Vitia Mirkine-Guetzevitch 1939 (died 1986); two s. one d.; m. 2nd Christiane Chabry 1987; war service 1941–45; Admin. Dir Secr. Gen., UN 1946–50; served in Foreign Ministry 1950–54; Asst to the Pres. 1954–55; Adviser to High Commr, Saigon 1955–57, Foreign Affairs Adviser, Algiers 1964–69; Asst Admin. UNDP 1970–72; Perm. Rep. to UN Office, Geneva 1977–81; mem. High Authority for Audiovisual Communication 1982–85; Chair. Asscn France-Algérie 1985; mem. Haut Conseil à l'intégration 1990–94, Haut Conseil à la Coopération Int. 1999–2001; Commdr, Légion d'honneur 1982, Grand Croix, Ordre nat. du Mérite, Croix de guerre 1939–45, Médaille des Evadés, Commdr des Palmes académiques; Hon. MBE. *Publications:* Danse avec le siècle (memoirs) 1996, Dix pas dans le nouveau siècle 2002. *Leisure interest:* Greek mythology. *Address:* 6 rue Antoine Chantin, 75014 Paris, France. *Telephone:* 1-45-42-81-97. *Fax:* 1-45-42-81-97.

HESTER, James McNaughton, DPhil; American university official; b. 19 April 1924, Chester, Pa; s. of James Montgomery Hester and Margaret (McNaughton) Hester; m. Janet Rodes 1953; three d.; ed Princeton and Oxford Univs.; Capt., US Marine Corps 1943–46, 1951–52; Civil Information Officer, Fukuoka Mil. Govt Team, Japan 1946–47; Rhodes Scholar, Oxford Univ. 1947–50; Asst to American Sec. to Rhodes Trustees Princeton 1950; Asst to Pres., Handy Assocs. Inc. (Management Consultants) NY 1953–54; Account Supervisor, Gallup & Robinson Inc. 1954–57; Provost, Brooklyn Center, LI Univ. 1957–60, Vice-Pres., Trustee LI Univ.; Prof. of History, Exec. Dean Arts and Sciences, Dean Grad. School of Arts and Sciences, NY Univ. 1960–61, Trustee 1962, Pres. 1962–75; Rector, UN Univ., Tokyo 1975–80; Pres. New York Botanical Garden 1980–89; Dir Union Carbide Corpn 1963–96, Alliance Fund and related funds 1983; Chair. Pres. Nixon's Task Force on Priorities in Higher Educ. 1969; mem. Asscn of American Rhodes Scholars 1962; Pres. Harry Frank Guggenheim Foundation 1989–; Trustee Lehman Foundation 1973; Hon. LLD (Princeton, Moorehouse Coll., Hofstra Univ., Lafayette Coll., Hahnemann Medical Coll., Fordham); Hon. LHD (Hartwick Coll., Pace Univ., Colgate, Pittsburgh, New York); Hon. DCL (Alfred Univ.); Chevalier, Légion d'honneur, First Class Order of the Sacred Treasure. *Portraits:* of Mary Bunting at Harvard Club, NY and of James Evans at Center Coll., Danville, Ky. *Leisure interest:* painting. *Address:* Harry Frank Guggenheim Foundation, 527 Madison Avenue, New York, NY 10022-4304 (Office); 45 E 89th Street, Apt. 39C, New York, NY 10128, USA (Home). *Telephone:* (212) 289-1673.

HESTER, Ronald Ernest, PhD, DSc, FRSC; British professor of chemistry; b. 8 March 1936, Slough, Bucks.; s. of Ernest Hester and Rhoda Lennox; m. Bridget Maddin 1958; two s. two d.; ed Royal Grammar School, High Wycombe, Univs. of London and Cambridge and Cornell Univ., USA; Asst Prof. Cornell Univ. 1962–65; Lecturer, Sr Lecturer, Reader, Univ. of York 1965–85, Prof. of Chem. 1985–2001; Prof. Emer. 2001–; European Ed. Biospectroscopy 1994–; mem. Council and various bds., Science & Eng Research Council (SERC). *Publications:* Physical Inorganic Chemistry 1964, Understanding Our Environment 1986, Advances in Spectroscopy (26 Vols) 1975–98, Spectroscopy of Biological Molecules 1991, Issues in Environmental Science and Technology 1994–; more than 300 research papers in int. journals. *Leisure interests:* squash, skiing, tennis, golf, travel. *Address:* Department of Chemistry, University of York, York, YO10 5DD (Office); The Old Rectory, Crayke, York, YO61 4TA, England (Home).

HESTON, Charlton; American actor; b. 4 Oct. 1924, Evanston, Ill.; s. of Russell Carter and Lilla Charlton Heston; m. Lydia Clark 1944; one s. one d.; ed Northwestern Univ., Evanston; first Broadway appearance in Antony and Cleopatra 1948; has starred in more than 50 films, Hollywood 1950–; Pres. Screen Actors Guild 1965–71; mem. Nat. Council of Arts 1967; Trustee American Film Inst. 1971–, Chair 1973; Chair. on Arts, Presidential Task Force on Arts and Humanities 1981–; Vice-Pres. Nat. Rifle Asscn 1997–98, Pres. 1998–; Acad. Award for Best Actor, Ben Hur 1959, Veterans of Foreign Wars Citizenship Medal 1982, Golden Medal of the City of Vienna 1995; Commdr Ordre des Arts et des Lettres. *Stage appearances include:* Macbeth 1954, 1959, 1976 (London), Mister Roberts 1954, Detective Story 1956, A Man for All Seasons 1965, 1987, Caine Mutiny Court Martial (also Dir), London 1985, Love Letters (London) 1999. *Television includes:* Chiefs (CBS) 1983, Nairobi Affair (CBS) 1984, The Colbys (ABC-TV), A Thousand Heroes 1991. *Films include:* Julius Caesar 1950, Dark City 1950, The Greatest Show on Earth 1952, The Savage 1952, Ruby Gentry 1952, The President's Lady 1953, Pony Express 1953, Arrowhead 1953, Bad for Each Other 1953, The Naked Jungle 1954, Secret of the Incas 1954, The Far Horizons 1955, Lucy Gallant 1955, The Private War of Major Benson 1955, Three Violent People 1956, The Ten Commandments 1956, Touch of Evil 1958, The Big Country 1958, The Buccaneer 1958, Ben Hur 1959, The Wreck of the Mary Deare 1959, El Cid 1961, The Pigeon that Took Rome 1962, Diamond Head 1962, 55 Days at Peking 1962, Major Dundee 1964, The Greatest Story Ever Told 1965, The Agony and the Ecstasy 1965, The War Lord 1965, Khartoum 1966, Counterpoint 1967, Will Penny 1967, Planet of the Apes 1967, Beneath the Planet of the Apes 1969, The Hawaiians 1970, Julius Caesar 1970, The Omega Man 1971, Antony and Cleopatra 1972, Skyjacked 1972, The Call of the Wild 1972, Soylent Green 1973, The Three Musketeers 1973, The Four Musketeers 1974, Earthquake 1974, Airport 1975, Midway 1975, Two Minute Warning 1976, The Last Hard Men 1976, The Prince and the Pauper 1976, Gray Lady Down 1978, The Awakening 1980, Mother Lode 1981, Caine Mutiny Court Martial (also Dir) 1988, Treasure Island 1989, Almost an Angel (cameo), Solar Crisis, Wayne's World 2 (cameo), True Lies 1994, In the Mouth of Madness, Alaska (also Dir), Hercules (voice) 1997, Any Given Sunday 1998, Town and Country 1998, Toscano 1999. *Publications:* The Actor's Life 1979, In the Arena 1995, Charlton Heston Presents the Bible 1997. *Leisure interests:* sketching, tennis. *Address:* c/o Jack Gilardi, ICM, 8942 Wilshire Boulevard, Beverly Hills, CA 90211, USA; c/o NRA, 11250 Waples Mill Road, Fairfax, VA 22030.

HETFIELD, James; American singer; b. 3 Aug. 1963; lead singer Metallica 1981–; Grammy Awards 1990, 1991, 1998. *Albums include:* Kill 'em All 1983, Ride the Lightning 1984, Master of Puppets 1986, ...And Justice For All 1988, Metallica 1991, Live Sh*t: Binge and Purge 1993, Kill 'Em All 1995, Load 1996, Reload 1997, Garage Inc. 1998, S & M 1999. *Address:* c/o Metallica Elektra Records, 75 Rockefeller Plaza, New York, NY 10019, USA (Office).

HEWISH, Antony, PhD, FRS, FRAS; British radio astronomer; b. 11 May 1924, Fowey, Cornwall; s. of the late Ernest W. Hewish and Grace F. L. Hewish (née Pinch); m. Marjorie E. C. Richards 1950; one s. one d.; ed King's Coll., Taunton and Gonville and Caius Coll., Cambridge; war service 1943–46; Research Fellow, Gonville and Caius Coll., Cambridge 1951–54, Supernumerary Fellow 1956–61; Univ. Asst Dir of Research 1953–61, lecturer 1961–69; Fellow, Churchill Coll. Cambridge 1962–; Reader in Radio Astronomy, Univ. of Cambridge 1969–71, Prof. 1971–89, Prof. Emer. 1989–; Prof. Royal Inst. 1977; Dir Mullard Radio Astronomy Observatory, Cambridge 1982–88; Vikram Sarabhai Prof., Ahmedabad 1988; Foreign Hon. mem. American Acad. of Arts and Sciences 1970; mem. Belgian Royal Acad. of Arts and Sciences 1989; mem. Emer. Academia Europaea 1996; Foreign Fellow Indian Nat. Science Acad.; Hon. ScD (Leicester) 1976, (Exeter) 1977, (Manchester) 1989, (Santa Maria, Brazil) 1989, (Cambridge) 1996, (Univ. Teknologi Malaysia) 1997; Hamilton Prize (Cambridge) 1951, Eddington Medal, Royal Astronomical Soc. 1968, Boys Prize, Inst. of Physics 1970, Dellinger Medal, Int. Union of Radio Science, Hopkins Prize, Cambridge Philosophical Soc. 1972, Michelson Medal, Franklin Inst. 1973, Holweck Medal and Prize, Soc. Française de Physique 1974, Nobel Prize for Physics (jtly with Sir Martin Ryle) 1974, Hughes Medal, Royal Soc. 1977, Vainu Bappu Prize, Indian Nat. Science Acad. 1998; Hon. Citizen of Kwangju, S Korea 1995. *Achievement:* discovery of pulsars. *Publications:* many papers in scientific journals; Ed.: Seeing Beyond the Invisible, Pulsars as Physics Laboratories. *Leisure interests:* listening to good music, gardening, cliff walking. *Address:* Cavendish Laboratory, Madingley Road, Cambridge, CB3 0HE (Office); Pryor's Cottage, Kingston, Cambridge, CB3 7NQ, England. *Telephone:* (1223) 337299 (Office); (1223) 262657. *Fax:* (1223) 354599 (Office). *E-mail:* ah120@mrao.cam.ac.uk (Office). *Website:* www.mrao.cam.ac.uk (Office).

HEWITT, Lleyton; Australian tennis player; b. 24 Feb. 1981, Adelaide; s. of Glynn Hewitt and Cherilyn Rumball; turned professional 1998; became youngest-ever season-ending world number one following Masters Cup victory over Pete Sampras (q.v.) 2001; winner Davis Cup 1999, finalist 2000, 2001; winner 17 singles titles (including US Open 2001, Wimbledon 2002), 2 doubles titles, to Dec. 2002. *Leisure interests:* Australian Rules football, golf. *Address:* Octagon Worldwide, PO. Box 3297, North Burnley, Victoria 3121, Australia (Office).

HEWITT, Patricia Hope, MA, FRSA; British politician; b. 2 Dec. 1948; d. of Sir (Cyrus) Lenox (Simson) Hewitt and Alison Hope Hewitt; m. William Birtles 1981; one s. one d.; ed Church of England Girls' Grammar School, Canberra, Australia, Australian Nat. Univ., Newnham Coll. Cambridge; Public Relations Officer, Age Concern 1971–73; Women's Rights Officer, Nat. Council for Civil Liberties (now Liberty) 1973–74, Gen. Sec. 1974–83; Labour Party cand. Leicester E, gen. elections 1983; Press and Broadcasting Sec. to Leader of Opposition 1983–88, Policy Co-ordinator 1988–89; Sr Research Fellow Inst. for Public Policy Research 1989, Deputy Dir 1989–94; Visiting Fellow Nuffield Coll. Oxford 1992–; Head, then Dir of Research, Andersen Consulting 1994–97; Labour MP for Leicester W 1997–; mem. Select Cttee on Social Security 1997–98; Econ. Sec. to the Treasury 1998–99, Minister of State, Dept of Trade and Industry 1999–2001, Sec. of State for Trade and Industry 2001–; Minister for Women 2001–; mem. Sec. of State's Advisory Cttee on Employment of Women 1977–84, Nat. Labour Women's Cttee 1979–83, Labour Party Inquiry into Security Services 1980–81, Editorial Advisory Panel, New Socialist 1980–90, Council, Campaign for Freedom of Information 1983–89, Bd, Int. League for Human Rights 1984–97, Exec. Cttee Fabian Soc. 1988–93, Council, Inst. for Fiscal Studies 1996–98; Co-Chair. Human Rights Network 1979–81; Deputy Chair. Comm. on Social Justice 1993–95; Vice-Chair. Healthcare 2000 1995–96, British Council 1997–98; Assoc. Newnham Coll. Cambridge 1984–97. *Publications:* Civil Liberties, the NCCL Guide (co-ed.) 1977, The Privacy Report 1977, Your Rights at Work 1981, The Abuse of Power 1981, Your Second Baby (jt author) 1990, About Time: The Revolution in Work and Family Life 1993. *Leisure interests:* reading, theatre, music, politics, gardening. *Address:* Department of Trade and Industry, 1 Victoria Street, London, SW1H 0ET (Office); 75 Ashleigh Road, Leicester, LE3 0FD, England (Home). *Telephone:* (20) 7215-5000 (Office); (116) 251-6160 (Home). *Fax:* (20) 7222-0612 (Office). *E-mail:* dti .enquiries@dti.gsi.gov.uk (Office). *Website:* www.dti.gov.uk (Office).

HEWSON, John Robert, AO, BEcons, PhD; Australian politician, professor of economics and business executive; b. 28 Oct. 1946, Sydney, NSW; s. of Donald Hewson and of the late Eileen Isabella Hewson (née Tippett); m. 1st Margaret Hewson; two s. one d.; m. 2nd Carolyn Judith Hewson 1988; one d.; ed Univ. of Sydney, Univ. of Saskatchewan, Canada and Johns Hopkins Univ. USA; Research Officer, Bureau of Census and Statistics, Treasury 1967–68; Teaching Fellow, Dept of Econs, Univ. of Saskatchewan 1968–69; Teaching Asst, Dept of Political Economy, Johns Hopkins Univ. 1969–71; Economist IMF 1973–74; Research Economist Reserve Bank of Australia 1975–76; Econ. Adviser to Fed. Treas. 1976–77, 1978–81, Chief of Staff 1981–82; Prof. of Econs, Univ. of NSW 1978–87, Head School of Econs 1983–87; MP for Wentworth, Fed. Parl. 1987–95; Shadow Minister for Finance 1988–89, Shadow Treas. 1989–90; Leader of the Opposition 1990–94; Shadow Minister for Industry, Commerce, Infrastrucuture and Customs 1994–95; Dir and Chair. ABN AMRO Australia Ltd 1995–98; Chair. The John Hewson Goup Pty Ltd 1995–, Network Entertainment Ltd 1996–97, Australian Bus Mfg Co. Ltd (now Universal Bus Co. Pty Ltd) 1999–, Global Renewables Ltd 2000–, Strategic Capital Man. Ltd 2000–, Belle Property Pty Ltd 2000–; Dir and Vice-Chair. TV Shopping Network Ltd 1996–98; Dir Churchill Resources NL Group 1996–98, Moran Health Care Group Pty Ltd 1998–2001; Deputy Chair. Miniproc Ltd 1998–2000; Fellow Australian Inst. of Co. Dirs.; Pres. Arthritis Foundation of Australia 1997–; Dir Positive Ageing Foundation 1999–; weekly columnist, Australian Financial Review opinion page. *Publications:* Liquidity Creation and Distribution in the Eurocurrency Market 1975, The Eurocurrency Markets and their Implications: A New View of International Monetary Problems and Monetary Reform (jtly) 1975, Offshore Banking in Australia 1981. *Leisure interests:* golf and most sports, classic cars and motor sports, jazz and musical comedies. *Address:* Level 29, ABN AMRO Tower, 88 Phillip Street, Sydney, NSW 2000, Australia. *Telephone:* (2) 8259-6204 (Office). *Fax:* (2) 8259-5430 (Office). *E-mail:* john.hewson@au.abnamro.com (Office).

HEY, John Denis, MA, MSc; British professor of economics and statistics; b. 26 Sept. 1944; s. of G. B. Hey and E. H. Hey; m. Marlene Bissett 1968 (divorced 1997); one s. two d.; ed Univs. of Cambridge and Edinburgh; econometrician, Hoare & Co. London 1968–69; Lecturer in Econs Univ. of Durham 1969–74, Univ. of St Andrew's 1974–75; Lecturer in Economic Statistics, Univ. of York 1975, Sr Lecturer, Prof. of Econs and Statistics 1984– (part-time 1998–), Co-Dir Centre for Experimental Econs 1986–; Hon. Prof. of Econs and Econometrics, Univ. of Vienna; Prof. Ordinario, Univ. of Bari 1998–. *Publications:* Statistics in Economics 1974, Uncertainty in Microeconomics 1979, Economics in Disequilibrium 1981, Data in Doubt 1984, Experiments in Economics 1991, Experimental Economics (Ed.) 1995, Economics of Uncertainty 1997. *Leisure interests:* walking, squash, opera, music. *Address:* Department of Economics and Related Studies, University of York, Heslington, York, YO1 5DD, England; Università degli Studi di Bari, via Camillo Rosalba 53, 70124 Bari, Italy. *Telephone:* (1904) 433786 (York) (Office); (080) 5049095 (Bari) (Office). *Fax:* (1904) 433759 (York) (Office); (080) 5049194 (Bari) (Office). *E-mail:* jdh1@york.ac.uk (Office); j.hey@dse.uniba.it (Office). *Website:* www .york.ac.uk/users/~jdh1 (Office).

HEYDE, Christopher Charles, PhD, DSc, FAA; Australian university professor and statistician; b. 20 April 1939, Sydney; s. of G. C. Heyde and A. D. Wessing; m. Elizabeth James 1965; two s.; ed Barker Coll., Hornsby, Sydney Univ. and Australian Nat. Univ.; Asst Prof. Mich. State Univ. 1964–65; lecturer Univ. of Sheffield, UK 1965–67; Special Lecturer Univ. of Manchester, UK 1967–68; Reader, Australian Nat. Univ. 1968–75; Chief Research Scientist CSIRO 1975–83; Prof. and Chair. Dept of Statistics, Univ. of Melbourne 1983–86; Prof. and Head Dept of Statistics, Inst. of Advanced Studies 1986–88, Dean School of Math. Sciences 1989–91; Prof. of Statistics, Inst. of Advanced Studies, Australian Nat. Univ. 1992–; Prof. of Statistics, Columbia Univ., New York 1993–; Dir Columbia Center for Applied Probability 1993–; Visiting Prof. Stanford Univ., Calif. 1972–73; Ed. Australian Journal of Statistics 1973–78, Stochastic Processes and Their Applications 1983–89, Journal of Advances in Applied Probability 1990–; Fellow Inst. of Mathematical Statistics 1973; Pres. Statistical Soc. of Australia 1979–80, also Hon. Life mem.; mem. Int. Statistical Inst. (Vice-Pres. 1985–87, 1993–95), Australian Acad. of Science (Vice-Pres. 1988–89, Treas. 1989–93); Hon. DSc (Sydney) 1998; Pitman Medallist, Statistical Soc. of Australia 1988, Thomas Ranken Lyle Medal, Australian Acad. of Sciences 1994, Inaugural Hannan Medal Australian Acad. of Sciences 1995. *Publications:* I. J. Bienaymé: Statistical Theory Anticipated (with E. Seneta) 1977, Martingale Limit Theory and Its Application (with P. Hall) 1980, Quasi-Likelihood and Its Application 1997, Statisticians of the Centuries (Ed. with E. Seneta) 2001; plus 190 articles on probability theory and mathematical statistics. *Address:* School of Mathematical Sciences, Australian National University, Canberra, ACT 0200; 22 Nungara Place, Aranda, ACT 2614, Australia (Home). *Telephone:* (2) 6125-2962 (Office).

HEYER, Stephen J.; American business executive; b. 1954; ed Cornell Univ.; fmr Sr Vice-Pres. and Man. Pnr Booz Allen & Hamilton; Pres. and COO Young & Rubicam Advertising Worldwide –1994; Pres. and COO AOL Time Warner Turner Broadcasting System Inc. (launched 14 TV networks and 19 websites for CNN, Cartoon Networks and Turner Classic Movies) and mem. AOL Time Warner Operating Cttee 1994–2001; Pres. and COO Coca-Cola Ventures –2001, Head of Latin American Operations 2002, Pres. and CEO Coca-Cola Co. Dec. 2002–; mem. Bd Dirs WPP Group PLC 2000–, Equifax Inc. 2002–, Coca-Cola Enterprises Inc., Coca-Cola FEMSA, Transora, Cable Advertising Bureau, Advisory Council, Atlanta History Center, Woodruff Arts Center, Atlanta Symphony Orchestra, Piedmont Hosp., Trinity School.

Address: The Coca-Cola Company, POB 1734, Atlanta, GA 30301, USA (Office). *Telephone:* (404) 676-2121 (Office). *Fax:* (404) 515-6428 (Office). *Website:* www.cocacola.com (Office).

HEYLIN, Angela Christine, OBE; British public relations consultant; b. 17 Sept. 1943, London; d. of the late Bernard Heylin and Ruth Victoria Heylin; m. Maurice Minzly 1971; one s.; ed Apsley Grammar School, Watford Coll.; CEO Charles Barker Lyons 1984, Charles Barker Watney & Powell 1986–, Charles Barker Traverse-Healy 1987–; Dir Charles Barker Group 1984, Chair. and CEO 1988; CEO Charles Barker PLC 1992–96, Chair. 1996–99; UK Pres. BSMG Worldwide 1999–; Dir Corp. Communications 1989, Mothercare PLC 1999–, Provident Financial PLC 1999–; mem. Citizen's Charter Advisory Panel 1993–97; Trustee Historic Royal Palaces 1999–, Austin Reed Group 2001–; Chair. The House of St Barnabas-in-Soho 2001–; Award for Outstanding Contrib. to Industry 1988. *Publication:* Putting It Across: The Art of Communicating, Presenting and Persuading 1991. *Leisure interests:* theatre, entertaining. *Address:* BSMG Worldwide, 110 St Martin's Lane, London, WC2N 4DY (Office); 46 St Augustine's Road, London, NW1 9RN, England (Home). *Telephone:* (20) 7841-5459 (Office); (20) 7485-4815 (Home). *Fax:* (20) 7841-5500 (Office); (20) 7482-3525 (Home). *E-mail:* acheylin@bsmg .com (Office); home@minzly.fsnet.co.uk (Home).

HEYMAN, David; British film producer; b. 1961; began career as production runner for film producers Milos Forman and David Lean; Creative Exec. Warner Bros., Los Angeles 1986–89, Vice-Pres. United Artists 1989; now working as ind. producer; returned to UK 1997, f. Heyday Films 1997. *Films produced include:* Juice, The Daytrippers, Harry Potter and the Philosopher's Stone 2001, Harry Potter and the Chamber of Secrets 2002. *Address:* Heyday Films, 5 Denmark Street, London, WC2H 8LP, England (Office). *Telephone:* (20) 7836-6333 (Office).

HEYMAN, Ira Michael, JD; American professor of law; b. 30 May 1930, New York City; s. of Harold A. Heyman and Judith Sobel; m. Therese Thau 1950; two s. (one deceased); ed Dartmouth Coll. and Yale Law School; Legislative Asst to Senator Irving M. Ives, Washington, DC 1950–51; mem. State Bar of NY 1956; Assoc. Carter, Ledyard & Milburn, New York 1956–57; Law Clerk, Court of Appeals for Second Circuit, New Haven, Conn. 1957–58; Chief Law Clerk, U.S. Supreme Court 1958–59; Acting Assoc. Prof. of Law, Univ. of Calif. (Berkeley) 1959–61, Prof. 1961–94, Prof. of Law and City and Regional Planning 1966–93, Prof. Emer. 1993–, Vice-Chancellor 1974–80, Chancellor 1980–90, Chancellor Emer. 1990–; Sec. Smithsonian Inst. 1994–99, Sec. Emer. 2000–; mem. State Bar. of Calif. 1961–; Visiting Prof. Yale Law School 1963–64, Stanford Law School 1971–72; Trustee Lawyers' Comm. for Civil Rights Under Law 1977, Chair. 1991; Chair. Dartmouth Coll. 1991; mem. Bd of Dirs., Pacific Gas & Electric Co. 1985–; Presidio Trust 2000–; other professional appts. and consultancies; Hon. LLD (Univ. of Pacific) 1981, (Md) 1986; Hon. DHumLitt (Hebrew Union Coll.) 1984; Chevalier, Légion d'honneur. *Publications:* numerous articles in journals, papers and legal documents in areas of civil rights, constitutional law, land planning, metropolitan Govt, housing, environmental law and man. *Leisure interests:* tennis, opera. *Address:* c/o Smithsonian Institution, 1000 Jefferson Drive, SW, Washington, DC 20560, USA. *E-mail:* heyman@law.berkeley.edu (Office).

HEYMANN, Daniel, PhD; Argentine professor of economics; b. 30 Dec. 1949, Buenos Aires; s. of Gunther Heymann and Marta Weil; m. Cristina Bramuglia 1976; two s.; ed Coll. Français de Buenos Aires, Univ. of Buenos Aires and Univ. of Calif. Los Angeles; Asst Prof. Univ. of Buenos Aires 1973–75; Research Asst ECLA, Buenos Aires Office 1974–78, Sr Economist 1982–; Prof. Instituto Torcuato Di Tella, Buenos Aires 1982–; Visiting Assoc. Prof. Univ. of Calif., LA 1987, Visiting Prof. 1991; Prof. Univ. of Buenos Aires 1987–. *Publications:* Fluctuations of the Argentine Manufacturing Industry 1980, Three Essays on Inflation and Stabilization 1986, The Austral Plan 1987, Notes on High Inflation and Stabilization 1990, Distributive Conflict and the Fiscal Deficit: Some Inflationary Games (jtly) 1991, On the Interpretation of the Current Account 1994, High Inflation (jtly.) 1995, Business Cycles from Misperceived Trends (jtly) 1996. *Address:* Instituto Torcuato Di Tella, Miñones 2159/77, 1428 Buenos Aires (Office); Paraguay 1178, 2do. Piso, 1057 Buenos Aires, Argentina. *Telephone:* (11) 4783-8630 (Office). *Fax:* (11) 4783-3061 (Office).

HEYMANN, Klaus; German business executive; m. Takako Nishizaki; one s.; Export Advertising and Promotion Man. Max Braun AG 1961–62; with The Overseas Weekly, Frankfurt 1962–67, ran Hong Kong Office 1967–69; f. Pacific Mail-Order System 1969; organized classical concerts in Hong Kong; mem. Bd Hong Kong Philharmonic Orchestra, later Chair. of Fund-Raising Cttee and Hon. Gen. Man.; f. Naxos. *Address:* HNH International Ltd., 6/F, Sino Industrial Plaza, 9 Kai Cheung Road, Kowloon Bay, Hong Kong Special Administrative Region, People's Republic of China (Office).

HEYZER, Noeleen, PhD; Singaporean international organization official; m.; two d.; ed Univ. of Singapore, Univ. of Cambridge, England; Fellow and Research Officer, Inst. of Devt Studies, Univ. of Sussex, England 1979–81; with Social Devt Div., ESCAP, Bangkok, Thailand; Dir Gender and Devt Programme, Asian and Pacific Devt Centre, Kuala Lumpur, Malaysia 1984–94; Substantive Co-ordinator for the Asia-Pacific NGO Working Group for the UN Fourth World Conf. on Women, Beijing, People's Repub. of China; Exec. Dir UN Devt Fund for Women 1994–; served on Bds. of several humanitarian orgs. including Devt Alternatives with Women for a New Era, the Global South, ISIS, Oxfam, Panos and Soc. for Int. Devt. *Publications*

include: Gender, Economic Growth and Poverty, The Trade in Domestic Workers, Working Women in South-East Asia. *Address:* United Nations Development Fund for Women, 6th Floor, 304 East 45th Street, New York, NY 10017, USA (Office). *Telephone:* (212) 906-6400 (Office). *Fax:* (212) 906-6705 (Office). *E-mail:* unifem@undp.org (Office). *Website:* www.unifem.undp .org (Office).

HIATT, Fred, BA; American journalist; b. 1955, Washington; City Hall reporter, Atlanta Journal-Constitution 1979–80; reporter, The Washington Star 1981; Va reporter, The Washington Post 1981–83, Pentagon reporter 1983–86, NE Asia Co-Bureau Chief 1987–90, Moscow Co-Bureau Chief 1991–95, editorial writer 1996–. *Publications:* The Secret Sun 1992 (novel), If I Were Queen of the World 1997 (children's book), Baby Talk 1999. *Address:* The Washington Post, 1150 15th Street, NW, Washington, DC 20071, USA (Office).

HIBBERT, Christopher, MC, MA, FRSL; British author; b. 5 March 1924, Enderby, Leics.; s. of the late Canon H. V. Hibbert; m. Susan Piggford 1948; two s. one d.; ed Radley Coll., Oriel Coll. Oxford; served in Second World War, Capt. London Irish Rifles (twice wounded) 1943–45; partner firm of land agents and auctioneers 1949–58; Hon. DLitt; Heinemann Award for Literature 1962, McColvin Medal Library Asscn 1989. *Publications:* The Destruction of Lord Raglan 1961, Corunna 1961, Benito Mussolini 1962, The Battle of Arnhem 1962, The Court at Windsor 1964, The Roots of Evil 1964, Agincourt 1965, Garibaldi and His Enemies 1966, The Making of Charles Dickens 1967, London: Biography of a City 1969, The Dragon Wakes: China and the West 1970, The Personal History of Samuel Johnson 1971, George IV (Vol. I) 1972, (Vol. II) 1973, The Rise and Fall of the House of Medici 1974, Edward VII 1976, The Great Mutiny: India 1857 1978, The French Revolution 1980, Rome: Biography of a City 1985, The English: A Social History 1986, The Grand Tour 1987, Venice: The Biography of a City 1988, The Encyclopaedia of Oxford (Ed.) 1988, The Virgin Queen: The Personal History of Elizabeth I 1990, Redcoats and Rebels: The War for America 1770–1781 1990, Cavaliers and Roundheads: The English at War, 1642–1649 1993, Florence: The Biography of a City 1993, Nelson: A Personal History 1994, Corunna 1996, A Soldier of the 71st 1996, Wellington: A Personal History 1997, No Ordinary Place: Radley College and the Public School System 1847–1997 1997, George III: A Personal History 1998, Queen Victoria: A Personal History 2000, The Marlboroughs: John and Sarah Churchill 2001; Napoleon: Wives and Women 2002. *Leisure interests:* gardening, cooking. *Address:* 6 Albion Place, West Street, Henley-on-Thames, Oxfordshire, RG9 2DT, England. *Telephone:* (1491) 575235.

HIBBIN, Sally, BA; British film producer; b. 3 July 1953, London; d. of Eric Hibbin and Nina Hibbin; ed Keele Univ. and Univ. Coll., London Univ.; researcher and sub-ed. The Movie 1978–81; freelance journalist (film and sports) 1981–93; documentary producer 1982–87; drama producer 1988–; Founder mem. and Dir Parallax Pictures Ltd; Jt Business Award, Women in TV and Film 1994. *Documentaries:* Live a Life 1982, The Road to Gdansk, Great Britain United. *TV and film productions:* A Very British Coup (BAFTA and Emmy Awards) 1987, Riff Raff (FELIX European Film Award) 1991, Raining Stones 1993, Bad Behaviour (exec. producer) 1993, Ladybird, Ladybird 1994, I.D. 1995, Land and Freedom (exec. producer) 1995, The Englishman Who Went Up a Hill But Came Down a Mountain (exec. producer) 1995, Carla's Song 1996, Hold Back the Night 1999, Liam (exec. producer) 2000, Innocence (exec. producer) 2001. *Television:* Stand and Deliver, BBC 1998, Dockers (drama), Channel 4 1999. *Publications:* Politics, Ideology and the State (ed.) 1978, The Making of Licence to Kill 1989, The Making of The Official History of the James Bond Films 1987, 1989, Back to the Future III 1990, The Official History of the Carry On Films 1988; contribs to various film journals, magazines and collections. *Leisure interests:* walking, cooking, Tottenham Hotspur Football Club. *Address:* Parallax Pictures Ltd, 7 Denmark Street, London, WC2, England. *Telephone:* (20) 7836-1478. *Fax:* (20) 7497-8062. *E-mail:* sally@parallaxpictures.freeserve.co.uk (Office). *Website:* parallaxpictures.co.uk (Office).

HICK, Graeme Ashley; Zimbabwean cricketer; b. 23 May 1966, Salisbury (now Harare); s. of John and Eve Hick; ed Banket Primary School, Prince Edward Boys' High School; right-hand batsman, off-break bowler, slip fielder; teams: Zimbabwe 1983–86, Worcs. 1984–, Northern Dists 1987–89, Queensland 1990–91; scored his first hundred when aged six (for Banket primary school); youngest player (17) to appear in 1983 World Cup and youngest to rep. Zimbabwe; 65 Tests for England 1991–97, scoring 3,383 runs (average 31.32), including 6 hundreds; youngest to score 2,000 first-class runs in a season (1986); scored 1,019 runs before June 1988, including a record 410 runs in April; fewest innings for 10,000 runs in county cricket (179); youngest (24) to score 50 first-class hundreds; toured Australia 1994–95; mem. England World Cup Squad 1996; 120 limited-overs ints for 3,846 runs (average 37.33) by Dec. 2002; scored 315 not out v. Durham June 2002 – highest championship innings of the season; Wisden Cricketer of the Year 1987. *Publication:* My Early Life (autobiog.) 1992. *Leisure interests:* golf, tennis, squash, indoor hockey, cinema, television, listening to music. *Address:* c/o Worcestershire County Cricket Club, New Road, Worcester, WR2 4QQ, England. *Telephone:* (1905) 748474.

HICK, John Harwood, PhD, DPhil, DLitt; British university teacher; b. 20 Jan. 1922, Scarborough, Yorks.; s. of Mark Day Hick and Mary Aileen Hirst; m. Joan Hazel Bowers 1953 (died 1996); three s. (one deceased) one d.; ed

Bootham School, York, Edinburgh Univ., Oxford Univ., Westminster Theological Coll., Cambridge; Minister, Belford Presbyterian Church, Northumberland 1953–56; Asst Prof. of Philosophy, Cornell Univ., USA 1956–59; Stuart Prof. of Christian Philosophy, Princeton Theological Seminary, USA 1959–64; Lecturer in Divinity, Cambridge Univ. 1964–67; H. G. Wood Prof. of Theology, Birmingham Univ. 1967–80, now Prof. Emer.; Danforth Prof. of Philosophy of Religion, Claremont Graduate Univ., USA 1980–92, Prof. Emer. 1992–, Chair., Dept of Religion, Dir Blaisdell Programs in World Religions and Cultures 1983–92; Gifford Lecturer, Edinburgh Univ. 1986–87; Guggenheim Fellow 1963–64, 1986–87; SA Cook Bye-Fellow, Gonville and Caius Coll., Cambridge 1963–64; Fellow Inst. for Advanced Research in Arts and Social Sciences, Birmingham Univ.; Vice-Pres. World Congress of Faiths, British Soc. for the Philosophy of Religion; Hon. Prof., Univ. of Wales; Hon. TheolDr (Uppsala) 1977; Hon. DD (Glasgow) 2002; Grawemeyer Award in Religion 1991. *Publications include:* Faith and Knowledge, Evil and the God of Love, God and the Universe of Faiths, Death and Eternal Life, Arguments for the Existence of God, Problems of Religious Pluralism, God Has Many Names, Philosophy of Religion, The Second Christianity, An Interpretation of Religion, Disputed Questions in Theology and the Philosophy of Religion, The Metaphor of God Incarnate, The Rainbow of Faiths, The Fifth Dimension; Ed. The Myth of God Incarnate, The Many-Faced Argument, The Myth of Christian Uniqueness, The Existence of God, Truth and Dialogue, Christianity and Other Religions, Faith and the Philosophers. *Leisure interests:* reading, sitting in the garden, discussing. *Address:* 144 Oak Tree Lane, Selly Oak, Birmingham, B29 6HU, England. *Telephone:* (121) 689-4803. *E-mail:* j.h.hick@bham.ac.uk (Home). *Website:* www.johnhick.org.uk (Home).

HICKEL, Walter Joseph; American fmr state governor and business executive; b. 18 Aug. 1919, nr Claflin, Kan.; s. of Robert A. Hickel and Emma Zecha; m. 1st Janice Cannon 1941 (died 1943); one s.; m. 2nd Ermalee Strutz 1945; five s.; ed public schools in Claflin; builder/owner, Traveler's Inn, Anchorage 1953–82, Fairbanks, Alaska 1955–82, Hickel Investment Co., Anchorage 1947–, Hotel Captain Cook, Anchorage, Northern Lights Shopping Center, Univ. Shopping Center, Anchorage, Valley River Shopping Center; Chair. Bd Hickel Investment Co.; Founder and fmr Chair. Yukon Pacific Corpn; Founder Inst. of the North, Alaska Pacific Univ. 1995; fmr mem. Bd of Dirs Rowan Cos., Inc.; fmr mem. world advisory council, Int. Design Science Inst.; fmr mem. Cttee on scientific freedom and responsibility AAAS; fmr mem. Bd of Dirs Salk Inst.; mem. Republican Nat. Cttee 1954–64; Sec. US Dept of Interior 1969–70; Gov. of Alaska 1966–69, 1990–94; Sec. Gen. The Northern Forum 1994–; several hon. degrees and other honours and distinctions. *Publications:* Who Owns America? 1971, Crisis in the Commons: The Alaska Solution 2002. *Leisure interests:* walking, travelling, boating in Prince William Sound. *Address:* 939 West Fifth Avenue, # 388 Anchorage, AK 99501 (Office); PO Box 101700, Anchorage, AK 99510; 1905 Loussac Drive, Anchorage, AK 99517, USA (Home). *Telephone:* (907) 343-2400 (Office); (907) 248-0013 (Home). *Fax:* (907) 343-2211 (Office). *E-mail:* wjhickel@gci.net (Office). *Website:* www.institutenorth.org (Office).

HICKEY, HE Cardinal James Aloysius, STD; American ecclesiastic; b. 11 Oct. 1920, Midland; s. of James P. Hickey and Agnes Ryan Hickey; ed Lateran Univ., Italy, Michigan State Univ.; ordained 1946, elected to the titular Church of Taraqua 1967, consecrated Bishop 1967, transferred to Cleveland 1974; Archbishop of Washington 1980–2000; Chancellor, Catholic Univ. America 1980–2000; Chair. Bd Trustees Nat. Shrine of Immaculate Conception 1980–2000, Bishop's Cttee on N American Colls. 1988–92, 1994–97; Episcopal Moderator Holy Childhood Asscn 1984–93; cr. Cardinal 1988. *Address:* Archdiocesan Pastoral Center, P.O. Box 29260, Washington, DC 20017, USA. *Telephone:* (301) 853-4585.

HICKOX, Richard Sidney, MA, FRCO, LRAM; British conductor; b. 5 March 1948, Stokenchurch, Bucks.; s. of Rev. S. E. Hickox and Jean Millar; m. 1st Frances Ina Sheldon-Williams 1976; one s.; m. 2nd Pamela H. Stephen 1995; one s.; ed Royal Grammar School, High Wycombe, Royal Acad. of Music, London and Queens' Coll. Cambridge (Organ Scholar); Dir of Music, High Wycombe Parish Church 1970–71, St Margaret's, Westminister 1972–82, Barbican Summer Festival 1984–85; Artistic Dir Woburn Festival 1967–89, Christ Church Spitalfields Festival 1978–94, St Endellion Festival 1974–, Truro Festival 1981–, Chester Summer Festival 1989–, City of London Festival 1994–; Artistic Dir Northern Sinfonia 1982–90, Prin. Guest Conductor 1990–; Music Dir, City of London Sinfonia and Richard Hickox Singers (now City of London Sinfonia Singers) 1971–, Bradford Festival Choral Soc. 1978–, London Symphony Chorus 1976–; Assoc. Conductor, London Symphony Orchestra 1985–; co-f. Opera Stage 1985; Prin. Conductor BBC Nat. Orchestra of Wales 2001–; has conducted opera at Covent Garden, ENO, Opera North and Scottish Opera; Gramophone Award for Best Choral Recording 1992, Royal Philharmonic Soc. Music Award 1995, Gramophone Opera Award 1995, Deutsche Schallplattenpreis, Diapason d'Or. *Recordings include:* Bach Masses, Albinoni Adagio, music by Finzi, Delius and Duruflé, Burgon Requiem, Haydn Nelson Mass (all for Decca, Argo Label), Gluck Armide, Handel Alcina, music by Vaughan Williams, Gilbert and Sullivan, Elgar Miniatures, Delius Miniatures and Berkeley Or Shall We Die? (all for EMI). *Leisure interests:* football, tennis, politics, surfing. *Address:* c/o Intermusica Artists' Management, 16 Duncan Terrace, London, N1 5BZ (Office); 35 Ellington Street, London, N7 8PN, England (Home). *Telephone:* (20) 7278-5455 (Office); (20) 7607-8984 (Home). *Fax:* (20) 7278-8434 (Office).

HIDAYAT, Bambang, PhD; Indonesian professor of astronomy; b. 18 Sept. 1934, Kundus, Cen. Java; m. (wife deceased); two c.; ed Case Inst. of Tech., Cleveland; Dir Bosscha Observatory 1968–83; Asst Prof. of Astronomy 1968, Assoc. Prof. 1974, Prof. 1976; Chair. Indonesian–Dutch Astronomy Programme 1982–, Indonesian–Japan Astronomy Programme 1980–94; Vice-Pres. Int. Astronomical Union 1994–2000; f. Indonesian Astronomical Soc. 1978, co-f. Indonesian Physics Soc.; mem. American Astronomical Soc., Royal Astronomical Soc., Indonesian Inst. of Sciences 1991; mem. Royal Comm. Al Albait Univ., Jordan 1993; Fellow Islamic Acad. of Sciences. *Publications:* several astronomy textbooks and more than 40 scientific papers. *Address:* Indonesian Institute of Sciences, Jl. Jendral Gatot Subroto no. 10, P.O. Box 250, Jakarta, Indonesia (Office). *Telephone:* (21) 5251542 (Office). *Fax:* (21) 5207226 (Office).

HIDE, Raymond, CBE, MA, ScD, CPhys, FInstP, FRS; British research geophysicist; b. 17 May 1929, Bentley near Doncaster; s. of the late Stephen Hide and Rose Edna Hide (née Cartlidge, later Mrs. T. Leonard); m. Phyllis Ann Licence 1958; one s. two d.; ed Percy Jackson Grammar School, Doncaster, Manchester and Cambridge Univs; Research Assoc. in Astrophysics, Yerkes Observatory, Univ. of Chicago 1953–54; Sr Research Fellow, Gen. Physics Div. AERE, Harwell 1954–57; Lecturer in Physics, King's Coll. Univ. of Durham 1957–61; Prof. of Geophysics and Physics at MIT 1961–67; Head of the Geophysical Fluid Dynamics Lab., Chief Scientific Officer (Individual Merit), Meteorological Office, Bracknell 1967–90; Gresham Prof. of Astronomy, Gresham Coll., City of London 1985–90; Dir Robert Hooke Inst. 1990–92 and Visiting Prof. of Physics, Oxford Univ. 1990–92, Research Prof., Dept of Physics 1992–94, Prof. Emer. of Physics, Oxford Univ. 1994–; Sr Research Investigator, Imperial Coll. London 2000–; Visiting Prof. Dept of Math., Univ. Coll., London 1969–84; Adrian Visiting Fellow, Univ. of Leicester 1981–83; Fellow Jesus Coll. Oxford 1983–97, Hon. Fellow 1997–; Hon. Fellow Gonville and Caius Coll., Cambridge 2001; mem. Council, Royal Soc. of London 1988–90; mem. Pontifical Acad. of Sciences, American Acad. of Arts and Sciences, Academia Europaea, Royal Astronomical Soc. (Pres. 1983–85), Royal Meteorological Soc. (Pres. 1974–76, Hon. mem. 1989), European Geophysical Soc. (Pres. 1982–84, Hon. mem. 1988), American Geophysical Union, Inst. of Physics, Int. Astronomical Union and numerous other socs and cttees; Chair. British Nat. Cttee for Geodesy and Geophysics, UK Chief Del. to Int. Union of Geodesy and Geophysics 1979–85; Hon. DSc (Leicester) 1985, (UMIST) 1994, (Paris) 1995; Charles Chree Medal and Prize of Inst. of Physics 1975, Holweck Medal and Prize, Société Française de Physique and Inst. of Physics 1982, Gold Medal, Royal Astronomical Soc. 1989, William Bowie Medal, American Geophysical Union 1997, Hughes Medal, Royal Soc. 1998, L. F. Richardson Medal, European Geophysical Soc. 1999. *Publications:* numerous scientific articles and papers. *Address:* Department of Mathematics, Imperial College, London, SW7 2BZ (Office); 17 Clinton Avenue, East Molesey, Surrey, KT8 0HS, England (Home). *Telephone:* (20) 8873-3366 (Home). *E-mail:* r.hide@ic.ac.uk (Office); r.hide@cwctv.net (Home).

HIEBERT, Erwin Nick, PhD; American professor of history of science; b. 27 May 1919, Saskatchewan, Canada; s. of Cornelius N. Hiebert and Tina Hiebert; m. Elfrieda Franz 1943; one s. two d.; ed Bethel Coll., N Newton, Kan., Univs. of Chicago and Wisconsin-Madison; Research Chemist, Standard Oil Co. of Indiana and the Manhattan Project 1943–46; Research Chemist, Inst. for Study of Metals, Univ. of Chicago 1947–50; Asst Prof. of Chem., San Francisco State Coll. 1952–55; Instructor in History of Science, Harvard 1955–57; Asst Prof., Assoc. Prof., Prof., History of Science, Univ. of Wis.-Madison 1957–70; Prof. of History of Science, Harvard 1970–90, Chair. 1977–84, Prof. Emer. 1990–; Pres. Div. of History of Science, Int. Union of History and Philosophy of Science 1982–84; Fellow, American Acad. of Arts and Sciences, Acad. Int. d'Histoire des Sciences; mem. Sächsische Akad. der Wissenschaften, Leipzig 1989–. *Publications:* Impact of Atomic Energy 1961, Historical Roots of the Principle of Conservation of Energy 1962, The Conception of Thermodynamics in the Scientific Thought of Mach and Planck 1967; and papers on history and philosophy of physics and chem. since 1800, science and religion, common frontiers between the exact sciences and the humanities, history of musical acoustics since 1850. *Leisure interests:* music, gardening. *Address:* c/o Harvard University, Widener Library 172, Cambridge, MA 02138, USA (Office). *E-mail:* ehiebert@fas.harvard.edu (Office).

HIERRO LÓPEZ, Luis; Uruguayan politician, teacher and journalist; b. 6 Jan. 1947, Montevideo; s. of Luis Hierro Gambardella and Celia Lopez; m. Ligia Armitran; four c.; journalist and newspaper 1965–84; history teacher 1968–73; researcher Museo Histórico Nacional 1974–84; mem. Nat. Exec. Cttee Colorado Party and Nat. Convention 1982–98, Chamber of Deputies (Pres. 1989) 1985–94; Chair. Cttees. on the Constitution, Gen. Legislation and Admin. and Human Rights, Special Cttee dealing with proposed anti-corruption legislation, Uruguayan Section of Jt Parl. Cttee of MERCOSUR; Senator, Colorado Party 1995–97; Vice-Pres. of Uruguay 2001–. *Publications:* Diario del Uruguay (co-author) 1975, Battle y la Reforma del Estado 1978. *Address:* Office of the Vice-President, Casa de Gobierno, Edif. Libertad, Avda Luis Alberto de Herrera 3350, esq. Avda José Pedro Varela, Montevideo, Uruguay (Office).

HIGGINS, Chester, Jr, BBA; American photographer; b. Nov. 1946, Lexington, Ky; s. of Varidee Loretta Young Higgins Smith and step-s. of Johnny Frank Smith; m. 1st Renalda Walker (divorced); one s. one d.; m. 2nd Betsy Kissam; ed Tuskegee Inst., Ala (now Tuskegee Univ.); became photographer 1967; photographer for Look magazine 1970; part-time photography instructor, New York Univ. School of Fine Arts 1975–78; staff photographer, New York Times 1975–; photographs have appeared in Art News, Look, New York Times Magazine, Life, Newsweek, Fortune, Ebony, Essence, Archaeology; UN Award, American Graphic Design Award, Art Dirs of New York Award. *Exhibitions include:* Int. Center of Photography, Smithsonian Inst., Museum of African Art, Museum of Photographic Arts, Schomberg Center, Newark Museum, Nat. Civil Rights Museum, Field Museum of Natural History, Metropolitan Museum of Art, New York Museum of Modern Art. *Publications include:* The Black Woman 1970, Drums of Life 1974, Some Time Ago: A Historical Portrait of Black Americans 1850–1950 1980, Feeling the Spirit: Searching the World for the People of Africa 1994, Elder Grace: The Nobility of Aging 2000. *Address:* c/o New York Times, 229 W 43rd Street, New York, NY 10036-3959, USA (Office).

HIGGINS, Jack (see Patterson, Harry).

HIGGINS, Dame Julia Stretton, DBE, DPhil, FRS, F.R.ENG.; British polymer scientist; b. 1 July 1942, London; d. of George Stretton Downes and Sheilah Stretton Downes; ed Ursuline Convent School, Wimbledon, Somerville Coll., Oxford; physics teacher Mexborough Grammar School 1966–68; Research Assoc. Manchester Univ. 1968–72, Centre de Recherche sur les Macromolécules, Strasbourg, France 1972–73; physicist, ILL, Grenoble, France 1973–76; mem. academic staff Imperial Coll., London 1976–, Prof. of Polymer Science 1989–; Foreign mem. Nat. Acad. of Eng, USA. *Publications:* 200 articles in scientific journals. *Leisure interests:* theatre, opera, travel. *Address:* Department of Chemical Engineering, Imperial College, London, SW7 2BY, England (Office). *Telephone:* (20) 7594-5565 (Office). *Fax:* (20) 7594-5638 (Office). *E-mail:* j.higgins@ic.ac.uk (Office).

HIGGINS, Michael D., BComm, MA; Irish politician and writer; b. April 1941, Limerick; m. Sabina Coyne; three s. one d.; ed Univ. Coll. Galway, Indiana Univ. and Univ. of Manchester; fmr Lecturer in Sociology and Politics, Univ. Coll. Galway; Senator 1973–77; mem. Galway Co. Council 1974–85; Alderman, Galway Borough Council 1974–85, Mayor of Galway 1982–83; mem. Galway City Council 1985–93; many other public appts.; mem. Dáil 1981–82, 1987–; Chair. The Labour Party 1978–87; Minister for Arts, Culture and the Gaeltacht 1993–97; fmr Pres. European Council of Culture Ministers; Pres. Council of Broadcasting Ministers; mem. Sociological Asscn of Ireland, American Sociological Asscn, PEN, Irish Writers' Union. *Address:* c/o Department of Arts, Culture and the Gaeltacht, 43–49 Mespil Road, Dublin 4, Ireland. *Telephone:* (1) 6670788. *Fax:* (1) 6670825.

HIGGINS, Dame Rosalyn, DBE, JSD, QC, FBA; British judge and professor of international law; b. 2 June 1937; d. of the late Lewis Cohen and Fay Inberg; m. Rt Hon Terence L. (now Lord) Higgins 1961; one s. one d.; ed Burlington Grammar School, London, Girton Coll. Cambridge and Yale Law School; UK Intern, Office of Legal Affairs, UN 1958; Commonwealth Fund Fellow 1959; Visiting Fellow, Brookings Inst. Washington, DC 1960; Jr Fellow in Int. Studies, LSE 1961–63; staff specialist in int. law, Royal Inst. of Int. Affairs 1963–74; Visiting Fellow, LSE 1974–78; Prof. of Int. Law, Univ. of Kent at Canterbury 1978–81; Prof. of Int. Law, LSE 1981–95; Judge of Int. Court of Justice 1995–; mem. UN Cttee on Human Rights 1985–95; Visiting Prof. Stanford Univ. 1975, Yale Univ. 1977; Vice-Pres. American Soc. of Int. Law 1972–74; Dr. hc (Paris XI); Hon. DCL (Dundee) 1994, (Durham, LSE) 1995, (Cambridge, Sussex, Kent, City Univ., Greenwich, Essex) 1996, (Birmingham, Leicester, Glasgow) 1997, (Nottingham) 1999, (Bath, Paris II, Sorbonne) 2001; Ordre des Palmes académiques 1988, Yale Law School Medal of Merit 1997, Manley Hudson Medal (ASIC) 1998. *Publications include:* The Development of International Law Through the Political Organs of the United Nations 1963, Conflict of Interests 1965, The Administration of the United Kingdom Foreign Policy Through the United Nations 1966, Law in Movement—Essays in Memory of John McMahon (ed., with James Fawcett) 1974, UN Peacekeeping: Documents and Commentary: (Vol. I) Middle East 1969, (Vol. II) Asia 1971, (Vol. III) Africa 1980, (Vol. IV) Europe 1981, Problems and Process—International Law and How We Use It 1994; articles in law journals and journals of int. relations. *Leisure interests:* sport, cooking, eating. *Address:* International Court of Justice, Peace Palace, 2517 KJ The Hague, Netherlands. *Telephone:* (70) 3022415 (Office). *Fax:* (70) 3022409 (Office). *E-mail:* mail@icj-cij.org (Office). *Website:* www.icj-cij.org (Office).

HIGGINS, Stuart; British journalist; b. 26 April 1956; m. Jenny Higgins; one s. one d.; ed Chase School for Boys, Filton Tech. Coll., Arblaster's of Bristol, Cardiff Coll. of Food, Tech. and Commerce; Dist reporter, The Sun, Bristol 1979, fmr NY corresp., Royal reporter, Features Ed., Exec. News Ed., Deputy Ed. 1991–93, Ed. 1994–98; public relations consultant 1998–; Acting Ed. News of the World 1993–94.

HIGGS, Peter Ware, PhD, FRSE, FRS; British professor of theoretical physics; b. 29 May 1929, Newcastle-upon-Tyne; s. of Thomas W Higgs and Gertrude M. Higgs (née Coghill); m. Jo Ann Williamson 1963; two s.; ed Cotham Grammar School, Bristol and King's Coll. London; Sr Research Fellow, Univ. of Edinburgh 1955–56; ICI Research Fellow, Univ. Coll. London 1956–57, Imperial Coll. London 1957–58; Lecturer in Math. Univ. Coll., London 1958–60; Lecturer in Math. Physics, Univ. of Edinburgh 1960–70, Reader 1970–80, Prof. of Theoretical Physics 1980–96; Fellow King's Coll. London 1998; Hon. FInstP 1998; Hon. DSc (Bristol) 1997, (Edin.) 1998, (Glasgow) 2002; Hughes Medal, Royal Soc. 1981, Rutherford Medal, Inst. of Physics 1984, James Scott Prize, Royal Soc. of Edin. 1994, Paul Dirac Medal and Prize, Inst. of Physics 1997, High Energy and Particle Physics Prize, European

Physical Soc. 1997, Royal Medal, Royal Soc. of Edin. 2000. *Publications:* papers in scientific journals. *Leisure interests:* walking, swimming, listening to music. *Address:* 2 Darnaway Street, Edinburgh, EH3 6BG, Scotland. *Telephone:* (131) 225-7060.

HIGHAM, John, PhD; American professor of history; b. 26 Oct. 1920, New York; s. of Lloyd Stuart Higham and Margaret (née Windred) Higham; m. Eileen Moss 1948; two s. two d.; ed Johns Hopkins Univ. and Univ. of Wisconsin; Instructor in History, Univ. of Calif., LA 1948–50, Asst Prof. 1950–54; Assoc. Prof., Rutgers Univ. 1954–58, Prof. 1958–60; Prof. Univ. of Mich., Ann Arbor 1961–67, Moses Coit Tyler Univ. Prof. 1968–71, 1972–73; John Martin Vincent Prof. of History, Johns Hopkins Univ. 1971–72, 1973–89, Prof. Emer. 1989–; Newman Prof. of American Civilization, Cornell Univ. 1991–92; Pres. Immigration and Ethnic History Soc. 1979–82, Org. of American Historians 1973–74; Assoc. Dir of Studies, Ecole des Hautes Etudes en Sciences Sociales 1981–82; mem. American Acad. of Arts and Sciences; Fulbright-Hays Lecturer, Kyoto American Studies Seminar 1974, Mellon Sr Fellow, Nat. Humanities Center 1988–89; Founding Ed. American Historical Asscn's Guide to Historical Literature; Dunning Prize, American Historical Asscn 1956, American Historical Asscn Award for Distinguished Scholarship 2003. *Publications:* Strangers in the Land 1955, History: Humanistic Scholarship in America 1965, Writing American History 1970, Send These to Me 1975, The Politics of Ethnicity (with others) 1982, American Immigrants and Their Generations 1990, Civil Rights and Social Wrongs 1997, Hanging Together: Unity and Diversity in American Culture 2001. *Address:* 3900 N. Charles St Apt 1402, Baltimore, MD 21218, USA (Home). *Telephone:* (410) 243-0112 (Home). *E-mail:* jhigham@jhu.edu (Office).

HIGHTOWER, John B.; American museum director; b. 23 May 1933, Atlanta, Georgia; s. of Edward A. Hightower and Margaret K. Hightower; m. 2nd Martha Ruhl 1984; one s. one d. (from 1st marriage); ed Yale Univ.; Gen. Asst to Pres. and Publisher, American Heritage Publishing Co. 1961–63; Exec. Dir New York State Council on the Arts 1964–70; Dir Museum of Modern Art, New York 1970–72; Pres. Assoc. Councils of Arts, New York 1972–74; Pres. South St Seaport 1977–84; Exec. Dir Richard Tucker Music Foundation 1977–89, The Maritime Center, Norwalk 1984–89; adviser to arts councils throughout USA, Cultural Adviser to Presidential Latin American Comm. 1969; Founder and Chair., Advocates for the Arts 1974–77; Instructor, Arts Man., Wharton School 1976–77, New School 1976–77; Chair. Planning Corpn for the Arts; Dir Planning and Devt of the Arts, Univ. of Va 1989–93; Interim Dir Bayly Museum, Univ. of Va 1990–91; Pres., CEO The Mariners' Museum, Va 1993–; NY State Award 1970. *Leisure interests:* gardening, cooking, travel. *Address:* 101 Museum Parkway, Newport News, VA 23606, USA (Home). *E-mail:* jhightower@mariner.org (Office).

HIGHTOWER, Rosella; American/French dance teacher, choreographer and artistic director; b. 30 Jan. 1920, Ardmore, USA; d. of Charles Hightower and Ula Fanning; m. Jean Robier 1955; one d.; worked with Léonide Massine at Ballets Russes from 1938; later soloist, American Ballet Theater; created roles in Balanchine's Apollo, Tudor's Pillar of Fire, etc.; Leading Dancer with Marquise de Cuevas' Ballet 1947–61; Founder, Centre de Danse Int. (for training of dancers from around the world) 1961; Artistic Dir Ecole Supérieure de Danse de Cannes Rosalind Hightower 1991–2001 (retd); also Dir of ballet at Marseilles Opéra, Grand Théâtre de Nancy, Paris Opéra and La Scala, Milan; Officier, Légion d'honneur, Commdr Ordre nat. du Mérite; other awards include Prix Porselli 1993, Lys d'Or 1994, Oklahoma Treasures 1997. *Address:* Villa Piège de Lumière, Parc Fiorentina, avenue de Vallauris, 06400 Cannes, France (Home).

HIGHWATER, Jamake; American writer and art critic; adopted at age of seven; writer on Native American and popular cultures; Founder and Dir Native Arts Festival, Houston, Tex. 1986; Gen. Dir Festival Mythos 1991; Visiting Scholar Columbia Univ. 1985; writer/host/producer several TV documentaries, including The Native Americans (10 parts; WNET-NY) 1985, Native Land (PBS) 1990; Creative Adviser, Star Trek: Voyager, Paramount Pictures 1993–; adviser to several orgs. including American Poetry Center 1991–; lecturer New York Univ. School of Continuing Educ. 1980–85, also Columbia Univ.; Wheless-Trotter Guest Prof. Univ. of Tex. Health Science Center, Houston 1985; Lecturer, Entertainment and Performing Arts Dept, Univ. of Calif. at LA 1999–; guest lecturer at many univs.; contrib. to numerous books, newspapers and magazines, including The Grove Dictionary of American Music, Stereo News, The Christian Science Monitor, The New York Times, The New York Times Book Review, Dance Magazine, Vogue, etc.; consultant Myth Quest PBS 2000–; mem. Advisory Bd visions magazine 1992–; Hon. DFA (Minneapolis Coll. of Art and Design 1986); numerous awards and prizes including Newbery Honor Award, American Library Asscn, for Anpao 1977, Best Film of the Year, Nat. Educational Film Festival, for Primal Mind 1984 and many awards for best book of the year from Int. Reading Asscn, New York Public Library and other orgs. 1977–95. *Recordings include:* Rock and Other Four Letter Words, Anpao, Rama. *Publications include:* (novels) Mick Jagger: The Singer Not the Song; (non-fiction) Rock and Other Four Letter Words, Myth and Sexuality 1990, The Language of Vision 1994, The Mythology of Transgression 1997. *Address:* Native Lands Foundation, 8491 W Sunset Boulevard, Los Angeles, CA 90069, USA. *E-mail:* nativeland@earthlink.net (Office).

HIJIKATA, Takeshi; Japanese business executive; b. 18 March 1915, Ena City, Gifu Prefecture; s. of Kikusaburo and Sue Hijikata; m. Michiko Kumakura; two s. one d.; ed Tokyo Imperial Univ.; joined Sumitomo Chemical Co. Ltd 1941, Dir 1971, Man. Dir 1973, Exec. Vice-Pres. 1977, Pres. 1977, Chair. 1985–93, Counsellor 1993–; Chair. Japan Tobacco Inc.; Dir Fuji Oil Co. Ltd, Sumitomo Seika Chemicals Co. Ltd, Japan Cttee for Econ. Devt; Dir and Counsellor Sumitomo Pharmaceuticals Co. Ltd; Dir Sumitomo Bakelite Co. Ltd, Inabata and Co. Ltd; Adviser and Hon. mem. Fed. of Econ. Orgs. (Keidanren); Adviser Japan Chem. Industry Asscn; Standing Dir Japan Fed. of Employees' Asscn, Kansai Econ. Fed.; mem. Trade Conf., Prime Minister's Office, Atomic Energy Comm., Science and Tech. Agency, Japan Singapore Asscn. *Leisure interests:* golf, reading. *Address:* Sumitomo Chemical Co. Ltd, 5-33 Kitahama, 4-chome, Chuo-ku, Osaka 541; 27-1, Shinkawa, 2-chome, Chuo-ku, Tokyo 104, Japan.

HILBE, Alfred J., DEcon; Liechtenstein politician; b. 22 July 1928, Gmunden, Austria; s. of Franz and Elisabeth (née Glatz) Hilbe; m. Virginia Joseph 1951; one d.; ed classical secondary schools in Vaduz and Zürich, Ecole Nationale des Sciences Politiques, Paris and Univ. of Innsbruck; several posts in pvt. business 1951–54; in foreign service 1954–65, Counsellor, Liechtenstein Embassy, Berne –1965; Deputy Head of Govt of Liechtenstein 1965–70, Head of Govt 1970–74; Financial Consultant 1974–; Grosskreuz of Liechtenstein Order of Merit, Grosses Silbernes Ehrenzeichen am Bande (Austria) 1975, Order of St Gregory (Vatican); Fatherland Union Party. *Leisure interests:* skiing, tennis, photography. *Address:* 9494 Schaan, Garsill 11, Principality of Liechtenstein. *Telephone:* 2322002 (Home); 2328320 (Office).

HILDENBRAND, Werner; German professor of economics; b. 25 May 1936, Göttingen; lecturer Univ. of Heidelberg 1964–66; Visiting Asst Prof. Univ. of Calif., Berkeley 1966–67, Visiting Assoc. Prof. 1967–68; Research Prof. Univ. of Louvain, Belgium 1968–76; Prof. of Econs Univ. of Bonn 1969–; Visiting Prof. of Econs, Berkeley and Stanford 1970, Berkeley 1973–74, Visiting Ford Prof. Berkeley 1985–86, European Univ. Inst., Florence 1989–, Univ. of Calif., San Diego 1986–91; Chaire Européenne Coll. de France 1993–94; Fellow Econometric Soc. 1972; mem. Rhein-West Akademie der Wissenschaften 1981–, Academia Europaea 1985–, Berlin-Brandenburgischen Akademie der Wissenschaften 1993–; Dr hc (Univ. Louis Pasteur Strasbourg) 1988, (Bern) 2002; Leibniz-Preis Deutsche Forschungsgemeinschaft 1987, Max-Planck-Forsch-Preis 1995, Alexander-von-Humboldt-Preis 1997, Gay-Lussac-Preis 1997. *Publications:* Core and Equilibria of a Large Economy 1974, Lineare ökonomische Modelle (with K. Hildenbrand) 1975, Introduction to Equilibrium Analysis (with A. Kirman) 1976, Equilibrium Analysis (with A. Kirman) 1988, Market Demand: Theory and Empirical Evidence 1994; numerous papers. *Address:* University of Bonn, Wirtschaftstheorie II, Lennestr. 37, 53113 Bonn, Germany. *Telephone:* (228) 739242. *Fax:* (228) 737940 (Office). *E-mail:* with2@wiwi.uni-bonn.de (Office). *Website:* www.wiwi .uni-bonn.de (Office).

HILDRETH, Eugene A., BS, MD, FRSM; American physician and university professor; b. 11 March 1924, St Paul, Minn.; s. of Eugene A. Hildreth and Lila K. Hildreth; m. Dorothy Ann Meyers 1946; two s. two d.; ed Washington and Jefferson Coll., Univ. of Virginia School of Medicine, Johns Hopkins Hosp., Baltimore, Md, Univ. of Pennsylvania; Research in Dept of Research Medicine, Univ. of Pa, Philadelphia 1957–60, Markle Scholar in Academic Medicine 1958–63, Assoc. Dean, Univ. of Pa 1964–67, Prof. of Clinical Medicine 1971–90, Prof. Emer. 1990–; Dir Dept of Medicine, The Reading Hosp. and Medical Center, Reading, Pa; Chair. Allergy and Immunology Subspeciality Bd 1966–72, American Bd of Allergy and Immunology 1971–72, American Bd of Internal Medicine 1975–82, Federated Council of Internal Medicine 1981–82, American Coll. of Physicians (ACP) Cttee on Developing Criteria and Standards for Delineation of Clinical Privileges 1986–90, Regent ACP 1985–92, Chair. Bd of Regents 1989–91, Pres. ACP 1991–92, Master 1992–, mem. nominating Cttee 1997–; mem. Federated Council of Internal Medicine, Fed. of the American Socs. for Experimental Biology, AAAS, ACP Cttee on Ethics, ACP Cttee on Int. Medicine, Inst. of Medicine (IOM), NAS, Council of IOM, Nominations Cttee of IOM, Bower Award Cttee of Franklin Inst. 1994, working group on disability of US Presidents 1994–2000. *Publications:* numerous scientific papers, chapters in books, reviews etc. *Leisure interests:* reading, white water kayaking, backpacking, museums, farming. *Address:* 5285 Sweitzer Road, Mohnton, PA 19540, USA (Home).

HILDREW, Bryan, CBE, MSc, DIC, FCGI, FREng; British engineer; b. 19 March 1920, Sunderland, Co. Durham; s. of Alexander William Hildrew and Sarah Jane Hildrew; m. Megan Kathleen Lewis; two s. one d.; ed Bede Collegiate School, Sunderland, Sunderland Tech. Coll., City and Guilds Coll., London Univ.; Principal Surveyor Engineering Investigations, Lloyds Register of Shipping 1961–65, Deputy Chief Engineer Surveyor 1965–67, Chief Engineer Surveyor 1967–70, Tech. Dir 1970–77, Man. Dir 1977–85; Pres. Inst. Mech. Engs. 1980–81; Chair. Council of Eng Insts. 1981–82; Pres. Inst. Marine Engs. 1983–85; Chair. Abbeyfield Orpington Soc. 1985–; Hon. DEng (Newcastle-upon-Tyne) 1987; Hon. DUniv (Surrey) 1994. *Leisure interests:* walking, orienteering. *Address:* 8 Westholme, Orpington, Kent, BR6 0AN, England.

HILFIGER, Tommy; American men's fashion designer; b. Elmira, NY; m. Susie Hilfiger; four c.; opened first store, People's Place, Elmira 1969; owned ten clothes shops throughout NY State by 1978; became full-time designer 1979; launched own sportswear label 1984; acquired fashion business from Mohan Muranji, cr. Tommy Hilfiger Corpn 1989; mem. Bd Fresh Air Fund, Race to Erase Multiple Sclerosis; winner From the Catwalk to the Sidewalk Award, VH-1 Fashion and Music Awards 1995, Menswear Designer of the

Year, Council of Fashion Designers of America 1995. *Leisure interests:* fishing, scuba diving, skiing. *Address:* Tommy Hilfiger USA Inc., 485 Fifth Avenue, New York, NY 10017, USA (Office); c/o Lynne Franks PR, 327–329 Harrow Road, London, W9 3RB, England. *Telephone:* (20) 7724-6777. *Fax:* (20) 7724-8484.

HILL, Anthony (Achill Redo); British artist; b. 23 April 1930, London; s. of Adrian Hill and Dorothy Whitley; m. Yuriko Kaetsu 1978; ed Bryanston School, St Martin's School of Art, Cen. School of Arts and Crafts; works in nat. collections GB, USA, France, Israel, Denmark; Leverhulme Fellowship 1971–72, Hon. Research Fellow, Dept of Mathematics, Univ. Coll. 1971–72, Hon. Research Assoc. 1972–; mem. The London Math. Soc. 1979–; First Prize, Norwegian Print Biennale 1999. *One-man exhibitions:* Inst. of Contemporary Arts, London 1958, Exhbn (with Gillian Wise) 1963; Exhbn Kasmin Gallery, London 1966, 1969, exhbns. (with Redo) 1969, 1980; retrospective Exhbn Hayward Gallery, London 1983; one-man Exhbn Mayor Gallery 1994. *Publications:* Data: Directions in Art, Theory and Aesthetics (Ed.) 1968, Duchamp: Passim 1994; numerous articles in art and mathematical journals. *Leisure interest:* erotology. *Address:* 24 Charlotte Street, London, W.1, England. *Telephone:* (20) 7636-5332 (Office); (20) 7636-5332 (Home). *Fax:* (20) 7636-5332 (Office); (20) 7636-5332 (Home).

HILL, Rt Rev Christopher John, BD, MTh; British ecclesiastic; b. 10 Oct. 1945; s. of Leonard Hill and Frances Hill; m. Hilary Ann Whitehouse 1976; three s. one d.; ed Sebright School, Worcs. and King's Coll., London; ordained (Diocese of Lichfield) 1969; Asst Chaplain to Archbishop of Canterbury for Foreign Relations 1974–81, Sec. for Ecumenical Affairs 1981–89; Anglican Sec. Anglican-Roman Catholic Int. Comm. I and II 1974–91; Anglican-Lutheran European Comm. 1981–82; Hon. Canon Canterbury Cathedral 1982–89; Chaplain to Queen 1987–96; Canon Residentiary of St Paul's Cathedral, London 1989–96; Area Bishop of Stafford, Diocese of Lichfield 1996–, Hon. Canon Lichfield Cathedral 1996–; mem. Gen. Synod 1999–, House of Bishops 1999–; mem. Church of England-German Churches Conversations 1987–89, Church of England-Nordic-Baltic Conversations 1989–93, Church of England Legal Advisory Comm. 1991–, Faith and Order Advisory Group of Gen. Synod 1997– (Vice-Chair. 1998–); mem. Council for Christian Unity 1992–97; Co-Chair. London Soc. of Jews and Christians 1991–96, Church of England-French Protestant Conversations 1993–98; Vice-Chair. Ecclesiastical Law Soc. 1993–2002, Chair. 2002–; Chair. Cathedrals' Precentors Conf. 1994–96; Anglican Co-Chair. Meissen Theological Conf. 1999–2001; mem. London Soc. for the Study of Religion 1990–2000, Working Party on Women in the Episcopate 2001–; Assoc. King's Coll., London. *Publications:* Anglicans and Roman Catholics: the Search for Unity (Co-Ed.), The Documents in the Debate. A Retrospect on the Papal Decision on Anglican Orders 1896 (Co-Ed.) 1996; ecumenical articles. *Leisure interests:* music, walking, reading. *Address:* Ash Garth, 6 Broughton Crescent, Barlaston, Stoke On Trent, ST12 9DD, England. *Telephone:* (1782) 373308. *Fax:* (1782) 373705. *E-mail:* bishop.stafford@lichfield.anglican.org (Office).

HILL, Christopher R., MA; American diplomatist; b. Little Compton, RI; ed Bowdoin Coll., Maine, Naval War Coll.; with Peace Corps in Cameroon; joined Foreign Service; overseas assignments in Yugoslavia, Albania, S Korea and Poland; Sr Country Officer for Polish Affairs, Dept of State; Amb. to Macedonia, to Poland 2000–; Sr Dir Southeast European Affairs, Nat. Security Council; several State Dept awards including Robert S. Frasure Award and Distinguished Service Award. *Address:* Embassy of USA, al. Ujazdowskie 29/31, 00–540 Warsaw, Poland (Office). *Telephone:* (22) 6283041. *Fax:* (22) 6288298. *Website:* www.usaemb.pl.

HILL, Damon Graham Devereux, OBE; British motor racing driver; b. 17 Sept. 1960, Hampstead, London; s. of the late Graham Hill (fmr Formula One world champion) and of Bette Hill; m. Georgie Hill 1988; two s. two d.; ed Haberdashers' Aske's School, London; first drove a car aged 5 years; first drove in motorcycle racing 1979; driver with Canon Williams team 1993, Rothmans Williams Renault team 1994–96, Arrows Yamaha team 1997, Benson and Hedges Jordan team 1998–99; first motor racing victory in Formula Ford 1600, Brands Hatch 1984; first Formula One Grand Prix, Silverstone 1992; winner, driving Williams-Renault FW15C, Hungarian Grand Prix 1993, winner, Belgian and Italian Grands Prix 1993, 1994; third place, Drivers' World Championship 1993; winner, Spanish Grand Prix, Barcelona 1994, British Grand Prix, Silverstone 1994, Portuguese Grand Prix 1994, Japanese Grand Prix 1994, 1996, French Grand Prix 1996, Spanish Grand Prix 1996, Argentine Grand Prix 1995, 1996, San Marino Grand Prix 1995, 1996, Hungarian Grand Prix 1995, Brazilian Grand Prix 1996, German Grand Prix 1996, Australian Grand Prix 1995, 1996, Canadian Grand Prix 1996, Belgian Grand Prix 1998; second place, Drivers' World Championship 1994, 1995, world champion 1996; 84 Grand Prix starts, 22 wins, 20 pole positions, 19 fastest laps, 42 podium finishes; retd end of 1999 season; British Competition Driver of the Year Autosport Awards 1995; numerous racing and sports personality awards. *Publications:* Damon Hill Grand Prix Year 1994, Damon Hill: My Championship Year 1996, F1 Through the Eyes of Damon Hill. *Leisure interests:* motorcycles, guitar playing, music, skiing, running, mountain biking, surfing, being outdoors. *Address:* c/o Michael Breen, Clyde & Co., 51 Eastcheap, London, EC3M 1JP, England.

HILL, Debra; American film director, producer and scriptwriter; b. Philadelphia, Pa; began film career as script supervisor and Asst Dir; producer and co-scriptwriter Halloween 1980, The Fog, Halloween II; work for TV includes

Adventures in Babysitting, El Diablo, Monsters, Dream On, Girls in Prison. *Films:* Halloween, The Fog, Escape from New York, Halloween II, Halloween III, Season of the Witch, The Dead Zone, Head Office, Adventures in Babysitting, Big Top Pee-Wee, Heartbreak Hotel, Gross Anatomy, The Fisher King, Escape from LA, Replacement Killers, Crazy in Alabama.

HILL, Geoffrey (William), MA, FRSL; British poet and university professor; b. 18 June 1932; s. of William George Hill and Hilda Beatrice Hill (née Hands); m. 1st Nancy Whittaker 1956 (divorced 1983); three s. one d.; m. 2nd Alice Goodman 1987; one d.; ed County High School, Bromsgrove and Keble Coll., Oxford; mem. acad. staff Univ. of Leeds 1954–80, Prof. of English Literature 1976–80; Univ. Lecturer in English and Fellow of Emmanuel Coll., Cambridge 1981–88; Univ. Prof. of Literature and Religion Boston Univ. 1988–; Co-Dir Editorial Inst., Boston Univ. 1998–; Churchill Fellow Univ. of Bristol 1980; Clark Lecturer Trinity Coll., Cambridge 1986; Tanner Lecturer Brasenose Coll. Oxford 2000; Fellow American Acad. of Arts and Sciences 1996; Hon. Fellow Keble Coll., Oxford 1981, Emmanuel Coll., Cambridge 1990; Hon. DLitt (Leeds) 1988; Whitbread Award 1971, RSL Award (W. H. Heinemann Bequest) 1971, Loines Award, American Acad. and Inst. of Arts and Letters 1983, Ingram Merrill Foundation Award in Literature 1985, Kahn Award 1998, T. S. Eliot Prize, Ingersoll Foundation 2000. *Publications:* poetry: For the Unfallen 1959 (Gregory Award 1961), King Log 1968 (Hawthornden Prize 1969, Geoffrey Faber Memorial Prize 1970), Mercian Hymns 1971 (Alice Hunt Bartlett Award 1971), Somewhere is Such a Kingdom: Poems 1952–71 1975, Tenebrae 1978 (Duff Cooper Memorial Prize 1979), The Mystery of the Charity of Charles Péguy 1983, Collected Poems 1985, New and Collected Poems 1952–1992 1994, Canaan 1996; The Triumph of Love 1998, Speech! Speech! 2000; The Orchards of Syon 2002; poetic drama: Henrik Ibsen, Brand: a version for the English stage 1978 (produced at Nat. Theatre, London 1978), 3rd (revised) edn 1996; criticism: The Lords of Limit: essays on literature and ideas 1984, The Enemy's Country 1991. *Address:* University Professors, Boston University, 745 Commonwealth Avenue, Boston, MA 02215, USA. *Telephone:* (617) 353-2000. *Telex:* (617) 353-2053. *Website:* www.bu.edu (Office).

HILL, Michael William, MA, MSc, MRSC, FIInfSc, FCILIP; British information consultant, research chemist and library director; b. 27 July 1928, Ross-on-Wye; s. of Geoffrey Hill and Dorothy Hill; m. 1st Elma Jack Forrest (died 1967); one s. one d.; m. 2nd Barbara Joy Youngman; ed King Henry VIIIth School, Coventry, Nottingham High School, Lincoln Coll., Oxford; Research Chemist, Laporte Chemicals Ltd 1953–56; Tech. and Production Man., Morgan Crucible Group 1956–64; Asst Keeper, British Museum 1964–68, Deputy Librarian Nat. Reference Library of Science and Invention (NRLSI) 1965–68, Keeper 1968–73; Dir, Science Reference Library, British Library 1973–86; Assoc. Dir Science. Tech. and Industry, British Library 1986–88; Hon. Pres. Fed. Int. d'Information et de Documentation 1985–90; fmr Chair. Circle of State Librarians; fmr Vice-Pres. Int. Asscn of Tech. Univ. Librarians; Co-founder European Council of Information Asscns; Hon. Fellow Fed. Int. d'Information et de Documentation 1992–, European Council of Information Asscns. 1996–. *Publications:* Patent Documentation (with Wittmann and Schiffels) 1979, Michael Hill on Science, Technology and Information 1988, National Surveys of Library and Information Services: 2: Yugoslavia (with Tudor Silovic), National Information Policies and Strategies 1994, The Impact of Information on Society 1998; Jt Series Ed. Saur Guides to Information Sources. *Leisure interests:* golf, theatre, music, Scottish dancing. *Address:* Jesters, 137 Burdon Lane, Cheam, Surrey, SM2 7DB, England. *Telephone:* (20) 8642-2418.

HILL, Polly, PhD; British economic anthropologist; b. 10 June 1914, Cambridge; d. of A.V. Hill, CH and Margaret N. Hill (née Keynes); m. Kenneth Humphreys 1953 (divorced 1961, died 1985); one d.; ed Newnham Coll., Cambridge; mem. editorial staff Economic Journal, Cambridge 1936–38; Research Asst, Fabian Soc., London 1938–39; temporary civil servant successively Treasury, Bd of Trade and Colonial Office 1940–51; mem. editorial staff West Africa, London 1951–53; mem. academic staff Univ. of Ghana, Legon 1954–65; field work in northern Nigeria, writing in Cambridge 1966–72; Smuts Reader in Commonwealth Studies, Univ. of Cambridge 1973–79, Reader Emer. 1979–; field work in India 1977–78, as Leverhulme Fellow Emer. 1981–82; Fellow Clare Hall, Cambridge 1966–81, Fellow Emer. 1981–; Hon. Fellow SOAS 1998. *Publications:* The Unemployment Services 1940, The Gold Coast Farmer 1956, The Migrant Cocoa Farmers of Southern Ghana 1963, Studies in Rural Capitalism in West Africa 1970, Rural Hausa: A Village and a Setting 1972, Population, Prosperity and Poverty: Rural Kano, 1900 and 1970 1977, Dry Grain Farming Families: Hausaland (Nigeria) and Karnataka (India) compared 1982, Development Economics on Trial: the Anthropological Case for a Prosecution 1986, Lydia and Maynard: The Letters of L. Lopokova and J. M. Keynes (ed. with R. Keynes) 1989, Who Were the Fen People? 1993 and many other publs. *Leisure interest:* embroidery.

HILL, Robert Lee, PhD; American university professor; b. 8 June 1928, Kansas City, Mo.; s. of William Alfred Hill and Geneva Eunice Sculock Hill; m. 1st Helen Root Hill 1948 (divorced); m. 2nd Deborah Anderson Hill 1982; one s. three d. (from previous marriage); ed Kansas Univ.; Research Instructor, Univ. of Utah, Salt Lake City 1956–57, Asst Research Prof. 1957–60, Assoc. Research Prof. 1960–61; Assoc. Prof., Duke Univ., Durham, NC 1961–65, Prof. 1965–74, Chair. Dept of Biochem. 1969–93, James B. Duke Prof. 1974–; Fellow, American Acad. of Arts and Sciences 1974–; mem. NAS

1975–; Pres. American Soc. of Biological Chemists 1976–77; Pres. Asscn of Medical Depts. of Biochem. 1982–83; Gen. Sec. Int. Union of Biochem. 1985–91. *Publications:* Principles of Biochemistry (co-author) 1978, The Proteins (co-ed.) (Vol. 1 1975, Vol. V 1982). *Address:* Department of Biochemistry, Duke University Medical Center, Durham, NC 27710, USA. *Telephone:* (919) 684-5326.

HILL, Robert Murray, BA, LLM; Australian politician; b. 25 Sept. 1946; s. of C. M. Hill; m. Diana Jacka 1969; two s. two d.; ed Scotch Coll., S Australia, Univ. of Adelaide, Univ. of London, UK; barrister and solicitor 1970–; Liberal Party Campaign Chair. 1975–77, Chair. Constitutional Cttee 1977–81; Vice-Pres. Liberal Party, S Australian Div. 1977–79; Senator for S Australia 1981–; Shadow Minister for Foreign Affairs –1993, for Defence 1993–94, for Public Admin. 1993–94, for Educ., Science and Tech. 1994–96; Leader of Opposition in Senate 1993–96; Leader of Govt in Senate 1996–, Minister for the Environment 1996–98, for the Environment and Heritage 1998–2001, for Defence 2002–; mem. Law Soc., S Australia. *Leisure interests:* Australian and Asian history. *Address:* Commonwealth Parliament Offices, 100 King William Street, Adelaide, SA 5000; MA 68, Parliament House, Canberra, ACT 2600, Australia (Office). *Telephone:* (2) 6277-7640 (Office). *Fax:* (2) 6273-6101 (Office).

HILL, Rodney, MA, PhD, ScD, FRS; British professor of mechanics of solids (retd); b. 11 June 1921; s. of Harold H. Hill; m. Jeanne K. Wickens 1946; one d.; ed Leeds Grammar School and Pembroke Coll., Cambridge; Armament Research Dept 1943–46; Cavendish Lab. Cambridge 1946–48; British Iron and Steel Research Asscn 1948–50; Research Fellow, Univ. of Bristol 1950–53, Reader 1953; Prof. of Applied Math. Univ. of Nottingham 1953–62; Professorial Research Fellow 1962–63; Berkeley Bye-Fellow, Gonville and Caius Coll. Cambridge 1963–69, Fellow 1972–88, Life Fellow 1988–; Reader, Univ. of Cambridge 1969–72, Prof. of Mechanics of Solids 1972–79; Hon. DSc (Manchester) 1976, (Bath) 1978; Von Karman Medal, American Soc. of Civil Engineers 1978, Gold Medal and Int. Modesto Panetti Prize, Turin Acad. of Sciences 1988, Royal Medal, The Royal Soc., London 1993. *Publications:* Principles of Dynamics 1964, Mathematical Theory of Plasticity 1950. *Leisure interests:* field botany and mycology, pianoforte, chess, rockery gardening. *Address:* Gonville and Caius College, Cambridge, CB2 1TA, England.

HILL, Susan Elizabeth, BA, FRSL; British author and playwright; b. 5 Feb. 1942; d. of the late R. H. Hill and Doris Hill; m. Prof. Stanley W. Wells 1975; two d. (and one d. deceased); ed grammar schools in Scarborough and Coventry and King's Coll. London; literary critic, various journals 1963–; numerous plays for BBC 1970–; Fellow, King's Coll. London 1978; presenter, Bookshelf, BBC Radio 1986–87; Founder and Publr Long Barn Books 1996–. *Publications:* The Enclosure 1961, Do Me a Favour 1963, Gentleman and Ladies 1969, A Change for the Better 1969, I'm the King of the Castle 1970, The Albatross 1971, Strange Meeting 1971, The Bird of the Night 1972, A Bit of Singing and Dancing 1973, In the Springtime of the Year 1974, The Cold Country and Other Plays for Radio 1975, The Ramshackle Company (play) 1981, The Magic Apple Tree 1982, The Woman in Black 1983 (stage version 1989), One Night at a Time (for children) 1984, Through the Kitchen Window 1984, Through the Garden Gate 1986, Mother's Magic (for children) 1986, The Lighting of the Lamps 1987, Lanterns Across the Snow 1987, Shakespeare Country 1987, The Spirit of the Cotswolds 1988, Can it be True? (for children) 1988, Family (autobiog.) 1989, Susie's Shoes (for children) 1989, Stories from Codling Village (for children) 1990, I've Forgotten Edward (for children) 1990, I Won't Go There Again (for children) 1990, Pirate Poll (for children) 1991, The Glass Angels 1991, Beware! Beware! 1993, King of Kings 1993, Reflections from a Garden (with Rory Stuart) 1995, Contemporary Women's Short Stories 1995 (Ed., with Rory Stuart), Listening to the Orchestra 1996 (short stories), The Second Penguin Book of Women's Short Stories 1997, The Service of Clouds 1998. *Leisure interests:* walking in the English countryside, friends, reading, broadcasting. *Address:* Longmoor Farmhouse, Ebrington, Chipping Campden, Glos., GL55 6NW, England. *Telephone:* (1386) 593352. *Fax:* (1386) 593443.

HILL, Terrell Leslie, PhD; American biophysicist and chemist; b. 19 Dec. 1917, Oakland, Calif.; s. of George Leslie Hill and Ollie Moreland Hill; m. Laura Etta Gano 1942; one s. two d.; ed Univ. of California at Berkeley and Harvard Univ.; Instructor in Chem., Western Reserve Univ. 1942–44; Research Assoc., Radiation Lab., Univ. of Calif. at Berkeley 1944–45; Research Assoc. in Chem., then Asst Prof. of Chem., Univ. of Rochester 1945–49; Chemist, US Naval Medical Research Inst. 1949–57; Prof. of Chem., Univ. of Oregon 1957–67; Prof. of Chem., Univ. of Calif. at Santa Cruz 1967–71, Vice-Chancellor, Sciences 1968–69, Adjunct Prof. of Chem. 1977–89, Prof. Emer. 1989–; Sr Research Chemist, Nat. Insts of Health 1971–88, Scientist Emer. 1988–; mem. NAS, ACS, Biophysical Soc., American Civil Liberties Union, Nat. Asscn for Advancement of Colored People, etc.; Guggenheim Fellow, Yale 1952–53; Sloan Foundation Fellow 1958–62; Arthur S. Flemming Award, US Govt 1954, Distinguished Civilian Service Award, US Navy 1955, Award of Washington Acad. of Sciences 1956, Kendall Award, ACS 1969, Superior Service Award, US Public Health Service 1981, Distinguished Service Award, Univ. of Oregon 1983. *Publications:* Statistical Mechanics 1956, Statistical Thermodynamics 1960, Thermodynamics of Small Systems Vol. I 1963, Vol. II 1964, Matter and Equilibrium 1965, Thermodynamics for Chemists and Biologists 1968, Free Energy Transduction in Biology 1977, Cooperativity Theory in Biochemistry 1985, Linear Aggregation Theory in Cell Biology 1987, Free Energy Transduction and

Biochemical Cycle Kinetics 1989; also 260 research papers. *Leisure interests:* reading, walking, music. *Address:* 3400 Paul Sweet Road, Apt C220, Santa Cruz, CA 95065, USA (Home).

HILL-NORTON, Baron (Life Peer), cr. 1979, of South Nutfield in the County of Surrey; **Adm. of the Fleet Peter John Hill-Norton,** GCB; British naval officer; b. 8 Feb. 1915, Germiston; s. of Martin J. and Margery B. Norton; m. Margaret E. Linstow 1936; one s. one d.; ed Royal Naval Coll., Dartmouth and Royal Naval Coll., Greenwich; went to sea 1932; commissioned 1936; served Arctic convoys, NW Approaches and Admiralty Naval Staff, Second World War 1939–45; Commdr 1948; Captain 1952; Naval Attaché, Argentine, Uruguay, Paraguay 1953–55; in command HMS Decoy 1956–57, HMS Ark Royal 1959–61; Asst Chief of Naval Staff 1962–64; Flag Officer, Second-in-Command Far East Fleet 1964–66; Deputy Chief of the Defence Staff (Personnel and Logistics) 1966; Second Sea Lord and Chief of Naval Personnel Jan.–Aug. 1967; Vice-Chief of Naval Staff 1967–68; C-in-C, Far East 1969–70; Chief of Naval Staff and First Sea Lord 1970–71; Chief of the Defence Staff 1971–74; Chair. North Atlantic Mil. Cttee 1974–77; Pres. Sea Cadet Asscn 1977–84; Vice-Pres. Royal United Service Inst. 1977; Pres. Friends of Osborne House 1980; Chair. Partridge, Muir & Warren 1982–; Pres. British Maritime League 1982–85; Chair. British Greyhound Racing Bd 2000–; Liveryman, Worshipful Company of Shipwrights 1973; Freeman of the City of London 1974. *Publications:* No Soft Options 1978, Sea Power 1982. *Leisure interests:* golf, shooting, cooking, travel. *Address:* British Greyhound Racing Board, 32 Old Burlington Street, London, W15 3AT (Office); Cass Cottage, Hyde, Fordingbridge, Hampshire, SP6 2QH, England. *Telephone:* (1425) 652392. *E-mail:* jennic@hill-norton. freeserve. co.uk.

HILL SMITH, Marilyn, AGSM; British soprano opera singer; b. 9 Feb. 1952, Carshalton, Surrey; d. of George Smith and Irene Smith; ed Nonsuch High School, Ewell and Guildhall School of Music and Drama; cabaret, pantomime, concerts 1971–74; toured Australia and NZ with Gilbert & Sullivan for All 1974, USA and Canada 1976; Prin. Soprano, ENO Opera 1978–84; Covent Garden début in Peter Grimes 1981; has appeared at several major European music festivals including Versailles, Granada, Aldeburgh, London Promenade Concerts etc., also with New Sadlers Wells Opera, Canadian Opera Co., Welsh Nat. Opera, Scottish Nat. Opera, New D'Oyly Carte Opera, Lyric Opera of Singapore, etc. and on television and radio and has made several recordings particularly of operetta; Patron Cen. Festival Opera, Epsom Light Opera; Hon. Life mem. Johann Strauss Soc. of GB; Young Musician of the Year 1975 and other prizes. *Leisure interests:* cooking, gardening, sleeping. *Address:* c/o Music International, 13 Ardilaun Road, Highbury, London, N5 2QR, England. *Telephone:* (20) 7359-5183.

HILLARY, Sir Edmund Percival, KG, KBE; New Zealand explorer, bee farmer and diplomatist; b. 20 July 1919, Auckland; s. of Percival Augustus and Gertrude Hillary; m. 1st Louise Mary Rose 1953 (died 1975); one s. two d. (one deceased); m. 2nd June Mulgrew 1989; ed Auckland Grammar School and Univ. of Auckland; served RNZAF (on Catalinas in the Pacific) 1944–45; went to Himalayas on NZ Garwhal expedition 1951, when he and another were invited to join the British reconnaissance over Everest under Eric Shipton; took part in British expedition to Cho Oyu 1952 and in British Mount Everest Expedition under Sir John Hunt 1953, when he and Tenzing reached the summit on May 29th; Leader NZ Alpine Club Expedition to Barun Valley 1954; NZ Antarctic Expedition 1956–58, reached South Pole Dec. 1957; Leader Himalayan Expeditions 1961, 1963, 1964; Pres. Volunteer Service Abroad in New Zealand 1963–64; built a hospital for Sherpa tribesmen, Nepal 1966; Leader climbing expedition on Mount Herschel, Antarctica 1967; River Ganges Expedition 1977; High Commr to India (also Accred to Bangladesh and Nepal) 1984; Hon. Pres. Explorers Club of New York; Consultant to Sears Roebuck & Co., Chicago; UNICEF Special Rep. Children of the Himalayas 1991–; Hon. LLD (Victoria Univ., BC, Canada, Victoria Univ., New Zealand) and other hon. degrees; Hubbard Medal 1954, Polar Medal 1958; Gurkha Right Hand (1st Class), Star of Nepal (1st Class), Founders' Gold Medal, Royal Geographical Soc., James Wattie Book of the Year Award, NZ 1975. *Publications:* High Adventure 1955, The Crossing of Antarctica (with Sir Vivian Fuchs) 1958, No Latitude for Error 1961, High in the Thin Cold Air (with Desmond Doig) 1963, Schoolhouse in the Clouds 1965, Nothing Venture, Nothing Win (autobiog.) 1975, From the Ocean to the Sky: jet-boating up the Ganges 1979, Two Generations (with Peter Hillary) 1983, Sagarmatha, The View from the Summit (autobiog.) 1998. *Leisure interests:* walking, fishing, camping. *Address:* 278A Remuera Road, Auckland 5, New Zealand (Home).

HILLEL, Shlomo; Israeli politician; b. Selim Hillel, 1923, Baghdad, Iraq; s. of Aharom Hillel and Hanini Hillel; m. Tmima Rosner 1952; one s. one d.; ed Herzliah High School, Tel Aviv and Hebrew Univ., Jerusalem; mem. Ma'agan Michael Kibbutz 1942–58; Jewish Agency for Palestine—mission to countries in Middle East 1946–48, 1949–51; Israel Defence Forces 1948–49; Prime Minister's Office 1952–53; mem. of Knesset 1953–59, 1974–; Amb. to Guinea 1959–61, to Ivory Coast, Dahomey, Upper Volta and Niger 1961–63; mem. Perm. Mission to UN with rank of Minister 1964–67; Asst Dir-Gen. Ministry of Foreign Affairs 1967–69; Minister of Police 1969–77; Co-ordinator of political contacts with Arab leadership in administered territories 1970–77; Minister of the Interior June–Oct. 1974, 1996–97; Chair. Ministerial Cttee for Social Welfare 1974–77, Cttee of the Interior and Environment 1977–81, of Foreign Affairs and Defence 1981–84; Perm. Observer to Council of Europe 1977–84; Speaker of the Knesset 1984–88; Chair. Sephardi Fed. 1976–; World Chair. Keren Hayesod United Israel Appeal 1989–; Pres. Council for Preser-

vation of Historical Sites in Israel 1996–; Chair. Zalman Shazar Center, Jerusalem; Dr. hc (Hebrew Univ.) 1995, (Ben-Gurion Univ.) 1997, (Tel-Aviv) 1998; Israel Prize for Life Achievement 1998; Commdr Nat. Order of Repubs. of Ivory Coast, Upper Volta and Dahomey. *Publication:* Operation Babylon 1988. *Leisure interests:* tennis, gardening. *Address:* 14 Gelber Street, Jerusalem 96755, Israel. *Telephone:* 2-6411416 (Home). *Fax:* 2-6436612.

HILLEMAN, Maurice Ralph, PhD, DSC; American virologist; b. 30 Aug. 1919, Miles City, Mont.; s. of Robert A. Hilleman and Edith M. (Matson) Hilleman; m. 1st Thelma L. Mason 1943 (deceased); m. 2nd Lorraine Witmer 1963; two c.; ed Montana State Coll. and Univ. of Chicago; Asst Bacteriologist, Univ. of Chicago 1942–44; Research Assoc., Virus Laboratories, E. R. Squibb & Sons 1944–47; Chief Virus Dept 1947–48; Medical Bacteriologist and Asst Chief, Virus and Rickettsial Diseases, Army Medical Service Graduate School, Walter Reed Army Medical Center 1948–56; Chief, Respiratory Diseases, Walter Reed Army Inst. of Research, Washington 1956–57; Dir Virus and Cell Biology Research, Merck Inst. for Therapeutic Research, Merck & Co. Inc. 1958–66, Exec. Dir 1966–70; Dir Virus and Cell Biology Research, Vice-Pres. Merck Sharp and Dohme Research Laboratories 1970–78, Sr Vice-Pres. 1978–84; Dir Merck Inst. for Vaccinology 1984–; Visiting Lecturer in Bacteriology, Rutgers Univ. 1947; Visiting Investigator, Hosp. of Rockefeller Inst. for Medical Research 1951; Visiting Prof. Dept of Bacteriology, Univ. of Maryland 1953–57; Adjunct Prof. of Virology in Pediatrics, School of Med., Univ. of Pa 1962–; Consultant, Surgeon-Gen. US Army 1958–63; Children's Hosp. of Philadelphia 1968–; mem. Expert Advisory Panel on Virus Diseases, WHO 1952–, Cttee on Influenza 1952, Cttee on Respiratory Diseases 1958, Scientific Group on Measles Vaccine Studies 1963, on Viruses and Cancer 1964, on Human Viral and Rickettsial Vaccines 1965, on Respiratory Diseases 1967; mem. Study Section, Microbiology and Immunology Grants-in-Aid Program 1953–61; mem. Editorial Bd Int. Soc. of Cancer 1964–71, Inst. for Scientific Information 1968–70, American Journal of Epidemiology 1969–75, Infection and Immunity 1970–76, Excerpta Medica 1971–, Proceedings of the Soc. for Experimental Biology and Medicine 1976, Editorial and Publs Cttee 1977–; mem. Council, Tissue Culture Asscn 1977–; mem. Council for Div. of Biological Sciences, Pritzker School of Medicine 1977–; mem. American Type Culture Collection Virology Dept Review Cttee 1980; mem. Overseas Medical Research Labs. Cttee, Dept of Defense 1980; Editorial Bd, Antiviral Research 1980–; mem. Bd of Dirs, W. Alto Jones Cell Science Center 1980–82, The Joseph Stokes Jr Research Inst., Univ. of Pa 1986–, Nat. Foundation for Infectious Diseases; mem. Advisory Bd Inst. of Biomedical Sciences, Taiwan, 1982–; mem. NAS Cttee on a Nat. Strategy for AIDS 1986–87, Nat. Vaccine Advisory Cttee of Nat. Vaccine Program 1988–; mem. Cttee on New Vaccine Development NAS 1983–; mem. AIDS Vaccine R & D Working Group, NIH 1992–; mem. Scientific Council of Paul Ehrlich Foundation 1993–; mem. numerous US and int. medical socs; John Herr Musser Lecturer, Tulane Univ. School of Med. 1969; 19th Graugnard Lecturer 1978; Fellow, American Acad. of Microbiology, American Acad. of Arts and Sciences; mem. NAS, American Philosophical Soc.; Foreign Corresp. mem. Acad. Nationale de Pharmacie, Paris; Hon. DSc (Montana Univ.) 1966, (Maryland Univ.) 1968, (Washington and Jefferson Coll.) 1992; Dr hc (Univ. Leuven) 1984; many awards including Distinguished Civilian Service Award given by Sec. of Defense 1957, Washington Acad. of Sciences Award for Scientific Achievement in the Biological Sciences 1958, Walter Reed Army Medical Center Incentive Award 1960, Merck Dirs Scientific Award 1969, 1984, Dean M. McCann Award for Distinguished Service 1970, Procter Award 1971, American Acad. of Achievement, Golden Plate Award 1975, Industrial Research Inst. Achievement Award 1975, Gold Medal for Service to Humanity, Hellenic Red Cross 1982, American Medical Asscn Scientific Achievement Award 1983, Albert Lasker Medical Research Award 1983, Howard Taylor Ricketts Award, Univ. Chicago 1983, Sabin Medal, German Soc. for Social Paediatrics 1988, Nat. Medal of Science, Pres. of USA 1988, Alumni Medal, Univ. of Chicago 1989, Robert Koch Gold Medal, Germany 1989, San Marino Medical Award 1989, Special Lifetime Achievement Award Children's Vaccine Initiative of WHO 1996, Sabin Gold Medal, Lifetime Achievement Award, Sabin Vaccine Foundation 1997, Maxwell Finland Award, Nat. Foundation for Infectious Diseases 1998. *Publications:* more than 490 original publications on virology, immunology and public health. *Leisure interests:* work, history. *Address:* Merck Institute for Vaccinology, Merck Research Laboratories, WP 53C-350, West Point, PA 19118, USA. *Telephone:* (215) 652-8913. *Fax:* (215) 652-2154.

HILLENBRAND, Martin Joseph, PhD; American diplomatist; b. 1 Aug. 1915, Youngstown, Ohio; s. of Joseph Hillenbrand and Maria Hillenbrand; m. Faith Stewart 1941; two s. one d.; ed Univs. of Dayton and Columbia; Vice-Consul, Zürich 1939, Rangoon 1940, Calcutta 1942, Lourenço Marques 1944, Bremen 1944; Consul, Bremen 1946; Bureau of German Affairs, State Dept 1950–52; First Sec., Paris 1952–56; U.S. Political Adviser, Berlin 1956–58; Dir Office of German Affairs, State Dept 1958–62; Head of "Berlin Task Force" 1962–63; Deputy Chief of Mission, Bonn 1963–67; Chair. Fulbright Comm. for Germany 1963–67; Amb. to Hungary 1967–69; Asst Sec. of State for European Affairs 1969–72; Amb. to FRG 1972–76; Dir-Gen. Atlantic Inst. for Int. Affairs, Paris 1977–82; Dean Rusk Prof. of Int. Relations, Univ. of Ga 1982–97, Prof. Emer. 1997–, Dir Global Policy Studies 1983–91; Chair. Bd, Southern Center for Int. Studies, Atlanta 1988–90; Co-Dir Center for Int. Trade and Security (fmrly Center for East–West Trade Policy), Univ. of Ga 1987–97; Dir Mercedes-Benz NA 1990–94; Grand Order of Merit (FRG) and many other honours. *Publications:* Power and Morals 1948, Zwischen Politik und Ethik (co-author) 1968, The Future of Berlin (co-author and ed.) 1980, Global Insecurity: A Strategy for Energy and Economic Growth (co-ed.) 1982, Germany in an Era of Transition 1983, Fragments of Our Time: Memoirs of a Diplomat 1998 and numerous articles. *Leisure interests:* reading, walking. *Address:* Center for International Trade and Security, University of Georgia, Athens, GA 30602, USA. *Telephone:* (706) 542-2111. *Fax:* (706) 542-4421.

HILLER, Susan, MA; American/British artist; b. 7 March 1940, New York City; d. of Paul Hiller and Florence Ehrich; m. David Coxhead 1962; one s.; ed Smith Coll. and Tulane Univ.; Lecturer, Slade School of Art, London 1982–91; Artist-in-Residence, Univ. of Sussex 1975; Assoc. Prof. of Arts, Dept of Fine and Applied Arts, Univ. of Ulster 1991–96; Baltic Chair. in Contemporary Art, Newcastle Univ. 2000–; Hon. Fellow Dartington Coll. of Arts 1998; Guggenheim Fellowship 1998–99, D.A.A.D. Berlin Fellowship 2002; Gulbenkian Foundation Visual Artists Award 1976, 1977. *Exhibitions:* one-woman exhbns. at galleries in London and other British cities, Toronto, New York, Zürich, Warsaw, Adelaide, Sydney, etc. since 1973; has participated in numerous group shows in Britain and abroad, also numerous solo exhbns.; mid-career retrospective Tate Gallery, Liverpool 1998; UK rep. Habana Bienale 2000. *Publications:* Dreams—Visions of the Night (co-author), The Myth of Primitivism (ed.), Thinking about Art: Conversations wth Susan Hiller, After the Freud Museum, Witness, Dream Machines. *Address:* 25 Artesian Road, London, W2, England (Office). *Telephone:* (20) 7229-5259 (Home). *E-mail:* aceposible@aol.com (Home).

HILLERY, Patrick John, BSc, MB, BCh, BAO, DPH, MRIA; Irish fmr Head of State and politician; b. 2 May 1923, Miltown Malbay, Co. Clare; s. of Dr. Michael Joseph Hillery and Ellen Hillery (née McMahon); m. Mary Beatrice Finnegan 1955; one s. one d.; ed Miltown Malbay Nat. School, Rockwell Coll., Cashel and Univ. Coll., Dublin; worked in Gen. Children's Tuberculosis and Psychiatric Hosp.; mem., Health Council 1955–57; Medical Officer, Miltown Malbay 1957–59; Coroner for West Clare 1958–59; mem. Dáil 1951–73; Minister for Educ. 1959–65, for Industry and Commerce 1965–66, for Labour 1966–69, of Foreign Affairs 1969–72; Vice-Pres. Comm. of European Communities with special responsibility for Social Affairs 1973–76; Pres. of Ireland 1976–90; Freeman City of Dublin; Hon. Fellow Royal Coll. of Surgeons (Ireland), Faculty of Dentistry, Royal Coll. of Surgeons (Ireland), All-India Inst. of Medical Sciences, Royal Coll. of Physicians (Ireland), Royal Coll. of Gen. Practitioners, Pharmaceutical Soc. of Ireland 1984; Hon. LLD (Nat. Univ. of Ireland, Trinity Coll., Dublin, Univ. of Melbourne, Pontifical Univ. of Maynooth, Limerick); Robert Schumann Gold Medal (France), Grand-Croix, Légion d'honneur and other decorations. *Leisure interests:* golf, painting, reading, travel. *Address:* Grasmere, Greenfield Road, Sutton, Dublin 13, Ireland.

HILLIER, Bevis, FRSA; British writer and editor; b. 28 March 1940; s. of the late Jack Ronald Hillier and of Mary Louise Palmer; ed Reigate Grammar School and Magdalen Coll., Oxford; Editorial Staff, The Times 1963–68, Antiques Corresp. 1970–84, Deputy Literary Ed. 1981–84; Ed. British Museum Soc. Bulletin 1968–70; Guest Curator, Minn. Inst. of Arts 1971; Ed. the Connoisseur 1973–76; Assoc. Ed., Los Angeles Times 1984–88; Ed. Sotheby's Preview 1990–93. *Publications:* Master Potters of the Industrial Revolution: The Turners of Lane End 1965, Pottery and Porcelain 1700–1914 1968, Art Deco of the 1920s and the 1930s 1968, Posters 1969, Cartoons and Caricatures 1970, The World of Art Deco 1971, 100 Years of Posters 1972, Austerity-Binge 1975, The New Antiques 1977, Greetings from Christmas Past 1982, The Style of the Century 1900–1980 1983, John Betjeman: A Life in Pictures 1984, Young Betjeman 1988, Early English Porcelain 1992, Art Deco Style; A Tonic to the Nation: The Festival of Britain (co-ed.) 1951 1976. *Leisure interests:* piano, collecting, awarding marks out of ten for suburban front gardens. *Address:* c/o The Maggie Noach Literary Agency, 21 Redan Street, London, W14 0AB, England.

HILLS, Carla Anderson, AB, LLD; American government official and lawyer; b. 3 Jan. 1934, Los Angeles; d. of Carl Anderson and Edith (Hume) Anderson; m. Roderick Maltman Hills 1958; one s. three d.; ed Stanford Univ., Calif., St Hilda's Coll., Oxford, UK, Yale Law School; Asst U.S. Attorney, Civil Div., LA, Calif. 1958–61; Partner, Munger, Tolles, Hills & Rickershauser (law firm) 1962–74; Adjunct Prof., School of Law, Univ. of Calif., Los Angeles 1972; Asst Attorney-Gen. Civil Div., U.S. Dept of Justice 1974–75; Sec. of Housing and Urban Devt 1975–77; Partner, Latham, Watkins & Hills (law firm) 1978–86, Weil, Gotshal and Manges, Washington 1986–88, Mudge Rose Gutherie Alexander & Ferdon 1994; Chair., CEO Hills & Co. 1993–; U.S. Trade Rep., Exec. Office of the Pres. 1989–93; Co-Chair. Alliance to Save Energy 1977–89; Vice-Chair. Bar of Supreme Court of the U.S., Calif. State and DC Bars, Council Section of Anti-trust Law, American Bar Asscn 1974, American Law Inst. 1974–, Fed. Bar Asscn (LA Chapter, Pres. 1963), Women Lawyers Asscn (Pres. 1964), LA County Bar Asscn, Chair. of various cttees. including Standing Cttee on Discipline, Calif. 1970–74; mem. Bd of Dirs. American Int. Group (AIG), Lucent Technologies Inc., Bechtel Enterprises, Trust Co. of the West Group Inc., AOL Time-Warner Inc. 1993–, Chevron Corp. 1993–; mem. Carnegie Comm. on the Future of Public Broadcasting 1977–78, Sloan Comm. on Govt and Higher Educ. 1977–79, Advisory Cttee Woodrow Wilson School of Public and Int. Affairs 1977–80, Yale Univ. Council 1977–80, Fed. Accounting Standards Advisory Council 1978–80, Trilateral Comm. 1977–82, 1993–, American Cttee on East–West Accord 1977–79, Int. Foundation for Cultural Cooperation and Devt 1977, Editorial Bd, Nat. Law Journal 1978, Calif. Gov.'s Council of Econ. Policy Advisers 1993–, Council on Foreign Relations 1993–; Co-Chair. Int. Advisory Bd, Center for Strategic and Int. Studies; Chair. Nat. Cttee on U.S.–China Relations 1993–; Contributing Ed., Legal Times 1978–88; Fellow, American Bar Foundation 1975; Trustee, Pomona Coll. 1974–79, Norton Simon Museum of Art 1976–80, Brookings Inst. 1977, Univ. of S. Calif. 1977–79; Advisor, Annenberg School of Communications, Univ. of S. Calif. 1977–78; Chair. Urban Inst. 1983; Dir Time Warner 1993; Vice-Chair. Interamerican Dialogue 1997–; mem. Bd of Trustees Asia Soc., Inst. for Int. Econs, Americas Soc.; Hon. degrees from Pepperdine Univ., Calif. 1975, Washington Univ., Mo. 1977, Mills Coll., Calif. 1977, Lake Forest Coll. 1978, Williams Coll., Notre Dame Univ., Wabash Coll. *Publications:* Federal Civil Practice (co-author) 1961, Antitrust Adviser (Ed. and co-author) 1971. *Leisure interest:* tennis. *Address:* Hills & Company, 1200 19th Street, NW, Suite 201, Washington, DC 20036; 3125 Chain Bridge Road, NW, Washington, DC 20016, USA (Home).

HILLY, Francis Billy; Solomon Islands politician; b. 1947; ed Univ. of S. Pacific; joined pre-independence govt working under Solomon Mamaloni; later worked for a pvt. co. in Gizo; mem. Parl. 1976–84, 1993–; fmr Premier of Western Prov.; Prime Minister of the Solomon Islands 1993–94. *Address:* c/o Office of the Prime Minister, Legakiki Ridge, Honiara, Solomon Islands.

HILSKÝ, Martin, PhD, MBE; Czech translator and professor of English literature; b. 8 April 1943, Prague; s. of Václav Hilský and Vlasta Hilská; m. Kateřina Hilská; two s. one d.; ed Charles Univ., Prague; Asst Prof. Charles Univ., Prague 1965–, Prof. 1993–, Dir Inst. of English 1988–98; Jr Research Fellow Oxford Univ. 1968–69; IREX grant, USA 1985; Jungmann's Translation Prize 1997. *Achievements:* Shakespeare translations performed throughout the Czech Republic. *Publications:* Contemporary English Novel (Rector's Prize) 1992, Modernists 1995; over 80 papers on English and American literature; translations of works by J. M. Synge, D. H. Lawrence, T. S. Eliot, J. Goldman and Shakespeare, 23 plays (including the Sonnets). *Leisure interests:* literature, theatre, arts, good wine, skiing, jogging, gardening. *Address:* FFKU, Charles University, Jana Palacha 2, 116 38 Prague (Office); Tychonova 10, 160 00 Prague 6, Czech Republic (Home). *Telephone:* (22) 1619341 (Office); (22) 4315722 (Home). *E-mail:* martin.hilsky@ff.cuni.cz (Office); hilsky@volny.cz (Home).

HILSUM, Cyril, CBE, PhD, FREng, FIEE, FIEEE, FRS; British research scientist; b. 17 May 1925, London; s. of Ben Hilsum and Ada Hilsum; m. Betty Hilsum 1947 (died 1987); one d. (one d. deceased); ed Raines School, London and Univ. Coll., London; H.Q. Admiralty 1945–47; Admiralty Research Lab., Teddington 1947–50; Services Electronics Research Lab., Baldock 1950–64; Royal Signals and Radar Establishments, Malvern 1964–83; Visiting Prof., Univ. Coll., London 1988–; Chief Scientist, Gen. Electric Co. (GEC) Research Labs. 1983–85; Dir of Research, GEC PLC 1985–92, Corporate Research Adviser 1992–; Pres. Inst. of Physics 1988–90; mem. Science and Eng Research Council 1984–88; Hon. DEng (Sheffield) 1992, (Nottingham Trent) 1998; Hon. FInstP; recipient of several awards. *Publications:* Semiconducting III-V Compounds 1961; over 100 scientific and technical papers. *Leisure interests:* tennis, chess, ballroom dancing. *Address:* 12 Eastglade, Moss Lane, Pinner, Middx, HA5 3AN, England. *Telephone:* (20) 8866-8323. *Fax:* (20) 8933-6114.

HILTON, Janet; British musician; b. 1 Jan. 1945, Liverpool; d. of H. Hilton and E. Hilton; m. David Richardson 1968; two s. (one deceased) one d.; ed Belvedere School, Liverpool, Royal Northern Coll. of Music, Vienna Konservatorium; BBC concerto début 1963; appearances as clarinet soloist with maj. British orchestras including Royal Liverpool Philharmonic, Scottish Nat., Scottish Chamber, City of Birmingham Symphony, Bournemouth Symphony, Bournemouth Sinfonietta, City of London Sinfonia, BBC Scottish and Welsh Symphony, BBC Philharmonic; guest at Edinburgh, Aldeburgh, Bath, Cheltenham, City of London Festivals, Henry Wood Promenade concerts; appearances throughout Europe and N America; Prin. Clarinet Scottish Chamber Orchestra 1974–80, Kent Opera 1984–88; teacher Royal Scottish Acad. of Music and Drama 1974–80, Royal Northern Coll. of Music 1983–87; Head of Woodwind, Birmingham Conservatoire 1992–; Head of Woodwind, RCM, London 1998–; Prof., Univ. of Cen. England (UCE) 1993; Dir Camerata Wind Soloists; several recordings for Chandos, including all Weber's music for clarinet with the CBSO, Lindsay Quartet and Keith Swallow, the Neilsen and Copland Concertos with the Scottish Nat. Orchestra, Stanford Clarinet Concerto with Ulster Orchestra, Mozart Clarinet Quintet with the Lindsay Quartet 1998; recordings of McCabe, Harper, Maconchy and Hoddinott concertos with BBC Scottish Symphony Orchestra on Clarinet Classics 2001; dedicatee of works by Iain Hamilton, John McCabe, Edward Harper, Elizabeth Maconchy, Alun Hoddinott, Malcolm Arnold. *Leisure interests:* cookery, reading. *Address:* 5B Belsize Park Gardens, London, NW3 4ND, England. *Telephone:* (20) 7586-7374. *E-mail:* jhilton@rcm.ac.uk (Office).

HIMMELFARB, Gertrude, PhD, FBA; American professor of history and author; b. 8 Aug. 1922, New York City; d. of Max Himmelfarb and Bertha (Lerner) Himmelfarb; m. Irving Kristol 1942; one s. one d.; ed Brooklyn Coll. and Univ. of Chicago; Distinguished Prof. of History, Graduate School, City Univ. New York 1965–88, Prof. Emer. 1988–; Fellow, American Philosophical Soc., American Acad. of Arts and Sciences, Royal Historical Soc., etc.; many public and professional appts.; Guggenheim Fellow 1955–56, 1957–58; Nat. Endowment for the Humanities Fellowship 1968–69, American Council of Learned Socs. Fellowship 1972–73, Woodrow Wilson Int. Center Fellowship 1976–77, Rockefeller Foundation, Humanities Fellowship 1980–81, and other fellowships; numerous hon. degrees including Hon. DHumLitt (Boston) 1987, (Yale) 1990; Hon. DLitt (Smith Coll.) 1977; Rockefeller Foundation Award 1962–63. *Publications:* Lord Acton: A Study in Conscience and Politics 1952, Darwin and the Darwinian Revolution 1959, Victorian Minds 1968, On Liberty and Liberalism: The Case of John Stuart Mill 1975, The Idea of Poverty 1984, Marriage and Morals Among the Victorians 1986, The New History and the Old 1987, Poverty and Compassion: The Moral Imagination of the Late Victorians 1991, On Looking Into the Abyss: Untimely Thoughts on Culture and Society 1994, The De-Moralization of Society From Victorian Virtues to Modern Values 1995, One Nation, Two Cultures 1999. *Address:* 2510 Virginia Avenue, NW, Washington, DC 20637, USA.

HINAULT, Bernard; French cyclist; b. 14 Nov. 1954, Yffiniac, Côtes du Nord; s. of Joseph and Lucie (Guernion) Hinault; m. Martine Lessard 1974; two s.; competitive cycling début 1971; French jr champion 1972; French champion 1978; world champion 1980; winner, Tour de France 1978, 1979, 1981, 1982, 1985, Tour d'Italie 1980, 1982, 1985, Tour d'Espagne 1978, 1983, Grand Prix des Nations 1978, 1982, 1984, Luis Puig Trophy 1986, Coors Classic, USA 1986 and many other int. racing events; retd from racing 1986; Technical Adviser, External Relations Dir Tour de France 1986–; Sports Dir French team 1988–; Dir-Gen. Ouest Levure 1992–; Chevalier, Légion d'honneur, Ordre Nat. du Mérite. *Publications:* Moi, Bernard Hinault (with others) 1979, Le Pentolou des souvenirs, Cyclisme sur route, technique, tactique, entraînement, Vélo tout terrain, découverte, technique et entraînement. *Address:* c/o Fédération française de cyclisme, Bâtiment Jean Monet, 5 rue de Rome, 93561 Rosny-sous-Bois, cedex (Office); Ouest Levure, 7 rue de la Sauvaie, 21 Sud-est, 35000 Rennes, France.

HINCH, Edward John, PhD, FRS; British academic; b. 4 March 1947, Peterborough; s. of Joseph Edward Hinch and Mary Grace Hinch (née Chandler); m. Christine Bridges 1969; one s. one d.; ed Cambridge Univ.; Fellow Trinity Coll., Cambridge 1971–; Asst lecturer Cambridge Univ. 1972–75, lecturer 1975–94, Reader in Fluid Mechanics 1994–98, Prof. 1998–; Chevalier, Ordre nat. du Mérite 1997. *Publications:* Perturbation Methods 1991; various papers in learned journals on fluid mechanics and its application. *Address:* Trinity College, Cambridge, CB2 1TQ, England. *Telephone:* (1223) 338427. *Fax:* (1223) 338564. *E-mail:* e.j.hinch@damtp.cam.ac.uk (Office).

HINCHCLIFFE, Peter Robert Mossom, CVO, CMG, MA; British diplomatist (retd); b. 9 April 1937, Mahableshwar, India; s. of Peter Hinchcliffe and Jeannie Hinchcliffe; m. Archbold Harriet Siddall 1965; three d.; ed Radley Coll., Trinity Coll., Dublin; British Army 1955–57; HMOCS Aden Protectorate 1961–67; First Sec. FCO 1969–71; mem. UK Mission to UN 1971–74; Head of Chancery, British Embassy, Kuwait 1974–76, FCO 1976–78, Deputy High Commr, Dar es Salaam 1978–81, Consul Gen., Dubai 1981–85; Head of Information Dept FCO 1985–87, Amb. to Kuwait 1987–90; High Commr in Zambia 1990–93; Amb. to Jordan 1993–97; Chair. Hutton and Paxton Community Council 2001–; Sr Research Fellow, Queen's Univ., Belfast; Hon. Fellow, Edinburgh Univ.; Adjunct Fellow Curtin Univ. Perth WA. *Publications:* Time to Kill Sparrows (anthology of diplomatic verse) 1999, Jordan: A Hashemite Legacy 2001, History of Conflicts in the Middle East Since 1945 2001. *Leisure interests:* golf, tennis, cricket, hill walking, writing poetry. *Address:* Antrim House, Kirk Lane, Hutton, Berwick-upon-Tweed, TD15 1TS, England. *Telephone:* (1289) 386121. *Fax:* (1289) 386122. *E-mail:* phinchcliffe@compuserve.com (Home); rah15@cam.ac.uk (Office).

HINCK, Walter, DPhil; German professor of language and literature; b. 8 March 1922, Selsingen; s. of Johann and Anna (née Steffens) Hinck; m. Sigrid Graupe 1957; one d.; ed Univ. of Göttingen; Prof. of Modern German Language and Literature, Literary Criticism, Univ. of Cologne 1964–; mem. Rheinisch-Westfälischen Akad. der Wissenschaften 1974–, (Vice-Pres. 1986–87), Sektion Bundesrepublik Deutschland des Internationalen PEN-Clubs 1986–; Kasseler Literaturpreis 1992. *Publications:* Die Dramaturgie des späten Brecht 1959, Das deutsche Lustspiel des 17. und 18. Jahrhunderts und die italienische Komödie 1965, Die deutsche Ballade von Bürger bis Brecht 1968, Das moderne Drama in Deutschland 1973, Von Heine zu Brecht—Lyrik im Geschichtsprozess 1978, Goethe—Mann des Theaters 1982, Germanistik als Literaturkritik 1983, Heinrich Böll: Ausgewählte Erzählungen 1984, Das Gedicht als Spiegel der Dichter 1985, Theater der Hoffnung, Von der Aufklärung bis zur Gegenwart 1988, Die Wunde Deutschland, Heinrich Heines Dichtung 1990, Walter Jens. Un homme de lettres 1993, Magie und Tagtraum. Das Selbstbild des Dichters in der deutschen Lyrik 1994, Geschichtsdichtung 1995, Im Wechsel der Zeiten: Leben und Literatur (autobiog.) 1998, Jahrhundertchronik, Deutsche Erzählungen des 20. Jahrhunderts 2000, Stationen der deutschen Lyrik von Luther bis in die Gegenwart. 100 Gedichte mit Interpretation 2000, Literatur als Gegenspiel. Essays zur deutschen Literatur von Luther bis Böll 2001. *Address:* Am Hammergraben 13/15, 51503 Rösrath, (Hoffnungsthal) bei Cologne, Germany. *Telephone:* (1) 22055147.

HINCKLEY, Gordon Bitner, BA; American religious leader; b. 23 June 1910, Salt Lake City, Utah; s. of Bryant S. Hinckley and Ada Bitner; m. Margorie Pay 1937; two s. three d.; ed Univ. of Utah; Asst to Quorum of the Twelve 1958, mem. Quorum 1961, Counselor in First Presidency 1981, Pres. The Church of Jesus Christ of Latter-day Saints 1995–; Dr hc (Utah, Brigham Young, Utah State, Southern Utah, Westminster Coll.); Distinguished Citizenship Award, Sons of American Revolution 1990, Silver Buffalo Award,

Boy Scouts of America 1994. *Publications:* Faith: The Essence of True Religion 1989, Teachings of Gordon B. Hinckley 1997, Standing for Something 2000. *Address:* Office of the President, The Church of Jesus Christ of Latter-day Saints, 47 East South Temple Street, Salt Lake City, UT 84150, USA (Office). *Telephone:* (801) 240-1000 (Office). *Fax:* (801) 240-2033 (Office).

HINDE, Robert Aubrey, CBE, DPhil, ScD, FRS, FBA; British biologist and psychologist; b. 26 Oct. 1923, Norwich; s. of Ernest B. Hinde and Isabella Hinde; m. 1st Hester Cecily Coutts (divorced); two s. two d.; m. 2nd Joan Stevenson 1971; two d.; ed Oundle School, St John's Coll., Cambridge, Balliol Coll., Oxford; pilot, RAF Coastal Command 1940–45; Curator, Ornithological Field Station, Dept of Zoology, Univ. of Cambridge 1960–64, Fellow of St John's Coll. 1951–54, 1958–, Master 1989–94; Royal Soc. Research Prof. 1963–89; Hon. Dir MRC Unit of Devt and Integration of Behaviour 1970–89; Hitchcock Prof., Univ. of Calif. 1979; mem. Acad. Europaea 1990; Croonian Lecturer (Royal Soc.) 1990; Foreign Hon. mem. AAAS 1974; Hon. Fellow American Ornithologists' Union 1976; Hon. Foreign Assoc. NAS 1978; Hon. Fellow Royal Coll. of Psychiatry 1988; Hon. Fellow, British Psychological Soc. 1981; Hon. Fellow Balliol Coll. Oxford 1986, Trinity Coll. Dublin 1990; Hon. ScD (Univ. Libre, Brussels) 1974, (Nanterre) 1978, (Gothenburg) 1991; Dr. hc (Stirling) 1991, (Edin.) 1992, (W Ont.) 1996, (Oxford) 1998; Frink Medal, Zoological Soc. of London 1992, Royal Medal, Royal Soc. 1996, Soc.'s Medal, Asscn for the Study of Animal Behaviour 1997; numerous other awards. *Publications:* Animal Behaviour: A Synthesis of Ethology and Comparative Psychology 1966, Social Behaviour and its Development in Sub-human Primates 1972, Biological Bases of Human Social Behaviour 1974, Towards Understanding Relationships 1979, Ethology 1982, Individuals, Relationships and Culture 1987, Relationships: A Dialectical Perspective 1997, Why Gods Persist 1999, Why Good is Good 2002; Bird Vocalizations (Ed.) 1969, Primate Social Behaviour 1983; Short-term Changes in Neural Activity and Behaviour (Jt Ed.) 1970, Constraints on Learning (Jt Ed.) 1973, Growing Points in Ethology (Jt Ed.) 1976, Social Relationships and Cognitive Development (Jt Ed.) 1985, Relationships Within Families (Jt Ed.) 1988, Aggression and War: Their Biological and Social Bases (Jt Ed.) 1988, Education for Peace (Jt Ed.), Co-operation and Prosocial Behaviour (Jt Ed.) 1991; The Institution of War (Ed.) 1991, War: A Cruel Necessity? (Jt Ed.) 1994; numerous articles in learned journals. *Leisure interests:* ornithology, reading, walking. *Address:* St John's College, Cambridge, CB2 1TP, England. *Telephone:* (1223) 339356. *Fax:* (1223) 337720.

HINDE, Thomas (see Chitty, Sir Thomas Wiles).

HINDERY, Leo Joseph, Jr, MBA; American business executive; b. 31 Oct. 1947, Springfield, Ill.; s. of Leo Joseph Hindery and E. Marie Whitener; m. Deborah Diane Sale 1980; one s.; ed Seattle Univ. and Stanford Univ.; U.S. Army 1968–70; Asst Treasurer Utah Int., San Francisco 1971–80; Treas. Natomas Co., San Francisco 1980–82; Exec. Vice-Pres. Finance Jefferies and Co., LA 1982–83; Chief Finance Officer AG Becker Paribas, New York 1983–85; Chief Officer Planning and Finance Chronicle Publishing Co., San Francisco 1985–88; Man. Gen. Partner Intermedia Partners, San Francisco 1988–97; Pres. TCI Cable Vision 1998–2000; Chair. and CEO Global Crossing Ltd 2000–; mem. Bd Dirs DMX Inc., NETCOM On-Line Comm. Services Inc., Nat. Cable TV Asscn, Cable Telecommunications Asscn, C-Span. *Leisure interest:* golf. *Address:* Global Crossing–Frontier Global Centre, 2831 Mission College Boulevard, Santa Clara, CA95054-1838, USA (Office).

HINDLIP, 6th Baron (cr. 1886); Charles Henry Allsopp; British business executive; b. 5 April 1940; s. of the late Baron Hindlip and Cecily Valentine Jane Borwick; m. Fiona Victoria Jean Atherley McGowan 1968; one s. three d.; ed Eton Coll.; served in Coldstream Guards 1959–62; joined Christie's 1962, Gen. Man. New York 1965–70, Chair. 1996–; Dir Christie Manson & Wood 1970–, Deputy Chair. 1985–86, Chair. 1986–96; Chair. Christie's Int. 1996–. *Leisure interests:* painting, shooting, skiing. *Address:* Christie's, 8 King Street, St James's, London, SW1Y 6QT (Office); 32 Maida Avenue, London, W2 1ST; Lydden House, King's Stag, Sturminster Newton, Dorset, DT10 2AU, England. *Telephone:* (20) 7839-9060 (Office); (20) 7389-2061.

HINDS, Samuel Archibald Anthony, BSc; Guyanese politician; b. 27 Dec. 1943, Mahaicony, E Coast, Demerara; m.Yvonne Zereder Burnett 1967; three c.; ed Queen's Coll. Georgetown and Univ. of New Brunswick; various positions with Bauxite Co., Linden, Guyana 1967–92; mem. Science and Industry Cttee Nat. Science Research Council 1973–76; fmr Chair. Guyanese Action for Reform and Democracy (GUARD); Prime Minister of Guyana 1992–97, 1997–99, April 2001–; also Minister of Communications; leader CIVIC (special political movt of business people and execs.). *Address:* Office of the Prime Minister, Wights Lane, Georgetown (Office); CIVIC, New Garden Street, Georgetown, Guyana . *Telephone:* 227-3101 (Office). *Fax:* 226-7563 (Office).

HINDUJA, Gopichand Parmanand; British (born Indian) businessman; b. 29 Feb. 1940; s. of Parmanand Deepchand Hinduja and Jamuna Parmanand Hinduja; brother of Srichand Hinduja (q.v.); m. Sunita Hinduja; two s. one d.; ed Jai Hind Coll., Mumbai; joined family business 1958; Pres. Hinduja Foundation and Hinduja Group of Cos. 1962–; Head of Hinduja Group Operations in Iran –1978; Chair. of Gurnanank Trust, Tehran; mem. Advisory Council, Hinduja Cambridge Trust 1991, Advisory Cttee Prince's Trust, Duke of Edin.'s Fellowship; patron Balaji Temple, Swaminaryan Hindu Mission, London; charged in connection with an arms bribery case in India Nov. 2002; Hon. LLD (Univ. of Westminster) 1996; Hon. DEcon (Richmond

Coll.). *Leisure interests:* Indian music, travel, sailing, yoga. *Address:* Hinduja Group of Companies, New Zealand House, 80 Haymarket, London, SW1Y 4TE, England (Office). *Telephone:* (20) 7839-4661 (Office). *Fax:* (20) 7839-5992 (Office). *E-mail:* gph@hindujagroup.com (Office). *Website:* www.hindujagroup .com (Office).

HINDUJA, Srichand Parmanand; Indian businessman; b. 28 November 1935; s. of Parmanand Deepchand Hinduja and Jamuna Parmanand Hinduja; brother of Gopichand Hinduja (q.v.); m. Madhu Srichand Hinduja; two d.; ed Nat. Coll., Mumbai, Davar Coll. of Commerce, Mumbai; joined family business; Chair. Hinduja Foundation and Hinduja Group of Cos. 1962–; Global Co-ordinator IndusInd 1962; Pres. IndusInd Int. Fed. 1996; mem. Advisory Council, Dharam Hinduja Indic Research Centres in Columbia, USA and UK, Advisory Council, Hinduja Cambridge Trust, Corpn of Mass. Gen. Hosp., Duke of Edin.'s Award Fellowship; patron Centre of India–US Educ., Asia Soc.; charged in connection with an arms bribery case in India Nov. 2002; Hon. LLD (Univ. of Westminster) 1996; Hon. DEcon (Richmond Coll.) 1997. *Publications:* Indic Research and Contemporary Crisis 1995, Conceptualiser of Series of Paintings Theorama 1995, The Essence of Vedic Marriage For Success and Happiness 1996. *Leisure interests:* tennis, volleyball, cricket, Indian classical music. *Address:* Hinduja Group of Companies, New Zealand House, 80 Haymarket, London, SW1Y 4TE, England (Office). *Telephone:* (20) 7839-4661 (Office). *Fax:* (20) 7839-5992 (Office).

HINE, Air Chief Marshal Sir Patrick, GCB, GBE, FRAeS, CBIM; British air force officer; b. 14 July 1932, Chandlers Ford, Hants.; s. of Eric Graham Hine and Cecile Grace Hine (née Philippe); m. Jill Adèle Gardner 1956; three s.; ed Sherborne House Preparatory School 1937–41, Peter Symonds School, Winchester 1942–49; fighter pilot and mem. RAF 'Black Arrows' and 'Blue Diamonds' Formation Aerobatic Teams 1957–62; Commdr No. 92 Squadron 1962–64 and 17 Squadron 1970–71, RAF Germany Harrier Force 1974–75; Dir RAF Public Relations 1975–77; Asst Chief of Air Staff for Policy 1979–83; C-in-C RAF Germany and Commdr NATO's 2nd Allied Tactical Air Force 1983–85; Vice-Chief of the Defence Staff 1985–87; Air mem. for Supply and Organization, Air Force Bd 1987–88; Air Officer Commanding-in-Chief, Strike Command, C-in-C UK Air Forces 1988–91; Jt Commdr British Forces in Gulf Conflict, Aug. 1990–April 1991; with reserve force, rank of Flying Officer 1991–; Mil. Adviser to British Aerospace 1992–99; King of Arms, Order of the British Empire 1997–. *Leisure interests:* golf, mountain walking, skiing, photography, caravanning, travel.

HINGIS, Martina; Swiss tennis player; b. 30 Sept. 1980, Košice, Czechoslovakia; d. of Karol Hingis and Mélanie Molitor; competed in first tennis tournament 1985; family moved to Switzerland at age eight; winner French Open Jr championship 1993, Wimbledon Jr Championship 1994; turned professional and won first professional tournament Filderstadt (Germany) 1996; winner Australian Open 1997 (youngest winner of a Grand Slam title), 1998, 1999 (singles and doubles), beaten finalist 2000, 2001, 2002; won US Open 1997, beaten finalist 1998, 1999; Wimbledon singles champion 1997; Swiss Fed. Cup Team 1996–98; semi-finalist US Open 2001; by end of 2002 had won 76 tournament titles including five Grand Slam singles and nine doubles titles; elected to WTA Tour Players' Council 2002; WTA Tour Most Impressive Newcomer 1995, Most Improved Player 1996, Player of the Year 1997. *Leisure interests:* horse-riding, roller-blading, skiing, swimming, going to musicals. *Address:* c/o AM Seidenbaum 17, 9377 Truebbach, Switzerland.

HINSON, David R.; American airline executive; b. 2 March 1933; m. Ursula Hinson; three c.; fighter pilot USN 1956–60, airline and Eng pilot 1960–72; Founder, Dir Midway Airlines Inc. 1979–91, Chair., CEO 1985–91; Admin. Fed. Aviation Admin. 1993–96; Dir several cos; Operations Award, Aviation Week and Space Tech. 1997. *Leisure interests:* aviation history, collecting aviation art. *Address:* c/o Federal Aviation Administration, 800 Independence Avenue, SW, Washington, DC 20591, USA.

HIQUILY, Philippe; French sculptor; b. 27 March 1925, Paris; s. of Jules Hiquily and Madeleine Velvet; m. Meei-Yen Wo 1985; two s.; ed secondary school and Ecole Nat. Supérieure des Beaux-Arts Paris; mil. service in Indochina 1943–47; since 1951 has concentrated on sculpture in metal, influenced by primitive art; Chevalier des Arts et des Lettres; Ordre Royal de Louang-Brabang (Laos). *Leisure interests:* fishing, agriculture, viticulture. *Address:* 21 rue Olivier-Noyer, Paris, France. *Telephone:* 1-45-39-30-25.

HIRAMATSU, Morihiko, LLB; Japanese civil servant; b. 12 March 1924, Oita; s. of the late Oriji Hiramatsu and Kun Hiramatsu; m. 1st Chizuko Ueda 1949; m. 2nd Teruko Mihara 1976; two d.; ed Kumamoto No. V. High School and Tokyo Univ.; employee Ministry of Commerce and Industry 1949–64; Dir Industrial Pollution Div. Enterprises Bureau, Ministry of Int. Trade and Industry 1964–65, Petroleum Planning Div. Mining Bureau 1965–67, Export Insurance Div. Trade Promotion Bureau 1967–69, Electronics Policy Div. Heavy Industries Bureau 1969–73, Co-ordination Office Basic Industries Bureau 1973–74; Counsellor Secr. Land Agency 1974–75; Vice-Gov. of Oita Pref. 1975–79; Gov. 1979–; Chair. Kyushu Govs'. Asscn 1991–, Nat. Expressway Construction Promotion Council 1995–, Nat. Port Devt & Promotion Council 1998–; Ramon Magsaysay Award for Govt Service (Philippines) 1995; Gran Cruz da Legião de Honra Giuseppe Garibaldi (Brazil) 1987, Commdr, Ordem do Infante D. Enrique (Portugal) 2001, Kt, Order of Orange Nassau (Netherlands) 2001; Friendship Award (People's Repub. of China) 2002. *Publications:* Talks on Software, Exhortations to One Village One Product, Challenging Technopolis, Age of Decentralised Management, Let's

Try What's Impossible in Tokyo, Think Globally and Act Locally, Locally Generated Ideas, The Road to the 'United States of Japan', My Views on the 'United States of Japan', A Better Tomorrow for Rural Regions, Hot Disputes over the 'United States of Japan'. *Leisure interests:* reading, golf, early morning walks. *Address:* Oita Prefectural Office, 3-1-1 Ohte-machi, Oita City, Oita Prefecture 870-8501 (Office); Official Residence, 8-20 Niage-machi, Oita City, Oita Prefecture 870-0046, Japan (Home). *Telephone:* (97) 532-2851 (Office); (97) 532-2001 (Home). *Fax:* (97) 532-5650 (Office); (97) 533-1234 (Home). *E-mail:* hiramatu@pref.oita.jp (Office). *Website:* www.pref.oita.jp (Office).

HIRANUMA, Takeo; Japanese politician; fmr Parl. Vice-Minister of Finance; Deputy Chair. LDP Policy Research Council, Chair. LDP Nat. Org. Cttee; mem. House of Reps.; Minister of Transport 1995–96; currently Minister of Economy, Trade and Industry. *Address:* Ministry of Economy, Trade and Industry, 1-3-1, Kasumigaseki, Chiyoda-ku, Tokyo 100-8901, Japan (Office). *Telephone:* (3) 3501-1511 (Office). *Fax:* (3) 3501-6942 (Office). *E-mail:* webmail@meti.go.jp (Office). *Website:* www.meti.go.jp (Office).

HIRSCH, Georges-François; French opera administrator; b. 5 Oct. 1944, Paris; s. of Georges Hirsch; stage-hand, Théâtre des Capucines 1960; later stage man. Théâtre de la Culture de l'Ile de France; Dir Théâtre de Limoges 1969–74; directed various productions especially in USA 1974–79; Dance Admin. Paris Opéra 1979–82; mem. directing team, RTLN 1982–83; Dir Théâtre des Champs-Elysées 1983–89; Gen. Admin. Opéra Bastille 1989–92, Opéra de Paris (Garnier Bastille) 1991–92; mem. council CSA 1993–96; Gen. Dir Orchestre de Paris 1996–; Chair. Syndicat nat. des orchestres et théâtres lyriques subventionnés de droit privé 1999–; Vice-Chair. French Asscn of Orchestras 2000–; Officier, Légion d'honneur, Chevalier, Ordre nat. du Mérite, Commdr des Arts et Lettres. *Address:* Orchestre de Paris, 25 rue de Mogador, 75009 Paris, France. *Telephone:* 1-56-35-12-01. *Fax:* 1-56-35-12-25.

HIRSCH, Judd, BS; American actor; b. 15 March 1935, New York; s. of Joseph S. Hirsch and Sally Kitzis; m. Bonni Chalkin 1992; ed City Coll. of New York; has appeared in numerous TV plays, series, films etc; mem. Screen Actors Guild. *Stage appearances include:* Barefoot in the Park 1966, Knock Knock 1976 (Drama Desk Award), Scuba Duba 1967–69, King of the United States 1972, Mystery Play 1972, Hot L Baltimore 1972–73, Prodigal 1973, Chapter Two 1977–78, Talley's Folly 1979 (Obie Award), The Seagull 1983, I'm Not Rappaport 1985–86 (Tony Award), Conversations with My Father (Tony Award) 1992, A Thousand Clowns 1996, Below the Belt 1996, Death of a Salesman 1997, Art 1998, I'm Not Rappaport (revival) 2002. *Television appearances include:* Delvecchio (series) 1976–77, Taxi (series) 1978–83 (Emmy Award), Dear John (series) 1988–92 (Golden Globe Award), George and Leo (series) 1997, Welcome to New York (episode) 2000, The Law (episode) 2001 and many TV movies. *Films include:* King of the Gypsies 1978, Ordinary People 1980, Without a Trace 1983, Teachers 1984, The Goodbye People 1984, Running on Empty 1988, Independence Day 1996, Man on the Moon 1999, A Beautiful Mind 2002. *Address:* c/o J. Wolfe Provident Financial Management, 10345 West Olympic Boulevard, Los Angeles, CA 90064, USA.

HIRSCH, Leon; American business executive; b. 20 July 1927, Bronx, New York; s. of the late Roslyn Hirsch and Isidor Hirsch; m. 2nd Turi Josefsen 1969; two s. one d. from 1st m.; ed Bronx School of Science; Chair. and CEO United States Surgical Corpn 1964–; inventor and developer of Auto Suture surgical staplers; Chair. Advisory Bd American Soc. of Colon and Rectal Surgeons Research Foundation; mem. American Business Conf.; Dir Americans for Medical Progress; mem. Bd of Trustees, Boston Univ.; Gordon Grand Fellow, Yale Univ.; Surgery Award Nessim Habif, Univ. of Geneva. *Leisure interests:* fishing, horseback riding, skiing, tennis. *Address:* 150 Glover Avenue, Norwalk, CT 06856, USA. *Telephone:* (203) 845-1401. *Fax:* (203) 845-4133.

HIRSCH, Sir Peter Bernhard, Kt, PhD, FRS; British professor of metallurgy; b. 16 Jan. 1925, Berlin; s. of Ismar Hirsch and Regina Meyersohn; m. Mabel A. Kellar (née Stephens) 1959; one step-s. one step-d.; ed Univ. of Cambridge; Lecturer in Physics, Univ. of Cambridge 1959–64; Reader 1964–66; Fellow, Christ's Coll., Cambridge 1960–66, Hon. Fellow 1978; Isaac Wolfson Prof. of Metallurgy, Univ. of Oxford 1966–92, Prof. Emer. 1992, Fellow, St Edmund Hall 1966–92, Fellow Emer. 1992–; Chair. Metallurgy and Materials Cttee, SRC 1970–73; mem. Council, Inst. of Physics 1968–72, Inst. of Metals 1968–73, Electricity Supply Research Council 1969–82, Council for Scientific Policy 1970–72, Metals Soc. Council 1978–82, Council Royal Soc. 1977–79; Royal Soc. UK-Canada Lecture 1992; mem. Bd (part-time) UKAEA 1982–94, Chair. 1982–84; mem. Tech. Advisory Cttee Advent 1982–89; Dir Cogent 1985–89, Rolls-Royce Assocs. 1994–98; Dir (non-exec.) OMIA 2000–01; mem. Tech. Advisory Cttee Monsanto Electronic Materials 1985–88; Chair. Isis Innovation Ltd 1988–96, Tech. Advisory Group on Structural Integrity 1993–2002, Materials and Processes Advisory Bd Rolls-Royce PLC 1996–2000; Assoc. mem. Royal Acad. of Sciences, Letters and Fine Arts of Belgium 1996; Foreign Assoc. Nat. Acad. of Eng, USA 2001; Hon. Fellow, St Catharine's Coll., Cambridge 1982, Royal Microscopical Soc. 1977, Japan Soc. of Electron Microscopy 1979, Japan Inst. of Metals 1989, Inst. of Materials 2002; Fellow, Imperial Coll., London 1988; Hon. mem. Materials Research Soc., India 1990; Hon. DSc (Newcastle Univ.) 1979, (City Univ.) 1979, (Northwestern Univ.) 1982, (East Anglia Univ.) 1983, Hon. DEng (Liverpool) 1991, (Birmingham) 1993; Rosenhain Medal, Inst. of Metals 1961, Boys' Prize, Inst. of Physics and Physical Soc. 1962, Clamer Medal, Franklin

Inst. 1970, Wihuri Int. Prize 1971, Hughes Medal of the Royal Soc. 1973, Platinum Medal of the Metals Soc. 1976, Royal Medal of Royal Soc. 1977, A.A. Griffith Medal, Inst. of Materials 1979, Arthur Von Hippel Award, Materials Research Soc. 1983, Wolf Prize in Physics 1984, Distinguished Scientist Award, Electron Microscopy Soc. of America 1986, Holweck Prize, Inst. of Physics and French Physical Soc. 1988, Gold Medal, Japan Inst. of Metals 1989, Acta Metallurgica Gold Medal 1997, Heyn Medal of German Soc. for Materials Science 2002. *Publications:* Electron Microscopy of Thin Crystals (jt author) 1965, The Physics of Metals, 2, Defects (ed.) 1975, Progress in Materials Science, Vol. 36 (co-ed.) 1992, Topics in Electron Diffraction and Microscopy of Materials (ed.) 1999, Fracture, Plastic Flow and Structural Integrity (co-ed.) 2000; and numerous articles in learned journals. *Leisure interest:* walking. *Address:* Department of Materials, University of Oxford, Parks Road, Oxford, OX1 3PH (Office); 104A Lonsdale Road, Oxford, OX2 7ET, England (Home). *Telephone:* (1865) 273773 (Office); (1865) 559523 (Home). *Fax:* (1865) 273764. *E-mail:* peter.hirsch@materials.ox.ac.uk (Office).

HIRSCH, Robert Paul; French actor; b. 26 July 1925; s. of Joachim Hirsch and Germaine Anne Raybois; mem. Comédie Française 1952–74; Prix Jean-Jacques Gautier 1987. *Stage appearances include:* La belle aventure, Le prince travesti, Monsieur de Pourceaugnac, Les temps difficiles, La double inconstance, Le dindon, Amphitryon, Britannicus, Crime et Châtiment, La faim et la soif, Monsieur Amilcar, L'abîme et la visite, Le Piège, Deburau, Chacun sa vérité, Les dégourdis de la 11e 1986, Mon Faust 1987, Moi, Feuerbach 1989, Le Misanthrope 1992, Une Folie 1993, Le Bel air de Londres 1998. *Films include:* Le dindon, Votre dévoué Blake, En effeuillant la marguerite, Notre-Dame de Paris, Maigret et l'affaire Saint-Fiacre, 125 rue Montmartre, Par question le samedi, Monnaie de singe, Martin soldat, Toutes folles de lui, Les Cracks, Appelez-moi Mathilde, Traitement de choc, Chobizenese, Le crime 1983, Hiver 54 1989, Mortel transfert 2001; Officier des Arts et des Lettres, Jean-Jacques Goutier Prize 1987, César Best Supporting Actor (for Hiver 54) 1990, Brig. d'honneur 1992. *Leisure interests:* painting, dancing. *Address:* Agence JFPM, 11 rue Chanez, 75016 Paris; 1 place du Palais Bourbon, 75007 Paris, France.

HIRSCH BALLIN, Ernst, LLD; Netherlands politician and lawyer; b. 15 Dec. 1950, Amsterdam; s. of Ernst D. Hirsch Ballin and Maria Koppe; m. Pauline van de Grift 1974; two c.; ed Univ. of Amsterdam; mem. Faculty of Law, Amsterdam Univ. 1974–77; Legal Expert, Ministry of Justice 1977–81; Prof. of Constitutional and Admin. Law, Tilburg Univ. 1981–89, Prof. of Int. Law 1994–; Minister of Justice and Netherlands Antillean and Aruban Affairs 1989–94; MP (Lower House) 1994–95, (Upper House) 1995–2000; Councillor of State 2000–; Pres. Catholic Univ. of Theology, Utrecht; Pres. Centre for Int. Legal Co-operation; Christian Democrat; Grand Cross, Orden del Libertador (Venezuela), Kt Order of Holy Sepulchre of Jerusalem; G.A. van Poelje Prize 1980. *Publications:* Publiekrecht en beleid 1979, Rechtstaat en beleid 1992; 300 other publs on int. and comparative law, legal theory, constitutional and admin. law. *Leisure interests:* Brazilian music, philosophy, tennis. *Address:* Council of State, PO Box 20019, 2500 EA The Hague (Office); Bruggenrijt 12, 5032 BH Tilburg, Netherlands (Home). *Telephone:* (70) 4264657 (Office). *Fax:* (13) 5920687 (Home). *E-mail:* ballin@kub.nl (Office).

HIRSCHFIELD, Alan J., BS, MBA; American business executive; b. 10 Oct. 1935, Oklahoma City; ed Univ. of Okla and Harvard Univ.; Vice-Pres. Allen and Co. 1959–67; Vice-Pres. (Finance) and Dir Warner Bros. Seven Arts Inc. 1967–68; Vice-Pres. and Dir American Diversified Enterprises Inc. 1968–73; Pres. and CEO, Columbia Pictures Industries Inc. 1973–79; Consultant, Warner Communications Inc. 1979; Vice-Chair. and COO, 20th Century-Fox Film Corpn 1979–81, Chair., CEO and COO 1981–84; CEO Data Broadcasting Corpn 1990–2000, Dir 2000–; Pres. Jackson Hole Land Trust, Cantel, Inc., CPP Belwin, Conservation Int., Trout Unlimited; Dir Straight Arrow Publishing Co., John B. Coleman Co., Motion Picture Asscn of America, New York State Motion Picture and TV Advisory Bd, Film Soc. of Lincoln Cen., Will Rogers Memorial Fund, George Gustav Heye Center, Nat. Museum of the American Indian 1997–, CBSmarket.com, Jackpot Inc. 1998–, Vice-Chair. JNet Enterprises 2000–; Trustee, Cancer Research Inst. (Sloan-Kettering). *Address:* P.O. Box 7443, Jackson, WY 83002, USA.

HIRSCHMAN, Albert Otto, D.ECON.SC.; American political economist; b. 7 April 1915, Berlin, Germany; s. of Carl Hirschmann and Hedwig Marcuse; m. Sarah Chapiro 1941; one d. (one d. deceased); ed Lycée Français, Berlin, Ecole des Hautes Etudes Commerciales, Paris, London School of Econs, Univ. of Trieste, Italy; Research Fellow in Int. Econs, Berkeley, Calif., USA 1941–43; Economist, Fed. Reserve Bd, Washington, DC 1946–52; Econ. Adviser and Consultant, Bogotá, Colombia 1952–56; Prof. of Econs, Yale Univ. 1956–58, Columbia Univ. 1958–64, Harvard Univ. 1964–74; Prof. of Social Science, Inst. for Advanced Study, Princeton 1974–85, Prof. Emer. 1985–; mem. NAS; Distinguished Fellow American Econ. Asscn; Corresp. Fellow British Acad.; Foreign mem. Accademia Nazionale dei Lincei, Italy; 15 hon. degrees and several prizes and awards including Toynbee Prize 1998, Thomas Jefferson Medal 1998. *Publications include:* National Power and the Structure of Foreign Trade 1945, The Strategy of Economic Development 1958, Journeys Towards Progress: Studies of Economic Policy-Making in Latin America 1963, Development Projects Observed 1967, Exit, Voice and Loyalty 1970, A Bias for Hope: Essays on Development and Latin America 1971, The Passions and the Interests 1977, Essays in Trespassing 1981, Shifting Involvements: Private Interest and Public Action 1982, Getting Ahead Collectively: Grassroots Experiences in Latin America 1984, Rival Views of Market Society and Other Recent Essays 1986, The Rhetoric of Reaction: Perversity, Futility, Jeopardy 1991, A Propensity to Self-Subversion 1995, Crossing Boundaries: Selected Writings and an Interview 1998. *Leisure interests:* art and art history. *Address:* c/o Institute for Advanced Study, Princeton, NJ 08540 (Office); 16 Newlin Road, Princeton, NJ, USA (Home). *Telephone:* (619) 734-8252 (Office). *Fax:* (609) 951-4457.

HIRST, Damien; British artist; b. 1965, Bristol; two s.; ed Goldsmiths Coll., London; winner Turner Prize 1995; various awards. *Solo exhibitions include:* Inst. of Contemporary Arts (ICA), London 1991, Emmanuel Perrotin, Paris 1991, Cohen Gallery, New York 1992, Regen Projects, LA 1993, Galerie Jablonka, Cologne 1993, Milwaukee Art Museum 1994, Dallas Museum 1994, Kukje Gallery, Seoul 1995, White Cube/Jay Jopling, London 1995, Prix Eliette von Karajan 1995, Max Gandolph-Bibliothek, Salzburg, Gasogian Gallery, New York 1996, Bruno Bischofberger, Zurich 1997, Astrup Fearnley, Oslo 1997, Tate Gallery, London 1999, Gagosain Gallery, New York 2000. *Group exhibitions include:* ICA, London 1989, Glasgow 1989, Building One, London 1990, The Cornerhouse, Manchester 1991, Serpentine Gallery, London 1991, 1993, 1994, Saatchi Collection, London 1992, Arolsen, Germany 1992, Rome 1992, Karsten Schubert, London 1992, Luis Campaña Gallery, Frankfurt 1992, Anthony d'Offay Gallery, London 1992, Barbara Gladstone Gallery, New York 1992, Tate Gallery, London 1992, Istanbul 1992, Galerie Metropol, Vienna 1992, Museum Fridericianum, Kassel 1993, Aperto Section, Venice 1993, Cohen Gallery, New York 1993, Nat. Gallery of Australia, Canberra 1994, Reina Sofia, Madrid 1994, Centre for Contemporary Art, Glasgow 1994, South Bank Centre, London 1994, Irish Museum of Modern Art, Dublin 1994, Kunsthaus, Zurich 1995, Contemporary Fine Arts, Berlin 1995, Museum Sztuki, Poland 1995, Tate Gallery (Turner Prize Exhbn), South Bank Centre, Waddington Galleries, London 1995, Musée d'Art Moderne, Jeu de Paume, Paris 1996, ICA, Hayward Gallery, London 1996, RA, London 1997, Museum of Contemporary Art, Sydney 1997, Bohen Foundation, New York 1997, Southampton City Art Gallery 1998, Deichtorhallen, Hamburg 1998, Gagosian Gallery, New York 2000 and many others. *Television:* Channel 4 documentary about Damien Hirst and Exhbn at Gagosian Gallery, directed by Roger Pomphrey 2000. *Publication:* I Want to Spend the Rest of My Life Everywhere, One to One, Always, Forever 1997, Theories, Models, Methods, Approaches, Assumptions, Results and Findings 2000. *Leisure interests:* losing myself, pub lunches. *Address:* Science Ltd, 2 Bloomsbury Place, London, WC1A 2QA (Office); The White Cube Gallery, 44 Duke Street, St James's, London, SW1Y 6DD, England. *Telephone:* (20) 7637-3994 (Office); (20) 7930-5373 (White Cube). *Fax:* (20) 7637-3995 (Science Ltd) (Office); (20) 7930-9973 (White Cube). *E-mail:* enquiries@science.ltd.uk (Office).

HIRST, Paul Heywood, MA; British academic; b. 10 Nov. 1927, Huddersfield; s. of Herbert Hirst and Winifred Hirst; ed Huddersfield Coll., Trinity Coll. Cambridge and Univ. of London; school teacher of math. 1948–55; Lecturer and Tutor, Dept of Educ., Univ. of Oxford 1955–59; Lecturer in Philosophy of Educ., Inst. of Educ., Univ. of London 1959–65; Prof. of Educ., King's Coll., Univ. of London 1965–71; Prof. of Educ. and Head Dept of Educ., Univ. of Cambridge 1971–88, Emer. Prof. 1988–; Fellow Wolfson Coll., Cambridge 1971–88, Fellow Emer. 1988–; Visiting Prof., Univs of BC, Alberta, Malawi, Otago, Melbourne, Sydney, Puerto Rico, London 1988–; Vice-Chair. Cttee for Educ., CNAA 1975–81, Chair. Cttee for Research 1988–92; Chair. Univs Council for Educ. of Teachers 1985–88; Hon. Vice-Pres. Philosophy of Educ. Soc. 1979–; mem. Swann Cttee on Educ. of Children of Ethnic Minorities 1981–85; Hon. DEd (CNAA) 1992, Hon. DPhil (Cheltenham and Gloucester Coll. of Higher Educ.) 2000, Hon. DLitt (Huddersfield) 2002. *Publications:* Logic of Education (with R. S. Peters) 1970, Knowledge and the Curriculum 1974, Moral Education in a Secular Society 1974, Educational Theory and its Foundation Disciplines (Ed.) 1983, Initial Teacher Training and the Role of the School (with others) 1988, Philosophy of Education: Major Themes in the Analytic Tradition (Jt Ed.), 4 Vols 1998; numerous articles in educational and philosophical journals. *Leisure interest:* music (especially opera). *Address:* Flat 3, 6 Royal Crescent, Brighton, BN2 1AL, England (Home). *Telephone:* (1273) 684118.

HIRZEBRUCH, Friedrich Ernst Peter, Dr rer. nat; German professor of mathematics; b. 17 Oct. 1927, Hamm, Westf.; s. of Dr. Fritz Hirzebruch and Martha Hirzebruch (née Holtschmit); m. Ingeborg Spitzley 1952; one s. two d.; ed Westfälische Wilhelms-Univ., Münster and Technische Hochschule, Zürich; Scientific Asst Univ. of Erlangen 1950–52; mem. Inst. for Advanced Study, Princeton, NJ, USA 1952–54; Dozent, Univ. of Münster 1954–55; Asst Prof., Princeton Univ., NJ 1955–56; Full Prof., Bonn Univ. 1956–93, Dean, Faculty of Math. and Natural Sciences 1962–64; Dir Max-Planck-Inst. für Mathematik, Bonn 1981–95; Pres. German Math. Soc. 1961–62, 1990, European Math. Soc. 1990–94; mem. Leopoldina, Heidelberg, Mainz, Netherlands and Nordrheinwestf. Acads., NAS, Bayerische Akad. der Wissenschaften, Finnish Acad. of Sciences, Russian (fmrly USSR) Acad. of Sciences, Acad. des Sciences (Paris), Akad. der Wissenschaften, Göttingen, American Acad. of Arts and Sciences, Ukrainian Acad., Sächsische Akad., Berlin-Brandenburgische Akad., Royal Soc., Royal Irish Acad., Polish Acad. of Sciences, Acad. Europaea, European Acad. of Arts and Sciences, Austrian Acad. of Sciences; Dr. hc (Univs. of Warwick, Göttingen, Wuppertal, Notre Dame, Trinity Coll. Dublin, Athens, Potsdam, Konstanz, Humboldt-Berlin, Bar-Ilan, Oslo); Hon. DSc (Oxford) 1984; Silver Medal, Swiss Fed. Inst. of Technology 1950, Wolf

Prize in Mathematics 1988, Lobachevskii Prize, USSR Acad. of Sciences 1989, Seki Prize, Japanese Mathematical Soc. 1996, Cothenius Gold Medal Leopoldina 1997, Lomonosov Gold Medal, Russian Acad. of Sciences 1997, Albert Einstein Medal 1999, Stefan Banach Medal, Polish Acad. of Sciences, Krupp-Wissenschaftspreis 2000; Orden pour le Mérite 1991, Grosses Verdienstkreuz mit Stern 1993, Order of the Holy Treasure, Gold and Silver (Japan) 1996. *Publications:* Neue topologische Methoden in der algebraischen Geometrie 1956, Collected Papers (2 Vols) 1987. *Address:* Max-Planck-Institut für Mathematik, Vivatsgasse 7, 53111 Bonn (Office); Thüringer Allee 127, 53757 St Augustin, Germany (Home). *Telephone:* (228) 4020 (Office); (2241) 332377 (Home). *Fax:* (228) 402277 (Office). *E-mail:* hirzebruch@mpim-bonn.mpg.de (Office).

HISLOP, Ian David, BA; British editor, writer and broadcaster; b. 13 July 1960; s. of the late David Atholl Hislop and of Helen Hislop; m. Victoria Hamson 1988; one s. one d.; ed Ardingly Coll. and Magdalen Coll., Oxford; joined Private Eye (satirical magazine) 1981, Deputy Ed. 1985–86, Ed. 1986–; Columnist The Listener magazine 1985–89, The Sunday Telegraph 1996–; TV critic The Spectator magazine 1994–96; BAFTA Award for Have I Got News for You 1991, Editors' Editor, British Soc. of Magazine Eds. 1991, Magazine of the Year, What the Papers Say 1991, Ed. of the Year, British Soc. of Magazine Eds. 1998. *Radio:* The News Quiz 1985–90, Fourth Column 1992–95, Lent Talk 1994, Gush (scriptwriter, with Nick Newman) 1994, Words on Words 1999, The Hislop Vote 2000, A Revolution in 5 Acts 2001, The Patron Saints 2002. *TV scriptwriting:* Spitting Image 1984–89, The Stone Age (with Nick Newman) 1989, Briefcase Encounter 1990, The Case of the Missing 1991, He Died a Death 1991, Harry Enfield's Television Programme 1990–92, Harry Enfield and Chums 1994–97, Mangez Merveillac 1994, Dead on Time 1995, Gobble 1996, Sermon from St. Albion's, Granada 1998, Confessions of a Murderer 1999, My Dad is the Prime Minister 2003. *TV performer:* Have I Got News for You 1990–, Great Railway Journeys, BBC 1999. *TV presenter:* Canterbury Tales, Channel 4 1996, School Rules, Channel 4 1997, Pennies from Bevan, Channel 4 1998. *Publications:* various Private Eye collections 1985–, contribs. to newspapers and magazines on books, current affairs, arts and entertainment. *Address:* c/o Private Eye, 6 Carlisle Street, London, W1V 5RG, England. *Telephone:* (20) 7437-4017.

HITAM, Tan Sri Dato' Musa bin; Malaysian politician (retd); b. 18 April 1934, Johor; ed English Coll., Johor Baharu Univ. of Malaya and Univ. of Sussex; Assoc. Sec. Int. Student Conf. Secr. (COSEC), Leiden 1957–59; civil servant 1959–64; political sec. to Minister of Transport 1964; MP 1968–90; Asst Minister to Deputy Prime Minister 1969; studied in UK 1970, subsequently lectured at Univ. of Malaya; Chair. Fed. Land Devt Authority 1971; Deputy Minister of Trade and Industry 1972–74; Minister of Primary Industries 1974–78, of Educ. 1978–81; Deputy Prime Minister and Minister of Home Affairs 1981–86; Deputy Pres. UMNO 1981–86; Special Envoy to UN 1990–91; Malaysia's Chief Rep. to UN Comm. on Human Rights 1994–; Special Envoy of the Prime Minister to Commonwealth Ministerial Action Group. *Address:* No. 12, Selekoh Tunku, Bukit Tunku, 50480, Kuala Lumpur, Malaysia.

HITE, Shere D., MA; American writer; b. St Joseph, Mo.; m. Friedrich Hoericke 1985; ed Univ. of Florida, Columbia Univ.; Dir feminist sexuality project NOW, New York 1972–78; Dir Hite Research Int., New York 1978–; instructor in female sexuality, New York Univ. 1977–; lecturer Harvard Univ., McGill Univ., Columbia Univ., also numerous women's groups, int. lecturer 1977–89; mem. Advisory Bd Foundation of Gender and Genital Medicine, Johns Hopkins Univ.; Consultant Ed. Journal of Sex Educ. and Therapy, Journal of Sexuality and Disability; mem. NOW, American Historical Asscn, American Sociological Asscn, AAAS, Acad. of Political Science, Women's History Asscn, Society for Scientific Study of Sex, Women's Health Network; Visiting Prof. Nihon Univ., Japan 1998; f. Nike Prize for Women's Non-Fiction Writing, Frankfurt 1997. *Publications:* Sexual Honesty: By Women For Women 1974, The Hite Report: A Nationwide Study of Female Sexuality 1976, The Hite Report on Male Sexuality 1981, Hite Report on Women and Love: A Cultural Revolution in Progress 1987, Good Guys, Bad Guys (with Kate Colleran) 1989, Women as Revolutionary Agents of Change: The Hite Reports and Beyond 1993, The Hite Report on the Family: Growing Up Under Patriarchy 1994, The Divine Comedy of Ariadne and Jupiter 1994, The Hite Report on Hite: A Sexual and Political Autobiography 1996, How Women See Other Women 1998. *Address:* 2 Soho Square, London, W1V, England (Office).

HJELM-WALLÉN, Lena, MA; Swedish politician; b. 14 Jan. 1943, Sala; d. of Elly Hjelm-Wallén and Gustaf Hjelm; m. Ingvar Wallén 1965; one d.; ed Univ. of Uppsala; teacher in Sala 1966–69; active in Social Democratic Youth League; elected to 2nd Chamber of Parl. 1968; mem. Exec. Cttee Västmanland br. of Socialdemokratiska Arbetarepartiet (Social Democratic Labour Party—SDLP) 1968, mem. SDLP Parl. Exec. 1976–82, SDLP Spokeswoman on Schools, mem. Bd SDLP 1978–87, SDLP Spokeswoman on Educ. 1991–94; Minister without Portfolio, with responsibility for schools 1974–76; Minister of Educ. and Cultural Affairs 1982–85, of Int. Devt Co-operation 1985–91, for Foreign Affairs 1994–98; Deputy Prime Minister 1998–2002. *Leisure interests:* nature, books, gardening, family. *Address:* c/o Rosenbad 4, 103 33 Stockholm, Sweden (Office).

HJÖRNE, Lars Goran; Swedish newspaper editor and publisher; b. 20 Oct. 1929, Gothenburg; s. of the late Harry Hjörne; m. Lena Hjörne (née Smith);

one s. one d.; Chief Ed. Göteborgs-Posten 1969–89, Chair. 1969–95, Hon. Chair. 1995–; Hon. British Consul-Gen. in Gothenburg 1991–98; Hon. OBE. *Address:* Polhemsplatsen 5, 405 02 Gothenburg (Office); Stora Vägen 43, 26043 Arild, Sweden (Home). *Telephone:* (31) 62-40-00 (Office); (42) 34-68-03 (Home).

HJÖRNE, Peter Lars; Swedish newspaper editor and publisher; b. 7 Sept. 1952, Gothenburg; s. of Lars Hjörne and Anne Gyllenhammar; m. 2nd Karin Linnea Tufvesson Hjörne 1995; four d.; ed Göteborgs Högre Samskola and Univ. of Gothenburg; Man. Trainee John Deere Co., USA 1978–79; Exec. Asst Göteborgs-Posten 1979–82, Deputy Man. Dir 1983–85, Man. Dir 1985–93, Publisher and Chief Ed. 1993–. *Leisure interests:* sailing, literature, music, art. *Address:* Göteborgs-Posten, Polhemsplatsen 5, 405 02 Gothenburg, Sweden. *Telephone:* 31-62-40-00 (Office). *Fax:* 31-15-76-92.

HLAWITSCHKA, Eduard, DPhil; German university professor; b. 8 Nov. 1928, Dubkowitz; s. of Ernst Hlawitschka and Emilie Tschwatschal; m. Eva-Marie Schuldt 1958; one s. one d.; ed Univs. of Freiburg and Saarbrücken; Prof. Univ. of Düsseldorf 1969, Univ. of Munich 1975–; Pres. Sudetendeutsche Akad. der Wissenschaften und Künste 1991–94; Sudetendeutscher Kulturpreis für Wissenschaft 1987, Prix de Liechtenstein, Conf. Int. de Généalogie et d'Héraldique 1991. *Publications:* Franken, Alemannen, Bayern und Burgunder in Oberitalien 1960, Studien zur Äbtissinnenreihe von Remiremont 1963, Lotharingien und das Reich an der Schwelle der deutschen Geschichte 1968, Die Anfänge des Hauses Habsburg-Lothringen 1969, Libri memoriales I 1970, Vom Frankenreich zur Formierung der europäischen Staaten- und Völkergemeinschaft 840–1046 (1986), Untersuchungen zu den Thronwechseln der ersten Hälfte des 11. Jahrhunderts und zur Adelsgeschichte Süddeutschlands 1987, Stirps Regia 1988, Andechser Anfänge 2000. *Address:* Panoramastrasse 25, 82211 Herrsching/Ammersee, Germany. *Telephone:* (18152) 4991.

HLINKA, Ivan; Czech ice hockey player; b. 26 Jan. 1950, Litvinov; m. 2nd 1998; one s.; ed Univs, Prague; Gen. Man. HC Chemopetrol Litvinov; fmr mem. nat. ice hockey team (132 goals in 256 appearances), winner medal World Championships 1972, 1976, 1977; coached gold medal-winning nat. ice hockey team, Winter Olympics Nagano 1998, World Championships, Norway 1999; Head Coach Pittsburg Penguins 2000–01; Gen. Man. Czech nat. ice hockey team, Winter Olympics, Salt Lake City 2002; Head Coach Omsk, Russia 2002–; Medal of Merit, Czech Repub. 1999, Int. Ice Hockey Fed. Hall of Fame 2002. *Leisure interest:* gardening. *Address:* Zimní Stadion, 43 601 Litvínov, Czech Republic (Office).

HO, Edmund H. W., BA; Macao business executive and politician; b. March 1955; s. of Ho Yin and Chan Keng; m.; one s. one d.; ed York Univ., Canada; chartered accountant and certified auditor 1981–; worked for accounting firm in Toronto, Ont. 1981–82; Gen. Man. Tai Fung Bank 1983, CEO 1999–; mem. CPPCC 1986–; elected Deputy to Nat. People's Congress (NPC) 1988, elected to 8th and 9th standing cttees.; mem. Legis. Ass. of Macao 1988–, Vice-Pres. 1988–99; Vice-Pres. Macao Chamber of Commerce; Chair. Macao Asscn of Banks 1985–; Chief Exec. Macao Special Admin. Region (MSAR) May 1999–; Vice-Chair. All-China Fed. of Industry and Commerce, Econ. Council of the Macao Govt, Kiang Wu Hosp. Bd of Charity, Tung Sin Tong Charitable Inst.; Vice-Pres. Drafting Cttee of the Basic Law of the MSAR 1988, Consultative Cttee of the Basic Law of the MSAR 1989, Preparatory Cttee of the MSAR 1998; Convenor of Land Fund Investment Comm. of the MSAR; Chair. Bd of Dirs. Univ. of Macao; Vice-Chair. Bd of Dirs. Jinan Univ., Guangzhou; Pres. Exec. Cttee Macao Olympic Cttee; Pres. Macao Golf Asscn. *Address:* Palácio do Governo, Rua da Praia Grande, Macao Special Administrative Region, People's Republic of China (Office). *Telephone:* 726886 (Office). *Fax:* 725468 (Office). *Website:* www.macau.gov.mo (Office).

HO, Peng-Yoke, PhD, DSc, CPhys, FInstP, FAHA; Australian professor of Chinese; b. 4 April 1926, Malaysia; s. of the late Tih-Aun Ho and Yeen-Kwai Ng; m. Lucy Mei-Yiu Fung 1955; one s. four d.; ed Raffles Coll., Singapore and Univ. of Malaya, Singapore; Asst Lecturer in Physics Univ. of Malaya, Singapore 1951–54, Lecturer in Physics 1954–60, Reader Dept of Physics 1960–64; Prof. of Chinese Studies, Univ. of Malaya, Kuala Lumpur 1964–73, Dean of Arts 1967–68; Foundation Prof. Griffith Univ., Queensland 1973–89, Foundation Chair. School of Modern Asian Studies 1973–78, Prof. Emer. 1989–; Prof. of Chinese, Univ. of Hong Kong 1981–87, Master Robert Black Coll. 1984–87; mem. Acad. Sinica; Dir Needham Research Inst., Cambridge 1990–; Professorial Research Assoc., SOAS, London Univ.; Hon. Prof., Chinese Acad. of Science, Beijing, Univ. of Science and Tech., Beijing, North-West Univ., Xian, China; Hon. DLitt (Edinburgh). *Publications:* The Astronomical Chapters of the Chin Shu 1966, Li, Qi and Shu: An Introduction to Chinese Science and Civilization 1985, Science and Civilization in China (with Joseph Needham), Vol. 5, Part 3 1976, Part 4 1980, Part 7 1986. *Leisure interest:* chess. *Address:* Needham Research Institute, 8 Sylvester Road., Cambridge, CB3 9AF (Office); 2B Sylvester Rd., Cambridge, CB3 9AF, England (Home); 8 Holdway Street, Kenmore, Queensland 4069, Australia (Home). *Telephone:* (1223) 311545 (Cambridge) (Office). *Fax:* (1223) 362703 (Cambridge) (Office).

HO, Stanley Hung Sun, OBE; Chinese business executive; b. 25 Nov. 1921, Hong Kong; ed Univ. of Hong Kong; Group Exec. Chair. Shun Tak Holdings Ltd (operator of world's largest jetfoil fleet); Founder and Man. Dir Sociedade de Turismo e Diversões de Macao, (SARL—tourism and entertainment, banking, property, airport and airline); Man. Dir Sociedade de Jogos de Macao, SA; Pres. Real Estate Developers' Asscn 1984–; Chair. Univ. of Hong

Kong Foundation for Educational Devt and Research 1995–; mem. Court of Univ. of Hong Kong 1982–, Council 1984–; Vice-Patron Community Chest 1986–; Vice-Pres. Basic Law Drafting Cttee, Macao Special Admin. Region 1988–93, Vice-Pres. Preparatory Cttee, Macao Special Admin. Region 1988–99; mem. Selection Cttee for First Govt of Hong Kong Special Admin. Region 1996–97; mem. Standing Cttee CPPCC Cttee 1998–; Co-Chair. Int. Cttee Franklin Delano Roosevelt Memorial Comm. 1994–97; mem. Economic Council of Macao SAR 2000–; Hon. DScS (Univ. of Macau) 1984, (Univ. of Hong Kong) 1987; Comendador da Ordem de Benemerência (Portugal) 1970; Comendador da Ordem de Infante Dom Henrique (Portugal) 1981; CStJ 1983; Chevalier, Légion d'honneur 1983, Grande-Oficial da Ordem do Infante Dom Henrique (Portugal) 1985, Order of the Sacred Treasure (Japan) 1987, Equitem Commendatorem Ordinis Sancti Gregorii Magni 1989, Darjah Dato Seri Paduka Mahkota Perak (Malaysia) 1990, Grã-Cruz, Ordem do Mérito (Portugal) 1990, Medalha Naval de Vasco da Gama (Portugal)1991, Cruz de Plata de la Medalla de la Solidaridad (Spain) 1993, Grã-Cruz, Ordem do Infante Dom Henrique (Portugal) 1995, Hon. Order of the Crown of Terengganu Darjah Seri' Paduka Mahkota Terengganu (Malaysia) 1997, Nuno Gonçalo Vieira Matias (Portugal) 1999, Global Award for Outstanding Contribution for the Development of Int. Trade and Relations, Priyadashni Acad. India 2000, Gold Medal of Merit in Tourism (Portugal) 2001; Hon. Citizen of Beijing 2001. *Leisure interests:* ballroom dancing, swimming, playing tennis. *Address:* Shun Tak Holdings Ltd, 39/F, West Tower, Shun Tak Centre, 200 Connaught Road Central, Hong Kong Special Administrative Region, People's Republic of China (Office). *Telephone:* (852) 28593111 (Hong Kong) (Office); (853) 566065 (Macao) (Office). *Fax:* (852) 28581014 (Hong Kong) (Office); (853) 371981 (Macao) (Office).

HO, Tao, BA, MArch, LHD; Chinese architect, urban planner and artist; b. 17 July 1936, Shanghai, China; s. of Ping-Yin Ho and Chin-Hwa Chiu; m. 1st Chi-Ping Lu 1960, one s. two d.; m. 2nd Irene Lo 1978, one d.; ed Pui Ching Middle High School, Hong Kong 1950–56, Williams Coll., Williamstown, Mass. and Harvard Univ., USA; Research Asst, Albright-Knox Art Gallery, Buffalo, NY 1959; Architectural Asst to Walter Gropius 1963–64; Visiting Lecturer, Fine Arts Dept, Chinese Univ., Hong Kong 1965–67; f. own practice, Taoho Design Architects, Hong Kong 1968–; co-founder, Hong Kong Arts Centre 1969, Chair. Visual Arts Cttee, Hong Kong Arts Centre 1972–77; Visiting Critic, Harvard Univ. Graduate School of Design 1975; External Examiner of Art, Chinese Univ., Hong Kong 1975–79; Visiting Critic, Design Dept, Hong Kong Polytechnic 1979–; Hon. lecturer, School of Architecture, Hong Kong Univ. 1979–; Chair. Hong Kong Designers Asscn 1981; Hon. Adviser, City Hall Museum, Hong Kong 1981–; Chinese Govt Advisor for Hong Kong Affairs 1995; mem. Bd of Architects, Singapore 1981–; Assoc. mem. Chartered Inst. of Arbitrators 1979–; core mem. Asian Planning and Architectural Consultants Ltd 1975–; Founder, Dir Vision Press Ltd, Hong Kong 1982–; Fellow, Hong Kong Inst. of Architects 1971–; mem. Singapore Inst. of Architects 1988; L'Ordre des Architectes, France, 1992; Founding mem. Hong Kong Artists' Guild 1987; f. Philharmonic Soc. of Hong Kong Professionals 1991; has organized more than 20 exhbns for Hong Kong Arts Centre 1972–; Arthur Lehman Fellow, Harvard Univ. 1960–63; Forum Fellow of World Econ. Forum at Davos 1997–2001; Justice of Peace of Hong Kong 1997–; mem. Political Consultative Cttee of Pudong, Shanghai 2001; Hon. FAIA 1988–; Hon. Fellow, Philippines Inst. of Architects 1993–; Hon. DHumLitt (Williams Coll., Mass., USA) 1979; Design Merit Award (Chinese Manufacturers' Asscn), Silver Medal (Hong Kong Inst. of Architects), Bicentennial Medal (Williams Coll., USA). *Radio:* 17-programme weekly radio series 'Tao Ho on Music' for RTHK 1987; regular panellist on 'Free as the Wind' (RTHK) 1997–. *Major works include:* Hong Kong Govt Pavilion, C.M.A. Exhbn, Hong Kong 1969; Hong Kong Int. Elementary School 1975, Hong Kong Arts Centre 1977, residential Devt, Shouson Hill, Hong Kong (with K. C. Lye) 1979, Planning and Urban design of 3 major Chinese cities: Xiamen, Qingdao and Harigzhou 1985–86, 6A Bowen Road Apt 1983 (HKIA Silver Medal), Bayview Residential Devt 1988, (HKIA Design Award), Hong Kong Baptist Coll. Redevt. 1988–89; revitalization of Western Market, Hong Kong 1992; Eng Bldg, Chinese Univ. of Hong Kong 1993; renovation of Hong Kong Govt House 1993; designed commemorative stamps for Hong Kong Govt 1975; commissioned by SWATCH to design art clock tower to represent Hong Kong at 1996 Olympic Games, Atlanta, USA; one-man painting exhbns at China Art Gallery, Beijing 1993, La Maison de Verre, Paris 1993, Hong Kong Univ. Museum 1995, Villa Turque, La Chaux-de-Fonds, Switzerland; China Construction Bank Headquarters, Beijing 1998, Giant Panda Habitat, Hong Kong 1999, Pentecostal Holiness Wing Kwong Church (including stained glass design), Hong Kong 2000, Industrial and Commercial Bank Data Centre, Beijing 2002; light sculpture 'BIG BANG' created for the new headquarters of the World Econ. Forum, Geneva. *Publications:* Taoho Building Dreams 2000; numerous papers on theory and practice of art and architecture. *Leisure interests:* collecting art, writing about art, listening to music, painting, reading in cosmology and philosophy of science, sculpture. *Address:* 8/B, 499 King's Road, North Point, Hong Kong Special Administrative Region, People's Republic of China. *Telephone:* (852) 28118780. *Fax:* (852) 28110337. *Website:* www.taoho.com (Office).

HOAGLAND, Edward, AB; American author; b. 21 Dec. 1932, New York; s. of Warren Eugene Hoagland and Helen Kelley Morley; m. 1st Amy J. Ferrara 1960 (divorced 1964); m. 2nd Marion Magid 1968 (died 1993); one d.; ed Harvard Univ.; faculty mem. New School for Social Research, New York 1963–64, Rutgers Univ. 1966, Sarah Lawrence Coll., Bronxville, New York

1967, 1971, City Univ. 1967, 1968, Univ. of Iowa 1978, 1982, Columbia Univ. 1980, 1981, Brown Univ. 1988, Bennington Coll., Bennington, Vt 1987–2002, Univ. of Calif. at Davis 1990, 1992, Beloit Coll., Wis. 1995; Gen. Ed. Penguin Nature Library 1985–; Houghton Mifflin Literary Fellow 1954; American Acad. of Arts and Letters Travelling Fellow 1964; Guggenheim Fellow 1964, 1975; mem. American Acad. of Arts and Letters; Longview Foundation Award 1961; O Henry Award 1971; Brandeis Univ. Citation in Literature 1972; New York State Council on Arts Award 1972; American Acad. of Arts and Letters Harold D. Vursell Award 1981; Nat. Endowment Arts Award 1982, Lannan Foundation Award 1993. *Publications:* Cat Man 1956, The Circle Home 1960, The Peacock's Tail 1965, Notes from the Century Before: A Journal from British Columbia 1969, The Courage of Turtles 1971, Walking the Dead Diamond River 1973, The Moose on the Wall: Field Notes from the Vermont Wilderness 1974, Red Wolves and Black Bears 1976, African Calliope: A Journey to the Sudan 1979, The Edward Hoagland Reader 1979, The Tugman's Passage 1982, City Tales 1986, Seven Rivers West 1986, Heart's Desire 1988, The Final Fate of the Alligators 1992, Balancing Acts 1992, Tigers and Ice 1999, Compass Points 2001; numerous essays and short stories. *Address:* P.O. Box 51, Barton, VT 05822, USA (Home).

HOAR, Gen. Joseph P., MA; American marine corps officer (retd); b. 30 Dec. 1934, Boston, Mass.; s. of Joseph J. Hoar (deceased) and Marion J. Hoar; m. Charlene Hoar 1956; one s. four d.; ed Tufts Univ., George Washington Univ.; 2nd Lt Marine Corps 1957, rifle platoon Commdr 5th Marines, battalion staff officer 1st Bn 1st Marines, platoon Commdr, later guard company Commdr Marine Barracks Yorktown, VA., Asst G-1 Marine Corps Base, Camp Lejeune, NC, Bn operations officer 2nd Marine Div., Bn and brigade adviser Vietnamese Marines 1966–68, special Asst to Asst Commdt Marine Corps, Exec. Officer 1st Battalion 9th Marines 1968–71, instructor Marine Corps Command and Staff Coll. 1972–76, served Personnel Man. Div. HQ U.S. Marine Corps 1976–77; Commdr 3rd Battalion 1st Marines 1977–79, promoted Col Regimental Commdr 1st Marines 1979–81; commanded 31st Marine Amphibious Unit on board USS Belleau Wood 1981–84; Asst Chief-of-Staff G-1 Marine Corps Recruit Depot, San Diego 1984–85; rank of Brig.-Gen. 1984; Asst Div. Commdr 2nd Marine Div., Dir Facilities and Services Div. Installations and Logistics Dept HQ Marine Corps Washington 1985–87; commanding Gen. Marine Corps Recruit Depot and Eastern Recruiting Region Parris Island 1987–88; promoted Maj.-Gen. 1987, Chief-of-Staff U.S. Cen. Command 1988–90; Deputy Chief-of-Staff Plans, Policies and Operations 1990–91; rank of Lt-Gen. 1990; C-in-C U.S. Cen. Command 1991–94; Pres. J. P. Hoar and Assoc. Inc. 1994–; Co-Chair. Middle East Panel, Council on Foreign Relations 1994–; rank of Gen. 1991; Fellow World Econ. Forum; three Defense Distinguished Service Medals, Bronze Star Medal with Combat "V" and Gold Star, Meritorious Service Medal with Gold Star and other decorations; awards from nine foreign govts. *Leisure interest:* tennis. *Address:* 386 13th Street, Del Mar, CA 92014, USA. *Telephone:* (858) 794-0546. *Fax:* (858) 794-0531.

HOARE, Sir Charles Antony Richard, Kt, FRS; British computer scientist; b. 11 Jan. 1934, Colombo, Ceylon (now Sri Lanka); s. of the late Henry S. M. and Marjorie F. Hoare; m. Jill Pym 1962; one s. one d.; ed Dragon School, Oxford, King's School, Canterbury, Merton Coll., Oxford, Unit. of Biometry, Oxford and Moscow State Univ.; with Elliott Bros. (London) Ltd 1960–68; Prof. of Computing Science, Queen's Univ. Belfast 1968–77; Prof. of Computation, Univ. of Oxford 1977–93; James Martin Prof. of Computing, Univ. of Oxford 1993–99, Prof. Emer. 1999–; Sr Researcher, Microsoft Research Ltd 1999–; Fellow Wolfson Coll. 1977–99; mem. Acad. Europea; Foreign mem. Acad. Lincei, Italy; Corresp. mem. Bavarian Acad. of Sciences; Distinguished Fellow of British Computer Soc.; Hon. Fellow, Kellogg Coll. Oxford 1998, Darwin Coll. Cambridge 2001; Hon. DSc (Univ. of S. Calif., Warwick, Pennsylvania, Queen's, Belfast); Hon. DUniv (York) 1989, (Essex) 1991, (Bath) 1993, (Oxford Brookes) 2000; AM Turing Award 1980, Harry Goode Memorial Award, Faraday Medal 1985, Kyoto Prize 2000. *Publications:* Structured Programming (co-author) 1972, Communicating Sequential Processes 1985, Essays in Computing Science 1989, Unifying Theories of Programming (co-author) 1998. *Leisure interests:* walking, music, reading, travel, gardening. *Address:* Microsoft Research Ltd., 7 J. J. Thomson Avenue, Cambridge, CB3 0FB, England (Office). *Telephone:* (1223) 479800 (Office). *Fax:* (1223) 479999 (Office). *E-mail:* thoare@microsoft.com (Office). *Website:* www .research.microsoft.com (Office).

HOBAN, Russell Conwell, FRSL; American author; b. 4 Feb. 1925, Lansdale, Pa; s. of Abram Hoban and Jenny Hoban (née Dimmerman); m. 1st Lillian Aberman 1944 (divorced 1975, died 1998); one s. three d.; m. 2nd Gundula Ahl 1975; three s.; ed Lansdale High School and Philadelphia Museum School of Industrial Art; served US Infantry, Italy 1943–45; held various jobs including gen. illustration with Wexton co., New York 1945–51; TV Art Dir BBDO Advertising, NY 1951–56; freelance illustrator 1956–65; copywriter, Doyle Dane Bernbach, New York 1965–67; novelist and author of children's books 1967–; Whitbread Prize for How Tom Beat Captain Najork and His Hired Sportsmen (children's book) 1974; John W. Campbell Memorial Award and Australian Science Fiction Achievement Award for Riddley Walker 1983. *Publications and other works:* novels: The Mouse and His Child 1967, The Lion of Boaz-Jachin and Jachin-Boaz 1973, Kleinzeit 1974, Turtle Diary 1975, Riddley Walker 1980, Pilgermann 1983, The Medusa Frequency 1987, Fremder 1996, The Trokeville Way 1996, Mr Rinyo-Clacton's Offer 1998, Angelica's Grotto 1999, Amaryllis Night and Day 2001, The Bat Tattoo

2002, Her Name was Lola 2003; 66 children's picture books and two books of verse for children since 1959; collection of poems The Last of the Wallendas 1997; text for The Carrier Frequency (theatre piece, Impact Theatre Co-operative) 1984; stage version of Riddley Walker (Manchester Royal Exchange Theatre Co.) 1986; The Moment under the Moment (a collection including stories, essays and a libretto) 1992; The Second Mrs Kong (opera text, music by Birtwistle) 1994 (premiere Glyndebourne 1994); radio play: Perfect and Endless Circles 1995; short stories performed on Radio 3 and 4; various essays and pieces for Granta and The Fiction Magazine. *Leisure interest:* writing. *Address:* c/o David Higham Associates Ltd, 5–8 Lower John Street, Golden Square, London, W1R 4HA, England (Office). *Telephone:* (20) 7437-7888 (Office). *Fax:* (20) 7437-1072 (Office). *E-mail:* noctys@globalnet.co .uk (Home).

HOBDAY, Sir Gordon (Ivan), Kt, PhD, FRSC, CChem, DL; British business executive (retd); b. 1 Feb. 1916, Derbyshire; s. of the late Alexander Thomas Hobday and Frances Cassandra Hobday (née Meads); m. 1st Margaret Jean Joule 1940 (died 1995); one d.; m. Patricia Shaw (née Birge) 2002; ed Long Eaton Grammar School, Univ. Coll., Notts.; joined The Boots Co. Ltd 1939, Dir of Research 1952–68, Deputy Man. Dir 1968–70, Man. Dir 1970–72, Chair. 1973–81; Dir The Metal Box Co. Ltd 1976–81; Dir Lloyds Bank 1981–86; Deputy Chair. Price Comm. 1977–78; Chair. Cen. Independent Television Co. Ltd 1981–85; Chancellor Univ. of Nottingham 1979–91 (Pres. of the Council 1973–82); Pres. Portland Coll. 1990–93; Lord Lt and Keeper of the Rolls for Nottinghamshire 1983–91; Hon. LLD. *Leisure interests:* handicrafts, gardening. *Address:* Newstead Abbey Park, Nottingham, NG15 8GD, England.

HOBERMAN, Brent, MA; British business executive; ed Univ. of Oxford; Sr Consultant, Media and Telecoms Spectrum Strategy Consultants, LineOne; Gen. Man., Head of Business Devt and Founder mem. QXL; co-f. with Martha Lane Fox (q.v.) and CEO Lastminute.com 1998–. *Address:* Lastminute.com PLC, Park House, 4th Floor, 116 Park Street, London, W1K 6NR, England (Office). *Telephone:* (20) 7802-4200 (Office). *Fax:* (20) 7659-4909 (Office). *Website:* www.lastminute.com (Office).

HOBHOUSE OF WOODBOROUGH, Baron (Life Peer), cr. 1998, of Woodborough in the County of Wiltshire; **Rt Hon. Sir John Stewart, Lord Justice Hobhouse,** Kt, PC; British judge; b. 31 Jan. 1932; ed Christ Church Coll., Oxford; called to Bar Inner Temple 1955, QC 1973; Judge of High Court, Queen's Bench Div. 1982–93; Lord Justice of Appeal 1993–98, a Lord of Appeal in Ordinary 1998–. *Address:* House of Lords, London, SW1A 0PW, England. *Telephone:* (20) 7219-3202.

HOBSBAWM, Eric John Ernest, CH, PhD, FBA; British university professor; b. 9 June 1917, Alexandria; s. of Leopold Percy Hobsbawm and Nelly Gruen; m. Marlene Schwarz 1962; one s. one d.; ed Cambridge Univ.; Lecturer, Birkbeck Coll. 1947–59, Reader 1959–70, Prof. of Econ. and Social History 1970–82, Prof. Emer. 1982–; Fellow, King's Coll., Cambridge 1949–55, Hon. Fellow 1973–; Andrew D. White Prof.-at-Large, Cornell Univ. 1976–82; Prof., New School for Social Research, New York 1984–97; Hon. Foreign Mem. American Acad. of Arts and Sciences; Foreign mem. Hungarian Acad. of Sciences, Accad. delle Scienze, Turin; Dr hc (Stockholm) 1970, (Chicago) 1976, (East Anglia) 1982, (New School) 1982, (York Univ., Canada) 1986, (Pisa) 1987, (London) 1993, (Essex) 1996, (Columbia Univ.) 1997, (Buenos Aires, Univ. of ARCIS, Santiago, Chile) 1998, (Univ. de la República, Montevideo, Uruguay) 1999, (Turin) 2000, (Oxford) 2001, (Pennsylvania) 2002; Chevalier des Palmes académiques, Order of the Southern Cross (Brazil) 1996. *Publications:* Primitive Rebels 1959, The Age of Revolution 1962, Labouring Men 1964, Industry and Empire 1968, Captain Swing 1969, Bandits 1969, Revolutionaries 1973, The Age of Capital 1975; Ed. Storia del Marxismo (5 Vols) 1978–82, Worlds of Labour 1984, The Age of Empire 1875–1914 1987, Politics for a Rational Left: Political Writing 1989, Nations and Nationalism since 1780 1990, Echoes of the Marseillaise 1990, The Jazz Scene 1992, The Age of Extremes 1914–1991 1994, On History (essays) 1997, Uncommon People: Resistance, Rebellion and Jazz 1998, On the Edge of the New Century 2000, Interesting Times 2002. *Address:* Birkbeck College, Malet Street, London, WC1E 7HX, England.

HOCH, Orion, PhD; American business executive; b. 21 Dec. 1928, Canonsburg, Pa; m. 1st Jane Lee Ogan 1952 (died 1978); one s. two d.; m. 2nd Catherine Nan Richardson 1980; one s.; ed Carnegie Mellon Univ., Univ. of Calif. Los Angeles and Stanford Univ.; engaged in research and Devt Hughes Aircraft 1952–54; various positions, Electron Devices Div. Litton Industries Inc. 1957–68; Vice-Pres. Litton Components Group 1968–70; Corp. Vice-Pres. Litton Industries Inc. 1970, Sr Vice-Pres. 1971, Deputy Head, Business Systems and Equipment Group 1973–74; Pres. Advanced Memory Systems (later Intersil Inc.) 1974–81; Pres. Litton Industries Inc. 1982–88, Dir and COO 1982, CEO 1986–93, Chair. 1988–94, Chair. Emer. 1994–; Chair. Exec. Cttee, Dir Western Atlas Inc. 1994–98. *Address:* UNOVA Inc. 21, 900 Burbank Boulevard, Woodland Hills, CA 91367, USA.

HOCHHUTH, Rolf; Swiss playwright; b. 1 April 1931; m.; three s.; fmr publisher's reader; Resident Municipal Playwright, Basel 1963; mem. PEN of FRG. *Publications:* plays: The Representative 1962, The Employer 1965, The Soldiers 1966, Anatomy of Revolution 1969, The Guerillas 1970, The Midwife 1972, Lysistrata and the NATO 1973, A German Love Story (novel) 1980, Judith 1984, The Immaculate Conception 1989. *Address:* P.O. Box 661, 4002 Basel, Switzerland.

HOCKNEY, David, CH, RA; British artist; b. 9 July 1937, Bradford; s. of the late Kenneth Hockney and Laura Hockney; ed Bradford Coll. of Art and Royal Coll. of Art; taught at Maidstone Coll. of Art 1962, Univ. of Iowa 1964, Univ. of Colo 1965, Univ. of Calif. (Los Angeles) 1966, Hon. Chair. of Drawing 1980, (Berkeley) 1967; has travelled extensively in Europe and USA; first one-man Exhbn, Kasmin Gallery, London 1963; subsequent one-man exhbns at Museum of Modern Art, New York 1964, 1968, Laundau-Alan Gallery, New York 1964, 1967, Kasmin Gallery 1965, 1966, 1968, 1969, 1970, 1972, Stedeljik Museum, Amsterdam 1966, Palais des Beaux-Arts, Brussels 1966, Studio Marconi and Galleria dell'Ariete, Milan 1966, Galerie Mikro, Berlin 1968, Whitworth Art Gallery, Manchester 1969, André Emmerich Gallery, New York 1972–96, Gallery Springer, Berlin 1970, Kestner-Ges., Hanover 1970, Whitechapel Gallery (retrospective exhbn), London 1970, Kunsthalle, Bielefeld 1971, Musée des Arts Décoratifs, Louvre, Paris 1974, Galerie Claude Bernard, Paris 1975, Nicholas Wilder, Los Angeles 1976, Galerie Neundorf, Hamburg 1977, Warehouse Gallery 1979, Knoedler Gallery 1979, 1981, 1982, 1983, 1984, 1986, Tate Gallery (retrospective Exhbn) 1980, 1986, 1988, 1992, Hayward Gallery (Photographs) 1983, 1985, Museo Tamayo, Mexico City 1984, LA County Museum of Art (retrospective) 1988, 1996, The Metropolitan Museum of Art (retrospective) NY 1988, Knoedler Gallery, London 1988, LA Louver Gallery, Calif. 1986, 1989–, Venice 1982, 1983, 1985, 1986, 1988, Nishimura Gallery, Tokyo, Japan 1986, 1989, 1990, 1994, Royal Acad. of Arts, London 1995, Hamburger Kunsthalle 1995, Manchester City Art Galleries (retrospective exhbn) 1996, Nat. Museum of American Art, Washington, DC 1997, 1998, Museum Ludwig, Cologne 1997, Museum of Fine Arts, Boston 1998, Centre Georges Pompidou, Paris 1999, Musée Picasso, Paris 1999, Annely Juda Fine Art 2003, Nat. Portrait Gallery 2003; Assoc. mem. Royal Acad. 1985; group exhbns include ICA, Second and Third Paris Biennales of Young Artists, Musée d'Art Moderne 1961, 1963, Third Inst. Biennale of Prints, Nat. Museum of Art, Tokyo 1962, London Group Jubilee Exhbn 1914–1964, Tate Gallery 1964, Painting and Sculpture of a Decade, Gulbenkian Foundation, Op and Pop, Stockholm and London 1965, Fifth Int. Exhbn of Graphic Art, Ljubljana 1965, First Int. Print Biennale, Cracow 1966, São Paulo Biennale 1967, Venice Biennale 1968, Pop Art Redefined, Hayward Gallery, London 1969, 150 Years of Photography, Nat. Gallery, Wash., DC 1989–90; touring show of prints and drawings Munich, Madrid, Lisbon, Tehran 1977, Saltaire, Yorks, New York, LA 1994, Royal Acad. (drawings) 1995–96; designed sets for Rake's Progress, Glyndebourne 1975, La Scala 1979, The Magic Flute, Glyndebourne 1978, L'Enfant et les sortilèges, Nightingale, Covent Garden 1983, Tristan and Isolde, LA Music Centre Opera, LA 1987, Turandot, Lyric Opera 1992–, San Francisco 1993, Die Frau Ohne Schatten, Covent Garden, London 1992, LA Music Centre Opera 1993; designer of costumes and sets, Metropolitan Opera House, New York 1980, of sets Varii Capricci 1983; appeared in autobiographical documentary film A Bigger Splash 1974; Hon. PhD (Aberdeen) 1988, (Royal Coll. of Art) 1992: Hon. DLitt (Oxford) 1995; Guinness Award 1961, Graphic Prize, Paris Biennale 1963, First Prize 8th Int. Exhbn of Drawings and Engravings, Lugano 1964, prize at 6th Int. Exhbn of Graphic Art, Ljubljana 1965, Cracow 1st Int. Print Biennale 1966, First Prize 6th John Moores Exhbn 1967, Hamburg Foundation Shakespeare Prize 1983, Praemium Imperiale, Japan Art Asscn 1989, Fifth Annual Gov.'s Award for Visual Arts in Calif. 1994. *Publications:* Hockney by Hockney 1976, David Hockney, Travel with Pen, Pencil and Ink 1978 (autobiog.), Paper Pools 1980, Photographs 1982, China Diary (with Stephen Spender), 1982, Hockney Paints the Stage 1983, David Hockney: Cameraworks 1984, Hockney on Photography: Conversations with Paul Joyce 1988, David Hockney: A Retrospective 1988, Hockney's Alphabet (ed. by Stephen Spender) 1991, That's the Way I See It 1993 (autobiog.), Off the Wall: Hockney Posters 1994, David Hockney's Dog Days 1998, Hockney on Art: Photography, Painting and Perspective 1999, Hockney on "Art": Conversation with Paul Joyce 2000, Secret Knowledge: Rediscovering the Lost Techniques of the Old Masters 2001; illustrated Six Fairy Tales of the Brothers Grimm 1969, The Blue Guitar 1977, Hockney's Alphabet 1991. *Address:* c/o 7508 Santa Monica Boulevard, Los Angeles, CA 90046-6407, USA.

HOCQ, Nathalie; French business executive; b. 7 Aug. 1951, Neuilly (Hauts-de-Seine); d. of Robert Hocq and Christiane Arnoult; m. Patrick Choay; one d.; ed École Mary Mount, Neuilly, Cours Victor-Hugo, Paris and Univ. of Paris-Dauphine; Publicity Asst, Havas-conseil 1970; in charge of duty-free network, Briquet Cartier 1970; Exec. Cartier SA 1974, Gen. Man. 1977, Man. Dir Devt 1979–81; Vice-Chair. Cartier Int. 1981; Pres., Dir-Gen. and CEO Poiray Joailliers Paris 1988–, René Boivin Joaillier 2000–; Prix de L'Innovation dans le Commerce (France). *Leisure interests:* riding, tennis, skiing and swimming. *Address:* Poiray Joailliers, 1 rue de la Paix, 75002 Paris, France.

HODDINOTT, Alun, CBE, DMus; Welsh composer; b. 11 Aug. 1929, Bargoed, S. Wales; s. of Thomas Ivor Hoddinott and Gertrude Jones; m. Beti Rhiannon Huws 1953; one s.; ed Gowerton Grammar School and Univ. Coll., Cardiff; Lecturer, Cardiff Coll. of Music and Drama 1951–59; Lecturer Univ. Coll., Cardiff 1959–65, Reader 1965–67, Prof. of Music 1967–87; Artistic Dir Cardiff Festival of Twentieth Century Music 1966–89, Pres. 1989–; Fellow, Royal Northern Coll. of Music 1980, Univ. Coll., Cardiff 1981, Welsh Coll. of Music and Drama 1990; Hon. mem. RAM; Hon. DMus (Sheffield) 1993; Walford Davies Prize 1954, Bax Medal 1957, Hopkins Medal of the St David's Soc. of New York 1981, Glyndŵr Medal 1997. *Works include:* seven symphonies 1955–77; four sinfoniettas, eleven concertos 1951–69, six piano sonatas 1959–72, four violin sonatas 1969–76, sonatas for harp, cello, clarinet, horn, sonata for Cello and Piano 1977, Welsh Dances, Investiture Dances, Black Bart, Dives and Lazarus 1965, Variants 1966, Fioriture 1968, The Tree of Life 1971, Ritornelli 1974, The Beach at Falesa (opera) 1974, The Magician (opera), Ancestor Worship, Five Landscapes (song cycles), A Contemplation upon Flowers (songs for soprano and orchestra), What the Old Man Does is Always Right (opera), Passaggio for orchestra 1977, Dulcia Iuventutis 1977, Sonata for Organ, Voyagers (for baritone solo, male voices and orchestra) Sonatina for guitar, Sonatina for two pianos, The Rajah's Diamond (opera), Scena for string quartet, Ritornelli for brass quintet, Hymnus Ante Somnum, Nocturnes and Cadenza for solo 'cello, The Heaventree of Stars (for violin and orchestra) 1980, The Trumpet Major (opera in three acts) 1981, Nocturnes and Cadenzas for solo flute, Ritornelli for four double basses, Te Deum (for mixed voices and organ), Lanterne des Morts (for orchestra), Six Welsh Folk Songs (soprano and piano), Doubles (for oboe, harpsichord and strings), Five Studies (for orchestra), Four Scenes from the Trumpet Major (for orchestra), Quodlibet for orchestra 1982, Quodlibet for brass quintet 1983, Masks (oboe, bassoon and piano) 1983, Ingravescentem aetatem (chorus and piano duet) 1983, Lady and Unicorn: Cantata for mixed voices and piano, Piano Trio No. 2, Bagatelles for oboe and harp, String Quartet No. 2, Piano Sonata No. 7, Scenes and Interludes: Concertante for trumpet, harpsichord and strings, Symphony No. 6, Hommage à Chopin (orchestra), Bells of Paradise: Cantata for baritone, mixed chorus and orchestra 1984, Welsh Dances, Third Suite (orchestra), Divertimenti for flute, bassoon, double bass and percussion, Scena for string orchestra, Sonata for two pianos, The Silver Hound: Cycle for tenor and piano, Passacaglia and Fugue for organ, Fanfare with Variants for brass band, Green Broom: Ballad for male voices and piano, Sonata for four clarinets, Sing a New Song (anthem for mixed voices and organ) 1985, Flower Songs (women's voices and piano), Concerto for violin, cello and orchestra, Sonata No. 8 for piano, Divisions: Concertante for horn, harpsichord and strings, Concerto for orchestra, Concerto for clarinet and orchestra 1986, Aspiciens A Longe (anthem for mixed voices and organ) 1987, Welsh Dances (for brass band) 1987, Cantata: Legend of St Julian 1987, String Quartet No. 3 1988, Dr. Faustus: Scena (for mixed voices and brass) 1988, lines from Marlowe's Dr. Faustus 1988, Noctis Equi (cello and orchestra), Songs of Exile, Piano Sonata No. 9, Star Children, Piano Sonata No. 10, Symphony for organ and orchestra 1989, Emynau Pantycelyn (cantata) 1990, Three Advent Carols 1990, Novelette for flute, oboe and piano 1991, Sonata for flute and piano 1991, Sonata No. 5 for violin and piano 1992, Vespers Canticle 1992, Symphony for brass and percussion 1992, Chorales, Variants and Fanfares for organ and brass quintet 1992, Gloria 1992, A Vision of Eternity 1992, Three Motets for chorus and organ 1993, Wind Quintet 1993, Sonata No. 11 for piano 1993, Mass for St David 1994, Sonata No. 12 for piano 1994, Six Bagatelles for string quartet 1994, Three Hymns for mixed chorus and organ 1994, Shakespeare Songs for unaccompanied chorus 1994, The Silver Swimmer for soprano and ensemble 1994, Five Poems of Gustavo Adolfo Bécquer for baritone and piano 1994, One Must Always Have Love (song for high voice and piano) 1994, Mistral (concerto for violin and orchestra) 1995, Shining Pyramid (concerto for trumpet and orchestra) 1995, Sonata for oboe and harp 1995, Tymhorau (four poems for Gwyn Thomas for baritone and piano) 1995, The Poetry of Earth (songs for mixed choir and piano duet) 1995, Camargue Mass 1996, Sonata No. 3 (cello and piano) 1996, Magnificat and Nunc Dimittis 1996, String Quartet No. 4 1996, Piano Trio No. 3 1996, Sonata No. 2 (clarinet and piano) 1996, Sonata No. 6 (violin and piano) 1997, Tempi: Sonata for Harp 1997, The Poetry of Earth (songs for baritone and harp) 1997, Island of Dragons (variants for cello) 1998, Dragon Fire (concertante for timpani, percussion and orchestra), Grongor Hill (scena for baritone, string quartet and piano), Lizard (variants for recorder), Tower (opera in three acts) 1998–99, Celebration Dances (orchestra), To the Poet (Pushkin songs for baritone and piano), Symphony No. 10 1999–2000, La Serenissima (songs for baritone and piano), Quintet for oboe, piano and string trio, Concerto for percussion and brass; Piano Sonata No. 13 2000; String Quartet No. 5 2001; Dream Wanderer for violin, horn and piano 2001, Bagatelles for 11 instruments 2001, Concerto for euphonium and orchestra 2001, Three Welsh Folk Songs (cello and piano) 2002, Lizard (concerto for orchestra) 2002. *Leisure interest:* travelling. *Address:* 64 Gowerton Road, Three Crosses, Swansea, SA4 3PX, Wales. *Telephone:* (1792) 873702 (Home). *E-mail:* hoddinott@croesau.fsnet.co.uk (Home).

HODDLE, Glenn; British professional footballer and football manager; b. 27 Oct. 1957, London; s. of Derek Hoddle and Teresa Roberts; m. Christine Anne Stirling (divorced 1999); one s. two d.; ed Burnt Mill School, Harlow; player with Tottenham Hotspur 1976–86, AS Monaco, France 1986; (12 Under-21 caps, 53 full caps on England nat. team 1980–88, played in World Cup 1982 and 1986); player/man. Swindon Town 1991–93 (promoted to FA Premier League 1993); player/man. Chelsea 1993–96; coach English nat. team 1996–99; Man. Southampton 2000–2001, Tottenham Hotspur 2001–; FA Cup winners' medal (Tottenham Hotspur) 1981 and 1982, UEFA Cup winners' medal (Tottenham Hotspur) 1984, French Championship winners' medal (Monaco) 1988. *Publications:* Spurred to Success (autobiog.), Glenn Hoddle: The 1998 World Cup Story 1998. *Leisure interests:* tennis, golf, reading. *Address:* Tottenham Hotspur Football Club Ltd, 748 High Road, Tottenham, London, N17 0AD, England. *Telephone:* (20) 8365-5000.

HODEL, Donald Paul, JD; American government official; b. 23 May 1935, Portland, Ore.; s. of Philip E. Hodel and Theresia R. (Brodt) Hodel; m. Barbara B. Stockman 1956; two s. (one deceased); ed Harvard Coll. and Univ. of Oregon; admitted to Oregon Bar 1960; Attorney, Daview, Biggs, Strayer, Stoel & Boley 1960–63; Georgia Pacific Corpn 1963–69; Deputy Admin., Bonneville Power Admin. 1969–72, Admin. 1972–77; Pres. Nat. Elec. Reliability Council, Princeton, NJ 1978–80; Pres. Hodel Assocs. Inc. 1978–81; Under-Sec. Dept of Interior 1981–83; Sec. of Energy 1982–85, of the Interior 1985–89; Republican.

HODGE, Sir James William, KCVO, CMG, MA; British diplomatist; b. 24 Dec. 1943; s. of the late William Hodge and Catherine Hodge (née Carden); m. Frances Margaret Coyne 1970; three d.; ed Holy Cross Acad., Edin., Univ. of Edin.; entered FCO 1966, Rhodesia Political Dept 1966–67, Second Sec. (Information), Tokyo 1967–72, FCO Marine and Transport Dept 1972–73, UN Dept 1973–75, First Sec. (Devt and later Chancery), Lagos 1975–78, FCO Personnel Operations Dept 1978–81, First Sec. (Econ.) and later Counsellor (Commercial), Tokyo 1981–86, Head of Chancery, Copenhagen 1986–90, FCO Security Dept 1990–93, attached to Royal Coll. of Defence Studies 1994; Minister Consular Gen. and Deputy Head of Mission, Beijing 1995–96; Amb. to Thailand 1996–2000; Consul-Gen. to Hong Kong Special Admin. Region, People's Repub. of China (concurrently non-resident Consul-Gen. to Macao) Aug. 2000–. *Leisure interests:* books, music. *Address:* British Consulate-General, 1 Supreme Court Road, Hong Kong, People's Republic of China (Office). *Telephone:* (852) 2901-3000. *Fax:* (852) 2901-3066. *E-mail:* information@britishconsulate.org.hk. *Website:* www.britishconsulate.org.hk.

HODGE, Patricia; British actress; b. 29 Sept. 1946, Grimsby; d. of the late Eric Hodge and Marion Phillips; m. Peter Owen 1976; two s.; ed London Acad. of Music and Dramatic Art; won Eveline Evans Award for Best Actress, Olivier Award for Best Supporting Actress 1999; Hon. DLitt (Hull) 1996, (Brunel) 2001. *Stage appearances include:* No-one was Saved, All My Sons, Say Who You Are, The Birthday Party, The Anniversary, Popkiss, Two Gentlemen of Verona, Pippin, Maudie, Hair, The Beggar's Opera, Pal Joey, Look Back in Anger, Dick Whittington, Happy Yellow, The Brian Cant Children's Show, Then and Now, The Mitford Girls, As You Like It, Bene-factors, Noel and Gertie, Separate Tables, The Prime of Miss Jean Brodie, A Little Night Music (Royal Nat. Theatre), Heartbreak House 1997, Money (Royal Nat. Theatre) 1999 (Olivier Award 2000), Summer-folk (Royal Nat. Theatre) 1999, Noises Off (Royal Nat. Theatre and tour) 2000–01. *Film appearances:* The Disappearance, Rose Dixon—Night Nurse, The Waterloo Bridge Handicap, The Elephant Man, Heavy Metal, Betrayal, Sunset, Just Ask for Diamond, The Secret Life of Ian Fleming, The Leading Man 1996, Prague Duet 1996, Jilting Joe 1997, Before You Go 2002. *TV appearances:* Valentine, The Girls of Slender Means, Night of the Father, Great Big Groovy Horse, The Naked Civil Servant, Softly, Softly, Jackanory Playhouse, Act of Rape, Crimewriters, Target, Rumpole of the Bailey, The One and Only Mrs Phyllis Dixey, Edward and Mrs Simpson, Disraeli, The Professionals, Holding the Fort, The Other 'Arf, Jemima Shore Investigates, Hayfever, The Death of the Heart, Robin of Sherwood, O.S.S., Sherlock Holmes, Time for Murder, Hotel du Lac, The Life and Loves of a She Devil, Rich Tea and Sympathy 1991, The Cloning of Joanna May 1991, The Legacy of Reginald Perrin 1996, The Moonstone 1996, The Falklands Play 2002. *Address:* c/o I.C.M., Oxford House, 76 Oxford Street, London, W1N 0AX, England. *Telephone:* (20) 7636-6565. *Fax:* (20) 7323-0101.

HODGES, Jim, BS, JD; American state governor and politician; b. 19 Nov. 1956, Lancaster, SC; m. Rachel Gardner; two s.; ed Davidson Coll., Univ. of South Carolina; Lancaster Co. Attorney, Gen. Counsel, Springs Co.; mem. SC House of Reps. 1986–97; Gov. of SC 1999–; Legislator of the Year, SC Chamber of Commerce 1993, Compleat Lawyer Silver Medallion 1994, Guardian of Small Business Award, Nat. Fed. of Ind. Businesses 1996, Special Service Award, Common Cause 1998. *Address:* Office of the Governor, P.O. Box 11829, Columbia, SC 29211, USA (Office). *Telephone:* (803) 734-9400 (Office). *Fax:* (803) 734-9413 (Office). *Website:* www.state.sc.us/governor (Office).

HODGKIN, Sir Howard, Kt, CH, CBE, DLitt; British painter; b. 6 Aug. 1932; m. Julia Lane 1955; two s.; ed Camberwell School of Art and Bath Acad. of Art; Trustee, Tate Gallery 1970–76, Nat. Gallery 1978–85; first one-man show of paintings Arthur Tooth & Sons, London 1962 since when numerous one-man shows of paintings and prints in UK, USA, Europe and Australia; retrospective Exhbn Metropolitan Museum of Art, New York 1995, then Modern Art Museum, Fort Worth, Der Kunstverein, Düsseldorf and Hayward Gallery, London 1995–97, Galerie Lawrence Rubin, Zurich 1997, Gagosian Gallery, New York 1998, Haas and Fuchs Galerie, Berlin 1998, Anthony d'Offay Gallery 1999–2000, Galleria Lawrence Rubin, Milan 2001, Dulwich Picture Gallery, London 2001; has participated in numerous group exhbns. worldwide; British rep., Venice Biennale 1984; works in many public collections including Tate Gallery, London, Museum of Modern Art, New York, Nat. Gallery of Washington, Metropolitan Museum of Art, New York, Nat. Gallery of S. Australia, Adelaide, Walker Art Center, Minneapolis; mem. Cttee Nat. Art Collections Fund 1989–90; Hon. Fellow, Brasenose Coll., Univ. of Oxford 1988, London Inst. 1999; Hon. DLitt (Birmingham) 1997, (Oxford) 2000; Tate Gallery Turner Prize 1985, Shakespeare Prize, Alfred Toepfer Stiftung FVS, Germany 1997. *Address:* c/o Anthony d'Offay Gallery, 9, 20, 23–24 Dering Street, London, W1S 1AJ, England (Office). *Telephone:* (20) 7580-7970.

HODGKINSON, Mike, BA; British business executive; b. 7 April 1944, Essex; m.; three c.; ed Hornchurch Grammar School, Nottingham Univ.; Ford Grad. Training Programme 1965; Finance and Admin. Dir Leyland Cars (Eng Div.) 1973–77; Man. Dir Land Rover 1978–82; Man. Dir Express Dairy Group 1985; CEO GM Foods Europe, Grand Metropolitan Group 1986–91; Group

Airports Dir BAA 1992–99, CEO 1999–2003; Dir Airports Council Int.; Dir (non-exec.) FKI, Transport for London, Royal Mail Holdings PLC 2002–; Chair. The Post Office 2003–; mem. ACI World Gov. Bd, Advisory Bd Essex Econ. Partnership 2001–; Chair. Hayes West Drayton Partnership. *Leisure interests:* golf, theatre. *Address:* The Post Office, Royal Mail Group PLC, 148 Old Street, London, EC1V 9HQ, England (Office). *Website:* www.royalmail .com.

HODGSON, Sir Maurice Arthur Eric, Kt, MA, BSc, FIChemE, F.R.ENG., CChem, FRSC; British company executive; b. 21 Oct. 1919, Bradford; s. of the late Walter Hodgson and of Amy (née Walker) Hodgson; m. Norma Fawcett 1945; one s. one d.; ed Bradford Grammar School and Merton Coll., Oxford; joined ICI Ltd, Fertilizer and Synthetic Products Group 1942; seconded to ICI (New York) Ltd 1955–58; Head of Technical Dept, ICI Ltd 1958, Devt Dir Heavy Organic Chemicals Div. 1960 (Deputy Chair. 1964), Gen. Man. Co. Planning 1966, Commercial Dir and Planning Dir 1970, Deputy Chair. 1972–78, Chair. 1978–82; Dir Carrington Viyella Ltd 1970–74, Imperial Chemicals Insurance Ltd 1970–78 (Chair. 1972–78), Chair. British Home Stores PLC 1982–87; Dir (non-exec.) Storehouse PLC 1985–89; Nominated mem. Council of Lloyd's 1987–94; mem. Court of British Shippers' Council 1978–82, Council, CBI 1978–82, Pres.'s Cttee, The Advertising Asscn 1978–90, Int. Council, The Salk Inst. 1978–97, Int. Advisory Cttee, Chase Manhattan Bank 1980–83, Int. Advisory Bd AMAX Inc. 1982–85, European Advisory Council Air Products and Chemicals Inc. 1982–84; Dir (non exec.) Dunlop Holdings PLC 1982–83, Chair. Jan.–Nov. 1984; Visiting Fellow, School of Business and Organizational Studies, Univ. of Lancaster 1970–80; Trustee, The Civic Trust 1978–82; mem. of Court, Univ. of Bradford 1979–94; Gov., London Graduate School of Business Studies 1978–87; Pres. Merton Soc. 1986–89; Chair. Civil Justice Review Advisory Cttee 1985–88; Hon. DUniv (Heriot-Watt) 1979; Hon. DTech (Bradford) 1979; Hon. DSc (Loughborough Univ. of Technology) 1981; Messel Medal, Soc. of Chemical Industry 1980, George E. Davis Medal, Inst. of Chemical Eng 1982; Hon. Fellow, Merton Coll., Oxford 1979; Hon. Fellowship UMIST 1979. *Leisure interests:* horse-racing, swimming, fishing. *Address:* Suite 75/76, Kent House, 87 Regent Street, London, W1R 7HF, England. *Telephone:* (20) 7734-7777.

HODGSON, Thomas R., M.S.E., MBA; American business executive; b. 17 Dec. 1941, Lakewood, Ohio; s. of Thomas J. Hodgson and Dallas L. Hodgson; m. Susan Cawrse 1963; one s. two d.; ed Purdue Univ., Univ. of Mich. and Harvard Univ.; Devt engineer DuPont 1964; Assoc. Booz-Allen & Hamilton 1969–72; with Abbott Labs. 1972–, Gen. Man. Faultless Div. 1976–78, Vice-Pres. and Gen. Man. Hosp. Div. 1978–80, Pres. Hosp. Div. 1980–83, Group Vice-Pres. and Pres. Abbott Int. Ltd 1983–84, Exec. Vice-Pres. 1985–80, Pres. and COO Abbott Labs. Oct. 1990–; Visiting Prof. Purdue Univ. 1996–. *Leisure interests:* skiing, scuba, wind-surfing, racquetball, tennis, kayaking. *Address:* Abbott Laboratories, 100 Abbott Park Road, Abbott Park, North Chicago, IL 60064 (Office); 1015 Ashley Road, Lake Forest, IL 60045, USA (Home). *Telephone:* (708) 688-8288.

HØEG, Peter; Danish writer; b. 1957, Copenhagen; m.; two d.; ed Univ. of Copenhagen; worked as sailor, ballet dancer, athlete and actor before becoming full-time writer; f. Lolwe Foundation 1996. *Publications:* The History of Danish Dreams 1988, Tales of the Night (short stories) 1990, Miss Smilla's Feeling for Snow 1992 (film 1997), Borderliners 1994, The Woman and the Ape 1996. *Address:* c/o H. Rosinante, Ryesgade 27, P.O. Box 24, 2200 Copenhagen N, Denmark (Office).

HOEVEN, John, MBA; American state official; m. Mical (Mikey) Hoeven; one s. one d.; ed Dartmouth Coll., Northwestern Univ.; fmr Exec. Vice-Pres. First Western Bank, Minot; Pres. and CEO Bank of North Dakota 1993; Gov. of North Dakota 2000–; mem. Souris Valley Humane Soc.; Dir Minot Kiwanis Club. *Address:* Office of the Governor, 600 East Boulevard Avenue, Bismark, ND 58505-0001, USA (Office).

HOEY, Rt. Hon. Catharine (Kate) Letitia, PC, BSc; British politician; b. 21 June 1946; d. of Thomas Henry Hoey and Letitia Jane Hoey; ed Ulster Coll., City of London Coll.; lecturer, Southwark Coll. 1972–76; Sr Lecturer, Kingsway Coll. 1976–85; Councillor London Borough of Hackney 1978–82, of Southwark 1988; Educational Adviser, London Football Clubs 1985–89; MP for Vauxhall 1989–; Opposition Spokeswoman Citizens' Charter and Women 1992–93; Parl. Pvt. Sec. to Minister of State (Minister for Welfare Reform), Dept of Social Security 1997; Parl. Under-Sec. of State, Home Office 1998–99, Dept of Culture, Media and Sport 1999–2001; mem. Labour Party. *Leisure interests:* keeping fit, watching football. *Address:* House of Commons, London, SW1A 0AA, England (Office). *Telephone:* (20) 7219-3000 (Office). *E-mail:* hcinfo@parliament.co.uk (Office).

HOFFENBERG, Sir Raymond (Bill), KBE, MA, MD, PhD, FRCP (UK), FRCP(E), FRCP(I); British physician (retd); b. 6 March 1923, Port Elizabeth, S Africa; s. of Benjamin Hoffenberg and Dora Hoffenberg; m. Margaret Rosenberg, 1949; two s.; ed Grey High School, Port Elizabeth, Univ. of Cape Town Medical School; Sr Lecturer in Medicine, Groote Schuur Hosp., Cape Town 1955–68; MRC Scientist and Consultant Physician, Nat. Inst. for Medical Research and Royal Free Hosp., London, England 1968–70; at MRC Clinical Research Centre and Northwick Park Hosp. 1970–72; Prof. of Medicine Univ. of Birmingham 1972–85; Pres. Royal Coll. of Physicians, London 1983–89, Wolfson Coll. Oxford 1985–93, Mental Health Foundation 1989–; Prof. of Medical Ethics Univ. of Queensland 1993–95; Hon. Fellow, American Coll. of Physicians; Hon. FRACP; Hon. FACP; Hon. FRCPC; Hon. FFOM; Hon.

FFPM; Hon. FRCPsych; Hon. FRCS(E); Hon. FRCPCH; Hon. mem. Acad. of Medicine of Malaysia; Hon. DSc (Leicester, City Univ., London, Witwatersrand, Cape Town, Imperial Coll., London Univ.); Hon. MD (Bristol). *Publications:* numerous chapters and articles on plasma protein metabolism, thyroid function and other aspects of endocrinology. *Leisure interests:* walking, golf. *Address:* c/o Wolfson College, Oxford, OX2 6UD, England. *Telephone:* (1451) 844545. *Fax:* (1451) 844874.

HOFFMAN, Alan Jerome, AB, PhD; American mathematician and educator; b. 30 May 1924, New York; s. of Jesse Hoffman and Muriel Hoffman; m. 1st Esther Walker 1947 (died 1988); two d.; m. 2nd Elinor Hershaft 1990; ed George Washington High School, Columbia Univ.; mem. U.S. Army Signal Corps 1943–46; mem. Inst. for Advanced Study 1950–51; Mathematician, Nat. Bureau of Standards 1951–56; Scientific Liaison Officer, Office of Naval Research, London 1956–57; Consultant, Gen. Electric Co. 1957–61; Adjunct Prof. City Univ. of New York 1965–75; Research Staff mem. IBM Research Center 1961–; IBM Fellow 1977–; Visiting Prof., Yale Univ. 1975–80, Rutgers Univ. 1990–96, Georgia Inst. of Tech. 1992–93; Consulting Prof., Stanford Univ. 1981–91; Fellow, New York Acad. of Sciences, American Acad. of Arts and Sciences; mem. NAS; Hon. DSc (Technion) 1986; Von Neumann Prize (Operations Research Soc. and Inst. of Man. Science) 1992. *Publications:* numerous articles in mathematical journals. *Leisure interests:* table tennis, music. *Address:* IBM T.J. Watson Research Center, Box 218, Yorktown Heights, NY 10598, USA.

HOFFMAN, Dustin Lee; American actor; b. 8 Aug. 1937, Los Angeles, Calif.; s. of Harry Hoffman; m. 1st Anne Byrne 1969 (divorced); two d.; m. 2nd Lisa Gottsegen 1980; two s. two d.; ed Santa Monica City Coll.; worked as an attendant at a psychiatric inst.; demonstrator Macy's toy Dept; First stage role in Yes is for a Very Young Man (Sarah Lawrence Coll., Bronxville, NY); Broadway debut in A Cook for Mr. General 1961; Officier Ordre des Arts et des Lettres; Britannia Award (BAFTA) 1997, Golden Globe Lifetime Achievement Award 1997. *Other stage appearances in:* Harry, Noon and Night 1964, Journey of the Fifth Horse (Obie Award) 1966, Star Wagon 1966, Fragments 1966, Eh? (Drama Desk, Theatre World, Vernon Rice Awards) 1967, Jimmy Shine 1968, Death of a Salesman 1984, The Merchant of Venice 1989; Asst Dir A View from the Bridge; Dir All Over Town 1974. *Films include:* The Tiger Makes Out 1966, Madigan's Millions 1966, The Graduate 1967, Midnight Cowboy 1969, John and Mary 1969, Little Big Man 1970, Who is Harry Kellerman...? 1971, Straw Dogs 1971, Alfredo Alfredo, Papillon 1973, Lenny 1974, All the President's Men 1975, Marathon Man 1976, Straight Time 1978, Agatha 1979, Kramer vs. Kramer 1979 (Acad. Award 1980, New York Film Critics Award), Tootsie (New York Film Critics Award, Nat. Soc. of Film Critics Award) 1982, Ishtar 1987, Rain Man (Acad. and Golden Globe Awards) 1988, Family Business 1989, Dick Tracy 1990, Hook 1991, Billy Bathgate 1991, Hero 1992, Outbreak 1995, American Buffalo, Sleeper 1996, Wag the Dog 1997, Mad City 1997, Sphere 1997, Joan of Arc 1999, The Messenger: the Story of Joan of Arc 1999, Being John Malkovich 1999. *TV appearance in:* Death of a Salesman 1985. *Leisure interests:* tennis, piano, photography, reading. *Address:* Punch Productions, 1926 Broadway, Suite 305, New York, NY 10023, USA.

HOFFMAN, Grace; American mezzo-soprano singer; b. 14 Nov. 1925, Cleveland, Ohio; d. of Dave Hoffman and Hermina Hoffman; ed Western Reserve Univ. and Manhattan School of Music, New York; completed musical studies in Italy (Fulbright Scholarship); appeared at Maggio Musicale, Florence; guest performance as Azucena (Il Trovatore) Zürich Opera and subsequently mem. of this company for two years; debut at La Scala, Milan as Fricka (Die Walküre); with Stuttgart Opera 1955–; given titles Württembergische Kammersängerin 1960, Austrian Kammersängerin 1980; has appeared at Edinburgh and Bayreuth festivals; numerous guest appearances in leading roles at Teatro Colón, Buenos Aires, San Francisco Opera, Chicago Lyric Opera, Covent Garden, Metropolitan Opera, the Vienna Opera, in Berlin, Brussels, etc.; numerous oratorio and concert appearances in the maj. European music centres; Prof. of Voice, Hochschule für Musik, Stuttgart 1978; Vercelli Prize, Medal of State of Baden-Württemberg 1978. *Leisure interests:* her house and furnishing it. *Address:* c/o Staatstheater Stüttgart, Oberer Schlossgarten 6, 7000 Stuttgart 1 (Office); Bergstrasse 19, 72666 Neckartailfingen, Germany (Home).

HOFFMAN, Jerzy; Polish film director; b. 15 March 1932, Cracow; m. (deceased); one d.; ed All-Union State Inst. of Cinematography, Moscow; has directed 27 documentaries with Edward Skórzewski including Remembrance of Kalwaria (Oberhausen and Florence Film Festival awards), Two Aspects of God, and others 1955–62; mem. Acad. of Fine Arts, Ukraine; Great Cross with Star, Order of Polonia Restituta; numerous Polish and int. film prizes including Minister of Culture and Arts Prize (four times). *Films include:* Gangsters and Philanthropists (feature film debut with Edward Skórzewski) 1962, Michał Wołodyjowski, Deluge, Medicine Man, With Fire and Sword (Polish Eagles for Best Film Producer) 2000. *Leisure interests:* historical books, bridge, cooking, swimming. *Address:* Zodiak Jerzy Hoffman Production, ul. Puławska 61, 02-595 Warsaw, Poland (Office). *Telephone:* (22) 845-20-47 (Office).

HOFFMAN, Philip Seymour; American actor; b. 1968, Fairport, New York; ed Tisch School of Drama, New York. *Films include:* Scent of a Woman 1992, My New Gun 1993, When a Man Loves a Woman 1994, Nobody's Fool 1994, The Getaway 1994, Twister 1996, Montana 1997, Boogie Nights 1997, Hard

Eight 1997, The Big Lebowski 1998, Patch Adams 1998, The Talented Mr Ripley 1999, Magnolia 1999, Flawless 1999, Almost Famous 2000, State and Main 2000, Red Dragon 2002, Love Liza 2002, 25th Hour 2002. *Address:* c/o Phil's Phans, P.O. Box 249, Penfield, NY 14526, USA (Office).

HOFFMANN, Adriana; Chilean environmentalist; leading environmentalist in various pressure groups such as Lahuen, Defenders of the Native Forests and Protege; plays leading role in the Chilean Science Soc., Biology Soc. of Chile, Earth Foundation, Asscn of Chilean Female Leaders, UICN (Int. Union for Conservation); Head Nat. Environmental Comm. (CONAMA) 2000–. *Publications:* Flora silvestre de Chile 1983, El árbol urbano en Chile 1989, Cactáceas en la flora silvestre de Chile 1990, De cómo Margarita Flores puede cuidar su salud y ayudar a salvar el planeta (with Marcelo Mendoza) 1992. *Address:* Obispo Donoso 6, Castilla 520 via Correo 21, Providencia, Santiago, Chile (Office). *Telephone:* 240-5600 (Office). *Fax:* 244-1262 (Office). *E-mail:* informaciones@conama.cl (Office).

HOFFMANN, Baron (Life Peer), cr. 1995, of Chedworth in the County of Gloucestershire; **Rt Hon. Leonard Hubert Hoffmann,** Kt, MA, PC; British judge; b. 8 May 1934; s. of B.W. Hoffmann and G. Hoffmann; m. Gillian Sterner 1957; two d.; ed South African Coll. School, Cape Town, Univ. of Cape Town and Queen's Coll. Oxford; Advocate, Supreme Court of S Africa 1958–60; called to Bar, Gray's Inn, London 1964, Bencher 1984; QC 1977; Judge, Courts of Appeal of Jersey and Guernsey 1980–85; Judge, High Court of Justice, Chancery Div. 1985–92; Lord Justice of Appeal 1992–95; a Lord of Appeal in Ordinary 1995–; Judge Court of Final Appeal, Hong Kong Special Admin. Region 1997–; Dir ENO 1985–90, 1991–94; Stowell Civil Law Fellow, Univ. Coll. Oxford 1961–73; Pres. British-German Jurists Asscn 1991–; Hon. Fellow, Queen's Coll. Oxford 1992; Hon DCL (City) 1992, (Univ. of West of England) 1995. *Publication:* The South African Law of Evidence 1963. *Address:* c/o House of Lords, London, SW1A 0PW (Office); Surrey Lodge, 23 Keats Grove, London, NW3 2RS, England.

HOFFMANN, Luc, D.PHIL; Swiss biologist; b. 23 Jan. 1923, Basel; s. of Dr. Emanuel Hoffmann and Marie-Anne Hoffmann (née Stehlin); m. Daria Razumovsky 1953; one s. three d.; ed Gymnasium Basel and Flim, Grisons, Univ. of Basel; f. Station Biologique de la Tour du Valat 1954, Man. Dir 1954–84, Chair. of Bd Fondation Tour du Valat 1974–; f. World Wildlife Fund (WWF) (later World Wide Fund for Nature) 1961, Vice-Pres. of Bd 1961–88 (Exec. Vice-Pres. 1971–78, Vice-Pres. Emer. 1989); Vice-Pres. of Bd Int. Union for Conservation of Nature (IUCN) 1966–69; Dir Int. Wildfowl Research Bureau (IWRB) 1962–69; Hon. Dir Wetlands Inst. (fmrly IWRB); Vice-Pres. Wildfowl Trust 1979, Hon. Life Fellow 1983; mem. Exec. Cttee Int. Council for Bird Preservation (ICBP) 1984–90; f. Fondation Int. du Banc d'Arquin (FIBA) 1985, Pres. 1985–2000; Hon. Pres. 2000–; Vice-Pres. Bd of Dirs. Hoffmann-La Roche and Co., Basel 1990–96; Pres. WWF France 1996–2000, Hon. Pres. 2001–; Dr. hc (Basel), (Thessaloniki); Commdr Order of the Golden Ark (Netherlands) 1988, Croix du Mérite pour les Sciences et les Arts (Austria), Chevalier, Légion d'honneur, Officier, Ordre du Mérite Nat. de la Répub. Islamique du Mauritanie 1998, Duke of Edin. Conservation Medal 1999, Officier, Ordre de l'Honneur (Greece) 1999. *Publications:* Camargue (with K. Weber) 1968; 60 Publs in the fields of ornithology, wetland ecology and conservation. *Leisure interests:* contemporary art, bird watching. *Address:* La Tour du Valat, Le Sambuc, 13200 Arles, France (Office); Le Petit Essert, 1147 Montricher, Switzerland (Home). *Telephone:* (4) 90-72-20-13 (Office); (21) 8645977 (Home). *Fax:* (4) 90-97-20-19 (Office); (21) 8644230 (Home). *E-mail:* l.hoffmann@tour-du-valat.com (Office); l.hoffmann@tour-du-valat.com (Home). *Website:* www.tour-du-valat.com (Office).

HOFFMANN, Roald, PhD; American professor of chemistry; b. 18 July 1937, Złoczów, Poland; s. of Hillel Safran and Clara Rosen, step-s. of Paul Hoffmann; m. Eva Börjesson 1960; one s. one d.; ed Columbia and Harvard Univs; Jr Fellow, Soc. of Fellows, Harvard Univ. 1962–65; Assoc. Prof. of Chem., Cornell Univ. 1965–68, Prof. 1968–74, John A. Newman Prof. of Physical Science 1974–96, Frank M. Rhodes Prof. of Humane Letters 1996–; mem. American Acad. of Arts and Sciences, NAS, American Philosophical Soc.; Foreign mem. Royal Soc., Indian Nat. Acad. of Sciences, Royal Swedish Acad. of Sciences; mem. USSR (now Russian) Acad. of Sciences, Societas Scientarum Fennica 1986; Hon. DTech. (Royal Inst. of Technology, Stockholm) 1977; Hon. DSc (Yale) 1980, (Columbia) 1982, (Hartford) 1982, (City Univ. of New York) 1983, (Puerto Rico) 1983, (Uruguay) 1984, (La Plata) 1984, (Colgate) 1985, (State Univ. of New York at Binghamton) 1985, (Ben Gurion Univ. of Negev) 1989, (Lehigh) 1989, (Carleton) 1989, (Md) 1990, (Ariz.) 1991, (Bar-Ilan Univ.) 1991, (Central Fla) 1991, (Athens) 1991, (Thessaloniki) 1991, (St Petersburg) 1991, (Barcelona) 1992, (Northwestern Univ.) 1996, (The Technion) 1996, (Durham) 2000; ACS Award 1969, Fresenius Award 1969, Harrison Howe Award 1969, Annual Award of Int. Acad. of Quantum Molecular Sciences 1970, Arthur C. Cope Award, ACS 1973, Linus Pauling Award 1974, Nichols Medal 1980, shared Nobel Prize for Chemistry 1981, Inorganic Chemistry Award, ACS 1982, Nat. Medal of Science 1984, Nat. Acad. of Sciences Award, in Chemical Sciences 1986, Priestley Medal 1990. *Play:* Oxygen (with Carl Djerassi). *Publications:* Conservation of Orbital Symmetry 1969, The Metamict State 1987, Solids and Surfaces 1988, Gaps and Verges 1990, Chemistry Imagined (jtly.)1993, The Same and Not the Same 1995, Old Wine, New Flasks (jtly.) 1997, Memory Effects 1999, Soliton 2002, Catalísta (Spanish) 2002. *Address:* Department of Chemistry and Chemical Biology, Cornell University, Ithaca, NY 14853, USA. *Telephone:* (607) 255-3419 (Office). *Fax:* (607) 255-5707 (Office). *E-mail:* rh34@cornell.edu (Office).

HOFMANN, Peter; German tenor; b. 12 Aug. 1944, Marienbad; ed Hochschule für Musik, Karlsruhe; operatic début as Tamino, Lübeck 1972; mem. Stuttgart Opera 1973–; sang Siegmund, centenary production of The Ring, Bayreuth 1976, Covent Garden London 1976; U.S. début as Siegmund, San Francisco Opera 1977; début Metropolitan New York (Lohengrin) 1980; pop artist 1984–; seven week tour across Germany performing Phantom of the Opera 1999. *Address:* c/o Fritz Höfman, Schloss Schönreuth 8581, Germany.

HOFMANN, Werner, DPhil; Austrian museum administrator (retd) and author; b. 8 Aug. 1928, Vienna; s. of Leopold Hofmann and Anna Hofmann (née Visvader); m. Jacqueline Hofmann (née Buron) 1950; ed Univ. of Vienna; Asst Albertina, Vienna 1950–55; Dir Museum of the 20th Century, Vienna 1962–69, Hamburger Kunsthalle 1969–90; Guest Lecturer Barnard Coll., NY 1957; Guest Prof. Berkeley, Calif. 1961, Harvard Univ. 1981, 1982, Columbia Univ. 1984, New York Univ. 1991, Vienna Univ. 1991; Gold Ehren-Medaille City of Vienna 1988, Sigmund-Freud-Preis 1991; Commdr des Arts et des Lettres. *Publications:* Die Karikatur von Leonardo bis Picasso 1956, Die Plastik des 20. Jahrhunderts 1958, Das irdische Paradies-Kunst im 19. Jahrhundert 1960, Grundlagen der modernen Kunst 1966, Turning Points in 20th Century Art 1969, Gustav Klimt und die Wiener Jahrhundertwende 1970, Nana, Mythos und Wirklichkeit 1973, Kataloge der Ausstellungsreihe "Kunst um 1800" 1974–80, Edouard Manet: Das Frühstück im Atelier 1985, Ausstellungskatalog "Zauber der Medusa" 1987, Une Époque en rupture 1750–1830 1995, Die Moderne im Rück-Spiegel. Hauptwege der Kunstgeschichte 1998, Caspar David Friedrich 2000. *Address:* Sierichstr. 154, 22299 Hamburg, Germany (Home). *Telephone:* 464711. *Fax:* 464711.

HOFMEKLER, Ori, BFA; Israeli painter; b. 12 March 1952, Israel; s. of Daniel Hofmekler and Rina Kune; m. Ilana Wellisch 1977; one s. one d.; ed Bezalel Acad., Jerusalem and Jerusalem Univ.; Shtrouk Prize 1976. *Publications:* Hofmekler's People 1983; contribs. to Penthouse Magazine since 1983 and to magazines in France, Germany and USA. *Leisure interests:* reading, sports and travel.

HOGAN, Linda, MA; American poet, novelist and essayist; b. 16 July 1947, Denver; d. of Charles Henderson and Cleo Henderson; two d.; ed Univ. of Colorado; Assoc. Prof. Univ. of Colo, Prof. 1989–; American Book Award. *Publications:* Mean Spirit 1980, Savings, Red Clay (poems and stories), Solo Storms (novel), Stories We Hold Secret, Book of Medicines (poetry), From Women's Experience to Feminist Theology. *Address:* University of Colorado, Central Office, Boulder, CO 80309, USA.

HOGAN, Paul, AO; Australian film actor; b. 8 Oct. 1940, Lightening Ridge; m. 1st Noelene Hogan (divorced 1989); five c.; m. 2nd Linda Kozlowski 1990; one s.; ed Parramatta High School; fmr rigger on Sydney Harbour Bridge; host of TV shows A Current Affair, The Paul Hogan Show; filmed TV specials on location in England 1983; commercials for Australian Tourist Comm., Fosters Lager. *Films:* Crocodile Dundee (Golden Globe Award) 1986, Crocodile Dundee II 1989, Almost An Angel 1993, Lightning Jack 1994, Flipper 1996, Sorrow Floats 1997, Crocodile Dundee in Los Angeles 2001. *TV:* Anzacs: The War Down Under. *Address:* c/o Silverstream Management, GPO Box 3950, Sydney, NSW 2001 (Office).

HOGG, Sir Christopher Anthony, Kt, MA, MBA; British business executive; b. 2 Aug. 1936, London, England; s. of Anthony Wentworth Hogg and Monica Mary Gladwell; m. 1st Anne Patricia Cathie 1961 (divorced 1997); two d.; m. 2nd Dr. Miriam Stoppard 1997; ed Marlborough Coll., Trinity Coll., Oxford and Harvard School of Business Administration, USA; Nat. Service, Parachute Regt 1955–57; Research Assoc. Institut pour l'Etude des Méthodes de Direction de l'Entreprise (business school), Lausanne, Switzerland 1962–63; with Philip Hill, Higginson, Erlangers Ltd (later Hill Samuel & Co. Ltd) 1963–66; staff mem. Industrial Reorganisation Corpn 1966–68; joined Courtaulds Group 1968, Man. Dir 1971, Dir (non-exec.) British Celanese Ltd 1971–72, Chair. 1972–75, Dir Courtaulds Ltd 1973–96, a Deputy Chair. 1978–80, Chief Exec. 1979–91, Chair. Courtaulds PLC 1980–96, Courtaulds Textiles PLC 1990–95; Deputy Chair. Allied Domecq 1995–96, Chair. 1996–; Dir (non-exec.) Reuters Group PLC 1984– (Chair. 1985–), SmithKline Beecham PLC 1993–2000, GlaxoSmithKline 2000– (Chair. 2002–); Air Liquide SA 2000–; Chair. (non-exec.) Royal Nat. Theatre 1995–; Trustee Ford Foundation 1987–99; mem. Dept of Industry Industrial Devt Advisory Bd 1976–81, Cttee of Award for Harkness Fellowships 1980–86, Int. Council J. P. Morgan 1988–, Court, Bank of England 1992–96; Foreign Hon. mem. American Acad. of Arts and Services 1991; Hon. Fellow Trinity Coll. Oxford 1982, London Busiess School 1992, City and Guilds of London Inst. 1992; Hon. FCSD 1987; Hon. DSc (Cranfield Inst. of Tech.) 1986, (Aston) 1988; BIM Gold Medal 1986, Centenary Medal, Soc. of Chemical Industry 1989; Hambro Businessman of the Year 1993. *Publication:* Masers and Lasers 1962. *Leisure interests:* theatre, reading, walking. *Address:* Reuters Group PLC, 85 Fleet Street, London, EC4P 4AJ, England (Office). *Telephone:* (20) 7542-7029 (Office). *Fax:* (20) 7542-5874 (Office).

HOGG, Baroness (Life Peer), cr. 1995, of Kettlethorpe in the County of Lincolnshire; **Sarah Elizabeth Mary Hogg;** British economist; b. 14 May 1946; d. of Lord Boyd-Carpenter; m. Rt Hon Douglas M. Hogg QC, MP 1968; one s. one d.; ed St Mary's Convent, Ascot and Lady Margaret Hall, Oxford Univ.; staff writer, The Economist 1967, Literary Ed. 1970, Econs Ed. 1977; Econs Ed. Sunday Times 1981; Presenter, Channel 4 News 1982–83; Econs Ed. and Deputy Exec. Ed. Finance and Industry, The Times 1984–86; Asst Ed. and Business and City Ed. The Independent 1986–89; Econs Ed. The Daily

Telegraph 1989–90; Head Policy Unit, 10 Downing Street (rank Second Perm. Sec.) 1990–95; Chair. London Econs 1997–99 (Dir 1995–97), Frontier Econs 1999–; mem. Int. Advisory Bd, Nat. Westminster Bank 1995–97, Advisory Bd, Bankinter 1995–98, House of Lords Select Cttee on Science and Tech. 1995–98, House of Lords Select Cttee on Monetary Policy 2000, Council, Royal Econ. Soc. 1996–, Council, Hansard Soc. 1996–; Dir London Broadcasting Co. 1982–90, Royal Nat. Theatre 1988–91, Foreign & Colonial Smaller Cos. Investment Trust 1995– (Chair. 1997–), Nat. Provident Inst. 1996–99, GKN 1996–, 3i 1997– (Deputy Chair. 2000, Chair. 2001–), P&O 1999–2000, P&O Princess Cruises 2000–, Martin Currie Portfolio Investment Trust 1999–; Gov. BBC 2000; Fellow, Eton Coll. 1996–; Hon. Fellow, Lady Margaret Hall, Oxford 1994; Gov. Centre for Econ. Policy Research 1985–92; Hon. MA (Open Univ.) 1987; Hon. DLitt (Loughborough Univ.) 1992; Wincott Foundation Financial Journalist of the Year 1985. *Publication:* Too Close to Call (with Jonathan Hill) 1995. *Address:* 3iGroup PLC, 91 Waterloo Road, London, SE1 8XP (Office); House of Lords, London, SW1A 0PW, England. *Website:* www .3igroup.com (Office).

HOGGART, Richard, MA, DLitt; British educator (retd) and writer; b. 24 Sept. 1918, Leeds; s. of Tom Longfellow Hoggart and Adeline Emma Hoggart (née Long); m. Mary Holt France 1942; two s. one d.; ed Leeds Univ.; Royal Artillery 1940–46; Staff Tutor and Sr Staff Tutor, Univ. Coll. of Hull and Univ. of Hull 1946–59; Sr Lecturer in English, Univ. of Leicester 1959–62; Visiting Prof. Univ. of Rochester, NY 1956–57; Prof. of English, Birmingham Univ. 1962–73; Pres. British Asscn of fmr UN Civil Servants 1978–86; Chair. European Museum of the Year Award Cttee 1977–, Broadcasting Research Unit 1980–90; mem. Albemarle Cttee on Youth Services 1958–60, Youth Service Devt Council 1960–62, Pilkington Cttee on Broadcasting 1960–62; Gov. Birmingham Repertory Theatre 1963–70; Dir Centre for Contemporary Cultural Studies 1964–73; mem. BBC Gen. Advisory Council 1959–60, 1964–70, Arts Council of GB 1976–81, Culture Advisory Cttee of UK Nat. Comm. to UNESCO 1966–70, Communications Advisory Cttee of UK Nat. Comm. to UNESCO 1977–79, Wilton Park Academic Council 1983–; Chair. Arts Council Drama Panel 1977–80, Vice-Chair. Arts Council 1980–81, Chair. Advisory Council for Adult and Continuing Educ. 1977–83, The Statesman and Nation Publishing Co. Ltd 1978–81; Gov. Royal Shakespeare Theatre 1966–88; Asst Dir-Gen. for Social Sciences, Humanities and Culture UNESCO 1970–75; Warden of Goldsmiths' Coll. 1976–84; Chair. Book Trust 1995–97; Pres. Nat. Book Cttee 1997–; Hon. Visiting Prof., Univ. of E Anglia 1985–, Univ. of Surrey 1985–; BBC Reith Lecturer 1971; Hon. Fellow Sheffield City Polytechnic 1983, Goldsmiths' Coll. 1987, Ruskin Coll. Oxford 1994; Hon. DUniv (Open Univ.) 1972, (Surrey) 1981; Hon. DèsSc (Bordeaux) 1974, (Paris) 1987; Hon. LLD (CNAA) 1982, (York Univ., Toronto) 1988; Hon. LittD (E Anglia) 1986; Hon. DLitt (Leicester Univ.), (Hull Univ.) 1988, (Univ. of Keele) 1995, (Metropolitan Univ. of Leeds) 1995, (Univ. of Westminster) 1996, (Sheffield Univ.) 1999, (Univ. of London) 2000; Hon. EdD (Univ. of E London) 1998. *Publications:* Auden 1951, The Uses of Literacy 1957, W. H. Auden—A Selection 1961, Teaching Literature 1963, How and Why Do We Learn 1965, Essays in Literature and Culture 1969, Speaking to Each Other 1970, Only Connect 1972, An Idea and Its Servants 1978, An English Temper 1982, The Future of Broadcasting (ed. with Janet Morgan) 1978, An Idea of Europe (with Douglas Johnson) 1987, A Local Habitation 1988, Liberty and Legislation (Ed.) 1989, A Sort of Clowning 1990, An Imagined Life 1992, Townscape with Figures 1994, The Way We Live Now 1995, First and Last Things 1999, Hoggart en France 1999, Between Two Worlds 2001. *Leisure interests:* family, reading, writing. *Address:* 19 Mount Pleasant, Norwich, NR2 2DH, Norfolk, England (Home). *Telephone:* (1603) 250398. *Fax:* (1603) 250398. *E-mail:* maryandrichard.hoggart@virgin.net (Office); maryandrichard.hoggart@virgin.net (Home).

HOGWOOD, Christopher Jarvis Haley, CBE, MA, FRSA; British musician, conductor, musicologist, keyboard player, writer and editor; b. 10 Sept. 1941, Nottingham; s. of Haley Evelyn and Marion Constance (née Higgott) Hogwood; ed Cambridge Univ., Charles Univ., Prague, Czechoslovakia; Keyboard Continuo, The Acad. of St Martin-in-the-Fields 1965–76, keyboard soloist 1970–76, Consultant Musicologist 1971–76; Founder-mem. Early Music Consort of London 1965–76; Writer and Presenter, The Young Idea (BBC Radio) 1972–82; Founder and Dir Acad. of Ancient Music 1973–; mem. Faculty of Music, Cambridge Univ. 1975–; Artistic Dir. King's Lynn Festival, England 1976–80; Series Ed., Music for London Entertainment 1983–97; Dir Handel and Haydn Soc., Boston, USA 1986–2001, Conductor Laureate 2001–; Hon. Prof. of Music, Keele Univ. 1986–90; Dir of Music, St Paul Chamber Orchestra, Minn., USA 1987–92, Prin. Guest Conductor 1992–98; Visiting Artist, Harvard Univ. 1988–89, Tutor, Mather House 1991–93; Artistic Adviser, Australian Chamber Orchestra 1989–93; Int. Prof. of Early Music Performance, RAM, London 1992–; Visiting Prof. Dept of Music, King's Coll., London 1992–96; Ed. Bd Early Music (Oxford Univ. Press) 1993–97; Artistic Dir Summer Mozart Festival, Nat. Symphony Orchestra, USA 1993–2001; Assoc. Dir Beethoven Acad., Antwerp 1998–2002; Chair. Advisory Bd CPE Bach Complete Works 1999–; Prin. Guest Conductor, Kammerorchester Basel, Switzerland 2000–; Prin. Guest Conductor, Orquesta de Granada 2001–; Hon. Fellow, Jesus Coll., Cambridge 1989, Pembroke Coll., Cambridge 1992; Hon. Prof. of Music, Cambridge Univ. 2002–; Hon. mem. RAM 1995; Hon. DMus (Keele) 1991; Walter Willson Cobbett Medal (Worshipful Co. of Musicians) 1986, Freeman Worshipful Co. of Musicians 1989, Univ. of Calif. at LA Award for Artistic Excellence 1996, Scotland on Sunday Music Prize, Edin. Int. Festival 1996, Distinguished Musician Award (Inc. Soc. of Musi-

cians) 1997, Martinu Medal (Bohuslav Martinu Foundation) Prague 1999; Handel & Haydn Soc. Fellowship named "The Christopher Hogwood Historically Informed Performance Fellowship". *Publications:* Music at Court 1977, The Trio Sonata 1979, Haydn's Visits to England 1980, Music in Eighteenth Century England (co-author) 1983, Handel 1984, Holmes' Life of Mozart (ed.) 1991; many edns. of musical scores; contribs. to The New Grove Dictionary of Music and Musicians 1980 and 2000; numerous recordings. *Address:* 10 Brookside, Cambridge, CB2 1JE, England. *Telephone:* (1223) 363975. *Fax:* (1223) 327377. *E-mail:* office@hogwood.org (Office). *Website:* www.hogwood .org (Office).

HOHLER, Erla Bergendahl, DPhil, FSA; Norwegian archaeologist and art historian; b. 20 Nov. 1937, Oslo; m. Christopher Hohler 1961; three c.; ed Univ. of Oslo, Courtauld Inst., London; Asst Prof. Inst. of Art History, Univ. of Oslo 1975; Keeper Medieval Dept, Univ. Museum of Nat. Antiquities, Oslo 1987; Prof. Inst. of Archaeology, Art History and Numismatics, Oslo Univ. 1993–; Prof. of Art History Univ. of Tromsø 1994; mem. Soc. of Antiquaries of London 1986, Det Norske Videnskapsakademi 1994. *Publications:* The Capitals of Urnes Church 1975, Stavkirkene 1981, Stilentwicklung in der Holzkirchen Architektur 1981, Norwegian Stave Church Carving 1989, Norwegian Stave Church Sculpture I-II 1999, Catalogue Raisonné 1999. *Address:* Universitetets Kulturhistoriske Museer, Frederiks Gt. 3, 0164 Oslo (Office); Lyder Sagens Gt. 23, 0358 Oslo, Norway. *Telephone:* 22-85-95-36 (Office); 22-46-57-32 (Home). *E-mail:* erla.hohler@ukm.uio.no (Office).

HOHOFF, Curt, DPhil; German writer; b. 18 March 1913, Emden; s. of Caspar Hohoff and Elisabeth (née Waterman) Hohoff; m. Elfriede Federhen 1949; four s. one d.; ed Univs. of Münster, Munich, Cambridge and Berlin; journalist Rheinischer Merkur, Koblenz 1948–49, Süddeutsche Zeitung, Munich 1949–50, freelance 1950–; mem. Akad. der Künste, Berlin 1956, Bayerische Akad. der Künste, Munich 1958; Bundesverdienstkreuz 1992. *Publications:* Woina-Woina, Russisches Tagebuch 1951, Geist und Ursprung (essays) 1954, Heinrich von Kleist (biog.) 1957, Schnittpunkte (essays) 1963, Die Märzhasen (novel) 1966, Munich 1970, Jakob M. R. Lenz (biog.) 1977, Grimmelshausen (biog.) 1978, Unter den Fischen (memoirs) 1982, Die verbotene Stadt (novel) 1986, Besuch bei Kalypso, Landschaften und Bildnisse 1988, J. W. von Goethe, Dichtung und Leben (biog.) 1989, Scheda—im Flug vorbei (novel) 1993, Veritas christiana (essays) 1994, Glanz der Wirklichkeit, Gelehrte Prosa als Kunst (essays) 1998. *Address:* Adalbert-Stifter-Strasse 27, 81925 Munich, Germany. *Telephone:* (89) 9828980.

HOLBOROW, Leslie Charles, BPhil, MA; New Zealand fmr. university vice-chancellor; b. 28 Jan. 1941, Auckland; s. of George Holborow and Ivah V. Holborow; m. Patricia L. Walsh 1965; one s. two d.; ed Henderson High School, Auckland Grammar School and Univs. of Auckland and Oxford; Jr Lecturer, Univ. of Auckland 1963; Lecturer, Sr Lecturer, Univ. of Dundee (until 1967 Queen's Coll. Univ. of St Andrew's) 1965–74; Prof. of Philosophy, Univ. of Queensland, Brisbane 1974–85, Pres. Professorial Bd 1980–81, Pro-Vice-Chancellor (Humanities) 1983–85; Vice-Chancellor, Victoria Univ. of Wellington 1985–98, now Prof. Emer.; Chair. NZ Vice-Chancellors' Cttee 1990, 1996; Council mem. Asscn of Commonwealth Univs. 1990–91, 1996; Pres. Australasian Asscn of Philosophy 1977; Nat. Pres. NZ Inst. of Int. Affairs 1987–90, Standing Cttee 2002–; mem. NZ Cttee for Pacific Econ. Co-operation 1986–94, Educ. Sub-Cttee of NZ Nat. Comm. for UNESCO 1996–99; Trustee NZ String Quartet 1990–; Hon. LLD (VUW) 1998. *Publications:* articles in philosophical journals. *Leisure interests:* tramping, sailing, listening to music. *Address:* 29 Upoko Road, Hataitai, Wellington, New Zealand (Home). *Telephone:* (4) 386-4427 (Home); (4) 905-8867. *Fax:* (4) 386-4427 (Home). *E-mail:* leshol@xtra.co.nz (Office); leshol@xtra.co.nz (Home).

HOLBROOKE, Richard C.; American diplomatist; b. 24 April 1941, New York; s. of Dan Holbrooke and Trudi Moos Kearl; two s.; m. 2nd Kati Marton 1995; ed Brown Univ. and Woodrow Wilson School, Princeton Univ.; Foreign Service Officer in Viet Nam and related posts 1962–66; White House Viet Nam staff 1966–67; Special Asst to Under-Secs. of State Katzenbach and Richardson and mem. U.S. del. to Paris peace talks on Viet Nam 1967–69; Fellow Woodrow Wilson School, Princeton Univ. 1969–70; Dir Peace Corps, Morocco 1970–72; Man. Ed. Foreign Policy (quarterly magazine) 1972–76; consultant, Pres.'s Comm. on Org. of Govt for Conduct of Foreign Policy and contributing Ed. Newsweek 1974–75; coordinator of nat. security affairs, Carter-Mondale campaign 1976; Asst Sec. of State for E Asian and Pacific Affairs 1977–81; Vice-Pres. Public Strategies (consulting firm) 1981–85; Man. Dir Lehman Brothers 1985–93; Amb. to Germany 1993–94; Asst Sec. of State for European and Canadian Affairs 1994–96; Chief Negotiator for Dayton Peace Accord in Bosnia 1995; Vice-Chair. Credit Suisse First Boston Corpn 1996–99; Adviser Baltic Sea Council 1996–98; Special Presidential Envoy for Cyprus 1997–98, to Yugoslavia; Perm. Rep. to UN 1999–2000, Amb. to UN 1999–2001; currently Dir Council on Foreign Relations; Chair. Bipartisan Comm. on Reorganizing Govt for Foreign Policy 1992; Chair. Refugees Int., American Acad. in Berlin, Nat. Advisory Council of Harriman Inst., Asia Soc. 2002–; mem. Bd of Dirs. of numerous orgs.; recipient of 12 hon. degrees; numerous awards including Distinguished Public Service Award, Dept of Defense 1994, 1996, Humanitarian of the Year Award, American Jewish Congress 1998, Dr. Bernard Heller Prize, Hebrew Union Coll. 1999. *Publications:* Counsel to the President (co-author) 1991, To End a War 1998; articles and essays on foreign policy. *Leisure interest:* tennis. *Address:* Council on Foreign Relations, The Harold Pratt House, 58 East 68th Street, New York, NY 10021, USA. *Telephone:* (212) 434-9400. *Fax:* (212) 434-9800. *Website:* www.cfr.org.

HOLDEN, Bob, BS; American state official; m. Lori Hauser; two s.; ed Southwest Mo. State Univ., Harvard Univ.; fmr Admin. Asst to Congressman Richard Gephardt (q.v.), St. Louis; mem. Mo. House of Reps. 1983–89; State Treas. of Mo. 1993–, Gov. of Mo. 2001–; mem. Bd Fund Commrs., Mo. State Employees Retirement System, Mo. Rural Opportunities Council, Holden Scholarship Fund, Leadership St. Louis, Council of State Govts., Nat Asscn State Treas.; Vice-Chair. Mo. Cultural Trust. *Address:* Office of the Governor, Capitol Building, Room 216, POB 720, Jefferson City, MO 65102-6720, USA (Office).

HOLDEN, Roberto; Angolan nationalist leader; b. 1925, São Salvador, Northern Prov.; ed Belgian Congo (now Democratic Republic of the Congo); worked in Finance Dept, Belgian Admin., Léopoldville (now Kinshasa), Stanleyville (now Kisangani) and Bukavu; f. União das Populações de Angola (UPA) 1954; travelled widely in Africa and Europe; attended first and second All African Peoples Confs. Accra 1958, Tunis 1960; elected to the Steering Cttee, Tunis; f. La Voix de la Nation Angolaise, a fortnightly newspaper; assumed leadership of guerrilla liberation operations against the Portuguese in Angola; made several trips to USA 1961; became leader of Frente Nacional de Libertação de Angola (FNLA) when UPA merged with Partido Democrático Angolano (PDA) March 1962; Premier of Angolan Govt in exile, Governo Revolucionário de Angola no Exílio (GRAE) 1962; leader of defeated FNLA forces in Angolan civil war after Portuguese withdrawal Nov. 1975; exiled to Zaire then Senegal; expelled from Senegal 1979; living in Paris 1980.

HOLDER, Eric H., BA, JD; American prosecutor; b. 21 Jan. 1951, New York; s. of Eric Holder and Miriam R. Yearwood; ed Columbia Coll.; Trial Attorney Public Integrity Section, US Dept of Justice 1976–88, US Attorney 1993–97, US Deputy Attorney-Gen. 1997–2001; Assoc. Judge Superior Court, Washington 1988–93. *Address:* c/o Department of Justice, 950 Pennsylvania Avenue NW, Washington DC 20530, USA.

HOLDER, Rt. Rev. John Walder Dunlop, BA, STM, PhD; ecclesiastic; b. 16 Feb. 1948, Barbados; m. Betty Lucas-Holder; one s.; ed Codrington Coll., Barbados, Univ. of the West Indies, The School of Theology (Univ. of the South), King's Coll., London; ordained priest 1975; tutor in Biblical Studies, Codrington Coll. 1977–81, Lecturer 1984–93, Acting Prin. Sept.–Dec. 1988, Sr Lecturer 1993–99, Deputy Prin. 1999–; Visiting Lecturer in Religious Studies, Erdiston Teacher Training Coll., Barbados; Lecturer in Biblical Studies, Lay Training Programme, Diocese of Barbados 1984–90; Visiting Lecturer at Barbados Community Coll. 1985; Visiting Sabbatical Prof. Gen. Theological Seminary, New York March–May 1988; Chair. Ministry of Educ. Cttee on Religious and Moral Educ. Syllabus for the primary schools of Barbados 1992–94; Visiting Lecturer Bucknell Univ. Summer Programme 1996–98; Curate St George's Cathedral, St Vincent, West Indies 1975–77; Asst Priest, St John's Parish Church, Barbados 1977–81, Priest-in-Charge 1990–92; Hon. Chaplain, Univ. Church of Christ the King, London 1981–84; Asst Priest, St Michael's Cathedral, Barbados 1984–86, St Augustine 1986–89, Priest-in-Charge 1989–90; Priest-in-Charge, St Mark and St Catherine, Barbados 1992–93, St Mark 1993–94, Holy Trinity 1994–95, Holy Cross 1995–; Hon. Canon Diocese of Barbados 1996; Bishop of Barbados 2000–; Long and Dedicated Service Award, Codrington Coll. 1994. *Television:* Religion in Barbados During the First Twenty-Five Years of Independence 1966–91 CBC 1990, CBC presentation on professions 1994. *Publications:* Christian Commitment 1985, Set the Captives Free: The Challenge of the Biblical Jubilee 1987, A Layman's Guide to the Bible (Vols I & II) 1989, The Intertestamental Period 1994, Biblical Reflections on the Book of Hosea 1999. *Address:* Diocesan Office, Mandeville House, Bridgetown, Jamaica (Office). *Telephone:* 426-2761 (Office). *Fax:* 427-5867 (Office).

HOLDGATE, Sir Martin Wyatt, Kt, CB, MA, PhD, FIBiol; British biologist; b. 14 Jan. 1931, Horsham; s. of the late Francis W. Holdgate and Lois M. Holdgate (née Bebbington); m. Elizabeth M. Weil (née Dickason) 1963; two s.; ed Arnold School, Blackpool and Queens' Coll. Cambridge; Research Fellow, Queens' Coll. Cambridge 1953–56; Jt Leader Gough Island Scientific Survey 1955–56; Lecturer in Zoology, Univ. of Manchester 1956–57, Univ. of Durham 1957–60; Leader, Royal Soc. Expedition to Southern Chile 1958–59; Asst Dir of Research, Scott Polar Research Inst. Cambridge 1960–63; Chief Biologist, British Antarctic Survey 1963–66; Deputy Dir (Research), The Nature Conservancy (UK) 1966–70; Dir Central Unit on Environmental Pollution, Dept of Environment 1970–74; Dir Inst. of Terrestrial Ecology 1974–76; Dir-Gen. of Research, Dept of Environment 1976–81; Chief Scientist and Deputy Sec. (Environment Protection), Dept of Environment and Chief Scientific Adviser, Dept of Transport 1981–88; Dir-Gen. Int. Union for Conservation of Nature and Natural Resources (now World Conservation Union) 1988–94; Pres. Zoological Soc. of London 1994–; Co-Chair. Intergovernmental Panel on Forests, UN Comm. on Sustainable Devt 1995–97; mem. Royal Comm. on Environmental Pollution 1994–2002; Chair. Int. Inst. for Environment and Devt 1994–2000, Governing Council, Arnold School 1997–; Pres. Freshwater Biological Asscn 2002–; Hon. mem. British Ecological Soc. 1996; Hon. mem. Int. Union for the Conservation of Nature and Natural Resources 2000; Hon. DSc (Durham) 1991, Sussex (1993), (Lancaster) 1995; Bruce Medal, Royal Soc. of Edinburgh and Royal Scottish Geog. Soc., Silver Medal, UNEP, UNEP Global 500 1988, Commdr Order of the Golden Ark 1991, Patrons Medal,

Royal Geographical Soc. 1992; Livingstone Medal, Royal Scottish Geographical Soc., Int. Conservationist of the Year Award, Nat. Wildlife Fed., USA 1993. *Publications include:* Mountains in the Sea: The Story of the Gough Island Expedition 1958, A Perspective of Environmental Pollution 1979, From Care to Action 1996, The Green Web: A Union for World Conservation 1999. *Leisure interests:* natural history, climbing hills. *Address:* Fell Beck, Hartley, Kirkby Stephen, Cumbria, CA17 4JH, England. *Telephone:* (17683) 72316. *Fax:* (17683) 72548.

HOLDING, Clyde, LLB; Australian politician; b. 27 April 1931, Melbourne; m. 1st Margaret Sheer (divorced); two s. one d.; m. 2nd Judith Crump; one d.; ed Melbourne Univ.; solicitor; mem. Victorian Parl. for Richmond 1962–77; Leader State Parl. Labor Party and Leader of Opposition 1967–77; mem. Fed. Parl. for Melbourne Ports 1977–; Minister for Aboriginal Affairs 1983–86, for Arts and Territories 1988–89, of Employment Services and Youth Affairs and Minister Assisting the Treasurer 1987–88, Minister, assisting the Minister for Immigration, Local Govt and Ethnic Affairs 1988–89, assisting the Prime Minister 1988–89; Minister for Arts, Tourism and Territories 1989–90; Pres. Victorian Labor Party 1977–79. *Leisure interests:* swimming, surfing, films, reading. *Address:* 58 Milton Street, Elwood, Vic. 3184, Australia; 117 Fitzroy Street, St Kilda, Vic. 3183. *Telephone:* (3) 9534-8126. *Fax:* (3) 9534-1575.

HOLDSWORTH, Sir (George) Trevor, Kt, CVO, FCA; British business executive and accountant; b. 29 May 1927, Bradford; m. 1st Patricia June Ridler 1951 (died 1993); three s.; m. 2nd Jenny Watson 1995; ed Hanson Grammar School, Bradford, Keighley Grammar School; with Rawlinson, Greaves and Mitchell (accountants), Bradford 1944–51; with Bowater Corpn 1952–63, becoming Dir and Controller of UK paper-making subsidiaries; Deputy Chief Accountant, Guest Keen and Nettlefolds Ltd 1963–64, Group Chief Accountant 1965–67, Gen. Man. Dir, GKN Screws and Fasteners Ltd 1968–70, Dir and Group Controller 1970–72, Group Exec. Vice-Chair., Corpn Controls and Services 1973–74, Deputy Chair. 1974, Man. Dir and Deputy Chair. 1977, Chair. 1980–88; Chair. British Satellite Broadcasting 1987–90; Dir Thorn EMI PLC 1977–86, Equity Capital for Industry Ltd 1976–83, Midland Bank PLC 1979–88, Prudential Corpn 1986–96 (Deputy Chair. 1988–92); Chair. Allied Colloids Group PLC 1983–96; Dir Opera Now Enterprises Ltd 1988; Dir (non-exec.) Owens-Corning 1994–98; mem. Council, British Inst. of Man. 1974–84, Vice-Chair. 1978–80, Chair. 1980, Vice-Pres. 1982; mem. Council CBI 1974–90, Econ. and Financial Policy Cttee CBI 1976–80, Pres. CBI 1988–90; Chair. (part-time) Nat. Power 1990–95, Beauford PLC 1991–99; Chancellor Bradford Univ. 1992–97; Council, Inst. of Dirs 1978–80, Steering Group on Unemployment 1982, Programmes Unit 1982, Bd of Govs Ashridge Man. Coll. 1978–92; Chair. Tax Reform Working Party 1984–86 (Deputy Pres. 1987–88), Lambert Howarth Group PLC 1993–98; Chair. Wigmore Hall Trust 1992–99; Vice-Pres. Eng Employers' Fed. 1980; mem. Exec. Cttee Soc. of Motor Mfrs and Traders 1980–83; mem. Eng Industries Council 1980; mem. Advisory Bd LEK Partnerships 1992–99; Trustee, Anglo-German Foundation for the Study of Industrial Soc. 1980–92; mem. British North American Cttee 1981–85, European Advisory Council AMF Inc. 1982–85, Council Royal Inst. of Int. Affairs 1983–88; Vice-Pres. Ironbridge Gorge Museum Devt Trust 1981–; Trustee, Royal Opera House Trust 1981–84; mem. Duke of Edinburgh's Award (Business and Commercial Enterprises Group) 1980, Int. Trustee 1987–94, UK Trustee 1988–96; mem. Council Foundation for Mfg and Industry; Liveryman, Worshipful Co. of Chartered Accountants in England and Wales; Freeman, City of London; Hon. D.Tech. (Loughborough) 1981; Hon. DSc (Aston) 1982, (Sussex) 1988; Hon. DBA (Inst. Man. Centre from Buckingham) 1986; Hon. DEng (Bradford) 1983, (Birmingham) 1992; British Inst. Man. Gold Medal 1987; City and Guilds Insignia Award in Tech. (hc) 1989; Chartered Accountants Founding Societies' Centenary Award 1983. *Leisure interests:* music, theatre. *Address:* The Athenaeum, Pall Mall, London, SW1, England.

HOLKERI, Harri Hermanni, M.POL.SC.; Finnish politician; b. 6 Jan. 1937, Oripää; s. of Antti Edvard Holkeri and Maire Kyllikki Ahlgren; m. Marja-Liisa Lepisto 1960; one s. one d.; Sec. Nat. Coalition Party Youth League 1959–60, Information Sec. 1960–62; Information Sec. Nat. Coalition Party 1962–64, Research Sec. 1964–65, Party Sec. 1965–71, Chair. 1971–79; mem. Helsinki City Council 1969–88, Chair. 1981–87; mem. Parl. 1970–78; mem. Bd Bank of Finland 1978–97; Chair. of Standing Finnish-Soviet Intergovernmental Comm. for Econ. Co-operation 1989–91; Prime Minister of Finland 1987–91; mem. Int. Body addressing the decommissioning of illegal weapons in NI 1995–98; Pres. 55th Session of the UN Gen. Ass. (Millennium Ass.) 2000–01; Hon. KBE. *Address:* United Nations, United Nations Plaza, New York, NY 10017, USA (Office).

HOLLAMBY, David James; British diplomatist; b. 19 May 1945; s. of Reginald William Hollamby and Eva May Hollamby (née Ponman); m. Maria Helena Guzmán 1971; two step-s.; ed Albury Manor School, Surrey; joined Foreign Office 1964; Beirut 1967–69; Latin American Floater 1970–72; Third Sec. and Vice Consul Asunción 1972–75; Second Sec. FCO 1975–78; Vice Consul (Commercial) New York 1978–82; Consul (Commercial) Dallas 1982–86; First Sec. FCO 1986–90, Rome 1990–94; Asst Head, Western European Dept, FCO 1994–96, Deputy Head, W Indian and Atlantic Dept 1996–98, Dept Head, Overseas Territories Dept 1998–99; Gov. and C-in-C, St Helena and Dependencies 1999–. *Leisure interests:* music, skiing, travel, reading. *Address:* c/o Foreign and Commonwealth Office, King Charles Street, London, SW1A 2AH, England (Office).

HOLLÁN, R. Susan; Hungarian professor of haematology; b. 26 Oct. 1920, Budapest; d. of Dr. Henrik Hollán and Dr. Malvin Hornik; m. Dr. György Révész; one s. one d.; ed Univ. Medical School, Budapest; Internal Med., Rokus Hospital, Budapest 1945–50; Research Fellow, Univ. Med. School, Budapest 1950–54; Science Adviser, Inst. for Experimental Medical Research 1954–91; Dir Nat. Inst. of Haematology and Blood Transfusion 1959–85, Dir-Gen. 1985–90; Prof. of Haematology, Postgraduate Med. School 1970–90; Corresp. mem. Hungarian Acad. of Sciences 1973, mem. 1982– (mem. of Presidium 1976–84); fmr Pres. Int. Soc. of Haematology and Vice-Pres. Int. Soc. of Blood Transfusion; mem. WHO Global AIDS Research Steering Cttee; mem. WHO Expert Cttee on Biological Standardization; mem. Clinical and Immunological Work Cttee of Hungarian Acad. of Sciences; Pres. Bd of Special Cttee for Clinical Sciences; Exec. mem. Hungarian Medical Research Council; Ed.-in-Chief Hungarian Medical Encyclopaedia and Haematologia (quarterly); mem. HSWP Cen. Cttee 1975–89; Foreign Corresp. mem. Soc. de Biologie, Collège de France, Paris; Vice-Pres. Nobel Prize Award, Int. Physicians Prevention of Nuclear War 1983–89; Hon. mem. American Soc. of Hematology, Polish Soc. of Haematology, German Soc. of Haematology (FRG), Purkinje Soc. (Czechoslovakia), Turkish Soc. of Haematology, All-Union Scientific Soc. of Haematology and Blood Transfusion (USSR); Hon. Pres. Hungarian Soc. of Human Genetics; Hungarian Academic Award 1970; State Prize 1974; Socialist Hungary Medal. *Publications:* Basic Problems of Transfusion 1965, Haemoglobins and Haemoglobinopathies 1972, Genetics, Structure and Function of Blood Cells 1980, Management of Blood Transfusion Services 1990; over 300 papers in Hungarian and int. medical journals. *Leisure interest:* fine arts, sport. *Address:* Daróczi ut 24, 1113 Budapest (Office); Palánta u. 12, 1025 Budapest, Hungary (Home). *Telephone:* (1) 372-4210 (Office); (1) 326-0619 (Home). *Fax:* (1) 372-4352. *E-mail:* hollan@ella.hu (Office).

HOLLAND, Agnieszka; Polish film director and screenwriter; b. 28 Nov. 1948, Warsaw; m. Laco Adamik; one d.; ed FAMU film school, Prague; Asst to Krzysztof Zanussi in filming of Illumination 1973; mem. production group 'X' led by Andrzej Wajda in Warsaw 1972–81; Dir first TV film 1973; subsequently worked in theatre in Cracow; co-Dir (with Jerzy Domaradzki and Paweł Kędzierski) film Screen Test 1977; co-scripted Wajda's film Rough Treatment 1978; also worked with Wajda on A Love in Germany, Man of Marble, Man of Iron, The Orchestra Conductor, Korczak, Danton 1982; wrote screenplay for Yurke Bocayevicz's Anna; has also made documentaries for French TV; directs plays for TV theatre (with Laco Aolamik); mem. Polish Film Asscn, European and American Acad. Award; Las Vegas Film Festival Award 1999, Officer's Cross, Order of Polonia Restituta 2001. *Films directed include:* Provincial Actors 1979 (Critics' Award, Cannes), The Fever 1980 (Gdańsk Golden Lions 1981), The Lonely Woman 1981, Angry Harvest (Germany) 1985, To Kill a Priest (France) 1987, Europe, Europe (Germany, France) 1990, (Golden Globe 1991), Oliver, Oliver (France) 1992, Secret Garden (USA) 1993, Total Eclipse (England, France) 1995, Washington Square (USA) 1997, The Third Miracle (USA) 1999, Shot in the Heart (USA) 2001, Julie Walking Home (Poland–Canada–Germany) 2002. *Plays:* Dybuk (Polish TV) 1999. *Publications:* Magia i pieniadze (Magic & Money) – Conversations with Maria Komatowska, ZNAK Poland 2002. *Address:* Agence Nicole Cann, 1 rue Alfred de Vigny, 75008 Paris, France. *Telephone:* 1-44-15-14-21.

HOLLAND, Julian Miles (Jools); British pianist and broadcaster; b. 24 Jan. 1958; s. of Derek Holland and June Rose Lane; one s. two d.; ed Invicta Sherington School, Shooters' Hill School; pianist 1975–78; keyboard player with pop group Squeeze (hits: Take Me I'm Yours, Cool for Cats, Up The Junction etc.) 1978–; regularly tours UK and USA, concerts at Madison Square Garden and Royal Albert Hall; actor and writer TV play The Groovy Fellers 1988; wrote and produced TV films Walking to New Orleans 1985 and Mr Roadrunner 1991; wrote film score for Milk 1999. *Films include:* (writer and producer): Spiceworld The Movie 1997, Beat Route 1998, Jools Meets The Saint 1999. *Solo albums:* A World of His Own 1990, Full Compliment 1991, A–Z of Piano 1993, Live Performance 1995, Solo Piano 1995, Lift the Lid 1997, Sunset Over London 1999, Hop the Wag 2000, Small World Big Band – Friends 2001, Small World Big Band Vol. 2 – More Friends; guest performances with numerous artists including Elvis Costello, George Harrison. *Radio:* Presenter BBC Radio 2. *Television:* Presenter The Tube 1981–86, Juke Box Jury 1989, Sunday Night (with David Sanborn) 1990, The Happening 1990, Later With Jools Holland 1993– (now in 20th series); Hootenanny (10th, New Year's Eve 2002). *Achievements:* regularly performs with his 17–piece rhythm & blues orchestra. *Publication:* Beat Route 1998. *Leisure interests:* sketching, giving advice. *Address:* One-Fifteen, 1 Prince of Orange Lane, Greenwich, London, SE10 8JQ (Office), Helicon Mountain Ltd, Helicon Mountain, Station Terrace Mews, London, SE3 7LP, England. *Telephone:* (20) 8293-0999 (Office); (20) 8858-0984. *Fax:* (20) 8293-4555. *E-mail:* info@joolsholland.com (Office). *Website:* www.joolsholland.com (Office).

HOLLANDER, John, PhD; American poet and professor of English; b. 28 Oct. 1929, New York; s. of Franklin and Muriel (Kornfeld) Hollander; m. 1st Anne Loesser 1953 (divorced 1977); two d.; 2nd Natalie Charkow 1981; ed Columbia Univ., Harvard Univ. and Indiana Univ.; Lecturer in English, Connecticut Coll. 1957–59; Instructor in English, Yale Univ. 1959–61, Asst Prof. of English 1961–64, Assoc. Prof. 1964–66, Prof. 1977–85, A. Bartlett Giamatti Prof. 1986–95, Sterling Prof. of English 1995–2002, Sterling Prof. Emer. 2002–; Prof. of English, Hunter Coll., New York 1966–77; Christian

Gauss Seminarian, Princeton Univ. 1962; Visiting Prof., School of Letters and Linguistic Inst., Indiana Univ. 1964; Visiting Prof. Seminar in American Studies, Salzburg, Austria 1965; Clark Lecturer, Trinity Coll., Cambridge 2000; editorial assoc. for Poetry Partisan Review 1959–65; mem. Poetry Bd Wesleyan Univ. Press 1959–62; mem. Editorial Bd Raritan 1981–; Fellow, American Acad. of Arts and Sciences; mem. American Acad. of Arts and Letters (Sec. 2000–03), Asscn of Literary Scholars and Critics (Pres. 2000); Fellow Ezra Stiles Coll., Yale Univ. 1961–64; Overseas Fellow Churchill Coll., Univ. of Cambridge 1967–68; Fellow Nat. Endowment for Humanities 1973–, Silliman Coll. 1977–; Guggenheim Fellow 1979–80; Chancellor, Acad. of American Poets 1981–, MacArthur Fellow 1990–95; Hon. D.Litt (Marietta Coll.) 1982; Hon. DHL (Indiana) 1990, (CUNY Grad. Center) 2001; Hon. DFA (Maine Coll. of Art) Levinson Prize 1964, Nat. Inst. of Arts and Letters Award 1963; Bollingen Prize 1983, Robert Penn Warren–Cleanth Brooks Award 1998. *Publications include:* A Crackling of Thorns 1958, The Untuning of the Sky 1961, Movie-Going and Other Poems 1962, Visions from the Ramble 1965, Types of Shape 1969 (enlarged edn) 1991, The Night Mirror 1971, Town and Country Matters 1972, Selected Poems 1972, The Head of the Bed 1974, Tales Told of the Fathers 1975, Vision and Resonance 1975, Reflections on Espionage 1976, Spectral Emanations 1978, In Place 1978, Blue Wine 1979, The Figure of Echo 1981, Rhyme's Reason 1981 (enlarged edn) 1989, Powers of Thirteen 1983, In Time and Place 1986, Harp Lake 1988, Some Fugitives Take Cover 1988, Melodious Guile 1988, William Bailey 1991, Tesserae 1993, Selected Poetry 1993, The Gazer's Spirit 1995, The Work of Poetry 1997, The Poetry of Everyday Life 1998, Figurehead 1999; contributor of numerous poems and articles to journals; ed. and contributing ed. of numerous books including: Poems of Ben Jonson 1961, The Wind and the Rain 1961, Jiggery-Pokery 1966, Poems of Our Moment 1968, Modern Poetry: Essays in Criticism 1968, American Short Stories Since 1945 1968, The Oxford Anthology of English Literature (with Frank Kermode, q.v.), 1973, For I. A. Richards: Essays in his Honor 1973, Literature as Experience (with Irving Howe and David Bromwich) 1979, The Essential Rossetti 1990, American Poetry: the Nineteenth Century 1993, Animal Poems (ed.) 1994, Garden Poems (ed.) 1996, Marriage Poems (ed.) 1997, Frost (ed.) 1997, Committed to Memory (ed.) 1999, Figurehead and Other Poems 1999, War Poems 1999, Sonnets 2001, A Gallery of Poems 2001; contributing ed. Harper's magazine 1969–71. *Address:* Department of English, Yale University, PO Box 208302, New Haven, CT 06520, USA. *Telephone:* (203) 432-4566. *Fax:* (203) 387-3497. *E-mail:* john.hollander@yale.edu (Office).

HOLLANDER, Samuel, OC, PhD, FRSC; British/Canadian/Israeli professor of economics; b. 6 April 1937, London, England; s. of Jacob Hollander and Lily Hollander; m. Perlette Kéroub 1959; one s. one d.; ed Gateshead Talmudical Acad., Hendon Tech. Coll., Kilburn Polytechnic, London School of Econs; Princeton Univ., NJ; emigrated to Canada 1963; Asst Prof., Univ. of Toronto 1963–67, Assoc. Prof. 1967–70, Prof. 1970–84, Univ. Prof. 1984–98, Univ. Prof. Emer. 1998–; Research Dir Univ. of Nice (CNRS) 1999–2000; Visiting Prof. Florence Univ., Italy 1973–74, London Univ. 1974–75, Hebrew Univ., Jerusalem 1979–80, 1988, La Trobe Univ., Melbourne, Australia 1985, Auckland Univ., NZ 1985, 1988, Sorbonne 1997, Ben Gurion Univ. 2000–, Nice Univ. 2001; several guest lectureships; Fulbright Fellowship 1959; Guggenheim Fellowship 1968–69; emigrated to Israel 2000; Hon. LLD (McMaster) 1999; Social Science Fed. of Canada 50th Anniversary Book Award 1990. *Publications:* The Sources of Increased Efficiency 1965, The Economics of Adam Smith 1973, The Economics of David Ricardo 1979, The Economics of J. S. Mill 1985, Classical Economics 1987, Ricardo—The New View: Collected Essays I 1995, The Economics of T. R. Malthus 1997, The Literature of Political Economy: Collected Essays II 1998, John Stuart Mill on Economic Theory and Method: Collected Essays III 2000. *Address:* Department of Economics, Ben Gurion University of the Negev, 84105, Beer Sheva (Office); 2 Rehov Sapir, 89066 Arad, Israel (Home). *Telephone:* 8-9771664 (Home). *Fax:* 8-6472941. *E-mail:* sholland@bgumail.bgu.ac.il (Office).

HOLLEIN, Hans, MArch; Austrian architect; b. 30 March 1934, Vienna; ed Acad. of Graphic Arts, Vienna, Ill. Inst. of Technology, Univ. of Calif. at Berkeley; Visiting Prof., Univ. of Washington, USA 1963–64, 1966; worked in architectural offices in Australia, S. America, Sweden and Germany; work as ind. architect in Vienna 1964–; Prof., Acad. of Fine Arts, Düsseldorf, Germany 1967–82; Dir Inst. of Design, Vienna 1976–; Visiting Prof., Yale Univ. 1979; Austrian Rep., Venice Biennale, Visual Arts 1978–90, Architecture 1991, 1996, Dir Architecture Sector 1994–; mem. Austrian Art Senate, American Inst. of Architects 1980; Hon. mem. Royal Swedish Acad., Koninklijke Acad. van Beeldende Kunsten, Netherlands, RIBA 1995, Bund Deutscher Architekten 1996; Reynolds Memorial Award, USA 1966, 1984, Vienna City Prize 1974, Deutscher Architekturpreis 1983, Pritzker Architecture Prize 1985, Chicago Architecture Award 1990. *Buildings designed include:* Rettl Kerzenladen, Vienna 1965, Headquarters, Siemens AG, Monaco 1972, Museum of Glass and Ceramics, Tehran 1977–88, Haas Haus, Vienna 1985–90, Headquarters, Banco Santander, Madrid 1988–93, Donau-City, Vienna 1993, Lichtforum Zumtobel, Vienna 1995–96. *Exhibitions include:* Galerie St Stephan, Vienna 1963, Museum of Modern Art, New York 1968, Centre Georges Pompidou, Paris 1987, 1994, Nat. Gallery, Berlin 1987–88, Ciudad del Arquitecto, Barcelona 1994, Historisches Museum der Stadt, Vienna 1995. *Address:* La Biennale di Venezia, Settore Architettura, Ca Giustinian San Marco 1364, 30124 Venice, Italy (Office). *Telephone:* (41) 5218860 (Office). *Fax:* (41) 5200569 (Office). *E-mail:* pressoffice@labiennale.com (Office).

HÖLLERER, Walter Friedrich, DPhil; German writer and critic; b. 19 Dec. 1922, Sulzbach-Rosenberg, Bavaria; s. of Hans Höllerer and Christine Höllerer (née Pürkner); m. Renate von Mangoldt 1965; two s.; ed Univs. of Erlangen, Göttingen and Heidelberg; Dozent in German Studies, Frankfurt Main Univ. 1958, Münster Univ. 1959; Ord. Prof. of Literature, Berlin Technical Univ. 1959–, Dir Inst. für Sprache im Technischen Zeitalter 1961–; Steuben Visiting Prof., Univ. of Wis. 1960; Dir Literarisches Colloquium, Berlin 1963; Prof. Univ. of Ill., Urbana 1973–; Ed. Akzente: Zeitschrift für Dichtung 1954 (now co-Publr), Sprache im technischen Zeitalter 1961 (now Publr); Publr Literatur als Kunst; mem. German PEN Club, Akad. für Sprache und Dichtung, Berlin Acad. of Arts, Group 1947, Communità Europea degli Scrittori, Schutzverband der Schriftsteller deutscher Sprache; Fontane Prize, Johann Heinrich Merck Prize, Horst-Bienek-Preis für Lyrik, Ernst Reuter Plakette 1994, Friedrich Baur Prize 1997. *Publications:* Der andere Gast (poems) 1952, 1964, Transit: Lyrikbuch der Jahrhundertmitte (anthology) 1956, Zwischen Klassik und Moderne: Lachen und Weinen in der Dichtung einer Übergangszeit (essays) 1958, Junge amerikanische Lyrik 1961, Spiele in einem Akt 1962, Gedichte 1964, Theorie der modernen Lyrik 1965, Modernes Theater auf kleinen Bühnen 1966, Ein Gedicht und sein Autor (poems and essays) 1967, Ausserhalb der Saison (poems) 1967, Systeme (poems) 1969, Elite und Utopie 1969, Dramaturgisches (correspondence with Max Frisch 1969, Die Elephantenuhr (novel) 1973, 1975, Hier wo die Welt anfing 1974, Geschichte, die nicht im Geschichtsbuch steht 1976, Alle Vögel alle (comedy) 1978, Berlin: Übern Damm und durch die Dörfer (essays) 1978, Gedichte 1942–82 1982, Autoren im Haus, Zwanzig Jahre Literatur in Berlin 1982, Die Leute von Serendip erkunden die Giftfabrik, Sprache 97 1986, Walter Höllerers Oberpfälzische Weltei-Erkundungen 1987, Zurufe, Widerspiele (essays) 1992. *Address:* Heerstrasse 99, 14055 Berlin, Germany. *Telephone:* 3045879.

HOLLICK, Baron (Life Peer), cr. 1991, of Notting Hill in the Royal Borough of Kensington and Chelsea; **Clive Richard Hollick,** BA; British business executive; b. 20 May 1945, Southampton; s. of Leslie George Hollick and Olive Mary Hollick (née Scruton); m. Susan Mary Woodford 1977; three d.; ed Univ. of Nottingham; joined Hambros Bank 1968, Dir 1973; CEO MAI PLC (fmrly Mills & Allen Int. PLC) 1974–96, Shepperton Studios 1976–84, Garban Ltd (USA) 1983–97, United Business Media PLC 1996–, CEO; Dir Logica PLC 1987–91, Meridian Broadcasting 1991–96, British Aerospace 1992–97, Anglia TV Ltd 1994–97, TRW Inc. 2000–, Diageo PLC 2001; mem. Nat. Bus Co. 1984–91, Applied Econs Dept Advisory Cttee (Univ. of Cambridge) 1989–97, Financial Law Panel 1993–97; Special Adviser to Dept of Trade and Industry 1997–98; Chair. South Bank Centre, London 2002–; Founder and Trustee Inst. for Public Policy Research 1988–; Hon. LLD (Nottingham) 1993. *Leisure interests:* cinema, countryside, reading, tennis, theatre. *Address:* United Business Media plc, Ludgate House, 245 Blackfriars Road, London, SE1 9UY (Office); House of Lords, London, SW1A 0PW, England. *Telephone:* (20) 7921-5000 (Office). *Website:* www.unitedbusinessmedia.com (Office).

HOLLIDAY, Charles O., Jr, BS; American business executive; b. 9 March 1948, Nashville; s. of Charles O. Holliday, Sr and Ann Hunter; m. Ann Holliday; two s.; ed Univ. of Tenn.; joined DuPont Fibers Dept as engineer, Old Hickory, Tenn. 1970, Business Analyst, Wilmington, Del. 1974, later product planner, Asst Plant Man., Seaford, Del. 1978; joined DuPont Corp. Planning Dept 1984, Global Business Man. for Nomex 1986, Global Business Dir for Kevlar 1987; Dir of Marketing DuPont Chemicals and Pigments Dept 1988; Vice-Pres., then Pres. DuPont Asia-Pacific 1990, Chair. 1995; Sr Vice-Pres. DuPont 1992, Exec. Vice-Pres., mem. Office of Chief Exec. 1995, Dir 1997–, Pres. Oct. 1997–, CEO Feb. 1998–, Chair. Dec. 1998–; Dir DuPont Photomasks Inc., Pioneer Hi-Bred Int. Inc., Analog Devices Inc.; Sr mem. Inst. of Industrial Engineers; mem. Chancellor's Advisory Council for Enhancement Univ. of Tenn., Knoxville. *Address:* E.I. DuPont De Nemours and Co., 1007 Market Street, Wilmington, DE 19898, USA. *Telephone:* (302) 774-1000.

HOLLIDAY, Sir Frederick (George Thomas), Kt, CBE, FIBiol, FRSE; British fmr university vice-chancellor, zoologist and business executive; b. 22 Sept. 1935; s. of the late Alfred Holliday and Margaret Holliday; m. Philippa Davidson 1957; one s. one d.; ed Bromsgrove County High School and Univ. of Sheffield; Fisheries Research Training Grant (Devt Comm.), Marine Lab. Aberdeen 1956–58, Scientific Officer 1958–61; Lecturer in Zoology, Univ. of Aberdeen 1961–66; Prof. of Biology, Univ. of Stirling 1967–75, Deputy Prin. 1972, Acting Prin. 1973–75; Prof. of Zoology, Univ. of Aberdeen 1975–79; Vice-Chancellor and Warden, Univ. of Durham 1980–90; Dir Shell UK 1980–99; mem. Bd Northern Investors Ltd 1984–90, BRB 1990–94 (Chair. BR (Eastern) 1986–90), Union Railways 1992–97, Lyonnaise des Eaux 1996–97, Suez Lyonnaise des Eaux 1997–, Wise Speke PLC 1997–98, Brewin Dolphin PLC 1998–; mem. Northern Regional Bd Lloyd's Bank 1985–91, Chair. 1986–89, Deputy Chair. 1989–91; Independent Chair. Jt Nature Conservation Cttee 1991; mem. numerous cttees. etc.; Chair. Northumbrian Water Ltd. 1993–, Ondeo Services UK Ltd 2001–, Council, Water Aid 1995–97, Northern Venture Capital Fund 1996–, Go-Ahead Group PLC 1997–, Northumbrian Water Ltd 2000–; Pres. British Trust for Ornithology 1996–2001; Chair. South Bank Centre 2002–; Hon. DUniv (Stirling) 1984; Hon. DSc (Sheffield) 1987, (Cranfield) 1991; Hon. DCL (Durham) 2002. *Publications:* Wildlife of Scotland (ed. and contrib.) 1979; numerous Pubs on fish biology and wildlife conservation in Advanced Marine Biology, Fish Physiology, Oceanography and Marine Biology etc. *Leisure interests:* walking, gardening, ornithology.

Address: Northumbrian Water Limited, Abbey Road, Durham, DH1 5FJ, England. *Telephone:* (191) 301-6462 (Office). *Fax:* (191) 301-6272 (Office). *E-mail:* susan.dishman@nwl.co.uk (Office). *Website:* www.nwl.co.uk (Office).

HOLLIDAY, Robin, PhD, FRS; British geneticist; b. 6 Nov. 1932, Palestine; s. of Clifford Holliday and Eunice Holliday; m. 1st Diana Collet Parsons 1957 (divorced 1983); one s. three d.; m. 2nd Lily I. Huschtscha 1986; one d.; ed Hitchin Grammar School and Univ. of Cambridge; mem. scientific staff, Dept of Genetics, John Innes Inst. Bayfordbury, Herts. 1958–65; mem. EMBO; mem. scientific staff, Div. of Microbiology, Nat. Inst. for Medical Research 1965–70, Head, Div. of Genetics 1970–88; Chief Research Scientist CSIRO 1988–97; Foreign Fellow, Indian Nat. Science Acad. 1995; proposed DNA 'Holliday Structure' 1964; Fulbright Scholar 1962; Lord Simon Prize 1987. *Art Exhibitions:* bronze sculptures exhibited in and around Sydney 1998–. *Publications:* The Science of Human Progress 1981, Genes, Proteins and Cellular Ageing 1986, Understanding Ageing 1995, Slaves and Saviours 2000; about 250 research publs. *Leisure interests:* sculpture, writing. *Address:* 12 Roma Court, West Pennant Hills, NSW 2125, Australia (Home). *Telephone:* (2) 9873-3476 (Home). *Fax:* (2) 9871-2159. *E-mail:* randl.holliday@bigpond.com (Home).

HOLLIGER, Heinz; Swiss oboist and composer; b. 21 May 1939, Langenthal; m. Ursula Holliger; ed in Berne, Paris and Basel under Emile Cassagnaud (oboe) and Pierre Boulez (composition); Prof. of Oboe, Freiberg Music Acad. 1965–; has appeared at all the maj. European music festivals and in Japan, USA, Australia, Israel, etc.; conducted Chamber Orchestra of Europe, London 1992, London Sinfonietta 1997; Composer-in-Residence, Lucerne Festival 1998; recorded over 80 works, mainly for Philips and Deutsche Grammophon; recipient of several int. prizes. *Compositions include:* Der magische Tänzer, Trio, Siebengesang, Wind Quintet, Dona nobis pacem, Pneuma, Psalm, Cardiophonie, Kreis, String Quartet, Atembogen, Die Jahreszeiten, Come and Go, Not I. *Address:* c/o Ingpen & Williams, 26 Wadham Road, London, SW15 2LR, England (Office); Konzertgesellschaft, Hochstrasse 51/Postfach, 4002 Basel, Switzerland.

HOLLINGHURST, Alan James, BA, M.LITT.; British writer; b. 26 May 1954, Stroud; s. of the late James Kenneth Hollinghurst and of Elizabeth Lilian Hollinghurst (née Keevil); ed Canford School, Dorset, Magdalen Coll., Oxford; with Times Literary Supplement 1982–95, Deputy Ed. 1985–90; Somerset Maugham Award 1988; American Acad. of Arts and Letters E. M. Forster Award 1989; James Tait Black Memorial Prize 1994. *Publications include:* The Swimming-Pool Library 1988, The Folding Star 1994, The Spell 1998. *Leisure interests:* music, architecture. *Address:* c/o Antony Harwood Ltd, Office 109, Riverbank House, 1 Putney Bridge Approach, London, SW6 3JD, England.

HOLLINGS, Ernest F., BA, LLB; American politician and lawyer; b. 1 Jan. 1922, Charleston, SC; s. of Adolph G. Hollings and Wilhlemine D. Meyer; m. 2nd Rita Liddy 1971; two s. two d. (by previous marriage); ed Charleston Public Schools, The Citadel and Univ. of S. Carolina; served US Army 1942–45; admitted to S Carolina Bar 1947; mem. S Carolina House of Reps. 1948–54, Speaker *pro tem.* 1951–53; Lt-Gov. of S Carolina 1955–59, Gov. of S Carolina 1959–63; law practice, Charleston 1963–66; Senator from S Carolina 1966–; Chair. Democratic Senatorial Campaign Cttee 1971–73; mem. Hoover Comm. on Intelligence Activities 1975–55, President's Advisory Comm. on Intergovernmental Relations 1959–63, on Federalism 1981–; mem. Senate Cttees. on Appropriations, Commerce, Budget, Chair. Budget Cttee 1980, Commerce Cttee 1982; mem. Democratic Policy Cttee, Office of Tech. Assessment, Nat. Ocean Policy Study; Democrat; numerous awards. *Publication:* The Case against Hunger: A Demand for a National Policy 1970. *Address:* US Senate, 125 Russell Senate Office Building, Washington, DC 20510, USA (Office).

HOLLINGS, (George) Leslie, AM; British/Australian journalist; b. 25 Feb. 1923, Hull; s. of the late John Hollings and Elizabeth (Singleton) Hollings; m. Joan Gwendoline Pratt 1951; two s.; ed NE Tech. School of Art, Colchester, Essex; Sub-Ed. The Daily Telegraph, London 1957–59; Sub-Ed. The Times, London 1959–65; Ed. The Australian 1975–80, Man. Ed. 1980–82, Ed.-in-Chief 1983–88; Dir News Ltd 1987–89; Deputy Chair. The Sydney Inst. 1989–93; Counsellor Cttee for Econ. Devt of Australia 1993–; mem. Policy Cttee, Bureau of Meteorology 1983–87; mem. Council of Australian Nat. Gallery 1985–92, Deputy Chair. 1987–92. *Leisure interests:* reading, opera, ballet, gardening, walking. *Address:* 19 Hillcrest Avenue, Mona Vale, NSW 2103, Australia (Home).

HOLLINGWORTH, Clare, OBE; British journalist; b. 10 Oct. 1911; d. of John Albert Hollingworth and Daisy Gertrude Hollingworth; m. 1st Vyvyan Derring Vandeleur Robinson 1936 (divorced 1951); m. 2nd Geoffrey Spence Hoare 1952 (died 1966); ed Girls' Collegiate School, Leicester, Grammar School, Ashby-de-la-Zouch, School of Slavonic Studies, Univ. of London; mem. staff League of Nations Union 1935–38; worked in Poland for Lord Mayor's Fund for Refugees from Czechoslovakia 1939; Corresp. for Daily Telegraph Poland, Turkey, Cairo (covered Desert Campaigns, troubles in Persia and Iraq, Civil War in Greece and events in Palestine) 1941–50, for Manchester Guardian (covered Algerian War and trouble spots including Egypt, Aden and Vietnam), based in Paris 1950–63; Guardian Defence Corresp. 1963–67; foreign trouble-shooter for Daily Telegraph (covering war in Vietnam) 1967–73, Corresp. in China 1973–76, Defence Corresp. 1976–81; Far Eastern Corresp. in Hong Kong for Sunday Telegraph 1981–; Research Assoc. (fmrly

Visiting Scholar), Centre for Asian Studies, Univ. of Hong Kong 1981–; Hon. DLitt (Leicester) 1993; Journalist of the Year Award and Hannan Swaffer Award 1963; James Cameron Award for Journalism 1994. *Publications:* Poland's Three Weeks War 1940, There's A German Just Behind Me 1945, The Arabs and the West 1951, Mao and the Men Against Him 1984, Front Line 1990. *Leisure interests:* visiting second-hand furniture and bookshops, collecting modern pictures and Chinese porcelain, music. *Address:* 302 Ridley House, 2 Upper Albert Road, Hong Kong Special Administrative Region, People's Republic of China. *Telephone:* 2868-1838 (Hong Kong).

HOLLINGWORTH, Rt Rev. Peter, AC, OBE, MA, TH.L, FAIM; Australian Govenor-General and ecclesiastic; b. 10 April 1935, Adelaide; m. Kathleen Ann Turner 1960; three d.; ed Trinity Coll. Univ. of Melbourne; Deacon-in-Charge then Priest-in-Charge, St Mary's, N Melbourne 1960–64; Chaplain to the Brotherhood of St Laurence 1964–90, Assoc. Dir 1970, later Dir of Social Services, Exec. Dir 1980–90; Hon. Curate, St Silas's, North Balwyn, later Hon. Curate at St Faith's, Burwood and Priest-in-Charge, St Mark's, Fitzroy; recipient of travelling bursary 1967; elected Canon, St Paul's Cathedral 1980; Bishop of the Inner City 1985–90, Archbishop of Brisbane 1990–2001; Gov.-Gen. of the Commonwealth of Australia June 2001–; Prior to Order of St John of Jerusalem; Chair. Int. Year of Shelter for the Homeless, Nat. Cttee of Non-Governmental Orgs. 1986–88, Anglican Social Responsibilities Comm. of Gen. Synod 1990–98, Anglicare in diocese of Brisbane; Pres. Victorian Council of Social Services 1969; mem., Hon. Chair. Centenary of Fed. Council, Constitutional Convention (as non-parl. Rep.); Fellow Trinity Coll. Melbourne; Hon. LLD (Monash Univ.) 1986, (Melbourne) 1990; Hon. DUniv (Griffith Univ.) 1993, (Queensland Univ. of Tech.) 1994, (Cen. Queensland) 1995; Hon. DLitt (Univ. of Southern Queensland) 1999; Victorian Rostrum Award of Merit 1985, Advance Australia Award 1988, Paul Harris Fellowship, Rotary Club 1989, Australian of the Year 1992, Nat. Living Treasure of Australia (Nat. Trust) 1997. *Publications:* The Powerless Poor 1972, The Poor: Victims of Affluence? 1974, Australians in Poverty 1979, Kingdom Come 1991, Public Thoughts of an Archbishop 1996. *Leisure interests:* swimming, Australian Rules football, theatre, reading. *Address:* Government House, Canberra, ACT 2600, Australia.

HOLLÓ, Janos; Hungarian chemical engineer; b. 20 Aug. 1919, Szentes; s. of Gyula Holló and Margit Mandl; m. 1st Hermina Milch (1944); m. 2nd Vera Novák 1956; two s. one d.; ed Tech. Univ., Budapest; Tech. Dir Budapest Breweries 1948; Prof. Agricultural and Chemical Tech., Budapest Tech. Univ. 1952–90, Dean Chemical Eng Faculty 1955–57, 1963–72, Prof. Emer. 1991–; Dir Hungarian Acad. of Sciences Cen. Research Inst. of Chemistry 1972–91, Prof. of Research 1991–; Pres. Comm. Int. des Industries Agricoles et Alimentaires (CIIA); Chair. Cereals and Pulses Cttee, Int. Org. for Standardization (ISO) 1960–99, Agricultural and Food Products Cttee 1971–98; Gen. Sec. Scientific Asscn of Hungary Food Industry 1949, Chair., Pres. 1981–91, Hon. Pres. 1991–; Pres. Int. Soc. for Fat Research (ISF) 1964–66, 1982–83, Exec. mem. 1964–; Chief Ed. Acta Alimentaria, Journal of Food Investigations, Biotechnology and Environmental Protection Today and Tomorrow; mem. numerous editorial bds; mem. Hungarian Acad. of Sciences 1967; Foreign mem. Finnish Acad. of Tech. Sciences 1984, German Acad. of Sciences 1984, Polish Acad. of Sciences 1991, New York Acad. of Sciences 1994, Int. Acad. of Food Science Tech. 1998; Hon. mem. Polish Science Asscn of Food Industries 1971, Austrian Soc. for Food and Biochemistry 1983; Dr hc (Tech. Univ. of Vienna) 1973, (Berlin, Charlottenburg) 1984, (Tech. Univ. Budapest) 1991, (Univ. of Horticulture and Food Industry, Budapest) 1991; Hon. Dip. (Int. Standards Organization) 1999; Commdr Ordre du Mérite pour la recherche et l'invention 1962; medal of French Starch Syndicate 1963; Chevalier des Palmes académiques 1967; Labour Order of Merit 1971, 1979; Saare Medal 1972; Premio d'Oro Interpetrol 1973; Copernicus Medal 1974; State Prize 1975; Prix d'honneur de l'Acad. Int. du Lutèce 1978; Chevreul Medal 1986; Normann Medal 1986; Award for Outstanding Paper Presentation (American Oil Chem. Soc.) 1992. *Publications:* numerous books (with others) including Technology of Malting and Brewing, Biotechnology of Food and Feed Production, Bioconversion of Starch, Aliments non-conventionnels à destination humaine, Automatization in the Food Industry, The Application of Molecular Distillation; co-author of some 600 articles for professional journals. *Address:* Central Research Institute for Chemistry of the Hungarian Academy of Sciences, 1025 Budapest, Pusztaszeri ut 59/67, Hungary. *Telephone:* (1) 325-7750. *Fax:* (1) 325-7750.

HOLLOWAY, Bruce William, AO, PhD, FAA, FTSE; Australian professor of genetics; b. 9 Jan. 1928, Adelaide; s. of Albert Holloway and Gertrude C. Walkem; m. Brenda D. Gray 1952; one s. one d.; ed Scotch Coll., Adelaide, Univ. of Adelaide and Calif. Inst. of Tech.; Lecturer in Plant Pathology, Waite Agric. Research Inst. 1949–50; Research Fellow in Microbial Genetics, John Curtin School of Medicine, Australian Nat. Univ. 1953–56; Sr Lecturer 1956–60, then Reader in Microbial Genetics, Univ. of Melbourne 1956–67; Foundation Prof. of Genetics, Monash Univ. 1968–93, Head Dept of Genetics and Devt Biology 1968–93, Chair. Bd CRC for Vertebrate Biological Control 1994–99; Project Co-ordinator, Crawford Fund 1994–; Visiting Lecturer in Microbiology and Fellow, MIT 1962–63; Sec. Biological Sciences, Australian Acad. of Science 1982–86; Visiting Prof. Univ. of Newcastle-upon-Tyne 1977–78; Chair. Nat. Biotechnology Program Research Grants Scheme 1983–86; mem. Industry and Research Devt Bd 1986–89; Kathleen Barton–Wright Lecturer, Soc. for Gen. Microbiology, UK 1998; Hon. Professorial Fellow 1994–. *Publications:* over 160 papers on genetics and micro-

biology in scientific journals and conf. proc. *Leisure interests:* music, reading, tennis. *Address:* 22 Reading Avenue, North Balwyn, Victoria, 3104, Australia (Home). *Telephone:* (3) 9819-7383 (Home). *Fax:* (3) 9857-8756 (Home). *E-mail:* hollowab@ozemail.com.au (Home).

HOLLOWAY, Adm. James Lemuel, III; American naval officer (retd); b. 23 Feb. 1922, Charleston, S Carolina; s. of Admiral James L. Holloway, Jr and the late Jean Hagood; m. Dabney Rawlings 1942; one s. (died 1964), two d.; ed US Naval Acad., Md; Commissioned Ensign in US Navy 1942, served on destroyers in Atlantic and Pacific Theatres, World War II; Gunnery Officer USS Bennion, took part in Battle of Surigao Straits; Exec. Officer of Fighter Squadron Fifty-two, USS Boxer, Korean War 1952–54; Commdr Attack Squadron Eighty-three, USS Essex, Sixth Fleet during Lebanon landings 1958; Nat. War Coll. 1961; nuclear training under Admiral Rickover 1963; Commdg Officer USS Enterprise (first nuclear-powered carrier) Viet Nam War 1965–67; promoted to rank of Rear-Adm. 1967; Dir Strike Warfare Div., Program Coordinator Nuclear Attack Carrier Program, Office of Chief of Naval Operations; Commdr Sixth Fleet Carrier Striking Force, directed operations in E Mediterranean during Jordanian crisis 1970; Deputy C-in-C Atlantic and US Atlantic Fleet, Vice-Adm. 1971; Commdr Seventh Fleet during combat operations in Viet Nam 1972–73; Vice-Chief of Naval Operations 1973–74; Chief of Naval Operations 1974–78; mem. Jt Chiefs of Staff 1974–78; Chair. Special Operations Review Group, Iranian Hostage Rescue 1981; Special Envoy of Vice-Pres. of USA to Bahrain 1986; mem. Pres.'s Comm. on Merchant Marine and Defense 1986; Pres. Council of American Flagship Operators 1981–87; Chair. of Bd Asscn of Naval Aviation; Chair. Academic Advisory Bd to US Naval Acad.; Exec. Dir, Vice-Pres.'s Task Force on Combating Terrorism 1985; Pres.'s Blue Ribbon Comm. on Defense Man. 1985–86; Commr, Comm. on Merchant Marine and Defense 1987, Comm. on Integrated Long-Term Strategy 1987; mem. Bd of Dirs US Life Insurance Co. 1985–95, UNC Inc. 1987–98, George Marshall Foundation 1988–98, Atlantic Council 1990–98; mem. Bd of Govs, St John's Coll. 1996–99; Pres. Naval Historical Foundation 1984–98 (Chair. 1998–); Chair. Emer. Bd Historic Annapolis Foundation 1998–; Chair. Emer. Naval Acad. Found. 1994–2000; Chair. Emer. Bd of Trustees, St James School, Md 2000; Tech. Adviser for film Top Gun 1985; awarded numerous medals for meritorious service including Defense Distinguished Service Medal (twice), Navy Distinguished Service Medal (four times), Legion of Merit, Distinguished Flying Cross, Bronze Star Medal with Combat "V", Air Medal (four times), Modern Patriot Award 1994, US Navy League Annual Award for Distinguished Civilian Leadership 1997, Sons of the Revolution Distinguished Patriot Award 1999, Distinguished Grad. Award, Naval Acad. 1999, 2000, US Nat. Wrestling Hall of Fame 1999 and many foreign decorations including Commdr., Légion d'honneur, Grand Cross of Germany (First Class), Order of The Rising Sun (Japan) (First Class), Italian Grand Cross. *Film:* stunt pilot in Bridges at Toko-Ri 1955. *Publications:* numerous articles on aviation, sealift and defence organization. *Leisure interest:* sailing. *Address:* 1694 Epping Farms Lane, Annapolis, MD 21401, USA. *Telephone:* (410) 849-2115. *Fax:* (410) 849-2115.

HOLLOWAY, Rt. Rev. Richard Frederick, BD, STM, FRSE; British ecclesiastic; b. 26 Nov. 1933, Glasgow; s. of Arthur Holloway and Mary Holloway; m. Jean Holloway 1963; one s. two d.; ed Kelham Theological Coll., Edinburgh Theological Coll. and Union Theological Seminary, New York; Curate, St Ninian's, Glasgow 1959–63; Priest-in-Charge, St Margaret's and St Mungo's, Gorbals, Glasgow 1963–68; Rector, Old St Paul's, Edin. 1968–80, Church of the Advent, Boston, Mass. 1980–84; Vicar, St Mary Magdalen's, Oxford 1984–86; Bishop of Edin. 1986–2000; Primus, Scottish Episcopal Church 1992–2000; Prof. of Divinity, Gresham Coll. London 1997–; mem. Human Fertilisation and Embryology Authority, UK 1991–97; Broadcasting Standards Comm., UK 2001–04; Hon. DUniv (Strathclyde) 1994; Hon. DD (Aberdeen) 1994, (Glasgow) 2001; Hon. DLitt (Napier) 2001; Winifred M. Stanford Award for The Killing 1984. *Television:* Holloway's Road (BBC) 2000. *Publications include:* Beyond Belief 1981, The Killing 1984, Paradoxes of Christian Faith and Life 1984, The Sidelong Glance 1985, The Way of the Cross 1986, Seven to Flee, Seven to Follow 1986, Crossfire 1988, Another Country, Another King 1991, Who Needs Feminism? 1991, Anger, Sex, Doubt and Death 1992, The Stranger in the Wings 1994, Churches and How To Survive Them 1994, Behold Your King 1995, Limping Towards the Sunrise 1996, Dancing on the Edge 1997, Godless Morality 1999, Doubts and Loves 2001, On Forgiveness 2002. *Leisure interests:* walking, movies, reading, cooking. *Address:* 6 Blantyre Terrace, Edinburgh, EH10 5AE, Scotland (Home). *Telephone:* (131) 446-0696 (Home). *E-mail:* doc.holloway@virgin.net (Home).

HOLLOWAY, Robin Greville, PhD, DMus; British composer, writer on music and professor of musical composition; b. 19 Oct. 1943, Leamington Spa; s. of Robert Charles Holloway and Pamela Mary Holloway (née Jacob); ed St Paul's Cathedral Choir School, King's Coll. School, Wimbledon, King's Coll., Cambridge and New Coll., Oxford; Lecturer in Music, Univ. of Cambridge 1975–, Reader in Musical Composition 1999–, Prof. 2001–; Fellow of Gonville and Caius Coll., Cambridge 1969–. *Compositions include:* Garden Music opus 1 1962, Scenes from Schumann opus 13 1970, Evening with Angels opus 17 1972, Domination of Black opus 23 1973, Clarissa opus 30 1976, Second Concerto for Orchestra opus 40 1979, Brand opus 48 1981, Women in War opus 51 1982, Seascape and Harvest opus 55 1983, Viola Concerto opus 56 1984, Double Concerto opus 68, The Spacious Firmament opus 69, Violin Concerto opus 70 1990, Boys and Girls Come Out To Play 1991, Frost at Midnight opus 78, Third Concerto for Orchestra opus 80 1994, Clarinet

Concerto opus 82 1996, Peer Gynt opus 84 1984–97, Scenes from Antwerp opus 85 1997, Symphony 1999, Missa Caiensis 2001, Spring Music opus 96 2002. *Publications:* Wagner and Debussy 1978; numerous articles and reviews. *Leisure interest:* cities, architecture, books. *Address:* Gonville and Caius College, Cambridge, CB2 1TA, England. *Telephone:* (1223) 335424. *E-mail:* rgh1000@cam.ac.uk (Home).

HOLM, Erik, PhD; Danish foundation director and political economist; b. 6 Dec. 1933, Hobro; s. of Carl Holm and Anne Margrethe Holm (née Nielsen); m. Annie Jacoba Kortleven 1960 (died 1984); two s. two d.; ed Univ. of Copenhagen; Economist, Cen. Statistical Office, Copenhagen 1961–65; Lecturer in Econs, Univ. of Copenhagen 1962–65, in Political Science 1971–81; Economist, IMF, Washington, DC 1965–69; Sr Economist, Ministry of Econ. Affairs, Copenhagen 1969–72; Adviser on European Affairs to Prime Minister 1972–82; Prin. Adviser (econ. and financial affairs), EC Comm., Brussels 1982–87; Visiting Scholar, Inst. of Int. Studies, Univ. of Calif., Berkeley 1987–89; Dir The Eleni Nakou Foundation, London 1989–. *Publications:* Stabilitet og Uligevagt 1986, Money and International Politics 1991, Union eller Nation 1992, Europe, a Political Culture? Fundamental Issues for the 1996 IGC 1994, The European Anarchy: Europe's Hard Road into High Politics 2001; articles in Danish and int. publications on European econ. and political affairs. *Address:* Xylografensvej 4, 3220 Tisvildeleje, Denmark (Summer) (Home); Wiedeweltsgade 27, 2100 Copenhagen, Denmark (Home). *Telephone:* 48-70-97-15 (Tisvildeleje) (Home); 35-42-03-62 (Copenhagen) (Home). *E-mail:* erholm@attglobal.net (Home).

HOLM, Sir Ian, Kt, CBE; British actor; b. 12 Sept. 1931, Ilford; s. of Dr. James Harvey Cuthbert and Jean Wilson Cuthbert; m. 1st Lynn Mary Shaw 1955 (divorced 1965); two d.; m. 2nd Bee Gilbert; one s. one d.; m. 3rd Sophie Baker 1982 (divorced 1986); one s.; m. 4th Penelope Wilton 1991 (divorced); one step-d.; ed Chigwell Grammar School, Essex, RADA (Royal Acad. of Dramatic Art); joined Shakespeare Memorial Theatre 1954; Worthing Repertory 1956; on tour with Lord Olivier in Titus Andronicus 1957; mem. RSC 1958–67; Laurence Olivier Award 1998, Evening Standard Award for Best Actor 1993 and 1997. *Roles include:* Puck, Ariel, Lorenzo, Henry V, Richard III, The Fool (in King Lear), Lennie (in The Homecoming); appeared in Moonlight 1993, King Lear 1997, Max in The Homecoming 2001. *Films include:* Young Winston, Oh! What a Lovely War, Alien, All Quiet on the Western Front, Chariots of Fire, The Return of the Soldier, Greystoke 1984, Laughterhouse 1984, Brazil 1985, Wetherby 1985, Dance with a Stranger 1985, Dreamchild 1985, Henry V 1989, Another Woman 1989, Hamlet 1990, Kafka 1991, The Hour of the Pig 1992, Blue Ice 1992, The Naked Lunch 1992, Frankenstein 1993, The Madness of King George 1994, Loch Ness 1994, Big Night 1995, Night Falls on Manhattan 1995, A Life Less Ordinary 1996, The Sweet Hereafter 1997, The Fifth Element 1997, eXistenZ 1998, Simon Magus 1998, Esther Kahn 1999, Joe Gould's Secret 1999, Beautiful Joe 1999, From Hell 2000, The Emperor's New Clothes 2000, The Lord of the Rings 2001. *Television appearances include:* The Lost Boys 1979, We, the Accused 1980, The Bell 1981, Strike 1981, Inside the Third Reich 1982, Mr. and Mrs. Edgehill 1985, The Browning Version 1986, Game, Set and Match 1988, The Endless Game 1989, The Last Romantics 1992, The Borrowers 1993, The Deep Blue Sea 1994, Landscape 1995, Little Red Riding Hood 1996, King Lear 1997, Alice Through the Looking Glass 1998. *Leisure interest:* tennis, walking. *Address:* Markham & Froggatt Ltd, Julian House, 4 Windmill Street, London, NW1T 2HZ, England.

HOLM, Richard H., PhD; American professor of chemistry; b. 24 Sept. 1933, Boston, Mass.; m. Florence L. Jacintho 1958; four c.; ed Univ. of Mass. and MIT; Asst Prof. of Chem., Harvard Univ. 1960–65; Assoc. Prof. of Chem. Univ. of Wisconsin 1965–67; Prof. of Chem. MIT 1967–75, Stanford Univ. 1975–80; Prof. of Chem. Harvard Univ. 1980–83, Higgins Prof. 1983–, Chair. Dept of Chem. 1983–86; mem. American Acad. of Arts and Sciences, NAS; Hon. AM; Hon. DSc; Chemical Sciences Award 1993, several awards for research in inorganic chem. *Publications:* numerous research papers in professional journals in the fields of inorganic chem. and biochem. *Address:* Department of Chemistry, Harvard University, Cambridge, MA 02138 (Office); 483 Pleasant Street, #10, Belmont, MA 02139, USA (Home). *Telephone:* (617) 495-0853 (Office). *E-mail:* holm@chemistry.harvard.edu (Office). *Website:* www.chem.harvard.edu (Office).

HOLME OF CHELTENHAM, Baron (Life Peer), cr. 1990, of Cheltenham in the County of Gloucestershire; **Richard Gordon Holme,** CBE, PC, MA; British politician, publisher and business executive; b. 27 May 1936, London; s. of Jack Richard Holme and Edna Holme (née Eggleton); m. Kay Powell 1958; two s. two d.; ed Royal Masonic School, St John's Coll. Oxford, Harvard Business School, USA; served in 10th Gurkha Rifles in Malaya 1954–56; Marketing Man., Unilever 1959–64; Dir Penguin Books 1964–66; Chair. BPC Publishing 1966–70; Pres. CRM Books, Calif., USA 1970–74; Dir Nat. Cttee for Electoral Reform 1976–84; Chair. Constitutional Reform Centre 1985, Threadneedle Publishing Group 1988–, Hollis Directories 1989–98, Prima Europe 1992–1995, Brasseys Ltd 1996–98; Pres. Liberal Party 1980–81; Liberal Democrat Parl. Spokesman on NI, House of Lords 1992–99; Chair. Broadcasting Standards Comm. 1999–2000; Chair. of Govs. English Coll., Prague; Chair. Hansard Soc. for Parl. Govt2000–; Dir Rio Tinto PLC 1995–98; Chancellor Univ. of Greenwich 1998–; Chair. Advisory Bd British-American Project 2000–. *Publications:* No Dole for the Young 1975, A Democracy Which

Works 1978, The People's Kingdom (Jt Ed.) 1987, 1688–1988: Time for a New Constitution 1988. *Leisure interests:* walking, opera. *Address:* House of Lords, London, SW1A 0PW, England. *Telephone:* (20) 7753-2454.

HOLMES, George Arthur, PhD, FBA; British historian; b. 22 April 1927, Aberystwyth, Wales; s. of the late John Holmes and Margaret Holmes; m. Evelyn Anne Klein 1953; two s. (one deceased), two d.; ed Ardwyn County School, Aberystwyth, Univ. Coll. Aberystwyth and St John's Coll. Cambridge; Fellow, St John's Coll. Cambridge 1951–54; Tutor, St Catherine's Coll. Oxford 1954–62, Fellow and Tutor 1962–89, Vice-Master 1969–71, Emer. Fellow 1990–; Chichele Prof. of Medieval History and Fellow, All Souls Coll., Oxford 1989–94, Emer. Fellow 1994–; Visiting Prof., Harvard Univ. Center for Italian Renaissance Studies, Florence 1995–; mem. Inst. for Advanced Study, Princeton, NJ, USA 1967–68; Chair. Victoria County History Cttee, Inst. of Historical Research 1979–89; Jt Ed. English Historical Review 1974–81; Del., Oxford Univ. Press 1982–92; Fellow Emer., Leverhulme Trust 1996–98; Serena Medal for Italian Studies, British Acad. 1993. *Publications:* The Estates of the Higher Nobility in Fourteenth-Century England 1957, The Later Middle Ages 1962, The Florentine Enlightenment 1400–1450 1969, Europe: Hierarchy and Revolt 1320–1450 1975, The Good Parliament 1975, Dante 1980, Florence, Rome and the Origins of the Renaissance 1986, The Oxford Illustrated History of Medieval Europe (ed.) 1988, The First Age of the Western City 1300–1500 1990, Art and Politics in Renaissance Italy (ed.) 1993, Renaissance 1996, The Oxford Illustrated History of Italy (ed.) 1997. *Leisure interests:* country walking, looking at pictures. *Address:* Highmoor House, Primrose Lane, Weald, Bampton, Oxon., OX18 2HY, England. *Telephone:* (1993) 850408.

HOLMES, Sir John Eaton, KBE, CMG, CVO; British diplomatist; b. 29 April 1951, Preston; s. of Leslie Holmes and Joyce Holmes; m. Penelope Morris 1976; three d.; ed Preston Grammar School, Balliol Coll., Oxford; joined FCO 1973; with Embassy, Moscow 1976–78; First Sec. FCO 1978–82; Asst Pvt. Sec. to Foreign Sec. 1982–84; First Sec. Embassy, Paris 1984–87; Asst Head Soviet Dept, FCO 1988–89; seconded to Thomas De La Rue & Co. 1989–91; counsellor British High Comm., India 1991–95; Prin. Pvt. Sec. to Prime Minister 1996–99; Amb. to Portugal 1999–2001, to France 2001–. *Leisure interests:* reading, music, sport. *Address:* Embassy of the UK, 35 rue du Faubourg Saint Honoré, 75383 Paris Cedex 08, France (Office); c/o Foreign and Commonwealth Office, King Charles Street, London, SW1A 2AH, England. *Telephone:* 1-44-51-32-02 (Office); 1-44-51-33-51 (Home). *Website:* www.amb-grandebretagne.fr (Office).

HOLMES, Kenneth Charles, MA, PhD, FRS; British research biophysicist; b. 19 Nov. 1934, London; s. of Sidney C. and Irene M. (née Penfold) Holmes; m. Mary Lesceline Scruby 1957; one s. three d.; ed Chiswick County School, St John's Coll., Cambridge and Birkbeck Coll., London; Research Asst, Birkbeck Coll. 1955–59; Research Assoc., Children's Hosp., Boston 1960–62; scientific staff, MRC Lab. of Molecular Biology, Cambridge 1962–68; Dir Dept of Biophysics, Max-Planck-Inst. for Medical Research, Heidelberg 1968–; Prof. of Biophysics, Heidelberg Univ. 1972–. *Publications:* articles in scientific books and journals. *Leisure interests:* rowing, singing. *Address:* Max-Planck-Institute for Medical Research, Abt. Biophysik, Jahnstrasse 29, 69120 Heidelberg (Office); Mühltalstrasse 117b, 6900 Heidelberg, Germany (Home). *Telephone:* (6221) 486270 (Office); (6221) 471313 (Home).

HOLMES, Larry; American boxer; b. 3 Nov. 1949, Cuthbert, Georgia; s. of John and Flossie Holmes; m. Diana Holmes; one s. four d.; ed Easton, Pa; amateur boxer 1970–73; 22 amateur fights, 19 wins; lost by disqualification to Duane Bobick in finals of American Olympic trials 1972; won World Boxing Council version of world heavyweight title from Ken Norton June 1978; made nine defences, all won inside scheduled distance (breaking previous record held by Joe Louis); became first man to stop Muhammad Ali Oct. 1980; stripped of World Boxing Council version 1983; lost Int. Boxing Fed. version to Michael Spinks 1985, beaten again by Spinks 1986; defeated by Mike Tyson (q.v.) in attempts to win WBA, WBC and IBF heavyweight titles 1988; beaten by Evander Holyfield (q.v.) 1992 and by Oliver McCall 1995; was undefeated for record 13 years; still fights occasionally (five contests since 1997); record at end of 2002 is 67 wins, 6 defeats (44 KOs); runs an Internet casino business. *Leisure interests:* food, sport and self-education. *Address:* c/o Holmes Enterprises Inc., 704 Alpha Bldg, Easton, PA 18042, USA.

HOLMES, Richard Gordon Heath, OBE, MA, FBA, FRSL; British writer; b. 5 Nov. 1945, London; s. of Dennis Patrick Holmes and Pamela Mavis Gordon; ed Downside School, Churchill Coll., Cambridge; historical features writer, The Times 1967–92; Visiting Fellow, Trinity Coll., Cambridge 2000; Prof. of Biographical Studies, Univ. of E Anglia Jan. 2001–; Somerset Maugham Award 1977, James Tait Black Memorial Prize 1994, Whitbread Book of the Year Prize 1989, Duff Cooper Prize 1998; Hon. D.Litt. (E Anglia) 2000, (Tavistock Inst.) 2001. *Radio:* BBC Radio: Inside the Tower 1977, To the Tempest Given 1992, The Nightwalking (Sony Award) 1995, Clouded Hills 1999, Runaway Lives 2000, The Frankenstein Project 2002. *Publications:* Shelley: The Pursuit 1974, Footsteps: Adventures of a Romantic Biographer 1985, Coleridge: Early Visions 1989, Dr. Johnson & Mr. Savage 1993, The Romantic Poets and their Circle 1997, Coleridge: Darker Reflections 1998, Sidetracks: Explorations of a Romantic Biographer 2000. *Address:* c/o HarperCollins, 77 Fulham Palace Road, London, W6 8JB, England (Office).

HOLMES À COURT, Janet, AO, BSc; Australian business executive; b. 1943, Perth; m. Robert Holmes à Court (died 1990); one d. three s.; ed Perth Modern

School and Univ. of Western Australia; fmr science teacher; Exec. Chair. Heytesbury Pty Ltd (family-owned co. which includes Heytesbury Beef Ltd, Vasse Felix (Vineyards), Heytesbury Thoroughbreds, John Holland Group and Key Transport); Chair. John Holland Group, Australian Children's TV Foundation, Black Swan Theatre Co., W Australian Symphony Orchestra; Dir Goodman Fielder Ltd. 1998–; fmr Pro-Chancellor, Univ. of W Australia; mem. Bd Man. Festival of Perth; British Business Woman of the Year 1996. *Leisure interest:* the arts. *Address:* Heytesbury Pty Ltd, 27/140 St. George's Terrace, Perth, WA 6000, Australia (Office).

HOLMES À COURT, Peter, BA; Australian business executive; b. 1969; s. of the late Robert Holmes à Court and of Janet Lee Holmes à Court; m.; two s.; ed Oxford Univ., UK and Middlebury Coll., Vt, USA; employed in family business Heytesbury 1990–92; Financial Analyst James D. Wolfensohn, USA 1992–93; Founder and Man. Dir Back Row Productions 1993–2000; Chief Exec. The Australian Agric. Co. (AACo) 2001–; Dir Stoll Moss Theatres, London until 1999; mem. Arts Advisory Bd, Middlebury Coll. *Address:* Level 25, Chifley Tower, 2 Chifley Place, Sydney, NSW 2000, Australia (Office). *Telephone:* (2) 9293-2880 (Office). *Fax:* (2) 9293-2828 (Office).

HOLOMISA, Maj.-Gen. Bantubonke Harrington (Bantu); South African politician and army officer; b. 25 July 1955, Mqandull, Transkei; s. of the late Chief B. Holomisa; m. Tunyelwa Dube 1981; one s. two d.; ed Army Coll. of South Africa; joined Transkei Defence Force 1976, Lt Platoon Commdr 1978–79, Capt. Training Wing Commdr 1979–81, Lt-Col Bn Command 1981–83, Col SS01 Operations and Training 1984–85, rank of Brig., Chief of Staff, Transkei Defence Force 1985–87, Commdr 1987–94; Leader of Transkei 1987–94; mem. A.N.C. Nat. Exec. Cttee 1994; Deputy Minister of Environmental Affairs, Govt of Nat. Unity 1994–96; Pres. United Democratic Movt 1997–; several military medals. *Publications:* Future Plan for South Africa, Comrades in Corruption (booklet). *Leisure interests:* soccer, rugby, cricket, athletics, wildlife gaming resorts. *Address:* P.O.B. 15, Parliament, Cape Town 8000 (Office); No. 6 Falcon's End, Hebert Street, Arcadia, Pretoria 0007, South Africa (Home). *Telephone:* (21) 4033921 (Cape Town) (Office); (12) 3210010 (Pretoria) (Office); (82) 5524156 (Pretoria) (Home). *Fax:* (21) 4032525 (Cape Town) (Office); (12) 3210015 (Pretoria) (Home). *E-mail:* info@udm.org .za (Office); info@holomisa.org.za (Home). *Website:* www.udm.org.za (Office).

HOLOUBEK, Gustaw; Polish theatre director and actor; b. 21 April 1923, Cracow; s. of Gustaw and Eugenia Holoubek; m. 1st Danuta Kwiatkowska; m. 2nd Maria Wachowiak; m. 3rd Magdalena Zawadzka; one s. two d.; ed State Higher Dramatic School, Cracow; actor in Cracow theatres 1947–49; at Wyspiański Theatre, Katowice, Artistic Man. 1954–56; at Polish Theatre, Warsaw 1958–59; actor Dramatic Theatre, Warsaw 1959–63 and 1969–82, Dir and Artistic Man. 1972–82, Nat. Theatre, Warsaw 1963–68, Polish Theatre, Warsaw 1969–82, Ateneum Theatre, Warsaw 1989–96, Dir and Artistic Man. 1996–; Assoc. Prof. State Higher Theatrical School 1991–; Vice-Chair. SPATIF (Asscn of Polish Theatre and Film Actors) 1963–70, Chair. 1972–81; Hon. Pres. of ZASP (Polish Actors Asscn) 1981; Deputy to Sejm (Parl.) 1976–82; Senator 1989–91; mem. Presidential Council for Culture 1992–95; numerous decorations including State Prize 1953, 1966, 1978 (1st Class), Order of Banner of Labour 2nd Class, Kt's Cross of Polonia Restituta Order, Award Meritorious Activist of Culture 1972, Warsaw City Prize 1975, Cttee for Polish Radio and TV Award 1980, Prix Italia 1994. *Films directed:* Mazepa 1976, A Book of Great Wishes 1997. *Theatre roles include:* Judge Caust in Leprosy at the Palace of Justice, Baron Goetze in Le diable et le bon Dieu (Sartre), Gustaw-Konrad in Dziady (A. Mickiewicz), Violinist in Rzeźnia (S. Mrózek), Beggar in Electra (J. Giraudoux), Hick in The Iceman Cometh (O'Neill), King Lear, Oedipus, Hamlet, Richard II, Hadrian VII (Peter Luke), Gen. Wincenty Krasiński in November Night (Wyspiański), Count Szarma in Operetka (Gombrowicz) 1980, Regent in Revenge 1990 (also Dir), Count Respect in Fantazy 1994 (also Dir), Shylock in The Merchant of Venice 1996, Sir in Dresser, Father in Madhouse 1998. *Television:* plays directed include Mazepa 1969, 1993, Fantazy 1971, Hamlet 1974, Dwa teatry (Two Theatres) 1998, Skiz 2000, Gra miłości i przypadku (Le jeu de l'amour et du hasard) 2001. *Publication:* Wspomnienia z niepamięci 1999. *Leisure interest:* sports.

HOLROYD, Michael, CBE; British author; b. 27 Aug. 1935, London; s. of Basil Holroyd and Ulla Holroyd (née Hall); m. Margaret Drabble 1982; ed Eton Coll.; Chair. Soc. of Authors 1973–74, Nat. Book League 1976–78; Pres. English Centre of PEN 1985–88; Chair. Strachey Trust 1990–95, Public Lending Right Advisory Cttee 1997–2000, Royal Soc. of Literature 1998–2001; mem. Arts Council (Chair. Literature Panel) 1992–95; Governor, Shaw Festival Theatre, Niagara-on-the-Lake 1993–; Trustee Laser Foundation 2001–; Hon. DLitt (Ulster) 1992, (Sheffield, Warwick) 1993, (East Anglia) 1994, (London School of Econs) 1998. *Publications:* Hugh Kingsmill 1964, Lytton Strachey 1967–68, Unreceived Opinions 1973, Augustus John 1974–75 (new Edn 1996), Bernard Shaw: Vol. 1: The Search for Love 1988, Vol II: The Pursuit of Power 1989, Vol. III: The Lure of Fantasy 1991, Vol. IV: The Last Laugh 1992, Vol. V: The Shaw Companion 1992, Bernard Shaw 1997 (one-vol. biog.), Basil Street Blues 1999, Works on Paper 2002. *Leisure interests:* music, stories. *Address:* c/o A. P. Watt Ltd, 20 John Street, London, WC1N 2DL, England. *Telephone:* (20) 7405-6774. *Fax:* (20) 7831-2154.

HOLST, Per; Danish film producer; b. 28 March 1939, Copenhagen; s. of Rigmor Holst and Svend Holst; m. 1st Anni Møller Kjeldsen 1962–72; m. 2nd Kristina Holst 1976; four s.; entered film industry with Nordisk Film 1957; Film Man. and copywriter, WA Advertising Agency 1962; Nordisk Film 1965; established Per Holst Filmproduktion ApS 1965; numerous film awards including Palme d'Or, Cannes Film Festival and Acad. Award (Oscar) for Pelle the Conqueror 1988. *Films:* Afskedens Time 1967, Benny's Bathtub 1967, Kaptajn Klyde og Hans Venner vender tilbage 1981, The Tree of Knowledge 1982, Zappa 1983, Beauty and the Beast 1983, The Boy Who Disappeared 1984, Twist and Shout 1984, Element of Crime 1984, Up on Daddy's Hat 1985, Coeurs Flambés 1986, Pelle the Conqueror 1987, The Redtops 1988, Aarhus by Night 1989, Sirup 1990, War of the Birds 1990, Cassanova 1990, The Hideaway 1991, Pain of Love 1992, Jungle Jack 1993, All Things Fair 1996. *Leisure interest:* golf.

HOLT, Sir James Clarke, Kt, DPhil, FBA, FSA; British historian and university professor; b. 26 April 1922, Bradford, Yorks.; s. of the late Herbert Holt and Eunice Holt; m. Alice Catherine Elizabeth Suley 1950 (died 1998); one s.; ed Bradford Grammar School and Queen's Coll., Oxford; served in army 1942–45; Harmsworth Sr Scholar, Merton Coll., Oxford 1947–49; Lecturer, Univ. of Nottingham 1949–62, Prof. of Medieval History 1962–66; Prof. of History, Univ. of Reading 1966–78, Dean of Faculty of Letters and Social Sciences 1972–76; Professorial Fellow, Emmanuel Coll., Cambridge 1978–81, Prof of Medieval History, Cambridge Univ. 1978–88, Master of Fitzwilliam Coll., Cambridge 1981–88; Visiting Prof., Univ. of Calif., Santa Barbara, USA 1977; Visiting Hinkley Prof., Johns Hopkins Univ., USA 1983; Raleigh Lecturer, British Acad. 1975; Visiting Prof., Japan 1986; mem. Advisory Council on Public Records 1974–81; Pres. Royal Historical Soc. 1980–84; Vice-Pres. British Acad. 1986–88; Pres. Lincoln Record Soc. 1987–96, Pipe Roll Soc. 1999–; Corresp. Fellow Medieval Acad. of America; Hon. Fellow, Emmanuel Coll. 1985–, Fitzwilliam Coll. 1988–, The Queen's Coll. 1996–, Merton Coll., Oxford 2001–; Hon. DLitt (Reading) 1984, (Nottingham) 1996; Comendador de la Orden del Mérito Civil 1988. *Publications:* The Northerners: A Study in the Reign of King John 1961, Praestia Rolls 14–18 John 1964, Magna Carta 1965, The Making of Magna Carta 1966, Magna Carta and the Idea of Liberty 1972, The University of Reading: The First Fifty Years 1977, Robin Hood 1982, War and Government in the Middle Ages (Ed. with John Gillingham), Magna Carta and Medieval Government 1985; Hand-list of Acta Henry II and Richard I surviving in British Repositories (with Richard Mortimer) 1986, Domesday Studies (Ed.) 1987, Colonial England 1066–1215 1997; papers in English Historical Review, Past and Present, Economic History Review, trans. Royal Historical Soc. *Leisure interests:* music, mountaineering, cricket, fly-fishing. *Address:* 5 Holben Close, Barton, Cambridge, CB3 7AQ, England. *Telephone:* (1223) 332041.

HOLT, Peter Malcolm, DLitt, FBA, FSA, FRHistS; British professor of history; b. 28 Nov. 1918, Leigh, Lancs.; s. of Rev. Peter Holt and Elizabeth Holt; m. Nancy Bury (née Mawle) 1953; one s. one d.; ed Univ. Coll., Oxford; Sudan Civil Service, Ministry of Educ. 1941–53, Govt Archivist 1954–55; joined SOAS 1955, Prof. of Arab History 1964–75, Prof. of the History of the Near and Middle East 1975–82, Prof. Emer. 1982–, Hon. Fellow 1985. *Publications:* The Mahdist State in the Sudan 1958, 1970, Studies in the History of the Near East 1973, The Memoirs of a Syrian Prince 1983, The Age of the Crusades 1986, Early Mamluk Diplomacy 1995, The Sudan of the Three Niles 1999; Co-Ed. The Cambridge History of Islam 1970. *Leisure interest:* walking. *Address:* Dryden Spinney, Bletchington Road, Kirtlington, Kidlington, Oxford, OX5 3HF, England. *Telephone:* (1869) 350477.

HOLTON, A. Linwood, Jr, BA, LLB; American politician and lawyer; b. 21 Sept. 1923, Big Stone Gap, Va; s. of Abner Linwood Holton and Edith Holton (née Van Gorder); m. Virginia Harrison Rogers 1953; two s. two d.; ed public schools in Big Stone Gap, Washington and Lee Univ. and Harvard Law School; Partner, Eggleston, Holton, Butler and Glenn (law firm); served submarine force during Second World War; fmr Chair. Roanoke City Republican Cttee; Vice-Chair. Virginia Republican State Cen. Cttee 1960–69; del. to Republican Nat. Convention 1960, 1968, 1972; mem. Nat. Nixon for Pres. Cttee 1967; Regional Co-ordinator for Nixon for Pres. Cttee; Gov. of Virginia 1970–74; Asst Sec. of State for Congressional Relations, Dept of State 1974–75; Partner in law firm of Hogan and Hartson 1975–78; Vice-Pres., Gen. Counsel American Council Insurance, Washington 1978–84; Chair. Burket Miller Center for Public Affairs, Univ. of Va 1979–; Pres. Supreme Court Historical Soc. 1980–89; Chair. Metropolitan Washington Airports Authority 1987–93; Pres. Centre for Innovative Tech., Herndon, Va 1988–94; Partner in law firm of McCandlish Holton 1994–. *Address:* McCandlish Holton, PC, 1111 East Main Street, Suite 1500, P.O. Box 796, Richmond, VA 23218 (Office); 3883 Black Stump Road, Weems, VA 22576, USA (Home). *Telephone:* (804) 775-3817 (Office); (804) 435-0604.

HOLTON, Gerald, PhD; American physicist and historian of science; b. 23 May 1922, Berlin, Germany; s. of Dr. Emanuel Holton and Regina (Rossmann) Holton; m. Nina Rossfort 1947; two s.; ed Wesleyan Univ., Middletown, Conn., Harvard Univ.; Harvard Univ. staff, officers' radar course and lab. for Research on Sound Control 1943–45, various faculty posts 1945–, Mallinckrodt Prof. of Physics and Prof. of History of Science 1975–; Visiting Prof., MIT 1976–94; Nat. Science Foundation Faculty Fellow, Paris 1960–61; Exchange Prof., Leningrad Univ. 1962; Founder and Ed.-in-Chief, Daedalus 1958–61; Morris Loeb Lecturer Harvard Univ. 1993; Rothschild Lecturer Harvard Univ. 1997; mem. Council, History of Science Soc. 1959–61, Pres. 1982–84; Fellow, American Physical Soc. (Chair. Div. History of Physics 1992–93), American Acad. of Arts and Sciences (mem. Council 1991–95), AAAS, American Philosophical Soc., American Asscn for the Advancement of Science, Acad. Internationale d'Histoire des Sciences (Vice-Pres. 1982–89), Deutsche

Akad. der Naturforscher Leopoldina, Acad. Internationale de Philosophie des Sciences; Visiting mem. Inst. for Advanced Study, Princeton 1964, 1967; mem. Nat. Acad. of Sciences Cttee on Communication with Scholars in the People's Repub. of China 1969–72, US Nat. Comm. on IUHPS 1982–88 (Chair. 1988); mem. German American Acad. Council Kuratorium 1997–2000; mem. Bd of Govs, American Inst. of Physics 1969–74; Fellow, Center for Advanced Study in Behavioral Sciences, Stanford, Calif. 1975–76; mem. US Nat. Comm. on UNESCO 1975–80, Library of Congress Council of Scholars 1979–98, US Nat. Comm. on Excellence in Educ. 1981–83, Advisory Bd Nat. Humanities Center 1989–93; Herbert Spencer Lecturer, Oxford 1979, Jefferson Lecturer 1981; 8 hon. degrees; Robert A. Millikan Medal 1967, Oersted Medal 1980, Guggenheim Fellowship 1980–81, Presidential Citation for Service to Educ. 1984, McGovern Medal 1985, Andrew Gemant Award 1989, George Sarton Medal 1989, Bernal Prize 1989, Joseph Priestley Award 1994, Joseph H. Hazen Prize of the History of Science Soc. 1998. *Film:* People and Particles (co-producer), The Life of Enrico Fermi (co-producer). *Publications:* Introduction to Concepts and Theories in Physical Science 1952, Thematic Origins of Scientific Thought 1973, 1988, Scientific Imagination 1978, Limits of Scientific Inquiry (Ed.) 1979, Albert Einstein, Historical and Cultural Perspectives (Ed.) 1982, The Advancement of Science and its Burdens 1986, Science and Anti-Science 1993, Einstein, History and Other Passions 1995, Gender Differences in Science Careers (co-author) 1995, Who Succeeds in Science? The Gender Dimension (co-author) 1995, Physics, the Human Adventure (co-author) 2001, Ivory Bridges: Connecting Science and Society (co-author) 2002, Understanding Physics (co-author) 2002; mem. Editorial Bd Collected Papers of Albert Einstein. *Leisure interests:* music, kayaking. *Address:* 358 Jefferson Physical Laboratory, Harvard University, Cambridge, MA 02138 (Office); 64 Francis Avenue, Cambridge, MA 02138, USA (Home). *Telephone:* (617) 495-4474 (Office); (617) 868-9003 (Home). *Fax:* (617) 495-0416 (Office); (617) 868-9003 (Home). *E-mail:* holton@physics.harvard.edu (Office).

HOLTZMAN, Wayne H(arold), MS, PhD; American psychologist; b. 16 Jan. 1923, Chicago, Ill.; s. of Harold H. Holtzman and Lillian Manny; m. Joan King 1947; four s.; ed Northwestern and Stanford Univs; Asst Prof. Univ. of Texas at Austin 1949–53, Assoc. Prof. 1954–59, Prof. of Psychology 1959–, Dean Coll. of Educ. 1964–70, Hogg Prof. of Psychology and Educ. 1964–; Assoc. Dir Hogg Foundation for Mental Health 1955–64, Pres. 1970–93, Special Counsel 1993–; Dir Science Research Assocs. 1974–89; Population Resource Center 1980–; Pres. Int. Union of Psychological Science 1984–88; other professional affiliations; Faculty Research Fellow, Social Science Research Council 1953–54, Center for Advanced Study in Behavioral Sciences 1962–63; Hon. LHD (Southwestern) 1980. *Publications:* Tomorrow's Parents (with B. Moore) 1964, Computer Assisted Instruction, Testing and Guidance 1971, Personality Development in Two Cultures (with others) 1975, Introduction to Psychology 1978, School of the Future (with others) 1992, History of the International Union of Psychological Science (with others) 2000. *Leisure interests:* travel, photography, gardening. *Address:* Hogg Foundation for Mental Health, The University of Texas, P.O. Box 7998, Austin, TX 78713-7998 (Office); 3300 Foothill Drive, Austin, TX 78731, USA (Home). *Telephone:* (512) 471-5041 (Office); (512) 452-8296 (Home).

HOLUM, John, BA; American government official; b. 4 Dec. 1940, Highmore, S. Dak.; m. Barbara P. Pedersen; one c.; ed Northern State Teachers' Coll. and George Washington Univ.; mem. staff of Sen. George McGovern 1965–79; mem. Policy and Planning Staff, U.S. State Dept 1979–81; attorney, O'Melveny & Myers (law firm) 1981–93; defence and foreign policy adviser to Bill Clinton during 1992 presidential campaign; Dir Arms Control and Disarmament Agency (ACDA) 1993–97; Acting Under-Sec. of State for Arms Control and Int. Security 1997–2001; Democrat. *Leisure interests:* flying, scuba diving, playing bluegrass and country music. *Address:* c/o Office of the Under-Secretary, 2201 C Street, NW, Room 7208, Washington, DC 20520, USA.

HOLYFIELD, Evander; American boxer; b. 19 Oct. 1962, Atlanta, Ga; s. of Anna Laura Holyfield; Bronze Medal, 1984 Olympic Games; World Boxing Asscn (WBA) cruiserweight title 1986; Int. Boxing Fed. cruiserweight title 1987; World Boxing Council (WBC) cruiserweight title 1988; world heavyweight champion 1990–92, 1993–94, 1996–99 (following defeat of Mike Tyson, q.v. Nov. 1996), defended title against Tyson 1997 (Tyson disqualified for biting off part of Holyfield's ear); defended IBF heavyweight title against Michael Moorer 1997; defended WBA and IBF titles and contested WBC title, against Lennox Lewis (q.v.) March 1999, bout declared a draw; lost to Lennox Lewis Nov. 1999; 2000–01 WBA heavyweight champion; record at end of 2002 – 38 wins, 6 losses, 2 draws; f. Real Deal Record Label 1999; f. Holyfield Foundation to help inner-city youth; Espy Boxer of the Decade 1990–2000. *Leisure interests:* all kinds of music, American football. *Address:* Main Events, 390 Murray Hill Parkway, East Rutherford, NJ 07073, USA.

HOLZER, Jenny, MFA; American artist; b. 29 July 1950, Gallipolis, Ohio; d. of Richard Vornholt Holzer and Virginia Beasley Holzer; m. Michael Andrew Glier 1984; one d.; ed Ohio Univ., Rhode Island School of Design, Whitney Museum of American Art Ind. Study Program; became working artist in New York 1977; special projects and comms. 1978– include "Green Table", Univ. of Calif., San Diego 1993, "Lustmord", Süddeutsche Zeitung Magazin, no. 46, Germany, "Black Garden", Nordhorn, Germany 1994, "Allentown Benches", Allentown, Pa 1995, "Erlauf Peace Monument", Erlauf, Austria 1995, installation at Schiphol Airport, Amsterdam, Netherlands 1995, Biennale di Firenze, Florence, Italy 1996, installation for Hamburger Kunsthalle, Hamburg, Germany 1996, perm. installation at Guggenheim Museum, Bilbao, Literaturhaus Munich, Germany, Oskar Maria Graf Memorial 1997, Kunsthalle Zürich, Switzerland; Fellow American Acad., Berlin 2000; Hon. D. Arts (Ohio Univ.) 1994, (Williams Coll. 2000); Golden Lion Award for Best Pavilion, 44th Venice Biennale, Italy 1990, Gold Medals for Title and Design, Art Directors' Club of Europe 1993, Skowhegan Medal for Installation, New York 1994, Crystal Award, for outstanding contrib. to cross-cultural understanding, World Econ. Forum, Switzerland 1996. *Solo exhibitions include:* Rüdiger Schöttle Gallery, Munich, Germany 1980, Barbara Gladstone Gallery, New York 1983, Dallas Museum of Art, Texas 1984, Des Moines Art Center, Iowa 1986, Am Hof, Vienna, Austria 1986, Rhona Hoffman Gallery, Chicago 1987, Contemporary Arts Museum, Houston 1987, Brooklyn Museum, New York 1988, American Pavilion, 44th Venice Biennale, Italy 1990, Art Tower Mito, Japan 1994, Bergen Museum of Art, Norway 1994, Williams Coll. Museum of Art, Williamstown, Mass. 1995, Kunstmuseum Kartause Ittingen, Warth, Switzerland 1996, Index Gallery, Osaka, Japan 1997, Yvon Lambert Gallery, Paris 1998, Inst. Cultural Itau, São Paulo 1998, Centro Cultural Banco do Brasil, Rio de Janeiro 1999, Neue Nationalgaleri, Berlin 2001, Musee d'Art Contemporain de Bordeaux 2001, Baltic Centre, Gateshead 2001. *Group exhibitions include:* Museum of Modern Art, New York 1988, 1990, 1996, Guggenheim Museum, New York 1996, Centre Pompidou, Paris, France 1996, Nat. Gallery Australia, Canberra 1998, Rhona Hofman Gallery, USA 1998, Oslo Museum of Contemporary Art 2000. *Publications:* A Little Knowledge 1979, Black Book 1980, Eating Through Living 1981, Truisms and Essays 1983. *Leisure interests:* reading, riding. *Address:* 80 Hewitts Road, Hoosick Falls, NY 12090, USA. *Telephone:* (518) 686-9323 (Office). *Fax:* (518) 686-9019 (Office). *E-mail:* jh@jennyholzer.com, gallery@cheimread.com (Office).

HOMBACH, Bodo; German politician and business executive; b. 19 Aug. 1952, Mülheim; m. 1977; ed Düsseldorf Polytechnic, Duisberg Comprehensive Univ., Hagen Correspondence Univ.; fmrly trainee telecommunications worker, youth affairs spokesman and youth worker; Sec. German TU Fed. (DGB) North Rhine Westphalia 1974–76; Educ. Policy Sec. Educ. and Sciences TU North Rhine Westphalia 1976–77, Regional Business Man. 1977–79; Deputy State Business Man. German Social Democratic Party (SPD) North Rhine Westphalia 1979–81, Business Man. 1981–91, Deputy Chair. Mülheim Dist 1993, Deputy Chair. Niederrhein Dist 1998; Fed. Minister Without Portfolio and Head Fed. Chancellery 1998–99; mem. North Rhine Westphalia Landtag 1990–98, Chair. Parl. Inquiry Comm. 1992–94, Parl. Econ. Affairs Spokesman 1994–98, State Minister for Econ. and Medium Industry, Tech. and Transport June–Oct. 1998; Dir Marketing, Org. and Co. Strategy Preussag Handel GmbH (fmrly Salzgitter Stahl AG), Man. 1992–98, Business Man. Preussag Int. GmbH 1995–98; Special Co-ordinator of the Stability Pact for S. Eastern Europe 1998–2001; Man. Westdeutsche Allgemeine Zeitung press group 2001–. *Publications include:* Der SPD von innen, Die Zukunft der Arbeit, Aufruf für eine Geschichte des Volkes in Nordrhein-Westfalia, Die Lokomotive in voller Fahrt der Räder wechseln, Anders Leben, Sozialstaat 2000, Die Kraft der Region: Nordrhein-Westfalia in Europa, The Politics of the New Centre 2002. *Address:* Zeitungsverlagsgesellschaft E. Brost und J. Funke GmbH & Co., Friedrichstr. 34-38, 45123 Essen, Germany. *Telephone:* (201) 804-0. *Fax:* (201) 804-2841. *Website:* www2.waz.de.

HOME, 15th Earl of, cr. 1605; **David Alexander Cospatrick Douglas-Home,** CVO, CBE, MA; British banker; b. 20 Nov. 1943, Coldstream, Scotland; s. of the late Rt. Hon. Alexander Frederick, Lord Home of the Hirsel and Elizabeth Hester Alington; m. Jane Margaret Williams-Wynne; one s. two d.; ed Eton Coll., Christ Church Oxford; Dir. Morgan Grenfell & Co. Ltd. 1974–99; Chair. Coutts & Co. 1999–, MAN Ltd. 2000–; Trustee The Grosvenor Estate 1993–. *Address:* Coutts & Co., 440 Strand, London, WC2R 0QS (Office); 99 Dovehouse Street, London, SW3 6JZ, England (Home). *Telephone:* (20) 7753-1000 (Office); (20) 7352-9060 (Home). *Fax:* (20) 7753-1066 (Office).

HONDROS, Ernest Demetrios, CMG, DSc, FRS; British scientist; b. 18 Feb. 1930, Kastellorizo, Dodecanese, Greece; s. of Demetrios Hondros and Athanasia Paleologos; m. Sissel Kristine Garder-Olsen 1968; two s.; ed Univ. of Melbourne, Australia, Univ. of Paris; CSIRO Tribophysics Lab., Melbourne 1955–59; Research Fellow, Laboratoire de Chimie Minérale, Univ. of Paris 1959–62; Sr Research Fellow, Nat. Physical Lab. 1962, Prin. Research Fellow 1965, Sr Prin. Research Fellow 1974, Supt Materials Div. 1979–85; Dir Petten Establishment, EC (now EU) Jt Research Centre, Netherlands 1985–95, Dir Inst. for Advanced Materials 1989–95; Visiting Prof. Imperial Coll. of Science, Tech. and Medicine 1988–; Hatfield Memorial Lecturer, Univ. of Sheffield 1986; Hon. mem. Soc. Française de Metallurgie; Hon. DSc (Univ. of London) 1997; Rosenhain Medal, Howe Medal, Griffiths Medal. *Publications:* Energetics of Solid-Solid Interfaces 1969, Grain Boundary Segregation (with M. P. Seah) 1973. *Leisure interest:* reading. *Address:* 37 Ullswater Crescent, London, SW15 3RG, England. *Telephone:* (20) 8549-9526. *Fax:* (20) 8549-9526.

HONECKER, Margot; German politician; b. (as Margot Feist), 17 April 1927, Halle; m. Erich Honecker 1953 (deceased); one d.; Co-Founder Anti-Fascist Youth Cttee, Halle 1945; mem. CP 1945–89; Sec., Freie Deutsche Jugend (FDJ) Cttee, Sachsen-Anhalt; Chair. Young Pioneers and Sec., Cen. Council, FDJ 1949–53; mem. Volkskammer 1949–54, 1967–89; mem. Cen. Cttee Socialist Unity Party (SED) 1963–89; univ. training in USSR 1953–54; Head Teacher Training Dept, Ministry of Educ. 1955–58, Deputy Minister of Educ. 1958–63, Minister of Educ. 1963–89; with husband in Moscow 1991, sought asylum in Chilean Embassy, Moscow Dec. 1991; left Embassy for Chile July 1992; mem. Acad. of Pedagogical Sciences; Dr. hc; Karl-Marx-Orden, Vaterländischer Verdienstorden in Gold, Held der Arbeit and other decorations. *Publication:* On Educational Policy and Pedagogics in the German Democratic Republic 1986. *Address:* c/o Rheinisch-Westfälische Akademie der Wissenschaften, Philosophy Section, Palmenstrasse 16, 4000 Düsseldorf, Germany (Office).

HONEGGER, Eric; Swiss business executive and politician; b. 29 April 1946, Zürich; m.; ed Univ. of Zürich; Sec. for City and Canton of Zürich, Free Democratic Party (FDP) 1975–79; with Gesellschaft zur Förderung der Schweizerischen Wirtschaft (Soc. for the Promotion of Swiss Trade and Industry) 1980–81; Dir Swiss printing industry employers' Asscn 1982–87; rep. of Zürich Canton on Bd of Dirs. SAirGroup 1993, mem. Bd Exec. Cttee 1995, Chair. 2000–; municipal councillor, Rüschlikon 1974–78; Zürich Cantonal Councillor (FDP) 1979–87; Cantonal Govt Councillor 1987–99, Minister of Public Works 1987–91, of Finance 1991; Prime Minister of Zürich Cantonal Govt 1993–94, 1998–99; Pres. Cantonal Govts' Conf. 1993–95; Col Transport Corps 1994–. *Address:* SAirGroup, P.O. Box 8058, Zürich Airport, Switzerland (Office). *Telephone:* (1) 8125600 (Office). *Fax:* (1) 8129071 (Office). *E-mail:* ehonegge@sairgroup.com (Office).

HONEYCOMBE, Sir Robert William Kerr, Kt, PhD, DSc, F.R.ENG., FRS; Australian professor of metallurgy; b. 2 May 1921, Melbourne; s. of William Honeycombe and Rachael (Kerr) Honeycombe; m. June Collins 1947; two d.; ed Geelong Coll. and Univ. of Melbourne; research officer CSIRO (Australia) 1942–47; ICI Research Fellow, Cavendish Lab., Cambridge 1948–49; Royal Soc. Armourers and Brasiers' Research Fellow, Cavendish Lab. 1949–51; Sr Lecturer in Physical Metallurgy, Univ. of Sheffield 1951–55, Prof. 1955–66; Goldsmiths' Prof. of Metallurgy, Univ. of Cambridge 1966–84, Prof. Emer. 1984–; Fellow, Trinity Hall, Cambridge 1966–73, Hon. Fellow 1975–; Pres. Clare Hall, Cambridge 1973–80, Fellow 1980–88, Fellow Emer. 1988–; Pres. Inst. of Metallurgists 1977, Metals Soc. 1980–81; Treasurer and Vice-Pres. Royal Soc. 1986–92; several hon. degrees; Rosenhain Medallist (Inst. of Metals) 1959, Beilby Gold Medallist 1963, St Claire Deville Medallist 1971, R. J. Mehl Medallist 1976. *Publications:* The Plastic Deformation of Metals 1968, Steels: Microstructure and Properties 1981. *Leisure interests:* walking, gardening, music, photography. *Address:* Department of Materials Science and Metallurgy, University of Cambridge, Pembroke Street, Cambridge, CB2 3QZ (Office); Barrabool, 46 Main Street, Hardwick, Cambridge, CB3 7QS, England (Home). *Telephone:* (1223) 334300 (Office); (1954) 210501 (Home). *Fax:* (1954) 334567 (Office).

HONEYMAN, Janice Lynne; South African actress, director and writer; b. 14 Jan. 1949, Cape Town; d. of Frank Gordon Honeyman and Marie Evelyn Honeyman; ed Univ. of Cape Town (performers diploma); Dir and actress with Market Theatre Co. and Performing Arts Council of Transvaal 1970–; Dir Dogge's Troupe-Interaction, London 1977–78; Founder mem. Market Theatre Co., Resident Dir 1984–85, Trustee Market Theatre Foundation 1985–; Trustee Foundation for Equality 1993–; Exec. and Artistic Dir Johannesburg Civic Theatre 1993–2000, Artistic Dir 2000–; freelance Dir RSC 1988–89 and of opera, operetta and musicals; Assoc. Artist PACT; Ernest Oppenheimer Award for Resident Dir, Market Theatre, SA Young Artists Award; Breytenbach Epathalon, A. A. Vita Award for directing; Gallo Award for Best Performance, Johnnie Walker Black Label Achievers Award. *Publications:* This is for Keeps (with V. Cooke and D. Keogh) 1984, Knickerbocker Knockabout 1988. *Leisure interests:* reading, opera, swimming, snorkelling, travelling. *Address:* 8A Seymour Street, Westdene, Johannesburg 2092, South Africa. *Telephone:* (11) 4033408 (Office); (11) 4777626 (Home). *Fax:* (11) 4033412.

HONG GUOFAN; Chinese molecular biochemist; b. Dec. 1939, Ningbo, Zhejiang Prov.; ed Fudan Univ., Shanghai; researcher, Biochemical Research Inst., Chinese Acad. of Sciences 1964–; researcher, MRC Molecular Biological Lab. in UK 1979–83; Research Prof. Shanghai Inst. of Biochemistry; Fellow, Chinese Acad. of Sciences 1997; Dir Nat. Genetics Research Centre 1993–; now Prof. Coll. of Pharmaceuticals and Biotech., Tianjin Univ. *Address:* Dept of Molecular and Cellular Pharmacology, College of Pharmaceuticals and Biotechnology, Tianjin University, 92 Weijin Road, Tianjin 300072; Chinese Academy of Sciences, 17 Zhongguacun Lu, Beijing 100864, People's Republic of China (Office). *Telephone:* (22) 27906148. *Fax:* (22) 23358706. *Website:* www.tjn.edu.cn.

HONG HU; Chinese politician; b. June 1940, Jinzhai Co., Anhui Prov.; ed Beijing Industrial Inst.; joined CCP 1965; Vice-Sec.-Gen., Sec.-Gen. State Comm. for Econ. Restructuring 1982–91; Vice-Dir State Comm. for Econ. Restructuring 1991–98; mem. Comm. of Securities of the State Council 1992–98; mem. CCP Cen. Cttee for Discipline Inspection 1992; mem. 15th CCP Cen. Cttee 1997–; Deputy Gov. Shanxi Prov. 1998–99, Gov. 1999; Gov. Jilin Prov. 1999–. *Address:* Office of the Governor, Jilin Provincial People's Government, Changchun, Jilin Province, People's Republic of China.

HONG JAE-HYONG; South Korean politician; b. Cheongju City, N Chungcheong Prov.; ed Seoul Nat. Univ.; joined Foreign Exchange Bureau, Ministry of Finance 1963; later worked at IBRD, Washington, DC; Admin., Korean Customs Admin.; Pres. Export-Import Bank of Korea, Korea Exchange Bank; Minister of Finance 1993; Deputy Prime Minister, Minister of Finance and Econs 1994–96. *Address:* c/o Ministry of Finance, 1 Jungang-dong, Gwacheon City, Gyeouggi Province, Republic of Korea.

HONG QIAN, (Tscha Hung), PhD; Chinese philosopher and university professor; b. 21 Oct. 1909, Fuki; mem. Vienna Circle 1931–36; Research Fellow, New Coll. Oxford, UK 1945–47, Visiting Fellow Queen's Coll. 1980, 1984, Trinity Coll. 1980; Dir Philosophy Inst., Beijing Univ. 1984–; Hon. Pres. Chinese Soc. of Contemporary Foreign Philosophy 1980–, Sino-British Summer Coll. in Beijing 1988–; mem. Editorial Advisory Bd Vienna Circle Collection, Dordrecht, Netherlands 1990–; Dr. hc (Vienna) 1984. *Publications:* Ayer and The Vienna Circle, in The Philosophy of Ayer 1992, Das Kausalproblem in der heutigen Physick, in Studien zur Österreichen Philosophie Verlag. *Address:* 2nd Apt. No. 232, Zhong Quan Yuan, Beijing University, 100871 Beijing, People's Republic of China.

HONG SONG NAM; North Korean politician; b. 1924, Kangwon Prov.; ed Kimilsung Univ.; Chief of a Korean Workers' Party Cen. Cttee Dept 1970; Deputy Premier and Chair. State Planning Comm. 1973, 1986; Assoc. mem., Politburo 1982, Sec. of Party chapter, S. Pyongan Prov. 1982, Full mem. of Politburo and First Deputy Premier 1986, Assoc. mem. 1989; Acting Premier of the Democratic People's Repub. of Korea Feb. 1997–Sept. 1998, Premier Sept. 1998–. *Address:* Office of the Premier, Pyongyang, Democratic People's Republic of Korea (Office).

HONG XUEZHI, Gen.; Chinese army officer; b. 1913, Jinzhai Co., Anhui Prov.; joined CCP 1929; Deputy Commdr, army corps, 4th Field Army 1949; Commdr Guangdong Mil. Region 1949–50; mem. Guangzhou Mil. Control Comm. 1949–50; Political Commissar, 16th Corps 1950; Dir Logistics Dept Chinese People's Volunteers in Korea 1952; mem. Nat. Defence Council 1954–59; Deputy Dir PLA Logistics Dept 1954–56, Dir 1956–59; alt.-mem. 8th Cen. Cttee of CCP 1956; mem. Standing Cttee, 5th NPC 1978; Dir, Gen. Office for Nat. Defence Industry 1978–79; Dir 2nd Office of Nat. Defence 1979–80; Vice-Chair. Cttee to Examine Proposals, 2nd Session, 5th NPC 1979; mem. 11th Cen. Cttee of CCP 1979; mem. 12th Cen. Cttee CCP 1982–85; Dir PLA Gen. Logistics Dept 1980–85, Political Commr 1985–87; mem. and Deputy Sec.-Gen. Cen. Mil. Comm. 1982–; mem. Cen. Party Consolidation Guidance Comm. 1983; Vice-Chair. Cen. Patriotic Public Health Campaign Cttee 1983; Head Leading Group of All-Army Financial and Econ. Discipline Inspection, CCP Cen. Mil. Comm. 1986; Chair. PLA Greening Cttee 1984; Vice-Chair. Cen. Greening Cttee 1983; Hon. Vice-Pres. Beijing Social Welfare Foundation 1984; promoted Gen. PLA 1988; Sr Adviser China Soc. of Mil. Sciences 1991–; mem. Presidium 14th CCP Nat. Congress 1992, Vice-Chair. 8th Nat. Cttee CPPCC 1993–98, Hon. Pres. Handball Asscn. *Address:* Office of the Director, People's Liberation Army General Logistics Department, Beijing, People's Republic of China.

HONIG, Edwin, MA; American professor of comparative literature and poet; b. 3 Sept. 1919, New York; s. of Abraham David Honig and Jane Freundlich; m. 1st Charlotte Gilchrist 1940 (died 1963); m. 2nd Margot S. Dennes 1963 (divorced 1978); two s.; ed Univ. of Wisconsin; Instructor in English Purdue Univ. 1942–43, New York Univ. and Ill. Inst. Tech. 1946–47, Univ. of NM 1947–48, Claremont Coll. 1949, Harvard Univ. 1949–52, Briggs-Copeland Asst Prof. of English, Harvard 1952–57; mem. Faculty Brown Univ. 1957, Prof. of English 1960–82, of Comparative Literature 1962–82, Chair. Dept of English 1967, Prof. Emer. 1983–; Visiting Prof. Univ. of Calif., Davis 1964–65; Mellon Prof. Boston Univ. 1977; Dir Copper Beech Press; Guggenheim Fellow 1948, 1962; Amy Lowell Travelling Poetry Fellow 1968; Golden Rose Award New England Poetry Club 1961, Poetry Prize, Saturday Review 1956, Nat. Inst. of Arts and Letters Award 1966, NEA Award (in poetry) 1980, (in transl.) 1983, Columbia Univ. Translation Center Nat. Award 1985; Kt of St James of the Sword, Portugal 1987, Kt of Queen Isabel, Spain 1996. *Publications:* (poems) The Moral Circus 1955, The Gazebos 1960, Survivals 1964, Spring Journal 1968, Four Springs 1972, Shake a Spear With Me, John Berryman 1974, At Sixes 1974, The Affinities of Orpheus 1976, Selected Poems (1955–1976) 1979, Interrupted Praise 1983, Gifts of Light 1983, God Talk 1992, The Imminence of Love: Poems 1962–92 1993; (plays) The Widow 1953, The Phantom Lady 1964, Life is a Dream, Calisto and Melibea (play/libretto) 1972, Ends of the World and Other Plays 1983, Calderón: Six Plays 1993; (selected prose of Fernando Pessoa) Always Astonished 1988; (criticism) García Lorca 1944, Dark Conceit: The Making of Allegory 1959, Calderón and the Seizures of Honor 1972, The Poet's Other Voice 1985; (stories) Foibles and Fables of an Abstract Man 1979; (anthologies) (with Oscar Williams): The Mentor Book of Major American Poets 1961, The Major Metaphysical Poets 1968; Spenser 1968; also translations of works by García Lorca, Calderón de la Barca, Fernando Pessoa, Miguel Hernández and Lope de Vega; produced opera Calisto and Melibea 1979, play Life is a Dream 1988, The Phantom Lady; A Glass of Green Tea With Honig 1993. *Leisure interests:* trees, ponds, woods, travel abroad: Spain, Portugal, China. *Address:* Brown University, Box 1852, Providence, RI 02912 (Office); 229 Medway Street, Apt. 305, Providence, RI 02906, USA (Home). *Telephone:* (401) 831-1027.

HONJO, Tasuku, MD, PhD; Japanese academic; b. 27 Jan. 1942, Kyoto; s. of Shoichi Honjo and Ryu Honjo; m. Shigeko Kotani 1969; one s. one d.; ed Ube High School and Kyoto Univ.; Fellow, Carnegie Inst. of Washington, Baltimore 1971–73; Visiting Fellow and Assoc. Lab. of Molecular Genetics, Nat. Insts. of Health 1973–74; Asst Prof. Dept of Physiological Chem. and Nutrition, Faculty of Medicine, Univ. of Tokyo 1974–79; Prof. Dept of Genetics, Osaka Univ. School of Medicine 1979–84; Prof. Dept of Medical Chem. Faculty of Medicine Kyoto Univ. 1984–, Dir Center for Molecular Biology and Genetics 1989–97; Hon. mem. American Asscn of Immunologists; Asahi Award 1981; Erwin von Baelz Award 1985; Takeda Medical Award 1988; Behring-Kitsato

Prize 1992, Japan Acad. Award 1996. *Publications:* Immunoglobulin Genes (ed.) 1989, Seppuku and Autoimmunity 1992. *Address:* Department of Medical Chemistry, Kyoto University, Yoshida-Honmachi, Sakyo-ku, Kyoto 606-8501, Japan. *Telephone:* (75) 753-7531. *Fax:* (75) 753-4388. *Website:* www .kyoto-u.ac.jp (Office).

HONKAPOHJA, Seppo Mikko Sakari, DSocSc; Finnish professor of economics; b. 7 March 1951, Helsinki; m. Sirkku Anna-Maija Honkapohja 1973; one s. one d.; ed United World Coll. of the Atlantic, UK, Univ. of Helsinki; Scientific Dir Yrjö Jahnsson Foundation 1975–87; Prof. of Econs, Turku School of Econs and Business Admin. 1987–91, Prof.-at-Large (Docent) 1992–; Prof.-at-Large (Docent) of Econs, Univ. of Helsinki 1981–91, Acting Prof. of Econs (Econometrics) 1985–87, Prof. of Econs 1992–; Visiting Lecturer and Scholar, Harvard Univ., USA 1978–79; Visiting Assoc. Prof. of Econs, Stanford Univ., USA 1982–83; Sr Fellow Acad. of Finland 1982–83, Acad. Prof. 1989–95; Man. Ed. Scandinavian Journal of Econs 1984–88; Ed. European Econ. Review 1993–; mem. Bd Finnish Econ. Asscn 1989–91, Finnish Soc. for European Studies 1994–; mem. Council, European Econ. Asscn 1985–86, 1999–2003; Vice-Chair. Kansallis Foundation for Financial Research 1989–96; mem. Governing Body The Finnish Cultural Foundation 1994–, Chair. 1997–2001; mem. Advisory Bd Journal of Econ. Surveys 1994–; mem. Supervisory Bd, Okopankki Ltd 1996–, Chair 1997–; mem. Finnish Acad. of Science and Letters, Academia Europaea; Fellow of the Econometric Soc.; Jaakko Honko Medal (Helsinki School of Economics and Business Administration) 1998. *Publications:* Limits and Problems of Taxation 1985; Ed. several books including The State of Macroeconomics 1990, Macroeconomic Modelling and Policy Implications 1993, Learning and Expectations in Macroeconomics 2001; numerous articles in journals. *Leisure interest:* fishing. *Address:* Faculty of Social Sciences, P.O. Box 54, Unioninkatu 37, University of Helsinki, FIN-00014, Finland. *Telephone:* (9) 19124876. *Fax:* (9) 19124877. *Website:* www.valt.helsinki.fi (Office).

HONORÉ, HE Cardinal Jean, DTheol; French ecclesiastic; b. 13 Aug. 1920, Saint Brice en Coglès; ed Collège de St Malon, Grand Séminaire de Rennes, Inst. Catholique de Paris, Ecole Pratique des Hautes Etudes, Paris; fmr. Archbishop of Tours, Archbishop Emer. 1997–; cr. Cardinal 2001; Prof. of Letters and Theology, Rector, Université Catholique d'Angers; Dr. hc (Louvain la Neuve); Commdr Légion d'honneur 2001. *Publications:* Itinéraire spirituel de Newman 1964, La fidélité d'une conscience 1987, La pensée christologique de Newman 1996, Fais paraître ton jour 2000. *Address:* 1 Allée de la Rocaille, 37390 La Membrolle sur Ch., France (Home). *Fax:* (2) 47-41-15-83 (Home).

HOOD, Leroy Edward, MD, PhD; American biologist; b. 10 Oct. 1938, Missoula, Mon.; s. of Thomas Edward Hood and Myrtle Evylan Wadsworth; m. Valerie A. Logan 1963; one s. one d.; ed Calif. Inst. of Tech. and Johns Hopkins School of Medicine; NIH Predoctoral Fellowship, Calif. Inst. of Tech. 1963–64, NIH Postdoctoral Fellowship 1964–67; Sr Investigator, Immunology Branch, GL&C, NCI, Nat. Insts. of Health, Bethesda, Md 1967–70; Asst Prof. of Biology Calif. Inst. of Tech. 1970–73, Assoc. Prof. 1973–75, Prof. 1975–77, Bowles Prof. of Biology 1977–92, Chair. Div. of Biology 1980–89, Dir Cancer Center 1981; Gates Prof. and Chair. of Molecular Biotech. Univ. of Wash. 1992–99; Dir NSF Science and Tech. Center for Molecular Biotech. 1989–2000; Founder, Pres. and Dir Inst. for Systems Biology 1999–; Fellow American Acad. of Microbiology; mem. NAS, American Acad. of Arts and Sciences, AAAS, American Asscn of Immunologists, American Philosophical Soc., American Soc. for Clinical Investigation, American Soc. of Biological Chemists, Asscn of American Physicians, Int. Soc. of Molecular Evolution, Sigma Xi, Soc. for Integrative and Comparative Biology; Hon. DSc (Montana State) 1986, (Mt Sinai School of Medicine, City Univ. of New York) 1987, (Univ. of British Columbia) 1988, (Univ. of S Calif.) 1989, (Wesleyan) 1992, (Whitman Coll.) 1995, (Bates Coll.) 1999; Hon. DHumLitt (Johns Hopkins) 1990; Albert Lasker Basic Medical Research Award 1987, Commonwealth Award of Distinguished Service 1989, Cetus Award for Biotechnology 1989, American Coll. of Physicians Award 1990, Ciba-Geigy/Drew Award 1993, Lynen Medal 1994, Distinguished Alumnus Award, Johns Hopkins Univ. 1994, Beckman Lecturer Award 1998, Distinguished Service Award, American Asscn for Clinical Chem. 1998. *Publications:* co-author of more than 40 books on immunology and biochemistry and of more than 500 papers in learned journals. *Leisure interests:* mountaineering, climbing, running, photography, science fiction. *Address:* Institute for Systems Biology, 4225 Roosevelt Way, NE, Suite 200, Seattle, WA 98105, USA (Office). *Telephone:* (206) 732-1201 (Office). *Fax:* (206) 732-1254 (Office). *E-mail:* lhood@systemsbiology .org (Office). *Website:* www.systemsbiology.org (Office).

't HOOFT, Gerardus; Netherlands professor of theoretical physics; b. 5 July 1946, Den Helder; s. of H. 't Hooft and M. A. van Kampen; m. Albertha A. Schik 1972; two d.; ed Dalton Lyceum Gymnasium beta, The Hague, Rijks Universiteit, Utrecht; Fellow CERN (Theoretical Physics Div.), Geneva 1972–74; Asst Prof., Univ. of Utrecht 1974–77, Prof. of Theory of Solids 1977–; mem. Koninklijke Acad. van Wetenschappen, Letteren en Schone Kunsten v. Belgïe, Koninklijke Nederlandse Acad. van Wetenschappen; Foreign Assoc. NAS; Foreign Hon. mem. American Acad. of Arts and Sciences, Acad. des Sciences; Fellow and CPhys Inst. of Physics (London) 2000; Dr hc (Chicago) 1981, (Leuven) 1996, (Bologna) 1998; W. Prins Prize 1974, Akzo Prize 1977, Dannie Heineman Prize 1979, Wolf Prize 1982, Spinoza Premium 1995, Pius XI Medal 1983, Lorentz Medal 1986, Franklin Medal 1995, G. C. Wick Medal 1997, High Energy Physics Prize (European Physical Soc.) 1999, Nobel Prize

for Physics (jtly) 1999. *Publications:* Under the Spell of the Gauge Principle 1994, In Search of the Ultimate Building Blocks 1996; papers on Renormalization of Yang-Mills Fields, magnetic monopoles, Instantons, Gauge theories, quark confinement, quantum gravity and black holes. *Address:* Faculty of Physics and Astronomy, University of Utrecht, Prinetonplein 5, 3584 CC Utrecht (Office); University of Utrecht, Spinoza Institute, PO Box 80.195, 3508 TD Utrecht, Netherlands. *Telephone:* (30) 2533284 (Office); (30) 2537549; (30) 2535928. *Fax:* (30) 2539282 (Office); (30) 2535937. *Website:* www.phys.uu.nl/~thooft (Home).

HOOGENDOORN, Piet; Netherlands business executive; b. 1946; Man. Partner Deloitte & Touche Netherlands 1990–2001; Vice-Chair. Deloitte Touche Tohmatsu Global Bd 1999–2000, Chair. July 2000–. *Address:* Deloitte Touche Tohmatsu, 1633 Broadway, New York, NY 10019, USA (Office). *Telephone:* (212) 492-4000 (Office). *Fax:* (212) 492-4111 (Office).

HOOGLANDT, Jan Daniel, DSc; Netherlands steel manufacturing executive; b. 15 Feb. 1926, Tangier, Morocco; m.; four c.; ed Hilversum Gymnasium, Municipal Univ. of Amsterdam; joined Koninklijke Nederlandsche Hoogovens en Staalfabrieken NV 1954 as Asst in Econ. Dept 1954; retd 1988 as Chair. Bd Hoogovens Groep BV; Chair. Supervisory Bd ABN/AMRO –1996, Ned. Participatie Maatschappij NV; mem. Supervisory Bd Koninklijke Nederlandsche Hoogovens en Staalfabrieken NV –1996, NV Koninklijke Nederlandse Petroleum Maatschappij –1996, Heineken NV; Order of the Netherlands Lion 1976; Commdr Order Oranje Nassau 1988. *Address:* Zwartweg 16, 2111 AJ Aerdenhout, Netherlands.

HOOKER, Charlie (Charles Raymond); British artist; b. 1 June. 1953, London; s. of Raymond C. Hooker and Daphne Hooker; m. Stephanie J. Burden 1980; one s.; ed Purley Grammar School, Croydon Coll. of Art and Brighton Polytechnic; Founder mem. The Artistics (music ensemble) 1972–75, 2B Butlers Wharf (art space) 1974–75; Visiting Lecturer, Chelsea, Croydon, Winchester, Trent, Cardiff, Central, Brighton, Newport, Newcastle, Camberwell Schools of Art/Polytechnics 1977–; part-time lecturer Brighton Polytechnic 1990–92; External Examiner, Chelsea School of Art 1995–; Sr Lecturer Camberwell Coll. 1990–92; Sr Lecturer/Area Leader—Sculpture, Univ. of Brighton 1992–; Artist in Residence at Amherst Jr and Hatcham Wood Secondary Schools 1985; Co-ordinator, Artists' Open Week, Camberwell School of Art 1989; several one-man and group shows of maquettes and drawings and numerous installations and performances in UK, Europe, America and Australia 1975–; works in Arts Council collection and pvt. collections and perm. public outdoor work in UK; Art/Science projects with Science Museum, London and Herstmonceux Science Centre 1995; published discussions in Performance and in Aspects 1980, 1984, 1986, De Appel 1987. *Radio interviews:* BBC Radio Nottingham 1981, BBC Radio Cambridge 1986, Warsaw Radio 1988. *TV interviews:* BBC Look North 1983, Anglia TV 1985, W Australia TV News 1985; published video recording 'Charlie Hooker Talks to Mike Archer' (Havering Educational) 1988. *Audio recordings:* Restricted Movement 1982, Transitions 1984, Charlie Hooker and Performers 1987, Wave-Wall/Dust and a Shadow 1991 for Audio Arts, Separate Elements 1992. *Leisure interest:* walking. *Address:* 28 Whippingham Road, Brighton, Sussex, BN2 3PG, England. *Telephone:* (1273) 600048. *Fax:* (1273) 643128.

HOOKER, Morna Dorothy, MA, DD, PhD; British professor of divinity; b. 19 May 1931, Surrey; d. of P. F. Hooker and L. Hooker (née Riley); m. Rev. Dr. W. D. Stacey 1978 (died 1993); one step-s. two step-d.; ed Univ. of Bristol; Research Fellow, Univ. of Durham 1959–61; Lecturer in New Testament, King's Coll. London 1961–70, Fellow 1979–; Lecturer in Theology, Univ. of Oxford 1970–76, Keble Coll. Oxford 1972–76; Fellow, Linacre Coll. Oxford 1970–76, Hon. Fellow 1980–; Visiting Fellow, Clare Hall, Cambridge 1974; Lady Margaret Prof. of Divinity, Univ. of Cambridge 1976–98, Prof. Emer. 1998–; Fellow, Robinson Coll. Cambridge 1977–; Jt Ed. Journal of Theological Studies 1985–; Pres. Soc. for New Testament Studies 1988–89; Visiting Prof. McGill Univ. 1968, Duke Univ. NC 1987, 1989; Hon. Fellow, Westminster Coll., Oxford 1995–; Hon. DLitt (Bristol) 1994; Hon. DD (Edinburgh) 1997. *Publications:* Jesus and the Servant 1959, The Son of Man in Mark 1967, Pauline Pieces 1979, Studying the New Testament 1979, The Message of Mark 1983, Continuity and Discontinuity 1986, From Adam to Christ 1990, A Commentary on the Gospel According to St Mark 1991, Not Ashamed of the Gospel 1994, The Signs of a Prophet 1997, Beginnings: Keys that Open the Gospels 1997. *Leisure interests:* molinology, music, walking. *Address:* Robinson College, Cambridge, CB3 9AN, England. *Telephone:* (1223) 339100. *Fax:* (1223) 351794. *E-mail:* mdh1000@cus.cam.ac.uk (Office).

HOOKWAY, Sir Harry Thurston, Kt, PhD; British administrator and librarian; b. 23 July 1921, London; s. of William Hookway and Bertha Hookway; m. Barbara Butler 1956; one s. one d.; ed Trinity School of John Whitgift and London Univ.; Asst Dir Nat. Chem. Lab. 1959; Dir UK Scientific Mission (N America), Scientific Attaché, Embassy, Washington, Scientific Adviser, High Comm., Ottawa 1960–64; Head, Information Div. Dept of Scientific and Industrial Research 1964–65; Chief Scientific Officer, Dept of Educ. and Science 1966–69, Asst Under-Sec. of State 1969–73; Deputy Chair. and Chief Exec. British Library Bd 1973–84; Pro-Chancellor Loughborough Univ. of Tech. 1987–93; mem. Royal Comm. on Historical Monuments (England) 1981–88; Chair. Publrs Data Bases Ltd 1984–87, LA Publishing Ltd 1986–89; Pres. The Library Asscn 1985; Dir Arundel Castle Trustees 1976–; Hon. Fellow Inst. of Information Scientists; Hon. LLD; Hon. DLitt;

Hon. FLA; Gold Medal Int. Asscn of Library Asscns 1985. *Publications:* papers in learned and professional journals. *Leisure interests:* music, travel. *Address:* 3 St James Green, Thirsk, North Yorks., YO7 1AF, England.

HOOLEY, Christopher, PhD, FRS; British university professor; b. 7 Aug. 1928, Edin.; s. of Leonard Joseph Hooley and Barbara Hooley; m. Birgitta Kniep 1954; two s.; ed Abbotsholme School and Corpus Christi Coll. Cambridge; Capt., Royal Army Educational Corps 1948–49; Fellow, Corpus Christi Coll. 1955–58; Lecturer in Math., Univ. of Bristol 1958–65; Prof. of Pure Math., Univ. of Durham 1965–67; Prof. of Pure Math. 1967–95, Distinguished Research Prof. 1995–, Head of Dept of Math. Wales Univ., Coll. of Cardiff (fmrly Univ. Coll. Cardiff) 1988–96, Dean of Faculty of Science 1973–76, Deputy Prin. Univ. Coll. Cardiff 1979–81, Wales Univ. Coll. of Cardiff 1991–94; Visiting mem., Inst. for Advanced Study, Princeton, USA on several occasions since 1970, Institut des Hautes Etudes Scientifiques, Paris 1984; Adam's Prize, Cambridge 1973, Sr Berwick Prize, London Math. Soc. 1980. *Publications:* Applications of Sieve Methods to the Theory of Numbers 1976, Recent Progress in Analytic Number Theory (Ed. with H. Halberstam) 1981. *Leisure interests:* antiquities and classic cars. *Address:* Rushmoor Grange, Backwell, Bristol, BS19 3BN, England. *Telephone:* (1275) 462363.

HOON, Rt. Hon. Geoffrey William, PC, MA; British politician; b. 6 Dec. 1953; s. of Ernest Hoon and June Hoon; m. Elaine Ann Dumelow 1981; one s. two d.; ed Jesus Coll., Cambridge; labourer at furniture factory 1972–73; Lecturer in Law, Leeds Univ. 1976–82; Visiting Prof. of Law, Univ. of Louisville 1979–80; called to the Bar, Gray's Inn 1978; in practice in Nottingham 1982–84; MP for Ashfield 1992–; Opposition Whip 1994–95; Opposition Spokesman on Information Tech. 1995–97; Parl. Sec., Lord Chancellor's Dept 1997–98, Minister of State 1998–99, Sec. of State for Defence 1999–; mem. for Derbyshire, European Parl. 1984–94, mem. Legal Affairs Cttee 1984–94; Vice-Chair. and Gov., Westminster Foundation 1994–97; mem. Labour Party. *Leisure interests:* cinema, cricket, football, music. *Address:* House of Commons, London, SW1A 0AA (Office); 8 Station Street, Kirby-in-Ashfield, Notts., NG17 7AR, England (Home). *Telephone:* (20) 7219-3477 (London) (Office); (1623) 720399 (Home). *Fax:* (20) 7219-2428 (London) (Office); (1623) 720398 (Home). *E-mail:* hcinfo@parliament.co .uk (London) (Office).

HOPE, Bob; American comedian; b. 29 May 1903, Eltham, England; m. Dolores Reade 1934; two adopted s. two adopted d.; first film 1938; since then has appeared in numerous films and radio and TV productions; numerous hon. degrees and awards including American Congressional Medal of Honor 1963, Award of Entertainment Hall of Fame 1975, four special Acad. Awards, American Hope Award 1988, Medal of Liberty, Hon. KBE and 48 hon. doctorates (1999), Nat. Medal of Arts 1995; Order of St Gregory the Great. *Films include:* College Swing, Big Broadcast, Give Me A Sailor, Thanks for the Memory 1938, Never Say Die, Some Like it Hot, Cat and the Canary 1939, Road to Singapore 1940, Nothing But the Truth, Road To Zanzibar, Louisiana Purchase, Caught in the Draft 1941, My Favourite Blonde, Star Spangled Rhythm, Road to Morocco 1942, They've Got Me Covered, Let's Face It 1943, Princess and the Pirate 1944, Road to Utopia 1945, Monsieur Beaucaire 1946, My Favourite Brunette 1947, Road To Rio, The Paleface 1948, Sorrowful Jones, The Great Lover 1949, Fancy Pants 1950, My Favourite Spy, Lemon Drop Kid 1951, Son of Paleface 1952, Off Limits, Here Come the Girls 1951, Road to Bali 1953, Casanova's Big Night 1954, Seven Little Foys 1955, Iron Petticoat, That Certain Feeling 1956, Beau James 1957, Paris Holiday 1958, Alias Jesse James 1959, The Facts of Life 1960, Bachelor in Paradise 1961, Road to Hong Kong 1962, Call Me Bwana 1963, A Global Affair 1964, I'll Take Sweden 1965, Boy, Did I Get a Wrong Number! 1966, Eight on the Lam 1967, Private Life of Sgt O'Farrell 1968, How to Commit Marriage 1969, The Road to Ruin 1972, Cancel My Reservation 1972, The Bob Hope Christmas Special 1987, The Bob Hope Birthday Special 1988, Bob Hope's Yellow Ribbon Party 1991, Bob Hope: A 90th Birthday Celebration 1993, Bob Hope: Laughing with the Presidents 1996. *Publications:* They've Got Me Covered 1941, I Never Left Home 1944, So This Is Peace 1946, Have Tux, Will Travel 1954, I Owe Russia $1200 1963, Five Women I Love 1966, The Last Christmas Show 1974, Road to Hollywood 1977, Confessions of a Hooker 1985, Don't Shoot, It's Only Me 1990, Dear Prez, I Wanna Tell Ya! 1996. *Address:* Hope Enterprises Inc., 210 North Pass Avenue, Suite 101, Burbank, CA 91505, USA (Office).

HOPE, Christopher, MA, FRSL; South African writer; b. 26 Feb. 1944, Johannesburg; s. of Dudley Mitford Hope and Kathleen Mary Hope; m. Eleanor Marilyn Klein; two s.; Cholmondeley Award 1972, David Higham Award 1981, Whitbread Prize for Fiction for Kruger's Alp 1985, C.N.A. Literary Award (S. Africa) 1989. *Publications:* A Separate Development 1981, Private Parts 1982, The King, the Cat and the Fiddle (with Yehudi Menuhin) 1983, Kruger's Alp 1984, The Dragon Wore Pink 1985, The Hottentot Room 1986, Black Swan 1987, White Boy Running 1988, My Chocolate Redeemer 1989, Moscow! Moscow! 1990, Serenity House 1992, The Love Songs of Nathan J. Swirsky 1993, Darkest England 1996. Poetry: Cape Drives 1974, In the Country of the Black Pig 1981, Englishman 1985, Me, the Moon and Elvis Presley 1997, Signs of the Heart 1999, Heaven Forbid 2002. *Leisure interest:* getting lost. *Address:* c/o Rogers, Coleridge & White, 20 Powis Mews, London, W11 1JN, England. *Telephone:* (20) 7221-3717. *Fax:* (20) 7229-9084.

HOPE, Most Rev. and Rt Hon David Michael, KCVO, PC, DPhil; British ecclesiastic; b. 14 April 1940; ed Wakefield Grammar School, Nottingham Univ., Linacre Coll. Oxford; Curate, St John's, Tuebrook, Liverpool 1965–70; Chaplain, Church of Resurrection, Bucharest 1967–68; Vicar, St Andrew's, Warrington 1970–74; Prin. St Stephen's House, Oxford 1974–82; Warden, Community of St Mary the Virgin, Wantage 1980–87; Vicar, All Saints', Margaret Street, London 1982–85; Bishop of Wakefield 1985–91, of London 1991–95; Archbishop of York 1995–; Prelate of the Order of the British Empire 1991–95; Dean of the Chapels Royal 1991–95. *Publications:* The Leonine Sacramentary 1971, Living the Gospel 1993. *Address:* Bishopthorpe, York, YO23 2GE, England. *Telephone:* (1904) 707021. *Fax:* (1904) 709204.

HOPE, Maurice; British boxer; b. 6 Dec. 1951, Antigua, West Indies; s. of Norris Hope and Sarah Andrew Hope; m. Patricia Hope; one s. two d.; ed Hackney Secondary Modern School, London; came to Britain 1961; rep. England and Great Britain as amateur boxer with Repton Amateur Boxing Club; quarter-finalist at Olympic Games, Munich 1972; professional boxer June 1973–1982; won British light-middleweight title from Larry Paul Nov. 1974, retained it v. Paul (Sept. 1975) and Tony Poole (April 1976); won Lonsdale Belt outright and became Commonwealth champion by beating Poole; lost to Bunny Sterling for vacant British middleweight title, June 1975; won European light-middleweight title from Vito Antuofermo, Rome Oct. 1976; drew with Eckhard Dagge for World Boxing Council (WBC) version of world light-middleweight title, Berlin March 1977; retained European title v. Frank Wissenbach, Hamburg (May 1977) and Joel Bonnetaz, Wembley (Nov. 1977); relinquished European title Sept. 1978; won WBC version of world light-middleweight title from Rocky Mattioli, San Remo March 1979; retained it v. Mike Baker (Sept. 1979), Mattioli (July 1980) and Carlos Herrera (Nov. 1980), lost it to Wilfredo Benitez (May 1981); 35 fights, 30 wins, one draw; now a trainer; flag carrier at 2002 Commonwealth Games opening ceremony. *Leisure interests:* table tennis, snooker, pool.

HOPE-CROSBY, Polly, FRSA; British artist, designer, writer and photographer; b. 21 June 1933, Colchester; d. of Gen. Sir Hugh Stockwell and Lady Stockwell; m. 1st John Hope 1953; one s.; m. 2nd Theo Crosby 1990; ed Heatherley, Chelsea and Slade Schools of Art; trained as a classical ballet dancer; has completed various commissions including pointillist mural for Barbican Centre, London, four life-size terracotta figures for Shakespeare's Globe Theatre; collaborated on bldg Shakespeare's Globe Theatre, vestments for Wakefield Cathedral 1999–2000 and many other public works; works with several composers writing librettos; has composed Greek song cycles; has written film scripts, made videos, films and animated films. *Solo exhibitions include:* Spaces and Places, London, Italy, Cyprus 1998, Dhaka, Bangladesh 2000, South Bank Art Centre, London, Shakespeare's Globe, London, Los Angeles, Calif. and many other shows. *Animated film:* Memories, Memories 1995. *Productions include:* Il Giardino degli Uccelli (1 act opera, music by Quentin Thomas) 1999, Death of Lord Byron (1 act opera, music by Quentin Thomas) 2000, Bran's Singing Head (music by Geoffrey Alvarez) 1996, The Bird Garden, Oper-am-Rhein, Düsseldorf (sets, libretto and book), Antony and Cleopatra 2002–03. *Plays include:* Freedom and Death 1992, General Hughie 1993. *Publications include:* Here Away From it All 1969, Us Lot 1970, The Immaculate Misconception 1972, A Baker's Dozen of Greek Folk Songs 1994, Songs My Parrot Taught Me 1994, Egyptian Love Songs and Songs for Aphrodite 1998, Il Giardino degli Uccelli 1999. *Leisure interests:* music, sitting in the sun and sleeping. *Address:* 5A & B Heneage Street, Spitalfields, London, E1 5LJ, England. *Telephone:* (20) 7247-3450. *Fax:* (20) 7247-3450. *E-mail:* polly@doxy.demon.co.uk (Office); polly@doxy.demon.co.uk (Home). *Website:* www.hopeart.com (Office).

HOPE OF CRAIGHEAD, Baron (Life Peer), cr. 1995, of Banff in the District of Perth and Kinross; **Rt Hon. James Arthur David Hope,** PC, MA, LLB; British judge; b. 22 June 1938, Edinburgh, Scotland; s. of Arthur Henry Cecil Hope and Muriel Ann Neilson Hope; m. Katharine Mary Kerr 1966; two s. one d.; ed The Edinburgh Acad., Rugby School, St John's Coll. Cambridge; nat. service, Seaforth Highlanders 1957–59; admitted to Faculty of Advocates, to practise at Scottish Bar 1965; Standing Jr Counsel to Bd of Inland Revenue in Scotland 1974–78; apptd. QC in Scotland 1978; Advocate-Depute, Crown Office, Edinburgh 1978–82; Chair. and Legal Chair. Medical Appeal Tribunals 1985–86; Dean Faculty of Advocates 1986–89; Lord Justice Gen. of Scotland and Lord Pres. of Court of Session 1989–96; a Lord of Appeal in Ordinary 1996–; Chair. Subcttee E (Law and Insts), House of Lords Select Cttee on the EU 1998–2001; Pres. Stair Soc. 1993–, Int. Criminal Lawyers Asscn 2000–; Chancellor, Univ. of Strathclyde 1998–; Hon. Prof. of Law, Univ. of Aberdeen 1994–; Hon. Fellow St John's Coll., Cambridge 1995; American Coll. of Trial Lawyers 2000; Hon. LLD (Aberdeen) 1991, (Strathclyde) 1993, (Edin.) 1995. *Publications:* Gloag & Henderson's Introduction to the Laws of Scotland (jt ed.) 1968, (asst ed.) 1980, 1987, 2001, Armour on Valuation for Rating (jt ed.) 1971, 1985, The Rent (Scotland) Act (jtly) 1984, 1986, Stair Memorial Encyclopedia of Scots Law (contrib.). *Leisure interests:* walking, ornithology, music. *Address:* House of Lords, London, SW1A 0PW, England; 34 India Street, Edinburgh, EH3 6HB, Scotland. *Telephone:* (20) 7219-3202 (London); (131) 225-8245 (Edinburgh). *E-mail:* hopejad@parliament.uk (Office).

HOPKINS, Sir Anthony, Kt, CBE; American (b. British) actor; b. 31 Dec. 1937, Port Talbot, Wales; s. of Richard Hopkins and Muriel Hopkins; m. 1st Petronella Barker 1967 (divorced 1972); one d.; m. 2nd Jennifer Lynton 1973 (divorced 2002); m. 3rd Stella Arroyave 2003; ed Cowbridge Grammar School, S Wales, Welsh Coll. of Music and Drama, Cardiff, Royal Acad. of Dramatic Art; mil. training and service: clerk Royal Artillery Unit, Bulford 1958–60; joined Manchester Library Theatre, Asst Stage Man. 1960; then at Nottingham Repertory Co.; joined Phoenix Theatre, Leicester 1963; then Liverpool Playhouse, then Hornchurch Repertory Co.; joined Nat. Theatre Co. 1967; Film debut The Lion in Winter 1967; film, TV, stage actor in UK and USA 1967–, in USA 1974–84; Hon. Fellow St David's Coll., Lampeter 1992; Hon. DLitt (Univ. of Wales) 1988; Commdr, Ordre nat. des Arts et Lettres; BAFTA TV Actor Award 1972, Emmy Awards 1976, 1981, Variety Club Film Actor of the Year (The Bounty) 1984, Stage Actor of the Year (Pravda) 1985, Soc. of West End Theatres. The Observer Award for Pravda 1985, Best Actor, Moscow Film Festival, for 84 Charing Cross Road 1987, BAFTA Award and Acad. Award for Best Actor for The Silence of the Lambs 1992, BAFTA Award for Best Actor in The Remains of the Day 1994, US Film Advisory Bd Special Career Achievement Award for US Work 1994, BAFTA (US) Britannia Award for Outstanding Contrib. to the Int. Film and TV Industry 1995 and numerous others worldwide. *Stage appearances include:* title role in Macbeth, Nat. Theatre 1972, Dr Dysart in Equus, Plymouth Theatre, New York 1974, 1975, Huntingdon Hartford Theatre, Los Angeles (also Dir) 1977, Prospero in The Tempest, Los Angeles 1979, Old Times, New York 1983, The Lonely Road, Old Vic Theatre, London 1985, Pravda, Nat. Theatre 1985, King Lear (title role), Nat. Theatre 1986, Antony and Cleopatra (title role), Nat. Theatre 1987, M. Butterfly 1989, August (also Dir) 1994. *Film appearances include:* The Lion in Winter 1967, The Looking Glass War 1967, Claudius in Hamlet 1969, When Eight Bells Toll 1969, Torvald in A Doll's House 1972, The Girl from Petrovka 1973, Juggernaut 1974, A Bridge Too Far 1976, Audrey Rose 1976, International Velvet 1977, Magic 1978, The Elephant Man 1979, A Change of Seasons 1980, Capt. Bligh in The Bounty 1983, The Good Father 1985, 84 Charing Cross Road 1987, The Old Jest 1987, A Chorus of Disapproval 1988, The Tenth Man 1988, Desperate Hours 1989, The Silence of the Lambs 1990, Spotswood 1990, One Man's War 1990, Howard's End 1991, Freejack 1991, Bram Stoker's Dracula 1991, Chaplin 1992, The Trial 1992, The Innocent 1992, The Remains of the Day 1992, Shadowlands 1993, Legends of the Fall 1993, The Road to Wellville 1993, August (also Dir) 1994, Nixon 1995, Surviving Picasso 1995, The Edge 1996, The Mask of Zorro 1997, Meet Joe Black 1998, Amistad 1998, Instinct 1999, Titus 1999, Mission Impossible 2, Hannibal 2001, Hearts in Atlantis 2001, The Devil and Daniel Webster 2001, Bad Company 2002, Red Dragon 2002. *TV appearances include:* A Heritage and its History, A Company of Five 1968, The Three Sisters, The Peasants Revolt 1969, title roles in Dickens, Danton, Astrov in Uncle Vanya, Hearts and Flowers 1970, Pierre in War and Peace 1971–72, title role in Lloyd George 1972, QB VII 1973, A Childhood Friend, Possessions, All Creatures Great and Small, The Arcata Promise 1974, Dark Victory, The Lindbergh Kidnapping Case (Emmy Award) 1975, Victory at Entebbe 1976, title role in Kean 1978, The Voyage of the Mayflower 1979, The Bunker (Emmy Award), Peter and Paul 1980, title role in Othello, Little Eyolf, The Hunchback of Notre Dame 1981, A Married Man 1982, Strangers and Brothers 1983, Old Times, The Arch of Triumph, Mussolini and I, Hollywood Wives, Guilty Conscience 1984, Blunt (role of Guy Burgess) 1987, Heartland 1989, Across the Lake (Donald Campbell) 1989, Great Expectations (Magwitch) 1989, To Be the Best 1990, A Few Selected Exits (Gwyn Thomas) 1993, Big Cats 1993. *Leisure interests:* music, playing the piano, reading philosophy and European history. *Address:* c/o The Peggy Thompson Office, 296 Sandycombe Road, Kew, Surrey, TW9 3NG, England.

HOPKINS, Antony, CBE, FRCM; British musician, author and broadcaster; b. 21 March 1921, London; s. of the late Hugh Reynolds and Marjorie Reynolds; m. Alison Purves 1947 (died 1991); ed Berkhamsted School and Royal Coll. of Music; composed incidental music for theatre (Old Vic, Stratford-upon-Avon), radio and cinema; composed music for winning entries, Italia Prize 1952 and 1957; radio broadcaster in series Talking about Music; Hon. Fellow RAM, Robinson Coll. (Cambridge) 1980; Hon. DUniv (Stirling) 1980; City of Tokyo Medal 1973, Grand Prix, Besançon Film Festival for John and the Magic Music Man, Chappell Gold Medal, Cobbett Prize, Royal Coll. of Music. *Compositions:* Five studies for voices, Psalm 42, songs, recorder pieces, two ballets, Magnificat and Nunc Dimittis (for girls' choir), A Time for Growing, Early One Morning, Three's Company, Dr. Musikus, Partita (for solo violin), John and the Magic Music Man (for narrator and orchestra; filmed 1976), three piano sonatas and others. *Publications:* Talking about Symphonies 1961, Talking about Concertos 1964, Talking about Sonatas 1971, Music Face to Face, Downbeat Guide 1977, Understanding Music 1979, The Nine Symphonies of Beethoven 1980, Songs for Swinging Golfers 1981, Sounds of Music 1982, Beating Time (autobiog.) 1982, Pathway to Music 1983, The Concertgoer's Companion Vol. I 1984, Vol. II 1986, The Seven Concertos of Beethoven 1997. *Leisure interest:* watching TV. *Address:* Woodyard Cottage, Ashridge, Berkhamsted, Herts., HP4 1PS, England. *Telephone:* (1442) 842257.

HOPKINS, Godfrey Thurston; British photojournalist and writer; b. 16 April 1913, London; s. of Sybil Beatrice Bately and Robert Thurston Hopkins; m. Grace Fyfe Robertson 1955; one s. one d.; ed Salesian RC School, Burwash, Sussex, Montpelier Coll., Brighton, Brighton Coll. of Art; trained as magazine illustrator, then as photographer; photographer with RAF Italy and N Africa 1939–45; freelance photographer in Europe 1946–49; mem. staff Picture Post, assignments worldwide 1949–57 and particular interest in aspects of British life; worked for London advertising agencies 1958–68; tutor, Studies in Photojournalism, Guildford School of Photography, W Surrey Coll. of Art and Design 1970–78; work in public collections including Victoria and Albert Museum, Arts Council, Museum of London, Metropolitan Museum of Art, New York, Helmut Gernsheim Collection, Switzerland, J. Paul Getty Museum, USA, Museum of Photographic Arts, San Diego, CA, USA; Encyclopaedia Britannica Award (twice). *Exhibitions:* one-man Exhbn, Arts Council of GB, toured UK 1976–77, Zelda Cheatle Gallery, London 1993; group Exhbn British Art 1940–80, Hayward Gallery, London 1980, Victoria and Albert Museum, London 1994; All Human Life: Great Photographs from the Hulton Deutsch Collection, Barbican Art Gallery, London 1994; Europa de Posguerra 1945–65, Barcelona, 1995. *Publication:* Thurston Hopkins 1977. *Leisure interests:* painting, writing. *Address:* Wilmington Cottage, Wilmington Road, Seaford, East Sussex, BN25 2EH, England. *Telephone:* (1323) 897656. *Fax:* (1323) 897656.

HOPKINS, Sir Michael John, Kt, CBE, FRIBA, RA; British architect; b. 7 May 1935, Poole, Dorset; s. of the late Gerald Hopkins and Barbara Hopkins; m. Patricia Wainwright 1962; one s. two d.; ed Sherborne School, Architectural Asscn and RIBA; partnership with Norman Foster 1969–75; f. Michael Hopkins & Partners 1976–; Consultant Architect Victoria & Albert Museum 1985; Vice-Pres. Architectural Asscn 1987–93, Pres. 1997–99; mem. Royal Fine Art Comm. 1986–99; Trustee Thomas Cubitt Trust 1987–, British Museum 1993–; mem. RIBA Council, London Advisory Cttee to English Heritage, Architectural Advisory Group, Arts Council; Hon. mem. Bund Architekten; Hon. FAIA 1996; Hon. Fellow, Royal Incorporation of Architects of Scotland 1996; Hon. DLitt (Nottingham) 1995; Hon. DTech (London Guildhall); RIBA Award 1977, 1980, 1988, 1989, 1994, 1996; Civic Trust Award 1979, 1988, 1990, 1997; Financial Times Award 1980, 1982; Structural Steel Award, 1980, 1988; Royal Acad. Architectural Award 1982, co-winner (with wife Patricia Hopkins) RIBA Gold Medal for Architecture 1994. *Major works include:* Patera Bldg System 1984, Research Centre for Schlumberger, Cambridge 1984, Bicentenary Stand, Lord's Cricket Ground 1987, redevelopment of Bracken House for Ohbayashi Corpn 1987–91, R&D Centre, Solid State Logic 1988, Glyndebourne Opera House 1987–94, Portcullis House, Westminster 1989–2000, Westminster Underground Station 1990–99, The William Younger Centre 1990–99, Inland Revenue Centre, Nottingham 1992–95, Office Bldg for IBM at Bedfont Lakes, The Queen's Bldg, Emmanuel Coll., Cambridge 1993–95, Dynamic Earth, Edinburgh 1990–99, Jubilee Campus, Nottingham 1996–99, Saga Group Headquarters 1994–99, Hampshire Co. Cricket Club 1994–2001, Wildscreen @ Bristol 2,000 1996–99, Goodwood Racecourse 1997–2001, Haberdashers' Hall 1996–2002, The Forum, Norwich 1996–2001, Manchester City Art Gallery 1994–, Nat. Coll. of School Leadership, Nottingham 2000–02. *Works in progress include:* Evelina Children's Hosp., The Wellcome Trust Headquarters. *Leisure interests:* sailing, Catureglio, Black Heath. *Address:* 27 Broadley Terrace, London, NW1 6LG (Office); 49A Downshire Hill, London, NW3 1NX, England (Home). *Telephone:* (20) 7724-1751 (Office); (20) 7435-1109 (Home). *Fax:* (20) 7723-0932 (Office); (20) 7794-1494 (Home). *E-mail:* mail@hopkins.co.uk (Office). *Website:* www.hopkins.co.uk (Office).

HOPKINS, P. Jeffrey, BA, PhD; American professor of religious studies; b. 30 Sept. 1940, Providence, RI; s. of Charles E. Hopkins and Ora Adams; m. Elizabeth S. Napper 1983 (divorced 1990); ed public school in Barrington, RI, Pomfret School, Conn., Harvard Univ., Univ. of Wis.-Madison and Lamaist Buddhist Monastery of America; Asst Prof. of Religious Studies, Univ. of Va 1973–77, Assoc. Prof. 1977–89, Prof. 1989–, Dir Center for South Asian Studies 1979–82, 1985–94; Pres. Inst for Asian Democracy 1994–2000; Visiting Prof. Univ. of BC 1983–84; Yehan Numata Distinguished Visiting Prof. of Buddhist Studies, Univ. of Hawaii 1995; Chief Interpreter to Dalai Lama (q.v.) on overseas tours 1979–89; Fulbright Scholar, India and Germany 1971–72, 1982. *Achievement:* organized and directed the Nobel Peace Laureates Conf., Univ. of Virginia 1998. *Publications:* Meditation on Emptiness 1973, Emptiness Yoga 1987, Fluent Tibetan 1993, Emptiness in the Mind-Only School of Buddhism 1999; author or trans. of 20 other books including eight in collaboration with the Dalai Lama; over 20 articles. *Leisure interests:* meditation, walking in woods. *Address:* Department of Religious Studies, University of Virginia, 104 Cocke Hall, Charlottesville, VA 22904 (Office); 7330 Harris Mountain Lane, Dyke, VA 22935, USA (Home). *Telephone:* (804) 924-6716 (Office); (804) 973-3256 (Home). *Fax:* (804) 924-1467.

HOPKINS, Patricia Anne (Lady Hopkins); British architect; b. 7 April 1942, Staffs.; d. of Denys Wainwright; m. (now Sir) Michael Hopkins 1962; one s. one d.; ed Wycombe Abbey School, Architectural Asscn, London; Co-Founder and Pnr Michael Hopkins and Pnrs 1976–; Assessor for Civic Trust Award Schemes 1993–2000; Gov. Queen's Coll., Hailey St 1998–; mem. Arts Council Nat. Lottery Advisory Bd 1994–99, Architectural Asscn 150 Campaign Bd 1994–99; Trustee Nat. Gallery, London 1998–; Hon. Fellow Royal Inst. of Architects in Scotland 1996; Hon. DTech (London Guildhall) 1996. *Architectural works include:* Hopkins House, Hampstead (RIBA Award 1997) 1996, Hopkins Office, Marylebone 1985, Fleet Velmead School, Hants (RIBA Award, Civic Trust Award 1988) 1986, Victoria and Albert Museum (Consultant Architect and Masterplan) 1988, Glyndebourne Opera House (RIBA Award, Royal Fine Art Comm. Award 1994, Civic Trust Award, FT Award 1995) 1994, Queen's Bldg, Emmanuel Coll. Cambridge (RIBA Award, Royal Fine Art Comm. Award 1996) 1995, Jewish Care Home for the Elderly 1996, Preacher's Court, Charterhouse 2000, Wildscreen at Bristol (Civic Trust Award, DTLR Urban Design Award 2001) 2001, Manchester Art Gallery 2002, Haberdasher's Hall 2002. *Leisure interests:* family and friends at Catoreglio and Blackheath. *Address:* Michael Hopkins and Partners, 27 Broadley Terrace, London, NW1 6LG (Office); 49A Downshire Hill, London,

NW3 INX, England (Home). *Telephone:* (20) 7724-1751 (Office); (20) 7794-1494 (Home). *Fax:* (20) 7723-0932 (Office); (20) 7794-1494 (Home). *E-mail:* patty.h@hopkins.co.uk (Office). *Website:* www.hopkins.co.uk (Office).

HOPP, Dietmar; German computer executive; fmrly with IBM; co.-f. SAP, fmr Bd Spokesman, now Co-Chair. *Leisure interests:* beer, golf. *Address:* SAP AG, P.O. Box 1461, D-69185, Walldorf, Germany (Office). *Telephone:* (6227) 747474 (Office).

HOPPER, Dennis; American actor, author, photographer and film director; b. 17 May 1936, Dodge City, Kan.; m. 1st Brooke Hayward; one d.; m. 2nd Doria Halprin; one d.; m. 3rd Katherine La Nasa 1989; one s.; ed public schools in San Diego; numerous TV appearances include Loretta Young Show; has held several public exhbns of photographs; named Best New Dir, Cannes 1969; Best Film Awards at Venice 1971, Cannes 1980. *Film appearances include:* Rebel Without a Cause 1955, I Died a Thousand Times 1955, Giant 1956, Story of Mankind, Gunfight at the O.K. Corral 1957, Night Tide, Key Witness, From Hell to Texas 1958, Glory Stompers 1959, The Trip 1961, The Sons of Katie Elder 1962, Hang 'Em High 1966, Cool Hand Luke 1967, True Grit 1968, The American Dreamer 1971, Kid Blue 1973, The Sky is Falling 1975, James Dean—The First American Teenager 1976, Mad Dog Morgan 1976, Tracks 1979, American Friend 1978, Apocalypse Now 1979, Wild Times 1980, King of the Mountain 1981, Human Highway 1981, Rumble Fish 1983, The Osterman Weekend 1984, Black Widow 1986, Blue Velvet 1986, River's Edge 1987, Blood Red 1989, Flashback 1989, The American Wars 1989, Chattahoochie 1990, Motion and Emotion 1990, Superstar: The Life and Times of Andy Warhol 1990, Hot Spot 1990, True Romance, Boiling Point, Super Mario Bros 1993, Chasers 1994, Speed 1994, Waterworld 1995, Search and Destroy 1995, Basquiat 1996, Carried Away 1996, Star Truckers 1997, Blackout 1997, Tycus 1998, Sources 1999, Lured Innocence 1999, Justice 1999, EdTV 1999, Straight Shooter 1999; actor, writer, Dir Easy Rider 1969, The Last Movie 1971, Paris Trout 1990, The Indian Runner 1991; actor, Dir Out of the Blue 1980; Dir Colors 1988, The Hot Spot 1990, Catchfire 1991, Nails 1991. *Publication:* Out of the Sixties (photographs) 1988. *Address:* c/o Creative Artists Agency, 9830 Wilshire Blvd., Beverly Hills, CA 90212, USA.

HOPPER, Wilbert Hill (Bill), OC, BSc, MBA; Canadian business executive; b. 14 March 1933, Ottawa, Ont.; s. of the late Wilbert C. Hopper and Eva (Hill) Hopper; m. Patricia M. Walker 1957; two s.; ed American Univ. and Univ. of Western Ontario; Petroleum Geologist, Imperial Oil 1955–57; Petroleum Economist, Foster Assocs. 1959–61; Sr Energy Economist, Nat. Energy Bd 1961–64; Sr Petroleum Consultant, Arthur D. Little, Cambridge, Mass. 1964–73; Asst Deputy Minister, Energy Policy, Dept of Energy, Mines and Resources 1973–75; Pres., CEO and Dir Petro-Canada 1976–79, Chair., CEO and Dir 1979–; Chair. and Dir Westcoast Energy Inc.; Vice-Chair. and Dir Panartic Oils Ltd; mem. Bd of Bi-Provincial Upgrader Jt Venture; Dir Syncrude Canada Ltd, Canada-China Trade Council, Petro-Canada Int. Assistance Corpn; mem. Bd of Govs. Acadia Univ., NS, Schooner Bluenose Foundation, Oxford Inst. for Energy Studies, Ashbury Coll., Ottawa; Int. Advisory Council, Centre for Global Energy Studies; mem. numerous socs., cttees. and asscns; Hon. LLD (Wilfrid Laurier). *Address:* 500 Eau Claire Ave., South West, Apartment H302, Calgary, Alberta, T2P 3R8, Canada.

HOPWOOD, Sir David (Alan), Kt, MA, PhD, FRS, FIBiol; British professor of genetics; b. 19 Aug. 1933, Kinver, Staffs.; s. of Herbert Hopwood and Dora Grant; m. 1962 Joyce Lilian Bloom; two s. one d.; ed Purbrook Park County High School, Hants., Lymm Grammar School, Cheshire, St John's Coll., Cambridge; John Stothert Bye-Fellow, Magdalene Coll., Cambridge 1956–58, Research Fellow, St John's Coll. 1958–61, Univ. Demonstrator 1957–61; Lecturer in Genetics, Univ. of Glasgow 1961–68; Prof. of Genetics, Univ. of E Anglia Norwich 1968–98, Prof. Emer. 1999–; Head of Genetics Dept, John Innes Centre 1968–98, Fellow Emer. 1999–; Hon. Prof., Chinese Acad. of Medical Science, Inst. of Microbiology and Plant Physiology, Chinese Acad. of Sciences, Huazhong Agricultural Univ., Wuhan, China; fmr Pres. Genetical Soc. of GB; Foreign Fellow, Indian Nat. Science Acad.; Pres. Soc. of Gen. Microbiology 2000–03; Hon. mem. Hungarian Acad. of Sciences, Soc. for Gen. Microbiology, Spanish Soc. of Mircobiology; Hon. Fellow UMIST, Magdalene Coll. Cambridge; Hon. Dr ETH (Zürich, Switzerland); Dr hc (Univ. of E Anglia, Norwich); Medal for Research in New Bioactive Compounds, Kitasato Inst. (Japan) 1988, Hoechst Award for Research in Antimicrobial Chemotherapy, American Soc. for Microbiology 1988, Chiron Biotech. Award, American Soc. for Microbiology 1992, Mendel Medal, Czech Acad. of Sciences 1995, Gabor Medal, Royal Soc. 1995. *Publications:* Genetics of Bacterial Diversity 1989 (Ed. D. A. Hopwood and K. F. Chater); 270 articles and chapters in scientific journals and books. *Leisure interests:* gardening and cooking. *Address:* John Innes Centre, Norwich Research Park, Colney, Norwich, NR4 7UH (Office); 244 Unthank Road, Norwich, NR2 2AH, England (Home). *Telephone:* (1603) 450000. *Fax:* (1603) 450778. *E-mail:* david.hopwood@bbsrc.ac.uk (Office). *Website:* www.micron.ac.uk/people/david-hopwood/hopwood.html (Office).

HORBULIN, Volodymyr Pavlovych, DTech; Ukrainian politician and space scientist; b. 17 Jan. 1939, Zaporozhya; ed Dnipropetrovsk State Univ.; with CB Yuzhnoye (Southern Design Bureau), Dnipropetrovsk 1962–77; mem. admin. staff, Cen. Cttee CP of Ukraine 1977–90, Chief of Missile and Aviation Section 1980; Gen. Dir Nat. Space Agency 1992; Sec. Nat. Security Council, Adviser to Pres. on nat. security issues 1994, Sec. Nat. Security and Defence Council 1996–99; Chair. State Comm. for Defence and Industrial Complex 2000–; Leader, Democratic Union Party, Chair. Party Council 2001–; fmr Head Ukraine-NATO Inter-Agency Comm.; mem. Ukrainian Nat. Acad. of Sciences 1997–; Ukrainian Nat. Acad. of Sciences Prize 1988, USSR State Prize 1990; Order of Red Banner of Labour 1976, 1982, First Class Order of Yaroslav the Wise 1997. *Leisure interests:* music, literature, theatre. *Address:* State Commission for Defence and Industrial Complex of Ukraine, Moskovska Str., 45/1, Kiev, 01011, Ukraine (Office). *Telephone:* (44) 254-37-91 (Office). *Fax:* (44) 254-48-72 (Office).

HORECKER, Bernard L., BS, PhD; American biochemist; b. 31 Oct. 1914, Chicago, Ill.; s. of Paul Horecker and Bessie Horecker; m. Frances Goldstein 1936; three d.; ed Univ. of Chicago; Research Assoc., Dept of Chem., Univ. of Chicago 1939–40; Examiner US Civil Service Comm., Washington, DC 1940–41; Biochemist US Public Health Service (USPHS) Nat. Insts. of Health (NIH) Industrial Hygiene Research Lab. 1941–47, Nat. Inst. of Arthritis and Metabolic Diseases 1947–53, Chief, Section on Enzymes and Cellular Biochemistry, NIH Nat. Inst. of Arthritis and Metabolic Diseases 1953–56; Head Lab. of Biochemistry and Metabolism 1956–59; Prof. and Chair. Dept of Microbiology, New York Univ. School of Medicine 1959–63, Dept of Molecular Biology Albert Einstein Coll. of Medicine 1962–71, Dir Div. of Biol. Sciences 1970–72, Assoc. Dean for Scientific Affairs 1971–72; Vice-Chair. Div. of Biological Chem., ACS 1975–76, Chair. 1976–77; mem. Roche Inst. of Molecular Biology 1972–84, Head Lab. of Molecular Enzymology 1977–84; professorial lecturer on Enzymes, George Washington Univ. 1950–57; Visiting Prof., Univ. of Calif. 1954, Univ. of Ill. 1957, Univ. of Paraná, Brazil, 1960, 1963, Cornell Univ. 1964, Univ. of Rotterdam 1970; Visiting Investigator, Pasteur Inst. 1957–58, Indian Inst. of Science, Bangalore 1971; Ciba Lecturer, Rutgers Univ. 1962; Phillips Lecturer, Haverford Coll. 1965; Reilly Lecturer, Notre Dame Univ. 1969; Visiting Prof., Albert Einstein Coll. of Medicine 1972–84; Adjunct Prof., Cornell Univ. Medical Coll. 1972–84, Prof. of Biochemistry 1984–89, Prof. Emer. 1989, Dean Graduate School of Medical Sciences 1984–92; Hon. Prof. Fed. Univ. of Paraná, Brazil 1981–; Ed. Biochemical and Biophysical Research Communications 1959–89; Chair. Editorial Cttee Archives of Biochemistry and Biophysics 1968–84; Ed. Current Topics in Cellular Regulation 1969–89; mem. Scientific Advisory Bd, Roche Inst. of Molecular Biology 1967–70, Chair. 1970–72; Dir Academic Press 1968–73; mem. Comm. on Personnel, American Cancer Soc. 1969–73; Medical Scientist Training Program Study Section NIH 1970–72; mem. Scientific Advisory Comm. for Biochem. and Chemical Carcinogenesis, American Cancer Soc. 1974–78, Council for Research and Clinical Investigation Awards, American Cancer Soc.; Pres. American Soc. of Biological Chem. 1968–69, Harvey Soc. of New York 1970–71; Vice-Chair. Pan American Asscn of Biochemical Socs. 1971, Chair. 1972; mem. NAS; Prof. hc (Univ.of Paraná, Brazil) 1982; Hon. mem. of Swiss, Japanese, Spanish Socs., Hellenic Biochemical and Biophysical Soc., Greece, Brazilian Acad. Sciences; Fellow, American Acad. of Arts and Sciences; mem. Indian Nat. Acad. of Science; Corresp. mem. Argentine Acad. of Science; Hon. DSc (Univ. of Urbino, Italy); Paul Lewis Labs. Award in Enzyme Chem. 1952, Fed. Security Agency's Superior Accomplishment Award 1952, Hillebrand Prize, ACS 1954, Washington Acad. of Sciences Award in Biological Sciences 1954, Rockefeller Public Service Award 1957, Fulbright Travel Award 1963, Commonwealth Fund Fellow 1967, Merck Award (American Soc. of Biological Chemists) 1981, Carl Neuberg Medal (Virchow-Pirquet Med. Soc.) 1981. *Leisure interests:* gardening, ornithology. *Address:* 16517 Cypress Villa Lane, Fort Myers, FL 33908, USA. *Telephone:* (914) 267-5578. *E-mail:* blhorecker@aol.com (Home).

HORI, Kosuke; Japanese politician; mem. House of Reps.; fmr Chair. LDP Diet Affairs Cttee; Parl. Vice-Minister for Agric., Forestry and Fisheries; fmr Minister for Educ.; Minister of Home Affairs, Chair. Nat. Public Safety Comm. 1999–2000. *Address:* c/o Ministry of Home Affairs, 2-1-1, Kasumigaseki, Chiyoda-ku, Tokyo 100, Japan (Office).

HORINOUCHI, Hisao; Japanese politician; mem. House of Reps.; fmr Minister of Agric., Forestry and Fisheries; Minister of Posts and Telecommunications 1996–98. *Address:* c/o Ministry of Posts and Telecommunications, 1-3-2, Kasumigaseki, Chiyoda-ku, Tokyo 100, Japan (Office).

HORLOCK, Sir John Harold, Kt, ScD, FREng, FRS; British university administrator and engineer; b. 19 April 1928, Edmonton; s. of Harold E Horlock and Olive M. Horlock; m. Sheila J. Stutely 1953; one s. two d.; ed Latymer School, Edmonton and St John's Coll., Cambridge; design engineer, Rolls-Royce Ltd 1949–51; Demonstrator, Lecturer in Eng, Univ. of Cambridge 1952–58, Prof. of Eng 1967–74; Harrison Prof. of Mech. Eng, Univ. of Liverpool 1958–67; Vice-Chancellor, Univ. of Salford 1974–80, Open Univ. 1981–90; Fellow, Open Univ. 1991–; Treas. and Vice-Pres. Royal Soc. 1992–97; Pro-Chancellor UMIST 1995–2001; Pres. Asscn for Science Educ. 1999; Hon. Fellow UMIST, St John's Coll. Cambridge; Hon. DSc (Heriot Watt, Salford, CNAA, East Asia, De Montfort, Cranfield); Hon. DEng (Liverpool); Hon. DUniv (Open Univ.); Hawksley Gold Medal (Inst. of Mech. Eng), R. T. Sawyer Award (American Soc. of Mech. Eng) 1997, Ewing Medal (Inst. of Civil Eng.) 2001. *Publications:* Axial Flow Compressors 1958, Axial Flow Turbines 1967, Actuator Disc Theory 1978, Thermodynamics and Gas Dynamics of I.C. Engines (Ed.) Vol. I 1982, Vol. II 1986, Cogeneration: Combined Heat and Power 1987, Combined Power Plants 1992. *Leisure interests:* music, sport. *Address:* 2 The Avenue, Ampthill, Bedford, MK45 2NR, England (Home). *Telephone:* (1525) 841307. *E-mail:* j.h.horlock@talk21.com (Home).

HORN, Sir Gabriel, Kt, MA, MD, ScD, FRS; British neuroscientist and university professor; b. 9 Dec. 1927, Birmingham; s. of the late Abraham Horn and Anne Horn; m. 1st Ann L. D. Soper 1952 (divorced 1979); two s. two d.; m. 2nd Priscilla Barrett 1980; ed Handsworth Tech. School and Coll., Birmingham Coll. of Tech., Univ. of Birmingham; served in RAF 1947–49; house appts in Birmingham hosps. 1955–56; demonstrator in Anatomy, Univ. of Cambridge 1956–62, Lecturer 1962–72, Reader in Neurobiology 1972–74, Fellow, King's Coll. 1962–74, 1978–92, 1999–; Prof. and Head Dept of Anatomy, Univ. of Bristol 1974–77; Prof. of Zoology, Univ. of Cambridge 1978–95, Head of Dept 1979–94, Prof. Emer. 1995–; Master Sidney Sussex Coll., Cambridge 1992–99, Fellow Emer. 1999–; Deputy Vice-Chancellor, Univ. of Cambridge 1994–98; Chair. Animal Sciences and Psychology Research Cttee Biotech. and Biochem. Research Council 1994–96; Chair. Cambridge Univ. Govt Policy Prog. 1998–; Chair. Review Cttee on Origin of BSE 2001; Sr Research Fellow in Neurophysiology, Montreal Neurological Inst., McGill Univ. 1957–58; Leverhulme Research Fellow Laboratoire de Neurophysiologie Cellulaire, France 1970–71; visiting professorships and lectureships Canada, Hong Kong, USA, UK and Uganda 1963–90; mem. Biological Sciences Cttee, SRC 1973–75, Research Cttee Mental Health Foundation 1973–78; Dir Co. of Biologists 1980–93; mem. Agricultural and Food Research Council 1991–94; Chair. Cttee on Biology of Spongiform Encephalopathies 1991–94; Foreign mem. Georgian Acad. of Sciences; Hon. mem. Anatomical Soc.; Hon. DSc (Birmingham) 1999, (Bristol) 2003; Kenneth Craik Award 1962, Royal Medal of Royal Soc. 2001. *Publications:* Short-Term Changes in Neural Activity and Behaviour (Ed. with R. A. Hinde) 1970, Memory, Imprinting and the Brain 1985, Behavioural and Neural Aspects of Learning and Memory (Ed. with J. R. Krebs) 1991; papers in scientific journals, mainly on neuroscience topics. *Leisure interests:* walking, cycling, riding, music, wine. *Address:* Sub-Department of Animal Behaviour, University of Cambridge, Madingley, Cambridge, CB3 8AA, England (Office). *Telephone:* (1223) 741813 (Office); (1223) 338815. *Fax:* (1223) 330869. *E-mail:* gh105@cus.cam.ac.uk (Office).

HORN, Gyula, DEcon; Hungarian politician and economist; b. 5 July 1932, Budapest; s. of Géza Horn and Anna Horn (née Csörnyei); m. Anna Király; one s. one d.; ed Rostov Coll. of Econs (USSR) and Political Acad. of Hungarian Socialist Workers' Party; staff mem., Ministry of Finance 1954–59; Desk Officer, Ministry of Foreign Affairs 1959–61, Perm. Sec. 1985–89, Minister for Foreign Affairs 1989–90; Embassy Sec., Sofia 1961–63, Belgrade 1963–69; staff mem. to Head of Int. Dept, Hungarian Socialist Workers' Party 1969–85; mem. of Parl. 1990–; Chair. Foreign Affairs Standing Cttee of Parl. 1990–93; Prime Minister of Repub. of Hungary 1994–98; Founding mem. of Hungarian Socialist Party 1989, Pres. 1990–98; mem. European Honorary Senate 1991–; Regional Vice-Pres., Socialist Int. (New York) 1996; Gold Medal, Stresemann Soc. (Mainz, Germany) 1990, Karl Prize for work towards European unification (Aachen, Germany) 1991; Golden Order of Labour, Grand Cross of Germany, Sharp Blade Award, Solingen 1991, Humanitarian Award of German Freemasons 1992, Gold Europe Award 1994, Kassel Glass of Understanding Award 1995. *Publications:* Yugoslavia: Our Neighbour, Social and Political Changes in Albania Since World War II, Development of East–West Relations in the 70s, Pikes (autobiog.) 1991, Those Were the '90s... 1999; co-author of over 100 articles published in tech. journals. *Leisure interests:* tennis, swimming, jogging. *Address:* Hungarian Parliament, 1055 Budapest, Kossuth Lajos tér 1/3, Hungary. *Telephone:* (1) 441-4059. *Fax:* (1) 441-4888 (Office). *E-mail:* gyhorn@mszp.hu (Office).

HORN, Heinz, Dr rer. pol; German company executive; b. 17 Sept. 1930, Duisberg; s. of Heinrich and Elisabeth (née Eckernkamp) Horn; m.; two s. two d.; ed Univ. of Frankfurt, Univ. of Munster; fmrly with Mannesmann for 6 years; Financial Dir, Erschweiler Bergweks-Verein 1965–68, mem. Bd and later Pres. 1974–83; mem. Bd, Krupp 1968–72; Deputy Chair. of the Bd, Ruhrkohle AG, Essen 1983–85, Chair. Man. Bd 1985–95; Chair. Supervisory Bd Rütgerswerke AG, EBV 1989–95.

HORNBY, Sir Simon (Michael), Kt; British business executive; b. 29 Dec. 1934; s. of the late Michael Hornby and Nicolette Ward; m. Sheran Cazalet 1968; ed Eton Coll., New Coll. Oxford and Harvard Business School; entered W. H. Smith & Son 1958, Dir 1965; Dir W. H. Smith & Son (Holdings) 1974–1994, Group Chief Exec. 1978–82; Chair. W. H. Smith Group PLC 1982–94; Dir Pearson PLC 1978–97, Lloyds Bank 1988–99; Chair. Lloyds Abbey Life 1992–97; Chair. Nat. Book League 1978–80 (Deputy Chair. 1976–78), Pres. Book Trust 1990–96, Chelsea Soc. 1994–2000; Chair. Design Council 1986–92, Asscn for Business Sponsorship of the Arts 1988–97, Nat. Literacy Trust 1993–2001; mem. Council, Royal Horticultural Soc. 1992–2001 (Pres. 1994–2001); Trustee British Museum 1978–88; Hon. DUniv (Stirling) 1992; Hon. DLitt (Hull) 1994; Hon. LLD (Reading) 1996. *Leisure interests:* gardening, golf, reading, cooking. *Address:* The Ham, Wantage, Oxon., OX12 9JA, England. *Telephone:* (1235) 770222. *Fax:* (1235) 768763 (Home).

HORNE, Donald Richmond, AO; Australian author and lecturer; b. 26 Dec. 1921, Sydney; s. of David Horne and Florence Carpenter; m. Myfanwy Gollan 1961; one s. one d.; ed Univ. of Sydney, Univ. Coll., Canberra; Ed. The Observer 1958–61, The Bulletin 1961–62, 1967–72; Co-Ed. Quadrant 1963–66; Contributing Ed. Newsweek Int. 1973–77; mem. Advisory Bd The Australian Encyclopedia 1973–89, Chair. 1987–89; served Advisory Council for NSW Cultural Affairs 1976–80; mem. Council, Soc. of Authors 1982–, Pres. 1984–85; Chair. Copyright Agency Ltd 1983–84; Chair. The Australia Council 1985–90; Research Fellow, Univ. of NSW 1973–74, Sr Lecturer 1975–79, Assoc. Prof. 1980–84, Prof. 1984–86, Prof. Emer. 1987–, Chair. Arts Faculty 1982–86, Council 1983–86; Chancellor Univ. of Canberra 1991–95; Chair.

Ideas for Australia Programme 1991–94, NSW Centenary of Fed. Cttee 1998–2001; mem. Australian Citizenship Council 1998–2000; Fellow, Australian Acad. of Humanities; Hon. DLitt (Univ. of NSW) 1986; Hon. D. Univ. (Griffith Univ.), (Canberra). *Publications:* The Lucky Country 1964, The Permit 1965, The Education of Young Donald 1967, God is an Englishman 1969, The Next Australia 1970, But What If There Are No Pelicans? 1971, The Australian People 1972, Death of the Lucky Country 1976, Money Made Us 1976, His Excellency's Pleasure 1977, Right Way, Don't Go Back 1978, In Search of Billy Hughes 1979, Time of Hope 1980, Winner Take All 1981, The Great Museum 1984, Confessions of a New Boy 1985, The Public Culture 1986, The Lucky Country Revisited 1987, Portrait of an Optimist 1988, Ideas for a Nation 1989, The Coming Republic 1992, The Intelligent Tourist 1993, The Avenue of the Fair Go 1997, An Interrupted Life 1998, Into the Open 2000, Looking for Leadership 2001. *Leisure interest:* writing. *Address:* 53 Grosvenor Street, Woollahra, NSW 2025, Australia (Home). *Telephone:* 9389-4212 (Home).

HORNE, Marilyn; American mezzo-soprano; b. 16 Jan. 1934, Bradford, Pa; d. of Bentz and Berneice Horne; m. 1st Henry Lewis (divorced); one d.; ed Univ. of Southern California (under William Vennard); performed with several German opera cos in Europe 1956; debut, San Francisco Opera 1960; has since appeared at Covent Garden, London, the Chicago Lyric Opera, La Scala, Milan, Metropolitan Opera, New York; repertoire includes Eboli (Don Carlo), Marie (Wozzeck), Adalgisa (Norma), Jane Seymour (Anna Bolena), Amneris (Aida), Carmen, Rosina (Barbiere di Siviglia), Fides (Le Prophète), Mignon, Isabella (L'Italiana in Algeri), Romeo (I Capuletti ed i Montecchi), Tancredi (Tancredi), Orlando (Orlando Furioso); many recordings; numerous hon. doctorates; Nat. Medal of Arts 1992, Kennedy Center Honor 1995, Musical American Musician of the Year 1995. *Publication:* My Life (autobiog., with Jane Scorell). *Leisure interests:* needlepoint, swimming, reading, sightseeing. *Address:* c/o Colombia Artists Management Inc., Wilford Division, 165 West 57th Street, New York, NY 10019, USA.

HORNER, James; American film music composer; b. 1953, Los Angeles, Calif.; ed Royal Coll. of Music, London, Univ. of S. Carolina, Univ. of Calif. at Los Angeles. *Film scores:* The Lady in Red, Battle Beyond the Stars, Humanoids from the Deep, Deadly Blessing, The Hand, Wolfen, The Pursuit of D. B. Cooper, 48 Hours, Star Trek II: The Wrath of Khan, Something Wicked This Way Comes, Krull, Brainstorm, Testament, Gorky Park, The Dresser, Uncommon Valor, The Stone Boy, Star Trek III: The Search for Spock, Heaven Help Us, Cocoon, Volunteers, Journey of Natty Gann, Commando, Aliens, Where the River Runs Black, The Name of the Rose, An American Tail (Grammy Award for song Somewhere Out There), P.K. and the Kid, Project X, Batteries Not Included, Willow, Red Heat, Vibes, Cocoon: The Return, The Land Before Time, Field of Dreams, Honey I Shrunk the Kids, Dad, Glory (Grammy Award for instrumental composition), I Love You to Death, Another 48 Hours, Once Around, My Heroes Have Always Been Cowboys, Class Action, The Rocketeer, An American Tail: Fievel Goes West, Thunderheart, Patriot Games, Unlawful Entry, Sneakers, Swing Kids, A Far Off Place, Jack the Bear, Once Upon a Forest, Searching for Bobby Fischer, The Man Without a Face, Bopha!, The Pelican Brief, Clear and Present Danger, Legend of the Fall, Braveheart, Casper, Apollo 13, Jumanji, Courage Under Fire, Ransom, To Gillian on Her 37th Birthday, Titanic (Acad. Award, Grammy Award), Mighty Joe Young, The Mask of Zorro, Deep Impact. *Address:* c/o Gorfaine Schwartz Agency, 13245 Riverside Drive, Suite 450, Sherman Oaks, CA 91423, USA.

HORNHUES, Karl-Heinz, Dr rer. pol; German politician; b. 10 June 1939, Stadtlohn; m. Ellen Buss 1965; two s.; ed Univ. of Münster; Adviser, Catholic Adult Educ. Center, Ludwig-Windthorst-Hause, Holthausen 1966–71, Dir 1970–71; Educ. and Teaching Dir Hofmann-La Roche AG, Grenzbach 1971; Assoc. Prof. of Social Econs and Political Science 1974, Prof. 1977; mem. Bundestag 1972–; Deputy Chair. of CDU/CSU Parl. Party in Bundestag in charge of foreign policy, defence policy and European affairs 1989–94; Chair. Foreign Affairs Cttee 1994–98; Chair. German Del., Ass. of WEU 2000–; Chair. German African Foundation; mem. Ass., Council of Europe; Kommendeurkreuz 1999. *Address:* Friedrichstr. 83, 10117 Berlin (Office); Piusstr. 19, 49134 Wallenhorst, Germany. *Telephone:* (30) 22794348. *Fax:* (30) 22796888 (Office).

HÖRNLUND, Börje; Swedish politician; b. 17 June 1935, Nordmaling, Västerbotten; Regional Forestry Man. Forest Owners' Asscn Västerbotten 1963–67, Inspector of Forests; mem. Exec. Cttee Centre Party Youth League 1963, Centre Party Nat. Bd 1977–; Municipal Councillor Skellefteå and mem. Västerbotten County Council 1966; mem. Bd Swedish Fed. of County Councils 1972–, Chair. 1977–80; MP 1976–; Minister of Labour 1991–94; fmr Chair. Official Cttee on Health and Medical Care, mem. Regional Econ. Cttee; mem. Bd of Govs. Bank of Sweden. *Address:* c/o Centre parteit Bergsgt 7B, P.O. Box 22107, Stockholm 104 22, Sweden.

HOROI, Rex Stephen, MA, BEd; Solomon Islands diplomatist and educator; b. 8 Sept. 1952; m.; three c.; ed Univ. of South Pacific, Univ. of Papua New Guinea, Univ. of Sydney; teacher, St Joseph Catholic Secondary School 1978–79, Deputy Prin. 1983–84; consultant, Univ. of Hawaii 1979–80; Sr Lecturer in English, Solomon Islands Coll. of Higher Educ. 1987–89, Head English Dept 1987, Diploma Course Co-ordinator 1988, Dir 1989–92; Perm. Rep. to UN 1992–2001; Exec. Dir Foundation for the Peoples of the South Pacific Int. 2001–. *Publications:* Peace Corps Language Handbook (co-author); handbooks on grammar, communications and culture; articles and papers. *Address:* c/o Ministry of Foreign Affairs, P.O. Box G10, Honiara, Solomon Islands (Office).

HOROVITZ, Joseph, MA, BMus, FRCM; British composer-conductor; b. 26 May 1926, Vienna; ed New Coll., Oxford Univ. and Royal Coll. of Music, London and studied with Nadia Boulanger, Paris; resident in UK 1938–; Music Dir Bristol Old Vic 1949–51; Conductor Festival Gardens Orchestra and open-air ballet, London 1951; Co-Conductor Ballets Russes, English season 1952; Assoc. Dir Intimate Opera Co. 1952–63; Asst Conductor Glyndebourne Opera 1956; Prof. of Composition, RCM 1961–; mem. Council, Composers' Guild 1970–, Council, Performing Right Soc. 1969–96; Pres. Int. Council of Composers and Lyricists of Int. Fed. of Socs. of Authors and Composers 1981–89; Commonwealth Medal Composition 1959, Leverhulme Music Research Award 1961, Gold Order of Merit of Vienna 1996, Nino Rota Prize (Italy) 2002. *Compositions:* 16 ballets including Alice in Wonderland, Les Femmes d'Alger, Miss Carter Wore Pink, Concerto for Dancers; one-act operas: The Dumb Wife, Gentlemen's Island; concertos for violin, trumpet, jazz harpsichord, oboe, clarinet, bassoon, percussion, tuba; other orchestral works include Horizon Overture, Jubilee Serenade, Sinfonietta for Light Orchestra, Fantasia on a Theme of Couperin, Toy Symphony; brass band music includes a euphonium concerto, Sinfonietta, Ballet for Band, Concertino Classico, Theme and Co-operation, The Dong with a Luminous Nose; music for wind band includes a divertimento Bacchus on Blue Ridge, Windharp, Fête Galante, Commedia dell'Arte, Dance Suite and Ad Astra in commemoration of the Battle of Britain; choral music includes Samson, Captain Noah and his Floating Zoo (Ivor Novello Award for Best British Music for Children 1976), Summer Sunday, Endymion, Sing Unto the Lord a New Song, 3 choral songs from As You Like It; vocal music includes Lady Macbeth (mezzo-soprano and piano) and works for the King's Singers (e.g. Romance); chamber music includes 5 string quartets, oboe sonatina, oboe quartet and clarinet sonatina; contribs. to Hoffnung Concerts: Metamorphoses on a Bed-Time Theme and Horrortorio for chorus, orchestra and soloists; numerous scores for theatre productions, films and TV series (Ivor Novello Award for Best TV Theme of 1978 for the series Lillie); productions of Son et Lumière include St Paul's Cathedral, Canterbury Cathedral, Brighton Pavilion, English Harbour Antigua, Bodiam Castle. *Address:* Royal College of Music, Prince Consort Road, London, SW7 2BS, England.

HOROWITZ, Norman Harold, PhD; American biologist; b. 19 March 1915, Pittsburgh, Pa; s. of Joseph Horowitz and Jeanette Miller; m. Pearl Shykin 1939 (died 1985); one s. one d.; ed Univ. of Pittsburg and Calif. Inst. of Technology; National Research Council Fellow 1939–40; Research Fellow, Calif. Inst. of Technology, Pasadena 1940–42, Assoc. Prof. of Biology 1947–53, Prof. 1953–, Prof. Emer. 1982–, Chair., Division of Biology 1977–80; Research Assoc. Stanford Univ. 1942–46; Chief, Bioscience Section, Jet Propulsion Lab., Pasadena 1965–70; Fulbright and Guggenheim Fellow, Univ. of Paris 1954–55; mem. NAS; Fellow, American Acad. of Arts and Sciences; NASA Public Service Medal 1977, Bicentennial Medal of Distinction, Univ. of Pittsburg 1987, T. H. Morgan Medal, Genetics Soc. of America 1998. *Publications:* To Utopia and Back: The Search for Life in the Solar System 1986, numerous tech. articles on genetics, biochem. and space exploration. *Leisure interests:* gardening, music. *Address:* Biology Division, Mail Stop 156-29, California Institute of Technology, Pasadena, CA 91125, USA (Office). *Telephone:* (626) 395-4926 (Office). *E-mail:* nhorowit@its.caltech.edu (Office).

HORROCKS, Jane; British actress; b. 18 Jan. 1964, Lancs.; d. of John Horrocks and Barbara Horrocks; partner Nick Vivian; one s. one d.; ed Royal Acad. of Dramatic Art. *Stage appearances include:* The Rise and Fall of Little Voice, Cabaret. *Television:* Road 1987, Absolutely Fabulous 1992–2001, Bad Girl 1992, Suffer the Little Children (Royal TV Soc. Award) 1994. *Films:* The Dressmaker 1989, Life is Sweet (Best Supporting Actress LA Critics Award) 1991, Little Voice 1998, Chicken Run 2002. *Address:* Conway van Gelder Ltd, 18–21 Jermyn Street, London, SW17 6HP1, England. *Telephone:* (20) 7287-0077.

HORROCKS, Paul John; British editor; b. 19 Dec. 1953; s. of Joe Horrocks and Eunice Horrocks; m. Linda Jean Walton 1976; two s. one d.; ed Bolton School; reporter Daily Mail 1974–75; reporter Manchester Evening News 1975–80, crime corresp. 1980–87, news ed. 1987–91, Asst Ed. 1991–95, Deputy Ed. 1995–97, Ed. 1997–; mem. Bd Dirs. UK Soc. of Eds.; mem. Organizing Cttee, Commonwealth Games Manchester 2002; Vice-Pres. Community Foundation for Greater Manchester; patron Francis House Children's Hospice; mem. Manchester Enterprises Partners' Council. *Address:* Manchester Evening News, 164 Deansgate, Manchester, M60 2RD, England (Office). *Telephone:* (161) 2112465 (Office). *Fax:* (161) 8399115 (Office). *E-mail:* joanne.watchorn@man.news.co.uk (Office). *Website:* www .manchesteronline.co.uk (Office).

HORTON, Frank Elba, MS, PhD; American university president; b. 19 Aug. 1939, Chicago; s. of Elba E. Horton and Mae P. Prohaska; m. Nancy Yocom 1960; four d.; ed Western Ill. and Northwestern Univs; mem. Faculty, Univ. of Ia 1966–75, Prof. of Geography 1966–75, Dir Inst. of Urban and Regional Research 1968–72, Dean of Advanced Studies 1972–75; Vice-Pres. for Acad. Affairs and Research, Southern Ill. Univ. 1975–80; Chancellor, Univ. of Wis., Milwaukee 1980–85; Pres. Univ. of Oklahoma 1985–88; Pres. and Prof. of Geography and Higher Educ., Univ. of Toledo 1988–98, Pres. Emer. 1999–; Prin. Horton and Assocs 1999–; Trustee Toledo Symphony Orchestra 1989–, Toledo Hosp. 1989–, Public Broadcasting Foundation, NW Ohio 1989–93, Soc. Bank and Trust 1990–; Vice-Chair. Toledo Chamber of Commerce 1991–93; mem. Bd of Dirs, Inter-State Bakeries, GAC Corp.; Interim Pres. Southern Ill. Univ. 2001; Interim Dean School of Biological Sciences, Univ. of Missouri 2002–03. *Publications:* Geographic Perspectives on Urban Systems with Integrated Readings (with B. J. L. Berry) 1970, Urban Environmental Management Planning for Pollution Control 1974. *Leisure interests:* hiking, skiing, golf, jogging. *Address:* Horton & Associates, 13171 East Saddlerock Road, Tucson, AZ 85749 (Office); 288 River Ranch Circle, Bayfield, CO 81122, USA (Home). *Telephone:* (520) 760-2420 (Office); (970) 884-2102 (Home).

HORTON, Sir Robert Baynes, Kt, BSc, SM, FRSA, CBIM; British business executive; b. 18 Aug. 1939, London; s. of the late William H. Horton and of Dorothy Joan Baynes; m. Sally Doreen Wells 1962; one s. one d.; ed King's School, Canterbury, St Andrew's Univ., Massachusetts Inst. of Technology; with British Petroleum Ltd (now BP PLC) 1957–86, 1988–92, Gen. Man. BP Tankers 1975–76, Gen. Man. Corporate Planning 1976–79, Man. Dir and CEO BP Chemicals 1979–83, BP Bd 1983–86, Deputy Chair. 1989–90, Chair. and CEO 1990–92; Chair., CEO Standard Oil Co. 1986–88; Vice-Chair. British Railways Bd 1992–94; Chair. Railtrack PLC 1993–99, Chubb PLC 2002–; Dir (non-exec.) ICL PLC 1982–84, Pilkington Bros. 1985–86, Emerson Electric 1987–, Partner Re 1993–2003, Premier Farnell PLC 1995–, Six Continents; Pres. Chemical Industries Asscn 1982–84, BESO 1993–97; Vice-Chair. BIM 1984–90, Business in the Arts (ABSA) 1988–98; Gov. King's School, Canterbury 1984–; Chair. Sloan School (MIT) Visiting Cttee; mem. MIT Corpn 1987–97; Chancellor, Kent Univ. 1990–95; Chair. Bodleian and Oxford Univ. Libraries Devt 1999–; Chair. Tate Gallery Foundation 1988–92; Hon. FCGI; Hon. FIChemE; Hon. FCIMgT; Hon. LLD (Dundee) 1988; Hon. DCL (Kent) 1990, (Aberdeen) 1992; Hon. DSc (Cranfield Inst. of Tech.) 1992, (Kingston) 1993; Hon. DBA (N London) 1991; Hon. DUniv (Open Univ.) 1993; Corporate Leadership Award, MIT 1987. *Leisure interests:* music, country activities, reading. *Address:* Chubb PLC, Cleveland House, 33 King Street, London, SW1Y 6RJ (Office); Stoke Abbas, South Stoke, Oxon., RG8 0JT, England (Home). *Telephone:* (20) 7766-4800. *E-mail:* info@chubbplc.com (Office). *Website:* www.chubbplc.com (Office).

HORVAT, Branko Anthony, PhD; Croatian university professor and economist; b. 1928, Petrinja; s. of Artur Horvat and Dolores Horvat (Stöhr); m. Ranka Peašinović 1952; two d.; ed Zagreb Univ., Victoria Univ. of Manchester, Harvard Univ., MIT; partisan 1944–45; Researcher, Inst. of Petroleum, Inst. of Econ., Zagreb 1952–55; Research Dir Fed. Planning Bureau, Belgrade 1958–62; Visiting Research Fellow, Inst. of Int. Econs Stockholm 1973–74; f. and Dir Inst. of Econ. Sciences, Belgrade 1963–70; mem. Fed. Econ. Council, Fed. Cttee for Market and Prices 1963–71; Econ. Adviser, govts. of Yugoslavia, Peru and Turkey 1970–74, 1979–80; Visiting Prof. in Econ. Theory, Planning, Comparative Social Systems or Political Theory, Univs. of Belgrade, Ljubljana, Sarajevo, Mich., Fla, Stockholm, Paris, Dar es Salaam, American Univ., Univ. of S. Calif., Univ. Católica de Chile, Univ. of Notre Dame, Yale Univ., Cambridge Univ.; Prof. of Econs, Univ. of Zagreb 1975–; Regents Prof., Univ. of Calif. at Berkeley 1993; Pres. Asscn for Yugoslav Democratic Initiative 1989–90, Social-Democratic Union 1992–; mem. shadow cabinet 1990; Bd mem. Econ. Soc.; Chair. Scientific Soc. of Economists; Founder Pres. Int. Asscn for the Econ. of Self-Man.; f. Ed. Econ. Analysis and Workers' Man.; mem. Yugoslav Govt dels. on planning to UN, Poland, USSR, Int. Foundation for Devt Alternatives, Centre International de Coordination des Recherches sur l'Autogestion; councils of various int. asscns. and bds.; lecturer at over 80 int. educational and scientific establishments; Ford Foundation Fellowship 1964; Fulbright Prof. 1978, 1984–85; Medal of Merit, May Festival Prizes, Zagreb 1948, 1949, 1950, Manchester Statistical Soc. Prize 1956, Book of the Year (USA) 1983, M. Mirković Econs Prize 1986, Int. Festschrift 2001. *Publications include:* Economics of the Petroleum Industry (4 Vols) 1954–65, Towards a Theory of Planned Economy 1961, Interindustry Analysis 1962, Economic Models 1962, Economic Science and National Economy 1968, An Essay of Yugoslav Society 1969, Business Cycles in Yugoslavia 1969, Economic Analysis 1972, Economic Policy of Stabilization 1976, Self-Governing Socialism (co-author) 1976, Political Economy of Socialism 1982, Yugoslav Economy 1967–83, 2 Vols 1984, Social Crisis 1985, The Labour Theory of Prices and Other Unsolved Problems of Economic Theory 1986, The Kosovo Question 1988, Foundations of Yugoslav Socialism 1989, Entrepreneurship and the Market Transformation of 'Social' Ownership 1990, The Theory of Value, Interest and Capital 1994, The Theory of International Trade 1998, Economics of Fast Development 2001, Essays in Economic Planning 2001, The State We Have and the One We Need 2002; 300 articles in numerous int. prof. journals; works have been translated into 18 languages. *Leisure interests:* manual labour, horticulture. *Address:* Institute for Advanced Studies, 32 Gornji Lukšić, Zagreb, Croatia. *Telephone:* (1) 3738411. *Fax:* (1) 3738411. *E-mail:* branko.horvat4@zg.hinet.hr (Home).

HORVITZ, H. Robert, MA, PhD; American professor of biology; b. 8 May 1947; ed Harvard Univ.; Asst Prof. of Biology, MIT, Cambridge, MA 1978, Assoc. Prof. 1981, Prof. 1986–, Investigator Howard Hughes Medical Inst. 1988–; mem. Nat. Acad. of Sciences 1991–; numerous awards and honours including Spencer Award in Neurobiology 1986, US Steel Foundation Award in Molecular Biology 1988, Hans Sigrist Award 1994, Gairdner Foundation Int. Award 1999, Segerfalk Award 2000, Bristol-Myers Squibb Award for Distinguished Achievement in Neuroscience 2001, Genetics Society of America Award 2001, Nobel Prize in Physiology or Medicine (jt recipient)

2002. *Address:* Department of Biology, Massachusetts Institute of Technology, 77 Massachusetts Avenue, Cambridge, MA 02139, USA (Office). *Telephone:* (617) 253-3162 (Office). *Fax:* (617) 253-8126 (Office). *E-mail:* horvitz@mit.edu (Office). *Website:* www.mit.edu (Office).

HOSKING, Geoffrey Alan, PhD, FBA, FRHistS; British academic; b. 28 April 1942, Troon, Ayrshire; s. of Stuart Hosking and Jean Smillie; m. Anne Lloyd Hirst 1970; two d.; ed Maidstone Grammar School, Moscow State Univ., Kings Coll., Cambridge, St Antony's Coll., Oxford; Lecturer in Govt Univ. of Essex 1966–71, Lecturer in History 1972–76, Sr Lecturer and Reader in History 1976–84; Prof. of Russian History, School of Slavonic Studies, Univ. of London 1984–99, Leverhulme Research Prof. 1999–; Deputy Dir School of Slavonic and East European Studies, Univ. of London 1996–98; Visiting Prof. in Political Science Univ. of Wis. (Madison), USA 1971–72, Slavisches Institut, Univ. of Cologne, Germany 1980–81; BBC Reith Lecturer 1988; mem. Booker Prize Jury for Russian Fiction 1993; Dr hc (Russian Acad. of Sciences); LA Times History Book Prize 1986, US Ind. Publrs History Book Prize 2001. *Publications:* The Russian Constitutional Experiment 1973, Beyond Socialist Realism 1980, The First Socialist Society: A History of the Soviet Union from Within 1985, The Awakening of the Soviet Union 1990, The Road to Post-Communism: Independent Political Movements in the Soviet Union 1985–91 (with J. Aves and P. Duncan) 1992, Russia: People and Empire (1552–1917) 1997, Ed. (with George Schöpflin) Myths and Nationhood 1997, Ed. (with Robert Service) Russian Nationalism Past and Present 1998, Ed. (with Robert Service) Reinterpreting Russia 1999, Russia and the Russians: A History from Rus to Russian Federation 2001. *Leisure interests:* music, walking, chess. *Address:* School of Slavonic and East European Studies, University College London, Senate House, Malet Street, London, WC1E 7HU, England. *Telephone:* (20) 7862-8571. *Fax:* (20) 7862-8643 (Office). *E-mail:* g.hosking@ ssees.ac.uk (Office).

HOSKINS, Bob (Robert William); British actor; b. 26 Oct. 1942; s. of Robert Hoskins and Elsie Lillian Hoskins; m. 1st Jane Livesey 1970; one s. one d.; m. 2nd Linda Banwell 1984; one s. one d.; ed Stroud Green School; several stage roles at Nat. Theatre; numerous awards including Best Actor Award, Cannes Film Festival, Variety Club Best Actor Award 1997. *Films include:* National Health 1973, Royal Flash 1974, Zulu Dawn 1980, The Long Good Friday 1980, The Wall 1982, The Honorary Consul 1983, Lassiter 1984, The Cotton Club 1984, Brazil 1985, The Woman Who Married Clark Gable 1985, Sweet Liberty 1985, Mona Lisa 1986 (New York Critics Award, Golden Globe Award, Best Actor Award, Cannes Festival), A Prayer for the Dying 1987, The Lonely Passion of Judith Hearne 1987, Who Framed Roger Rabbit? 1987, The Raggedy Rawney (Dir, acted in and wrote) 1988, Mermaids 1989, Shattered 1990, Heart Condition 1990, The Projectionist 1990, The Favour, The Watch and the Very Big Fish 1990, Hook 1991, The Inner Circle 1992, Super Mario Brothers 1992, Nixon 1995, The Rainbow 1996 (also Dir), Michael 1996, Cousin Bette 1996, Twenty-four-seven 1998, The Secret Agent 1998, Felicia's Journey 1999, Parting Shots 1999, Enemy at the Gates 2001, Last Orders 2001. *Television appearances include:* Omnibus – It Must be Something in the Water 1971, Villains 1972, Thick as Thieves 1972, Schmoedipus 1974, Shoulder to Shoulder 1974, Pennies from Heaven 1975, Peninsula 1975, Sheppey 1980, Flickers 1980, Othello 1981, The Beggars' Opera 1983, Mussolini and I 1984, The Changeling 1993, World War Two: Then There Were Giants 1993, David Copperfield 1999, The Lost World (film) 2001. *Stage:* Old Wicked Songs 1996. *Leisure interests:* photography, gardening, playgoing. *Address:* c/o Hutton Management, 200 Fulham Road, London, SW10 9PN, England (Office).

HOSKYNS, Sir John Austin Hungerford Leigh, Kt; British business executive; b. 23 Aug. 1927, Farnborough, Hants.; s. of the late Lt-Col Chandos Hoskyns and Joyce Hoskyns; m. Miranda Jane Marie Mott 1956; two s. one d.; ed Winchester Coll.; Capt. British Army 1945–57; with IBM UK Ltd 1957–64; Chair. and Man. Dir Hoskyns Group Ltd 1964–75; Part-time Policy Adviser to Opposition 1975–77, Full-time Adviser to Rt Hon Margaret Thatcher (q.v.) and Shadow Cabinet 1977–79, Head, Prime Minister's Policy Unit 1979–82; Dir-Gen. Inst. of Dirs 1984–89; Chair. Burton Group 1990–98 (Dir 1990–98), EMAP 1994–98 (Dir 1993–98), Arcadia Group PLC 1998–; Dir ICL PLC 1982–84, AGB Research PLC 1983–88, Clerical Medical and Gen. Life Assurance Soc. 1983–98, McKechnie Brothers PLC 1983–93, Ferranti PLC 1986–94; Hon. DSc (Salford) 1986; Dr hc (Essex) 1987. *Publication:* Just In Time 2000. *Leisure interests:* opera, shooting. *Address:* c/o Child & Co., 1 Fleet Street, London, EC4Y 1BD, England.

HOSNI, Naguib, DenD; Egyptian professor of criminal law and politician; b. 5 Nov. 1928, Cairo; m. Fawzia Ali 1957; two s. one d.; ed Cairo Univ. and Univ. of Paris, France; Asst Prof. of Criminal Law, Cairo Univ. 1959, Prof. 1964–, Vice-Dean Faculty of Law 1970–73, Dean 1977–83, Pres. 1987–89; Visiting Prof., Arab Univ. of Beirut, Lebanon, 1967–70, Univ. of UAE 1974–76, Univ. of Paris (12) 1991; Pres. Bd of Legal Studies 1987–, African Univs. 1989–; Dir Centre for the Prevention of Crime and Treatment of Offenders, Cairo Univ. 1993–; mem. Int. Soc. of Penal Law, Int. Soc. of Criminology, Int. Soc. of Social Defence; Senator 1989–; State Prize 1961, 1967, Medal of Science 1960, 1979, Medal of the Republic 1976, State Award 1991, Palmes Académiques (France) 1979. *Publications include:* International Criminal Law 1960, Abnormal Criminals 1967, Criminal Participation 1969, Criminal Intent 1988, Treatment of Mentally Ill Offenders 1992, The Constitution and Criminal Law 1992. *Leisure interests:* reading, music. *Address:* 30 Aden Street, Mohandessin, Giza, Egypt. *Telephone:* 3490555; 3490857.

HOSOKAWA, Morihiro; Japanese politician; b. 14 Jan. 1938, Tokyo; m. Kayoko Hosokawa; one s. two d.; ed Sophia Univ., Tokyo; reporter The Daily Asahi Shimbun; mem. House of Councillors 1971–83; Gov. of Kumamoto 1983–91; Founder, Chair. Japan New Party 1992; mem. House of Reps. 1993; Prime Minister 1993–94; fmr mem. Liberal Democratic Party (LDP); retd from politics 1998; Special Adviser to Japan Times. *Leisure interests:* skiing, golf. *Address:* 6F Sankyu-Bldg 3-6-14, Kasumigaseki, Chiyoda-ku, Tokyo 100-0013, Japan (Office). *Telephone:* (3) 3592-0711 (Office). *Fax:* (3) 3592-0665 (Office).

HOSPITAL, Janette Turner, MA; Australian author and professor of English; b. 12 Nov. 1942, Melbourne; d. of Adrian Charles Turner and Elsie Turner; m. Clifford Hospital 1965; one s. one d.; ed Univ. of Queensland, and Queen's Univ., Canada; high school teacher, Queensland 1963–66; librarian, Harvard Univ. 1967–71; Lecturer in English, St Lawrence Coll., Kingston, Ont., in maximum and medium-security fed. penitentiaries for men 1971–82; professional writer 1982–; Writer-in-Residence and lecturer Writing Program, MIT 1985–86, 1987, 1989, Writer-in-Residence Univ. of Ottawa, Canada 1987, Univ. of Sydney, Australia 1989, Queen's Univ. at Herstmonceux Castle, UK 1994; Adjunct Prof. of English, La Trobe Univ., Melbourne 1990–93; Visiting Fellow and Writer-in-Residence Univ. of E Anglia, UK 1996; O'Connor Chair. in Literature, Colgate Univ., Hamilton, NY 1999; Dickey Prof. and Distinguished Writer-in-Residence, Univ. of S. Carolina 1999–; Dr hc Griffith Univ. (Queensland) 1995, Hon. DLitt (Univ. of Queensland) 2003; several awards for novels and short stories; Gold Medal, Nat. Magazine Awards (Canada) 1991 (for travel writing), First Prize, Magazine Fiction, Foundation for the Advancement of Canadian Letters 1982. *Publications:* The Ivory Swing (Seal First Novel Award) 1982, The Tiger in the Tiger Pit 1983, Borderline 1985, Charades 1988, The Last Magician 1992, Oyster 1996, Due Preparations for the Plague 2003; (short story collections) Dislocations (Fiction Award, Fellowship of Australian writers 1988) 1986, Isobars 1990, Collected Stories 1995, North of Nowhere, South of Loss 2003; crime thriller (under pseudonym Alex Juniper) A Very Proper Death 1991; numerous articles. *Leisure interests:* hiking, mountain climbing, music, gardening. *Address:* Department of English, University of South Carolina, Columbia, SC 29208, USA (Office); c/o Barbara Mobbs, P.O. Box 126, Edgeclif, Sydney, NSW 2027, Australia; c/o Mic Cheetham, 11–12 Dover Street, London, W1X 3PH, England. *E-mail:* jthospital@sc.edu (Office).

HOSS, Selim al-, MBA, PhD; Lebanese politician and professor of economics; b. 20 Dec. 1929; s. of Ahmad El-Hoss and Wadad Hoss; m. Leila Hoss (died 1990); one d.; ed American Univ. of Beirut, Indiana Univ., USA; Teacher, later Prof. of Business, American Univ. of Beirut 1955–69; Financial Adviser, Kuwait Fund for Arab Econ. Devt, Kuwait 1964–66; Pres. Banking Supervision Comm. 1967–73; Chair. of Bd and Gen. Man. Nat. Bank for Industrial Devt 1973–76; Prime Minister 1976–80, remaining as Prime Minister in caretaker capacity July–Oct. 1980, Minister of the Econ. and Trade and Information 1976–79, of Industry and Petroleum 1976–77, of Labour, Fine Arts and Educ. 1984–85 (resgnd); Adviser to Arab Monetary Fund, Abu Dhabi, UAE 1983; Chair. of Bd Banque Arabe et Int. d'Investissement, Paris 1982–85; Head, Arab Dinar Study Group, Arab Monetary Fund 1984–85; Minister of Educ. 1985–87; Head, Arab Experts Team commissioned by Arab League 1986–87; Prime Minister 1987–90, also Minister of Foreign and Expatriate Affairs; elected Deputy to Parl. 1992–2000; Pres. of Council of Ministers (Prime Minister of Lebanon) 1976–80, 1987–90, 1998–2000; mem. Bd of Trustees, American Univ. of Beirut 1991–; mem. Consultative Council, Int. Bank for the Middle East and North Africa 1992–. *Publications:* The Development of Lebanon's Financial Markets 1974, Lebanon: Agency and Peace 1982 and six books in Arabic; numerous articles on economics and politics. *Address:* Aïsheh Bakkar, Beirut (Office); Aisheh Bakkar, Beirut, Lebanon (Home). *Telephone:* 736000. *Fax:* 354929.

HOSSAIN, Kemaluddin, LLB; Bangladeshi judge; b. 31 March 1923, Calcutta, India; ed Ballygunge Govt High School, Calcutta, St Xavier's Coll. and Calcutta Univ. Law Coll.; Advocate, High Court, Dacca 1950–69; Sr Advocate Supreme Court, Pakistan 1966–69; Deputy Attorney-Gen., Pakistan 1968–69; Judge, High Court, Dacca 1969–72; Judge, High Court, Bangladesh 1972–75, Appellate Div. 1975–78; Chief Justice, Bangladesh 1978–82; Negotiator, Indus Water Treaty 1960; part-time law lecturer, City Law Coll., Dacca 1956–68; Chair. Law Cttee 1978; attended several int. law confs. including Commonwealth Chief Justices Conf., Canberra May 1980. *Address:* c/o Chief Justice's House, 19 Hare Road, Dhaka, Bangladesh. *Telephone:* 243585 (Office); 404849 (Home).

HOSSAIN, Shah Moazzem, MA; Bangladeshi politician; b. 10 Jan. 1939, Munsigonj Dist; m.; one s. one d.; ed Dhaka Univ.; Gen. Sec. East Pakistan Students League 1959–60, Pres. 1960–63; Chair. the All-Party Action Cttee 1962; political prisoner for many years between 1953 and 1978; Chief Whip, Bangladesh Parliament 1972–73; co-f. Democratic League 1976, Gen. Sec. 1977–83; Minister of Land Admin. and Land Revenue 1973–75, in charge of Ministry of Labour and Manpower 1984–85, of Information 1985–86, of Local Govt, Rural Devt and Co-operatives 1986–88, of Labour and Manpower 1988–90, of Food 1990; Deputy Prime Minister 1987–90. *Publication:* Nitta Keragarey 1976.

HOSSEIN, Robert; French actor and director; b. 30 Dec. 1927, Paris; s. of Amin Hossein and Anna Mincovschi; m. 1st Marina de Poliakoff 1955 (divorced); two s.; m. 2nd Caroline Eliacheff 1962 (divorced); one s.; m. 3rd

Candice Patou 1976; one s.; stage actor, Dir and playwright, film Dir and producer, scriptwriter and actor; Chair. and Man. Dir Sinfonia Films 1963–; Founder and Dir Théâtre Populaire de Reims and of Théâtre-Ecole de Reims 1971; Artistic Dir Théâtre de Paris-Théâtre Moderne 1975–, Théâtre Marigny 2000–; Prix Orange 1963; Commdr, Ordre nat. du Mérite, Officier, Légion d'honneur, Commdr des Arts et des Lettres, Médaille de Vermeil de la Ville de Paris, Molière d'honneur 1995, Prix Grand siècle Laurent Perrir 2000. *Plays include:* La neige était sale, Haute surveillance, Les voyous (writer), La P. respectueuse, Huis-Clos, Vous qui nous jugez (writer), Les six hommes en question (co-writer with Frédéric Dard and producer), La moitié du plaisir (producer), Crime et châtiment, Les bas-fonds, Roméo et Juliette, Pour qui sonne le glas, La maison des otages, Hernani (produced for the Comédie Française) 1974, La maison de Bernada (produced at the Odéon) 1975, Le cuirassé Potemkine (Dir at Palais des Sports) 1975, Des souris et des hommes, Shéhérazade (ballet) 1975, Procès de Jeanne d'Arc (producer) 1976, Pas d'orchidées pour Miss Blandish (producer and actor) 1977, Notre-Dame de Paris (producer) 1978, Le cauchemar de Bella Manningham (producer) 1978, Danton et Robespierre (producer) 1979, Lorna et Ted 1981, Un grand avocat 1983, Les brumes de Manchester 1986, Liberty or Death and the Heritage of the French Revolution (Dominique Prize for Best Dir) 1988, Dans la nuit la liberté (producer) 1989, Cyrano de Bergerac (producer) 1990, Jésus était son nom 1991, Les bas-fonds 1992, Je m'appelais Marie-Antoinette 1993, La nuit du crime (producer and actor) 1994, Angélique, Marquise des anges (director and actor) 1995, Ouragan sur le Caine 1997, La Vie en bleu 1997, Surtout ne coulez pas (producer) 1997, De Gaulle, celui qui a dit non (producer) 1999, Jésus, la Résurrection 2000, Coupable ou non coupable 2001, Lumières et ténèbres 2002. *Films include:* Quai des blondes, Du rififi chez les hommes, Crime et châtiment, Toi le venin (script-writer and producer), Le jeu de la vérité (writer), Le goût de la violence (script-writer and producer), Le repos du guerrier, Le vice et la vertu, Les yeux cernés, Angélique marquise des anges, Banco à Bangkok, La marquise de Düsseldorf, Le tonnerre de Dieu, La seconde vérité, J'ai tué Raspoutine (writer and producer), Indomptable Angélique, Don Juan 1973, Prêtres interdits, Le protecteur, Le faux cul 1975, Les uns et les autres, Le professionnel 1981, Les Misérables (producer) 1982, Un homme nommé Jésus (director) 1983, Jules César 1985, Les brumes de Manchester 1986, Un homme et une femme, vingt ans déjà 1986, Les Enfants du désordre 1989, L'Affaire 1994, la Nuit du Crime 1994, L'Homme au masque de cire 1996, Vénus beauté 1999. *Publications:* La sentinelle aveugle 1978, Nomade sans tribu 1981, En désespoir de cause (memoirs) 1987, La Nostalgie (autobiog.) 2001. *Leisure interest:* skiing. *Address:* Théâtre Marigny, Carré Marigny, 75008 Paris (Office); c/o Mme. Ghislaine de Wing, 10 rue du Docteur Roux, 75015 Paris, France.

HOTTER, Hans; German singer; b. 19 Jan. 1909, Offenbach; m. Helga Fischer 1936; one s. one d.; ed Munich; concert debut 1929, opera debut 1930; mem. Vienna, Hamburg and Munich Opera cos.; has appeared in concerts and operas in maj. cities in Europe, Australia and the USA and in Festivals at Salzburg, Bayreuth and Edin.; renowned for Wagnerian roles; retd 1974. *Address:* c/o Bayerische Staatsoper, 80539 Munich, Germany.

HOU, Hsiao-hsien; Taiwanese film director; b. 8 April 1947, Meihsien, Canton Prov.; ed Taipei Nat. Acad. of Arts film and drama Dept; worked as an electronic calculator salesman; entered film industry in 1973; Asst to several dirs. from 1974. *Films include:* Chiu shih liu-liu-te t'a (Cute Girl) 1981, Feng-erh t'i-t'a-ts'ai (Cheerful Wind) 1982, Tsai na ho-pan ch'ing-ts'ao-ch'ing (Green Grass of Home) 1982, Erh-tzu-te ta wan-ou (The Sandwich Man) 1983, Feng-kuei-lai-te jen (The Boys from Fengkuei/All the Youthful Days) 1983, Tung-tung-te chia-ch'i (A Summer at Grandpa's) 1984, T'ung-nien wang-shih (The Time to Live and the Time to Die) 1985, Lien-lien feng-ch'en (Dust in the Wind/Rite of Passage) 1986, Ni-lo-ho nü-erh (Daughter of the Nile) 1987, Pei-ch'ing ch'eng-shih (A City of Sadness) 1989 (winner of Golden Lion at the Venice Film Festival).

HOU RUNYU; Chinese orchestral conductor; b. 6 Jan. 1945, Kunming; s. of Hou Zhu and Zhu Bangying; m. Su Jia 1971; one s. one d.; ed Music Middle School of Shanghai Conservatory, Shanghai Conservatory (conducting); studied at Musikhochschule, Cologne, FRG and Mozarteum, Salzburg, Austria 1981–85; started playing piano aged 7, debut, Kunming 1954; Prin. Conductor Shanghai Symphony Orchestra 1990–; debut Carnegie Hall, New York 1990; Hon. mem. Richard Wagner Verband, Cologne. *Leisure interests* sport, literature. *Address:* 105 Hunan Road, Shanghai (Office); 1710-3-602 Huai-Hai-Zhong Road, Shanghai, People's Republic of China. *Telephone:* 64316474.

HOU YUNDE, D.M.SC.; Chinese virologist; b. 13 July 1929, Changzhou, Jiangsu Prov.; ed Tongji Univ. Medical Coll., Russian Inst. of Medical Sciences; Fellow Chinese Acad. of Eng; Dir Inst. of Virology, Chinese Acad. of Preventive Medicine 1985–; Dir Virus Research Centre of WHO, researches on para-influenza and the structure and function of virus gene; Vice-Pres. Chinese Acad. of Eng 1998–; Dir Nat. Key Research Lab. for Virogenetic Eng 1998–; now Dir Inst. of Virology, Chinese Acad. of Preventive Medicine; Chair. Board of Tri-Prime Gene 1998–; Assoc. Chief Ed. Chinese Medical Sciences Journal; 21 prizes including one First Prize and two Second Prizes of Nat. Science and Tech. Advancement Award, He Liang & He Li Medical Prize 1994, China Medical Science Award 1996. *Publications:* 9 monographs and over 200 scientific treatises. *Address:* Virology Research Institute of Chinese Academy

of Preventative Medical Science, 100 Yingxin Street, Xuanwu District, Beijing 100052, People's Republic of China (Office). *Telephone:* (10) 63529224 (Office). *Fax:* (10) 63532053 (Office). *E-mail:* engach@mail.cae.ac.cn (Office).

HOU ZONGBIN; Chinese administrator; b. 1929, Nanhe Co., Hebei Prov.; one s. one d.; joined CCP 1946; Vice-Gov., Gansu Prov. 1983–88; Deputy Sec. of Gansu Prov. CP 1986–88; Deputy Sec. Shaanxi Prov. CP 1989–90; Gov. Shaanxi Prov. 1989–90; Sec. Henan Prov. CP 1990–92; a Deputy Sec. Cen. Comm. for Discipline Inspection; Chair. Internal Affairs and Judicial Cttee of 9th NPC 1998–; mem. 14th CCP Cen. Cttee 1992–97. *Address:* c/o Standing Committee of National People's Congress, Beijing, People's Republic of China.

HOUBEN, Francine, MSc; Netherlands architect; b. 2 July 1955, Sittard; m.; two d. one s.; ed Delft Univ. of Tech.; architect with Mecanoo Architecten; Chair., Prof. of Aesthetics of Mobility, Delft Univ. of Tech., Università della Svizzera Italiana, Switzerland; fmr Visiting Prof. and Lecturer at univs. in Germany, Philadelphia, USA, Univ. of Calgary, Canada, Berlage Inst., Amsterdam; Hon. Fellow RIBA; numerous prizes include Rotterdam-Maaskant Prize for Young Architects 1987, National Staalprijs 1998, Chorus Construction Award for the Millennium 2000, Bouwkwaliteitsprijs, Rotterdam 2000, TECU Architecture Award 2001. *Exhibitions:* Mecanoo Blue—Composition, Contrast, Complexity (4 Bienal Internacional de Arquitectura's Award) 2000. *Publications include:* Mecanoo architecten (with P. Volland and L. Waaijers) 1998, Maliebaan, een huls om in te werken 2000, Composition, Contrast Complexity 2001. *Address:* Mecanoo Architecten, Oude Delft 203, 2611 HD Delft, Netherlands. *Telephone:* (31) 152798100 (Office). *Fax:* (31) 152798111 (Office). *E-mail:* info@mecanoo.nl (Office). *Website:* www.mecanoo.nl (Office).

HOUELLEBECQ, Michel, DipAgr; French novelist and poet; b. 26 Feb. 1958, Réunion; m. 1st 1980 (divorced); one s.; m. 2nd Marie-Pierre Gauthier 1998; first works (poetry) published in Nouvelle Revue de Paris 1985; Grand Prix Nat. des Lettres Jeune Talent 1998. *Publications include:* Contre le monde, contre la vie 1991, Rester vivant 1991, La poursuite de bonheur (Prix Tristan Tzara) 1992, Extension du domaine à la lutte 1994, Le sens du combat (Prix de Flore) 1996 , Interventions, Les Particules élémentaires (Prix Novembre), Renaissance 1999, Lanzarote 2000, Plateforme (Impac Prize) 2002. *Address:* c/o Flammarion, 26 rue Racine, 75006 Paris, France (Office).

HOUGH, Stephen Andrew, MMus, FRNCM; British pianist; b. 22 Nov. 1961, Heswall, Cheshire; ed Chetham's School of Music, Royal Northern Coll. of Music and Juilliard School, New York; regular guest performer with London Symphony, Philharmonia, Royal Philharmonic and London Philharmonic Orchestras; Visiting Prof. RAM; regular appearances with maj. orchestras in USA, Europe, Australia, Far East and at int. music festivals; MacArthur Foundation Fellowship 2001; Dayas Gold Medal (Royal Northern Coll. of Music), Terence Judd Award 1982, Naumburg Int. Piano Competition 1983; Gramophone Record of the Year 1996, 2002. *Recordings include:* complete Beethoven violin sonatas (with Robert Mann), Hummel piano concertos, recitals of Liszt and Schumann, Brahms concerto nos. 1 and 2, The Piano Album Vol I, II, Britten Music for One and Two Pianos, Scharwenka and Sauer concertos, Grieg, Liszt, Rubinstein cello sonatas (with Steven Isserlis), Brahms violin sonatas (with Robert Mann), York Bowen piano music, Franck piano music, Mompou piano music, Liebermann piano concertos, Mendelssohn piano and orchestral works, Schubert sonatas and New York Variations, Brahms Clarinet Trio, The New Piano Album, Liszt Sonata, Mozart Piano and Wind Quintet, Brahms F minor Sonata, Saint-Saëns Complete Music for Piano and Orchestra, English Piano Album. *Compositions:* Transcriptions, Suite R-B and Other Enigmas, Piano Album. *Leisure interest:* reading. *Address:* c/o Harrison Parrott Ltd, 12 Penzance Place, London, W11 4PA, England. *Website:* www.stephenhough.com (Home).

HOUGHTON, James Richardson, AB, MBA; American business executive (retd); b. 6 April 1936, Corning, New York; s. of the late Amory Houghton and Laura Richardson Houghton; m. May Kinnicutt 1962; one s. one d.; ed St Paul's School, Concord, NH, Harvard Coll. and Harvard Univ. Business School; worked in investment banking, Goldman, Sachs and Co., New York 1959–61; in production and finance, Corning Glass Works, Danville, Ky and Corning, New York 1962–64; Vice-Pres. and Area Man., Corning Glass Int., Zurich and Brussels 1964–68; Vice-Pres. and Gen. Man. Consumer Products Div., Corning Glass Works (Corning Inc. since 1989), Corning, New York 1968–71, Vice-Chair. of Bd 1971–83, Chair. of Bd and CEO 1983–96, also fmr Chair. Exec. Cttee; Dir Exxon Mobil, Corning Inc., Metropolitan Life Insurance Co.; Trustee Corning Glass Works Foundation, Corning Museum of Glass, Metropolitan Museum of Art, Pierpont Morgan Library; mem. Council on Foreign Relations, The Business Council, Harvard Corpn. *Address:* c/o Corning Inc., 80 E Market Street, Suite 201, Corning, NY 14830; The Field, 2649B Spencer Hill Road, Corning, NY 14830, USA (Home).

HOUGHTON, Sir John, Kt, CBE, MA, DPhil, FRS; British physicist; b. 30 Dec. 1931, Dyserth, Clwyd; s. of Sidney Houghton and Miriam Houghton (née Yarwood); m. 1st Margaret E. Broughton 1962 (died 1986); one s. one d.; m. 2nd Sheila Thompson 1988; ed Rhyl Grammar School and Jesus Coll., Oxford; Research Fellow, Royal Aircraft Establishment. Farnborough 1954–57; Lecturer in Atmospheric Physics, Univ. of Oxford 1958–62, Reader 1962–76, Prof. 1976–83, Fellow, Jesus Coll. 1960–83, Hon. Fellow 1983–; Dir Appleton, Science and Eng Research Council 1979–83; Chair. Earth Observation Advisory Cttee, European Space Agency 1980–93; Chair. Jt Scientific Cttee, World Climate Research Prog. 1981–83; Dir-Gen. Meteorological Office

1983–90, Chief Exec. 1990–91; mem. Exec. Cttee WMO 1983–91, Vice-Pres. 1987–91; Pres. Royal Meteorological Soc. 1976–78; Chair. (or Co-Chair.) Scientific Assessment Working Group, Intergovernmental Panel on Climate Change 1988–2002, Royal Comm. on Environmental Pollution 1992–98, Jt Scientific and Technical Cttee, Global Climate Observing System 1992–95; mem. UK Govt Panel on Sustainable Devt 1994–2000; Chair. John Rey Initiative 1997–; Hon. Scientist Rutherford Appleton Lab. 1992–; Fellow Optical Soc. of America; mem. Acad. Europaea; Trustee Shell Foundation 2000–; Hon. FRIBA 2001; Hon. mem. Royal Meteorological Soc., American Meteorological Soc.; Hon. DSc (Univ. of Wales) 1991, (Stirling) 1992, (East Anglia) 1993, (Leeds) 1995, (Heriot-Watt) 1997, (Greenwich) 1997, (Glamorgan) 1998, (Reading) 1999, (Birmingham) 2000, (Gloucestershire) 2001, (Hull) 2002; Charles Chree Medal and Prize (Inst. of Physics) 1979, jt recipient Rank Prize for opto-electronics 1989, Glazebrook Medal (Inst. of Physics) 1990, Symonds Gold Medal, Royal Meteorological Soc. 1991, Bakerian Lecturer, Royal Soc. 1991, Global 500 Award, UNEP 1994, Gold Medal, Royal Astronomical Soc. 1995, Int. Meteorological Org. Prize 1998. *Publications:* Infra Red Physics (with S. D. Smith) 1966, The Physics of Atmospheres 1977, Remote Sounding of Atmospheres (with F. W. Taylor and C. D. Rodgers) 1984, Does God Play Dice? 1988, The Search for God: Can Science Help? 1995, Global Warming: The Complete Briefing 1997. *Address:* Hadley Centre, Meteorological Office, Bracknell, Berks., RG12 2SY, England. *Fax:* (1344) 856912.

HOUGRON, Jean (Marcel), LenD; French writer; b. 1 July 1923, Caen; s. of Jean Hougron and Denise Grude; m. 1st Noëlle Desgouille (divorced); two s. two d.; m. 2nd Victoria Sanchez 1974; one s.; ed Faculty of Law, Univ. of Paris; schoolmaster 1943–46; commercial employment in export-import firm, Saigon 1946–47; lorry driver 1947–49; trans. in American Consulate 1950; news ed. Radio France Asie 1951; returned to France to write 1952; bookseller in Nice 1953–54; lived in Spain 1958–60; Grand Prix du Roman, Acad. Française 1953; Prix Populiste 1965; Grand Prix de la Science-Fiction for Le Naguen 1982; Chevalier des Arts et des Lettres. *Publications:* Tu récolteras la tempête 1950, Rage blanche 1951, Soleil au ventre 1952, Mort en fraude (film) 1953, La nuit indochinoise 1953, Les portes de l'aventure 1954, Les Asiates 1954, Je reviendrai à Kandara (film) 1955, La terre du barbare 1958, Par qui le scandale 1960, Le signe du chien 1961, Histoire de Georges Guersant 1964, Les humiliés 1965, La gueule pleine de dents 1970, L'homme de proie 1974, L'anti-jeu 1977, Le Naguen 1979, La chambre (novel) 1982, Coup de soleil 1984, Beauté chinoise 1987. *Address:* c/o Editions J'ai hu, 84 rue de Grenelle, 75007 Paris (Office); 1 rue des Guillemites, 75004 Paris, France (Home).

HOUMADI, Halifa; Comoran politician; Prime Minister of Comoros 1994–95; mem. Rassemblement pour la Démocratie et le Renouveau (RDR). *Address:* c/o Office of the Prime Minister, BP 421, Moroni, Comoros.

HOUNGBÉDJI, Adrien; Benin politician and lawyer; sentenced to death in absentia March 1975 after alleged involvement in attempted coup; Speaker of Nat. Ass. 1991–96; Prime Minister 1996–98; Leader Parti du renouveau démocratique (PRD). *Address:* Parti du renouveau démocratique, B.P. 281, Cotonou, Benin (Office). *Telephone:* 33-94-88 (Office). *Fax:* 33-94-89 (Office). *Website:* www.prd-by.net (Office).

HOUNSFIELD, Sir Godfrey Newbold, Kt, CBE, FRS; British research scientist; b. 28 Aug. 1919; s. of Thomas Hounsfield; ed Magnus Grammar School, Newark, City and Guilds Coll., London and Faraday House Electrical Eng Coll.; served RAF 1939–46; with EMI Ltd 1951–, Head of Medical Systems section 1972–76, Chief Staff Scientist 1976–77, Sr Staff Scientist, Cen. Research Labs. of EMI (now THORN EMI Central Research Labs.) 1977–86, Consultant to Labs. 1986–; inventor EMI-scanner computerized transverse axial tomography system for X-ray examination; Professorial Fellow in Imaging Sciences, Univ. of Manchester 1978–; Consultant (part-time) Nat. Heart and Chest Hospitals 1986–; Hon. FRCP; Hon. Fellow Royal Coll. of Radiologists; Hon.Dr. Med. (Basel) 1975; Hon. DSc (City Univ., London) 1976, (London) 1976; Hon. D. Tech. (Loughborough) 1976; Dr. hc (Cambridge) 1992; MacRobert Award 1972; Wilhelm-Exner Medal, Austrian Industrial Asscn 1974; Ziedses des Plantes Medal, Physikalisch-Medizinische Gesellschaft, Würzburg 1974; Prince Philip Medal Award, City and Guilds of London Inst. 1975; ANS Radiation Award, Georgia Inst. of Tech. 1975; Lasker Award 1975; Duddell Bronze Medal, Inst. of Physics 1976; Golden Plate, American Acad. of Achievement 1976; Churchill Gold Medal 1976; Gairdner Foundation Award 1976; shared Nobel Prize in Medicine and Physiology 1979 with Prof. A. M. Cormack for Devt of computer-assisted tomography and other awards and prizes. *Publications:* articles in professional journals. *Leisure interests:* mountain walks and country rambles, music, playing piano. *Address:* EMI Central Research Laboratories, Dawley Road, Hayes, Middx, UB3 1HH (Office); 15 Crane Park Road, Whitton, Twickenham, TW2 6DF, Middx, England (Home). *Telephone:* (20) 8848-6404 (Office); (20) 8894-1746 (Home).

HOUSE, Lynda Mary; Australian film producer; b. 30 April 1949, Tasmania; d. of Graeme House and Patricia House; m. Tony Mahood 1993; mem. Bd Film Vic. 1993–96, Australian Film Finance Corpn 1997–2002. *Films include:* Proof (Australian Film Inst. Best Film 1991), Muriel's Wedding (Australian Film Inst. Best Film 1994), River Street 1996, Secret Brides-

maid's Business 2001, Ned Kelly 2002. *Leisure interests:* watching films, reading, gardening. *Address:* 117 Rouse Street, Port Melbourne, Vic. 3121, Australia. *Telephone:* (3) 9646-4025. *Fax:* (3) 9646-6336.

HOUSHIARY, Shirazeh, BA; British sculptor; b. 15 Jan. 1955, Iran; ed Tehran Univ., Chelsea School of Art and Cardiff Coll. of Art; sculptor at the Lisson Gallery, London; Jr Fellow Cardiff Coll. of Art 1979–80; Prof. London Inst. 1997–. *Solo exhibitions include:* Chapter Arts Centre 1980, Galleria Massimo Minini, Milan 1983, Valentina Moncada, Rome 1992, Camden Arts Centre, London, Fine Arts Centre, Univ. of Mass. 1993–94, Islamic Gallery, British Museum 1997. *Group exhibitions include:* The Sculpture Show (Arts Council of GB, Hayward Gallery, Serpentine Gallery), New Art (Tate Gallery London) 1983, Bruges La Morte Gallery, Belgium 1992, Sculptors' Drawings The Body of Drawing (Univ. of Warwick, Coventry and The Mead Gallery) 1993, Tate Gallery, London 1994, Sculpture at Goodwood 1994, 1997, Dialogues of Peace, Palais des Nations, Geneva 1995, Negotiating Rapture, Museum of Contemporary Art, Chicago 1996, Follow Me: Britische Kunst en der Unterelbe, Schloss Agathenburg 1997. *Address:* Lisson Gallery London Ltd, 67 Lisson Street, London, NW1 5DA, England. *Telephone:* (20) 7724-2739. *Fax:* (20) 7724-7124.

HOUSLAY, Miles Douglas, PhD, FRSE, FRSA, FIBiol; British professor of biochemistry; b. 25 June 1950, Wolverhampton; s. of Edwin Douglas Houslay and Georgina Marie Houslay (née Jeffs); m. Rhian Mair Gee 1972; two s. one d.; ed The Grammar School, Brewood, Staffs., Univ. Coll., Cardiff, King's Coll., Cambridge; ICI Postdoctoral Research Fellow, Univ. of Cambridge 1974–76, Research Fellow, Queen's Coll. 1975–76; Lecturer in Biochem., UMIST 1976–82, Reader 1982–84; Gardiner Prof. of Biochem., Univ. of Glasgow 1984–; Hon. Sr Research Fellow, Calif. Metabolic Research Foundation, La Jolla, USA 1980–91; Deputy Chair. Editorial Bd Biochemical Journal; Ed.-in-Chief, Cellular Signalling; mem. Editorial Bd Progress in Growth Factor Research 1988–93; external assessor Univ. of Malaysia 1991–; mem. Cttee, Biochemical Soc. 1982–86; Chair. MRC Cell Bd Research Grant Cttee A 1990–92, British Heart Foundation Research Grant Panel 1996–98; mem. MRC Cell Bd 1989–94; mem. Scottish Home and Health Dept Research Cttee 1991–94, Wellcome Trust Biochem. Cell Biology Grant Panel 1996–2000; Selby Fellow, Australian Royal Soc. 1984; Trustee British Heart Foundation 1996–2000; Colworth Medal, Biochemical Soc. 1985. *Publications:* Dynamics of Biological Membranes and over 370 scientific articles. *Leisure interests:* walking, music, cycling, sailing, driving. *Address:* Molecular Pharmacology Group, Division of Biochemistry and Molecular Biology, IBLS, Wolfson Building, University of Glasgow, Glasgow, G12 8QQ, Scotland. *Telephone:* (141) 330-5903. *Fax:* (141) 330-4365 (Office). *E-mail:* m.houslay@bio.gla.ac .uk. *Website:* www.gla.ac.uk/ibls/bmb/mdh (Home).

HOUSTON, Whitney; American singer and actress; b. 9 Aug. 1963, East Orange, NJ; d. of the late John Houston and of Cissy Houston; m. Bobby Brown 1992; one d.; trained under direction of mother; mem. Hew Hope Baptist Jr Choir 1974; backing vocalist for Chaka Khan and Lou Rawls 1978; appeared in Cissy Houston night club act; recording debut Hold Me (duet with Teddy Pendergrass) 1984; solo artist 1985–; first US and European tours 1986; Montreux Rock Festival 1987; Nelson Mandela Tribute Concert, Wembley, London 1988; US nat. anthem, Super Bowl XXV, Miami 1991; Speaker, HIV/AIDS rally, London 1991; Hon. HHD (Grambling Univ.); Grammy Award for Best Female Pop Performance 1985, 1987, for Best R & B Vocal Performance 2000; seven American Music Awards; Emmy 1986; Songwriter's Hall of Fame 1990. *Albums:* Whitney Houston 1985, Whitney 1986, I'm Your Baby Tonight 1990, My Love is Your Love 1998, Whitney: The Greatest Hits 2000, Love Whitney 2001, Just Whitney 2002. *Film soundtracks:* The Bodyguard 1992, Waiting to Exhale 1995, The Preacher's Wife 1996. *Singles:* You Give Good Love 1985, Saving All My Love For You 1985, How Will I Know 1986, Greatest Love of All 1986, I Wanna Dance With Somebody 1987, Didn't We Almost Have It All 1987, So Emotional 1987, Where Do Broken Hearts Go 1988, Love Will Save The Day 1988, I'm Your Baby Tonight 1990, All The Man That I Need 1991, Miracle 1991, My Name Is Not Susan 1991, I Will Always Love You 1992, I'm Every Woman 1993, I Have Nothing 1993, Run To You 1993, Queen of the Night 1994, Something In Common (with Bobby Brown) 1994, Exhale (Shoop Shoop) 1995, Count On Me (with CeCe Winans) 1996, Why Does It Hurt So Bad 1996, Step By Step 1997, I Believe In You And Me 1997, When You Believe (with Mariah Carey) 1998, It's Not Right But It's Okay 1999, My Love Is Your Love 1999, I Learned From The Best 1999, If I Told You That (with George Michael) 2000, Could I Have This Kiss Forever (with Enrique Iglesias) 2000, Heartbreak Hotel (with Faith Evans and Kelly Price) 2000, Whatchulookinat 2002, One Of Those Days 2002. *Films:* The Bodyguard 1992, Waiting to Exhale 1995, The Preacher's Wife 1996, Scratch the Surface 1997, Anything for You 2000. *Address:* c/o Arista Records, 6 West 57th Street, New York, USA (Office). *Website:* www.whitneyhouston.com.

HOUTHAKKER, Hendrik Samuel; American economist; b. 31 Dec. 1924, Amsterdam, Netherlands; s. of Bernard Houthakker and Marion (née Lichtenstein) Houthakker; m. Anna-Teresa Tymieniecka 1955; two s. one d.; ed Univ. of Amsterdam; Research Staff mem., Dept of Applied Econs, Univ. of Cambridge 1949–51; on Research Staff, Cowles Comm. for Research in Econs, Univ. of Chicago 1952–53; Prof. of Econs, Stanford Univ. 1954–60, Harvard Univ. 1960–94, Prof. Emer. 1994–, Chair. 1987–88; Sr Staff Economist, Council of Econ. Advisers 1967–68, mem. 1969–71; Vice-Pres. American Econ. Asscn 1972; Dir New York Futures Exchange 1979–; Fellow, Econometric Soc.

(Past Pres. and Council mem.); mem. NAS; Corresp. mem. Royal Netherlands Acad. of Sciences; Dr. hc (Amsterdam) 1972, (Fribourg) 1974; John Bates Clark Medal of American Econ. Asscn 1963. *Publications:* The Analysis of Family Budgets (with S. J. Prais) 1955, Consumer Demand in the United States (with L. D. Taylor) 1966, Economic Policy for the Farm Sector 1967, The World Price of Oil, 1976; also articles. *Address:* 348 Payson Road, Belmont, MA 02178 (Home); Department of Economics, Littauer Bldg, Harvard University, Cambridge, MA 02138 (Office); 348 Payson Road, Belmont, MA 02178, USA. *Telephone:* (617) 495-2111 (Office).

HOUTTE, Baron Jean van, DenD; Belgian politician and emeritus university professor; b. 17 March 1907, Ghent; s. of Hubert van Houtte; m. Cécile de Stella 1932; one s. three d.; ed Univ. of Ghent; Prof. Univ. of Liège 1931, Univ. of Ghent 1937; Head of Secretariat, Ministry of the Interior 1944–45; co-opted Senator 1949–68; Minister of Finance 1950–52, 1958–61; Prime Minister 1952–54; Minister of State 1966; Hon. Pres. Sabena Airlines; various Belgian and foreign decorations. *Publications:* Traité des sociétés de personnes à responsabilité limitée 1935, 1950, 1962, La responsabilité civile dans les transports aériens 1940, La réparation des dommages de guerre aux biens privés 1948, Formulierboek voor notarissen 1947, Principes du droit fiscal belge 1958, 1966, 1979. *Address:* 54 Boulevard St Michel, Brussels, Belgium. *Telephone:* 733-62-94.

HOVE, Andrew C., Jr; American finance official; b. 9 Nov. 1934, Minden, Neb.; s. of the late Andrew C. Hove and Rosalie Vopat; m. Ellen Matzke 1956; one s. two d.; ed Univ. of Nebraska and Univ. of Wisconsin Grad. School of Banking; US Navy 1956–60; Neb. Nat. Guard 1960–63; officer, Minden Exchange Bank & Trust Co. 1960–81, Chair. and CEO 1981–90, Vice-Chair. 1990–92; Vice-Chair. Fed. Deposit Insurance Corpn 1990–92, 1994–97, 1998–, Chair. 1992–94, 1997–98. *Address:* Federal Deposit Insurance Corporation, 550 17th Street, NW, Washington, DC 20429, USA.

HOVE, Chenjerai, BA; Zimbabwean journalist and writer; b. 9 Feb. 1956, Zvishavane; s. of R. Muza Hove and Jessie Muza Hove; m. Thecla Hove 1978; three s. two d.; ed Gweru Teacher's Coll.; high school teacher 1978–81; Ed. Mambo Press, Gweru 1981; Sr Ed. Zimbabwe Publishing house, Harare 1985; Ed. Cultural Features, Interpress Service 1988; Writer-in-Residence, Univ. of Zimbabwe 1991–94; Visiting Prof. Lewis and Clark Coll., Oregon, USA 1995; full-time writer 1999–; in exile in France 2002–; Democracy and Freedom of Speech in Africa Prize, Berlin 2001. *Publications:* Swimming in Floods of Tears (co-author) 1983, Red Hills of Home 1985, Bones (Zimbabwe Book Publishers Literary Award 1988, Noma Award for Publishing in Africa 1989) 1988, Shadows 1991, Guardians of the Soil 1996, Ancestors 1996, Shebeen Tales: Messages from Harare 1997, Rainbows in the Dust 1998. *Leisure interests:* gardening, reading, snooker, table tennis. *Address:* c/o Édition Actes Sud, BP 38, 13633 Arles Cedex, France (Office).

HOVERS, Joannes Coenradus Maria, PhD; Netherlands business executive; b. 29 July 1943, Beek; m. Ineke van der Heijde 1971; three s.; ed Michiel Lyceum, Geleen, Tilburg Univ.; with Océ NV 1967–76, Chair. Bd of Exec. Dirs. May 1998–; Chair. Man. Bd Teewen Group (Bldg materials), later Chair. Man. Bd Synres (synthetic resins) 1976–83; mem. Man. Bd Stork NV 1983–88, Exec. Vice-Pres. Man. Bd 1988–89, CEO Man. Bd 1989–98; Chair. Comm. of Int. Econ. Relations; Supervisory Dir De Nederlandsche Bank NV, Hoechst AG, Koninklijke Grolsch NV, Ericsson Telecommunicatie BV, Randstad Holding NV; mem. Supervisory Bd TIAS Training Inst., Gooi-Noord Regional Hosp.; Asscn of European Man. Publrs. Award 1973. *Address:* Océ NV, P.O. Box 101, 5900 MA Venlo, Netherlands. *Telephone:* (77) 3592205. *Fax:* (77) 3595436.

HOVING, Thomas, PhD; American author and cultural administrator; b. 15 Jan. 1931, New York; s. of Walter Hoving and Mary Osgood Field; m. Nancy Bell 1953; one d.; ed The Buckley School, New York, Eaglebrook School, Deerfield, Mass., Exeter Acad., Exeter NH, The Hotchkiss School, Lakeville, Conn. and Princeton Univ.; Curatorial Asst of Medieval Art and The Cloisters, Metropolitan Museum of Art 1959–60, Asst Curator 1960–63, Assoc. Curator 1963–65, Curator of Medieval Art and The Cloisters 1965; Commr of Parks, New York 1966; Admin. of Recreation and Cultural Affairs, New York 1967; Dir Metropolitan Museum of Art 1966–77; Ed.-in-.Chief Connoisseur Magazine 1981–90; Arts and Entertainment Corresp. ABC News 20/20 1978–84; Pres. Hoving Associates Inc. (cultural affairs consulting); Fellowship, Nat. Council of Humanities 1955, Kienbusch and Haring Fellowship 1957; Hon. LLD (Pratt Inst.) 1967; Hon. DFA (New York) 1968; Hon. DHum(Princeton) 1968; Hon. DLitt (Middlebury Coll.) 1968; Distinguished Citizen's Award, Citizen's Budget Cttee 1967, Creative Leadership in Educ. Award, New York Univ. 1975, Woodrow Wilson Award, Princeton 1975. *Publications:* Guide to the Cloisters 1962, Tutankhamun, The Untold Story 1978, Two Worlds of Andrew Wyeth 1978, King of the Confessors 1981, Masterpiece 1986, Discovery 1989, Making the Mummies Dance, Inside the Metropolitan Museum of Art 1992, False Impressions: The Hunt for Big-Time Art Fakes 1996, Andrew Wyeth: Autobiography 1996, Greatest Works of Art of Western Civilization 1997, Art for Dummies 1999, The Art of Dan Namingha 2000. *Leisure interests:* sailing, skiing, bicycling, flying. *Address:* Hoving Associates Inc., 150 East 73rd Street, New York, NY 10021, USA. *Telephone:* (212) 734-1480 (Office). *Fax:* (212) 570-0348. *E-mail:* tomhoving@earthlink.net (Office).

HOWARD, Alan Mackenzie, CBE; British actor; b. 5 Aug. 1937, London; s. of the late Arthur John Howard and of Jean (Compton Mackenzie) Howard; m. 1st Stephanie Hinchcliffe Davies 1965 (divorced 1976); m. 2nd Sally

Beauman 1976; one s.; ed Ardingley Coll.; nat. service with RAF in Germany 1956–58; stage hand, Asst Stage Man., actor, Belgrade Theatre Coventry 1958–60; London West End debut, Duke of York's Theatre in Roots 1959; played in London at Royal Court, Arts, Mermaid, Strand, Phoenix theatres, also outside London 1960–65; with RSC 1966–, Assoc. Artist 1967–; Plays and Players London Theatre Critics Most Promising Actor Award 1969, Best Actor Award 1977; Soc. of West End Theatre Managers Best Actor in a Revival Award 1976, 1978; Evening Standard Drama Award for Best Actor 1978, 1981; Variety Club of Great Britain Best Actor Award 1980. *Plays include:* Twelfth Night, Revenger's Tragedy, As You Like It, The Relapse, King Lear, Troilus and Cressida, Much Ado About Nothing, Bartholomew Fair, Dr. Faustus, Hamlet, Midsummer Night's Dream, Enemies, Man of Mode, The Balcony, The Bewitched, Henry IV Parts 1 and 2, Henry V, Wild Oats, Henry VI Parts 1, 2 and 3, Coriolanus, Antony and Cleopatra, Children of the Sun, Richard II, Richard III, The Forest, Good 1981, 1982–83, Breaking the Silence 1985, The Silver King 1990, Scenes from a Marriage 1990, Pygmalion 1992, Macbeth 1993, La Grande Magia 1995, Rosencrantz and Guildenstern Are Dead 1995, Oedipus Plays 1996, Waiting for Godot 1997, King Lear 1997, Khludov in Flight 1998, The Play About the Baby 1998, Sloper in the Heiress 2000, Lulu 2001. *Films include:* The Return of the Musketeers, The Cook, The Thief, His Wife and Her Lover. *Television appearances include:* Coriolanus, Sherlock Holmes, A Perfect Spy. *Leisure interests:* reading, music. *Address:* c/o Julian Belfrage Associates, 46 Albemarle Street, London, W1X 4PP, England. *Telephone:* (20) 7491-4400.

HOWARD, Ann; British mezzo-soprano opera singer; b. 22 July 1936, Norwood, London; d. of William A. Swadling and Gladys W. Swadling; m. Keith Giles 1954; one d.; ed with Topliss Green and Rodolfa Lhombino, London and Dominic Modesti, Paris; repertoire includes Carmen, Dalila (Samson et Dalila), Dulcinée (Don Quichotte), Hélène (La Belle Hélène), Eboli (Don Carlo), Azucena (Il Trovatore), Amneris (Aida), Isabella (L' Italiana in Algeri), Proserpina (Orfeo), Ortrud (Lohengrin), Brangaene (Tristan und Isolde), Fricka (Das Rheingold and Die Walküre), Baba the Turk (The Rake's Progress), Katisha (The Mikado), Czipra (Gipsy Baron), Lilli Vanessi (Kiss Me Kate), Clytemnestra (Electra), La Grande Duchesse de Gerolstein, Stepmother (Into The Woods), Prince Orlofsky (Die Fledermaus), Old Lady (Candide), Auntie (Peter Grimes), Hostess (Boris Godunov), Jezi Baba (Rusalka), Marcellina (Marriage of Figaro), Emma Jones (Street Scene), performed in world premières of Mines of Sulphur (Bennett) 1970, Rebecca (Josephs) 1982, The Tempest (Eaton, USA) 1985, The Plumber's Gift (Blake) 1989, The Doctor of Myddfai (Maxwell Davies) 1996 and in UK première of Le Grand Macabre 1981; series of Gilbert and Sullivan operas Performing Arts Centre, NY State Univ. 1993–98; has appeared in UK, France, Canada, USA, Mexico, Chile, Portugal, Germany, Austria and Italy and on BBC radio and TV; teaches privately; The Worshipful Co. of Musicians Sir Charles Santley Memorial Award 2002. *Leisure interests:* gardening, cooking. *Address:* c/o Stafford Law Associates, 6 Barham Close, Weybridge, Surrey, KT13 9PR, England. *Telephone:* (1932) 854489. *Fax:* (1932) 858521.

HOWARD, Anthony Michell, CBE, MA; British journalist; b. 12 Feb. 1934, London; s. of the late Canon W. G. Howard and Janet Howard (née Rymer); m. Carol Anne Gaynor 1965; ed Westminster School and Christ Church, Oxford; on editorial staff Manchester Guardian 1959–61; Political Corresp. New Statesman 1961–64; Whitehall Corresp. Sunday Times 1965; Washington Corresp. Observer 1966–69; Asst Ed. New Statesman 1970–72, Ed. 1972–78; Ed. The Listener 1979–81; Deputy Ed. The Observer 1981–88; Presenter Face the Press, Channel Four 1982–85; Presenter, reporter BBC TV 1989–92; Obituaries Ed., The Times 1993–99; Harkness Fellow, USA 1960; Hon. LLD (Nottingham) 2001; Hon. DLitt (Leicester) 2003; Gerald Barry Award, What the Papers Say 1998. *Publications:* The Making of the Prime Minister (with Richard West) 1965; ed. The Crossman Diaries 1964–70, 1979, Rab: The Life of R. A. Butler 1987, Crossman: The Pursuit of Power 1990; ed. The Times Lives Remembered 1993. *Address:* 11 Campden House Court, 42 Gloucester Walk, London, W8 4HU; Dinham Lodge, Ludlow, Shropshire, SY8 1EH, England. *Telephone:* (20) 7937-7313 (London); (1584) 878457 (Shropshire).

HOWARD, Sir David Howarth Seymour, Bt, MA, DSc; British business executive; b. 29 Dec. 1945, Lincoln; s. of Sir Edward Howard, Bt; m. Valerie Picton Crosse 1968; two s. two d.; ed Radley Coll., Worcester Coll., Oxford; Chair. Charles Stanley & Co., Stockbrokers 1971–; mem. Sutton London Borough Council 1974–78; Common Councilman, City of London 1972–86, Alderman 1986–, Sheriff 1997–98, Lord Mayor of London 2000–01; Master, Gardeners' Co. 1990–91; Hon. FSI. *Leisure interest:* gardening. *Address:* Charles Stanley & Co. Ltd., 25 Luke Street, London, EC2A 4AR, England. *Telephone:* (20) 7739-8200. *Fax:* (20) 7739-7798.

HOWARD, Elizabeth Jane, CBE, FRSL; British novelist; b. 26 March 1923; d. of David Liddon and Katharine M. Howard; m. 1st Peter M. Scott 1942; one d.; m. 2nd James Douglas-Henry 1959; m. 3rd Kingsley Amis 1965 (divorced 1983, deceased); ed at home and at London Mask Theatre School; BBC TV modelling 1939–46; Sec. Inland Waterways Asscn 1947; then professional writer including plays for TV; Hon. Artistic Dir Cheltenham Literary Festival 1962; Artistic Co-Dir Salisbury Festival of Arts 1973; John Llewellyn Rhys Memorial Prize 1950, Yorkshire Post Prize 1982. *Film scripts:* Getting It Right 1985, The Attachment 1986, The Very Edge. *Television:* Our Glorious Dead, Sight Unseen, Skittles, adaptations of After Julius (3 plays for TV), Something in Disguise (6 plays for TV). *Publications:* The Beautiful Visit

1950, The Long View 1956, The Sea Change 1959, After Julius 1965, Something in Disguise 1969 (TV series 1982), Odd Girl Out 1972, Mr. Wrong 1975; Ed. A Companion for Lovers 1978; Getting it Right 1982 (Yorkshire Post Prize 1982), Howard and Maschler on Food: Cooking for Occasions (jtly.) 1987, The Light Years (1st vol. of The Cazalet Chronicle), Green Shades (gardening anthology) 1991, Marking Time (2nd vol. of The Cazalet Chronicle) 1991, Confusion (3rd vol. of The Cazalet Chronicle) 1993, Casting Off (4th vol. of the Cazalet Chronicle) 1995, Falling 1999, Slipstream (autobiog.) 2002. *Leisure interests:* music, gardening, enjoying all the arts, travelling, natural history, reading. *Address:* c/o Jonathan Clowes, Iron Bridge House, Bridge Approach, London, NW1 8BD, England.

HOWARD, Hon. John Winston, LLB; Australian politician; b. 26 July 1939, Sydney; s. of Lyall Falconer and Mona Jane Howard; m. Alison Janette Parker 1971; two s. one d.; ed Univ. of Sydney; solicitor to Supreme Court, NSW 1962; partner, Sydney solicitors' firm 1968–74; Liberal MP for Bennelong, NSW, Fed. Parl. 1974–; Minister for Business and Consumer Affairs 1975–77, Minister Assisting Prime Minister 1977, Fed. Treas. 1977–83; Deputy Leader of Opposition 1983–85, Leader 1985–89; Prime Minister of Australia March 1996–; Shadow Minister for Industrial Relations, Employment and Training, Shadow Minister Assisting the Leader on the Public Service and Chair. Manpower and Labour Market Reform Group 1990–95; mem. State Exec., NSW Liberal Party 1963–74; Vice-Pres., NSW Div., Liberal Party 1972–74; Leader Liberal Party 1985–1989, 1995–. *Leisure interests:* reading, cricket, tennis. *Address:* Parliament House, Canberra, ACT 2600 (Office); G.P.O. Box 59, Sydney, NSW 2001, Australia. *Telephone:* (2) 6277-7100 (ACT) (Office). *Fax:* (2) 6277-7749 (ACT) (Office). *Website:* www.dpmc.gov.au (Office).

HOWARD, Ken (James Kenneth), RA, RWS, RWA, ARCA; British painter; b. 26 Dec. 1932, London; s. of Frank Howard and Elizabeth Howard; m. 1st Ann Popham (divorced 1974); m. 2nd Christa Gaa (née Köhler; died 1992); m. 3rd Dora Bertolutti 2000; ed Kilburn Grammar School, Hornsey School of Art, Royal Coll. of Art; British Council Scholarship to Florence 1958–59; taught in various London art schools 1959–73; Official Artist for Imperial War Museum, NI 1973, 1978; painted for British Army in NI, Germany, Cyprus, Oman, Hong Kong, Brunei, Nepal, Canada, Norway, Belize, Beirut 1973–83; one-man exhbns. including New Grafton Gallery, London 1971–, Lowndes Lodge Gallery 1987–, Everard Read Gallery, Johannesburg 1998, Jersey, Hong Kong, Nicosia, Delhi, Richard Green Gallery 2002; works in public collections including Plymouth City Art Gallery, Ulster Museum, Imperial War Museum, Nat. Army Museum, Hove City Art Gallery, Guildhall Art Gallery; comms for UN, BAOR, Stock Exchange, London, States of Jersey, Banque Paribas, Drapers Co., Royal Hosp. Chelsea, Richard Green 2003; Pres. NEAC 1998; Hon. mem. Royal Inst. of Oil Painters, Royal Soc. of British Artists; First Prize Lord Mayor's Art Award 1965, Hunting Group Award 1982, Sparkasse Karlsruhe 1983; Prizewinner John Moores 1978, Annual N.E.A.C. Critics' Prize 2000. *Publications:* The Paintings of Ken Howard 1992, Ken Howard: A Personal Viewpoint 1998. *Leisure interests:* opera, cinema. *Address:* 8 South Bolton Gardens, London, SW5 0DH; St Clements Studio, Paul Lane, Mousehole, Cornwall, TR19 6TR, England. *Telephone:* (20) 7373-2912 (London); (1736) 731596 (Cornwall). *Fax:* (20) 7244-6246.

HOWARD, Rt Hon. Michael, PC, QC; British politician and barrister; b. 7 July 1941; s. of Bernard Howard and Hilda Howard; m. Sandra Clare Paul 1975; one s. one d. one step-s.; ed Llanelli Grammar School, Peterhouse, Cambridge; Pres. Cambridge Union 1962; called to Bar, Inner Temple 1964, Master of the Bench of Inner Temple 1992; Jr Counsel to the Crown (Common Law) 1980–82; a Recorder 1986–; Conservative parl. cand., Liverpool (Edge Hill) 1966, 1970; Chair. Bow Group 1970–71; MP for Folkestone and Hythe 1983–; Parl. Pvt. Sec. to Solicitor-Gen. 1984–85; Under-Sec. of State, Dept of Trade and Industry, Minister for Corp. and Consumer Affairs 1985–87; Minister of State, Dept of the Environment 1987–88, Minister of Water and Planning 1988–90; Sec. of State for Employment 1990–92, for the Environment 1992–93, Home Sec. 1993–97; Opposition Front-Bench Spokesman on Foreign and Commonwealth Affairs 1997–99; Shadow Chancellor of the Exchequer 2001–; Chair. Soc. of Conservative Lawyers, Atlantic Partnership. *Leisure interests:* watching football and baseball. *Address:* House of Commons, London, SW1A 0AA, England. *Telephone:* (20) 7219-5493. *Fax:* (20) 7219-5322.

HOWARD, Sir Michael Eliot, Kt, CBE, MC, DLitt, FBA, CH; British historian; b. 29 Nov. 1922, London; s. of the late Geoffrey Eliot Howard and of Edith Howard (née Edinger); ed Wellington Coll., Christ Church, Oxford; served in army 1942–45; Asst Lecturer, Lecturer in History, King's Coll., London 1947–53; Lecturer, Reader in War Studies, Univ. of London 1953–63; Prof. of War Studies, Univ. of London 1963–68; Fellow in Higher Defence Studies, All Souls Coll., Oxford 1968–77; Chichele Prof. of the History of War, Univ. of Oxford 1977–80; Regius Prof. of Modern History, Univ. of Oxford 1980–89, Prof. Emer. 1989–; Hon. Fellow, Oriel Coll. 1990; Hon. Student Christ Church 1990; Robert A. Lovett Prof. of Mil. and Naval History, Yale Univ. 1989–93; Leverhulme Lecturer 1996; Lee Kuan Yew Distinguished Visitor, Nat. Univ. of Singapore 1996; Founder and Pres. Emer. Int. Inst. for Strategic Studies; Foreign mem. American Acad. of Arts and Sciences; Hon. LittD (Leeds) 1979; Hon. DLitt (London) 1988; Duff Cooper Memorial Prize 1961, Wolfson Literary Award 1972, NATO Atlantic Award 1989; Chesney Memorial Gold Medal, R.U.S.I. *Publications:* The Franco-German War 1961, Grand Strategy, Vol. IV (in UK History of Second World War) 1972, The Continental Commitment 1973, War in European History 1976, trans. (with Peter Paret) Clau-

sewitz on War 1976, War and the Liberal Conscience 1978, Restraints on War 1979, The Causes of Wars 1983, Clausewitz 1983, Strategic Deception: British Intelligence in the Second World War 1990, The Lessons of History (essays) 1991, The Oxford History of the Twentieth Century (Ed. with W. R. Louis) 1998, The Invention of Peace 2000, The First World War 2001. *Leisure interests:* music, gardening. *Address:* The Old Farm, Eastbury, Hungerford, Berks., RG17 7JN, England (Home). *Telephone:* (1488) 71387.

HOWARD, Ron; American film actor and director; b. 1 March 1954, Duncan, Okla; s. of Rance Howard and Jean Howard; m. Cheryl Alley 1975; two s. two d.; ed Univ. of S Calif. and Los Angeles Valley Coll.; Dir, co-author, star, Grand Theft Auto 1977. *Television includes:* (series) The Andy Griffith Show 1960–68, The Smith Family 1971–72, Happy Days 1974 and many other TV appearances. *Films directed include:* Night Shift 1982, Splash 1984, Cocoon 1985, Gung Ho 1986, Return to Mayberry 1986, Willow 1988, Parenthood 1989, Backdraft 1991, Far and Away (also co-producer) 1992, The Paper 1994, Apollo 13 1995 (Outstanding Directorial Achievement in Motion Picture Award from Directors' Guild of America (DGA) 1996), A Beautiful Mind (Acad. Awards for Best Dir and Best Film (producer) 2002, DGA Best Dir Award 2002) 2001. *Film appearances include:* The Journey 1959, Five Minutes to Live 1959, Music Man 1962, The Courtship of Eddie's Father 1963, Village of the Giants 1965, Wild County 1971, Mother's Day, American Graffiti 1974, The Spikes Gang, Eat My Dust 1976, The Shootist 1976, More American Graffiti 1979, Leo and Loree (TV), Act of Love 1980, Skyward 1981, Through the Magic Pyramid (Dir, exec. producer) 1981, When Your Lover Leaves (co-exec. producer) 1983, Return to Mayberry 1986, Ransom 1996, Ed TV 1999. *Address:* c/o Peter Dekom Bloom, Dekom & Hergott, 150 South Rodeo Drive, Beverly Hills, CA 90212; Imagine Entertainment, 1925 Century Park East, Suite 230, Los Angeles, CA 90067, USA.

HOWARTH, Elgar, ARAM, DMus, FRCM, FRNCM; British musician; b. 4 Nov. 1935, Cannock, Staffs.; s. of Oliver Howarth and Emma Wall; m. Mary Bridget Neary 1958; one s. two d.; ed Eccles Grammar School and Manchester Univ.-Royal Northern Coll. of Music (Jt course); orchestral player 1958–70; Chair. Royal Philharmonic Orchestra 1968–70; Prin. Guest Conductor Opera North 1985–88; freelance orchestral conductor 1970–; Musical Adviser Grimethorpe Colliery Brass Band 1972–; compositions: Trumpet Concerto 1968, Trombone Concerto 1962, Music for Spielberg 1984, Songs for BL for brass band; Fellow, Welsh Coll. of Music and Drama; Hon. Fellow (Royal Northern Coll. of Music) 1999, (Royal Coll. of Music) 2001, (Univ. Coll. Salford); Hon. DUniv (Cen. England, York); Hon. DMus (Keele) 1996, (York) 2000; DLitt hc (Salford) 2003; Eddison Award 1977, Olivier Award for Outstanding Achievement in Opera 1997. *Leisure interests:* hypochondria, cricket, football. *Address:* 27 Cromwell Avenue, London, N6 5HN, England.

HOWARTH, Judith; British opera singer; b. 11 Sept. 1962, Ipswich; m. 1986; ed Royal Scottish Acad. of Music and Drama and studies with Patricia Macmahon; recipient of special bursary to join Royal Opera House, Covent Garden as prin. soprano in 1985–86 season; maj. roles with Royal Opera include Musetta, Ännchen (Der Freischütz), Gilda, Adela, Marguerite de Valois (Les Huguenots), Liu, Norina, Marzelline and Morgana (Alcina) 1989–96; now freelance; numerous concert and recital engagements in UK, USA, Far East, Australia and NZ; debut at Salzburg Festival in Mozart's Der Schauspieldirektor 1991; has also appeared with Florida Grand Opera, Drottningholm Festival, Opera North and Glyndebourne Touring Opera; debut with Deutsche Staatsoper, Berlin in Cavalli's La Didone 1996. *Leisure interest:* cooking. *Address:* c/o Askonas Holt, Lonsdale Chambers, 27 Chancery Lane, London, WC2A 1PF, England. *Telephone:* (20) 7379-7700. *Fax:* (20) 7242-1831.

HOWATCH, Susan, LLB; British writer; b. 14 July 1940, Leatherhead, Surrey; d. of G. S. Sturt; m. Joseph Howatch 1964; one d.; ed Sutton High School, King's Coll., London Univ.; emigrated to USA 1964, lived in Ireland 1976–80, returned to UK 1980; first book published 1965; Fellow King's Coll. London. *Publications:* (novels) Penmarric 1971, Cashelmara 1974, The Rich are Different 1977, Sins of the Fathers 1980, The Wheel of Fortune 1984, Glittering Images 1987, Glamorous Powers 1988, Ultimate Prizes 1989, Scandalous Risks 1991, Mystical Paths 1992, Absolute Truths 1994, A Question of Integrity (US title: The Wonder Worker) 1997, The High Flyer 1999, The Heartbreaker 2003. *Leisure interest:* theology. *Address:* c/o Gillon Aitken Associates, 29 Fernshaw Road, London, SW10 0TG, England. *Telephone:* (20) 7351-7561. *Fax:* (20) 7376-3594. *E-mail:* reception@aitkenassoc.demon.co.uk (Office).

HOWDEN, Timothy Simon; British business executive; b. 2 April 1937, London; s. of Phillip Alexander Howden and Rene Howden; m. 1st Penelope Mary Howden 1958 (divorced 1984); two s. one d.; m. 2nd Lois Chesney 1999; ed Tonbridge School; on staff of Reckitt & Colman in France, FRG and UK, ending as Dir Reckitt & Colman Europe 1962–73; Dir RH.M. Flour Mills 1973–75, Man. Dir RH.M. Foods Ltd 1975–80, Chair. and Man. Dir British Bakeries Ltd 1980–85, Planning Dir RH.M. PLC 1985–89, Man. Dir RH.M. PLC 1989–92; Group Chief Exec. for Europe, The Albert Fisher Group 1992–96, CEO for N America 1996–97; Dir (non-exec.) SSL Int. PLC 1994–, 1996–, FMMing Int. Inc. 1998–, Hyperion Insurance Group Ltd 2000–; Chair. Zwetshoot Ltd 2001–, Benchmark Dental Holdings Ltd. 2001–; Assoc. Dir Mahendra British Telecom Ltd. *Leisure interests:* skiing, scuba diving, tennis, sailing, opera. *Address:* Flat 72, Berkeley House, Hay Hill, London, W1X 7LH, England. *Telephone:* (1628) 484121. *Fax:* (1628) 478838 (Office). *E-mail:* timlwe@email.msn.com (Office).

HOWE, Brian Leslie, AM, MA; Australian politician; b. 28 Jan. 1936, Melbourne; s. of John Percy Howe and Lilian May Howe; m. Renate Morris 1962; one s. two d.; ed Melbourne Univ., McCormick Theological Seminary, Chicago; worked as Uniting Church Minister, Melbourne and Morwell, Victoria; fmr Sr Lecturer in Sociology and Chair. Dept of Social and Political Studies, Swinburne Inst. of Tech., Melbourne; joined Australian Labor Party 1961; MP for Batman, House of Reps. 1977–96; Minister for Defence Support 1983–84, for Social Security and assisting the Prime Minister for Social Justice 1984–90, for Health, Housing and Community Services and assisting the Prime Minister for Social Justice 1990–93, for Housing, Local Govt and Community (now Human) Services 1993–94, for Housing and Regional Devt 1994–96; Deputy Prime Minister 1991–95; Minister assisting the Prime Minister for Commonwealth Relations 1991–93; Professional Assoc. Centre for Public Policy and Dept of Social Work, Univ. of Melbourne 1996–; Visiting Research Fellow Woodrow Wilson School of Public Policy and Int. Affairs 1997, 1998; fmr Chair. Caucus Econs Cttee; fmr mem. Caucus Resources Cttee, Urban and Regional Affairs Cttee, House of Reps. Standing Cttee on the Environment, Jt House Cttee on Publs; Fellow Queen's Coll., Univ. Melbourne 2000. *Leisure interests:* Australian Rules football, tennis, films, reading. *Address:* Centre for Public Policy, 2/234 Queensberry Street, Carlton, Vic. 3053 (Office); 6 Brennand Street, North Fitzroy, Vic. 3068, Australia (Home). *Telephone:* (3) 8344-9469 (Office); (3) 9489-4787 (Home). *Fax:* (3) 9482-3202 (Home). *E-mail:* b.howe@arts.unimelb.edu.au (Office).

HOWE, Geoffrey Michael Thomas, MA; British business executive and solicitor; b. 3 Sept. 1949, Cambridge; s. of Michael Edward Howe and Susan Dorothy Howe (née Allan); m. Karen Mary Webber (née Ford); two d.; ed Manchester Grammar School, St John's Coll. Cambridge; with Stephenson Harwood law firm 1971–75 (qualified as solicitor 1973); joined Clifford Chance 1975, apptd Partner, Corp. Dept 1980, Man. Partner 1989–97; Dir and Gen. Counsel, Robert Fleming Holdings Ltd 1998–2000; Dir Fleming Overseas Investment Trust PLC 1999–; Chair. Railtrack Group plc March–Oct. 2002; Dir (non-exec.) Jardine Lloyd Thompson Group PLC 2002–; consultant to several financial and professional orgs. *Leisure interests:* opera, wine, tennis, paintings. *Address:* 11 Highbury Terrace, London, N5 1UP, England (Home). *E-mail:* geoffreymt.howe@lineone.net (Home).

HOWE OF ABERAVON, Baron (Life Peer), cr. 1992, of Tandridge in the County of Surrey; **(Richard Edward) Geoffrey Howe,** CH, PC, QC; British politician and lawyer; b. 20 Dec. 1926, Port Talbot, Glam.; s. of the late B. Edward Howe and of E. F. Howe; m. Elspeth R. M. Shand (cr. Baroness Howe of Idlicote 2001) 1953; one s. two d.; ed Winchester Coll. and Trinity Hall, Cambridge; called to the Bar, Middle Temple 1952, Bencher 1969; Deputy Chair. Glamorgan Quarter Sessions 1966–70; MP for Bebington 1964–66, for Reigate 1970–74, for East Surrey 1974–92; Solicitor-Gen. 1970–72; Minister for Trade and Consumer Affairs 1972–74; Opposition Spokesman for Social Services 1974–75, for Treasury and Econ. Affairs 1975–79; Chancellor of the Exchequer 1979–83; Sec. of State for Foreign and Commonwealth Affairs 1983–89; Lord Pres. of the Council, Leader of House of Commons and Deputy Prime Minister 1989–90; Visitor SOAS Univ. of London 1991–2001; Special Adviser on European and Int. Affairs to int. law firm Jones, Day, Reavis & Pogue 1991–2000; Herman Phleger Visiting Prof. Stanford Law School, USA 1992–93; Pres. GB-China Centre 1992–; Chair. Framlington Russian Investment Fund 1994–2003; a Gov. IMF 1979–83; Chair. Int. Cttee 1983; fmr Pres. British Overseas Trade Bd; Dir Sun Alliance and London Insurance Group 1974–79, BICC 1991–97, Glaxo 1991–96; Dir EMI Ltd 1974–79, AGB Research Ltd 1974–79; mem. Int. Advisory Councils, J. P. Morgan 1992–2001, Stanford Univ. Inst. for Int. Studies 1991–, Fuji Wolfensohn Int. European Advisory Bd 1996–98, Carlyle European Advisory Bd 1996–2001, Fuji Bank Advisory Council 1999–; Hon. Fellow American Bar Foundation 2000; Conservative; Hon. Fellow Trinity Hall 1992; Hon. LLD (Wales) 1988; Hon. DCL (City Univ.) 1993; Joseph Bech Prize 1993; Grand Cross Order of Merit (Portugal) 1987, (Germany) 1992; Order of Ukraine for Public Service 2001. *Publication:* Conflict of Loyalty 1994. *Leisure interest:* photography. *Address:* House of Lords, London, SW1A 0PW, England (Office). *Telephone:* (20) 7219-6986 (Office). *E-mail:* howeg@parliament.uk (Office).

HOWE YOON CHONG, BA, DSO; Singaporean politician and banker; b. 1923, China; m.; three c.; ed St Francis' Inst. Malacca, Raffles Coll. and Univ. of Malaya in Singapore; fmr civil servant; Sec. to Public Service Comm.; CEO Housing and Devt Bd 1960; Perm. Sec. Ministries of Finance and Nat. Devt; Deputy Chair. Econ. Devt Bd; Chair. and Pres. Devt Bank of Singapore, concurrently Chair. and Gen. Man. Port of Singapore Authority; Perm. Sec. Prime Minister's Office and Head of Civil Service; mem. Parl. 1979–84; Minister of Defence 1979–82, of Health 1982–84; Chair. and Chief Exec. Devt Bank of Singapore 1985–90, Straits Trading Co., Ltd 1992–; Chair. Great Eastern Life Assurance Co. Ltd 1992–2000; mem. Bd of Trustees, Eisenhower Exchange Fellowships Inc. 1980–90; Hon. DLitt (Singapore) 1971; Malaysia Medal, Meritorious Service Medal 1963. *Address:* Straits Trading Company Ltd, 9 Battery Road, 21-00 Straits Trading Building, Singapore 049910, Singapore. *Telephone:* 65354722 (Office). *Fax:* 65327939 (Office).

HOWELL, Francis Clark, PhD; American professor of anthropology; b. 27 Nov. 1925, Kansas City, Mo.; s. of E. Ray Howell and Myrtle M. Howell; m.

Betty Ann Tomsen 1955; one s. one d.; ed Univ. of Chicago; Instructor in Anatomy, Washington Univ. 1953–55; Asst Prof. of Anthropology, Univ. of Chicago 1955–59, Assoc. Prof. of Anthropology 1959–62, Prof. of Anthropology 1962–70; Prof. of Anthropology, Univ. of Calif., Berkeley 1970–92, Prof. Emer. 1992–; mem. NAS; Fellow American Philosophical Soc., Acad. of Arts and Sciences; Foreign mem. Acad. des Sciences Paris, Mitglied, Senckenbergische Naturforschende Gesellschaft, Frankfurt; Foreign Assoc., Royal Soc. of S Africa; Trustee, Fellow and fmr Pres., Calif. Acad. of Science; Hon. DSc (Chicago) 1992; Fellows Medal, Calif. Acad. of Sciences 1990; Leakey Prize 1998; Charles Robert Darwin Lifetime Achievement Award 1998. *Publications:* African Ecology and Early Man (ed.) 1963, Early Man 1965, Earliest Man and Environments in the Rudolf Basin (ed.) 1975; numerous papers on paleo-anthropology in professional journals. *Address:* Laboratory for Human Evolutionary Studies, Museum of Vertebrate Zoology, University of California, Berkeley, CA 94720 (Office); 1994 San Antonio, Berkeley, CA 94707, USA (Home). *Telephone:* (510) 642-1393 (Office); (510) 524-6243 (Home). *Fax:* (510) 643-8231 (Office).

HOWELL, Margaret, DipAD; British clothes and product designer; b. 5 Sept. 1946, Tadworth; d. of E. H. Howell; m. Paul Renshaw 1974 (divorced 1987); one s. one d.; ed Tadworth Primary School, Deburgh Co-Educational, Goldsmith's Coll., London; 1st Margaret Howell Collection 1972; opened first London shop 1977; opened flagship shop, Beauchamp Place, London 1987; opened Margaret Howell (France) 1996; over 50 retail outlets world-wide by end of 1996, opened main London outlet, Wigmore Street 2002; Co. Dir Margaret Howell Ltd 1985–; Designer of the Year. *Leisure interests:* films, art exhbns., visiting country houses and gardens, walking, the countryside. *Address:* 34 Wigmore Street, London W1, England.

HOWELL OF GUILDFORD, Baron (Life Peer), cr. 1997, of Penton Mewsey in the County of Hampshire; **David Arthur Russell Howell,** PC, BA; British politician, journalist and economist; b. 18 Jan. 1936, London; s. of the late Col Arthur Howell and of Beryl Howell; m. Davina Wallace 1967; one s. two d.; ed Eton Coll., King's Coll., Cambridge; Lt Coldstream Guards 1954–56; Econ. Section, HM Treasury 1959, resgnd 1960; Leader-writer The Daily Telegraph 1960; Chair. Bow Group 1961–62; fmr Crossbow; MP for Guildford 1966–97; a Lord Commr of Treasury 1970–71; with Civil Service Dept 1970–72; Parl. Under-Sec. Dept of Employment 1971–72; Minister of State, Northern Ireland Office 1972–74, Dept of Energy Jan.–Feb. 1974; Sec. of State for Energy 1979–81, for Transport 1981–83; Chair. House of Commons Foreign Affairs Cttee 1987–97, One Nation Group of Conservative MPs 1987–97, European Cttee on Common Foreign and Security Policy 1999–2000; Opposition Spokesman on Foreign and Commonwealth Affairs 2000–; Chair. UK–Japan 2000 Group 1989–2001; Dir Conservative Political Centre 1964–66; Dir Monks Investment Trust 1992–, John Laing Investments PLC 1997–2002; Advisory Dir UBS-Warburg 1996–2000; Sr Adviser Japan Cen. Railway Co. 2001–; Visiting Fellow, Nuffield Coll., Oxford 1993–; Gov. Sadler's Wells Trust 1995–98; Trustee Shakespeare's Globe Theatre 2000–; Foundation Scholar, King's Coll. Cambridge, Richmond Prize 1959; Grand Cordon of the Order of the Sacred Treasure (Japan) 2001. *Publications:* Principle in Practice (co-author) 1960, The Conservative Opportunity 1965, Freedom and Capital 1981, Blind Victory 1986, The Edge of Now 2000. *Leisure interests:* family life, writing. *Address:* House of Lords, Westminster, London, SW1A 0PW; Chalkcroft Farm, Penton Mewsey, Andover, Hampshire, SP11 0RL, England. *E-mail:* howelld@parliament.uk (Office). *Website:* www.lordhowell.com (Office).

HOWELLS, Anne Elizabeth, FRNCM; British opera and concert singer; b. 12 Jan. 1941, Southport, Lancs.; d. of Trevor Howells and Mona Howells; m. 1st Ryland Davies (q.v.) 1966 (divorced 1981); m. 2nd Stafford Dean 1981 (divorced 1998); one s. one d.; ed Sale County Grammar School, Royal Northern Coll. of Music; three seasons in Chorus with Glyndebourne Festival Opera 1964–66, took leading role at short notice in L'Ormindo (Cavalli) 1967; subsequent roles include Dorabella in Così fan tutte, Cathleen in world premiere Rising of the Moon (Nicholas Maw), Composer in Ariadne, Diana in Calisto; with Royal Opera House, Covent Garden 1969–71, appearing as Lena in world premiere of Victory (Richard Rodney Bennett), Rosina in The Barber of Seville, Cherubino in The Marriage of Figaro; Guest Artist with Royal Opera House 1973–; has also appeared with Welsh Nat. Opera, Scottish Opera, ENO, Chicago Opera, Geneva Opera, Metropolitan Opera, New York, Lyons Opera, Marseilles Opera, Nantes Opera, Netherlands Opera and in Naples, San Francisco and in Belgium and at La Scala and Salzburg Festival 1976 and 1980 (Tales of Hoffmann and film version of Clemenza di Tito) and in Hamburg and Berlin; Prof. RAM 1997–. *Leisure interests:* cinema, reading. *Address:* c/o IMG Artists, Media House, 3 Burlington Lane, London, W4 2TH, England. *Telephone:* (20) 8233-5800. *Fax:* (20) 8233-5801.

HOWELLS, William White, PhD, DSc, FSA; American anthropologist; b. 27 Nov. 1908, New York; s. of John Mead Howells and Abby MacDougall White; m. Muriel Gurdon Seabury 1929; one s. one d.; ed St Paul's School, Concord, NH and Harvard Univ; Asst Prof. to Prof., Univ. of Wis. 1939–54; Ed. American Journal of Physical Anthropology 1949–54; Prof. of Anthropology, Harvard Univ. 1954–74, Emer. 1974–; Curator of Somatology, Peabody Museum 1955–75, Honorary Curator 1975–; Pres. American Anthropological Assen 1951; FSA; mem. NAS, American Acad. of Arts and Sciences; Corresp. mem. Royal Soc. of SA, Austrian Acad. of Sciences, Anthropological Socs. of Paris and Vienna, Soc. of Antiquaries of London, Geographical Soc. of Lisbon, Spanish Soc. for Biological Anthropology; Hon. Foreign Fellow, Indian

Anthropological Asscn; Hon. Fellow, School of American Research 1975; Hon. DSc (Beloit College) 1975, (Witwatersrand Univ.) 1985; Viking Fund Medal in Physical Anthropology 1955, Distinguished Service Award, American Anthropological Asscn 1978, Darwin Lifetime Achievement Award, Physical Anthropologists Asscn 1992; Broca Prix du Centenaire, Anthropological Soc. of Paris 1980, Viking Fund Medal and Award 1954. *Publications:* Mankind So Far 1944, The Heathens 1948, Back of History (British Edn Man in the Beginning) 1954, Mankind in the Making 1959, Ideas on Human Revolution (ed.) 1962, The Pacific Islanders 1973, Cranial Variation in Man 1973, Evolution of the Genus Homo 1973, Multivariate Statistical Methods in Physical Anthropology 1984 (Ed.), Skull Shapes and the Map 1989, Getting Here 1993, Who's Who in Skulls 1995. *Address:* 11 Lawrence Lane, Kittery Point, ME 03905, USA. *Telephone:* (207) 439-1302. *Fax:* (207) 439-1380.

HOWIE, Archibald, CBE, PhD, FRS; British university professor emeritus and research physicist; b. 8 March 1934, Kirkcaldy, Scotland; s. of Robert Howie and Margaret Marshall McDonald; m. Melva Jean Scott 1964; one s. (deceased), one d.; ed Kirkcaldy High School, Univ. of Edinburgh, California Inst. of Tech., USA, Univ. of Cambridge; ICI Research Fellow (Cavendish Lab.) and Research Fellow (Churchill Coll., Cambridge) 1960–61; Demonstrator in Physics (Cavendish Lab.) 1961–65; Teaching Fellow and Dir of Studies in Physics (Churchill Coll.) 1961–86, Lecturer 1965–79, Reader 1979–86, Professorial Fellow 1986–2001, Pensioner Fellow 2001–, Head of Dept of Physics 1989–97; part-time Consultant Union Carbide Corpn 1977–78, World Bank China Univ. Devt Programme 1984, Norwegian Research Council 1986; Dir (non-exec.) NPL Man. Ltd 1995–2001; Pres. Royal Microscopical Soc. 1984–86, Int. Fed. of Socs. for Electron Microscopy 1999–2002; Hon. FRSE 1995; Hon. Fellow Royal Microscopical Soc. 1978; Hon. Dr. of Physics (Univ. of Bologna) 1989, (Univ. of Thessaloniki) 1995; C. V. Boys Prize (jtly), Guthrie Medal, Inst. of Physics 1992; Hughes Medal (jtly), Royal Soc. 1988, Distinguished Scientist Award and Hon. mem. Electron Microscopy Soc. of America, Royal Medal, Royal Soc. 1999; Hon. mem. Chinese Electron Microscopy Soc. 2000. *Publications:* Electron Microscopy of Thin Crystals (Jt author) 1965 and numerous articles on electron microscopy and related subjects in scientific journals. *Leisure interest:* making wine. *Address:* Cavendish Laboratory, Madingley Road, Cambridge, CB3 0HE (Office); 194 Huntingdon Road, Cambridge, CB3 0LB, England (Home). *Telephone:* (1223) 337334 (Office); (1223) 570977 (Home). *Fax:* (1223) 363263 (Office). *E-mail:* ah30@phy.cam.ac.uk (Office).

HOWIE, J. Robert, BA, BCL, QC; Canadian politician and lawyer; b. 29 Oct. 1929, Fredericton, New Brunswick; s. of James R. Howie and Mary L. Pond; m. Nancy Goulding 1955; one s. three d.; ed University of New Brunswick; solicitor, Oromocto 1962–72; Clerk of the New Brunswick Legislature 1970–72; mem. House of Commons 1972, 1974; Minister of State (Transport) 1979–80, 1984–88; Presiding mem. Veterans' Appeal Board 1990–93; lawyer, pvt. practice 1993; Progressive Conservative. *Leisure interests:* curling, hockey, theatre, swimming, writing. *Address:* 678 Churchill Row, Fredericton, New Brunswick, E3B 1P6, Canada. *Telephone:* (506) 458-9981 (Office); (506) 455-9320 (Home). *Fax:* (506) 455-6256 (Office). *E-mail:* jrh@nbnet.nb.ca (Office).

HØYEM, Tom, MA; Danish politician, teacher, journalist and fmr businessman; b. 10 Oct. 1941, Nykøbing, Falster; s. of Ove Charles Høyem and Karen Høyem; m. 1st Inge-Lise Bredelund 1969 (died 2000); one s. one d.; m. 2nd Gerlinde Martin 2002; ed Univ. of Copenhagen, Univ. of Bergen, Norway; schoolteacher 1960–64; teacher, Skt Jørgens Gymnasium 1964–80; Sr master, Foreningen Norden, Sweden 1967–68; businessman 1968–75; cofounder, Chair. Centre Democratic Party 1973; Asst Prof. of Danish Language and Literature, Univ. of Stockholm 1975–79; Danish corresp. for the Berlingske Tidende in Sweden 1975–80; headmaster Høng Gymnasium 1979; Sec. of State for Greenland 1982–87; Headmaster European School, Culham 1987–94, Munich 1994–2000, Karlsruhe 2000–; co-founder of European Folk High School, Møn, Denmark and of similar insts. in Sicily, Austria, Ireland and Luxembourg; Leader of European Movt West Zeeland, Denmark 1980–82; Hon. Pres. European Inst. Luxembourg 1983; election observer in Albania and Bosnia 1996; mem. "Let Bosnia Live" Goodwill Amb. for Copenhagen; mem. Ausländerbeirat, Munich 1997–2000; OSZE observer of elections in Bosnia, Albania and Montenegro; Kt of the Dannebrog. *Publications:* Avisens spiseseddel-avisens ansigt 1975, Tabloidetik i Norden 1976, Mulighedernes Samfund 1985, Laegaest 1985, Dagens Grønland 1986, There is Something Wonderful in the State of Denmark 1987, Gud, Konge, Faedreland 1987, Nordisk i Europa 1988, From My Office 1999. *Leisure interests:* politics, reading, skiing, golfing. *Address:* European School, Albert-Schweitzer-str. 1, 76139 Karlsruhe, Germany. *Telephone:* 72168009 (Office). *Fax:* 72168009 (Office). *E-mail:* hmtm@eursc.org (Office). *Website:* www.eskar.org (Office).

HOYLAND, John, RA; British artist; b. 12 Oct. 1934, Sheffield; s. of John Kenneth Hoyland and Kathleen Hoyland; m. Airi Karkainen 1958 (divorced 1968); one s.; ed Sheffield Coll. of Art and Crafts and Royal Acad. Schools; teacher Hornsey School of Art 1960–61; Chelsea School of Art 1962–70, Prin. Lecturer 1965–69; St Martin's School of Art 1974–77; Slade School of Fine Art 1974–77, 1979–89; Charles A. Dana Prof., Colgate Univ., Hamilton, NY, USA 1972; Artist in Residence, Studio School, New York 1978, Melbourne Univ., Australia 1979; has exhibited all over the world; exhibited ceramic and glass sculptures 1994; Selector, Hayward Annual and Silver Jubilee RA Exhbns. 1979; Faculty mem. and Visitor, British School at Rome 1984; Curator, Hans Hofman Exhbn, Tate Gallery, London 1988; Prof. of Painting, Royal Acad.

Schools 2000–; foreign painter Accademia Nat. di San Luca, Italy 2000; Young Artist Int. Award, Tokyo 1963; Gulbenkian Foundation Award 1963; Peter Stuyvesant Travel Award 1964; John Moores Exhbn Prize 1965; First Prize Edin. Open 100 1969; Chichester Nat. Art Award 1975; Arts Council of GB Purchase Award 1979; First Prize John Moores Exhbn 1982; Order of the Southern Cross (Brazil) 1986; First Prize Athena Award, Barbican Gallery, London 1987; Charles Wollaston Award 1998; Hon. Dr (Sheffield Hallam) 2002. *Solo exhibitions include:* Eva Cohen Gallery, Chicago 1991, Annendale Gallery, Sydney, Australia 1994, Royal Acad., London 1999, John Hoyland Retrospective, Graves Art Gallery, Sheffield 2001, Galerie Carinthia-Bohunousky, Austria 2002. *Address:* c/o Royal Academy of Arts, Piccadilly, London, W1V 0DS (Office); 41 Charterhouse Square, London, EC1M 6EA, England.

HRAWI, Elias; Lebanese politician and businessman; b. 1930, Zahle; Pres. of Lebanon 1989–98; fmr Maronite Christian deputy. *Address:* c/o Office of the President, Baabda, Beirut, Lebanon.

HRŮZA, Jiří, CSc; Czech architect; b. 31 May 1925; s. of the late Václav Hrůza and of Františksa Hrůza; m. 1st Emilie Hrůza (died 1991); one s. (deceased) one d.; m. 2nd Marta Opplová; ed Charles Univ., Prague; with Prague Inst. for Town Planning 1961–90, apptd Chair.; currently Chief Specialist Terplan, AS; Guest Lecturer Charles Univ. and Acad. of Graphic and Plastic Arts 1991; mem. German Acad. for Town Planning 1993; Herder's Prize, Univ. of Vienna 1979. *Publications:* Czech Towns 1960, Theory of Towns 1965, International History of City Development (co-author) 1972, The City of Prague 1990, The Development of Urbanism II 1996. *Leisure interests:* foreign languages, history, classical literature. *Address:* K Matěji 18, Prague 6, 16000; Inst. of Urbanism of Tech. Univ. Thákurova 7, Prague 6, 16000, Czech Republic. *Telephone:* (2) 33334648 (Office).

HSIAO WAN-CH'ANG, (Vincent C. Siew), MA; Taiwanese politician and civil servant; b. 3 Jan. 1939; m. Susan Chu; three d.; ed Nat. Chengchi Univ.; Vice-Consul, Kuala Lumpur 1966–69, Consul 1969–72; Section Chief Ministry of Foreign Affairs 1972; Deputy Dir, Dir 4th Dept Bd of Foreign Trade 1972–77, Deputy Dir-Gen. 1977–82, Dir-Gen. 1982–88; Vice-Chair. Council for Econ. Planning and Devt 1988–89, Chair. 1993–94; Dir Kuomintang Cen. Cttee Dept of Organizational Affairs 1989–90; Minister of Econ. Affairs 1990–93; mem. Kuomintang Cen. Cttee, Cen. Standing Cttee 1993–; Chair. Mainland Affairs Council 1994; rep. for Chiayi, Legis. Council; Eisenhower Exchange Fellow 1985. *Publication:* Research on Improvement of the Foreign Trade Structure. *Address:* 16th Floor, 4 Chung Hsiao W Road, Section 1, Taipei, Taiwan.

HSÜ, Kenneth Jinghwa, MA, PhD; Swiss professor of geology; b. Jinghwa Hsü, 28 June 1929, China; s. of Sin-wu Hsü and Su-lan; m. 1st Ruth Grunder 1958 (deceased); two s. one d.; m. 2nd Christine Eugster 1966; one s.; ed Chinese Nat. Univ., Nanking, Ohio State Univ., Univ. of Calif. at Los Angeles and ETH, Zürich; Research Geologist and Research Assoc. Shell Devt Co., Houston, Tex. 1954–63; Assoc. Prof. State Univ. of New York, Binghamton, NY 1963–64; Assoc. Prof. Univ. of Calif. Riverside 1964–67; Prof. Swiss Fed. Inst. of Tech. (ETH), Zürich 1967–94, Prof. Emer. 1994–; Pres. Tarim Assocs. AG 1994, Fengshui Water Tech. Ltd 1998–; Pres. Int. Asscn of Sedimentologists 1978–82; Chair. Int. Marine Geology Comm. 1980–89; Hon. Prof. Chinese Acad. of Sciences; mem. NAS, Acad. Sinica (Taiwan); Fellow, Inst. of Advanced Studies, Berlin 1995–96; Assoc. Fellow Third World Acad. of Sciences; Dr. hc (Nanjing Univ.) 1994; Wollaston Medal, Geological Soc. of London; Twenhofel Medal, American Sedimentological Soc., Penrose Medal, Geological Soc. of America, President's Award, American Asscn of Petroleum Geologists; Hon. mem. Int. Asscn of Sedimentologists. *Publications:* Ein Schiff revolutioniert die Wissenschaft 1982, The Mediterranean was a Desert 1984, The Great Dying 1986, Challenger at Sea 1994, Geology of Switzerland 1995, Tectonic Facies Map of China 1996, Geologic Atlas of China 1998, Klima macht Geschichte 2000; other books and more than 400 scientific articles. *Leisure interest:* Chinese aerophilately. *Address:* Fengshui Water Technology Ltd, Vaduz, Liechtenstein (Office); Frohburgstr. 96, 8006 Zürich, Switzerland (Home). *Telephone:* (1) 3621462. *Fax:* (1) 3423231. *E-mail:* hsu@fwt.li (Home).

HSU CHING-CHUNG, D.AGRIC.; Taiwanese politician (retd); b. 19 July 1907, Taipei; s. of Teh An Hsu and Shyh Iuan Hung; m. Huang Tsen; two s. one d.; ed Taipei Acad., Taipei Imperial Univ; Prof., Nat. Taiwan Univ. 1945–47; Dir Agricultural and Forestry Admin., Taiwan Provincial Govt 1947–49; Commr Dept of Agric. and Forestry, Taiwan Provincial Govt 1949–54, Commr 1954–57; mem. Cen. Planning and Evaluation Cttee, China Nationalist Party 1955–61, Deputy Sec.-Gen. Cen. Cttee 1961–66; Minister of the Interior 1966–72; Vice-Premier of Exec. Yuan 1972–81; mem. Standing Cttee, Taiwan Land Bank 1946–67, China Farmers' Bank 1967–72; Medal of Clouds and Banner. *Publications:* several studies on agricultural problems in Taiwan. *Leisure interests:* horticulture, reading, painting, golf. *Address:* 180 Yenping S. Road, Taipei, Taiwan.

HSU LI-TEH, LL.M, MPA; Taiwanese politician; b. 6 Aug. 1931, Loshan County, Honan; m.; two s.; ed Taiwan Provincial Coll. of Law and Commerce, Nat. Chengchi Univ. and Harvard Univ.; Dir Fifth Dept Exec. Yuan 1972–76; Admin. Vice-Minister of Finance 1976–78; Commr Dept of Finance, Taiwan Provincial Govt 1978–81; Minister of Finance 1981–84, of Econ. Affairs 1984–85; Chair. Lien-ho Jr Coll. of Tech., Global Investment Holding Co. Ltd 1986–88; Chair. Finance Comm. Cen. Cttee Kuomintang 1988–93; Deputy

Sec.-Gen. and Exec. Sec. Policy Coordination Comm. Cen. Cttee Kuomintang 1990–93; Vice-Premier of Taiwan 1993–97. *Address:* c/o National Assembly, Taipei, Taiwan.

HSU SHUI-TEH, MA; Taiwanese politician; b. 1 Aug. 1931, Kaohsiung City; m. Yang Shu-hua; two s.; ed Nat. Taiwan Normal Univ., Nat. Chengchi Univ. and Japan Univ. of Educ.; official, Pingtung County Govt 1968–70, Kaohsiung City Govt 1970–75; Commr Dept of Social Affairs, Taiwan Provincial Govt 1975–79; Dir Dept of Social Affairs, Cen. Cttee, Kuomintang 1979; Sec.-Gen. Kaohsiung City Govt 1979–82; Mayor of Kaohsiung 1982–85, of Taipei 1985–88; Minister of the Interior 1988–91; Rep. Taipei Econ. and Culture Rep. Office in Japan 1991–93; Hon. LLD (Lincoln Univ.) 1985. *Publications:* The Childhood Education of Emile, My Compliments—Recollections of Those Days Serving as Kaohsiung Mayor, A Thousand Sunrises and Midnights, My Scoopwheel Philosophy, A Study of Welfare Administration for the Aged, several works on psychology and educ. *Address:* c/o Kuomintang, 53 Jen Ai Road, Section 3, Taipei, Taiwan.

HU, Jason Chih-chiang, DPhil; Taiwanese politician; b. 15 May 1948, Yungchi Co., Kirin Prov., China; m. Shirley S. Hu; one s. one d.; ed Nat. Chengchi Univ., Univ. of Southampton, Univ. of Oxford; Exec. Sec. Nat. Union of Students 1966–68; Youth Rep. del. to second conf. of World League for Freedom and Democracy 1968; led del. to UN World Youth Asscn Congress 1970; fmr instructor Inst. of Int. Studies, Univ. of SC, USA; taught Oxford Overseas Studies Prog. 1982–83, Research Fellow St Antony's Coll., Univ. of Oxford 1985; Assoc. Prof. Nat. Sun Yat-sen Univ. 1986–90; Deputy Dir Sun Yat-sen Center for Policy Studies 1986–90; Chief Nat. Unification Council Conf. Dept 1990; Deputy Dir First Bureau, Office of the Pres. concurrently Presidential Press Officer 1991; Dir-Gen. Govt Information Office, Exec. Br. and Govt Spokesman 1991–96; fmr Rep. of Taipei Econ. and Cultural Office, Washington, DC; Minister of Foreign Affairs 1997–99; Campaign Man., Kuomintang 1999–2000, Dir Cultural and Communication Affairs Comm. 2000–01, Deputy Sec.-Gen. 2001–; Mayor of Taichung City 2001–; Deputy Sec.-Gen. Asian Pacific League for Freedom and Democracy 1986–89; Sec.-Gen. Repub. of China Chapter of World League for Freedom and Democracy 1989–91; Deputy Sec.-Gen. for Strategic Studies 1989; Dr hc (Southampton) 1997; Best Govt Spokesman Award 1993, Top Ten Chinese Award 1994, Outstanding Professional Achievement Award 1996. *Publications include:* On the Role of PLA in Post-Mao Chinese Politics, Chinese Politics After Mao 1977, numerous articles on Chinese and strategic affairs. *Address:* No. 99, Ming Chuan Road, Taichung, Taiwan (Office). *Telephone:* (2) 2228-8211 (Office). *Fax:* (2) 2229-1136 (Office).

HU FUGUO; Chinese administrator and engineer; b. 1937, Changzi Co., Shanxi Prov.; ed Fuxin Mining Coll.; Dir Xishan Coal Mining Admin. of Shanxi Prov., 1978–82, Gov. (a.i.) of Shanxi Prov. 1992–93; Sec. CPC 6th Shanxi Provincial Cttee 1993–99; Chair. CPC 7th Shanxi Provincial Cttee 1994–; Vice-Minister of Coal Industry 1982–88; Vice-Minister of Energy 1988; mem. State Econ. Examination Cttee 1983; mem. 14th CCP Cen. Cttee 1992–97, 15th CCP Cen. Cttee 1997–2002. *Address:* Shanxi Provincial Committee of CCP, Taiyuan, People's Republic of China.

HU HAN, PhD; Chinese academic; s. of Hu Yen Bo and Xiao Shi Xun; m. Dong Yu Shen; one d.; ed Central Univ., Zhongqing; Lab. of Genetics & Breeding, Dept of Biology Univ. of Leningrad, USSR; Asst Prof. of Inst. of Genetics, Academia Sinica 1964–78, Assoc. Prof. 1977–87, Dir 1978–96, Prof. 1992–; Chair. of Scientific Cttee of State Key Lab. of Plant Cell & Chromosome Eng; Vice-Pres. Genetics Soc. of China 1991; Ed. of Science in China and Chinese Sciences Bulletin 1978–91, of Theoretical Applied Genetics 1982–, of Plant Science 1992–; Nat. Science Congress Prize 1978, Maj. Prize, Academia Sinica 1978. *Publications:* (co-ed.) Haploids of Higher Plants in Vitro 1986, Plant Somatic Genetics and Crop Improvement 1988, Plant Cell Manipulation and Breeding 1990, numerous articles on androgenesis in cereals and chromosome eng of pollen-derived plants in wheat. *Address:* Institute of Genetics, Academia Sinica, Bei Sha Tan Building, Beijing 100101, People's Republic of China.

HU JINTAO; Chinese party and state official; b. Dec. 1942, Jixi Co., Anhui Prov.; ed Qinghua Univ.; joined CCP 1964; alt. mem. 12th CCP Cen. Cttee 1982, mem. 1985; Dir Construction Comm., Gansu Prov. Govt 1980–82; Sec. Gansu Prov. Br. Communist Youth League 1982; Sec. Communist Youth League 1982–85; mem. Standing Cttee, 6th NPC, mem. Presidium and mem. Standing Cttee, CPPCC 6th Nat. Cttee 1983–98; Vice-Pres. of People's Repub. of China 1998–2003, Pres. of People's Repub. of China 2003–; Vice-Chair. CCP Cen. Mil. Cttee 1999–; Sec. CCP Cttee, Guizhou 1985–88, Tibet 1988–92; mem. 13th CCP Cen. Cttee 1987–92, 14th CCP Cen. Cttee 1992–97, Sec., Secr. 1992–; mem. 15th CCP Cen. Cttee 1997–2002, 16th CCP Cen. Cttee 2002–; Pres. Cen. Party School 1993–; mem. CCP Politburo Standing Cttee 1992–, Head Cen. Leading Group for Party Bldg Work. *Address:* Office of the President, Zhong Nan Hai, Beijing, People's Republic of China.

HU KEHUI; Chinese politician; b. Feb. 1944, Anshun, Guizhou Prov.; ed Southwest Univ. of Political Science and Law; joined CCP 1971; Chief Procurator of Guizhou Prov. People's Procuratorate 1993–98; Vice-Chair. Supreme People's Procuratorate 1998–. *Address:* Supreme People's Procuratorate, Beijing, People's Republic of China.

HU PING; Chinese government official; b. 1930, Jiaxing Co., Zhejiang Prov.; ed Jiangsu Industry Inst.; joined CCP 1950; Vice-Gov. of Fujian 1981–83; Sec.

CCP Prov. Cttee Fujian 1982; Deputy Sec. CCP Prov. Cttee, Fujian 1982; Dir Fujian Cttee for Econ. Reconstruction 1983; alt. mem. 12th CCP Cen. Cttee 1982, mem. 1985; mem. 13th CCP Cen. Cttee 1987–92, 14th CCP Cen. Cttee 1992–; Sec. CCP Prov. Cttee 1982–83; Acting Gov. of Fujian 1983, Gov. 1983–87 (removed from post); Vice-Minister, State Planning Comm. 1987–88; Minister of Commerce 1988–93; Dir Special Econ. Zones Office 1993–96; Chair. Bd of Regents, Overseas Chinese Univ. 1986. *Address:* c/o Ministry of Commerce, 45 Fuxingmen Nei Dajie, Beijing 100801, People's Republic of China.

HU QIHENG; Chinese scientist and administrator; b. 15 June 1934, Beijing; d. of Shu Wei Hu and Wen Yi Fan; m. Yuan Jian Lian 1959; one s. one d.; ed in USSR; Dir Inst. of Automation, Academia Sinica 1980–89; a Vice-Pres., Chinese Acad. of Sciences 1988–96; mem. CPPCC 1993–; Vice-Pres., China Asscn for Science and Tech. 1996–; mem. Chinese Acad. of Eng; Outstanding Woman of China 1984, Award for contrib. to Nat. Hightech. Programme 863 1996. *Publications:* book chapters in Advances in Information Systems Science 1986; Processing of Pattern-Based Information, Parts I and II (with Yoh Han Pao). *Leisure interests:* reading novels, growing flowers, pets (kittens and guinea-pigs), bicycling, computer drawing. *Address:* Chinese Academy of Sciences, 52 Sanlihe Road, Beijing 100864, People's Republic of China. *Telephone:* (10) 68597535 (Office). *Fax:* (10) 68512458 (Office); (10) 68512458. *E-mail:* qhhu@cashq.ac.cn (Office).

HU QILI; Chinese politician; b. 1929, Yulin Co., Shaaxi Prov.; m.; one s. one d.; ed Beijing Univ.; joined CCP 1948; Sec. Communist Youth League (CYL) Cttee, Beijing Univ. 1954; Vice-Chair. Students' Fed. 1954; mem. Standing Cttee, Youth Fed. 1958; Sec. CYL 1964, 1978; Vice-Chair. Youth Fed. 1965; purged 1967; Vice-Pres. Qinghua Univ., Beijing 1978; Sec. CYL 1978; Chair. Youth Fed. 1979–80; mem. Standing Cttee, 5th CPPCC 1979–83; Mayor, Tianjin 1980–82; Sec. CCP Cttee, Tianjin 1980–82; Dir Gen. Office Cen. Cttee CCP 1982–87; mem. 12th CCP Cen. Cttee 1982–87, 13th CCP Cen. Cttee 1987–92, Politburo 1982–89, Politburo Standing Cttee 1987–89; Sec. Secr. CCP 1982–89; Vice-Chair. Cen. Party Consolidation Comm. 1983–89; mem. Presidium, 1st session 7th NPC; Vice-Minister of Electronics Industry and Machine-Bldg Industry 1991–93; Minister of Electronics Industry 1993–98; mem. 14th CCP Cen. Cttee 1992–97; Vice-Chair. 9th Nat. Cttee of CPPCC 1998. *Leisure interests:* tennis, cycling. *Address:* National Committee of Chinese People's Political Consultative Conference, 23 Taipingqiao Street, Beijing 100823, People's Republic of China.

HU TSU TAU, Richard, PhD; Singaporean politician; b. 30 Oct. 1926; m. Irene Tan Dee Leng; one s. one d.; ed Anglo-Chinese School, Univ. of California (Berkeley), USA, Univ. of Birmingham, UK; Lecturer in Chemical Eng, Univ. of Manchester, UK 1958–60; joined Shell (Singapore and Malaysia) 1960, Dir Marketing and Gen. Man. Shell (KL) 1970, with Shell Int. Petroleum Co., Netherlands 1973, Chief Exec. Shell Cos. (Malaysia) 1974, Chair. and Chief Exec. Shell Cos. (Singapore) 1977, Chair. 1982; Man. Dir The Monetary Authority of Singapore and Man. Dir Govt of Singapore Investment Corpn Pte. Ltd 1983–84; elected MP (People's Action Party) 1984; Chair. The Monetary Authority of Singapore, Chair. Bd of Commrs. of Currency 1985; Minister for Trade and Industry Jan.–May 1985, for Health 1985–87, for Finance 1985–2001, of Nat. Devt 1992. *Leisure interests:* golf, swimming. *Address:* c/o Ministry of Finance, 100 High Street, 09-01 The Treasury, Singapore 179434, Singapore.

HUA GUOFENG; Chinese politician; b. 1920, Shanxi; m. Han Chih-chun; Vice-Gov. Hunan 1958–67; Sec. CCP Hunan 1959; Vice-Chair. Hunan Revolutionary Cttee 1968, Chair. 1970; mem. 9th Cen. Cttee of CCP 1969; First Sec. CCP Hunan 1970–77; Political Commissar Guangzhou Mil. Region, PLA 1972; First Political Commissar Hunan Mil. Dist PLA 1973; mem. Politburo, 10th Cen. Cttee of CCP 1973; Deputy Premier and Minister of Public Security 1975–76, Acting Premier Feb.–April 1976, Premier 1976–81, Deputy Premier 1981; First Vice-Chair. Cen. Cttee of CCP April–Oct. 1976, Chair. 1976–81; Chair. CCP Mil. Affairs Comm. 1976–81; Chair. and mem. Politburo, 11th Cen. Cttee CCP 1977–81, Vice-Chair. 1981–82; mem. 12th CCP Cen. Cttee 1982–87, 13th CCP Cen. Cttee 1987–92, 14th CCP Cen. Cttee 1992–97, 15th CCP Cen. Cttee 1997–2002. *Address:* Central Committee, Zhongguo Gongchan Dang, Beijing, People's Republic of China.

HUANG, Rayson Lisung, CBE, JP, DPhil, DSc, FRCPE; Singaporean university vice-chancellor and retd professor of chemistry; b. 1 Sept. 1920, Shantou, China; s. of Rufus and Roseland Huang; m. Grace Wei Li 1949 (deceased); two s.; ed Munsang Coll., Hong Kong, Univs. of Hong Kong and Oxford; Demonstrator in Chemistry, Nat. Kwangsi Univ., Kweilin, China 1943; Post-Doctoral Fellow and Research Assoc., Univ. of Chicago 1947–50; Lecturer in Chem. Univ. of Malaya, Singapore 1951–54, Reader in Chem. 1955–59; Prof. of Chem. Univ. of Malaya, Kuala Lumpur 1959–69, Dean of Science 1962–65; Vice-Chancellor, Nanyang Univ., Singapore 1969–72, Univ. of Hong Kong 1972–86; Pres. Asscn of Southeast Asian Insts. of Higher Learning 1970–72, 1981–83; Chair. Council, Asscn of Commonwealth Univs 1980–81; unofficial mem. Legis. Council of Hong Kong 1977–83; Vice-Chair. of Council, Shantou Univ., China 1987–94; mem. Drafting Cttee and Vice-Chair. Consultative Cttee for Basic Law of the Hong Kong Special Admin. Region of the People's Repub. of China 1985–90; Life mem. of Court, Univ. of Hong Kong; Life mem. Bd of Trustees Croucher Foundation, Hong Kong, Rayson Huang Foundation, Kuala Lumpur; Dir Ming Pao Enterprise Corpn Ltd, Hong Kong 1990–94; Hon. DSc (Hong Kong); Hon. LLD (E Asia, Macao); Order of the Rising Sun

(Japan) 1986. *Publications:* The Chemistry of Free Radicals 1974, A Lifetime in Academia (autobiog.) 2000; about 50 research papers on chemistry of free radicals, molecular rearrangements and synthetic oestrogens. *Leisure interests:* opera, ballet, concerts, violin-playing. *Address:* Raycrest II, 10 The Stables, Selly Park, Birmingham B29 7JW, England. *Telephone:* (121) 472-0180 (Home).

HUANG AN-LUN, MM, F.T.C.L.; Chinese composer; b. 15 March 1949, Guangzhou City, Guangdong Prov.; s. of Huang Fei-Li and Zhao Fang-Xing; m. Ouyang Rui-Li 1974; one s.; ed Central Conservatory of Music, Beijing, Univ. of Toronto, Canada, Trinity Coll. of Music, London and Yale Univ., USA; started piano aged 5; studied with Shaw Yuan-Xin and Chen Zi; works have been widely performed in China, Hong Kong, Philippines, northern Africa, Australia, Europe, USA and Canada; Resident Composer, Cen. Opera House of China 1976–; Pres. Canadian Chinese Music Soc., Ont. 1987–; Deputy Dir State Bureau of Materials and Equipment 1987–88; Vice-Minister of Materials 1990; Fellowship in Composition, Trinity Coll. of Music, London 1983; Yale Alumni Asscn Prize, Yale Univ. 1986. *Compositions:* operas: Flower Guardian op. 26 1979, Yeu Fei op. 37 1986 and 6 others; symphonic, chamber, vocal, choral and film music, including: Symphonic Concert op. 25, Symphonic Overture, The Consecration of the Spring in 1976 op. 25a 1977, Piano Concerto in G op. 25b 1982, Symphony in C op. 25c 1984, The Sword (symphonic poem) op. 33 1982, Easter Cantata (text by Semuel Tang) op. 38 1986; Psalm 22-A Cantata in Baroque Style op. 43c 1988, Piano Concerto in G; ballets: The Little Match Girl op. 24 1978, A Dream of Dun Huang op. 29 1980, The Special Orchestra Album 1997. *Leisure interests:* reading, sport. *Address:* 15 Carlton Road, Markham, Ont., L3R 17E, Canada (Office); The Central Opera House of China, Zuojia Zhuang, Out of Dongzhimen Gate, Beijing, People's Republic of China. *Telephone:* (416) 423-6396.

HUANG ANREN; Chinese artist; b. 8 Oct. 1924, Yangjiang County, Guandong; s. of Huang Ting Jin and Lin Fen; m. Tan Su 1941; two s. two d.; fmr Vice-Sec.-Gen. Guangdong Br., Chinese Artists' Asscn; Chair. Guangzhou Hairi Research Inst. of Painting and Calligraphy; Adviser, Guangdong Writers' Asscn of Popular Science. *Publications:* Selected Paintings of Huang Anren, Album of Sketches by Huang Anren, On Arts: Collection of Commentaries by Huang Anren. *Leisure interests:* literature, music. *Address:* Room 602, No 871-2 Renminbei Road, Guangzhou, People's Republic of China.

HUANG DA, MA; Chinese economist and academic; b. 22 Feb. 1925, Tianjin; s. of Shu-ren and Gao Huang; m. Shu-zhen Luo 1952; two s.; ed Northern China United Univ.; Dir Finance Dept Renmin Univ. of China 1978–83, Vice-Pres. 1983–91, Pres. 1991–94; mem. Nat. People's Congress (NPC), NPC Cttee on Finance & Econ. 1993–98; mem. and head of econ. group, Academic Degrees Cttee of the State Council 1988–; mem. Monetary Policy Cttee of People's Bank of China 1997–; Dir Expert Advisory Cttee on Humanities and Social Sciences Studies, State Educ. Comm. 1997–; currently in charge of the Eighth 5-Year Plan key projects: Marketization of Income, Distribution & Social Security and Restructuring Mechanism of Transition from Saving to Investment in Socialist Market Econ. Systems; Vice-Chair. Chinese Soc. for Finance and Banking 1984–95 (Chair. 1995–), Chinese Soc. for Public Finance 1983–, Chinese Soc. for Prices 1986–, Chinese Soc. for Materials Circulation 1990–; Vice-Pres. China Enterprise Man. Asscn and the Securities Asscn of China 1987–; Council mem., Chinese Asscn for Int. Understanding 1982–; Chair. Chinese Cttee on Econs Educ. Exchange with USA 1985–. *Publications:* Money and Money Circulation in the Chinese Socialist Economy 1964, Socialist Fiscal and Financial Problems 1981, Introduction to the Overall Balancing of Public Finance and Bank Credit 1984, The Price Scissors on the Price Parities Between Industrial and Agricultural Products 1990, The Economics of Money and Banking 1992, Macro-economic Control and Money Supply 1997. *Leisure interests:* calligraphy, running. *Address:* Office of the President, Renmin University of China, Beijing 100872, People's Republic of China.

HUANG FANZHANG; Chinese economist; b. 8 Feb. 1931, Jiang-Xi; s. of Qi-Kun Huang and Yun-Jin Hua; m. Yue-Fen Xue 1959; two s.; ed Peking Univ.; Researcher, Inst. of Econs Chinese Acad. of Social Science (CASS) 1954–, Sr Researcher and Prof. 1979–, Deputy Dir 1982–85; Visiting Scholar, Harvard Univ. 1980–82, Stockholm Univ. 1982; Exec. Dir for China, IMF 1985–86; Visiting Research Assoc. Center for Chinese Studies, Univ. of Mich. 1986–87; Consultant to World Bank 1987–88; Dir Dept of Int. Econ. Studies, State Planning Comm. 1988–90; Vice-Pres. Economic Research Centre, State Planning Comm. 1990–97; Sr Researcher, State Devt Planning Comm. of People's Repub. of China 1997–; Consultant for a series of 100 books on current Chinese Economy 1994; CASS Prize 1985. *Publications:* Modern Economics in Western Countries (with others) 1963, The Evolution of Socialist Theories of Income Distribution 1979, Swedish Welfare State in Practice and its Theories 1987, The Reform in Banking System and The Role of Monetary Policy in China 1989, Joint Stock System – An Appropriate Form to China's Socialist Public Ownership 1989, The Characteristics of the World Economy in the 1980s, its Prospects for the 1990s and China's Countermeasures 1990, China's Exploration of the Theories of Economic Reform in the Last Ten Years (1979–89) 1991, Stock Ownership, Privatization, Socialization and Other Topics 1992, Foreign Direct Investment in China Since 1979 1992, On the Trend and Pattern of Economic Growth in East Asia and the Asia-Pacific Region 1993, East Asian Economics: Development, Prospects for Co-operation and China's Strategy 1993, China's Transitional Inflation 1994, China's Use of Foreign Direct Investment and Economic Reform 1995,

Selected Works of Huang Fan-Zhang (1980–93) 1995, White Paper on East Asian Economies 1996, Economic Globalization and Financial Supervision In Internationalization 1998, Whither Will the East Asian Economies Go? 1999, To Establish the Social Security Fund and the Fund's Ownership 2000, China's Reform: Opening to the Outside and Its International Environment 2002. *Leisure interest:* classical music. *Address:* Apartment 801, Building 13, Mu-Xi-Di, Bei-Li, Beijing 100038, People's Republic of China. *Telephone:* (10) 63261950. *Fax:* (10) 63908071.

HUANG HUA; Chinese diplomatist; b. 1913, Cixian Co., Hebei Prov.; m. He Liliang; two s. one d.; ed Yanqing Univ., Beijing; joined CCP 1936; fmr Dir, Foreign Affairs Bureau of Tianjin, Nanking and Shanghai; later Dir, West European Dept, Ministry of Foreign Affairs; Chief. Chinese del. at Panmunjom (Korean War political negotiations) 1953; Political adviser to Premier Zhou En-lai, Spokesman of Chinese Del. to Geneva Conf. on Indo-China and Korea 1954, First Afro-Asian Conf., Bandung 1955; Adviser, Sino-American negotiations, Warsaw 1958; Amb. to Ghana 1960–66, to Egypt 1966–69, to Canada July–Nov. 1971; Perm. Rep. to UN 1971–76; Minister of Foreign Affairs 1976–83; mem. 10th Cen. Cttee CCP 1974, 11th 1978, 12th 1983–87; a Vice-Premier, State Council 1980–82; State Councillor 1982–83; Vice-Chair. Standing Cttee, 6th NPC 1983–88; mem. Standing Cttee of Cen. Advisory Comm. 1987; mem. Presidium, 14th CCP Nat. Congress 1992; Pres. Exec. Cttee, China Welfare Inst. 1988; Pres. Chinese Asscn for Int. Friendly Contacts 1992–; Hon. Pres. China Int. Public Relations Asscn 1991–, Chinese Environmental Protection Foundation 1993–; Chair. Soong Ching Ling Foundation 1992–; Adviser Chinese Asscn for Promotion of the Population Culture; Head several int. dels.; Hon. Pres. Yenching Alumnae Assoc.; Pres. Smedley, Strong, Snow Soc. of China; mem. Policy Bd Interaction Council; Hon. DHumLitt (Missouri). *Leisure interests:* fishing, jogging. *Address:* Standing Committee, National People's Congress, Beijing, People's Republic of China.

HUANG HUANG; Chinese party official; b. 1933, Lianshui Co., Jiangsu Prov.; joined PLA 1946, CCP 1949; Leading Sec. CCP Cttee, Anhui Prov. 1983–86; mem. 12th CCP Cen. Cttee 1985–87; mem. Presidium 6th NPC 1986–; Deputy Gov. Jianxi Prov. 1987–90; Sec. CPC 7th Ningxia Hui Autonomous Regional Cttee 1990–; Political Commissar 1990–96; mem. 14th CCP Cen. Cttee 1992–.

HUANG JIANXIN; Chinese film director; b. 1954, Shenxian, Hebei Prov.; ed Northwest Univ., Beijing Motion Picture Acad. *Films include:* The Black Cannon Incident, Samsara, Stand Straight, Don't Collapse, Back to Back, Face to Face. *Address:* Xian Film Studio, Xian, People's Republic of China.

HUANG JU; Chinese party and government official; b. 1938; Deputy Dir First Bureau, Mechanical and Electrical Industry of Shanghai 1979–82; mem. Standing Cttee of Shanghai Municipal CCP Cttee 1983–, Deputy Sec. 1985–94; Vice-Mayor Shanghai 1986–91, Mayor 1991–95; alt. mem. 13th CCP Cen. Cttee 1987–92; Chair. People's Armament Cttee 1992–; mem. 14th CCP Cen. Cttee 1992–97, 15th CCP Cen. Cttee 1997–2002, 16th CCP Cen. Cttee 2002–; mem. CCP Politburo 1994–, mem. Standing Cttee, CCP Politburo 2002–; Sec. CPC 6th Shanghai Municipal Cttee 1994–; Vice-Premier State Council 2003–. *Address:* Central Committee of the Chinese Communist Party, Zhongguo Gongchan Dang, 1 Zhong Nan Hai, Beijing, People's Republic of China.

HUANG KUN; Chinese university professor; b. 1919, Zhejiang Prov.; Prof. of Physics, Beijing Univ. 1951; Deputy to NPC 1964; Dir Inst. of Semi-Conductors of the Chinese Acad. of Sciences 1977; mem. Standing Cttee of 5th, 6th and 7th CPPCC 1978; Pres. Chinese Soc. of Physics 1987–91; mem. Royal Swedish Acad. 1980. *Publications:* Dynamical Theory of Crystal Lattices (with Max Born), The Physics of Semiconductors (with Xie Xide), The Physics of Solid State. *Address:* P.O. Box 912, Beijing, People's Republic of China.

HUANG WEILU; Chinese engineer; b. 1916; ed Cen. Univ., Beijing, London Univ.; one of the pioneers of rocket science in China and later of Earth satellites 1959–; Chief Engineer of the Ministry of Astronautics Industry 1982–; Vice-Chair. Science and Tech. Cttee 1982–; Deputy 6th NPC 1983–87, 7th NPC 1988; Corresp. mem. Int. Acad. of Astronautics 1986–; Meritorious Service Medal 1999. *Address:* Science and Technology Committee, Beijing, People's Republic of China.

HUANG YONGYU; Chinese artist and poet; b. 1924, Fenghuang Co., Hunan Prov.; best known for his satirical picture of an owl with its left eye closed, produced during the 'Gang of Four' era; Vice-Chair. Chinese Artists' Asscn 1985–; mem. Nationalities Cttee 7th CPPCC; Commendatore (Italy) 1986. *Address:* Central Academy of Fine Arts, Beijing, People's Republic of China.

HUANG ZHENDONG; Chinese politician; b. 1940, Jiangsu Prov.; joined CCP 1981; Vice-Minister of Communications 1985–91, Minister 1991–2003; mem. 14th CCP Cen. Cttee 1992–97, 15th CCP Cen. Cttee 1997–2002, 16th CCP Cen. Cttee 2002–. *Address:* c/o Zhongguo Gongchan Dang (Chinese Communist Party), 1 Zhong Nan, Beijing, People's Republic of China.

HUANG ZHIQUAN; Chinese politician; b. Feb. 1942, Tongxiang, Zhejiang Prov.; ed Zhejiang Agricultural Univ.; joined CCP 1979; Deputy Dir Jiangxi Prov. Planning Comm., Dir, Asst Gov. 1980–92; Deputy Gov. Jiangxi Prov. 1993, Gov. 2001–; Deputy Sec. CCP Jiangxi Prov. Cttee 1995; mem. 15th CCP Cen. Cttee 1997–2002. *Address:* Jiangxi Provincial People's Government, 5 Beijing West Road, Nanchang 330046, People's Republic of China (Office).

HUBBARD, John, BA; American painter; b. 26 Feb. 1931, Ridgefield, Conn.; s. of G. Evans Hubbard and Dorothea Denys Hubbard; m. Caryl Whineray 1961; one s. one d.; ed Milton Acad., Harvard Univ. and Art Students' League; served U.S. army in Counter-Intelligence 1953–56; designed décor and costumes for Le Baiser de la Fée, Dutch Nat. Ballet 1968, Midsummer, Royal Ballet, London 1983 and Sylvia Pas de Deux, Royal Ballet, London 1985; mem. Advisory Panel, Tate Gallery, St Ives 1993–2000; Astra Award (Garden Design) 1992, Jerwood Prize 1996. *Exhibitions include:* nine at New Art Centre, London 1961–75, four at Fischer Fine Art, London 1979–91, Ten Americans, Rome 1959, British Painting in the Sixties, European Tour 1963, British Painting 1974, Hayward Gallery, London 1974, Jubilee Exhbn, RA, London 1977, Yale Center for British Art 1986, Purdy Hicks Gallery, London 1994, McLauren Gallery, Ayr, Scotland 1996, Fitzwilliam Museum 1998, Marlborough Fine Art, London 2000, Art in the Garden, Waddesdon Manor 2000 and others in London, Oxford and elsewhere. *Television:* The South Bank Show 1981. *Publications:* Second Nature 1984, The Tree of Life 1989. *Leisure interests:* walking and gardening. *Address:* Chilcombe House, Chilcombe, nr Bridport, Dorset, DT6 4PN, England. *Telephone:* (1308) 482234.

HUBBARD, Thomas C.; American diplomatist; b. 1943, Ky; m. Joan Magnusson Hubbard; two c.; ed Univ. of Alabama; joined Foreign Service 1965; Political/Econ. Officer, US Embassy, Santo Domingo 1966; Econ./Commercial Officer, Fukuoka, Japan; with Political Section, Tokyo 1971; Econ. Officer, Japan Desk, Dept of State 1973–75; Exec. Sec. to Del., then Energy Adviser, US Mission to OECD, Paris 1975–78; with Political Section, Tokyo 1978–81; Dir Training and Liaison Staff, Bureau of Personnel, State Dept, Deputy Dir, Philippine Desk 1984–85, Country Dir 1985–87; Deputy Chief of Mission, Kuala Lumpur 1987; Minister-Counsellor, Sr Foreign Service 1989; Minister and Deputy Chief of Mission, Manila 1990–93; Deputy Asst Sec., East Asian and Pacific Affairs, Dept of State 1993–96; Amb. to Philippines 1996–2000; Prin. Deputy Asst Sec. of State for E Asian and Pacific Affairs 2000–01; Amb. to Repub. of Korea 2001–. *Address:* American Embassy, 82 Sejong-no, Jongno-gu, Seoul, Republic of Korea (Office). *Telephone:* (2) 397-4114 (Office). *Fax:* (2) 725-8543 (Office).

HUBEL, David Hunter, MD; Canadian professor of neurobiology; b. 27 Feb. 1926, Windsor, Ont., Canada; s. of Jesse H. Hubel and Elsie M. Hunter; m. S. Ruth Izzard 1953; three s.; ed McGill Univ.; Prof. of Neurophysiology, Harvard Medical School 1965–67, George Packer Berry Prof. of Physiology and Chair. Dept of Physiology 1967–68, George Packer Berry Prof. of Neurobiology 1968–82, John Franklin Enders Univ. Prof. 1982–; George Eastman Prof., Univ. of Oxford 1991–92; First Annual George A. Miller Lecture, Cognitive Neuroscience Soc. 1995; mem. NAS, Leopoldina Acad., Bd of Syndics, Harvard Univ. Press 1979–83; Foreign mem. Royal Soc., London; Sr Fellow, Harvard Soc. of Fellows 1971–; Fellow American Acad. of Arts and Sciences; Hon. AM (Harvard) 1962; Hon. DSc (McGill) 1978, (Manitoba) 1983, (Oxford), (Univ. of Western Ont.) 1993, (Gustavus Adolphus Coll.) 1994, (Ohio State Univ.) 1995; Hon. DHumLitt (Johns Hopkins Univ.) 1990; Lewis S. Rosenstiel Award for Basic Medical Research (Brandeis Univ.) 1972, Friedenwald Award (Asscn for Research in Vision and Ophthalmology) 1975, Karl Spencer Lashley Prize (American Philosophical Soc.) 1977, Louisa Gross Horwitz Prize, (Columbia Univ.) 1978, Dickson Prize in Medicine, Univ. of Pittsburgh 1979, Soc. of Scholars, Johns Hopkins Univ. 1980, Ledlie Prize (Harvard Univ.) 1980, Nobel Prize in Medicine or Physiology 1981, New England Ophthalmological Soc. Award 1983, Paul Kayser Int. Award of Merit in Retina Research 1989, City of Medicine Award 1990, Gerald Award (Soc. for Neuroscience) 1993, Charles F. Prentice Medal (American Acad. of Optometry) 1993, Helen Keller Prize (Helen Keller Eye Research Foundation) 1995. *Publications:* Eye, Brain and Vision 1987; articles in scientific journals. *Leisure interests:* music, photography, astronomy, languages, weaving, amateur radio. *Address:* Department of Neurobiology, Harvard Medical School, 220 Longwood Avenue, Boston, MA 02115; 98 Collins Road, Newton, MA 02168, USA (Home). *Telephone:* (617) 432-1655 (Office); (617) 527-8774 (Home). *Fax:* (617) 432-0210 (Office).

HUBER, Karl, PhD; Swiss government official; b. 18 Oct. 1915, Häggenschwil; s. of Carl Huber and Mathilde Haessig; m. Elizabeth Fink 1945; one s. two d.; ed high school, St Gall and Univ. of Berne; entered Fed. Admin. 1941, mem. staff of Gen. Secr. of Ministry of Political Econ.; Sec.-Gen. Ministry of Political Econ. 1954; Fed. Chancellor of Swiss Confed. 1967–81. *Leisure interests:* history, swimming, walking. *Address:* Steingrubenweg 23, 3028 Spiegel, Switzerland.

HUBER, Robert, Drrer.nat, FRS; German biochemist; b. 20 Feb. 1937, Munich; s. of Sebastian Huber and Helene Huber; m. Christa Huber 1960; two s. two d.; ed Tech. Univ. Munich; fmr External Prof. Tech. Univ. Munich; Dir Max-Planck-Inst. für Biochemie 1972–; Assoc. Prof. Munich Tech. Univ. 1976–; Ed. Journal of Molecular Biology 1976–; Scientific mem., Max-Planck-Gesellschaft; mem. Bavarian Acad. of Sciences, Accad. Nazionale dei Lincei and numerous socs.; Fellow American Acad. of Microbiology; Assoc. Fellow Third World Acad. of Sciences, Trieste, Italy; Foreign Assoc. NAS; Dr hc (Louvain) 1987, (Ljubljana) 1989, (Tor Vergata, Rome) 1990, (Lisbon) 2000, (Barcelona) 2000; E. K. Frey Prize (German Surgical Soc.) 1972; Otto Warburg Medal (Soc. for Biological Chem.) 1977; Emil von Behring Prize (Univ. of Marburg) 1982; Keilin Medal (Biochemical Soc. London); Richard Kuhn Medal (Soc. of German Chemists) 1987; E. K. Frey-E. Werle Medal 1989, Kone Award (Asscn of Clinical Biochemists) 1990; Orden Pour le Mérite; Nobel Prize for Chemistry 1988; Sir Hans Krebs Medal 1992, Bayerischer Maximiliansorden für

Wissenschaft und Kunst 1993, Linus Pauling Medal 1993, Distinguished Service Award (Miami Winter Symposia) 1995, Max Tishler Prize (Harvard Univ.) 1997, Max-Bergmann-Medaille (Max-Bergmann-Kreises zur Förderung der peptidchemischen Forschung) 1997, Grosse Verdienstkreuz mit Stern und Schulterband 1997. *Leisure interests:* hiking, biking, skiing. *Address:* Max-Planck-Institut für Biochemie, Am Klopferspitz 18A, 82152 Martinsried (Office); Schlesierstr. 13, 82110 Germering, Germany (Home). *Telephone:* (89) 85782678 (Office); (89) 849153 (Home). *Fax:* (89) 85783516 (Office). *E-mail:* huber@biochem.mpg.de (Office); huber@biochem.mpg.de (Home).

HUBER-HOTZ, Annemarie; Swiss politician; b. 16 Aug. 1948, Baar, Canton Zug; m.; three c.; ed Univ. of Geneva, Swiss Fed. Inst. of Tech., Zurich; Head Secr. Dept for German Law, Faculty of Law, Univ. of Geneva, translator ILO, Geneva 1973–75; mem. staff Regional Planning Office, Canton of Zug 1976–77; Asst to Sec.-Gen. Fed. Ass. 1978–81, Dir Scientific Services 1989–99, Sec.-Gen. 1992–99; Chancellor of the Swiss Confed. 2000–; mem. Radical Free Democratic Party. *Address:* Federal Chancellery, Bundeshaus-West, 3003 Berne, Switzerland (Office). *Telephone:* (31) 3222111 (Office). *Fax:* (31) 3223706 (Office).

HÜBNER, Danuta; Polish politician and economist; b. 8 April 1948; ed Main School of Planning and Statistics, Warsaw; researcher Main School of Planning and Statistics, Warsaw (now Warsaw School of Econs) 1971–92; Deputy Dir Inst. of Devt and Strategic Studies 1991–94; Ed.-in-Chief Gospodarka Narodowa (monthly); Deputy Ed.-in-Chief Ekonomista (bi-monthly) 1992; Under-Sec. of State Ministry of Industry and Trade 1994–96; Sec. Cttee for European Integration 1996–97, 2001– Sec. of State for European Integration 1996–97; Head Chancellery of the Pres. of Poland 1997–98; Deputy Exec. Sec. UN Econ. Comm. for Europe 1998–2000, Exec. Sec. 2000–01, UN Under-Sec.-Gen. 2000–01; Under-Sec. of State Ministry of Foreign Affairs 2001–. *Address:* Ministry of Foreign Affairs, al. Szucha 23, 00-580 Warsaw (Office); Office of the Committee for European Integration, al. Ugazdowskie 9.00–918 Warsaw, Poland (Office). *Website:* www.msz.gov.pl (Office); www.ukie.gov.pl (Office).

HUCKABEE, Michael Dale, BA; American state governor and ecclesiastic; b. 24 Aug. 1955, Hope, Ark.; m. Janet McCain 1974; three s. one d.; ed Ouachita Baptist Univ., Arkadelphia, Ark., Southwestern Baptist Theological Seminary, Fort Worth; ordained to ministry 1974; pastor various Baptist churches 1974–, Beech St 1st Baptist Church, Texarkana, Ark. 1986–; Lt Gov. State of Ark. 1994–96, Gov. of Arkansas 1996–; Founder, Past-Pres. American Christian TV System, Pine Bluff; Pres. Ark. Baptist Convention 1989–91; columnist weekly newspaper Positive Alternatives. *Address:* Office of the Governor, Room 250, State Capitol, Little Rock, AR 72201 (Office); 1800 Center Street, Little Rock, AR 72206, USA (Home).

HUCKLE, Alan Edden, MA; British diplomatist; b. 15 June 1948, Penang, Malaya; s. of the late Albert Arthur Huckle and of Ethel Maud Pettifer Huckle (née Edden); m. Helen Myra Gibson 1973; one s. one d.; ed Harrow School, Univ. of Warwick; Personnel Man. Div., Civil Service Dept (CSD) 1971–74; Asst Pvt Sec. to Sec. of State for Belfast 1974–75, Machinery of Govt Div., CSD 1975–78; Asst Sec. NI Office 1978–80; with FCO 1980–83; Exec. Dir British Information Services, NY, USA 1983–87; Head of Chancery, Manila 1987–90; Head Dept of Arms Control and Disarmament, FCO 1990–92; Counsellor and Head Del. to CSCE, Vienna 1992–96; Head Dept Territories Regional Secr., Bridgetown 1996–98; with OSCE/Council of Europe Dept, FCO 1998–2001; Head Overseas Territories Dept, FCO and Commr (non-resident) British Antarctic Territory and British Indian Ocean Territory 2001–; Leverhulme Trust Scholar, British School at Rome 1971. *Leisure interests:* armchair mountaineering, hill-walking. *Address:* Head of Overseas Territories Department, Foreign and Commonwealth Office, King Charles Street, London, SW1A 2AH, England (Office). *Telephone:* (20) 7008-2741 (Office). *Fax:* (20) 7008-2108 (Office). *E-mail:* alan.huckle@fco.gov.uk (Office). *Website:* www.fco .gov.uk (Office).

HUCKNALL, Mick, BA; British singer and songwriter; b. Michael James Hucknall, 8 June 1960, Manchester; ed Manchester Polytechnic; fmrly with own punk band Frantic Elevators; founder, lead singer, Simply Red 1984–; world tours 1989–90, 1992; co-f. Blood and Fire (reggae music label) 1992; mem. Govt Task Force on the Music Industry 1997–; Hon. MSc (UMIST) 1997; Brit Awards (Best British Band 1991, 1992, Best Male Artist 1992), Ivor Novello Songwriter of the Year Award 1992, Mobo Award for Outstanding Achievement 1997, Manchester Making It Happen Award 1998. *Singles include:* Money's Too Tight To Mention 1985, Come To My Aid 1985, Holding Back The Years 1985, Jericho1986, Open Up The Red Box 1986, The Right Thing 1987, Infidelity 1987, Maybe Some Day 1987, Ev'ry Time We Say Goodbye 1987, I Won't Feel Bad 1988, It's Only Love 1989, If You Don't Know Me By Now 1989, A New Flame 1989, You've Got It 1989, Something Got Me Started 1991, Stars 1991, For Your Babies 1992, Thrill Me 1992, Your Mirror 1992, Fairground 1995, Remembering The First Time 1995, Never Never Love 1996, We're In This Together 1996, Angel 1996, Nightnurse 1997, Say You Love Me 1998, The Air That I Breathe 1998, Ghetto Girl 1998, Ain't That a Lot of Love 1999, Your Eyes 2000, Sunrise 2003. *Albums include:* Picture Book 1985, Men and Women 1987, A New Flame 1989, Stars 1991, Life 1995, Greatest Hits 1996, Blue 1997, Love and the Russian Winter 1999, It's Only Love (greatest hits) 2000, Home 2003. *Address:* PO Box 20197, London, W10 6YQ; c/o Silentway Ltd, Unit 61B, Pall Mall Deposit, 124-128 Barlby Road,

London, W10 6BL, England. *Telephone:* (20) 8969-2498 (Office). *Fax:* (20) 8969-2506 (Office). *E-mail:* info@simplyred.com (Office). *Website:* www .simplyred.com (Office).

HUCKSTEP, Ronald Lawrie, CMG, MA, MD, FRCS, FRCSE, FRACS, F.A.ORTH.A.; British/Australian consultant orthopaedic surgeon and university professor; b. 22 July 1926, Chefoo, China; s. of Herbert George Huckstep and Agnes Huckstep (née Lawrie-Smith); m. Ann Macbeth 1960; two s. one d.; ed Cathedral School, Shanghai, Queens' Coll., Cambridge, Middlesex, Royal Nat. Orthopaedic and St Bartholomew's Hosps., London; Registrar and Chief Asst, Orthopaedic Dept, St Bartholomew's Hosp. and various surgical appts., Middx and Royal Nat. Orthopaedic Hosps. 1952–60; Hunterian Prof., Royal Coll. of Surgeons 1959–60; Lecturer, Sr Lecturer and Reader in Orthopaedic Surgery, Makerere Univ., Kampala, Uganda 1960–67, Prof. 1967–72; Hon. Consultant Orthopaedic Surgeon, Mulago and Mengo Hosps. and Round Table Polio Clinic, Kampala 1960–72; Hon. Orthopaedic Surgeon to all Govt and Mission hosps. in Uganda and Adviser on Orthopaedic Surgery to Ministry of Health, Uganda 1960–72; Prof. and Head, Dept of Traumatic and Orthopaedic Surgery Univ. of NSW 1972–92 and fmr Rotating Chair., School of Surgery; Chair. Dept of Traumatic and Orthopaedic Surgery and Dir of Accident Services, Prince of Wales/Prince Henry Hosps. 1972–92, Consultant Orthopaedic Surgeon, Royal S. Sydney and Sutherland Hosps., Sydney 1974–92; Prof. Emer. of Traumatic and Orthopaedic Surgery, Univ. of NSW and Consultant Orthopaedic Surgeon, Prince of Wales and Prince Henry Hosps. 1993–; Visiting Prof. Univ. of Sydney 1995–; Hon. Adviser, Rotary Int., The Commonwealth Foundation, WHO and UN on starting services for the disabled in developing countries 1970–; Sr Medical Disaster Commdr, Dept of Health, NSW and Chair. and mem. of various disaster and emergency cttees. in Australia 1972–; Corresp. Ed. British and American Journals of Bone and Joint Surgery 1965–72, Injury, British Journal of Accident Surgery 1972; mem. Traffic Authority of NSW 1982–; Consultant to Archives of Orthopaedic Surgery 1984; Founder World Orthopaedic Concern 1973, numerous orthopaedic inventions including Huckstep nail, hip, femur, knee, shoulder, humerus, staple, circlip, plate, bone screw, caliper, wheelchairs and skelecasts; Hon. Fellow 1978; Patron Medical Soc. of Univ. of NSW 1976; Hon. Dir Orthopaedic Overseas, USA 1978; Vice-Pres. Australian Orthopaedic Asscn 1982; Pres. Coast Medical Asscn, Sydney 1985–86; Hon. Fellow Western Pacific Orthopaedic Asscn 1968, Asscn of Surgeons of Uganda 1993; Chair. or mem. of numerous other bodies; Hon. MD (Univ. of NSW) 1988; Irving Geist Award, Int. Soc. for Rehabilitation of the Disabled 1969, Melsome Memorial Prize, Cambridge 1948, Raymond Horton Smith Prize, Cambridge 1957, Betts Memorial Medal, Australian Orthopaedic Asscn 1983, James Cook Medal, Royal Soc. of NSW 1984, K. L. Sutherland Medal, Australian Acad. of Tech. Sciences 1986, Paul Harris Fellow and Medal, Rotary Int. and Rotary Foundation 1987, Humanitarian Award (Orthopaedics Overseas, USA) 1991, Vocational Service Award, Rotary Club of Sydney 1994. *Film:* Polio in Uganda 1966. *Publications:* Typhoid Fever and Other Salmonella Infections 1962, A Simple Guide to Trauma 1970, Poliomyelitis: A Guide for Developing Countries, Including Appliances and Rehabilitation 1975, A Simple Guide to Orthopaedics 1993, Picture Tests – Orthopaedics and Trauma 1994; numerous chapters in books and papers. *Leisure interests:* photography, designing orthopaedic appliances and implants, swimming and travel. *Address:* 108 Sugarloaf Crescent, Castlecrag, Sydney, NSW 2068, Australia (Home). *Telephone:* (612) 9958-1786. *Fax:* (612) 9967-2971. *Website:* www.worldortho.com (Office).

HUDEČEK, Václav; Czech violinist; b. 7 June 1952, Rožmitál pod Třemšínem, Příbram Dist; m. Eva Trejtnarová 1977; ed Faculty of Music, Acad. of Musical Arts, Prague 1968–73; worked with David Oistrakh, Moscow 1970–74; worked as musician 1974–; mem., Union of the Czech Composers and Concert Artists 1977–; individual concerts, 1967–; soloist with Czech Philharmonic Orchestra 1984–90; freelance musician 1990–; concert tours to Austria, GDR, Norway, Hungary, USSR, Switzerland, Turkey, USA, Yugoslavia, Japan, Italy, Iceland, Finland, Jordan; est. School for Talented Young Violinists in Czech Repub.; charity concerts after floods in Czech Repub. 2002; Concertino Praga int. radio competition 1967, Award for Outstanding Labour 1978, Artist of Merit 1981, Supraphon Gold Record Prize 1994. *Recordings include:* Carmen 1999, Tichá noc (Holy Night) (with others) 1999, album Souvenir (with pianist Petr Adamec), Antonín Dvořák's Compositions 2001. *Television:* Musical Nocturne (TV Prague) 2001. *Address:* Euroconcert, Bellebern 10A, 78234 Engen, Germany (Office); Londynska 25, 120 00 Prague 2, Czech Republic (Home). *Telephone:* (2) 24254010 (Home). *E-mail:* violin@ quick.cz.

HUDSON, Hugh; British film director and producer; b. 25 Aug. 1936; s. of the late Michael Donaldson-Hudson and Jacynth Ellerton; m. Susan Caroline Michie 1977; one s.; ed Eton; numerous awards and prizes. *Films include:* Chariots of Fire 1980 (5 BAFTA Awards, 4 Oscars, other awards), Greystoke: The Legend of Tarzan 1984, Revolution 1985 (BFI Anthony Asquith Award for Music), Lost Angels 1989, Son of Adam 1996, A Life So Far 1997, I Dreamed of Africa 1998; numerous documentaries, political films (for Labour Party) and over 600 advertisements. *Address:* Hudson Film Ltd, 24 St Leonard's Terrace, London, SW3 4QG, England (Office). *Telephone:* (20) 7730-0002 (Office). *Fax:* (20) 7730-8033 (Office). *E-mail:* hudsonfilm@aol.com (Office).

HUE, Robert; French politician and nurse; b. 19 Oct. 1946, Cormeilles-en-Parisis; s. of René Hue and Raymonde Gregorius; m. Marie-Edith Solard

1973; one s. one d.; ed Coll. d'Enseignement Technique and Ecole d'Infirmier; mem. Young Communists 1962; mem. French CP 1963–, mem. Secr. Fed. of Val d'Oise 1970–77, mem. Cen. Cttee 1987, mem. Politburo 1990, Nat. Sec. 1994–2001, Chair. 2001–03; Cand. of CP, French Presidential Election 1995; Mayor of Montigny-les-Cormeilles 1977–; Conseiller-Gén. Val d'Oise 1988–97; Deputy for Argenteuil-Bezons 1997–; MEP 1999–2000; Pres. Nat. Asscn of Communist and Republican elected mems. 1991–94; charged with electoral malpractice Oct. 1999. *Publications:* Histoire d'un village du Parisis des origines à la Révolution 1981, Du village à la ville 1986, Montigny pendant la Révolution 1989, Communisme: la mutation 1995, Il faut qu'on se parle 1997, Communisme: un nouveau projet 1999. *Leisure interests:* reading, painting, cinema, music (jazz and rock), walking, judo. *Address:* c/o Parti Communiste Français, 2 place du Colonel Fabien, 75167 Paris Cedex 19; 12 rue de Verdun, 95370 Montigny-les-Cormeilles, France (Home).

HUERTA DÍAZ, Vice-Adm. Ismael; Chilean diplomatist (retd) and naval officer; b. 13 Oct. 1916; s. of Rear-Adm. Ismael Huerta Lira and Lucrecia Díaz Vargas; m. Guillermina Wallace Dunsmore Aird 1942; two s. two d.; ed Sacred Heart School, Valparaíso, Naval Acad., Ecole Supérieure d'Electricité, Paris, Naval Polytechnic Acad., Chile; successive posts in Chilean Navy include Dir of Armaments, Dir of Instruction, Dir of Scientific Investigation, Dir of Naval Polytechnic Acad., Dir of Shipyards, Dir-Gen. of Army Services; Prof. of Electronics, Univ. de Concepción 1954, 1955, 1956; Prof. of Radionavigation, Univ. Católica de Valparaíso 1962–67; mem. Org. Cttee, Pacific Conf., Viña del Mar 1970, Pres. Centre of Pacific Studies 1970–72; Dir Compañia de Acero del Pacífico (CAP) 1970, 1971, 1972; Pres. Nat. Transport Cttee 1972; Minister of Public Works 1973, of Foreign Affairs 1973–74; Perm. Rep. to UN 1974–77; Rector Univ. Técnica Federico Santa María 1977–85; Chair. Bd Empresa Marítima del Estado 1978–; mem. Coll. of Chilean Engineers. Inst. of Mechanical Engineers of Chile; Decoration of Pres. of the Repub. (Chile), Grand Officer Order of Léopold II (Belgium), Gran Cruz de la Orden del Libertador San Martín (Argentina), Gran Cruz Extraordinaria de la Orden Nacional al Mérito (Paraguay), Medall Kim-Kank (Repub. of Viet Nam). *Publications:* The Role of the Armed Forces in Today's World 1968, Volvería a ser Marino (memoirs) 1988 and various technical articles.

HUF, Jaroslav, DipEng; Czech business executive; b. 24 May 1966, Zábreh; s. of František Huf and Jirina Huf; m. Lenka Huf; one s.; ed Tech. Univ. of Agric., Brno; various engineering positions 1989–95; Dir Finance Moravolen a.s. 1995–96, Man. Dir and Chair. Moravolen Holding a.s. 1996–. *Leisure interest:* sport. *Address:* Moravolen Holding a.s., M.R. Štefánika 1, 78701 Šumperk, Czech Republic (Office). *Telephone:* (5) 83387111 (Office). *Fax:* (5) 83387187 (Office). *E-mail:* hufj@moravolen.cz (Office). *Website:* www .moravolen.cz (Office).

HUG, Michel, PhD; French civil engineer; b. 30 May 1930, Courson; s. of René Hug and Marcelle (née Quenee) Hug; m. Danielle Michaud; one s. two d.; ed Ecole Polytechnique, Ecole Nationale des Ponts et Chaussées, State Univ. of Iowa; joined Electricité de France 1956, various positions at the Chatou Research and Test Centre 1956–66, Regional Man. (Southern Alps) 1967–68, Research and Devt Man. 1969–72, Planning and Construction Man. 1972–82; Gen. Man. Charbonnages de France (French Coal Bd) 1982–86; Prof. of Fluid Mechanics, Ecole Nationale des Ponts et Chaussées 1963–80; Chair. Bd Ecole Nationale Supérieure d'Electrotechnique, d'Electronique, d'Informatique et d'Hydraulique de Toulouse 1980–90; Chair. Bd CdF Chimie 1985–86; Deputy Admin. Org. des Producteurs d'Energie Nucléaire (OPEN) 1992–2000; mem. Applications Cttee of Acad. des Sciences 1987; Foreign mem. US Nat. Acad. of Eng 1979–; mem. American Nuclear Soc.; Hon. mem. Int. Assoc. of Hydraulics Research; Lauréat de l'Institut (Prix des Laboratoires) 1964; Commdr Ordre nat. du Merite 1980; Officier, Légion d'honneur 1977; Officier des Palmes académiques (Ministry of Educ.) 1986; Chevalier des Arts et Lettres 1981, du Mérite agricole. *Publications:* Mécanique des fluides appliquée aux problèmes d'aménagement et d'énergétique 1975, Organiser le changement dans l'entreprise—une expérience à E.D.F. 1975. *Leisure interests:* tennis, shooting, swimming, flying. *Address:* Design Stratégique, BP 14, 78115 Le Vésinet cedex (Office); 57 avenue Franklin Roosevelt, 75008 Paris, France. *E-mail:* michelhug@imaginet.fr (Office).

HUGH SMITH, Sir Andrew Colin, Kt, BA; British stockbroker; b. 6 Sept. 1931; s. of the late Lt-Commdr Colin Hugh Smith; m. Venetia Flower 1964; two s.; ed Ampleforth Coll. and Trinity Coll., Cambridge; called to Bar (Inner Temple) 1956; with Courtaulds Ltd 1960–68; joined Capel-Cure Carden (subsequently Capel-Cure Myers) 1968, became Partner 1970, Sr Partner 1979; Deputy Chair. ANZ McCaughan Merchant Bank 1985–90; Chair. Holland & Holland PLC 1987–95; elected to Council, The Stock Exchange 1981; Chair. The Int. Stock Exchange (now London Stock Exchange), London 1988–94; Chair. Penna PLC 1995–, Microtransfer Ltd 1995–, European Advisory Bd Andersen Consulting 1995–; Dir Matheson Lloyds Investment Trust 1994–97, (non-exec.) J. Bibby & Sons (now Barlow Int.) 1995–, Barbour Ltd 1998–; mem., Hon. Treas. Malcolm Sargent Cancer Fund for Children 1992–. *Leisure interests:* gardening, shooting, fishing, reading. *Address:* c/o National Westminster Bank PLC, 1 Princess Street, London, EC2R 8PA, England (Office).

HUGHES, Anthony Vernon, MA; Solomon Islands banking executive and civil servant; b. 29 Dec. 1936, England; s. of Henry Norman Hughes and Marjorie Hughes; m. 1st Carole Frances Robson 1961 (divorced 1970); one s.; m. 2nd Kuria Vaze Paia 1971; one s. one d. two adopted d.; ed Queen Mary's

Grammar School, Walsall, England, Pembroke Coll., Oxford and Bradford Univ.; Commr of Lands, Registrar of Titles, Solomon Islands 1969–70, Head of Planning 1974–76, Perm. Sec. Ministry of Finance 1976–81, Gov. Cen. Bank 1982–93; Devt Sec., Gilbert and Ellice Islands 1971–73; Regional Econ. Adviser UN Econ. and Social Comm. for Asia and the Pacific 1994–; Cross of Solomon Islands 1981. *Publications:* numerous articles on land tenure, econ. planning, Devt admin., foreign investment, expecially Jt ventures, with special emphasis on small countries. *Leisure interests:* working outside, sculling, sailing. *Address:* ESCAP, Pacific Operations Centre, PMB 004, Port Vilan, Vanuatu; P.O. Box 486, Honiara, Solomon Islands (Home).

HUGHES, Rev. Gerard Joseph, MA, STL, PhD; British ecclesiastic; b. 6 June 1934, Wallington, Surrey; s. of Henry Hughes and Margaret Hughes; ed St Aloysius Coll. Glasgow, London Inst. of Educ., Campion Hall, Univ. of Oxford, Heythrop Coll. Oxford and Univ. of Mich.; Chair. Dept of Philosophy, Heythrop Coll. Univ. of London 1973–96, Vice-Prin. 1986–98; mem. Senate and Academic Council, Univ. of London 1987–96; Vice-Provincial, British Prov. of Soc. of Jesus 1982–88; Austin Fagothey Prof. of Philosophy, Univ. of Santa Clara, Calif. 1988, 1992; Master Campion Hall, Univ. of Oxford 1998–. *Publications:* Authority in Morals 1978, Moral Decisions 1980, The Philosophical Assessment of Theology (ed.) 1987, The Nature of God 1995, Aristotle on Ethics 2001. *Leisure interests:* music, computer programming, crosswords, walking. *Address:* Campion Hall, Oxford, OX1 1QS, England (Office). *Telephone:* (1865) 286101 (Office). *Fax:* (1865) 286148 (Office). *E-mail:* gerard .hughes@campion.ox.ac.uk (Office).

HUGHES, H. Richard; British architect; b. 4 July 1926, London; s. of Major Henry Hughes and Olive Hughes (née Curtis); m. Anne Hill 1951; one s. two d.; ed Kenton Coll., Nairobi, Kenya, Hilton Coll., Natal, SA, Architectural Asscn School of Architecture, London; Corporal, Kenya Regt, attached to Royal Engineers 1944–46; Asst Architect Kenya and Uganda 1950–51; Architect, Hartford, Conn., USA 1953–55, Nairobi, Kenya 1955–57; Prin. Richard Hughes and Partners 1957–86; Chair. Kenya Branch, Capricorn Africa Soc. 1958–61, Environment Liaison Cen. 1976–78, Lamu Soc. 1977–79; UNEP Consultant on Human Settlements 1978; UN Cen. for Human Settlements Consultant on Bldg materials, construction tech. in developing countries 1979; Ed., Fireball Int. 1986–92; mem. Exec. Cttee, Friends of the Elderly, London 1987–92; mem. Zebra Housing Asscn Bd, London 1988–98, Trustee, Zebra Trust, London 1988 (Vice-Chair. 1994); Guide, The Tate Gallery, London 1988; NADFAS Lecturer 1995. *Exhibitions:* Overseas League and Imperial Inst., London 1953, Commonwealth Arts Festival, Cardiff 1965, German Africa Soc., Berlin and Bonn 1966, RIBA Architecture Overseas, London 1984, Gallery Watatu, Nairobi 1986. *Publications:* Jt author (with Graham Searle) Habitat Handbook 1982, In the Frame 1989, Capricorn – David Stirling's Second African Campaign 2003; and contribs to books on architecture and articles in New Commonwealth, Architectural Review, Architects Journal and Modern Painters; Ed. Living Paintings Trust Albums of Architecture for the Blind 1991, 1994. *Leisure interests:* collecting modern art, dinghy sailing. *Address:* 47 Chiswick Quay, London, W4 3UR, England. *Telephone:* (20) 8995 3109. *Fax:* (20) 8995 3109. *E-mail:* richard@cquay.f9.co .uk (Home).

HUGHES, John Lawrence, BA; American publisher; b. 13 March 1925, New York; s. of John C. Hughes and Margaret Kelly; m. Rose M. Pitman 1947; three s. one d.; ed Yale Univ.; reporter, Nassau Review Star, Rockville Centre, Long Island, NY 1949; Asst Sr Ed., Pocket Books, Inc. New York 1949–59; Vice-Pres. Washington Square Press 1958; Sr Ed., Vice-Pres., Dir William Morrow & Co. 1960–65, Pres. and CEO 1965–85; Pres. The Hearst Trade Book Group 1985–87, Chair., CEO 1988–90, Ed.-at-Large, Group Adviser 1990–; Consultant, Ed.-at-Large HarperCollins Publrs, NY 1999–; Trustee, Yale Univ. Press, Pierpont Morgan Library, Library of America, Acad. of American Poets; mem. Bd Asscn of American Publishers 1986–90 (Chair. 1988–90); mem. Bd Nat. Book Awards 1982–94 (Chair. 1988–89); mem. Publrs. Hall of Fame 1989. *Leisure interest:* golf. *Address:* HarperCollins Publishers, 10 East 53rd Street, New York, NY 10022-5299 (Office); P.O. Box 430, Southport, CT 06490, USA (Home). *Telephone:* (212) 207-7569 (Office); (203) 259-8957 (Home). *Fax:* (212) 207-7506 (Office); (203) 259-8142 (Home). *E-mail:* larry .hughes@harpercollins.com (Office). *Website:* www.harpercollins.com (Office).

HUGHES, John W.; American film producer, screenplay writer and director; b. 18 Feb. 1950, Detroit, Mich.; m. Nancy Ludwig; two s.; ed Univ. of Arizona; copywriter and Creative Dir Leo Burnett Co.; Ed. Nat. Lampoon magazine which led to writing screenplay of Nat. Lampoon's Class Reunion; Founder and Pres. Hughes Entertainment 1985–; Commitment to Chicago Award 1990, NATO/ShoWest Producer of the Year 1990. *Films:* National Lampoon's Class Reunion (screenplay) 1982, National Lampoon's Vacation (screenplay) 1983, Mr. Mom (screenplay) 1983, Nate and Hayes (screenplay) 1983, Sixteen Candles (screenplay and Dir) 1984, National Lampoon's European Vacation (screenplay) 1985, Weird Science (screenplay and Dir) 1985, The Breakfast Club (screenplay, Dir and producer) 1985, Ferris Bueller's Day Off (screenplay, Dir and producer) 1986, Pretty in Pink (screenplay and producer) 1986, Some Kind of Wonderful (screenplay and producer) 1987, Planes, Trains and Automobiles (screenplay, Dir and producer) 1987, The Great Outdoors (screenplay and producer) 1988, She's Having a Baby (screenplay, Dir and producer) 1988, National Lampoon's Christmas Vacation (screenplay and producer) 1989, Uncle Buck (screenplay, Dir and producer) 1989, Home Alone (screenplay and producer) 1990, Career Opportunities (screenplay and pro-

ducer) 1990, Dutch (screenplay and producer) 1991, Curly Sue (screenplay, Dir and producer) 1991, Only the Lonely (co-producer) 1991, Beethoven (screenplay, as Edmond Dantès) 1992, Home Alone 2: Lost in New York (screenplay and producer) 1992, Dennis the Menace (screenplay and producer) 1993, Baby's Day Out (screenplay and producer) 1994, Miracle on 34th Street (screenplay and producer) 1994, 101 Dalmatians (screenplay) 1996, Home Alone 1997, Reach the Rock 1998, New Port South 1999, 102 Dalmatians 2000, Just Visiting 2001. *Address:* c/o Jacob Bloom, Bloom and Dekom, 150 South Rodeo Drive, Beverly Hills, CA 90212; Hughes Entertainment, 10201 West Pico Boulevard, Los Angeles, CA 90064, USA.

HUGHES, Leslie Ernest, MB, DS, FRCS, FRACS; Australian professor of surgery; b. 12 Aug. 1932, Parramatta; s. of Charles J. Hughes and Vera D. (Raines) Hughes; m. Marian Castle 1955; two s. two d.; ed Parramatta High School and Univ. of Sydney; surgical trainee, Sydney 1955–59; Registrar, Derby and London, UK 1959–61; British Empire Cancer Research Campaign Research Fellow, King's College Hospital, London 1962–63; Reader in Surgery, Univ. of Queensland 1964–71; Eleanor Roosevelt Int. Scholar, Roswell Park Memorial Inst., Buffalo, NY 1969–71; Prof. of Surgery, Univ. of Wales Coll. of Medicine, Cardiff 1971–92, Prof. Emer. 1992–; Visiting Prof. Univs. of Queensland, Allahabad, Sydney, Witwatersrand, Cairo, Melbourne, Lund, Albany, New York and NSW; Pres. Welsh Surgical Soc. 1991–93, Surgical Research Soc. 1992–94; Chair. Editorial Cttee, European Journal of Surgical Oncology 1992–97; Pres. History of Medicine Soc. of Wales 1999–2000; Hon. Fellow Asscn of Coloproctology of GB and Ireland 2000. *Publications:* Benign Disorders and Diseases of the Breast 1989; more than 200 papers and book chapters dealing mainly with tumour immunology, disease of the breast, inflammatory bowel disease, surgical oncology, surgical pathology and wound healing. *Leisure interests:* history, gardening, travel. *Address:* 1 Cwrt Llyn, 74 Lake Road East, Cardiff, Wales.

HUGHES, Louis R., MBA; American motor executive; b. 10 Feb. 1949, Cleveland, O; m. Candice Ann Hughes 1972; two c.; ed Gen. Motors Inst. Flint, Mich. and Harvard Univ.; began career with Gen. Motors on financial staff in New York; Asst Treas 1982; Vice-Pres. of Finance, Gen. Motors of Canada 1985–86; Vice-Pres. for Finance, Gen. Motors (Europe), Zürich 1987–89; Chair., Man. Dir Adam Opel AG 1989–92; Exec. Vice-Pres. Gen. Motors Corpn (responsible for int. operations) 1992–; Pres. Gen. Motors (Europe) AG 1992–94; Chair. Bd Saab Automobile AB 1992–; Pres. Gen. Motors Int. Operations, Inc., Switzerland 1994–98; Exec. Vice-Pres. New Business Strategies, Gen. Motors Corpn, Detroit 1998–; mem. Supervisory Bd Deutsche Bank 1993–; mem. Bd of Dirs. AB Electrolux; Pres. Swiss-American Chamber of Commerce; Chair. European Council of American Chambers of Commerce; Order of Merit (Germany). *Leisure interests:* skiing, mountain climbing, antiques. *Address:* General Motors Corporation, 300 Renaissance Center, Detroit, MI 48265, USA.

HUGHES, Mervyn Gregory; Australian cricketer; b. 23 Nov. 1961, Euroa, Vic.; s. of Ian Hughes and Freda Hughes; m. Sue Hughes 1991; one d.; right-arm fast bowler and right-hand lower-order batsman; played for Victoria 1981–95, Essex 1983; 53 Test matches for Australia 1985–94, taking 212 wickets (average 28.3) and scoring 1,032 runs (average 16.6), took hat-trick v. W Indies, Perth 1988; toured England 1989, 1993; 33 limited-overs ints.; took 593 wickets (average 29.4) in first-class cricket; Wisden Cricketer of the Year 1994. *Leisure interests:* golf, relaxing at home, going to the beach, Australian Rules, basketball. *Address:* c/o Australian Cricket Board, 90 Jolimont Street, Jolimont, Vic. 3002, Australia.

HUGHES, Sean Patrick Francis, MS, FRCS, FRCS.Ed(ORTH.), FRCSI; British orthopaedic surgeon; b. 2 Dec. 1941, Farnham, Surrey; s. of Patrick Hughes and Kathleen E. Hughes; m. Felicity M. Anderson 1971; one s. two d.; ed Downside School and St Mary's Hosp. Medical School, Univ. of London; Asst Lecturer in Anatomy, St Mary's Hosp. Medical School 1969; Research Fellow, Mayo Clinic, USA 1975; Sr Registrar in Orthopaedics, Middlesex Hosp. London 1977; Sr Lecturer in Orthopaedics, Royal Postgrad. Medical School, London 1979; Prof. of Orthopaedic Surgery, Univ. of Edinburgh 1979–91, Royal Postgrad. Medical School 1991–; Hon. Consultant Orthopaedic Surgeon Hammersmith Hosps 1991–; Clinical Dir Surgery and Anaesthetics Hammersmith Hosps NHS Trust 1998–2002; Medical Dir Ravenscourt Park Hosp. Hammersmith Hosps NHS Trust 2002–; Prof. of Orthopaedic Surgery, Head of Div. Surgery, Anaesthetics and Intensive Care, Imperial Coll. London 1996–; Aris and Gale Lecturer, RCS 1976, Rahume Darwood Prof., E Africa 1993, Patrick Kelly Prof. May Clinic 1999; Hon. Civilian Consultant to RN; Hon. Consultant, Nat. Hosp. for Nervous Diseases, London 1994–. *Publications:* textbooks and scientific publications on orthopaedics, particularly bone blood flow, musculoskeletal infection, fractures and management of spinal disorders. *Leisure interests:* sailing, golf, walking, skiing, opera, ballet, watching Tottenham Hotspur. *Address:* Department of Musculoskeletal Surgery, Faculty of Medicine, Imperial College London, Charing Cross Campus, Fulham Palace Road, London, W6 8RF (Office); 24 Fairfax Road, London, W4 1EW, England (Home). *Telephone:* (20) 8846-1477 (Office); (20) 8383-0970 (academic) (Office); (20) 8995-2039 (Home). *Fax:* (20) 8383-0468 (Home). *E-mail:* s.hughes@imperial.ac.uk (Office); s.hughes@imperial.ac.uk (Home).

HUGHES, Simon Henry Ward, MA; British politician and barrister; b. 17 May 1951; s. of the late James Henry Annesley Hughes and of Sylvia Hughes (née Ward); ed Christ Coll., Brecon, Selwyn Coll., Cambridge, Inns of Court

School of Law; called to The Bar, Inner Temple 1974; trainee EEC, Brussels 1975–76; trainee and mem. Secr., Directorate and Comm. on Human Rights, Council of Europe, Strasbourg 1976–77; practising barrister 1978–; Vice-Chair. Bermondsey Liberal Asscn 1981–83; MP for Southwark and Bermondsey 1983–97 (Liberal 1983–88, Liberal Democrat 1988–97), Southwark N and Bermondsey 1997–; Vice-Chair. Parl. Youth Affairs Lobby 1984–; Vice-Pres. Southwark Chamber of Commerce 1987– (Pres. 1984–87); Liberal Spokesman on the Environment 1983–87, 1987–88; Alliance Spokesman on Health Jan.–June 1987; Liberal Democrat Spokesman on Educ. and Science 1988–90, on Environment 1988–94, on Natural Resources 1992–94, on Community and Urban Affairs and Young People 1994–95, on Social Welfare 1995–97, on Health 1995–99, on Home Affairs 1999–; Chair. Liberal Party Advisory Panel on Home Affairs 1981–83; mem. Accommodation and Works Select Cttee 1992–97; mem. Southwark Area Youth Cttee, Anti-Apartheid Movt; Hon. Fellow S. Bank Univ.; mem. Liberal Democrat Party. Publications: Across the Divide 1986, Pathways to Power 1992. Leisure interests: music, sport, theatre, the outdoors. Address: House of Commons, London, SW1A 0AA (Office); 6 Lynton Road, Bermondsey, London, SE1 5QR, England (Home). Telephone: (20) 7219-6256 (Office).

HUI, Ann; Chinese film director; b. 23 May 1947, Anshan, Liaoning Prov.; ed Hongkong Univ., London Film School; fmr Asst to Hu Jingquan; began career making TV documentaries and features; joined RTHK 1978, directed three segments of Beneath the Lion Rock (series). Films include: The Secret, The Spooky Bunch, The Story of Woo Viet, Boat People, Love in a Fallen City, Summer Show (Silver Bear Award, Berlin Film Festival), Ordinary Heroes. Publications: The Secret 1979, Boat People 1982, Romance of Book and Sword 1987, Yakuza Chase 1991, Summer Snow 1995.

HUI LIANGYU; Chinese politician and economist; b. 1944, Yushu Co., Jilin Prov.; ed Jilin Agricultural School, Party School of Communist Party of China Jilin Provincial Cttee; joined CCP 1966; Deputy Sec. CCP Yushu Co. Cttee 1974–77; Deputy Dir Jilin Prov. Agricultural Bureau, Prov. Agricultural and Animal Husbandry Dept; Deputy Sec. CCP Leading Group 1977–84; Deputy Sec. CCP Baichengzi Prefectural Cttee, Commr Baichengzi Admin. Office 1984–85; elected mem. Standing Cttee CCP Jilin Prov. Cttee 1985; Dir Rural Policy Research Office, Dir Rural Work Dept CCP Jilin Prov. Cttee 1985–87; apptd Vice-Gov. Jilin Prov. 1987; Deputy Dir CCPCC Policy Research Office 1990; Deputy Sec. CCP Hubei Prov. Cttee 1992; Chair. 1993 Hubei Prov. CPPCC Cttee, Deputy Sec. CCP Anhui Prov. Cttee. and Acting Gov. Anhui Prov. 1994–95, Gov. 1995–98; Sec. CCP Anhui Prov. Cttee 1998, Sec. CCP Jiangsu Prov. Cttee. 1999–2002; Rep. 15th CCP Congress; alt. mem. 14th CCP Cen. Cttee; mem. 15th CCP Cen. Cttee 1997–2002, 16th CCP Cen. Cttee 2002–; Rep. of 7th, 8th and 9th NPC; Vice-Premier State Council 2003–. Address: Zhongguo Gongchan Dang (Chinese Communist Party), 1 Zhong Nan Hai, Beijing, People's Republic of China (Office).

HUISGEN, Rolf, PhD; German academic; b. 13 June 1920, Gerolstein, Eifel; s. of Edmund Huisgen and Maria Flink; m. Trudl Schneiderhan 1945; two d.; ed Univs. of Bonn and Munich; Lecturer, Univ. of Munich 1947–49, Full Prof. of Organic Chem. 1952–88, Prof. Emer. 1988–; Assoc. Prof., Univ. of Tübingen 1949–52; Rockefeller Fellow, USA 1955; numerous guest professorships, USA, Israel, Japan, Spain and Switzerland; Hon. FRSC, London; mem. Bavarian Acad. of Science, Deutsche Akad. der Naturforscher Leopoldina; Foreign Assoc. NAS, Washington; Corresp. mem. Real Acad. de Ciencias Exactas, Madrid, Heidelberg Acad. of Sciences, Polish Acad. of Sciences; Hon. mem. American Acad. of Arts and Sciences, Soc. Chimique de France, Pharmaceutical Soc. of Japan, Gesellschaft Deutscher Chemiker, Accad. Nazionale dei Lincei (Italy), Istituto Lombardo, Polish Acad. Sciences; Hon. Prof. Univ. of St Petersburg; Dr hc (Univ. Complutense de Madrid) 1975; Hon. Dr rer. nat. (Freiburg) 1977, (Erlangen-Nuremberg) 1980, (Würzburg) 1984, (Regensburg) 1985, (St Petersburg) 1993; Liebig Medal, Gesellschaft Deutscher Chemiker 1961, Médaille Lavoisier, Soc. Chimique de France 1965, Roger Adams Award in Organic Chem., ACS 1975, Otto Hahn Award for Chem. and Physics 1979, Adolfo Quilico Medal, Italian Chemical Soc. 1987 and other awards; Bavarian Order of Merit; Bavarian Maximilian Order for Science and Art. Publications: The Adventure Playground of Mechanisms and Novel Reactions (autobiog.) 1994; more than 500 research papers on organic reaction mechanisms and cycloadditions. Leisure interests: modern art, archaeology. Address: Department Chemie, Universität München, Butenandtstr. 5–13, 81377 Munich (Office); Kaulbachstr. 10, 80539 Munich, Germany (Home). Telephone: (89) 218077712 (Office); (89) 281645 (Home). E-mail: rolf.huisgen@cup.uni-muenchen.de (Office).

HUISMANS, Sipko, BA; British business executive; b. 28 Dec. 1940, Ede, Netherlands; s. of Jouko Huismans and Roelofina Huismans; m. Janet Durston 1969; two s. one d.; ed Stellenbosch Univ., S Africa; joined Courtaulds as shift chemist with Ustu Pulp Co., Ltd 1961; Sales Man., later Gen. Man. Springwood Cellulose Co., Ltd 1968; Exec. responsible for Courtaulds trading interests in Eastern Europe and Far East 1974; apptd to Courtaulds Fibres Bd 1980, Man. Dir of Fibres 1982; apptd to Int. Paint Bd 1986, Chair. 1987; Chair. Courtaulds Chemical and Industrial Exec. 1988–96; responsible for films and packaging 1989; mem. Courtaulds Group Exec. 1986–96; Man. Dir Courtaulds PLC 1990–91, Chief Exec. 1991–96; Dir (non-exec.) Vickers PLC 1994–99, Imperial Tobacco Group PLC 1996–; Special Adviser to Chair. Texmaco, Indonesia 1996–. Leisure interests: motor racing, sailing and

'competition'. Address: Latchmore House, Brockenhurst, Hants., SO42 7UE, England. Telephone: (1590) 624419 (Office); (1590) 624229 (Home). Fax: (1590) 624453 (Office). E-mail: sipko@talk21.com (Office).

HUIZENGA, Harry Wayne; American entertainment corporation executive; b. 29 Dec. 1939, Evergreen Park, Ill.; s. of G. Harry Huizenga and Jean (Riddering) Huizenga; m. Martha Jean Pike 1972; three s. one d.; ed Calvin Coll.; Vice-Chair., Pres., COO Waste Man. Inc., Oak Brook, Ill. 1968–84; Prin. Huizenga Holdings. Inc., Fort Lauderdale, Fla 1984–; Chair. and CEO Blockbuster Entertainment Corpn, Fort Lauderdale 1987–94; owner Florida Marlins, Miami 1992–99; co-owner Miami Dolphins, Joe Robbie Stadium; Chair. Boca Resorts Inc. 1996–, Auto Nation Inc. 1999–; mem. Team Republican Nat. Cttee, Washington, DC 1988–90; Man. of Year, Billboard/Time Magazine 1990 and numerous other awards. Leisure interests: golf, collecting antique cars. Address: Huizenga Holdings, 450 E. Las Olas Boulevard, Suite 1500, Fort Lauderdale, FL 33301 (Office); Auto Nation, 110, S.E. 6th Street, Fort Lauderdale, FL 33301, USA.

HUIZENGA, John R., PhD, FAAS; American nuclear chemist and educator; b. 21 April 1921, Fulton, Ill.; s. of Harry M. Huizenga and Josie B. (Brands) Huizenga; m. Dorothy J. Koeze 1946; two s. two d.; ed Calvin Coll., Grand Rapids, Mich. and Univ. of Illinois, Urbana, Ill.; Lab. Supervisor, Manhattan Wartime Project, Oak Ridge 1944–46; Assoc. Scientist, Argonne Nat. Lab., Chicago 1949–57, Sr Scientist 1958–67; Prof of Chem. and Physics Univ. of Rochester, New York 1967–78, Tracy H. Harris Prof. of Chem. and Physics 1978–91, Prof. Emer. 1991–, Chair. Dept of Chem. 1983–88; Fulbright Fellow, Netherlands 1954–55; Guggenheim Fellow, Paris 1964–65; Berkeley, Munich and Copenhagen 1973–74; mem. NAS, ACS; Fellow American Acad. of Arts and Sciences, American Physical Soc., AAAS; E. O. Lawrence Award, Atomic Energy Comm. 1966, Award for Nuclear Application in Chem., ACS 1975, Leroy Grumman Medal 1991. Publications: Nuclear Fission (with R. Vandenbosch) 1973, Damped Nuclear Reactions (with W. U. Schröder), Treatise on Heavy-Ion Science, Vol. 2 1984, Cold Fusion: The Scientific Fiasco of the Century 1992; 275 articles in professional journals. Leisure interests: tennis, golf. Address: 43 McMichael Drive, Pinehurst, NC 28374, USA. Telephone: (910) 295-9539.

HULCE, Tom; American actor; b. 6 Dec. 1953, Detroit; ed N Carolina School of Arts. Plays include: The Rise and Rise of Daniel Rocket 1982, Eastern Standard 1988, A Few Good Men 1990. Films: September 30th 1955, National Lampoon's Animal House, Those Lips Those Eyes, Amadeus 1985, Echo Park 1985, Slam Dance 1987, Nicky and Gino 1988, Parenthood 1989, Shadowman, The Inner Circle, Fearless, Mary Shelley's Frankenstein 1994, Wings of Courage 1995, The Hunchback of Notre Dame (voice) 1996. Television includes: Emily Emily, St Elsewhere, Murder in Mississippi 1990, Black Rainbow, The Heidi Chronicles 1995. Address: c/o CAA, 9830 Wilshire Boulevard, Beverly Hills, CA 90212, USA.

HULL, Jane Dee, MSc; American lawyer and politician; b. 8 Aug. 1935, Kansas City; d. of Justin D. Bowersock and Mildred Swenson; m. Terrance Ward Hull 1954; two s. two d.; ed Kansas and Arizona Univs; House Maj. Whip, Ariz. House of Reps. 1987–88, Speaker of House 1989–93; Chair. Ethics Cttee, Econ. Devt Cttee 1993; mem. Legis. Council, Gov.'s Int. Trade and Tourism Advancement Bd, Gov.'s Strategic Partnership for Econ. Devt, Employment Implementation Task Force 1993; fmr Sec. of State of Arizona, Gov. 1997–2003; mem. Bd Dirs Morrison Inst. for Public Policy, Ariz. Town Hall, Ariz. Econ. Council; mem. Nat. Org. of Women Legislators, Nat. Repub. Legislators Asscn; Republican; Nat. Legislator of the Year Award 1989, Econ. Devt Award of Ariz. Innovation Network 1993. Address: c/o Office of the Governor, State Capitol, West Wing, 1700 West Washington Street, Phoenix, AZ 85007, USA.

HULME, Keri; New Zealand novelist; b. 9 March 1947, Christchurch, NZ; ed Canterbury Univ., Christchurch; worked as tobacco picker, fish and chip cook, TV Dir and woollen mill worker and studied law, before becoming full-time writer 1972; Writer-in-Residence Otago Univ. 1978, Univ. of Canterbury, Christchurch 1985; awarded New Zealand Book of the Year Award 1984, Mobil Pegasus Prize 1984, Booker McConnell Prize for Fiction, UK 1985. Publications: The Bone People 1984, The Windeater 1987, Homeplaces 1989, Strands (poems) 1991, Bait 1992. Address: c/o Hodder & Stoughton Ltd, 338 Euston Road, London, NW1 3BH, England; P.O. Box 1, Whataroa, South Westland, Aotearoa, New Zealand.

HULSE, Russell Alan, PhD; American research physicist; b. 28 Nov. 1950; s. of Alan Earle Hulse and Betty Joan Wedemeyer; ed The Cooper Union, New York and Univ. of Massachusetts; worked at Nat. Radio Astronomy Observatory 1975–77; researcher at Plasma Physics Lab., Princeton Univ. 1977–80, Prin. Research Physicist 1992–, Head Advanced Modelling Sciences Lab. 1994–; Fellow American Physical Soc. 1993, Distinguished Resident Fellow, Princeton Univ. 1994; Nobel Prize in Physics (Jt winner) 1993. Publications: papers in professional journals and conf. proceedings in fields of pulsar astronomy, controlled fusion plasma physics and computer modelling. Leisure interests: cross-country skiing, canoeing, nature photography, bird watching, other outdoor activities, target shooting, music. Address: Princeton University, Plasma Physics Laboratory, James Forrestal Research Campus, P.O. Box 451, Princeton, NJ 08543, USA. Telephone: (609) 243-2621.

HULTQVIST, Bengt Karl Gustaf, DrSci; Swedish space physicist; b. 21 Aug. 1927, Hemmesjö; s. of Eric Hultqvist and Elsa Hultqvist; m. Gurli Gustafsson

1953; two s. one d.; ed Univ. of Stockholm; Dir Kiruna Geophysical Observatory 1956–73, Kiruna Geophysical Inst. 1973–87, Swedish Inst. of Space Physics 1987–94, Int. Space Science Inst. (ISSI), Berne, Switzerland 1995–99; Sec.-Gen. Int. Asscn of Geomagnetism and Aeronomy 2001–; Chair. Swedish Space Science Cttee 1972–97, Swedish Nat. Cttee for Geodesy and Geophysics 1980–94, EISCAT Council 1987–88, Nordic Soc. for Space Research 1989–92, Space Science Advisory Cttee, European Space Agency 1998–2000, and others; Kt of the Northern Star Award 1965, Royal Swedish Acad. of Science Prize 1968, 1972, Gold Medal, Royal Swedish Acad. of Eng Sciences 1988, King's Medal 1991, Berzelius Medal, Royal Swedish Acad. of Science 1994, Julius Bartels Medal, European Geophysical Soc. 1996, Haunes Alfvén Medal, European Geophysical Soc. 2002, and other decorations. *Publications include:* Introduction to Geocosmophysics 1967, High Latitude Space Plasma Physics (ed.) 1983, Space, Science and I 1997, Magnetospheric Plasma Sources and Losses (ed.) 1999; more than 200 scientific papers on radiation and space physics. *Address:* Swedish Institute of Space Physics, Box 812, 981 28 Kiruna (Office); Grönstensv. 2, 98140 Kiruna, Sweden (Home). *Telephone:* (980) 790-60 (Office); (980) 843-40 (Home). *Fax:* (980) 790-91 (Office); (980) 843-40 (Home). *E-mail:* hultqv@irf.se (Office); hultqv@irf.se (Home).

HUME, Cameron R.; American diplomatist; m.; four d.; ed Princeton Univ., American Univ. School of Law; joined Foreign Service 1970, early assignments included Vice-Consul in Palermo, Adviser on Human Rights, USA Mission to UN, mem. planning staff Sec. of State, Desk Officer for SA; Political Counsellor in Damascas and Beirut; Dir Foreign Service Inst. field school, Tunis –1986; Adviser on Middle East, Mission to UN 1986–90, Sr Adviser 1990–91; Deputy Chief of Mission, Holy See and US Rep. to Mozambique Peace Talks 1991–94; Minister Counsellor for Political Affairs, Mission to UN 1994–97; Amb. to Algeria 1997–2000; Special Adviser to Perm. Rep. to UN 2000–01; Amb. to SA Nov. 2001–; Fellow Council on Foreign Relations 1975–76, Harvard Univ. Centre for Int. Affairs 1989–90; Guest Scholar US Inst. of Peace 1994. *Publications include:* (books) The United Nations, Iran and Iraq: How Peacemaking Changed 1994, Ending Mozambique's War 1994, Mission to Algiers: Diplomacy by Engagement 2001; numerous articles on diplomacy. *Address:* Embassy of USA, 877 Pretorius Street, Pretoria 0083, POB 9536, Pretoria 0001, South Africa (Office). *Telephone:* (12) 3421048 (Office). *Fax:* (12) 342244 (Office). *Website:* www.usembassy.state.gov/southafrica (Office).

HUME, Gary, RA; British artist; b. 1962, Tenterden, Kent; ed Goldsmiths Coll., Univ. of London; mem. RA Summer Exhibition Selection Cttee 2002. *Art exhibitions:* Group exhibitions include: Freeze, Part 2, Surrey Docks 1988, The British Art Show '90, East Country Yard Show 1990, Confrontations, Madrid 1991, New Voices, New Work, Brussels 1992, Unbound, Hayward Gallery, London 1994, General Release, Venice Biennale 1995, Such is Life 1996, Conclusions, Santa Fe 1997, Dimensions Variable, British Council Touring Exhbn. 1997, Distinctive Elements, S Korea 1998, Graphics! New Haven, Conn. 1999; Solo exhibitions include: Recent Works, London 1989, The Dolphin Paintings, London 1991, Tarpaulins, London 1991, Recent Paintings, Santa Monica, Calif. 1992, My Aunt and I Agree, London 1995, Gary Hume, Kunsthalle Bern 1995, XXIII Bienal de São Paulo, Brazil 1996, Matthew Marks Gallery, New York 1997, Sadler's Wells Theatre, London 1998, Dean Gallery, Scottish Nat. Gallery of Modern Art, Edin. 1999, Venice Biennale April–Nov. 1999. *Address:* Royal Academy of Arts, Burlington House, Piccadilly, London, W1J 0BD, England.

HUME, John, MA; Irish politician and fmr teacher; b. 18 Jan. 1937, Londonderry, N Ireland; s. of Samuel Hume and Anne Hume (née Doherty); m. Patricia Hone 1960; two s. three d.; ed St Colomb's Coll., Londonderry, St Patrick's Coll., Maynooth, Nat. Univ. of Ireland; Research Fellow, Trinity Coll., Assoc. Fellow, Centre for Int. Affairs, Harvard; Founder mem. Credit Union in NI, Pres. 1964–68; Non-violent Civil Rights leader 1968–69; rep. Londonderry in NI Parl. 1969–72, in NI Ass. 1972–73; Minister of Commerce, Powersharing Exec. 1974; rep. Londonderry in NI Convention 1975–76; elected to European Parl. 1979–; Leader, Social Democratic and Labour Party (SDLP) 1979–2001; mem. NI Ass. 1982–86; MP for Foyle 1983–; mem. for Foyle, NI Ass. 1998– (Ass. suspended 2002); mem. SDLP New Ireland Forum 1983–84, Irish Transport and General Workers Union, Bureau of European Parl. Socialist Group 1979–, Regional Policy and Regional Planning Cttee 1979–, EEC, Socialist Co-Chair. Intergroup on Minority Cultures and Languages; Co-Leader Int. Democratic Observers for 1986 Philippines Election; mem. Advisory Cttee on Pollution of the Sea (ACOPS) 1989; Sponsor, Irish Anti-Apartheid Movt; Dr hc (Massachusetts) 1985, (Catholic Univ. of America) 1986, (St Joseph's Univ., Phila) 1986, (Univ. of Mass., Catholic Univ. of America, Wash. DC, Tusculum Coll., Tenn.); Hon. LLD (Queen's) 1995, (Wales) 1996; Hon. DLitt (Ulster) 1998; Légion d'honneur; shared Nobel Peace Prize 1998; Martin Luther King Award 1999, Gandhi Peace Prize 2002. *Publication:* Politics, Peace and Reconciliation in Ireland 1996. *Address:* 5 Bayview Terrace, Derry, BT48 7EE, Northern Ireland (Office); House of Commons, London, SW1A 0AA, England. *Telephone:* (28) 7126-5340 (Office); (20) 7219-3000 (London). *Fax:* (28) 7136-3423 (Office).

HUMMES, HE Cardinal Cláudio; Brazilian ecclesiastic; b. 8 Aug. 1934, Montenegro; ordained priest 1958; Bishop 1975; Coadjutor Santo André 1975–96; Archbishop of Fortaleza 1996–98, of São Paulo 1998–; cr. Cardinal 2001. *Address:* Avenida Higienópolis 890, C.P. 1670, 01238-908 São Paulo, SP, Brazil (Office). *Telephone:* (11) 826-0133 (Office). *Fax:* (11) 825-6806 (Office).

HUMPHREYS, James Charles, BCom, MSc; Australian diplomatist; b. 6 Oct. 1934, Melbourne; s. of James Thomas Humphreys and Mary Charlotte Humphreys; m. Diane May Dummett 1962; two d.; ed Scotch Coll., Melbourne, Univs of Melbourne and London; with Dept of Trade and Customs 1951–62; Dept of Treasury 1963–71; Counsellor (Financial), Tokyo 1972–74; Dept of Foreign Affairs, Canberra 1974–78; Amb. to Denmark 1978–80, to OECD, Paris 1980–83; First Asst Sec. Dept of Foreign Affairs, Canberra 1984–86; First Asst Sec. Dept of Foreign Affairs and Trade, Canberra 1987–88; High Commr in Canada, also Accred to Bermuda 1989–91; Exec. Dir EBRD, London 1991–94; Consul-Gen. in USA, New York 1994–96; Chief Exec. Global Econs Ltd 1997–. *Leisure interests:* sailing, tennis, reading, music. *Address:* P.O. Box 4847, Kingston, ACT 2604, Australia.

HUMPHRIES, (John) Barry, AO; Australian entertainer and author; b. 17 Feb. 1934; s. of J. A. E. Humphries and L. A. Brown; m. 1st Rosalind Tong 1959; two d.; m. 2nd Diane Millstead; two s.; m. 3rd Lizzie Spender 1990; ed Melbourne Grammar and Univ. of Melbourne; repertory seasons Union Theatre, Melbourne 1953–54, Phillip Street Revue Theatre, Sydney 1956, Demon Barber Lyric, Hammersmith 1959, Oliver, New Theatre 1960; one-man shows (author and performer): A Nice Night's Entertainment 1962, Excuse I 1965, Just a Show 1968, A Load of Olde Stuffe 1971, At Least You Can Say That You've Seen It 1974, Housewife Superstar 1976, Isn't It Pathetic at His Age 1979, A Night with Dame Edna 1979, An Evening's Intercourse with Barry Humphries 1981–82, Tears Before Bedtime 1986, Back with a Vengeance, London 1987–88, Look at Me When I'm Talking to You 1993–94, Edna: The Spectacle 1998, Dame Edna: The Royal Tour, San Francisco 1998, Remember You're Out 1999; numerous plays, films and broadcasts; best-known for his comic characterizations of Dame Edna Everage, Sir Les Patterson and Sandy Stone; Pres. Frans de Boewer Soc. (Belgium); Vice-Pres. Betjeman Soc. 2001–. *Publications:* Bizarre 1964, Innocent Austral Verse 1968, The Wonderful World of Barry McKenzie (with Nicholas Garland) 1970, Bazza Holds His Own (with Nicholas Garland) 1972, Dame Edna's Coffee Table Book 1976, Les Patterson's Australia 1979, Treasury of Australian Kitsch 1980, A Nice Night's Entertainment 1981, Dame Edna's Bedside Companion 1982, The Traveller's Tool 1985, The Complete Barry McKenzie 1988, My Gorgeous Life: The Autobiography of Dame Edna Everage 1989, The Life and Death of Sandy Stone 1991, More Please: An Autobiography 1992, Women in the Background (novel) 1996. *Leisure interests:* reading secondhand booksellers' catalogues in bed, inventing Australia.

HUMPHRY, Richard George, AO, FCA, FAIM; Australian administrator and stock exchange official; b. 24 Feb. 1939, Perth; s. of Arthur D. Humphry and Enid G. Humphry; m. Rose Friel 1961; one s. one d.; ed Univ. of Western Australia; computer programmer in public service 1967–77; Asst Sec. Supply Computer Systems Br. 1978–79, Accounting Devt Br. 1979–81; Asst Sec. Defence Br. Commonwealth Dept of Finance 1981–82; First Asst Sec. Financial Man. and Accounting Policy Div. 1982–85; Deputy Sec. Commonwealth Dept of Aboriginal Affairs 1985; Auditor-Gen., Victoria 1986–88; Dir Gen. Premier's Dept of NSW 1988–94; Chair. Audit and Compliance Cttee, State Super Financial Services 1992–2001; Dir State Super Financial Services 1992–2001; Chair. NSW Financial Insts Comm. 1994–99; Man. Dir and CEO Australian Stock Exchange 1994–; Chair. Australian Financial Insts Comm. 1996–2000 (Dir 1992–96); Dir Garvan Medical Research Foundation 1997–; Deputy Chair. Zoological Parks Bd, NSW 1998–; Pres. Commonwealth Remuneration Tribunal 1998–; Ind. Reviewer Govt Information Tech. Outsourcing Initiative 2000; mem. Advisory Bd Nat. Office for Information Economy 1997–98, Financial Sector Advisory Cttee Taskforce 1998–, Foreign Affairs Council 2000–; Business Council of Australia 2000–; mem. Australian Computing Soc., Australasian Inst. of Banking and Finance; Fellow Australian Soc. of Certified Practising Accountants, Australian Inst. of Co. Dirs; Int. Fed. of Accountants Award 1988, Accountant of the Year (Public Sector Div.) 1989, Best Financial Services Exec. (Australian Banking and Finance Awards) 2000. *Leisure interests:* bush walking, reading, scuba diving. *Address:* Australian Stock Exchange Ltd, P.O. Box H224, Australia Square, Sydney, NSW 2000, Australia (Office). *Telephone:* (2) 9227-0400 (Office). *Fax:* (2) 9227-0007 (Office). *Website:* www.asx.com.au (Office).

HUMPHRYS, John; British broadcaster; b. 17 Aug. 1943; s. of Edward George Humphrys and Winifred Matthews; m. (divorced); two s. one d.; ed Cardiff High School; Washington corresp. BBC TV 1971–77, Southern Africa corresp. 1977–80, Diplomatic corresp. 1981; presenter, BBC Nine o'Clock News 1981–87; presenter, BBC Radio 4 Today Programme 1987–, On the Record, BBC TV 1993–, John Humphrys Interview Radio 4 1995–; Hon. Fellow Cardiff Univ. 1998; Hon. DLitt (Dundee) 1996; Hon. MA (Univ. of Wales) 1998; Hon. LLD (St Andrews) 1999. *Publication:* Devil's Advocate 1999. *Leisure interests:* cello, trees, books, farming, music. *Address:* BBC, News Centre, Wood Lane, London, W12, England.

HUN SEN, BA, PhD; Cambodian politician; b. 5 Aug. 1952, Stoeung Trang District, Kompang-Cham Prov.; m. Bun Rany 1975; three s. three d.; ed Lycée Indra Devi, Phnom Penh, Univ. of Phnom Penh, Nat. Political Acad., Hanoi; joined Khmer Rouges 1970, rising to Commdt; in Viet Nam with pro-Vietnamese Kampucheans 1977, returned to Kampuchea (now Cambodia) after Vietnamese-backed take-over; Founding mem. United Front for the Nat. Salvation of Kampuchea 1978; Minister for Foreign Affairs 1979–85; Deputy Prime Minister 1981–85; Chair. Council of Ministers of Cambodia (Prime Minister) 1985–91, Second Prime Minister Royal Govt of Cambodia 1993–98,

Prime Minister of Cambodia 1998–; Vice-Pres. Cambodian People's Party (CPP); Hon. PhD (Southern Calif. Univ.) 1995, (Iowa Wesleyan Coll.) 1996; Dr. hc (Dankook Univ., S. Korea) 2001, (Ramkhamhaeng, Thailand) 2001; awarded title Samdech by the King of Cambodia, World Peace Award, Int. Peace Center 'Lifting Up the World with a Oneness-Heart' Award 2001. *Address:* Council of Ministers, Phnom Penh, Cambodia.

HÜNER, Tomáš, DipEng; Czech business executive and engineer; b. 26 June 1959, Ostrava; s. of Julius Hüner and Olga Hüner; m. Katerina Trnková; two d.; ed Brno Univ. of Tech.; engineer 1985–90; Deputy-Dir Severomoravská Energetika a.s. (SME) Energy works 1990–94, CEO and Chair. SME 1994–; Chair. Supervisory Bd Aliatel a.s.; Chair. Energetika Vítkovice a.s., ePRIM, a.s.; Vice-Chair. Supervisory Bd Union Group a.s. *Publications include:* Chronicle of Corporate Heads, Historica Prague (Publr); papers in specialist journals. *Leisure interests:* skiing, tennis, surfing. *Address:* Severomoravská energetika a.s., 28. Rijna 152, 70902 Ostrava (Office); ul. Přátelství 269/15, 73601 Havírov, Czech Republic (Home). *Telephone:* (6) 96673201 (Office); (6) 96415491 (Home). *E-mail:* tomas.huner@sme.cz (Office). *Website:* www.sme .cz.

HUNGERFORD, John Leonard, MA, MB, BChir, FRCS; British ophthalmologist; b. 12 Oct. 1944; s. of Leonard Harold Hungerford and Violet Miriam Hungerford (née Bickerstaff); m. Yvonne Carole Rayment 1987; one d.; ed The Glyn School, Epsom, Gonville and Caius Coll. Cambridge, Charing Cross Hosp. Medical School; consultant surgeon, Moorfields Eye Hosp. 1983–; consultant Ophthalmic Surgeon, St Bartholomew's Hosp. 1983–; Fellow Royal Coll. of Ophthalmologists; Vice-Pres. Int. Soc. for Ocular Oncology 2001; Ridley Medal 1998, Gregg Medal 2001. *Publications:* several publns on ocular cancer. *Leisure interests:* travel, reading, music, gardening, architecture. *Address:* 114 Harley Street, London, W1N 1AG, England (Office). *Telephone:* (20) 7935-1565 (Office). *Fax:* (20) 7224-1752 (Office). *E-mail:* john .hungerford@moorfields.nhs.uk (Office); hungerford.england@btopenworld .co.uk (Home).

HUNKAPILLER, Michael W., PhD; American scientist; b. 1949; ed Oklahoma Baptist Univ., California Inst. of Tech.; joined Research and Devt Dept of Applied Biosystems Inc. 1983, Exec. Vice-Pres. 1995, Gen. Man. 1995–97; Vice-Pres. PE Corpn 1995–97, Sr Vice-Pres. and Pres. of Applied Biosystems Div. 1997–98, Pres. PE Biosystems Group June 1998–; Dir ACLARA Biosciences Inc. 2000–; mem. of numerous professional socs.; has received several awards for contribs. to chemistry. *Publications:* more than 100 publs. *Address:* 761 Main Avenue, Norwalk, CT 06859, USA (Office).

HUNLÉDÉ, Ayi Houénou, LenD; Togolese politician; b. 2 Feb. 1925, Anécho; ed Univ. of Montpellier, France; Asst Insp. of Schools, Northern Togo, then teacher at Ecole Normale d'Atakpamé 1953–56; worked for French Overseas Territories Admin. 1958; Asst Admin. Mayor, Lomé; Chief, admin. subdiv. of Tabligbo; Admin. Mayor of Tsévié 1958–60; Amb. to France, UK, EEC 1960–65; High Commr for Planning 1965–67; Minister of Foreign Affairs 1967–76; ordained pastor in Togolese Evangelical Church 1977; Commdr, Légion d'honneur, Great Cross of Merit (FRG), Commdr, Order of Liberia.

HUNT, Caroline Rose, PhD; American business executive; b. 8 Jan. 1923, El Dorado; d. of H. L. Hunt and Lyda Bunker; four s. one d.; ed Mary Baldwin Coll., Univs. of Texas and Charleston; beneficiary of Caroline Hunt Trust Estate which includes Corpn, Rosewood Properties, Rosewood Resources, Rosewood Hotels with interests in oil and gas properties, luxury hotels and resorts; owner Lady Primrose's Shopping Establishment Countryside, Lady Primrose's Royal Bathing and Luxuries; Hon. Chair. and Chair. numerous socs. and cttees.; Award for Excellence in Community Service in the Field of Business, Dallas Historic Soc. 1984, Les Femmes du Monde Award 1988, Grande Dame d'Escoffier 1989, Nat. Fragrance Council Award 1994, British American Commerce Award 1994, Texas Business Hall of Fame 1999, Silver Plume Outstanding Citizen 2000, Featured Author, Texas Book Festival 2001 and Dallas Historical Soc. Centennial 2002. *Publications:* The Compleat Pumpkin Eater 1980, Primrose Past, The 1848 Diary of Young Lady Primrose 2001. *Leisure interests:* antiques, writing. *Address:* 100 Crescent Court, Ste. 1700, Dallas, TX 75201, USA.

HUNT, Helen; American actress; b. 15 June 1963, LA; d. of Gordon Hunt and Jane Hunt. *Stage appearances include:* Been Taken, Our Town, The Taming of the Shrew, Methusalem. *Films include:* Rollercoaster, Girls Just Want to Have Fun, Peggy Sue Got Married, Project X, Miles From Home, Trancers, Stealing Home, Next of Kin, The Waterdance, Only You, Bob Roberts, Mr Saturday Night, Kiss of Death, Twister, As Good As It Gets (Acad. Award for Best Actress 1998), Twelfth Night, Pay It Forward 2000, Dr. T and the Women 2000, Cast Away 2000, What Women Want 2000, The Curse of Jade Scorpion 2001. *Television includes:* Swiss Family Robinson, Mad About You (Emmy Award 1996, 1997, Golden Globe Award 1997). *Address:* c/o Connie Tavel, 9171 Wilshire Boulevard, Suite 436, Beverly Hills, CA 90210, USA.

HUNT, James Baxter, Jr, BS(EDUC), MS(Econs); American politician and lawyer; b. 16 May 1937, Guilford Co., NC; s. of James Baxter and Elsie (Brame) Hunt; m. Carolyn Joyce Leonard 1958; one s. three d.; ed North Carolina State Univ., Univ. of North Carolina; called to Bar of NC 1964; Econ. Adviser to Govt of Nepal for Ford Foundation 1964–66; partner with Kirby, Webb and Hunt 1966–72, Poyner and Spruill, Raleigh, NC 1985–93; mem. Womble, Carlyle, Sandridge & Rice 2001–; Lt-Gov. N Carolina 1973–77, Gov. of N Carolina 1977–85, 1993–2000; Chair. Nat. Bd for Professional Teaching

Standards 1987–; mem. Bd of Dirs. Nat. Center for Educ. and the Economy; Democrat; 1st Annual Harry S. Truman Award Nat. Young Democrats 1975, Soil Conservation Honors Award 1986, Outstanding Govt Leader in US Conservation, Nat. Wildlife Fed. 1983 and other awards. *Address:* Womble, Carlyle, Sandridge & Rice, 150 Fayetteville Street Mall, Suite 2100, PO Box 831, Raleigh, NC 27602 (Office); c/o Office of the Governor, 116 West Jones Street, Raleigh, NC 27603, USA.

HUNT, Jonathan Lucas, PC, MA; New Zealand politician; b. 2 Dec. 1938, Lower Hutt; s. of H. Lucas Hunt and A. Z. Hunt; ed Auckland Grammar School, Auckland Univ.; teacher Kelston Boys' High School 1961–66; tutor, Univ. of Auckland 1964–66; mem. for New Lynn 1966–; Jr Govt Whip 1972, Chair. of Cttees. and Deputy Speaker of House of Reps. 1974–75, Acting Speaker 1975; Labour Opposition Spokesman on Health 1976–79, Constitution and Parl. Affairs 1978–81; Sr Opposition Whip 1980–84; Shadow Minister of Broadcasting 1982; Minister of Broadcasting and Postmaster-Gen. 1984–87, Minister of State 1987–89, Leader of the House 1987–90, Minister of Broadcasting 1988–90; Minister for Tourism 1988–89, of Housing 1989, of Communications Jan.–Oct. 1990; Sr Opposition Whip 1990–96; Shadow Leader of the House 1996–99; Speaker of House of Reps 1999–. *Leisure interests:* music, int. affairs, cricket, literature. *Address:* Parliament Buildings, Wellington; P.O. Box 15180, New Lynn, Auckland, 1232 (Office); Lone Kauri Road, Kare Kare, R.D.I., New Lynn, Waitakere City, New Zealand (Home). *Telephone:* (4) 471-9831 (Office); (9) 812-8864. *Fax:* (4) 472-2055 (Office); (9) 812-8864 (Home). *E-mail:* jonathan.hunt@parliament.govt.nz (Office); jonathan.hunt@parliament.govt.nz (Home).

HUNT, Sir Rex Masterman, Kt, CMG, BA; British diplomatist (retd); b. 29 June 1926, Redcar, Yorks.; s. of the late H. W. Hunt and of Ivy Masterman; m. Mavis Buckland 1951; one s. one d.; ed Coatham School, St Peter's Coll., Oxford; service with RAF 1944–48; with Overseas Civil Service 1951; Dist Commr, Uganda 1962; in Commonwealth Relations Office 1963–64; First Sec., Kuching, Malaysia 1964–65, Jesselton (now Kota Kinabalu), Malaysia 1965–67, Brunei 1967; First Sec., (Econ.), Embassy, Turkey 1968–70; First Sec. and Head of Chancery, Embassy, Indonesia 1970–72; Asst, Middle East Dept, FCO 1972–74; Counsellor, Embassy, S. Viet Nam 1974–75, Deputy High Commr, Malaysia 1976–79; Gov. and C-in-C Falkland Islands and Dependencies 1980–82, expelled after Argentine seizure of Falkland Islands April 1982, returned as Civil Commr June, after UK recapture of Islands; Civil Commr Falkland Islands 1982–Sept. 1985, Gov. Oct. 1985, High Comm. British Antarctic Territory 1980–85; Freeman of the City of London 1978, Freeman Stanley FC 1985. *Publication:* My Falkland Days 1992. *Leisure interests:* gardening, golf. *Address:* Old Woodside, Broomfield Park, Sunningdale, Berks., SL5 0JS, England. *Telephone:* (1344) 625563. *Fax:* (1344) 625563 (Home).

HUNT, Tim (Richard Timothy), PhD, FRS; British biochemist; b. 19 Feb. 1943, Neston, Wirral; s. of Richard William Hunt and Kit Rowland; m. Mary Collins; two d.; ed Dragon School, Oxford, Magdalen Coll. School, Oxford and Univ. of Cambridge; Research Fellow in Biochem., Univ. of Cambridge 1970–81, Univ. Lecturer 1982–90; Prin. Scientist, Imperial Cancer Research Fund 1990–; Nobel Prize for Physiology or Medicine 2001. *Publications:* Molecular Biology of the Cell – Problems Book (jtly.), The Cell Cycle: An Introduction (jtly.). *Address:* Imperial Cancer Research Fund, Clare Hall Laboratories, South Mimms, Herts., EN6 3LD (Office); Rose Cottage, Ridge, Herts., EN6 3LH, England (Home). *Telephone:* (20) 7269-3981 (Office); (1707) 646484 (Home). *Fax:* (20) 7269-3804 (Office); (20) 7323-5519 (Home). *E-mail:* tim.hunt@icrf.icnet.uk (Office). *Website:* www.icnet.uk/clarehall (Office).

HUNT OF KINGS HEATH, Baron (Life Peer), cr. 1997, of Birmingham in the County of West Midlands; **Philip Alexander Hunt,** OBE, BA; British politician; b. 19 May 1949, Birmingham; m.; five c.; ed City of Oxford High School, Oxford School and Univ. of Leeds; joined Oxford Regional Hosp. Bd 1972; with Nuffield Orthopaedic Centre 1974; Sec. Edgware and Hendon Community Health Council 1975–79; joined Nat. Asscn of Health Authorities 1978, Dir 1990; mem. House of Lords 1997–; apptd. Govt Whip and Spokesman on Educ. and Employment and Health, House of Lords 1998; Parl. Under-Sec. of State, Dept of Health 1999–2003; mem. Oxford City Council 1973–79, Birmingham City Council 1980–82; Jt Chair. All Party Care and Public Health Group 1997–98; Vice-Chair. All Party Group on AIDS 1997–98. *Leisure interests:* swimming, Birmingham City Football Club, music. *Address:* House of Lords, Westminster, London, SW1A 0PW (Office). *Telephone:* (20) 7210-5333 (Office). *Fax:* (20) 7210-5066 (Office).

HUNTEN, Donald Mount, PhD; American astronomer and physicist; b. 1 March 1925, Montreal, Canada; s. of Kenneth William Hunten and Winnifred Binnmore Mount; m. 1st Isobel Ann Rubenstein 1949 (divorced 1995); two s.; m. 2nd Ann Louise Sprague; ed Univ. of Western Ontario, McGill Univ.; Research Assoc. to Prof. Univ. of Sask., Saskatoon 1950–63; Physicist Kitt Peak Nat. Observatory 1963–78, Consultant to NASA 1964–, Science Adviser to NASA Assoc. Admin. for Space Science 1977–78; Prof. of Planetary Science Univ. of Ariz., Tucson 1978–88, Regents Prof. 1988–; mem. NAS; numerous awards including Space Science Award, Cttee. on Space Research 2000. *Publications:* Introduction to Electronics 1964, Theory of Planetary Atmospheres (with J. W. Chamberlain) 1987; several NASA publs, numerous papers in scientific journals. *Leisure interest:* music. *Address:* Department of Planetary Sciences, University of Arizona, Tucson, AZ 85721; 3445 W Foxes Den Drive, Tucson, AZ 85745, USA (Home). *Telephone:* (602) 621-4002 (Office). *Fax:* (602) 621-4933.

HUNTER, Evan, BA; American author; b. 15 Oct. 1926, New York; s. of Charles and Marie Lombino; m. 1st Anita Melnick 1949 (divorced); three s.; m. 2nd Mary Vann Finley 1973 (divorced); one step-d.; m. 3rd Dragica Dimitrijevic 1997; ed Cooper Union and Hunter Coll. *Publications:* The Blackboard Jungle 1954, Second Ending 1956, Strangers When We Meet 1958 (screenplay 1959), A Matter of Conviction 1959, Mothers and Daughters 1961, The Birds (screenplay) 1962, Happy New Year Herbie (short stories) 1963, Buddwing 1964, The Easter Man (play) 1964, The Paper Dragon 1966, A Horse's Head 1967, Last Summer 1968, Sons 1969, The Conjurer (play) 1969, Nobody Knew They Were There 1971, Every Little Crook and Nanny 1972, Fuzz (screenplay) 1972, The Easter Man (short stories) 1972, Come Winter 1973, Streets of Gold 1974, The Chisholms 1976, Me and Mr. Stenner 1976, The Chisholms (TV play) 1979, Walk Proud (screenplay) 1979, The Legend of Walks Far Woman (TV play) 1980, Love Dad 1981, 87th Precinct Mysteries, Far From the Sea 1983, Lizzie 1984, Dream West (TV play) 1986, Criminal Conversation 1994, Privileged Conversation 1996, Me and Hitch (memoir) 1997, Barking at Butterflies (short stories) 2000, Candyland: a novel in two parts 2001, The Moment She Was Gone 2002; under pseudonym Ezra Hannon: Doors 1975; under pseudonym Richard Marsten: Runaway Black 1954, Death of a Nurse 1955, Vanishing Ladies 1957, Big Man 1959, Even the Wicked 1958; under pseudonym Ed McBain: Cop Hater 1956, The Mugger 1956, The Pusher 1956, The Con Man 1957, Killer's Choice 1957, Killer's Payoff 1958, Lady Killer 1958, Killer's Wedge 1959, 'Til Death 1959, King's Ransom 1959, Give the Boys a Great Big Hand 1960, The Heckler 1960, See Them Die 1960, Lady, Lady, I Did It 1961, Like Love 1962, The Empty Hours (three novelettes) 1962, Ten plus One 1963, Ax 1964, He Who Hesitates 1965, Doll 1965, The Sentries 1965, Eighty Million Eyes 1966, Fuzz 1968 (screenplay 1972), Shotgun 1969, Jigsaw 1970, Hail, Hail, The Gang's All Here 1971, Sadie When She Died 1972, Let's Hear It for the Deaf Man 1972, Hail to the Chief 1973, Bread 1974, Where There's Smoke 1975, Blood Relatives 1975, So Long as You Both Shall Live 1976, Long Time No See 1977, Goldilocks 1977, Calypso 1979, Ghosts 1980, Rumpelstiltskin 1981, Heat 1981, Ice 1983, Beauty and the Beast 1983, Jack and the Beanstalk 1984, Lightning 1984, Snow White and Rose Red 1985, Eight Black Horses 1985, Cinderella 1986, Another Part of the City 1986, Poison 1987, Puss in Boots 1987, Tricks 1987, McBain's Ladies 1988, The House that Jack Built 1988, Lullaby 1989, Downtown 1989, Vespers 1990, Three Blind Mice 1990, Widows 1991, Kiss 1992, Mary, Mary 1992, Mischief 1993, There Was a Little Girl 1994, And All through the House 1994, Romance 1995, Gladly the Cross-Eyed Bear 1996, Nocturne 1997, The Last Best Hope 1998, The Big Bad City 1999, Driving Lessons 2000, The Last Dance 2000, Money Money Money 2001, Fat Ollie's Book: A Novel of the 87th Precinct 2003. *Leisure interest:* travel. *Address:* c/o Gelfman Schneider Literary Agency, Suite 2515, 250 West 57th Street, New York, NY 10107, USA. *E-mail:* evan@edmcbain.com. *Website:* www.edmcbain.com.

HUNTER, Holly, BFA; American actress; b. 20 March 1958, Atlanta, Ga; d. of Charles Hunter and Opal M. Catledge; m. Janusz Kaminski (q.v.) 1995; ed Carnegie-Mellon Univ.; Broadway appearances include Crimes of the Heart, The Wake of Jamey Foster, The Miss Firecracker Contest; other stage appearances include A Weekend Near Madison, The Person I Once Was, Battery (all in New York), A Lie of the Mind (Los Angeles) and in regional productions; Dir Calif. Abortion Rights Action League; Emmy Award for TV production Roe vs. Wade 1989; Best Actress Award, American TV Awards, for cable TV production of The Positively True Adventures of the Alleged Texas Cheerleader Murdering Mom 1993; Best Actress Award, Cannes Film Festival Award 1993 and Acad. Award 1994 for role in The Piano. *Films:* Broadcast News 1987, Raising Arizona 1987, Miss Firecracker 1989, Always 1989, Once Around 1990, The Piano 1993, The Firm 1993, Home for the Holidays, Copycat 1995, Crash 1996, Living Out Loud 1998, Time Code 2000, When Billie Beat Bobby 2001, Festival in Cannes 2001, Goodbye Hello 2002, Levity 2003.

HUNTER, Robert John, PhD, FAA, FRACI, CChem; Australian research chemist; b. 26 June 1933, Abermain, NSW; s. of Ronald J. Hunter and Elizabeth Dixon; m. Barbara Robson 1954 (divorced 1995); one s. one d.; ed Cessnock High School, NSW, New England Univ. Coll. and Univ. of Sydney; secondary school teacher 1953–54; Tech. Officer, CSIRO 1954–57, Research Officer 1960–64; Lecturer, Univ. of Sydney 1964, Assoc. Prof. of Physical Chem. 1972–90, Head, School of Chem. 1987–90, Hon. Research Assoc. 1990–; Dir Colloidal Dynamics Pty Ltd 1988–96; Chair. Nat. Science and Industry Forum 1991–93; Pres. Int. Asscn of Colloid and Interface Scientists 1992–94; Nat. Pres. Scientists for Global Responsibility (fmrly Scientists Against Nuclear Arms) 1986–88, 1990–92, 1996–; Alexander Memorial Lecturer 1987; Liversidge Lecturer of Royal Soc. of NSW 1988, to Australia and New Zealand Acad. of Arts and Sciences 2001; Archibald Ollé Prize 1982, 1993. *Publications:* Chemical Science 1976, Zeta Potential in Colloid Science 1981, Foundations of Colloid Science, (Vol. I) 1987, (Vol. 2) 1989, Introduction to Modern Colloid Science 1993. *Leisure interests:* music, drama, reading, lawn bowls. *Address:* School of Chemistry, The University of Sydney, NSW 2006 (Office); 26/20A Austin Street, Lane Cove, NSW 2066, Australia (Home). *Telephone:* (2) 9351-2220 (Office); (2) 9427-6261 (Home). *Fax:* (2) 9351-3329

(Office). *E-mail:* hunter_r@chem.usyd.edu.au (Office); sgr@hotkey.net.au (Home). *Website:* www.chem.usyd.edu.au/staffrjh.htm (Office); www.hotkey.net.au/~sgr (Home).

HUNTER, Tony (Anthony Rex), MA, PhD, FRS, FRSA; British molecular biologist and cell biologist; b. 23 Aug. 1943, Ashford, Kent; s. of Ranulph Rex Hunter and Nellie Ruby Elsie Hitchcock; m. 1st Philippa Charlotte Marrack 1969 (divorced 1974); m. 2nd Jennifer Ann Maureen Price 1992; two s.; ed Felsted School, Essex and Gonville and Caius Coll., Cambridge; Research Fellow Christ's Coll., Cambridge 1968–71, 1973–75; Research Assoc. Salk Inst., San Diego, Calif. 1971–73, Asst Prof. 1975–78, Assoc. Prof. 1978–82, Prof. 1982–; Adjunct Assoc. Prof. Dept of Biology Univ. of California, San Diego 1979–82, Adjunct Prof. 1982–; Fellow American Acad. of Arts and Sciences 1992; Assoc. mem. EMBO 1992; American Cancer Soc. Research Prof. 1992–; Foreign Assoc. Nat. Acad. of Sciences (USA) 1998; American Business Foundation for Cancer Research Award 1988; Katharine Berkan Judd Award (Memorial Sloan-Kettering Cancer Center) 1992, Hopkins Medal (Biochemical Soc.) 1994, Gairdner Foundation Int. Award 1994, General Motors Cancer Research Foundation Mott Prize 1994, Feodor Lynen Medal 1999, J. Allyn Taylor Int. Prize in Medicine 2000, Keio Medical Science Prize 2001, Sergio Lombroso Award in Cancer Research 2003. *Publications:* 425 papers and journal articles. *Leisure interests:* white-water rafting, desert camping. *Address:* Molecular and Cell Biology Laboratory, The Salk Institute, 10010 North Torrey Pines Road, La Jolla, CA 92037-1099, USA (Office); 4578 Vista de la Patria, Del Mar, CA 92014-4150, USA (Home). *Telephone:* (858) 453-4100 (Ext. 1385) (Office); (858) 792-1492 (Home). *Fax:* (858) 457-4765 (Office). *E-mail:* hunter@salk.edu (Office).

HUO DA; Chinese writer; b. 1945, Beijing; ed Beijing Constructional Eng Coll.; translator Beijing Bureau of Cultural Relics; screenplay writer Beijing TV Station and Beijing TV Art Centre; Vice-Chair. Chinese Soc. of Writers of Ethnic Minorities; The Burial Ceremony of Muslims (Mao Dun Prize for Literature), 4th Nat. Prize for Red Dust, 4th Nat. Prize for The Worry and Joy of Thousands of Households, Best Film Screenplay Award for Dragon Foal, Flying Apsaras Award for Magpie Bridge. *Publications:* Collected Works of Huo Da (6 Vols). *Address:* Beijing Television Station, Beijing 100089, People's Republic of China (Office).

HUO YINGDONG (also known as Henry Fok Ying-tung); Chinese politician and business executive; b. 10 May 1923, Panyu Co., Guangdong Prov.; Perm. mem. 5th and 6th CPPCC 1983–88; Perm. mem. 7th Standing Cttee NPC 1988–92; mem. Preparatory Cttee of the Hong Kong Special Admin. Region 1985–97; Vice-Chair. 8th Nat. Cttee CPPCC 1993–98, 9th Nat. Cttee 1998–; Vice-Chair. PWC; Chair. Yau Wing Co. Ltd; Chair. Henry Fok Estates Ltd 1955–; Dir China Int. Trust and Investment Corpn 1979–; Pres. Real Estate Developers Asscn of Hong Kong, Hong Kong Football Asscn; Vice-Pres. Chinese Gen. Chamber of Commerce, China Asscn for Advancement of Int. Friendship, All China Sports Fed.; mem. Exec. Cttee Fed. of Int. Football Asscns. *Address:* National Committee of Chinese People's Political Consultative Conference, 23 Taipingqiao Street, Beijing, People's Republic of China; Pedder Building, Central, Hong Kong Special Administrative Region, People's Republic of China.

HUONG, Tran Van (see Tran Van Huong).

HUPPERT, Herbert Eric, MA, PhD, ScD, FRS; Australian scientist; b. 26 Nov. 1943, Sydney; s. of Leo Huppert and Alice Huppert (née Neumann); m. Felicia Ferster 1966; two s.; ed Sydney Boys High School, Univ. of Sydney, Australian Nat. Univ. and Univ. of California, San Diego; ICI Research Fellow Cambridge Univ. 1968–69, Asst Dir Research Dept Applied Math. and Theoretical Physics 1970–81, Univ. Lecturer 1981–88, Reader Geophysical Dynamics 1988–89, Prof. of Theoretical Geophysics 1989–; Prof. of Math., Univ. of NSW 1991–95; BP Venture Unit Sr Research Fellow 1983–89; Fellow King's Coll., Cambridge 1970–; fmr Visiting Research Scientist Univs. of Calif., Canterbury, New South Wales and Australian Nat. Univ., MIT, Woods Hole Oceanographic Inst. and California Inst. of Tech.; Vice-Chair. Scientists for the Release of Soviet Refuseniks 1985–88, Co-Chair. 1988–92; mem. Council NERC 1993–98, Scientific Council, the Earth Centre 1995–, Council Royal Soc. 2001–; Ed. Journal of Soviet Jewry 1986–92; Assoc. Ed. Journal of Fluid Mechanics 1971–90; mem. Editorial Bd Philosophical Transactions of the Royal Soc. A 1994–99, Reports on Progress in Physics 1997–2000; Evnin Lecturer, Princeton University 1995, Mid-West Mechanics Lecturer 1996–97, Henry Charnock Distinguished Lecturer 1999, Smith Industries Lecturer, Oxford Univ. 1999. *Achievement:* played squash for Cambridgeshire 1970–72. *Publications:* over 180 papers on fluid motions associated with the atmosphere, oceans, volcanoes and the interior of the earth. *Leisure interests:* his children, squash, mountaineering, lawn tennis, music, travel. *Address:* Institute of Theoretical Geophysics, Department of Applied Mathematics and Theoretical Physics, University of Cambridge, Centre of Mathematical Sciences, Wilberforce Road, Cambridge, CB3 9EW (Office); 46 De Freville Avenue, Cambridge, CB3 0WA, England (Home). *Telephone:* (1223) 765900 (Office); (1223) 765900 (Home). *Fax:* (1223) 337918 (Office); (1223) 337918. *E-mail:* heh1@esc.cam.ac.uk (Office).

HUPPERT, Isabelle Anne; French actress; b. 16 March 1953, Paris; d. of Raymond Huppert and Annick Beau; two s. one d.; ed Lycée de St-Cloud, Ecole nat. des langues orientales vivantes; Pres. Comm. d'avances sur recettes 1994–; several theatre appearances including Mary Stuart (London) 1996, 4.48 Psychose (Paris) 2002; Prix Susanne Blanchetti 1976, Prix Bistingo 1976,

Prix César 1978 and for Best Actress (for la Cérémonie) 1996, Gold Palm, Cannes 1978, Prix d'Interpretation, Cannes 1978. *Films include:* Le bar de la Fourche, César et Rosalie, Les valseuses, Aloïse, Dupont la joie, Rosebud, Docteur Françoise Gailland, Le juge et l'assassin, Le petit Marcel 1976, Les indiens sont encore loin 1977, La dentellière, Violette Nozière 1978, Les soeurs Brontë 1978, Loulou 1980, Sauve qui peut (la vie), Les Héritières 1980, Heaven's Gate 1980, Coup de Torchon 1981, Dame aux Camélias 1981, Les Ailes de la Colombe 1981, Eaux Profondes 1981, Passion, travail et amour, La Truite 1982, Entre Nous 1984, My Best Friend's Girl 1984, La Garce 1984, Signé Charlotte, Sac de noeuds 1985, Cactus 1986, Sincerely Charlotte 1986, The Bedroom Window 1986, The Possessed 1988, Story of Women 1989, Milan Noir 1990, Madame Bovary 1991, Malina 1991, Après l'amour 1992, La Séparation 1994, Amateur 1994, L'Inondation 1994, La Cérémonie 1995, Les Affinités électives 1996, Rien ne va plus 1997, Les Palmes de M. Schutz 1997, L'Ecole de la chair 1998, Merci pour le chocolat 2000, Les Destineées Sentimentales 2000, La Fausse suivante et Saint-Cyr 2000, The Piano Teacher 2001 (Best Actress, Cannes Film Festival), 8 Femmes 2002. *Publication:* Madame Deshoulières 2001. *Address:* c/o VMA, 10 avenue George V, 75008 Paris, France.

HÜPPI, Rolf; Swiss financial services executive; b. 1943; joined Zurich Financial Services 1963, Man. India Office 1964–70, Zurich Office 1970–72, Regional Man. U.S. Office, Pittsburgh, PA 1972–74, mem. Group Exec. Bd 1983–, CEO for U.S. Br. 1983–87, Deputy COO 1987–88, COO 1988–91, Pres. and CEO 1991–98; mem. Bd of Dirs. Zurich Insurance Co. 1993–2002, Chair. 1995–2002; Chair. and CEO Zurich Financial Services Group (following merger) 1998–2002. *Address:* c/o Zurich Financial Services, Mythenquai 2, 8022 Zurich, Switzerland (Office).

HUQ, Muhammad Shamsul, MA; Bangladeshi social scientist and educationist; b. 2 Dec. 1910, Comilla; s. of the late M. Karimul Huq and Mahmuda Khatoon; m. Tayyeba Huq 1938; two s.; ed Univs. of Calcutta, Dhaka and London; Scholar-in-Residence, Advanced Projects, East-West Centre, Honolulu 1963–64; Vice-Chancellor Rajshahi Univ. 1965–69; Minister for Educ., Scientific and Technological Research of fmr Pakistan 1969–71; led Del. 25th Anniversary of ECOSOC, Paris 1970; mem. UNESCO Int. Experts Cttee on formulation of policy of training abroad, Paris 1971; Fellow, Woodrow Wilson Int. Center for Scholars, Smithsonian Inst., Washington, DC 1971–73; Vice-Chancellor Dhaka Univ. 1975–76; Chair. Planning Cttee Social Science Research Council 1977–82; mem. Pres.'s Council of Advisers in charge of Ministry of Foreign Affairs 1977–78; Foreign Minister 1978–82; Chair., Trustee Bangladesh Nat. Museum, Dhaka 1983–86; Chair. Bd Govs. Bangladesh Inst. of Int. and Strategic Studies 1982–89; Pres. Foundation for Research on Educational Planning and Devt 1973; Chair. Nat. Advisory Group, Asia-Pacific Network in Social Sciences 1988; led Del. to UN 1977, 1978, 1979, 1980, 1981; active in negotiation of Ganges Water Agreement with India 1977, repatriation of 200,000 Burmese refugees 1978, election of Bangladesh to Security Council, UN 1979–80, Commonwealth Conf. initiative on Zimbabwe, Lusaka 1978–79, the Middle East issue (mem. Ministerial Cttee on Jerusalem) and preparations for Cancún Summit March 1981 (attended Summit Oct. 1981); B.B. Gold Medal, Univ. of Calcutta 1933. *Publications:* Changing Education in England 1948, Compulsory Education in Pakistan 1954, Education and Development Strategy in South and South East Asia 1965, Education, Manpower and Development in South and South East Asia 1975, Higher Education and Employment in Bangladesh (jtly.) 1983, The Patterns of Education in South and South East Asia (in Encyclopaedia Britannica and German encyclopaedia Lexikon der Pedagogik), Tragedy in Lebanon, Geo-political Implications, Cancún and After: From Hope to Despair, Education and Development 1986, International Politics: A Third World Perspective 1987, The Dilemmas of the Weak States: Bangladesh in International Politics 1992, Aid, Development and Diplomacy: The Need for an Aid Policy (jtly.) 1999. *Leisure interests:* reading, writing, gardening. *Address:* Reema, 10 Eskatan Garden Road, Dhaka 1000, Bangladesh. *Telephone:* 503485 (Office); 414045 (Home).

HURD OF WESTWELL, Baron (Life Peer), cr. 1997, of Westwell in the County of Oxfordshire; **Douglas Richard Hurd,** CH, CBE, PC; British politician and diplomatist; b. 8 March 1930, Marlborough; s. of the late Baron Hurd and Stephanie Corner; m. 1st Tatiana Elizabeth Michelle Eyre 1960 (divorced 1982); three s.; m. 2nd Judy Smart 1982; one s. one d.; ed Eton Coll., Trinity Coll., Cambridge; joined diplomatic service 1952; served in Beijing 1954–56, UK Mission to UN 1956–60, Private Sec. to Perm. Under-Sec. of State, Foreign Office 1960–63, in British Embassy, Rome 1963–66; joined Conservative Research Dept 1966, Head of Foreign Affairs Section 1968; Private Sec. to Leader of the Opposition 1968–70, Political Sec. to the Prime Minister 1970–74; MP for Mid-Oxon 1974–83, for Witney 1983–97; Opposition Spokesman on European Affairs 1976–79, Minister of State, FCO 1979–83, Home Office 1983–84; Sec. of State for NI 1984–85; Home Sec. 1985–89; Sec. of State for Foreign and Commonwealth Affairs 1989–95; mem. Royal Comm. for Lords Reforms 1999–; Deputy Chair. NatWest Markets 1995–98; Dir NatWest Group 1995–99; Chair. British Invisibles 1997–2000; Deputy Chair. Coutts and Co. 1998–; Cand. for Conservative Leadership 1990; Chair. Prison Reform Trust 1997–2001; Chair. Booker Prize Cttee 1998, Sr Adviser to Hawkpoint 1999–; Chair. Council for Effective Dispute Resolution (CEDR) 2001–; High Steward Westminster Abbey 2000–; Jt Pres. Royal Inst. Int. Affairs 2002–; Spectator Award for Parliamentarian of the Year 1990. *Publications:* The Arrow War 1967, Send Him Victorious (with Andrew

Osmond) 1968, The Smile on the Face of the Tiger 1969, Scotch on the Rocks 1971, Truth Game 1972, Vote to Kill 1975, An End to Promises 1979, War Without Frontiers (with Andrew Osmond) 1982, Palace of Enchantments (with Stephen Lamport) 1985, The Last Day of Summer 1992, The Search for Peace 1997, The Shape of Ice 1998, Ten Minutes to Turn the Devil (short stories) 1999, Image in the Water 2001. *Leisure interests:* writing and broadcasting. *Address:* House of Lords, Westminster, London, SW1A 0PW, England. *Telephone:* (20) 7665-4538 (Office); (20) 7219-3000. *Fax:* (20) 7665-4694 (Office).

HURFORD, Peter (John), OBE, MusB, MA, FRCO; British organist; b. 22 Nov. 1930, Minehead, Somerset; s. of Hubert John Hurford and Gladys Winifred James; m. Patricia Mary Matthews 1955; two s. one d.; ed Blundell's School, Royal Coll. of Music (Open Foundation Scholar), Jesus Coll. Cambridge (organ scholar) and private studies with André Marchal, Paris; commissioned Royal Signals 1954–56; Organist and Choirmaster Holy Trinity Church, Leamington Spa 1956–57; Dir of Music, Bablake School, Coventry 1956–57; Master of the Music, Cathedral and Abbey Church of St Alban 1958–78; freelance concert and recording organist 1978–; Visiting Prof., Coll. Conservatory of Music, Cincinnati, USA 1967–68, Univ. of Western Ont., Canada 1976–77; Acting Organist, St John's Coll. Cambridge 1979–80; Visiting Artist-in-Residence, Sydney Opera House 1980–82; Prof. RAM 1982–88; John Betts Fellow, Univ. of Oxford 1992–93; Hon. Fellow in Organ Studies, Univ. of Bristol 1997–98; Decca recording artist 1977–: concerts in USA, Canada, Australia, NZ, Japan, Far East, E and W Europe 1958–98; f. Int. Organ Festival 1963, Artistic Dir 1963–79, Hon. Pres. 1981–; Pres. Inc. Asscn of Organists 1995–97; Council mem. Royal Coll. of Organists 1963–, Pres. 1980–82; Fellow Royal School of Church Music 1977; Hon. FRCM 1987; Hon. mem. RAM 1982; Hon. DMus (Baldwin-Wallace Coll., Ohio, USA) 1981, (Bristol Univ.) 1992; Gramophone Award 1979; Herald Angel Critics Award 1997. *Compositions include:* (organ music) Suite—Laudate Dominum, Chorale Preludes, (choral music) The Communion Service, Series III, The Holy Eucharist, Rite 2 (for American Episcopal Church), music for the Daily Office, miscellaneous anthems, songs, carols, etc. *Recordings include:* complete organ works of J. S. Bach, Handel, F. Couperin, P. Hindemith, music of Franck, Mendelssohn, etc.; numerous recitals for BBC including: 34 commentated programmes of J. S. Bach's complete organ works 1980–82. *Publications:* Making Music On The Organ 1988, sundry forewords, contribs. to journals. *Leisure interests:* walking and wine. *Address:* Broom House, St Bernard's Road, St Albans, Herts., AL3 5RA, England.

HURLEY, Alfred Francis, PhD; American university chancellor and professor of history; b. 16 Oct. 1928, Brooklyn, NY; s. of Patrick F. Hurley and Margaret C. Hurley; m. Joanna Leahy Hurley 1953; four s. one d.; ed St John's Univ., New York and Princeton Univ.; US Air Force Navigator, Planner and Educator; enlisted as Pvt., retd as Brig.-Gen.; served in Tex., Colo and Germany with brief assignments in Washington, DC and Viet Nam 1950–80; Instructor, Asst Prof. and Research Assoc. USAF Acad. 1958–63; Perm. Prof. of History and Head of History Dept, USAF 1966–80; Chair. Humanities Div. and mem. Acad. Bd USAF Acad. 1977–80; Vice-Pres. for Admin. Affairs, Univ. of N Tex. 1980–82, Prof. of History 1982–, Chancellor and Pres. 1982–2000, Chancellor 2000–, Guggenheim Fellow 1971–72; Eisenhower Inst. Fellow, Smithsonian Inst. 1976–77; Legion of Merit, USAF 1972; Oak Leaf Cluster 1980; Pres.'s Medal, St John's Univ. 1990. *Publications:* Billy Mitchell: Crusader for Air Power 1964, Air Power and Warfare (ed.) 1979. *Leisure interests:* jogging, reading, international travel. *Address:* Office of the Chancellor, University of North Texas Systems, Denton, TX 76203 (Office); 828 Skylark Drive, Denton, TX 76205, USA (Home). *Telephone:* (940) 565-2904 (Office).

HURLEY, Elizabeth Jane; British actress, producer and model; b. 10 June 1965; d. of the late Roy Leonard Hurley and of Angela Mary Hurley; one s.; producer for Simian Films and producer of Extreme Measures 1996, Mickey Blue Eyes 1999; Spokeswoman and model for Estée Lauder. *Television includes:* title role in Christabel (series), The Orchid House, Act of Will, Rumpole, Inspector Morse, The Young Indiana Jones Chronicles, Sharpe's Enemy. *Films include:* Aria 1987, Rowing With the Wind 1987, The Skipper 1989, The Long Winter of 39, Passenger '57 1992, Mad Dogs and Englishmen 1994, Dangerous Ground 1995, Samson and Delilah 1996, Austin Powers: International Man of Mystery (ShoWest Award for Best Supporting Actress 1997) 1996, Permanent Midnight 1997, My Favourite Martian 1999, Ed TV 1999, Austin Powers: The Spy Who Shagged Me 1999, Bedazzled 2000, Serving Sara 2002, The Weight of Water 2002, Double Whammy 2002. *Leisure interest:* gardening. *Address:* Simian Films, 3 Cromwell Place, London, SW7 2JE, England. *Telephone:* (20) 7589-6822. *Fax:* (20) 7589-9405.

HURLEY, Rev. Michael Anthony, SJ, STD; Irish ecumenical theologian and Jesuit priest; b. 10 May 1923, Ardmore, Co. Waterford; s. of Martin Hurley and Johanna Foley; ed Mount Melleray Seminary, Cappoquin, Univ. Coll., Dublin, Jesuit Theological Faculty, Louvain, Pontifical Gregorian Univ., Rome; entered Soc. of Jesus 1940; ordained priest 1954; Lecturer in Dogmatic Theology, Jesuit Theological Faculty, Dublin 1958–70; Dir Irish School of Ecumenics, Dublin 1970–80; mem. Columbanus Community of Reconciliation, Belfast 1983–93 (Leader 1983–91); Hon. LLD (Queen's Univ., Belfast) 1993, (Trinity Coll., Dublin) 1995. *Publications:* Church and Eucharist (Ed.) 1966, Ecumenical Studies: Baptism and Marriage (Ed.) 1968, Theology of Ecumenism 1969, John Wesley's Letter to a Roman Catholic (Ed.) 1968, Irish Anglicanism (Ed.) 1970, Beyond Tolerance: The Challenge of Mixed Marriage

(Ed.) 1975, Reconciliation in Religion and Society (ed.) 1994, Christian Unity: An Ecumenical Second Spring? 1998; articles in various periodicals. *Leisure interest:* reading. *Address:* Jesuit Community, Milltown Park, Dublin 6, Ireland. *Telephone:* 218-0237. *Fax:* 218-0279.

HURLEY, Dame Rosalinde, DBE, LL.B, MD, F.R.C.PATH, FRCOG; British professor of microbiology and barrister; b. 30 Dec. 1929, London; d. of the late William Hurley and Rose Hurley; m. Peter Gortvai 1963; ed Acad. of the Assumption, Wellesley Hills, Mass., Queen's Coll., London, Univ. of London, Inns of Court; Consultant Microbiologist 1962–75; Prof. of Microbiology, Royal Postgrad. Medical School's Inst. of Obstetrics and Gynaecology 1975–95, Prof. Emer. 1995–; Consultant Microbiologist, Queen Charlotte's Maternity Hosp., London 1963–95, Hon. Consultant 1995–; Vice-Chair. Cttee on Dental and Surgical Materials 1975–78, Chair. 1979–81; Chair. Medicines Comm. 1982–94; Pres. Assen of Clinical Pathologists 1984–; Chair. Assen of Profs. of Medical Microbiology 1987–94; European Parl. Rep., Man. Bd European Medicines Evaluation Agency 1994–; mem. Advisory Bd, Sheffield Inst. of Biotech. Law and Ethics 1995; Hon. F.F.P.M. 1990; Hon. FRSM 1996; Hon. FIBiol 1999; Hon. DUniv (Surrey) 1984; Baron C. ver Heyden de Lancey Prize 1991; Medal of Royal Coll. of Pathologists 1999. *Publications:* Candida Albicans 1964; numerous papers on candidosis and infections in pregnant women and the newborn. *Leisure interests:* reading, gardening. *Address:* 2 Temple Gardens, Temple, London, EC4Y 9AY, England. *Telephone:* (20) 7353-0577.

HURN, David; British photographer and lecturer; b. 21 July 1934, Redhill, Surrey; s. of Stanley Hurn and Joan Maynard; m. Alita Naughton 1964 (divorced 1971); one d.; ed Hardy's School, Dorchester and Royal Mil. Acad., Sandhurst; Asst Photographer to Michael Peto and George Vargas, Reflex Agency, London 1955–57; Freelance Photographer for The Observer, Sunday Times, Look, Life, etc. 1957, working from Wales 1971; mem. Magnum Photos co-operative agency, New York, Paris, London and Tokyo 1967–; Editorial Adviser Album Photographic magazine, London 1971; Head, School of Documentary Photography, Gwent Coll. of Higher Educ., Newport, Gwent 1973–90; Distinguished Visiting Artist and Adjunct Prof., Arizona State Univ., USA 1979–80; mem. Photographic Cttee, Arts Council of GB 1972–77, Arts Panel 1975–77, CNAA 1983–87; works in collections of Welsh Arts Council, Arts Council of GB, British Council, Bibliothèque Nationale, Paris, Int. Center of Photography, New York, San Francisco Museum of Modern Art, Museum of Modern Art, New York and others; Hon. Fellow, Univ. of Wales 1997; Welsh Arts Council Award 1971, Imperial War Museum Arts Award 1987–88; Kodak Photographic Bursary 1975; UK/USA Bicentennial Fellowship 1979–80; Bradford Fellow 1993–94; Arts Council of Wales Bursary 1995. *Exhibitions:* numerous individual and group exhbns., UK, France, FRG, The Netherlands, Spain, Sweden, Belgium, USA, Japan. *Publications:* David Hurn: Photographs 1956–1976 1979, On Being a Photographer 1997, Wales: Land of My Father 2000, On Looking at Photographs 2000. *Leisure interests:* music, looking, meeting people. *Address:* Prospect Cottage, Tintern, Monmouthshire, Wales. *Telephone:* (1291) 689358. *Fax:* (1291) 689464.

HURN, Sir (Francis) Roger, Kt; British business executive; b. 9 June 1938; s. of Francis James Hurn and Joyce Elsa (née Bennett) Hurn; m. Rosalind Jackson 1980; one d.; ed Marlborough Coll.; Eng apprentice, Rolls Royce Motors 1956; joined Smiths Industries PLC 1958, Export Dir Motor Accessory Div. 1969–74, Man. Dir Int. Operations 1974–75, Div. Man. Dir 1975–76, Exec. Dir 1976–; Man. Dir 1978–91, Chief Exec. 1981–96, Chair. 1991–98; Deputy Chair. Glaxo Wellcome PLC 1997–2000, GlaxoSmithKline 2000–; Chair. Gen. Electric Co. (now Marconi) PLC 1998–2001, Prudential PLC 2000–02; Dir (non-exec.) Ocean Transport and Trading 1982–88, Pilkington 1984–94, S. G. Warburg Group 1987–95, ICI PLC 1993–2001, Cazenove; Chair. of Govs. Henley Man. Coll. 1996– (Gov. 1986–); Liveryman, Coachmakers' and Coach Harness Makers' Co. 1979. *Leisure interests:* outdoor pursuits, travel. *Address:* GlaxoSmithKline, Stockley Park West, Uxbridge, Middx, UB11 1BT, England. *Website:* www.gsk.com.

HURNÍK, Ilja; Czech pianist and composer; b. 25 Nov. 1922, Ostrava-Poruba; m. Jana Hurníková 1966; one s.; ed Conservatoire, Prague; composition; Acad. of Music and Dramatic Arts, Prague 1948–52; self-employed artist 1942–; one-man concerts since 1942, Poland, Switzerland, FRG, Cuba, USA; Dr hc (Univ. of Ostrava) 1992; Czech Musical Fund Prize 1967, Supraphon Prize 1971, Grand Prix, Piano Duo Assen of Japan 1990, Int. Antonín Dvořák Prize 2001. *Works:* piano compositions: The First Melodies 1931, Concert for Oboe and Strings 59, Preludes for piano 1943, Studies for four hands 1975; chamber compositions: Sonata for viola and piano, Four Seasons of the Year for 12 instruments 1952, Sonata da camera, Moments musicaux for 11 wind instruments 1955, Esercizii for wind quartet 1963; vocal works: cantata Maryka 1948, Children's Tercets 1956, oratorio Noah 1959, Choirs about Mothers for mixed choir 1962, cantata Aesop, songs for alto and orchestra Sulamit 1965, Seasonal Madrigals 1984, Water, Water 1986, Oratorio for children's chorus and orchestra 1990; ballet: Ondráš 1950, Faux pas de quatre 1979; opera: The Lady and Robbers 1966, Oldřich a Boženka 1999; recorded complete works of Debussy. *Publications:* The Journey with a Butterfly, Marshland, Childhood in Silesia (memoirs), Laurel Leaves 1987; children's books, including Kterak psáti a řečniti (How to Write and Speak) 1997, Final Report 2000. *Address:* Český rozhlas, Vinohradská 12, 120 99, Prague 2; Národní třída 35, 110 00, Prague 1, Czech Republic. *Telephone:* (2) 2421-4226.

HURST, Sir Geoffrey Charles, Kt, MBE; British footballer and insurance executive; b. 8 Dec. 1941, Ashton-under-Lyne; s. of Charles Hurst and Evelyn Hurst; m. Judith Harries 1964; three d.; player West Ham United 1957–72, Stoke City 1972–74, West Bromwich Albion 1975–76; player and Man. Telford United 1976–79; Man. Chelsea 1979–81, England nat. team 1966–72; scored hat-trick in victory over W Germany, World Cup 1966 (only player to do so in a World Cup final); Dir Aon Warranty Group 1995–; Patron Ludlow Town Football Club. *Publication:* 1966 and All That 2001. *Leisure interest:* sport in general, family. *Address:* Dragonwyck, Old Avenue, St George's Hill, Weybridge, Surrey, KT13 0PY, England (Home).

HURT, John; British actor; b. 22 Jan. 1940, Chesterfield; s. of Rev. Arnould Herbert and Phyllis (née Massey) Hurt; m. 1st Annette Robertson; m. 2nd Donna Peacock 1984 (divorced 1990); m. 3rd Jo Dalton 1990 (divorced 1995); two s.; ed The Lincoln School, Lincoln and Royal Acad. of Dramatic Art; began as painter; stage debut, Arts Theatre, London 1962; Dir United British Artists 1982. *Stage appearances include:* Chips With Everything, Vaudeville Theatre 1962, The Dwarfs, Arts 1963, Hamp (title role), Edinburgh Festival 1964, Inadmissible Evidence, Wyndhams 1965, Little Malcolm and his Struggle against the Eunuchs, Garrick 1966, Belcher's Luck, (RSC), Aldwych 1966, Man and Superman, Gaiety, Dublin 1969, The Caretaker, Mermaid 1972, The Only Street, Dublin Festival and Islington 1973, Travesties (RSC), Aldwych and The Arrest, Bristol Old Vic 1974, The Shadow of a Gunman, Nottingham Playhouse 1978, The London Vertigo, Dublin 1991, A Month in the Country, Albery 1994, Krapp's Last Tape, New Ambassadors Theatre 2000, Gate Theatre, Dublin 2001, Afterplay, Gielgud Theatre 2002. *Films include:* The Wild and the Willing 1962, A Man for All Seasons 1966, Sinful Davey 1968, Before Winter Comes 1969, In Search of Gregory 1970, Mr. Forbush and the Penguins 1971, 10 Rillington Place, The Ghoul 1974, Little Malcolm 1974, East of Elephant Rock 1977, The Disappearance, The Shout, Spectre, Alien, Midnight Express (British Acad. Best Supporting Actor Award 1978, Golden Globe Best Supporting Actor Award 1978, Variety Club Best Actor Award 1978) 1978, Heaven's Gate 1980, The Elephant Man (British Acad. Best Actor Award 1980, Variety Club Best Film Actor Award 1980) 1980, Champions (Evening Standard Best Actor Award 1984) 1983, The Hit (Evening Standard Best Actor Award 1984) 1984, Jake Speed 1985, Rocinante 1986, Aria 1987, White Mischief 1987, Scandal 1988, From the Hip 1989, Frankenstein Unbound, The Field 1989, Windprints 1990, King Ralph 1991, Lapse of Memory 1991, Dark at Noon 1992, Monolith 1994, Even Cowgirls Get the Blues 1994, Wild Bill 1994, Rob Roy 1994, Two Nudes Bathing (Cable Ace Award 1995) 1995, Dead Man 1996, Wild Bill 1996, Contact 1997, Love and Death on Long Island 1998, All the Little Animals 1999, You're Dead 1999, The Love Letter 1999, Krapp's Last Tape 1999, Lost Souls 2000, Night Train 2000, Captain Corelli's Mandolin 2001, Harry Potter and the Philosopher's Stone 2001, Tabloid 2001, Bait 2001, Miranda 2001, Owning Mahony 2001. *Television appearances include:* The Waste Places 1968, Nijinsky—God of the Dance (Best Television Actor 1975) 1975, The Naked Civil Servant (British Acad. Award 1975, Emmy Award 1978) 1975, Caligula in I, Claudius 1976, Treats 1977, Raskolnikov in Crime and Punishment 1979, Poison Candy 1988, Deadline 1988, Who Bombed Birmingham? 1990, Journey to Knock 1991, Red Fox (Best Actor Monte Carlo TV Awards 1991) 1991, Six Characters in Search of an Author 1992, Prisoner in Time 1995, Saigon Baby 1995. *Address:* c/o Julian Belfrage Associates, 46 Albemarle Street, London, W1S 4DF, England. *Telephone:* (20) 7491-4400.

HURT, William; American actor; b. 20 March 1950, Wash.; m. 1st Mary Beth Hurt (divorced 1982); m. 2nd Heidi Henderson 1989; two s.; ed Tufts Univ., Juilliard School; appeared with Ore. Shakespeare Festival production of A Long Day's Journey Into Night, NY; mem. Circle Repertory Co., NY; recipient 1st Spencer Tracy Award 1988, for outstanding screen performances and professional achievement. *Stage appearances include:* Henry V 1976, Mary Stuart, My Life, Ulysses in Traction, Lulu, Fifth of July, Childe Byron, The Runner Stumbles, Hamlet, Hurlyburly, Beside Herself 1989, Ivanov 1991, others. *Films include:* Altered States, Eyewitness, Body Heat (Theatre World Award 1978), The Big Chill, Gorky Park, Kiss of the Spider Woman (Best Actor Award Cannes Film Festival 1985, Acad. Award for Best Actor 1985), Children of a Lesser God, Broadcast News 1987, A Time of Destiny 1988, The Accidental Tourist 1989, The Plastic Nightmare, I Love You to Death 1990, The House of Spirits 1990, The Doctor 1991, Until the End of the World 1991, Mr. Wonderful 1993, The Plague 1993, Trial by Jury 1994, Second Best 1994, Jane Eyre 1995, Secrets Shared With a Stranger, Smoke 1995, Michael, Loved, Lost in Space 1998, One True Thing 1998, The Proposition 1998, Dark City 1998, The Miracle Maker 2000, AI: Artificial Intelligence 2001, The Flamingo Rising 2001. *Address:* c/o Hilda Quille, William Morris Agency, 151 El Camino Drive, Beverly Hills, CA 90212, USA.

HURTADO LARREA, Oswaldo, BrerPol, DIur; Ecuadorean politician; b. 26 June 1939, Chambo, Chimborazo Prov.; s. of José Hurtado and Elina Larrea de Hurtado; m. Margarita Pérez Pallares; three s. two d.; ed Catholic Univ. of Quito; f. Ecuadorian Christian Democratic Party 1964; Pres. of Congress 1966; Prof. of Political Sociology, Catholic Univ., Quito; Dir Instituto Ecuatoriano de Desarrollo Social (INEDES) 1966; Under-Sec. of Labour 1969; Sub-Dean, Faculty of Econs and Dir Inst. of Econ. Research, Catholic Univ., Quito 1973; invited to form part of World Political Council of Christian Democracy 1975; joined with other political groups to form Popular Democracy 1978; Pres. Org. of Christian Democrats of America, Vice-Pres. Int. Christian Democrats; Pres. Comm. to prepare Law of Referendum of Elections and

Political Parties 1977; Vice-Pres. of Ecuador and Pres. Consejo Nacional de Desarrollo (Nat. Devt Council) 1979–81; Pres. of Ecuador 1981–84; Pres. Nat. Ass. 1998; Pres. Cordes (org. for study of Latin American Devt problems) (Quito); fmr Vice-Pres. Inst. for European Latin-American Relations, Madrid; mem. Council of ex-Pres., Atlanta, Interamerican Dialogue, Washington, S. American Peace Comm., Santiago, Raúl Prebisch Foundation, Buenos Aires, Latin American Popular Foundation, Caracas, Centre for Research and Promotion of Latin America–European Relations, Madrid; mem. various environmental comms.; Dr hc (Georgetown) and various foreign decorations. *Publications include:* El poder político en el Ecuador 1977, Dos mundos superpuestos 1969, La organización popular en el Ecuador 1974, Una constitución para el futuro 1998, Deuda y desarollo en el Ecuador contemporáneo 2002. *Leisure interests:* tennis and gardening. *Address:* Suecia 277 y Av. Los Shyris, Quito, Ecuador (Office); Tomás Chariove 405 y Agustín Zambrano (Home). *Telephone:* (5932) 2455701. *Fax:* (5932) 2446414. *E-mail:* cordes2@cordes.org.ec (Office). *Website:* www.cordes.org.ec (Office).

HURVICH, Leo M., PhD; American sensory psychologist; b. 11 Sept. 1910, Malden, Mass.; s. of Julius S. Hurvich and Celia Chikinsky; m. Dorothea Jameson 1948 (died 1998); ed Harvard Coll. and Harvard Univ.; Asst, Dept of Psychology, Harvard Univ. 1936–37, Instructor and Tutor 1937–40, Research Asst, Div. of Research, Graduate School of Business Admin. 1941–47; Research Psychologist, Color Tech. Div., Eastman Kodak Co. 1947–57; Prof. of Psychology, New York Univ. 1957–62; Prof. of Psychology, Dept of Psychology, Univ. of Pa 1962–79, Prof. Emer., mem. Inst. of Neurological Sciences, Dir Vision Training Program 1979–91; Visiting Prof. Columbia Univ. 1971–72, Univ. of Rochester, NY 1974; fmr Chair. Psychology Dept., Washington Square Coll. 1957–62; mem. Research Advisory Cttee, Lighthouse 1993–; mem. NAS, Int. Brain Research Org., Int. Colour Vision Soc., Asscn for Research in Vision and Ophthalmology; Fellow, Center for Advanced Study in the Behavioral Sciences, Stanford 1981–82; Fellow American Acad. of Arts and Sciences, American Psychological Asscn, Soc. of Experimental Psychologists 1958–, Optical Soc. of America, Guggenheim Fellow 1964–65, William James Fellow American Psychological Soc. 1989; Hon. DSc (State Univ. of NY); several awards including Howard Crosby Warren Medal for Outstanding Research, Soc. of Experimental Psychologists 1971, I. H. Godlove Award, Inter-Soc. Color Council, Distinguished Scientific Contrib. Award 1973, American Psychological Asscn 1972, Edgar D. Tillyer Medal, Optical Soc. of America, Deane B. Judd-AIC Award 1982, Asscn Internationale de la Couleur 1985, Helmholtz Prize 1987 (Cognitive Neuroscience Inst.). *Publications:* The Perception of Brightness and Darkness (with D. Jameson) 1966, Outlines of a Theory of the Light Sense (trans., with D. Jameson) 1964, Handbook of Sensory Physiology: Visual Psychophysics VII/4 (Ed., with D. Jameson) 1972, Color Vision 1981; contribs to Elsevier Encyclopedia of Neuroscience 1999 and American Psychological Asscn Encyclopedia of Psychology 2000. *Address:* Department of Psychology, University of Pennsylvania, 3815 Walnut Street, Philadelphia, PA 19104 (Office); 1 Fifth Avenue 2-J, New York, NY 10003, USA (Home). *Telephone:* (212) 673-5646 (Home); (215) 898-7313 (Office). *Fax:* (215) 898-7301 (Office); (212) 674-1586 (Home). *E-mail:* hurvich@cattell.psych.upenn.edu (Office); lhurvich@aol.com (Home).

HURWITZ, Emanuel, CBE, FRAM, FRSAMD, FRSA; British violinist; b. 7 May 1919, London; s. of the late Isaac Hurwitz and Sarah Gabrilovitch; m. Kathleen Crome 1948; one s. one d.; ed Royal Acad. of Music, London; Leader, Hurwitz String Quartet 1946–53, Melos Ensemble 1956–74; Leader Goldsborough Orchestra 1947–57, English Chamber Orch. 1957–69, New Philharmonia Orch. 1968–70, Aeolian String Quartet 1970–81; Prof. RAM 1968–; Visiting Lecturer Royal Scottish Acad. of Music and Drama 1987–, Univ. of Mich. 1995; recorded complete Haydn Quartets with Aeolian Quartet 1972–76; now active internationally in chamber music master classes; f. Emanuel Hurwitz Chamber Music Trust 1993; Pres. Inc. Soc. of Musicians 1995–96; Gold Medal, Worshipful Company of Musicians 1965. *Leisure interests:* collecting books and antique violin bows, listening to Beethoven piano works, Mozart operas and Schubert songs. *Address:* 25 Dollis Avenue, London, N3 1DA, England. *Telephone:* (20) 8346-3936. *Fax:* (20) 8343-1595.

HUSA, Karel; American composer and conductor; b. 7 Aug. 1921, Prague, Czech Repub.; s. of the late Karel Husa and Bozena Husova; m. Simone Husa (née Perault); four d.; ed Prague Conservatory of Music, Prague Acad. of Music, Paris Conservatory of Music, Ecole normale de musique de Paris; composer, conductor in Paris, guest conductor with European orchestras 1946–54, Kappa Alpha Prof. of Music, Cornell Univ. 1954, Asst Prof. 1954, Assoc. Prof. 1957, Prof. 1961; conductor of the univ. orchestras, teacher of composition (retd 1992), guest conductor with American orchestras and lecturer 1971; Prof. Ithaca Coll., School of Music 1967–86; mem. Belgian Royal Acad. of Arts and Sciences 1974–, American Acad. of Arts and Letters 1994–; hon. degrees include Coe Coll. 1976, Cleveland Inst. of Music 1985, Ithaca Coll. 1986, Baldwin-Wallace Coll. 1991, St. Vincent Coll. 1995, Hartwick Coll. 1997, New England Conservatory 1998, Masaryk Univ., Brno 2000, Acad. of Musical Arts, Prague 2000; awards include Pulitzer Prize 1969, Sudler Prize 1984, Friedheim Award 1985, Grawemeyer Award 1993, Guggenheim Award 1964, 1965, Sousa Order of Merit 1985, Czech Repub. Medal of Merit (First Class) 1995, Medal of Honor of the City of Prague 1998. *Dance:* Monodrama (ballet) for Butler Ballet, Indiana 1976, The Steadfast Tin Soldier for Boulder Philharmonic, Colorado 1974, The Trojan Women for Louisville Ballet, Kentucky 1980. *Film:* Young Generation 1946, Gen, Prague 2001, Karel Husa Comes Home 2002. *Music:* Music for Prague 1968, Apotheosis of this Earth 1972, four string quartets; concertos for piano, brass quintet, organ, viola, violin, cello, saxophone, percussion, trumpet, orchestra; symphonies (Mosaiques, Fantasies); chamber music includes quintets for wind, brass, works for piano, sonatas for violin, music for band. *Publications:* Music for Prague; Apotheosis of this Earth; Concerto for Orchestra; The Trojan Women; An American Te Deum; Concerto for Sax and Winds; Concerto for Wind Ensemble; Les couleurs fauves, Cayuga Lake; Four Quartets; Twelve Moravian Songs; Sonata a Tre; Symphony No.1; Evocation de Slovaquie; Serenade. *Leisure interests:* painting, poetry, tennis. *Address:* 4535 S. Atlantic Avenue, Apt. 2106, Daytona Beach, FL 32127 (Office); 1 Belwood Lane, Ithaca, NY 14850, USA (Home). *Telephone:* (386) 322-0635 (Winter) (Office); (607) 257-7018 (Summer) (Office). *Fax:* (386) 767-6786 (Winter) (Home); (607) 257-0616 (Summer) (Home).

HUSAIN, Maqbool Fida; Indian painter; b. 17 Sept. 1915, Sholapur, Maharashtra State; s. of Fida Husain and Zainub Husain; m. Fazila Abbasi 1943; four s. two d.; joined Progressive Artists Group, Bombay 1948; first one-man exhbn, Bombay 1950, later at Rome, Frankfurt, London, Zürich, Prague, Tokyo, New York, New Delhi, Calcutta, Kabul and Baghdad; mem. Lalit Kala Akademi, New Delhi 1954, Gen. Council Nat. Akademi of Art, New Delhi 1955; mem. Rajya Sabha 1986; First Nat. Award for Painting 1955; Int. Award, Biennale Tokyo 1959. *Major works:* Murals for Air India Int. at Hong Kong, Bangkok, Zürich and Prague 1957 and WHO Building, New Delhi 1963; Mural in Mosaic for Lever Bros. and Aligarh Univ. 1964; High Ceramic Mural for Indian Govt Building, New Delhi; Exhibitor "Art Now in India" Exhbn, London 1967; world's largest painting on canvas (240 ft. × 12 ft.) 1985; India Through the Lens of a Painter (photographic show), USSR 1988. *Film:* Through the Eyes of the Painter 1967 (Golden Bear Award, Berlin 1967), Gajagamini (producer) 2000. *Publications:* Husain's Letters 1962, Husain 1971, Poetry to be Seen 1972, Triangles 1976, Tata's Book Husain 1988. *Address:* 23 Canning Lane, New Delhi 11001, India.

HUSAR, Cardinal Lubomyr, MA, DTheol; Ukrainian ecclesiastic; b. 26 Feb. 1933, Lviv; ordained priest 1958; consecrated Bishop 1977; Auxiliary Bishop of the Greater Archiepiscopate of Lviv of the Ukrainians 1996–2001; cr. Cardinal 2001. *Address:* Ploscha Sviatoho Jura 5, 79000 Lviv, Ukraine (Office). *Telephone:* (32) 297-11-21 (Office). *Fax:* (32) 297-95-60 (Office).

HUSBANDS, Clifford (Straughn), GCMG, QC; Barbadian Governor-General and fmr judge; b. 5 Aug. 1926; s. of Adam Straughn Husbands and Ada Augusta Griffith; m. Ruby Parris 1959; one s. two d.; ed Parry School, Harrison Coll., Middle Temple, Inns of Court, London; called to Bar, Middle Temple 1952; in pvt. practice, Barbados 1952–54; Acting Deputy Registrar, Barbados 1954; Legal Asst to Attorney-Gen., Grenada 1954–56; magistrate, Grenada 1956–57, Antigua 1957–58; Crown Attorney, Magistrate and Registrar, Montserrat 1958–60; Acting Crown Attorney, St Kitts-Nevis-Anguilla 1959, Acting Attorney-Gen. 1960; Asst to Attorney-Gen., Barbados 1960–67 (legal draftsman 1960–63); Dir Public Prosecutions, Barbados 1967–76; QC Barbados 1968; Judge, Supreme Court, Barbados 1976–91; Justice of Appeal 1991–96; Gov.-Gen. of Barbados 1996–; Kt of St Andrew, Order of Barbados 1995. *Address:* Government House, St Michael, Barbados (Office). *Telephone:* 4292962 (Office).

HUSÉN, Torsten, PhD; Swedish educationist; b. 1 March 1916, Lund; s. of Johan Husén and Betty Husén (née Prawitz); m. Ingrid Joensson 1940 (died 1991); two s. one d.; ed Univ. of Lund; Research Asst, Inst. of Psychology, Univ. of Lund 1938–43; Sr Psychologist, Swedish Armed Forces 1944–51; Reader in Educational Psychology, Univ. of Stockholm 1947–52, Prof. 1953–56, Prof. of Educ. and Dir Inst. of Educ. Research, Univ. of Stockholm 1956–71, Prof. of Int. Educ. 1971–82; Fellow, Center for Advanced Study in the Behavioral Sciences, Stanford, Calif. 1965–66, 1973–74, Wissenschaftskolleg, Berlin 1984; Expert in Royal Comms. on Swedish School Reform 1957–65; mem. Panel of Scientific Advisers to Swedish Govt 1962–69; Chair. Int. Asscn for the Evaluation of Educ. Achievement 1962–78; Consultant to OECD and the World Bank 1968–85, United Nations Univ.; Co-Ed. in Chief, Int. Encyclopedia of Educ.; Chair. Governing Bd, Int. Inst. Educ. Planning, Paris 1970–81; mem. Governing Bd Max Planck Inst., Berlin 1964–82, Int. Council for Educ. Devt 1971–93; Chair. Int. Acad. of Educ. 1986–97; Chair. Int. Jury, Grawemeyer Award in Educ. 1988–90; Chair. Acad. Europaea Task Force on Educ. 1988–91; Visiting Prof., Univs. of Chicago 1959, Hawaii 1968, Ontario Inst. for Studies in Educ. 1971, Stanford Univ. 1981, California 1984; mem. Swedish Royal Acad. of Sciences 1972–, US Nat. Acad. of Educ. 1967–, Advisory Bd Int. Encyclopedia of the Social and Behavioral Sciences; Hon. Prof. (East China Normal Univ.) 1984; Hon. mem. American Acad. of Arts and Sciences, Acad. Europaea, USSR (now Russian) Acad. of Pedagogical Sciences; Hon. LLD (Chicago) 1967, (Glasgow) 1974; Hon. DTech (Brunel Univ.) 1974; Hon. LHD (Rhode Island Univ.) 1975; Hon. D.Ed. (Joensuu) 1979, (Amsterdam) 1982, (Ohio State Univ.) 1985; Medal for Distinguished Service in Int. Educ., Teachers Coll., Columbia Univ. 1970, Comenius Medal 1993. *Publications:* Psychological Twin Research 1959, Problems of Differentiation in Swedish Compulsory Schooling 1962, International Study of Achievement in Mathematics I-II 1967, Educational Research and Educational Change 1968, Talent, Opportunity and Career 1969, Talent, Equality and Meritocracy 1974, Social Influences on Educational Attainment 1975, The School in Question 1979, An Incurable Academic (autobiog.) 1983, Educational Research and Policy 1984, Becoming Adult in a Changing Society (with James Coleman) 1985, The Learning Society Revisited 1986, Higher Education and

Social Stratification 1987, Educational Research and School Reforms 1988, Education and the Global Concern 1990, Schooling in Modern European Society 1992, The Role of the University 1994, School and University Facing the 21st Century 1995, The Information Society 1999, Research on the Reserve of Ability 2000, Conversations with Torsten Husén 2001. *Leisure interest:* book collecting (old books). *Address:* Institute for International Education, Stockholm University, 10691 Stockholm (Office); Armfeltsgatan 10, 11534 Stockholm, Sweden (Home). *Telephone:* (8) 16-43-24 (Office); (8) 664-19-76 (Home). *E-mail:* torsten.husen@interped.su.se (Office).

HUSSAIN, Altaf; Pakistani politician; m.; Founder and Leader Muttahida Qaumi Movement (MQM); in exile in Britain 1990–2002, returned to Pakistan 2002. *Address:* MQM International Secretariat, 54–58, First Floor, Elizabeth House, High Street, Edgware, Middx, HA8 7EJ, England (Office). *Telephone:* (20) 8905-7300 (Office). *Fax:* (20) 8952-9282 (Office). *E-mail:* mqm@mqm.org (Office). *Website:* www.mqm.org (Office).

HUSSAIN, Ishrat, PhD; Pakistani economist; b. 17 June 1941, Allahabad, India; s. of the late Rahat Husain and Khursheed Rahat Husain; m. Shahnaz Husain; two d.; ed Williams Coll., Boston Univ. and Grad. Exec. Devt Programme (Harvard, Stanford and INSEAD); mem. Staff Sr Managerial, Planning and Devt Dept and Finance Dept, Govt of Sindh; Additional Deputy Commr for Devt, Chittagong, Bangladesh; mem. Govt of Pakistan's Panel of Economists; Adjunct Prof. of Econs Karachi Univ., Dir Poverty and Social Policy Dept; IBRD Resident Rep. for Nigeria 1986, Chief Economist for Africa, IBRD 1991–94, Chief Economist for E Asia and Pacific Region 1995, also Chief Debt and Int. Finance Div., Dir for Cen. Asian Repubs; Gov. State Bank of Pakistan 1999–; Hilal-e-Imtiaz. *Publications:* Pakistan: The Economy of an Elitist State, The Political Economy of Reforms: Case Study of Pakistan, Adjustment in Africa: Lessons from Case Studies: Dealing with Debt Crisis, African External Finance in the 1990s, The Economy of Modern Sindh; numerous articles and papers on debt, external finance and adjustment issues. *Leisure interests:* reading and writing economics, poetry. *Address:* State Bank of Pakistan, Central Directorate, I. I. Chundrigar Road, PO Box 4456, Karachi 2, Pakistan (Office); 12 Fatima Jinnah Road, Karachi, Pakistan (Home). *Telephone:* (21) 9212447 (Office); (21) 9206020 (Home). *Fax:* (21) 9212446 (Office). *E-mail:* governor.office@sbp.org.pk (Office); ishrat.husain@sbp.org.pk (Office). *Website:* www.sbp.org.pk (Office).

HUSSAIN, Nasser, OBE, BSc; British cricketer; b. 28 March 1968, Chenna, India; s. of Joe Hussain; m. Karen Hussain; two s.; ed Forest School, London, Durham Univ.; youngest-ever batsman to represent Essex Under-15 Schools 1980; right-hand batsman, right-hand leg-break bowler; England début against West Indies, Kingston 1989; Capt. England 'A' team in tour of Pakistan 1996; scored first Test centuries at Edgbaston and Trent Bridge against India 1996 and career-best 207 against Australia at Edgbaston 1997; 80 tests for 4,719 runs (average 36.58) to 26 Dec. 2002; scored 18,942 first-class runs (average 41.8) including 48 centuries to Jan. 2003; Capt. of Essex April 1999–; Capt. of England June 1999–; Cricket Writers' Club Young Cricketer of the Year Award 1989. *Leisure interests:* golf, football (Leeds United fan), reading. *Address:* c/o English Cricket Board, Lord's Cricket Ground, London, NW8 8QZ, England (Office). *Telephone:* (20) 7289-1611 (Office). *Website:* www.ecb.co.uk (Office).

HUSSEIN, Abdul-Aziz; Kuwaiti politician and diplomatist; b. 1921, Kuwait; m. 1948; two s. one d.; ed Teachers Higher Inst., Cairo and Univ. of London; fmr Dir "House of Kuwait", Cairo, Dir-Gen. Dept of Educ., Kuwait; Amb. to the UAR 1961–62; Perm. Rep. to Arab League Council; State Minister in Charge of Cabinet Affairs 1963–64; Minister of State for Cabinet Affairs 1971–85; Counsellor of HM the Amir of Kuwait 1985–. *Publication:* Lectures on Arab Society in Kuwait 1960. *Address:* Amari Diwan, Seif Palace, Kuwait City, Kuwait.

HUSSEIN, Saddam (see Saddam Hussein).

HUSSEINOV, Col Suret Davud ogly; Azerbaijani politician; b. 1959; m.; two s.; ed Gyanja Inst. of Tech.; worker, Asst foreman carpet factory, Gyanja 1982–83, sorter procurement station, Sheki 1984–86; Sr controller, foreman wool processing factory, Yevlakh 1987–, Dir 1989–; Pres. Consortium Azersherstprom 1983; mem. Parl. 1990, Vice-Prime Minister, plenipotentiary of Pres. in Nagorny Karabakh, Comm. of Nat. Army Corps 1992–93; rank of Col 1992; deprived of all his posts by order of the Pres. Feb. 1993; Prime Minister of Azerbaijan 1993–94; dismissed after organizing an abortive coup d'état 1994; lived in exile in Russia 1997; extradited to Azerbaijan 1997, sentenced to life imprisonment on 40 charges for involvement in coup Feb. 1999; Nat. Hero of Azerbaijan 1992.

HUSSEY OF NORTH BRADLEY, Baron (Life Peer), cr. 1996, of North Bradley in the County of Wiltshire; **Marmaduke James Hussey,** MA; British business executive; b. 29 Aug. 1923; s. of the late E. R. J. Hussey, CMG and Christine Hussey; m. Lady Susan K. Waldegrave 1959; one s. one d.; ed Rugby School and Trinity Coll., Oxford; served with Grenadier Guards, Italy 1939–45; joined Associated Newspapers 1949, Dir 1964; Man. Dir Harmsworth Publs 1967–70; mem. Thomson Org. Exec. Bd 1971; Chief. Exec. and Man. Dir Times Newspapers Ltd 1971–80, Dir 1982–86; Chair. Royal Marsden Hosp. 1985–98, Bd of Govs. BBC 1986–96; a Rhodes Trustee 1972–91; mem. Bd British Council 1993–96; Trustee Royal Acad. Trust 1988–96; Vice-Chair. Appeals Cttee B.L.E.S.M.A.; Dir Colonial Mutual Group PLC 1982–97; Wm. Collins PLC 1985–89; Jt Chair. Great Western Radio

1985–86; Chair. Ruffer Investment Man. Ltd 1995–, Cadweb 1996–; Pres. Somerset Royal British Legion 1999–; mem. Govt Working Party on Artificial Limb and Appliance Centres in England 1984–86, Man. Cttee and Educ. Cttee King Edward's Hosp. Fund for London 1987–99. *Address:* Waldegrave House, Chewton Mendip, near Bath, Somerset, BA3 4PD; Flat 15, 45/47 Courtfield Road, London, SW7 4DB, England. *Telephone:* (20) 7370-1414 (London).

HUSSON, Philippe Jean Louis Marie, DenD; French diplomatist; b. 22 July 1927, Nouméa, New Caledonia; s. of Jean Husson and Antoinette Leclerc; m. Christiane Marchand 1956; three s. two d.; ed Inst. d'Études Politiques; Ecole nat. d'admin.; Contrôleur Civil, Morocco 1954–56; Moroccan Desk, Foreign Ministry, Paris 1956–58; First Sec., French Embassy, Bucharest 1958–61, Moscow 1961–64, Second Counsellor, Washington, DC 1964–67; Deputy Dir Cultural and Scientific Relations, Foreign Ministry 1967–71; First Counsellor, French Embassy, Ottawa 1971–74, Minister-Counsellor, Moscow 1974–77; Deputy Perm. Rep. to the UN, New York 1977–81; Amb. to Finland 1981–84; Deputy Inspector-Gen., Foreign Ministry 1984–87; Amb. to Canada 1987–89; Dir Archives and Documentation, Foreign Ministry 1990–92; Govt Diplomatic Adviser 1992; mem. Comm. on Publ of French diplomatic documents 1992–, Comm. on archives of Ministry of Foreign Affairs 1995–; Officier, Légion d'honneur; Commdr, Ordre nat. du Mérite, Great Cross, Order of the Lion (Finland), Grand Officier, Ordre Equestre du St. Sépulcre de Jérusalem, Commdr Order of Merit (Malta). *Address:* c/o Ministry of Foreign Affairs, 37 quai d'Orsay, 75007 Paris (Office); 7 promenade Venezia, Grand Siècle, 78000 Versailles, France (Home). *E-mail:* phhusson@club-internet.fr (Office).

HUSTON, Anjelica; American actress; b. 8 July 1951, Los Angeles, Calif.; d. of the late John Huston and Enrica Huston (née Soma); m. Robert Graham 1992. *Films include:* Sinful Davey, A Walk with Love and Death 1969, The Last Tycoon 1976, The Postman Always Rings Twice 1981, Swashbuckler, This is Spinal Tap 1984, The Ice Pirates 1984, Prizzi's Honor (Acad. Award for Best Supporting Actress 1985, New York and Los Angeles Film Critics' Awards 1985), Gardens of Stone, Captain Eo, The Dead, Mr North, A Handful of Dust, The Witches, Enemies, A Love Story, The Grifters, The Addams Family, Addams Family Values, The Player, Manhattan Murder Mystery, The Crossing Guard 1995, The Perez Family 1995, Buffalo '66 1997, Phoenix 1997, Ever After 1998, Breakers 1999; Dir Bastard Out of Carolina 1995, Phoenix 1997, Agnes Browne 1999, The Golden Bowl 2001, The Royal Tenenbaums 2002. *Stage appearances include:* Tamara, Los Angeles 1985. *Television appearances include:* The Cowboy and the Ballerina (NBC-TV film) 1984, Faerie Tale Theatre, A Rose for Miss Emily (PBS film), Lonesome Dove (CBS mini-series), The Mists of Avalon (TNT mini-series) 2001. *Address:* c/o International Creative Management, 8942 Wilshire Boulevard, Beverly Hills, CA 90211, USA.

HUTAPEA, Eva Riyanti; Indonesian business executive; b. 1950; trained as accountant; fmr auditor; joined Indofood, worked through ranks to become CEO and Pres. Dir 1996–; CEO and Chair. P.T. Intiboga Sejahtera. *Address:* PT Indofood Sukses Makmur Tbk, Aristomo Central Building, 12th Floor, SI HR Rasuna Said X-2 Kav. 5, Jakarta 12950, Indonesia (Office). *Telephone:* (21) 522-8822 (Office). *Fax:* (21) 522-6014 (Office). *Website:* www.indofood.co .id (Office).

HUTCHINSON, (John) Maxwell; British architect; b. 3 Dec. 1948; s. of the late Frank M. Hutchinson and Elizabeth R. M. Wright; ed Oundle, Scott Sutherland School of Architecture, Aberdeen and Architectural School of Architecture; Founder, Hutchinson & Partners (Chartered Architects) 1972, Chair. Hutchinson & Partners Architects Ltd 1987–92; Dir The Hutchinson Studio Architects 1992–2000; Visiting Prof. of Architecture, Queen's Univ., Belfast 1988–93; Special Prof. of Architectural Design, Nottingham Univ. 1993–96; Visiting Prof. Westminster Univ. 1997–2001; Chair. Permarock Products Ltd, Loughborough 1985–96, London Br. Elgar Soc. 1987–93, East Midlands Arts Bd 1991–94, British Architectural Library Trust 1991–99, Schools of Architecture Accreditation Bd 1991–97; Chair. Industrial Bldg Bureau 1988–91; Vice-Chair. Construction Industry Council 1990–91; mem. Council, Royal Inst. of British Architects (RIBA) 1978–93, Sr Vice-Pres. 1988–89, Pres. 1989–91; Fellow Greenwich Univ.; mem. Council Royal School of Church Music 1997–2000; regular broadcaster on TV and radio; Hon. Fellow Royal Soc. of Ulster Architects 1992. *Compositions:* The Kibbo-Kift 1979, The Ascent of Wilberforce 111 1984, Requiem in a Village Church 1988, Christmas Cantata 1990. *Publications:* The Prince of Wales, Right or Wrong: An Architect Replies 1989, Number 57 – The Story of a House 2003. *Leisure interests:* composing, playing the guitar loudly, cooking, champagne. *Address:* 58 Hatton Garden, London, EC1N 8LX; 1 Back Hill, Clarkenwell, London, EC1R 5EN, England (Home). *Telephone:* (973) 795210. *E-mail:* maxwellh@dircon.co.uk (Office). *Website:* www.bbc.co.uk/londonlive ."maxfiles".

HUTCHISON, Clyde A., Jr, PhD; American university professor; b. 5 May 1913, Alliance, Ohio; s. of Clyde A. and Bessie G. Hutchison; m. Sarah Jane West 1937; two s. one d.; ed Ohio State Univ.; Nat. Research Council Fellow, Columbia Univ. 1937–38; Asst Prof. of Chem., Univ. of Buffalo 1939–45; Research Assoc., Univ. of Va 1942–43, Manhattan District Project 1943–45; Asst Prof. Enrico Fermi Inst., Univ. of Chicago 1945–50; Dept of Chem. 1948–50, Assoc. Prof. 1950–54, Prof. 1954–63, Carl William Eisendrath Prof. 1963–69, Carl. W Eisendrath Distinguished Service Prof. of Chem. 1969–83, Emer. 1983–, Chair. Dept of Chem. 1959–62; Consultant Argonne Nat. Lab.

1946–; Ed., Journal of Chemical Physics, American Inst. of Physics 1953–59; Visiting Prof. sponsored by Japan Soc. for the Promotion of Science 1975; Eastman Prof., Oxford Univ. 1981–82; Visiting Lecturer, Chinese Acad. of Sciences 1986; mem. NAS, ACS; Fellow, American Acad. of Arts and Sciences, American Physical Soc. (mem. Council 1967–71); Guggenheim Fellow, Oxford Univ. 1955–56, 1972–73; Hon. DSc (Cedarville); Ohio State Univ. Centennial Achievement Award 1970; Peter Debye Award, ACS 1972. *Publications:* 110 scientific papers, documents and contribs. to books. *Address:* Searle Laboratory, University of Chicago, 5735 Ellis Avenue, Chicago, IL 60637, USA. *Telephone:* (312) 702-7069. *Fax:* (312) 702-0805.

HUTCHISON, Kay Bailey, LLB; American politician; b. 22 July 1943, Galveston, Tex.; d. of Allan Bailey and Kathryn Bailey; m. Ray Hutchison; ed Univ. of Tex.; TV news reporter, Houston 1969–71; pvt. law practice 1969–74; Press Sec. to Anne Armstrong 1971; Vice-Chair. Nat. Transport Safety Bd 1976–78; Asst Prof. Univ. of Tex. Dallas 1978–79; Sr Vice-Pres., Gen. Counsel, Repub. of Tex. Corpn Dallas 1979–81; counsel, Hutchison, Boyle, Brooks & Fisher, Dallas 1981–91; mem. Tex. House of Reps. 1972–76; elected Treas. of Tex. 1990; Senator from Texas 1993–; Fellow, American Bar Foundation, Tex. Bar Foundation; mem. American Bar Asscn, State Bar of Tex.; Republican. *Address:* U.S. Senate, 370 Russell Senate Building, Washington, DC 20510, USA.

HUTT, Peter Barton, BA, LLM; American lawyer; b. 16 Nov. 1934, Buffalo, NY; s. of Lester Ralph Hutt and Louise Rich Fraser; ed Phillips Exeter Acad., Yale and Harvard Univs.; Assoc., Covington and Burling (law firm) 1960–68, Partner 1968–71, 1975–; Lecturer on Food and Drug Law, Harvard Law School 1994–; Stanford Law School 1998; Chief Counsel, US Food and Drug Admin. 1971–75; Counsel, Soc. for Risk Analysis, American Coll. of Toxicology; Chair. Alcoholic Beverage Medical Research Foundation 1986–92; Vice-Chair. Legal Action Center, New York 1984–, Foundation for Biomedical Research 1988–; mem. Inst. of Medicine, NAS 1970–, Advisory Bd, Tufts Center for Study of Drug Devt 1976–, Univ. Va Center for Advanced Studies 1982–, Nat. Cttee on New Drugs for Cancer and AIDS 1988–90; Inst. of Medicine Round Table on Drugs and Vaccines against AIDS 1988–95; mem. Bd of Dirs. of numerous cos.; mem. Advisory Bd of numerous other scientific, academic and financial orgs; Underwood-Prescott Award, MIT 1977 and numerous other honours and awards. *Publications:* Dealing with Drug Abuse (with Patricia M. Wald) 1972, Food and Drug Law: Cases and Materials (with Richard A. Merrill) 1980, 1991. *Leisure interests:* research on the history of Govt regulation of food and drugs. *Address:* Covington & Burling, 1201 Pennsylvania Avenue, NW, Washington, DC 20004 (Office); 402 Prince Street, Alexandria, VA 22314, USA (Home). *Telephone:* (202) 662-5522 (Office). *Fax:* (202) 778-5522 (Office). *E-mail:* phutt@cov.com (Office).

HUTTON, Baron (Life Peer), cr. 1997, of Bresagh in the County of Down; **Rt. Hon. Sir (James) Brian Edward Hutton,** Kt, PC; British judge; b. 29 June 1931, Belfast, Northern Ireland; s. of the late James Hutton and Mabel Hutton; m. Mary Gillian Murland 1975 (died 2000); two d.; ed Shrewsbury School, Balliol Coll. Oxford, Queen's Univ. of Belfast; called to NI Bar 1954, QC (NI) 1970, Bencher, Inn of Court of NI 1974, Sr Crown Counsel 1973–79, Judge of High Court of Justice 1979–88, Lord Chief Justice of NI 1988–97; a Lord of Appeal in Ordinary 1997–; mem. Jt Law Enforcement Comm. 1974, Deputy Chair. Boundary Comm. for NI 1985–88; Pres. NI Asscn for Mental Health 1983–; Visitor Univ. of Ulster 1999–; Hon. Fellow, Balliol Coll., Hon. Bencher, Inner Temple, King's Inns, Dublin. *Publications:* articles in Modern Law Review. *Address:* House of Lords, Westminster, London, SW1A 0PW, England.

HUTTON, Timothy; American actor; b. 16 Aug. 1960, Malibu, Calif.; s. of Jim Hutton and Maryline Hutton; m. Debra Winger (q.v.) 1986 (divorced); one s. *Plays:* Prelude to a Kiss, Broadway 1990, Babylon Gardens 1991. *Television appearances include:* Zuma Beach 1978, Best Place to Be, Baby Makes Six, Sultan and the Rock Star, Young Love, First Love, Friendly Fire 1979. *Films include:* Ordinary People 1980 (Oscar for Best Supporting Actor), Taps 1981, Daniel 1983, Iceman 1984, Turk 1985, The Falcon and the Snowman 1985, Made in Heaven 1987, A Time of Destiny 1988, Everybody's All-American 1988, Betrayed 1988, Torrents of Spring 1990, Q & A 1990, The Temp 1993, The Dark Half 1993, French Kiss 1995, City of Industry, Scenes From Everyday Life 1995, The Substance of Fire 1996, Mr and Mrs Loving 1996, Beautiful Girls 1996, City of Industry 1997, Playing God 1997, Deterrance 1998, The General's Daughter 1999, Just One Night 2000, Deliberate Intent 2000, Deterrence 2000. *Address:* CAA, 9830 Wilshire Boulevard, Beverly Hills, CA 90212, USA.

HUTTON, Will Nicholas, MBA; British newspaper editor and business executive; b. 21 May 1950, London; s. of the late William Hutton and Dorothy Haynes; m. Jane Atkinson 1978; one s. two d.; ed Chislehurst and Sidcup Grammar School, Univ. of Bristol and INSEAD; with Phillips & Drew (stockbrokers) 1971–77; Sr Producer Current Affairs, BBC Radio 4 1978–81; Dir and Producer The Money Programme, BBC2 1981–83; Econs Corresp. Newsnight, BBC2 1983–88; Ed. European Business Channel 1988–90; Econs Ed. The Guardian 1990–95, Asst Ed. 1995–96; Ed. The Observer 1996–98, Ed.-in-Chief 1998–2000; Chief Exec. The Work Foundation (fmrly The Industrial Soc. –2002) 2000–; Gov. LSE 2000–; Hon. DLitt (Kingston) 1995, (De Montfort) 1996; Political Journalist of the Year, What the Papers Say 1993. *Publications:* The Revolution That Never Was: An Assessment of Keynesian Economics 1986, The State We're In 1994, The State to Come 1997, The

Stakeholding Society 1998, The World We're In 2002. *Leisure interests:* family, reading, squash, tennis, cinema, writing. *Address:* The Work Foundation, Peter Runge House, 3 Carlton Terrace, London, SW1Y 5DG, England (Office). *Telephone:* (20) 7004-7100. *Fax:* (20) 7004-7111. *E-mail:* roconnor@theworkfoundation.com (Office). *Website:* www.theworkfoundation.com (Office).

HUXLEY, Sir Andrew Fielding, Kt, OM, ScD, FRS; British physiologist; b. 22 Nov. 1917, London; s. of Leonard Huxley and Rosalind Huxley (née Bruce); m. Jocelyn Richenda Gammell Pease 1947; one s. five d.; ed Univ. Coll. School, Westminster School and Trinity Coll., Cambridge; Operational Research, Anti-Aircraft Command 1940–42, Admiralty 1942–45; Fellow of Trinity Coll., Cambridge 1941–60, 1990–, Dir of Studies 1952–60, Hon. Fellow 1967–90, Master, Trinity Coll. 1984–90; Demonstrator, Dept of Physiology, Cambridge Univ. 1946–50, Asst Dir of Research 1951–59, Reader in Experimental Biophysics 1959–60; Jodrell Prof. of Physiology, Univ. Coll. London 1960–69; Royal Soc. Research Prof. 1969–83, Prof. Emer. of Physiology, Univ. of London 1983–; Pres. BAAS 1976–77; Chair. Medical Research Cttee of the Muscular Dystrophy Group 1974–80, Vice-Pres. Muscular Dystrophy Group 1980–; mem. Govt.'s Scientific Authority for Animals 1976–77, Agric. Research Council 1977–81, Nature Conservancy Council 1985–87, Home Office Animal Procedures Cttee 1987–95; mem. Council, Royal Soc. 1960–62, 1977–79, 1980–85; Pres. Royal Soc. 1980–85, Int. Union of Physiological Sciences 1986–93; mem. Leopoldina Acad. 1964, Royal Danish Acad. of Sciences and Letters 1964, American Philosophical Soc. 1975; mem. Emer. Acad. Europaea 1989; Trustee, British Museum (Natural History) 1981–91, Science Museum 1983–88; Croonian Lecturer, Royal Soc. 1967; First Florey Lecturer, Australia 1982; Romanes Lecturer, Oxford 1982–83; Fenn Lecturer, Sydney 1983; Davson Lecturer, American Physiological Soc. 1998; Fellow, Imp. Coll. of Science and Tech. 1980; Hon. Fellow Univ. Coll., London 1980; Foreign Fellow Indian Nat. Science Acad. 1985; Assoc. mem. Royal Acad. of Sciences, Letters and Fine Arts, Belgium 1978; Foreign Assoc. NAS 1979; Foreign mem. Dutch Soc. of Sciences 1984; Hon. mem. Royal Irish Acad. 1986, Japan Acad. 1988; Hon. Foreign mem. American Acad. of Arts and Sciences 1961, Royal Acad. of Medicine, Belgium 1978; Hon. Fellow Inst. of Biology 1981, Darwin Coll., Cambridge 1981, Royal Soc. of Edinburgh 1983, Fellowship of Eng 1986, Queen Mary Coll. 1987; Hon. MD (Saar) 1964, (Ulm) 1993, (Charles Univ., Prague) 1998; Hon. DSc (Sheffield) 1964, (Leicester) 1967, (London) 1973, (St Andrews) 1974, (Aston) 1977, (Oxford) 1983, (Keele) 1985, (Md) 1987, (Brunel) 1988, (Hyderabad) 1991, (Glasgow) 1993, (Witwatersrand) 1998; Hon. ScD (Cambridge) 1978, (Pennsylvania) 1988, (East Anglia) 1985; Hon. LLD (Birmingham) 1979, (Dundee) 1984; Dr. hc (Marseilles) 1979, (York) 1981, (W Australia) 1982, (Harvard Univ.) 1984, (Humboldt Univ.) 1985, (Toyama) 1995; Hon. DHL (New York) 1982; Nobel Prize for Physiology or Medicine (jtly.) 1963, Copley Medal (Royal Soc.) 1973, Swammerdam Medal (Soc. for Natural Science, Medicine and Surgery, Amsterdam) 1997; Grand Cordon of Sacred Treasure (Japan) 1995. *Publications:* Reflections on Muscle (Sherrington Lectures, Liverpool Univ.) 1977; papers on nerve conduction and muscle contraction, chiefly in Journal of Physiology. *Leisure interests:* walking, design of scientific instruments. *Address:* Manor Field, 1 Vicarage Drive, Grantchester, Cambridge, CB3 9NG, England. *Telephone:* (1223) 840207. *Fax:* (1223) 840207.

HUXLEY, George Leonard, MA, FSA, MRIA; British professor of Greek; b. 23 Sept. 1932, Leicester; s. of Sir Leonard Huxley and Lady Molly Huxley; m. Davina Iris Best 1957; three d.; ed Blundell's, Magdalen Coll., Oxford; commissioned into Royal Engineers 1951; Acting Operating Supt, Longmoor Military Railway 1951; Fellow All Souls Coll., Oxford 1955–61; Prof. of Greek, Queen's Univ., Belfast 1962–83, Prof. Emer. 1988–; Hon. Pres. Classical Asscn of Ireland 1999–2000; Dir Gennadius Library, American School of Classical Studies, Athens 1986–89; mem. Exec. NI Civil Rights Asscn 1971–72; mem. Man. Cttee ASCSA 1991–; mem. Irish Advisory Bd, Int. Irish Studies, Liverpool Univ. 1997–; Hon. Prof. Trinity Coll., Dublin 1989–; Sr Vice-Pres. Fédération Int. des Sociétés d'Etudes Classiques 1984–89; Irish mem., Humanities Cttee of European Science Foundation 1978–86; Vice-Pres. Royal Irish Acad. 1984–85, 1997–98, Hon. Librarian 1990–94, Special Envoy 1994–99, Senior Vice-Pres. 1999–2000; mem. Acad. Europaea 1990; mem. Int. Comm. Thesaurus Linguae Latinae, Munich 1999–2000; mem. Editorial Bd Dictionary of Mediaeval Latin from Celtic Sources 2001–; Patron Irish Inst. of Hellenic Studies, Athens 1998–; Hon. LittD (Dublin); Hon. DLitt (Belfast); Cromer Greek Prize 1963. *Publications:* Early Sparta 1962, Achaeans and Hittites 1960, The Early Ionians 1966, Greek Epic Poetry 1969, Kythera (Jt) 1972, Pindar's Vision of the Past 1975, On Aristotle and Greek Society 1979, Homer and the Travellers 1988; articles on Hellenic and Byzantine subjects. *Leisure interest:* siderodromophilia. *Address:* School of Classics, Trinity College, Dublin 2, Ireland (Office); Forge Cottage, Church Enstone, Oxfordshire, OX7 4NN, England (Home). *Telephone:* (1) 6764222 (Office); (1608) 677595 (Home). *Fax:* (1608) 677595 (Home).

HUXLEY, Hugh Esmor, MBE, PhD, DSc, FRS; British scientist; b. 25 Feb. 1924, Birkenhead, Cheshire; s. of Thomas Hugh Huxley and Olwen Roberts; m. Frances Fripp 1966; one d. two step-s. one step-d.; ed Park High School, Birkenhead and Christ's Coll., Cambridge; Radar Officer, RAF Bomber Command and Telecommunications Research Establishment, Malvern 1943–47; Research Student, MRC Unit for Molecular Biology, Cavendish Lab., Cambridge 1948–52; Commonwealth Fund Fellow, Biology Dept, MIT 1952–54; Research Fellow, Christ's Coll., Cambridge 1953–56; mem. of

External Staff of MRC and Hon. Research Assoc., Biophysics Dept, Univ. Coll. London 1956–61; mem. of Scientific Staff, MRC Lab. of Molecular Biology, Cambridge 1962–87, Jt Head, Structural Studies Div. 1976–87, Deputy Dir 1977–87; Prof. of Biology, Rosenstiel Basic Medical Sciences Research Center, Brandeis Univ., Boston, Mass. 1987–97, Prof. Emer. 1997– (Dir 1988–94); Fellow, King's Coll., Cambridge 1961–67, Churchill Coll., Cambridge 1967–87; Harvey Soc. Lecturer, New York 1964–65; Sr Visiting Lecturer, Physiology Course, Woods Hole, Mass. 1966–71; Wilson Lecturer, Univ. of Tex. 1968; Dunham Lecturer, Harvard Medical School 1969; Croonian Lecturer, Royal Soc. of London 1970; Ziskind Visiting Prof. of Biology, Brandeis Univ. 1971; Penn Lecturer, Univ. of Pa 1971; Mayer Lecturer, MIT 1971; Miller Lecturer, State Univ. of NY 1973; Carter-Wallace Lecturer, Princeton Univ. 1973; Pauling Lecturer, Stanford Univ. 1980; Jesse Beams Lecturer, Univ. of Va 1980; Ida Beam Lecturer, Univ. of Ia 1981; mem. Advisory Bd of Rosenstiel Basic Medical Sciences Center, Brandeis Univ. 1971–77; mem. Council of Royal Soc. of London 1973–75, 1984–86; mem. Scientific Advisory Cttee, European Molecular Biology Lab. 1975–81; mem. Bd of Trustees, Associated Univs Inc. 1987–90; mem. German Acad. of Science, Leopoldina 1964; Foreign Assoc. NAS 1978, American Asscn of Anatomists 1981, American Physiological Soc. 1981, American Soc. of Zoologists 1986; Foreign Hon. mem. American Acad. of Arts and Sciences 1965, Danish Acad. of Sciences 1971, American Soc. of Biological Chemists 1976; Hon. Fellow, Christ's Coll., Cambridge 1981; Hon. DSc (Harvard) 1969, (Univ. of Chicago) 1974, (Univ. of Pa) 1976, (Leicester) 1988; Feldberg Award for Experimental Medical Research 1963, William Bate Hardy Prize of the Cambridge Philosophical Soc. 1965, Louisa Gross Horwitz Prize 1971, Int. Feltrinelli Prize for Medicine 1974, Int. Award, Gairdner Foundation 1975, Baly Medal, Royal Coll. of Physicians 1975, Royal Medal, Royal Soc. of London 1977, E. B. Wilson Medal, American Soc. for Cell Biology 1983, Albert Einstein World Award of Science 1987, Franklin Medal 1990, Distinguished Scientist Award, Electron Microscopy Soc. of America 1991, Copley Medal Royal Soc. of London 1997. *Publications:* articles in scientific journals. *Leisure interests:* skiing, sailing, travel. *Address:* Rosenstiel Basic Medical Sciences Research Center, Brandeis University, Waltham, MA 02254; 349 Nashawtuc Road, Concord, MA 01742, USA (Home). *Telephone:* (617) 736-2490.

HUXTABLE, Ada Louise, AB; American writer and critic; b. New York; d. of Michael Louis and Leah (Rosenthal) Landman; m. L. Garth Huxtable 1942; ed Hunter Coll. and Inst. of Fine Arts, New York Univ.; Asst Curator of Architecture and Design, Museum of Modern Art, New York 1946–50; Fulbright Scholarship to study contemporary Italian architecture and design 1950, 1952; contributing ed. Progressive Architecture, Art in America, freelance writer on architecture and design 1952–63; architecture critic, New York Times 1963–82; mem. Times Editorial Bd 1973–82; independent architectural consultant and critic 1982–96; Architecture Critic, The Wall Street Journal 1996–; mem. Corpn Visiting Cttees on Architecture, Harvard Univ., MIT, Rockefeller Univ. Council, Smithsonian Council; mem. Soc. of Architectural Historians, American Acad. of Arts and Letters, American Philosophical Soc.; Fellow of American Acad. of Arts and Sciences; Guggenheim Fellowship for studies in American architecture 1958; Hon. mem. American Inst. of Architects; Hon. FRIBA; Hon. degrees from Univs. of Harvard, Yale, New York, Pennsylvania, Massachusetts, Nottingham, England, Fordham, Washington, Williams, Hamilton, Colgate, Trinity, Oberline, Smith, Skidmere, Mt Holyoke Coll. and others; numerous prizes and awards including Frank Jewett Mather Award of Coll. Art Asscn for Art Criticism 1967, Pulitzer Prize for Distinguished Criticism 1970, Architectural Criticism Medal of American Inst. of Architects 1969, Special Award of Nat. Trust for Historic Preservation 1970, Nat. Arts Club Medal for Literature 1971, Diamond Jubilee Medallion of the City of New York 1973, US Sec. of Interior's Conservation Award 1976, Thomas Jefferson Medal for Architecture 1977, Jean Tschumi Prize for Architectural Criticism, Int. Union of Architects 1987, Medal for Architectural Criticism (Acad. d'Architecture Française) 1988, MacArthur Prize Fellowship 1981–86, Henry Allen Moe Prize in the Humanities (American Philosophical Soc.) 1992. *Publications:* Pier Luigi Nervi 1960, Classical New York 1964, Will They Ever Finish Bruckner Boulevard? 1970, Kicked a Building Lately? 1976, The Tall Building Artistically Reconsidered: The Search for a Skyscraper Style 1985, Architecture, Anyone? 1986, Goodbye History, Hello Hamburger 1986, The Unreal America: Architecture and Illusion 1997. *Address:* 969 Park Avenue, New York, NY 10028, USA.

HUYGENS, Robert Burchard Constantijn, PhD; Netherlands professor of medieval Latin (retd); b. 10 Dec. 1931, The Hague; m. Caroline Sprey 1962; one s. two d.; ed Leiden Univ.; army service 1952–54; Lecturer in Medieval Latin, Univ. of Leiden 1964, Prof. 1968–96; Fellow, Dumbarton Oaks, Washington, DC 1982, Inst. for Advanced Study, Jerusalem 1983–84, Inst. for Advanced Study, Princeton, NJ 1986–87, Herzog August Bibliothek, Wolfenbüttel 1987; mem. Royal Netherlands Acad., Soc. des Antiquaires de France, Monumenta Germaniae Historica; Past Pres. Rotary Club Leiden. *Publications include:* Jacques de Vitry 1960, Accessus ad Auctores 1970, Vézelay 1976, William of Tyre 1986, Berengar of Tours 1988, Guibert of Nogent 1992, Serta mediaevalia 2000, Ars edendi 2001. *Address:* Witte Singel 28, 2311 BH Leiden, Netherlands. *Telephone:* (71) 5143798.

HVEDING, Vidkunn; Norwegian engineer, economist and politician; b. 27 March 1921, Orkdal; s. of Johan Hveding and Ida Marie Hveding (née Songlid); m. 1st Ellen Palmstrom 1948 (divorced 1963); m. 2nd Tone Barth 1963 (died 1980); m. 3rd Grete Blydt Quisler 1986; one s. three d.; ed

Norwegian Inst. of Tech. (N.T.H.), Univ. of Trondheim; Eng (design and supervision), various hydro-power projects 1946–54; Assoc. Prof. of Hydro-electric Eng, N.T.H. 1954–56, Prof. 1958–61; Adviser, Ethiopian Electric Light and Power Authority 1956–57; Man. Project Dept, Noreno Brasil SA, São Paulo 1957–58; Asst Dir-Gen. Norwegian Water Resources and Elec. Bd 1961–63; Adviser, Kuwait Fund for Arab Econ. Devt 1963–65; Sec.-Gen. Norwegian Ministry of Industry 1967–68; Chair. and Chief Exec., Norwegian Water Resources and Electricity Bd 1968–75; Planning Man. Industrial Bank of Kuwait 1975–77; Dir of various cos. in banking industry, shipping, consulting 1977–81, 1983–; Minister of Petroleum and Energy 1981–83; Commdr, Royal Order of St Olav. *Publications:* Comprehensive Energy Analysis Norway 1969, Hydropower Development in Norway 1992, articles on hydroelectric power tech., energy Econs, resource conservation and political philosophy. *Leisure interests:* skiing, sailing, woodwork. *Address:* Voksenkollv. 23B, 0790 Oslo, Norway (Home). *E-mail:* vidkunn@online.no (Home).

HVIDT, Gen. Christian, DFC; Danish air force officer; b. 15 July 1942, Copenhagen; m. 1st; three c.; m. 2nd Jane Hvidt; two step-c.; flying service (F-100 Super Sabre) 1962–69; test pilot on F-35 Draken at SAAB factories, Linköping, Sweden 1969–72; Deputy Squadron Commdr (F-35 Draken) 1972–74; Br. Chief Tactical Air Command, Denmark 1975–79; Squadron Commdr First Danish F-16 Squadron, Air Station Skrydstrup 1979–83; staff officer and Br. Chief Plans and Policy Div., HQ Chodden 1983–87; Commdg Officer Air Station Karup 1987–88; Chief of Staff Tactical Air Command, Denmark 1989–90; Deputy Chief of Staff Plans and Policy, Operations, Budget and Finance HQ Chodden 1991–93; Perm. Danish Rep., NATO Mil. Cttee 1994–96; Chief of Staff, HQ Chodden 1996; Chief of Defence 1996–2002; Grand Cross of the Order of Dannebrog, Danish Air Force Badge of Honour, Badge of Honour of the Danish Reserve Officers Asscn., Medal of Merit of the Home Guard, Commdr, Grand Cross, Royal Swedish Order of the Northern Star, Jordanian Military Order of Merit of the First Degree, Commdr, Cross with the Star of Merit of the Repub. of Poland, Commdr, Légion d'honneur, de l'Ordre Nat. du Mérite. *Address:* c/o Defence Command, PO Box 202, 2950 Vedbaek, Denmark (Office).

HVOROSTOVSKY, Dmitri; Russian singer (baritone); b. 16 Oct. 1962, Krasnoyarsk, Siberia; ed Krasnoyarsk High School of Arts; soloist with Krasnoyarsk Opera 1986–; debut Wigmore Hall, London 1989, Alice Tully Hall, New York, Washington Kennedy Center 1990, BBC Promenade Concerts 1993; appeared in Aix-en-Provence and Salzburg Festivals 1992; has performed recitals in Europe, USA and Russia; First Prize USSR Nat. Glinka Competition 1987, Toulouse Singing Competition 1988, BBC Cardiff Singer of the World Competition 1989. *Opera includes:* The Queen of Spades (Opéra de Nice) 1991, (Metropolitan Opera, New York) 1999, Eugene Onegin (La Fenice) 1991, (Covent Garden) 1993, Il Barbiere di Siviglia (San Francisco Opera) 1991, I Puritani (Covent Garden) 1992, Eugene Onegin (Châtelet, Paris) 1992, La Traviata (Chicago Lyric Opera) 1993, I Masnadieri (Covent Garden) 1998; *Recordings include:* Tchaikovsky and Verdi Arias, Cavalleria Rusticana, Eugene Onegin, Don Carlos. *Address:* c/o Philips/Polygram Artists, P.O. Box 1420, 1 Sussex Place, London, W6 9XS, England (Office).

HWANG IN-SUNG; South Korean politician; b. 9 Jan. 1926; ed Korea Mil. Acad. and Seoul Nat. Univ.; army officer 1960–68; Asst Minister without Portfolio 1970; Chief Sec. to Prime Minister 1973; Gov. N Cholla Prov. 1973–78; Minister, Ministry of Transport 1978; Pres. KNTC 1980; mem. Nat. Ass. 1981, 1985, 1992; Minister, Ministry of Agric., Forestry and Fisheries 1985–87; Chair. Asiana Air Lines 1988–93; Pres. Kumho Air Lines 1989–93; Chair. Political Cttee Democratic Liberal Party 1992; Prime Minister of Repub. of Korea March–Dec. 1993. *Address:* c/o Office of the Prime Minister, Seoul, Republic of Korea.

HYMAN, Timothy; British painter and writer on art; b. 17 April 1946, Hove; s. of Alan Hyman and Noreen Gypson; m. Judith Ravenscroft 1982; ed Charterhouse and Slade School of Fine Art; mounted Narrative Paintings at Arnolfini and ICA Galleries, etc. 1979–80; public collections include Arts Council, Bristol City Art Gallery, Museum of London, Contemporary Art Soc., British Museum, Govt Art Collection, Los Angeles Co. Museum; Visiting Prof. at Baroda, two British Council lecture tours 1981–83; Artist in Residence at Lincoln Cathedral 1983–84, Sandown Racecourse 1992; Purchaser for Arts Council Collection 1985; selector, John Moores Prize 1995; Lead curator Stanley Spencer retrospective exhbn, Tate Gallery, London 2001–; Leverhulme Award 1992, Rootstein Hopkins Foundation Award 1995, Wingate Award 1998. *Exhibitions:* started to exhibit at Blond 1980, one-man exhbns 1981, 1983 and 1985; Austin/Desmond (one-man exhbn 1990, 2001, 2003), Castlefield Gallery, Manchester 1993, Gallery Chemould, Bombay 1994, Gallery M, Flowers East 1994; group exhbns at Royal Acad., Hayward Gallery, Whitechapel Art Gallery, Nat. Portrait Gallery. *Publications:* Hodgkin 1975, Kitaj 1977, Beckmann 1978, Balthus 1980, Narrative Paintings 1979, English Romanesque 1984, Kiff 1986, Domenico Tiepolo 1987, Bhupen Khakhar (monograph) 1998, Bonnard (monograph) 1998, Carnivalesque (catalogue) 2000, Stanley Spencer (catalogue) 2001, Sienese Painting (monograph) 2003; numerous articles on contemporary figurative painting in London Magazine, Artscribe, Times Literary Supplement 1975–. *Leisure interests:* the novels of John Cowper Powys, reading, travel, cinema. *Address:* 62 Myddelton Square, London, EC1, England. *Telephone:* (20) 7837-1933.

HYND, Ronald; British choreographer; b. 22 April 1931, London; s. of William John Hens and Alice Louisa Griffiths; m. Annette Page 1957; one d.;

ed Holloway Coll., numerous wartime emergency schools, England; trained with Marie Rambert 1946; joined Ballet Rambert 1949, Royal Ballet (then known as Sadlers Wells Ballet) 1952 (Prin. Dancer 1959–70); Ballet Dir Bavarian State Opera 1970–73, 1984–86; freelance choreographer; ballets presented by numerous int. ballet cos., including English Nat. Ballet, Royal Sadler's Wells, La Scala Milan, Deutsche Oper Berlin, Vienna State Opera, Houston Ballet, Bavarian State Opera, American Ballet Theater, Australian Ballet, Tokyo Ballet, Canadian Nat. Ballet, Grands Ballets Canadiens, Dutch Nat. Ballet, Northern Ballet, Slovenian Nat. Ballet, South African State Theatre Ballet, Tulsa Ballet Theater, Royal Danish Ballet, Ballet Maggio Musicale, Florence and Pacific Northwest Ballet; TV productions of Merry Widow, Nutcracker and Sanguine Fan. *Works choreographed include:* Three Act Ballets: Merry Widow 1975, The Nutcracker 1976, Rosalinda 1978, Papillon 1979, Le Diable à Quatre 1984, Coppelia 1985, Ludwig II 1986, The Hunchback of Notre Dame 1988, The Sleeping Beauty 1993; one act ballets include: The Fairy's Kiss 1967, Dvorak Variations 1970, Wendekreise 1971, Mozartiana 1972, Das Telefon 1972, Marco Polo 1975, Sanguine Fan 1976, La Chatte 1978, La Valse 1981, Seasons 1982, Scherzo Capriccioso 1982, Fanfare 1985, Liaisons Amoureuses 1989, Ballade 1989. *Choreography for:* Galileo (film) 1974, La Traviata (BBC TV) 1974, Amahl and Night Visitors (BBC TV) 1975, ice ballets for John Curry 1977, The Sound of Music 1981, Camelot 1982, Sylvia for Princess Diana's 30th Birthday Banquet 1992. *Leisure interests:* gardens, music, travel. *Address:* Fern Cottage, Upper Somerton, Bury St Edmunds, Suffolk, IP29 4ND, England. *Telephone:* (1284) 789284. *Fax:* (1284) 789284.

HYNDE, Chrissie; American singer, songwriter and musician; b. 7 Sept. 1951, Akron, Ohio; one d. with Ray Davies; m.1st Jim Kerr (divorced); one d.; m. 2nd Lucho Brieva 1999; contrib. to New Musical Express; Co-Founder Chrissie Hynde and the Pretenders 1978, singer, songwriter and guitarist, new band formed 1983; tours in Britain, Europe and USA; platinum and gold discs in USA. *Singles include:* Stop Your Sobbing (debut) 1978, Kid 1979, Brass in Pocket 1979, I Go to Sleep 1982, Back on the Chain Gang 1982, Middle of the Road 1984, Thin Line Between Love and Hate, Don't Get Me Wrong, Hymn to Her. *Albums include:* Pretenders (debut) 1980, Pretenders II 1981, Extended Play 1981, Learn to Crawl 1985, Get Close 1986, The Singles 1987.

HYNES, Garry, BA; Irish theatre director; b. 10 June 1953, Ballaghaderreen, Co. Roscommon; d. of Oliver Hynes and Carmel Hynes; ed Dominican Coll., Galway, Univ. Coll. Galway; f. Druid Theatre Co. 1975, Artistic Dir 1994–; Artistic Dir Abbey Theatre, Dublin 1990–94; Hon. LLD (Nat. Council for Educ. Awards) 1987, (Nat. Univ. of Ireland) 1998; Fringe First, Edinburgh 1980, Harveys Award for Best Dir 1983, Time Out (London) Award for Direction 1988, People of the Year Award 1989. *Plays directed:* at Druid Theatre include The Playboy of the Western World, Conversations on a Homecoming 1985, Bailegangaire (with Siobhán McKenna) 1985, The Beauty Queen of Leenane (Tony Award for Best Dir. 1998), The Leenane Trilogy; plays directed at Abbey Theatre include A Whistle in the Dark, The Plough and the Stars 1991, The Power of Darkness, Famine, Portia Coughlan 1996, The Leenane Trilogy 1997, Mr Peter's Connections 1998; directed RSC,

Stratford and London 1988, 1989. *Leisure interests:* books, poker, food. *Address:* Druid Theatre Company, Chapel Lane, Galway, Ireland. *Telephone:* (91) 568617.

HYNES, Samuel, DFC, PhD, FRSL; American educator and author; b. 29 Aug. 1924, Chicago; s. of Samuel Lynn and Margaret (Turner) Hynes; m. Elizabeth Igleheart 1944; two d.; ed Univ. of Minnesota, Columbia Univ.; served USMCR 1943–46, 1952–53; mem. faculty, Swarthmore Coll. 1949–68, Prof. of English Literature 1965–68; Prof. of English Northwestern Univ., Evanston, Ill. 1968–76, Princeton Univ. 1976–90, Woodrow Wilson Prof. of Literature 1978–90, Prof. Emer. 1990–; Fulbright Fellow 1953–54; Guggenheim Fellow 1959–60, 1981–82; Bollingen Fellow 1964–65; American Council of Learned Socs. Fellow 1969, 1985–86; Nat. Endowment for Humanities Sr Fellow 1973–74, 1977–78. *Publications:* The Pattern of Hardy's Poetry (Explicator Award 1962), William Golding 1964, The Edwardian Turn of Mind 1968, Edwardian Occasions 1972, The Auden Generation 1976, Flights of Passage: Reflections of a World War Two Aviator 1988; Ed.: Further Speculations by T. E. Hulme 1955, The Author's Craft and Other Critical Writings of Arnold Bennett 1968, Romance and Realism 1979, Complete Poetical Works of Thomas Hardy, Vol. I 1982, Vol. II 1984, Vol. III 1985, Vols IV, V 1995, Thomas Hardy 1984, A War Imagined 1990, Complete Short Fiction of Joseph Conrad (Vol. I–III) 1992, (Vol. IV) 1993, The Soldiers' Tale 1997 (Robert F. Kennedy Book Award 1998), The Growing Seasons 2003. *Address:* 130 Moore Street, Princeton, NJ 08540, USA.

HYTNER, Nicholas Robert, MA; British theatre director; b. 7 May 1956, Manchester; s. of Benet A. Hytner and Joyce Myers; ed Manchester Grammar School and Trinity Hall, Cambridge; staff producer, ENO 1978–80; Assoc. Dir Royal Exchange Theatre, Manchester 1985–89; Assoc. Dir Royal Nat. Theatre 1989–97, Artistic Dir 2003–; Laurence Olivier Award for Xerxes 1985, Evening Standard Opera Award 1985, Evening Standard Best Dir Award 1989, Tony Award Best Dir of a Musical (for Carousel) 1994. *Theatre and opera productions include:* Wagner's Rienzi (ENO) 1983, Tippett's King Priam (Kent Opera) 1984, Handel's Xerxes (ENO), The Scarlet Pimpernel (Chichester Festival) 1985, As You Like It, Edward II, The Country Wife, Schiller's Don Carlos, (Royal Exchange) 1986, Handel's Giulio Cesare (Paris Opera), Measure for Measure (RSC) 1987, Tippett's The Knot Garden (Royal Opera), The Magic Flute (ENO), The Tempest (RSC) 1988, The Marriage of Figaro (Geneva Opera), Joshua Sobol's Ghetto (Nat. Theatre), Miss Saigon (Theatre Royal, Drury Lane) 1989, King Lear (RSC) 1990, The Wind in the Willows (Nat. Theatre) 1990, Volpone (Almeida) 1990, The Madness of George III (Nat. Theatre) 1991, The Recruiting Officer (Nat. Theatre) 1992, Carousel (Nat. Theatre) 1992, The Importance of Being Earnest, Aldwych 1993, Don Giovanni (Bavarian State Opera) 1994, The Cunning Little Vixen (Paris) 1995, The Cripple of Inishmaan 1997, The Crucible 1997, The Lady in the Van 1999, Cressida 2000, Orpheus Descending 2000, The Winter's Tale (Nat. Theatre) 2001, Mother Clap's Molly House (Nat. Theatre) 2001, Sweet Smell of Success (Broadway) 2002. *Films:* The Madness of King George 1994, The Crucible 1996, The Object of My Affection 1998. *Address:* c/o Royal National Theatre, South Bank, London, SE1 9PX, England.

I

IACOCCA, Lee A.; American automobile executive; b. 15 Oct. 1924, Allentown, Pa; s. of Nicola Iacocca and Antoinette Perrotto; m. 1st Mary McCleary 1956 (died 1983); two d.; m. 2nd Peggy Johnson 1986 (divorced); m. 3rd Darrien Earle 1991; ed Lehigh and Princeton Univs.; with Ford Motor Co. 1946; District Sales Man., Washington 1956; Ford Div. Truck Marketing Man. 1956; Car Marketing Man. 1957; Vice-Pres. and Gen. Man., Ford Div. 1960–65; Vice-Pres. Car and Truck Group 1965; Exec. Vice-Pres., North American Automotive Operations 1967; Exec. Vice-Pres., Ford Motor Co. and Pres. Ford North American Automotive Operations 1969–70, Pres. Ford Motor Co. 1970–78; Pres., COO, Chrysler Corpn 1978–79, Chair. 1979–93, CEO 1979–93, Dir –1993; Prin. Iacocca Partners 1994–; Acting Chair. Kro Koo Roo Inc. 1998–; Pres. Iacocca Assocs., LA 1994–; f. EV Global Motors; Fellow Princeton Univ.; mem. Soc. Automotive Engineers; Chair. of Presidential Comm. to restore Statue of Liberty 1982–86; mem. Nat. Acad. of Eng 1986–; Dr. hc (Muhlenberg Coll., Babson Inst.); Detroit's Man of the Year 1982; Jefferson Award 1985; Kt, Order of Labour (Italy) 1989. *Publications:* Iacocca, An Autobiography (with William Novak) 1984, Talking Straight 1988. *Address:* EV Global Motors, 10900 Wilshire Boulevard, Suite 310, Los Angeles, CA 90024, USA (Office).

IACOVOU, Georgios, MA, MSc; Cypriot politician and diplomatist; b. 19 July 1938, Peristeronopigi; s. of Kyriacos Iacovou and Maria Michalopoulou; m. Jennifer Bradley 1963; one s. three d.; ed Greek Gymnasium for Boys, Famagusta and Univ. of London; Eng, Cyprus Building and Road Construction Corpn Ltd 1960–61; Man. Electron Ltd, Nicosia 1961–63; with Operations Research and Finance Depts., British Railways Bd, London 1964–68; Sr Consultant (Man.), Price Waterhouse Assocs., London 1968–72; Dir Cyprus Productivity Centre, Nicosia 1972–76; Dir Special Service for Care and Rehabilitation of Displaced Persons 1974–76; Chief, E African Region, UNHCR, Geneva 1976–79; Amb. to FRG (also Accred to Austria and Switzerland) 1979–83; Dir-Gen. Ministry of Foreign Affairs Jan.–Sept. 1983; Minister of Foreign Affairs 1983–93, 2003–; Presidential Cand. 1998; Pres. Cttee of Ministers, Council of Europe 1983; participated in Commonwealth Heads of State and Govt Confs. in Delhi 1983, Bahamas 1985, Vancouver 1987, Kuala Lumpur 1989 and non-Aligned Summit, Harare 1986, Belgrade 1989; Chair. Ministerial Conf. of Non-Aligned Movt, Nicosia 1988; Hon. MA (Boston); Grosses Verdienstkreuz mit Stern und Schulterband (FRG), Grosses Goldenes Ehrenzeichen (Austria), Grand Cross, Order of Phoenix (Greece), Grand Cross of the Order of Isabella the Catholic (Spain), Grand Cross of the Order of Honour (Greece), Order of the Flag with Sash (Yugoslavia), Order of the Repub. First Class (Egypt), Grand Cross of Infante D. Henrique (Portugal). *Address:* Ministry of Foreign Affairs, 18–19 Dem. Severis Avenue, 1447 Nicosia, Cyprus. *Telephone:* (22) 300600. *Fax:* (22) 665778. *E-mail:* minforeign1@cytanet.com.cy. *Website:* www.mfa.gov.cy.

IAKOVOS, Archbishop; American ecclesiastic; b. 29 July 1911, Island of Imbros, Turkey; s. of Maria and Athanasios Coucouzis; baptismal name Demetrios; ed Theological School of Halki, Istanbul; Deacon 1934; ordained priest in Lowell, Mass., USA 1940; Dean Cathedral of the Annunciation, Boston 1942–54; Bishop of Malta 1954; Rep. of Patriarch of Constantinople to World Council of Churches, Geneva 1955; Primate, Archbishop, Greek Orthodox Church in N and S. America 1959–96; Exarch, Ecumenical Patriarchate of Constantinople; Pres. World Council of Churches 1959–68; fmr Dean Holy Cross Orthodox Theological School, Mass., now Pres.; numerous hon. degrees; Presidential Medal of Freedom 1980, Inaugural Award New York Univ. 1981, Great Cross of the Holy Sepulchre, Patriarchate of Jerusalem 1982, Gold Medal of Acad. of Athens 1985.

IANNELLA, Egidio, CPN; Argentine banker and consultant; b. 16 May 1921, Buenos Aires; s. of Antonio and Carmen Bárbaro; m. Isabel Rodríguez; one s. one d.; ed Escuela Nacional de Comercio, Buenos Aires, Univ. Nacional de Buenos Aires and Centro de Estudios Monetarios Latinoamericanos, Mexico; various positions in Banco Central de la República Argentina 1939–56, Gen. Man. 1967–69, Pres. 1969–70, 1981–82, 1989, Dir 1978–81; Gen. Man. Banco Argentino de Comercio 1956–66; Exec. Vice-Pres. Banco Federal Argentino 1971–77; Pres. Banco Nacional de Desarrollo 1978–81; Pres. Asociación Latinoamericana de Instituciones Financieras de Desarrollo (ALIDE), Lima 1979–81, 1989–90; mem. Bd Bolsa de Comercio de Buenos Aires 1992–98, Counsellor, Foundation of the Bolsa 1993–99; Prof., Pontificia Univ. Católica Argentina 1966–95; Pres. VISA Argentina SA 1983–99; Dir VISA Int., Miami, USA 1985–99; Pres. Rotary Club of Buenos Aires 1991–92. *Address:* Corrientes Ave., No 1437, 11th floor, Buenos Aires, Argentina. *Telephone:* (541) 325-1403; (541) 325-3091. *Fax:* (541) 325-3091.

IBARRETXE MARKUARTU, Juan José, BEcons; Spanish politician; b. 15 March 1957, Llodio, Alava; ed Llodio Secondary School, Univ. of the Basque Country; mem. Partido Nacionalista Vaso (PNV); Mayor of Llodio 1983–87; Pres. Alava Prov. Parl. 1986–91; mem. Basque Parl., Chair. Econ. and Budgetary Comm. 1986–90, 1991–94; Vice-Pres. Basque Govt and Minister for Inland Revenue and Public Admin 1995–98, Pres. June 1998–; fmr mem. Univ. of the Basque Country Social Council. *Address:* Palacio de Ajuria-Enea, Paseo Fray Francisco 5, 01007 Vitoria-Gasteiz (Office); Partido Nacionalista Vasco, Ibáñez de Bilbao 17 (Sabin Etxea), 48001 Bilbao, Spain. *Telephone:* (45) 017900 (Office). *Fax:* (45) 017832 (Office). *E-mail:* prensa-comun@ej-gv.es (Office); prensa@eaj-pnv.com (Office). *Website:* www.eaj.pnv.com (Office); www.euskadi.net (Office).

IBBS, Sir (John) Robin, Kt, KBE, MA, DSc, LLD, FCIB; British industrialist; b. 21 April 1926, Birmingham; s. of the late Prof. T. L. Ibbs and of Marjorie Bell; m. Iris Barbara Hall 1952; one d.; ed Gresham's School, Upper Canada Coll., Toronto, Univ. of Toronto, Trinity Coll., Cambridge and Lincoln's Inn; called to Bar 1952; Instructor Lt, RN 1947–49; C. A. Parsons & Co. Ltd 1949–51; joined ICI 1952, held various Eng, tech., production, commercial and gen. man. appointments at Head Office, Gen. Chemicals Div. and Metals Div.; Man. Planning Dept, Imperial Metal Industries Ltd 1969–74, Exec. Dir 1972–74, Non-Exec. Dir 1974–76; Gen. Man. Planning, ICI 1974–76, Exec. Dir 1976–80, 1982–88; Dir ICI Americas Inc. 1976–80; Dir ICI Australia Ltd 1982–87; Dir Lloyds Bank PLC 1985–97, Deputy Chair. 1988–93, Chair. 1993–97; Chair. Lloyds TSB Group PLC 1995–97; Chair. Lloyds Merchant Bank Holdings Ltd 1989–92; mem. Industrial Devt Advisory Bd, Dept of Industry 1978–80, Head Cent. Policy Review Staff, Cabinet Office 1980–82; mem. Council, Chemical Industries Assen 1976–80, 1982–88, Vice-Pres. 1983–87, Hon. mem. 1987; mem. Governing Body and Council, British Nat. Cttee, ICC 1976–80, Chair. Finance and Gen. Purposes Cttee 1976–80; mem. Top Salaries Review Body 1983–88; mem. Council, Royal Inst. of Int. Affairs, Chatham House 1983–89; mem. Court, Cranfield Inst. of Tech. 1983–88; Adviser to the Prime Minister on Efficiency and Effectiveness in Govt 1983–88; Trustee and Deputy Chair. Isaac Newton Trust 1988–99; Leader of review of House of Commons services 1990; Chair. Council, Univ. Coll., London 1989–95; mem. Council Foundation for Science and Tech. 1997–; Hon. Fellow Univ. Coll., London 1993; Hon. DSc (Bradford) 1986; Hon. LLD (Bath) 1993. *Leisure interests:* walking, natural history, gardening, social history, music and arts. *Address:* c/o Lloyds TSB Group, 71 Lombard Street, London, EC3P 3BS, England. *Telephone:* (20) 7626-1500.

IBERS, James Arthur, PhD; American professor of chemistry and educationist; b. 9 June 1930, Los Angeles; s. of Max Ibers and Esther Ibers (née Imerman); m. Joyce Audrey Henderson 1951; one s. one d.; ed Calif. Inst. of Tech.; NSF Post-doctoral Fellow, Melbourne, Australia 1954–55; chemist, Shell Devt Co. 1955–61, Brookhaven Nat. Lab. 1961–64; mem. Faculty Northwestern Univ. 1964–, Prof. of Chem. 1964–85, Charles E. and Emma H. Morrison Prof. of Chem. 1986–; mem. NAS, American Acad. of Arts and Sciences, ACS, American Crystallographic Assen; ACS Inorganic Chem. Award 1978, ACS Distinguished Service Award 1992, ACS Pauling Medal 1994, Distinguished Alumni Award, Calif. Inst. of Tech. 1997, American Crystallographic Assen Buerger Award 2002. *Address:* Department of Chemistry, Northwestern University, Evanston, IL 60208-3113 (Office); 2657 Orrington Avenue, Evanston, IL 60201-1760, USA (Home). *Telephone:* (847) 491-5449 (Office); (847) 869-6318 (Home). *Fax:* (847) 491-2976. *E-mail:* ibers@chem.northwestern.edu.

IBRAGIMBEKOV, Maksud Mamed Ibragim ogli; Azerbaijani/Russian writer, scriptwriter and playwright; b. 1935, Baku; s. of Mamed Ibragim Ibragimbekov and Fatima Alekper-kyzy Meshadibekova; m. Anna Yuryebna Ibragimbekova (née Gerulaitis); one s.; ed Baku Polytech. Inst., High Scenario and Directoral Courses, Moscow; Supt Aztyazhpromstroi 1960–62; freelance scriptwriter, theatre Dir 1964–; mem. USSR Union of Writers 1965–; mem. Azerbaijan Parl. 1985–(2005); Pres. PEN-CLUB of Azerbaijan 1991–; Chair. Nobility Ass. of Azerbaijan; Order of Labour Red Banner 1981, Order of Glory of Azerbaijan Repub. 1995; State Prize of Azerbaijan Repub. 1975, People's Writer of Azerbaijan 1998. *Films:* Latest Night of Childhood, Djabishmuallim, Who is Going to Travel to Truskavets?, Latest Interview. *Plays:* Mesozoic Story (Moscow Maly Theatre) 1975, Death of All the Good (Leningrad Theatre of Young Spectator) 1978, Men for Young Woman (Dramatic Theatre) 1992, The Oil Boom is Smiling on Everyone 2002. *Television:* Gold Voyage 1993, The History with Happy End 1998. *Publications:* Who is Going to Travel to Truskavets?, There Was Never a Better Brother, Let Him Stay With Us; novels and prose in magazines and separate editions. *Leisure interests:* travelling, gardening. *Address:* 28 Boyuk Qala str., 370004 Baku (Office); 38 Kutkashenli str., 370006 Baku, Azerbaijan (Home). *Telephone:* (12) 929843 (Office); (12) 975300 (Home). *Fax:* (12) 928459 (Office). *E-mail:* maksud@planet-az.com (Office); Maksud@azeurotel.com (Home).

IBRAGIMBEKOV, Rustam Mamed Ibragimovich; Azerbaijani/Russian film scriptwriter and writer; b. 5 Feb. 1939, Baku; s. of Mamed Ibragim Ibragimbekov and Fatima Alekper-kyzy Meshadibekova; m. Shokhrat Soltan-kyzy Ibragimbekova; one s., one d.; ed Azerbaijan State Inst. of Oil and Gas; Chair. Confed. Unions of Cinematographers of CIS and Baltic States; Sec. Union of Cinematographers of Russian Fed.; Chair. Jewish Film Festival in Moscow; Chair. Union of Cinematographers of Azerbaijan; mem. European Cinema Acad. Felix, American Acad. of Cinema Oscar; USSR State Prize 1981, State Prizes of Russian Fed. 1993, 1998, 1999, 2000, State Prize of Azerbaijan SSR 1980, Comsomol Prize 1979, Order for Service to Motherland, Commdr des Arts et des Lettres. *Film scripts include:* In This Young Town 1971, White Sun of the Desert 1971, Then I Said No 1974, Heart... Heart 1976, Country House for One Family 1978, Strategy of Risk 1979, Interrogation 1979, Mystery of Vessel Watch 1981, Birthday 1983, In Front of the Closed Door 1985, Save Me, My Talisman 1986, Free Fall, Other Life 1987, Cathedral of Air 1989, Hitchhiking, Taxi-Blues (producer) 1989, Seven Days After Murder, To See Paris and To Die 1990, Duba-Duba (producer) 1990, Urga Territory of Love (producer) 1992, Destroyed Bridges (also producer) 1993, Tired with the Sun 1994, The Man Who Tried (jtly) 1997, Barber of Siberia, Family (also dir and producer) 1998, East–West 1999; Mysteria 2000. *Plays:* 15 plays produced including A Woman Behind a Closed Door, Funeral in California, A House on the Sand, Like a Lion. *Publications:* 10 books and collections of stories including Ultimatum 1983, Woken Up with a Smile 1985, Country House 1988, Selected Stories 1989, Solar Plexus 1996. *Address:* Lermontova str. 3, Apt. 54, 370006 Baku, Azerbaijan (Home). *Telephone:* (12) 926313 (Home).

IBRAHIM, Abdul Latif, PhD; Bangladeshi professor of veterinary physiology; ed Bangladesh Agriculture Univ., Univ. of Hawai and Univ. of California; lecturer Faculty of Veterinary Medicine and Animal Science, Univ. of Pertanian, Malaysia 1973, later Dean and Prof.; known for research on Newcastle Disease; Fellow Islamic Acad. of Sciences, Malaysia Acad. of Sciences, Svon Brohult Award, First Int. Science Award (jtly.), Malaysia. *Publications:* over 120 Publs on animal science. *Address:* Islamic Academy of Sciences, P.O. Box 830036, Amman, Jordan (Office). *Telephone:* 5522104 (Office). *Fax:* 5511803 (Office).

IBRAHIM, Maj. Abu al-Qassim Mohammed; Sudanese politician and army officer; b. 1937, Omdurman; ed Khartoum Secondary School and Military Coll.; commissioned 1961; mem. Revolutionary Council 1969; Minister of Local Govt 1969–70; Asst Prime Minister for Services 1970; Minister of Interior 1970–71, of Health and Social Welfare 1971–73, of Agric., Food and Natural Resources 1974–76; mem. Political Bureau of Sudanese Socialist Union 1971–79, Deputy Sec.-Gen. 1975–76, Sec.-Gen. 1976–79; Commr for Khartoum Prov. 1976–79; First Vice-Pres. of Sudan 1977–79.

IBRAHIM, Encik Anwar bin, BA; Malaysian politician; b. 10 Aug. 1947; ed Univ. of Malaya; Pres. UMNO Youth Movt 1982–; Vice-Pres. UMNO 1982–; Head UMNO Permatang Pauh Div. 1982–; Deputy Minister, Prime Minister's Dept 1982; Minister of Sport, Youth and Culture 1983, of Agric. 1984–86, of Educ. 1986–91, of Finance 1991–98; Deputy Prime Minister 1993–98; arrested Sept. 1998; sentenced to six years' imprisonment for corruption April 1999; put on trial for sodomy 1999; sentenced to nine years' imprisonment and banned for 5 years from running for public office after release.

IBRAHIM, Izzat; Iraqi politician; b. 1942, al-Dour Shire; Ed. Voice of the Peasant 1968, Head Supreme Cttee for People's Work 1968–70; Minister of Agrarian Reform 1970–74; Vice-Pres. Supreme Agric. Council 1970–71, Head 1971–79; Minister of Agriculture 1973–74, of the Interior 1974–79; mem. Revolutionary Command Council, Vice-Pres. 1979–2003; Deputy Sec.-Gen. Regional Command of Arab Baath Socialist Party 1979–2003; mem. Nat. Command Arab Baath Socialist Party –2003.

IBRAHIM, Sid Moulay Abdullah; Moroccan politician; b. 1918; ed Ben Youssef Univ., Marrakesh and the Sorbonne, Paris; mem. Istiqlal (Independence) Party 1944–59; mem. Editorial Cttee Al Alam (Istiqlal organ) 1950–52; imprisoned for political reasons 1952–54; Sec. of State for Information and Tourism, First Moroccan Nat. Govt 1955–56; Minister of Labour and Social Affairs 1956–57; Prime Minister and Minister of Foreign Affairs 1958–60; Leader Union Nationale des Forces Populaires 1959–72.

IBRAHIMI, Bedredin, LLB; Macedonian politician and legal administrator; b. 25 Oct. 1952, Mala Recica, nr Tetovo; ed Pristina Univ.; fmr doctor; Sr Officer for Legal Affairs and Sec. of Poloska Kotlina Co., Tetovo Agric. Complex, Belgrade 1976–81; Officer in charge of Gen. Legal Affairs and Sec. Jelak Tetovo Co., Interpromet Complex 1981–89; with Tekom-Tetovo Trade Co. 1990–96; Sec. of Council, Municipality of Tetovo 1997–98; currently Gen. Sec. Democratic Party of Albania (DPA); Deputy Prime Minister of Macedonia 1998–2002, Minister of Labour and Social Welfare 1998–. *Address:* Ministry of Labour and Social Welfare, Dame Gruev 14, 1000 Skopje, Republic of Macedonia (Office). *Telephone:* (2) 117787 (Office). *Fax:* (2) 118242 (Office). *E-mail:* mtsp@mt.net.mk (Office). *Website:* www.mtsp.gov.mk (Office).

IBRAIMOVA, Elmira; Kyrgyzstan diplomatist and economist; b. 13 April 1962, Frunze (now Bishkek); ed Moscow State Univ.; Perm. Rep. to UN 1999–2002. *Address:* c/o Ministry of Foreign Affairs, Razzakova 59, 720050 Bishkek, Kyrgyzstan (Office).

ICAHN, Carl C.; American business executive; b. 1936, Queens; m. Liba Icahn; two c.; ed Princeton Univ. and New York Univ. School of Medicine; apprentice broker, Dreyfus Corpn, New York 1960–63; Options Man. Tessel, Patrick & Co., New York 1963–64; Gruntal & Co. 1964–68; Chair. and Pres. Icahn & Co., New York 1968–; Chair. and CEO ACF Industries Inc., Earth City, Mo. 1984–; Chair. Trans World Airlines Inc. 1986–99. *Address:* ACF Industries, 620 N 2nd Street, Saint Charles, MO 63301, USA (Office).

ICE-T; American rap singer and actor; b. (Tracy Marrow), Newark, NJ; m. Darlene Ortiz; one c. *Albums:* Rhyme Pays 1987, The Iceberg/Freedom of Speech, Just Watch What You Say 1989, O.G. Original Gangster 1991, Havin' a "T" Party (with King Tee) 1991, Body Count 1992, Home Invasion 1993, The Classic Collection 1993, Born Dead (with Body Count) 1994, 7th Deadly Sin 1999. *Films:* Breakin' 1984, New Jack City 1991, Ricochet 1991, Trespass 1992, Surviving the Game 1994, Tank Girl 1995, Johnny Mnemonic 1995, Below Utopia, Final Voyage 1999, Corrupt 1999, Leprechaun 5 2000, Sonic

Impact 2000, The Alternate 2000, Hip Hop 2000 2001, Out Kold 2001. *Publication:* The Ice Opinion 1994. *Address:* Priority Records, 6430 W Sunset Blvd., Los Angeles, CA 90028, USA. *Website:* www.mcicet.com (Office).

ICHIKAWA, Kon; Japanese film director; b. 1915; ed Ichioka Commercial School, Osaka. *Films include:* Poo-San 1953, A Billionaire 1954, The Heart 1954, Punishment Room 1955, The Burmese Harp 1956, The Men of Tohoku 1956, Conflagration 1958, Fires on the Plain 1959, The Key 1959, Bonchi 1960, Her Brother 1960, The Sin 1961, Being Two Isn't Easy 1962, The Revenge of Yuki-No-Jo 1963, Alone on the Pacific 1963, Tokyo Olympiad 1964, Seishun 1970, To Love Again 1971, The Wanderers 1973, Visions of Eight (co-Dir) 1973, Wagahai wa Neko de Aru 1975, The Ingunami's 1976, Gokumonto 1977, Joobachi 1978, Byoin-zaka no Kubikukuri no le 1979, Ancient City 1980, The Makioka Sisters 1983, Actress 1987, Fusa 1993, The Forty-Seven Ronin 1994.

IDEI, Nobuyuki; Japanese business executive; m. Teruyo Idei; one d.; ed Waseda Univ., Institut des hautes etudes internationales, Geneva, Switzerland ; joined Sony 1960, est. Sony of France, fmrly Head of Corp. Communications and Brand Image, Pres. and Rep. Dir Sony Corpn 1995–99, Pres. and CEO 1999–2000, Chair. and CEO 2000–; mem. bd General Motors 1999–, Nestlé SA 2001–; Chair. IT Strategy Council (advisory cttee to Japan's Prime Minister) July–Nov. 2000. *Leisure interests:* music, cinema, golf. *Address:* Sony Corporation, 7-35 Kitashinagawa 6-chome, Shinagawa-ku, Tokyo 141-0001, Japan (Office). *Telephone:* (3) 5448-2111. *Fax:* (3) 5448-2244. *Website:* www.sony.com (Office).

IDEMITSU, Yuji; Japanese business executive; b. 1 Jan. 1927, Fukuoka; m. Yoko Idemitsu 1956; two s.; ed Kyushu Teikoku Univ.; joined Idemitsu Kosan Co. 1948, Gen. Man. London Office 1974–77, Man. Dir and Gen. Man. Overseas Operations Dept 1981–83, Sr Man. Dir & Gen. Man. Chiba Refinery 1985–86, Exec. Vice-Pres. 1986–93, Pres. 1993–98; mem. Petroleum Asscn of Japan (Pres. 1995–), Fed. Econ. Orgs. (mem. Exec. Bd 1993–). *Leisure interests:* reading, golf, calligraphy. *Address:* c/o Idemitsu Kosan Co. Ltd, 1-1, 3 chome, Marunouchi, Chiyoda-ku, Tokyo 100, Japan. *Telephone:* (3) 3213-3110. *Fax:* (3) 3213-9340.

IDRAC, Anne-Marie, LenD; French politician and civic administrator; b. 27 July 1951, Saint-Brieuc, Côtes-du-Nord; d. of André Colin and Marguerite Médecin (née Laurent); m. Francis Idrac 1974; four d.; ed Univ. of Paris–II, Ecole Nat. d'Admin; civic administrator, Dept of Building and Public Works, Ministry of Supply 1974–77; Chargée de Mission to the Prefect of the Midi–Pyrenees 1977–79; Tech. Councillor in the Cabinets of Marcel Cavaillé (Sec. of State for Housing) and Michel d'Ornano (Minister of the Environment) 1979–81; Deputy Dir, Ministry of the Quality of Life 1981–83; Deputy Dir of Finance and Judicial Affairs 1983–87; Chief of Service and Deputy Dir, Dept of Construction, Ministry of Supply 1987–90, Dir-Gen. Public Devt in Cergy–Pontoise 1990–93; Dir. of Territorial Transport (DTT) 1993–95; Sec. of State for Transport 1995–97; elected Deputy of Yvelines (Union pour la démocratie française—UDF) June 1997; Sec.-Gen. of Force Démocrate; mem. Regional Council Ile-de-France 1998–; Pres. Mouvement Européen France 1999–; Vice-Pres., then Sec.-Gen. UDF 2001–; Pres. Régie Autonome des Transports Parisiens (RATP) 2002–; Chevalier, Ordre nat. du Mérite; Nat. Foundation for Public Enterprise Award 1977. *Address:* Régie Autonome des Transports Parisiens (RATP), 54 quai de la Rapée, 75599 Paris Cédex 12, France (Office). *Telephone:* 1-44-68-20-20 (Office). *Fax:* 1-44-68-31-60 (Office). *E-mail:* am.idrac@wanadoo.fr (Office). *Website:* www.ratp.fr (Office).

IDRIS, Kamil E., BA, PhD; Sudanese diplomatist and lawyer; ed Univs. of Cairo, Khartoum, Ohio and Geneva and Inst. of Public Admin., Khartoum; part-time journalist El-Ayam and El-Sahafa newspapers in Sudan 1971–79; lecturer Univ. of Cairo 1976–77, Ohio Univ. 1978, Univ. of Khartoum 1986; Asst Dir Arab Dept, Ministry of Foreign Affairs, Khartoum 1977–78, Asst Dir Research Dept Jan.–June 1978, Deputy Dir Legal Dept July–Dec. 1978; mem. Perm. Mission of Sudan to UN Office, Geneva 1979–82; Vice-Consul of Sudan, Switzerland 1979–82; Sr Program Officer, Devt Cooperation and External Relations Bureau for Africa, WIPO 1982–85; Dir Devt Cooperation and External Relations Bureau for Arab and Cen. and Eastern European Countries 1985–94, Deputy Dir-Gen. WIPO 1994–97, Dir-Gen. Nov. 1997–; mem. UN Int. Law Comm. (ILC) 1991–96 (Vice-Chair. 45th session 1993); served on numerous cttees. of int. orgs. including WHO, ILO, ITU, UNHCR, OAU, Group of 77 etc. and Sudanese del. to numerous int. and regional confs.; Prof. of Public Int. Law, Univ. of Khartoum; mem. African Jurists Asscn; Scholars and Researchers State Gold Medal (Sudan) 1983, Scholars and Researchers Gold Medal, Egyptian Acad. of Scientific Research and Tech. 1985. *Publications include:* State Responsibility in International Law 1977, North-South Insurance Relations: The Unequal Exchange 1984, The Law of Non-navigational Uses of International Water Courses; the ILC's draft articles: An Overview 1995, The Theory of Source and Target in Child Psychology 1996 and articles on law, economics, jurisprudence and aesthetics in newspapers and periodicals. *Address:* World Intellectual Property Organization, 34 chemin des Colombettes, 1211 Geneva 20, Switzerland (Office). *Telephone:* (22) 3389111 (Office). *Fax:* (22) 7335428 (Office). *E-mail:* wipo.mail@wipo.int (Office). *Website:* www.wipo.int (Office).

IDRISOV, Yerlan Abilfaizovich; Kazakhstan politician and diplomatist; b. 28 April 1959, Karkalinsk; m.; three c.; ed Moscow Inst. of Int. Relations, Diplomatic Acad., USSR Ministry of Foreign Affairs; rep. for Tyzahpromexport, Pakistan 1981–85; mem. of staff Ministry of Foreign Affairs 1985–90, trainee USSR Embassy, India 1991–92; First Sec. Perm. Mission to UN 1992–95; Head American Dept Kazakhstan Foreign Ministry 1995–96, Asst to Pres. on Int. Issues 1996–97; First Deputy Minister of Foreign Affairs 1997–99, 1999–2002, Minister Feb.–Oct. 1999; Amb. to UK 2002–. *Address:* Embassy of Kazakhstan, 33 Thurloe Square, London, SW7 2SD, England (Office). *Telephone:* (20) 7581-4646 (Office). *Fax:* (20) 7584-8481 (Office).

IEHSI, Ieske K., Noahs Pingelap (Traditional Leader), MPA; Micronesian politician; b. 4 Jan. 1955, Pingelap Atoll; five c.; ed Harvard Univ., USA; Asst Chief Clerk, Congress of Micronesia 1977–97, Man., Office of the Attorney-Gen. 1980–81; Special Asst to the Pres. 1981–87, Chief of Staff, Exec. Office of the Pres. 1987–92; Deputy Sec. of the Dept of Foreign Affairs 1997–2001, Sec. of Foreign Affairs March 2001–. *Address:* Department of Foreign Affairs, P.O.B. PS-123, Palikir, Pohnpei, Eastern Caroline Islands, FM 96941, Federated States of Micronesia (Office). *Telephone:* (691) 320-2641 (Office). *Fax:* (691) 320-2933 (Office). *E-mail:* foreignaffairs@mail.fm (Office).

IENG SARY; Cambodian politician; m. Khieu Thirith; ed Paris; fmr teacher; active in left-wing movts. and forced to flee Phnom Penh 1963; prominent in Khmer Rouge insurgent Movt 1963–75; Khmer Rouge liaison officer to Royal Govt of Nat. Union of Cambodia (GRUNC) in exile 1971–75; mem. Politburo Nat. United Front of Cambodia (FUNC) 1970–79; Second Deputy Prime Minister of Democratic Kampuchea (now Cambodia) with special responsibility for Foreign Affairs, GRUNC 1975–79; charged with genocide by Heng Samrin regime and sentenced to death in absentia Aug. 1979; Deputy Prime Minister in charge of Foreign Affairs of Democratic Kampuchean Govt in exile (Khmer Rouge) fighting Vietnamese forces 1979–82; rep. for Finance and Econ. Affairs (in coalition in exile) 1982–92; mem. Co-ordination Cttee Nat. Govt of Cambodia for Finance and Economy 1991; defected from Khmer Rouge Aug. 1996; granted amnesty Sept. 1996.

IGER, Robert A.; American broadcasting executive; b. 1951, New York City; m. Willow Bay 1995; two d. one s.; ed Ithaca Coll.; Studio supervisor ABC-TV 1974–76; various positions ABC-TV Sports 1976–85, Vice-Pres. Programme Planning and Devt 1985–87, Vice-Pres. Programme Planning and Acquisition 1987–88; Exec. Vice-Pres. ABC TV Network Group 1988–99, Pres. 1992–94; Pres. ABC Entertainment 1989–92; Exec. Vice-Pres. Capital Cities/ABC Inc., New York 1993–94, Pres. and COO 1994–96; Pres. ABC Inc., New York 1996–99; Chair. ABC Group 1999–; Pres. The Walt Disney Co., Calif. 1999–; Trustee Ithaca Coll. *Address:* The Walt Disney Co., 5005 Buena Vista Street, Burbank, CA 91521-0001, USA (Office).

IGLESIAS, Enrique; Spanish singer and songwriter; b. b.8 May 1975, Madrid; s. of Julio Iglesias; sings in English and Spanish; numerous tours; Grammy Award 1997; Eight Premios Los Nuestro; Billboard Awards, Artist of the Year, Album of the Year 1997; ASCAP Award, Songwriter of the Year 1998; American Music Award, Favourite Latin Artist 2002; Platinum and Gold discs. *Recordings include:* albums: Enrique Iglesias 1996, Vivir 1997, Cosas Del Amor 1998, Enrique 1999, Escape 2001, Quizás 2002; singles: Experienca Religiosa, No Llores Por Mi, Bailamos (No. 1 USA) 1999, Be With You (No. 1 USA) 2000, Hero (No. 1 UK) 2002. *Address:* Interscope Records, 2220 Colorado Avenue, Santa Monica, CA 90404, USA (Office). *Website:* www .enriqueiglesias.com (Office).

IGLESIAS, Enrique V.; Uruguayan international official; b. 26 July 1931, Asturias, Spain; s. of Isabel García de Iglesias; ed Univ. de la República, Montevideo; held several positions including Prof. Agregado, Faculty of Political Economy, Prof. of Econ. Policy and Dir Inst. of Econs, Univ. de la República, Montevideo 1952–67; Man. Dir Unión de Bancos del Uruguay 1954; Technical Dir Nat. Planning Office of Uruguay 1962–66; Pres. (Gov.), Banco Cent. del Uruguay 1966–68; Chair. Council, Latin American Inst. for Econ. and Social Planning (ILPES), UN 1967–72, Interim Dir Gen. 1977–78; Head, Advisory Mission on Planning, Govt of Venezuela 1970; Adviser UN Conf. on Human Environment 1971–72; Exec. Sec. Econ. Comm. for Latin America and the Caribbean (ECLAC) 1972–85; Minister of External Affairs 1985–88; Pres. Inter-American Devt Bank (IDB) 1988– (re-elected 1997); currently Pres. of Soc. for Int. Devt; Acting Dir-Gen. Latin American Inst. for Econ. and Social Planning 1973–78; Pres, Third World Forum 1973–76; mem. Steering Cttee, Soc. for Int. Devt 1973–92, Pres. 1989, Selection Cttee, Third World Prize 1979–82; Sec.-Gen. UN Conf. on New and Renewable Sources of Energy Feb.–Aug. 1981; Chair. UN Inter-Agency Group on Devt of Renewable Sources of Energy; mem. North-South Round Table on Energy; Chair. Energy Advisory Panel, Brundtland Comm. 1984–86; Hon. LLD (Liverpool Univ., UK) 1987, Hon. PhD (Univ. de Guadalajara, Mexico) 1994, (Candido Mendes Univ., Rio de Janeiro) 1994; Prince of Asturias Award 1982, UNESCO Pablo Picasso Award 1997; Order of Rio Branco, Grand Cross (Brazil), Grand Cross Silver Plaque, Nat. Order of Juan Mora Fernandez (Costa Rica), Commdr Legion of Honour, Commdr des Arts and des Lettres 1999 (France), Grand Cross of Isobel the Catholic (Spain); numerous other foreign decorations. *Leisure interests:* music, art. *Address:* Inter-American Development Bank, 1300 New York Avenue, NW, Washington, DC 20577, USA (Office). *Telephone:* (202) 623-1000 (Office). *Fax:* (202) 623-3096 (Office). *Website:* www .idab.org (Office).

IGNARRO, Louis J., PhD; American scientist; b. 31 May 1941, Brooklyn; ed Columbia Univ., Univ. of Minnesota; Postdoctoral Fellow, NIH 1966–68; Prof. Dept of Molecular and Medical Pharmacology, Univ. of Calif. at LA, School of Medicine; mem. NAS; Nobel Prize for Medicine (jtly.) 1998. *Publications:* numerous articles in scientific journals. *Address:* School of Medicine, Uni-

versity of California at Los Angeles, Department of Molecular and Medical Pharmacology, 23-315 CHS, 10833 Le Conte Avenue, Los Angeles, CA 90095-1735, USA (Office).

IGNATENKO, Vitaly Nikitich; Russian journalist; b. 19 April 1941, Sochi; m. Svetlana Ignatenko; one s.; ed Moscow Univ.; , corresp., Deputy Ed.-in-C. Komsomolskaya Pravda 1963–75; Deputy Dir-Gen. TASS (USSR Telegraph Agency) 1975–78; Deputy Head of Int. Information Section, CPSU Cen. Cttee 1978–86; Ed.-in-C. Novoe Vremya 1986–90; Asst to fmr Pres. Gorbachev, Head of Press Service 1990–91; Dir-Gen. Agency ITAR-TASS 1991–; Deputy Chair. Council of Ministers 1995–97; Pres., Chair. of Bd Russian Public TV (ORT) 1998–; Pres. World Asscn of Russian Press; mem. Int. Acad. of Information Science, Russian Fed. Comm. on UNESCO Affairs, Union of Russian Journalists, Union of Russian Cinematographers; Lenin Prize 1978, Prize of USSR Journalists' Union 1975; Order of the Friendship of Peoples (twice) 1996, Order of Merit to the Fatherland 1999. *Publications:* several books and more than 30 film scripts. *Leisure interest:* tennis. *Address:* ITAR-TASS, Tverskoy blvd 10, 103009 Moscow, Russia. *Telephone:* (095) 229-79-25. *Fax:* (095) 203-31-80.

IGNATIUS, David; American journalist, editor and novelist; b. 1950, Cambridge, Mass.; m. Eve Ignatius; three d.; ed Harvard Univ. and King's Coll. Cambridge, UK; Ed. The Washington Monthly magazine 1975; reporter The Wall Street Journal 1976–86, assignments included Steelworkers Corresp., Pittsburgh, Senate Corresp., Washington DC, Middle East Corresp., Chief Diplomatic Corresp.; Ed. Sunday Outlook, The Washington Post 1986–90, Foreign Ed. 1990–93, apptd Asst Managing Business Ed. 1993, then Assoc. Ed.; Exec. Ed. International Herald Tribune 2000–03; mem. Washington Post Writer's Group 2003–; Contrib. to The New York Times Magazine, The Atlantic Monthly, Foreign Affairs and The New Republic; Frank Knox Fellow, Harvard–Oxford Univs. 1973–75; Edward Weintal Prize for Diplomatic Reporting 1985, Gerald Loeb Award for Commentary 2000. *Publications include:* Agents of Innocence 1987, SIRO 1991, The Bank of Fear 1994, A Firing Offense 1997, The Sun King 1999. *Address:* Washington Post Writers Group, 1150 15th Street, NW Washington, DC 20071, USA (Office). *Telephone:* (202) 334-6375 (Office). *Fax:* (202) 334-5669 (Office). *E-mail:* writersgrp@ washpost.com. (Office). *Website:* www.postwritersgroup.com (Office).

IGNATIUS ZAKKA I IWAS, His Holiness Patriarch; Iraqi ecclesiastic; b. 21 April 1933, Mosul; ed St Aphrem Syrian Orthodox Theol. Seminary, Mosul, Gen. Theol. Seminary, New York and New York Univ.; ordained 1957; consecrated Metropolitan for Archdiocese of Mosul 1963, transferred to Archdiocese of Baghdad 1969; Patriarch of Antioch and All the East (Supreme Head of Universal Syrian Orthodox Church) 1980–; fmr mem. Iraq Acad. of Science, Arabic Acad. of Jordan; fmr mem. Cen. Cttee WCC; Fellow, Faculty of Syriac Studies, Lutheran School of Theology, Chicago 1981; Hon. DD (Gen. Theol. Seminary, NY). *Publications:* several books and articles. *Address:* Syrian Orthodox Patriarchate, Bab Touma, B.P. 914, Damascus, Syria. *Telephone:* (11) 447036.

IGNATYEV, Sergey Mikhailovich; Russian economist; b. 10 Jan. 1948, St Petersburg; m.; ed Leningrad Inst. of Energy, Moscow State Univ.; asst sr teacher, Leningrad Inst. of Soviet Trade 1978–88; sr teacher, docent Leningrad Inst. of Finance and Econs 1988–91; Deputy Minister of Econs and Finance 1991–92, Deputy Minister of Finance 1992–94, Deputy Minister of Econs 1993–96, First Deputy Minister of Finance 1997–; Deputy Chair., Cen. Bank of Russian Fed. 1992–93; asst to Pres. 1996–97; Hon. Diploma, Russian Govt 1998; 850th Anniversary of Moscow Medal 1997. *Publications:* numerous articles and papers on econs. *Address:* Ministry of Finance, Ilyinka str. 9, 103097 Moscow, Russia (Office). *Telephone:* (095) 913-45-91 (Office); (095) 298-98-74 (Office). *Fax:* (095) 298-51-88 (Office). *Website:* ww.minfin.ru/ org (Office).

IGRUNOV, Vyacheslav Vladimirovich; Russian politician; b. 28 Oct. 1948, Cheznitsky, Zhytomer region, Ukraine; m.; four c.; ed Odessa State Inst. of Nat. Econs; detained by KGB due to his protest against invasion of Soviet army into Czechoslovakia 1968, participated in dissident Movt 1960s, arrested 1975; released after campaign by Andrei Sakharov and Aleksandr Solzhenitsyn (q.v.) in his defence 1977; f. Samizdat Library; mem. staff 20th Century and World (bulletin) 1987; f. ideological Movt Memorial July 1987; f. Moscow Public Information Exchange Bureau M-BIO, newspaper Panorama 1988; Head of Programme Civil Soc. Foundation of Cultural Initiative 1990–92; Head of Analytical Centre in Goscomnats; Dir Int. Inst. of Humanitarian and Political Studies; mem. State Duma (Parl.) 1993–; Deputy Chair. Public Movt Yabloko 1996–2000; mem. faction Yabloko. *Publications:* Problematics of Social Movements, Informal Political Clubs in Moscow 1989, Economic Reform as One of the Sources of National Clashes 1993. *Leisure interests:* reading, gardening, talking with friends. *Address:* International Institute of Humanitarian and Political Studies, Gazetny per. 5, 103918 Moscow, Russia (Office). *Telephone:* (095) 232-26-43 (Office); (095) 940-83-32 (Home). *Fax:* (095) 232-26-43 (Office). *E-mail:* igrunov@igpi.ru (Office). *Website:* www.igrunov.ru (Office).

IHAMUOTILA, Jaakko, M.S.ENG.; Finnish business executive; b. 15 Nov. 1939, Helsinki; s. of Veikko Artturi Ihamuotila and Anna-Liisa (née Kouki) Ihamuotila; m. Tuula Elina Turja 1965; two s. one d.; ed Univ. of Tech., Helsinki; Asst in Reactor Tech. 1963–66, Acting Asst to Prof. of Physics 1964–66; with Canadian Gen. Electric Co. Ltd, Toronto 1966; Imatran Voima Oy 1966–68; Valmet Oy 1968–70, Asst Dir 1970–72, Dir of Planning 1972–73,

Man. Dir 1973–79, mem. Bd 1980–82; mem. Bd Neste Oy 1979–, Chair. and Chief Exec. 1980–; Chair. Bd of Dirs. Asko Oy, Silja Oy Ab, Chemical Industry Fed. of Finland; mem. Bd Pohjola Insurance Co.; mem. Supervisory Bd Merita Bank Ltd, MTV Finland, Finnish Cultural Foundation a.o.; mem. Bd Finnair, Confed. of Finnish Industry and Employers; mem. Council Econ. Orgs. in Finland, Nat. Bd of Econ. Defence, Council of Univ. of Tech.; Hon. DTech. *Leisure interests:* tennis, outdoor pursuits. *Address:* Neste Oy, Keilaniemi, 02150 Espoo, Finland (Office). *Telephone:* (20) 4501.

IHSANOĞLU, Ekmeleddin, PhD; Turkish professor of history of science and international administrator; b. 1943, Cairo, Egypt; m. Füsun Bilgiç 1971; three s.; ed Ankara Univ.; instructor and researcher Ain Shams Univ., Cairo 1966–70, Ankara Univ., Turkey 1971–75, Exeter Univ., England 1975–77; Assoc. Prof. Univ. of Ankara 1978–80; Dir Gen. Research Centre for Islamic History, Art and Culture, Org. of the Islamic Conf. 1980–, also Sec. Int. Comm. for Preservation of Islamic Cultural Heritage 1980–2000; Founder and Chair. Turkish Soc. for History of Science 1988–; Pres. Int. Union of History and Philosophy of Science/Div. of History of Science (IUHPS/DHS) 2001–; mem. numerous orgs. concerned with study of history of science and Islamic civilization, including Acad. Int. d'Histoire des Sciences, Paris, Cultural Centre of the Atatürk Supreme Council for Culture, Language and History, Ankara, Int. Soc. for History of Arabic and Islamic Sciences and Philosophy, Paris, Royal Acad. of Islamic Civilization Research, Jordan, Middle East and the Balkans, Research Foundation, Istanbul, Acad. of Arabic Language (Jordan, Egypt, Syria), Egyptian History Soc., Cairo, Tunisian Acad. of Sciences, Letters and Arts 'Bait al Hikma', Tunis, Int. Soc. for History of Medicine, Paris; apptd Amb. at Large by Govt of Bosnia-Herzegovina 1997; Order of Nat. Merit (Senegal) 2002; Dr hc (Mimar Sinan Univ., Istanbul) 1994, (Dowling Coll., New York) 1996, (Azerbaijan Acad. of Sciences) 2000, (Univ. of Sofia) 2001, (Univ. of Sarajevo) 2001; Distinction of the First Order Medal (Egypt) 1990, Certificate of Honour and Distinction, Org. of the Islamic Conf. 1995, Independence Medal of the First Order (Jordan) 1996, Medal of Distinguished State Service (Turkey) 2000. *Publications:* has written, edited and translated several books on Islamic culture and science; over 70 articles and papers. *Leisure interests:* reading and music, sponsoring and collecting Islamic works of art. *Address:* Research Centre for Islamic History, Art and Culture, Yıldız Sarayı, Seyir Köşkü, Barbaros Bulvarı, 80700 Beşiktaş, Istanbul (Office); Türk Bostani Sokak, Dostlar Sitesi 35, Yenikoy 80870 Istanbul, Turkey (Home). *Telephone:* (212) 2591742. *Fax:* (212) 2584365. *E-mail:* ircica@superonline.com (Office). *Website:* ircica.org (Office).

IKAWA, Motomichi, PhD; Japanese banking and finance executive; b. 10 Feb. 1947, Tokyo; m. Yoshiko Ikawa; ed Tokyo Univ., Univ. of California at Berkeley; economist Balance of Payments Div., OECD, Paris 1976–79; various man. posts Ministry of Finance, Tokyo 1979–85; Asst Regional Commr, C.I.D., Osaka Taxation Bureau 1985–86; Dir Budget, Personnel and Man. Systems Dept, Asian Devt Bank 1986–89; Asst Vice-Minister of Finance, Int. Affairs 1989–90; Dir Int. Org. Div., Int. Finance Bureau, Ministry of Finance 1990–91, Foreign Exchange and Money Market Div. 1991–92, Devt Policy Div. 1992–93, Co-ordination Div. 1993–94; Man. Dir Co-ordination Dept, Overseas Econ. Co-operation Fund 1994–96; Deputy Dir-Gen. Int. Finance Bureau 1996–97; Sr Deputy Dir-Gen. 1997–98; Exec. Vice-Pres. Multilateral Investment Guarantee Agency (MIGA), World Bank Group 1998–. *Publications:* Exchange Market Interventions during the Yen Depreciation 1980 1982, IMF Handbook 1990, The Role of the Overseas Economic Co-operation Fund Towards 2010 1994. *Leisure interests:* tennis, golf, hiking. *Address:* Multilateral Investment Guarantee Agency, 1818 H Street, NW, U12-001, Washington, DC 20433, USA. *Telephone:* (202) 473-6138. *Fax:* (202) 522-2620. *E-mail:* mikawa@worldbank.org (Office). *Website:* www.miga.org (Office).

IKEDA, Daisaku; Japanese Buddhist philosopher and author; b. 2 Jan. 1928, Tokyo; s. of Nenokichi Ikeda and Ichi Ikeda; m. Kaneko Shiraki 1952; two s.; ed Fuji Coll.; Pres. Soka Gakkai 1960–79, Hon. Pres. 1979–, Pres. Soka Gakkai Int. 1975–; founder of Soka Univ., Soka Univ. of America, Soka Women's Coll., Tokyo, Kansai Soka Schools, Soka Kindergartens (Sapporo, Japan, Hong Kong, Singapore, Malaysia and Brazil), Makiguchi Foundation for Educ., Inst. of Oriental Philosophy, Boston Research Center for the 21st Century, Toda Inst. for Global Peace and Policy Research, Tokyo, Shizuoka Fuji Art Museum, Min-On Concert Asscn, Victor Hugo House of Literature and Komeito Party; Poet Laureate, World Acad. of Arts and Culture, USA 1981–; Foreign mem., Brazilian Acad. of Letters 1993–; Hon. Prof. Nat. Univ. of San Marcos 1981, Beijing Univ. 1984 and others; Hon. Senator, European Acad. of Sciences and Arts 1997–; Hon. Adviser WFUNA 1999–; Hon. mem., The Club of Rome 1996–, Inst. of Oriental Studies of Russian Acad. of Sciences 1996–; Order of the Sun of Peru with Grand Cross 1984, Grand Cross, Order of Merit in May (Argentina) 1990, Nat. Order of Southern Cross (Brazil) 1990, Kt Grand Cross of the Most Noble Order of the Crown (Thailand) 1991, Hon. Cross of Science and the Arts (Austria) 1992, Kt Grand Cross of Rizal (Philippines) 1996 and others; inducted into Morehouse Coll.'s Martin Luther King, Jr Int. Collegiate of Scholars 2000; Dr hc (Moscow State Univ.) 1975, (Sofia) 1981, (Buenos Aires) 1990, (Univ. of the Philippines) 1991, (Ankara) 1992, (Fed. Univ. of Rio de Janeiro) 1993, (Glasgow) 1994, (Hong Kong) 1996, (Havana) 1996, (Univ. of Ghana) 1996, (Cheju Nat. Univ.) 1999, (Delhi) 1999, (Queens Coll. City Univ. of NY) 2000, (Univ. of Sydney) 2000 and others; UN Peace Award 1983, Kenya Oral Literature Award 1986, UNHCR Humanitarian Award 1989, Rosa Parks Humanitarian Award (USA) 1993, Simon

Wiesenthal Center Int. Tolerance Award (USA) 1993, Tagore Peace Award, The Asiatic Soc. (India) 1997 and others. *Exhibition:* Dialogue with Nature (photographic exhbn. shown in many countries 1988–). *Publications:* The Human Revolution Vols I–VI 1972–99, The Living Buddha (with A. Toynbee) 1976, Choose Life 1976, Buddhism: The First Millennium 1977, Glass Children and Other Essays 1979, La Nuit Appelle L'Aurore (with R. Huyghe) 1980, A Lasting Peace Vols I–II 1981, 1987, Life: An Enigma, a Precious Jewel 1982, Before It Is Too Late (with A. Peccei) 1984, Buddhism and Cosmos 1985, The Flower of Chinese Buddhism 1986, Human Values in a Changing World (with B. Wilson) 1987, Unlocking the Mysteries of Birth and Death 1988, The Snow Country Prince 1990, A Lifelong Quest for Peace (with L. Pauling) 1992, Choose Peace (with J. Galtung) 1995, A New Humanism: The University Addresses of Daisaku Ikeda 1996, The Wisdom of the Lotus Sutra, Vols I–VI (in Japanese) 1996–2000, Ikeda-Jin Yong Dialogue (in Japanese) 1998, The New Human Revolution, Vols I–XI (in Japanese) 1998–2002, The Way of Youth 2000, For the Sake of Peace 2000, Soka Education 2001, Diálog sobre José Martí (with C. Vitier) 2001, Dialogue pour la paix (with M. Gorbachev) 2001, The World is Yours to Change 2002, Choose Hope (with D. Krieger) 2002, Alborada del Pacífico (with P. Aylwin) 2002, On Being Human (with R. Simard and G. Bourgeault) 2002, Global Civilization: A Buddhist–Islamic Dialgoue (with M. Tehranian) 2003, and other writings on Buddhism, civilization, life and peace. *Leisure interests:* poetry, photography. *Address:* 32 Shinano-machi, Shinjuku-ku, Tokyo 160-8583, Japan (Office). *Telephone:* (3) 5360-9831 (Office). *Fax:* (3) 5360-9885 (Office). *Website:* www.sgi.org (Office).

IKEDA, Yukihiko; Japanese politician; b. 13 May 1937, Kobe City, Hyogo Pref.; ed Univ. of Tokyo; Overall Co-ordination Div. Minister's Secr., Ministry of Finance 1961; seconded to Ministry of Foreign Affairs (served four years as Vice-Consul, New York) 1964; Pvt. Sec. to Minister of Finance 1974; mem. House of Reps 1976–, House of Reps Budget Cttee; Deputy Chief Cabinet Sec. 1981; Chair. Prime Minister's Office Div., Policy Research Council of LDP 1983; Chair. House of Reps Cttee on Finance 1986, Cttee on Basic Policies of the Nation 2002; Dir-Gen. Man. and Co-ordination Agency June–Aug. 1989; Deputy Sec.-Gen. LDP March–Dec. 1990, Chair. Policy Research Council 1998–99, Gen. Council 1999–2000; Dir-Gen. Defence Agency 1990–91; Minister for Foreign Affairs 1996–97. *Address:* 1st Members' Office Building, House of Representatives #514, 2-2-1 Nagata-cho, Chiyoda-ku, Tokyo 100-8981 (Office); c/o Liberal-Democratic Party, 1-11-23, Nagata-cho, Chiyoda-ku, Tokyo 100, Japan. *Telephone:* (3) 3508-7244 (Office). *Fax:* (3) 3502-5032 (Office).

IKEHATA, Seiichi; Japanese politician; mem. House of Reps., fmr Dir Cttee on Social and Labour Affairs; fmr Chair. Special Cttee on Disasters; Minister of State, Dir-Gen. Nat. Land Agency 1995–96; mem. Social Democratic Party of Japan (SDPJ). *Address:* c/o Social Democratic Party of Japan, 1-8-1, Nagata-cho, Chiyoda-ku, Tokyo 100, Japan.

IKLÉ, Fred Charles, PhD; American government official and social scientist; b. 21 Aug. 1924, Fex, Switzerland; m. Doris Eisemann 1959; two d.; ed Univ. of Chicago; research scholar, Bureau of Applied Social Research, Columbia Univ. 1950–54; mem. Social Science Dept, Rand Corpn 1955–61, Head of Dept 1968–73; Research Assoc. in Int. Relations, Centre for Int. Affairs, Harvard Univ. 1962–63; Assoc. Prof., then Prof. of Political Science, MIT 1963–67; Dir US Arms Control and Disarmament Agency 1973–77; Under-Sec. of Defense for Policy 1981–88; Distinguished Scholar, Center for Strategic and Int. Studies 1988–; Dir Defense Forum Foundation 1988–; Dir Nat. Endowment for Democracy 1992–2001; Co-Chair. US Comm. on Integrated Long Term Strategy 1987–88; mem. Bd Int. Peace Acad. 1977–81; Chair. Council on Nat. Security of Republican Nat. Cttee 1977–79; Chair. CMC Energy Services 1978–81, 1988–, Telos Corpn 1995–; Gov. Smith Richardson Foundation 1996–; Chair. US Cttee for Human Rights in N Korea 2001–; Adviser Bd Rand Drug Policy Center 1988–; US Defense Dept Distinguished Public Service Awards 1975, 1987, 1988. *Publications:* The Social Impact of Bomb Destruction 1958, After Detection...What? 1961, How Nations Negotiate 1964, Every War Must End 1971, Can Nuclear Deterrence Last Out The Century? 1973 and many articles on int. affairs. *Address:* Center for Strategic and International Studies, 1800 K Street, NW, Washington, DC 20006 (Office); 7010 Glenbrook Road, Bethesda, MD 20814, USA (Home). *Telephone:* (202) 775-3155 (Office). *Fax:* (202) 775-3199 (Office); (301) 951-0286 (Home). *Website:* www.csis.org (Office).

IKOUEBE, Basile; Republic of the Congo diplomatist; b. 1 July 1946; m.; six c.; ed Int. Inst. of Public Admin., Paris, Inst. for Political Studies, Bordeaux; apptd. Chief Int. Orgs. Div., Minister of Foreign Affairs 1974, Prin. Pvt. Sec. to Minister 1975–77, Sec. to Ministry 1977–79; training assignment in France 1980–82; Diplomatic Adviser to Head of State 1982–92; Minister and Prin. Pvt. Sec. to Head of State 1987–94; Amb.-at-Large 1994–95; Sec. to Ministry of Foreign Affairs and Co-operation 1996–98; Perm. Rep. to UN 1998–. *Address:* Permanent Mission of the Republic of the Congo to the United Nations, 14 East 65th Street, New York, NY 10021, USA (Office). *Telephone:* (212) 744-7840 (Office). *Fax:* (212) 744-7975 (Office). *E-mail:* congo@un.int (Office).

ILETO, Rafael M.; Philippine politician; b. 24 Oct. 1920, Sn. Isidro, Nueva Ecija; s. of Francisco Ileto and Lorenza Manio; m. Olga Clemena Ileto 1945; three s. four d.; ed Univ. of the Philippines, Philippine and U.S. Mil. Acads.; served U.S. Army World War II; Officer in Philippine Army 1950, Founder and Head Scout Rangers 1950–55; Mil. Attaché in Laos and S. Vietnam

1955–59; Operations Chief, Nat. Intelligence Co-ordinating Agency 1959; fmr Commanding Gen. of Philippine Army and Deputy Chief of Staff; rank of Lt-Gen.; Amb. to Iran 1975, later Amb. to Thailand; Deputy Defence Minister Feb.–Nov. 1986, Defence Minister 1986–88; Pres. Adviser on Nat. Security Affairs 1989–. *Leisure interests:* golf, swimming. *Address:* c/o Office of the President, San Miguel, Metro Manila, The Philippines.

ILIĆ, Venceslav; Bosnia and Herzegovina judge; b. 10 Sept. 1937, Sarajevo; s. of Anto Ilić and Ema Ilić (née Uršić); m. Bogdanka Ilić (née Mioković); two d.; District Court Judge 1972–78; Public Prosecutor 1978–84; Supreme Court Judge 1984–87, 1992–96; Pres. Dist Court 1987–92; Supreme Court, Fed. of Bosnia and Herzegovina Sept. 1996–; Medallion of the City of Sarajevo. *Publications:* work on educ. of juridical personnel. *Leisure interests:* work for sports orgs., walking in the countryside. *Address:* Supreme Court of the Federation of Bosnia and Herzegovina, 71000 Sarajevo, Valtera Perića 15, Federation of Bosnia and Herzegovina (Office). *Telephone:* (33) 664754 (Office).

ILIESCU, Ion; Romanian politician; b. 3 March 1930, Oltenița, Ilfov District; m. Elena Iliescu 1951; ed Bucharest Polytechnic Inst. and Energy Inst., Moscow; researcher, Energy Eng Inst., Bucharest 1955; Pres. Union of Student Asscns. 1957–60; Alt. mem. Cen. Cttee of RCP 1965–68, mem. 1968–84; First Sec. Cen. Cttee of Union of Communist Youth and Minister for Youth 1967–71; Sec. RCP Cen. Cttee 1971; Vice-Chair. Timiş County Council 1971–74; Chair Iaşi County Council 1974–79; accused of 'intellectual deviationism' and kept under surveillance; Chair. Nat. Water Council 1979–84; Dir Tech. Publishing House, Bucharest 1984–89; Pres. Nat. Salvation Front 1989–90, Pres. Provisional Council for Nat. Unity Feb.–May 1990, Pres. of Romania 1990–96, Dec. 2000–; Senator 1996–; fmr Pres. Party of Social Democracy of Romania (merged with SDP to become Social Democratic Party 2001); Chevalier de la Légion d'honneur and other state decorations; hon. doctorates from numerous univs. *Publications:* Global Problems and Creativity, Revolution and Reform, Romania in Europe and in the World, Where is Romanian Society Going?, Romanian Revolution, Hope Reborn, Integration and Globalisation – A Romanian Vision; studies on water man. and ecology, political power and social relations. *Leisure interests:* global problems, political and economic sciences. *Address:* Office of the President, Cotroceni Palace, 76258 Bucharest, Romania.

ILLARIONOV, Andrei Nikolayevich, CAND.EC.SC.; Russian economist; b. 16 Sept. 1961, Leningrad; m. Alexandra Vacroux 1997; one s.; ed Leningrad Univ., Birmingham Univ., UK, Georgetown Univ., USA; Asst researcher Leningrad State Univ. 1983–89; Head of Sector St Petersburg Financial and Econ. Inst. 1989–94; Dir Inst. of Econ. Analysis 1994–; adviser to Pres. Putin on Econ. Problems 2000–. *Publications:* Russian Economic Reforms: Lost Year 1994, Financial Stabilization in Russia 1995, Russia in a Changing World 1997, Economic Freedom of the World (co-author and co-ed.) 2000. *Address:* Institute of Economic Analysis, Building 2, Slavyanskaya ploshchad 4, Moscow 103074, Russia (Office). *Telephone:* (095) 924-41-38 (Office). *Fax:* (095) 921-33-90 (Office). *E-mail:* ieamos@glasnet.ru (Office). *Website:* www.iea.ru (Office).

ILLNEROVÁ, Helena, DSc; Czech physiologist; b. 28 Dec. 1937, Prague; d. of the late Lagus Karel and Libuše Karel; m. Michal Illner; one s. one d.; ed Charles Univ., Prague; researcher Inst. of Physiology 1961–92; researcher Acad. of Sciences, Prague 1961–62, Vice-Pres. 1993–2001, Pres. 2001–; Sr Lecturer Charles Univ., Prague 1995–; mem. Czech Learned Society and numerous other academic and scientific orgs.; J. E. Purkyně Prize 1987. *Publications:* over 90 scientific publications. *Leisure interests:* literature, hiking, academic activities. *Address:* Academy of Sciences, Národní 3, 117 20 Prague 1, Czech Republic (Office). *Telephone:* (2) 41721151 (Office); (2) 66052067 (Home). *Website:* www.cas.cz (Office).

ILLUECA SIBAUSTE, Jorge Enrique, LLD; Panamanian politician and diplomatist; b. 17 Dec. 1918, Panama City; m.; four c.; ed Univ. de Panamá, Harvard Law School, Univ. of Chicago; Prof., Univ. de Panamá 1962–63, 1966–68; Pres. Nat. Bar Asscn 1963–64, 1966–68; Dir El Panamá América (newspaper) 1963–64, 1967–68; Special Amb. to USA to begin negotiations for new Panama Canal Treaty 1964, Special Envoy for negotiations on the treaty 1972; mem. del. to UN Gen. Ass. 1957, 1961, 1975, also to 3rd Special Emergency Session; Head of Del. to 1st Session of 3rd UN Conf. on Law of the Sea 1974, mem. Del. to 4th Session 1976; Deputy Perm. Rep. to UN 1957, Perm. Rep. 1960, 1976–81, 1994–97, Pres. 38th Session of UN Gen. Ass. Sept.–Dec. 1983; mem. Perm. Court of Arbitration, The Hague, Netherlands 1974–76; Foreign Minister 1983–84; Vice-Pres. of Panama 1982–83, Pres. Feb.–Oct. 1984; U Thant Award 1983. *Address:* c/o Ministry of Foreign Affairs, Panamá 4, Panama.

ILLYA II, Catholicos-Patriarch of all Georgia; Georgian ecclesiastic; b. 4 Dec. 1933, Sno, Kazbegi Region; ed Moscow Theological Seminary, Moscow Theological Acad.; took monastic vows 1957; Father-Superior 1960; Archimandrite 1961; Vicar of Catholicos-Patriarch 1963; entrusted with Tsum-Abkhaz Diocese 1977; Tsum-Abkhaz Mitropolite 1969; Rector Mtskheta Theological Acad. 1963–72; awarded Second Panagya 1972; enthroned as Catholicos-Patriarch of all Georgia 1977–; Pres. World Council of Churches 1978–83; Dr of Theology American St-Vladimir Theological Acad.; holder of highest awards of churches of Georgia, Constantinople, Alexandria, Antioch, Jerusalem, Russia, Czechoslovakia and Poland; Order of Friendship of Peoples.

ILOILO, Ratu Josefa; Fijian politician; b. 1920; fmr teacher, civil admin., prov. admin.; Vice-Pres. Methodist Church of Fiji and Rotuma 1997–98; fmr MP and Pres. of Senate; Vice-Pres. –2000, Acting Pres. Dec. 2000–01, Pres. of Fiji March 2001–; Pres. Bd Trustees Native Land Trust Bd 2001–. *Address:* Office of the President, P.O. Box 2513, Government Buildings, Suva, Fiji (Office). *Telephone:* 314244 (Office). *Fax:* 301645 (Office).

ILVES, Toomas Hendrik, MA; Estonian fmr government minister, diplomatist and scientist; b. 26 Dec. 1953, Stockholm, Sweden; m. Merry Bullock; two c.; ed Columbia Univ., New York, USA, Univ. of Pennsylvania, USA; Research Asst, Dept of Psychology, Columbia Univ. 1974–76, 1979; Asst to Dir and English Teacher, Center for Open Educ., Englewood, NJ 1979–81; Arts Admin. and Dir Vancouver Literary Centre, Canada 1981–82; Lecturer in Estonian Literature and Linguistics, Dept of Interdisciplinary Studies, Simon Fraser Univ., Vancouver 1983–84; Research Analyst, Radio Free Europe, Munich, Germany 1984–88, Dir Estonian Service 1988–93; Amb. of Estonia to USA (also Accred to Canada and Mexico) 1993–96; Minister of Foreign Affairs 1996–98, 1999–2001; Chair. Bd Estonian N Atlantic Trust 1998; mem. Riigi Kogu (Estonian State Ass.) 1999; Deputy Chair., then Chair. Moodukad Party 1999–. *Leisure interests:* reading, cooking, farming. *Address:* Ministry of Foreign Affairs, Islandi Väljak 1, Tallinn 15049, Estonia. *Telephone:* (2) 631-7000.

ILYASOV, Stanislav; Russian politician; b. 24 July 1953, Kizlyar, Repub. of Dagestan; m.; four c.; ed Leningrad Electricity Inst.; fmr nat. champion in free-style wrestling; served in armed forces 1972–75; supervisor Kizlyar power grid; deputy dir electrical equipment plant, Zaterechny; elected Deputy Chair. Kizlyar Municipal Exec. Cttee 1987, later Chair.; Gen. Dir Spetsenergoremont (repairs and construction co.), Makhachkala 1990–93; Gen. Dir Southern Grid, Unified Energy Systems (UES) 1993–94, Deputy CEO of a UES subsidiary, N. Caucasus 1994, later CEO, Vice-Pres. of UES May–August 1997; CEO Energoperetok Inc. 1997; apptd First Vice-Prime Minister of Stavropol Aug. 1997, Premier of Stavropol 1997–99; First Vice-Pres. Yediny Elektroenergeticheski Kompleks Rossiiskoi Federatsii Corpn 1999–2001; Prime Minister of Govt of Chechnya 2001–02; Fed. Minister for Chechen Affairs 2002–. *Address:* Office of the Government, Krasnopresnenskaya nab. 2, 103274 Moscow, Russia (Office).

ILYENKO, Yuriy Gerasimovich; Ukrainian cinematographer; b. 18 July 1936, Ukraine; s. of Gerasim Ilyenko and Maria Ilyenko; m. Liudmyla Yefymenko 1977; two s.; ed VGIK, Moscow; Head Sub-Faculty of Directing and Dramatic Composition, State Inst. of Theatrical Arts, Kiev; founder mem. Ukrainian Acad. of Arts 1996–; T. Sherchenko Prize 1991, People's Artist of Ukraine 1987. *Films include:* Shadows of Our Forgotten Ancestors (by Paradzhyanov) 1964 (16 int. prizes); (as director), A Spring for the Thirsty 1965, On the Eve of Ivan Kupalo Day 1968, A White Bird with a Black Mark 1971, In Defiance of All 1972, To Dream and to Live 1974, Baked Potato Festival 1977, The Forest Song 1981, Strip of Wild Flowers 1982, Legend of Queen Olga 1983, Straw Bells 1985, Swan Lake – The Zone 1990 (2 prizes, Cannes Film Festival). *Leisure interest:* painting (exhibited in Kiev, Munich and Vienna). *Address:* 9 Michail Kotzybinksy Str., Apt. 22, Kiev 252030, Ukraine. *Telephone:* (44) 224-75-40 (Home). *Fax:* (44) 224-75-40 (Home).

IL'YIN, Leonid Andreyevich, DMed; Russian toxicologist; b. 15 March 1928; ed First Leningrad Medical Inst.; worked as doctor in the navy, Head of Lab. of Irradiation Protection, Deputy Dir Leningrad Inst. of Irradiation Protection, USSR Ministry of Public Health 1961–67; Dir, Prof. Inst. of Biophysics, USSR Ministry of Public Health 1968–89; Dir Inst. of Radiation Medicine 1989–; mem. Russian Acad. of Medical Sciences 1982, Vice-Pres. 1984–90; Deputy Chair. Soviet Cttee Doctors Against the Nuclear Threat 1984–90; Hero of Socialist Labour; USSR State Prize, Pirogov Prize. *Publications:* more than 100 works on problems of toxicology and radiation medicine, including A Threat of Nuclear War (with E. Chazov). *Address:* Institute of Radiation Medicine, Zhivopisnaya Street 46, 123182 Moscow, Russia. *Telephone:* (095) 190-56-51.

ILYUMZHUNOV, Kirsan Nikolayevich; Kalmyk politician; b. 5 April 1962, Elista; m.; one s.; ed Moscow Inst. of Int. Relations; man. Japanese cos in Russia; f. a number of maj. enterprises in Kalmykya; Pres. Int. Corp. SAN 1991; People's Deputy of Russian Fed. 1990–93; Pres. of Kalmyk Repub. (Khalmg Tangch) 1993, mem. Russian Council of Fed. 1993–; Pres. Int. Chess Fed. (FIDE) 1995–, Master of Chess. *Address:* Office of the President, Lenina Sq. House of Government, 358000 Elista, Kalmykya, Russia (Office).

ILYUSHIN, Viktor Vasilyevich; Russian politician; b. 4 June 1947, Nizhny Tagil; m.; one s. one d.; ed Urals Polytech. Inst., Acad. of Social Science; metalworker Nizhny Tagil metallurgy plant; First Sec. Nizhny Tagil City Komsomol Cttee, then First Sec. Sverdlovsk Regional Komsomol Cttee, Asst to First Sec. Sverdlovsk Regional CPSU Cttee; First Sec. Leninsky Dist CPSU Cttee (Sverdlovsk); counsellor Cen. Cttee Afghanistan People's Democractic Party; Asst to Chair. Russian Supreme Soviet 1990–91; Head Pres. Yeltsin's Secr. 1991–92; First Asst Pres. of Russian Fed. 1991–96; First Deputy Prime Minister 1996–97; Chair. Bd of Dirs Gazprom-Media 1997–98; mem. Bd, Head Cooperation with Regions Dept, mem. Bd Gazprom 1997–. *Leisure interests:* tennis, mountain skiing, riding, jazz, cars, computers. *Address:* Gazprom, Nametkina str. 16, 117884 Moscow, Russia. *Telephone:* (095) 719-32-24.

IMAI, Nobuko; Japanese viola soloist; b. 18 March 1943, Tokyo; m. Aart van Bochove 1981; one s. one d.; ed Toho School of Music, Tokyo, Juilliard School and Yale Univ., USA; mem. Vermeer Quartet 1974–79; soloist with Berlin Philharmonic, London Symphony Orchestra, Royal Philharmonic, the BBC orchestras, Detroit Symphony, Chicago Symphony, Concertgebouw, Montreal Symphony, Boston Symphony, Vienna Symphony, Orchestre de Paris, Stockholm Philharmonic; festival performances include Marlborough, Salzburg, Lockenhaus, Casals, South Bank, Summer Music, Aldeburgh, BBC Proms, Int. Viola Congress (Houston), New York "Y", Festival d'Automne, Paris; conceived Int. Hindemith Viola Festival (London, New York, Tokyo) 1995; Prof. High School of Music, Detmold 1985–; Artistic Adviser, Casals Hall, Tokyo; over 20 recordings; First Prize Munich, Second Prize Geneva Int. Viola Competitions; Avon Arts Award 1993, Japanese Educ. Minister's Art Prize for Music 1993, Mobil Japan Art Prize 1995, Suntory Hall Prize 1996. *Leisure interest:* cooking. *Address:* c/o Irene Witmer Personal Management in Classical Music, Leidsegracht 42, 1016 CM Amsterdam, The Netherlands. *Telephone:* (20) 5244040. *Fax:* (20) 5244044.

IMAI, Takashi; Japanese business executive; b. 1929, Kamakura; ed Univ. of Tokyo; joined Fuji Iron & Steel 1952, Man. Raw Materials 1963; Deputy Gen. Man. Fuel and Ferrous Metals, Nippon Steel (formed by merger of Fuji Iron & Steel and Yawata Steel) 1970, Gen. Man. Iron Ore 1973, Man. Dir 1983, Exec. Vice-Pres. 1989, Pres. Nippon Steel 1992–99, Chair. 1999–. *Address:* Nippon Steel Corporation, 2-6-3 Otemachi, Chiyoda-ku, Tokyo 100-8071, Japan. *Telephone:* (3) 3242-4111. *Fax:* (3) 3275-5641. *E-mail:* www-info@www .nsc.co.jp (Office). *Website:* www.nsc.co.jp (Office).

IMAMURA, Shohei; Japanese film director; b. 15 Sept. 1926, Tokyo; ed Waseda Univ.; entered film industry in 1951 as an Asst Dir at Ofuna Studio; started directing 1958; opened film school Yokohama Hoso Eiga Seimon Gako where he teaches. *Films include:* Stolen Carnal Desire 1958, Lights of Night, The Endless Desire 1959, My Second Brother 1959, Hogs and Warships/The Flesh is Hot/The Dirty Girls 1961, The Insect Woman 1963, Unholy Desire 1964, Intentions of Murder 1964, The Pornographer/The Amorists 1966, A Man Vanishes 1967, Kuragejima—Legend from a Southern Island 1968, Postwar Japanese History 1970, Vengeance is Mine 1979, Eijaniko 1981, The Ballad of Narayama (Palme d'Or at Cannes) 1983, Zegen 1987, Kanzo Sensei 1988, Black Rain (Grand Prize for Tech. Excellence, Cannes Film Festival 1989) 1989, The Eel (Palme d'Or at Cannes 1997), Unagi 1997, Warm Water Under a Red Bridge 2002. *Address:* Toei Company Ltd, 3-2-17 Ginza, Chuo-Ku, Tokyo 104, Japan.

IMAN, (Iman Abdul Majid); Somali model; b. 25 July 1956, Somalia; m. 1st Spencer Haywood (divorced 1987); one c.; m. 2nd David Bowie 1992; ed Nairobi Univ.; fashion model 1976–90, has modelled for Claude Montana and Thierry Mugler; signed Revlon Polish Ambers contract (first black model to be signed by int. cosmetics co.) 1979; has made numerous TV appearances and has appeared in a Michael Jackson video. *Films include:* Star Trek VI: The Undiscovered Country 1986, Houseparty II 1991, Exit to Eden 1994, The Deli 1997, Omikron: The Nomad Soul 1999. *Television appearances include:* Miami Vice, The Cosby Show, In the Heat of the Night. *Address:* c/o Elite Model Management, 40–42 Parker Street, London WC2B 5PQ, England. *Telephone:* (20) 7333-0888.

IMANAKA, Hiroshi, LLD; Japanese university professor; b. 2 Dec. 1930, Fukuoka City; s. of the late Tsugumaro Imanaka; ed Univs. of Hiroshima and Nagoya; Lecturer, Faculty of Educ., Miyazaki Univ. 1960–65; Lecturer, Dept of Gen. Educ., Hiroshima Univ. 1965–67, Assoc. Prof. 1967–78, Prof. of Political Science, Faculty of Integrated Arts and Sciences 1978–81, Faculty of Law 1981–91, Prof. Emer. 1991–; Dean and Prof., Kinjogakuin Univ. 1991–2001; Prof. Emer. 2001–. *Publications:* Constitutional Law (co-author) 1971, George Lawson's Political Theory of Civil Government 1976, A Study of the History of English Political Thought 1977, Parliamentarism and its Origin in the Era of English Revolution, The English Revolution and the Modern Political Theory of George Lawson 2000. *Address:* 2-6-10 Yoshijima-Higashi, Naka-ku, Hiroshima Shi, Japan. *Telephone:* (82) 244-4756. *E-mail:* himanaka@do7.enjoy.ne.jp (Home).

IMANALIYEV, Muratbeck Sansyzbayevich, CAND.HIST.; Kyrgyzstan politician; b. 1956, Frunze (now Bishkek); m.; two c.; ed Inst. of Asian and African Countries, Moscow State Univ., Leningrad br. Inst. of Oriental Studies USSR Acad. of Sciences; Second Sec. on Press and Information Ministry of Foreign Affairs Kyrgyz SSR 1982–88, Head of Protocol Consulate Div. 1988–89, Head Consular Div. 1989–90, Minister of Foreign Affairs Kyrgyz Repub. 1991–93; Amb. to China 1993–96; Head Int. Div. Presidential Admin. 1996–97; Minister of Foreign Affairs 1997–. *Address:* Ministry of Foreign Affairs, Erkindik blvd 54, 720021 Bishkek, Kyrgyzstan (Office). *Telephone:* (3312) 22-05-45 (Office).

IMBALI, Faustino Fudut; Guinea-Bissau politician; cand. presidential election 1999; Minister of Foreign Affairs Jan.–March 2001, Prime Minister of Guinea-Bissau March–Dec. 2001. *Address:* c/o Office of the Prime Minister, Avda Unidade Africana, CP 137, Bissau, Guinea-Bissau (Office).

IMBERT, Baron (Life Peer), cr. 1999, of New Romney in the County of Kent; **Peter Michael Imbert,** QPM; British police officer and business executive; b. 27 April 1933, Folkestone, Kent; s. of the late William Henry Imbert and of Frances May Hodge; m. Iris Rosina Dove 1956; one s. two d.; ed Harvey Grammar School; Metropolitan Police 1953–93, Asst Chief Constable, Surrey Constabulary 1976–77, Deputy Chief Constable 1977–79, Chief Constable, Thames Valley Police 1979–85, Deputy Commr Metropolitan Police 1985–87, Commr 1987–93; Metropolitan Police Anti-Terrorist Squad 1973–75; Police negotiator in Balcombe Street (London) IRA Siege Dec. 1975; Sec. Nat. Crime Cttee, ACPO Council 1980–83, Chair. 1983–85; Chair. Vehicle Security Installation Bd 1994–96; Chair. (non-exec.) Retainagroup 1995–; Chair. Capital Eye Security Ltd 1997–; Dir (non-exec.) Securicor 1993–2000, Camelot Group 1994–; consultant CDR Int. 1997–2000; mem. Gen. Advisory Council, BBC 1980–87, Criminal Justice Consultative Cttee 1992–93; Chair. Surrey Co. Cricket Club Youth Trust 1993–96; mem. Ministerial Advisory Bd on Royal Parks 1993–2000, Public Policy Cttee of Royal Automobile Club 1993–; Trustee Help the Aged 1993–95, St Catherine's Foundation Cumberland Lodge; DL Greater London 1994–98, Lord Lt of Greater London 1998–; Hon. DLitt (Reading Univ.); Hon. MBA (Int. Man. Centre). *Leisure interests:* golf, bad bridge, watching good cricket, talking about his grandchildren. *Address:* The Lieutenancy Office, 18th Floor, City Hall, PO Box 240, Victoria Street, London, SW1E 6QP, England (Office). *Telephone:* (20) 7641-3259.

IMBUSCH, George Francis, DSc, PhD, FInstP, F.A.I.P., FIEE; Irish professor of experimental physics; b. 7 Oct. 1935, Limerick; s. of George Imbusch and Alice Neville; m. Mary Rita O'Donnell 1961; one s. one d.; ed Christian Brothers' School, Limerick, Univ. Coll. Galway and Stanford Univ.; mem. tech. staff, Bell Labs. USA 1964–67; Lecturer in Physics, Univ. Coll. Galway 1967–74, Prof. of Experimental Physics 1974–, Head, Dept of Physics 1986–89, Vice-Pres. Univ. Coll. Galway 1992–98; Science Sec., Royal Irish Acad. 1989–93; Visiting Prof. Univ. of Wis. 1978, Regensburg 1981, Utrecht 1988, Canterbury, NZ 1995, Georgia 1998. *Publications:* Optical Spectroscopy of Inorganic Solids (co-author) 1989; 100 scientific papers in journals. *Leisure interests:* painting, reading. *Address:* National University of Ireland, Galway (Office); Forramoyle West, Barna, Co. Galway, Republic of Ireland. *Telephone:* (91) 524411 (Office); (91) 592159 (Home). *Fax:* (91) 525700 (Office). *E-mail:* g.f .imbusch@nuigalway.ie (Office).

IMMELT, Jeffrey R., BS, MBA; American business executive; b. 1957; s. of Joseph Immelt and Donna Immelt; m. Andrea Immelt; one d.; ed Finneytown High School, Dartmouth Coll., Harvard Univ.; joined Gen. Electric Co. 1982, Corp. Marketing Dept 1982, various positions with GE Plastics 1982–89, Vice-Pres. 1992–93, Vice-Pres. GE Appliances 1989–91, Vice-Pres. Worldwide Marketing and Product Man. 1991, Vice-Pres. and Gen. Man. GE Plastics Americas 1993–97, Pres. and CEO GE Medical Systems 1997–2001, Chair. and CEO Gen. Electric Co. April 2001–. *Leisure interest:* golf. *Address:* General Electric Company, 3135 Easton Turnpike, Fairfield, CT 06431-0002, USA (Office). *Telephone:* (203) 373-2211 (Office). *Fax:* (203) 373-3131 (Office). *Website:* www.ge.com.

IMRAN KHAN NIAZI; Pakistani cricketer and politician; b. 25 Oct. 1952, Lahore; m. Jemima Goldsmith 1995; two s.; ed Aitchison Coll. and Cathedral School, Lahore, Worcester Royal Grammar School, England, Keble Coll. Oxford; right-arm fast bowler, middle-order right-hand batsman; played for Lahore 1969–71, Worcs. 1971–76, Oxford Univ. 1973–75 (Capt. 1974), Dawood 1975–76, PIA 1975–81, Sussex 1977–88, NSW 1984–85; 88 Test matches for Pakistan 1971–92, 48 as Capt., scoring 3,807 runs (average 37.6) and taking 362 wickets (average 22.8); toured England 1971, 1974, 1975 (World Cup), 1979 (World Cup), 1982, 1983 (World Cup), 1987; scored 17,771 first-class runs and took 1,287 first-class wickets; 175 limited-overs ints., 139 as Capt. (including 1992 World Cup victory); second player to score a century and take 10 wickets in a Test 1983; only third player to score over 3,000 Test runs and take 300 wickets; Special Rep. for Sports, UNICEF 1989; Ed.-in-Chief Cricket Life 1989–90; f. Imran Khan Cancer Hosp. Appeal 1991–; f. Movement for Justice; Hon. Fellow Keble Coll. Oxford 1988; Wisden Cricketer of the Year 1983, Hilal-e-Imtiaz 1993. *Publications:* Imran 1983, All-Round View (autobiog.) 1988, Indus Journey 1990, Warrior Race 1993; writes syndicated newspaper column. *Leisure interests:* shooting, films, music. *Address:* c/o Shankat Khanum Memorial Trust, 29 Shah Jamal, Lahore 546000, Pakistan.

IMRAN TUANKU JAAFAR, HRH Tunku, LLB; Malaysian business executive; b. 21 March 1948, Seremban, Negeri Sembilan; s. of HM Tuanku Ja'afar the fmr 10th King of Malaysia and HM Tuanku Najihah; m. HH Che Engku Mahirah; two s.; ed The King's School, Canterbury and Univ. of Nottingham; called to the Bar at Gray's Inn, London 1971; joined Malaysian Nat. Corp. (PERNAS) 1971, Rep. in Indonesia, later Group Co. Sec.; joined Haw Par Group, 1973, Man. Dir Haw Par Malaysia until 1976; CEO Anttah Group of Cos. 1977–2001; Exec. Chair. Petra Group 2001–; mem. Bd Dirs of several other publicly listed cos. in Malaysia and abroad; Dir Inst. of Strategic and Int. Studies (ISIS) Malaysia; mem. Malaysian Business Council and Malaysian-British Business Council (MBBC); Past Pres. Badan Warisan (Heritage of Malaysia Trust); Pres. Olympic Council of Malaysia; mem. Nat. Sports Council of Malaysia; Pres. Malaysian Cricket Asscn; Founding Chair. Foundation for Malaysian Sporting Excellence (SportExcel); Pres. Emer. World Squash Fed. (Pres. 1989–96); Exec. Bd mem. Int. Cricket Council (ICC); Vice-Pres. Commonwealth Games Fed.; Malaysia's first nat. squash champion 1973; Chef-de-Mission, Seoul Olympic Games 1988; Nat. Sports' Leadership Award 1991, Panglima Setia Mahkota, conferring the title Tan Sri 1992, Darjah Seri Urama Negeri Sembilan, conferring the title Dato' Seri Utama 1999. *Address:* 9th Floor, Wisma Antah, Off Jalan Semantan, Damansaia Heights, 50490 Kuala Lumpur (Office); No. 33, Jalan Semantan Dua, Damansaia Heights, 50490, Kuala Lumpur, Malaysia (Home). *Telephone:* (603) 2545144 (Office); (603) 2556031 (Home). *Fax:* (603) 2561044 (Office); (603) 2533641 (Home). *E-mail:* tunku-imran@antah.com.my (Office).

IMRAY, Sir Colin Henry, KBE, CMG, KStJ, MA; British diplomatist; b. 21 Sept. 1933, Newport, Mon.; s. of Henry Gibbon Imray and Frances Olive Badman; m. Shirley Margaret Matthews 1957; one s. three d.; ed Highgate School, London, Hotchkiss School, Conn., USA and Balliol Coll., Oxford; Second Lt Seaforth Highlanders, Royal W African Frontier Force 1952–54; Asst Prin. Commonwealth Relations Office 1957–58, 1961–63; Third then Second Sec. British High Comm., Canberra 1958–61; First Sec., Nairobi 1963–66; Asst Head Personnel Dept FCO 1966–70; British Trade Commr, Montreal 1970–73; Counsellor, Consul Gen. and Head of Chancery, Islamabad 1973–77; Royal Coll. of Defence Studies 1977; Commercial Counsellor British Embassy, Tel Aviv 1977–80; Deputy High Commr, Bombay 1980–84; Asst Under-Sec. of State (Chief Inspector and Deputy Chief Clerk) 1984–85; High Commr in Tanzania 1986–89, in Bangladesh 1989–93; Sec. Gen. O.St.J. 1993–97, Dir Overseas Relations 1997–98; mem. Cen. Council Royal Over-Seas League 1998–, Exec. Cttee 1999–, Chair. 2000–; High Steward of Wallingford 2001–; Freeman City of London 1994. *Leisure interests:* travel, walking. *Address:* Over-Seas House, Park Place, St James's Street, London, SW1A 1LR (Office); Holbrook House, Reading Road, Wallingford, Oxon., OX10 9DT, England. *Telephone:* (20) 7408-0214 (Office). *Fax:* (20) 7499-6738 (Office). *E-mail:* imray@rosl.org.uk (Office). *Website:* www.rosl.org.uk (Office).

IMRU HAILE SELASSIE, Lij Mikhail; Ethiopian politician; b. 1930; ed Oxford Univ., England; fmr Dir-Gen. Ministry of Defence and mem. Planning Bd, Ministry of Agriculture; fmr Amb. to U.S., then to USSR; Head Ethiopian Mission to UN Office, Geneva until 1974; Minister of Commerce and Industry March 1974; Minister in the Prime Minister's Office in charge of Econ. and Social Affairs April–July 1974; Prime Minister July–Sept. 1974; Minister of Information 1974–75; Chief Political Adviser to Head of State 1975–76.

INAGAKI, Jitsuo; Japanese politician; mem. House of Reps.; fmr Parl. Vice-Minister of Health and Welfare; Dir Gen. Hokkaido Devt Agency and Okinawa Devt Agency (State Minister) 1996–99. *Address:* c/o Hokkaido Development Agency, 3-1-1, Kasumigaseki, Chiyoda-ku, Tokyo 100, Japan (Office).

INAGAKI, Masao; Japanese advertising executive; b. 27 Oct. 1922, Aichi Pref.; s. of Gonpachi and Katsu Inagaki; m. Teruko Inagaki 1949; one d.; ed Training Inst., Ministry of Foreign Affairs; with Civil Property Bureau, Ministry of Foreign Affairs 1948–50; joined Sekai-Sha, apptd. Gen. Man., Advertising Div. 1950; Founder and Dir Daiichi-Tsushinsya; f. Asatsu Inc., CEO and Pres. 1956–. *Leisure interest:* writing poems. *Address:* 7-16-12, Ginza, Chuo-ku, Tokyo 104 (Office); 2-32-7 Matsugaoka, Nakano-ku, Tokyo 165, Japan (Home). *Telephone:* (3) 3547-2111 (Office); (3) 3951-8644 (Home). *Fax:* (3) 3547-2345 (Office).

INBAL, Eliahu; British/Israeli conductor; b. 16 Feb. 1936, Jerusalem; s. of Jehuda Joseph Inbal and Leah Museri Inbal; m. Helga Fritzsche 1968; three s.; ed Acad. of Music, Jerusalem, Conservatoire Nat. Supérieur, Paris; from 1963 guest conductor with numerous orchestras including Milan, Rome, Berlin, Munich, Hamburg, Stockholm, Copenhagen, Vienna, Budapest, Amsterdam, London, Paris, Tel Aviv, New York, Chicago, Toronto and Tokyo; Chief Conductor, Radio Symphony Orchestra, Frankfurt 1974–90, Hon. Conductor 1995–, Teatro La Fenice 1984–87; Hon. Conductor, Nat. Symphony Orchestra, RAI Torino 1996–; Chief Conductor Berlin Symphony Orchestra 2001–; has made numerous recordings, particularly of Mahler, Bruckner, Berlioz and Shostakovich; First Prize, Int. Conductors' Competition 'G. Cantelli' 1963; Officier des Arts de Lettres 1995; Goldenes Ehrenzeichen, Vienna 2001. *Leisure interests:* music reproduction, photography. *Address:* Hessischer Rundfunk, Bertramstrasse 8, 6000 Frankfurt, Germany. *Telephone:* (611) 1552371.

INDIANA, Robert, BFA; American artist; b. 13 Sept. 1928, New Castle, Ind.; ed John Herron School of Art, Indianapolis, Munson-Williams-Proctor Inst., Utica, New York, Art Inst. of Chicago, Skowhegan School of Painting and Sculpture, Univ. of Edinburgh and Edinburgh Coll. of Art; served USAAF 1946–49; Artist-in-Residence, Center of Contemporary Art, Aspen, Colo 1968; Hon. DFA (Franklin and Marshall Coll., Lancaster, Pa) 1970. *Group/Solo exhibitions include:* Painting and Sculpture of a Decade, Tate Gallery, London 1964, Twenty-ninth Biennial Exhbn of American Painting, Corcoran Gallery of Art, Washington, DC 1965, Pop Art and the American Tradition, Milwaukee 1965, White House Festival of the Arts, Washington 1965, American Painting Now, Expo 67, Montreal 1967, Annual Exhbns. of American Painting, Documenta IV, Kassel 1968, Art in the Sixties, Cologne 1969, San Francisco Museum of Art 1975, Royal Acad., London 1991, Museo Nacional Reina Sofía, Madrid 1992; numerous others including Stable Gallery, New York 1962, 1964, 1966, Walker Art Center, Minneapolis 1963, Inst. of Contemporary Art, Boston 1963, Rolf Nelson Gallery, LA 1965, Dayton's Gallery 1912, Minneapolis 1966, Galerie Alfred Schmela, Düsseldorf 1966, Stedelijk van Abbemuseum, Eindhoven 1966, Museum Hans Lange, Krefeld (FRG) 1966, Württembergischer Kunstverein, Stuttgart 1966, Inst. of Contemporary Art, Univ. of Pennsylvania 1968, Marion Koogler McNay Art Inst., San Antonio, Tex. 1968, Herron Museum of Art, Indianapolis 1968, Toledo Museum of Art, Ohio 1968, Hunter Gallery, Aspen, Colo 1968, Creighton Univ., Omaha 1969, St Mary's Coll., Notre Dame, Ind. 1969, Colby Coll. Art

Museum, Waterville, Maine 1969–70, Currier Gallery of Art, Manchester, NH 1970, Hopkins Center, Dartmouth Coll. Hanover, NH 1970, Bowdoin Coll. Museum of Art, Brunswick, Maine 1970, Brandeis Univ., Waltham, Mass. 1970, Heron Art Museum, Indianapolis 1977, Univ. of Texas 1977, Osuna Gallery, Washington 1981, Tex. Art Centre 1982, William A. Farnsworth Library and Art Museum, Maine 1982. *Address:* Press Box 464, Vinalhaven, ME 04863, USA.

INDJOVA, Reneta, PhD; Bulgarian economist and politician; b. 6 July 1953, Nova Zgora; m. Boyan Slavenkov 1977 (divorced 1990); one d.; ed Sofia Univ. of Nat. and World Economy; Univ. Asst Prof. of Political Economy and Econs 1975–89; a founder of Union of Democratic Forces (UDF), co-author UDF's platform 1990; Econ. Counsellor to Great Nat. Ass. 1990–91; Expert, Govt.'s Agency for Econ. Devt 1991–93; Head of Privatization Agency 1993, Exec. Dir 1994; Prime Minister 1994–95; Founder and Nat. Chair. political party "For Real Reforms" 1997; currently Co-Chair. Democratic Alliance party; Presidental Cand. 2001; Fellow, Eisenhower Exchange Program, Phila 1995; Trustee American Univ. of Blagoevgrad 1996–; Distinguished Speaker, Atlantic Club of Bulgaria 1995. *Leisure interests:* literature, music, tailoring. *Address:* Democratic Alliance, c/o National Assembly, Blvd. Narodno Sobraniye 3, Sofia 1000, Bulgaria.

INDURÁIN, Miguel; Spanish cyclist; b. 16 July 1964, Villava, Navarre; m. Marisa Induráin; one d.; mem. Reynolds team 1984–89, Banesto team 1989–96; five successive times winner, Tour de France 1991–95, 1995 winning time, 92 hrs. 44 min. 59 sec.; Gold Medal, Atlanta Olympics 1996; ranked No. 1 cyclist 1992, 1993; announced retirement Jan. 1997. *Address:* Villava, Pamplona, Spain.

INDYK, Martin S., BEcons, PhD; American diplomatist; b. 1 July 1951, London, England; ed Sydney Univ., Australian Nat. Univ.; Adjunct Prof. Johns Hopkins School of Advanced Int. Studies; Exec. Dir Washington Inst. for Near East Policy; Special Asst to the Pres. and Sr Dir for Near East and S Asian Affairs, Nat. Security Council; Prin. Adviser to the Pres. and Nat. Security Adviser on Arab–Israeli Issues, Iraq, Iran and S Asia; Sr mem. Warren Christopher's Middle East peace team; Amb. to Israel 1995–97, 2000–01; Asst Sec. for Near Eastern Affairs 1997–2000; Sr Fellow and Dir Saban Center for Middle East Policy, The Brookings Institution 2002–; mem. Int. Inst. for Strategic Studies, Middle East Inst. *Address:* The Brookings Institution, 1775 Massachusetts Avenue, NW, Washington, DC 20036, USA (Office). *Telephone:* (202) 797-6000. *Fax:* (202) 797-6004. *Website:* www.brook.edu.

INGAMELLS, John, BA; British museum director and art historian; b. 12 Nov. 1934, Northampton; s. of the late George H. Ingamells and Gladys L. (Rollett) Ingamells; m. Hazel Wilson 1964; two d.; ed Hastings and Eastbourne Grammar Schools and Fitzwilliam House, Cambridge; Art Asst York Art Gallery 1959–62; Asst Keeper of Art, Nat. Museum of Wales 1963–67; Curator, York Art Gallery 1967–77; Asst to Dir Wallace Collection 1977–78, Dir 1978–92; mem. Exec. Cttee Nat. Art Collections Fund 1992–97. *Publications:* The Davies Collection of French Art 1967, The English Episcopal Portrait 1981, Wallace Collection, Catalogue of Pictures (Vol. I) 1985, (Vol. II) 1986, (Vol. III) 1989, (Vol. IV) 1992, A Dictionary of British and Irish Travellers in Italy 1701–1800 (ed.) 1998, Allan Ramsay, A Complete Catalogue by A. Smart (ed.) 1999, The Letters of Sir Joshua Reynolds (ed.) 2000; numerous museum catalogues, Exhbn catalogues and articles in learned journals. *Address:* c/o Paul Mellon Centre for Studies in British Art, 16 Bedford Square, London, WC1B 3JA (Office); 39 Benson Road, London, SE23 3RL, England (Home). *Telephone:* (20) 7580-0311 (Office).

INGARDEN, Roman; Polish professor of physics; b. 1 Oct. 1920, Zakopane; m. Regina Urbanowicz; two s.; ed Jagiellonian Univ., Kraków; researcher Wrocław Univ., Sr Asst 1945–49, Asst Prof. 1949–54, Prof. 1954–66; Prof. Nicolaus Copernicus Univ., Toruń 1966–91, Prof. Emer. 1996–; Visiting Prof. univs. in the USA, Germany, France, Belgium, Canada, Japan; fmr Dir Research Centres of Geometrical Optics and Low Temperature Physics, Wrocław, then Centre of Mathematical Physics, Toruń; mem. Polish Socialist Party (PPS) 1936–44, Polish United Workers' Party (PZPR) 1954–90; mem. numerous scientific asscns.; Kt's Cross, Order of Polonia Restituta 1964, Officer's Cross 1972, Order of Saint Treasury with Ribbon (Japan) 1994, Maria Skłodowska-Curie Award, Polish Acad. of Sciences 1972. *Publications include:* The Theory of Sprays and Finsler Spaces with Applications in Physics and Biology 1993, Information Dynamics and Open Systems 1997. *Leisure interests:* Japanese language and culture, philosophy, history of physics. *Address:* ul. I. Kraszewskiego 22B m. 28, 87-100 Toruń, Poland (Office). *Telephone:* (56) 6223835 (Office).

INGE, Baron (Life Peer), cr. 1997, of Richmond in the County of North Yorkshire; **Field Marshal Peter Anthony Inge,** KG, GCB; British army officer; b. 5 Aug. 1935; s. of Raymond Albert Inge and the late Grace Maud Caroline Inge; m. Letitia Marion Beryl Thornton-Berry 1960; two d.; ed Summer Fields, Wrekin Coll., Royal Mil. Acad. Sandhurst; commissioned Green Howards 1956, ADC to G.O.C. 4 Div. 1960–61, Adjutant 1st Green Howards 1963–64, student Staff Coll. 1966, Ministry of Defence 1967–69, Co. Commdr 1st Green Howards 1969–70, student Jt Service Staff Coll. 1971, Brigade Maj. 11th Armoured Brigade 1972, Instructor Staff Coll. 1973–74, CO 1st Green Howards 1974–76, Commdt Jr Div. Staff Coll. 1977–79, Commdr 4th Armoured Brigade 1980–81, Chief of Staff HQ 1st (BR) Corps 1982–83, G.O.C. NEDIST and Commdr 2nd Infantry Div. 1984–86, Dir-Gen.

Logistic Policy (Army) 1986–87, Commdr 1st (BR) Corps 1987–89, Commdr NORTHAG and C.-in-C. BAOR 1989–92, Chief of Gen. Staff 1992–94, of the Defence Staff 1994–97, Constable of the Tower of London 1996–2000; ADC Gen. to the Queen 1991–94, Deputy Lt of N Yorks. 1994; Col The Green Howards 1982–94, Col Commdt RMP 1987–92, Col Commdt APTC 1988–97; Freeman City of London 1994. *Leisure interests:* cricket, walking, music, reading, military history. *Address:* House of Lords, London, SW1A 0PW, England.

INGHAM, Sir Bernard, Kt; British fmr civil servant; b. 21 June 1932, Halifax, Yorkshire; s. of Garnet Ingham and Alice Ingham; m. Nancy Hilda Hoyle 1956; one s.; ed Tech. Colls. of Todmorden, Halifax and Bradford; reporter Hebden Bridge Times 1948–52, The Yorkshire Post and Yorkshire Evening Post, Halifax 1952–59; with The Yorkshire Post, Leeds 1959–61, Northern Industrial Corresp. 1961; with The Guardian 1962–67, Labour Staff, London 1965–67; Press and Public Relations Adviser Nat. Bd for Prices and Incomes 1967–68; Chief Information Officer, Dept of Employment and Productivity 1968–72; Dir of Information Dept of Employment 1973; with Dept of Energy 1974–79, Dir of Information 1974-77, Under-Sec. and Head of Energy Conservation Div. 1978–79; Chief Press Sec. to the Prime Minister 1979–90; columnist, Daily Express 1991–98; Chair. Bernard Ingham Communications 1990–; Pres. British Franchise Asscn 1993–; Vice-Pres. Country Guardian 1991–; Dir (non-exec.) McDonald's Restaurants Ltd 1991–, Hill and Knowlton 1991–; Visiting Fellow and Hon. Dir Applied Policy Science Unit, Univ. of Newcastle-upon-Tyne 1991–; mem. Council Univ. of Huddersfield 1994–2000; Visiting Prof. Middlesex Univ. Business School 1997–, Sec. Supporters of Nuclear Energy 1998–; (Buckingham) 1997, (Middx) 1999. *Publication:* Kill the Messenger 1991, Yorkshire Millennium 1999, Yorkshire Castles 2001, Yorkshire Villages 2001, The Wages of Spin 2003. *Leisure interests:* walking, reading, gardening, visiting Yorkshire. *Address:* 9 Monahan Avenue, Purley, Surrey, CR8 3BB, England. *Telephone:* (20) 8660-8970. *Fax:* (20) 8668-4357.

INGHRAM, Mark Gordon, PhD; American professor and physicist; b. 13 Nov. 1919, Livingstone, Mont.; s. of Mark E. Inghram and Luella McNay Inghram; m. Evelyn M. Dyckman 1946; one s. one d.; ed Olivet Coll. and Univ. of Chicago; Physicist, Univ. of Minn. 1942, Manhattan Project, Columbia Univ. 1943–45; Sr Physicist Argonne Nat. Lab. 1945–49; Instructor in Physics, Univ. of Chicago 1947–49, Asst Prof. 1949–51, Assoc. Prof. 1951–57, Prof. of Physics 1957–69, Samuel K. Allison Distinguished Service Prof. of Physics 1969–84, Chair. Dept of Physics 1959–70, Assoc. Dean Div. of Physical Sciences 1964–71, 1981–84, Assoc. Dean, The College 1981–84, Master, Physical Sciences Collegiate Div. 1981–84, Samuel K. Allison Distinguished Service Prof. Emer. 1985–; mem. NAS; Lawrence Smith Medal of NAS 1957. *Publications:* over 150 research papers in scientific journals. *Address:* 3077 North Lakeshore Drive, Holland, MI 49424, USA. *Telephone:* (616) 399-8638.

INGLIS, Kenneth Stanley, MA, DPhil; Australian professor and university administrator; b. 7 Oct. 1929, Melbourne; s. of Stanley W Inglis and Irene (née Winning) Inglis; m. 1st Judy Betheras 1952 (deceased 1962); one s. two d.; m. 2nd Amirah Gust 1965; ed Univs. of Melbourne and Oxford; Sr Lecturer Univ. of Adelaide 1956–60, Reader 1960–62; Reader Australian Nat. Univ. 1963–65, Prof. 1965–66; Prof. Univ. of Papua New Guinea 1967–72, Vice-Chancellor 1972–75; Professorial Fellow A.N.V. 1975–76, Prof. of History, Research School of Social Sciences 1977–94, Prof. Emer. 1994–; Overseas Visiting Fellow St John's Coll., Cambridge 1990–91; Hon. DLitt (Melbourne) 1996; Ernest Scott Prize for History 1983–84, 1999, Fellowship of Australian Writers Prize for Literature 1999, NSW Premier's Prize for Australian History 1999; Nat. Centre for Cultural Studies Award 1999. *Publications:* The Stuart Case 1961, Churches and the Working Classes in Victorian England 1963, The Australian Colonists 1974, This is the ABC: The Australian Broadcasting Comm. 1932–1983, 1983, The Rehearsal 1985, Australians: A Historical Library, 11 Vols (Gen. Ed.) 1987–88, Nation: The Life of an Independent Journal of Opinion 1958–72, (Ed.) 1989, Sacred Places: War Memorials in the Australian Landscape 1998, Observing Australia 1959–99 1999. *Address:* P.O. Box 5, O'Connor, ACT 2602, Australia.

INGOLD, Keith Usherwood, OC, PhD, FRS, FRSC, FCIC; Canadian research chemist; b. 31 May 1929, Leeds, England; s. of Sir Christopher Kelk Ingold and Lady Edith Hilda Usherwood; m. Carmen Cairine Hodgkin 1956; one s. one d.; ed Univ. Coll., Univ. of London, Oxford Univ.; Postdoctoral Fellow Nat. Research Council of Canada 1951–53, Research Officer Div. of Chem. 1955–90, Head Hydrocarbon Chem. Section 1965–90, Assoc. Dir 1977–90; Postdoctoral Fellow Univ. of BC 1953–55; Distinguished Research Scientist, Steacie Inst. for Molecular Sciences 1990–2000, Nat. Research Council 2000–; Adjunct Prof. Dept of Biochem., Brunel Univ., UK 1983–94; Adjunct Prof. Dept of Chem. and Biochem. Univ. of Guelph, Ont. 1985–89; Adjunct Research Prof., Carleton Univ., Ottawa 1991–; Adjunct Prof. Dept of Chem., Univ. of St Andrews, Scotland 1997–; visiting scientist to numerous univs., numerous lectureships; Sr Carnegie Fellowship Univ. of St Andrews (Scotland) 1977; Fellow Univ. Coll. London 1987; mem. ACS Vice-Pres. Canadian Soc. for Chem. 1985–87, Pres. 1987–88; Hon. mem. Sociedad Argentina de Investigaciones en Química Orgánica; Dr. hc (Univ. degli Studi di Ancona) 1999; Hon. DSc (Guelph, Ontario) 1985, (St Andrews) 1989, (Carleton Univ.) 1992, (McMaster Univ., Ontario) 1995, (Dalhousie Univ., NS) 1996; Hon. LLD (Mount Allison) 1987; numerous awards including Chem. Inst. of Canada Medal 1981, Syntex Award in Physical Organic Chem. 1983, Royal Soc. of

Canada Centennial Medal 1982, Henry Marshall Tory Medal, Royal Soc. of Canada 1985, Pauling Award, ACS 1988, Alfred Bader Award in Organic Chem., Canadian Soc. for Chem. 1989, Humboldt Research Award 1989, Davy Medal, Royal Soc. 1990, Arthur C. Cope Scholar Award, ACS 1992, Izaak Walton Killam Memorial Prize, Canada Council 1992, James Flack Norris Award in Physical Organic Chem., ACS 1993, Angelo Mangini Medal, Italian Chemical Soc. 1997, Canada Gold Medal for Science and Eng, Natural Science and Eng Research Council 1998, Royal Medal A, Royal Soc. 2000. *Publications:* Free-Radical Substitution Reactions (with B. P. Roberts) 1971, Nitrogen-centered Radicals, Aminoxyl and Related Radicals (with J. C. Walton) 1994; over 480 publications in the open scientific literature. *Leisure interests:* skiing, water skiing. *Address:* National Research Council of Canada, 100 Sussex Drive, Ottawa, Ont., K1A 0R6, Canada. *Telephone:* (613) 822-1123 (Home); (613) 990-0938. *Fax:* (613) 941-8447. *E-mail:* keith.ingold@nrc.ca (Office).

INGÓLFSSON, Thorsteinn; Icelandic diplomatist; b. 9 Dec. 1944, Reykjavik; s. of Ingólfur Thorsteinsson and Helga Gudmundsdóttir; m. 1st Gudrún Valdís Ragnarsdóttir (divorced 1986); one s. one d.; m. 2nd Hólmfrídur Kofoed-Hansen 1994; ed Commercial Coll. of Iceland, Univ. of Iceland; First Sec. and Deputy Chief of Mission, Washington, DC 1973–78; Chief of Div., Ministry of Foreign Affairs 1978–85; Minister Counsellor 1981; Deputy Perm. Rep. to Int. Orgs., Geneva 1985–87, Acting Perm. Rep. Feb.–June 1987; rank of Amb. 1987; Dir Defence Dept Ministry for Foreign Affairs, 1987–90; Chair. Icelandic-American Defence Council 1987–90; Perm. Under-Sec. for Foreign Affairs 1990–94; Perm. Rep. to N Atlantic Council and WEU 1994–99; Perm. Rep. to UN 1999–; Amb. to Cuba 2001, to Barbados 2002, to Jamaica 2003 with residence in New York; Grande Croix, Légion d'honneur, Hon. GCMG, numerous decorations. *Address:* Permanent Mission of Iceland to the United Nations, 800 Third Avenue, 36th Floor, New York, NY 10022, USA (Office). *Telephone:* (212) 593-2700 (Office). *Fax:* (212) 593-6269 (Office).

INGRAHAM, Hubert Alexander; Bahamian politician; b. 4 Aug. 1947, Pine Ridge, Grand Bahama; m. Delores Velma Miller; six c.; ed Cooper's Town Public School, Southern Sr School and Govt High School Evening Inst. Nassau; called to the Bar, Bahamas 1972; Sr Partner, Christie, Ingraham & Co. (law firm); fmr mem. Air Transport Licensing Authority; fmr Chair. Real Property Tax Tribunal; mem. Nat. Gen. Council Progressive Liberal Party (PLP) 1975; Nat. Chair. and mem. Nat. Exec. Cttee PLP 1976; elected to House of Ass. as PLP mem. 1977, 1982; Minister of Housing, Nat. Insurance and Social Services 1982–84; Chair. Bahamas Mortgage Corpn 1982; alt. del. conf. of IDB, Uruguay 1983, IMF/IBRD 1979–84; expelled from PLP 1986; elected to Nat. Ass. as ind. 1987; Parl. Leader, Official Opposition 1990–92; Leader, Opposition Free Nat. Movt and of Official Opposition 1990; Prime Minister of the Bahamas 1992–2002, also of Housing and Local Govt 1995–97 and Trade and Industry 1995–97; fmrly Minister of Finance and Planning; Dr. hc (Buckingham) 2000. *Leisure interests:* reading, swimming. *Address:* c/o Office of the Prime Minister, Cecil V. Wallace-Whitfield Centre, P.O. Box CB-10980, Nassau, Bahamas (Office).

INGRAM, Christopher John; British advertising and marketing executive and entrepreneur; b. 9 June 1943; s. of Thomas Frank Ingram and Gladys Agnes Ingram (née Louttid); m. Janet Elizabeth Rye; one s. one d.; ed Woking Grammar School, Surrey; Media Dir KMP Partnership 1969–71; Man. Dir TMD Advertising 1972–75; Chair. CIA Group/Tempus Group PLC 1976–2002; Ernst & Young London Entrepreneur of the Year 2000, Ernst & Young UK Business-to-Business Entrepreneur of the Year 2000. *Leisure interests:* art, theatre, wildlife, travel in cold climates, entrepreneurship, the voluntary sector, Woking Football Club. *Address:* Tempus Group PLC, 1 Pemberton Row, London, EC4A 3BG, England (Office). *Telephone:* (20) 7803-2227 (Office). *Fax:* (20) 7803-2800 (Office). *E-mail:* cingram@tempusgroup .com (Office). *Website:* www.tempusgroup.com (Office).

INGRAM, James Charles, AO, B.A.(ECON.); Australian diplomatist and international civil servant; b. 27 Feb. 1928, Warragul; m. Odette Koven 1950; one s. two d.; ed De la Salle Coll., Melbourne Univ.; joined Dept of External Affairs 1946; Third Sec., Tel Aviv 1950; First Sec., Washington 1956; Chargé d'Affaires, Brussels 1959; Counsellor, Djakarta 1962, Australian Mission to UN 1964; Asst Sec. External Affairs, Canberra 1967; Amb. to Philippines 1970–73; High Commr in Canada, Jamaica, Barbados, Guyana, Trinidad and Tobago 1973–74; First Asst Sec. Australian Devt Assistance Agency 1975–76; Dir-Gen. Australian Devt Assistance Bureau, Dept of Foreign Affairs 1977–82; Exec. Dir UN World Food Programme 1982–92; Dir Australian Inst. of Int. Affairs 1992–93; Visiting Fellow, Centre for Int. and Public Law, ANU 1993–94; Chair., Australian Govt Advisory Cttee on Non-Govt Devt Orgs. 1995–; mem. Bd of Trustees, Int. Food Policy Research Inst. 1991–98, Crawford Fund for Int. Agric. Research, Melbourne 1994–99 (Chair. 1996–99), Int. Crisis Group, Brussels 1995–99; mem. Gov. Council, Soc. for Int. Devt 1988–94; mem. Commonwealth Intergovernmental Group on the Emergence of a Global Humanitarian Order, London 1994–95; Chair. UN Asscn of Australia (A.C.T. Div.) 1998–99; Alan Shawn Feinstein World Hunger Award (Brown Univ.) 1991. *Leisure interests:* music, reading, gardening, cycling. *Address:* 4 Stokes Street, Manuka, ACT 2603, Australia. *Telephone:* 6295-0446. *Fax:* 6295-0552.

INGRAM, Vernon M., PhD, DSc, FRS, FAAS; British professor of biochemistry; b. 19 May 1924, Breslau, Germany; s. of Kurt Immerwahr and Johanna Immerwahr; m. 1st Margaret Young 1950; one s. one d.; m. 2nd Elizabeth

Hendee 1984; ed Birkbeck Coll., Univ. of London; Research Chemist, Thos. Morson and Son 1941–45; Lecture Demonstrator, Birkbeck Coll., London 1945–47, Asst Lecturer 1947–50; Rockefeller Foundation Fellow, New York 1950–51; Coxe Fellow, Yale Univ. 1951–52; mem. staff, Molecular Biology Unit, Cavendish Lab., Cambridge 1952–58; Visiting Assoc. Prof. MIT 1958–59; Assoc. Prof. MIT 1959–61, Prof. of Biochem. 1961–, John and Dorothy Wilson Prof. of Biology 1988–; Guggenheim Fellow, Univ. of London 1967–68; Fellow American Acad. of Arts and Sciences. *Publications:* Haemoglobin and its Abnormalities 1961, The Haemoglobins in Genetics and Evolution 1963, The Biosynthesis of Macromolecules 1965, 1971. *Leisure interest:* music. *Address:* Department of Biology, Massachusetts Institute of Technology, 77 Massachusetts Avenue, Cambridge, MA 02139, USA. *Telephone:* (617) 253-1000. *Fax:* (617) 253-8000. *Website:* www.mit.edu (Office).

INGRAMS, Richard Reid; British journalist; b. 19 Aug. 1937, London; s. of Leonard St Clair and Victoria (née Reid) Ingrams; m. Mary Morgan 1962 (divorced 1993); two s. (one deceased) one d.; ed Shrewsbury School, Univ. Coll., Oxford; joined Private Eye 1962; Ed. 1963–86, Chair. 1974–; Founder and Ed. The Oldie 1992–; TV Critic The Spectator 1976–84; columnist, The Observer 1988–90, 1992–. *Publications:* Private Eye on London (with Christopher Booker and William Rushton) 1962, Private Eye's Romantic England 1963, Mrs. Wilson's Diary (with John Wells) 1965, Mrs. Wilson's Second Diary 1966, The Tale of Driver Grope 1968, The Bible for Motorists (with Barry Fantoni) 1970, The Life and Times of Private Eye (Ed.) 1971, Harris in Wonderland (as Philip Reid with Andrew Osmond) 1973, Cobbett's Country Book (Ed.) 1974, Beachcomber; the works of J. B. Morton (Ed.) 1974, The Best of Private Eye 1974, God's Apology 1977, Goldenballs 1979, Romney Marsh (with Fay Godwin) 1980, Dear Bill: The Collected Letters of Denis Thatcher (with John Wells) 1980, The Other Half 1981, Piper's Places (with John Piper) 1983, Dr. Johnson by Mrs. Thrale (Ed.) 1984, Down the Hatch (with John Wells) 1985, Just the One (with John Wells) 1986, John Stewart Collis: A Memoir 1986, The Best of Dear Bill (with John Wells) 1986, Mud in Your Eye (with John Wells) 1987, The Eye Spy Look-alike Book (ed.) 1988, The Ridgeway 1988, You Might As Well Be Dead 1988, England: An Anthology 1989, No. 10 1989, On and On . . . . Further Letters of Denis Thatcher (with John Wells) 1990; ed. The Oldie Annual 1993, The Oldie Annual II 1994, Malcolm Muggeridge 1995; ed. I Once Met 1996, ed. The Oldie Annual III 1997, Jesus: Authors Take Sides (anthology) 1999, ed. The Oldie Annual IV 1999. *Leisure interests:* music, book selling. *Address:* c/o The Oldie, 45/46 Poland Street, London, W1V 4AU, England. *Telephone:* (20) 7734-2225. *Fax:* (20) 7734-2226.

INGRAO, Pietro; Italian politician and journalist; b. 30 March 1915, Lenola, Latina; m. Laura Lombardo Radice 1944; one s. four d.; ed Univ. of Rome; began career as a journalist; active in anti-fascist student groups at Univ. of Rome 1939; joined Italian Communist Party (PCI) 1940; joined editorial staff of l'Unità (PCI newspaper) 1943; took part in resistance movement in Rome and Milan 1943–45; Ed. l'Unità 1947–57; mem. Nat. Exec. and Sec. of PCI 1956; mem. Chamber of Deputies (lower house of Parl.) for Rome, Latino, Frosinone, Viterbo 1948–58, for Perugia, Terni, Rieti 1958–63, 1968–, for Ancona and Perugia 1963–68; Pres. of PCI Parl. Group 1972–76; Pres. of Chamber of Deputies 1976–79; Pres. of Centre of Studies and Activities for the Reform of the State 1979. *Publications:* essays on political and social subjects in periodicals, incl. Rinascita, Critica Marxista 1945–, Masse e Potere 1977, Crisi e Terzavia 1978, Tradizione e Progetto 1982, Il Dubbio dei Vincitori (poetry) 1987. *Telephone:* 6784101.

INHOFE, James Mountain, BA; American politician; b. 17 Nov. 1934, Des Moines, Ia; s. of Perry Inhofe and Blanche Mountain; m. Kay Kirkpatrick 1958; two s. two d.; ed Univ. of Tulsa; mem. Okla House of Reps 1966–68; mem. Okla State Senate 1968–76, Minority Leader 1970–76; Mayor of Tulsa 1978–84; mem. US House of Reps., 1st Dist Okla 1987–94; Senator from Oklahoma Jan. 1995–; Pres. Fly Riverside Inc. 1978, Quaker Life Insurance Co.; Republican. *Address:* US Senate, 453 Russell Senate Building, Washington, DC 20510-0001, USA. *E-mail:* jim-inhofe@inhofe.senate.gov (Office).

INK, Claude; French business executive; b. 17 March 1928, Hussigny; s. of Gilbert Ink and Paule Rollin; m. Annie Beaurain-Verdollin 1952; two s. one d.; ed Ecole Polytechnique; engineer, Sollac 1952, Asst Dir-Gen. 1966, Vice-Pres., Dir-Gen. Sollac 1978; Dir-Gen. SCAC 1969; Pres. Bd of Dirs., Solmer 1980, Dir-Gen. 1985; Pres. and Dir-Gen. Solnetal, Vice-Pres. Sollac; Dir-Gen. Sacilor; Pres. Chambre syndicale Fer blanc 1986; Del. Gen. Fondation Ecole Polytechnique 1987–95, Conseilleur 1996; Pres. Asscn Professionnelle des Producteurs Européens de l'Acier pour l'Emballage Léger (A.P.E.A.L.) 1988–90; Pres. Comité Int. du titre de l'ingénieur 1996–99; Officier, Légion d'honneur, Chevalier des Palmes académiques. *Address:* Fondation de l'Ecole Polytechnique, place des Corolles, 92080 Paris-la-Défense (Office); 65 bis avenue du Belloy, 78110 Le Vesinet, France (Home). *Telephone:* 39-52-45-03 (Home). *E-mail:* claude.ink2@wanadoo.fr (Home).

INKELES, Alex, PhD; American professor of sociology; b. 4 March 1920, Brooklyn, New York; s. of Meyer Inkeles and Ray Gewer Inkeles; m. Bernadette Mary Kane 1942; one d.; ed Cornell and Columbia Univs., Washington School of Psychiatry; Social Science Research Analyst, Dept of State 1942–46, Int. Broadcasting Div. 1949–51; Instructor in Social Relations, Harvard Univ. 1948–49, Lecturer in Sociology 1948–57, Prof. 1957–71, Dir Russian Research Center Studies in Social Relations 1963–71, Dir Center of Int. Affairs Studies on Social Aspects of Econ. Devt 1963–71; Margaret Jacks

Prof. of Educ., Stanford Univ. 1971–78, Prof. of Sociology and, by courtesy, Educ. 1978–90, Emer. Prof. of Sociology 1995–; Sr Fellow, Hoover Inst. on War, Revolution and Peace 1978–, Prof. Emer. 1990–; numerous fellowships including Inst. for Advanced Study, Princeton, Guggenheim, Fulbright, Rockefeller Foundation, Bellagio, Italy, NAS Exchange Program with People's Repub. of China, Nankai Univ. 1983; mem. American Acad. of Arts and Sciences, NAS, AAAS, American Philosophical Soc., American Psychology Asscn; numerous awards. *Publications:* Public Opinion in Soviet Russia 1950, How the Soviet System Works 1956, The Soviet Citizen: Daily Life in a Totalitarian Society 1959, What is Sociology? 1964, Social Change in Soviet Russia 1968, Becoming Modern: Individual Change in Six Developing Countries 1974, Exploring Individual Modernity 1983, On Measuring Democracy: Its Consequences and Concomitants 1991, National Character: A Psycho-Social Perspective 1996, One World Emerging? Convergence and Divergence in Industrial Societies 1998. *Leisure interests:* travel, East Asian art collection, biking, swimming. *Address:* Hoover Institution, LHH-239, Stanford University, Stanford, CA 94305; 1001 Hamilton Avenue, Palo Alto, CA 94301, USA (Home). *Telephone:* (415) 723-4856 (Office); (415) 327-4197 (Home). *Fax:* (415) 723-0576 (Office). *E-mail:* inkeles@hoover.stanford.edu (Office). *Website:* www-hoover.stanford.edu/bios/inkeles.html (Office).

INNES OF EDINGIGHT, Sir Malcolm Rognvald, KCVO, KStJ; b. 25 May 1938; s. of the late Sir Thomas Innes of Learney and of Lady Lucy Buchan; m. Joan Hay 1963; three s.; ed Edinburgh Acad., Univ. of Edinburgh; Falkland Pursuivant Extraordinary 1957; Carrick Pursuivant 1958; Lyon Clerk and Keeper of the Records 1966; Marchmont Herald 1971, Lord Lyon King of Arms 1981–01; Secretary to Order of the Thistle 1981–01; Orkney Herald Extraordinary 2001–; mem. Queen's Body Guard for Scotland (Royal Company of Archers) 1971; Pres. Heraldry Soc. of Scotland; Grand Officer of Merit, Sovereign Mil. Order, Malta. *Leisure interest:* visiting places of historic interest. *Address:* Castleton of Kinnairdy, Bridge of Marnoch, Aberdeenshire, AB54 7RT, Scotland (Home). *Telephone:* (1466) 780866.

INNIS, Roy Emile Alfredo; American human rights organization executive and chemist; b. 6 June 1934, St Croix, Virgin Islands; s. of Alexander Innis and Georgianna Innis; m. Doris Funnye 1965; six s. (two deceased) two d.; ed City Coll., New York; joined US Army 1950, Sergeant 1951, discharged 1952; pharmaceutical research work, Vick Chemical Co., then medical research Montefiore Hosp. until 1967; active in Harlem Chapter of Congress of Racial Equality (CORE) 1963–, Chair. Harlem Educ. Cttee 1964, Chair. Harlem CORE 1965–67, Second Nat. Vice-Chair. 1967–68, Assoc. Nat. Dir CORE Jan–Sept. 1968, Nat. Dir 1968–70, Nat. Chair. 1982–; Founder Harlem Commonwealth Council, First Exec. Dir 1967–68, now mem. of Bd; Res. Fellow, Metropolitan Applied Research Center 1967–; Co-Publisher The Manhattan Tribune 1968–71; mem. Bd and Steering Cttee Nat. Urban Coalition; mem. of Bd New York Coalition, Haryou Inc., Bd of Dirs New Era Health Educ. and Welfare, Bd of Advisers Pan-African Journal; mem. Editorial Staff Social Policy Magazine; Publr The Correspondent; Co-Chair. Econ. Devt Task Force, New York Urban Coalition; Founder CORE Community School, South Bronx 1977. *Publications:* The Little Black Book 1971; chapters in: The Endless Crisis, Black Economic Development 1970, Integrating America's Heritage: A Congressional Hearing to Establish A National Commission on Negro History and Culture 1970, Profiles in Black 1976; articles and editorials in Manhattan Tribune, CORE Magazine, Business Weekly, etc. *Leisure interests:* reading, sports, music. *Address:* 817 Broadway, New York, NY 10003, USA (Office). *Telephone:* (212) 598-4000 (Office). *Fax:* (212) 529-3568 (Office). *E-mail:* corenyc@aol.com (Office). *Website:* www.core-online.org (Office).

INNOCENTI, HE Cardinal Antonio; Italian ecclesiastic; b. 23 Aug. 1915, Poppi, Fiesole, Tuscany; ordained 1938; consecrated Bishop, Titular See of Aeclanum 1968, then Archbishop; fmr Apostolic Nuncio in Spain; cr. Cardinal 1985; fmr Prefect of Congregation for the Clergy; Pres. of the Pontifical Comm. for the Conservation of the Artistic and Historic Heritage of the Church 1988–91; Pres. Pontifical Comm. 'Ecclesia Dei' 1991–99. *Address:* Piazza della Città Leonina 9, 00193 Rome, Italy. *Telephone:* (06) 6896789.

INNOCENTI, Luigi; Italian industrialist; b. 19 Dec. 1923; ed Massimo Coll., Rome and School of Engineering, Rome; Manager, Innocenti 1948–51, Gen. Vice-Dir 1951–58, Vice-Chair. 1958–66, Chair. 1966–. *Address:* Via Senato 19, Milan, Italy.

İNÖNÜ, Erdal, PhD; Turkish politician; b. 1926, Ankara; s. of the late İsmet İnönü (fmr Prime Minsiter and Pres. of Turkey); m.; ed Ankara Univ., California Inst. of Tech., USA; Prof. of Physics, Middle East Tech. Univ. 1960–74, also served as Dean, Science-Literature Faculty and Rector; Chair. Social Democratic Party (SODEP), subsequently Social Democratic Populist Party (SHP) 1963, merged with Repub. Peoples' Party 1995; elected deputy from İzmir 1986, 1987; Deputy Prime Minister and State Minister 1991–94; Minister of Foreign Affairs March–Sept. 1995.

INOUE, Kichio; Japanese politician; b. 1923, Kagoshima Pref.; worked as tech. expert with a mining firm; fmr mem. city and pref. assemblies; mem. House of Councillors; fmr Leader of LDP del. in Upper House; Dir-Gen. Hokkaido and Okinawa Devt Agencies 1998–99. *Leisure interests:* kendo, golf, reading. *Address:* c/o Okinawa Development Agency, 1-6-1, Nagata-cho, Chiyoda-ku, Tokyo 100, Japan.

INOUE, Yuko; Japanese viola player; b. Hamamatsu; ed Royal Northern Coll. of Music, Manchester; fmr Prin. Viola of Netherlands Chamber Orchestra; now soloist and chamber musician; Prof. at RAM, London; performed as soloist with Hungarian State Philharmonic Orchestra, Hallé, Orchestra, Netherlands Chamber Orchestra; performed as prin. with Philharmonia Orchestra, London Sinfonietta; has appeared at Lockenhaus, Kuhmo, Cheltenham, Bath and Aldeburgh Festivals; winner of 17th Budapest Int. Viola Competition.

INOUE, Yutaka, D.MED.SCI.; Japanese politician; b. 17 Nov. 1927, Chiba; m.; three d.; ed Tokyo Dental Coll.; mem. Chiba Prefectural Ass. 1963–72; mem. House of Reps. 1976–79; mem. House of Councillors 1980–, Pres. 2000–02; State Sec. for Finance 1983–84; Minister of Educ. 1990–91; Chair. Cttee on the Budget 1995–96; Chair. Research Cttee on Int. Affairs 1999–2000; Grand Cordon, Order of the Rising Sun. *Publication:* Major Airports in the World. *Leisure interests:* golf, comic story telling, Sumo. *Address:* c/o Secretariat of the House of Councillors, Kokkai, Nagata-cho, Chiyoda-ku, Tokyo, Japan (Office).

INOUYE, Daniel Ken, AB, JD; American politician and lawyer; b. 7 Sept. 1924, Honolulu, Hawaii; s. of Hyotaro Inouye and Kame Imanaga Inouye; m. Margaret Shinobu Awamura 1949; one s.; ed Univ. of Hawaii and George Washington Univ. Law School; US Army 1943–47; Majority Leader, Territorial House of Reps 1954–58, mem. Territorial Senate 1958–59; mem. US Congress 1959–62; US Senator from Hawaii 1962–; Democrat; mem. Senate Cttee on Appropriations, Commerce Cttee, Asst Majority Whip 1964–76; mem. Democratic Senatorial Campaign Cttee, Senate Select Cttee on Indian Affairs; Chair. Senate Appropriations Subcttee on Foreign Operations; Chair. Senate Commerce Subcttee on Merchant Marine and Tourism; Chair. Senate Select Cttee on Intelligence 1976–77; Chair. Senate Sub-Cttee on Budget Authorizations 1979–84, Head Special Cttee on Iran Affairs 1986; Temp. Chair. and Keynoter 1968 Dem. Nat. Convention; Sec. Dem. Conf. 1977; Purple Heart with Cluster; Horatio Alger Award 1989, Medal of Honour with Blue Ribbon, (Japan) 1989. *Address:* US Senate, 722 Hart Senate Office Building, Washington, DC 20510-0001 (Office); 469 Ena Road, Honolulu, HI 96815-1749, USA. *Telephone:* (202) 224-3934 (Office).

INOUYE, Minoru, BL; Japanese banker; b. 1924, Tokyo; m.; one s.; ed Univ. of Tokyo; joined Bank of Tokyo 1947, Deputy Agent, New York 1964–66, Deputy Gen. Man. Int. Funds and Foreign Exchange Div. 1966–67, Deputy Gen. Man. Planning and Co-ordination Div. 1967–70, Gen. Man. 1970–72, Dir and Gen. Man. London Office 1972–75, Resident Man. Dir for Europe 1975, Man. Dir 1975–79, Sr Man. Dir 1979–80, Deputy Pres. 1980–85, Pres. 1985–90, Adviser 1990, Advisor, Bank of Tokyo-Mitsubishi, Ltd 1996–; Orden Mexicana del Aguila Azteca, Mexico 1986, Medal of Honour, with Blue Ribbon, Japan 1989, Ordem Nacional de Cruzeiro do Sul, Brazil 1989, Chevalier, Légion d'honneur 1990, Order of the Rising Sun, Gold and Silver Star, Japan 1994. *Leisure interests:* golf, travel. *Address:* The Bank of Tokyo-Mitsubishi, Ltd, 3–2 Nihombashi Hongokucho 1-chome, Chuo-ku, Tokyo 103-0021, Japan (Office).

INSANALLY, Rudy, BA; Guyanese diplomatist; b. 23 Jan. 1936; ed Univs. of London and Paris; teacher of modern languages Kingston Coll., Jamaica, Queen's Coll., Guyana and Univ. of Guyana 1959–66; Counsellor at Guyanese Embassy, Washington, DC 1966–69; Chargé d'affaires at Embassy, Venezuela 1970, Amb. 1972–78; Deputy Perm. Rep. of Guyana to UN, New York 1970–72, Perm. Rep. 1987–; Perm. Rep. to EEC 1978–81; Amb. to Belgium (also accred to Sweden, Norway and Austria) 1978–81, to Colombia 1982–86; Head of Political Div. I Ministry of Foreign Affairs of Guyana 1982–86; High Commr to Barbados, Trinidad and Tobago and the Eastern Caribbean 1982–86; Minister of Foreign Affairs 2001–; mem. Bd of Govs. Inst. of Int. Relations, Trinidad and Tobago 1982–86. *Address:* Ministry of Foreign Affairs, Takuba Lodge, 254 South Road and New Garden Street, Georgetown, Guyana (Office). *Telephone:* 226-1606 (Office). *Fax:* 225-9192 (Office). *E-mail:* minfor@sdnp.org.gy (Office). *Website:* www.minfor.gov.gy (Office).

INSULZA SALINAS, José Miguel; Chilean politician and lawyer; b. 1943; m. Georgina Núñez J.; four c.; ed St George's Coll., Santiago, Law School, Universidad de Chile, Facultad Latinoamericana de Ciencias Sociales and Univ. of Michigan, USA; Prof. of Political Theory, Universidad de Chile, of Political Sciences, Pontifícia Universidad Católica de Chile –1973; Political Adviser to Ministry of Foreign Relations, Dir Diplomatic Acad. –1973; researcher, then Dir Instituto de Estudios de Estados Unidos, Centro de Investigación y Docencia Económicas, Mexico 1981–88; Prof., Universidad Autónoma de México; Head Multilateral Econ. Affairs Dept, Ministry of Foreign Relations, Deputy Chair. Int. Co-operation Agency 1990–94; Under-Sec. for Foreign Affairs 1994, Minister 1994–99; Minister of the Interior 2000–; mem. Bd of Dirs. Instituto de Fomento de Desarrollo Científico y Tecnológico; mem. Consejo Chileno de Relaciones Internacionales, Consejo de Redacción, Nexos Magazine, Mexico, Corporación de Desarrollo Tecnológico Empresarial. *Address:* Ministry of the Interior, Palacio de la Moneda, Santiago, Chile. *Telephone:* (2) 690-4000 (Office). *Fax:* (2) 699-2165 (Office).

INTRILIGATOR, Michael David, PhD; American economist and educator; b. 5 Feb. 1938, New York; s. of Allan Intriligator and Sally Intriligator; m. Devrie Shapiro 1963; four s.; ed MIT, Yale Univ.; Asst Prof. Econs Univ. of Calif. at LA (UCLA) 1963–66, Assoc. Prof. 1966–72, Prof. Dept of Econs 1972–, Prof. Dept of Political Science 1981–, Prof. Dept of Political Studies 1994–, Dir Center for Int. and Strategic Affairs 1982–92, 2000–02; Dir Jacob Marschak Interdisciplinary Coll. 1977–; Dir Burkle Center for Int. Relations 2000–02; Assoc. Ed. Conflict Man. and Peace Science 1980–; Co-Ed. Handbooks in Econs 1980–, Advanced Textbooks in Econs 1972–; mem. Council on Foreign Relations (NY), Int. Inst. for Strategic Studies (London); Fellow Econometric Soc.; Sr Fellow The Milken Inst.; Sr Fellow Gorbachev Foundation of N America. *Publications include:* Mathematical Optimization and Economic Theory 1971, Economic Models, Techniques and Applications 1978, A Forecasting and Policy Simulation Model of the Health Care Sector 1979, East-West Conflict: Elite Perceptions and Political Opinions (jtly) 1988, Co-operative Models in International Relations Research (ed., with U. Luterbacher) 1994. *Leisure interests:* travel and art collecting, classical music. *Address:* Department of Economics, UCLA, Los Angeles, CA 90095-0001 (Office); 140 Foxtail Drive, Santa Monica, CA 90402, USA (Home). *Telephone:* (310) 825-4144 (Office); (310) 395-7909 (Home). *Fax:* (310) 825-9528 (Office). *E-mail:* intriligator@econ.ucla.edu (Office).

IOFFE, Boris Lazarevich, MS; Russian theoretical physicist; b. 6 July 1926, Moscow; s. of Lazar Iof and Pesia Ioffe; m. 1st Svetlana Mikhailova 1957 (divorced 1974); one s.; m. 2nd Nina Libova 1990; ed Moscow Univ.; Jr Scientist, Inst. of Theoretical and Experimental Physics (ITEP), Moscow 1950–55, Sr Scientist 1955–77, Head of Lab. 1977–, Prof. 1977–, Chair. ITEP Scientific Council 1990–97; Deputy Ed. Moscow Physics Soc. Journal; mem. High Energy Physics Scientific Policy Cttee (Russia) 1992, Russian Nuclear Soc. –1990; Corresp. mem. USSR (now Russian) Acad. of Sciences 1990; mem. Exec. Cttee United Physical Soc. of Russian Fed. 1998; Fellow American Physical Soc. 1995; Order of Honour of USSR 1954, 1974, Veteran of Labour Medal 1985, USSR Award for Discovery 1986, 1989, Alexander von Humboldt Award (Germany) 1994, 850 Years of Moscow Medal 1997, Novy Mir Magazine Prize 1999. *Publications:* Hard Processes 1984; 250 articles. *Leisure interests:* mountaineering (especially in Cen. Asia and Far East), skiing. *Address:* Institute of Theoretical and Experimental Physics, Bolshaya Cheremushkinskaya 25, 117259 Moscow (Office); Bolotnikovskaya Street 40, Korp 4, Apt. 16, 113209 Moscow, Russia (Home). *Telephone:* (095) 123-31-93 (Office); (095) 121-44-38 (Home). *Fax:* (095) 883-96-01. *E-mail:* ioffe@vitep5.itep.ru (Office).

IORDACHE, Ştefan; Romanian actor; b. 3 Feb. 1941, Bucharest; s. of Traian Iordache and Elena Iordache; m. Michaela Tonitza 1970; ed Theatre and Cinema Art Inst., Bucharest; with Nat. Theatre, Craiova and Nottara Theatre, Little Theatre and Nat. Theatre, Bucharest; Salvo Randone Excellence Prize, Karlovy Vary Award (Best Actor) 1967, Romanian Acad. Prize (Best Actor) 1993. *Stage roles include:* Hamlet 1977, Apemantus in Timon of Athens 1978, Master in Master and Margaret 1980, Richard III 1982, Titus in Titus Andronicus 1992, Cearnota in The Run (Bulgakov) 1995, Barrymore in Barrymore 1999. *Films:* The Stranger 1964, Glissando 1982, Luxurious Hotel 1991, The Most Beloved on Earth 1992, My Name Is Adam 1996, The Man of Today 1997. *Radio roles include:* Prometheus in Prometheus Bound, Richard III, Serebriakov in Uncle Vanya. *Television roles include:* Don Juan in Don Juan by Molière, King John in King John by Dürrenmatt and Jack Worthing in The Importance of being Earnest. *Leisure interest:* life. *Address:* 16 George Cantilli Street, Bucharest, Romania (Home). *Telephone:* (1) 2118242.

IOSIFESCU, Marius Vicenţiu Viorel, PhD, DSc; Romanian mathematician; b. 12 Aug. 1936, Piteşti; s. of the late Victor Iosifescu and Ecaterina Iosifescu; m. Ştefania Eugenia Zamfirescu 1973; one s.; ed Bucharest Univ.; consultant Cen. Statistical Bd 1959–62; Asst Prof. Bucharest Polytech. Inst. 1961–63; Research Mathematician Inst. of Math. and Centre for Math. Statistics of the Romanian Acad., Bucharest 1963–76, Dir 1976–; Visiting Prof. Univs. of Paris 1974, 1991, 1996, 1998, Mainz 1977–78, Frankfurt am Main 1979–80, Bonn 1981–82, Melbourne 1991, Lille 1997, Bordeaux 1998, 1999; Overseas Fellow Churchill Coll., Cambridge Univ. 1971; mem. editorial bds. Biometrical Journal, Bulletin Mathématique de la Soc. des Sciences Mathématiques de Roumanie, Mathematica, Revue d'Analyse Numérique et de Théorie de l'Approximation; Deputy Chief Ed. Revue Roumaine de Mathématiques Pures et Appliquées; mem. Int. Statistical Inst., Bernoulli Soc. for Mathematical Statistics and Probability (mem. council 1975–79), American Math. Soc.; Corresp. mem. Romanian Acad. 1991, Titular mem. 2000; Romanian Acad. Prize 1965, 1972; Bronze Medal Helsinki Univ. 1975; Chevalier, Ordre des Palmes Académiques 1993. *Publications:* Random Processes and Learning (with R. Theodorescu) 1969, Stochastic Processes and Applications in Biology and Medicine, Vol. I Theory, Vol. II Models (with P. Tăutu) 1973, Finite Markov Processes and Their Applications 1980; ed. Proceedings of Braşov Conference on Probability Theory 1971, 1974, 1979, 1982, Dependence with Complete Connections and its Applications (with Ş. Grigorescu) 1982, 1990; ed. Studies in Probability and Related Topics 1983, Elements of Stochastic Modelling (with Ş. Grigorescu, G. Oprişan and G. Popescu) 1984, From Real Analysis to Probability: Autobiographical Notes 1986, Metrical Theory of Continued Fractions (with C. Kraaikamp) 2002. *Leisure interests:* music, playing violin. *Address:* Centre for Mathematical Statistics, Casa Academiei Romane, Calea 13 Septembrie nr 13, 76117 Bucharest 5 (Office); Str. Dr. N Manolescu 9–11, 76222 Bucharest 35, Romania (Home). *Telephone:* (1) 4114900 (Office); (1) 4103523 (Home). *Fax:* (1) 2116608 (Office). *E-mail:* miosifes@csm.ro (Office); miosifes@valhalla.racai.ro (Home). *Website:* www.csm.ro (Office).

IOVINE, Jimmy; American record company executive and producer; fmr engineer; Co-founder Interscope Records 1989; Co-Chair. Interscope Geffen

A&M; Co-founder (with Doug Morris), Chair. and CEO Jimmy and Doug's Farm Club (project comprising a record label, website and cable TV show) 1999–; has worked with Dr Dre, Marilyn Manson, Stevie Nicks, Nine Inch Nails, No Doubt, 2Pac, Tom Petty, The Pretenders, Brian Setzer Orchestra, Patti Smith and U2; Producer of the Year, Rolling Stone Magazine (twice). *Address:* Interscope Records, 2220 Colorado Avenue, Santa Monica, CA 90404, USA (Office). *Website:* www.interscope.com (Office); www.farmclub .com (Office).

IRAN, fmr. Empress of (see Pahlavi, Farah Diba).

IRANI, Jamshed Jiji, PhD; Indian business executive; b. 2 June 1936, Nagpur; s. of Jiji D. Irani and Khorshed Irani; m. Daisy Irani 1971; one s. two d.; ed Sheffield Univ.; worked for British Iron and Steel Research Asscn 1963–67; Tata Iron and Steel Co. Ltd 1968–, Gen. Man. 1979–81, Deputy Man. Dir 1981–83, Vice-Pres. (Operations) 1983–85, Pres. 1985–88, Jt Man. Dir 1988–92, Man. Dir 1992–; Dir of numerous cos.; Nat. Metallurgist Award 1974, Platinum medal of I.I.M. 1988; Hon. KBE 1997. *Publications:* numerous tech. papers. *Leisure interests:* philately, photography. *Address:* 3 C Road, Northern Town, Jamshedpur, 831001 Jharkhand, India. *Telephone:* (657) 431024 (Office); (657) 431025 (Home). *Fax:* (657) 431818 (Office).

IRANI, Ray R., DSc; American business executive; b. 15 Jan. 1935, Beirut, Lebanon; s. of Rida Irani and Naz Irani; m. Ghada Irani; two s. one d.; ed Univ. of S Calif.; Sr Research Leader, Monsanto Co. 1957–67; Assoc. Dir New Products, later Dir of Research, Diamond Shamrock Corpn 1967–73; joined Olin Corpn 1973, Pres. Chemicals Group 1978–80, Dir and Corp. Pres. 1980–83; Exec. Vice-Pres. Occidental Petroleum Corpn, Los Angeles 1983–84, Pres. and COO 1984–91, Chair., CEO, Pres. 1991–96, Chair. and CEO 1996–, also Dir; CEO Occidental Chemical Corpn, 1983–91, Chair. 1983–94; Chair. Canadian Occidental Petroleum, Ltd, Calgary 1987–99; mem. Bd of Dirs, American Petroleum Inst.; mem. ACS, American Inst. of Chemists, Scientific Research Soc., American Industrial Research Inst. *Publications:* Particle Size; numerous papers in field of particle physics. *Address:* Occidental Petroleum Corporation, 10889 Wilshire Blvd., Los Angeles, CA 90024-4201, USA. *Telephone:* (310) 208-8800 (Office). *Fax:* (310) 443-6690.

IRELAND, Norman Charles, CA, FCMA; British business executive; b. 28 May 1927, Aden; s. of Charles Ireland and Winifred A. Ireland; m. Gillian M. Harrison 1953; one s. one d.; ed in UK, USA and India; Chartered Man. Accountant with Richard Brown & Co. 1944–50, Brown Fleming & Murray 1950–54, Avon Rubber Co. 1955–64; Chief Accountant, United Glass 1964–66; Finance Dir BTR PLC 1967–87, Chair. 1993–96; Chair. Bowater PLC 1987–93, The Housing Finance Corpn 1988–93, Intermediate Capital Group 1989–93, Meggitt 1987–93. *Leisure interests:* gardening, ballet, opera, music.

IRHAYIM, Tarik al-, PhD; Iraqi petroleum engineer and business executive; b. 3 Feb. 1937, Mosul; m. Amel Ahmed Omar 1962; four s. two d.; ed Al-Idadiya High School, Guildford Tech. Coll., Univ. of Birmingham; Chief Petroleum Engineer North Oil Co. 1971–80, Project Man. Underground Storage 1980–87, Man. Laboratories 1987–90, Deputy Fields Dir 1990–92, Fields Dir 1992–95, Consultant 1995; apptd Dir Euphrates Consulting Bureau 1996; Order of Merit. *Publications:* Bulk Storage of Crude Oil 1963, Thermal Analogue Studies 1966, Quality Assurance in Oil Field Operations 1989. *Leisure interests:* bridge, swimming, reading, world affairs. *Address:* c/o Euphrates Consulting Bureau, Sector 101, Sadoon, Street 87, Ahmed Bldg No. 21, Suite 14H/9, Batawen, Baghdad, Iraq. *Telephone:* 7181927. *Telex:* 212252.

IRIGOIN, Jean, DèsSc; French professor of Greek; b. 8 Nov. 1920, Aix-en-Provence; s. of Paul Irigoin and Isabelle Gassier; m. Janine Garaud 1954; two s. two d.; ed Collège St-Louis-de-Gonzague, Paris, Sorbonne and Ecole Pratique des Hautes Etudes, Paris; Prof. Univ. de Poitiers 1953–65, Univ. of Paris X 1965–72, Univ. de Paris IV 1972–85; Collège de France (Chaire de Tradition et Critique des Textes Grecs) 1985–92; mem. Institut de France 1981, Acads. of Athens, Göttingen, Munich, Naples, Rome; Pres. Fédération Internationale des Etudes Classiques 1989–94; Chevalier Légion d'honneur. *Publications:* Histoire du texte de Pindare 1952, Règles et recommandations pour les éditions critiques 1972, Bacchylide 1992, Tradition et critique des textes grecs 1997, Le livre grec des origines à la Renaissance 2001. *Address:* 11 Place Marcelin-Berthelot, F-75231 Paris Cedex 05, France. *Telephone:* 1-44-27-10-18. *Fax:* 1-44-27-11-09.

IRIMESCU, Ion; Romanian sculptor and teacher; b. 27 Feb. 1903, Preutești, Suceava County; s. of Petru Irimescu and Maria Irimescu; m. Eugenia Melidon 1932; ed School of Fine Arts, Bucharest and Académie Grande Chaumière, Paris; Prof. Fine Arts Inst. N Grigorescu, Bucharest 1966–; Vice-Chair. Romanian Artists' Union 1963–68; Chair. Romanian Artists' Union 1978–90; exhbns. in Bucharest, Cluj-Napoca, Iași, Athens, Oslo, Moscow, Anvers-Middleheim, Paris, Barcelona, Zürich, Sofia, Budapest, Berlin, Ankara, Cairo, Belgrade; perm. sculptures in Modern Art Museum, Tel Aviv, Pushkin Art Museum, Moscow, Biblioteca Ambroisana, Milan, Middelheim, Anvers and numerous works (sculptures and drawings) in Romanian museums, including 314 sculptures and more than 1,000 graphic works at the Ion Irimescu Museum at Fălticeni, Suceava County; religious frescoes at the Church of the Holy Archangels, Fălticeni; Citizen of Honour of Fălticeni, Iași and Cluj; Dr. hc ('George Enescu' Superior Acad. of Art, Iași); State Prize 1954, 1955; Prize of Romanian Acad. 1943; People's Artist 1964; Mem. of Hon. of the

Romanian Acad. 1992; The Star of Romania with Degree of Great Officer 2000; Prize of Excellence in Romanian Culture 2001. *Publications:* Ed. fire albums of the art of Ton Trimescu. *Leisure interest:* classical music, travels. *Address:* Muzeul de Artă 'Ion Irimescu', str. Mihai Eminescu nr 2, Fălticeni 5750, Suceava County (Home); Uniunea Artistilor Plastici, Str. Nicolae Iorga 42, Bucharest, Romania. *Telephone:* (30) 541606 (Home); 6332751.

IRIMO, Antonio Barrera de; Spanish business executive and politician; Pres. Telefonica 1964–73; fmr Vice-Pres. of Spain and Minister of Finance; fmr Chair. Sema Group PLC; Chair. Bull Int. Oct. 2002–; fmr Chair. Bd Pechiney and Générale des Eaux; fmr mem. Bd Banco Hispano Americano. *Address:* Bull (España) SA, Paseo de las Doce Estrellas 2, Campo de las Naciones, 28042 Madrid, Spain (Office). *Telephone:* (91) 3939393 (Office). *Fax:* (91) 3939395 (Office). *Website:* www.bull.com (Office).

IRINEOS I, His Holiness Patriarch; Greek Orthodox ecclesiastic; b. 1939, Samos; rep. of church of Jerusalem in Athens 1972–81; Bishop and mem. Holy Synod in Jerusalem 1981–; elected Greek Orthodox Patriarch of Jerusalem 2001. *Address:* P.O. Box 19632-633, Greek Orthodox Patriarchate Street, Old City, Jerusalem, Israel (Office). *Telephone:* (2) 6271657 (Office). *Fax:* (2) 6282048 (Office).

IROBE, Yoshiaki; Japanese banker; b. 18 July 1911, Tokyo; s. of Tsuneo and Tsuneko (Hirohata) Irobe; m. Kiyoko Kodama 1939; three s. one d.; ed Tokyo Imperial Univ.; Man., Matsuyama Branch, The Bank of Japan 1954, Deputy Chief, Personnel Dept 1956, Chief Sec. and Chief, Foreign Relations Dept 1959, Chief, Personnel Dept 1962, Man. Nagoya Branch 1963; Sr Man. Dir, The Kyowa Bank Ltd (now Asahi Bank) 1966, Deputy Pres. 1968, Pres. 1971–80; Chair. 1980–86, Adviser 1986–, Hon. Chair. 1986–. *Leisure interests:* 'Go', travel, reading. *Address:* 26-6, Saginomiya 6-chome, Nakano-ku, Tokyo, Japan (Home). *Telephone:* 999-0321 (Home).

IRONS, Jeremy; British actor; b. 19 Sept. 1948, Isle of Wight; s. of the late Paul Dugan Irons and Barbara Sharpe; m. 1st (divorced); 2nd Sinead Cusack 1978; two s.; ed Bristol Old Victoria Theatre School; TV debut 1968; mem. Gaia Foundation, European Film Acad.; Patron Prison Phoenix Trust, Archway Foundation; Officier Ordre des arts et des lettres, European Film Acad. Special Achievement Award 1998. *Television appearances include:* Notorious Woman, Love for Lydia, Langrishe Go Down, Voysey Inheritance, Brideshead Revisited, The Captain's Doll, Tales from Hollywood 1991, Longitude 2000. *Films:* Nijinsky 1980, The French Lieutenant's Woman 1980, Moonlighting 1981, Betrayal 1982, The Wild Duck 1983, Swann in Love 1983, The Mission 1986, A Chorus of Disapproval 1988, Dead Ringers (New York Critics Best Actor Award 1988) 1988, Australia 1989, Danny, The Champion of the World 1989, Reversal of Fortune (Acad. Award 1991) 1990, Kafka 1991, Damage 1991, Waterland 1992, M. Butterfly 1994, House of the Spirits 1994, Die Hard with a Vengeance 1995, Stealing Beauty 1996, Lolita 1996, The Man in the Iron Mask 1997, Chinese Box 1998, Dungeons and Dragons 2000, The Time Machine 2001. *Stage appearances:* The Real Thing, Broadway 1984 (Tony Award), Rover 1986, The Winter's Tale 1986, Richard II, Stratford 1986. *Leisure interests:* skiing, riding, sailing. *Address:* c/o Hutton Management, 4 Old Manor Close, Askett, Bucks., HP27 9NA, England.

IRSHAIDAT, Salah, BA; Jordanian lawyer; b. 1919, Irbid; s. of Al Jaibari; m. Lamis Sulaiman 1959; one s. two d.; ed Damascus Coll., Univ. of Syria; conciliation judge 1942; land settlement judge, later Public Prosecutor, Asst Attorney Gen., Pres. Attorney Gen., mem. Court of First Instance; mem. Court of Appeal, Pres.; Deputy Minister of Justice; Judge Supreme Court of Justice; Pres. Court of Cassation and High Justice 1989–. *Publication:* Publ on history of Andalusia. *Leisure interest:* reading law books.

IRVINE, Ian Alexander, FCA, CBIM, FRGS, FRSA; British business executive; b. 2 July 1936, Derby; m. Elizabeth Noelle; one d. one s.; ed Surbiton County Grammar School and London School of Econs; joined Touche Ross & Co. 1961, Partner 1965; Man. Dir Fleet Holdings PLC 1982–85, also Dir Express Newspapers PLC and Morgan-Grampian PLC (subsidiaries); consultant to United Newspapers PLC –1985; Dir (non-exec.) Capital Radio 1982–2002, Chair. 1992–2002; Dir TV-AM PLC 1983, Chair. 1988–90; Chief Exec. Octopus Publishing Group 1986, with responsibility for Butterworths 1989; Chair. British Sky Broadcasting 1990–91; Chief Exec. Reed Int. Books 1990–94; Dir Reed Int. PLC 1987, Chair. 1994–97; mem. Exec. Cttee Reed Elsevier 1993–96, Chair. 1994–96, Co-Chair. 1996–99; Chair. (non-exec.) Video Networks 1997–, Dawson Int. PLC 1998–, Van Tulleken Co. 2003–; Freeman of the City of London. *Leisure interest:* scuba diving. *Address:* Van Tulleken Company, 33 Lowndes Street, London, SW1X 9HX, England (Office). *Telephone:* (20) 7235-1099 (Office). *Fax:* (20) 7235-7956 (Office). *E-mail:* london@vantulleken.com (Office). *Website:* www.vantulleken.com (Office).

IRVINE, John Maxwell, PhD, CPhys, FInstP, FRAS, FRSA, FRSE, CIMgt, DL; British theoretical physicist; b. 28 Feb. 1939, Edinburgh; s. of John Mac-Donald Irvine and Joan Paterson Irvine; m. Grace Ritchie 1962; one s.; ed George Heriot's School, Edinburgh, Univs of Edinburgh, Manchester, Michigan; Asst Lecturer in Theoretical Physics, Univ. of Manchester 1964–66, Lecturer 1968–73, Sr Lecturer 1973–76, Reader 1976–83, Prof. 1983–91, Dean of Science 1989–91; Prin. and Vice-Chancellor Univ. of Aberdeen 1991–96; Prin. and Vice-Chancellor Univ. of Birmingham 1996–2001; Prof. of Physics Univ. of Manchester 2001–; Chair. Scottish Advisory Group on the Academic Year 1993–96, Cttee of Scottish Univ. Prins 1994–96; Research

Assoc., LNS, Cornell Univ., USA 1966–68; Head of Nuclear Theory, SERC Daresbury Lab. 1974–78; Dir Rowett Research Inst. 1992–96, Cobuild Ltd 1996–2001, Barber Trust 1996–2001; mem. Bd Scottish Council Devt and Industry 1991–96, Grampian Enterprise Ltd 1992–96; Council mem. Inst. of Physics 1981–87, 1988–92 (Vice-Pres. 1982–87), European Physical Soc. 1989–92; mem. Nuclear Physics Bd and Chair. Nuclear Structure Cttee SERC 1984–88; mem. Scottish Econ. Council 1993–96, Council Asscn of Commonwealth Univs. 1993– (Chair. 1994–95, Treas. 1998–), BT Scottish Advisory Forum 1993–96, British Council (Scotland) 1993–96, Council CVCP 1995–98, Bd HEQC 1994–97, UCEA 1995–2001, UCAS 1995–2001, Birmingham Chamber of Commerce and Industry 1996–2001, Public Health Laboratories Service 1997–, Commonwealth Scholarships Comm. 2002–, Educ. Consultancy Service of the British Council 2002–; Chair. West Midlands Regional Innovation Strategy Group 1996–2001, Jt Information Structure Cttee 1998–; Gov. English Speaking Union 1998–; Hon. FRCSE 1995; Hon. DSc (William and Mary) 1995; Hon. DEd (RGU) 1995; Hon. DUniv (Edin.) 1995; Hon. LLD (Aberdeen) 1997. *Publications:* The Basis of Modern Physics 1967, Nuclear Structure Theory 1972, Heavy Nuclei, Superheavy Nuclei and Neutron Stars 1975, Neutron Stars 1978; more than 100 research publns on physics. *Leisure interests:* hill walking, tennis. *Address:* Schuster Laboratory, University of Manchester, Manchester, M13 9PL (Office); 27 Belfield Road, Manchester, M20 6BJ, England (Home). *Telephone:* (161) 275-4158 (Office); (161) 445-1434. *E-mail:* j.m.irvine@man.ac.uk (Office); j.m.irvine@man.ac.uk (Home).

IRVINE OF LAIRG, Baron (Life Peer), cr. 1987, of Lairg in the District of Sutherland; **Alexander Andrew Mackay Irvine,** QC, MA, LLB; British lawyer; b. 23 June 1940; s. of Alexander Irvine and Margaret Christina Irvine; m. 1st Margaret Veitch (divorced 1973); m. 2nd Alison Mary McNair 1974; two s.; ed Inverness Acad., Hutcheson's Boys' Grammar School, Univ. of Glasgow, Christ's Coll., Cambridge; lecturer, LSE 1965–69; called to the Bar, Inner Temple 1967, Bencher 1985; a Recorder 1985–88; Deputy High Court Judge 1987–97; Shadow Spokesman on Legal Affairs and Home Affairs 1987–92; Shadow Lord Chancellor 1992–97, Lord High Chancellor of GB 1997–; Pres. Magistrates' Asscn; Jt Pres. House of Lords British-American Parl. Group, Commonwealth Parl. Asscn, Inter-Parl. Union; Pres. NI Youth and Family Courts Asscn 1999; Hon. Bencher Inn of Court of NI 1998; Vice-Patron World Fed. of Mental Health; Trustee Whitechapel Art Gallery 1990–, Hunterian Collection 1997–; Hon. Fellow LSE; Hon. LLD (Glasgow) 1997; Laurea hc (Siena) 2000. *Leisure interests:* cinema, theatre, art, travel. *Address:* House of Lords, Westminster, London, SW1A 0PW, England. *Telephone:* (20) 7219-3245 (Office); (20) 7219-6790 (Office). *Fax:* (20) 7219-4711 (Office). *E-mail:* lordchancellor@lcdhq.gsi.gov.uk (Office).

IRVING, Amy; American actress; b. 10 Sept. 1953, Palo Alto, Calif.; m. Steven Spielberg (q.v.) 1985 (divorced); one s.; one s. by Bruno Barreto; ed American Conservatory Theater and London Acad. of Dramatic Art; frequent TV appearances. *Stage appearances include:* Juliet in Romeo and Juliet, Seattle Repertory Theater 1982–83, on Broadway in Amadeus 1981–82, Heartbreak House 1983–84, off Broadway in The Road to Mecca 1988. *Films include:* Carrie, The Fury, Voices, Honeysuckle Road, The Competition, Yentl, Mickey and Maude, Rumpelstiltskin, Crossing Delancey, A Show of Force, Benefit of the Doubt, Kleptomania, Acts of Love (also co-exec. producer), I'm Not Rappaport, Carried Away, Deconstructing Harry, One Tough Cop 1998, Blue Ridge Fall 1999, The Confession, The Rage: Carrie 2 1999, Trafffic 2000, Bossa Nova 2000.

IRVING, Edward (Ted), ScD, FRS, FRSC; Canadian research scientist (retd); b. 27 May 1927, Colne, Lancs.; s. of George E. Irving and Nellie Irving; m. Sheila A. Irwin 1957; two s. two d.; ed Colne Grammar School and Univ. of Cambridge; army service 1945–48; Research Fellow, Fellow and Sr Fellow, ANU 1954–64; Dominion Observatory, Canada 1964–66; Prof. of Geophysics, Univ. of Leeds 1966–67; Research Scientist, Dominion Observatory, later Earth Physics Br. Dept of Energy, Mines and Resources, Ottawa 1967–81; Research Scientist, Pacific Geoscience Centre, Sidney, BC 1981–92, Research Scientist Emer. 1992–; Adjunct Prof. Carleton Univ. Ottawa 1975–81, Univ. of Vic. 1985–95; Fellow, American Geophysical Union; Hon. DSc (Carleton Univ.) 1979, (Memorial Univ.) 1986, (Victoria Univ.) 1999; Fellow, Foreign Assoc. NAS; Hon. Fellow Geological Soc. of London; Distinguished Fellow Geological Asscn of Canada. *Publications:* Palaeomagnetism 1964; contributions to learned journals. *Leisure interests:* gardening, carpentry, choral singing. *Address:* Pacific Geoscience Centre, 9860 West Saanich Road, PO Box 6000, North Saanich, BC, V8L 4B2; 9363 Carnoustie Crescent, R.R.2, North Saanich, BC, V8L 5G7, Canada (Home). *Telephone:* (250) 656-9645 (Home). *Fax:* (250) 363-6565 (Office). *E-mail:* tirving@pgc-gsc.nrcan.gc.ca (Office).

IRVING, John Winslow, BA, MFA; American author; b. 2 March 1942, Exeter, NH; s. of Colin F. N. Irving and Frances Winslow; m. 1st Shyla Leary 1964 (divorced 1981); two s.; m. 2nd Janet Turnbull 1987; one s.; ed Univs. of Pittsburgh, Vienna, New Hampshire and Iowa; Asst Prof. of English, Mt. Holyoke Coll. 1967–72, 1975–78; writer-in-residence, Univ. of Iowa 1972–75; with Bread Loaf Writers' Conf. 1976; Rockefeller Foundation grantee 1971–72; Nat. Endowment for Arts Fellow 1974–75, Guggenheim Fellow 1976–77; mem. American Acad. of Arts and Letters 2001; Nat. Book Award 1980, O. Henry Award 1981, Acad. Award for the best adapted screenplay (The Cider House Rules) 2000. *Publications:* novels including: Setting Free the Bears 1969, The Water-Method Man 1972, The 158-Pound Marriage 1974, The World According to Garp 1978, The Hotel New Hampshire 1981, The

Cider House Rules 1985 (later screenplay), An Introduction to Great Expectations 1986, A Prayer for Owen Meany 1989, A Son of the Circus 1994, Trying to Save Piggy Sneed 1996 (a collection of memoirs, short stories and essays), An Introduction to A Christmas Carol 1996, A Widow for One Year 1998, My Movie Business (memoir) 1999, The Fourth Hand (novel) 2001; short stories and reviews in other Publs. *Address:* c/o Turnbull Agency, PO Box 757, Dorset, VT 05251, USA.

IRWIN, Flavia, (Lady de Grey), RA; British artist; b. 15 Dec. 1916, London; d. of Clinton Irwin and Everilda Irwin; m. Sir Roger de Grey 1942; two s. one d.; ed Hawnes School, Ampthill, Beds. and Chelsea School of Art; taught gen. design at Medway Coll. of Art 1970–75; Sr tutor, Decorative Arts Course, City & Guilds of London Art School, Kennington, London 1975–; solo Exhbn Ansdell Gallery, RA Friends' Room 2001 and Arups Gallery; several group exhbns: RA of Arts Summer Exhbn, Gallery 10, Grosvenor St, Studio 3 Group Show, Shad Thames Group Show; work in collections including Westminster Conf. Centre, London, Midland Montague Morgan Grenfell, Carlisle City Art Gallery, Dept of the Environment, Govt Art Collection; Hon. Academician, Royal West of England Acad., Bristol. *Leisure interests:* swimming, reading. *Address:* 5 Camer Street, Meopham, Kent, DA13 0XR, England. *Telephone:* (1474) 812327.

IRYANI, Abd al-Karim al-, PhD; Yemeni politician and economist; b. 12 Oct. 1934, Eryan; m.; three s. three d.; ed Univ. of Georgia, Yale Univ., USA; worked in an agricultural project in Yemen 1968–72; Chair. Cen. Planning Org. 1972–76; Minister of Devt 1974–76, of Educ. and Rector San'a Univ. 1976–78; Adviser, Kuwait Fund for Arab Econ. Devt 1978–80; Prime Minister 1980–83; Deputy Prime Minister and Minister of Foreign Affairs 1984–90, 1994–98; Minister of Foreign Affairs 1990–93, of Planning and Devt 1993–94; Prime Minister of Yemen 1998–2001; Sec.-Gen. Gen. People's Congress party (GPC); Chair. Council for the Reconstruction of Earthquake Areas 1983–84. *Address:* General People's Congress, San'a, Republic of Yemen (Office). *E-mail:* gpc@y.net.ye (Office). *Website:* www.gpc.org.ye.

ISA, Pehin Dato Haji; Brunei politician; trained as barrister in UK; fmrly Gen. Adviser to Sultan of Brunei, now Special Adviser, with ministerial rank in Prime Minister's Office; Minister of Home Affairs 1988–95, Special Adviser to the Prime Minister –1995. *Address:* c/o Ministry of Home Affairs, Bandar Seri Begawan, Brunei.

ISAACS, Sir Jeremy Israel, Kt, MA; British arts administrator; b. 28 Sept. 1932; s. of Isidore Isaacs and Sara Jacobs; m. 1st Tamara (née Weinreich) 1958 (died 1986); one s. one d.; m. 2nd Gillian Widdicombe 1988; ed Glasgow Acad., Merton Coll., Oxford; TV Producer, Granada TV (What the Papers Say, All Our Yesterdays) 1958, Associated Rediffusion (This Week) 1963, BBC TV (Panorama) 1965; Controller of Features, Associated Rediffusion 1967; with Thames TV 1968–78, Producer, The World at War 1974, Cold War 1998; Dir of Programmes 1974–78; special independent consultant TV series Hollywood, ITV, A Sense of Freedom, ITV, Ireland, a Television Documentary, BBC, Battle for Crete, NZ TV, Cold War, Turner Broadcasting; CEO, Channel Four TV Co. 1981–88; Gen. Dir Royal Opera House 1988–96 (Dir 1985–97); Chief Exec. Jeremy Isaacs Productions 1998–; Gov. British Film Inst. 1979–84; Chair., BFI Production Bd 1979–81, Artsworld Channels Ltd 2000–; James MacTaggart Memorial Lecturer, Edin. TV Festival 1979; Fellow, Royal Television Soc. 1978, BAFTA 1985, BFI 1986; Hon. DLitt (Strathclyde) 1983, (Bristol) 1988; Dr. hc (Council for Nat. Academic Awards) 1987, (RCA) 1988; Hon. LLD (Manchester) 1998; Desmond Davis Award for Outstanding Creative Contrib. to TV 1972; George Polk Memorial Award 1973; Cyril Bennett Award 1982; Lord Willis Award for Distinguished Service to TV 1985. *Publications:* Storm Over Four: A Personal Account 1989, Cold War (jtly.) 1999, Never Mind the Moon 1999. *Leisure interests:* books, walks, sleep. *Address:* Jeremy Isaacs Productions, Awdry House, 11 Kingsway, London, WC2B 6XF, England (Office). *Telephone:* (20) 7240-9942 (Office).

ISAACSON, Walter Seff, MA; American journalist; b. 20 May 1952, New Orleans, La.; s. of Irwin Isaacson and Betsy Isaacson; m. Cathy Wright 1984; one d.; ed Harvard Univ., Pembroke Coll., Univ. of Oxford; reporter Sunday Times, London 1976–77, States-Item, New Orleans 1977–78; staff writer Time magazine, New York 1978–79, political corresp. 1979–81, Assoc. Ed. 1981–84, Sr Ed. 1985–91, Asst Man. Ed. 1991–93, Man. Ed. 1995–2000; Editorial Dir Time Inc. 2000–01; Chair. and CEO CNN Newsgroup 2001–03; Ed. New Media Time, Inc. 1993–96; Pres. and CEO Aspen Inst. 2003–; mem. Council on Foreign Relations, Century Asscn; Overseas Press Club Award, NY 1981, 1984, 1987; Harry Truman Book Prize 1987. *Publications:* Pro and Con 1983, Kissinger: A Biography 1992, The Wise Men (jtly.) 1986. *Address:* The Aspen Institute, Suite 700, One Dupont Circle, NW, Washington, DC 20036-1133, USA (Office). *Telephone:* (202) 736-5800 (Office). *Fax:* (202) 467-0790 (Office). *Website:* www.aspeninstitute.org (Office).

ISAAKOV, Yuri Fedorovich, DM; Russian surgeon; b. 28 June 1923, Kovrov, Vladimir Region; s. of Fedor Fedorovich Isaakov and Kladvia Fedorovna Isaakov; m. Tamara Gennadievna Isaakov; one s.; ed Russian State Medical Univ.; Asst, docent, prof. 1953–65, Head of Chair of Children Surgery Russian State Medical Univ. 1966–; Vice-Pres. Russian Acad. of Medical Sciences; Chair. Russian Asscn of Children Surgeons; mem. Int. Soc. of Surgeons; mem. Presidium of Russian Soc. of Surgeons; expert of WHO on scientific directions in public health. *Publications:* more than 300 scientific works, including 13 monographs on plastic and reconstructive surgery, surgery of intestine and lungs. *Leisure interests:* sports. *Address:* Russian

Academy of Medical Sciences, Solyanka str. 14, 103001 Moscow (Office); Frunzenskaya nab. 50, apt. 89, 119270 Moscow, Russia (Home). *Telephone:* (095) 254-10-77 (Office); (095) 242-46-15 (Home).

ISAKOV, Col-Gen. Vladimir Ilyich; Russian military officer; b. 21 July 1950, Voskresenskoye, Kaluga region; ed Moscow Mil. School of Civil Defence, Mil. Acad. of Home Front Transport, Mil. Acad. of Gen. Staff; Platoon Commdr of Civil Defence Forces; served in Group of Soviet Armed Forces in Germany; Deputy Regt Commdr, then Deputy Army Commdr of Home Front.; Deputy Commdr Div. of Home Front, Siberian Mil. Command 1982–84, 40th Army in Afghanistan 1984–86; Deputy Army Commdr, then Head of Home Front, Kiev Mil. Command 1988–89; Head of Gen. Staff of Home Front, W Group of Armed Forces 1989–94; Head of Chair. Mil. Acad. of Gen. Staff 1994–; Head of Gen. Staff Armed Forces of Russian Fed. 1996, First Deputy Head of Home Front 1996–97, Head 1997–; Deputy Minister of Defence 1997–. *Address:* Ministry of Defence, ul. Znamenka 19, 103160 Moscow, Russia (Office). *Telephone:* (095) 296-84-37.

ISAMUDDIN, Riduan (Hambali); Indonesian religious leader; b. 1966, Sukamanah, W Java; m. Noral Wizaah Lee; active in opposition to Suharto regime 1970s and 1980s; sought exile in Malaysia 1985; fought as mujahideen guerilla against Soviet occupation, Afghanistan 1988; recruited Muslim supporters to join a jihad (holy war) in order to est. a Pan-Asian Islamic State, Malaysia 1990; believed to have co-f. Jemaah Islamiah (JI—Islamic Community) network with Abu Bakar Bashir with operations throughout SE Asia 1990; returned to Indonesia to recruit supporters 2000; mem. consultative council al-Qaeda; alleged liaison officer between al-Qaeda and radical Islamic groups in SE Asia; allegedly funded numerous mil. terrorist groups fighting jihad, in particular in Maluko Islands 1999; wanted by Govts of Indonesia, Malaysia, Singapore and The Philippines as key suspect for involvement in series of bomb attacks on World Trade Center 1993, Philippine airliner 1994, USS Cole, Yemen 2000, Christian church bombings, Indonesia 2000, Manila bombings 2000, Sept. 11 attacks in USA 2001, Operation Jabril (attempted mass terrorist attacks on US targets in Malaysia, Singapore and Philippines) 2001, Bali nightclub 2002.

ISARD, Walter, PhD, FAAS; American economist; b. 19 April 1919, Philadelphia, Pa; s. of Lazar Isard and Anna (Podolin) Isard; m. Caroline Berliner 1943; four s. four d.; ed Temple, Harvard and Chicago Univs; Instructor Wesleyan Univ. 1945, MIT 1947; Visiting Lecturer Tufts Coll. 1947; Assoc. Prof. of Econs, Assoc. Dir of Teaching, Inst. of Econs, American Univ. 1948–49; Research Fellow and Lecturer, Harvard Univ. 1949–53; Assoc. Prof. of Regional Econs, Dir Urban and Regional Studies, MIT 1953–56; Prof. of Econs, Chair. Dept of Regional Science, Univ. of Pa 1956–75, Head Dept of Peace Science 1975–77; Visiting Prof. of Regional Science, Yale Univ. 1960–61, of Landscape Architecture and Regional Science, Harvard Univ. 1966–71; Chair. Graduate Group in Peace Research and Peace Science Unit 1970–78; Sr Research Assoc., Visiting Prof. of Econs, Regional Science and Policy Planning, Cornell Univ. 1971–79, Prof. 1979–; Distinguished Visiting Prof., Inst. für Regionalwissenschaft, Karlsruhe 1972; Consultant, Tenn. Valley Authority 1951–52, Resources for the Future Inc. 1954–58, Ford Foundation 1955–56; Founder Regional Science Asscn 1954, Ed., Co-Ed. Papers 1954–58, Pres. 1959, Hon. Chair. 1960–; Ford Foundation Fellow in Econs and Business Admin. 1959–60; Ed., Co-Ed., Journal of Regional Science 1960–; Chair. OEEC Econ. Productivity Agency Conf. on Regional Econs and Planning, Bellagio, Italy 1960; Founder Peace Science Soc. (Int.) 1963, Co-Ed. Papers 1963–, Exec. Sec. 1964–, Pres. 1968; Pres. World Acad. of Art and Science 1977–81; Dir ECAAR 1989–, (Trustee 2001); Assoc. Ed. Quarterly Journal of Econs 1968–71, Peace Economics, Peace Science and Public Policy 1994–; mem. Editorial Bd Journal of Conflict Resolution 1972–; mem. NAS, Fellow, American Acad. of Arts and Sciences 1980; Hon. Prof. (Peking Univ., Northwest Univ.) 1993; Dr. hc (Poznan Acad. of Econ.) 1976, (Erasmus Univ.) 1978, (Karlsruhe) 1979, (Umeå) 1980, (Univ. of Ill.) 1982, (Binghamton Univ.) 1997, (Geneva) 2002; August Lösch Ring 1988. *Publications:* Atomic Power: An Economic and Social Analysis 1952, Location Factors in the Petrochemical Industry 1955, Location and Space Economy 1956, Municipal Costs and Revenues Resulting from Community Growth 1957, Industrial Complex Analysis and Regional Development 1959, Methods of Regional Analysis 1960, Regional Economic Development 1961, General Theory: Social, Political, Economic and Regional 1969, Regional Input-Output Study 1971, Ecologic-Economic Analysis for Regional Planning 1971, Spatial Dynamics and Optimal Space-Time Development 1979, Conflict Analysis and Practical Conflict Management Procedures 1982, Arms Races, Arms Control and Conflict Analysis 1988, Practical Methods of Regional Science and Empirical Applications 1990, Location Analysis and General Theory 1990, Economics of Arms Production and the Peace Process 1992, The Science of Peace 1992, Commonalities in Art, Science and Religion 1997, Methods of Interregional and Regional Analysis 1998. *Leisure interests:* music, dancing. *Address:* Department of Economics, 436 Uris Hall, Cornell University, Ithaca, NY 14853 (Office); 3218 Garrett Road, Drexel Hill, PA 19026, USA (Home). *Telephone:* (607) 255-3306 (Office). *Fax:* (607) 255-2818. *E-mail:* will@cornell.edu (Office).

ISĂRESCU, Constantin Mugurel, PhD; Romanian economist; b. 1 Aug. 1949, Drăgășani, Vâlcea Co.; s. of Constantin Isărescu and Aritina Isărescu; m. Elena Isărescu; one s. one d.; ed Acad. of Econs; research fellow Inst. for World Econ. 1971–90; Asst lecturer Acad. of Econs, Bucharest 1975–89, Prof. 1996–; Prof. Timișoara West Univ. 1994–96; fmrly Prof. Banking Coll. of

Romanian Banking Inst.; First Sec. Embassy, Washington 1990; Gov. Nat. Bank of Romania 1990–99, 2001–; Chair. Romanian Chess Fed.; Chair. for Romania, Club of Rome; Vice-Pres. Cent. Banks' Govs.' Club; mem. Bd Romanian American Enterprise Fund; Prime Minister of Romania 1999–2000; Honour Medal (Architects' World Forum). *Publications:* Financial Crisis 1979, Gold, Myth and Reality 1981, Stock Exchange 1982, Recent Developments in Romania 1990, Monetary Policy, Macroeconomic Stability and Banking Reform in Romania 1995, Banking System in Romania: Recent Developments and Prospects 1996, Reform of Financial System in Romania and European Integration 1996, Monetary Policy After 1989 1997. *Leisure interests:* literature, history. *Address:* National Bank of Romania, 25 Lipscani Street, Bucharest 70421, Romania. *Telephone:* (1) 312-62-32. *Fax:* (1) 312-49-34.

ISAYEV, Alexander Sergeyevich; Russian biologist and forester; b. 26 Oct. 1931, Moscow; m. Lidia Pokrovskaya 1953; two d.; ed Leningrad Forestry Acad.; mem. CPSU 1965–91; Deputy Chair. Council for Protection of the Environment and Rational Exploitation of Resources in USSR Supreme Soviet 1979–89; mem. USSR (now Russian) Acad. of Sciences 1984; Dir V. N Sukachev Forestry Inst., Krasnoyarsk, Chair. Krasnoyarsk Div., Siberian Dept of USSR Acad. of Sciences 1977–88; Pres. GOSKOMLES (State Comm. on Forestry) 1988–91; Chair. Higher Ecological Council at Russian Fed. Supreme Soviet 1992–93; Dir Centre for Ecological Problems and Productivity of Forests 1991–; Pres. Int. Forestry Inst. 1991–; Hon. Diploma (UNEP Programme) 1989; Gold Medal (Int. Union of Forestry Research Orgs.) 1976, Gold Medal (Russian Acad. of Sciences) 1992. *Publications:* eight books, over 270 articles. *Leisure interests:* fishing, hunting. *Address:* Novocheremushkinskaya str. 69, 117418 Moscow, Russia. *Telephone:* (095) 332-86-52. *Fax:* (095) 332-29-17. *E-mail:* isaev@cepl.rssi.ru (Office).

ISCHINGER, Wolfgang; German diplomatist; b. 4 June 1946, Beuren, Stuttgart; two c.; ed Univs of Bonn and Geneva, Fletcher School of Law and Diplomacy, Harvard Univ. Law School, USA; mem. cabinet staff of UN Sec.-Gen., New York 1973–75; joined Foreign Service 1975, mem. Policy Planning Staff 1977–79; posted to Washington, DC 1979–82; mem. cabinet staff, Minister of Foreign Affairs, Bonn 1982–90, Pvt. Sec. to Minister 1985–87, Dir Cabinet and Parl. Affairs 1987–90; Minister-Counsellor, Head Political Section, German Embassy, Paris 1990–93; Dir Policy Planning Staff, Bonn 1993–95, Dir-Gen. for Political Affairs 1995–98, State Sec. 1998–2001, 2000–01; Amb. to USA 2001–; mem. High Level German-Russian Strategy Group; mem. Bd East-West Inst., New York, American Field Service Germany; Chair. Ambs' Advisory Bd, Exec. Council on Diplomacy, Washington, DC. *Publications:* numerous articles on foreign policy, security and arms control policy, European policy issues. *Leisure interests:* skiing, mountaineering, flying. *Address:* Embassy of Germany, 4645 Reservoir Road, NW, Washington, DC 20007, USA (Office). *Telephone:* (202) 298-4000 (Office). *Fax:* (202) 471-5559 (Office). *E-mail:* ge-embus@ix.netcom.com (Office). *Website:* www.germany-info.org (Office).

ISHIBASHI, Kanichiro; Japanese business executive; b. 1 March 1920, Kurume-shi, Fukuoka-ken; s. of Shojiro and Masako Ishibashi; m. Saeko Ishibashi 1944; one s. two d.; ed Faculty of Law, Univ. of Tokyo; naval service 1943–45; joined Bridgestone Tire Co. Ltd (now called Bridgestone Corpn) 1945, Dir 1949–, Vice-Pres. 1950–63, Pres. 1963–73, Chair. 1973–85, Hon. Chair. 1985–; Exec. Dir Fed. of Econ. Orgs., Japan Fed. of Employers' Asscns.; fmr Pres. Japan Rubber Mfrs Asscn. *Leisure interests:* pictures, photography, music, golf. *Address:* 1 Nagasaka-cho, Azabu, Minato-ku, Tokyo, Japan (Home). *Telephone:* (3) 583-0150 (Home).

ISHIGURO, Kazuo, OBE, MA, DLitt; British author; b. 8 Nov. 1954, Nagasaki, Japan; s. of Shizuo Ishiguro and Shizuko Ishiguro; m. Lorna Anne Macdougall 1986; one d.; ed Woking Grammar School, Univs. of Kent and East Anglia; fmr community worker, Renfrew; writer 1980–; Chevalier des Arts et des Lettres 1998; Premio Scanno 1995, Premio Mantova 1998. *Publications include:* A Pale View of Hills (Winifred Holtby Prize) 1982, An Artist of the Floating World (Whitbread Book of the Year Fiction Prize) 1986, A Profile of Arthur J. Mason (TV Play), The Remains of the Day (Booker Prize 1989) 1989, The Unconsoled (Cheltenham Prize 1995) 1995, When We Were Orphans 2000. *Address:* c/o Rogers, Coleridge and White Ltd, 20 Powis Mews, London, W11 1JN, England. *Telephone:* (20) 7221-3717. *Fax:* (20) 7229-9084.

ISHIHARA, Nobuteru; Japanese politician; b. 1957; s. of Shintaro Ishihara; MP (Liberal Democratic Party); Minister of State (Admin. Reform, Regulatory Reform) 2001–. *Address:* c/o Cabinet Office, 1-6-1, Nagata-cho, Chiyoda-ku, Tokyo, Japan (Office). *Website:* www.cao.go.jp

ISHIHARA, Shintaro; Japanese politician; b. Sept. 1932, Kobe; brother of Yujiro Ishihara; m.; four s.; ed Hitotsubashi Univ.; mem. House of Councillors 1972; mem. House of Reps 1972–95; Minister of State, Dir-Gen. Environment Agency 1976; Minister of Transport 1987–88; mem. Liberal-Democratic Party; leftnat. politics 1995; Gov. of Tokyo 2002–. *Publications include:* Season of the Sun (Akutagawa Prize for Literature) 1955, The Tree of the Young Man, The Forest of Fossils, The Japan that Can Say No (with Akio Morita) 1989. *Leisure interests:* yachting, skiing. *Address:* Office of the Governor of Tokyo, 2-8-1, Nishishinjuku, Shinjuku-ku, Tokyo 163-8001, Japan.

ISHII, Hajime, MA; Japanese politician; b. 17 Aug. 1934, Kobe; m. Tomoko Sugiguchi 1961; one s.; ed Konan Univ., Stanford Univ. Graduate School;

mem. House of Reps. 1969–; fmr Parl. Vice-Minister of Transport; Minister of State, Dir-Gen. Nat. Land Agency 1989–; Minister of Home Affairs 1994; fmr Chair. Liberal-Democratic Party Nat. Org. Cttee; fmr Chair. LDP Research Comm. on Foreign Affairs; Chair. Special Cttee on Political Reform (House of Reps.). *Publications:* The Dream of Young Power, Dacca Hijacking, The Future of Kobe, A Distant Country Getting Closer. *Leisure interests:* golf, saxophone, scuba diving. *Address:* 4-1-12 Kitanagasa-dori, Chuo-ku, Kobe 650-0012 (Office); No. 1 Diet Bldg, Room 220, 2-2-1 Nagata-cho, Chiyoda-ku, Tokyo 100, Japan. *Telephone:* (3) 3508-7220 (Office); (78) 333-0050. *Fax:* (3) 3502-5383 (Office); (78) 332-0074. *E-mail:* pin@po.sphere.ne.jp (Office). *Website:* www.infomax-kobe.com/hajime/ (Office).

ISHII, Kazuhiro; Japanese architect; b. 1 Feb. 1944, Tokyo; s. of Toshio Ishii and Kyoko Ishii; m. Noriko Nagahama 1988; two d.; ed Univ. of Tokyo and Yale Univ.; lecturer, Waseda Univ.; Univ. of Tokyo 1992–, Japan Inst. of Architecture Prize 1989;. *Major works include:* Noshima Educational Zone 1970–82, Tanabe Agency Bldg 1983, Gyro-Roof 1987, Sukiya Mura 1989, Kitakyu-shu City Hall 1991. *Publications:* Rebirth of Japanese-style Architecture 1985, Thought on Sukiya 1985, My Architectural Dictionary 1986. *Leisure interests:* golf, music (playing saxophone). *Address:* 4-14-27 Akasaka, Minato-ku, Tokyo 107 (Office); 7-5-1-303 Akasaka, Minato-ku, Tokyo 107, Japan (Home). *Telephone:* (3) 3505-0765 (Office); (3) 3584-0779 (Home).

ISHII, Michiko; Japanese politician; mem. House of Councillors; fmr Parl. Vice-Minister of Labour; Dir Gen. Environment Agency (State Minister) 1996–98.

ISHIKAWA, Shigeru, DEcon; Japanese economist; b. 7 April 1918; m. Michiko Ishikawa; ed Tokyo Univ. of Commerce (now Hitotsubashi Univ.); attached to Jiji Press News Agency 1945–56, Hong Kong Corresp. 1951–53; Asst Prof., Inst. of Econ. Research, Hitotsubashi Univ. 1956–63, Prof. 1963–82, Dir 1972–74, Prof. Emer. 1982–; Far Eastern Fellow, East Asian Research Center, Harvard Univ. 1957–58; Visiting Prof. SOAS, Univ. of London 1980, Hon. Fellow 1991; Prof. School of Int. Politics, Econs and Business, Aoyama Gakuin Univ. 1982–94, Prof. Emer. 1994–, Dir Univ. Library 1996–98, mem. Japan Acad. 1998–, Visiting Prof. Josai Univ. 1994–; Order of Friendship (Vietnam) 1997–. *Publications:* National Income and Capital Formation in Mainland China 1965, Economic Development in Asian Perspective 1967, Agricultural Development Strategies of Asia 1970, Labor Absorption in Asian Agriculture 1978, Essays on Technology, Employment and Institutions in Economic Development: Comparative Asian Experience 1981, Basic Issues in Development Economics 1990. *Address:* 19-8, 4 chome Kugayama, Suginami-ku, Tokyo 168-0082, Japan. *Telephone:* (3) 3332-8376. *Fax:* (3) 3332-0877.

ISHIKAWA, Tadao, LLD; Japanese academic; b. 21 Jan. 1922, Tokyo; s. of Chukichi Ishikawa and Yoshi Ishikawa; m. Yoshiko Ishikawa (deceased); one s. three d.; ed Keio Univ., Harvard Univ. and Univ. of Calif. at Berkeley, USA; mem. Faculty of Law, Keio Univ., 1946–87, Prof. 1955–87, Dean 1971–77, Vice-Pres. Keio Univ. 1965–69, Pres. 1977–93; mem. Bd Int. Asscn of Univ. Pres. 1980–85; Pres. Japan Asscn of Pvt. Univs. and Colls. 1983–88; Vice-Chair. Prov. Council on Educ. Reform 1984–87; Chair. Univ. Council, Ministry of Educ. 1987–99, Tokyo Metropolitan Bd of Educ. 1988–96, The Juvenile Problem Council 1989–99; Chair. Japan-China Friendship Cttee for the 21st Century 1984–97; Chair. Lower House Election Redistricting Council 1994–; Dr. hc (Western Mich. Univ., USA); Hon. LLD (York Univ., Toronto); Award for Cultural Merit, Japanese Govt 1991, Grand Cordon, Order of the Rising Sun 1995, Order of Cultural Merit 2002 and many other awards. *Publications include:* A History of the Chinese Constitution 1952, A Study of the History of the Chinese Communist Party 1959, International Politics and Red China 1968, Contemporary Issues of Present Day China 1970, My Dreams and My Choice 1993, Future-Creating Mind 1998; numerous articles. *Address:* Ishikawa Doko-Bunseki Kenkyujo, Izumi-kan Kioi-cho Building 5F, 4-9 Kioi-cho, Chiyoda-ku, Tokyo 102 (Office); 4-1-10-209 Hiroo, Shibuya-ku, Tokyo 150, Japan (Home). *Telephone:* (3) 3288-3496 (Office); (3) 3486-4317 (Home). *Fax:* (3) 3288-3497 (Office).

ISHIMARU, Akira, PhD, FIEEE, FInstP; American professor of electrical engineering (retd); b. 16 March 1928, Fukuoka, Japan; s. of Shigezo Ishimaru and Yumi Ishimaru (née Yamada); m. Yuko Kaneda 1956; two s. two d.; ed Univ. of Tokyo, Univ. of Washington, USA; Asst Prof., Univ. of Washington 1958–61, Assoc. Prof. 1961–65, Prof. of Electrical Eng 1965; Boeing Martin Prof. 1993, also Adjunct Prof. of Applied Math.; Visiting Assoc. Prof. Univ. of Calif. at Berkeley 1963–64; Ed. Radio Science 1978–82; mem. Editorial Bd Proc. IEEE 1973–83; mem. Nat. Acad. of Eng 1996–; Ed.-in-Chief Waves in Random Media 1990–; Fellow Optical Soc. of America 1982, Acoustical Soc. of America 1997; IEEE Centennial Medal 1984, Distinguished Achievement Award 1995, 1998, IEEE Heinrich Hertz Medal 1999, U.R.S.I. John Dellinger Gold Medal 1999, IEEE Third Millennium Medal 2000. *Publications:* Wave Propagation and Scattering in Random Media, Vols 1 and 2 1978, Electromagnetic Wave Propagation, Radiation and Scattering 1991. *Address:* 2913 165th Place, NE, Bellevue, WA 98008, USA (Home). *Telephone:* (206) 543-2169 (Office); (425) 885-0018 (Home). *Fax:* (206) 543-3842 (Office); (425) 881-1622 (Home). *E-mail:* ishimaru@ee.washington.edu (Office).

ISHIOKA, Eiko; Japanese designer; ed Nat. Univ. of Fine Arts, Tokyo; fmr Art Dir Shiseido cosmetics co.; designer of advertising posters, television commercials and stage sets; created designs for film Mishima, play M.

Butterfly and opera The Making of the Representative for Planet 8; designed cover for a Miles Davis album (Grammy award). *Publication:* Eiko by Eiko: Eiko Ishioka, Japan's Ultimate Designer 1990.

ISHIZAKA, Kimishige, MD, PhD; Japanese biomedical research scientist; b. 12 March 1925, Tokyo; m. Teruko Ishizaka 1949; one s.; ed Univ. of Tokyo; Chief, Dept of Serology, Div. of Immunoserology, Tokyo 1953–62; Chief, Dept of Immunology, Children's Asthma Research Inst. and Hosp., Denver, Colo 1962–70; Assoc. Prof. of Medicine and Microbiology, Johns Hopkins Univ. 1970–81, Dir Subdept. of Immunology 1981–88, O'Neill Prof. of Immunology and Medicine 1981–89; Scientific Dir and Head, Div. of Immunobiology, La Jolla Inst. of Allergy and Immunology, La Jolla, Calif. 1989–; Emperor's Award 1974; Pioneer of Modern Allergy Award 1982; Distinguished Scientist Award, Japanese Medical Soc. of America 1989. *Publications:* numerous contribs. to scientific journals.

ISHLINSKY, Aleksandr Yulyevich; Russian applied mathematician; b. 6 Aug. 1913, Moscow; s. of Yuliy Eduardovich Ishlinsky and Sofia Ivanovna Kirillova; m. 1st Natalia Vladimirovna Zaporozhets 1943 (deceased); ed Moscow Univ.; mem. CPSU 1940–91; Prof., Moscow Univ. 1944–48, Prof. and Head of Dept 1955–64; Prof. Kiev Univ. 1949–55; Dir Inst. for Problems in Mechanics, USSR (now Russian) Acad. of Sciences 1964–88, hon. Dir 1989–; mem. Ukrainian Acad. of Sciences 1948, USSR (now Russian) Acad. of Sciences 1960–; Chair. USSR Union of Scientific and Eng Socs 1970; Regional mem. Int. Fed. Scientific Workers; Deputy to Supreme Soviet USSR 1974–89; Pres. World Fed. of Eng Orgs 1987; Foreign mem. Mexican Eng Acad. 1976, Czechoslovakia Acad. 1977, Polish Acad. 1977; Hon. mem. Int. Acad. of Science History 1981; Lenin Prize 1960, Hero of Socialist Labour 1961 and other decorations. *Publications:* The Dynamics of Ground Masses 1954, The Theory of the Horizon Compass 1956, On the Equation of Problems Determining the Position of Moving Objects by Using a Gyroscope and Measuring Acceleration 1957, The Mechanics of Gyroscopic Systems 1963, Inertial Guidance of Ballistic Rockets 1968, Orientation, Gyroscopes and Inertial Navigation 1976, Applied Problems in Mechanics 1986, Classical Mechanics and Inertia Forces 1987. *Leisure interests:* radiotechnique, chess. *Address:* Institute for Problems in Mechanics, Russian Academy of Sciences, prospekt Vernadskogo 101, Korp. 1, Moscow 117526, Russia. *Telephone:* (095) 434-34-65.

ISKANDER, Fazil Abdulovich; Russian/Abkhaz author; b. 6 March 1929, Sukhumi, Georgian SSR; m.; one s. one d.; ed Maxim Gorky Inst. of Literature, Moscow; first works Publ 1952; USSR People's Deputy 1989–91; Pres. Asscn of Authors and Publrs against Piracy; Head, World of Culture Asscn; Vice-Pres. Russian Acad. of Arts; Academician of RAN, Natural Sciences Dept, Bayerische Akad. der Khönen Künste; Dr hc (Norwich Univ., USA); Malaparti Prize (Italy) 1985, USSR State Prize 1989, State Prize of Russia 1993, A. Sakharov Prize, A. Pushkin Prize (Germany) 1994, Moscow-Penne Prize (Italy) 1996, Triumph Prize (Russia) 1998. *Films include:* Time of Lucky Finds, Crime Kings 1986, A Little Giant of Big Sex, A Night with Stalin. *Plays:* Djamchuch – A Son of a Deer 1986, A Greeting from Zürüpa (The One Who Thinks About Russia) 1999. *Publications include:* Green Rain 1960, Youth of the Sea 1964, Goatibex Constellation 1966, Forbidden Fruit 1966 (English trans. 1972), Summer Forest 1969, Time of Lucky Finds 1970, Tree of Childhood and Other Stories 1970, Sandro from Chegem 1978, Metropol (co-ed.) 1979, Small Giant of the Big Sex 1979, Rabbits and Boa Constrictors 198, The Path (poems) 1987, School Waltz or the Energy of Shame 1990, Poets and Tsars 1991, Man and His Surroundings 1992, Pshada 1993, Sofichka 1996, The One Who Thinks About Russia and the American 1997, Poet 1998, The Swallow's Nest 2000 and other stories. *Leisure interest:* reading fiction. *Address:* Leningradski prosp. 26, korp. 2, Apt. 67, 125040 Moscow, Russia. *Telephone:* (095) 973-94-53 (Office); (095) 212-73-60. *Fax:* (095) 973-94-53 (Office).

ISLAM, A. K. M. Nurul; Bangladeshi politician and judge; b. 1925, Khajilpur, Dhaka Dist m. Jahanara Arjoo; two s. two d.; ed in Calcutta; Advocate, Dhaka High Court 1951, Supreme Court 1956; Additional Judge, Dhaka High Court 1968, Judge 1970; Chief Election Commr of Bangladesh 1977, 1982; Founder and Sr Prof. City Law Coll. Dhaka; active in independence Movt 1971; Vice-Pres. of Bangladesh 1986–88, 1989, also Minister of Law and Justice 1986–89.

ISLAM, Nurul, PhD; Bangladeshi economist; b. 1 April 1929, Chittagong; s. of Abdur Rahman and Mohsena Begum; m. Rowshan Ara 1957; one s. one d.; ed Univ. of Dhaka and Harvard Univ.; Reader in Econs Dhaka Univ. 1955–60, Prof. 1960–64; Dir Pakistan Inst. of Devt Econs, Karachi 1964–72; Visiting Prof. Econ. Devt Inst., World Bank 1967–68; Professorial Research Assoc., Yale Econ. Growth Cen. 1968 and 1971; Deputy Chair. Bangladesh Planning Comm. (with ministerial status) 1972–75; Chair. Bangladesh Inst. of Devt Studies, Dhaka 1975–77; mem. Bd of Trustees Int. Rice Research Inst., Manila 1973–77, Exec. Cttee Third World Forum 1974–, Bd of Govs. Int. Food Policy Research Inst. 1975–87 (Research Fellow Emer. 1987–), UN Cttee on Devt Planning 1975–77; Asst Dir-Gen. Econ. and Social Policy Dept, Food and Agric. Org. of UN 1977–; mem. Editorial Bd The World Economy, London, Research Advisory Cttee, World Bank 1980, Advisory Group, Asian Devt Bank, Manila 1981–82, Advisory Cttee, Inst. of Int. Econ., Washington, DC; Consultant with various UN Cttees., ESCAP, UNESCO, UNCTAD etc.; Nuffield Foundation Fellow at Univs. of London and Cambridge 1958–59; Rockefeller Fellow, Netherlands School of Economics 1959. *Publications:* A

Short-Term Model of Pakistan's Economy: An Econometric Analysis 1964, Studies in Foreign Capital and Economic Development 1960, Studies in Consumer Demand 1965, Studies in Commercial Policy and Economic Growth 1970, Development Planning in Bangladesh—A Study in Political Economy 1977, Development Strategy of Bangladesh 1978, Interdependence of Developed and Developing Countries 1978, Foreign Trade and Economic Controls in Development: The Case of United Pakistan 1980, Aid and Influence: The Case of Bangladesh (co-author) 1981, Agriculture Towards 2000 (co-author) 1981, The Fifth World Food Survey 1985, Agriculture Price Policies 1985. *Leisure interests:* reading political and historical books, movies. *Address:* International Food Policy Research Institute, 2033 K Street, N.W., Washington, DC 20006, U.S.A. *Telephone:* 202-862-5600. *Fax:* 202-467-4439. *Website:* www.ifpri.org.

ISLAMI, Kastriot, MA, DSc; Albanian politician; b. 18 Feb. 1952, Tirana; s. of Selman Islami; m.; one s. one d.; ed Univ. of Tirana, Univ. of Paris XI, Orsay, France; Vice-Dean Faculty of Natural Sciences, Univ. of Tirana 1987–91; Minister of Educ. 1991; Speaker (Chair.) of Albanian Parl. 1991–92; Head Parl. Comm. for Preparation of Draft of Albanian Constitution 1991–96; Minister of State to Prime Minister of Albania 1997–98; Deputy Prime Minister 1998–2002; Minister of Finance 2002–. *Publications include:* The Basis of Quantum Mechanics Vol. 1 1989, Vol 2 1990; publs on nat. and int. media. *Address:* Ministria e Financave, Bulevardi Deshmoret e Kombit, Tirana (Office); Rruga: Dora D'Istria, Pallati R 8-Katesh, Tirana, Albania (Home). *Telephone:* (5) 4228405 (Office); (5) 4240669 (Home). *Fax:* (5) 4228494 (Office). *E-mail:* minister@minfin.gov.al (Office); kislami@icc-al.org (Home). *Website:* www.minfin.gov.al (Office).

ISMAIL, Mohamed Ali, MA; Malaysian investment banker; b. 16 Sept. 1918, Port Kelang, Selangor; s. of Haji Mohamed Ali bin Taib and Hajjah Khadijah binti Haji Ahmad; m. Maimunah binti Abdul Latiff 1949; two s.; ed Univ. of Cambridge and Middle Temple, London; joined Malayan Civil Service 1946; Asst State Sec., Selangor State 1948–50; Asst Sec. Econ. Div. of Fed. Treasury 1950–53; Econ. Officer, Penang 1954–55; Controller, Trade Div., Ministry of Commerce and Industry 1955–57; Minister Malaysian Embassy, Washington, DC 1957–58, Econ. Minister 1958–60; Exec. Dir IBRD, Int. Finance Corpn, Int. Devt Asscn 1958–60; Deputy Gov. Cen. Bank of Malaysia 1960–62, Gov. 1962–80; Chair. Capital Issues Cttee 1968–80, Malaysian Industrial Devt Finance Bhd. 1969–2000; Pres. Malaysian Inst. of Man. 1966–68; Chair. Nat. Equity Corpn 1979–; Chair. of Council, Malaysia Inst. of Bankers 1978–80; mem. Nat. Devt Planning Cttee 1962–80, Council of Univ. of Malaya 1962–72; Adviser, Nat. Corpn (PERNAS) 1971–80; mem. Foreign Investment Cttee 1974–80; mem. Bd of Govs., Asian Inst. of Man., Manila 1971–; Dir Sime, Darby Berhad 1980–; Chair. Guthrie Corpn Ltd 1982–, Harrisons Malaysian Plantations Berhad 1982–; Malaysian Nat. Reinsurance Berhad 1985, Commodities Trading Comm. 1981–, Panglima Mangku Negara 1964, Order of Panglima Negara Bintang Sarawak 1976; Hon. LLD (Univ. of Malaya) 1973, (Univ. of Singapore) 1982; Hon. DEcon (Univ. Kebangsaan Malaysia) 1982; Seri Paduka Mahkota Selangor Award 1977; Seri Paduka Mahkota Johor Award 1979; Tun Abdul Razak Foundation Award 1980. *Leisure interests:* golf, swimming. *Address:* National Equity Corporation, P.O.B. 745, Kuala Lumpur (Office); 23 Jalan Natesa, off Cangkat Tunku, Kuala Lumpur, Malaysia (Home). *Telephone:* (3) 2425597 (Home).

ISMAIL, Dato Razali, BA; Malaysian diplomatist; b. 1939, Kedah; m.; three c.; joined Ministry of Foreign Affairs 1962; served Delhi 1963–64; Asst High. Commr in Madras 1964–66; Second Sec. Paris 1966–68; Prin. Asst Sec. Ministry of Foreign Affairs 1968–70; Counsellor, London 1970–72; various posts at Ministry of Foreign Affairs and Chargé d'affaires, Vientiane 1972–78; Amb. to Poland 1978–82; High Commr in India 1982; Deputy Sec.-Gen. Ministry of Foreign Affairs 1985–88; Perm. Rep. to UN 1988, Pres. UN Gen. Ass. 1996–97; apptd. Special Adviser to Prime Minister 1998; UN Special Envoy to Myanmar 1998–. *Address:* c/o Ministry of Foreign Affairs, Wisma Putra, Jalan Wisma Putra, 50602 Kuala Lumpur, Malaysia.

ISMAIL AMAT; Chinese politician; b. 1935, Xinjiang; active in People's Commune Movt –1960; Deputy Sec. CCP Cttee, a country admin., Xinjiang 1960; Deputy Dir Dept of Political Work in Culture and Educ. Xinjiang 1960; mem. 10th CCP Cen. Cttee 1973–77; Sec. CCP Cttee, Xinjiang 1974–79; Vice-Chair. Aubnavan Regional Revolutionary Cttee, Xinjiang 1974–79; Political Commissar, Xinjiang Mil. Region 1976–85; First Deputy Dir Party School, Xinjiang 1977–85; Chair People's Govt, Xinjiang 1979–85; mem. 12th CCP Cen. Cttee 1982–87, 13th CCP Cen. Cttee 1987–92, 14th CCP Cen. Cttee 1992–97, 15th CCP Cen. Cttee 1997–2002, 16th CCP Cen. Cttee 2002–; Minister of State Nationalities Affairs Comm. 1986–98; State Councillor 1993–; Minister in Charge of State Nat. Ethnic Affairs Comm. 1993–98; Dir China Comm. of Int. Decade for Disaster Reduction 1998–2000, China Comm. for Int. Disaster Reduction 2000–; Pres. China-Turkey Friendship Asscn; Hon. Pres. Chinese Asscn of Ethnic Minorities for External Exchanges. *Address:* The State Council, Zhongnanhai, Beijing, People's Republic of China (Office).

ISOKALLIO, Kaarlo, MSc; Finnish business executive; b. 13 May 1948, Helsinki; m. Ammi Kristiina; one d.; ed Univ. of Tech., Helsinki; Project Engineer Wärtsilä Corpn 1972–74; Marketing Dir IBM (Finland) 1974–81; Man. Dir Kabmatik AB, Sweden 1981–83; with Nokia Corpn 1983–, Dept Man. Cables Dept, Machinery Div., 1983–85, Pres. Electronics, Information Systems 1985–86, Pres. Information Systems 1986–88, Exec. Pres. Nokia

Data Group 1988–90, Pres. and COO Nokia Corpn 1990–91, Deputy to CEO, Vice-Chair. Group Exec. Bd 1990; mem. Bd of Dirs. Oy Lindell Ab 1987–, Taloudellinen Tiedotustoimisto 1991–; mem. Supervisory Bd Mecrastor Oy 1987–, Oy Rastor Ab 1987–, Helsinki Univ. Cen. Hosp. Foundation 1991–; mem. Bd Econ. Information Bureau 1991–, ICL PLC 1991–; mem. Tech. Del., Ministry of Trade and Industry 1990; Chair. Bd MTV (Finnish commercial TV) 1991; mem. Acad. for Tech. Sciences 1991.

ISOZAKI, Arata; Japanese architect; b. 23 July 1931, Oita City; s. of Soji Isozaki and Tetsu Isozaki; m. Aiko Miyawaki 1974; two s.; ed Univ. of Tokyo; with Kenzo Tange's team 1954–63; Pres. Arata Isozaki and Assocs. 1963–; juror, Pritzker Architecture Prize 1979–84, Concours Int. de Parc de la Villette 1982, The Peak Int. Architectural Competition 1983, R. S. Reynolds Memorial Award 1985, The Architectural Competition for the New Nat. Theatre of Japan 1986, competitions for Passenger Terminal Bldg, Kansai Int. Airport 1988, Triangle de la Folie, Paris 1989, Int. Architects' competition, Vienna EXPO '95 1991, Kyoto Station Bldg Renovation Design competition 1991; visiting prof. at numerous univs. including Harvard, Yale and Columbia; numerous prizes; Hon. Fellow Acad. Tiberina, AIA, RIBA 1994–; Hon. Academician Royal Acad. of Arts 1994; Hon. mem. B.D.A.; Chevalier Ordre des Arts et des Lettres. *Works include:* Expo '70, Osaka 1966–70, Oita Medical Hall 1959–69, Annex 1970–72, Oita Prefectural Library 1962–66, head office of Fukuoka Mutual Bank 1968–71, Museum of Modern Art, Gunma 1971–74, Kitakyushu City Museum of Art 1972–74, Kitakyushu Cen. Library 1972–74, Shuko-sha Bldg 1974–75, Kamioka Town Hall 1975–78, Gymnasium and Dining Hall, NEG Co. 1978–80, Los Angeles Museum of Contemporary Art 1981–86, Tsukuba Centre Bldg 1978–83, Palladium, New York 1983–85, Sports Hall, Barcelona 1983–90, Brooklyn Museum 1986, Art Tower, Mito 1986–90, Bond Univ., Australia 1987–89, Hara Museum—ARC 1987–88, Kitakyushu Int. Conf. Center 1987–90, Team Disney Bldg 1987–90, Tokyo Univ. of Art and Design 1986–90, Guggenheim Museum, USA 1991–92, Centre for Advanced Science and Tech., Hyogo 1993, Japanese Art and Tech. Centre, Kraków 1994, Museum of Contemporary Art, Nagi 1994, B-Con Plaza (int. conf. centre) 1995, Toyonokuni Libraries for Cultural Resources 1995, Kyoto Concert Hall 1995, Domus: la casa del hombre, La Coruña, Spain 1995, Akiyoshidai Int. Art Village 1998, Nara Centennial Hall 1998, COSI, Columbus 1999. *Publications include:* Kukane 1971, Kenchiku no Kaitai 1975, Shūho ga 1979, Kenchiku no Shūji 1979, Kenchiku no Seijigaku 1989, Image Game 1990, Arata Isozaki Architecture 1960–90 1991, Kenchiku to iu Keishiki 1991, GA Architect 6 – Arata Isozaki (Vol. 1) 1991, Arata Isozaki – Works 30 1992, Arata Isozaki – Four Decades of Architecture 1998, GA Architect 15 – Arata Isozaki 2000, UNBUILT 2001. *Address:* Arata Isozaki and Associates, 6-17, Akasaka 9-chome, Minato-ku, Tokyo 107, Japan (Office); 5-12, Akasaka 9-chome, Minato-ku, Tokyo 107-0052 (Home). *Telephone:* (3) 3405-1526 (Office). *Fax:* (3) 3475-5265 (Office).

ISRAEL, Werner, OC, PhD, FRSC, FRS; Canadian professor of physics; b. 4 Oct. 1931, Berlin, Germany; s. of Arthur Israel and Marie Kappauf; m. Inge Margulies 1958; one s. one d.; ed Univ. of Cape Town, SA and Trinity Coll., Dublin, Ireland; Asst Prof., then Full Prof. of Math., Univ. of Alberta 1958–71, Prof. of Physics 1971–96, Univ. Prof. 1986–; Adjunct Prof. of Physics, Univ. of Victoria, BC 1997–; Pres. Int. Soc. of General Relativity and Gravitation 1997–2001; Research Scholar, Dublin Inst. for Advanced Studies 1956–58; Sherman Fairchild Scholar, Caltech. 1974–75; Fellow Canadian Inst. for Advanced Research 1986–; Hon. DSc (Queen's Univ.) 1987, (Univ. of Vic.) 1999; Dr hc (Univ. de Tours) 1994; Izaak Walton Killam Prize 1983, Tomalla Prize (Tomalla Foundation for Gravitational Research, Switzerland) 1996, (Vic.) 1999. *Publications:* Relativity, Astrophysics and Cosmology (Ed.) 1973, (Co-Ed. with S. W. Hawking,) General Relativity, an Einstein Centenary Survey 1979, 300 Years of Gravitation 1987; numerous papers on black hole theory, general relativity, statistical mechanics. *Leisure interest:* music. *Address:* Department of Physics and Astronomy, University of Victoria, PO Box 3055, Victoria, BC, V8W 3P6; Suite 401, 2323 Hamiota Street, Victoria, BC, V8R 2N1, Canada (Home). *Telephone:* (250) 721-7708 (Office). *E-mail:* israel@uvic.ca (Office).

ISRAELACHVILI, Jacob Nissim, PhD, FAA, FRS; Australian/Israeli university professor; b. 19 Aug. 1944, Tel-Aviv; s. of Haim Israelachvili and Hela Israelachvili; m. Karin Haglund 1971; two d.; ed Univ. of Cambridge; Postdoctoral Research Fellow, Cavendish Lab. Cambridge 1971–72; European Molecular Biology Org. Research Fellow, Univ. of Stockholm 1972–74; Prof. Fellow, Inst. of Advanced Studies, ANU, Canberra 1974–86; Professor of Chemical Eng and Materials Science, Univ. of Calif. at Santa Barbara 1986–; Debye Lecturer, Cornell Univ. 1987; Foreign Assoc. Nat. Acad. of Eng (USA) 1999; Pawsey Medal, Australian Acad. of Science 1977. *Publications:* Intermolecular and Surface Forces 1985; numerous scientific Publs on surface forces in liquids and biological membrane structure and interactions. *Leisure interest:* history of science. *Address:* Department of Chemical Engineering, University of California, Santa Barbara, CA 93106 (Office); 2233 Foothill Lane, Santa Barbara, CA 93105, USA (Home). *Telephone:* (805) 893-8407 (Office); (805) 963-2768 (Home). *Fax:* (805) 893-7870.

ISSAD, Mohand; Algerian lawyer; b. 1939; ed Univ. de Rennes; lawyer specializing in commercial law, Algiers 1965–; lecturer Faculty of Law, Ben-Aknoun Univ. 1965–99; Chair. Nat. Comm. for Judicial Reform 2000, Comm. investigating disturbances in Kabylia 2001. *Address:* c/o Faculté de Droit, Université de Ben-Aknoun, rue Doudou Mokhtar, Algiers, Algeria (Office). *Telephone:* (2) 79-23-23 (Office).

ISSELBACHER, Kurt Julius, MD; American professor of medicine; b. 12 Sept. 1925, Wirges, Germany; s. of Albert Isselbacher and Flori Isselbacher; m. Rhoda Solin 1950; one s. three d.; ed Harvard Univ. and Harvard Medical School; Chief. Gastrointestinal Unit, Mass. Gen. Hosp. 1957–88, Chair. Research Cttee 1967, Dir Cancer Center 1987–; Prof. of Medicine Harvard Medical School 1966–, Mallinckrodt Prof. of Medicine 1972–97, Distinguished Mallinckrodt Prof. 1998–, Chair. Exec. Cttee Medicine Depts. 1968–, Chair. Univ. Cancer Cttee 1972–87; mem. Governing Bd Nat. Research Council 1987–90; Ed.-in-Chief, Harrison's Principles of Internal Medicine 1991–; mem. NAS (Chair. Food and Nutrition Bd 1983–88, Exec. Cttee and Council 1987–90); Hon. DSc (Northwestern Univ.) 2001; Distinguished Achievement Award, American Gastroenterological Asscn (AGA) 1983; Friedenwald Medal, AGA 1985, John Phillips Memorial Award, American Coll. of Physicians 1989, Bristol-Myers Squibb Award for Distinguished Achievement in Nutrition Research 1991; Kober Medal, Asscn of American Physicians 2001; Jewish Nat. Fund Tree of Life award 2001. *Leisure interest:* tennis. *Address:* Massachusetts General Hospital Cancer Center, 139 13th Street, Charlestown, MA 02129-2023 (Office); 20 Nobscot Road, Newton, MA 02459-1323, USA (Home). *Telephone:* (617) 726-5610 (Office).

ISSERLIS, Steven John, CBE; British cellist; b. 19 Dec. 1958, London; s. of George Isserlis and the late Cynthia Isserlis; m. Pauline Mara; one s.; ed City of London School, Int. Cello Centre, Scotland, Oberlin Coll., Ohio, USA; London début Wigmore Hall 1977; London concerto début 1980; concerts and recitals throughout the world; Artistic Dir IMS Prussia Cove; Dir concert series Wigmore Hall, London, Salzburg Festival 1997, Berlin and Vienna 2000–01; featured soloist in Channel 4 TV series with Dudley Moore; TV documentary about Schumann and performance of Schumann's cello concerto, Channel 4 TV; numerous recordings; Hon. mem. RAM; Piatigorsky Award 1993, Royal Philharmonic Soc. Award 1993; Schumann Prize, Zwickau 2000. *Publications:* transcription Beethoven Variations in D arranged for violin or cello and piano or harpsichord, Edn of Saint-Saëns pieces for cello and piano, Steven Isserlis's Cello World, Unbeaten Tracks, Why Beethoven Threw the Stew 2001. *Leisure interests:* books, films, gossip, e-mail, eating too much, avoiding exercise, wishing I was fitter, wondering why I have so few worthwhile hobbies. *Address:* c/o Harrison Parrott Ltd, 12 Penzance Place, London, W11 4PA, England. *Telephone:* (20) 7229-9166. *Fax:* (20) 7221-5042. *E-mail:* info@harrisonparrott.co.uk (Office). *Website:* www.harrisonparrott.com (Office).

ISSING, Otmar, PhD; German economist and banker; b. 27 March 1936, Würzburg; ed Humanistisches Gymnasium, Würzburg, Univ. of Würzburg; Prof. of Econs Univ. of Erlangen-Nuremberg 1967–73, Univ. of Würzburg 1973–90; mem. Council of Experts for Assessment of Overall Econ. Trends at Fed. Ministry of Econs 1988–90; mem. Directorate Deutsche Bundesbank 1990–98; mem. Exec. Bd European Cen. Bank 1998–; mem. Acad. of Sciences and Literature, Mainz, Acad. Europaea, Salzburg; Hon. Prof. Univ. of Würzburg 1991–; Co-founder and Co-ed. of the scientific journal WiSt; mem. Verein für Socialpolitik, American Econ. Asscn, List Gesellschaft, Arbeitskrers Europäische Integration, European Acad. of Arts and Sciences, Acad. of Sciences and Literature, Walter Eucken Inst.; Dr hc (Bayreuth) 1996, (Konstanz) 1998, (Frankfurt am Main) 1999. *Publications:* Introduction to Monetary Policy (6th Edn) 1996, Introduction to Monetary Theory (11th Edn) 1998, Monetary Policy in the Euro Arena (jtly.) 2001. *Address:* Kaiserstr. 29, 60311 Frankfurt am Main, Germany (Office). *Telephone:* (69) 13440 (Office). *Fax:* (69) 13446000 (Office). *E-mail:* info@ecb.int (Office). *Website:* www.ecb.int (Office).

ISSOUFOU, Mahamadou; Niger politician; b. 1952, Illéla; Pres. Parti nigérien pour la démocratie et le socialisme (PNDS); Prime Minister of Niger 1993–94; Chief Economist 1999; Presidential Cand. 1999. *Address:* c/o Office of the Prime Minister, Niamey, Niger.

ISTOMIN, Eugène George; American pianist; b. 26 Nov. 1925, New York; s. of George T. Istomin and Assia Chavin; m. Marta Montanez Casals 1975; ed Curtis Inst., Philadelphia; studied under Kyriena Silote, Rudolf Serkin; Concert pianist 1943–; toured with Adolf Busch Chamber Players 1944–45; first European appearance 1950; charter mem. Casals Prades and Puerto Rico festivals 1950–; several world tours; f. Trio with Isaac Stern and Leonard Rose 1961; numerous recordings of solo, orchestral and chamber works; Leventritt Award 1943. *Leisure interests:* archaeology, history, painting, baseball. *Address:* c/o ICM Concerts, 40 West 57th Street, New York, NY 10019, USA (Office).

ITO, Toyo; Japanese architect; b. 1941; ed Tokyo Univ.; began career with Kiyonori Kikutake Architects and Assocs 1965; est. studio Urban Robot (Urbot), Tokyo 1971 (renamed Toyo Ito and Assocs 1979); fmr Guest Prof. Columbia Univ., New York, USA; Hon. Prof. Univ. of N London, UK; AA Interarch '97 Grand Prix Gold Medal, Union of Bulgarian Architects 1997; Art Encouragement Prize, Ministry of Educ. 1998; Arnold W. Brunner Memorial Prize, American Acad. of Arts and Letters 2000; Gold Prize, Japanese Good Design Award 2001; Golden Lion for Lifetime Achievement Award, Venice Biennale 2002. *Architectural works include:* White U 1976, Silver Hut (Architecture Inst. of Japan Award 1986) 1984, A Dwelling for the Tokyo Nomad Woman 1985, Tower of Winds 1986, Egg of Winds 1991, Yatsushiro Municipal Museum (33rd Mainrich Art Award 1992) 1991, Old People's Home, Yatsushiro 1994, Sendai Mediatheque (multi-resource public cultural centre), Sendai 2001. *Exhibitions include:* 'Vision of Japan', Victoria

& Albert Museum, London, (UK) 1991, 'Vision and Reality', Louisiana Museum of Modern Art, (USA) 2000, 'Blurring Architecture', travelling exhbn in Japan, Netherlands and NZ 1999–2000, 'Toyo Ito Architetto', Basilica Palladiana, Vicenza, (Italy) 2001. *Publication:* Toyo Ito Architetto 2001. *Address:* Toyo Ito & Associates, Fujima Building, 19-4-1-Chome, Shibuya, Shibuya-ku, Tokyo, 150-0002, Japan (Office).

ITZIK, Dalia, BA; Israeli politician and teacher; b. 1952, Jerusalem; m.; three c.; ed Hebrew Univ., Interdisciplinary Centre, Herzliya; fmr Deputy Mayor of Jerusalem in charge of Educ.; fmr Chair. Legis. Panel of Labour Party; fmr mem. Labour Party Cen. Cttee, Bd of Govs. of Israel Broadcasting Authority, Bd of Jerusalem Theatre, Gerard Behar Centre; mem. Knesset 1992–; served in Finance Cttee 1992–96, Educ. and Culture Cttee 1992–99 (Chair. 1995–96), Cttee on Status of Women 1992–99; Chair. Special Cttee for Research and Scientific Technological Devt 1997–99; Minister of the Environment 1999–2001, of Industry and Trade March 2001–. *Address:* Ministry of Industry and Trade, P.O. Box 299, 30 Rehov Agron, Jerusalem 94190, Israel (Office). *Telephone:* 2-6220661 (Office). *Fax:* 2-6222412 (Office). *E-mail:* dover@moit.gov.il (Office). *Website:* www.tamas.gov.il (Office).

IVANCHENKO, Aleksander Vladimirovich, DJur; Russian lawyer; b. 8 Jan. 1954, Krasnodar; m.; one d.; ed Higher School of Ministry of Internal Affairs; worked in Moscow militia forces; lecturer, Higher School of Ministry of Internal Affairs 1983–88; on staff Supreme Soviet Russian Fed. 1988–93; Deputy Chair., Cen. Election Comm. of Russian Fed. 1993–96, Chair. 1996–99; Founder and Dir Inst. of Election Tech. Studies 1999–; mem. State Duma/JCP faction 1999–; Chair. Cttee on Fed. Affairs 2000. *Publications:* papers and articles on problems of political rights and freedom, on election law. *Leisure interests:* tennis, walks in the countryside. *Address:* State Duma, Okhotny Ryka 1, 103265 Moscow, Russia. *Telephone:* (095) 292-97-75 (Office). *Fax:* (095) 292-51-40 (Office).

IVANENKO, Sergey Victorovich, CAND.ECON.; Russian politician and economist; b. 12 Jan. 1959, Russia; ed Moscow State Univ.; researcher, teacher Moscow State Univ. –1990; Chief Expert State Comm. on Econ. Reform RSFSR Council of Ministers 1990–91; leading researcher Cen. of Econ. and Political Studies 1991–92; mem. State Duma 1993–, Chair. Cttee on Property, Privatisation and Econs 1993–95; mem. Cttee on Ecology 1995–99, Deputy Chair. Yabloko faction. *Address:* State Duma, Okhotny Ryad 1, 109265 Moscow, Russia (Office). *Telephone:* (095) 292-91-24 (Office).

IVANENKO, Maj.-Gen. Victor Valentinovich; Russian oil executive and intelligence officer; b. 19 Sept. 1947, Koltsovka, Tyumen region; m.; three c.; ed Tyumen State Industrial Inst., Higher KGB Courses; mem. staff KGB, Tyumen region 1970-86, Sr Inspector, Head of Div., Deputy Head of Dept USSR KGB 1986-91, Chair. RSFSR KGB 1991; Dir-Gen., with rank of Minister, Russian Agency of Fed. Security 1991-1992; Vice-Pres., then First Vice-Pres. YUKOS (Jt Stock Oil Co.) 1993–; mem. Bd of Dirs. ROSPROM (Jt Stock Co.) 1996-; adviser Ministry of Taxation and Revenues 1998-99; Vice-Pres. Foundation for Devt of Parl. in Russia 2000-; mem. Otechestvo Movt; mem. Moscow English Club; Order Red Star, 6 medals. *Address:* Joint Stock Oil Co. YUKOS, Zagorodnoye shosse 5,113152 Moscow, Russia (Office). *Telephone:* (095) 232-31-61 (Office).

IVANIĆ, Mladen, MA, PhD; Bosnia and Herzegovina (Serb) politician, economist and academic; b. 16 Sept. 1958, Sanski Most, Bosnia; m.; two c.; ed Faculties of Econs, Banja Luka and Belgrade, Univ. of Meinheim, Germany and Univ. of Glasgow, UK; journalist Radio Banja Luka 1981–85; Asst Prof. of Political Economy, Faculty of Econs, Banja Luka 1985–88, Docent 1988–, Head of Post-Grad. Study of Reconstruction and Transition (held in conjunction with Univs of Bologna, Sussex and LSE); Teacher Faculty of Econs, Sarajevo 1990–92; Teacher Faculty of Econs, Srpsko Sarajevo 1992–98; Lecturer Univ. of Glasgow, UK 1998; mem. Presidency of Yugoslav Repub. of Bosnia and Herzegovina 1988–91; Founder and Leader Party of Democratic Progress 1999–; mem. Govt Econ. Council 1999; Prime Minister of Serb Repub. of Bosnia and Herzegovina Jan. 2001–03; Minister of Foreign Affairs, Council of Ministers of Bosnia and Herzegovina 2003–; Head Deloitte & Touche Consultancy Office –2001; mem. Editorial Bd Ideje magazine, Belgrade 1988–91, Aktuelnosti magazine, Banja Luka 1999–98; Del. to OSCE sessions 1991; participant World Forum, Davos, Switzerland 1999, 2000; Pres. Serb Intellectual Forum. *Publications include:* Political Economy, Principles of Political Economy; numerous contribs. to newspapers and magazines including Savremenost (Modernity), Pregled (Overview), Ideje (Ideas), Opredjeljenja (Determinations), Lica (Faces), Aktuelnosti (Updates); author or co-author of several programmes for World Bank, UNDP and other int. orgs. *Address:* Ministry of Foreign Affairs, Musala 2, 71000 Sarajevo, Bosnia and Herzegovina. *Telephone:* (33) 281101. *Fax:* (33) 472188. *E-mail:* info@mvp.gov.ba. *Website:* www.mvp.gov.ba.

IVANIŠEVIĆ, Goran; Croatian tennis player; b. 13 Sept. 1971, Split; s. of Srdjan Ivanišević and Gorana Ivanišević; won US Open Jr doubles with Nargiso 1987; turned professional 1988; joined Yugoslav Davis Cup squad 1988; semi-finalist, ATP World Championship 1992; bronze medal, men's doubles, Barcelona Olympic Games 1992; runner-up, Wimbledon Championship 1992, 1994, 1998; winner Wimbledon Championship 2001; winner of numerous ATP tournaments, including Kremlin Cup, Moscow 1996; winner of 22 tours singles and nine doubles titles, and over US$19 million prize money as at end of 2002; Pres. of the Children in Need Foundation, which he established in 1995; BBC Overseas Sports Personality of the Year Award 2001. *Leisure interests:* football, basketball, reading, music, cinema. *Website:* www.goranivanisevic.com.

IVANOV, Igor Sergeyevich; Russian diplomatist; b. 23 Sept. 1945, Moscow; m.; one d.; ed Moscow Pedagogical Inst. of Foreign Languages; Jr researcher Inst. of World Econs and Int. Relations, USSR Acad. of Sciences 1969–73; diplomatic service 1973–; Second, then First Sec., Counsellor, Counsellor-Envoy USSR Embassy, Spain 1973–83; expert First European Dept, Ministry of Foreign Affairs 1983–84; Counsellor of Minister 1984–85; Asst Minister 1985–86; Deputy Chief, then Chief of Dept 1987–92; Chief Gen. Sec., mem. of Bd 1989–91; Russian Amb. to Spain 1991–93; First Deputy Minister of Foreign Affairs 1994–98, Minister 1998–; Perm. mem. Security Council of Russia 1998–; Co-Chair. EU-Russia Co-operation Council 1998–. *Publications:* New Russian Diplomacy 2001; numerous papers and articles. *Address:* Ministry of Foreign Affairs, Smolenskaya-Sennaya str. 32/34, 121200 Moscow, Russia. *Telephone:* (095) 244-40-56; (095) 244-41-19.

IVANOV, Ivan Dmitriyevich, DR.ECON.; Russian politician and economist; b. 1934, Moscow; m.; two c.; ed Moscow Inst. of Foreign Trade; Head of Div. Inst. of USA and Canada, USSR Acad. of Sciences 1971–76; Deputy Dir, Prof. Inst. of World Econs and Int. Relations USSR Acad. of Sciences 1977–86; Head Dept of Int. Econ. Relations USSR Ministry of Foreign Affairs, Chair. USSR State Comm. on Foreign Econ. Orgs. 1986–91; Deputy Dir Inst. of Foreign Econ. Research 1991–94; Russian Trade Rep. to Belgium 1994–96, Deputy Perm. Russian Rep. to EU in Brussels 1996–99; Deputy Minister of Foreign Affairs 1999–. *Address:* Ministry of Foreign Affairs, Smolenskaya-Sennaya str. 32/34, 121200 Moscow, Russia (Office). *Telephone:* (095) 244-95-20 (Office). *Fax:* (095) 244-16-06 (Office). *Website:* www.mid.ru (Office).

IVANOV, Mikhail Vladimirovich; Russian microbiologist; b. 6 Dec. 1930; m.; ed Moscow State Univ.; researcher Inst. of Microbiology, USSR Acad. of Sciences, head of lab., Deputy Dir Inst. of Biochem. and Physiology of Plants and Micro-organisms; Dir Inst. of Microbiology 1984–; Corresp. mem. USSR (now Russian) Acad. of Sciences 1981, mem. 1987; research in geochem. activities of microorganisms and biotech., marine microbiology, global ecology and biogeochem.; Ed.-in-Chief Microbiology journal; S. Vernadsky Prize. *Leisure interest:* coin collecting. *Address:* Institute of Microbiology, Russian Academy of Sciences, 60-letiya Oktyabrya pr., 7 kor. 2, 117811 Moscow, Russia. *Telephone:* (095) 135-21-39 (Office); (095) 299-63-17 (Home).

IVANOV, Lt-Gen. Sergey Borisovich; Russian politician; b. 31 Jan. 1953, Leningrad (now St Petersburg); m.; two c.; ed Leningrad State Univ., Yu V. Andropov Inst. at KGB; various posts in intelligence service and missions abroad 1976–97; Deputy Dir Fed. Service of Security, 1998–99; Head Dept of Analysis, Prognosis and Strategic Planning 1998–99; Sec. Security Council of Russian Fed. 1999–2000; Minister of Defence 2001–. *Leisure interests:* fishing, reading detective stories in English and Swedish. *Address:* Ministry of Defence, ul. Znamenka 19, 103160 Moscow, Russia. *Telephone:* (095) 296-84-37; (095) 296-39-66. *Website:* www.mil.ru.

IVANOV, Vadim Tikhonovich; Russian biochemist; b. 18 Sept. 1937; s. of Tikhon Timofeevitch Ivanov and Lidia Ivanovna Ivanova; m. Raisa Alexandrovna Ivanova (née Osadchaya); one s. one d.; ed Moscow State Univ.; Jr, Sr researcher, head of lab., Deputy Dir, Dir Shemyakin-Ovchinnikov Inst. of Bio-organic Chem. Russian Acad. of Sciences; Corresp. mem. USSR (now Russian) Acad. of Sciences 1976, mem. 1987, Academician-Sec. Dept of Biochem. and Biophysics 1996–; research in chem. of proteins and peptides, structure and functions of neuropeptides, synthetic vaccines; Chair. Council New Problems of Bioeng.; Lenin Prize, USSR State Prize, Russian Govt Prize. *Publications include:* Membrane active complexones 1974, The Way to Protein Synthesis 1982. *Leisure interests:* chess, nature. *Address:* Institute of Bio-organic Chemistry, Russian Academy of Sciences, Miklukho-Maklay str. 16/10, 117437 Moscow, Russia. *Telephone:* (095) 330-56-38 (Office). *Fax:* (095) 310-70-07.

IVANOV, Col Victor Petrovich; Russian administrator; b. 12 May 1950, Novgorod; m.; one s. one d.; ed Leningrad Bonch-Bruyevich Electrical Inst. of Communications; engineer Scientific-Production co. Vektor 1971–77; employee in nat. security orgs. rising to Head of Div., Dept of Fed. Service of Security of St Petersburg and Leningrad region 1977–94, Head of Dept 1998, Deputy Dir, concurrently Head Dept of Econ. Security 1999–2000; Head of Admin., Office of Mayor of St Petersburg 1994–98; Deputy Head of Admin., Office of the Pres. Jan. 2000–; participated in mil. operations in Afghanistan 1987–94; Medal for Mil. Service. *Address:* Administration of President of Russian Federation, Staraya pl. 4, 103132 Moscow, Russia (Office). *Telephone:* (095) 206-34-17 (Office).

IVANOV, Vladimir; Bulgarian physician; b. 6 June 1923, Simeonovgrad; s. of Boris Ivanov and Maria Ivanova; m. Liliana Kirova 1948; one s.; ed Univ. of Sofia, Acad. of Medical Sciences, Moscow and Univ. of London; Deputy Dir Scientific Psychoneurological Inst. Sofia 1956–63; Asst Prof. and Head Dept of Psychiatry and Medical Psychology, Varna 1963–67, Prof. 1967–85; Deputy Rector, Higher Medical Inst. Varna, 1964–66, Rector 1966–72; Dir Scientific Inst. of Neurology, Psychiatry and Neurosurgery, Medical Acad. Sofia and Head, First Psychiatric Clinic 1985–88; Ed.-in-Chief Neurology, Psychiatry and Neurosurgery 1987–91; Adviser Medical Univ., Sofia 1988–; Pres. Bulgarian Scientific Soc. of Psychosomatic Medicine 1989; mem. Admin. Bd, Union of Scientific Medical Socs. of Bulgaria 1991–95; mem. Council, Neuro-

sciences and Behaviour Foundation 1991–; Ed.-in-Chief Psychosomatic Medicine 1993–; mem. Bulgarian Nat. Acad. of Medicine 1995–; several awards and medals. *Publications:* some 16 monographs and numerous articles in professional journals. *Leisure interests:* philosophy, poetry. *Address:* Medical University, 1 Psychiatric Clinic, Sofia 1431 (Office); Praga 26, Sofia 1606, Bulgaria (Home). *Telephone:* (2) 52-03-33 (Office); (2) 52-42-68 (Home).

IVANOV, Vyacheslav Vsevolodovich, DPhil; Russian philologist and translator; b. 21 Aug. 1929, Moscow; s. of Vsevolod Vyacheslavovich Ivanov; m.; one s.; ed Moscow State Univ.; Dir of the Library of Foreign Literature in Moscow 1991–94; People's Deputy of the USSR 1989–91; Dir Inst. of World Culture 1990–94; Prof. UCLA 1994–; mem. Russian Acad. of Sciences 2000; Lenin Prize 1988; Hon. mem. American Linguistics Soc. 1968, British Acad. *Publications:* works on Indo-European linguistics, Slavic and general linguistics, semiotics, including: Indo-European, Praslavic and Anatolian Linguistic Systems 1965, Slavic Linguistic Modelling Systems (with V. Toporov) 1965, Studies in the Field of Slavic Antiquities (with V. Toporov) 1974, Indo-European Language and Indo-Europeans Vols 1–2 (with T. Gamrekelidze) 1984, Balkan Peninsula in the Mediterranean Context 1986, The Ethnolinguistics of the Text 1988, The Category of Passivity in Slavic and Balkan Languages 1989, Novelties in Linguistics 1990; ed. works on Balto-slavic spiritual culture. *Address:* Slavic Department, University of California at Los Angeles, Los Angeles, CA 90024, USA. *Telephone:* (310) 825-4321.

IVANOVA, Ludmila Nikolayevna, MD; Russian physiologist; b. 10 Feb. 1929, Novosibirsk; ed Novosibirsk Inst. of Med.; Head of lab., Inst. of Cytology and Genetics Siberian br. Russian Acad. of Sciences 1971–; Corresp. mem., Russian Acad. of Sciences 1991, mem. 1997–; main research in cellular and molecular mechanisms of regulation of permeability of biological membranes; L. A. Orbeli Award, Russian Acad. of Sciences. *Leisure interests:* music, cookery. *Address:* Institute of Cytology and Genetics, Akademika Lavretyeva prosp. 10, Novosibirsk, Russia. *Telephone:* (3832) 34-24-74 (Office). *Fax:* (3832) 33-12-78 (Office). *E-mail:* ludiv.bionet.nsc.ru.

IVANS, Dainis; Latvian politician; b. 25 Sept. 1955, Madona; s. of Evalds Ivans and Ilga Ivans; m. Elvira Chrschenovitch 1979; two s. two d.; school teacher and journalist; Reporter Latvian TV 1980–85; organized opposition to hydro-electric scheme nr Daugavpils 1986; Ed. School and Family magazine 1986–88; Pres. of Latvian People's Front 1988–90; USSR People's Deputy 1989–90; mem. Latvian Supreme Soviet 1990–, Vice-Chair. 1990–91; Gen. Sec. Latvian Comm. of UNESCO 1992–, Sec. Writers Union 1994–. *Leisure interests:* Oriental philosophy, literature, fishing. *Address:* Bruninieku Str. 89, Apt. 6, Riga, Latvia. *Telephone:* (2) 323142 (Office); (2) 274644 (Home).

IVANTER, Ernest Viktorovich; Russian biologist; b. 15 Nov. 1935, Moscow; s. of Victor S. Ivanter and Irina F. Riss; m. Tatyana Matusevich 1960; one s. one d.; ed Moscow K. Timiryazev Acad. of Agric.; Sr lab., Jr researcher Kivach Karelian br. USSR Acad. of Sciences 1958–60; Jr researcher Inst., of Biology Karelian br. of USSR Acad. of Sciences 1960–63; Asst, Docent, Prof., Dean Petrozavodsk Univ. 1965–; Chair. Dept of Zoology and Ecology Petrozavodsk Univ. 1987–; Corresp. mem. USSR (now Russian) Acad. of Sciences 1991; research in ecology, biocenology, morphophysiology and evolutional ecology of animals; mem. Scientific Council for Biological Fundamentals of Protection and Rational Use of Fauna; mem. USA Zoological Soc.; Hon. mem. Finnish Soc. of Teriologues. *Publications include:* Population Ecology of Small Mammals 1975, Adaptive Peculiarities of Mammals 1985, Fauna of Karelia 1988, Statistical Methods for Biologists 1992, Zoogeography 1993; numerous articles in scientific journals. *Leisure interests:* books, sport, tourism. *Address:* Petrozavodsk University, pr. Lenina 33, 185640 Petrozavodsk (Office); ul. Amuhina la Kv. 5, 185035 Petrozavodsk, Russia (Home). *Telephone:* (8142) 76-38-64 (Office); (8142) 78-17-41 (Home). *Fax:* (8142) 78-21-08.

IVANY, J. W. George, MA, PhD; Canadian university president; b. 26 May 1938, Grand Falls, Newfoundland; s. of Gordon Ivany and Stella Skinner; m. Marsha Gregory 1983; one s. three d.; ed Memorial Univ. of Newfoundland, Columbia Univ. and Univ. of Alberta; Head of Science Dept Prince of Wales Coll. St John's, Newfoundland 1960–63; Grad. Teaching Fellow, Univ. of Alberta 1963–64, Asst Prof. of Elementary Educ. 1965–66; Asst Prof. of Natural Science, Teachers Coll. Columbia Univ. 1966–68, Assoc. Prof. 1968–74, Head, Dept of Science Educ. 1972–74; Visiting Fellow, Inst. of Educ., Univ. of London 1972–73; Dean and Prof. Faculty of Educ., Memorial Univ. of Newfoundland 1974–77; Dean and Prof. Faculty of Educ., Simon Fraser Univ. 1977–84, Vice-Pres. (Academic) 1984–89; Pres. and Vice-Chancellor, Univ. of Sask. 1989–99; Chair. Bd Nat. Inst. of Nutrition 1995–98; various public appts.; Hon. LLD (Memorial Univ. Newfoundland) 1991. *Publications include:* High School Teaching: A Report on Current Practices 1972, Today's Science: A Professional Approach to Teaching Elementary School Science 1975, Who's Afraid of Spiders: Teaching Science in the Elementary School 1988; textbooks; articles in professional journals. *Address:* c/o University of Saskatchewan, 105 Administration Place, Saskatoon, Saskatchewan, S1N 5A2, Canada.

IVANYAN, Eduard Aleksandrovich, DR.HIST.; Russian journalist and political scientist; b. 14 June 1938, Tbilisi, Georgia; m.; one s. one d.; ed Moscow State Inst. of Int. Relations; mem. staff Ministry of Culture 1955–60, UN Secr., Geneva and New York 1961–71; Head of Sector, Div. Inst. of USA and Canada, USSR (now Russian) Acad. of Sciences 1971–98; Ed.-in-Chief USA and Canada: Economics, Politics and Culture (journal) 1998–. *Pub-*

lications: over 100 scientific Publs including 25 books on the history of USA, presidential power in USA, Russian-American relations. *Address:* USA-Canada Journal, Khlebny per. 2/3, 121814 Moscow, Russia (Office). *Telephone:* (095) 291-20-56 (Office).

IVASHOV, Col-Gen. Leonid Grigoryevich, CAND.HIST.SC; Russian business executive and security officer; b. 1943; m.; ed Tashkent Commdr School, M. Frunze Mil. Acad.; army service 1964, various positions 1964–76; with cen. staff, Ministry of Defence 1976–, Head Admin. Dept 1987–92; Sec. Council of Defence Ministers, CIS Countries 1992–96; Head of Dept, Int. Mil. Co-operation 1996–2001, Head of Staff, Co-ordination of Mil. Co-operation, CIS Countries 1999–2001; Adviser to Minister of Defence 2001–; Order Red Star, 6 medals. *Address:* Ministry of Defence, ul. Znamenka 19, 103160 Moscow, Russia (Office). *Telephone:* (095) 296-84-37 (Office). *Website:* www.mil.ru.

IVEROTH, C. Axel; Swedish business executive; b. 4 Aug. 1914, Ekerö; s. of Carl Carlsson Iveroth and Jenny Iveroth; m. Inger Dorthea Iveroth; two s. two d.; ed Stockholm School of Econ.; Producer, Swedish Broadcasting Corpn 1937–41; Sec. Industrial Inst. for Econ. and Social Research 1939–44; Industrial Counsellor, Swedish Embassy, Washington, DC 1944–45; Man. Dir Cementa 1945–52; Chair. and Man. Dir Cembureau (Cement Statistical and Tech. Asscn) 1949–57; Dir-Gen. Fed. of Swedish Industries 1957–77, Vice-Chair. 1977; Chair. Int. Council of Swedish Industry 1977–81; Ed.-in-Chief Industria 1946, Swedish-American News Exchange 1952–66; Chair. and Founder Industrial Council for Social and Econ. Studies 1948–60; Chair. Advisory Bd European Productivity Agency, Paris 1954–56; Chair. Swedish Productivity Council 1957–65; Bd mem. Gen. Export Asscn of Sweden 1961, Chair. and Exec. Bd mem. 1971–81; Chair. Sweden-America Foundation 1970–88; Chair. Integration Cttee of European Industrial Feds. 1958–; Sec.-Gen. Business and Industry Advisory Cttee to OECD (BIAC) 1962–63, Vice-Chair. 1974–82; Chair. Swedish Nat. Cttee of the European League for EEC Co-operation 1965; Vice-Chair. Union des Industries de la Communauté européenne, Brussels 1977–79; mem. Bd Royal Swedish Acad. of Eng Sciences 1957–; Chair. Securitas Int. AB 1950–83, Banque nat. de Paris, Sweden 1986–88, AIM AB 1985–, Sweden-Japan Foundation 1979–87 (Hon. Chair. 1987–); Chair. Asscn of Swedish Chambers of Commerce Abroad 1979–; Int. Adviser Swedish Business Group, Japan 1987–; Chair. Swedish Section of the European League for Econ. Co-operation 1975–, Swedish Mastership in Exports 1985–; Kt Commdr of the Royal Order of Vasa (Sweden); Hon. CBE; Officier Ordre de la Couronne (Belgium), Officier, Légion d'honneur, Commdr Ordine al Merito della Repubblica Italiana, Order of the White Rose of Finland, Third Degree of the Rising Sun (Japan). *Publications:* Handicraft and Small Industries in Sweden 1943, The Good Society 1980; numerous articles on politics and economics in press and professional journals. *Leisure interests:* angling, skiing.

IVERSEN, Leslie Lars, PhD, FRS; British scientist; b. 31 Oct. 1937; s. of Svend Iversen and Anna Caia Iversen; m. Susan Diana (née Kibble) Iversen 1961; one s. one d. (one d. deceased); ed Cambridge, Harkness Fellow, USA; with Nat. Inst. of Mental Health and Dept of Neurobiology, Harvard Medical School 1964–66; Locke Research Fellow of Royal Soc., Dept of Pharmacology, Cambridge 1967–71, Dir MRC Neurochemical Pharmacology Unit 1971–82; Exec. Dir Merck, Sharp and Dohme Neuroscience Research Centre 1982–95; Visiting Prof., Dept of Pharmacology, Univ. of Oxford 1995–96, Visiting Prof. of Pharmacology 1996–99; Visiting Prof. of Pharmacology, Univ. of Oxford 1996–, Imperial Coll. School of Medicine 1997–; Prof. of Pharmacology, Dir Wolfson Centre for Age-Related Diseases, King's Coll., London 1999–; Fellow Trinity Coll., Cambridge 1964–84; Foreign Assoc. NAS 1986. *Publications:* The Uptake and Storage of Noradrenaline in Sympathetic Nerves (with S. D. Iversen) 1967, Behavioural Pharmacology 1975, The Science of Marijuana 2000. *Leisure interests:* reading, gardening. *Address:* Department of Pharmacology, University of Oxford, Mansfield Road, Oxford, OX1 3QT, England (Office).

IVERSON, Ann; American retail executive; b. 1944; d. of John Earl Van Eenenaam and Dorothy Ann Knight; m. 4th (divorced); one s. one d.; ed Arizona State Univ.; Arizona Univ.; with Bullock's Dept Store, LA, Harzfield's, Kan. City, T.H. Mandy, Va; Operating Vice-Pres. Bloomingdale's (two main brs.) 1984; Sr Vice-Pres. of Stores, Region Vice-Pres. Bonwit Teller, NY 1989–90; joined Storehouse (UK retailer group) 1989, Stores Dir British Home Stores (BHS), Chief Exec. Mothercare; Chief Exec. Kay-Bee Toys, Laura Ashley 1995–97.

IVORY, James Francis, MFA; American film director; b. 7 June 1928, Berkeley, Calif.; s. of the late Edward Patrick Ivory and Hallie Millicent De Loney; ed Univs of Oregon and Southern California; began to work independently as a film maker 1952; dir, writer and cameraman in first films; Partner (with Indian producer Ismail Merchant, q.v.), Merchant Ivory Productions 1962–; has collaborated on screenplay of numerous films with author Ruth Prawer Jhabvala (q.v.); Guggenheim Fellow 1974; D. W. Griffith Award (Dirs Guild of America) 1995; Commdr des Arts et des Lettres; BAFTA Fellowship 2002. *Films:* documentaries: Venice, Theme and Variations 1957, The Sword and the Flute 1959; feature films: The Householder 1963, Shakespeare Wallah 1965, The Guru 1969, Bombay Talkie 1970, Savages 1972, The Wild Party 1975, Roseland 1977, The Europeans 1979, Quartet 1981, Heat and Dust 1983, The Bostonians 1984, A Room with a View 1986, Maurice 1987, Slaves of New York 1989, Mr and Mrs Bridge 1990, Howards End 1992, The Remains of the Day 1993, Jefferson in Paris 1995,

Surviving Picasso 1996, A Soldier's Daughter Never Cries 1998, The Golden Bowl 2000; TV films: Adventures of a Brown Man in Search of Civilisation 1971, Autobiography of a Princess 1975 (also published as a book 1975), Hullabaloo over Georgie and Bonnie's Pictures 1978, The Five Forty-Eight 1979, Jane Austen in Manhattan 1980. *Leisure interest:* looking at pictures. *Address:* Merchant-Ivory Productions, 250 West 57th Street, New York, NY10107 (Office); 18 Patroon Street, Claverack, NY 12513, USA. *Telephone:* (212) 582-8049 (Office); (518) 851-7808 (Home). *E-mail:* contact@ merchantivory.com.

IVRY, David, BS; Israeli diplomatist; b. 1934, Gedera; m. Ifra Ivry; three c.; ed Technion—Israel Inst. of Tech.; Chief Rep. U.S.-Israel Strategic Dialogue 1986–88; Dir-Gen. Ministry of Defence 1986–96, Prin. Asst Minister of Defence for Strategic Affairs 1996–99; Nat. Security Adviser to Head of Nat. Security Council 1999–2000; Amb. to USA 2000–02; Head Inter-ministerial Steering Cttee on Arms Control 1986–96; Head Israeli Del. to Multilateral Working Group on Arms Control and Regional Security 1986–96; mem. Bd of Dirs. El-Al 1978–82, Israel Aircraft Industries 1982–92; mem. Bd of Govs. Technion, Haifa 1987–; Maj.-Gen., Commdr Israel Air Force 1977–82; Legion of Merit (USAF), Distinguished Service Order (Singapore), Amitai Distinction Award for Ethical Admin. and Conduct. *Address:* c/o Ministry of Foreign Affairs, Hakirya, Romena, Jerusalem 91950, Israel (Office).

IWAN, Dafydd, BArch; Welsh politician, singer-composer and record company manager; b. Dafydd Iwan Jones, 24 Aug. 1943, Brynaman, Wales; s. of Rev. Gerallt Jones and Elizabeth Jane Jones; m. 1st Marion Thomas 1968 (divorced 1986); two s. one d.; m. 2nd Bethan Jones 1988; two s.; ed Aman Valley Grammar School, Ysgol Ty Tan Domen, Y Bala, Univ. Coll. of Wales, Aberystwyth and Welsh School of Arch., Cardiff; f. Sain (Recordiau) Cyf (now Wales' leading record co.) 1969; Man. Dir 1984–; f. Tai Gwynedd Housing Asscn 1971; founder-trustee, Nant Gwrtheyrn Language Centre 1975; Chair. Welsh Language Soc. 1968–71; parl. cand. 1974, 1983, 1984; Chair. Plaid Cymru (Nationalist Party of Wales) 1982–84, Vice-Pres. 1984–95; Plaid Cymru mem. of Gwynedd Unitary Authority 1995–; Chair. Planning and Economic Devt Cttee, Cyngor Gwynedd Council 1995–, mem. Exec. Cttee responsible for Planning, Highways and Environment 1999–; Trustee Portmeirion Foundation; composer of over 200 songs; Gold Disc for services to Welsh music; over 40 records, cassettes, CDs and video of live concert 1965–; nonconformist lay preacher; Hon. mem. Gorsedd of Bards for services to Welsh language; Hon. Fellow Univ. of Wales, Bangor and Aerstwyth 1998. *Television:* Yma Mae Ngân, S4C (three series introducing own songs). *Publications:* Dafydd Iwan (autobiog.) 1982, 100 O Ganeuon (collection of songs) 1983, Caneuon Dafydd Iwan (2nd collection of songs) 1991. *Leisure interests:* composing songs, sketching, reading. *Address:* SAIN, Llandwrog, Caernarfon, Gwynedd, LL54 5TG (Office); Carrog, Rhos-Bach, Caeathro, Caernarfon, Gwynedd, LL55 2TF, Wales (Home). *Telephone:* (1286) 831111 (Office); (1286) 676004 (Home). *Fax:* (1286) 831497 (Office); (1286) 676004 (Home). *E-mail:* dafydd@sain.wales.com (Office). *Website:* www.sain.wales .com (Office).

IYANAGA, Shokichi; Japanese professor of mathematics; b. 2 April 1906; s. of Katsumi Iyanaga and Kiyono (née Shidachi) Iyanaga; m. Sumiko Kikuchi 1936; three s. one d.; ed First High School, Univ. of Tokyo and Athénée Français, Tokyo; Assoc. Prof., Univ. of Tokyo 1935–42, Prof. 1942–67, Prof. Emer. 1967–; Visiting Prof., Chicago Univ. 1960–61; Dean Faculty of Science, Univ. of Tokyo 1965–67; Prof., Gakushuin Univ. 1967–77; Assoc. Prof., Univ. of Nancy 1967–68; Pres. Math. Soc. of Japan, Int. Comm. on Math. Instruction 1975–78, Vice-Pres. Council of Admin. Maison franco-japonaise 1978–91; Adviser, Maison franco-japonaise 1991–; Pres. Council of Admin. Tsuda Coll. 1993–95; mem. Science Council of Japan 1948–58, Exec. Cttee Int. Math. Union 1952–55, Japan Acad. 1978–, Council of Admin. Tsuda Coll. 1995–; Officier, Ordre Palmes académiques, Officier Légion d'honneur, Order of Rising Sun (2nd Class) 1976. *Publications:* Introduction to Geometry 1968, Theory of Numbers (Ed.) 1969, Encyclopaedic Dictionary of Mathematics (Ed.-in-Chief) 1954, Collected Papers 1994. *Leisure interests:* literature and western music. *Address:* 12-4 Otsuka 6-chome, Bunkyo-ku, Tokyo 112-0012, Japan. *Telephone:* (3) 3945-5977. *Fax:* (3) 3945-9246.

IZETBEGOVIĆ, Alija, PhD; Bosnia and Herzegovina politician; b. 8 Aug. 1925, Bosanski Šamac; m.; one s. two d.; ed Sarajevo Univ.; legal adviser PUT Co., Traffic Inst., Sarajevo; imprisoned for nationalist activities for three years 1945, for pan-Islamic activities 1983, released 1988; Founder and fmr. Chair. Party of Democratic Action (PDA) 1990; elected to Presidency of Bosnia and Herzegovina Nov. 1990, Pres. of the Presidency 1990–96, Co-Pres. 1996–2000. *Publications:* Islamic Declaration 1970, Islam between East and West 1976, Problems of Islamic Revival 1981, Meditation in Prison 1995; several articles and essays. *Address:* c/o Office of the Presidency, 71000 Sarajevo, Musala 5, Bosnia and Herzegovina (Office).

IZMEROV, Nikolay Fedorovich, MD; Russian medical official; b. 19 Dec. 1927, Frunze, Kirghizia; ed Tashkent Medical School and Moscow Cen. Inst. for Advanced Medical Training; worked as doctor in Khavast rural areas, Tashkent Dist; Postgraduate training, Moscow 1952–53; Sr Insp. USSR Ministry of Health 1953–55; Postgraduate training (Municipal Hygiene) 1955–58; doctor in Moscow City Sanitary Epidemiological Station 1956–59; Deputy Dir (Int. Health), Dept of External Relations, USSR Ministry of Health 1960–62; Vice-Minister of Health of RSFSR, Moscow and Chief Sanitary Insp. 1962–64; Asst Dir-Gen. WHO 1964–71; Dir Inst. of Occupational Health of the USSR (now Russian) Acad. of Medical Sciences 1971–; Corresp. mem. Russian Acad. of Medical Sciences 1980, mem. 1986, Acad.-Sec. Dept of Preventive Medicine 1990–. *Address:* Institute of Occupational Health of the Russian Academy of Medical Sciences, 31 Prospekt Budennogo, Moscow 105275, Russia. *Telephone:* (095) 365-02-09. *Fax:* (095) 365-02-09.

IZRAEL, Yuri Antonievich, DR.PHYS.-MATH.SC.; Russian geophysicist and ecologist; b. 15 May 1930, Tashkent; s. of Antony I. Izrael and Antonina S. Shatalina; m. Elena Sidorova 1958; one s. one d.; ed Tashkent State Univ.; engineer, research assoc. Geophysics Inst. of USSR Acad. of Sciences 1953–63; Deputy Dir, Dir of Inst. of Applied Geophysics 1963–70; First Deputy Head of Main Admin. of Hydrometeorological Service of USSR 1970–74; Head 1974–78; Corresp. mem. USSR (now Russian) Acad. of Sciences 1974, mem. 1994, Acad.-Sec., Dept of Oceanography, Atmospheric Physics and Geography 1996–; mem. Russian Acad. of Ecology 1994; Chair. USSR State Cttee for Hydrometeorology and Environmental Control 1978–88; Chair. USSR State Cttee for Hydrometeorology 1988–91, Dir Research Inst. of Global Climate and Ecology 1990–; Deputy to Supreme Soviet 1979–89; Sec. and First Vice-Pres. World Meteorological Org. 1975–87; Vice-Chair. Intergovernmental Panel on Climate Change 1994–; mem. Int. Acad. of Astronautics 1990; Hon. mem. Int. Radiological Union 1999; State Prize in the field of Environment 1981, Gold Medal of USSR Acad. of Sciences in the field of Ecology 1983, Gold Medal (per Chernobyl) of Int. Centre 'Ettore Majorana' (Italy) 1990, Gold Medal of Soviet State Exhbn 1991, UN-UNEP Sasakawa Environmental Prize 1992, Gold Medal and Prize of Int. Meteorological Org. 1992, Renowned Scientist of the Russian Fed. 1996; state orders. *Publications:* Peaceful Nuclear Explosions and Environment 1974, Ecology and Control of Environment 1983, Global Climatic Catastrophes 1986, Anthropogenic Climate Change 1987, Anthropogenic Ecology of the Ocean 1989, Chernobyl: Radioactive Contamination of the Environment 1990, Earth's Ozone Shield and its Changes (co-author) 1992, Radioactive Fallout after Nuclear Explosions and Accidents 1996; and numerous other scientific books and articles. *Leisure interests:* organ music, mountaineering, philately. *Address:* Institute of Global Climate and Ecology, Glebovskaya str. 20B, 107258 Moscow (Office); Dept of Oceanology, Atmospheric Physics and Geography, Russian Academy of Sciences, Leninsky pr. 32A, 117993 Moscow (Office); Apt. 84, Romanov per. 3, 84, Moscow, Russia (Home). *Telephone:* (095) 169-24-30 (Office); (095) 938-14-63 (Office). *Fax:* (095) 160-08-31 (Office); (095) 938-18-59 (Office).

IZRAELEWICZ, Erik, DEcon; French journalist; b. 6 Feb. 1954, Strasbourg; ed Haute Ecole de Commerce, Centre de Formation des Journalistes and Univ. de Paris I; journalist, L'Expansion 1981–85; Banking Finance Ed. Le Monde 1986–88, Head of Econ. Service 1989–92, Deputy Ed.-in-Chief 1992–94, New York corresp. 1993–94, Econs reporter, Europe 1994–95, leader writer 1994, Ed.-in-Chief 1996; currently Ed.-in-Chief Les Echos. *Address:* Les Echos, 46 rue de la Boétie, 75381, Paris, Cedex 08, France.

IZZO, Lucio; Italian economist and financial executive; b. 5 April 1932, Rome; m. Marga Berg; two d.; ed Univ. of Oxford and MIT; Econ. Research Dept, Bank of Italy 1958–60, 1962–63; Rockefeller Fellow, Dept of Econs, MIT 1960–62; Asst Prof. of Econs, Univ. of Rome 1963–66; Assoc. Prof., then Prof. of Econs, Univ. of Siena 1966–74; Visiting Prof. of Econs, LSE 1971–72; Prof. of Econs, Univ. of Rome 1975; Econ. Adviser to Minister of the Budget 1974–78, to Minister of the Treasury 1980–82; Vice-Pres. and Vice-Chair. Bd of Dirs. European Investment Bank (EIB) 1982; Italian Rep. OECD Working Party 3, Econ. Policy Cttee 1976–81; mem. American Econ. Asscn, American Finance Asscn, Econometric Soc.; Pres. of Italy's Gold Medal for studies in field of public finance 1978.

JAAFAR ALBAR, Datuk Seri Syed Hamid bin Syed; Malaysian politician; b. 15 Jan. 1944, Kampong Melayu Air Hitam, Penang; m. Datin Seri Sharifah Aziah bte Syed Zainal Abidin; three s. three d.; ed Monash Univ., Melbourne, Australia; Magistrate and Pres. of Sessions Court, Kuala Lumpur 1970–72; Head of Legal Dept, Bank Bumiputra Malaysia Bhd (BBMB) 1972, Legal Adviser and later Sr Man. 1972–78, Asst Sec. and Sec. to Man. 1974–79, first Gen. Man. of Bahrain Br. 1979–80, Gen. Man. of London Br., transferred to Kuala Lumpur as Head of Int. Banking Div. (Credit Supervision) 1980–82, Chief Gen. Man. and Sec. of the Bank 1985–86; Sec. Kewangan Bumiputra and Bank Pembangunan Malaysia Bhd 1976–79, Inst. of Bankers 1978–79; Dir and CEO Bumiputra Merchant Bankers 1982–85; Dir Koperasi Usaha Bersatu 1983–88, Kewangan Bumiputra Malaysia Bhd, Bumiputra Lloyds Leasing Bhd, Bumiputra Merchant Bankers, Syarikat Nominee Sdn Bhd, BBMB Properties 1985–86; Advocate and Solicitor-Gen. Partner, Albar Zulkifly and Yap 1986–90; Chair. Shamelin Holdings 1989–90, Koperasi Shamelin Bhd 1989–90; MP for Kota Tinggi (Johor) 1990; Minister of Justice in Prime Minister's Dept (in charge of oil and gas affairs) 1990–92; Minister of Law and Minister in Prime Minister's Dept 1992–95; Minister of Defence 1995–99, of Foreign Affairs 1999–. *Address:* Ministry of Foreign Affairs, Wisma Putra, 1 Jalan Wisma Putra, 50602 Kuala Lumpur, Malaysia (Office). *Telephone:* (3) 8887400 (Office). *Fax:* (3) 88891717 (Office). *E-mail:* webmaster@kln.gov.my (Office). *Website:* www.kln.gov.my (Office).

JÄÄTTEENMÄKI, Anneli Tuulikki, LLM; Finnish politician; b. 11 Feb. 1955, Lapua; m. Jorma Melleri 1994; Acting Lawyer, Office of the Local Authorities Negotiating Del. 1981–82; Temporary Asst Ministry for Foreign Affairs 1982, Ministerial Political Adviser 1983–84; Legis. Sec. to Centre Party Parl. Faction 1986, Deputy Chair. Centre Party Parl. 1991–94, 1999–2000, Deputy Chair. Centre Party 2000–02, Chair. 2002–; Mem. Parl. 1987–; mem. Finnish Del. to the Nordic Council 1987–94; mem. Parl. Cttee for Constitutional Law 1987–99, Cttee for Ordinary Law 1987–91, Minister of Justice 1994–95; Parl. Gov. Bank of Finland 1991–92, mem. Parl. Council Bank of Finland 1992–94, 1995–, Parl. Trustee 1993–94, First Deputy Parl. Trustee 1993, 1999–, Second Deputy Parl. Trustee 1991–93, 1995–99; mem. and Deputy Chair. Finnish Del. to Parl. Ass. of Council of Europe 1996–; mem. Parl. Cttee for Foreign Affairs 1999–; mem. Parl. Grand Cttee 1999–; Prime Minister of Finland April 2003–; mem. Equal Opportunities Comm. 1987–91, Advisory Bd for Prison Affairs 1988–91 (Chair. 1991–94), Helsinki Inst. for Criminal Policy (HEUNI) 1996–; Deputy Chair. Paasikivi Soc. 1994–. *Publications:* Oikeus Voittaa (Justice Wins) 1999, Sillanrakentaja 2002. *Address:* Prime Minister's Office, POB 23, 00023 Government, Helsinki, Finland (Office). *Telephone:* (9) 1601 (Office). *Fax:* (9) 478711 (Office). *E-mail:* kirjaamo@vnk.vn.fi (Office). *Website:* www.vn.fi/vnk (Office).

JACAMON, Jean-Paul; French business executive; b. 5 Aug. 1947, Thaon-les-Vosges; m. Colette Jacquier; four c.; ed Ecole Polytechnique de Paris and Ecole des Mines de Paris; mem. staff Ministry of Industry 1975, Sr civil servant, French Regional Land Use Planning Comm. (DATAR) –1981; Exec. Asst Groupe Schneider 1981, various positions with Spie Batignolles (electrical Eng construction subsidiary) 1983–, Man. of 'Ferrière la Grande' plant, Vice-Pres. Eng and Gen. Contracting Div., Vice-Pres. Electric and Nuclear Power Div. 1988, Vice-Pres. responsible for electrical contracting activities, Chair. and CEO Spie-Trindel (local contracting for electrical and electro-mechanical projects) –1993, COO Spie Batignolles 1993–94; Exec. Vice-Pres. European Div., Groupe Schneider (now Schneider Electric 1999–2002) 1995, COO 1996–2002, Vice-Chair. 1999–2002; ind. consultant 2002–; Dir (non-exec.) AMEC PLC 2002–, Péchiney 2002–, Carbonne Louane 2003–; Chevalier, Ordre nat. du Mérite 1994. *Leisure interests:* golf, bridge. *Address:* Marly conseil, 23 rue d'Aumale, 75009 Paris (Office); 64 route de l'Etang la Ville, 78750 Mareil-Marly, France (Home). *Telephone:* 6-07-25-46-79 (Office); 1-39-16-14-68 (Home). *Fax:* 1-39-16-89-21 (Office). *E-mail:* jp.jacamon@wanadoo.fr (Home).

JACK, James Julian Bennett, PhD, FRCP, F.MED.SC., FRS; New Zealand neurophysiologist; b. 25 March 1936, Invercargill; ed Univ. of Otago, Univ. of Oxford, UK; Rhodes Scholarship 1960–63; Foulerton Gift Researcher 1964–68; demonstrator, Univ. Lecturer then Reader, Univ. Laboratory of Physiology, Oxford 1968–; Prof. of Cellular Neuroscience, Oxford Univ.; Fellow Univ. Coll. Oxford; Gov. Wellcome Trust 1987– (Deputy Chair. 1994–99); Hon. FRSNZ 1999, Hon. DSc (Univ. of Otago) 1999. *Address:* University Laboratory of Physiology, Parks Road, Oxford, OX1 3PT, England. *Telephone:* (1865) 282491 (Office); (1865) 790637 (Home). *Fax:* (1865) 282498.

JACK, Kenneth Henderson, OBE, FRS; British professor of applied crystal chemistry; b. 12 Oct. 1918, North Shields, Northumberland (now Tyne and Wear); s. of late John Henderson Jack and Emily Jack (née Cozens); m. Alfreda Hughes 1942 (died 1974); two s.; ed Tynemouth Municipal High School, King's Coll., Univ. of Durham, Fitzwilliam Coll., Univ. of Cambridge; Experimental Officer Ministry of Supply 1940–41; Lecturer in Chem., Univ. of Durham 1941–45, 1949–52, 1953–57; Sr Scientific Officer British Iron and Steel Research Asscn 1945–49; Research at Cavendish Lab., Cambridge 1947–49; Research Engineer Westinghouse Electrical Corpn, Pittsburgh, Pa, USA 1952–53; Research Dir Thermal Syndicate Ltd, Wallsend 1957–64; Prof. of Applied Crystal Chem. Univ. of Newcastle-upon-Tyne 1964–84, Prof. Emer. 1984–; Dir Wolfson Research Group for High-Strength Materials 1970–84; Leverhulme Research Fellow 1984–87; Consultant Cookson Group PLC 1986–94; Hon. Prof. Univ. of Wales, Swansea 1996–; Fellow American Ceramic Soc. 1984; mem. Acad. of Ceramics 1989; Hon. mem. Soc. Française de Métallurgie 1984, Materials Research Soc. (India) 1991, Ceramic Soc. of Japan 1991; American Ceramic Soc. Sosman Lecturer 1989; numerous awards and prizes including Prince of Wales Award for Industrial Innovation and Production 1984, Royal Soc. Armourers and Brasiers Award 1988, Inst. of Metals Griffith Medal 1989, Centennial Award, Ceramic Soc. of Japan 1991. *Publications:* papers on solid state chem., crystallography, metallurgy, ceramic science and glass tech. in scientific journals and conference proceedings. *Leisure interest:* walking. *Address:* 147 Broadway, Cullercoats, North Shields, Tyne and Wear, NE30 3TA, England (Home). *Telephone:* (191) 257-3664 (Home).

JACKAMAN, Michael Clifford John, MA; British businessman; b. 7 Nov. 1935; s. of Air Commodore Clifford Thomas Jackaman and Lily Margaret Jackaman; m. Valerie Jane Pankhurst 1960; one s. one d.; ed Felsted School, Essex, Jesus Coll., Cambridge; with Yardley Ltd 1959–60, Beecham Foods Ltd 1960–63, John Harvey & Sons Ltd 1963–65, Findus Ltd 1965, Harveys of Bristol 1966–92 (Chair. 1984–93); Marketing Dir Allied Breweries Ltd 1978–80, Deputy Man. Dir 1978–83; Chair. Allied Vintners Ltd 1983–88; Chair. and CEO Hiram Walker-Allied Vintners Ltd 1988–91; Chair. Allied-Lyons (now Allied Domecq) PLC 1991–96; Chair. Grand Appeal, Royal Hosp. for Sick Children, Bristol 1996–; Dir Rank Group PLC 1992–97, Kleinwort Benson Group 1994–98, Theatre Royal, Bath 1999–; Hon. D.B.A. (Univ. of West of England). *Leisure interests:* opera, gardening, tennis, walking, oriental antiques, theatre. *Address:* Appeal Office, Royal Hospital for Children, 24 Upper Maudlin Street, Bristol, BS2 8DJ, England. *Telephone:* (117) 927-3888. *Fax:* (117) 929-3718.

JACKLIN, Bill, MA, RA; British artist and painter; b. 1 Jan. 1943, Hampstead; s. of Harold Jacklin and Alice Jacklin; m. 1st Lesley Berman 1979 (divorced 1993); m. 2nd Janet Russo 1993; ed Walthamstow School of Art, London and Royal Coll. of Art; teacher at numerous art colls. 1967–75; moved to New York 1985. *Paintings included in following collections:* Arts Council of GB, British Council, British Museum, Metropolitan Museum of Art, New York, Museum of Modern Art, New York, Tate Gallery, Victoria and Albert Museum; Artist-in-Residence British Council, Hong Kong 1993–95. *Solo exhibitions include:* Nigel Greenwood, Inc. 1970, 1971, 1975, Hester van Royen Gallery 1973, 1977, Marlborough Fine Art 1980, 1983, 1988, 1992, 1997, 2000, Marlborough Gallery, New York 1985, 1987, 1990, 1997, 1999, 2002, "Urban Portraits", Museum of Modern Art, Oxford 1992, Hong Kong Art Centre 1995, L'Ecole de Londres Musée Maillol, Paris 1998–99. *Leisure interest:* walking. *Address:* c/o Marlborough Fine Art, 6 Albemarle Street, London, W1X 4BY, England.

JACKLIN, Tony, CBE; British golfer; b. 7 July 1944, Scunthorpe; s. of Arthur David Jacklin and Doris Lillian Jacklin; m. Vivien Jacklin 1966 (died 1988); two s. one. d.; m. 2nd Astrid May Waagen 1988; one s. one step-s. one step-d.; Lincolnshire Open champion 1961; professional 1962–85, 1988–; won British Asst Professionals' title 1965; won Dunlop Masters 1967, 1973; first British player to win British Open since 1951 1969; US Open Champion 1970; first British player to win US Open since 1920 and first since 1900 to hold US and British Open titles simultaneously; Greater Greensboro Open champion, USA 1968, 1972; won Italian Open 1973, German Open 1979, Venezuelan Open 1979, Jersey Open 1981, British PGA champion 1982 and 15 maj. tournaments in various parts of the world; played in eight Ryder Cup matches and four times for England in World Cup; Capt. of 1983 GB and Europe Ryder Cup Team; Capt. of victorious European Ryder Cup team 1985 (first win for Europe since 1957), 1987; BBC TV golf commentator; moved to Sotogrande, Spain from Jersey 1983; Commr of Golf, Las Aves Club, Sotogrande 1983–; Dir of Golf, San Roque Club 1988–; now golf course designer; Hon. Life Pres. British Professional Golfers' Asscn; Hon. Fellow, Birmingham Polytechnic 1989. *Publications:* Golf With Tony Jacklin 1969, The Price of Success 1979, Jacklin's Golfing Secrets (with Peter Dobereiner), The First Forty Years (with Renton Laidlaw) 1985, Your Game and Mine (with Bill Robertson) 1999. *Address:* Tony Jacklin Golf Academy, Plaza del Rio Office Centre, 101 Riverfront Boulevard, Suite 610, Bradenton, FL 34205, USA (Office).

JACKSON, Alan Robert, A.O.; Australian business executive; b. 30 March 1936, Drovin, Vic.; m.; four d.; ed Hemmingway Robertson Inst., Harvard School of Business, USA; clerk, accountant, Co. Sec., then Finance Dir and Man. Dir Mather & Platt Pty Ltd 1952–77; Man. Dir BTR Nylex Ltd 1977–91, Chair. 1991–97; Dir BTR PLC 1984–97, Man. Dir and Chief Exec. 1991–96, Chair. BTR Inc. USA 1991–96; Chair. Sanshin Holdings, Japan 1985–95, Nylex Malaysia Berhad 1985–96, CGPC Group, Taiwan 1986–96; Chair. and Chief Exec. Austrim Nylex Ltd 1990–; Chair. ACI Glass Co. Ltd 1993–96, ACI Guandong Glass Co. Ltd 1994–96, Dir Reserve Bank of Australia 1991–2001, Seven Network Ltd 1995–, Titan Petrochemicals and Polymers Berhad, Malaysia 1997–; Chair. Australian Trade Comm. 1995–; mem. Econ. Planning Advisory Council 1990–; Dir St Frances Cabrini Hosp. 1995–; mem. Inst. of Chartered Accountants in Australia, Australian Soc. of Accountants, Australian Inst. of Man.; Advance Australia Award for Services to Industry

1990 and other awards. *Address:* Office of the Chairman, Austrade, AIDC Tower, 201 Kent Street, Sydney, NSW 2000, Australia (Office); Level 4 East Tower, 608 St. Kilda Road, Melbourne, Vic. 3004. *Telephone:* (2) 9390-2002 (Office). *Fax:* (2) 9390-2106 (Office). *Website:* www.austrade.gov.au (Office).

JACKSON, Betty, MBE; British couturier; b. 24 June 1949, Lancashire; d. of Arthur Jackson and Phyllis Gertrude Jackson; m. David Cohen 1985; one s. one d.; ed Bacup and Rawtenstall Grammar School and Birmingham Coll. of Art and Design; Chief Designer Quorum 1975–81; f. Betty Jackson Ltd 1981, Dir 1981–; opened Betty Jackson retail shop 1991; Fellow Birmingham Polytech. 1989, Univ. of Cen. Lancashire 1993; Hon. Fellow RCA 1989, part-time tutor 1982–, Visiting Prof. 1999; Designer of the Year 1985, Royal Designer for Industry (Royal Soc. of Arts) 1988, 1989, Fil d'Or, Int. Linen 1989, Contemporary Designer of the Year 1999. *Leisure interests:* reading, listening to music. *Address:* Betty Jackson Ltd, 1 Netherwood Place, Netherwood Road, London, W14 0BW, England. *Telephone:* (20) 7602-6023. *Fax:* (20) 7602-3050. *E-mail:* info@bettyjackson.com (Office). *Website:* www.bettyjackson.com (Office).

JACKSON, Colin Ray, OBE; British athlete; b. 18 Feb. 1967, Cardiff; World-class 110m hurdler; holds the 60m world indoor record and 110m outdoor record (as at end of 2002); 110m hurdles achievements include: silver medal European Jr Championships 1985, gold medal World Jr Championships 1986, silver medal Commonwealth Games 1986, silver medal European Cup 1987, bronze medal World Championships 1987, silver medal Olympic Games 1988, silver medal World Cup 1989, gold medal European Cup 1989, 1993, gold medal Commonwealth Games 1990, gold medal World Cup 1992, gold medal (and new world record) World Championships 1993 (silver medal 4x100m relay); achievements (60m hurdles): silver medal World Indoor Championships 1989, 1993, gold medal European Indoor Championships 1989 (silver medal 1987), 1994, gold medals European and Commonwealth Championships 1994, gold medal European Championships 1998, 2002, gold medal World Championships 1999; in world's top ten at 110m each year from 1986–; set to become the most capped British athlete ever (70 vests), Glasgow Feb. 2003; 25 medals total; announced intention to retire March 2003; mem. Brecon Athletics Club, UK Int. 1985–; numerous Welsh, UK, European and Commonwealth records; Hon. BA (Aberystwyth) 1994, Hon. BSc (Univ. of Wales) 1999; Athlete of the Decade, French Sporting Council, Hurdler of the Century, German Athletic Asscn (DLV), Athlete of the Year 1993–94, British Athletics Writers, Sportsman of the Year 1994, Sports Writers Asscn. *Address:* c/o MTC (UK) Ltd, 20 York Street, London, W1V 6PU, England; 4 Jackson Close, Rhoose, Vale of Glamorgan, CF62 3DQ, Wales. *Telephone:* (20) 7935-8000 (MTC). *Fax:* (1446) 710642 (Home). *Website:* www.mtc-uk.com.

JACKSON, Daryl Sanders, AO, DIP.ARCH., BArch, L.F.R.A.I.A., ARIBA; Australian architect; b. 7 Feb. 1937, Clunes, Victoria; s. of Cecil John Jackson and Doreen May Sanders; m. Kay Parsons 1960; one s. three d.; ed Wesley Coll., Melbourne, Royal Melbourne Inst. of Tech., Univ. of Melbourne; Asst, Edwards, Madigan and Torzillo, Sydney 1959, Don Henry Fulton, Melbourne 1960, Chamberlin, Powell and Bon, London 1961–63, Paul Rudolph, New Haven, Conn. 1963–64, Skidmore, Owings and Merrill, San Francisco 1964; Partner, Daryl Jackson, Evan Walker Architects, Melbourne 1965–79; Dir Daryl Jackson Pty Ltd Architects 1979–; Dir Daryl Jackson, Robin Dyke Pty Ltd (Sydney) 1985–; Prof. Assoc. Architecture Melbourne Univ. 1985–; Pres. Wesley Coll. Council, Melbourne 1993–; Dir Daryl Jackson Alastair Swayn Pty Ltd (Canberra); Dir Daryl Jackson Int. Ltd (London) 1989–; Dir RAIA Victorian Chapter Housing Service 1966–69; mem. RAIA Victorian Chapter Council 1967–77, Victorian Tapestry Workshop Cttee 1975–84, Parl. House Construction Authority, Canberra 1985–89, Victorian Arts Centre Trust 1991, Melbourne Cricket Club 1992– (Vice-Pres. 1997–); Trustee, Nat. Gallery of Vic. 1983–95; Chair. Australian Film Inst. 1990–94, Melbourne Major Events Co. Ltd 1991–; Assoc. RIBA; Life Fellow Royal Australian Inst. of Architects; Hon. FAIA; numerous architectural and design awards. *Major works:* YWCA Community Resource Centre, Suva, Fiji 1973, Princes Hill High School, Melbourne 1973, Methodist Ladies' Coll., Library Resource Centre, Melbourne 1973, City Edge Housing Devt, Melbourne 1976, School of Music, Canberra 1976, Asscn for Modern Educ. School, Canberra 1977, Emu Ridge Govt Housing Devt, Canberra 1978, School of Art, Canberra 1980, McLachlan Offices, Canberra 1980, The Walter and Eliza Hall Inst. of Medical Research, Melbourne 1982, Nat. Sports Centre, Swimming Training Hall, Bruce, ACT 1982, Australian Chancery Complex, Riyadh, Saudi Arabia 1987, Hyatt Hotel, Canberra, Bond Univ., Gold Coast 1989, Commercial Union Office Bldg, Melbourne 1990, Melbourne Cricket Ground Southern Stand 1991, 120 Collins Street, Melbourne, Methodist Ladies' Coll. Music School, Kew 1994, Subiaco Oval Redevelopment, Perth 1994, Wesley Coll. Pre-Preparatory School, Prahran 1995, Brisbane Cricket Ground Redevelopment, 'The Gabba' 1995. *Publications:* Daryl Jackson Architecture: Drawings and Photos 1984, Daryl Jackson, The Master Architect 1996; numerous articles and papers. *Address:* 161 Hotham Street, East Melbourne, Vic. 3002, Australia (Home).

JACKSON, Edwin Sydney, FSA, FCIA, BCom; Canadian financial executive; b. 17 May 1922, Regina, Sask.; s. of late Edwin and Dorothy Hazel (née Bell) Jackson; m. Nancy Joyce (née Stovel) 1948; three d.; ed Univ. of Manitoba; joined Mfrs Life Insurance Co. 1948, Pres. and CEO 1972, Chair. and CEO 1985–87, Chair. 1987–90, Vice-Chair. 1990–; Pres. Canadian Inst. of Actuaries 1966–67; Chair. Life Office Man. Asscn 1982–83; Chair. Canadian Life and Health Insurance Asscn 1977–78; Dir American Coll. of Life Insurance;

Dir Manufacturers Life Capital Corpn Inc.; mem. Soc. of Actuaries; Past Pres. Ont. Div. Canadian Arthritis and Rheumatism Soc.; Dir Canadian Centre for Philanthropy. *Leisure interests:* skiing, curling, golf. *Address:* 101 Stratford Crescent, Toronto, Ont., M4N 1C7, Canada.

JACKSON, Francis Alan, DMus, FRCO; British organist and composer; b. 2 Oct. 1917, Malton, Yorks.; s. of William Altham Jackson and Eveline May (née Suddaby); m. Priscilla Procter 1950; two s. one d.; ed York Minster Choir School and with Sir Edward Bairstow; Organist Malton Parish Church 1933–40; war service with 9th Lancers in N Africa and Italy 1940–46; Asst Organist York Minster 1946, Master of the Music 1946–82, Organist Emer. 1988–; Conductor York Musical Soc. 1947–82, York Symphony Orchestra 1947–80; now freelance organist and composer; Patron, Whitlock Trust; Hon. Fellow Royal School of Church Music, Westminster Choir Coll., Princeton, NJ, USA, Royal Northern Coll. of Music; Order of St William of York 1983; Hon. DUniv (York) 1983. *Music:* published works include Symphony in D minor 1957, Organ Concerto 1985, Eclogue for piano and organ 1987, Recitative and Allegro for trombone and organ 1989, organ music including 4 sonatas, 3 duets, church music, songs and monodramas, Blessed City: The Life and Works of Edward C. Bairstow 1996, Sonatina Pastorale for recorder and piano 1999. *Leisure interests:* gardening, art and architecture. *Address:* Nether Garth, East Acklam, Malton, North Yorkshire, YO17 9RG, England. *Telephone:* (1653) 658395.

JACKSON, Frank Cameron, PhD, FAHA, FASSA, FBA; Australian professor of philosophy; b. 31 Aug. 1943, Melbourne; s. of Allan C. Jackson and Ann E. Jackson; m. Morag E. Fraser 1967; two d.; ed Melbourne and La Trobe Univs.; Prof. of Philosophy, Monash Univ., Vic. 1978–86, 1991; Prof. of Philosophy, ANU 1986–90, 1992–, Dir Inst. of Advanced Studies 1998–2001. *Publications:* Perception 1978, Conditionals 1986, The Philosophy of Mind and Cognition 1996, From Metaphysics to Ethics 1998, Mind, Method and Conditionals 1998. *Leisure interests:* reading, tennis. *Address:* Philosophy Program, Australian National University, ACT 0200; 33 David Street, O'Connor, ACT 2602, Australia. *Telephone:* (2) 6125-2146 (Office). *Fax:* (2) 6125-3294. *E-mail:* frank.jackson@anu.edn.av (Office).

JACKSON, Glenda, CBE; British actress and politician; b. 9 May 1936, Birkenhead, Cheshire; d. of Harry and Joan Jackson; m. Roy Hodges 1958 (divorced 1976); one s.; ed Royal Acad. of Dramatic Art; fmr mem. Royal Shakespeare Co. where roles included Ophelia in Hamlet and Charlotte Corday in Marat/Sade (in London and New York); played Queen Elizabeth I in TV series Elizabeth R; Pres., Play Matters (fmrly. Toy Libraries Asscn) 1976–; Dir United British Artists 1983–; Labour MP for Hampstead and Highgate 1992–; Parl. Under-Sec. of State, Dept for the Environment and Transport 1997–99; Adviser on Homelessness, GLA 2000–; Hon. D.Litt (Liverpool) 1978, Hon. LLM (Nottingham) 1992; Hon. Fellow, Liverpool Polytechnic 1987; Acad. Award for Women in Love 1971, for A Touch of Class 1974. *Plays include:* Marat/Sade, New York and Paris 1965, The Investigation 1965, Hamlet 1965, US 1966, Three Sisters 1967, Collaborators 1973, The Maids 1974, Hedda Gabler 1975, The White Devil 1976, Antony and Cleopatra 1978, Rose 1980, Strange Interlude 1984, Phaedra 1984, 1985, Across from the Garden of Allah 1986, Strange Interlude 1986, The House of Bernarda Alba 1986, Macbeth 1988, Scenes from an Execution 1990, Mermaid 1990, Mother Courage 1990, Mourning Becomes Electra 1991. *Films include:* Marat/Sade 1966, Negatives 1968, Women in Love 1969, The Music Lovers 1970, Sunday, Bloody Sunday 1971, The Boy Friend 1971, Mary, Queen of Scots 1971, The Triple Echo 1972, Bequest to the Nation 1972, A Touch of Class 1973, The Romantic Englishwoman 1975, The Tempter 1975, The Incredible Sarah 1976, The Abbess of Crewe 1976, Stevie 1977, Hedda 1977, House Calls 1978, The Class of Miss McMichael 1978, Lost and Found 1979, Hopscotch 1980, The Return of the Soldier 1982, Giro City 1982, Summit Conference 1982, Great and Small 1983, And Nothing But the Truth 1984, Turtle Diary 1985, Beyond Therapy 1985, Business as Usual 1986, Salome's Last Dance 1988, The Rainbow 1989, The Secret Life of Sir Arnold Bax 1992. *Leisure interests:* gardening, reading, listening to music. *Address:* House of Commons, London, SW1A 0AA, England. *Telephone:* (20) 7219-4008.

JACKSON, Rev. Jesse Louis; American clergyman and civic leader; b. 8 Oct. 1941, Greenville, N Carolina; s. of Charles Henry and Helen Jackson; m. Jacqueline Lavinia Brown 1964; three s. two d. one d. by Karin Stanford; ed Univ. of Illinois, Illinois Agricultural and Tech. Coll., Chicago Theological Seminary; ordained to Ministry Baptist Church 1968; active Black Coalition for United Community Action 1969; Co-Founder Operation Breadbasket S. Christian Leadership Conf.; Co-ordinating Council Community Orgs., Chicago 1966, Nat. Dir 1966–77; Founder and Exec. Dir Operation PUSH (People United to Save Humanity), Chicago 1971–96, Pres. Rainbow PUSH Coalition (formed with merger with Rainbow Coalition) 1996–; unsuccessful cand. for Democratic nomination for US Presidency 1983–84, 1987–88; TV Host, Voices of America 1990–; Pres. Award Nat. Medical Asscn 1969; Humanitarian Father of the Year Award Nat. Father's Day Cttee 1971. *Address:* c/o Rainbow PUSH Coalition, 930 E 50th Street, Chicago, IL 60615, USA.

JACKSON, John B. H.; British business executive; Dir (non-exec.) Hilton Group PLC 1980, Vice-Chair. 1991–94, Chair. 1994–; Chair. Celltech, Xenova, Wyndham Press; Chair. (non-solicitor) Mishcon de Reya; Dir (non-exec.) WPP Group, Billiton. *Address:* Maple Court, Central Park, Reeds Crescent, Watford, Herts., WD24 4QQ, England (Office). *Telephone:* (20) 7856-8000 (Office). *Fax:* (20) 7856-8001 (Office). *Website:* www.hiltongroup.com (Office).

JACKSON, (Kevin) Paul, BA, FID; British television producer and executive; b. 2 Oct. 1947, London; s. of the late T. Leslie Jackson and Jo Spoonley; m. Judith E. Cain 1981; two d.; ed Gunnersbury Grammar School and Univ. of Exeter; stage man. Marlowe Theatre, Canterbury 1970, Thorndike Theatre, Leatherhead 1971; production work for BBC TV: Two Ronnies, 3 of a Kind, Carrott's Lib, The Young Ones, Happy Families 1971–82; freelance producer and Dir Canon and Ball, Girls on Top 1982–84; Producer and Chair. Paul Jackson Productions: Red Dwarf, Don't Miss Wax, Saturday Live 1984–86; Exec. Producer, Appointments of Dennis Jennings (Acad. Award 'Oscar' for Best Live Action Short 1989); Man. Dir NGTV 1987–91; Dir of Progs. Carlton TV 1991–93, Man. Dir Carlton TV 1993–94, Carlton UK Productions 1994–96; Controller BBC Entertainment 1997–2000; currently CEO Granada Productions; Chair. Comic Relief 1987–98; Vice-Chair. Charity Projects 1990–92, Chair. 1992–98; Chair. RTS 1994–96; Stanford Exec. Programme 1993; Fellow Inst. of Dirs; BAFTA 1983, 1984; Hon. Fellow (Exeter) 1999. *Leisure interests:* theatre, rugby, travel, food and wine, friends and family. *Address:* Granada Productions, Fox Studios Australia, 34 Driver Avenue, Moore Park, NSW 1363, Australia (Office); Room 4152, BBC Television Centre, Wood Lane, London, W12 7RJ, England. *Telephone:* (612) 9383-4361 (Office). *Fax:* (612) 9383-4367 (Office). *E-mail:* paul.jackson@granadaproductions.com.au (Office).

JACKSON, Michael, BA; British broadcasting executive; b. 11 Feb. 1958; s. of Ernest Jackson and Margaret Jackson (née Kearsley); ed King's School, Macclesfield, Polytechnic of Cen. London; Organizer Channel 4 Group 1979; Producer The Sixties 1982; ind. producer Beat Productions Ltd 1983–87; Ed. The Late Show, BBC TV (BFI Award) 1988–90; with Late Show Productions 1990–91; Head of Music and Arts BBC TV 1991–93, Controller BBC2 1993–96, Controller BBC1 and BBC Dir of TV 1996–97; CEO Channel 4 1997–2001, Dir of Programmes 1997–98; Chair. Film Four Ltd 1997–2001; Dir (non-exec.) EMI Group 1999–; Pres., CEO USA Entertainment Group 2001–02; Chair. Universal Television Group 2002–; Hon. DLitt (Westminster) 1995. *Programmes produced include:* Whose Town is it Anyway?, Open the Box, The Media Show, The Nelson Mandela Tribute, Tales from Prague (Grierson Documentary Award), Moving Pictures, The American Late Show (Public Broadcasting Service, USA), Naked Hollywood (BAFTA Best Factual Series Award), Sounds of the Sixties, The Lime Grove Story, TV Hell. *Leisure interests:* reading, walking. *Address:* Universal Television Group, 100 Universal City Plaza, Bldg 1280/12th Floor, Universal City, CA 91608, USA (Office). *Telephone:* (818) 777-0283 (Office). *Fax:* (818) 866-1345 (Office). *E-mail:* michael.jackson@unistudios.com (Office).

JACKSON, Gen. Sir Michael David (Mike), KCB, DSO, ADC; British military officer; b. 21 March 1944; s. of George Jackson and Ivy Jackson (née Bower); m. Sarah Coombe 1985; two s. one d.; ed Stamford School, Sandhurst Mil. Acad., Birmingham Univ.; joined Command Intelligence Corps 1963; transferred to Parachute Regt 1970, attended Staff Coll.1976–78, Chief of Staff Berlin Infantry Brigade 1977–78, commanded a parachute co., NI 1979–81, mem. Directing Staff, Staff Coll. 1981–83, Commdr 1st Bn Parachute Regt 1984–86; with Sr Defence Staff, Jt Service Defence Coll., Greenwich 1986–88; Services Fellow Wolfson Coll. Cambridge 1989; Commdr 39 Infantry Brigade, NI 1989–92; Dir-Gen. of Personnel Services, Ministry of Defence (Army) 1992–94; Commdr 3rd Div. 1994–96, Commdr Implementation Force Multinational Div. SW, Bosnia and Herzegovina 1995–96; Dir-Gen. of Devt and Doctrine, Ministry of Defence 1996–97; rank Lt-Gen. 1997; Commdr ACE Rapid Reaction Force 1997–2000; Commdr Kosovo Force to Macedonia March–Oct. 1999; C-in-C Land Command 2000–03; Chief of the Gen. Staff 2003–; Freeman City of London 1988. *Address:* Office of the Chief of the General Staff, Ministry of Defence, Main Building, Whitehall, London, SW1A 2HB, England (Office). *Telephone:* (20) 7218-9000 (Office). *E-mail:* webmaster@dgics.mod.uk (Office). *Website:* www.mod.uk (Office).

JACKSON, Michael Joseph; American singer; b. 29 Aug. 1958, Gary, Ind.; s. of Joseph W. Jackson and Katherine E. Jackson (née Scruse); m. 1st Lisa Presley 1994 (divorced 1996); m. 2nd Debbie Rowe 1996 (divorced 1999); two s. one d.; ed privately; lead singer, family singing group Jackson Five (later The Jacksons) 1969–75; solo artist 1971–; performed at Silver Jubilee of HM Queen Elizabeth II 1977; world tours include Bad Tour 1987, Dangerous World Tour 1992; has recorded with numerous artists including Minnie Ripperton, Carol Bayer Sager, Donna Summer (q.v.), Paul McCartney (q.v.); Founder, Heal The World Foundation (children's charity); Owner, ATV Music Co. (including rights for John Lennon and Paul McCartney songs); Owner, MJJ record label; Hon. Dir Exeter City Football Club 2002–; numerous Grammy Awards 1980– (including seven awards 1984, Song of the Year 1986, Legend Award 1993); numerous American Music Awards 1980– (including 11 awards 1984, Special Award of Achievement 1989, Artist of the Century 2002); Brit Awards: Best Int. Artist 1984, 1988, 1989, Artist of a Generation 1996; Soul Train Awards 1988–; MTV Video Vanguard Award 1988; 2 NAACP Image Awards 1988; Entertainer of the Decade, American Cinema Awards Foundation 1990; First recipient, BMI Michael Jackson Award 1990; 3 World Music Awards 1993. *Albums include:* with Jackson Five/Jacksons: Diana Ross Presents The Jackson Five 1969, ABC 1970, Third Album 1970, Goin' Back To Indiana 1971, Maybe Tomorrow 1971, Looking Through The Windows 1972, Farewell My Summer 1973, Get It Together 1973, Skywriter 1973, Dancing Machine 1974, Moving Violation 1975, Joyful Jukebox Music 1976, The Jacksons 1976, Goin' Places 1977, Destiny 1978, Triumph 1980, Boogie 1980, Live 1981, Victory 1984; solo albums: Got To Be There 1971, Ben 1972,

Music and Me 1973, Forever Michael 1975, The Best of Michael Jackson 1975, The Wiz (film soundtrack) 1978, Off The Wall 1979, ET (film soundtrack) 1982, Thriller (listed in Guinness Book of Records as the most successful album in record history—50 million copies sold world-wide) 1982, BAD 1987, Dangerous 1991, HIStory: Past, Present and Future, Book 1 1995, Invincible 2001. *Singles include:* with Jackson Five/Jacksons: I Want You Back 1969, ABC 1970, The Love You Save 1970, I'll Be There 1970, Never Can Say Goodbye 1971, Maybe Tomorrow 1971, Looking Through The Windows 1972, Doctor My Eyes 1973, Dancing Machine 1973, Enjoy Yourself 1976, Show You The Way To Go 1977, Blame It On The Boogie 1978, Shake Your Body Down To The Ground 1979, Lovely One 1980, Can You Feel It? 1981, Walk Right Now 1981, State of Shock 1984; solo singles: Got To Be There 1971, Rockin' Robin 1972, Ain't No Sunshine 1972, Ben 1972, Don't Stop Till You Get Enough 1979, Off The Wall 1979, Rock With You 1980, One Day In Your Life 1981, She's Out of My Life 1980, The Girl Is Mine (duet with Paul McCartney) 1982, Billie Jean 1983, Beat It 1983, Wanna Be Startin' Somethin' 1983, Human Nature 1983, Say Say Say (duet with Paul McCartney) 1983, Thriller 1983, PYT 1984, Farewell My Summer Love 1984, I Can't Stop Loving You (with Siedah Garrett) 1987, Bad 1987, The Way You Make Me Feel 1988, The Man In the Mirror 1988, Dirty Diana 1988, Another Part of Me 1988, Smooth Criminal 1988, Leave Me Alone 1989, Liberian Girl 1989, Black and White 1991, Remember The Time 1992, In The Closet 1992, Jam 1992, Heal The World 1992, Give In To Me 1992, Scream (with Janet Jackson) 1995, You Are Not Alone 1995, Earth Song 1995, They Don't Care About Us 1996, Ghosts 1997, Stranger in Moscow 1997, Blood on the Dance Floor 1997, You Rock My World 2001, Cry 2001. *Film appearances include:* The Wiz 1978, Captain Eo 1986, Moonwalker 1988. *Television appearances include:* The Jacksons 1976, The Simpsons (guest voice as John Jay Smith) 1991. *Publications:* Moonwalk (autobiog.) 1988, Dancing the Dream: Poems and Reflections 1992. *Address:* Bob Jones, MJJ Productions, 10960 Wilshire Boulevard, Suite 2204, Los Angeles, CA 90024, USA. *Website:* www.michaeljackson.com.

JACKSON, Peter; New Zealand film director; b. New Zealand. *Films:* Meet the Feebles, Bad Taste, Dead Alive, Heavenly Creatures, The Frighteners, Contact (special effects only), The Lord of the Rings: the Fellowship of the Ring (BAFTA Award for Best Dir) The Lord of the Rings: the Two Towers 2002, The Lord of the Rings: the Return of the King 2003. *Address:* c/o ICM, 8942 Wilshire Boulevard, Beverly Hills, CA 90211, USA.

JACKSON, Peter John, BSc; British business executive; b. 16 Jan. 1947, Sheffield; s. of Jack Jackson and Joan Jackson; m. Anne Campbell 1974; two s. one d.; ed Univ. of Leeds; personnel and industrial relations positions at British Steel, Comm. on Industrial Relations, Guthrie Industries 1968–76; Dir Personnel and Employee Relations, Deputy Man. Dir Perkins Engines (Shrewsbury), Perkins Engines Group 1976–87; Personnel Dir British Sugar PLC 1987–88, Deputy Man. Dir 1988–89, Man. Dir 1989–93, Chief Exec. 1994–99; Chief Exec. Associated British Foods PLC 1999– (Dir 1992–). *Leisure interests:* garden, Sheffield United. *Address:* Associated British Foods PLC, Weston Centre, Bowater House, 68 Knightsbridge, London, SW1X 7LQ, England (Office). *Telephone:* (20) 7589-6363 (Office).

JACKSON, Rashleigh Esmond; Guyanese diplomatist; b. 12 Jan. 1929, New Amsterdam, Berbice; two s. two d.; ed Queen's Coll., Georgetown, Univ. Coll., Leicester, England, Columbia Univ., New York; entered public service 1948; Master, Queen's Coll. 1957; Prin. Asst Sec., Ministry of Foreign Affairs 1965, Perm. Sec. 1969–73; Perm. Rep. to UN 1973–78; Minister for Foreign Affairs 1978–90; consultant 1992–; Pres. UN Council for Namibia 1974; Chair. Caribbean Task Force on Environment 1991–92; Man. Dir Public Affairs Consulting Enterprise (PACE) 1993–; mem. Bd of Dirs. Environmental Protection Agency Guyana 1997–. *Address:* c/o Ministry of Foreign Affairs, Takuba Lodge, 254 South Road and New Garden Street, Georgetown (Office); 182 Republic Park, East Bank, Demerara, Guyana. *Telephone:* (2) 72847. *Fax:* (2) 55512.

JACKSON, Samuel L., BA; American actor; b. 21 Dec 1948, Washington; m. LaTanya Richardson; one d.; ed Morehouse Coll., Atlanta; co-f. and mem. Just Us theatre co., Atlanta. *Stage appearances:* Home, A Soldier's Story, Sally/ Prince, Colored People's Time, Mother Courage, Spell No. 7, The Mighty Gents, The Piano Lesson, Two Trains Running, Fences. *Television appearances:* (series) Movin' On 1972, Ghostwriter 1992; (films) The Trial of the Moke 1978, Uncle Tom's Cabin 1987, Common Ground 1990, Dead and Alive: The Race for Gus Farace 1991, Simple Justice 1993, Assault at West Point 1994, Against the Wall 1994. *Films include:* Together for Days 1972, Ragtime 1981, Eddie Murphy Raw 1987, Coming to America 1988, School Daze 1988, Do The Right Thing 1989, Sea of Love 1989, A Shock to the System 1990, Def by Temptation 1990, Betsy's Wedding 1990, Mo' Better Blues 1990, The Exorcist III 1990, GoodFellas 1990, Return of the Superfly 1990, Jungle Fever 1991 (Best Actor Award, Cannes Int. Film Festival, New York Film Critics' Award), Strictly Business 1991, Juice 1992, White Sands 1992, Patriot Games 1992, Johnny Suede 1992, Jumpin' at the Boneyard 1992, Fathers and Sons 1992, National Lampoon's Loaded Weapon 1 1993, Amos & Andrew 1993, Menace II Society 1993, Jurassic Park 1993, True Romance 1993, Hail Caesar 1994, Fresh 1994, The New Age 1994, Pulp Fiction 1994, Losing Isaiah 1995, Kiss of Death 1995, Die Hard With a Vengeance 1995, Fluke (voice) 1995, The Great White Hype 1996, A Time to Kill 1996, The Long Kiss Goodnight 1996, One Eight Seven 1996, Trees Lounge 1996, Hard Eight 1996, Eve's Bayou (also producer) 1997, Jackie Brown 1997, Out of Sight 1998, The Negotiator 1998, Sphere 1998, Star Wars Episode I: The Phantom Menace 1999, Deep

Blue Sea 1999, Rules of Engagement 1999, Any Given Wednesday 2000, Shaft 2000, Unbreakable 2000, The Caveman's Valentine 2001, The 51st State 2001, Changing Lanes 2002, Star Wars Episode II: Attack of the Clones 2002, The House on Turk Street 2002, XXX 2002, Basic 2003. *Address:* c/o ICM, 8942 Wilshire Boulevard, Beverly Hills, CA 90211, USA.

JACOB, François, MD, DSc; French professor of genetics; b. 17 June 1920, Nancy; m. 1st Lise Bloch 1947 (died 1984); three s. one d.; m. 2nd Geneviève Barrier 1999; ed Lycée Carnot and Univ. de Paris à la Sorbonne; Officer Free French Forces 1940–45; with Inst. Pasteur 1950–, Asst 1950–56, Head of Laboratory 1956–60, Head of Cellular Genetics Unit 1960–91, Pres. 1982–88; Prof. of Cellular Genetics Coll. de France 1965–92; mem. Acad. des Sciences 1977, Acad. française 1996; Foreign mem. Royal Danish Acad. of Sciences and Letters 1962, American Acad. of Arts and Sciences 1964; Foreign Assoc. Nat. Acad. of Sciences (USA) 1969; Foreign mem. Royal Soc., London 1973, Acad. Royale Médicale Belgique 1973, Acad. of Sciences of Hungary 1986, Royal Acad. of Sciences of Madrid 1987; Dr. hc of several univs.; Prix Charles Léopold Mayer, Acad. des Sciences 1962, Nobel Prize for Medicine (jointly with A. Lwoff and J. Monod) 1965; Croix de la Libération, Grand-Croix Légion d'honneur. *Publications:* The Logic of Life 1970, The Possible and the Actual 1981, The Statue Within 1987, La Souris, la mouche et l'homme 1997; and over 200 scientific papers. *Address:* Institut Pasteur, 25 rue de Dr. Roux, 75724 Paris Cedex 15; 15 rue de Condé, 75006 Paris, France (Home). *E-mail:* fjacob@pasteur.fr (Office).

JACOB, Gilles; French film festival director; Gen. Del. Cannes Film Festival 1978–2000, Pres. 2000–. *Address:* Association française du festival international du film, 3 rue Amélie, 75007 Paris, France (Office). *Telephone:* 1-53-59-61-00 (Office). *Fax:* 1-53-59-61-10 (Office). *E-mail:* festival@festival-cannes.fr (Office). *Website:* www.festival-cannes.com (Office).

JACOB, Lieut.-Gen. J. F. R., MSc; Indian politician and army officer; b. 2 May 1921, Calcutta; s. of E. Jacob; ed Madras Univ., Fort Sill, USA; commissioned into Indian Artillery 1942; active service in Middle East, Burma, Sumatra; fmrly commanded infantry and artillery brigades, the Artillery School, an infantry div., a corps and the Eastern Army; Chief of Staff Eastern Army during intervention in East Pakistan (now Bangladesh); retd 1978; Gov. of Goa 1998–99, of Punjab 1999–. *Address:* Raj Bhavan, Chandigarh, Punjab, India (Office). *Telephone:* (172) 740740 (Office); (172) 740768 (Home).

JACOB, Mathew Mundakaal, BEcons, LLB, MA; Indian politician; b. 9 Aug. 1928, Ramapuram; s. of Mathew Jacob; m. Achamma Jacob; four d.; advocate High Court of Cochin, specializing in taxation; involved in youth training in various parts of India for Bhoodan Movt for redistribution of land; Sec. Gen. Bharat Sevak Samaj org. to encourage popular participation in nat. Devt, Kerala 1956–66; led youth Work Camp Movt in India and co-leader int. work camps in Bangalore and Calcutta overseen by UNESCO; Indian Rep. World Youth Festival, Moscow 1957, World Ass. of Youth Confs., Delhi 1958; Convenor Student and Youth Affairs Cttee for Nat. Defence, Kerala State Govt 1962; State Sec. Sadachar Samiti, Kerala; mem. Exec. Cttee India Red Cross, Kerala State; Organizer Youth Hostel Movt, Kerala State and served as Sec. Gen. Youth Hostel Asscn of India; experience as social worker; mem. Bd of Govs. Inst. of Social Work directly after inception; Chair. Plantation Corpn of Kerala 1974–78; first Chair. Oil Palm India Ltd (Jt PCK-Govt initiative); Pres. Kerala State Co-operative Rubber Marketing Bd, Cochin for six years; Dir Indian Overseas Bank 1976–82; f. and Dir, then Chair. Chitralekha Film Cooperative, Trivandrum; Publr Bharat Sevak social work journal 1958–67; Man. Dir and Publr Congress Review newspaper 1977–86; Man. Dir Veekshanam (Malayalam daily) newspaper 1978–82; fmr Sec. Gen. Congress Party, Kerala State; fmr mem. All India Congress Cttee (AICC); mem. Indian Parl. (Senate) 1982–94; Chair. Parl. Cttee on Subordinate Legislation 1983–85; Deputy Chair. Senate 1986–87; Minister of State for Parl. Affairs 1987–93, Minister of State for Water Resources 1988–89, Minister of State for Home Affairs, Council of Ministers 1991–93, Chair. Parl. Standing Cttee on Home Affairs 1993–94; Gov. of Meghalaya, Shillong 1995–, of Arunachal Pradesh 1996; Del. to UN Gen. Ass. 1985, 1993, to UN/IPU World Disarmament Symposium 1985, UN World Human Rights Conf. 1993, to Commonwealth, IPU and rubber producers' confs. *Address:* Office of the Governor of Meghalaya, Raj Bhavan, Shillong-793001, India. *Telephone:* (364) 223001 (Office); (364) 225352 (Home). *Fax:* (364) 223338 (Office).

JACOBI, Sir Derek George, Kt, CBE, MA; British actor; b. 22 Oct. 1938, London; s. of Alfred George Jacobi and Daisy Gertrude Masters; ed Leyton County High School and St John's Coll., Cambridge; Birmingham Repertory Theatre 1960–63 (first appeared in One Way Pendulum 1961); National Theatre 1963–71; Prospect Theatre Co. 1972, 1974, 1976–78, Artistic Assoc. 1976–91; Old Vic Co. 1978–79; joined RSC April 1982; Vice-Pres., Nat. Youth Theatre 1982–; Artistic Dir Chichester Festival Theatre 1995–96; Hon. Fellow St John's Coll., Cambridge; Variety Club Award 1976, British Acad. Award 1976, Press Guild Award 1976, Royal Television Soc. Award 1976, Hamburg Shakespeare Award 1998. *Television appearances include:* She Stoops to Conquer, Man of Straw, The Pallisers, I Claudius, Philby, Burgess and Maclean, Tales of the Unexpected, A Stranger in Town, Mr. Pye, Brother Cadfael 1994. *Films:* Odessa File, Day of the Jackal, The Medusa Touch, Othello, Three Sisters, Interlude, The Human Factor, Charlotte 1981, The Man who went up in Smoke 1981, The Hunchback of Notre Dame 1981, Inside the Third Reich 1982, Little Dorrit 1986, The Tenth Man 1988, Henry V, The

Fool 1990, Dead Again, Hamlet 1996, Love is the Devil (Evening Standard Award for Best Actor 1998) 1997, Gladiator 2000, Gosford Park 2002. *Plays include:* The Lunatic, Lover and the Poet 1980, The Suicide 1980, Much Ado about Nothing, Peer Gynt, The Tempest 1982, Cyrano de Bergerac 1983, Breaking the Code 1986, Richard II 1988, Richard III 1989, Kean 1990, Becket 1991, Mad, Bad and Dangerous to Know, Ambassadors 1992, Macbeth 1993, Hadrian VII, Playing the Wife 1995, Uncle Vanya 1996, God Only Knows 2000; Dir Hamlet 1988, 2000. *Leisure interests:* gardening, reading, looking for the next job. *Address:* c/o ICM Ltd, Oxford House, 76 Oxford Street, London, W1N 0AX, England. *Telephone:* (20) 7636-6565. *Fax:* (20) 7323-0101.

JACOBOVITS de SZEGED, Adriaan; Netherlands diplomatist; b. 27 Dec. 1935, Vienna, Austria; s. of Giulio Jacobovits de Szeged and Eveline Tak van Poortvliet; m. Françoise S. Montant 1968; two s.; ed Univ. of Leyden; Master of Netherlands Law; Ministry of Finance 1963; joined Foreign Service 1964; postings at Embassy, Moscow, Perm. Mission to UN and other int. orgs., Geneva, Embassy, London, Embassy, Nairobi, Perm. to EC, Brussels; Dir Econ. Co-operation, Ministry of Foreign Affairs 1978–82; Dir-Gen. Political Affairs 1982–86; Perm. Rep. to UN, New York 1986–89; Perm. Rep. to NATO, Brussels 1989–93; Amb. to USA 1993–97; Pres. Int. Comm. for the Protection of the River Rhine 1999–2001; Personal Rep. of the OSCE Chair.-in-Office for Moldova 2002–03; Kt, Order of the Netherlands Lion; Grosses Verdienstkreuz (Germany); Commdr Légion d'honneur. *Address:* Riouwstraat 76, 2585 HD The Hague, Netherlands.

JACOBS, Adrianus Gerardus, M.ECON.; Netherlands business executive; b. 28 May 1936, Rotterdam; m. C. M. M. de Haas 1963; two s. one d.; ed Univ. of Rotterdam; joined De Nederlanden van 1845 1962 (Nationale-Nederlanden since 1963), Gen. Man. 1979, mem. Exec. Bd 1988, mem. Exec. Bd ING Group 1991, Vice-Chair. Exec. Bd ING Group 1992, Chair. 1992; Chair. Exec. Bd ING Insurance N.V. July 1992; Dir Nederlandse Participatie Mij. N.V., N.V. Struktongroep, Nat. Investeringsbank N.V.; Kt Order of Netherlands Lion.

JACOBS, Francis Geoffrey, DPhil; British lawyer; b. 8 June 1939, Cliftonville; s. of the late Cecil Sigismund Jacobs and Louise Jacobs (née Fischhof); m. 1st Ruth Freeman 1964; m. 2nd Susan Felicity Gordon Cox 1975; two s. three d.; ed City of London School, Christ Church, Oxford and Nuffield Coll., Oxford; lecturer in Jurisprudence, Univ. of Glasgow 1963–65; lecturer in Law, LSE 1965–69; Prof. of European Law, King's Coll., London 1974–88, Fellow, King's Coll. 1990; Secr. European Comm. of Human Rights and Legal Directorate, Council of Europe 1969–72; Legal Sec. Court of Justice of the EC 1972–74, Advocate Gen. 1988–; Barrister, Middle Temple 1964, QC 1984, Bencher 1990; Gov. Inns of Court School of Law 1996–; Commdr, Ordre de Mérite 1983; Hon. LLD (Birmingham) 1996; Hon. DCL (City Univ., London) 1997. *Publications include:* several books on European law and Yearbook of European Law (founding ed.) 1981–88. *Address:* Palais de la Cour de Justice, 2925 Luxembourg (Office); Wayside, 15 St Alban's Gardens, Teddington, Middx, TW11 8AE, England (Home). *Telephone:* 4303-2215 (Luxembourg); (20) 8943-0503 (England).

JACOBS, Louis, CBE, PhD; British rabbi; b. 17 July 1920, Manchester; s. of Harry Jacobs and Lena Jacobs; m. Sophie Lisagorska 1944; two s. one d.; ed Manchester Cen. High School, Manchester Talmudical Coll. and Univ. Coll. London; Rabbi, Cen. Synagogue, Manchester 1948–54, New West End Synagogue 1954–60; Dir Soc. for Study of Jewish Theology 1960–64; Rabbi, New London Synagogue 1964–; Visiting Prof. Lancaster Univ. 1987–; Hon. LLD; Hon. DHL. *Publications include:* Principles of the Jewish Faith, A Jewish Theology, God, Torah, Israel, Jewish Mystical Testimonies, The Structure and Form of the Babylonian Talmud, Hasidic Prayer, Religion and the Individual, The Jewish Religion: a companion, Concise Companion to Judaism 1999, Beyond Reasonable Doubt 1999. *Leisure interests:* walking, theatre, cinema. *Address:* 27 Clifton Hill, St John's Wood, London, NW8 0QE, England.

JACOBS, Marc; American fashion designer; b. New York City; ed High School of Art and Design, New York; f. Jacobs Duffy Designs (with Robert Duffy) 1984; initiated Marc Jacobs design label 1986; joined Perry Ellis 1989; promoted 'grunge' fashion, early 1990s; Artistic Dir Louis Vuitton 1997–; CFDA Perry Ellis Award for New Talent 1987, CFDA Women's Designer of the Year Award 1992, VH1 Women's Designer of the Year Award, CFDA Accessory Designer of the Year. *Address:* 163 Mercer Street, New York, NY 10012, USA (Office). *Telephone:* (212) 343-0222 (Office). *Fax:* (212) 343-2960 (Office). *Website:* www.marcjacobs.com (Office).

JACOBS, Peter Alan, BSc; British business executive; b. 22 Feb. 1943, Ayrshire; m. Eileen Dorothy Naftalin 1966; two s. one d.; ed Glasgow and Aston Univs; Production Man. Pedigree Petfoods 1981–83; Sales Dir Mars Confectionery 1983–86; Man. Dir British Sugar PLC 1986–91; Dir S. and W Berisford PLC 1986–91; CEO British United Provident Asscn 1991–98; Chair. Healthcall 1998–2001; Chair. L. A. Fitness 1999–, W.T. Foods; Dir (non-exec.) Hillsdown Holdings 1998–99, Bank Leumi (UK) 1998–, Allied Domecq 1998–. *Leisure interests:* tennis, squash, music, theatre, fund-raising. *Address:* 2 Norfolk Road, London, NW8 6AX, England. *E-mail:* peter@peatonhouse.co.uk (Office).

JACOBSON, Dan, BA, FRSL; British (b. South African) writer; b. 7 March 1929, Johannesburg; s. of Hyman Michael and Liebe (Melamed) Jacobson; m. Margaret Pye 1954; two s. one d.; ed Boys' High School, Kimberly, Univ. of Witwatersrand, S. Africa; worked in business and journalism in S. Africa, settled in England 1955; Fellow in Creative Writing, Stanford Univ., Calif. 1956–57; Prof. of English, Syracuse Univ., New York 1965–66; Visiting Fellow, State Univ. of NY 1971, Humanities Research Centre, Australian Nat. Univ., Canberra 1981; Lecturer Univ. Coll., London 1975–79; Reader in English, Univ. of London 1979–87; Prof. of English, Univ. Coll., London 1988–94, Prof. Emer. 1995–; Hon. DLitt (Witwatersrand) 1997; John Llewelyn Rhys Award 1958, W. Somerset Maugham Award 1961, Jewish Chronicle Award 1971, H. H. Wingate Award 1978, J. R. Ackerley Award for Autobiography 1986, Mary Eleanor Smith Poetry Prize 1992. *Publications:* novels: The Trap 1955, A Dance in the Sun 1956, The Price of Diamonds 1957, The Evidence of Love 1960, The Beginners 1965, The Rape of Tamar 1970, The Wonder-Worker 1973, The Confessions of Josef Baisz 1977, Her Story 1987, Hidden in the Heart 1991, The God-Fearer 1992; short stories: Inklings 1973; criticism: The Story of the Stories 1982; Adult Pleasures 1988; autobiography: Time and Time Again 1985; travel: The Electronic Elephant 1994, Heshel's Kingdom 1998; A Mouthful of Glass (trans.) 2000; Ian Hamilton in Conservation with Dan Jacobson (interview) 2002. *Address:* c/o A. M. Heath & Co., 79 St Martin's Lane, London, WC2, England. *Telephone:* (20) 7836-4271.

JACOBY, Ruth; Swedish international civil servant; b. 13 Jan. 1949, New York, USA; d. of Erich Jacoby and Lotte Jacoby; m. Bjorn Meidal 1976; two s.; ed Univ. of Uppsala; First Sec., Ministry for Foreign Affairs, Stockholm 1972, Deputy Asst Under-Sec. 1984–88, Asst Under-Sec. and Head of Dept 1990–94, Dir-Gen. for Devt Co-operation 2002–; mem. Swedish del. to OECD, Paris 1980–84; Deputy Asst Under-Sec., Ministry of Finance 1988–90; Exec. Dir World Bank 1994–97; Amb. for Econ. and Social Affairs, Perm. Mission of Sweden to the UN 1997–2002; Co-Chair. Preparatory Cttee of the Int. Conf. on Financing for Devt (FfD) 2001–02. *Address:* Ministry of Foreign Affairs, Gustav Adolfstorg 1, 10339 Stockholm, Sweden (Office); Malmgardsvagen 6, 11638 Stockholm, Sweden. *Telephone:* (8) 405-10-00. *Fax:* (8) 723-11-76. *E-mail:* meidal@swipnet.se (Home). *Website:* www.ud.se (Office).

JACOMB, Sir Martin Wakefield, Kt, MA; British banker; b. 11 Nov. 1929, Chiddingfold, Surrey; s. of Felise Jacomb and Hilary W. Jacomb; m. Evelyn Heathcoat Amory 1960; two s. one d.; ed Eton Coll. and Worcester Coll. Oxford; practised at the Bar 1955–68; Kleinwort, Benson Ltd 1968–85, Vice-Chair. 1976–85; Dir Hudson's Bay Co., Canada 1971–86; Chair. The Merchants Trust PLC 1974–85, Transatlantic Fund Inc. 1978–85; Dir Christian Salvesen PLC 1974–88, British Gas PLC 1981–88; Deputy Chair. Securities and Investments Bd Ltd 1985–87; a Deputy Chair. Barclays Bank PLC 1985–93; Chair. Barclays de Zoete Wedd 1986–91, British Council 1992–98; Dir Commercial Union Assurance Co. PLC 1984–93 (Deputy Chair. 1988–93); Dir Bank of England 1986–95, Daily Telegraph 1986–95, RTZ Corpn PLC (now Rio Tinto PLC) 1988–2000; Chair. Postel Investment Man. Ltd 1991–95; Dir Marks and Spencer 1991–2000, Canary Wharf Group PLC 1999–, Minorplanet Systems PLC 2000–; Deputy Chair. (non-exec.) Delta PLC 1993–94, Chair. 1993–; Chair. Prudential Corpn 1995–2000 (Dir 1994–2000), Share PLC 2001–; Dir Royal Opera House Covent Garden Ltd 1987–92, Oxford Playhouse Trust Ltd 1994, Oxford Playhouse Ltd 1994; External mem., Finance Cttee, Oxford Univ. Press 1971–95; Hon. Master of the Bench of the Inner Temple 1987; Trustee, Nat. Heritage Memorial Fund 1982–97; Chancellor Univ. of Buckingham 1998–; Hon. Fellow Worcester Coll. Oxford 1994; Dr. hc (Buckingham, Oxford) 1997. *Leisure interests:* theatre, family, bridge, tennis. *Address:* c/o Delta PLC, 1 Kingsway, London, WC2B 6XF, England (Office). *Telephone:* (20) 7420-3945 (Office). *Fax:* (20) 7420-3931 (Office).

JACQUEMARD, Simonne; French novelist; b. 6 May 1924, Paris; d. of André and Andrée (Raimondi) Jacquemard; m. 2nd Jacques Brosse 1955; ed Inst. Saint-Pierre, Univ. of Paris; teacher of music, Latin and French; collaborator, Laffont-Bompiani Dictionaries; contributor to Figaro Littéraire, La Table Ronde; travelled in USSR, Egypt, Greece, Italy, N Africa and Spain; Prix Renaudot 1962, Grand prix Thyde-Monnier 1984; Officier Ordre des Arts et des Lettres, Chevalier Légion d'honneur 1999. *Publications:* Les fascinés 1951, Sable 1952, La leçon des ténèbres 1954, Judith Albarès 1957, Planant sur les airs 1960, Compagnons insolites 1961, Le veilleur de nuit 1962 (Prix Renaudot 1962), L'oiseau 1963, L'orangerie 1963, Les derniers rapaces 1965, Dérive au zénith 1965, Exploration d'un corps 1965, Navigation vers les îles 1967, A l'état sauvage 1967, L'éruption du Krakatoa 1969, La thessalienne 1973, Des roses pour mes chevreuils 1974, Le mariage berbère 1975, Danse de l'orée 1979, Le funambule 1981, Lalla Zahra 1983, La fête en éclats 1985, Les belles échappées 1987, L'huître dans la perle 1993, Le Jardin d'Hérodote 1995, L'Éphèbe couronné de lierre 1995, La Gloire d'Ishwara 1996, Vers l'estuaire ébloui 1996, Trois mystiques grecs 1997, Orphée ou l'initiation mystique (jtly) 1998, L'Oiseau 1998 (Prix Jacques Lacroix, l'Académie française 1999). *Leisure interests:* studies on music (with Lucette Descave) and on bird life and observation of wild animals. *Address:* Le Verdier, 24620 Sireuil, France.

JACQUES, Paula (pseudonym of Paula Abadi); French author and broadcaster; b. 8 May 1949, Cairo; d. of Jacques Abadi and Esther Sasson; m. (divorced 1970); worked as comedienne in Africa; joined Radio France Internationale as reporter, worked on Après-midi de France-Culture, L'Oreille en coin 1975–90; presenter Nuits-noires France-Inter radio 1997–, Cosmopolitaine 2000–; sometime writer F Magazine; mem. Prix Femina jury 1996–. *Play:* Zanouba. *Publications:* Lumière de l'oeil 1980, Un baiser froid comme la lune 1983, L'Heritage de Tante Carlotta 1987, Deborah et les anges

dissipés (Prix Femina 1991), La Déscente au Paradis 1995, Les femmes avec leur amour 1997. *Address:* France-Inter, 116 avenue du Président Kennedy, 75220 Paris cedex 16, France.

JACQUET, Michel Antoine Paul Marie; French business executive; b. 28 March 1936, Dijon; s. of André Jacquet and Marie-Antoinette Baut; m. 2nd Marie-Agnès Corbière 1976; one s. and one s. one d. by first m.; ed Lycée Rouget de Lisle, Lons-le-Saulnier, Lycée du Parc, Lyons and Ecole Polytechnique; Dir-Gen. Crédit Lyonnais d'Espagne 1971–77; Dir-Gen. Paribas Gabon and Pres. Sogapar 1977–79; Deputy Dir Banque Paribas 1980–84; CEO Paribas New York 1985–88; Pres. Nord-Est and Magnésia 1989–95, Hon. Pres. Nord-Est 1995–; now Man. Ledo-Salina; Croix de valeur militaire, Chevalier Légion d'honneur. *Address:* Ledo-Salina, 46-48 rue Lauriston, 75116 Paris (Office); 15 rue Raynouard, 75016 Paris, France (Home).

JAENICKE, Lothar, DPhil, DiplChem; German biochemist; b. 14 Sept. 1923, Berlin; s. of Johannes Jaenicke and Erna Jaenicke (née Buttermilch); m. Dr. Doris Heinzel 1949; two s. two d.; ed Univs. of Marburg, Tübingen; taught Univ. of Marburg 1946–57, Munich 1957–62, Cologne 1962, apptd. Prof. Cologne Univ. 1963, also Dir Inst. of Biochem. 1988; now Prof. Emer.; Visiting Scientist All India Inst. of Medicine, New Delhi 1961, Univ. of Texas, Austin 1977, 1992, 1994, 1996; Visiting Prof. American Univ. of Beirut 1971, Ain Shams Univ., Cairo 1974, Indian Inst. of Science, Bangalore 1980; mem. Rheinisch-Westfälische Akademie der Wissenschaften, Deutsche Akademie der Naturforscher Leopoldinae; Corresp. mem. Bayerische Akad. der Wissenschaften, Academia Europea; Fellow, Wissenschaftskolleg Berlin 1986–87; Hon. mem. Gesellschaft für Biochemie und Molekular Biologie, Gesellschaft der Naturforschung und Ärzte; Paul Ehrlich/Ludwig-Darmstaedter-Preis 1963, Otto Warburg Medal 1979, Richard Kuhn Medal 1984, Lorenz Oken Medal 2000. *Publications:* c. 250 original papers on enzymology and biochemical signalling in scientific journals. *Address:* Kaesenstr. 13, 50677 Cologne, Germany (Home); University of Cologne Institute of Biochemistry, Zülpicherstr. 47, 50674 Cologne (Office). *Telephone:* (221) 4706452 (Office); (221) 315725 (Home). *Fax:* (221) 4706431 (Office).

JAFFE, Harold W., AB, MD; American epidemiologist; b. 26 April 1946, Newton, Mass.; ed Univ. of California at Berkeley and at Los Angeles; Jr doctor at Univ. of Calif. at LA Hosp. 1971–74; Clinical Research Investigator, Venereal Disease Control Div., Centers for Disease Control (CDC), Atlanta 1974–77, 1980–81, Epidemic Intelligence Service Officer for AIDS Activity 1981–83, f. (with James W. Curran and others) Kaposi's Sarcoma-Opportunistic Infections Task Force, Center for Infectious Diseases to study causes of immune-deficiency disease in homosexual men 1981, Chief, Epidemiology Br. of AIDS Programme, CDC 1983–; Head of HIV, STD and TB prevention laboratory, Acting Dir 2001–; Fellow in Infectious Diseases, Univ. of Chicago 1977–80; Visiting Prof., Chester Beatty Labs, Inst. of Cancer Research and Dept of Medicine, Hammersmith Hosp., London, 1988–90; Clinical Instructor of Medicine, Emory Univ. School of Medicine, Atlanta; Assoc. Ed. American Journal of Epidemiology, mem. Editorial Bd AIDS journal; Commendation Medal for work on HIV/AIDS, US Public Health Service 1984, Meritorious Service Medal 1986, Distinguished Service Medal 1992. *Publications:* book chapters and over 90 articles in scientific journals, including Epidemiologic Aspects of the Current Outbreak of Kaposi's Sarcoma and Opportunistic Infections, in New England Journal of Medicine Jan. 1982, The Epidemiology of AIDS: Current Status and Future Prospects, in Science Sept. 1985 (co-author), HIV Infection and AIDS in the United States, in Science Feb. 1989 (co-author). *Address:* Centers for Disease Control, Mailstop G-29, 1600 Clifton Road, Atlanta, GA 30333, USA.

JAFFE, Stanley Richard, BEcons; American film producer and director; b. 31 July 1940, New York; s. of Leo Jaffe and Dora Bressler; m. Melinda Long; two s. two d.; ed Wharton School, Univ. of Pennsylvania; with Seven Arts Assoc. Corpn 1962–67, exec. Asst to Pres. 1964; Dir E Coast programming, Seven Arts TV 1963–64, Dir programming 1965–67; Exec. Vice-Pres., Chief. Corp. Officer, Paramount Pictures Corpn 1969–70, Pres. Corpn also Pres. Paramount TV 1970–71; Pres. Jaffilms Inc. 1971; Exec. Vice-Pres. worldwide production, Columbia Pictures Corpn 1965–76; Pres. and COO Paramount Communications, New York 1991–94; Gov., Pres., COO NY Knicks 1991–94; Gov. NY Rangers 1991–94; owner Jaffilms LLC 1994–. *Films include:* The Professionals 1963, Goodbye Columbus 1968, Bad Company 1971, Man on A Swing 1973, Bad News Bears 1974, Kramer vs Kramer 1979, Taps 1981, Without a Trace 1983, Racing with the Moon 1984, Firstborn 1984, Fatal Attraction 1987, The Accused 1988, Black Rain 1989, School Ties 1992, The Firm 1993, Madeleine 1998, I Dreamed of Africa 2000.

JAFFRÉ, Philippe Serge Yves, LenD; French business executive; b. 2 March 1945, Charenton-le-Pont; s. of Yves-Frédéric Jaffré and Janine Alliot; m. Elisabeth Coulon 1974; one s. two d.; ed Institut d'Etudes Politiques, Paris and Ecole Nat. d'Admin; Inspecteur des Finances 1977; Dept of Treasury 1977–88; Gen. Sec. Comité Interministériel pour l'Aménagement des Structures Industrielles (CIASI) 1978; Tech. Adviser to Minister of Economy 1979; Deputy Dir Dept of Govt Holdings 1984; Head, Dept for Monetary and Financial Affairs 1986; Dir Banque Stern 1988; Pres. CEO, Caisse Nat. de Crédit Agricole 1988–93; Chair. and CEO Elf Aquitaine 1993–99; Insp.-Gen. of Finances 1994; Chair. Advisory Bd Zebank 1999–2002, Europ@web 2001–02; Adviser to the CEO Alstom 2002–; Chevalier, Légion d'Honneur,

Chevalier, Ordre du Mérite, Officier, Ordre du Mérite Agricole. *Leisure interest:* golf. *Address:* Alstom Co., 25 avenue Kléber, 75795 Paris, France (Office). *Telephone:* 1-47-55-20-00 (Office). *Website:* www.alstom.com (Office).

JAFFRELOT, Christophe, PhD; French political scientist; ed Institut d'études politiques, Univ. Paris I – Sorbonne, Institut nat. des langues et civilisations orientales; Lecturer in South Asian Politics, Institut d'études politiques, Univ. Paris I – Sorbonne and Institut nat. des langues et civilisations orientales; Dir Centre d'études et de recherches internationales (CERI); Ed. Critique internationale. *Publications:* The Hindu Nationalist Movement and Indian Politics 1996, L'Inde contemporaine de 1950 à nos jours (ed.) 1997, La démocratie en Inde – Religion, caste et politique 1998, BJP – The Compulsions of Politics (co-ed.) 1998, Le Pakistan, carrefour de tensions régionales (ed.) 1999, Démocraties d'ailleurs: démocraties et démocratisations hors d'Occident (ed.) 2000, Le Pakistan (ed.) 2000, Dr Ambedkar 2000. *Address:* CERI, 56 rue Jacob, 75006 Paris, France (Office). *Telephone:* 1-58-71-70-00 (Office). *Fax:* 1-58-71-70-90 (Office). *E-mail:* info@ceri-sciencespo.org (Office). *Website:* www.ceri-sciencespo.com (Office).

JAGAN, Janet, OE; Guyanese politician and author; b. 20 Oct. 1920, Chicago, Ill., USA; d. of Charles and Kathryn Rosenberg; m. Cheddi Jagan 1943 (died 1997); one s. one d.; Gen. Sec. People's Progressive Party (PPP) 1950–70; Ed. Thunder 1950–56; Deputy Speaker House of Assembly 1953; six months' political imprisonment 1954; Minister of Labour, Health and Housing 1957–61; Minister of Home Affairs 1963–64; mem. Elections Comm. 1967–68; Ed. Mirror 1969–72, 1973–97; Int. Sec. PPP 1970–84, Exec. Sec. 1984–90; mem. Nat. Ass. 1953, 1957–61, 1976–97, Senate 1963–64; Amb. at Large and acting Amb. to the UN Oct.–Dec. 1993; First Lady of Guyana 1992–97; Prime Minister of Guyana March–Dec. 1997; Pres. of Guyana 1997–1999; Pres. Women's Progressive Org., Union of Guyanese Journalists; fmr Chair. Comm. on Rights of the Child; Chair. Man. Cttee Castellani House (nat. art collection); Trustee and Chair. Cheddi Jagan Research Centre; mem. Council of Women Leaders; Outstanding Woman Award, Univ. of Guyana 1989, Mahatma Gandhi Award, UNESCO, for contrib. to democracy, peace and women's rights; Order of Excellence 1993, Order of the Liberator (Venezuela) 1998. *Publications:* History of the People's Progressive Party 1971, Army Intervention in the 1973 Elections in Guyana 1973, An Examination of National Service 1976, When Grandpa Cheddi Was a Boy and other stories (children's) 1993; children's books: Patricia the Baby Manatee and other stories 1995, Children's Stories of Guyana's Freedom Struggles 1995, Anastasia, the Ant Eater and other stories 1997, The Dog Who Loved Flowers 2000, The Alligator Ferry Service and other stories 2000, Anthology of Children's Stories by Guyanese Writers 2002. *Leisure interests:* swimming, writing children's stories. *Address:* Freedom House, 41 Robb Street, Georgetown, Guyana. *Telephone:* 72095 (Office). *Fax:* 72096 (Office). *E-mail:* ppp@guyana.net.gy (Office).

JAGDEO, Bharrat, MEconSc; Guyanese politician and fmr government official; b. 23 Jan. 1964, Unity Village, East Coast Demerara; ed Moscow State Univ.; mem. People's Progressive Party (PPP); fmrly Dir Guyana Water Authority; a Dir for Caribbean Devt Bank, Nat. Bank of Industry and Commerce, Gov. for Guyana, World Bank; Sr Finance Minister; Pres. of Guyana 2000–. *Address:* Office of the President, New Garden Street and South Road, Georgetown, Guyana (Office). *Telephone:* (2) 51330 (Office). *Fax:* (2) 63395 (Office).

JAGENDORF, André Tridon, PhD; American professor of plant physiology; b. 21 Oct. 1926, New York; s. of Moritz A. Jagendorf and Sophie S. Jagendorf; m. Jean Whitenack 1952; two d. one s.; ed Cornell and Yale Univs.; Post-doctoral Fellow, Univ. of Calif., Los Angeles 1951–53; Asst Prof., Johns Hopkins Univ. 1953–58, Assoc. Prof. 1958–65, Prof. of Biology 1966; Prof. of Plant Physiology, Cornell Univ. 1966–, Liberty Hyde Bailey Prof. of Plant Physiology 1981–96, Emer. Prof. 1997–; mem. NAS 1980; Pres. American Soc. of Plant Physiologists; Merck Fellow in Natural Sciences 1951–53; Weizmann Fellow 1962; AAAS Fellow 1964; Fellow American Acad. of Arts and Sciences 1972; Outstanding Young Scientist Award, Md Acad. of Sciences 1961, Kettering Research Award 1963, C. F. Kettering Award in Photosynthesis, American Soc. of Plant Physiologists 1978, Charles Reid Barnes Award 1989. *Publications:* 162 papers in scientific journals. *Leisure interests:* music, ballet, art. *Address:* c/o Plant Biology Department, Plant Sciences Building, Cornell University, Ithaca, NY 14853 (Office); 455 Savage Farm Drive, Ithaca, NY 14850, USA (Home). *Fax:* (607) 255-5407 (Office); (607) 266-8703 (Home). *E-mail:* atj1@cornell.edu (Office).

JAGGER, Sir Mick, KBE; British singer, song writer and actor; b. 26 July 1943, Dartford, Kent; s. of Joe Jagger and the late Eva Jagger; m. 1st Bianca Pérez Morena de Macías 1971 (divorced 1979); one d.; m. 2nd Jerry Hall (q.v.) 1990 (divorced 1999); two s. two d.; one d. by Marsha Hunt; one c. by Luciana Morad; ed London School of Econs, London Univ.; began singing career with Little Boy Blue and the Blue Boys while at LSE; appeared with Blues Inc. at Ealing Blues Club, Singer with Blues Inc. at London Marquee Club 1962; formed Rolling Stones 1962; wrote songs with Keith Richards under pseudonyms Nanker, Phelge until 1965, without pseudonyms 1965–; first own composition to reach no. 1 in UK charts The Last Time 1965; first maj. UK tour 1964; maj. U.S. tours 1964, 1966, 1969, 1972, 1973, 1975, 1981; toured Europe 1973, 1982, the Americas 1975; recent tours with Rolling Stones 1989, 1994; title role in film Ned Kelly 1969, appeared in Performance 1969, Gimme Shelter 1972, Free Jack 1991; lived in France for some years; Pres. LSE Students' Union 1994–. *Film produced:* Enigma 2001. *Singles include:* Come On 1963, I Wanna Be Your Man 1963, It's All Over Now 1964, Little Red Rooster 1964, Satisfaction 1965, Jumping Jack Flash 1968, Honky Tonk Women 1969, Brown Sugar 1971, Miss You 1978, Emotional Rescue 1980, Beast of Burden, She's So Cold, Dancing in the Street (with David Bowie for Live Aid Appeal) 1985, Voodoo Lounge 1994. *Albums include:* The Rolling Stones 1964, The Rolling Stones No. 2 1965, Out of Our Heads 1965, Aftermath 1966, Between the Buttons 1967, Their Satanic Majesties Request 1967, Beggar's Banquet 1968, Let it Bleed 1969, Get Yer Ya-Ya's Out 1969, Sticky Fingers 1971, Exile on Main Street 1972, Goat's Head Soup 1973, It's Only Rock'n'Roll 1974, Black and Blue 1976, Some Girls 1978, Emotional Rescue 1980, Still Life 1982, She's the Boss (solo) 1985, Primitive Cool 1987, Steel Wheels 1989 (also co-producer), Flashpoint 1991, Bent 1997, Goddess in the Doorway 2001. *Address:* c/o Marathon Sounds, 5 Church Row, Wandsworth Plain, London SW18 1ES, England.

JAGIELIŃSKI, Roman; Polish politician; b. 2 Jan. 1947, Wichradz, Radom Prov.; m.; two s.; ed Horticulture Dept Main School of Farming, Warsaw; runs fruit farm in village of Świniokierz Dworski, Piotrków Trybunalski Prov.; Pres. Polish Fruit-Growers' Union; mem. United Peasants' Party (ZSL) 1970–89; mem. Polish Peasants' Party "Rebirth" 1989–90; mem. Polish Peasants' Party (PSL) 1990–97; co-f. and leader Peasant Democratic Party 1997–, Chair. 1998–; Deputy to Sejm (Parl.) 1991–, Vice-Chair. Parl. Comm. for Small and Medium Enterprises 1997–; Vice-Pres. Polish Peasants' Party Parl. Club 1991-96; Deputy Prime Minister and Minister of Agric. and Food Economy 1995–97; Chair. Soc. of Econ. and Educ. Initiatives. *Address:* Sejm RP, ul. Wiejska 4/6/8, 00-902 Warsaw, Poland. *Telephone:* (22) 6941602.

JAGLAND, Thorbjørn; Norwegian politician; b. 5 Nov. 1950; m. Hanne Grotjord 1975; two c.; ed Univ. of Oslo; Exec. Sec. Norwegian Labour League of Youth (AUF) 1977–81; Project and Planning Officer, Norwegian Labour Party 1981–86, Acting Gen. Sec. 1986, Gen. Sec. 1987, Chair. 1992–; mem. Storting; Chair. Labour Party Parl. Group; Prime Minister of Norway 1996–97; Minister of Foreign Affairs 2000–01; Chair. Parl. Standing Cttee on Foreign Affairs 2001–. *Publications include:* Min europeiske drøm 1990, Ny solidaritet 1993, Brev 1995, Vår sårbare verden 2002, For det blir for sent (co-author) 1982; articles on defence, nat. security and disarmament. *Address:* Stortinget, 0026 Oslo, Norway (Office). *Telephone:* 23313055 (Office). *Fax:* 23313818 (Office). *E-mail:* thorbjorn.jagland@stortinget.no (Office).

JAGNE, Baboucarr-Blaise Ismaila, MA; Gambian diplomatist; b. 11 Feb. 1955, Banjul; m.; four c.; ed Univs. of Dakar, Grenoble and Paris; Asst Sec., Foreign Ministry 1980–84, Sec. to Pres. of Gambia, Chair. Islamic Peace Cttee on Iran–Iraq War 1984–88, Sr Asst Sec. for Political Legal Affairs 1986–89, Prin. Asst Sec. 1989–92; Deputy Perm. Sec. for Educ. 1992–93, for Political Affairs 1993–95; Minister of External Affairs 1995–97; Amb. to Saudi Arabia 1997–98; Perm. Rep. to UN 1998–2001; Sec. of State for Foreign Affairs 2001–. *Address:* Department of State for Foreign Affairs, 4 Col Muammar Ghadaffi Avenue, Banjul, The Gambia (Office).

JAHN, Helmut, FAIA; German architect; b. 4 Jan. 1940, Nuremberg; s. of Wilhelm Anton Jahn and Karolina Wirth; m. Deborah Lampe 1970; one s.; ed Technische Hochschule, Munich and Illinois Inst. of Tech.; C. F. Murphy Assocs. 1967–73, Exec. Vice-Pres. and Dir of Planning and Design 1973; corp. mem. American Inst. of Architects 1975; registered architect, NCARB 1975; mem. German Chamber of Architects, State of Hesse 1986; Prin. Murphy/Jahn 1981, Pres. 1982, Pres. and CEO 1983–; Visiting Prof. Harvard Univ. 1981, Yale Univ. 1983; numerous other lectureships at univs. and professional socs. 1989–93; participant in numerous architectural exhbns.; completed bldgs. include libraries, exhbn halls, court bldgs., office and leisure bldgs., university bldgs., hotels, apts. and airport terminals in USA, Europe and Far East; Hon. DFA (St Mary's Coll. Notre Dame, Ind.); Chevalier des Arts et des Lettres (France), Bundesverdienstkreuz Erster Klasse (Germany); numerous professional awards. *Leisure interests:* sailing, skiing. *Address:* Murphy/Jahn, Inc., Suite 300, 35 East Wacker Drive, Chicago, IL 60601, USA. *Telephone:* (312) 427-7300. *Fax:* (312) 332-0274.

JAHN, Martin, M.B.A.; Czech business executive; b. 21 Jan. 1970, Prague; s. of Vladimír Jahn and Hana Jahn; m. Karolina Jahn; two d.; ed Univ. of Econs, Prague, DePaul Univ., Chicago, USA; Dir American Operations, Czechinvest 1996–99, CEO 1999–; mem. Bd CMC Celákovice; mem. Czech–American Chamber of Commerce, Czech–Canadian Chamber of Commerce 2000–. *Leisure interests:* tennis, squash, skiing, film, literature, music. *Address:* Czechinvest, Štěpánská 15, 12000 Prague 2, Czech Republic (Office). *Telephone:* (2) 96342501 (Office). *Fax:* (2) 96342502 (Office). *E-mail:* jahn@czechinvest.org (Office). *Website:* www.czechinvest.org (Office).

JAHN, Robert George, MA, PhD; American professor of aerospace sciences; b. 1 April 1930, Kearny, NJ; s. of George Jahn and Minnie Holroyd; m. Catherine Seibert 1953; one s. three d.; ed Princeton Univ.; Teaching Asst Princeton Univ. 1953–55; Instructor Lehigh Univ. Bethlehem, Pa 1955–56, Asst Prof. 1956–58; Asst Prof. of Jet Propulsion, Calif. Inst. of Tech. Pasadena 1958–62; Asst Prof. of Aeronautical Eng Princeton Univ. 1962–64, Assoc. Prof. 1964–67, Prof. of Aerospace Sciences 1967–, Dean, School of Eng and Applied Science 1971–86; mem. various NASA research cttees.; numerous professional appts. etc.; Fellow, American Physical Soc., American Inst. of Aeronautics and Astronautics; Hon. ScD (Andhra) 1986; Cirtis W. McGraw Award, American Soc. for Eng Educ. 1969. *Publications:* Physics of Electric Propulsion 1968, Margins of Reality (with B. J. Dunne) 1987. *Leisure interests:*

his dog, sports, music. *Address:* Mechanical and Aerospace Engineering Department, Princeton University, Princeton, NJ 08544, USA (Office). *Telephone:* (609) 258-4550 (Office). *Fax:* (609) 258-1993. *E-mail:* rgjahn@princeton.edu. *Website:* www.princeton.edu/~pear (Office).

JAKHAR, Bal Ram; Indian politician; b. 23 Aug. 1923, Panjkosi, Ferozepur Dist, Punjab; s. of Chaudhri Raja Ram Jakhar; m. Rameshwari Jakhar; three s. two d.; elected to Punjab Ass. 1972, Deputy Minister of Co-operatives and Irrigation 1972–77, Leader of Opposition 1977–79; Speaker, Lok Sabha (House of the People) 1980–89; Pres. Indian Parl. Group, Indian Group of IPU, Indian Br., CPA 1979–; Minister of Agric. 1991–96; Chair. Bharat Krishak Samaj 1979; led numerous Indian parl. dels. overseas 1980. *Publication:* People, Parliament and Administration. *Address:* 11 Race Course Road, New Delhi 110011, India.

JAKOBSEN, Mimi; Danish politician; b. 19 Nov. 1948, Copenhagen; d. of Erhard Jakobsen; Lecturer in German Philology and Phonetics, Univ. of Copenhagen; MP 1977–; Minister for Cultural Affairs. 1982–86, for Social Affairs 1986–88, of Business Affairs 1993–96, of Industry 1994–96; Leader Centre Democrats party 1989–. *Address:* Centrum-Demokraterne, Folketinget, Christiansborg, 1240 Copenhagen K, Denmark. *Telephone:* 33-37-48-77. *Fax:* 33-37-48-56. *E-mail:* cd@ft.dk (Office). *Website:* www.centrumdemokraterne. dk (Office).

JAKUBISKO, Juraj, MFA; Slovak film director, producer, scriptwriter and artist; b. 30 April 1938, Kojšov; m. Horváthová Jakubisko; one d. one s.; ed Prague Film Acad.; films censored by Communist regime late 1970s (Birds, Orphans and Fools, See You in Hell, My Friends); blacklisted and banned from producing films for ten years; retrospective tour of his work in USA, Canada and Europe 1991; mem. Twentieth Century Acad. 1999–; Pribina Cross, Second Class (Slovakia) 2003; over 80 nat. and int. awards. *Films:* 15 feature films 1967–99, including Silence (Brussels Film Acad. Award, Knokke Experimental Film Festival, Belgium), Waiting for Godot (Best Short Film Award, Oberhausen, Simone Dubroilh Award, Mannheim) 1968, Birds, Orphans and Fools (banned 1968, Fipresci Prize 1991), The Millennial Bee (Golden Phoenix Award, Venice Film Festival) 1983, The Feather Fairy 1985, Frankenstein's Aunt 1986, A Rose Story 1990, See You in Hell, My Friends (originally made but banned in 1968) 1991, It's Better to Be Wealthy and Healthy Than Poor and Ill 1992 (re-released 2002), An Ambiguous Report About the End of the World (also TV series) 1999. *Leisure interests:* painting, golf. *Address:* Jakubisko Film Asscn Ltd, Palác Lucerna, Vodičkova 36, 116 02 Prague 1, Czech Republic (Office). *Telephone:* (2) 96236383 (Office). *Fax:* (2) 96236353 (Office). *E-mail:* info@jakubiskofilm.com (Office). *Website:* www.jakubiskofilm.com.

JALAL, Mahsoun B., PH.D.(ECON.); Saudi Arabian businessman; b. 26 June 1936; m. Michæle Marie Garein 1967; three s. one d.; ed Univ. of Cairo, Egypt, Rutgers Univ., New Brunswick, NJ, USA, Univ. of California, USA; Prof., Chair. Dept of Econs, Riyadh Univ. 1967–75; Consultant to various Govt agencies 1967–75; formed the Consulting Centre 1969 (Pres. 1981–); Vice-Chair. and Man. Dir Saudi Fund for Devt 1975–79; mem. Civil Service Council 1977–78; Dir Saudi Int. Bank, London 1975–; Chair. Saudi Int. Bank, Nassau, Bahamas 1979–81; Chair. Saudi Investment Banking Corpn 1977–82, OPEC Special Fund (now OPEC Fund) 1979–82; Dir Saudi Basic Industries Corpn 1975–87; Exec. Dir IMF 1978–81; Chair. Saudi United Commercial Bank 1983–85; Chair. Eastern Petrochemical Co. 1981–86; Chair. Tunisian-Saudi Devt Investment Co. 1981–; Chair. and CEO Nat. Industrialization Co. 1984–90, Man. Dir 1990–94; Chair. and Man. Dir Nat. Co. for Glass Industries 'Zoujaj' 1990–; Man. Dir Motazah Le Cote de Cartage Co., Tunis 1995; Chair. various investment cos.; Golden Star, First Class (Taiwan) 1973, Tanda Mahputera (Indonesia) 1978, Chevalier Ordre National (Mali) 1978, Order of the Repub., First Class (Tunisia) 1985. *Publications:* Principles of Economics; other books and articles on econ. Devt and econ. theory. *Leisure interests:* travel, sports. *Address:* P.O. Box 88646, Riyadh 11672, Saudi Arabia (Office). *Telephone:* 47700456 (Office). *Fax:* 4770087.

JALALI, Ali Ahmad; Afghanistan/American politician; m.; mil. studies in Afghanistan, UK and Turkey; army col Afghan Armed Forces –1978; Dir Islamic Unity of Afghan Mujahideen and Sr Mil. Commdr during rebellion against Soviet occupation 1980s; obtained American citizenship 1987; Dir, Broadcaster and Head of Pashtu and Persian Services, Voice of America (int. radio station), Washington DC –2003; Minister of Internal Affairs Jan. 2003–. *Publications include:* The Other Side of the Mountain (co-author) 1998, three-vol. mil. history of Afghanistan, several other books. *Address:* Ministry of Internal Affairs, Shar-I-Nau, Kabul, Afghanistan (Office).

JALAN, Bimal, PhD; Indian economist; ed Cambridge, Oxford and Bombay Univs.; various positions at IMF, World Bank, Pearson Comm. 1964–70; Chief Economist, Industrial Credit and Investment Corpn of India 1970–73; Econ. Adviser, Ministry of Finance and of Industry, India 1973–79; Chief Econ. Adviser, Ministry of Finance 1981–88, Sec. for Banking 1985–88; Dir Econ. Affairs, Commonwealth Secr., London 1979–81; Exec. Dir IMF 1988–90; fmr Exec. Dir IBRD; Gov. Reserve Bank Nov. 1997–. *Publications include:* Essays in Development Policies, Problems and Policies in Small Economies (ed.). *Address:* Reserve Bank of India, Central Office Building, Shahid Bhagate Singh Road, P.O. Box 406, Mumbai, 400 023, India. *Telephone:* (22) 2861602 (Office). *Fax:* (22) 2861784 (Office). *E-mail:* rbiprd@giasbm.01.vsnl.net.in (Office). *Website:* www.rbi.org.in (Office).

JALANG'O, Bob Francis, BSc; Kenyan diplomatist and information technology specialist; b. 5 Feb. 1945, Siaya; two s. four d.; ed Makerere Univ., Kampala, Uganda; systems programmer, Olivetti Co. 1970–74; with Caltex Oil Kenya, Computer Systems Man. for six East African countries 1974–88; MP 1988–92; Amb. to Zambia, Malawi, Botswana, Italy, Greece, Poland 1993–2000; Perm Rep. to UN, New York 2000–; Moran of the Burning Spear, Presidential Award 2000. *Leisure interests:* international travel, sports. *Address:* Permanent Mission of Kenya to the United Nations, 866 United Nations Plaza, Suite 486, New York, NY 10017, USA (Office); 643 Sore Drive, P.O. Box 41553, Nairobi, Kenya (Home). *Telephone:* (212) 421-4740 (Office). *Fax:* (212) 486-1985 (Office). *E-mail:* jalango@un.int (Office); balozinewyork@hotmail.com (Home). *Website:* www.un.int/kenya (Office).

JALLOUD, Maj. Abd as-Salam; Libyan politician and army officer; b. 15 Dec. 1944; ed Secondary School, Sebha, Mil. Acad., Benghazi; mem. of Revolutionary Command Council 1969–77, Gen. Secr. of Gen. People's Congress 1977–79; Minister of Industry and the Econ., Acting Minister of the Treas. 1970–72; Prime Minister 1972–77; Second-in-Command to Revolutionary Leader Col Gaddafi 1997–. *Address:* c/o General Secretariat of the General People's Congress, Tripoli, Libya.

JALOLOV, Abdulkhafiz, DPhil; Uzbekistan politician; b. 1 June 1947, Namangan; m. Jalolova Zarifahon; two s. one d.; ed Tashkent State Univ.; mil. service 1969–71; Lecturer of Philosophy Tashkent Univ. 1971–72; researcher Philosophy and Law Inst., Uzbekistan Acad. of Sciences 1972–77, Dir 1993–2001; Chair.of Philosophy, State Inst. of Physical Culture 1977–81; Asst Prof., Deputy Dir Social Science Lecturers' Skills Level Raising Inst., Tashkent State Univ. 1981–93; Second Sec. of Gen. Council, People's Democratic Party of Uzbekistan 1991–94, First Sec. 1994–. *Publications include:* Mustakillik Mas'uliyati 1996, Istikbol Ufklari 1998, Demokratiya: mashakkatli surur 2000. *Address:* People's Democratic Party of Uzbekistan, pl. Mustakillik, 5/1, 700029 Tashkent, Uzbekistan (Office). *Telephone:* (71) 139-8311 (Office). *Fax:* (71) 133-5934 (Office).

JAMAL, Amir Habib, BComm (ECON.); Tanzanian politician; b. 26 Jan. 1922, Dar es Salaam; s. of Habib Jamal and Kulsum Thawer; m. 1st Zainy Kheraj; m. 2nd Shahsultan Cassam 1967; three s. one d.; ed primary school, Mwanza, secondary school, Dar es Salaam and Univ. of Calcutta, India; elected mem. Tanganyika Legis. Council 1958; Minister of Urban Local Govt and Works 1959, of Communication, Power and Works 1960; Minister of State, President's Office, Directorate of Devt 1964; re-elected MP 1965; Minister of Finance 1965–72; Minister for Commerce and Industries 1972–75, of Finance and Econ. Planning 1975–77, of Communications and Transport 1977–79, of Finance 1979–83, without Portfolio 1983–84, Minister of State for Cabinet Affairs, Pres.'s Office 1984–85; Head, Perm. Mission to the UN, Geneva 1985–; Chair. Interpress Service, Third World, Rome; Chair. Governing Council Sokoine Univ. of Agric., Morogoro; Hon. Exec. Dir South Centre, Geneva; mem. Nat. Exec. CCM Party; mem. Brandt Comm. 1977–80, Trustee Dag Hammarskjöld Foundation; mem. Advisory Panel, World Inst. for Devt Economics Research; Dr. hc (Uppsala) 1973, (Dar es Salaam) 1980. *Leisure interests:* gardening, reading, bridge, swimming.

JAMALI, Mir Zafarullah Khan, MA; Pakistani politician; b. 1 Jan. 1944, Rowjhan, Baluchistan; s. of Mir Zafarullah Khan Jamali; m.; four s. one d.; ed Murree Royal Coll., Aitchison Coll., Lahore, Punjab Univ.; tribal elder from SW Prov. of Baluchistan; joined Pakistan People's Party (PPP) 1970s; elected mem. Prov. Ass., Baluchistan 1977, Minister for Food and Information; Minister for Food and Agric. 1982, for Local Govt, for Water and Power 1985, for Railways 1986; mem Nat. Ass. 1985–89; Chief Minister for Baluchistan 1988–89; Rep. to UN 1991; elected Ind. mem. Nat. Ass. 1993–, mem. Cabinet 1997–; Senator, Islamabad 1997; Sr mem. Pakistan Muslim League (PML-N) –1999; currently mem. Pakistan Muslim League-Quaid-e-Azam (PML-Q); Prime Minister of Pakistan Nov. 2002–. *Leisure interest:* hockey. *Address:* Office of the Prime Minister, Constitution Avenue, Islamabad, Pakistan (Office). *Telephone:* (51) 9210360 (Office). *Fax:* (51) 9206907 (Office).

JAMBREK, Peter, MA, PhD; Slovenian judge; b. 14 Jan. 1940, Ljubljana; ed Grammar School, Ljubljana, Ljubljana Univ. and Univ. of Chicago; Prof. Dept of Theory of Law and State, Ljubljana; Judge, Constitutional Court of Repub. of Slovenia 1990, Pres. 1991–95; Judge, European Court of Human Rights 1993–99; currently ind. consultant and author. *Publications:* Development and Social Change in Yugoslavia: Crises and Perspectives of Building a Nation 1975, Participation as a Human Right and as a Means for the Exercise of Human Rights 1982, Contributions for the Slovenian Constitution 1988, Constitutional Democracy 1992. *Address:* Ceste v Megre 4, 64260 Bled, Slovenia (Home). *Telephone:* (64) 77449 (Home).

JAMES, Clive Vivian Leopold; Australian author, broadcaster and journalist; b. 7 Oct. 1939; s. of Albert A. James and Minora M. Darke; ed Sydney Technical High School, Sydney Univ. and Pembroke Coll. Cambridge; Pres. of Footlights at Cambridge; television critic, The Observer 1972–82, feature writer 1972–; Dir Watchmaker Productions 1994–; as lyricist for Pete Atkin, record albums include: Beware of the Beautiful Stranger, Driving Through Mythical America, A King at Nightfall, The Road of Silk, Secret Drinker, Live Libel, The Master of the Revels; also songbook, A First Folio (with Pete Atkin). *Television series include:* Cinema, Up Sunday, So It Goes, A Question of Sex, Saturday Night People, Clive James on Television, The Late Clive James, The Late Show with Clive James, Saturday Night Clive, Fame in the 20th Century, Sunday Night Clive, The Clive James Show; numerous TV documentaries including Clive James meets Katherine Hepburn 1986, Clive James meets Jane Fonda, Clive James meets Mel Gibson 1998, Clive James meets the Supermodels 1998, Postcard series 1989–. *Publications:* non-fiction: The Metropolitan Critic 1974, The Fate of Felicity Fark in the Land of the Media 1975, Peregrine Prykke's Pilgrimage through the London Literary World 1976, Britannia Bright's Bewilderment in the Wilderness of Westminster 1976, Visions Before Midnight 1977, At the Pillars of Hercules 1979, First Reactions 1980, The Crystal Bucket 1981, Charles Charming's Challenges on the Pathway to the Throne 1981, From the Land of Shadows 1982, Glued to the Box 1982, Flying Visits 1984, Snakecharmers in Texas 1988, The Dreaming Swimmer 1992, Fame 1993, The Speaker in Ground Zero 1999; novels: Brilliant Creatures 1983, The Remake 1987; autobiog.: Unreliable Memoirs 1980, Falling Towards England: Unreliable Memoirs Vol. II 1985, Unreliable Memoirs Vol. III 1990, May Week was in June 1990, Brrm! Brrm! or The Man from Japan or Perfume at Anchorage 1991, Fame in the 20th Century 1993, The Metropolitan Critic 1993; three Vols of poetry; criticism: Clive James on Television 1993, The Silver Castle 1996 (novel). *Address:* Peters, Fraser & Dunlop, 503/4 The Chambers, Chelsea Harbour, London, SW10 0XF, England.

JAMES, Rt Rev Colin Clement Walter, MA; British ecclesiastic; b. 20 Sept. 1926, Cambridge; s. of late Canon Charles CH James and Gwenyth M. James; m. Margaret J. (Sally) Henshaw 1962 (deceased); one s. two d.; ed Aldenham School, King's Coll. Cambridge and Cuddesdon Theological Coll.; Asst Curate, Stepney Parish Church 1952–55; Chaplain, Stowe School 1955–59; BBC Religious Broadcasting Dept 1959–67; Religious Broadcasting Organizer, BBC South and West 1960–67; Vicar of St Peter with St Swithin, Bournemouth 1967–73; mem. Gen. Synod 1970–95; Bishop Suffragan of Basingstoke 1973–77; Canon Residentiary of Winchester Cathedral 1973–77; Bishop of Wakefield 1977–85; Bishop of Winchester 1985–95; Pres. Woodward Corpn 1978–93, RADIUS 1980–93; Chair. Church Information Cttee 1976–79, Central Religious Advisory Cttee, BBC and IBA 1979–84, United Soc. for the Propagation of the Gospel 1985–88, Liturgical Comm. 1986–93; Hon. DLitt (Southampton) 1996. *Leisure interests:* theatre, travelling. *Address:* 35 Christchurch Road, Winchester, SO23 9SY, England. *Telephone:* (1962) 868874. *E-mail:* colinjames@btinternet.com (Home).

JAMES, Sir Cynlais (Kenneth) Morgan, KCMG, MA; British diplomatist (retd); b. 29 April 1926, Resolven; s. of Thomas Ellis James and Lydia Ann (Morgan) James; m. Teresa Girouard 1953; two d.; ed St Marylebone Grammar School, Durham Univ., Trinity Coll., Cambridge; in RAF 1944–47; Sr Branch of Foreign Service 1951, in Tokyo 1953, Brazil 1956, Cultural Attaché, Moscow 1959, Foreign Office 1962, Paris 1965, Saigon 1969; FCO, Head of Western European Dept 1971–75; NATO Defence Coll. 1975–76; Minister, Paris 1976–81; Amb. to Poland 1981–83; Asst Under-Sec. of State 1983; Amb. to Mexico 1983–86; Dir Thomas Cook Group 1986–91; Dir-Gen. Canning House 1987–92; Dir Darwin Instruments, Latin American Investment Trust 1991–96; Foreign and Colonial Emerging Markets Investment Trust PLC 1991–98, Polish Investment Trust (SECAV), Euro Principals Ltd; Adviser to Amerada Hess; Chair. British-Mexican Soc. 1987–90, Inst. of Latin-American Studies 1992–; mem. Franco-British Council 1986–99, Young Concert Artists' Trust; Dr. hc (Mexican Acad. of Int. Law); Order of the Aztec Eagle (Mexico), Order of Andrés Bello (Venezuela), Order of Merit (Chile), Chevalier, Légion d'honneur. *Leisure interests:* history, music, tennis, cricket. *Address:* 63 Eccleston Square, London, SW1V 1PH, England. *Telephone:* (20) 7828–8527.

JAMES, Edison Chenfil, MSc; Dominican politician and agronomist; b. 18 Oct. 1943, Marigot; s. of David James and Patricia James; m.; one s. two d.; ed North East London Polytechnic, Reading Univ., Imperial Coll. (Univ. of London); teacher St Mary's Acad. Sept.–Dec. 1973; agronomist Ministry of Agric. 1974–76; Farm Improvement Officer Caribbean Devt Bank (attached to Dominica Agricultural and Industrial Devt Bank) 1976–80, Loans Officer 1976–80; Co-ordinator Coconut Rehabilitation and Devt Project; Chief Exec. (Gen. Man.) Dominica Banana Marketing Corpn 1980–87; Adviser to Dirs. Bd of Windward Islands Banana Growers Asscn (WINBAN) 1980–87; Man. Dir Agricultural Man. Corpn Ltd (AMCROP) 1987–95; Leader Dominica United Workers Party (UWP) and Parl. Leader of the Opposition 1990–95, 2000–; Prime Minister of Dominica 1995–2000, also Minister of Legal and Foreign Affairs and Labour; leading negotiator with several int. aid agencies; served on numerous public service cttees. *Leisure interests:* cricket, football, int. affairs, politics, table tennis. *Address:* Dominica United Workers Party, 37 Cork Street, Roseau, Dominica (Office).

JAMES, Geraldine; British actress; b. 6 July 1950; d. of Gerald Trevor Thomas and Annabella Doogan Thomas; m. Joseph Sebastian Blatchley 1986; one d.; ed Downe House, Newbury, Drama Centre London Ltd; Royal TV Soc. Award for Best Actress 1978, Venice Film Festival Award for Best Actress 1989, Drama Desk (New York) Award for Best Actress 1990. *Stage appearances:* repertory, Chester 1972–74, Exeter 1974–75, Coventry 1975, Passion of Dracula 1978, The White Devil 1981, Turning Over 1984, When I was a Girl I used to Scream and Shout 1987, Cymbeline 1988, Merchant of Venice 1989 (and Broadway 1990), Death and the Maiden 1992, Lysistrata 1993, Hedda Gabler 1993, Give Me Your Answer Do 1998, Faith Healer 2001–02. *TV series:* The History Man 1980, Jewel in the Crown 1984, Blott on the Landscape 1985, Echoes 1988, Stanley and the Women 1991, Kavanagh QC 1995, Band of Gold 1995, Over Here 1995, Band of Gold 1996, Drovers' Gold 1996, Gold 1997, Kavanagh QC 1997, The Sins 2000, White Teeth 2002, Hearts of Gold 2002.

Television films: Dummy 1977, She's Been Away 1989, Inspector Morse 1990, The Doll's House 1991, Ex 1991, The Healer 1994, Doggin Around 1994, Rebecca 1996, See Saw 1997, Hans Christian Andersen 2001, Crime and Punishment 2002, The Hound of the Baskervilles 2002. *Films:* Sweet William 1978, Night Cruiser 1978, Gandhi 1981, The Storm 1985, Wolves of Willoughby Chase 1988, The Tall Guy 1989, If Looks Could Kill 1990, The Bridge 1990, Losing Track 1991, Prince of Shadows 1991, No Worries 1992, Words on the Window Pane 1993, Moll Flanders 1996, The Man Who Knew Too Little 1996, Testimony of Taliesin Jones 1999, First Love 1999, The Luzhin Defence 2000, Tom and Thomas 2001, Odour of Chrysanthemums 2002, An Angel for May 2002, Calendar Girls 2002. *Leisure interest:* music. *Address:* c/o Julian Belfrage Associates, 46 Albemarle Street, London, W1, England. *Telephone:* (20) 7491-4400 (Office).

JAMES, Ioan Mackenzie, MA, DPhil, FRS; British professor of geometry; b. 23 May 1928; s. of Reginald D. James and Jessie A. James; m. Rosemary G. Stewart 1961; ed St Paul's School and Queen's Coll. Oxford; Commonwealth Fund Fellow, Princeton, Univ. of Calif. Berkeley and Inst. for Advanced Study 1954–55; Tapp Research Fellow, Gonville & Caius Coll. Cambridge 1956; Reader in Pure Math., Univ. of Oxford 1957–69, Sr Research Fellow, St John's Coll. 1959–69, Savilian Prof. of Geometry 1970–95, Prof. Emer. 1995–, Fellow, New Coll. 1970–95, Emer. Fellow 1995–, Leverhulme Emer. Fellow 1996–98; Ed. Topology 1962–; Hon. Prof. Univ. of Wales 1989; Hon. Fellow St John's Coll., Oxford 1988, New Coll., Oxford 1996; Hon. DSc (Aberdeen) 1993; Whitehead Prize and Lecturer 1978. *Publications:* The Mathematical Works of J.H.C. Whitehead 1963, The Topology of Stiefel Manifolds 1976, Topological Topics 1983, General Topology and Homotopy Theory 1984, Aspects of Topology 1984, Topological and Uniform Spaces 1987, Fibrewise Topology 1988, Introduction to Uniform Spaces 1989, Handbook of Algebraic Topology 1995, Fibrewise Homotopy Theory 1998, Topologies and Uniformities 1999, History of Topology 1999, Remarkable Mathematicians 2003; numerous papers in mathematical journals. *Address:* Mathematical Institute, 24–29 St Giles, Oxford, OX1 3LB, England. *Telephone:* (1865) 735389. *Fax:* (1865) 273583 (Office). *E-mail:* imj@maths.ox.ac.uk (Office).

JAMES, Michael Leonard (pen name Michael Hartland), MA, FRSA; British government official, writer and broadcaster; b. 7 Feb. 1941; s. of the late Leonard James and Marjorie James; m. Jill Tarján 1975; two d.; ed Christ's Coll., Cambridge; entered Govt service (GCHQ) 1963; Pvt. Sec. to Rt Hon Jennie Lee, Minister for the Arts 1966–68; DES 1968–71; Planning Unit of Rt Hon Margaret Thatcher, Sec. of State for Educ. and Science 1971–73, Asst Sec. 1973; Deputy Chief Scientific Officer 1974; Adviser to OECD, Paris and UK Gov., Int. Inst. for Man. of Tech., Milan 1973–75; Int. negotiations on non-proliferation of nuclear weapons 1975–78; Dir, IAEA Vienna 1978–83; Adviser Int. Relations 1983–85 (Consultant 1985–) to Comm. of the European Union, Brussels; a Chair. Civil Service Selection Bds. 1983–93; Chair. The Hartland Press Ltd 1985–2001, Wade Hartland Films Ltd 1991–2000; Hon. Fellow Univ. of Exeter 1985–; Gov. East Devon Coll. of Further Educ., Tiverton 1985–91, Colyton Grammar School 1985–90, Sidmouth Community Coll. 1988–, Chair. Bd of Govs 1998–2001; Chair. Bd of Govs Axe Vale Further Educ. Coll. Seaton 1987–91; mem. Immigration Appeal Tribunal 1987–, Devon and Cornwall Rent Assessment Panel 1990–, Gen. Medical Council Professional Conduct Cttee 2000–; Feature Writer and Book Reviewer for The Times (thriller critic 1990–91), Sunday Times, Guardian and Daily Telegraph (thriller critic 1993–). *TV and radio include:* Sonja's Report (ITV documentary) 1990, Masterspy: interviews with KGB defector Oleg Gordievsky (BBC Radio 4) 1991. *Publications:* Internationalization to Prevent the Spread of Nuclear Weapons (Co-author) 1980; novels (under pen-name Michael Hartland): Down Among the Dead Men 1983, Seven Steps to Treason 1985 (South West Arts Literary Award, dramatized for BBC Radio 4 1990), The Third Betrayal 1986, Frontier of Fear 1989, The Year of the Scorpion 1991; (under pen-name Ruth Carrington) Dead Fish 1998. *Address:* Cotte Barton, Branscombe, Devon, EX12 3BH, England. *Telephone:* (1297) 680382. *Fax:* (1297) 680381.

JAMES, P. D. (See James of Holland Park).

JAMES, Thomas Garnet Henry, CBE, MA, FBA; British museum curator (retd); b. 8 May 1923, Neath, Wales; s. of Thomas Garnet James and Edith James (née Griffiths); m. Diana Margaret Vavasseur-Durell 1956 (died 2002); one s.; ed Neath Grammar School and Exeter Coll. Oxford; served in army (RA) 1942–45; Asst Keeper, British Museum 1951–74; Laycock Student, Worcester Coll. Oxford 1954–60; Keeper of Egyptian Antiquities, British Museum 1974–88; Chair. Egypt Exploration Soc. 1983–89, Vice-Pres. 1990; Chair. Advisory Cttee, Freud Museum 1987–98; Wilbour Fellow, The Brooklyn Museum 1964; Visiting Prof., Collège de France 1983; Visiting Prof. Memphis State Univ. 1990; Pres. Asscn for the Study of Travellers in Egypt and the Near East 1998–; mem. German Archaeological Inst.; Hon. Fellow Exeter Coll. Oxford 1998; Correspondant Etranger de l'Inst. de France 2000. *Publications:* The Mastaba of Khentika 1953, The Hekanakhte Papers 1962, Hieroglyphic Texts in the British Museum, I (revised) 1961, 9 1970, Archaeology of Ancient Egypt 1972, Corpus of Hieroglyphic Inscriptions in The Brooklyn Museum, 1 1974, Pharaoh's People 1984, Egyptian Painting 1985, Ancient Egypt: The Land and Its Legacy 1988, Egypt: The Living Past 1992, Howard Carter: The Path to Tutankhamun 1992, A Short History of Ancient Egypt 1995, Egypt Revealed: Artist-Travellers in an Antique Land 1997, Tutankhamun: The Eternal Splendour of the Boy Pharaoh 2000, Ramesses

II 2002. *Leisure interests:* music, cooking. *Address:* 113 Willifield Way, London, NW11 6YE, England (Home). *Telephone:* (20) 8455-9221 (Home). *Fax:* (20) 8731-6303.

JAMES OF HOLLAND PARK, Baroness (Life Peer), cr. 1991, of Southwold in the County of Suffolk; **P(hyllis) D(orothy) James,** OBE, JP, FRSL, FRSA; British author; b. 3 Aug. 1920, Oxford; d. of Sidney Victor James and Dorothy Amelia Hone; m. Connor Bantry White 1941 (deceased); two d.; ed Cambridge Girls' High School; Admin., Nat. Health Service 1949–68; Prin., Home Office 1968; Police Dept 1968–72; Criminal Policy Dept 1972–79; JP, Willesden 1979–82, Inner London 1984; Chair. Soc. of Authors 1984–86, Pres. 1997–; a Gov. of BBC 1988–93; Assoc. Fellow Downing Coll., Cambridge 1986; mem. Bd of British Council 1988–93, Arts Council; Chair. Arts Council Literary Advisory Panel 1988–92; mem. Church of England Detection Club; mem. Church of England Liturgical Comm. 1991–; Hon. Fellow, St Hilda's Coll., Oxford 1996, Downing Coll., Cambridge 2000, Girton Coll., Cambridge 2000; Hon. DLitt (Buckingham) 1992, (Herts.) 1994, (Glasgow) 1995, (Durham) 1998, (Portsmouth) 1999; Hon. LitD (London) 1993; Dr hc (Essex) 1996; 'Grand Master' Award of the Mystery Writers of America 1999. *Publications:* Cover Her Face 1962, A Mind to Murder 1963, Unnatural Causes 1967, Shroud for a Nightingale 1971, The Maul and the Pear Tree (with T. A. Critchley) 1971, An Unsuitable Job for a Woman 1972, The Black Tower 1975, Death of an Expert Witness 1977, Innocent Blood 1980, The Skull Beneath the Skin 1982, A Taste for Death 1986, Devices and Desires 1989, The Children of Men 1992, Original Sin 1994, A Certain Justice 1997, Time To be in Earnest 1999, Death in Holy Orders 2001, The Murder Room 2003. *Leisure interests:* exploring churches, walking by the sea. *Address:* c/o Greene & Heaton Ltd, 37A Goldhawk Road, London, W12 8QQ, England.

JAMIR, S. C., BA, LLB; Indian politician; b. 17 Oct. 1931, Ungma, Nagaland; s. of Shri Senayangba; m. Alemia Jamir 1959; three s. two d.; ed Univ. of Allahabad; mem. Interim Body of Nagaland, then Jt Sec. Naga People's Convention; Vice-Chair. Mokokchung Town Cttee 1959–60; MP 1961–70; Parl. Sec., Ministry of External Affairs, Govt of India 1961–67; Union Deputy Minister of Railways, of Labour and Rehabilitation, of Community Devt and Co-operation, Food and Agric. 1968–70; elected mem. to Nagaland Legis. Ass. 1971–73, re-elected mem. from Aonglenden Constituency 1974; subsequently apptd. Minister of Finance, Revenue and Border Affairs; re-elected 1977 and apptd. Deputy Chief Minister in UDF Ministry; Chief Minister of ULP Ministry April 1980; resgnd when NNDP Ministry came to power June 1980; Leader of Opposition Congress (I) in State Legis. Ass. 1980–82; elected from 26 Aonglenden Constituency, Gen. Elections 1982; unanimously elected Leader Congress (I) Legislature Party, Chief Minister Nagaland 1982–86, 1989–92, 1993–; MP Rajya Sabha 1987–89. *Address:* Chief Minister's Secretariat, Kohima, Nagaland, India. *Telephone:* (370) 222171 (Office); (370) 222222 (Home).

JAMMEH, Col Yahya A. J. J.; Gambian Head of State and army officer (retd); b. 25 May 1965, Kanilai Village, Foni Kansala Dist, Western Div.; m. Zineb Yahya-Jammeh (née Soumah); one d.; ed Gambia High School; joined fmr Gambia Nat. Gendarmerie as Pvt. 1984; with Special Intervention Unit, Gambia Nat. Army 1984–86, Sergeant 1986, Escort Training Instructor, Gendarmerie Training School 1986–89, Cadet Officer 1987, commissioned 1989, Second Lt 1989, in charge of Presidential Escort, Presidential Guards 1989–90, CO Mobile Gendarmerie Jan.–June 1991, Mil. Police Unit June–Aug. 1991, Lt 1992, Commdr Gambia Nat. Army Mil. Police Aug.–Nov. 1992, Capt. 1994, Col 1996; became Chair. Armed Forces Provisional Ruling Council, Head of State 1994–; elected Pres. of The Gambia 1996–; Chair., Pres. Alliance for Patriotic Reorientation and Construction (APRC) 1996–; Chair. Inter-states Cttee for Control of Drought in the Sahel 1997–2000; 1st Vice-Chair. Org. of the Islamic Conf. 2000–; numerous awards. *Leisure interests:* playing tennis, soccer, hunting, reading, correspondence, driving and riding motorcycles, music, films and animal rearing. *Address:* Office of the President, State House, Banjul, The Gambia (Office); Alliance for Patriotic Reorientation and Construction, GAMSTAR Building, Banjul. *Telephone:* 227881 (Office). *Fax:* 227034 (Office). *Website:* www.jammeh2001.org (Office).

JANABIL; Chinese party official; b. April 1934, Khaba Co., Xinjiang; s. of Simagul Janabil and Ajikhan Janabil; m. Zubila Janabil 1955; two s. two d.; alt. mem. 10th CCP Cen. Cttee 1973; Vice-Chair. Revolutionary Cttee, Xinjiang Autonomous Region 1975–79; Chair. Revolutionary Cttee and First Sec. CCP Cttee, Ili Autonomous Kazakh Pref. 1975–80; Deputy Sec. CCP Cttee, Xinjiang 1977–83, Sec. 1983–85; Vice-Chair. Xinjiang 1979–83; Deputy Sec. CCP 4th Xinjiang Uyghur Autonomous Regional Cttee 1983–; Chair. CPPCC 7th Xinjiang Uygur Autonomous Regional Cttee 1993; Pres. Xinjiang Br. Futurology Soc. 1980; alt. mem. 12th CCP Cen. Cttee 1982, 13th Cen. Cttee 1987, 14th Cen. Cttee 1992–. *Address:* c/o Xinjiang Autonomous Regional Chinese Communist Party, Urumqi, Xinjiang, People's Republic of China.

JANCSÓ, Miklós; Hungarian film director; b. 27 Sept. 1921, Vác; s. of Sándor Jancsó and Angela Poparád; m. 1st Katalin Wowesny 1949; one s. one d.; m. 2nd Márta Mészáros 1958; one s.; m. 3rd Zsuzsa Csákány 1981; one s.; studied legal sciences and ethnography at Kolozsvár (now Cluj), Romania and Budapest Coll. of Cinematographic Art; worked at newsreel studio 1953–58; Documentary film studio 1962; Chief Producer, Hunnia Film Studio 1963–; Grand Prix of San Francisco 1961, Prize of Fédération Internationale de la Presse Cinématographique (FIPRESCI), Balázs Béla prize 1965, Merited

artist 1970, Eminent Artist of the Hungarian People's Repub. 1980, Best Dir Award, Cannes Festival 1972, Kossuth Prize (2nd Degree) 1973, Prize for Oeuvre Complet (Cannes) 1982, Prize for Oeuvre Complet (Venice) 1990, Best Dir Award, Montreal 1992. *Films:* A harangok Rómába mentek (The Bells have gone to Rome) 1959, Oldás és Kötés (Cantata) 1963, Igy Jöttem (My Way Home) 1965, Szegény Legények (The Round-Up) 1966, Csillagosok–Katonák (The Red and the White) 1967, Csend és Kiáltás (Silence and Cry) 1968, Fényes Szelek (The Confrontation) 1969, Sirókkó (Winter Wind) 1969, La Pacifista 1970, Agnus Dei 1971, Red Psalm 1972, Elektreia (Electra) 1975, Private Vices, Public Virtues 1976, Hungarian Rhapsody 1978, Allegro Barbaro 1978, The Tyrant's Heart or Boccaccio in Hungary 1981, Omega 1984, The Dawn 1985, Season of Monsters 1987, The God is Going Backwards 1990, The Blue Danube Waltz 1991; for Italian TV: Il Tecnico e il Rito, Roma rivuole Cesare, La Pacifista. *Stage productions:* Jack the Ripper (Budapest) 1977, Nostoi (Seoul) 1988. *Opera directed:* Otello (Florence) 1980. *Address:* Eszter u. 17, 1022 Budapest, Hungary (Home). *Telephone:* 135-3761 (Home).

JANDA, Krystyna; Polish actress and film and theatre director; b. 18 Dec. 1952, Starachowice; m.; two s. one d.; ed State Higher School of Drama, Warsaw; actress Atheneum Theatre, Warsaw 1976–88, Powszechny Theatre, Warsaw 1988–; acting on TV and performing in cabaret; numerous awards in Poland and abroad; over 50 leading roles in classic and contemporary plays and over 50 leading roles in film and TV; Best Actress 40th Int. Film Festival, San Sebastián. *Films include:* Man of Marble 1976, Without Anaesthetic 1978, The Border 1978, The Conductor 1979, Die Grünen Vögel 1979, Golem 1979, Mephisto 1980, War Between Worlds 1980, Man of Iron 1981, Espion lève toi 1981, Interrogation 1982, Ce fut un bel été 1982, Bella Donna 1983, Gluth 1983, Der Bulle und das Mädchen 1984, Vertige 1985, My Mother's Lovers 1985, Laputa 1986, Short Film About Killing 1987, II Decalogue, V Decalogue 1988, Ownership 1989, Polish Kitchen 1991, Relieved of the Life 1992, As 1995, Pestka (actress and Dir) 1996, Mother's Mother 1996, Unwritten Principles 1997, Last Chapter 1997, David Weissen 1999, Żółtyszalik (Yellow Muffler) 2000, Przedwiośnie 2000, Życie jako śmiertelna choroba prienoszona drogą płciową (Life as a Fatal Sexually Transmitted Disease) 2000. *Stage appearances include:* Bal manekinów 1974, Edukacja Rity 1984, Z życia glist 1984, Biała bluzka 1987, Medea 1988, Shirley Valentine 1990, Kobieta zawiedziona 1996, Kotka na gorącym blaszanym dachu 1997, Maria Callas – Lekcja śpiewu (Song Lesson) 1997, Harry i ja (Harry and Me) 1998, Opowiadania zebrane (Collected Stories) 2001, Mała Steinberg (Spoonfeed Steinberg) 2001, Kto się boi Virginii Woolf (Who's Afraid of Virginia Woolf) 2002. *Plays directed include:* Hedda Gabler 1999, Związek otwarty (Friendship Opened) 2000, Zazdrość (Jealousy) 2001. *TV series:* Mierzejewska 1989, From Time to Time 1999. *Address:* Teatr Powszechny, ul. Zamoyskiego 20, Warsaw, Poland (Office). *Website:* www .krystynajanda.com.

JANEWAY, Elizabeth Hall, AB; American author; b. 7 Oct. 1913, Brooklyn, New York; d. of Charles H. and Jeannette F. (Searle) Hall; m. Eliot Janeway 1938 (died 1993); two s.; ed Barnard Coll.; Assoc. Fellow Yale Univ.; educator's award Delta Kappa Gamma, 1972; mem. Council, Authors Guild, Council Authors League America, PEN; Chair. NY State Council for the Humanities; Assoc. Fellow Yale; Fellow AAAS; Hon. PhD (Simpson Coll., Cedarcrest Coll., Villa Maria Coll., Hon DHL (Russell Sage Coll., Fla Int. Univ., Simmons Coll. 1989); Medal of Distinction, Barnard Coll. 1981. *Publications:* The Walsh Girls 1943, Daisy Kenyon 1945, The Question of Gregory 1949, The Vikings 1951, Leaving Home 1953, Early Days of the Automobile 1956, The Third Choice 1959, Angry Kate 1963, Accident 1964, Ivanov Seven 1967, Man's World, Women's Place 1971, Between Myth and Morning: Women Awakening 1974, Harvard Guide to Contemporary American Writing 1979, Powers of the Weak 1980, contribs. to Comprehensive Textbook of Psychology 1974, 1980, Cross Sections from a Decade of Change 1982, Improper Behavior 1987. *Address:* 350 East 79th Street, New York, NY 10021, USA.

JANEWAY, Richard, AB, MD; American physician and medical school administrator; b. 12 Feb. 1933, Los Angeles, Calif.; s. of VanZandt Janeway and Grace Eleanor Bell Janeway; m. Katherine Esmond Pillsbury 1955; one s. two d.; ed Colgate Univ., Univ. of Pennsylvania School of Medicine; Instructor in Neurology, Bowman Gray School of Medicine of Wake Forest Univ. (now Wake Forest Univ. School of Medicine) 1966–67, Asst Prof. 1967–70, Assoc. Prof. 1970–71, Prof. 1971–, Dean 1971–85, Exec. Dean 1985–94, Vice-Pres. for Health Affairs 1983–90, Exec. Vice-Pres. 1990–97, Univ. Prof. of Medicine and Man. 1997–, Exec. Vice-Pres. Emer. for Health Affairs 1997–; mem. Winston-Salem Foundation Bd 1994–2002 (Chair. 1997–98); Dir Idealliance 1999–; Chair. Asscn of American Medical Colls. 1984–85; mem. Dir B&T Corpn 1995– (Exec. Cttee 2000–, Chair. 2001–), S. Nat. Corpn 1989–95; mem. Nat. Asscn for Biomedical Research 1993–96, Americans for Medical Progress Inc. 1993–97; mem. Bd of Trustees Colgate Univ., 1988–95, Winston-Salem State Univ. 1991–95; mem. Inst. of Medicine of NAS, American Medical Asscn, American Heart Asscn, American Neurological Asscn, Soc. for Neuroscience, Soc. of Medical Admins., American Clinical and Climatological Asscn; Fellow American Acad. of Neurology; Life Fellow American Coll. of Physicians; John and Mary R. Markle Scholar in Academic Medicine 1968–73; Distinguished Service mem. Asscn of American Medical Colls. 1991; Medallion of Merit, Wake Forest Univ. 2000. *Leisure interests:* golf, photography, gardening, travel. *Address:* Wake Forest University, School of Medicine, Medical Center Blvd., Winston-Salem, NC 27157

(Office); 2710 Old Town Club Road, Winston-Salem, NC 27106, USA (Home). *Telephone:* (336) 716-1825 (Office); (336) 727-7537 (Home). *Fax:* (336) 716-1822. *E-mail:* djaneway@wfubmc.edu (Office).

JANICOT, Daniel Claude Emmanuel, LenD; French international official; b. 20 May 1948, Neuilly; s. of François-Xavier Janicot and Antoinette Mauxion; m. 2nd Catherine Lachenal 1991; one s.; two d. from previous marriage; ed Ecole Nat. d'Admin., Inst. d'Etudes Politiques and Faculté de Droit, Paris; Auditeur, Conseil d'Etat 1975–, Deputy Sec.-Gen. 1978–82, Maître des requêtes 1979; Maître de Confs. Insts. d'Etudes Politiques, Paris and Bordeaux and Ecole Nat. des Ponts et Chaussées; mem. Admin. Council, Public Information Library, Beaubourg 1979; Del.-Gen. American Center 1980–90; Vice-Pres. Bibliothèque-Nationale 1981; Maître de séminaire, Ecole Nat. d'Admin. 1982–83; Del.-Gen. Union Centrale des Arts Décoratifs 1982–86; Special Adviser Office of Dir-Gen. of UNESCO 1990–91, Dir of Exec. Office of Dir-Gen. 1991–94, Asst Dir-Gen. 1994–99; mem. Conseil d'état 1995–; Chair. Bd, Centre Nat. d'Art Contemporain de Grenoble 1995–; Vice-Chair. Bd, Institut Français de Gestion 1996–; Dir Musée des arts premiers; Chevalier, Ordre Nat. du Mérite, Ordre des Arts et des Lettres, Légion d'honneur. *Address:* Conseil d'Etat, 1 place du Palais-Royal, 75100, Paris 01 SP (Office); 6 rue Casimir-Périer, 75007 Paris, France (Home). *Telephone:* 1-45-68-13-00 (Office). *Fax:* 1-47-34-85-87.

JANIK, Krzysztof, PhD; Polish politician; b. 11 June 1950, Kielce; m. Jadwiga Cisło; one s.; ed Jagiellonian Univ., Kraków; Sec. Voiv. Bd Union of Rural Youth (ZMW), Cracow 1971–75; researcher Silesian Univ. 1975–81; Vice-Chair. Polish Socialist Youth Union 1981–86; mem. Cen. Cttee Polish United Workers' Party (PZPR) 1986–90; mem. Social Democracy of the Rep. of Poland (SdRP) 1990–99; Deputy to Sejm (Parl.) 1993–; Under-Sec. of State Chancellery of the Pres. of Poland 1995–97; Gen. Sec. Democratic Left Alliance (SLD) 1999–; Minister of Interior Affairs and Admin. 2001–. *Leisure interests:* bridge, books. *Address:* Ministry of Internal Affairs and Administration, ul. Stefana Batorego 5, 02-514 Warsaw, Poland (Office). *Telephone:* (22) 6210251 (Office). *Fax:* (22) 8497494 (Office). *E-mail:* wp@mswia.gov.pl (Office). *Website:* www.mswia.gov.pl (Office).

JANION, Maria; Polish academic; b. 24 Dec. 1926, Mońki; d. of Cyprian Janion and Ludwika Kudryk; ed Łódź Univ., Warsaw Univ.; researcher Inst. of Literary Research, Polish Acad. of Sciences (PAN), Warsaw 1946–96, mem. Scientific Bd 1957–; Asst Warsaw Univ. 1951–52, lecturer 1981–87, apptd. Prof. 1987; researcher Higher Pedagogic School, Gdańsk 1957–69, Prof. 1963–70; Prof. Inst. of Polish Studies, Gdańsk Univ. 1970–81, 1984–90; lecturer Inst. of Philosophy and Sociology School of Social Research, PAN 1992–; Ed.-in-Chief Historia i teoria literatury. Studia (series) 1968–78, Bibliteka Romanistyczna (series) 1978–; mem. Cttee of Literary Research, PAN 1996–; ordinary mem. Polish Acad. of Arts and Sciences 1990–; corresp. mem. PAN 1991, mem. 1998–; mem. jury Nike Literature Award 1997–, Chair. 2000–; Dr. hc (Gdańsk Univ.) 1994; Alfred Jurzykowski Foundation Award 1980, Culture Foundation Great Prize for the Year 1998, Chair. of Council of Ministers Award 2001, Kazimierz Wyka Award 2001. *Publications include:* Gorączka romantyczna 1975, Romantyzm i historia (with M. Żmigrodzka) 1978, Transgresje (7 vol. series, also co-ed.) 1981–88, Wobec zła 1989, Życie Pośmiertne Konrada Wallenroda 1990, Kobiety i duch inności 1996, Płacz generała. Eseje o wojnie 1998, Do Europy tak, ale razem z naszymi umarłymi 2000, Żyjąc tracimy życie. Niepokojące tematy egzystencji 2001. *Address:* ul. J.U. Niemcewicza 24 m. 24, 02-306 Warsaw, Poland (Office). *Telephone:* (22) 8228468 (Office).

JANKLOW, William John, BS, JD; American politician and lawyer; b. 13 Sept. 1939, Chicago, Ill.; s. of Arthur Janklow and LouElla Gulbranson; m. Mary Dean Thom 1960; one s. two d.; ed Flandreau High School, South Dakota, Univ. of South Dakota; Staff Attorney and Chief Officer, S Dakota Legal Services 1966–67; Directing Attorney and Chief Officer, S Dakota Legal Services 1967–72; Chief Trial Attorney, S Dakota Attorney Gen.'s Office 1973–74; Attorney Gen. of S Dakota 1975–79; Gov. of S Dakota 1979–87, 1995–2003; Dir Nat. Legal Services Corpn; mem. Exec. Cttee of the Nat. Governors' Asscn; Republican; Nat. award for legal excellence and skill 1968; various awards. *Leisure interests:* waterskiing, collecting 1950s music. *Address:* c/o Office of the Governor, 500 E Capitol Avenue, Pierre, SD 57501-5070, USA.

JANKOWITSCH, Peter, DDL; Austrian diplomatist and politician; b. 10 July 1933, Vienna; s. of Karl and Gertrude (née Ladstaetter) Jankowitsch; m. 1st Odette Prevor 1962 (divorced); one s.; m. 2nd Silvia Lahner 2001; ed Vienna Univ. and The Hague Acad. of Int. Law; fmr lawyer; joined foreign service 1957, worked in Int. Law Dept; Private Sec., Cabinet of Minister of Foreign Affairs 1959–62; posted to London 1962–64; Chargé d'affaires, Dakar, Senegal 1964–66; Head of Office of Bruno Kreisky, Chair. Austrian Socialist Party 1967; Chief of Cabinet of Fed. Chancellor (Kreisky) 1970–72; Perm. Rep. to UN 1972–78; Chair. UN Cttee on Peaceful Uses of Outer Space 1972–91; Vice-Chair. of Bd, Int. Energy Agency 1979–83; Rep. for Austria to UN Security Council 1973–75, Pres. Security Council 1973, Vice-Pres. 29th Gen. Assembly; Vice-Pres. 7th Special Session of Gen. Assembly 1975; mem. UN Security Council Mission to Zambia 1973; Perm. Rep. to OECD 1978–82; Deputy Perm. Under-Sec., Chief of Cabinet, Fed. Ministry of Foreign Affairs 1982–83; Fed. Minister for Foreign Affairs 1986–87; mem. Austrian Nat. Ass. (Nationalrat) 1983–90 (Chair. Foreign Relations Cttee 1987–90), 1992–93; Minister of State for Integration and Devt Co-operation 1990–92; Perm. Rep.

to OECD and ESA 1993–98; Chair. OECD Devt Centre 1994–98; Chair. Jt Cttee European Parl.–Austrian Parl.; Sec.-Gen. Franco-Austrian Centre for East–West Encounters 1998–; Int. Sec. Soc. Dem. Party of Austria 1983–90; Chair. Human Rights Cttee Socialist Int. 1987–97, Vice-Chair. Socialist Int. Cttee on Econ. Affairs 1997–99; Pres. Cttee of Parliamentarians of EFTA 1989–90; Hon. Pres., Austrian Soc. for European Policy 1996–; mem. Bd Austrian Foreign Policy Soc, Austrian Inst. for Int. Politics, Vienna Inst. for Devt, Austrian UN League (fmrly Vice-Pres.), Int. Acad. of Astronautics 1998; Pres. Austrian Nat. Cttee for Unispace 1999; Chair. Austrian Space Agency 1998–; Pres. Austria–Vietnam Soc. 1999–, Jerusalem Foundation, Austria 2002–; Assoc. Ed. Acta Astronomica 2003–; Hon. mem. Bd Int. Inst. of Space Law; Commdr Légion d'honneur; Allan D. Emil Memorial Award for Int. Co-operation in Astronautics 1981, Social Sciences Award, Int. Acad. of Astronautics 2001, and many other awards. *Publications:* Kreisky's Era in Austrian Foreign Policy (Ed. with E Bielka and H. Thalberg) 1982, Red Markings–International (Ed. with H. Fischer) 1984, The European Integration Process and Neutral Austria 1994, Austria and the Non-Aligned 2002; and papers and articles on Austria and on econ. and political Devt of the Third World; contrib. to Wörterbuch des Völkerrechts 1960. *Leisure interests:* history and baroque music. *Address:* Salzgries 19, 1010 Vienna, Austria. *Telephone:* (1) 5352335. *Fax:* (1) 5338927. *E-mail:* jankowitsch@nextra.at (Office). *Website:* www.oefz.at.

JANOWITZ, Gundula; Austrian opera singer; b. 2 Aug. 1937, Berlin, Germany; d. of Theodor and Else (née Neumann) Janowitz; m.; one d.; ed Acad. of Music and Performing Arts, Graz; Début with Vienna State Opera 1960; has sung with Deutsche Oper, Berlin 1966, Metropolitan Opera, New York 1967, Salzburg Festival 1968–81, Teatro Colón, Buenos Aires 1970, Munich State Opera 1971, Grand Opera, Paris 73, Covent Garden Opera 1976, La Scala 1978; concerts in maj. cities throughout the world, appearances at Bayreuth, Aix-en-Provence, Glyndebourne, Spoleto, Salzburg, Munich Festivals; Opera Dir at Graz 1990–91; mem. Vienna State Opera, Deutsche Oper, Berlin; recordings with Deutsche Grammophon, EMI, Decca. *Leisure interest:* modern literature. *Address:* 3072 Kasten 75, Austria.

JANOWSKI, Gabriel, DAgric; Polish politician; b. 22 April 1947, Konstantów; s. of Jan Janowski and Józefa Nocuń; m. Elżbieta Radomyska 1974; one s. two d.; ed Lycée Błonie, Warsaw Agricultural Univ., Int. Agric. Center, Wageningen, Netherlands, Georgetown Univ., Washington, DC; scientific worker and tutor, Warsaw Agricultural Univ. 1971–80, 1983–91; Founder and Vice-Pres. Solidarity Workers' Union of Farmers 1980–81, Pres. 1989–91; interned 1981–82; Co-organizer Farmers' Pastorate 1983–89; lecturer, people's univs 1983–89; Co-organizer and Vice-Pres. Warsaw Econ. Soc. 1986; Founder and Vice-Chair. Econ. Union 1989; Senator 1989–91; Vice-Pres. Citizens' Parl. Caucus 1989–91; Founder Bank of Econ. Union 1991; Deputy to Sejm (Parl.) 1991–93, 1997–; Minister of Agric. and Food Economy 1991–93; Pres. Polish Peasants' Party–People's Alliance (PSL–PL) 1992–2001; Chair. Parl. Cttee on Agric. and Rural Devt 1997–2001; mem. Parl. Cttee on European Integration 1997–2001, Parl. European Cttee 2001–; Pres. Alliance for Poland (PdP) 2001–02, merged with four other parties to form League of Polish Families 2002; mem. Parl. Ass. of the Council of Europe 1997–2000, 2001–. *Leisure interests:* history, gardens. *Address:* Faszczyce Stare 18, 05-870 Błonie, Poland (Home). *Telephone:* (22) 7254754 (Home).

JANOWSKI, Marek; German conductor; b. 18 Feb. 1939, Warsaw, Poland; ed Cologne Musikhochschule; studied in Italy and Fed. Repub. of Germany; Music Dir Freiburg and Dortmund operas 1973–79; regular Guest Conductor Paris, West Berlin, Hamburg, Cologne and Munich opera houses; has also conducted at Metropolitan Opera, New York and Chicago, San Francisco, Dresden and Vienna State operas and Teatro Colón, Buenos Aires and Orange Festival, France; has conducted concerts with Berlin Philharmonic, Chicago Symphony, London Symphony Orchestra, Philharmonia, NHK (Tokyo), Dresden Staatskapelle, Boston Symphony Orchestra, Stockholm Philharmonic and BBC Symphony Orchestra; Artistic Adviser, Royal Liverpool Philharmonic Orchestra 1983–86; Chief Conductor Orchestre Philharmonique de Radio France 1984–; Gurzenich-Orchester, Cologne 1986–. *Recordings include:* Wagner's Der Ring des Nibelungen, Weber's Euryanthe and Strauss's Die Schweigsame Frau, Penderecki's The Devils of Loudun and Bruckner's Symphony No. 6. *Address:* c/o IMG Atists Europe, Lovell House, 616 Chiswick High Road, London, W4 5RX, England (Office).

JANSEN, Jan Kristian Schøning, DrMed; Norwegian professor of physiology; b. 16 Jan. 1931, Oslo; s. of Jan Jansen and Helene Schøning; m. Helen Troye 1981; three s. two d.; ed Oslo Univ.; Rockefeller Foundation Research Fellow, Univ. of Oxford 1959–60; Asst Prof. Dept of Physiology, Oslo Univ. 1968–79, Prof. of Physiology 1979–96; Visiting Prof. Harvard Medical School 1970–71; Sr Research Fellow, Norwegian Research Council 1995–; Anders Jahres Prize 1967, Monrad Krohn Legat 1982, Fridtjof Nansen Award 1996. *Publications:* articles in professional journals. *Address:* c/o Institute of Physiology, University of Oslo, P.B. 1103, Blindern, 0317 Oslo 3, Norway.

JANSONS, Maris; Latvian conductor; b. 14 Jan. 1943, Riga; s. of Arvid Jansons and Erhaida Jansons; m. Irina Jansons 1967; one d.; ed by father (also conductor), then Leningrad Conservatory (under N. Rabinovich), Vienna Conservatory (with Hans Swarovsky) and Salzburg (under von Karajan); Prin. Guest Conductor of Leningrad (now St Petersburg) Philharmonic Orchestra, Chief Conductor of Oslo Philharmonic 1979–2002; Guest Conductor of Welsh Symphony Orchestra 1985–88; Prin. Guest Conductor of

London Philharmonic Orchestra –1997; Chief Conductor of Pittsburgh Symphony Orchestra 1997–2002; Musical Dir Bavarian Radio Symphony Orchestra 2002–; has appeared all over world, with Berlin Philharmonic, Royal Concertgebouw Orchestra, Vienna Philharmonic and maj. British and US orchestras; world-wide tours with Oslo Philharmonic, St Petersburg Philharmonic and Pittsburgh Symphony Orchestra; RSFSR People's Artist 1986; Commdr with Star Royal Norwegian Order of Merit. *Leisure interests:* arts, theatre, films, sports. *Address:* c/o IMG Artists Europe, Media House, 616 Chiswick High Road, London, W4 5RX, England.

JANSSEN, Baron Daniel, ING., LIC., MBA; Belgian business executive; b. 15 April 1936, Brussels; s. of Baron Charles-Emmanuel Janssen and Marie-Anne (née Boël) Janssen; m. Thérèse Bracht 1970; three s.; ed Univ. of Brussels, Harvard Univ.; Asst Sec. Euratom Comm., Brussels 1959–60; Prof. Brussels Univ. 1965–71; mem. Club of Rome 1968–87; Bd of Dirs. Brussels Univ. 1969–70; mem. of Bd Inst. pour l'Encouragement de la Recherche Scientifique dans l'Industrie et l'Agriculture (IRSIA) 1971–77, Vice-Chair. 1974–77; mem. of Bd Belgian Fed. of Chemical Industries 1972–76, Chair. 1976–79; mem. European Cttee for R & D, EEC 1974–79; Chair. Exec. Cttee UCB 1975–84, Fed. of Belgian Enterprises 1981–84; CEO, Solvay & Cie SA 1986–, now Chair. Bd; holds non-exec. functions on numerous enterprises; recipient of Alumni Achievement Award, Harvard Business School. *Leisure interests:* tennis, skiing, shooting. *Address:* Solvay & Cie SA, 33 rue du Prince Albert, 1050 Brussels (Office); La Roncière, 108 avenue Ernest Solvay, 1310 La Hulpe, Belgium (Home).

JANSSEN, Baron Paul-Emmanuel, LLD; Belgian banker; b. 22 Feb. 1931, Brussels; s. of Baron Charles-Emmanuel Janssen and Marie-Anne (née Boël) Janssen; m. Cecilia Löfgren; one s. one d.; ed Univ. Libre de Bruxelles, Harvard Business School of Admin., Boston, USA; fmr Chair. Générale de Banque SA (now Hon. Chair.), Belgium, Belgian Banking Asscn; fmr Dir Solvay, Solvac, Boël, Atlas Copco, European Banking Fed., Belgian Fed. of Enterprises; Commdr Ordre de la Couronne, Commdr Ordre de Léopold, Officier Légion d'honneur. *Leisure interests:* riding, hunting, forestry, music. *Address:* Le Bonnier, 79 rue Gaston, Bary B 1310, La Hulpe, Belgium (Home). *Telephone:* (2) 653-88-08 (Office); (2) 652-03-50 (Home). *Fax:* (2) 652-12-29 (Office); (2) 652-07-38 (Home).

JANSSON, Jan-Magnus, PhD; Finnish professor and publisher; b. 24 Jan. 1922, Helsinki; s. of Carl Gösta and Anna-Lisa Jansson (née Kuhlefelt); m. 1st Kerstin Edgren 1948 (divorced 1970); m. 2nd Marita Hausen 1970 (divorced 1975); m. 3rd Siv Dahlin 1976; two d.; ed Helsinki Univ.; Prof. of Political Science, Helsinki Univ. 1954–74; Minister of Trade and Industry 1973–74; Ed.-in-Chief Hufvudstadsbladet 1974–87; Chair. Bd Finnish Inst. of Foreign Affairs 1959–85; Chair. Paasikivi Soc. 1964–66, 1975–85, Swedish People's Party in Finland 1966–73, Parl. Defence Comms. 1970–71, 1975–76, 1980–81, mem. Governmental Comms. for Constitutional Reform 1983–90; mem. Bd Int. Political Science Assoc. 1958–61; Chancellor Åbo Akad. (Swedish Univ. of Finland) 1985–90; mem. Regia Societas Humaniorum Litterarum, Lund; Commdr Order of the White Rose of Finland, Commdr Grand Cross of the Order of the Lion of Finland, Cross of Liberty; Hon. LLD (Helsinki) 1990. *Publications:* Hans Kelsens statsteori 1950, Frihet och jämlikhet 1952, Politikens teori 1969, Idé och verklighet i politiken 1972, Ledare 1981, Från splittring till samverkan: parlamentarismen i Finland 1992, Tidiga Möten (memoirs) 1996, Från Regeringsformen till Grundlagen 2000; and two collections of poetry. *Leisure interest:* literature. *Address:* Mannerheimvägen 42 B 27, 00260 Helsinki 26, Finland (Home). *Telephone:* (9) 493424 (Home). *Fax:* (9) 493424 (Home).

JANVIER, Gen. Bernard Louis Antonin; French army officer; b. 16 July 1939, La Voulte-sur-Rhône, Ardèche; s. of Pierre Janvier and Eugénie Bernard; m. Denise Diaz 1963; two s. one d.; ed Lycée de Nice, Coll. d'Orange, Lycée Bugeaud, Algiers, Univ. of Rennes and Ecole Spéciale Militaire de Saint-Cyr; commissioned 2nd Lt 1960; served in Algeria 1962–64, Madagascar and Comoros 1964–67; Co. Commdt 9th Parachute Regt 1968–70; Commdt in charge of trainee officers, Ecole Spéciale Militaire de Saint-Cyr 1970–72; Bn Chief 1974; training course, Ecole Supérieure de Guerre 1974–76; Lt-Col 1978; Second-in-Command, Bureau of Operations-Instruction 1981; Col 1982; Chef de Corps, 2nd Overseas Parachute Regt 1982–84; Head, Office of Personnel, Chief of Ground Forces 1984–87; Deputy to Gen. Commdt 6th Armoured Div. 1987–89; Brig.-Gen. 1988; Chief. Org.-Logistic Div. of Army Chief of Staff 1989–91; Commdt Operation Requin, Port Gentil, Gabon 1991; Commdt Daguet Div. Saudi Arabia and Iraq 1991; Div. Gen. 1991; Commdt 6th Armoured Div. Nîmes 1991–93; Army Chief of Staff, Operational Planning (Emia) 1993–95; Gen. Army Corps 1994; apptd. Army Chief of Staff 1995; Dir Centre des hautes études militaires, Inst. des hautes études de la défense nat. 1996–98; Commdt UN Peace Forces in fmr Yugoslavia 1995; Commdr Légion d'honneur, Ordre Nat. du Mérite, Legion of Merit (USA); numerous other decorations including medals from Kuwait and Saudi Arabia. *Leisure interests:* history of Provence, running. *Address:* 6 place de l'Eglise, 83310 Grimaud, France (Home).

JANZEN, Daniel Hunt, PhD; American professor of biology; b. 18 Jan. 1939, Millwaukee, Wis.; s. of Daniel Hugo Janzen and Floyd Foster Janzen; m. twice, divorced twice; one s. one d. from 1st marriage; ed Univ. of Minnesota and Univ. of California, Berkeley; Asst and Assoc. Prof., Univ. of Kansas 1965–68; Assoc. Prof., Univ. of Chicago 1969–72; Assoc. Prof. and Prof. of Ecology and Evolutionary Biology, Univ. of Mich. 1972–76; Prof. of Biology, Univ. of Pa, Philadelphia 1976–; teacher Org. for Tropical Studies in Costa Rica 1965–; field research in tropical ecology, supported mainly by grants from Nat. Science Foundation, USA 1963; MacArthur Fellow 1989; Gleason Award, American Botanical Soc. 1975; Crafoord Prize, Coevolutionary Ecology, Swedish Royal Acad. of Sciences 1984. *Publications:* Herbivores (Ed., with G. A. Rosenthal) 1979, Costa Rican Natural History (Ed.) 1983 and over 250 papers in scientific journals. *Leisure interest:* tropical ecology. *Address:* Department of Biology, University of Pennsylvania, Philadelphia, PA 19104, USA; Parque Nacional Santa Rosa, Apdo. 169, Liberia, Guanacaste Province, Costa Rica. *Telephone:* (215) 898-5636 (USA); 69-55-98 (Costa Rica).

JAPAN, H.M. Emperor of (see Akihito).

JÁRAI, Zsigmond; Hungarian economist and central banker; b. 29 Dec. 1951, Biharkeresztes; m. Marianna Kiss; one s. one d.; ed Univ. of Econs, Budapest; banker, State Devt Bank, Hungary 1976–89; Deputy Minister of Finance and Dir of State Bank Supervision 1989–90; Sr Exec. for Eastern Europe, James Capel & Co., London 1990–92; Man. Dir Samuel Montagu Financial Consultant and Securities Co., Budapest 1993–95; Chair. and CEO ABN AMRO (Magyar) Bank (fmrly Hungarian Credit Bank) 1995–98; Chair. Hungarian Stock Exchange 1996–98; Minister of Finance 1998–2000; Pres. Nat. Bank of Hungary 2001–. *Address:* Magyar Nemzeti Bank, Szabadság tér 8–9, 1850 Budapest, Hungary (Office). *Telephone:* (1) 428-2708 (Office). *Fax:* (1) 428-2578 (Office). *E-mail:* jaraizs@mnb.hu (Office). *Website:* www.mnb.hu (Office).

JARAY, Tess, DFA; British artist; b. 31 Dec. 1937, Vienna; d. of Dr. Francis F. and Pauline Jaray; m. 1960 (divorced 1983); two d.; ed Alice Ottley School, Worcester, St Martin's School of Art and Slade School of Fine Art; French Govt scholarship 1961; teacher Hornsey Coll. of Art 1964–88, Slade School of Art 1968–; commissioned to paint mural for British Pavilion, Expo '67, Montreal, terrazzo floor Victoria Station, London 1985, Centenary Square, Birmingham 1988, Cathedral Precinct Wakefield 1989, Hosp. Square, Leeds 1998, forecourt new British Embassy, Moscow 1999; Hon. FRIBA 1995. *Exhibitions:* individual exhbns. Grabowski Gallery, London 1963, Hamilton Galleries, London 1965, 1967, Axiom Gallery, London 1969, Whitechapel Gallery, London 1973, Adelaide Festival Centre 1980, Whitworth Art Gallery, Manchester and Ashmolean Museum, Oxford 1984, Serpentine Gallery 1988; numerous group exhbns. in Rome, Liverpool, London, Bern, etc. *Address:* 29 Camden Square, London, NW1, England. *Telephone:* (20) 7485-5057.

JARDIM GONÇALVES, Jorge Manuel, BCE; Portuguese banker; b. 4 Oct. 1935, Funchal, Madeira Island; ed Univ. of Oporto; military service, Army Eng Corps 1960–63; engineer in Angola; lecturer, Eng School of Oporto –1970; joined Banco de Agricultura 1970, later apptd. to Bd of Dirs; employee Compañia de Gestion de Industrias (subsidiary of Banco Popular Español) 1975–76; Exec. Dir Banco Português do Atlântico 1977, Chair. 1979–85; Chair. Banco Comercial de Macao and Dir Companhia de Seguros de Macao 1979–85; Chair. Banco Comercial Português (BCP) 1985–. *Address:* Banco Comercial Português (BCP), Rua Augusta n° 62/96, 2°, 1149-023 Lisbon, Portugal (Office). *Telephone:* (21) 3211100 (Office). *Fax:* (21) 3211102 (Office). *Website:* www.bcp.pt (Office).

JARMUSCH, Jim; American film director; b. 1953, Akron, Ohio; ed Medill School of Journalism, Northwestern Univ., Evanston, Ill., Colombia Coll., SC; Teaching Asst to Nicholas Ray at New York Univ. Graduate Film School 1976–79; has worked on several films as sound recordist, cameraman and actor. *Films written and directed include:* (feature films) Permanent Vacation (also ed. and producer) 1980, Stranger Than Paradise (also co-ed.) (Camera d'Or Award, Cannes Film Festival 1984), Down By Law 1986, Mystery Train 1989, Night on Earth (also producer) 1992, Dead Man 1995, Year of the Horse (Dir and cinematographer) 1997, Ghost Dog: The Way of the Samurai (also producer) 1999; (short films) Coffee and Cigarettes 1986, Coffee and Cigarettes (Memphis Version) 1989, Coffee and Cigarettes (Somewhere in California) 1993; (music videos) The Lady Don't Mind (Talking Heads) 1986, Sightsee MC! (Big Audio Dynamite) 1987, It's Alright With Me (Tom Waits) 1991, I Don't Wanna Grow Up (Tom Waits) 1992, Dead Man Theme (Neil Young) 1995, Big Time (Neil Young and Crazy Horse) 1996.

JAROCKI, Jerzy; Polish theatre director; b. 11 May 1929, Warsaw; s. of Bohdan Jarocki and Leokadia Jarocka; m. 1st 1962; one d.; m. 2nd Danuta Maksymowicz 1980; ed State Higher School of Drama, studies in drama production in Cracow and in USSR; Dir Teatr Śląski, Katowice 1957–62, Stary Teatr, Cracow 1962–98; scientific worker, State Higher Dramatic School, Cracow 1965–; Dir Teatr Polski, Wrocław 1998–2000, Teatr Narodowy, Warsaw 2000–; directs plays mainly by Polish writers S. Witkiewicz, W. Gombrowicz, T. Różewicz and S. Mrożek, also by Shakespeare and Chekhov; mem. Presidential Council for Culture 1992–95; mem. Polish Acad. of Arts and Science, Cracow 1994–; productions abroad, including Amsterdam, Zürich, Munich, Chelyabinsk, Nuremberg, Wuppertal, Belgrade, Novi Sad, Bonn; teacher, State Higher School of Drama, Cracow 1963–, Asst Prof. 1965–85, Extraordinary Prof. 1985–; has directed over 100 plays including: Ślub (The Wedding) 1960, 1973, 1974, 1991, Cymbeline 1967, Moja córeczka (My Little Daughter) 1968, Stara kobieta wysiaduje (Old Woman Brooding) 1969, Three Sisters 1969, 1974, Pater Noster 1971, Szewcy (The Shoemakers) 1972, On All Fours 1972, Matka (The Mother) 1966, 1974, The Trial 1973, The Cherry Orchard 1975, Rzeźnia (The Slaughterhouse) 1975, Bal manekinów (Mannequins Ball) 1976, King Lear 1977, White Glove 1978, Twilight 1979, The Dream of the Sinless 1979, The Inspector General 1980,

Murder in the Cathedral 1982, Pieszo (On Foot) 1981, La Vida es Sueño 1983, Sceny z Jaffy (Scenes from Jaffa) 1984, Samobójca (The Suicide) 1987, Portret (Portrait) 1988, (in Germany) 1996, Słuchaj Izraelu (Listen, Israel) 1989, Pułapka (Trap) 1992, Sen srebrny Salomei (Silver Dream of Salome) 1993, Płatonow 1993, Kasia z Heilbronnu (Kate from Heilbronn) 1994, Grzebanie 1996, Płatonow akt pominięty (Płatonow the Missed Act) 1996, Faust 1997, Historia PRL wg Mrożka (PPR History by Mrożek) 1998; Gold Cross of Merit 1968, Commdr's Cross, Order of Polonia Restituta 1996, Gold Award of City of Cracow, Minister of Culture and Arts Prize (1st Class) 1971, 1997, Contact-Int. Theatre Festival (3rd Prize) 1994, Baltic House Int. Film Festival, St Petersburg 1997 and others. *Address:* ul. Moniuszki 33, 31-523 Cracow, Poland.

JARRATT, Sir Alexander Anthony, Kt, CB; British company executive; b. 19 Jan. 1924, London; s. of Alexander Jarratt and Mary Jarratt; m. (Mary) Philomena Keogh 1946; one s. two d.; ed Royal Liberty Grammar School, Essex and Birmingham Univ.; mil. service in Fleet Air Arm; Asst Prin. Ministry of Power 1949–53, Prin. 1953–54; Treasury 1954–55; Prin. Pvt. Sec. to Minister of Fuel and Power 1955–59; Asst Sec. in Oil Div. of Ministry 1959–63, Under-Sec. in Gas Div. 1963–64; Cabinet Office 1964–65; First Sec., Nat. Bd for Prices and Incomes 1965–68; Deputy Under-Sec. of State, Dept of Employment and Productivity 1968; Deputy Sec. Ministry of Agric. 1970; mem. Bds of IPC and Reed Int. Ltd 1970; Man. Dir IPC 1970–74, Chair. 1974–, also of IPC Newspapers 1974; Chair. and CEO Reed Int. Ltd 1974–85; Chair. CBI Econ. Policy Cttee 1972–74, Industrial Soc. 1975–79; mem. Supervisory Bd, Thyssen-Bornemisza 1972–89; non-exec. Dir ICI Ltd 1975–91, Smith's Industries 1984–96 (Chair. (non-exec.) 1985–91); Dir and Deputy Chair. Midland Bank 1980–91; Jt Deputy Chair. Prudential Corpn 1987–91, 1992–94 (Dir 1985–94); Chair. Admin. Staff Coll., Henley 1976–89, Centre for Dispute Resolution 1990–2000 (Pres. 2001–); Pres. Advertising Asscn 1979–83; Chair. CBI Employment Policy Cttee 1982–86; Pres. Periodical Publishers Asscn 1983–85; Vice-Pres. Inst. of Marketing 1982; Chancellor Birmingham Univ. 1983–2002; Gov. Ashridge Man. Coll.; mem. Council CBI; Hon. DSc (Cranfield); Hon. DUniv (Brunel, Essex); Hon. DLL (Birmingham); DL (Essex) 1995. *Leisure interests:* countryside pursuits, theatre, music, reading. *Address:* Barn Mead, Fryerning, Essex, CM4 0NP, England.

JARRE, Jean Michel André, LèsL; French composer; b. 24 Aug 1948, Lyon; s. of Maurice Jarre (q.v.) and France Jarre (née Pejot); m. 2nd Charlotte Rampling (q.v.) 1978; one s. and one s. one d. from previous marriage; ed Lycée Michelet, Université de la Sorbonne, Conservatoire de musique de Paris; composer of electronic music 1968–; int. concerts include shows in China, Europe and USA; shows incorporate state-of-the-art sound and vision tech.; Composer for ballet Aor and Opera de Paris 1971; UNESCO Goodwill Amb. 1993; spokesperson European Music Industry 1998–, Int. Fed. for Phonographic Industry 1998–2000; Officier des Arts et des Lettres; Officer, Legion d'honneur; Soc. des auteurs, compositeurs et éditeurs de musique Gold Medal 1980. *Albums include:* Oxygène 1976, Equinoxe 1978, Magnetic Fields 1980, The China Concerts 1982, Music for Supermarkets 1983, Zoolook 1984, Rendez-vous 1986, Revolutions 1987, Jarre Live 1989, (Best Instrumental Album, Victoire de la Musique 1986); Concert d'Images 1989 (Exhibition), Waiting for Cousteau 1990, Chronologie 1993, Oxygène 7–13 1997. *Publications:* Concert d'Images 1989, Paris-la-Défense, une ville en concert 1990, Europe in Concert 1994, Paris-Tour Eiffel, Concert pour la Tolérance 1995. *Address:* c/o Cream-Creative Management, 8 rue de Lévis, 75017 Paris (Office); B.P. 58, 78290 Croissy-sur-Seine, France. *E-mail:* jmj@f-cream.com (Office).

JARRE, Maurice Alexis; French composer; b. 13 Sept. 1924, Lyons; s. of André Jarre and Gabrielle Boullu; m. 1st France Pejot 1946; one s.; m. 2nd Dany Saval 1965; one d.; m. 3rd Laura Devon 1967; m. 4th Khong Fui Fong 1984; ed Lycée Ampère, Lyons and Conservatoire Nat. Supérieur de Musique; musician attached to Radiodiffusion Française 1946–50; Dir of Music, Théâtre Nat. Populaire (TNP) 1950–63; work includes symphonic music, music for theatre and ballet including Roland Petit's Notre-Dame de Paris (created at Paris Opéra 1966) and numerous film scores including: Lawrence of Arabia (Acad. Award) 1963, Dr. Zhivago (Acad. Award) 1965, Ryan's Daughter 1970, Shogun 1980, Doctors in Love 1982, A Passage to India (Acad. Award) 1985, The Mosquito Coast 1987, Tai-pan 1987, Gaby 1988, Gorillas in the Mist 1989, Dead Poets Society 1990, Fatal Attraction, Ghost, Les vendanges de feu 1994, Sunchaser 1996, Le jour et la nuit 1996, Sunshine 1999, I Dreamed of Africa 2000; Officier, Légion d'honneur, Commdr des Arts et des Lettres, Commdr Ordre Nat. du Mérite; Prix Italia 1955, 1962; Grand Prix du Disque, Acad. Charles Cros 1962; Hollywood Golden Globe 1965, 1984, People's Choice Award 1988, etc. *Leisure interests:* athletics, football. *Address:* Sacem, 225 avenue Charles de Gaulle, 92521 Neuilly-sur-Seine, France.

JARRETT, Keith; American pianist and composer; b. 8 May 1945, Allentown, Pa; ed Berklee School of Music; gave first solo concert aged 7, followed by professional appearances; 2-hour solo concert of own compositions 1962; led own trio in Boston; worked with Roland Kirk, Tony Scott and others in New York; joined Art Blakely 1965; toured Europe with Charles Lloyd 1966; with Miles Davis 1970–71; soloist and leader of own groups 1969–; Officier, des Arts et des Lettres, Guggenheim Award 1972, Prix du Prés. de la République 1991; Polar Prize, Royal Swedish Acad. of Music 2003. *Albums include:* Personal Mountains, Nude Ants, The Cure 1990, Bye Bye Black 1991, At the Dear Head Inn 1992, Bridge of Light 1993, At the Blue Note 1994, La

Scala 1995, Tokyo '96, Melody at Night With You 1999, Always Let Me Go 2002. *Address:* Vincent Ryan, 135 West 16th Street, New York, NY 10011, USA.

JARUZELSKI, Gen. Wojciech; Polish politician and army officer; b. 6 July 1923, Kurów, Lublin Prov.; s. of Władysław Jaruzelski and Wanda Jaruzelska; m. Barbara Jaruzelska 1961; one d.; ed Infantry Officers' School and Karol Świerczewski Gen. Staff Acad., Warsaw; served with Polish Armed Forces in USSR and Poland 1943–45; various sr army posts 1945–57; Commdr Armoured Div. 1957–60; Chief of Cen. Political Bd of the Armed Forces 1960–65; Chief of Gen. Staff 1965–68; Minister of Nat. Defence 1968–83; Chair. Council of Ministers 1981–85; First Sec. Cen. Cttee PZPR 1981–89; Brig.-Gen. 1956, Divisional-Gen. 1960, Gen. of Arms 1968, Gen. of Army 1973; mem. PZPR 1948–90, mem. PZPR Cen. Cttee 1964–89, mem. Political Bureau 1971–89; Deputy to Sejm (Parl.) 1961–89; Vice-Pres. Chief Council of Union of Fighters for Freedom and Democracy 1972–88; Chair. Comm. for Econ. Reform 1981–86; Chair. Mil. Council for Nat. Salvation 1981–83; mem. Presidium All-Poland Cttee of Nat. Unity Front 1981–83, Provisional Nat. Council of Patriotic Movt for Nat. Rebirth (PRON) 1982–83, mem. Nat. Council PRON 1983–89; Chair. Country Defence Cttee 1983–90, Supreme Commdr of the Armed Forces of Polish People's Repub. for Wartime 1983–90; Chair. Council of State (Head of State) 1985–89, Pres. of Polish People's Repub. (Polish Repub.) 1989–90; charged with murder of shipyard workers in 1970, 2001; decorations include Order of Builders of People's Poland, Order of Banner of Labour (First Class), Kt's Cross of Order of Polonia Restituta, Silver Cross of Virtuti Militari and Cross of Valour, Medals of 30th and 40th Anniversary of People's Poland, Hon. Miner of People's Repub., Order of Lenin 1968, 1983, Commdr's Cross Order of the Crown (Belgium) 1967, Order of the October Revolution (USSR) 1973, Scharnhorst Order (GDR) 1975, Grand Cross Order of Henry the Navigator (Portugal) 1975, Order of the State Banner (Dem. People's Repub. of Korea) 1977, Order of Suche Bator (Mongolia) 1977, Order of the Red Banner (Hungary) 1977, Order of the Red Banner (USSR) 1978, Order of the White Lion (Czechoslovakia) 1979, Order of Klement Gottwald (Czechoslovakia) 1983, Karl Marx Order (GDR) 1983, Order of the Star of the Socialist Repub. (First class with Riband) (Romania) 1983, Order of the Golden Star (Vietnam) 1983, Order of Georgi Dimitrov (Bulgaria) 1983, Order of the Red Battle Banner (Mongolia) 1983, Order of the Banner (First Class with Diamonds) (Hungary) 1983, Order of José Martí (Cuba) 1983, Grand Cross of Order of the Holy Saviour (Greece) 1987, Officier Légion d'honneur 1989. *Publications:* Stan Wojenny: Dlaczego 1993, Różnić się mądrze 2000. *Leisure interests:* history, military affairs. *Address:* Biuro Byłego Prezydenta RP Wojciecha Jaruzelskiego, Al. Jerozolimskie 91, 02-001 Warsaw, Poland. *Telephone:* (22) 6289942. *Fax:* (22) 6875773.

JÄRVI, Neeme; Estonian conductor; b. 7 June 1937, Tallinn; s. of August Järvi and Elss Järvi; m. Liilia Järvi 1961; two s. one d.; ed Tallinn Music School, Leningrad Conservatorium and Leningrad Post-Graduate Studium; studied with N. Rabinovich and Y. Mravinsky; Conductor Estonian Radio Symphony Orchestra –1963; Chief Conductor Estonian State Opera House 1963–76; Chief Conductor Estonian State Symphony Orchestra 1976–80; emigrated to USA 1980; Prin. Guest Conductor City of Birmingham Symphony Orchestra, England 1981–83; Prin. Conductor Royal Scottish Nat. Orchestra 1984–88, Conductor Laureate 1988–; Prin. Conductor Gothenburg Orchestra, Sweden 1982–; Music Dir Detroit Symphony Orchestra, USA 1990–; Guest Conductor of many int. symphony orchestras including New York Philharmonic, Boston, Chicago, Royal Concertgebouw, Philharmonia, London Symphony, London Philharmonic; conducted Eugene Onegin 1979, 1984, Samson and Delilah 1982 and Khovanshchina 1985 at Metropolitan Opera House, New York; many recordings include all Prokoviev, Sibelius, Grieg, Nielsen, Dvorak, Shostakovich, Franz Berwald and Stenhammar symphonies; Dr. hc (Aberdeen, Tallinn Music Conservatory Estonia, Wayne State Univ., USA); Hon. mem. Royal Swedish Acad. of Music; First Prize, Accademia Nazionale di Santa Cecilia Conductors' Competition 1971, Gramophone Magazine's Artist of the Year 1991; Kt Commdr of North Star Order, Sweden, Sash, Insignia, Coat of Arms, Tallinn 1997. *Address:* c/o Harrison Parrott Ltd, 12 Penzance Place, London, W11 4PA, England. *Telephone:* (20) 7229-9166. *Fax:* (20) 7221-5042.

JARVIK, Robert Koffler, MD; American physician; b. 11 May 1946, Midland, Mich.; s. of Norman Eugene and Edythe Jarvik (née Koffler); m. Marilyn vos Savant 1987; one s. one d.; ed Syracuse Univ., New York, Univ. of Bologna, New York Univ., Univ. of Utah; research Asst, Div. of Artificial Organs, Univ. of Utah 1971–77; Acting Dir Old St Mark's Hosp., Div. of Artificial Organs 1977–78, Asst Dir 1978–82; Pres. Symbian Inc., Salt Lake City 1981–87, Jarvik Research Inc. 1987–; Asst Research Prof. of Surgery, Univ. of Utah 1979–87; mem. American Soc. for Artificial Internal Organs, Int. Soc. for Artificial Organs; Hon. DSc (Syracuse) 1983, (Hahnemann Univ.) 1985; awards include Inventor of the Year 1983, Outstanding Young Men of America 1983, Gold Heart Award 1983, Par Excellence Award (Univ. of Utah). *Publication:* Ed. (US Section) The International Journal of Artificial Organs. *Address:* 1 Columbus Place, New York, NY 10019-8200, USA.

JASKIERNIA, Jerzy Andrzej, DJur; Polish diplomatist, politician and professor of law; b. 21 March 1950, Kudowa Zdrój; s. of Zofia Jaskiernia and Mieczysław Jaskiernia; m. Alicja Słowińska 1980; one s. one d.; ed Jagiellonian Univ., Cracow; academic teacher Law and Admin. Faculty of Jagiellonian Univ., Cracow 1972–81; mem. Main Bd of Socialist Youth Union 1973–76; mem. Polish Socialist Youth Union (ZSMP) 1976–85; mem. Main

Arbitration Bd 1976–80, Chair. 1980–81, Chair. ZSMP Gen. Bd 1981–84; mem. Polish United Workers' Party (PZPR) 1970–90, deputy mem. PZPR Cen. Cttee 1982–86, Vice-Chair., Youth Comm. of PZPR Cen. Cttee 1981–86; mem. Inter-party Problems Comm. of PZPR Cen. Cttee 1986–88, Nat. Council of Patriotic Movt for Nat. Rebirth 1983–89, Sec.-Gen. 1984–87; Adviser to Minister of Foreign Affairs 1987–88; Counsellor, Embassy in Washington 1988–90; mem. Scientific Bd, Research Inst. of Youth Problems (Warsaw) 1984–89; mem. Social Democracy of the Repub. of Poland (SdRP) 1990–99, SdRP Cen. Exec. Cttee 1991–92 (Head Parl. and Self-Govt Affairs Dept 1990–91), SdRP Presidium of the Main Council 1993–97, Chair. Cttee on Int. Co-operation 1998–99; Deputy to Sejm (Parl.) 1985–89, 1991–; mem. Nat. Ass. Constitutional Cttee 1992–95; Chair. Legis. Cttee of the Sejm 1993–95, 1996–97; Minister of Justice and Attorney-Gen. 1995–96; Prof. Świętokrzyska Acad., Kielce 1995–; Deputy Chair. Democratic Left Alliance (SLD), Parl. Caucus 1996–2001, Chair. 2001–; mem. Parl. Ass. of Council of Europe 1994–, Chair. Subcttee on Human Rights 1998–2001, Chair. Subcttee on Criminal Law and Criminology 2001–03, Deputy Chair. Cttee on Legal Affairs and Human Rights 2003–; Chair. Polish-British Parl. Group 1993–, Deputy Chair. Cttee on European Integration 1997–2001, Chair. Cttee on Foreign Affairs 2001–; mem. SLD Nat. Cttee 1999–, SLD Nat. Exec. Bd 2000–; Corresp. mem. European Acad. of Science, Arts and Literature, Paris 2002–. *Publications:* Pozycja stanów w systemie federalnym USA 1979, Dylematy młodych 1984, Dialog naszą szansą 1985, (co-author) System polityczny PRL w procesie przemian 1988, Problemy pluralizmu, porozumienia narodowego i consensusu w systemie politycznym PRL 1989, Stany Zjednoczone a współczesne procesy i koncepcje integracji europejskiej 1992, Zasada równości w prawie wyborczym USA 1992, Wizja parlamentu w nowej Konstytucji Rzeczypospolitej Polskiej 1994, Zasady demokratycznego państwa prawnego w sejmowym postepowaniu ustawodawczym 1999, Zgromadzenie Parlamentarne Rady Europy (English trans.: The Parliamentary Assembly of the Council of Europe 2003) 2000. *Address:* Sejm RP, ul. Wiejska 4/6/8, 00-902 Warsaw, Poland. *Telephone:* (22) 6942256. *Fax:* (22) 6218423 (Office).

JASON, David, OBE; British actor; b. 2 Feb. 1940; s. of Arthur White and Olwyn Jones; one d.; started acting career in repertory; awards include Best Actor Award, BAFTA 1988; BAFTA Fellowship 2003. *Theatre includes:* Under Milk Wood 1971, The Rivals 1972, No Sex Please . . . We're British! 1972, Darling Mr London (tour) 1975, Charley's Aunt (tour) 1975, The Norman Conquests 1976, The Relapse 1978, Cinderella 1979, The Unvarnished Truth (Mid/Far East tour) 1983, Look No Hans! (tour and West End) 1985. *Films:* Under Milk Wood 1970, Royal Flash 1974, The Odd Job 1978, Only Fools and Horses, Wind in the Willows 1983. *Television includes:* Do Not Adjust Your Set 1967, The Top Secret Life of Edgar Briggs 1973–74, Mr Stabbs 1974, Ronnie Barker Shows 1975, Open All Hours 1975, Porridge 1975, Lucky Feller 1975, A Sharp Intake of Breath 1978, Del Trotter in Only Fools and Horses 1981–2001, Porterhouse Blue 1986, Jackanory 1988, A Bit of A Do 1988–89, Single Voices: The Chemist 1989, Amongst Barbarians 1989, Pa Larkin in The Darling Buds of May 1990–92, A Touch of Frost 1992, 2001, The Bullion Boys 1993, Micawber 2001. *Voice work:* Dangermouse, Count Duckula, The Wind in the Willows, The B.F.G. *Leisure interests:* diving, flying, motorcycles. *Address:* c/o Richard Stone Partnership, 2 Henrietta Street, London, WC2E 8PS, England.

JASRAI, Puntsagiin; Mongolian politician; b. 26 Nov. 1933; ed Moscow Inst.; teacher then headmaster of primary school, Gobi-Altai Aimag (Prov.) 1950–54; Insp. of the Exec. Bd People's deputies of Gobi-Altai Aimag 1954–56; lecturer at the Inst. of Econs 1961–65; Deputy Chief Cen. Statistical Bd of the MPR 1966–70; Chair. State Prices Cttee 1970–75, State Prices and Standard 1975–76; Head Dept of the Cen. Cttee of the MPRP 1976–78; First Deputy Chair. State Planning Comm. MPRP 1978–84; Deputy Chair. Council of Ministers, Chair. State Planning Comm. 1984; Deputy Chair. Council of Ministers, Chair. State Planning and Economy Cttee 1988; Prime Minister of Mongolia 1992–96; mem. MPRP Conf.; mem. State Great Hural (Parl.); Dir Asscn of Mongolian Consumers' Co-operatives 1990. *Address:* c/o Office of the Prime Minister, Ulan Bator, Mongolia.

JASTROW, Robert, PhD; American physicist and writer; b. 7 Sept. 1925, New York; s. of Abraham Jastrow and Marie Jastrow; Asst Prof., Yale Univ. 1953–54, Consultant nuclear physics, US Naval Research Lab. 1958–62; Head Theoretical Div., Goddard Space Flight Center, NASA 1958–61, Chair. Lunar Exploration Comm. 1959–60, Dir Goddard Inst. Space Studies 1961–81; Adjunct Prof. of Astronomy, Columbia Univ., New York 1961–77, of Earth Sciences, Dartmouth Coll., Hanover, NH 1973–92, of Geology and Astronomy, Columbia Univ. 1977–81; Pres. G. C. Marshall Inst. 1985–, Chair. 2002–; Chair., Dir Mount Wilson Inst. 1991–; Hon. DSc (Manhattan Coll.) 1980; Arthur S. Flemming Award 1965; NASA Medal for exceptional scientific achievement 1968. *Publications:* Red Giants and White Dwarfs, The Origin of the Solar System 1963, The Evolution of Stars, Planets and Life 1967, Astronomy: Fundamentals and Frontiers 1972, The Venus Atmosphere 1969, Until the Sun Dies 1977, God and the Astronomers 1978, The Enchanted Loom 1981, How to Make Nuclear Weapons Obsolete 1985, Journey to the Stars 1989. *Address:* Mount Wilson Observatory, Hale Solar Laboratory, 740 Holladay Road, Pasadena, CA 91106-4115, USA (Office). *E-mail:* jastrow@mtwilson.edu (Office).

JATOI, Ghulam Mustafa; Pakistani politician and landowner; b. 14 Aug. 1932, New Jatoi; s. of Ghulam Rasool Jatoi; m. 1st 1951; m. 2nd 1965; five s. three d.; elected Pres. Nawabshah Dist Council 1954, Sindh Prov.; elected mem. W Pakistan Ass. 1956, Nat. Ass. of Pakistan 1962, 1965, 1970, 1977, 1989, 1990, 1993, 1997; del. to UN Gen. Ass. 1962, 1965, to IPU Conf., Ottawa (elected Vice-Pres. of Conf.) 1965; Fed. Minister for Communications, Political Affairs, Railways and Natural Resources 1971; Special Envoy of Pres. to Indonesia, Malaysia, Japan 1972, of Prime Minister to Turkey 1976; founder mem. People's Party (PPP); fmr aide to late Zulfikar Ali Bhutto, Prime Minister of Pakistan; fmr Chief Minister of Sindh; imprisoned for political activities 1977; led Movt for Restoration of Democracy against mil. regime; founder Nat. People's Party (NPP); Leader of Opposition 1988; Leader of Combined Opposition Parties (COP) 1989–90; Leader of Islamic Democratic Alliance for 1990 election; caretaker Prime Minister of Pakistan Aug.–Nov. 1990; Chair. Grand Nat. Alliance for 2002 election. *Leisure interest:* hunting. *Address:* Jatoi House, 18 Khayaban-e-Shamsheer Defence Housing Authority, Phase V, Karachi, Pakistan. *Telephone:* (21) 585-4522. *Fax:* (21) 583-6884.

JAUDEL, Jean Emmanuel; French publisher; b. 6 Jan. 1910, Strasbourg; s. of Armand Jaudel and Lucie Jaudel; m. Nicole Weill 1946; one s. one d.; ed Faculty of Law of Paris Univ., Ecole libre des sciences politiques, Ecole des hautes études internationales, Geneva; Man. Dir Atlantique française 1945–; Chair. La Revue des Deux Mondes, publrs. of La Revue des Deux Mondes (monthly review) 1969, Pres. Supervisory Bd 1988–; Pres. Asscn Presse-Enseignement 1981–; Officier Légion d'honneur, Commdr Ordre nat. du Mérite, Médaille militaire, Croix de guerre, other French and foreign awards. *Leisure interest:* riding. *Address:* 31 rue de Penthièvre, 75008 Paris, France (Home).

JAUHO, Pekka Antti Olavi; Finnish scientist and consultant; b. 27 April 1923, Oulu; s. of Antti Arvid Jauho and Sylvi Jauho (née Pajari); m. Kyllikki Hakala 1948; one s.; ed Univ. of Helsinki; Chief Mathematician, Insurance Co. Kansa 1951–54; Assoc. Prof., Tech. Univ. of Helsinki 1955–57 (now Helsinki Univ. of Tech.), Prof. of Tech. Physics 1957–70; Dir-Gen. The State Inst. for Tech. Research (Tech. Research Centre of Finland since 1972) 1970–87; consultant to many Finnish and foreign cos.; mem. Acad. of Finland, American Nuclear Soc., European Physical Soc., RILEM, Finnish Acad. of Sciences, IVA (Swedish Acad. of Tech. Sciences) and several Finnish socs.; Commdr Order of White Rose, Order of Lion (First Class, Finland), Commdr des Palmes académiques, Officier Légion d'honneur; Hon. Prize of YDIN Power Asscn, Hon. Prize of VILAMO Foundation 1996. *Publications:* about 140 articles. *Leisure interest:* music, tennis. *Address:* Otakaari 1, 02150 Espoo 15 (Office); Tuohikuja 9E, 02130 Espoo, Finland (Home). *Telephone:* (9) 4513132 (Office); (9) 427705 (Home). *Fax:* (9) 427705. *E-mail:* pekka.jauho@kolumbus.fi (Home).

JAUMOTTE, Baron André; Belgian university official and mechanical engineer; b. 8 Dec. 1919, Jambes; s. of Jules Jaumotte and Marie Braibant; m. Valentine Demoulin 1946; ed Free Univ. of Brussels; Head Depts. of Applied Mechanics and Aerodynamics, Free Univ. of Brussels 1958–86, Rector 1968–73, Pres. 1974–81; Chair. von Karman Inst. of Fluid Dynamics 1994; Pres. A-VN; mem. Bd UN Univ., Tokyo 1980–86; Hon. Pres. Asscn des Universités partiellement ou entièrement de langue française (AUPELF) 1981–84; mem. Royal Acad., Belgium, Royal Acad. of Overseas Science, European Acad. of Sciences, Letters and Arts, Int. Acad. of Astronautics, Academia Europaea; Foreign mem. Czechoslovak Acad. of Science; mem. Nat. Acad. of Air and Space, France; Foreign mem. Acad. des Sciences (Paris) 1989, Romanian Acad. 1994; Commdr Légion d'honneur 1981, Grand Officier Ordine al Merito della Repubblica Italiana 1973, Commdr Ordre du Mérite (Gabon), Grand Officier Ordre de la Couronne (Belgium) 1983, Grand Officier Ordre de Léopold 1988, Order of the Sacred Treasure, Gold and Silver Stars (Japan); Hon. Dr hc (Free University, Brussels), (Laval Univ., Québec), (Univ. of Cluj, Romania), (Tech. Univ., Bucharest). *Publications:* Rocket Propulsion 1967, Choc et Ondes de Choc 1971, 1973, Un demi-siècle de nucléaire en Belgique 1994, Mosaïque: Fragments du tout 2000; and 300 articles on internal aerodynamics and thermodynamics of turbomachines. *Leisure interests:* painting and sculpture. *Address:* Université Libre de Bruxelles, avenue Franklin Roosevelt 50, CP 160/25, 1050 Brussels; 33 avenue Jeanne Bte. 17, B1050 Brussels, Belgium (Home). *Telephone:* (2) 650-32-71 (Office); (2) 647-54-13 (Home). *Fax:* (2) 650-45-99. *E-mail:* bstephanik@admn.ULB.ac.be (Office).

JAVED MIANDAD KHAN; Pakistani cricketer; b. 12 June 1957, Karachi; m.; ed CMS Secondary School, Karachi; Asst Vice-Pres. Habib Bank of Pakistan; right-hand middle-order batsman, leg-break and googly bowler; played for Karachi 1973–76, Sind 1973–76, Sussex 1976–79, Habib Bank 1976–94, Glamorgan 1980–85; 124 Test matches for Pakistan 1976–94, 34 as Capt., scoring 8,832 runs (average 52.5) including 23 hundreds; scored over 28,000 first-class runs (80 hundreds); toured England 1975, 1979 (World Cup), 1982, 1983 (World Cup), 1987, 1992 (Capt.); holds record for most appearances (7) in Cricket World Cup; 233 limited-overs ints. for 7,381 runs (average 41.7); Pakistan Nat. Team Coach; Wisden Cricketer of the Year 1982. *Leisure interests:* hockey, soccer, swimming, reading sports books, television, spending time with family. *Address:* National Stadium, National Stadium Road, Karachi, Pakistan.

JAVIERRE ORTAS, HE Cardinal Antonio María, S.D.B.; Spanish ecclesiastic; b. 21 Feb. 1921, Siétamo, Huesca, Spain; ordained 1949, elected 1976, consecrated titular Archbishop of Meta 1976; Sec. of the Congregation for Catholic Educ.; cr. Cardinal 1988; Archivist and Librarian of the Holy Roman

Church 1988–91; Prefect of Congregation for Divine Worship and the Discipline of the Sacraments 1991; mem. Congregations for Doctrine of Faith, of Bishops, of Catholic Educ., Pontifical Council for the Laity. *Address:* Via Rusticucci 13, 00193 Rome, Italy.

JAWARA, Hon. Alhaji Sir Dawda Kairaba, Kt, FRCVS, DTVM; Gambian politician and fmr Head of State; b. 16 May 1924, Barajally; s. of Almamy Jawara and the late Mama Jawara; ed Achimota Coll., Glasgow Univ.; Principal Veterinary Officer, Gambian Civil Service 1957–60; entered politics 1960; Minister of Educ. 1960–61; Premier 1962–65; Prime Minister 1965–70; Pres. of Repub. of The Gambia 1970–94 (overthrown in coup); Vice-Pres. of Confed. of Senegambia 1982; Minister of Defence 1985; Pres. Comité Inter-Etats de Lutte contre la Sécheresse du Sahel; mem. Board Peutinger Coll. (FRG); Hon. GCMG 1974; decorations from Senegal, Mauritania, Lebanon, Grand Master Nat. Order of the Repub. of Gambia 1972, Peutinger Gold Medal 1979; numerous other decorations. *Leisure interests:* golf, gardening, sailing. *Address:* 15 Birchen Lane, Haywards Heath, West Sussex, RH16 1RY, England (Office). *Telephone:* (1444) 456168 (Home). *E-mail:* dawda@kjawara .freeserve.co.uk (Home).

JAWORSKI, HE Cardinal Marian, DTheol, DPhil, DPhilR; Polish ecclesiastic; b. 21 Aug. 1926, Lviv; ed Jagiellonian Univ., Kraków, Catholic Univ. of Lublin, Warsaw Theological Acad.; ordained priest 1950; consecrated Titular Bishop of Lambesi 1984; apptd. Metropolitan Archbishop of Lviv 1991; cr. Cardinal (secretly) 1998, (openly) 2001; currently Pres. Bishops Conf. of Ukraine; Dr hc (Bochum) 1985, (Cardinal Stefan Wysujnski Univ., Warsaw) 2002. *Publications:* three books, 31 monographs, two textbooks, over 160 scientific articles. *Address:* Metropolis Curia of Archdiocese of Lviv of the Roman Catholic Church, Katedralna Square, 79008 Lviv, Ukraine (Office). *Telephone:* (322) 76-94-15 (Office). *Fax:* (322) 96-61-14 (Office). *E-mail:* AB@rkc .lviv.ua (Office). *Website:* www.rkc.lviv.ua (Office).

JAY, Sir Michael Hastings, KCMG, MA, MSc; British diplomatist; b. 19 June 1946, Shawford, Hants.; s. of the late Alan Jay and of Felicity Vickery; m. Sylvia Mylroie 1975; ed Winchester Coll., Magdalen Coll. Oxford and SOAS, Univ. of London; Ministry of Overseas Devt 1969–73, 1976–78; UK Del. IMF, IBRD, Washington, DC 1973–75; First Sec. New Delhi 1978–81; FCO 1981–85; Cabinet Office 1985–87; Counsellor, Paris 1987–90; Asst Under-Sec. of State for EC Affairs, FCO 1990–93, Deputy Under-Sec. of State (Dir for EC (now EU) and Econ. Affairs) 1994–96; Amb. to France 1996–2001; Perm. Under-Sec. of FCO and Head Diplomatic Service 2002–. *Address:* Foreign and Commonwealth Office, King Charles Street, London, SW1A 2AH, England (Office). *Telephone:* (20) 7270-3000 (Office). *Website:* www.fco.gov.uk (Office).

JAY, Peter, MA; British economic journalist and fmr diplomatist; b. 7 Feb. 1937, London; s. of the late Lord Jay; m. 1st Margaret Ann Callaghan (now Baroness Jay, q.v.), d. of Lord Callaghan (q.v.), 1961 (divorced 1986); one s. two d.; one s. by Jane Tustian; m. 2nd Emma Thornton 1986; three s.; ed Winchester Coll. and Christ Church, Oxford; Midshipman and Sub-Lt, RDVR 1956–57; Asst Prin., HM Treasury 1961–64, Pvt. Sec. to Jt Perm. Sec. 1964, Prin. 1964–67; Econs Ed. The Times 1967–77, Assoc. Ed. Times Business News 1969–77; Presenter, Weekend World, ITV 1972–77, The Jay Interview 1975–77; Amb. to USA 1977–79; Consultant, Economist Group 1979–81; Dir The Economist Intelligence Unit (EIU) 1979–83; Columnist The Times 1980; Dir New Nat. Theatre, Washington, DC 1979–81; Chair. TV-AM 1980–83, TV-AM News 1982–83, Pres. TV-AM 1983; Presenter, A Week in Politics, Channel 4 1983–86; Chief of Staff to Robert Maxwell 1986–89; Econs Ed., BBC 1990–2001; Sr Econ. Consultant, Man. Dir Banking World BPCC, Editor Banking World 1983–86, Supervising Ed. 1986–89; Chair. United Way of GB 1982–83, Feasibility Study 1982–83; Chair. Nat. Council for Voluntary Orgs. 1981–86; Visiting Scholar, Brookings Inst., Washington, DC 1979–80; Copland Memorial Lecturer, Australia 1980; Gov. Ditchley Foundation 1982–; Hon. DH (Ohio State Univ.) 1978; Political Broadcaster of Year 1973, Royal TV Soc.'s Male Personality of Year (Pye Award) 1974, Shell Int. TV Award 1974, Wincott Memorial Lecturer 1975. *Publications:* The Budget 1972, Foreign Affairs, America and the World 1979 (contrib.) 1980, The Crisis for Western Political Economy and other essays 1984, Apocalypse 2000 (with Michael Stewart) 1987, Road to Riches, or The Wealth of Man 2000; numerous newspaper and magazine articles. *Leisure interest:* sailing. *Address:* Hensington Farmhouse, Woodstock, Oxon, OX20 1LH, England. *Telephone:* (1993) 811222. *Fax:* (1993) 812861. *E-mail:* peter@jay.prestel.co.uk (Office).

JAY OF PADDINGTON, Baroness (Life Peer), cr. 1992, of Paddington, in the City of Westminster; **Margaret Ann Jay,** PC; British politician; b. 18 Nov. 1939; d. of James Callaghan (now Lord Callaghan of Cardiff, Prime Minister 1976–79) (q.v.); m. 1st Peter Jay (q.v.) 1961 (divorced 1986); one s. two d.; m. 2nd M. W. Adler 1994; ed Somerville Coll. Oxford; Dir Nat. AIDS Trust 1988–92; Prin. Opposition Spokesperson on Health, House of Lords 1995–97, Minister of State, Dept of Health 1997–98, Leader House of Lords, Minister for Women 1998–2001; Dir (non-exec.) Carlton TV 1996–, Scottish Power 1996–97, British Telecommunications (BT) PLC 2002–; mem. Kensington, Chelsea and Westminster Health Authority 1992–97; Chair. Nat. Assen Leagues of Hosp. Friends 1994. *Publication:* Battered – The Story of Child Abuse (co-author) 1986. *Address:* c/o House of Lords, London, SW1A 0PW, England (Office).

JAYAKUMAR, Shanmugam, LLM; Singaporean diplomatist; b. 12 Aug. 1939, Singapore; m. Dr. Lalitha Rajhram 1969; two s. one d.; ed Univ. of

Singapore and Yale Univ.; Dean, Law Faculty, Univ. of Singapore 1974–80, Prof. of Law; Perm. Rep. of Singapore to UN 1971–74, High Commr to Canada 1971–74; MP 1980–; Minister of State for Law and Home Affairs 1981–83; Minister of Labour 1983–85, of Home Affairs 1985–94, of Foreign Affairs 1994–, of Law 1994–. *Publications:* Constitutional Law Cases from Malaysia and Singapore 1971, Public International Law Cases from Malaysia and Singapore 1974, Constitutional Law (with documentary material) 1976 and articles in journals. *Address:* Ministry of Foreign Affairs, Tanglin, Singapore 248163. *Telephone:* 3798000 (Office). *Fax:* 4747885 (Office). *E-mail:* mfa@mfa .gov.sg (Office). *Website:* www.mfa.gov.sg (Office).

JAYALALITHA, C. Jayaram; Indian politician and fmr film actress; b. 24 Feb. 1948, Mysore City; d. of R. Jayaram; has appeared in over 100 films; joined All-India Anna Dravida Munnetra Kazhagam (AIADMK) 1983, Propaganda Sec. 1983, Deputy Leader, Leader; elected mem. Rajya Sabha (parl.) 1984; Chief Minister, Tamil Nadu 1991–96, 2001–; Kalaimamani Award 1971–72. *Publications:* numerous Publs. *Address:* Poes Garden, Chennai, India.

JAYAWARDENA, Amarananda Somasiri, BA, MSc, MPA; Sri Lankan economist, academic, civil servant and banker; b. 3 Aug. 1936, Matale, Sri Lanka; s. of P. de S. Jayawardena and Emaline Weerasinghe; m. Lalitha Subasinghe 1968; one s. one d.; ed Univ. of Ceylon, London School of Econs, Harvard Univ.; joined Cen. Bank of Sri Lanka 1958, Gov. and Chair. Monetary Bd 1995–; Visiting Lecturer, Univ. of Vidyodaya, Colombo 1968–75; Gen. Man. Bank of Ceylon 1977, Chair. 1989; Alt. Exec. Dir IMF 1981–86; Sec. Ministry of Industries, Science & Tech. 1989–93, Ministry of Finance & Planning 1994–95. *Radio:* frequent commentator on radio and TV. *Publications:* numerous Publs on the econs. of the world tea industry, evaluation of public enterprise performance and econ. aspects of privatization. *Leisure interests:* gardening, reading, the arts. *Address:* Central Bank of Sri Lanka, World Trade Centre, West Tower Echlan Square, P.O. Box 590, Colombo 1 (Office); Bank House, 206 Bauddhaloka Mawatha, Colombo 00700, Sri Lanka (Home). *Telephone:* (1) 346 251 (Office); (941) 502068 (Home). *Fax:* (1) 346 252 (Office). *E-mail:* cbslgen@sri.lanka.net (Office); jayawar@ccom.lk (Home). *Website:* www.centralbanklanka.org (Office).

JAYSTON, Michael, FGSM; British actor; b. 29 Oct. 1935, Nottingham; s. of Aubrey Jayston and Edna Myfanwy Llewelyn; m. 1st Lynn Farleigh 1965 (divorced 1970); m. 2nd Heather Mary Sneddon (divorced 1977); m. 3rd Elizabeth Ann Smithson 1978; three s. one d.; with the RSC 1965–69, Nat. Theatre 1976–79. *Films include:* Cromwell 1970, Nicholas and Alexandra 1971, Follow Me 1972, Bequest to the Nation 1972, Tales That Witness Madness 1973, Craze 1973, The Internecine Project 1974. *TV appearances include:* Power Game, Charles Dickens, Beethoven, Solo–Wilfred Owen, Quiller 1975, Tinker, Tailor, Soldier, Spy 1979, Dr. Who 1986, A Bit of a Do 1988, Kipling's Sussex 1989, About Face 1989, Darling Buds of May 1992, Outside Edge 1995–96, Only Fools and Horses 1996. *Theatre appearances include:* Private Lives 1980, Sound of Music 1981, Way of the World 1984–85, Woman in Mind, Beethoven Readings with Medici String Quartet 1989, Dancing at Lughnasa 1992, Wind in the Willows, Nat. Theatre 1994, Racing Demon, Chichester Prod. in Toronto 1998, Easy Virtue, Chichester 1999. *Leisure interests:* cricket, darts, chess. *Address:* c/o Michael Whitehall Ltd, 125 Gloucester Road, London, SW7 4TE, England. *Telephone:* (20) 7244-8466. *Fax:* (20) 7244-9060.

JAZAIRY, Idriss, MA, MEcons, MPA; Algerian international administrator and diplomatist; b. 29 May 1936, Neuilly-sur-Seine, France; three s. one d.; ed Univ. of Oxford, UK, Ecole Nat. d'Admin., Paris, France, Harvard Univ., USA; Chief Econ. and Social Dept Algiers 1963–71; Dir Int. Co-operation, Ministry of Foreign Affairs 1963–71; Adviser to Pres. of Repub. 1971–77; Under-Sec.-Gen. Ministry of Foreign Affairs 1977–79; Amb. to Belgium, Luxembourg and EEC 1979–82; Amb.-at-large specializing in int. econ. affairs, Ministry of Foreign Affairs 1982–84; Pres IFAD 1984–93; Exec. Dir Agency for Co-operation and Research in Devt (ACORD) 1993–99; Sr Consultant to UNDP 1994–98; Amb. to USA 1999–; Pres. Bd of Govs. African Devt Bank 1971–72; Chair. UN Gen. Ass. Cttee of the Whole on North–South Dialogue 1978–79; organized first World Summit on the Econ. Advancement of Rural Women 1992; Grand Officer Order of Merit (Italy), Officer of the Wissam Alaouite (Morocco); Medal of Independence (Jordan); numerous other foreign decorations and awards. *Publication:* The State of World Rural Poverty 1992. *Leisure interests:* jogging, skiing, riding. *Address:* Embassy of Algeria, 2118 Kalorama Road, Washington, DC 20008, USA. *Telephone:* (202) 265-2800. *Fax:* (202) 667-2174. *E-mail:* embalgus@cais.com; ijazairi@aol.com. *Website:* www.algeria-us.org.

JEAMBAR, Denis; French journalist; mem. staff Paris-Match 1970–73, Le Point 1973–95 (Ed. 1993–95); Ed. Radio station Europe 1 1995–96; Ed.-in-Chief weekly L'Express 1996. *Publications include:* Sur la route de Flagstaff, George Gershwin, Dieu s'amuse, Le poisson pourrit par la tête, Daisy. *Leisure interests:* painting, cinema, literature, travel. *Address:* c/o L'Express, 61 avenue Hoche, 75411 Paris cedex 08, France. *Telephone:* 1-40-54-30-00. *Fax:* 1-42-67-72-93.

JEAN BENOÎT GUILLAUME MARIE ROBERT LOUIS ANTOINE ADOLPHE MARC D'AVIANO, HRH fmr. Grand Duke of Luxembourg, Duke of Nassau, Prince of Bourbon-Parma; b. 5 Jan. 1921, Colmar Berg; s. of Felix, Prince of Bourbon-Parma and Prince of Luxembourg and Charlotte, Grand Duchess of Luxembourg; m. Princess Josephine-Charlotte of Belgium

April 1953; three s. two d.; Lt-Rep. of Grand Duchess 1961–64; became Grand Duke of Luxembourg on abdication of Grand Duchess Charlotte Nov. 1964, abdicated Oct. 2000; Col of the Irish Guards; mem. Int. Olympic Cttee; Chief Scout, Luxembourg Boy Scouts' Asscn; Col Regt Irish Guards 1984–; Dr. hc (Strasbourg, Miami); numerous decorations. *Leisure interests:* photography and natural history. *Address:* Grand Ducal Palace, 2013 Luxembourg.

JEANCOURT-GALIGNANI, Antoine; French business executive; b. 12 Jan. 1937, Paris; s. of Paul Jeancourt-Galignani and Germaine Verley; m. 1st Brigitte Auzouy 1961 (divorced 1983); three s. one d.; m. 2nd Hannelore Wagner 1983; one d.; ed Mount St Mary's Coll. Spinkhill, UK, Ecole St Louis de Gonzague, Faculté de Paris, Ecole Nat. d'Admin; Inspecteur de Finances 1965; Asst Sec., Office of Minister of Finance 1968–70, Treasury Dept of Ministry of Finance 1970–71; with Chase Manhattan Bank, New York 1972; Sr then Exec. Vice-Pres. in charge of int. and corp. banking, Crédit Agricole 1973–79; joined Banque Indosuez 1979, Pres. 1980–81, 1982–88, Chair. and CEO 1981–82, 1988–94; Chair. Assurances Générales de France 1994–2001; Chair. Gecina 2001–; Dir Société Générale, Bouygues 1989–99, Total 1994–, Euro Disney (Chair. Supervisory Bd 1995–); Officier, Légion d'honneur, Ordre nat. du Mérite, Chevalier du Mérite agricole, Croix de la valeur militaire. *Publication:* La Finance Déboussolée 2001. *Address:* 3 avenue Bosquet, 75007 Paris, France (Home). *Telephone:* 1-40-40-52-44 (Office). *E-mail:* jeangal@gecina.fr (Office).

JEANMAIRE, Renée Marcelle (Zizi); French actress, dancer and singer; b. 29 April 1924, Paris; d. of Marcel Jeanmaire; m. Roland Petit (q.v.) 1954; one d.; student, Paris Opera Ballet 1933–40, Dancer 1940–44; with Ballets de Monte-Carlo, Ballets Colonel de Basil, Ballets Roland Petit; Dir (with Roland Petit) Casino de Paris 1969–; leading role in three concerts, Zénith 1995, nine concerts, Opéra Bastille 2000; music hall appearances; Chevalier Légion d'honneur, Chevalier des Arts et des Lettres, Officier, Ordre nat. du Mérite. *Films:* Hans Christian Andersen, Anything Goes, Folies Bergère, Charmants Garçons, Black Tights, La Revue, Zizi je t'aime; musical: The Girl in Pink Tights (Broadway). *Leading roles in:* Aubade, Piccoli, Carmen, La Croqueuse de Diamants, Rose des Vents, Cyrano de Bergerac, La Dame dans la Lune, La Symphonie Fantastique 1975, Le loup, La chauve-souris 1979, Hollywood Paradise Show 1985, Java for ever 1988, Marcel et la Belle Excentrique 1992. *Address:* c/o Ballets Roland Petit, 20 boulevard Gabès, 13008 Marseille, France.

JEANNENEY, Jean-Marcel, LèsL, DenD; French politician and economist; b. 13 Nov. 1910, Paris; s. of Jules Jeanneney (fmr Pres. of the Senate and Minister); m. Marie-Laure Monod 1936; two s. (and one s. deceased) five d.; ed Ecole Libre des Sciences Politiques, Paris; Prof. of Political Economy, Grenoble Univ. 1937–51, Dean of Law Faculty 1947–51; Prof. of Social Econs Paris Univ. 1951–56, of Financial Econs 1957–59, of Political Econs 1970–80; Dir du Cabinet of his father, Jules Jeanneney, Minister of State, de Gaulle Prov. Govt 1944–45; mem. Admin. Council, Ecole nat. d'admin. 1945–58; Dir Econ. Activity Study Service, Fondation Nat. des Sciences Politiques 1952–58; Consultant to OEEC 1953; mem. Rueff Cttee 1958; Rapporteur and del. to numerous confs.; Minister of Industry, (Debré Cabinet) 1959–62; Amb. to Repub. of Algeria 1962–63; Chair. French Cttee on Co-operation with Developing Countries 1963; mem. and French Rep. to UN Econ. and Social Council 1964–66; Minister of Social Affairs 1966–68; Deputy June 1968; Minister of State 1968–69; Pres. L'Observatoire français des Conjonctures économiques 1981–89; Dir Nat. Foundation for Political Sciences 1981–; Commdr Légion d'honneur, Grand-Croix Ordre Nat. du Mérite, Commdr des Palmes académiques. *Publications:* Essai sur les mouvements des prix en France depuis la stabilisation monétaire (1927–1935) 1936, Economie et droit de l'électricité (with C. A. Colliard) 1950, Les commerces de détail en Europe occidentale 1954, Forces et faiblesses de l'économie française 1945–1956, Textes de droit économique et social français 1789-1957 (with Perrot), Documents économiques (2 Vols) 1958, Economie politique 1959, Essai de comptabilité interrégionale française pour 1954, 1969, Régions et sénat 1969, A mes amis gaullistes 1973, Pour un nouveau protectionnisme 1978, Les économies occidentales du XIXème siècle à nos jours 1985, L'Economie française depuis 1967, La traversée des turbulences mondiales 1989, Vouloir l'emploi 1994, Ecoute la France qui gronde 1996, Une Mémoire Républicaine 1997, Que vive la constitution de la cinquième république 2002. *Address:* 69 quai d'Orsay, 75007 Paris (Office); 102 rue d'Assas, 75006 Paris (Home); Rioz 70190, France (Home). *Telephone:* 1-43-26-39-46 (Paris); 3-84-91-82-52 (Rioz).

JEANNENEY, Jean-Noël, DèsSc; French politician and professor; b. 2 April 1942, Grenoble; s. of Jean-Marcel Jeanneney (q.v.) and Marie-Laure Jeanneney (née Monod); m. 2nd Annie-Lou Cot 1985; two s.; ed Lycées Champollion and Louis-le-Grand, Ecole normale supérieure, Inst. d'études politiques de Paris; Lecturer in Contemporary History, Univ. de Paris X 1969–77, lecturer 1968; Univ. Prof. Inst. d'études politiques de Paris 1977–; Pres., Dir-Gen. Radio-France and Radio-France Int. 1982–86; Pres. Bicentenary of the French Revolution 1988–89; mem. Bd of Dirs, Agence France-Presse 1982–84, Télédiffusion de France 1982–86, La Sept 1986, Seuil Publs 1987–91, 1993–; Chair. Scientific Council, Inst. d'Histoire du Temps Présent 1991–2000; Sec. of State for External Trade 1991–92, for Communication 1992–93; Regional Councillor, Franche-Comté 1992–98; Chair. Advisory Cttee for 'Histoire' (cable TV) 1997–; Pres. Europartenaires 1998–, Bibliothèque nationale de France 2002–; Chevalier, Légion d'honneur; Officier, Ordre nat. du Mérite. *Radio:* Concordance des temps (weekly programme on French culture) 1999–. *Television:* historical films for French TV: Léon Blum ou la fidélité 1973, Eamon de Valera 1975, Le Rhin 1996, Les Grandes Batailles de la République 1996–99, Senghor entre deux mondes 1998, Histoire des présidentielles 1965–1995 2002. *Publications:* Le Riz et le Rouge, cinq mois en Extrême-Orient 1969, Le Journal politique de Jules Jeanneney 1939–42 1972, François de Wendel en République, l'Argent et le Pouvoir 1976, Leçon d'histoire pour une gauche en pouvoir, La Faillite du Cartel 1924–26 1977, Le Monde de Beuve-Méry ou le métier d'Alceste (co-author) 1979, L'Argent caché, milieux d'affaires et pouvoirs politiques dans la France du XXe Siècle 1981, Télévision nouvelle mémoire, les magazines de grand reportage 1959–68 (with others) 1982, Echec à Panurge, l'audiovisuel public au service de la différence 1986, Concordances des temps, chroniques sur l'actualité du passé 1987, Georges Mandel, l'Homme qu'on attendait 1991, L'Avenir vient de loin (essay) 1994, Une histoire des médias des origines à nos jours 1996–2000, Le Passé dans le prétoire, l'historien, le juge et le journaliste 1998, L'Echo du siècle, Dictionnaire historique de la radio et de la télévision en France 1999, La République a besoin d'histoire, interventions 2000, L'Histoire va t'elle plus vite? Variations sur un vertige 2001. *Address:* Bibliothèque nationale de France, Site François Mitterand, Quai François Mauriac, 75013 Paris (Office); 48 rue Galande, 75005 Paris, France (Home). *Telephone:* 1-53-79-48-48 (Office). *Fax:* 1-40-51-08-87 (Office). *E-mail:* jean-noel.jeanneney@bnf.fr (Office).

JEANNIOT, Pierre Jean, OC, MSc; Canadian/French air transport official (retd); b. 9 April 1933, Montpellier, France; ed Sir George Williams Univ., McGill Univ. and Univ. de Montréal; designer of aircraft and marine instrumentation, Sperry Gyroscope of Canada 1952–55; various positions in research, Devt and man., Air Canada 1955–68; contributed to Devt of the 'black box'; Vice-Pres. Computers and Communications, Univ. du Québec 1969; Vice-Pres. Computer and Systems Services, Air Canada 1970–76; subsequently held other sr positions in Air Canada; Exec. Vice-Pres. and COO Air Canada 1983, Pres. and CEO 1984–90; Pres. and CEO JINMAG Inc. 1990–92; Dir-Gen. and CEO IATA 1992–2002; Dir Bank of Nova Scotia; Chair. Bd Univ. of Québec 1971–77, Chancellor 1996–; Chevalier, Légion d'honneur, Independence Medal of First Order (Jordan); Dr hc (Québec) 1988, (Concordia) 1997; Man. Achievement Award, McGill Univ. 1989. *Publications:* numerous technical papers. *Address:* c/o International Air Transport Association, Route de l'Aéroport 33, P.O. Box 416, 1215 Geneva 15-Airport, Switzerland.

JEEVES, Malcolm Alexander, CBE, MA, PhD, FMedSci, FBPsS, PPRSE; British professor of psychology and author; b. 16 Nov. 1926, Stamford; s. of Alexander Frederic Thomas Jeeves and Helena May Jeeves (née Hammond); m. Ruth Elisabeth Hartridge 1955; two d.; ed Stamford School, St John's Coll., Cambridge, Harvard Univ.; commd. Royal Lincs. Regt, served with 'Desert Rats' in First Bn Sherwood Foresters, BAOR 1945–48; Research Exhibitioner St John's Coll., Cambridge 1952; Rotary Foundation Fellow, Harvard Univ. 1953; lecturer Leeds Univ. 1956; Prof. of Psychology Adelaide Univ. 1959–69, Dean 1962–64; Vice-Prin. St Andrews Univ. 1981–85; Dir MRC Cognitive Neuroscience Research Group, St Andrews 1984–89; Ed.-in-Chief Neuropsychologia 1990–93; mem. Psychology Cttee SSRC 1972–76, Biology Cttee SERC 1980–84, Science Bd 1985–89, Council 1985–89, Neuroscience and Mental Health Bd, MRC 1985–89, Manpower Sub-Cttee, ABRC 1991–93, Council Royal Soc. of Edin. 1984–88, Exec. 1985–87, Vice-Pres. Royal Soc. of Edin. 1990–93, Pres. 1996–99; Pres. Section J, BAAS 1988; Founding Fellow Acad. of Medical Sciences 1998; Hon. Research Prof. St Andrews Univ. 1993–; Hon. Sheriff Fife 1986–; Hon. DUniv (Stirling); Hon. DSc (Edin.) 1993, (St. Andrews) 2000; Abbie Memorial Lecture, Adelaide Univ. 1981, Cairns Memorial Lecture, 1986, 1987; Burney Student, Kenneth Craik Award (St John's Coll., Cambridge), Gregg Bury Prize, Cairns Medal 1986. *Publications:* Thinking in Structures (with Z. P. Dienes) 1965, The Effects of Structural Relations upon Transfer (with Z. P. Dienes) 1968, The Scientific Enterprise and Christian Faith 1969, Experimental Psychology: An Introduction for Biologists 1974, Psychology and Christianity: The View Both Ways 1976, Analysis of Structural Learning (with G. B. Greer) 1983, Free to be Different (with R. J. Berry and D. Atkinson) 1984, Behavioural Science: a Christian Perspective 1984, Psychology – Through the Eyes of Faith (with D. G. Myers) 1987, Mind Fields 1994, Callosal Agenesis (ed. with M. Lassonde) 1994, Human Nature at the Millennium 1997, Science, Life and Christian Belief (with R. J. Berry) 1998, From Cells to Souls – and Beyond (ed. and contrib.) 2003; papers on neuropsychology and cognition in scientific journals. *Leisure interests:* music, fly fishing, walking. *Address:* School of Psychology, University of St Andrews, St Andrews, Fife, KY16 9JU (Office); 7 Hepburn Gardens, St. Andrews, Fife, KY16 9DE, Scotland (Home). *Telephone:* (1334) 462072 (Office); (1334) 473545 (Home). *Fax:* (1334) 477441 (Office); (1334) 472539 (Home). *E-mail:* maj2@st-andrews.ac.uk (Office).

JEEWOOLALL, Sir Ramesh, Kt, LLB; Mauritian politician and lawyer; b. 20 Dec. 1940; m.; two c.; ed Middle Temple, London; lawyer 1969–71; magistrate 1971–72; Chair. Tea Devt Authority 1976; elected to Legis. Ass. (Labour Party) 1976, Deputy Speaker 1976–79, Speaker 1979–82, 1996–2001; elected to Legis. Ass. (Alliance Party) 1987; Minister of Housing, Lands and Environment 1987–90. *Address:* c/o National Assembly, Port Louis; 92 Belle Rose Avenue, Quatre Bornes, Mauritius.

JEFFARES, Alexander Norman, AM, MA, PhD, DPhil; British professor of English; b. 11 Aug. 1920, Dublin; s. of Cecil N. Jeffares and Agnes Jeffares (née Fraser); m. Jeanne A. Calembert 1947; one d.; ed The High School,

Dublin, Trinity Coll., Dublin and Oriel Coll., Oxford; Lecturer in Classics, Trinity Coll., Dublin 1943–45; lector in English, Groningen Univ., Netherlands 1946–48; lecturer in English Literature, Univ. of Edin. 1949–51; Prof. of English Language and Literature, Univ. of Adelaide 1951–57; Prof. of English Literature, Univ. of Leeds 1957–74; Prof. of English, Univ. of Stirling 1974–86, Hon. Prof. 1986–; Hon. Research Fellow Royal Holloway Coll., Univ. of London 1997–; Man. Dir Academic Advisory Services Ltd 1974–; Dir Colin Smythe Ltd 1975–; mem. Scottish Arts Council 1979–84, Vice-Chair. 1980–84; Chair. Book Trust, Scotland 1986–89; Pres. Scottish PEN 1986–89; mem. Arts Council of GB 1980–84; mem. Council, Royal Soc. of Edin. 1986–89, Vice-Pres. 1988–89; Dir Edin. Book Festival 1982–90; mem. Exec. Cttee Scots Australian Council 1992–; Hon. Fellow, Trinity Coll. Dublin; Hon. DUniv (Lille), (Stirling) 2002; Hon. DLitt (Ulster). *Publications:* W. B. Yeats: man and poet 1949, Seven Centuries of Poetry 1955, The Circus Animals 1970, Restoration Drama (4 Vols) 1974, A History of Anglo-Irish Literature 1982, Poems of W. B. Yeats: a new selection 1984, A New Commentary on the Poems of W. B. Yeats 1984, Brought up in Dublin (poems) 1987, Brought up to Leave (poems) 1987, An Irish Childhood (with A. Kamm) 1987, A Jewish Childhood (with A. Kamm), W. B. Yeats: A New Biography 1988, Yeats's Poems 1989, Yeats's Vision 1990, W. B. Yeats, The Love Poems 1990, W. B. Yeats, Poems of Place 1991, Always your Friend: Letters between Maud Gonne and W. B. Yeats 1893–1938 (with Anna MacBride White) 1992, Jonathan Swift, Selected Poems 1992, Joycechoyce (with Brendan Kennelly) 1992, Ireland's Women: Writings Past and Present (with Katie Donovan and Brendan Kennelly) 1994, Maud Gonne MacBride, A Servant of the Queen (with Anna MacBride White) 1994, Collins Dictionary of Quotations (with Martin Gray) 1995, Images of Invention: Essays on Irish Writing 1996, Victorian Love Poems 1996, A Pocket History of Irish Literature 1997, Irish Love Poems 1997, The Irish Literary Movement 1998, The Secret Rose: Love Poems by W. B. Yeats 1998, Ireland's Love Poems: Wonder and a Wild Desire 2000, The Poems and Plays of Oliver St John Gogarty 2001. *Leisure interests:* drawing, restoring old houses. *Address:* Craighead Cottage, Fife Ness, Crail, Fife, KY10 3XN, Scotland. *Telephone:* (1333) 450898. *Fax:* (1333) 450898.

JEFFERSON, Sir George Rowland, Kt, CBE, F.R.ENG., FIEE, FRAeS, FRSA, CBIM, FCGI; British/Australian business executive; b. 26 March 1921; s. of Harold Jefferson and Eva Elizabeth Ellen; m. 1st Irene Watson-Browne 1943 (died 1998); three s.; m. 2nd Bridget Anne Reilley 1999; ed Dartford Grammar School, Kent; Eng apprentice, Royal Ordnance Factory, Woolwich 1937–42; with RAOC and REME 1942; Anti-Aircraft Command and Armament Design Dept, Fort Halstead 1942–45; Ministry of Supply, Fort Halstead 1945–52; joined Guided Weapons Div., English Electric Co. Ltd 1952, Chief Research Engineer 1953, Deputy Chief Engineer 1958; Dir English Electric Aviation Ltd 1961; with British Aircraft Corpn (BAC), Dir and CEO, BAC (Guided Weapons) Ltd 1963, Deputy Man. Dir 1964, mem. Bd 1965–77; Dir British Aerospace, Chair. and CEO its Dynamics Group 1977–80; Chair. BAC (Anti-Tank) 1968–78; Deputy Chair. Post Office 1980–87; Chair. British Telecommunications 1981–87, CEO –1986; Dir Babcock Int. 1980–87, Lloyds Bank 1986–89; Chair. Matthew Hall PLC 1987–88; Chair. City Centre Communications Ltd 1988–90, Videotron Corpn 1990–97; Dir AMEC PLC 1988–90; mem. Nat. Enterprise Bd 1979–80, Governing Council Business in the Community Ltd 1984–87; Freeman of the City of London; Hon. FIMechE; Hon. BScEng; Hon. DSc (Bristol); Hon. DUniv (Essex). *Address:* 12 Ocean Shore's Edge, Connolly, Perth, WA 6027, Australia. *Telephone:* (8) 9300-6414 (Home). *Fax:* (8) 9300-8777. *E-mail:* georgejefferson@dingoblue.net.au (Home).

JEFFORDS, James Merrill, BS, LLB; American politician; b. 11 May 1934, Rutland, Vt; s. of Olin M. Jeffords and Marion Hausman; m. Elizabeth Daley; one s. one d.; ed Yale and Harvard Univs.; admitted to Vermont Bar 1962; law clerk, Judge Ernest Gibson, Vt District 1962; Partner, Bishop, Crowley & Jeffords 1963–66, Kinney, Carbine & Jeffords 1967–68; mem. Vt Senate 1967–68; Attorney-Gen. State of Vt 1969–73; Partner, George E. Rice, Jr and James M. Jeffords 1973–74; mem. 94th–100th Congresses from Vt; Senator from Vermont 1989–; Chair. Environment Cttee 2001–; Republican –2001, Ind. 2001–. *Address:* US Senate, 728 Hart Building, Washington, DC 20510-4503, USA. *E-mail:* vermont@jeffords.senate.gov (Office).

JEFFREY, Richard Carl, PhD; American university professor; b. 5 Aug. 1926, Boston, Mass.; s. of Mark M. Jeffrey and Jane Markovitz; m. Edith Kelman 1955; one s. one d.; ed Univs. of Boston, Chicago and Princeton; lecturer in computer design MIT 1952–55, Asst Prof. of Electrical Eng, MIT 1958–59, Asst Prof. of Philosophy, Stanford Univ. 1959–63, visiting mem. Inst. for Advanced Study 1963, Assoc. Prof. of Philosophy City Coll. of New York 1964–67, Prof. of Philosophy, Univ. of Pa 1967–74, Princeton Univ. 1974–99. *Publications:* The Logic of Decision 1965, Formal Logic: Its Scope and Limits 1967, Computability of Logic (jtly with Geo Borlos) 1974, Studies in the Inductive Logic of Probability (Vol. I) 1970, (Vol. II) 1979 (Jt Ed.), Probability and the Art of Judgement 1991, Logic, Logic and Logic 1998. *Address:* 55 Patton Avenue, Princeton, NJ 08540-5251, USA (Home). *Telephone:* (609) 924-9139.

JEFFREY, Robin Campbell, BSc, PhD, FREng, FIChemE, FIMechE; British engineer and business executive; b. 19 Feb. 1939; s. of Robert Jeffrey and Catherine McSporran; m. Barbara Robinson 1962; two s. one d.; ed Kelvinside Acad., Royal Technical Coll. Glasgow, Pembroke Coll., Cambridge; with Babcock Int. 1956–79; with South of Scotland Electricity Bd 1979–89, Project Man. Torness AGR Station 1980–88, Chief Engineer, Generation Design and Construction 1988–89; Man. Dir Eng Resources, Scottish Power 1990–92; CEO Scottish Nuclear Ltd 1992–98, Chair. 1995–98; Jt Deputy Chair. British Energy PLC 1995–2001, Chair., CEO 2001–02; Visiting Prof. Strathclyde Univ.; mem. London Transport Bd. *Address:* c/o British Energy PLC, 10 Lochside Place, Edinburgh, EH12 9DF, Scotland (Office).

JEFFREYS, Sir Alec John, Kt, MA, FRCPath, FRS, FLS, FMedSci, CBiol; British university professor; b. 9 Jan. 1950, Oxford; s. of Sidney Victor Jeffreys and Joan Jeffreys (née Knight); m. Susan Miles 1971; two d.; ed Luton Grammar School, Luton Sixth Form Coll., Merton Coll., Oxford; European Molecular Biology Org. Postdoctoral Research Fellow, Univ. of Amsterdam 1975–77; lecturer, Dept of Genetics, Univ. of Leicester 1977–82, Lister Inst. Research Fellow 1982–91, Reader in Genetics 1984–87, Prof. of Genetics 1987–, Royal Soc. Wolfson Research Prof. 1991–; Inventor of Genetic Fingerprinting; FFSc (India), Hon. FRCP, Hon. FIBiol, Hon. mem. American Acad. of Forensic Sciences 1998; Hon. DUniv (Open Univ.) 1991; Hon. DSc (St Andrews) 1996, (Strathclyde) 1998; Analytica Prize, German Soc. of Clinical Chemistry 1988, Australia Prize 1998; Press, Radio and TV awards for the Midlander of the Year 1988, 1989; Hon. Freeman (Leicester) 1993; Colworth Medal Biochemical Soc. 1985, Linnean Bicentenary Medal for Zoology, Linnean Soc. 1987, Carter Medal, Clinical Genetics Soc. 1987, Davy Medal, Royal Soc. 1987, Gold Medal for Zoology, Linnean Soc. 1994, Sir Frederick Gowland Hopkins Memorial Medal, Biochemical Soc. 1996, Albert Einstein World of Science Award, World Cultural Council Award, Baly Medal, Royal Coll. of Physicians 1997, Soc. of Chemical Industry Medal 1997, Sir George Stokes Medal, Royal Soc. of Chemistry 2000, Edward Buchner Prize, Soc. for Biochem. and Molecular Biology (Germany) 2001. *Publications:* numerous articles on human molecular genetics. *Leisure interests:* walking, swimming, postal history, reading unimproving novels. *Address:* Department of Genetics, Adrian Building, University of Leicester, University Road, Leicester, LE1 7RH, England. *Telephone:* (116) 252-3435.

JEFFRIES, Lionel; British actor and director; b. Lionel Charles Jeffries, 10 June 1926; s. of Bernard Jeffries and Elsie Jeffries (née Jackson); m. Eileen Walsh; one s. two d.; ed Queen Elizabeth's Grammar School, Wimborne, Dorset, Royal Acad. of Dramatic Art; began career in film industry 1947; writer and dir The Railway Children, The Amazing Mr Blunden, Wombling Free; Dir Baxter, The Water Babies; Burma Star, Kendal Award, Royal Acad. of Dramatic Art. *Stage appearances include:* (London) Hello Dolly 1983–84, See How They Run, Two into One 1984–85, The Wild Duck 1990, (New York) Pygmalion 1989. *Films include:* Bhowani Junction, The Nun's Story, Law and Disorder, Life is a Circus, Idle on Parade, Jazzboat, Please Turn Over, Two-Way Stretch, Trials of Oscar Wilde, Fanny, The Hellions, Operation Snatch, Mrs Gibbon's Boys, Wrong Arm of the Law, Call Me Bwana, The Long Ships, First Men in the Moon, Secret of my Success, Murder Ahoy, You Must be Joking, Journey to the Moon, Camelot, Chitty Chitty Bang Bang, Ménage à trois, Danny Champion of the World. *TV films include:* Ending Up 1989, First and Last, Heaven on Earth 1997. *Leisure interest:* painting. *Address:* c/o Liz Hobbs, MBE, 68 Castlegate, Newark, Notts., NG24 1BG, England. *Telephone:* (1636) 703342 (Office); (20) 7287-8870. *Fax:* (1636) 703343 (Office); (20) 7287-8871.

JEKER, Robert A.; Swiss business executive; b. 26 Aug. 1935, Basel; m. Vreni Jeker 1967; one s. two d.; ed Univ. of Massachusetts, Amherst; head Spalenberg br. Credit Suisse, Basel 1968–72, Head Credit Suisse, Basel 1972–76, mem. Exec. Bd 1976–83, Pres. 1983–93; Man. Dir Unotec, Anova and Nueva Holdings 1993–96; now Chair. Bd Swiss Steel, Emmenbrücke, Batigroup AG, Basel, MCH Messe Schweiz, Basel. *Leisure interests:* sports, concerts, travel. *Address:* c/o MCH Messe Schweiz AG, 4021 Basel (Office); Waldrain 2, 4103 Bottmingen, Switzerland (Home). *Telephone:* (58) 2062010 (Office); (61) 4013067 (Home). *Fax:* (58) 2062009 (Office); (61) 4013075 (Home). *E-mail:* robertjeker@messe.ch.

JELE, Khiphusizi Josiah; South African diplomatist; b. 1 May 1930, Johannesburg; m. 1976; one s. two d.; ed Mil. Acad. Odessa and Moscow Political Science Acad., USSR; studied public admin., Great Britain and USA; African Nat. Congress (ANC) Political Commissar, Dir of Broadcasting, Chief Rep., Dar es Salaam, Tanzania 1967–71, ANC Rep. World Peace Council Secr., Helsinki, Finland 1971–77, Dir, ANC Int. Affairs Dept, Lusaka, Zambia 1978–83, Chair. ANC Political Cttee, Lusaka 1983–85, Sec. to ANC Political Mil. Council, Lusaka 1985–91, mem. ANC Nat. Elections Comm. 1991–92, mem. ANC Civil Service Unit 1992–94; mem. ANC Exec. Cttee 1977–94; MP 1994; Perm. Rep. of South Africa to UN 1994–99; mem. Hon. Ambassadorial Cttee, Congress of Racial Equality; Phelps-Stokes Fund Annual Award 1995 (Hon. mem. Bd of Fund); Freedom of City of Memphis. *Publications:* (papers) Racism in South Africa 1973, Population Explosion in Africa 1974; Western Military Collaboration with South Africa (booklet). *Leisure interests:* soccer, boxing, jazz, classical music, reading. *Address:* c/o Ministry of Foreign Affairs, Union Building, E Wing, Government Avenue, Pretoria 0002, South Africa.

JELINEK, Otto John; Canadian politician; b. 1940, Prague, Czechoslovakia; m. Leata Mary Bennett 1974; two s.; ed Oakville, Ont., Swiss Alpine Business Coll., Davos, Switzerland; business exec.; MP 1972–93; apptd. Parl. Sec. to Minister of Transport 1979; fmr mem. Caucus Cttee on Trade, Finance, Econ. Affairs, fmr mem. Standing Cttee on Transport and Communications, on External Affairs; fmr mem. Parl. Cttee on Miscellaneous Estimates, Minister of State (Fitness and Amateur Sport) 1984–88, for Multiculturalism 1985–86, of Supply and Services and Receiver Gen. of Canada 1988–89;

Acting Minister of Public Works 1988–89, Minister of Nat. Revenue 1989–93; Pres. Jelinek Int. Inc. 1993–; mem. Bd Dirs. Hummingbird Communications Ltd, Canbra Foods Ltd; Chair. Canada-Taiwan Friendship Cttee; mem. Big Brothers' Asscn of Canada, Olympic Club of Canada, Canadian Sports Hall of Fame; Fed. Progressive Conservative Party.

JELLICOE, 2nd Earl, (cr. 1925); **George Patrick John Rushworth Jellicoe,** KBE, PC, DSO, MC, FRS; British politician, diplomatist and businessman; b. 4 April 1918, Hatfield; s. of 1st Earl Jellicoe (Admiral of the Fleet); m. 1st Patricia O'Kane 1944; m. 2nd Philippa Ann Bridge 1966; three s. four d.; ed Winchester and Trinity Coll., Cambridge; mil. service (Coldstream Guards, Special Air Service (SAS) and CO Special Boat Service (SBS)) 1939–45; joined Foreign Office 1947; First Sec. Washington, Brussels, Baghdad; Deputy Sec.-Gen. Baghdad Pact; Lord-in-Waiting 1961; Jt Parl. Sec., Ministry of Housing and Local Govt 1961–62; Minister of State, Home Office 1962–63; First Lord of Admiralty 1963–64; Minister of Defence for the Royal Navy 1964; Deputy Leader of the Opposition, House of Lords 1967–70; Lord Privy Seal, Leader of House of Lords and Minister for Civil Service Dept 1970–73; Dir. S. G. Warburg 1966–70, 1973–88, Smiths Industries 1973–87, Tate and Lyle 1974–93 (Chair. 1978–83), Chair. Booker Tate Ltd 1988–91; Life Peer 2000–; Chair. Anglo-Hellenic League 1978–86, Davy Corpn 1985–90, European Capital 1991–95; Dir Morgan Crucible 1974–88, Sotheby's (Holdings) 1973–93; Pres. Nat. Fed. of Housing Socs 1965–70, London Chamber of Commerce and Industry 1979–82, Parl. and Scientific Cttee 1980–83, Crete Veterans Asscn 1990–2001, British Heart Foundation 1992–95, SAS Asscn 1996–2001, Royal Geographical Soc. 1993–97; Chancellor Univ. of Southampton 1984–96; Chair. Council of King's Coll., Univ. of London 1977–84, Medical Research Council 1982–90, British Overseas Trade Bd 1983–86; Pres. East European Trade Council (Chair. 1986–90); Pres. Kennet and Avon Canal Trust 1980–93, Vice-Pres. 1999–; Freeman City of Athens; Hon. LLD (Southampton Univ.) 1985, (Southampton Coll., Long Island) 1987 (King's Coll. London); Croix de guerre, Légion d'honneur, Grand Commdr Greek Order of Honour, Greek War Cross. *Leisure interest:* travel. *Address:* Tidcombe Manor, Tidcombe, Nr. Marlborough, Wilts, SN8 3SL; 97 Onslow Square, London, SW7, England. *Telephone:* (1264) 731225 (Wilts.); (20) 7584-1551 (London). *Fax:* (1264) 731418.

JELVED, Marianne, M.ED.; Danish politician; b. 5 Sept. 1943, Charlottenlund; m.; teacher in public schools 1967–89, Royal Danish School of Educ. Studies 1979–87; Deputy Mayor of Gundsø 1982–85; mem. Folketing 1988–; Chair. Social Liberal mems. of Parl. 1988, currently Leader; Minister for Econ. Affairs 1993–2001, also for Nordic Cooperation 1994–2001, also Deputy Prime Minister. *Publications:* BRUD: Radikale vaerdier i en forandret tid (co-author) 1994. *Address:* Folketing, Christiansborg, 1240 Copenhagen K, Denmark (Office). *Telephone:* 33-37-55-00. *Fax:* 33-32-85-38. *E-mail:* folketinget@folketinget.dk. *Website:* www.folketinget.dk.

JENCKS, Charles, MA, PhD; American architectural historian and designer; b. 1939, Baltimore, Md; m. Maggie Keswick (deceased); ed Harvard Univ., Univ. of London, UK; studied under Siegfried Giedon and Reyner Banham; with Architectural Asscn 1968–88; Lecturer UCLA 1974–; has lectured at over forty univs including Univs of Peking, Shanghai, Paris, Tokyo, Milan, Venice, Frankfurt, Montréal, Oslo, Warsaw, Barcelona, Lisbon, Zurich, Vienna, Edin., Columbia, Princeton, Yale and Harvard; producer of furniture designs for Sawaya & Moroni, Milan 1986–; currently Ed. Consultant Architectural Design and Ed. Academy Editions, London; contrib. to Sunday Times Magazine, Times Literary Supplement, The Observer, The Independent (all UK); mem. Selection Cttee Venice Biennale 1980; Juror for Phoenix City Hall 1985; Curator Wight Art Centre, LA and Berlin 1987; mem. Royal Soc. of Arts, London, Acad. Forum of Royal Acad., London; Fulbright Scholarship (London Univ.) 1965–67; NARA Gold Medal for Architecture 1992. *Furniture designs include:* 'Architecture in Silver': Tea and Coffee Service, Alessi, Italy 1983, Symbolic Furniture exhibition, Aram Designs, London 1985; other furniture and drawings collected by museums in Japan and Victoria & Albert Museum, London. *Architectural works include:* Garagia Rotunda, Truro, MA 1976–77, The Elemental House (with Buzz Yudell), LA, The Thematic House (with Terry Farrell), London 1979–84, The Garden of Six Senses 1998. *Television includes:* two feature films written for BBC on Le Corbusier and Frank Lloyd Wright. *Publications include:* Meaning in Architecture (co-ed.) 1969, Architecture 2000: Predictions and Methods 1971, Adhocism (co-author) 1972, Modern Movements in Architecture 1973, Le Corbusier and the Tragic View of Architecture 1974, The Language of Post-Modern Architecture 1977, The Daydream Houses of Los Angeles 1978, Bizarre Architecture 1979, Late-Modern Architecture 1980, Signs, Symbols and Architecture (co-author) 1980, Skyscrapers-Skycities 1980, Architecture Today 1982, Kings of Infinite Space 1983, Towards a Symbolic Architecture 1985, What is Post-Modernism? 1987, Post-Modernism. The New Classicism in Art and Architecture 1987, The Prince, The Architects and New Wave Monarchy 1988, The New Moderns 1990, The Post-Modern Reader (ed.) 1992, The Architecture of the Jumping Universe 1995, Theories and Manifestos of Contemporary Architecture 1997, New Science—New Adventure? 1997, The Chinese Garden (with Maggie Keswick). *Address:* c/o Royal Academy Forum, Royal Academy of Arts, Burlington House, Piccadilly, London, W1J 0BD, England (Office).

JENCKS, William Platt, MD; American biochemist; b. 15 Aug. 1927, Bar Harbor, Me; s. of Gardner Jencks and Elinor Melcher Cheetham; m. Miriam Ehrlich Jencks 1950; one s. one d.; ed Harvard Coll. and Harvard Medical School; Intern, Peter Bent Brigham Hosp., Boston, Mass. 1951–52; mem. staff, Dept of Pharmacology, Army Medical Service Graduate School 1953–54, Chief, Dept of Pharmacology 1954–55; Life Insurance Medical Research Fund Postdoctoral Fellow, Mass. Gen. Hosp. 1955–56; US Public Health Service Postdoctoral Fellow, Dept of Chem., Harvard 1956–57; Asst Prof. of Biochem., Brandeis Univ. 1957–60, Assoc. Prof. of Biochem. 1960–63, Prof. of Biochem. 1963–96, of Biochem. and Molecular Pharmacodynamics 1977–96, Prof. Emer. 1996–; Guggenheim Memorial Foundation Fellow 1973–74; Fellow AAAS, American Acad. of Arts and Sciences; mem. Nat. Acad. of Sciences, American Soc. of Biological Chemists, American Philosophical Soc.; Foreign mem. Royal Soc. (UK); American Chem. Soc. Award in Biological Chem. 1962, American Soc. of Biological Chemists Merck Award 1993, James Flack Norris Award 1995, Repligen Award 1996. *Publications:* Catalysis in Chemistry and Enzymology 1969, Biochemistry (co-author) 1992; and over 380 articles in journals. *Leisure interest:* music. *Address:* Brandeis University, Graduate Department of Biochemistry, Waltham, MA 02254 (Office); 11 Revere Street, Lexington, MA 02420, USA (Home). *Telephone:* (781) 736-2315 (Office); (781) 862-8875 (Home). *Fax:* (781) 736-2349.

JENKIN OF RODING, Baron (Life Peer), cr. 1987, of Wanstead and Woodford in Greater London; **(Charles) Patrick (Fleeming) Jenkin,** PC, MA; British politician; b. 7 Sept. 1926, Edin.; s. of the late C. O. F. Jenkin and Margaret E. Jenkin (née Sillar); m. Alison Monica Graham 1952; two s. two d.; ed Clifton Coll., Bristol, Jesus Coll., Cambridge; called to the Bar, Middle Temple 1952; Adviser Distillers Co. Ltd 1957–70; Hornsey Borough Council 1960–63; MP for Wanstead and Woodford 1964–87; Opposition Spokesman on Finance, Econs and Trade 1965–66, 1967–70; Financial Sec. to Treasury 1970–72, Chief Sec. 1972–74; Minister for Energy Jan.–March 1974; mem. Shadow Cabinet 1974–79; Opposition Spokesman on Energy 1974–76, on Social Services 1976–79; Sec. of State for Social Services 1979–81, for Industry 1981–83, for the Environment 1983–85; mem. House of Lords Select Cttee on Science and Tech. 1997–2001 (Chair. Sub-Cttee II on Science and Soc. 1999–2000); Dir (non-exec.) Tilbury Contracting Group Ltd 1974–79, Royal Worcs. Co. Ltd 1975–79; Dir Continental and Industrial Trust Ltd 1975–79; Adviser Arthur Andersen 1985–96; Dir Friends Provident Life Office 1986–88, Chair. 1988–98; Chair. Lamco Paper Sales Ltd 1987–93; Dir UK-Japan 2000 Group 1986–99 (Chair. 1986–90); Chair. Crystalate Holdings PLC 1988–90, Target Finland Ltd 1991–96 (Dir 1989–91); Vice-Pres. Local Govt Asscn 1987–, Nat. Asscn of Local Councils 1987–2000, Greater London Area Conservatives 1987–89, Pres. 1989–92; mem. UK Advisory Bd Nat. Econ. Research Assocs. Inc. 1985–98; Dir UK Council for Econ. and Environmental Devt Ltd 1987–; Council mem. Guide Dogs for the Blind Asscn 1987–97; Chair. Westfield Coll. Trust 1988–2000; Adviser Sumitomo Trust and Banking Co. Ltd 1989–; Pres. British Urban Regeneration Asscn 1990–96; Chair. Forest Healthcare NHS Trust 1991–97; mem. Advisory Bd PPRU, Queen Mary and Westfield Coll. 1991–97 (Fellow 1991–), Supervisory Bd Achmea Holding NV 1991–98; Council mem. Imperial Cancer Research Fund 1991–97 (Deputy Chair. 1994–97); Patron Stort Trust 1991, St Clare West Essex Hospice Care Trust 1991–; Jt Pres. MIND (Nat. Asscn of Mental Health) 1991–93, Asscn of London Govt 1995–; Vice-Pres., Nat. Housing Fed. 1991–99; Sr Vice-Pres. World Congress on Urban Growth and Devt 1992–94; Pres. London Boroughs Asscn 1992–95; Adviser Thames Estuary Airport Co. Ltd 1992–; mem. Int. Advisory Bd Marsh & McLennan Cos Inc. (US) 1993–99, Nijenrode Univ., Netherlands 1994–98; Vice-Pres., Foundation for Science and Tech. 1996–97, Chair. 1997–; Pres. Asscn for Science Educ. 2002–03; Conservative; Hon. Fellow Coll. of Optometrists 2003; Hon. mem. BAAS 2001–; Freeman City of London, Hon. Freeman London Borough of Redbridge; Hon. FRSE 2001–; Hon. LLD (Univ. of the South Bank) 1997; Hon. DSc (Univ. of Ulster) 2001. *Leisure interests:* music, gardening, sailing, D.I.Y. *Address:* House of Lords, London, SW1A 0PW, England. *Telephone:* (20) 7219-6966. *Fax:* (20) 7219-0759. *E-mail:* jenkinp@parliament.uk.

JENKINS, Sir Brian Garton, GBE, MA, FCA; British business executive; b. 3 Dec. 1935, Beckenham; m. (Elizabeth) Ann Jenkins; one s. one d.; ed Tonbridge, Trinity Coll., Oxford; with RA, Gibraltar 1955–57; partner Coopers & Lybrand 1960–95; Chair. Woolwich PLC 1995–2000; Deputy Chair. Barclays PLC 2000–; Pres. Inst. of Chartered Accountants in England and Wales 1985–86, London Chamber of Commerce and Industry 1996–98, British Computer Soc. 1997–98; Chair. Charities Aid Foundation 1998–; Lord Mayor of London 1991–92; Hon. Bencher Inner Temple; Hon. mem. Baltic Exchange. *Publication:* An Audit Approach to Computers 1978. *Address:* 54 Lombard Street, London, EC3P 3AH, England. *Telephone:* (20) 7699-4170 (Office). *Fax:* (20) 7699-3690 (Office). *E-mail:* brian.jenkins@barclays.co.uk (Office). *Website:* www.barclays.com (Office).

JENKINS, Rt Rev David Edward, MA; British ecclesiastic; b. 26 Jan. 1925, London; s. of Lionel C. Jenkins and Dora K. Jenkins (née Page); m. Stella M. Peet 1949; two s. two d.; ed St Dunstan's Coll., Catford, Queen's Coll., Oxford, Lincoln Theological Coll.; Capt. RA 1945–47; priest 1954; Succentor Birmingham Cathedral 1953–54; Fellow and Chaplain and Praelector in Theology, Queen's Coll., Oxford 1954–69; Hon. Fellow 1990; Dir Humanum Studies, WCC, Geneva 1969–73; Dir William Temple Foundation, Manchester 1973–78; Prof. of Theology Leeds Univ. 1979–84, Prof. Emer. 1984–; Bishop of Durham 1984–94; Asst Bishop of Ripon 1994–; Hon. Prof. of Divinity, Durham 1994–; Hon. Fellow Queen's Coll. Oxford, Sunderland Univ.; Hon. DD (Durham, Aberdeen, Trinity Coll., Toronto, Leeds, Birmingham); Hon. DLit (Teesside); Hon. DCL (Northumbria). *Publications:* The

Glory of Man 1967, Living With Questions 1969, What is Man? 1970, The Contradiction of Christianity 1979, God, Miracles and the Church of England 1987, God, Politics and the Future 1988, God, Jesus and Life in the Spirit 1988, Still Living With Questions 1990, Free to Believe (with Rebecca Jenkins) 1991, Market Why and Human Wherefores 2000, The Calling of a Cuckoo 2003. *Leisure interests:* music (opera and church music), walking, birdwatching, nature and conservation, travel and books. *Address:* Ashbourne, Cotherstone, Barnard Castle, Co. Durham, DL12 9PR, England. *Telephone:* (1833) 650804 (Home). *Fax:* (1833) 650714 (Home).

JENKINS, Elizabeth, OBE; British writer; b. 31 Oct. 1905; ed Newnham Coll. Cambridge. *Publications:* The Winters 1931, Lady Caroline Lamb: a Biography 1932, Portrait of an Actor 1933, Harriet (Femina Vie Heureuse Prize) 1934, The Phoenix Nest 1936, Jane Austen–a Biography 1938, Robert and Helen 1944, Young Enthusiasts 1946, Henry Fielding, English Novelists Series 1947, Six Criminal Women 1949, The Tortoise and the Hare 1954, Ten Fascinating Women 1955, Elizabeth the Great 1958, Elizabeth and Leicester 1961, Brightness 1963, Honey 1968, Dr. Gully 1972, The Mystery of King Arthur 1975, The Princes in the Tower 1978, The Shadow and the Light: A Life of Daniel Dunglass Home 1983, A Silent Joy (novel) 1992. *Address:* 121 Greenhill, Hampstead, London, NW3 5TY, England. *Telephone:* (20) 7435-4642.

JENKINS, Hugh, CBE, FRICS, F.P.M.I.; British business executive; b. 9 Nov. 1933; m. Beryl Kirk 1988; ed Llanelli Grammar School, Coll. of Estate Man.; valuer, London Co. Council 1956–62; Asst Controller Coal Industry (Nominees) Ltd 1962–68, Man. Dir 1968–72; Dir.-Gen. Investments, Nat. Coal Bd 1972–85; Vice-Chair. Nat. Asscn of Pension Funds 1979–80; CEO Heron Financial Corpn 1985–86; Group Investment Dir, Allied Dunbar Asscn 1986–89; Deputy Chair. and Chief Exec. Allied Dunbar Unit Trusts 1986–89; Chair. and Chief Exec. Allied Dunbar Asset Man. 1987–89; Chair. Dunbar Bank 1988–89; Chair. and Chief Exec. Prudential Portfolio Mans. 1989–95; Dir Prudential Corpn 1989–95; Chair. Falcon Property Trust 1995–, Devt Securities PLC 1999–; Deputy Chair. Thorn PLC 1996–97, Chair. 1997–98; Dir Unilever Pensions Ltd 1985–89, IBM Pensions Trust PLC 1985–89, Heron Int. 1985–89, EMI 1995–, Rank Org. 1995–, Johnson Matthey 1996–; Chair. Property Advisory Group, Dept of the Environment 1990–96; mem. City Capital Markets Cttee 1982, Pvt. Financial Panel 1994–95; Lay mem. Stock Exchange 1984–85. *Leisure interests:* golf, theatre. *Address:* c/o Development Securities PLC, Portland House, Stag Place, London, SW1E 5DS, England (Office); 41 Tower Hill, London, EC3N 4HA. *Telephone:* (20) 7597-3071.

JENKINS, Dame (Mary) Jennifer, DBE; British administrator; b. 18 Jan. 1921; d. of the late Sir Parker Morris; m. Roy Jenkins, the late Lord Jenkins of Hillhead 1945; two s. one d.; ed St Mary's School, Calne, Girton Coll., Cambridge; with Hoover Ltd 1942–43; Ministry of Labour 1943–46; Political and Econ. Planning 1946–48; part-time extra-mural lecturer 1949–61; part-time teacher Kingsway Day Coll. 1961–67; Chair. Consumers Asscn 1965–76; mem. Exec. Bd British Standards Inst. 1970–73, Design Council 1971–74, Cttee of Man. Courtauld Inst. 1981–84, Exec. Cttee, Nat. Trust 1985–91 (Chair. 1986–90), Ancient Monuments Bd 1982–84, Historic Bldgs and Monuments Comm. 1984–85; Chair. Historic Bldgs Council for England 1975–84, Royal Parks Review Group 1991–96, Architectural Heritage Fund 1994–97, Expert Panel, Heritage Lottery Fund 1995–99; Pres. Ancient Monuments Soc. 1985– (Sec. 1972–75); Chair. N Kensington Amenity Trust 1974–77; Trustee Wallace Collection 1977–83; Dir J. Sainsbury Ltd 1981–86, Abbey Nat. PLC 1984–91; JP London Juvenile Courts 1964–74; Hon. Fellow Landscape Inst. 1995; Hon. FRIBA, Hon. FRICS, Hon. MRTPI; Hon. LLD (Univ. of London) 1988, (Bristol) 1990; Hon. DCL (Univ. of Newcastle-upon-Tyne) 1992; Hon. DUniv (York) 1990, (Strathclyde) 1993; Hon. DArch (Oxford Brookes) 1993, (Greenwich) 1998. *Publication:* From Acorn to Oak Tree: The Growth of the National Trust 1994. *Address:* 11 Hereford Mansions, Hereford Road, London, W2 5BA; St Amand's House, East Hendred, Oxon., OX12 8LA, England.

JENKINS, Sir Michael Romilly Heald, KCMG, BA; British diplomatist and business executive; b. 9 Jan. 1936, Cambridge; s. of Prof. Romilly Jenkins and Celine J. Jenkins (née Haeglar); m. Maxine L. Hodson 1968; one s. one d.; ed King's Coll., Cambridge; entered Foreign (subsequently Diplomatic) Service 1959; served in Paris, Moscow and Bonn; Deputy Chef de Cabinet 1973–75, Chef de Cabinet to George Thomson, EEC 1975–76; Prin. Adviser to Roy Jenkins, the late Lord Jenkins of Hillhead, Jan.–Aug. 1977; Head, European Integration Dept (External), FCO 1977–79; Head, Cen. Advisory Group, EEC 1979–81; Deputy Sec.-Gen., Comm. of the European Communities 1981–83; Asst Under-Sec. of State (Europe), FCO 1983–85; Minister, British Embassy, Washington 1985–87; Amb. to the Netherlands 1988–93; Exec. Dir Kleinwort Benson Group PLC 1993–96, Vice-Chair. Dresdner Kleinwort Benson 1996–2000, Dresdner Kleinwort Wasserstein 2001–03; Chair. British Group, Trilateral Comm. 1995–99, Action Centre for Europe (ACE) 1995–, DataRoam Ltd 2000–02; Dir Aegon NV 1994–2001; Adviser Sage Int. Ltd (later SELS Ltd) 1998–; Chair. MCC 2000–02; Pres. Boeing UK 2003–; mem. Council Britain in Europe 2000–, The Pilgrims 2001–, Advisory Council Prince's Trust 2002–. *Publications:* Arakcheev, Grand Vizir of the Russian Empire 1969, A House in Flanders 1992. *Address:* c/o Dresdner Kleinwort Wasserstein, 20 Fenchurch Street, London, EC3P 3DB, England.

JENKINS, Simon David, BA; British journalist; b. 10 June 1943, Birmingham; s. of Daniel Jenkins; m. Gayle Hunnicutt 1978; one s. one step-s.;

ed Mill Hill School, St John's Coll., Oxford; worked for Country Life Magazine 1965; News Ed. Times Educ. Supplement 1966–68; Leader-Writer, Columnist, Features Ed. Evening Standard 1968–74; Insight Editor, Sunday Times 1974–76; Ed. Evening Standard 1977–78; Political Ed. The Economist 1979–86; columnist Sunday Times 1986–90, The Spectator 1992–95, The Times 1992–; Ed. The Times 1990–92; Dir Faber and Faber (Publrs.) Ltd 1981–90; mem. Bd, Old Vic Co. 1979–81; Part-time mem. British Rail Bd 1979–90, London Regional Transport Bd 1984–86; founder and Dir Railway Heritage Trust 1985–90; Gov. Museum of London 1984–87, Bryanston School 1986–94; Dir The Municipal Journal 1980–90; Deputy Chair. Historic Bldgs and Monuments Comm. 1985–90, English Heritage; Trustee World Monuments Funds 1995–; mem. South Bank Bd 1985–90; mem. Millennium Comm. 1994–2000; Chair. Comm. for Local Democracy 1993–95, Bldg Books Trust 1994–, Booker Prize Judges 2000; mem. Human Fertilization and Embryology Authority 2001–; Hon. DLitt (Univ. of London, City Univ.); Edgar Wallace Prize 1997, Rio Tinto David Watt Memorial Prize 1998; Journalist of the Year, Granada Awards 1988, Columnist of the Year 1993. *Publications:* A City at Risk 1971, Landlords to London 1975, Newspapers: The Power and the Money 1979, The Companion Guide to Outer London 1981, Images of Hampstead 1982, The Battle for the Falklands 1983, With Respect, Ambassador 1985, The Market for Glory 1986, The Selling of Mary Davies and other writings 1993, Against the Grain 1994, Accountable to None: The Tory Nationalization of Britain 1995, The Thousand Best Churches in England 1999. *Leisure interests:* architecture, history of London. *Address:* c/o The Times, 1 Pennington Street, London, E98 1TT, England.

JENNINGS, Sir John (Southwood), Kt, CBE, PhD, FRSE, FGS; British business executive; b. 30 March 1937, Oldbury, Worcs.; s. of the late George Southwood Jennings and of Irene Beatrice (née Bartlett) Jennings; m. 1st Gloria Ann Griffiths 1961 (divorced 1996); one s. one d.; m. 2nd Linda Elizabeth Baston 1997; ed Oldbury Grammar School, Univs. of Birmingham and Edin.; joined Royal Dutch/Shell 1958, various posts, including Gen. Man. and Chief Rep. of Shell cos in Turkey 1976–78, Man. Dir Shell UK Exploration and Production 1979–84, Exploration and Production Co-ordinator, Shell Internationale Petroleum Mij., The Hague 1985–90; Dir The Shell Transport and Trading Co. PLC 1987–2001 (Man. Dir Royal Dutch/Shell Group of Cos. 1987–97, Chair. Shell Transport and Trading Co. 1993–97); Chair. EME (Emerging Market Econs) 2000–, Intelligent Energy 2001, Spectron 2002–; Dir Det Norske Veritas 1997–2001, Robert Fleming Holdings Ltd 1998–2000, the Mitie Group 1998–, Norseman Tectonics 1998–; Vice-Chair. Governing Body London Business School 1993–97 (mem. 1990–97); Vice-Pres. Liverpool School of Tropical Medicine 1991–97; mem. Council Royal Inst. of Int. Affairs 1994–97; Adviser JPMorgan Chase 2000–; Trustee, Edin. Univ. Devt Trust 1996, Exeter Univ. Council 1997–2000, Int. Advisory Bd Toyota Corpn 1997–, Bd of Counsellors Bechtel Corpn 1997–; Hon. DSc (Edin.) 1991, (Birmingham) 1997; Commdr, Ordre Nat. du Mérite (Gabon). *Leisure interests:* fishing, travel, music, wine. *Address:* South Kenwood, Kenton, Exeter, EX6 8EX, England (Office).

JENNINGS, Hon. Mr. Justice John R. R., BA, LLB, QC; Canadian judge; b. 10 July 1937, Toronto, Ont.; s. of Robert D. Jennings and Mary Rogers; m. Eyton Margaret Embury 1964; two s.; ed Upper Canada Coll., Univ. of Toronto and Osgoode Hall Law School, Toronto; past mem. York Co. Legal Aid Area Cttee; mem. and past mem. Council, Medico-Legal Soc.; Chair. Nat. Family Law Section 1974–76; Pres. Co. of York Law Asscn 1976; Chair. Bd, Windsor-Essex-Mediation Centre 1981–85; Dir Canadian Bar Insurance Asscn 1987–89; Pres. Advocates' Soc. 1987, Canadian Bar Asscn 1989–90, Canadian Bar Foundation 1989–90, CBANET Inc. 1989–90; Judge, Superior Court of Justice, Ont.; Hon. mem. Law Soc.; Fellow, American Coll. of Trial Lawyers. *Leisure interests:* tennis, travel. *Address:* Osgoode Hall, 130 Queen Street W, Toronto, Ont., M5H 2N5 (Office); 70 Montclair Avenue, Apartment 703, Toronto, Ont., M5P 1P7, Canada (Home). *Telephone:* (416) 327-5284 (Office). *Fax:* (416) 327-5417 (Office). *E-mail:* jjennings@judicom.cc.ca.

JENNINGS, Sir Robert Yewdall, Kt, MA, LLB; British judge of the International Court of Justice (retd); b. 19 Oct. 1913, Idle, Yorks.; s. of Arthur Jennings and Edith Schofield Jennings; m. Christine Dorothy Bennett 1955; one s. two d.; ed Belle Vue Secondary School, Bradford, Downing Coll., Cambridge, Harvard Univ.; war service (army) 1940–46; Asst Lecturer in Law, LSE 1938–39, Lecturer 1946–55; called to the Bar, Lincoln's Inn 1943, Hon. Bencher 1970–; QC 1969; Whewell Prof. of Int. Law, Cambridge Univ. 1955–81; Reader in Int. Law, Council of Legal Educ. 1959–70; Ed. Int. and Comparative Law Quarterly 1957–59, British Yearbook of Int. Law 1959–81, Sr Ed. 1974–81; Assoc. Inst. of Int. Law 1957, mem. 1967, Vice-Pres. 1979–81, Pres. 1981–83, Hon. mem. 1985–; Judge, Int. Court of Justice, The Hague 1982–95 (Pres. 1991–94); mem. Perm. Court of Arbitration 1982–; Appointing Authority Iran–USA Claims Tribunal, The Hague 1999–; fmr legal consultant to numerous govts.; counsel in several int. arbitrations; Fellow Jesus Coll., Cambridge 1939–, Sr Tutor 1949–55, fmr Pres., Hon. Fellow 1982–; Hon. mem. American Soc. of Int. Law 1989; Hon. Fellow Downing Coll. 1982–, LSE 1994–; Hon. LLD (Hull) 1987, (Cambridge) 1993, (Leicester) 1995; Hon. DJur (Saarland), (Rome–Sapienza) 1990; Hon. DCL (Oxford) 1996; Manley O. Hudson Medal 1993. *Publications:* The Acquisition of Territory 1963, General Course on International Law 1967, Oppenheim's International Law (9th ed. with Sir Arthur Watts) 1992, Collected Writings (2 Vols) 1998; and numerous articles and monographs. *Leisure interests:* music, reading, walking in Lake District. *Address:* Jesus College, Cambridge, CB5 8BL, England (Office).

JENRETTE, Richard Hampton, MBA; American insurance executive; b. 5 May 1929, Raleigh, NC; s. of Joseph M. Jenrette and Emma Love; ed Univ. of N Carolina and Harvard Grad. School of Business Admin.; New England Life Insurance Co. 1951–53; Brown Bros. Harriman & Co. 1957–59; with Donaldson, Lufkin & Jenrette Inc. 1959–, Chair. 1986–; Chair. Bd of Dirs. Equitable Life Assurance Soc. 1987–94, Chair Exec. Cttee 1994–, Chair., CEO Equitable Investment Corpn (now Credit Suisse First Boston) 1986–90; Dir Advanced Micro Devices, Sunnyvale, Calif.; Trustee, The Rockefeller Foundation, many other public affiliations and appts; Hon. DLitt (Univ. of SC) and other awards. *Address:* Credit Suisse First Boston, 18th Floor, 277 Park Avenue, New York, NY 10172 (Office); 67 East 93rd Street, New York, NY 10128, USA (Home).

JENS, Walter (Walter Freiburger; Momos), DPhil; German critic, philologist and novelist; b. 8 March 1923, Hamburg; s. of Walter and Anna (Martens) Jens; m. Inge Puttfarcken 1951; two s.; ed Hamburg and Freiburg im Breisgau Univs.; Asst Univs. of Hamburg and Tübingen 1945–49; Dozent Univ. of Tübingen 1949–56, Prof. of Classical Philology and Rhetoric 1956–88; Prof. Emer. 1988–; Visiting Prof. Univ. of Stockholm 1964, Univ. of Vienna 1984; Dir Seminar für Allgemeine Rhetorik (Tübingen) 1967–; mem. Gruppe 47 1950, German PEN 1961– (Pres. 1976–82, Hon. Pres. 1982–), Berliner Akad. der Künste 1961–, Deutsche Akad. für Sprache und Dichtung 1962–, Deutsche Akad. der Darstellenden Künste (Frankfurt) 1964–, Freie Akad. der Künste (Hamburg) 1964; Pres. Akad. der Künste Berlin-Brandenburg 1989–97, Hon. Pres. 1997–; Hon. DPhil; Prix Amis de la Liberté 1951, Schleussner Schüller Prize 1956, Kulturpreis der deutschen Industrie 1959, Lessing Prize 1968, DAG Prize 1976, Heinrich-Heine Prize 1981, Adolf-Grimme 1984, Theodor-Heuss Prize, (with I. Jens) 1988, Alternativer Büchnerpreis 1989, Hermann-Sinsheimer Prize 1989, Österreichischer Staatspreis für Kulturpublizistik 1990, Frankfurter Poetik-Vorlesungen 1992; Tübinger Universitätsmedaille 1979, Österreichisches Verdienstzeichen 1993, Bruno-Snell-Plakette (Univ. of Hamburg) 1997, Ernst-Reuter-Plakette 1998, Deutscher Predig und Preis 2002. *Publications include:* Nein–Die Welt der Angeklagten (novel) 1950, Der Blinde (novel) 1951, Vergessene Gesichter (novel) 1952, Der Mann, der nicht alt werden wollte (novel) 1955, Die Stichomythie in den frühen griechischen Tragödie 1955, Hofmannsthal und die Griechen 1955, Das Testament des Odysseus (novel) 1957, Statt einer Literaturgeschichte (Essays on Modern Literature) 1957, Moderne Literatur—moderne Wirklichkeit (essay) 1958, Die Götter sind sterblich (Diary of a Journey to Greece) 1959, Deutsche Literatur der Gegenwart 1961, Zueignungen 1962, Herr Meister (Dialogue on a Novel) 1963, Euripides-Büchner 1964, Von deutscher Rede 1969, Die Verschwörung (TV play) 1970, Am Anfang der Stall, am Ende der Galgen 1973, Fernsehen-Themen und Tabus 1973, Der tödliche Schlag (TV play) 1974, Der Prozess Judas (novel) 1975, Der Ausbruch (libretto) 1975, Republikanische Reden 1976, Eine deutsche Universität, 500 Jahre Tübinger Gelehrtenrepublik 1977, Zur Antike 1979, Die Orestie des Aischylos 1979, Warum ich Christ bin (Ed.) 1979, Ort der Handlung ist Deutschland (essays) 1979, Die kleine grosse Stadt Tübingen 1981, Der Untergang (drama) 1982, In letzter Stunde (Ed.) 1982, Aufruf zum Frieden 1983, In Sachen Lessing 1983, Kanzel und Katheder 1984, Momos am Bildschirm 1984, Dichtung und Religion (with H. Küng) 1985, Roccos Erzählung 1985, Die Friedensfrau 1986, Theologie und Literatur 1986, Das A und das O–die Offenbarung der Johannes 1987, Deutsche Lebensläufe 1987, Feldzüge eines Republikaners 1988, Juden und Christen in Deutschland 1988, Reden 1989, Schreibschule 1991, Die sieben letzten Worte am Kreuz 1992, Die Friedensfrau 1992, Mythen der Dichter 1993, Am Anfang das Wort 1993, Menschenwürdig sterben 1995, Macht der Erinnerung 1997, Aus gegebenem Anlass 1998, Wer am besten red't ist der reinste Mensch 2000, Der Römerbrief 2000, 'Der Teufel lebt nicht mehr, mein Herr' Erdachte Monologe – imaginäre Gespräche 2001. *Address:* Sonnenstrasse 5, 72076 Tübingen, Germany. *Fax:* (7071) 600693.

JENSEN, Arthur Robert, PhD; American educational psychologist; b. 24 Aug. 1923, San Diego, Calif.; s. of Arthur Alfred Jensen and Linda Schachtmayer; m. Barbara Jane Delarme 1960; one d.; ed Calif. (Berkeley), Columbia and London Univs.; Asst in Medical Psychology, Univ. of Maryland 1955–56; Research Fellow, Inst. of Psychiatry, London Univ. 1956–58; Asst Prof. to Prof. of Educational Psychology, Univ. of Calif., Berkeley 1958–94, Prof. Emer. 1994–; Research Psychologist, Inst. of Human Learning 1962–; Guggenheim Fellow 1964–65; Fellow, Center for Advanced Study in the Behavioral Sciences 1966–67; Visiting Lecturer, Melbourne, La Trobe, Adelaide and Sydney Univs. 1977, various univs in India 1980, China and Taiwan 2002; Galton Lecture, London 1999; Distinguished Research Contrib. Award, Int. Soc. for the Study of Individual Differences 2003. *Publications:* Genetics and Education 1972, Educability and Group Differences 1973, Educational Differences 1973, Bias in Mental Testing 1980, Straight Talk About Mental Tests 1981, The g Factor 1998. *Leisure interests:* classical music, swimming. *Address:* School of Education, University of California, Berkeley, CA 94720 (Office); 30 Canyon View Drive, Orinda, CA 94563, USA. *Telephone:* (510) 642-4201 (Office).

JENSEN, Elwood V., PhD; American academic and director of research; b. 13 Jan. 1920, Fargo, ND; s. of Eli A. Jensen and Vera Morris Jensen; m. 1st Mary Collette 1941 (died 1982); one s. one d.; m. 2nd Hiltrud Herborg 1983; ed Wittenberg Coll. and Univ. of Chicago; Guggenheim Fellowship E.T.H. Zürich 1946–47; Asst Prof. Dept of Surgery, Univ. of Chicago 1947–51, Asst Prof. Ben May Lab. for Cancer Research and Dept of Biochemistry 1951–54,

Assoc. Prof. 1954–60, Prof. Ben May Lab. for Cancer Research 1960–63, American Cancer Soc. Research Prof. Ben May Lab. and Dept of Physiology 1963–69, Prof. Dept of Physiology 1969–73, Dept of Biophysics and Theoretical Biology 1973–84, Dept of Physiological and Pharmacological Sciences 1977–84, Dept of Biochemistry 1980–90, Dir Ben May Lab. for Cancer Research 1969–82, Charles B. Huggins Distinguished Service Prof. Univ. of Chicago 1981–90, Prof. Emer. 1990–; Research Dir Ludwig Inst. for Cancer Research, Zürich 1983–87; scholar-in-residence Fogarty Int. Center NIH 1988–2001, Cornell Univ. Medical Coll. 1990–91; Visiting Scientist Inst. for Hormone and Fertility Research, Hamburg, Germany 1991–97; Visiting Prof. Karolinska Inst., Sweden 1998–2001, STINT Visiting Scientist 1998–99, Prof. Emer. 1999–2001; Visiting Scientist NICH/NIH 2001; Visiting Prof. Univ. of Cincinnati Medical Centre 2002–; mem. Research Advisory Bd Clinical Research Inst., Montreal 1987–96; mem. Scientific Advisory Bd Klinik für Tumorbiologie, Freiburg 1993–, Strang Cancer Prevention Center, New York 1994–98; mem. NAS (mem. Council 1981–84), American Acad. of Arts and Sciences; Hon. DSc (Wittenberg Univ.) 1963, (Acadia Univ.) 1976, (Medical Coll. Ohio) 1991; Hon. MD (Hamburg Univ.) 1995; Nobel Ass. Fellowship 1998, American Asscn for Cancer Research Dorothy P. Landon prize 2002, and numerous other awards and prizes. *Publications:* 227 articles and reviews since 1945. *Leisure interests:* tennis, squash, riding. *Address:* Department of Cell Biology, University of Cincinnati, Vontz Center for Molecular Studies, 3125 Eden Avenue, Cincinnati, OH 45267-0521, USA (Office); c/o Department of Medical Nutrition, Karolinska Institute, Novum, 141 86 Huddinge, Sweden. *E-mail:* jensene@mail.nih.gov (Office).

JENSEN, Hans Peter, PhD, DSc; Danish research director; b. 11 June 1943, Copenhagen; m. Helle Rønnow Olesen 1965; two s. one d.; ed Univ. of Copenhagen, Chalmers Univ. of Tech., Gothenburg; Asst Prof. Tech. Univ. of Denmark 1969, Assoc. Prof. 1972, Head of Chem. Dept A. 1980–83, Dean of Chem. Faculty 1983–86, Rector 1986–2001; Deputy Dir Inst. of Food Safety and Nutrition 2001–; Research Assoc. Univ. of Oregon 1974–75, Visiting Prof. 1978, 1984; mem. Danish Natural Science Research Council 1984–92, Danish Acad. of Tech. Sciences, Cttee on Higher Educ. and Research (Council of Europe) 1986–2001, Evaluation Group of European Postgrad. Training Programme 1989–93, Cultural Foundation between Denmark and Finland 1989–97, Fulbright Comm. of Denmark 1990–2001; Chair. Danish Rectors' Conf. 1993–2000; Chair. Asscn of Nordic Univ. Rectors' Confs. 1995–2001; mem. Bd of Govs, Jt Research Centre of EU 2001–; Kt First Degree Order of Dannebrog 1999; Dr hc (Shenandoah Univ., USA) 1993, (Helsinki Univ. of Tech.) 1998, (State Univ. of NY) 1998. *Publications:* General Chemistry (textbook) 1985; articles in professional journals. *Leisure interests:* music, literature. *Address:* Institute of Food Safety and Nutrition, Danish Veterinary and Food Administration, Moerkhoej Bygade 19, 2860 Soeborg (Office); Resedavej 9, 2820 Gentofte, Denmark (Home). *Telephone:* 33-95-60-82 (Office); 39-65-34-29 (Home). *Fax:* 33-95-60-01 (Office); 39-65-34-77 (Home). *E-mail:* hpj@fdir.dk (Office). *Website:* www.foedevaredirektoratet.dk (Office).

JENSEN, Ole Vig; Danish politician; b. 17 May 1936, Frederikssund; fmr teacher; mem. Folketing (Parl.) 1971–73, 1978–, mem. Presidium 1984–; mem. Gen. Council, Social Liberal Party 1968–, Exec. Council 1974–, Deputy Chair. Parl. Group 1979–; mem. Cen. Land Bd 1983–; Chair. Parl. Cttee for Agric. and Fisheries 1979–84; Deputy Chair. Parl. Educ. Cttee 1979–82; Minister of Cultural Affairs 1988–90, of Educ. 1993–98. *Address:* c/o Ministry of Education and Research, Frederiksholms Kanal 21, 1220 Copenhagen K, Denmark.

JEONG SE-HYUN; South Korean politician; ed Seoul Nat. Univ.; entered Ministry of Unification 1977, Vice-Minister of Unification 1998–99, Minister 1999–; represented S Korea during inter-Korean talks on Seoul's provision of fertilizer aid to N Korea and reunion of separated families 1998; Special Adviser to Head of Nat. Intelligence Service 2001–. *Address:* Ministry of Unification, 77-6, Sejong-no, Jongno-gu, Seoul 110-760, Republic of Korea (Office). *Telephone:* (2) 720-2424 (Office). *Fax:* (2) 720-2149 (Office). *Website:* www.unikorea.go.kr (Office).

JERUSALEM, Siegfried; German tenor; b. 17 April 1940, Oberhausen; m. 1980; one s. one d.; studied violin and piano at Folkwang Hochschule, Essen; played bassoon in German orchestras, including Stuttgart Radio Symphony Orchestra; studied voice and started singing career in Zigeunerbaron 1975; début Metropolitan New York 1980, La Scala 1981, Vienna State Opera 1979; sang Loge and Siegfried, Wagner's Ring Cycle, Metropolitan New York 1990, Tristan, Bayreuth 1993, Wagner's Ring Cycle, Vienna 1994, Wagner's Rienzi, Vienna 1997, Tristana, Berlin Staatsoper 2000; Grammy for Wagner's Ring Cycle 1992, Grammy for Rheingold 1991, Bundesverdienstkreuz (1st Class) 1996. *Leisure interests:* video, tennis, photography, golf. *Address:* Hochschule für Musik Nuremberg-Augsburg, Am Katharinenklaster 6, 90403 Nuremberg (Office); c/o Dr. G. Hilbert (Agent), Maximillianstrasse 22, 80538 Munich, Germany. *E-mail:* m.s.jerusalem@t-online.de (Office).

JERVIS, Simon Swynfen, MA, FSA; British art historian; b. 9 Jan. 1943, Yoxford; s. of the late John Swynfen Jervis and of Diana Parker (née Marriott); m. Fionnuala MacMahon 1969; one s. one d.; ed Downside School, Corpus Christi Coll., Cambridge; with Leicester Museum and Art Gallery 1964–66; Asst Keeper, Furniture Dept, Vic. and Albert Museum 1966–75, Deputy Keeper 1975–79, Acting Keeper 1989, Curator 1989–90; Dir Fitzwilliam Museum, Cambridge 1990–95; Dir of Historic Bldgs, Nat. Trust 1995–2002; mem. Council, Soc. of Antiquaries 1986–88 (Pres. 1995–2001),

Royal Archaeological Inst. 1987–91, Walpole Soc. 1990–95, Kelmscott Cttee 2001–; Chair. Nat. Trust Arts Panel 1987–95; Ed. Furniture History Soc. 1987–91, Chair. 1998–; Dir Burlington Magazine 1993–, Trustee 1997–; Guest Scholar, J. Paul Getty Museum 1988–89; Trustee, Royal Collection Trust 1993–2001, Leche Trust 1995–, Sir John Soane's Museum 1999–. *Publications:* Victorian Furniture 1968, Victorian and Edwardian Decorative Art: the Handley Read Collection 1972, Printed Furniture Designs Before 1650 1974, High Victorian Design 1974, The Penguin Dictionary of Design and Designers 1984, Furniture from Austria and Hungary in the Victoria and Albert Museum 1986. *Leisure interests:* churches, tennis. *Address:* 45 Bedford Gardens, London, W8 7EF, England (Office). *Telephone:* (20) 7727-8739 (Home). *Fax:* (20) 7727-8739 (Home).

JESIH, Boris; Slovenian artist and poet; b. 8 Aug. 1945, Škofja Loka; s. of Svetoslav and Kristina Jesih; m. Bojana Žokalj 1970 (divorced 1981); one s. one d.; ed Acad. of Fine Arts, Ljubljana, Berlin; works appear in numerous collections; has published several books of poetry; 10 nat. and 10 int. awards. *Exhibitions include:* 37th Biennale, Venice 1978, Premio le Arti 1971, 11–15th Biennale of Graphic Arts, Ljubljana 1975–83, 6–10th Biennale of Graphic Art, Cracow 1976–84, Premio Biella 1976, British Print Biennale, Bradford 1980, 1982, 1984, Die Kunst vom Stein, Vienna 1985. *Leisure interests:* basketball, fishing. *Address:* Valjavčeva 17, 61000 Ljubljana, Slovenia.

JESZENSZKY, Géza, PhD; Hungarian historian and politician; b. 10 Nov. 1941, Budapest; s. of Zoltán Jeszenszky and Pálma Miskolczy-Simon; m. Edit Héjj; one s. one d.; ed Eötvös Loránd Univ. Budapest; subject specialist with Nat. Széchényi Library 1968–76; Sr lecturer 1976–81, reader 1981–; Dean of the School of Political and Social Sciences, Budapest Univ. of Econs 1989–90, Head, Faculty of Int. Relations 1990–91; Visiting Prof. Univ. of Santa Barbara, Calif. 1984–86 and Univ. of Calif. at LA 1986; Visiting De Roy Prof., Univ. of Michigan, Ann Arbor 1996; Founding mem. Hungarian Democratic Forum 1988–96, Head Foreign Affairs Cttee 1988–90, mem. Presidency 1990–94; Minister of Foreign Affairs 1990–94; mem. Parl. 1994–98; Amb. to USA 1998–; numerous decorations. *Publications:* Prestige Lost, The Changing Image of Hungary in Great Britain 1894–1918 1986, The Hungarian Question in British Politics 1848–1914 1986, István Tisza: Villain or Tragic Hero? 1987, Lessons of Appeasement 1994, More Bosnias? National and Ethnic Tensions in the Post-Communist World 1997; other studies in Hungarian and English. *Leisure interests:* literature, jazz, dedicated skier. *Address:* Embassy of Hungary, 3910 Shoemaker Street, NW, Washington, DC 20008, USA. *Telephone:* (202) 362-3284. *Fax:* (202) 966-8135. *E-mail:* HuAmbassad@aol.com (Office).

JETTOU, Driss; Moroccan politician; b. 24 May 1945, El Jadida; m.; four c.; ed Lycée El Khawarizmi de Casablanca, Univ. of Rabat, Cordwainers Coll., London, UK; fmr Pres. Moroccan Fed. of Leather Industries (FEDIC); fmr Vice-Pres. Moroccan Asscn of Exporters (ASMEX); Minister of Trade and Industry 1994–95, of Culture and Foreign Trade 1995–97, of Trade, Industry and Culture 1997–98, of the Interior 1998–2002; Prime Minister of Morocco Oct. 2002–; apptd Pres. Office Cherifien des Phosphates (OCP) Aug. 2002; fmr mem. Gen. Confed. of Moroccan Enterprises (CGEM); Grande Chevalier, Wissam du Trône. *Address:* Office of the Prime Minister, Palais Royal, Le Méchouar, Rabat, Morocco (Office). *Telephone:* (3) 7762709 (Office). *Fax:* (3) 776995 (Office). *Website:* www.pm.gov.mor (Office).

JEUNET, Jean-Pierre; French film director; b. 1955, Roanne; worked as telecommunications engineer; Dir of TV commercials and short films. *Films:* L'évasion 1978, Le manège (César Award) 1980 (both co-Dir with Marc Caro), Le bunker de la dernière rafale 1981, Pas de repos pour Billy Brakko 1984, Foutaises (César Award) 1989, Delicatessen (César Award) 1991, Le cité des enfants perdus 1995, Alien: Resurrection 1997, Le fabuleux destin d'Amélie Poulain (Amélie) 2001.

JEWISON, Norman Frederick, OC, BA; Canadian film director; b. 21 July 1926, Toronto; s. of Percy Joseph and Dorothy Irene (née Weaver) Jewison; m. Margaret Dixon 1953; two s. one d.; ed Malvern Collegiate High School, Toronto, Victoria Coll., Univ. of Toronto; stage actor, Toronto; TV actor 1950–52; TV Dir for CBC 1953–58, CBS 1958–61; film Dir 1961–; Faculty mem. Inst. for American Studies, Salzburg, Austria 1969; Pres. D'Avoriaz Film Festival 1981–; Dir Centre for Advanced Film Studies 1987–; Dir TV shows for Harry Belafonte, Andy Williams, Judy Garland and Danny Kaye; mem. Electoral Bd, Dirs. Guild of America; mem. Canadian Arts Council; Hon. LLD (Univ. of Western Ont.) 1974; Acad. of Canada Special Achievement Award 1988, Emmy Award 1960, Golden Globe Award 1966, Best Dir, Berlin Film Festival for Moonstruck 1988, Irving Thalberg Memorial Prize 1999. *Films include:* Forty Pounds of Trouble, The Thrill of It All 1963, Send Me No Flowers 1964 (all for Universal Studios), Art of Love, The Cincinnati Kid 1965, The Russians are Coming (also producer) 1966, In the Heat of the Night (Acad. Award 1967), The Thomas Crown Affair (also producer) 1967, Gaily, Gaily 1968, The Landlord (producer) 1969, Fiddler on the Roof (also producer) 1970, Jesus Christ Superstar (also producer) 1972, Billy Two Hats (producer) 1972, Rollerball 1974, F.I.S.T. (also producer) 1977, And Justice for All 1979, Best Friends 1982, A Soldier's Story 1984, Agnes of God 1985, Moonstruck 1987, In Country 1989, Other People's Money 1991, Only You 1994, Bogus 1996, The Hurricane 1999, Dinner with Friends 2001. *Leisure interests:* skiing, yachting, tennis. *Address:* Yorktown Productions Ltd, 300 West Olympic Boulevard, Santa Monica, CA 90404, USA.

JEWKES, Sir Gordon Wesley, KCMG; British diplomatist; b. 18 Nov. 1931; s. of the late Jesse Jewkes; m. Joyce Lyons 1954; two s.; ed Barrow Grammar School, Magnus Grammar School, Newark-on-Trent; joined Colonial Office 1948; with army 1950–52; with Gen. Register Office 1950–63, 1965–68; mem. Civil Service Pay Research Unit 1963–65; joined FCO 1968; Commercial Consul, Chicago 1969–72, Consul-Gen. 1982–85; Deputy High Commr Port of Spain 1972–75; Head of Finance Dept, FCO and Finance Officer of Diplomatic Service 1975–79; Consul-Gen. Cleveland 1979–82; Gov. Falkland Islands, Commr S Georgia and S Sandwich Islands, High Commr British Antarctic Territory 1985–88; Consul-Gen., NY and Dir-Gen. Trade and Investment, USA 1989–91; mem. Bd of Dirs Hogg Group PLC 1992–94, Slough Estates PLC 1992–2002; Exec. Dir The Walpole Cttee 1992–96; mem. Council Univ. of Buckingham 1996–2001, Marshall Aid Commemoration Comm. 1996–99, Salvation Army London Advisory Bd 1996–2001. *Leisure interests:* music, travel, walking. *Address:* Apt 5, Boyne House, 9 Grove Road, Beaconsfield, Bucks., HP9 1UN, England.

JEYARETNAM, J. B., LLB; Singaporean politician and lawyer; b. 5 Jan. 1926, Ceylon; ed Muar, Johore, Malaysia, St Andrew's School, Singapore, Univ. Coll. London; barrister-at-law, Gray's Inn, London; joined Singapore legal service 1952; Head Subordinate Judiciary 1963, resgnd after two months; legal practice 1963–2000; Sec.-Gen. Workers' Party 1971–2000; mem. Parl. for Anson 1981–86; fined and jailed for one month on charge of fraud, charge (and subsequent disbarment from legal practice) overturned by Judicial Cttee of the Privy Council 1988; first opposition mem. Parl. to be elected for 15 years 1997–2001. *Address:* c/o Workers' Party, 411B Jalan Besar, Singapore 209014. *Website:* www.wp.org.sg (Office).

JHABVALA, Ruth Prawer, CBE, MA; British/American writer; b. 7 May 1927, Cologne, Germany; d. of Marcus Prawer and Eleonora Cohn; sister of Siegbert Salomon Prawer (q.v.); m. C. S. H. Jhabvala 1951; three d.; ed Hendon Co. School and London Univ.; born in Germany of Polish parentage; refugee to England 1939; lived in India 1951–75, in USA 1975–; Neill Gunn Int. Fellowship 1979; Booker Award for best novel 1975, MacArthur Foundation Award 1984, Acad. Award for Best Screenplay 1986, 1992. *Publications:* novels: To Whom She Will 1955, Nature of Passion 1956, Esmond in India 1958, The Householder 1960, Get Ready for Battle 1962, A Backward Place 1962, A New Dominion 1971, Heat and Dust 1975, In Search of Love and Beauty 1983, Three Continents 1987, Poet and Dancer 1993, Shards of Memory 1995; short story collections: A Stronger Climate 1968, An Experience of India 1970, How I Became a Holy Mother 1976, Out of India: Selected Stories 1986, East into Upper East 1998; film scripts (for James Ivory, q.v.): Shakespeare Wallah 1965, The Guru 1969, Bombay Talkie 1971, Autobiography of a Princess 1975, Roseland 1977, Hullabaloo over Georgie and Bonnie's Pictures 1978, The Europeans 1979, Jane Austen in Manhattan 1980, Quartet 1981, The Bostonians 1984, A Room with a View 1986, Madame Sousatzka 1988, Mr and Mrs Bridge 1989, Howards End 1992, The Remains of the Day 1993, Jefferson in Paris 1995, Surviving Picasso 1996, The Golden Bowl 2000. *Address:* 400 East 52nd Street, New York, NY 10022, USA.

JI CHAOZHU, BSc; Chinese diplomatist; b. 30 July 1929, China; s. of Prof. Chi Kungchuan; m. Wang Xiangtong 1957; two s.; ed Harvard Univ., USA, Tsinghua Univ., Beijing; stenographer and typist at Panmunjom for Chinese People's Volunteers 1952–54; English interpreter for Mao Zedong, Zhou Enlai and others 1955–73; Counsellor at Liaison Office of China in Washington, DC 1973–75; Deputy Dir Dept for Int. Orgs. and Confs., Ministry of Foreign Affairs 1975–79, Deputy Dir of American and Oceanic Affairs 1979–82; Minister-Counsellor of Chinese Embassy in Washington, DC 1982–85; Amb. to Fiji, Kiribati and Vanuatu 1985–87; Amb. to UK 1987–91; UN Under-Sec. for Tech. Co-operation for Devt 1991–92; Under-Sec.-Gen., Dept of Econ. Devt 1992–96 (now Dept for Devt, Support and Man. Services); Vice-Chair. All-China Fed. of Returned Overseas Chinese 1997–; Sr Consultant China Inst. of Int. Strategic Studies 1997–. *Leisure interests:* swimming, archaeology, history. *Address:* 112-01 Queens Boulevard, Apartment 18D, Forest Hills, NY 11375, USA.

JI XIANLIN; Chinese university professor; b. 6 Aug. 1911, Shandong Prov.; one s. one d.; ed Tsinghua Univ., Beijing, Univ. of Göttingen, Fed. Repub. of Germany; Prof., Dir Dept of Oriental Languages, Beijing Univ. 1946; disappeared during Cultural Revolution; Vice-Pres. Beijing Univ. 1978–84; Dir South Asian Inst., Chinese Acad. of Social Sciences 1978–85; Pres. Foreign Languages Research Soc. 1981; Pres. Soc. of Linguistics 1986, Soc. for Study of Africa and Asia, Dunhuang-Turpan Soc.; Vice-Pres. China Educ. Asscn for Int. Exchanges 1988–; Adviser, Chinese Writers' Asscn 1996–. *Publications include:* Collected Papers on the History of Cultural Relations Between China and India 1982, Studying the Ramayana 1981, Selected Papers on the Languages of Ancient India 1982 and trans. of various Indian classics including 7 Vols of Valmiki's Ramayana 1980, Problems of the Language of Primitive Buddhism 1985. *Address:* Department of Oriental Studies, Beijing University, Beijing, People's Republic of China. *Telephone:* 2501578.

JI YUNSHI; Chinese politician; b. 26 Sept. 1945, Haimen, Jiangsu Prov.; m. Lu Guohong; one d.; ed Shandong Univ.; joined CCP 1975; Vice-Gov. Jiangsu Prov. 1989–99, Gov. Feb. 1999–. *Address:* Jiangsu Provincial People's Government, 68 West Beijing Road, Nanjing, Jiangsu Province (Office); 29 Xikang Road, Nanjing, People's Republic of China (Home). *Telephone:* (25) 339-6639 (Office); (25) 339-6800 (Home). *Fax:* (25) 330-5325; (25) 330-5325 (Home).

JIA CHUNWANG; Chinese state official; b. 1938, Beijing; ed Qinghua Univ.; Vice-Chair. Tibet Autonomous Regional People's Govt 1984–85; Minister of State Security 1985–98; Minister of Public Security 1998–2003; mem. 12th CCP Cen. Cttee 1985, 13th Cen. Cttee 1987–92; mem. Cen. Comm. of Political Science and Law 1991–, 14th CCP Cen. Cttee 1992–97, 15th CCP Cen. Cttee 1997–2002, 16th CCP Cen. Cttee 2002–. *Address:* c/o Chinese Communist Party Central Committee, Quanguo Renmin Daibiao Dahui, Zhongguo Gongchan Dang, 1 Zhongnanhai, Beijing, People's Republic of China (Office).

JIA PINGWA; Chinese writer; b. 21 Feb. 1952, Danfeng Co., Shaanxi Prov.; s. of Jia Yanchun and Zhouzhue; m.; one d.; ed Dept of Chinese Language, Northwest Univ., Xian; Ed., Shaanxi People's Publishing House 1975–; Chief Ed. magazine Mei Wen (Beautiful Essays); mem. Writers' Asscn 1979–; Prize for Nat. Literature (3 times), Pegasus Prize for Literature. *Publications:* more than 60 works; including novels Turbulence, The Corrupt and Waning, White Night; short stories and essays; works have been translated in many languages. *Leisure interest:* painting, collecting antiques. *Address:* No. 2 Lian Hu Xiang, Xian City, Shaanxi, People's Republic of China.

JIA QINGLIN; Chinese engineer and government official; b. 1940, Jiaohe Co., Hebei Prov.; ed Hebei Coll. of Eng; joined CCP 1959; Deputy Sec. Fujian Prov. CCP Cttee 1985–93, Sec. 1993–; Gov. of Fujian Prov. 1991–94; Mayor of Beijing 1997–99; Chair. Standing Cttee Fujian Provincial 8th People's Congress 1994–; mem. 14th CCP Cen. Cttee 1992–97, 15th CCP Cen. Cttee 1997–2002; mem. Standing Cttee CCP Politburo 2002–; Sec. CCP Beijing Municipal Cttee 1997–; mem. CCP Politburo 1997–. *Address:* Standing Committee, CCP Politburo, Quanguo Renmin Diabiao Dahui, Zhongguo Gongchan Dang, 1 Zhongnanhai, Beijing, People's Republic of China.

JIA ZHIJIE; Chinese party and government official; b. 1935, Fuyu Co., Jilin Prov.; ed USSR; joined CCP 1960; Dir Lanzhou Petrochemical Machinery Plant; Deputy Sec. Plant CCP Cttee; Deputy Sec. Gansu Prov. CCP Cttee 1983–92; Gov. Gansu Prov. 1986–92; Gov. of Hubei Prov. 1992–94; Sec. CCP Cttee Hubei Prov. 1994–2001; Sec.-in-Chief Hubei Mil. District CCP Cttee 1994–; alt. mem. CCP 13th Cen. Cttee 1987–92; mem. 14th CCP Cen. Cttee 1992–97, 15th CCP Cen. Cttee 1997–2002. *Address:* Office of Provincial Governor, 1 Beihuan Road, Wuhan, Hubei Province, People's Republic of China. *Telephone:* (27) 87814585. *Fax:* (27) 87816148.

JIAGGE, Annie Ruth, LLD; Ghanaian fmr judge and voluntary worker; b. 7 Oct. 1918, Lomé, Togo; d. of the late Rev. R. D. Baëta and Henrietta L. Baëta; m. F. K. A. Jiagge 1953; ed Achimota Training Coll., London School of Econs, Lincoln's Inn; Headmistress of Keta Presbyterian Sr Girls' School for 5 years; admitted to bar, Ghana 1950, practised law 1950–55; Dist Magistrate 1955–57, Sr Magistrate 1957–59; Judge, Circuit Court 1959–61, High Court 1961–69, Court of Appeal 1969–83 (Pres. 1980–83); Ghanaian Rep. on UN Comm. on the Status of Women 1962–72, Chair. 1968; author of basic draft of 1968 UN Declaration on Elimination of Discrimination against Women; Chair. Comm. on Investigation of Assets 1966, Ghana Council on Women and Devt 1975–80; Moderator WCC Programme to Combat Racism 1984–91; Pres. Cttee of Churches' Participation in Devt 1985–93; mem. Court, Univ. of Legon 1968–; fmr Pres. Y.W.C.A. of Ghana, mem. Exec. Cttee for 12 years and fmr Vice-Pres. of World Y.W.C.A.; mem. Presidium World Council of Churches 1975–83; mem. Int. Advisory Bd, Noel Foundation 1990–; mem. Cttee of Experts to prepare the draft of the 1992 Constitution of Ghana; mem. Pres.'s Transitional Cttee 1993; mem. Council of State 1993; Hon LLD (Legon) 1974; Gimbles' Int. Award for Humanitarian Work 1969, Ghana Grand Medal 1969. *Leisure interests:* music, gardening, crafts. *Address:* 8 Onyasia Crescent, Roman Ridge, P.O. Box 5511, Accra North, Ghana. *Telephone:* (21) 772046.

JIANG, Li-Jin, PhD; Chinese organic chemist and academician; b. 15 April 1919, Beijing; d. of Jiong-Shang Jiang and Shu-Duan Li; m. Guo-Zhi Xu 1954; two s.; ed Univ. of Minnesota, USA; Prof. and Sr Research Fellow, Inst. Photographic Chem., Acad. Sinica 1978–; mem. Standing Cttee 6th CPPCC 1983–87, 7th CPPCC 1988–92, 8th CPPCC 1993–97; mem. Standing Cttee of Chem. Div., Acad. Sinica 1981–93, Academician Acad. Sinica 1994–. *Publications:* The Chemistry and Phototherapeutic Mechanism of Hypocrellins (Second Prize, Natural Science Award, Acad. Sinica 1990), The Relationship between the Structures of the Phycobiliproteins and the Evolution of the Algal Species, The Study of the Mechanism of Energy Transfer (Second Prize, Natural Science Award, Acad. Sinica 1993), The Photochemical, Photophysical and Photodynamical Actions of the Naturally Occurring Perylenohydroxylquinones (Second Prize, Natural Science Award, Acad. Sinica 1996). *Leisure interests:* tennis, travelling. *Address:* Institute of Photographic Chemistry, Academia Sinica, Bei Sha Tan, De Wai, Beijing 100101 (Office); Apartment 804, Building 812, Huang Zhuang, Haidian Qu, Beijing 100080, People's Republic of China (Home). *Telephone:* (10) 64888068 (Office); (10) 62569291 (Home). *Fax:* (10) 62029375.

JIANG BAOLIN; Chinese artist; b. 20 Jan. 1942, Penglai Co., Shandong Prov.; s. of the late Jiang Chunfu and Dai Shuzhi; m. Ling Yunhua 1970; one s. one d.; ed Dept of Traditional Chinese Painting, Inst. of Fine Arts, Zhejiang, Cen. Acad. of Fine Arts, Beijing; worked in Cultural House, Fenghua Co. 1967–79; Dir Zhejiang Artists' Gallery 1982–84; Vice-Pres. Zhejiang Landscape Painting Research Inst. 1982–; mem. Council of Zhejiang Br. of Chinese Painters' Asscn 1984–; mem. Bd Zhejiang Painting Acad. 1984–; Visiting Prof. Beijing Cen. Fine Arts Acad. 1996–; Tutor Acad. of Arts, Qinghua Univ., Beijing, mem. Council, Cui Zifan Art Foundation Int.; Hon. Adviser, Research Bd of Advisers, American Biographical Inst. 1992–; mem. Chinese Artists'

Asscn; numerous exhbns. 1987–, including Contemporary Chinese Paintings in celebration of Hong Kong's return to China, Beijing, Shanghai, Tianjin 1997; Silver Medal, 9th Nat. Art Exhbn 1999. *Paintings include:* Spring in Remote Valley 1972, Pear Blossoms in Spring Rain 1981, He Lan Mountain 1983, Cottages in Si Ming 1983, Autumn Jubilation in She Village, Mountains and Rocks in Home Village, Rainy Season, Autumn Flavour 1984, Grapes 1986, Moonlight, Hurricane, Bumper Harvest 1987, Spring Wind Again 1999. *One-man exhibitions:* Beijing 1987, Taipei, Taiwan 1987, Gaoxiong, Taiwan 1989, Bonn 1991, Paris 1991, Hong Kong 1994, Seoul, Korea 1996, Beijing, Hangzhou, Qinan, Yantai 1999, Johnson, Vt, USA 1999. *Group exhibitions:* Chinese Ink-Wash Paintings, Beijing 1988 (Prize for outstanding works), Selected Chinese Ink-Wash Paintings, Hong Kong 1989, Monte Carlo 1992 (Prince's Prize), Shenzhen 1992, 8th Nat. Art Exhbn (mem. Adjudicators' Cttee), Nat. Symposium of City Landscape, Shenzheng 1995, 9th Nat. Art Exhbn 1999; 72 paintings in collection Asian Art Gallery, Seoul, Korea. *Publications:* Collections of Jiang Baolin's Paintings 1984, Jiang Baolin's ink-wash paintings 1989, Signatur Objekt 15, Jiang Baolin 1991, Jiang Baolin's Paintings (Publ in France) 1991, A selection of Jiang Baolin's Bird and Flower Paintings 1992, The World of Jiang Baolin's Ink & Wash Painting 1994, The Art World of Jiang Baolin (Publ in Korea) 1996, Series on Modern Chinese Artists 2000. *Leisure interests:* Beijing Opera, literature, music, gardening. *Address:* 201 Building 11, 2nd District, Nandu Huayuan Wenyi Road, Hangzhou, People's Republic of China. *Telephone:* (571) 8850096. *Fax:* (571) 8850096.

JIANG, Boju; Chinese mathematician; b. 4 Sept. 1937, Tianjin City; m. Chuanrong Xu 1968; two d.; ed Peking Univ.; Assoc. Prof. Math. Peking Univ. 1978–82, Prof. 1983–, Dean School of Math. Sciences 1995–98; mem. Chinese Acad. of Sciences 1980; Fellow, Third World Acad. of Sciences 1985; HLHL Math. Prize 1996, Nat. Scientific Award of China 1982, 1987, S. S. Chern Mathematics Award 1988, L. K. Hua Math. Award 2002. *Address:* Department of Mathematics, Peking University, Haidian Road, Beijing 100871, People's Republic of China. *Telephone:* (10) 62751804. *Fax:* (10) 62751801.

JIANG CHUNYUN; Chinese party official; b. April 1930, Laixi Co., Shandong Prov.; ed Teachers Training Coll., Laixi Co.; fmr primary school teacher; Clerk of CCP Maren District Cttee, Sec., CCP Laixi Co. Cttee 1946–49; joined Chinese Communist Party (CCP) 1947; Dir of Gen. Office Laixi Co. CCP Cttee 1949–57; Deputy Section Chief Qingdao br., China Export Corpn for Local Products 1957–60; with Foreign Trade Bureau, Qingdao City 1957–60; Instructor and Chief Insp. and Deputy Dir of Gen. Office, Propaganda Dept Shandong Prov. CCP Cttee 1960–66; manual work in village in Huimin Co. during Cultural Revolution, sent to cadre school, Qihe Co. 1969; worked under Revolutionary Cttee Shandong Prov. 1970–75; Deputy Dir, Gen. Office Shandong Prov. CCP Cttee 1975–77, Deputy Sec.-Gen., then Sec.-Gen. 1977–83, Deputy Sec. 1983–84; Sec. Ji'nan Municipal CCP Cttee 1984–87; Acting Gov. Shandong Prov. 1987–88, Gov. 1988–89; Pres. Shandong Prov. Party School 1989–92; First Sec. Shandong Mil. Dist CCP Cttee 1989–94; Vice-Premier of State Council (in charge of agricultural work) 1995–; mem. CCP Politburo 1992–, CCP Cen. Cttee Secr. 1994–98; Head State Flood-Control and Drought Relief HQ; mem. 13th CCP Cen. Cttee, 14th CCP Cen. Cttee, 15th CCP Cen. Cttee 1997–2002; Vice-Chair. Standing Cttee of 9th NPC 1998–; Pres. of China Family Planning Asscn 1998–; Prof. (part time) Shandong Univ.; Hon. Prof. China Agric.Univ. *Address:* Standing Committee of National People's Congress, Beijing, People's Republic of China.

JIANG ENZHU; Chinese diplomatist; b. 14 Dec. 1938, Jiangsu Prov.; s. of Jiang Guohua and Yu Wen Guizhen; m. Zhu Manli; one s.; ed Beijing Foreign Languages Univ.; entered Ministry of Foreign Affairs as translator 1964; Attaché, Third and Second Sec. London during 1970s; Deputy Dir-Gen., then Dir-Gen. Dept of West European Affairs, Ministry of Foreign Affairs 1984–90, Asst Foreign Minister 1990–91, Vice-Minister 1991–95; Chief Negotiator for People's Repub. of China in Sino-British talks over future of Hong Kong; Deputy Head Preliminary Working Cttee of Preparatory Cttee of Hong Kong Special Admin Region; Amb. to UK 1995–97; Dir Hong Kong br. Xinhua News Agency 1997–99; mem. 15th CCP Cen. Cttee 1997–; mem. Standing Cttee 9th Nat. People's Congress 1998–; Dir (Minister) Liaison Office of People's Republic of China to Hong Kong Special Administrative Region 2000–. *Address:* Liaison Office of the Central People's Government, 160 Connaught Road West, Hong Kong Special Administrative Region, People's Republic of China.

JIANG FUTANG, Lt-Gen.; Chinese army officer; b. Oct. 1941, Rongcheng Co., Shandong Prov.; ed PLA Political Acad.; joined PLA 1959; joined CCP 1960; Vice-Divisional Political Commissar; Dir Army Political Dept 1980; Army Political Commissar 1980; Dir Political Dept of PLA Ji'nan Mil. Area Command; Vice-Political Commissar and Dir Political Dept of PLA Chengdu Mil. Area Command 1985–95; Commissar PLA Shenyang Mil. Area Command 1995–; rank of Maj.-Gen. 1988, Lt-Gen. 1993–; mem. 15th Cen. Cttee 1997–. *Address:* PLA Shenyang Military Area Command, Shenyang City, Liaoning Province, People's Republic of China.

JIANG MINKUAN; Chinese party and state official; b. 1930, Suzhou City, Jiangsu Prov.; ed Shanghai Polytechnic School; joined CCP 1961; fmr technician, workshop Dir, factory Dir and chief engineer, Southwest China Aluminium Processing Factory 1966–79; Deputy Sec. CCP Cttee, Sichuan Prov. 1982–85; Vice-Gov., Sichuan 1983–85, Gov. 1985–88; Vice-Chair. State Science and Tech. Comm. 1988–90; mem. 12th CCP Cen. Cttee 1985, 13th

CCP Cen. Cttee 1987–92; mem. 14th Cen. Cttee CCP 1992–97, 15th Cen. Cttee; Dir State Patent Bureau 1988–89; Deputy Dir United Front Work Dept, CCP Cen. Cttee 1990–95, Exec. Deputy Head 1995–98; Vice-Pres. China Asscn of Inventions 1991–; Vice-Chair. 7th Exec. Cttee All China Fed. of Industry and Commerce 1993, China Chamber of Commerce 1993–; mem. Standing Cttee 7th to 9th CPPCC Nat. Cttees. 1988–; Vice-Chair. Science, Educational Culture, Public Health and Physical Culture Cttee, 9th Nat. Cttee of CPPCC 1998–. *Address:* c/o National Committee of Chinese People's Political Consultative Conference, 23 Taipingqiao Street, Beijing, People's Republic of China.

JIANG WEN; Chinese actor and film director; b. 1963, Tangshan, Hebei Prov.; ed Cen. Acad. of Drama; joined China Youth Arts Theatre 1984; now actor at Cen. Acad. of Drama; acted in Furong Town, Red Sorghum, directed The Days of Splendid Sunshine, Devils on the Doorstep 2000. *Address:* Central Academy of Drama, Beijing, People's Republic of China.

JIANG XI; Chinese government official; b. (Qing Jong), Jan. 1923, Shanghai; fmr Vice-Minister of Commerce; Pres. China Gen. Commercial 1994–, World Asscn of Chinese Cuisine. *Address:* c/o Ministry of Commerce, 45 Fuxingmennei Street, Beijing 100801, People's Republic of China. *Telephone:* (10) 66094602 (Office); (10) 63467719 (Home). *Fax:* (10) 66062700 (Office). *E-mail:* www.ccas.com.ch (Office).

JIANG XINXIONG; Chinese party and government official; b. 6 July 1931; ed Nankai Univ., Tianjin; joined CCP 1956; Dir nuclear fuel plant 1979–82; Vice-Minister of Nuclear Industry 1982–83, Minister 1983; Chair. Bd of Dirs., China Isotopes Co. 1983–98; Pres. Nat. Nuclear Corpn 1988–98; Chair. China Atomic Energy Authority 1994–99; Deputy Head Leading Group for Nuclear Power Plants; Vice-Chair Finance and Econ. Cttee of 9th NPC 1998–; Pres. China-Canada Friendship Asscn of NPC 1998–; alt. mem. 12th CCP Cen. Cttee 1982, 13th CCP Cen. Cttee 1985–92, 14th CCP Cen. Cttee 1992–97. *Address:* c/o Standing Committee of National People's Congress, Beijing, People's Republic of China. *Telephone:* (10) 68533923.

JIANG ZEMIN; Chinese government official and fmr head of state; b. 17 Aug. 1926, Yangzhou City, Jiangsu Prov.; ed Jiaotong Univ., Shanghai; joined CCP 1946; worked in Shanghai Yimin No. 1 Foodstuffs Factory, Shanghai Soap Factory, First Ministry of Machine-Bldg Industry; trainee, Stalin Automobile Plant, Moscow, USSR 1955–56; Deputy Chief Power Div., Deputy Chief Power-Engineer, Dir, Power Plant, Changchun No. 1 Auto Works 1957–62; Deputy Dir Shanghai Electric Equipment Research Inst., Dir and Acting Party Sec. Wuhan Thermo-Tech. Machinery Research Inst., Deputy Dir, Dir Foreign Affairs Bureau of First Ministry of Machine-Bldg Industry 1962–80; Vice-Chair. and Sec.-Gen. State Comm. on Admin. of Imports and Exports and State Comm. on Admin. of Foreign Investment 1980–82; First Vice-Minister Electronics Industry 1982–83, Minister 1983–85; Mayor of Shanghai 1985–88; Deputy Sec., Sec. Shanghai Municipal Party Cttee 1985–89; mem. 12th Nat. Congress CCP Cen. Cttee 1982, Politburo 1st Plenary Session of 13th Cen. Cttee 1987, Gen. Sec. 4th Plenary Session 1989, Chair. Mil. Cttee 5th Plenary Session 1989; mem. Standing Cttee Politburo, Gen. Sec. and Chair. Mil. Cttee 14th and 15th CCP Cen. Cttees 1992–2002; Chair. Cen. Mil. Comm. 1990–; Pres. People's Repub. of China 1993–2003; Hon. Chair. Red Cross Soc. of China; Hon. Pres. Software Industry Asscn. *Address:* Chinese Communist Party, Zhongguo Gongchan Dang, 1 Zhongnanhai, Beijing, People's Republic of China.

JIANG ZHENGHUA; Chinese politician; b. Oct. 1937, Hangzhou City, Zhejiang Prov.; ed Xian Jiaotong Univ., Int. Population Science Coll., Bombay, India 1982; Vice-Minister State Family Planning Comm. 1991–; joined Chinese Peasants' and Workers' Democratic Party 1992; Vice-Chair. Chinese Peasants' and Workers' Democratic Party 1992, Chair. 1997–; mem. Standing Cttee 8th CPPCC 1993–98; Vice-Chair. Standing Cttee of 9th NPC 1998–; now Prof. of Systems Eng, Econometrics and Demography; Outstanding Expert at Nat. Level of China 1985, Nat. Advanced Worker of China 1989, First Class Nat. Science and Tech. Progress Prize 1987. *Publications:* Economic Development Planning Models 1981, Country Report on Population of China 1997, Sustainable Development of China 1999. *Address:* Standing Committee of National People's Congress, Beijing 100805, (Office); 11 Min Zu Yuan Road, Room 601, Beijing 100029, People's Republic of China (Home). *Telephone:* (10) 63091615 (Office); (10) 62357120 (Home). *Fax:* (10) 63091614 (Office). *E-mail:* jenjenny@sina.com (Office).

JIANG ZHUPING; Chinese engineer and administrator; b. 1937, Yixing Co., Jiangsu Prov.; ed Faculty of Missile Eng, Harbin Mil. Eng Inst.; joined CCP 1960; with Design Inst. of Ministry of Nat. Defence 1963–65; Deputy Dir Design Inst. of Nanchang Aircraft. Mfg Plant 1978–82, Deputy Sec. plant's Party Cttee 1982–84; Sec. Party Cttee of Depts. under Ministry of Aeronautics Industry 1984–85; Vice-Gov. of Jiangxi Prov. 1985–88; Deputy Sec. CCP Jiangxi Prov. Cttee 1988–95; Gov. of Hubei Prov. 1995–2001; Sec. CCP Hubei Prov. Cttee 2001; Vice-Chair. NPC Educ., Science, Culture and Health Cttee 2001–; mem. 14th CCP Cen. Cttee 1992–97, 15th CCP Cen. Cttee 1997–; Deputy Dir Civil Aviation Gen. Admin. of China 1991–95. *Address:* National People's Congress, Tiananmen, Beijing, People's Republic of China.

JIANG ZILONG; Chinese writer; b. 2 June 1941, Cang Xian, Hebei; s. of Jiang Junsan and Wei Huanzhang; m. Zhang Qinglian 1968; one s. one d.; worker Tianjin Heavy Machinery Plant 1958; navy conscript 1960–65; Vice-Chair. Chinese Writers' Asscn 1996–; Nat. Short Story Prize 1979. *Pub-*

lications: A New Station Master 1965, One Day for the Chief of the Bureau of Electromechanics 1976, Manager Qiao Assumes Office 1979, Developer 1980, Diary of a Plant Secretary 1980, All the Colours of the Rainbow 1983, Yan-Zhao Dirge 1985, Serpent Deity 1986, Jiang Zi Long Works Collection (8 Vols) 1996, Human Vigour 2000, Ren Qi 2000, Empty Hole 2001. *Leisure interests:* swimming, Beijing opera. *Address:* No. 7 Dali Road, Heping District, Tianjin (Home); Tianjin Writers' Association, Tianjin, People's Republic of China. *Telephone:* (22) 23304153 (Office); (22) 23306250 (Home). *Fax:* (22) 23304159 (Office); (22) 23306250 (Home). *E-mail:* jzltj@hotmail.com (Home).

JIČINSKÝ, Zdeněk, DJur; Czech politician, university professor and jurist; b. 26 Feb. 1929, Ostřešany; m. Nada Jičínská 1961; two s.; ed Charles Univ., Prague; mem. Czech. CP 1951–69; on staff of Inst. of Social Sciences, Cen. Cttee of Czech. CP 1954–60; Prof., Law Faculty, Charles Univ. 1964–70; mem. Scientific Law Council, Charles Univ. 1962–69; mem. Legal Comm., Cen. Cttee of Czech. CP 1964; mem. Expert Comm. of Govt Cttee for Constitutional Regulation of Repub. 1968; Deputy Chair. Czech. Nat. Council 1968; mem. Chamber of Nations, Fed. Ass. of CSSR 1969; forced to leave public life and university 1969; lawyer in insurance co. 1969–77; signed Charter 77; Rep. Civic Forum 1989; Deputy Chair. Fed. Ass. 1989–90, First Deputy Chair. 1990–92; Deputy and mem. Presidium Fed. Ass. 1992–; mem. Civic Movt 1991–92; mem. Czechoslovak Social Democratic Party 1992–; mem. Parl. 1996–2002, Deputy Chair., Parl. Constitutional Juridical Cttee 1996–2002; mem. Standing Del. to Interparl. Union 1996–98; political commentator, Právo newspaper (fmrly Rudé Právo) 1992–. *Publications:* Political Ideology of the First Czechoslovak Republic 1961, On the Development of Thinking in Czechoslovakia in the Sixties 1991, Developments in Czechoslovak Parliament since November 1989 1993, The Extinction of Czechoslovakia in 1992 from a Constitutional Viewpoint 1993, Problems of Czech Politics 1994, Charter 77 and Society Governed by the Law 1995, Constitutional and Political Problems of the Czech Republic 1995; numerous works on politics, theory of state and law and institutional law. *Address:* Pařížská 12, 110 00 Prague 1, Czech Republic (Home). *Telephone:* (2) 2312560 (Home).

JIMENEZ, Menardo R., B.SC.(COM); Philippine business executive; b. 6 Dec. 1932, Manila; s. of late Marcelo A. Jimenez and Emiliana Rodriguez-Jimenez; m. Carolina L. Gozon 1962; two s. two d.; ed Far Eastern Univ., qualified as certified accountant; worked for Abaca Corpn of Philippines (Abacorp) 1956–70; Pres. and CEO Repub. Broadcasting Inc. (GMA-7); Chair. MA Jimenez Enterprises Inc., Majalco Finance & Investment Corpn, Cable Entertainment Corpn; Pres. Albay-Agro Industrial Devt Corpn, Justitia Realty & Devt Corpn, GMA Marketing & Productions Inc.; Dir many cos.; Chair. and Trustee Kapwa Ko Mahal Ko Foundation; Chair. Bd Philippine Constitution Asscn; Chair. Prison Fellowship Philippines Inc.; Gov. Philippine Nat. Red Cross; Dir Philippine Chamber of Commerce and Industry; Dir or Trustee many other bodies. *Leisure interest:* stamp collection. *Address:* Republic Broadcasting System Inc., 2nd Floor, Sagittarius Bldg, H.V. dela Costa Street, Salcedo Village, Makati City, 1200, Philippines. *Telephone:* 8163883; 8122922. *Fax:* 8133223; 8163042.

JIMÉNEZ-BELTRÁN, Domingo; Spanish environmental executive; b. 2 April 1944, Zaragoza; s. of Mariano Jiménez and María Gloria Beltrán; m. Elin Solem; one c.; ed High Tech. School of Industrial Engineers and Polytechnic Univ. Madrid; lecturer, Polytechnic Univ. Madrid 1978–86; Exec. Adviser to Minister for Public Works and Planning 1983–85; Deputy Dir-Gen. for Int. and EU Relations and with Ministry of Public Works and Urban Planning 1985–86; Attaché for Environment and Public Works, Perm. Mission to EU, Brussels 1986–87; Head of Div. Health, Physical Safety and Quality, Consumers Policy Service, European Comm. 1987–91; Dir-Gen. for Environmental Policy, Sec. of State for Environment and Housing, Ministry of Public Works, Transport and Environment 1991–94; Exec. Dir European Environment Agency, Copenhagen 1994–2002. *Publications:* author and ed. of various Publs and articles. *Address:* c/o European Environment Agency, Kongens Nytorv 6, 1050 Copenhagen K, Denmark.

JIN CHONGJI; Chinese historian; b. 13 Dec. 1930, Qingpu, Jiangsu Prov.; ed Fudan Univ.; joined CCP 1948; lecturer, admin., Fudan Univ. 1951–65; researcher, Ministry of Culture 1965–73; Deputy Chief Ed., Chief Ed. Cultural Relics Press 1973–81; researcher, Assoc. Exec. Dir, Exec. Dir CCP Cen. Cttee Historical Documents Research Office 1981–; Vice-Dir Cultural and Historical Documents Cttee, CPPCC; Chair. All-China Asscn of Historians. *Publications:* Xinhai Geming de Qian Qian Hou Hou (A History of the 1911 Revolution), Sun Zhongshan he Xinhai Geming (Sun Yat-sen and the 1911 Revolution), Biography of Zhou En-lai (1898–1976), Biography of Mao Zedong (1893–1949). *Leisure interest:* reading books. *Address:* Historical Documents Research Office of Chinese Communist Party Central Committee, 1 Maojiawan, Xisi Bei Qian, Beijing 100017 (Office); Wanshoulu Jia-15, 7th Zone, 4th Building, 101th Room, Beijing 100036, People's Republic of China (Home). *Telephone:* (10) 63095701 (Office); (10) 68218172 (Home). *Fax:* (10) 63094431 (Office).

JIN LUXIAN, Rt Rev Louis; Chinese Catholic bishop; b. 20 June 1916, Shanghai; s. of Luc Jin and Lucy Chang; ed Xuhui seminary in Shanghai, seminaries in France and Rome; Bishop, Shanghai Diocese 1984–; Dir Sheshan Catholic Seminary in Shanghai 1985–; mem. Standing Cttee CPPCC 8th Nat. Cttee 1993. *Leisure interest:* collecting stamps. *Address:* Sheshan

Catholic Seminary, Shanghai; Bishop's Residence, 158 Pu Xi Road, Shanghai 200030, People's Republic of China. *Telephone:* (21) 64398913. *Fax:* (21) 64398913.

JIN NYUM; South Korean politician; b. 1940; ed Coll. of Commerce, Seoul Nat. Univ., Washington Univ., Stanford Univ.; with Econ. Planning Bd (EPB); fmr Minister of Labour; fmr Minister of Energy and Resources, of Maritime Affairs and Fisheries; Deputy Prime Minister for Finance and the Economy 2000–02 (resgnd). *Address:* c/o Ministry of Finance and Economy, 1 Jungang-dong, Gwacheon City, Gyeonggi Province, Republic of Korea (Office).

JIN RENQING; Chinese politician; b. July 1944, Suzhou, Jiangsu Prov.; ed Cen. Inst. of Finance and Banking; joined CCP 1973; Vice-Minister of Finance; Vice-Mayor of Beijing; Vice-Sec. CCP Beijing Municipal Cttee 1991–98; Dir State Tax Bureau 1998–2003; alt. mem. CCP 15th Cen. Cttee 1997–2002, mem. CCP 16th Cen. Cttee 2002–; Minister of Finance 2003–. *Address:* Ministry of Finance, 3 Nansangxiang, Sanlihe, Xicheng Qu, Beijing 100820, People's Republic of China. *Telephone:* (10) 68551888. *Fax:* (10) 68533635. *E-mail:* webmaster@mof.gov.cn. *Website:* www.mof.gov.cn.

JIN SHANGYI; Chinese artist; b. 1934, Jiaozuo City, Henan Prov.; ed Cen. Fine Arts Acad., Beijing; known as the forerunner of classicism in Chinese Art; Pres. Cen. Inst. of Fine Arts 1987–; Chair. Chinese Artists' Asscn; Vice-Chair. China Fed. of Literary and Art Circles 2001. *Works include:* Mao Zedong Leads the Red Army on the Long March 1964, A Maiden 1981, A Tajik Girl 1983. *Address:* Central Institute of Fine Arts, 5 Xiaowei Hutong, East District, Beijing 100730, People's Republic of China (Office). *Telephone:* 65254731 (Office).

JIN XIANGWEN; Chinese administrator; b. Oct. 1939, Shanghai; ed Wuhan Surveying and Mapping Inst.; joined CCP 1966; Dir State Bureau of Surveying and Mapping 1988–2000. *Address:* c/o State Bureau of Surveying and Mapping, Beijing, People's Republic of China.

JIN YONG; Chinese writer and newspaper publisher; b. (Cha Liangyong), 1923, Haining, Zhejiang Prov.; ed Dongwu Law School; founder of Ming Bao newspaper in Hong Kong. *Publications:* 14 kung-fu novels.

JIN YONGJIAN; Chinese diplomatist and international official; b. 15 Sept. 1934; s. of Jin Zhiying and Bo Canzhang; m. Wang Youping 1955; two s.; ed Beijing Univ. of Foreign Studies; officer People's Inst. of Foreign Affairs of China 1954–63; Attaché Embassy, Nairobi 1964–67; officer African Dept Ministry of Foreign Affairs, Beijing 1967–71, Deputy Dir-Gen., Dir-Gen. 1984–88, Dir-Gen. Dept of Int. Orgs. and Conferences 1988–90; Third Sec., Second Sec. Embassy, Lagos 1971–76; Second Sec., First Sec., Counsellor Perm. Mission to UN, NY, Alt. Rep. to UN Security Council, Rep. to Security Council Special Cttee on Decolonization, UN Council for Namibia 1977–84, Deputy Perm. Rep., Amb. to UN, Deputy Rep. to Security Council 1990–92; Amb., Perm. Rep. to UN, Geneva, also accred to other int. orgs. in Switzerland 1992–96; Under-Sec.-Gen. for Devt Support and Man. Services, UN 1996–97, for Gen. Ass. Affairs and Conf. Services 1997–. *Leisure interests:* walking, Chinese chess, bridge. *Address:* United Nations Headquarters, Room S-2963-A, New York, NY 10017 (Office); 8 Peter Cooper Road, Apartment 8H, New York, NY 10010, USA (Home). *Telephone:* (212) 963-8362. *Fax:* (212) 963-8196. *E-mail:* jin@un.org (Office).

JING SHUPING; Chinese industrialist; b. 1918, Shangyu Co., Zheijiang Prov.; ed St John's Univ., Shanghai; Deputy Man. Xinzhong Factory, Shanghai 1940–42; Man. Changxing Trade Co. 1943–50; Deputy Sec.-Gen. Fed. of Industry and Commerce 1963; mem. Bd of Dirs. China Int. Trust and Investment Corpn (CITIC) 1979, Vice-Pres. 1984–89, Exec. Dir, Chair. Bd Dirs. 1988–; Chair. Bd Dirs. China Minsheng Banking Corpn 1993–; Pres. China Int. Econ. Consultants Inc. 1981–; Vice-Chair. Exec. Cttee of All-China Fed. of Industry and Commerce 1988–93, Chair. 1993–; mem. Standing Cttee 6th NPC 1986; Deputy Sec.-Gen. 8th Nat. Cttee of CPPCC 1993–98; Vice-Chair. 9th Nat. Cttee of CPPCC 1998–; mem. NPC Preliminary Working Cttee of Preparatory Cttee of Hong Kong Special Admin. Region 1993–97; Vice-Chair. Asscn for Relations Across the Taiwan Straits 1991–; Vice-Pres. Taiwan Studies Soc. 1988–. *Address:* China International Trust and Investment Corporation (CITIC), Beijing, People's Republic of China.

JIRICNA, Eva Magdalena, CBE, RIBA, RA; British architect; b. 3 March 1939, Zlin, Czechoslovakia; d. of late Josef Jiricny and of Eva Jiricna; ed Univ. of Prague, Prague Acad. of Fine Arts; worked with the GLC's School Div. 1968; Louis de Soissons Partnership 1969–78, Project Architect; went into practice with David Hodges 1978; team leader at Richard Rogers Partnership 1982–84; formed her own practice 1984, re-formed as Eva Jiricna Architects 1986–; External Examiner for RCA and the Schools of Architecture at Leicester, Sheffield, Oxford, Bath, Humberside and Plymouth Univs. and for RIBA; Hon. Fellow Royal Coll. of Art 1990; R.D.I. 1991; Hon. Fellow Royal Inc. of Architects in Scotland 1996; mem. American Hall of Fame 1998; lectures worldwide; Hon. DTech (Southampton, Brno Czech Repub.) 2000, Hon. DLitt (Sheffield) 2000; Design Prize, RA 1994. *Major commissions include:* the Gehry Bldg, Prague, the new Orangery, Prague, Canada Water bus station, London, Faith Zone, Millennium Dome 1999, Amec PLC HQ, London, Devt of masterplan for Vic. and Albert Museum, London. *Television:* Tales from Prague, BBC2, Architecture of the Imagination: Staircases, BBC2 1990, The Late Show – Czech Modernism 1994, Wideworld, Anglia TV 1997, The Dome: Trouble at the Big Top, BBC2 1999. *Publications:* Eva Jiricna: Design in Exile, The Joseph Shops: Eva Jiricna, Staircases. *Address:* Eva Jiricna Architects,

Third Floor, 38 Warren Street, London, W1T 6AE, England (Office). *Telephone:* (20) 7554-2400 (Office). *Fax:* (20) 7388-8022 (Office). *E-mail:* mail@ejal .com (Office). *Website:* www.ejal.com (Office).

JISCHKE, Martin C., PhD; American administrator; b. 7 Aug. 1941, Chicago, Ill.; m. Patricia Fowler Jischke; one s. one d.; ed Ill. Tech. Inst. Chicago, Ill., MIT Cambridge; Asst to Transportation Sec. US Transportation Dept 1975–76; Dir, Prof. School of Aerospace, Mechanical & Nuclear Eng 1977–81; Dean Eng Coll. Okla Univ. 1981–86, Acting Pres. 1985; Chancellor Mo.-Rolla Univ. 1986–91; Pres. Iowa State Univ. 1991–2000, Purdue Univ. 2000–; Pres. Asscn of Big Twelve Univs. 1994–; mem. Bd of Dirs Bankers Trust 1995–, American Council on Educ. 1996–, Nat. Merit Scholarship Corpn 1997–; Founding Pres. Global Consortium of Higher Educ. and Research for Agric. 1999; numerous awards. *Publications:* articles in specialist journals. *Leisure interests:* golf, reading, travel. *Address:* Office of the President, Purdue University, West Lafayette, IN 47907 (Office); 500 McCormick Road, West Lafayette, IN 47906, USA (Home).

JO MYONG ROK, Vice Marshal; North Korean politician; b. 1924, Manchuria; ed Mangyougdae Revolutionary School; Commdr Korean Air Force 1977–95; mem. Worker's Party of Korea Cen. Mil. Cttee 1980–, Chief of Gen. Political Bureau, Korean People's Army 1995–, First Vice Chair. Nat. Defence Cttee 1998–, del. to Russia 1994, to Cuba 1994, 1997, to Pakistan 1995, to Syria 1998, to People's Repub. of China 2000, Special Envoy to USA Oct. 2000. *Address:* National Defence Cttee, Pyongyang, Democratic People's Republic of Korea (Office).

JOBS, Steven Paul; American business executive; b. 1955; adopted s. of Paul J. and Clara J. Jobs; m. Laurene Powell 1991; ed Reed Coll.; with Hewlett-Packard, Palo Alto, Calif.; designer, video games, Atari Inc. 1974; Chair. of Bd Apple Computer Inc., Cupertino, Calif. 1975–85, Consultant 1997–; Interim CEO 1997–; Pres. NeXT Inc., Calif. 1985–96; Chair., CEO Pixar Animation Studios 1986–; co-designer (with Stephan Wozniak), Apple I Computer 1976; Nat. Medal of Tech. *Address:* Pixar Animation Studios, 1200 Park Avenue, Emeryville, CA 94608-3677, USA.

JODICE, Mimmo; Italian photographer and professor of fine arts; b. 29 March 1934, Naples; m. Angela Jodice; two s. one d.; Prof. Acad. of Fine Arts, Naples 1970–96; first photographic exhibition in Milan (with text of Cesare Zavattini) 1970; exhibited in many major museums including San Francisco Museum of Art, Philadelphia Museum of Art, Museo di Capodimonte, Cleveland Museum of Art, Castello di Rivoli, Turin 1970–. *Exhibitions include:* La Città Invisibile, Castel Sant'Elmo, Naples 1990, Mediterraneo, Philadelphia Museum of Art (USA) 1995, Eden, Palazzo Ducale, Mantova 1998, Paris, Maison Europeenne de la Photographie (France) 1998, Anni '70, Galleria Arte Moderna, Modena 2000, Boston, Mass. Coll. of Art, Boston (USA) 2001. *Publications include:* La Città Invisibile 1990, Mediterranean 1995, Paris 1998, Eden 1998, Isolario Mediterraneo 2000, Anni Settanta 2000, Boston 2001, Mare 2003. *Leisure interest:* classical music. *Address:* Baudoin Lebon Gallery, 38 rue St Croix de la Bretonnerie, 75004 Paris, France (Office); Salita Casale 24, 80123 Naples, Italy (Office). *Telephone:* (081) 2466144 (Office). *Fax:* (081) 2466144 (Office). *E-mail:* mimmo.jodice.@ inwind.it (Office).

JOEL, Billy (William Martin Joel); American pop singer; b. 9 May 1949, Bronx, New York; s. of Howard Joel and Rosalind Nyman; m. Christie Brinkley 1985 (divorced 1994); one d.; popular recording artist 1972–; first tour of USSR by American popular music artist 1987; Summer tour with Elton John (q.v.) 1994, Spring tour with Elton John 1995, Asian and European Tour with Elton John 1998; Dr hc (Berkee Coll. of Music) 1993; recipient of numerous Grammy Awards, American Music Awards Award of Merit 1999, inducted into Rock and Roll Hall of Fame 1999. *Singles include:* Just the Way You Are 1978, Honesty 1979, We Didn't Start the Fire 1989. *Albums include:* Piano Man, Streetlife Serenade, Turnstiles, The Stranger, 52nd Street, Glass Houses 1980, Songs in the Attic, The Nylon Curtain 1982, An Innocent Man, Greatest Hits (Vols I & II) 1985, The Bridge 1986, Live From the Soviet Union (concert) 1987, Storm Front 1989, River of Dreams 1993, 2000 Years: Millennium Concert 2000. *Address:* Maritime Music Inc., 2nd Floor, 280 Elm Street, Southampton, NY 11968, USA.

JOFFE, Josef, PhD; German journalist, editor and international relations scholar; ed Harvard Univ.; Foreign and Editorial Page Dir Suddeutsche Zeitung; fmr Foreign Corresp. Die Zeit newspaper, Ed. and Publr 2000–; Visiting Lecturer Harvard Univ., Princeton Univ., Stanford Univ., Texas A & M Univ., USA; Contrib. The National Interest, Foreign Affairs; Assoc. Olin Inst. for Strategic Studies, Harvard Univ. *Publications include:* The Limited Partnership: Europe, the United States and the Burdens of Alliance 1987, The Great Powers 1998; numerous articles in scholarly journals and chapters in books. *Address:* Die Zeit, Speersort 1, Pressehaus, 20095 Hamburg, Germany (Office). *Telephone:* (40) 32800 (Office). *Fax:* (40) 32711 (Office). *Website:* www .zeit.de (Office).

JOFFE, Roland I. V.; British film director; b. 17 Nov. 1945, London; m. Jane Lapotaire (divorced); one s.; ed Carmel Coll., Berks. and Univ. of Manchester; Prix Italia 1978, Prix de la Presse, Prague 1978, Premio San Fidele 1985. *Films:* The Killing Fields 1984, The Mission 1986, Fat Man and Little Boy 1989, City of Joy 1991, Super Mario Bros (producer only), The Scarlet Letter 1995, Goodbye Lover 1999, Vatel 2000. *Television includes:* Spongers 1978,

No Mama No 1980, United Kingdom 1981, 'Tis Pity She's a Whore 1982, Shadow Makers 1990, The Stars Look Down (series). *Address:* William Morris Agency, 151 S. El Camino Drive, Beverly Hills, CA 90212, USA.

JOHANNS, Michael O., BA, JD; American state official; b. 18 June 1950, Osage, Iowa; s. of John Robert Johanns and Adeline Lucy Johanns (née Royek); m. Constance J. Weiss 1972 (divorced 1985); one s. one d.; m. Stephanie A. Suther 1986; ed St. Mary's Coll., Minn., Creighton Univ.; law clerk Neb. Supreme Court, Lincoln 1974–75; assoc. lawyer, Cronin & Hannon, Neb. 1975–76; partner Nelson Johanns, Lincoln 1976–91; Mayor of Lincoln 1991–98; Gov. of Neb. 1999–; mem. Lancaster County Bd, Lincoln 1983–87, City Council, Lincoln 1989–91, Neb. Bar Asscn. *Leisure interests:* skiing, cycling, reading. *Address:* Office of the Governor, POB 94848, Lincoln, NE 68509-4848, USA (Office).

JÓHANNSSON, Kjartan, CE, PhD; Icelandic politician and diplomatist; b. 19 Dec. 1939, Reykjavik; s. of Jóhann and Astrid Dahl Thorsteinsson; m. Irma Karlsdóttir 1964; one d.; ed Reykjavik Coll., Tech. Univ. of Stockholm, Sweden, Univ. of Stockholm, Illinois Inst. of Tech., Chicago; Consulting Eng in Reykjavik 1966–78; Teacher in Faculty of Eng and Science, later Prof. in Faculty for Econs and Business Admin., Univ. of Iceland 1966–78, 1980–89; Chair. Org. for Support of the Elderly, Hafnarfjördur; mem. Bd of Dir Icelandic Aluminium Co. Ltd 1970–75; Chair. Fisheries Bd of Municipal Trawler Co., Hafnarfjördur 1970–74; mem. Municipal Council, Hafnarfjördur 1974–78; mem. Party Council and Exec. Council, Social Democratic Party 1972–89, Vice-Chair. of Social Democratic Party 1974–80, Chair. 1980–84; mem. Althing (Parl.) 1978–89, Speaker of the Lower House 1988–89; Minister of Fisheries 1978–80, also Minister of Commerce 1979–80; Amb. and Perm. Rep. to UN and other int. orgs Geneva 1989–94; Sec.-Gen. EFTA 1994–2001; mem. staff External Trade Department, Ministry of Foreign Affairs 2002; Amb. to Belgium, Liechtenstein, Luxembourg and Chief of Mission to the EU 2002–. *Address:* Icelandic Mission to the EU, 74 Rue de Trèves, 1040 Brussels, Belgium. *Telephone:* (2) 286-17-00 (Office). *Fax:* (2) 286-17-70 (Office). *E-mail:* kjartan.johannsson@utn.stjr.is.

JOHANSEN, Hans Christian, DrOec; Danish professor of economic history; b. 27 June 1935, Aarhus; s. of Vilhelm Johansen and Clara Andersen; m. Kirstine Madsen 1967; one s. one d.; ed Univ. of Aarhus; Danish Foreign Service 1963–64; Sr Lecturer, Univ. of Aarhus 1964–70; Prof. of Econ. History, Univ. of Odense 1970–; Dir Danish Centre for Demographic Resarch 1998–. *Publications:* books and articles on Danish and int. econ. and social history in the 18th, 19th and 20th centuries. *Address:* Anne Maries Alle 4A, 5250 Odense SV, Denmark. *Telephone:* 66-17-21-05. *E-mail:* hcj@demfo.sdu.dk (Office).

JOHANSEN, John MacLane, MArch; American architect; b. 29 June 1916, New York; s. of John C. and Jean MacLane Johansen; m. 1st Mary Lee Longcope 1945; m. 2nd Beate Forberg 1981; one s. one d.; ed Harvard Coll. and Harvard Grad. School of Design; self-employed architect 1947, est. office in New York 1950, est. firm of Johansen-Bhavnani 1973, pvt. practice, New York 1989–; Pres. Architectural League 1968–70; Prof. Pratt Inst.; Prof. of Architecture at Yale Univ. at various times and has taught for short periods at MIT, Columbia and Harvard Univs. and Univ. of Pa; Architect in Residence, American Acad. in Rome 1975; mem. American Acad. of Arts and Letters; Hon. DFA (Maryland Inst. and Clark Univ.); Brunner Award 1968; Gold Medal, New York Chapter, American Inst. of Architects 1976. *Publications:* An Architecture for the Electronic Age, The Three Imperatives of Architecture, Observations and Deductions, John M. Johnnsen – A Life in the Continuum of Modern Architecture 1995. *Leisure interests:* painting, writing, music, building construction, sport, travel. *Address:* 821 Broadway, New York, NY 10003, USA.

JOHANSEN, Peter, PhD; Danish professor of computer science; b. 29 Jan. 1938, Copenhagen; s. of Paul Johansen and Grethe Johansen (née Smith); m. Jytte Jepsen 1963; one s. two d.; ed Univ. of Copenhagen; Asst Prof. Tech. Univ. 1964–67; mem. Research Staff MIT 1967–69; Asst Prof. of Computer Science, Univ. of Copenhagen 1969–74, Prof. 1974–, Dean of Faculty 1988–90; Visiting Prof. Univ. of Manoa, Hawaii 1977–78; mem. Danish Natural Science Research Council 1981–84, Royal Danish Acad. of Sciences 1984–; Kt First Class Order of Dannebrog. *Publications:* An Algebraic Normal Form for Regular Events 1972, The Generating Function of the Number of Subpatterns 1979, Representing Signals by their Toppoints in Scale Space 1986, Inductive Inference of Ultimately Periodic Sequences 1988, On the Classification of Toppoints in Scale Space 1994, On-line string matching with feedback 1995, Adaptive Pattern Recognition 1997, Branch Points in One-dimensional Gaussian Scale Space 2000, Products of Random Matrices 2002. *Address:* DIKU, Universitetsparken 1, 2100 Copenhagen (Office); Ørnebakken 72, 2840 Holte, Denmark. *Telephone:* 35-32-14-42 (Office); 805302. *E-mail:* peterjo@diku.dk.

JOHANSON, Donald Carl, PhD; American physical anthropologist; b. 28 June 1943, Chicago; s. of Carl Torsten and Sally Eugenia (Johnson) Johanson; m. 1st Chris Boner 1967 (divorced); m. 2nd Susan Whelan 1981 (divorced); one step-s. one step-d.; m. 3rd Lenora Carey 1988; one s.; ed Univ. of Illinois, Univ. of Chicago; mem. Dept of Physical Anthropology, Cleveland Museum of Natural History 1972–81, Curator 1974–81; Adjunct Prof. Case Western Reserve Univ. 1982; Prof. of Anthropology, Stanford Univ. 1983–89, Ariz. State Univ. 1997; host, Nature series, Public Broadcasting Service TV 1982; host-narrator three-part Nova series In Search of Human Origins 1994; Pres.

Inst. of Human Origins, Berkeley 1981–97; Dir Inst. of Human Origins, Tempe, Ariz. 1997–; Fellow, AAAS, Royal Geographical Soc., California Acad. of Sciences; Hon. DSc (John Carroll) 1979, (The College of Wooster) 1985; Fregene Prize 1987, American Book Award 1982, Distinguished Service Award, American Humanist Asscn 1983, Golden Plate American Acad. of Achievement 1976, Professional Achievement Award 1980, Outstanding Achievement Award 1979, Golden Mercury Int. Award 1982, Alumni Achievement Award, Univ. of Ill. 1995, Anthropology in Media Award, American Asscn of Anthropologists 1999. *Television:* The First Family 1981, Lucy in Disguise 1982, In Search of Human Origins 1994. *Publications:* The Beginnings of Humankind (with M. A. Edey) 1981 (American Book Award), Blueprints: Solving the Mystery of Evolution (with M. A. Edey) 1989, Lucy's Child: The Discovery of a Human Ancestor (with James Shreeve) 1989, Journey from the Dawn (with Kevin O'Farrell) 1990, Ancestors: In Search of Human Origins (with L. E. Johanson and Blake Edgar) 1994, From Lucy to Language (with Blake Edgar) 1997, Ecce Homo (ed. with G. Ligabue) 1999, The Skull of Australopithecus afarensis (with W. H. Kimbel and Y. Rak) 2003; many scientific articles, papers and reviews. *Leisure interests:* photography, tennis, fly-fishing, classical music (including opera), golf. *Address:* Institute of Human Origins, Arizona State University, P.O. Box 874101, Tempe, AZ 85287, USA. *Telephone:* (480) 727-6580 (Office). *Fax:* (480) 727-6570. *E-mail:* johanson.iho@asu.edu (Office). *Website:* www.becominghuman.org (Office).

JOHANSSON, (Erik) Lennart Valdemar; Swedish industrialist; b. 3 Oct. 1921, Gothenburg; s. of Waldemar and Alma Johansson (née Nordh); m. Inger Hedberg 1944; two s. one d.; ed Tech. Coll.; Production Engineer AB SKF 1943, Man. of Mfg 1961, Gen. Man. 1966, Deputy Man. Dir 1969, Pres. and Group CEO 1971–95, Chair. 1985–92, Hon. Chair. 1992–; mem. Royal Swedish Acad. of Eng Sciences 1971; DTech. hc (Chalmers Univ. of Tech., Gothenburg) 1979; Hon. DTech (Sarajevo) 1983; King of Sweden's Medal; Commdr Merito della Repub. Italiana, Commdr Royal Order of Vasa, Yugoslav Star Medal with Golden Garland, Das grosse Bundesverdienstkreuz, Kt Commdr's Cross (1st Class), Finnish Order of the Lion, John Ericsson Medal 1986. *Leisure interests:* sailing, swimming. *Address:* Berzeliigatan 11-65, 412 53 Gothenburg, Sweden (Home).

JOHANSSON, Leif; Swedish business executive; b. 30 Aug. 1951, Gothenburg; s. of Lennart Johansson (q.v.) and Inger Johansson; m. Eva Birgitta Fjellman; two s. three d.; ed Ed. Chalmers Univ. of Tech.; joined Electrolux 1978, Chief Exec. 1994; Pres., CEO AB Volvo, Gothenburg 1997–; Dir Confed. of Swedish Enterprise; mem. Royal Swedish Acad. of Eng Sciences. *Address:* AB Volvo, SE-405 08, Göteborg, Sweden (Office). *Telephone:* (31) 66-00-90 (Office). *Fax:* (31) 54-33-72 (Office). *E-mail:* leif.johansson@volvo.com. *Website:* www.volvo.com (Office).

JOHANSSON, Olof; Swedish politician; b. 1937, Ljungby, Kalmar; m. Inger Johansson; two s.; non-commissioned reserve officer 1959; farm-worker, journalist, office worker, teacher 1953–65; mem. Stockholm City Council 1966–70; Sec. Centre Party's Parl. Group 1966–69, Chair. Youth League 1969–71; MP 1971–; mem. Nat. Bd Centre Party 1971–, Asst Deputy Leader 1979–86, Deputy Leader 1986–87, Leader 1987; Minister for Energy and Tech. Devt 1976–78, for Civil Service Affairs and Personnel 1979–82, for the Environment 1991–94; mem. Council of Europe 1986–, Nordic Council 1986–, Advisory Council on Foreign Affairs 1987–. *Address:* c/o Centre Party, Bergsgt. 7B, P.O. Box 22107, 104 22 Stockholm, Sweden.

JOHN, Sir David Glyndwr, KCMG, MA, MBA, CIMgt, FRSA; British business executive; b. 20 July 1938, Pontypridd; s. of William G. John and Marjorie John; m. Gillian Edwards 1964; one s. one d.; ed Christ's Coll. Cambridge, Columbia Univ. New York and Harvard Univ.; trainee man. British Steel; later worked for RTZ and Redland; joined Gray Mackenzie (Inchcape Group) 1981, Chief Exec. 1986; Chief Exec. Inchcape Berhad 1987, Chair. 1990; mem. Bd Inchcape PLC 1988–95; Exec. Chair. Inchcape Toyota Motors 1995, Premier Oil PLC 1998–; Dir (non-exec.) BOC Group PLC 1993– (Chair. 1996–2002), The St Paul Cos. Inc., Minn., USA 1996–, Balfour Beatty PLC 2000–, Welsh Devt Agency 2001–. *Leisure interests:* reading, gardening. *Address:* c/o Samuel Montagu and Co. Ltd., 31 Hill Street, London, WIX 7FD, England.

JOHN, Sir Elton Hercules, Kt, CBE; British musician; b. (as Reginald Kenneth Dwight), 25 March 1947, Pinner, Middx; s. of Stanley Dwight and Sheila Farebrother; m. Renata Blauel 1984 (divorced 1988); ed Pinner Co. Grammar School; began piano lessons 1951; played piano in Northwood Hills Hotel bar 1964; joined local group Bluesology 1965; began writing songs with Bernie Taupin 1967; recording contract with DJM Records 1967; first single I've Been Loving You 1968, first LP Empty Sky 1969; concerts in Los Angeles 1970; formed Rocket Record Co. with Bernie Taupin 1973; frequent tours in UK, USA, Japan, Australia 1971–76; Vice-Pres. Nat. Youth Theatre of GB 1975–; first int. star to perform concerts in USSR 1979; first album released by Rocket Record Co. 1976; produced records with Clive Franks for Kiki Dee, Blue, Davey Johnstone's China 1976–77; Chair. Watford Football Club 1976–90, 1997–, Life Pres. 1990–; f. Elton John AIDS Foundation 1993, Rocket Pictures; Trustee Wallace Collection 1999–; Chair. The Old Vic Theatre Trust 2002–; Hon. mem. Royal Acad. of Music 1997; Dr hc Royal Acad. of Music 2002; Ivor Novello Awards 1976, 1977 and silver and gold discs in various countries for singles and albums; US Grammy Awards 1991, 1998, 2000; Acad. Award for Best Original Song (Can You Feel the Love Tonight?) 1995, Grammy Lifetime, Achievement Award 2000. *Singles include:* Lady

Samantha, It's Me That You Need, Border Song, Rock and Roll Madonna, Your Song, Friends, Rocket Man, Honky Cat, Crocodile Rock, Daniel, Saturday Night's Alright (for fighting), Goodbye Yellow Brick Road, Step into Christmas, Candle in the Wind, Don't Let the Sun Go Down on Me, The Bitch is Back, Lucy in the Sky with Diamonds, Philadelphia Freedom, Someone Saved My Life Tonight, Island Girl, Grow Some Funk of Your Own, Pinball Wizard, Don't Go Breaking My Heart (with Kiki Dee), Sorry Seems to be the Hardest Word, Crazy Water, Bite Your Lip, Ego, Part Time Love, Song for Guy, Are You Ready for Love, Victim of Love, Johnny B. Goode, Little Jeanie, Sartorial Eloquence, Nobody Wins, Just like Belgium, Blue Eyes, I'm Still Standing, Empty Garden, Princess, All Quiet on the Western Front, I Guess that's Why They Call It the Blues, Sad Songs (Say So Much), Passengers, Who Wears these Shoes, Breaking Hearts, Act of War, Nikita, Wrap Her Up, Cry to Heaven, Heartache All Over the World, Slow Rivers, Your Song, Candle in the Wind, I Don't Wanna Go On With You Like That, Healing Hands, Sacrifice. *Albums include:* Empty Sky, Elton John, Tumbleweed Connection, Friends (film soundtrack), 17-11-70, Madman Across the Water, Honky Chateau, Don't Shoot Me I'm Only the Piano Player, Goodbye Yellow Brick Road (double), Caribou, Elton John's Greatest Hits (2 Vols), Captain Fantastic and the Brown Dirt Cowboy, Rock of the Westies, Here and There, Blue Moves (double), A Single Man, Victim of Love, Lady Samantha, 21 at 33, The Fox, Jump Up, Love Songs, Too Low for Zero, Breaking Hearts, Ice on Fire 1985, Leather Jackets 1986, Live in Australia 1987, Reg Strikes Back 1988, Sleeping with the Past 1989, The Very Best of Elton John 1990, The One 1992, Made in England 1995, Love Songs 1995, The Big Picture 1997, Aida 1999, El Dorado 2000, Songs From the West Coast 2001, Elton John – Greatest Hits 1970–2002 2002. *Films:* Goodbye to Norma Jean 1973, To Russia with Elton 1980, The Rainbow 1989; played Pinball Wizard in Tommy 1973. *Achievements:* Wrote music for film The Lion King 1994, stage musical The Lion King plays at six theatres worldwide 2001. *Leisure interests:* football, collecting records, tennis, all sports. *Address:* c/o Simon Prytherch, Elton John Management, 7 King Street Cloisters, Clifton Walk, London, W6 0GY, England. *Telephone:* (20) 7348-4800.

JOHN, Patrick; Dominican politician; b. 7 Jan. 1937; fmr mem. Parl.; Leader Dominica Labour Party 1974–83, Deputy Leader 1983–84; Minister of Communications and Works 1970–73, Deputy Premier and Minister of Finance 1974, Premier of Dominica 1974–78, Prime Minister 1978–79, Minister for Housing, Security and Devt 1978–79; Gen. Sec. Labour Party of Dominica 1985; MP July–Nov. 1985; arrested 1981, tried and acquitted May 1982, re-tried Oct. 1985; sentenced to 12 years' imprisonment for conspiracy to overthrow Govt.

JOHN PAUL II, His Holiness Pope (Karol Wojtyła); Polish ecclesiastic; b. 18 May 1920, Wadowice; s. of Karol Wojtyła and Emilia Kaczorowska; ed Jagiellonian Univ., Cracow, Angelicum – St Thomas Pontifical Univ., Rome; ordained Priest 1946; Prof. of Moral Theology at Jagiellonian Univ. and Metropolitan Ecclesiastic Seminary, Cracow, Catholic Univ. of Lublin (KUL); Chair. Dept of Ethics, Catholic Univ. of Lublin; Titular Bishop of Ombi and Vicar-Gen. of Archdiocese of Cracow 1958–64, Archbishop of Cracow 1964–78; cr. HE Cardinal by Pope Paul VI 1967; elected Pope Oct. 1978; Hon. Freeman of Dublin 1979; Hon. Citizen of Warsaw 1996; Dr hc (Mainz) 1977, (Coimbra) 1982, (Salamanca) 1982, (Cracow) 1983, (Lublin) 1983. *Publications:* (as Karol Wojtyła) Love and Responsibility 1960, In Front of the Jeweller's Shop (play) 1960, The Acting Person 1969, Sources of Renewal – The Implementation of the Second Vatican Council 1972, Sign of Contradiction 1976, Brother of Our Lord (play) 1979, Collected Poems 1982, The Collected Plays and Writings on Theater (transl. B. Taborski) 1987; (as John Paul II) Redemptor hominis (The Redeemer of Man) 1979, Dives in misericordia (On the Mercy of God) 1980, Laborem (On Human Work) 1981, The Role of the Christian Family in the Modern World 1981, Be Not Afraid 1982, Reconciliatio et paenitentia (On Reconciliation and Penance) 1982, Salvifici doloris (Christian Meaning of Human Suffering) 1984, Slavorum Apostoli (The Apostles of the Slavs) 1985, Dominum et vivificantem (The Lord, the Giver of Life) 1986, Redemptoris Mater (Virgin Mary) 1987, Redemptoris missio (Missionary Mandate) 1990, Centesimus Annus 1991, Pastores olabo vobis (Formation of Priests) 1992, Catholic Catechism 1992, Veritatis splendor (The Shine of Truth) 1993, Gratissimam sane (Letter to Families) 1994, Ordination sacerdotalis (Priestly Ordination) 1994, Tertio Millennio Adveniente (The Jubilee of 2000) 1994, Crossing the Threshold of Hope 1994, Letter to Children 1994, Evangelium vitae (The Gospel of Life) 1995, Eastern Church 1995, Ut Unum Sint (They Should Be One) 1995, Letter to Women 1995, Ecclesia in Africa (Church in Africa) 1995, The Gift and Mystery 1996, Vita consecrata (On Consecrated Life) 1996, New Hope for Lebanon 1997, Fides et ratio (Faith and Mind) 1998, Letter to the People Well On in Years 1999, Agenda for the Third Millennium 1999, Incarnationis Mysterium 2000, Novo millenio ineunte 2000, Rosarium Virginis Mariae 2002, Roman Triptych (poetry) 2003. *Address:* Palazzo Apostolico Vaticano, 00120 Città del Vaticano, Rome, Italy.

JOHNOVÁ, Adriena; Czech painter; b. 6 Aug. 1926, Prague; d. of the late Václav Šimota and Milena Šimota; m. Jiři John 1923 (died 1972); one s.; ed Univ. of Industrial Arts; Grand Prix for Graphics, Ljubljana 1979, Grand Prix Int. for Drawings, Wrocław, Gottfried von Herder Prize, Vienna; Medal of Merit, Prague 1997. *Solo exhibitions include:* Prague 1960, Uppsala, Sweden 1978, Baumgartner, W Berlin 1983, Riverside Studios, London 1983, Galerie de France, Paris 1991, Gallery Gema, Prague, Berlin 1997. *Group exhibitions include:* New York 1980, Osaka and Kyoto 1981, Munich 1983, Washington

1988, Repub. of Korea 1988, Denmark 1984, Prague Castle 1996. *Leisure interests:* human relations, literature, music, nature. *Address:* Nad Královskou oborou 15, 170 00 Prague 7 (Studio); Na Podkovce 14, 140 00 Prague 4, Czech Republic. *Telephone:* (2) 41430393.

JOHNS, Anthony Hearle, PhD, FAHA; Australian/British professor of Islamic studies; b. 28 Aug. 1928, Wimbledon, UK; s. of the late Frank Charles Johns and of Ivy Doris Kathleen Johns (née Hearle); m. Yohanni Bey 1956; four s. one d.; ed St Boniface's Coll., Plymouth, UK and School of Oriental and African Studies, Univ. of London; lecturer Ford Foundation-sponsored Training Project, Indonesia 1954–58; Sr Lecturer in Indonesian Languages and Literatures, Australian Nat. Univ. 1958–63, Prof. 1963–, Chair. and Head. Dept 1963–83, Dean Faculty of Asian Studies 1963–64, 1965–67, 1975–79, 1988–91, Head Southeast Asia Centre 1983–88; Visiting Prof., Univ. of Toronto (Dept of Religious Studies and Dept of Middle East and Islamic Studies) 1989; Special Foreign Visiting Prof. in Islamic Studies Chiba Univ., Tokyo 1991; Visiting Scholar, Oxford Centre for Hebrew and Jewish Studies, UK 1993–94; Visiting Fellow, Research School Pacific and Asian Studies, Australian Nat. Univ., Canberra 1994–96, 1997–2000; Fellow Inst. for Advanced Studies, Hebrew Univ. of Jerusalem 1984–85; Univ. of London Sr Studentship 1953–54; Rhuvon Guest Prize in Islamic Studies, SOAS 1953–54, Centenary Medal for Service to Australian Society and the Humanities 2003. *Publications:* The Gift Addressed to the Spirit of the Prophet 1965, A Road with No End (trans. and Ed.) 1968, Cultural Options and the Role of Tradition 1981, Islam in Asia II Southeast and East Asia (Ed. and contrib. with R. Israeli) 1984, Reflections on the Dynamics and Spirituality of Sūrat al-Furqān in Literary Structures of Religious Meaning in the Qur'an (contrib.) 2000. *Leisure interests:* music, literature. *Address:* Division of Pacific and Asian History, Research School of Pacific and Asian Studies, Australian National University, Canberra, ACT 0200 (Office); 70 Duffy Street, Ainslie, Canberra, ACT 2602, Australia (Home). *Telephone:* (2) 6125-3106 (Office); (2) 6249-6574 (Home). *Fax:* (2) 62125-5525 (Office). *E-mail:* ahyj@coombs.anu.edu.au (Office); ah_yjohns@netspeed.com.au (Home).

JOHNS, Jasper; American painter; b. 15 May 1930, Augusta; s. of Jasper Johns Sr and Jean Riley; ed Univ. of South Carolina; works in following collections: Tate Gallery, London, Museum of Modern Art, New York, Albright-Knox Art Gallery, Buffalo, NY, Museum Ludwig, Cologne, Hirshhorn Museum and Sculpture Garden, Washington, DC, Whitney Museum of American Art, Stedelijk Museum, Amsterdam, Moderna Museet, Stockholm, Dallas Museum of Fine Arts, Art Inst. of Chicago, Baltimore Museum of Art, Kunstmuseum Basel, Cleveland Museum of Art, Nat. Gallery of Art, Washington, DC, San Francisco Museum of Modern Art, Va Museum of Fine Arts, Walker Art Center, Minneapolis; mem. American Acad. of Arts and Letters; Hon. RA (London); Prize, Pittsburgh Int. 1958, Wolf Foundation Prize 1986, Gold Medal (American Acad. and Inst. of Arts and Letters) 1986, Int. Prize, Venice Biennale 1988, Nat. Medal of Arts 1990, Officier, Ordre des Arts et des Lettres 1990, Praemium Imperiale Award (Japan) 1993. *Solo exhibitions include:* Leo Castelli Gallery, New York 1958, 1960, 1961, 1963, 1966, 1968, 1976, 1981, 1984, 1987, 1991, Nat. Acad. of Design, New York 1996 and numerous other galleries in Canada, France, Germany, Italy, Japan, Spain, Switzerland, UK and USA, Nat. Acad. of Design, NY 1996, Philadelphia Museum of Art 1999, Art Inst. of Chicago 1999. *Address:* P.O. Box 642, Sharon, CT 06069, USA.

JOHNS, Air Chief Marshal Sir Richard Edward, GCB, CBE, LVO, FRAeS; British air force officer; b. 28 July 1939, Horsham, Sussex; s. of the late Lt Col Herbert Edward Johns and Marjory Harley Johns (née Everett); m. Elizabeth Naomi Anne Manning 1965; one s. two d.; ed Portsmouth Grammar School, RAF Coll. Cranwell; commissioned 1959; Night Fighter/Fighter Reconnaissance Squadrons, UK, Cyprus, Aden 1960–67; Flying Instructor 1968–71, Flying Instructor to HRH the Prince of Wales 1970–71; Officer Commanding 3 (Fighter) Squadron (Harrier) 1975–77; Dir Air Staff Briefing 1979–81; Station Commdr and Harrier Force Commdr, RAF Gütersloh 1982–84; ADC to HM The Queen 1983–84; at Royal Coll. of Defence Studies 1985; Sr Air Staff Officer RAF HQ, Germany 1985–88; Sr Air Staff Officer HQ Strike Command 1989–91; Air Officer Commanding No. 1 Group 1991–93; Chief of Staff, Deputy C-in-C Strike Command and UK Air Forces 1993–94; Air Officer Commanding in Chief Strike Command 1994; C-in-C Allied Forces NW Europe 1994–97; Chief of Air Staff and Air ADC to HM The Queen 1997–2000; Constable and Gov. of Windsor Castle 2000–; Chair. Bd of Trustees, RAF Museum; Hon. Air Commodore, RAF Regiment. *Leisure interests:* military history, rugby, cricket, equitation. *Address:* Norman Tower, Windsor Castle, Windsor, SL4 1NJ, England. *Telephone:* (1753) 868286 (Office); (1753) 856106 (Home). *Fax:* (1753) 854910.

JOHNSON, Ben, MA, RCA; British artist; b. 24 Aug 1946, Llandudno, Wales; s. of Harold Johnson and Ivy Lloyd Jones; m. Sheila Kellehar 1976; two s.; ed Royal Coll. of Art; has exhibited internationally since 1969; has undertaken direct commissions from Centre Pompidou, Paris and Museum of London; work represented in public and corp. collections at Boymans van Beuningen Museum, Rotterdam, British Council, London, Tate Gallery, London, Contemporary Arts Soc., London, RIBA, London, City Art Gallery, Glasgow, Whitworth Gallery, Manchester, Centre Pompidou, Paris, Victoria & Albert Museum, London, Deutsche Bank, British Petroleum, Guildhall Art Gallery, Corpn of London, Special Admin. Regional Govt of Hong Kong, New Convention & Exhbn Centre, Hong Kong, Regional Services Council Museum, Hong Kong, British Museum, London; Hon. FRIBA. *Leisure interests:* architecture, cities. *Address:* 4 St Peter's Wharf, Hammersmith Terrace, London, W6 9UD, England. *Telephone:* (20) 8563-8768. *Fax:* (20) 8563-8768. *Website:* www.benjohnsonartist.com (Office).

JOHNSON, Ben; Canadian (b. Jamaican) athlete; b. 30 Dec. 1961, Falmouth, Jamaica; emigrated with family to Canada 1976; began athletics career coached by Charlie Francis 1977; finished last, Commonwealth Games 100 metres trial, Canada 1978; won Canadian Jr title, became Canadian citizen 1979; selected for Olympic Games, Moscow, but Canada boycotted Games 1980; came sixth in 100m, Pan-American Jr Games 1980, second, Commonwealth Games 1982; semi-finalist, World Championships 1983; bronze medallist, Olympic Games, LA, USA 1984; won World Cup 1985, Commonwealth title 1986, indoor 60m in record time 1987; gold medallist, World Championships, with time of 9.83 seconds, Rome 1987; came first in final, Olympic Games, in world record 9.79 seconds, Seoul 1988; medal withdrawn after allegations concerning drug-taking; stripped of world record Sept. 1989, life ban from Canadian nat. team lifted Aug. 1990; failed second drugs test and banned from athletics for life March 1993; IAAF rejected petition for reinstatement Aug. 1999.

JOHNSON, Betsey Lee, BA; American fashion designer; b. 10 Aug. 1942, Hartford, Conn.; d. of John Herman Johnson and Lena Virginia Johnson; m. 1st John Cale 1966; one d.; m. 2nd Jeffrey Olivier 1981; ed Pratt Inst., New York, Syracuse Univ.; editorial Asst Mademoiselle magazine 1964–65; partner and co-owner Betsey, Bunky & Nini, New York 1969–; shops in New York, LA, San Francisco, Coconut Grove, Fla, Venice, Calif., Boston, Chicago, Seattle; Prin. Designer for Paraphernalia 1965–69; designer Alvin Duskin Co., San Francisco 1970; Head Designer Alley Cat by Betsey Johnson (div. of LeDamor, Inc.) 1970–74; freelance designer for Jr Womens' div., Butterick Pattern Co. 1971, Betsey Johnson's Kids Children's Wear (div. of Shutterbug Inc.) 1974–77, Betsey Johnson for Jeanette Maternities, Inc. 1974–75; designer for Gant Shirtmakers Inc. (women's clothing) 1974–75, Tric-Trac by Betsey Johnson (women's knitwear) 1974–76, Butterick's Home Sewing Catalog 1975– (children's wear); Head Designer Jr sportswear co.; designed for Star Ferry by Betsey Johnson and Michael Miles (children's wear) 1975–77; owner and Head Designer B.J., Inc., designer wholesale co., New York 1978; Pres. and Treas. B.J. Vines, New York; opened Betsey Johnson store, New York 1979; mem. Council of Fashion Designers, American Women's Forum; Merit Award, Mademoiselle magazine 1970, Coty Award 1971, two Tommy Print Awards 1971. *Address:* 110 East 9th Street, Suite A889, Los Angeles, CA 90079, USA.

JOHNSON, Boris (Alexander Boris de Pfeffel); British journalist; b. 19 June 1964; s. of Stanley Patrick Johnson and Charlotte Fawcett; m. 1st Allegra Mostyn-Owen; m. 2nd Marina Wheeler 1993; two s. two d.; ed Eton, Balliol Coll., Oxford; journalist with The Times 1987–88; EC Corresp., The Daily Telegraph 1989–94, Asst Ed. and Chief Political Columnist 1994–99; Ed. The Spectator 1999–; MP (Conservative) for Henley 2001–. *Publication:* Friends, Voters, Countrymen 2001. *Address:* The Spectator, 56 Doughty Street, London, WC1N 2LL, (Office); House of Commons, London, SW1A 0AA, England. *Telephone:* (20) 7405-1706 (Office). *Fax:* (20) 7242-0603 (Office). *E-mail:* editor@spectator.co.uk (Office). *Website:* www.spectator.co.uk (Office).

JOHNSON, Brian Frederick Gilbert, PhD, FRS, FRSC, FRSE; British professor of inorganic chemistry; b. 11 Sept. 1938; s. of Frank Johnson and Mona Johnson; m. Christine Draper 1962; two d.; ed Northampton Grammar School, Univ. of Nottingham; Reader in Chem., Univ. of Cambridge 1978–90, Fellow Fitzwilliam Coll. 1970–90, Hon. Fellow 1990–, Master 1999–; Crum Brown Prof. of Inorganic Chem., Univ. of Edin. 1991–95; Prof. of Inorganic Chem., Univ. of Cambridge 1995–; Tilden Lecturer, RSC; Corday Morgan Medal, RSC, Frankland Medal and Prize, RSC. *Publications:* Transition Metal Clusters 1982, over 1,000 academic papers and review articles. *Leisure interests:* walking, painting, riding. *Address:* Department of Chemistry, Lensfield Road, CB2 1EW, Cambridge; Fitzwilliam College, Cambridge, CB3 0DG, England (Home). *Telephone:* (1223) 336337. *E-mail:* bfgj1@cus.cam.ac.uk (Office).

JOHNSON, Charles Richard, MA; American author; b. 23 April 1948, Evanston, Ill.; m. Joan New 1970; one s. one d.; ed Southern Illinois Univ.; fmr cartoonist and filmmaker; lecturer, Univ. of Washington, Seattle 1975–79, Assoc. Prof. of English 1979–82, Prof. 1982–; Co-Dir Twin Tigers (martial arts studio); recipient of U.S. Nat. Book Award for Middle Passage 1990. *Publications include:* novels: Faith and the Good Thing 1974, Oxherding Tale 1982, Middle Passage 1990; The Sorcerer's Apprentice (short stories) Being and Race: Black Writing Since 1970 1988, The Middle Passage 1990, All This and Moonlight 1990, In Search of a Voice (with Ron Chernow) 1991; Black Humor, Half-Past Nation Time (drawings), Booker, Charlie Smith and the Fritter Tree (broadcast plays); numerous reviews, essays and short stories. *Address:* c/o Atheneum Publishers, Macmillan Publishing Company, 866 3rd Avenue, New York, NY 10022; c/o University of Washington, Department of English, Engl. G N-30, Seattle, WA 98105, USA. *Telephone:* (206) 543-2100. *Website:* www.washington.edu (Office).

JOHNSON, David T., BEcons; American diplomatist; b. Georgia; m. Scarlett M. Swan; two d. one s.; ed Emory Univ., Canadian National Defence Coll.; Asst Nat. Trust Examiner, Treasury Dept; joined US Foreign Service 1977; Vice-Consul, Consulate-Gen., Ciudad Juárez, Mexico 1978–79; Econ. Officer, US Embassy, Berlin 1981–83; Deputy Dir, State Dept Operations Center 1987–89; Consul.-Gen., Vancouver 1990–93; Deputy Spokesman, State Dept; Dir State Dept Press Office 1993–95; Deputy Press Sec. for Foreign Affairs at the White House and Spokesman for Nat. Sec. Council 1995–97; Chief (with rank of Amb.), US Mission to OSCE 1998–. *Address:* Organization for Security and Co-operation in Europe, Obersteinergasse 11, 1190 Vienna, Austria (Office). *Telephone:* (1) 514-36-0 (Office). *Fax:* (1) 514-36-105 (Office). *E-mail:* info@osce.org (Office). *Website:* www.osce.org (Office).

JOHNSON, David Willis, BEcons, MBA; Australian business executive; b. 7 Aug. 1932, Tumut, NSW; s. of Alfred Ernest Johnson and Eileen Melba Johnson (née Burt); m. Sylvia Raymonda Wells 1966; three s.; ed Univs. of Sydney and Chicago; Exec. Trainee Ford Motor Co., Geelong; Man. Trainee Colgate-Palmolive, Sydney 1959–60; Product Man. 1961, Asst to Man. Dir 1962, Brands Man. 1963, Gen. Products Man. 1964-65; Asst Gen. Man. and Marketing Dir, Colgate-Palmolive, Johannesburg 1966, Chair. and Man. Dir 1967–72; Pres. Warner-Lambert/Parke Davis Asia, Hong Kong 1973–76, Personal Products Div., Warner-Lambert Co., Morris Plains, NJ 1977, Exec. Vice-Pres. and Gen. Man. Entenman's Div., Bay Shore, NY 1979, Pres. Speciality Foods Group, Morris Plains, NJ 1980-81, Vice-Pres. 1980–82; Pres. and CEO Entenman's Div., Bay Shore 1982, Vice-Pres. Gen. Foods Corpn, White Plains, NY 1982–87, Pres., CEO Entenman's Inc., Bay Shore 1982–87; Chair., Pres. and CEO Gerber Products Co., Fremont, Mich. 1987–89, Chair. and CEO 1989–90; Pres., CEO and Dir Campbell Soup Co., Camden, NJ 1990–97, 2000–01, Chair. Bd of Dirs. 1993–; mem. Bd Dirs. Colgate-Palmolive Co., Exec. Advisory Bd Donaldson, Lufkin & Jenrette Merchant Banking Partners; mem. Advisory Council Univ. of Notre Dame Coll. of Business Admin., Univ. of Chicago Grad. School of Business; fmr Dir American Bakers Asscn, Nat. Food Producers' Asscn, Grocery Mfrs America; Distinguished Alumnus Award, Univ. of Chicago 1992; Dir of Year Award, Nat. Asscn of Corp. Dirs 1997. *Address:* Campbell Soup Company World Headquarters, Campbell Place, Camden, NJ 08103, USA. *Telephone:* (609) 342-4800.

JOHNSON, Douglas William John, BA, BLitt; British historian; b. 1 Feb. 1925, Edinburgh; s. of John Thornburn Johnson and Christine Douglas-Mair; m. Madeleine Rébillard 1950; one d.; ed Royal Grammar School, Lancaster, Worcester Coll. Oxford, Ecole Normale Supérieure, Paris; lecturer in History, Univ. of Birmingham 1949–63, Prof. of Modern History and Head History Dept 1963–68; Prof. of French History, Univ. Coll. London 1968–90, Prof. Emer. 1990–, Dean of Faculty of Arts 1979–82; Visiting Prof. French Dept, King's Coll. 1993–; mem. Franco-British Council 1973–, Comm. Tocqueville, Paris, Jury for Award of Guizot Prize, Val-Richer, France; Officier, Légion d'honneur, Chevalier, Ordre nat. du mérite, Commdr des Palmes académiques; Hon. DSc (Univ. of Aston) 1997. *Publications:* Guizot: Aspects of French History 1963, France and the Dreyfus Affair 1966, A Concise History of France 1970, French Society and the Revolution 1976, The Age of Illusion (with Madeleine Johnson) 1987, An Idea of Europe (with Richard Hoggart) 1987, The Permanent Revolution (with Geoffrey Best) 1988, Michelet and the French Revolution 1990, How European are the French? 1996, A Day in June (with Anne Corbett) 2000. *Leisure interests:* French politics, music. *Address:* 29 Rudall Crescent, London, NW3 1RR, England; 12 rue Delambre, 75014 Paris, France. *Telephone:* (20) 7435-6668 (London); 1-43-27-69-81 (Paris).

JOHNSON, Earvin (Magic Johnson); American professional basketball player; b. 14 Aug. 1959, Lansing, Mich.; s. of Earvin Johnson and Christine Johnson; m. Cookie Kelly; one s.; ed Mich. State Univ.; professional basketball player Los Angeles Lakers Nat. Basketball Asscn (NBA) 1979–91 (retd), returned to professional sport 1992; later announced abandonment of plans to resume sporting career; Vice-Pres., co-owner Los Angeles Lakers 1994–, Head Coach 1994; resumed career Feb. 1996, retd July 1996; Chair. Johnson Devt Corpn 1993–, Magic Johnson Entertainment 1997–; presenter TV show The Magic Hour 1998–; mem. NCAA Championship Team 1979, Nat. Basketball All-Star Team 1980, 1982–89, Nat. Basketball Asscn Championship Team 1980, 1982, 1985, 1987, 1988; fmr mem. Nat. Aids Asscn, rejoined 1993; commentator NBC-TV 1995–96; named most valuable player NBA Playoffs 1980, 1982, 1987, NBA 1987, 1989, 1990, Player of the Year (Sporting News) 1987, J. Walter Kennedy Citizenship Award, Naismith Memorial Basketball Hall of Fame 2002. *Publications:* Magic 1983, What You Can Do to Avoid AIDS 1992, My Life (autobiog.) 1992. *Address:* Magic Johnson Foundation, Suite 1080, 1600 Corporate Pointe, Culver City, CA 90230 (Office); Johnson Development Corporation, 9100 Wilshire Boulevard, Beverly Hills CA 90212, USA.

JOHNSON, Frank Robert; British journalist; b. 20 Jan. 1943; s. of late Ernest Johnson and of Doreen Johnson (née Skinner); m. Virginia Johnson 1998; two step-s. two step-d.; ed Chartesey Secondary School, Shoreditch Secondary School; messenger boy, Sunday Express 1959–60; reporter local and regional newspapers 1960–69; mem. political staff Sun newspaper 1969–72; parl. sketch writer and leader writer Daily Telegraph 1972–79; columnist Now! magazine 1979–81; parl. sketch writer The Times 1981–83, 1986–87, Paris diarist 1984, Bonn Corresp. 1985–86, Assoc. Ed. 1987–88; Assoc. Ed. The Sunday Telegraph 1988–93, Deputy Ed. (Comment) 1993–94, Deputy Ed. 1994–95; Ed. The Spectator 1995–99; Parl. Sketch Writer of the Year, Granada, What The Papers Say 1977, Columnist of the Year, British Press Awards 1981. *Publications:* Out of Order 1982, Frank Johnson's Election Year 1983. *Leisure interests:* opera, ballet. *Address:* c/o The Spectator, 56 Doughty Street, London, WC1N 2LL, England.

JOHNSON, Frederick Ross, BComm, MBA; Canadian business executive; b. 13 Dec. 1931, Winnipeg, Man.; s. of Frederick H. Johnson and Caroline Green; m. Laurie A. Graumann 1979; two s. (from previous marriage); ed Univs. of Manitoba and Toronto; Vice-Pres. Merchandising, T. Eaton Co. (Canada) 1965–66; Exec. Vice-Pres. and COO, GSW Ltd 1966–71; Pres. and CEO, Standard Brands Ltd, Canada 1971–74; Dir Standard Brands Inc. 1974–, Sr Vice-Pres. 1974–75, Pres. 1975–76, Chair. and CEO 1977–81; Pres. and COO Nabisco Brands Inc. 1981–83, Vice-Pres. and CEO 1984–85, Chief Exec. R.J.R. Nabisco 1987–89 (after take over of Nabisco by Reynolds), Pres. and COO R. J. Reynolds Industries 1985–87, Pres. and CEO 1987–89; Chair. and CEO RJM Group Inc. 1989–; Dir Wosk's Ltd, Vancouver, Bank of Nova Scotia, Toronto; mem. Advisory Council, Columbia Univ., New York; Trustee, Econ. Club of New York; Chair. Multiple Sclerosis Soc., New York br.; Hon. Dr. (St Francis Xavier Univ., Antigonish, NS) 1978, (Univ. of Newfoundland) 1980. *Leisure interests:* golf, skiing, tennis. *Address:* RJM Group, 200 Galleria Parkway, Suite 970, Atlanta, GA 30339, USA.

JOHNSON, Gabriel Ampah, DD'ÉTAT; Togolese professor of biology and administrator; b. 13 Oct. 1930, Aneho; s. of William K. A. Johnson and Rebecca A. Ekue-Hettah; m. Louise Chipan 1962; three s. three d.; ed Univ. of Poitiers, France; Teaching Asst, Univ. of Poitiers until 1956; Research Fellow, CNRS, France 1958–60; Deputy Dir of Educ., Togo 1959-60; Asst Prof. Nat. Univ. of Ivory Coast, Abidjan 1961–64, Assoc. Prof. 1965–66, Prof., Chair. of Biology 1966–, Asst Dean, Faculty of Science 1963–68, Founding Dir Nat. Centre for Social Services 1964–68; Founding Rector, Univ. du Bénin, Lomé, Togo 1970–86; Dir of Higher Educ., Togo 1970–75; Pres. Nat. Planning Comm. of Togo 1973; Pres. Asscn of African Univs. 1977–80; mem. Exec. Bd UNESCO 1997–; mem. Bd of Admin., Asscn of Partially or Fully French-Speaking Univs. 1975–, Pan African Inst. for Devt 1977–, Int. Cttee of Bioethics 2001; mem. Cen. Cttee Togo People's Rally (ruling party) 1976–; Founding Pres. Africa Club for an Integrated Devt 1980–; mem. Zoological Soc. of France 1956, Biological Soc. of France 1962, Endocrinological Soc. of France 1966; Hon. Vice-Pres. Gold Mercury Int. 1983; Chevalier Ordre national de la Côte d'Ivoire 1966, Officier Légion d'honneur 1971, Commdr Order of Cruzeiro do Sul (Brazil) 1976, Commdr Order of Merit (France) 1983, Ordre des Palmes Académiques, (France) 1986, Commdr Ordre du Mono (Togo) 2000; Dr hc Sherbrooke, (Canada) 1979, (Lille) 1983, (Bordeaux) 1986; Medal of Honour, Univ. of São Paulo, Brazil 1980; Gold Mercury Int. Award 1982, Gold Medal of Honour, Univ. of Benin. *Publications:* several articles in scientific journals. *Leisure interests:* reading, classical and modern music, swimming, farming (cattle breeding). *Address:* B.P. 7098, Lomé, Togo. *Telephone:* (2) 21-53-65 (Home).

JOHNSON, Gary Earl, BA; American business executive and politician; b. 1 Jan. 1953, Minot, ND; s. of Earl W. Johnson and Lorraine B. Bostow; m. Dee Sims 1976; one s. one d.; ed Univ. of New Mexico; Pres. and CEO Big J Enterprises, Albuquerque 1976–99; Gov. of New Mexico 1995–2003; mem. Bd Dirs Entrepreneurship Studies programme Univ. of NM 1993–95, Albuquerque Chamber of Commerce 1993–95; Republican; Entrepreneur of the Year 1995. *Leisure interests:* rock and mountain-climbing, skiing, flying, athletics. *Address:* c/o Office of the Governor, Room 400, State Capitol, Santa Fe, NM 87503, USA.

JOHNSON, Graham Rhodes, OBE, FRAM, FGSM; British concert accompanist; b. 10 July 1950, Bulawayo, Rhodesia (now Zimbabwe); s. of the late John Edward Donald Johnson and of Violet May Johnson; ed Hamilton High School, Bulawayo, Rhodesia, Royal Acad. of Music, London; Artistic Adviser, accompanist Alte Oper Festival, Frankfurt 1981–82; Prof. of Accompaniment, Guildhall School of Music 1986–; Song Adviser, Wigmore Hall 1992–; Artistic Dir The Songmakers' Almanac; guest lecturer in several countries; writer, presenter BBC Radio 3 series on Poulenc, BBC TV series on Schubert 1978, Liszt 1986; concert début, Wigmore Hall 1972; has accompanied numerous singers including Dame Elisabeth Schwarzkopf, Jessye Norman, Victoria de los Angeles, Dame Janet Baker, Sir Peter Pears, Dame Felicity Lott, Ann Murray, Matthias Goerne, Christine Schäfer, Dorothea Roeschmann, François Le Roux; has appeared at festivals in Edin., Munich, Hohenems, Salzburg, Bath, Hong Kong, Bermuda; Chair. Jury Wigmore Hall Int. Singing Competition 1997, 1999, 2001; mem. Royal Swedish Acad. of Music 2000; numerous recordings; Chevalier des Arts et des Lettres 2002; Gramophone Award 1989, 1996, 1997, Royal Philharmonic Prize for Instrumentalist 1998. *Publications:* contrib. The Britten Companion 1984, Gerald Moore: The Unashamed Accompanist, The Spanish Song Companion 1992, The Songmakers' Almanac Reflections and Commentaries 1996, A French Song Companion 2000, articles and reviews. *Leisure interests:* dining out, book collecting. *Address:* 83 Fordwych Road, London, NW2 3TL, England. *Telephone:* (20) 8452-5193. *Fax:* (20) 8452-5081 (Home).

JOHNSON, Hugh Eric Allan, MA; British author, editor and broadcaster; b. 10 March 1939, London; s. of the late Guy F. Johnson and Grace Kittel; m. Judith Eve Grinling 1965; one s. two d.; ed Rugby School, King's Coll., Cambridge; feature writer Condé Nast Magazines 1960–63; Ed. Wine and Food Magazine 1963–65; wine corresp. Sunday Times 1965–67, Travel Ed. 1967; Ed. Queen Magazine 1968–70; Wine Ed. Gourmet Magazine 1971–72; Wine Ed. Cuisine Magazine (New York) 1983–84; Chair. Winestar Productions Ltd 1984–, The Hugh Johnson Collection Ltd, The Movie Business; Pres. Sunday Times Wine Club 1973–, Circle of Wine Writers 1997–; founder mem. Tree Council 1974, founder The Plantsman (quarterly) 1979; Dir Château Latour 1986–2001; Editorial Consultant The Garden (Royal Horti-

cultural Soc. Journal) 1975–; Sec. Wine and Food Soc. 1962–63; Gardening Corresp. New York Times 1986–87; Hon. Chair. 'Wine Japan' 1989–93; Hon. Pres. Int.Wine and Food Soc.; Fellow Commoner King's Coll. Cambridge 2001; Hon. Freeman of the Vintner's Co. 2003; Dr hc (Essex) 1998; André Simon Prize 1967, 1989, Glenfiddich Award 1972, 1984, 1989, Marqués de Cáceres Award 1984, Wines and Vines Trophy 1982, Grand Prix de la Communication de la Vigne et du Vin 1992, 1993, Decanter Magazine Man of the Year 1995, Von Rumor Award, Gastronomische Akad., Germany 1998, Gold Veitch Memorial Medal, Royal Horticultural Soc. 2000. *TV includes:* Wine–A User's Guide (series) 1986, Vintage—A History of Wine (series) 1989, Return Voyage 1992. *Publications:* Wine 1966, Frank Schoonmaker's Encyclopaedia of Wine (Ed. of English Edn) 1967, The World Atlas of Wine 1971, The International Book of Trees 1973, The California Wine Book (with Bob Thompson) 1975, Understanding Wine (Sainsbury Guide) 1976, Hugh Johnson's Pocket Wine Book (annually since 1977), The Principles of Gardening 1979, revised Edn with new title, Hugh Johnson's Gardening Companion 1996, Hugh Johnson's Wine Companion 1983, How to Handle a Wine (video) 1984; Hugh Johnson's Cellar Book 1986, The Atlas of German Wines 1986, How to Enjoy Your Wine 1985, The Wine Atlas of France (with Hubrecht Duijker) 1987, The Story of Wine 1989, The Art and Science of Wine (with James Halliday) 1992, Hugh Johnson on Gardening: The Best of Tradescant's Diary 1993, The New German Wine Atlas (with Stuart Pigott) 1995, Tuscany and Its Wines 2000. *Leisure interests:* travel, trees, gardening, pictures. *Address:* 73 St James's Street, London, SW1A 1PH; Saling Hall, Great Saling, Essex, CM7 5DT, England; Domaine des Boutons, 03190 Hérisson, Allier, France.

JOHNSON, Adm. Jay; American naval officer; b. 1946, Great Falls, Mont.; m. Garland Hawthorne; one c.; ed U.S. Naval Acad.; joined U.S. Navy 1968; fmr Asst to Chief of Naval Personnel; fmr Commdr Naval Group Eight, Theodore Roosevelt Battle Group 1992; Commdr Second Fleet Striking Fleet Atlantic, Jt Task Force 120 1994; fmr Vice-Chief Naval Operations; aircraft-carrier combat pilot during Viet Nam war; Chief of Naval Operations 1996–2000; numerous medals and awards. *Address:* c/o The Pentagon, Washington, DC 20350, USA.

JOHNSON, John H.; American publisher; b. 19 Jan. 1918, Arkansas; m. Eunice Johnson; one s. (deceased) one d.; ed DuSable High School and Chicago and Northwestern Univs.; Asst Ed. 1936, later Man. Ed. of employees' publication, Supreme Life Insurance Co. of America; CEO, Chair. Johnson Publishing Co. 1942–; founded Ebony 1945, Jet 1951; first Black businessman to be selected as one of the "ten outstanding young men of the year" by U.S. Jr Chamber of Commerce 1951; accompanied Vice-Pres. Nixon at Ghana Independence celebrations 1957, appointed Special Amb. representing the U.S. at Ivory Coast Independence celebrations 1961 and Kenya Independence ceremony 1963; Chair. and CEO Supreme Life Insurance Co.; Dir Marina City Bank of Chicago, Service Fed. Savings and Loan Asscn, Chicago, Greyhound Corpn, Zenith, Bell & Howell, Arthur D. Little Corpn, 20th Century-Fox Corpn, United Negro Coll. Fund, etc.; Trustee, Inst. of Int. Educ., Tuskegee Inst., Howard and Fisk Univs.; Dir Chicago Asscn of Commerce; Hon. LLD of several univs. and colls.; Horatio Alger Award 1966, named Publr of the Year by Magazine Publrs.' Asscn 1972, Presidential Medal of Freedom 1996, Lifetime Achievement Award, American Advertising Foundation 1996 and numerous other awards. *Publication:* Succeeding Against the Odds 1989. *Address:* 1270 Avenue of the Americas, New York, NY 10020; 1750 Pennsylvania Avenue, NW, Washington, DC 20006, USA.

JOHNSON, III, Joseph Eggleston, MD; American professor of medicine and administrator; b. 17 Sept. 1930, Elberton, Ga; s. of Joseph Eggleston Johnson and Marie Johnson (née Williams); m. Judith H. Kemp 1956; one s. two d.; ed Vanderbilt Univ., Nashville, Tenn., Johns Hopkins Univ.; Instructor in Medicine, Johns Hopkins Univ. School of Medicine 1961–62, Physician, Johns Hopkins Hosp 1961–66, Asst Prof. of Medicine 1962–66, Asst Dean for Student Affairs 1963–66; Assoc. Prof. of Medicine, Univ. of Fla Coll. of Medicine 1966–68, Chief, Div. of Infectious Disease 1966–72, Prof. of Medicine 1968–72, Assoc. Dean 1970–72; Prof. and Chair. Dept of Medicine, Bowman Gray School of Medicine 1972–85; Chief of Medicine, NC Baptist Hosp. 1972–85; Dean, Univ. of Mich. Medical School 1985–90, Prof. of Internal Medicine 1985–93; Sr Vice-Pres. American Coll. of Physicians 1993–, interim exec. Vice-Pres. 1994–95; mem. accreditation comm. on grad. medical educ. 1988–93; Markle Scholar, Royal Soc. of Medicine; mem. Johns Hopkins Soc. of Scholars, Int. Soc. of Internal Medicine (Pres. 2000–02). *Publications:* 100 articles and book chapters on infectious disease, immunology and internal medicine. *Address:* American College of Physicians, Independence Mall West, Sixth Street at Race, Philadelphia, PA 19106 (Office); 15-C-44, The Philadelphian, 2401 Pennsylvania Avenue, Philadelphia, PA 19130, USA (Home). *Telephone:* (215) 351-2690 (Office).

JOHNSON, Dame Louise Napier, DBE, PhD, FRS; British university professor; b. 26 Sept. 1940, Worcester; d. of George Edmund Johnson and Elizabeth Johnson (née King); m. (husband deceased); one s. one d.; ed Wimbledon High School, Univ. Coll. London, Royal Institution, London; Research Asst, Yale Univ. 1996; demonstrator, Zoology Dept, Univ. of Oxford 1967–73, Lecturer in Molecular Biophysics 1973–90, David Phillips Prof. of Molecular Biophysics 1990–, Additional Fellow Somerville Coll. 1973–90, Hon. Fellow 1991–, Professorial Fellow Corpus Christi Coll. 1990–; mem. European Molecular Biology Org. 1991–; Assoc. Fellow Third World Acad. of Sciences 2000–; mem. Council, Royal Soc. 1998–2001, Scientific Advisory Council, European Molecular Biology Lab. 1994–2000, Council for the Central

Lab. of the Research Councils 1998–2001; Trustee Cambridge Crystallographic Data Centre; Gov. Westminster School 1994–2001; Hon. DSc (St Andrews) 1992; Linderström-Lang Prize 1989, Charmian Medal, Royal Soc. of Chem. 1997, Datta Medal, Fed. of European Biochemical Soc. 1998. *Publications:* Protein Crystallography (with T.L. Blundell) 1976, Glycogen Phosphorylase (co-author) 1991; more than 150 scientific papers on lysozyme, phosphorylase protein kinases, allosteric mechanisms, cell cycle proteins, protein crystallography. *Leisure interests:* family, horses. *Address:* Laboratory of Molecular Biophysics, Department of Biochemistry, University of Oxford, Oxford, OX1 3QU, England (Office). *Telephone:* (1865) 275365 (Office). *Fax:* (1865) 285353 (Office). *E-mail:* louise@biop.ox.ac.uk (Office). *Website:* www.biop.ox.ac.uk (Office).

JOHNSON, Luke; British business executive; ed Univ. of Oxford; stockbroking analyst Kleinwort Benson Securities; Chair. PizzaExpress PLC, Signature Restaurants PLC; co-Man. Intrinsic Value PLC; f. and Dir New-Media SPARK PLC; mem. Bd of Dirs Nightfreight PLC, Integrated Dental Holdings PLC. *Address:* Signature Restaurants PLC, 52 Brook's Mews, London, W1K 4EE, England (Office). *Telephone:* (20) 7499-5311 (Office). *Fax:* (20) 7499-5312 (Office). *E-mail:* lukej@riskcapitalpartners.co.uk (Office).

JOHNSON, Manuel H., Jr.; American economist; b. 10 Feb. 1949, Troy, Alabama; s. of Manuel Holman Johnson Sr and Ethel Lorraine Jordan; m. Mary Lois Wilkerson 1972; two s.; ed Troy State Univ., Florida State Univ., George Mason Univ., Fairfax, Va; Asst Sec. of Treasury for Econ. Policy 1982–86; mem. Fed. Reserve Bd 1985–90, Vice-Chair. 1986–90; Dir Centre for Global Market Studies, George Mason Univ. 1990–94; Co-Chair., Sr Partner Johnson Smick Int., Washington 1990–. *Publications:* (co-author) Political Economy of Federal Government Growth 1980, Better Government at Half Price 1981, Deregulating Labor Relations 1981. *Address:* Johnson Smick International, 1133 Connecticut Avenue, NW, # 901, Washington, DC 20036, USA.

JOHNSON, Martin O., OBE; British rugby football player; b. 9 March 1970, Solihull; joined Leicester 1988, won Premiership honours 1999–2001; toured Australia with England Schoolboys side 1990; int. debut England versus France 1993; captained British Lions on SA tour 1997, winning 2–1 Test series; apptd Capt. England team in Six Nations Championships 2000, re-apptd 2001; first player ever to captain two British Lions tours; won Heineken Cup 2001, 2002; 70 caps as at Dec. 2002. *Publication:* Agony and Ecstasy. *Address:* c/o Rugby Football Union, 21 Rugby Road, Twickenham, TW1 1DS, England (Office). *Telephone:* (20) 8892-2000 (Office).

JOHNSON, Michael; American athlete; b. 13 Sept. 1967, Dallas; m. Kerry Doyen 1998; one s.; ed Baylor Univ.; world champion 200m. 1991, 400m and 4×400m 1993, 200m, 400m and 4×400m (world record) 1995, 400m 1997, 400m (world record) and 4×400m. 1999; Olympic champion 4×400m (world record) 1992, 200m, 400m 1996, world record holder 400m (indoors) 44.63 seconds 1995, 4×400m (outdoors) 2:55.74 1992, 2:54.29 1993; undefeated at 400m from 1989–97; first man to be ranked World No. 1 at 200m and 400m simultaneously 1990, 1991, 1994, 1995; Olympic champion 200m (world record), 400m, Atlanta 1996; Olympic Champion 400m and 4×400m, Sydney 2000; announced retirement 2001; Jesse Owens Award (three times), Track and Field US Athlete of the Year (four times), Asscn of American Univs. (AAU)/Sullivan Award 1996. *Publications:* Slaying The Dragon (autobiog.) 1996, Michael Johnson: Sprinter Deluxe. *Leisure interest:* piano. *Address:* IMG, 600 17th Street, Suite 2420 South, Denver, CO 80202 (Office); USA Track and Field, P.O. Box 120, Indianapolis, IN 46206, USA. *Telephone:* (303) 573-0600 (Office). *Fax:* (303) 573-0605 (Office).

JOHNSON, Paul (Bede), BA; British journalist, historian and broadcaster; b. 2 Nov. 1928, Barton; s. of William Aloysius and Anne Johnson; m. Marigold Hunt 1957; three s. one d.; ed Stonyhurst and Magdalen Coll., Oxford; Asst Exec. Ed. Réalités, Paris 1952–55; Asst Ed. New Statesman 1955–60, Deputy Ed. 1960–64, Ed. 1965–70, Dir 1965; DeWitt Wallace Prof. of Communications, American Enterprise Inst., Washington, DC 1980; mem. Royal Comm. on the Press 1974–77, Cable Authority 1984–90; freelance writer; Book of the Year Prize, Yorkshire Post 1975, Francis Boyer Award for Services to Public Policy 1979, King Award for Excellence (Literature) 1980, Pilkington Literary Award 2003. *Publications:* The Offshore Islanders 1972, Elizabeth I: a Study in Power and Intellect 1974, Pope John XXIII 1975, A History of Christianity 1976, Enemies of Society 1977, The National Trust Book of British Castles 1978, The Civilization of Ancient Egypt 1978, Civilizations of the Holy Land 1979, British Cathedrals 1980, Ireland: Land of Troubles 1980, The Recovery of Freedom 1980, Pope John Paul II and the Catholic Restoration 1982, Modern Times 1983 (revised 1991), History of the Modern World: From 1917 to the 1980s 1984, The Pick of Paul Johnson 1985, Saving and Spending 1986, The Oxford Book of Political Anecdotes (ed.) 1986, The History of the Jews 1987, Intellectuals 1988, The Birth of the Modern: World Society 1815–1830 1991, Wake Up Britain! 1994, The Quest for God 1996, To Hell with Picasso and other essays 1996, A History of the American People 1997, The Renaissance 2000, Napoleon 2002. *Leisure interests:* painting, hill walking. *Address:* 29 Newton Road, London, W2 5JR; The Coach House, Over Stowey, nr Bridgwater, Somerset, TA5 1HA, England. *Telephone:* (20) 7229-3859 (London); (1278) 732393 (Somerset). *Fax:* (20) 7792-1676 (London).

JOHNSON, Philip Cortelyou, AB; American architect; b. 8 July 1906; ed Harvard Univ.; Dir Dept of Architecture and Design, Museum of Modern Art 1932–54, Trustee 1958–; with Johnson/Burgee Architects 1967–; assoc. with the late Mies van der Rohe in design of Seagram Building, New York; mem. Acad. of Arts and Letters; Bronze Medallion (City of New York) 1980; Pritzker Prize 1979, Fellows Award RI School of Design 1983. *Works include:* the Annexe and Sculpture Court, Museum of Modern Art and the Glass House, New Canaan, Conn., Lincoln Center Theater. *Publications:* The International Style, Architecture since 1922 (with H. R. Hitchcock, Jr) 1932, Machine Art 1934, Mies van der Rohe 1947, Architecture 1949–1965 1966. *Address:* 15 West 53rd Street, New York, NY 10019, USA (Home).

JOHNSON, Pierre Marc, BA, LLL, MD, FRSC; Canadian politician and lawyer; b. 5 July 1946, Montreal; s. of late Daniel Johnson and Reine (Gagné) Johnson; m. Marie-Louise Parent 1973; one s. one d.; ed Coll. Jean-Brébeuf, Montreal, Univ. de Montreal and Univ. de Sherbrooke; called to Québec Bar 1971; admitted Québec Coll. of Physicians and Surgeons 1976; elected to Québec Nat. Ass. 1976; mem. Nat. Exec. Council, Parti Québécois 1977–79, Pres. Parti Québécois 1985–87; Minister of Labour and Manpower, Québec 1977–80, of Consumer Affairs, Cooperatives and Financial Insts. 1980–81, of Social Affairs 1981–84, of Justice, Attorney-Gen. and Minister Responsible for Canadian Intergovernmental Affairs 1984–85; Premier of Québec Oct.–Dec. 1985; Leader of Opposition, Québec Nat. Ass. 1985–87; Sr Counsel Heenan Blaikie Attorneys, Montreal; Dir Unimedia, Innovitech Inc., CRC Sofema, EETINA (Mexico), Int. Union for Conservation of Nature (Geneva); Hon. PhD (Lyon). *Publication:* The Environment and NAFTA: implementing and understanding New Continental Law 1995. *Leisure interests:* skiing, swimming, music. *Address:* 1250 René Levesque blvd West, Suite 2500, Montreal, Que., H3B 4Y1, Canada. *Telephone:* (514) 846-2200. *Fax:* (514) 846-3427.

JOHNSON, Richard Keith; British actor and producer; b. 30 July 1927, Upminster, Essex; s. of Keith Holcombe and Frances Louisa Olive Johnson (née Tweed) Johnson; m. 1st Sheila Ann Sweet 1957 (divorced); one s. one d.; m. 2nd Kim Novak 1965 (divorced); m. 3rd Marie-Louise Nordlund 1982 (divorced); one s. one d.; ed Parkfield School, Felsted School, Royal Acad. of Dramatic Art; Nat. Theatre Player, Assoc. Artist RSC; first stage appearance in Hamlet, Opera House, Manchester 1944; Founder, Chair. and CEO United British Artists 1982–90; mem. Council British Acad. Film and Television Arts 1976–78, Council Royal Acad. of Dramatic Art (RADA) 2001–. *Plays:* major parts include Marius Tertius (The First Victoria) 1950, Pierre (The Madwoman of Chaillot) 1951, Demetrius (A Midsummer Night's Dream) 1951, George Phillips (After My Fashion) 1952, Beauchamp, Earl of Warwick (The Lark) 1955, Laertes (Hamlet) 1955, Jack Absolute (The Rivals) 1956, Lord Plynlimmon (Plaintiff in a Pretty Hat) 1956, Orlando (As You Like It), Mark Antony (Julius Caesar), Leonatus (Cymbeline), Ferdinand (The Tempest), Romeo (Romeo and Juliet), Sir Andrew Aguecheek (Twelfth Night), title-role in Pericles, Don Juan (Much Ado About Nothing) 1957–58, Ferdinand (The Tempest) 1957, Romeo (Romeo and Juliet), Sir Andrew Aguecheek (Twelfth Night), Moscow and Leningrad 1959, The Prince (Ondine), Grandier (The Devils), RSC 1960–62, Charles (Blithe Spirit), Pinchwife (The Country Wife), Pilate (The Passion), title-role in The Guardsman all at Nat. Theatre 1975–78; UK tour, Death Trap 1982, An Inspector Calls 1992, The Rivals 1994, Long Day's Journey Into Night 1996, Uncle Vanya 1996, Staying On 1997, To Kill a Mockingbird 1997, Plenty 1999, The Seagull (RSC) 2000. *Films:* Never so Few 1959, The Haunting 1963, The Pumpkin Eater 1964, Operation Crossbow 1965, Khartoum 1966, Deadlier Than the Male 1966, Oedipus the King 1967, Hennessy 1975, Turtle Diary 1984, Treasure Island 1989, Milk 1998, Tomb Raider 2001. *TV films:* Man for All Seasons 1988, Voice of the Heart 1988, The Camomile Lawn, Anglo-Saxon Attitudes 1992, Heavy Weather 1995, The Echo 1998, The Whistle Blower 2000; leading roles in productions including Rembrandt, Antony and Cleopatra, Hamlet (Claudius), The Member for Chelsea (Sir Charles Dilke), Cymbeline. *Productions include:* The Biko Inquest, Serjeant Musgrave's Dance, The Playboy of the Western World, Old Times, Turtle Diary, Castaway, The Lonely Passion of Judith Hearne, Tales From Hollywood 2001, Hock and Soda Water 2001, Gates of Gold 2002. *Publication:* Hennessy 1974. *Leisure interests:* photography, music, travel, cooking, gardening. *Address:* c/o Conway, Van Gelder, Robinson Ltd, 18–21 Jermyn Street, London, SW1Y 6HP, England. *Telephone:* (20) 7287-0077. *Fax:* (20) 7287-1940.

JOHNSON, Thomas S., AB, MBA; American bank executive; b. 19 Nov. 1940, Racine, Wis.; s. of H. Norman Johnson and Jane Agnes McAvoy; m. Margaret Ann Werner 1970; two s. one d.; ed Trinity Coll., Harvard; Head Graduate Business Program, Instructor Finance and Control Ateneo de Manila Univ. 1964–66; Special Asst to Controller, Dept of Defense 1966–69; with Chemical Bank and Chemical Banking Corpn 1969–89, Exec. Vice-Pres. 1979, Sr Exec. Vice-Pres. 1981, Pres. 1983–89; Pres., Dir Corp. and Mfrs Hanover Trust Co. 1989–91, Olympia and York Devts Ltd 1992–; Chair. Pres. CEO GP Financial Corpn, GreenPoint Savings Bank, Flushing, NY 1993–; Chair. Bd of Dirs. Union Theological Seminary, Harvard Business School Club of Greater New York; Bank Capital Market Asscn.'s Cttee for Competitive Securities Market; Dir Bond Club of New York Inc.; Vice-Pres. and Bd mem. Cancer Research Inst. of America; Bd mem. Texas Commerce Bancshares Inc., Pan Atlantic Re, Inc., Phelps Stokes Fund, Montclair Art Museum; mem. Council on Foreign Relations, Inc., Financial Execs Inst. Asscn of Reserve City Bankers, The Group of Thirty; Trustee Trinity Coll.; mem. Business Cttee, Museum of Modern Art, Consultative Group on Int. Econ. and Monetary Affairs. *Address:* GreenPoint Financial Corporation, 90 Park Avenue, New York, NY 10016-1301, USA.

JOHNSON, Timothy Peter, MA, JD; American politician; b. 28 Dec. 1946, Canton, S.D.; s. of Vandal Johnson and Ruth Ljostveit; m. Barbara Brooks 1969; two s. one d.; ed Univ. of South Dakota and Michigan State Univ.; called to bar, S. Dakota 1975, US Dist Court, S. Dakota 1976; fiscal analyst, Legis. Fiscal Agency, Lansing, Mich. 1971–72; sole practice, Vermillion, S. Dakota 1975–86; mem. S. Dakota House of Reps. 1978–82, S. Dakota Senate 1982–86; mem. 101st–103rd US Congresses 1987–97; Senator from S. Dakota 1997–; Democrat. *Address:* United States Senate, 324 Hart Senate Office Building, Washington, DC 20510-0001, USA (Office). *E-mail:* tim@johnson.senate.gov (Office).

JOHNSON, Sir Vassel (Godfrey), Kt., CBE, JP; British banking executive and business executive; b. 18 Jan. 1922, Cayman Islands; s. of the late Charles McKintha Johnson and of Theresa Virginia Johnson (née McDoom); m. Rita Joanna Hinds 1952; three s. (one deceased) four d.; ed Govt Secondary School, Grand Cayman and Bennet Coll., Wolsey Hall, Sussex Univ., UK; entered civil service, Cayman Islands 1942; with Cayman Co. of Jamaica Home Guard 1942–45; Clerical Officer Dept of Treasury, Customs and PO 1945–55; Asst to Deputy Treas. 1955–59; Clerk of Courts 1959–60; Public Recorder 1962–76; Treas. and Collector of Taxes 1965–82; Head of Exchange Control 1966–80; Insp. of Banks and Trust Cos 1966–73; Chair. Cayman Islands Currency Bd 1971–82; mem. Exec. Council, responsible for Finance and Devt 1972–82; Acting Gov. of Cayman Islands 1977; Chair. Govt Vehicles Funding Scheme 1977–82; retd from civil service 1982; Dir British American Bank 1983–; Chair. Public Service Comm. 1983–84; MLA, George Town 1984–88; mem. Exec. Council, responsible for Devt and Nat. Resources 1984–88; Founding Dir Cayman Airways Ltd 1968, Chair. 1971–77, 1984–85; Chair. Cayman Islands Corpn (Airways) 1969–77; Trustee Swiss Bank & Trust Corpn 1983–97; Man. Dir Montpellier Properties (Cayman) Ltd 1983–97; Chair. Bd of Govs Cayman Preparatory School 1982–84, 1993–95; Silver Jubilee Medal 1977. *Publications include:* Cayman Islands Economic and Financial Review 1904–1981 1982, As I See It: How the Cayman Islands Became a Leading Financial Centre (autobiog.) 2001. *Leisure interests:* bridge, church-related activities (Sr Elder, United Church). *Address:* POB 78G, Grand Cayman, Cayman Islands (Office). *Telephone:* 9499217 (Office). *Fax:* 9459326 (Office).

JOHNSON, William, DSc, FRS, FREng, FIMechE; British professor of engineering (retd); b. 20 April 1922, Manchester; s. of James Johnson and Elizabeth Riley; m. Heather Marie Thornber 1946; three s. two d.; ed Univ. of Manchester and Univ. Coll. London; Prof. of Mechanical Eng UMIST 1960–75, Visiting Prof. of Mechanical Eng and History of Science 1992–94; Prof. of Mechanics, Eng Dept Univ. of Cambridge 1975–82, Prof. Emer. 1982–; Visiting Prof., Industrial Eng Dept, Purdue Univ., Ind., USA 1984–85, United Technologies Distinguished Prof. of Eng 1988–89; Founder, Ed. Int. Journal of Mechanical Sciences 1960–87, Int. Journal of Impact Eng 1983–87; Foreign Fellow Acad. of Athens 1982; Foreign mem. Russian Acad. of Science (Ural Br.) 1993, Indian Nat. Acad. of Eng 1999; Fellow of Univ. Coll. London 1981; Hon. DTech (Bradford) 1976, Hon. DEng (Sheffield) 1986, (UMIST) 1995; T. Bernard Hall Prize 1965, 1966, James Clayton Fund Prize 1972, 1977, Safety in Mechanical Eng Prize 1980, 1990, James Clayton Prize, Inst. Mechanical Engineers 1987, Silver Medal Inst. Sheet Metal 1987, AMPT Gold Medal, Dublin 1995, American Soc. of Mechanical Engineers Engineer-Historian Award 2000. *Publications:* (with various co-authors) Plasticity for Mechanical Engineers 1962, Mechanics of Metal Extrusion 1962, Bibliography of Slip Line Fields 1968, Impact Strength of Materials 1972, Engineering Plasticity 1973, Engineering Plasticity: Metal-Forming Processes 1978, Crashworthiness of Vehicles 1978, A Source Book of Plane Strain Slip Line Fields 1982, Collected Works on B. Robins and C. Hutton 2003, Record and Services Satisfactory (memoir) 2003. *Leisure interests:* gardening, walking, music, reading. *Address:* 62 Beach Road, Carlyon Bay, St Austell, Cornwall, PL25 3PJ, England. *Telephone:* (1726) 813179.

JOHNSON-LAIRD, Philip Nicholas, PhD, FRS, FBA; British/American psychologist; b. 12 Oct. 1936, Leeds, Yorks.; s. of Eric Johnson-Laird and Dorothy Johnson-Laird (née Blackett); m. Maureen Mary Sullivan 1959; one s. one d.; ed Culford School, Univ. Coll. London; left school at age 15 and worked as quantity surveyor and in other jobs before univ.; Asst Lecturer, Dept of Psychology, Univ. Coll., London 1966, Lecturer 1967–73; Visiting mem. Inst. for Advanced Study, Princeton, USA 1971–72; Reader in Experimental Psychology, Univ. of Sussex 1973, Prof. 1978–82; Asst Dir, MRC Applied Psychology Unit, Cambridge 1982–89; Fellow Darwin Coll. Cambridge 1984–89; Visiting Fellow, Cognitive Science, Stanford Univ., USA 1980, Visiting Prof. of Psychology 1985, Visiting Prof. of Psychology, Princeton Univ., USA 1986, Prof. 1989–, Stuart Prof. of Psychology 1994–; Dr hc (Gothenburg) 1983; Laurea hc (Padua) 1997; Hon. DSc (Univ. of Dublin Trinity Coll.) 2000; Hon. D.Psych., (Universidad Nacional de Educación a Distancia, Madrid) 2000, (Ghent) 2002; Rosa Morison Memorial Medal, Univ. Coll. London, James Sully Scholarship; Spearman Medal, British Psychological Soc. 1974, Pres.'s Award 1985, Fyssen Foundation Int. Prize 2002. *Publications:* Thinking and Reasoning (Ed. with P. C. Wason) 1968, Psychology of Reasoning (with P. C. Wason) 1972, Language and Perception (with G. A. Miller) 1976, Thinking (Ed. with P. C. Wason) 1977, Mental Models 1983, The Computer and the Mind 1988, Deduction (with R. M. J. Byrne) 1992, Human and Machine Thinking 1993; numerous articles in psychological journals; reviews. *Leisure interests:* arts and music, talking and

arguing. *Address:* Department of Psychology, Princeton University, Princeton, NJ 08544, USA. *Telephone:* (609) 258-4432. *E-mail:* phil@princeton.edu (Office).

JOHNSON SIRLEAF, Ellen; Liberian politician and civil servant; ed Harvard Univ.; Asst Minister of Finance 1964–69, Deputy Minister of Finance 1977–80; Sr Loan Officer, IBRD, Washington, DC 1973–77, 1980–81; fmr Pres. Liberian Bank for Devt Investment; Vice-Pres. Citibank Regional Office for Africa, Nairobi 1981–85; Vice-Pres. and mem. Bd of Dirs. Equator Holders, Equator Bank Ltd, Washington, DC until 1992; Asst Admin. UNDP and Dir Regional Bureau for Africa 1992–97; Presidential Cand. 1997; Leader Unity Party (UP). *Address:* Unity Party, Monrovia, Liberia (Office).

JOHNSSON, Anders B., LLM; Swedish international organization official; b. 1948, Lund; m.; three c.; ed Univs. of Lund and New York; mem. staff UNHCR, posts in Honduras, Pakistan, Sudan and Viet Nam, then Prin. Legal Adviser to High Commr, Geneva 1976–91; Under-Sec.-Gen. IPU 1991–94, Deputy Sec.-Gen. and Legal Adviser 1994–98, Sec.-Gen. 1998–. *Address:* Inter-Parliamentary Union, CP 330, 1218 Le Grand-Saconnex/Geneva, Switzerland (Office). *Telephone:* (22) 9194150 (Office). *Fax:* (22) 9194160 (Office). *E-mail:* postbox@mail.ipu.org (Office). *Website:* www.ipu.org (Office).

JOHNSTON, David Lloyd, CC, LLB; Canadian professor of law; b. 28 June 1941, Sudbury, Ont.; s. of Lloyd Johnston and Dorothy Stonehouse; m. Sharon Downey 1964; five d.; ed Sault Collegiate Inst., Sault Ste. Marie, Ont., Harvard Univ., Univ. of Cambridge and Queen's Univ., Kingston; Asst Prof. Faculty of Law, Queen's Univ., Kingston 1966–68; Asst Prof. Faculty of Law, Univ. of Toronto 1968–69, Assoc. Prof. 1969–72, Prof. 1972–74; Dean and Prof. Faculty of Law, Univ. of W Ont. 1974–79; Prof. of Law, McGill Univ. 1979–, Prin. and Vice-Chancellor 1979–94; Pres. and Vice-Chancellor, Univ. of Waterloo 1999–; Pres. Harvard Univ. Bd of Overseers 1997–98; recipient of 12 hon. degrees. *Publications:* Computers and the Law 1968, Canadian Securities Regulation 1977, The Law of Business Associations (with R. Forbes) 1979, Canadian Companies and the Stock Exchange 1980, If Québec Goes: The Real Cost of Separation (with Marcel Côté) 1995, Getting Canada On Line: Understanding the Information Highway (co-author) 1995, Cyberlaw 1997, Communications Law of Canada 1999; numerous articles in academic journals. *Leisure interests:* jogging, skiing. *Address:* University of Waterloo, 200 University Avenue W, Waterloo, Ont., N2L 3G1 (Office); R. R. #1, St Clements, Ont., N0B 2M0, Canada (Home). *Telephone:* (519) 888-4400 (Office); (519) 699-4877 (Home). *Fax:* (519) 888-6337 (Office). *E-mail:* president@waterloo.ca (Office).

JOHNSTON, Hon. Donald J., PC, QC, BA, BCL; Canadian politician, lawyer and international civil servant; b. 26 June 1936, Cumberland, Ont.; s. of Wilbur Austin Johnston and Florence Jean Moffat Tucker; m. Heather Bell Maclaren; four d.; ed McGill Univ. and Univ. of Grenoble; joined Stikeman, Elliott (int. law firm) 1961; subsequent f. own law firm, Johnston, Heenan & Blaikie; teacher of law, McGill Univ. 1963–76; mem. Parl. 1978–88; Pres. Treasury Bd 1980–82; Minister for Econ. Devt and Minister of State for Science and Tech. 1982–83; Minister of State for Econ. Devt and Tech. 1983–84; Minister of Justice and Attorney-Gen. June–Sept. 1984; elected Pres. Liberal Party of Canada 1990, re-elected 1992; Counsel, Heenan, Blaikie (law firm), Montreal 1988–96; Sec.-Gen. OECD 1996–; Hon. DCL; Hon. DEcon. *Publications:* Up the Hill (political memoirs) 1986; one book on taxation; numerous professional papers. *Leisure interests:* tennis, piano, writing. *Address:* Organisation for Economic Co-operation and Development, 2 rue André-Pascal, 75775 Paris Cedex 16, France. *Telephone:* 1-45-24-80-10. *Fax:* 1-45-24-80-12. *E-mail:* donald.johnston@oecd.org (Office). *Website:* www.oecd.org (Office).

JOHNSTON, Jennifer; Irish writer; b. 12 Jan. 1930, Dublin; d. of Denis Johnston and Shelah Richards; m. 1st Ian Smyth; two s. two d.; m. 2nd David Gilliland; ed Park House School, Dublin, Trinity Coll., Dublin; Hon. Fellow Trinity Coll., Dublin; Hon. DLitt (New Univ. of Ulster, Queen's Univ., Belfast, Trinity Coll., Dublin); Whitbread Prize 1980, Giles Cooper Award 1989. *Plays:* The Desert Lullaby, Moonlight and Music; several radio and TV programmes. *Publications:* How Many Miles to Babylon?, The Old Jest, The Christmas Tree, The Invisible Worm 1991, The Illusionist 1995, Two Moons, The Railway Station Man 1986, Shadows on Our Skin, The Gingerbread Woman, The Porch 1986, The Invisible Man 1986, The Desert Lullaby 1996, This is Not a Novel 2003. *Leisure interests:* reading, theatre, cinema. *Address:* Brook Hall, Culmore Road, Derry, BT48 8JE, Northern Ireland (Home). *Telephone:* (28) 7135-1297 (Home).

JOHNSTON, J(ohn) Bennett, Jr.; American politician; b. 10 June 1932, Shreveport, La.; s. of J. Bennett Johnston; m. Mary Gunn; two s. two d.; ed Byrd High School, Washington and Lee Univ., U.S. Mil. Acad. and Louisiana State Univ. Law School; School of Law; mil. service in Judge Advocate Gen. Corps La.; State Senator 1968–72; Senator from Louisiana 1972–96; Chair. Democratic Senatorial Campaign Cttee 1975–76; mem. Senate Cttee on Energy and Natural Resources, on Appropriations, Senate Budget Cttee, mem. Senate Bldg Cttee; partner Johnston & Assocs. 1996–; Democrat. *Leisure interest:* tennis. *Address:* Johnston & Associates, 1455 Pennsylvania Avenue, NW, Suite 200, Washington, DC, 20004, USA.

JOHNSTON, Ronald John, PhD, FBA; British geographer; b. 30 March 1941, Swindon; s. of Henry Louis Johnston and Phyllis Joyce (née Liddiard) Johnston; m. Rita Brennan 1963; one s. one d.; ed The Commonweal Co.

Secondary Grammar School, Swindon, Univ. of Manchester; Teaching Fellow, then lecturer, Dept of Geography, Monash Univ., Australia 1964–66; lecturer then Reader, Dept of Geography, Univ. of Canterbury, NZ 1967–74; Prof. of Geography, Univ. of Sheffield 1974–92, Pro-Vice-Chancellor for Academic Affairs 1989–92; Vice-Chancellor Univ. of Essex 1992–95; Prof. of Geography, Univ. of Bristol 1995–; Co-Ed. Environment and Planning 1979–, Progress in Human Geography 1979–; mem. Acad. of Learned Socs for the Social Sciences; Hon. DUniv (Essex) 1996; Hon. LLD (Monash, Australia) 1999; Hon. DLitt (Sheffield) 2002; Murchison Award, Royal Geographical Soc. (RGS) 1984, Victoria Medal (RGS) 1990, Hons Award for Distinguished Contribs, Asscn of American Geographers 1991, Prix Vautrin Lud 1999. *Publications:* author or co-author of more than 30 books, including Geography and Geographers, Philosophy and Human Geography, City and Society, The Geography of English Politics, A Nation Dividing?, Bell-ringing: the English Art of Change-Ringing, An Atlas of Bells; Ed. or Co-Ed. of more than 20 books, including Geography and the Urban Environment (six vols), The Dictionary of Human Geography; author or co-author of more than 500 articles in academic journals. *Leisure interests:* bell-ringing, walking. *Address:* School of Geographical Sciences, University of Bristol, Bristol, BS8 1SS (Office); 123 The Close, Salisbury, SP1 2EY, England (Home). *Telephone:* (117) 928-9116 (Office). *Fax:* (117) 928-7878 (Office). *E-mail:* r.johnston@bris.ac.uk (Office). *Website:* www.bris.ac.uk/geog (Office).

JOHNSTON, Very Rev. William Bryce, MA, BD, DD, DLitt; British ecclesiastic; b. 16 Sept. 1921, Edinburgh; s. of William B. Johnston and Isabel W. Highley; m. Ruth M. Cowley 1947; one s. two d.; ed George Watson's Coll. Edinburgh and Univ. of Edinburgh; Chaplain to HM Forces 1945–49; Minister, St Andrew's Bo'ness 1949–55, St George's Greenock 1955–64, Colinton Parish Church, Edin. 1964–91; Chaplain to HM The Queen in Scotland 1981–91, Extra Chaplain 1991–; Moderator of Gen. Ass. of Church of Scotland 1980–81, Chair. Judicial Comm. 1987–91; Visiting Lecturer in Social Ethics, Heriot-Watt Univ. 1966–87; Cunningham Lecturer, New Coll. Edin. 1968–71. *Leisure interests:* organ music, bowls. *Address:* 15 Elliot Road, Edinburgh, EH14 1DU, Scotland. *Telephone:* (131) 441-3387.

JOHNSTONE, D. Bruce, PhD; American university administrator and educator; b. 13 Jan. 1941, Minneapolis, Minn.; s. of Donald Bruce and Florence Elliott Johnstone; m. Gail Eberhardt 1965; one s. one d.; ed Harvard Univ. and Univ. of Minnesota; Admin. Asst to Senator Walter F. Mondale (q.v.) 1969–71; Project Specialist, Ford Foundation 1971–72; Exec. Asst to Pres. and Vice-Pres., Univ. of Pa 1972–77, Adjunct Assoc. Prof. of Educ. 1976–79, Vice-Pres. for Admin. 1977–79; Pres. State Univ. Coll., Buffalo 1979–88; Chancellor State Univ. of New York 1988–94; Prof., Univ. at Buffalo 1994–; Dr hc (D'Youville Coll.) 1995, (Calif. State Univ.) 1997; Nat. Asscn of Student Financial Aid Admin's Golden Quill Award. *Publications:* Sharing The Costs of Higher Education: Student Financial Assistance in The United Kingdom, The Federal Republic of Germany, France, Sweden and the United States 1986; other works on the Econs and man. of higher educ. *Leisure interests:* writing, wilderness canoeing, wildflower botany. *Address:* 468 Baldy Hall, University at Buffalo, Buffalo, NY 12246, USA (Office); 284 Rivermist Drive, Buffalo, NY 14202, USA (Home). *Telephone:* (716) 645-3168. *Fax:* (716) 645-2481. *E-mail:* dbj@acsu.buffalo.edu (Office).

JOHNSTONE, Peter; British diplomatist and administrator; b. 30 July 1944; m. Diane Claxton 1969; one s. one d.; joined Foreign Office 1962, postings abroad include Berne 1965–66, Benin City 1966–68, Budapest 1968–69, Maseru 1969–72, Dhaka 1977–79; First Sec. Dublin 1979–82, Harare 1986–89; Consul-Gen. Edmonton 1989–91; Counsellor for Commercial Devt, Jakarta 1995–2000; Gov. of Anguilla and Chair. Exec. Council 2000–. *Address:* Office of the Governor, Government House, P.O. Box 60, The Valley, Anguilla, West Indies (Office). *Telephone:* 497-2622 (Office). *Fax:* 497-3314 (Office).

JOHORE, HH Sultan of, Sultan Mahmood Iskandar ibni Al-Marhum Sultan Ismail; Malaysian Ruler; b. 8 April 1932, Johore Bahru, Johore; s. of Sultan Tengku Ismail of Johore; m. 1st Josephine Trevorrow 1956; m. 2nd Tengku Zanariah Ahmad Zanariah Ahmad 1961; ed Sultan Abu Bakar English Coll., Johore Bahru, Trinity Grammar School, Sydney, Australia, Devon Tech. Coll., Torquay, UK; Tengku Makota (Crown Prince) 1959–61, 1981; Raja Muda (second-in-line to the throne) 1966–81; fifth Sultan of Johore 1981–; Col-in-Chief, Johore Mil. Forces 1981–; Yang di-Pertuan Agung (Supreme Head of State) 1984–89; f. Mado's Enterprises and Mados-Citoh-Daiken (timber cos.). *Leisure interests:* hunting, tennis, golf, flying, water sports.

JOKIPII, Liisa, MD; Finnish university teacher and medical doctor; b. 26 March 1943, Helsinki; m. Anssi Jokipii 1968; two s. two d.; ed Univ. of Helsinki; Asst, Dept of Serology and Bacteriology, Univ. of Helsinki 1973, Dozent in Clinical Microbiology and Immunology 1977–; Prof. of Clinical Microbiology and Immunology, Univ. of Oulu 1977; Prof. of Bacteriology and Serology, Univ. of Turku 1978. *Publications:* scientific articles on cell-mediated immunity, bacteriology and parasitology; textbook chapters on parasitology. *Leisure interests:* classical music (opera), old Finnish handicrafts and design. *Address:* Vanhaväylä 37, 00830 Helsinki, Finland (Home). *Telephone:* (0) 783827 (Home).

JOKLIK, Wolfgang Karl, DPhil; American professor of microbiology and immunology; b. 16 Nov. 1926, Vienna, Austria; s. of Karl F. Joklik and Helene Joklik (née Giessl) ; m. 1st Judith V. Nicholas 1955 (died 1975); one s. one d.; m. 2nd Patricia H. Downey 1977; ed Sydney and Oxford Univs.; Research Fellow, Australian Nat. Univ. 1954–56, Fellow 1957–62; Assoc. Prof. of Cell Biology, Albert Einstein Coll. of Medicine, New York 1962–65, Siegfried Ullman Prof. 1966–68; Prof. and Chair. Dept of Microbiology and Immunology Duke Univ. 1968–92, James B. Duke Distinguished Prof. 1972–96, James B. Duke Distinguished Prof. Emer. 1996–; Pres. Virology Div. American Soc. for Microbiology 1966–69; Chair. Virology Study Section Nat. Insts of Health 1973–75; Pres. American Medical School Microbiology Chairs.' Asscn 1979; Pres. American Soc. for Virology 1982–83; Ed.-in-Chief Virology 1975–93, Microbiological Reviews 1991–95; Assoc. Ed. Journal of Biological Chem. 1978–88; mem. NAS, mem. NAS Inst. of Medicine; Humboldt Prize 1986, ICN Int. Prize in Virology 1992. *Publications:* Contrib. to and Sr Ed. specialist books, including Zinsser Microbiology, Principles of Animal Virology, The Reoviridae; more than 200 articles in specialist journals. *Leisure interests:* travel, photography, music, golf, tennis and squash. *Address:* Department of Molecular Genetics and Microbiology, P.O. Box 3020, Duke University Medical Center, Durham, NC 27710, USA. *Telephone:* (919) 684-2042. *Fax:* (919) 684-8735.

JOKŪBONIS, Gediminas; Lithuanian sculptor; b. 8 March 1927, Kupiškis; s. of Albinas Jokūbonis and Domicėlė Jokūbonienė; m. Bronė Valantinaitė 1953; two s. one d.; ed Kaunas Inst. of Decorative and Applied Arts, Inst. of Arts, Lithuanian SSR; lecturer, Vilnius Inst. of Arts (now Acad. of Arts) 1965–, Prof. 1974–; mem. USSR (now Russian) Acad. of Arts 1983; author of monumental sculptures in Lithuania, including Mother (Memorial Complex, Pirciupiai) 1960, Monuments to the singer Kipras Petrauskas, Vilnius 1974, to the poet Maironis, Kaunas 1977, to A. Miczkevic, Vilnius 1984, to poet Vienažindys Mažeikiai 1987, to Grand Duke of Lithuania Vytautas, Vytautas church in Kaunas 1991, to Martynas Mažvydas, Nat. Library, Vilnius 1996, to the poet Antanas Baranauskas, Seinai, Poland 1999; People's Artist of Lithuania 1977; Lithuanian State Prize, Lenin Prize. *Group exhibitions include:* Moscow, Russia, Rīga, Latvia, Tallinn, Estonia, Tbilisi, Georgia, Baku, Azerbaijan; Young Artists exhbn, Paris 1962, 32nd Biennale, Venice, Expo '67, Montreal; Osaka, Japan, Rostock, Germany 1998, Amsterdam 1998. *Leisure interests:* archaeology, history. *Address:* VDA, Maironio str. 6, 2600 Vilnius (Office); V. Kudirkos 4–3, 2009 Vilnius, Lithuania. *Telephone:* (2) 253632 (Office); (2) 330714 (Home).

JOLIE, Angelina; American actress; b. 1975; d. of Jon Voight (q.v.) and Marcheline Bertrand; m. 1st Jonny Lee Miller 1996 (divorced 1999); m. 2nd Billy Bob Thornton 2000; one adopted s.; ed Lee Strasberg Inst., New York Univ.; apptd. Goodwill Amb. by UNHCR 2001; Golden Globes for George Wallace 1998, for Gia 1999, Screen Actors Guild Award for Gia 1999. *Films include:* Lookin' to Get Out 1982, Cyborg II: Glass Shadow 1995, Hackers 1995, Foxfire 1996, Mojave Moon 1996, Love is All There is 1996, True Women 1997, George Wallace 1997, Playing God 1997, Hell's Kitchen 1998, Gia 1998, Playing by Heart 1999, Tomb Raider 2001, Original Sin 2001. *Address:* c/o Richard Bauman & Associates, Suite 473, 5757 # Wilshire Boulevard, Los Angeles, CA 90036, USA.

JOLIOT, Pierre Adrien, D. ÈS SC.; French scientist; b. 12 March 1932, Paris; s. of Frédéric Joliot and Irène Joliot Curie; m. Anne Gricouroff 1961; two s.; ed Faculté des Sciences de Paris; researcher, Centre Nat. de la Recherche Scientifique 1954–81, Dir of Research 1974–; Prof., Collège de France 1981–; Chef de Service, Institut de Biologie Physico-Chimique 1975–94, Admin. 1994–97; Dir Dept of Biology, Ecole Normale Supérieure 1987–92; Scientific Adviser to Prime Minister 1985–86; Pres. Science Ethics Cttee, CNRS 1998–; mem. Comité nat. d'évaluation de la recherche, CNER, 1989–92; mem. de l'Institut (Acad. des Sciences, Paris) 1982; mem. NAS (USA), Academia Europaea, Acad. Européenne des Sciences, des Arts et des Lettres; Prix André Policard-Lacassagne 1968, Charles F. Kettering Award for excellence in photosynthesis 1970, Prix du Commissariat à l'Energie Atomique 1980, Gold Medal CNRS 1982; Officier Légion d'honneur; Commdr de l'Ordre du mérite. *Publications:* scientific works on bioenergetics and photosynthesis. *Leisure interests:* tennis, sailing, skiing. *Address:* Institut de Biologie Physico-Chimique, 13 rue Pierre et Marie Curie, 75005 Paris (Office); 16 rue de la Glacière, 75013 Paris, France (Home). *Telephone:* 1-58-41-50-11 (Office); 1-43-37-22-56 (Home). *E-mail:* pjoliot@ibpc.fr (Office).

JOLLEY, Elizabeth Monica, AO; British/Australian writer and lecturer; b. 4 June 1923, Birmingham; d. of Charles Knight and Margarethe Knight; m. Leonard Jolley 1945 (died 1994); one s. two d.; ed Friends' School, Sibford; trained as a nurse Queen Elizabeth Hosp., Birmingham 1940–46; moved to W Australia with family 1959; held a variety of occupations; lecturer School of Communication and Cultural Studies, Curtin Univ. of Tech.1978–, Prof. of Creative Writing 1998–; Hon. DTech (W.A.I.T., now Curtin), Hon. DLitt (Macquarie Univ.), (Queensland) 1997; novels Mr Scobie's Riddle and My Father's Moon won Age Book of the Year Award, novel The Well won Miles Franklin Award (film 1997), novel The Sugar Mother won France-Australia Literary Translation Award, novel Milk and Honey won Premier of NSW Prize and the collection of essays Central Mischief won Premier of WA Prize; ASAL Gold Medal for contrib. to Australian Literature. *Publications:* 14 novels including The Orchard Thieves 1995, Lovesong 1997, An Accommodating Spouse 1999, one vol. of poetry, one vol. of essays, one vol. of radio plays. *Leisure interests:* orchardist and goose farmer, reading, walking. *Address:* School of English, Curtin University of Technology, P.O. Box U1987, Perth, WA 6001; 28 Agett Road, Claremont 6010, Western Australia. *Telephone:* (8) 9384-7879.

JOLLY, Robert Dudley, BVSc, DSc, PhD, FRSNZ; New Zealand veterinary pathologist; b. 1 Oct. 1930, Hamilton; s. of Thomas D. Jolly and Violet Mills; m. Aline C. Edwards 1958; two s. two d.; ed King's Coll., NZ and Univs. of Auckland and Sydney; mixed veterinary practice, Rotorua 1955–59; Teaching Fellow, Univ. of Sydney 1960–63; Assoc. Prof. Univ. of Guelph, Canada 1963–65; Sr Lecturer, Massey Univ. 1965–68, Reader 1968–85, Prof. in Veterinary Pathology and Public Health 1985–96, Prof. Emer. 1997–; Hon. mem. American Coll. of Veterinary Pathologists; Hon. Fellow Australian Coll. of Veterinary Science; Hon. FRCPA; Hector Medal 1996. *Publications:* 150 publs in scientific books and journals. *Leisure interests:* gardening, trout fishing. *Address:* Institute of Veterinary, Animal and Biomedical Science, Massey University, Palmerston North (Office); 136 Buick Crescent, Palmerston North, New Zealand (Home). *Telephone:* (6) 356-9099 (Office); (6) 354-5852 (Home). *E-mail:* r.d.jolly@massey.ac.nz (Office).

JOLOWICZ, John Anthony, QC, MA; British professor of law and barrister; b. 11 April 1926, London; s. of H. F. Jolowicz and Ruby Wagner; m. Poppy Stanley 1957; one s. two d.; ed Oundle School and Trinity Coll., Cambridge; army service 1944–48; called to the Bar 1952; QC 1990; Fellow, Trinity Coll. Cambridge 1952–; Asst lecturer, lecturer in law, Univ. of Cambridge 1955–72, Reader in Common and Comparative Law 1972–76, Prof. of Comparative Law 1976–93, Prof. Emer. 1993–, Chair. Faculty of Law 1985–87; Pres. Soc. of Public Teachers of Law 1986–87; Visiting Prof. Chicago 1957, Mexico 1965, 1968, Paris 1976, Bologna 1992, Trento 1995; Bencher, Gray's Inn, London; a Vice-Pres. Int. Acad. of Comparative Law 1999–; Corresp. Acad. des Sciences Morales et Politiques; Chevalier Légion d'honneur 2002; Dr hc (Nat. Univ. Mexico) 1985, (Buckingham) 2000. *Publications:* Winfield & Jolowicz on Tort, H. F. Jolowicz's Lectures on Jurisprudence 1963, Public Interest Parties and the Active Role of the Judge (with M. Cappelletti) 1975, Droit Anglais (with others) 1992, Recourse Against Judgments in The European Union (with others, also Man. Ed.) 1999, On Civil Procedure 2000; numerous legal articles. *Leisure interests:* music, reading, travel, grandchildren. *Address:* Trinity College, Cambridge CB2 1TQ (Office); West Green House, Barrington, Cambs., CB2 5SA, England (Home). *Telephone:* (1223) 338400 (Office); (1223) 870495 (Home). *Fax:* (1223) 338461 (Office); (1223) 872852 (Home). *E-mail:* jaj1000@hermes.cam.ac.uk (Home).

JOLY, Alain; French business executive; b. 18 April 1938, Nantes; s. of Albert Joly and Yvonne Poyet Rolin; m. Marie-Hélène Capbern-Gasqueton 1966; two s. one d.; ed Lycée Louis Le Grand, Paris and Ecole Polytechnique Paris; Engineer, L'Air Liquide 1962–67; Dir of Operations, Canadian Liquid Air 1967–73; Dir Corp. Planning, Société L'Air Liquide 1973–76, Regional Man. 1976–78, Gen. Sec. 1978–81, Vice-Pres. 1981, Dir 1982, Chair. and CEO 1995–, Chair. Supervisory Bd 2001–; Dir Lafarge Coppée (now Lafarge) 1993–, Banque Nat. de Paris 1995–; mem. Int. Council, JP Morgan; Croix de la Valeur Militaire, Officier, Légion d'honneur. *Leisure interests:* sailing, golf. *Address:* L'Air Liquide SA, 75 Quai d'Orsay, 75007 Paris, France. *Telephone:* 1-40-62-55-55.

JOLY, Eva, DenD; Norweigan judge; b. 1945, Oslo; m. (husband died 2001); one s. one d.; legal counsellor in a psychiatric hosp.; apptd regional judge, Orleans 1981, Asst to Public Prosecutor 1981–83; High Court Judge, Evry 1983–89, currently First Examining Judge; legal specialist, Interministerial Cttee for Industrial Reconstruction, Ministry of Finance, Paris 1989, Deputy Sec.-Gen. –1993; investigating magistrate for financial affairs, Palais de Justice, Paris 1993–, led to conviction of Bernard Tapie 1994, Roland Dumas 1998, forty exec. mems. of Elf Aquitaine including Chair. Lok Le Floch-Prigent 1995–2002, employees of Pechiney, Crédit Lyonnaise and other high-ranking politicians and businessmen; employed by Ministry of Justice to draft int. conventions against corruption, Oslo 2002–(05); Transparency Int. Integrity Award 2001, European of the Year, Reader's Digest 2002. *Publication:* Notre Affaire à Tous (This Concerns All of Us) (autobiog.) 2000. *Address:* c/o Ministry of Defence, Myntgt. 1, POB 8126 Dep., 0032 Oslo, Norway (Office).

JONAS, Sir Peter, Kt, CBE, BA, LRAM, FRCM, FRNCM, FRSA; British arts administrator and opera company director; b. 14 Oct. 1946, London; s. of Walter Adolf and Hilda May Jonas; m. Lucy Hull 1989 (divorced 2001); ed Worth School, Univ. of Sussex, Royal Northern Coll. of Music, Manchester, Royal Coll. of Music, London, Eastman School of Music, Univ. of Rochester, USA; Asst to Music Dir, Chicago Symphony Orchestra 1974–76, Artistic Admin. 1976–85; Dir of Artistic Admin., The Orchestral Asscn, Chicago 1977–85; Gen. Dir English Nat. Opera 1985–93; Staatsintendant (Gen. and Artistic Dir) Bavarian State Opera, Munich 1993–; mem. Bd of Man. Nat. Opera Studio 1985–93; mem. Council Royal Coll. of Music 1988–95; mem. Council of Man., London Lighthouse 1990–92; mem. Kuratorium Richard Strauss Gesellschaft 1993–; mem. Advisory Bd Bayerische Vereinsbank 1994–; mem. Rundfunkrat, Bayerische Rundfunk 1999–; Queen's Lecture, Berlin 2001; Bayerische Verdienstorden (Germany) 2001; Hon. DMus (Sussex) 1993; Bavarian Constitutional Medal 2001. *Publications:* Powerhouse (with M. Elder and D. Pountney) 1993, Eliten und Demokratie 1999. *Leisure interests:* 20th century architecture, cinema, theatre, skiing, mountain hiking, wine, old master paintings. *Address:* c/o Bayerische Staatsoper, Nationaltheater, Max-Joseph-Platz 2, 80539 Munich, Germany. *Telephone:* (89) 21851001 (Office); (89) 21851000. *Fax:* (89) 21851003 (Office); (89) 21851003. *E-mail:* peter.jonas@st-oper.bayern.de (Office); sirpeterjonas@t-online.de (Home).

JONES, Alan Stanley, OBE; Australian racing driver; b. 2 Nov. 1946, Melbourne; s. of Stan Jones (fmr Australian champion racing driver); m. Beverly Jones 1971; one adopted s.; ed Xavier Coll., Melbourne; began racing in 1964 in Australia, raced in Britain from 1970; World Champion 1980, runner-up 1979; CanAm Champion 1978; Grand Prix wins: 1977 Austrian (Shadow-Ford), 1979 German (Williams-Ford), 1979 Austrian (Williams-Ford), 1979 Dutch (Williams-Ford), 1979 Canadian (Williams-Ford), 1980 Argentine (Williams-Ford), 1980 French (Williams-Ford), 1980 British (Williams-Ford), 1980 Canadian (Williams-Ford), 1980 US (Williams-Ford), 1981 US (Williams-Ford); announced retirement in 1981; started to compete in Amsterdam Touring Car Championships 1990; participated in launch of Australian Motor Sports Acad.; apptd to Bd Australian Grand Prix Corpn 1995; TV commentator. *Leisure interests:* collecting interesting cars, farming in Australia, boating.

JONES, Allen, RA, FRBS; British artist; b. 1 Sept. 1937, Southampton; s. of William and Madeline Jones; m. 1st Janet Bowen 1964 (divorced 1978); two d.; m. 2nd Deirdre Morrow 1994; ed Hornsey School of Art, Royal Coll. of Art; Sec., Young Contemporaries, London 1961; lived in New York 1964–65; Tamarind Lithography Fellowship, Los Angeles 1966; Guest Prof. Dept of Painting, Univ. of S Florida 1969; Hochschule für Bildende Künste, Hamburg 1968–70, Hochschule der Künste, Berlin 1982–83; Guest Lecturer Univ. of Calif. 1977; first one-man exhbn, London 1963, one-man exhbns in UK, USA, Switzerland, Germany, Italy, Australia, Japan, Netherlands, Belgium, Austria, Spain, China, Argentina, Brazil, Czech Repub., Cyprus, Norway, Finland, Estonia 1963–; many group exhbns. of paintings and graphic work, worldwide 1962–; first travelling retrospective, Europe 1979–80; Welsh Arts Council-sponsored sculpture exhbn 1992; British Council Print Retrospective 1995–98; Commercial Mural Project, Basel 1979; designs for TV and stage in Fed. Repub. of Germany and UK; sculptures commissioned for Liverpool Garden Festival 1984, Cotton's Atrium, Pool of London 1987, Sterling Hotel, Heathrow 1990, Riverside Health Authority, Westminster and Chelsea Hosp., London 1993, Swire Properties, Hong Kong 1997, Goodwood 1998, GSK World HQ, London 2001–02; works in many public and pvt. collections in UK and elsewhere including Tate Gallery, London, Victoria & Albert Museum, London, Museum of 20th Century, Vienna, Stedelijk Museum, Amsterdam, Museum of Modern Art, New York, Hirshhorn Museum, Washington DC, Chicago Museum of Art, Moderna Museet, Stockholm, Yale Center for British Art, Whitney Museum of American Art, New York; Trustee British Museum 1990–99; Prix des Jeunes Artistes, Paris Biennale 1963, Art and Work Award, Wapping Arts Trust 1989, Heitland Foundation Award 1995. *Publications:* Allen Jones Figures 1969, Allen Jones Projects 1971, Waitress 1972, Ways and Means 1977, Sheer Magic (Paintings 1959–79) 1979, UK 1980, Allen Jones (painting and sculpture) 1963–93 1993, Allen Jones Prints 1995, Allen Jones 1997, Allen Jones Sculptures 1965–2002 2002. *Leisure interest:* gardening. *Address:* 41 Charterhouse Square, London, EC1M 6EA, England. *Telephone:* (20) 7606-2984 (Home). *Fax:* (20) 7600-1204. *E-mail:* aj@ajstudio.demon.co.uk (Home).

JONES, Rt. Rev. Alwyn Rice, MA; Welsh ecclesiastic; b. 25 March 1934, Capel Curig, Gwynedd; s. of the late John Griffith Jones and Annie Jones (née Roberts); m. Meriel Ann Jones 1967; one d.; ed Llanrwst Grammar School, Univ. of Wales, Lampeter, Fitzwilliam Coll., Cambridge; ordained Diocese of Bangor, deacon 1958, priest 1959; Asst curate Llanfairisgaer, Bangor 1958–62; sec. and chaplain Student Christian Movt Colls. Wales 1962–65; chaplain St Winifred's School, Llanfairfechan 1965–67; Diocesan Dir of Educ. Diocese of Bangor 1965–75, youth chaplain 1967–72, warden of ordinands 1970–75; Asst tutor in Religious Studies Univ. Coll. of North Wales 1973–76; Hon. Canon Bangor Cathedral 1975; vicar of St Mary's with Battle 1979–82; Bishop of St Asaph 1982–99; Archbishop of Wales 1991–99; Chair. Religious Panel S4C TV 1987; Pres. Council of Churches for Britain and Ireland 1997–2000; mem. Religious Advisory Panel IBA 1973–75. *Leisure interests:* music, walking. *Address:* Curig, 7 Llwyn Onn, Bishop's Walk, St Asaph, Denbighs., LL17 0SQ, Wales. *Telephone:* (1745) 584621. *Fax:* (1745) 584301.

JONES, Barry Owen, AO, MA, LLD, DSc, DLitt, DUniv, FAA, FAHA, FTSE, FRSA, FAIM; Australian politician, fmr public servant, teacher, university lecturer and lawyer; b. 11 Oct. 1932, Geelong, Vic.; s. of Claud Edward Jones and Ruth Marion (née Black) Jones; m. Rosemary Hanbury 1961; ed Melbourne High School, Melbourne Univ.; MP Victorian Parl. 1972–77, House of Reps 1977–98; Minister for Science 1983–90, Minister for Technology 1983–84, Minister Assisting the Minister for Industry, Tech. and Commerce 1984–87, Minister for Science, Customs and Small Business 1988–90; Minister Assisting the Prime Minister for Science and Tech. 1989–90; Visiting Prof. Wollongong Univ. 1991–98, Victoria Univ. of Tech. 1994–; Adjunct Prof. Monash Univ. 1999–; Chair. Port Arthur Historic Site, Tasmania 2000–; mem. Nat. Comm. for UNESCO 1990–99, Exec. Bd of UNESCO, Paris 1991–95; Chair. House of Reps Cttee on Long Term Strategies 1990–96, Victorian Schools Innovation Comm. 2001–; Nat. Pres. Australian Labor Party 1992–2000; Chair. Australian Film and TV School 1973–75, Australian Film Inst. 1974–80; Deputy Chair. Australian Council for the Arts 1969–73, Australian Constitutional Convention 1997–98; Vice-Pres., World Heritage Cttee 1995–96, Australia ICOMOS Inc. 1998–2000; mem. Australian Film Devt Corpn 1970–75, Australian Nat. Library Council 1996–98; Visiting Fellow Trinity Coll., Cambridge, England 2000–; Australian Labor Party; Raymond Longford Award (Australian Film Inst.) 1986, Redmond Barry Award (ALIA) 1996, John Curtin Medal 2001. *Publications include:* Macmillan Dictionary of Biography 1981, Sleepers, Wake!: Technology and the Future of Work 1982, Managing Our Opportunities 1984, Living by Our Wits 1986, Dictionary of World Biography 1994, A Thinking Reed 2004. *Leisure interests:* films, music, travel, collecting autographed documents, antique terracottas and paintings, reading. *Address:* 2 Treasury Place, East Melbourne, Victoria 3002 (Office); GPO Box 496, Melbourne, Victoria 3001, Australia. *Telephone:* (3) 9637-3595 (Office); (418) 399196. *E-mail:* jones .barry.o@edumail.vic.gov.au (Office); barry.jones@alp.org.au (Home).

JONES, Bill T.; American dancer and choreographer; b. 15 Feb. 1952, Bunnell, Fla; ed State Univ. of New York, Binghamton; Co-Founder American Dance Asylum 1973; Co-Founder, Artistic Dir Bill T. Jones/Arnie Zane Dance Co. 1982–; Choreographer (with Arnie Zane) Pas de Deux for Two 1974, Across the Street 1975, Whosedebabedolbabedoll 1977, Monkey Run Road 1979, Blauvelt Mountain 1980; Choreographer Negroes for Sale (soloist) 1973, Track Dance 1974, Everybody Works/All Beasts Count 1976, De Sweet Streak to Loveland 1977, The Runner Dreams 1978, Stories, Steps and Stomps 1978, Progresso 1979, Echo 1979, Naming Things Is Only the Intention to Make Things 1979, Floating the Tongue 1979, Sisyphus Act I and II 1980, Open Spaces 1980, Tribeca, Automation, Three Wise Men, Christmas 1980, Secret Pastures 1984, History of Collage 1988, D-Man in the Waters 1989, Dances 1989, Last Supper at Uncle Tom's Cabin/The Promised Land 1991, Love Defined 1991, Aria 1992, Last Night on Earth 1992, Fête 1992, Still/Here 1993 (Edin. Festival 1995), Achilles Loved Patroclus 1993, War Between the States 1993, Still/Here 1994, We Set Out Early . . . Visibility Was Poor 1997; Dir, Choreographer of operas include: New Year 1990 (Co-Dir BBC TV production), The Mother of Three Sons, Lost in the Stars; Dir Guthrie Theatre, Minneapolis 1994; Assoc. Choreographer Lyons Opera Ballet 1995–; MacArthur Foundation Grant; NY Dance and Performance (Bessie) Award (with Arnie Zane) 1986, Bessie Award for D-Man in the Waters 1989, Dorothy B. Chandler Performing Arts Award 1991, Dance Magazine Award 1993, Edin. Festival Critics' Award (presented to Jones/Zane Dance Co.) 1993; Hon. Dr. (Bard Coll.) 1996. *Publication:* Last Night on Earth 1995. *Address:* Bill T. Jones/Arnie Zane Dance Company, 853 Broadway, Suite 1706, New York, NY 10003, USA.

JONES, Bobby Louis, BEd, MA, PhD; American gospel singer, television broadcaster and lecturer; b. 1939, Hindreas, Tenn.; m. Ethel Williams Jones; ed Tenn. State Univ. and Vanderbilt Univ., Nashville; teacher elementary schools in Tenn. and Missouri; textbook consultant for educational publr; Instructor in Reading and Study Skills, Tenn. State Univ. 1973–85; began performing as gospel singer 1970s; Producer and Host Fun City 5 (children's programme), WTBF, Nashville; formed gospel group 'New Life' 1975; cr. first Black Expo, Nashville 1976; signed contract for first TV gospel show (Channel 4) 1976; Producer and Host The Bobby Jones Gospel Hour (BET) 1980–, Bobby Jones World (BET) 1978–84, Video Gospel (BET) 1989, Bobby Jones Gospel Explosion (BET) 1989–, Bobby Jones Presents...Gospel on Stage, Bobby Jones Presents...Gospel on Classics (Word Network) 2001–, radio programme The Bobby Jones Gospel Countdown (Sheridan Network); composed and acted in gospel opera 'Make a Joyful Noise' (Gabriel Award, Int. Film Festival Award) 1980; co-ordinator Exec. Int. Record Label Gospel Artists Retreat; Hon. PhD (Payne Theological Seminary, Wilberforce, Ohio) 1991; Commonwealth Award, Gospel Music Assen 1990. *Recordings include:* New Life albums: Sooner or Later 1976, There Is Hope in This World 1978, Caught Up 1979, Tin Gladje 1981, Soul Set Free 1982, Come Together (Dove Award, Gospel Music Asscn) 1984, I'll Never Forget 1990, Bring It to Jesus 1993, Another Time 1996, Just Churchin' (featuring the Nashville Superchoir) 1998; singles: I'm So Glad I'm Standing Here Today (with Barbara Mandrell, Grammy Award) 1984. *Television includes:* Sister Sister (film) 1982. *Publication:* Make a Joyful Noise: My 25 Years in Gospel Music (autobiog.) 2000. *Address:* c/o Millennium Entertainment, 1314 Fifth Avenue N, Nashville, TN 37208, USA (Office). *Website:* www.bobbyjonesgospel.com (Office).

JONES, Bryn Terfel (see Terfel Jones, Bryn).

JONES, Catherine Zeta; British actress; d. of David James Jones.; m. Michael Douglas (q.v.) 2000; one s. one d. *Stage appearances include:* The Pyjama Game, Annie, Bugsy Malone, 42nd Street, Street Scene. *Television appearances include:* Darling Buds of May, Out of the Blue, Cinder Path 1994, Return of the Native 1995, Titanic 1996. *Films include:* Scheherazade, Coup de Foudre, Splitting Heirs 1993, Blue Juice 1995, The Phantom 1996, The Mask of Zorro 1997, Entrapment 1998, The Haunting 1999, Traffic 2000, America's Sweethearts 2001, Chicago (Best Supporting Actress, BAFTA Awards 2003, Screen Actors Guild Awards 2003, Acad. Awards 2003) 2002, Monkeyface 2003. *Address:* c/o ICM Ltd, Oxford House, 76 Oxford Street, London, W1N 0AX, England. *Telephone:* (20) 7636-6565. *Fax:* (20) 7323-0101.

JONES, Gen. David Charles, DFC; American air force officer (retd); b. 9 July 1921, Aberdeen, S Dak.; s. of Maurice Jones and Helen Meade; m. Lois M. Tarbell 1942; one s. two d.; ed Univ. of North Dakota and Minot State Coll., N Dak., USAF Flying School, Nat. War Coll.; Commdr 22nd Air Refueling Squadron 1953–54, 33rd Bomb Squadron 1954; Operations Planner, Bomber Mission Branch, HQ Strategic Air Command Sept.–Dec. 1954, Aide to C-in-C, SAC 1955–57; Dir of Material, later Deputy Commdr for Maintenance, 93rd Bomb Wing 1957–59; Chief, Manned Systems Branch, Deputy Chief and later Chief, Strategic Div., DCS/Operations, HQ USAF 1960–64; Commdr 33rd Tactical Fighter Wing March–Oct. 1965; Insp.-Gen. HQ United States Air Forces in Europe 1965–67, Chief of Staff Jan.–June 1967, Deputy Chief

of Staff, Plans and Operations 1967–69; Deputy Chief of Staff, Operations, HQ 7th Air Force, Repub. of Viet Nam 1969, Vice-Commdr 7th Air Force, Tan Son Nhut Airfield, Repub. of Viet Nam 1969; Commdr 2nd Air Force 1969–71; Vice-C-in-C USAFE, later C-in-C USAFE and Commdr 4th Allied Tactical Air Forces, Ramstein Air Base, Fed. Repub. of Germany 1971–74; Chief of Staff, US Air Force 1974–78, Chair. Jt Chiefs of Staff 1978–82; Dir USAir, Radio Corpn of America, Nat. Broadcasting Co., Kemper Group 1982, US Steel, Nat. Educ. Corpn; Chair. Bd Hay Systems Inc.; Hon. DHumLitt (Nebraska) 1974; Hon. DLaws (Louisiana Tech. Univ.) 1975; Distinguished Service Medal with Oak Leaf Cluster, Legion of Merit, Distinguished Flying Cross, Bronze Star Medal, Air Medal W/I OLC and many other decorations. *Leisure interests:* jogging, skiing, racquetball, flying, historical novels. *E-mail:* dcji@aol.com (Office).

JONES, (David) Huw, MA, FRTS; British broadcasting executive; b. 5 May 1948, Manchester; s. of late Idris Jones and of Olwen Edwards; m. Siân Marylka Miarczynska 1972; one s. one d.; ed Cardiff High School for Boys, Jesus Coll., Oxford; pop singer, recording artist, TV presenter 1968–76; Dir, Gen. Man. Sain Recording Co. 1969–81; Chair. Barcud Cyf (TV Facilities), Caernarfon 1981–93; Man. Dir, Producer Teledu'r Tir Glas Cyf (ind. production co.) 1982–93; first Chair. Teledwyr Annibynnol Cymru (Welsh Ind. Producers) 1984–86; Chief Exec. S4C (Welsh Fourth Channel) 1994–; Chair. Celtic Film and TV Festival 2001, Skillset Cymru; Dir Sgrin Cyf, SDN Ltd, Skillset Ltd, Nat. Ass. of Wales Broadcasting Co. Ltd, mem. British Screen Advisory Council, Future Skills Wales Employers Group; Hon. Fellow Univ. of Wales, Aberystwyth. *Leisure interests:* reading, cycling, walking. *Address:* S4C, Parc Ty Glas, Llanishen, Cardiff, CF14 5DU, Wales. *Telephone:* (29) 2074-1400. *Fax:* (29) 2068-0863 (Office); (29) 2075-4444. *E-mail:* huw.jones@ s4c.co.uk (Home). *Website:* www.s4c.co.uk (Office).

JONES, Dean Mervyn; Australian cricketer; b. 24 March 1961, Coburg, Vic.; m. Jane Jones 1986; one d.; ed Mt. Waverley High School, Vic.; right-hand batsman; played for Victoria 1981–82 to 1997–98; (Capt. 1993–94 to 1995–96), Durham 1992, Derbyshire (Capt.) 1996 to 1997, resigning mid-way through season and returning home; played in 52 Tests for Australia 1983–84 to 1992–93, scoring 3,631 runs (average 46.5) including 11 hundreds; toured England 1989; scored 19,188 first-class runs (55 hundreds); 164 limited-overs ints; Wisden Cricketer of the Year 1990. *Publication:* Deano: My Call 1995. *Leisure interests:* golf, baseball, looking after his two Rottweilers.

JONES, Digby Marritt, LLB, FRSA, CIMgt; British lawyer and financial services executive; b. 28 Oct. 1955, Birmingham; s. of Derek Jones and Bernice Jones; m.; ed Bromsgrove School, Univ. Coll. London; joined Edge & Ellison (corp. law firm) 1978, Partner 1984, Deputy Sr Partner 1990, Sr Partner 1995; joined KPMG as Vice-Chair. Corp. Finance 1998; Dir-Gen. CBI 2000–; Sr Dir (non-exec.) iSOFT PLC; mem. Int. Advisory Bd Buchanan Ingersoll (law firm), USA; mem. City of Birmingham Symphony Orchestra Devt Trust; Chair. Birmingham St Mary's Hospice Appeal 1998. *Leisure interests:* theatre, skiing, cycling, rugby, military history. *Address:* CBI, Centre Point, 103 New Oxford Street, London, WC1A 1DU (Office); 58 Elizabeth Court, 1 Palgrave Gardens, London, NW1 6EJ, England (Home). *Telephone:* (20) 7379-7400 (Office); (20) 7224-8592 (Home). *Fax:* (20) 7240-1578 (Office); (20) 7723-5807 (Home). *E-mail:* digby.jones@cbi.org.uk (Office). *Website:* www.cbi.org.uk (Office).

JONES, Douglas Samuel, MBE, MA, DSc, CMath, CEng, FRS, FRSE, FIMA, FIEE; British professor of mathematics; b. 10 Jan. 1922, Corby, Northants.; s. of Jesse Dewis Jones and Bessie Streather; m. Ivy Styles 1950; one s. one d.; ed Wolverhampton Grammar School, Corpus Christi Coll., Univ. of Oxford; Flight Lt, RAF Volunteer Reserve 1941–45; Commonwealth Fellow, Mass. Inst. of Tech. 1947–48; Asst Lecturer, then Lecturer, Univ. of Manchester 1948–54, Sr Lecturer 1955–57; Visiting Prof., New York Univ. 1955, 1962–63; Prof. of Math., Univ. of Keele 1957–64; Ivory Prof. of Math., Univ. of Dundee 1965–92, Emer. Prof. 1992–; mem. Univ. Grants Cttee 1976–86, Chair. Math. Sciences sub-Cttee 1976–86; mem. Computer Bd 1976–82; mem. Open Univ. Visiting Cttee 1982–87; mem. Council, Inst. of Math. and its applications 1982–97 (Pres. 1988–90); Hon. Fellow, Corpus Christi Coll., Univ. of Oxford; Hon. DSc (Strathclyde) 1975; Van Der Pol Gold Medal, Int. Scientific Radio Union 1981; Keith Prize, RSE 1974, Naylor Prize of London Math. Soc. 1987. *Publications include:* Electrical and Mechanical Oscillations 1961, The Theory of Electromagnetism 1964, Generalised Functions 1966, Introductory Analysis (vol.1) 1969, (vol.2) 1970, Methods in Electromagnetic Wave Propagation 1979, 1994, Elementary Information Theory 1979, The Theory of Generalised Functions 1982, Differential Equations and Mathematical Biology 1983, Acoustic and Electromagnetic Waves 1986, Assembly Programming and the 8086 Microprocessor 1988, 80x86 Assembly Programming 1991, Introduction to Asymptotics 1997. *Leisure interest:* avoiding e-mail. *Address:* Department of Mathematics, The University, Dundee, DD1 4HN (Office); 1 The Nurseries, St Madoes, Glencarse, Perth, PH2 7NX, Scotland (Home). *Telephone:* (1382) 344486 (Office); (1738) 860544 (Home). *Fax:* (1382) 345516 (Office). *E-mail:* dross@mcs.dundee.ac.uk (Office).

JONES, (Everett) Le Roi (Imamu Baraka); American poet and dramatist; b. 7 Oct. 1934, Newark, NJ; s. of Coyette L. Jones and Anna Lois (Russ) Jones; m. 1st Hettie R. Cohen 1958 (divorced 1965); two step-d.; m. 2nd Sylvia Robinson (Bibi Amina Baraka) 1966; five c.; one step-c.; ed Howard Univ., New School and Columbia Univ.; served with USAF; taught poetry at New School Social Research, drama at Columbia Univ., literature at Univ. of

Buffalo; Visiting Prof., San Francisco State Univ.; began publishing 1958; founded Black Arts Repertory Theater School, Harlem 1964, Spirit House, Newark 1966; Whitney Fellowship 1963, Guggenheim Fellowship 1965; Fellow, Yoruba Acad. 1965; Visiting Lecturer, Afro-American Studies, Yale Univ. 1977–78; Asst Prof. of African Studies State Univ. of New York 1980–83, Assoc. Prof. 1983–85, Prof. 1985–; mem. Int. Co-ordinating Cttee of Congress of African Peoples; mem. Black Acad. of Arts and Letters. *Publications include:* Preface to a Twenty Volume Suicide Note 1961, Dante 1962, Blues People 1963, The Dead Lecturer 1963, Dutchman 1964, The Moderns 1964, The System of Dante's Hell 1965, Home 1965, Jello 1965, Experimental Death Unit 1965, The Baptism–The Toilet 1966, Black Mass 1966, Mad Heart 1967, Slave Ship 1967, Black Music 1967, Tales 1968, Great Goodness of Life 1968, Black Magic, Four Black Revolutionary Plays 1969, Black Art 1969, In Our Terribleness 1970, Junkies are Full of Shhh ..., Bloodrites 1970, Raise 1971, It's Nation Time 1971, Kawaida Studies 1972, Spirit Reach 1972, Afrikan Revolution 1973, Hard Facts: Excerpts 1975, Spring Song 1979, AM/TRAK 1979, In the Tradition: For Black Arthur Blythe 1980, Reggae or Not! Poems 1982, The Autobiography of Le Roi Jones/Amiri Baraka 1984, Thornton Dial: Images of the Tiger 1993, Shy's, Wise, Y's: The Griot's Tale 1994; several film scripts; ed. Hard Facts 1976. *Address:* c/o State University of New York, Department of African Studies, Stony Brook, NY 11794, USA.

JONES, George; American country music singer; b. 12 Sept. 1931, Saratoga, Texas; s. of George Jones and Clara Washington Jones; m. 3rd Tammy Wynette 1969 (divorced 1975, died 1998); m. 4th Nancy Sepulvado 1983; began singing for money on streets in Beaumont aged 11; performed on local radio and bars; began recording career with single No Money in This Deal 1954; has recorded over 200 albums; Grammy Award for Choices 1999. *Publication:* I Lived to Tell It All (autobiog.). *Address:* Razor & Tie, 214 Sullivan Street, Suite 4A, New York, NY 10012, USA.

JONES, Grace; American singer, model and actress; b. 19 May 1952, Spanishtown, Jamaica; d. of Robert and Marjorie P. Jones; one s.; m. Atila Altaunbay 1996; went to New York at age of 12; abandoned Spanish studies at Syracuse Univ. for first stage role, Phila; became fashion model in New York, then Paris; made first album, Portfolio, for Island Records 1977; debut as disco singer New York 1977; opened La Vie en Rose restaurant, New York 1987. *Films include:* Conan the Destroyer, A View to a Kill 1985, Vamp, Straight to Hell, Siesta, Boomerang 1991. *Albums include:* Fame, Muse, Island Life, Slave to the Rythym. *Address:* c/o Island Pictures Inc., 8920 Sunset Boulevard, 2nd Floor, Los Angeles, CA 90069, USA (Office).

JONES, Dame Gwyneth, DBE, FRCM; British soprano; b. 7 Nov. 1936, Pontnewynydd, Mon., Wales; d. of the late Edward George Jones and Violet Webster; one d.; ed Royal Coll. of Music, London, Accad. Chigiana, Siena, Zürich Int. Opera Centre; with Zürich Opera House 1962–63; a Prin. Dramatic Soprano Royal Opera House, Covent Garden 1963–; with Vienna State Opera House 1966–, Deutsche Oper Berlin 1966–, Bavarian State Opera 1967–; guest performances in numerous opera houses throughout the world including La Scala, Milan, Rome Opera, Berlin State Opera, Munich State Opera, Hamburg, Paris, Metropolitan Opera, New York, San Francisco, Los Angeles, Zürich, Geneva, Dallas, Chicago, Teatro Colón, Buenos Aires, Tokyo, Bayreuth Festival, Salzburg Festival, Arena di Verona, Edin. Festival and Welsh Nat. Opera; Kammersängerin in Austria and Bavaria; known for many opera roles including Leonora, Il Trovatore, Desdemona, Otello, Aida, Aida (Verdi), Leonore, Fidelio (Beethoven), Senta, The Flying Dutchman (Wagner), Medea, Medea (Cherubini), Sieglinde, Die Walküre (Wagner), Lady Macbeth, Macbeth (Verdi), Elizabeth, Don Carlos (Verdi), Madame Butterfly (Puccini), Tosca (Puccini), Donna Anna, Don Giovanni (Mozart), Salome (R. Strauss), Kundry, Parsifal and Isolde, Tristan und Isolde (Wagner), Helena, Aegyptische Helena (R. Strauss), Färberin, Frau ohne Schatten, Elektra, Elektra (R. Strauss), Elizabeth/Venus, Tannhäuser (Wagner), Marschallin, Der Rosenkavalier (R. Strauss), Brünnhilde, Der Ring des Nibelungen (Wagner), Ortrud, Lohengrin (Wagner), Minnie, Fanciulla del West (Puccini), Norma (Bellini), Erwartung (Schoenberg), La voix humaine (Poulenc); Pres. Richard Wagner Soc., London 1990; masterclasses in UK, Germany, France, the Netherlands and Switzerland; recordings for Decca, DGG, Philips, Chandos, EMI, CBS; Hon. mem. Vienna State Opera 1989; Bundesverdienstkreuz (FRG) 1988, Commdr des Arts et Lettres (France) 1993, Verdienst-Kreuz, First Class (Austria) 1998; Hon. DMus (Wales) 1998; Shakespeare Prize, Hamburg 1987, Gold Medal of Honour, Vienna 1991. *Television films:* Fidelio, Aida, Flying Dutchman, Leonore, Beethoven 9th Symphony, Tannhäuser, Poppea (Monteverdi), Rosenkavalier (R. Strauss), Die Walküre, Siegfried, Götterdämmerung, Die lustige Witwe. *Address:* PO Box 2000, 8700 Küsnacht, Switzerland.

JONES, James Earl; American actor; b. 17 Jan. 1931, Miss.; s. of Robert Earl Jones and Ruth Williams; m. Cecilia Hurt 1982; ed Univ. of Mich.; numerous stage appearances on Broadway and elsewhere include Master Harold ... And the Boys, Othello, King Lear, Hamlet, Paul Robeson, A Lesson From Aloes, Of Mice and Men, The Iceman Cometh, A Hand is on the Gate, The Cherry Orchard, Danton's Death, Fences; frequent TV appearances; cast as voice of Darth Vader in films Star Wars, The Empire Strikes Back and The Return of the Jedi; Hon. DFA (Princeton, Yale, Mich.); Tony Award for role in stage version and Golden Globe Award for role in screen version of The Great White Hope, numerous other awards. *Films include:* Matewan, Gardens of Stone, Soul Man, My Little Girl, The Man, The End of the Road, Dr Strangelove, Conan the Barbarian, The Red Tide, A Piece of the Action, The Last Remake

of Beau Geste, The Greatest, The Heretic, The River Niger, Deadly Hero, Claudine, The Great White Hope, The Comedians, Coming to America, Three Fugitives, Field of Dreams, Patriot Games, Sommersby, The Lion King (voice), Clear and Present Danger, Cry the Beloved Country, Lone Star, A Family Thing, Gang Related, Rebound, Summer's End 1998, Undercover Angel 1999, Quest for Atlantis 1999, Our Friend Martin (voice) 1999, On the Q.T. 1999, Finder's Fee 2001, Recess Christmas: A Miracle on Third Street (voice) 2001. *Address:* Horatio Productions, PO Box 610, Pawling, NY 12564-0610, USA.

JONES, Gen. James L., BSc; American army official; ed Georgetown Univ. School of Foreign Service, Basic and Amphibious Warfare Schools, Quantico, Va, Nat. War Coll., Washington DC; Second Lt Marine Corps 1967; Platoon Commdr and Co. Commdr Co. G, 2nd Bn, 3rd Marines, Viet Nam 1967–68; rank of First Lt 1968; Co. Commdr Camp Pendleton, Calif. 1968–70, Marine Barracks, Washington DC 1970–73, Co. H, 2nd Bn, 9th Marines, 3rd Marine Div., Okinawa 1974–75; served in Officer Assignments Section HQ Marine Corps, Washington DC 1976–79; rank of Maj. 1977; Marine Corps Liaison Officer to US Senate 1979–84; rank of Lt-Col 1982; Commdr 3rd Bn, 9th Marines, 1st Marine Div., Camp Pendleton 1985–87; Sr Aide to Commdr of Marine Corps 1987–89; rank of Col 1988; Mil. Sec. to Commdt 1989–90; CO 24th Marine Expeditionary Unit, Camp Lejeune, NC 1990–92; rank of Brig.-Gen. 1992; Deputy Dir J-3, US European Command, Stuttgart, Germany 1992–94; Chief of Staff Jt Task Force Provide Promise, Operations in Bosnia and Herzegovina and Macedonia 1992–94; rank of Maj.-Gen. 1994; Commanding Gen. 2nd Marine Div., Marine Forces Atlantic, Camp Lejeune 1994–96; Dir Expeditionary Warfare Div., Office of the Chief of Naval Operations 1996; Deputy Chief of Staff for Plans, Policies and Operations, HQ Marine Corps 1996; rank of Lt-Gen. 1996; Mil. Asst to Sec. of Defense 1997–99; rank of Gen. 1999; 32nd Commdt Marine Corps 1999–2003; Commdr US European Command and 14th Supreme Allied Commdr Europe, NATO 2003–; Defense Distinguished Service Medal, Silver Star Medal, Legion of Merit with 4 gold stars, Bronze Star Medal with Combat V, Combat Action Ribbon. *Address:* Nato Allied Commander Europe, NATO Headquarters, boulevard Léopold III, 1110 Brussels, Belgium (Office). *E-mail:* natodoc@hq.nato.int (Office). *Website:* www.nato.int (Office).

JONES, James Larkin (Jack), CH, MBE; British trade unionist; b. 29 March 1913, Liverpool; s. of George Jones and Anne Jones; m. Evelyn Mary Taylor 1938 (died 1998); two s.; ed Liverpool; worked in eng and dock industries 1927–39; served in Spanish Civil War; Midlands Official, Transport and Gen. Workers' Union 1939–63, Exec. Officer 1963–69, Gen. Sec. 1969–78; Dist Sec. Confed. of Shipbuilding and Eng Unions 1939–63; mem. Labour Party Nat. Exec. Cttee 1964–67; Deputy Chair. Nat. Ports Council 1967–78; mem. Council, Trades Union Congress 1968–78; Chair. Int. Cttee, TUC 1972–78; mem. Exec. Bd Int. Confed. of Free Trade Unions, European Trade Union Confed., Pres. EFTA Trade Union Council 1973–; British Overseas Trade Bd 1975–78, Advisory, Conciliation and Arbitration Service (ACAS) 1975–78; mem. Royal Comm. on Criminal Procedure 1978–; mem. NEDC 1969–78; mem. Econ. and Social Cttee, EEC 1975–78; Pres. Retd. Mems. Asscns., TGWU 1978–, Nat. Pensioners' Convention 1992–; Vice-Pres. Int. Transport Workers Fed. 1974–80, Age Concern (England), Anti-Apartheid Movement, European Fed. of Retd. and Elderly Persons 1990–; Chair. Nat. Museum of Labour History 1990–; Fellow, Nuffield Coll., Oxford 1970–78, Chartered Inst. of Transport 1971; Assoc. Fellow LSE 1978; Hon. mem. Int. Longshoremen's Asscn (USA) 1973, Union Gen. de Trabajadores de España (Spain) 1975; Hon. Fellow John Moores Univ., Liverpool 1988, Lancashire Cen. Univ. 1993; Freeman City of London; Dimbleby Lecture, BBC-TV 1977; Hon. DLitt (Warwick); Dr hc (Open Univ.) 2000, (Coventry); City of Coventry Medal of Merit. *Publications:* Incompatibles 1968, A to Z of Trade Unionism and Industrial Relations 1982, A Union Man (autobiog.) 1986. *Leisure interests:* walking, painting. *Address:* 74 Ruskin Park House, Champion Hill, London, SE5 8TH, England (Home). *Telephone:* (20) 7274-7067.

JONES, James Robert, LLB; American diplomatist and attorney; b. 5 May 1939, Muskogee, Okla; s. of Robert Jones and Margaret Wich; m. Olivia Barclay 1968; two s.; ed Univ. of Oklahoma and Georgetown Univ.; Asst to Pres. Johnson, White House, Washington, DC 1965–69; practising lawyer and business consultant, Tulsa, Okla 1969–73; mem. US Congress 1973–87; partner, Dickstein, Shapiro & Moran (law firm), Washington, DC 1987–89; Chair. and CEO American Stock Exchange, New York 1989–93; Amb. to Mexico 1993–97; Pres. Warnaco Int. 1997–98; Sr Counsel to Manatt, Phelps and Phillips 1998–; Steiger Award 1979, Humanitarian Award, Anti Defamation League 1990, Aztec Eagle Award (Mexico) 1997. *Leisure interests:* golf, reading. *Address:* 1501 M Street NW, Suite 700, Washington, DC 20005-1737, USA. *E-mail:* jjones@manatt.com (Office).

JONES, Rt Rev James Stuart, BA; British ecclesiastic; b. 18 Aug. 1948; s. of Maj. James Stuart Anthony Jones and Helen Deans Dick Telfer (née McIntyre); m. Sarah Caroline Rosalind Marrow 1980; three d.; ed Univ. of Exeter and Wycliffe Hall, Oxford; Asst master Sevenoaks School 1971–74; producer Scripture Union 1975–81; Asst curate Christ Church, Clifton 1982–84, Assoc. Vicar 1984–90; Vicar Emmanuel Church, Croydon 1990–94; Bishop of Hull 1994–98; Bishop of Liverpool 1998–; Hon. DD (Univ. of Hull) 1999; Hon. DLitt (Univ. of Lincolnshire and Humberside) 2001. *Television:* The Word on the Street 1999. *Publications include:* Following Jesus 1984, Finding God 1987, Why Do People Suffer? 1993, The Power and the Glory 1994, The People of the Blessing 1998, The Moral Leader 2002. *Leisure* *interests:* swimming, opera and holidays in France. *Address:* Bishop's Lodge, Woolton Park, Woolton, Liverpool, L25 6DT, England. *Telephone:* (151) 421-0831. *Fax:* (151) 428-3055.

JONES, Le Roi (see Jones, (Everett) Le Roi).

JONES, Marion; American athlete; b. 12 Oct. 1975, Los Angeles; m. C. J. Hunter 1998 (divorced); ed Rio Mesa High School, Thousand Oaks High School, Calif., N Carolina Coll.; gold medal (100m), World Championships 1997, 1999; three gold medals (100m, 200m and 4×400m relay) and two bronze medals (long-jump and 4×100m relay), Olympic Games, Sydney 2000; gold medal (200m), World Championships 2001, gold medal (100m) World Cup 2002; Jesse Owens Award (three times), Associated Press Female Athlete of the Year 2000, Laurens World Sportswoman of the Year 2000. *Address:* c/o USA Track and Field, 1 RCA Dome, Suite 140, Indianapolis, IN 46225-1023, USA (Office).

JONES, Mark Ellis Powell, MA, FSA, FRSE; British museum administrator; b. 5 Feb. 1951; s. of John Ernest Powell-Jones and Ann Paludan; m. Ann Camilla Toulmin 1983; two s. two d.; ed Eton Coll., Worcester Coll., Oxford and Courtauld Inst. of Art; Asst Keeper Dept of Coins and Medals, British Museum 1974–90, Keeper 1990–92; Dir Nat. Museums of Scotland 1992–2001; Dir Victoria and Albert Museum, London 2001–; Ed. The Medal 1983–94; Pres. Féd. Int. de la Médaille 1994–2000, British Art Medal Soc. 1998– (Sec. 1982–94); co-f. Scottish Cultural Resources Access Network 1994–96, mem. Bd 1996–; mem. Royal Mint Advisory Cttee 1994–, Arts and Humanities Data Service Steering Cttee 1997–99, Focus Group Nat. Cultural Strategy 1999–2000; Dir Edin. and Lothians Tourist Bd 1998–2000; Hon. Prof. (Edin.) 1997. *Publications include:* The Art of the Medal 1977, Impressionist Painting 1979, Contemporary British Medals 1986, Fake?: the Art of Deception (ed.) 1990, Why Fakes Matter (ed.) 1992, Designs on Posterity (ed.) 1994. *Address:* The Victoria and Albert Museum, Cromwell Road, South Kensington, London, SW7 2RL, England (Office). *Telephone:* (20) 7942-2171 (Office). *E-mail:* mark.jones@vam.ac.uk (Office). *Website:* www.vam.ac.uk (Office).

JONES, Mervyn Thomas, BA; British diplomatist; b. 23 Nov. 1942; s. of William Clifford Jones and Winifred Mary Jones (née Jenkins); m. Julia Mary Newcombe 1965; two s.; ed Univ. Coll., Swansea; entered Diplomatic Service 1964; FCO 1964–66; Calcutta 1966, Bonn 1966–70, Warsaw 1970–73, FCO 1973–77, Oslo 1977–80; First Sec. (Man.), then Head of Chancery, Bangkok 1981–85; on secondment to Commonwealth Secr. as Asst Dir Int. Affairs Div. 1985–90; Deputy Consul Gen. and Consul (Commercial) LA 1990–94; Asst Head, Migration and Visa Dept, FCO 1994–96; Counsellor (Commercial and Econ.) Brussels (also Accred to Luxembourg) 1996–99; Consul Gen. and Deputy Head of Mission, Brussels 1999; Gov. Turks and Caicos Islands 2000–02. *Leisure interests:* reading, walking, cinema, music. *Address:* c/o Foreign and Commonwealth Office, King Charles Street, London, SW1A 2AH, England (Office).

JONES, Michael Frederick; British journalist; b. 3 July 1937, Gloucester; s. of late Glyn F. Jones and Elizabeth Coopey; m. Sheila Dawes 1959; three s.; ed Crypt Grammar School, Gloucester; reporter on provincial newspapers 1956–64; Financial Times 1964–65; Daily Telegraph 1965–67; Business News Asst Ed. The Times 1967–70; Man. Ed. The Asian, Hong Kong 1971; News Ed. Sunday Times 1972, Political Corresp. 1975, Political Ed. 1984, Assoc. Ed. 1990–95, Assoc. Ed. (Politics) 1995–2002; Chair. Parl. Press Gallery, House of Commons 1989–91; Visiting Fellow Goldsmith's Coll., London Univ. 2000–02. *Publication:* Betty Boothroyd: The Autobiography (collab.) 2001. *Leisure interest:* Anglo-American history. *Address:* 115 Cliffords Inn, Fetter Lane, London, EC4A 1BX, England (Home). *Telephone:* (20) 7430-0443 (Home). *E-mail:* micjon1937@aol.com (Home).

JONES, Philip James, DPhil, FBA; British historian and academic; b. 19 Nov. 1921, London; s. of John David Jones and Caroline Susan Jones (née Davies); m. Carla Susini 1954; one s. one d.; ed St Dunstan's Coll., London and Wadham Coll., Oxford; Asst Lecturer in Modern History, Glasgow Univ. 1949–50; Lecturer in Medieval History, Leeds Univ. 1950–61, Reader 1961–63; Fellow and Tutor in Modern History, Brasenose Coll., Oxford 1963–89, Librarian 1965–89, Emer. Fellow 1989–; Amy Mary Read Studentship 1946–47; Bryce Research Studentship 1947–48; Eileen Power Memorial Studentship 1956–57; Corresp. mem. Deputazione Toscana di Storia Patria 1975–; Serena Medal for Italian Studies 1988. *Publications:* The Malatesta of Rimini 1974, Economia e Società nell'Italia medioevale 1980; contribs. to Cambridge Economic History I 1966, Storia d'Italia, II 1974, Storia d'Italia, Annali, I 1978, The Italian City-State: from commune to signoria 1997, articles. *Address:* 167 Woodstock Road, Oxford, OX2 7NA, England. *Telephone:* (1865) 557953.

JONES, Quincy; American composer, arranger, conductor and trumpeter; b. 14 March 1933, Chicago; s. of Quincy Delight and Sarah Jones; m. 2nd Peggy Lipton; two d.; three c. by previous m.; one d. with Nastassja Kinski (q.v.); ed Seattle Univ., Berklee School of Music and Boston Conservatory; trumpeter, arranger, Lionel Hampton Orchestra 1950–53; arranger for orchestras and singers inc. Frank Sinatra, Dinah Washington, Count Basie, Sarah Vaughan and Peggy Lee; organizer and trumpeter, Dizzy Gillespie Orchestra, Dept of State tour of Near and Middle East and S. America 1956; Music Dir Barchlay Disques, Paris; led own European tour 1960; Music Dir Mercury Records 1961, Vice-Pres. 1964; conductor of numerous film scores; composer, actor in

film Blues for Trumpet and Koto; producer recordings of Off the Wall 1980 by Michael Jackson (q.v.), Thriller 1982, Bad, videotape Portrait of An Album: Frank Sinatra with Quincy Jones and Orchestra 1986; composer The Oprah Winfrey Show 1989–; producer Fresh Prince of Bel Air 1990–; Dr hc (Berklee Music Coll.) 1983; (Hebrew Univ.) 1993, (Clark Univ.) 1993; German Jazz Fed. Award; Edison Int. Award (Sweden); Downbeat Critics Poll Award; Downbeat Readers Poll Award; Billboard Trendsetters Award 1983; Martell Foundation Humanitarian Award 1986, Lifetime Achievement Award, Nat. Acad. Songwriters 1989, Jean Hersholt Humanitarian Award 1995; several Grammy Awards, Scopus Award, Producers' Guild of America Award 1999, Crystal Award, World Econ. Forum 2000, Marian Anderson Award 2001, Ted Arison Prize, Nat. Foundation for Advancement in the Arts 2001, Kennedy Center Honor 2001. *Albums include:* Body Heat 1974, The Dude 1981, Back on the Block 1989. *Address:* Rogers and Cowan, 3800 Barham Boulevard, Suite 503, Los Angeles, CA 90068, USA.

JONES, Roy, Jr; American boxer; b. 16 Jan. 1969, Pensacola, Fla; three s.; undisputed lighheavyweight champion of the world (47 wins, 1 loss, 38 knockouts as at Nov. 2002); voted Outstanding Boxer of the Olympic Games 1988; won IBF (Int. Boxing Fed.) middleweight crown beating Bernard Hopkins 1993; moved up to super middleweight, won IBF title from James Toney 1994; moved up to light heavyweight div. winning WBC (World Boxing Council) (1997), WBA (World Boxing Asscn) (1998) and IBF (1999) titles; winner WBA heavyweight title 2003 (first fmr middleweight champion since 1897 to win title); professional basketball player for five years with the Sarasota Sun Dogs; f. Body Head Entertainment 1998; has appeared in numerous films and TV programmes; Boxing Writers' Asscn of America Fighter of the Decade (for 1990s), The Ring Fighter of the Year 1994, WBC Lifetime Achievement Award 2001. *Leisure interests:* music, basketball, hunting, fishing, raising livestock. *Website:* www.royjonesjr.com (Office).

JONES, Stephen John Moffat, BA; British milliner; b. 31 May 1957, West Kirby, Cheshire; s. of Gordon Jones and Margaret Jones; ed Liverpool Coll., St Martin's School of Art; milliner 1980–, collaborating with int. designers including Jean-Paul Gaultier, Comme des Garçons, Claude Montana, John Galliano, Christian Dior (Paris) 1997–; colour creator for Shiseido Cosmetics; licences in Japan for gloves, sunglasses, kimonos, scarves, handkerchiefs, handbags; hats in perm. collections of Victoria and Albert Museum, London, Brooklyn Musuem, New York, Kyoto Costume Inst., Australian Nat. Gallery, Canberra. *Leisure interest:* sculpture. *Address:* Stephen Jones Millinery Ltd, 36 Great Queen Street, London, WC2B 5AA, England (Office). *Telephone:* (20) 7242-0770 (Office). *Fax:* (20) 7242-0796 (Office). *E-mail:* stephenjonesmillinery@msn.com (Office). *Website:* www .stephenjonesmillinery.com (Office).

JONES, Steve, PhD; British scientist; b. 24 March 1944, Aberystwyth, Wales; ed Wirral Grammar School; fmr Head Galton Lab.; Prof. of Genetics Univ. Coll., London; column writer The Daily Telegraph; Reith Lecturer 1991; Rhône-Poulenc Science Prize 1994, Faraday Medal, Royal Soc. 1997, Natural World Book Prize 2000. *Publications:* The Language of the Genes 1993, In the Blood 1997, Almost Like a Whale 1999. *Address:* c/o University College, London, Gower Street, London, WC1E 6BT, England. *Telephone:* (20) 7679-7416. *Fax:* (20) 7383-2048.

JONES, Tom, OBE; British singer; b. (as Thomas Jones Woodward), 7 June 1940, Treforest, Glamorgan; s. of Thomas Woodward and Freda Woodward (née Jones); m. Melinda Trenchard 1956; one s.; fmr bricklayer, factory worker; sang in clubs and dance halls billing himself as Tommy Scott, singing with the Senators and with self-formed group The Playboys; changed his name to Tom Jones, signed contract with Decca as solo artist 1963; first hit record It's Not Unusual 1965; toured USA 1965; appeared in Ed Sullivan Show at Copacabana, New York and in variety show This Is Tom Jones in UK and USA 1969; other TV appearances include Beat Room, Top Gear, Thank Your Lucky Stars, Sunday Night at the London Palladium, The Right Time (series) 1992; score for musical play Matador 1987; acted and sang in live performance of Dylan Thomas' Under Milkwood 1992; performed in Amnesty Int. 40th Anniversary Special 2001, Pavarotti and Friends 2001, Prince's Trust Party in the Park 2001; Hon. Fellow Welsh Coll. of Music and Drama 1994; mem. Screen Actors Guild, American Fed. of TV and Radio Artists, American Guild of Variety Artists; Britain's Most Popular Male Singer in Melody Maker Poll 1967, 1968; Hon. Fellow Welsh Coll. of Music and Drama 1994; MTV Video Award 1988, BRIT Award for Best British Male Solo Artist 2000, Nadnoff Robbins Music Therapy Silver Clef Award 2001, Q Magazine Merit Prize 2002, Brit Award for Outstanding Contrib. to Music 2003. *Films:* The Jerky Boys—The Movie 1995, Mars Attacks! 1996, Agnes Browne 1999, The Emperor's New Groove (voice) 2000. *Albums:* Along Came Jones 1965, A-Tom-Ic Jones 1966, From The Great 1966, Green Green Grass of Home 1966, Live At The Talk Of The Town 1967, Delilah 1968, Help Yourself 1968, Tom Jones Live In Las Vegas 1969, This Is Tom Jones 1969, Tom 1970, I Who Have Nothing 1970, Tom Jones Sings She's A Lady 1971, Tom Jones Live At Caesar's Palace, Las Vegas 1971, Close Up 1972, The Body And Soul Of Tom Jones 1973, Somethin' 'Bout You Baby I Like 1974, Memories Don't Leave Like People 1975, Say You'll Stay Until Tomorrow 1977, Rescue Me 1980, Darlin' 1981, Matador: The Musical Life Of El Cordorbes 1987, At This Moment 1989, After Dark 1989, Move Closer 1989, Carrying A Torch 1991, The Lead And How To Swing It 1994, Reload 1999, Mr Jones 2002, Reload 2 2002. *Singles include:* It's Not Unusual 1965, What's New Pussycat 1965, Thunderball 1966, Green Green Grass of Home 1966, Detroit City 1967,

Funny Familiar Forgotten Feelings 1967, I'll Never Fall In Love Again 1967, I'm Coming Home 1967, Delilah 1968, Help Yourself 1968, Love Me Tonight 1969, Without Love 1969, Daughter of Darkness 1970, I Who Have Nothing 1970, She's A Lady 1971, Till 1971, The Young New Mexican Puppeteer 1972, Can't Stop Loving You, Letter To Lucille 1973, Somethin' 'Bout You Baby I Like 1974, Say You Stay Until Tomorrow 1976, A Boy From Nowhere 1987, Kiss (with Art of Noise) 1988, All You Need Is Love 1993, If I Only Knew 1994, Burning Down The House (with The Cardigans) 1999, Baby It's Cold Outside (with Cerys Matthews) 1999, Mama Told Me Not To Come (with Stereophonics) 2000, Sex Bomb (with Mousse T) 2000, You Need Love Like I Do (with Heather Small) 2000, Tom Jones International 2002. *Publications:* The Fantasticks (screenplay) 2000. *Leisure interests:* history, music. *Address:* c/o Tom Jones Enterprises, 10100 Santa Monica Blvd., Suite 348, Los Angeles, CA 90067, USA (Office). *Telephone:* (310) 552-0044 (Office). *Fax:* (310) 552-0714 (Office). *E-mail:* tjeoffice@aol.com (Office). *Website:* www.tomjones.com.

JONES, Tommy Lee; American actor; b. 15 Sept. 1946, San Saba, Tex.; s. of Clyde L. Jones and Lucille Marie Scott; m. 1st Kimberlea Cloughley 1981; m. 2nd Dawn Laurel 2001; ed Harvard Univ.; Broadway debut in A Patriot for Me; other Broadway appearances include Four in a Garden, Ulysses in Night Town, Fortune and Men's Eyes; Emmy Award for TV role as Gary Gilmon in The Executioner's Song. *Films include:* Love Story 1970, Eliza's Horoscope, Jackson County Jail, Rolling Thunder, The Betsy, Eyes of Laura Mars, Coal Miner's Daughter, Back Roads, Nate and Hayes, River Rat, Black Moon Rising, The Big Town, Stormy Monday, The Package, Firebirds, JFK, Under Siege, House of Cards, The Fugitive, Blue Sky, Heaven and Earth, Natural Born Killers, The Client, Blue Sky, Cobb, Batman Forever, Men In Black 1997, Volcano 1997, Marshals 1997, Small Soldiers (voice) 1998, Rules of Engagement 1999, Double Jeopardy 1999, Space Cowboys 2000, Men in Black II 2002. *Television appearances include:* The Amazing Howard Hughes, Lonesome Dove, The Rainmaker, Cat on a Hot Tin Roof, Yuri Nosenko, KGB, April Morning.

JONES-MORGAN, Judith, LL.M; Saint Vincent and the Grenadines attorney-at-law; b. 7 Sept. 1957, Trinidad and Tobago; d. of Rita Jones; m. Desmond Carlos Richardson Morgan; ed Univ. of E London and Jesus Coll. Cambridge, UK; accounts technician Ministry of Finance and Treasury, Trinidad and Tobago 1976–80; legal clerk Nat. Energy Corpn, Trinidad and Tobago 1980–84; legal Asst Graham Ritchie & Co., UK 1988–89; pupil barrister Chancery/Commercial Chambers, UK 1991; Crown Counsel in Chambers of Attorney-Gen., Saint Vincent and the Grenadines 1992–93, Sr Crown Counsel 1993–99; registrar High Court 2000–01, Attorney-Gen. of Saint Vincent and the Grenadines 2001–; mem. Interim Study Programme for Judicial Educators 2000; mem. Bar of England and Wales, Saint Vincent and the Grenadines, Trinidad and Tobago; mem. Hon. Soc. of the Middle Temple, UK; Fellow Cambridge Commonwealth Soc. 1990; Cambridge Commonwealth Award, Maxwell Law Prize, UKCOSA Essay Competition. *Leisure interests:* politics, drama, public speaking, cricket, jogging, travel. *Address:* Office of the Attorney-General, Government Buildings, Kingstown (Office); P.O.B. 78, Mount Pleasant, Argyle, Saint Vincent and the Grenadines (Home). *Telephone:* (784) 457-2807 (Office); (784) 458-2010 (Home). *Fax:* (784) 457-2898 (Office); (784) 457-2420 (Home). *E-mail:* att.gen.chambers@vincysurf.com (Office); judithmorgan_ag@hotmail.com (Home).

JONES PARRY, Sir Emyr, KCMG, PhD; British diplomatist; b. 21 Sept. 1947, Carmarthen, Wales; s. of Hugh Jones Parry and Eirwen Jones Parry; m. Lynn Jones Parry; two s.; ed Gwendraeth Grammar School, Univ. Coll., Cardiff, St Catharine's Coll., Cambridge; joined FCO 1973; Deputy Chef du Cabinet and Pres. of the European Council 1987–89; Head EC Dept (External) FCO 1989–93; Minister, British Embassy, Madrid 1993–96; Deputy Political Dir FCO 1996–97; Dir EU, FCO 1997–98; Political Dir FCO 1998–2001; Perm. Rep. to N Atlantic Council, NATO 2001–03, to UN 2003–. *Leisure interests:* gardening, theatre, reading, sport. *Address:* c/o Foreign and Commonwealth Office (UK Mission, New York), Whitehall, London, SW1A 2AH, England (Office).

JONG, Erica Mann, MA; American author and poet; b. 26 March 1942, New York; d. of Seymour Mann and Eda (Mirsky) Mann; m. 1st Michael Worthman; m. 2nd Allan Jong (divorced 1975); one d.; m. 3rd Jonathan Fast 1977 (divorced 1983); one d.; m. 4th Kenneth David Burrows 1989; ed Barnard Coll. and Columbia Univ., New York; mem. Faculty, English Dept City Univ. of New York 1964–65, 1969–70; Overseas Div. Univ. of Md 1967–69; mem. Literature Panel, NY State Council on Arts 1972–74; mem. Faculty Salzburg Seminar, Salzburg, Austria 1993; Hon. Fellow (Welsh Coll. of Music and Drama) 1994; Bess Hokin Prize, Poetry magazine 1971, Alice Faye di Castagnola Award, Poetry Soc. of America 1972, Prix Littéraire, Deauville Film Festival 1997; Nat. Endowment Arts grantee 1973. *Publications:* poems: Fruits & Vegetables 1971, Half-Lives 1973, Loveroot 1975, At the Edge of the Body 1979, Ordinary Miracles 1983, Becoming Light 1991; novels: Fear of Flying 1973, How to Save Your Own Life 1977, Fanny 1980, Parachutes and Kisses 1984, Serenissima; a Novel of Venice 1987 (reissued as Shylock's Daughter 1995), Any Woman's Blues 1990, Inventing Memory 1997; nonfiction: Witches 1981, Megan's Book of Divorce (for children) 1984, The Devil at Large: Erica Jong on Henry Miller 1993, Fear of Fifty 1994, What Do Women Want? 1998; Composer Zipless: Songs of Abandon from the Erotic Poetry of Erica Jong 1995. *Leisure interests:* sailing, flying. *Address:* c/o K. D.

Burrows, Erica Jong Productions, 425 Park Avenue, New York, NY 10022-3506, USA. *Telephone:* (212) 980-6922. *Fax:* (212) 421-5279. *E-mail:* erica@ericajong.com. *Website:* www.ericajong.com (Office).

JONG, Petrus J. S. de, DSC; Netherlands politician and naval officer; b. 3 April 1915, Apeldoorn; m. Anna Geertriida Jacoba Henriette Bartels; three c.; ed Royal Naval Coll.; entered Netherlands Royal Navy 1931, commissioned 1934; submarine Commdr during Second World War; Adjutant to Minister for Navy 1948; Capt. of frigate De Zeeuw 1951; Staff Officer on staff Allied Commdr-in-Chief, Channel, Portsmouth 1953; Adjutant to Queen of Netherlands 1955; Capt. of destroyer Gelderland 1958; State Sec. for Defence 1959–63; Minister of Defence 1963–67; Prime Minister and Minister of Gen. Affairs 1967–71; mem. First Chamber (Parl.) 1971–74; Catholic Party.

JONSEN, Albert R., MA, PhD, STM; American professor of ethics in medicine; b. 4 April 1931, San Francisco; s. of Albert R. Jonsen and Helen C. Sweigert; m. Mary E. Carolan 1976; ed Gonzaga Univ., Spokane, Wash., Santa Clara Univ., Calif. and Yale Univ.; Instructor in Philosophy, Loyola Univ. of Los Angeles 1956–59; Instructor in Divinity, Yale Univ. 1966–67; Asst, Assoc. Prof. in Philosophy and Theology, Univ. of San Francisco 1968–73, Pres. 1969–72; Prof. of Ethics in Medicine and Chief, Div. of Medical Ethics, Univ. of Calif., San Francisco 1973–87; Prof. of Ethics in Medicine, Chair. Dept of Medical History and Ethics, Univ. of Wash., Seattle 1987–99, Prof. Emer. 1999–2000; Commr US Nat. Comm. for Protection of Human Subjects of Biomedical and Behavioral Research 1974–78; Commr President's Comm. for Study of Ethical Problems in Medicine and in Biomedical and Behavioral Research 1979–82; mem. Artificial Heart Assessment Panel, Nat. Heart and Lung Inst. 1972–73, 1984–86; mem. Nat. Bd of Medical Examiners 1985–88; Consultant American Bd of Internal Medicine 1978–84; mem. NAS Inst. of Medicine; mem. Cttee on AIDS Research NAS; Chair. NAS Panel on the Social Impact of AIDS 1989–92, Nat. Advisory Bd on Ethics and Reproduction 1991–96; Pres. Soc. for Health and Human Values 1986; Guggenheim Fellowship 1986–87; Visiting Prof. Yale Univ. 1999–2000, Stanford Univ. School of Medicine 2002, Univ. of Va Law School 2002; mem. Ethics Advisory Bd GERON Corpn 2000–; Davies Award, American Coll. of Physicians 1987, Convocation Medal, American Coll. of Surgeons 1988, Lifetime Achievement Award, American Soc. for Bioethics and Humanities 1999. *Publications:* Responsibility in Modern Religious Ethics 1968, Ethics of Newborn Intensive Care 1976, Clinical Ethics (with M. Siegler and W. Winslade) 1982, The Abuse of Casuistry (with S. Toulmin) 1986, The Old Ethics and the New Medicine 1990, The Impact of AIDs on American Society (with J. Stryker) 1993, The Birth of Bioethics 1997, A Short History of Medical Ethics 2000. *Leisure interests:* sketching, swimming, walking, music. *Address:* Department of Medical History and Ethics, Box 357120, University of Washington, Seattle, WA 98195; 1333 Jones Street, # 502 San Francisco, CA 94109, USA. *E-mail:* arjonsen@cs.com.

JOPLING, Baron (Life Peer), cr. 1997, of Ainderby Quernhow in the County of North Yorkshire; **(Thomas) Michael Jopling,** PC, BSc, DL; British politician and farmer; b. 10 Dec. 1930, Ripon, Yorks.; s. of Mark Bellerby Jopling; m. Gail Dickinson 1958; two s.; ed Cheltenham Coll. and King's Coll., Newcastle-upon-Tyne; mem. Thirsk Rural Dist Council 1958–64; Conservative MP for Westmorland 1964–83, Westmorland and Lonsdale 1983–97; Jt Sec. Conservative Parl. Agric. Cttee 1966–70; Parl. Pvt. Sec. to Minister of Agric. 1970–71; an Asst Govt Whip 1971–73; Lord Commr of the Treasury 1973–74; an Opposition Spokesman on Agric. 1974–75, 1976–79; Shadow Minister of Agric. 1975–76; Parl. Sec. to HM Treasury and Chief Whip 1979–83; Minister of Agric., Fisheries and Food 1983–87; mem. Nat. Council, Nat. Farmers' Union 1962–64, UK Exec., Commonwealth Parl. Asscn 1974–79, 1987–97, Vice-Chair. 1977–79, Int. Exec. 1988–89; Chair. Select Cttee on Sittings of the House 1991–92; mem. Select Cttee on Agric. 1967–69, on Foreign Affairs 1987–97; mem. NATO Parl. Ass. 1987–97, 2001–; Leader UK Del. to Parl. Ass., OSCE 1990–97, mem. 2000–01; mem. Lords Sub-Cttee 'C' European Defence and Security 1999– (Chair. 2000–); Pres. Auto-Cycle Union 1989–; DL Cumbria 1991–97, N Yorks. 1998–; Hon. Sec. British American Parl. Group 1987–2001; Hon. DCL (Newcastle) 1992. *Address:* Ainderby Hall, Thirsk, North Yorks., YO7 4HZ, England. *Telephone:* (1845) 567224.

JORDA, Claude Jean Charles; French judge and international official; b. 16 Feb. 1938, Bône, Algeria; ed Inst. d'Etudes Politiques and School of Law, Univ. of Toulouse, Ecole Nat. de la Magistrature (ENM), Univ. of Aix-en-Provence; called to Bar, Toulouse 1961; Auditeur de Justice (magistrate in training) 1963–66; Magistrate, Cen. Admin. Services Dept, Ministry of Justice 1966–70; Deputy Dir for Legal Org. and Regulations 1976–78, Dir Legal Services 1982–85; Sec.-Gen. ENM 1970–76; Vice-Pres. Tribunal de Grande Instance, Paris 1978–82; Prosecutor-Gen. Court of Appeals, Bordeaux 1985–92, Paris 1992–94; Judge at Int. Criminal Tribunal for fmr Yugoslavia (ICTY) 1994–96, Pres. Trial Chamber I 1995–99, Pres. ICTY 1999–; Officier, Légion d'honneur 1993, Commdr, Ordre nat. du Mérite 2000, Commdr des Palmes académiques, Commdr du Mérite agricole; Médaille de l'Educ. Surveillée (for services to young people in difficulty and in prison). *Publications:* Un nouveau statut pour l'accusé dans la procédure du Tribunal pénal international pour l'ex-Yougoslavie (essays) 2000; academic contribs., book chapters and conf. proc., articles on ICTY. *Address:* UN International Criminal Tribunal for the former Yugoslavia, Public Information Unit, P.O.

Box 13888, 2501 The Hague, The Netherlands (Office). *Telephone:* (70) 5125318 (Office). *Fax:* (70) 5125307 (Office). *Website:* www.un.org/icty (Office).

JORDAN, Hamilton (see Jordan, W. H. M.).

JORDAN, Michael Hugh, MSChemE; American broadcasting and media executive; b. 15 June 1936, Kansas City, Mo.; m. Kathryn Hiett 1961 (divorced); one s. one d.; m. Hilary Cecil 2000; ed Yale and Princeton Univs.; consultant prin. McKinsey & Co. 1964–74; Dir Financial Planning PepsiCo 1974–76, Sr Vice-Pres. Planning and Devt 1976–77, Sr Vice-Pres. Mfg Operations Frito-Lay Div. PepsiCo Int. 1977–82, Pres., CEO 1983–85, Pres. PepsiCo Foods Int. 1982–83, Exec. Vice-Pres., Chief Financial Officer PepsiCo Inc. 1985–86, Pres. 1986, also Bd Dirs., Pres., CEO PepsiCo Worldwide 1987–92; Chair., CEO Westinghouse Electric Corpn 1993–98; Chair. Centre for Excellence in Ed. 1988–92; Chair., Bd Dirs, partner Clayton, Dubilier and Rice 1992–93; now Chair. CBS; mem. Bd Dirs Melville Corpn, Rhone-Poulenc Rorer, Aetna, Dell Computers Inc., United Negro Coll. Fund 1986–. *Address:* CBS Gateway Center, 51 West 52nd Street, New York, NY 10019, USA.

JORDAN, Michael Jeffery; American basketball and baseball player; b. 17 Feb. 1963, Brooklyn, NY; s. of the late James Jordan and of Delores Jordan; m. Juanita Vanoy 1989; two s. one d.; ed Univ. of NC; player for Chicago Bulls, Nat. Basketball Asscn (NBA) 1984–93 1995–98 (NBA Champions 1991, 1992, 1993, 1996, 1997, 1998), Birmingham Barons baseball team 1993; mem. NCAA championship team 1982, U.S. Olympic team 1984, NBA All-Star team 1985–91; with Nashville Sounds 1994–95; holds record for most points in NBA playoff game with 63 and for highest points-scoring average (33.4); named world's highest paid athlete, Forbes Magazine 1992; retd 1998; Pres. Basketball Operations, Washington Wizards 1999–; came out of retirement to play for Washington Wizards 2001–; extensive business interests include a record co., automotive group and restaurants; supports numerous children's charities; Seagram's NBA Player of the Year 1987; Most Valuable Player, NBA All-Star Game 1988, NBA Most Valuable Player 1988, 1991, 1992, 1996, 1998. *Publications:* Rare Air: Michael on Michael (autobiog.) 1993, I Can't Accept Not Trying: Michael Jordan on the Pursuit of Excellence. *Address:* Washington Wizards, 718 7th Street, NW, Washington DC 20001, USA.

JORDAN, Neil, BA; Irish writer and director; b. 25 Feb. 1950, Sligo; two d. three s.; ed St Paul's Coll. Raheny, Dublin and Univ. Coll. Dublin; co-f. Irish Writers' Cooperative 1974; Guardian Fiction Award 1997, London Critics' Circle 1984, Evening Standard Award 1982, Los Angeles Film Critics Award 1992, NY Film Critics Award 1992, BAFTA 1992, 2000, Golden Lion, Venice Film Festival 1996, Silver Bear, Berlin Film Festival 1997. *Directed films:* Angel 1981, Company of Wolves 1984, Mona Lisa 1986, High Spirits 1988, We're No Angels 1989, The Miracle 1991, The Crying Game 1992, Interview with a Vampire 1994, Michael Collins 1995 (Golden Lion, Venice 1996), The Butcher Boy 1997, In Dreams 1999, The End of the Affair 1999, Double Dawn 2001. *Publications:* novels, plays and film-scripts including Night in Tunisia and Other Stories 1976, The Past 1980, The Dream of a Beast 1983, Sunrise with Sea Master 1995, Nightlines 1995. *Leisure interest:* music. *Address:* c/o Jenne Casarotto Co. Ltd, National House, 60-66 Wardour Street, London, WIV 3HP, England; 2 Martello Terrace, Bray, Co. Wicklow, Ireland.

JORDAN, Mgr Thierry; French ecclesiastic; b. 31 Aug. 1943, Shanghai, China; ed Lycée Hoche, Grand Séminaire de Versailles, Institut catholique de Paris, Gregorian Univ., Rome; ordained priest, Versailles 1966; Chaplain Church of Saint-Louis-des-Français, Rome, then Sec. to Cardinal Jean Villot, Vatican 1967–79; curate, Vésinet, Versailles 1980–84; Vicar-Episcopal, Saint-Quentin-en-Yvelines 1984–87; Vicar-Gen. Versailles diocese 1986–88; Bishop of Pontoise (Val-d'Oise) 1988–99; Archbishop of Rheims 1999–; Chair. Comm. épiscopale de la vie consacrée of Conf. of French Bishops 1993–96.

JORDAN, Vernon Eulion, Jr; American lawyer and investment banker; b. 15 Aug. 1935, Atlanta; s. of Vernon Eulion Jordan and Mary Jordan (née Griggs); m. 1st Shirley M. Yarbrough 1958 (died 1985); one d.; m. 2nd Ann Dibble Cook 1986; ed DePauw Univ., Howard Univ.; mem. Bar, Ga 1960, Ark. 1964; law practice, Atlanta 1960–61; Ga Field Dir NAACP 1961–63; law practice, Pine Bluff, Ark. 1964–65; Dir Voter Educ. Project Southern Regional Council 1964–68; Attorney Office of Econ. Opportunity, Atlanta 1969; Exec. Dir United Negro Coll. Fund 1970–71; Pres. Nat. Urban League 1972–81; Sr Partner Akin, Gump, Strauss, Hauer & Feld 1981–2000, of Counsel Akin, Gump, Strauss, Hauer & Feld LLP 2000–; Chair. Clinton Pres. Transition Bd; joined Lazard Freres and Co. LLC 2000, Sr Man. Dir 2000–; fmr mem., trustee and Dir numerous orgs. including Presidential Clemency Bd, Urban Inst., American Express Co., Revlon Group Inc.; over 50 hon. degrees, including Princeton Univ., Harvard Univ. *Leisure interests:* golf, tennis, yoga. *Address:* Lazard Freres & Co. LLC, 30 Rockefeller Plaza, New York, NY 10112-0002 (Office); 2940 Benton Place, NW, Washington, DC 20008, USA (Home). *Telephone:* (212) 632-6190 (Office). *Fax:* (212) 332-1640; (212) 667-1794 (Home). *E-mail:* jeannie.sotomayor@lazard.com (Office).

JORDAN, (William) Hamilton (McWhorter), BA; American politician; b. 21 Sept. 1944, Charlotte, NC; s. of Richard and Adelaide Jordan; m. 1st Nancy Jordan (divorced); m. 2nd Dorothy A. Henry 1981; one s.; served in S. Viet Nam with Int. Voluntary Services 1967–68; Youth Co-ordinator in Jimmy Carter's campaign for Governorship of Ga 1966, Man. 1970; Campaign Dir for Nat. Democratic Party Campaign Cttee 1973–74, for Carter's Pres. Campaign 1975–76, for Carter's re-election campaign 1980; an Asst to Pres. 1977–81;

White House Chief of Staff 1979–81; Distinguished Visiting Fellow, Emory Univ. 1981–82; political commentator Cable News Network 1981–; consultant in Corp. and int. communications 1984–; Pres., COO Whittle Communications 1991–92, Vice-Chair. 1992. *Publications:* Crisis: The Last Year of the Carter Presidency 1982, No Such Thing as a Bad Day 2000.

JORDAN, (Zweledinga) Pallo, PhD; South African politician; b. 22 May 1942, Kroonstad, OFS; s. of Dr. Archibald Jordan and Priscilla Ntantala; m. Carolyn Roth 1972; one d.; ed Athlone High School, Cape Town, Univs. of Cape Town and Wisconsin and London School of Econs.; joined African Nat. Congress (ANC) 1960; worked full time for ANC in London 1975–77; Head, Radio Freedom, Luanda, Angola 1977–79; in Lusaka, Zambia 1980–90; Mem. ANC Nat. Exec. Cttee (NEC) 1985–, Deputy Sec. of Information 1985, Admin. Sec. of NEC Secr. –1988, Head Dept. of Information and Publicity 1989–; MP 1994–; Minister of Posts, Telecommunications and Broadcasting 1994–96, of Environmental Affairs and Tourism 1996–99; Head Foreign Affairs Cttee. 2002–. *Publications:* articles and papers on South African political questions. *Address:* c/o African National Congress, 54 Sauer Street, Johannesburg 2001, South Africa.

JORDAN OF BOURNVILLE, Baron (Life Peer), cr. 2000, of Bournville in the County of West Midlands; **William Brian Jordan,** CBE; British trade union official; b. 28 Jan. 1936, Birmingham; s. of Walter Jordan and Alice Jordan; m. Jean Livesey 1958; three d.; ed Secondary Modern School, Birmingham; machine-tool fitter 1961; joined eng union and served as shop steward; convenor of shop stewards, Guest Keen & Nettlefolds 1966, later Dist Pres.; Div. Organizer for West Midlands AUEW 1977; Pres. Amalgamated Eng and Electrical (fmrly Amalgamated and Electrical) Union 1986–95; mem. TUC Gen. Council 1986–95 (Chair. Cttee on European Strategy 1988–95); mem. NEDC (Chair. Eng Industry Cttee) 1986–92, Energy Industry Training Bd 1986–91, Council, Industrial Soc. 1987–, Advisory, Conciliation & Arbitration Service (ACAS) 1987–95, Nat. Training Task Force 1989–92, Eng Training Authority 1991–, Foundation for Manufacturing and Industry; Gen. Sec. ICFTU 1994–2002; fmr Pres. European Metalworkers' Fed.; fmr Exec. mem. Int. Metalworkers' Fed.; fmr mem. European Trade Union Confed., Bd Govs BBC, Nat. Advisory Council for Educ. and Training Targets, UK Skills Council; mem. Victim Support Advisory Cttee, Bd English Partnership, Winston Churchill Trust; a Gov. of LSE, Ashridge Man. Coll.; mem. Royal Soc. of Arts; Dr hc (Univ. of Cen. England) 1993, (Univ. of Cranfield) 1995. *Leisure interests:* reading, sports (especially football, Birmingham City Football Club supporter). *Address:* c/o ICFTU, Boulevard Emile Jacqmain 155, 1210 Brussels, Belgium.

JORDÁN-PANDO, Roberto; Bolivian diplomatist and economist; b. 21 Feb. 1930; m.; five c.; ed Universidad Real y Pontífica San Francisco Xavier, Sucre, Universidad Mayor San Andrés, La Paz; Deputy Minister for Rural and Farming Affairs 1955–56, Minister 1960–63; Amb.-del. to UN Gen. Ass. 1956–57, to first UN Conf. on Law of the Sea 1958; Head. Bolivian del. to UNCTAD 1964; fmr consultant FAO, OAS, UNDP and other orgs.; Pres. Financial de Consultoria S.r.l. 1984–; consultant on investment projects, PEMECO Ltd 1993–95; Prof., Latin American Faculty of Social Sciences 1990–91; Rector Universidad Privada Franz Tamayo 1996–98; Perm. Rep. to UN 1998–2001. *Address:* c/o Ministry of Foreign Affairs, Calle Ingavi, esq. Junin, La Paz, Bolivia (Office).

JØRGENSEN, Anker; Danish politician and trade unionist; b. 13 July 1922, Copenhagen; s. of Johannes Jørgensen; m. Ingrid Jørgensen 1948; four c.; ed School for Orphans and evening classes; messenger, shipyard worker, warehouse worker 1936–50; Vice-Pres. Warehouse Workers' Union 1950, Pres. 1958–62; Group Sec. Transport and Gen. Workers' Union 1962–68, Pres. 1968–72; mem. Folketing (Parl.) 1964–94; mem. Bd of Dirs., Workers' Bank of Denmark 1969–; Prime Minister 1972–73; Parl. Leader, Social Democratic Group 1973–75; Prime Minister 1975–82; Chair. Social Democratic Party, Social Democratic Parl. Group 1972–87; mem. European Cttee Against Racism 1994–. *Publication:* Memoirs (Vol. I) 1994. *Address:* Borgbjergsvej 1, 2450 S.V. Copenhagen, Denmark.

JØRGENSEN, Bo Barker, PhD; Danish biologist; b. 22 Sept. 1946, Copenhagen; s. of Carl C. B. Jørgensen and Vibeke Balslev Smidt; m. Inga M. Vestergaard 1971; two s. one d.; ed Univs. of Copenhagen and Aarhus; lecturer, Dept of Ecology and Genetics, Univ. of Aarhus 1973–77, Sr lecturer 1977–87, Prof. 1987–92; Dir Max Planck Inst. for Marine Microbiology, Bremen, Germany 1992–97; Prof., Univ. of Bremen, Germany 1993; Adjunct Prof., Univ. of Aarhus 1993–; research, Marine Biology Lab., Eilat, Israel 1974, 1978, NASA—ARC, Moffett Field, Calif. 1984–85. *Publications:* more than 200 scientific publs in int. journals in the field of ecology, microbiology and geochemistry. *Leisure interests:* photography, music. *Address:* Auf den Hornstücken 25, 28359 Bremen, Germany. *Telephone:* (421) 242336.

JØRGENSEN, Sven-Aage, MA; Danish professor of German philology; b. 22 July 1929, Herstedvester; s. of Aage Julius Jørgensen and Emma Lydia (née Eriksen) Jørgensen; m. Elli Andresen 1957 (divorced 1985); two s. one d.; ed Birkerød Statsskole, Univ. of Copenhagen, Univ. of Würzburg and Warburg Inst., London; lecturer Univ. of Copenhagen 1961, Prof. of German Philology 1968; Research Prof. Univ. of Bielefeld 1980–81; Visiting Prof. Heidelberg 1973, Regensburg 1985, Kiel 1986, Cologne 1990; Visiting Fellow ANU 1975; mem. Royal Danish Acad. of Sciences and Letters 1986, Akad. der Wissenschaften in Göttingen 1998; Kt of Order of Dannebrog; Alexander von Humboldt Prize 1995, Univ. Gold Medal 1957. *Publications:* J. G. Hamann's

Fünf Hirtenbriefe 1962, J. G. Hamann's Sokratische Denkwurdigkeiten und Aesthetica in Nuce 1962, Th. Fontane's Unwiederbringlich 1971, J. G. Hamann 1976, Deutsch-dänische Literaturbeziehungen im 18. Jhdrt. (co-ed.) 1977, Dänische 'guldalderliteratur' und deutsche Klassik (co-ed.) 1982, Tysk et sprog Fire Stater–Fire Kulturer 1989, Wieland's Oberon 1990, Geschichte der deutschen Literatur 1740–1789 (co-author) 1990, Zentrum der Aufklärung: Kopenhagen–Kiel Altona (co-ed.) 1992, Verfilmte Litteratur (co-ed.) 1993, Fortschritt ohne Ende–Ende des Fortschritts? (ed.) 1994, Wieland Epoche-Werk-Wirkung (co-author) 1994, C. M. Wieland's Die Abenteuer des Don Sylvio von Rosalva 2001; numerous articles. *Leisure interests:* jogging, swimming. *Address:* Ny Kongensgade 20, 3, 1557 Copenhagen V, Denmark. *Telephone:* 33-15-76-04 (Home). *E-mail:* sven.aage@get2net.dk (Home).

JORGENSON, Dale W., PhD; American economist; b. 7 May 1933, Bozeman, Mont.; s. of Emmett B. Jorgenson and Jewell T. Jorgenson; m. Linda Ann Mabus 1971; one s. one d.; ed Reed Coll. and Harvard Univ.; Asst Prof. of Econs Univ. of Calif., Berkeley 1959–61, Assoc. Prof. 1961–63, Prof. 1963–69; Ford Foundation Research Prof. of Econs Univ. of Chicago 1962–63; Prof. of Econs Harvard Univ. 1969–80, Frederic Eaton Abbe Prof. of Econs 1980–2002, Samuel W. Morris Univ. Prof. 2002–, Frank William Taussig Research Prof. of Econs 1992–94, Chair. Dept of Econs 1994–97; Dir Program on Tech. and Econ. Policy, Kennedy School of Govt, Harvard Univ. 1984–; mem. Science Advisory Cttee, Gen. Motors Corpn 1996–2002; Visiting Prof. of Econs Hebrew Univ., Jerusalem 1967, Stanford Univ. 1973; Visiting Prof. of Statistics Oxford Univ. 1968; Chair. Section 54, Econ. Sciences, Nat. Acad. of Sciences 2001–; mem. Bd on Science, Tech. and Econ. Policy, Nat. Research Council 1991–98, Chair. 1998–; Consulting Ed., North-Holland Publishing Co., Amsterdam, Netherlands 1970–2002; Fellow, AAAS, American Acad. of Arts and Sciences, American Statistical Asscn, Econometric Soc. (Pres. 1987); mem. NAS, American Econ. Asscn (Pres. 2000), Royal Econ. Soc., Econ. Study Soc., Conf. on Research in Income and Wealth, Int. Asscn for Research in Income and Wealth, American Philosophical Soc.; Foreign mem. Royal Swedish Acad. of Sciences; several fellowships including Nat. Science Foundation Snr. Postdoctoral Fellowship, Netherlands School of Econs, Rotterdam 1967–68; lectures include Shinzo Koizumi, Keio Univ., Tokyo, Japan 1972, Fisher-Schultz, 3rd World Congress, Econometric Soc. 1975, Frank Paish, Asscn of Univ. Teachers of Econs Conf., UK 1980, Erik Lindahl Lectures, Uppsala Univ. 1987, Inst. Lecture, Inst. of Industrial Econs, Univ. of Toulouse 2001, Astra Zeneca/Ericsson Lecture, Research Inst. of Industrial Econs, Stockholm 2002; Hon. DPhil (Oslo), (Uppsala) 1991; prizes include John Bates Clark Medal, American Econ. Asscn 1971, Outstanding Contrib. Award, Int. Asscn of Energy Economists 1994. *Publications:* Technology and Economic Policy (with R. Landau) 1986, Productivity and U.S. Economic Growth 1987, Technology and Capital Formation 1989, General Equilibrium Modeling and Economic Policy Analysis 1990, Tax Reform and the Cost of Capital (with K.-Y. Yun) 1991, Tax Reform and the Cost of Capital: An International Comparison (with R. Landau) 1993, Postwar U.S. Economic Growth 1995, International Comparisons of Economic Growth 1995, Capital Theory and Investment Behavior 1996, Tax Policy and the Cost of Capital 1996, Improving America's Schools 1996, Aggregate Consumer Behavior 1997, Measuring Social Welfare 1997, Econometric General Equilibrium Modeling 1998, Energy, the Environmental and Economic Growth 1998, Lifting the Burden (with K.-Y. Yun) 2001; over 200 papers and contribs to learned journals and collections of essays. *Address:* Department of Economics, Harvard University, Littauer 122, Cambridge, MA 02138 (Office); 1010 Memorial Drive, Cambridge, MA 02138, USA (Home). *Telephone:* (617) 495-4661 (Office); (617) 491-4069 (Home). *Fax:* (617) 495-4660 (Office); (617) 491-4105 (Home). *E-mail:* djorgenson@harvard.edu (Office).

JORRITSMA-LEBBINK, Annemarie; Netherlands politician; b. 1 June 1950, Hengelo; d. of Berend-Jan Lebbink and Maria Wilhelmina Lebbink (née Tulp); m. Gerlog Jorritsma 1971; two s.; ed Baudartius Coll., Zutphen and Tourism Training Coll., Breda; admin. with Wolvega (travel agency) 1969–71; Sec. to Export Man., Bk-Beccon-Edy, Dieren 1971–74; mem. Volkspartij voor Vrijheid en Democratie (VVD, People's Party for Freedom and Democracy) 1973; mem. Bolsward Council 1978–89; mem. Second Chamber 1982–; Minister of Transport and Public Works 1996; Deputy Prime Minister and Minister of Econ. Affairs; mem. cttees. on Traffic and Water, Educ., Emancipation, Housing and Spatial Order, Social Affairs and Agric. *Address:* Ministry of Economic Affairs, Bezuidenhoutseweg 30, P.O. Box 20101, 2500 EC The Hague, Netherlands. *Telephone:* (70) 3798911 (Office). *Fax:* (70) 3474081 (Office).

JORTNER, Joshua, PhD; Israeli professor of physical chemistry; b. 14 March 1933, Tarnow, Poland; s. of Arthur Jortner and Regina Jortner; m. Ruth Sanger 1960; one s. one d.; ed Hebrew Univ. of Jerusalem; Instructor Dept of Physical Chemistry, Hebrew Univ. of Jerusalem 1961–62, Sr lecturer 1963–65; Research Assoc. Univ. of Chicago 1962–64, Prof. 1965–71; Assoc. Prof. of Physical Chem., Tel Aviv Univ. 1965–66, Prof. 1966–, Head Inst. of Chem. 1966–72, Deputy Rector 1966–69, Vice-Pres. 1970–72, Heinemann Prof. of Chem. 1973–; Visiting Prof. H.C. Orsted Inst., Univ. of Copenhagen 1974, Visiting Prof. of Chem. 1978; Visiting Prof. UCLA-Berkeley 1975; Vice-Pres. Israeli Acad. of Sciences and Humanities 1980–86, Pres. 1986–95, mem. Council 1996–; Vice-Pres. IUPAC 1996–97, Pres. 1998–99; Int. Acad. of Quantum Science Award 1972, Weizmann Prize 1973, Rothschild Prize 1976, Kolthof Prize 1976, Israel Prize in Chem. 1982, Wolf Prize 1988, Hon. J. Hejrovsky Gold Medal 1993, August Wilhelm von Hofmann Medal 1995,

Joseph O. Hirschfelder Prize in Theoretical Chem. 1999. *Publications:* Intramolecular Radiationless Transitions (with M. Bixon) 1968, Energy Gap Law for Radiationless Transitions (with E. Englman) 1970, Electronic Excitations in Condensed Rare Gases (with N. Schwentner and E. E. Koch) 1985, Cluster Size Effects 1992; The Jerusalem Symposia on Quantum Chemistry and Biochemistry (Ed. with Bernard Pullman) Vols 15–27 1982–93. *Leisure interest:* science policy. *Address:* School of Chemistry, Tel Aviv University, Ramat Aviv, 69978 Tel Aviv, Israel. *Telephone:* 3-6408322. *Fax:* 3-6415054.

JORY, Edward John, PhD, FAHA; British/Australian professor of classics; b. 20 June 1936, England; s. of E Jory; m. Marie McGee 1965; three s.; ed Humphry Davy Grammar School, Penzance and Univ. Coll., London; lecturer Dept of Classics and Ancient History, Univ. of Western Australia 1959–65, Sr Lecturer 1966–73, Assoc. Prof. 1974–78, Dean of Faculty of Arts 1976–79, Prof. and Head of Dept 1979–84, 1988–89, Head of Div. of Arts and Architecture 1990–93, Exec. Dean Faculty of Arts 1994–2000; Visiting Prof. Inst. of Classical Studies, Univ. of London 1990; Fellow Australian Acad. of Humanities, Alexander von Humboldt Fellow 1974, 1980, Kommission für Alte Geschichte und Epigraphik, Munich 1974, T. B. L. Webster Fellow, Inst. of Classical Studies 2000. *Publications:* contrib. to Corpus Inscriptionum Latinarum 1974, 1989; numerous articles on the Roman theatre. *Leisure interests:* cricket, skin diving, golf. *Address:* Department of Classics and Ancient History, University of Western Australia, Crawley, WA 6009 (Office); 36 Marita Road, Nedlands, WA 6009, Australia. *Telephone:* 9380-7073 (Office); 9386-2714. *Fax:* 9380-1009 (Office). *E-mail:* ejjory@arts.uwa.edu.au (Office).

JOSEPH, Cedric Luckie, MA; Guyanese diplomatist (retd) and historian; b. 14 May 1933, Georgetown; s. of late Frederick McConnell Joseph and Cassie Edith Joseph, née Austin; m. Dona Avril Barrett 1973; two s. (adopted); ed LSE, Univ. Coll. of Wales, Aberystwyth; taught history at a London Comprehensive School 1962–66; Lecturer in History, Univ. of the W Indies, Kingston, Jamaica 1966–71; Prin. Asst Sec., Ministry of Foreign Affairs, Guyana 1971–74; Deputy High Commr for Guyana in Jamaica 1974–76; Counsellor, Embassy of Guyana, Washington, DC 1976; Deputy Perm. Rep., Perm. Mission of Guyana to the UN 1976–77; High Commr for Guyana in Zambia (also accred to Angola, Botswana, Mozambique, Tanzania and Zimbabwe) 1977–82, in the UK (also Accred as Ambassador to France, the Netherlands, Yugoslavia and UNESCO) 1982–86; Chair. Commonwealth Cttee on Southern Africa 1983–86; Head of the Presidential Secretariat 1986–91; Sec. to the Cabinet 1987–91; Sr Amb., Ministry of Foreign Affairs 1991–94; Foreign policy analyst 1995–; Cacique's Crown of Honour, 1983. *Publications include:* The Manning Initiative 1993; in Guyana Review: Intervention in Haiti 1994, Reconstruction of the Caribbean Community 1994, Dependency and Mendicancy 1995, Transition and Guyana 1995, Caribbean Community–Security and Survival 1997, Anglo-American Diplomacy and the Reopening of the Guyana/Venezuela Boundary Controversy 1961–1966 1998. *Leisure interests:* the fine arts, reading, walking. *Address:* 332 Republic Park, Peter's Hall, East Bank Demerara, Guyana. *Telephone:* 233-5751. *Fax:* 233-5751. *E-mail:* clmdj@networksgy.com (Home).

JOSEPHSON, Brian David, PhD, FInstP, FRS; British physicist; b. 4 Jan. 1940, Cardiff; s. of Abraham and Mimi Josephson; m. Carol Anne Olivier 1976; one d.; ed Cardiff High School, Cambridge Univ.; Fellow, Trinity Coll., Cambridge 1962–; Research Asst Prof. Univ. of Illinois 1965–66; Asst Dir of Research, Cambridge Univ. 1967–72, Reader in Physics 1972–74, Prof. of Physics 1974–; faculty mem. Maharishi European Research Univ. 1975; Hon. mem. Inst. of Electrical and Electronic Engineers; Foreign Hon. mem. American Acad. of Arts and Sciences; New Scientist Award 1969, Research Corpn Award 1969, Fritz London Award 1970, Hughes Medal Royal Soc. 1972, shared Nobel Prize for Physics 1973. *Publications:* Co-ed. Consciousness and the Physical World 1980, The Paranormal and the Platonic Worlds (in Japanese) 1997; research papers on superconductivity, critical phenomena, theory of intelligence, science and mysticism. *Leisure interests:* walking, ice skating, photography, astronomy. *Address:* Cavendish Laboratory, Madingley Road, Cambridge, CB3 0HE, England (Office). *Telephone:* (1223) 337260 (Office). *Fax:* (1223) 337356 (Office). *E-mail:* bdj10@cam.ac.uk (Office).

JOSEPHSON, Erland; Swedish actor and theatre director; b. 15 June 1923, Stockholm; at Municipal Theatre, Helsingborg 1945–49, Gothenburg 1949–56, Royal Dramatic Theatre, Stockholm 1956–; Dir of Royal Dramatic Theatre, Stockholm 1966–75; American stage début in The Cherry Orchard 1988. *Film appearances include:* Montenegro 1981, Fanny and Alexander 1983, After the Rehearsal 1984, The Unbearable Lightness of Being 1988, Hanussen 1989, Meeting Venus, The Ox, Sofie, Ulysses' Gaze, Vendetta, Waiting for Sunset, Kristin Lauransdatter. *Publications include:* Cirkel 1946, Spegeln och en portvakt 1946, Spel med bedrövade artister 1947, Ensam och fri 1948, Lyssnarpost 1949, De vuxna barnen 1952, Utflykt 1954, Sällskapslek 1955, En berättelse om herr Silberstein 1957, Kungen ur leken 1959, Doktor Meyers sista dagar 1964, Kandidat Nilssons första natt 1964, Lejon i Övergångsåldern (pjas Dromaten) 1981, En talande tystnad (pja's Dramaten) 1984, Loppaus Kvällsvard 1986, Kameleonterna 1987, Järgen 1988, Rollen 1989. *Address:* c/o Royal Dramatic Theatre, Nybroplan, Box 5037, 102 41 Stockholm, Sweden.

JOSHI, Damayanti, BA; Indian classical dancer; b. 5 Dec. 1932, Mumbai; d. of Ramchandra Joshi and Vatsala Joshi; ed numerous Schools of Classical

Dancing; leading exponent of Kathak Dance; has choreographed numerous productions, holding dance seminars throughout India and touring extensively in Asia, Africa and Europe; acts as examiner in music and dance for numerous Indian univs.; holds numerous public service posts connected with the dance; Chair. Dancers' Guild, Bombay; Life mem. numerous dance socs.; Visiting Prof. IndiraKala Sangeet Vishwavidyalaya, Khairagarh, also conducts teachers' workshops; has performed before Heads of State of Nepal, Afghanistan, USSR, Laos, Yugoslavia, Indonesia, Philippines, Mexico; TV appearances and film Damayanti Joshi on Kathak Dance; lecture demonstrations in GB, Germany, China and India; Sangeet Nathak Award 1968. *Publications:* Madame Menaka (monograph), articles for art magazines, weeklies, dailies. *Leisure interests:* reading, writing, sitar. *Address:* D-1, Jeshtharam Baug, Tram Terminus, Dadar, Mumbai 400013, India. *Telephone:* 4141589.

JOSPIN, Lionel Robert; French politician; b. 12 July 1937, Meudon, Hauts-de-Seine; s. of Robert Jospin and Mireille Dandieu; m. 2nd Sylviane Agacinski 1994; one s. one d. (from previous m.), one step-s.; ed Institut d'études politiques de Paris, École nat. d'administration; Sec. Ministry of Foreign Affairs 1965–70; Prof. Econ. Inst. universitaire de tech. de Paris-Sceaux, also attached to Univ. de Paris XI 1970–81; Nat. Sec. Socialist Party, mem. steering Cttee 1973–75, spokesman on Third World Affairs 1975–79, Int. Relations 1979–81, First Sec. 1981–88, Head 1995–97; Councillor for Paris (18e arrondissement) 1977–86; Socialist Deputy to Nat. Ass. for Paris (27e circ.) 1981–86, for Haute-Garonne 1986–88; mem. Gen. Council Haute-Garonne 1988–; Conseiller régional, Midi-Pyrénées 1992–98; Minister of State, Nat. Educ., Research and Sport May–June 1988; Minister of State, Nat. Educ., of Youth and Sport 1988–91, Minister of Nat. Educ. 1991–92; Presidential Cand. 1995, 2002; Prime Minister of France 1997–2002; Trombinoscope Politician of the Year 1997. *Publications:* L'Invention du Possible 1991, 1995–2000: Propositions pour la France 1995, Le Temps de répondre 2002. *Leisure interests:* basketball, tennis. *Address:* c/o Office of the Prime Minister, Hôtel Matignon, 57 rue de Varenne, 75700 Paris, France.

JOSSELIN, Charles; French politician; b. 31 March 1938, Pleslin-Trigavou; s. of Charles Josselin and Marie Hamoniaux; m. 2nd Evelyne Besnard 1987; four c.; fmr attaché, financial secr., Banque de l'Union Parisienne, economist, Soc. centrale pour l'équipement du transitoire; Parti Socialiste (PS) Nat. Ass. Deputy for 2nd Côtes d'Armor Constituency (Dinan) 1973–78, 1981–85, 1986–92; Minister of State for Transport 1985–86, for the Sea 1992–93; Sec. of State attached to Minister of Foreign Affairs, with responsibility for Co-operation 1997, for Co-operation and Francophonie 1997–98, Deputy Minister for Co-operation and Francophonie 1998–2002, Minister of State 1998–2002; Mayor of Pleslin-Trigavou 1977–97; mem. European Parl. 1979–81; Chair. Nat. Council for Regional Economies and Productivity 1982–86, Nat. Ass.'s EC Select Cttee 1981–85, 1988–92, Vice-Chair. EU Select Cttee 1993–; Chair. Parl. Study Group on int. aid orgs.; mem. Côtes d'Armor Gen. Council for Ploubalay canton 1973–, Chair. 1976–97; mem. Nat. Council for Town and Country Planning, Local Finance Cttee, EU Cttee of the Regions. *Address:* c/o Ministry of Co-operation, 20 rue Monsieur, 75700 Paris, France.

JOULWAN, Gen. George Alfred, BS, MA; American army officer; b. 16 Nov. 1939, Pottsville, Pa; m. Karen E. Jones; three d.; ed U.S. Mil. Acad. West Point, Loyola Univ., Chicago, US Army War Coll., Washington, DC; served in Vietnam as Co. Commdr and Operations Officer, 1st Bn, 26th Infantry, 1st Infantry Div. and as Brigade Operations Officer and Deputy Div. Operations Officer, 101st Airborne Div. (Air Assault); Aide-de-Camp to Vice-Chief of Staff, US Army; Special Asst to the Pres. 1973–74, to Supreme Allied Commdr, Europe 1974–75; Bn Commdr, US Army, Europe 1975–77; Dir Political and Economic Studies, US Army War Coll., Pa 1978–79; Commdr 2nd Brigade, 3rd Infantry Div. (Mechanized), US Army, Europe 1979–81; Chief of Staff 1981–82; Exec. Officer to Chair., Jt Chiefs of Staff, Washington, DC 1982–85; Dir Force Requirements (Combat Support Systems), Office of Deputy Chief of Staff for Operations and Plans, Washington, DC 1985–86; Deputy Chief of Staff for Operations, US Army, Europe and Seventh Army 1986–88, Commdg Gen., 3rd Armored Div. 1988–89, V Corps, 1989–90; C-in-C, US Southern Command, Quarry Heights, Panama 1990–93, US European Command, Stuttgart/Vaihingen, Germany 1993–97; Supreme Allied Commdr, Europe, SHAPE, Belgium 1993–97; numerous decorations including Defense Distinguished Service Medal (with Oak Leaf Cluster), Defense Superior Service Medal, Silver Star (with Oak Leaf Cluster); numerous orders including Légion d'honneur, Hessian Order of Merit (Germany). *Address:* Supreme Headquarters, Allied Powers Europe, B7010 SHAPE, Belgium.

JOVANOVIĆ, Vladislav, LLB; Serbia and Montenegro (Serbian) diplomatist; b. 9 June 1933, Prokuplje; s. of Milorad Jovanović and Dragica Jovanović; m. Mirjana Jovanović (née Borić) 1985; one s.; ed Belgrade Univ.; joined Foreign Service 1957; served in Belgium, Turkey and UK 1960–79, Amb. to Turkey 1985–89; various Sr posts in Fed. Ministry for Foreign Affairs 1990–91; Head Yugoslav Dels. to Disarmament and Human Dimension confs. of CSCE 1990–91; Minister of Foreign Affairs, Repub. of Serbia 1991–92; Fed. Minister for Foreign Affairs of Yugoslavia 1992, 1993–95; Amb. and Perm. Rep. of Yugoslavia to UN 1995–2002; Légion d'honneur and other decorations. *Publications:* two books of poetry. *Leisure interest:* chess. *Address:* c/o Ministry of Foreign Affairs, 11000 Belgrade, Kneza Milosa 24, Serbia and Montenegro (Office).

JOVANOVIĆ, Živadin; Serbia and Montenegro (Serbian) politician; b. 14 Nov. 1938, Oparic, Rekovać Dist; ed Belgrade Univ.; legal adviser, Novi Beograd Dist Council 1961–64; with Ministry of Foreign Affairs 1964–; Yugoslavian Amb. to Angola 1988–93; Asst to Minister of Foreign Affairs 1994–97; Deputy Chair. Socialist Party of Serbia 1997–, currently Pres. (acting); mem. Parl. (Narosna Skuptina) of Serbia 1997–; Minister of Foreign Affairs of Yugoslavia 1998–2000. *Address:* Socialist Party of Serbia, bul. Lenjina 6, 11000 Belgrade, Serbia and Montenegro. *Telephone:* (11) 634921 (Office). *Fax:* (11) 628642.

JOWELL, Rt. Hon. Tessa Jane Helen Douglas, PC, MA; British politician; b. 17 Sept. 1947, London; d. of Kenneth Palmer and Rosemary Palmer; m. 1st Roger Jowell 1970 (divorced 1978); m. 2nd David Mills 1979; one s. one d. and one step-s. two step-d.; ed St Margaret's School, Aberdeen, Univs of Aberdeen and Edinburgh; childcare officer, social worker, community care Dir; Asst Dir MIND 1974–86; Dir Community Care Special Action Project 1987–90, Joseph Rowntree Foundation Community Care Programme 1990–92; mem. Labour Party 1969–; Councillor, London Borough of Camden 1971–86; MP for Dulwich 1992–97, for Dulwich and W. Norwood 1997–; Opposition Whip, responsible for Trade and Industry 1994–95, Opposition Spokeswoman on Women 1995–96, on Health 1996–97; Minister of State for Public Health 1997–99, for Employment 1999–2001; Minister for Women, House of Commons 1998–2001; Sec. of State for Culture, Media and Sport 2001–; Chair. Social Services Cttee, Housing Man. Cttee, Staff Cttee, Asscn of Metropolitan Authorities 1978–86; mem. Mental Health Act Comm. 1985–90, Health Select Cttee 1992–94; Gov. Nat. Inst. of Social Work 1985–97; Visiting Fellow Nuffield Coll., Oxford. *Publications:* numerous papers on social policy and community care. *Address:* Department for Culture, Media and Sport, 2–4 Cockspur Street, London, SW1Y 5DH, England (Office). *Telephone:* (20) 7211-6000 (Office). *Fax:* (20) 7211-6210 (Office). *E-mail:* enquiries@culture.gov.uk (Office). *Website:* www.culture.gov.uk (Office).

JOXE, Pierre Daniel, LenD; French politician; b. 28 Nov. 1934, Paris; s. of Louis Joxe and Françoise-Hélène Halevy; m. 3rd Valérie Cayeux 1981; two s. two d. from previous m.; ed Lycée Henri IV, Faculté de droit and Ecole Nat. d'Admin; Mil. Service 1958–60; Auditor, later Counsellor Cour des Comptes; mem. Exec. Bureau and Exec. Cttee, Socialist Party 1971–93; Deputy for Saône and Loire 1973, 1978, 1981, 1986, 1988; Minister of Industry and Admin. May–June 1981, of the Interior, Decentralization and Admin. July 1984 and March 1986, of the Interior 1988–91, of Defence 1991–93; First Pres. Cour des Comptes (audit court) 1993–2001; mem. Conseil Constitutionnel 2001–; mem. European Parl. 1977–79; Pres. Regional Council, Burgundy 1979–82, Socialist Parl. Group 1981–84, 1986–88; Commdr Ordre nat. du Mérite, Hon. KBE. *Publications:* Parti socialiste 1973, Atlas du Socialisme 1973, L'édit de Nantes (Literary Prize, Droits de l'homme) 1998, A propos de la France 1998. *Address:* Conseil Constitutionnel, 2 rue de Montpensier, 75100 Paris, France (Office).

JOY-WAY ROJAS, Victor, BEng, MA, M.ECON.; Peruvian politician; ed Univ. Nac. de Ingeniería, Escuela Superior de Admin. Pública, Peru, Williams Coll., Mass. and Harvard Univs, USA; Man. Dir number of overseas trade and int. business cos.; consultant to UN and OAS on foreign trade; Head Andean Plan for the Promotion of Exports, Cartagena Accord Group; Pres. Org. of Peruvian Importers and Exporters; Co-ordinator China-Latin America Econ. Cooperation Programmes; Dir Corpn Andina de Fomento; Ministry of Industry, Tourism, Integration and Int. Commercial Negotiations 1991–92; mem. Democratic Constituent Congress 1992–, Third Vice-Pres. 1993, Second Vice-Pres. 1994–95, First Vice-Pres. 1995–96, Pres. 1996–97, 1998; fmr Vice-Pres. Amazonian Parl.; Pres. Council of Ministers and Minister of the Economy 1999; under investigation for fraud allegedly committed while in office, 2001; Rep. of Pres. of Peru to External Debt Cttee; Pres. Econ. Comm. 1995–96, Foreign Affairs Comm. 1997–98, Peruvian Congress; Pres. Peru-China Friendship League, Peru-Brazil Friendship League; mem. Privatization Cttee (COPRI). *Address:* c/o Oficina del Presidente, Lima, Peru.

JOYNER-KERSEE, Jacqueline, BA; American athlete; b. 3 March 1962, E St Louis, Ill.; d. of Alfred Joyner and the late Mary Joyner; m. Bobby Kersee 1986; ed Univ. of Calif. at Los Angeles (UCLA); specializes in heptathlon; coached by husband; world record heptathlon scores: 7,158 points, Houston, 1986; 7,215 points, US Olympic trial, Indianapolis 1988 (still world record as at Dec. 2002); 7,291 points, Seoul 1988; 7,044 points (gold medal), Olympic Games, Barcelona 1992; 3 Olympic gold medals, 4 world championships; long jump: gold medal, World Championships 1987, gold medal, Olympic Games, Seoul 1988, bronze medal, Olympic Games, Barcelona 1992, bronze medal, Olympic Games, Atlanta 1996; winner IAAF Mobil Grand Prix 1994; Chair. St Louis Sports Comm. 1996–; played basketball for Richmond Rage, American Basketball League 1996; business interests include gold medal Rehab (sports medicine); CEO Elite Int. Sports Marketing; f. Jackie Joyner-Kersee Youth Foundation; motivational speaker; Hon. DHL (Spellman Coll.) 1998, (Howard Univ.) 1999, (George Washington Univ.) 1999; numerous honours including Associated Press Female Athlete of the Year 1988, first woman to win Sporting News Man of the Year Award, Jim Thorpe Award 1993, Jackie Robinson Robie Award 1994, Jesse Owens Humanitarian Award 1999. *Publication:* A Kind of Grace (autobiog.) 1997. *Address:* Elite International Sports Marketing Inc., 1034 South Brentwood Boulevard, Suite 1530, St Louis, MO 63117, USA. *Website:* www.sportsstarsusa.com.

JU MING; Taiwanese sculptor; b. 20 Jan. 1938, Taiwan; apprenticeship with Master Chin-chuan Lee 1953–57; trained in modern sculpture by Yu Yu Yang 1968–76; moved to USA and made debut in int. arena 1981; produced two series: Taichi Series in wood and bronze and Living World Series in wood, bronze, sponge and stainless steel; Sculpture Award Chinese Sculptors and Artists Asscn 1976, Nat. Culture Award, Repub. of China Nat. Culture Foundation 1976, Award for Ten Outstanding Young People 1987, Achievement Award of Fok Ying Tung, Hong Kong 1999. *Exhibitions include:* Nat. History Museum, Taipei 1976, Tokyo Cen. Museum 1976, Hong Kong Arts Centre 1979, Max Hutchinson Gallery, New York 1981, Ayala Museum, Manila 1984, Birashri Inst. of Modern Art, Bangkok 1984, Nat. Museum of Singapore 1986, Taipei Fine Art Museum 1987, South Bank Centre, London 1991, Browses & Darby Gallery, London 1991, Yorkshire Sculpture Park 1991, Musée d'art contemporain de Dunkerque, France 1991, Mistukoshi Dept Store, Tokyo, 1992, Hakone Open-air Museum, Japan 1995, Place Vendôme, Paris 1997, Luxembourg City 1999, Brussels, Belgium 2000. *Address:* 208 No. 2 She-shi-hu, Chin-shan, Taipei (Office); 111 No. 28, Lane 460, Sec. 2, Chih-shan Road, Taipei, Taiwan (Home). *Telephone:* (2) 24989940 (Office); (2) 28412011 (Home). *Fax:* (2) 24988529 (Office); (2) 28413000 (Home). *E-mail:* www.juming.org.tw (Office).

JUAN CARLOS I, King of Spain; b. 5 Jan. 1938, Rome; s. of the late HRH Don Juan de Borbón y Battenberg, Count of Barcelona and of the late HRH Doña María de las Mercedes de Borbón y Orleans and grandson of King Alfonso XIII and Queen Victoria Eugenia of Spain; m. Princess Sophia, d. of the late King Paul of the Hellenes and of Queen Frederica, 1962; heir, Crown Prince Felipe, b. Jan. 1968; daughters Princess Elena, Princess Cristina; ed privately in Fribourg (Switzerland), Madrid, San Sebastián, Inst. of San Isidro, Madrid, Colegio del Carmen, Gen. Mil. Acad., Zaragoza and Univ. of Madrid; spent childhood in Rome, Lausanne, Estoril and Madrid; commissioned into the three armed forces and undertook training in each of them 1957–59; studied the org. and activities of various Govt ministries; named by Gen. Franco as future King of Spain 1969, inaugurated as King of Spain 22 Nov. 1975, named as Capt.-Gen. of the Armed Forces Nov. 1975; Foreign mem. Académie des sciences morales et politiques, Assoc. mem. 1988; Dr. hc (Strasbourg) 1979, (Madrid), (Harvard) 1984, (Sorbonne) 1985, (Oxford) 1986, (Trinity Coll., Dublin) 1986, (Bologna) 1988, (Cambridge) 1988, (Coimbra) 1989, (Tokyo, Bogotá, Limerick, Tufts, Chile) 1990, (Toronto) 1991, (Jerusalem) 1993; Charlemagne Prize 1982, Bolívar Prize (UNESCO) 1983, Gold Medal Gore 1985, Candenhove Kalergi Prize, Switzerland 1986, Nansen Medal 1987, Humanitarian Award Elie Wiesel, USA 1991, shared Houphouët Boigny Peace Prize (UNESCO) 1995, Franklin D. Roosevelt Four Freedoms Award 1995. *Address:* Palacio de la Zarzuela, 28071 Madrid, Spain.

JUANTORENA, Alberto; Cuban athlete (retd), sports administrator and politician; b. 3 Dec. 1950, Santiago; m.; five c.; ed Havana to train under Polish coach Zgymunt Zabierzowski 1971; gold 400m. (45.36) Dominica Cen. American Games 1974; gold 800m. (1:43.50), gold 400m. (44.26) Montreal Olympic Games 1976; gold 800m. (1:44.01), gold 400m. (45.36) Dusseldorf World Cup 1977; gold 400m. (44.27), gold 800m. (1:47.78) Columbia Cen. American Games 1978; fmr Vice-Minister of Sports for Cuba, Vice-Pres. Cuban Olympic Cttee, Vice-Pres. for Latinamerica UNESCO, Sr Vice-Pres. Cuban Olympic Cttee; mem. Council IAAF; Track & Field News Athlete of the Year 1976, 1977; Olympic Order. *Address:* c/o Cubadeportes S.A., Calle 20 No. 710 e/ 7ma y 9na, Miramar, Playa, Havana, Cuba (Office). *Telephone:* 24-09-45 (Office). *Fax:* 24-19-14 (Office). *E-mail:* cdp@inder.co.cu (Office).

JUDA, Annely, CBE; German art dealer; b. 23 Sept. 1914, Kassel; d. of Kurt Brauer and Margarete Brauer; m. Paul A. Juda 1939 (dissolved 1955); one s. two d.; ed grammar school; opened Molton Gallery, London 1960; f. Hamilton Gallery 1963; started (with her son David) under her own name Annely Juda Fine Art 1967; Cologne Prize 1993. *Publications:* numerous art catalogues. *Leisure interests:* theatre, music. *Address:* Annely Juda Fine Art, 23 Dering Street, London, W1R 9AA (Office); 74 Windermere Avenue, London, N3 3RA, England (Home). *Telephone:* (20) 7629-7578 (Office). *Fax:* (20) 7491-2139 (Office). *E-mail:* ajfa@annelyjudafineart.co.uk (Office).

JUGNAUTH, Rt Hon. Sir Anerood, KCMG, PC, QC; Mauritian politician and lawyer; b. 29 March 1930, Palma; m. Sarojni Devi Ballah; one s. one d.; ed Church of England School, Palma, Regent Coll., Quakre, Borneo, Lincoln's Inn, London; called to Bar 1954; won seat on Legis. Ass., Mauritius 1963; Minister of State and Devt 1965–67, of Labour 1967; Dist Magistrate 1967; Crown Counsel and Sr Crown Counsel 1971; co-founder and Pres. Mouvement Militant Mauricien with Paul Bérenger Dec. 1971–; Leader of Opposition 1976; Prime Minister of Mauritius 1982–95, other portfolios include Minister of Finance 1983–84, of Defence and Internal Security and Reform Insts., Information, Internal and External Communications and the Outer Islands, of Justice; Prime Minister and Minister of Defence and Home Affairs and of External Communications Sept. 2000–; Order of the Rising Sun (Japan) 1988, Grand Officier, Légion d'honneur 1990; Hon. DCL (Mauritius) 1985; Hon. LLD (Madras) 2001; Dr hc (Aix-en-Provence) 1985. *Leisure interests:* football, reading. *Address:* Office of the Prime Minister, Government Centre, Port Louis, Mauritius; La Caverne No. 1, Vacoas, Mauritius (Home). *Telephone:* 202-9000 (Office). *Fax:* 211-7907 (Office). *Website:* ncb.intnet.mu/pmo.htm (Office).

JUILLET, Alain; French intelligence officer and fmr business executive; b. 1943; ed Centre de perfectionnement des affaires, Institut des hautes études de défense nationale, Paris, Stanford Univ., USA; fmr employee Pernod-Ricard, Jacobs-Suchard, Union Laitière Normande, France Champignon; Chief Exec. French Operations, Marks & Spencer Ltd –2001; Head of Information, Direction Générale de la Sécurité Extérieure (DGSE) 2002–. *Address:* DGSE, Caserne des Tourelles, 128 Boulevard Mortier, 75020 Paris, France (Office).

JULESZ, Bela, PhD; American experimental psychologist and university professor; b. 19 Feb. 1928, Budapest, Hungary; s. of Jeno Julesz and Klementin Fleiner; m. Margit Fasy 1953; ed Tech. Univ. Budapest and Hungarian Acad. of Sciences; Asst Prof. Dept of Communication, Tech. Univ. Budapest 1950–51; mem. tech. staff, Telecommunication Research Inst. Budapest 1951–56; mem. tech. staff, Bell Labs, Murray Hill, NJ 1956–64, head, sensory and perceptual processes 1964–83; research head, visual perception research, AT & T Bell Labs Murray Hill, NJ 1984–89; Prof. of Psychology, Dir Lab. of Vision Research, Rutgers Univ., NJ 1989–99; Visiting Prof. Dept of Biology Calif. Inst. of Tech. 1985–94; retd 1999; Fellow, American Acad. of Arts and Sciences, AAAS; mem. NAS; corresp. mem. Göttingen Acad.; hon. mem. Hungarian Acad.; MacArthur Fellow Award, H.P. Heineken Prize, Royal Netherlands Acad. of Arts and Sciences 1985. *Publications:* Foundations of Cyclopean Perception, Dialogues on Perception; 200 scientific papers on visual perception. *Address:* 30 Valleyview Road, Warren, NJ 07059-5229, USA (Home).

JULIANA, HRH Princess (Louise Emma Marie Wilhelmina), former Queen of the Netherlands; Princess of the Netherlands, Princess of Orange-Nassau, Duchess of Mecklenburg, Princess of Lippe-Biesterfeld; b. 30 April 1909; d. of Queen Wilhelmina and Prince Henry of Mecklenburg-Schwerin; m. Prince Bernhard of Lippe-Biesterfeld (later Prince of the Netherlands, q.v.), 1937; daughters Princess Beatrix Wilhelmina Armgard (now Queen Beatrix), b. Jan. 1938, Princess Irene Emma Elisabeth, b. Aug. 1939, Princess Margriet Francisca, b. Jan. 1943, Princess Maria Christina, b. Feb. 1947; went to Canada after German occupation 1940; in England 1944; returned to Netherlands 1945; Princess Regent Oct.–Dec. 1947, May–Aug. 1948; Queen of Netherlands 1948–80 (abdicated 30 April 1980). *Address:* c/o Palace of Soestdijk, Amsterdamsestraatweg 1, 3744 AA Baarn, Netherlands.

JULIEN, Claude Norbert; French journalist; b. 17 May 1925, Saint-Rome de Cernon (Aveyron); s. of Henri Julien and Léontine (née Gau); m. Jacqueline Tannery 1949; two s. two d.; ed Ecole primaire de Labruguière, Univ. of Notre Dame, Ind., USA; Ed.-in-Chief Vie catholique illustrée 1949–50, Dépêche Marocaine à Tanger 1950–51; Foreign Ed. Le Monde 1951, Asst Head Foreign Service 1960–69, Head 1969–73, Ed.-in-Chief Le Monde diplomatique 1973–82, Dir 1982–90 (Man. Le Monde 1981–82); Admin. Canadian Inst. for Int. Peace and Security (Ottawa), La Maison de l'Amérique latine; Pres. Cercle Condorcet, Paris, Ligue française de l'enseignement, Paris, Festival international des francophonies, Paris and Limoges; mem. Bd of Dirs., Action des chrétiens pour l'abolition de la torture (ACAT), Paris; Foreign mem. Royal Soc. of Canada; Dr hc (Univ. de Mons-Hainaut, Belgium) 1996; Officier, Légion d'honneur; Prix Aujourd'hui for book L'Empire américain. *Publications:* L'Amérique en révolution (with J. Julien) 1956, Le Nouveau Nouveau Monde 1960, La Révolution cubaine 1962, God's Trombones 1960, Le Canada–dernière chance de l'Europe 1968, L'Empire américain 1968, Le suicide des démocraties 1972, Le Rêve et l'histoire–deux siècles d'Amérique 1976, Le devoir d'irrespect 1979. *Leisure interest:* gardening. *Address:* Le Buguet-Haut, 47500 Sauveterre-la-Lémance, France (Home). *Telephone:* (5) 53-40-62-71.

JULIEN, Michael Frederick, FCA, FCT; British business executive and accountant; b. 22 March 1938, London; s. of late Robert A. F. Julien and Olive R. Evans; m. Ellen Martinsen 1963; one s. two d.; ed St Edward's School, Oxford; Price Waterhouse & Co. 1958–67; other commercial appts 1967–76; Group Finance Dir BICC (now Balfour Beatty PLC) 1976–83; Exec. Dir Finance and Planning, Midland Bank (now HSBC Bank PLC) 1983–86; Man. Dir Finance and Admin. Guinness PLC (now Diageo PLC) 1987–88; Dir (non-exec.) 1988–97; Group Chief Exec. Storehouse PLC (now Mothercare PLC) 1988–92; Chair. Owners Abroad PLC (now First Choice Holidays PLC) 1993–97; Dir Medeva PLC 1993–98; Deputy Chair. Oxford English Training Ltd 1999–. *Leisure interests:* family, travel, computing (including video editing). *Address:* Glenhaven, 1 Beechwood Avenue, Weybridge, Surrey, KT13 9TF, England. *Telephone:* (1932) 831286. *Fax:* (1932) 831287. *E-mail:* mfjulien@julienco.com (Home). *Website:* www.julienco.com (Home).

JULIUS, Anthony Robert, PhD; British lawyer; b. 16 July 1956; s. of Morris Julius and Myrna Julius; m. 1st Judith Bernie 1979 (divorced 1998); two s. two d.; m. 2nd Dina Rabinovitch 1999; ed City of London School, Jesus Coll., Cambridge, Univ. Coll. London; partner Mishcon de Reya 1984–98 (Head of Litigation 1988–98), Consultant 1998–; Chair. Diana, Princess of Wales Memorial Fund 1997–99, Trustee 1997–; Chair. Law Panel, Inst. of Jewish Policy Research (reporting on Holocaust Denial Legislation) 1997–; Chair. Man. Bd Centre for Cultural Analysis, Theory and History, Univ. of Leeds 2001–; mem. Appeals Cttee Dermatrust 1999–. *Publications:* T. S. Eliot, Anti-Semitism and Literary Form 1995, (contrib.) Law and Literature 1999, Idolising Pictures 2000, Transgressions 2002. *Leisure interest:* cooking. *Address:* Mishcon de Reya, 21 Southampton Row, London, WC1B 5HS, England (Office). *Telephone:* (20) 7440-7000 (Office). *Fax:* (20) 7404-2376 (Office). *E-mail:* anthony.julius@mishcon.co.uk (Office).

JULIUS, DeAnne, CBE, PhD; American/British economist; b. 14 April 1949; d. of Marvin Julius; m. Ian A. Harvey 1976; one s. one d.; ed Iowa State Univ. and Univ. of California at Davis; Econ. Adviser for Energy, IBRD 1975–82; Man. Dir Logan Assocs., Inc. 1983–86; Dir of Econs Royal Inst. of Int. Affairs, London 1986–89; Chief Economist Shell Int. Petroleum Co., London 1989–93, British Airways 1993–97; mem. Monetary Policy Cttee, Bank of England 1997–2001, Dir Bank of England Court 2001–; Chair. British Airways Pension Investment Man. Ltd 1995–97; Dir (non-exec.) Lloyds TSB 2001–, BP (British Petroleum) 2001–, Serco Group 2001–, Roche 2002–; Chair. Royal Inst. of Int. Affairs July 2003–. *Publications:* The Economics of Natural Gas 1990, Global Companies and Public Policy: The Growing Challenge of Foreign Direct Investment 1990, Is Manufacturing Still Special in the New World Order? (jtly) 1993 (Amex Bank Prize); and articles on int. econs. *Leisure interests:* skiing, windsurfing, bonsai. *Address:* Royal Institute of International Affairs, Chatham House, 10 St James's Square, London, SW1Y 4LE, England (Office). *Telephone:* (20) 7957-5700 (Office). *Fax:* (20) 7957-5710 (Office). *E-mail:* contact@riia.org (Office). *Website:* www.riia.org (Office).

JULLIEN, François, DèsSc; French professor of philosophy; b. 2 June 1951, Embrun, Hautes-Alpes; s. of Raymond Jullien and Marie Cler; m. Odile Sournies 1974; one s. two d.; ed Ecole normale supérieure and Univ. of Shanghai; Head French Sinology Unit, Hong Kong 1978–81; Resident Maison franco-japonaise, Tokyo 1985–87; Sr Lecturer Univ. de Paris VIII-Saint-Denis 1981–87, Prof. 1987–90; Prof. Univ. de Paris VII-Denis Diderot 1990–, Dir Inst. Marcel Granet; Pres. Asscn française des études chinoises 1988–90; Pres. Collège Int. de philosophie 1995–; Dir Oriental collection, P.U.F.; mem. Editorial Cttee Critique journal. *Publications:* Fleurs du matin cueillies le soir 1976, Sous le dais fleuri 1978 (both translations of the Chinese texts of Lu Xun), La Valeur allusive 1985, Procès ou création 1989, Eloge de la fadeur 1991, La Propension des choses 1991, Figures de l'immanence 1993, Le Détour et l'accès 1995, Fonder la morale 1995, Traité de l'efficacité 1997, Un sage est sans idée ou l'autre de la philosophie 1998, De l'essence ou du nu 2000, Penser d'un dehors (la Chine) 2000, Du "temps": éléments d'une philosophie du vivre 2001. *Address:* Université Paris VII-Denis Diderot, 2 place Jussieu, 75251 Paris cedex 05 (Office); 8 rue Tournefort, 75005 Paris, France (Home). *Telephone:* 1-44-27-82-95 (Office).

JULLIEN, Mgr Jacques; French ecclesiastic; b. 7 May 1929, Brest; s. of Pierre Jullien and Jeanne Maudon; ed Grand-Séminaire de Quimper, Univ. Catholique d'Angers, Univ. Catholique de Paris et Hautes-Etudes, Paris; ordained priest 1954; Vicar, Locmaria-Quimper; Prof. of Moral Theology, Grand-Séminaire de Quimper 1957–69; Curé, Saint-Louis de Brest 1969–78; Bishop of Beauvais 1978–84; Coadjutor Bishop to HE Cardinal Gouyon 1984; Archbishop of Rennes, Dol and Saint-Malo 1985–98, Emer. 1998–; Chevalier, Légion d'honneur. *Publications:* Le Chrétien et la politique 1963, Les Chrétiens et l'état (Co-author) 1967, La régulation des naissances, Humanae Vitae 1968, Pour vous, qui est Jésus-Christ? (Co-author) 1968, Faire vivre, livre blanc sur l'avortement (Co-author) 1969, Les prêtres dans le combat politique 1972, L'homme debout 1980, En paroles et en actes 1983, La Procréation artificielle: des motifs d'espérer (Co-author), Demain la Famille 1992, Trop petit pour ta grâce 1996. *Address:* Communauté des Augustines, 4 rue Adolphe Leray, 35044 Rennes cedex, France.

JULY, Serge; French journalist; b. 27 Dec. 1942, Paris; one s.; journalist Clarté 1961–63; Vice-Pres. Nat. Union of Students 1965–66; French teacher Coll. Sainte-Barbe, Paris 1966–68; Asst Leader Gauche prolétarienne 1969–72 (disbanded by the Govt); f. with Jean-Paul Sartre, Jean-Claude Vernier and Philippe Gavi Libération Feb. 1973, Chief Ed. 1973–, Publishing Dir 1974–75, Jt Dir 1981, Man. Dir 1987–; Reporter Europe 1 April 1983; mem. Club de la presse Europe 1 Oct. 1976–. *Publications:* Vers la guerre civile (with Alain Geismar and Erlyne Morane) 1969, Dis maman, c'est quoi l'avant-guerre? 1980, Les Années Mitterrand 1986, La Drôle d'Année 1987, Le Salon des artistes 1989, La Diagonale du Golfe 1991, Entre quatre z'yeux (with Alain Juppé). *Address:* Libération, 11 rue Béranger, 75003 Paris, France (Office). *Telephone:* 1-42-76-19-78 (Office).

JUMA, Omar Ali; Tanzanian politician; fmr Govt official; Chief Minister of Zanzibar 1988–95; Vice-Pres. of Tanzania 1995–2001. *Address:* c/o Office of the Vice-President, P.O. Box 776, Zanzibar, Tanzania.

JUMBE, (Mwinyi) Aboud; Tanzanian politician (retd); b. 14 June 1920, Zanzibar; s. of Jumbe Mwinyi and Sanga Mussa; m. Khadija Ibrahim 1947, Zeyena Rashid 1976, Fatma Muhammed 1980; fourteen s. four d.; ed secondary school, Zanzibar and Makerere Univ. Coll., Uganda; Teacher 1946–60; fmr mem. Zanzibar Township Council; mem. Afro-Shirazi Party (ASP) 1960–77, later Organizing Sec., Head 1972–77; Vice-Chair. Chama Cha Mapinduzi (formed by merger of TANU and ASP) 1977–84; mem. Nat. Assembly of Zanzibar (ASP) 1961–84; Opposition Whip 1962–64; Minister of Home Affairs, Zanzibar Jan.–April 1964; Minister of State, First Vice-President's Office, Tanzania 1964–72, concurrently responsible for Ministry of Health and Social Services 1964–67; First Vice-Pres. of Tanzania 1972–77, Vice-Pres. 1977–84; Chair. Zanzibar Revolutionary Council 1972–84; fmr Vice-Chair. Revolutionary Party of Tanzania; has resgnd all Govt and party positions and now resides as a villager; engaged in small-scale fishing, animal husbandry and land cultivation. *Leisure interests:* reading and writing Islamic materials. *Address:* Mjimwema, P.O. Box 19875, Dar es Salaam, Tanzania. *Telephone:* 33969; 31359.

JUMBE, Philbert Alexander; Zimbabwean business executive; b. 22 Oct. 1946, Bindura; m. Bernadette Stembeni 1974; one s. five d.; ed Bradley Inst., Bindura; Man. Dir Zimbabwe Bearings (Pvt) Ltd, Harare 1980–; Chief Exec. PAJ Holdings (Pvt) Ltd, Zimbabwe Bearings Manufacturing (Pvt) Ltd; Pres. Zimbabwe Nat. Chamber of Commerce (ZNCC) 1989–90, 1990–91 (Chair. Harare Branch 1986); mem. Council, Zimbabwe Asscn of Pension Funds 1980–81; Chair. Machembere Creche, Highfield 1978; Chair. and Founder-mem. Rusununguko School Students' Asscn 1987; Life mem. Jairosi Jiri Asscn 1985, Zimbabwe Council for Welfare of Children 1986; Award for outstanding services to ZNCC 1985, 1989. *Leisure interests:* tennis, squash, jogging. *Address:* Zimbabwe Bearings (Pvt) Ltd, P.O. Box 4600, Harare, Zimbabwe. *Telephone:* (4) 792688, 729248, 729249.

JUMINER, Bertène Gaëtan, LicMed; French professor of medicine; b. 6 Aug. 1927, Cayenne, French Guiana; s. of Félix Juminer and Marie-Léone Placide; m. 2nd Bernadette Stephenson 1977; one s. one d.; (two s. three d. from previous m.); Head Lab. of Exotic Pathology, Faculty of Medicine, Montpellier 1956–58; Head of Lab. Inst. Pasteur, Tunis 1958–66; Maître de Conf. Agrégé and Hosp. Biologist, Faculty of Medicine, Meched, Iran 1966–67; Prof. and Hosp. Biologist, Faculty of Medicine, Dakar, Senegal 1967–73; Prof. and Hosp. Biologist Faculty of Medicine, Amiens, Univ. of Picardie 1972–81; Rector of Acad. des Antilles et de la Guyane and Chancellor of Univ. 1982–87; Prof., Head of Univ. Hosp. Centre Point-à-Pitre 1988–97; Pres. Société immobilière de la Guadeloupe; Vice-Pres. Regional Econ. and Social Council 1998–; mem. Int. Human and Animal Mycology Asscn Comm. of French Repub. for Educ., Science and Culture (UNESCO), Nat. Council of Univs. 1992–98, other nat. and int. professional bodies; Chevalier, Légion d'honneur; Officier de l'Ordre national du Mérite; Prix des Caraibes 1981. *Publications:* Les Bâtards 1961, Au seuil d'un nouveau cri 1963, La revanche de Bozambo 1968, Les héritiers de la presqu'île 1979, La fraction de seconde 1990; about 120 articles on parasitology, epidemiology, medical mycology and medical entomology. *Leisure interest:* jazz music. *Address:* la Bertenière, Bellemont, 97114 Trois-Rivières, Guadeloupe.

JUNCKER, Jean-Claude; Luxembourg politician; b. 9 Dec. 1954, Redange-sur-Attert; s. of Jos Juncker and Marguerite Hecker; m. Christiane Frising 1979; ed Univ. of Strasbourg; Parl. Sec. to Christian Social Party 1979–82; Sec. of State for Labour and Social Affairs 1982–84, Minister of Labour, Minister in charge of Budget 1984–89, Minister of Labour, of Finance 1989–94; Prime Minister of Luxembourg Jan. 1995–, also Minister of State, of Finance and the Treasury, of Labour and Employment 1995–99, of State and of Finance 1999–; Chair. Christian Social Party 1990–95. *Leisure interest:* reading. *Address:* Hôtel de Bourgogne, 4 rue de la Congrégation, 2910 Luxembourg, Luxembourg. *Telephone:* 478-1. *Fax:* 46-17-20.

JUNG, Andrea; American retail executive; ed Princeton Univ.; fmr Sr Vice-Pres. Gen. Merchandising, I. Magnin; Exec. Vice-Pres. Neiman Marcus –1994; joined Avon Products Inc. 1994, Sr Vice-Pres. 1994–97, mem. Bd of Dirs 1998–, Pres. and COO 1998–2000, CEO 1999–, Chair. 2001–; Chair. The Cosmetic, Toiletry and Fragrance Asscn (CTFA); mem. Bd of Dirs Gen. Electric Co., Princeton Univ., Fashion Institute of Technology, Fragrance Foundation, Cosmetic Exec. Women, Sales Corpn Donna Karan Int.; mem. Int. Advisory Council, Salomon Smith Barney. *Address:* Avon Products, Inc. Headquarters, 1345 Avenue of the Americas, New York, NY 10105-0302, USA (Office). *Telephone:* (800) 367-2866 (Office). *Website:* www.avoncompany.com (Office).

JUNG, Roland Tadeusz, BChir, MA, MB, MD, FRCP, FRCPE; British physician; b. 1948, Glasgow; m.; one d.; ed Pembroke Coll., Cambridge, St Thomas' Hosp. Medical School, London; MRC Clinical Scientist, Dunn Nutrition Unit, Cambridge 1977–80; Sr Registrar, Royal Postgrad. Medical School, London 1980–82; Consultant Physician Ninewells Hosp. and Medical School, Dundee 1982–91, Clinical Dir of Medicine 1991–97; Dir Tayside Research & Devt NHS Consortium, Dundee 1997–2000; Chair. Scottish Hosp. Endowments Research Trust 2000–01; Chief Scientist Health Dept, Scottish Exec. 2001–; Card Medal, Asscn of Physicians of GB and Ireland 1987. *Publications:* Endocrine Problems in Oncology 1984, Colour Atlas of Obesity 1990. *Leisure interest:* gardening. *Address:* Scottish Executive Health Department, St Andrew's House, Regent Road, Edinburgh, EH1 3DG, Scotland (Office). *Website:* www.show.scot.nhr.uk/cso (Office).

JÜNGEL, Eberhard Klaus, DTheol; German professor of theology; b. 5 Dec. 1934, Magdeburg; s. of Kurt Jüngel and Margarete Rothemann; ed Humboldt-schule, Magdeburg, Katechetisches Seminar, Naumburg/Saale, Kirchliche Hochschule, Berlin and Univs. of Zürich and Basel; Asst Kirchliche Hoch-schule (Sprachenkonvikt), East Berlin 1959–61, lecturer in New Testament 1961–63, lecturer in Systematic Theology 1963–66; ordained priest of the Evangelical Church 1962; Prof. of Systematic Theology and History of Dogma, Univ. of Zürich 1966–69; Prof. of Systematic Theology and Philosophy of Religion and Dir Inst. für Hermeneutik (interpretation of scripture), Univ. of Tübingen 1969–, Dean, Faculty of Evangelical Theology 1970–72, 1992–94; Ephorus Evangelisches Stift, Tübingen 1987–; Guest Prof. of Systematic Theology, Univ. of Halle-Wittenberg 1990–93, Univ. of Berlin 1994; Fellow Inst. for Advanced Study, Berlin; various appts. within Evangelical Church, etc.; mem. Heidelberg and Norwegian Acads., Academia Scientiarum et Artium Europaea, Salzburg, Akademie der Wissenschaften, Göttingen; Hon. DD (Aberdeen) 1985, Dr. hc (Greifswald) 2000, Karl Barth Prize 1986; Orden pour le mérite 1992, Grosses Verdienstkreuz mit Stern des Verdienstordens

1994, Verdienstmedaille des Landes Baden-Württemberg. *Publications:* more than 20 books including Paulus und Jesus 1962, Gottes Sein ist im Werden 1965, Unterwegs zur Sache 1972, Gott als Geheimnis der Welt 1977, Entsprechungen 1980, Glauben und Verstehen, Zum Theologiebegriff Rudolf Bultmanns 1985, Wertlose Wahrheit. Zur Identität und Relevanz des christlichen Glaubens 1990, Das Evangelium von der Rechtfestigung des Gottlosen als Zentrum des Glaubens 1998, Indikative der Gnade-Imperative d. Freiheit 2000, (Ed.) Religion in Geschichte und Gegenwart and five Vols of sermons. *Address:* Institut für Hermeneutik, Liebermeisterstrasse 12, 72076 Tübingen; Schwabstrasse 51, 72074 Tübingen, Germany.

JUNGERIUS, Pieter Dirk, DSc; Netherlands professor of geography; b. 10 June 1933, Rÿnsburg; ed Gymnasium B, Leiden and Univ. of Amsterdam; Asst Univ. of Amsterdam 1955–59; Scientific Officer, Soil Survey of England and Wales 1959–63; on secondment to Soil and Land Use Survey, Ghana 1959, Ministry of Agric. E Nigeria 1960–63; Sr Lecturer in Physical Geography, Univ. of Amsterdam 1963–70; seasonal staff mem. Ministry of Mines and Tech. Surveys, Canada 1965–67; Prof. of Physical Geography, Climatology and Cartography, Univ. of Amsterdam 1970–; mem. Royal Netherlands Acad. of Sciences 1987. *Publications:* Soil Evidence of Tree Line Fluctuations, Alberta, Canada 1969, Quarternary Landscape Developments, Río Magdalena, Colombia 1976, Soils and Geomorphology 1985, Perception and Use of the Physical Environment in Peasant Societies 1986, Dunes of the European Coast: Geomorphology, Hydrology, Soils.

JUNZ, Helen B., PhD; American economist and consultant; d. of Samson Bachner and Dobra Bachner (née Mandelbaum); ed Univ. of Amsterdam and New School of Social Research; Acting Chief, Consumer Price Section, Nat. Industrial Conf. Bd, New York 1953–58; Research Officer, Nat. Inst. of Social and Economic Research, London 1958–60; Economist, Bureau of Economic Analysis, Dept of Commerce, Washington 1960–62; Adviser, Div. of Int. Finance, Bd of Govs., Fed. Reserve System 1962–77; Adviser, OECD, Paris 1967–69; Sr int. economist, Council of Econ. Advisers, The White House, Washington 1975–77; Deputy Asst Sec., Office of Asst Sec. for Int. Affairs, Dept of the Treasury, Washington, 1977–79; Vice-Pres. and Sr Adviser, First National Bank of Chicago 1979–80; Vice-Pres. Townsend Greenspan and Co. Inc., New York 1980–82; Sr Adviser, European Dept, IMF, Washington 1982–87, Deputy Dir Exchange and Trade Relations Dept 1987–89, Special Trade Rep. and Dir, Geneva Office 1989–94, Dir Gold Econ. Service, World Gold Council, Geneva and London 1994–96; Pres. HBJ Int., London 1996–. *Publications:* Where Did All the Money Go? 2002; numerous articles in professional journals. *Address:* HBJ International, 23 Warwick Square, London, SW1V 2AB, England. *Telephone:* (20) 7630-9727. *Fax:* (20) 7630-9727.

JUPPÉ, Alain Marie; French politician and government finance official; b. 15 Aug. 1945, Mont-de-Marsan, Landes; s. of Robert Juppé and Marie (Darroze) Juppé; m. 1st Christine Leblond 1965; one s. one d.; m. 2nd Isabelle Legrand-Bodin 1993; one d.; ed Lycée Louis-le-Grand, Paris, Ecole normale supérieure, Inst. d'études politiques, Paris and Ecole Nat. d'Admin; Insp. of Finance 1972; Office of Prime Minister Jacques Chirac June–Aug. 1976; Technical adviser, Office of Minister of Cooperation 1976–78; Nat. del. of RPR 1976–78; Tech. Adviser, Office of Mayor of Paris (Jacques Chirac) 1978; Dir-Gen. with responsibility for finance and econ. affairs, Commune de Paris 1980; Councillor, 18th arrondissement, Paris 1983–95; Second Asst to Mayor of Paris in charge of budget and financial affairs 1983–95; Deputy to Nat. Ass. from Paris 1988–97, from Gironde 1997–; Mayor of Bordeaux 1995–2001; Nat. Sec. of RPR with responsibility for econ. and social recovery 1984–88, Sec.-Gen. 1988–95, Acting Pres. 1994–95, Pres. 1995–97; MEP 1984–86, 1989–93; Deputy to Minister of Economy, Finance and Privatization with responsibility for budget 1986–88; Minister of Foreign Affairs 1993–95; Prime Minister of France 1995–97; cleared of embezzlement charges 1999; Pres. Union pour la majorité presidentielle (UMP) 2002–; Grand Cross of Merit, Sovereign Order of Malta. *Publications:* La Tentation de Venise 1993, Entre Nous 1996, Montesquieu, Le moderne 1999, Entre quatre z'yeux (with Serge July, q.v.),. *Address:* Union pour la majorité presidentielle (UMP), 11 rue St Dominique, 75007 Paris (Office); Mairie, place Pey-Berland, 33077 Bordeaux cedex, France.

JURGENSON, Sven, BSc; Estonian diplomatist; b. 2 April 1962; m.; two c.; ed Tallinn Tech. Univ., Inst. Int. d'Admin. Publique, Paris, Ingenieurhochschule, Dresden; Jr Research Assoc. and lecturer in Data Processing, Tallinn Tech. Univ. 1987–90; Sr Assoc., Estonian Inst. 1990–91; Counsellor, Chargé d'affaires, Helsinki, Counsellor, Office for Estonian Culture, Helsinki 1991–93; Minister-Counsellor, Chargé d'affaires, Embassy, Vienna 1993–95; Deputy Political Dir, Ministry of Foreign Affairs, then Dir Div. for Int. Orgs and Security Policy 1995–96, Dir-Gen. Political Dept 1996–98; Amb. to Turkey 1996–98; Perm. Rep. to UN 1998–2000; Amb. to USA Jan. 2000–. *Address:* Embassy of Estonia, 2131 Massachusetts Avenue, NW, Washington, DC 20008, USA (Office). *Telephone:* (202) 588-0101 (Office). *Fax:* (202) 588-0108 (Office). *E-mail:* info@estemb.org (Office). *Website:* www.estemb.org.

JURINAC, Sena; Austrian singer (retd); b. Srebrenka Jurinac, 24 Oct. 1921, Travnik, Yugoslavia; d. of Dr Ljudevit Jurinac and Christine Cerv-Jurinac; m. Dr Josef Lederle; ed Gymnasium and Music Acad., Zagreb, Yugoslavia; studied under Maria Kostrenćić; first appearance as Mimi, Zagreb 1942; mem. Vienna State Opera Co. 1944–82; now works as a voice teacher; has sung at Salzburg, Glyndebourne Festivals, etc.; sang in Der Rosenkavalier

1966 and 1971, Tosca 1968, Iphigénie en Tauride 1973, Covent Garden; Austrian State Kammersängerin 1951; numerous tours and recordings; subject of biog. by Ursula Tamussino 2001; Ehrenkreuz für Wissenchaft und Kunst 1961, Grosses Ehrenzeichen für Verdienste um die Republik Österreich 1967, Ehrenring der Wiener Staatsoper 1968, Ehrenmitglied der Wiener Staatsoper 1971, Silver Rose of the Vienna Philharmonic Orchestra 2001. *Films:* Lisinski 1943, Der Rosenkavalier 1960. *Television:* Schwester Angelica (Puccini) (ORF) 1959, Otello (Verdi) (ORF) 1965, Wozzeck (Berg) (ZDF) 1970, Hänsel und Gretel (ORF) 1981. *Recordings:* Fidelio, Orfeo, Così fan tutte, Don Giovanni, Idomeneo, Le Nozze di Figaro, Ariadne auf Naxos, Der Rosenkavalier, Eugene Onegin, Lieder by Schumann and Richard Strauss. *Leisure interests:* gardening, cats. *Address:* c/o Wehrgasse 11A, 1050 Vienna, Austria. *Telephone:* (1) 5879295. *Fax:* (1) 5879295.

JURKOVIČ, Pero, PhD; Croatian economist; b. 4 June 1936, Brštanica, Neum, Bosnia and Herzegovina; ed Univs. of Sarajevo, Skopje and Zagreb; chief accountant, construction materials industry Neretva, Čapljina 1956–57; Officer for Planning, Municipality of Čapljina 1960–61, Chief Officer for Agric. 1961–63; Dir Inst. of Economy, Mostar 1963–67; Assoc. to Adviser, Econ. Inst., Zagreb (also Assoc. Prof., Foreign Trade School and Faculties of Econs Zagreb and Mostar) 1967–80; Prof., Faculty of Econs, Zagreb 1980–92; Gov. Nat. Bank of Croatia 1992–96; apptd. Chief Econ. Adviser to Pres. of Croatia 1997; mem. Int. Inst. for Financing, Saarbrücken, Int. Asscn of Economists; Guest Lecturer, Univs. of Rotterdam, London, Lexington and Fla; B. Adžija and M. Mirkovic awards. *Publications:* about 150 including System of Public Financing (with Ksente Bogoev) 1977, Introduction to the Theory of Economic Policy 1984, Fundamentals of the Economics of Public Services 1987, Commercial Finances 1987, Fiscal Policy 1989. *Address:* c/o Presidential Palace, Pautovčak 241, 10000 Zagreb, Croatia.

JUROWSKI, Vladimir; Russian conductor and music director; b. 1972, Moscow; ed Music Acad., Berlin and Dresden; int. debut, Wexford Festival 1995; since then has conducted in major venues world-wide, including Metropolitan Opera, NY, Opera Bastille, Paris, Komische Oper, Berlin, Teatro Comunale, Bologna, Teatro Real, Madrid, Royal Opera House, London, Welsh Nat. Opera, Cardiff, English Nat. Opera, London and Edin. Festival; Chief Conductor Sibelius Orchestra, Berlin 1993–96; f. Ensemble Berlin, for performance of modern music; Prin. Guest Conductor Orchestra Sinfonica Verdi, Milan, Teatro Comunale, Bologna; Musical Dir Glyndebourne Festival Opera 2001–. *Recordings include:* Werther by Massenet. *Address:* c/o Glyndebourne Festival Opera, Lewes, Sussex, BN8 5UU, England (Office).

JUSKO, Marián, DPhil; Slovak banker; b. 24 March 1956, Prešov; m.; one c.; ed Univ. of Econs, Bratislava; lecturer Univ. of Econs, Bratislava 1979–90, adviser, Slovak Nat. Council 1990; Head of Banking Analyses and Prognoses, State Bank of Czechoslovakia 1991; Deputy Minister, Ministry of Admin. and Privatization of Nat. Property of Slovak Repub.; Chair. Bd Nat. Property Fund 1991–92; mem. man. team State Bank of Czechoslovakia for Slovakia, Bratislava 1992; Vice-Gov. Nat. Bank of Slovakia 1993–99, Gov. 1999–. *Address:* National Bank of Slovakia, Imricha Karvaša 1, 813 25 Bratislava, Slovakia (Office). *Telephone:* (2) 5787-2011 (Office). *Fax:* (2) 5787-1101 (Office). *Website:* www.nbs.sk (Office).

JUSYS, Oskaras; Lithuanian diplomatist; b. 13 Jan. 1954, Anyksciai Region; m.; one s.; ed Vilnius Univ., V. Lomonosov Univ., Moscow; Sr Lecturer, Faculty of Law, Vilnius Univ. 1981–1985, Assoc. Prof. 1986–90; Scientific Scholarship, IREX Exchange Programme, Law School, Columbia Univ., New York, USA 1985–86; Dir Legal Dept, Ministry of Foreign Affairs 1990–92, Counsellor to Minister of Foreign Affairs 1993–94; Amb., Perm. Rep. of Lithuania to UN 1994–2000; Deputy Minister of Foreign Affairs 2000–; Dir Lithuanian Br. of US law firm McDermott, Will & Emery 1993–94. *Leisure interests:* jazz, basketball. *Address:* Ministry of Foreign Affairs, J. Tumo-Vaižganto 2, Vilnius 2660, Lithuania (Office). *Telephone:* (2) 36-24-15 (Office). *Fax:* (2) 31-30-90 (Office).

JUTIKKALA, Eino Kaarlo Ilmari, PhD; Finnish historian; b. 24 Oct. 1907, Sääksmäki; s. of Kaarle Fredrik Rinne and Hilma Maria Hagelberg; ed Helsinki Univ.; Docent, Helsinki Univ. 1933, Prof. of Finnish History 1947–50, 1954–74, Prof. of Econ. History 1950–54, Dean of Faculty of Arts 1966–69; Chair. State Comm. for the Humanities 1967–70; mem. Culture Foundation for Finland and Sweden 1960–71; Academician, Finnish Acad. 1972; Hon. PhD (Stockholm); Hon. PolD (Helsinki); Dr hc (Helsinki Commercial Univ.), (Tampere). *Publications include:* Suomen talonpojan historia 1942, Atlas of Finnish History 1949, Turun kaupungin historia 1856-1917 1957, A History of Finland (jtly.) 1962, Pohjoismaisen yhteiskunnan historialliset juuret 1965, Bonden adelsmannen kronan i Norden 1550–1750 1979, Tampereen kaupungin historia 1905–45 1979, Desertion in the Nordic Countries 1300–1600 (with others) 1982, Kuolemalla on aina syynsä 1987, Valtion tiedoituslaitoksen salainen sotakronikka 1997; studies dealing with demographic, agrarian and parliamentary history, the history of communications, etc.; editor of several historical works and learned journals (Historiallinen Aikakauskirja 1970–82). *Address:* Merikatu 3B, Helsinki 14, Finland.

JUTTERSTROEM, Christina, BA; Swedish journalist and academic; b. Christina Lewell, 27 March 1940, Stockholm; d. of Siri Lewell and Gosta Lewell; m. 1st Stig Jutterstroem 1962; m. 2nd Ingemar Odlander 1978; two d.; political reporter Swedish Radio and TV 1967–75, Africa Corresp. 1975–77,

Man. Ed. Radio News and Commentaries 1977–81; Ed.-in-Chief Dagens Nyheter 1982–95, Expressen 1995–96; Prof. of Journalism, Univ. of Gothenburg 1997; Dir-Gen. Swedish TV 2001–. *Address:* Swedish Television, 10510 Stockholm (Office); Bjursattergard, 64032 Malmköping, Sweden. *Telephone:* (8) 784-80-50 (Office); (157) 442-22 (Home). *E-mail:* christina.jutterstrom@svt .se (Office). *Website:* www.svt.se (Office).

JYRÄNKI, Antero, DIur; Finnish professor of constitutional law; b. 9 Aug. 1933, Hamina; two s. one d.; ed Univ. of Helsinki; Assoc. Prof. of Public Law, Univ. of Tampere 1966–70; Gen. Sec. to the Pres. of the Repub. 1970–73; Sr Research Fellow, Acad. of Finland 1974–77; Vice-Chair., Comm. on the Revision of the Constitution 1970–74; Assoc. Prof. of Public Law, Univ. of Tampere 1977–79; Prof. of Constitutional and Int. Law, Univ. of Turku 1980–98, Dean, Law Faculty 1981–83, 1991–93; Research Prof., Acad. of Finland 1983–87; Pres. Finnish Asscn of Constitutional Law 1982–88; mem. Council of the Int. Asscn of Constitutional Law 1983–, mem. Exec. Cttee 1993–; mem. Admin. Bd Finnish Broadcasting Corpn 1983–99, Finnish Acad. of Science 1987–; Perm. Expert for the Constitutional Comm. of Parl. 1982–. *Publications:* Sotavoiman ylin päällikkyys (The Commander-in-Chief of the Armed Forces) 1967, Yleisradio ja sananvapaus (The Freedom of Expression and Broadcasting) 1969, Perustuslaki ja yhteiskunnan muutos (The Constitution and the Change of Society) 1973, Presidentti (The President of the Republic) 1978, Lakien laki (The Law of the Laws) 1989, Kolme vuotta linnassa (Three Years in the Presidential Castle) 1990, Valta ja vapaus (Power and Freedom) 1994, Uusi perustuslakimme (Our New Constitution) 2000. *Leisure interests:* languages, literature, problems of mass communication. *Address:* Faculty of Law, University of Turku, 20014 Turku, Finland.

K

KA, Ibra Deguène; Senegalese diplomatist; b. 4 Jan. 1939, Koul-Mecke, Thies Region; ed Ecole Nationale d'Admin. et de Magistrature; Chief Div. of UN Affairs, Ministry of Foreign Affairs 1969–72, Chef de Cabinet 1972–73, Exec. Sec. Senegalo-Gambian Interministerial Cttee 1973–78; Amb. to several countries, including Algeria, Tunisia, Liberia, USA, Argentina, Mexico and Switzerland 1978–96; Perm. Rep. to UN 1996–2001; mem. UN Special Cttee investigating Israeli activities in the Occupied Territories 1994; Founding mem. UN Asscn Senegal; Commdr Nat. Order of Merit and other decorations. *Address:* c/o Ministry of Foreign Affairs, African Unity and Senegalese Abroad, 1 place de l'Indépendence, Dakar, Senegal (Office).

KAAS, Patricia; French singer; b. 5 Dec. 1966, Stiring Wendel, nr Forbach; tea-dance and night-club appearances aged 13; first single, Jalouse, aged 17; first maj. success with Mademoiselle Chante le Blues; toured Viet Nam and Cambodia 1994; has made four world tours; has sold 14 million albums. *Albums include:* Café noir 1996, Rendez-vous 1998, Le Mot de passe 1999, Les Chansons commencement 2000. *Address:* c/o Talent sorcier, 3 rue des Petites Ecuries, 75010 Paris, France. *Telephone:* 1-44-59-99-00 (Office). *Fax:* 1-44-59-99-01 (Office).

KABA, Sidiki; Senegalese human rights organization executive and lawyer; human rights lawyer assoc. with cases in Senegal, Chad, Côte d'Ivoire, Guinea; Pres. Nat. Org. for Human Rights, Senegal; Vice-Pres. Int. Fed. of the League for Human Rights, Paris, Pres. 2001–. *Address:* Fédération Internationale des Ligues des Droits de l'Homme, 17 Passage de la Main d'Or, 75011 Paris, France (Office). *Telephone:* 1-43-55-25-28 (Office). *Fax:* 1-43-55-18-80 (Office). *E-mail:* fidh@csi.com (Office). *Website:* www.fidh.imaginet.fr (Office).

KABAKOV, Alexander Abramovich; Russian writer and journalist; b. 22 Oct. 1943, Novosibirsk; m.; one d.; ed Dniepropetrovsk Univ.; engineer space rocket production co. 1965–70; journalist Gudok 1972–88; columnist, then Deputy Ed.-in-Chief Moscow News 1988–97; special corresp. Commersant Publishing 1997–2000, Departmental Ed. 2000–; columnist New Media Publishing Group 2002–; first literary Publ 1975; Moscow Journalists' Union Prize 1989, Best Pens of Russia Award 1999, Short Story of the Year Award 1999. *Publications:* Cheap Novel 1982, Cafe Yunost 1984, Oil, Comma, Canvas 1986, Approach of Kristapovich (triology) 1985, Obviously False Fabrications (collection of short stories) 1989, No Return 1989, Story-Teller 1991, Imposter 1992, The Last Hero (novel) 1995, Selected Prose 1997, One Day from the Life of a Fool 1998, The Arrival Hall 1999, Youth Café 2000, The Journey of an Extrapolator 2000, The Tardy Visitor 2001, Qualified as Escape 2001, Survivor 2003. *Leisure interest:* jazz. *Address:* New Media Publishing Group, Pyatnitzkaya str. 55, Moscow, Russia (Office). *Telephone:* (095) 411-63-90 (Office); (095) 994-83-45 (Home); (095) 101-77-24.

KABANOV, Victor Aleksandrovich; Russian chemist; b. 15 Jan. 1934, Moscow; s. of Alexander Nikolaevich Kabanov and Brainina Matilda Yakovlevna; m. Nersesova Astguik Aramovna 1961; one s.; ed Moscow State Univ.; Jr researcher, Head of Lab. Moscow State Univ. 1956–70, Prof., Head of Chair 1970; Corresp. mem. USSR (now Russian) Acad. of Sciences 1968, mem. 1987; Academic Sec. Dept of Gen. and Tech. Chemistry; Ed.-in-Chief Doklady Akademii Nauk (periodical); Ed.-in-Chief Encyclopedia of Polymers; Chair. Scientific Council on High-Molecular Compounds; mem. American Chemical Soc.; Foreign mem. Royal Acad. of Sciences of Belgium; mem. Acad. Europaea; Lenin Prize and other distinctions. *Publications include:* scientific works on polymerization mechanisms, polyelectrolyte complexes, polymers of medical application, including Polymerization of Ionizing Monomers 1975, New Class of Complex Water-Soluble Polyelectrolites 1982, Complex Radial Polymerization 1987. *Address:* Russian Academy of Sciences, Dept of General Chemistry, Leninsky prosp. 32A, 117993 Moscow, Russia (Office). *Telephone:* (095) 938-17-39 (Office).

KABARITI, Abdul Karim A., BA; Jordanian politician; b. 15 Dec. 1949, Amman; m.; two c.; ed St Edward's Univ., Austin, Tex., USA, American Univ. of Beirut, Lebanon; licensed financial adviser, New York –1986; proprietor of a money exchange co.; mem. Bd of dirs. of many cos.; mem. House of Reps. for Governorate of Ma'an 1989–93, 1993–95, Minister of Tourism 1989–92, of Labour 1992–93, of Foreign Affairs 1995–96, Prime Minister, Minister of Defence and of Foreign Affairs 1996–97; currently Chair. and CEO Jordan Kuwait Bank; fmr. Chair. Foreign Relations Cttee of House of Reps.; fmr. Head, Royal Court; Chair. Bd Social Security Corpn 1992–93; Chair. Bd Vocational Training Corpn 1992–93. *Leisure interests:* water skiing, music. *Address:* Jordan Kuwait Bank, POB 9776, Amman 11194, Jordan.

KABBAH, Alhaji Ahmed Tejan, BEcons; Sierra Leonean Head of State and civil servant; b. 16 Feb. 1932, Pendembu, Kailahun Dist, Eastern Prov.; m. Patricia Tucker (deceased); four c.; ed St Edward's School, Freetown, Cardiff Coll. of Tech., Univ. Coll. Aberystwyth, Wales; called to the Bar (Gray's Inn), London; fmr Dist Commr Moyamba, Kono, Bombali and Kambia Dists., Deputy Sec., Ministry of Social Welfare and Perm. Sec., Ministries of Educ. and of Trade and Industry; joined staff of UN, served as UNDP Rep. Lesotho 1973, Tanzania and Uganda 1976, temporarily assigned to Zimbabwe 1980, apptd head of Eastern and Southern Africa Div. 1979, Deputy Personnel Dir, then Dir, Div. of Admin. and Man. 1981–92; mem. Sierra Leone People's Party (SLPP) 1954–; Chair. Nat. Advisory Council 1992–96; Pres. of Sierra Leone 1996–97, March 1998–, also Minister of Defence and C-in-C of Armed Forces;

Chancellor Univ. of Sierra Leone; Grand Commdr Order of the Repub. of Sierra Leone; Hon. LLD (Univ. of Sierra Leone), (Southern Connecticut State Univ.) 2001. *Address:* Office of the President, Freetown, Sierra Leone. *Fax:* (22) 231404 (Office).

KABBAJ, Omar; Moroccan international organization official; mem. Exec. Bd IMF; econ. affairs specialist Prime Minister's Office; Exec. Pres., Chair. Bd of Dirs. African Devt Bank (ADB) 1995–. *Address:* African Development Bank, rue Joseph Anoma, 01 BP 1387, Abidjan 01, Côte d'Ivoire (Office). *Telephone:* 20-20-44-44 (Office). *Fax:* 20-20-40-06 (Office). *E-mail:* comuadb@afdb.org (Office). *Website:* www.afdb.org (Office).

KABBARA, Muhammad Bashar, PhD; Syrian banker and economist; b. 1944, Damascus; s. of M. Jamil and Hikmat Kouatly; m. 1968; three c.; ed American Univ. Washington, DC, Western Illinois Univ. and American Univ. of Beirut; Section Head, Office of Gen. Studies, The Presidency 1973–74; Economist, Econ. Bureau, The Presidency 1974–77, Sr Economist 1977–82; Adviser/Dir Econ. Bureau of Pres. of Syria 1982–95; Gov. Cen. Bank of Syria 1995–, Arab Monetary Fund; Chief Ed. The Syrian Econ. Journal 1975–84; Alt. Gov. IMF; Alt. Exec. Dir Arab Fund for Econ. and Social Devt, Programme for Financing Arab Trade; mem. Syrian Higher Planning Bd; Washington-Lincoln Honor Award 1968, Hall of Nations Award 1969–70, Union of Arab Banks Award 1996. *Publications:* more than 20 papers and articles in professional journals and contribs. to The Arabic Encyclopedia. *Leisure interests:* historical reading, antiquities, agronomy, sports. *Address:* Central Bank of Syria, POB 2254, At-Tajrida al-Mughrabia Square, Damascus, Syria. *Telephone:* (11) 2212642; (11) 2220550. *Fax:* (11) 2227103. *E-mail:* mrksybabn@mail.net.sy (Office); comukabb@mail.sy (Home). *Website:* www.syrecon.org (Office).

KABILA, Maj.-Gen. Joseph; Democratic Republic of the Congo politician and army officer; b. 1970, East Africa; s. of the late Laurent-Désiré Kabila; mil. training in People's Repub. of China; Army Chief; Pres. of Democratic Repub. of the Congo and Minister of Defence Jan. 2001–. *Address:* Office of the President, Hôtel du Conseil Exécutif, ave de Lemera, Kinshasa-Gombé, Democratic Republic of the Congo (Office). *Telephone:* (12) 30892 (Office).

KABORÉ, Roch Marc-Christian; Burkinabè politician; Minister of State in charge of Relations with Insts. 1990–94; Prime Minister of Burkina Faso 1994–96; mem. Organisation pour la démocratie populaire/Mouvement du travail (ODP/MT), First Vice-Pres., then Exec. Sec. Congrès pour la démocratie et le progrès (CDP) (new party f. 1996 as successor to ODP/MT) 1996–. *Address:* Congrès pour la démocratie et le progrès, 01 BP 1605, Ouagadougou, Burkina Faso. *Telephone:* 31-50-18. *E-mail:* cdp@cenatrin.bf (Office). *Website:* www.cdp.bf (Office).

KABUA, Imata; Marshall Islands politician and fmr Head of State; Pres. of the Marshall Islands 1994–2000. *Address:* c/o Office of the President, POB 2, Majuro, MH 96960, Marshall Islands (Office).

KAC, Eduardo; American artist and writer; pioneer of holopoetry, telepresence art, biotelematics, transgenic art; Asst Prof. of Art and Tech., School of Art, Inst. of Chicago; mem. Editorial Bd Leonardo (journal); Shearwater Foundation Holography Award 1995, Leonardo Award for Excellence 1998, award for telepresence work Uirapuru, InterCommunication Centre Biennale, Tokyo 1999. *Exhibitions:* In USA, Europe, S America; works in perm. collections including: Museum of Modern Art, New York, Museum of Holography, Chicago, Museum of Modern Art, Rio de Janeiro. *Publications:* New Media Poetry: Poetic Innovation and New Technologies (anthology) 1996; articles in periodicals. *Address:* Art and Technology Department, School of the Art Institute of Chicago, 112 S Michigan Avenue, 4th Floor, Chicago, IL 60603, USA (Office). *Telephone:* (312) 345-3567 (Office). *Fax:* (312) 345-3565 (Office). *E-mail:* ekac@artic.edu (Office). *Website:* www.ekac.org (Office).

KACHORNPRASART, Maj.-Gen. Sanan; Thai politician; b. 7 Sept. 1944, Phichit; ed Chulachomklao Royal Mil. Acad.; aide-de-camp to Gen. Chalard Hiranyasiri; involved in attempted coup 1981; Democrat Party MP for Phichit 1983, 1986, 1988; Deputy Communications Minister 1986; Minister of Agric. and Co-operatives 1989, of the Interior 1998–2000; Deputy Prime Minister 1990–91; Sec.-Gen. Democrat Party. *Address:* Democrat Party, 67 Thanon Setsiri, Samsen Nai, Phyathai, 10400, Bangkok, Thailand.

KACZMAREK, Jan, DrTSc; Polish scientist; b. 2 Feb. 1920, Pabianice; s. of Władysław Kaczmarek and Zofia Kaczmarek; m. Olga Steranka 1946; one s. one d.; ed Acad. of Mining and Metallurgy, Cracow; Asst to Asst Prof. Acad. of Mining and Metallurgy, Cracow 1947–58; Head, Dept of Metal Working, Cracow Tech. Univ. 1958–68, Asst Prof. 1958–62, Prof. 1962–89, Pro-Rector and Rector 1966–68; with Research Inst. of Metal Cutting (IOS) 1949–68, Dir 1958–68; Pres. State Cttee for Science and Tech. 1968–72; Deputy to Sejm (Parl.) 1972–75, 1985–89; Minister of Science, Higher Educ. and Tech. and mem. Govt Presidium 1972–74; Prof. Inst. for Fundamental Problems of Tech. 1978–, Head Dept of Mechanical Systems 1980–90, Leader State research projects 1975–2001, Head Lab. for Surface Layer of Solids 1990–95; Pres. Supervisory Bd SIGMA-NOT Ltd (publrs), Warsaw 1991–; Corresp. mem.

Polish Acad. of Sciences (PAN) 1962, Ordinary mem. 1971–, Scientific Sec. 1972–80, mem. Presidium 1972–80, 1984–87, Chair. Scientific Cttee of Machines Construction 1982–93; mem. Gen. Council Fed. of Polish Scientific-Tech. Asscns. (NOT) 1972–90, Vice-Chair. 1976–80, Chair. 1980–82, Vice-Pres. 1982–84, Pres. 1984–90; mem. Polish Acad. of Knowledge and Art, Cracow (PAU) 1989–, Polish Acad. of Eng 1991– (mem. Exec. Cttee 1991–, Vice-Pres. 1992–97, Hon. mem. 1998–); Ed.-in-Chief Advances in Manufacturing Science and Tech. 2001–; Foreign mem. Nat. Acad. of Eng (USA) 1976–, Bulgarian Acad. of Sciences 1977–, Royal Acad. of Sciences, Literature and Arts, Belgium 1978–, Cen. European Acad. of Science and Arts 1998; Foreign Hon. mem. Groupement pour l'Avancement des Mécaniques Industrielles (GAMI), France 1979–; mem. Int. Inst. for Production Eng Research (CIRP) 1961–, Pres. 1973–74, mem. Senate 1975–, Hon. mem. 1990–; mem. numerous other Polish, foreign and int. scientific socs; Hon. mem. Polish Soc. of Mechanical Eng 1976– (Hon. Pres. 1998); Kt's and Commdr's Cross of Order of Polonia Restituta, Gold Order of Palmes académiques 1971, Grand Officier Légion d'honneur 1972, Hon. Citizen of City of Pabianice 2002, and other decorations; Dr hc (Tech. Univ. Chemnitz) 1973, (Moscow Tech. Univ.) 1974, (Tech. Univ. of Poznań) 2001, (Tech. Univ. of Koszalin) 2002; N. Copernicus Medal 1980. *Publications:* numerous publs on production eng and theory of machining and science of science, including (in Polish) Principles of Metals Cutting 1956, Theory of Machining by Cutting: Abrasion and Erosion 1970, (in English) 1976, On Principles of Science Policy 1972, (in French) 1972. *Leisure interests:* gardening and classical music. *Telephone:* (22) 8269806 (Office). *E-mail:* jankacz@interia.pl (Office).

KACZMAREK, Wiesław; Polish politician; b. 1 Jan. 1958, Wrocław; m.; two d.; ed Warsaw Univ. of Technology; Sr Asst Mechanics and Tech. Dept, Warsaw Univ. of Tech. 1984–89; Deputy Dir Industrial & Commercial Chamber of Foreign Investors 1989–91; co-f. and mem. Social Democracy of the Repub. of Poland (SdRP) 1990–99; Deputy to Sejm (Parl.) 1989–; Man. Warsaw Br., First Commercial Bank SA, Lublin 1991–93; Minister of Privatization 1993–96, of the Economy 1997, of the Treasury 2001–03; mem. Nat. Bd Democratic Left Alliance (SLD) 1999–. *Leisure interests:* diving, sailing (Pres. Polish Sailing Association), hunting, skiing, photography. *Address:* c/o Ministry of the Treasury, ul. Krucza 36, 00-522 Warsaw, Poland (Office).

KACZMAREK, Zdzisław; Polish scientist; b. 7 Aug. 1928, Poznań; s. of Edward and Klara Kaczmarek; m. Imelda Kaczmarek 1950; two s. one d.; ed Warsaw Univ. of Tech.; scientific worker in Warsaw Univ. of Tech. 1947–78, Doctor of Tech. Sciences 1958, Assoc. Prof. 1961–67, Extraordinary Prof. 1967–72, Ordinary Prof. 1972–; fmr Dir of Inst. of Environmental Eng in Dept of Water and Sanitary Eng; Chief of Div. in the State Hydro-Meteorological Inst. (PIH-M), Warsaw 1957–60, Vice-Dir 1960–63, Gen. Dir of Hydro-Meteorological Inst. 1963–66; Dir of Inst. for Meteorology and Water Economy, Warsaw 1976–80; Head, Water Resources Dept, Inst. of Geophysics, Warsaw 1981–; Chair. of Cttee of Water Economy, Polish Acad. of Sciences (PAN); mem. Polish United Workers' Party (PZPR) 1951–90; Deputy mem. of Warsaw Cttee of PZPR 1955–57, worked in Dept of Science and Educ. of Central Cttee. of PZPR, Deputy Chief of Dept 1966–71; mem. of Comm. of Science in Cen. Cttee of PZPR, mem. of Cen. Cttee 1986–89; former mem. of Gen. Bd of Polish Teachers' Asscn (ZNP); First Deputy Minister of Science, Higher Educ. and Tech. 1972–74; Project Leader, Int. Inst. of Applied Systems Analysis, Austria 1974–76, 1989–91; Deputy Chair. of Cen. Qualifying Comm. for Scientific Personnel, attached to Chair. of Council of Ministers 1989; Chair. State Council for Environmental Protection 1981–86; Poland 2000 Cttee for Prognosis on Country Devt 1984–88, Cttee on Water Resources, Cttee on Global Change 1996–; mem. Comm. for Hydrology, WMO 1993–, Nat. Council for Water Resources 2002–; Corresp. mem. Polish Acad. of Sciences 1969–, mem. 1980–, Deputy Scientific Sec. Polish Acad. of Sciences 1971–72, Sec. of VII Dept of Polish Acad. of Sciences 1978–80, Sec.-Gen. Polish Acad. of Sciences 1981–88; Int. Hydrological Prize 1990; Silver and Gold Cross of Merit, Commdr's Cross and Officer's Cross of Order of Polonia Restituta, Order of Banner of Labour (1st Class), Order of Friendship of Nations (USSR), Silver Star of Order of Friendship (GDR) and other decorations. *Publications:* numerous works on hydrology and water resources, on impacts of climate change and variability, on organization of scientific research and on co-operation of science and national economy. *Leisure interests:* sightseeing and tourism. *Address:* Water Resource Department, Institute of Geophysics, Polish Academy of Sciences, ul. Ks. Janusza 64, 01-452, Warsaw (Office); al. J. Ch. Szucha 16 m. 51, 00-582 Warsaw, Poland (Home). *Telephone:* (22) 6915851 (Office); (22) 6291057 (Home). *Fax:* (22) 6915915 (Office). *E-mail:* kaczmar@igf.edu.pl (Office).

KACZYŃSKI, Jarosław Aleksander, DJur; Polish politician and lawyer; b. 18 June 1949, Warsaw; s. of Rajmund Kaczyński and Jadwiga Kaczyńska; brother of Lech Kaczyński (q.v.); ed Warsaw Univ.; Asst, Sr Asst in Inst. of Science and Higher Educ. 1971–76; collaborator, Workers' Defence Cttee (KOR) 1976–80; scientific worker, Białystok br. of Warsaw Univ. 1977–81; ed. Głos (independent magazine) 1980–82; warehouseman 1982; mem. Solidarity Trade Union 1980–90; Sec. Nat. Exec. Comm. of Solidarity 1986–87; took part in Round Table talks in Comm. for Political Reforms Feb.–April 1989; Ed.-in-Chief Solidarność (weekly) 1989–90; Dir Office of Pres. and Minister of State 1990–91; Deputy to Senate 1989–91; Deputy to Sejm (Parl.) 1991–93, 1997–; Chair. Centre Alliance 1990–98; Mem. Main Bd Law and Justice (PiS) 2001–; mem. Helsinki Comm. in Poland 1982–89. *Leisure interests:* reading, history of Poland. *Address:* Sejm RP, ul. Wiejska 4/6/8, 00-902 Warsaw (Office); Prawo i Sprawiedliwość, ul. Nowogrodzka 84/86, 02-018 Warsaw, Poland (Office). *Telephone:* (22) 6215035 (Office). *Fax:* (22) 6216767 (Office). *E-mail:* biuro .organizacyjne@pis.org.pl (Office).

KACZYŃSKI, Lech Aleksander, PhD; Polish civic trade union leader and lawyer; b. 18 June 1949, Warsaw; s. of Rajmund Kaczyński and Jadwiga Kaczyńska; brother of Jarosław Kaczyński (q.v.); m. Maria Mackiewicz 1978; one d.; ed Warsaw, Gdańsk Univ.; Asst, Sr Asst in Labour Law Dept, Gdańsk Univ. 1971–97; adviser to striking workers in Gdańsk Aug. 1980; mem. Solidarity Ind. Self-governing Trade Union 1980–; head Group for Current Analysis and Intervention Bureau of Founding Cttee of Solidarity Trade Union, then head regional Centre for Social and Professional Work, Gdańsk 1980–81; mem. Regional Bd of Solidarity, Gdańsk 1981; interned 1981–82; assoc. of Lech Wałęsa (q.v.) 1982–91 and Provisional Co-ordinating Comm. of Solidarity 1983–84, its rep. in Gdańsk Jan.–July 1986, Sec. 1986–87; sec. Nat. Exec. Comm. of Solidarity 1988–90; took part in Round Table talks in Comm. for Trade Union Pluralism Feb.–April 1989; mem. Presidium Nat. Exec. Comm. of Solidarity 1989–90, First Deputy Chair. Nat. Comm. May 1990–91, Assoc. Workers' Defence Cttee (KOR) 1977–78, Free Trade Unions on the Seacoast 1978–80; Citizens' Cttee of Solidarity Chair. 1988–91; Senator 1989–91, Minister of State for Nat. Security Affairs in Chancellery of Pres. of Poland March–Nov. 1991; Pres. Cen. Audit Comm. 1992–95; Deputy to Sejm (Parl.) 1991–93, 2001–, Chair. Comm. of Admin. and Interior Affairs 1991-93; Vice-Leader Programme Bd of Public Affairs Inst., Warsaw 1996–; mem. EUROSAI Governing Bd 1993–95, Admin. Bd of ILO; Prof. Acad. of Catholic Theology (now Cardinal S. Wyszyński Univ.), Warsaw 1998–; Minister of Justice and Prosecutor-Gen. 2000–01; Chair. Law and Justice 2001–; Mayor of Warsaw 2002–. *Publications:* Social Pension 1989 and some 15 works on labour law and social insurance. *Leisure interests:* reading, family, history, philosophy. *Address:* pl. Bankowy 3/5, 00-142 Warsaw, Poland (Office). *Telephone:* (22) 6956254/60 (Office).

KADAKIN, Alexander Mikhailovich; Russian diplomatist; b. 22 July 1949, Kishinev, Moldova; ed Moscow Inst. of Int. Relations; translator Special Construction Bureau Vibpribor, Kishinev 1966–67; joined diplomatic service 1972; with USSR Embassy, India 1972, Attaché 1972–75, Third Sec. 1975–78; Second Sec. Secr., First Deputy to USSR Minister of Foreign Affairs 1978–80, First Sec., Secr.Secr. 1980–83, Asst 1983–86, Asst to Deputy Minister 1986–88, Asst First Deputy Minister 1988–89; Minister-Counsellor USSR Embassy, India 1989–91; First Deputy Head of Dept USSR Ministry of Foreign Affairs 1991; counsellor Embassy, India 1991–93; Amb. to Nepal 1993–97; mem. Collegium, Dir of Linguistic Support Dept, Ministry of Foreign Affairs 1997–99; Amb. to India 1999–; Asst Prof. Dept of Indian Studies Moscow State Inst. of Int. Relations 1978–83. *Address:* Russian Embassy, Shanti Path, Chanakyapuri, New Delhi 110 021, India (Office). *Telephone:* (911) 6110565 (Office); (911) 6110642 (Home). *Fax:* (11) 6876823 (Office). *E-mail:* indrusem@dc12.vsnl.net.in (Office). *Website:* www.india.mid .ru (Office).

KADANNIKOV, Vladimir Vasilievich; Russian manager; b. 3 Sept. 1941, Gorky (now Nizhny Novgorod); m.; two d.; ed Gorky Polytech. Inst.; fitter, foreman, then area man., Gorky Automotive Plant 1959–67; Deputy Workshop Man., Volga Automotive Works 1967–76; Deputy Dir-Gen. PO AvtoVAZ in charge of production 1976–86, First Deputy Dir-Gen., then Dir R&D Centre 1986–88, Dir-Gen. PO AvtoVAZ 1988–93, Pres. and Dir-Gen. joint stock co. AvtoVAZ Inc. 1993–96; First Deputy Prime Minister of Russia Jan.–Aug. 1996; Chair., Bd of Dirs. AvtoVAZ Inc. 1996–; Chair. Council for Industrial Policy; Hon. Prof. Samara State Univ.; mem. Presidential Consultative Council; mem. Int. Eng Acad., Russian Eng Acad.; fmr People's Deputy of the USSR; Hero of Socialist Labour. *Publications:* scientific articles on cold sheet stamping by stretch forming; book chapters. *Leisure interest:* reading, basketball. *Address:* Yuzhnoe Shosse 36, 445633 Togliatti, Russia. *Telephone:* (8482) 37-71-25. *Fax:* (848) 378-74-50.

KADANOFF, Leo Philip, PhD; American physicist; b. 14 Jan. 1937, New York; s. of Abraham Kadanoff and Celia (Kibrick) Kadanoff; m. Ruth Ditzian 1979; four d.; ed Harvard Univ.; postdoctoral research at Bohr Inst. for Theoretical Studies, Copenhagen 1960–62; Asst Prof. of Physics, Univ. of Ill. 1962–63, Assoc. Prof. 1963, Prof. 1965–69; Visiting Prof., Cambridge Univ., England 1965; Univ. Prof. of Physics, Brown Univ. 1969–78, Prof. of Eng 1971–78; Prof. of Physics, Univ. of Chicago 1978–82, John D. and Catherine T. MacArthur Distinguished Service Prof. of Physics and Math. 1982–; Alfred P. Sloan Foundation Fellow 1962–67; mem. Editorial Bd Annals of Physics 1982–, Nuclear Physics 1980–; mem. NAS 1978 American Philosophical Soc. 1997; Fellow American Acad. of Arts and Sciences, American Physical Soc.; Ryerson Lectureship, Univ. of Chicago 2000; Buckley Prize, American Physical Soc. 1977, Onsager Prize, American Physical Soc. 1998; Wolf Foundation Award 1980, Elliott Cresson Medal, Franklin Inst. 1986, IUPAP Boltzmann Medal 1989, Quantrell Award, Univ. of Chicago 1990, Centennial Medal, Harvard Univ. 1990, Grande Médaille de'or, Acad. des Sciences de l'Inst. de France 1998, Nat. Medal of Science 2000. *Publications:* Quantum Statistical Mechanics (with G. Baym) 1962, From Order to Chaos: Essays Critical Chaotic and Otherwise 1993, Statistical Physics: Statics, Dynamics and Renormalization 2000. *Address:* James Franck Institute, University of Chicago, 5640 South Ellis Avenue, Chicago, IL 60637 (Office); 5421 South Cornell Avenue, Chicago, IL 60615, USA (Home). *E-mail:* leop@uchicago.edu.

KÁDÁR, Béla, PhD, DSc; Hungarian politician and economist; b. 21 March 1934, Pécs; s. of Lajos Kádár and Teréz Schmidt; m. Patricia Derzső; one s.; ed Budapest Univ. of Economy; with int. econ. Dept Nat. Bank of Hungary; Elektro-impex Foreign Trading Co.; Dept head and research man. Business and Market Research Inst.; Hungarian Acad. of Sciences Research Inst. of World Economy 1965–88; lecturer Eötvös Loránd Univ. of Budapest; Visiting Prof. Santiago de Chile and San Marcos Univ. of Lima; Dir Econ. Planning Inst. 1988–90; Minister of Int. Econ. Relations 1990–94; mem. Parl. 1994–98; Chair. Cttee on Budget and Finances; Vice-Chair. Hungarian Asscn of Economists 1990–2000, Chair. 2002–; Univ. Prof. 1998–; Pres. Hungarian Import-Export Bank 1998–99; Vice-Pres. Hungarian Soc. of Foreign Affairs 1998–; Amb. to OECD 1999–2003; mem. Monetary Council of Hungarian Nat. Bank 1999–; Chair. Hungarian Group in Trilateral Comm. 1999–; Academician Budapest Univ. of Economy 2001; Dr hc (San Marcos Univ., Lima) 1970, (Budapest) 1999; Grand Prix Hungarian Acad. of Sciences 1984; Econ. Policy Club (Bonn) Prize for Social Market Econ. 1993. *Publications:* author of 8 books, 400 papers. *Leisure interests:* music, literature. *Address:* Budapest 1124, Mártonhegyi u. 38/B, Hungary. *Telephone:* 1-35-57-98-7. *Fax:* 1-35-57-98-7.

KADARÉ, Ismail; Albanian author; b. 28 Jan. 1936, Gjirokaster; s. of Halit Kadaré; m. Elena Gushi 1963; two c.; ed Univ. of Tirana, Gorky Inst. Moscow; full-time writer since 1963; works translated into more than 30 languages; sought political asylum in Paris 1990; mem. Albanian Acad.; corresponding, then Assoc. foreign mem. Académie des sciences morales et politiques; mem. Acad. of Arts, Berlin, Acad. Mallarmé; Dr. hc (Grenoble III) 1992, (St Etienne) 1997; Prix Mondial Cino del Duca 1992. *Publications include:* Chronicle in Stone (novel) 1971, The Great Winter (novel) 1973, The Twilight 1978, The Three-Arched Bridge 1978, The Niche of Shame 1978, The Palace of Dreams 1981, Broken April 1982, Invitation to an official concert and other Stories 1985, Who Brought Back Doruntine? 1986, The Concert 1988, Eschyle or The Eternal Loser 1988, The H Dossier 1989, Albanian Spring 1991, Le Monstre 1991, La Pyramide 1992, La grande Muraille 1993, Le Firman aveugle 1993, Clair de Lune 1993, L'Ombre 1994, L'Aigle 1996, Spiritus 1996, Oeuvres 1993–97 (5 Vols) 1997, Temps barbares, de l'Albanie au Kosovo 1999, Il a fallu ce deuil pour se retrouver 2000, Froides fleurs d'avril 2000; poetry including The Sixties, Insufficient Time. *Address:* c/o Librairie Arthème Fayard, 75 rue des Saints Pères, 75006 Paris (Office); 63 blvd Saint-Michel, 75005 Paris, France.

KADDOUR, Muhammad Ghassan al-; Syrian civil engineer; b. 1952, El-Bab; m. Myriam Koudsi; one s. two d.; ed Univ. of Aleppo; with Milihouse Corpn 1976–80; in business 1981–83; Chair.-Dir Gen. Syrian Railways 1983–98. *Leisure interest:* sport. *Address:* c/o Syrian Railways, POB 182, Aleppo, Syria.

KADHAFI, Col Mu'ammar Muhammed al- (see Gaddafi, Col Mu'ammar Muhammed al-).

KADUMA, Ibrahim Mohamed, B.SC.(ECON.), BPhil; Tanzanian politician and economist; b. 1937, Mtwango Njombe, Iringa Region; s. of the late Mohamed Maleva Kaduma and of Mwanaidza Kaduma; m. Happiness Y. Mgonja 1969; four s. one d.; ed Makerere Univ. Coll. Uganda and Univ. of York, UK; Accounts Clerk, the Treasury 1959–61, Accounts Asst 1961, Asst Accountant 1962–65, Economist 1965–66, Dir of External Finance and Technical Co-operation 1967–69, Deputy Sec. Treasury 1969–70; Principal Sec. Ministry of Communications, Transport and Labour, 1970–72, Treasury 1972–73; Dir Inst. of Devt Studies, Univ. of Dar es Salaam 1973–75, Centre on Integrated Rural Devt for Africa 1982–85; Minister for Foreign Affairs 1975–77, of Trade 1980–81, of Communications and Transport 1981–82; Vice-Chancellor Univ. of Dar es Salaam 1977–80; Gen. Man. Tanzania Sisal Devt Bd 1985–; Arts Research Prize, Makerere Univ., Uganda 1964–65. *Leisure interests:* tennis, squash, gardening, dairy farming. *Address:* POB 277, Tanga, Tanzania. *Telephone:* (53) 44401 (Office); (53) 46224 (Home).

KADYROV, Akhmed-Khadzhi Abdulkhamidovich; Russian ecclesiastic and politician; b. 23 Aug. 1950, Karaganda, Kazakh. SSR; ed Bukhara Medrese, Novosibirsk Bldg Inst., Islamic Univ. in Tashkent; f. and Rector in N Caucasus Islamic Univ. 1989–94; elected Mufti (Head of Chechen Moslems) 1995; from the start of mil. operations fought against fed. armed forces; in late 1990s supported Russian Admin. against supporters of Pres. Maskhadov; apptd. Head of Chechen Admin. by Russian Govt 2000–. *Address:* Administration of Chechen Republic, Gudermes-Grozny, Chechen Republic, Russia (Office).

KAFELNIKOV, Yevgeny Aleksandrovich; Russian tennis player; b. 18 Feb. 1974, Sochi; m. two d.; ed Krasnodar Pedagogical Inst.; ATP professional since 1992; won ATP tournaments including Milan, St Petersburg, Gstaad, Long Island; won French Open (singles and doubles) 1996; won Moscow Kremlin Cup 1997, 1999; won Australian Open 1999; mem. Russian Fed. Davis Cup Championship Team 1993, winner (with Russian team) 2002; has appeared in top 10 men's ranking list since 1995; runner-up World Championship, Hanover 1997; highest ATP rating 1st (May 1999); Olympic champion (singles), Sydney 2000; winner of 51 pro titles by the end of 2002. *Leisure interests:* fishing, flying, golf. *Address:* All-Russian Tennis Association, Luzhnetskaya nab. 8, 119871 Moscow, Russia.

KAFI, Ali; Algerian politician and army officer; b. Al Harroch; rank of Col in independence Movt, controlled a Dist 1954–62; fmr Amb. to Egypt, Tunisia; mem. State Council Jan. 1992–; Pres. of Algeria 1992–94; mem. Nat. Liberation Front; Sec.-Gen. Nat. Asscn of War Veterans. *Address:* c/o Front de libération nationale, 7 rue du Stade, Hydra, Algiers, Algeria.

KAFKA, Alexandre; Brazilian professor of economics; b. 25 Jan. 1917; s. of the late Bruno Kafka and Jana Kafka (née Bondy de Bondrop); m. Rita Petschek 1947; two d.; ed Law School German Univ., Prague, Grad. School of Int. Studies, Geneva, Balliol Coll. Oxford, England; Prof. of Econs, Univ. de São Paulo 1941–46; Adviser to Brazilian Del. to Preparatory Cttee and Conf. of Int. Trade Org. 1946–48; Asst Div. Chief, Int. Monetary Fund (IMF) 1949–51, Exec. Dir 1966–98, Vice-Chair. Deputies of Cttee on Reform of Int. Monetary System and Related Matters 1972–74; Adviser, Superintendency of Money and Credit (now Banco Central do Brasil); Dir of Research, Brazilian Inst. of Econs 1951–56, Dir 1961–63; Chief Financial Inst. and Policies Section, UN 1956–59; Prof. of Econs, Univ. of Va, US 1959–60, 1963–75, lecturer Law School 1977–87; lecturer, George Washington Univ. 1989, Visiting Prof. of Econs, Boston Univ. 1975–79; Adviser to Minister of Finance 1964; Comendador Ordem do Rio Branco (Brazil) 1973, Grand Cross (Colombia), Order de Boyaca (Colombia), Grand Officer (Peru), Order del sol (Peru). *Publication:* IMF Governance, in G-24: commemorating 50th year after Bretton Woods Conf. 1994. *Address:* 4201 Cathedral Avenue, NW, (Apt. 805E), Washington, DC 20016, USA. *Telephone:* (202) 623-7870 (Office); (202) 362-1737 (Home).

KAFRAWY, Hasaballah el-, BEng; Egyptian politician; b. 22 Nov. 1930; s. of Mohamed El-Kafrawy; m. Elham Abd El-Aziz Fouad 1961; three s.; ed Alexandria Univ.; with southern region of High Dam electricity lines until 1966; Chair. Canal Gen. Contracting Co.; Vice-Pres. of exec. organ for reconstruction of Suez Canal region 1974, Pres. 1975; Gov. of Damietta 1976; Deputy Minister for Reconstruction, then Minister of Devt, Housing and Land Reclamation 1977–86; supervised planning of satellite cities and public utilities of Sadat, Ramadan 10, October 6, May 15, Cairo Sanitary Project, Damietta Port etc.; Minister of Devt, New Communities, Housing and Public Utilities 1986–93; mem. Egyptian People's Ass. 1979–93; Chair. and CEO El rehab Saudi-Egyptian Group of cos 1997–; Pres. Egyptian Eng Asscn 1990–; Perm. mem. Int. Org. of Metropolis; UN Prize for Housing 1992; Nile Sash 1994, Egyptian Order of Merit (First Class) 1964, 1975, 1980, Medal for Championship of Labour (USSR) 1964, Order of Merit (First Class) (France) 1983. *Address:* 21 Gamal Eldin Aboulmahasen Street, Garden City, POB 11451, Cairo, Egypt. *Telephone:* (2) 3555505. *Fax:* (2) 3556255.

KAGAME, Maj.-Gen. Paul; Rwandan politician and army officer; b. 1957; m.; two c.; ed Fort Leavenworth, USA; escaped to Uganda with family from anti-Tutsi persecution 1960; joined Ugandan Rebel Army 1982, Chief of Intelligence Ugandan Army 1986; formed rebel army of Tutsi exiles 1990, Leader campaign in Rwanda 1990–94, helped broker cease-fire 1993; Head Rwandan Patriotic Front Party (FPR) 1990–, Vice-Pres. and Minister of Nat. Defence 1994–2000; Pres. of Rwanda March 2000–. *Address:* Office of the President, BP 15, Kigali, Rwanda (Office). *Telephone:* 75432 (Office).

KAGEL, Mauricio; Argentine composer; b. 21 Dec. 1931, Buenos Aires; ed Univ. of Buenos Aires; Artistic Dir Agrupación Nueva Música 1949; Co-founder, Cinemathèque Argentine 1950; Dir and Conductor, Teatro Colón, Buenos Aires 1955; emigrated to Germany 1957; f. Kölner Ensemble für Neue Musik, Cologne 1959; Slee Prof. of Composition, State Univ. of New York 1964–65; Visiting Lecturer, Berlin Acad. of Film and TV 1967; Dir Scandinavian Courses for New Music, Gothenburg 1968–69; Dir Courses for New Music, Cologne 1969–75; Prof. of New Music and Theater, Cologne Conservatory 1974–97; numerous awards and prizes. *Compositions include:* Música para la Torre 1953, Sur Scène 1959, Le Bruit 1960, Phonophonie 1963, Mirum 1965, Hallelujah 1968, Tactil 1970, Mare Nostrum 1975, Kantrimiusik 1975, An Tasten 1977, Die Erschöpfung der Welt 1980, Fragen 1982, Old/New 1986, Tantz-Schul 1988, Nah und Fern 1993, Playback Play 1997, Entführung aus dem Konzertsaal 2000. *Television includes:* Sur Scène 1963, Match 1966, Duo 1968, Tactil 1971, Pas de Cinq 1978, Blue's Blue 1980, Dressur 1985, Repertoire 1989, Die Erschöpfung der Welt 2000. *Address:* c/o Universal Edition, Bösendorferstrasse 12, Postfach 3, 1015 Vienna, Austria.

KAHALANI, Avigdor, BA; Israeli politician and army officer; b. 1944, Israel; m.; three c.; ed Tel Aviv Univ., Haifa Univ., Command and Gen. Staff Coll.; Fort Leavenworth, Kan., USA, Nat. Defence Coll.; fmr career officer in Israeli Defence Forces, to rank of Brig.-Gen.; mem. Knesset (Parl.) 1992– (Labour Party 1992–96, The Third Way Party 1996–), mem. Knesset Foreign Affairs and Defence Cttee, Educ. and Culture Cttee 1992–96; a founder-mem. The Third Way, led party in 1996 elections; Minister of Internal Security 1996–2000; DSM, Medal of Valour. *Publications:* The Heights of Courage: A Tank Leader's War, On the Golan 1975, A Warrior's Way 1989. *Address:* c/o Ministry of Public Security, P.O. Box 18182, Kiryat Hamemshala, Jerusalem 91181, Israel (Office).

KAHIN, Dahir Riyale; Somali politician; Vice-Pres. self-proclaimed Repub. of Somaliland (N-Western Somalia) –2002, Pres. May 2002–. *Address:* Office of the President of the Republic of Somaliland, Hargeysa, Somalia (Office). *Website:* www.somalilandgov.com.

KAHN, Alfred E(dward), PhD; American economist and fmr government official; b. 17 Oct. 1917, Paterson, NJ; s. of the late Jacob M. Kahn and Bertha Orlean Kahn; m. Mary Simmons 1943; one s. two d.; ed New York Univ. and Graduate School, Univ. of Missouri, Yale Univ.; Research Staff of Brookings

Inst. 1940, 1951–52; joined US Govt Service with Antitrust Div., Dept of Justice, Dept of Commerce, War Production Bd 1941–43; Research Staff, 20th Century Fund 1944–45; Asst Prof. Dept of Econs, Ripon Coll., Wis. 1945–47; joined Dept of Econs, Cornell Univ., Ithaca, NY, as Asst Prof. 1947, Chair. Econs Dept 1958–63, Robert Julius Thorne Prof. of Econs 1966–89, Emer. Prof. 1989–, mem. Bd of Trustees 1964–69, Dean Coll. of Arts and Sciences 1969–74; Chair. New York Public Service Comm. 1974–77, Civil Aeronautics Bd 1977–78; Adviser to the Pres. on Inflation and Chair. Council on Wage and Price Stability 1978–80; Special Consultant, Nat. Econ. Research Associates 1980–; Chair. Int. Inst. for Applied Systems Analysis Advisory Cttee on Price Reform and Competition in the USSR 1990–91, Blue Ribbon Panel to Study Pricing in the Calif. Electricity Market 2000; Vice-Pres. American Econ. Asscn 1981–82; mem. American Acad. of Arts and Sciences; Fellow, American Acad. of Arts and Sciences 1977–; AEI Brookings Joint Center First Distinguished Lecturer 1999; Hon. LLD (Colby Univ., Ripon Coll., Univ. of Mass., Northwestern Univ., Colgate Univ.), Hon. DHL (State Univ. of New York) 1985; Distinguished Alumni Award, Univ. of New York 1976, L. Welch Pogue Award for Lifetime Contribs. to Aviation 1997, Sovereign Fund Award 1997, J. Rhoads Foster Award for achievements in econ. regulation 1999; Wilbur Cross Medal, Yale Univ. 1995. *Publications:* Great Britain in the World Economy 1946, (co-author) Fair Competition, the Law and Economics of Antitrust Policy 1954, (co-author) Integration and Competition in the Petroleum Industry 1959, The Economics of Regulation (two vols) 1970, 1971, 1988, Letting Go: Deregulating the Process of Deregulation 1998, Whom the Gods Would Destroy, or How Not to Deregulate 2001. *Leisure interests:* sports, dramatics, music. *Address:* 308 N Cayuga Street, Ithaca, NY 14850 (Office); 221 Savage Farm Drive, Ithaca, NY 14850, USA (Home). *Telephone:* (607) 277-3007 (Office); (607) 266-8340 (Home). *Fax:* (607) 277-1581 (Office). *E-mail:* alfred.kahn@nera.com (Office).

KAHN, Jacob Meyer, BA, MBA; South African business executive; b. 29 June 1939, Pretoria; m. Lynette Sandra Asher 1968; two d.; ed Brits High School, Univ. of Pretoria; Dir South African Breweries Ltd 1981, Group Man. Dir 1983, Exec. Chair. 1990–, Group Chair. 1999–; Chair. SAB MIWWER PLC 1999–; Chief. Exec. South African Police Service 1997–99; Prof. Extraordinaire 1989, DComm hc 1991; Marketing Man. of the Year 1987, Business Man of the Year 1990; Award for Business Excellence 1991; Police Star of Excellence 2000. *Leisure interests:* reading, golf. *Address:* SAB MIWWER PLC, 2 Jan Smuts Avenue, P.O. Box 1099, Johannesburg; 4 East Road, Morningside, Sandton, Johannesburg, South Africa (Home). *Telephone:* (11) 4071800 (Office); (11) 7836061 (Home). *Fax:* (11) 4031857 (Office); (11) 7836061 (Home). *E-mail:* cdccastro@sab.co.za (Office).

KAHN-ACKERMANN, Georg; German politician, journalist and broadcaster; b. 4 Jan. 1918, Berlin-Charlottenburg; s. of Lucian Kahn-Ackermann and Maria Gretor; m. Rosemarie Müller-Diefenbach 1945; one s. two d.; ed Starnberg Grammar School; mem. Social Democratic Party (Sozialdemokratische Partei Deutschlands–SPD) 1946; mem. Bundestag 1953–57, 1962–69, 1970–74; Vice-Pres. Admin. Council Deutschlandfunk; Pres. Political Comm., Western European Union; Vice-Pres. Assembly, Council of Europe 1973–74: Sec.-Gen. Council of Europe 1974–79; Pres. V. G. Wort 1979, Hon. Pres. 1980–; Vice-Pres. Deutsche Welthungerhilfe 1968–89; mem. Bd Asscn of fmr mems. of Bundestag 1982–; Pres. European Comm. of German Journalists Asscn 1991–. *Leisure interest:* cookery. *Address:* Sterzenweg 3, 82541 Münsing, Germany. *Telephone:* (8177) 206. *Fax:* (8177) 1303.

KAHNEMANN, Daniel, PhD; Israeli/American psychologist; b. 1934, Tel-Aviv; m. Anne Treisman; ed The Hebrew Univ., Jerusalem, Univ. of Calif. at Berkeley; Lecturer in Psychology The Hebrew Univ. 1961–66, Sr Lecturer 1966–70, Assoc. Prof. 1970–73, Prof. 1973–78; Lecturer in Psychology Harvard Univ. 1966–67; Prof. of Psychology Univ. of British Columbia, Canada 1978–86; Prof. of Psychology Univ. of Calif. at Berkeley 1986–94; Eugene Higgins Prof. of Psychology Princeton Univ. 1993–, Prof. of Public Affairs Woodrow Wilson School 1993–; Visiting Scientist Univ. of Michigan 1965–66, Applied Psychological Research Unit, Cambridge, UK 1968–69; Fellow Centre for Cognitive Studies 1966–67, Centre for Advanced Studies in the Behavioural Sciences 1977–78, Centre for Rationality, The Hebrew Univ. 2000–; Assoc. Fellow Canadian Inst. for Advanced Research 1984–86; Visiting Scholar Russell Sage Foundation 1991–92; Fellow American Acad. of Arts and Sciences, Econometric Soc., American Psychological Asscn, American Psychological Soc., Canadian Psychological Asscn; mem. Nat. Acad. of Sciences, Soc. of Experimental Psychologists, Psychonomic Soc., Soc. for Econ. Science, Soc. for Judgement and Decision Making (Pres. 1992–93); mem. Ed. Bd Journal of Behavioral Decision Making, Journal of Risk and Uncertainty, Thinking and Reasoning, Economics and Philosophy; pioneered integration of research about decision-making into field of econs; Hon. DrSc (Univ. of Penn.) 2001; Distinguished Scientific Contrib. Award, American Psychological Soc. 1982, Distinguished Scientific Contrib. Award, Soc. of Consumer Psychology 1992, Warren Medal, Soc. of Experimental Psychologists 1995, Hilgard Award for Lifetime Contrib. to Gen. Psychology 1995, Nobel Prize for Econ. Sciences 2002. *Publications include:* Attention and Effort 1973, Human Engineering of Decisions in Ethics in an Age of Uncertainty 1980, Well-Being: Foundations of Hedonic Psychology (co-ed.) 1999, Choices, Values and Frames (co-ed.) 2000, Heuristics and Biases: The Psychology of Intuitive Judgement (co-ed.) 2002; author or co-author of over 120 articles in professional journals and

chapters in books. *Address:* Woodrow Wilson School, Princeton University, Princeton, NJ 08544-1013, USA (Office). *E-mail:* kahnemann@princeton.edu (Office). *Website:* www.princeton.edu (Office).

KAIFU, Toshiki; Japanese politician; b. 1932; m. Sachiyo Kaifu; elected to House of Reps six times; Parl. Vice-Minister of Labour; Chair. Steering Cttee of House of Reps.; various posts in admin. of the late Takeo Miki 1974–76, including Deputy Chief Cabinet Sec., Chair. of Diet Policy Cttee of Liberal Democratic Party (LDP); Minister of Educ. 1976–77, 1985–86; Prime Minister of Japan 1989–91; leader New Frontier Party (opposition coalition) 1994–95. *Address:* House of Representatives, Tokyo, Japan.

KAIN, Karen, CC; Canadian ballet dancer; b. 28 March 1951, Hamilton, Ont.; d. of Charles A. Kain and Winifred Mary Kelly; m. Ross Petty 1983; ed Nat. Ballet School; joined Nat. Ballet 1969, Prin. 1970; has danced most of major roles in repertoire; appeared as Giselle with Bolshoi Ballet on USSR tour, Aurora in the Sleeping Beauty with Festival Ballet in UK and Australia, in Swan Lake with Vienna State Opera Ballet; toured Japan and Korea with Ballet national de Marseille 1981; created roles of Chosen Maiden in The Rite of Spring for Nat. Ballet 1979, Giuletta in Tales of Hoffman for Ballet national de Marseille 1982, the Bride in The Seven Daggers/Los Siete Puñales and roles in Glen Tetley's Alice 1986, La Ronde 1987, Daphnis and Chlöe 1988, Tagore 1989, Musings 1991, James Kudelka's The Actress 1994; appeared in CBC-TV productions of Giselle, La Fille Mal Gardée, The Merry Widow, Alice, La Ronde; Pres. The Dancer's Transition Centre; Artistic Assoc., Nat. Ballet of Canada 1999–2000; hon. degrees, York, McMaster and Trent Univs.; Officier des Arts er des Lettres; Silver Medal, Second Int. Ballet Competition, Moscow 1973; Int. Emmy Award for Karen Kain: Dancing in the Moment. *Publication:* Movement Never Lies (autobiog.) 1994. *Address:* The Walter Carsen Centre for The National Ballet of Canada, 470 Queens Quay, Toronto, Ont., M5V 3K4, Canada.

KAISER, Karl, PhD; German professor of political science; b. 8 Dec. 1934, Siegen; s. of Walther Kaiser and Martha Müller; m. Deborah Strong 1967; two s. one d.; ed Univs. of Cologne, Bonn and Grenoble and Nuffield Coll. Oxford; lecturer, Harvard Univ. 1963–67, Univ. of Bonn 1968–69, Johns Hopkins Univ. Bologna Center 1968–69; Prof. of Political Science, Univ. of the Saarland 1969–74, Univ. of Cologne 1974–91, Univ. of Bonn 1991–; Dir Research Inst. of German Soc. for Foreign Affairs, Bonn 1973–; Prix Adolphe Bentinck 1973; NATO Atlantic Award 1986; Hon. CBE 1989; Officier, Légion d'honneur, Bundesverdienstkreuz Erster Klasse 1999. *Publications:* EEC and Free Trade Area 1963, German Foreign Policy in Transition 1968, Europe and the USA 1973, New Tasks for Security Policy 1977, Reconciling Energy Needs and Proliferation 1978, Western Security: What Has Changed, What Can be Done? 1981, Atomic Energy Without Nuclear Weapons 1982, German–French Security Policy 1986, British–German Co-operation 1987, Space and International Politics 1987, Germany's Unification, The International Aspects 1991, Germany and the Iraq Conflict 1992, Foreign Policies of the New Republics in Eastern Europe 1994, Germany's New Foreign Policy, Vol. 1 1994, Vol. 2 1995, Vol. 3 1996, The Foreign Policies of the New Democracies in Central and Eastern Europe 1994, Acting for Europe, German-French Co-operation in a Changing World 1995, World Politics in a New Era 1996, Interests and Strategies 1996, Institutions and Resources 1998, The Future of German Foreign Policy 1999. *Leisure interests:* music, sailing. *Address:* Forschungsinstitut der Deutschen Gesellschaft für Auswärtige Politik e.V., 53113 Bonn, Adenauerallee 131 (Office); 10787 Berlin, Rauchstrasse 18 (Office); 53173 Bonn, Kronprinzenstrasse 68, Germany (Home). *Telephone:* (228) 2675150 (Bonn) (Office); (228) 25423100 (Berlin) (Office). *Fax:* (228) 2675173.

KAISER, Michael M., MA; American arts administrator; ed Brandeis Univ. and Sloan School of Man., MIT; f. and Dir Michael M. Kaiser Assocs (consultancy) 1981–85, Kaiser/Engler (arts man. consultancy) 1994, Pres. 1994–95; Exec. Dir Alvin Ailey Dance Theater Foundation 1991–93, American Ballet Theatre 1995–98, Royal Opera House, London 1998–2000; Pres. John F. Kennedy Center for Performing Arts, Washington DC 2000–; Adjunct Prof. of Business Admin., Rockhurst Coll., Kan. 1985–86, then Adjunct Prof. of Arts Admin., New York Univ.; US Del. advisory comm. on arts funding policies of S African Govt 1994–95; Visiting Prof. of Arts Admin., Univ. of Witwatersrand 1995; Assoc. Dir State Ballet of Mo. 1985–87, Pierpoint Morgan Library 1987–89; mem. Bd Dirs New York Foundation for the Arts; fmr Dir Washington Opera, Ensemble Studio Theater, PS 122. *Publications:* Understanding the Competition: A Practical Guide to Competitive Analysis 1981, Developing Industry Strategies: A Practical Guide to Industry Analysis 1983, Strategic Planning in the Arts: A Practical Guide 1995. *Address:* John F. Kennedy Center for Performing Arts, 2700 F. Street, NW, Washington, DC 20566, USA (Office).

KAISER, Philip M., AB, MA; American diplomatist, publisher and banker; b. 12 July 1913, New York; s. of Morris and Temma Kaiser; m. Hannah Greeley 1939; three s.; ed Univ. of Wisconsin and Balliol Coll., Oxford (Rhodes Scholar); Fed. Reserve System 1939–42, Bd of Econ. Warfare 1942–46; joined Research Planning Div. Dept of State 1946; Exec. Asst to Asst Sec. of Labor (Int. Labor Affairs) 1946–47; Dir Office of Int. Labor Affairs, Dept of Labor 1947–49; Asst Sec. of Labor 1949–53; US Govt mem., Governing Body, Int. Labor Org. 1949–53; Labor Adviser, Comm. for Free Europe 1953–54; Special Asst to Gov. of New York 1955–58; Prof. of Int. Relations, American Univ. 1958–61; Amb. to Senegal and Mauritania 1961–64; Minister, American

Embassy in London 1964–69; Amb. to Hungary 1977–80, to Austria 1980–81; Professorial Lecturer Johns Hopkins School for Advanced Int. Studies 1981–83; Chair. and Man. Dir Encyclopaedia Britannica Int. Ltd, London 1969–75; Sr Consultant SRI Int. 1981–97; mem. Bd, Guinness Mahon Holdings Ltd 1975–77, Weidenfeld and Nicolson 1969–77, American Ditchley Foundation 1981–, Council of American Ambs 1984–, Franklin & Eleanor Roosevelt Inst. 1985–, Weizmann Inst. of Science, Asscn of Diplomatic Studies 1987–, Partners for Democratic Change, American Acad. of Diplomacy 1996–; mem. Council on Foreign Relations, Washington Inst. of Foreign Affairs; Kt Commdr Order of Austria 1992, Order of Merit, Return of Crown of St. Stephen (Hungary) 1998. *Publication:* Journeying Far and Wide: A Political and Diplomatic Memoir 1993. *Leisure interests:* tennis, swimming, music, ballet, theatre. *Address:* 2101 Connecticut Avenue, NW, Washington, DC 20008, USA (Home). *Telephone:* (202) 667-6095 (Home). *Fax:* (202) 332-6124 (Home).

KAJANTIE, Keijo Olavi, PhD; Finnish professor of physics; b. 31 Jan. 1940, Hämeenlinna; m. Riitta Erkiö 1963; one s. one d.; ed Univ. of Helsinki; Visiting Scientist CERN, Geneva 1966–67, 1969–70, 1995–98; Assoc. Prof. of Physics, Univ. of Helsinki 1970–72, Prof. 1973–; Visiting Prof., Univ. of Wis., Madison 1975; Research Prof. Acad. of Finland 1985–90; Sr Scientist, Acad. of Finland 2002–03. *Publications:* more than 180 publs in the field of elementary particle physics. *Address:* Department of Physics, P.O. Box 64, 00014 University of Helsinki, Finland; Liisankatu 12D 26, 00170 Helsinki, Finland (Home). *Telephone:* (9) 19150622 (Univ.); (9) 1352232 (Home). *E-mail:* keijo.kajantie@helsinki.fi (Office).

KAJIYAMA, Seiroku; Japanese politician; b. 27 March 1926, Ibaraki Pref.; m. Harue Kajiyama; one s. one d.; ed Nihon Univ.; mem. Ibaraki Prefectural Ass. 1955–69, Speaker 1967–69; mem. House of Reps 1969–; Deputy Chief Cabinet Sec. 1974; Parl. Vice-Minister for Construction 1976, for Int. Trade and Industry 1979; Chair. House of Reps Standing Cttee on Commerce and Industry 1983; Chair. Exec. Council of Liberal Democratic Party (LDP) 1986; Minister of Home Affairs 1987–88, of Trade and Industry 1989; Chief Cabinet Sec. 1996–97. *Leisure interests:* golf, shogi (4th dan), reading. *Address:* Kudun Shukusha, 2-14-3 Fujimi, Chiyoda-ku, Tokyo 102, Japan.

KAKLAMANIS, Apostolos; Greek politician and lawyer; b. 7 Sept. 1936, Lefkas; s. of Christos Kaklamanis and Evageloula Kaklamanis; m. Athina-Anna Gavera 1972; one s. one d.; ed Athens Univ.; Gen. Sec. Ministry of Welfare 1964–65; political prisoner during colonels' dictatorship; founding mem. Pasok and mem. Cen. Cttee and Exec. Cttee; MP 1974–; Minister of Labour 1981–82, of Educ. and Religious Affairs 1982–86, of Justice 1986–87, Minister in charge of the Prime Minister's Office 1987–88, Minister of Health, Welfare and Social Services 1988–89, of Labour 1989–90; Speaker Parl. 1993–96, 1996–2000, 2000–. *Address:* Solumou 58, 10682, Athens, Greece. *Telephone:* (1) 3608640.

KÁKOSY, László; Hungarian Egyptologist; b. 15 Aug. 1932, Budapest; s. of Károly Kákosy and Ilona Vámos; m. Éva Grigássy; ed Eötvös Loránd Univ. of Arts and Sciences; lecturer Eötvös Loránd Univ. of Arts and Sciences, Prof. 1960, head Dept of Egyptology 1972-98; lecturer, Pázmány Peter Catholic Univ. 1996–; Chair. of Working Cttee on History of Ancient Sciences Hungarian Acad. of Sciences 1987; mem. Cttee of Oriental Studies; Pres. Soc. of Classical Studies 1997–, research in religion, culture, archaeology of Ancient Egypt, Egyptian-Greek Relations; mem. of the Nubian Expedition of Hungarian Acad. of Sciences 1964; participated in the planning of a new museum for Cairo 1983; Dir Hungarian excavations in Thebes 1983–; Corresp. mem. Acad. of Sciences, Heidelberg, Germany 1996–, Acad. of Sciences, Budapest 1998–; Research Fellow of the Lexikon der Ägyptologie of Wiesbaden 1975; Kuzsinszky Commemorative Medal, Ábel Jenő Commemorative Medal, Széchenyi Award 1992. *Publications:* Varázslás az ókori Egyiptomban Magic in Ancient Egypt 1969, Egy évezred a Nilus völgyében with Edith Varga, A Millennium in the Nile Valley 1970, Egyiptom és antik csillaghit Egypt and Ancient Belief in Stars 1978, Ré fiai Sons of Re 1979, Fény és káosz Light and Chaos 1984, La magia in Egitto ai tempi dei faraoni 1985, Dzsehutimesz sirja Thébában The Tomb of Djehutimes in Thebes 1989, Zauberei im alten Ägypten 1989, Egyptian Healing Statues in Three Museums in Italy 1999. *Leisure interests:* astronomy, chess. *Address:* Eötvös Loránd University of Arts and Sciences, 1088 Budapest, Múzeum krt. 4., B. ép. Hungary. *Telephone:* (1) 266-0860/2933.

KAKOURIS, Constantine; Greek judge; b. 16 March 1919, Pyrgos; s. of Nicolas and Helen Kakouris; ed Univs of Athens and Paris; called to Bar, Athens 1942; Auxiliary Judge, Supreme Admin. Court 1951–62, Asst Judge 1962–70, Judge 1970–83; Judge, Court of Justice of EEC 1983–97; several times mem. or Pres. High Council of the Judiciary and High Council of Diplomatic Corps, Chief Inspector for Admin. Tribunals; Pres. or mem. several cttees.; Corresp. mem. Acad. of Athens 1996–; Dr. hc (Univ. of Athens Law School) 1992. *Publications:* A study of General Theory of Law on Judiciary Power and the Mission of the Courts; articles and reviews in legal and philosophical journals. *Leisure interest:* philosophy. *Address:* 52, Skoufa Street, 106.72 Athens, Greece. *Telephone:* (1) 3635588.

KALAM, Aavul Pakkiri Jainulabidin Abdul, PhD; Indian head of state and nuclear scientist; b. 15 Oct. 1931, Dhanushkodi, Rameswaram Dist; ed Madras Inst. of Tech.; mem. staff Space Dept 1960s and 1970s, later Defence Lab., Hyderabad; launched India's first satellite 1980, masterminded integrated guided missile devt and nuclear programmes, developed Agni, Trishul and Prithvi missiles, responsible for carrying out underground nuclear tests 1998; fmr Cabinet Minister and Prin. Scientific Adviser to Govt –1999; Chair. Tech. Information, Forecasting and Assessment Council (TIFAC); head of an agricultural devt agency; Pres. of India 2002–; Padma Bhusan 1981, Padma Vibhushan 1990, Bharat Ratna 1997. *Publications include:* Yenudaya Prayana (Tamil poems), Wings of Fire (bestselling autobiog.) 1999, Eternal Quest (children's novel), Ignited Minds: Unleashing the Power Within India 2001. *Address:* President's Office, Rashtrapati Bhavan, New Delhi 110 004, India (Office). *Telephone:* (11) 3015321 (Office). *Fax:* (11) 3017290 (Office). *E-mail:* poi_gen@rb.nic.in. *Website:* presidentofindia.nic.in (Office).

KALAMANOV, Vladimir Avdashevich, DrHist; Russian politician; b. 1951, Moscow; ed Moscow State Inst. of Int. Relations; Head of Dept Ministry of Problems with Nationalities; Plenipotentiary Rep. of Pres. in Repubs. of N Ossetia and of Ingushetia 1997–99; Dir Fed. Migration Service of Russian Fed. 1999–2002; Special Rep. of Pres. to supervise observance of human rights and freedom in Chechen Repub. 2000; Rep. of Russian Fed. at UNESCO 2002–. *Address:* 1 rue Miollis, 75732, Paris, Cedex 15, France. *Telephone:* 1-45-68-26-82; 1-45-04-37-52. *Fax:* 1-42-67-51-99. *E-mail:* unerus@club-internet.fr.

KALANTARI, Isa, PhD; Iranian politician and agriculturalist; b. 1952, Marand; s. of Mohammad Hussein Kalantari and Kobra Kalantari (née Esfandi); m. 1982; one s. one d.; ed Univs. of Urmiya, Nebraska and Iowa State; Head Agricultural Extension Org. 1982, Plant and Seed Improvement Research Inst. 1983, Deputy Minister for Agricultural Research, Educ. and Extension 1983–85, Man. Dir and Head Bd of Dirs. Moghan Stock-farming and Agro-Industry Complex, Ministry of Agric. 1985–88; Minister of Agric. 1988–2001; Pres. World Food Council 1991–95. *Publications:* A Policy for Reforming Nutrition Patterns: Nutrition Physiology and Foodstuff Economics 1997; series of articles in journal Agricultural Economics and Development. *Leisure interests:* reading, sport. *Address:* c/o Ministry of Agriculture, 20 Malaei Avenue, Vali-e-Asr Square, Tehran, Iran.

KALASHNIKOV, Anatoliy Ivanovich; Russian wood-engraver; b. 5 April 1930, Moscow; s. of Ivan Nikiforovich Kalashnikov and Vera Alekseevna Kalashnikova; m. 1st Iulia Kaizer 1957 (died 1980); m. 2nd Ludmila Chembrovskaya 1980 (died 1994); m. 3rd Ludmila Fyodorova 1994; ed Moscow Art Inst. (fmrly Stroganoff Art School), pupil of Ivan Pavlov, Dmitry Sobolev and Mikhail Matorin; freelance designer for many Soviet publishing houses and Ministry of Communications (postal designs) 1950–90; designed over 100 postage stamps, 500 commemorative envelopes and over 950 bookplates; 160 solo exhbns. worldwide; elected Academician, Int. Acad. of the Book and Art of the Book, Moscow 1992; Hon. mem. Royal Society of Painter-Etchers and Engravers, London 1988, Soc. of Wood Engravers, London 1991; Merited Artist of Russia 1983; 20 prizes in int. bookplate design competitions, Italy, Spain, Hungary, Denmark, Poland, Germany, USA. *Publications include:* Canton Ticino 1978, Anglo-Russian Relations 1983, Lombardia 1991, War and Peace: A suite of Wood Engravings based on the novel by Leo Tolstoy 1991, 500 Ex-libris 1993, Frankonia 1993, The Dostoyevsky Suite 1994, Omar Khayam in Wood engravings by A. Kalashnikov 1994, Sensuality and the Bookplate 1996, Golden Ring of Russia 1997, The Bookplate Designs of A. I. Kalashnikov: A Catalogue in Four Volumes 2003; many albums and suites. *Leisure interest:* travelling. *Address:* Leninsky prospekt 44, Apt. 124, 117334 Moscow, Russia. *Telephone:* (095) 137-37-30.

KALASHNIKOV, Lt-Gen. Mikhail Timofeyevich, DTechSc; Russian military engineer; b. 10 Nov. 1919, Kurya, Altaizay Kpai Region; s. of Timofei Aleksandrovich Kalashnikov and Aleksandra Frolovna; m. (deceased); one s. two d.; served World War II; inventor of new types of armaments since 1940s, of machine guns RPK, PK, PKT and of automatic machine carbines AK, AKM (total number of machine carbines produced designed by Kalashnikov exceeds 55 million); Chief constructor Head of Constructor's Bureau at Izhmash; Deputy of USSR Supreme Soviet 1950–54, 1966–69, 1970–73, 1974–78, 1979–83, 1984–88; Andrey Pezvozvany Order 1998, Peter the Great Order 2001; USSR State Prize 1949, Lenin Prize 1964, State Prize 1998; Hero of Socialist Labour 1958, 1976. *Publications:* Notes of a Weapon Designer, From a Stranger's Doorstep to the Kremlin's Gates, We Went With You by One Road. *Leisure interests:* hunting, fishing, gardening, reading historical books. *Address:* AO 'Izhmash', 426006 Izhevsk; Sovietskaya ul. 21A, KV 46, 426076 Izhevsk, Russia (Home). *Telephone:* (3412) 49-52-49 (Office); (3412) 52-41-85 (Home). *Fax:* (3412) 78-17-80.

KALASHNIKOV, Sergey Vyacheslavovich, DPsych; Russian politician; b. 3 July 1951, Akmolinsk, Kazakh SSR; m. Natalia Kalashnikova; three c.; ed Leningrad State Univ., Inst. of Psychology, USSR (now Russian) Acad. of Sciences, Acad. of Nat. Econs USSR Council of Ministers, Russian Diplomatic Acad.; Head, Social-Psychological service of the Research Inst., USSR Ministry of Defence Industry, concurrently Chair. Inst. of Advanced Studies, USSR Ministry of Oil and Chemical Industry, Dir Intermanager State Enterprise 1979–91; Chair., Bd Dirs. European-Asian Bank; concurrently Dir-Gen. Asscn of Defence against Unemployment and Poverty, Chair. Cttee on Labour and Social Policy in the State Duma, Deputy of the Duma, Chair. Perm. Cttee on Social Policy, Interparl. Ass. of CIS 1993–98; Minister of Labour and Social Devt 1998–2000; Deputy Sec.-Gen. Union of Russia and Belarus; mem., Int. Acad. of Informatics, Russian Acad. of Science. *Pub-*

lications: over 50 works including 2 monographs and textbook Social Psychology of Management. *Address:* Union of Russia and Belarus, Minsk, Belarus. *E-mail:* zzur@mail.ru (Home).

KALETSKY, Anatole, MA; journalist; b. 1 June 1952, Moscow, Russia; s. of Jacob Kaletsky and Esther Kaletsky; m. Fiona Murphy 1985; two s. one d.; ed Melbourne High School, Westminster City School, King's Coll., Cambridge and Harvard Univ.; Hon. Sr Scholar King's Coll., Cambridge 1973–74; Kennedy Scholar Harvard Univ. 1974–76; financial writer The Economist 1976–79; leader writer Financial Times 1979–81, Washington Corresp. 1981–83, Int. Econs Corresp. 1984–86, Chief New York Bureau 1986–90, Moscow Assignment 1990; Econs Ed. The Times 1990–96, Assoc. Ed. and econ. commentator 1992–; Dir Kaletsky Econ. Consulting 1997–; mem. Advisory Bd UK Know-How Fund for E Europe and fmr Soviet Union 1991–, Royal Econs Soc. 1999–; Specialist Writer of the Year, British Press Awards 1980, 1992, Press Awards Commentator of the Year 1995, What the Papers Say 1996, Financial Journalist of the Year, Wincott Foundation Award 1997. *Publications:* The Costs of Default 1985, In the Shadow of Debt 1992. *Leisure interests:* playing the violin, cinema, family life. *Address:* The Times, 1 Pennington Street, London, E1 9XN, England. *Telephone:* (20) 7782-5000. *Fax:* (20) 7782-5229.

KALICHSTEIN, Joseph, MSc; American/Israeli concert pianist; b. 15 Jan. 1946, Tel-Aviv; s. of Isaac Kalichstein and Mali Kalichstein; m. Rowain (née Schultz) Kalichstein; two c.; ed Juilliard School, New York; New York debut 1967; European debut 1970; appearances with all the world's leading orchestras; recent engagements include Nat. Symphony Orchestra, Washington, DC, Cincinnati Symphony, US tour with Jerusalem Symphony and Lawrence Foster, and return tours to Japan and Scandinavia; mem. Piano Faculty of Juilliard School 1985–; First Prize, Leventritt Int. Competition 1969, Edward Stevermann Memorial Prize 1969. *Leisure interests:* reading, chess. *Address:* c/o Harrison Parrott Ltd., 12 Penzance Place, London, W11 4PA, England (Office).

KALILOMBE, Rt Rev Patrick-Augustine, STL, SSL, PhD; Malawian ecclesiastic and lecturer; b. 28 Aug. 1933, Dedza; s. of Pierre Kalilombe and Helena Mzifei; ed Kasina Seminary, Kachebere Theological Coll., Gregorian Univ., Rome, Graduate Theological Union, Berkeley, USA; trained as White Father, Algeria and Tunisia 1954–58; ordained priest 1958; teacher and Rector, Kachebere Major Seminary 1964–72; Bishop of Lilongwe 1972–78; Fellow and Lecturer in Third World Theologies, Selly Oak, Birmingham, UK 1982–86, Dir Centre for Black and White Christian Partnership Selly Oak 1985–, Sr Lecturer, Third World Theologies 1982–87; Vice-Pres. East African Episcopal Confs 1974–76, Ecumenical Asscn of Third World Theologians 1976–78, Ecumenical Asscn of African Theologians 1985–; Cttee mem. Symposium of Episcopal Confs of Africa and Madagascar 1974–76; mem. Council, Malawi Univ. 1974–76. *Publications:* Christ's Church in Lilongwe 1973, From Outstations to Small Christian Communities 1983. *Address:* Selly Oak Colleges, Bristol Road, Birmingham, B29 61Q (Office); Flat 10, Elizabeth Court, 107 Metchley Lane, Harborne B17 0JH, England (Home). *Telephone:* (121) 472-4231; (121) 426-1738 (Home).

KALINOWSKI, Jarosław; Polish politician; b. 12 April 1962, Wyszków; m.; two d. three s.; ed Warsaw Agricultural Univ., Inst. of Law Sciences of the Polish Acad. of Sciences; owner farm, Jackowo Górne; mem. Union of Rural Youth (ZMW) 1981–89; Admin. Somianka village 1990–97; Deputy to Sejm (Parl.) 1993–; Deputy Prime Minister and Minister of Agric. and Food Economy (later Rural Devt) 1997, 2001–; Chair. Polish Peasant Party (PSL) 1997–; Chair. Caucus 2000–01; Chair. PSL Parl. Club 2000–; Deputy to Local Ass. of the Voivodship of Mazovia 1998–2000. *Leisure interests:* culture and folk music. *Address:* Ministry of Agriculture and Rural Development, ul. Wspólna 30, 00-930 Warsaw, Poland (Office). *Telephone:* (22) 6231000 (Office). *Fax:* (22) 6232750 (Office). *Website:* www.minrol.gov.pl (Office).

KALLAS, Siim; Estonian politician and banker; b. 2 Oct. 1948, Tallinn; s. of Udo Kallas and Rita Kallas; m. Kristi Kallas (née Kartus) 1972; one s. one d.; ed Tartu State Univ.; Chief Specialist Ministry of Finance Estonian SSR 1975–79; Gen. Man. Estonian Savings Banks 1979–86; Deputy Ed. Rahva Haal 1986–89; Chair. Asscn of Estonian Trade Unions 1989–91; Pres. Eesti Pank (Bank of Estonia) 1991–95; Founder and Chair. Estonian Reform Party (Eesti Reformierakond) 1994: elected to Riigikogu (Parl.) 1995–99, also mem. Parl. Nat. Defence Cttee; Minister of Foreign Affairs 1995–96; Minister of Finance 1999–2002; Prime Minister of the Repub. of Estonia 2002–03; currently Visiting Prof. Tartu State Univ. *Leisure interests:* tennis, history, reading, cycling, theatre. *Address:* c/o Prime Minister's Office, State Chancellery, The Stenbock House, 3 Rahukohtu str., Tallinn 15161, Estonia.

KALLIO, Heikki Olavi, LLM; Finnish administrator; b. 9 June 1937, Turku; m. 1st Liisa Toivonen 1961 (divorced 1995); three s. one d.; m. 2nd Anneli Hämäläinen 1997; ed Helsinki Univ.; Chief Admin. Officer Univ. of Turku 1963–71; Admin. Dir Acad. of Finland 1971–72, Exec. Vice-Pres. (Admin.) 1973–; Admin. Dir State Tech. Research Centre 1973. *Leisure interests:* sailing, navigation, safety and security at sea. *Address:* Vilhonvuorenkatu 6, 00500 Helsinki, Finland. *Telephone:* (9) 77488230. *Fax:* (9) 77488379. *E-mail:* heikki.kallio@aka.fi (Office). *Website:* www.aka.fi (Office).

KALLSBERG, Anfinn; Faroe Islands politician; Prime Minister and Minister of Constitutional Affairs, Foreign Affairs and Municipal Affairs 1998–;

mem. People's Party. *Address:* Løgmansskrivstovan, Tinganes, P.O. Box 64, 110 Tórshavn, Faroe Islands (Office). *Telephone:* 351010 (Office). *Fax:* 351015 (Office). *E-mail:* fl@fl.fo (Office). *Website:* www.fl.fo (Office).

KALMAN, Jozef, RSDr; Slovak politician and trade union official; b. 18 April 1951, Pohorelá, Banská Bystrica Dist; s. of Jozef Kalman and Lucia Kalmanová; m. Mária Kalmanová 1972; two d.; official of Metal Workers' Trade Union; Vice-Prime Minister, Govt of Slovak Repub. 1994–98; Vice-Chair. Movt for a Democratic Slovakia (HZDS) 2000–. *Address:* Movement for a Democratic Slovakia, Tomášikova 32A, Bratislava, Slovakia. *Telephone:* (12) 43330144.

KALMS, Sir (Harold) Stanley, Kt; British business executive; b. 21 Nov. 1931; s. of Charles Kalms and Cissie Kalms; m. Pamela Jimack 1954; three s.; ed Christ's Coll., Finchley; began career with Dixons 1948 working in father's photographic store; opened 16 shops; Dixons Photographic floated 1962, Man. Dir 1962–72, Chair. Dixons Group PLC 1972–2001, acquired Currys and PC World, launched Freeserve 1998; Dir British Gas 1987–97; Chair. King's Healthcare NHS Trust 1993–96; Dir Centre for Policy Studies 1991– (Treasurer 1993–98), Business for Sterling 1998–; Treas. Conservative Party 2001–; Visiting Prof. Business School, Univ. of N London 1991; Gov. Nat. Inst. of Econ. and Social Research 1995; Hon. Fellow London Business School 1995; Hon. DLitt (CNAA) 1991, Hon. DUniv (N London) 1994, Hon. DEcon (Richmond) 1996. *Leisure interests:* ballet, communal activities, opera. *Address:* Dixons Group PLC, 29 Farm Street, London, W1X 7RD (Office); Conservative and Unionist Party, 32 Smith Square, London, SW1P 3HH, England. *Telephone:* (20) 7499-3494 (Dixons) (Office); (20) 7222-9000. *Fax:* (20) 7499-3436 (Dixons) (Office); (20) 7222-1135. *Website:* www.conservatives.com (Office).

KALNIETE, Sandra, MA; Latvian diplomatist and politician; b. 22 Dec. 1952, Togur, Tomsk Region, Russia; m. (divorced); ed Latvian Acad. of Arts, Leeds Univ., UK, Geneva Univ., Switzerland; Sec.-Gen. Latvian Artists' Union 1987–88; Sec.-Gen., Deputy Chair. Co-ordinating Council, Latvian Popular Front (LPF) 1988–90; Chief of Protocol Dept, Deputy Foreign Minister, Ministry of Foreign Affairs 1990–93; Amb. to UN, Geneva, Switzerland 1993–97; Amb. to France 1997–2002; Minister of Foreign Affairs Nov. 2002–; Commdr, Order of the Three Stars 1995, Commdr, Légion d'Honneur 2001, Commdr des Palmes académiques 2002; Latvian Cabinet Ministers' Award. *Address:* Ministry of Foreign Affairs, Brivibas blvd. 36, Riga LV 1395, Latvia (Office). *Telephone:* 701-6210 (Office); 701-6201 (Office). *Fax:* 782-8121 (Office). *E-mail:* info@mfa.gov.lv (Office). *Website:* www.mfa.gov.lv/ (Office).

KALOMOH, Tuliameni; Namibian diplomatist; b. 18 Feb. 1948, Onamutai; m.; three c.; ed Indian Acad. of Int. Law and Diplomacy, New Delhi, India; Special Asst to Regional Election Dir, Oshakati; Chief Rep. to W Africa, SW Africa People's Org. (SWAPO) 1976–81, Chief Rep. to France 1981–86, SWAPO Amb. to India 1986–90; Amb. to USA (concurrently High Commr to Canada) 1991–96; Under-Sec. for Political and Econ. Affairs 1990–91, Acting Minister for Foreign Affairs 2000–01, Deputy Minister for Foreign Affairs 2001–; UN Special Rep. for Liberia 1997–2002; UN Asst Sec.-Gen. for Political Affairs 2002–. *Address:* Department of Political Affairs, United Nations, New York, NY 10017, USA (Office). *Telephone:* (212) 963-1234 (Office). *Fax:* (212) 963-4879 (Office). *Website:* www.un.org (Office).

KALORKOTI, Panayiotis; British artist; b. 11 April 1957, Cyprus; one s.; ed Univ. of Newcastle-upon-Tyne, RCA, Koninklijke Akad. voor Kunst en Vormgeving, 's-Hertogenbosch; artist in residence Leeds Playhouse 1985, Cleveland Co. 1992, The Grizedale Soc., Cumbria 1994; Bartlett Fellow in Visual Arts, Univ. of Newcastle-upon-Tyne 1988; commissioned by Imperial War Museum, London 1988, Nat. Garden Festival, Gateshead 1989–90; now part-time tutor and visiting lecturer at various Art Depts.; has exhibited at Hatton Gallery, Newcastle-upon-Tyne 1988–89 (also touring Exhbn), Imperial War Museum 1990, Cleveland Gallery, Middlesbrough 1992 (also touring Exhbn), Gallery K, London 1994 (also touring Exhbn), Gallery in the Forest, Grizedale 1995, Design Works, Gateshead 1997, Shipley Art Gallery, Gateshead 1998–99 (also touring Exhbn); Granada Prize for Northern Young Contemporaries, Whitworth Art Gallery, Manchester 1983. *Publications include:* Kalorkoti 1988, A Retrospective of Etchings and Screenprints 1990, A Retrospective View 1985–91 1992, Etchings and Drawings 1992, Retrospective (Etchings 1983–93) 1994, Reflections of Grizedale (Acrylics, Watercolours, Etchings) 1995, An Exhibition of Acrylics, Watercolours and Etchings 1997, Heads, Faces and Figures 1998. *Leisure interests:* music, films, malt whisky, travel.

KALPAGÉ, Stanley, PhD; Sri Lankan diplomatist and agricultural chemist; b. 30 Aug. 1925, Colombo; s. of late Andrew Christopher Perera Kalpagé and Gimara Agnes Kalpagé (née Perera); m. Chithranganie Herat 1963; two s.; ed Univ. of Ceylon, Colombo, Univs of Leeds and London, UK; held academic posts, Depts. of Agric. and Agricultural Chem., Univ. of Peradeniya 1951–74; mem. Upper House 1965–71; Adviser to Ministry of Educ. 1977–78; Sec. Ministry of Higher Educ. and Chair. Univ. Grants Comm. 1978–89; High Commr in India 1989–91; Perm. Rep. to UN, New York 1991–94; Chair. Sri Lanka's del. to 46th (1991) and 47th (1992) Gen. Ass., Special Political and Decolonization Cttee of 48th Gen. Ass., Open-ended Working Group on Revitalization of Work of Gen. Ass., Special Comm. to Investigate Israeli Practices affecting the Human Rights of the Palestinian People and other Arabs of the Occupied Territories, ad hoc Comm. of Gen. Ass. on Indian Ocean as a Zone of Peace, Sri Lanka's del. to 10th Ministerial Meeting of Non-Aligned

Movt, Accra, Ghana 1991; Rep. of Sri Lanka, UN Gen. Ass. Third Cttee (Social, Humanitarian and Cultural) 1967, 1968, 1969; mem. Jt Select Cttee of Parl. for Revision of Constitution 1968–69; mem. UN Univ. Council 1980–86, Bd of Trustees Asian Inst. of Tech. 1980–89; mem. Bd of Man., Postgraduate Inst. of Archaeology, Postgrad. Inst. of Man. 1986–89; columnist The Sunday Island newspaper; Gen. Pres. Sri Lanka Asscn for the Advancement of Science 1993; Visiting Prof. Bandaranaike Center for Int. Studies, Bandaranaike Int. Diplomatic Training Inst., Ranjan Wijeratne Acad. for Political Educ.; Fellow Nat. Acad. of Sciences of Sri Lanka 1986–, Inst. of Chem., Sri Lanka 1977–; Nuffield Fellowship in Natural Sciences, UK 1961, Int. Cooperation Admin. Fellowship, USA 1961, Int. Visitor Program Fellowship, USA 1985; Hon. DSc (Peradeniya) 1985, (Ruhuna) 1987; Deshamanya Award for outstanding and distinguished service to the Nation 1993. *Publications:* Tropical Soils–Their Classification, Fertility and Management, 1974, 1976, 1983, Soils and Fertilizer Use in Malaysia 1979, Higher Education: Themes and Thoughts 1988, Mission to India: From Confrontation to Co-operation, Asia at the End of the Twentieth Century 2000; numerous scientific articles. *Leisure interests:* public speaking, farming, writing, reading, walking. *Address:* 33/1 Pagoda Road, Nuge-godo, Sri Lanka. *Telephone:* (1) 853-754. *Fax:* (1) 853-754. *E-mail:* skalpage@eureka.lk (Home).

KALPOKAS, Donald; Ni-Vanuatu politician; fmr Minister of Educ. and Judicial Services; Pres. Vanuaaku Pati (VP); Prime Minister of Vanuatu Sept.–Dec. 1991, 1998–99, also Minister of Comprehensive Reform Programme 1998–99, the Public Service, of Foreign Affairs and acting Minister of Agric., Forestry and Fisheries, Deputy Prime Minister and Minister of Educ. 1996–97. *Address:* Vanuaaku Pati, P.O. Box 472, Port Vila, Vanuatu (Office). *Telephone:* 22413 (Office). *Fax:* 22863 (Office).

KALUGIN, Maj.-Gen. Oleg Danilovich; Russian intelligence officer and politician; b. 6 Sept. 1934, Leningrad; m.; two d.; ed Leningrad Univ., Columbia Univ.; on staff of KGB 1958–89; corresp. Soviet Radio, New York 1959–65; Second, then First Sec. Embassy, Washington 1965–70; Chief Dept of External Intelligence Service KGB 1973–80; First Deputy Chief of KGB for City of Leningrad and Leningrad Region 1980–87; returned to Moscow 1987, forced to retire for participation in democratic movt and criticism of KGB 1989, deprived of all decorations and titles by order of Pres. Gorbachev 1990; prosecuted, all charges lifted at end of 1991; USSR People's Deputy 1990–91; gave evidence on activities of KGB in courts and mass media; consultant, Information Service Agency; mem. Fed. Democratic Movt 1995–; Economics, Politics and Law in Russia; has lived in USA since 1996; Man. Dir CIS Dept Cannistraro Asscn 1998–; sentenced in absentia by Russian court to 15 years' imprisonment for treason after disclosing Russian agents in USA 2001–; awarded many decorations. *Publications:* A Look from Lubianka, My 32 Years of Espionage Against the West; numerous articles. *Leisure interests:* hunting, fishing, swimming. *Telephone:* (202) 347-2624 (Office); (301) 431-0093 (Home).

KALULE, Ayub; Ugandan boxer; b. 6 Jan. 1954, Kampala; m.; three d.; amateur boxer 1967–76; lightweight gold medal, Commonwealth Games 1974; inaugural winner of world amateur light-welterweight championship 1974; professional boxer April 1976–86; won Commonwealth middleweight title May 1978 (first Ugandan to win a Commonwealth championship); defended it Sept. 1978; won World Boxing Asscn version of world light-middleweight title from Masashi Kudo, Akita, Japan Oct. 1979; retained title v. Steve Gregory Dec. 1979, Emiliano Villa April 1980, Marijan Benes June 1980 and Bushy Bester Sept. 1980; first Ugandan to win a world title; won all 35 fights before losing to Sugar Ray Leonard (q.v.) 1981; career record: 46 wins, 4 defeats; now lives in Denmark. *Leisure interest:* table tennis. *Address:* c/o Palle, Skjulet, Bagsvaert 12, Copenhagen 2880, Denmark.

KALYAGIN, Aleksander Aleksandrovich; Russian actor; b. 25 May 1942, Malmysh, Kirov Region; m. Glushenko Yevgeniya Konstantinovna; one s. one d.; ed Shchukin Higher School of Theatre Art; actor Taganka Theatre and Yermolova Theatre in Moscow 1966–71; Moscow Art Theatre 1971–93; master classes in Russia and in Europe; Chair. Union of Theatre Workers of Russia 1996–; People's Artist of Russia 1983, State Prize 1981, 1983. *Roles in productions:* Dark Lady of the Sonnets by G. B. Shaw, Don Quixote by A. Morfov after Cervantes, Old New Year by M. Roshchin, Notes of the Lunatic and Marriage by Gogol, Galileo by Brecht, Tartuffe by Molière, several plays by A. Gelman, M. Shatrov, A. Galin and other contemporary dramatists; in cinema since 1967. *Films include:* Untimely Man 1973, One's Own Among Strangers 1974, Slave of Love 1976, Interrogation 1979, Aesop 1982, Prokhindiada or Run on the Spot 1985, How Are You Doing, Crucians? 1992; f. and artistic Dir Et Cetera Theatre in Moscow 1992–. *Leisure interests:* collecting art books, museums. *Address:* Union of Theatre Workers, Strastnoy blvd 10, 103031 Moscow, (Office); 1905 Goda str., 3 Apt 91, 123100 Moscow, Russia (Home). *Telephone:* (095) 209-28-46 (Office); (095) 205-26-54 (Home). *Fax:* (095) 230-22-58 (Office). *E-mail:* stdrf@rc.ru.

KALYUZHNII, Viktor Ivanovich; Russian politician; b. 18 April 1947, Birsk, Bashkiria; ed Ufa Inst. of Oil; Mgr, then Deputy Head Tomskneft Co. 1970–78, First Deputy Dir.-Gen. 1993–97; Chief Engineer Dept of Oil and Gas Vasyuganneft Co., Strezhevoy; Sec. CP Cttee Strezhevoyneft Co. 1980–84, later Deputy Dir; Second Sec. Strezhevoy Town CP Exec. Cttee 1984–86; Deputy Dir USSR Ministry of Oil Industry 1986; Chief Engineer, then Dir Priobneft Co., Nizhevartovsk Tumen 1986–90; Dir Vietsovpetro, Vu Tan, Viet Nam 1990–93; First Vice-Pres. Vostochnaya Neftyanaya Komapniya, Tomsk

1997–98; First Deputy Minister of Fuel and Power Industry 1998–99, Minister 1999–2000; Special Rep. of Pres. for Caspian Sea with rank of Deputy Minister of Foreign Affairs 2000–. *Address:* Ministry of Foreign Affairs, Sadovaya-Sennaya 52/54, Moscow, Russia (Office). *Telephone:* (095) 244-17-07 (Office).

KAMALI, Norma; American fashion designer; b. 27 June 1945, New York; d. of Sam Arraez and Estelle Galib; m. M. H. Kamali (divorced); ind. fashion designer, New York 1965–; opened first shop in East 53rd Street 1968, moving to Madison Avenue 1974; retitled business OMO (On My Own) and moved to 56th Street 1978; second boutique opened Spring Street, New York 1986; OMO Home opened 1988; collaboration with Bloomingdale's on production of exclusive collections 1988–; OMO Tokyo opened 1990; awards include Coty American Fashion Critics' Winnie Award 1981, 1982, Outstanding Women's Fashion Designer of the Year Award, Council of Fashion Designers of America 1982, American Success Award 1989, Pencil Award 1999, Fashion Outreach Style Award 1999. *Address:* 11 W 56th Street, New York, NY 10019, USA.

KAMANDA WA KAMANDA, LenD; Democratic Republic of the Congo politician, administrator and lawyer; b. 10 Dec. 1940, Kikwit; s. of Raphaël Kamanda and Germaine Kukikidika; two s. one d.; ed Coll. St Ignace de Kiniati, Coll. Notre Dame de Mbansa Boma, Univ. Lovanium, Kinshasa; Lawyer, Court of Appeal 1964; Legal Adviser, Féd. congolaise des travailleurs 1964–65; Prof. Inst. Nat. d'Etudes Politiques 1965–66; Legal Adviser to Presidency of Repub. 1965–66, Sec.-Gen. 1966–67; Prin. Adviser with responsibility for legal, admin., political and diplomatic affairs to Presidency of Repub.; Dir de Cabinet to Sec.-Gen. of Org. of African Unity 1967–72, Asst Sec.-Gen. 1972–78; Perm. Rep. to UN 1979–82; State Commr for Foreign Affairs and Int. Co-operation 1982–83, for Justice 1983–84; Deputy Sec.-Gen. MPR 1987; f. Mouvement populaire de la revolution (MPR) 1997; Assoc. mem. Office Nat. de la Recherche Scientifique et du Développement; Vice-Pres. Zairian section, Soc. Africaine de la Culture; del. to several int. confs; Deputy Prime Minister 1994–97, in charge of Institutional Reforms, Justice and Keeper of the Seals 1994–96, of Interior 1996–97. *Publications:* Essai-critique du système de la criminalité d'emprunt 1964, Négritude face au devenir de l'Afrique 1967, L'université aujourd'hui en Afrique 1969, L'intégration juridique et le développement harmonieux des nations africaines 1969, L'incidence de la culture audio-visuelle sur le phénomène du pouvoir 1970, Les organisations africaines Vol. I: L'OUA ou la croisade de l'unité africaine 1970, Vol. II: 1970, Le défi africain–une puissance économique qui s'ignore 1976, L'enracinement—culture et progrès 1976. *Address:* Mouvement populaire de la revolution, Kinshasa, Democratic Republic of the Congo.

KAMARCK, Andrew Martin, BS, MA, PhD; American international bank official; b. 10 Nov. 1914, Newton Falls, New York; s. of Martin Kamarck and Frances Earl; m. Margaret Goldenweiser Burgess 1941; one s. two d.; ed Harvard Univ.; Int. Section, Fed. Reserve Bd 1939–40; US Treasury 1940–42; US Army 1942–44; Allied Control Comm., Italy 1943–44; Allied Control Council, Germany 1945; Office of Int. Finance, US Treasury, Chief of Nat. Advisory Council on Int. Monetary and Financial Problems (NAC) Div., Financial Policy Cttee preparing Marshall Plan 1945–48; US Treasury Rep., Rome 1948–50; Chief of Africa section, Econ. Dept, World Bank 1950–52; Econ. Adviser, Dept of Operations, Europe, Africa and Australasia, World Bank, Chief of Econ. Missions to 14 countries, 1952–64; Dir Econ. Dept, World Bank 1965–71; Dir Econ. Devt Inst. 1972–77, Sr Fellow 1977–78; mem. American Econ. Asscn, Council on Foreign Relations; Dir African Studies Asscn 1961–64; Visiting Fellow, Harvard Inst. Int. Devt 1977–86; Regents Prof., Univ. of Calif. 1964–65; mem. Council, Soc. for Int. Devt 1967–70, 1973–76; Pres. Housing Assistance Corpn of Cape Cod 1980–83; US War Dept Certificate of Merit 1945. *Publications:* The Economics of African Development 1967, Capital Movements and Economic Development (co-author) 1967, The Tropics and Economic Development 1976, La Politica Finanziaria degli Alleati in Italia 1977, Economics and the Real World 1983, Health, Nutrition and Economic Crises (co-author) 1988, The Role of the Economist in Government (co-author) 1989, The Bretton Woods-GATT System (co-author) 1995, Economics for the Twenty-First Century 2001, Economics as a Social Science 2002. *Leisure interests:* walking, music. *Address:* 118 Pine Ridge Road, Brewster, MA 02631, USA. *Telephone:* (508) 385-8221. *E-mail:* rdg118pine@aol.com (Home).

KAMBA, Walter Joseph, BA, LLB, LLM; Zimbabwean administrator and professor; b. 6 Sept. 1931, Marondera; s. of Joseph Mafara and Hilda Kamba; m. Angeline Saziso Dube 1960; three s. (one deceased); ed Univ. of Cape Town, Yale Law School; Attorney High Court of Rhodesia (now Zimbabwe) 1963–66; Research Fellow Inst. of Advanced Legal Studies, London Univ. 1967–68; Lecturer then Sr Lecturer in Comparative Law and Jurisprudence, Univ. of Dundee 1969–80, Dean Faculty of Law 1977–80; Legal Adviser ZANU (PF) 1977–80; Prof of Law, Univ. of Zimbabwe 1980–, Vice-Prin. 1980–81, Vice-Chancellor 1981–91; Vice-Chair. Zimbabwe Broadcasting Corpn 1980–87, Chair. 1987; Inaugural UNESCO Africa Prof., Univ. of Utrecht 1992–96; Founding Dean and UNESCO Prof. of Human Rights, Democracy and Law, Univ. of Namibia 1994–2000, legal adviser, Prof. 1995–; Trustee Zimbabwe Mass Media Trust 1981–, Conservation Trust of Zimbabwe 1981–87, Zimbabwe Cambridge Trust 1987–; mem. Bd Gov.'s Rauche House Coll. Harare 1980–; mem. Working Party on Future Policy of Asscn of Commonwealth Univs 1981; mem. Council, Exec. Cttee and Budget Review Cttee Asscn of Commonwealth Univs 1981–83; mem. Council UN Univ. for Peace, Costa Rica 1982–86, Univ. of Zambia 1982–86, Commonwealth Standing Cttee on

Student Affairs 1982–88, UN Univ., Tokyo 1983–89, Zimbabwe Nat. Comm. for UNESCO 1987–, Bd of Govs Zimbabwe Inst. of Devt Studies 1982–, Chair. 1986–, Exec. Bd Asscn African Univs 1984–; Chair. Electoral Supervisory Comm. 1984, Kingston's (Booksellers and Distributors) 1984–, Asscn of Eastern and Southern African Univs 1984–87; Chair. Council UN Univ., Tokyo 1985–87; Vice-Pres. Int. Asscn of Univs 1985–90, Pres. 1990–; Trustee, African-American Inst. (New York) 1985–; mem. Int. Bd, United World Colls 1985–87, Bd of Govs, Int. Devt Research Centre, Canada 1986–, Nat. Cttee Law and Population Studies Project 1986–, Swaziland Univ. Planning Comm. 1986, Bd, Commonwealth of Learning 1988, Int. Cttee for Study of Educ. Exchange 1988–; Patron, Commonwealth Legal Education Asscn 1986–; Hon. LLD (Dundee) 1982, (Natal) 1995, (Zimbabwe) 1998; Officer, Ordre des palmes académiques. *Publications:* articles in law journals. *Leisure interest:* tennis. *Address:* International Association of Universities, 1 rue Miollis, 75732 Paris cedex 15, France (Office); Faculty of Law, University of Namibia, Private Bag 13301, 340 Mandume Ndemufayo Avenue, Pioneerspark, Windhoek, Namibia.

KAMEI, Masao; Japanese business executive; b. 20 April 1916, Kobe City, Hyogo Pref.; s. of Einosuke Kamei and Sei Kamei; m. Hanae Kamei; two s. one d.; ed Tokyo Univ.; Dir Sumitomo Electric Industries Ltd 1964–66, Man. Dir 1966–69, Sr Man. Dir 1969–71, Exec. Vice-Pres. 1971–73, Pres. 1973–82, Chair. 1982–91, Sr Adviser 1991–; Exec. Dir Fed. of Econ. Orgs (Keidanren) 1973–91, Kansai Econs Fed. 1974–; Vice-Pres. Japan Fed. of Employers' Asscns (Nikkeiren) 1977–91; Commr Local Govt System Investigation Council 1977–88, Employment Council 1986–, Advisory Council on Election System 1989–91; Chair. Cttee for the Promotion of Political Reform 1992–; Chair. Japanese Nat. Railways Reform Comm. 1983–87; Chair. Assets Disposal Council of Japan Nat. Railways Settlement Corpn 1991–; Vice-Chair. Japan Productivity Center 1987–92, Chair. 1992–; Chair. Kansai Int. Airport Co. Ltd, Osaka, Japan 1988–95; Chair. Housing and Bldg Land Council 1988–, New Media Devt Asscn 1989–, Japan Housing Asscn 1991–; Blue Ribbon Medal 1976, Order of the Sacred Treasure (First Class) 1986. *Leisure interests:* paintings, golf. *Address:* 34-11, Kyodo 1-chome, Setagaya-ku, Tokyo 156, Japan.

KAMEI, Shizuka; Japanese politician; Parl. Vice-Minister of Transport, Minister 1994–95, of Construction 1996; mem. House of Reps for Hiroshima; Chair. LDP Nat. Org. Cttee and Acting Chair. LDP Policy Research Council. *Address:* c/o Liberal-Democratic Party, 1-11-23, Nagata-cho, Chiyoda-ku, Tokyo 100, Japan.

KAMEL AHMED, Kamal El-Din, MB, CH.B., D.M.SC., MD; Egyptian pathologist; b. 20 Jan. 1927, Mehella El-Kobra; m. Naguia Abd-El Khalek Safwat 1954; one s.; ed medical schools of Cairo and Ain Shams Univs. and Max Planck Inst., Fed. Repub. of Germany; WHO mission, Iran; Prof. and Head Dept of Pathology, Mansoura Medical School 1969–80, Dean of Medical School 1971–80; Vice-Pres. Mansoura Univ. 1980–82, Pres. 1983–87; Prof. Emer. Mansoura Medical School 1987–; Distinguished Service Medal 1987, Mansoura Univ. Award 1988. *Publications:* A Study of Carcinoma of the Urinary Bladder 1958, A New Application of Van Gieson Stain in the Diagnosis of Tumours of the Nervous System 1962, A Scheme for the Histological Diagnosis of Tumours of the Nervous System during Operations 1965, Modern Pathology 1989. *Leisure interest:* member of Gezira Sporting Club, Cairo. *Address:* 33 Ramsis Street, Apartment 144, Cairo, Egypt. *Telephone:* 5741307.

KAMEN, Dean; American inventor, physicist and engineer; ed Worcester Polytechnic Inst., Mich.; while undergrad. invented wearable infusion pump; f. AutoSyringe Inc. 1976; developed first portable pump to dispense insulin 1978; est. Science Enrichment Encounters (SEE) museum 1985; f. FIRST (For Inspiration and Recognition of Science and Tech.) 1989; developed portable dialysis machine 1993; created the Segway Human Transporter (motorized, low-energy scooter) 2001; mem. Nat. Acad. of Eng; Pres. and owner DEKA Research and Devt Corpn 1992–; holds more than 100 US patents; Hon. DSc (Rensselaer Polytechnic Inst.), (Worcester Polytechnic Inst.); Engineer of the Year (Design News Magazine) 1994, Hoover Medal 1995, NH Business Leader of the Year 1996, Nat. Medal of Tech. 2000. *Address:* DEKA Research and Development Corporation, Technology Center, 340 Commercial Street, Manchester, NH 03101, USA (Office). *Telephone:* (603) 669-5139 (Office). *Fax:* (603) 624-0573 (Office). *Website:* www.dekaresearch.com (Office).

KAMINSKI, Janusz, BA; Polish cinematographer and film director; b. 27 June 1959, Ziembice; m. Holly Hunter (q.v.) 1995; ed Columbia Coll., Chicago, American Film Inst., Washington, DC; mem. American Soc. of Cinematographers; Acad. Award Best Cinematographer for Schindler's List 1994. *Films include:* All the Love in the World 1990, Trouble Bound 1993, Schindler's List 1993, Jerry Maguire 1996, Amistad 1997, The Lost World: Jurassic Park 1997, Saving Private Ryan 1998, AI: Artificial Intelligence 2001; *Film directed:* Lost Souls 2000. *Address:* 1223 Wilshire Boulevard, #645 Santa Monica, CA 90403, USA (Office).

KAMIŃSKI, Gen. Józef; Polish army officer and politician; b. 3 March 1919, Brzęzany, Tarnopol Dist; s. of Antoni and Tekla (née Szpakowska) Kamińska; m. Krystyna Kamińska (née Podlaszewska); one s. one d.; ed Infantry Training Centre, Rembertów; during Second World War in USSR, served in Red Army unit in the Far East 1940–43 in Polish Army 1943–; soldier of Tadeusz Kościuszko First Infantry Div. Platoon Commdr, subsequently Co. and Battalion Commdr; Deputy C-in-C, 34th Infantry Regt, 8th Infantry Div.;

took part in fighting against armed underground Ukrainian org. in Bieszczady Mountains 1946; Commdr of Regt then of Infantry Div. and Armoured Div.; Brig.-Gen. 1954; Armoured Corps Commdr 1954–64; Commdr, Pomeranian Mil. Dist 1964–71, Silesian Mil. Dist 1971–76; rank of Gen. 1974; Deputy Chief of Staff of United Armed Forces of Warsaw Treaty, then Commdt of Karol Świerczewski Gen. Staff Acad. of Polish Army, Warsaw; mem. Union of Fighters for Freedom and Democracy (ZBoWiD), fmr mem. ZBoWiD Voivodship Bd, Bydgoszcz, mem. ZBoWiD Chief Council, Pres. ZBoWiD Gen. Bd; Pres. Union of Veterans of Polish Repub. and Fmr. Political Prisoners 1990–99, Hon. Pres. 1999–; Order of Banner of Labour (1st and 2nd Class), Grunwald Cross (3rd Class), Order Polonia Restituta (4th and 5th Class), Order of Lenin, Order of Friendship among the Nations, Virtuti Militari Cross (5th Class). *Leisure interest:* military history. *Address:* ul. Szarkowników 12, 04-410 Warsaw, Poland. *Telephone:* (2) 6119680 (Office).

KAMIŃSKI, Marek; Polish explorer; b. 24 March 1964, Gdańsk; s. of Zdzisław Kamiński and Maria Kamińska; Founder Game San SA and Marek Kamiński Foundation; mem. The Explorers Club 1996–; Hon. mem. Polar Research Cttee Polish Acad. of Sciences; Finalist World Young Business Achiever 1994; Man of the Year 1995, Życie Warszawy daily; Kt's Cross Order of Polonia Restituta, Gold Medal for Outstanding Achievments in Sport, Chopin Award. *Expeditions to:* Mexico, Guatemala, crossing of Spitsbergen, crossing of Greenland (twice); attempted solo crossing of Antarctica; first man who reached alone both North and South Poles in the same year 1995; climbed Mount Vinson (Antarctica) 1998; crossed Gibson Desert 1999; sailed yacht across the Atlantic (twice); participated in expedition to sources of the Amazon 2000 and North Pole expedition 2001, 2002. *Publication:* Not only a Pole 1996, My Poles. Diaries from Expeditions 1990–98 1998 (Artus Award for the Best Book of the Year), My Expeditions 2001. *Leisure interests:* travelling to the coldest places in the world, sailing, philosophy. *Address:* ul. Dickmana 14/15, 80-339 Gdańsk, Poland. *Telephone:* (58) 5544522. *Fax:* (58) 5523315. *E-mail:* mkaminski@gamasan.pl (Office). *Website:* www.kaminski.pl (Home).

KAMLANG-EK, Gen. Arthit; Thai politician; b. Bangkok; ed Chulachomklao Royal Mil. Acad.; Supreme Commdr of the Armed Forces and C-in-C of the Army 1983–86; Senator 1977, 1986; Thai People's Party MP for Loei 1988; Deputy Prime Minister 1990–91. *Address:* c/o Government House, Nakhom Pathan Road, Bangkok 10300, Thailand.

KAMOUGUÉ, Lt-Col Wadal Abdelkader; Chadian politician and army officer; b. 20 May 1939, Bitam, Gabon; s. of Terkam Kamougue and Jeannette Kinel; m. 1st Eve-Marie Baba 1967; m. 2nd Martine Rondoh 1983; nine c.; Minister of Foreign Affairs and Co-operation, mem. of Supreme Mil. Council in Govt of Brig.-Gen. Félix Malloum 1975–78; Commdr of Gendarmerie 1978–79; mem. Provisional State Council following Kano peace agreement March–May 1979, in charge of Agric. and Animal Resources; Leader of Front Uni du Sud (later Forces Armées Tchadiennes, Forces Unifiées) 1979; Vice-Pres. of Transitional Gov. of Nat. Unity (GUNT) 1979–82; Pres. of State Council 1980–82; fled to Cameroon, then Gabon Sept.–Oct. 1982, after defeat by forces of FAN; Leader Mouvement révolutionnaire du peuple (MRP), Brazzaville, Congo 1983–87; returned to N'Djamena Feb. 1987; Minister of Agric. 1987–89, of Justice 1989–90, of Trade and Industry 1990; mem. Conseil Provisoire de la République (CPR) 1991–92; Pres. Union pour le renouveau et la démocratie (URD) 1992–; Minister of Civil Service and Labour 1993–94; Pres. Assemblée Nat. (Parl.) 1997; Général de Brigade 1992–; Commdr Ordre nat. avec Palme d'Or Chevalier du Mérite Civique, Commdr Ordre nat. du Tchad, Chevalier Ordre nat. du Mérite (France), Commdr Ordre nat. Centrafricain (Central African Repub.), Commdr Ordre Coréen (Repub. of Korea). *Leisure interests:* volleyball, basketball, reading, table tennis, athletics. *Address:* Union pour le renouveau et la démocratie, B.P. 92, N'Djamena, Chad. *Telephone:* 51-44-23. *Fax:* 51-41-87.

KAMPELMAN, Max M., JD, PhD; American diplomatist; b. 7 Nov. 1920, New York; s. of Joseph Kampelmacher and Eva Gottlieb; m. Marjorie Buetow 1948; two s. three d.; ed New York and Minnesota Univs; Partner, Fried, Frank Harris, Shriver and Kampelman, Washington 1956–85, Fried, Frank Harris, Shriver and Jacobson 1989–91, Counselor 1991–; Visiting Prof. Political Science, Claremont Coll., Calif. 1963; Sr Adviser, US Del. to the UN 1966–67; Chair. Emer., Greater Washington Telecommunications Asscn (WETA-TV); Co-Chair., US Del. to observe the Elections in El Salvador 1984; Bd of Dirs, US Inst. of Peace 1985–86; Amb., Head of US Del. to the Negotiations on Nuclear and Space Arms 1985–89; Counselor Dept of State 1987–89; Amb. and Chair. US Del. to the Conf. on Security and Co-operation in Europe (CSCE), Madrid 1980–83; Amb., Head US del. to Geneva Meeting on Ethnic Minorities of the CSCE 1991; Amb., Head US del. to Moscow Meeting of Conf. on Human Dimension of the CSCE 1991; Legis. Counsel to Senator H. H. Humphrey 1949–55; Bd of Trustees Woodrow Wilson Int. Center for Scholars 1979–90 (Chair. 1979–81); Chair. Freedom House 1983–85, 1989–; Kt Commdr's Cross of the Order of Merit (FRG) 1984; Dr hc (Hebrew Univ. of Jerusalem) 1982, (Hebrew Union Coll.) 1984, (Georgetown Univ.) 1984, (Bates Coll.) 1986, (Minn.) 1987, (Bar Ilan) 1987, (Adelphi Univ.) 1988, (Yeshiva Univ.) 1990, (Ben Gurion Univ.) 1992, (Florida Int. Univ.) 1993, (Brandeis Univ.) 1993; Hon. DIur (Jewish Theological Seminary of NY) 1988, (NY Univ.) 1988; The Anatoly Scharansky Award 1981; Vanderbilt Gold Medal, New York Univ. Law Center 1982; Human Rights Award, American Fed. of Teachers 1983; Masaryk Award, Czechoslovak Nat. Council of America 1983; Golden Plate Award, American Acad. of Achievement 1984;

Henry M. Jackson Award (JINSA) 1987; Sec. of State's Distinguished Service Award 1988; Trainar Award for Distinction in the Conduct of Diplomacy, Georgetown Univ. 1988 Pres.'s Citizens' Medal 1989. *Publications:* The Communist Party vs. the C.I.O.: A Study in Power Politics 1957, Three Years at the East-West Divide 1983; Co-Author: The Strategy of Deception 1963; contrib. to Congress Against the President 1976, Entering New Worlds: The Memoirs of a Private Man in Public Life 1991. *Address:* Fried, Frank Harris, Shriver and Jacobson, Suite 800, 1001 Pennsylvania Avenue, NW, Washington, DC 20004 (Office); 3154 Highland Place, NW, Washington, DC 20008, USA (Home). *Fax:* (202) 639-7008.

KAMPOURIS, Emmanuel Andrew, MA; Greek business executive; b. 14 Dec. 1934, Alexandria, Egypt; s. of Andrew G. Kampouris and Euridice A. Caralli; m. Myrto Stellatos 1959 (deceased); two s.; ed King's School, Bruton, UK, Oxford Univ. and N Staffs. Coll. of Tech.; Plant Man. and Dir KEREM, Athens 1962–64; Dir HELLENIT, Athens 1962–65; Vice-Pres. and Group Exec. (Int. and Export), American Standard Inc., Piscataway, NJ 1979–84, Sr Vice-Pres. (Bldg Products) 1984–89; Pres. and CEO American Standard Inc. New York 1989–99, Chair. 1993–; mem. Bd of Dirs Click Commerce Inc. *Leisure interests:* golf, tennis, classical music. *Address:* American Standard Inc., 1 Centennial Avenue, Piscataway, NJ 08854, USA; Click Commerce Inc., 200 East Randolph Drive, Suite 4900, Chicago, IL 60601 (Office).

KAMU, Okko; Finnish conductor and violinist; b. 7 March 1946, Helsinki; m. Susanne Kamu 1987; three s. three d.; ed Sibelius Acad.; leader, Suhonen Quartet 1964; began professional career with Helsinki Philharmonic Orchestra 1965; subsequently appointed leader, Finnish Nat. Opera Orchestra 1966–69, Third Conductor 1967; guest conductor, Swedish Royal Opera, Stockholm 1969; Chief Conductor, Finnish Radio Symphony Orchestra 1971–77; Music Dir Oslo Philharmonic 1975–79, Helsinki Philharmonic 1981–89; Prin. Conductor, Netherlands Radio Symphony 1983–86; Prin. Guest Conductor, City of Birmingham Symphony Orchestra 1985–88; Prin. Conductor, Sjaelland Symphony Orchestra, Copenhagen 1988–94; Music Dir Stockholm Sinfonietta 1989–93; Prin. Conductor Helsingborg Symphony Orchestra 1991–2000; First Guest Conductor, Singapore Symphony Orchestra 1995–2001; Music Dir Finnish Nat. Opera, Helsinki 1996–2000; Prin. Guest Conductor Lausanne Chamber Orchestra 1999–2002; conducted world premières of Sallinen's operas The Red Line and The King Goes Forth to France; numerous engagements with orchestras and opera houses worldwide; mem. Royal Swedish Acad. of Music 1996; First Prize, First Int. Karajan Conductor Competition, Berlin 1969. *Leisure interests:* sailing, fishing, underwater photography, diving, golf, gastronomy, family life. *Address:* Villa Arcadia, Calle Mozart 7, Rancho Domingo, 29639 Benalmedina Pueblo, Spain.

KAMYNIN, Mikhail Leonidovich; Russian diplomatist; b. 13 Aug. 1956, Moscow; m.; one d. one s.; ed Moscow Inst. of Int. Relations, Diplomatic Acad. of Ministry of Foreign Affairs; various positions Embassy in Mexico 1978–82, 1987–91; Press Sec. Ministry of Foreign Affairs (MFA) 1991–92; Counsellor Embassy in Spain 1992–97; Asst Dir of Press and Information, MFA 1997–99; Minister Counsellor Embassy in Cuba 1999–2002; Asst Dir European Affairs, MFA 2002; Amb. to Spain 2002–; del. to numerous int. meetings; mem. Russian Union of Journalists. *Address:* Russian Embassy, Velázquez 155, Madrid, Spain (Office). *Telephone:* (91) 4115625 (Office). *Fax:* (91) 5629712 (Office). *E-mail:* embrues@infonegocio.com (Office).

KAN, Naoto; Japanese politician; fmr patent attorney; Minister of Health and Welfare Jan.–Nov. 1996; mem. House of Reps; mem. New Party Sakigake (NPS), now Sakigake; Founder mem. Democratic Party of Japan 1998, Pres. 1998–99, 2002–, Sec.-Gen. 2000–02. *Address:* Headquarters, Democratic Party of Japan, 1-11-1 Nagata-cho, Chiyoda-ku, Tokyo 100-0014, Japan. *Telephone:* (3) 3595-7312 (Office); (3) 3595-9981 (Office). *Fax:* (3) 3595-9922 (Office). *E-mail:* dpjenews@dpj.or.jp (Office). *Website:* www.dpj.or.jp (Office).

KAN, Yuet Wai, MD, DSc, FRCP, FRS; American physician and investigator; b. 11 June 1936, Hong Kong; s. of Tong Po Kan and Lai Wai Li; m. Alvera Lorraine Limauro 1964; two d.; ed Wah Yan Coll., Hong Kong and Univ. of Hong Kong Medical School; Asst Prof. of Pediatrics, Harvard Medical School, USA 1970–72; Assoc. Prof., Dept of Medicine, Univ. of Calif. San Francisco 1972–77, Prof. of Lab. Medicine, Medicine 1977–, Louis K. Diamond Prof. of Hematology 1991–, Investigator, Howard Hughes Medical Inst. 1976–; Head Div. of Molecular Medicine and Diagnostics 1989–; Dir and Hon. Prof. Inst. of Molecular Biology, Univ. of Hong Kong 1994–; mem. Research Grants Council, Hong Kong 1990–94; mem. NIH Blood Diseases and Resources Advisory Cttee 1985–89, Nat. Inst. of Digestive and Kidney Disease Advisory Council, NIH 1991–95; mem. Scientific Advisory Bd, St Jude's Children's Hosp. 1994–97, Qiu Shi Science and Technologies Foundation, Hong Kong 1994–, Nat. Heart, Lung & Blood Inst. 1995–96, Thalassemia Int. Fed. 1995–; Trustee Croucher Foundation 1992–, Chair. 1997–; mem. NAS, Academia Sinica; Assoc. Fellow, Third World Acad. of Sciences; Foreign mem. Chinese Acad. of Sciences; Damashek Award, American Soc. of Hematology 1979, Stratton Lecture Award, Int. Soc. of Hematology 1980, George Thorn Award, Howard Hughes Medical Inst. 1980, Gairdner Foundation Int. Award 1984, Allan Award, American Soc. of Human Genetics 1984, Lita Annenberg Hazen Award for Excellence in Clinical Research 1984, Waterford Award in Biomedical Sciences 1987, NIH Merit Award 1987, American Coll. of Physicians Award 1988, Sanremo Int. Award for Genetic Research 1989, Warren Alpert Foundation Prize 1989, Albert Lasker Clinical Medical Research

Award 1991, Christopher Columbus Discovery Award in Biomedical Research 1992, City of Medicine Award 1992, Cotlove Award, Acad. of Clinical Lab. Physicians and Scientists 1993, Merit Award, Fed. of Chinese Canadians Educ. Foundation 1994, Helmut Horten Research Award 1995. *Publications:* more than 240 articles and chapters in many scientific journals and books. *Address:* Room U-432, University of California, 533 Parnassus Avenue, San Francisco, CA 94143-0793, USA. *Telephone:* (415) 476-5841. *Fax:* (415) 476-2956 (Office). *E-mail:* kanyuet@labmed2.ucsf.edu.

KANAAN, Taher Hamdi, PhD; Jordanian politician, economist and civil servant; b. 1 March 1935, Nablus, Palestine; s. of Hamdi and Najiah (née Quttainah) Kanaan; m. Ilham Kahwaji 1960; three s.; ed American Univ. of Beirut, Trinity Coll., Cambridge; Econ. Adviser, Ministry of Planning, Iraq 1964–65; Dir of Programmes at Arab Fund for Econ. and Social Devt, Kuwait 1973–76; Consultant in Industrial Devt, Ministry of Planning, Morocco 1977–78; Chief External Financing and Devt, UNCTAD, Geneva 1979–83; Dir and Econ. Adviser Arab Fund 1983–85; Minister of Occupied Territories Affairs 1985, of Planning 1986–89; Gen. Man. Industrial Devt 1989–92; World Bank Resident Rep. in Ghana 1992–94; Hon. Prof. Univ. of Warwick 1994; World Bank Chief Thought Forum, Bd of Higher Educ., Jordan, Bd of Dirs., Arab Soc. for and Chief Economist 1996–97; T. H. Lee Prof. of World Affairs and Prof. of Econs Cornell Univ., Ithaca, NY 1997. *Leisure interest:* swimming, music, history, philosophy and watching TV. *Address:* Industrial Development Bank, P.O. Box 1982, Amman, Jordan.

KANANIN, Roman Grigorevich; Russian architect; b. 19 June 1935, Moscow; s. of Grigoriy Kananin and Maria Kananin; m. 1959; one d.; ed Moscow Architectural Inst.; Corresp. mem. Russian Acad. of Architecture and Bldg Sciences 2001–; Lenin Prize 1984, Honoured Architect of Russia 1993, Honoured Builder of Moscow 1999. *Works include:* Patrice Lumumba Univ. (now Univ. of People's Friendship), Moscow (with others) 1969–73, residential blocks on Lenin Prospekt, Moscow 1965–70, multi-storey brick residential complex, Noviye Cheremushky 1973–84, memorial complex to war veterans in Novorossiysk 1982, various monuments in Moscow and Magnitogorsk, including monument to Gerzen and Ogarev, Vorobyevy Hils, Moscow, Palace of Youth, Moscow 1978, IRIS Pulman Hotel and apartments, Moscow 1991, Parus Business Centre, Tverskaya-Yamskaya St, Moscow 1994, exclusive multi-storey residential bldgs, Krasnoproletarskaya str., vl. 7 1999, Dolgorukovskaya str., vl. 24–30 2001, B. Gruzinskaya str., vl. 37 2001; Head of Atelier No. 3. of 'Mosproyekt–1' 1972–. *Leisure interests:* sport, travelling. *Address:* Joint-Stock Company Mosproyekt, 13/14, 1-st Brestkaya str., GSP, 125190 Moscow, Russia. *Telephone:* (095) 209-61-22, 250-46-99. *Fax:* (095) 209-50-02.

KANAWA, Dame Kiri (see Te Kanawa, Dame Kiri).

KANBUR, Ravi, MA, DPhil; British economist; b. 28 Aug. 1954, Dharwar, India; s. of Prof. M. G. Kanbur and M. M. Kanbur; m. Margaret S. Grieco 1979; ed King Edward VII Camp Hill School, Birmingham, Gonville & Caius Coll. Cambridge and Merton and Worcester Colls. Oxford; Prize Fellow, Nuffield Coll. Oxford 1978–79; Fellow in Econs Clare Coll. Cambridge 1979–83; Prof. of Econs Univ. of Essex 1983–85; Visiting Prof. Princeton Univ. 1985–87; Prof. of Econs and Dir Devt Econs Research Centre, Univ. of Warwick 1987–89; Sr Adviser and Ed. World Bank Economic Review and World Bank Research Observer, IBRD, Washington, DC 1989–92; World Bank Resident Rep. in Ghana 1992–94; Hon. Prof. Univ. of Warwick 1994; World Bank Chief Economist for Africa 1994–96; World Bank Prin. Adviser to Sr Vice-Pres. and Chief Economist 1996–97; T. H. Lee Prof. of World Affairs and Prof. of Econs Cornell Univ., Ithaca, NY 1997–; Hon. Prof. (Warwick) 1994; American Agricultural Econs Asscn Research Award (jtly with L. Haddad) 1991. *Publications:* articles in learned journals. *Leisure interest:* watching TV. *Address:* 309 Warren Hall, Cornell University, Ithaca, NY 14853, USA. *Telephone:* (607) 255-7966. *Fax:* (607) 255-9984.

KANCHELI, Giya (Georgy); Georgian composer; b. 10 Aug. 1935, Tbilisi; s. of Alexander Kancheli and Agnessa Kancheli; m. Valentina Djikia; one s. one d.; ed Tbilisi State Conservatory with I. Tuskia; Prof. Tbilisi Conservatory 1970–90; Music Dir Rustaveli Drama Theatre 1971–; First Sec. Georgian Composers' Union 1984–89; Composer in Residence, Berlin (German Academic Exchange Service) 1991–92; Composer in Residence, Royal Flemish Philharmonic Orchestra, Antwerp 1995–96; USSR State Prize 1976, USSR People's Artist 1988, State Prize of Georgia 1982, Nika Prize for film music 1987, Triumph Prize Moscow 1998. *Compositions include:* symphonies: First 1967, Second 1970, Third 1973, Fourth (in Memoriam Michelangelo) 1975, Fifth 1977, Sixth (In Memory of Parents) 1980, Seventh (Epilogue) 1986; other symphonic works: Mourned by the Wind for orchestra and viola 1989, Lament (in memory of Luigi Nono), for violin, soprano and orchestra 1995; opera: Music for the Living 1984; chamber works: Life Without Christmas 1989–90 (cycle of four works for chamber ensembles), Magnum Ignotum, for wind ensemble and tape 1994, Exil, for soprano, small ensemble and tape 1994; music to plays by Shakespeare, including King Lear, Richard III and other productions of Rustaveli Drama Theatre, incidental music. *Address:* Tovstonogov str. 6, 380064 Tbilisi, Georgia; Consience Straat 14, 2018 Antwerp, Belgium. *Telephone:* (3) 295-03-39 (Tbilisi); (3) 230-85-53 (Antwerp).

KANDBORG, Lt.-Gen. Ole Larson; Danish army officer and international organization official; b. 16 May 1941, nr Skanderborg; m.; two c.; ed Viborg, Army Officers' Acad., Copenhagen, Canadian Forces' Staff Coll., Toronto, Canada, NATO Defence Coll., Rome, Italy; nat. service with Prince's Life

Regiment, Viborg, Sergeant, Lt; First Lt, Capt. of mechanized infantry Bn 1966–72; Instructor, Danish Combat Arms School 1974–77; Staff Officer, HQ of the UN Peace-keeping Force in Cyprus 1977–78; Co. Commdr, Skive, G3 of Mechanized Brigade 1978–82; at Faculty of Danish Defence Coll. 1982–84; Instructor, annual Nordic UN Staff Officers' Course (Sweden), Chief Instructor; Lt-Col, Commdr of 1st Tank Bn, Jutland Dragoon Regt, Holstebro 1984–85; Public Information Adviser and Deputy to Chief of Defence, Defence HQ, Copenhagen 1986–89, Deputy Chief of Staff for Plans and Policy 1992; Col, Commdr 2nd New Zealand Brigade, Vordingborg 1989–90; Maj.-Gen., Commdr Jutland Div., Fredericia 1990–92; Commdr of Danish Operational Command based in Aarhus and Kamp 1993–96; Danish Mil. Rep. to NATO Mil. Cttee April–Sept. 1996, Dir Int. Mil. Staff, NATO Sept. 1996–; Commdr Order of Dannebrog, Mil. Good Service Medal, Reserve Officers' Asscn's Good Service Medal, Commdr 1st Degree Order of the Swedish North Star, Legion of Merit (Degree of Commdr), UN Medal 7. *Address:* North Atlantic Treaty Organization, blvd Léopold III, 1110 Brussels, Belgium (Office). *Telephone:* (2) 707-41-11 (Office). *Fax:* (2) 707-45-79 (Office).

KANDEL, Eric Richard, BA, MD; American biologist; b. 7 Nov. 1929, Vienna, Austria; m. 1956; two c.; ed Harvard Coll., New York Univ.; New York Univ. School of Medicine 1956; Resident in Psychiatry, Harvard Medical School 1960–64, staff psychiatrist 1964–65; Assoc. Prof. of Physiology, NYU 1965–74; Prof. of Physiology and Psychiatry, Columbia Univ. 1974–, Prof. of Biochemistry 1992–; Sr Investigator, Howard Hughes Medical Inst. 1983–; mem. NAS, American Acad. of Arts and Sciences, Soc. of Neurosciences (Pres. 1980–81), Int. Brain Research Org., New York Acad. of Sciences; numerous awards and prizes include Nat. Medal of Science 1988, Warren Triennial Prize 1992, Harvey Prize 1993, Mayor Award for Excellence in Science and Tech. 1994, New York Acad. of Medicine Award 1996, Heineken Prize 2000; Nobel Prize for Medicine (Jt recipient) 2000. *Address:* Howard Hughes Medical Institute, Columbia University, 722 West 168th Street, New York, NY 10032, USA (Office). *Telephone:* (212) 960-2202 (Office). *Fax:* (212) 960-2410 (Office). *E-mail:* erk@columbia.edu (Office).

KANEKO, Hisashi, MSc; Japanese business executive; b. 19 Nov. 1933, Tokyo; s. of Shozo Kaneko and Toshi Kaneko; m. Mokoto Washino; three c.; ed Tokyo Univ., Univ. of Calif., Berkeley; joined NEC Corpn 1956, Pres. NEC America 1989–91, NEC Corpn 1994–99. *Address:* NEC Corporation, 7-1 Shiba 5-chome, Minato-ku, Tokyo 108-01, Japan.

KANERVA, Ilkka Armas Mikael, M.POL.SC.; Finnish politician; b. 28 Jan. 1948, Lokalahti; mem. Turku City Council 1972–; Party Man., Nat. Coalition Party 1972–93 (mem. Exec. Cttee 1975–93), Chair. Nat. Coalition Party Youth League 1972–76; MP 1975–, Minister of State (attached to Office of the Council of State) 1987–90; Minister at the Ministry of Finance 1989–91, 1991; Minister of Transport and Communications 1990–91, of Labour 1991–94. *Address:* c/o National Coalition Party, Kansakoulukija 3, 00100 Helsinki, Finland.

KANG, Dong-Suk; American violinist; b. 28 April 1954, Seoul, S Korea; m. Martine Schittenhelm; one s. one d.; ed Juilliard School, New York and Curtis Inst. Philadelphia (under Ivan Galamian); prize winner, Queen Elisabeth of the Belgians, Montreal, San Francisco Symphony Foundation and Carl Flesch competitions; has appeared with maj. orchestras throughout USA, UK, Europe and Far East and at music festivals around the world including BBC Promenade concerts (debut 1987). *Recordings include:* complete repertoire for violin and orchestra by Sibelius, Nielsen Violin Concerto, Elgar Violin Concerto, Bruch Violin Concerto, Walton Violin Concerto. *Address:* 23 rue Daumesnil, 9430 Vincennes, France (Office); c/o Clarion/Seven Muses, 47 Whitehall Park, London, N19 3TW, England. *Telephone:* (20) 7272-4413. *Fax:* (20) 7281-9687.

KANG, Young Hoon, MA, PhD; South Korean politician and diplomatist; b. 30 May 1922; m. Hyo-Soo Kim 1947; two s. one d.; ed Univs of Manchuria and S California; Mil. Attaché to Embassy, Washington, DC 1952–53; Div. Commdr 1953, Corps Commdr 1959–60; retd rank of Lt-Gen. 1961; Asst Minister of Defence 1955–56; Staff mem. Research Inst. on Communist Strategy and Propaganda, Univ. of S. California 1968–69; Dir Research Inst. on Korean Affairs, Silver Spring, Md 1970–76; Dean Grad. School, Hankuk Univ. of Foreign Studies 1977–78; Chancellor Inst. of Foreign Affairs and Nat. Security, Ministry for Foreign Affairs 1978–80; Amb. to UK 1981–84, to the Holy See 1985–88; Prime Minister of the Repub. of Korea 1988–91; numerous mil. medals.

KANG SOK JU; North Korean politician; b. 4 Aug. 1939, Pyongwan, S Pyongan Prov.; First Vice-Minister, Admin Council, Ministry of Foreign Affairs 1986–87, First Vice-Minister of Foreign Affairs 1987–, Del. to UN following N Korean accession to UN 1991, Head of Del. to Negotiations with USA 1993, attended meeting of Kim Il Sung and US Pres. Jimmy Carter 1994, signed nuclear agreement with US, Geneva 1994, accompanied Kim Jong Il to Russia 2001, to summit with Japanese Prime Minister Junichiro Koizumi 2002; mem. Cen. Cttee Korean Workers' Party 1991–. *Address:* Ministry of Foreign Affairs, Pyongyang, Democratic People's Republic of Korea (Office).

KANI, John; South African actor; fmrly worked on a car ass. line; began acting in amateur production; many stage tours abroad and appearances in S. Africa particularly at Market Theatre, Johannesburg; appeared in Waiting for Godot, Miss Julie, Othello 1987; Tony Award for Broadway performance in Athol Fugard's Sizwe Banzi is Dead. *Address:* c/o Market Theatre, Johannesburg, South Africa.

KANIS, Pavol, DPhil, CSc; Slovak politician; b. 27 Aug. 1948; m.; two c.; ed Charles Univ., Prague; has held various positions in Party of the Democratic Left; mem. Slovak Nat. Council; Minister of Defence 1998–2001. *Leisure interests:* reading, gardening. *Address:* Slovak National Council, Mudronova 1, 812 80 Bratislava, Slovakia.

KANN, Peter Robert; American journalist; b. 13 Dec. 1942, New York; s. of Robert Kann and Marie Breuer; m. 1st Francesca Mayer 1969 (died 1983); m. 2nd Karen House 1984; one s. three d.; ed Harvard Univ.; with The Wall Street Journal 1964–; journalist, New York 1964–67, Vietnam 1967–68, Hong Kong 1968–75, Publr and Ed. Asian Edn 1976–79, Assoc. Publr 1979–88; Exec. Vice-Pres. Dow Jones & Co. 1986, Pres. int. and magazine groups 1986–89, mem. Bd of Dirs. 1987; Publr and Editorial Dir The Wall Street Journal 1989–2002; Pres. Dow Jones & Co. New York 1989–91, Chair., CEO 1991–; Chair. Bd Far Eastern Econ. Review 1987–89; Trustee Asia Soc. 1989–94, Inst. for Advanced Study, Princeton 1990–, Aspen Inst. 1994–; mem. Pulitzer Prize Bd 1987–96; recipient, Pulitzer Prize for int. reporting 1972. *Address:* Wall Street Journal, 200 Liberty Street, New York, NY 10281, USA.

KANOVITZ, Howard, BS; American painter; b. 9 Feb. 1929, Fall River, Mass.; s. of Meyer J. Kanovitz and Dora (Rems) Kanovitz; m. Mary Rattray 1961 (divorced 1992); one d.; ed Providence Coll., Rhode Island School of Design, New School for Social Research, New York Univ. Inst. of Fine Arts; works in numerous public collections; DAAD Fellowship Berlin 1979. *Exhibitions:* one-man exhbns New York, Fall River, Cologne, Malmö, Utrecht, Duisburg, Berlin, Hanover, Freiburg, Rottweil, Chicago, Frankfurt, Seoul 1962–; numerous group exhbns 1953–. *Stage design:* Die Bakchen, Mülheim an der Ruhr, Germany 1988. *Leisure interests:* music, fishing. *Address:* 237 East 18th Street, New York, NY 10003 (Office); 361 No. Sea Mecox Road, Southampton, NY 11968, USA. *Telephone:* (212) 505-8958; (631) 283-7179. *Fax:* (631) 283-4625 (Office). *E-mail:* nero@optonline.net (Office). *Website:* howardkanovitz.com (Office).

KANTOR, Mickey; American corporate lawyer; b. 1939; m. 1st (died 1978); two s. (died 1988) one d.; m. 2nd 1982; one d.; ed Vanderbilt Univ., Georgetown Univ. Law School; served USN; began career as lawyer protecting rights of migrant farm workers; partner LA law firm 1993; mem. Bd of Legal Services Corpn in Carter Admin.; mem. Comm. investigating LA Riots 1992; Chair. Bill Clinton's Presidential Campaign 1992; US Trade Rep. 1993–97; Sec. of Commerce 1996–99; Partner Mayer, Brown, Roewe & Maw, Washington 1997–; also mem. Bd of Dirs Monsanto Corpn, Pharmacia Corpn, Korea First Bank, Int. Advisory Bd Fleishman-Hillard, Bd of Visitors, Georgetown Univ. Law Center; chief negotiator NAFTA, Uruguay Round, Free Trade Areas of America, APEC; Order of Southern Cross (Brazil); Distinguished Public Service Medal, Center for Study of Presidency. *Address:* Mayer, Brown, Rowe & Maw, 1909 K Street, NW, Washington, DC 20006, USA. *Telephone:* (202) 263-3000. *Fax:* (202) 263-3300. *Website:* www.mayerbrown.com.

KANTROWITZ, Adrian, MD; American heart surgeon; b. 4 Oct. 1918, New York City; s. of Bernard Abraham Kantrowitz and Rose Kantrowitz (née Esserman); brother of Arthur Robert Kantrowitz; m. Jean Rosensaft 1947; one s. two d.; ed New York Univ. and Long Island Coll. of Medicine; Cleveland Teaching Fellow in Physiology, Western Reserve Univ. School of Medicine 1951–52; Instructor in Surgery, New York Medical Coll. 1952–55; Asst Prof. of Surgery, New York Downstate Medical Center 1955–57, Assoc. Prof. of Surgery 1957–64, Prof. of Surgery 1964–70; Adjunct Surgeon, Montefiore Hospital, Bronx, New York 1951–55; Dir (full-time) Cardiovascular Surgery, Maimonides Hospital 1955–64; Attending Surgeon, Maimonides Medical Center 1955–64; Dir Surgical Services (full-time), Maimonides Medical Center and Coney Island Hospital, Brooklyn 1964–70; Chair. Dept of Surgery, Sinai Hospital, Detroit 1970–73, Chair. Dept of Cardiovascular-Thoracic Surgery 1973; Prof. Surgery, Wayne State Univ. School of Medicine 1970–; Pres. Brooklyn Thoracic Soc. 1967–68; Pres. American Soc. of Artificial Internal Organs 1968–69; mem. Editorial Bd Journal of Biomedical Materials Research 1966–, Scientific Review Bd Medical Research Eng 1966–; performed first human implantation of a partial mechanical heart 1966; performed first US human heart transplantation 1967 and installed first human intra-aortic balloon pump 1968; Henry L. Moses Research Prize 1949; New York State Medical Soc., First Prize, Scientific Exhibit 1957, First Prize Maimonides Hospital Research Soc. for work in Bladder Stimulation 1963, Gold Plate Award, American Acad. of Achievement 1966, Max Berg Award for Outstanding Achievement in Prolonging Human Life 1966, Brooklyn Hall of Fame Man of Year Award for Science 1966, Theodor and Susan B. Cummings Humanitarian Award, American Coll. of Cardiology 1967. *Publications:* numerous articles and films on heart surgery. *Leisure interests:* flying, skiing, sailing, music. *Address:* 300 River Place, Detroit, MI 48207 (Office); 70 Gallogly Road, Auburn Hills, MI 48326, USA. *Telephone:* (313) 446-2800 (Office). *Fax:* (313) 446-2801. *E-mail:* adriank3ak@aol.com (Office).

KANTROWITZ, Arthur Robert, PhD; American physicist and university professor; b. 20 Oct. 1913, New York; s. of Bernard Abraham Kantrowitz and Rose Kantrowitz (née Esserman); brother of Adrian Kantrowitz; m. 1st Rosalind Joseph 1943 (divorced 1973); three d.; m. 2nd Lee Stuart 1980; ed Columbia Univ.; Physicist and Chief of Gas Dynamics Section Nat. Advisory Cttee for Aeronautics 1935–46; Prof. Aero Eng and Eng Physics Cornell Univ.

1946–56; Fulbright and Guggenheim Fellow Cambridge and Manchester Univs. (UK) 1953–54; Founder and CEO Avco Everett Research Lab. Inc., Everett, Mass. 1955–78, Sr Vice-Pres. and Dir Avco Corpn 1956–79; Prof. of Eng Thayer School of Eng, Dartmouth Coll. 1978–; mem. Presidential Advisory Group on Anticipated Advances in Science and Tech., 'Science Court' Task Force Chair. 1975–76; mem. Bd of Dir Hertz Foundation; Hon. Prof. Huazhong Inst. of Tech., Wuhan, People's Repub. of China 1980; mem. NAS, Nat. Acad. of Eng, American Inst. of Physics; Fellow American Acad. of Arts and Sciences, American Physical Soc., American Inst. of Aeronautics and Astronautics (Hon. Fellow 1998), Int. Acad. of Astronautics, American Inst. for Medical and Biological Eng; Messenger Lecturer, Cornell Univ. 1978; achievements include high-energy lasers, heart assist devices, MHD generators, re-entry from space, notable early work in fusion and molecular beams; Hon. Life mem. Bd of Govs, The Technion; Theodore Roosevelt Medal of Science 1967, M. H. D. Faraday Medal, UNESCO 1983, First Int. Symposium on Beamed Energy Propulsion Award 2002. *Publications:* co-author Fundamentals of Gas Dynamics 1958, author or co-author of more than 200 scientific and professional articles. *Address:* 4 Downing Road, Hanover, NH 03755, USA (Home). *Telephone:* (603) 643-3639 (Home). *E-mail:* ark@ dartmouth.edu (Office).

KANYA, Mary M.; Swazi diplomatist; ed Zombodze Nat. School; fmr teacher Swaziland Teacher Training Coll., Univ. of Swaziland; tutored children of King Sobhuza II; f. royal school; fmr Sr Insp. of Schools; became Swaziland's first female Amb. 1990; Amb. to Canada 1990–94, to USA 1994–. *Address:* Embassy of Swaziland, 3400 International Drive, NW, Washington, DC 20008, USA (Office). *Telephone:* (202) 234-5002 (Office). *Fax:* (202) 234-8254 (Office).

KANZAKI, Takenori, LLB; Japanese politician; b. 15 July 1943, Tien-Tsin, People's Repub. of China; ed Tokyo Univ.; public prosecutor 1968–76; lawyer 1982–; mem. House of Reps; mem. Komeito, Chair. Foreign Affairs Cttee; Chair. Diet Policy Cttee; Minister of Posts and Telecommunications 1993–94; Rep. New Komeito 1998–. *Publication:* Prohibition of Profit Granting (co-author). *Leisure interests:* shogi (Japanese chess), reading, travelling, theatre. *Address:* New Komeito Headquarters, 17 Minamimoto-Machi, Shinjuku-ku, Tokyo 160-0012 (Office); Room No. 201, No. 6 Green Building, 2-12-7 Hakata-Ekimae, Hakata-ku, Fukuoka-shi 812, Fukuoka Prefecture, Japan (Home). *Telephone:* (3) 3353-0111 (Office); (3) 3581-5111. *Fax:* (3) 3353-9746 (Office); (3) 3503-2388.

KAO, Charles, PhD; American (b. Chinese) academic; b. 4 Nov. 1933, Shanghai, China; s. of the late Chun-Hsian and Tsing-Fong King; m. May-Wan Wong 1959; one s. one d.; ed Univ. of London; engineer, Standard Telephones and Cables Ltd, UK 1957–60, Research Scientist/Research Man., Standard Telecommunications Labs. Ltd./ITT Cen. European Lab., Essex, UK 1960–70; Chair. Dept of Electronics, Chinese Univ. of Hong Kong 1970–74; Chief Scientist and Dir of Eng Electro-Optical Products Div. ITT, Roanoke, Va 1974–81, Vice-Pres. and Dir of Eng 1981–88; Exec. Scientist and Corporate Dir of Research, ITT Advanced Tech. Centre, Conn. 1983–87; Vice-Chancellor The Chinese Univ. of Hong Kong 1987–96; Chair. and CEO Transtech Services Ltd 1996–2001, ITX Services Ltd 2000–; Hon. DSc (Chinese Univ. of Hong Kong) 1985, (Sussex) 1990, (Durham) 1994, (Hull) 1998, (Yale) 1999; Dr hc (Soka) 1991; Hon. DEng (Glasgow) 1992; Hon. Dr of Telecommunications Eng (Padova, Italy) 1996; numerous awards and prizes including Alexander Graham Bell Medal, Inst. of Electrical & Electronic Engs. (USA) 1985, Marconi Int. 1985, Faraday Medal, Inst. of Electronic Engs. (UK) 1989; Hon. CBE 1993, Japan Prize 1996, Charles Stark Draper Prize, Nat. Acad. of Eng (USA) 1999; Asian of the Century in Science and Tech., Asiaweek (magazine) 1999. *Publications:* Optical Fiber Technology II 1981, Optical Fiber Systems: Technology, Design and Applications 1982, Optical Fibre 1988, A Choice Fulfilled–The Business of High Technology 1991. *Leisure interests:* tennis, hiking, pottery-making. *Address:* S. K. Yee Foundation, Unit 1708, Office Tower, Convention Plaza, 1 Harbour Road, Wan Chai, Hong Kong Special Administrative Region, People's Republic of China. *Telephone:* 26037643. *Fax:* 26037663. *E-mail:* ckao@ie.cuhk.edu.hk (Home).

KAO, Chin-Yen; Chinese business executive; b. 24 May 1929, Taiwan; m. Lai-Kwan Kao; one d.; ed Tainan Co. Tienchow Elementary School; Sales Man. Tainan Fabric Corpn 1957–67; Pres. Enterprises Corpn 1967–89, Vice-Chair. and Pres. 1989–, CEO Pres. Enterprises Group 1989–, Chair. Pres. Enterprises Chain Store Corpn 1986–; Chair. Ztong Yee Industrial Co. Ltd 1977–, Ton Yi Industrial Corpn 1979–; mem. Cen. Standing Cttee, Kuomintang 1994–; Hon. PhD (Lincoln) 1983. *Address:* 301 Chung Cheng Road, Yungkang, Tainan County, Taiwan.

KAPARTIS, Costas, MA; Cypriot labour relations official; b. 28 Sept. 1933, Nicosia; m. Anna Kapartis; three c.; ed Webster and Cornell Univs.; various positions in Ministry of Labour and Social Insurance 1957–65; Dir-Gen. Cyprus Employers' Fed. 1965–75; Exec. Sec. Int. Org. of Employers (IOE) 1975, Deputy Sec.-Gen. 1980–90, Sec.-Gen. 1990–2001. *Address:* 9 chemin A. Pasteur, 1209 Geneva, Switzerland (Home).

KAPIL DEV; Indian cricketer; b. 6 Jan. 1959, Chandigarh; m. Romi Dev; ed Punjab Univ.; right-hand middle-order batsman, right-arm fast-medium bowler; played for Haryana 1975–76 to 1991–92, Northamptonshire 1981–83, Worcestershire 1984–85; played in 131 Tests for India 1978–79 to 1993–94, 34 as Capt., scoring 5,248 runs (average 31.0) including 8 hundreds and

taking record 434 wickets (average 29.6); youngest to take 100 Test wickets (21 years 25 days); hit four successive balls for six v. England, Lord's 1990; scored 11,356 runs (18 hundreds) and took 835 wickets in first-class cricket; toured England 1979, 1982, 1983 (World Cup), 1986 and 1990; 225 limited-overs internationals; Indian Nat. Coach 1999–2000; Wisden Cricketer of the Year 1983, Electrolux Kelvinator Wisden Indian Cricketer of the Century 2002. *Publication:* Kapil Dev — Triumph of the Spirit 1995. *Leisure interests:* hunting, riding, dancing. *Address:* 39 Sunder Nagar, New Delhi 110 003 India. *Telephone:* (11) 4698333. *Fax:* (11) 3719776.

KAPITSA, Sergey Petrovich, DPhysMathSc; Russian physicist; b. 14 Feb. 1928, Moscow; s. of the late Pyotr Kapitsa; m. Tat'yana Alimovna Kapitsa; one s. two d.; ed Moscow Aviation Inst.; engineer Cen. Inst. of Aerohydrodynamics 1949–51; Jr researcher Inst. of Geophysics 1951–53; researcher, head of lab., leading researcher, chief researcher, Head of Div. Inst. of Physical Problems USSR (now Russian) Acad. of Sciences 1953–; Prof., Head of Dept Moscow Inst. of Physics and Tech. 1965–; mem. Russian Acad. of Natural Sciences 1990, Vice-Pres. 1995–; mem. World Acad. of Sciences and Arts, European Acad.; Pres. Eurasian Physical Soc., Int. Inst. of Sciences, Int. Fed. of Aeronautics, Manchester Literary and Philosophical Soc.; mem. Ed. Bd Public Understanding of Science, Sceptical Inquirer and other Publs; Kalinga Prize of UNESCO 1979; USSR State Prize 1989. *Television:* broadcaster Obvious-Unbelievable (series) 1973–94, Obvious-Unbelievable XXI century 1997–. *Leisure interest:* underwater swimming. *Address:* Russian Academy of Sciences, 117901 Moscow, Leninsky pr. 14, Moscow, Russia (Office). *Telephone:* (095) 954-29-05 (Office). *Fax:* (095) 954-33-20 (Office).

KAPLAN, Jeremiah; American publishing executive; b. 15 July 1926, New York; s. of Samuel Kaplan and Fannie Brafman; m. Charlotte R. Larsen 1945; one s. three d.; Vice-Pres. Free Press Glencoe Inc., Ill. 1947–60, Pres. 1960–64; Editorial Dir Gen. Publishing Div. Crowell Collier Publishing Co. 1960–62, Vice-Pres. 1962–67, Sr Vice-Pres. 1967–; Chair. Bd Science Materials Inc. 1962–63; Vice-Pres. Macmillan Co. 1960–63, Exec. Vice-Pres. 1963–65, Pres. 1965–73, 1977–86, Chair. 1983–87; Exec. Vice-Pres. Crowell Collier Div. Macmillan Inc. 1968–86; Head, Product Devt Corp. Marketing Planning, Crowell Collier & Macmillan Inc. 1972–, also mem. Bd Dirs.; Chair. Collier Macmillan Int. 1973; Exec. Vice-Pres. and Dir Macmillan Inc. 1979–86; Chair. Bd Macmillan Publishing Co., Inc. 1980–86; Special Adviser to Chair. Simon & Schuster, Inc. New York 1987, Pres. 1987–90.

KAPLAN, Jonathan Stewart (Cutter Delacroix); American film writer, film director, television producer and television director; b. 25 Nov. 1947, Paris; s. of Sol Kaplan and Frances Heflin; m. Julie Selzer 1987 (divorced 2001); one d.; ed Univ. of Chicago, New York Univ. and New World Pictures Roger Corman Postgrad. School of Film Making, Hollywood; mem. tech. staff, Bill Graham's Fillmore East, New York 1969–71; appeared in The Dark at the Top of the Stairs, Broadway 1956–57; Best Male Vocal Concept Video, Billboard 1986. *Films:* Night Call Nurses 1972, Student Teachers 1973, The Slams 1973, Truck Turner 1974, White Line Fever 1974, Mr Billion 1976, Over the Edge 1978, 11th Victim 1979, Muscle Beach 1980, Gentleman Bandit 1981, White Orchid 1982, Heart Like a Wheel 1983, Project X 1986, The Accused 1987, Immediate Family 1989, Love Field 1990, Unlawful Entry 1992, Bad Girls 1994, Rebel Highway 1994, Picture Windows 1995, Fallen Angels 1996, Brokedown Palace 1999. *Video films:* directed 15 music videos for John Mellencamp, two for Rod Stewart (q.v.), one for Barbra Streisand (q.v.) and one for Paula Abdul. *TV series:* producer/director of ER (NBC) 1999–2001. *Address:* Industry Entertainment, 953 Carillo Drive, Suite 300, Los Angeles, CA 90048, USA (Office).

KAPLICKY, Jan; Czech architect; b. 1937, Prague; living in UK 1968–; Co-founder (with David Nixon) of design studio—Future Systems 1979; Exhbn in Prague 1998; co-operation with NASA on projects for satellite systems; with partner Amanda Levete 2nd in competition for the Bibiothèque de France (Paris); Stirling Prize 1999.

KAPOOR, Anish, MA; Indian sculptor; b. 12 March 1954, Bombay; s. of Rear-Adm. Kapoor and Mrs D. C. Kapoor; m. Susanne Spicale 1995; one d. one s.; ed Hornsey Coll. of Art, Chelsea Coll. of Art and Design, London; teacher, Wolverhampton Polytechnic 1979; Artist-in-Residence, Walker Art Gallery, Liverpool 1982; one-man exhbns in Paris 1980, 1998, London 1981, 1982, 1983, 1985, 1988, 1989–90, 1990–91 (Anish Kapoor Drawings, Tate Gallery, London), 1993, 1995–96, 1998, 2000, 2002 (Unilever Series, Tate Modern), Liverpool 1982, 1983, Rotterdam, Lyon 1983, New York 1984, 1986, 1989, 1990, 1993, 1998, Basel 1985, Oslo, Univ. of Mass. Amherst 1986, Sydney 1987, Nagoya, Japan 1989, 1994, Venice 1990, Grenoble 1990–91, Madrid 1991, 1992, Hanover 1991, Ushimado, Japan 1991, Cologne 1991, 1996–97, Los Angeles 1992, San Diego 1992–93, Tel Aviv 1993, Ljubljana 1994, Tokyo 1995, 1998, Tillburg 1995, Milan 1995–96, Turku, Finland 1996, Cambridge, England 1996, Brescia, Italy 1996, 1998, San Francisco 1996, Bordeaux 1998, Santiago de Compostela, Spain 1998; travelling exhbn USA and Canada 1992–93; and has participated in group exhbns since 1974 throughout Britain and in Europe, North America, Japan, Australia, New Zealand, Mexico, Morocco and Brazil; works in public collections including Tate Gallery, London, Hirshhorn Museum and Sculpture Garden, Washington, DC, Museum of Modern Art, New York, Art Gallery of NSW, Australia, Contemporary Art Soc., London, Nat. Gallery, Ottawa, Hara Museum of Contemporary Art, Tokyo, Auckland City Art Gallery, NZ, Tel-Aviv Museum of Art, Groeningen Exhbn, Neues Museum, Bremen, Lyon Biennale, Lisson

Gallery, London and many others; public comms: Cast Iron Mountain, Tachikawa Art Project, Tokyo 1994; outdoor comms; Toronto 1995, Israel Museum, Jerusalem 1997, Bordeaux 1998–99; Hon. Fellow London Inst. 1997; Hon. DLitt (Leeds) 1993; Premio Duemila, Venice Biennale 1990, Turner Prize, Tate Gallery, London 1991. *Address:* c/o Lisson Gallery, 67 Lisson Street, London, NW1 5DA, England. *Telephone:* (20) 7724-2739. *Fax:* (20) 7724-7124.

KAPOOR, Shashi; Indian actor and producer; b. 18 March 1938, Calcutta; s. of late Prithviraj Kapoor; m. Jennifer Kendal 1958 (died 1984); three c.; joined Shakespeareana co. 1955 and toured India, Pakistan and Malaysia; producer with Junoon 1978–. *Films include:* Awaara 1951, Char Diwari 1960, Householder 1962, Shakespeare Wallah 1965, Jab Jab Phool Khile 1965, Waqt 1967, Aa Gale Lag Jaa 1973, Deewar 1975, Siddhartha 1978, Heat and Dust 1983, Utsav 1984, Sammie and Rosie Get Laid 1987, The Deceivers, Nomads, Ajuba 1988, In Custody 1994, Side Streets. *Films produced include:* Junoon 1979 (Nat. Award), Kalyug, 36 Chowringhee Lane 1981, Vijeta 1982, Do Aur Do Paanch, New Delhi Times, Suhaag, Basera, Kala Patthar, Shaan, Kabhie Kabhie, Dusra Admi. *Address:* 112, Atlas Apartments, Mumbai 400006, India (Home); Film Walas, Janki Kutir, Juhu Church Road, Mumbai 400049. *Telephone:* (22) 6142922 (Office); (22) 3697710 (Home).

KAPTEYN, Paul Joan George, LLD; Netherlands lawyer; b. 31 Jan. 1928, Laren, NH; s. of Paul J. Kapteyn and Picaine (Schröder) Kapteyn; m. Ieteke Streef 1956; one s. one d.; ed Univ. of Leiden, Inst. des Hautes Etudes Int., Paris; Asst Prof. of Int. Law, Univ. of Leiden 1953–60; with Foreign Office, The Hague 1960–63; Prof. of Law of Int. Orgs., Univ. of Utrecht 1963–74, Univ. of Leiden 1972–76; mem. Council of State 1976–90, Pres. Judicial Section 1984–90; mem. Int. Comm. of Jurists 1976–90; Pres. Netherlands Asscn of Int. Law 1987–93; Judge, Court of Justice of the EC 1990–99; mem. Royal Netherlands Acad. of Sciences. *Publications:* The Common Assembly of the European Coal and Steel Community 1960; Co-author: An Introduction to the Law of the European Communities 4 edns. 1970–87. *Leisure interests:* tennis, reading, travelling.

KAPUR, Shekhar, CA; Indian film director; b. 1945, Lahore, Pakistan; m. Suchitra Krishnamurthy; one d. *Films include:* Masoom 1983, Joshilar, Mr India, Bandit Queen 1994, Time Machine 1995, Dushmani, Dil Se 1998, Elizabeth 1998, Long Walk to Freedom, The Four Feathers 2002, The Guru (Exec. Producer) 2002. *Address:* 42 New Sital Apartments, A. B. Nair Road, Juhu, Mumbai 400449, India (Home). *Telephone:* (22) 6204988 (Home).

KAPUŚCIŃSKI, Ryszard, MA; Polish journalist; b. 4 March 1932, Pińsk; s. of Józef Kapuściński and Maria Bobka Kapuścińska; m. Alicja Mielczarek 1952; one d.; ed Faculty of History, Warsaw Univ.; began career with Sztandar Młodych 1951, with Polityka 1957–61; later Corresp. Polish Press Agency (PAP) in Africa and Latin America 1962–72; Kultura 1974–81; Deputy Chair. Poland 2000 Cttee, Polish Acad. of Sciences 1981–85; mem. Presidential Council of Culture 1992–95; mem. Polish Journalists Asscn 1982–; Sr Assoc. mem. St Antony's Coll., Oxford 1985; Visiting Scholar Bangalore Univ. 1973, Univ. of Caracas 1978, Columbia Univ. 1983, Temple Univ., Phila 1988; mem. Bd of Advisers, New Perspectives Quarterly; mem. European Acad. of Science and Art 1993–; mem. Polish Acad. of Art and Science 1998–; mem. Polish PEN Club 1998–; Gold Cross of Merit, Kt's Cross, Order of Polonia Restituta 1974; Dr hc (Silesian Univ.) 1997, (Univ. of Wrocław) 2001, (Univ. of Sofia) 2002; B. Prus Prize 1975, Julian Brun Prize, Int. Prize of Int. Journalists Org. five times, State Prize (Second Class) 1976, Prize of German Publishers and Booksellers for European Understanding, Leipzig 1994, Prix d'Astrolabe, Paris 1995, Jan Parandowski PEN Club Prize 1996, J. W. Goethe Prize, Hamburg, 1999, S. B. Linde Literary Prize, Toruń-Göttingen, 1999; Alfred Jurzykowski Foundation Award in the Field of Literature, New York 1994, Turański Foundation Award, Toronto 1996, Josef Conrad Literature Award (J. Piłsudski Inst. of America), New York 1997, Ikar Award 1999, Journalist of the Century (Press monthly), 1999, Premio Internazionale Viareggio (Italy) 2000, Premio Omegna (Italy) 2000, Orcola Award, (Italy) 2000, Premio Feudo di Maida (Italy) 2000, Prix Tropiques (France) 2002, Liberpress (Spain) 2002, Premio Grinzane Cavour (Italy) 2003. *Publications:* Busz po polsku 1962, Czarne gwiazdy 1963, Kirgiz schodzi z konia 1968, Gdyby cała Afryka... 1969, Dlaczego zginął Karl von Spreti? 1970, Chrystus z karabinem na ramieniu 1975, Jeszcze dzień życia 1976, Cesarz 1978, Wojna futbolowa 1978, Szachinszach 1982, Notes (poems) 1986, Lapidarium 1990, Imperium 1992, Vol. II 1995, Vol. III 1997, Lapidaria 1993, Heban 1998, Z Afryki 2000, The Shadow of the Sun 2001, Lapidarium Vol. IV 2000, Vol. V 2002. *Leisure interest:* photography. *Address:* ul. Prokuratorska 11 m. 2, 02-074 Warsaw, Poland. *Telephone:* (22) 8252223. *Fax:* (22) 8252223.

KARA-MURZA, Alexei Alexeyevich, Dr rer. pol, DPhil; Russian politician; b. 1956; ed Moscow State Univ.; Dir Cen. for Theoretical Studies of Russian Reforms, Inst. of Philosophy, Russian Acad. of Sciences; Co-Pres. Moscow Foundation of Freedom and Human Rights (now Moscow Liberal Fund) 1992–; worked as scientific researcher; Head of Dept of Social and Political Philosophy, Russian Acad. of Sciences 1995–; Deputy Chair. Union of Right Forces party 2000–; mem. Council of Trustees Obshchaya Gazeta (weekly). *Publications:* scientific publs on modern philosophy and politology. *Address:* Centre for Theoretical Studies of Russian Reforms, Russian Academy of Sciences, Volkhonka str. 14 Bldg 5, 119842 Moscow, Russia (Office). *Telephone:* (095) 203-91-09 (Office). *E-mail:* edit@sps.ru (Office).

KARACHENTSOV, Nikolai Petrovich; Russian actor; b. 24 Oct. 1944, Moscow; m. Svetlana Porgina; one s.; ed Studio School, Moscow Art Theatre; with Lenkom Theatre 1967–; People's Artist of Russia 1989. *Films include:* Elder Son, Déjà Vu, Underground of the Witches, A Woman for All, Petersburg Secrets. *Theatre includes:* Til in Til Eulenspiegel, Zvonarev in Sorry, Lev Zudin in Czech Photo, Rezanov in Yunona and Avos. *Address:* Voznesensky per. 16/4, Apt. 59, 103009 Moscow, Russia. *Telephone:* (095) 229-30-65.

KARADJORDJEVIC, HRH Crown Prince Alexander (see ALEXANDER KARADJORDJEVIC, HRH Crown Prince).

KARADŽIĆ, Radovan; Serbia and Montenegro (Serbian) political leader and psychiatrist; b. 19 June 1945, Montenegro; m. Lilyan Karadžić; one s. one d.; worked in state hosps (specialized in neuroses and depression); with Unis Co.; Co.-f. Serbian Democratic Party 1990; leader of self-declared Serbian Repub. (in Bosnia and Herzegovina), elected Pres., resgnd 1996, int. arrest warrant issued for him July 1996; attended ceasefire talks in London Aug. 1992, Geneva Jan. 1993, after outbreak of hostilities; named as war crimes suspect by UN Tribunal for fmr Yugoslavia April 1995; formally charged with genocide and crimes against humanity by Int. War Crimes Tribunal for fmr Yugoslavia 1995; now in hiding; mem. Order of St Dionysus of Xanthe (First Rank); received main literary award of Montenegro for book of poetry Slavic Guest 1993; Risto Ratkovic Prize for Literature; Mikhail Sholokhov prize for Poetry (Russian Writers' Union) 1994. *Publications:* three books, children's poetry. *Leisure interest:* composes music.

KARAGANOV, Sergei Aleksandrovich, DHist; Russian defence and foreign affairs specialist; b. 12 Oct. 1952, Moscow; divorced; one d.; ed Moscow State Univ., postgraduate study in USA; Jr Fellow, Sr Fellow, Head of Section, USA and Canada Studies Inst. 1978–88; Research Fellow, Perm. Mission of USSR at UN 1976–77; Head of Dept, Deputy Dir Inst. of Europe of Russian Acad. of Sciences 1988–; mem. Foreign Policy Council, Ministry of Foreign Affairs of Russia 1991; Founder and Chair. Bd Council of Foreign and Defence Policy 1991–; mem. Presidential Council of Russia 1992–99; Adviser to Presidential Admin.; mem. Consulting Council to Security Council of Russia 1993–; mem. Consultative Council of Fed. 1996–; Chair. Dept on World Politics, State Univ. Higher School of Econs 2002–; Chair. Editorial Bd Russia in Global Affairs magazine 2002–; mem. Inst. of Strategic Studies, London. *Publications:* author or Ed. of 17 books including: Tactical Nuclear Weapons in Europe 1990, Security of the Future Europe 1991, Russia: The New Foreign Policy and Security Agenda. A View from Moscow 1993, What Has Gone Wrong With Western Aid to Russia? 1993, Damage Limitation or Crisis? Russia and the Outside World, Russia's Economic Role in Europe 1995, Russian–American Relations on the Threshold of Two Centuries (co-author) 2000, Strategy for Russia: Agenda for the President (Ed.) 2000, Strategy for Russia: Ten Years of CFDP (Ed.) 2002; over 250 articles. *Leisure interests:* athletics, literature, cooking. *Address:* Mokhovaya Street 11-3B, 103873 Moscow (Office); Chernyahovskogo, 9/5 Apt. 387, 125139 Moscow, Russia (Home). *Telephone:* (095) 203-68-34 (Office); (095) 152-99-82 (Home). *Fax:* (095) 200-42-98 (Office). *E-mail:* cfdp@online.ru (Office); kar@ok.ru (Home). *Website:* www.svop.ru.

KARAGEORGHIS, Vassos, PhD, FSA, FRSA; Cypriot archaeologist; b. 29 April 1929, Trikomo; s. of George and Panagiota Karageorghis; m. Jacqueline Girard 1953; one s. one d.; ed Pancyprian Gymnasium, Nicosia, Univ. Coll. and Inst. of Archaeology, London Univ.; Asst Curator, Cyprus Museum 1952–60, Curator 1960–63, Acting Dir, Dept of Antiquities, Cyprus 1963–64, Dir 1964–89; Dir Archaeological Research Unit, Prof. of Archaeology, Univ. of Cyprus 1992–96; excavations at Salamis 1952–73, Akhera and Pendayia 1960, Kition 1962–81, Maa-Palaeokastro, Pyla-Kokkinokremos 1979–87; Dir d'Etudes, Ecole Pratique des Hautes Etudes, Sorbonne, Paris 1983–84; Adjunct. Prof. of Classical Archaeology, State Univ. of New York, Albany 1973–; Geddes-Harrower Prof. of Classical Art and Archaeology, Univ. of Aberdeen 1975; Visiting Mellon Prof., Inst. for Advanced Study, Princeton 1989–90; adviser to the Pres. of Cyprus on cultural heritage 1989–92; mem. Council, A. G. Leventis Foundation (mem. Governing Body 1997–), Cultural Foundation of the Bank of Cyprus; mem. Royal Swedish Acad., Accademia dei Lincei, Acad. des Inscriptions et Belles Lettres, German Archaeological Inst., Acad. of Athens; Corresp. mem. Austrian Acad. of Sciences, Royal Acad. of Spain 1997; Hon. mem. Soc. for Promotion of Hellenic Studies, Archaeological Inst. of America, Council, Greek Archaeological Soc.; Visiting Fellow, Merton Coll., Oxford 1979, 1988, Sr Research Fellow 1980, Hon. Fellow 1990; Visiting Fellow, All Souls Coll., Oxford 1982; Visiting Scholar Harvard Univ. 1997–; Fellow, Royal Soc. of Humanistic Studies, Lund, Univ. Coll., London, Royal Soc. of Arts; Corresp. Fellow, British Acad.; Hon. Fellow, Soc. of Antiquaries, London; mem. Nat. Olympic Cttee Greece 1998; Order of Merit (1st Class), FRG 1980, Commdr Royal Order of Polar Star (Sweden) 1990, Commdr des Arts et des Lettres 1990, Commdr Order of Merit (Italy) 1990, Austrian Decoration for Arts and Sciences 1997, Officier Légion d'honneur 1998; Dr hc (Lyon, Göteborg, Athens, Birmingham, Toulouse, Brock, Brussels, Oxford, Dublin); Prix de la Soc. des Etudes Grecques, Sorbonne 1966, R. B. Bennett Commonwealth Prize 1978, Onassis Prize 'Olympia' 1991, Premio Internazionale 'I Cavalli d'Oro di San Marco' 1996; Award for Excellence in Science and Arts, Govt of Cyprus 1998. *Publications include:* Treasures in the Cyprus Museum 1962, Corpus Vasorum Antiquorum 1963, 1965, Nouveaux documents pour l'étude du bronze récent à Chypre 1964, Sculptures from Salamis, Vol. I 1964, Vol. II 1966, Excavations in the Necropolis of Salamis, Vol. I 1967, Vol. II 1970, Vol. III 1973, Vol. IV 1978, Mycenaean Art from Cyprus 1968,

Cyprus (Archaeologia Mundi) 1968, Salamis in Cyprus 1969, Altägäis und Altkypros (with H. G. Buchholz) 1971, Cypriot Antiquities in the Pierides Collection, Larnaca, Cyprus 1973, Fouilles de Kition I 1974, Kition, Mycenaean and Phoenician discoveries in Cyprus 1976, The Civilization of Prehistoric Cyprus 1976, La céramique chypriote de style figuré Indash;III (with Jean des Gagniers) 1974–79, Vases et figurines de l'Age du Bronze (with Jean des Gagniers) 1976, Fouilles de Kition II (with J. Leclant and others) 1976, Hala Sultan Tekké I (with P. Åström, D. M. Bailey) 1976, Fouilles de Kition III (with M. G. Guzzo Amadasi) 1977, Two Cypriot sanctuaries of the end of the Cypro-Archaic period 1977, The Goddess with Uplifted Arms in Cyprus 1977, Cypriot Antiquities in the Medelhavsmuseet, Stockholm (with C. G. Styrenius and M.-L. Winbladh) 1977, Mycenaean Pictorial Vase Painting (with Emily Vermeule) 1981, Excavations at Kition IV (with J. N. Coldstream and others) 1981, Cyprus from the Stone Age to the Romans 1982, Palaepaphos-Skales. An Iron Age Cemetery in Cyprus 1983, Pyla-Kokkinokremos–A late 13th Century BC fortified settlement in Cyprus (with M. Demas) 1984, Cyprus at the close of the Late Bronze Age (with J. D. Muhly, eds.) 1984, Ancient Cypriot Art in the Pierides Foundation Museum (with others) 1985, Archaeology in Cyprus 1960–85 (ed.) 1985, Excavations at Kition V (with M. Demas) 1985, La Nécropole d'Amathonte III: Les Terres Cuites 1987, Excavations at Maa-Palaeokastro 1979–86, 1988 (with M. Demas), Blacks in Ancient Cypriot Art 1988, The End of the Late Bronze Age in Cyprus 1990, Tombs at Palaepaphos 1990, Les anciens Chypriotes: entre orient et occident 1990, The Coroplastic Art of Ancient Cyprus (Vol. I) 1991, (Vol. II) 1993, (Vol. III) 1993, (Vol. IV) 1995, (Vol. VI) 1996, Cyprus in the Eleventh Century BC (Ed.) 1994, Cyprus and the Sea (Ed. with D. Michaelides) 1995, The Evolution of the Economy of Cyprus from the Prehistoric Period to the Present Day (Ed. with D. Michaelides) 1996, The Potters' Art of Ancient Cyprus (with Y. Olenik) 1997, Greek Gods and Heroes in Ancient Cyprus 1998, Cypriot Archaeology Today: Achievements and Perspectives 1998, Excavating at Salamis in Cyprus, 1952–74 1999, Ayia Paraskevi Figurines in the Univ. of Pa Museum (with T. P. Brennan) 1999, Die Sammlung zyprischer Antiken im Kunsthistorischen Museum 1999, Ancient Cypriot Art in the Severis Collection 1999, The Art of Ancient Cyprus in the Fitzwilliam Museum, Cambridge (with E. Vassilika and P. Wilson) 1999, Ancient Art from Cyprus. The Cesnola Collection (with J. R. Mertens, M. E. Rose), Céramiques mycéniennes Ras Shamra – Ougarit XIII (with M. Yon, N. Hirschfeld), Ancient Cypriot Art in Copenhagen. The Collections of the Nat. Museum of Denmark and the NY Carlsberg Glyptotek (with Bodil Bundgaard Rasmussen et al.), Defensive Settlements of the Aegean and Eastern Mediterranean after c. 1200 B.C. (with Christine Morris), Italy and Cyprus in Antiquity, 1500-450 B.C. (with L. Bonfante), Ancient Cypriot Art in Berlin (with S. Brehme et al.), Greek and Cypriot Antiquities in the Archaeological Museum of Odessa (with V.P. Vanchugov et al.), Early Cyprus, Crossroads of the Mediterranean; and more than 380 articles in Greek, German, American, English and French journals. *Leisure interests:* gardening, photography. *Address:* c/o Foundation Anastasios G. Leventis, 40 Gladstonos Street, 1095 Nicosia, Cyprus. *Telephone:* (2) 2667706, (2) 2674018. *Fax:* (2) 2675002. *E-mail:* leventcy@zenon.logos.cy.net (Office). *Website:* www .leventisfoundation.org (Office).

KARAMANOV, Alemdar Sabitovich; Ukrainian/Crimean Tatar composer; b. 10 Sept. 1934, Simferopol; ed Moscow State Conservatory (pupil of S. Bogatyrev and D. Kabalevsky); author of numerous symphonic compositions including 24 symphonies 1954–94, vocal-orchestral compositions of secular and religious character, including Requiem 1991, Mysteria of Khersones 1993, 3 piano concertos, 2 violin concertos, Nat. Anthem of Crimea Repub. 1992, chamber ensembles, piano music, choruses and vocal compositions; most of his music not performed up to late 1980s. *Address:* Voykova str. 2, Apt. 4, Simferopol, Crimea, Ukraine (Home).

KARAMI, Omar; Lebanese politician; fmr Minister of Educ. and the Arts; Prime Minister of Lebanon 1990–92. *Address:* c/o Office of the Prime Minister, Beirut, Lebanon.

KARAN, Donna; American fashion designer; b. 2 Oct. 1948, Forest Hills, New York; m. 1st Mark Karan (divorced 1978); one d.; m. 2nd. Stephan Weiss 1983 (died 2001); ed Parsons School of Design, New York; designer, Anne Klein & Co., then Addenda Co. until 1968; returned to Anne Klein 1968, Assoc. Designer 1971, Dir of Design (in collaboration with Louis Dell'Olio, q.v.) 1974–84; owner, designer Donna Karan Co., New York 1984–96, Chair., Head designer Donna Karan Int. (public co.) 1996–2001; Chief Designer LVMH 2001–; mem. Fashion Designers of America; Coty Awards 1977, 1981, Fashion Designers of America Women's Wear Award 1996. *Address:* Donna Karan International, 15th Floor, 550 Seventh Avenue, New York, NY 10018, USA.

KARAOSMANOGLU, Attila, PhD; Turkish economist; b. 20 Sept. 1932, Manisa; s. of Ibrahim Ethem Karaosmanoglu and Fatma Eda Karaosmanoglu; m. Sukriye Ozyet 1960; one s.; ed Univs. of Ankara and Istanbul, Harvard and New York Univs., USA; faculty mem. Middle East Tech. Univ. and Ankara Univ. 1954–63; Head Econ. Planning Dept, State Planning Org. of Turkey 1960–62; Adviser, Fed. of Turkish Trade Unions, Consultant, Turkish Scientific and Tech. Research Council 1963–65; Consultant, Directorate for Scientific Affairs, OECD 1965–66; Economist, then Sr Economist, World Bank 1966–71; Deputy Prime Minister in Charge of Econ. Affairs and Chair. of the High Planning Council, Turkish Govt 1971; mem. Exec. Bd, Is Bank, Turkey 1972; Chief Economist, World Bank 1973–75, Dir of Devt Policy 1975–79, Dir of Europe, Middle East and N Africa Region Country Programmes 1979–82, Vice-Pres. E Asia and Pacific Region 1983–87, Asia Region 1987–91 (IBRD), Man. Dir World Bank (IBRD) 1991–95; Chief Adviser, Istanbul Chamber of Industry 1995–; mem. Bd Scientific and Technological Research Council of Turkey 1995–, Alt. Bank of Turkey 1996–; Chair. Bd Nat. Inst. of Metrology 1997–. *Publications:* Towards Full Employment and Price Stability (OECD Publ, with others) 1977, Poverty and Prosperity–The Two Realities of Asian Development 1989, Diversity and Consensus–The Emergence of an Asian Development Paradigm 1991. *Address:* Dr. Faruk Ayanoglu Cad. 37 D.5, 81030 Fenerbahce, Istanbul, Turkey. *Telephone:* (216) 363-6953. *Fax:* (216) 369-4076.

KARASIN, Grigory Borisovich; Russian diplomatist; b. 23 Aug. 1949, Moscow; m.; two d.; ed Moscow Inst. of Oriental Languages, Moscow State Univ.; diplomatic service since 1972; translator, attaché USSR Embassy, Senegal 1972–76; attaché First African Div., USSR Ministry of Foreign Affairs 1976–77; sec. to Deputy Minister of Foreign Affairs 1977–79; Second, First Sec. Embassy, Australia 1979–85; First Sec., Counsellor Second European Div. Ministry of Foreign Affairs 1985–88; Counsellor USSR Embassy, UK 1988–92; Head of Dept of Africa, Ministry of Foreign Affairs of Russia 1992–93, Head. Dept of Information and Press 1993–96; Deputy Minister of Foreign Affairs 1996–2000; Amb. to UK March 2000–. *Address:* Russian Embassy, 13 Kensington Palace Gardens, London, W8, England. *Telephone:* (20) 7229-3620 (Office). *Fax:* (20) 7229-5804 (Office). *E-mail:* karasingb@ hotmail.com. *Website:* www.great-britain.mid.ru (Office).

KARDASHEV, Nikolai Semenovich; Russian astronomer; b. 25 April 1932; m.; one d.; ed Moscow State Univ.; lab., sr lab., jr, sr researcher State Astronomical Inst. 1955–67; head of lab., Deputy Dir Inst. of Space Studies USSR Acad. of Sciences 1967–90; Dir Astronomical Cen. Lebedev Physical Inst., USSR Acad. of Sciences 1990–; corresp. mem. USSR (now Russian) Acad. of Sciences 1976, mem. 1994; research in radiophysics, radioastronomy, radio radiation of galaxies and quasars; USSR State Prize. *Publications include:* Pulsars and nonthermal Radio Sources 1970, Strategy and Future Projects 1977; numerous articles in scientific journals. *Address:* Astronomical Centre of Lebedev Physical Institute, Russian Academy of Sciences, Profsoyuznaya str. 84/32, 117810 Moscow, Russia. *Telephone:* (095) 333-21-89 (Office).

KAREFA-SMART, John Musselman, BA, BSc, MD, CM, DTM, MPH, FRSH, FAPHA, FRSA; Sierra Leonean politician and physician; b. 17 June 1915, Rotifunk; s. of Rev. James Karefa-Smart and May Karefa-Smart (née Caulker); m. Rena Joyce Weller 1948; one s. two d.; ed Fourah Bay and Otterbein Colls., McGill and Harvard Univs.; lecturer, Union Coll., Bunumbu 1936–38; ordained Elder of Evangelical United Brethren Church 1938; Medical Officer, RCAMC 1943–45; Sierra Leone Missions Hosps 1946–48; Lecturer, Ibadan Univ. Coll. (Nigeria) 1949–52; Health Officer, WHO 1952–55, Leader del. to WHO 1956 and 1959; mem. House of Reps 1957–64; Minister of Lands and Survey 1957–59; Africa Consultant, World Council of Churches 1955–56; Minister for External Affairs 1960–64; Asst Prof. Columbia Univ. 1964–65; Asst Dir-Gen. WHO, Geneva 1965–70; Visiting Prof. of Int. Health, Harvard Univ. 1971–73, Lecturer Harvard Medical School 1973–81; Medical Dir Roxbury Health Centre 1973–78, Health and Devt Consultant 1978–; Clinical Prof. Boston Univ. 1976–; Visiting Prof. Harvard Univ. 1977–; returned to Sierra Leone 1990; f. United Democratic Party; Pres. United Nat. People's Party (UNPP)–1997; mem. of Parl., Leader of Opposition 1996–99; Hon. LLD (Otterbein, McGill, Boston), Hon. DSc (Sierra Leone); Commdr Order of Star of Africa (Liberia), Kt Grand Band, Order of African Redemption (Liberia), Grand Cordon, Order of the Cedar (Lebanon). *Publications:* The Halting Kingdom 1959, Evaluating Health Program Impact 1974. *Leisure interests:* photography, stamps. *Address:* 20 Damba Road, Freetown, Sierra Leone. *Telephone:* (22) 272163. *E-mail:* tonkolili@aol.com.

KAREKIN II, His Holiness (Ktrich Nerssisian); Armenian ecclesiastic; b. 21 Aug. 1951, Etchmiadzin; ed Kevorkian Theological Seminary, Univ. of Vienna, Univ. of Bonn; Asst Dean, Kevorkian Theological Seminary; ordained priest 1972; pastor in Germany 1975; Asst to Vicar-Gen. of Araratian Patriarchal Diocese 1980, Vicar-Gen., Bishop 1983, later Archbishop; mem. Supreme Spiritual Council of Catholicosate of All Armenians 1990–; Supreme Patriarch and Catholicos of All Armenians 1999–; f. Vazkenian Seminary, Sevan 1989, Christian Educ. Centre 1990; Dr. hc (Artsakh); Kawkab Medal (First Class) Jordan 2000, Bethlehem 2000 Award (Palestinian Nat. Authority) 2000, Star of Romania 2000. *Address:* Mother See of Holy Etchmiadzin, Vagharsapat, Residence of the Catholicosate of All Armenians, Etchmiadzin, Armenia. *Telephone:* (2) 28-86-66, (1) 28-57-37. *Fax:* (2) 15-10-77, (1) 15-10-77. *E-mail:* mairator@arminco.com, holysee@etchmiadzin.am.

KARELIN, Col Aleksander Aleksandrovich; Russian politician and wrestler; b. 19 Sept. 1967, Novosibirsk; ed Novosibirsk Pedagogical Inst.; turned professional 1978; unbeaten for 12 years until the Sydney Olympics; world champion (nine times), European champion (12 times); Olympic champion 1988, 1992, 1996; Olympic silver medallist, Sydney 2000; mem. of team Dynamo; now works for tax police; co-founder and co-leader Yedinstvo; mem. State Duma 1999–; USSR Merited Master of Sports, Hero of Russia 1997. *Leisure interests:* poetry, literature, classical music. *Address:* State Duma, Yedinstvo Faction, Okhotny Ryad 1, 103265 Moscow, Russia (Office). *Telephone:* (095) 292-56-97 (Office).

KARGBO, Tom Obakeh, BA, DipEd, MSc, PhD; Sierra Leonean diplomatist; b. 17 July 1945, Mabonto; s. of Pa Yamba Kargbo and Leah Susannah Kargbo; m. Mary Kargbo 1980; one s. two d.; ed Fourah Bay Coll., Univ. of Sierra Leone and Univ. of Salford, Manchester, England; Lecturer St Augustine's Teachers' Coll., Makeni 1969–72; Sr teacher Muslim Brotherhood Secondary School, Freetown 1973–75; Lecturer Dept of Environmental Studies and Geography, Njala Univ. Coll., Univ. of Sierra Leone 1984–87; Perm. Rep. of Sierra Leone to UN, New York 1987–92; Amb. to USA 1993–94. *Publications:* numerous papers including two for UNICEF (on disability) and one for FAO (on rural issues). *Leisure interests:* reading, games (outdoor). *Address:* c/o Department of Foreign Affairs and International Co-operation, Gloucester Street, Freetown, Sierra Leone.

KARHILO, Aarno, LLM; Finnish diplomatist; b. 22 Nov. 1927, Helsinki; m.; two c.; ed Univ. of Helsinki; entered diplomatic service 1952; served in Helsinki, Washington and Rio de Janeiro; First Sec., Rome 1961; Counsellor and Deputy Chief of Mission, UN 1963–65, Moscow 1966–68; Adviser to del. at UN Gen. Ass. 1959–60, 1963–65, 1969–71, Vice-Chair. 1972–76, 1988–92; Amb. to Japan 1971–72; Perm. Rep. to UN 1972–77; Perm. Rep. to UNESCO and Amb. to France 1977–82, to USSR 1983–88; Under-Sec. of State for Political Affairs, Ministry for Foreign Affairs, Helsinki 1988–92, Acting Sec. of State 1992–93; Vice-Chair. ECOSOC 1973, Pres. 1974; Chair. Finnish del. for ECOSOC Sessions 1972–74; Pres. Bd of Finnish Nat. Opera 1990–95; Chair. Council of Finnish Design Forum 1989–95; mem. Council for Naantali Music Festival 1985–, Editorial Bd Nat. Defence (periodical) 1989–, Council, Red Cross of Finland 1991–. *Publications:* articles on foreign policy and cultural policy. *Leisure interest:* the arts.

KARIEVA, Bernara; Uzbekistan ballerina; b. 28 Jan. 1936, Tashkent; d. of Rakhim Kariev; m. Kulakhmat Rizaev; two d.; ed Tashkent Choreography School (under N. A. Dovgelli and L. A. Zass) 1947–51 and Moscow School of Choreography (under M. A. Kozhukhova); Prin. ballerina with Navoi Theatre, Tashkent 1955–96, Bolshoi Ballet Moscow 1957–, Dir Bolshoi Navoi Theatre of Opera and Ballet 1994–; mem. CPSU 1967–91; dances frequently with the Bolshoi Ballet, Moscow and has given many performances abroad; Prof. of Choreography; USSR People's Deputy 1989–91; mem. UNESCO Nat. Comm. on Culture, Uzbekistan, Asscn of Actors of Uzbekistan 1984–98; Adviser to Minister of Culture 2003–; Awards include Uzbek State Prize 1970, People's Artist of USSR 1973, USSR State Prize 1982; Uzbek Order of Dustlike; 200th Anniversary of Pushkin Medal. *Roles include:* Odette/Odile (Swan Lake by Tchaikovsky), Giselle (by Adan), Anna Karenina (by Shchedrin), Donna Anna (Don Juan), Zarriny (Love and the Sword by Ashrify), Dea (by Gugo), Madame Bovary (by Flaubert), Spartacus (by Khachaturian), Maskarad, Neznakomka (by Blok), Othello, Hamlet. *Ballets include:* Ballet Princess. *Film appearances:* I'm a Ballerina, Born Miniatures, Variations. *Leisure interests:* piano music, visually discovering the world. *Address:* Ministry of Culture, 51 Khamza Street, Tashkent, Uzbekistan. *Telephone:* (371) 136-14–15 (Office); (371) 132-10-20 (Home). *Fax:* (371) 133-46-58 (Office). *Website:* gabt-uz.narod.ru (Home).

KARIM, Mustai (pseudonym of Mustafa Safich Karimov); Russian (Bashkir) writer and poet; b. 20 Oct. 1919, Kliashevo, Bashkiria; s. of Safa Karimov and Vazifa Karimova; m. Rauza Saubanova 1941; one s. one d.; ed Bashkir Pedagogical Inst. 1940; first Publ 1935; mem. CPSU 1944–91, Soviet Army 1941–45; Chair. Bashkir Writers' Union 1951–62; Sec. Russian Writer's Union 1964–80; Hon. mem. Acad. of Sciences of Bashkortostan 1991; People's Poet of Bashkortostan 1963, State Prize (USSR) 1972, Hero of Socialist Labour 1979, Lenin Prize 1984, Int. Sholokhov Prize 1999; 10 state orders of USSR and Russia. *Plays include:* The Wedding Feast Goes On 1947, Lonely Birch 1950, Abduction of a Girl 1959, A Song Unsung 1961, On the Night of the Lunar Eclipse 1964, Salavat 1973, Prometheus 1975, A Horse to Dictator! 1980, Evening Meal 1993. *Publications include:* The Detachment Moves Off 1938, Spring Voices 1941, December Song 1942, The Girls from Our Kolkhoz 1948, Sabantui 1953, Europe-Asia 1951–54, Poems on Viet Nam 1956–57, Viet Nam Is Not Far 1958, Selected Works (two vols) 1969, Year by Year 1971, A Long-Long Childhood 1972–78, Collected Works 1983, Homeland, Bread, Love 1985, Forgiveness 1985, The Village Advocates 1989, Flashes of Life 1991, Evening Meal 1993, The Return 1994, Daddy Yalaletdin 1996, Collected Works (five vols) 1996–99, Memoirs 2002. *Leisure interests:* fishing, playing preference, Bashkit folk songs. *Address:* Engels St. 5, Fl. 17, Ufa 450077, Russia. *Telephone:* (3472) 51-65-52. *E-mail:* karim@anrb.ru.

KARIM-LAMRANI, Mohammed; Moroccan politician and government official; b. 1 May 1919, Fez; m.; four c.; econ. adviser to HM King Hassan II; Dir-Gen. Office Chérifien des Phosphates 1967–90; Chair. Crédit du Maroc; Minister of Finance April–Aug. 1971; Prime Minister 1971–72, 1983–86, 1992–94; Pres. Crédit du Maroc, Phosphates de Boucraa, Société Marocaine de Distillation et Rectification; f. and Pres. Soc. Nat. d'Investissements 1966–; Ouissam de Grand Officier de l'Ordre du Trône, Légion d'honneur, Order of Rising Sun (Japan). *Address:* Rue du Mont Saint Michel, Anfa Supérieur, Casablanca 21300, Morocco.

KARIMOV, Dzhamshed Khilolovich, DEcon; Tajikistan politician; b. 4 Aug. 1940, Dushanbe; m.; two c.; ed Moscow Technological Inst. of Light Industry; researcher Cen. Research Inst. of Econs and Math., USSR Acad. of Sciences; Asst Chair of Econ. on Industry Tajik State Univ., Jr researcher, Head of Div. of Optimal Planning Inst. of Econ., Tajik Acad. of Sciences 1962–72, Deputy Dir, Dir Research Inst. of Econ. and Econ.-Mathematical

Methods of Planning, State Planning Cttee, Tajik SSR 1972–81; Corresp. mem. Tajik Acad. of Sciences; Deputy Chair. State Planning Cttee 1981–88; Deputy Chair. Council of Ministers, Chair. State Planning Cttee 1988–89; First Sec. Dushanbe City Cttee of CP Tajikistan 1989–91; USSR People's Deputy 1989–92; Deputy, First Deputy Chair. Council of Ministers Tajik Repub. 1991–92; represented Repub. of Tajikistan in Russia 1992–93; Chief Adviser on Econ. to Pres. Sept.–Nov. 1994; Prime Minister of Tajikistan 1994–96; Adviser to Pres. Rakhmonov 1996–97; Amb. to People's Repub. China 1997–. *Address:* c/o Ministry of Foreign Affairs, Rudaki prosp. 42, 734051 Dushanbe, Tajikistan.

KARIMOV, Islam, CAND.ECON.SC.; Uzbekistan politician; b. 30 Jan. 1938, Samarkand; m. Tat'yana Karimova; two d.; ed Cen. Asian Polytechnic and Tashkent Econs Inst.; mem. CPSU 1964–91; work in Tashkent aviation construction factory 1960–66; Sr specialist, head of section, Vice-Chair. of Uzbekistan Gosplan 1966–83; Minister of Finance, Deputy Chair. of Council of Ministers, Uzbek SSR 1983–86; First Sec. of Kashkadarinsk Dist Cttee (obkom) 1986–89; First Sec. Cen. Cttee Uzbek CP 1989–91; USSR People's Deputy 1989–91; Mem. Cen. Cttee CPSU and Politburo 1990–91; Pres. of Uzbek SSR 1990; Chair. People's Democratic Party of Uzbekistan 1991–96; Pres. of Uzbekistan 1991–, concurrently Chair. Cabinet of Ministers; Hon. Chair. Fund of Friendship of Cen. Asia and Kazakhstan; various decorations. *Publications:* Uzbekistan's Way of Restoration and Progress, To Complete the Noble Cause, Uzbekistan's Way of Strengthening Economic Reforms 1995, Stability and Reforms 1996, Uzbekistan on the Threshold of the Twenty-First Century 1997. *Address:* Office of the President, Uzbekistansky str. 43, 700163 Tashkent, Uzbekistan. *Telephone:* (3712) 139-53-00; (3712) 139-54-56. *Fax:* (3712) 139-55-25.

KARINA, Anna (Hanne Karin Bayer); French film actress; b. 22 Sept. 1940, Fredriksburg, Solbjerg, Denmark; d. of Carl Johann Bayer and of Elva Helvig Frederiksen; m. 1st Jean-Luc Godard (q.v.) (divorced); m. 2nd Pierre-Antoine Fabre 1968 (divorced); m. 3rd Daniel Georges Duval 1978; Prix Orange. *Films include:* She'll Have To Go 1961, Une femme est une femme 1961, Vivre sa vie 1962, Le petit soldat 1963, Bande à part 1964, Alphaville 1965, Made in the USA 1966, La religieuse 1968, The Magus 1968, Before Winter Comes 1968, Laughter in the Dark 1969, Justine 1969, The Salzburg Connection 1972, Living Together 1974, L'assassin musicien 1975, Les oeufs brouillés 1976, Boulette chinoise 1977, L'ami de Vincent 1983, Ave Maria 1984, Dernier été à Tanger 1987, Cayenne Palace 1987, L'Oeuvre au noir 1988, Last Song 1989, L'Homme qui voulait être coupable 1990, Une Histoire d'amour 2000; has also appeared on television and in theatre. *Album:* Une histoire d'amour 2000. *Publications:* Golden City 1983, On n'achète pas le soleil (novel) 1988. *Address:* c/o Ammédia, 20 avenue Rapp, 75007 Paris (Office); Orban éditions, 76 rue Bonaparte, 75006 Paris, France.

KARLE, Isabella, PhD; American chemist; b. Isabella Helen Lugoski, 2 Dec. 1921, Detroit, Mich.; d. of Zygmunt A. Lugoski and Elizabeth Lugoski (née Graczyk); m. Jerome Karle (q.v.) 1942; three d.; ed Univ. of Michigan; Assoc. Chemist, Univ. of Chicago 1944; Instructor in Chem., Univ. of Mich. 1944–46; Physicist, Naval Research Lab., Washington, DC 1946–; mem. NAS, American Crystallographic Asscn American Chem. Soc., American Physical Soc., American Biophysical Soc., American Peptide Soc., American Philosophical Soc., American Acad. of Arts and Sciences; Hon. DSc (Mich.) 1976, (Wayne State) 1979, (Md) 1986, (Athens) 1997, (Univ. of Pa) 1999, (Harvard) 2001, (Jagiellonian Univ., Kraków) 2002; Hon. DHumLitt (Georgetown) 1984, Lifetime Achievement Award (Women in Science and Eng) 1986, Gregori Aminoff Prize (Swedish Royal Acad. of Sciences) 1988, Bijvoet Medal (Univ. of Utrecht, The Netherlands) 1990, Bower Award in Science (Franklin Inst.) 1993, Chemical Sciences Award (NAS) 1995, Nat. Medal of Science (Pres.'s Award, USA) 1995, and other awards and honours. *Publications:* over 300 scientific articles, chapters and reviews. *Leisure interests:* swimming, ice skating, needlework. *Address:* Naval Research Laboratory, Code 6030, Washington, DC 20375 (Office); 6304 Lakeview Drive, Falls Church, VA 22041, USA (Home). *Telephone:* (202) 767-2624 (Office). *Fax:* (202) 767-6874 (Office).

KARLE, Jerome, PhD; American government scientist; b. 18 June 1918, Brooklyn, New York; s. of Louis Karfunkle and Sadie Helen Kun; m. Isabella Karle (née Lugoski) 1942; three d.; ed Abraham Lincoln High School, City Coll. of New York, Harvard Univ. and Univ. of Mich.; Head, Electron Diffraction Section, Naval Research Lab. 1946–58, Head, Diffraction Branch 1958–68, Chief Scientist, Lab. for the Structure of Matter 1968–; Prof. (part-time), Univ. of Maryland 1951–70; Pres. American Crystallographic Asscn 1972; Chair. US Nat. Cttee for Crystallography of NAS and Nat. Research Council 1973–75; Pres. Int. Union of Crystallography 1981–84; Charter mem. Sr Exec. Service 1979; Fellow, American Physical Soc.; mem. NAS; jt recipient of Nobel Prize for Chem. 1985, for devt of methods to determine the structures of crystals and several other awards. *Publications:* one book and about 200 research and review articles on theoretical and experimental topics associated with the study of the structures of materials by diffraction methods. *Leisure interests:* stereo-photography, swimming, ice-skating. *Address:* Naval Research Laboratory for the Structure of Matter, Code 6030, Washington, DC 20375, USA. *Telephone:* (202) 767-2665.

KARLIC, Mgr Estanislao Esteban; Argentine ecclesiastic; b. 7 Feb. 1926, Oliva; ordained priest 1954; ordained Bishop and apptd Auxiliary Bishop of Córdoba 1977; Coadjutor Archbishop of Paraná 1983, Archbishop of Paraná 1986–; Pres. Exec. Comm. of Episcopal Conf. of Argentina; mem. Special

Council for America of Gen. Secr. of Synod of Bishops. *Address:* Conferencia Episcopal Argentina, Suipacha 1034, 1008 Buenos Aires, Argentina (Office). *Telephone:* (11) 4328-0993 (Office). *Fax:* (11) 4328-9570 (Office). *E-mail:* seccea@cea.org.ar (Office). *Website:* www.cea.org.ar (Office).

KARLIN, Samuel, PhD; American mathematician; b. 8 June 1924, Yanova, Poland; m. Elsie Karlin (divorced); two s. one d.; ed Illinois Inst. of Technology and Princeton Univ.; Proctor Fellow, Univ. of Princeton 1945; Bateman Research Fellow, Calif. Inst. of Tech. 1947–48, Instructor 1948–49, Asst Prof. of Math. 1949–52; Visiting Asst Prof. of Math., Univ. of Princeton 1950–51; Assoc. Prof., Calif. Inst. of Tech. 1952–55, Prof. 1955–56; Prof. of Math., Univ. of Stanford 1956–; Elected Fellow, Inst. of Math. Statistics 1956, Wald Lecturer 1957–; Guggenheim Fellow 1959–60; Nat. Science Sr Fellow 1960–61; Elected Fellow, Int. Statistical Inst. 1964; mem. American Acad. of Arts and Sciences 1970; mem. NAS; Andrew D. White Prof.-at-Large, Cornell Univ. 1975–81; Wilks Lecturer, Univ. of Princeton 1977; Pres. Inst. of Math. Statistics 1978–79; Commonwealth Lecturer, Univ. of Massachusetts 1980; Fellow, AAAS 1981; Gibbs Lecturer, First Mahalanobis Memorial Lecturer, Indian Statistical Inst., Fisher Memorial Lecturer, London 1983; Britton Lecturer, McMaster Univ., Canada; mem. Human Genome Org. 1990, American Philosophical Soc. 1995; Cockerham Lecturer, North Carolina State Univ. 1996; mem. editorial bds. of numerous learned journals; Hon. DSc (Technion-Israel Inst. of Tech.) 1985; John Von Neumann Theory Prize, Operations Research Soc. of America 1987; Nat. Acad. of Sciences Award for Applied Math. 1973, Lester R. Ford Award, American Math. Asscn 1973, Robert Grimmett Chair of Math., Univ. of Stanford 1978; US Nat. Medal of Science 1989, Karlin Prize in Mathematical Biology, Stanford Univ. 1992. *Publications:* Sex Ratio Evolution (with Sabin Lessard) 1986, Evolutionary Processes and Theory (Ed. with E. Nevo) 1986, over 430 articles in various journals on topics of pure and applied probability theory, game theory, decision theory and statistical methodology, mathematical analysis and mathematical biology. *Address:* Department of Mathematics, Stanford University, Building 380, Stanford, CA 94305-2125, USA. *Telephone:* (650) 723-2204. *Fax:* (650) 725-2040. *E-mail:* karlin@math.stanford.edu (Office).

KARLOV, Nikolai Vasilyevich; Russian physicist; b. 15 Oct. 1929, Leningrad; m.; one s. one d.; ed Moscow State Univ.; worker aviation plant, Moscow 1943–47; Jr, then Sr researcher, then Head of Sector Lebedev Physical Inst., USSR Acad. of Sciences 1955–83, Head of Sector, then Head of Div. Inst. of Gen. Physics 1983–87; Rector Moscow Inst. of Physics and Tech. 1987–97; USSR People's Deputy 1989–91; Chair. Higher Attestation Cttee 1992–98; Adviser to Russian Acad. of Sciences 1999–; corresp. mem. Russian Acad. of Sciences 1984; USSR State Prize 1976, Order of Friendship. *Publications:* 13 scientific books including Intense Resonant Interactions in Quantum Electronics (with V. M. Akulin) 1992, Lectures on Quantum Electronics 1993, Laser Thermo-Chemistry (with others) 2000; over 300 articles in scientific journals. *Leisure interests:* history of Russia, old Russian literature, foreign languages. *Address:* Moscow Institute of Physics and Technology, Institutsky per. 9, 141700 Dolgoprudny, Moscow, Russia (Office). *Telephone:* (095) 408-81-54 (Office); (095) 135-13-86 (Home). *Fax:* (095) 408-81-54 (Office). *E-mail:* karlov@peterl.culture.mipt.ru (Office).

KARLSSON, Jan O., BA; Swedish government minister, international organization official and fmr civil servant; b. 1 June 1939, Stockholm; ed Univ. of Stockholm; Admin. Officer, Head of Section, Ministry of Agric. 1962–68; Political Adviser, Cabinet Office 1968–73, Co-ordinating Adviser 1990–91; Sec. to City Commr, Stockholm City Council 1973–77; Deputy Sec. to Presidium, Nordic Council 1977–82; Under-Sec. of State to Minister for Nordic Co-operation 1982–85; Under-Sec. of State, Ministry of Finance 1985–88; Chair. Comm. on Metropolitan Problems 1988–90; Prime Minister's Personal Rep. on Nordic Co-operation in connection with membership of EEA and EU 1991–92; Negotiator and Adviser, Social Democratic Party 1992–94; Dir-Gen. Ministry for Foreign Affairs 1994; Minister for Devt Co-operation, Migration and Asylum Policy 2002–; mem. European Court of Auditors 1995, Pres. 1999–; mem. editorial staff TIDEN periodical 1974–82, Ed.-in-Chief 1978–82; mem. Bd Nordic Investment Bank 1983–89, Nat. Pharmacy Corpn 1986–91; Chair. Bd Swedish Nat. Housing Finance Corpn 1986–89; Chair. OECD Project Group on Housing, Social Integration and Liveable Environments in Cities 1991–93; fmr mem. Bd Stockholm Philharmonic. *Address:* Ministry for Foreign Affairs, 10339 Stockholm, Sweden (Office). *Telephone:* (8) 405-55-37 (Office). *Fax:* (8) 405-55-87 (Office). *E-mail:* jan.karlsson@ foreign.ministry.se (Office). *Website:* www.ud.se (Office).

KARMAPA, The (Urgyen Trinley Doje); Tibetan Buddhist leader; Living Buddha of the White Sect, Tibet; Seventeenth Incarnation; enthroned 1992; now living in exile in Dharamsala, India.

KARMAZIN, Mel; American media executive; b. 1944; stage man. CBS Radio 1960–70, Chair., CEO CBS Station Group 1996–, now Pres., COO CBS Corpn; Vice Pres., Gen. Man. Metromedia Inc. 1970–81; Pres. Infinity Broadcasting Corpn 1981–96, CEO 1988–96; Pres., COO Viacom Inc. May 2000–. *Address:* CBS Corporation, 51 West 52nd Street, New York, NY 10019, USA.

KARMEL, Peter Henry, AC, CBE, BA, PhD; Australian academic administrator; b. 9 May 1922, Melbourne; s. of Simeon Karmel and Ethel Karmel; m. Lena Garrett 1946; one s. five d.; ed Univ. of Melbourne, Trinity Coll., Cambridge; Research Officer, Commonwealth Bureau of Census and Statistics 1943–45; Lecturer in Econs, Univ. of Melbourne 1946, Sr Lecturer

1948–49; George Gollin Prof. of Econs and Dean of Faculty of Econs, Univ. of Adelaide 1950–62, Prin. (desig.), Univ. of Adelaide at Bedford Park (later Flinders Univ. of S. Australia) 1961–66, Vice-Chancellor 1966–71; Visiting Prof., Queen's University, Belfast 1957–58; Chair., Interim Council, Univ. of Papua New Guinea 1965–69, Chancellor 1969–70; Chair., Australian Univs Comm. 1971–77, Interim Cttee for Schools Comm. 1972–73, Australia Council 1974–77, Commonwealth Tertiary Educ. Comm. 1977–82; Pres., Australian Council for Educational Research 1979–99; Vice-Chancellor, Australian Nat. Univ. 1982–87; Chair., Commonwealth Govt Quality of Educ. Review Cttee 1984–85, Australian Inst. of Health 1987–92; Pres. Acad. of Social Sciences in Australia 1987–90; Exec. Chair., Canberra Inst. of the Arts 1988–91; Chair. Australian Nat. Council on AIDS 1988–91, Chair. Bd of Nat. Inst. of the Arts, Australian Nat. Univ. 1992–; Fellow Acad. of the Social Sciences in Australia 1952–, Australian Coll. of Educ. 1969–; Hon. LLD (Univ. of Papua New Guinea) 1970, (Melbourne) 1975; Hon. DLitt (Flinders) 1971, (Murdoch) 1975, (Macquarie) 1992; Hon. DUniv (Newcastle, NSW) 1978; Dr hc (Queensland) 1985; Mackie Medal 1975, Australian Coll. of Educ. Medal 1981. *Publications include:* 3 textbooks on econs and statistics; 115 papers in learned journals, etc. *Address:* 4/127 Hopetoun Circuit, Yarralumla, ACT 2600, Australia. *Telephone:* (2) 6285-2414 (Home); (2) 6125-5701 (Office). *Fax:* (2) 6282-7778 (Home); (2) 6125-5705 (Office).

KARMI, Ram; Israeli architect; b. 1931, Jerusalem; m.; three s. three d.; ed Architectural Asscn School, London; joined father's architectural office in partnership Karmi-Meltzer-Karmi 1956; est. (with sister) office of Ram Karmi, Ada Karmi-Melamed, Karmi Assoc. 1962; est. Karmi Assoc. (br. office), New York 1972; Chief Architect, Ministry of Housing 1975–79; Partner, Karmi Architects & Co., Tel-Aviv 1979–; various teaching posts at Faculty of Architecture and Town Planning, Technion since 1964, Assoc. Prof. 1987–94; Visiting Prof. Princeton Univ. 1969, MIT 1972; projects include univ. bldgs (Faculty of Humanities, Hebrew Univ., Mt Scopus), schools, hotels (Holyland Compound, Jerusalem), pvt. homes, large housing projects (Giloh, Jerusalem), public bldgs (Museum of Children of the Holocaust, Supreme Court, Jerusalem) and industrial complexes; numerous awards and competition prizes including Israel Prize for Architecture 2002. *Publications:* articles in professional journals. *Address:* Ram Karmi Architects, 17 Kaplan Street, Tel-Aviv 64734, Israel. *Telephone:* (3) 6913646. *Fax:* (3) 6913508. *E-mail:* office@karmi.co.il.

KARMOKOV, Khachim Mukhamedovich, DEcon; Russian economist and politician; b. 2 May 1941, Zayukovo, Kabardin-Balkar Autonomous Repub.; m.; one d.; ed Kabardin-Balkar State Univ., Moscow Inst. for Eng and Econs; Eng and managerial posts in construction industry 1963–67, 1978–81; teacher, docent Kabardin-Balkar State Univ. 1967–78; Financial Dir Trust Kabbalpromstroi 1981–90; Deputy Chair. Council of Ministers, Kabardin-Balkar Repub. 1990–91; Chair. Supreme Soviet Kabardin-Balkar Repub. 1991–93; Chair. Accounts Chamber of Russian Fed. 1994–; mem. State Duma Russian Fed. 1993–95; Rep. of Kabardino-Balkan Repub. in Council of Fed. 2001–; mem. Russian Acad. of Natural Sciences, Int. Acad. of Informatization. *Leisure interest:* hunting. *Address:* Council of Federation, B. Dmitrovka 26, 103426 Moscow (Office); Lenina Prospect 27, Suite 327, Nalchik 360028, Kabardino-Balkaria, Russia (Office). *Telephone:* (095) 291-11-50 (Moscow) (Office); (86622) 74050 (Nalchik) (Office).

KARMOUL, Akram Jamil, PhD; Jordanian business executive and consultant; b. 13 Aug. 1939, W Bank; m. Huda Abu-Errub 1964; two s. two d.; ed Assiut Univ., Strathclyde Univ., Imperial Coll., London; geologist, geophysicist and mining engineer 1961–72; Dir Industry, later Dir Science and Tech. Ministry of Planning 1972–80; Dir Gen. of Industry Ministry of Industry and Trade 1980–87; Dir, Man. Industrial, Commercial and Agric. Co. 1987; Exec. Dir, Asst Man. Dalla-Al-Baraka Saudi Group, Jeddah 1988–89; Dir of Industry Dept UN-ESCWA Comm. for W Asia 1989–93; Gen. Man. United Textile Group 1995; Assoc. Consultant Arab Consulting Centre and Assignments UNDP 1996–; Cand. Gen. Man. for a public firm 1996–; Science Award for Outstanding Persons. *Publications:* numerous works on mineral wealth and industrial tech. of Jordan, public enterprises. *Leisure interests:* reading, swimming.

KARNAD, Girish, MA; Indian playwright, film-maker and actor; b. 19 May 1938, Matheran; s. of Raghunath Karnad and Krishnabai Karnad; m. Saraswarthy Ganapathy 1980; one s. one d.; ed Karnatak Coll., Dharwad and Univ. of Oxford; Rhodes Scholar, Oxford 1960–63; Pres. Oxford Union Soc. 1963; Asst Man. Oxford Univ. Press, Madras 1963–69, Man. 1969–70; Homi Bhabha Fellow 1970–72; Dir Film & TV Inst. of India, Pune 1974, 1975; Visiting Prof. and Fulbright Scholar-in-Residence Univ. of Chicago 1987–88; Indian Co-Chair., Media Cttee, Indo-US Subcomm. 1984–93; Chair. Sangeet Natak Akademi (Nat. Acad. of Performing Arts) 1988–93; Dir The Nehru Centre, London 2000; Fellow Sangeet Natak Acad. 1994; Hon. DLitt (Univ. of Karnataka) 1994; several awards for film work; Padma Bhushan 1992, Bharatiya Jnanapith Award 1999, Sahitya Acad. Award 1994. *Plays:* Yayati 1961, Tughlaq 1964, Hayavadana 1971, Anjumallige 1976, Nagamandala 1988, Taledanda 1990, Agni Mattu Male 1995, Tipu Sultan Kanda Kanasu 2000, Bali 2002. *Films:* Vamsha Vriksha 1971, Kaadu 1973, Tabbaliyu Neenade Magane 1977, Ondanondu Kaaladalli 1978, Utsav 1984, Cheluvi 1992, Kanooru Heggadithi 1999. *Radio:* Ma Nishada 1986, The Dreams of Tipu Sultan 1997. *TV:* Antaraal 1996, Swarajnama 1997, Kanooru Ki Thakurani 1999, wrote and presented The Bhagavad Gita for BBC Two 2002. *Address:* The Nehru Centre, 8 South Audley Street, London, W1K 1HF,

England (Office); 697, 15th Cross, JP Nagar Phase II, Bangalore 560 078, India (Home). *Telephone:* (20) 7491-3567, (20) 7493-2019 (Office); (80) 659 0463 (Bangalore); (20) 7355-2069 (Home). *Fax:* (20) 7409-3360 (Office); (80) 659-0019 (Bangalore). *E-mail:* gkarnad38@aol.com (Home); nerhucentre@aol .com (Office). *Website:* www.nehrucentre.org.

KAROUI, Hamed, PhD; Tunisian politician; b. 30 Dec 1927, Sousse; m.; four c.; ed Faculté de Médecine de Paris; doctor at Sousse Regional Hosp. 1957–; active in the Destour Movt from 1942, including responsibility for Al Kifah journal; Pres. Féd. Destourienne de France; Municipal Councillor, Sousse 1957–72, Mayor 1985; Deputy to the Nat. Ass. 1964, re-elected 1981 and 1989; Vice-Pres. Chamber of Deputies 1983–86; Minister for Youth and Sports 1986–87; Dir Parti Socialiste Destourien (renamed Rassemblement constitutionnel démocratique, 1988) 1987, now Vice-Chair.; Minister for Justice 1988–89; Prime Minister 1989–99; Grand Cordon Ordre de l'Indépendance et de la République (Tunisia). *Address:* Rassemblement constitutionnel démocratique, blvd 9 avril 1938, Tunis, Tunisia. *E-mail:* info@rcd.tn (Office). *Website:* www.rcd.tn (Office).

KARPLUS, Martin, PhD; American professor of chemistry; b. 15 March 1930, Vienna, Austria; s. of Hans Goldstern and Isabella Goldstern; m. Marci Hazard 1981; one s. two d.; ed Harvard Univ. and California Inst. of Tech.; Nat. Science Foundation Postdoctoral Fellow, Mathematical Inst., Oxford; Asst Prof., Dept of Chem., Univ. of Illinois 1955–59; Assoc. Prof. 1960; Prof. of Chem., Columbia Univ. 1960–66, Harvard Univ. Cambridge, Mass. 1966–, Theodore William Richards Prof. of Chem., Harvard Univ. 1979–99, Research Prof. 1999–; Visiting Prof. Univ. of Paris 1972–73, 1980–81 (Prof. 1974–75), Collège de France 1980–81, 1987–88; Prof. Conventionné Louis Pasteur Univ. 1992, 1994–; Theodore William Richards Research Prof., Harvard Univ. 1999–, Eastman Prof., Univ. of Oxford 1999–2000; mem. European Acad. of Arts, Sciences and Humanities, NAS, American Acad. of Arts and Sciences, Int. Acad. of Quantum Molecular Science; Foreign mem. Netherlands Acad. of Arts and Science; Dr. hc (Sherbrooke) 1998; Joseph O. Hirschfelder Prize in Theoretical Chem. (Univ. of Wisconsin) 1995; Harrison Howe Award, American Chem. Soc. (Rochester Section) 1967, Award for Outstanding Contrib. to Quantum Biology (Int. Soc. of Quantum Biology) 1979, Distinguished Alumni Award (Calif. Inst. of Tech.) 1986, Irving Langmuir Award (American Physical Soc.) 1987, Nat. Lecturer (Biophysical Soc.) 1991, Theoretical Chem. Award (ACS, first recipient) 1993, Anfinsen Award, Portein Soc. 2001. *Publications:* Atoms and Molecules (with R. N Porter) 1970, A Theoretical Perspective of Dynamics, Structure and Thermodynamics (with C. L. Brooks III and B. M. Pettitt) 1988; over 600 articles in the field of theoretical chemistry. *Address:* Laboratoire de Chimie Biophysique, ISIS, Université Louis Pasteur, 67000 Strasbourg, France (Office); Department of Chemistry, Harvard University, 12 Oxford Street, Cambridge, MA 02138, USA.

KARPOV, Anatoliy Yevgenievich, DEcon; Russian chess player; b. 23 May 1951, Zlatoust; s. of Yevgeniy Stepanovich Karpov and Nina Karpov; m. 1st Irina Karpov; one s.; m. 2nd Natalia Bulanova; one d.; ed Leningrad Univ.; mem. CPSU 1980–91; USSR Candidate Master 1962, Master 1966; European Jr Champion 1967, 1968, World Jr Champion 1969; Int. Master 1969, Int. Grandmaster 1970; USSR Champion 1976, 1983, 1988; world champion 1975–85; became world champion when the holder Bobby Fischer (q.v.) refused to defend the title and he retained his title against Viktor Korchnoi in 1978 and in 1981; defended against Garry Kasparov (q.v.) in Moscow Sept. 1984; the match later adjourned due to the illness of both players; lost to the same player in 1985; unsuccessfully challenged Kasparov 1986, 1987, 1990; won World Championship title under FIDE after split in chess orgs. 1993, 1996, 1998; has won more tournaments than any other player (over 160); first player to become a millionaire from playing chess; People's Deputy of USSR 1989–91; Pres. Soviet Peace Fund (now Int. Asscn of Peace Funds) 1982–; Pres. Chernobyl-Aid org. 1989–; UNICEF Amb. for Russia and E Europe 1998–; Chair. Council of Dirs. Fed. Industrial Bank, Moscow; mem. Soviet (now Russian) UNESCO Affairs Comm.; mem. Bd Int. Chess Fed.; Ed.-in-Chief Chess Review 64 (magazine) 1980–91; Winner of Oscar Chess Prize 1973–77, 1979–81, 1984, 1994, Fontany di Roma Prize for humanitarian achievements 1996; Hon. Texan, Hon. Citizen of Tula, Zlatoust, Orsk and other cities in Russia, Belarus and Ukraine. *Publications:* Chess is My Life 1980, Karpov Teaches Chess 1987, Karpov on Karpov 1991, How to Play Chess and 47 other books. *Leisure interest:* philately. *Address:* International Peace Fund, Prechistenka 10, Moscow, Russia. *Telephone:* (095) 202-41-71, 202-42-36.

KARPOV, Vladimir Vasilyevich; Russian author and editor; b. 28 July 1922, Orenburg; s. of Vasiliy Karpov and Lydia Karpov; m. Evgenia Vasilievna Karpov 1956; one s. two d.; ed Military Acad., Moscow and Gorky Literary Inst.; arrested 1941, sent to camp, released to join a penal Bn, subsequently distinguishing himself in mil. reconnaissance work; mem. CPSU 1943–91; started publishing (novels, stories, essays) 1948–; Deputy Ed. of Oktyabr 1974–77; Sec. of Presidium of USSR Union of Writers 1981–86, First Sec. 1986–91; Chief Ed. of Novy mir 1981–86; Deputy to the Presidium of the USSR Supreme Soviet 1984–89; mem. CPSU Cen. Cttee 1988–90, USSR People's Deputy 1989–91; mem. Acad. of Mil. Sciences; Hon. DLitt (Strathclyde Univ.); State Prize 1986, Hero of Soviet Union 1944. *Publications:* The Marshal's Baton 1970, Take Them Alive 1975, The Regimental Commander 1982–84, The Eternal Struggle 1987, Marshal Zhukov, (Vol. I) 1989, (Vol. II) 1992, (Vol. III) 1995, Selected Works (3 Vols), The Destiny of

a Scout (novel) 1999, The Executed Marshals 2000. *Leisure interests:* collecting books, especially on mil. history. *Address:* Kutozovsky prosp. 26, Apt. 94, Moscow, Russia. *Telephone:* (095) 249-26-12. *Fax:* (095) 200-02-93.

KARRUBI, Mahdi; Iranian politician; b. 1937; mem. of the Iranian Parl., Speaker 1989–92, May 2000–; mem. Asscn of Militant Clerics. *Address:* Majlis-e-Shura e Islami, Tehran, Iran (Office).

KARSENTI, René, MS, MBA, PhD; French international finance official; b. 27 Jan. 1950, Tlemcen, Algeria; s. of Leon Karsenti and Mireille Benham; m. Hélène Dayan 1978; two d.; ed ESCIL, Lyons, Paris Business School and Sorbonne, Paris; researcher in finance and Econs Univ. of Calif. Berkeley 1973; investment analyst/portfolio man. Caisse des Dépôts, Paris 1975–79; Finance Officer, World Bank (IBRD), Washington, DC 1979–83, Financial Adviser 1983–85, Div. Chief 1985–87, Sr Man. Finance Dept Treasury 1987–89; Treas., Dir Financial Policy Dept Int. Finance Corpn World Bank Group, Washington, DC 1989–91; Treas. European Bank for Reconstruction and Devt (EBRD) 1991–95; Dir-Gen. Finance, European Investment Bank 1995–; Chevalier Légion d'honneur. *Publications:* Research in Pharmaceutical Industry 1977; various financial lectures and articles on int. finance, capital markets and European Monetary Union. *Leisure interests:* swimming, antiques, opera. *Address:* European Investment Bank, 100 blvd Konrad Adenauer, 2950 Luxembourg. *Telephone:* 43-79-52-69 (Office). *Fax:* 43-79-52-62 (Office). *E-mail:* r.karsenti@eib.org (Office). *Website:* www.eib.org (Office).

KARSOU, Omar; Palestinian banker and politician; b. 1960, Nablus; m.; four c.; with family, est. foreign exchange business, Ramallah, set up offices in the West Bank, Jordan, Kuwait and Abu Dhabi (Ramallah offices ransacked by Israeli troops 2002); est. online foreign exchange business (after first co. assets frozen by Jordanian Govt 1986); advocate of democratic reform and a Palestinian constitution; Founder Democracy in Palestine Movt (to promote a rule of law in the Palestinian Authority) 2002; held talks with mems of US Admin. 2002; participated in political panel discussion, Hudson Inst., Washington DC Oct. 2002.

KARTASHKIN, Vladimir Aleksandrovich, DJur; Russian politician; b. 4 March 1941; m. Elena Kovanova 1991; one s. one d.; ed Moscow State Univ.; Chief Scientific Researcher Inst. of State and Law 1957–63, Chief Researcher, Prof. 1985–; with Div. of Human Rights UN 1969–73; Consultant UN Dir-Gen. on Juridical Problems 1979–85; Chair. Comm. on Human Rights Russian Presidency 1996–2002; Prof. Int. Inst. of Human Rights, Strasbourg, Cornell Univ., Santa-Clair Univ.; Univ. of Peoples' Friendship, Moscow. *Publications:* over 150 books and articles including Human Rights in International and State Law. *Leisure interests:* tennis, swimming. *Address:* Institute of State and Law, Russian Academy of Sciences, Znemaenka str. 10, 119841, Moscow, Russia (Office). *Telephone:* (095) 291-34-90 (Office).

KARTOMI, Margaret Joy, AM, BA, BMus, DPhil, FAHA, AUA; Australian musicologist; b. 24 Nov. 1940, Adelaide; d. of George Hutchesson and Edna Hutchesson; m. Hidris Kartomi 1961; one d.; ed Univ. of Adelaide, Humboldt Univ.; Lecturer Monash Univ. Music Dept 1969–70, Sr Lecturer 1971–73, Reader 1974–88, Prof. of Music 1986–, Head of Music Dept 1989–; Dir Inst. of Contemporary Asian Studies, Monash Univ. 1989–91; Dir Monash-ANZ Centre for Int. Briefing 1989–90, Monash Asia Inst. 1988–90; Dir-at-large Int. Musicology Soc. 1993–; Visiting Prof., Univ. of Calif., Berkeley 1986–87; Dir Symposium of Int. Musicological Soc., Melbourne 1988, 2004; Alexander Clarke Prize for Pianoforte Performance 1960, Dr Ruby Davy Prize for Musical Composition 1961, Fed. German Record Critics' Prize 1983, 1998. *Publications:* On Concepts and Classifications of Musical Instruments 1990, 14 other books (author or Ed.); numerous articles and 300 articles in the New Grove Dictionary of Musical Instruments 1989, The Gamelan Digul and the Prison Camp Musician Who Built It: An Australian Link with the Indonesian Revolution 1992. *Leisure interests:* tennis, badminton, concerts, theatre. *Address:* School of Music, Monash University, Wellington Rd. Clayton, Vic. 3168, Australia (Office). *Telephone:* (3) 9905-3230 (Office). *Fax:* (3) 9905-3241 (Office). *E-mail:* m.kartomi@arts.monash.edu.au (Office). *Website:* www.arts .monash.ed.au/music/about/Kartomi.html (Office).

KARUKUBIRO-KAMUNANWIRE, Perezi, PhD; Ugandan diplomatist; b. 25 July 1937, Mbarara; m.; two c.; ed Columbia Univ.; Chair. Uganda People's Congress Youth League 1958–63; Pres. and Chair. Pan-African Students' Org. in the Americas 1965–70; Prof. City Univ. of New York 1974–86; Amb. to Austria, Fed. Repub. of Germany and the Holy See and Perm. Rep. to int. orgs. in Vienna 1986–88; Perm. Rep. to UN, New York 1988–95; Chair. UN Gen. Ass. Special Political Cttee 1990–95. *Address:* c/o Ministry of Foreign Affairs, P.O. Box 7048, Kampala, Uganda.

KARUME, Amani Abeid; Tanzanian politician; b. 1948; s. of the late Abeid Amani Karume; fmr Minister of Communications and Transport, Zanzibar; Chair. and Pres. Supreme Revolutionary Council of Zanzibar 2000–; mem. Chama Cha Mapunduzi (CCM – Revolutionary Party of Tanzania). *Address:* State House, P.O. Box 776, Zanzibar, Tanzania (Office). *Telephone:* (54) 31822 (Office). *Fax:* (54) 33788 (Office).

KARUNANIDHI, Muthuvel (known as Kalaignar); Indian politician and playwright; b. 3 June 1924, Thirukkuvalai, Thanjavur; s. of Muthuvel Karunanidhi and Anjuham Karunanidhi; m. Dayalu Karunanidhi; four s. one d.; ed Thiruvarur Bd High School; Ed.-in-Charge Kudiarasu; journalist and stage and screen playwright in Tamil, acting in his own plays staged to collect party funds; has written over 35 film-plays including the screen version of the

Tamil classic Silappadhikaram, stage plays and short stories; started first student wing of the Dravidian movement called Tamilnadu Tamil Manavar Mandram; one of the founder mems. of Dravida Munnetra Kazhagam Legislative Party (DMK) 1949, Treas. 1961, Deputy Leader 1968, Pres. 1969–; founder-editor of the Tamil daily organ of the DMK Murasoli; represented Kulittalai in State Assembly 1957–62, Thanjavur 1962–67, Saidapet 1968; led the Kallakkudi Agitation and was imprisoned for six months; fmr Minister of Public Works; Chief Minister of Tamil Nadu (Madras) 1969–76 (presidential rule imposed), 1989–90, 1996–2001; arrested on corruption charges 2001, then released; Thamizha Vell (Patron of Tamil), Asscn of Research Scholars in Tamil 1971; Hon. DLitt (Annamalai Univ., Tamil Nadu) 1971. *Address:* Chief Minister's Secretariat, Fort St Georges, Chennai (Office); 7A S. Gopalapuram, IV Street, Chennai 600086, India (Home). *Telephone:* (44) 5362345 (Office); (44) 8275225 (Home).

KARZAI, Hamid; Afghanistan politician and head of state; b. 24 Dec. 1957, Popolzai; s. of the late Abdul-Ahad Karzai, Chief of Popolzai tribe, assassinated in Quetta 1999; ed in India; official rep. of deposed Afghan king, Zahir Shah; Deputy Foreign Minister 1992–96; went into exile 1996–2001; Chief of Popolzai tribe, S Afghanistan 1999–; consultant Union Oil Co. of Calif. (UNOCAL), USA; mem. Del. to Future of Afghanistan Govt Talks, Bonn Nov. 2001; Chair. Afghan Interim Authority Dec. 2001–June 2002; Pres. (elected by Loya Jirga—grand tribal council) June 2002–.

KASAHARA, Yukio, BEng; Japanese business executive; b. 27 Jan. 1925, Tokyo; m. Yuri Tsumura 1983; ed Tokyo Univ.; joined Nippon Mining Co. 1949, mem. Bd of Dirs 1974, Man. Dir and Gen. Man. Petroleum Group 1976, Sr Man. Dir and Gen. Man. Petroleum Group 1979, Exec. Vice-Pres. and Gen. Man. of Planning and Devt Group and Petroleum Group 1981, Pres. and Rep. Dir 1983–89, Chair. and Rep. Dir June 1989–; fmr Chair. Japan Energy Corpn. *Leisure interests:* reading, model railroading. *Address:* Nippon Mining Co. Ltd, 10-1, Toranomon 2-chome, Minato-ku, Tokyo, 107 (Office); 3–6–1201, Okubo 2-chome, Shinjuku-ku, Tokyo 169, Japan (Home). *Telephone:* (3) 3505-8111 (Office); (3) 202-3119 (Home).

KASAL, Jan; Czech politician; b. 6 Nov. 1951, Nove Město na Moravě; m. Jaroslava Ranecká; three d.; ed Czech Tech. Univ.; ind. research worker in hydraulic systems 1975–90; mem. Czechoslovak People's Party 1986–89; Vice-Chair. Christian Democratic Union–Czechoslovak People's Party 1992–99, 2001–(Chair. 1999–2001); mem. of Parl. 1990–, Vice-Chair. of Parl. 1990–98; Pres. European Acad. for Democracy 1993–. *Leisure interests:* history, literature, music. *Address:* Parliament Buildings, Sněmovni 4, 118 26 Prague 1, Czech Republic (Office). *Telephone:* (2) 57172095 (Office). *Fax:* (2) 57173637 (Office). *E-mail:* kasal@psp.cz (Office). *Website:* www.psp.cz (Office).

KASATKINA, Natalya Dmitriyevna; Russian ballet dancer and choreographer; b. 7 June 1934, Moscow; d. of Dmitriy A. Kasatkin and Anna A. Kardashova; m. Vladimir Vasilyov 1956; one s.; ed Bolshoi Theatre Ballet School; with Bolshoi Theatre Ballet Company 1954–76, main roles including Frigia (Spartacus), Fate (Carmen), The Possessed (The Rite of Spring); Choreographer (with V. Vasilyov) of Vanina Vanini 1962, Geologists 1964, The Rite of Spring 1965, Tristan and Isolde 1967, Preludes and Fugues 1968, Our Yard 1970, The Creation of the World 1971, Romeo and Juliet 1972, Prozrienie 1974, Gayane 1977, Mayakovsky (opera) 1981, Adam and Eve (film ballet) 1982, The Magic Cloak 1982, The Mischiefs of Terpsichore 1984, Blue Roses for a Ballerina (film ballet) 1985, Pushkin 1986, The Faces of Love 1987, Petersburg's Twilights 1987, The Fairy's Kiss 1989, Don Quixote (film ballet) 1990; TV Film: Choreographic Novels; Head (with V. Vasilyov); Moscow State Classical Ballet Theatre 1977–; wrote libretto and produced operas Peter I 1975, Così fan Tutte (with V. Vasilyov) 1978; choreographed (with V. Vasilyov) Spartacus (Khachaturian) 2002; State Prize of USSR 1976, People's Actress of RSFSR 1984. *Leisure interests:* drawing, cooking. *Address:* Karetny Riad 5/10, Apt. 37, 103006 Moscow, Russia. *Telephone:* (095) 299-95-24. *Fax:* (095) 921-31-27.

KASDAN, Lawrence Edward, BA, MA; American film director and screenwriter; b. 14 Jan. 1949, Miami Beach, Florida; s. of Clarence Norman Kasdan and Sylvia Sarah (née Landau) Kasdan; m. Meg Goldman 1971; two s.; ed Univ. of Mich.; copywriter W. B. Doner and Co. (Advertising), Detroit 1972–75, Doyle, Dane Berbach, LA 1975–77; Freelance Screenwriter 1977–80; Motion Picture Dir, screenwriter, LA 1980–; Co-Screenwriter, The Empire Strikes Back 1980; Screenwriter, Continental Divide 1981, Raiders of the Lost Ark 1981; Writer, Dir, Body Heat 1981; Co-screenwriter, Return of the Jedi 1982; Co-screenwriter, Dir, Exec. Producer, The Big Chill 1983, Silverado 1985, The Accidental Tourist 1989, I Love You to Death 1989; Producer, Cross My Heart 1987; Grand Canyon (Dir, co-screenwriter), The Body Guard (screenwriter exec. producer), Wyatt Earp (Dir, co-producer, co-screenwriter), French Kiss (Dir), Mumford (Dir) 1999; mem. Writers Guild, American West, Dirs Guild, American West; Recipient Clio awards for Advertising, Writers Guild Award for The Big Chill 1983.

KASEL, Jean-Jacques; Luxembourg diplomatist; b. 1947; ed Inst. Etudes Politiques, Paris; joined Foreign Ministry 1973, Embassy in Paris (also Deputy Perm. Rep. to OECD) 1976–79; Pvt. Sec. to Gaston Thorn (q.v.) 1979–81; Dir for Budget and Staff Regulation, Gen. Secr. EC Council 1981–84; Chargé Special Missions, Perm. Mission of Luxembourg to EC 1984–86; Dir Political and Cultural Affairs, Foreign Ministry 1986–89; Amb. to Greece (resident in Luxembourg) 1989; Perm. Rep. to EU 1991–98, Chair. Perm. Reps

Cttee of Council of Ministers of EU 1997–98; Perm. Rep. to NATO 1998–2003. *Address:* c/o Ministry of Foreign Affairs and Trade, 5 rue Notre Dame, 2240 Luxembourg, Luxembourg (Office).

KASER, Michael Charles, MA, DLitt; British economist; b. 2 May 1926, London; s. of Joseph Kaser and Mabel Blunden; m. Elizabeth Anne Mary Piggford 1954; four s. one d.; ed King's Coll., Cambridge; with Econs Section Ministry of Works, London 1946–47; HM Foreign Service 1947–51, Second Sec., Moscow 1949; UN Econ. Comm. for Europe, Geneva 1951–63; lecturer in Soviet Econs, Univ. of Oxford 1963–72, Chair. Faculty Bd 1974–76, mem. Gen. Bd of Faculties 1972–78, Chair. Advisory Council of Adult Educ. 1972–78, Univ. Latin Preacher 1982; Gov. Plater Coll., Oxford 1968–95, Emer. Gov. 1995–; Visiting Prof. of Econs, Univ. of Mich., USA 1966; Visiting Lecturer, European Inst. of Business Admin., Fontainebleau 1959–82, 1988–92, Univ. of Cambridge 1967–68, 1977–78, 1978–79; Reader in Econs and Professorial Fellow, St Antony's Coll., Oxford 1972–93, Sub-Warden 1986–87, Reader Emer. 1993–; Dir, Inst. of Russian, Soviet and E European Studies, Univ. of Oxford 1988–93; Assoc. Fellow Templeton Coll., Oxford 1983–; Visiting Faculty mem. Henley Man. Coll. 1987–2002; Vice-Chair. Social Science Research Council Int. Activities Cttee 1980–84; Special Adviser House of Commons Foreign Affairs Cttee 1985–87; Chair. Co-ordinating Council, Area Studies Asscns 1986–88 (mem. 1980–93, 1995), Wilton Park Academic Council (FCO) 1986–92 (mem. 1985–2001); Pres. British Asscn of Slavonic and E European Studies 1988–91, Vice-Pres. 1991–93; Prin. Charlemagne Inst., Edin. 1993–94, Hon. Fellow Divinity Faculty, Univ. of Edin. 1993–96; mem. Int. Social Science Council (UNESCO) 1980–91, Council Royal Inst. of Int. Affairs 1979–85, 1986–92 (mem. Meetings Cttee 1976-88, Chair. Central Asian and Caucasus Advisory Bd 1993), Royal Econ. Soc. 1975–86, 1987–90, Council School of Slavonic and East European Studies 1981–87, Cttee Nat. Asscn for Soviet and East European Studies 1965–88, Steering Cttee Königswinter Anglo-German Confs 1969–90, Exec. Cttee Int. Econ. Asscn 1974–83, 1986– (Gen. Ed.), also various editorial bds, Anglo-Soviet, British-Mongolian, Anglo-Polish, British-Bulgarian, British-Yugoslav (Chair.), Canada-UK, British-Romanian and UK-Uzbek Round Tables, British-Polish Mixed Comm.; Sec. British Nat. Cttee of AIESEE 1988–93; Pres. British Asscn of Fmr UN Civil Servants 1994–2001, Albania Soc. of Britain 1992–95; Chair. Council, the Keston Inst., Oxford 1994–2002; Trustee Foundation of King George VI and Queen Elizabeth, St Catharine's (Chair. Academic Consultative Cttee 1987–2002), Sir Heinz Koeppler Trust (Chair. 1992–2001); mem. Higher Educ. Funding Council for England Advisory Bd on Eastern European Studies 1995–2000, CAFOD East Europe Cttee 2001–; Hon. Prof. Inst. for German Studies, Univ. of Birmingham 1994–; Kt Order of St Gregory the Great 1990, Order of Naim Frashëri (Albania) 1995, Kt Order of Merit (Poland) 1999; Hon. DSocSc (Birmingham) 1996. *Publications:* Comecon: Integration Problems of the Planned Economies 1965, Planning in East Europe (with J. Zielinski) 1970, Soviet Economics 1970, Health Care in the Soviet Union and Eastern Europe 1976, Economic Development for Eastern Europe 1968, Planning and Market Relations (with R. Portes) 1971, The New Economic Systems of Eastern Europe (jointly) 1975, The Soviet Union since the Fall of Khrushchev (with A. H. Brown) 1975, Soviet Policy for the 1980s (with A. H. Brown) 1982, Economic History of Eastern Europe, Vols I–III (with E. A. Radice) 1985–86, Early Steps in Comparing East-West Economies (with E. A. G. Robinson) 1991, Reforms in Foreign Economic Relations of Eastern Europe and the Soviet Union 1991, The Macroeconomics of Transition in Eastern Europe (with D. Morris) 1992, The Central Asian Economies after Independence (with S. Mehrotra) 1992, Education and Economic Change in Eastern Europe and the Former Soviet Union (with D. Phillips) 1992, Cambridge Encyclopedia of Russia and the Former Soviet Union (jtly) 1994, Privatization in the CIS 1996, The Economies of Kazakstan and Uzbekistan 1997; articles in econ. and Slavic journals. *Address:* 31 Capel Close, Oxford, OX2 7LA, England (Home). *Telephone:* (1865) 515581. *Fax:* (1865) 515581. *E-mail:* michael.kaser@economics.ox.ac.uk (Office).

KASHIWAGI, Yusuke, LLB; Japanese banker; b. 17 Oct. 1917, Dalian, China; s. of Hideshige Kashiwagi and Kiyo Yamada; m.; two s. two d.; ed Tokyo Imperial Univ.; entered Ministry of Finance 1941; Foreign Exchange Bureau 1941, Minister's Secr. 1945, Budget Bureau 1948, Sr Budget Examiner 1951, Dir Research Section of Foreign Exchange Bureau 1954, Dir Planning Section 1956; Financial Sec. Embassy in Washington, DC 1958; Financial Counsellor, Ministry of Finance 1961; Financial Commr 1965; Dir-Gen. Int. Finance Bureau 1966; Vice-Minister of Finance for Int. Affairs 1968; resgnd from Ministry of Finance 1971; Special Adviser to Minister of Finance 1971–72; Deputy Pres. Bank of Tokyo Ltd 1973–77, Pres. 1977–82, Chair. Bd of Dirs. 1982–92, Sr Adviser 1992–96; Sr Adviser The Bank of Tokyo-Mitsubishi 1996–; Dir Sony Corpn 1976–92; mem. Exec. Cttee Trilateral Comm. 1973–92; Adviser, Int. Finance Corpn, Washington, DC 1979–92; mem Int. Monetary Conf. 1977–92; mem. business advisory Cttee EBRD 1991–; Dir Meiji Seika Kaisha, Tokyo 1983–97; Chair. BIAC Japan 1985–93, BIAC OECD 1988–90; Adviser Robeco Group, Rotterdam 1985–95; Grand Cordon, Order of the Sacred Treasure 1989. *Leisure interests:* golf, travel. *Address:* The Bank of Tokyo-Mitsubishi Ltd, 3-2, Nihonbashi Hongokucho 1-Chome Chuo-ku, Tokyo 103-0021, Japan.

KASHLEV, Yuriy Borisovich, DHist; Russian diplomatist; b. 13 April 1934, Tejen; s. of Boris and Olga Kashlev; m. 1957; one s. one d.; ed Moscow Inst. of Int. Relations; fmr mem. CPSU; worked for Soviet Cttee for Youth Orgs.

1961–65; CPSU Cen. Cttee 1965–68; Counsellor, USSR Ministry of Foreign Affairs 1968–70; served in Embassy, UK 1970–71, Counsellor, Head of Sector, Deputy Head, Dept of Information, Ministry of Foreign Affairs 1971–78, Head Dept 1982–86; Sec.-Gen. USSR Comm. for UNESCO 1978–82; Head Dept of Humanitarian and Cultural Relations 1986–89, Deputy First Vice-Minister, USSR Ministry of Foreign Affairs 1986–90; mem. or head of Soviet dels. to CSCE confs Geneva, Berne, Vienna, Paris; Russian Amb. to Poland 1990–96; Rector, Prof. Diplomatic Acad., Foreign Ministry 1996–2000, First Vice-Rector 2001–; 11 state awards (orders and medals), USSR, Poland and Bulgaria. *Publications:* Détente in Europe: from Helsinki to Madrid, International Information Exchange, After Fourteen Thousand Wars, Mass Media and International Relations, Ideological Struggle or Psychological War; and other books on int. affairs. *Leisure interests:* tennis, journalism. *Address:* Diplomatic Academy, Ostozhenka str. 53/2, 119021, Moscow, Russia. *Telephone:* (095) 973-07-74 (Home); (095) 245-39-43 (Office). *Fax:* 095) 244-18-78 (Office). *E-mail:* yuri.kashlev@dipacademy.ru.

KASICH, John R., BA; American politician; b. 13 May 1952, McKees Rocks, Pa; ed Ohio State Univ.; Admin. Asst Ohio State Senate 1975–77; mem. Ohio Legislature 1979–82; mem. 98th–104th Congress from 12th Ohio Dist, Washington 1983–2001; mem. Nat. Security Cttee; mem. House Budget Cttee, now Chair.; Chair. New Century Project, Columbus 2001–. *Address:* c/o House of Representatives, 309 Cannon H.O.B., Washington, DC 20515, USA.

KASMIN, John; British art dealer; b. 24 Sept. 1934, London; s. of David Kosminsky and Vera D'Olzewski; m. Jane Nicholson 1959 (divorced 1975); two s.; ed Magdalen Coll. School, Oxford; worked for Gallery One, Soho, London; Dir New London Gallery, Bond St 1960–61; f. Kasmin Gallery, Man. Dir Kasmin Ltd 1961–, Knoedler Kasmin Ltd 1977–92. *Leisure interests:* literature, art, walking, museums. *Address:* c/o Kasmin Ltd, 34 Warwick Avenue, London, W9 2PT, England. *Fax:* (020) 7289-0746.

KASPAROV, Garry Kimovich; Russian-Armenian chess player; b. (as Garry Weinstein), 13 April 1963, Baku; s. of late Kim Weinstein and of Klara Kasparova; m. 1st Maria Arapova (divorced); one d.; m. 2nd Yulia Vovk 1996; one s.; ed Azerbaijan Pedagogical Inst. of Foreign Languages; started playing chess in 1967; Azerbaijan Champion 1976; USSR Jr Champion 1976; Int. Master 1978, Int. Grandmaster 1980; World Jr Champion 1980; won USSR Championship 1981, subsequently replacing Anatoliy Karpov (q.v.) at top of world ranking list; won match against Viktor Korchnoi, challenged Karpov for World Title in Moscow Sept. 1985, the match being adjourned due to the illness of both players; won rescheduled match to become the youngest-ever world champion in 1985; successfully defended his title against Karpov 1986, 1987, 1990; series of promotional matches in London Feb. 1987; won Times World Championship against Nigel Short 1993; stripped of title by World Chess Fed. 1993; winner Oscar Chess Prize 1982–83, 1985–89, World Chess Cup 1989; highest-ever chess rating of over 2800 1992–; f. Professional Chess Asscn (PCA) 1993; won PCA World Championship against V. Anand 1995, lost title against V. Kramnik 2000; won match against Deep Blue computer 1996, lost 1997; defeated in four-game match of rapid chess against Karpov, New York 2002; Deputy Leader Democratic Party of Russia 1990–91; f. The Kasparov Foundation, Moscow; actively promotes use of chess in schools as an educational subject; f. Kasparov Int. Chess Acad.; Order of Red Banner of Labour. *Publications:* New World Chess Champion 1985, The Test of Time 1986, Child of Change (with Donald Trelford) 1987, London-Leningrad Championship Games 1987, Unlimited Challenge 1990. *Leisure interests:* history (new chronology), politics, computers, literature, walking, weight training, swimming, rowing, most sports. *Address:* Mezhdunarodnaya-2, Suite 1108, Krasnopresnenskaya nab. 12, 123610 Moscow (Office); Gagarinsky per. 26, Ap. 12, 121002 Moscow, Russia (Home). *Telephone:* (095) 258-15-36 (Office); (095) 241-82-80 (Home). *Fax:* (095) 258-15-39 (Office); (095) 241-95-96 (Home). *E-mail:* maiavia@dol.ru (Office); gk@totalchess.ru (Home). *Website:* www.kasparovchess.com (Home).

KASPER, HE Cardinal Walter Josef, DTheol; German Catholic theologian; b. 5 March 1933, Heidenheim/Brenz; s. of Josef Kasper and Theresia Bacher; ed Univs. of Tübingen and Munich; ordained Priest 1957; Prof. of Dogmatic Theology, Univ. of Münster 1964–70, Univ. of Tübingen 1970–89; Bishop of Rottenburg-Stuttgart 1989–99; Chair. Comm. for World Church Affairs 1991–99, Comm. for Doctrine of Faith, German Bishops Conf. 1996–99; Special Sec. Synod of Bishops 1985; mem. Heidelberger Akad. der Wissenschaften, Academia Scientiarum et Artium Europaea; mem. Congregation for the Doctrine of Faith, Pontifical Council for Culture 1998; Sec. Pontifical Council for Unity 1999, Pres. 2001–; cr. Cardinal 2001–; Dr. hc (Catholic Univ. of America, Washington, DC) 1990, (St Mary's Seminary and Univ., Baltimore) 1991, (Marc Bloch Univ., Strasbourg 2000; Prof. hc (Eberhard-Karls Univ., Tübingen) 2001; Bundesverdienstkreuz, Landesverdienstmedaille. *Publications:* Die Tradition in der Römischen Schule 1962, Das Absolute in der Geschichte 1965, Glaube und Geschichte 1970, Einführung in den Glauben 1972 (An Introduction to Christian Faith 1980), Jesus der Christus 1974, Der Gott Jesu Christi 1982, Theologie und Kirche 1987 (Theology and Church 1989), The Christian Understanding of Freedom and the History of Freedom in the Modern Era 1988, Wahrheit und Freiheit in der Erklärung über die Religionsfreiheit des II. Vatikanischen Konzils 1988, Lexikon für Theologie und Kirche 1993–2001, Theologie und Kirche II 1999. *Leisure interest:* climbing. *Address:* Pontificio Consiglio per l'Unita dei Cristiani, Via dell'Ersa 1, V-00120, Città del Vaticano, Rome, Italy. *Fax:* (06) 69885365 (Office). *E-mail:* office1@chrstuni.va. *Website:* www.vaticano.va.

KASPSZYK, Jacek; Polish conductor; b. 1952; ed Acad. of Music, Warsaw; conducting debut at age 14; debut Warsaw Opera 1975, Visiting First Conductor Deutsche Oper am Rhein, Düsseldorf 1976–77; Prin. Conductor Polish Nat. Radio Symphony Orchestra 1977–81, Music Dir 1980–82; debut Berlin Philharmonic and New York 1978, London (with Philharmonia) 1982; conducted French Nat., Stockholm Philharmonic, Bavarian Radio Symphony, Rotterdam, Czech Philharmonic Orchestras; conducted Detroit Opera and San Diego Symphony Orchestra 1982; concerts at La Scala, Milan 1982; Australian tour with Chamber Orchestra of Europe 1983; conducted UK orchestras 1983–; debut Henry Wood Promenade Concerts 1984; Prin. Conductor and Artistic Adviser North Netherlands Orchestra 1991–95; Prin. Guest Conductor English Sinfonia 1992–; Prin. Guest Conductor Polish Philharmonic 1996-; Artistic and Musical Dir Great Theatre-Nat. Opera Warsaw 1998–. *Music:* operas conducted include: A Midsummer Night's Dream (Lyon) 1983, Eugene Onegin (Bordeaux) 1985, The Magic Flute (Opéra Comique, Paris and Stockholm) 1986, Seven Deadly Sins (Lyon) 1987, Die Fledermaus (Scottish Opera), Flying Dutchman (Opera North, UK) 1988, Barber of Seville (English Nat. Opera) 1992, Der Rosenkavalier (Great Theatre – Nat. Opera Warsaw) 1997, Don Giovanni (Great Theatre – Nat. Opera Warsaw) 1999; recordings with London Symphony Orchestra, London Philharmonic Orchestra, Royal Philharmonic, Philharmonic Orchestras, Warsaw Symphony Orchestra; several other recordings. *Address:* Teatr Wielki, pl. Teatralny 1, 00-077, Warsaw, Poland. *Telephone:* (22) 8275640.

KASRASHVILI, Makvala; Georgian soprano; b. 13 March 1948, Kutaisi; d. of Nina Nanikashvili and Filimon Kasrashvili; m. (divorced); ed Tbilisi Conservatory; joined Bolshoi Co., Moscow 1968, Dir Bolshoi Theatre Opera Dept 2002–; has performed internationally, including Covent Garden London, Metropolitan Opera New York, Verona, Vienna State Opera etc.; People's Artist of the USSR 1986; Grand Prix, Montreal Vocal Competition. *Roles include:* Lisa, Tatyana, Maria, Tosca, Lauretta, Donna Anna, Leonora, Aida, Turandot, Amelia. *Leisure interest:* car driving. *Address:* Bolshoi Theatre, Teatralnaya Pl. 1, Moscow, Russia. *Telephone:* (095) 200-58-00 (Home).

KASSEBAUM BAKER, Nancy Landon, MA; American politician; b. 29 July 1932, Topeka; d. of Alfred M. Kassebaum and Theo Landon; three s. one d.; m. 2nd Howard Baker 1996; ed Univs of Kansas and Mich.; mem. Washington staff of Senator James B. Pearson of Kansas 1975–76; Senator from Kansas 1979–97; mem. several senate cttees; mem. Bd Trustees Robert Wood Johnson Foundation 1997–; Co-Chair. The Presidential Appointee Initiative Advisory Bd, Brookings Inst.; Republican. *Address:* Presidential Appointee Initiative, 1720 Rhode Island Avenue, NW, Suite 301, Washington, DC 20036 (Office); c/o Robert Wood Johnson Foundation, College Road East, P.O. Box 2316, Princeton, NJ 08543, USA.

KASSEM, Abdul-Rauf al-, D.ARCH.; Syrian politician; b. 1932, Damascus; ed Damascus Univ. School of Arts, Istanbul and Geneva Univs.; teacher of architecture, School of Fine Arts Damascus, Dean 1964–70, Head, Architecture Dept, School of Civil Engineering Damascus Univ. 1970–77, Rector 1977–79; concurrently engineer 1964–77; Gov. of Damascus 1979–80; elected mem. Baath party Regional Command Dec. 1979, Cen. Command of Progressive Nat. Front April 1980; Prime Minister 1980–87; mem. Higher Council for Town Planning 1968–; mem. Nat. Union of Architects' Perm. Comm. on Town Planning 1975–; Hon. Prof. Geneva Univ. 1975–. *Address:* c/o Office of the Prime Minister, Damascus, Syria.

KASTEN, Robert W., Jr., BA; American politician; b. 19 June 1942, Milwaukee, Wis.; s. of Robert W. Kasten and Mary Kasten (née Ogden); m. Eva J. Nimmons 1986; one d.; ed Univ. of Arizona and Columbia Univ., New York; with Genesco, Nashville, Tenn. 1966–68; Dir and Vice-Pres. Gilbert Shoe Co., Thiensville, Wis. 1968–75; mem. Wis. Senate 1972–75; Joint Finance Cttee 1973–75, Chair. Joint Survey Cttee on Tax Exemptions 1973–80; Designee Eagleton Inst. of Politics 1973; mem. House of Reps 1975–79 from 9th Dist, Wis., mem. Govt Operations Cttee, Small Businesses Cttee; alt. del. Republican Nat. Convention 1972, del. 1976, Co-Chair. 1988; Senator from Wis. 1980–93; founder Kasten & Co, Thiensville, Wis. 1993–; Sr Assoc. Center for Strategic and Int. Studies, Washington 1993–; served on Appropriations, Budget, Commerce, Science and Transportation Cttee and Small Business Cttee. *Address:* Kasten & Co., #700, 888 16th Street, N.W., Washington, DC 20006; Strategic and International Studies Center, 1800 K Street N.W., Washington, DC 20006, USA.

KASTNER, Elliott; American film producer; b. 7 Jan. 1933, New York; s. of Jack Kastner and Rose Kastner; m. Tessa Kennedy; four s. one d. *Films include:* Harper (The Moving Target), Kaleidoscope 1965, The Bobo, Laughter in the Dark, Night of the Following Day, Where Eagles Dare 1968, The Walking Stick, A Severed Head, When Eight Bells Toll, Tam Lin, Villain, X Y and Zee, The Nightcomers, Big Truck and Poor Clare, Face to the Wind, Fear is the Key, The Long Goodbye, Cops and Robbers, Jeremy, 11 Harrowhouse, Spot, Rancho Deluxe, 92 in the Shade, Farewell My Lovely, Russian Roulette, Breakheart Pass, The Missouri Breaks, The Swashbuckler, A Little Night Music, Equus, Black Joy, The Stick-Up, The Medusa Touch, The Big Sleep, Absolution, Golden Girl, Yesterday's Hero, North Sea Hijack, The First Deadly Sin, Death Valley, Man Woman and Child, Oxford Blues, Garbo Talks, Nomads, White of the Eye, Heat, Angel Heart, Zits, The Blob, Jack's Back, Never on Tuesday, Zombie High, A Chorus of Disapproval, Homeboy, The

Last Party, Love is All There Is, Sweet November. *Address:* Cinema Seven Productions Ltd, Pinewood Studios, Iver Heath, Iver, Bucks., SL0 0NH, England.

KASTRUP, Dieter; German diplomatist (retd); b. b. March 1937, Bielefeld; m.; two c.; ed Univ. of Cologne; Third Sec. to First Sec. Embassy, Tehran 1967–71, Counsellor, then Deputy Div. Head, Ministry of Foreign Affairs, Bonn 1971–75, Embassy, Washington, DC 1975–78, Perm. Rep., Consulate-Gen., Houston, Tex. 1978–80, Head Div., Ministry of Foreign Affairs 1980–85, Head Directorate 1985–88, Dir-Gen. 1988–91, State Sec. 1991–95; Amb. to Italy 1995–98; Perm. Rep. to UN 1998–2001; Foreign and Security Policy Adviser to Fed. Chancellor 2002. *E-mail:* Dieterkastrup@aol.com.

KASYANOV, Mikhail Mikhailovich; Russian politician; b. 8 Dec. 1957, Solntsevo, Moscow Region; ed Moscow Inst. of Automobile Transport; leading posts RSFSR State Planning Comm., then Ministry of Econs 1981–90; Head Dept of Overseas Credits, Ministry of Finance 1993–95, Deputy Minister of Finance 1995–99, First Deputy Minister, then Minister 1999–2000; main negotiator with Western financial orgs on problems of Russian Liabilities; Deputy Man. for Russian Fed., EBRD 1999–; First Deputy Prime Minister Jan. 2000, Acting Prime Minister, then Prime Minister May 2000–; mem. Presidium of Russian Govt 1999–, Security Council 1999–. *Address:* House of Government, Krasnopresnenskaya nab. 2, 103274 Moscow, Russia (Office). *Telephone:* (095) 205-54-56 (Office). *Fax:* (095) 205-50-55 (Office).

KATANANDOV, Sergey Leonidovich; Russian politician and businessman; b. 21 April 1955, Petrozavodsk; m.; two s.; ed Petrozavodsk State Univ., NW Acad. of State and Municipal Service; worked as Head of sector, Sr engineer, Petrozavodskstroi 1977–91; mem. Petrozavodsk City Exec. Cttee, Chair. City Soviet 1991–98, Mayor of Petrozavodsk 1994–98; elected Chair. Karelian Govt 1998–; Merited Worker of Nat. Economy of Repub. of Karelia 1995, Order of Honour of Russian Fed. 2000. *Publications include:* articles in Russian and Finnish journals and newspapers. *Leisure interests:* fishing, hunting. *Address:* Government of Karelia, Lenina prosp. 19, Petrozavodsk 185020, Karelia (Office); Andropova av. 30, Petrozavodsk, Karelia, Russia. *Telephone:* (8142) 76-41-41 (Office). *Fax:* (8142) 76-41-48 (Office). *E-mail:* government@karelia.ru (Office). *Website:* www.gov.karelia.ru.

KATES, Robert William, PhD; American professor of geography; b. 31 Jan. 1929, Brooklyn, New York; s. of Simon J. Kates and Helen G. Brener; m. Eleanor C. Hackman 1948; one s. two d.; ed Univ. of Chicago; Asst Prof. Graduate School of Geography, Clark Univ. 1962–65, Assoc. Prof. 1965–67, Prof. 1968–92, Univ. Prof. 1974–80, Univ. Prof. and Dir Alan Shawn Feinstein World Hunger Program 1986–92, Prof. Emer. 1992–; Dir Bureau of Resource Assessment and Land Use Planning, Univ. Coll., Dar es Salaam 1967–68; Hon. Research Prof. Univ. of Dar es Salaam 1970–71; Fellow, Woodrow Wilson Int. Center for Scholars 1979; mem. Assen of American Geographers (Pres. 1993–94); many other professional appointments; mem. NAS, AAAS, several awards. *Publications include:* Risk Assessment of Environmental Hazard 1978, The Environment as Hazard (with Ian Burton and Gilbert F. White) 1978; co-ed. of 18 books; monographs and articles on environmental topics. *Address:* c/o Brown University, 182 George Street, Providence, RI 02912, USA (Office).

KATHRADA, Ahmed, BA; South African politician; b. 21 Aug. 1929, Schweizer Reneke; joined Young Communist League 1941; first imprisoned for participation in Passive Resistance 1946, subsequently imprisoned several times during 1950s and 1960s; first banned in 1954, accused in treason trial 1956–61, placed under house arrest Oct. 1962; sentenced to life imprisonment, Rivonia Trial 1964, unconditionally released 1989; rep. SA in World Fed. of Democratic Youth 1951–52; involved in Defiance Campaign 1952, Congress of People's Campaign 1955; Sec. first Free Mandela Cttee 1962; mem. ANC del. to Talks about Talks with South African Govt 1990, Nat. Exec. Cttee ANC 1991–, Internal Leadership Cttee of ANC, Head Public Relations Dept; MP Govt of Nat. Unity 1994–; Parl. Counsellor in Office of Pres. 1994–; Chair. Robben Island Museum Council; Chair. Ex-Political Prisoners' Cttee.; Fellow Mayibuye Centre, Univ. of Western Cape; Patron Trauma Centre, Cape Town. *Address:* House of Assembly, Cape Town, South Africa. *Telephone:* (21) 4642121 (Cape Town); (12) 3191620 (Pretoria). *Fax:* (21) 4642123 (Cape Town); (12) 3251270 (Pretoria).

KATILI, John (Younis) Ario, DSc; Indonesian professor of geology and politician; b. 9 June 1929, Gorontalo, Sulawesi; m. Iliana Syarifa Uno; one s. one d.; ed Univ. of Indonesia, Inst. of Tech., Bandung, Univ. of Innsbruck, Austria; fmr Prof. of Structural and Tectonic Geology, Head Dept of Geology and Dean Faculty of Mineral Tech., of Inst. of Tech. Bandung (ITB); Vice-Pres. of ITB 1961; Deputy Chair. Indonesian Inst. of Sciences –1973; Dir-Gen. of Mines 1973-84, of Geology and Mineral Resources 1984-89; fmr Sr Adviser to State Minister of Research and Tech. and to Minister of Mines and Energy; fmr Vice-Chair. Indonesian Nat. Research Council; Vice-Speaker House of Reps. (Parl.) and Vice-Chair. People's Consultative Ass. 1992–97; Amb. to Russian Fed., Turkmenistan, Kazakhstan and Mongolia 1999–; First Pres. Southeast Asia Union of Geological Sciences 1984; Vice-Pres. Indonesian Acad. of Sciences 1998; mem. Nat. Geographic Soc.; Foreign mem. Russian Acad. of Natural Sciences 2000; Fellow Islamic Acad. of Sciences; Hon. mem. RGS, Indonesian Assen of Geologists, Geological Soc. of Sweden, Royal Geological Soc. and Mining Soc. of the Netherlands; Dr. hc (Stockholm) 1988; Commdr Ordre Nat. du Mérite 1988, Order of Orange Nassau 1995; Van Waterschoot van der Gracht Medal 1995. *Publications:* 12 books; over 150

scientific and policy papers in English and Indonesian. *Address:* Embassy of Indonesia, ul. Novokouznetskaya 12/14, 109017 Moscow, Russia (Office). *Telephone:* (095) 951-95-50 (Office). *Fax:* (095) 230-64-31 (Office). *E-mail:* kbrimos@online.ru.

KATIN, Peter Roy, FRAM, ARCM; British pianist; b. 14 Nov. 1930, London; s. of the late Jerrold Katin and Gertrude Katin; m. Eva Zweig 1954; two s.; ed Henry Thornton School, Royal Acad. of Music, Westminster Abbey; London debut, Wigmore Hall 1948; extensive concert tours in UK, Europe, Africa, Canada, USA and Far East; special interest in Chopin; recordings for Decca, EMI, Unicorn, Everest, Philips, CFP, Lyrita and Pickwick Int., Claudio, Olympia, Simax, Athene; Prof. Royal Acad. of Music 1956–60, Univ. of Western Ont. 1978–84, Royal Coll. of Music 1992–2001; Founder Katin Centre for Advanced Piano Studies 1991, Katin Trio 1997; Pres. Camerata of London 1991–; Hon. DMus (De Montfort) 1994; Eric Brough Memorial Prize 1944; Chopin Arts Award (New York) 1977. *Leisure interests:* writing, tape-recording, theatre, reading, photography. *Address:* c/o TRANSART, 8 Bristol Gardens, London, W9 2JG (Office); 4 Clarence Road, Croydon, Surrey, CR0 2EN, England (Home). *Telephone:* (20) 7286-7526 (Office). *Fax:* (20) 7266-2687 (Office). *E-mail:* transart@transartuk.com (Office); peter_katin@compuserve.com (Home). *Website:* ourworld.compuserve.com/homepages/peter_katin (Home).

KATO, Susumu, PhD; Japanese professor of atmospheric physics; b. 27 Aug. 1928, Saitama; s. of late Nimpei Kato and Minoru Kato; m. Kyoko Kojo; ed Kyoto Univ.; lecturer, Faculty of Eng, Kyoto Univ. 1955–61, Asst Prof. Ionosphere Research Lab. 1961–62, Assoc. Prof. 1964–67, Prof. 1967–81, Dir and Prof. Radio Atmospheric Science Center 1981–92, Prof. Emer. 1992–; Research Officer, Upper Atmosphere Section, CSIRO, NSW, Australia 1962–64; Visiting Scientist, High Altitude Observatory, NCAR, Colo 1967–68, 1973–74; Visiting Prof., Dept of Meteorology, UCLA, LA 1973–74, Bandung Inst. of Tech., Indonesia 1994–97; Vice-Chair. Japan-Indonesia Science and Tech. Forum 1992–96; AGU Fellow 1991; Foreign Assoc. Nat. Acad. of Eng USA 1995–; Fellow Int. Inst. for Advanced Studies 1998; Tanakadate Prize 1959, Yamaji Science Prize 1974, Appleton Prize 1987, Hasegawa Prize 1987, Fujiwara Prize 1989, Japan Acad. Award 1989. *Publications:* Dynamics of the Upper Atmosphere 1980, Dinamika Atmosfer 1998; over 100 scientific papers on atmospheric tidal theory, observation of atmospheric waves by MST radar. *Leisure interests:* reading, music, jogging, swimming, Japanese calligraphy. *Address:* 22-15 Fujimidai, Otsu, Shiga Prefecture 520-0846, Japan (Home). *Telephone:* (77) 534-1177 (Home). *Fax:* (77) 533-4013 (Home). *E-mail:* kato@kurasc.kyoto-u.ac.jp (Home).

KATONA, Tamás; Hungarian politician and historian; b. 2 Feb. 1932, Budapest; s. of Tibor Katona and Magdolna Halász; m. Klára Barta; one s. two d.; ed Archiepiscopal High School (Rákóczianum), Budapest, Eötvös Loránd Univ. Budapest; Head public libraries 1954–61; ed. Magyar Helikon Publishing House and Európa Publishing House 1961–86; lecturer on 19th-century Hungarian history at Eötvös Coll. 1980–85, at József Attila Univ. of Szeged 1986–90; mem. of Parl. 1990–98; Sec. of State for Foreign Affairs 1990–92; Sec. of State, Prime Minister's Office 1992–94; First Vice-Pres. IPU, Hungary; Mayor, Castle Dist Budapest 1994–98; Prof. Károlic Gáspár Protestant Univ. 1998–; Amb. to Poland 2000–; Chair. Hungarian Scout Assen 1994–98, Manfred Wörner Foundation 1998–; Ed. serial Publs Bibliotheca Historica and Pro Memoria (pocket library of history and cultural history); joined Hungarian Democratic Forum, later joined Hungarian Democratic People's Party. *Publications:* Az aradi vértanúk 1979, 1983, 1991 (The Martyrs of Arad), A korona kilenc évszázada (Nine Centuries of the Crown) 1979, A tatárjárás emlékezete (The Mongol Invasion) 1981, 1987, Budavár bevételének emlékezete, 1849 (Capture of Fort Buda in 1849) 1991, Csány László erdélyi főkormánybiztos (László Csány High Commissioner of Transylvania) 1991. *Leisure interests:* tennis, music. *Address:* Fortuna-utca 13, 1014 Budapest, Hungary. *Telephone:* (1) 201-13-65.

KATRITZKY, Alan Roy, MA, DPhil, PhD, ScD, FRS; British/American professor of chemistry, researcher and consultant; b. 18 Aug. 1928, London; s. of Frederick C. Katritzky and Emily C. Katritzky (née Lane); m. Agnes Kilian 1952; one s. three d.; ed Oxford and Cambridge Univs.; Univ. Lecturer, Cambridge 1958–63; Fellow Churchill Coll., Cambridge 1959–63; Prof. of Chem., Univ. of East Anglia 1963–80, Dean, School of Chemical Sciences 1963–70, 1976–80; Kenan Prof. Univ. of Fla 1980–; Dir Florida Inst. of Heterocyclic Compounds 1986–; Assoc. Ed. Journal für praktische Chemie 1997-99; Foreign mem. Polish Acad. of Sciences, Royal Catalan Acad. of Sciences, Slovenian Acad. of Arts and Sciences; Hon. Fellow, Italian Chem. Soc., Polish Chem. Soc.; Hon. Prof. Beijing Inst. of Tech., Xian Modern Univ.; Tilden Lecturer, Chem. Soc.; Hon. DSc (Madrid, Poznan, Gdansk, E Anglia, Toulouse, St Petersburg, Bucharest, Rostov, Ghent, Bundelkhand); Kametani Prize (Japan); Heterocyclic Award, Royal Soc. of Chem., Sr Humboldt Award (Germany), Cope Senior Scholar Award, American Chemical Soc.; Cavaliere ufficiale (Italy); Heyrowsky Medal, Czech Acad. of Science, Gold Medal, Partnership for Peace Foundation, Moscow. *Publications:* seven books and 1600 papers in heterocyclic chemistry; Ed. Advances in Heterocyclic Chemistry (80 vols) and Comprehensive Heterocyclic Chemistry, 1st edn (eight vols), 2nd edn (ten vols), Organic Functional Group Transformations (seven vols). *Leisure interests:* walking, wind surfing. *Address:* Department of Chemistry, University of Florida, Gainesville, FL 32611 (Office); 1221 SW

21st Avenue, Gainesville, FL 32601, USA (Home). *Telephone:* (352) 392-0554 (Office); (352) 378-1221 (Home). *Fax:* (352) 392-9199. *E-mail:* katritzky@chem.ufl.edu (Office). *Website:* ark.chem.ufl.edu/.

KATSAV, Moshe; Israeli head of state; b. 5 Dec. 1945, Iran; m. Gila Katsav; four s. one d.; ed Hebrew Univ. of Jerusalem; reporter for Yediot Aharonot (newspaper) 1966–68; Mayor of Kiryat Malachi 1969, 1974–81; mem. Knesset 1977–; mem. Interior and Educ. Cttees. 1977–81; Deputy Minister of Housing and Construction 1981–84; Minister of Labour and Social Affairs 1984–88, of Transportation 1988–92; mem. Cttee on Defence 1988–92, 1996–99; Chair. Likud faction in the Knesset, Parl. Cttee of Chinese–Israeli Friendship League 1992–96; Deputy Prime Minister 1996–99, also Minister of Tourism, for Israeli Arab Affairs; Pres. 2000–; Chair. Cttee for Nat. Events 1996–99; mem. Foreign Affairs and Defence Cttee 1999–2000; mem. Bd of Trustees Ben-Gurion Univ. 1978–; Hon. Dr. (Neb.) 1998, (George Washington) 2001, (Hartford) 2001. *Address:* Office of the President, Beit Hanassi, 3 Hanassi Street, Jerusalem 92188, Israel (Office). *Telephone:* (2) 6707211 (Office). *Fax:* (2) 5611033 (Office).

KATTAN, Mohammed Imad, BSc, MCD; Jordanian architect and planner; b. 3 Sept. 1951, Amman; s. of Mahmoud Kamal and Ilham Hamzah; m. 1st Leen M. Halawa 1983; m. 2nd Nawal Radi Abdulla 1987; one s.; ed Bath and Liverpool Univs, UK; architect-planner, CH2M Hill, Portland, Ore., USA 1977–81; lecturer, Jordan Univ., Amman 1981–84; Dir UBMC, Amman 1982–95; Chair. and Man. Dir UDC, Amman 1982–; Man. Dir ASCO (Architectural Systems Co. Ltd), Amman 1997–99; Chair. SOS Children's Village Asscn, Jordan 1999– mem. Joradanian Engineers' Asscn. *Leisure interests:* tennis, jogging, photography, scuba diving. *Address:* P.O. Box 950846, Amman 11195, Jordan. *Telephone:* (6) 4648530. *Fax:* (6) 4648043, 4619715. *E-mail:* udc@go.com.jo (Office).

KATTAN, Naim, OC, FRSC; Canadian writer; b. 26 Aug. 1928, Baghdad, Iraq; s. of the late Nessim and Hela Kattan; m. Gaetane Laniel 1961; one s.; ed Univ. of Baghdad and Sorbonne, Paris; newspaper corresp. in Near East and Europe, broadcaster throughout Europe; emigrated to Canada 1954; Int. Politics Ed. for Nouveau Journal 1961–62; fmr teacher at Laval Univ.; fmr Sec. Cercle Juif de langue française de Montreal; freelance journalist and broadcaster; Prof., Univ. of Québec, Montreal; Assoc. Dir Canada Council; mem. Académie Canadienne-Française; Pres. Royal Soc. of Canada; Chevalier Légion d'honneur; Officier des Arts et Lettres de France; Chevalier Ordre nat. du Québec. *Publications:* (novels) Adieu Babylone 1975, Les Fruits arrachés 1981, La Fiancée promise 1983, La Fortune du passager 1989, La Célébration 1997, L'Anniversaire 2000; (essays) Le Réel et le théâtral 1970, Ecrivains des Amériques, Tomes I-III, Le Repos et l'Oubli 1987, Le Père 1990, Farida 1991, La Reconciliation 1992, A. M. Klein 1994, La Distraction 1994, Culture: Alibi ou liberté 1996, Idoles et images 1996, Figures bibliques 1997, L'Amour reconnu 1999, Le Silence des adieux 1999, Les Villes de naissance, L'Ecrivain migrant; also numerous short stories and criticisms. *Address:* 2463 rue Sainte Famille No. 2114, Montreal, Québec, H2X 2K7, Canada. *Telephone:* (514) 499-2836. *Fax:* (514) 499-9954. *E-mail:* kattan.naim@uqom.

KATZ, Michael, AB, MD, FAAS; American pediatrician and educator; b. 13 Feb. 1928, Lwów, Poland; s. of Edward Katz and Rita Gluzman; m. Robin J. Roy 1986; one s.; ed Univ. of Pennsylvania, State Univ. of New York, Brooklyn, Columbia Univ. School of Public Health; Intern, Univ. of Calif., Los Angeles, Medical Center 1956–57; Resident, Presbyterian Hosp. New York 1960–62, Dir Pediatric Service 1977–92; Hon. Lecturer in Paediatrics, Makerere Univ. Coll., Kampala, Uganda 1963–64; Instructor in Pediatrics, Columbia Univ. 1964–65, Prof. in Tropical Medicine, School of Public Health 1971–92, Prof. Emer. 1992–, Prof. of Pediatrics, Coll. of Physicians and Surgeons 1972–77, Reuben S. Carpentier Prof. and Chair. Dept of Pediatrics 1977–92, Prof. Emer. 1992–; Asst Prof. of Pediatrics, Univ. of Pa 1966–71; Vice-Pres. for Research, March of Dimes Birth Defects Foundation 1992–; Pres. World Alliance of Orgs. for the Prevention of Birth Defects 1995–; Assoc. mem. Wistar Inst., Philadelphia 1965–71; Consultant, WHO regional offices, Guatemala, Venezuela, Egypt, Yemen; mem. US Del. to 32nd World Health Ass., Geneva 1979; Consultant, UNICEF, New York and Tokyo; mem. numerous medical socs. including Inst. of Medicine, NAS; Jurzykowski Foundation Award in Medicine 1983, Alexander von Humboldt Foundation Sr US Scientist Award 1987, Bard Coll. *Publications:* contributions to numerous journals and medical works. *Address:* 1 Griggs Lane, Chappaqua, NY 10514, USA (Home); 1275 Mamaroneck Avenue, White Plains, NY 10605. *Telephone:* (914) 997-45-55. *Fax:* (914) 997-45-60. *E-mail:* mkatz@modimes.org (Office); robinroy@optonline.net (Home). *Website:* www.modimes.org (Office).

KATZ, Samuel Lawrence, MD; American professor of pediatrics; b. 29 May 1927, Manchester, NH; s. of Morris Katz and Ethel Lawrence Katz; m. 1st Betsy Jane Cohan 1950 (divorced 1971); four s. (one s. deceased) three d.; m. 2nd Catherine Minock Wilfert 1971; two step-d.; ed Dartmouth Coll. and Harvard Univ.; hosp. appts, Boston, Mass. 1952–56; Exchange Registrar, Pediatric Unit, St Mary's Hosp. Medical School, London, England 1956; Research Fellow in Pediatrics, Harvard Medical School at Research Div. of Infectious Diseases, Children's Hosp. Medical Center, Boston 1956–58, Research Assoc. 1958–68; Pediatrician-in-Chief, Beth Israel Hosp., Boston 1958–61, Visiting Pediatrician 1961–68; Assoc. Physician, Children's Hosp. Medical Center, Boston 1958–63, Sr Assoc. in Medicine 1963–68, Chief, Newborn Div. 1961–67; Instructor in Pediatrics, Harvard Medical School, Boston 1958–59, Assoc. 1959–63, Tutor in Medical Sciences 1961–63, Asst

Prof. of Pediatrics 1963–68; Co-Dir Combined Beth Israel Hosp.-Children's Hosp. Medical Center, Infectious Disease Career Training Program 1967–68; Prof. and Chair. Dept of Pediatrics, Duke Univ. School of Medicine, Durham, NC 1968–90, Wilburt C. Davison Prof. of Pediatrics 1972–97, Wilburt C. Davison Prof. Emer. 1997–; prin. activities involve research on children's vaccines and on pediatric AIDS; mem. Bd of Dirs. Georgetown Univ. 1987–93, Hasbro Foundation 1988–, Burroughs Wellcome Fund 1991–99, (Chair. Bd of Dirs 1995–99), Scientific Advisory Bd, St Jude Children's Research Hosp.; Consultant, Nat. Insts. of Health (NIH), AIDS Exec. Cttee 1986–89, mem. NIH Pediatric AIDS Exec. Cttee 1994–97; mem. Editorial Bd Pediatric Infectious Diseases Report; fmr mem. Editorial Bd Annual Review in Medicine, Postgraduate Medicine, Reviews of Infectious Diseases, Current Problems in Pediatrics, Ped Sat (TV Educ.); Fellow American Acad. of Pediatrics, Infectious Diseases Soc. of America, AAAS; mem. Soc. for Pediatric Research, American Soc. for Microbiology, American Asscn of Immunologists, American Public Health Asscn, American Soc. for Clinical Investigation, American Pediatric Soc., American Epidemiological Soc., American Soc. for Virology, American Fed. for Clinical Research, Inst. of Medicine; Hon. DSc (Georgetown Univ.) 1996, (Dartmouth Coll.) 1998; Distinguished Physician Award (Pediatric Infectious Diseases Soc.) 1991, Bristol Award and Soc. Citation Infectious Diseases Soc. of America 1993, Needleman Medal and Award, American Public Health Asscn 1997, Howland Award, American Pediatric Soc. 2000 and other awards; Presidential Medal of Dartmouth Coll. for Leadership and Achievement 1991. *Publications:* numerous articles in scientific journals, textbooks of pediatrics and infectious diseases. *Leisure interests:* jazz drumming (Joe Butterfield Dixieland Jazz Concert 1994–), cycling, reading, opera. *Address:* Duke University Medical Center, P.O. Box 2925, Durham, NC 27710 (Office); 1917 Wildcat Creek Road, Chapel Hill, NC 27516, USA (Home). *Telephone:* (919) 684-3734 (Office); (919) 968-0008 (Home). *Fax:* (919) 681-8934 (Office); (919) 968-0447 (Home). *E-mail:* katz0004@mc.duke.edu (Office); slkatz@mindspring.com (Home).

KATZENBACH, Nicholas deBelleville; American government official and lawyer; b. 17 Jan. 1922, Philadelphia; s. of Edward and Marie Katzenbach; m. Lydia King Phelps Stokes 1946; two s. two d.; ed Philips Exeter Acad., Princeton and Yale Univs. and Balliol Coll., Oxford; US Army Air Force 1941–45; admitted to NJ Bar 1950, Conn. Bar 1955, New York Bar 1972; with firm Katzenbach Gildea and Rudner, Trenton, NJ 1950; Attorney-Adviser, Office of Gen. Counsel, Air Force 1950–52, part-time Consultant 1952–56; Assoc. Prof. of Law, Yale Univ. 1952–56; Prof. of Law, Univ. of Chicago 1956–60; Asst Attorney-Gen., US Dept of Justice 1961–62, Deputy Attorney-Gen. 1962–64, Attorney-Gen. 1965–66; Under-Sec. of State 1966–69; Sr Vice-Pres. and Gen. Counsel, IBM Corpn 1969–86; Partner Riker, Danzig, Scherer, Hyland and Perretti 1986–91, Counsel 1991–94; mem. American Bar Asscn, American Judicature Soc., American Law Inst.; Democrat; hon. degrees from Rutgers Univ., Univ. of Bridgeport (Conn.), Tufts Univ., Georgetown Univ., Princeton, Northeastern Univ., Brandeis Univ., Bard Coll. *Publications:* The Political Foundations of International Law (with Morton A. Kaplan) 1961, Legal Literature of Space (with Prof. Leon Lipson) 1961. *Address:* 33 Greenhouse Drive, Princeton, NJ 08540, USA. *Telephone:* (609) 924-8536. *Fax:* (609) 924-6610. *E-mail:* NKatzenbcc@aol.com (Office).

KATZENBERG, Jeffrey; American film executive; b. 1950; m. Marilyn Siegal; one s. one d.; Asst to Chair., CEO Paramount Pictures, New York 1975–77; Exec. Dir Marketing, Paramount TV, Calif. 1977, Vice-Pres. Programming 1977–78; Vice-Pres. feature production, Paramount Pictures 1978–80, Sr Vice-Pres. production, motion picture div. 1980–82, Pres. production, motion pictures and TV 1982–94; Chair. Walt Disney Studios, Burbank, Calif. 1994–; Co-founder and Chair. Dream works SKG 1994–. *Address:* Dreamworks SKG, 100 Flower Street, Glendale, CA 91201, USA.

KATZIR, Ephraim, MSc, PhD; Israeli fmr Head of State, scientist, teacher and administrator; b. (as Ephraim Katchalski), 16 May 1916, Kiev, Russia; s. of Yehuda and Tsila Katchalski; m. Nina Gotlieb 1938 (deceased); one s.; ed Hebrew Univ., Jerusalem; Prof. and Head, Dept of Biophysics, Weizmann Inst. of Science 1951–73; Chief Scientist, Ministry of Defence 1966–68; Pres. of Israel 1973–78; Prof. Weizmann Inst. of Science 1978–, Prof. Tel Aviv Univ. 1978–; first incumbent Herman F. Mark Chair in Polymer Science, Polytechnic Inst. of New York 1979; Pres. World ORT Union (Org. for Rehabilitation Through Training) 1987–90, COBIOTECH Int. Scientific Cttee for Biotech. 1989–95; mem. Israel Acad. of Sciences and Humanities, NAS, USA, Leopoldina Acad. of Science, German Democratic Repub., The Royal Soc. of London (Foreign mem.), Int. Union of Biochemistry, Acad. des Sciences, France (Foreign mem.), American Acad. of Microbiology and many other orgs.; mem. American Soc. of Biological Chemists (Hon.), American Acad. of Arts and Sciences (Foreign Hon. mem.), Royal Inst. of Great Britain (Hon. mem.); Hon. Prof. Polytechnic Inst., New York; Commdr Légion d'honneur 1990; Hon. PhD (Brandeis, Michigan, Harvard, Northwestern, Jerusalem Hebrew, McGill, Thomas Jefferson, Oxford, Miami Univs., Weizmann Inst., Israel Technion and Hebrew Union Coll., Jerusalem, Eidgenossische Technische Hochschule, Univ. of Buenos Aires); Tchernikhovski Prize 1948; Weizmann Prize 1950; Israel Prize Natural Sciences 1959; Rothschild Prize Natural Sciences 1961; first recipient of Japan Prize, Science and Tech. Foundation of Japan 1985; Underwood Prescott Award, MIT 1982; Enzyme Eng Award 1987; Linderstrøm-Lang Gold Medal 1969; Hans Krebs Medal 1972. *Publications:* numerous papers and articles on proteins and polyamino acids, polymers structure and function of living cells and enzyme engineering.

Leisure interest: swimming. *Address:* Department of Biological Chemistry, Weizmann Institute of Science, P.O. Box 26, Rehovot 76100, Israel. *Telephone:* 8-9343947 (Office); 8-9343525 (Home). *Fax:* 8-9468256 (Office). *E-mail:* ephraim.katzir@weizmann.ac.il (Office).

KAUFMAN, Rt Hon Gerald Bernard, PC, MA, MP; British politician; b. 21 June 1930; s. of Louis and Jane Kaufman; ed Leeds Grammar School and Queen's Coll., Oxford; Asst Gen. Sec. Fabian Soc. 1954–55; political staff, Daily Mirror 1955–64; political corresp. New Statesman 1964–65; Parl. Press Liaison, Labour Party 1965–70; MP for Manchester, Ardwick 1970–83; for Manchester, Gorton 1983–; Under-Sec. of State for the Environment 1974–75, for Industry 1975; Minister of State, Dept of Industry 1975–79; mem. Parl. Cttee of Labour Party 1980–92; Opposition Spokesman for Home Affairs 1983–87; Shadow Foreign Sec. 1987–92; Chair. House of Commons Nat. Heritage Select Cttee 1992–97, Culture, Media and Sport Select Cttee 1997–; mem. Labour Party Nat. Exec. Cttee 1991–92; mem. Royal Comm. on House of Lords Reform 1999; Chair. Booker Prize Judges 1999. *Publications:* How to Live under Labour (co-author) 1964, To Build the Promised Land 1973, How to be a Minister 1980 (revised edn 1997), Renewal: Labour's Britain in the 1980's 1983, My Life in the Silver Screen 1985, Inside the Promised Land 1986, Meet Me in St Louis 1994. *Leisure interests:* cinema, opera, records, theatre, concerts, travel. *Address:* House of Commons, London, SW1; 87 Charlbert Court, Eamont Street, London, NW8, England. *Telephone:* (20) 7219-5145. *Fax:* (20) 7219-6825.

KAUFMAN, Henry, BA, MS, PhD; American banker; b. 20 Oct. 1927, Wenings, Germany; s. of Gustav and Hilda (née Rosenthal) Kaufman; m. Elaine Reinheimer 1957; three s.; ed New York and Columbia Univs.; went to USA 1937; Asst Chief Economist, Research Dept, Fed. Reserve Bank of New York 1957–61; with Salomon Bros., New York 1962–88, Gen. Partner 1967–88, mem. Exec. Cttee 1972–88, Man. Dir 1981–88, also Chief Economist, in charge Bond Market Research, Industry and Stock Research and Bond Portfolio Analysis Research Depts.; f. Henry Kaufman & Co., NY 1988–; Pres. Money Marketeers, New York Univ. 1964–65; Dir Lehman Bros. 1995–; Trustee, Hudson Inst.; mem. Bd of Govs, Tel Aviv Univ.; mem. American Econ. Asscn, American Finance Asscn, Conf. of Business Economists, Econ. Club, New York (also Dir); UN Asscn (also Dir); Council on Foreign Relations. *Publication:* Interest Rates, the Markets and the New Financial World 1986. *Address:* Henry Kaufman & Co., 65 E 55th Street, New York, NY 10022, USA.

KAUFMAN, Philip; American film writer and director; b. 23 Oct. 1936, Chicago, Ill.; s. of Nathan Kaufman and Betty Kaufman; m. Rose Kaufman; one s.; ed Univ. of Chicago and Harvard Law School; fmr teacher in Italy. *Films:* Goldstein (co-screenplay, co-Dir and co-producer) (Prix de la Nouvelle Critique, Cannes 1964), Fearless Frank 1965, The Great Northfield Minnesota Raid 1971, The White Dawn (Dir only) 1973, Invasion of the Body Snatchers (Dir only) 1977, The Wanderers (co-screenplay and Dir) 1979, The Right Stuff (Dir and screenplay) 1983 (winner of four Acad. Awards), The Unbearable Lightness of Being (Dir and co-screenplay) 1988, (Orson Welles Award for Best Filmmaker-Writer/Dir. 1988, Nat. Soc. of Film Critics Award for Best Dir 1988), Henry & June (Dir and co-scriptwriter) 1990, Rising Sun (Dir and co-screenplay) 1993, China: The Wild East (narrator and exec. producer) 1995. *Address:* c/o William Morris Agency, 151 El Camino Drive, Beverly Hills, CA 90212, USA.

KAUFMANN, Arthur, DrIur; German university professor; b. 10 May 1923, Singen; s. of Edmund Kaufmann and Elisabeth (née Gsell) Kaufmann; m. Dorothea Helffich 1949; one s. three d.; ed Univs. of Frankfurt and Heidelberg; judge at Landgericht Karlsruhe 1951–57; Docent Univ. of Heidelberg 1957–60; Ordinary Prof. Univ. of Saarbrücken 1960–69, Univ. of Munich 1969–, now Emer.; fmr Dir Inst. for Legal Philosophy and Legal Information, Univ. of Munich; Ordinary mem. Bayerische Akademie der Wissenschaften 1980–; mem. many other academies and orgs.; Hon. Pres. German Section Int. Asscn for Philosophy of Law and Social Philosophy 1982–, Hon. Pres. Int. Asscn for Philosophy of Law and Social Philosophy 1991–; numerous hon. degrees; Dr. hc (Munich); Hon. mem. Inst. for Advanced Studies in Jurisprudence, Univ. of Sydney. *Publications:* Naturrecht und Geschichtlichkeit 1957, Das Schuldprinzip 1976, Analogie und 'Natur der Sache' 1982, Schuld und Strafe 1983, Strafrecht zwischen Gestern und Morgen 1983, Rechtsphilosophie im Wandel 1984, Beiträge zur Juristischen Hermeneutik 1984, Gerechtigkeit, der vergessene Weg zum Frieden 1986, Gustav Radbruch 1987, Rechtsphilosophie in der Nach Neinzeit 1990, Vom Ungehorsam gegen die Obrigkeit 1991, Das Gewissen und das Problem der Rechtsgeltung 1991, Über Gerechtigkeit 1993, Grundprobleme der Rechtsphilosophie 1994, Einführung in Rechtsphilosophie und Rechtstheorie der Gegenwart 1994, Rechtsphilosophie 1997, Das Verfahren der Rechtsgewinnung 1999; more than 700 articles and trans. into 18 languages. *Leisure interests:* music, literature, theology. *Address:* Longinusstrasse 3, 81247 Munich, Germany. *Telephone:* (89) 8111723. *Fax:* (89) 8111723.

KAUL, Pratap Kishen, MA; Indian diplomatist; b. 3 July 1929, Calcutta; s. of late K. K. Kaul; m. Usha Kaul; three d.; ed Allahabad and Harvard Univs.; Deputy Sec., Ministries of Home Affairs and Finance 1965–66, Joint Sec. Ministry of Finance 1967–73, Finance Sec. and Sec. Economic Affairs 1983–85; Joint Sec. Ministry of Steel and Mines 1975–76; Chief Controller, Imports and Exports, Ministry of Commerce Jan.–July 1976, Additional Sec. 1976–80, Sec. (Export Devt) Feb.–May. 1980, Sec. (Textiles) July–Sept. 1980,

Sec. 1980–81; Chair. State Trading Corpn 1980–81; Defence Sec. Ministry of Defence 1981–83; Cabinet Sec. 1985–86; Amb. to the USA 1986–89. *Leisure interests:* reading, sports.

KAULA, Prithvi Nath, MA, MLibrSc; Indian professor of library science; b. 13 March 1924, Srinagar; s. of Damodar Kaula; m. Asha Kaula 1941; two s. three d.; ed S.P. Coll., Srinagar, Punjab Univ., Delhi Univ., Banaras Hindu Univ.; mem. Council, Indian Library Asscn 1949–53, 1956–62, Pres. 1996–98; Man. Ed. Annals, Bulletin and Granthalays of Indian Library Asscn 1949–53; Sec. Ranganathan Endowment for Library Science 1951–61; Gen. Sec. Delhi Library Asscn 1953–55, 1958–60, Vice-Pres. 1956–58; Visiting lecturer in Library Science, Aligarh Muslim Univ. 1951–58; Reader Dept of Library Science, Univ. of Delhi 1958–60; Vice-Pres. Govt of India Libraries Asscn 1958–61; mem. Review Cttee on Library Science, Univ. Grants Comm. 1961–63, mem. Panel on Library and Information Science 1978–80, 1982–84, Chair. 1990–92; Chair. Curriculum Devt Cttee (UGC) 1991–93; Visiting Prof. Documentation, Research and Training Centre, Bangalore 1962, 1965; Ed. Library Herald 1958–61, Herald of Library Science 1962–; Pres. Fed. of Indian Library Asscns. 1966–83; mem. Governing Council, Nat. Library of India 1966–69; UNESCO Expert, UNESCO Regional Centre in the Western Hemisphere, Havana 1967–68; Founder and Gen. Sec. Indian Asscn of Teachers of Library Science 1969, Pres. 1973–85, Patron 1986–; Ed. Granthalaya Vijnana 1970–; Librarian, Banaras Hindu Univ. and Prof. of Library Science 1971–78, Dean Faculty of Arts 1980–82; Prof. Emer. Kashi Vidyapith 1983–, UGC Prof. Emer. Lucknow Univ. 1985–; Ed. Research Journal of the Banaras Hindu Univ. 1980–, Ed. Progress in Library and Information Science 1980–; Ed.-in-Chief International Information, Communication and Education 1982–; Chair. Council of Literacy and Adult Educ. 1971–; Pres. Indian Library Asscn 1996–98; Vice-Pres. Indian Asscn of Special Libraries and Information Centres; UNESCO expert and consultant, UNESCO Regional Centre for the Western Hemisphere (Latin American countries) 1967–68; Dir UNESCO Training Programme on Library Science and Documentation, Havana, Cuba 1968, Modernisation of Library and Information Service, Nat. Library, Bangkok, Thailand 1978; Bureau for Promotion of Urdu Library Science 1980–84; mem. State Library Cttee, Uttar Pradesh 1981–85, Acad. Council, Aligarh Muslim Univ. 1996–2000, Acad. Council, Dr Ambedkar Univ. 1997–99; mem. Raja Rammohun Roy Library Foundation 1974–77, 1996–99; Bd of Studies in Library and Information Science of 16 univs; Expert mem. UNESCO Advisory Group on Comparability of Higher Degrees in Library Science 1973–75, Nat. Review Cttee on Univ. and Coll. Libraries 1996–; Dir Int. Inst. of Higher Studies in Educ., Knowledge and Professional Training 1992–; mem. Bd Trustees, Nat. Book Trust 1999–; Patron Indian Coll. Library Asscn, Nat. Music Acad., Library Council; Visiting Prof. 35 Indian Univs, 11 American Univs, Univ. of Havana, Hebrew Univ., Jerusalem and Univs in France, Cuba, Canada, Germany, Denmark, Italy, Hungary, Mexico, Spain, Thailand, Brazil, Singapore, the former USSR and the UK; Consultant and Adviser on Library Science to several int. orgs and nat. asscns; Organizing Sec. and Pres. of numerous confs; f. several professional bodies and trusts; est. Kaula Endowment for Library and Information Science 1975; Regional Pres. World Council of Vocational Educ. 1995–; Founder-Ed. of six journals, currently Ed. of three journals; Founder Delhi Library Asscn 1953, Jammu and Kashmir Library Asscn 1966, Indian Asscn for Teachers of Library and Information Science 1969, Nat. Book Museum 2000, Ranganathan Soc. for Book Culture, Library and Informatics Studies 2002; Fellow Raja Rammohun Roy Foundation 2002–; Hon. Adviser, Libraries, AP Govt 1972–79; Hon. Fellow Int. Council for Professional Educ. 1992, RRR Library Foundation 2001; Int. Kaula Gold Medal awarded to 21 recipients 1975–, Ranganathan-Kaula Gold Medal to 10 recipients 1980–, honoured by Int. Festschrift Cttee 1974, 1984, 1994, Indian Library Movt Award 1974, Pro Mundi Beneficio Medal (India) 1975, Deutsche Bücherei Medal (Germany) 1981, Commemorative Medal of Honour (USA) 1985, Kaula Gold Medal instituted at six univs; Kaula-Bashiruddin Chair instieud at Aligarh Univ.; numerous other awards. *Publications:* 60 books and monographs and numerous other publs including over 1,000 technical papers and book reviews on library science, labour problems and student unrest. *Leisure interests:* reading, writing, the study of library and information science. *Address:* Lucknow University, C-239 Indira Nagar, Lucknow 226016, India. *Telephone:* (522) 351172.

KAUNDA, Kenneth David; Zambian politician; b. Buchizya, 28 April 1924, Lubwa; m. Betty Banda 1946; six s. (two s. deceased) two d. one adopted s.; ed Lubwa Training School and Munali Secondary School; schoolteacher at Lubwa Training School 1943, Headmaster 1944–47; Sec. Chinsali Young Men's Farming Asscn 1947; welfare officer, Chingola Copper Mine 1948; school teaching 1948–49; Founder-Sec. Lubwa branch, African Nat. Congress (ANC) 1950, district organizer 1951, prov. organizer 1952, Sec.-Gen. for N Rhodesia 1953; imprisoned for possession of prohibited literature Jan.–Feb. 1954; broke away from ANC to form Zambia African Nat. Congress 1958; imprisoned for political offences May 1959–Jan. 1960; Pres. United Nat. Independence Party 1960–92, 1995–2000; Minister of Local Govt and Social Welfare, N Rhodesia 1962–64; Prime Minister of N Rhodesia Jan.–Oct. 1964; Pres. Pan-African Freedom Movt for East, Central and South Africa (PAF-MECSA) 1963; First Pres. of Zambia 1964–91 and Minister of Defence 1964–70, 1973–78; Head of Sub-Cttee for Defence and Security 1978–91; Minister of Foreign Affairs 1969–70, also of Trade, Industry, Mines and State Participation 1969–73; Chair. Mining and Industrial Devt Corpn of Zambia 1970; Chair. Org. of African Unity (OAU) 1970–71, 1987–88, Non-Aligned

Nations Conf. 1970–73, fmr Chair. ZIMCO; Chancellor, Univ. of Zambia 1966–91, Copperbelt Univ. 1988; f. Peace Foundation 1992; charged with 'misprison of treason' over alleged involvement in attempted coup d'état 1997; freed after six months of house arrest after charges dropped June 1998; deprived of citizenship March 1999; citizenship restored by Supreme Court 2000; Founder and Chair. Kenneth Kaunda Children of Africa Foundation 2000; Freeman of the Municipality of Chipata 1994; Order of the Collar of the Nile, Kt of the Collar of the Order of Pius XII, Order of the Queen of Sheba; Hon. LLD (Fordham, Dublin, Windsor (Canada), Wales, Sussex, York and Chile Univs); Dr hc (Humboldt State Univ., Calif.) 1980; Jawaharlal Nehru Award for Int. Understanding, Quaide Azam Human Rights Inst. Prize (Pakistan) 1976; honoured for his Keynote Address on Conflict Resolution in Africa and for Distinguished Leadership of African People for Over Half A Century, African Studies Coalition, Calif. State Univ., Sacramento 1995. *Publications:* Black Government 1961, Zambia Shall Be Free 1962, A Humanist in Africa (with Colin Morris) 1966, Humanism in Zambia and a Guide to its Implementation 1967, Humanism Part II 1977, Letter to my Children 1977, Kaunda On Violence 1980. *Address:* Office of the First President of the Republic of Zambia, 21 A Serval Road, PO E 501, Lusaka, Zambia. *Telephone:* (1) 260327 (Office); (1) 260323 (Home). *Fax:* (1) 220805 (Office); (1) 220805 (Home).

KAUR, Bibi Jagir; Indian religious leader; m. (husband deceased); two d.; fmr maths teacher; fmr Minister in Punjab State Govt; fmr Pres. Shiromani Gurudwara Prabandhak Cttee (Sikh body). *Address:* Bhulath, Dist Kapurthala, Punjab, India. *Telephone:* (1822) 48051 (Home); (172) 687652.

KAUR, Prabhjot (see Prabhjot Kaur).

KAURISMÄKI, Aki; Finnish film maker; b. 4 April 1957; co-founder film production co-operative Filmtotal; Man. Dir and Jt owner (with brother Mika Kaurismäki) film production co. Villealfa; jtly runs distribution co. Senso Film. *Films:* (Co-writer and Asst Dir) The Liar 1980, The Worthless 1982, The Clan: Tale of the Frogs 1984, Rosso 1985; (Co-Dir) The Saimaa Gesture 1981; (Dir) Crime and Punishment 1985, Calamari Union (Special Award, Hong Kong Int. Film Festival) 1985, Shadows in Paradise (Jussi Award for Best Finnish Film) 1986, Hamlet 1987, Ariel 1988, Leningrad Cowboys Go Home 1989, The Match Factory Girl 1989, I Hired a Contract Killer 1990, La Vie Bohème, Leningrad Cowboys Meet Moses 1993, Take Care of Your Scarf, Tatiana 1995, Drifting Clouds 1996, The Man Without a Past (Cannes Film Festival Best Actress Award 2002) 2002. *Rock videos:* Rock'y VI, Thru', The Wire, LA Woman 1986. *Address:* c/o The Finnish Film Foundation, K.13, Kanavakatu 24, SF-00160 Helsinki, Finland.

KAUZMANN, Walter Joseph, PhD; American professor of chemistry (retd); b. 18 Aug. 1916, Mount Vernon, New York; s. of Albert Kauzmann and Julia Kahle; m. Elizabeth Flagler 1951; two s. one d.; ed Cornell, Princeton Univs; Research Fellow, Westinghouse Co.; with Nat. Defense Council Explosives Research Lab.; worked on Atomic Bomb project, Los Alamos Labs, New Mexico 1944–46; Asst Prof. Princeton Univ. 1946–51, Assoc. Prof. 1951–60, Prof. 1960–83, David B. Jones Prof. of Chem. 1963–83, Chair. Dept of Chemistry 1963–68, Dept of Biochemical Sciences 1980–82; Visiting Scientist, Nat. Resources Council of Canada, Halifax 1983; mem. NAS, American Acad. of Arts and Sciences, American Chem. Soc., American Physical Soc., AAAS, Fed. of American Scientists, American Soc. of Biochemists, American Geophysical Union; Guggenheim Fellow 1957, 1974–75; Visiting Lecturer Kyoto Univ. 1974, Ibadan Univ. 1975; Hon. PhD (Stockholm Univ.) 1992; Stein and Moore Award (Protein Soc.) 1993; first recipient Kaj Ulrik Linderstrøm-Lang Medal 1966. *Publications:* Introd. to Quantum Chemistry 1957, Thermal Properties of Matter (2 Vols) 1966, 1967, Structure and Properties of Water 1969. *Address:* 301 North Harrison Street, PMB 152, Princeton, NJ 08540, USA (Home); c/o Department of Chemistry, Princeton University, Princeton, NJ 08544.

KAVAN, Jan Michael, BSc; Czech politician and journalist; b. 17 Oct. 1946, London; s. of Pavel Kavan and Rosemary Kavanová (née Edwards); m. Lenka Mázlová 1991; one s. three d.; ed Charles Univ., Prague, London School of Econs and St Antony's Coll., Oxford; journalist Univerzita Karlova, Prague 1966–68; Ed. East European Reporter, London 1985–90; Dir Palach Press Ltd, London 1974–90, Deputy Dir Jan Palach Information and Research Trust 1982–90; Vice-Pres. East European Cultural Foundation, London 1985–90; mem. Parl., Foreign Affairs Cttee, Fed. Ass., Czech Repub. 1990–92; Chair. Helsinki Citizens' Ass. in Czech Rep. 1990–95, Policy Centre for the Promotion of Democracy, Prague 1992–98; Senator Parl. of Czech Repub. 1996–2000, 2002–; Minister of Foreign Affairs 1998–2002, Deputy Prime Minister 1999–2002; Deputy Chair. State Security Council 1999–2002; Chair. Council for Intelligence Activities 1999–2002; lecturer Adelphi Univ., New York 1993, Amherst Coll., Mass. 1994, Hon. Prof. Faculty of Int. Relations, Mongolia State Univ. 1999; Pres. 57th Session UN Gen. Ass. 2002–03; Hon. Fellow LSE 2001; Hon. DHumLitt (Adelphi, NY) 2001; TGM Medal of Honour 2001. *Publications:* Czechoslovak Socialist Opposition 1976, Voices of Czechoslovak Socialists 1977, Voices from Prague 1983, Justice with a Muzzle 1996, McCarthyism Has a New Name: Castration in Transition to Democracy 2002. *Leisure interests:* int. politics, good literature, film, theatre. *Address:* United Nations, Room C-204, 1st Avenue, New York, NY 10017, USA (Office); Klausova 9, Prague 5, 155 00, Czech Republic (Home). *Telephone:* (212) 963-5067 (Office). *Fax:* (212) 963-3301 (Office).

KAVÁNEK, Pavel; Czech banker; two c.; ed Prague School of Econs, Georgetown Univ., USA; staff mem. Foreign Exchange Dept, Ceskolovenská Obchodní Banka (CSOB) 1972–76, Chief Dealer of Dept 1977–90, mem. Bd of Dirs 1990–93, Chair. and CEO 1993–; with Zivnostenská Banka, London, UK 1976–77; Vice-Pres. Asscn of Banks, Prague; Pew Econ. Freedom Fellowship, Georgetown Univ. 1992. *Address:* Ceskolovenská Obchodní Banka, Na Prikope 14, 11520 Prague 1, Czech Republic (Office).

KAVINDELE, Enoch Percy; Zambian politician; Vice-Pres. Movt for Multi-Party Democracy; Minister of Health –2001; Vice-Pres. of Zambia May 2001–; Mem. Nat. Assembly for Kabompo West. *Address:* Office of the Vice-President, P.O. Box 30208, Lusaka, Zambia (Office). *Telephone:* (1) 218282 (Office).

KAWAGUCHI, Yoriko, PhD; Japanese politician and economist; b. 14 Jan. 1941, Tokyo; m.; two c.; ed Univ. of Tokyo, Yale Univ., USA; joined Ministry of Int. Trade and Industry 1965, apptd Dir-Gen. Econ. Co-operation Dept 1990, Deputy Dir-Gen. for Global Environmental Affairs 1992; fmr economist World Bank (IBRD); apptd Minister, Embassy in Washington DC 1990; Man. Dir Suntory Ltd 1993–2000; apptd Minister of State and Dir-Gen. of the Environment Agency 2000; Minister of the Environment 2001–02, of Foreign Affairs 2002–; fmr mem. Regulatory Reform Cttee, Cen. Council for Educ., Univ. Council; fmr mem. Bd Dirs Japan Centre for Int. Exchange; mem. Trilateral Comm.; special mem. Japan Asscn of Corp. Execs. *Address:* Ministry of Foreign Affairs, Shiba Koen 2-11-1, Minato-ku, Tokyo 105-8519, Japan (Office). *Telephone:* (3) 3580-3311 (Office). *Fax:* (3) 3581-2667 (Office). *E-mail:* webmaster@mofa.go.jp (Office). *Website:* www.mofa.go.jp (Office).

KAWAI, Ryoichi; Japanese business executive; b. 18 Jan. 1917; s. of Yoshinari Kawai and Chieko Kawai; m. 1st Kiyoko Kawai 1942 (died 1973); three s.; m. 2nd Junko Kawai 1976; ed Tokyo Univ.; fmr Pres. Komatsu Ltd, Chair. 1982–95, Dir and Counsellor 1995, Counsellor June 1997–. *Leisure interest:* golf. *Address:* Komatsu Building, 3-6, Akasaka 2-chome, Minato-ku, Tokyo, Japan.

KAWAKUBO, Rei; Japanese couturier; b. 1943, Toyko; m. Adrian Joffe; ed Keio Univ., Tokyo; joined Asahikasei 1964; freelance designer 1966; launched Comme des Garçons Label 1969; f. and Pres. Comme des Garçons Co. Ltd 1973; Japan Comme des Garçons Collection presented twice a year, Tokyo; 395 outlets in Japan, 5 Comme des Garçons shops and 550 outlets outside Japan; currently has 11 lines of clothing, 1 line of furniture and a perfume; opened 1st overseas Comme des Garçons Boutique in Paris 1982; joined Fed. Française de la Couture 1982; f. Six magazine 1988; cr. costumes and stage design for Merce Cunningham's Scenario 1997; Dr. hc (RCA, London) 1997; Mainichi Newspaper Fashion Award 1983, 1988; Chevalier Ordre des Arts et des Lettres. *Address:* c/o Comme des Garçons Co. Ltd, 5-11-5 Minamiaoyama, Minatoku, Tokyo, Japan.

KAWALEROWICZ, Jerzy; Polish film director and screenwriter; b. 19 Jan. 1922, Gwoździec; m.; one s. two d.; ed Acad. of Fine Arts, Cracow 1946, Film Inst., Cracow 1948; Film Dir 1950–; Artistic Man. Film Group KADR 1956–68, 1989–; Assoc. Prof. State Higher Film, TV and Theatre School, Łódź 1980; mem. Nat. Council of Culture 1986–90; mem. ZASP (Union of Polish Stage Artists) 1960–; Chair. of SFP (Polish Film Union) 1966–78; mem. Polish United Workers' Party (PZPR) 1954–90; Deputy to Sejm (Parl.) 1985–89; numerous State distinctions; Hon. Chair. of SFP (Polish Film Union) 1978; Great Cross Order of Polonia Restituta 1997; Dr hc (Sorbonne) 1998, (State Higher Film, TV and Theatre School, Łódź) 2000; Minister of Culture and Arts Prize 1997. *Films:* Gromada 1951, Celuloza 1953, Pod gwiazdą frygijską 1954, Cień 1956, Prawdziwy koniec wielkiej wojny 1957, Pociąg 1959, Matka Joanna od Aniołów 1960, Faraon 1965, Gra 1968, Magdalena 1971, Śmierć prezydenta 1977, Spotkanie na Atlantyku 1980, Austeria 1982, Jeniec Europy 1989, Bronsteins Kinder 1990, Za co? 1995,Quo Vadis? 2001. *Leisure interest:* sport. *Address:* Studio Filmowe KADR, ul. Puławska 61, 02-595 Warsaw (Office); ul. Marconich 5 m. 21, 02-954 Warsaw, Poland (Home). *Telephone:* (22) 8454923 (Office). *Fax:* (22) 8454923 (Office).

KAWAMATA, Tadashi, MFA; Japanese visual artist; b. 1953, Hokkaido; ed Tokyo Nat. Univ. of Fine Art and Music; works exhibited at Venice Biennale 1982, Int. Youth Triennale of Drawing, Nuremberg 1983, Documenta 8 1987, São Paulo Biennale 1987, Tyne Int. Exhbn for Contemporary Art, Newcastle-upon-Tyne and Gateshead, UK 1990; apartment projects: Takara House Room 205, Tokyo 1982, Slip in Tokorozawa 1983, Tetra House N-3 W-26, Sapporo 1983; construction site projects: Spui Project, The Hague 1986, La Maison des Squatters, Grenoble 1987, Nove de Julho Cacapave, São Paulo 1987, Fukuroi Project 1988; urban projects: P.S.1 Project, New York 1985, Destroyed Church, Kassel 1987, Toronto Project at Colonial Tavern Park, Toronto 1989, Project at Begijnhof St Elisabeth, Kortrijk, Belgium 1989–90; projects are the subject of several catalogues; Asian Cultural Council Fellowship Grant (worked in New York 1984–86); Grand Prix Int. Youth Triennale 1983.

KAWARA, Tsutomu; Japanese politician; mem. House of Reps; fmr Deputy Chief Cabinet Sec.; fmr Dir.-Gen. Defence Agency; fmr Construction Minister; Dir.-Gen. Defence Agency 1999–2000. *Address:* c/o Defence Agency, 9-7-45, Akasaka, Minato-ku, Tokyo 107-8513, Japan (Office).

KAWASAKI, Jiro; Japanese politician; b. Mie; s. of Hideji Kawasaki; ed Keio Univ.; with Matsushita Electric Industrial Co. 1973–80; mem. for Tokai, House of Reps. 1980–; fmr Parl. Vice-Minister of Posts and Telecommunications; Minister of Transport 1988–99; fmr Head Public Relations Dept of LDP. *Leisure interests:* reading, tennis. *Address:* c/o Ministry of Transport, 2-1-3, Kasumigaseki, Chiyoda-ku, Tokyo 100, Japan.

KAWAWA, Rashidi Mfaume; Tanzanian politician; b. 1929, Songea; ed Tabora Secondary School; fmr Pres. of the Tanganyikan Fed. of Labour; Minister of Local Govt and Housing 1960–61; Minister without Portfolio 1961–62; Prime Minister Jan.–Dec. 1962, Vice-Pres. 1962–64; Second Vice-Pres., United Republic of Tanzania 1964–77, also Prime Minister 1972–77; Minister of Defence and Nat. Service 1977–80, Minister without Portfolio 1980; fmr Vice-Pres. of TANU (Tanganyika African Nat. Union); Sec.-Gen. Chama Cha Mapinduzi 1982–93.

KAY, John Anderson, MA, FBA; British economist; b. 3 Aug. 1948, Edinburgh; s. of the late James Kay and Allison Kay; m. Deborah Freeman 1986 (divorced 1995); ed Royal High School, Edin., Univ. of Edin. and Nuffield Coll. Oxford; Fellow, St John's Coll. Oxford 1970–; lecturer in Econs Univ. of Oxford 1971–79; Research Dir Inst. for Fiscal Studies 1979–82, Dir 1982–86; Dir Centre for Business Strategy, London Business School 1986–91; Chair. London Econs 1986–96; Dir Said Business School, Univ. of Oxford 1997–99, Undervalued Assets Trust PLC 1994–; Dir (non-exec.) Halifax Bldg Soc. 1991–97, Foreign & Colonial Special Utilities Investment Trust PLC 1993–, Value and Income Trust PLC 1994–, Halifax PLC 1997–2000. *Publications:* The Business of Economics, The British Tax System, Foundations of Corporate Success, Why Firms Succeed; co-author of Concentration in Modern Industry, The Reform of Social Security, The Economic Analysis of Accounting Profitability; articles in scholarly journals. *Leisure interests:* walking, travel. *Address:* johnkay.com Ltd, P.O. Box 4036, London, WIA 6NZ, England (Home). *Telephone:* (20) 7224-8797. *Fax:* (20) 7402-1368. *E-mail:* johnkay@johnkay.com (Office). *Website:* www.johnkay.com (Office).

KAYE, Harvey Jordan, PhD; American professor of social change and development; b. 9 Oct. 1949, Englewood, NJ; s. of Murray N. Kaye and Frances Kaye; m. Lorna Stewart 1973; two d.; ed Paramus High School, Rutgers Univ., Univ. of Mexico, Univ. of London, UK and Louisiana State Univ.; Asst Prof. of Interdisciplinary Studies, St Cloud Univ., Minn. 1977–78; Asst Prof. of Social Change and Devt, Univ. of Wis., Green Bay 1978–83, Assoc. Prof. 1983–86, Head of Dept 1985–88, Prof. 1986–, Ben and Joyce Rosenberg Prof. of Social Change and Devt 1990–, Dir Center for History and Social Change 1991–; Visiting Fellow, Univ. of Birmingham, UK 1987; mem. Editorial Bd Marxist Perspectives 1978–80, The Wisconsin Sociologist, Wis. Sociological Asscn 1985–87, Rethinking History 1996–; Consulting Ed., Verso Publishers, London 1988–94; NYU Press 1996–; Series Ed., American Radicals (Routledge) 1992–98; columnist Times Higher Educational Supplement 1994–2001, Tikkun magazine 1996–, Index on Censorship 1996–; mem. Exec. Bd, Center for Democratic Values 1996–, Scholars, Artists and Writers for Social Justice 1997–; mem. American Historical Asscn, American Sociological Asscn, American Studies Asscn, Org. of American Historians; Nat. Endowment for Humanities Fellowship 2002–03; Isaac Deutscher Memorial Prize 1993; Founders' Award for Scholarship 1985; Best Book for the Teen Age, New York Public Library 2001. *Publications:* The British Marxist Historians 1984, The Powers of the Past 1991, The Education of Desire 1992, Why do Ruling Classes Fear History? 1996, Thomas Paine 2000, Are We Good Citizens? 2001; (Ed.) History, Classes and Nation-States 1988, The Face of the Crowd: Studies in Revolution, Ideology and Popular Protest 1988, Poets, Politics and the People 1989, E. P. Thompson: Critical Perspectives (with K. McClelland) 1990, The American Radical (with M. Buhle and P. Buhle) 1994, Imperialism and its Contradictions 1995, Ideology and Popular Protest 1995; numerous articles on history and historians. *Leisure interests:* travel, films, friendship and conversation. *Address:* Social Change and Development Department, University of Wisconsin-Green Bay, 2420 Nicolet Drive, Green Bay, WI 54311, USA (Office). *Telephone:* (920) 465-2355/2755 (Office). *Fax:* (920) 465-2791. *E-mail:* kayeh@uwgb.edu (Office).

KAYENKIKO, Anatole; Burundian politician and engineer; b. Ngozi Prov.; ed Caen Univ.; fmr Mayor of Bujumbura; Minister of Public Works and Equipment –1994; Prime Minister of Burundi 1994–95; mem. Union pour le Progrès Nat. (UPRONA). *Address:* c/o Union pour le Progrès National, BP 1810, Bujumbura, Burundi.

KAYSEN, Carl, AB, MA, PhD; American economist; b. 5 March 1920, Philadelphia; s. of Samuel and Elizabeth Resnick; m. 1st Annette Neutra 1940 (died 1990); two d.; m. 2nd Ruth A. Butler 1994; ed Overbrook High School, Philadelphia, Univ. of Pennsylvania and Harvard Univ.; Nat. Bureau of Econ. Research 1940–42; Office of Strategic Services, Washington, DC 1942–43; US Army (Intelligence) 1943–45; Teaching Fellow in Econs, Harvard Univ. 1947, Jr Fellow, Soc. of Fellows 1947–50, Asst Prof. in Econs 1950–55, Assoc. Prof. 1955–57, Prof. 1957–66, Assoc. Dean, Graduate School of Public Admin. 1960–66, Lucius N. Littauer Prof. of Political Economy 1964–66; Dir, Inst. of Advanced Study, Princeton 1966–76, Dir Emer. 1976–, Prof. of Social Science 1976–77; David W. Skinner Prof. Political Econ., MIT 1976–90, Prof. Emer. 1990–, Sr Research Scientist 1992–; Dir Program in Science, Tech. and Soc. 1981–86; Vice-Chair. and Dir Research, Sloan Comm. on Govt and Higher Educ. 1977–79; Sr Fulbright Research Scholar, London School of Econs 1955–56; Econ. Consultant to Judge Wyzanski, Fed. District Court of Mass. 1950–52; Deputy Special Asst to Pres. for Nat. Security Affairs 1961–63. *Publications:* United States v. United Shoe Machinery Corporation, an Economic Analysis of an Anti-Trust Case 1956, The American Business Creed

(with others) 1956, Anti-Trust Policy (with D. F. Turner) 1959, The Demand for Electricity in the United States (with Franklin M. Fisher) 1962, The Higher Learning, the Universities and the Public 1969, Nuclear Power, Issues and Choice, Nuclear Energy Policy Study Group Report (with others) 1977, A Program for Renewed Partnership, Report of the Sloan Commission on Government and Higher Education (with others) 1980, Emerging Norms of Justified Intervention 1993, Peace Operations by the United Nations (with George Rathjens) 1996, The American Corporation Now (ed.) 1996, The United States and the International Criminal Court (ed. with S. Sewall) 2000. *Address:* Massachusetts Institute of Technology Program in Security Studies, 292 Main Street, E38-614 Cambridge, MA 02139, USA. *Telephone:* (617) 253-4054. *Fax:* (617) 253-9330.

KAZAN, Elia (Elia Kazanjoglous), AB, MFA; American film and stage director; b. 7 Sept. 1909, Istanbul, Turkey; s. of George and Athena (Sismanoglou) Kazan; m. 1st Molly Day Thacher 1932 (died 1963); two s. two d.; m. 2nd Barbara Loden 1967 (died 1980); one s.; m. 3rd Frances Rudge 1982; ed Williams Coll. and Yale Dramatic School; Apprentice and Stage Man. with Group Theatre; acted on stage 1935–41 in Waiting for Lefty, Golden Boy, Gentle People, Fire-Alarm Waltz, Liliom and in two films City for Conquest and Blues in the Night 1941; fmr Dir of Actors Studio; Best Picture of Year Award, New York Film Critics 1948, 1952, 1955; D. W Griffith Award, Dirs. Guild of America 1987, Hon. Golden Bear Award 1996, Hon. Acad. Award 1999. *Films include:* A Tree Grows in Brooklyn 1945, Gentlemen's Agreement (Academy Award) 1947, Boomerang 1947, Pinky 1949, Panic in the Streets 1950, Streetcar Named Desire 1951, Viva Zapata 1952, Man on a Tightrope 1953, On the Waterfront (Acad. Award) 1954, East of Eden 1955, Baby Doll 1956, A Face in the Crowd 1957, Wild River 1960, Splendor in the Grass 1961, America, America 1963, The Arrangement 1969, The Visitors 1972, The Last Tycoon 1976. *Theatre includes:* Skin of Our Teeth (Drama Critics Award), One Touch of Venus, Harriet, Jacobowsky and the Colonel (Drama Critics Award), Streetcar Named Desire, Death of a Salesman (Drama Critics Award), Tea and Sympathy, Cat on a Hot Tin Roof (Drama Critics Award), The Dark at the Top of the Stairs, J. B., Sweet Bird of Youth, for Lincoln Center Repertory Theatre After the Fall, But for Whom Charlie, The Changeling. *Publications:* America, America 1962, The Arrangement 1967, The Assassins 1972, The Understudy 1974, Acts of Love 1978, The Anatolian 1982, A Life (autobiog.) 1988, Beyond the Aegean 1994.

KAZANKINA, Tatyana Vassilyevna; Russian athlete; b. 17 Dec. 1951, Petrovsk, Saratov Region; d. of Vasily Kazankin and Maria Kazankina; m. Alexandre Kovalenko 1974; one d.; int. athlete since 1972; competed in Olympic Games Montreal 1976, winning gold medals at 800m and 1500m, Moscow 1980, won gold medal at 1500m; European Indoor silver medallist 1975; world records at 800m, 1500m (three times), 2000m, 3000m, 4×800m; world bronze medal 1983; suspended for life by IAAF for refusing to take a blood test 1984, reinstated 1985; economist, Leningrad; Asst Prof. St Petersburg Acad. of Physical Culture; Pres. St Petersburg Union of Athletes; mem. Union of Right Forces party 2000–; Hon. Master of Sport 1976; Hon. PhD 1992. *Leisure interests:* travelling, human contacts. *Address:* c/o Light Athletic Federation, Millionnaia 22, St Petersburg (Office); Hoshimina Street 11-1-211, St Petersburg, Russia (Home). *Telephone:* (812) 114-69-31 (Office); (812) 595-09-40 (Home). *Fax:* (812) 315-97-95.

KAZANNIK, Aleksei Ivanovich, DIur; Russian lawyer; b. 26 July 1941, Perepis, Chernigov Region; m.; two s.; ed Irkutsk Univ.; teacher Irkutsk Univ. 1975–79; Prof., Head of Chair, Omsk Univ. 1979–89, 1994–; forbidden to give public lectures because of criticism of Soviet invasion of Afghanistan; USSR People's Deputy 1989–91; fmr mem. USSR Supreme Soviet; active participant Movt Democratic Russia; mem. Interregional Group of Deputies; mem. Cttee on ecology problems and rational use of natural resources, USSR Supreme Soviet; mem. Pres.'s Council 1993–94; Prosecutor-Gen. of Russia 1993–94 (resgnd); Founder and Chair. Party of People's Conscience 1995–; Chair. Cttee on problems of nationalities, religions and public orgs of Omsk Region 1996–; Deputy Gov. Omsk Region 1999–. *Publications:* legal aspects of regional problems of nature preservation, numerous articles on ecology, law, pamphlets. *Address:* Administration of Omsk Region, Krasny Put str. 1, 644002 Omsk; Omsk State University, Mira Prosp. 55A, 644077 Omsk, Russia. *Telephone:* (3812) 23-49-26 (Administration). *E-mail:* eshish@univer.omsk.ru.

KAZANTSEV, Aleksei Nikolayevich; Russian playwright, actor and director; b. 11 Dec. 1945, Moscow; s. of Prof. of Moscow State Univ.; m. Natalya Vyacheslavovna Somova; one s.; ed Moscow State Univ., Leningrad Acad. of Theatre, Music and Cinema, Studio of Moscow Art Theatre; Founder and Artistic Dir (with M. Roshchin) Dramaturg magazine 1992. *Plays include:* Anton and Others 1975, Old House 1976, And The Silver Thread Will Break 1979, Great Buddha, Help Them 1988, Yevgenya's Dreams 1990, This That World 1992, Running Stages 1996. *Stage productions include:* Strawberry Field, Nest of a Wood-Grouse, Riga Drama Theatre, If I Stay Alive, Moscow Mossoviet Theatre. *Address:* Palikha str. 7-9, korp. 2, apt. 54, 103055 Moscow, Russia (Home). *Telephone:* (095) 972-65-85 (Home).

KAZANTSEV, Col-Gen. Victor Germanovich; Russian army officer; b. 22 Feb. 1946, Kokhanovo, Vitebsk Region, Belarus; m. Tamara Valentinovna Kazantseva; ed Leningrad Higher School of Gen. Army, M. Frunze Mil. Acad., Mil. Acad. of Gen. Staff; officer in Caucasian, Middle-Asian, Turkestan, Baikal Mil. Commands, Cen. Army Group in Czechoslovakia, First Deputy

Commdr of Army N Caucasian Mil. Command; Chief of Staff to Commdr of troops N Caucasian Mil. Command 1996–97, Commdr 1997–99; Commdr group of Fed. forces in N Caucasus 1999–2000; Rep. of Russian Pres. to N Caucasian Fed. Dist 2000–; Hero of Russia for operations in Dagestan and Chechnya 1999. *Address:* Office of the Representative of the President to North Caucasian Federal District, Bolshaya Sadovaya str. 73, 344006 Rostov-on-Don, Russia (Office). *Telephone:* (8632) 44-16-16 (Rostov-on-Don) (Office); (095) 206-63-85 (Moscow) (Office). *Fax:* (8632) 40-39-40 (Rostov-on-Don), (095) 206-70-73 (Moscow).

KAZARNOVSKAYA, Lubov Yurievna; Russian soprano; b. 18 July 1956; m. Robert Roszik; ed Moscow Gnessin School of Music and Moscow State Conservatory; as student became soloist Moscow Stanislavsky and Nemirovich-Danchenko Musical Theatre 1981–86; soloist Leningrad Kirov (now Mariinsky) Opera Theatre 1986–89; debut outside USSR in Un Ballo in Maschera, Zürich Opera 1989, Desdemona in Otello, Covent Garden, London March 1990; moved to Vienna 1989; has performed in maj. opera houses of the world, in opera productions with Herbert von Karajan, Carlos Kleiber, Claudio Abbado, Riccardo Muti, Daniel Barenboim, James Conlon; also performs in concerts, including Requiem (Verdi), La Voix humaine by Poulenc and at festivals in Salzburg, Bregenz, Edin. and others; prize winner All-Union competition of singers 1981, int. competition in Bratislava 1984. *Music:* Operatic roles include leading parts in Eugene Onegin, Iolanthe, La Bohème, Pagliacci, Faust, Marriage of Figaro, Falstaff, Force of Destiny, Boris Godunov, La Traviata, Salome. *Address:* Hohenbergstrasse 50, A-1120 Vienna, Austria. *Telephone:* (1) 839106 (Vienna) (Home); (095) 249-17-13 (Moscow) (Home).

KAZHEGELDIN, Akezhan Magzhanovich; Kazakhstan politician and economist; b. 27 March 1952, Georgiyevka, Semipalatinsk Region; m. Bykova Natalia Kazhegeldina; one s. one d.; ed Semipalatinsk Pedagogical Inst., Almaty Inst. of Nat. Econs; Chair. Regional Exec. Cttee of Semipalatinsk 1983; Dir Ore-enriching Factory, Deputy Head Admin. of Semipalatinsk Region 1991–94; Pres. Kazakhstan Union of Industrialists and Entrepreneurs 1992–; First Deputy Prime Minister of Kazakhstan 1993–94, Prime Minister 1994–97; Adviser to Pres. Nazarbayev May–Oct. 1998; Chair. Bd Republican Party 1998–2001; mem. Politburo Bd United Democratic Party 2001; in opposition to Pres. Nazarbayev 1999–; now lives abroad, sentenced to 10 years' imprisonment in absentia 1999. *Publications include:* six books including Kazakhstan in the Conditions of Reforms, Problems of State Regulation in the Conditions of Socio-Economic Transformation, Socio-Economic Problems of Development of Kazakhstan in the Conditions of Reforms 1999, Opposition to Middle Ages 2000.

KAZIBWE, Speciosa Wandira, MB, CH.B.; Ugandan politician; b. 1 July 1955, Iganga Dist; ed Makerere Univ., Kampala; mem. Nat. Resistance Movt (NRM); MP for Kigulu S Iganga Dist; Deputy Minister for Industry 1989–91; fmr Minister for Gender and Community Devt; fmr Minister of Agric., Animal Industry and Fisheries; Vice-Pres. of Uganda 1994–. *Address:* Office of the Vice-President, P.O. Box 7359, Kampala, Uganda (Office). *Telephone:* (41) 236563 (Office). *Fax:* (41) 236778 (Office).

KAZMIN, Andrei Ilyich, PhD; Russian banker; b. 1958, Moscow; m.; ed Moscow Inst. of Finance; Economist, State Bank of the USSR 1982–83; Asst Prof., then Deputy Dean Faculty of Credit, Moscow Inst. of Finance 1983–88; Sr Researcher USSR (now Russian) Acad. of Sciences 1988–91; Sr Research Fellow Alexander von Humboldt Foundation, Inst. for Int. Politics and Security, Ebenhausen, Germany 1991–93; training at German Ministry of Finance and German banks 1992–93; Deputy Minister of Finance, Russian Fed. 1993–96; Chair. of Bd and CEO Savings Bank of Russian Fed. (Sperbank) 1996–; mem. Supervising Cttee Agency on Housing Credits 1996–; Vice-Pres. World Savings Banks Inst. 2000–; mem. Bd Dirs Europay International (Eastern Europe) 2000–; Order of Honour 2002. *Publications:* more than 40 publs. *Leisure interest:* theatre, literature, sports. *Address:* Sberbank, Vavilova str. 19, 117997 Moscow, Russia (Office). *Telephone:* (095) 957-57-25 (Office). *Fax:* (095) 957-57-31 (Office). *E-mail:* sbrf@sbrf.ru (Office). *Website:* www.sbrf.ru (Office).

KE TING-SUI, (Ge Tingsui), PhD; Chinese scientist; b. 3 May 1913, Shantung; m. He Yizhen 1941; one s. one d.; ed Univ. of California Berkeley; mem. staff Spectroscopy and Radiation Lab. MIT 1943–45; Research Assoc. Inst. for the Study of Metals, Univ. of Chicago 1945–49; Prof. Physics, Tsinghua Univ. 1949–52; Prof., Deputy Dir Inst. Metal Research, Acad. Sinica 1952–80; f., Prof., Dir Inst. of Solid State Physics 1980–86, Prof. and Hon. Dir 1986–, Dir Lab. of Internal Friction and Defects in Solids 1985–93; current research: grain boundary relaxation, point defect-dislocation interaction, nonlinear anelasticity; Prof. of Physics, Univ. of Science and Tech. of China 1987–93, concurrently Prof., Tsinghua Univ. 1993–95; Guest Research Prof., Inst. Metal Research, Shenyang, Chinese Acad. of Sciences 1995–; Visiting Prof. Max-Planck Inst. for Metals, Stuttgart 1979–80; Guest Prof. Nat. Inst. of Applied Science, Lyon 1980–81; lecturer TMS Inst. of Metals; Deputy 3rd NPC 1963–74, 5th NPC 1978–83, 6th NPC 1983–88, 7th NPC 1988–93; Sr mem. Chinese Acad. of Sciences; Hon. mem. Japan Inst. of Metals; R. R. Hasiguti Prizes 1996, Ho Leung Ho Lee Prize 1996; C. Zener Medallist 1989; Robert Franklin Mahl Award 1999. *Publications:* 250 scientific papers, Proceedings of Ninth Int. Conference on Internal Friction and Ultrasonic Attenuation in Solids (ed.) 1990, Grain Boundary Relaxation and Grain Boundary Structure 1998, Internal Friction and Defects in Solids 1999,

Materials Damping 2000. *Address:* Institute of Solid State Physics, Chinese Academy of Sciences, Hefei 230031, Anhui, People's Republic of China. *Telephone:* (551) 5591415; (551) 5591429. *Fax:* (551) 5591434.

KEACH, Stacy; American actor and director; b. 2 June 1941, Savannah, Ga; s. of Walter Edmund Keach and Dora Stacy; m. Malgossia Tomassi 1986; two d.; stage debut in Joseph Papp's production of Hamlet, Cen. Park 1964; other stage appearances include A Long Day's Journey into Night, Macbird (Vernon Rice Drama Desk Award), Indians, Deathtrap, Hughie, Barnum, Cyrano de Bergerac, Peer Gynt, Henry IV (Parts I & II), Idiot's Delight, The King and I 1989, Love Letters 1990–93, Richard III 1991, Stieglitz Loves O'Keefe 1995; numerous TV appearances; Dir Incident at Vichy and Six Characters in Search of an Author for TV; mem. Artists Cttee Kennedy Center Honors 1986–; Hon. Chair. American Cleft Palate Foundation 1995–; recipient of three Obie Awards, Pasadena Playhouse Alumni Man of the Year 1995, Pacific Pioneers Broadcasters' Asscn Diamond Circle Award 1996. *Films include:* The Heart is a Lonely Hunter, End of the Road, The Travelling Executioner, Brewster McCloud, Doc, Judge Roy Bean, The New Centurions, Fat City, The Killer Inside Me, Conduct Unbecoming, Luther, Street People, The Squeeze, Gray Lady Down, The Ninth Configuration, The Long Riders, Road Games, Butterfly, Up in Smoke, Nice Dreams, That Championship Season, The Lover, False Identity, The Forgotten Milena, John Carpenter's Escape from LA 1996, Prey of the Jaguar 1996, The Truth Configuration 1998, American History X 1998. *Publication:* Keach, Go Home! 1996 (autobiog.). *Address:* c/o Palmer & Associates, #950, 23852 Pacific Coast Highway, Malibu, CA 90265, U.S.A. (Office).

KEAN, Thomas H., MA; American fmr politician and university president; b. 21 April 1935, New York; m. Deborah Bye; two s. one d.; ed Princeton Univ., Columbia Univ. Teachers' Coll.; fmr teacher of history and Govt; mem. NJ Ass. 1967–77, Speaker 1972, Minority Leader 1974; Acting Gov. of NJ 1973, Gov. 1982–90; Pres. Drew Univ., Madison, NJ 1990–; mem. White House Conf. on Youth 1970–71; fmr Chair. Carnegie Corpn of New York, Educate America, Nat. Environmental Educ. and Training Foundation; Chair. Newark Alliance, Nat. Campaign to Prevent Teen Pregnancy, Nat. Comm. on Terrorist Attacks upon the US (9-11 Comm.) 2002–; mem. Bd Robert Wood Johnson Foundation, Nat. Council World Wildlife Fund; regular columnist, The Star Ledger. *Publications include:* The Politics of Inclusion. *Address:* Office of the President, Drew University, 36 Madison Avenue, Madison, NJ 07940; National Commission on Terrorist Attacks Upon the United States, c/o GSA Agency Liaison Division, 701 D Street SW, Room 7120, Washington, DC 20407, USA. *Telephone:* (973) 408-3100 (Drew Univ.). *Fax:* (973) 408-3080 (Drew Univ.). *E-mail:* tomkean@drew.edu. *Website:* www.drew.edu (Office); www.9-11commission.gov.

KEANE, Fergal Patrick, OBE; Irish journalist and broadcaster; b. 6 Jan. 1961; s. of the late Eamon Brendan Keane and of Mary Hasset; m. Anne Frances Flaherty 1986; one s.; ed Terenure Coll., Dublin and Presentation Coll., Cork; trainee reporter Limerick Leader 1979–82; reporter Irish Press Group, Dublin 1982–84; Radio Telefis Eireann, Belfast 1986–89 (Dublin 1984–86); Northern Ireland Corresp. BBC Radio 1989–91, South Africa Corresp. 1991–94, Asia Corresp. 1994–97, Special Corresp. 1997–; presenter Fergal Keane's Forgotten Britain (BBC) 2000; Hon. DLitt (Strathclyde) 2001, (Staffs.) 2002; James Cameron Prize 1996, Bayeux Prize for war reporting 1999; Reporter of the Year Sony Silver Award 1992 and Sony Gold Award 1993, Int. Reporter of the Year 1993, Amnesty Int. Press Awards, RTS Journalist of the Year 1994, BAFTA Award 1997. *Publications:* Irish Politics Now 1987, The Bondage of Fear 1994, Season of Blood: A Rwandan Journey 1995, Letter to Daniel 1996, Letters Home 1999, A Stranger's Eye 2000. *Leisure interests:* fishing, golf, poetry. *Address:* c/o BBC Television, Wood Lane, London, W12 7RJ, England.

KEATING, Francis Anthony, II, JD; American politician and lawyer; b. 10 Feb. 1944, St Louis; s. of Anthony Francis Keating and Anne Martin; m. Catherine Dunn Heller 1972; one s. two d.; ed Georgetown and Oklahoma Univs.; called to the bar, Okla 1969; Special Agent with FBI 1969–71; Asst Dist Attorney, Tulsa Co. 1971–72; mem. Okla House of Reps. 1972–74, Okla Senate 1974–81; attorney, Northern Dist, Okla 1981–84; Asst Sec. US Treasury Dept, Washington 1985–88, Assoc. Attorney-Gen. Dept of Justice 1988–89, Gen. Counsel and Acting Deputy Sec. Dept of Housing and Urban Devt 1989–93; attorney in pvt. practice, Tulsa 1993–95; Gov. of Oklahoma 1995–2003; mem. Okla Bar Asscn. *Address:* c/o Office of the Governor, 212 State Capitol Bldg, Oklahoma City, OK 73105, USA.

KEATING, Henry Reymond Fitzwalter, FRSL; British writer; b. 31 Oct. 1926, St Leonards-on-Sea, Sussex; s. of John Hervey Keating and Muriel Keating; m. Sheila Mary Mitchell 1953; three s. one d.; ed Merchant Taylors' School, Trinity Coll., Dublin; journalist 1952–59; Chair. Crime Writers Asscn 1970–71, Soc. of Authors 1983, 1984; Pres. The Detection Club 1985–2001; Gold Dagger Award 1964, 1980, Diamond Dagger Award 1996. *Publications:* Death and the Visiting Firemen 1959, The Perfect Murder 1964, Inspector Ghote's Good Crusade 1966, Inspector Ghote Caught in Meshes 1967, Inspector Ghote Hunts the Peacock 1968, Inspector Ghote Plays a Joker 1969, Inspector Ghote Breaks an Egg 1970, Inspector Ghote Goes by Train 1971, The Strong Man 1971, Inspector Ghote Trusts the Heart 1972, Bats Fly Up for Inspector Ghote 1974, The Underside 1974, Murder Must Appetize 1976, Filmi, Filmi Inspector Ghote 1976, A Long Walk to Wimbledon 1978, Sherlock Holmes, the Man and his World 1979, The Murder of the Maharajah 1980, Go

West, Inspector Ghote 1981, The Lucky Alphonse 1982, The Sheriff of Bombay 1983, Under a Monsoon Cloud 1984, Dead on Time 1988, Inspector Ghote, His Life and Crimes 1989, The Iciest Sin 1990, Cheating Death 1992, The Rich Detective 1993, Doing Wrong 1994, The Good Detective 1995, Asking Questions 1996, The Soft Detective 1997, Bribery, Corruption 1999, Jack, the Lady Killer 1999, The Hard Detective 2000, Breaking and Entering 2000, A Detective in Love 2001, A Detective Under Fire 2002, The Dreaming Detective 2003. *Address:* 35 Northumberland Place, London, W2 5AS, England. *Telephone:* (20) 7229-1100.

KEATING, Hon. Paul John; Australian politician; b. 18 Jan. 1944, Sydney; s. of Matthew Keating and Min Keating; m. Anna Van Iersel 1975; one s. three d.; ed De la Salle Coll., Bankstown; Research Officer Federated Municipal and Shire Council Employees' Union of Australia 1967; elected to the House of Reps. for the Fed. Seat of Blaxland 1969–96; Minister for N Australia Oct.–Nov. 1975; Opposition Spokesman on Agric. Jan.-March 1976; on Minerals and Energy 1976–83, on Treasury Matters Jan.–March 1983; Fed. Treas. 1983–91; Leader Australian Labor Party 1991–96; Deputy Prime Minister 1990–91; Prime Minister of Australia 1991–96; Chair. Australian Inst. of Music 1999–; Bd of Architects of NSW 2000–; Hon. UD (Keio Univ. Tokyo), (Nat. Univ. of Singapore). *Publication:* Engagement: Australia Faces the Asia Pacific 2000. *Leisure interests:* classical music, architecture, swimming. *Address:* GPO Box 2598, Sydney, NSW 2001, Australia.

KEATING, Ronan; Irish singer and songwriter; b. 3 March 1977, Dublin; s. of Gerry Keating and the late Marie Keating; m. Yvonne Keating; one s. one d.; mem. Boyzone (with Stephen Gately, Keith Duffy, Shane Lynch and Mikey Graham) 1993–; solo singer 1999–. *Singles:* Love Me for a Reason 1994, Key to my Life 1995, So Good 1995, Father and Son 1995, Coming Home 1996, Words 1996, A Different Beat 1996, Isn't it a Wonder 1997, Picture of You 1997, Baby Can I Hold You 1997, All that I Need 1998, No Matter What 1998, I Love the Way you Love Me 1998, When the Goin' Gets Tough 1999, You Needed Me 1999, When You Say Nothing At All (solo, from film Notting Hill) 1999, Everyday I Love You 1999, Life is a Rollercoaster (solo) 2000, The Way You Make Me Feel (solo) 2000, Lovin' Each Day (solo) 2001, If Tomorrow Never Comes (solo) 2002, I Love The Way We Do (solo) 2002, We've Got Tonight 2002. *Albums:* Said and Done 1995, A Different Beat 1996, Where We Belong 1998, By Request – The Greatest Hits 1999, Ronan (solo) 2000, Destination 2002. *Publications:* No Matter What 2000, Life is a Rollercoaster 2000. *Address:* The Outside Organization, 180–182 Tottenham Court Road, London, W1P 9LE, England. *Telephone:* (20) 7436-3633. *Fax:* (20) 7436-3632.

KEATINGE, William Richard, MA, MB, BChir, PhD, FRCP; British professor of physiology; b. 18 May 1931, London; s. of Edgar Mayne Keatinge and Katherine Lucille Keatinge; m. Margaret Ellen Annette Hegarty 1955; one s. two d.; ed Univ. of Cambridge, St Thomas's Hosp. Medical School; Dir of Studies in Medicine, Pembroke Coll., Cambridge 1956–60; Fellow of Cardiovascular Research Inst., San Francisco 1960–61; Dept of Regius Prof. of Medicine, Oxford, MRC appointment 1961–68; Fellow and Tutor in Physiology, Pembroke Coll., Oxford 1956–68; Reader in Physiology, London Hosp. Medical Coll. 1968–71; Prof. 1971–90; Prof. of Physiology, Queen Mary and Westfield Coll. 1990–96, Prof. Emer. 1996–; Oliver-Sharpey Lecturer, Royal Coll. of Physicians 1986; Dean of Basic Medical Sciences, Queen Mary and Westfield Coll. 1991–94. *Achievements:* Co-ordinator of European Union 'Eurowinter' Project and related projects on winter mortality, 1993–98. *Publications:* Survival in Cold Water: The Physiology and Treatment of Immersion Hypothermia and Drowning 1970, Local Mechanisms Controlling Blood Vessels (with C. Harman) 1980; numerous articles and papers. *Leisure interests:* archaeology, sailing. *Address:* Biomedical Sciences, Queen Mary and Westfield College, Mile End Road, London, E1 4NS, England. *E-mail:* w.r.keatinge@qmw.ac.uk (Office).

KEATON, Diane; American actress; b. 5 Jan. 1946, Calif.; student Neighbourhood Playhouse, New York; New York stage appearances in Hair 1968, Play It Again Sam 1971, The Primary English Class 1976. *Films include:* Lovers and Other Strangers 1970, Play It Again Sam 1972, The Godfather 1972, Sleeper 1973, The Godfather Part 2 1974, Love and Death 1975, I Will-I Will-For Now 1975, Harry and Walter Go To New York 1976, Annie Hall 1977, (Acad. Award for Best Actress and other awards), Looking for Mr. Goodbar 1977, Interiors 1978, Manhattan 1979, Reds 1981, Shoot the Moon 1982, Mrs Soffel 1985, Crimes of the Heart 1986, Trial and Error 1986, Radio Days 1987, Heaven (Dir) 1987, Baby Boom 1988, The Good Mother 1988, The Lemon Sisters 1989, Running Mates 1989, The Godfather III, Wildflower (Dir) 1991, Heaven (Dir), Secret Society (Dir), Manhattan Murder Mystery 1993, Unsung Heroes (Dir) 1995, Father of the Bride 2 1995, Marvin's Room, The First Wives Club 1996, The Only Thrill 1997, Hanging Up (also Dir) 1999, The Other Sister 1999, Town and Country 1999, Sister Mary Explains It All 2001. *Publications:* Reservations, Still Life (Ed.). *Address:* c/o John Burnham, William Morris Agency, 151 El Camino Drive, Beverly Hills, CA 90212, USA.

KEATON, Michael; American actor; b. 9 Sept. 1951, Pittsburgh, Pa; m. Caroline MacWilliams (divorced); one s.; ed Kent State Univ.; with comedy group, Second City, LA. *Films:* Night Shift 1982, Mr Mom 1983, Johnny Dangerously 1984, Touch and Go 1987, Gung Ho 1987, Beetlejuice 1988, Clean and Sober 1988, The Dream Team 1989, Batman 1989, Much Ado About Nothing 1992, My Life, The Paper 1994, Speechless 1994, Multiplicity, Jackie Brown 1997, Desperate Measures 1998, Jack Frost 1999. *Television appearances include:* All in the Family, Maude, Mary Tyler Moore Show, Working

Stiffs, Report to Murphy, Roosevelt and Truman (TV film), Body Shots (producer) 1999. *Address:* c/o ICM Management, 8942 Wilshire Boulevard, Beverly Hills, CA 90211, USA.

KEAVENEY, Raymond, MA; Irish gallery director and art historian; b. 1947, Carlanstown, Co. Meath; ed Franciscan Coll., Gormanston, University Coll. Dublin; worked and studied abroad 1975–78; Curator, Nat. Gallery of Ireland, Dublin 1979–81, Asst Dir 1981–88, Dir 1988–; specializes in Italian art and Old Master drawings. *Publications:* Master European Drawings 1983, Views of Rome 1988. *Address:* National Gallery of Ireland, Merrion Square West, Dublin 2, Ireland. *Telephone:* (1) 6615133 (Office); (1) 6615133. *Fax:* (1) 6615372. *E-mail:* info@ngi.ie (Office). *Website:* www.nationalgallery.ie (Office).

KEBICH, Vyacheslau Frantsavich; Belarus politician; b. 10 June 1936, Konyushevshchina, Minsk Dist; s. of Frants Karlovich Kebich and Tatyana Vasilyevna Kebicha; m. Yelena Kebicha 1970; one s. one d.; ed Belarus Polytechnic Inst., Higher Party School; mem. CPSU 1962–91, Cen. Cttee 1980–91; engineer, man. in Minsk 1973–80; party official 1980–85; Deputy Chair. Council of Ministers, Chair. State Planning Cttee 1985–90; USSR People's Deputy 1989–91; Chair. Council of Ministers (Prime Minister) of Byelorussia (now Belarus) 1990–94; Presidential Cand. 1994; Pres. Belarus Trade and Finance Union 1994–; mem. Supreme Soviet (Parl.) 1980–96, MP 1996–; Corresp. mem. Int. Eng Acad.; Belarus State Prize. *Leisure interest:* fishing. *Address:* National Assembly, K. Marksa str. 38, Dom Urada, 220016 Minsk, Belarus. *Telephone:* (17) 229-33-13.

KEDAH, HRH The Sultan of; **Tuanku Haji Abdul Halim Mu'adzam Shah ibni Al-Marhum Sultan Badlishah,** DK, DKH, DKM, DMN, DUK, DK (KELANTAN), DK (PAHANG), DK (SELANGOR), DK (PERLIS), DK (JOHORE), DK (TRENGGANU), DP (SARAWAK), SPMK, SSDK, DHMS; b. 28 Nov. 1927, Alor Setar; m. Tuanku Bahiyah binti Al-marhum, Tuanku Abdul Rahman, d. of 1st Yang di Pertuan Agong of Malaya, 1956; three d.; ed Sultan Abdul Hamid Coll., Alor Setar and Wadham Coll., Oxford; Raja Muda (Heir to Throne of Kedah) 1949, Regent of Kedah 1957, Sultan 1958–; Timbalan Yang di Pertuan Agong (Deputy Head of State of Malaysia) 1965–70, Yang di Pertuan Agong (Head of State) 1970–75; Col Commdt Malaysian Reconnaissance Corps 1966; Col-in-Chief of Royal Malay Regiment 1975; Kt St J. First Class Order of the Rising Sun (Japan) 1970, Bintang Maha Putera, Klas Satu (Indonesia) 1970, Kt Grand Cross of the Bath (UK) 1972, Most Auspicious Order of the Rajamithrathorn (Thailand) 1973. *Leisure interests:* golf, billiards, photography, tennis. *Address:* Istana Anak Bukit, Alor Setar, Kedah, Darul Aman, Malaysia.

KEDDAFI, Col Mu'ammar al- (see Gaddafi, Col Mu'ammar al-).

KEDERIS, Konstadinos; Greek athlete; b. 11 June 1973, Mitilini; winner 200m. Olympic Games, Sydney 2000, World Championships, Edmonton 2001, European Championships (19.85 seconds), Munich 2002—reigning World, Olympic and European 200m. champion (as at end 2002). *Address:* c/o Greek Athletics Federation, Univiversity of Thessaly, Department of Physical Education and Sport Science, Karyes, Trikala 42100, Greece (Office).

KEDIKILWE, Ponatshego, MA; Botswana politician; b. 4 Aug. 1938, Sefhophe; ed Univ. of Connecticut, Syracuse Univ.; joined Govt 1970; Prin. Finance Officer, Finance Ministry 1974–76; Sec. for Financial Affairs 1976; Perm. Sec., Ministry of Works, Transport and Communications 1977–79; Dir Public Service Man., Office of the Pres. 1979–84; MP 1984–; Deputy Minister of Finance 1984; Minister of Presidential Affairs and Public Admin. 1985–89, 1994–98, of Commerce and Industry 1989–94, of Finance and Devt Planning 1998, of Educ. 1999–2000; currently Chair. Botswana Democratic Party; Presidential Order of Honour 1992. *Leisure interests:* soccer, ranching, debating, gardening, speech writing, traditional music, folklore and poetry. *Address:* P.O. Box 2, Sefhophe, Botswana (Home).

KEE, Robert, CBE, MA; British journalist, author and broadcaster; b. 5 Oct. 1919, Calcutta, India; s. of late Robert and Dorothy F. Kee; m. 1st Janetta Woolley 1948 (divorced 1950); one d.; m. 2nd Cynthia Judah 1960 (divorced 1989); one s. (and one s. deceased) one d.; m. 3rd Catherine M. Trevelyan 1990; ed Rottingdean School, Stowe School and Magdalen Coll., Oxford; journalist, Picture Post 1948–51; picture ed. Who 1952; foreign corresp. Observer 1956–57, Sunday Times 1957–58; literary ed. Spectator 1957; TV reporter Panorama, BBC 1958–62; TV Reporters Int., This Week, Faces of Communism (four parts, also for Channel 13, USA) ITV 1962–78; Ireland: a TV history (13 parts, also for Channel 13, USA), Panorama, BBC 1979–82; TVam 1982–83, Presenter 7 Days (Channel 4), ITV 1984–88; numerous BBC radio broadcasts 1946–97; BAFTA Richard Dimbleby Award 1976. *Publications:* A Crowd Is Not Company 1947, The Impossible Shore 1949, A Sign of the Times 1955, Broadstrop in Season 1959, Refugee World 1960, The Green Flag 1972, Ireland: A History 1980, The World We Left Behind 1984, The World We Fought For 1985, Trial and Error 1986, Munich: The Eleventh Hour 1988, The Picture Post Album 1989, The Laurel and the Ivy: Parnell and Irish Nationalism 1993. *Leisure interests:* swimming, music. *Address:* c/o Rogers, Coleridge and White, 20 Powis Mews, London, W11 1JN, England. *Telephone:* (20) 7221-3717.

KEEBLE, Sir (Herbert Ben) Curtis, GCMG; British diplomatist (retd); b. 18 Sept. 1922, London; s. of Herbert Keeble and Gertrude Keeble; m. Margaret Fraser 1947; three d. (one deceased); ed Clacton County High School, London Univ.; served Royal Irish Fusiliers 1942–47; entered Foreign Service 1947;

served in Batavia (now Jakarta, Indonesia) 1947–49; Foreign Office 1949–51, 1958–63; Berlin 1951–54; Washington 1954–58; Counsellor and Head of European Econ. Orgs. Dept 1963–65; Counsellor (Commercial), Berne 1965–68; Minister, Canberra 1968–71; Asst Under-Sec. of State, FCO 1971–74; Amb. to GDR 1974–76; Deputy Under-Sec. of State, FCO 1976–78; Amb. to USSR 1978–82; Chair. GB-USSR Asscn 1985–92, Britain-Russia Centre 1993–2000, Foundation for Accountancy and Financial Man. 1993–2000; Gov. of BBC 1985–90; mem. Royal Inst. of Int. Affairs 1947– (mem. Council 1984–90), Council of the School of Slavonic and East European Studies; Consultant to FCO 1984–97. *Publications:* The Soviet State: The Domestic Roots of Soviet Foreign Policy 1985, Britain and the Soviet Union 1917–1989 1990, Britain, the Soviet Union and Russia 2000; articles on yachting. *Leisure interests:* sailing, painting. *Address:* Dormers, St Leonards Road, Thames Ditton, Surrey, England. *Telephone:* (20) 8398-7778 (Home). *E-mail:* keeble@sagainternet.co.uk (Home).

KEEFFE, Barrie Colin; British dramatist, novelist and director; b. 31 Oct. 1945, London; s. of the late Edward Thomas Keeffe and Constance Beatrice Keeffe (née Marsh); m. 1st Sarah Dee (Truman) 1969 (divorced 1975); m. 2nd Verity Eileen Bargate 1981 (died 1981); two step-s.; m. 3rd Julia Lindsay 1983 (divorced 1991); ed East Ham Grammar School; fmrly actor with Nat. Youth Theatre, journalist; has written plays for theatre, TV and radio; fmrly resident writer Shaw Theatre, London, RSC; assoc. writer Theatre Royal, Stratford East, also mem. Bd; Assoc. Soho Theatre Co.; Winter Mentor, Nat. Theatre 1999–; tutor, City Univ., London 2001–; UN Amb., 50th Anniversary Year 1995; French Critics Prix Révélation 1978, Giles Cooper Award Best Radio Plays, Mystery Writers of America Edgar Alan Poe Award 1982. *Theatre plays include:* Only a Game 1973, A Sight of Glory 1975, Scribes 1975, Here Comes the Sun 1976, Gimme Shelter 1977, A Mad World My Masters 1977, Barbarians 1977, Frozen Assets 1978, Sus 1979, Bastard Angel 1980, She's So Modern 1980, Black Lear 1980, Chorus Girls 1981, Better Times 1985, King of England 1988, My Girl 1989, Not Fade Away 1990, Wild Justice 1990, I Only Want to Be With You 1995, Shadows on The Sun 2001. *Plays directed include:* A Certain Vincent, A Gentle Spirit, Talking of Chekov (Amsterdam and London), My Girl (London and Bombay), The Gary Oldman Fan Club (London). *Film:* The Long Good Friday (screenplay). *Television plays include:* Substitute 1972, Not Quite Cricket 1977, Gotcha 1977, Nipper 1977, Champions 1978, Hanging Around 1978, Waterloo Sunset 1979, No Excuses (series) 1983, King 1984. *Radio plays include:* On the Eve of the Millennium 1999, Feng Shui and Me 2000, The Five of Us 2002. *Publications:* (novels) Gadabout 1969, No Excuses 1983; (screenplay) The Long Good Friday 1998; (plays) Barrie Keeffe Plays I 2001. *Leisure interests:* playing tennis, watching soccer. *Address:* 110 Annandale Road, London, SE10 0JZ, England.

KEEFFE, Bernard, BA; British conductor, broadcaster and professor; b. 1 April 1925, London; s. of Joseph Keeffe and Theresa Keeffe (née Quinn); m. Denise Walker 1954; one s. one d.; ed St Olave's Grammar School and Clare Coll., Cambridge; served in Intelligence Corps 1943–47; mem. Glyndebourne Opera Co. 1951–52; BBC Music Staff 1954–60; Asst Music Dir, Royal Opera House 1960–62; Conductor BBC Scottish Orchestra 1962–64; Prof., Trinity Coll. of Music 1966–89; freelance conductor and broadcaster on radio and TV, concerts with leading orchestras 1966–; mem. int. juries, competitions in Sofia, Liège, Vienna and London; Warden solo performers section, Inc. Soc. of Musicians 1971; Chair. Anglo-Austrian Music Soc.; Hon. Fellow Trinity Coll. of Music 1968. *Radio:* Music in Japan (BBC World Service). *Television:* Elgar and the Orchestra (Best Music Programme of the Year) (BBC) 1979. *Publications:* Harrap's Dictionary of Music and Musicians (Ed.), ENO Guide to Tosca. *Leisure interests:* photography, languages. *Address:* 153 Honor Oak Road, London, SE23 3RN, England. *Telephone:* (20) 8699-3672.

KEEGAN, Sir John, Kt, OBE; British military historian and journalist; b. 1934, London; s. of Francis Joseph Keegan and Eileen Mary Bridgman; m. Susanne Keegan; two s. two d.; ed privately and Balliol Coll. Oxford; awarded travel grant to study American Civil War in USA; writer of political reports for US Embassy, London, 1957–59; lecturer, Sr lecturer War Studies Dept Royal Mil. Acad. Sandhurst 1959–86; war correspondent for The Atlantic Monthly Telegraph, Beirut 1984; Defence Ed., Daily Telegraph 1986–; Delmas Prof. of History, Vassar Coll. 1997–98; contributing ed. US News and World Report 1986–; Dir E Somerset NHS Trust 1991–97; Commr Commonwealth War Graves Comm. 2000–; Trustee Heritage Lottery Fund 1994–2000; BBC Reith Lecturer 1998; Hon. Fellow Balliol Coll. Oxford; Hon. LLD (New Brunswick) 1997; Hon. LittD (Queen's Univ. Belfast) 2000; Hon. DLitt (Bath) 2001; Samuel Eliot Morrison Prize US Soc. for Mil. History 1996. *Publications include:* The Face of Battle 1976, The Nature of War 1981, Six Armies in Normandy: From D-Day to the Liberation of Paris 1982, Zones of Conflict: An Atlas of Future Wars 1986, Soldiers: A History of Men in Battle 1986, The Mask of Command 1987, Who's Who in Military History (with A. Wheatcroft) 1987, The Price of Admiralty: The Evolution of Naval Warfare 1989, The Second World War 1990, Churchill's Generals (ed.) 1991, A History of Warfare 1993, Warpaths: travels of a military historian in North America 1995, Who's Who in World War 2 1995, The Battle for History: Re-fighting World War II 1995, Warpaths 1996, The First World War 1998, The Penguin Book of War 1999; ed. and co-ed. of several mil. reference works. *Address:* The Manor House, Kilmington, nr Warminster, Wilts., BA12 6RD, England. *Telephone:* (1985) 844856.

KEEGAN, Kevin Joseph, OBE; British professional football manager and player; b. 14 Feb. 1951, Armthorpe; s. of the late Joseph Keegan; m. Jean

Woodhouse 1974; two d.; player Scunthorpe United, Liverpool 1971–77 (won League Championship three times, FA Cup 1974, European Cup 1977, UEFA Cup 1973, 1976), SV Hamburg 1977–80, Southampton 1980–82, Newcastle United 1982–84 (retd); scored 274 goals in approx. 800 appearances; capped for England 63 times (31 as Capt.), scoring 21 goals; Man. Newcastle United 1992–97, Fulham 1998–99, England nat. team 1999–2000, Manchester City May 2001–; Footballer of the Year 1976, European Footballer of the Year 1978, 1979. *Publications:* Kevin Keegan 1978, Against the World: Playing for England 1979, Kevin Keegan: My Autobiography 1997. *Address:* c/o Manchester City Football Club, Maine Road, Moss Side, Manchester, M14 7WN, England (Office).

KEEL, Alton G., Jr, PhD; American diplomatist, civil servant, engineer and banker; b. 8 Sept. 1943, Newport, Va; s. of Alton G. Keel and Ella Kennedy; m. 1st Franmarie Kennedy-Keel 1982; one d.; m. 2nd Lynn Matti Keel; ed Univ. of Virginia and Univ. of California, Berkeley; Facility Man. Naval Weapons Center 1971–77; Sr Official Senate Armed Services Cttee, US Senate 1977–81; Asst Sec. Air Force for Research, Devt and Logistics, The Pentagon 1981–82; Assoc. Dir Nat. Security and Int. Affairs, Exec. Office of Pres. 1982–86; Exec. Dir Pres. Comm. on Space Shuttle Challenger Accident 1986; Acting Asst to the Pres. for Nat. Security Affairs 1986; Perm. Rep. to NATO 1987–89; Pres., Man. Dir Carlyle Int., The Carlyle Group 1992–94; Chair. Carlyle SEAG 1994–95, Chair., Man. Dir Atlantic Partners L.L.C. Washington 1992–; Chair., CEO Land-5 Corpn 1999–2002; mem. Dean's Advisory Bd, Univ. of Va 1996–; mem. Bd Dirs InoStor Corpn 2002–, Digital Atlantic 2002–; Nat. Congressional Science Fellow AIAA 1977; Youth Scientist Award 1976, Air Force Decoration for Exceptional Civilian Service 1982; NASA Group Achievement Award 1987, Distinguished Alumnus Award (Univ. of Va) 1987. *Publications:* numerous scientific and tech. articles, foreign policy and nat. security publs. *Leisure interests:* running, golf, sailing, physical fitness. *Address:* Atlantic Partners, 2891 South River Road, Stanardsville, VA 22973, USA.

KEILIS-BOROK, Vladimir Isaakovich, DSc; Russian geophysicist and applied mathematician; b. 31 July 1921, Moscow; s. of Isaak Moiseyevich and Kseniya Ruvimovna Keilis-Brook; m. L. N. Malinovskaya 1955; one d.; ed S. Ordzhonikidze Inst. of Geological Prospecting, O. Schmidt Inst. of Earth Physics, USSR Acad. of Sciences; Chair. Dept of Computational Geophysics 1960–89; Dir Int. Inst. Earthquake Prediction Theory and Mathematical Geophysics 1989–98, Hon. Dir 1998–; mem. USSR (now Russian) Acad. of Sciences 1987–; Foreign Assoc. NAS; Foreign Hon. mem. American Acad. of Arts and Sciences; Assoc. Royal Astronomical Society; mem. Bd of several int. journals 1987–91; fmr Pres. Int. Union of Geodesy and Geophysics. *Publications:* Computational Seismology series, Vols 1–24 1966–91; other works on global seismology and tectonics. *Leisure interests:* mountaineering, sociology. *Address:* International Institute of Earthquake Prediction Theory and Mathematical Geophysics, Moscow 113556, Warshavskoye sh. 79, Kor. 2, Russia. *Telephone:* (095) 110-77-95 (Office); (095) 936-55-88 (Home). *Fax:* (095) 956-70-95.

KEILLOR, Garrison Edward, BA; American writer and broadcaster; b. 7 Aug. 1942, Anoka, Minn.; s. of John P. Keillor and Grace R. (Denham) Keillor; m. Jenny Lind Nilsson; one s. one d.; ed Univ. of Minnesota; cr. radio show A Prairie Home Companion 1974–87, 1993–, American Radio Co. 1989; Grammy Award for best non-musical recording (Lake Wobegon Days) 1987, Ace Award for best musical host (A Prairie Home Companion) 1988, Nat. Humanities Medal 1999. *Publications:* Happy to Be Here 1982, Lake Wobegon Days 1985, Leaving Home 1987, We Are Still Married: Stories and Letters 1989, WLT: A Radio Romance 1991, The Book of Guys 1993, Cat, You Better Come Home (children's book) 1995, The Man Who Loved Cheese 1996, The Sandy Bottom Orchestra 1996, Wobegon Boy 1997, Me 1999, Lake Wobegon Summer 1956 2001. *Address:* A Prairie Home Companion, 45 7th Street E, St Paul, MN 55101, USA.

KEINÄNEN, Eino, M.POL.SC.; Finnish fmr civil servant and business executive; b. 17 Nov. 1939; ed Univ. of Helsinki; credit official, Kansallis-Osake-Pankki 1962–64; Head of Section, Finnish State Computer Centre and Planning Organ for State Accounting 1965–68; various posts, Budget Dept, Ministry of Finance 1969–85, Head Budget Dept 1985–87, Perm. Under-Sec. 1987–89, Perm. State Sec. 1989–95; Gen. Man. and mem. Bd Postipankki Ltd 1995–96, Chair and Chief Exec. March 1996–; mem. Bd of Dirs. Finnish State Treasury 1985–89, Finnish Tourist Bd 1985–89, Finnish Foreign Trade Asscn 1985–89, Cen. Statistical Office of Finland 1985–89; mem. Investment Fund of Finland 1985–89; Vice-Pres. Supervisory Bd Finnish Export Credit Ltd 1987–, Finnish Fund for Industrial Devt Co-operation Ltd (Finnfund) 1994–; Pres. Bd of Dirs. State Computer Centre 1988–; mem. Supervisory Bd Slot Machine Asscn 1989–, Regional Devt Fund of Finland Ltd 1989–, Finnish Grain Bd 1989–; mem. Bd of Admin. Alko Ltd 1989–; Pres. Supervisory Bd Finnish Ice-Hockey Asscn 1989–. *Address:* Postipankki Ltd, Unioninkati 22, 00007 Helsinki, Finland. *Fax:* (0) 6221019.

KEINO, Kipchoge A. (Kip); Kenyan athlete; b. 1940, Kipsamo; m. Phyllis Keino; fmr physical training instructor in police force; began int. running career in 1962; set two world records at 3000m and 5000m 1964; winner 1500m and 5000m, African Games 1964, 1965; winner one mile and three miles, Commonwealth Games 1966; gold medallist 1500m, silver medallist 5000m, Olympic Games, Mexico City 1968; gold medallist 3000m steeplechase, silver medallist 1500m, Olympic Games, Munich 1972; retd from int. running 1973; Pres. Kenyan Olympic Cttee; mem. IOC; helped establish high-altitude training as a technique to improve running time at any altitude; helped coach Kenyan track-and-field teams; ran in London Marathon for Oxfam 2002; acquired a farm in Kenya (with wife Phyllis), est. an orphanage on farm land; Laureus World Sports Acad. 'Sport for Good' Award. *Address:* Kenyan Olympic Committee, POB 46888, Garden Plaza, 11th Floor, Moi Avenue, Nairobi, Kenya. *Telephone:* (2) 210797. *Fax:* (2) 336827. *E-mail:* nock@iconnect.co.ke.

KEITA, Ibrahima Boubacar; Malian politician; Minister of Foreign Affairs 1993–94; Prime Minister of Mali 1994–2000; fmr Chair. of External Relations, Alliance pour la démocratie au Mali (ADEMA); Leader Rassemblement pour le Mali 2001–, Presidential Cand. 2002. *Address:* Rassemblement pour le Mali, Bamako, Mali (Office).

KEITA, Modibo, PhD; Malian politician; b. 13 Jan. 1953, Bamako; m.; two s.; ed Tübingen Univ., Germany; Prof. of Higher Educ., École normale supérieure de Bamako 1984–86; Minister of Foreign Affairs 1986–89; f. Cabinet d'études pour l'éduc. et le développement (CED) 1987 (renamed Cabinet d'études Keita Kala Saba 1997–); Dir Boutique de gestion, d'échanges et de conseils – Promotion de l'artisanat 1993–94; apptd Urban Waste Expertise Programme (UWEP) Co-ordinator 1996; Prime Minister of Mali March–June 2002. *Address:* Cabinet d'Etudes Keita Kala Saba (CEK), BP 9014, Bamako, Mali (Office). *Telephone:* 23-84-12 (Office). *Fax:* 23-84-13 (Office). *E-mail:* cek@spider.toolnet.org.

KEITA, Salif; Malian singer; b. 25 Aug. 1949, Djoliba; began musical career in Bamako 1967; joined govt-sponsored group Rail Band, later renamed Les Ambassadeurs Internationaux; moved to Paris to begin solo career as a singer 1984; first solo album 1987; Grande Parade du Jazz de Nice 1992; WOMAD festivals: Reading 1992, Adelaide 1993, Las Palmas 1993; tour of Japan 1993, Australia 1993, Canada 1994, USA 1994, Africa (including South Africa) 1994; annual European tour including summer festivals; Montreux Jazz Festivals 1993, 1995; Parkpop Festival, The Hague, Holland 1995; Chevalier des Arts et Lettres; Chevalier, Order of the Nation (Mali), Nat. Order of Guinea 1977, Grammy Award. *Albums include:* Seydou Bathili 1982, 69-80, Soro 1987, Ko-Yan 1989, Destiny of a Noble Outcast 1991, Amen 1991, L'enfant Lion 1992, Mansa of Mali 1994, Folon 1995, Rail Band 1996, Seydou Bathili 1997, Papa 1999, Sosie 2001, Compilation 1969–80 2001, Moffou 2002. *Address:* c/o Mad Minute Music, 5–7 rue Paul Bert, 93400 St Ouen, France. *Website:* www.salifkeita.net.

KEITEL, Harvey; American actor; b. 13 May 1939; m. Lorraine Bracco (divorced); one d.; ed Actors Studio; served US Marines; starred in Martin Scorsese's student film Who's That Knocking at My Door?; stage appearances in Death of a Salesman, Hurlyburly. *Films:* Mean Streets, Alice Doesn't Live Here Anymore, That's the Way of the World, Taxi Driver, Mother Jugs and Speed, Buffalo Bill and the Indians, Welcome to LA, The Duellists, Fingers, Blue Collar, Eagle's Wing, Deathwatch, Saturn 3, Bad Timing, The Border, Exposed, La Nuit de Varennes, Corrupt, Falling in Love, Knight of the Dragon, Camorra, Off Beat, Wise Guys, The Men's Club, The Investigation, The Pick-up Artist, The January Man, The Last Temptation of Christ, The Two Jakes, Two Evil Eyes (The Black Cat), Thelma & Louise, Tipperary, Bugsy, Reservoir Dogs, Bad Lieutenant, Mean Streets, The Assassin, The Young Americans, The Piano, Snake Eyes, Rising Sun, Monkey Trouble, Clockers, Dangerous Game, Pulp Fiction, Smoke, Imaginary Crimes, Ulysses' Gaze 1995, Blue in the Face 1995, City of Industry, Cop Land 1996, Head Above Water, Somebody to Love 1996, Simpatico 1999, Little Nicky 2000, U-571 2000, Holy Smoke 2000. *Address:* c/o William Morris Agency, 151 South El Camino Drive, Beverly Hills, CA 90212, USA.

KEITH, Rt Hon Sir Kenneth James, KBE, PC, LLM, QC; New Zealand judge; b. 19 Nov. 1937; s. of Patrick James Keith and Amy Irene Keith (née Witheridge); m. Jocelyn Margaret Buckett 1961; two s. two d.; ed Auckland Grammar School, Auckland Univ., Victoria Univ. of Wellington, Harvard Law School; with Dept of External Affairs, Wellington 1960–62; with Law Faculty, Vic. Univ. 1962–64, 1966–91, Prof. 1973–91, Dean 1977–81; UN Secr. Office of Legal Affairs 1968–70; with NZ Inst. of Int. Affairs 1971–73; Judge Courts of Appeal of Samoa 1982–, Cook Islands 1982–, Niue 1995–, NZ 1996–; mem. NZ Law Comm. 1986–91, Pres. 1991–96; Assoc. mem. Inst. of Int. Law 1997; Hon. LLD (Auckland), Commemoration Medal 1990. *Publications:* Advisory Jurisdiction of the International Court 1971, Essays on Human Rights (Ed.) 1968; numerous Law Comm. publs and papers on constitutional law in legal journals. *Leisure interests:* family, walking, reading. *Address:* Court of Appeal, P.O. Box 1606, Wellington; 11 Salamanca Road, Kelburn, Wellington, New Zealand. *Telephone:* (4) 914-3540 (Court of Appeal); (4) 472-6664. *Fax:* (4) 914-3570 (Court of Appeal); (4) 472-6664. *E-mail:* k.keith@courts.govt.nz.

KEITH, Penelope Anne Constance, OBE; British actress; b. 2 April 1940, Sutton, Surrey; d. of Frederick Hatfield and Constance Mary Keith; m. Rodney Timson 1978; ed Annecy Convent, Seaford, Sussex, Convent Bayeux, Normandy, Webber Douglas School, London; first professional appearance, Civic Theatre, Chesterfield 1959; repertory, Lincoln, Salisbury, Manchester 1960–63, Cheltenham 1967; RSC, Stratford 1963, Aldwych 1965; Pres. Actors Benevolent Fund 1990–; Gov. Queen Elizabeth's Foundation for the Disabled 1989–, Guildford School of Acting 1991–; Trustee Yvonne Arnaud Theatre 1992–; High Sheriff of Surrey 2002; Best Light Entertainment Performance (British Acad. of Film and TV Arts) 1976, Best Actress 1977, Show Business Personality (Variety Club of GB) 1976, BBC TV Personality 1979, Comedy

Performance of the Year (Soc. of West End. Theatre) 1976, Female TV Personality, T.V. Times Awards 1976–78, BBC TV Personality of the Year 1978–79, TV Female Personality (Daily Express) 1979–82. *Stage appearances include:* Suddenly at Home 1971, The Norman Conquests 1974, Donkey's Years 1976, The Apple Cart 1977, The Millionairess 1978, Moving 1980, Hobson's Choice, Captain Brassbound's Conversion 1982, Hay Fever 1983, The Dragon's Tail 1985, Miranda 1987, The Deep Blue Sea 1988, Dear Charles 1990, The Merry Wives of Windsor 1990, The Importance of Being Earnest 1991, On Approval 1992, Relatively Speaking 1992, Glyn and It 1994, Monsieur Amilcar 1995, Mrs Warren's Profession 1997, Good Grief 1998, Star Quality 2001. *TV appearances include:* The Good Life (Good Neighbors in USA) 1974–77, Private Lives 1976, The Norman Conquests 1977, To the Manor Born 1979–81, On Approval 1980, Spider's Web, Sweet Sixteen, Waters of the Moon, Hay Fever, Moving, Executive Stress, What's my Line? 1988, Growing Places, No Job for a Lady 1990, Law and Disorder 1994, Next of Kin, Coming Home 1999. *Leisure interest:* gardening. *Address:* London Management, 2–4 Noel Street, London, W1V 3RB, England. *Telephone:* (20) 7287-9000. *Fax:* (20) 7287-3036.

KEITH OF CASTLEACRE, Baron (Life Peer), cr. 1980, of Swaffham in the County of Norfolk; **Kenneth Alexander Keith,** FRSA; British industrialist and banker; b. 30 Aug. 1916; s. of late Edward Charles Keith; m. 1st Lady Ariel Olivia Winifred Baird 1946 (divorced 1958); one s. one d.; m. 2nd Nancy (Slim) Hayward (née Gross) 1962 (divorced 1972, died 1990); m. 3rd Marie-Luz Hanbury (née Dennistoun-Webster) 1973; ed Rugby and Dresden; trained as Chartered Accountant, London 1934–39; Army Service 1939–45; Asst to Dir-Gen. Political Intelligence Dept, Foreign Office 1945–46; Asst to Man. Dir Philip Hill & Partners, London 1946–48, Dir 1947; Dir Philip Hill Investment Trust 1949, Man. Dir 1951; Man. Dir Philip Hill, Higginson & Co. Ltd 1951–59, Philip Hill, Higginson, Erlangers Ltd 1959–62, Chair. 1962–65; Deputy Chair. and Chief Exec. Hill Samuel & Co. 1965–70, Group Chair. 1970–80; Chair. and Chief Exec. Rolls-Royce 1972–80; Chair. Arlington Securities PLC 1982–90; mem. Bd Standard Telephone and Cables 1977–85, Chair. 1985–89; Vice-Chair. Beecham Group Ltd 1970–85, Chair. 1985–87; Vice-Chair. BEA 1964–71, Dir British Airways 1971–72; Dir Bank of Nova Scotia 1958–86, Eagle Star Insurance Co. 1955–75, Nat. Provincial Bank 1967–69, Times Newspapers Ltd 1967–81, Guinness Peat Aviation Group 1983; Pres. British Standards Inst. 1989–94; mem. Nat. Econ. Devt Council 1964–71; Chair. Econ. Planning Council for East Anglia 1965–70; Gov. Nat. Inst. of Econ. and Social Research; Council mem. Manchester Business School; Pres. Royal Norfolk Agricultural Asscn 1989, RoSPA 1989–92; Hon. Companion Royal Aeronautical Soc.; Croix de Guerre with Silver Star. *Leisure interests:* shooting, farming, golf. *Address:* The Wicken House, Castle Acre, Norfolk, PE32 2BP, England. *Telephone:* (1760) 755225.

KEKILBAYEV, Abish Kekilbayevich (pseudonym Abish Tagan); Kazakhstan politician and writer; b. 6 Dec. 1939, Ondy, Mangystau Region; s. of Kekilbay Kokimov and Aysaule Kokimova; m. Klara Zhumabaeva; four c.; ed Kazakh State Univ.; schoolteacher of Kazakh language; worked for newspapers Kazakh Adebieti and Leninshil Zhas; Ed.-in-Chief Studio Kazakhfilm; CP official in Alma-Ata; Deputy Minister of Culture Kazakh SSR; Sec. Man. Cttee Kazakh Writers' Union; Chair. Presidium of Kazakh Soc. for Protection of Monuments of History and Culture 1962–89; Chair. Cttee on Nat. Policy, Language and Culture Devt, Kazakhstan Supreme Soviet 1991–93; Ed.-in-Chief Egemen Kazakhstan (newspaper) 1992–93; State Counsellor 1993–94; Chair. Supreme Council of Repub. 1994–95; State Counsellor to Pres. of Repub. 1995–; Deputy to Majlis (Parl.) 1995–; State Sec. Rep. of Kazakhstan 1996–. *Publications:* author of novels, short stories, critical reviews, translations. *Address:* Office of the President, Beibitshilik str. 11, 473000 Astana (Office); Zheltokstan str. 16/1 Apt. 4, 473000 Astana, Kazakhstan (Home). *Telephone:* (3172) 32-27-04 (Office); (3172) 39-17-44 (Home). *Fax:* (3172) 32-23-83 (Home).

KELAM, Tunne; Estonian politician and historian; b. 10 July 1936, Taheva, Valgamaa Region; m.; one d.; ed Tallinn State Univ.; Sr Researcher Cen. History Archives 1959–64; Sr Ed. Estonian Encyclopaedia 1965–75; Sr Bibliographer F. R. Kreutzwald State Library of Estonian SSR 1975–79; employee Ranna State farm 1980–88; with journal Akadeemia 1988–90; mem. Bd Int. Policy Forum 1991; Chair. Supervisory Bd Nat. Library 1996–99; f. Estonian Nat. Ind. Party (ENIP) 1988, Chair. 1993–95, Deputy Chair 2001; mem. Riigikogu (Parl.) 1998–; mem. Bd of Dirs Inst. for Human Rights 1997–, Kistler-Ritso Foundation 1998–; Deputy Chair. Estonian European Movt 1998–; Pres. Estonian Scout Asscn 1996–; Paul Harris Fellowship; Hon. Citizen of Maryland, USA; Rotary Int. Award, Estonian Newspapers' Union Award 1996, Baltic Ass. Award. *Address:* Riigikogu, Tompea Castle, Lossi plats 1a, 0100 Tallinn, Estonia (Office). *Telephone:* (2) 631-6321 (Office). *E-mail:* tunne.kelam@riigikogu.ee (Office). *Website:* www.riigikogu.ee/parliament (Office).

KELCHE, Gen. Jean-Pierre; French army officer; b. 19 Jan. 1942, Macon; m.; two c.; ed Mil. Acad. Saint Cyr; served in Côte d'Ivoire, then Djibouti 1971–73, Jr Staff Course, Staff Coll., then with French Caribbean and Guiana Territorial Command 1979–81; Commdr 5th Combined Bn, Djibouti 1985–87; Staff Officer, Doctrine and Devt Div., rank of Brig.-Gen. 1991; Deputy Commdr 5th Armoured Div., Landau, Germany 1991; Chief Plans, Programmes and Evaluation Div., Gen. Staff 1992–95; Chief of Prime Minister's Mil. Cabinet 1995–96; Vice-Chief of Defence Staff 1996–98, Chief of Defence

Staff, rank of Gen. 1998–; Commdr, Légion d'honneur, Officier, Ordre nat. du Mérite. *Address:* c/o Ministry of Defence, 14 rue St Dominique, 75007 Paris, France (Office).

KELDYSH, Leonid Venyaminovich, DPhysMathSc; Russian physicist; b. 7 April 1931, Moscow; s. of Benjamin L. Granovskii and Lyudmila V. Keldysh; m. Galina S. Krasnikova 1983; one s.; ed Moscow State Univ.; Jr then Sr researcher, Head of Sector, Head of Dept, Lebedev Physical Inst. USSR (now Russian) Acad. of Sciences 1954–89, Dir 1989–93, Sr Researcher 1993–; Prof. Moscow State Univ. 1965–; Pres. Physical Soc. of Russian Fed. 1998–; Corresp. mem. USSR Acad. of Sciences 1968, mem. 1976; Academic-Sec., Dept of Gen. Physics; main research on solid state theory, physics of semiconductors, interaction of radiation with matter; Fyzika i Tekhnika Poluprovodnikov; Foreign Assoc. Nat. Acad. of Sciences (USA) 1995–; Lenin Prize, Lomonosov Prize, Hewlett-Packard Prize 1975; A. V. Humboldt Research Award 1975. *Publications:* Coherent Exciton States 1972, Absorption of Ultrasound by Electron-Hole Drops 1976; articles in scientific journals. *Address:* P.N. Lebedev Physical Institute, Leninski Prospect 53, 117924 Moscow V-333, Russia. *Telephone:* (095) 135-30-33. *Fax:* (095) 938-22-51.

KELETI, György; Hungarian politician and army officer; b. 18 May 1946, Losonc; m. Erzsébet Petrik; three c.; ed Zalka Máté Mil. Tech. Coll., Zrinyi Miklós War Coll.; co. Commdr, then later deputy Commdr of a Bn in Vác Dist 1969–74; posts in Ministry of Defence 1980; Press Spokesman of Ministry of Defence 1977; mem. Hungarian Socialist Party (HSP) 1992; mem. Parl. 1992–; mem. of Nat. Security Cttee of Parl.; Minister of Defence 1994–98; rank of Col in army reserve; Order of Star (with swords), Silver Cross of Merit. *Address:* c/o Honvédelmi Minisztérium, 1055 Budapest, Balaton u. 711, Hungary.

KELLENBERGER, Jakob; Swiss diplomatist; m. Elisabeth Kellenberger-Jossi 1973; two d.; ed Univ. of Zurich, Univ. of Tours, Univ. of Granada; joined Swiss diplomatic service 1974, worked in Madrid, Brussels and London; State Sec. Fed. Dept of Foreign Affairs 1992–99; Pres. Int. Cttee of the Red Cross (ICRC) Jan. 2000–. *Address:* International Committee of the Red Cross, 19 avenue de la Paix, 1202 Geneva, Switzerland (Office). *Telephone:* (22) 7346001 (Office). *Fax:* (22) 7332057. *E-mail:* press.gva@icrc.org (Office). *Website:* www.icrc.org (Office).

KELLER, Evelyn Fox, PhD; American historian and professor of philosophy of science; b. 20 March 1936, New York; m. Joseph B. Keller 1964 (divorced); one s. one d.; ed Radcliffe Coll., Brandeis and Harvard Univs.; Asst Research Scientist, New York Univ. 1963–66, Assoc. Prof. 1970–72; Assoc. Prof., State Univ. of New York, Purchase 1972–82; Prof. of Math. and Humanities, Northwestern Univ. 1982–88; Prof. Univ. of Calif., Berkeley 1988–92; Prof. of History and Philosophy of Science, MIT 1992–; mem. Inst. of Advanced Studies, Princeton 1987–88; Visiting Fellow, later Scholar, MIT 1979–84, Visiting Prof. 1985–86; Pres. West Coast History of Science Soc. 1990–91; MacArthur Fellow 1992–97; Guggenheim Fellowship 2000–01; numerous awards including Hon. DHumLitt (Rensslaer Polytechnic Inst.) 1995, (New School Univ. Allegheny Coll.) 2000, (Wesleyan Univ.) 2001, Hon. LHD (Holyoak Coll.) 1991, Dr hc (Amsterdam) 1993, Hon. DTech (Luleå) 1996; Mina Shaughnessey Award 1981–82, Radcliffe Graduate Soc. Medal 1985. *Publications include:* A Feeling for the Organism 1983, Reflections on Gender and Science 1985, Secrets of Life, Secrets of Death 1992, Keywords in Evolutionary Biology (Ed.) 1994, Refiguring Life 1995, Feminism and Science (co-author) 1996, The Century of the Gene 2000, Making Sense of Life 2002. *Address:* Massachusetts Institute of Technology, E51-171, 77 Massachusetts Avenue, Cambridge, MA 02139, USA (Office). *Telephone:* (617) 253-8722 (Office). *Fax:* (617) 253-8118 (Office). *Website:* web.mit.edu.sts (Office).

KELLER, Joseph Bishop, PhD; American professor of mathematics and mechanical engineering; b. 31 July 1923, Paterson, NJ; s. of Isaac Keller and Sally Bishop; m. Evelyn Fox 1963 (divorced 1976); one s. one d.; ed New York Univ.; Prof. of Math. Courant Inst. of Math. Sciences, New York Univ. 1948–79, Chair. Dept of Math., Univ. Coll. of Arts and Sciences and Graduate School of Eng and Sciences 1967–73; Prof. of Math. and Mechanical Eng Stanford Univ. 1979–; Hon. Prof. of Math. Sciences (Univ. of Cambridge) 1990–; Research Assoc. Woods Hole Oceanographic Inst. 1965–; mem. NAS, Foreign mem. Royal Soc.; Hon. DTech (Tech. Univ. of Denmark) 1979; Hon. DSc (Northwestern Univ.) 1988, (Crete) 1993, (New Jersey Inst. Tech.) 1995, (Carlos Tercero de Madrid) 1995; Nemmers Prize 1996, shared Wolf Prize 1997; Nat. Medal of Science 1988, NAS Award in Applied Math. and Numerical Analysis 1995, numerous awards and lectureships. *Publications:* over 400 articles in professional journals. *Leisure interests:* hiking, skiing. *Address:* Department of Mathematics, Stanford University, Stanford, CA 94305 (Office); 820 Sonoma Terrace, Stanford, CA 94305, USA (Home). *Telephone:* (415) 723-0851 (Office).

KELLER, Thomas A.; American chef; b. 1961, Southern Calif.; fmr chef La Reserve and Restaurant Raphael, New York; served an estagiare apprentice in France in restaurants of Guy Savoy, Michael Pasquet, Gerard Besson, also Taillevant, Le Toit de Passey, Chiberta and Le Pre Catalan; est. restaurant Rakel, New York; Exec. Chef Checkers Hotel, LA; acquired The French Laundry, Yountville, Calif. 1994, currently chef and owner; Founder and owner EVO Inc. (retail line of olive oils and vinegar); spokesperson for Calif. Milk Advisory Bd 1997–98; Ivy Award, Restaurants and Insts 1996; named Best American Chef: Calif., James Beard Foundation 1996; Oustanding Chef: America 1997; World's Best Chef, Wedgewood 2002. *Address:* The French Laundry, 6640 Washington Street, Yountville, CA 94559, USA (Office).

KELLEY, Harold H., PhD; American professor of psychology; b. 16 Feb. 1921, Boise, Idaho; s. of Harry H. Kelley and Maude M. Kelley; m. Dorothy Drumm 1942; one s. two d; ed Univ. of Calif., Berkeley and MIT; Study Dir and lecturer, Dept of Psychology, Univ. of Mich. 1948–50; Asst Prof., Dept of Psychology, Yale Univ. 1950–55; Assoc Prof., then Prof., Dept of Psychology, Univ. of Minn. 1955–61; Prof. Dept of Psychology, Univ. of Calif., Los Angeles 1961–91, Prof. Emer. 1991–; Fellow NAS, American Acad. of Arts and Sciences; Distinguished Sr Scientist, Soc. for Experimental Social Psychology; Distinguished Scientific Contribution Award, American Psychological Asscn; Kurt Lewin Memorial Award (Soc. for the Psychological Study of Social Issues); Cooley-Mead Award, American Sociological Asscn. *Publications:* The Social Psychology of Groups (with J. W. Thibaut) 1959, Attribution (co-author) 1972, Interpersonal Relations (with J. W. Thibaut) 1978, Personal Relationships 1979, Close Relationships (co-author) 1983, Atlas of Interpersonal Situations 2002. *Leisure interests:* music, gardening. *Address:* 21634 Rambla Vista Street, Malibu, CA 90265, USA.

KELLY, Donald P.; American business executive; b. 24 Feb. 1922, Chicago; s. of Thomas Nicholas Kelly and Ethel M. Healy; m. Byrd M. Sullivan 1952; two s. one d.; ed De Paul, Loyola and Harvard Univs.; Man. Data Processing, Swift & Co. 1953, Asst Controller 1965, Controller 1967, Vice-Pres. Corp. Devt 1968, Financial Vice-Pres. and Dir 1970–; Financial Vice-Pres. and Dir Esmark April–Oct. 1973, Pres., COO 1973–77, Pres. and CEO 1977–82, Chair., Pres. and CEO 1982–84; Chair. Kelly Briggs and Assocs., Inc. 1984–86; Chair., CEO BCI Holdings Corpn 1986–87; Chair. and CEO EII Holdings Inc. 1987–88; Chair. Beatrice Co., Chicago March–Oct. 1988; Pres. and CEO D.P. Kelly Assocs. L.P. 1988–; Dir, Chair., Pres., CEO Envirodyne Industries Inc. 1989–96. *Address:* D.P. Kelly and Associates, 701 Harger Road, Suite 190, Oak Brook, IL 60521, USA.

KELLY, Ellsworth; American painter and sculptor; b. 31 May 1923, Newburgh, NY; ed Boston Museum Fine Arts School and Ecole des Beaux Arts, Paris; works exhibited, Salon de Réalités Nouvelles, Paris 1950, 1951, Carnegie Int. 1958, 1961, 1964, 1967, São Paulo Biennale 1961, Tokyo Int. 1963, Documenta III and IV, Germany 1964, 1968, Venice Biennale 1966, Guggenheim Int. 1967, Corcoran Annual, Washington, DC 1979, etc.; works in numerous perm. collections including Museum of Modern Art, Whitney Museum, Carnegie Inst., Chicago Art Inst., Guggenheim Museum, Tate Gallery, London, Musée d'Art Moderne, Paris, Stedelijk Museum, Amsterdam; mem. Nat. Inst. of Arts and Letters; recipient of numerous art prizes; Chevalier Ordre des Arts et des Lettres 1993; Mayor of Barcelona Medal 1993. *Solo exhibitions include:* Galerie Arnaud 1951, Betty Parsons Gallery, New York 1956, 1957, 1959, 1961, 1963, Galerie Maeght, Paris 1958, 1964, Tooth Gallery, London 1962, Washington Gallery of Modern Art 1964, Inst. of Contemporary Art, Boston 1964, Sidney Janis Gallery, New York, 1965, 1967, 1968, 1971, Dayton's Gallery 12, Minn. 1971, Albright Art Gallery 1972, Leo Castelli Gallery, New York, 1973, 1975, 1977, 1981, 1982, 1984, 1985, 1989, 1990, New York Museum of Modern Art 1973, 1978, Blum/Helman Gallery, New York, 1975, 1977, 1979, 1981, 1982, 1984, 1985, 1986, 1988, 1989, 1992, Stedelijk Museum, Amsterdam 1979, Hayward Gallery, London 1980, Whitney Museum of Modern Art, New York 1982, St Louis Museum of Art 1983, Anthony d'Offay Gallery, London 1992, 1994, Art Inst., Chicago 1999, Kunstmuseum, Winterthur 1999, Kunstmuseum, Bonn 1999, Smithsonian 2000, Whitney Museum of American Art 2000.

KELLY, Gregory Maxwell, PhD, FAA; Australian professor of pure mathematics; b. 5 June 1930, Sydney; s. of Owen S. Kelly and Rita M. (née McCauley) Kelly; m. Constance Imogen Kelly 1960; three s. one d.; ed Univs of Sydney and Cambridge, England; Lecturer in Pure Math. Univ. of Sydney 1957–60, Sr Lecturer 1961–65, Reader 1965–66; Prof. of Pure Math. Univ. of NSW 1967–72, Univ. of Sydney 1973–94, Prof. Emer. and Professorial Fellow 1994–; Ed. Journal of Pure and Applied Algebra 1971–, Applied Categorical Structures 1992–, Theory and Applications of Categories 1995–. *Publications:* An Introduction to Algebra and Vector Geometry 1972, Basic Concepts of Enriched Category Theory 1981; numerous learned papers. *Leisure interests:* bridge, music, tennis, swimming. *Address:* University of Sydney, School of Mathematics and Statistics, FO7, Sydney, NSW 2006 (Office); 5 Bolton Place, Pymble, NSW 2073, Australia (Home). *Telephone:* (2) 9351-3796 (Office); (2) 9983-9985 (Home). *Fax:* (2) 9351-4534 (Office). *E-mail:* maxk@maths.usyd.edu.au (Office).

KELLY, James A., BS, MBA; American politician; m. Audrey Pool Kelly; two c.; ed Harvard Univ., US Naval Acad., Nat. War Coll.; served in US Navy 1959–83, retd from active duty as Capt., Supply Corps; Deputy Asst Sec. of Defence for Int. Security Affairs (E Asia and Pacific), Pentagon 1983–86; Special Asst for Nat. Security Affairs to Pres. Ronald Reagan and Sr Dir of Asian Affairs, Nat. Security Council 1986–89; Pres. EAP Assocs Inc. (int. business consultants), Honolulu 1989–94; Pres. The Pacific Forum, Center for Strategic and Int. Studies (CSIS), Honolulu 1994–2001; Asst Sec. of State for E Asian and Pacific Affairs May 2001–. *Address:* Bureau of East Asian and Pacific Affairs, Department of State, 2201 C Street, NW, Washington, DC 20520, USA (Office). *Telephone:* (202) 647-5291 (Office). *Fax:* (202) 647-6738 (Office). *Website:* www.state.gov/index.html (Office).

KELLY, Jim; American journalist; b. 15 Dec. 1953, Brooklyn, New York; m. Lisa Henricksson; one s.; ed Princeton Univ.; joined Time magazine 1977 as writer Nation section, Foreign Ed. early 1990s, Deputy Man. Ed. 1996–2000, Man. Ed. 2001–, Ed. Corporate Welfare series 1998, Visions 21 series 1999–2000. *Address:* Office of the Managing Editor, Time, Time-Life Building, Rockefeller Center, 1271 Avenue of the Americas, New York, NY 10020-1393, USA (Office). *Telephone:* (212) 522-1212 (Office). *Fax:* (212) 522-0323 (Office). *Website:* www.time.com (Office).

KELLY, John Hubert, BA; American diplomatist; b. 20 July 1939, Fond du Lac, Wis.; m. Helena Marita Ajo; one s. one d.; ed Emory Univ., Atlanta; Second Sec. US Embassy, Ankara 1966–67; American Consul, Songkhla, Thailand 1969–71; First Sec. U.S. Embassy, Paris 1976–80; Deputy Exec. Sec., Dept of State, Washington DC 1980–81, Sr Deputy Asst Sec. of State for Public Affairs 1982–83, Prin. Deputy Asst Sec. of State for European Affairs 1983–85; Amb. to Lebanon 1986–88, to Finland 1991–94; Prin. Deputy Dir of Policy Planning Staff 1988–89; Asst Sec. for Near Eastern and SE Asian Affairs 1989–93; Man. Dir Int. Equity Partners, Atlanta 1995–98; Pres. John Kelly Consulting Inc. 1999–; Dir Finnish-American Chamber of Commerce 1998, American Int. Petroleum Co. 1999; Trustee Lebanese-American Univ. 1997; Amb.-in-Residence Georgia Inst. of Tech. 1999–. *Address:* John Kelly Consulting, Inc., 1808 Over Lake Drive SE, Suite D, Conyers, GA 30013, USA (Office). *Telephone:* (770) 918-9957 (Office). *Fax:* (770) 483-3090 (Office).

KELLY, John Philip, CMG, LVO, MBE; British diplomatist; b. 25 June 1941, Tuam, Ireland; s. of William Kelly and Norah Kelly (née Roche); m. Jennifer Anne Buckler 1964; one s.; joined HM Diplomatic Service 1959; worked at Embassies in Kinshasa (fmrly Léopoldville) 1962–65, Cairo 1965–67, Bonn 1967–70; with FCO 1970–73, 1986–89, 1994–96; with High Comm. Canberra 1973–76, Consulate-Gen. Antwerp 1977–78; with Dept of Trade 1980–82; Rep. to Grenada 1982–86; Deputy Gov. of Bermuda 1989–94; Gov. Turks and Caicos Islands 1996–2000; Chair. Victoria League for Commonwealth Friendships 2002–. *Leisure interests:* golf, reading, walking. *Address:* The Laurels, 56 Garden Lane, Royston, Herts., SG8 9EH, England. *Telephone:* (1763) 245128 (Home). *E-mail:* johnandjenniferkelly@btinternet.com.

KELLY, Most Rev. Patrick Altham, STL, PhL; British ecclesiastic; b. 23 Nov. 1938, Morecambe; s. of John Kelly and Mary (née Altham) Kelly; ed Preston Catholic Coll., Venerable English Coll., Rome; Asst Priest, Lancaster Cathedral 1964–66; Prof. of Dogmatic Theology, Oscott Coll., Birmingham 1966–79, Rector 1979–84; Bishop of Salford 1984–96; Archbishop of Liverpool, Metropolitan of the Northern Prov. 1996–. *Address:* Archbishop's House, Lowood, Carnatic Road, Mossley Hill, Liverpool L18 8BY, England. *Telephone:* (151) 724-6398. *Fax:* (151) 724-6405. *E-mail:* archbishop.liverpool@rcaolp.co.uk (Office). *Website:* www.archdiocese-of-liverpool.co.uk (Office).

KELLY, Ros, BA; Australian politician; b. 25 Jan. 1948, Sydney; d. of M. Raw and P. Raw; m. David Morgan; one s. one d.; ed Univ. of Sydney; high-school teacher, NSW and ACT 1969–74; consultant and mem. ACT Consumer Affairs Council 1974–79; mem. ACT Legal Aid Comm. 1976–79; fmr mem. ACT Legis. Ass.; mem. Fed. Parl. 1980–95; Sec. Fed. Labor Party Parl. Caucus 1981–87; Minister for Defence, Science and Personnel 1987–89, for Telecommunications and Aviation Support 1989–90, for Sport, the Environment and Territories 1990–94, for the Arts 1990–93, Assisting the Prime Minister for the Status of Women 1993–94; mem. Int. Advisory Council Normandy Ltd 1995–; Dir ERM 2000–; mem. Bd Theiss, External Sustainable Devt Advisory Group. *Leisure interests:* reading, films, aerobics. *Address:* 22 The Crescent, Vaucluse, NSW 2030, Australia. *E-mail:* rkelly1@attglobal.net.

KELLY, Sharon Pratt, BA, JD; American politician and lawyer; b. 30 Jan. 1944, Washington, DC; d. of Carlisle E. Pratt; m. 1st Arrington L. Dixon 1967 (divorced 1982); two d.; m. 2nd James Kelly III 1991; ed Roosevelt High School, Washington, DC and Howard Univ.; Assoc. Pratt & Queen (law firm) 1971; teaching post, Antioch School of Law, Washington, DC 1972–76; Assoc. Gen. Counsel, Potomac Electric Power Co. (PEPCO) 1976, Dir of Consumer Affairs 1979, Vice-Pres. 1983, Vice-Pres. for Public Policy 1986–89; mem. Democratic Nat. Cttee 1977; Treas. Democratic Party 1989; Mayor of Washington, DC 1991–95; Dr hc (Howard, George Washington and Georgetown Univs and St Mary's Coll.). *Address:* 1525 Iris Street, NW, Washington, DC 20012, USA.

KELMAN, Charles D., BS, MD; American ophthalmologist; b. 23 May 1930, Brooklyn, New York; s. of Eva and David Kelman; m. 2nd Ann Gur-Arie 1989; one s. and one s. and two d. from previous marriage; ed Tufts Univ., Univ. of Geneva Medical School, Switzerland; Residency in Ophthalmology, Wills Eye Hosp., Pa 1956–60; Attending Surgeon, Manhattan Eye, Ear and Throat Hosp., New York 1967–, New York Eye and Ear Infirmary 1983–; Attending Ophthalmologist, Riverside Gen. Hosp., Secaucus, NJ 1979; developed new techniques for cataract removal and lens implantation and invented surgical instruments for these operations 1962–67; has taught method to over 4,000 ophthalmologists from hospitals throughout world; Founder and Pres. Autogenesis Technologies Inc. (medical research co.); Pres. David J. Kelman Research Foundation; Clinical Prof. NY Medical Coll., Valhalla 1980–; Hon. Chair. European Soc. for Phaco- and Related Techniques; Arthur J. Bedell Memorial Lecturer 1991; Co-founder Aura Medical Systems (medical tech. co.); Hon. Pres. World Congress on Lens Implant Surgery 1994; Hon. LittD (Jefferson Univ.) 2000; Physician's Recognition Award, American Medical Assocn, American Acad. of Achievement Gold Plate Award, American Acad. of Ophthalmology Sr Honor Award, Ridley Medal, Int. Congress of Oph-

thalmology, Nat. Medal of Tech. Award and numerous other awards. *Publications:* Atlas of Cryosurgical Techniques in Ophthalmology 1966, Phacoemulsification and Aspiration: The Kelman Technique of Cataract Removal 1975, Cataracts–What You Must Know About Them 1982, Through My Eyes (autobiog.) 1985; and numerous articles. *Leisure interests:* golf, saxophone, composing, flying. *Address:* Eye Centre, 220 Madison Avenue, New York, NY 10116, USA.

KELMAN, James; British author; b. 1946, Glasgow; m. Marie Connors; two d.; ed Greenfield Public School, Govan; Cheltenham Prize for Greyhound for Breakfast 1987, James Tait Black Memorial Prize for A Disaffection 1989, Scottish Arts Council Book Award for The Burn, Booker Prize for How Late It Was, How Late 1994, Spirit of Scotland Award. *Plays:* Hardie and Baird, The Last Days 1991, One, Two – Hey (R and B musical, toured 1994). *Radio:* The Art of the Big Bass Drum (BBC Radio 3) 1998. *Publications include:* Not Not While the Giro (short stories), The Bus Conductor Hines, A Chancer, Greyhound for Breakfast, A Disaffection (novel) 1989, The Burn (short stories) 1991, How Late It Was, How Late (novel) 1994, The Good Times (Scottish Writer of the Year Award 1998) 1998, Translated Accounts 2001, And the Judges Said (essays) 2002. *Address:* c/o Rodgers, Coleridge and White Ltd, 20 Powis Mews, London, W11 1JN, England (Office). *Telephone:* (20) 7240-3444.

KELSO, Adm. Frank Benton II; American naval officer; b. 11 July 1933, Fayetteville, Tenn.; s. of Thomas Benton Kelso and Wista Muse; m. Landess McCown 1956; four c.; ed US Naval Acad.; Commdr ensign USN 1956; Office of Program Appraisal 1983; Office, Sec. for the Navy 1985; rank of Adm. 1986; Commdr US Sixth Fleet 1985–86; Commdr-in-Chief, US Atlantic Fleet, Norfolk, Va 1986–88; Supreme Allied Commdr, Atlantic Commdr-in-Chief, Atlantic Command, Norfolk 1988–90; Chief of Naval Operations, Washington, DC 1990–94; Acting Sec. of Navy 1993; retd 1994.

KELTOŠOVÁ, Olga, BSc; Slovak politician; b. Olga Suchalová, 27 Feb. 1943, Pezinok; m. (divorced); one d. one s.; ed Komenský Univ. Bratislava; collaborated with various students' magazines later banned in 1968; worked as translator and interpreter 1970–89; Press Sec. Democratic Party 1989; Deputy Chair. to Nat. Council 1990–92; expelled from Democratic Party 1991; joined Movt for Democratic Slovakia (now Political Party for Democratic Slovakia) 1991–; Minister of Labour, Social Affairs and Family Matters 1992–94, 1995–98; Chair. Co-ordination Cttee for Issues of Handicapped 1995, Co-ordinating Body for Problems of Women 1996–; mem. Parl. 1998–; A. Hlinka Order 1998. *Leisure interests:* classical ballet, gardening. *Address:* Political Party for Democratic Slovakia (HZDS), Tomášikova 32/A, Bratislava 1, (Office); Národné Rada Sr, Ném A. Dubčecka 1, 812 80 Bratislava, Slovakia. *Telephone:* (2) 5934-1347 (Office); (2) 4333-0144. *Fax:* (2) 5441-6337 (Office); (2) 6478-9330 (Home).

KELVEDON OF ONGAR, Baron (Life Peer), cr. 1997, of Ongar in the County of Essex; **(Henry) Paul Guinness Channon,** PC, MA; British politician; b. 9 Oct. 1935; s. of late Sir Henry Channon and Lady Honor (née Guinness) Svejdar; m. Ingrid Olivia Georgia Wyndham 1963; one s. two d. (one d. deceased); ed Eton Coll., Oxford Univ.; 2nd Lt Royal Horse Guards; MP for Southend West 1959–97; Parl. Pvt. Sec. to Minister of Power 1960, to the Home Sec. and later to the Foreign Sec. 1961–64; Opposition Spokesman on the Arts 1967–70; Parl. Sec., Ministry of Housing 1970–72; Minister of State, Northern Ireland Office April–Nov. 1972; Minister for Housing and Construction 1972–74; Opposition Spokesman on Prices and Consumer Affairs June–Oct. 1974, on the Environment 1974–75; Minister of State, Civil Service Dept 1979–81; Minister of State, Dept of Education and Science (responsible for the Arts 1981–83; Minister of State for Trade, Dept of Trade and Industry 1983–86; Sec. of State for Trade and Industry 1986–87, for Transport 1987–89; Chair. House of Commons Finance and Services Cttee 1992–97, Transport Select Cttee 1993–97; Sponsor, Royal Comm. on Historical Monuments 1983–; Conservative. *Address:* c/o House of Lords, London, SW1A 0PW (Office); c/o Iveagh Trustees Ltd, 41 Harrington Gardens, London, SW7 4JU; Kelvedon Hall, Brentwood, Essex, England. *Telephone:* (1277) 362180.

KEMAL, Yashar; Turkish writer and journalist; b. 1923, Adana; m. Thilda Serrero 1952; one s.; self-educated; mem. Académie Universelle des Cultures, Paris; Dr hc (Strasbourg) 1991, (Akdeniz Univ., Antalya) 1991, (Mediterranean Univ.) 1992, (Free Univ., Berlin) 1998; Prix Mondial Cino del Duca 1982, VIII Premi Internacional Catalunya, Barcelona 1996, Peace Prize of German Book Trade 1997, Prix Nonino, Percoto, Italy 1997, Stig Dagerman Prize, Sweden 1997, Norwegian Authors Union Prize 1997, Prix Ecureuil de littérature étrangère, Bordeaux 1998; Hellman-Hammett Award, New York 1996; Commdr, Légion d'honneur 1984. *Publications:* (in English) Memed, My Hawk 1961, The Wind from the Plain 1963, Anatolian Tales 1968, They Burn the Thistles 1973, Iron Earth, Copper Sky 1974, The Legend of Ararat 1975, The Legend of the Thousand Bulls 1976, The Undying Grass 1977, The Lords of Akchasaz (Part I), Murder in the Ironsmiths' Market 1979, The Saga of a Seagull 1981, The Sea-Crossed Fisherman 1985, The Birds Have Also Gone 1987, To Crush the Serpent 1991, Salman the Solitary 1997, The Story of an Island Vols I–IV 1998; novels, short stories, plays and essays in Turkish. *Leisure interest:* folklore. *Address:* P.K. 14, Basinköy, Istanbul, Turkey.

KÉMOULARIA, Claude de; French international administrator and diplomatist; b. 30 March 1922, Paris; s. of Joseph de Kémoularia; m. Chantal Julia de Kémoularia 1951; one d.; ed Coll. Carnot, Fontainebleau, Faculté de Droit, Univ. de Paris and Ecole Libre des Sciences Politiques; early career with

Ministry of Interior 1945, Office of Gov.-Gen. French Zone of Occupied Germany 1946–47, Ministry of Finance 1948; Parl. Sec. to Paul Reynaud 1948–56; Personal Asst to Sec.-Gen. of UN, Dag Hammarskjöld 1957–61, in charge of World Refugee Year 1959–60; Dir European Information Services of UN 1961; entered pvt. business 1962; Dir Forges de Chatillon-Commentry 1962–79, Paribas North America 1979–82, S. G. Warburg 1980–82; Sr Consultant to Administrator, UN Devt Programme 1964–82; Pvt. Adviser to Prince Rainier of Monaco 1965–67; financial adviser for int. operations (Banque de Paris et des Pays-Bas) 1968–82; Hon. Chair. Soc. Néo-Calédonienne de Dévt. et Participations, Soc. Gabonaise de Participations; Amb. to Netherlands 1982–84; Perm. Rep. to UN 1984–87; UN Goodwill Amb. for Population Matters 1987–92, Vice-Chair. SGS Holding France 1994–; Dir Sociéte générale de surveillance 1987–94, Nina Ricci, Eurocopter, Bank Dofar Al Omani Al Fransi, Baiduri Bank Brunei; Pres. Paribas Netherlands 1988–92, Hon. Pres. 1992; Dir Revue politique et parlementaire 1989–; mem. Nat. Cttee European Movt; Hon. Pres. French UN Asscn; Chair. Friends of the French Repub. Asscn; Officier Légion d'honneur, Commdr des Arts et des Lettres, Grand Officier Orange Nassau and other decorations. *Address:* IEPM-Club de Monaco, 73 avenue des Champs Elysées, 75088 Paris (Office); 41 boulevard du Commandant Charcot, 92200 Neuilly-sur-Seine; Lascours, 24200 Carsac-Aillac, France.

KEMP, Rt Rev Eric Waldram, MA, DD, DLitt, FRHistS; British ecclesiastic (retd); b. 27 April 1915, Grimsby; s. of Tom Kemp and Florence L. Waldram; m. Leslie Patricia Kirk 1953; one s. four d.; ed Brigg Grammar School, Lincs., Exeter Coll., Oxford and St Stephen's House; ordained Deacon 1939; Priest 1940; Curate St Luke's, Southampton 1939–41; Librarian Pusey House, Oxford 1941–46; Chaplain Christ Church, Oxford 1941–46; Acting Chaplain St John's Coll., Oxford 1943–45; Fellow, Chaplain, Tutor and Lecturer in Theology and Medieval History Exeter Coll. 1946–69; Emer. Fellow Exeter Coll. 1969; Dean of Worcester 1969–74; Lord Bishop of Chichester 1974–2001; Canon and Prebendary of Caistor in Lincoln Cathedral 1952–2000; Hon. Provincial Canon of Cape Town 1960; Bampton Lecturer 1959–60; Chaplain to the Queen 1967–69; Chanoine d'honneur Chartres Cathedral 1998; Hon. Fellow Univ. Coll. Chichester 2001; Hon. DLitt (Sussex) 1986; Hon. DD (Berne) 1987. *Publications:* Canonization in the Western Church 1948, 25 Papal Decretals Relating to the Diocese of Lincoln 1954, N.P.Williams 1954 (biog.), An Introduction to Canon Law in the Church of England 1957, Life and Letters of K. E. Kirk 1959, Counsel and Consent 1961, Man: Fallen and Free 1969, Square Words in a Round World 1980. *Leisure interests:* music, travel and medieval history. *Address:* 5 Alexandra Road, Chichester, W Sussex, PO19 7LX, England.

KEMP, Martin John, MA, DLitt, FBA, FRSA, FRSE; British historian of art and science; b. 5 March 1942, Windsor; s. of Frederick Maurice Kemp and Violet Anne (née Tull) Kemp; m. Jill Lightfoot 1966 (separated 1995); one s. one d.; ed Windsor Grammar School, Downing Coll., Cambridge and Courtauld Inst. of Art, London Univ.; Lecturer in History of Western Art, Dalhousie Univ., NS, Canada 1965–66; Lecturer in History of Fine Art, Univ. of Glasgow 1966–81; Prof. of Fine Arts, Univ. of St Andrew's 1981–90; Prof. of History, Royal Scottish Acad. 1985–; Prof. of History and Theory of Art, Univ. of St Andrew's 1990–95; Prof. of History of Art, Univ. of Oxford 1995–; Fellow Trinity Coll. Oxford 1995–; Provost St Leonard's Coll., Univ. of St Andrew's 1991–95; mem. Inst. for Advanced Study, Princeton, NJ, USA 1984–85; Slade Prof., Univ. of Cambridge 1987–88; Benjamin Sonenberg Visiting Prof., Inst. of Fine Arts, New York Univ. 1988; Wiley Visiting Prof., Univ. of N Carolina, Chapel Hill 1993; British Acad. Wolfson Research Prof. 1993–98; Trustee Nat. Galleries of Scotland 1982–87, Vic. and Albert Museum, London 1986–89, British Museum 1995–, Ashmolean Museum 1995–; Pres. Leonardo da Vinci Soc. 1988–97; Chair. Asscn of Art Historians 1989–92; mem. Exec. Scottish Museums Council 1990–95; Dir and Chair. Graeme Murray Gallery 1990–92; Dir Wallace Kemp/Artakt 2001; mem. Bd Interalia 1992–, Bd Museum Training Inst. 1993–98; Council British Soc. for the History of Science 1994–97; mem. Visual Arts Advisory Panel, Arts Council of England 1996–; Visiting mem., Getty Center, Los Angeles 2002; Hon. mem. American Acad. of Arts and Sciences 1996–; Mitchell Prize 1981; Armand Hammer Prize for Leonardo Studies 1992; Pres.'s Prize, Italian Asscn of America 1992. *Publications:* Leonardo da Vinci, The Marvellous Works of Nature and Man 1981, Leonardo da Vinci (Co-Author) 1989, The Science of Art, Optical Themes in Western Art from Brunelleschi to Seurat 1990, Behind the Picture. Art and Evidence in the Italian Renaissance 1997, Immagine e Verità 1999, The Oxford History of Western Art (Ed.) 2000, Spectacular Bodies (with Marina Wallace) 2000, Visualizations The Nature Book of Science and Art 2001. *Leisure interest:* sport, especially hockey. *Address:* Department of History of Art, Centre for Visual Studies, 2nd floor, Littlegate House, St Ebbes, Oxford, OX1 1PT (Office); Trinity College, Oxford, OX1 3BH; 2 Harrisons Lane, Woodstock, OX20 1SS, England (Home). *Telephone:* (1865) 286831 (Office); (1993) 811364 (Home). *Fax:* (1865) 286830 (Office); (1993) 811364 (Home). *E-mail:* martin.kemp@trinity.ox.ac.uk (Office).

KEMP-WELCH, Sir John, Kt, FRSA; British stock exchange executive; b. 31 March 1936, Hertford; s. of Peter Kemp-Welch and Peggy Kemp-Welch; m. Diana Leishman 1964; one s. three d.; ed Winchester Coll.; Hoare & Co. 1954–58; Cazenove & Co. 1959–93, Jt Sr Partner 1980–93; Dir Savoy Hotel PLC 1985–98; Dir London Stock Exchange 1991–2000, Chair. 1994–2000; Chair. Scottish Eastern Investment Trust 1994–99, Claridge's Hotel 1995–97; Deputy Chair. Financial Reporting Council 1994–2000; Vice-Chair.

Fed. of European Stock Exchanges 1996–98; Dir Royal and Sun Alliance Insurance Group PLC 1994–99, British Invisibles 1994–98, Securities and Futures Authority 1994–97, ProShare 1995–97, Accountancy Foundation 2000–. *Leisure interests:* the hills of Perthshire, Impressionist Paintings, Champagne. *Address:* 12 Tokenhouse Yard, London, EC2R 7AN, England.

KEMPTHORNE, Dirk Arthur, BS; American politician; b. 29 Oct. 1951, San Diego; s. of James Henry Kempthorne and Maxine Jesse (Gustason) Kempthorne; m. Patricia Jean Merrill 1977; one s. one d.; ed Univ. of Idaho; Exec. Asst to Dir Idaho Dept Lands, Boise 1975–78; Exec. Vice-Pres. Idaho Home Builders' Asscn 1978–81; Campaign Man., Batt for Gov., Boise 1981–82; Idaho Public Affairs Man. FMC Corpn, Boise 1983–86; Mayor of Boise 1986–93; Senator from Idaho 1993–99; Gov. of Idaho 1999–; Chair. US Conf. of Mayors Standing Cttee on Energy and Environment 1991–93, mem. Advisory Bd 1991–93; Sec. Nat. Conf. of Republican Mayors and Municipal Elected Officials 1991–93; mem. Bd of Dirs. Parents and Youth Against Drug Abuse 1987–; Republican; numerous awards. *Address:* Office of the Governor, P.O. Box 83720, Boise, ID 83720, USA.

KENDAL, Felicity, CBE; British actress; b. 25 Sept. 1946; d. of Geoffrey and Laura Kendal; m. 1st (divorced); one s.; m. 2nd Michael Rudman 1983 (divorced 1991); one s.; ed six convents in India; first appeared on stage 1947, at age nine months in A Midsummer Night's Dream; grew up touring India and Far East with parents' theatre co., playing pageboys at age eight and Puck at age nine, graduating to roles such as Viola in Twelfth Night, Jessica in The Merchant of Venice and Ophelia in Hamlet; returned to England 1965; Variety Club Most Promising Newcomer 1974, Best Actress 1979, Clarence Derwent Award 1980, Evening Standard Best Actress Award 1989, Variety Club Best Actress Award 2000. *Stage roles include:* London debut as Carla in Minor Murder, Savoy Theatre 1967, Katherine in Henry V, Lika in The Promise, Leicester 1968, Amaryllis in Back to Methuselah, Nat. Theatre, Hermia in A Midsummer Night's Dream, Hero in Much Ado About Nothing, Regent's Park, London 1970, Anne Danby in Kean, Oxford 1970, London 1971; Romeo and Juliet, 'Tis Pity She's a Whore and The Three Arrows 1972; The Norman Conquests, London 1974, Viktosha in Once Upon a Time, Bristol 1976, Arms and The Man, Greenwich 1978, Mara in Clouds, London 1978; Constanza Mozart in Amadeus, Desdemona in Othello; On the Razzle 1981, The Second Mrs. Tanqueray, The Real Thing 1982, Jumpers 1985, Made in Bangkok 1986, Hapgood 1988, Ivanov 1989, Much Ado About Nothing 1989, Hidden Laughter 1990, Tartuffe 1991, Heartbreak House 1992, Arcadia 1992, An Absolute Turkey 1994, Indian Ink 1995, Mind Millie for Me 1996, The Seagull 1997, Waste 1997, Alarms and Excursions 1998, Fallen Angels 2000, Humble Boy 2002. *TV appearances include:* four series of The Good Life; Solo; The Mistress; The Woodlanders; Edward VII; plays and serials including Viola in Twelfth Night 1979, The Camomile Lawn 1992, The Mayfly and the Frog, Boy meets Girl, The Tenant of Wildfell Hall, Crimes of Passion, The Dolly Dialogues, Now is Too late, Deadly Earnest, The Marriage Counsellor, Home and Beauty, Favourite Things, How Proust Can Change Your Life 2000. *Films include:* Shakespeare Wallah 1965, Valentino 1976, Parting Shots. *Publication:* White Cargo (memoirs) 1998. *Address:* c/o Chatto and Linnit, 123A Kings Road, London, SW3 4PL, England. *Telephone:* (20) 7352-7722. *Fax:* (20) 7352-3450.

KENDALL, David William, FCA; British business executive; b. 8 May 1935; s. of William Jack Kendall and Alma May Kendall; m. 1st Delphine Hitchcock 1960 (divorced); one s. one d.; m. 2nd Elisabeth Rollison 1973; one s. one d.; ed Enfield Grammar School, Southend High School; with Elles Reeve & Co. 1955–62, Shell-Mex & BP Ltd 1963–68; Finance Dir Irish Shell & BP Ltd 1969–70; Crude Oil Sales Man. British Petroleum Co. Ltd 1971–72, Man. Bulk Trading Div. 1973–74, mem. Org. Planning Cttee 1975; Gen. Man. BP NZ Ltd 1976–79, Man. Dir and CEO 1980–82; Chair. BP South West Pacific 1979–82; Finance and Planning Dir BP Oil Ltd 1982–85, Man. Dir and CEO 1985–88; Dir BP Chemicals Int. 1985–88, BP Oil Int. 1985–88, BP Detergents Int. 1985–88; Deputy Chair. British Coal Corpn 1989–90; Dir (non-exec.) Bunzl PLC 1988–90, Chair. 1990–93; Dir STC PLC 1988–90; Chair. Ruberoid PLC 1993–2000, Whitecroft PLC 1993–1999, Meyer Int. PLC 1994–95, Celtic Energy Ltd 1994–, Wagon PLC 1997–; Non-exec. Dir Blagden Industries PLC 1993–94 (Chair. 1994–2000), British Standards Inst. 2000–; Dir Danka Business Systems PLC 1993–2000 (Chair. 1998–2000), Gowrings 1993–, South Wales Electricity PLC 1993–96; Pres. UK Petroleum Industries Asscn 1987–88, Oil Industries Club 1988. *Leisure interests:* golf, music. *Address:* 41 Albion Street, London, W2 2AU, England. *Telephone:* (20) 7258-1955.

KENEALLY, Thomas Michael, AO, FRSL; Australian author; b. 7 Oct. 1935, Sydney; s. of Edmund Thomas and Elsie Margaret Keneally; m. Judith Mary Martin 1965; two d.; Lecturer in Drama, Univ. of New England, Armidale, NSW 1968–70; Visiting Prof. Univ. of Calif., Irvine 1985; Berg Prof., Dept of English, New York Univ. 1988; Pres. Nat. Book Council of Australia –1987; Chair. Australian Soc. of Authors 1987–90, Pres. 1990–; Prof. Dept of English and Comparative Literature, Univ. of Calif. at Irvine 1991–95; mem. Literary Arts Bd 1985–; mem. Australia-China Council; mem. American Acad. of Arts and Sciences; Founding Chair. Australian Republican Movt 1991–93; Hon. DLit (Univ. of Queensland), (Nat. Univ. of Ireland) 1994; Hon. DLitt (Fairleigh Dickenson Univ., USA) 1996, (Rollins Coll., USA) 1996; Royal Soc. of Literature Prize, Los Angeles Times Fiction Prize 1983. *Publications:* Bring Larks and Heroes 1967, Three Cheers for the Paraclete 1968, The Survivor 1969, A Dutiful Daughter 1970, The Chant of Jimmie Blacksmith 1972, Blood Red, Sister Rose 1974, Gossip from the Forest 1975, Season in Purgatory

1976, A Victim of the Aurora 1977, Passenger 1978, Confederates 1979, Schindler's Ark (Booker Prize 1982) 1982, Outback 1983, The Cut-Rate Kingdom 1984, A Family Madness 1985, Australia: Beyond the Dreamtime (contrib.) 1987, The Playmaker 1987, Towards Asmara 1989, Flying Hero Class 1991, Now and in Time to Be: Ireland and the Irish 1992, Woman of the Inner Sea 1992, The Place Where Souls Are Born: A Journey into the American Southwest 1992, Jacko: The Great Intruder 1993, The Utility Player – The Story of Des Hassler (non-fiction) 1993, Our Republic (non-fiction) 1993, A River Town 1995, Homebush Boy: A Memoir 1995, The Great Shame: And the Triumph of the Irish in the English-Speaking World 1998, Bettany's Book 2000, An American Scoundrel: The Life of the Notorious Civil War General Dan Sickles (non-fiction) 2002, An Angel in Australia 2002, Abraham Lincoln 2003, The Office of Innocence 2003. *Leisure interest:* cross-country skiing. *Address:* Curtis Brown (Aust.) Pty Ltd, P.O. Box 19, Paddington, NSW 2021, Australia.

KENGO WA DONDO, Leon, LLD; Democratic Republic of the Congo politician, lawyer and diplomatist; b. 1935; fmr Procurator-Gen. and Pres. of Judicial Council of Zaire; Minister of Justice 1979–80; Amb. to Belgium 1980–82; First State Commr 1982–86, 1988–90; State Comm. for Foreign Affairs 1986–87; elected Prime Minister of Zaire (now Democratic Repub. of the Congo) by Parl. of Transition and High Council of Repub. 1994–97.

KENILOREA, Rt. Hon. Sir Peter, PC, DipEd; Solomon Islands politician; b. 23 May 1943, Takataka, Malaita; m. Margaret Kwanairara 1971; two s. two d.; ed Teachers' Coll. in New Zealand; Schoolmaster, King George VI Secondary School 1968–70; Asst Sec. Finance 1971; Admin. Officer, Dist admin. 1971–73; Lands Officer 1973–74; Deputy Sec. to Cabinet and to Chief Minister 1974–75; District Commr, Eastern Solomons 1975–76; mem. Legis. Assembly 1976–78; MP for East Are-Are 1976–91; f. United Democratic Party 1980, Pres. 1989–; Chief Minister of the Solomon Islands 1976–78; Prime Minister of Solomon Islands 1978–81, 1984–86; Deputy Prime Minister 1986–89, Minister of Foreign Affairs 1988–89, of Foreign Affairs and Trade Relations 1990; Ombudsman 1996–; Dir S Pacific Forum Fisheries Agency 1991–94; Queen's Silver Jubilee Medal 1977. *Publications:* numerous articles for political and scientific publications. *Leisure interests:* reading, sports. *Address:* Kalala House, P.O. Box 535, Honiara, Guadalcanal, Solomon Islands.

KENNAN, George Frost, AB; American diplomatist and scholar; b. 16 Feb. 1904, Milwaukee, Wis.; m. Annelise Sørensen 1931; one s. three d.; ed Princeton Univ.; Vice-Consul Hamburg 1927, Tallinn 1928; Third Sec. Riga, Kovno and Tallinn 1929; Language Officer, Berlin 1929; Third Sec. Riga 1931, Moscow 1934; Consul Vienna 1935, Second Sec. 1935; Second Sec. Moscow 1935; Dept of State 1937; Second Sec. Prague 1938, Consul 1939; Second Sec. Berlin 1939, First Sec. 1940; Counsellor, Lisbon 1942; Counsellor to US del. European Advisory Comm. London 1944; Minister-Counsellor Moscow 1945; Deputy for Foreign Affairs, Nat. War Coll., Washington 1946; Policy Planning Staff, Dept of State 1947; Chief, Policy Planning Staff, Dept of State 1949–50; on leave, at Inst. for Advanced Study, Princeton, NJ 1950–51, Prof. 1956; Amb. to USSR 1952–53; retd from Foreign Service 1953; Charles R. Walgreen Foundation Lecturer, Univ. of Chicago 1951; Stafford Little Lecturer, Princeton 1954; George Eastman Visiting Prof. Oxford Univ. 1957–58; Reith Lecturer on Russia, The Atom and the West 1957; Visiting Lecturer, History, Harvard Univ. 1960, Yale Univ. 1960; Amb. to Yugoslavia 1961–63; Prof. Inst. for Advanced Study, Princeton 1963–74, Prof. Emer. 1974–; Prof. Princeton Univ. 1964–66; mem. Nat. Inst. of Arts and Letters (Pres. 1965–68); American Acad. of Arts and Letters (Pres. 1967–71); Univ. Fellow in History and Slavic Civilizations; Harvard Univ. 1966–70; Fellow, All Souls Coll., Oxford 1969; Fellow, Woodrow Wilson Int. Center for Scholars, Smithsonian Inst. 1974–75; Nat. Book Award, Bancroft Prize, Pulitzer Prize history 1956, biography 1968, Francis Parkman Prize; LLD hc (Yale, Dartmouth, Colgate, Notre Dame, Kenyon, Princeton, Michigan, Northwestern, Brandeis, Denison, Harvard, Rutgers, Wisconsin Univs., Lake Forest, Clark, Oberlin, Brown, William & Mary Coll., Columbia, New York), Hon. DCL (Oxford) 1969; Hon. degrees (Univ. of Helsinki) 1986, (Rider Coll.) 1988; Benjamin Franklin Fellow of the Royal Soc. of Arts, London 1968; Albert Einstein Peace Prize 1981; Grenville Clarke Prize 1981; Peace Prize of the W German Book Trade 1982, Union Medal, Union Theological Seminary 1982, American Acad. and Inst. of Arts and Letters Gold Medal for History 1984, Freedom from Fear Medal, Franklin D. Roosevelt Foundation, Physicians for Social Responsibility Annual Award 1988, Toynbee Award 1988, Encyclopedia Britannica Award 1989, Presidential Medal of Freedom 1989, Gov.'s Award (of NJ) 1989. *Publications:* American Diplomacy 1900–1950 1952, Das Amerikanisch-Russische Verhältnis 1954, Realities of American Foreign Policy 1954, Soviet-American Relations 1917–1920, Vol. I, Russia Leaves the War 1956, Vol. II, The Decision to Intervene 1958, Russia, The Atom and the West (Reith Lectures) 1958, Soviet Foreign Policy 1917–45 1960, Russia and the West under Lenin and Stalin 1961, On Dealing with the Communist World 1963, Memoirs 1925–1950 1967, Democracy and the Student Left 1968, From Prague After Munich: Diplomatic Papers 1938–1940 1968, The Marquis de Custine and his "Russia in 1839" 1971, Memoirs 1950–1963 1972, The Cloud of Danger 1977, The Decline of Bismarck's European Order: Franco-Russian Relations 1875–1890 1979, The Nuclear Delusion: Soviet-American Relations in the Atomic Age 1982, The Fateful Alliance 1984, Sketches from a Life 1989,

Around the Cragged Hill, A Personal and Political Philosophy 1993, At a Century's Ending: Reflections 1982–95 1996. *Address:* Institute for Advanced Study, Princeton, NJ 08540, USA.

KENNARD, Olga, OBE, ScD, FRS; British research scientist; b. 23 March 1924, Budapest, Hungary; d. of Joir Weisz and Catherina Weisz; m. 1st David Kennard 1948 (divorced 1961); m. 2nd Sir Arnold Burgen 1992; ed schools in Hungary, Prince Henry VIII Grammar School, Evesham and Newnham Coll. Cambridge; Research Asst Cavendish Lab. Cambridge 1944–48; MRC Scientific Staff, London 1948–61; MRC External Scientific Staff, Univ. of Cambridge 1961–89; Dir Cambridge Crystallographic Data Centre 1965–97; MRC Special Appt. 1969–89; Visiting Prof., Univ. of London 1988–90; mem. Academia Europaea, Council, Royal Soc. 1995–97; Royal Soc. of Chem. Prize for Structural Chem. 1980. *Publications:* about 200 papers in scientific journals and books on X-ray crystallography, molecular biology, information technology; 20 scientific reference books. *Leisure interests:* swimming, music, modern architecture and design. *Address:* Keelson, 8A Hills Avenue, Cambridge, CB1 7XA, England. *Telephone:* (1223) 415381.

KENNARD, William E.; American business executive, lawyer and government official; b. 19 Jan. 1957, Los Angeles; s. of Robert A. Kennard and Helen Z. King; m. Deborah D. Kennedy 1984; ed Stanford Univ., Yale Law School.; fmrly with Nat. Assen of Broadcasters; fmr Partner and mem. Bd Dirs Verner, Liipfert, Bernhard, McPherson and Hand law firm; Gen. Counsel to Fed. Communications Comm. 1993–97, Chair. 1997–2001; Man. Dir (Global Telecommunications and Media Investment Strategy) The Carlyle Group 2001–. *Address:* The Carlyle Group, 1001 Pennsylvania Ave NW, Washington, DC 20004, USA (Office). *Telephone:* (202) 347-2626 (Office). *E-mail:* inquiries@thecarlylegroup.com (Office). *Website:* www.thecarlylegroup.com (Office).

KENNEDY, Anthony M., LLB; American judge; b. 23 July 1936, Sacramento; s. of Anthony J. Kennedy and Gladys Kennedy; m. Mary Davis; two s. one d.; ed Stanford and Harvard Univs. and London School of Econs and Political Science; mem. Calif. Bar 1962, US Tax Court Bar 1971; Assoc. Thelen, Marrin, Johnson & Bridges, San Francisco 1961–63; sole practice, Sacramento 1963–67; partner, Evans, Jackson & Kennedy (law firm) 1967–75; Prof. of Constitutional Law, McGeorge School of Law, Univ. of Pacific 1965; Judge, US Court of Appeals, 9th Circuit, Sacramento 1976–88; Judge Supreme Court of USA Jan. 1988–. *Address:* Supreme Court Building, 1 First Street, NE, Washington, DC 20543, USA.

KENNEDY, Rt Hon. Charles Peter, MA; British politician, journalist and broadcaster; b. 25 Nov. 1959, Inverness; s. of Ian Kennedy and Mary McVarish MacEachen; ed Lochaber High School, Fort William and Univ. of Glasgow; journalist, BBC Highland, Inverness 1982; Fulbright Scholar and Assoc. Instr. Dept of Speech Communication, Indiana Univ. Bloomington Campus 1982–83; MP for Ross, Cromarty and Skye 1983–97, for Ross, Skye and Inverness W 1997–; mem. Social Democratic Party 1983–88, Liberal Democrats 1988– (spokesperson on Trade and Industry 1988–89, on Health 1989–92, on Europe and E–W relations 1992–97, on Agric. and Rural Affairs 1997–99); Pres. Liberal Democrats 1990–94, Leader Aug. 1999–; Dr hc (Glasgow) 2002. *Publication:* The Future of Politics 2000. *Address:* House of Commons, London, SW1A 0AA, England. *Telephone:* (20) 7219-6226 (Office). *Fax:* (20) 7219-4881 (Office). *E-mail:* kennedy@parliament.uk (Office). *Website:* www.charleskennedy.org.uk (Office).

KENNEDY, Donald, MA, PhD; American academic; b. 18 Aug. 1931, New York; s. of William D. and Barbara (Bean) Kennedy; m. 1st Jane J. Dewey 1953; two d.; m. 2nd Robin Beth Wiseman 1987; two step-s.; ed Harvard Univ.; Asst Prof. Syracuse Univ. 1956–59, Assoc. Prof. 1959–60; Asst Prof. Stanford Univ. 1960–62, Assoc. Prof. 1962–65, Prof. 1965–77, Chair. Dept of Biological Sciences 1965–72, Benjamin Crocker Prof. of Human Biology 1974–77, Vice-Pres. and Provost 1979–80, Pres. 1980–92, Pres. Emer. and Bing Prof. of Environmental Science 1992–; Sr Consultant, Office of Science and Tech. Policy, Exec. Office of the Pres. 1976–77; Commr of Food and Drug Admin. 1977–79; Ed.-in-Chief Science 2000–; Fellow, American Acad. of Arts and Sciences; mem. NAS; Hon. DSc (Columbia Univ., Williams Coll., Michigan, Rochester, Ariz., Whitman Coll., Coll. of William and Mary); Dinkelspiel Award 1976. *Publications:* The Biology of Organisms (with W. M. Telfer) 1965, Academic Duty 1997; over 60 articles in scientific journals. *Leisure interests:* skiing, fly fishing, natural history. *Address:* Stanford University, Institute for International Studies, Encina Hall 401, Stanford, CA 94305 (Office); 532 Channing Avenue, #302, Palo Alto, CA 94301, USA (Home). *E-mail:* kennedyd@stanford.edu (Office).

KENNEDY, Edward Moore, AB, LLB; American politician and lawyer; b. 22 Feb. 1932, Boston, Mass.; s. of late Joseph Kennedy and of Rose Kennedy; brother of late Pres. John F. Kennedy; m. 1st Virginia Joan Bennett 1958 (divorced 1982); two s. one d.; m. 2nd Victoria Annie Reggie 1992; ed Milton Acad., Harvard Coll. and Univ. of Virginia Law School; US Army, Infantry, Private 1st Class 1951–53; Reporter, Int. News Service, N Africa 1956; Man. Western States, John F. Kennedy Presidential Campaign 1960; fmr Asst District Attorney, Mass.; Senator from Mass. 1962–; Asst Majority Leader, US Senate 1969–71; Chair. Senate Judiciary Comm. 1979–81, ranking Democrat Labour and Human Resources Cttee 1981–; Pres. Joseph P. Kennedy Jr Foundation 1961–; Trustee, Boston Univ., Boston Symphony, John F. Kennedy Library, Lahey Clinic, Boston, John F. Kennedy Center for the Performing Arts, Robert F. Kennedy Memorial Foundation; Bd mem. Fletcher School of Law and Diplomacy, Mass. Gen. Hospital; mem. Bd

Advisers, Dunbarton Oaks Research Library and Collections; Democrat; numerous hon. degrees; Order of the Phoenix (Greece) 1976; Harvard Univ. John F. Kennedy School of Govt Medal 1986. *Publications:* Decisions for a Decade 1968, In Critical Condition 1972, Our Day and Generation 1979, Freeze: How You Can Help Prevent Nuclear War (with Senator Mark Hatfield, q.v., 1979). *Address:* US Senate, Senate Office Building, 315 Russell Senate Building, Washington, DC 20510, USA.

KENNEDY, Eugene Patrick, BSc, PhD; American professor of biological chemistry; b. 4 Sept. 1919, Chicago; s. of Michael and Catherine Frawley Kennedy; m. Adelaide Majewski 1943; three d.; ed De Paul Univ. and Univ. of Chicago; Asst Prof., Ben May Lab., Univ. of Chicago 1952–55, Assoc. Prof. 1955–56, Prof. of Biological Chem. 1956–60; Prof. and Head, Dept of Biological Chem., Harvard Medical School 1960–65, Hamilton Kuhn Prof. of Biological Chem., Harvard Medical School 1960–; Assoc. Ed. Journal of Biological Chemistry 1969; Pres. American Soc. of Biol. Chemists 1970–71; mem. NAS, American Acad. of Arts and Sciences, American Philosophical Soc.; Hon. DSc (Chicago) 1977; George Ledlie Prize (Harvard) 1976, Heinrich Wieland Prize 1986; Glycerine Research Award 1956; Paul-Lewis Award, American Chem. Soc. 1959, Lipid Chem. Award of the American Oil Chemists Soc. 1970, Josiah Macy, Jr Foundation Faculty Scholar Award 1974, Gairdner Foundation Award 1976, Sr US Scientist Award, Alexander von Humboldt Foundation 1983, Passano Award 1986. *Address:* Department of Biological Chemistry, Harvard Medical School, 25 Shattuck Street, Boston, MA 02115; 221 Mount Auburn Street, Cambridge, MA 02138, USA.

KENNEDY, George Danner, B.A; American business executive; b. 30 May 1926, Pittsburgh, Pa; s. of Thomas Reed and Lois (Smith) Kennedy; m. Valerie Putis 1972; three s. one d.; ed Williams Coll.; Scott Paper Co. 1947–52; Champion Paper Co. 1952–65; Pres. Brown Co. 1965–71; Exec. Vice-Pres., IMCERA (fmrly Int. Minerals & Chemical Corpn) 1971–78, Dir 1975, Pres. 1978–86, CEO 1983–93, Chair. of Bd IMCERA (now Mallinckrodt Group) 1986–; Dir SCM Corpn 1978–82; Dir Brunswick Corpn 1979; Dir, Exec. Cttee, Kemper Group and Foundation 1982; Dir Ill. Tool Works 1988; Bd Chair. Children's Memorial Hosp., Chicago; Vice-Pres., Dir NE Ill. Boy Scout Council; Trustee Nat. Comm. Against Drunk Driving, Chicago Symphony. *Address:* P.O. Box 559, Winnetka, IL 60093, USA.

KENNEDY, James C., B.B.A.; American publishing and media executive; b. 1947; m.; ed Univ. of Denver; with Atlanta Newspapers 1976–79; Pres. Grand Junction Newspapers 1979–80; Publr Grand Junction Daily Sentinel 1980–85; Vice-Pres. newspaper Div. Cox Enterprises Inc. 1985–86, Exec. Vice-Pres., Pres. 1986–87, COO, Chair. 1987–; Chair., CEO Cox Enterprises Inc. 1988–. *Address:* Cox Enterprises Inc., P.O. Box 105357, Atlanta, GA 30348 (Office); 1601 W Peachtree Street North East, Atlanta, GA 30309, USA (Home).

KENNEDY, Sir Ludovic Henry Coverley, Kt, MA, FRSL; British writer and broadcaster; b. 3 Nov. 1919, Edinburgh; s. of late Capt. E. C. Kennedy, RN and of Rosalind Kennedy; m. Moira Shearer King 1950; one s. three d.; ed Eton Coll., Christ Church, Oxford; served in RN 1939–46 (attained rank of Lt); Pvt. Sec. and ADC to Gov. of Newfoundland 1943–44; Librarian, Ashridge (Adult Educ.) Coll. 1949; Ed., feature, First Reading (BBC Third Programme) 1953–54; Lecturer for British Council, Sweden, Finland, Denmark 1955, Belgium, Luxembourg 1956; contested Rochdale by-election 1958, gen. election 1959 as Liberal candidate; Pres. Nat. League of Young Liberals 1959–61, mem. Liberal Party Council 1965–67; TV and radio: introduced Profile, ATV 1955–56; newscaster, ITV 1956–58; introducer On Stage, Associated Rediffusion 1957, This Week, Associated Rediffusion 1958–59; Chair. BBC features: Your Verdict 1962, Your Witness 1967–70; commentator BBC's Panorama 1960–63, Television Reports Int. (also producer) 1963–64; introducer BBC's Time Out 1964–65, World at One 1965–66; presenter Liberal Party's Gen. Election TV Broadcasts 1966, The Middle Years, ABC 1967, The Nature of Prejudice, ATV 1968, Face The Press, Tyne-Tees 1968–69, 1970–72, Against the Tide, Yorkshire TV 1969, Living and Growing, Grampian TV 1969–70, 24 Hours, BBC 1969–72, Ad Lib, BBC 1970–72, Midweek, BBC 1973–75, Newsday, BBC 1975–76, Tonight, BBC 1976–80, A Life with Crime BBC 1979, presenter Lord Mountbatten Remembers 1980, Change of Direction 1980, Did You See? BBC 1980–88, Great Railway Journeys of the World BBC 1980, Chair. Indelible Evidence BBC 1987, 1990, A Gift of the Gab BBC 1989, Portrait BBC 1989; mem. Council Navy Records Soc. 1957–70; Pres. Sir Walter Scott Club, Edin. 1968–69; Chair. Royal Lyceum Theatre Co. of Edin. 1977–84; Chair. Judges, NCR Book Award 1990–91; Pres. Voluntary Euthanasia Soc. 1995–; FRSA 1974–76; Voltaire Memorial Lecturer 1985; Hon. DL (Strathclyde) 1985, (Southampton) 1993; Dr hc (Edin.) 1990, (Stirling) 1991; Richard Dimbleby Award (BAFTA) 1989, Bar Council Special Award 1992; Cross First Class, Order of Merit (Fed. Repub. of Germany). *Films include:* The Sleeping Ballerina, The Singers and the Songs, Scapa Flow, Battleship Bismarck, Life and Death of the Scharnhorst, U-Boat War, Target Tirpitz, The Rise of the Red Navy, Lord Haw-Haw, Who Killed the Lindbergh Baby?, Elizabeth: The First Thirty Years, A Life of Richard Dimbleby, Happy Birthday, dear Ma'am, Murder in Belgravia: The Lucan Affair, Princess to Queen. *Publications:* Sub-Lieutenant 1942, Nelson's Band of Brothers 1951, One Man's Meat 1953, Murder Story 1956, Ten Rillington Place 1961, The Trial of Stephen Ward 1964, Very Lovely People 1969, Pursuit: the Chase and Sinking of the Bismarck 1974, A Presumption of Innocence: the Amazing Case of Patrick Meehan 1975, The Portland Spy Case 1978, Wicked Beyond Belief: The Luton Post Office Murder Case 1980, Menace: The Life and Death of the

Tirpitz 1979, The Airman and the Carpenter: The Lindbergh Case and the Framing of Richard Hauptmann 1985, On My Way to the Club (autobiog.) 1989, Euthanasia: The Good Death 1990, Truth to Tell (collected writings) 1991, In Bed with an Elephant: A Journey through Scotland's Past and Present 1995, All in the Mind: A Farewell to God 1999; Gen. Ed. The British at War 1973–77; Ed. A Book of Railway Journeys 1980, A Book of Sea Journeys 1981, A Book of Air Journeys 1982, 36 Murders and Two Immoral Earnings 2002. *Address:* c/o Rogers, Coleridge and White, 20 Powis Mews, London, W11 1JN, England.

KENNEDY, Michael, CBE, MA, CRNCM; British journalist and critic; b. 19 Feb. 1926, Manchester; s. of Hew G. and Marian F. Kennedy; m. 1st Eslyn Durdle 1947 (died 1999); m. 2nd Joyce Bourne 1999; ed Berkhamsted School; staff music critic, The Daily Telegraph 1950–, Northern Ed. 1960–86; music critic, The Sunday Telegraph 1989–; Gov. Royal Northern Coll. of Music; Hon. mem. Royal Manchester Coll. of Music 1971; Hon. MA (Manchester) 1975. *Publications:* The Hallé Tradition 1960, The Works of Ralph Vaughan Williams 1964, Portrait of Elgar 1968, History of Royal Manchester College of Music 1971, Barbirolli 1971, Portrait of Manchester 1971, Mahler 1974, Strauss 1976, Britten 1980, Concise Oxford Dictionary of Music 1980, Oxford Dictionary of Music 1985, Adrian Boult 1987, Portrait of Walton 1989, Music Enriches All: The First 21 Years of the RNCM, Manchester 1973–94 1994, Richard Strauss, Man, Musician, Enigma 1999. *Leisure interest:* cricket. *Address:* The Bungalow, 62 Edilom Road, Manchester, M8 4HZ, England. *Telephone:* (161) 740-4528 (Home). *Fax:* (161) 720-7171 (Home). *E-mail:* majkennedy@bungalow62.fsnet.co.uk.

KENNEDY, Nigel; British violinist; b. 28 Dec. 1956; s. of John Kennedy and Scylla Stoner; partner Eve Westmore; one s.; ed Yehudi Menuhin School, Juilliard School of Performing Arts; chosen by the BBC as the subject of a five-year documentary on the Devt of a soloist following his début with the Philharmonia Orchestra 1977; has since appeared with all the maj. British orchestras; has made appearances at all the leading UK festivals and in Europe at Stresa, Lucerne, Gstaad, Berlin and Lockenhaus; début at the Tanglewood Festival with the Boston Symphony under André Previn 1985, at Minn. with Sir Neville Marriner, at Montreal with Charles Dutoit; has given concerts in the field of jazz with Stephane Grappelli at Carnegie Hall and Edin. and runs his own jazz group; recordings include the Elgar Sonata with Peter Pettinger (Chandos Records), Tchaikovsky, Sibelius, Vivaldi, Mendelssohn, Bruch, Walton Viola and Violin Concertos and the Elgar Concerto with the London Philharmonic Orchestra (EMI/Eminence); Sr Vice-Pres. Aston Villa FC 1990–; Hon. DLitt (Bath) 1991; for his recording of the Elgar Concerto he received the Record of the Year nomination by Gramophone Magazine Feb. 1985 and received the Best Classical Disc of the Year award, London 1985. *Publication:* Always Playing 1991. *Leisure interests:* cricket, golf, football. *Address:* c/o Ellie Page, First Floor, No. 5, 119 Church Street, Malvern, Worcs., WR14 2AJ (Office); c/o Russells (Solicitors), Regency House, 1–4 Warwick Street, London, W1R 5WB, England. *Telephone:* (1684) 560040 (Office). *Fax:* (1684) 561613 (Office).

KENNEDY, Rt Hon. Sir Paul (Joseph Morrow); Rt Hon. Lord Justice Kennedy, PC, MA, LLB; British judge; b. 12 June 1935, Sheffield; m. Virginia Devlin 1965; two s. two d.; ed Ampleforth Coll., York, Gonville & Caius Coll., Cambridge; called to Bar Gray's Inn 1960, Bencher 1982, Treas. 2002; Recorder of Crown Court 1972–83; QC 1973; Judge High Court of Justice, Queen's Bench Div. (QBD) 1983–92, Vice-Pres. QBD 1997–2002; Presiding Judge NE Circuit 1985–89; Lord Justice of Appeal 1992–; Chair. Criminal Cttee Judicial Studies Bd 1993–96; Hon. Fellow Gonville & Caius Coll. 1998; Hon. LLD (Sheffield) 2000. *Leisure interests:* family, walking, occasional golf. *Telephone:* (20) 7947-6688 (Office).

KENNEDY, Paul Michael, CBE, MA, DPhil, FRHistS; British historian; b. 17 June 1945, Wallsend; s. of John Patrick Kennedy and Margaret (née Hennessy) Kennedy; m. 1st Catherine Urwin 1967 (died 1998); three s.; m. 2nd Cynthia Farrar 2001; ed St Cuthbert's Grammar School, Newcastle-upon-Tyne, Univ. of Newcastle and Oxford Univ.; Research Asst to Sir Basil Liddell Hart 1966–70; lecturer, Reader and Prof., Univ. of E Anglia 1970–83; J. Richardson Dilworth Prof. of History Yale Univ. 1983–, Dir Int. Security Studies 1988–; Visiting Fellow Inst. for Advanced Study, Princeton 1978–79; Fellow Alexander von Humboldt Foundation, American Philosophical Soc., American Acad. of Arts and Sciences; Hon. DHL (New Haven, Alfred, Long Island, Connecticut); Hon. DLitt (Newcastle, East Anglia); Hon. LLD (Ohio); Hon. MA (Yale, Union, Quinnipiac); Dr hc (Leuven). *Publications:* The Samoan Tangle 1974, The Rise and Fall of British Naval Mastery 1976, The Rise of the Anglo-German Antagonism 1980, The Realities Behind Diplomacy 1981, Strategy and Diplomacy 1983, The Rise and Fall of the Great Powers 1988, Grand Strategy in War and Peace 1991, Preparing for the Twenty-First Century 1993, Pivotal States: A New Framework for US Policy in the Developing World (Ed.) 1998. *Leisure interests:* soccer, hill-walking, old churches. *Address:* Department of History, Yale Univ., P.O. Box 208324, New Haven, CT 06520, USA. *Telephone:* (203) 432-6246 (Office).

KENNEDY, William Joseph, BA; American author and professor of English; b. 16 Jan. 1928, Albany, New York; s. of William J. Kennedy and Mary E. McDonald; m. Ana Segarra 1957; one s. two d.; ed Siena Coll., New York; Asst Sports Ed., columnist, Glens Falls Post Star, New York 1949–50; reporter, Albany Times-Union, New York 1952–56, special writer 1963–70; Asst Man. Ed., columnist, P.R. World Journal, San Juan 1956; reporter, Miami Herald

1957; corresp. Time-Life Publs, Puerto Rico 1957–59; reporter, Knight Newspapers 1957–59; Founding Man. Ed. San Juan Star 1959–61; lecturer, State Univ. of New York, Albany 1974–82, Prof. of English 1983–; Visiting Prof. Cornell Univ. 1982–83; founder, NY State Writers' Inst. 1983; Nat. Endowment for Arts Fellow 1981, MacArthur Foundation Fellow 1983; several hon. degrees; Gov. of New York Arts Award 1984, Creative Arts Award, Brandeis Univ. 1986; Pulitzer Prize and Nat. Book Critics Circle Award 1984 for Ironweed. *Publications include:* The Ink Truck 1969, Legs 1975, Billy Phelan's Greatest Game 1978, Ironweed 1983, O Albany! (non-fiction) 1983, Charlie Malarkey and the Belly Button Machine (children's book) 1986, Quinn's Book 1988, Very Old Bones 1992, Riding the Yellow Trolley Car 1993, Charlie Malarkey and the Singing Moose (children's book) 1994, The Flaming Corsage 1996, Grand View (play) 1996, Roscoe 2002; film scripts, The Cotton Club 1984, Ironweed 1987; also short stories, articles in professional journals. *Address:* NYS Writers Institute, Washington Avenue, Albany, NY 12222, USA.

KENNEDY OF THE SHAWS, Baroness (Life Peer) cr. 1997, of Cathcart in the City of Glasgow; **Helena Ann Kennedy,** QC, FRSA; British lawyer; b. 12 May 1950; d. of Joshua Kennedy and Mary Jones; partner (Roger) Iain Mitchell 1978–84; one s.; m. Dr. Iain L. Hutchison 1986; one s. one d.; ed Holyrood Secondary School, Glasgow and Council of Legal Educ.; called to the Bar, Gray's Inn 1972; mem. Bar Council 1990–93; mem. CIBA Comm. into Child Sexual Abuse 1981–83; mem. Bd City Limits Magazine 1982–84, New Statesman 1990–96, Counsel Magazine 1990–93; mem. Council, Howard League for Penal Reform 1989–, Chair. Comm. of Inquiry into Violence in Penal Insts for Young People (report 1995); Commr BAFTA inquiry into future of BBC 1990, Hamlyn Nat. Comm. on Educ. 1991–; Visiting lecturer, British Postgrad. Medical Fed. 1991–; Adviser, Mannheim Inst. on Criminology, LSE 1992–; Leader of inquiry into health, environmental and safety aspects of Atomic Weapons Establishment, Aldermaston (report 1994); Chancellor, Oxford Brookes Univ. 1994–2001; Chair. British Council 1998–, Human Genetics Comm. 2000–; author of official report (Learning Works) for Further Educ. Funding Council on widening participation in further educ. 1997; mem. Advisory Bd, Int. Centre for Prison Studies 1998; Chair. London Int. Festival of Theatre, Standing Cttee for Youth Justice 1992–97; Charter 88; Pres. London Marriage Guidance Council, Birth Control Campaign, Nat. Children's Bureau, Hillcroft Coll.; Vice-Pres. Haldane Soc., Nat. Ass. of Women; mem. British Council's Law Advisory Cttee Advisory Bd for Study of Women and Gender, Warwick Univ., Int. Bar Asscn's Task Force on Terrorism; presenter of various programmes on radio and TV and creator of BBC drama series Blind Justice 1988; Patron, Liberty; mem. Acad. de Cultures Internationales; Hon. Fellow Inst. of Advanced Legal Studies, Univ. of London 1997; Hon. mem. Council, Nat. Soc. for Prevention of Cruelty to Children; 18 hon. LLDs from British and Irish Univs; Women's Network Award 1992, UK Woman of Europe Award 1995; Campaigning and Influencing Award, Nat. Fed. of Women's Insts 1996, Times Newspaper Lifetime Achievement Award in the Law (jtly) 1997; Spectator Magazine's Parl. Campaigner of the Year 2000. *Publications:* The Bar on Trial (jtly) 1978, Child Abuse within the Family (jtly) 1984, Balancing Acts (jtly) 1989, Eve was Framed 1992; articles on legal matters, civil liberties and women. *Leisure interests:* theatre, spending time with family and friends. *Address:* House of Lords, London, SW1A 0PW, England. *Telephone:* (1708) 379482. *Fax:* (1708) 379482.

KENNET, (2nd Baron) cr. 1935, of the Dene; **Wayland Young,** MA, FRIBA; British writer and politician; b. 2 Aug. 1923, London; s. of Edward Hilton Young (Lord Kennet) and Kathleen Bruce; m. Elizabeth Ann Adams 1948; one s. five d.; ed Stowe School, Trinity Coll., Cambridge, Univ. for Foreigners, Perugia; Royal Navy 1942–45; Foreign Office 1946–47, 1949–51; Corresp. for Observer newspaper in Italy 1953–55; mem. Parl. Assemblies Council of Europe and Western European Union Africa 1962–65; Chair. British Cttee for International Co-operation Year 1965; Parl. Sec. Ministry of Housing and Local Govt 1966–70; Chair. Int. Parl. Confs on the Environment 1971–78; Chair. Advisory Cttee on Oil Pollution of the Sea 1970–74; Chair. Council for the Protection of Rural England 1971–72; Opposition Spokesman on Foreign Affairs and Science Policy, House of Lords 1971–74; Dir Europe Plus Thirty Project 1974–75; mem. European Parl. 1978–79; Chief Whip SDP, House of Lords 1981–83, Spokesman on Foreign Affairs and Defence 1981–90; Vice-Chair. Parl. Office of Science and Tech. 1989–93; Vice-Pres. Parl. and Scientific Cttee 1989–98; rejoined Labour Party 1990; Pres. Architecture Club 1984–94; mem. North Atlantic Ass. 1997–2000. *Publications:* The Italian Left 1949, The Deadweight 1952, Now or Never 1953, Old London Churches (with Elizabeth Young) 1956, The Montesi Scandal 1957, Still Alive Tomorrow 1958, Strategy for Survival 1959, The Profumo Affair 1963, Eros Denied 1965, Preservation 1972, The Futures of Europe 1976, London's Churches (with Elizabeth Young) 1986, Northern Lazio: An Unknown Italy (with Elizabeth Young) 1990; Ed. Disarmament and Arms Control 1963–65, The Rebirth of Britain 1982, Parliaments and Screening 1994. *Leisure interests:* sailing, swimming, music. *Address:* 100 Bayswater Road, London, W2 3HJ, England. *E-mail:* waylandkennet@gn.apc.org (Office).

KENNEY, Edward John, MA, FBA; British professor of Latin; b. 29 Feb. 1924, London; s. of George Kenney and Emmie Carlina Elfrida Schwenke; m. Gwyneth Anne Harris; ed Christ's Hosp. and Trinity Coll. Cambridge; served in Royal Signals, UK and India 1943–46; Asst Lecturer, Univ. of Leeds 1951–52; Research Fellow, Trinity Coll., Cambridge Univ. 1952–53, Fellow of Peterhouse 1953–91, Asst Lecturer in Classics, Cambridge Univ. 1955–60, Lecturer 1960–70, Reader in Latin Literature and Textual Criticism 1970–74, Kennedy Prof. of Latin 1974–82, Emer. Prof. 1982–; Jt Ed. Classical Quarterly 1959–65; Jt Ed. Cambridge Greek and Latin Classics 1970–; Pres. Jt Asscn of Classical Teachers 1977–79, Classical Asscn 1982–83; Treas. and Chair. Council of Almoners, Christ's Hosp. 1984–86; Foreign mem. Royal Netherlands Acad. of Arts and Sciences. *Publications:* P. Ovidi Nasonis Amores, etc. 1961, Lucretius, De Rerum Natura III 1971, The Classical Text 1974, The Cambridge History of Classical Literature, Vol. II, Latin Literature (Ed. and Contrib.) 1982, The Ploughman's Lunch (Moretum) 1984, Ovid, Metamorphoses–Introduction and Notes 1986, Ovid, The Love Poems–Introduction and Notes 1990, Apuleius, Cupid & Psyche 1990, Ovid, Sorrows of an Exile (Tristia)–Introduction and Notes 1992, Ovid, Heroides xvi–xxi 1996, Apuleius, The Golden Ass – Trans. with Introduction and Notes 1998; numerous articles and reviews. *Leisure interests:* cats, books. *Address:* Peterhouse, Cambridge, CB2 1RD, England.

KENNY, Sir Anthony John Patrick, Kt, DPhil, FBA; British philosopher and university teacher; b. 16 March 1931, Liverpool; s. of John and Margaret (Jones) Kenny; m. Nancy Caroline Gayley 1966; two s.; ed Gregorian Univ., Rome, St Benet's Hall, Oxford; ordained Catholic priest, Rome 1955; Curate, Liverpool 1959–63; returned to lay state 1963; Asst Lecturer, Univ. of Liverpool 1961–63; Lecturer in Philosophy, Exeter and Trinity Colls, Oxford 1963–64; Tutor in Philosophy, Balliol Coll., Oxford 1964, Fellow 1964–78, Sr Tutor 1971–72, 1976–77, Master 1978–89; Warden Rhodes House 1989–99; Professorial Fellow St John's Coll., Oxford 1989–99; Pro-Vice-Chancellor, Univ. of Oxford 1984–99; Pro-Vice Chancellor for Devt, Univ. of Oxford 1999–2001; Wilde Lecturer in Natural and Comparative Religion, Oxford 1969–72; Joint Gifford Lecturer, Univ. of Edin. 1972–73; Stanton Lecturer, Univ. of Cambridge 1980–83; Speaker's Lecturer in Biblical Studies, Univ. of Oxford 1980–83; Visiting Prof. Stanford and Rockefeller Univs, Univs of Chicago, Washington, Mich., Cornell; Vice-Pres. British Acad. 1986–88, Pres. 1989–93; Chair. Bd British Library 1993–96 (mem Bd 1991–96); Del. and mem. of Finance Cttee, Oxford Univ. Press 1986–93; Ed. The Oxford Magazine 1972–73; mem. Royal Norwegian Acad. 1993–, American Philosophical Soc. 1994–; Hon. Bencher, Lincoln's Inn 1999; Hon. DLitt (Bristol) 1982, (Denison Univ.) 1986, (Liverpool) 1988, (Glasgow) 1990, (Lafayette) 1990, (Trinity Coll., Dublin) 1992, (Hull) 1993, (Belfast) 1994; Hon. DCL (Oxford) 1987; Hon. DLit (London) 2002. *Publications:* Action, Emotion and Will 1963, Responsa Alumnorum of English College, Rome (two Vols) 1963, Descartes 1968, The Five Ways 1969, Wittgenstein 1973, The Anatomy of the Soul 1974, Will, Freedom and Power 1975, Aristotelian Ethics 1978, Freewill and Responsibility 1978, The God of the Philosophers 1979, Aristotle's Theory of the Will 1979, Aquinas 1980, The Computation of Style 1982, Faith and Reason 1983, Thomas More 1983, The Legacy of Wittgenstein 1984, A Path from Rome 1985, The Logic of Deterrence 1985, The Ivory Tower 1985, Wyclif–Past Master 1985, Wyclif's De Universalibus 1985, Rationalism, Empiricism and Idealism 1986, Wyclif in His Times 1986, The Road to Hillsborough 1986, Reason and Religion (essays) 1987, The Heritage of Wisdom 1987, God and Two Poets 1988, The Metaphysics of Mind 1989, Mountains 1991, What is Faith? 1992, Aristotle on the Perfect Life 1992, Aquinas on Mind 1992, The Oxford Illustrated History of Western Philosophy (ed.) 1994, Frege 1995, A Life in Oxford 1997, A Brief History of Western Philosophy 1998, Essays on the Aristotelian Tradition 2001, Aquinas on Being 2002. *Address:* St John's College, Oxford, OX1 3JP, England.

KENNY, Gen. Sir Brian (Leslie Graham), GCB, CBE; British army officer (retd.); b. 18 June 1934; s. of late Brig. James W. Kenny, CBE and Aileen A. G. Swan; m. Diana C. J. Mathew 1958; two s.; ed Canford School; commissioned into 4th Hussars (later Queen's Royal Irish Hussars) 1954; served British Army of the Rhine (BAOR), Aden, Malaya, Borneo and Cyprus; pilot's course 1961; Ministry of Defence 1966–68; Instructor Staff Coll. 1971–73; CO Queen's Royal Irish Hussars, BAOR and UN, Cyprus 1974–76; Col G.S. 4 Armoured Div. 1977–78; Command, 12 Armoured Brigade (Task Force D) 1979–80; Royal Coll. of Defence Studies 1981; Commdr 1st Armoured Div. 1982–83; Dir Army Staff Duties, Ministry of Defence 1983–85; Command, 1st British Corps 1985–87; C-in-C BAOR and Commdr NATO's Northern Army Group 1987–89; Deputy Supreme Allied Commdr Europe 1989–93; Col Commandant RAVC 1983–95; Col QRIH 1985–93; Col Commandant RAC 1988–93; Gov. Royal Hosp. Chelsea 1993–99, Canford School 1988–; Chair. ABF 1993–99; Gov. (non-exec.) Dorset Ambulance Trust 2000–; Bath King of Arms 1999–. *Leisure interests:* theatre, cricket, tennis, golf, shooting, racing. *Address:* c/o Lloyds Bank, Camberley, Surrey, GU15 3SE, England.

KENSIT, Patsy, (Patricia Jude Kensit); British film actress; b. 4 March 1968, London; m. 1st Dan Donovan; m. 2nd Jim Kerr (divorced 1996); one s.; m. 3rd Liam Gallagher (divorced 2000) 1997; one s.; childhood film actress; also appeared in commercials; with brother James Kensit's band Eighth Wonder made successful pop album Fearless; Best Actress Ind. Spirit Awards 1992. *Films include:* The Great Gatsby, The Bluebird, Absolute Beginners, Chorus of Disapproval, The Skipper, Chicago Joe and The Showgirl, Lethal Weapon II, Twenty-One, The Skipper, Prince of Shadows, Does This Mean We're Married, Blame It On The Bellboy, The Turn of the Screw, Beltenebros, Bitter Harvest, Prince of Shadows, Angels and Insects, Grace of My Heart, Human Bomb, Janice Beard, Pavillions 1999, Best, Things Behind the Sun 2000, Bad Karma, Who's Your Daddy 2001, The One and Only 2001. *TV appearances:* Great Expectations, Silas Marner, Tycoon: The Story of a

Woman, Adam Bede, The Corsican Brothers (US TV), Aladdin. *Leisure interests:* horse-riding, skiing. *Address:* c/o Steve Dagger, 14 Lambton Place, London, W11 2SH, England. *Telephone:* (20) 7792-1040 (Office). *Fax:* (20) 7221-7625. *E-mail:* daggerents@aol.com (Office).

KENT, Bruce Eric, PhD; Australian historian; b. 15 Feb. 1932, Melbourne; s. of Rev. Eric Deacon Kent and Beatrice Maude Kent; m. Ann Elizabeth Garland 1966; two s.; ed Geelong Grammar School, Melbourne Univ., Univ. of Oxford, UK, ANU; Tutor in History, Melbourne Univ. 1954–55; lecturer in History, ANU 1962–70, Sr Lecturer 1970–90, Reader 1990–, Acting Head History Dept 1984, Visiting Fellow, Dept of Econ. History 1998; Fulbright Visiting Fellow, Hoover Inst., Stanford Univ. and History Dept, Princeton Univ., USA 1970; Visiting Lecturer, E China Normal Univ., Shanghai 1975–76; Pres. Australian Asscn of European Historians 1984–86; Visiting Fellow, Center of Int. Studies, Princeton Univ., USA, 1996; Victorian Rhodes Scholar 1955. *Publication:* The Spoils of War: the Politics, Economics and Diplomacy of Reparations, 1918–1932 1989. *Leisure interests:* violin, cricket, surfing. *Address:* School of Economics, Faculty of Economics and Commerce, Australian National University, Canberra, ACT 0200; 70 Dominion Circuit, Deakin, ACT 2600, Australia (Home). *Telephone:* (2) 6125-4721 (Office); (2) 6273-1019 (Home). *Fax:* (2) 6125-5792 (Office). *E-mail:* bruce.kent@anu.edu.au (Office).

KENT, HRH Prince Edward George Nicholas Paul Patrick, the Duke of; the Earl of St Andrew's and the Baron Downpatrick, KG, GCMG, GCVO, ADC; b. 9 Oct. 1935; s. of the late Duke of Kent (fourth s. of King George V) and Princess Marina (d. of late Prince Nicholas of Greece); m. Katherine Worsley 1961; two s. (George, Earl of St Andrew's and Lord Nicholas Windsor) one d. (Lady Helen Windsor); ed Eton Coll. and Le Rosey, Switzerland; Second Lt, Royal Scots Greys 1955; attended Army Staff Course 1966, later on staff, GOC Eastern Command, Hounslow, Major 1967; Lt-Col Royal Scots Dragoon Guards 1972, Maj. Gen. 1983, Deputy Col-in-Chief 1993–; rank of Field Marshal 1993; Ministry of Defence 1972–76; Chair. Nat. Electronics Council 1977–; Vice-Chair. British Overseas Trade Bd 1976–; Pres. All-England Lawn Tennis Club 1969–, Commonwealth War Graves Comm., RNLI 1969–, Football Asscn 1971–, Automobile Asscn 1973–, RAF Benevolent Fund 1974–, Scout Asscn 1975–, Royal Inst. of Great Britain 1976–, Business and Technicians Educ. Council 1984–, Eng Council 1989–, British Menswear Guild 1989–; Hon. Pres. Royal Geographical Soc. 1969–; Dir Vickers; Chancellor Univ. of Surrey 1977–; Patron Inst. of Export 1977–, Kent Opera 1978–, The London Philharmonic 1980–, Anglo-Jordanian Soc. 1982–, The Hanover Band 1992–, Anglo-German Asscn 1994; as Queen's Special Rep. has visited Sierra Leone 1961, Uganda 1962, The Gambia 1965, Guyana and Barbados 1966, Tonga 1967; ADC to HM The Queen 1967; Grand Master of the United Grand Lodge of England 1967–; Col-in-Chief Royal Regt of Fusiliers 1969–, Devonshire and Dorset Regt 1978–, Lorne Scots Regt 1978–; Col Scots Guards 1974; Hon. DCL (Durham), Hon. LLD (Leeds), DUniv (York); decorations from Greece, Nepal, Liberia and Jordan. *Leisure interests:* skiing, shooting, photography, opera. *Address:* York House, St James's Palace, London, SW1A 1BQ, England.

KENT, Francis William, PhD, DipEd, FAHA; Australian university teacher; b. 30 March 1942, Melbourne; m. 1st Dale V. Kent 1964 (divorced 1984); one d.; m. 2nd Carolyn James 1987; one s. one d.; ed Univ. of Melbourne and Univ. of London; Lecturer, Sr Lecturer and Reader in History, Monash Univ. 1971–, Personal Chair. 1989–, Prof. of History 1989–; Dir Monash Univ. in Prato 2000–; Fellow Harvard Univ. at Centre for Italian Renaissance Studies, Florence 1977–78, Visiting Scholar 1982, Visiting Prof. 1986–87; Robert Lehman Visiting Prof. 1995–96; Shouler Lecturer in History, Johns Hopkins Univ. 1999; Foundation Co-Ed. I Tatti Studies: Essays in the Renaissance 1982; Gen. Ed. Correspondence of Lorenzo de' Medici 2001–; Chair. Australian Foundation for Studies in Italy; Socio Straniero Deputazione di Storia Patria per la Toscana. *Publications:* Household and Lineage in Renaissance Florence 1977, A Florentine Patrician and His Palace (with others) 1981, Neighbours and Neighbourhood in Renaissance Florence (with D. V. Kent) 1982, Patronage, Art and Society in Renaissance Italy (ed. with P. Simons) 1987, Bartolomeo Cederni and his Friends (with G. Corti) 1991; numerous articles. *Leisure interests:* reading, gardening, travel. *Address:* 19 Downshire Road, Elsternwick, Vic. 3185, Australia.

KENTRIDGE, Sir Sydney, KCMG, QC, MA; British lawyer; b. 5 Nov. 1922, Johannesburg, South Africa; s. of Morris Kentridge and May Kentridge; m. Felicia Geffen 1952; two s. two d.; ed King Edward VII School, Johannesburg, Univ. of the Witwatersrand and Exeter Coll., Oxford; war service with S African forces 1942–46; Advocate, SA 1949, Sr Counsel 1965; called to Bar, Lincoln's Inn, London 1977, Bencher 1986; Queen's Counsel, England 1984; Judge, Court of Appeal, Jersey and Guernsey 1988–92; mem. Court of Appeal, Botswana 1981–89, Constitutional Court, SA 1995–97; Roberts Lecturer, Univ. of Pa 1979; Hon. Fellow American Coll. of Trial Lawyers 1998; Hon. Fellow Exeter Coll., Oxford 1986; Hon. mem. Bar Asscn New York City 2001; Hon. LLD (Leicester) 1985, (Cape Town) 1987, (Natal) 1989, (London) 1995, (Sussex) 1997, (Witwatersrand) 2000; Granville Clark Prize, USA 1978. *Leisure interests:* opera, theatre. *Address:* 7–8 Essex Street, London, WC2R 3LD, England. *Telephone:* (20) 7379-3550. *Fax:* (20) 7379-3558.

KENWORTHY, Duncan, OBE; British film producer; b. 9 Sept. 1949; worked as producer for Henson Org. 1979–95; Man. Dir Toledo Productions 1995–; Co-Chair. DNA Films Ltd 1997–; mem. Council BAFTA 1996–; Film Finance Forum 1998–; Dir Film Council 1999–; Chair. Film and TV Advisory Cttee, British Council 1999–, UK–China Forum 2000–01; British Producer of the Year, London Film Critics 1994. *Films produced include:* Dark Crystal 1982, Dream Child 1985, Four Weddings and a Funeral 1994, Gulliver's Travels 1996, Lawn Dogs 1997, Notting Hill 1998 (BAFTA Orange Audience Award 2000), The Parole Officer 2001, Love Actually 2003. *Address:* DNA Films, 75–77 Margaret Street, London, W1W 8BH, England (Office). *Telephone:* (20) 7291-8050 (Office). *Fax:* (20) 7291-8060 (Office).

KENWRIGHT, Bill, CBE; British theatre producer; b. 4 Sept. 1945; s. of Albert Kenwright and Hope Kenwright (née Jones); ed Liverpool Inst.; actor 1964–70; theatre producer 1970–; Vice-Chair. Everton Football Club; Dr hc (Liverpool John Moores) 1994; numerous awards. *Films directed include:* Stepping Out, Don't Go Breaking My Heart 1999. *Plays directed include:* Joseph and The Amazing Technicolor Dreamcoat 1979, The Business of Murder 1981, A Streetcar Named Desire 1984, Stepping Out 1984, Blood Brothers 1988, Shirley Valentine 1989, Travels With My Aunt 1993, Piaf 1993, Lysistrata 1993, Medea 1993, Pygmalion 1997, A Doll's House, An Ideal Husband, The Chairs 2000, Blood Brothers, Ghosts, The Female Odd Couple. *Leisure interest:* football. *Address:* Bill Kenwright Ltd, 106 Harrow Road, London, W2 1RR, England (Office). *Telephone:* (20) 7446-6200 (Office). *Fax:* (20) 7446-6222 (Office).

KENYATTA, Uhuru; Kenyan politician; b. 1961; s. of the late fmr Pres. Jomo Kenyatta; Chair. Kenya Tourism Bd 1999; nominated MP by Pres. Daniel arap Moi (q.v.); apptd Minister of Local Govt 2001; Vice-Chair. of Kenya African Nat. Union (KANU) 2002–; named heir apparent by Pres. Moi July 2002, failed to be elected in presidential elections Dec. 2002. *Address:* c/o Ministry of Local Government, Jogoo House 'A', Taifa Road, PO Box 30004, Nairobi, Kenya (Office). *Telephone:* (2) 217475 (Office). *E-mail:* mlog@form-net.org (Office).

KENYON, Nicholas Roger, CBE, BA; British broadcasting executive; b. 23 Feb. 1951; s. of Thomas Kenyon and Kathleen Holmes; m. Marie-Ghislaine Latham-Koenig 1976; three s. one d.; ed Balliol Coll., Oxford; music critic, The New Yorker 1979–82, The Times 1982–85, The Observer 1985–92; Music Ed., The Listener 1982–87; Controller, BBC Radio 3 1992–98, Dir BBC Proms 1996–, Controller, BBC Proms and Millennium Programmes 1998–2000, BBC Proms, Live Events and TV Classical Music 2000–; Royal Philharmonic Soc. Awards for Fairest Isle (BBC Radio 3) 1996 and Sounding the Century 2000. *Publications:* The BBC Symphony Orchestra 1930–80 1981, Authenticity and Early Music (ed.) 1988, The Viking Opera Guide (jtly) 1993, The Penguin Opera Guide (jtly) 1995, Simon Rattle: From Birmingham to Berlin 2001, Musical Lives (ed.) 2001. *Address:* c/o BBC, Broadcasting House, London, W1A 1AA, England (Office). *Telephone:* (20) 7765-4928 (Office). *Fax:* (20) 7765-0612 (Office).

KENZO (pseudonym of Kenzo Takada); Japanese fashion designer; b. 1940, Kyoto; ed art school in Japan; after graduating designed patterns for a Tokyo magazine; moved to Paris 1964; created own freelance collections and sold designs to Louis Féraud 1964–70; opened own shop Jungle Jap 1970; noted for translating traditional designs into original contemporary garments and for ready-to-wear knitwear.

KEOBOUNPHAN, Gen. Sisavat; Laotian politician; b. 1928, Houaphanh Prov.; Political Chief, then Head of mil. force, Rassavong armed unit 1949–52; Founding mem. Lao People's Revolutionary Party (LPRP) 1955, mem. Cen. Cttee 1955, 1972–75; Party Sec., Samneua Rallying Zone 1956–60; mem. admin. Bd for Supreme Command and Chief of Supreme Gen. Staff of Lao People's Army 1960–72; Minister attached to Prime Minister's Office and Minister of the Interior 1975–91; Maj. of Vientiane Municipality Admin. 1975–91; Minister of Agric. and Forestry 1991–96; Vice-Pres. of Laos 1996–98, Prime Minister of Laos 1998–2001. *Address:* c/o Office of the Prime Minister, Vientiane, Laos (Office).

KEOGH, James; American government official and journalist; b. 29 Oct. 1916, Nebraska; s. of David J. Keogh and Edith Dwyer Keogh; m. Verna Marion Pedersen; one s. one d.; joined Omaha Herald 1938, rising to Ed. 1948–51; contrib. to Time 1951, Ed. 1956–68; chief of research, Presidential election campaign 1968; special Asst to Pres. Nixon 1969–70; Dir US Information Agency 1973–76; Exec. Dir, Business Roundtable 1976–86; Dir The Philadelphia Fund 1987–2003; Trustee Taft Inst. 1987–92. *Publications:* This is Nixon 1956, President Nixon and the Press 1972, One of a Kind 1995, Living By Our Wicks 1999. *Leisure interest:* duplicate bridge. *Address:* 202 West Lyon Farm Drive, Greenwich, CT 06831, USA.

KEOGH, Lainey; Irish designer; b. 20 Sept. 1957; d. of Peter Keogh and Patricia Byrne; worked in medical sciences –1983; began to work with yarn in 1983; recognized for work by Int. Wool 1987; mem. Secr. Int. Festival du Lin 1989, British Fashion Council 1994; Man. Dir Lainey Keogh 1986–; developed fabrics for Dior couture studio 1998; Prix De Coeur (France) 1987; Cable Ace Award for Costume Design for film Two Nudes Bathing 1995, People of the Year Award (Ireland) 1997, Prix de Coeur (France) 1997. *Leisure interests:* sky, walking, looking. *Address:* 42 Dawson Street, Dublin 2, Ireland. *Telephone:* (1) 6793299. *Fax:* (1) 6794975.

KEOHANE, Robert Owen, PhD; American professor of political science; b. 3 Oct. 1941, Chicago, Ill.; s. of Robert Emmet Keohane and Marie Irene Keohane (née Pieters); m. Nannerl Overholser 1970; three s. one d.; ed Shimer Coll., Illinois, Harvard Univ.; Fellow Harvard Univ., Woodrow Wilson School of Public and Int. Affairs, Princeton Univ. 1961–62; mem. Woodrow Wilson Award Cttee 1982, Chair. Nominating Cttee 1990–91, Chair. Minority Identification Project 1990–92; Instructor, then Assoc. Prof. Swathmore Coll. 1965–73; Assoc. Prof., then Prof. Stanford Univ. 1973–81; Ed. Int. Org. 1974–80, mem. Bd Eds 1968–77, 1982–88, 1992–97, 1998–, Chair. 1986–87; Prof. Brandeis Univ. 1981–85; Pres. Int. Studies Asscn 1988–89, Chair. Nominations Cttee 1985; Prof., then Stanfield Prof. of Int. Peace, Harvard Univ. 1985–96, Chair. Dept of Govt 1988–92; Pres. American Political Science Asscn 1999–2000; currently James B. Duke Prof. of Political Science, Duke Univ.; Sherill Lecturer Yale Univ. Law School 1996; Research Fellow German Marshall Fund 1977–78; Fellow Council on Foreign Relations 1967–69, Center for Advanced Study in Behavioral Sciences 1977–78, 1987–88, American Acad. of Arts and Sciences 1983–, Guggenheim Foundation 1992–93; Sr Foreign Policy Fellow Social Science Research Council 1986–88; Bellagio Resident Fellow 1993; Frank Kenan Fellow Nat. Endowment for the Humanities 1995–96; Hon. PhD (Univ. of Aarhus, Denmark) 1988; Grawemeyer Award for Ideas Improving World Order 1989, First Mentorship Award, Soc. for Women in Int. Political Economy 1997. *Publications include:* After Hegemony: Cooperation and Discord in the World Political Economy 1984, Neorealism and Its Critics 1986, International Institutions and State Power: Essays in International Relations Theory 1989; (as co-Ed.): Transnational Relations and World Politics 1972, The New European Community: Decision-Making and Institutional Change 1991, Ideas and Foreign Policy 1993, From Local Commons to Global Interdependence 1994, Institutions for Environmental Aid: Pitfalls and Promises 1996, Internationalization and Domestic Politics 1996, Imperfect Unions: Security Institutions Across Time and Space 1999, Exploration and Contestation in the Study of World Politics 1998, Legalization and World Politics 2000; (as co-author): Power and Interdependence: World Politics in Transition 1977, Institutions for the Earth: Sources of Effective International Environmental Protection 1993, After the Cold War: State Strategies and International Institutions in Europe, 1989–91 1993, Designing Social Inquiry: Scientific Inference in Qualitative Research 1994. *Address:* Department of Politics, Duke University, Durham, NC 27708-0204 (Office); 1508 Pinecrest Road, Durham, NC 27705-5817, USA (Home). *Telephone:* (919) 660-4322 (Office). *Fax:* (919) 419-0289 (Office). *E-mail:* rkeohane@acpub.duke (Office).

KEOUGH, Donald Raymond, BS; American business executive (retd); b. 4 Sept. 1926, Maurice, Ia; s. of Leo H. Keough and Veronica (née Henkels) Keough; m. Marilyn Mulhall 1949; three s. three d.; ed Creighton Univ.; with Butter-Nut Foods Co., Omaha 1950–61, Duncan Foods Co., Houston 1961–67; Vice-Pres. and Dir Marketing Foods Div., The Coca-Cola Co., Atlanta, Ga 1967–71, Pres. 1971–73; Exec. Vice-Pres. Coca-Cola USA 1973–74, Pres. 1974–76; Exec. Vice-Pres. The Coca-Cola Co., Atlanta, Ga 1976–79, Sr Exec. Vice-Pres. 1980–81, Pres., COO and Dir 1981–93; Chair. Bd of Dirs., Coca-Cola Enterprises Inc., Atlanta, Ga 1986–93, Adviser to Bd 1993–98; Chair. Bd Allen & Co., Inc. 1993–, Convera 2002–; fmr Chair. Bd of Trustees, Univ. of Notre Dame, now Trustee Emer. *Address:* 200 Galleria Parkway, Suite 970, Atlanta, GA 30339, USA (Office).

KERDEL-VEGAS, Francisco, MD, MSc; Venezuelan dermatologist, physician and diplomatist; b. 3 Jan. 1928, Caracas; s. of Osvaldo F. Kerdel and Sofia Vegas de Kerdel; m. Martha Ramos de Kerdel 1977; two s. four d.; ed Liceo Andrés Bello, Caracas, Universidad Central de Venezuela, Harvard Univ. and New York Univ., USA; Prof. of Dermatology, Universidad Central de Venezuela 1954–77; Visiting Scientist, Dept of Experimental Pathology, ARC Inst., Cambridge, UK, mem. Trinity Coll. Cambridge; Scientific Attaché, Venezuelan Embassy, London 1966–67; Vice-Chancellor Simón Bolívar Univ. 1969–70; Amb. to UK 1987–92, to France (also Accred to UNESCO) 1995–99; Visiting Prof. United Medical and Dental Schools of Guy's and St Thomas's Hosps., Univ. of London 1990; mem. Nat. Research Council, Venezuela 1969–79; mem. Bd Universidad Metropolitana, Caracas 1970–, Int. Foundation of Dermatology 1987– (fmr Pres.); Co-Chair. Pan-American Medical Asscn 1990; Prosser White Oration, Royal Coll. of Physicians 1972; Fellow Venezuelan Acad. of Medicine, Venezuelan Acad. of Sciences, American Coll. of Physicians, American Acad. of Dermatology; Hon. Fellow Acad. of Medicine, Brazil, Chile; Hon. mem. Royal Soc. of Medicine, British Asscn of Dermatologists and Socs. of Dermatology of 15 other countries; Hon. DSc (Calif. Coll. of Podiatric Medicine) 1975, (Cranfield Inst. of Tech., UK) 1991; Orders of Andrés Bello, Cecilio Acosta, Francisco de Miranda, Diego de Losada, El Libertador; Hon. CBE; Chevalier, Légion d'honneur. *Publications:* Tratado de Dermatología 1959; chapters in textbooks on dermatology. *Leisure interests:* travelling, swimming, photography, reading. *Address:* c/o Ministry of Foreign Affairs, Edif. MRE, Avda Urdaneta, Esq. Carmelitas, Caracas 1010, Venezuela (Office).

KÉRÉKOU, Brig.-Gen. Mathieu (Ahmed); Benin politician and army officer; b. 2 Sept. 1933, Natitingou; ed Saint-Raphael Mil. School, France; served French Army until 1961; joined Dahomey Army 1961; Aide-de-camp to Pres. Maga 1961–63; took part in mil. coup d'état which removed Pres. Christophe Soglo 1967; Chair. Mil. Revolutionary Council 1967–68; continued studies at French mil. schools 1968–70; Commdr Ouidah Paratroop Unit and Deputy Chief of Staff 1970–72; leader of the mil. coup d'état which ousted Pres. Ahomadegbe Oct. 1972; Pres. and Head of Mil. Revolutionary Govt, Minister of Nat. Defence 1972–91, fmr Minister of Planning, of Co-ordination of Foreign Aid, Information and Nat. Orientation; Pres. of Benin 1996–;

Chair. Cen. Cttee Parti de la révolution populaire du Bénin. *Leisure interests:* cycling, football. *Address:* Présidence de la république, P.O. Box 1288, Cotonou, Benin. *Telephone:* 30-02-28. *Fax:* 30-06-36.

KERIMOV, Makhmud; Azerbaijani physicist; b. 18 Oct. 1948, Baku; m.; two c.; ed Baku State Univ.; mem. staff Inst. of Physics, Azerbaijan Nat. Acad. of Sciences 1979–, Prof. 2000–, mem. 2001, Pres. 2001–; mem. Int. Eco-Energy Acad. *Publications:* over 116 scientific papers and patents on chemical physics, radiation physics, chem. of condensed matter, electron spin resonance spectroscopy, environmental studies. *Address:* Azerbaijan National Academy of Sciences, Istiglaiyyat str. 10, 370001 Baku, Azerbaijan (Office). *Telephone:* (12) 92-35-29 (Office). *Fax:* (12) 92-56-99 (Office). *E-mail:* president@aas.ab.az (Office).

KERIN, John Charles, AM, BA, BEcons; Australian politician; b. 21 Nov. 1937, Bowral, NSW; s. of late Joseph Sydney and Mary Louise (née Fuller) Kerin; m. 1st Barbara Elizabeth Large (divorced 1981); one d.; m. 2nd Dr. June Rae Verrier 1983; ed Univ. of New England, Australian Nat. Univ.; Econs Research Officer in wool marketing, Bureau of Agricultural Econs 1971, 1975–78; MP for Macarthur, House of Reps 1972–75, for Werriwa 1978–93; Minister for Primary Industry 1983–87, for Primary Industries and Energy 1987–91, Treas. for Trade and Overseas Devt 1991–93; resgnd from Parl. 1993; Chair. Australian Meat and Livestock Corpn 1994–97; Dir Coal Mines Australia Ltd 1994–2001; Chair. Biologic Int. Ltd 1996–98; fmr Deputy Chancellor Univ. of Western Sydney, now mem. Bd of Trustees and Chair. Macarthur Council of the Univ.; Chair. NSW Forestry Comm. and Chair. or mem. of various pvt. and public orgs; Fellow Australian Inst. of Agricultural Science and Tech., Australian Acad. of Tech. Sciences and Eng; Australian Labor Party; Dr hc (New England) 1992, (Western Sydney) 1995, (Tasmania) 2001. *Leisure interests:* opera, bush-walking, classical music, reading. *Address:* P.O. Box 3, Garran, ACT 2605, Australia. *Telephone:* (6) 285-2480 (Home). *Fax:* (6) 282-5778 (Home). *E-mail:* kerrier1@bigpond.net.au.

KERKAVOV, Rovshen Bairamnazarovich; Turkmenistan politician and economist; b. 1961, Ashgabat; ed Novosibirsk Inst. of Electrotech.; engineer Turkmenpromsvyazstroi Co. 1983–84; engineer Ashgabat Gen. Post Office 1986; econ., Head of Div., Ashgabat Glavpochtamt Co. 1991–93; First Deputy Dir-Gen., then Dir-Gen. State Co. of Post Communications, Turkmenpochta 1995–97; Minister of Telecommunications Repub. of Turkmenistan 1997–2001; Deputy Chair. Cabinet of Ministers 2001; Order of Galkynysh. *Address:* c/o Cabinet of Ministers, Ashgabat, Turkmenistan (Office).

KERKELING, Hans-Peter; German comedian, writer, actor and television broadcaster; b. 9 Dec. 1964, Recklinghausen; ed Marie Curie Gymnasium, Recklinghausen; presenter, writer WDR TV 1985–87, BR TV 1988–89, RB TV 1989–91; actor, Dir NDR TV 1991–94; presenter, writer RTL TV 1994–95, SAT 1 TV 1998–; host SAT 1 show Darüber lacht die Welt. *Films:* Kein Pardon (cinema) 1992, Club Las Piranjas (NDR TV) 1995, Willi U.D. Winzors (NDR TV) 1996, Oma ist tot (NDR TV) 1997. *Recordings include:* Das ganze Leben ist ein Quiz 1991, Hurz 1991, Helsinki is Hell 1999; (albums) Ariola 1984, Kerkelings Kinderstunde 1985–87, Känguru, Comedy 1989–91; Goldene Kamera, Bronze Rose of Montreux, Grimme Preis, Telestar, Golden Gong, Europa 1991–93. *Publications:* Hannilein & Co. 1992, Kein Pardon 1993, Cheese 1994. *Address:* Postfach 32 06 30, 40421 Düsseldorf, Germany.

KERKORIAN, Kirk; American business executive; b. 6 June 1917, Fresno, Calif.; m. 1st Hilda Schmidt 1942 (divorced 1951); m. 2nd Jane Hardy 1954 (divorced); two d.; m. 3rd Lisa Bonder 1998 (divorced 1998); one d.; commercial airline pilot 1940; Capt. Transport Command, RAF 1942–44; f. LA Air Services (later Trans Int. Airlines Group) 1948, Int. Leisure Corpn 1968; CEO M.G.M. Inc. 1973–74, Chair. Exec. Cttee, Vice-Chair. M.G.M. 1974–79, controlling stockholder M.G.M./U.A. Communications Co., consultant 1979–; majority shareholder M.G.M. Grand. *Address:* M.G.M./U.A. Communications Co., 2500 Broadway Street, Santa Monica, CA 90404, USA.

KERMODE, Sir (John) Frank, Kt, MA, FBA, FRSL; British university professor; b. 29 Nov. 1919, Douglas, Isle of Man; s. of John Pritchard Kermode and Doris Kennedy; m. Maureen Eccles 1947 (divorced); one s. one d.; ed Liverpool Univ.; John Edward Taylor Prof., Manchester Univ. 1958–65; Winterstoke Prof., Bristol Univ. 1965–67; Lord Northcliffe Prof., Univ. Coll., London 1967–74; King Edward VII Prof., Cambridge Univ. 1974–82; Julian Clarence Levi Prof., Humanities Dept, Univ. of Columbia New York 1983, 1985; Charles Eliot Norton Prof. of Poetry, Harvard Univ. 1977–78; Foreign mem. American Acad. Arts and Sciences, Academia dei Lincei, Rome 2002; Hon. mem. American Acad. of Arts and Letters 1999–; Officier, Ordre des Arts et des Sciences; Hon. DHL (Chicago); Hon. DLitt (Liverpool) 1981, (Amsterdam) 1994; Yale 1995, (Wesleyan) 1997, (London) 1997. *Publications:* Romantic Image 1957, Wallace Stevens 1960, The Sense of an Ending 1967, Lawrence 1973, The Classic 1975, The Genesis of Secrecy 1979, The Art of Telling 1983, Forms of Attention 1985, History and Value 1988, The Literary Guide to the Bible (ed. with Robert Alter) 1989, An Appetite for Poetry 1989, Poetry, Narrative, History 1989, The Uses of Error 1991, The Oxford Book of Letters (with Anita Kermode) 1995, Not Entitled: A Memoir 1995, Shakespeare's Language 2000, Pleasing Myself 2001, Pieces of My Mind 2003. *Leisure interest:* music. *Address:* 9 The Oast House, Grange Road, Cambridge, CB3 9AP, England. *Telephone:* (1223) 357931. *Fax:* (1223) 303790. *E-mail:* frankkermode@lineone.net (Home).

KERNAN, Roderick Patrick, PhD, DSc, MRIA; Irish professor of physiology; b. 20 May 1928, Dublin; s. of Dermod Kernan and Pauline (Hickey) Kernan; m. Mary Cecily Kavanagh 1956; one s. one d.; ed Synge Street Boys' School, Univ. Coll. Dublin; Research Assoc., Dept of Reproductive Physiology, Rockefeller Inst., New York, USA 1957–58; Sr Fellow Medical Research Council of Ireland 1958–66; Rae Prof. of Biochemistry, Royal Coll. of Surgeons in Ireland 1965–67; Assoc. Prof. of Gen. Physiology Univ. Coll. Dublin 1966–93, Emer. Prof. 1993; Visiting Prof. of Physiology, George Washington Univ., Washington, DC 1969–70; elected mem. Royal Irish Acad. 1965, mem. Council 1977–81, 1986–90, 1993–, Vice-Pres. 1978, 1986, Sec. for Science 1993–2000; elected mem. Physiological Soc. 1963. *Publications:* Cell K 1965, Cell Potassium 1980. *Leisure interests:* hill walking, photography, gardening, painting, music. *Address:* Royal Irish Academy, 19 Dawson Street, Dublin 2 (Office); 37 Templeville Drive, Dublin 6W, Ireland (Home). *Telephone:* (1) 6762570 (Office). *Fax:* (1) 6762346.

KERNAN, Gen. William F., MA; American army officer; b. Fort Sam Houston, Tex.; m. Marianne Purnell; one s.; ed US Army Command and Gen. Staff Coll., US Army War Coll.; commissioned Infantry Officer 1968; commanded two Airborne Cos, two Ranger Cos, an Airborne Infantry Battalion, the 75th Ranger Regt; exchange officer 3rd Battalion, Parachute Regt, UK; Asst Div. Commdr (Manoeuvre) 7th Infantry Div.; Dir Plans, Policy and Assessments, J5, US Special Operations Command; Commdr 101st Airborne Div. (Air Assault), XVIII Airborne Corps and Fort Bragg; combat tours Viet-Nam, Grenada, Panama; rank of Gen. 2000; Supreme Allied Commdr, Atlantic (SACLANT) and C-in-C US Jt Forces Command, Norfolk, Va 2000–; Defense Distinguished Service Medal, Distinguished Service Medal (with oak leaf cluster), Legion of Merit (with 3 oak leaf clusters), Bronze Star Medal with "V" device, Bronze Star Medal (with oak leaf cluster), Purple Heart, Meritorious Service Medal (with 3 oak leaf clusters), Air Medal and other medals and badges. *Address:* Office of Supreme Allied Commander, Atlantic, 7857 Blandy Road, Suite 100, Norfolk, VA 23551-2490, USA (Office). *Website:* www.saclant .nato.int (Office).

KERR, David Nicol Sharp, CBE, MSc, FRCP, FRCPE; British physician; b. 27 Dec. 1927, London; s. of William Kerr and Elsie Ransted; m. (Mary) Eleanor Jones 1960; two s. one d.; ed George Watson's Boys' School and Univs of Edinburgh and Wisconsin; Surgeon-Lt RDVR 1953–55; Surgeon Lt-Commdr RNR 1993–95; Prof. of Medicine, Univ. of Newcastle-upon-Tyne 1968–83; Dean, Royal Postgrad. Medical School 1984–91; Prof. of Renal Medicine, Univ. of London 1986–93, Prof. Emer. 1993–; medical adviser and trustee Nat. Kidney Research Fund 1999–, Chair. 2000–; Postgrad. Medical Adviser, North Thames Regional Health Authority, later Nat. Health Service (NHS) Exec. N Thames Regional Office 1991–97; Medical Awards Admin. Commonwealth Scholarships Comm. 1993–98; Ed. Journal of Royal Coll. of Physicians 1994–98; mem. Council, British Heart Foundation 1991–97; Hon. consultant renal physician, Hammersmith Hosp.; Volhard Medal (German Medical Foundation), Distinguished Overseas Medal (Nat. Kidney Foundation of USA) etc. *Publications:* Oxford Textbook of Clinical Nephrology (ed.); other books, book sections and articles in professional journals. *Leisure interests:* walking, theatre, opera, church. *Address:* 22 Carbery Avenue, London, W3 9AL, England (Home); National Kidney Research Fund, Kings Chambers, Priestgate, Peterborough, PE1 1FG, England (Office). *Telephone:* (20) 8992-3231 (Home); (1733) 704-664 (Office). *Fax:* (20) 8992-3231; (1733) 704-660 (Office). *E-mail:* enquiries@nkrf.org.uk (Office); DNSKerr@aol.com (Home). *Website:* www.nkrf.org.uk (Office).

KERR, Deborah Jane, CBE; British actress; b. 30 Sept. 1921, Helensburgh, Dunbarton, Scotland; d. of Arthur Kerr Trimmer and Colleen Smale; m. 1st Anthony Bartley 1945 (divorced 1959); two d.; m. 2nd Peter Viertel 1960; one step-d.; ed Rossholme Prep., Weston-super-Mare, Northumberland House, Bristol; began acting career at Open Air Theatre, Regent's Park 1939; first film Contraband, first major role as Jenny Hill in film Major Barbara; went to Hollywood 1946; film awards include four New York Drama Critics' Awards, 1947 (two), 1957, 1960; Hollywood Foreign Press Asscn Awards 1956 (for The King and I), 1958; Variety Club of GB Award 1961; six Acad. Award Nominations; awards for plays include Donaldson and Sarah Siddons Awards for Tea and Sympathy; BAFTA Special Award 1991; Hon. Acad. Award 1994. *Films include:* Major Barbara 1940, Love on the Dole 1940, Penn of Pennsylvania 1940, Hatter's Castle 1941, The Day Will Dawn 1941, The Life and Death of Colonel Blimp 1942, Perfect Strangers 1944, Black Narcissus 1945, I See a Dark Stranger 1945, The Hucksters 1946, If Winter Comes 1947, Edward My Son 1948, The Prisoner of Zenda 1948, Young Bess 1949, King Solomon's Mines 1950, Quo Vadis 1950, Rage of The Vulture 1951, Dream Wife 1952, From Here to Eternity 1953, The End of the Affair 1954, The Proud and the Profane 1955, The King and I 1956, Heaven Knows Mr. Allison 1957, An Affair to Remember 1957, Separate Tables 1957/58, The Journey 1958, The Blessing 1958, Beloved Infidel 1960, The Sundowners 1960, The Innocents 1961, The Chalk Garden 1963, The Night of the Iguana 1963, Marriage on the Rocks 1965, Gypsy Moths 1968, The Arrangement 1968/69, The Assam Garden 1984, Reunion at Fairborough 1984. *Plays:* Heartbreak House 1943, Tea and Sympathy 1953 (US tour 1954/55), The Day After the Fair (US tour 1973/74), Seascape 1974/75, Souvenir 1975, Long Day's Journey Into Night (US) 1977, Candida (London) 1977, The Last of Mrs. Cheyney (US tour 1978), The Day After the Fair (Australian tour 1979), Overheard (London and UK tour 1981), The Corn is Green (London) 1985. *Television:* A Song at Twilight

1981, Witness for the Prosecution (TV film) 1982, Ann & Debbie, 1984, A Woman of Substance 1984, Hold the Dream 1986. *Leisure interests:* painting, gardening. *Address:* Klosters, 7250 Grisons, Switzerland.

KERR, Sir John Olav, GCMG; British diplomatist and international public servant; b. 22 Feb. 1942, Grantown-on-Spey, Scotland; s. of Dr and Mrs J. D. O. Kerr; m. Elizabeth Kalaugher 1965; two s. three d.; ed Glasgow Acad. and Pembroke Coll. Oxford; entered diplomatic service 1966; served Moscow and Rawalpindi; Pvt. Sec. to Perm. Under-Sec. FCO 1974–79; Head DM1 Div. HM Treasury 1979–81; Prin. Pvt. Sec. to Chancellor of Exchequer 1981–84; Head of Chancery, Washington, DC 1984–87; Asst Under-Sec. of State, FCO 1987–90; Amb. and Perm. Rep. of UK to EC (now EU), Brussels 1990–95; Amb. to USA 1995–97; Perm. Under-Sec. of State and Head of HM Diplomatic Service 1997–2002; Sec.-Gen. European Convention 2002; Dir Shell Transport and Trading, Scottish-American Investment Trust; Trustee Rhodes Trust, Oxford, Nat. Gallery, London; Hon. LLD (St Andrews) 1996, (Glasgow) 1999. *Address:* c/o Council Secretariat, 175 rue de la Loi, 1048 Brussels, Belgium. *Telephone:* (2) 285-5071 (Office).

KERR, Philip Ballantyne, LLM; British writer and novelist; b. 22 Feb. 1956, Edin.; s. of William Kerr and Ann Brodie; m. Jane Thynne 1991; two s. one d.; ed Northampton Grammar School and Birmingham Univ.; Prix de Romans L'Aventures, Deutsches Krimi Prize. *Play:* Bluesbreakers 2002. *Publications:* March Violets 1989, The Pale Criminal 1990, The Penguin Book of Lies 1990, A German Requiem 1991, Fights, Feuds and Heartfelt Hatreds 1992, A Philosophical Investigation 1992, Dead Meat 1993, Gridiron 1993, Esau 1996, A Five Year Plan 1997, The Second Angel 1998, The Shot 1999, Dark Matter 2002. *Leisure interest:* cinema. *Address:* c/o A. P. Watt Literary Agents, 20 John Street, London, WC1N 2DR, England. *Telephone:* (20) 7405-6774. *Fax:* (20) 7430-1952. *E-mail:* philip.kerr@dial.pipex.com (Office); philip.kerr@dsl .pipex.net (Home).

KERREY, Bob (J. Robert), BS; American politician; b. 27 Aug. 1943, Lincoln, Neb.; s. of James Kerrey and Elinor Kerrey; m. 1st; one s. one d.; m. 2nd Sarah Paley 2001; one s.; ed Univ. of Nebraska; owner, founder, developer, outlets in Omaha and Lincoln, Grandmother's Skillet Restaurant 1972–75; owner, founder fitness enterprises, including Sun Valley Bowl and Prairie Life Fitness Center, Lincoln, Neb.; Gov. of Nebraska 1983–87; Partner, Printon, Kane & Co., Lincoln 1987; Senator from Nebraska 1989–2001; Pres. New School Univ., New York 2001–; Democrat; Medal of Honor; Bronze Star; Purple Heart. *Address:* New School University, Johnson and Kaplan Building, 66 W 12th Street, New York, NY 10011, USA (Office).

KERRUISH, Sir (Henry) Charles, Kt, OBE; Manx politician and farmer; b. 23 July 1917, Isle of Man; s. of Henry Howard Kerruish and Clara May Kewin; m. 1st Margaret Gell 1944; one s. three d.; m. 2nd Kay Warriner 1975; three step-d.; ed Ramsey Grammar School; mem. House of Keys, Isle of Man 1946–90, Speaker 1962–90; First Pres. of Tynwald and of Legislative Council, Isle of Man 1990–; fmr Chair. Health Services Bd, Tynwald and mem. Gov.'s Exec. Council; Regional Councillor Commonwealth Parl. Asscn 1975–77, Pres. 1983–84; mem. Court, Liverpool Univ. 1974–90; Pres. Manx Loaghtan Sheep Breed Soc.; Capt. Parish of Maughold; Order of Merit (Norway); Hon. DIur (Lancaster Univ.) 1990. *Leisure interests:* horse breeding, motor cycling, reading. *Address:* Ballafayle, Maughold, Isle of Man. *Telephone:* (1624) 812293.

KERRY, John Forbes, JD; American politician; b. 11 Dec. 1943, Denver; s. of Richard J. and Rosemary (Forbes) Kerry; m. 1st Julia S. Thorne 1970; two d.; m. 2nd Teresa Heinz 1995; ed Yale Univ. and Boston Coll.; US Navy 1966–70; called to Bar, Mass. 1976; Nat. co-ordinator, Vietnam Veterans Against The War 1969–71; Asst Dist Attorney, Middx County, Mass. 1976–79; Partner, Kerry & Sragow, Boston 1979–82; Lieut Gov. State of Mass. 1982–84; Senator from Massachussetts 1985–; Democrat; awarded Bronze Star, Silver Star, 3 Purple Hearts. *Publications:* The New Soldier 1971, The New War: the Web of Crime That Threatens America's Security 1997. *Address:* United States Senate, 304 Russell Senate Office Building, Washington, DC 20510, USA.

KERTÉSZ, Imre; Hungarian author and translator; b. 9 Nov. 1929, Budapest; m.; deported to Auschwitz, then Buchenwald during Second World War 1944; worked for newspaper Világosság, Budapest 1948–51 (dismissed when it adopted CP line); mil. service 1951–53; ind. writer and translator of German authors such as Nietzsche, Schnitzler, Freud, Roth, Wittgenstein and Canetti 1953–; has also written musicals for the theatre; his works have been translated into French, Swedish, German and English; Brandenburger Literaturpreis 1995, Leipziger Buchpreis zur Europäischen Verständigung 1997, WELT-Literaturpreis 2000, Ehrenpreis der Robert-Bosch-Stiftung 2001, Hans-Sahl-Preis 2002, Nobel Prize in Literature 2002. *Publications include:* Sorstalanság (Fateless 1992) 1975, A nyomkeresö (The Pathfinder) 1977, A kudarc (Fiasco) 1988, Kaddis a meg nem született gyermekért (Kaddish for a Child not Born 1997) 1990, Az angol labogó (The English Flag) 1991, Gályanapló (Galley Diary) 1992, A Holocaust mint kultúra (The Holocaust as Culture) 1993, Jegyzökönyv 1993, Valaki más: a változás kró'nikája (I, Another: Chronicle of a Metamorphosis) 1997, A gondolatnyi csend, amig kivégzöoztag újratölt (Moment of Silence while the Execution Squad Reloads) 1998, A számüzött nyelv (The Exiled Language) 2001. *Address:* c/o Magvetö Press, Balassi B.U. 7, 1055 Budapest, Hungary (Office); c/o Northwestern University Press, 625 Colfax Street, Evanston, IL 60208-4210, USA (Office).

KERTZER, David I., PhD; American historian; b. 20 Feb. 1948, New York City; ed Brown Univ., Brandeis Univ.; Asst Prof. of Anthropology Bowdoin Coll. 1973–79, Assoc. Prof. 1979–84, Prof. 1984–89, William R. Kenan Jr Prof. 1989–92, Chair. Dept of Sociology and Anthropology 1979–81, 1984–86, 1987–88, 1992; Paul Dupee Jr Univ. Prof. of Social Science, Brown Univ. 1992–, also Prof. of Anthropology 1992–, of History 1992–2001, of Italian Studies 2001–; Fulbright Sr Lecturer, Univ. of Catania 1978; Professore a contratto Univ. of Bologna 1987; Visiting Fellow Trinity Coll. Cambridge 1991; Visiting Scholar Posthumous Inst. and Univ. of Amsterdam 1994; Visiting Dir of Studies Ecole des Hautes Etudes en Sciences Sociales, Paris 1994; Prof. of Educ. American Acad. of Rome 1999; Fulbright Chair. Univ. of Bologna 2000; Visiting Prof. Ecole Normale Superieure, Paris 2002; guest lecturer at over 40 univs across the world; Co-Founder and Co-Ed. Journal of Modern Italian Studies 1994–; Ed. Book Series: New Perspectives in Anthropological and Social Demography 1996–; Pres. Soc. for the Anthropology of Europe 1994–96; mem. Ed. Bd Social Science History 1987–96, 2001–(04), Journal of Family History 1990–, Continuity and Change 1996–2000, Int. Studies Review 1998–2002; mem. Jury Lynton History Prize 2000–01; mem. Exec. Bd American Anthropological Asscn 1995–96, Nat. Inst. of Health Population Review Cttee 1996–99, Social Science History Asscn Publs Cttee 1998–, Nat. Research Council Cttee on Population 1999–, German Marshall Fund Advisory Bd 2000–02; contrib. to numerous nat. and state newspapers; Guggenheim Fellowship 1986, Nat. Endowment for the Humanities Fellowship 1995, Rockefeller Foundation Fellowship, Bellagio, Italy 2000. *Publications include:* Comrades and Christians: Religion and Political Struggle in Communist Italy 1980, Famiglia Contadina e Urbanizzazione 1981, Family Life in Central Italy 1880–1910: Sharecropping, Wage Labour and Coresidence (Marraro Prize, Soc. for Italian Historical Studies 1985) 1984, Ritual, Politics and Power 1988, Family, Political Economy and Demographic Change (Marraro 1990) 1989, Sacrificed for Honor: Italian Infant Abandonment and the Politics of Reproductive Control 1993, Politics and Symbols: The Italian Communist Party and the Fall of Communism, 1996, The Kidnapping of Edgardo Mortara (Nat. Jewish Book Award 1997, Best Book of the Year, Publishers Weekly, Toronto Globe and Mail 1997; stage version 'Edgard Mine' by Alfred Uhry premiered 2002) 1997, The Popes Against the Jews (UK edn The Unholy War 2002) 2001; contrib., ed. or co-ed. of numerous books; author of over 60 journal articles and 50 academic papers. *Address:* Department of Anthropology, Box 1921, Brown University, Providence, RI 02912, USA (Office). *Telephone:* (401) 863-3251 (Office). *Fax:* (401) 863-7588 (Office). *E-mail:* David_Kertzer@Brown.edu (Office). *Website:* www.davidkertzer.com (Office).

KERWIN, Larkin, CC, DSc, LLD, FRSC; Canadian physicist; b. 22 June 1924, Québec City; s. of Timothy Kerwin and Catherine Kerwin (née Lonergan); m. Maria G. Turcot 1950; five s. three d.; ed St Francis Xavier Univ., Massachusetts Inst. of Tech., Laval Univ.; research physicist, Geotech. Corpn, Cambridge 1945–46; Asst Prof. of Physics, Laval Univ. 1948–51, Assoc. Prof. 1951–56, Prof. 1956, Chair. Physics Dept 1961–67, Vice-Dean, Faculty of Sciences 1967–69, Vice-Rector 1969–72, Rector 1972–77, Prof. Emer. 1991–; Vice-Pres. Natural Sciences and Eng Research Council, Canada 1978–80; Pres. Nat. Research Council of Canada 1980–89; Pres. Canadian Space Agency 1989; developed an ion optics theory; invented inflection mass spectrometer; developed electron selector; discovered P8 and numerous excited states in various atoms and molecules; research into determination of isotopic abundance ratios; Pres. Canadian Asscn of Physicists 1954–55, Int. Scientific and Tech. Affiliations Cttee of Nat. Research Council 1972–80, Acad. of Science, Royal Soc. of Canada 1973–74, Asscn of Univs. and Colls. of Canada 1974–75, Royal Soc. of Canada 1976; Sec.-Gen. Int. Union of Pure and Applied Physics 1972–84, First Vice-Pres. 1984–87, Pres. 1987–90; mem. Bd of Dirs., Canada-France-Hawaii Telescope Corpn 1973–78; mem. Acad. des Grands Québecois 1995–; Fellow, Canadian Acad. of Engineers 1987; Allan Lecturer, Univ. of Alberta 1987; Ordre nat. du Québec 1988; Officier, Légion d'honneur 1989; Hon. LLD (St Francis Xavier) 1970, (Toronto) 1973, (Concordia) 1976, (Alberta) 1983, (Dalhousie) 1983; Hon. DSc (British Columbia) 1973, (McGill) 1974, (Memorial, Newfoundland) 1978, (Ottawa) 1981, (Royal Mil. Coll.) 1982, (Winnipeg) 1983, (Windsor) 1984, (Moncton) 1985; Hon. DCL (Bishop's) 1978; Hon. DUniv (Montreal) 1991; Prix David 1951, Centennial Medal 1967, Medal of Canadian Asscn of Physicists 1969, Silver Jubilee Medal 1977, Laval Alumni Medal (Gloire de l'Escolle) 1978, Canadian Council of Professional Engineers Gold Medal 1982, Médaille Rousseau, ACFAS 1983, Golden Jubilee Medal 2002. *Publications:* Atomic Physics: An Introduction 1963; and 50 scientific articles. *Address:* 2166 Bourbonière Park, Sillery, Québec, G1T 1B4, Canada (Home). *Telephone:* (418) 527-7949 (Home). *Fax:* (418) 527-2844 (Home).

KERZNER, Sol(omon); South African business executive; b. 23 Aug. 1935, Johannesburg; s. of Morris Kerzner; two s. three d.; ed Athlons High School, Univ. of Witwatersrand; Founder and CEO Southern Sun Hotels 1969–83; CEO Sun Int. Hotels (South Africa) 1983–87, Chair. 1994–; Chair. World Leisure Group 1989–94; rep. Univ. of Witwatersrand for boxing and wrestling 1954–55; Inst. of Marketing Man. Marketing Award of the Year 1978–80, Jewish Businessman of the Year 1993.

KESTELMAN, Sara; British actress; d. of late Morris Kestelman and Dorothy Mary Creagh; ed Cen. School of Speech and Drama; joined Liverpool Playhouse; subsequently moved to Library Theatre, Manchester; roles included Abigail in The Crucible and Cecily in The Importance of Being Earnest; joined Royal Shakespeare Co. (RSC) 1969; roles for RSC included Mariana in Measure for Measure, Jessie Tate in The Silver Tassle, Margaret in Much Ado About Nothing, Cassandra in Troilus and Cressida, Natasha in Subject to Fits, Titania in A Midsummer Night's Dream and Cleopatra in Gorky's Enemies; other stage appearances have included Messalina in I Claudius (Queen's Theatre, London), Lady Macbeth and Ruth in The Homecoming (Birmingham Repertory Theatre), Prudence in Plunder and Ilyena in Uncle Vanya (Bristol Old Vic), Nine (Donmar) 1996, Hamlet 2000; has appeared in several TV plays. *Film:* Zardoz. *Television includes:* Tom Jones 1997, Kavanagh QC 1997, Anna Karenina 2000. *Publication:* A Two Hander (poems, with Susan Penhaligon) 1996. *Leisure interests:* drawing, photography, writing.

KESWICK, Sir Chippendale (Chips) (see Keswick, Sir J. C. L.).

KESWICK, Henry Neville Lindley; British business executive; b. 29 Sept. 1938; s. of late Sir William Keswick and of Mary Lindley; a brother of Sir (John) Chippendale Keswick (and of Simon Lindley Keswick, q.v.); m. Lady Tessa Reay 1985; ed Eton Coll., Cambridge Univ.; Nat. Service 1956–58; Dir Sun Alliance and London Insurance PLC 1975–96, Sun Alliance Group PLC 1989–, Deputy Chair. 1993–96, Dir Royal and Sun Alliance Insurance Group PLC 1996–2000; Dir Robert Fleming Holdings Ltd 1975–2000, Rothmans Int. 1988–94, Hongkong Land Co. 1988–, Mandarin Oriental Int. 1988–, Dairy Farm Int. Holdings 1988–, The Daily Telegraph 1990–2001; Chair. Matheson & Co. 1975–, Jardine Matheson Holdings Ltd, Hong Kong 1972–75, 1989– (Dir 1967–), Jardine Strategic Holdings 1989– (Dir 1988–); Chair. Hong Kong Asscn 1988–2001; mem. 21st Century Trust 1987–97; Propr The Spectator 1975–81; Trustee Nat. Portrait Gallery 1982–2001 (Chair. 1994–2001). *Leisure interest:* country pursuits. *Address:* Matheson & Co. Ltd, 3 Lombard Street, London, EC3V 9AQ, England. *Telephone:* (20) 7816-8100. *Fax:* (20) 7623-5024 (Office).

KESWICK, Sir (John) Chippendale Lindley, (Chips), Kt; British merchant banker; b. 2 Feb. 1940; s. of late Sir William Keswick and of Mary Lindley; brother of Henry N. L. Keswick and Simon L. Keswick, q.v.; m. Lady Sarah Ramsay 1966; three s.; ed Eton Coll., Univ. of Aix-Marseilles; with Glyn Mills & Co. 1961–65; Jt Vice-Chair. Hambros PLC 1986, Jt Deputy Chair. 1990–97, Group Chief Exec. 1995–97; Chair. Hambros Bank Ltd 1986–95, Chair. (non-exec.) 1995–98, Chair. Hambros PLC 1997–98; Sr Banking and Capital Markets Adviser Société Générale 1998–; Dir Persimmon PLC 1984–, De Beers 1993–, Bank of England 1993–2000, Edin. Investment Trust PLC 1992–, IMI PLC 1994–, Anglo American Corpn of S Africa Ltd 1995; Vice-Counsellor Cancer Research Campaign 1992–, Chair. Investec Bank Ltd 2000–; Hon. Treas. Children's Country Holidays Fund; mem. Queen's Body Guard for Scotland, Royal Co. of Archers 1976–. *Leisure interests:* bridge, country pursuits. *Address:* 17 Charterhouse Street, London, EC1N 6RA (Office); De Beers, 17 Charterhouse Street, London, EC1N 6RA, England. *Telephone:* (20) 7430-3553 (Office). *Fax:* (20) 7430-8670 (Office).

KESWICK, Simon Lindley, FRSA; British business executive; b. 20 May 1942; s. of late Sir William Keswick and of Mary Lindley; brother of Henry N. L. Keswick and Sir John Chippendale Lindley Keswick (q.v.); m. Emma Chetwode 1971; two s. two d.; ed Eton Coll. and Trinity Coll., Cambridge; Dir Fleetways Holdings Ltd, Australia 1970–72, Greenfriar Investment Co. 1979–82, Matheson & Co. Ltd 1978–82; Chair. Jardine Matheson Insurance Brokers 1978–82; Dir Jardine Matheson & Co. Ltd, Hong Kong 1972–, Man. Dir 1982, Chair. 1983–89; Chair. Hongkong Land Holdings Ltd 1983–, Hongkong & Shanghai Banking Corpn 1983–88, Jardine Matheson Holdings Ltd 1984–89 (Dir 1972–), Mandarin Oriental Int. 1984–, Dairy Farm Int. Holdings Ltd 1984–, Jardine Strategic Holdings Ltd 1987–89, (Dir 1987–), Fleming Mercantile Investment Trust 1990– (Dir 1988–), Jardine Int. Motor Holdings 1990–97, Trafalgar House PLC 1993–96; Dir Hanson PLC 1991–; Dir Jardine Lloyd Thomson Group PLC 2001–; Dir (non-exec.) Wellcome 1995–; Trustee British Museum 1989–. *Leisure interests:* country pursuits, Tottenham Hotspur. *Address:* May Tower 1, 5–7 May Road, Hong Kong Special Administrative Region, People's Republic of China; Rockcliffe, Upper Slaughter, Cheltenham, Glos., GL54 2JW, England. *Telephone:* (1451) 30648 (England).

KESWICK, Tessa; British administrator and fmr civil servant; b. Anabel Therese Fraser, 15 Oct. 1942, Beauly, Scotland; d. of 15th Lord Lovat and Rosamund Broughton; m. 1st Lord Reay 1964 (divorced 1978); two s. one d.; m. 2nd Henry Keswick (q.v.) 1985; ed Sacred Heart Convent, Woldingham, Surrey; Conservative Councillor, Royal Borough of Kensington and Chelsea 1982–86; Conservative Cand. for Inverness 1987; special policy adviser to Rt Hon Kenneth Clarke at Dept of Health 1989, Dept of Educ., Home Office, Treasury –1995; Dir Centre for Policy Studies 1995–. *Leisure interests:* art, music, breeding horses. *Address:* Centre for Policy Studies, 57 Tufton Street, London, SW1P 3QL, England. *Telephone:* (20) 7222-4488. *Fax:* (20) 7222-4388. *Website:* www.cps.org.uk.

KETELAAR, Jan Arnold Albert, PhD; Netherlands university professor (retd); b. 21 April 1908, Amsterdam; s. of Albert Jan Ketelaar and L. C. M. Struycken; m. Sytske Bessem 1949 (deceased); three s.; ed Univ. of Amsterdam and California Inst. of Technology, Pasadena; Priv Doz Chemical Crystallography, Univ. of Leiden 1936–40, Lecturer in Physical Chemistry 1940–41; Prof. of Physical Chemistry and Chemical Thermodynamics, Univ. of Amsterdam 1941–60; Visiting Prof. of Chemistry, Brown Univ., Providence, RI 1958–59; Prof. of Electrochemistry, Univ. of Amsterdam 1960–78; mem.

Nat. Bd of Educ. 1960–78; mem. Royal Netherlands Acad. of Sciences. *Publications:* Monomorphe overgangen in de kristalstructuren van zilverwikjodide, natriumnitraat en aluminium fluoride 1933, De Chemische Binding 1947, 1952, 1966, Physische Scheikunde 1950, Chemical Constitution 1953, 1958, Liaisons et propriétés chimiques 1960, Chemische Konstitution 1964, Chemical History in Fuel Cell Systems 1993. *Address:* Tusseler 115, 7241 KD Lochem, Netherlands (Home). *Telephone:* (573) 54480.

KETTANI, M. Ali, PhD; Moroccan professor of electrical engineering; b. 27 Sept. 1941, Fez; m.; four c.; ed Swiss Fed. Inst. of Tech., Geneva and Lausanne Univs., Carnegie Mellon Univ.; instructor Ecole d'Ingenieurs, Rabat 1964; Asst Prof. Electrical Eng Dept, Univ. of Pittsburgh 1966–68; Assoc. Prof. Electrical Eng Dept, Univ. of Riyadh 1968–69, Univ. of Petroleum and Minerals, Dhahran 1969–73, Head of Dept 1972–74, Prof. 1973–82; Visiting Prof. MIT 1975–76; Dir Gen. Islamic Foundation for Science, Tech. and Devt 1981–89; Fellow, Sec. Gen. Islamic Acad. of Sciences 1986–94, Vice-Pres. 1994–; f. Ibn Rushd Int. Islamic Univ., Córdoba; mem. Bd Int. Fed. of Insts of Advanced Studies, Stockholm; mem. Energy Research Group, Ottawa, Exec. Cttee Islamic Educ., Science and Culture Org. 1982–86, Arab Thought Forum, Amman. *Publications:* 12 books in English and Arabic and more than 150 articles on energy issues. *Address:* Islamic Academy of Sciences, P.O. Box 830036, Amman, Jordan (Office). *Telephone:* 5523385 (Office). *Fax:* 5511803 (Office). *E-mail:* secretariat@ias-worldwide.org (Office). *Website:* www .ias-worldwide.org (Office).

KETTERLE, Wolfgang, MSc, PhD; German physicist; b. 21 Oct. 1957, Heidelberg; m.; three c.; ed Univ. of Heidelberg, Univ. of Munich, Max-Planck Inst. for Quantum Optics, Garching; Research Asst Max-Planck Inst. for Quantum Optics, Garching 1982–85; Staff Scientist 1985–88; Research Scientist Dept of Physical Chemistry, Univ. of Heidelberg 1989–90; Research Assoc. Dept of Physics, MIT, Mass. 1990–93, Faculty mem. 1993–, Asst Prof. of Physics 1993–97, Prof. of Physics 1997–98, John D. MacArthur Prof. of Physics 1998–; Fellow American Physical Soc. 1997, American Acad. of Arts and Sciences 1999; mem. German Physical Soc., Optical Soc. of America; Michael and Philip Platzman Award, MIT 1994, Gustav-Hertz Prize, German Physical Soc. 1997, Rabi Prize, American Physical Soc. 1997, Discover Magazine Award for Tech. Innovation 1998, Fritz London Prize 1999, Benjamin Franklin Medal in Physics 2000, Nobel Prize in Physics (jt recipient) 2001. *Address:* Massachusetts Institute of Technology, Room 26–243, 77 Massachusetts Avenue, Cambridge, MA 02139 (Office); 24 Grassmere Road, Brookline, MA 02467, USA (Home). *Telephone:* (617) 253-6815 (Office); (617) 327-7421 (Home). *Fax:* (617) 253-4876 (Office). *E-mail:* ketterle@mit.edu (Office).

KEUTCHA, Jean; Cameroonian politician, civil servant and diplomatist; b. June 1923, Bangangté; m.; three c.; ed École supérieure d'agriculture de Yaoundé; Chef de Cabinet, Minister of State with Special Responsibilities 1957, subsequently Chef de Cabinet, Sec. of State with responsibility for Information, Posts and Telecommunications; Asst to Chief of Bamiléké Region 1959; Sub-Prefect, Bafoussam 1960; Prefect of Mifi, subsequently of Menoua 1962–64; Sec. of State for Public Works 1964, subsequently Sec. of State for Rural Devt and Sec. of State for Educ.; Minister of Foreign Affairs 1971–72, 1975–80, of Agric. 1972–75; Amb. to EEC 1984–85, to People's Repub. of China 1985–88; Pres. Caisse nationale de réassurances (CNR); Commdr Ordre Camerounais de la Valeur, Grand Officier, Légion d'honneur, Grand Officier de l'Ordre National Gabonais, etc. *Publication:* Le Guide pratique pour la taille du Caféier Arabica. *Address:* Caisse nationale de réassurances, avenue Foch, BP 4180, Yaoundé, Cameroon. *Telephone:* 22-37-99. *Fax:* 23-36-80.

KÉVÉS, György; Hungarian architect; b. 20 March 1935, Osi; s. of Sándor Kévés and Silányi Piroska; m. Éva Földvári 1966; ed Tech. Univ., Budapest; designer for firms, Agroterv and Eliti, Budapest 1959–61, Iparterv, Budapest 1961–69, Studio 'R' 1983–; private practice with Éva Földvári 1966–; teacher, Faculty of Architecture, Tech. Univ., Budapest 1966–73; Sr Architect and Prof., Architectural Masterschool, Budapest 1974–; with Káva Architects 1987–, Kévés Architects SA; organizes confs and exhbns Masterschool, including exhbns of post-modern architecture and Mario Bótta's works 1980–; organized lectures by Rob Krier and Mario Bótta, Hungary 1980; Visiting Lecturer, Washington Univ., St Louis, USA 1981; exhbns: Budapest, Milano Triennale 1973, Stuttgart 1977, Canada 1978, Washington Univ. St Louis 1983; Ybl Prize; Hungarian State Prize; several first prizes in architecture competitions. *Publications include:* Architecture of the 70s, Architecture of the 20th century; numerous articles in architectural magazines. *Leisure interest:* all kinds of art. *Address:* Kévés és Épitésztársai Rt. 1121 Budapest, Melinda u. 21, Hungary.

KEYFITZ, Nathan, PhD, FRSC; American demographer; b. 29 June 1913, Montreal, Canada; s. of Arthur Keyfitz and Anna (née Gerstein) Keyfitz; m. Beatrice Orkin 1939; one s. one d.; ed McGill Univ. and Univ. of Chicago, USA; Statistician, then Sr Research Statistician, Dominion Bureau of Statistics, Ottawa 1936–56; Lecturer in Sociology, McGill Univ. 1948–51; Adviser to Indonesian Planning Bureau, Jakarta 1952–53; Prof. of Sociology, Univ. of Montreal 1962–63, Univ. of Toronto 1959–63, Univ. of Chicago 1963–68, Chair. Dept of Sociology 1965–67; Prof. of Demography, Univ. of Calif., Berkeley 1968–72; Andelot Prof. of Sociology and Demography, Harvard Univ. 1972–83, Prof. Emer. 1983–, Chair. Dept of Sociology 1978–80; Lazarus Prof. of Social Demography, Ohio State Univ. 1981–83, Prof. Emer. 1983–;

Visiting Fellow Statistics Canada 1983–; Leader Population Programme, Deputy Dir, Int. Inst. for Applied Systems Analysis, Laxenburg, Austria 1984–93; Consultant, Dept of Finance, Jakarta, Indonesia 1984–90; researcher Initiatives on Children, American Acad. of Arts and Sciences 1994–2000; mem. NAS, Int. Statistical Inst.; Fellow American Statistical Asscn; Pres. Population Asscn of America 1970; Life Trustee, Nat. Opinion Research Center; hon. mem. Canadian Statistical Soc. 1980–; Hon. MA (Harvard), Hon. LLD (Western Ont., Montreal, McGill, Alberta, Edmonton, Siena, Carleton). *Publications:* Applied Mathematical Demography 1985, Introduction to the Mathematics of Population 1977, Population Change and Social Policy 1982, World Population Growth and Aging (jtly) 1990. *Leisure interests:* computers, foreign languages. *Address:* 1580 Massachusetts Avenue, Apt. 7C, Cambridge, MA 02138, USA (Home). *Telephone:* (617) 491 2845 (Home). *Fax:* (617) 491 7396 (Home).

KEYNES, Richard Darwin, CBE, MA, PhD, ScD, FRS; British scientist; b. 14 Aug. 1919, London; s. of late Sir Geoffrey Keynes and Margaret Elizabeth Darwin; m. Anne Pinsent Adrian; four s. (one deceased); ed Oundle School and Trinity Coll., Cambridge; Temporary Experimental Officer, Anti-Submarine Establishment and Admiralty Signals Establishment 1940–45; Demonstrator, later Lecturer in Physiology Univ. of Cambridge 1949–60; Research Fellow, Trinity Coll., Cambridge 1948–52; Fellow of Peterhouse, Cambridge and Dir of Studies in Medicine 1952–60; Head of Physiology Dept, Agricultural Research Council Inst. of Animal Physiology, Babraham 1960–65, Dir of Inst. 1965–73; Prof. of Physiology, Univ. of Cambridge 1973–86; Sec.-Gen. of Int. Union for Pure and Applied Biophysics 1972–78, Vice-Pres. 1978–81, Pres. 1981–84; Chair. ICSU/UNESCO Int. Biosciences Networks 1982–93; Pres. Fed. European Physiological Socs. 1991–94; Foreign mem. Royal Danish Acad. 1971, American Philosophical Soc. 1977, American Acad. of Arts and Sciences 1978, Acad. Brasileira de Ciências 1995; Fellow of Churchill Coll., Cambridge 1961–, Fellow of Eton 1963–78; Hon. Fellow Peterhouse, Cambridge 1989; Dr hc (Brazil) 1968, (Rouen) 1995, (Nairobi) 1999; Ordem Nacional do Mérito Científico (Brazil) 1997. *Publications:* The Beagle Record (ed.) 1979, Nerve and Muscle (with D. J. Aidley) 1981, Charles Darwin's Beagle Diary 1988, Lydia and Maynard: the letters between Lydia Lopokova and John Maynard Keynes (co-ed.) 1989, Charles Darwin's Zoology Notes and Specimen Lists from HMS Beagle 2000, Fossils, Finches and Fuegians: Charles Darwin's Adventures and Discoveries on the Beagle, 1832–1836 2002. *Leisure interest:* pre-Columbian antiquities. *Address:* 4 Herschel Road, Cambridge, CB3 9AG; Primrose Farm, Wiveton, Norfolk, NR25 7TQ, England. *Telephone:* (1223) 353107; (1263) 740317. *E-mail:* rdk12@cam.ac.uk (Home).

KHACHATRYAN, Armen; Armenian politician and philologist; b. 13 Aug. 1957, Yerevan; s. of Avag Khachatryan and Johanna Hovakimyan; m. Larisa Khachatryan; one s. two d.; ed Yerevan State Pedagogical Inst.; Instructor Shaumyan Regional CP Cttee and Yerevan City Comsomol Cttee 1981–87; Dir Yerevan School 191 1987–90; Founder and Vice-Pres. for Science and Educ. Yerevan Univ. of Hrachya Asharyan, Prof. 1991–99; Deputy, Chair. Standing Cttee on Foreign Relations, People's Chair. Nat. Ass. 1999–; Prof. New York Acad. of Sciences; Academican NY Acad. of sciences; Sodruzhestvo Award, Council Inter-Parl. Ass. of CIS 2001, Saint Andreas Order, Patriarch of Constantinople. *Address:* National Assembly, 19 M. Baghramyan Avenue, 375095 Yerevan, Armenia (Office). *Telephone:* (3741) 524614 (Office). *Fax:* (3741) 529826 (Office). *E-mail:* lata@parliament.am. *Website:* www .parliament.am.

KHADDAM, Abd al-Halim; Syrian politician; Minister of the Economy and Foreign Trade 1969–70; Deputy Prime Minister and Minister of Foreign Affairs 1970–84; Vice-Pres. for Political and Foreign Affairs 1984–; mem. Regional Command, Baath Party 1971–84. *Address:* Office of the President, Damascus, Syria. *Website:* www.assad.org (Office).

KHADDURI, Majid, BA, LHD, PhD, LLD; Iraqi writer and educationalist; b. 27 Sept. 1909, Mosul, Iraq; m. Majdia Khadduri 1942 (died 1972); one s. one d.; ed American Univ. of Beirut and Univ. of Chicago; Sec.-Treas. Baghdad PEN Club; mem. American Soc. of Int. Law; Iraqi del. to the 14th Conf. of the PEN Clubs in Buenos Aires 1936; mem. the Iraq del. at the San Francisco Conf. 1945; Visiting Lecturer in Near Eastern Politics at Indiana Univ. 1947–48; fmr Prof. Modern Middle-Eastern History at the Higher Teachers' Coll., Baghdad, taught Middle East politics at Chicago and Harvard Univs 1949–50; Prof. Middle East Studies, Johns Hopkins Univ. 1950–80, Prof. Emer. 1980–; Dir of Research and Education, Middle East Inst. 1950–80; Visiting Middle East Prof., Columbia Univ.; mem. American Political Science Asscn and Pres. Shaybani Soc. of Int. Law (Washington); Corresp. mem. Acad. of Arabic Language, Cairo, Iraqi Acad.; Order of Rafidain (Iraq), Order of Merit, 1st Class (Egypt). *Publications:* The Liberation of Iraq from the Mandate (in Arabic) 1935, The Law of War and Peace in Islam 1941, The Government of Iraq 1944, The System of Government in Iraq (in Arabic) 1946, Independent Iraq 1951, War and Peace in the Law of Islam 1955, Islamic Jurisprudence 1961, Modern Libya 1963, The Islamic Law of Nations 1966, Republican Iraq 1969, Political Trends in the Arab World 1970, Arab Contemporaries 1973, Socialist Iraq 1978, Arab Personalities in Politics 1981, The Islamic Conception of Justice 1983, The Gulf War 1988, War in the Gulf 1990–91 1997, Contemporary Iraq 2001. *Leisure interest:* long-distance walking. *Address:* 1740 Massachusetts Avenue, NW, Washington, DC 20036 (Office); 4454 Tindall Street, NW, Washington, DC 20016, USA (Home). *Telephone:* (202) 966-2702.

KHADJIEV, Salambek Naibovich, DChemSc; Russian/Chechen professor of chemistry and politician; b. 7 Jan. 1941, Rovnoye, Kazakh SSR; m.; one s. two d.; ed Grozny Oil Inst., Moscow Univ.; Sr researcher, Hon. Dir Inst. of Oil 1983–87; Dir Scientific Production Union Grozneftekhim 1987-91; USSR People's Deputy 1989-91; Minister of Petroleum Refining and Petrochemicals, USSR 1991; Chair. Democratic Reforms Movt in Chechen Rep. 1991–93; Chair. State Cttee of Industrial Policy, Russian Fed. 1995–96, Vice-Pres. Asscn of Financial and Industrial Groups 1996–; Chair. Bd Ecotec-oil Co. Moscow; Corresp. mem. Russian Acad. of Sciences 1990–; Ed.-in-Chief Petroleum Chemistry magazine; Chair. Scientific Bd of Petrochemistry, Russian Acad. of Sciences; Fellow Islamic Acad. of Sciences in Amman; Hon. Oil-Chemist of the USSR 1990. *Publications:* Cracking of Oil – Fractions over Zeolite Catalysts; more than 250 scientific publs and more than 120 inventions. *Address:* Institut Neftekhimsintes, Leninski prosp. 29, 117912 Moscow (Office); bld. 12 42/44 Mytnaya Street, 115035 Moscow, Russia. *Fax:* (095) 236-12-62 (Home). *E-mail:* ecotek@dol.ru (Office). *Website:* khadzhiev@ipsac .ru.

KHAIN, Viktor Yefimovich, DSc; Russian geologist; b. 26 Feb. 1914, Baku; s. of Sophia and Yefim Khain; m. Valentina Kuzmina 1949; two s.; ed Azerbaijan Industrial Inst.; geologist at oil fields, Azerbaijan 1935–39; Assoc. Azerbaijan Oil Research Inst. 1939–41; army service 1941–45; mem. CPSU 1943–90; Sr Assoc., Inst. of Geology, Acad. of Sciences, Azerbaijan SSR 1945–54; Prof. Azerbaijan Industrial Inst. 1949–54; Head of Dept Museum of Earth Sciences, Moscow Univ. 1954–60; Senior Assoc., Vernadsky Inst. of Geochemistry and Analytical Chem., USSR Acad. of Sciences 1957–71; Prof. Geology Dept, Moscow Univ. 1961–94, Prof. Emer. 1994–; Sec.-Gen. Subcomm. for the Tectonic Map of the World, Int. Geological Congress 1972–87, Pres. 1988–; Senior Assoc., Geological Inst., USSR Acad. of Sciences 1972–91, Inst. of the Lithosphere, Russian Acad. of Sciences 1991–; Corresp. mem. USSR Acad. of Sciences 1966–87, mem. 1987; mem. New York Acad. of Sciences 1994; Hon. mem. Moscow Soc. of Naturalists, Bulgarian Geological Soc., Acad. Europaea 1994; Foreign mem. Soc. Géologique de France, Geological Soc. of London, Georgian Acad. of Sciences 1996; Hon. Prof. of Earth Sciences, Changchun Univ. 1996; Hon. DSc (Univ. P. et M. Curie, Paris) 1977; State Prize, USSR 1987, Prestwich Prize, Soc. Géologique de France 1990, Steinmann Medaille, Geologische Vereinigung (GDR) 1991, Karpinsky Gold Medal (USSR Acad. of Sciences) 1991, Fourmarier Medaille d'Or (Acad. Royale de Belgique) 1993, Lomonosov Prize (Moscow Univ.) 1993, State Prize, Russia 1995. *Publications include:* Geotectonic Principles of Oil Prospecting 1954, The Geology of Caucasus (with E. E. Milanovsky) 1963, General Geotectonics 1964, Regional Geotectonics (5 Vols) 1971–85, Geology of USSR 1985, General Geology 1988 (co-author), Historical Geotectonics (Vol. 1) 1988 (with N. A. Bozhko), (Vol. 2) 1991 (with K. B. Seslavinsky), (Vol. 3) 1993 (with A. .N Balukhovsky), Geology of Northern Eurasia 1994, Main Problems of Modern Geology 1994, Geotectonics and Principles of Geodynamics (with M. G. Lomize) 1995, History and Methodology of Geological Sciences (with A. G. Ryabunkin) 1996, Historical Geology (with N. V. Koronovsky and N. A. Yasamanov) 1997. *Address:* Institute of the Lithosphere of Marginal Seas, 22 Staromonetny per., 109180 Moscow (Office); 54 Frunzenskaya emb., apt. 18, 119270 Moscow, Russia (Home). *Telephone:* (095) 939-11-09; (095) 203-81-23 (Office); (095) 242-44-47 (Home). *Fax:* (095) 233-55-90.

KHAIRULLAYEV, Saidullo Khairullayevich; Tajikistan politician; b. 10 Aug. 1945, Garm region; ed Tashkent Higher CPSU School, Tajik Inst. of Agric.; engineer, Chief Engineer, then Head of Div. Garm irrigation system 1969–75; Chair. Exec. Cttee Garm Regional Soviet of People's Deputies 1975–77, Chair. Regional Soviet 1979–85; First Sec. Soviet region CP of Tajikistan 1985–88; Sec. Ktalon Regional CP Cttee 1988–90; Deputy Prime Minister of Tajikistan 1991–92; Minister of Environmental Protection, then Minister of Nature Protection 1992–94; Chair. Govt Cttee on Precious Metals 1994–95, Govt Cttee on Land Construction and Land Reform 1999–2000; Pres. Majlisi Namoyandagon (House of Reps of Majlisi Oli–Parl.) April 2000–. *Address:* Majlisi Oli, Majlisi Namoyandagon, Rudaki prosp. 42, 734051 Dushanbe, Tajikistan (Office). *Telephone:* (3772) 21-22-53 (Office).

KHAKAMADA, Irina Mutzuovna, Cand.Econ.; Russian politician; b. 13 April 1955, Moscow; m. 3rd Vladimir Sirotinsky; three c.; ed Univ. of Friendship of Peoples in Moscow; mem. Research Inst. State Planning Cttee 1981–85; teacher Tech. Inst. of Automobile Factory 1985–89; Sr expert Russian Stock Exchange of Raw Materials 1990; mem. Party of Econ. Freedom 1992, Sec.-Gen and Co-Chair. 1992–94; Pres. Liberal Women's Foundation 1994; mem. State Duma 1993–97, 1999–, Head, Right Forces faction, Deputy Chair. 2000–; Leader pre-election union Obshcheye Delo 1995; Chair. State Cttee for Support of Small Enterprises 1997–98; Founder and Co-Leader pre-election union Pravoye Delo, transformed later into Union of Right Forces party 1999, Co-Chair. 2000–. *Publications:* The Maiden Name, Peculiarities of National Politics; and numerous articles. *Address:* State Duma, Okhotny Ryad 1, 103265 Moscow, Russia. *Telephone:* (095) 292-80-41 (Office). *Fax:* (095) 292-44-38 (Office).

KHALATNIKOV, Isaac Markovich, DPhysMathSc; Russian theoretical physicist; b. 17 Oct. 1919, Dniepropetrovsk; m. Valentina Nikolaevna Shchors; two d.; ed Dniepropetrovsk State Univ., USSR Acad. of Sciences; Jr researcher, Sr researcher, head of div. Inst. of Physical Problems USSR Acad. of Sciences 1945–65; Dir L.D. Landau Inst. of Theoretical Physics, USSR (now Russian) Acad. of Sciences 1965–92, Hon. Dir 1992–; Adviser Russian Acad. of Sciences 1993–; Prof. Moscow Inst. of Physics and Tech. 1954–; Prof., Tel-

Aviv Univ. School of Physics and Astronomy 1993–; f., Pres. Landau Network Centro Volta, Como, Italy 1995; Corresp. mem. USSR Acad. of Sciences 1972, mem. 1984; Foreign mem. Royal Soc. 1994; USSR State Prize 1953, Landau Prize in Physics 1976, Alexander von Humboldt Award 1989, Kiwani Club Int. Prize 1999. *Publications:* more than 150 papers on solid state physics, relativistic cosmology, quantum field theory. *Leisure interests:* chess, draughts. *Address:* Landau Institute, Kosygina str. 2, 117940 Moscow, Russia. *Telephone:* (095) 137-32-44.

KHALID, Dato' Ghazzali Sheikh Abdul, BEcons; Malaysian diplomatist; b. 20 March 1946; ed Univ. of La Trobe, Australia; Deputy Perm. Rep. to UN and Security Council, NY; Deputy High Commr to UK; High Commr to Zimbabwe; Dir-Gen. Inst. of Diplomacy and Foreign Relations, Malaysia; Deputy Sec.-Gen. Ministry of Foreign Affairs; currently Amb. to USA. *Leisure interests:* reading, walking. *Address:* Embassy of Malaysia, 3516 International Court, NW, Washington, DC 20008, USA (Office). *Telephone:* (202) 572-9700 (Office). *Fax:* (202) 572-9882 (Office). *E-mail:* malwashdc@kln.gov.my (Office).

KHALID, Mansour, LLD; Sudanese diplomatist and lawyer; b. 13 Dec. 1931, Omdurman; s. of Khalid Mohammed and Sara Sawi; ed Univs. of Khartoum, Pennsylvania and Paris; began his career as an attorney, Khartoum 1957–59; Legal officer, UN, New York 1962–63; Deputy UN resident rep., Algeria 1964–65; Bureau of Relations with Member States, UNESCO, Paris 1965–69; Visiting Prof. of Int. Law, Univ. of Colo 1968, Univ. of Khartoum 1982; Minister of Youth and Social Affairs, Sudan 1969–71; Chair. of del. of Sudan to UN Gen. Ass., Special Consultant and Personal Rep. of UNESCO Dir-Gen. for UNWRA fund-raising mission 1970; Perm. Rep. of Sudan to UN 1971; Pres. UN Security Council; Minister of Foreign Affairs 1971–75, of Educ. 1975–77, of Foreign Affairs Feb.–Sept. 1977; Asst to Pres. for Co-ordination and Foreign Affairs 1976, Asst to Pres. for Co-ordination 1977; fmr mem. Political Bureau and Asst Sec.-Gen., Sudan Socialist Union 1978; resgnd from all political posts July 1978 but remained mem. of Gen. Congress of the Sudan Socialist Union; Chair. Bureau of Trilateral Co-operation, Khartoum 1978–80; Personal Rep. for Exec. Dir of UNEP Anti-desertification Programme 1981–82; UN Special Consultant on Co-ordination of UN Information System 1982; Chair. Univ. Devt Cttee, Univ. of Khartoum 1982; Fellow, Woodrow Wilson Center, Smithsonian Inst. 1978–80, Financial and Investment Consultant 1980–; Loyal Son of Sudan and numerous foreign decorations. *Publications:* Private Law in Sudan 1970, The Nile Basin, Present and Future 1971, Solution of the Southern Problem and its African Implications 1972, The Decision-Making Process in Foreign Policy 1973, Sudan Experiment with Unity 1973, A Dialogue with the Sudanese Intellectuals, Nimeiri and the Revolution of Dis-May 1985, 1985, The Government They Deserve: the role of the elite in Sudan's political evolution 1990. *Leisure interests:* music, gardening. *Address:* P.O. Box 2930, Khartoum, Sudan (Home); 9 Jubilee Palace, London, SW3, England.

KHALIFA, HM Sheikh Hamad bin Isa al-, King of Bahrain; b. 28 Jan. 1950, Bahrain; s. of the late Sheikh Isa bin Salman al- Khalifa; m. Sheikha Sabeeka bint Ibrahim Al-Khalifa 1968; six s. four d.; ed Secondary School, Manama, Bahrain, Leys School, Cambridge Univ., Mons Officer Cadet School, Aldershot, England and US Army Command and Gen. Staff Coll., Fort Leavenworth, Kan., USA; formed Bahrain Defence Force 1968, Commdr-in-Chief 1968–, also C-in-C Nat. Guard, raised Defence Air Wing 1978; mem. State Admin. Council 1970–71; Minister of Defence 1971–88; Deputy Pres. Family Council of Al-Khalifa 1974–; succeeded as Ruler on the death of his father March 1999; introduced constitutional monarchical system and assumed title of King Feb. 2002; created Historical Documents Centre 1976; Founder mem. and Pres. Bahrain High Council for Youth and Sports 1975–; initiated Al-Areen Wildlife Parks Reserve 1976; f. Salman Falcon Centre 1977, Amiri Stud, Bahrain 1977; f. Bahrain Equestrian and Horse Racing Asscn, Pres. 1977–; f. Bahrain Centre for Studies and Research 1989; Hon. mem. Helicopter Club of GB; Orders of the Star of Jordan (1st Class) 1967, Al-Rafidain of Iraq (1st Class) 1968, National Defence of Kuwait (1st Class) 1970, Al-Muhammedi of Morocco (1st Class) 1970, Al-Nahdha of Jordan (1st Class) 1972, Qiladat Gumhooreeya of Egypt (1st Class) 1974, The Taj of Iran (1st Class) 1973, King Abdul-Aziz of Saudi Arabia (1st Class) 1976, Repub. of Indonesia (1st Class) 1977, Repub. of Mauritania (1st Class) 1969, El-Fateh Al-Adheem of Libya (1st Class) 1979, Kuwait Liberation 1994, Hon. KCMG (UK), Ordre nat. du Mérite de la République française (1st Class) 1980, Grand Cross of Isabel la Católica of Spain (1st Class) 1981; Freedom of the City of Kansas 1971, US Army Certificate of Honour 1972. *Leisure interests:* horse riding, golf, study of ancient history and prehistory of Bahrain, water skiing, swimming, fishing, falconry, shooting, football, tennis. *Address:* P.O. Box 555, Ritala Palace, Manama, Bahrain.

KHALIFA, Brig.-Gen. Khalifa bin Ahmed al-; Bahraini army officer; b. 20 June 1945, Muharraq, Bahrain; ed Royal Mil. Acad., Sandhurst; platoon Commdr; training co. Commdr; Infantry Co. Commdr; Bn second in command; Battalion Commdr; fmr Chief of Staff, Bahrain Defence Force. *Address:* c/o Ministry of Defence, P.O. Box 245, West Rifaa, Bahrain. *Telephone:* 661-656.

KHALIFA, Sheikh Khalifa bin Sulman al-; Bahraini politician; b. 1935; s. of the late Sheikh Sulman and brother of the ruler, Sheikh Isa; Dir of Finance and Pres. of Electricity Bd 1961; Pres. Council of Admin. 1966–70; Pres. State Council 1970–73, Prime Minister 1973–; fmr Chair. Bahrain

Monetary Agency. *Address:* Office of the Prime Minister, P.O. Box 1000, Government House, Government Road, Manama, Bahrain. *Telephone:* 253361. *Fax:* 533033.

KHALIFA, Sheikh Muhammad bin Mubarak bin Hamad al-, BA; Bahraini politician; b. 1935; s. of Sheikh Mubarak bin Hamad al-Khalifa; m.; two c.; ed American Univ. of Beirut, Oxford Univ. and Univ. of London; attended Bahrain Courts as cand. for the bench, Dir of Information 1962; head Political Bureau 1968 (now Dept of Foreign Affairs); State Council 1970; Minister of Foreign Affairs 1971–. *Address:* Ministry of Foreign Affairs, P.O. Box 547, Government House, Government Road, Manama, Bahrain. *Telephone:* 227555. *Fax:* 212603.

KHALIFA, Sheikh Salman bin Hamad al-, BPA, MA; Bahraini Crown Prince and politician; s. of HH Sheikh Hamad bin Isa Al-Khalifa; ed American Univ., Washington, DC, USA, Cambridge Univ., UK; Under-Sec. for Defence 1995–99, Crown Prince and C-in-C Bahrain Defence Force 1999–; Chair. Bd of Trustees Bahrain Centre for Studies and Research 1995–. *Address:* Ministry of Defence, P.O. Box 245, West Rifa'a, Bahrain (Office). *Website:* www.bahrainembassy.org/rulingfam (Office).

KHALIFA BIN HAMAD AL-THANI, Sheikh (see Thani, Sheikh Khalifa bin Hamad al-).

KHALIKYAR, Fazle Haq; Afghanistan politician; b. 1934, Shahr-e Naw, Herat; s. of Gholam Yahya; ed Kabul Univ.; Govt employee in Ministry of Planning 1958–60; Ministry of Internal Affairs 1962–64, Ministry of Communications 1966–67; Gen. Auditor, Kabul Prov.; Admin. Pres. Ministry of Finance 1969; Gov. Baghlan Prov. 1971; Deputy Minister of Finance 1971–72, First Deputy Minister of Finance 1972–81; Minister Counsellor, Council of Ministers and Gov.-Gen. North-Western Zone 1981–90; Prime Minister of Afghanistan 1990; Hero of the Republic.

KHALIL, Idriss, PhD; Moroccan professor of mathematics; b. 20 Dec. 1936, El Jadida; m.; two c.; ed Rabat Univ., Univ. of Bordeaux, Univ. of Nancy, Univ. of Paris; Asst lecturer, Univ. of Bordeaux 1963–65; Asst lecturer, then Sr lecturer, then prof., Univ. Mohammed V, Rabat Univ. 1966–; Jr lecturer, Univ. of Nancy 1968–70; research Asst CNRS 1968–72; lecturer, Bielefeld Univ. 1973; Dean, Faculty of Sciences, Univ. Mohammed V, Rabat Univ. 1974–85; Prof. Univ. of Nancy, MIT, Ecole Polytechnique, Paris and Paris-Sud Univ. 1979–85; fmr Minister of Educ. and Higher Educ.; Ed. Afrika Mathematika 1979; founder mem. Math. Africa Union 1976, African Asscn for the Advancement of Science and Tech.; Corresp. mem. Int. Asscn for Peace (PUGWASH) 1979; mem. Royal Acad. of Morocco 1982, Int. Asscn of French-Speaking Communities; Founding Fellow Islamic Acad. of Sciences; Chevalier Palmes Académiques 1979, Ordre Nat. du Mérite 1982, Ordre du Trône (Morocco) 1982. *Address:* Université Mohammed V, BP 554, 3 rue Michlifen, Agdal, Rabat, Morocco (Office). *Telephone:* 67-13-18 (Office). *Fax:* 67-14-01 (Office).

KHALIL, Mustafa, MSc, DPhil; Egyptian politician, engineer and banker; b. 18 Nov. 1920, El Kalyoubieh; ed Univ. of Cairo, Illinois Univ., USA; served in Egyptian State Railways 1941–47, 1951–52; training with Chicago-Milwaukee Railways (USA) 1947; lecturer in Railways and Highway Engineering, Ain Shams Univ., Cairo 1952; Tech. Consultant to Transport Cttee, Perm. Council for Nat. Production 1955; Minister of Communications and Transport 1956–64, of Industry, Mineral Resources and Electricity 1965–66; Deputy Prime Minister 1964–65; resgnd. from Cabinet 1966; Head of Broadcasting Corpn 1970; Prime Minister 1978–80, also Minister of Foreign Affairs 1979–80; Deputy Chair. Nat. Democratic Party May 1980; Chair. Arab Int. Bank, Cairo 1980–. *Leisure interest:* music. *Address:* Arab International Bank, P.O. Box 1563, 35 Sharia Abd al-Khalek Sarwat Street, Cairo (Office); 9A El Maahad El Swisry Street, Zamalek, Cairo, Egypt (Home). *Telephone:* (2) 3918794 (Office); 3416111 (Home). *Fax:* (2) 3916233.

KHALILI, Abdul Karim; Afghanistan politician; Leader Hezb-i-Wahdat-i-Islami (Unity Party, UP) an alliance of anti-Taliban fighters from Hazara ethnic minority, located in Bamian prov.; driven out of Cen. Afghanistan by Taliban 1998; Leader Bamian prov. 2001–.

KHALILOV, Erkin Khamdamovich, CAND. JUR.; Uzbekistan politician; b. 1955, Bukhara, Uzbekistan; m.; three s.; ed Tashkent State Univ.; engineer Research-Production Unit Cybernetics 1977–79; Jr, then Sr researcher, Head of Div. Inst. of Philosophy and Law Uzbek Acad. of Sciences, 1979–90; Deputy, then Chair. Cttee on Law, Deputy Chair. Oliy Majlis (Supreme Soviet, later Supreme Ass.) 1990–93; Acting Chair. 1993–95, Chair. 1995–, re-elected 2000. *Address:* Oliy Majlis, House of Government, 700008 Tashkent, Uzbekistan (Office). *Telephone:* (712) 139-87-40, (712) 139-87-49.

KHALILZAD, Zalmay; American (born Afghanistan) political adviser; b. 1951, Mazar-i-Sharif; ed Univ. of Chicago; Official in US Dept of State 1980s; fmr Under-Sec. of Defence under Pres. George Bush Sr; risk analyst and adviser to Unocal (US oil co. involved in deals with Taliban to construct gas and oil pipelines in Afghanistan) 1997; fmr Defence Analyst for Rand Corpn; Chief Adviser on Afghanistan Affairs, Nat. Security Council (urged US Admin. to re-engage with Taliban regime to foster attractive econ. climate); condemned Taliban as sponsors of terrorism after Embassy bombings in Africa 1998; Amb.-at-Large; apptd US Special Envoy to Kabul, Afghanistan

2002, to Iraqi Nat. Congress, Iraqi Opposition 2003. *Address:* c/o National Security Council, Eisenhower Executive Office Building, 17th Street and Pennsylvania Avenue, Washington, DC 20504, USA (Office).

KHAMA, Lt-Gen. (Seretse) Ian; Botswana politician; s. of the late Sir Seretse Khama, Pres. of Botswana 1966–80; fmr Commdr Botswana Defence Force (BDF); Minister of Presidential Affairs and Public Admin. March–July 1998; elected mem. Nat. Ass. 1998; Vice-Pres. of Botswana 1998–2000, Sept. 2000–. *Address:* c/o Office of the President, Private Bag 001, Gaborone, Botswana (Office).

KHAMENEI, Ayatollah Sayyed Ali; Iranian politician and religious leader; b. 1940, Mashad, Khorassan; m. 1964; four s. one d.; ed Qom; studied under Ayatollah Khomeini; returned to Mashad 1964; imprisoned six times 1964–78, once exiled in 1978; fmr, personal rep. of Ayatollah Khomeini, Supreme Defence Council; Friday Prayer Leader, Tehran 1980–; Sec.-Gen. (and Pres. Cen. Cttee) Islamic Republican Party 1980–87; Pres. of Iran 1981–89; Wali Faqih (Religious Leader) 1989–; mem. Revolutionary Council until its dissolution Nov. 1979; Rep. of Revolutionary Council, Ministry of Defence 1980; Commdr Revolutionary Guards 1980; Sec.-Gen. and Pres. Cen. Cttee Islamic Republican Party 1980–87; survived assassination attempt June 1981; Pres. Islamic Repub. of Iran 1981–89. *Leisure interests:* reading, art, literature. *Address:* Office of the Wali Faqih, Tehran, Iran.

KHAN, Ali Akbar; Indian classical musician; b. 14 April 1922, Shivpur (now in Bangladesh); s. of Dr Allauddin Khan and Medina Khan; m. Mary J. Khan; début Allahabad 1936; world tours since 1955; Founder Ali Akbar Coll. of Music, Calcutta 1956, San Rafael, Calif. 1968, Basel, Switzerland 1982; Musical Dir of many films including award-winning Hungry Stones; numerous appearances at concerts and maj. festivals, world-wide; musical collaboration with Yehudi Menuhin, Ravi Shankar (q.v.), Duke Ellington and others; lecture recitals at maj. univs, incl. Montreal, McGill, Washington, San Diego and Tennessee; composer of concerti, orchestra pieces and several ragas, notably Chandranandan, Gauri Manjari, Alamgiri, Medhavi; Propr Alam Madina Music Productions (record co.); f. Ali Akbar Khan Foundation 1994; MacArthur Foundation Fellowship 1991; Nat. Heritage Fellowship 1997; recipient Meet the Composer/Arts Endowment Commissioning Music grant 1996; Hon. DLitt (Rabindra Bharati Univ., Calcutta) 1974; Dr Arts, Calif. Inst. of Arts 1991; Pres. of India Award 1963, 1966, Grand Prix du Disque 1968, Padma-bhibhushan Award 1989, Kalidas Award 1992, Bill Graham Lifetime Award, BAM 1993, Asian Paints Shiromani Award 1997, Nat. Acad. of Recording Arts and Science Gov.'s Award for Outstanding Achievement 1998, Asiatic Soc. of Calcutta Indira Gandhi Gold Plaque 1998; Ustad Ali Akbar Khan Day f. San Francisco, 18 Oct. 1998. *Address:* Ali Akbar College of Music, 215 West End Avenue, San Rafael, CA 94901, USA. *Telephone:* (415) 454-6264.

KHAN, Amjad Ali; Indian musician and composer; b. 9 Oct. 1945, Gwalior, Madhya Pradesh; s. of the late Hafiz Ali Khan and Rahat Jahan Begum; m. Subhalakshmi Barooah 1976; two s.; ed Modern School, New Delhi; sarod player; numerous concert performances including Pakistan 1981, China 1981, Hong Kong Arts Festival 1982, Festival of India (London) 1982; numerous recordings for maj. recording cos. in India and abroad; recording Raag Bhairav named one of best CDs in world, BBC Music Magazine 1996; mem. World Arts Council, Geneva; Founder-Pres. Ustad Hafiz Ali Khan Memorial Soc. (promotion of Indian classical music and dance); Visiting Prof. Univ. of York, UK 1995, Univ. of Pa, Univ. of NM; Hon. DUniv (York) 1997, (Delhi) 1998; awards include UNESCO Award, Int. Music Forum 1970, 1975, Special Honour, Sahitya Kala Parishad, Delhi 1977, Musician of Musicians, Bhartiya Vidhya Bhavan, Nagpur 1983, Amjad Ali Khan Day (Mass.) 1984, Acad. Nat. Award (Tirupathi) 1987, Raja Ram Mohan Roy Teacher's Award 1988, Sangit Natak Acad. Award 1989, Tansen Award, Nat. Cultural Org., New Delhi 1989, Vijaya Ratna Award, India Int. Friendship Soc., New Delhi 1990, Crystal Award, World Econ. Forum 1997; Hon. Citizen Nashville, Tenn. 1997, Houston, Tex. 1997; Padma Shree 1975, Padma Bhusan 1991, Sarod Samrat, Gwalior 1993, Padma Vibhushan 2001. *Compositions include:* many ragas; music for Kathak ballets Shan E Mughal, Shahajahan Ka Khwab, Ganesh; orchestral compositions Ekta Se Shanti, Ekta Ki Shakti, Tribute to Hong Kong (for Hong Kong Philharmonic Orchestra). *Radio includes:* promenade concert, BBC 1995. *Leisure interests:* music, television, light reading, long walks. *Address:* 3 Sadhna Enclave, Panchsheel Park, New Delhi 110 017, India. *Telephone:* (11) 6017062 (Office). *Fax:* (11) 6018011. *Website:* music@sarod.com (Office).

KHAN, Ghulam Ishaq; Pakistani politician and civil servant; b. 20 Jan. 1915, Bannu; s. of the late Ghulam Muhammad Khan; m. Shamin Ishaq 1950; one s. five d.; ed Islamia Coll., Peshawar and Punjab Univ.; North-West Frontier Province (NWFP) Civil Service (India) 1940–47, Sub-Divisional Officer, Treasury Officer and Magistrate First Class 1940–44; Bursar and Sec. to Council of Management of Islamia Coll., Peshawar; Sec. to Chief Minister, NWFP 1947; Home Sec. Food and Dir Civil Supplies to Govt NWFP 1948; Devt and Admin. Sec. for Agriculture, Animal Husbandry, Forests, Industries, Co-operatives and Village Aid 1949–52; Devt Commr and Sec. to Devt Dept, NWFP 1953–56; Sec. for Devt and Irrigation, Govt of W Pakistan 1956–58; mem. W Pakistan Water and Power Devt Authority 1958–61, Chair. 1961–66; mem. Land Reforms Comm. 1958–59, Chair. 1978–; Sec. Finance, Govt of Pakistan 1966–70; Cabinet Sec. Govt of Pakistan 1970; Gov. State Bank of Pakistan 1971–75; Sec.-Gen. Ministry of Defence 1975–77; Sec.-Gen.-

in-Chief (status of Fed. Minister), Adviser for Planning and Co-ordination 1977–78; Adviser to Chief Martial Law Administrator 1978; Minister for Finance and Co-ordination 1978–79, for Finance, Commerce and Co-ordination 1979–85; Chair. Econ. Co-ordination Cttee of the Cabinet 1978–85; Chair. Exec. Cttee Nat. Econ. Council 1978; Deputy Chair. of Planning Comm. 1979–82, Chair. 1982; Chair. of Senate 1985–88; Pres. of Pakistan (a.i.) Aug.–Nov. 1988, Pres. 1988–93; Chair. of Jt Ministerial Cttee of Bd of Govs. of World Bank and IMF 1982–88; Chair. Org. of Islamic Conf. Standing Cttee on Scientific and Technological Co-operation 1988; Life Pres. Soc. for Promotion of Eng Sciences and Tech. in Pakistan; Pres. Bd of Govs GIK Inst. of Eng Sciences and Tech.; Tamgha-i-Pakistan 1959, Sitara-i-Pakistan 1962, Halal-i-Quaid-i-Azam 1968, Int. Asscn of Lions Clubs Head of State Medal, Int. Sword of Islam Award, Islamic Foundation, USA 1993, Millennium Gold Medal, Sarhad Arts Soc. 2000; Grand Croix, Légion d'honneur. *Leisure interest:* social and educational work. *Address:* Ghulam Ishaq Khan Institute of Sciences and Technology, Topi 23460, District Swabi, NWFP, Pakistan. *Telephone:* (938) 7185861. *Fax:* (521) 841966. *E-mail:* gik@brain.net.pk (Office).

KHAN, Hameed Ahmed, PhD; Pakistani professor of physics; b. 1942, Rangoon, Burma; ed Punjab Univ., Birmingham Univ.; joined Pakistan Atomic Energy Comm. (PAEC) 1965; helped to commission country's first research reactor; on staff of teaching and research faculties, Birmingham Univ. until 1974; Chief Scientist PAEC and Dir Gen. Pakistan Inst. of Nuclear Science and Tech.; fmr Chief Ed. Nucleus; Fellow Islamic Acad. of Sciences, Pakistan Acad. of Sciences; First Prize in Physics (Nat. Book Foundation of Pakistan) 1991, 1992, 1993, Khawarizmi Prize (Iranian Research Org. for Science and Tech.) 1993, Prize in Tech. (Third World Network of Scientific Orgs.) 1998, Sitara-i-Imtiaz Award. *Address:* Pakistan Institute of Nuclear Science and Technology, P.O. Nilore, Islamabad, Pakistan (Office). *Telephone:* (51) 9204276 (Office). *Fax:* (51) 9204908 (Office).

KHAN, Imran (see Imran Khan Niazi).

KHAN, Irene Zubaida; Bangladeshi United Nations official and international organization executive; b. 24 Dec. 1956, Dhaka; one d.; joined UNHCR 1980, adviser to local project offices, worked in Pakistan, SE Asia, UK, Ireland and numerous crisis deployments 1980–90, Chief of Comm. in India 1995, Head of Documentation and Research Centre 1998–99, Head of Comm. in fmr Yugoslav Repub. of Macedonia 1999, Deputy Dir Dept for Int. Legal Protection; Sec.-Gen. Amnesty Int. (AI) Aug. 2001–. *Address:* Amnesty International, 1 Easton Street, London, WC1X 0DN, England (Office). *Telephone:* (20) 7413-5500 (Office). *Fax:* (20) 7956-1157 (Office). *E-mail:* amnestyis@amnesty.org (Office). *Website:* www.amnesty.org (Office).

KHAN, Ismail; Afghanistan politician; b. 1947; fmr Mujahideen Commdr during Soviet occupation; joined Islamic Soc. of Afghanistan; led uprising and liberated Herat from Soviet control; Gov. of Herat 1992–1997, 2001–; taken prisoner by Taliban following re-occupation of Herat 1997; escaped in 2000; mem. Northern Alliance.

KHAN, Khurshed Alam, MA; Indian politician; b. 5 Feb. 1919, Kaimganj; s. of Jan Alam; elected to Rajya Sabha 1974, 1980, Lok Sabha 1984; Minister of State for Commerce 1980, for Tourism and Civil Aviation 1982, 1983–84, for Tourism 1982–83, for External Affairs 1984, for Commerce 1985, for Textiles 1985–86, Gov. of Goa 1989–91, of Karnataka 1991–99; fmr Chancellor Jamia Milia Islamia; Vice-Pres. Zakir Hussain Educ. and Cultural Foundation; mem. Zakir Hussain Memorial Trust. *Address:* Pitaura (Kaimganj), Farrukhabad District, Uttar Pradesh, India (Home).

KHAN, Niazi Imran (see Imran Khan Niazi).

KHAN, Shahrukh; Indian film actor; b. 2 Nov. 1965, New Delhi; s. of Taj Khan; m. Gauri Chibber Khan; one s. one d.; ed Hansraj Coll., Jamia Milia Islamia, New Delhi; actor in more than 40 films 1992–. *Films include:* Deewana 1992, Baazigar 1993, Darr 1993, Karan Arjun 1995, Trimurti 1995, Dilwale Dulhania le Jayenge 1995, Koyla 1996, Yes Boss 1997, Dil to Pagal Hai 1997, Kuch Kuch Hota Hai 1998, Josh 2000, Mohabbatein 2000, Asoka 2001. *Leisure interests:* computer games, acting. *Address:* 603 Amrit Bandar (West), Mumbai 400050, India (Office). *Telephone:* (22) 6486116/6281413 (Office). *E-mail:* dreamzandfilms@hotmail.com (Office).

KHANE, Abd-El Rahman, MD; Algerian politician, administrator and physician; b. 6 March 1931, Collo; m. 1955; three s. one d.; ed Univ. of Algiers; served as officer in Nat. Liberation Army until Algerian independence 1962; Sec. of State, provisional Govt (GPRA) 1958–60; Gen. Controller Nat. Liberation Front 1960–61; Head of Finance Dept, GPRA 1961–62; Pres. Algerian-French tech. org. for exploiting wealth of Sahara sub-soil 1962–65; Pres. Electricité et Gaz d'Algérie July–Oct. 1964; mem. Bd Dirs. Nat. Petroleum Research and Exploitation Co. 1965–66; Minister of Public Works and Pres. Algerian-French Industrial Co-operation Org. 1966–70; Physician, Cardiology Dept, Univ. Hosp. of Algiers 1970–73; Sec.-Gen. OPEC 1973–74; Exec. Dir UNIDO 1975–85; founding mem., mem. Bd Worldwatch Inst., now mem. Emer. *Address:* 42 chemin B. Brahimi, El Biar, Algiers, Algeria. *Telephone:* (21) 924483.

KHANH, Emanuelle (pseudonym of Renée Nguyen); French fashion designer; b. 12 Sept. 1937, Paris; m. Manh Khanh Nguyen 1957; one s. one d.; fmr fashion model for various Paris houses including Balenciaga and Givenchy; designer of jr sportswear for Cacharel, Paris 1962–67; established own co., launching Missoni knitwear etc. Paris 1970; f. own label, specializing in embroidered clothes, accessories etc. 1971. *Leisure interest:* music. *Address:* Emanuelle Khanh International, 45 Avenue Victor Hugo, 75116 Paris, France. *Telephone:* 1-44-17-31-00.

KHARITONOV, Mark Sergeyevich; Russian writer; b. 31 Aug. 1937, Zhitomir, Ukraine; m. Galina Edelman; one s. two d.; ed Moscow Pedagogical Inst.; teacher of secondary school; exec. sec. of newspaper; of publishing house 1960–69; freelance 1969–; trans. Kafka, Stefan Zweig, Elias Canetti, Herman Hesse, Thomas Mann and others; works banned in official press until 1988; first Booker Russian Novel Prize for Lines of Fate or Milashevich's Trunk 1992, Prix du Meilleur Livre Etranger Essai (France) 1997. *Publications include:* Prokor Menshutin 1971 (published 1988), Provincial Philosophy 1977 (published 1993), Two Ivans 1980 (published 1988), Lines of Fate or Milashevich's Trunk 1985 (published 1992), Storozh 1994, The Voices 1994, Return from Nowhere 1995, Seasons of Life 1998, A Mode of Existence 1998, The Approach 1998, Amores Novi 1999, The Conveyor 2000, Stenography of the End of the Century 2002, A Professor of Lie 2002. *Address:* Bazhova str. 15, corp. 1, Apt. 182, 129128 Moscow, Russia. *Telephone:* (095) 187-56-92. *Fax:* (095) 187-56-92 (Home). *E-mail:* mkharitonov@mail.ru (Home).

KHARITONOV, Col Nikolai Mikhailovich; Russian politician; b. 30 Oct. 1948, Rezino, Novosibirsk Region; m.; four d.; ed Novosibirsk Inst. of Agric., Acad. of Nat. Econs; agronomist sovkhoz Novosibirsk Region 1972–76; Dir sovkhoz 1976–94; deputy Novosibirsk Regional Exec. Cttee; RSFSR People's Deputy, mem. Cttee on Agrarian Problems Supreme Soviet Russian Fed. 1990–93, mem. faction Agrarian Union 1990; mem. State Duma 1993–; leader Agrarian Group (now Agrarian-Industrial Group); Deputy Chair. Agrarian Party of Russia; mem. Parl. Ass. of European Council. *Leisure interest:* sports. *Address:* Agrarian Party of Russia, Malaya Kaluzhskaya str. 15, Moscow, Russia (Office). *Telephone:* (095) 292-89-01 (Office). *Fax:* (095) 292-89-00 (Office).

KHARRAT, Edwar al-, LLB; Egyptian author; b. 16 March 1926, Alexandria; s. of Kolta Faltas Youssef Al-Kharrat; m. 1958; two s.; ed Alexandria Univ.; storehouse Asst Royal Navy Victualling Dept, Alexandria 1944–46; clerk Nat. Bank of Egypt 1946–48; clerk Nat. Insurance Co. 1950–55; Dir of Tech. Affairs Afro-Asian People's Solidarity Org. 1959–67, Asst Sec.-Gen. 1967–73, Pres. 1967–; mem. Afro-Asian Writers' Asscn (Asst Sec.-Gen. 1967–72), Egyptian Writers' Union, Egyptian PEN; trans. and broadcaster for Egyptian Broadcasting Service; Assoc. Sr mem. St Antony's Coll. Oxford 1979; Ed. The Lotus, Afro-Asian Writings; Franco-Arab Friendship Prize 1991, Ali Al Owais Award (for fiction) 1996, Cavifis Prize 1998, State Merit Award 2000. *Publications include:* short stories: High Walls 1959, Hours of Pride 1972 (State Prize), Suffocations of Love and Mornings 1983; novels: Rama and the Dragon 1979, The Railway Station 1985, The Other Time 1985, Saffron Dust 1986, The Ribs of Desert 1987, Girls of Alexandria 1990, Creations of Flying Desires 1990, Waves of the Nights 1991, Stones of Bobello 1992, Penetrations of Love and Perdition 1993, My Alexandria 1994, Ripples of Salt Dreams 1994, Fire of Phantasies 1995, Soaring Edifices 1997, Certitude of Thirst 1997, Throes of Facts and Folly 1998, Boulders of Heaven 2000; poetry: Cry of the Unicorn 1998, Seven Clouds 2000; literary criticism: Transgeneric Writing 1994, The New Sensibility 1994, From Silence to Rebellion 1994, Hymn to Density 1995, Beyond Reality 1998, Voices of Modernity in Fiction 1999, Modernist Poetry in Egypt 2000. *Leisure interest:* travel. *Address:* 45 Ahmad Hishmat Street, Zamalek, Cairo, Egypt. *Telephone:* (2) 7366367. *Fax:* (2)7366367.

KHARRAZI, Kamal; Iranian diplomatist and fmr university professor; b. 1 Dec. 1944, Tehran; s. of Mehdi Kharrazi and Kobra Kharrazi; m. Mansoureh Kharrazi; two c.; ed Tehran Univ., Univ. of Houston, USA; Teaching Fellow, Univ. of Houston 1975–76; Man. of Planning and Programming, Nat. Iranian TV 1979; Man. Dir Centre for Intellectual Devt of Children and Young Adults 1979–81; Deputy Foreign Minister for Political Affairs 1979–80, Minister of Foreign Affairs 1997–; Man. Dir Islamic Repub. News Agency 1980–89; mem. Supreme Defence Council, Head War Information HQ 1980–89; Prof. of Man. and Psychology, Tehran Univ. 1983–89; Perm. Rep. to UN, New York 1989–97; Founding mem. Islamic Research Inst., London; mem. American Asscn of Univ. Profs. *Publications:* textbooks and articles in journals. *Address:* Ministry of Foreign Affairs, Koushake Mesri Avenue, UN Street,Tehran, Iran (Office). *Telephone:* (21) 3211 (Office); (21) 3903873 (Home). *Fax:* (21) 3116276 (Office). *E-mail:* ravanchi@mfa.gov.ir (Office). *Website:* www.mfa.gov.ir.

KHASAWNEH, Awn Shawkat al-, MA, LLM; Jordanian judge; b. 22 Feb. 1950, Amman; ed Islamic Educational Coll. of Amman, Queens' Coll. Cambridge, England; entered diplomatic service 1975; with Perm. Mission to UN 1976–80, later as First Sec.; with Ministry of Foreign Affairs 1980–90, Head of Legal Dept 1985–90; Legal Adviser to Crown Prince 1990–95, Adviser to the King 1995, Chief of the Royal Hashemite Court 1996–98; mem. (Judge) Int. Court of Justice Feb. 2000–; mem. Arab Int. Law Comm. 1982–89; mem. Subcomm. on Prevention of Discrimination and Protection of Minorities (Chair. 1993), Comm. on Human Rights 1984–93, Special Rapporteur of Comm. on Human Rights on the human rights dimensions of forcible population transfer; mem. Int. Law Comm. 1986–; mem. Royal Jordanian Comm. on Legislative and Admin. Reform 1994–96; Istiqlal Order 1st Class 1993, Kawkab Order 1st Class 1996, Nahda Order 1st Class 1996, Grand Officier Légion d'honneur 1997. *Address:* International Court of Justice,

Peace Palace, Carnegieplein 2, 2517 KJ The Hague, Netherlands (Office). *Telephone:* (70) 302-23-23 (Office). *Fax:* (70) 364-99-28 (Office). *E-mail:* information@icj-cij.org (Office).

KHASBULATOV, Ruslan Imranovich, DEconSc; Russian/Chechen politician and economist; b. 22 Nov. 1942, Grozny; m.; one s. one d.; ed Kazakh State Univ., Moscow State Univ.; instructor Cen. Cttee of Comsomol 1970–72, head of information sector Inst. of Social Sciences USSR Acad. of Sciences 1972–74, head of sector Research Inst. of Higher Educ. 1974–79, lecturer, Prof., Head, Chair of Int. Economy Plekhanov Inst. (now Acad.) of Econs 1979–90, 1995–; People's Deputy of Russia 1990–93, First Vice-Chair., then Acting Chair. Supreme Soviet 1990–91, Chair. 1991–93; Chair. Interparl. Ass. of CIS 1992–93; charged with inciting mass disorder Oct. 1993; released Feb. 1994; one of the leaders of opposition to Pres. Dudaev in Chechen crisis 1994–95 and to mil. policy of Kremlin; Corresp. mem. Russian Acad. of Sciences 1991. *Achievement;* Il Golpe di Agosto 1992. *Publications:* Bureaucracy and Socialism 1989, Russia: Time of Change 1991, International Economic Relations (two Vols) 1991, Power 1992, The Struggle for Russia 1993, Les Ombres au-dessus de la Maison Blanche (France) 1993, Great Russian Tragedy 1994, World Economy 1994, World Economy (two Vols) 2001, Crisis of Commonwealth of Independent States and Positive Experience of European Union 2002. *Leisure interests:* fishing, hunting, playing chess. *Address:* Russian G. Plekhanov Academy of Economics, Stremyanny per. 36, 113054 Moscow (Office); Granatnay per. 10/35, Moscow, Russia (Home). *Telephone:* (095) 958-50-15 (Office); (095) 203-53-92 (Home). *Fax:* (095) 202-84-84 (Home); (095) 958-46-22 (Office). *E-mail:* hasbulatov@zea.ru.

KHASHOGGI, Adnan M.; Saudi Arabian business entrepreneur; b. 1935, Mecca; s. of Mohammad Khashoggi; m. 1st Soraya Khashogi (divorced 1980); four s. one d.; m. 2nd Laura Biancolini 1978; one s.; ed Victoria Coll., Egypt and Calif. State Univ.; businessman in Seattle 1953–56; contract to sell trucks to Saudi Arabian Army 1956; Sales Agent in Saudi Arabia for Chrysler, Fiat, Westland Helicopters Ltd and Rolls-Royce 1962, for Lockheed, Northrop and Raytheon 1964; came to prominence with oil-boom in mid-1970s, founding his own co. Triad, based in the USA; owns houses in Marbella, Paris, Cannes, Madrid, Rome, Beirut, Riyadh, Jeddah, Monte Carlo and the Canary Islands; arrested in Berne over illegal property deals April 1989, acquitted 1990.

KHATAMI, Hojatoleslam Sayed Muhammad, B.PHIL; Iranian politician; b. 1943, Ardkan, Yazd; s. of Ayatollah Seyyed Rooh Allah Khatami (religious scholar); m. 1974; one s. two d.; ed Qom and Isfahan seminaries and Univ. of Tehran; Man. Islamic Centre, Hamburg; mem. for Ardakan and Meibod, first Islamic Consultative Ass. (Parl.); rep. of Imam Khomeini and Dir Kayhan newspaper; fmr Minister of Culture and Islamic Guidance; Cultural Deputy HQ of C-in-C and Head Defence Publicity Cttee; fmr Minister of Culture and Islamic Guidance; fmr Adviser to Pres. Rafsanjani and Pres. Nat. Library of Iran; fmr mem. High Council of Cultural Revolution; Pres. of Iran May 1997–. *Publications:* Fear of Wave, From World of City to World City, Faith and Thought Trapped by Selfishness; and numerous articles and speeches. *Address:* Office of the President, Pastor Avenue, Tehran, Iran. *Telephone:* 6162440. *Fax:* 6162824.

KHATIB, Hisham, PhD; Jordanian energy and environmental consultant and former politician; b. 5 Jan. 1936, Acre, Palestine; s. of Mohamed Khatib and Fahima Khatib; m. Maha Khatib 1968; two s. one d.; ed Univs of Cairo, Birmingham, London; Chief Engineer Jerusalem Electricity Co. 1965–73; Deputy Dir Gen. Jordanian Electricity Authority 1974–76; Sr Energy Expert Arab Fund, Kuwait 1976–80; Dir Gen. Jordan Electricity Authority 1980–84; Minister of Energy 1984–90; Vice-Chair. World Energy Council 1989–92; int. energy consultant 1990–93; Minister of Water and Planning 1993–95; Chair. Cttee for Developing Countries World Energy Council 1992–95; int. consultant 1995–; Hon. Vice-Chair. World Energy Council; Achievement Medal, Inst. of Electrical Engineers (UK) 1998; decorations from Jordan, Sweden, Italy, Indonesia, Austria and the Vatican. *Exhibitions:* numerous art exhbns in Europe and Jordan on the Holy Land and Jerusalem (from his collection). *Publications:* Economics of Reliability 1978, Financial and Economic Evaluation of Projects 1997, Palestine and Egypt under the Ottomans 2003; numerous articles in professional journals. *Leisure interest:* collecting nineteenth-century Jerusalem and Holy Land artefacts. *Address:* P.O. Box 925387, Amman 11110, Jordan. *Telephone:* (6) 5621532 (Office); (6) 5815316 (Home). *Fax:* (6) 5698556. *E-mail:* khatib@nets.com.jo (Office).

KHATTAK, Vice-Adm. Taj Muhammad, MSc; Pakistani naval officer; b. 20 Feb. 1948, Sahiwal; s. of Karra Khan Khattak and Gul Begum; m. Nasim Khattak; two s.; ed Cadet Coll., Hassan Abdal; joined Pakistan Navy 1965, fought Indo-Pak War 1971 (POW in India for two years), appointments include Flag Officer of Sea Training, Additional Secr./Dir-Gen. Ports and Shipping Wing, Ministry of Communications, Commdr Pakistan Fleet, Deputy Chief of Naval Staff (Projects), Deputy Chief of Naval Staff (Material), Chief of Staff, Naval HQ, Islamabad; apptd Rear Adm. 1997, Vice-Adm. 2002; currently Chair. Port Qasim Authority, Karachi; Sword of Honour 1969, Sitara-e-Jurrat (Gallantry Award) 1971, Sitara-e-Imtiaz 1996, Hilal-e-Imtiaz 2001. *Publications include:* Amphibious Threat to Pakistan, Indian Nuclear Threat. *Leisure interests:* reading, golf. *Address:* Office of the Chairman, Port Qasim Authority, Bin Qasim, Karachi 75020 (Office); 12 B/1 3rd Gizri Street, DHA, Phave-IV Karachi 75020, Pakistan (Home). *Telephone:* (21) 9204271 (Office); (21) 5898382 (Home). *E-mail:* tajmkhattak@hotmail.com (Home).

KHAVIN, Vladimir Yosifovich; Russian architect; b. 29 July 1931, Moscow; s. of Yosif Efimovich Khavin and Sophya Danilovna Khavina; m. Nadezhda Ermakova; one s.; ed Moscow Architectural Inst.; Head of Workshop no. 12 of Mosproekt-1; teacher, Moscow Inst. of Architecture 1976–; Corresp. mem. Int. Acad. of Architecture 1999; Lenin Prize 1984; Honoured Architect of Russia 1988. *Works include:* Circus Bldg on Vernadsky St, Moscow 1963–71, October Square 1972, Intourist Hotel Complex by Kakhovskaya Metro Station 1980, Monument to Frunze, Frunze 1965, The Rear to the Front Monument, Magnitogorsk 1972–79, memorial complex To the Heroes of the Civil War and the Great Patriotic War, Novorosiysk 1982, Moscow townbuilding exhbn, Brestskaya St 1985, Palace of Youth on Komsomolskaya Avenue, Moscow 1988, new residential Dist Yushnoye Buruvo 1990–, reconstruction of Cheryomushkinski Dist, Moscow 1990–, Russian Jt-Stock Co. complex GASPROM 1995, apt houses, Namyotkina str. 1997. *Leisure interest:* painting. *Address:* Glavmosarchitektura, Triumfalnaya Square 1, 103001 Moscow (Office); Novocheryomushkinskaya str. 71/82, Apt 259, 123056 Moscow, Russia (Home). *Telephone:* (095) 251-61-72 (Office); (095) 719-97-16 (Home). *Fax:* (095) 251-61-72.

KHAYOYEV, Izatullo; Tajikistan economist; b. 22 June 1936, Khodzhaikhok, Kulyab Dist, Tajik SSR; m. several s.; ed Tajik Univ., Higher Party School; mem. CPSU 1961–91; worked in financial insts 1954–61; Head of Dept, Ministry of Agric. 1961–63; Chair. of collective farm 1963–65; Sr posts in state and CP insts 1966–78; Minister of Meat and Dairy Industry, Tajik SSR 1978–83; First Sec. Kulyab Dist 1983–86; Deputy, USSR Supreme Soviet 1984–89; cand. mem. CPSU Cen. Cttee 1986–91; Chair. Council of Ministers, Tajik SSR 1986–90, Vice-Pres. Tajik SSR 1990–91; Prime Minister 1991–92; Minister of Foreign Econ. Relations 1992–94; Head of Staff of Pres. Rakhmonov 1994–96; in pvt. business 1999–; orders and medals of USSR and Repub. of Tajikistan. *Leisure interests:* saddle-horse riding, reading fiction, science fiction and literature. *Address:* Prospect Rudaki, 1 proezd k. 75/2, Dushanbe, Tajikistan (Home). *Telephone:* 24-75-35 (Home).

KHAZANOV, Gennady Viktorovich; Russian comedian and actor; b. 1945, Moscow; m. Zlata Khazanov; one d.; ed State High School of Circus and Variety Actors; worked in radio equipment factory; debut as actor Moscow Univ. Students' Theatre Nash Dom; compere L. Utyosov Orchestra; on professional stage since 1969 in solo productions, first production Trifles of Life 1981; variety programmes Evident and Unbelievable 1987, Little Tragedies 1987, Selected 1988; leading role Gamblers of XXI Century Moscow Art Theatre; leading role in film Little Giant of Large Sex; performed in America, Australia, Israel, Germany, Canada; Artistic Dir Variety Theatre Mono 1991–96; Dir, Artistic Dir Moscow Variety Theatre 1997–; First Prize All-Union Competition of Variety Artists; State Prize 1995. *Address:* Variety Theatre, Bersenevskaya Nab. 20/2, 109072 Moscow, Russia. *Telephone:* (095) 230-18-68.

KHIATI, Mostafa, PhD; Algerian professor of medicine and academic administrator; ed Algerian Medical Inst.; fmr Head, Dept of Pediatrics, El-Harrach Hosp.; Pres., Nat. Foundation for Health Progress and Medical Research Devt in Algeria 1990–; mem. Medical Soc. of Algeria, Algerian Soc. of Pediatrics 1983–86, Int. Asscn of Pediatrics; fmr consultant, Ministry of Health; Fellow Islamic Acad. of Sciences; Shoman Award for Clinical Sciences 1984, Maghrebian Medicine Award 1986, Chadli Benjedid Award 1989, Union of Arab Physicians Award. *Address:* Islamic Academy of Sciences, P.O. Box 830036, Amman, Jordan (Office). *Telephone:* 5522104 (Office). *Fax:* 5511803 (Office).

KHIEM, Gen. Trân Thien (see Trân Thien Khiem, Gen.).

KHIEU, Samphan; Cambodian politician; b. 1932, Svay Rieng Prov.; m. Khieu Ponnary; ed Paris Univ.; f. French-language journal, Observer, Cambodia; Deputy, Nat. Ass. in Prince Sihanouk's party, Sangkum Reastr Nyum (Popular Socialist Community); served as Sec. of State for Commerce; left Phnom Penh to join Khmer Rouge 1967; Minister of Defence in Royal Govt of Nat. Union of Cambodia (GRUNC) 1970–76, Deputy Prime Minister 1970–76 (in exile 1970–75, in Phnom Penh 1975–76); mem. Politbureau Nat. United Front of Cambodia (FUNC) 1970–79; C-in-C Khmer Rouge High Command 1973–79; Pres. of State Presidium (Head of State) 1976–79; Prime Minister of the Khmer Rouge opposition Govt fighting Vietnamese forces 1979–91; Vice-Pres. of Govt of Democratic Kampuchea (in exile) June 1982–91 (responsibility for Foreign Affairs); Pres. Khmer Rouge 1985–91, returned to Cambodia Nov. 1991; apptd "Prime Minister" of illegal Provisional Govt of Nat. Unity (fmrly Khmer Rouge) 1994; Chair. Party of Democratic Kampuchea; Pres. and founder Nat. Solidarity Party May 1997; mem. Supreme Nat. Council 1991–97; Vice-Pres. in charge of Foreign Affairs, Nat. Govt of Cambodia 1991; Chair. Cambodian Nat. Union Party (CNUP) 1993–97; surrendered to govt Dec. 1997, at liberty pending charges relating to activities of Khmer Rouge regime Jan. 1998–.

KHIZHA, Georgy Stepanovich, DTechSc; Russian politician and manager; b. 2 May 1938, Ashkhabad; m.; two d.; ed Leningrad Polytech. Inst., Acad. of Nat. Econ.; engineer, head of div., Chief Engineer, Dir-Gen. Leningrad Engels Factory (now Svetlana Asscn) 1961–91; Deputy Mayor of Leningrad 1991–92; Deputy Prime Minister of Russia 1992–93, Chair. Expert Council of Govt 1993–, Int. Cttee for Econ. Reforms and Co-operation 1993–96. *Publications:* more than 60 papers and about 50 licensed inventions. *Leisure interests:* hunting and diving. *Address:* Expert Council, Krasnopresnenskaya nab. 2, 103274 Moscow, Russia. *Telephone:* (095) 205-59-67, (095) 205-56-32.

KHLEFAWI, Gen. Abdel Rahman; Syrian army officer; b. 1927, Damascus; m.; four c.; ed schools in Damascus; entered Mil. Coll. 1949, graduated as Lt 1950; promoted to Maj.-Gen. 1971; attended courses abroad, especially in France and the USSR; served in Syrian Arab Army; Gov. Deraa, Chair. of Municipality and Chief of its Police; later Gov. of Hama; Rep. of Syria, Jt Arab Command, Cairo 1965–67; Chief of Martial Court; Chief, Dept of Officers' Affairs 1968–70; Minister of the Interior, Deputy Martial Judge 1970–71; mem. House of People 1971; Prime Minister 1971–72, 1976–78; mem. Progressive Nat. Front; elected as mem. in Regional Leadership of Socialist Arab Ba'ath Party and Chief of Econ. and Financial Bureau.

KHLOPONIN, Aleksander Gennadyevich; Russian politician and banking official; b. 6 March 1965, Colombo, Sri Lanka; m.; one d.; ed Moscow Inst. of Finance; army service 1983–85; with Vneshtorgbank 1989–92; Deputy, First Deputy Chair., Chair., Pres., Commercial Bank Int. Financial Co. 1992–; Acting Deputy Chair., mem. Bd of Dirs, Norilsky Nikel 1996–; mem. Advisory Council, Fed. Comm. 1997–; mem. Bd of Dirs Kolskaya Mine Co., Murmansk 1998–; Gov., Taimyr Autonomous Territory 2001–02; Gov. of Krasnoyarsk Territory Sept. 2002–; Order of Honour 1998. *Address:* Office of the Governor, Mira prosp. 110, 66009 Krasnoyarsk, Russia (Office). *Telephone:* (3912) 49-30-26 (Office). *Fax:* (3912) 22-11-78 (Office). *E-mail:* kds@adm-kr.krasnoyarsk.su (Office).

KHLYSTUN, Viktor Nikolayevich, DEcon; Russian agricultural engineer and politician; b. 19 March 1946, Dmitrievka, Kokchetav Region, Kazakhstan; m.; two c.; ed Moscow Inst. of Agric. Eng (MIIZ); metalworker, worker sovkhoz 1963–65; Asst, Sr teacher, docent, Prof., Dean Moscow Inst. of Agric. Eng 1971–90, 1998–, Sec. CP Bureau 1977–80, Pro-rector 1980–90; Chair. RSFSR State Cttee on Land Reform 1990–91; Minister of Agric. 1991–93, 1995–98; Deputy Chair. Agroprombank 1994–96; Deputy Chair. of Russian Govt responsible for agric. problems 1997–98; Dir-Gen. Inst. of Agrarian Market Research, Moscow 1998–; Corresp. mem. Russian Acad. of Agricultural Sciences; Vice-Pres. Razgulyai-Ukzross Corpn 1998–. *Address:* Institute of Agricultural Engineering, 2nd Institutskaya str. 6, 109428 Moscow, Russia (Office). *Telephone:* (095) 171-29-50. *Fax:* (095) 171-29-50.

KHODAKOV, Aleksander Georgyevich; Russian diplomatist; b. 8 March 1952, Moscow; m.; two s.; ed Moscow State Inst. of Int. Relations, Algiers Univ., Algeria; worked in USSR Embassy, Gabon 1974–79; Legal and Treaty Dept, Ministry of Foreign Affairs 1980–85, Deputy Dir Legal Dept 1992–94, Dir 1994–97; First Sec., then Second Sec. Perm. Mission of USSR to UN, New York 1985–91; Perm. Rep. to Org. for banning Chemical Armaments, The Hague; Amb. to the Netherlands 1997–. *Address:* Embassy of the Russian Federation, Andries Bickerweg 2, 2517 JP, The Hague, Netherlands (Office). *Telephone:* (70) 3451300 (Office). *Fax:* (70) 3617960 (Office). *E-mail:* ambrusnl@euronet.nl (Office).

KHODORKOVSKY, Mikhail Borisovich; Russian businessman; b. 26 June 1963, Moscow; m.; two s.; ed D. Mendeleev Moscow Inst. of Chemistry and Tech.; Head Centre of Interfield Research Programmes (NTTM), USSR State Cttee for Science and Tech. (now Menatep Asscn) 1986–93; Chair. Bd of Dirs, Menatep Bank 1993–; Chair. Bd Commercial Innovation Bank of Scientific Progress 1989–90; Econ. Counsellor to Chair. of Russian Council of Ministers 1990–91; Deputy Minister of Fuel and Energy Industry 1991; Chair. Bd of Dirs Rosprom co. 1995–; Vice-Pres. YUKOS Asscn 1996, Chair. United Bd Rosprom-YUKOS Co. 1997–2000, Exec. Cttee OAO NK YUKOS, Man. Cttee YUKOS-Moscow 2000–. *Address:* YUKOS Co., 26 Ulansky Lane, 113152 Moscow, Russia.

KHORANA, Har Gobind, PhD, MSc; Indian-born scientist; b. 9 Jan. 1922, Raipur; s. of Sri Ganpat Rai and Shiramati Krishna Khorana; m. Esther Elizabeth Sibler 1952; one s. two d.; ed Punjab Univ.; began career as organic chemist; worked with Sir Alexander Todd on building nucleotides, Cambridge 1950–52; later worked with Nat. Research Inst., Canada, until 1960; Prof. and Co-Dir Inst. of Enzyme Chem., Univ. of Wis. 1960–64, Conrad A. Elvehjem Prof. in Life Sciences 1964–70; Andrew D. White Prof.-at-Large, Cornell Univ., Ithaca 1974–80; Alfred P. Sloan Prof. MIT 1970–97, Prof. Emer. and Sr Lecturer 1997–; visiting Prof. Rockefeller Inst. 1958–; mem. NAS; Foreign Academician USSR Acad. of Sciences 1971; Foreign mem. Royal Soc. London 1978; Pontifical Acad. of Sciences 1978; numerous hon. degrees, Nobel Prize for Medicine and Physiology (with Holley and Nirenberg) for interpretation of genetic code and its function in protein synthesis 1968, Louisa Gross Horwitz Prize for Biochem. 1968, American Chem. Soc. Award for creative work in Synthetic Chem. 1968, Lasker Foundation Award 1968, American Acad. of Achievement Award 1971, Willard Gibbs Medal 1974, Gairdner Foundation Annual Award 1980, Nat. Medal of Science 1987, Paul Kayser Int. Award of Merit 1987. *Publications:* Some Recent Developments in the Chemistry of Phosphate Esters of Biological Interest 1961; articles on Biochemistry in various journals. *Leisure interests:* music, hiking. *Address:* Departments of Biology and Chemistry, Massachusetts Institute of Technology, 77 Massachusetts Avenue, Room 68-680, Cambridge, MA 02139. USA.

KHOUNA, Cheikh el Avia Ould Mohamed; Mauritanian politician; mem. Democratic and Social Republican Party (DSRP); fmr Minister of Fisheries and Marine Economy; Prime Minister of Mauritania 1996–97, Nov. 1998–. *Address:* Office of the Prime Minister, Nouakchott, Mauritania.

KHRENNIKOV, Tikhon Nikolayevich; Russian composer; b. 10 June 1913, Yelets, Lipetsk region; s. of Nikolay Khrennikov and Varvara Kharla-
mova; m. Klara Arnoldovna Vax (Khrennikova) 1936 (deceased); one d.; ed Moscow Conservatoire; Dir of Music Central Theatre of Soviet Army 1941–54; Gen. Sec. Soviet Composers' Union 1948–57, First Sec., then Chair. 1957–91; Chair. Int. Asscn of Composers Unions 1991–92, Hon. Chair. 1995–; Pres. Tchaikovsky Int. Competition 1978–90, 1994–; Prof. Moscow Conservatory 1966–; mem. CPSU 1947–91; Deputy to USSR Supreme Soviet 1962–89; mem. Cttee USSR Parl. Group; mem. Cen. Auditing Comm., CPSU 1961–76; cand. mem. CPSU Cen. Cttee 1976–87; USSR People's Deputy 1989–91; Hon. mem. Santa Cecilia Acad., Tiberiana Acad. (Italy); State Prize 1942, 1946, 1951, 1967, 1979, People's Artist of the RSFSR 1955, of the USSR 1963; Hero of Socialist Labour 1973, Lenin Prize 1974, UNESCO Prize 1977, Glinka Prize 1983, Commdr des Arts et des Lettres (France). *Principal compositions:* four piano concertos 1933, 1971, 1983, 1991, Five Pieces for Piano 1933, First Symphony 1935, Three Pieces for Piano 1935, Suite for Orchestra from Music for Much Ado About Nothing, In the Storm (opera) 1939, Second Symphony 1941, incidental music for play Long Ago 1942, Frol Skobeyev (opera) 1950, Mother (opera) 1956, Concerto for Cello and Orchestra 1959, A Hundred Devils and One Girl (operetta) 1961, two Concertos for Violin 1964, 1976, White Nights (operetta) 1967, Boy Giant (opera for children) 1969, Our Courtyard (ballet for children) 1970, Much Ado About Hearts (chamber opera) 1974, Third Symphony 1975, Love for Love (ballet) 1976, The Hussars' Ballad (Ballet) 1980, Dorothea (opera) 1982–83, The Golden Calf 1985 (opera), Napoleon Buonaparte (ballet) 1995, Captain's Daughter (ballet, after A. Pushkin) 1997; numerous popular songs and incidental music. *Address:* Plotnikov per. 10/28, Apt. 19, 121200 Moscow, Russia. *Telephone:* (095) 244-71-72.

KHRUSHCHOV, Nikolai Grigoryevich; Russian biologist; b. 23 June 1932; m.; one d.; ed 2nd Moscow Inst. of Medicine; Jr, then Sr Researcher, Head of Div. Deputy Dir, currently Dir Koltsov Inst. of Biology of Devt USSR (now Russian) Acad. of Sciences; corresp. mem. Russian Acad. of Sciences 1979, mem. 1990, mem. Presidium 1994, Academician Sec. Dept of Gen. Biology; Mechnikov Prize. *Publications:* main scientific research and numerous scientific Publs on problems of biology of Devt of tissue and cellular systems. *Address:* Koltsov Institute of Biology of Development, Russian Academy of Sciences, Vavilova str. 26, 117808 Moscow, Russia (Office). *Telephone:* (095) 938-16-91 (Office), (095) 938-51-90 (Acad.) (Office).

KHRZHANOVSKY, Andrei Yurevich; Russian film maker and scriptwriter; b. 30 Nov. 1939, Moscow; s. of Yuriy Borisovich Khrzhanovsky and Vera Mihayilovna Khrzhanovsky; m. Mariya Newman 1972; one s.; ed VGIK; worked with 'Soyuzmultfilm' since 1962; Chair. Bd Higher Refresher Animation School-Studio 'Shar'; Prof.VGIK; Hon. Artist of Russia; State Prize 1986, 1999. *Films include:* Once upon a time there lived a man by the name of Kozyavin 1966, The Glass Harmonica 1968, The Cupboard 1971, The Butterfly 1972, In the World of Fables 1973, A Wonderful Day 1975, The House that Jack Built 1976, I Fly to You in Memory (trilogy of films based on Pushkin's doodles) 1977, 1981, 1982, The King's Sandwich 1985, The School of Fine Arts (part 1 – A Landscape with Juniper 1987, part 2 – The Return 1990), The Lion with the Grey Beard 1994, Oleg Kagan: Life After Life (documentary) 1996, The Long Journey (based on Federico Fellini's drawings) 1997, The Dreams About MKHAT (documentary) 1999, Studys About Pushkin, Lullaby for Cricket 1999, Pushkin Take-off 2002, I Love You 2002, A Cat and a Half (based on Joseph Brodsky's drawings) 2002. *Address:* Vasilyevskaya str. 7, Apt 56, 123056 Moscow, Russia. *Telephone:* (095) 254-51-75. *Fax:* (095) 253-87-09.

KHUB DASS, Rt Rev. Smart, MA; Pakistani educator and religious leader; b. 20 Dec. 1938, Lahore; s. of the late Rev. Khub Dass; ed Univ. of Punjab, Univ. of Nashville Tenn., USA; fmr youth leader; fmr Prin. Intermediate Colls, Co-ordinator of Educ.; fmrly Gen. Sec. (Synod) Church of Pakistan, now Moderator; Bishop of Hyderabad 1997–; Exec. mem. World Methodist Conf., mem. Educ. Cttee. *Publications include:* History of the Church of Pakistan, Seven Words on the Cross, Sunday School Lessons (Sarmaya–I–Hayat). *Leisure interest:* reading. *Address:* 27 Liaqat Road, Civil Lines, Hyderabad 71000, Sindh, Pakistan (Office). *Telephone:* (221) 780-221 (Office). *Fax:* (221) 28772 (Office). *E-mail:* dohcop@hyd.netasia.co.pk (Office).

KHUBLARYAN, Martin Gaykovich; Russian hydrologist; b. 5 March 1935; m. Servenik A. Gabrielyan 1968; two d.; ed Armenian Inst. of Agric.; Sr researcher, head of lab., Deputy Dir Inst. of Water Problems USSR, Acad. of Sciences 1968–88, Dir 1988–; Corresp. mem. USSR (now Russian) Acad. of Sciences 1984, mem. 1994; research in hydromechanics, hydrology, hydrogeology; mem. American Soc. of Hydrology; Ed.-in-Chief Water Resources Journal; Russian Acad. of Sciences Award for Terrestrial Waters Sciences. *Publications include:* Chemical substance transport in soil and its effect on groundwater quality 1989, Water Streams: Models of flow and quality surface water 1991, The Caspian Sea Phenomenon 1995, The Application of Nonlinear Models to the Analysis of Water Level Fluctuations in Reservoirs 1996; numerous other publications. *Leisure interests:* reading memoirs, painting, classical music, chess. *Address:* Water Problems Institute of the Russian Academy of Sciences, 3 ul. Gubkina, 117971 Moscow, Russia. *Telephone:* (095) 135-54-56. *Fax:* (095) 135-54-15. *E-mail:* martin@iwapr.msk.su (Office).

KHUDAIBERDYEV, Narmankhonmadi Dzhurayevich; Uzbekistan politician; b. 1928, Uzbekistan; ed Uzbek Agric. Inst.; mem. CPSU 1948–91; Dept head, sec. of a Regional Uzbek Komsomol Cttee; Lecturer, Assistant Prof. Agric. Inst., Samarkand 1943–54; leading CPSU and state posts 1954–; Sec.

Bukhara Dist Cttee of Uzbek CP, Head Agric. Dept of Cen. Cttee of Uzbek CP; Second Sec. Bukhara Dist Cttee 1956–60; Deputy to Supreme Soviet of Uzbek SSR 1959–63, 1967; mem. Cen. Cttee of Uzbek CP 1960; Deputy Chair. Council of Ministers of Uzbek SSR 1960–61; First Sec. Surkhan-Darya Dist Cttee of Uzbek CP 1961–62; Prime Minister of Uzbekistan 1971–85; cand. mem. Cen. Cttee of CPSU 1961–66, mem. 1971; mem. Foreign Affairs Comm. of Soviet of the Union, USSR Supreme Soviet 1962–66; Sec. and mem. Presidium of the Cen. Cttee of the Uzbek CP 1962–65, Chair. Agric. Bureau 1962–64; Chair. Council of Ministers of Uzbek SSR 1971–84; mem. Politburo of Cen. Cttee of Uzbek CP 1971–84; sentenced to nine years in a labour camp for bribery Sept. 1989, released 1992.

KHUDONAZAROV, Davlatnazar; Tajikistan film director and politician; b. 13 March 1944; ed All-Union Inst. of Cinematography; film Dir and cameraman in documentary cinema 1965–77; debut in feature film The First Morning of Youth 1979; Chair. Confed. of Cinema Unions 1990–; USSR People's Deputy, mem. of Supreme Soviet 1989–91; mem. Inter-regional Deputies' Group; Cand. for Pres. of Tajikistan; moved to Moscow after civil war 1992; adviser, Social and Political Union Focus 1999–; State Prize of Tajikistan 1972 and other awards. *Films include:* Dzura Sarkor, Tale about Rustam, Rustam and Sokhrab, One Life is not Enough, Tale about Siyavush, A Brook Ringing in Melted Snow (Prize of All-Union Film Festival 1983). *Address:* Confederation of Cinema Unions, Vasilyevskaya str. 13, 123825 Moscow, Russia. *Telephone:* (095) 250-41-14 (Office).

KHUDYAKOV, Konstantin Pavlovich; Russian film director; b. 13 Oct. 1938, Moscow; m. Irina Mikhailovna Ivanova; one s.; ed All-Union Inst. of Cinematography; film Dir 1970–; with Mosfilm Studio 1970–; mem. Union of Cinematographers 1975; Prof., Head of Studio Higher Courses of Film Dirs.; Prof. All-Union Inst. of Cinematography 1995–; Chair. State Attestation Comm. of Russian Inst. of Cinematography 1998–; Crystal Box for Pages of Life 1971, Prize Moscow Film Festival for Who Will Pay for Luck 1980, Grand Prix Barcelona Film Festival 1986, Golden Tulip Prize Istanbul Film Festival 1986, Prize of the 1st Washington Film Festival 1986, Prize of the Royal Acad. of Cinema (Stockholm) for Success 1986, Prize of European Community for From Evening to Noon 1983, Prize of the Jerusalem Film Festival for Mother of Jesus 1988. *Films include:* Pages of Life, To Live Your Own Way, Ivatsov, Petrov, Sidorov, Success, From Evening to Noon, Death in Cinema, Contender, Mother of Jesus, Without the Return Address, Michel, The Shadows of Fabergé. *Televisions productions:* Presence, Behind the Stone Wall, The Sun of the Wall, Such a Long Short Life, Girl without Dowry, Game, Tango for Two Voices, Impostors. *Leisure interests:* avant-garde and jazz music. *Address:* 1812 Iear str. 3, Apt 40, 121293 Moscow, Russia (Home). *Telephone:* (095) 148-33-37 (Home).

KHURANA, Sundar Lal, MA; Indian politician; b. 28 Feb. 1919, Jhang (now in Pakistan); s. of A. L. Khurana; m. 1955; two s.; ed Govt Coll., Lahore; joined Defence Forces as Civilian Officer in 1943, subsequently obtaining regular comm.; joined Indian Admin. Service 1949; various posts in Rajasthan 1950–55; Deputy Sec., Ministry of Community Devt, Govt of India and mem. Exec. Cttee Cen. Social Welfare Bd 1955–59; Sr UN Adviser to Govt of Afghanistan 1959–62; Collector and Dist Magistrate, Commr for Border Dists., Rajasthan 1963–66; Chair. Rajasthan State Electricity Bd 1966–70; Commr for Home Affairs, Sec. for Jails, Transport and Information and Public Relations Depts., Rajasthan 1970–71; Chief. Sec. to Govt and Sec. various Depts., Rajasthan 1971–75; Sec., Ministry of Home Affairs and Sec. Justice Dept, Govt of India 1975–77; Exec. Pres. Hindustan Times Groups of Publs 1979–80 and 1980–81; Adviser to Gov. of Rajasthan March–June 1980; Lt-Gov. of Delhi 1981–82; Gov. of Tamil Nadu 1982–88; Past Nat. Pres. All India Inst. of Marketing Man.; Vice-Pres. All India Inst. of Public Admin. *Publication:* Towards a New Order.

KHURSHID, Ahmed, MA, LLB, PhD; Pakistani economist and politician; b. 22 March 1932, Delhi, India; Chair. Inst. of Policy Studies, Islamabad 1979–; Vice-Pres. Islamic Research Acad. 1979–; Fed. Minister of Planning Devt and Statistics 1978–79, mem. Hiira Cttee 1978–83; Senator 1985–97; Chair. Islamic Foundation, UK 1978–, Int. Inst. of Islamic Econs., Int. Islamic Univ. 1983–87; mem. Bd Trustees, Islamic Centre, Nigeria 1976–, Bd Trustees, Int. Islamic Univ., Islamabad 1980–, Foundation Council, Royal Acad. for Islamic Civilization, Jordan 1987–, and numerous academic advisory cttees.; Islamic Devt Bank Award 1988, King Faisal Int. Prize for Services to Islam 1990, 5th Annual Prize, American Finance House 1998. *Address:* Institute of Policy Studies, Nasr Chambers, Block-19, Markaz F-7, Islamabad 44000, Pakistan (Office). *Telephone:* (51) 2650971 (Office). *Fax:* (51) 2650704 (Office). *E-mail:* khurshid@ips.net.pk (Office).

KHUSH, Gurdev Singh, PhD, FRS; Indian agricultural research scientist and plant breeder; b. 22 Aug. 1935, Rurkee; s. of Kartar Singh and Pritam Kaur; m. Harwant Kaur Grewal 1961; one s. three d.; ed Punjab Univ., Chandigarh, Univ. of California, Davis, USA; Research Asst, Univ. of Calif., Davis 1957–60, Asst Geneticist 1960–67; Plant Breeder, Int. Rice Research Inst., Manila, Philippines, 1967–72, Head of Plant Breeding Div./Genetics and Biochem. 1972–; mem. Indian Nat. Science Acad., Third World Acad. of Sciences, NAS (USA); Borlaug Award 1977, Japan Prize 1987, Int. Agronomy Award 1989, World Food Prize 1996, Rank Prize 1998, Wolf Prize 2000. *Achievements:* noted for his role in developing high-yielding varieties of rice, which led to doubling of world rice production between 1966 and 1990. *Publications:* Cytogenetics of Aneuploids 1974, Plant Breeding Lectures 1984, Host Plant Resistance to Insects 1995; 152 research papers and 40 book chapters. *Leisure interests:* world history, human rights. *Address:* International Rice Research Institute, P.O. Box 3127, Makati City 1271 (Office); IRRI Staff Housing, Los Bamos, Laguna, Philippines (Home). *Telephone:* (2) 845-0563, ext. 734 (Office); (2) 845-0563, ext. 251 (Home). *Fax:* (2) 891-1292 (Office); (2) 891-1292 (Home). *E-mail:* g.khush@cgiar.org (Office).

KHUSSAIBY, Salim Bin Mohammed Bin Salim al-; Omani diplomatist; b. 11 March 1939; m.; three c.; ed Teachers Coll., Zanzibar and Police Officers Coll., Kenya; teacher Secondary School, Dubai 1964–70; joined Royal Omani Police 1970, apptd Deputy Inspector Gen. of Police and Customs; Minister Plenipotentiary Ministry of Foreign Affairs 1976, later Chargé d'affaires Omani Embassy, Nairobi; Consul Gen. Bombay 1979; Amb. to Kuwait 1980, to Pakistan, (also Accred to Nepal, Bangladesh, Brunei, Darussalam, Indonesia and Malaysia) 1982–87; Perm. Rep. to the UN 1987–99.

KHUWEITER, Abd al-Aziz al-Abdallah al-; Saudi Arabian politician; b. 1927, Onaizah; s. of Abdullah Khuweiter and Moodi al-Khuweiter; m. Fatima al-Khuweiter 1963; one s. three d.; Vice-Rector King Saud Univ.; Head Directorate Supervision and Follow-up; fmr Minister of Health; Minister of Educ. 1987–95; of State 1995–; King Abdulaziz Order of Merit (Second Class), Republican Order, Sudan (First Class). *Publications:* Fi Turuk al Bahth, Tarikh Shafi Ibn Ali (Ed.), Al-Malik al-Zahir Baybars (in Arabic and English), Al-Rawd al Zahir (Ed.), Min Hatab al-Layl, Ayy-Bunayy, Qiraah Fi Diwan al-Sha'ir Muh. Uthaymin. *Leisure interest:* reading. *Address:* Council of Ministers, Murabba Riyadh 11121, Saudi Arabia.

KHVOROSTOVSKY, (Hvorostovsky), Dmitry Alexandrovich; Russian baritone; b. 17 Oct. 1962, Krasnoyarsk; m. Svetlana Khvorostovskaya; ed Krasnoyarsk Inst. of Arts; début as opera singer 1984; soloist Krasnoyarsk Opera Theatre 1984–90; winner All-Union Glinka Competition 1987; winner int. competitions in Toulouse, Nice, Cardiff; has gained worldwide reputation after his recitals in London, New York 1989–90; début in Moscow 1990; performances in La Scala, Liceo, Metropolitan Opera and others; roles include Eugene Onegin, Figaro (Barber of Seville), Robert (Iolanthe), Germont (Traviata), Silvio (Pagliacci), Eletsky (The Queen of Spades); State Prize of Russia 1991; People's Artist of Russia 1995. *Address:* c/o Askonas Holt Company, 6 Henrietta Street, London, WC2E 8LA, England; c/o Elen Victorova, Mosfilmovskaya 26, apt. 5, Moscow, Russia. *Telephone:* (20) 7379-7700.

KHVOSTOV, Mikhail Mikhaylavich; Belarus diplomatist; b. 27 June 1949, Vytebsk Region; m.; two c.; ed Minsk Inst. of Foreign Languages, Belarus State Univ.; with Ministry of Foreign Affairs 1982–91; Sr diplomatic officer Perm. Mission of Belarus to UN, New York 1991–92; Sr diplomatic officer Belarus Embassy to USA 1992–93; Head State Protocol Dept Ministry of Foreign Affairs 1993–94, Deputy Minister of Foreign Affairs 1994–97; Amb. to Canada 1997–2000; Asst to Pres. for Foreign Policy Problems Aug.–Nov. 2000; Deputy Prime Minister 2000–01, Minister of Foreign Affairs 2000–. *Address:* Ministry of Foreign Affairs, Lenina str. 19, 220030 Minsk, Belarus (Office). *Telephone:* (172) 272922 (Office). *Fax:* (172) 274521 (Office). *Website:* www.mfa.gov.by (Office).

KIANO, Julius Gikonyo, MA, PhD; Kenyan politician and economist; b. 1 June 1926, Weithaga, Kenya; s. of Jonathan Kiano and Damari Wanjiru Kiano; m. Jane Mumbi Kiano 1966; two s. three d.; ed Alliance High School, Kikuyu, Makerere Univ. Coll., Uganda, Antioch Coll. Ohio, Stanford Univ. and Univ. of California at Berkeley, USA; lecturer in Econs and Constitutional Law at Royal Tech. Coll., Kenya (now Univ. of Nairobi) 1956–58; elected mem. Kenya Legis. Council 1958–63; mem. Indian Govt Cultural Scholarships Cttee and US Scholarship Cttee 1959–62; mem. Kenya Advisory Council on Tech. Educ. and Vocational Training 1960–62; mem. Kenya Parl. 1963–79; Minister of Commerce and Industry 1963–66, Minister of Labour 1966–67, Minister of Educ. 1968–70, Minister of Local Govt 1970–73, Minister of Commerce and Industry 1973–76, Minister of Water Devt 1976–79; Chair. African Ministers of Educ. Conf. 1968, African Ministers of Industry Conf. 1975; mem. Common Market and Econ. Consultative Council of the East African Community 1973–76; Pres. UN Conf. on Desertification Aug.–Sept. 1977; Man. Dir Industrial Devt Bank of Kenya 1980–83; mem. Freedom from Hunger Council 1976–; mem. Governing Council UNEP 1977–79; mem. Council, Univ. of Nairobi 1976–, Exec. Cttee Kenya African Nat. Union (KANU) 1978–79, Sec. KANU Parl. Group 1978–79; mem. Council, Univ. of Nairobi 1976–, exec. Cttee Assoc. of African Devt Finance Insts. 1981–83; Chair. Nat. Oil Corpn of Kenya 1983–; Chair. Kenya Petroleum Refineries Ltd 1988–89, Kenya Broadcasting Corpn 1989–; Hon. DLitt (Univ. of Nairobi) 1997; Haas Int. Award for fmr Foreign Students, Univ. of Calif. 1989; Elder of Golden Heart, Kenya. *Leisure interests:* social welfare, reading, broadcasting, international relations. *Address:* Kenya Broadcasting Corporation, Broadcasting House, Harry Thuku Road, P.O. Box 30456, Nairobi; P.O. Box 40125, Nairobi (Office); Forest Edge Road, Langata, Nairobi, Kenya (Home). *Telephone:* (2) 334567 (Office); (2) 891747 (Home). *Fax:* (2) 220675 (Office). *E-mail:* kbc@swiftkenya.com (Office). *Website:* www.kbc.co.ke (Office).

KIAROSTAMI, Abbas, BA; Iranian film director, producer, writer and editor; b. 22 June 1940, Tehran; m. (divorced); two s.; ed Tehran Coll. of Fine Arts; worked as designer and illustrator (commercials, film credit titles and children's books); involved in establishment of film making dept at Inst. for Intellectual Devt of Children and Young Adults (Kanoon); ind. film maker from early 1990s; has made over twenty films including shorts, educational films, documentaries; more than 50 int. prizes including special prize of the Pasolini Foundation 1995, UNESCO Fellini Medal 1997. *Films directed include:* Bread and Alley (short) 1970 (debut production of Kanoon film Dept), The Traveller 1973, So Can I (short) 1975, Two Solutions for One Problem (short) 1975, The Report (Gozaresh) 1977, The Toothache (public-service film) 1980, Chorus (short) 1982, Fellow Citizen 1983, First Graders (documentary) 1985, Earthquake Trilogy: Where Is the Friend's House? 1987, Homework (documentary) 1989, Close Up (documentary) 1990, And Life Goes On 1992 (Rossellini Prize, Cannes Film Festival), Through the Olive Trees 1994, Taste of Cherry 1997 (Palme d'Or, Cannes Film Festival), The Wind Will Carry Us (Grand Jury Prize, Venice Film Festival) 1999, ABC Africa 2001, Ten 2002, The Deserted Station 2002. *Film screenplays:* The Key 1987, The Journey 1995, The White Balloon 1995 (Caméra d'Or, Cannes Film Festival). *Publications:* Walking with the Wind: Poems 2001. *Address:* c/o Zeitgeist Films Ltd, 247 Center Street, 2nd Floor, New York, NY 10013, USA.

KIBAKI, Mwai, BA, BSc (Econs); Kenyan politician; b. 15 Nov. 1931, Gatuyaini, Othaya; s. of the late Kibaki Githinji and Teresia Wanjiku; m. Lucy Muthoni; three s. one d.; ed Man'gu High School, Makerere Univ., LSE; Lecturer in Econs, Makerere Univ. Coll. 1959–60; Nat. Exec. Officer Kenya African Nat. Union (KANU) 1960–64; elected by Legis. Council as one of Kenya's nine reps. in E African Legis. Ass. of E African Common Services Org. 1962; mem. House of Reps. for Nairobi Doonholm 1963–74; Parl. Sec. to Treasury 1963–64; Asst Minister of Econ. Planning and Devt 1964–66; Minister for Commerce and Industry 1966–69, of Finance 1969–70, of Finance and Econ. Planning 1970–78, of Finance 1978–82, of Home Affairs 1978–88, of Health 1988–91; Vice-Pres. of Kenya 1978–88; Vice-Pres. KANU 1978–91; Pres. Democratic Party 1991–; Leader of the official Opposition 1998–2003; Pres. of Kenya and C-in-C of the Armed Forces Dec. 2002–. *Leisure interests:* reading, golf. *Address:* Office of the President, Harambee House, Harambee Avenue, PO Box 30510, Nairobi, Kenya. *Telephone:* (20) 227411. *Website:* www .officeofthepresident.go.ke.

KIBEDI, Wanume, LLB; Ugandan politician and lawyer; b. 3 Aug. 1941, Busesa; s. of Mr. and Mrs. EM Kibedi; m. Elizabeth Kibedi (née Amin) 1970; one d.; ed Busoga Coll. and Univ. of London; articled with Waterhouse and Co., London 1961–66, admitted solicitor 1966; worked in office of Attorney-Gen., Uganda 1968; Partner, Binaisa and Co. (advocates) 1969–70; Minister of Foreign Affairs 1971–73 (resgnd); del. to UN Gen. Ass. 1971; Perm. Rep. to the UN 1986–89. *Leisure interests:* chess, tennis, reading. *Address:* c/o Ministry of Foreign Affairs, P.O.B. 7048, Kampala, Uganda.

KIBEDI VARGA, Aron, PhD; Netherlands professor of French literature and poet; b. 4 Feb. 1930, Szeged, Hungary; m. 1st T. Spreij 1954; m. 2nd K. Agh 1964; m. 3rd S. Bertho 1991; four s. one d.; ed Univs. of Amsterdam, Leiden, Sorbonne; lecturer in French Literature, Free Univ. of Amsterdam 1954–66, Prof. 1971–; Prof. of French Literature, Univ. of Amsterdam 1966–71; Visiting Prof. Iowa Univ. 1971, Yale Univ. 1975, Princeton Univ. 1980, Rabat Univ. 1985, Coll. de France 1992; mem. Cttee Int. Soc. for the History of Rhetoric 1979–83; Pres. Int. Asscn Word and Image Studies 1987–93; mem. Royal Netherlands Acad. of Sciences 1981–; mem. Hungarian Acad. of Sciences 1990–; Dr. hc (Pécs) 1994. *Publications:* Criticism: Les Constantes du Poème 1963, Rhétorique et Littérature 1970, Théorie de la Littérature (Ed.) 1981, Discours récit, image 1989, Les Poétiques du classicisme (Ed.) 1990, Le Classicisme 1998, Szavak, világok 1998, Noé könyvei 1999, Amszterdami krónika 2000; Poetry (in Hungarian): Kint és Bent 1963, Téged 1975, Szépen 1991, Hantani, fosztani 2000. *Address:* Department of French, Vrije Universiteit, Amsterdam, Netherlands. *Telephone:* (20) 4446456 (Office). *Fax:* (20) 4446500 (Office).

KIBIROV, Timur Yuryevich; Russian poet; b. (Zapoyev), 15 Feb. 1955, Shepetovka, Ukraine; m. Yelena Ivanovna Borisova; one d.; ed Krupskaya Moscow Regional Pedagogical Inst.; jr researcher All-Union Research Inst. of Arts 1981–93; ed. Tsikady (Publr) 1993–; first poems published in Yunost and Continent 1989; Pushkin Prize (Germany) 1993, Prize of Druzhba Narodov (magazine) 1993. *Publications:* collections of poetry: Calendar 1990, Verses about Love 1993; Sentiments 1994; verses in leading literary journals. *Address:* Ostrovityanova str. 34, korp. 1, Apt. 289, Moscow, Russia (Home). *Telephone:* (095) 420-6175 (Home).

KIBRIA, Shah A. M. S., MA; Bangladeshi politician and fmr United Nations official; b. 1 May 1931, Sylhet; m.; one s. one d.; ed Univ. of Dhaka, Fletcher School of Law and Diplomacy, Boston, Mass., USA; joined diplomatic service of Pakistan 1954; served various embassies until 1971; declared allegiance to Bangladesh and joined Bangladesh mission, Washington, DC 1971; Dir-Gen. Political Affairs Dept, Ministry of Foreign Affairs 1972; Sec. Ministry of Foreign Affairs 1972–73; High Commr in Australia (also Accred to New Zealand and Fiji) 1973–76; Perm. Rep. to UN Offices, Geneva 1976–78; Chair. Preparatory Cttee, Group of 77 for UNCTAD V, Geneva 1978; Foreign Sec., Ministry of Foreign Affairs 1978–81; Exec. Sec. UN Econ. and Social Comm. for Asia and the Pacific (ESCAP) 1981–92; Special Rep. of UN Sec.-Gen. for Co-ordination of Cambodian Humanitarian Assistance Programmes 1987; Political Adviser to Pres. of Awami League 1994–; Minister for Finance 1996–2001; Mem. Parl. (Awami League) 2001–. *Publications:* Mridhubason (essays on contemporary political, econ. and social issues) 1997, Bangladesh at the Crossroads (essays on int. and nat. issues) 1999, The Emerging New World Order 2000. *Leisure interests:* music, golf, fishing. *Address:* House No.

58, Road No. 3/A, Dhanmondi Residential Area, Dhaka 5, Bangladesh. *Telephone:* (2) 8616950 (Home). *Fax:* (2) 8615847 (Home). *E-mail:* hfmoff@ bdmail.net (Office).

KIBRICK, Anne, EdD; American professor of nursing; b. 1 June 1919, Palmer, Mass.; d. of Martin Karlon and Christine Grigas Karlon; m. Sidney Kibrick 1949; one s. one d.; ed Boston Univ., Columbia Univ., Harvard Univ.; Head Nurse, Worcs. Hahnemann Hosp. 1941–43; Staff Nurse, Children's Hosp. Medical Center, Boston 1943–45; Educ. Dir, Charles V. Chapin Hosp., Providence, RI 1945–47; Asst Educ. Dir, Veterans Admin. Hosp. 1948–49; Asst Prof. Simmons Coll., Boston 1949–55; Dir Graduate Programmes in Nursing, Boston Univ. 1958–63, Prof. and Dean 1963–70; Dir Graduate Programs in Nursing, Boston Coll. 1970–74; Chair. School of Nursing Boston State Coll. 1974–82; Dean Coll. of Nursing Univ. of Mass., Boston 1982–88, Prof. 1988–93, Prof. Emer. 1993–; Consultant Nat. Student Nurses Asscn 1985–88; Consultant, Hadassah Medical Org., Israel, Cumberland Coll. of Health Sciences, NSW, Australia, Menonfia Univ., Shebin El-Kam, Egypt; Fellow American Acad. of Nursing 1973–; mem. Inst. of Medicine, Nat. Acad. of Sciences 1972–, Brookline Town Meeting 1995–2000; Charter mem. Nat. Acads. of Practice 1985–; mem. Bd of Dirs. Post-Grad. Medical Inst., Mass. Medical Soc. 1983–96, Exec. Cttee 1988–96; Dir Landy-Kaplan Nurses Council 1992– (Treasurer 1994–98); DHL (St Joseph's Coll.); Mary Adelaide Nutting Award, Distinguished Service Award and Isabel Stewart Award, Nat. League for Nursing, Service Award, Nat Hadassah Org. and other awards; Chancellor's Medal, Univ. of Mass., Boston 1992; Hall of Fame, Nursing, Teacher's Coll., Univ. of Columbia 1999, Mass. Nurses Asscn 2000. *Publications:* (with H. Wechsler) Explorations in Nursing Research 1979; numerous professional articles. *Leisure interests:* reading, travel. *Address:* 130 Seminary Avenue, #312, Auburndale, MA 02466, USA (Home). *Telephone:* (617) 969-3225 (Home).

KIDD, Hon. Douglas Lorimer (Doug), DCNZM, LLB; New Zealand politician and lawyer; b. 12 Sept. 1941, Levin; s. of Lorimer Edward Revington Kidd and Jessie Jean Kidd (née Mottershead); m. Jane Stafford Richardson 1964; one s. two d.; ed Horowhenua Coll., Vic. Univ., Wellington; partner, Wisheart Macnab & Partners (law firm) 1964–78; fmr part-time mussel farmer, Marlborough Sounds; Nat. Party MP for Marlborough/Kaikoura 1978–99; Minister of State-Owned Enterprises and Assoc. Minister of Finance 1990–91; Minister of Fisheries 1990–96; Minister of Maori Affairs 1991–93; Minister of Energy, of Labour and for Accident Rehabilitation and Compensation Insurance 1993–96; Speaker of House of Reps and Chair. of Parl. Service Comm. 1996–99; fmr Foundation Pres. Marlborough Forest Owners' Asscn; Nat. Party List MP 1999–; Opposition Spokesman on Fisheries; Chair. Regulations Review Select Cttee; mem. Privileges and Maori Affairs Select Cttee 1999–; mem. Bd New Zealand Business and Parl. Trust Hon. Col of Canterbury, Nelson, Marlborough, West Coast Regt 1997–; Commonwealth Medal 1990, Chief of Gen. Staff's Commendation for Outstanding Service to NZ Army 1999. *Leisure interests:* fishing, reading, travel. *Address:* Parliament Buildings, Wellington, New Zealand. *Telephone:* (4) 471-9939 (Office). *Fax:* (4) 471-2455 (Office). *E-mail:* doug.kidd@national.org.nz (Office). *Website:* www.national.org.nz (Office).

KIDD, Jodie; British fashion model; b. 1979, Surrey; great granddaughter of Lord Beaverbrook; ed St Michael's School, W Sussex; spent much of childhood in Barbados; has modelled for numerous fashion magazines; also top int. catwalk model for designers including Gucci, Prada, Karl Lagerfeld, Yves Saint Laurent, Chanel, John Galliano, Calvin Klein and Yohji Yamamoto; make-up model for Chanel 1999 season; fmr Nat. Jr Athletics Champion; holder of Under-15s High Jump record for Sussex; many awards as a jr show jumper. *Leisure interests:* riding, polo. *Address:* c/o IMG Models, Bentinck House, 3–8 Bolsover Street, London, W1P 7HG, England. *Telephone:* (20) 7580-5885.

KIDMAN, Dame Fiona Judith, DNZM, OBE; New Zealand writer; b. 26 March 1940, Hawera; d. of Hugh Eric Eakin and Flora Cameron Eakin (née Small); m. Ian Kidman 1960; one s. one d.; ed small rural schools in the north of NZ; Founding Sec./Organizer NZ Book Council 1972–75; Sec. NZ Centre, PEN 1972–76, Pres. 1981–83; Pres. NZ Book Council 1992–95, Pres. of Honour 1997–; f. Writers in Schools, Words on Wheels (touring writing co.), Writers Visiting Prisons; teaches creative writing; many literary prizes including NZ Book Awards (fiction category), Queen Elizabeth II Arts Council Award for Achievement, Victoria Univ. Writers' Fellow; NZ Scholarship in Letters; A. W. Reed Award for Lifetime Achievement 2001. *Publications:* A Breed of Women 1979, Mandarin Summer 1981, Mrs. Dixon and Friend (short stories) 1982, Paddy's Puzzle 1983, The Book of Secrets 1986, Unsuitable Friends (short stories) 1988, True Stars 1990, Wakeful Nights (poems selected and new) 1991, The Foreign Woman (short stories) 1994, Palm Prints (autobiog. essays) 1995, Ricochet Baby 1996, The House Within 1997, The Best of Fiona Kidman's Short Stories 1998, New Zealand Love Stories; An Oxford Anthology (Ed.) 1999, A Needle in the Heart (short stories) 2002. *Leisure interests:* theatre, film, gardening. *Address:* P.O. Box 14-401, Kilbirnie, Wellington, New Zealand. *Fax:* (4) 386-1895. *E-mail:* fionakidman@ compuserve.com (Home).

KIDMAN, Nicole; Australian actress; b. 20 June 1967, Hawaii, USA; d. of Dr Antony Kidman and Janelle Glenny; m. Tom Cruise 1990 (divorced 2001); one adopted s. and one adopted d.; ed St Martin's Youth Theatre, Melbourne, Australian Theatre for Young People, Sydney and Philip Street Theatre;

acting début in Australian film aged 14; Australian Film Inst. Best Actress Award for role in TV mini-series Bangkok Hilton; voted Best Actress of Year in Australia for role in Vietnam. *Films include:* The Emerald City, The Year My Voice Broke, Flirting, Dead Calm, Days of Thunder, Far and Away, Billy Bathgate, Malice, My Life, Batman Forever, To Die For, Portrait of a Lady, The Peacemaker, Eyes Wide Shut 1998, Practical Magic 1999, Moulin Rouge (Golden Globe for Best Actress in a Musical) 2001, The Others 2001, Birthday Girl 2001, The Hours (Golden Globe for Best Dramatic Actress 2003, BAFTA Award for Best Actress in a Leading Role 2003, Acad. Award for Best Actress 2003) 2002, Dogville 2003, The Human Stain 2003. *Play:* The Blue Room 1998–99. *Address:* c/o Ann Churchill Brown, Shanahan Management, PO Box 478, Kings Cross, NSW 2011, Australia.

KIDWAI, Akhlaq R., PhD; Indian politician, educationist, scientist and administrator; b. b. 1 July 1920, Baragaon; Prof. and Head of Dept of Chem., Dean Faculty of Science, Aligarh Muslim Univ. 1951–67, Chancellor 1983–92; Chair. of Union Public Service Comm. 1967–79; Gov. of Bihar 1979–85, 1993–98, of W Bengal 1998–99; Chair. Dr. Ambedkar Centre for Biomedical Research, Univ. of Delhi 1998–; Chair. Bombay Mercantile Coop. Bank 1999–; mem. Rajya Sabha (Upper House of Parl.) 2000–; Chair. Inst. of Marketing and Man. 2001–; Pres. Vocational Educ. Soc. for Women 1985–; Hon. Fellow Inst. of Engineers, India. *Publications:* more than 40 research papers. *Address:* 196 Zakir Bagh, Okhla Road, New Delhi, 110 025; 15 AB Pandara Road, New Delhi 110 003, India (Home). *Telephone:* (11) 3073214 (Office); (11) 3073400 (Home); (11) 6838004. *Fax:* (11) 3073403 (Home). *E-mail:* arkidwai@sansad.nic.in (Office); arkidwai@mantraonline.com (Home).

KIDWAI, Mohsina; Indian politician; b. 1 Jan. 1932, Banda Dist, Uttar Pradesh; d. of Qutubuddin Ahmed; m. Khalilur Rahman Kidwai 1953; three d.; ed Women's Coll., Aligarh; mem. UP Legis. Council 1960–74, Legis. Ass. 1974–77, Lok Sabha 1978–79, 1980–84; Minister of State for Food and Civil Supplies, Govt of UP 1973–74, Minister of Harijan and Social Welfare 1974–75, of Small-Scale Industries 1975–77; Union Minister of State for Labour and Rehabilitation 1982–83, for Health and Family Welfare 1983–84, for Rural Devt Aug.–Oct. and Nov.–Dec. 1984; Minister of Health and Family Welfare 1984–88, of Urban Devt 1988–90; Pres. UP Congress Cttee (I) 1976–80, 1982, now Pres. UP Congress Exec. (I); mem. Congress Working Cttee and Gen. Sec. All India Congress Cttee 2000–; mem. Population Control Bd, Govt of India; Founder Patron Nat. Girls' Higher Secondary School, Bara Banki and other insts. helping women, children and destitutes, including Harijans. *Leisure interests:* reading biographies and other literary works, music, badminton. *Address:* All India Congress Committee, 24 Akbar Road, New Delhi 110D11 (Office); B-124, Sector 26, Noida, Uttar Pradesh, India (Home); Civil Lines, Bara Banki, Uttar Pradesh. *Telephone:* (11) 3010366 (New Delhi) (Office); (11) 8-4543633 (Noida) (Home). *Fax:* (11) 3017047 (New Delhi) (Office); (11) 8-4530030 (Noida) (Home).

KIEBER, Walter, DJur; Liechtenstein politician and lawyer; b. 20 Feb. 1931, Feldkirch, Austria; s. of Alfons and Elisabeth Kieber; m. Selma Ritter 1959; one s. one d.; ed Grammar School in Bregenz, Austria, Univ. of Innsbruck; lawyer in Vaduz 1955–59, 1981–; entered civil service as Head of the Govt Legal Office 1959; Chief of Presidential Office 1965–; Sec.-Gen. of Govt 1969, Deputy Head of Govt 1970–74, Head of Govt 1974–78, Deputy Head of Govt 1978–80; Pres. Liechtenstein Bar Asscn 1993–; Progressive Citizens' Party; Grand Cross, Liechtenstein Order of Merit, Grosses Goldenes Ehrenzeichen am Bande für Verdienste um die Republik Österreich (Austria). *Address:* Heiligkreuz 6, 9490 Vaduz (Office); Landstrasse 22, 9494 Schaan, Liechtenstein (Home). *Telephone:* 2358181 (Office); 2322529 (Home).

KIEFER, Anselm; German artist; b. 8 March 1945, Donaueschingen; m.; three c.; ed Univ. of Freiburg and Freiburg Acad., Karlsruhe Acad.; first one-man exhbn, Galerie am Kaiserplatz, Karlsruhe 1969; first one-man Exhbn in USA, Marian Goodman Gallery, New York; retrospective exhbns. Städtische Kunsthalle, Düsseldorf, Musée d'Art Moderne, Paris and Israel Museum, Jerusalem 1984, Stedelijk Museum, Amsterdam 1986, US tour 1987–89; first group Eexhbn, Deutscher Künstlerbund, Kunstverein, Hanover 1969; has also exhibited Kunstverein, Frankfurt 1976, Kassel Documenta 1977, 1982, 1987, Biennale de Paris 1977, Venice Biennale 1980; other group exhbns. include Expressions: New Art from Germany, touring exhbn USA 1983–84, touring exhbn Moscow and Leningrad 1983, 1984 Museum of Modern Art survey of int. art, Fifth Biennale of Sydney, Australia 1984; works in many pvt. collections including Saatchi Collection, London and in many public galleries including Art Inst. of Chicago, Museum of Modern Art, Phila Museum of Art, Hirshhorn Museum, Washington, DC, LA Museum of Contemporary Art and San Francisco Museum of Modern Art, Praemium Imperiale 1999; Wolf Foundation Prize 1990. *Publication:* A Book by Anselm Kiefer 1988.

KIELMANSEGG, Gen. Johann Adolf, Graf von; German army officer (retd); b. 30 Dec. 1906, Hofgeismar; s. of the late Adolf Graf von Kielmansegg and the late Eva Graefin von Kielmansegg (née von Werner); m. Mechthild Freiin von Dincklage 1933; two s. two d.; ed Monastic School, Rossleben; Army Service 1926, Officer 1930; War Acad., Berlin 1937–39; Gen. Staff, 1st and 6th Panzer Div. 1939–42; OKH (High Command of the Army) 1942–44, CO Armed Infantry Regiment 111 1944–45; journalistic activities 1945–50; Office of the Fed. Chancellor 1950–55; Mil. Rep. of Fed. Repub. of Germany to SHAPE, Paris 1955–58; Second-in-Command, 5th Panzer Div. 1959–60, CO 10th Panzer Div. 1960–63; Defence Ministry, Bonn until 1963; promoted to rank of Gen. 1963; C-in-C Allied Land Forces, Cen. Europe 1963–66; C-in-C Allied Forces, Cen. Europe 1966–68; now writer on politico-military matters; mem. Int. Inst. for Strategic Studies (London), German Asscn for Foreign Affairs, Inst. for Foreign Policy Analysis, Cambridge, Mass.; fmr mem. US Strategic Inst. Washington, DC; fmr Chair. Advisory Bd Inst. for Research into Military History; Freiherr vom Stein Preis 1968; Iron Cross (First Class), Grand Cross of the Fed. Repub. with Ribbon and Star, Commdr Légion d'honneur, Commdr Legion of Merit. *Publications:* Der Fritsch–Prozess 1938, Unbesiegbar? China als Militärmacht 1985. *Leisure interests:* history, political science. *Address:* Parkstift St Ulrich Hebelstr. 18, 79189 Bad Krozingen, Germany. *Telephone:* (7633) 403-325 (Home).

KIELY, Rory; Irish politician; b. May 1934; m. Eileen Kiely (née O'Connor); two s. two d.; ed Univ. Coll. Cork; Senator 1977–82, 1983–; elected Chair. (Cathaoirleach) of Seanad Éireann Sept. 2002–. *Address:* Cathaoirleach, Seanad Èireann, Leinster House, Kildare Street, Dublin 2 Dublin 2, Ireland (Office). *Telephone:* (1) 6183227 (Office). *Fax:* (1) 6184101 (Office). *E-mail:* rory.kiely@oireachtas.ie (Office). *Website:* www.oireachtas.ie (Office).

KIEP, Walther Leisler, CBE; German politician and business executive; b. 5 Jan. 1926, Hamburg; s. of the late Louis Leisler Kiep and Eugenie vom Rath; m. Charlotte ter Meer 1950; three s. (one deceased) two d.; ed Hamburg, Istanbul, Frankfurt; with Ford Motor Co., then Insurance Co. of North America 1948–55, joined Gradmann and Holler 1955–, man. partner 1968–98; Advisory Council of Deutsche Bank 1972–2001; mem. CDU 1961–, mem. Bundestag 1965–80, 1980–81; fmr Chair. Parliamentary Cttee on Foreign Aid, Treasurer, mem. Exec. Cttee 1971–; Lower Saxony Minister for Econs and Finance 1976–80, concurrently Special Envoy for Turkish aid; Deputy to Leader of Opposition 1980–81; Chair. Atlantik-Brücke, Berlin 1984–2000; mem. Int. European Advisory Bd Fuji-Wolfensohn, New York 1989–98; Chair. ZENECA GmbH, Plankstadt 1993–98; Chair. Int. Advisory Bd, J. & H. Marsh & McLennan Cos. New York 1993–99; Chair. Supervisory Bd IABG, Ottobrunn 1994–2000; Pres. European Business School, Oestrich-Winkel 1994–2000; mem. Int. Advisory Bd, Coll. Univ., New York 1997–, Int. Advisory Bd, Fuji Bank Ltd, Tokyo 1999–; Bundesverdienstkreuz mit Stern und Schulterband, Grosses Verdienstkreuz des Niedersächsischen Verdienstordens. *Publications:* Goodbye Amerika–Was Dann? 1972, A New Challenge for Western Europe 1974, Was bleibt ist grosse Zuversicht 1999. *Leisure interest:* history. *Address:* Holzhecke 31, 60528 Frankfurt a.M., Germany. *Telephone:* (69) 67-73-38-84. *Fax:* (69) 67-73-38-72.

KIERANS, Eric William, OC; Canadian politician and economist; b. 2 Feb. 1914, Montreal; s. of Hugh Kierans and Lena (née Schmidt); m. Teresa Catherine Whelan 1938; one s. one d.; ed Loyola Coll., Montreal and McGill Univ., Montreal; Prof. of Commerce and Finance 1953–60; Dir McGill School of Commerce 1953–60; Pres. Montreal and Canadian Stock Exchanges 1960–63; Minister of Revenue, Québec 1963–65; Minister of Health, Québec 1965–66; Pres. Québec Liberal Fed. 1966–68; Postmaster-Gen. and Minister responsible for Dept of Communications 1968–69; Minister of Communications 1969–71; Consultant to Manitoba Govt on Resources Policy 1972; Dir Savings and Trust Corpn of BC 1975, Sidbec-Dosco Ltée. 1978; Prof. of Econs, McGill Univ. 1972–80; Chair. Canadian Adhesives Ltd 1980; Prof. of Econs, Dalhousie Univ., Halifax 1983–84; mem. Council NS Barristers' Soc. 1990–94; Hon. LLD (McGill Univ.) 1981, (Concordia Univ.) 1987, (Dalhousie Univ.) 1991; Liberal. *Publications:* Challenge of Confidence: Kierans on Canada 1967, Natural Resources Policy in Manitoba 1973. *Leisure interest:* sports. *Address:* 3200 Cedar Avenue, Westmount, Quebec, Canada.

KIERES, Leon; Polish politician and professor of law; b. 26 May 1948, Kolonia Zielona; s. of Józef Kieres and Helena Kieres; m. Anna Kieres; one s. one d.; ed Wroclaw Univ.; Jr Librarian Wroclaw Univ. 1970, Research Asst 1971–73, Sr Asst 1973–75, Lecturer in Law 1975–85, Asst Prof. 1985–91, Extraordinary Prof. 1991–96, Ordinary Prof., Faculty of Law and Admin. 1996–; councillor, Wroclaw Town Council 1990–98; Pres. Self-governmental Council of Wroclaw Voivodship 1990–98; mem. Local Govt Council at the Chancellory of the Pres. 1994; Vice-Pres. Congress of Local and Regional Authorities of Council of Europe 1995–, mem. Parl. Ass. 1998–2000, involved in Council of Europe mission in Bosnia and Herzegovina 1998; Senator, Vice-Pres. Senate Local Govt and Public Admin. Cttee, mem. Foreign Affairs and European Integration Cttee; Pres. int. group of local Govt observers in Croatia 1997; councillor, Dolnoslaskie Voivodship Council, Pres. Culture, Science and Educ. Cttee 1998–2002; Pres. Inst. of Nat. Remembrance 2000–; Vice-Pres. Polish–German Co-operation Foundation 1993; mem. Polish Teachers' Asscn 1970–80, NSZZ Solidarnosc 1980–2000; Bronze Cross of Merit 1978, Kt's Cross, Order of Polonia Restituta 1996; Walerian Panka Award 1997, St Silvester Order of the Pope 1998, St George Medal 2002. *Publications include:* Zalecenia RWPG w sprawie koordynacji narodowych planów gospodarczych i ich realizacja w PRL (Recomendations of Council for Mutual Economic Aid on Coordination of National Economic Schemes and Their Realisation in Poland) 1978, Zagraniczne przedsiebiorstwo socjalistyczne w Polsce (Foreign Socialist Enterprises in Poland) 1986, Struktura Centralnego aparatu gospodarczego i jego funkcje (Structure of Central Economic Machinery and its Functions—Ed.) 1989, Tworzenie i funkcjonowanie spólek: zagadnienia cywilnoprawne i administracyjne (Establishment and Functioning of Companies: Civil and Administrative Law Issues—Ed.) 1989, Region samorzadowy (Local-governmental Region) 1991, Podejmowanie dzialalnosci gospodarczej przez inwestorów zagranicznych (Foreign Investors' Establishment) 1993, Prawo administracyjne (Administrative Law—co-author); over 40 scientific Publs and numerous articles in nat. and foreign magazines on public admin. law, econ. law and law of local Govt. *Leisure interests:* supporting football teams, watching good films. *Address:* Institute of National Remembrance—Commission for the Prosecution of Crimes against the Polish Nation, ul. Towarowa 28, 00-839 Warsaw (Office); ul. Obornicka 34 m. 15, 51-113 Wroclaw, Poland (Home). *Telephone:* (22) 5818500 (Office). *Fax:* (22) 5818524 (Office). *E-mail:* sekretariat@ipn.gov.pl (Office). *Website:* www.ipn.gov.pl (Office).

KIJIMA, Torazo, BEcons; Japanese business executive; b. 18 Dec. 1901; ed Tokyo Imperial Univ. (now Univ. of Tokyo). Dir Japanese Nat. Railways 1950–52; mem. House of Councillors 1953–59; Pres. Hinomaru Ceramic Industry Co. Ltd 1953, Aito Vehicles Industries Co. Ltd; Chair. Bd of Dirs. Nippon Express Co. Ltd 1968–; Second Grand Order of Sacred Treasure (Japan) 1972, Commdr, Grand Order (Madagascar) 1973.

KIKABIDZE, Vakhtang Konstantinovich; Georgian actor and singer; b. 19 July 1938, Tbilisi; s. of Konstantin Kikabidze and Manana Bagrationi; m. Irene Kebadze 1964; one s.; soloist and leader of Georgian pop-group Orero 1966–; film début in 1967 with Meeting in the Hills; solo career since 1988; USSR State Prize 1978, People's Artist of Georgian SSR 1980, Order of Honour, special award (Georgia) 1994, Order of Konstantine (Russia) 1997, Order of St Nicholaus 1998, Golden Gramophone Prize 1998, Leonid Utesov Prize for Achievement in field of Music 2000. *Films include:* Meeting in the Hills 1967, Don't Grieve 1968, I'm a Detective 1969, The Stone of the First Water 1970, Pen-name Lukach, The Melodies of Verikysky Block 1973, Lost Expedition 1973, Completely Gone 1972, Mimino 1978, TASS is Authorized to Inform, Hi! Friend (TV film) 1981, To Your Health Dear (Dir, scriptwriter, actor) 1983, Man and all the Others (scriptwriter, producer, actor) 1985, Fortuna (actor) 2000. *Music:* albums: My Years, My Wealth 1994, Larisa Ivanovna Please! 1995, Letter to Friend 1996, Tango of Love 1999, Greatest Hits 2000. *Leisure interest:* fishing. *Address:* S. Chikovani Street 20, Apt. 38, 380015 Tbilisi, Georgia. *Telephone:* (32) 98-90-14; 23-08-67 (Home).

KIKOIN, Konstantin Abramovich, PhD; Russian theoretical physicist; b. 9 Aug. 1945, Tver; s. of Abram Kikoin and Ekaterina Sosenkova; m. Larisa Markina 1969; one s. one d.; ed Ural State Univ. (Sverdlovsk/Ekaterinburg), Physical-Tech. Inst. Moscow; Jr Scientific Researcher, Inst. of Optical-Physical Measurements, Moscow 1971–74; Sr Scientific Researcher I.V. Kurchatov Inst. of Atomic Energy, Moscow 1974–85, Leading Scientific Researcher Vice-Head Solid State Theory Dept 1985–; Deputy Chair. Exec. Bd Moscow Physical Soc. 1989–, Assoc. Ed. Journal of Moscow Physical Soc. 1990–; Assoc. Ed. Journal of Experimental and Theoretical Physics 1991–; Rep. of American Inst. of Physics in Moscow 1992–; mem. Expert Council of Supreme Attestation Cttee 1994–; lives in Israel. *Publications:* more than 70 papers in scientific journals. *Leisure interest:* translating poetry from Russian into English. *Address:* c/o I.V. Kurchatov Institute, Kurchatov Square 46, 123182 Moscow (Office); Vasilevsky str. 9/5, Apt. 21, 123182 Moscow, Russia (Home). *Telephone:* (095) 196-91-48 (Office); (095) 196-60-87 (Home).

KIKUTAKE, Kiyonori, BA, FAIA; Japanese architect; b. 1 April 1928, Kurume; s. of Kiyoshi and Masue Kikutake; m. Norie Sasaki 1953; one s. two d.; ed Waseda Univ.; est. Kiyonori Kikutake & Assocs (Architects) 1953, now Rep. Dir; Prof. Dept of Architecture, Waseda Univ. 1959; Vice-Pres. Japan Fed. of Professional Architects Asscns, Tokyo Professional Architects' Asscn, Japan Architects' Asscn 1982–; now Exec. Dir Tokyo YMCA Inst. of Design; mem. Bd Architectural Inst. of Japan 1962–; Visiting Prof. Univ. of Hawaii 1971; del. to UNESCO Int. Conf., Zürich 1970; Hon. Fellow, American Inst. of Architects 1971; several awards including Ministry of Educ. Arts Award 1964, Architectural Inst. of Japan Award 1964, Pan Pacific Architectural Citation of the Hawaii Chapter, AIA 1964, Cultural Merits of Kurume City 1975, Auguste Perret Award UIA 1978, XXI Mainichi Art Awards 1979. *Major works include:* Shimane Prefectural Museum 1958, Sky House 1958, Admin. Building for Izumo Shrine, Tatebayashi City Hall 1963, Hotel Tokoen, Yonago-City, Miyakonojo City Hall, Pacific Hotel, Chigasaki 1966, Iwate Prefectural Library 1967, Shimane Prefectural Library, Hagi Civic Centre 1968, Kurume Civic Centre 1969, Expo Tower for Expo 70, Osaka 1970, Pasadena Heights (tiered mass housing) 1974, Aquapolis (floating module for ocean), Ocean Expo 75 1975, Hagi City Hall 1975, Redevelopment of Yamaga city centre 1975, Tsukuba Academic New Town, Pedestrian Deck Network and the Symbol Tower 1976, Otsu Shopping Centre 1976, branches of Kyoto Community Bank 1971–, Tanabe Museum, Matsue City 1979, Darumaya-Seibu Dept Store 1980, Treasury of Izumo Shrine 1981, Seibu-Yaow Shopping Centre 1981, Karuizawa Art Museum 1981, Kuamoto Pref. Arts and Crafts Centre 1982, Fukuoka City Hall (Ass. Hall) 1982; Edo Tokyo Museum 1992, Kurume City Hall 1994. *Publications:* Metabolism 1960 1960, Taisha Ken-chiku-ron (Metabolic Architecture) 1968, Ningen-no-Kenchiku (Human Architecture) 1970, Ningen-no-Toshi (A Human City) 1970, Essence of Architecture 1973, Floating City 1973, Kiyonori Kikutake—Works and Methods 1956–70 1973, Community and Civilization 1978, Kiyonori Kiku-take-Concepts and Planning 1978, Ningen-no-Kankyo (Human Environment) 1978, Community and City 1978, Tight Spaces, Macro-Engineering 1982. *Leisure interests:* swimming, photography, reading, travel. *Address:* 1-11-15 Ohtsuka, Bunkyo-ku, Tokyo, Japan. *Telephone:* (3) 941-9184; (3) 941-0830.

KILAR, Wojciech; Polish composer; b. 17 July 1932, Lvov; m. Barbara Pomianowska; ed State Higher School of Music, Katowice, (student of B.

Woytowicz) Nadia Boulanger School; mem. Cttee Int. Festival of Contemporary Music Warszawska Jesień 1975, Polish Composers Union 1953–; mem. Polish Acad. of Arts and Sciences 1998–; Dr hc (Opole Univ.) 1999; numerous awards in Poland and abroad. *Works include:* Mała uwertura 1955, I Symfonia 1955, II Symfonia 1956, Oda Bela Bartok in Memoriam 1957, Riff 62 1962, Générique 1963, Diphthongs 1964, Springfield Sonnet 1963, Solenne 1967, Upstairs Downstairs 1971, Przygrywka i Kolęda 1972, Krzesany 1974, Bogurodzica 1975, Kościelec 1909 1976, Siwa mgła 1979, Exodus 1981, Victoria 1983, Angelus 1984, Orawa 1986, Prelude for Strings 1988, Dracula 1991, Piano Concerto 1997, Missa pro pace 2000; music for about 30 plays and 150 films including Illumination 1973, The Promised Land 1974, Death and the Maiden 1994, Portrait of a Lady 1997, The Ninth Gate 1999, The Pianist 2002. *Leisure interests:* books about mountains and cats, travels, home, cars. *Address:* ul. Kościuszki 165, 40-524 Katowice, Poland. *Telephone:* (32) 2514965.

KILBY, Jack St Clair, MS, FIEEE; American scientist; b. 8 Nov. 1923, Jefferson City, Mo.; ed Univ. of Illinois, Univ. of Wisconsin; Centralab Div., Globe Union Inc. 1947–58; Texas Instruments (TI), Dallas 1958–70 (invented the first microchip while at TI in 1958); worked as ind. inventor 1970–78; Distinguished Prof. of Electrical Eng, Texas A&M Univ. 1978–84; holder of over 60 US patents; mem. Nat. Acad. of Eng; Nat. Medal of Science 1970, Nat. Inventors Hall of Fame 1982, Nobel Prize in Physics (Jt recipient) 2000. *Address:* Suite 155, 6600 Lyndon B. Johnson Freeway, Dallas, TX 75240 (Office); 7723 Midbury Drive, Dallas, TX 75230, USA (Home).

KILEY, Robert R.; American business executive; b. 16 Sept. 1935, Minneapolis; m. Rona Kiley; ed Univ. of Notre Dame, Ind., Harvard Univ., Mass.; Staff Asst CIA 1963–70; Assoc. Dir Police Foundation, Washington, DC 1970–72; Deputy Mayor of Boston, MA 1972–75; Chair. and CEO Mass. Bay Transportation Authority 1975–79; Vice-Pres. Gemini Consulting (man. analysis centre), Cambridge, Mass. 1979–83; Chair. and CEO Metropolitan Transportation Authority (MTA), New York 1983–90; with Kohlberg & Co.; Pres. Fischbach Corpn 1991–94, Chair. 1994; Pres. and CEO New York City Partnership and Chamber of Commerce 1995–2000; Chair. London Transport, UK Jan.–July 2001; Commr of Transport for London, UK 2001–; mem. Council on Foreign Relations; mem. Bd Salzburg Int. Seminar, American Repertory Theater, MONY Group Inc., Princeton Review Inc., Edison Schools Inc.; mem. Advisory Bd, Harvard Univ. Center for State and Local Govt. *Address:* Transport for London, Windsor House, 42–50 Victoria Street, London, SW1H 0TL, England (Office). *Telephone:* (20) 7941-4500. *Website:* www.tfl.gov.uk.

KILGUS, Martin A., MA, PhD; German journalist; b. 15 March 1963, Stuttgart; s. of Alfred Kilgus and Charlotte-Pauline Hofmann; ed Wirtemberg-Gymnasium, Stuttgart, Univ. of Stuttgart and The American Univ., Washington, DC; traineeship, NBC Radio; joined Dept for Ethnic Broadcasting, SDR Radio & TV, Stuttgart 1989; worked as ed. for migrants' audio broadcasts; 1991; now Ed. with SWR (fmrly SDR) Radio & TV; special field of research and activity: Digital Audio Broadcasting (DAB) and multi-lingual broadcasts; Chair. Int. Educ. Information Exchange (IEIE e.V.), Stuttgart 1996–; mem. German Asscn for the UN; Caritas Prize for Journalism. *Leisure interests:* arts, literature, cooking, snowboarding. *Address:* SWR Radio & TV, 70178 Stuttgart, Christophstrasse 10, Germany. *Telephone:* (711) 6075065. *Fax:* (711) 600499.

KILLICK, Sir John Edward, GCMG; British diplomatist; b. 18 Nov. 1919, Isleworth; s. of late Edward W. J. Killick and Doris M. Stokes; m. 1st Lynette de Preez 1949 (died 1984); m. 2nd Irene M. H. Easton, OBE 1985 (died 1995); ed Latymer Upper School, Univ. Coll., London and Univ. of Bonn; Mil. Service 1939–46; Control Comm. for Germany 1946; entered diplomatic service 1946; Foreign Office 1946–48, Berlin, Frankfurt and Bonn 1948–51; Foreign Office 1951–53; British Embassy, Addis Ababa 1953–57; Nat. Defence Coll. of Canada 1957–58; Foreign Office 1958–61; Imperial Defence Coll. 1962; British Embassy, Washington 1963–68; Asst Under-Sec. of State, FCO 1968–71; Amb. to USSR 1971–73; Deputy Under-Sec. of State, FCO 1973–75; Perm. Rep. to NATO 1975–79; Dir Dunlop SA 1980–85; Pres. British Atlantic Cttee 1985–92; Vice-Pres. Atlantic Treaty Asscn 1991–93; Chair. SA Club 1986–89. *Address:* 5 Norstead Gardens, Southborough, Kent, TN4 0VE, England. *Telephone:* (1892) 545702 (Home). *Fax:* (1892) 545702 (Home). *E-mail:* john_killick@hotmail.com (Home).

KILLION, Redley (Rere), MA (Econs); Micronesian politician and economist; b. 23 Oct. 1951, Weno, Chuuk State; m. Jacinta Killion; nine c.; ed Mizpah High School, Weno, Marist High School, Eugene, Oregon, Univ. of Hawaii, Vanderbilt Univ., Nashville, Tenn.; economist, Dept of Resources and Devt, Trust Territory Govt 1974–79; Dir Dept of Resources and Devt, Chuuk State Govt 1979–86; Nat. Senator 1987–99, Vice-Pres. Federated States of Micronesia 1999–; Congress of Micronesia Scholarship Awards 1969–70; UN Fellowship for Graduate Studies at Vanderbilt Univ. 1977–78. *Address:* P.O. Box PS-53, Palikir, Pohnpei State, FSM 96941 (Office); P.O. Box PS 237, Palikir, Pohnpei State, FSM 96942, Micronesia (Home). *Telephone:* (691) 320-2228 (Office); (691) 320-2833 (Home). *Fax:* (691) 330-4360 (Office); (691) 320-2930 (Home).

KILLIP, Christopher David; British photographer; b. 11 July 1946, Isle of Man; s. of Allen Killip and Mary Quirk; one s.; ed Douglas High School for Boys; photography in Isle of Man 1969–71; Prof. of Visual Studies, Harvard Univ. 1991–; *exhbns include:* Isle of Man, Arts Council of GB (ACGB) Tour of

UK 1980–82, Serpentine Gallery 1985, Nat. Museum of Photography, Bradford 1986, Art Inst. of Chicago 1986, Victoria & Albert Museum 1988, Landesmuseum, Munster 1988, Princesshof Museum, Netherlands 1989, IVAM, Valencia 1990, Palais de Tokyo, Paris 1990; *group exhbns include:* Royal Acad. 1989, Barbican Centre, London 1989, Photography until now, Museum of Modern Art (MOMA), New York 1990; works in many public collections including Victoria & Albert Museum, George Eastman House, USA, Stedelijk Museum, Amsterdam, Nat. Gallery of Australia; ACGB Photography Awards 1973–74; Northern Arts Photography Fellow 1975–76; ACGB Bursary Award 1977; Henri Cartier-Bresson Award, Paris 1989. *Publications:* Isle of Man (portfolio), Isle of Man (book) 1980, In flagrante 1988, Fifty-five 2001. *Address:* Harvard University, 24 Quincy Street, Cambridge, MA 02138, USA.

KILLY, Jean-Claude; French Olympic skier and business executive; b. 30 Aug. 1943, St-Cloud, Seine-et-Oise; s. of Robert Killy and Madeleine de Ridder; m. Danièlle Gaubert 1973 (died 1987); one d., two step-c.; ed Ecole de Val-d'Isère, Lycées in Chambéry, Grenoble, Saint-Jean-de-Maurienne, Bourg-Saint-Maurice; French champion 1964, 1965, 1966; won three gold medals at Winter Olympics, Grenoble, France 1968; retd from competitive skiing 1968 but returned in 1972 to become professional world champion in 1973; customs officer 1965–68; Publicity Agent Gen. Motors 1968; Marketing Consultant (concerning skiing information) United Air Lines 1969; settled in Geneva 1969 and moved into the sports clothing business with the co. Veleeda-Killy; Tech. Adviser Dynamic 1981–; Pres. World Sport Marketing (now Amaury Sport Org.) 1992–2000, Société du Tour de France; Co-Pres. Winter Olympics, Albertville 1992; mem. Admin Bd Coca-Cola 1993–, Coca-Cola Enterprises 1997–, Int. Olympic Cttee 1995–; Dir Rolex Watch Co.; Pres. Co-ordination Cttee for 2006 Olympic Games in Turin; Commdr, Légion d'honneur; IOC Olympic Order; Export Oscar 1982. *Film:* Snow Job. *Publications:* Skiez avec Killy 1969, Le Ski 1978. *Leisure interests:* flying, reading, cycling, walking, swimming, snowboarding. *Address:* 13 chemin Bellefontaine, 1223 Cologny-GE, Switzerland.

KILMER, Val; American actor; b. 31 Dec. 1959, Los Angeles; m. Joanne Whalley (q.v.) 1988 (divorced 1996); one d.; ed Hollywood's Professional School, Juilliard; appears on TV. *Films:* Top Secret 1984, Real Genius 1985, Top Gun 1986, Willow 1988, Kill Me Again 1989, The Doors 1991, Thunderheart 1991, True Romance 1993, The Real McCoy 1993, Tombstone 1993, Wings of Courage 1995, Batman Forever 1995, Heat 1995, The Saint 1996, The Island of Dr. Moreau 1996, The Ghost and the Darkness 1996, Dead Girl 1996, Joe the King 1999, At First Sight 1999, Planet Red 2000, Pollock 2000. *Stage appearances include:* Electra and Orestes, Henry IV Part One 1981, As You Like It 1982, Slab Boys (Broadway debut) 1983, Hamlet 1988, 'Tis Pity She's A Whore 1992. *Address:* c/o CAA, 9830 Wilshire Boulevard, Beverly Hills, CA 90212, USA. *Website:* www.valkilmer.org (Office).

KIM, Anatoly Andreyevich; Russian writer; b. 15 June 1939, S Kazakhstan; ed Literary Inst., Moscow; freelance writer 1973–; Prof. of Russian Language and Literature, Inst. of Journalism, Moscow; lecturer in S Korea 1991–95. *Publications include:* more than 20 books including novels: Gatherers of Herbs 1976, Litis 1980, Squirrel 1984, Forest-Father 1989, Onlyrya 1995, Mushroom Picking with Bach's Music 1997, The Wall 1998, Twins 2000; numerous short stories; film scripts: My Sister Lucy, Revenge, To Go Out of the Forest. *Address:* Akademika Pavlova str. 36, apt. 112, 121552 Moscow, Russia (Home). *Telephone:* (095) 140-15-31 (Home).

KIM, HE Cardinal Stephen Sou-hwan; South Korean ecclesiastic; b. 8 May 1922, Daegu; ed Sophia Univ., Tokyo, Major Seminary, Seoul and Sociology Dept, Univ. of Munster, Germany; ordained priest 1951; Pastor of Andong, Archdiocese of Taegu 1951–53; Sec. to Archbishop of Taegu 1953–55; Pastor of Kimchon (Daegu) 1955–56; Dir Sung-Eui Schools, Kimchon 1955–56; sociology studies, Univ. of Munster, Germany 1956–64; Editor-in-Chief Catholic Shibo (weekly) 1964–66; Bishop of Masan 1966–68; Archbishop of Seoul 1968–98, Archbishop Emer. 1998–; cr. HE Cardinal 1969; Pres. Bishops' Conf. of Korea until 1987, Pres. Follow-up Cttee for Fed. of Asian Bishops' Conf. 1971–74; Apostolic Admin. for Pyongyang 1975–98; Dr hc (Sogang Univ. Seoul) 1974, (Notre Dame Univ., USA) 1977, (Sophia Univ., Tokyo) 1988, (Korea Univ.) 1990, (Seaton Hall Univ., USA) 1990, (Yonsei Univ.) 1994, (Fu-Jen Univ., Taiwan) 1995, (Ateneo Univ., Philippines) 1997, (Seoul Nat. Univ.) 1999. *Leisure interests:* music, literature. *Address:* Bishop's House, Catholic University, 90-1 Hyehwa-Dong, Jongno-gu, Seoul, Republic of Korea. *Telephone:* (2) 3675-2278 (Office). *Fax:* (2) 3675-2279 (Office).

KIM DAE-JUNG, MA, PhD; South Korean politician; b. 3 Dec. 1925, Hugwang-ri, S Jeolla Prov.; m. Lee Lee Ho; ed Mokpo Commercial High School, Korea and Kyunghee Univs., Diplomatic Acad. of Foreign Ministry of Russia; Pres. Mokpo Merchant Ship Co. 1948; arrested by N Korean Communists, escaped from jail 1950; Pres. Mokpo Daily News 1950; Deputy Commdr S. Jeolla Region, Maritime Defence Force 1950; Pres. Heungkuk Merchant Shipping Co. 1951; Pres Dae-yang Shipbldg. Co. 1951; mem. Cen. Cttee Democratic Party 1957, Spokesman 1960, Spokesman, Nat. Alliance to Protect Human Rights 1958; elected to 5th Nat. Ass. 1961, 6th Nat. Ass. 1963; Spokesman, People's Party 1965, Chair. Policy Planning Council and mem. Cen. Exec. Bd 1966; Spokesman, New Democratic Party and mem. of Party Cen. Exec. Bd 1967; elected to 7th Nat. Ass. 1967, 8th Nat. Ass. 1971; injured in assassination attempt 1971; in exile, organized anti-dictatorship movts. in Japan and USA 1972; abducted from Japan by Korean CIA agents, survived

two assassination attempts, forcibly returned to Seoul, placed under house arrest 1973; arrested for criticizing Constitution 1976; sentenced to five years' imprisonment 1977; sentence suspended; released from jail, placed under house arrest 1978; house arrest lifted 1979; amnesty granted, civil rights restored; rearrested, charged with treason, sentenced to death 1980; sentence commuted to life imprisonment 1981; sentence reduced to 20 years, later suspended 1982; went into exile in USA 1982; f. Korean Inst. for Human Rights, Va 1983; returned to Korea 1985; under intermittent house arrest 1985–87; Co-Chair. Council for Promotion of Democracy 1985; Standing Adviser, Reunification Democratic Party 1987; f. Party for Peace and Democracy, Pres. 1987–91; reappointed to 13th Nat. Ass. 1988; f., Pres. New Democratic Party April–Sept. 1991; f. Democratic Party, Co.-Chair. 1991–92; reappointed to 14th Nat. Ass., later retd from politics 1992; f. Kim Dae-Jung Peace Foundation for Asia-Pacific Region, Chair. Bd of Dirs. 1994; ended retirement from politics 1995; f. Nat. Congress for New Politics 1995; Pres. of Repub. of Korea 1997–2003; Pres. Millennium Democratic Party 2000–01; Co-Pres. Forum of Democratic Leaders in Asia-Pacific 1994; Visiting Fellow Clare Hall Coll., Univ. of Cambridge, UK 1993, Life Fellow 1993; mem. Int. Ecological Acad. Moscow 1994–; Adviser, Int. Cttee for Relief of Victims of Torture, USA 1984–, Union Theological Seminary, USA 1984–; Visiting Fellow, Centre for Int. Affairs, Harvard Univ., USA 1983–84; Trustee, Fed. of Unions of Korean Shipbldg. Agents 1951; Ed.-in-Chief, Centre for Study of Korean Labour 1995; Hon. Prof. (Moscow Univ.) 1992, (Chinese Acad. of Social Sciences, Nankai Univ., Fudan Univ., People's Repub. of China) 1994; Hon. LLD (Emory Univ., USA) 1983, (Catholic Univ. of America) 1992; Hon. Dr of Political Science (Wonkwang Univ.) 1994; numerous honours and awards including Bruno Kreisky Human Rights Award, Austria 1981, Union Medal, Union Theol. Seminary, USA 1994; awarded Nobel Peace Prize 2000. *Publications include:* Conscience in Action 1985, Prison Writings 1987, Building Peace and Democracy 1987, Kim Dae-jung's Views on International Affairs 1990, In the Name of Justice and Peace 1991, Korea and Asia 1994, The Korean Problem: Nuclear Crisis, Democracy and Reunification 1994, Unification, Democracy and Peace 1994, Mass Participatory Economy: Korea's Road to World Economic Power 1996. *Address:* c/o Office of the President, Chong Wa Dae, 1 Sejongno, Jongno-gu, Seoul, Republic of Korea (Office).

KIM DONG-SHIN, Gen., BA, MS; South Korean politician and army general (retd); b. 13 March 1941, Kwangju City; ed Seoul Nat. Univ., Korean Mil. Acad. and Hannam Univ.; Regimental Commdr, Army of Repub. of Korea 1983; apptd Chief, Foreign Policy Div., Ministry of Nat. Defence 1984; Deputy Dir of Strategic Planning, Jt Chief of Staff 1989–90; Commanding Gen. 51st Infantry Div. 1990–92; Dir of Force Planning 1992–93; Commanding Gen. Capital Corps, 3rd Army 1993–94; Chief Dir of Operations, Jt Chiefs of Staff 1995–96; Deputy Commdr-in-Chief, Repub. of Korea–US Combined Forces Command 1996–98; Army Chief of Staff 1998–99; Adviser, Nat. Security Cttee 2000; Minister of Nat. Defence 2001–02; Silver Star Medal 1972, Order of Nat. Security Merit (Samil Medal 1983, Gukson Medal 1993, Tangil Medal 1997), Order of Mil. Merit 1991, US Army Meritorious Service Medal 1999, Legion of Merit 2001. *Address:* c/o Ministry of National Defence 1, 3-ga, Yonsan-don, Yongsan-gu, Seoul, Republic of Korea (Office).

KIM HAK-SU, PhD; South Korean international civil servant and economist; b. Wonju; ed Yonsei Univ., Edin. Univ. and Univ. of South Carolina; economist Cen. Bank 1960; Sec. to Minister of Commerce and Industry 1969; London Rep. Bank of Korea 1971–73; Exec. Dir Daewoo Corpn 1977; Pres. ACWOO Int. Corpn; Chief Planning Officer, Chief Tech. Advisor UN Dept for Tech. Co-operation and Devt 1980s; Sr Research Fellow Korea Inst. for Int. Econ. Policy 1989–93; Pres. Hanil Banking Inst. 1993–95; Sec.-Gen. of the Colombo Plan, Sri Lanka 1995–99; UN Amb. for Int. Econ. Affairs 1999; Exec. Sec. ESCAP 2000–. *Address:* Economic and Social Commission for Asia and the Pacific, United Nations Building, Rajdamnern Avenue, Bangkok, 10200, Thailand (Office). *Telephone:* (2) 288-1234 (Office). *Fax:* (2) 288-1000 (Office). *E-mail:* unisbkk.unescap@un.org (Office). *Website:* www.unescap.org (Office).

KIM IL CHOL, Vice-Marshal; North Korean politician; b. 1928, Pyongyang; ed Mangyongdae Revolutionary School, Navy Acad., USSR; apptd Commdr East Sea Fleet 1970; mem. Party Cen. Cttee 1980–; Deputy in Supreme People's Ass. 1982; apptd Commdr of Navy 1982; rank of Lt-Gen. 1982, Col-Gen. 1985, Gen. 1992, Vice-Marshal 1997; First Minister of the People's Armed Forces 1997–98, Minister 1998–; Vice-Chair. Nat. Defence Comm. 1998–; Kim Il Sung medal 1982, Nat. Flag Order, Hero title 1995. *Address:* Office of the Minister, Ministry of the People's Armed Forces, Pyongyang, Democratic People's Republic of Korea (Office).

KIM JONG IL, Marshal; North Korean Head of State; b. 16 Feb. 1942, secret camp on Mt. Paekdu; s. of the late Kim Il Sung (named Eternal Pres. 1998) and Kim Jong Suk; ed Kim Il Sung Univ., Pyongyang; Officer, then Section Chief, then Deputy Dir, then Dir a Dept of Cen. Cttee Workers' Party of Korea 1964–73; mem. Cen. Cttee 1972, Sec. 1973; mem. Political Comm. Cen. Cttee 1974, mem. Presidium of Politburo of Cen. Cttee of Workers' Party of Korea 1980–, Gen. Sec. 1997–; Chair. Nat. Defence Comm. (Head of State) Sept. 1998–; mem. Mil. Comm. Cen. Cttee at Sixth Party Congress 1980; Deputy to Supreme People's Assembly 1982; First Vice-Chair. Nat. Defence Comm. 1990–93, Chair. 1993–; Supreme Commdr Korean People's Army 1991–; Marshal of the Democratic People's Repub. of Korea 1992–; Hon. Prof. Inca Garsilaso, Vega Univ., Peru 1986; Kim Il Sung Order (three times), title of Marshal; Orden de Solidaridad, Cuba, Grand Croix de l'Ordre Nat. des Mille

Collines, Rwanda, Necklace Order of Egypt; Dr hc (Chiclayo Univ., Peru) 1986; Kim Il Sung Prize; Hero of Democratic People's Repub. of Korea (three times), and many other foreign and domestic awards and honours. *Publications include:* Kim Jong Il Selected Works (13 Vols), For the Completion of the Revolutionary Cause of Juche (10 Vols). *Address:* Central Committee of the Workers' Party of Korea, Pyongyang, Democratic People's Republic of Korea.

KIM JONG-PIL, Brig.-Gen.; South Korean politician; b. 7 Jan. 1926, Puyo; m. Park Young Ok (niece of the late Pres. Park Chung Hee); one s. one d.; ed High School, Gyeongju, Seoul Nat. Univ. and Korean Military Acad.; served in Korean war; Dir Korean Central Intelligence Agency 1961–63; mem. Nat. Assembly 1963–68, 1971–80; Chair. Democratic Republican Party 1963–68; Senior Adviser to Pres. 1970; Vice-Pres. Democratic Republican Party 1971, Pres. 1979–80 (banned from political activity 1980); Pres. New Democratic Republican Party 1987; Jt Pres. Democratic Liberal Party (DLP) 1990–93, Chair. 1993; Hon. Chair. United Liberal Democrats, Pres. 2000–; Prime Minister 1971–75, 1998–99; mem. Spanish Nat. Acad., Korean Acad.; Hon. LLD (Long Island Univ., NY) 1964, (Chungang Univ., Seoul) 1966, (Fairleigh Dickinson Univ.) 1968; Hon. DHumLitt (Westminster Coll., Fulton, Mo.) 1966; Hon. PhD (Hongik Univ.) 1974; numerous awards from Korean and foreign govts. *Leisure interests:* painting, music. *Address:* 103-4, Shinsu-dong, Mabo-gu, Seoul (Office); 340-38, Shindang 4-dong, Jung-gu, Seoul, Republic of Korea (Home). *Telephone:* (2) 701-3355 (Office); (2) 783-7061-2 (Home). *Fax:* (2) 707-1637 (Office); (2) 782-9185 (Home). *E-mail:* www.jamin.or.kr (Office).

KIM JUNG-TAE, BSc; South Korean banker; ed Seoul Nat. Univ.; began career with Daehan Merchant Bank 1969; with Daeshin Securities 1975; Exec. Dir Dongwon Securities 1982, Dir of Venture Capital 1991, Vice-Pres. –1997, CEO 1997–98; Vice-Chair., Pres. and CEO Housing and Commercial Bank (H&CB) 1998–2001; Pres. and CEO Kookmin Bank 2001– (merged with H&CB 2001 becoming Repub. of Korea's biggest bank). *Address:* Kookmin Bank, 9-1 Namdaemunro 2-ga, Jung-gu, Seoul, Republic of Korea. *Telephone:* (2) 3172114 (Office).

KIM JUNG-WON; South Korean business executive; b. 3 March 1948; ed Kyungnam Sr High School, Guilford Coll., New York; joined Hanil Synthetic Fiber Ind. Co. Ltd 1972, Exec. Man. Dir 1974, Vice-Pres. 1975, Pres. 1979–; Pres. Hanhyo Co. Ltd 1977, Chair. 1984–; Pres. Hanhyo Devt Co. Ltd 1978, Chair. 1984–; Pres. Kyungnam Woollen Textile Co. Ltd 1979; First Chair. Hanhyo Acad. 1982; Pres. Korean Amateur Volleyball Asscn 1983, Vice-Pres. Asian Volleyball Asscn 1983; awarded Saemaul Decoration 1974; First Hon. Consul Kingdom of the Netherlands 1985. *Address:* Kukje-ICC Corpn, C.P.O. Box 747, Seoul, Republic of Korea.

KIM MAHN-JE, DEcon; South Korean politician and economist; b. 3 Dec. 1934, Sonsan; ed Univs. of Denver and Missouri, USA; Assoc. Prof., Sogang Univ., Seoul 1965–70, Prof. 1982–; mem. Legis. Ass. 1980–; Minister of Finance 1983–86; Deputy Prime Minister and Minister of Econ. Planning 1986–88; Pres. Korean Devt Inst. 1971–82, Korean Int. Econ. Inst. (KIEI) 1981, Koram Bank 1983–84; apptd. Pres. Pohang Iron & Steel Co. 1994; Sr Policy Researcher, Policy Research Inst. of Democratic Justice Party (DJP) 1982; mem. Monetary Bd 1975–, Econ. Planning Bd Advisory Cttee 1982. *Address:* c/o Pohang Iron and Steel Co. Ltd., 1, Gyeongsang Buk-do, Pohangshi, Kyongbuk, Republic of Korea.

KIM SUK-JOON, BA; South Korean business executive; b. 9 April 1955, Gyeongsang Prov.; m.; two s. one d.; ed Korea Univ., Seoul; mil. service Repub. of Korea Marine Corps 1972–75; planning office SsangYong Corpn 1977–79, NY and LA br. offices SsangYong (USA) Inc. 1979–82, Dir Planning and Project Man. Div. SsangYong Eng and Construction Co. Ltd 1982–83, CEO 1983–95, Pres. 1983–92, Chair. 1992–95, Vice-Chair. SsangYong Business Group 1991–93, 1994–95, CEO 1991–93, 1994–, Chair. 1995–, Chair., CEO SsangYong Motor Co. 1994–95, Chair., CEO SsangYong Cement Industrial Co. 1995–; Co-Chair. Korean Party Korea-France High-Level Businessmens' Club, Korean Party Korea-Singapore Econ. Co-operation Cttee; Vice-Chair. Korea-Japan Econ. Asscn, Fed. of Korean Industries, Korean Employers' Fed.; mem. Korea Chamber of Commerce and Industries; Dir Bd of Trustees Kookmin. Univ.; Baden-Powell World Fellow World Scout Foundation; Order of Industrial Service Merit Gold Tower 1991. *Address:* SsangYong Business Group, 24-1, 2-ga, Jeo-dong, Jung-gu, Seoul 100-748, Republic of Korea. *Telephone:* (2) 270-8155. *Fax:* (2) 273-0981. *Website:* www.cemtecasia.com.sg (Office).

KIM SUK-SOO; South Korean politician and judge; b. 20 Nov. 1932; ed Yonsei Univ., Seoul; admitted to Korean Bar 1958; Judge Advocate, Repub. of Korea Army HQ 1960–63; Judge Masan Br. Court of Pusan Dist Court 1963–67, Pusan Dist Court 1967–69, Incheon Br. Court of Seoul Civil and Criminal Dist Court 1969–70, Seoul Criminal Dist Court 1970–71, Seoul High Court 1971–73; Research Judge Supreme Court 1973–74; Presiding Judge Pusan Dist Court 1974–77, Sungbook Br. Court of Seoul Dist. Court 1977–79, Seoul Civil Dist Court 1979–80; Chief Judge Incheon Br. Court of Suwon Dist Court 1980–81; Presiding Judge Seoul High Court and Chief Judge Nambu Br. of Seoul Dist. Court 1981–83; Sr Presiding Judge Seoul High Court 1983–86; Chief Judge Pusan Dist Court 1986–88; Vice-Minister of Court Admin 1988–91; Supreme Court Justice 1991–97; Chair. Nat. Election Comm. 1993–97; Chair. Judicial Officers' Ethics Cttee of Supreme Court 1997–2001; Chair. Korea Press Ethics Comm. 2000–02; Chair. Govt Public Service Ethics Cttee 2002; Prime Minister of Repub. of Korea Oct. 2002–;

Auditor Bd of Dirs Yonsei Univ. Foundation 1997–2002; Dir Samsung Electronics Co. 1999–2001, Yonsei Law Promotion Foundation 2002; Order of Service Merit (Blue Stripes) 1997; Hon. PhD (Yonsei Univ.) 1997. *Address:* Office of the Prime Minister, 77 Sejong-no, Jongno-gu, Seoul, Republic of Korea (Office). *Telephone:* (2) 737-0094 (Office). *Fax:* (2) 737-0109 (Office). *Website:* www.opm.gov.kr (Office).

KIM TAEK-JIN, MSc; South Korean computer engineer and business executive; ed Seoul Nat. Univ.; co-author of Hangul (Korean-language word-processing programme) while at Univ. 1989; cr. Hanmesoft (computer software) 1989; staff mem. Research and Devt Centre, Hyundai Electronics Industries Co. (now Hynix) 1991–92, Head of Devt Team for Shinbiro (S Korea's first internet service provider), 1994; cr. Lineage (online fantasy computer game) 1997, expanded to Taiwan markets 2000, has signed up five million users –2002; Founder, Pres. and CEO NCSoft Corpn 1997–, est. subsidiaries and jt ventures in USA, Japan, Hong Kong and China; Regional Dir Microsoft Corpn 1998; Man of the Year, Computer Reporters Asscn. 1989; New Venture Age Leader, Naeway Economic Daily 2000; Industrial Medal, Soft Expo/Digital Contents Fair 2001; Best Contrib. to Cultural Industry, Ministry of Culture and Tourism 2001. *Address:* NCSoft Corpn, Seung Kwang Building, 143-8, Samsung-dong, Kangnam-gu, Seoul 135-090, Republic of Korea (Office). *Telephone:* (2) 2186-3300 (Office). *Website:* www.ncsoft.co.kr (Office).

KIM WOO-CHOONG, BA; North Korean business executive; b. 19 Dec. 1936, Daegu; s. of Yong-Ha Kim and In-Hang Chun; m. Hrrja Chung 1964; four c.; ed Kyunggi High School, Seoul, Yonsei Univ.; with Econ. Devt Council; with Hansung Industrial Co. Ltd, Dir –1967 (resgnd); Founder, Daewoo Industrial Co. Ltd (textile co.) 1967, Chair. Daewoo Group, includes Daewoo Shipbldg. & Heavy Machinery Ltd, Daewoo Motor Co., etc.; Founder, Daewoo Foundation 1978; under investigation for fraud 1999–; in exile 1999–, to be charged with fraud when located; Dr hc (Yonsei Univ., Korea Univ., George Washington Univ., USA, Univ. of South Carolina, Russian Econ. Acad., Univ. Santiago de Cali/Univ. del Valle, Colombia); numerous honours and awards including Int. Business Award, Int. Chamber of Commerce 1984; Commdr., Légion d'honneur 1996. *Publications:* It's Big World and There's Lots To Be Done 1989, Every Street is Paved With Gold: The Road to Real Success.

KIM YONG CHUN, Gen.; North Korean army official; b. 1922; assoc. mem. Workers' Party Cen. Cttee (WPCC) –1980, Deputy Chief of Dept, WPCC 1980–83; rank of Gen. 1992, Vice Marshall 1995; Chief of Staff North Korean People's Party 1995–; mem. Nat. Defence Comm. Sept. 1998–. *Address:* Korean People's Army, Pyongyang, People's Republic of Korea (Office).

KIM YONG NAM; North Korean politician; b. 1925; ed Kim Il Sung Univ., Moscow Univ.; mem. Cen. Cttee Workers' Party of Korea (WPK) 1970, Political Commissar 1977, mem. Political Bureau 1980–; Vice-Premier and Minister of Foreign Affairs 1983–98; Del. to Supreme People's Ass.; Pres. Presidium of the Supreme People's Ass. 1998–. *Address:* Choe ko in min hoe ui (Supreme People's Assembly), Pyongyang, Democratic People's Republic of Korea (Office).

KIM YOUNG-SAM, BA; South Korean politician; b. 20 Dec. 1927, Koje-gun, South Gyeongsang Prov.; s. of Kim Hong-Jo and late Park Bu-ryon; m. Sohn Myoung-Soon; two s. three d.; ed Kyongnam High School, Busan and Seoul Nat. Univ.; mem. Nat. Ass. 1954–79; Founder-mem. Democratic Party 1955; re-elected Pres. New Democratic Party 1974, 1979; expelled from Nat. Ass. for opposition to regime of Pres. Park 1979; arrested under martial law 1980–81; banned from political activity Nov. 1980; again under house arrest 1982–83; staged 23-day hunger strike demanding democracy May–June 1983; Co-Chair. Council for Promotion of Democracy 1984; played leading role in org. of New Korea Democratic Party (absorbing Democratic Korea Party) which won large number of seats in 1985 election; political ban lifted May 1985; Presidential Cand. 1987 elections; Founder-Pres. Reunification Democracy Party 1987–90; Exec. Chair. Democratic Liberal Party (DLP) 1990–97, Pres. 1992–97; Pres. of Repub. of Korea 1992–97; Dr hc (Towson State Univ., Baltimore) 1974; Martin Luther King Peace Prize 1995. *Publications:* There is No Hill We Can Depend On, Politics is Long and Political Power is Short, Standard-Bearer in his Forties, My Truth and My Country's Truth 1984, My Resolution 1987, Democratization, the Way of Salvation of my Country 1987, New Korea 2000. *Leisure interests:* calligraphy, mountain climbing, jogging, swimming. *Address:* 7-6 Sangdo 1-dong, Dongjak-gu, Seoul, Republic of Korea.

KIMBALL, Warren Forbes, PhD; American professor of history; b. 24 Dec. 1935, Brooklyn, New York; s. of Cyril S. Kimball and Carolyn F. Kimball; m. Jacqueline Sue Nelson 1959; one s. two d.; ed Villanova and Georgetown Univs.; served USNR 1958–65; Instructor, US Naval Acad. 1961–65; Asst Prof., Georgetown Univ. 1965–67, Univ. of Georgia 1967–70; Assoc. Prof., Rutgers Univ. 1970–85, Prof. II 1985–93, Robert Treat Prof. of History 1993–; Pitt Prof. of American History, Corpus Christi, Cambridge Univ., UK 1988–89. *Publications:* 'The Most Unsordid Act': Lend-Lease, 1939–1941 1969, Swords or Ploughshares? The Morgenthau Plan 1976, Churchill and Roosevelt: The Complete Correspondence (3 Vols) 1984, The Juggler: Franklin Roosevelt as Wartime Statesman 1991, Forged in War: Roosevelt, Churchill and the Second World War 1997. *Address:* Department of History, Rutgers University, Newark, NJ 07102 (Office); 2540 Otter Lane, John's Island, SC 29455, USA (Home). *Telephone:* (843) 768-3879 (Home). *E-mail:* wkimball@andromeda.rutgers.edu (Office).

KINAKH, Col Anatoliy Kyrilovich; Ukrainian politician; b. 4 Aug. 1954, Moldova; m. Marina Volodimirovna Kinakh 1960; three d.; ed Leningrad Vessel Construction Inst.; worked on vessel construction and vessel repair plants in Tallinn and Nikolayev 1978–92; mem. Verkhovna Rada (Parl.); mem. Comm. on Econ. Reform and Nat. Econ. Man. 1990; Presidential Rep. in Nikolayev region, then Head of Nikolayev Regional Admin. 1992–94; Head Nikolayev Regional Council of People's Deputies 1994–95; mem. Political Council People's Democratic Party, Deputy Chair. 1996; Deputy Prime Minister of Ukraine for Problems of Industrial Policy 1995–96; Presidential Adviser on Industrial Policy, then Pres. Ukrainian Union of Businessmen 1996–97; First Deputy Head Council of Int. Congress of Businessmen 1997–; mem. Higher Econ. Council at Ukrainian Presidency, Head of Co-ordination Council on Privatization of Industrial Enterprises of Strategic Importance 1997–; mem. Nat. Council of Ukraine on Problems of Quality 1997–2001; Head Cttee on Industrial Policy Verkhovna Rada (Parl.) 1998–2001; Chair. Nat. Cttee of Int. Trade Chamber 1998–2001; First Deputy Prime Minister of Ukraine Aug.–Dec. 1999; Prime Minister of Ukraine 2001–02; currently Chair. Party of Industrialists and Entrepreneurs of Ukraine (Partiya promyslovtsiv i pidpryyemtsiv Ukrainy); mem. Parl. 2002–; mem. Acad. of Cybernetics. *Leisure interest:* classical music. *Address:* Partiya promyslovtsiv i pidpryyemtsiv Ukrainy, vul. Baseyna 30–46, 01023 Kiev, Ukraine (Office). *E-mail:* pppu@ukr.net (Office). *Website:* pppu.com.ua (Office).

KINCAID, Jamaica; Antigua and Barbuda writer; b. 25 May 1949, St John's; d. of Annie Richardson; one s. one d.; staff writer The New Yorker 1976; teaches at Harvard Univ.; lives in Vt, USA; numerous hon. degrees. *Publications include:* At the Bottom of the River (short stories; American Acad. and Inst. of Arts and Letters Morton Dauwen Zabel Award) 1983, Annie John (novel) 1985, A Small Place (non-fiction) 1988, Lucy (novel) 1990, My Brother 1997, My Favorite Plant 1998, My Garden (non-fiction) 1999, Talk Stories 2001, Mr. Potter 2002. *Leisure interest:* gardening. *Address:* c/o Farrar Straus & Giroux, 19 Union Square West, New York, NY 10003, USA.

KINCSES, Veronika; Hungarian soprano and opera and concert singer; d. of György Kincses and Etelka Angyal; m. József Vajda; one s.; ed Liszt Ferenc Music Acad. Budapest and Accademia Santa Cecilia, Rome; soloist State Opera, Budapest; song-recitals, also oratorio performances; guest performances USA, Argentina, Venezuela, Hong Kong, Singapore etc. 1997–98; operatic roles include Madame Butterfly, Mimi (La Bohème), Manon Lescaut, Liu (Turandot), Le Villi (Puccini), Contessa (Le Nozze di Figaro), Fiordiligi (Così fan Tutte), Vitellia (La Clemenza di Tito), Elvira (Don Giovanni), Amelia (Simone Boccanegra), Leonora (La Forza del destino), Micaela (Carmen), Marguerita (Faust), Silvana (Fiamma–Respighi), Eva (Meistersinger von Nürnberg), Adriana (Adriana Lecouvreur), Tosca, Judit (Bluebeard's Castle); Liszt Prize, Kossuth Prize, Merited Artist title, Grand Prix du Disque, Paris. *Leisure interest:* teaching singers. *Address:* International Management of the Hungarian State Opera, Andrássy ut 22, 1061 Budapest, Hungary; Robert Lombardo Associates, 61 West 62nd Street, New York, NY 10023, USA. *Telephone:* (1) 332-7372 (Hungary); (212) 586-4453 (New York).

KIND, Dieter Hans, DrIng; German electrical engineer; b. 5 Oct. 1929, Reichenberg, Bohemia; s. of Hans Kind and Gerta Kind; m. Waltraud Wagner 1954; three c.; ed Technical Univ., Munich; Prof. and Dir High-Voltage Inst., Technical Univ., Braunschweig 1962–75, Prof. Emer. 1975–; Pres. Physikalisch-Technische Bundesanstalt, Braunschweig and Berlin 1975–95, Comité Int. des Poids et Mesures, Sèvres/Paris 1975–95; Fellow IEEE; Dr hc (Tech. Univ. Munich); Ehrenring VDE 1988, Dong-Baeg Medal (Korea) 1988, Ordem do Mérito Científico (Brazil) 1995, Grosses Bundesverdienstkreuz. *Publications:* An Introduction to High-Voltage Experimental Technique 1978, High-Voltage Insulation Technology 1985, Herausforderung Metrologie 2002; about 50 scientific articles. *Leisure interests:* sport, literature. *Address:* Knappstrasse 4, 38116 Braunschweig, Germany. *Telephone:* (531) 511497. *Fax:* (531) 5160239.

KINDLEBERGER, Charles Poor, MA, PhD; American economist; b. 12 Oct. 1910, New York; s. of E. Crosby Kindleberger and Elizabeth Randall McIlvaine Kindleberger; m. Sarah Bache Miles 1937; two s. two d.; ed Kent School, Univ. of Pennsylvania and Columbia Univ.; research economist, US Treasury 1936; Fed. Reserve Bank of New York 1936–39; Bank for Int. Settlements 1939–40; Fed. Reserve Bd 1940–42; Office of Strategic Services 1942–45; Capt. and Maj. US Army 1944–45; Dept of State 1945–48; Assoc. Prof. and Prof. MIT 1948–81, now Prof. Emer.; Visiting Prof. Middlebury Coll. 1982–83, Brandeis Univ. 1983–87; Consulting Fellow British Acad.; mem. American Philosophical Soc., American Acad. of Arts and Sciences; Bronze Star 1944; Legion of Merit 1956; Dr hc (Paris) 1966, (Ghent) 1977, (Pennsylvania) 1984, (Basel) 1997; Harms Prize, Inst. für Weltwirtschaft 1978. *Publications:* 30 books including: The World in Depression 1929–39 1973, Manias, Panics and Crashes 1978, A Financial History of Western Europe 1984, The Life of an Economist: An Autobiography 1991, Mariners and Markets 1992, World Economic Primacy 1500–1990 1996, Essays in History 1999, Comparative Political Economy: A Retrospective 2000. *Address:* Brookhaven at Lexington A-406, 1010 Waltham Street, Lexington, MA 02421, USA. *Telephone:* (781) 863-2540. *Fax:* (781) 863-9944 (Home).

KINELEV, Vladimir Georgiyevich, DTechSc; Russian politician; b. 28 Jan. 1945, Ust-Kalmanka, Altay Region; m.; one d.; ed Bauman Higher Tech. School; worked Cen. Bureau of Experimental Machine-Construction, Asst, Prof., Pro-rector Bauman Higher Tech. School; First Deputy Chair. State Cttee on Science and Higher School 1990–91; Chair. Cttee on Higher School Ministry of Science, Higher School and Tech. Policy of Russian Fed., concurrently First Deputy Minister 1992–93; Chair. State Cttee on Higher Educ. 1993–96; Deputy Chair. Russian Govt 1996; Minister of Gen. and Professional Educ. 1996–98; Dir UNESCO Inst. for Information Technologies in Educ. (IITE) 1998–; Academician Russian Acad. of Educ., Russian Eng Acad.; Prize of USSR Govt 1990, State Prize of Russia 1997; Order of Honour, Russian Fed. 1995. *Publications:* The Objective Necessity 1995, Education and Culture in the History of Civilization 1998. *Address:* UNESCO Institute for Information Technologies in Education, Kedrova str. 8, 117096 Moscow, Russia (Office). *Telephone:* (095) 129-19-98 (Office). *Fax:* (095) 718-07-66 (Office). *E-mail:* kinelev@iite.ru (Office). *Website:* www.iite.ru.

KING, Angela; Jamaican United Nations official; with Perm. Mission of Jamaica to UN, New York –1966; joined UN Secr. 1966, worked in Br. for the Promotion of Equality Between Men and Women, del. to UN Conf. on Women, Mexico City 1975, Copenhagen 1980, Beijing 1995; Chief of UN Observer Mission in S Africa (UNOMSA) 1992–94; fmr Deputy to Asst Sec. for Human Resources and Man. and Dir of Operational Services Div.; Dir Div. of Advancement of Women; Chair. Inter-Agency Cttee on Women and Gender and Equality; Asst Sec.-Gen., Special Adviser on Gender Issues and the Advancement of Women 1997–. *Address:* United Nations, Department of Economic and Social Affairs, United Nations Plaza, New York, NY 10017, USA (Office). *Telephone:* (212) 963-1234. *Fax:* (212) 963-4879. *Website:* www.un.org.

KING, Angus S., Jr, JD; American lawyer, broadcaster and politician; b. 31 March 1944; m. Mary J. Herman; four s. one d.; ed Dartmouth Coll. and Pennsylvania Univ.; called to the Bar, Maine 1969; staff attorney Pine Tree Legal Assistance, Showhegan, Me 1969–72; Chief Counsel, Office of Senator William D. Hathaway, US Senate Subcttee on Alcoholism and Narcotics, Washington 1972–75; fmr partner Smith, Lloyd & King, Brunswick, Me; Gov. of Maine 1995–2003; TV host Maine Watch 1977–; Vice-Pres. and Gen. Counsel Swift River/Hafslund Co. 1983; f. and Pres. NE Energy Man. Inc. 1989–94. *Address:* c/o Office of the Governor, State House, Station 1, Augusta, ME 04333, USA.

KING, Anthony Stephen, DPhil; Canadian professor of government; b. 17 Nov. 1934; s. of the late Harold King and Marjorie King; m. 1st Vera Korte 1965 (died 1971); m. 2nd Jan Reece 1980; ed Queen's Univ., Kingston, Ont., Magdalen and Nuffield Colls, Oxford; Fellow Magdalen Coll., Oxford 1961–65; Sr Lecturer Univ. of Essex 1966–68, Reader 1968–69, Prof. of Govt 1969–; Visiting Prof. Wis. Univ. 1967, Princeton Univ. 1984; Fellow, Center for Advanced Study in Behavioral Sciences, Stanford Univ., Calif. 1977–78; elections commentator for BBC; Daily Telegraph mem. Cttee on Standards in Public Life 1994–98, Royal Comm. on House of Lords Reform 1999; Hon. Foreign mem. American Acad. of Arts and Sciences 1993. *Publications:* The British General Election of 1964 (jtly) 1965, The British General Election of 1966 (jtly) 1966, British Politics: People, Parties and Parliament (Ed.) 1966, The British Prime Minister (Ed.) 1969, Westminster and Beyond (jtly) 1973, British Members of Parliament: A Self-portrait 1974, Why is Britain Becoming Harder to Govern? (Ed.) 1976, Britain Says Yes: The 1975 Referendum on the Common Market 1977, The New American Political System (Ed.) 1978, Both Ends of the Avenue: the Presidency of the Executive Branch and Congress in the 1980s (Ed.) 1983, Britain at the Polls 1992 (Ed.) 1992, SDP: The Birth, Life and Death of the Social Democratic Party (jtly) 1995, Running Scared: Why America's Politicians Campaign Too Much and Govern Too Little 1997, New Labour Triumphs: Britain at the Polls (Ed.) 1997, British Political opinion 1937–2000 (Ed.) 2001, Does the United Kingdom Still Have a Constitution? 2001, Britain at the Polls 2001 (Ed.) 2001, Leaders' Personalities and the Outcomes of Democratic Elections (Ed.) 2002; numerous papers in British and American journals. *Leisure interests:* holidays, music, theatre, walking. *Address:* Department of Government, University of Essex, Wivenhoe Park, Colchester, Essex, CO4 3SQ (Office); The Mill House, Lane Road, Wakes Colne, Colchester, Essex, CO6 2BP, England (Home). *Telephone:* (1206) 873393 (Office); (1787) 222497 (Home).

KING, B. B. (Riley B. King); American singer and guitarist; b. 16 Sept. 1925, Itta Bena, Miss.; began teaching himself guitar 1945; later studied Schillinger System; fmr disc jockey and singer, Memphis radio stations; numerous int. appearances; founding mem. John F. Kennedy Performing Arts Center 1971; Co-Chair. Foundation for Advancement of Inmate Rehabilitation and Recreation 1972–; toured USSR 1979; performance at closing ceremonies, Summer Olympics, Atlanta, Ga 1996; Hon. LHD (Tougaloo Coll. Miss.) 1973; Hon. D. Mus. (Yale) 1977; numerous awards including Grammy Lifetime Achievement Award 1987; Grammy Award: Best Traditional Blues Album (for Blues Summit 1994); Kennedy Center Honours 1995, Living Legend Award, Trumpet Awards 1997. *Films include:* When We Were Kings 1996, Blues Brothers 1998, 2000. *Albums include:* King of the Blues 1989, Indianola Mississippi Seeds 1989, Blues is King 1990, Live at the Apollo 1991, Spotlight on Lucille 1992, Singin' the Blues 1993, Blues on the Bayou 1998, Let the Good Tune Roll 1998, numerous other recordings. *Address:* c/o Sidney A. Seidenberg, 1414 Avenue of the Americas, New York, NY 10019, USA.

KING, Billie Jean; American tennis player; b. 22 Nov. 1943, Long Beach, Calif.; d. of Willard J. Moffitt; m. Larry King 1965 (divorced); ed Los Angeles State Univ.; amateur player 1958–67, turned professional 1967; Australian champion 1968; Italian champion 1970; French champion 1972; Wimbledon champion 1966, 1967, 1968, 1972, 1973, 1975; US Open champion 1967, 1971, 1972, 1974; FRG champion 1971; South African champion 1966, 1967, 1969; won record 20 Wimbledon titles (6 singles, 10 doubles, 4 mixed) and played more than 100 matches; had won 1,046 singles victories by 1984; sports commentator, ABC-TV 1975–78; f. Women's Tennis Asscn 1973; Publisher, Women Sports 1974–; Commr, US Tennis Team 1981–; CEO World Team-Tennis 1985–; Capt. US Fed. Cup Team 1995–; Women's Olympic Tennis Coach 1996, 2000; Consultant Virginia Slims Championship Series; nat. amb. for AIM children's charity; Top Woman Athlete of the Year Award 1973; Lifetime Achievement Award, March of Dimes 1994, Sarah Palfrey Danzig Award 1995, Flo Hyman Award 1997. *Publications:* Tennis to Win 1970, Billie Jean (with Kim Chapin) 1974, We Have Come a Long Way: The Story of Women's Tennis 1988. *Leisure interests:* ballet, movies. *Address:* c/o World TeamTennis, 445 North Wells, Suite 404, Chicago, IL 60610, USA.

KING, Coretta Scott, AB, MusB; American singer and civil rights campaigner; b. 27 April 1927, Marion, Ala; d. of Obidiah Scott and Bernice McMurray; m. Martin Luther King, Jr 1953 (assassinated 1968); two s. two d.; ed Antioch Coll., New England Conservatory of Music; concert début as singer, Springfield, Ohio 1948; numerous concerts throughout USA; performed in India 1959 and at Freedom Concert, USA; Voice Instructor, Morris Brown Coll., Atlanta, Ga 1962; Del. to White House Conf. on Children and Youth 1960; sponsor, Cttee for Sane Nuclear Policy, Cttee on Responsibility, Mobilization to End War in Viet Nam 1966–67; mem. Southern Rural Action Project, Inc.; Pres. Martin Luther King Jr Foundation; Chair. Comm. on Econ. Justice for Women; mem. Exec. Cttee, Nat. Cttee of Inquiry; Co-Chair. Clergy and Laymen Concerned about Viet Nam, Nat. Comm. for Full Employment 1974; Pres. Martin Luther King Jr Center for Social Change; Co-Chairperson Nat. Cttee for Full Employment; mem. Exec. Bd Nat. Health Insurance Cttee; mem. Bd Southern Christian Leadership Conf., Martin Luther King Jr Foundation, UK; Trustee, Robert F. Kennedy Memorial Foundation, Ebenezer Baptist Church; sponsor, Margaret Sanger Memorial Foundation; commentator, Cable News Network, Atlanta 1980–; lecturer and writer; Hon. LHD (Boston Univ.) 1969, (Marymount-Manhattan Coll., New York) 1969, (Morehouse Coll., Atlanta) 1970; Hon. HHD (Brandeis Univ., Waltham, Mass.) 1969, (Wilberforce Univ., Ohio) 1970, (Bethune-Cookman Coll., Daytona Beach, Fla) 1970, (Princeton Univ.) 1970; Hon. LLD (Bates Coll., Lewiston, Me) 1971; Hon. MusD (New England Conservatory of Music, Boston) 1971; numerous awards including Universal Love Award, Premio San Valentine Cttee 1968, Wateler Peace Prize 1968, Dag Hammarskjöld Award 1969, Pacem in Terris Award, Int. Overseas Service Foundation 1969, Leadership for Freedom Award, Roosevelt Univ. 1971, Martin Luther King Memorial Medal 1971, Int. Viareggio Award 1971. *Publications:* My Life With Martin Luther King, Jr 1969; articles in magazines. *Address:* Martin Luther King Jr Center for Nonviolent Social Change, 449 Auburn Avenue, NE, Atlanta, GA 30312; 671 Beckwith Street, SW, Atlanta, GA 30314, USA.

KING, Sir David Anthony, Kt, PhD, ScD, FRSC, FInstP, FRS; British professor of physical chemistry, research scientist and science policy consultant; b. 12 Aug. 1939, Durban, South Africa; s. of Arnold King and Patricia Vardy; m. Jane Lichtenstein 1983; three s. one d.; ed St John's Coll., Johannesburg, Univ. of Witwatersrand, Johannesburg, Imperial Coll. London; Lecturer in Chemical Physics, Univ. of E Anglia, Norwich 1966–74; Brunner Prof. of Physical Chemistry, Univ. of Liverpool 1974–88, Head Dept of Inorganic, Physical and Industrial Chem. 1983–88; 1920 Prof. of Physical Chem., Dept of Chem., Cambridge Univ. 1988–, Head Dept of Chem. 1993–2000; Fellow St John's Coll. 1988–95; Master of Downing Coll. 1995–2000; Chief Scientific Adviser to UK Govt 2000–; Head, Office of Science and Tech. 2000–; Ed. Chemical Physics Letters 1990–; Pres. Asscn of Univ. Teachers 1976–77; Chair. British Vacuum Council 1982–85; mem. Comité de Direction, Centre Cinétique et Physique, Nancy 1974–81, Research Awards Advisory Cttee Leverhulme Trust 1980–91 (Chair. 1995–), Direction Cttee (Beirat) Fritz Haber Inst., Berlin 1981–93; Chair. European Science Foundation Programme 'Gas–Surface Interactions' 1991–96, Kettle's Yard Gallery, Cambridge 1989–; Shell Scholar 1963–66; Assoc. Fellow Third World Acad. of Sciences 2000; Hon. Fellow Indian Acad. of Sciences, Downing Coll., Univ. of Cardiff 2001; Tilden Lectureship 1988; Hon. DSc (Liverpool) 2001, (E Anglia) 2001; Royal Soc. of Chem. Awards, Surface Chem. 1978, Medal for Research, British Vacuum Council 1991, Liversidge Lectureship and Medal 1997–98. *Publications:* The Chemical Physics of Solid Surfaces and Heterogeneous Catalysis, 7 Vols (Ed. with D. P. Woodruff) 1980–94; over 350 original Publs in the scientific literature. *Leisure interests:* photography, art, philosophy. *Address:* 70 Whitehall, London, SW1A 2AS (Office); Department of Chemistry, University of Cambridge, Lensfield Road, Cambridge, CB2 1EN; 20 Glisson Road, Cambridge, CB1 2EW, England (Home). *Telephone:* (20) 7271-2010 (Office); (1223) 315629 (Home); (1223) 336338. *Fax:* (20) 7271-2003 (Office); (1223) 762829. *E-mail:* eld1000@ens.cam.ac.uk (Office).

KING, Don; American boxing promoter; b. 20 Aug. 1931, Cleveland; s. of Clarence King and Hattie King; m. Henrietta King; two s. one d.; convicted of manslaughter and justifiable homicide; boxing promoter 1972–; owner Don King Productions Inc. 1974–; fighters promoted include: Muhammad Ali, Sugar Ray Leonard (q.v.), Mike Tyson (q.v.), Ken Norton, Joe Frazier, Larry Holmes (q.v.), Roberto Durán (q.v.), Tim Witherspoon, George Foreman (q.v.), Evander Holyfield (q.v.); f. The Don King Foundation and actively supports

other charities including The Martin Luther King Jr Foundation; Int. Boxing Hall of Fame 1997. *Address:* c/o Don King Productions Inc., 501 Fairway Drive, Deerfield Beach, FL 33441, USA (Office).

KING, Francis Henry, CBE, OBE, MA, FRSL; British writer; b. 4 March 1923, Adelboden, Switzerland; s. of the late Eustace Arthur Cecil King and Faith Mina Read; ed Shrewsbury School and Balliol Coll., Oxford; served in British Council 1948–62, Regional Dir, Kyoto, Japan 1958–62; theatre critic Sunday Telegraph 1978–88; Pres. English PEN 1978–86, Int. PEN 1986–89; Vice-Pres. Int. PEN 1989–; Somerset Maugham Prize 1952, Katherine Mansfield Short Story Prize 1965, Yorkshire Post Prize 1984. *Publications:* novels: To the Dark Tower 1946, Never Again 1947, The Dividing Stream 1951, The Widow 1957, The Man on the Rock 1957, The Custom House 1961, The Last of the Pleasure Gardens 1965, The Waves Behind the Boat 1967, A Domestic Animal 1970, Flights 1973, A Game of Patience 1974, The Needle 1975, Danny Hill 1977, The Action 1978, Act of Darkness 1983, Voices in an Empty Room 1984, Frozen Music (novella) 1987, The Woman Who Was God 1988, Punishments 1989, The Ant Colony 1991, Secret Lives 1991, The One and Only 1994, Ash on an Old Man's Sleeve 1996, Dead Letters 1997, Prodigies 2001, The Nick of Time 2003; short stories: So Hurt and Humiliated 1959, The Japanese Umbrella 1964, The Brighton Belle 1968, Hard Feelings 1976, Indirect Method 1980, One is a Wanderer 1985, A Hand at the Shutter 1996; biography: E. M. Forster and His World 1978, My Sister and Myself: The Diaries of J. R. Ackerley 1982; travel: Florence 1982, Florence: A Literary Companion 1991, Yesterday Came Suddenly (autobiog.) 1993. *Leisure interests:* ikebana, pictures and music. *Address:* 19 Gordon Place, London, W8 4JE, England. *Telephone:* (20) 7937-5715. *E-mail:* fhk@dircon.co.uk (Home).

KING, Ivan Robert, PhD; American astronomer; b. 25 June 1927, New York; s. of Myram King and Anne (Franzblau) King; m. Alice Greene 1952 (divorced 1982); two s. two d.; ed Woodmere Acad., Hamilton Coll., Harvard Univ.; served USNR 1952–54; Methods Analyst, US Dept of Defence 1952–56; Asst Prof., then Assoc. Prof., Univ. of Ill. 1956–64; Assoc. Prof. of Astronomy Univ. of Calif. at Berkeley 1964–66, Prof. 1966–93, Prof. Emer. 1993–; Chair. Astronomy Dept 1967–70; Pres. American Astronomical Soc. 1978–80; mem. AAAS, Fellow, Chair. Astronomy Section 1973; mem. NAS. *Publications:* The Universe Unfolding 1976, The Milky Way as a Galaxy 1990; 100 articles in scientific journals. *Address:* Astronomy Department, University of California, Berkeley, CA 94720-3411, USA. *E-mail:* king@astron.berkeley.edu.

KING, Larry; American broadcaster; b. 19 Nov. 1933, Brooklyn; s. of Eddie Zeiger and Jennie Zeiger; m. 1st Alene Akins 1961 (divorced 1963, remarried 1967, divorced 1971); one d.; m. 2nd Sharon Lepore 1976 (divorced 1982); m. 3rd Julia Alexander 1989; one s.; m. 4th Shawn Southwick 1997; disc jockey with various radio stations, Miami, Fla 1957–71; freelance writer and broadcaster 1972–75; radio personality, Station WIOD, Miami 1975–78; writer, entertainment sections of Miami Herald for seven years; host, The Larry King Show (radio talk show) 1978–, 1990 Goodwill Games, WLA-TV Let's Talk, Washington, DC; columnist, USA Today, Sporting News; appeared in films Ghostbusters 1984, Lost in America 1985; recipient of numerous broadcasting and journalism awards. *Publications:* Mr King, You're Having a Heart Attack (with B. D. Colen) 1989, Larry King: Tell Me More, When You're from Brooklyn, Everything Else is Tokyo 1992, On the Line (jtly) 1993, Daddy Day, Daughter Day (jtly) 1997. *Address:* c/o CNN Larry King Live, 820 1st Street, NE, Washington, DC 20002, USA.

KING, Mary Elizabeth; British horserider; b. 8 June 1961, Newark; d. of Lt-Commdr M. D. H. Thomson; m. David King 1995; one s. one d.; ed Manor House School, Honiton, King's Grammar School, Ottery St Mary, Evendine Court (Cordon Bleu); team gold medals 1991, 1994, 1995, 1997; rep. GB at Barcelona, Atlanta and Sydney Olympics; British Open champion 1991, 1992, 1996; winner Badminton Horse Trials 1992, 2000, Burghley Horse Trials 1996; broke her neck in 2001, but has made full recovery; Watch Leader 'Sir Winston Churchill'. *Publications:* Mary Thomson's Eventing Year 1993, All the King's Horses 1997, William and Mary 1998. *Leisure interests:* tennis, snow and water skiing. *Address:* Old Barn Cottage, Salcombe Regis, Sidmouth, Devon, EX10 0JQ (Office); Matford Park Farm, Exminster, Exeter, Devon, EX6 8AT, England (Home). *Telephone:* (1395) 514882 (Office). *Fax:* (1392) 432531 (Office). *E-mail:* eluk@eluk.co.uk. *Website:* www.eluk.co.uk/maryking (Office).

KING, Maurice Athelstan, LLB; Barbadian politician and lawyer; b. 1 Jan. 1936; s. of James Cliviston King and Caroline Constance King; m. Patricia A. Williams; one s. one d.; ed Harrison Coll., Barbados, Univ. of Manchester and Gray's Inn, London; lawyer in pvt. practice 1960–; Chair. Natural Gas Corpn 1964–76; mem. Barbados Senate 1967–75; Gen. Sec. Democratic Labour Party 1968–69; Amb. to USA and OAS Jan.–Sept. 1976; mem. Parl. 1981–; Attorney-Gen. and Minister of Legal Affairs 1986–91, Attorney-Gen. 1991–94 and Minister of Foreign Affairs 1991–93, of Justice and CARICOM Affairs 1993–94. *Leisure interests:* music, tennis, reading, swimming. *Address:* c/o Ministry of Justice, Marine House, Hastings, Christ Church, Barbados.

KING, Mervyn Allister, BA, FBA; British economist and professor of economics; b. 30 March 1948; s. of Eric Frank King and Kathleen Alice Passingham; ed Wolverhampton Grammar School, King's Coll., Cambridge; Jr Research Officer, Dept of Applied Econs, Cambridge Univ., mem. Cambridge Growth Project 1969–73, Research Officer 1972–76, lecturer, Faculty of Econs 1976–77; Esmée Fairbairn Prof. of Investment, Univ. of Birmingham

1977–84; Prof. of Econs, LSE 1984–95; Exec. Dir Bank of England 1991–98, Chief Economist 1991–98, Deputy Gov. (Monetary Policy) 1998–2003, Gov. 2003–; Pres. Inst. of Fiscal Studies 1999–2003; Research Officer, Kennedy School at Harvard Univ., USA 1971–72, Visiting Prof. of Econs 1982; Visiting Prof. of Econs MIT 1983–84, LSE 1996–; Co-Dir LSE Financial Markets Group 1987–91; Man. Ed. Review of Economic Studies 1978–83; founder mem. Monetary Policy Cttee 1997; mem. City Capital Markets Cttee; Bd mem. The Securities Asscn; mem. Council and Exec. Cttee Royal Econ. Soc. 1981–86, 1992–; Fellow Econometric Soc.; mem. Acad. Europaea 1992; mem. Council, European Econ. Asscn (Pres. 1993); Research Assoc. Nat. Bureau of Econ. Research; Assoc. mem. Inst. of Fiscal and Monetary Policy, Ministry of Finance, Japan 1986–91; mem. The Group of Thirty 1997, Advisory Council of the London Symphony Orchestra 2001; Chair. of OECD's Working Party 3 (WP3) Cttee 2001–03; Visiting Fellow, Nuffield Coll. Oxford 2002–03; Hon. Sr Scholarship and Richards Prize, King's Coll. Cambridge 1969; Hon. Fellow St John's Coll., Cambridge 1997; Foreign Hon. mem. American Acad. of Arts and Sciences 2000; Dr hc (London Guildhall Univ.) 2001, (Birmingham) 2002, (City Univ., London) 2002; Wrenbury Scholarship, Cambridge Univ. 1969; Stevenson Prize, Cambridge Univ. 1970; Kennedy Scholarship and Harkness Fellowship 1971; Medal of Univ. of Helsinki 1982. *Publications:* Public Policy and the Corporation 1977, The British Tax System (with J. A. Kay), Indexing for Inflation (Ed. with T. Liesner) 1975, The Taxation of Income from Capital Growth (Co-Author) 1984; numerous articles in various journals. *Address:* Bank of England, Threadneedle Street, London, EC2R 8AH, England. *Telephone:* (20) 7601-4444. *Fax:* (20) 7601-3047. *Website:* www.bankofengland.co .uk.

KING, Michael, OBE, DLitt, DPhil; New Zealand writer and historian; b. 15 Dec. 1945, Wellington; s. of Lewis King and Eleanor King (née Smith); m. Maria Jungowska 1987; one s. one d.; ed Victoria Univ., Wellington and Waikato Univ., Hamilton; Sr Journalist Waikato Times, Hamilton 1968–71; tutor in Journalism, Wellington Polytechnic 1972–74; Lahara Lecturer in Journalism, Univ. of Papua New Guinea, Port Moresby 1976; Research Fellow Centre for Maori Studies and Research, Univ. of Waikato 1978; Postdoctoral Fellow in History, Univ. of Auckland 1980; Fellowship in Humanities, Univ. of Waikato 1991–93; Sr Research Fellow in Humanities Univ. of Auckland 1996–97; Burns Fellow Otago Univ. 1998–99; Sr Research Fellow, Univ. of Waikato 2002–; Medal for Services to New Zealand Literature 1990, NZ Literary Fund Award for Achievement 1989, Buckland Literary Award 1996 and many other awards and writer's fellowships. *Publications:* Te Puea 1977, New Zealanders at War 1981, The Collector: A Biography of Andreas Reischek 1981, Maori: A Photographic and Social History 1983, Whina: A Biography of Whina Cooper 1983, Being Pakeha: An Encounter with New Zealand and the Maori Renaissance 1985, Death of the Rainbow Warrior 1986, New Zealand 1987, Mortiori: A People Rediscovered 1989, A Land Apart: The Chatham Islands of New Zealand 1990, Being Pakeha Now: Reflections and Recollections of a White Native 1999, Wrestling with the Angel: A Biography of Janet Frame 2000. *Leisure interests:* reading, fishing, planting trees. *Address:* P.O. Box 109, Whangamata, New Zealand. *Telephone:* (7) 865-9095. *Fax:* (7) 865-9095. *E-mail:* jungking@xtra.co.nz (Home).

KING, Phillip, CBE, MA (CANTAB); British sculptor; b. 1 May 1934, Tunis, Tunisia; s. of the late Thomas J. King and Gabrielle Liautard; m. 1st Lilian Odelle 1957 (divorced 1987); one s. (deceased); m. 2nd Judith Corbalis 1991; ed Mill Hill School, Christ's Coll., Cambridge, St Martin's School of Art, London; Asst to Henry Moore 1957–59; taught at St Martin's School of Art 1959–74; Prof. of Sculpture, Royal Coll. of Art 1980–90, Prof. Emer. 1991–; Prof. of Sculpture, RA 1990–99, Pres. 1999–; Trustee, Tate Gallery 1967–69; mem. Art Panel, Arts Council 1977–79; Hon. Fellow Christ Coll., Cambridge 2002–; 1st Prize Int. Sculpture exhbn, Piestany (Czechoslovakia) 1968. *Exhibitions:* One-man exhbn, Whitechapel Gallery 1968, British Pavilion at Venice Biennale with Bridget Riley (q.v.) 1968, British Council touring exhbn, Kröller-Müller (Netherlands), Düsseldorf, Bern, Paris and Belfast 1974–75, Arts Council Exhbn, Hayward Gallery, Forte Belvedere, Florence, 1981. *Leisure interest:* holidays in Corsica close to both land and sea. *Address:* Royal Academy of Arts, Piccadilly, London, W1J 0BD, England.

KING, Poppy; Australian business executive; b. 24 May 1972, Melbourne; d. of late Graham Nathan King and of Rachelle King; ed Wesley Coll., Melbourne; f. Poppy Industries cosmetics co. aged 18, CEO 1992–; Founding mem. Australian Republican Movt 1993–; Young Australian of the Year 1995. *Leisure interests:* art, literature, film, antiques. *Address:* Poppy Industries Pty Ltd, P.O. Box 4354, Melbourne, Vic. 3000, Australia (Office). *E-mail:* poppyk@ poppy.com.au (Office).

KING, Stephen Edwin, BS; American author; b. 21 Sept. 1947, Portland, Me; s. of Donald King and Nellie R. (Pillsbury) King; m. Tabitha J. Spruce 1971; two s. one d.; ed Univ. of Maine; teacher of English, Hampden Acad., Me 1971–73; writer-in-residence, Univ. of Maine at Orono 1978–79; mem. Authors' Guild of America, Screen Artists' Guild, Screen Writers of America, Writers' Guild. *Publications:* novels include Carrie 1974, Salem's Lot 1975, The Shining 1976, The Stand 1978, Fire Starter 1980, Danse Macabre 1981, Cujo 1981, Different Seasons 1982, The Dark Tower: The Gunslinger 1982, Christine 1983, Pet Sematary 1983, Cycle of the Werewolf 1985, Skeleton Crew 1986, It 1987, Misery 1988, Horror: 100 Best Books (Jt Ed.) 1988, The Dark Half 1989, Four Past Midnight 1990, The Stand 1990, Needful Things 1991, Gerald's Game 1992, Dolores Claiborne 1992, Nightmares and Dreamscapes 1993, Rose Madder 1995, The Green Mile 1996, Desperation 1996, The

Regulators 1996, Wizard and Glass 1997, Bag of Bones 1997; Night Shift (short story collection) 1978 and numerous other short stories; as Richard Bachman: Rage 1977, The Long Walk 1979, Roadwork 1981, The Running Man 1982, Thinner 1984, Insomnia 1993, Hearts in Atlantis 1999, The Girl Who Loved Tom Gordon 1999, Storm of the Century (adapted into mini-series) 1999, Riding the Bullet 2000, On Writing 2000, Dreamcatcher 2001, Everything's Eventual 2002. *Address:* 49 Florida Avenue, Bangor, ME 04401, USA (Office). *Website:* www.stephenking.com (Office).

KING, Dame Thea, DBE, FRCM, ARCM, FGSM; British clarinettist; b. 26 Dec. 1925, Hitchin, Herts.; d. of Henry W. M. King and Dorothea L. King; m. Frederick J. Thurston 1953 (died 1953); ed Bedford High School and Royal Coll. of Music; Sadler's Wells Orchestra 1950–52; Portia Wind Ensemble 1955–68; London Mozart Players 1956–84; Prof. Royal Coll. of Music 1961–87, Guildhall School of Music 1988–; now mem. English Chamber Orchestra, Melos Ensemble of London, Robles Ensemble; frequent soloist, broadcaster and recitalist. *Recordings include:* works by Mozart, Brahms, Spohr, Mendelssohn, Bruch, Finzi, Stanford and 20th-century British music. *Publications:* Clarinet Solos (Chester Woodwind Series) 1977, Arrangement of J. S. Bach: Duets for Two Clarinets 1979, Schumann for the Clarinet 1991, Mendelssohn for the Clarinet 1993, The Romantic Clarinet: A Mendelssohn Collection 1994, Tchaikovsky 1995. *Leisure interests:* skiing, cows, pillowlace. *Address:* 16 Milverton Road, London, NW6 7AS, England. *Telephone:* (20) 8459-3453.

KING-HELE, Desmond George, MA, FRS; British author and scientist; b. 3 Nov. 1927, Seaford, Sussex; s. of late S. G. King-Hele and Mrs B. King-Hele; m. Marie Newman 1954 (separated 1992); two d.; ed Epsom Coll. and Trinity Coll., Cambridge; Royal Aircraft Establishment, Farnborough 1948–88 (research on earth's gravity field and upper atmosphere by analysis of satellite orbits), Deputy Chief Scientific Officer, Space Dept 1968–88; mem. Int. Acad. of Astronautics 1961–; Chair. British Nat. Cttee for the History of Science, Medicine and Tech. 1985–89, History of Science Grants Cttee 1990–93; Ed. Notes and Records of the Royal Soc. 1989–96; Bakerian Lecturer, Royal Soc. 1974, Wilkins Lecturer, Royal Soc. 1997; Hon. DSc (Univ. of Aston) 1979, Hon. DUniv (Univ. of Surrey) 1986; Soc. of Authors' Medical History Prize 1999; Eddington Medal, Royal Astronomical Soc. 1971, Chree Medal, Inst. of Physics 1971, Nordberg Medal, Int. Cttee on Space Research 1990. *Radio:* dramas: A Mind of Universal Sympathy 1973, The Lunaticks 1978. *Publications:* Shelley: His Thought and Work 1960, Satellites and Scientific Research 1960, Erasmus Darwin 1963, Theory of Satellite Orbits in an Atmosphere 1964, Observing Earth Satellites 1966, Essential Writings of Erasmus Darwin 1968, The End of the Twentieth Century? 1970, Poems and Trixies 1972, Doctor of Revolution 1977, Letters of Erasmus Darwin 1981, Animal Spirits 1983, The R.A.E. Table of Earth Satellites 1957–1989, 1990, Erasmus Darwin and the Romantic Poets 1986, Satellite Orbits in an Atmosphere 1987, A Tapestry of Orbits 1992, John Herschel 1992, Erasmus Darwin: A Life of Unequalled Achievement 1999, Antic and Romantic 2000, Charles Darwin's The Life of Erasmus Darwin 2002; more than 300 scientific or literary papers in various learned journals. *Leisure interests:* playing tennis, savouring the beauties of nature, cross-country running. *Address:* 7 Hilltops Court, 65 North Lane, Buriton, Hants., GU31 5RS, England. *Telephone:* (1730) 261646.

KING, Baron (Life Peer), cr. 2001, of Bridgwater in the County of Somerset; **Thomas (Tom) Jeremy King,** PC, CH, MA; British politician; b. 13 June 1933, Glasgow; s. of John H. King and Mollie King; m. Elizabeth J. Tilney 1960; one s. one d.; ed Rugby School and Emmanuel Coll., Cambridge; in packaging and printing industry 1958–70; MP for Bridgwater 1970–2001; Parl. Private Sec. to Rt Hon Christopher Chataway 1970–74; Shadow Spokesman for Energy 1976–79; Minister for Local Govt 1979–83; Sec. of State for the Environment Jan.–June 1983 for Transport June–Oct. 1983, for Employment 1983–85, for Northern Ireland Sept. 1985–89, for Defence 1989–92; Chair. Intelligence and Security Cttee 1994–97; Chair. London Int. Exhbn Centre, Docklands; Dir (non-exec.) Electra Investment Trust 1992–; mem. Nolan Cttee on Standards in Public Life 1994–97; Conservative. *Leisure interests:* cricket, skiing, forestry. *Address:* c/o House of Lords, Westminster, London, SW1A 0PW, England (Office).

KING OF WARTNABY, Baron (Life Peer), cr. 1983, of Wartnaby in the County of Leicestershire; **John Leonard King,** Kt, FBIM; British business executive; b. 29 Aug. 1918; s. of Albert John and Kathleen King; m. 1st Lorna Kathleen Sykes 1941 (died 1969); three s. one d.; m. 2nd Isabel Monckton 1970; f. Whitehouse Industries Ltd 1945 and Ferrybridge Industries Ltd (subsequently Pollard Ball & Roller Bearing Co.), Man. Dir 1945, Chair. 1961–69; Chair. Dennis Motor Holdings Ltd 1970–72, FKI Babcock PLC (fmrly Babcock and Wilcox, subsequently Babcock Int. Group PLC) 1970–94 (Hon. Pres. 1994–), British Airways 1981–93 (Pres. 1993–97, Pres. Emer. 1997–); Dir SKF (UK) Ltd 1976–89, R. J. Dick Inc. (USA), Dick Corpn (USA), Dick Precismeca Inc. (USA), The Daily Telegraph PLC 1990–; mem. NEDC Cttee on Finance for Investment 1976–78, Review Bd for Govt Contracts 1975–78; Chair., British Olympic Appeals Cttee 1975–78; Vice-Pres. Nat. Soc. for Cancer Relief; Fellow Inst. of Chartered Transport; Hon. Fellow The Coke Oven Man. Assoc.; Commdr Royal Order of the Polar Star (1983); Hon. Dr.Hum. (Gardner-Webb Coll., USA) 1980; Dr. hc (City Polytechnic) 1991. *Leisure interests:* hunting, field sports, racing. *Address:* Wartnaby, Melton

Mowbray, Leicestershire, LE14 3HY, England (Home); British Airways PLC, Berkeley Square House, Berkeley Square, London, W1X 6BA. *Telephone:* (20) 7930-4915.

KINGMAN, Sir John Frank Charles, Kt, ScD, CStat, FRS; British mathematician and statistician; b. 28 Aug. 1939, Beckenham; s. of the late Frank E. T. and Maud Elsie (née Harley) Kingman; m. Valerie Cromwell 1964; one s. one d.; ed Christ's Coll., Finchley, London, Pembroke Coll., Cambridge; Asst Lecturer in Math., Univ. of Cambridge 1962–64, Lecturer 1964–65; Reader in Math. and Statistics, Univ. of Sussex 1965–66, Prof. 1966–69; Prof. of Math., Univ. of Oxford 1969–85; Chair. Science and Eng Research Council 1981–85; Vice-Chancellor Univ. of Bristol 1985–2001; Chair. Statistics Comm. 2000–03; Dir Isaac Newton Inst. for Mathematical Sciences 2001–; mem. council British Tech. Group 1984–92; mem. Bd British Council 1986–91; Pres. London Math. Society 1990–92; Hon. Fellow, St Anne's Coll., Oxford, Pembroke Coll., Cambridge; Hon. DSc (Sussex) 1983, (Southampton) 1985, Hon. LLD (Bristol) 1989, (Queen's Univ., Ont.) 1999; Officier des Palmes académiques. *Publications:* Introduction to Measure and Probability (with S. J. Taylor) 1966, The Algebra of Queues 1966, Regenerative Phenomena 1972, Mathematics of Genetic Diversity 1980, Poisson Processes 1993. *Address:* c/o Senate House, University of Bristol, Tyndall Avenue, Bristol, B58 1TH (Office); Isaac Newton Institute for Mathematical Sciences, 20 Clarkson Road, Cambridge, CB3 0EH, England. *Telephone:* (117) 928-7499 (Office); (1223) 335999. *Fax:* (117) 930-4263 (Office); (1223) 330508.

KINGSDOWN, Baron, (Life Peer), cr. 1993, of Pemberton in the County of Lancashire; **Robert (Robin) Leigh-Pemberton,** KG, PC, MA, DCL; British banker, barrister and landowner; b. 5 Jan. 1927, Lenham; s. of the late Robert Douglas Leigh-Pemberton, MBE, MC and Helen Isabel Payne-Gallwey; m. Rosemary Davina Forbes 1953; five s. (one deceased); ed St Peter's Court, Broadstairs, Eton Coll., Trinity Coll., Oxford; Oppidan Scholar, Eton 1940–45; Grenadier Guards 1945–48; practised at the Bar 1953–60; Dir Univ. Life Assurance Soc. 1968–78; Dir Birmid-Qualcast PLC, Deputy Chair. 1970–75, Chair. 1975–77; Dir Redland PLC 1972–83, Equitable Life Assurance Soc. 1978–83, Vice-Pres. 1982; Dir Nat. Westminster Bank PLC 1972–74, Deputy Chair. 1974–77, Chair. 1977–83; Gov. Bank of England 1983–93; Dir BIS 1983–; mem. Kent County Council 1961–77, Leader 1964–69, Chair. 1972–75; JP for Kent 1961–76; Deputy Lt for Kent 1969, Vice-Lord Lt 1972–82, Lord Lt 1982–2002; Gov. Wye Coll., London Univ. 1968–77; Hon. Master of the Bench, Inner Temple 1983; Deputy Pro-Chancellor of Kent Univ. 1969–78, Pro-Chancellor 1977–83; mem. Medway Ports Authority 1972–77, SE Econ. Planning Council 1971–74, Prime Minister's Cttee on Standards in Local Govt 1973–74, Cttee of Enquiry into Teachers' Pay 1974, Cttee to review Police Conditions of Service 1977–79, NEDC 1981–92; Chair. City Communications Centre 1979–82, Cttee of London Clearing Bankers 1982–83; Pres. Royal Agric. Soc. of England 1989–90; Dir (non-exec.) Glaxo Wellcome 1993–96, (non-exec.) Hambros 1993–98, Redland 1972–83, 1993–98, (non-exec.) Foreign & Colonial Investment Trust; Hon. DCL (Kent) 1983, Hon. MA (Trinity Coll., Oxford) 1984; Hon. DLitt (City of London) 1988, (Loughborough) 1989, (City Polytechnic) 1990; KStJ 1983, Order of Aztec Eagle, Mexico (First Class) 1985. *Leisure interests:* English country life, skiing, the arts. *Address:* Hambros PLC, 41 Tower Hill, London, EC3N 4HA; Torry Hill, Sittingbourne, Kent ME9 0SP, England (Home).

KINGSLEY, Sir Ben, Kt; British actor; b. 31 Dec. 1943; s. of Rahimtulla Harji Bhanji and Anna Leina Mary Bhanji; m.; three s. one d.; ed Manchester Grammar School; with RSC 1970–80; Nat. Theatre 1977–78; Assoc. Artist, RSC; Hon. MA (Salford Univ.); awarded Padma Shri (Govt of India); Evening Standard Best Film Actor 1983, European Film Awards Best European Actor 2001. *Stage appearances include:* A Midsummer Night's Dream, Occupations, The Tempest, Hamlet (title role), The Merry Wives of Windsor, Baal, Nicholas Nickleby, Volpone, The Cherry Orchard, The Country Wife, Judgement, Statements After An Arrest, Othello (title role), Caracol in Melons, Waiting for Godot. *Television appearances include:* The Love School 1974, Kean, Silas Marner, The Train 1987, Murderous Amongst Us 1988, Anne Frank (Screen Actors' Guild Award for Best Actor 2002), several plays. *Films:* Gandhi (two Hollywood Golden Globe Awards 1982, New York Film Critics' Award, two BAFTA Awards, Acad. Award, Los Angeles Film Critics' Award 1983), Betrayal 1982, Harem 1985, Turtle Diary 1985, Without A Clue 1988, Testimony 1988, Pascali's Island 1988, Bugsy 1991, Sneakers 1992, Innocent Moves 1992, Dave 1992, Schindler's List 1993, Death and the Maiden 1994, Species 1995, Twelfth Night 1996, Photographing Fairies 1997, The Assignment 1998, Weapons of Mass Destruction 1998, Sweeney Todd 1998, The Confession 1999, Sexy Beast (Best Actor, British Ind. Film Awards 2001) 1999, Rules of Engagement 1999, What Planet Are You From? 1999, Spooky House 1999, A.I. 2000, Triumph of Love 2000, Anne Frank 2000, Tuck Everlasting 2001, Sound of Thunder 2002, Suspect Zero 2002, House of Sand and Fog 2002. *Address:* c/o ICM, 76 Oxford Street, London, WIN 0AX, England. *Telephone:* (20) 7636-6565. *Fax:* (20) 7323-0101.

KINGSOLVER, Barbara, MS; American writer; b. 8 April 1955, Annapolis, Md; m. Steven Hopp; two d.; ed DePauw Univ., Indiana, Univ. of Arizona; scientific writer, Office of Arid Land Studies, Univ. of Ariz. 1981–85; freelance journalist 1985–87, novelist 1987–; book reviewer NY Times 1988–, LA Times 1989–, San Francisco Chronicle, The Nation, The Progressive, The Washington Post, Women's Review of Books, and others; Woodrow Wilson Foundation/Llia Wallace Fellowship 1992; established The Bellwether Prize for Fiction: In Support of a Literature of Social Change 1997; Hon. LittD

(DePauw) 1994; Nat. Writers Union Andrea Egan Award 1998, Arizona Civil Liberties Union Award 1998, Nat. Humanities Medal 2000, Best American Science and Nature Writing 2001, Gov.'s Nat. Award in the Arts, Kentucky 2002, John P. McGovern Award for the Family 2002, Physicians for Social Responsibility Nat. Award 2002, Acad. of Achievement Golden Plate Award 2003. *Publications:* The Bean Trees (Enoch Pratt Library Youth-to-Youth Books Award) 1988, Holding the Line 1989, Homeland and Other Stories 1989, Animal Dreams (Edward Abbey Award for Ecofiction, PEN/USA West Fiction Award) 1990, Another America 1992, Pigs in Heaven (Mountains and Plains Booksellers Award for Fiction, Los Angeles Times Fiction Prize) 1993, High Tide in Tucson 1995, The Poisonwood Bible (Village Voice Best Books 1998, New York Times Top Ten Books 1998, Los Angeles Times Best Books for 1998, Independence Publisher Brilliance Audio 1999, Booksense Prize 1999, Nat. Book Award (SA) 2000) 1998, Prodigal Summer 2000, Small Wonder 2002, Last Stand 2002. *Leisure interests:* human rights, environmental conservation, natural history, farming. *Address:* PO Box 31870, Tucson, AZ 85751 (Office); c/o Harper Collins, 10 East 53rd Street, New York, NY 10022, USA.

KINGSTON, Arthur Edward, PhD, FRAS, FInstP, MRIA; British professor of theoretical autoimic physics; b. 18 Feb. 1936, Armagh, N Ireland; s. of Arthur Kingston and Henrietta Duff; m. Helen McCann 1962; one s. one d.; ed Royal School Armagh and Queen's Univ. Belfast; Research Fellow, Queen's Univ. 1959–60, Sr Research Fellow 1960–61; Asst Lecturer, Liverpool Univ. 1961–62, lecturer 1962–63; Visiting Fellow, Univ. of Colorado, USA 1963–64; lecturer, Queen's Univ. 1964–68, Sr Lecturer 1968–71, Reader 1971–83, Prof. of Theoretical Atomic Physics 1983–, Dean, Faculty of Science 1989–94, Provost for Science and Agric. 1994, Prof. Emer. 2000–; mem. Int. Acad. of Astronautics. *Publications:* more than 260 papers in atomic physics and astrophysics. *Address:* 25 Cadogan Park, Belfast, BT9 6HH (Home); School of Mathematics and Physics, The Queen's University of Belfast, University Road, Belfast, BT7 1NN, N Ireland. *Telephone:* (28) 9027-3175 (Office); (28) 9066-9658 (Home). *Fax:* (28) 9023182. *E-mail:* a.kingston@qub.ac.uk (Office).

KINGSTON, Maxine Hong, BA; American author; b. 27 Oct. 1940, Stockton, Calif.; d. of Tom Kingston and Ying Lan (Chew) Hong; m. Earll Kingston 1962; one s.; taught English, Sunset High School, Hayward, Calif. 1965–66, Kahuku High School, Hawaii 1967, Kahaluu Drop-In School 1968, Kailua High School 1969, Honolulu Business Coll. 1969, Mid-Pacific Inst., Honolulu 1970–77; Prof. of English, Visiting Writer, Univ. of Hawaii, Honolulu 1977; Thelma McCandless Distinguished Prof., Eastern Mich. Univ., Ypsilanti 1986; Chancellor's Distinguished Prof., Univ. Calif., Berkeley 1990–; Mademoiselle Magazine Award 1977, Anisfield-Wolf Book Award 1978, Stockton (Calif.) Arts Comm. Award 1981, Hawaii Award for Literature 1982; NEA Writing Fellow 1980; Guggenheim Fellow 1981; named Living Treasure of Hawaii 1980, American Acad. and Inst. Award in Literature 1990; Nat. Humanities Medal 1998, Fred Cody Lifetime Achievement Award 1998, Commonwealth Club Silver Medal 2001, California Gold Medal 2002. *Publications:* The Woman Warrior: Memoirs of a Girlhood Among Ghosts 1976 (Nat. Book Critics Circle Award for non-fiction), China Men 1981 (Nat. Book Award), Hawai'i One Summer 1987, Ka Palapola Po'okela Award 1999, Through The Black Curtain 1988, Tripmaster Monkey–His Fake Books 1989 (PEN USA West Award in Fiction); The Literature of California (Ed.); short stories, articles and poems. *Address:* Department of English, University of California, 322 Wheeler Hall, Berkeley, CA 94720, USA.

KINIGI, Sylvie; Burundian politician and civil servant; fmr exec. officer of structural adjustment programme; Prime Minister of Burundi 1993–94; fmr mem. Union pour le progrès nat. (UPRONA). *Address:* c/o Office of the Prime Minister, Bujumbura, Burundi.

KINKEL, Klaus, LLD; German politician and lawyer; b. 17 Dec. 1936, Metzingen; s. of Ludwig Kinkel and Charlotte Klaus; m. Ursula Vogel 1961; one s. three d.; ed Bonn, Cologne, Tübingen Univs; lawyer 1962–70; Personal Aide to Hans Dietrich Genscher (q.v.) 1970–79; State Sec. Justice Ministry 1982–83, 1987–91, Justice Minister 1991–92; Minister of Foreign Affairs 1992–98; (mem. 1991–) Fed. Vice-Chancellor 1992–99; Head of External Intelligence Service 1982–87; Chair. Free Democratic Party 1993–95; Sr Adviser, Lehman Brothers Europe 2003–. *Leisure interests:* jogging, tennis. *Address:* c/o Lehman Brothers Europe, One Broadgate, London, EC2M 7HA, England.

KINNELL, Galway, MA; American writer; b. 1 Feb. 1927, Providence, RI; s. of James S. Kinnell and Elizabeth Mills; m. 1st Inés Delgado de Torres 1965; (divorced) one s. two d.; m. 2nd Barbara K. Bristol 1997; ed Princeton Univ. and Univ. of Rochester; mem. Nat. Inst., Acad. of Arts and Letters; Guggenheim Fellow 1963–64, 1974–75, MacArthur Fellow 1984; Dir Writing Programme New York Univ. 1981–84, Samuel F. B. Morse Prof. of Arts and Sciences 1985–92, Erich Maria Remarque Prof. of Creative Writing 1992–; named Vt State Poet 1989–93; Award of Nat. Inst. of Arts and Letters 1962, Cecil Hemley Poetry Prize 1969, Medal of Merit 1975, Pulitzer Prize 1983, Nat. Book Award 1983, Frost Medal 2001. *Publications:* poetry: What a Kingdom it Was 1960, Flower Herding on Mount Monadnock 1963, Body Rags 1966, The Book of Nightmares 1971, The Avenue Bearing the Initial of Christ into the New World 1974, Mortal Acts, Mortal Words 1980, Selected Poems 1982, The Past 1985, Imperfect Thirst 1994; novel: Black Light 1966; children's story: How the Alligator Missed Breakfast 1982; trans.: The Poems of François Villon 1965, On the Motion and Immobility of Douve by Yves

Bonnefoy 1968, The Lackawanna Elegy by Yvan Goll 1970, The Essential Rilke; interviews: Walking Down the Stairs 1977. *Address:* 1218 Town Road 16, Sheffield, VT 05866, USA (Home).

KINNEY, Catherine R.; American finance executive; b. 1952; m.; ed Iona Coll., New Rochelle, Harvard Graduate School of Business; joined NY Stock Exchange 1974, responsible for trading-floor operations and tech. 1986–95, Group Exec. Vice-Pres. 1995–2002, Pres., Exec. Vice-Chair. and mem. Bd of Dirs. 2002–; mem. Bd Securities Industry Automation Corpn 1988–97, mem. exec. Cttee 1994–97; mem. Bd NY Univ. Downtown Hosp., Bd of Regents, Georgetown Univ.; Trustee Iona Coll.; Woman of the Year (Financial Women's Asscn) 2001. *Address:* New York Stock Exchange, 11 Wall Street, New York, NY 10005, USA (Office).

KINNOCK, Rt Hon. Neil Gordon, PC, BA; British politician; b. 28 March 1942, Tredegar, S Wales; s. of Gordon Kinnock and Mary Howells; m. Glenys Elizabeth Parry 1967; one s. one d.; ed Lewis School, Pengam, Univ. Coll., Cardiff; Pres. Univ. Coll., Cardiff Students' Union 1965–66; Tutor Organizer in Industrial and Trade Union Studies, Workers' Educational Asscn 1966–70; MP for Bedwellty 1970–83, for Islwyn 1983–95; mem. Welsh Hosp. Bd 1969–71; Parl. Pvt. Sec. to Sec. of State for Employment 1974–75; mem. Gen. Advisory Council BBC 1976–80; mem. Nat. Exec. Cttee, Labour Party 1978–94 (Chair. 1987–88); Leader of Labour Party 1983–92; Leader of the Opposition 1983–92; EU Commr with responsibility for Transport 1995–99, Vice-Pres. European Comm. 1999–(2004); Pres. Cardiff Univ. 1998–; Hon. LLD (Wales) 1992. *Publications:* Wales and the Common Market 1971, Making Our Way 1986, Thorns and Roses 1992; contribs. in newspapers, periodicals and books including The Future of Social Democracy 1999. *Leisure interests:* male voice choral music, opera, theatre, reading, grandchildren, rugby, soccer, cricket. *Address:* European Commission, 200 rue de la Loi, 1049 Brussels, Belgium. *Telephone:* (2) 296-32-20 (Office). *Fax:* (2) 296-07-49 (Office).

KINSELLA, Thomas; Irish poet; b. 4 May 1928, Dublin; s. of John Paul and Agnes Casserly Kinsella; m. Eleanor Walsh 1955; one s. two d.; Irish Civil Service 1946–65, resgnd as Asst Prin. Officer, Dept of Finance 1965; Artist-in-Residence, Southern Ill. Univ. 1965–67, Prof. of English 1967–70; Prof. of English, Temple Univ., Philadelphia 1970–90; Dir Dolmen Press Ltd, Cuala Press Ltd, Dublin; founded Peppercanister (pvt. publishing enterprise), Dublin 1972; mem. Irish Acad. of Letters 1965–, American Acad. of Arts and Sciences 2000–; Guggenheim Fellowship 1968–69, 1971–72; Hon. DLitt (Nat. Univ. of Ireland) 1985; Guinness Poetry Award 1958, Irish Arts Council Triennial Book Award 1960, Denis Devlin Memorial Award 1966, 1969, 1992, First European Poetry Award 2001. *Publications:* Poems 1956, Another September (poems) 1958, Downstream (poems) 1962, Nightwalker and Other Poems 1966, Notes from the Land of the Dead (poems) 1972, Butcher's Dozen 1972, New Poems 1973, Selected Poems 1956–1968 1973, Song of the Night and Other Poems 1978, The Messenger (poem) 1978, Fifteen Dead (poems) 1979, One and Other Poems 1979, Poems 1956–1973, Peppercanister Poems 1972–1978 1979; Songs of the Psyche (poems) 1985, Her Vertical Smile (poem) 1985, St Catherine's Clock (poem) 1987, Out of Ireland (poems) 1987, Blood and Family (collected poems from 1978) 1988, Poems from Centre City 1990, Personal Places (poems) 1990, One Fond Embrace (poem) 1990, Madonna and other Poems 1991, Open Court (poem) 1991, Butcher's Dozen (anniversary reissue) 1992, From Centre City (collected poems from 1990) 1994, The Dual Tradition: an Essay on Poetry and Politics in Ireland 1995, Collected Poems 1956–94, The Pen Shop (poem) 1997, The Familiar (poems) 1999, Godhead (poems) 1999, Citizen of the World (poems) 2001, Littlebody (poem) 2001; The Táin (trans.) 1969; Selected Poems of Austin Clarke 1976; co-ed. Poems of the Dispossessed 1600–1900 (with 100 translations from the Irish) 1981; Ed. Ireland's Musical Heritage: Sean O'Riada's Radio Talks on Irish Traditional Music 1981, The New Oxford Book of Irish Verse (including all new trans. from the Irish) 1986. *Leisure interests:* history, publishing. *Address:* 639 Addison Street, Philadelphia, PA 19147, USA. *Telephone:* (267) 671-0536.

KINSELLA, William Patrick, BA, MFA; Canadian author; b. 25 May 1935, Edmonton, Alberta; s. of John M. Kinsella and Olive M. Elliot; m. 1st Myrna Salls 1957; m. 2nd Mildred Heming 1965; m. 3rd Ann Knight 1978; m. 4th Barbara L. Turner 1999, three d.; ed Eastwood High School, Edmonton and Univs of Victoria and Iowa; recipient Houghton Mifflin Literary Fellowship 1982; Books in Canada First Novel Award 1982; Canadian Authors' Asscn Award for Fiction 1982; Writers Guild Alberta Award for Fiction 1982, 1983; Vancouver Award for Writing 1987; Stephen Leacock Award for Humour 1987; Canadian Booksellers Asscn Author of the Year 1987. *Publications:* stories: Dance Me Outside 1977, Scars 1978, Shoeless Joe Jackson Comes to Iowa 1980, Born Indian 1981, The Moccasin Telegraph 1983, The Thrill of the Grass 1984, The Alligator Report 1985, The Fencepost Chronicles 1986, Five Stories 1987, Red Wolf, Red Wolf 1987, The Further Adventures of Slugger McBatt (reissued as Go the Distance 1995) 1988, The Miss Hobbema Pageant 1988, Dixon Cornbelt League 1993, Brother Frank's Gospel Hour 1994, The Secret of the Northern Lights 1998, The Silas Stories 1998, Japanese Baseball 2000; novels: Shoeless Joe 1982, The Iowa Baseball Confederacy 1986, Box Socials 1991, The Winter Helen Dropped By 1995, If Wishes Were Horses 1996, Magic Time 1998; other works: The Ballad of the Public Trustee 1982, The Rainbow Warehouse (poetry, with Ann Knight) 1989, Two Spirits Soar: The Art of Allen Sapp 1990, Even at this Distance (poetry, with Ann Knight)

1993. *Leisure interests:* baseball, sumo wrestling, Scrabble. *Address:* 9442 Nowell, Chilliwack, BC, V2P 4X7, Canada (Office); PO Box 3067 Sumas, WA 98295, USA .

KINSKI, Nastassja; German actress; b. (Nastassja Nakszynski), 24 Jan. 1961, W Berlin; d. of the late Klaus Kinski and of Ruth Brigitte Kinski; m. Ibrahim Moussa 1984; one s. one d.; one d. by Quincy Jones (q.v.); film début in Falsche Bewegung 1975; Bundespreis 1983. *Films include:* Stay As You Are 1978, Tess 1978, One From The Heart 1982, Cat People 1982, Moon In The Gutter 1983, Spring Symphony 1983, Unfaithfully Yours 1984, The Hotel New Hampshire 1984, Maria's Lovers 1984, Paris, Texas 1984, Revolution 1985, Harem, Torrents of Spring 1989, On a Moonlit Night 1989, Magdalene 1989, The King's Future 1989, The Secret, Night Sun 1991, Faraway, So Close!, Terminal Velocity 1994, One Night Stand 1997, Little Boy Blue 1997, Father's Day 1997, Somebody is Waiting 1997, Sunshine 1998, Your Friends and Neighbors 1999, The Magic of Marciano 1999, The Intruder 1999, Town and Country 1999, The Lost 1999, The Claim 2000, The Day the World Ended 2001, An American Rhapsody 2001. *Address:* c/o Peter Levine, William Morris Agency, 151 South El Camino Drive, Beverly Hills, CA 90212 (Office); 888 Seventh Avenue, New York, NY 10106, USA.

KINTANAR, Roman, MA, PhD; Philippine scientist, government official and university professor; b. 13 June 1929, Cebu City; s. of Augustin Y. Kintanar and Pureza Lucero; m. Generosa Perez-Kintanar 1959; two s. one d.; ed Univ. of the Philippines, Univ. of Texas; Prof. of Physics, Univ. of the Philippines 1955–56, Feati Univ. 1958–65; Professorial lecturer, Ateneo de Manila Univ. 1966–68; Chief Geophysicist, Philippine Weather Bureau 1953–58, Dir 1958–72; Admin. Philippine Atmospheric, Geophysical and Astronomical Services Admin. (PAGASA) 1972–77, Dir-Gen. 1977–; Chair. Scientific and Tech. Cttee, UN Int. Decade for Natural Disaster Reduction 1994; Chair. of Bd, Typhoon Cttee Foundation 1996–; Pres. ROMAROSA Realty Devt Corpn Inc. 1996–; del. or invited participant to 57 Regional or Int. Scientific Confs. 1959–79; Co-ordinator, WMO/ESCAP Typhoon Cttee Secr. 1967–79; Perm. Rep. to WMO 1958; Vice-Pres. Regional Asscn V for SW Pacific (WMO-RA V) 1966–74, Pres. 1974–78; Vice-Pres. WMO 1978–79, Pres. 1979; Vice-Chair. Manila Observatory Inc. 1996–; mem. Philippine Asscn for the Advancement of Science, Nat. Research Council of the Philippines, Philippine Meteorological Soc., Int. Asscn of Seismology and Physics of the Earth's Interior, UNESCO/UNDRO Int. Advisory Cttee on Earthquake Damage and Mitigation and many other scientific socs.; Fulbright Smidthmundt Scholarship (US Educational Foundation); Office of the Pres. Ecology Award, Budiras Award for Outstanding Performance (Bureau Dirs. Asscn); Parangal ng PAGASA Award, Lingkod Bayan Award 1982, Padre Faura Astronomy Medal 1982, Presidential Citation 1995, Int. Meteorological Org. Prize 1995. *Publications:* A Study of Typhoon Microseisms 1958 and many articles in scientific journals. *Leisure interests:* playing golf, chess. *Address:* 100 Don Primitivo Street, Don Antonio Heights, Quezon City, Philippines. *Telephone:* 9317069; 3733443. *Fax:* 3733419 (Office); 9318484. *E-mail:* fcs@philonline .com (Office).

KIPKETER, Wilson; Kenyan/Danish athlete; b. 12 Dec. 1970, Kapchemoiywo, Kenya; m. Pernille Kipketer 2000; ed St Patrick's High School, Iten, Kenya; world outdoor record-holder for 800m (1 minute and 41.11 seconds) 1997 and indoor record (1 minute and 42.67 seconds) 1997; set new world indoor record for 1000m (2 minutes and 14.36 seconds), Birmingham, UK 2000; coached by Slawomir Nowak; resident in Denmark since 1990, qualified to compete for Denmark May 1995; gold medal World Championships 1995, 1997, 1999; gold medal World Indoor Championships 1997; Olympic silver medal 800m, Sydney 2000; European champion 800m, Munich 2002. *Website:* www.dansk.atletik.dk.

KIPPENHAHN, Rudolf; German astronomer; b. 24 May 1926, Bärringen; s. of Rudolf Kippenhahn and Alma Belz; m. Johanna Rasper 1955; three d.; ed Graslitz and St Joachimsthal Schools, Univs of Halle and Erlangen; Scientific Asst Bamberg Observatory 1951–57; staff mem. Max-Planck-Inst. für Physik und Astrophysik, Inst. für Astrophysik 1957–65, mem. of directorate 1963, Dir 1975–91; Visiting Prof. Caltech, Pasadena and Princeton Univs. 1961–62; Prof. Univ. Observatory, Göttingen 1965–75; Visiting Prof. Univ. of Calif., LA 1968, Ohio State Univ. 1979, Univ. Observatory, Hamburg 1986–87; Hon. Prof. Univ. of Munich 1975–; Assoc. mem. Royal Astronomical Soc., London; mem. Bayerische Akademie der Wissenschaften, Munich; Carus-Medal (Leopoldina, Halle); Carus Prize (City of Schweinfurt); Verdienstkreuz (1st Class) (Fed. Repub. Germany); Lorenz-Oken-Medal (Gesellschaft Deutscher Naturforscher und Ärzte). *Publications:* One Hundred Billion Suns: The Birth, Life and Death of the Stars 1983, Licht vom Rande der Welt 1984, Light from the Depth of Time 1987, Unheimliche Welten 1987, Stellar Structure and Evolution 1990, Der Stern von dem wir Leben 1990, Abenteuer Weltall 1991, Discovering the Secrets of the Sun 1994; and numerous articles in astronomical and astrophysical journals. *Address:* Rautenbreite 2, 37077 Göttingen, Germany. *Telephone:* (551) 24714. *Fax:* (551) 22902.

KIRALY, Karch; American professional volleyball player; b. 3 Nov. 1960, Jackson, MI; s. of Lazlo Kiraly; m. Janna Miller; two s.; ed UCLA; led UCLA to Nat. Collegiate Athletic Asscn (NCAA) championships 1979, 1981, 1982; played on nat. team, winning gold medals, Olympic Games 1984, 1988, world championship titles 1982, 1986; won inaugural gold medal for Olympic beach volleyball (with Kent Steffes) 1996; record for most pro beach titles (143); f.

Karch Kiraly Scholarship Fund; Fédération Internationale de Volleyball (FIVB) Player of the Century; Assen of Volleyball Professionals (AVP) Sportsman of the Year 1995, 1997, 1998. *Publications include:* co-author (with Byron Shewman) Beach Volleyball, The Sand Man (autobiog.). *Address:* c/o Association of Volleyball Professionals (AVP), 1600 Rosecrans Avenue Suite 310, Building 7, Manhattan Beach, CA 90266, USA.

KIRBY, Anthony John, PhD (CANTAB.), FRS, FRSC; British university teacher and research scientist; b. 18 Aug. 1935, Welwyn Garden City, Herts.; s. of Samuel A. Kirby and Gladys R. (née Welch) Kirby; m. Sara Nieweg 1962; one s. two d.; ed Eton Coll., Gonville and Caius Coll., Cambridge; NATO Research Fellow, Brandeis Univ., Mass. 1963–64; demonstrator, lecturer, Organic Chem., Univ. of Cambridge 1968–85, Reader 1985–95, Prof. of Bio-organic Chem. 1995–, Tutor 1967–75, Dir of Studies in Natural Sciences, Gonville & Caius Coll., Cambridge 1968–96; Coordinator European Network on Artificial Nucleases 2000–; Fellow Gonville and Caius Coll. 1962–; Royal Soc. of Chemistry Award in Organic Reaction Mechanisms 1983, Tilden Lecturer of Royal Soc. of Chem. 1987, Ingold Lecturer of Royal Soc. of Chem. 1996. *Publications:* The Organic Chemistry of Phosphorus (with S. G. Warren) 1967, Stereoelectronic Effects at Oxygen 1983, Stereoelectronic Effects 1996; over 250 articles on mechanistic bioorganic chemistry. *Address:* University Chemical Laboratory, Cambridge, CB2 1EW (Office); 14 Tenison Avenue, Cambridge, CB1 2DY, England (Home). *Telephone:* (1223) 336370 (Office); (1223) 359343 (Home). *Fax:* (1223) 336362 (Office). *E-mail:* ajk1@cam.ac.uk (Office). *Website:* www.ch.cam.ac.uk/cucl/staff/ajk.html (Office).

KIRBY, Hon. Justice Michael Donald, AC, CMG, LLM, BA, BEcons; Australian judge; b. 18 March 1939, Sydney; s. of Donald Kirby and the late Jean Kirby (née Knowles); partner Johan van Vloten 1969; ed Fort Street Boys' High School and Univ. of Sydney; Fellow, Senate, Univ. of Sydney 1964–69; mem. NSW Bar Council 1974; Deputy Pres., Australian Conciliation & Arbitration Comm. 1975–83; Chair. Australian Law Reform Comm. 1975–84, OECD Expert Group on Privacy and Int. Data Flows 1978–80, Cttee of Counsellors, Human and People's Rights UNESCO 1985, UNESCO Expert Group on the Rights of Peoples 1989; mem. Admin. Review Council of Australia 1976–84; mem. Council, Univ. of Newcastle, NSW 1977–83, Deputy Chancellor 1978–83; mem. Australian Nat. Comm. for UNESCO 1980–84, 1997–, Australian Inst. of Multicultural Affairs 1979–83; Judge Fed. Court of Australia 1983–84; mem. Exec. CSIRO 1983–86; Chancellor, Macquarie Univ., Sydney 1984–93; Pres. Court of Appeal, Supreme Court of NSW 1984–96; Acting Chief Justice of NSW 1988, 1990, 1993, 1995; Admin. (Acting Gov.) NSW 1991; Justice, High Court of Australia 1996–; Commr WHO Global Comm. on Aids 1989–91; mem. Int. Comm. of Jurists, Geneva 1985–99, mem. Exec. Cttee 1989–95, Chair. 1992–95, Pres. 1995–98, Pres. Australian Section 1989–96; Special Rep. of Sec.-Gen. of UN on Human Rights for Cambodia 1993–96; Pres. Court of Appeal of Solomon Islands 1995–96; Pres. Australian Acad. of Forensic Sciences 1987–89; mem. Ethics Cttee of Human Genome Org. 1995–; mem. Council of the Australian Opera; mem. ILO Fact-Finding and Conciliation Comm. on Freedom of Assen Inquiry on South Africa 1991–92; mem. Perm. Tribunal of Peoples' Session on Tibet 1992; Trustee AIDS Trust of Australia 1987–93; Gov. Int. Council for Computer Communications, Washington 1984–; mem. UNESCO Jury for Prize for Teaching of Human Rights 1994–96, UNESCO Int. Bioethics Cttee 1996–, American Law Inst.; Rapporteur Int. Group on Judicial Integrity (UNHCH) 2001, UNAIDS Global Panel on HIV/AIDS and Human Rights 2003–; Co-Chair. Expert Group on Bioethics and Human Rights, High Commr of Human Rights 2002–; Chair. UNAIDS Expert Group on HIV Testing in UN Peacekeeping Operations 2001–02, Jt UNAIDS/High Commr for Human Rights Expert Group on Revision of UN Guidelines on HIV/AIDS and Human Rights 2002–; mem. Advisory Bd Int. Human Rights Inst., De Paul Univ., Chicago, USA; Hon. Fellow, NZ Research Foundation, Australian Acad. of Social Sciences 1996; Hon. DLitt (Newcastle, NSW) 1987, (Ulster) 1998; Hon. LLD (Macquarie Univ.) 1995, (Sydney Univ.) 1996, (Buckingham Univ.) 2000; Hon. DUniv (S Australia) 2001; Loewenthal Medal, Sydney Univ., Australian Human Rights Medal 1991, Laureate, UNESCO Prize for Human Rights Educ. 1998. *Publications:* Industrial Index to Australian Labour Law 1978, 1984, Reform the Law 1983, The Judges 1984, Jt Ed. A Touch of Healing 1986, Through the World's Eye 2000. *Leisure interest:* work. *Address:* Judge's Chambers, High Court of Australia, Canberra, ACT 2600, Australia (Office). *Telephone:* (2) 6270-6969 (Office). *Fax:* (2) 6270-6970 (Office).

KIRBY, Peter Maxwell, MA, MBA; Australian business executive; b. 2 Aug. 1947, South Africa; s. of Robert Maxwell Kirby and May Kirby; m. Erica Anne Ebden; one s.; ed Rhodes Univ., Natal Univ., Manchester Univ., Univ. of the Witwatersrand, Harvard Business School; Man. Dir Dulux Paints 1991–92; CEO ICI Paints Asia Pacific 1992–95, ICI Paints 1995–98; Man. Dir and CEO CSR Ltd Jan. 1998–. *Leisure interests:* boating, cars. *Address:* CSR Ltd, Level 1, 9 Help Street, Chatswood, NSW 2067, Australia. *Telephone:* (2) 9235-8080. *Fax:* (2) 9235-8130.

KIRBY, Ronald Hubert, BArch; Zambian architect and urban designer; b. 3 Jan. 1936, Lusaka, N Rhodesia; s. of Hubert Rowland Kirby and May Elizabeth Kirby (née Hinds); m. Davina Anne Roderick 1985; one d.; ed Muir Coll., Uitenhage, Univ. of Cape Town, Univ. of Witwatersrand; architect, commissions include: Queen Victoria Memorial Library, Zimbabwe 1960, Ndola Civic Centre, Zambia 1975, UAE Nat. Ass., Abu Dhabi 1977, Oppenheimer Life Sciences Bldg, Johannesburg 1979, Zimbabwe Parl. Bldg, Harare 1984; external examiner Univs of Cape Town and Pretoria 1985, rep. Zambia

and Africa at confs in various countries; Chair. Transvaal Prov. Inst. of Architecture PR and Press Communication 1985–87; Prof. of Architecture and Head of Dept Univ. of Witwatersrand 1991–94; Dir Zambia Nat. Housing Authority 1991–92; mem. S Africa Council of Architects Educational Inspection Comm. to Univ. of Witwatersrand 1985–, Transvaal Prov. Inst. of Architecture Commn. 1983–87; fmr Pres. Zambia Inst. of Architecture; Zambia Inst. of Architecture Industrial Award 1964, Commercial Awards 1964, 1968, Civic Award 1968, Institutional Awards 1971, 1973, 1983, Inst. of S African Architecture Awards of Merit 1983, 1987, RIBA Bronze Medal, Rhodesia 1963, Habitation Space Int. Award 1981. *Publications:* numerous articles in professional journals. *Address:* P.O. Box 337, Melville, 2109 Johannesburg, South Africa. *Telephone:* (271) 482-2323. *Fax:* (271) 482-1218. *E-mail:* plandesign@icon.co.za (Office).

KIRCH, Leo, PhD; German media executive; b. 21 Oct. 1926; ed Univ. of Würzburg; f. Beta Film (film and TV programme library) 1959, TaurusFilm 1963; Founder and Chair. KirchGruppe (production and marketing of films and TV programmes, rights trading, film tech., digital TV); Chair. Taurus Holding (KirchGruppe's holding co.), three sub-holdings KirichMedia (filed for insolvency April 2002), KirchPayTV, KirchBeteiligungs; responsible for establishment of pay-per-view TV and infrastructure for digital TV in Germany. *Address:* Kirchgruppe, Robert-Bürkle-Strasse 2, 85737 Ismaning, Germany (Office).

KIRCHNER, Alfred; German theatre director; b. 22 May 1937, Göppingen; s. of Julius Kirchner and Alice (née Bonatz) Kirchner; two d.; ed Max Reinhardt Schule, Berlin; Chief Producer, Staatstheater, Stuttgart 1972–79; mem. Bd of Dirs. and Chief Producer, Schauspielhaus, Bochum 1979–86, Burgtheater, Vienna 1986–89; Gen. Dir Staatliche Schauspielbühnen, Berlin 1990–97; guest producer at Residenztheater, Munich, Hamburg Schauspielhaus, Hamburg State Opera, Frankfurt Opera, Holland Festival, Brussels Opera, Vienna State Opera, Santa Fé Opera, etc.; has directed operas by Udo Zimmermann, Bernd Alois Zimmermann, Hans Zender, Hans Werner Henze, Mozart, Verdi, Mussorgsky, Tchaikovsky; Dir Der Ring des Niebelungen, Bayreuth 1994–98, La Bohème, Frankfurt 1998, Rosenkavalier, Leipzig 1998, Rigoletto, Leipzig 1999, Peter Grimes, Strasbourg 1999, Manon Lescaut, Frankfurt 1999; producer of work for radio and TV. *Publications:* newspaper articles.

KIRCHNER, Néstor Carlos; Argentine politician and lawyer; b. 1950; m. Cristina Fernandez de Kirchner; fmr lawyer; mem. Peronist party; jailed briefly during 1976-83 military dictatorship; Gov. Prov. of Santa Cruz 1991–2003; Pres. of Argentina 2003–. *Address:* Office of the President, Balcarce 50, 1064 Buenos Aires, Argentina (Office). *Telephone:* (11) 4344-3662 (Office). *Fax:* (11) 4344-3789 (Office). *E-mail:* secgral@presidencia.net.ar (Office).

KIRCHSCHLAGER, Angela; Austrian mezzo-soprano; b. Salzburg; ed Musisches Gymnasium, Salzburg and Vienna Music Acad.; studied with Walter Berry in Vienna 1984; first performance in Die Zauberflöte, Vienna Kammeroper; concert performances in Austria, France, Germany, Italy, Czech Repub., Denmark, USA and Japan; recent recitals in London, Edin., Amsterdam, Cologne, Frankfurt, Hohenems, Graz, Bilbao and in Scandinavia; composed Jonathan Miller production, Lausanne Opera 1998–99; sang with London Symphony Orchestra, NY Chamber Orchestra and Vienna Symphony Orchestra 1999–2000; feature appearances on Austrian Nat. Radio and TV (ORF); participated in film production about Hugo Woolf in role of Frieda Zerny 1992; signed exclusive contract with Sony label 1997; winner of three prizes, Int. Belvedere Competition, Vienna 1991. *Operatic title roles include:* Le nozze di Figaro, Schloss Schönbrunn, Vienna, Der Rosenkavalier, Geneva, Hänsel und Gretel, Graz, The Merry Widow, Vienna, Palestrina, Vienna, Die Lustige Witwe, Vienna, Don Giovanni, Ravenna and Milan, Les Contentes d'Hoffman, Paris, Ariadne auf Naxos, London. *Recordings include:* album of lieder by Alma Mahler, Gustav Mahler and Erich Wolfgang Korngold (solo debut) 1997; featured on recording of Mendelssohn with Claudio Abbado and Berlin Philharmonic; When Night Falls (solo recital). *Address:* c/o Sony Music Entertainment (UK) Head Office/European Regional Office, 10 Great Marlborough Street, London, W1F 7LP, England (Office). *Telephone:* (20) 7911-8200 (Office). *Website:* www.sonymusic.co.uk (Office).

KIRIYENKO, Sergey Vladilenovich; Russian politician; b. 27 July 1962, Sukhumi, Georgia; m.; one s. one d.; ed Gorky (now Nizhny Novgorod) Inst. of Water Transport Eng, Acad. of Econs; mem. CPSU 1980–91; army service 1984–86; Sec. Comsomol Cttee Krasnoye Sormovo shipyard, Gorky 1986–90; Founder and Dir A.M.K. (firm) 1988–91; Pres. Nizhny Novgorod Bank Garantia 1991–96; Pres. Norsi Oil Co. 1996–97; First Deputy Minister of Fuel and Energy Aug.–Nov. 1997, Minister 1997–98; First Deputy Prime Minister, Acting Chair. of Govt March–April 1998, Chair. (Prime Minister) April–Aug. 1998; f. Novaya Sila (New Force) political Movt 1998; leader of pre-election block Union of Right Forces 1999; mem. State Duma 1999–2000 (resgnd); Pres.'s Rep. Privolzhsky Fed. District 2000–; cand. for Mayor of Moscow 1999. *Address:* Office of the Plenipotentiary Representative of the President, Kremlin, Korp. 1, 603082 Nizhny Novgorod, Russia (Office). *Telephone:* (8312) 31-46-07; 31-46-14. *Fax:* (8312) 31-47-51 (Office).

KIRK, Kent Sand; Danish politician and fishing captain; b. 29 Aug. 1948, Esbjerg; s. of Sand and Brynhild Kirk; m. Ruth Henriksen 1971; three s. one d.; Master's certificate; capt. of fishing boat 1971–; Gen. Man. K. and K. Kirk Ltd 1973–; Chair. Bd Fishermen's Assen, Esbjerg 1975–; mem. Bd Danish

Deep Sea Fishing Fed., Danish Fishermen's Producers' Org., Esbjerg Harbour Council 1976–; mem. European Parl. 1979–84; mem. Folketing 1984–98; Minister for Fisheries 1989–93; mem. Bd Danish Conservative Party 1980–84; Vice-Pres. European Democratic Group 1981–83; Partner, Esvagt Ltd (Stand-by vessels) 1981–; Chair. Bd Int. School, Esbjerg 1982–. *Leisure interests:* skiing, reading. *Address:* c/o Ministry of Fisheries, Stormgade 2, 1470 Copenhagen K, Denmark. *Telephone:* 33-96-38-52.

KIRK, Paul Grattan, Jr, AB, LLB; American political official and lawyer; b. 18 Jan. 1938, Newton, Mass.; s. of Paul G. Kirk and Josephine Kirk (née O'Connell); m. Gail Loudermilk 1974; ed Harvard Univ.; partner, Sullivan & Worcester, Boston and Washington 1977–90, Counsel 1990–; Chair. Kirk & Assocs. Inc. 1990–; Special Asst to Senator Edward Kennedy (q.v.); Nat. Political Dir Kennedy for Pres. Cttee 1980; Treas. Democratic Nat. Cttee 1983–85, Chair. 1985–89; Visiting Lecturer, Mass. Continuing Legal Educ. Program, New England Law Inst., J. F. Kennedy Inst. of Politics, Harvard Univ.; Chair., Bd of Dirs J. F. Kennedy Library Foundation, Nominating Cttee Harvard Bd of Overseers 1993, Nat. Democratic Inst. for Int. Affairs 1992–2001; mem. Bd of Dirs ITT Corpn 1989–97, Bradley Real Estate Inc. 1992–99, Hartford Life Insurance Co.1995–2000, Hartford Financial Services Group 1994–, Rayonier Corpn 1993–; mem. Bd of Trustees, Stonehill Coll. 1984–, St Sebastian's School 1992–; Co-Chair. Comm. on Pres. Debates 1987–; Visiting Commr on Harvard Athletics 2000–; Hon. LLD (Stonehill Coll. 2002); W. Averell Harriman Democracy Award 1988. *Leisure interest:* athletics. *Address:* Sullivan and Worcester, One Post Office Square, Suite 2400, Boston, MA 02109, USA (Office). *Telephone:* (617) 338-2800 (Office). *Fax:* (617) 338-2880 (Office).

KIRKBY, Emma, OBE, MA, F.G.S.M.D.; British singer; b. 26 Feb. 1949, Camberley, Surrey; d. of late Capt. Geoffrey Kirkby and of Beatrice Daphne Kirkby; one s. by Anthony Rooley; ed Sherborne School for Girls and Somerville Coll., Oxford and pvt. singing lessons with Jessica Cash; specialist singer of renaissance, baroque and classical repertoire; started full-time professional singing 1975; since mid-1970s involved in revival of performances with period instruments and the attempt to recreate the sounds the composers would have heard; performances at the Proms 1977–; works as freelance with many groups and orchestras in the UK and Germany; Hon. DLitt (Salford) 1985; Hon. DMus (Bath) 1994, (Sheffield) 2000; Handel Prize, Halle, Germany 1997. *Recordings include:* Complete songs of John Dowland 1976–77, Messiah (Handel) 1979, 1988, Madrigals by Monteverdi, Wert, Scarlatti and other Italians, Schütz, Grabbe, Wilbye, Ward and other English composers, Monteverdi Vespers, Mass in B Minor (Bach), Handel's Athalia, Joshua, Judas Maccabaeus, Sequences by Hildegarde of Bingen (Hyperion), Arie Antiche and Songs of Maurice Greene, Dido and Aeneas, Handel's German Arias, Italian Cantatas: Songs by Arne and Handel, Stabat Mater (Pergolesi), Haydn's Creation, Mozart Motets, Mozart Concert Arias, Vivaldi Opera Arias, Handel Opera Arias, Christmas Music with Westminster Abbey Choir, Christmas Music with London Baroque, Bach Cantatas with Freiburger Barockorchester. *Telephone:* (20) 8444-6565. *Fax:* (20) 8444-1008. *E-mail:* consort@easynet.co.uk (Office).

KIRKINEN, Heikki, PhD; Finnish university professor (retd); b. 22 Sept. 1927, Liperi; s. of Sulo A. Kirkinen and Anna Hirvonen; m. Maire Mirjam Rehvonen 1953; one s.; ed Joensuu Lycée, Univ. of Helsinki; lecturer in History and Finnish, Orthodox Seminary of Finland 1953–59; lecturer in History, Univ. of Jyvaskyla 1960–62; Researcher, Acad. of Finland 1962–66; Assoc. Prof. Sorbonne, Paris 1966–70; Prof. of History, Univ. of Joensuu 1970, Rector 1971–81, Prof. and Dir Inst. of History 1981–90; Assoc. Prof., Sorbonne Nouvelle 1984–85; Assoc. Dir of Studies, Ecole Pratique des Hautes Etudes, Paris 1988–89; mem. History Soc., Finnish Literature Soc., Acad. of Sciences of Finland; mem. Acad. Européenne des Sciences, des Arts et des Lettres; Hon. mem. Kalevala Soc.; Commdr, Order of the White Rose; Commdr, Ordre des Palmes Académiques, Officier, Ordre Nat. du Mérite (France). *Publications:* Les Origines de la conception moderne de l'homme-machine 1960, Karelia between East and West, I. Russian Karelia in the Renaissance (1478–1617) 1970, Karelia on the Battlefield. Karelia between East and West, II 1976, Problems of Rural Development in Finland and in France (Ed.) 1982, Europas födelse. Bonniers varldshistoria 7 1984, The Kalevala, an Epic of Finland and all Mankind (with H. Sihvo) 1985, History of Russia and the Soviet Union (Ed.-in-Chief) 1986, Le Monde kalévaléen en France et en Finlande avec un regard sur la tradition populaire et l'épopée brétonnes (Ed. with Jean Perrot) 1987, Byzantine Tradition and Finland 1987, Structures and Forces in History 1987, The Roots of the Kalevala Tradition in North Karelia 1988, Europe of Regions and Finland 1991, History of the Karelian People (with others) 1994, Provincial Government 1996, Termite or Angel? – Reflections on Cultural Evolution 2002. *Leisure interests:* music, fishing. *Address:* University of Joensuu, B.P. 111, 80101 Joensuu (Office); Roskildenkatu 4D7, 80140 Joensuu, Finland (Home). *Telephone:* (13) 801143.

KIRKLAND, Gelsey; American ballerina; b. 1953, Bethlehem, Pa; m. Greg Lawrence; ed School of American Ballet; youngest mem. of New York Ballet at 15 in 1968, Soloist 1969–72, Prin. Dancer 1972–74; American Ballet Theater 1974–81, 1982–84, teacher, coach American Ballet Theatre 1992–; Guest Dancer, Royal Ballet, London 1980, 1986, Stuttgart Ballet 1980; appeared in TV show The Nutcracker 1977. *Ballets include:* Firebird, The Goldberg Variations, Scherzo fantastique, An Evening's Waltzes, The Leaves are Fading, Hamlet, The Tiller in the Field, Four Bagatelles, Stravinsky Symphony in C, Song of the Nightingale Connotations, Romeo and Juliet and

others. *Publications:* Dancing on My Grave (autobiog.) 1987, The Shape of Love (with Greg Laurence) 1990, The Little Ballerina and Her Dancing Horse 1993. *Address:* c/o Dubé Zakin Management Inc., 67 Riverside Drive, Apartment 3B, New York, NY 10024, USA.

KIRKPATRICK, Jeane Duane Jordan, MA, PhD; American diplomatist and professor of political science; b. 19 Nov. 1926, Duncan, Okla; d. of Welcher F. and Leona (Kile) Jordan; m. Evron M. Kirkpatrick 1955; three s.; ed Stephens Coll., Columbia, Mo., Barnard Coll., Columbia Univ., New York and Inst. de Science Politique, Univ. of Paris; Research Analyst, Dept of State 1951–53; Research Assoc., George Washington Univ., Washington, DC 1954–56, Fund for the Republic 1956–58; Asst Prof. of Political Science, Trinity Coll., Washington, DC 1962–67; Assoc. Prof. of Political Science, Georgetown Univ., Washington, DC 1967–73, Prof. 1973–; Leavey Prof. in Foundations of American Freedom 1978–; Sr Fellow American Enterprise Inst. for Public Policy Research 1977–; Perm. Rep. to UN 1981–85; fmr mem. Democratic Nat. Comm.; Vice-Chair. Comm. on Vice-Presidential Selection 1972–74; mem. Nat. Comm. on Party Structure and Presidential Nomination 1975; mem. Int. Research Council Cen. for Strategic and Int. Studies, Georgetown Univ.; Pres. Helen Dwight Reid Educ. Foundation 1990–; Earhart Fellow 1956–57; fmr Democrat, joined Republican Party 1985; Hon. LHD (Georgetown Univ., Univ. of Pittsburgh, Univ. of Mich., Tel Aviv Univ., Coll. of William and Mary, St John's Univ., St Anselm's Univ., Syracuse Univ.); Prix Politique (France) 1984; Distinguished Alumna Award, Stephens Coll. 1978, Distinguished Alumna Medal, Barnard Coll. 1983, B'nai B'nith Award 1982; Pres. Medal of Freedom 1985, Hubert Humphrey Award (American Political Science Asscn) 1988, Hungarian Presidential Gold Medal 1999, Grand Officier du Wissam Al Alaoui Medal, King of Morocco 2000. *Publications:* Foreign Students in the United States: A National Survey 1966, Mass Behavior in Battle and Captivity 1968, Leader and Vanguard in Mass Society: The Peronist Movement in Argentina 1971, Political Woman 1974, The Presidential Elite 1976, Dismantling the Parties: Reflections on Party Reform and Party Decomposition 1978, Dictatorships and Double Standards 1982, The Reagan Phenomenon 1983, Legitimacy and Force (2 Vols) 1988, Foreign Affairs: America and the World 1989–90, The Withering Away of the Totalitarian State 1990; ed. and contrib. to several others; also articles in political journals. *Leisure interests:* contemporary fiction, Bach, gourmet cooking. *Address:* American Enterprise Institute, 1150 17th Street, NW, Washington, DC 20036, USA. *E-mail:* jkirkpatrick@aei.org (Office).

KIRKUP, James Harold, BA, FRSL; British writer; b. 23 April 1918, South Shields; s. of James Harold Kirkup and Mary Johnson; ed Durham Univ.; Gregory Fellow in Poetry, Leeds Univ. 1950–52; Visiting Poet, Bath Acad. of Art 1953–56; travelling lectureship from Swedish Ministry of Education 1956–57; Prof. of English Language and Literature, Salamanca (Spain) 1957–58; Prof. of English Literature, Tohoku Univ. 1959–61; Visiting Prof. of English Literature, Japan Women's Univ., Tokyo 1964–69; Visiting Prof. and Poet in Residence, Amherst Coll. Mass. 1968–69; Prof. of English Literature, Univ. of Nagoya, Japan 1969–72; Morton Visiting Prof. in Int. Literature, Ohio Univ. 1975–76; Playwright in Residence, Sherman Theatre, Univ. Coll., Cardiff 1976–77; Prof. of English Literature, Kyoto Univ. of Foreign Studies 1977–89; Tutor, Arvon Foundation 1979; obituarist for The Independent and The Guardian newspapers 1989–; Literary Ed. Orient-West Magazine, Tokyo 1963–65; founder Pres. The British Haiku Soc. 1991–96; Literary Adviser Ko Haiku Magazine, Nagoya, Japan; trans. of poetry on www.brindin.com; Atlantic Award in Literature (Rockefeller Foundation) 1959, Japan Festival Foundation Award for A Book of Tanka 1997, Scott-Moncrieff Prize for Translation 1997. *Music:* libretto for An Actor's Revenge (music by Minoru Miki) 1975. *Plays:* trans. The Prince of Homburg (Kleist), Don Carlos (Schiller), The Physicists (Friedrich Dürrenmatt), The True Mystery of the Nativity, The True Mystery of the Passion. *Radio:* Poetry Please (BBC Radio). *Publications:* The Cosmic Shape 1947, The Drowned Sailor 1948, The Creation 1950, The Submerged Village 1951, A Correct Compassion 1952, A Spring Journey 1954, Upon This Rock, The Dark Child, The Triumph of Harmony 1955, The True Mystery of the Nativity, Ancestral Voices, The Radiance of the King 1956, The Descent into the Cave, The Only Child (autobiography) 1957, The Peach Garden, Two Pigeons Flying High (TV plays), Sorrows, Passions and Alarms (autobiography) 1960, The True Mystery of the Passion, The Prodigal Son (poems) 1956–60, These Horned Islands (travel) 1962, The Love of Others (novel) 1962, Tropic Temper (travel) 1963, Refusal to Conform, Last and First Poems 1963, The Heavenly Mandate 1964, Japan Industrial, Vols I and II 1964–65, Tokyo (travel) 1966, Bangkok (travel) 1967, Paper Windows 1967, Michael Kohlhaas 1967, Filipinescas (travel) 1968, One Man's Russia (travel) 1968, Streets of Asia (travel) 1969, Hong Kong (travel) 1969, White Shadows, Black Shadows: Poems of Peace and War 1969, The Body Servant: Poems of Exile 1971, Japan Behind the Fan 1970, Streets of Asia 1969, Insect Summer (novel) 1971, A Bewick Bestiary 1971, Transmental Vibrations 1972, Brand (Ibsen) 1972, The Magic Drum (play for children) 1972, (story for children) 1973, Peer Gynt 1973, The Winter Moon, Selected Poems of Takagi Kyozo, Cyrano de Bergerac 1974, Play Strindberg 1974, The Conformer 1975, Don Carlos 1975, Heaven, Hell and Hara-Kiri 1975, Background to English Literature 1975, An English Traveller in Japan 1975, Frank the Fifth, Portrait of a Planet 1976, Scenes from Sesshu 1977, Modern Japanese Poetry (anthology) 1978, Dengoban Messages: One-line Poems, Zen Contemplations, Enlightenment 1979, Cold Mountain Poems, The Guardian of the Word, Aspects of Europe, Countries and Customs, British Traditions and Superstitions 1980, James Kirkup's Tales from Shakespeare

1969–84, Scenes from Sutcliffe 1981, The British Lady and Gentleman, I am Count Dracula 1981, Ecce Homo 1981, To The Unknown God 1982, The Bush Toads 1982, Folktales Japanesque 1982, To the Ancestral North (poems for autobiog.) 1983, The Glory that was Greece 1984, The Sense of the Visit 1984, Hearn in my Heart 1984; An Actor's Revenge (opera) 1979, Friends in Arms, Shunkinsho 1980, No More Hiroshimas 1982, 1995, The Damask Drum (opera) 1984, Trends and Traditions 1985, Dictionary of Body Language 1985, English with a Smile 1986, Fellow Feelings (poems) 1986, Portraits and Souvenirs 1987, The Mystery and Magic of Symbols 1987, The Cry of the Owl: Native American Folktales and Legends 1987, I of All People, Scenes from American Life, I Remember America, Everyday English Superstitions 1988, The Best of Britain 1989, Everyday English Proverbs 1989, Gaijin on the Ginza 1992, A Poet Could Not But Be Gay 1992, Throwback (Poems) 1992, First Fireworks (Poems) 1992, Me All Over: Memoirs of a Misfit (autobiog.) 1993, Queens Have Died Young and Fair (novel) 1993, Strange Attractors (poems) 1994, Blue Bamboo (Haiku) 1994, Words or Contemplation (poems) 1993, Noems, Koans & A Navel Display 1995, A Certain State of Mind 1995, Blindsight (trans. Hervé Guibert) 1995, Paradise (trans. Hervé Guibert) 1996, Collected Longer Poems 1996, Selected Shorter Poems 1996, Counting to 9,999 1996, Look at it This Way! (Poems for young people) 1995, A Child of the Tyne (autobiography) 1996, A Book of Tanka 1996, The Patient Obituarist: New Poems 1996, Burning Giraffes: Modern Japanese Poets 1996, Broad Daylight: Poems East and West 1996, Figures in a Setting 1996, Utsusemi (tanka) 1996, Two Classic German Dramas: Kleist's Prince of Homburg and Schiller's Don Carlos 1997, The Nativity and the Passion: Two Mystery Plays 1997, How to Cook Women: Selected Poetry and Prose by Takagi Kyozo 1997, He Dreamed He Was a Butterfly 1998, Pikadon: An Epic 1998, Tanka Tales 1998, One-Man Band: Poems Without Words 1999, Tokonoma (haiku and tanka, with woodcuts by Naoko Matsubara), Tankalphabet 2001, A Tiger in Your Tanka 2001, In Thickets of Memory: Tanka by Saito Fumi (trans.), 2002, Pages from the Seasons: Tanka by Fumiko Miura 2002, Shields Sketches 2002, An Island in the Sky: Poems for Andora 2003; numerous poems, plays and essays and trans. from French, German, Japanese, Italian and Norwegian. *Leisure interests:* macrobiotic diet, Zen Buddhist meditation, listening to good jazz. *Address:* Atic D. Edifici Les Bons, Avingcuda de Rouillac 7, Les Bons, Encamp, Andorra (Home). *Telephone:* (376) 831065 (Home). *Fax:* (376) 831065 (Home).

KIRKWOOD, Thomas Burton Loram, BA, MSc, PhD, FMedSci; British professor of gerontology; b. 6 July 1951; s. of the late Kenneth Kirkwood and of Deborah Burton Kirkwood (née Collings); m. 1st Betty Rosamund Bartlett 1973 (divorced 1975); one s. one d.; m. 2nd Jane Louise Bottomley 1995; ed Dragon School, Oxford, Magdalen Coll. School, Oxford, St Catharine's Coll., Cambridge, Worcester Coll., Oxford; initially qualified as a mathematician; developed 'disposable soma' theory of ageing; Scientist, Nat. Inst. for Biological Standards and Control 1973–81, Sr Scientist 1981–88; Head, Laboratory of Math. Biology 1988–93; Prof. of Biological Gerontology Univ. of Manchester 1993–99 (first in GB); Prof. of Medicine and Head of Dept of Gerontology, Univ. of Newcastle upon Tyne 1999–; Chair. British Soc. for Research on Ageing 1992–99; Dir Jt Centre on Ageing, Univs of Manchester and Newcastle upon Tyne 1996–; Gov. Research Advisory Council, Research into Ageing 1998–2001, Chair. 1999–2000; Chair. Foresight Task Force on Health Care of Older People 1999–2001; mem. WHO Expert Advisory Panel on Biological Standardization 1985–, UK Human Genome Mapping Project Cttee 1991–93, Basic Scis Interest Group, Wellcome Trust 1992–97, Biotech. and Biological Sciences Research Council 2001–; Co-Ed. Mechanisms of Ageing and Development 2000–; Pres. Int. Biometric Soc. (British Region) 1998–2000; Fellow Inst. for Advanced Study, Budapest 1997; Heinz Karger Prize 1983, Fritz Verzár Medal 1996, British Geriatrics Soc. Dhole-Eddlestone Prize 2001, Royal Inst. Henry Dale Prize 2002. *Radio:* BBC Reith Lectures 2001. *Publications:* (jtly): Accuracy in Molecular Processes: Its Control and Relevance to Living Systems 1986, Time of Our Lives: The Science of Human Ageing 1999, Sex and Longevity: Sexuality, Gender, Reproduction, Parenthood 2001; (with C. E. Finch): Chance, Development and Aging 2000, The End of Age 2001; numerous scientific articles in learned journals. *Leisure interests:* gardening, hill-walking, running, pottery. *Address:* Department of Gerontology, Institute for Ageing and Health, Wolfson Research Centre, University of Newcastle upon Tyne, Newcastle General Hospital, Westgate Road, Newcastle upon Tyne, NE4 6BE (Office); Roughlees, Ewesley, Morpeth, Northumberland, NE61 4PH, England (Home). *Telephone:* (191) 256-3319 (Office). *Fax:* (191) 219-5074 (Office). *E-mail:* tom.kirkwood@ncl.ac.uk (Office).

KIRPAL, Prem Nath, MA, LLB; Indian educationist; b. 30 April 1909, Moga, Punjab; s. of Raibahadur Ishwardas and Bibi Kesari; ed Punjab Univ. and Balliol Coll., Oxford; Lecturer, then Prof. of History and Political Science 1934–45; Educ. Adviser, Indian High Comm., London 1945–48; Deputy Sec. Ministry of Educ. and Sec.-Gen. Indian Nat. Comm. for UNESCO 1948–52; Deputy Dir then Dir UNESCO Dept of Cultural Activities 1952–57; Joint Sec. Ministry of Educ. and Joint Educ. Adviser to Govt of India 1957–60; Sec. Ministry of Educ. 1960–69; Sr Specialist, East-West Centre, Honolulu Hawaii 1969; Dir Int. Study of Private Philanthropy 1969–; Pres. Exec. Board, UNESCO 1970–72; Founder, Pres., Inst. of Cultural Relations and Devt Studies, New Delhi 1971–; Pres. Indian Council of Peace Research 1972–; Pres. Int. Educational Consortium, New Delhi 1979–81; Consultant, World Bank, Washington, DC; mem. Exec. Council, Delhi Univ.; Chair. Delhi Public Library, Delhi School of Social Work; Pres. Forum of Educ., India; Hon. LLD (Temple Univ.), Hon. DSc (Leningrad), Hon. DLitt (Punjab Univ.); UNESCO Gold Medal 1972, 30th Anniversary Award, UNESCO 1976 and other awards; Orders of Repub. of Egypt and of UAR 1972. *Publications:* East India Company and Persia 1800–1810: A Study in Diplomatic Relations, Memoirs of Wollebrant de Jong 1624, Life of Dyal Singh Majithia, Main Trends in Cultural Development of India, A Decade of Indian Education 1958–68, Indian Education–Twenty-five Years of Independence, Youth Values and Established Culture, Education and Development, In Quest of Humanity, The Cosmic Sea and other Poems 1980, Songs of Psyche, Spirit's Musings, Songs of Eternity (philosophical poems), Voices from the Deep 1986, From Near and Far (poems) 1988, Autumn offerings (poems) 1989, Foundations of Education for Free India 1990, Education and International Cooperation 1991, Dreams and Solitudes 1990, Mind and Modes 1990, Monsoon Breezes 1991, Roses in December 1991 (all poems), Quests and Celebrations (poems), Heart's Offerings (poems), A Decade of Education in India, Culture and Development, Reconstituting the Human Community; and over 20 articles on educ., culture and int. co-operation. *Leisure interests:* hiking, painting, poetry and meditation. *Address:* F-63, Sujan Singh Park, New Delhi 110003, India (Home). *Telephone:* (11) 388158.

KIRPICHNIKOV, Mikhail Petrovich, DBiolSc; Russian politician; b. 9 Nov. 1945, Moscow; m.; one d.; ed Moscow Inst. of Physics and Tech.; with Inst. of Molecular Biology 1972–89; Deputy Head, Head of Div., USSR Cttee on Science and Tech. 1989–91; Head of Div., Head of Dept, Ministry of Science and Tech. Policy of Russian Fed. 1991–93; Head, Div. of Science, Educ., High School and Tech., Russian Govt 1993–94; Head, Dept of Science and Educ. 1994–98; First Deputy Minister of Science and Tech. July–Sept. 1998, Minister 1998–2001; Prof. Inst. of Bio-organic Chemistry, Russian Acad. of Sciences 2000–; mem., Russian Acad. of Sciences 1997–. *Publications:* over 200 books, articles and papers on biology. *Address:* Institute of Bio-organic Chemistry, Mirlukho-Maklaya str. 16/10, 117871 GSP-7 Moscow, Russia. *Telephone:* (095) 335-28-88 (Office).

KIRPICHNIKOV, Valery Aleksandrovich; Russian politician; b. 29 June 1946, Rostov-on-Don; m.; two c.; ed Leningrad Polytech. Inst.; army service, Lt, air defence forces 1969–71; engineer, sr engineer, Deputy Head of lab., S. Vavilov State Inst. of Optics, Leningrad Region br. 1971–81; chief engineer, Research Inst. of Complex Tests 1981–88; Deputy Chair., Chair., Exec. Cttee Sosnovy Bor Town Soviet 1988–92; RSFSR Peoples' Deputy 1990, mem. Supreme Soviet 1990–93; mem. State Duma 1993–98; Deputy Gov. Leningrad Region 1996–98; Pres. Union of Russian Towns 1993–98; Minister of Regional Policy of Russian Fed. 1998–99; First Deputy Minister of Fed., Nat. and Migration Policy 2000–; f. Russian Union of Local Self-Man. *Publications:* scientific works, patents. *Address:* Ministry of Federation, National and Migration Policy, Trubnikovsky per. 19, 121819 GSP2 Moscow, Russia. *Telephone:* (095) 202-53-05 (Office).

KIRSCHNER, Marc W., PhD; American cell biologist; ed Northwestern Univ., Univ. of California, Berkeley; postdoctoral research at Univ. of Calif., Berkeley and Oxford Univ.; Asst Prof. Princeton Univ. 1972; Prof. Univ. of Calif., San Francisco; Founder and Chair. Dept of Cell Biology and Carl W. Walter Prof. of Cell Biology, Harvard Medical School; Co-Founder Inst. for Chemistry and Cell Biology, Harvard Univ. 1999; mem. NAS, American Acad. of Arts and Sciences; Foreign mem. Royal Soc. 1999–. *Publication:* Cells, Embryos and Evolution (co-author) 1997. *Address:* Department of Cell Biology, Harvard Medical School, 240 Longwood Avenue, Boston, MA 02115, USA (Office). *Telephone:* (617) 432-2250 (Office). *Fax:* (617) 432-0420 (Office). *E-mail:* marc@hms.harvard.edu (Office). *Website:* www.harvard.edu (Office).

KIRSCHSTEIN, Ruth L., AB, MD; American physician and administrator; b. 12 Oct. 1926, Brooklyn, New York; d. of Julius and Elizabeth (Berm) Kirschstein; m. Alan S. Rabson 1950; one s.; ed Long Island Univ., New York and Tulane Univ., New Orleans, La; Hosp. intern and resident 1951–54; Instructor in Pathology, Tulane Univ. 1954–55; Medical Officer, Resident in Pathology, then Pathologist, Lab. of Viral Products, Nat. Insts. of Health 1956–60, Chief, Section of Pathology, Lab. of Viral Immunology 1960–62, Asst Chief, Lab. of Viral Immunology 1962–64, Acting Chief, Lab. of Pathology 1964–65, Chief 1965–72; Asst Dir Div. of Biologics Standards, Nat. Insts. of Health 1971–72, Acting Deputy Dir, Bureau of Biologics 1972–73, Deputy Assoc. Commr for Science 1973–74; Dir Nat. Inst. of Gen. Medical Sciences, NIH 1974–93; Deputy Dir NIH 1993–, Acting Dir 2000–; mem. Inst. of Medicine of NAS; Co-Chair. PHS Co-ordinating Comm. on Women's Health Issues 1990–; Co-Chair. Special Emphasis Oversight Comm. on Science and Tech. 1989–; Hon. LLD (Atlanta) 1985; DSc hc (Mount Sinai School of Medicine) 1984, (Medical Coll. of Ohio) 1986; Hon. Dr (School of Medicine, Tulane Univ.) 1997; Presidential Meritorious Exec. Rank Award 1980, Distinguished Exec. Service Award Sr Exec. Asscn 1985, Presidential Distinguished Exec. Rank Award 1985, 1995 and numerous other awards. *Publications:* numerous scientific papers. *Address:* National Institutes of Health, Building 1, Room 126, 1 Center Drive, MSC 0148, Bethesda, MD 20892-0148 (Office); 6 West Drive, Bethesda, MD 20814, USA (Home). *Telephone:* (301) 496-2433 (Office). *Fax:* (301) 402-2700 (Office). *E-mail:* execsec1@od.nih.gov (Office). *Website:* www.nih.gov (Office).

KIRST, Michael, MPA, PhD; American professor of education; b. 1 Aug. 1939, West Reading, Pa; s. of Russell Kirst and Marian (Weile) Kirst; m. Wendy Burdsall 1975; one s. one d.; ed Dartmouth Coll. and Harvard Univ.; Assoc. Dir President's Comm. on White House Fellows, Nat. Advisory Council on

Educ. of Disadvantaged Children 1966; Dir Program Planning and Evaluation, Bureau of Elementary and Secondary Educ., US Office of Educ. 1967; Staff Dir US Senate Sub-Cttee on Manpower, Employment and Poverty 1968; Prof. of Educ. and Business Admin. Stanford Univ. 1968–; Pres. Calif. State Bd of Educ. 1977–81; Chair. Bd of Int. Comparative Studies in Educ., NAS 1994–; mem. Nat. Acad. of Educ., USA, Int. Acad. of Educ. and numerous other educ. bds, cttees, etc. *Publications include:* Schools in Conflict: Political Turbulence in American Education (with F. Wirt) 1992, Contemporary Issues in Education: Perspectives from Australia and USA (with G. Hancock and D. Grossman) 1983, Who Controls Our Schools: American Values in Conflict 1984, Political Dynamics of American Education 2001. *Address:* School of Education, Stanford University, Stanford, CA 94305, USA. *Telephone:* (650) 723-4412. *Fax:* (650) 725-7412.

KIRSZENSTEIN-SZEWIŃSKA, Irena, MEcon; Polish athlete and sports official; b. 24 May 1946, Leningrad, USSR (now St Petersburg, Russia); m. Janusz Szewinsk; two s.; ed Warsaw Univ.; coached by Janusz Szewinsk; athlete 1961–80 (100m, 200m, long jump, 4×100m relay, 4×400m relay); set 38 Polish records; won seven Olympic medals in five different events; took part in Olympic Games, Tokyo 1964 (silver medals for long jump and 200m, gold medal for 4×100m relay), Mexico City 1968 (bronze medal for 100m, gold medal for 200m), Munich 1972 (bronze medal for 200m), Montreal 1976 (gold medal for 400m); ten times world record-holder, for 100m, 200m and 400m; Pres. Polish Women's Sport Asscn 1994–, Polish Athletic Asscn 1997–; Vice-Pres. Polish Olympic Cttee 1988–, Polish Olympians Asscn 1993–, World Olympians Asscn 1995–99, Council mem. 1999–; mem. Council European Athletic Asscn 1995–, Women's Cttee, Int. Assoc. of Athletic's Fed., Int. Olympic Cttee (IOC) 1998–, IOC Co-ordination Comm. Athens (2004)–, Sport for All Comm. 1999–; Pres. Irena Szewińska Foundation—Vita-Aktiva 1998–; Gold Cross of Merit 1964, Officer's Cross, Order of Polonia Restituta 1968, Commdr's Cross, Order of Polonia Restituta 1972, with Star 1999, Order of Banner of Labour (2nd Class) 1976. *Leisure interests:* jogging, books, theatre. *Address:* Polish Athletic Association, ul. Cegłowska 68/70, 01-809 Warsaw, Poland. *Telephone:* (22) 6397015. *Fax:* (22) 6397016.

KIRWAN, William E., PhD; American university president and professor of mathematics; b. 14 April 1938, Louisville, Ky; s. of Albert Dennis Kirwan and Elizabeth H. Kirwan; m. Patricia Harper 1960; one s. one d.; ed Univ. of Kentucky, Rutgers Univ.; Asst Instructor, Rutgers Univ. 1963–64; Asst Prof., Dept of Math., Univ. of Maryland 1964–68; Visiting Lecturer, Royal Holloway Coll., London Univ., UK 1966–67; Assoc. Prof., Dept of Math., Univ. of Md at Coll. Park 1968–72, Prof. 1972–, Chair. Dept of Math. 1977–81, Vice-Chancellor for Academic Affairs 1981–88, Acting Chancellor 1982, Vice-Pres. for Academic Affairs and Provost 1986–88, Acting Pres. 1988–89, Pres. 1989–98; Pres. Ohio State Univ. 1998–; Chair. Nat. Asscn of State Univs. and Land Grant Colls. 1995–; several other appointments; Ed. Proc. of American Math. Soc. 1979–85; NDEA Fellow 1960–63; Nat. Science Foundation Grants 1965–82; Officier, Order of Leopold II, Belgium 1989. *Publications:* Advances in Complex Analysis (Co-Ed. with L. Zalcman) 1976; numerous published research articles and seminar talks. *Leisure interests:* classical music, tennis. *Address:* Ohio State University, 190 North Oval Mall, 205 Bricker, Columbus, OH 43210, USA. *Telephone:* (614) 292-2424. *Website:* www.acs.ohio-state.edu (Office).

KISELEV, Anatoly Ivanovich; Russian aviation engineer; b. 29 April 1938, Moscow; m.; one s. one d.; ed Moscow Inst. of Aviation Tech.; fmr electrician, then Eng, tester, head of lab., head of workshop, Deputy Dir Moscow Khrunichev Machine Construction Factory 1956–72, Dir 1975–93, involved in merger of Moscow Khrunichev Machine Construction Factory and Salut Construction Bureau, Dir United State Scientific Production Cen. 1993–; Deputy Head, then First Chief of Dept USSR Ministry of Gen. Machine Construction 1972–75; Dir Russian-American Lokhid-Khrunichev (Int. Launch Services) 1994–2001, mem. Bd Dirs 2001–; Lenin's Prize; Order for Service to Motherland, Hero of Socialist Labour and numerous other orders and medals. *Address:* United State Scientific Production Centre, Novozavodskaya str. 18, 121309 Moscow, Russia (Office). *Telephone:* (095) 145-88-54 (Office).

KISELEV, Oleg Vladimirovich, CandTechSci; Russian politician and engineer; b. 1 June 1953, Divnoye, Stavropol territory; m.; one s.; ed Moscow State Inst. of Construction; teacher Inst. of Steel and Alloys 1981–86; Deputy Dir Inst. of Chem. Physics USSR (now Russian) Acad. of Sciences 1986–88; Founder and Head Alfa-Eco co-operative, then Jt Venture Alfa-Eco, then Alfa production-finance co. including Alfa Bank and other affiliates 1988–91; Founder, Pres. and Chair. Bd Dirs Mosexpo Co. 1991–; co-f. IMPEX Bank 1993, Pres. and Chair. Bd Dirs 1993–2001; mem. Bd Dirs Russian Bank of Reconstruction and Devt 2001–; Man. Dir, Chair. Bd Metalloinvest (holding co.) 2001–; mem. Int. Asscn of Business Dirs 1989–; Chair. Council on Foreign Econ. Relations, Ministry of Foreign Affairs 1992; mem. Govt Union on Business 1993–94, Pres. Council 1994, Bd Dirs Russian-American Foundation of Support of Business 1994–, Public Council on Foreign and Defence Policy, Bd Asscn of Russian Banks 1999–. *Address:* Metalloinvest Co., Yefremova str. 12a, 119048 Moscow, Russia (Office). *Telephone:* (095) 245-72-10 (Office).

KISELEV, Yevgeny Alekseyevich; Russian broadcaster; b. 15 June 1956, Moscow; s. of Aleksei Kiselev and Anna Kiselev; m. Masha Shakhova 1974; one s.; ed Inst. of Asian and African Studies, Moscow State Univ.; teacher of Persian (Farsi) language, Higher School of KGB 1981–84; corresp., Radio Moscow Middle Eastern Dept 1984–86; TV journalist 1987–; regular host '120 Minutes' breakfast show 1987–90, staff corresp. news div. Gosteleradio (fmr USSR State Cttee for TV and radio broadcasting) 1989–90; made series of documentaries on everyday life in Israel 1989, 1990; joined newly founded Russian TV 1991, anchorman 'Vesti' late-night news programme; joined Ostankino State TV co. 1992; started 'Itogi' weekly news and current affairs programme 1992, on TNT station 2001–; Co-Founder and Vice-Pres. NTV independent broadcasting co. 1993–2000, Gen. Dir 2000–01; Co-founder, NTV-Plus Co. (direct satellite broadcasting) 1996; Gen. Dir TV-6 Independent Broadcasting Co. 2001–02; Ed.-in-Chief TVS Broadcasting 2002–; mem. Acad. of Russian TV; Journalist of the Year, Moscow Journalistic Union 1993, included on list of 100 most influential people in Russia, Publ monthly by Nezavisimaya Gazeta 1993–; Int. Press Freedom Award, Cttee to Protect Journalists, New York 1995. *Leisure interest:* playing tennis. *Address:* Moscow Independent Broadcasting Company TVS, Ilyinka str. 15, bldg 1 Moscow, Russia (Office). *Telephone:* (095) 206-92-98; 206-02-85 (Office).

KISHIMOTO, Tadamitsu; Japanese university president; b. 7 May 1939, Osaka; s. of Tadanobu Kishimoto and Yasuko Kishimoto; ed Osaka Univ. Medical School; Research Fellow Dept of Medicine, Johns Hopkins Univ. School of Medicine 1970–73, Asst Prof. 1973–74; Asst Prof., Dept of Medicine III, Osaka Univ. Medical School 1974–79, Prof. and Chair. 1991–98, Prof. Dept of Pathology and Medicine 1979–83, Prof. Inst. for Molecular and Cellular Biology 1983–91, Dean Osaka Univ. Medical School 1995–97, Pres. Osaka Univ. 1997–; Foreign Assoc. NAS, USA 1991; Hon. mem. American Asscn of Immunologists 1992, American Soc. of Hematology 1997; mem. Japan Acad. 1995; Asahi Prize 1988, Imperial Prize, Japan Acad. 1992; Person of Cultural Merit 1990, Order of Culture 1998. *Address:* Office of the President, Osaka University, 1-1 Yamadaoka, Suita, Osaka 565-0871 (Office); 3-5-31, Nankano-cho, Tondabayashi City, Osaka, Japan (Home). *Telephone:* (6) 6879-7004 (Office); (7) 2124-0532 (Home). *Fax:* (6) 6879-7006 (Office). *E-mail:* kishimot@emed3.med.osaka-u.ac.jp (Office). *Website:* www.osaka-u.ac.jp (Office).

KISHLANSKY, Mark Alan, PhD, FRHistS; American professor of history; b. 10 Nov. 1948, Brooklyn, NY; s. of Morris Kishlansky and Charlotte Katz; m. Jeanne Thiel 1975; two s.; ed Commack High School, State Univ. of New York at Stony Brook and Brown Univ.; Prof. of History, Univ. of Chicago 1975–91, Northwestern Univ. 1983, Harvard Univ. 1991–, Frank Baird Jr Prof. of History 1997–; Mellon Visiting Prof. of History, Calif. Inst. of Tech. 1990; mem. Cttee on Social Thought 1990–91; various research awards and other distinctions. *Publications:* The Rise of the New Model Army 1979, Parliamentary Selection: Social and Political Choice in Early Modern England, Early Modern Europe: The Crisis of Authority (ed. with C. M. Gray and E. Cochrane) 1987, Civilization in the West (with P. Geary and P. O'Brien) 1991, Sources of the West (ed.) 1991, Societies and Cultures in World Civilizations (with P. Geary, P. O'Brien, R. B. Worg) 1995, A Monarchy Transformed 1996. *Leisure interests:* Shakespeare, baseball, comedy. *Address:* Department of History, Harvard University, Cambridge, MA 02138, USA. *Telephone:* (617) 496-3427. *Fax:* (617) 496-3425. *Website:* www.harvard.edu (Office).

KISHTMAND, Sultan Ali; Afghanistan politician; b. 1935; ed univ.; mem. of Hazara ethnic minority; a founder mem. People's Democratic Party of Afghanistan (PDPA) and mem. Cen. Cttee 1965; with Parcham faction when PDPA split 1967; Minister of Planning April–Aug. 1978; tried on charges of conspiracy and sentenced to death 1978; sentence commuted by Pres. Amin. Oct. 1978; fmr Vice-Pres. of Revolutionary Council; Deputy Prime Minister and Minister of Planning after Soviet intervention 1979–81; Prime Minister of Afghanistan and Chair. Council of Ministers 1981–88, 1989–90; First Vice-Pres. 1990–91.

KISIM, Marwan al-, PhD; Jordanian politician; b. 12 May 1938, Amman; ed Eastern Michigan, Columbia and Georgetown Univs., USA; joined Ministry of Foreign Affairs 1962; Consul-Gen., New York 1964–65; Deputy Dir of Protocol 1966; Political Officer, Jordanian Embassy, Beirut 1967–68, USA 1968–72; Sec. to Crown Prince Hassan 1972–75; Dir-Gen. Royal Hashemite Court 1975–76, Chief 1988; Minister of State 1976; Minister of Supply 1977–79; Minister of State for Foreign Affairs 1979–80, Minister of Foreign Affairs 1980–83; Deputy Prime Minister and Minister of Foreign Affairs 1988–90; Jordanian, Syrian, Mexican, Lebanese, Chinese and Italian decorations. *Address:* c/o Ministry of Foreign Affairs, Amman, Jordan.

KISLOV, Aleksander Konstantinovich, DHist; Russian political scientist; b. 11 Sept. 1929, Moscow; m.; one s. two d.; ed Moscow Inst. of Int. Relations; corresp., head of div., head of sector, Deputy Ed.-in-Chief Foreign Information Dept TASS News Agency 1956–71; head of sector Inst. of USA and Canada, USSR Acad. of Sciences 1971–86, Deputy-Dir Inst. of World Econs and Int. Relations 1986–96; fmr consultant Dept of Planning Int. Events, USSR Ministry of Foreign Affairs; Peace Research Inst. 1990–96; Head Peace Research Centre IMEMO RAN 1996–; mem. editorial Bd numerous journals; mem. Russian Acad. of Nat. Sciences 1992–. *Publications:* USA and the Islamic World, Contemporary Foreign Policy of the USA (two Vols, ed. and co-author). *Address:* IMEMO, Profsoyuznaya str. 23, 117997 Moscow (Office); Apt 374, prospekt Vernadskogo 127, 117571 Moscow, Russia (Home). *Telephone:* (095) 128-93-89 (Office); (095) 438-61-59 (Home). *Fax:* (095) 120-65-75 (Office). *E-mail:* imemoran@online.ru (Office).

KISSIN, Yevgeny Igorevich; Russian pianist; b. 10 Oct. 1971, Moscow; ed Moscow Gnessin Music School, studied piano with Anna Kantor; lives in USA. *Performances include:* début with Moscow Philharmonic 1984, in Europe 1988; toured Europe, USA, Japan as child prodigy, played and recorded with orchestras under Herbert von Karajan, Seiji Ozawa, Claudio Abbado, Mstislav Rostropovich; participates in numerous European festivals; returned to Moscow for concerts 1997, 2001. *Address:* c/o Harold Holt Ltd, 31 Sinclair Road, London, W14 0NS, England. *Telephone:* (20) 7603-4600 (Agent) (Office); (212) 580-5296 (New York) (Home).

KISSINGER, Henry Alfred, MA, PhD; American university professor, international consultant and government official; b. 27 May 1923, Fuerth, Germany; s. of Louis Kissinger and Paula Stern; m. 1st Anne Fleisher 1949 (divorced 1964); one s. one d.; m. 2nd Nancy Maginnes 1974; ed George Washington High School, Harvard Coll., Harvard Univ.; went to USA 1938; naturalized US Citizen 1943; US Army 1943–46; Dir Study Group on Nuclear Weapons and Foreign Policy, Council of Foreign Relations 1955–56; Dir Special Studies Project, Rockefeller Brothers Fund 1956–58; Consultant, Weapons System Evaluation Group, Joint Chiefs of Staff 1956–60, Nat. Security Council 1961–63, US Arms Control and Disarmament Agency 1961–69, Dept of State 1965–68 and to various other bodies; Faculty mem. Harvard Univ. 1954–69; Dept of Govt and Center for Int. Affairs ; faculty Harvard Univ. Center for Int. Affairs 1960–69; Dir Harvard Int. Seminar 1951–69, Harvard Defense Studies Program 1958–69, Asst to Pres. of USA for Nat. Security Affairs 1969–75; Sec. of State 1973–77; prominent in American negotiations for the Viet Nam settlement of Jan. 1973 and in the negotiations for a Middle East ceasefire 1973, 1974; Trustee, Center for Strategic and Int. Studies 1977–; Chair. Kissinger Assocs, Inc. 1982–; mem. Pres.'s Foreign Intelligence Advisory Bd 1984–90; Chair. Nat. Bipartisan Comm. on Cen. America 1983–84; Counsellor to J. P. Morgan Bank and mem. of its Int. Advisory Council; Hon. Gov. Foreign Policy Asscn; Sr Fellow, Aspen Inst., syndicated columnist LA Times 1984–; Adviser to Bd of Dirs American Express, Forstmann Little & Co., Dir Emer. Freeport McMoran Copper and Gold Inc., Conti Group Cos Ltd, The TCW Group, Hollinger Int. Inc., US Olympic Cttee, Int. Rescue Cttee; Chair. American Int. Group, Int. Advisory Bd; mem. Exec. Cttee Trilateral Comm.; Chair. Eisenhower Exchange Fellowships; Chancellor The Coll. of William and Mary; Hon. Chair. World Cup USA 1994; Woodrow Wilson Book Prize 1958, American Inst. for Public Service Award 1973, Nobel Peace Prize 1973, American Legion Distinguished Service Medal 1974, Wateler Peace Prize 1974, Presidential Medal of Freedom 1977, Medal of Liberty 1986, Hon. KCMG 1995, and many other awards and prizes. *Publications:* Nuclear Weapons and Foreign Policy 1956, A World Restored: Castlereagh, Metternich and the Restoration of Peace 1812–22 1957, The Necessity for Choice: Prospects of American Foreign Policy 1961, The Troubled Partnership: A Reappraisal of the Atlantic Alliance 1965, American Foreign Policy (3 essays) 1969, White House Years 1979, For the Record 1981, Years of Upheaval 1982, Observations: Selected Speeches and Essays 1982–84 1985, Diplomacy 1994, Years of Renewal 1999, Does America Need a Foreign Policy? 2001; and numerous articles on US foreign policy, international affairs and diplomatic history. *Address:* 350 Park Avenue, New York, NY 10022; Suite 400, 1800 K Street, NW, Washington, DC 20006, USA.

KISTLER, Darci; American ballerina; b. 4 June 1964, Riverside, Calif.; d. of Jack B. Kistler and Alicia Kistler (née Kinner); m. Peter Martins (q.v.) 1991; ed School of American Ballet; joined corps de ballet New York City Ballet as prin. dancer under Balanchine 1980; injured 1982–85; teacher School of American Ballet 1994–; New York Women's Award, Golden Plate Award, Dance Magazine Award. *Ballets:* studied with Irina Kosmovska in Los Angeles; performances include: prin. role in Haydn Concerto 1979, Swan Queen in Lev Ivanov's choreographing of Swan Lake 1979, leading roles in Brahms-Schönberg Quartet, Divertimento no. 15, Symphony in C, Raymonda Variations, Walpurgisnacht Ballet, Valse fantaisie, Tchaikovsky Suite no. 3, Dew Drop and the Sugar Plum Fairy in The Nutcracker 1980; new roles created for her in Suite from Soldier's Tale and Tchaikovsky Symphony no. 1 1980; leading roles in Who Cares?, Balanchine's Chaconne, Jacques d'Amboise's Irish Fantasy, Robbins' Prélude à l'après-midi d'un Faune, Martin's The Magic Flute 1981–82; shepherdess in Jacques d'Amboise's Pastorale 1982, siren in Peter Martins' Piano Rag-Music 1982; returned to New York Theater in Prélude à l'après-midi d'un Faune 1985; subsequent roles include: Titania in Balanchine's A Midsummer Night's Dream and the siren in his Prodigal Son, strip-tease girl in Slaughter on Tenth Avenue, man-eating door in Variations pour une porte et un soupir, title role in La Sonnambula 1986; recent work includes: Balanchine's Serenade, Ivesiana, Danses Concertantes, Mozartiana and Jewels 1988–89; Jerome Robbins' The Four Seasons 1989; Balanchine's Allegro brillante, Tchaikovsky Suite no. 3, Robbins' The Goldberg Variations, Other Dances, Dances at a Gathering, In G Major 1989–90, Balanchine Celebration 1993, Symphonic Dances 1994, Apollo 1994; début in Balanchine's La Valse Feb. 1991, Peter Martins' The Sleeping Beauty, Peter Martins' Swan Lake (full length) 1999. *Films:* Balanchine's Ballerinas – Ann Belle 1988, The Nutcracker 1993. *Publication:* Ballerina: My Story 1993. *Leisure interests:* piano, painting, tennis, skiing, cooking. *Address:* c/o The New York City Ballet Inc., New York State Theater, 20 Lincoln Center, New York, NY 10023, USA.

KITAJ, R. B. (Ronald), RA; American artist; b. 29 Oct. 1932, Ohio; s. of the late Walter Kitaj and Jeanne Brooks Kitaj; m. (deceased); three c.; m. 2nd Sandra Fisher 1983 (died 1994); ed New York, Vienna and Royal Coll. of Arts,

London; has lived in London since 1960; Guest Prof. Univ. of Calif., Berkeley 1967–68, Univ. of Calif., LA 1970–71; retrospective tour Hirshhorn Museum, Washington, Cleveland Museum and Kunsthalle, Düsseldorf 1981; retrospective exhbns., Tate Gallery, London 1994, LA Co. Museum of Art 1994, Metropolitan Museum of Art, New York 1995; work in public collections in museums in Australia, Denmark, Germany, Netherlands, Norway, Sweden, Switzerland, UK and USA; mem. American Inst. of Arts and Letters 1982; Hon. LHD (Univ. of London) 1982; Dr hc (Royal Coll. of Art) 1991; Hon. Dr. (Calif. Coll. of Art and Craft) 1995, (Univ. of Durham) 1996; 1st Prize for Painting (Golden Lion), Venice Biennale 1995; Order of Arts and Letters (France) 1996. *Solo exhibitions include:* Marlborough New London Gallery 1963, 1970, Marlborough Gerson Gallery, New York, LA County Museum of Art 1965, Stedelijk Museum, Amsterdam, Museum of Art, Cleveland and Univ. of Calif., Berkeley 1967, Berlin and tour of Fed. Germany 1969–70, Kestner Gesellschaft, Hanover, Boymans-van-Beuningen Museum, Rotterdam 1970, Cincinnati Art Museum, Ohio (with James Dine, q.v.) 1973, Marlborough, New York 1974, 1978, Marlborough, Zürich 1977, Marlborough, London 1977, 1980, 1985. *Publications:* David Hockney: A Retrospective (with others) 1988, First Diasporist Manifesto 1989. *Address:* c/o Marlborough Fine Art Ltd, 6 Albemarle Street, London, W1X 3HF, England. *Telephone:* (20) 7629-5161.

KITAMURA, Hiroshi; Japanese diplomatist and university president; b. 20 Jan. 1929, Osaka; m. Sachiko Kitamura 1953; two d.; ed Tokyo Univ., Fletcher School of Law and Diplomacy, Mass., USA; joined Foreign Affairs Ministry 1953, served in Washington, New York, Delhi; First Sec. Japanese Embassy, London 1963–66; with Japanese Mission to OECD, Paris 1971–74; Exec. Asst to Prime Minister 1974–76; Deputy Dir-Gen. American Affairs Bureau 1977–79, Dir-Gen. 1982–84, Deputy Vice-Minister of Foreign Affairs 1984–87, Deputy Minister 1987–88; Consul-Gen. San Francisco 1979–82, Amb. to Canada 1988–90, to the UK 1991–94; Corp. Adviser, Mitsubishi Corpn 1994–99; Pres. Shumei Univ. 1998–2001; Prime Minister's Personal Rep. to Venice Summit 1987, Toronto Summit 1988; Fellow, Center for Int. Affairs, Harvard Univ. 1970; Chair. Japan–British Soc. 1994–; Gold and Silver Star, Order of the Rising Sun 1999; Hon. LLD (Northumbria) 1993. *Publications include:* Psychological Dimensions of US–Japanese Relations 1971, Between Friends (co-author) 1985, The UK Seen through an Ambassador's Eyes (in Japanese), Diplomacy and Food (in Japanese), An Ambassador and his Lhasa Apso (in Japanese). *Leisure interests:* Japanese classical music, food and wine, golf. *Address:* 1-15-6 Jingumae, Shibuya-ku, Tokyo, Japan. *Telephone:* (3) 3470-4630. *Fax:* (3) 3470-4830.

KITAMURA, So; Japanese playwright; b. 5 July 1952, Ohtsu-shi; m. Konomi Kitamura; one d.; leader Project Navi 1986–; Awards include Kishida Gikyoku-sho 1984, Kinoleuni-ya engeki-sho 1989. *Publications:* plays include: Hogiuta, So-Ko Gingatetsudo no yoru. Novels include: Kaijin nijumenso den (Shincho sha), Seido no majin (Shincho sha), Kenji (Kadokawa). *Leisure interest:* movies. *Address:* Project Navi, 11–13 Imaike-Minami, Chikusa-ku, Nagoya-shi, Aichi 464, Japan. *Telephone:* (52) 731-2867.

KITANO, Takeshi; Japanese film director, actor and comedian; b. 18 Jan. 1948, Tokyo; ed Meiji Univ. *Films include:* Sonatine 1993, Johnny Mnemonic 1995, Hana-bi (Golden Lion, Venice Film Festival 1997), Kikujiro no natsu, Tokyo Eyes 1998, Kikujiro Summer 1999, Brother 2000, Battle Royal 2001, Dolls 2003. *Leisure interest:* writing.

KITAYENKO, Dmitriy Georgievich; Russian conductor; b. 18 Aug. 1940, Leningrad; ed Leningrad Conservatory; postgrad. study Moscow Conservatory (under Khazanov and Ginzburg); further study at Acad. of Music, Vienna 1966–67; conductor, Nemirovich-Danchenko Theatre 1969–, prin. conductor 1970–76; chief conductor, Moscow Philharmonic 1976–89; numerous appearances in Europe and USA; teacher at Moscow Conservatory 1969–, Prof. 1986–90; Music Dir, Frankfurt Radio Orchestra 1990–95; Bern Symphony Orchestra 1994–; Perm. Conductor, Music Adviser, Bergen Philharmonic Orchestra 1991–; USSR People's Artist 1984; RSFSR State Prize 1988. *Address:* Münzgraben 2, 3000 Bern 7 (Office); Chalet Kalimor, 1652 Botterens, Switzerland (Home). *Telephone:* (31) 3118321. *Fax:* (31) 3116257.

KITBUNCHU, HE Cardinal Michael Michai; Thai ecclesiastic; b. 25 Jan. 1929, Samphran, Nakhon Pathom; ordained priest 1959; Archbishop of Bangkok 1973–; cr. Cardinal 1983. *Address:* Assumption Cathedral, 40 Thanon Charoenkrung, Bangrak, Bangkok 10500 (Office); Bishop's Conference of Thailand, 122/6-7 Soi Naaksuwan, Thanon Nonsi, Yannawa, Bangkok 10120, Thailand. *Telephone:* (2) 233-8712 (Office); (2) 681-5361. *Fax:* (2) 237-1033 (Office); (2) 681-5370. *E-mail:* cbct@ksc.th.com (Office).

KITE, Thomas O., Jr; American golfer; b. 9 Dec. 1949, Austin, Tex.; m. Christy Kite; two s. one d.; ed Univ. of Texas; won Walker Cup 1971; professional golfer PGA 1972–2000; won Ryder Cup 1979, 1981, 1983, 1985, 1987, 1989, 1993, European Open 1980, US Open, Pebble Beach, Calif. 1992; LA Open 1993; 10 US PGA wins; apptd Capt. US team for 1997 Ryder Cup, Valderrama, Spain; joined Sr PGA Tour 2000, wins include The Countryside Tradition 2000, MasterCard Championship 2002; spokesman for Chrysler Jr Golf Scholarship programme. *Leisure interest:* landscaping. *Address:* c/o PGA Tour, 112 Tpc Boulevard Ponte Vedra Beach, FL 32082, USA.

KITOVANI, Tengiz; Georgian politician and army officer; Commdr Georgian Nat. Guard; fmr supporter of fmr Pres. Gamsakhurdia, but opposed subordination of his command to Ministry of Internal Affairs Sept. 1991; Head opposition mil. forces Dec. 1991, Jt Head Mil. Council Jan. 1992–; Head Georgian Nat. Guard; mem. Georgian State Council Mar.–Oct. 1992; mem. Supreme Soviet 1992–; Minister of Defence 1992–93; arrested in 1995, charged with conspiracy against the State; sentenced to eight years' confinement 1996, released on parole 1999.

KITSIKIS, Dimitri, MA, PhD, FRSC; Canadian/French/Greek poet and university professor; b. 2 June 1935, Athens; s. of the late Nikolas Kitsikis and Beata Petychakis; m. 1st Anne Hubbard 1955 (divorced 1973); one s. one d.; m. 2nd Ada Nikolaros 1975; one s. one d.; ed American Coll. Athens, Ecole des Roches, Normandy, Lycée Lakanal and Lycée Carnot, Paris and Sorbonne, Paris; Research Assoc. Grad. Inst. of Int. Studies, Geneva 1960–62, Centre for Int. Relations, Nat. Foundation of Political Science, Paris 1962–65, Nat. Centre for Scientific Research, Paris 1965–70; Assoc. Prof. of History of Int. Relations, Univ. of Ottawa 1970–83, Prof. 1983–96, Emer. Prof. 1996–; Sr Research Scholar, Nat. Centre of Social Research, Athens 1972–74; founder, Ed. Intermediate Region (journal) 1996–; adviser to govts of Greece and Turkey; numerous visiting professorships and other appts; First Prize in Poetry, Abdi Ipekçi Peace and Friendship Prize 1992. *Publications:* author of 26 books including; Propaganda and Pressure in International Politics 1963, The Role of the Experts at the Paris Peace Conference of 1919 1972, A Comparative History of Greece and Turkey in the 20th Century 1978, History of the Greek-Turkish Area 1981, The Ottoman Empire 1985, The Third Ideology and Orthodoxy 1990, The Old Calendarists 1995, Turkish-Greek Empire 1996, The Byzantine Model of Government 2001; co-author of 33 other books; six vols of poetry; over 80 scholarly articles. *Leisure interests:* art, science fiction, study of languages. *Address:* Department of History, University of Ottawa, Ont. K1N 6N5, Canada (Office); 29 Travlantoni, Zographou, Athens 157.72, Greece. *Telephone:* (613) 562-5800 (Ottawa) (Office); (613) 834-4634 (Ottawa) (Home); (210) 777-6937 (Athens). *Fax:* (613) 562-5995 (Ottawa) (Office). *E-mail:* dkitsiki@uottawa.ca (Office); dkitsiki@rogers.com (Home). *Website:* members.rogers.com/dimitri-kitsikis (Office).

KITSON, Linda Frances, MA; British artist and teacher; b. 17 Feb. 1945, London; granddaughter of Capt. James B. Kitson and Hon. Frances Margaret Palmer (née Howard); ed West Preston Manor School, Rustington, Tortington Park, Arundel, Ecole des Beaux Arts, Lyons, St Martin's School of Art and Royal Coll. of Art; visiting tutor, Royal Coll. of Art, St Martin's School of Art 1972–78, Chelsea School of Art, Camberwell School of Art and Crafts, City & Guilds of London Art School 1972–82; Lecturer, Royal Coll, of Art 1979–82, visiting tutor 1984; Official War Artist, Falkland Islands Task Force 1982; several one-man exhbns. and contrib. to Royal Acad. Summer Exhbn. 1971–; Pres. Army Arts and Crafts Soc. 1983; South Atlantic Medal (with rosette) 1983. *Publication:* The Falklands War: A Visual Diary 1982, The Plague 1985, Sun, Wind, Sand and Stars 1989. *Leisure interests:* rock-dancing, music. *Address:* 1 Argyll Mansions, Kings Road, London, SW3 5ER, England. *Telephone:* (20) 7584-5020.

KITT, Eartha Mae; American singer and actress; b. 26 Jan. 1928, North, SC; d. of John Kitt and Anna Kitt; m. William McDonald 1960 (divorced); one d.; ed high school; soloist with Katherine Graham Dance Group 1948; int. night club singer 1949–; numerous TV appearances; records for RCA; Woman of the Year, Nat. Asscn of Negro Musicians 1968. *Films include:* New Faces 1953, Accused 1957, St Louis Blues 1957, Anna Lucasta 1958, Mark of the Hawk 1958, Saint of Devil's Island 1961, Synanon 1965, Up the Chastity Belt 1971, Dragonard, All By Myself (documentary) 1982, Boomerang 1992, Fatal Instinct 1993. *Stage appearances include:* Dr Faustus, Paris 1951, New Faces of 1952, New York, Mrs Patterson, New York 1954, Shinbone Alley, New York 1957, Timbuktu 1978, Blues in the Night 1985, The Wizard of Oz 1998, The Wild Party 2000. *Publications:* Thursday's Child 1956, A Tart is Not a Sweet, Alone with Me 1976, I'm Still Here 1990, Confessions of a Sex Kitten 1991, Down to Earth (jtly) 2000, How to Rejuvenate: It's Not Too Late (jtly) 2000. *Address:* c/o Eartha Kitt Productions, Flat 37, 888 7th Avenue, New York, NY 10106, USA.

KITTEL, Charles, PhD; American professor of physics and author; b. 18 July 1916, New York; s. of George Paul Kittel and Helen Kittel; m. Muriel Agnes Lister 1938; two s. one d.; ed Massachusetts Institute of Technology and Univs. of Cambridge and Wisconsin; Prof. of Physics, Univ. of Calif. at Berkeley 1951–78, Prof. Emer. 1978–; mem. NAS, American Acad. of Arts and Sciences; Buckley Prize for Solid State Physics, Berkeley Distinguished Teaching Award, Oersted Medal, American Asscn of Physics Teachers. *Publications:* Quantum Theory of Solids 1963, Thermal Physics 1980, Introduction to Solid State Physics 1996. *Leisure interests:* friends, wine. *Address:* Department of Physics, University of California, Berkeley, CA 94720, USA (Office). *Telephone:* (510) 525-5356. *E-mail:* kittel@uclink4.berkeley.edu (Office).

KITTIKACHORN, Field Marshal Thanom; Thai politician and army officer; b. 11 Aug. 1911, Tak; ed Wat Kokplu School (Tak) and Military Acad. Bangkok; entered Mil. Survey Dept as student officer 1931, assigned to Planning Section 1934; Lt in Mil. Educ. Dept 1935, Instructor 1936–38, 1939–41, 1944–46; Capt. 1938, student officer in Infantry School, active service in Shan State 1941; Major 1943, Lt-Col 1944; Instructor Mil. Acad. technical branch 1946–47; Commdr 21st Infantry Regt 1947; Colonel, Commdr 11th Infantry Regt 1948; Deputy Commdr 1st Infantry Div. 1949, Commdr 1950; Major-Gen., Deputy Commdr 1st Army 1951; Commdr 1st Army 1954; Lt-Gen., mem. Defence Coll. 1955; Deputy Minister of Co-

operatives 1955; Asst C-in-C of Army 1957; Deputy Minister of Defence April 1957, Minister Sept. 1957; Prime Minister, Minister of Defence, General 1958; Deputy Prime Minister and Minister of Defence 1959–63; Prime Minister 1963–71, 1972–73; Minister of Defence and Foreign Affairs 1973; Chair. Nat. Exec. Council Dec. 1971–72; Special ADC to King; Chair. United People's Party 1968–73; in USA 1973–74; detained upon return to Bangkok Dec. 1974; exile in Singapore 1976; returned to Bangkok Sept. 1976; served as monk Sept. 1976–Feb. 1977.

KITTIKHOUN, Alounkèo; Laotian diplomatist; b. 10 Oct. 1951, Pakse, Champasark; m. Dr Kongpadith Kittikhoun; two s.; ed Royal Inst. of Law and Admin., Vientiane, Univ. of Paris I (Panthéon-Sorbonne), Int. Inst. of Public Admin., Paris; joined Foreign Ministry 1977; Second Sec., then First Sec. and Counsellor, Perm. Mission to UN 1980–90, Perm. Rep. 1993–; Chair. Landlocked Developing Countries Group at the UN 1999–2003 and of numerous other UN bodies and cttees; Deputy Dir Dept of Int. Orgs, Foreign Ministry 1990–92, Dir 1992–93. *Leisure interests:* golf, reading, eating, relaxing with family. *Address:* Permanent Mission of Laos to the United Nations, 317 East 51st Street, New York, NY 10022, USA (Office). *Telephone:* (212) 832-2734 (Office). *Fax:* (212) 750-0039 (Office). *E-mail:* laos@un.int (Office); alkktk@hotmail.com (Home). *Website:* www.un.int/lao/ (Office).

KITZHABER, John Albert, MD; American doctor and politician; b. 5 March 1947, Colfax, WA; s. of Albert Raymond Kitzhaber and Annabel Reed Wetzel; ed Dartmouth Coll. and Univ. of Ore.; intern Gen. Rose Memorial Hosp., Denver 1976–77; Emergency Physician Mercy Hosp., Roseburg, Ore. 1974–75; mem. Ore. House of Reps 1979–81, Ore. Senate 1981–95, Pres. 1985, 1987, 1989, 1991; Gov. of Ore. 1995–2003; Assoc. Prof., Ore. Health & Science Univ. 1986–; mem. American Coll. of Emergency Physicians, Physicians for Social Responsibility, American Council of Young Political Leaders; Democrat. *Address:* c/o Office of the Governor, Capitol Bldg, Room 254, 900 Court Street NE, Salem, OR 97301, USA.

KITZINGER, Sheila Helena Elizabeth, MBE, MLitt; British birth educator, author, social anthropologist and lecturer; b. 29 March 1929, Taunton, Somerset; d. of Alex Webster and Clare Webster; m. Uwe Kitzinger (q.v.) 1952; five d.; ed Bishop Fox's Girls' School, Taunton, Ruskin Coll. and St Hugh's Coll., Oxford; Research Asst Dept of Anthropology, Univ. of Edin. 1952–53; Course Team Chair. Open Univ. 1981–83; Man. Cttee Midwives' Information and Resource Service 1985–87, Editorial Cttee 1987–; Chair. Steering Cttee Int. Homebirth Movt; mem. Bd Int. Caesarean Awareness Network; Consultant, Int. Childbirth Educ. Asscn; Adviser, Baby Milk Coalition, Maternity Alliance; Patron of the Seattle School of Midwifery; Dir Birth Crisis Network; Module Leader, Univ. of Sheffield Online Masters in Midwifery; Hon. Prof., Thames Valley Univ. 1993–; Joost de Blank Award for Research 1971–73. *Publications:* The Experience of Childbirth 1962, Education and Counselling for Childbirth 1977, Women as Mothers 1978, The Place of Birth (ed. with John Davis) 1978, Birth at Home 1979, The Good Birth Guide 1979, The Experience of Breastfeeding 1979, Pregnancy and Childbirth 1980, Some Women's Experiences of Episiotomy (with Rhiannon Walters) 1981, 1983, Episiotomy: physical and emotional aspects 1981, The New Good Birth Guide 1983, Women's Experience of Sex 1983, (ed. with Penny Simkin) Episiotomy and the Second Stage of Labour 1984, Being Born 1986, Celebration of Birth 1987, Freedom and Choice in Childbirth 1987, Some Women's Experiences of Epidurals 1987, Giving Birth: How it Really Feels 1987, The Midwife Challenge (ed.) 1988, The Crying Baby 1989, Breastfeeding Your Baby 1989, Talking with Children about Things that Matter (with Celia Kitzinger) 1989, Pregnancy Day by Day (with Vicky Bailey) 1990, Homebirth and Other Alternatives to Hospital 1991, Ourselves as Mothers 1993, Birth over Thirty-Five 1994, The Year after Childbirth 1994, The New Pregnancy and Childbirth 1997, Becoming a Grandmother 1997, Breastfeeding 1998, Rediscovering Birth 2000, Midwifery Guidelines on Water Birth (with Ethel Burns) 2000, Birth Your Way: Choosing Birth at Home or in a Birth Centre 2002, Pregnancy and Childbirth: Choices and Challenges 2003. *Leisure interest:* painting. *Address:* The Manor, Standlake, Oxon., OX29 7RH, England. *Telephone:* (1865) 300266. *Fax:* (1865) 300438. *E-mail:* info@sheilakitzinger.com (Home). *Website:* www.sheilakitzinger.com (Office).

KITZINGER, Uwe, CBE, MLitt, MA; British academic; b. 12 April 1928, Nuremberg, Germany; s. of the late Dr G. and Lucy Kitzinger; m. Sheila Helena Elizabeth Webster (Sheila Kitzinger, q.v.) 1952; five d.; ed Watford Grammar School, Balliol and New Colls, Oxford; Foundation Scholar, New Coll., Oxford; Pres. of Oxford Union 1950; Econ. Section, Council of Europe 1951–58; Research Fellow, Nuffield Coll., Oxford 1956–62, Official Fellow and Investment Bursar 1962–76, Emer. Fellow 1976–; Dean, European Inst. of Business Admin. (INSEAD), Fontainebleau 1976–80; Dir Oxford Centre for Man. Studies 1980–84; first Pres. Templeton Coll., Oxford 1984–91; Founding Ed., Journal of Common Market Studies 1962–; Visiting Prof. Univ. of West Indies 1964–65; Visiting Prof. and Assoc., Centre for Int. Affairs, Harvard 1969–70; Visiting Prof. Univ. of Paris VIII 1970–73; Adviser to the late Lord Soames (Vice-Pres. Comm. of the European Communities), Brussels 1973–75; Sr Research Fellow Atlantic Council 1993–; Visiting Scholar Harvard Univ. 1993–; Founding Chair. Cttee on Atlantic Studies 1967–70; Founding Chair. Major Projects Asscn 1981–86; Pres. Int. Asscn of Macro-Eng Socs. 1987–92, 1996–, Féd. Britannique des Alliances Françaises 1998–; Council mem. European Movt 1974–76, Royal Inst. of Int. Affairs 1976–85, Oxfam 1981–84, Fondation Jean Monnet 1990–; Chair. Oxfordshire Radio Ltd 1988; mem. Conflict Man. Group, Cambridge, Mass., Inst. for Transition to Democracy,

Zagreb, Asian Disaster Reparation Centre, Bangkok; co-f. Lentils for Dubrovnik 1991; Hon. Fellow, Templeton Coll. 2001; Hon. LLD; Order of Morning Star (Croatia) 1997. *Publications:* German Electoral Politics 1960, The Challenge of the Common Market 1961, Britain, Europe and Beyond 1964, The Second Try 1968, Diplomacy and Persuasion 1973, Europe's Wider Horizons 1975, The 1975 Referendum (with David Butler) 1976, Macro-Engineering and the Earth (Jt Ed. with Ernst Frankel) 1998. *Leisure interest:* cruising under sail. *Address:* The Manor, Standlake, Oxon., England; La Rivière, 11100 Bages, France; Lowell House, Cambridge, MA 02138, USA. *Telephone:* (1865) 300266 (England); (617) 495-3495 (USA). *Fax:* (1865) 300438 (England); 4-68-41-70-13 (France); (617) 495-3495 (USA). *E-mail:* kitzing@fas.harvard.edu (Office).

KIVRIKOGLU, Gen. Huseyin; Turkish army officer; b. Dec. 1934, Bozuyuk, Bilecik; m.; one s.; ed Isiklar Mil. School, Army Acad., Army War Coll., Armed Forces Coll., NATO Defence Coll., Rome, Italy; served as platoon and battery commdr in various artillery units 1957–65, Staff Officer 9th Infantry Div. in Sarikamis 1967–70; Planning Officer Allied Forces S Europe Operations Div., Italy 1979–72; Instructor Army War Coll. 1972–73; Section Chief of Gen. Staff and Br. Chief of Land Forces Command; Commdr of Cadet Regt, Army Acad., Ankara 1978–80; rank of Brig.-Gen. 1980; Chief of Operations Centre, Supreme HQ Allied Powers in Europe (SHAPE), Belgium 1980–83; Commanding Officer 3rd and 11th Brigades 1983–84; rank of Maj. Gen. 1984; Chief of Staff NATO Allied Land Forces SE Europe (CLSE), Izmir 1984–86; Commanding Officer 9th Infantry Div. 1986–88; rank of Lt-Gen. 1988; Asst Chief of Staff, Gen. Staff HQ; Commanding Officer 5th Corps and Under-Sec. Ministry of Nat. Defence 1990–93; promoted to Four Star 1993; Commdr CLSE 1993–96, First Army, Istanbul 1996–97, Land Forces 1997–98; C-in-C Armed Forces and Chief of Gen. Staff 1998–2002; Armed Forces Distinguished Service Medal, Grand Cross and Golden Honour Medal (Turkey), Star of Romania, Order of Merit (USA), Order of Distinction Medal (Pakistan); numerous Army Acad. Badges, NATO Service Badge, Commdr Armed Forces Identification Badge. *Address:* c/o Ministry of National Defence, Milli Savunma Bakanligi, 06100 Ankara, Turkey (Office).

KIZIM, Col.-Gen. Leonid Denisovich, CandMilSc; Russian cosmonaut; b. 5 Aug. 1941, Krasny Liman, Ukraine; m.; one s. one d.; ed Chernigov Higher Mil. Aviation School, Gagarin Mil. Aircraft Acad., Mil. Gen. Staff Acad.; with cosmonaut team 1965–87; took part in space flights on Soyuz-3, orbital station Salyut-6 1980, Soyuz T-10, T-11, orbital station Salyut-7, orbital complex Mir 1984; Chair. NW Regional Br. Russian Fed. of Cosmonauts; Deputy Commdr of Space Mil. Forces, Ministry of Defence 1987–99; Head A. F. Mozhaisky Mil. Acad. of Space and Eng 1999–; Order of Lenin (3), other decorations. *Address:* A. F. Mozhaisky Military Academy of Space Engineering, Moscow, Russia (Office).

KJAERSGAARD, Pia; Danish politician; b. 23 Feb. 1947, Copenhagen; d. of Poul Kjaersgaard and Inge Munch Jensen; m. Henrik Thorup; two c.; ed Gentofte Lower Secondary School, Copenhagen School of Commerce; office Asst for insurance and advertising co. 1963–67; home help 1978–84; Mem. Parl. 1984–; leader of Fremskridtspartiet 1985–94; mem. Ministry of Justice's Road Safety Comm. 1986–87; Chair. Parliament's Health Cttee 1988–91; mem. Bd of Danish Nat. Bank 1989–96; mem. Nordic Council 1990–94, 1998–, Deputy Chair. Liberal group 1990–94; mem. Defence Comm. 1997; Deputy Chair. Council of Foreign Affairs; mem. Bd of Political Foreign Affairs and OSCE; mem. Comm. of the Intelligence Service, Political-Econ. Bd; mem. Justice Comm.; mem. Bd of Danish–Taiwan Asscn; Jt founder and Party Chair. Danish People's Party 1995–; Kosan Prize 1986, Politician of the Year 1989, Golden Post Horn 1992, Medal of Honour of the Friends of Overseas Chinese Asscn 1999, Special Medal of Diplomacy (Taiwan) 2003. *Publication:* Men udsigten er god... (But the view is excellent...) 1998. *Leisure interests:* gardening, music, physical fitness. *Address:* Dansk Folkeparti, Christiansborg, 1240 Copenhagen K (Office); Kaermindevej 31, 2820 Gentofte, Denmark (Home). *Telephone:* 33-37-51-07 (Office). *Fax:* 33-37-51-93 (Office). *E-mail:* df@ft.dk (Office). *Website:* www.danskfolkeparti.dk (Office).

KJELLEN, Bo, MPolSc; Swedish diplomatist; b. 8 Feb. 1933, Stockholm; s. of John Kjellen and Elsa Kjellen; m. 1st Margareta Lindblom 1959 (died 1978); m. 2nd Gia Boyd 1980; four c.; ed Univ. of Stockholm; entered Foreign Service 1957, posted to Rio de Janeiro, Brussels, Stockholm 1959–69; Prin. Pvt. Sec. to Sec.-Gen., OECD 1969–72; Deputy Head of Mission Del. to EEC, Brussels 1972–74; Amb. to Viet Nam 1974–77; Head Multilateral Dept for Devt Co-operation, Ministry of Foreign Affairs 1977–81; Under-Sec. Admin. and Personnel 1981–85; Amb. to OECD and UNESCO 1985–91; Chief Negotiator, Ministry of Environment 1991–98; Negotiator Climate Convention 1991–2001; Chair. Swedish Research Council for Environment, Agricultural Sciences and Spatial Planning 2001–; Hon. DSc (Cranfield, UK) 1997; Hon. PhD (Gothenburg) 1999; Elizabeth Haub Prize for Environmental Diplomacy 1999, GEF Award for Environmental Leadership 1999. *Address:* Ministry of Environment, Tegelbacken 2, 10333 Stockholm, Sweden. *Telephone:* (8) 405-21-75; (18) 71-03-07 (Home). *Fax:* (8) 468-21-16-90. *E-mail:* bo.kjellen@environment.ministry.se.

KJER, Bodil; Danish actress; b. 2 Sept. 1917; has appeared at Royal Theatre of Denmark in more than 100 roles; numerous awards including four awards from Danish film critics (Bodil award named after her); Commdr Order of Dannebrog. *Films include:* Elly Petersen, The Invisible Army, Jenny and the Soldier, Meet Me on Cassiopeia, The Missing Clerk, Copper, Mirror, Mirror,

Tradition, Up Yours!, Babette's Feast (Academy Award), Sunset Boys. *Address:* Vestre Pavilion, Frydenlund, Frydenlunds Allé 19, 2950 Vedbaek, Denmark.

KJETSAA, Geir, DPhil; Norwegian professor of Russian literature; b. 2 June 1937, Oslo; s. of Thorleif Kjetsaa and Marit Kjetsaa; m. Gerd Margit 1959; one d.; ed Univ. of Oslo and Moscow State Univ.; Asst Dept of Slavic and Baltic Studies, Univ. of Oslo 1966–70, Prof. 1971–; Pres. Asscn of Norwegian Slavists 1977–80, 1982–87, Asscn of Scandinavian Slavists 1984–87; Vice-Pres. Int. Dostoevsky Soc. 1983–; mem. Norwegian Acad. of Sciences and Letters 1984–; Bastian Prize 1978, Fritt Ords Honnør 2000, Premija imeni F.M. Dostoevskogo 2001. *Publications:* Evgenij Baratynskij 1973, The Authorship of The Quiet Don 1984, Dostoevsky and His New Testament 1984, Prinadlezhnost Dostoevskomu 1986, Fyodor Dostoevsky: A Writer's Life 1987, Nikolaj Gogol: Den gåtefulle dikteren 1990, Maxim Gorki: Eine Biographie 1996, Lew Tolstoj: Dichter und Religionsphilosoph 2001. *Address:* Universitetet i Oslo, P.O. Box 1030, Blindern, 0315 Oslo (Office); Lybekkveien 12a, Oslo 0772, Norway (Home).

KJØNSTAD, Asbjørn, DJur; Norwegian professor of law; b. 6 Feb. 1943, Levanger; s. of late Arne Kjønstad and of Nelly Stavern Kjønstad; m. 1st Lise-Lena Stubberød 1971–81 (divorced); one d.; m. 2nd Ayala Orkan 1995 (divorced 2002); Legal Adviser, Nat. Insurance Admin. 1970–72; Research Fellow, Univ. of Oslo 1972–78, Prof. of Pvt. Law 1978–84, Head, Inst. of Pvt. Law 1983–84, Prof. of Social Law 1985–, Dean of Faculty of Law 1986–88, mem. Bd of Univ. of Oslo 1986–88, 1999–2001; Chair. Royal Comm. on Social Security Law 1982–90; Chair. Governmental Comm. on Co-ordination of Pension Schemes 1991–95, on Transfer of Pension Rights 1999–; Vice-Pres. European Inst. of Social Security 1993–97; mem. Bd Nat. Council on Tobacco and Health 1972–93, 1997–, Head Research Project on Tobacco Products Liability 1998–; mem. Norwegian Acad. of Science 1987; Hon. JuD (Lund Univ., Sweden) 1996. *Publications:* 35 scientific reports and books and some 130 articles on social security law, medical law and tort law including: Social Security and Compensation for Personal Injuries 1977, The Industrial Injuries Insurance 1979, Constitutional Protection of Social Security 1984, Medical Law 1987, Norwegian Social Law 1987, A Simplified National Insurance Act 1990, The National Insurance Disablement Pension 1992, Health Priority and Patient's Rights (co-ed.) 1992, Social Services and the Rule of Law (co-author) 1993, Constitutional Protection of Social Security Benefits (co-author) 1994, Aspects of Health Law (co-author) 1994, Welfare Law I (co-author) 1997, Law, Power and Poverty (co-ed.) 1997, Introduction to Social Security Law 1998, Social Security Act with commentary (ed.)1998, European Social Security Law (ed.) 1999, Social Services and the Rule of Law (co-author) 2000, Welfare Law (Vol. I, co-author) 2000, Confidentiality About Children 2001, Welfare Law II – Social Services (co-author and co-ed.) 2003. *Leisure interests:* outdoor exercise, skiing, jogging, marathon running. *Address:* University of Oslo, Karl Johann gs 47, PO Box 6706, 0130 Oslo (Office); Lillevannsveien 37c, 0788 Oslo, Norway (Home). *Telephone:* 22-85-94-80 (Office); 22-13-80-75 (Home). *Fax:* 22-85-94-20 (Office); 22-49-64-51 (Home). *E-mail:* asbjorn.kjonstad@jus.uio.no (Office).

KLAASTE, Aggrey Zola, BA; South African journalist; b. 6 Jan. 1940, Kimberley; s. of late T. P. Klaaste; m. Valetta Kubugane Makgele; three s.; ed Madibane High School, Univ. of Witwatersrand; journalist Trust 1970–71; News Ed. The World 1974–77, Post 1978–82; Asst Ed. The Sowetan 1982, now Ed.; mem. Ed. Bd Black Focus 1985, Viewpoint 1985; mem. Shield Unit Salvation Army 1984–; Hon. PhD et Litt. (Transkei). *Leisure interests:* martial arts, reading, music. *Address:* Sowetan, 61 Commando Road, Industria West, P.O. Box 6663, Johannesburg 2000, South Africa (Office). *Telephone:* (11) 4714000 (Office). *Fax:* (11) 4748834 (Office). *E-mail:* swtnedit@sowetan.co.za (Office). *Website:* sowetan.co.za (Office).

KLAMMER, Franz; Austrian skier; b. 3 Dec. 1953, Mooswald; 26 World Cup race wins, including downhill titles 1975, 1976, 1977, 1978, 1983; gold medal, downhill race, Winter Olympics 1976; retd from skiing 1985; took up car racing; won European Championship Touring Car race, Nurburgring, Germany; f. Franz Klammer Foundation; guest speaker for Qwest Communications Inc.; UN Goodwill Amb.; mem. Laureus World Sports Acad. *Leisure interests:* golf. *Address:* c/o Qwest Communications International Inc., 1801 California Street, Denver, CO 80202, USA (Office).

KLAS, Eri; Estonian conductor; b. 7 June 1939, Tallinn; s. of Eduard Klas and Anna Klas; m.; one d.; ed Tallinn State Conservatory, Leningrad State Conservatory; Asst conductor to Boris Khaikin Bolshoi Theatre, Moscow 1960–72; conductor Orchestra of Estonian Radio 1964–70; conductor Nat. Opera Theatre Estonia 1965–, Music Dir 1975–95, Laureate conductor 1996–; conducted more than 100 symphony orchestras in 40 different countries; Music Dir Royal Opera, Stockholm 1985–89; Prin. Guest Conductor, Finnish Nat. Opera 1990–; Chief Conductor Aarhus Symphony Orchestra, Denmark 1991–96; Prof. Sibelius Acad. Helsinki 1994–; Music Dir Orchestra of Dutch Radio 1996–; Artistic Dir and Prin. Conductor Tampere Philharmonic Orchestra 1998–; Musical Adviser Israel Sinfonietta 1999–; Chair. Bd Estonia Nat. Cultural Foundation 1991–; conducted at the Nobel Prize Ceremonial Concert in Stockholm 1989; Dr hc (Estonian Acad. of Music) 1994; Order of Nordsternier Sweden. *Repertoire includes:* more than 50 operas, operettas, musicals and ballets. *Address:* Nurme str. 54, 11616 Tallinn, Estonia. *Telephone:* (2) 504-3444. *Website:* www.erkt.ee (Office).

KLAUS, Václav, PhD; Czech politician and economist; b. 19 June 1941, Prague; s. of Václav Klaus and Marie Klausová; m. Livia Klausová 1968; two s.; ed Prague School of Econs, Cornell Univ.; researcher Inst. of Econs Czechoslovak Acad. of Sciences until 1970; various positions Czechoslovak State Bank 1971–86; head Dept of Macroeconomic Policy, Inst. of Forecasting, Acad. of Sciences 1987–; f. Civic Forum Movt (Chair. 1990–91); Minister of Finance 1989–92; Chair. Civic Democratic Party 1991–2002; Deputy Prime Minister 1991–92; Prime Minister of the Czech Republic 1992–97; Chair. State Defence Council 1993–97; Chair. Govt Cttee for Integration of Czech Repub. in NATO 1997; Chair. Chamber of Deputies 1998–2002; Pres. of the Czech Republic 2003–; mem. Scientific Council, Palacký Univ. 1997–; Hon. Prof. Univ. Guadalajara 1993; Hon. Chair. ODS (Civic Democratic Party) 2002–; Hon. DHumLitt (Suffolk Univ.) 1991, Dr hc (Rochester Inst. of Tech.) 1991, (Univ. Francisco Marroquín, Guatemala) 1993, (Jacksonville, USA) 1995, (Buckingham, UK) 1996, (Prague School of Econs) 1994, (Belgrano Univ., Argentina) 1994, (Tufts Univ., USA) 1994, (Univ. of Aix-Marseilles) 1994, (Tech. Univ. of Ostrava) 1997, (Toronto, Canada) 1997, (Arizona) 1997, (Dallas) 1999, (Chicago) 1999; Schumpeter Prize for Econs, Freedom Award (New York) 1990, Max Schmidheiny Freedom Prize, St Gallen 1992, Ludwig Erhard Prize, Germany 1993, Poeutinger Collegium Prize 1993, Hermann Lindrath Prize (Hanover) 1993, Konrad Adenauer Prize (Prague) 1993, Club of Europe Award 1994, Prix Transition (Fondation du Forum Universal) 1994, Adam Smith Award (Libertas, Copenhagen) 1995, Int. Democracy Medal (Center for Democracy, Washington, DC) 1995, Transatlantic Leadership Award (European Inst., Washington, DC) 1995, Prognos Award (Prognos Forum, Basel) 1995, James Madison Award (James Madison Inst., Jacksonville, USA) 1995, Karel Engliš Prize (Universitas Masarykiana Foundation, Brno) 1995, European Prize for Craftsmanship, Germany 1996, Goldwater Medal for Econ. Freedom, Phoenix, USA 1997, Bernhard Harms Medal (Kiel Inst. of World Econs) 1999. *Publications:* A Road to Market Economy 1991, Tomorrow's Challenge 1991, Economic Theory and Economic Reform 1991, Why am I a Conservative? 1992, Dismantling Socialism: A Road to Market Economy II 1993, The Year–How much is it in the History of the Country? 1993, The Czech Way 1994, Rebirth of a Country: Five Years After 1994, Counting Down to One 1995, Between the Past and the Future: Philosophical Reflections and Essays 1996, The Defence of Forgotten Ideas 1997, Tak pravil Václav Klaus (So Said Václav Klaus, conversations with J. Klusáková), Why I Am Not a Social Democrat 1998, Země, kde se již dva roky nevládne (The Land that has not been Governed for 2 years) 1999, Cesta z pasti (The Way Out of the Trap) 1999 From the Opposition Treaty to the Tolerance Patent 2000, Evropa pohledem politika a pohledem ekonoma (Europe, The View of the Politician and the View of the Economist) 2001, Conversations with Vaclav Klaus 2001, Klaus v Bruselu (Klaus in Brussels) 2001; numerous articles. *Leisure interests:* tennis, skiing, basketball, volleyball, jazz. *Address:* Office of the President, Prague Castle, 119 08 Prague 1 (Office). *Telephone:* (2) 2437-1111 (Office). *Fax:* (2) 2437-3300 (Office). *Website:* www.hrad.cz (Office); www.klaus.cz (Home).

KLEBANOV, Ilya Iosifovich; Russian politician; b. 7 May 1951, Leningrad; m. Yevgenya Yakovlevna Klebanova; one s. one d.; ed Leningrad Polytech. Inst.; Eng electrophysicist Electron scientific production unit 1974–77; engineer, then Sr master, Head of Construction Bureau, later Head of Div. Leningrad Optical-Mechanical Complex (LOMO) 1977–92, Dir-Gen. 1992–97; First Vice-Gov. St Petersburg 1997–98; Deputy Chair. of Russian Govt 1999–2002, Minister of Industry, Science and Tech. (Minpromnauki) 2001–. *Leisure interest:* classical music. *Address:* Minpromnauki, Miusskaya Pl. 3, 125889 Moscow, Russia (Office). *Telephone:* (095) 251-50-01 (Office).

KLEBE, Giselher; German composer; b. 28 June 1925, Mannheim; s. of Franz Klebe and Gertrud Michaelis Klebe; m. Lore Schiller 1946; two d.; ed Berlin Conservatoire and with Boris Blacher; Composer in Berlin until 1957; Prof. of Composition and Theory of Music, Nordwestdeutsche Musik-Akademie, Detmold 1957–; mem. Acad. of Arts, Berlin and Hamburg, Bavarian Acad. of Fine Arts 1978; Pres. Berlin Acad. of Arts 1986–89; Bundesverdienstkreuz (1st Class) 1975, Grosses Bundesverdienstkreuz 1999; Berliner Kunstpreis 1952, Preis Musik im XX Jahrhundert, Rome 1954, Mauricio Fürst Prize (Sweden) 1959, Rompreis Villa Massimo 1962, Premio Marzotto, Valdiagno 1964. *Principal works:* Operas: Die Räuber (Schiller) 1957, Die tödlichen Wünsche (Balzac) 1959, Die Ermordung Cäsars (Shakespeare) 1959, Alkmene (Kleist) 1961, Figaro lässt sich scheiden (Ödön von Horvath) 1963, Jacobowsky und der Oberst (Werfel) 1965, Das Märchen von der Schönen Lilie (nach Goethe) 1969, Ein wahrer Held (Synge/Böll) 1975, Das Mädchen aus Domrémy (Schiller) 1976, Rendezvous (Sostshenkov) 1977, Der jüngste Tag (Ödön von Horwath) 1980, Die Fastnachtsbeichte (nach Zuckmayer) 1983, Gervaise Macquart (after Zola) 1995; Ballets: Signale 1955, Menagerie 1958, Das Testament (nach F. Villon) 1970; Orchestral Works: Zwitschermaschine 1950, Deux Nocturnes 1952, 6 symphonies 1952, 1953, 1967, 1971, 1977, 1995, Adagio und Fuge (with theme from Wagner's Walküre) 1962, Herzschläge (for Beatband and Symphony Orchestra), Konzert für Cembalo mit elektrischen Klangveränderungen und kleines Orchester 1972, Orpheus (Dramatic scenes for orchestra) 1976, Salutations 1981, Boogie Agitato 1981, Concerto for Clarinet and Orchestra op. 92; Songs: Fünf Lieder 1962, Vier Vocalisen für Frauenchor 1963, La Tomba di Igor Stravinsky (for oboe and chamber orch.) 1979, Concerto for organ and orchestra 1980, Concerto for harp and orchestra 1988, Concerto for 'cello and orchestra 1989, Poema Drammatico 1999, Mignon, concerto for violin and orchestra 2000; Church music: Missa (Miserere Nobis) 1964, Stabat Mater 1964, Messe (Gebet einer armen Seele) 1966, Beuge dich, du Menschenseele (after S. Lagerlöf) for Baritone and Organ, Choral und Te deum for Solo Soprano, Choir and Orchestra 1978, Weihnachtsoratorium 1989; Chamber Music: 3 String Quartets 1949, 1963, 1981, 2 Solo Violin Sonatas 1952 and 1955, 2 Sonatas for Violin and Piano 1953 and 1974, 'Römische Elegien' 1953, Piano Trio Elegia Appassionata 1955, Introitus, Aria et Alleluja for Organ 1964, Quintet for Piano and Strings quasi una fantasia 1967, Fantasie und Lobpreisung (for organ) 1970, Variationen über ein Thema von Hector Berlioz (for organ and three drummers) 1970, Sonate für Kontrabass und Klavier 1974, 'Nenia' for solo violin 1975, Der Dunkle Gedanke for Clarinets and Piano 1980, Klavierstücke für Sonya (piano) 1980, Feuersturz für Klavier (op. 91) 1983, Otto canti con rime di Michelangelo 2000, Poema Drammatico, Concerto per due pianoforti ed orchestra (op. 130) 2000, Poema Lirico per violino e pianoforte con orchestra d'archi (op. 136) 2001. *Leisure interest:* photography. *Address:* Bruchstrasse 16, 32756 Detmold, Germany (Home). *Telephone:* (30) 3900070 (Office); (5231) 23414 (Home).

KLEIHUES, Josef Paul; German architect and professor; b. 11 June 1933, Rheine; s. of Heinrich Kleihues and Paula Krüselmann Kleihues; m. Sigrid Müller 1961; two s. two d.; ed Tech. Univs of Stuttgart and Berlin; in pvt. practice; Dir New Construction Planning, Int. Bldg Exhbns. Berlin 1979–87; Prof. of Design and Architectural Theory, Univ. of Dortmund 1973–86, of Design and Town Planning 1986–94; Prof. of Architecture, Kunstakademie Düsseldorf 1994–98, Prof. Emer. 1998–; Irwin S. Chanin Distinguished Int. Prof., The Cooper Union, New York 1986–90; Visiting Eero Saarinen Prof., Grad. School of Architecture, Yale Univ., USA 1987; Young Generation Art Prize, Berlin 1967, Berlin Architecture Prize 1994, German Natural Stone Prize 1995; Order of Fed. Repub. of Germany (1st Class) 1988, Order of Merit, Land Berlin 2000. *Solo exhibitions:* The Museum Projects, Cooper Union, New York 1989, City of Architecture – Architecture of the City, Berlin 1900–2000, New Museum, Berlin 2000. *Principal works:* Cen. Workshops Municipal Dept of Refuse Collection, Berlin 1969–74, Block 270, Berlin 1971–77, New Hosp., Berlin-Neukoelln 1973–86, German Blades Museum, Solingen 1979–89, Archaeological Museum, Frankfurt Main 1980–88, Kant Triangle, Berlin-Charlottenburg 1984–94, Lütze Museum and Municipal Gallery, Sindelfingen 1986–89, Henninger Museum and Municipal Gallery, Kornwestheim 1987–89, House 7, Block 7, Berlin 1986–89, San Clemente, Santiago de Compostela, Spain 1988–94, Hamburger Bahnhof, Museum of Contemporary Art, Berlin 1989–96, Museum of Contemporary Art, Chicago 1991–96, Houses Sommer and Liebermann, Pariser Platz, Berlin 1992–98, Media Port, Berlin-Wedding 1994–96, Ministry of Labour, Berlin 1996–99. *Publications:* Berlin Atlas zu Stadtbild und Stadtraum (compiler) 1971–73, Dortmunder Architekturhefte (Ed.) 1975–99, Park Lenné. Ein innerstädtische Wohnform 1977, Dokumente und Projekte, Die Neubaugebiete (Ed.) 1979–, Das Kant Dreieck, Museum of Contemporary Art Chicago, Hamburger Bahnhof, Museum für Gegenwat Berlin. *Address:* Helmholtzstrasse 42, 10587 Berlin (Office); Fasanenstr. 26, 10719 Berlin, Germany (Home). *Telephone:* (30) 3997790 (Office). *Fax:* (30) 39977977 (Office). *E-mail:* berlin@kleihues.com (Office). *Website:* www.kleihues.com (Office).

KLEIN, Calvin Richard; American fashion designer; b. 19 Nov. 1942, New York; s. of Leo Klein and Flore Klein (née Stern); m. 1st Jayne Centre 1964 (divorced 1974); one d.; m. 2nd Kelly Rector 1986; ed Fashion Inst. of Tech., New York and High School of Art and Design; started own fashion business 1968; Pres./Designer Calvin Klein Ltd 1969–; Consultant Fashion Inst. of Tech. 1975–; mem. Council of Fashion Designers; Coty Award 1973, 1974, 1975; Coty Hall of Fame, FIT Pres.'s Award, Outstanding Design Council of Fashion Designers of America (four womenswear, two menswear). *Address:* Calvin Klein Industries Inc., 205 West 39th Street, New York, NY 10018, USA.

KLEIN, George, MD, DSc, PhD; Swedish tumour biologist; b. 28 July 1925, Budapest, Hungary; s. of Henrik Klein and Ilona Engel; m. Eva Fischer 1947; one s. two d.; ed medical schools at Pécs, Szeged and Budapest, Hungary and Stockholm, Sweden; Instructor Histology, Budapest Univ. 1945, Pathology 1946; Research Fellow, Karolinska Inst. 1947–49, Asst Prof. of Cell Research 1951–57; Prof. of Tumour Biology and Head of the Dept for Tumour Biology, Karolinska Inst. Med. School, Stockholm 1957–93, Research Group Leader, Microbiology and Tumour Biology Centre, Karolinksa Inst. 1993–; Guest Investigator, Inst. for Cancer Research, Philadelphia, Pa 1950; Visiting Prof., Stanford Univ. 1961; Fogarty Scholar, NIH 1972; Dunham Lecturer, Harvard Medical School 1966; Visiting Prof., Hebrew Univ., Jerusalem 1973–93; Harvey Lecturer 1973; Donald Wae Waddel Lecturer, Univ. of Arizona 1991; mem. Scientific Advisory Council of Swedish Medical Bd, Royal Swedish Acad. of Sciences; mem. Bioethics Cttee, UNESCO; Corresp. mem. American Asscn of Cancer Research; Foreign Assoc. NAS of United States; Fellow, New York Acad. of Science; Ed. Advances in Cancer Research; Hon. mem. American Asscn of Immunologists, of Cancer Research, French Soc. of Immunology, Hungarian Acad. of Sciences, American Acad. of Arts and Sciences; Hon. DSc (Univ. of Chicago) 1966, (Univ. of Neb.) 1991; Hon. MD (Univ. of Debrecen) 1988; Hon. PhD (Hebrew Univ., Jerusalem) 1989, (Tel-Aviv Univ.) 1994, (Osaka Univ.) 2001; Bertha Goldblatt Teplitz Award (jointly) 1960; Rabbi Shai Shacknai Prize in Tumour Immunology 1972; Bertner Award 1973; Award of American Cancer Soc. 1973; Prize of Danish Pathological Soc.; Harvey Prize 1975; Prize of Cancer Research Inst. 1975; Gairdner Prize 1976; Behring Prize 1977; Annual Award Virus Cancer Program 1977, Gen. Motors Sloan Prize for Cancer Research, Björkén Award of Uppsala Univ. 1979,

Award of the Santa Chiara Acad., Italy, 1979, Erik Fernström Prize (with Eva Klein) 1983, Anniversary Prize of the Swedish Med. Asscn 1983, Letterstedt Prize, Royal Swedish Acad. of Sciences 1989, Doblong Prize, Swedish Acad. of Literature 1990, Lisl and Leo Eitinger Prize, Oslo Univ. 1990, Robert Koch Gold Medal 1998, Lifetime Achievement Award, Inst. of Human Virology 1998 and many others. *Publications include:* more than 1,000 papers in fields of experimental cell research and cancer research; The Atheist and the Holy City 1990, Hack i häl på Minerva (with Lars Gyllensten) 1993, Pietà 1993, Live Now 1997, Korpens Blick 1998. *Address:* MTC, Karolinska Institutet, Box 280, 171 77 Stockholm (Office); Kottlavagen 10, 181 61 Lidingo, Sweden. *Telephone:* (8) 728-67-30 (Office). *Fax:* (8) 33-04-98.

KLEIN, Herbert George; American journalist and fmr government official; b. Herbert George Klein, 1 April 1918, Los Angeles; s. of George J. and Amy Cordes Klein; m. Marjorie Galbraith 1941; two d.; ed Univ. of S Calif; journalist 1940–42; US Naval Reserve 1942–46; Political Reporter and News Ed., Post Advocate 1946; Feature Writer, San Diego Evening Tribune 1950, Editorial Writer 1951; Chief Editorial Writer, San Diego Union 1951, Ed. 1959; mem. office staff of Vice-Pres. Nixon 1959–60; Dir of Communications for the Exec. Branch 1969–73; publicist and press sec. for many of Richard Nixon's election campaigns; Vice-Pres. Corp. Relations Metromedia Inc. 1973–77; Pres. H. G. Klein Media Consultants 1977–80; Ed.-in-Chief, Vice-Pres. Copley Newspapers, San Diego 1980–; Trustee, Univ. S Calif., LA; Hon. Dr (Univ. of San Diego). *Television:* guest in numerous public affairs programmes, including Meet the Press, Face the Nation and 20-20 with Barbara Walters. *Publication:* Making It Perfectly Clear 1980. *Leisure interests:* golf, reading, gardening, spectator sports. *Address:* Copley Press Inc., 350 Camino De La Reina, San Diego, CA 92108 (Office); 5110 Saddlery Square, P.O. Box 8935, Rancho, Santa Fe, CA 92067, USA (Home). *Telephone:* (619) 293-1111 (Office). *Fax:* (619) 293-2878 (Office). *E-mail:* herb.klein@uniontrib.com (Office).

KLEIN, Maj.-Gen. Jacques Paul; American international organization official; fmr Air Force Officer (retd as Maj.-Gen.); joined Foreign Service in Operations Center of Exec. Secr. of Sec. of State 1971; Consular Officer Consulate-Gen., Bremen; Political Officer Office of Southern European Affairs, Dept of State; Counsellor Officer, Berlin; Political Officer American Embassy, Bonn; Man. Analysis Officer Office of Dir-Gen. of Foreign Service; seconded to Dept of Defense as Adviser on Int. Affairs to Sec. of Air Force with rank of Deputy Asst Sec.; Dir Office of Strategic Tech. Matters, Bureau of Politico-Mil. Affairs, Dept of State; Asst Deputy Under-Sec. of Air Force for Int. Affairs, Dept of Defense 1989–90; Prin. Adviser to Dir-Gen. Foreign Service 1990–93; Political Adviser to C-in-C, US European Command, Stuttgart 1993–96; Prin. Deputy High Rep., Bosnia and Herzegovina 1997–99; UN Transitional Admin. for Eastern Slavonia, Baranja and Western Sirmium, rank of Under-Sec.-Gen. 1996–97; Special Rep. of Sec.-Gen. to Bosnia and Herzegovina, rank of Under-Sec.-Gen. 1999–; Air Force Distinguished Service Medal, Legion of Merit (with oak leaf cluster), Bronze Star, Distinguished Honor Award, Dept of State, Defense Medal for Outstanding Public Service, Grand Cross of Merit, FRG and other honours. *Address:* c/o UN Department of Peace-keeping Operations, Room S-3727-B, United Nations, New York, NY 10017, USA (Office).

KLEIN, Jonathan D.; American financial executive; with Hambros Bank Ltd 1983–93, Dir 1989–93; co-f. Getty Investment Holdings 1993–95; Jt Chair. Getty Communications PLC 1995–96, CEO and Dir 1996–98; co-f., CEO and Dir Getty Images 1998–; mem. Bd of Dirs Getty Investments, Conservation Corpn. *Address:* Getty Images, 701 N 34th Street, Seattle, WA 98103, USA (Office).

KLEIN, Lawrence Robert, PhD; American economist; b. 14 Sept. 1920, Omaha, Neb.; s. of Leo Byron Klein and Blanche Monheit; m. Sonia Adelson 1947; one s. three d.; ed Univ. of Calif. at Berkeley, MIT, Lincoln Coll., Oxford; joined Faculty, Univ. of Chicago 1944–47; Research Assoc., Nat. Bureau of Econ. Research, Cambridge, Mass. 1948–50; with Univ. Michigan 1949–54; Research Assoc., Survey Research Center 1949–54; Oxford Inst. Statistics 1954–58; mem. faculty, Univ. of Pennsylvania 1958–; Prof. 1958–, Univ. Prof. 1964–; Benjamin Franklin Prof. 1968–; Visiting Prof., Osaka Univ. 1960, Univ. of Colorado 1962, City Univ., New York 1962–63, Hebrew Univ. of Jerusalem 1964, Princeton Univ. 1966, Stanford Univ. 1968, Univ. of Copenhagen 1974; Ford Visiting Prof. Univ. of Calif. at Berkeley 1968; Visiting Prof. Inst. for Advanced Studies, Vienna 1970–74; Econ. Consultant to Canadian Govt 1947, UNCTAD 1966, 1967, 1975, McMillan Co. 1965–74, E. I. du Pont de Nemours 1966–68, State of NY 1969, American Telephone and Telegraph Co. 1969, Fed. Reserve Bd 1973, UNIDO 1973–75, Congressional Budget Office 1977–82, Council of Econ. Advisers 1977–80; Adviser State Planning Comm., People's Repub. of China; Chair. Bd of Trustees, Wharton Econometrics Forecasting Assoc. Inc. 1969–80, Chair. Professional Bd 1980–92; Dir Uni-Coll Corpn; Dir W. P. Carey & Co. 1984–; Trustee, Maurice Falk Inst. for Econ. Research, Israel, 1969–75; mem. Advisory Council, Inst. for Advanced Studies, Vienna 1977–; Chair. Econ. Advisory Cttee Gov. of Pa 1976–78; mem. Cttee on Prices, Fed. Reserve Bd 1968–70; Prin. Investigator, Econometric Model Project of Brookings Inst., Washington, DC 1963–72, Project LINK 1968–, Sr Adviser Brookings Panel on Econ. Activity 1970–; co-ordinator Jimmy Carter's Econ. Task Force 1976; mem. Advisory Bd, Strategic Studies Center, Stanford Research Inst. 1974–76; Ed. International Economic Review 1959–65, Assoc. Ed. 1965–92; mem. Editorial Bd Empirical Economics 1976–; Fellow, Econometrics Soc., American Acad. of Arts and Sciences, NAS, Social Sciences Research Council, American Economics Asscn, Eastern Econ. Asscn; Corresp. Fellow British Acad. 1991; Hon. Prof., Shanghai Acad. of Social Sciences 1994; Univ. of Nankai, People's Repub. of China 1993, Chinese Acad. of Social Science 2000; Hon. LLD (Mich.) 1977, (Dickinson) 1981; Hon. DLitt (Glasgow) 1991; Hon. ScD (Widener Coll.) 1977; Hon. DSc (Elizabeth Town) 1981, (Ball State) 1982, (Technion) 1982, (Nebraska) 1983, (Nat. Cen., Taiwan) 1985, (Rutgers) 1991; Hon. DHumLitt (Bard) 1986, (Bilkent) 1989, (St Norbert) 1989; Hon. Dr Ed. (Villanova) 1978; Dr hc(Vienna) 1977, Bonn Univ., Free Univ. of Brussels and Univ. of Paris) 1979, (Univ. of Madrid) 1980, (Helsinki) 1986, (Łooz) 1990, (Bar Ilan) 1994, (Carleton, Canada) 1997, (Piraeus, Greece) 2000, J. B. Clark Medal, American Econ. Asscn 1959, William F. Butler Award, New York Asscn of Business Economists 1975; Golden Slipper Club Award 1977; Nobel Prize in Econ. Science for work on econometric models 1980. *Publications:* The Keynesian Revolution 1947, Textbook of Econometrics 1953, An Econometric Model of the United States 1929–1952 1955, Wharton Econometric Forecasting Model 1967, Essay on the Theory of Economic Prediction 1968, Brookings Quarterly Econometric Model of U.S. Econometric Model Performance (author-ed.) 1976, The Economics of Supply and Demand 1983, Lectures in Econometrics 1983, Comparative Performance of US Econometric Models 1991. *Address:* University of Pennsylvania McNeil Bldg, Room 335, 3718 Locust Walk, Philadelphia, PA 19104 (Office); 101 Cheswold Lane, Harverford, PA 19041, USA (Home).

KLEIN, Peter Wolfgang, PhD; Netherlands professor of history; b. 10 Dec. 1931, Vienna, Austria; ed Netherlands School of Econs, Rotterdam; Asst Prof. of Econ. History 1959–65; Reader in Social History 1965–67; Prof. of Econ. and Social History, Erasmus Univ., Rotterdam 1969–85, Part-time Prof. of Econ. History 1969–74, Vice-Chancellor 1974–75, Dean Faculty of Econs 1977–78, Head History Dept 1979–81; Prof. of Early Modern History, State Univ. Leiden 1985–, Head History Dept 1986–88; Pres. Dutch Historical Soc. 1987–; mem. State Cttee for Nat. History 1981–, Bd State Inst. for History Second World War 1972–89, Scientific Cttee Inst. of Econ. History Francesco Datini 1986–, Cttee Int. Asscn of Econ. History 1985–, Royal Netherlands Acad. of Arts and Sciences 1979 (Chair. Arts Dept); Founding mem. Academia Europaea. *Publication:* Dr. Trippen in de 17e. eeuw 1965. *Address:* Vakgroep Geschiedenis, Doelensteeg 16, 2311VL Leiden (Office); Oude Herengracht 24, Leiden, Netherlands (Home); Universitet Leiden, Stationsweg 46, P.O. Box 9500, 2399, RA Leiden. *Telephone:* (71) 272759 (Office); (71) 5272727. *Fax:* (71) 5273118.

KLEISTERLEE, Gerard J.; German business executive; b. 1946; ed Eindhoven Technical Univ.; joined Philips in Medical Systems Div. 1974, several posts in mfg man., Gen. Man. Professional Audio Systems product group (now part of Consumer Electronics) 1981, joined Philips Components 1986, later Gen. Man. Philips Display Components for Europe, Man. Dir. Philips Display Components Worldwide 1994, Pres. Philips Taiwan and Regional Man. Philips Components in Asia-Pacific 1996, responsible for Philips Group in China 1997–98, Pres. and CEO Philips Components 1999–2000 (also mem. Group Man. Cttee), Exec. Vice-Pres. Royal Philips Electronics (also mem. Bd of Man.) 2000–, COO Philips 2000–, Pres. of Philips and Chair. Bd of Man. 2001–; Chair. Supervisory Bd Eindhoven Technical Univ. 2001–. *Address:* Investor Relations, Breitner Center, HBT 12-8, Amstelplein 2, POB 77900, 1070 MX Amsterdam, Netherlands (Office). *Telephone:* (20) 5977221 (Office). *Fax:* (20) 5977220 (Office). *Website:* www.philips.com (Office).

KLEMPERER, Paul David, BA, MBA, PhD, FBA; British professor of economics; b. 15 Aug. 1956; s. of the late Hugh G. Klemperer and Ruth Jordan; m. Margaret Meyer 1989; two s. one d.; ed King Edward's School, Birmingham, Peterhouse, Cambridge, Stanford Univ., USA; Consultant Arthur Andersen & Co. 1978–80; Harkness Fellow of Commonwealth Fund 1980–82; Lecturer in Operations Research and Math. Econs, Univ. of Oxford 1985–90, Reader in Econs 1990–95, Edgeworth Prof. of Econs 1995–, John Thomson Fellow and Tutor St Catherine's Coll. 1985–95, Fellow Nuffield Coll. 1995–; Visiting Lecturer MIT 1987, Univ. of Calif. at Berkeley 1991, 1993, Stanford Univ. 1991, 1993, Yale Univ. 1994, Princeton Univ. 1998; consultant to Dept of Trade and Industry 1997–2000, US Fed. Trade Comm. 1999–2001, Dept for Energy, Transport and the Regions 2000–01, Dept for the Environment, Food and Rural Affairs 2001–02 and pvt. cos; mem. UK Competition Comm. 2001–; Ed. RAND Journal of Econs 1993–99; assoc. or mem. editorial Bd Oxford Econ. Papers 1986–, Review of Econ. Studies 1989–97, Journal of Industrial Econs 1989–96, Int. Journal of Industrial Org. 1993–2000, European Econ. Review 1997–2001, Review of Econ. Design 1997–2000, Econ. Policy 1998–99, Econ. Journal 2000–01, Frontiers in Econs 2000–, Journal of Econ. Analysis and Policy 2001–; Fellow Econometric Soc. 1994. *Publications:* The Economic Theory of Auctions 1999; articles in econs journals. *Address:* Nuffield College, Oxford, OX1 1NF, England (Office). *Telephone:* (1865) 278588 (Office). *E-mail:* paul.klemperer@economics.ox.ac.uk (Office).

KLEMPERER, William, PhD; American professor of chemistry; b. 6 Oct. 1927, New York; s. of Paul Klemperer and Margit (Freund) Klemperer; m. Elizabeth Cole 1949; one s. two d.; ed New Rochelle High School, NY, Harvard Univ. and Univ. of California, Berkeley; US Navy Air Corps 1944–46; Instructor, Berkeley Feb.–June 1954; Instructor, Harvard Univ. 1954–57, Asst Prof. 1957–61, Assoc. Prof. 1961–65, Prof. 1965–; Asst Dir, Nat. Science Foundation (for math. and physical sciences) 1979–81; mem. American Physical Soc., NAS, American Acad. of Arts and Sciences, American Chemical Soc.; several memorial lectures; Wetherill Medal, Franklin Inst. Hon. DSc (Univ. of Chicago) 1996; Irving Langmuir Award, American Chemical Soc.;

Earle Plyler Award, American Physical Soc.; Distinguished Service Medal, Nat. Science Foundation–; Bornem Michelson Award, Coblentz Soc.; Remsen Award, Maryland Section of American Chemical Soc.; Peter Debye Award in Physical Chem., American Chemical Soc.; Faraday Medal, Royal Soc. of Chem. *Address:* Department of Chemistry and Chemical Biology, Harvard University, 12 Oxford Street, Cambridge, MA 02138 (Office); 53 Shattuck Road, Watertown, MA 02172, USA (Home). *Telephone:* (617) 495-4904 (Office); (617) 924-5775 (Home). *Fax:* (617) 496-5175 (Office).

KLEPPE, Johan; Norwegian politician and veterinarian; b. 29 Sept. 1928, Bjørnskinn, Andøya; s. of Jon Kleppe and Alvhild Caroliussen Kleppe; m. Inger Johansen 1961; one s. one d.; ed Veterinary Coll. of Norway; Veterinarian 1954–63, Dist Veterinarian, Andøy 1963–76, Supervisory Veterinarian 1966–76; Regional Veterinary Officer of North Norway 1976–94; mem. Bjørnskinn Municipal Council 1956–64; Deputy Mayor of Andøy 1964–66, Mayor 1966–68, 1975–78, mem. Exec. Cttee Andøy municipality 1964–78; Deputy mem. of Parl. 1967; Parl. Under-Sec. of State, Ministry of Agriculture 1968–69; Liberal mem. of Parl. for Nordland 1969–73, mem. Bd of Liberal Parl. faction 1969–73; mem. Liberal Party's Cttee on Oil Policy and EC Cttee, mem. Prin. Planning Cttee; Minister of Defence 1972–73; mem. Liberal Nat. Exec. 1966–72; Leader, Norwegian del., FAO confs, Rome and Malta 1969; Norwegian Del., UN Gen. Ass., New York 1971; fmr Bd mem. Nordland Co. Liberal Asscn; fmr Chair. Students Liberal Asscn, Oslo and Bjørnskinn and Andøy Liberal Asscn; Chair. of Board, Directorate of State Forests 1969–77, Chair. Nat. Council on Sheep-breeding 1969–82; Chair. of Bd Nordlandsbanken A/S, 8480 Andenes 1974–90, State Veterinary Laboratory for Northern Norway 1976–91, Vesteraalen Intermunicipal Planning Office 1978–88; Vice-Chair. Cttee Norwegian Veterinary Asscn 1981–84, Chair. 1984–91; Chair. of Bd Andøyposten a/s 1981–90, Troms Population Acad. Asscn 1987–94; mem. Bd Norwegian Nat. Programme for Sea Ranching 1990–94. *Address:* 8484 Risøyhamn, Norway. *Telephone:* 76-14-76-30. *Fax:* 76-14-76-30.

KLEPSCH, Egon Alfred, DPhil; German politician; b. 30 Jan. 1930, Bodenbach/Elbe; s. of Egon Klepsch and Hermine Hölzl; m. Anita Wegehaupt 1952; three s. three d.; joined CDU 1951, mem. Bureau 1977–94; Fed. Chair. Young Christian Democrats 1963–69; Chair. European Union of Young Christian Democrats 1964–70; mem. Bundestag 1965–80; mem. Parl. Assemblies of Council of Europe and of WEU 1969–80; MEP (not directly elected) 1973–79, elected MEP 1979–94, Vice-Pres. European Parl. 1982–84, Pres. 1992–94; Vice-Pres. European People's Party (EPP) 1977–92, mem. Bureau 1992–94, Chair. EPP Group 1977–82, 1984–92; Chair. Europa-Union Deutschland 1989–97; Vice-Chair. German Council of European Movt 1990–99 (Hon. mem. 1999–); mem. Bd of Govs. Deutschlandfunk 1991–; Bundesverdienstkreuz mit Stern und Schulterband and decorations from Italy, Luxembourg, Argentina, Chile and Greece. *Publications:* several books on European policy and military topics. *Leisure interest:* chess. *Address:* c/o Christian-Democratic Union, Konrad-Adenauer-Haus, Friedrich-Ebert Allee 73–75, 53115 Bonn, Germany.

KLERIDES, Glavkos John, BA, LLB; Cypriot politician and lawyer; b. 24 April 1919, Nicosia; s. of the late Yiannis Klerides and Elli Klerides; m. Lilla-Irene Erulkar 1946; one d.; ed Pancyprian Gymnasium, Nicosia, King's Coll., London Univ.; served with RAF 1939–45, POW 1942–45; called to Bar, Gray's Inn 1951; practised law in Cyprus 1951–60; Minister of Justice 1959–60; Head Greek Cypriot Del., Jt Constitutional Comm. 1959–60, Greek Cypriot Del., London Conf. 1964, Rep. Negotiator Greek Cypriot Community Intercommunal Talks 1968; mem. House of Reps. 1960–76, 1981–93, Pres. 1960–76; Acting Pres. of Cyprus July–Dec. 1974, Pres. 1993–2003; Pres. Red Cross 1961–63 (Hon. Certificate and Hon. Life mem., Recognition of Distinguished Service); f. Unified Party 1969, Democratic Rally 1976; leading mem. Unified Party, Progressive Front and Democratic Nat. Front 1976; Gold Medal (Order of Holy Sepulchre), Recognized Services and Understanding of Roman Catholic Religious Group (by approval of His Holiness Pope John XXIII); Grand Cross of the Saviour (Greece). *Publications:* My Deposition (4 vols.). *Address:* c/o Presidential Palace, Nicosia; 5 Ioannis Clerides Street, Nicosia, Cyprus.

KLERIDES, Takis; Cypriot politician and accountant; b. 21 Aug. 1951, Nicosia; m. Nancy Hak 1976; one s. one d.; ed Birmingham Polytechnic, UK; joined KPMG Cyprus 1977, partner 1983–97, Sr Partner 1997–; Minister of Finance 1999–2003; mem. Monopolies Comm. 1998–99, Cyprus Olympic Cttee 1996–99; Chair. Cyprus Basketball Fed. 1988–98; Fellow Chartered Asscn of Certified Accountants; mem. Inst. of Certified Public Accountants of Cyprus (mem. Council 1984–99). *Leisure interest:* sports. *Address:* c/o Ministry of Finance, Ex-Secretariat Compound, 1439 Nicosia, Cyprus (Office).

KLESTIL, Thomas, DEcon; Austrian Head of State and diplomatist; b. 4 Nov. 1932; m. 1st; two s. one d.; m. 2nd Margot Löffler 1999; ed Economic Univ., Vienna; Office for Econ. Co-ordination in Fed. Chancellery, Vienna 1957–59; mem. of Austrian Del. to OECD, Paris 1959–62; Embassy, Washington DC 1962–66; Sec. to Fed. Chancellor 1966–69; Consul Gen. of Austria in LA, Calif. 1969–74; Perm. Rep. of Austria to UN 1978–82; Amb. to USA 1982–87; Sec.-Gen. for Foreign Affairs 1987–92; Pres. of Austria July 1992–. *Publication:* Themen Meines Lebens. *Address:* Präsidentschaftskanzlei, Hofburg, 1010 Vienna, Austria (Office). *Telephone:* (1) 534-22-0 (Office). *Fax:* (1) 535-65-12 (Office). *Website:* hofburg.at (Office).

KLEY, Max Dietrich; German business executive; b. 1940, Berlin; ed Univs of Munich and Heidelberg; joined legal Dept BASF AG 1969, Head of Tax Dept

1977–82, CEO Gewerkschaft Auguste Vic., Marl 1982–87, Pres. Energy and Coal Div. 1987–90, mem. Bd Exec. Dirs. 1990–, Deputy Chair. 1999–; mem. Supervisory Bd Bayerische Hypo- und Vereinsbank AG 1990–, Gerling Konzern Speziale-Kreditversicherungs-AG 1992–, Landesbank Rheinland-Pfalz 1993–, Lausitzer Braunkohle AG 1995–, Mannesmann Demag Krauss Maffei AG 1995–, Winterhall AG 1996–, BASF Coatings AG 1999–; Chair. Industrial Energy and Power Asscn 1991–97; Pres. German Inst. for Share Promotion 1998–. *Address:* BASF AG, Charlottenstr. 59, 10117 Berlin, Germany (Office). *Telephone:* (30) 20629500 (Office). *Fax:* (30) 206295020 (Office). *Website:* www.basf.de (Office).

KLIBI, Chedli, BA; Tunisian politician and international official; b. 6 Sept. 1925, Tunis; s. of Hassouna Klibi and Habiba Bannani; m. Kalthoum Lasram 1956; one s. two d.; ed Sadiki Coll., Tunis, Sorbonne, Paris; successively high school teacher, lecturer, Univ. of Tunis and journalist 1951–57; Dir-Gen. Tunisian Radio and TV 1958–61; Minister of Information and Cultural Affairs 1961–64, 1969–73, of Cultural Affairs 1976–78, of Information Sept. 1978; Minister, Dir Cabinet of Pres. 1974–76; Sec.-Gen. League of Arab States 1978–90; Mayor of Carthage 1963–; mem. Political Bureau and Cen. Cttee, Neo Destour (Parti Socialiste Destourien) 1979–; mem. Cairo Arabic Language Acad.; Grand Cordon, Order of Independence and Order of Repub. (Tunisia) and several foreign decorations. *Publications include:* The Arabs and the Palestinian Question, Islam and Modernity, Culture is a Civilisational Challenge, Orient–Occident, la paix violente. *Leisure interest:* reading. *Address:* Carthage, Tunisia. *Telephone:* 734-535. *Fax:* 734-820.

KLÍMA, Ivan, MA; Czech author; b. 14 Sept. 1931, Prague; m. Helena Malá-Klímová 1958; one s. one d.; ed Charles Univ., Prague; Ed. Československy spisovatel (publishing house) 1958–63; Ed. Literárni noviny 1963–67, Literárni Listy 1968, Listy 1968–69; Visiting Prof. Univ. of Mich. Ann Arbor 1969–70; freelance author publishing abroad 1970–89; mem. Council, Czech Writers 1989–, Ed.'s Council, Lidové noviny 1996–97; Exec. Pres. Czech PEN Centre 1990–93; Hostovský Award, New York 1985, George Theiner Prize (UK) 1993, Franz Kafka Prize 2002. *Publications:* Ship Named Hope 1968, A Summer Affair 1972, My Merry Mornings (short stories) 1979, My First Loves (short stories) 1985, Love and Garbage 1987, Judge on Trial 1987, Waiting for the Dark, Waiting for the Light, My Golden Trades (short stories) 1992, The Island of Dead Kings 1992, The Spirit of Prague (essays, jtly) 1994, The Ultimate Intimacy (novel) 1997, Solo for Jug and Two Female Voices, No Saints or Angels 1999, Between Security and Insecurity: Prospects for Tomorrow 2000, Lovers for a Day: New and Collected Stories on Love 2000, Karel Capek: Life and Work 2002; plays: The Castle 1964, The Master 1967, The Sweetshop Myriam 1968, President and the Angel, Klara and Two Men 1968, Bridegroom for Marcela 1968, The Games 1975, Kafka and Felice 1986; contribs to magazines. *Leisure interests:* tennis, gathering mushrooms. *Address:* České Centrum Mezinárodního, PEN Klubu, ul. 28, října 9, 11000 Prague 1, Czech Republic. *Telephone:* (2) 24221926 (Office).

KLIMA, Viktor; Austrian politician and business executive; b. 4 June 1947, Vienna; s. of Viktor Klima and Anna Varga; m. Sonja Holzinger 1995; one s. one d.; ed Vienna Tech. Univ., Univ. of Vienna; worked at Inst. for Automation and Scientific Business Consultancy; joined staff of Österreichische Mineralöl-Verwaltungs AG (ÖMV) 1970, Head Organizational Div. 1980–85, Dir Cen. Personnel Office and group's Prokuriet (holder of a gen. power of attorney) 1986–, mem. Man. Bd with responsibility for finance, control, accountancy and acquisitions (subsequently also chemical div.) 1990–92; Minister of Public Economy and Transport 1992–96, of Finance 1996–97, Fed. Chancellor of Austria 1997–2000; mem. several supervisory and advisory bds, Governing Bd Fed. of Public Economy and Utility Enterprises; Chair. Fed. Econ. Chamber's Petroleum Industry Labour Law Cttee, Cttee on Public and Utility Enterprises. *Address:* c/o Ballhauspl. 2, 1014 Vienna, Austria.

KLIMMT, Reinhard; German politician and historian; b. 16 Aug. 1942; mem. of Landtag 1975–; Chair. Sozialdemokratische Partei Deutschlands (SPD) Landtag Party, mem. SPD Party Exec., Chair. Media Comm. of SPD Party Exec. –1998; Minister-Pres. of Saarland 1998–99; Minister of Regional Planning, Urban Devt, Construction and Transport 1999–2000. *Address:* Krausenstrasse 17–20, 10117 Berlin, Germany.

KLIMOV, Dmitri Mikhailovich; Russian expert on mechanics; b. 13 July 1933; m.; ed Moscow State Univ.; researcher Research Inst. of Applied Mech. 1958–67; head of lab., head of div.; Deputy Dir Inst. for Problems in Mechanics USSR Acad. of Sciences 1967–89, Dir 1989–; Corresp. mem USSR (now Russian) Acad. of Sciences 1981, mem. 1992, Academician-Sec. Div. for Problems of Machine Engineering, Mechanics and Control Processes 1996–; main research in mechanics, gyroscopic and navigation systems, gen. and analytical mechanics, mechanics of deformable solid bodies; Deputy Chair. Scientific Council on Problems of Man. of Navigation Movt; USSR State Prize 1976, Russian State Prize 1994. *Publications:* Inertial Navigation on the Sea 1984, Applied Methods in Oscillations Theory 1988, Methods of Computer Algebra in Problems of Mechanics 1989; numerous articles. *Leisure interest:* chess. *Address:* Institute for Problems in Mechanics, Vernadskogo prosp. 101, 117526 Moscow, Russia (Office). *Telephone:* (095) 434-46-10 (Office); (095) 938-14-04 (Academy). *Fax:* (095) 938-20-48 (Office).

KLIMOV, Elem Germanovich; Russian film director; b. 9 July 1933; m. Larisa Shepit'ko (died 1981); ed Aviation Inst., All-Union State Cinematography Inst. (VGIK), Moscow; First Sec. USSR Union of Film Makers 1986–90. *Films include:* The Fiancée, Careful–Banality!, Look, the Sky!

(shorts) 1962–64; Welcome 1964, Adventures of a Dentist 1967, Sport, Sport, Sport 1971, Agony (on Rasputin) 1981 (with Alexei Petrenko), Farewell 1983, Come and See 1985. *Address:* Frunzenskaya nab. 24/1, Apt. 30, 119146 Moscow, Russia. *Telephone:* (095) 242-42-47.

KLIMOVSKI, Savo, LLD; Macedonian politician; b. 1947, Skopje; m. Radmila Klimovski; one s. one d.; ed Skopje Univ., Ljubljana Univ.; Lecturer, Asst Prof., Prof., Dean of Law Faculty, Pres., St Cyril and Methodius Univ., Skopje; mem. Exec. Council, Macedonian Ass.; Pres. Macedonian Cttee for Educ., Culture and Physical Culture; f. Democratic Alternative (political party) 1998–; mem. Govt Coalition For Changes; Pres. Ass. of Repub. Macedonia; Pres. Cttee for Constitutional Issues, Council for Interethnic Relations; Pres. Repub. of Macedonia Nov.–Dec. 1999. *Publications:* Constitutional and Political System, Politics and Institutions, Political Philosophy, Parliamentary Law. *Address:* Bul. 'Patizanski odredi' nr. 3/II-19, Skopje, Macedonia (Home); Sobranje, Oktomyri blvd 11, 91000 Skopje. *Telephone:* (2) 227549 (Office); (2) 227228 (Home). *Website:* www.klimovski.com.mk (Home).

KLIMUK, Col-Gen. Piotr Ilyich, DTechSc; Russian cosmonaut; b. 10 July 1942, Komarovka, Brest Region; m. Lilia Vladimirovna Klimuk; one s.; ed Chernigov Higher Mil. Aviation School, Air Force Acad., Lenin Mil. Political Acad.; three space flights 1973–78; Deputy Head, Head Political Dept Yuriy Gagarin Centre for Cosmonauts Training 1978–91, Head 1991–; USSR People's Deputy 1989–91; Hero of Soviet Union 1973, 1975; Tsiolkovsky Gold Medal, USSR State Prize 1978, 1981, Gold Medal (Polish Acad. of Sciences). *Publications:* Next to the Stars, Attacking Weightlessness. *Address:* Yuriy Gagarin Centre for Cosmonauts Training, Zvezdny Gorodok, Moscow Region, Russia. *Telephone:* (095) 526-35-33.

KLINE, Kevin Delaney, BA; American actor and director; b. 24 Oct. 1947, St Louis; s. of Robert J. Kline and Peggy Kirk; m. Phoebe Cates 1989; one s. one d.; ed Indiana Univ. and Juilliard School Drama Div. New York; founding mem. The Acting Co. New York 1972–76; Obie Award for sustained achievement, Will Award for classical theatre; Joseph Papp Award 1990, John Houseman Award 1993, Gotham Award 1997. *Films include:* Sophie's Choice 1982, Pirates of Penzance 1983, The Big Chill 1983, Silverado 1985, Violets are Blue 1985, Cry Freedom 1987, A Fish Called Wanda (Acad. Award for Best Supporting Actor 1989) 1988, The January Man 1989, I Love You to Death 1989, Soapdish 1991, Grand Canyon 1991, Consenting Adults 1992, Chaplin 1992, Dave 1993, Princess Caraboo 1994, French Kiss 1995, The Hunchback of Notre Dame (voice) 1996, Fierce Creatures 1996, The Ice Storm 1997, In and Out 1997, A Midsummer Night's Dream 1999, Wild Wild West 1999, The Road to El Dorado (voice) 2000, The Anniversary Party 2001, Life as a House 2001, Orange County 2002, The Emperor's Club 2002, The Hunchback of Notre Dame II (voice) 2002. *Theatre:* Broadway appearances in On the Twentieth Century 1978 (Tony Award 1978), Loose Ends 1979, Pirates of Penzance 1980 (Tony Award 1980), Arms and the Man 1985; off-Broadway appearances in Richard III 1983, Henry V 1984, Hamlet (also Dir) 1986, 1990, Much Ado About Nothing 1988, Measure for Measure 1995, The Seagull 2001. *Address:* c/o William Morris Agency, 1325 Avenue of the Americas, New York, NY 10019, USA.

KLINGENBERG, Wilhelm; German professor of mathematics; b. 28 Jan. 1924, Rostock; s. of Paul Klingenberg and Henny Klingenberg; m. Christine Kob 1953; two s. one d.; ed Kiel Univ.; Asst Hamburg Univ. 1952–55; Asst Prof., Assoc. Prof. Göttingen Univ. 1955–63; Prof. Univ. of Mainz 1963–66; Prof. of Math. Univ. of Bonn 1966–; mem. Acad. of Science and Literature, Mainz; Dr hc (Leipzig) 2001. *Publications:* A Course in Differential Geometry 1978, Lectures on Closed Geodesics 1978, Riemannian Geometry 1982, 1995, Der weite Weg zum Kailas 1992, Tibet 1997. *Leisure interests:* piano, horseback riding, Chinese art, art of Albrecht Dürer. *Address:* Am Alten Forsthaus 42, 53125 Bonn, Germany. *Telephone:* (288) 251529.

KLINSMANN, Jürgen; German footballer; b. 30 July 1964, Göppingen; m. Debbie Klinsmann 1995; one s.; centre-forward, began career with Stuttgarter Kickers before moving to VfB Stuttgart 1984–89 (79 goals); mem. winning team, World Cup 1990, UEFA Cup with Inter Milan 1991 and Bayern Munich 1996; with Inter Milan 1989–92 (34 goals); AS Monaco 1992–94 (29 goals) with Tottenham Hotspur 1994–95, 1997–98; played for Bayern Munich 1995–97 (31 goals), Sampdoria 1997; scored 47 goals in 108 int. games for Germany; Int. Amb. for SOS Children's Villages in partnership with FIFA; f. children's care charity AGAPEDIA; Vice-Pres. SoccerSolutions (sports marketing and business devt consultancy); now lives in Calif.; European Footballer of Year 1988, German Footballer of the Year 1988, 1994, English Footballer of the Year 1995. *Leisure interests:* travel, cinema, music. *Address:* Soccer Solutions LLC, 744 SW Regency Place, Portland, OR 97225, USA. *Telephone:* (503) 297-0844. *Website:* www.soccersolutions.com.

KLJUŠEV, Nikola, DEconSc; Macedonian politician, economist and poet; b. 2 Oct. 1927, Stip; s. of Emanuel Kljušev and Lenka Kljušev; m. 1956; one s. one d.; ed Belgrade Univ.; Asst Researcher Inst. for Industrial Scientific Research, Skopje 1953–60; Sr Researcher Inst. of Econs, Skopje 1960–67; Prof. Skopje Univ. 1968–91; mem. Macedonian Acad. of Arts and Sciences; Ed.-in-Chief, Economic Interview 1971–78; Prime Minister of Macedonia 1991–92; researcher 1992–98; Minister of Defence 1998–99; Pres. Council VMRO-DPMNE independent; Golden Wreath Award, 13 Nov. Prize. *Publications:* (books on Econs): Period of Activization of Investment 1963, Criteria and Methods for Evaluation of Economic Efficiency of Investments 1965, Usage of Productive Capacity in Industry 1967, Policy and Economics of

Investment in Companies 1968, Efficiency of Investment in Macedonian Industry 1969, Selected Problems of Theory and Policy of Economic Development 1978, Theory and Policy of Economic Development 1979, Investments (Theory, Economics, Policy) 1980; (books of poetry): Stone Island 1994, Antithesis 1994, The Power of the Word 1994, Ode to the Word 1995, Non-germinated Seed 1996; Selected Works (6 Vols) 1997; (Essays): trilogy: I Faith and Delusion, II Unslept Nights, III Visions 1997–2000; Dictionary of the Heart 2001. *Leisure interests:* hunting, skiing. *Address:* Dimitar Mirasciev 19, Skopje, Macedonia. *Telephone:* (2) 773003.

KLOSE, Hans-Ulrich; German politician and lawyer; b. 14 June 1937, Breslau; two s. two d.; ed gymnasium in Bielefeld, High School, Clinton, Iowa and Univs of Freiburg and Hamburg; fmr lawyer in Hamburg; mem. Social Democratic Party (SPD) 1964–; mem. Public Services and Transport Workers' Union 1968; mem. Hamburger Bürgerschaft 1970, Chair. SPD Parl. Group 1972; Senator of the Interior 1973; Mayor of Hamburg 1974–81 (resgnd); mem. (Constituency 18, Hamburg-Harburg) Bundestag 1983–; Vice-Pres. 1994–98), Chair. Foreign Affairs Cttee 1998–2002, Vice-Chair. 2002–; Chair. German–American Parl. Group 2003–; Treas. SPD 1987–91; Chair. SPD Parl. Party 1991–94; Hon. Citizen of Lima 1981. *Publications:* Charade (poems), Charade 2 (poems), Das Altern der Gesellschaft, Altern ist Zukunft. *Leisure interests:* early American cultures, art and antiques, painting, literature. *Address:* Bundeshaus, 11011 Berlin, Germany (Office). *Telephone:* (30) 22771222; (30) 22770110. *E-mail:* hans-ulrich.klose@bundestag.de (Office).

KLOSSON, Michael, MA, MPA; American diplomatist; b. 22 Aug. 1949, Washington; s. of Boris H. Klosson and Harriet F. C. Klosson; m. Boni Klosson; two d.; ed Hamilton Coll. and Princeton Univ.; teacher of English and modern Chinese history, Hong Kong Baptist Coll. 1971–72; joined Foreign Service 1972, served with Bureau of E Asian and Pacific Affairs, State Dept, Washington and Taipei and with Office of Japanese Affairs 1975–81; Special Asst to Secs. of State Alexander Haig and George Schultz 1981–83; Deputy Dir Office of European Security and Political Affairs, Dir Secr. Staff, Office of Sec. of State 1984–90; Deputy Chief of Mission and Chargé d'Affaires, US Embassy, Stockholm and The Hague 1990–96; Prin. Deputy Asst Sec. of State for Legis. Affairs 1996–99; Consul-Gen. for Hong Kong and Macao 1999–; Herbert H. Lehman Fellowship, Winston Churchill Fellowship; six Superior Honor Awards, US Dept of State. *Music:* Behold the Word 1968. *Leisure interests:* photography, music, running, scuba diving. *Address:* United States Consulate-General, Psc 464, Box 30, F.P.O. AP 96522, USA (Office). *E-mail:* klossonm@state.gov (Office). *Website:* www.usconsulate.org.hk (Office).

KLOSTER, Einar, BA; Norwegian business executive; b. 22 Sept. 1937, Oslo; s. of Knut Utstein Kloster and Ingeborg (née Ihlen) Kloster; m. Elizabeth (née Hajan) Blake 1961; two d.; ed Dartmouth Coll. and Harvard Univ.; Marketing Man. Philips Norway 1961–68, Philips Head Office, Netherlands 1968–70; Marketing Dir Philips Japan 1970–74; CEO Philips East Africa 1974–77, Philips Norway 1978–82, Philips Brazil 1982–85; Exec. Vice-Pres. North American Philips Corpn 1985–86, Pres. 1989; Chair. and CEO Kloster Cruise Ltd 1986–88, Pres. and CEO 1989–; Chair. Norsk Hydro June 1997–. *Leisure interests:* golf, tennis, skiing. *Address:* Norsk Hydro AS, Bygdoy Alle 2, 0240 Oslo, Norway. *Telephone:* 22-43-21-00. *Fax:* 22-43-27-25.

KLOTZ, Irving Myron, PhD; American professor of chemistry and biochemistry; b. 22 Jan. 1916, Chicago, Ill.; s. of Frank and Mollie Nasatir Klotz; m. Mary S. Hanlon 1966; two s. one d.; ed Univ. of Chicago; Research Assoc., Northwestern Univ. 1940–42, Instructor in Chem. 1942–46, Asst Prof. of Chem. 1946–47, Assoc. Prof. of Chem. 1947–50; Prof. of Chem. and Biochemistry 1950–, Morrison Prof. 1963–86, Prof. Emer. 1986–; Fellow, American Acad. of Arts and Sciences; mem. NAS; Eli Lilly Award 1949, Midwest Award 1970 (ACS), W. C. Rose Award (American Soc. of Molecular Biology) 1993. *Publications:* Chemical Thermodynamics 1950, 1964, 1972, 1986, 1994, 2000, Energy Changes in Biochemical Reactions 1957, 1967, Introduction to Biomolecular Energetics 1986, Diamond Dealers, Feather Merchants: Tales from the Sciences 1986, Ligand-Receptor Energetics: A Guide for the Perplexed 1997; over 300 research papers. *Address:* c/o Department of Chemistry, Northwestern University, Evanston, IL 60208-3113 (Office); 1500 Sheridan Road, Unit 7D, Wilmette, IL 60091-1844, USA (Home). *Telephone:* (847) 491-3546 (Office). *Fax:* (847) 491-7713 (Office). *E-mail:* i-klotz@northwestern.edu (Office); chemdept@chem.northwestern.edu (Office).

KLUG, Sir Aaron, Kt, OM, ScD, FRS; British biochemist; b. 11 Aug. 1926; s. of Lazar Klug and Bella Silin; m. Liebe Bobrow 1948; two s. (one deceased); ed Durban High School and Univs of the Witwatersrand, Cape Town and Cambridge; Jr Lecturer 1947–48; Research Student, Cavendish Lab., Cambridge 1949–52; Rouse-Ball Research Studentship, Trinity Coll., Cambridge 1949–52; Colloid Science Dept, Cambridge 1953; Nuffield Research Fellow, Birkbeck Coll., London 1954–57; Dir Virus Structure Research Group, Birkbeck Coll. 1958–61; mem. staff, MRC Lab. of Molecular Biology, Cambridge 1962–, Jt Head, Div. of Structural Studies 1978–86, Dir 1986–96; Pres. Royal Soc. 1995–2000; Fellow of Peterhouse 1962–93; Hon. Fellow Peterhouse, Cambridge 1993–; Royal Coll. of Pathologists 1991, Birkbeck Coll. 1994; Hon. Prof. Univ. of Cambridge 1989; Foreign Assoc. NAS; Foreign mem. Max Planck Gesellschaft 1984, Acad. des Sciences, Paris 1989, Japan Acad. 1999; Foreign Hon. mem. American Acad. of Arts and Sciences; Hon. Fellow, Trinity Coll., Cambridge, Royal Coll. of Physicians 1987; Hon. DSc (Chicago) 1978, (Columbia) 1978, (Witwatersrand 1984), (Hull) 1985, (Jerusalem) 1985, (St Andrews) 1987, (Western Ont.) 1991, (Warwick) 1994, (Cape Town) 1997,

(London) 1999, (Oxford) 2001; Dr hc (Strasbourg) 1978, (Stirling) 1998; Hon. Dr Fil. (Stockholm) 1980; Hon. LittD (Cantab.) 1998; Hon. DLitt (Cambridge) 1998; Heineken Prize, Royal Netherlands Acad. of Science 1979; Louisa Gross Horwitz Prize (Columbia Univ.) 1981; Nobel Prize for Chemistry 1982, Copley Medal, Royal Soc. 1985, Harden Medal, Biochemical Soc. 1985, Baly Medal, Royal Coll. of Physicians 1987; William Bate Hardy Prize, Cambridge Philosophical Soc. 1996. *Publications:* articles in scientific journals. *Leisure interests:* reading, ancient history. *Address:* MRC Laboratory of Molecular Biology, Cambridge, CB2 2QH (Office). *Telephone:* (1223) 248011 (Office).

KLUGE, John Werner, BA; American broadcasting and advertising company executive; b. 21 Sept. 1914, Chemnitz, Germany; s. of Fritz Kluge and Gertrude (Donj) Kluge; one s. one d.; ed Wayne and Columbia Univs.; with Otten Bros Inc., Detroit 1937–41; served US Army 1941–45; Pres., Dir WGAY Radio Station, Silver Spring, Md 1946–59, St Louis Broadcasting Corpn, Brentwood, Mo. 1953–58, Pittsburgh Broadcasting Co. 1954–59; Pres., Treas., Dir Capitol Broadcasting Co., Nashville 1954–59, Assoc. Broadcasters Inc., Fort Worth, Dallas 1957–59; partner, Western NY Broadcasting Co., Buffalo 1957–60; Pres., Dir Washington Planagraph Co. 1956–60, Mid-Fla Radio Corpn, Orlando 1952–59; Treasurer, Dir Mid-Fla TV Corpn 1957–60; owner, Kluge Investment Co., Washington, DC 1956–60; partner, Nashton Properties, Nashville 1954–60, Texworth Investment Co., Fort Worth 1957–60; Chair. Bd Seaboard Service System Inc. 1957–58; Pres. New England Fritos, Boston 1947–55, New York Inst. of Dietetics 1953–60; Chair. Bd, Treas., Dir, Kluge, Finkelstein & Co., Baltimore; Chair. Bd, Treas., Tri-Suburban Broadcasting Corpn, Washington, Kluge & Co.; Chair. Bd, Pres., Treas., Silver City Sales Co., Washington; Dir Marriott-Hot Shoppes Inc., and other cos.; Vice-Pres. Bd Dirs. United Cerebral Palsy Research and Educational Foundation 1972–; Chair. Bd, Pres., CEO Metromedia Inc., Secaucus, N.J. 1959–86, now Chair. Pres. Metromedia Co., E. Rutherford, NJ. *Address:* Metromedia Inc., 1 Meadowlands Plaza, East Rutherford, NJ 07073, USA.

KLUTSE, Kwassi; Togolese politician; fmr Minister of Planning and Territorial Devt; Prime Minister, Minister of Planning and Territorial Devt 1996–99. *Address:* c/o Office of the Prime Minister, Lomé, Togo.

KNACKSTEDT, Günter Wilhelm Karl, PhD; German diplomatist; b. 29 July 1929, Berlin; s. of Willi and Anni Knackstedt; m. (divorced); two s.; m. 2nd Marianne Fischbach 1984; ed Univs. of Frankfurt, Paris, Cincinnati and Harvard; Ed. at Cincinnati Enquirer 1958–59; Chief Ed. You and Europe, Wiesbaden 1959–61; joined diplomatic service 1961; Press Attaché, Havana 1963, Caracas 1963–66; Ministry of Foreign Affairs 1966–74, Sec. for Parl. Affairs 1976–79; Political Counsellor, Madrid 1974–76; Amb. to Luxembourg 1979–84, to Council of Europe, Strasbourg 1985–88, to Chile 1988–89, to Poland 1989–92, to Portugal 1992–94. *Publications:* Compendium of World History 1954, Living with Venezuelans 1968. *Leisure interests:* skiing, tennis, collecting old clocks. *Address:* 7 val Ste Croix, 1371 Luxembourg. *Telephone:* 453701 (Office); 225530 (Home). *Fax:* 453706 (Office).

KNAIFEL, Alexander Aronovich; Russian composer; b. 28 Nov. 1943, Tashkent; s. of Aron Iosifovich Knaifel and Muza Veniaminovna Shapiro-Knaifel; m. Tatiana Melentieva 1965; one d.; ed Moscow and Leningrad Conservatoires; freelance composer; mem. Composers Union 1967, Cinematographers Union 1987–; Honoured Art Worker of Russia 1996. *Compositions:* Diada (Two Pieces) 1962, Classical Suite 1963, Ostinati 1964, Five Poems by Mikhail Lermontov 1964, Angel 1964, Musique militaire 1964, The Coming City of the Seeking After 1964, Passacaglia 1965, The Canterville Ghost 1965–66, Disarmament 1966, 150 000 000 1966, Lamento 1967, The Petrograd Sparrows 1967, Monodia 1968, Medea 1968, Argumentum de jure 1969, Joan 1970–78, A prima vista 1972, Status nascendi 1975, Ainana 1978, Rafferti 1980, Vera (Faith) 1980, Solaris 1980, Da (Yes) 1980, A Silly Horse 1981, A Chance Occurrence 1982, Pagan Fate 1982, Nika 1983–84, Counteraction 1984, God 1985, Agnus Dei 1985, Wings of a Serf 1986, Madness 1987, Through the Rainbow of Involuntary Tears 1987–88, Litania 1988, Shramy marsha (Scars of March) 1988, Voznosheniye (The Holy Oblation) 1991, Svete Tikhiy (O Gladsome Light) 1991, Postludia 1992, Once Again on the Hypothesis 1992, Scalae Iacobis 1992, Chapter Eight 1993, Maranatha 1993, Cantus 1993, Butterfly 1993, In Air Clear and Unseen 1994, Prayers to the Holy Spirit 1994–95, Alice in Wonderland 1994–2002, Psalm 51 (50) 1995, Amicta sole 1995, The Beatitudes 1996, Bliss 1997, Lux aeterna 1997, This Child 1997, Tabernacle 1998, With the White on the White 1998, Snowflake on a Spiderthread 1998, Daylight 1999, Small Blue Fealthers 2001, Morning Prayers 2001, Entrance 2001, Fairytale of a Fisherman and a Fish 2002; incidental music for 40 films. *Leisure interests:* photography, shooting video films. *Address:* Skobelevski pr. 5, apt. 130, 194214 St Petersburg, Russia (Home). *Fax:* (812) 553-82-68 (Home). *Fax:* (812) 553-53-97; (812) 373-48-92. *E-mail:* zair_matchball@hotmail.com (Office); knaifel@yahoo.de (Home). *Website:* www.ceo.spb.ru/rus/music/knaifel (Office).

KNAPP, Charles, MA, PhD; American university president; b. 13 Aug. 1946, Ames, Ia; s. of Albert B. Knapp and Anne Marie Knapp; m. Lynne Vickers Knapp 1967; one d.; ed Iowa State Univ. and Univ. of Wisconsin; Asst Prof. of Econs Univ. of Tex., Austin 1972–76; Special Asst to US Sec. of Labor 1976–79; Deputy Asst Sec. of Labor for Employment Training 1979–81; Visiting Faculty, George Washington Univ. 1981–82; Senior Vice-Pres. Tulane Univ. 1982–85, Exec. Vice-Pres. 1985–87; Pres., Prof. of Econs Univ. of Georgia 1987–97; Pres. Aspen Inst. 1997–99, partner Heidrick & Struggles

Int. Inc., Atlanta 2000–; Dir AFLAC, Inc. *Publications:* A Human Capital Approach to the Burden of the Military Draft 1973, Earnings and Individual Variations in Postschool Human Investment 1976, Employment Discrimination 1978. *Address:* Heidrick & Struggles International Inc., 303 Peachtree Street, NE, Suite 3100, Atlanta, GA 30308, USA.

KŇAŽKO, Milan; Slovak politician and actor; b. 28 Aug. 1945, Horné Plachtince, Velký Krtíš Dist; m. Eugenia Kňažková; three s.; ed Acad. of Performing Arts, Bratislava, Univ. of Nancy, France; mem. drama company, Theatre on the Promenade, Bratislava 1970–71; actor, New Theatre, Bratislava 1971–85; mem. Slovak Nat. Theatre Drama Company, Bratislava, 1985–; co-founder, Public Against Violence (political Movt) Nov. 1989, rally speaker 1989–90; adviser to Pres. of Czechoslovakia 1989–90; deputy to House of People, Fed. Ass. 1990–92; Minister of Slovak Repub. 1990; Minister for Foreign Affairs, Govt of Slovak Repub. 1990–91; mem. Movt for Democratic Slovakia 1991–93 (resgnd) (Vice-Chair. 1991–93); Deputy Prime Minister, Slovak Repub. 1992–93, Minister for Foreign Affairs 1992–93, of Culture 1998–; Chair. Govt Council of Slovak Republic for Ethnic Groups 1992–93; Chair. Alliance of Democrats 1993–94, Independent Deputies Club 1993–; First Deputy Chair. Democratic Union of Slovakia 1994–2000; Vice-Chair. Slovak Democratic and Christian Union (SDCHU) 2000–; numerous roles on stage, in films, on TV, on radio; Merited Artist Award 1986 (returned award 1989). *Leisure interests:* family, sport, culture, theatre, golf. *Address:* Úrad vlády SR, nám. Slobody 1, 813 70 Bratislava 1, Slovakia. *Telephone:* (2) 544 10 978 (Ministry of Culture).

KNEALE, (Robert) Bryan (Charles), RA; British sculptor; b. 19 June 1930, Douglas, Isle of Man; s. of the late William Kneale and Lilian Kewley; m. Doreen Lister 1956 (died 1998); one s. (deceased) one d.; ed Douglas High School, Douglas School of Art, Isle of Man, Royal Acad. Schools; Tutor, RCA Sculpture School 1964, Sr Tutor 1980–85, Head Dept of Sculpture 1985–90; Head of Sculpture School, Hornsey 1967; Assoc. Lecturer, Chelsea School of Art 1970; Fellow RCA 1972, Sr Tutor 1980–85, Head of Sculpture Dept 1985–90; Prof. of Drawing, Royal Coll. of Art 1990–95, Sr Fellow 1995; Master of Sculpture RA 1982–85, Prof. 1985–90; mem. Fine Art Panels, Nat. Council for Art Design 1964–71, Arts Council 1971–73, CNAA 1974–82; Chair. Air and Space 1972–73; organized Sculpture '72, RA 1972, Battersea Park Silver Jubilee Sculpture 1977, Sade exhbn, Cork 1982, Sculpture for Westminster Cathedral 1999; exhbns at Redfern Gallery, John Moores, Sixth Congress of Int. Union of Architects, Art Aujourd'hui, Paris, Battersea Park Sculpture, Tate Gallery, Whitechapel Gallery, Hayward Gallery, Serpentine Gallery, Compass Gallery, Glasgow, 51 Gallery, Edin., Arts Council Tours 1966–71, Nat. History Museum, Royal Coll. of Art, Sala Uno, Rome, Royal West of England Acad., etc.; Collections Arts Council of GB, Contemporary Art Soc., Manx Museum, Nat. Galleries of Victoria, S Australia and NZ, City Art Galleries York, Nottingham, Manchester, Bradford, Leicester, Tate Gallery, Beaverbrook Foundation, Fredericton, Museum of Modern Art, São Paulo, Brazil, Bahía Museum, Brazil, Oriel Coll., Oxford, Museum of Modern Art, New York, Fitzwilliam Museum, Cambridge, New Arts Centre, Roche Court 2000, Mandria Park, Turin 2000, Bronze 2000, Holland Park, London 2000, Hart Gallery 2002; Rome Prize 1949, Leverhulme Award 1952, Young Artist Competition Prize 1955, Arts Council Purchase Award 1978. *Address:* 10A Muswell Road, London, N10 2BG, England. *Telephone:* (20) 8444-7617. *Fax:* (20) 8444-7617.

KNEŽEVIĆ, Stojan, DenM, DèsSc; Croatian professor of internal medicine; b. 6 Dec. 1923, Split; s. of Stevo Knežević and Marija Knežević; m. Jelena Konstantinović 1947; one s. one d.; ed Univ. of Zagreb; country doctor DZ-Sisak 1952–54; Specialist in Internal Medicine 1954–57; Asst Clinic for Internal Medicine, Zagreb 1957–63; interim St Antoine Hosp., Paris; Asst Prof., then Prof. of Medicine, Univ. of Zagreb-Croatia 1963–; Head of Gastroenterology Inst., Univ. of Zagreb; Ed.-in-chief, Acta Medica Croatica 1996–; mem. Senate, mem. Soc. européene de culture; Hon. mem. Croatian Acad. of Medical Sciences, Hrvatski Liječnički Zbor; Czecho-Slovak Medical Asscn, Croatian Anthropological Soc.; Award of the City of Zagreb 1966, Order of Danice Hrvatske (Rudjer Bošković) 2001. *Publications:* Klinička medicina 1959, Interna medicina 1970, Etika i medicina 1976, San je java snena 1977 (literary), Medicinske razglednice 1985, Slike koje pamtim 1989 (poetry), Medicinski susreti 1990, Medicina Starije Dobi 1990, Udžbenik Interne Medicine 1991, Veliki Medicinski Savjetnik, Misli i Poruke (Aforizmi) 1998, Izronci iz Tmine (poetry) 1999, Moje Dvorište u Ratu 2002, Navoji Vatre i Dima 2003. *Leisure interests:* writing, poetry, philosophy. *Address:* Smičiklasova 19, 10000 Zagreb, Croatia. *Telephone:* (1) 4614856.

KNIGHT, Andrew Stephen Bower; British editor and newspaper executive; b. 1 Nov. 1939; s. of M. W. B. Knight and S. E. F. Knight; m. 1st Victoria Catherine Brittain 1966 (divorced); one s.; m. 2nd Begum Sabiha Rumani Malik 1975 (divorced 1991); two d.; Ed. The Economist 1974–86; Chief Exec. Daily Telegraph 1986–89, Ed.-in-Chief 1987–89; Chair. News Int. PLC 1990–94; Chair. Ballet Rambert 1984–87; Chair. Times Newspaper Holdings 1990–94; Dir News Corpn 1991–, Rothschild Investment Trust CP 1996–; Chair. Shipston House Nursing 1996–; mem. Advisory Bd Center for Econ. Policy Research, Stanford Univ., USA 1981–; Gov. mem. Council of Man. Ditchley Foundation 1982–; Trustee Jerwood Charitable Foundation 2001–; now farms in Warwicks. and Dannevirke, NZ. *Address:* Compton Scorpion Manor, Shipston-on-Stour, Warwickshire, CV36 4PJ, England (Home).

KNIGHT, Douglas Maitland, PhD; American educational and corporate administrator; b. 8 June 1921, Cambridge, Mass.; s. of Claude Rupert and Fanny Sarah Douglas Brown Knight; m. Grace Wallace Nichols 1942; four s.; ed Yale Univ; Instructor of English, Yale 1946–47; Asst Prof. of English Literature, Yale 1947–53; Morse Research Fellow 1951–52; Pres. Lawrence Univ., Appleton, Wisconsin 1954–63; Pres. Duke Univ., Durham, N Carolina 1963–69, Pres. Emer. 1992–; Chair. Woodrow Wilson Nat. Fellowship Foundation; Chair. Nat. Library Comm. 1966–67; Div. Vice-Pres. Educational Devt, RCA, New York 1969–71, Div. Vice-Pres. Educ. Services 1971–72, Staff Vice-Pres. Educ. and Community Relations 1972–73, Consultant 1973–75; Pres. RCA, Iran 1971–72, Dir 1971–73; Pres. Social Econ. and Educ. Devt Inc. 1973–76, Questar Corpn 1976–99, Chair. 1999; Dir Near East Foundation 1975–80; Co-Founder and Trustee, Questar Library of Science and Art 1982– (Pres. 1996–99); Pres. Delaware River Mill Soc. 1992–97, Emer. 1997; mem. Nat. Comm. on Higher Educ. Issues 1981–84; Trustee, Solebury School, American Asscn for the Advancement of the Humanities; numerous hon. degrees. *Publications:* Alexander Pope and the Heroic Tradition 1951, The Dark Gate (poems) 1971; Ed. and contrib.: Medical Ventures and the University 1967; Ed. The Federal Government and Higher Education 1960; Joint Ed. Twickenham Edn of Iliad and Odyssey (trans. by Alexander Pope) 1965, Libraries at Large 1968, Street of Dreams: The Nature and Legacy of the 1960s 1989, Journeys in Time (poems) 1993, Education and the Civil Order: A History of the Woodrow Wilson National Fellowship Foundation 1995, The Dancer and the Dance: A Journey in Liberal Learning 2003. *Leisure interests:* farming, sailing. *Address:* Questar Corporation, 6204 Ingham Road, New Hope, PA 18938 (Office); Heritage Towers, #816, 200 Veterans Lane, Doylestown, PA 18901, USA (Home). *Telephone:* (215) 862-5277 (Office). *Fax:* (215) 862-5012 (Office).

KNIGHT, Sir Harold Murray, Kt, KBE, DSC, MComm; Australian banker; b. 13 Aug. 1919, Melbourne; s. of W. H. P. Knight; m. Gwenyth Catherine Pennington 1951; four s. one d.; ed Scotch Coll., Melbourne and Melbourne Univ; Commonwealth Bank of Australia 1936–40, 1946–55; served Australian Imperial Forces and Royal Australian Navy 1940–45 (awarded DSC); Statistics Div., Research and Statistics Dept of IMF 1955–59, Asst Chief 1957–59; Research Economist, Reserve Bank of Australia 1960, Asst Man. Investment Dept 1962–64, Man. Investment Dept 1964–68, Deputy Gov. Reserve Bank of Australia and Deputy Chair. of Bank's Bd 1968–75, Gov. and Chair. of Bd 1975–82; Dir Western Mining Corpn 1982–91, Mercantile Mutual Group 1983–89, Chair. 1985–89; Chair. I.B.J. Australia Bank Ltd 1985–92; Dir Angus and Coote Holdings Ltd 1986–93; mem. Police Bd, NSW 1988–89, 1991–93; Pres. Scripture Union, NSW 1983–2002; Hon. Visiting Fellow, Macquarie Univ. 1983–86, Councillor 1984–87, 1990–93; Hon. DLitt (Macquarie Univ.) 1995. *Publication:* Introducción al Análisis Monetario 1959. *Address:* 13 Tryon Road, Lindfield, NSW 2070, Australia.

KNIGHT, Malcolm, MA, PhD; Canadian economist; b. Windsor, Ont.; ed Univ. of Toronto, LSE, UK; teacher of econs Univ. of Toronto and LSE 1971–75; joined Research Dept., IMF 1975, served successively as economist in Financial Studies Div., Chief of External Adjustment Issues, Asst Dir of Research Dept for Developing Country Studies, Deputy Dir of Middle East Dept, Monetary and Exchange Affairs Dept, European Dept; fmrly COO Bank of Canada, Sr Deputy Gov. May 1999–; mem. Bd of Govs; fmrly adjunct Prof. Centre for Canadian Studies, Johns Hopkins Univ. School of Advanced Int. Studies, Virginia Polytechnic and State Univ.; academic visitor Centre for Labour Econs, LSE 1985–86; mem. Editorial Bd IMF Staff Papers 1987–97. *Publications include:* numerous publs in fields of macroecons, int. finance and banking. *Address:* Bank of Canada, 234 Wellington Street, Ottawa, Ont. K1A 0G9, Canada (Office). *Website:* www.bank-banque-canada.ca (Office).

KNIGHT, Philip H(ampson), MBA; American business executive; b. 24 Feb. 1938, Portland, Ore.; s. of William W. Knight and Lota Hatfield; m. Penelope Parks 1968; two s.; ed Univ. of Oregon, Stanford Univ.; First Lt US Army 1959–60; Chair., CEO, fmr Pres. Nike Inc., Beaverton, Ore. 1969–; Dir US–Asian Business Council, Washington; mem. American Inst. of Certified Public Accountants; Ore. Businessman of the Year 1982. *Leisure interests:* sports, reading, movies. *Address:* Nike Inc., 1 SW Bowerman Drive, Beaverton, OR 97005, USA (Office); One Bowerman Dr., Beaverton, OR 97005, USA (Home). *Telephone:* (503) 671-3598 (Office). *Fax:* (503) 644-6655 (Office). *E-mail:* lisa.mckillips@nike.com (Office).

KNIPPING VICTORIA, Eladio, LLB; Dominican diplomatist; b. 28 June 1933, Santiago de los Caballeros; s. of Elpidio Knipping and Luz Victoria; m. Soledad Knipping 1963; one s. one d.; ed Autonomous University of Santo Domingo, Diplomatic School of Spain, School of Int. Affairs, Madrid; Asst to Madrid Consulate 1963–65, Econ. Attaché, Netherlands 1966–68; Sec. Consultative Comm. Ministry of Foreign Affairs; Minister-Counsellor and Deputy Chief of Div. of UN Affairs, OAS and Int. Orgs. 1966–68, 1969–74; Minister-Counsellor Perm. Mission to UN, New York 1968–69, Amb. to Honduras 1974–78; Perm. Rep. to OAS 1979–83, 1987–95; Amb. (non-resident) to Barbados, Jamaica, St Lucia and Trinidad and Tobago 1990–, to Haiti 1995–97, to Panama 1997–2001; Perm. Rep. to UN, New York 1983–87; Pres. Juridical and Political Comm., OAS Perm. Council 1981–82, 1992–93; Dominican mem. Int. Court of Arbitration, The Hague; Del. UN III Conf. of Law of the Sea; Lecturer in Int. Law Pedro Henríquez Ureña Univ. 1969; f. Inst. Comparative Law; mem. Spanish-Portuguese-American and Philippine Inst. of Int. Law (Pres. 1990–92); UN Adlai Stevenson Fellow. *Leisure interests:*

reading, listening to music. *Address:* c/o Secretariat of State for External Relations, Avda Independencia 752, Santa Domingo, ON, Dominican Republic.

KNÍŽÁK, Milan; Czech multimedia artist, writer, art theorist and musician; b. 19 April 1940, Plzeň; s. of Karel Knížák and Emilie Knížáková; m. 1st Soňa Švecová 1967; m., 2nd Jarka Charvátová 1970; m., 3rd Marie Geislerová 1975; ed Acad. of Fine Arts, Charles Univ., Prague; f. Aktual group; prosecuted and imprisoned on numerous occasions 1957–89 mostly for his art activities; in USA (at invitation of Fluxus group of artists) 1968–70; Univ. Prof.; Rector Acad. of Fine Arts, Prague 1990–97; Dir Gen. Nat. Gallery Prague 1999–; mem. Czech TV Council 2001–; awards include DAAD Berlin, Barkenhoff Worpswede, Germany, Schloss Bleckede, Germany, Schloss Solitude, Germany, 5th Inter-Triennale Wrocław, Poland; Medal 1st Degree, Ministry for Educ. and Physical Training 1997. *Exhibitions include:* Prague 1998, 2000 and c. 100 one-man shows in Germany, Italy, USA, Poland, Belgium, Hungary, Slovakia, France, Australia, Austria, Czech Repub.; numerous group exhbns. *Films:* Stone Ceremony, Material Events, Kill Yourself and Fly. *Albums:* Broken Music 1979, Obřad hořící mysli (The Rite of a Burning Mind) 1992, Navrhuju krysy (I Propose the Rats) 2002. *Plays:* Also in my Belly Grows a Tree, Heads. *Radio Play:* Adamits. *Television:* Kill Yourself and Fly (a film about M. Knížák) 1991. *Publications:* Zeremonien 1971, Action as a Life Style 1986, Neo Knížák 1991, Nový ráj (New Paradise) 1996, Bez důvodu (Without Reason) 1996, Jeden z možných postojů, jak být s umění (One Way to Exist with Art) 1998, Skutečnost, že jsem se narodil, beru jako výzvu (The Fact I was Born I Take as a Challenge) 1999, Tady ve Skotsku (Here in Scotland) 2000, Básně 1974–2001 (Poems 1974–2001) 2001, Vedle umění (Close to the Arts) (with J. Lancaster) 2002, and many others. *Leisure interests:* collecting old marionettes and scientific research on them. *Address:* AVU, U Akademie 4, 17000 Prague 7, Czech Republic; Národní galerie v Praze, Palác Kinských, Staroměstské naměstí 12, 11015 Prague 1 (Office). *Telephone:* (22) 2329331 (Office); (602) 321208 (Home). *Fax:* (22) 2324641 (Office); (22) 4919782 (Home). *E-mail:* genreditel@ngprague.cz (Office). *Website:* www.ngprague.cz (Office); www.avu.cz (Office).

KNOLL, József; Hungarian pharmacologist; b. 30 May 1925, Kassa; s. of Jakab Knoll and Blanka Deutscher; m. Dr Berta Knoll; one d.; ed Medical Univ., Budapest; Asst Lecturer Univ. Pharmacological Inst.; Lecturer Medical Univ. 1958, Prof. and Head 1962–95, Vice-Rector 1964–70; Corresp. mem. Hungarian Acad. of Sciences 1970, mem. 1979–; Gen. Sec. Hungarian Pharmacological Soc. 1962–67, Pres. 1967–83, Hon. Pres. 1984–; Chair. Nat. Drug Admin. Cttee and Drug Research Cttee of the Acad. of Sciences; Vice-Pres. Medical Sciences Section, Hungarian Acad. of Sciences 1967–76; mem. Leopoldina Deutsche Akad. der Naturwissenschaften, Halle 1974–; councillor Int. Union of Pharmacological Sciences 1981–84, First Vice-Pres. 1984–87; Foreign mem., Polish Acad. of Arts and Sciences 1995; mem. editorial bd of numerous int. pharmacological periodicals; Hon. mem. Pharmacological Socs. of Czechoslovakia, Bulgaria, Poland and of Italy; Hon. FRSM 1990; Dr hc (Medizinische Akad., Magdeburg) 1984, (Bologna Univ.) 1989; Nat. Prize of Hungary 1985, Award for Distinguished Service in European Pharmacology 1999, Award for Outstanding Contribs to Anti-Aging Medicine 2001. *Achievements:* devt of (-)-deprenyl (Selegiline) – a drug used worldwide. *Publications:* Theory of Active Reflexes 1969, Handbook of Pharmacology, nine edns. since 1965; over 800 papers in int. trade journals; 53 patents. *Leisure interest:* visual arts. *Address:* Semmelweis University, Faculty of General Medicine, Department of Pharmacology and Pharmacotherapy, Budapest 1089, Nagyvárad tér 4, Hungary. *Telephone:* (1) 210-4405 (Office); (1) 329-3805 (Home). *Fax:* (1) 210-4405. *E-mail:* jozsefknoll@hotmail.com (Office).

KNOPF, Alfred, Jr., AB; American publisher (retd); b. 17 June 1918, New York; s. of Alfred A. Knopf and Blanche Wolf; m. Alice Laine 1952; one s. two d.; ed Union Coll.; with Atheneum Publishers 1959–88, Chair. 1964–88; fmr Vice-Chair. Scribner Book Co.; fmr Sr Vice-Pres. Macmillan Publishing Co. *Address:* 530 East 72nd Street, Apartment 18F, New York, NY 10021, USA (Home).

KNOPFLER, Mark, OBE; British guitarist and songwriter; b. 12 Aug. 1949; s. of late Erwin Knopfler and of Louisa Knopfler; m. Lourdes Salomone 1983; ed Leeds Univ.; fmr journalist Yorkshire Evening Post; f. Dire Straits 1977, guitarist; first concert 1977; group has since toured worldwide; albums include: Making Movies, Brothers in Arms, On Every Street; best-known songs include Romeo and Juliet, Money For Nothing, Calling Elvis; has also toured with Eric Clapton and recorded with Chet Atkins; formed own ad hoc band, Notting Hillbillies; Hon. DMus (Leeds) 1995; awards: Ivor Novello, BRIT, MTV, Grammy. *Address:* c/o Damage Management, 16 Lambton Place, London, W11 2SH, England. *Telephone:* (20) 7229-2992. *Fax:* (20) 7229-2213.

KNOPOFF, Leon, MS, PhD; American professor of physics and geophysics; b. 1 July 1925, Los Angeles, California; m. Joanne Van Cleef 1961; one s. two d.; ed California Inst. of Tech; Asst Prof., Assoc. Prof. of Physics, Miami Univ. 1948–50; mem. staff Univ. of Calif. (LA) 1950–, Prof. of Geophysics 1957–, of Physics 1961–, Research Musicologist 1963–, Assoc. Dir Inst. of Geophysics and Planetary Physics 1972–86; Prof. of Geophysics, Calif. Inst. of Tech. 1962–92; Visiting Prof. Technische Hochschule, Karlsruhe (Germany) 1966; Chair. US Upper Mantle Cttee 1963–71, Sec.-Gen. Int. Upper Mantle Cttee 1963–71; Nat. Science Foundation Sr Postdoctoral Fellow 1960–61; Guggenheim Foundation Fellowship (Cambridge) 1976–77; Visiting Prof., Harvard Univ. 1972, Univ. of Chile, Santiago 1973; Chair. Int. Cttee on Mathematical

Geophysics 1971–75; H. Jeffreys Lecturer, Royal Astronomical Soc. 1976; mem. NAS, American Philosophical Soc., American Physical Soc., Royal Astronomical Soc.; Fellow, American Acad. of Arts and Sciences, American Geophysical Union; Hon. mem. Seismological Soc. of America; Int. Co-operation Year Medal (Canada) 1965, Wiechert Medal, German Geophysical Soc. 1978, Gold Medal of the Royal Astronomical Soc. 1979, Medal of the Seismological Soc. of America 1990. *Publications:* The Crust and Upper Mantle of the Pacific Area (co-ed.) 1968, The World Rift System (co-ed.); chapters in Physics and Chemistry of High Pressures (ed. R. L. Bradley) 1963, Physical Acoustics (ed. W. P. Mason) 1965, The Earth's Mantle (ed. T. Gaskell) 1967, The Megatectonics of Oceans and Continents (ed. H. Johnson and B. L. Smith); more than 300 papers in professional journals. *Leisure interests:* mountaineering, gardening, playing piano and harpsichord. *Address:* Institute of Geophysics and Planetary Physics, University of California, Los Angeles, CA 90095, USA. *Telephone:* (310) 825-1885.

KNORRE, Dmitri Georgievich; Russian chemist and biochemist; b. 28 July 1926, Leningrad; s. of Georgy F. Knorre and Elena A. Knorre; m. Valeria L. Knorre 1959 (died 1996); one s. two d.; ed Moscow Chemical-Technological Inst.; worked in USSR (now Russian) Acad. of Sciences Inst. of Chemical Physics 1947–61, then in all grades to Head Dept of Biochem. at Acad. of Sciences, Inst. of Organic Chem. 1961–84, Dir at Acad. Sciences Inst. of Bio-organic Chem., Novosibirsk 1984–96; Adviser to Pres. Acad. of Sciences 1996–; also Prof. of Univ. of Novosibirsk 1961–, Dean 1961–83; Corresp. mem. of Acad. 1968–81, mem. 1981, Acad.-Sec. Dept of Biochem. and Biophysics 1988–99; Hon. PhD Chem. Science (Novosibirsk Univ.) 1967; Lenin Prize, M. Shemyakin Prize and other awards. *Publications:* Chemical Kinetics, Physical Chemistry, Biological Chemistry. *Leisure interest:* hiking. *Address:* Institute of Bio-organic Chemistry, Prospekt Lavrenteva 8, 630090 Novosibirsk (Office); ul. Voyevodskogo 7, 630090 Novosibirsk, Russia (Home). *Telephone:* (3832) 36-06-32 (Office); (3832) 35-57-03 (Home). *Fax:* (3832) 33-36-77 (Office).

KNOWLES, Jeremy Randall, CBE, MA, DPhil, FRS; British/American professor of chemistry and biochemistry; b. 28 April 1935, Rugby; s. of the late Kenneth G. J. C. Knowles and of Dorothy H. Swingler; m. Jane S. Davis 1960; three s.; ed Magdalen Coll. School, Balliol Coll., Merton Coll. and Christ Church Oxford; Research Assoc. Calif. Inst. of Tech. 1961–62; Fellow, Wadham Coll. Oxford 1962–74 (Hon. Fellow 1990); Univ. Lecturer, Univ. of Oxford 1966–74; Amory Houghton Prof. of Chem. and Biochem. (fmrly of Chem.), Harvard Univ. 1974–, Dean Faculty of Arts and Sciences 1991–2002; Fellow, American Acad. of Arts and Sciences 1982; Foreign Assoc. NAS 1988; mem. American Philosophical Soc. 1988; Hon. Fellow Balliol Coll. 1984, Wadham Coll. 1990, Royal Soc. of Chem. 1991; Dr hc (Univ. of Edinb 1992, (ETH, Zurich) 2001; Charmian Medal, Royal Soc. of Chem. 1980, Alfred Bader Award (USA) 1989, Cope Scholar Award (USA) 1989, Prelog Medal 1989, Davy Medal, Royal Soc. 1991, Repligen Award (USA) 1992, Robert A. Welch Award in Chem. 1995, Nakanishi Prize (USA) 1999, Harvard Medal 2002. *Publications:* research papers and reviews in learned journals. *Address:* Wadsworth House, Harvard University, Cambridge, MA 02138 (Office); 67 Francis Avenue, Cambridge, MA 02138, USA (Home).

KNOWLES, Tony, BA; American politician and retailer; b. 1 Jan. 1943, Tulsa; m. Susan Morris; two s. one d.; ed Yale Univ.; US Army, Vietnam 1961–65; owner and Man. The Works, Anchorage 1968–, Downtown Deli, Anchorage 1978–; Mayor Municipality of Anchorage 1981–87; Gov. of Alaska 1994–2002; mem. Citizen's Cttee for Planned Growth and Devt of Anchorage 1972, Borough Ass., Anchorage 1975–79; Bd dirs. KAKM TV Station, Anchorage Chamber of Commerce; mem. numerous sports cttees; Child Advocate of the Year, American Child Welfare League 1999. *Address:* c/o Office of the Governor, PO Box 110001, Juneau, AK 99811, USA.

KNOWLES, William S.; American scientist; b. 1917, Taunton, Mass.; m. Nancy Knowles 1945; ed Harvard and Columbia Univs.; chemist with Monsanto Co. 1942–86; during career made breakthrough in Devt of drug treatment for Parkinson's Disease; Nobel Prize in Chemistry Nov. 2001 (Jt recipient). *Leisure interests:* cycling, environmental issues. *Address:* c/o Monsanto Company, 800 North Lindbergh Boulevard, St Louis, MO 63167, USA (Office). *Telephone:* (314) 694-1000 (Office). *Website:* www.monsanto.com (Office).

KNOWLING, Robert E., Jr; American computer engineer and business executive; b. 1955, Ind.; m.; four c.; ed Wabash Coll.; staff mem. Indiana Bell (now part of Ameritech) 1970s; Head of Eng. Devt Team Ameritech 1992, later Vice-Pres. Network Operations; Exec. Vice-Pres. of Operations and Techs US West; Pres. and CEO Covad Communications, Calif. 1998–2001; Chair. and CEO Information Access Technologies (IAT) Inc. 2001–; mem. Bd Dirs Hewlett-Packard Co. Inc., Broadmedia, Ariba, Heidrick & Struggles Int., Juvenile Diabetes Foundation Int. *Leisure interest:* YMCA volunteer. *Address:* Internet Access Technologies Inc., 5450 Northwest Central, Suite 300, Houston, TX 77092, USA (Office). *Website:* www.iat.com (Office).

KNOX, Selby Albert Richard, PhD, DSc, CChem, FRSC; British professor of chemistry; b. 24 Sept. 1944, Newcastle-upon-Tyne; s. of George H. Knox and Elsie Knox; m. Julie D. Edwards 1979; one s. two d.; ed Rutherford Grammar School, Newcastle-upon-Tyne and Univ. of Bristol; Research Fellow, Univ. of Calif. Los Angeles 1970–71; lecturer, Univ. of Bristol 1972–83, Reader 1983–90, Prof. of Inorganic Chem. 1990–96, Head Dept of Chem. 1992–2001, Head Inorganic and Materials Chem. 2001–, Alfred Capper Pass Prof. of

Chem. 1996–; Corday-Morgan Medal and Prize 1980; Royal Soc. of Chem. Award for Chem. of Noble Metals and their compounds 1986; Royal Soc. of Chem. Tilden Lecturer 1992–93. *Publications:* over 160 scientific papers in organometallic chemistry. *Leisure interests:* fly fishing, sailing, skiing. *Address:* School of Chemistry, University of Bristol, Bristol, BS8 1TS (Office); 50 Druid Stoke Avenue, Stoke Bishop, Bristol, BS9 1DQ, England (Home). *Telephone:* (117) 928-7650 (Office); (117) 9685397 (Home). *Fax:* (117) 929-0509. *E-mail:* selby.knox@bris.ac.uk.

KNUSSEN, (Stuart) Oliver, CBE; British composer and conductor; b. 12 June 1952, Glasgow; s. of Stuart Knussen and Ethelyn Jane Alexander; m. Susan Freedman 1972; one d.; ed Watford Field School, Watford Boys Grammar School, Purcell School; pvt. composition study with John Lambert 1963–68; conducted first performance of his First Symphony with London Symphony Orchestra 1968; Fellowships to Berkshire Music Center, Tanglewood, USA 1970, 1971, 1973; Caird Travelling Scholarship 1971; Head of Contemporary Music Activities, Tanglewood Music Center 1986–93; Co-Artistic Dir Aldeburgh Festival 1983–98; Music Dir London Sinfonietta 1998–2002; Hon. mem. American Acad. of Arts and Letters 1994, Royal Philharmonic Soc. 2002; Dr hc (Royal Scottish Acad. of Music and Drama) 2002; Countess of Munster Awards 1964, 1965, 1967; Peter Stuyvesant Foundation Award 1965; Watney-Sargent Award for Young Conductors 1969; Margaret Grant Composition Prize (for Symphony No. 2), Tanglewood 1971; Arts Council Bursaries 1979, 1981; winner, first Park Lane Group Composer Award 1982. *Compositions include:* operas: Where the Wild Things Are 1979–81, Higglety Pigglety Pop! 1984–85; symphonies: Symphony in one movement 1969, No. 2 (soprano and small orchestra) 1970–71, No. 3 1973–79; other works for chamber ensemble and for voice and ensemble, for orchestra and for piano. *Leisure interests:* cinema, record collecting, whale watching. *Address:* c/o Harrison/Parrott Ltd, 12 Penzance Place, London, W11 4PA (Office); c/o Faber Music Ltd, 3 Queen Square, London, WC1N 3AR, England.

KNUTH, Donald Ervin, MS, PhD; American professor of computer science; b. 10 Jan. 1938, Milwaukee, Wis.; s. of Ervin Henry Knuth and Louise Marie (née Bohning) Knuth; m. Nancy Jill Carter 1961; one s. one d.; ed Case Inst. of Tech., California Inst. of Tech.; Asst Prof. Math. Calif. Inst. of Tech. 1963–66, Assoc. Prof. 1966–68; Prof. of Computer Science, Stanford Univ. 1968–77, Fletcher Jones Prof. of Computer Science 1977–89, Prof. of Art of Computer Programming 1990–93, Prof. Emer. 1993–; mem. NAS, Nat. Acad. of Eng; Foreign mem. French, Norwegian, Bavarian Science Acads; 27 hon. degrees, including (Paris) 1986, (Oxford) 1988, (St Petersburg) 1992; Nat. Medal of Science 1979; Steele Prize, American Math. Soc. 1986; Franklin Medal, Franklin Inst. of Philadelphia 1988, Harvey Prize, Israel Inst. of Tech. 1995; numerous awards, John Von Neumann Medal, IEEE 1995; Kyoto Prize 1996. *Publications:* The Art of Computer Programming, (Vol. 1) 1968, (Vol. 2) 1969, (Vol. 3) 1973, Surreal Numbers 1974, Mariages Stables 1976, Computers and Typesetting (5 Vols) 1986, Concrete Mathematics 1988, 3:16 Bible Texts Illuminated 1990, Literate Programming 1992, The Stanford Graph-Base 1993, Selected Papers on Computer Science 1996, Digital Typography 1999, MMIXware 1999, Selected Papers on Analysis of Algorithms 2000, Things a Computer Scientist Rarely Talks About 2001, Selected Papers on Computer Languages 2003, Selected Papers on Discrete Mathematics 2003. *Leisure interests:* piano and organ playing, browsing in libraries. *Address:* Computer Science Department, Stanford University, Stanford, CA 94305, USA (Office). *Telephone:* (650) 723-4367 (Office). *Website:* www-cs-faculty.stanford.edu/~knuth (Office).

KOBAYASHI, Taiyu; Japanese company executive; b. 13 June 1912, Hyogo Prefecture; m. Nagae Sano 1938; two s.; ed Kyoto Univ.; joined Fuji Electric Co. 1935; joined Fujitsu Ltd 1935, Dir 1964, Man. Dir 1969, Exec. Dir 1972, Exec. Vice-Pres. 1975, Pres. 1976–81, Chair 1981; Pres. Communications Industries Asscn of Japan 1976–78; Pres. Japan Electronic Industry Devt Asscn 1979–; Chair. Eng Research Asscn of Opto-Electronics Applied System 1981–; Purple Ribbon Award with Medal of Honour, Blue Ribbon Award with Medal of Honour. *Leisure interests:* gardening, golf. *Address:* 674 Nitta Kannami-cho, Tagata-gun, Shizuoka, Japan (Home).

KÖBBEN, André J. F., PhD; Netherlands professor of cultural anthropology and administrator; b. 3 April 1925, 's-Hertogenbosch; m. Agatha M. van Vessem 1953; one s. two d.; ed Municipal Gymnasium and Univ. of Amsterdam; Prof. of Cultural Anthropology, Univ. of Amsterdam 1955–76; Visiting Prof. Univ. of Pittsburgh 1972; Cleveringa Prof. Univ. of Leiden 1980–81; Prof. Erasmus Univ. 1981–90; Dir Centre for the Study of Social Conflicts 1976–90; Curl Bequest Prize, Royal Anthropological Inst. 1952; mem. Royal Netherlands Acad. of Science 1975; Hon. mem. Anthropological Soc. 1986. *Publications:* Le Planteur noir 1956, Van primitieven tot medeburgers 1964, Why exceptions? The logic of cross-cultural analysis 1967, Why Slavery? 1997, De Onwelkome Boodschap (The Unwelcome Message) 1999, Goldhagen Versus Browning 2002, Het Gerecht met de Engel (The Struggle with the Angel) 2003, and many others. *Address:* Libellenveld 2, 2318 VG Leiden, Netherlands. *Telephone:* (71) 5215369.

KOBZON, Iosif Davydovich, DPhil; Russian singer and politician; b. 11 Sept. 1937, Chasov Yar, Ukraine; m. Nelly Kobzon; one s. one d.; ed Moscow Gnessin Pedagogical Inst. of Music; army service 1956–59, soloist Ensemble of Dance and Song of Caucasian Mil. command 1957–59; soloist All-Union Radio and TV Co. 1959–62; soloist Moskonzert 1962–89; Artistic Dir and Chair., Vocal and Variety Show Faculty Gnessin Inst. (now Acad.) of Music

1989–, Prof. 1992; soloist and Artistic Dir Concert Co. Moskva; retd from concert activity 1997; Pres. Jt Stock Co. Moscovit 1990–97; USSR People's Deputy 1989–92; mem. State Duma (Parl.) 1997–98 (suspended membership in protest against anti-Semitic declarations by Communist deputies), 1999–; Deputy Chair. Comm. on Culture; mem. Regions of Russia group; Order of Courage 2002; People's Artist of USSR, Russia, Ukraine, Checheno-Ingushetia and Dagestan Autonomous Repub.; USSR State Prize 1984. *Address:* State Duma, Okhotny Ryad 1, 103265 Moscow, Russia (Office). *Telephone:* (095) 292-17-53 (Office); (095) 292-17-53 (Home). *Fax:* (095) 292-73-85 (Office).

KOÇ, Rahmi M.; Turkish business executive; Chair. Koç Holdings AS; fmr Pres. ICC. *Address:* Koç Holdings AS, Nakkaştepe Aziz Bey Sok. 1, 80207 Kuzguncuk, Istanbul, Turkey.

KOČÁRNÍK, Ivan, CSc; Czech politician and business executive; b. 29 Nov. 1944, Třebonín, Kutna Hora Dist; m.; two d., one s.; ed Prague Inst. of Econs; worked at Research Inst. of Financial and Credit System until 1985; Dir Research Dept Fed. Ministry of Finance 1985–89; Deputy Minister of Finance of Czechoslovakia 1990; mem. Civic Democratic Party (ODS); Vice-Premier and Minister of Finance of Czech Repub. 1992–97; Chair. Council of Econ. and Social Agreement 1992–97; Chair. Bd Czech Insurance Co. 1997–2001, Chair. Supervisory Bd 2000–; Best Minister of Finance in 1994, awarded by magazine Central European 1995. *Leisure interests:* tennis, skiing, hiking, music. *Address:* Česká pojišťovna a.s. (Czech Insurance Company), Na Pankráci 1658/121, 140 21 Prague 4, Czech Republic. *Telephone:* (2) 61319139 (Office). *Fax:* (2) 61319289 (Office). *E-mail:* ikocarnik@cpoj.cz (Office).

KOCH, Edward I., LLB; American politician, local government official and lawyer; b. 12 Dec. 1924, New York; s. of Louis Koch and Joyce Silpe; ed City Coll. of New York and New York Univ. Law School; served Second World War in US Army; admitted to New York bar 1949; sole practice law, New York 1949–64; Sr partner Koch, Lankenau, Schwartz & Kovner 1965–69; mem. Council, New York 1967–68, Mayor 1978–90; partner Robinson, Silverman, Pearce, Aronsohn and Berman, New York 1990–; mem. US House of Reps. from New York, 17th Dist 1969–72, 18th District 1973–77; mem. House Appropriations Cttee; Sec. New York Congressional Del.; Democratic Dist Leader, Greenwich Village 1963–65, mem. Village Ind. Democrats; Visiting Fellow, Urban Research Center, New York Univ. 1990–91; TV commentator for Fox 5; columnist New York Post 1990–; film critic for 4 newspapers; appears in film segment Oedipus Wrecks 1989. *Publications:* Mayor (autobiog.) 1984, Politics 1985, His Eminence and Hizzoner (with HE Cardinal J. O'Connor) 1989, All the Best: Letters from a Feisty Mayor 1990, Citizen Koch 1991, Ed Koch on Everything 1994, Murder at City Hall 1995, Murder on Broadway 1996, Murder on 34th Street 1997, The Senator Must Die 1998, Giuliani Nasty Man 1999, I'm Not Done Yet 1999. *Address:* Robinson, Silverman, Pearce, Aronsohn and Berman, 1290 Avenue of the Americas, New York, NY 10104, USA.

KOCH, Marita; German athlete; b. 18 Feb. 1957, Wismar; m. Wolfgang Meier 1987; holds world record for 400m (47.60) Canberra 1985; set world indoor records for 50m and 60m; became second fastest-ever female 100m runner (10.83); set four world records for 200m (best was 21.71 in 1979 and 1984), seven world records for 400m; winner Olympic gold medal 400m 1980, world title 200m 1983; retd 1987; owner of sports shop.

KOCH, Roland; German politician and lawyer; b. 24 March 1958; m.; two c.; Fed. State Chair. CDU Hessen 1998–; Minister-Pres. Hessen 1999–. *Publications:* Gemeinsam Chancen nutzen, Vision 21, Aktive Bürgergesellschaft (Hsg) *Address:* Bierstadter Str. 2, 65189 Wiesbaden, Germany. *E-mail:* r .koch@ltg.hessen.de (Office). *Website:* www.roland-koch.de (Office).

KOCHARIAN, Robert Sedrakovich; Armenian politician; b. 31 Aug. 1954, Stepanakert; s. of Sedrack S. Kocharian and Emma A. Dhanian; m. Bella L. Kocharian; two s. one d.; ed Erevan Polytech. Inst.; engineer and electrotechnician Karabakh Silk Production Factory, Stepanakert 1981–87; concurrently sec. factory CP Cttee 1987–89; one of founders Karabakh Movt; Deputy to Armenian Supreme Council 1989–94; left CP 1989; after proclamation of 'Nagorny-Karabakh Repub.' in Azerbaijan 2 Sept. 1991 and Referendum 10 Dec. 1991 elected to Supreme Council 'Nagorny-Karabakh Repub.' in Azerbaijan; Chair. State Cttee of Defence and Leader of Repub. 1992–94; elected First Pres. of 'Nagorny-Karabakh Repub.' in Azerbaijan by Supreme Council 1994–; Prime Minister of Repub. of Armenia 1997–98, Pres. 1998–. *Leisure interests:* basketball, jazz. *Address:* House of Government, Marshal Bagramian prosp. 19, 375016 Yerevan, Armenia. *Telephone:* (2) 52-54-00; (2) 52-02-04. *Fax:* (2) 15-11-52.

KOCHERGA, Anatoly Ivanovich; Ukrainian opera singer (bass); b. 9 July 1947, Vinnitsa; s. of Ivan Kocherga and Maria Kocherga; m. Lina Kocherga 1985; one d.; ed Kiev Conservatoire; studied at La Scala, Milan; soloist, Shevchenko Opera and Ballet, Kiev 1972–, also Vienna State Opera 1990–; Glinka Prize 1971, Tchaikovsky Prize 1974, USSR People's Artist 1983. *Major roles include:* Boris Godunov, Galitsky (Borodin's Prince Igor), Don Basilio (Barber of Seville), Mephistopheles (Gounod's Faust), Don Carlos (Verdi), Don Giovanni (Mozart), Khovanshchina (Mussorgsky), Dosiphey (Khovanshchina), Nilakanta (Lakmé); USSR People's Artist 1983. *Leisure interest:* tennis. *Address:* Gogolevskaho 37, Korp. 2, Apt. 47, Kiev 254053, Ukraine.

KOCHERGIN, Eduard Stepanovich; Russian theatrical designer; b. 22 Sept. 1937, Leningrad; s. of Stepan Kochergin and Bronislava (née Odinets)

Kochergina; m. Inna Gabai 1962; one s.; ed Leningrad Theatre Art Inst., theatre production faculty (pupil of N. Akimov and T. Bruni); chief set-designer in various Leningrad theatres 1960–; chief set-designer at Gorky (now Tovstonogov) Bolshoi Drama Theatre 1972; worked as set-designer, Maly Drama Theatre and in Japan, USA, Poland, Germany, Finland, Canada, France; Prof. Y.I. Repin Inst. of Painting 1983–; mem. Russian Acad. of Fine Arts 1991; State Prize 1974, 1978; three Golden and two Silver awards, int. exhbns. theatre design Novisad 1975, 1978, Prague 1975, 1979, 1987; Honoured Artist of Russia. *Leisure interest:* research in Russian pre-Christian culture and symbolism. *Address:* Tovstonogov Bolshoi Drama Theatre, Fontanka 65, 191023 St Petersburg, Russia. *Telephone:* (812) 352-89-33 (Office); (812) 351-23-79 (Home). *Fax:* (812) 110-47-10.

KOCHETKOV, Nikolay Konstantinovich; Russian chemist; b. 18 May 1915, Moscow; s. of Konstantin Kochetkov and Marie Kochetkova; m. Dr. Vera Volodina 1945; one s. one d.; ed M. V. Lomonosov Inst. of Fine Chem. Tech.; Asst, Chemistry Dept of Moscow Univ. 1945–52, Dozent 1952–56, Prof. 1956–60; Head of Dept of Organic Synthesis, Inst. of Pharmacology 1953–60; Deputy Dir, Head of Nucleic Acids and Carbohydrates Laboratory, Inst. of Natural Products 1960–66; Dir, Head of Carbohydrates Laboratory, Zelinsky Inst. of Organic Chem. 1966–88, Dir Emer. 1988–; Corresp. mem. USSR (now Russian) Acad. of Medical Sciences 1957–; Corresp. mem. USSR (now Russian) Acad. of Sciences 1960–79, mem. 1979–; mem. Soc. de Chimie 1972–, Polish Acad. of Sciences 1988; Haworth Medal (Royal Soc. of Chem.) 1989, Lenin Prize 1989, Nat. Prize of Demidov Foundation 1993, Order of Lenin, Hero of Socialist Labour, Lomonosov Great Gold Medal, Russian Acad. of Science 1995 and other decorations. *Publications:* Chemistry of Natural Products 1961, Chemistry of Carbohydrates 1967, Organic Chemistry of Nucleic Acids 1970, Radiation Chemistry of Sugars 1973, Carbohydrates in the Synthesis of Natural Products 1984, Synthesis of Polysaccharides 1995. *Address:* Zelinsky Institute of Organic Chemistry, Leninsky Prospekt 47, Moscow B-334; Leninsky Prospekt 13,6 Moscow, Russia (Home). *Telephone:* (095) 137-61-48 (Office); (095) 237-48-16 (Home). *Fax:* (095) 135-53-28.

KOCHI, Jay K., PhD; American professor of chemistry; b. 17 May 1927, Los Angeles; s. of Tsuruzo Kochi; m. Marion K. Kiyono 1961; one s. one d.; ed Cornell and Iowa State Univs.; Instructor Harvard Univ. 1952–55; Nat. Inst. of Health Special Fellow, Univ. of Cambridge (UK) 1955–56; Shell Devt Co. Emeryville, Calif. 1956–62; Case Western Univ., Cleveland, Ohio 1962–69; with Ind. Univ. 1969–84; Robert A. Welch Distinguished Prof. of Chem. Univ. of Houston, Tex. 1984–; chemical consultant 1964–; mem. NAS; J. F. Norris Award, American Chem. Soc. 1981; A. C. Cope Scholar Award, American Chem. Soc. *Publications:* three books and more than 500 research papers. *Address:* Department of Chemistry, University of Houston, University Park, Houston, TX 77204-5641; 4372 Faculty Lane, Houston, TX 77004, USA (Home). *E-mail:* jkochi@mail.uh.edu (Office).

KOCK, Manfred; German ecclesiastic; b. 14 Sept. 1936, Burgsteinfurt; s. of Walter Kock and Erika Braunschweig; m. Gisela Stephany 1960; two s. one d.; ed Univs. of Bethel, Münster and Tübingen; pastor, Recklinghausen 1962–70, Cologne 1970–97; Chair. Evangelical Church in the Rhineland 1997–, Council of the Evangelical Church in Germany 1997–. *Address:* Herrenhäuser Str. 12, 30419 Hanover, Germany (Office). *Telephone:* (511) 27960 (Office). *Fax:* (511) 2796755 (Office). *E-mail:* rv@ekd.de (Office). *Website:* www.ekd.de (Office).

KOCSIS, Zoltán; Hungarian pianist, conductor and composer; b. 30 May 1952, Budapest; s. of Ottó Kocsis and Mária Mátyás; m. 1st Adrienne Hauser 1986; one s. one d.; m. 2nd Erika Tóth 1997; one s.; ed Budapest Music Acad. (under Pál Kadosa); Asst Prof. Music Acad. Budapest 1976–79, Prof. 1979–; Producer of Archive Section of Hungaroton (record co.); Co-founder, Artistic Co-Dir Budapest Festival Orchestra 1983–96; Music Dir Hungarian Nat. Philharmonic Orchestra 1998–; First Prize, Beethoven Piano Competition, Hungarian Radio and Television 1970, Liszt Prize 1973, Kossuth Prize 1978; Merited Artist's title 1984. *Performances:* has appeared with Berlin Philharmonic Orchestra and performed in Germany, USSR, Austria and Czechoslovakia 1971; toured USA together with Dezsö Ranki (q.v.) and Budapest Symphony Orchestra (under George Lehel) 1971; recitals in Netherlands, Paris, London and Ireland 1972; concerts in Norway, with Svyatoslav Richter in France and Austria, with Claudio Abbado and London Symphony Orchestra and at BBC Promenade Concerts in London and Festival Estival, Paris 1977, Edin. Festival 1978. *Publications:* Miscellaneous Publs, Arrangements for Piano and 2 Pianos, etc. *Leisure interest:* photography. *Address:* Hungarian National Philharmonic Orchestra, 1051 Budapest V, Vörösmarty tér I (Office); Ringló u. 60/A, 1116 Budapest, Hungary (Home). *Telephone:* (1) 4116620; (1) 4116624 (Office). *Fax:* (1) 4116624 (Office); (1) 424-5917 (Home). *E-mail:* z.kocsis@elender.hu (Office).

KODAMANOĞLU, Nuri, MSc; Turkish politician; b. 16 Aug. 1923, Ulukişla-Niğde; s. of Fazil and Hatice Kodamanoğlu; m. Ayten Unal Kodamanoğlu 1951; ed Istanbul Univ.; fmr civil servant, Ministry of Educ.; later Under-Sec. Ministry of Educ.; Deputy to Grand Nat. Assembly; Minister of Energy and Natural Resources 1972; Adviser to the Prime Minister 1988–; Chief Adviser to the Pres. 1991–; mem. Business Admin. Inst., Faculty of Political Science, Univ. of Ankara; mem. Ataturk Research Centre; mem. Bd of Dirs. Turkish Petroleum Corpn; mem. Consultative Cttee Asscn of Turkish Parliamentarians 1995–; Consultant, Asscn of Turkish Chambers of Commerce, Chambers of Ind. and Exchange. *Publications:* Principles of New Education 1954,

Education in Turkey 1963; various articles and reports. *Leisure interests:* handicrafts, gardening. *Address:* Bükreş Sokak No. 6 Daire 8, Cankaya, 06680 Ankara, Turkey. *Telephone:* (312) 427-15-15.

KODEŠ, Jan; Czech tennis player; b. 1 March 1946, Prague; s. of Jan Kodeš and Vlasta Richterová-Kodešová; m. 1st Lenka Rösslerová-Kodešová 1967 (divorced 1988); one s. one d.; m. 2nd Martina Schlonzová; one d.; ed Univ. of Econs, Prague; first Czech national to win a Grand Slam title; Wimbledon Singles Champion 1973, French Open Singles Champion 1970 and 1971, runner-up US Championships 1971, 1973, Italian Championships 1970, 1971, 1972; mem. Czechoslovak Davis Cup Team 1964–80, incl. 1975 (runners-up), 1980 (winners), non-playing Capt. 1982–87; Czechoslovak No. 1 player 1966–77; Bd mem. Czechoslovak Tennis Asscn (CTA), 1982–98; mem. ETA Men's Cttee 1990–93; mem. ITF Davis Cup European Cttee 1997–; Founder and Tournament Dir Czech Open, Prague 1982–98; Pres. Czech Tennis Asscn 1994–98; Dir Czechoslovak Tennis Centre 1986–92; part-owner and CEO Prague CZ Fashion sro 1994–; Meritorious Master of Sports 1971, State Decoration for Outstanding Work 1973, ITF Award for Services to the Game 1988, Int. Tennis Hall of Fame 1990. *Leisure interests:* football, other sports, stamp collecting, films. *Address:* Hugo Boss Shop, Pařížská Street 28, Prague 1, 110 00 (Office); Hugo Boss Shop, Jungmanovo Square 18, Prague 1, 110 00 (Office); Na Bérance 20, Prague 6, 160 00 Czech Republic. *Telephone:* (2) 2231-4584 (Office); (2) 3332-1536 (Home). *Fax:* (2) 2231-4583 (Office); (2) 3332-1535 (Home). *E-mail:* Praguefashion@iol.cz (Office).

KODJO, Edem; Togolese politician and administrator; b. 23 May 1938, Sokodé; m. 1962; two s. two d.; ed Coll. St Joseph, Univ. of Rennes, Ecole Nat. d'Administration, Paris; worked as admin. for Office de Radiodiffusion-Télévision Française (ORTF) 1964–67; returned to Togo 1967; Sec.-Gen., Ministry of Finance, Economy and Planning 1967–72; Administrator, Banque Centrale des Etats de l'Afrique de l'Ouest 1967–76, Pres. of Admin. Council 1973–76; Dir-Gen. Société Nat. d'Investissement 1972–73; Minister of Finance and Economy 1973–76, of Foreign Affairs 1976–77, of Foreign Affairs and Co-operation 1977–78; Sec.-Gen. of the OAU 1978–84; Assoc. Prof. Sorbonne, Paris 1985–90; Prime Minister of Togo 1994–96; Founder and Chair. Pan-African Inst. of Int. Relations (IPRI); Ed. Afrique 2000; mem. Rassemblement du Peuple Togolaise (RPT), RPT Political Bureau (Sec.-Gen.) 1967–71); leader Togolese Union for Democracy (UTD) –1999, Pres. Convergence patriotique panafricaine 1999–; mem. Club of Rome; Gov. for Togo, IMF 1973–76; fmr Chair. OAU Council of Ministers, Afro-Arab Perm. Comm. on Co-operation, OAU Cttee of Ten; Dr. hc (Univ. of Bordeaux I); Commdr, Ordre du Mono, Togo, Univ. of Sorbonne Medal, Officier, Légion d'honneur; decorations from many African countries. *Address:* Convergence patriotique panafricaine, B.P. 12703, Lomé, Togo (Office).

KODJO, Messan Abgéyomé; Togolese politician; b. 12 Oct. 1954, Tokpli, Yoto Pref.; m.; ed Higher School of Sciences and Tech., Univ. of Benin, Univ. of Poitiers, France; fmr Sales Man. SONACOM; Minister for Youth, Sports and Culture 1988–91, for Territorial Admin. and Security 1991; organized Constitutional Referendum; Gen. Man. Port Authority of Lomé 1993–99; elected Deputy 1999; Prime Minister of Togo 2000–02. *Address:* c/o Bureau du Premier Ministre, B.P. 5618, Lomé, Togo (Office).

KOENIG, Pierre Francis, BArch; American architect; b. 17 Oct. 1925, San Francisco; s. of Harold Koenig and Blanche Chige; m. 1st Sue Thompson 1953 (divorced 1959); one s.; m. 2nd Gaile Carson 1960 (divorced 1975); one s.; m. 3rd Gloria Kaufman 1984; ed Univ. of Utah, Pasadena City Coll. and Univ. of S Calif.; opened own architectural office, Glendale, Calif. 1952; Instructor Architectural Design Studio, Univ. of S Calif. 1962–69, Assoc. Prof. of Architecture 1970, now Distinguished Prof. of Architecture; Dir Chemehuevi Reservation Comprehensive Planning Program 1971–76; visiting lecturer at numerous univs, insts etc.; designed Case Study Houses No. 21 and 22 (Arts and Architecture Magazine Case Study House Program 1959–60); work exhibited at Whitney Museum 1985–86, Museum of Contemporary Art, Los Angeles 1989–90 and in many other architectural exhbns; Fellow AIA; Hon. FRIBA 2000; prizewinner, São Paulo Bienal 1957; Architectural League of NY Award 1957; American Inst. of Steel Award 1963; Gold Medal AIA LA 1999; Gold Medal from Tau Sigma Delta Soc. 2000; AIACC 25-year Award 2001; numerous awards from American Inst. of Architects etc. *Exhibitions:* work exhibited at Whitney Museum 1985–86, Museum of Contemporary Art, Los Angeles 1989–90 and at Form Zero Gallery, Santa Monica, Univ. of Texas, Calif. Polytechnic Univ., Univ. of S Calif. and in many architectural exhbns. *Publications:* The Chemehuevi Project (with others) 1971, The Chemehuevi Future 1973, This Is Our Land 1974, Remaking the Homeland 1975, The Chemehuevi Today 1976, Graphic Communication 1977, Prefabricated Building Systems, Pierre Koenig by James Steel and David Jenkins. *Leisure interests:* music, drawing, photography, running. *Address:* 12221 Dorothy Street, Los Angeles, CA 90049, USA. *Telephone:* (310) 826-1414. *E-mail:* pfkoenig@mizar.usc.edu (Office). *Website:* www-rcf.usc.edu/~pfkoenig (Office); www.pierrekoenig.org (Home).

KOEPP, David; American screenplay writer. *Film screenplays:* Apartment Zero 1989, Bad Influence 1990 (with Martin Donovan), Toy Soldiers (with Daniel Petrie, Jr) 1991, Death Becomes Her (with Martin Donovan) 1992, Jurassic Park (with Michael Crichton) 1993, Carlito's Way 1993, The Paper (with Stephen Koepp) 1994, The Shadow 1994. *Address:* U.T.A., 9560 Wilshire Blvd., Fl. 5, Beverly Hills, CA 90212, USA.

KOFFIGOH, Joseph Kokou; Togolese politician; b. 1948, Kpele Dafo; m.; three s. one d.; ed Univs of Abidjan and Poitiers, France; called to the Bar, Poitiers, France; joined Viale Chambers, Togo; f. Togo Bar Asscn 1980, Pres. 1990; founder mem. Observatoire panafricain de la démocratie (OPAD) 1991, Ligue togolaise des droits de l'homme 1990; founder mem. and Vice-Pres. FAR (Asscn for reform); Vice-Pres. Nat. Sovereign Conf.; Prime Minister of Togo 1991–94, also Minister of Defence, Minister of Foreign Affairs and Co-operation 1999–2001, of Regional Integration responsible for relations with Parl. 2001–; Pres. Coordination nat. des forces nouvelles. *Leisure interests:* lawn tennis, basketball, shadow-boxing. *Address:* Ministry of Regional Integration, Lomé, Togo (Office).

KOFLER, Georg; German (b. Italian) television executive; b. 26 April 1957, Brunico, Italy; m. José Kofler; two s.; ed Univ. of Vienna; fmrly mem. staff Austrian state broadcasting co. Österreichischer Rundfunk (ORF); with Eureka TV 1987–89; co-founder (with Gerhard Ackermans and Thomas Kirch) and Chair. Pro 7 TV network 1989–2000. *Address:* Medienallee 7, 85767 Unterföhring, Germany. *Telephone:* (89) 95070.

KOGAN, Pavel Leonidovich; Russian violinist and conductor; b. 6 June 1952, Moscow; s. of Leonid Kogan and Elizaveta Gilels; m. (divorced); one s.; ed Moscow State Conservatory; studied conducting in Leningrad with I. Mussin and in Moscow with Leo Ginzburg; performances 1970–; Conductor Moscow Chamber Orchestra 1980–83; Chief Conductor and Music Dir Zagreb Philharmonic 1988–90, Moscow State Academic Symphony Orchestra 1988–; Prin. Guest Conductor, Utah Symphony Orchestra, USA 1998–99; winner Int. Jean Sibelius Competition Helsinki, 1970. *Performances:* performed in maj. concert halls of Europe, America and Japan as soloist, also in ensembles with parents and pianist Nina Kogan (sister); performed with symphony orchestras in USSR (Russia), USA and countries of Europe and Asia since 1983. *Leisure interest:* automobiles. *Address:* Bryusov per. 8/10, Apt. 19, 103009 Moscow, Russia (Home). *Telephone:* (095) 292-13-95 (Home).

KOGAN, Richard Jay, MBA; American business executive; b. 6 June 1941, New York; m. Susan Linda Scher 1965; ed City Coll. of City Univ. of New York and Stern School of Business, New York Univ.; fmr Pres. US Pharmaceuticals Div. Ciba-Geigy Corpn; Exec. Vice-Pres. Pharmaceutical Operations, Schering-Plough Corpn 1982–86, Pres. and COO 1986–95, Pres. and CEO 1996–98, Chair. Bd Dirs., CEO 1999–; mem. Bd Dirs. Atlantic Mutual Cos., Colgate-Palmolive Co., Bank of New York Co. Inc.; mem. Council on Foreign Relations. *Address:* Schering-Plough Corporation, 2000 Galloping Hill Road, Kenilworth, NJ 07033, USA. *Telephone:* (201) 822-7000. *Fax:* (201) 822-7000.

KOGURE, Gohei, BEcons; Japanese business executive; b. 19 Sept. 1924, Gunma Pref.; s. of Goro Kogure and Hiro Kogure; m. Noriko Shigehara 1951; one s. one d.; ed Univ. of Tokyo; joined Dentsu Inc. 1947, Exec. Dir 1971–73, Man. Dir 1973–79, Sr Man. Dir 1979–85, Pres. and CEO 1985–93, Chair. 1993–97, now Sr Corp. Adviser; Chair. Japan Advertising Agencies Asscn 1987–; Trustee Keizai Doyukai (Japan Asscn of Corp. Execs); Hon. Life mem. Int. Advertising Asscn; Kt Commdr Order of St Sylvester Pope with Star (Vatican); Grand Cordon of the Order of the Sacred Treasure 2001; All Japan Advertising Award 1989. *Leisure interests:* golf, haiku. *Address:* Dentsu Inc., 1-8-1 Higashi-shimbashi, Minato-ku, Tokyo 105-7001, Japan (Office). *Telephone:* (3) 6216-5111 (Office).

KOH, Tommy Thong Bee, LLD; Singaporean diplomatist and law professor; b. 12 Nov. 1937, Singapore; s. of Koh Han Kok and Tsai Ying; m. Siew Aing 1967; two s.; ed Univ. of Singapore and Harvard and Cambridge Univs.; Asst lecturer, Univ. of Singapore 1962–64, lecturer 1964–71; Sub-Dean, Faculty of Law, Univ. of Singapore 1965–67, Vice-Dean 1967–68; Perm. Rep. of Singapore to UN 1968–71, concurrently High Commr to Canada 1969–71; Assoc. Prof. of Law and Dean, Faculty of Law, Singapore Univ. 1971–74; Perm. Rep. to UN, (also Accred to Canada and Mexico) 1974–84; Amb. to USA 1984–90; Amb.-at-Large, Ministry of Foreign Affairs 1990–; Dir Inst. of Policy Studies 1990–97; Exec. Dir Asia-Europe Foundation 1997–; Pres. Third UN Law of the Sea Conf. (Chair. Singapore Del. to Conf.) 1981–82; Chair. Preparatory Cttee, Chair. Main Cttee UN Conf. on Environment and Devt 1990–92; UN Sec.-Gen.'s Special Envoy to Russian Fed., Latvia, Lithuania and Estonia Aug.–Sept. 1993; Chair. Nat. Arts Council 1991–96; Chair. Nat. Heritage Bd. 2002–; Hon. LLD (Yale) 1984; Adrian Clarke Memorial Medal 1961, Leow Chia Heng Prize 1961, Public Service Star 1971, Meritorious Service Medal 1979, Wolfgang Friedman Award 1984, Jackson H. Ralston Prize 1985, Annual Award of the Asia Soc., New York, 1985, Int. Service Award, Fletcher School of Law and Diplomacy, Tufts Univ., USA 1987, Jit Trainor Award for Distinction in Diplomacy, Georgetown Univ., USA 1987, Elizabeth Haub Prize, Univ. of Brussels and Int. Council on Environmental Law 1997; Fok Ying Tung Southeast Asia Prize, Hong Kong 1993; Distinguished Service Order Award 1990, Commdr Order of the Golden Ark, The Netherlands 1993, Grand Cross of Order of Bernardo O'Higgins, Chile 1997. *Publications:* United States and East Asia: Conflict and Cooperation 1995, The Quest for World Order: Perspectives of a Pragmatic Idealist 1998. *Leisure interests:* sport, reading, music. *Address:* c/o Ministry of Foreign Affairs, 250 North Bridge Road, #39-00 Raffles City Tower, Singapore 179101, Singapore. *Telephone:* 3305600. *Fax:* 3381908.

KOHÁK, Erazim, PhD; Czech philosopher, educationist and author; b. 21 May 1933, Prague; s. of Dr Miloslav Kohák and Dr. Zdislava Koháková; m. 3rd Dorothy Koháková; three d. from 1st m.; ed Yale Univ.; exiled with parents to USA 1948; lecturer Univ. Boston Univ. 1960–72, Prof. 1972–90, Prof. Emer. 1994–; returned to Czechoslovakia 1990; Prof. Charles Univ., Prague 1990–2001, Prof. Emer. 2000–; mem. Metaphysical Soc. of America, American Theological Soc., Czech TV Council 2001–; Josef Vavroušek Prize for Ecology 1997, Medal of Merit (Czech Repub.) 1998, Great Gold Medal, Charles Univ., Hlávka Medal, Czechoslovak Acad. of Science. *Publications include:* Národ v nás 1978, Idea and Experience 1978, The Embers and the Stars 1984, Jan Patočka: His Thought and Writings 1989, Dopisy přes oceán 1992 Pražské přednášky 1992 Jan Patočka: filosofický životopis 1993, P.S. Psoŭ 1993, Člověk, dobro a zlo 1993, Pruvodce demokracii 1997, Zelená svatozář 1998, Hesla mladých svišťů 1999, The Green Halo 2000, Poutník po hvězdách 2001, Orbis bene vivendi; numerous articles in philosophical journals. *Leisure interests:* hiking, railways, ecology. *Address:* Faculty of Philosophy, Charles University, 116 38 Prague 1; (Office); Czech Television, Kavčí hory, 140 70 Prague 4 (Office); Babákova 2200, 148 00 Prague 414, Czech Republic (Home). *Telephone:* (2) 21619306 (Office); (2) 72935586 (Home); (606) 662280. *E-mail:* kohak.e@ecn.cz (Home).

KOHL, Helmut, DPhil; German politician; b. 3 April 1930, Ludwigshafen; s. of Hans and Cäcilie (née Schnur) Kohl; m. Hannelore Renner 1960 (died 2001); two s.; ed Univs of Frankfurt and Heidelberg; Mem. of man. of an industrial union 1959; Chair. Christian Democrat Party (CDU), Rhineland-Palatinate 1966–73, Deputy Chair. CDU Deutschlands 1969–73, Chair. 1973–98, Hon. Chair. 1998–2000; Minister-Pres. Rhineland-Palatinate 1969–76; Leader of the Opposition in the Bundestag 1976–82; Fed. Chancellor, Fed. Repub. of Germany 1982–98; Adviser on Foreign Policy 2000–; mem. Bundestag 1976–; Dr hc (Cambridge) 1998, Prof. hc (Tongji Univ., China) 1993; numerous hon. degrees; Karlspreis (Aachen) 1988, 1991; Jawaharlal Nehru Award 1990; Konrad Adenauer Prize 1994, Leo Baeck Prize 1996; Grosses Bundesverdienstkreuz 1979, Bundesverdienstkreuz 1998, Grand Cross of Dutch Lion 1999, Grand Cross, Order of Merit. *Publication:* Mein Tagebuch 1998–2000. *Leisure interests:* reading, music, walking and swimming. *Address:* c/o Deutsche Bundestag, 11011 Berlin (Office); Marbacher Strasse 11, 67071 Ludwigshafen Rhein-Oggersheim, Germany (Home).

KÖHLER, Horst, Dr rer. pol; German banker; b. 22 Feb. 1943, Skierbieszow, Poland; m.; two c.; ed Univ. of Tübingen; Sec. of State, Ministry of Finance, Bonn 1990–93; Pres. Deutsche Sparkassen- und Giroverband, Bonn 1993–98; Deputy German Gov. IBRD and EBRD, Pres. EBRD 1998–2000; Pres. European Asscn of Savings Banks 1994–97; Man. Dir IMF 2000–; Grosses Verdienstkreuz der Bundesrepublik Deutschland 1992; Commdr de l'Ordre Grand-ducal de la Couronne de Chêne 1994; Officier, Légion d'honneur 1995; Verdienstmedaille des Landes Baden-Württemberg 2002. *Address:* IMF, 700 19th Street NW, Washington DC 20431, USA (Office). *Telephone:* (202) 623-7300 (Office). *Fax:* (202) 623-4661 (Office). *Website:* www.imf.org (Office).

KOHLHAUSSEN, Martin, German banker; b. 6 Nov. 1935, Marburg/Lahn; m.; three c.; ed Univs of Frankfurt am Main, Freiburg and Marburg; bank training, Deutsche Bank, Frankfurt am Main; Man. Lloyds Bank, Frankfurt am Main 1974–76; Man. Tokyo Br. Westdeutsche Landesbank Girozentrale 1976–78, New York Br. 1979–81; mem. Bd Man. Dirs. Commerzbank AG 1982–, Chair. Exec. Cttee 1991–2001, Chair. Supervisory Bd 2001–; Pres. Bundesverband Deutscher Banken 1997–2000; Dr hc (Technische Univ., Chemnitz) 1998. *Address:* Commerzbank AG, Kaiserplatz, 60261 Frankfurt am Main, Germany. *Telephone:* (69) 13620.

KOHN, Walter, PhD; American professor of physics; b. 9 March 1923, Vienna, Austria; s. of Solomon Kohn and Gusti Rappaport; m. 1st Lois Mary Adams 1948 (divorced); three d.; m. 2nd Mara Schiff 1978; ed Toronto and Harvard Univs; served with Canadian Infantry 1944–45; Instructor Harvard Univ. 1948–50; Asst Prof., Assoc. Prof., then Prof., Carnegie Mellon Inst. of Tech. 1950–60; Prof. Univ. of Calif. at San Diego 1960–79, Chair. Dept of Physics 1961–63, Dir Inst. for Theoretical Physics 1979–84; Prof. of Physics, Univ. of Calif. at Santa Barbara 1984–91, Prof. Emer. and Research Prof. 1991–, Research Physicist Centre for Quantized Electronic Structures 1991–; mem. revision cttee reactor div. NIST, Md 1994–; Visiting Prof., Univs of Mich. and Pa 1957–58, Imperial Coll. of Science and Tech. London 1960; Nat. Research Council Fellow, Inst. of Theoretical Physics, Copenhagen 1951–52; Guggenheim Fellow and Visiting Prof. Ecole Normale Supérieure Paris 1963–64; Nat. Science Foundation Sr Postdoctoral Fellow Univ. of Paris 1967; Fellow AAAS; Councillor-at-Large, American Physical Soc. 1968–72; Visiting Prof. Hebrew Univ., Jerusalem 1970 and Univs of Washington, Paris, Copenhagen, ETH (Zurich); mem. Bd Govs. Weizmann Inst. 1996–; Fellow American Acad. of Arts and Sciences; mem. Int. Acad. of Quantum Molecular Sciences; mem. NAS; Foreign mem. Royal Soc.; Hon. LLD (Toronto) 1967; Hon. DSc (Univ. of Paris) 1980, (Queen's Univ., Canada) 1986, Hon. DPhil (Brandeis Univ.) 1981; (Hebrew Univ. of Jerusalem) 1981 and others; Oliver E. Buckley Prize in Solid State Physics 1960; Davisson-Germer Prize in Surface Physics 1977, Nat. Medal of Science 1988, Feenberg Medal 1991, Nobel Prize for Chemistry (jt winner) 1998, UNESCO Gold Medal 1998. *Publications:* 200 scientific articles in professional journals 1945–92. *Leisure interests:* flute, reading, sports. *Address:* Department of Physics, University of California, Santa Barbara, CA 93106, USA (Office); 236 La Vista Grande, Santa Barbara, CA 93103, USA (Home). *Telephone:* (805) 893-3061 (Office); (805) 962-1489 (Home). *Fax:* (805) 893-5816 (Office); (805) 962-1489 (Home). *E-mail:* kohn@physics.ucsb.edu (Office).

KOHONEN, Teuvo Kalevi, DEng, FIEEE; Finnish physicist; b. 11 July 1934, Lauritsala; s. of Väinö Kohonen and Tyyne E Koivunen; m. Elvi Anneli Trast 1959; two s. two d.; ed Helsinki Univ. of Tech.; Teaching Asst in Physics, Helsinki Univ. of Tech. 1957–59; Research Assoc. Finnish Atomic Energy Comm. 1959–62; Asst Prof. in Physics, Helsinki Univ. of Tech. 1963–65, Prof. of Tech. Physics 1965–93; on leave as Visiting Prof. Univ. of Washington, Seattle 1968–69; Research Prof. Acad. of Finland 1975–78, 1980–99, Prof. Emer. 1999–; Pres. European Neural Network Soc. 1991–92; Vice-Chair. Int. Asscn for Pattern Recognition (IAPR) 1982–84; mem. Acad. Scientiarum et Artium Europaea, Finnish Acad. of Sciences, Finnish Acad. of Eng Sciences; Dr hc (Univ. of York, Åbo Akademi, Univ. of Dortmund); Emil Aaltonen Prize 1983; Cultural Prize, Finnish Commercial TV (MTV) 1984, IEEE Neural Networks Pioneer Award 1991, Int. Neural Network Soc. Lifetime Achievement Award 1992, Finnish Cultural Foundation Prize 1994, Tech. Achievement Award, IEEE Signal Processing Soc. 1995, King-Sun Fu Prize, Int. Asscn for Pattern Recognition 1996, Centennial Prize, Finnish Asscn of Grad. Engineers (TEK) 1996, Medal of Finnish Acad. of Eng Sciences 1997, SEFI Leonardo da Vinci Medal, European Soc. for Eng Educ. 1998, Jubilee Prize Finnish Foundation of Tech. 1999, Italgas Prize 1999, Caianiello Int. Award 2000, Third Millennium Medal, IEEE Signal Processing Soc. 2000, Academician 2000; Commdr Order of Lion of Finland; Kt, Order of White Rose of Finland. *Publications:* Digital Circuits and Devices 1972, Associative Memory: A System Theoretical Approach 1977, Content-Addressable Memories 1982, Self-Organization and Associative Memory 1984, Self-Organizing Maps 1995. *Leisure interests:* philosophy of music, literature. *Address:* Helsinki University of Technology, Laboratory of Computer and Information Science, P.O. Box 5400, 02015 TKK; Mellstenintie 9 C 2, 02170 Espoo, Finland (Home). *Telephone:* (9) 4513268.

KOIRALA, Girija Prasad; Nepalese politician; Gen. Sec. Nepali Congress Party (NCP), currently Pres.; Prime Minister of Nepal, also responsible for Defence, Foreign Affairs and Royal Palace Affairs 1991–94; Prime Minister of Nepal 1998–99, 2000–01; fmr. Minister of Royal Palace Affairs, Defence and Foreign Affairs, numerous other portfolios. *Address:* Nepali Congress Party, Bhansar Tole, Teku, Kathmandu, Nepal (Office).

KOIVISTO, Mauno Henrik, PhD; Finnish politician; b. 25 Nov. 1923, Turku; s. of Juho and Hymni Sofia Koivisto (née Eskola); m. Taimi Tellervo Kankaanranta 1952; one d.; ed Turku University; Man. Dir Helsinki Workers' Savings Bank 1959–67; Gov. Bank of Finland 1968–82; Minister of Finance 1966–67; Prime Minister 1968–70, 1979–82; Minister of Finance and Deputy Prime Minister Feb.–Sept. 1972; Pres. of Finland 1982–94; Chair. Bd of Postipankki 1970–82, Mortgage Bank of Finland Ltd 1971–82, Bd of Admin. of Co-operative Soc. ELANTO 1966–82; mem. Bd of Admin. of Co-operative Union KK 1964–82; Gov. for Finland IBRD 1966–69; Gov. for Finland IMF 1970–79. *Publications:* Sosiaaliset suhteet Turun satamassa (doctoral thesis) 1956, Landmarks: Finland in the World 1985, Foreign Policy Standpoints 1982–92: Finland and Europe 1992, Witness to History 1997; 11 books on econs and social politics. *Leisure interest:* volleyball. *Address:* c/o Presidential Palace, Helsinki, Finland.

KOIVULEHTO, Jorma Juhani, PhD; Finnish professor emeritus of Germanic philology; b. 12 Oct. 1934, Tampere; m. Marja-Liisa Pakarinen 1963; one s. one d.; ed Univ. of Helsinki and German Dialect Research Centre of Marburg/Lahn, Fed. Repub. of Germany; Assoc. Prof. of Germanic Philology, Univ. of Helsinki 1973–83, Prof. 1983–98, Prof. Emer. 1998–; Research Prof., Acad. of Finland 1988–93; mem. Finnish Acad. of Sciences; corresp. mem. Akad. der Wissenschaften, Gottingen, Österreichische Akad. der Wissenschaften; Hon. mem. Finno-Ugrian Soc. (Helsinki) 1997–. *Publications include:* 'Jäten' in deutschen Mundarten 1971, Idg. Laryngale und die finnisch-ugrische Evidenz 1988, Uralische Evidenz für die Laryngaltheorie 1991, Indogermanisch-Uralisch: Lehnbezie-hungen oder (auch) Urverwandtschaft? 1994, Verba mutuata 1999, Finno-Ugric Reflexes of North-West Indo-European and Early Stages of Indo-Iranian 2000, The Earliest Contacts Between Indo-European and Uralic Speakers in the Light of Lexical Loans 2001. *Address:* University of Helsinki, Department of Germanic Philology, Box 4 (Vuorikatu 6 A 10), 00014 Helsinki (Office); Sallatunturintie 1 D 24, 00970 Helsinki, Finland (Home). *Telephone:* (9) 19124027 (Office); (9) 3256081 (Home). *Fax:* (9) 19123069 (Office). *E-mail:* jorma.koivulehto@helsinki.fi (Office).

KOIZUMI, Junichiro; Japanese politician; b. 8 Jan. 1942; m. (divorced); mem. House of Reps from Kanagawa; fmr Parl. Vice-Minister of Finance and of Health and Welfare; Minister of Posts and Telecommunications 1992–93; Chair. House of Reps. Finance Cttee; mem. Mitsuzuka Faction of LDP; Minister of Health and Welfare 1996–98, Prime Minister of Japan April 2001–; Pres. Jiyu Minshuto (Liberal-Democratic Party) Aug. 2001–. *Address:* Jiya Minshuto, 1-11-23, Nogata-che, Chiyoda-ku, Tokyo 100-8910 (Office); Office of the Prime Minister, 1-6-1 Nagata-cho, Chiyoda-ku, Tokyo 100-8914, Japan. *Telephone:* (3) 3581-6211; (3) 3581-2361. *Fax:* (3) 3581-1910. *E-mail:* koho@ldp.jimin.or.jp (Office). *Website:* www.kantei.go.jp; www.jimin.jp (Office).

KOJIMA, Kiyoshi, PhD; Japanese economist; b. 22 May 1920, Nagoya; m. Keiko Kojima 1947; ed Tokyo Univ. of Commerce and Econs, Leeds Univ., UK and Princeton Univ., USA; Asst Prof. of Int. Econs, Hitotsubashi Univ. 1945–60, Prof. 1960–84, Prof. Emer. 1984–; Secr. (Dir) for UN Conf. on Trade and Devt 1963; Prof. Int. Christian Univ. 1984–91, Surugadai Univ. 1991–97;

mem. Science Council of Japan 1985; British Council Scholarship 1952–53, Rockefeller Foundation Fellowship 1953–55; Second Order of the Sacred Treasure 1996. *Publications:* (in Japanese): Theory of Foreign Trade 1950, Japan's Economic Development and Trade 1958, Japan in Trade Expansion for Developing Countries 1964 (in English), Japan and a Pacific Free Trade Area 1971, Japan and a New World Economic Order 1977, Direct Foreign Investment 1978, Japanese Direct Investment Abroad 1990, Trade, Investment and Pacific Economic Integration 1996; Ed. Papers and Proceedings of a Conference on Pacific Trade and Development 1968, 1969, 1973; also articles in English on int. trade. *Leisure interests:* golf, Noh (Utai). *Address:* 3-24-10 Maehara-cho, Koganei-shi, Tokyo 184-0013, Japan. *Telephone:* (3) 381-1041.

KOK, Willem (Wim); Netherlands politician; b. 29 Sept. 1938, Bergambacht; m.; three c.; ed Nijenrode Business School; Asst. Int. Officer Netherlands Fed. of Trade Unions (Construction Sectors) 1961–67, Sec. 1967–69; Sec. Netherlands Fed. of Trade Unions (NVV) 1969–73, Chair. (later renamed Fed. of Netherlands Trade Unions, FNV) 1973–85; Chair. European Trade Union Confed. 1979–82; mem. Parl. 1986–2002, Party Leader Labour Party 1986–2002; Deputy Prime Minister and Minister of Finance 1989–94; Prime Minister of the Netherlands and Minister for Gen. Affairs 1994–2002; Deputy Chair. Socialist Int. 1989–; Vice-Chair. De Nederlandsche Bank; Adviser to European Comm. *Address:* c/o Labour Party, Herengracht 54, P.O. Box 1310, 1000 BH Amsterdam, Netherlands.

KOKH, Alfred Reingoldovich, CandEconSci; Russian media executive; b. 28 Feb. 1961, Zyryanovsk, Kazakhstan; m.; two d.; ed Leningrad Inst. of Finance and Econs; Sr Researcher Prometey Inst.; Asst Leningrad Polytech. Inst. 1987–90; elected Chair. Sestroretsk Dist Exec. Cttee, Leningrad 1990–91; Deputy Dir Cttee on Man. of State Property of St Petersburg 1991–93; First Deputy Chair. State Cttee on Property in Russian Fed. 1993–96, Chair. 1996–97; Vice-Chair. Russian Fed. Govt responsible for Privatization and Budget 1997; resigned 1997; Chair. Bd of Dirs. Montes Auri Investment Co. 1997–; Dir-Gen. Gasprom-Media 1998–2001; Chair. Bd of Dirs. NTV Broadcasting 2001. *Publications:* History of Privatization in Russia (with A. Chubais and M. Boyko) 1997, Sale of Soviet Empire 1998. *Address:* Montes Auri Co., Gazetny per. 3, 103918 Moscow, Russia (Office). *Telephone:* (095) 229-03-04 (Office).

KOKOSHIN, Andrei Afanasievich, DHisSc; Russian politician; b. 26 Oct. 1945, Moscow; m.; two d.; ed Bauman Moscow Higher Tech. Univ.; scientific researcher, Head of Dept, Deputy Dir Inst. of USA and Canada Acad. of Sciences 1974–92; First Deputy Minister of Defence of the Russian Fed. 1992–97; Chair. Interagency Cttee on Defence Security, Security Council of the Russian Fed. 1993–97; mem. Govt Council on Industrial Policy 1993–; Sec. Council of Defence of Russian Fed.; Chief Military Inspector of Russian Fed.; Sec. Security Council of Russian Fed. March–Oct. 1998; mem. State Duma 1999– (mem. Otechestvo–All Russia faction), Vice-Chair. Cttee on Industry, Construction and High Technologies 1999–; mem. Russian Acad. of Sciences 1987 (Vice-Pres. 2000), Russian Acad. of Social Sciences 1993, Russian Acad. of Artillery and Rocket Science and Eng 1993–, Russian Acad. of Natural Sciences; Chair. Bd High Tech. Foundation/Gorbachev Project 2001, Russian Public Bd for Educ. Devt 2001; mem. Scientific Advisory Council, Inst. for Int. Studies, Stanford Univ. 2000, Cen. Political Council, Unity-Otechestvo (United Russia) Party 2001–, Bd Dirs. Nuclear Threat Initiative 2001–, Russian Interagency Governmental Cttee on Biotechnologies, Bd of Trustees Russian–American Business Council 2002, Nat. Anticorruption Comm. 2002, Russian Interagency Governmental Cttee on Biotechnologies; Hon. Chair. Russian Rugby Football League 1992–; Services for the Fatherland, Mark of Honour, Military Comradeship 1987, 1997, 2000. *Publications:* 17 books (including 6 as co-author) on nat. security, int. affairs, Russian nat. industrial policy and econs including Forecasting and Foreign Policy 1975, The USA in the System of International Relations in the 1980s 1984, Weapons in Space: Security Dilemma 1986, National Industrial Policy of Russia 1992, Soviet Strategic Thought 1918–1991 1999, The National Industrial Policy and the National Security of Russia (jtly) 2001, Deterrence in the Second Nuclear Age (jtly) 2001, Types and Categories of Nuclear Conflicts in the XXI Century 2003; more than 150 articles and papers. *Address:* State Duma, Okhotny Ryad 1, 103265 Moscow, Russia. *Telephone:* (095) 292-52-18 (Office); (095) 938-18-92 (Office). *Fax:* (095) 272-99-91 (Office); (095) 938-18-93 (Office).

KOKOV, Valery Mukhamedovich, CandEconSc; Russian politician; b. 18 Oct. 1941, Tyrnauz; s. of Mukhammed Kambotovich Kokov and Zamirat Akhmedovna Kokova; m. Violetta Taubievna Oshnokova 1968; one s. one d.; ed Kabardino-Balkarian Univ., Higher School of Cen. CP Cttee in Rostov; chief agronomist in kolkhoz 1964–66; postgrad. student All-Union Research Inst. of Econ. of Agric. 1966–70; Sr economist, head of div. Ministry of Agric. Kabardino-Balkar Autonomous Repub., Dir of sovkhoz Leskensky 1970–74; First Sec. Urvansk Regional CP Cttee 1974–83; Chair. State Cttee on Material-Tech. Provision of the Repub. 1983–85; Sec. Kabardino-Balkar Regional CP Cttee 1985–88, Second Sec. 1988–90, First Sec. 1990–91; Chair. Supreme Soviet Kabardino-Balkar ASSR 1990–91; Pres. of Kabardino-Balkariya Repub. 1992–; mem. Pres. Council of Russia 1994–98; People's Deputy of Russian Fed. 1990–93; mem. Council of Fed. of Russia 1993–2001, Deputy Chair. 1996–2001; mem. Cttee. for Internal Affairs, mem. Parl. Ass. of Black Sea Econ. Co-operation 1996–2001. *Address:* Office of President, Lenina 27, 360028, Nalchik, Kabardino-Balkariya (Office); Karashaeva 15/23, 360028 Nalchik, Kabardino-Balkariya, Russia (Home). *Telephone:* (86622) 720-64 (Office); (86622) 221-52 (Office). *Fax:* (86622) 761-74 (Office).

KOŁAKOWSKI, Leszek, DPhil, FBA; Polish/British professor of philosophy; b. 23 Oct. 1927, Radom; s. of Jerzy Kołakowski and Lucyna (née Pietrusiewicz) Kołakowska; m. Tamara Dynenson 1949; one d.; ed Łódź and Warsaw Univs.; Asst (logic), Łódź Univ. 1947–49; Asst Warsaw Univ. 1950–54, Chair. Section of History of Philosophy 1959–68 (expelled by Govt for political reasons); Visiting Prof. McGill Univ., Montreal 1968–69; Prof. Univ. of Calif., Berkeley 1969–70; Sr Research Fellow, All Souls Coll., Oxford 1970–, Fellow Emer.; Prof. Yale Univ. 1975, Univ. of Chicago 1981–94; mem. American Acad. of Arts and Sciences, Bayerische Akad. der Künste, Institut Int. de Philosophie, Acad. Europaea, Acad. Universelle des Cultures, Polish Acad. of Sciences; mem. PEN Club, Polish Philosophical Soc., Polish Writers Asscn; mem. Philosophical Soc., Oxford, UK; Dr hc (Bard Coll., New York, Reed Coll., Portland, USA, State Univ. of New York, Adelphi Univ., New York, Łódź, Gdańsk, Sczecin, Wroclaw); several prizes including Alfred Jurzykowski Award 1969, Friedenpreis des deutschen Buchhandels 1977, Prix Européen d'Essai 1980, Prix d'Erasme and McArthur Foundation Prize 1983, Jefferson Award 1986, Prix Tocqueville 1994, Bloch Prize 1995, White Eagle Order 1997, Premio Nonino 1998. *Publications include:* Individual and Infinity (in Polish) 1958, Chrétiens sans église 1968, Positivist Philosophy 1970, Die Gegenwärtigkeit des Mythos 1973, Husserl and the Search for Certitude 1975, Leben trotz Geschichte 1977, Main Currents of Marxism 1976–78, Religion If There Is No God 1982, Bergson 1985, Metaphysical Horror 1988, Modernity on Endless Trial 1990, God Owes Us Nothing 1994, My Correct Views on Everything (in Polish) 1999, Mini-Lectures on Maxi-Issues (3 vols in Polish, trans in various languages), In Praise of Inconsistency (3 vols in Polish); several fairy tales, dramas and Biblical stories. *Address:* 77 Hamilton Road, Oxford, OX2 7QA, England.

KOLESNIKOV, Gen. Mikhail Petrovich; Russian army officer; b. 30 June 1939, Yeisk, Krasnodar Dist; m.; one s.; ed Omsk Tank Tech. School, Gen. Staff Acad.; started mil. service as Commdr of platoon 1975, then Commdr of co., Bn, Regt 1975–77, Head of Staff and Deputy Commdr of Div. 1977–79, Commdr of tank div. 1979–83, Commdr of corps, Commdr of Army in Transcaucasian Command 1983–87, Head of Staff and First Deputy Commdr of troops in Siberian Command 1987–89, Head of Staff and First Deputy C-in-C of Southern Command 1988–90, Head of Gen. Staff and First Deputy C-in-C of land troops 1990–91, Deputy Head of Staff of Armed Forces of Russian Fed. 1991–92, First Deputy Minister of Defence, Head of Gen. Staff of Russian Fed. 1992–96; Chair. Cttee Heads of Staff CIC Armed Forces 1996–98, Pres.'s State Tech. Comm. 1998–2000. *Address:* c/o Gostekhkomissiya, Znamenka str. 19, 103160 Moscow, Russia. *Telephone:* (095) 924-68-08 (Office).

KOLESNIKOV, Lt-Gen. Vladimir Ilyich; Russian criminal investigator; b. 1938; m.; two c.; ed Rostov State Univ., Acad. of Ministry of Internal Affairs; worked as investigator, Deputy Head, Dept of Criminal Investigation; Deputy Head, Dept of Internal Affairs; Head, Main Dept of Criminal Investigation 1991–; First Deputy Minister of Internal Affairs 1995–2000; Adviser to Gen. Public Prosecutor of Russia 2000–. *Address:* Bolshaya Dmitrovka str. 15A, 103793 Moscow, Russia. *Telephone:* (095) 292-88-69 (Office).

KOLFF, Willem Johan, MD, PhD; American professor of surgery; b. 14 Feb. 1911, Leiden, Netherlands; s. of Jacob and Adriana Pieternella Kolff; m. Janke Cornelia Huidekoper 1937; four s. one d.; ed Univs of Leiden and Groningen; Asst Pathological Anatomy, Univ. of Leiden 1934–36; Asst Medical Dept Univ. of Groningen 1938–41; Head, Medical Dept, Municipal Hosp., Kampen 1941–50; Privaat Docent, Univ. of Leiden Medical School 1949–51; mem. of staff, Research Div., Cleveland Clinic Foundation 1950–63; Asst Prof., later Prof. of Clinical Investigation, Educ. Foundation of Cleveland Clinic Foundation 1950–67; mem. staff, Surgical Div., Cleveland Clinic Foundation 1958–67, Head, Dept of Artificial Organs 1958–67, Scientific Dir Artificial Organs Program 1966–67; Prof. of Surgery, Head of Div. of Artificial Organs, Univ. of Utah Coll. of Medicine 1967–86, Distinguished Prof. of Medicine and Surgery 1979–, also Research Prof. of Eng, Prof. of Internal Medicine 1981–, Dir Kolff's Lab. 1986–; developed artificial kidney for clinical use; mem. Nat. Acad. of Eng 1989; Foreign mem. Hollandsche Maatschappij der Wetenschappen; Hon. mem. Peruvian Urological Soc., Greek Soc. of Cardiology, Sociedad Médica de Santiago, Austrian Soc. for Nephrology, Fundación Favaloro, Buenos Aires, Argentina 1981–; Hon. DSc (Allegheny Coll.) 1960, (Tulane Univ.) 1975, (City Univ. New York) 1982, (Temple Univ. Philadelphia) 1983, (Univ. of Utah) 1983; Hon. MD (Rostock) 1975, (Univ. of L'Aquila, Italy) 1981, (Univ. of Bologna) 1983; Commdr Order of Orange-Nassau, Orden de Mayo al Mérito en el Grado de Gran Oficial (Argentina) 1974; numerous medals, awards and prizes from several countries including Francis Amory Award (American Acad. of Arts and Sciences) 1948, Cameron Prize (Univ. of Edin.) 1964, Gairdner Prize (Gairdner Foundation, Toronto) 1966, Gold Medal (Netherlands Surgical Soc.) 1970, Benjamin Franklin Fellow (Royal Soc. of Arts, London) 1972, Leo Harvey Prize (Technion Inst. of Israel) 1972, Ray C. Fish Award and Medal Tex. Heart Inst. 1975, Senior U.S. Scientist Award, Alexander von Humboldt Foundation 1978, Gewerbevereins Wilhelm-Exner Award (Austria) 1980, American Medical Asscn.'s Scientific Achievement Award for Outstanding Work 1982, Japan Prize, Science and Tech. Foundation of Japan 1986, ANNA Hon. mem. 1987, First Jean Hamburger Award in Clinical Nephrology, Int. Soc. of Nephrology 1987, Christopher Columbus Award, Washington 1992, "Father of Artificial

Organs" Award and Medal, World Conf. of ISAO, Montreal 1992, Legacy of Life Award, LDS Hosp.-Deseret Foundation's Heart and Lung Inst. 1995, Lifetime Achievement Award, Ahmedabad, India 1996, numerous other awards. *Publications:* De Kunstmatige Nier 1946, New Ways of Treating Uraemia 1947; over 600 articles in learned journals and chapters in books on organ replacement, etc. *Leisure interests:* bird-watching, hiking, camping. *Address:* Kolff's Laboratory/Bioengineering, University of Utah, 2460-A Merrill Engineering Building, Salt Lake City, UT 84112 (Office); 2894 Crestview Drive, Salt Lake City, UT 84108, USA (Home). *Telephone:* (801) 581-6296 (Office); (801) 582-3056 (Home).

KOLINGBA, André; Central African Republic politician and army officer; fmr Chief of Staff; overthrew Pres. David Dacko (q.v.) in coup Sept. 1981; Pres. Mil. Cttee for Nat. Recovery 1981–85; Pres. of Cen. African Repub. 1981–93, Minister of Defence and of War Veterans 1981–83, 1984–85, Prime Minister and Minister of Defence and War Veterans 1985–91; Pres. Cand. in Aug. 1993 election; rank of Gen. revoked March 1994; sentenced to death in absentia for his role in failed coup in 2001, Aug. 2002.

KOLLEK, Theodore (Teddy); Israeli politician and public administrator; b. 27 May 1911, Vienna; s. of S. Alfred and Margaret Fleischer Kollek; m. Tamar Schwartz 1937; one s. one d.; ed secondary school, Vienna; founder mem. Kibbutz Ein Gev 1937; Political Dept Jewish Agency for Palestine 1940; established Jewish Agency office, Istanbul, for contact with Jewish underground in Europe 1942; Mission to USA for Haganah 1947–48; Head of US Div., Israel Foreign Ministry 1950; Minister, Washington 1951–52; Dir-Gen. of Prime Minister's Office, Jerusalem 1952–65; Chair. Israel Govt Tourist Corpn 1955–65; Chair. Israel Govt Water Desalination Joint Project with US Govt 1964–66; f. and Chair. Bd of Govs Israel Museum, Jerusalem 1964; Chair. Africa-Israel Investment Co. Ltd 1964–65, Int. Chair. Jerusalem Foundation; Mayor of Jerusalem 1965–93; mem. Advisory Bd Inst. on Global Conflict and Co-operation 1982–92; Hon. Doctorate (Hebrew Univ., Jerusalem) 1977, (Univ. of Notre Dame) 1981, (Brown Univ.) 1983, (Jewish Theological Seminary, Harvard Univ.) 1984, (Ben Gurion Univ.) 1985, (Hebrew Union Coll.) 1986, (Weizmann Inst. of Science) 1986, (Tel Aviv Univ.) 1989; Hon. Pres. Israel Museum, numerous prizes and awards. *Publications:* Jerusalem: A History of Forty Centuries (Co-Author), Pilgrims to the Holy Land 1970 (Co-Author), For Jerusalem (autobiography) 1978, My Jerusalem; Twelve Walks in the World's Holiest City (Co-Author); 180 scientific articles. *Leisure interests:* archaeology, reading, collecting ancient maps and books on Holy Land. *Address:* 3 Guatemala Street, Jerusalem 96704, Israel (Home). *Telephone:* 6751704 (Office); 6435690 (Home).

KOLLER, Arnold; Swiss politician; b. 29 Aug. 1933, Appenzell; m. Erica Brauder 1972; two c.; fmr univ. prof. of law, Univ. of St Gallen; mem. Swiss Parl. 1971–85; Pres. Nat. Council 1984–85; mem. Bundesrat (Fed. Council) 1986–99, Head of Fed. Mil. (Defence) Dept 1986–89; Head Fed. Dept of Justice and Police 1989–99; Pres. of Switzerland 1990, 1997; Pres. Int. Conf. on Federalism 2002; Christian Democratic Party; DrIur hc (Bern) 2002. *Publications:* Die unmittelbare Anwendbarkeit volkerrechtlicher Verträge und des EWG-Vertrags 1971, Für eine starke und solidarische Schweiz 1999. *Leisure interests:* skiing, tennis. *Address:* Steinegg, Gschwendes 8, 9050 Appenzell, Switzerland (Home). *Telephone:* (71) 7872290 (Home). *Fax:* (71) 7875590 (Home). *E-mail:* arnold.koller@bluemail.ch (Home).

KOLLO, René; German opera singer; b. 20 Nov. 1937, Berlin; s. of the late Willi and of Marie-Louise Kollodzieyski; m. 1st Dorthe Larsen 1967; one d.; m. 2nd Beatrice Bouquet 1982; began career with Staatstheater, Brunswick 1965; First Tenor, Deutsche Oper am Rhein 1967–71; Dir Metropol Theater, Berlin 1996–97; guest appearances with numerous leading opera cos. and at annual Bayreuth Wagner festival; Bundesverdienstkreuz, Goldene Kamera Award, Hörzu 2000. *Performances include:* The Flying Dutchman 1969, 1970, Lohengrin 1971, Die Meistersinger von Nürnberg 1973, 1974, Parsifal 1975, Siegfried 1976, 1977, Tristan (Zürich) 1980, (Bayreuth) 1981. *Publication:* Imre Fabian im Gespräch mit René Kollo 1982. *Leisure interests:* sailing, tennis, flying. *Address:* c/o Pran Event GmbH, Ralf Sesselberg, An der Brücke 18, 26180 Rastede, Germany (Office). *Telephone:* (4) 402-8687 (Office).

KOLOBOV, Yevgeny Vladimirovich; Russian conductor; b. 19 Jan. 1946, Leningrad; m. Natalia Popovich; one s. one d.; ed Sverdlovsk (now Ekaterinburg) Conservatory class of M. Paverman; debut 1969, conductor Sverdlovsk Opera Theatre 1974–77, Chief Conductor 1977–81, conductor of Leningrad Kirov Theatre of Opera and Ballet 1981–87; Artistic Dir and Chief Conductor K. Stanislavsky and V. Nemirovich-Danchenko Musical Theatre, Moscow 1988–90; f. and Artistic Dir Moscow Municipal Theatre New Opera 1990–; People's Artist of Russia 1983; Triumph Prize 1995. *Productions include:* Maria Stuarda, Il Pirata, La Wally, I Due Foscari, Hamlet, thematic productions devoted to Mozart, Salieri, Rossini. *Address:* Moscow Municipal Theatre New Opera, Karetny Ryad 3, 103006 Moscow, Russia (Office). *Telephone:* (095) 200-08-68 (Office); (095) 251-53-94 (Home).

KOLODKIN, Anatoliy Lazarevich, DCL; Russian specialist on law of sea and int. law; b. 27 Feb. 1928, Leningrad; s. of Lazar Kolodkin and Nadezhda Kolodkina; m. Berta Levina 1958; one s.; ed Leningrad Univ.; mem. numerous USSR dels to int. confs on maritime affairs; headed USSR dels at confs of Int. Maritime Satellite Org. (INMARSAT) 1981; participated in creation of Russian maritime satellite org. 'Morsvyassputnik'; Deputy Dir, Prof. Scientific Research Inst. of Maritime Transport 1981–; Spokesman and Co-ordinator Group D, E European states, at UN Conf. for elaboration UN

Convention on conditions of registration of ships 1982–86; co-author draft Convention on legal status of Ocean Data Acquisition Systems; Prof. of Law of Sea, Moscow State Legal Acad. 1994–; mem. Perm. Court of Arbitration, The Hague 1990–; mem. (Judge) UN Int. Tribunal for Law of Sea 1996–; has lectured extensively on law of sea in Russia and abroad; Pres. Maritime Law Asscn of USSR (now CIS) 1981–, Russian Int. Law Asscn 1994–; Chair. Nat. Cttee of Russian Fed. on UN Decade of Int. Law 1996–; Co-Chair. Consultative Council of State Duma (Parl.) for Int. Law 1996–; Deputy Chair. 'Peace for the Oceans' Cttee 1990–, Union of Lawyers; Hon. Vice-Pres., Int. Maritime Cttee 1994–; mem. Council, Int. Oceanic Inst. "Pacem in Maribus", Malta 1971–; mem. acad. councils, Law Faculty, Moscow Univ. 1975–, Inst. of State and Law, Russian Acad. of Sciences 1993–; mem. Higher Degree Cttee, Expert Council on Legal Sciences of Russian Fed. 1985–; mem. World Acad. of Science and Art 1989–; mem. Council, Law of the Sea Inst. (USA) 1989–95; mem. group of experts of State Duma for elaboration of new Russian marine legislation 1994–; Hon. Medal of Free Univ. of Brussels. *Publications:* 250 scientific articles in Russia and other countries. *Address:* Bolshoi Koptevsky per. 3, 125319 Moscow, Russia. *Telephone:* (095) 151-75-88. *Fax:* (095) 152-09-16.

KOŁODKO, Grzegorz Witold; Polish politician and professor of economics; b. 28 Jan. 1949, Tczew; m.; two d.; ed Warsaw School of Econs; Prof. Warsaw School of Econs 1972–2001, Dir Inst. of Finance 1989–94; Prof. of Econs, Leon Kozminski Acad. of Entrepreneurship and Man. (WSPiZ), Warsaw 2002–; fmr consultant, World Inst. for Devt Econs Research of UN, Helsinki; IMF and World Bank expert 1991–92, 1999–2000; First Deputy Prime Minister 1994–97, 2002–; Minister of Finance 1994–97, 2002–; Dir Transformation, Integration and Globalization Economic Research (Tiger) 2000–; Visiting Prof. Yale Univ., Univ. of Calif., LA, John C. Evans Prof. in European Studies, Univ. of Rochester, NY 1998–; numerous prizes and awards including Polish Broadcasting Award 1985, Polish TV Best Politician Award 1997, Commdr's Medal, Order of Polonia Restituta 1997. *Publications:* more than 300 publications in 20 languages on econ. theory and policy, including: Strategy for Poland 1994, The Polish Alternative: Old Myths, Hard Facts and New Strategies in Successful Transformation of the Polish Economy 1997, Equity Issues in Policy-making in Transition Economies 1998, From Shock to Therapy: The Political Economy of Postsocialist Transformations 2000, Post-Communist Transition: The Thorny Road 2000, Globalization and Transformation: Illusions and Reality 2001, Globalization and Catching-up in Transition Economies 2001, Emerging Market Economies – Globalization and Development 2003. *Leisure interests:* classical music, sport (marathon runner), travelling (more than 100 countries), nature. *Address:* Ministry of Finance, ul. Swietokrzyska 12, 00-916 Warsaw, Poland (Office). *Telephone:* (22) 6945555 (Office). *Fax:* (22) 8260180 (Office). *E-mail:* info@mofnet.gov.pl (Office). *Website:* www.mofnet.gov.pl (Office); kolodko.tiger.edu.pl (Office).

KOLOKOLOV, Boris Leonidovich; Russian diplomatist; b. 9 Nov. 1924; m. (wife deceased); one d.; ed Moscow Inst. of Int. Relations; army service, took part in mil. operations 1942–45; diplomatic service, UN, Geneva 1956–62; mem. Protocol Dept USSR Ministry of Foreign Affairs 1962–69, Chief of Protocol Dept 1969–73; Amb. to Tunisia 1973–81; Deputy Minister of Foreign Affairs of RSFSR (now Russia) 1981–96, Amb. Extraordinary and Plenipotentiary and consultant on int. problems, Ministry of Foreign Affairs 1996–; Prof., Academician Int. Science Acad. of Information, Information Processes and Technologies; numerous nat. and int. honours and awards inclduing Honoured Diplomatist of the Russian Fed. 1999. *Publication:* Profession–Diplomatist (memoirs) 2000. *Address:* Ministry of Foreign Affairs, Smolenskaya-Sennaya 32/34, Moscow, Russia. *Telephone:* (095) 244-92-30. *Fax:* (095) 253-90-81.

KOLPAKOVA, Irina; Russian ballerina; b. 22 May 1933, Leningrad; m. Vladilen Semenov 1955; one d.; ed Leningrad Choreographic School; Prima Ballerina, Kirov Theatre of Opera and Ballet, Leningrad (now Mariinsky Theatre, St Petersburg) 1957–91; Ballet mistress, American Ballet Theatre 1991–, Ballet Internationale, Indianapolis Ind. 1997–, then Asst Dir; Prof. Acad. of Russian Ballet 1995–; People's Artist of the USSR 1965, Grand Prix de Ballet, Paris 1966, USSR State Prize 1980, Hero of Socialist Labour 1983. *Main ballet roles:* Aurora (Sleeping Beauty), Juliet (Romeo and Juliet), Desdemona (Othello), Tao Khao (The Red Poppy), Maria (Fountain of Bakhchisarai), title roles in Giselle, Cinderalla, Raymonda and La Sylphide, Chopiniana (Les Sylphides), Kitri (Don Quixote), Natalie Pushkin (Pushkin), Eve (Creation of the World); cr. role of Katerina (The Stone Flower) and Shirin (Legends of Love). *Television:* main roles: The Lady (The Lady and the Houligan), Woman (The House by the Roadside), Aurora (Sleeping Beauty), Raymonda (Raymonda). *Address:* c/o American Ballet Theater, 890 Broadway, New York, NY 10003, USA.

KOLTAI, Ralph, CBE FRSA; British stage designer; b. 31 July 1924, Berlin, Germany; s. of Alfred Koltai and Charlotte Koltai (née Weinstein); m. Annena Stubbs 1954 (divorced 1976); ed Cen. School of Art and Design, London; Head of Theatre Design Dept, Cen. School of Art and Design 1965–72; Assoc. Artist RSC 1964–66, 1976–; Opera Dir The Flying Dutchman, Hong Kong Arts Festival 1987 and La Traviata 1990; over 200 productions of opera, drama and dance throughout Europe, the USA, Canada and Australia; Fellow Acad. of Performing Arts, Hong Kong, London Inst., Rose Bruford Coll. Art; Royal Design for Industry, London Drama Critics' Award (for As You Like It) 1967, Gold Medal (Prague Quadriennale) 1975, Soc. of West End Theatres Designer of the Year (for Brand) 1978, Golden Triga (Prague) 1979, 1991, London

Drama Critics' Award (for The Love Girl and The Innocent) 1981, Designer of the Year Award (for Cyrano de Bergerac) 1989, Silver Medal, Prague (for Othello) 1987, Distinguished Service to Theater, US Inst. of Theater Tech. 1993. *Exhibition:* retrospective exhbn London 1997, touring Asia, Europe 1998–99. *Designs include:* musical Metropolis 1989 (London), The Planets (Royal Ballet) 1990, The Makropulos Affair (Norwegian Opera) 1992, My Fair Lady (New York) 1993, La Traviata (Stockholm) 1993, Hair (London) 1993, Othello (Essen) 1994, (Tokyo) 1995, Madame Butterfly (Tokyo) 1995, Twelfth Night (Copenhagen) 1996, Carmen (Royal Albert Hall, London) 1997, Simon Boccanegra (Wales) 1997, Timon of Athens (Chicago) 1997, Nabucco (Festival Orange, France) 1998, Suddenly Last Summer (also Dir, Nottingham Playhouse) 1998, Dalibor (Edin. Festival) 1998, A Midsummer Night's Dream (Copenhagen 1998), Don Giovanni (St Petersburg) 1999, Genoveva (Edin. Festival) 2000, Katya Kabanova (La Fenice, Venice) 2003. *Publication:* Ralph Koltai: Designer for the Stage 1997. *Leisure interest:* wildlife photography. *Address:* c/o London Management, 2–4 Noel Street, London W1; Suite 118, 78 Marylebone High Street, London, W1U 5AP, England. *Telephone:* (20) 7287-9000. *Fax:* (20) 7287-3436.

KOLVENBACH, Peter-Hans, SJ; Netherlands ecclesiastic; b. 30 Nov. 1928, Druten (Gelderland); s. of Gerard A. J. Kolvenbach and Jacqueline J. P. Domensino; ed Canisius Coll., Nijmegen, language studies in Netherlands and in Beirut, Inst. of Oriental Languages, Paris, Schools of Ancient Oriental Languages, Sorbonne; theological studies in Beirut, spiritual theology in Pomfret, Conn.; entered Soc. of Jesus 1948, ordained as a priest 1961; Prof. of General Linguistics and Armenian, Inst. of Oriental Languages and Faculty of Humanities, St Joseph's Univ., Beirut 1968–81; Prof. of Gen. Linguistics, then, Dir Inst. of Philosophical Studies and Prof. of Hermeneutics, St Joseph's Univ. 1968–74; del. to 32nd Gen. Congregation of Society of Jesus 1974; Provincial, Jesuit Vice-Province of the Near East 1974–81; Rector, Pontifical Oriental Inst., Rome 1981–83; Superior Gen. of the Society of Jesus Sept. 1983–. *Publications:* Men of God: Men for Others, A Most Pleasant Mission, El Padre Kolvenbach en Colombia, Kolvenbach en México, Cinco mensajes universitarios; numerous articles and reviews primarily in the field of linguistics and spiritual theology. *Address:* Borgo Santo Spirito 4, C.P. 6139, 00195 Rome, Italy. *Telephone:* 689771.

KOLYADA, Nikolai Vladimirovich; Russian actor, writer and playwright; b. 4 Dec. 1957, Presnogorkovka, Kustanai region, Kazakhstan; ed ed. Sverdlovsk Higher School of Theatre Arts; actor Sverdlovsk Drama theatre 1972–77; mem. USSR Writers' Union 1989–; teacher Yekaterinburg Inst. of Theatre Arts 1998–; Ed.-in-Chief Ural Journal 1999–; Sverdlovsk Komsomol Cttee Prize 1978, Teatralnaya Zhizn (magazine) Prize 1988, Schloss Solitude Academy Award, Stuttgart, Germany 1992. *Plays:* Forfeits, Our Unsociable Sea or A Fool's Vessels, Barakb Lashkaldak, Parents' Day, Slingshot, Chicken, Polonaise, Mannequin, A Tale About the Dead Tsarina, Persian Lilac; *Theatre:* Chicken Blindness. *Publications:* Plays for Beloved Theatre 1994. *Address:* Ural Journal, Malysheva str. 24, 620219 GSP 352, Yekaterinburg, Russia. *Telephone:* (3432) 759754. *Fax:* (3432) 769741. *E-mail:* editor@mail.ur/ru. *Website:* www.koljada.uralinfo.ru/.

KOMAROV, Igor Sergeyevich, DrSc; Russian geologist; b. 29 Jan. 1917, Kiev; s. of Sergey Ivanovich Komarov and Nathalia Yosifovna Komarova; m. Nathalya Khaime 1968; one s. one d.; ed Moscow Geological Prospecting Inst.; prospecting work 1938–43; served in Soviet Army 1943–47; on staff of Moscow Geological Prospecting Inst. (now Acad.), Asst Prof., Dean, then Prof. of Eng Geology 1948–; Lenin Prize for work on Eng Geology of the USSR (8 Vols) 1982. *Publications:* Multimeasured Statistical Analysis in Engineering Geology 1976, Application of Aeromethods in Engineering Geology 1978, Engineering Geology of the USSR (8 Vols) 1976–80, Engineering Geology of the Earth 1989, Engineering Geology of Platform Regions of the USSR 1991. *Leisure interests:* skiing, bridge. *Address:* Moscow Geological Prospecting Academy, 23 Micklucho–Macklai Street, 117873 Moscow (Office); Millionshchikova Street 15, Apt. 198, 115487 Moscow, Russia (Home). *Telephone:* (095) 433-64-66 (Office); (095) 112-05-90 (Home). *E-mail:* ikomarov@space.ru (Home).

KOMATSU, Koh, BEcons; Japanese banker; b. 14 March 1921, Kobe City; s. of Masanori and Sumi Komatsu; m. Setsuko Itoh 1948; one s. two d.; ed Tokyo Univ.; joined Sumitomo Bank Ltd 1946, Dir 1971–, Man. Dir 1973–77, Sr Man. Dir 1977–81, Deputy Pres. 1981–83, Pres. 1983–87, Deputy Chair. 1987; Dir Fed. of Bankers Asscns of Japan 1983–; Standing Dir Kansai Econ. Fed. 1984–. *Leisure interest:* literature. *Address:* Sumitomo Bank, 3-2 Marunouchi 1-chome, Chiyoda-ku, Tokyo 100 (Office); 301 Higashimatsubara Terrace, 24-15, Daita 4-chome, Setagaya-ku, Tokyo, Japan (Home). *Telephone:* (3) 282-5111 (Office); (3) 323-3154 (Home).

KOMILOV, Abdulaziz H., PhD; Uzbekistan diplomatist; b. 16 Nov. 1947, Yangiyul; m.; one s.; ed Moscow Inst. of Oriental Languages; Diplomatic Acad. USSR Ministry of Foreign Affairs; diplomatic service 1972; Attaché USSR Embassy, Lebanon 1973–76; Second Sec. USSR Embassy Syria 1980–84; mem. Div. of Near E, USSR Ministry of Foreign Affairs 1984–88; Sr researcher Inst. of World Econs and Int. Affairs, USSR Acad. of Sciences 1988–91; Counsellor Uzbekistan Embassy, Russian Fed. 1991–92; Deputy Chair. Security Service of Uzbekistan Repub. 1992–94; First Deputy Minister of Foreign Affairs Jan.–Aug. 1994, Minister of Foreign Affairs 1994–. *Address:*

Ministry of Foreign Affairs, Uzbekistansky prosp. 9, 700029 Tashkent, Uzbekistan. *Telephone:* (71) 133-64-75 (Office). *Fax:* (71) 139-15-17 (Office). *E-mail:* root@relay.tiv.uz (Office). *Website:* www.tiv.uz (Office).

KOMISARJEVSKY, Christopher, MBA; American public relations executive; b. 16 Feb. 1945, New Haven, Conn., USA; ed Union Coll., Univ. of Freiburg, Univ. of Connecticut School of Business, Wharton School; Capt. US Army (helicopter pilot) 1967–72, combat service in Viet Nam, 1st Cavalry Div. 1969–70; Sr Vice-Pres. Hill & Knowlton 1974–85, Deputy Man. Dir Hill & Knowlton Int. 1985–86, COO 1986–87, Pres. and CEO of Europe/Middle East/Africa operations 1987–88, Exec. Vice-Pres. and Man. Dir corp. and financial counselling office, USA 1990–91, Exec. Vice-Pres. and Gen. Man., New York and Eastern USA, 1991–93; Pres. and CEO Carl Byoir and Assocs. 1988–90; Pres. and CEO Gavin Anderson & Co. 1993–95; Pres. and CEO Burson Marsteller, USA, 1995–98, Pres. and CEO Burson Marsteller (Worldwide) 1998–; Trustee EQ Advisors Trust; mem. Univ. of Miami Rosenstiel School, Asscn for the Help of Retarded Children; mem. Arthur Page Soc.; lectured on communications and business in Spain, Switzerland and New York; Ellis Island Medal of Honor 1996. *Publications:* Peanut Butter & Jelly Management 2000 (with Reina Komisarjevsky); numerous articles on public relations topics. *Address:* Burson Marsteller Worldwide, 230 Park Avenue, New York, NY 10003, USA (Office). *Telephone:* (212) 614-5008 (Office). *Fax:* (212) 598-6914 (Office). *E-mail:* christopher_komisarjevsky@nyc.bm.com (Office). *Website:* www.bm.com (Office).

KOMLEVA, Gabriela Trofimovna; Russian ballerina; b. 27 Dec. 1938, Leningrad; d. of Trofim Ivanovich Komlev and Lucia Petrovna Komleva; m. Arkady Andreevich Sokolov-Kaminsky 1970; ed Leningrad Ballet School (teacher Kostrovitskaya) and Leningrad Conservatoire; with Kirov (now Mariinsky) Ballet 1957–, teacher 1978–; teacher Leningrad Conservatoire 1987–, Prof. 1994; regular masterclasses in Europe and USA 1994–; Presenter Terpsichore's Finest Points, Leningrad TV 1985–89; numerous awards including People's Artist of USSR 1983. *Major roles:* Odette-Odile in Swan Lake, Aurore in Sleeping Beauty, Nikiya in La Bayadère, Raimonda, Giselle, Kitry in Don Quixote, Cinderella, Sylphide, Sylphides, Firebird, Paquita, Pas de Quatre and many modern ballets. *Films:* Don Quixote, La Bayadère, The Sleeping Beauty, Paquita, Pas de Quatre, Cinderella, The Moor's Pavane, The Firebird, Leningrad Symphony, Furious Isadora. *Publication:* Dance–My Happiness and My Suffering, The Memoirs of a St Petersburg Ballerina 2000. *Leisure interests:* painting, music. *Address:* Fontanka Nab. 116, Apt. 34, 190005 St Petersburg, Russia. *Telephone:* (812) 110-10-83. *Fax:* (812) 110-10-83.

KOMLÓS, Péter; Hungarian violinist; b. 25 Oct. 1935, Budapest; s. of László Komlós and Franciska Graf; m. 1st Edit Fehér 1960, two s.; m. 2nd Zsuzsa Árki 1984, one s.; ed Budapest Music Acad.; f. Komlós String Quartet 1957; First Violinist, Budapest Opera Orchestra 1960; Leader Bartók String Quartet 1963; 1st Prize, Int. String Quartet Competition, Liège 1964, Liszt Prize 1965, Gramophone Record Prize of Germany 1969, Kossuth Prize 1970, 1997, Eminent Artist Title 1980, UNESCO Music Council Plaque 1981; Order of Merit, Middle Cross of Repub. of Hungary 1995. *Performances:* extensive concert tours to USSR, Scandinavia, Italy, Austria, German Democratic Repub. Czechoslovakia 1958–64, USA, Canada, NZ and Australia 1970, including Human Rights Day concert, UN HQ New York, Japan, Spain and Portugal 1971, Far East, USA and Europe 1973; performed at music festivals of Ascona, Edin., Adelaide, Spoleto, Menton, Schwetzingen, Lucerne, Aix-en-Provence. *Recordings:* recordings of Beethoven's string quartets for Hungaroton, Budapest and of Bartók's string quartets for Erato, Paris. *Leisure interest:* watching sports. *Address:* 2083 Solymár, Sport-u. 6, Hungary. *Telephone:* (6) 26-360-697. *Fax:* (6) 26-360-772.

KOMMANDEUR, Jan, PhD; Netherlands professor of physical chemistry (retd); b. 29 Nov. 1929, Amsterdam; s. of Jan Kommandeur and Rika Jorna; m. Elizabeth Eickholz 1951; two s.; ed Univ. of Amsterdam; Postdoctoral Fellow, Research Council, Ottawa 1955–57; research scientist, Union Carbide Corpn, Cleveland, Ohio 1958–61; Prof. of Physical Chem. Univ. of Groningen 1961–94; mem. Royal Netherlands Acad. of Science 1981, Science Advisory Council of the Netherlands; Kt Order of Lion 1993. *Publications:* Photoconductivity in Aromatic Hydrocarbons 1958, Electric Conductivity in Organic Complexes 1961, Ions in Iodine 1966, Natural Gas in Europe: How much, for how long? 1977, Radiationless Transitions 1988. *Leisure interests:* literature, theatre, popularizing science. *Address:* P. J. Noel Baker Straat 180, 9728 WG, Groningen, Netherlands (Home). *Telephone:* (50) 5267053. *Fax:* (50) 5267053. *E-mail:* j.kommandeur@home.nl (Home).

KOMOROWSKI, Stanislaw, DSc; Polish diplomatist; b. 18 Dec. 1953, Warsaw; s. of Henryk Komorowski and Helena Komorowska; m. Ewa Komorowska; three s.; ed Warsaw Univ.; researcher, Inst. of Physical Chem., Polish Acad. of Sciences 1978–90, lecturer 1987–89; lecturer, Univ. of Utah, USA 1989; Dir Dept of Western Europe, Ministry of Foreign Affairs 1991–94; Amb. to The Netherlands 1994–98, to UK 1999–; Dir Secr. of Minister of Foreign Affairs 1998–99; Grand Cross of the Order of Orange Nassau 1988. *Leisure interests:* tennis, photography, skiing. *Address:* Embassy of Poland, 47 Portland Place, London W1B 1JH (Office); 4 Templewood Avenue, London NW3 7XA, England (Home). *Telephone:* (20) 7580-4324 (Office). *Fax:* (20) 7323-4018 (Office). *E-mail:* polishembassy@polishembassy.org.uk (Office). *Website:* www.polishembassy.org.uk (Office).

KOMURA, Masahiko; Japanese politician; fmr Parl. Vice-Minister Defence Agency; Minister of State, Dir-Gen. Econ. Planning Agency 1994–95; mem. House of Reps for Yamaguchi; Deputy Sec.-Gen. LDP, Chair. LDP Special Cttee on Disasters; Minister of Foreign Affairs 1999, then Minister of Justice –2001. *Address:* c/o Liberal-Democratic Party, 1-11-23, Nagata-cho, Chiyoda-ku, Tokyo 100-8910.

KON, Igor Semenovich, DPhil; Russian psychologist; b. 21 May 1928, Leningrad; ed Leningrad Pedagogical Inst.; Prof., Chair. of Philosophy Leningrad State Univ. 1950–68; Head of Div. Inst. of Concrete Social Studies, USSR Acad. of Sciences 1968–75, mem. of staff Inst. of Ethnography (now Inst. of Ethnology and Anthropology) 1975–; mem. Russian Acad. of Educ. 1989; Hon. Prof. Cornell Univ. *Publications:* Sociology of Personality, Introduction to Sexology, Sexual Revolution in Russia, Faces and Masks of Unisexual Love; and numerous articles on psychology, sociology and sexology. *Address:* N. Miklukho-Maklai Institute of Ethnology and Anthropology, Leninsky prosp. 32a, korp. B, 117334 Moscow, Russia (Office). *Telephone:* (095) 938-17-47 (Office).

KONARÉ, Alpha Oumar, PhD; Malian politician; b. 1946, Kayes; m. Adam Ba; four c.; ed Ecole nat. supérieure, Univ. of Warsaw, Poland; teacher; Dir Inst. for Human Sciences, Bamako 1974, Historic and Ethnographic Div., Ministry of Culture 1975–78; Minister for Youth, Sports and Culture 1978–80 (resgnd); Research Fellow, Institut supérieur de formation et de recherche appliquée, Bamako 1980–89; f. Jamana, a cultural co-operative 1983; f. daily Les Echos, monthly for young people, Grin Grin and news service on tape cassettes for rural population 1989; Pres. of Mali 1992–2002. *Publications:* Le Concept du pouvoir en Afrique, Bibliographie archéologique du Mali, Les grandes dates du Mali (with Adam Ba), Sikasso Tata, Les Constitutions du Mali, Les Partis politiques au Mali. *Address:* c/o Office of the President, B.P. 1463, Koulouba, Bamako, Mali (Office).

KONDIĆ, Novak, MA; Bosnia and Herzegovina (Serb) politician and economist; b. 20 July 1952, Banja Luka; s. of Vlado Kondić and Gospa Kondić; m. Nevenka Predragović 1980; two s.; ed Univ. of Banja Luka; Head Co. Accountancy Dept, Serbian Devt Bank, Banja Luka 1977–86, Head of Inspectorate Control and Information Analysis 1986–90, Dir Municipal Admin. of Public Revenues 1990–92, mem. Municipal Exec. Bd 1990–92; Deputy Dir-Gen. Payment Transaction Services for Repub. of Srpska 1992–95, for Banja Luka 1997–; Minister of Finance Repub. of Srpska 1995–97, 1998–2000; Rep. of Bosnia and Herzegovina to IMF 1998; Medal for Mil. Valour. *Leisure interests:* beekeeping, gardening, vineyard cultivation, fruit farming. *Address:* Kolubarska 11, 78000 Banja Luka, Republic of Srpska, Bosnia and Herzegovina. *Telephone:* (78) 212 871.

KONDO, Seiichi, BA; Japanese international organization official; m.; one d.; ed Univ. of Tokyo, St Catherine's Coll., Oxford, UK; seconded by Foreign Ministry to Ministry of Int. Trade and Industry 1977–80, to Int. Energy Agency, OECD 1980–83; Deputy Dir OECD Desk, Foreign Ministry 1983–86, Deputy Head Korea Desk 1986–87, Chef de Cabinet, Vice-Minister of Foreign Affairs 1987–88, Dir Int. Press Div. 1988–90; Head of Chancery, Manila 1990–92; Counsellor for Public Affairs, Washington, DC 1992–95, Minister 1996; Head Co-ordination and Logistics Office for G8 Summits, Asia-Pacific Econ. Co-operation and Asia-Europe Meeting 1996–97; Deputy Dir-Gen. Econ. Affairs Bureau 1998–99; Deputy Sec.-Gen. OECD 1999–. *Publications:* Image of Japan in the American Media 1994, The Distorted Image of Japan – The Perception Game Inside The Beltway 1997; many articles in Japanese and English-language magazines. *Address:* OECD, 2 rue André-Pascal, 75775 Paris cédex 16, France (Office). *Telephone:* 1-45-24-82-00 (Office). *Fax:* 1-45-24-85-00 (Office). *E-mail:* webmaster@oecd.org (Office). *Website:* www.oecd.org (Office).

KONDOR, Katalin; Hungarian journalist; b. 27 Oct. 1946, Debrecen; d. of Lajos Kondor and Erzsébet Kuhár; ed Budapest Economics Univ., Budapest Univ. of Arts and Sciences (ELTE), School of Journalism; joined Hungarian Radio 1973, TV and radio presenter 1990–, Ed.-in-Chief Kossuth Radio 1999–2001; Pres. Hungarian Radio 2001–. *Publications:* Szerda reggel (Wednesday Morning) (radio interviews with Prime Minister Viktor Orbán, co-ed by János Hollós) Vol. 1 2001, Vol. 2 2002. *Leisure interests:* theatre, opera, music, travel, reading and animals. *Address:* Magyar Rádió (Hungarian Radio), Bródy Sándor u. 5–7, 1800 Budapest, Hungary (Office). *Telephone:* (1) 328-7621/3 (Office). *Fax:* (1) 328-7355 (Office). *E-mail:* kondorka@radio.hu (Office). *Website:* www.radio.hu (Office).

KONDRATYEV, Col-Gen. Georgy Grigorievich; Russian army officer; b. 17 Nov. 1944, Klintsy, Bryansk Region; m.; two c.; ed Kharkov Guards Tank School, Mil. Acad. of Armoured Forces, USSR Gen. Staff Acad.; served as Commdr of tank platoon, Bn, Commdr Regt, Gen. Staff 1973–74; Regt Commdr 1974–76; Deputy Commdr, Div. Commdr 1976–85; Deputy C-in-C Turkestan Army Mil. Command 1985–87, Commdr 1987–89; First Deputy C-in-C Turkestan Mil. Command 1989–91, Commdr 1991–92; Deputy Minister of Defence of Russian Fed. 1992–95; Deputy Minister Ministry of Emergencies and Natural Disasters 1995–99, Chief. Mil. Expert 1999–. *Address:* Ministry of Emergencies and Natural Disasters, Teatralny per. 4, 103012 Moscow, Russia. *Telephone:* (095) 926-38-57 (Office).

KONDRAT'YEVA, Marina Viktorovna; Russian ballet dancer; b. 1 Feb. 1934; ed Bolshoi Theatre Ballet School; with Bolshoi Ballet Co. 1953–80; coach at Bolshoi Theatre 1980–; People's Artist of RSFSR 1976. *Main roles*

include: Cinderella (Cinderella), Maria (Fountain of Bakhchisaraï), Aurora (Sleeping Beauty), Juliet (Romeo and Juliet), Katerina (Stone Flower), Giselle (Giselle), Gayane (Gayane), Odette-Odile (Swan Lake), Shirin (Legend of Love). *Address:* c/o Bolshoi Theatre, Teatralnaya Ploshchad 1, Moscow, Russia. *Telephone:* (095) 291-27-97.

KONDRUSEVIC, Tadeusz Ignatyevich, DTheol; Russian Roman Catholic ecclesiastic; b. 3 Jan. 1946; ed Vilnius Polytech. Inst., Kaunas Ecclesiastical Seminary; with St Therese Church, Ostra Brama Church, Vilnius 1981–87; Dean Cathedral of God's mother–Angels' Tsarina, Grodno 1988–89; Titular Bishop and Apostle Admin. of Minsk, First Bishop of Belarus Catholics 1989; currently Titular Archbishop of Hippo Diarrhytus and Apostolic Admin. for Catholics of the Latin Rite in Northern European Russia, Moscow. *Address:* Church of St Ludovic, M. Lubyanka str. 12, 101000 Moscow, Russia (Office). *Telephone:* (095) 925-20-34 (Office).

KONG JIESHENG; Chinese writer; b. 1952, Guangzhou City, Guangdong Prov.; Vice-Chair., Guangzhou Br. of Writers' Asscn 1985–. *Publications:* My Marriage 1978, Story Investigations 1985. *Address:* Guangzhou Branch of Writers' Association, Guangzhou City, Guangdong Province, People's Republic of China.

KONIDARIS, Ioannis (John), DrIur; Greek professor of law; b. 10 Sept. 1948, Chios; s. of Marinos Konidaris and Ioanna Konidaris; m. Ersi Mantakas 1975, one d.; ed Univs of Athens, Thessaloniki and Munich; mil. service 1971–73; mem. Bar Asscn of Athens 1974–; Asst Faculty of Law, Univ. of Frankfurt 1978–81; Lecturer in Ecclesiastical Law 1985; mem. editorial Bd of official journal of Bar Asscn of Athens 1985–; Prof. of Ecclesiastical Law, Univ. of Athens 1989–; Research Scholarship, Max Planck Inst. for European History of Law, Frankfurt am Main 1989–90; Dir Research Centre for the History of Greek Law, Acad. of Athens 1994–2000, Ed. the Centre's Yearbook (Vol. 31) 1995, (Vol. 32) 1996, (Vol. 33) 1997, (Vol. 34) 1998; columnist on ecclesiastical issues, BHMA newspaper; adviser on religious subjects to Minister of Foreign Affairs 1996–99, 2001; Sec.-Gen. for Religious Affairs, Ministry of Nat. Educ. and Religious Affairs 2001–; Founder and Ed. Nomokanonika 2002–. *Publications include:* Monastic Property Law Between 9th and 12th Centuries 1979, Legal Aspects of Monastery 'Typika' 1984, Legal Theory and Praxis concerning Jehovah's Witnesses in Greece 1987, 1988, 1991, Law 1700/1987 and the Recent Crisis Between the Orthodox Church and the Greek State 1988, 1991, Subjects of Byzantine and Ecclesiastical Law 1991, Church and State in Greece 1993, The Conflict between Law and Canon and the Establishment of Harmony Between Them 1994, Ekklesiastika Atakta 1999, Basic Legislation of State-Church Relations 1999, A Manual of Ecclesiastical Law 2000, Regulations of the Church of Greece 2001, Regulations of the Monasteries of the Church of Greece (two vols) 2002, Mount Athos Avaton 2003; numerous articles on ecclesiastical law and history of law, especially Byzantine law. *Address:* 45 Akadimias Street, 10672 Athens (University); 107 Asklipiou Street, 11472 Athens (Private Office); 20 Bizaniou Street, 15237 Filothei/Athens, Greece (Home). *Telephone:* 3688607 (University); 3630391 (Private Office); 6742896 (Home). *Fax:* 6772225 (Home); 3630391 (Private Office). *E-mail:* imkonidaris@law.uoa.gr (Office).

KÖNIG, HE Cardinal Franz; Austrian ecclesiastic; b. 3 Aug. 1905, Rabenstein, Pielach; ed Univs of Rome, Vienna and Lille; ordained 1933; Dozent, Vienna Univ. 1946; Prof., Faculty of Theology, Salzburg 1948; Titular Bishop of Livias 1952; Archbishop of Vienna 1956–85; cr. Cardinal by Pope John XXIII 1958; fmr Pres. Secr. for Non-Believers, Rome; Pres. Pax Christi Int. 1985–90. *Publications include:* Christus und die Religionen der Erde, Religionswissenschaftliches Wörterbuch, Zarathustras Jenseitsvorstellungen und das Alte Testament 1964, Die Stunde der Welt 1971, Aufbruch zum Geist 1972, Das Zeichen Gottes 1973, Der Mensch ist für die Zukunft angelegt 1975, Kirche und Welt 1978, Glaube ist Freiheit 1981, Der Glaube der Menschen (Herausgeber) 1985, Der Weg der Kirche 1988, Lexikon der Religionen 1987, Juden und Christen haben eine Zukunft 1988 (König/Ehrlich). *Address:* Wollzeile 2, 1010 Vienna, Austria. *Telephone:* (1) 515-52-223.

KONO, Yohei; Japanese politician; b. 15 Jan. 1937; ed Waseda Univ., Stanford Univ.; mem. House of Reps from Kanagawa; fmr Parl. Vice-Minister of Educ., Dir-Gen. Science and Tech. Agency; Chief Cabinet Sec. (State Minister) 1992–93; Chair. LDP Research Comm. on Foreign Affairs, Pres. 1993–99; Minister of Foreign Affairs 1999–2001; Deputy Prime Minister and Minister of Foreign Affairs 1994–96; left LDP to co-found New Liberal Club (now defunct) 1976–86; mem. Miyazawa faction of LDP. *Address:* Liberal Democratic Party (Jiyu-Minshuto), 1-11-23, Nagata-cho, Chiyoda-ku, Tokyo 100-8910, Japan. *Telephone:* (3) 3581-6211. *E-mail:* koho@ldp.jimin.or.jp (Office). *Website:* www.jimin.jp (Office).

KONOVALOV, Aleksander Nikolayevich, MD; Russian neurosurgeon; b. 12 Dec. 1933, Moscow; s. of Nikolai Konovalov and Ekaterina Konovalova; m. Inna Konovalova 1957, one s.; ed First Moscow Medical Inst.; intern, researcher, Deputy Dir N. N. Burdenko Research Inst. of Neurosurgery 1957–75, Dir 1975–; mem. Russian Acad. of Medical Sciences 1992, Russian Acad. of Sciences 2000; conducted unique operation on separation of the heads of Siamese twins 1989; Ed.-in-Chief Voprosi Neurochirurgii; USSR State Prize; Orden Druzba Narodov. *Publications:* more than 215 works on problems of surgery. *Leisure interests:* tennis, skiing. *Address:* N. N. Burdenko Institute of Neurosurgery, Fadeeva str. 5, 125047 Moscow (Office); Novoslobodskaya str. 57/65, Apt. 33, 103055 Moscow, Russia (Home). *Telephone:* (095) 251-65-26 (Office); (095) 978-76-18 (Home). *Fax:* (095) 975-22-28.

KONRÁD, György; Hungarian novelist and essayist; b. 2 April 1933, Debrecen; s. of József Konrád and Róza Klein; m. Judit Lakner; three s. two d.; ed Eötvös Loránd Univ., Budapest; Ed. Életképek 1956; social worker, Budapest 7th Dist Council 1959–65; Ed. Magyar Helikon 1960–66; urban sociologist on staff of City Planning Research Inst. 1965–73; full-time writer 1973–; Pres. Akad. der Künste Berlin-Brandenburg; numerous scholarships; visiting Prof. of Comparative Literature, Colorado Springs Coll. 1988; Corresp. mem. Bayerische Akad., Munich; fmr Pres. Int. PEN; Herder Award, Vienna-Hamburg 1984, Charles Veillon European Essay, Zürich 1986, Fredfonden Peace Foundation, Copenhagen 1986, Fed. Critics' Prize for Novel of the Year (Fed. Repub. of Germany) 1986, Kossuth Prize, Friedens-Preis des Deutschen Buchhandels 1991, Karlspreis zu Aachen 2001. *Publications include:* (novels) A látogató (The Case Worker) 1969, A városlapitó (The City Builder) 1977, A cinkos (The Loser) 1983, Kerti mulatságok (Feast in the Garden) 1987, Kóóra (Stone Clock) 1994; (Essays): Az értelmiség utja az osztályhatalomhoz (The Intellectuals on the Road to Class Power) 1978, Az autonómia kisértése (The Temptation of Autonomy) 1980, Antipolitics 1986, The Melancholy of Rebirth 1991, Esszék 91–93 (Essays 1991–93) 1993, Várakozás (Expectation) 1995, Áramló leltár 1996, Láthatatlan hang (The Invisible Voice) 1997. *Address:* 1026 Budapest, Torockó utca 3, Hungary. *Telephone:* (1) 560-425.

KONTIĆ, Radoje, DTechSc; Serbia and Montenegro (Montenegrin) politician and engineer; b. 31 May 1937, Nikšić; s. of Milivoje Kontić and Vidoslava Kontić; m. Mara Kontić; three c.; ed High School of Chemical Eng; specialized in France in ferrous metallurgy; Tech. Dir Niksic Steel Co.; Prof. School of Tech. and Metallurgy Univ. of Podgorica; Minister Fed. Govt; Prime Minister of Yugoslavia 1993–97. *Publications include:* univ. textbook on metallurgy.

KONTOGEORGIS, Georgios; Greek politician and public servant; b. 21 Nov. 1912; m.; Prin. Admin., Ministry of Economy and of Trade 1941–52; Dir-Gen. Ministry of Trade until 1967; Sec. of State for Econ. Co-ordination and Planning 1974–77; mem. Parl. (New Democracy Party) 1977; Minister for Relations with the EEC 1977 (led negotiations for Greece's entry); Commr for Transport, Fisheries and Co-ordination of Tourism, Comm. of European Communities 1981–85; Minister for Nat. Economy and Tourism 1989–90. *Publication:* The Association of Greece with the European Community 1961, Greece in Europe 1985, The European Idea: The European Union, Greece: History, Present, Perspectives 1995. *Address:* 26–28 Anagnostopoulou Street, 106 73 Athens, Greece. *Telephone:* 3616844.

KONTOS, Constantine William; American government official; b. 10 Aug. 1922, Chicago, Ill.; s. of William C. and Irene Thomas Kontos; m. Joan Fultz 1948; two s.; ed Univ. of Chicago and London School of Econs; Special Asst to Dir of Econ. Co-operation Admin., Mission to Greece 1949–53; Program Budget Officer, Foreign Operations Admin., Washington, DC 1953–55; Sr Man. Officer Int. Co-operation Admin., Washington, DC 1955–57; Exec. Officer, Bureau of Africa and Europe 1957–59; Deputy Dir US Agency for Int. Devt (USAID) Mission, Ceylon 1959–61; Deputy Dir USAID Mission, Nigeria 1961–64; attended Nat. War Coll. 1964–65; Dir Personnel USAID 1965–67; Dir USAID Mission, Pakistan 1967–69; Dir Office of Program Evaluation, USAID 1969–72; Deputy Commr-Gen. UN Relief and Works Agency (UNRWA) 1972–74; mem. policy planning staff, State Dept, Washington 1974–76; special rep. of Pres., Dir Sinai support mission, Washington 1976–80; Amb. to Sudan 1980–83; mem. Policy Planning Council, Dept of State 1983–86, Exec. Dir Advisory Cttee to Sec. of State on South Africa 1986–87, Policy Planning Staff 1987; Sr Vice-Pres. Exec. Council on Foreign Diplomats 1988–90; ind. consultant 1990–; Vice-Pres. Global Business Access Inc. 1992–; Dept of State Superior Honor Award 1971. *Address:* 3606 Warren Street, NW, Washington, DC 20008, USA. *Telephone:* (202) 966-8578 (Home).

KONUK, Nejat; Turkish-Cypriot politician, lawyer and writer; b. 1928, Nicosia; ed Turkish Lycée, Cyprus and Law Faculty of Ankara Univ., Turkey; Legal Adviser in Turkish Civil Service, Turkey; Sec.-Gen. and Acting Dir-Gen. of Turkish Communal Chamber, Cyprus; Under-Sec. to Rauf Denktaş (q.v.) 1968–69; Minister of Justice and Internal Affairs, Turkish Cypriot Admin. 1969–75; mem. for Nicosia, Turkish Communal Chamber, Constituent Ass., Turkish Cypriot Leg. Ass. 1970–; founder mem. Nat. Unity Party 1975, Leader 1976–78; Prime Minister "Turkish Federated State of Cyprus" 1976–78; Leader of the Democratic People's Party 1979–82 (resgnd); Pres. Legis. Ass. "Turkish Federated State of Cyprus" July–Dec. 1981, 1982–83; Prime Minister "Turkish Repub. of N Cyprus" 1983–85. *Publications:* essays on literature, various papers on Cyprus, political articles 1953–77. *Leisure interests:* reading, swimming. *Address:* Kumsal, Lefkoşa, Mersin 10, Turkey.

KONUMA, Michiji, DS; Japanese professor of physics; b. 25 Jan. 1931, Tokyo; s. of Haruo Konuma and Taka Konuma; m. Masae Shinohara 1960; one s. one d.; ed Musashi High School and Univ. of Tokyo; Research Assoc. Univ. of Tokyo 1958–67 (leave of absence 1963–67); Research Fellow, Consiglio Nazionale Ricerche, Italy and Visiting Prof. Scuola Normale Superiore, Pisa 1963–65; Visiting Prof. Catholic Univ. of Louvain, Belgium 1965–67; Assoc. Prof. Kyoto Univ. 1967–83; Prof. Keio Univ. 1983–96, Prof. Emer. 1996–; Prof. and Dean, Faculty of Environmental and Information Studies, Musashi Inst. of Tech., Yokohama 1996–2001, Adviser 2001–03; Visiting Prof. Univ. of the Air 1992–2001; mem. Physics Action Council, UNESCO 1994–96; mem. and fmr Pres. Physical Soc. of Japan; Pres. Asscn of Asia Pacific Physical Socs 1994–97, Special Adviser 2001–; mem. Council, Pugwash Confs on Science and World Affairs 1992–2002; other professional appts; Hon. mem. Roland

Eötvös Physical Soc., Hungary 1997; Hon. mem. Hungarian Acad. of Sciences 1998. *Publications:* numerous articles on theoretical particle physics, history of modern physics and physics educ. *Address:* Musashi Institute of Technology, Ushikubonishi 3-3-1, Tsuzuki-ku, Yokohama 224-0015 (Office); 200-9 Kudencho, Sakaeku, Yokohama 247-0014, Japan (Home). *Telephone:* (45) 910-2500 (Office); (45) 891-8386 (Home). *Fax:* (45) 891-8386. *E-mail:* konuma@yc.musashi-tech.ac.jp. *Website:* www.yc.musashi-tech.ac.jp.

KONWICKI, Tadeusz; Polish writer and film director; b. 22 June 1926, Nowa Wilejka, USSR (now in Lithuania); m. Danuta Lenica (deceased); ed Jagiellonian Univ., Cracow, Warsaw Univ.; Partisan, Home Army detachment 1944–45; mem. Polish Writers' Asscn 1949–, Editorial Staff of Nowa Kultura (weekly) 1950–57; Officer's Cross, Order of Polonia Restituta 1964; State Prize, 3rd Class 1950, 1954, 1st Class 1966; Mondello Prize for Literature 1981 and many other awards and prizes at int. film festivals, including Venice 1958. *Films directed:* Ostatni dzień lata (Last Day of Summer) 1958, Zaduszki 1962, Salto 1965, Jak daleko stąd jak blisko 1972, Dolina Issy 1982, Lawa 1989. *Publications:* novels: Władza 1954, Godzina smutku 1954, Z oblężonego miasta 1955, Rojsty 1956, Dziura w niebie 1959, Sennik współczesny (A Dreambook of Our Time) 1963, Ostatni dzień lata (filmscript) 1966, Wniebowstąpienie 1967, Zwierzoczłekoupiór 1969, Nic albo nic 1971, Kronika wypadków miłosnych 1974, Kalendarz i klepsydra (The Calendar and the Sand-Glass) 1976, Kompleks polski 1977, Mała apokalipsa 1979, Wschody i zachody Księżyca 1982, Rzeka podziemna, podziemne ptaki 1985; Nowy Świat i okolice 1986, Bohiń 1987, Zorze wieczorne 1991, Czytadło 1994, Pamflet na samego siebie 1995; filmscripts: Zimowy zmierzch (Winter Twilight), Matka Joanna od aniołów 1961, Faraon 1965, Jowita 1968, Austeria 1988. *Address:* ul. Górskiego 1 m. 68, 00-033 Warsaw, Poland.

KONYUKHOV, Fedor Filippovich; Russian explorer; b. 12 Dec. 1951, Chkalovo, Zaporizhye Region, USSR (now Ukraine); m.; two c.; ed Kronstadt Marine Higher School, Bobruysk School of Arts; completed solo expedition to North Pole 1989; completed project Seven Mountain Peaks of the World (one-man ascent of seven peaks of seven continents) 1997; f. School of Travellers 1991; Plenipotentiary Rep. of UNEP (UN programme on Environmental Protection) 1997–; mem. Russian Union of Artists; Hon. Citizen Terni, Italy 1991, Taipei, Taiwan 1995, Nakhodka, Russia 1996; Order of Friendship of Peoples, UNESCO Order; Merited Master of Sports of Russia 1989. *Address:* Tourism and Sports Union of Russia, Studeniy proyezd 7, 129282 Moscow, Russia. *Telephone:* (095) 478-63-02 (Office).

KOOGLE, Timothy K., MS; American communications executive; b. 1952; m. (divorced); ed Univ. of Virginia, Stanford Univ.; Pres. Intermec Corpn; Corp. Vice-Pres. Western Atlas Inc.; with Motorola Inc.; CEO Yahoo! Corpn 1992–99, Chair., CEO 1999–2001; Chair. Bd Dirs AIM. *Leisure interests:* vintage guitars, cars. *Address:* c/o Yahoo! Corporation, 3400 Central Expressway, Santa Clara, CA 95051, USA (Office).

KOOIJMANS, Pieter Hendrik, DJur; Netherlands politician and lawyer; b. 6 July 1933, Heemstede; m. A. Kooijmans-Verhage; four c.; ed Free Univ. Amsterdam; mem. Faculty of Law, Free Univ. of Amsterdam 1960–65, Prof. of European Law and Public Int. Law 1965–73; State Sec. for Foreign Affairs 1973–77; Prof. of Public Int. Law, Univ. of Leiden 1978–92, 1995–; Minister for Foreign Affairs 1993–94; mem. (Judge) Int. Court of Justice 1997–; Chair. or mem. numerous orgs. including Chair. Bd Carnegie Foundation, Netherlands Disaster Relief Agency; Head Netherlands del. to UN Comm. on Human Rights 1982–85, 1992, Chair. Comm. 1984–85, Special Rapporteur on questions relevant to torture 1985–92; mem. various UN and CSCE missions to fmr Yugoslavia 1991–92. *Publications:* various textbooks and articles on int. law and human rights. *Address:* c/o International Court of Justice, Peace Palace, Carnegieplein 2, 2517 KJ The Hague, Netherlands. *Telephone:* (70) 3022323 (Office). *Fax:* (70) 3649928 (Office). *E-mail:* information@icj-cij-org (Office). *Website:* www.icj-cij.org (Office).

KOOLHAAS, Rem; Netherlands architect; b. 1944; ed Architectural Asscn School; fmr journalist Haagse Post, Amsterdam; fmr screenplay writer; co.-f. Office of Metropolitan Architecture (OMA); f. Grosztstadt Foundation; Visiting Scholar, The Getty Center, LA 1993; now Prof. of Architecture and Urban Design, Harvard Univ. Grad. School of Design; Progressive Architecture Award (jtly) 1974, Le Moniteur, Prix d'Architecture 1991, Antonio Gaudi Prize 1992, Pritzker Prize 2000, Chevalier, Légion d'honneur 2001. *Major works include:* Congrexpo, Lille, Kunsthal, Rotterdam, Educatorium, Univ. of Utrecht, Cardiff Bay Opera House, Wales, extension of the Tate Gallery, London, Miami Performing Arts Center, Hypo-Theatiner-Zentrum, Munich, Yokohama Urban Ring, Japan, New Seoul Int. Airport, extension of The Hague's Parl. Bldg, Guggenheim Heritage 2001, Guggenheim Las Vegas 2001. *Exhibitions include:* The Sparkling Metropolis, Guggenheim Museum 1978, OMA 1972–88, ArchitecturMuseum, Basel 1988, OMA. The First Decade, Boymans Museum, Rotterdam 1989, OMA, Museum of Modern Art, New York 1994, Light Construction, Museum of Modern Art, New York 1995. *Publications:* The Berlin Wall as Architecture 1970, Exodus, or the Voluntary Prisoners of Architecture 1972, Delirious New York, a Retrospective Manifesto for Manhattan, OMA: S, M, L, XL. *Address:* Harvard University Graduate School of Design, Cambridge, MA 02138, USA (Office). *Telephone:* (617) 495-1000 (Office). *E-mail:* webmaster@harvard.edu (Office). *Website:* www.harvard.edu (Office).

KOOLMAN, Olindo; Aruban politician; Gov. of Aruba 1992–. *Address:* Office of the Governor, Plaza Henny Eman 3, Oranjestad, Aruba (Office).

KOONS, Jeff; American artist; b. 1955, York, Pa; m. Ilona Staller (La Cicciolina) 1991 (divorced 1994); fmr commodity broker, Wall Street. *One-man exhibitions include:* New Museum of Contemporary Art, New York 1980, Daniel Weinberg Gallery, LA 1986, Max Hetzler Gallery, Cologne 1988, Venster Gallery, Rotterdam 1989, Lehmann Gallery, Lausanne 1992, San Francisco Museum of Modern Art 1992, 1993, Museum of Contemporary Art, Sydney 1996. *Group exhibitions include:* Barbara Gladstone Gallery, New York 1981, Whitney Museum, New York 1985, 1987, 1989, 1990, Galerie Crousel-Hussenot, Paris 1985, Museo Nacional Centro de Arte Reina Sofía, Madrid 1987, Saatchi Collection, London 1987, 1988, Centre Pompidou, Paris 1988, Kunsthalle, Düsseldorf 1988, Biennale, Venice 1990, Anthony d'Offay Gallery, London 1992. *Address:* Koons Production, 433 W 14th Street, Floor 6, New York, NY 10014, USA (Office).

KOONTZ, Dean R(ay) (also writes under pseudonyms David Axton, Brian Coffey, Deanna Dwyer, K. R. Dwyer, John Hill, Leigh Nichols, Anthony North, Richard Paige and Owen West); American author; b. 9 July 1945, Everett, Pa; s. of Raymond Koontz and Florence Logue; m. Gerda Ann Cerra 1966; fmr teacher of English; freelance author 1969–; work includes novels, short stories, science fiction/fantasy, social commentary/phenomena and journalism. *Publications:* recent work (under various names) includes: The Voice of the Night 1980, Whispers 1980, The Funhouse 1980, The Eyes of Darkness 1981, The Mask 1981, House of Thunder 1982, Phantoms 1983, Darkness Comes 1984, Twilight 1984, Strangers 1986, Shadow Fires 1987, Watchers 1987, Twilight Eyes 1987, Oddkins 1988, Servants of Twilight 1988, Midnight 1989, The Bad Place 1990, Moon 1993, The House of Thunder 1993, Dark Rivers of the Heart 1994, Mr Murder 1994, Fun House 1994, Strange Highways 1994, Icebound 1995, Intensity 1995, The Key to Midnight 1995, Ticktock 1996, Sole Survivor 1996, Fear Nothing 1997, Demon Seed 1997, Seize the Night 1998, False Memory 1999, From the Corner of His Eye 2001.

KOOP, C. Everett, AB, MD, ScD; American surgeon; b. 14 Oct. 1916, New York; s. of J. Everett Koop and Helen Apel; m. Elizabeth Flanagan 1938; three s. one d.; ed Dartmouth Coll., Cornell Medical School and Graduate School of Medicine, Univ. of Pennsylvania; Surgeon-in-Chief, Children's Hosp. of Philadelphia 1948–81; Prof. of Pediatric Surgery, Univ. of Pa 1959–85; Prof. of Pediatrics 1976–85; US Surgeon Gen. 1981–89; Deputy Asst Sec. for Health and Dir Office of Int. Health, US Public Health Service (USPHS) 1982; Consultant, USN 1964–84; Ed. of various medical journals 1961–; now with C. Everett Koop Inst.; McInerny Prof., Dartmouth Coll. 1994–; mem. Asscn Mil. Surgeons (Pres. 1982, 1987); special qualifications in pediatric surgery, American Bd. of Pediatric Surgery; 35 hon. degrees; Hon. FRCS; Denis Browne Gold Medal (British Asscn of Paediatric Surgeons) 1971, Duarte, Sanchez and Mella Award of the Dominican Repub., Drexel Univ. Eng and Science Day Award 1975, Chevalier, Légion d'honneur 1980, USPHS Distinguished Service Medal 1983, Department of Health and New Human Services, Secretary's Recognition Award 1986, Harry S Truman Award 1990, Presidential Medal of Freedom 1995, Heinz Foundation Award 1995, Medal of Hon., American Cancer Soc. 2000 and other USPHS awards; Emmy Award for 5-part documentary series 'C. Everett Koop, MD'. *Publications:* 230 papers and monographs; several books including Koop: The Memoirs of the Former Surgeon General 1991, Let's Talk 1992. *Leisure interest:* lapidary art. *Address:* C. Everett Koop Institute at Dartmouth, 7025 Strasenburgh, Hanover, NH 03755, USA (Office). *Telephone:* (603) 650-1450 (Office). *Fax:* (603) 650-1452 (Office).

KOOPMAN, Antonius (Ton) Gerhardus Michael; Netherlands musician, professor of harpsichord and conductor; b. 2 Oct. 1944, Zwolle; m. Christine H. H. Mathot 1975; three d.; ed Amsterdam Conservatory and Univ. of Amsterdam; Prof. of Harpsichord, Royal Conservatory, The Hague; f. Amsterdam Baroque Orchestra 1979, Amsterdam Baroque Choir 1992; appears on concert platforms around the world and on radio and TV; has made over 200 recordings of harpsichord and organ works by Bach, Handel etc.; f. his own record label Antoine Marchand (Sub-label of Challenge Classics); Hon. mem. RAM, London; Dr hc (Utrecht) 2000; winner of several prizes. *Publications:* Interpretation of Baroque Music 1985 and a small book about J. S. Bach 1985; (co-) The Harpischord in Dutch Paintings. *Leisure interests:* art and culture of the Renaissance and Baroque period. *Address:* Meerweg 23, 1405 BC Bussum, Netherlands. *Telephone:* (35) 6913676. *Fax:* (35) 6939752. *E-mail:* ton.koopman@wxs.nl (Office). *Website:* www.tonkoopman.nl (Office).

KÖÖRNA, Arno, PhD; Estonian economist; b. 2 Feb. 1926, Tartu; s. of Artur and Anna Köörna; m. Eha Lind 1946; two c.; ed Tartu Univ.; lecturer Tartu Univ. 1953–65, Prof. 1971; Corresp. mem. Estonian Acad. of Sciences 1972, mem. 1975; Scientific Dir Inst. of Econs Estonian Acad. of Sciences 1965–66, Dir 1966–73; Chief Scientific Sec. Presidium of Estonian Acad. of Sciences 1973–82, Vice-Pres. 1978–82, Pres. 1990–94; Prof. Emer., Eurouniversity, Tallinn 1998–. *Publications:* Science in Estonia 1993, Introduction to the Theory of Innovation 1997, In the Service of Prometheus 2002. *Address:* Estonian Academy of Sciences, Kohtu str. 6, 10130 Tallinn (Office); Kapi str. 9-22, 10136 Tallinn, Estonia (Home). *Telephone:* (2) 6442129 (Office); (2) 6620628 (Home). *Fax:* (2) 6451805 (Office). *E-mail:* riho@tan.ee (Office); arno.koorna@mail.ee (Home). *Website:* www.akadeemia.ee (Office).

KÖPECZI, Béla; Hungarian politician and historian; b. 16 Sept. 1921, Nagyenyed (Aiud in Romania); s. of Árpád Köpeczi and Anna Tomai; m. Edit Bölcskei 1951; ed Budapest and Paris Univs.; Publr 1949–53; Vice-Pres., Hungarian Council of Publishing 1953–55; Chair. Hungarian Bd of Pub-

lishing 1955; Head, Cultural Dept Hungarian Socialist Workers' Party 1964–66; Prof. Univ. of Budapest 1964, Vice-Rector 1967; mem. Hungarian Acad. of Sciences, Deputy Gen. Sec. 1970–72, Gen. Sec. 1972–75, Deputy Sec.-Gen. 1975–82; Minister of Culture and Educ. 1982–88; Dr hc (Paris) 1979, (Rome); State Prize 1980; Commdr Palmes académiques (France). *Publications:* La France et la Hongrie au début du XVIIIe siècle 1971, Révolté ou révolutionnaire 1973, L'Autobiographie d'un prince rebelle 1977, Staatsräson und christliche Solidarität 1983, Hongrois et Français de Louis XIV à la Révolution française 1983, A francia felvilágosodás (The Age of French Enlightenment) 1986, History of Transylvania (ed.) 1986, A bujdosó Rákóczi (Prince Rákóczi in exile) 1991, Histoire de la culture hongroise 1994, Nemzetképkutatás és XIX. századi román irodalom magyarság képe (The Search for National Identity and Hungarian Image in Romanian Literature of the 19th Century) 1995, Brenner Domoko 1996, Az emberisors és a XX századii francia regény (The Human Condition and the French Novel in the 20th century) 1997, Correspondance diplomatique de François II Rákóczi 1711–1735 1999, Egy ecselszövö diplomata, Klement János Mihály 2000, Vetési Kökenygesdi László 2001, Rákóczi Teran Dúlpolitilidyu (Foreign Policy of Rákóczi) 2002, Erdelyn tordenetele (Stories of Transylvania) 2002. *Leisure interests:* literature, music, travelling. *Address:* Tulipán-u. 5, 1022 Budapest, Hungary (Home).

KOPELSON, Arnold, BS, JD; American film producer; b. 14 Feb. 1935, New York; m. Anne Kopelson; ed New York Univ., New York Law School; with Anne Kopelson exec. producer, producer, packager, developer and distributor of over 100 films; Co-Chair. and CEO Kopelson Entertainment; Variety Showbiz Expo Hall of Fame 1986, NATO/ShoWest Producer of the Year 1994, Cinema Expo Int. Lifetime Achievement in Film-making Award, Nat. Asscn of Theater Owners Producer of the Year Award, Publicists Guild of America Motion Picture Showmanship Award, New York Law School Distinguished Alumnus Award for Lifetime Achievement. *Television:* series: The Fugitive 2000, Thieves 2001. *Films produced:* Lost and Found (exec. producer) 1979, The Legacy (exec. producer) 1979, Night of the Juggler (exec. producer) 1980, Foolin' Around 1980, Final Assignment (exec. producer) 1980, Dirty Tricks (exec. producer) 1981, Platoon 1986 (Acad. Award for Best Picture), Warlock (exec. producer and int. distributor) 1989, Triumph of the Spirit 1989, Fire Birds (exec. producer) 1990, Out for Justice 1991, Falling Down 1993, The Fugitive 1993, Outbreak 1995, Seven 1995, Eraser 1996, Murder at 1600 1997, Mad City 1997, The Devil's Advocate 1997, U.S. Marshals 1998, Perfect Murder 1998, Don't Say a Word 2001, Joe Somebody 2001, Blackout 2003. *TV film:* Past Tense. *Address:* Kopelson Entertainment, 8560 Sunset blvd, Los Angeles, CA 90069, USA. *Telephone:* (310) 360-3222 (Office). *Fax:* (310) 360-3242 (Office).

KOPONEN, Harri; Finnish business executive; b. 6 Dec. 1962, Lahti; s. of Onni Koponen and Aili Ikonen; m.; four c.; ed Commercial Coll. of Turku, Helsinki Univ., Helsinki School of Econs; fmr Educ. Officer, Finnish Defence Force; fmr Office Man. Oy Shell AB; fmr Head Telecom Sales, Hewlett-Packard; Global Account Exec., Ericsson; currently Pres. and CEO Sonera. *Leisure interests:* hockey, golf, coaching. *Address:* Sonera, Teollisuuskatu 15, 00051 Helsinki, Finland (Office). *Telephone:* 204054110 (Office). *Fax:* 204054112 (Office). *E-mail:* harri.koponen@sonera.com (Office). *Website:* www.sonera.com (Office).

KOPPEL, Ted, MA; American journalist; b. 8 Feb. 1940, Lancs., England; m. Grace A. Dorney; four c.; ed Syracuse and Stanford Univs; went to USA 1953; news corresp., writer, WMCA, New York 1963–; with ABC News 1963, fmr news corresp. Vietnam; Chief, Miami Bureau, ABC News; Chief, Hong Kong Bureau; diplomatic corresp. Hong Kong Bureau, ABC News, Washington; anchorman, ABC News Nightline 1980–, Ed. Man. 1980–; corresp. for TV specials including The People of People's China 1973, Kissinger: Action Biography 1974, Second to None 1979, The Koppel Reports 1988–90; co-author with Marvin Kalb, TV special: In the National Interest (Overseas Press Club Award); numerous awards. *Publications:* The Wit and Wisdom of Adlai Stevenson 1985, In The National Interest 1977, Nightline: History In the Making 1996. *Address:* c/o Nightline, 1717 De Sales Street, NW, Washington, DC 20036, USA.

KOPPER, Hilmar; German banker; b. 13 March 1935; CEO Deutsche Bank AG –1997, Chair. Supervisory Bd 1997–99; Chair. of Supervisory Bd Daimler-Benz AG, Stuttgart, Lincas GmbH, Hamburg; mem. Supervisory Bd Akzo, Arnhem, Netherlands, Bayer AG, Leverkusen, Deutsche Lufthansa AG, Cologne, Deutsche Bank, Frankfurt, Mannesmann AG, Düsseldorf, Municher Rückversicherungs-Gesellschaft, Munich, VEBA AG, Düsseldorf; Chair. Advisory Bd Brauerei Beck & Co., Bremen, Frowein GmbH & Co. KG, Wuppertal, Leopold Kostal GmbH & Co. KG, Lüdenscheid, DaimlerChrysler AG (mem. Chair.'s Council 2001–); mem. Advisory Bd Solvay & Cie SA, Brussels; fmr Deputy Chair. Bd Morgan Grenfell Group PLC, London; mem. Bd St Helens. *Leisure interests:* reading, collecting the wrappings that encase citrus fruits in greengrocers' shops. *Address:* DaimlerChrysler AG, 70546 Stuttgart, Germany.

KOPTEV, Yuri Nikolayevich, Cand.TechSc; Russian engineer and manager; b. 13 March 1940, Stavropol; m.; two s.; ed Bauman Higher Tech. School; worked as engineer Lavochkin Science-Tech. Corpn 1965–69; author of a number of space-rocket projects; Sr Engineer, Head of Dept, then Deputy Minister, Ministry of Gen. Machine Construction 1969–91; Vice-Pres. Rosobshchemash Corpn 1991–92; Dir-Gen. Russian Space Agency 1992–99,

Russian Aviation and Space Agency 1999–; Chair. Bd Dirs Tupolev Corpn 1999–; Co-Chair. Space Cttee Russian-American Comm. for Econ. and Tech. Co-operation 1993–; Prof. Bauman Moscow State Tech. Univ.; mem. Tsiolkovsky Acad. of Cosmonautics and Presidium, Cosmonautics Fed. of Russia and Presidium, Int. Acad. of Eng; three state prizes 1997, 1993, 1999, four state awards. *Address:* Russian Aviation and Space Agency, 42 Shchepkina str., 129857 Moscow, Russia (Office). *Telephone:* (095) 971-80-21 (Office). *Fax:* (095) 288-90-63 (Office).

KORALEK, Paul George, CBE, RA, RIBA; British architect; b. 7 April 1933, Vienna, Austria; s. of the late Ernest Koralek and Alice (née Müller); m. (Audrey) Jennifer Koralek 1956; one s. two d.; ed Aldenham, Architectural Asscn; Partner and Dir Ahrends, Burton & Koralek, Architects 1961–; Fellow Royal Inst. of the Architects of Ireland (FRIAI); Winner Int. Competition for New Library, Trinity Coll., Dublin 1961, Competition for Nat. Gallery Extension 1982–85, Int. Competition for Devt Plan, Grenoble Univ. 1991, RIBA Architecture Award 1978, 1996, 1999, RIBA Housing Award 1977, Structural Steel Design Award 1976, 1980, 1985, Financial Times Award 1976 (Commendation 1986, 1987), Civic Trust Award 1986, 1992, RIAI Award 1999. *Buildings include:* new British Embassy, Moscow 1999; Docklands Light Railway Extension Stations; Templeton Coll., Oxford 1969, Nebenzahl House, Jerusalem 1972, Warehouse and Showroom for Habitat, Wallingford 1974, residential bldg for Keble Coll., Oxford 1976, Arts Faculty bldg Trinity Coll., Dublin 1979, factory for Cummins Engines, Shotts 1983, supermarket J. Sainsbury, Canterbury 1984, Retail HQ, W.H. Smith, Swindon 1985, 1995, dept store John Lewis, Kingston 1990, St Mary's Hosp., Newport, Isle of Wight 1990, White Cliffs Heritage Centre, Dover 1991, Dublin Dental Hosp. 1998–, Techniquest Science Discovery Centre, Cardiff 1995, Insts of Tech. Tralee, Waterford, Blanchardstown 1997–, Offaly Co. Council HQ 1999–, Tipperary N Riding County Offices 2000, Convent Lands Devt Plan, Dublin 2000. *Publications:* Ahrends, Burton & Koralek 1991, Collaborations – The Architecture of ABK 2002. *Address:* Unit 1, 7 Chalcot Road, London, NW1 8LH, England. *Telephone:* (20) 7586-3311. *Fax:* (20) 7722-5445. *E-mail:* abk@abclondon.com.

KÖRBER, Manfred J.; German public relations executive and bank official; b. 15 Sept. 1939, Berlin; ed Univs of Bonn and Hamburg; with Mobil Oil Deutschland AG 1966–67; cen. staff Dept Hoechst AG 1967–73; with Deutsche Bundesbank, 1973–98, Head of Press and Information, Public Relations Div. 1984–87, Head of Dept of Press and Public Relations, Library and Archives, Language Services, Press Spokesman 1987–98, Dir of Communications and Press Spokesman. *Address:* European Central Bank, Kaiserstr. 29, Postfach 160319, 60066 Frankfurt a.M., Germany (Office). *Telephone:* (69) 13447312 (Office). *Fax:* (69) 13447404 (Office). *E-mail:* manfred.korber@ecb.int (Office). *Website:* www.ecb.int (Office).

KORD, Kazimierz; Polish conductor; b. 18 Nov. 1930, Pogórze nr. Cieszyn; m.; ed Acad. of Music in Leningrad (piano with Wladimir Nilsen); State Higher School of Music in Cracow (conducting with Artur Malawski) 1956–60; Artistic Man. Music Theatre, Cracow 1962–69; Man. and Music. Man. Great Symphonic Orchestra of Polish Radio and TV in Katowice 1969–73; Artistic Dir. and Principal Conductor, Warsaw Philharmonic 1977–2001; Chief Conductor Südwestfunk Orchestra in Baden Baden 1980–86; six years' co-operation with Metropolitan Opera, New York; conducted in all important music centres of the world, toured in 57 countries; Critics Award at Music Biennale in Berlin 1971; Gold Orpheus Prize of Polish Musicians Union 1972, Star of the Year, Munich 1975, Minister of Culture and Arts Prize (1st Class) 1977, 1998. *Recordings:* complete Beethoven symphonies, Górecki's Symphony No. 3 and works by Szymanowski, Penderecki, Panufnik and Szymański. *Leisure interest:* astronomy. *Address:* ul. Nadarzyńska 37A, 05-805 Kanie-Otrebusy, Poland (Home). *Telephone:* (601) 544000. *E-mail:* kama .kord@t-online.de (Home).

KORDA, Michael Vincent, BA; American publishing executive; b. 8 Oct. 1933, London, England; s. of Vincent Korda and Gertrude (née Musgrove) Korda; m. Carolyn Keese 1958; one s.; ed Magdalen Coll., Oxford; served RAF 1952–54; joined Simon and Schuster, New York 1958–, firstly as Ed., then Sr Ed., Man. Ed., Exec. Ed., now Sr Vice-Pres. and Ed.-in-Chief; mem. Nat. Soc. of Film Critics, American Horse Shows Asscn. *Publications:* Male Chauvinism: How It Works 1973, Power: How to Get It, How to Use It 1975, Success! 1977, Charmed Lives 1979, Worldly Goods 1982, The Fortune 1989. *Address:* Simon and Schuster, 1230 Avenue of the Americas, New York, NY 10020, USA.

KORDA, Petr; Czech tennis player; b. 23 Jan. 1968, Prague; s. of Petr Korda and Jana Korda; m. Regina Rajchrtová 1992; two d. one s.; coached by his father until age 18; coached by Tomáš Petera 1991–; winner Wimbledon Jr Doubles 1986; turned professional 1987; runner-up French Open 1992; winner Grand Slam Cup 1993; winner Stuttgart Open 1997, Australian Open 1998, Qatar Open 1998; mem. Czechoslovak Davis Cup Team 1988, 1996; lives in Monte Carlo; received one-year ban after testing positive for nandrolone in Wimbledon Championship 1998; retd in 1999 having won 20 professional titles (including 10 singles titles); now plays in Srs Tour; runner-up to Guy Forget 2001; won Honda Challenge 2002; Chair. Bd of Supervisors Karlštejn golf resort, Czech Repub. 2000–. *Leisure interest:* golf.

KORHONEN, Keijo Tero, PhD; Finnish diplomatist; b. 23 Feb. 1934, Paltamo; s. of Hannes Korhonen and Anna née Laari; m. 1st Anneli (née Torkkila) 1958, three s.; m. 2nd Anita (née Uggeldahl) 1990; ed Turku Univ.;

Prof. of Int. Relations, Univ. of Arizona 1964–; Deputy Dir for Political Affairs, Ministry of Foreign Affairs 1971–74; Prof. of Political History, Univ. of Helsinki 1974–77; Minister of Foreign Affairs 1976–77; Under-Sec. of State for Political Affairs, Ministry of Foreign Affairs 1977–83; Perm. Rep. to UN 1983–88; Special Adviser to Prime Minister 1988–89; Ed.-in-Chief Kainuun Sanomat 1989–94; Presidential cand. (ind.) 1994. *Publications:* four books about Finnish–Soviet and Finnish–Russian relations since 1808; Finland in the Russian Political Thought of the 19th century 1966, An Ambassador's Journal, Urho Kekkonen, the Leader and the Man, The Reverse Side of the Coin 1989, This Country Is Not For Sale 1991, An Accidental Corporal (memories) 1999. *Leisure interests:* reading, jogging, horse riding. *Address:* HC 1, Box 611, Tucson, AZ 85736, USA. *Telephone:* (520) 822-2705. *Fax:* (520) 822-2706.

KORMILTSEV, Col-Gen. Nikolai Viktorovich; Russian army officer; b. 14 March 1946, Omsk; ed Omsk Higher Military General Army School, Moscow M.V. Frunze Military Acad., Moscow Military Acad. of General Staff; Commdr of Army corpus, Turkestan Mil. Command until 1994; Deputy Commdr, then Commdr of Armed Forces, Baikal Mil. Command 1994–98; Commdr of Armed Forces, Siberian Mil. Command 1998–2001; C-in-C Land Armed Forces 2001–; Deputy Minister of Defence 2001–. *Address:* Ministry of Defence, Znamenka str. 19, 103160 Moscow, Russia (Office). *Telephone:* (095) 923-38-54 (Office).

KORNAI, János, DrSc; Hungarian economist; b. 21 Jan. 1928, Budapest; m. Zsuzsa Dániel 1971; two s. one d.; ed Univ. of Budapest; Econ. Ed. 1947–55; Research Assoc. Inst. of Econs, Hungarian Acad. of Sciences 1955–58, Inst. of Textile Industry 1958–63; Sr Research Assoc., Computer Centre, Hungarian Acad. of Sciences 1963–67; Research Prof., Inst. of Econs, Hungarian Acad. of Sciences 1967–; Allie S. Freed Prof. of Econs, Harvard Univ. 1986–2002, Allie S. Freed Prof. Emer. 2002–; Perm. Fellow, Collegium Budapest 1992–; Visiting Prof., LSE 1964, Univ. of Sussex 1966, Stanford Univ. 1968, Yale 1970, Princeton and Stanford 1972–73, Stockholm 1976–77, Geneva 1981, Munich 1983, Princeton 1983–84, Harvard 1984–85; Pres. Int. Econ. Asscn 2002–; mem. Hungarian Acad. of Sciences; Corresp. mem. British Acad.; Foreign mem. Royal Swedish Acad., Finnish Acad., Russian Acad. of Sciences;; Hon. mem. American Acad. of Arts and Sciences, American Econ. Asscn; Officier, Légion d'honneur 1997; Commdr's Cross, Order of Merit of the Hungarian Repub. 2002; Dr hc (Paris) 1978, (Poznań) 1978, (London) 1990, (Amsterdam), (Budapest) 1992, (Wrocław) 1993, (Turin) 1993, (Debrecen) 2001, (Stockholm) 2001; Seidman Award 1982, Hungarian State Prize 1983, Humboldt Prize 1983, Széchenyi Prize 1994. *Publications:* Overcentralization in Economic Administration 1959, Mathematical Planning of Structural Decisions 1967, Anti-Equilibrium 1971, Rush versus Harmonic Growth 1972, Economics of Shortage 1980, Non-Price Control 1981, Growth, Shortage and Efficiency 1982, Contradictions and Dilemmas 1985, The Road to a Free Economy 1990, Vision and Reality 1990, The Socialist System 1992, Highways and Byways 1995, Struggle and Hope 1997, Welfare, Choice and Solidarity in Transition (with K. Eggleston) 2001. *Address:* Collegium Budapest, Institute for Advanced Study, Szentháromság utca 2, 1014 Budapest (Office); Toboz utca 10A, 1037 Budapest, Hungary (Home); 130 Mount Auburn Street, Cambridge, MA 02138, USA (Home). *Telephone:* (1) 224-8312 (Hungary) (Office). *Fax:* (1) 224-8328 (Hungary) (Office). *E-mail:* kornai@colbud.hu (Office).

KORNBERG, Arthur, MD, DSc, LLD, LHD; American biochemist; b. 3 March 1918, New York; s. of Joseph and Lena Katz Kornberg; m. 1st Sylvy R. Levy 1943 (died 1986); three s.; m. 2nd Charlene W Levering 1988 (died 1995); ed City Coll. of New York and Univ. of Rochester; commissioned Officer, US Public Health Service 1941–42; Nat. Insts of Health, Bethesda, Md 1942–52; Prof. and Chair. Dept of Microbiology, Washington Univ. School of Medicine 1953–59; Prof., Dept of Biochemistry, Stanford Univ. School of Medicine 1959–88, Prof. Emer. 1988–, Head 1959–69; mem. NAS, American Philosophical Soc., American Acad. of Arts and Sciences, Foreign mem. Royal Soc. 1970; Hon. LLD, City Coll. of New York 1960, DSc (Notre Dame, Washington, Rochester and Pennsylvania), LHD (Yeshiva Univ.) 1962, DSc (Princeton) 1970, DSc (Colby Coll.) 1970, MD (Univ. of Barcelona) 1970; Nobel Prize in Medicine and Physiology (with Prof. Ochoa) 1959 and many other awards. *Publications:* For the love of Enzymes: the odyssey and a biochemist (autobiog.) 1989; numerous original research papers and reviews on subjects in biochemistry, particularly enzymatic mechanisms of biosynthetic reactions. *Address:* Department of Biochemistry, Stanford University Medical Center, Stanford, CA 94305 (Office); 365 Golden Oak Drive, Portola Valley, CA 94025, USA (Home). *E-mail:* akornberg@cmgm.standord.edu (Office).

KORNBERG, Sir Hans (Leo), Kt, MA, DSc, ScD, PhD, FRS, FRSA, FIBiol; British professor of biochemistry; b. 14 Jan. 1928, Herford, Germany; s. of Max and Margarete (née Silberbach) Kornberg; m. 1st Monica M. King 1956 (died 1989); twin s. two d.; m. 2nd Donna Haber 1991; ed Queen Elizabeth Grammar School, Wakefield and Univ. of Sheffield; John Stokes Research Fellow, Univ. of Sheffield 1952–53; mem. Medical Research Council Cell Metabolism Research Unit, Univ. of Oxford 1955–61; Lecturer in Biochem., Worcester Coll., Oxford 1958–61; Prof. of Biochem., Univ. of Leicester 1961–75; Sir William Dunn Prof. of Biochem., Univ. Cambridge 1975–95; Univ. Prof. and Prof. of Biology, Boston Univ., Boston, Mass., USA 1995–; Fellow Christ's Coll., Cambridge 1975–, Master 1982–95; Chair. Science Bd, SRC 1969–72, mem. 1967–72; Chair. Royal Comm. on Environmental Pollution 1976–81; mem. Agric. and Food Research Council 1980–84; mem. Priorities Bd for

Research and Devt in Agric. 1984–90; Chair. Advisory Cttee Genetic Modification 1986–95, Jt Policy Group Agric. and Environment 1986–89; mem. of Bd NIREX 1986–95; Pres. Int. Union of Biochem. and Molecular Biology 1991–94, The Biochemical Soc. 1990–95 (Hon. mem. 2001–); mem. Advisory Council for Applied Research and Devt 1982–85; Scientific Advisory Cttee Inst. for Molecular Biology and Medicine, Monash Univ. 1987–; Commonwealth Fund Fellow (Yale Univ. and Public Health Research Inst., New York) 1953–55; mem. German Acad. of Sciences Leopoldina 1982; Foreign Assoc. NAS 1986; mem. Acad. Europaea 1988; Fellow, American Acad. of Microbiology 1992; Foreign mem. American Philosophical Soc. 1993, Accad. Nazionale dei Lincei, Italy 1997; Vice-Pres. Inst. of Biology 1969–72; Vice-Chair. European Molecular Biological Org. 1978–81; Pres. British Asscn for the Advancement of Science 1984–85 (Hon. mem. 2003–); Pres. Asscn for Science Educ. 1991–92; Leeuwenhoek Lecturer, Royal Soc. 1972; Man. Trustee, Nuffield Foundation 1973–93; Trustee, Wellcome Trust 1990–95; Hon. mem. Soc. Biological Chem. (USA) 1972, Japanese Biochem. Soc. 1981; Foreign Hon. mem. American Acad. of Arts and Sciences 1987; Hon. FRCP 1989; Hon. Fellow Worcester Coll., Oxford, Brasenose Coll., Oxford, Wolfson Coll., Cambridge; Hon. ScD (Cincinnati) 1974, Hon. DSc (Warwick) 1975, (Leicester) 1979, (Sheffield) 1979, (Bath) 1980, (Strathclyde) 1985, (South Bank) 1994, (Leeds) 1995, (La Trobe) 1997; Hon. DUniv (Essex) 1979; Hon. MD (Leipzig) 1984; Hon. LLD (Dundee) 1999; Colworth Medal (Biochemical Soc.) 1963, Warburg Medal (Gesellschaft für biologische Chemie der Bundesrepublik, FRG) 1973. *Publications:* numerous articles in scientific journals. *Leisure interests:* conversation, cooking. *Address:* The University Professors, Boston University, 745 Commonwealth Avenue, Boston, MA 02215, USA.

KORNBLUM, John Christian, BA; American diplomatist and investment banker; b. 6 Feb. 1943, Detroit, Mich.; s. of Samuel Christian Kornblum and Ethelyn Kornblum (née Tonkin); m. Helen Sen 1987; two s.; ed Michigan State Univ., Georgetown Univ., DC; Officer-in-Charge of Berlin and Eastern Affairs, Bonn 1970–73; mem. policy planning staff Dept of State 1973–75, Officer-in-Charge of European Regional Political Affairs 1977–79, Dir of Cen. European Affairs 1981; political adviser to US mission, Berlin 1979–81, Minister and Deputy Commdt 1985; Deputy Rep. to NATO, Brussels 1987; Amb., Rep. to CSCE 1991; Sr Deputy Asst Sec. of State for European Affairs 1994; Asst Sec. of State for European and Canadian Affairs 1996; Amb. to Germany 1997–2001; Chair. Lazard & Co. GmbH 2001–; mem. US Del. to Quadripartite Negotiations, Berlin 1970–72; co-ordinator meeting of 1977, Chair. US Del. to Helsinki 1992, Head US Del. to Vienna 1992; Kt.'s Cross, Germany 1991, Order of Merit, Austria 1994, Distinguished Alumni Award, Michigan State Univ. 1999, Silver Award, American Chamber of Commerce (Germany) 2000. *Leisure interests:* music, sports, gardening, travel. *Address:* Lazard & Co. GmbH, Postfach 080544, 10005 Berlin, Germany (Office). *Telephone:* (30) 72610190 (Office). *Fax:* (30) 726101910 (Office). *E-mail:* john.kornblum@lazard.com (Office).

KORNUKOV, Col.-Gen. Anatoly Mikhailovich; Russian army officer (retd); b. 10 Jan. 1942, Stakhanovo, Lugansk Region; m.; one s. one d.; ed Chernigov Higher Mil. Aviation School, Zhukov Mil. Acad., Mil. Gen. Staff Acad.; Commdr of fighter squadron, Aviation Regt of Fighter Div. in Far E; qualified as Mil. Pilot-Sniper; Commdr Anti-Aircraft Defence Forces of Moscow Command 1991–97; C-in-C Mil. Aircraft Forces of Russian Fed. 1998–2002 (resgnd); on staff of Ministry of Defence 2002–. *Leisure interests:* nature, music. *Address:* c/o General Air Force Staff, B. Pirogorskaya str. 23, K-160 Moscow, Russia (Office). *Telephone:* (095) 296-18-00 (Office).

KOROLEV, Mikhail Antonovich, DEconSc; Russian statistician; b. 12 Sept. 1931, Almaty; s. of A. I. Korolev and T. A. Ivanova; m. Letalina Koroleva 1957; one d.; ed Moscow Plekhanov Inst. of Nat. Econ.; Asst Dean, Dept Head, Moscow Inst. of Econs and Statistics 1954–66, Rector 1966–72, Prof. 1967–; Deputy, First Deputy Dir Cen. Statistics Board of USSR 1972–85, Dir 1985–87; Pres. USSR State Cttee on Statistics 1987–89; Adviser to Prime Minister of USSR 1991; Pres. Interstate Statistical Cttee of the CIS 1992–; cand. mem. of CPSU Cen. Cttee 1986–90; Deputy to USSR Supreme Soviet 1986–89; Chair. Statistical Comm. of UN 1979–81, Vice-Chair. 1976–79, 1989–91; mem. Int. Statistical Inst., Int. Informatics Acad.; Hon. Scientist. *Publications:* 20 books, numerous articles. *Address:* Interstate Statistical Committee of the Commonwealth of Independent States, 39, Bldg 1, Myasnitskaya Street, 107450 Moscow, Russia (Office). *Telephone:* (095) 921-19-73 (Office). *Fax:* (095) 207-45-92 (Office). *E-mail:* korolev@cisstat.com (Office); mkorolev@netscape.net (Home); *Website:* www.cisstat.com (Office); mikhailkorolev.narod.ru.

KOROMA, Abdul G.; Sierra Leonean diplomatist and lawyer; ed King's Coll., Univ. of London, Kiev State Univ.; barrister and Hon. Bencher (Lincoln's Inn) and legal practitioner, High Court of Sierra Leone; joined Sierra Leone Govt service 1964, Int. Div., Ministry of External Affairs 1969; del., UN Gen. Assembly; mem. Int. Law Comm. (Chair. 43rd Session); mem. of dels to 3rd UN Conf. on the Law of the Sea, UN Conf. on Succession of States in Respect of Treaties, UN Comm. on Int. Trade Law, Special Cttee on the Review of the UN Charter and on the Strengthening of the Role of the Org. Cttee on the Peaceful Uses of Outer Space; Vice-Chair. UN Charter Cttee 1978; Chair. UN Special Cttee of 24; Deputy Perm. Rep. of Sierra Leone to the UN 1978–81, Perm. Rep. 1981–85; fmr Amb. to S Korea, to Cuba and to EEC and Perm. Del. to UNESCO; Amb. to France, Belgium, Netherlands, Luxembourg and to Ethiopia and OAU 1988; Perm. Rep. to UN –1994; Judge Int. Court of Justice 1994–; High Commr in Zambia, Tanzania and Kenya; Chair.

UN 6th Cttee (Legal); Vice-Pres. African Soc. of Int. and Comparative Law, African Soc. of Int. Law; Pres. Henry Dunant Centre for Humanitarian Dialogue, Geneva; del. to numerous int. confs; lecturer at numerous univs; mem. Int. Planning Council of Int. Ocean Inst.; mem. American Soc. of Int. Law; Hon. LLD; Insignia of Commdr of Rokel 1991. *Publications:* numerous articles on int. law. *Leisure interests:* reading, music, sports. *Address:* International Court of Justice, Peace Palace, Carnegieplein, 2517 KJ The Hague, Netherlands. *Telephone:* (70) 3022323. *Fax:* (70) 3022409.

KOROMA, Sorie Ibrahim; Sierra Leonean politician; b. 30 Jan. 1930, Port Loko; m.; c.; ed Govt Model School, Freetown, Bo Govt School and Co-operative Coll., Ibadan, Nigeria; worked in Co-operative Dept 1951–58; in pvt. business 1958–62; First Sec.-Gen. Sierra Leone Motor Transport Union 1958; MP 1962–65, 1967; Councillor and Deputy Mayor of Freetown 1964; Minister of Trade and Industry 1968–69, of Agric. and Nat. Resources 1969–71; Vice-Pres. of Sierra Leone 1971–79, First Vice-Pres. 1981–86, Prime Minister 1971–75, Minister of the Interior 1971–73, 1981–82, of Finance 1975–78, of Devt and Econ. Planning 1977–78, of State Enterprises 1978–79; Vice-Chair. FAO Conf., Rome 1971; Rep. of Sierra Leone to OAU Summit Conf., Addis Ababa 1971, Morocco 1972; Commdr of the Republic of Sierra Leone; decorations from Lebanon, People's Repub. of China, Ethiopia, Liberia. *Leisure interests:* reading, football, sport. *Address:* c/o Office of the First Vice-President, Tower Hill, Freetown, Sierra Leone. *Telephone:* 2757.

KOROMO, Momodu, MSC; Sierra Leonean politician; b. 12 Sept. 1956; m.; five c.; ed Njala Univ. Coll., Univ. of Nairobi, Kenya, Univ. of Reading, UK, Int. Centre for Theoretical Physics, Trieste, Italy; Govt Minister 1996–; currently Minister of Foreign Affairs and Int. Cooperation. *Leisure interests:* tennis, sight-seeing. *Address:* Ministry of Foreign Affairs, Gloucester Street, Freetown (Office); MQ8 Spur Road, Wilberforce, Freetown, Sierra Leone (Home). *Telephone:* 229710 (Office); 232873 (Home). *Fax:* 225615 (Office). *E-mail:* mforeign@securicomsl.com (Office); graceful@sierratel.se (Home).

KOROTCHENYA, Ivan Mikhailovich; Belarus politician; ed Minsk Agric. Acad.; worked as chief agronomist, Chair. collective farm, Chair. Regional Union of Collective Farms, Chair. Viley Dist Soviet of People's Deputies; Deputy of Belarus Supreme Soviet, mem. Accord faction 1994–96; mem. Presidium; Chair. Comm. on Problems of Glasnost, Mass Media and Human Rights 1990–92; elected coordinator of Workgroup at Council of Leaders of States and Leaders of Govts CIS Countries after disintegration of USSR 1992–98; Deputy Exec. Sec. CIS Secr. 1998–2001. *Address:* Secretariat of Russia and Belarus Union, Kirova str. 17, 220050 Minsk, Belarus (Office).

KOROTEYEV, Anatoly Sazonovich; Russian physicist; b. 22 July 1936, Moscow Region; s. of Sazon Z. Koroteyev and Maria P. Koroteyeva; m.; one s.; ed Moscow Aviation Inst.; engineer, Sr engineer, head of div., First Deputy Dir Research Inst. of Thermal Processes (now Keldysh Research Centre) 1959–88, Dir 1988–; Corresp. mem. USSR (now Russian) Acad. of Sciences 1990, mem. 1994; research in generation and diagnostics of low-temperature plasma; USSR State Prize 1982, Order for Service to Fatherland 1996. *Publications:* Generator of low-temperature plasma 1966, Applied Dynamics of Thermal Plasma 1975, Plasmotrons: Structures, Characteristics, Calculation 1993, Space and New Power Sources 1996, New Propulsion for Advanced Launchers 1998, Solar Power Propulsion System with Electrically Heated Thermal Accumulator 1999, Electric Plasma Propulsion Today and Tomorrow 2000; numerous articles. *Leisure interests:* history, skiing. *Address:* M. Keldysh Research Centre, Onezhskaya str. 8/10, 125438 Moscow, Russia. *Telephone:* (095) 456-46-08. *Fax:* (095) 456-82-28.

KOROTYCH, Vitaliy Alekseyevich; Russian/Ukrainian writer and poet; b. 26 May 1936, Kiev; s. of Aleksey Korotych and Zoa Korotych; m. Zinaida Korotych 1958; two s.; ed Kiev Medical Inst.; physician 1959–66; Ed. Ukrainian literary journal Ranok 1966–77; Ed.-in-Chief Vsesvit magazine 1978–86; Ed.-in-Chief Ogonyok weekly magazine 1986–91; Sec. of Ukrainian Writers' Union 1966–69; mem. USSR Writers' Union 1981–90; USSR People's Deputy 1989–91; Prof. Boston Univ., USA 1991–98; returned to Moscow; ed. Boulevard magazine and others 1998–; two State Prizes, USSR, A. Tolstoy Prize 1982, Int. Julius Fuchik Prize 1984, Wiental Prize, Georgetown Univ. (USA) 1987, Int. Ed. of the year, W P Revue (USA) 1989. *Publications include:* Golden Hands 1961, The Smell of Heaven 1962, Cornflower Street 1963, O Canada! 1966, Poetry 1967, Metronome (novel) 1982, The Face of Enmity (novel) 1984, Memory, Bread and Love 1986, Le Visage de la haine (travel essays) 1988, Glasnost und Perestroika 1990, The Waiting Room (memoirs, Vol. I) 1991, On My Behalf (memoirs, Vol. II) 2000; many translations from English into Ukrainian and other Slavonic languages. *Address:* Trifonovskaya str. 11, Apt. 156, 127018 Moscow, Russia. *Telephone:* (095) 289-03-84. *Fax:* (095) 289-03-84.

KORS, Michael; American fashion designer; b. 9 Aug. 1959, Mineola, NY; s. of William Kors and Joan L. Kors; ed Fashion Inst. of Tech.; f., proprietor Kors Co. 1981, Pres. 1981–; Dupont American Original Prize. *Publications:* articles in Vogue, The New York Times and other newspapers and magazines. *Leisure interests:* theatre, film, travel. *Address:* 550 7th Ave, 7th Floor, New York, NY 10018, USA.

KORTHALS ALTES, Frederik; Netherlands lawyer and politician; b. 15 May 1931, Amsterdam; s. of Everhardus Joannes Korthals Altes and Mary s'Jacob; ed Leiden Univ.; practised as solicitor 1958–89; mem. First Chamber, States-Gen. 1981–82, 1991–2001; Minister of Justice 1982–89; Chair. Volkspartij voor Vrijheid en Democratie (VVD) 1975–81, Floor Leader in First Chamber, States-Gen. 1995–97, Pres. 1997–2001; partner, Nauta Dutilh law firm 1990–96; Hon. Minister of State 2001–; Hon. mem. Volkspartij voor Vrijheid en Democratie (VVD) 1997; Grand Officier, Légion d'honneur 1984, Grosses Verdienskreuz des Verdienstordens 1985, Commdr of the Order of Orange-Nassau, Grand Cross Ordem do Mérito 1989, Grand Cross Ordre nat. du Mérite, Grand Cross of Sacred Treasure, Japan 2000; Prof. E.M. Meijers Medal of Law Faculty (Leiden) 1988, Nat. Police Award 1990. *Address:* Oudorpweg 9, NL 3062 RB, Rotterdam, Netherlands (Home). *Telephone:* (10) 4526163 (Home). *Fax:* (10) 4529491 (Home). *E-mail:* fka@planet.nl (Home).

KORTLANDT, Frederik H. H., PhD; Netherlands professor of linguistics; b. 19 June 1946, Utrecht; ed Univ. of Amsterdam; Asst Prof. of Slavic Linguistics, Univ. of Amsterdam 1969–72; Assoc. Prof. of Balto-Slavic Languages, Univ. of Leiden 1972–74, Prof. 1974–; Prof. of Descriptive and Comparative Linguistics 1985–; mem. Royal Netherlands Acad. 1986–; Spinoza Prize Laureate 1997. *Publications:* Modelling the phoneme 1972, Slavic Accentuation 1975; numerous articles on linguistics and Slavic, Baltic, Germanic, Celtic, Armenian, Japanese and other languages. *Leisure interest:* classical music. *Address:* Faculty of Letters, P.O. Box 9515, 2300 RA Leiden (Office); Cobetstraat 24, 2313 KC Leiden, Netherlands (Home). *Telephone:* (71) 527-2501. *Fax:* (71) 527-7569 (Office). *E-mail:* f.kortlandt@let.leidenuniv.nl (Office). *Website:* www.kortlandt.nl (Office).

KORTÜM, Franz-Josef; German business executive; b. 18 Aug. 1950, Billerbeck, Coesfeld; m.; three c.; ed studies in Münster and Regensburg; employed in family car retailing co. Billerbeck 1975; car sales exec. Bielefeld subsidiary of Daimler-Benz AG 1976; Head, Passenger Car Field Sales, Used Vehicle Sales and Truck Sales, Berlin subsidiary of Daimler-Benz AG 1979; Asst to Dir of Sales Org. Germany, Daimler-Benz AG, Stuttgart-Untertürkheim 1985; Dir Saarbrücken subsidiary of Daimler-Benz AG 1987; Dir Cen. Admin. Daimler-Benz AG 1989; Man. Dir Mercedes-Benz-owned co. Rheinische Kraftwagengesellschaft (RKW), Bonn 1990; mem. Man. Bd AUDI AG 1992, Chair. 1993–95. *Address:* c/o AUDI AG, Postfach 10 02 20, 8070 Ingolstadt, Germany.

KORVALD, Lars; Norwegian politician; b. 29 April 1916, Nedre Eiker; s. of Engebret Korvald and Karen Wigen; m. Ruth Borgersen 1943; one s. four d.; ed Coll. of Agriculture; Teacher, Tomb School of Agric. 1943–48; Chief Adviser, League of Norwegian Agricultural Clubs 1948–52; Headmaster, Tomb School of Agric. 1952–61; mem. Storting 1961–81; del. to UN Gen. Assembly 1963, 1968; mem. Advisory Assembly, Council of Europe 1965–70; mem. Nordic Council 1966–81, Vice-Pres. 1979–81; Chair. Christian Dem. Party 1967–75, 1977–79; Pres. Lagting (Upper House of Storting) 1969–72; Prime Minister 1972–73; Gov. Østfold Dist 1981–86; Commdr St Olav's Order (Norway) 1986. *Publication:* Politics and Christianity (memoirs, with Per Øyvind Heradstveit) 1982. *Leisure interests:* skiing, literature. *Address:* Vinkelgt. 6, 3050 Mjondalen, Norway.

KORZENIOWSKI, Robert; Polish athlete; b. 30 July 1968, Lubaczów; m. Agnieszka Fiedziukiewicz; one d.; ed Acad. of Physical Education, Cracow; winner gold medal 20km walk Olympic Games, Atlanta 1996, 20km walk and 50km walk, Sydney 2000; winner 20km walk European Cup, La Coruña 1996; winner gold medal 50km walk World Championships, Athens 1997, Edmonton 2001; winner gold medal 50km walk European Championships 1998, Munich 2002; Sport and Fair Play Amb. to European Council, Strasbourg 1997–; Officer's Cross, Order of Polonia Restituta 2000; Gold Medal for Outstanding Achievement in Sport 1996. *Publication:* Chodu sportowego. *Leisure interests:* books, cinema, cooking, history, politics. *Address:* Korzeniowski i Sport Promocja, ul. Bociana 6, 31-231 Cracow, Poland (Office). *Telephone:* (12) 420-03-30 (Office). *Fax:* (12) 415-88-65 (Office). *E-mail:* korzeniowski@korzeniowski.pl (Office). *Website:* www.korzeniowski.pl (Office).

KORZHAKOV, Lt-Gen. Aleksander Vasilyevich; Russian army officer; b. 31 Jan. 1950, Moscow; m.; two d.; ed All-Union Inst. of Law; mem. Dept 9 State Security Cttee 1970–; personal bodyguard of First Sec. Moscow CPSU Cttee Boris Yeltsin (q.v.) 1986–87; f. and Chief Security Service of Russian Supreme Soviet 1990–91; Head Security Service of Pres. of Russia 1991–96, Deputy Chief Main Admin. of Bodyguards 1992–96 (discharged); participated in suppression of attempted coup of Aug. 1991 and confrontation of Oct. 1993; mem. State Duma (Parl.) 1997–; joined Otechestvo-All Russia faction 2000. *Publication:* Boris Yeltsin: From Dawn to Decline (memoirs) 1997. *Leisure interest:* tennis. *Address:* State Duma, Okhotny Ryad 1, 103009 Moscow, Russia. *Telephone:* (095) 292-87-78. *Fax:* (095) 292-87-78.

KORZHAVIN, Naum (pseudonym of Naum Moiseyevich Mandel); Russian author and poet; b. Mandel Emmanuel Moiseyevich Korzhavin, 14 Oct. 1925, Kiev; ed Karaganda Mining Inst. and Gorky Inst. of Literature, Moscow 1959; first publication 1941; exiled to West (USA) 1974; revisited Moscow 1989; citizenship and membership of Writers' Union restored 1990. *Publications include:* The Years 1963, Where Are You? 1964, Bread, Children in Auschwitz, Autumn in Karaganda, Verse 1981, Selected Verse 1983, Interlacements 1987, Letter to Moscow 1991, The Time is Given 1992, To Myself 1998; contributor to émigré dissident journal Kontinent. *Address:* 28c Colborne Road, Apt 2, Brighton, MA 02135, USA.

KORZHEV-CHUVELYOV, Gely Mikhailovich; Russian artist; b. 7 July 1925, Moscow; ed Surikov State Inst. of Arts, Moscow; professional artist 1950–; has participated in many Soviet and foreign exhbns 1950–; Prof. Moscow Higher Artist-Tech. Inst. 1966–; mem. USSR (now Russian) Acad. of Arts 1970; Chair. Bd Artists' Union of RSFSR (now Russia) 1968–75; Sec. Bd Dirs Artists' Union of USSR (now Russia); Merited Worker of Arts of the RSFSR; Repin State Prize of USSR; People's Artist of the RSFSR 1972. *Address:* Bolshoi Devyatinski per. 5, Apt 45, Moscow, Russia. *Telephone:* (095) 212-55-29.

KOSAI, Akio, BA; Japanese business executive; b. 19 April 1931, Okayama; ed Univ. of Tokyo; joined Sumitomo Chemical Co., Ltd 1954, Dir and Gen. Man. Industrial Chemicals and Fertilizers Div. 1983; Pres. Petrochemical Corpn of Singapore (Pte) Ltd 1984–87; Man. Dir Sumitomo Chemical Co., Ltd 1987, Sr Man. Dir 1991, Pres. 1993–. *Address:* Sumitomo Chemical Co., Ltd, 2-27-1, Shinkawa, Chuo-ku, Tokyo, 104-8260, Japan. *Telephone:* (3) 5543-5102. *Fax:* (3) 5543-5901. *Website:* www.sumitomo-chem.co.jp (Office).

KOSÁRY, Domokos; Hungarian historian; b. 31 July 1913, Selmecbánya; m. Klára Huszti 1937; one d.; ed Univ. of Budapest, Eötvös Coll., Budapest, Sorbonne Paris, Inst. of Historical Research, London; Prof. Eötvös Coll. 1937–50; Dir Inst. of History, Teleki Inst. 1945–49; Founder and Ed.-in-Chief Revue d'Histoire Comparée (Budapest) 1943–48; Prof. of Modern History Univ. of Budapest 1946–49; divested of functions by the authorities 1949; Pres. Revolutionary Council of Historians 1956; sentenced to four years imprisonment 1957, released 1960; archivist, later scientific researcher, then scientific counsellor Inst. of History Hungarian Acad. of Sciences, corresp. mem. 1982; mem. Hungarian Acad. of Sciences 1985–, Pres. 1990–96; mem. Academia Europaea, London, Académie Européenne, Paris, British Acad., London, Croatian Acad. of Sciences and Arts, Zagreb, Romanian Acad., Bucharest; Pres. Nat. Cttee of Hungarian Historians 1985–90; Pres. Hungarian Historical Soc. 2000–; Officier des Palmes académiques 1988, Officier, Légion d'honneur 1996; Grand Cross (Hungary) 1993; Laureate of Hungarian State Prize 1988; Széchenyi Grand Prize (Hungary); Gold Medal, Slovak Acad. of Science 1997. *Publications:* numerous works include: Introduction to the Sources and Literature of Hungarian History (3 Vols) 1951–58, Culture in 18th-Century Hungary 1980, Small States Facing Cultural, Political and Economic Changes, from 1750 to 1914 1985, History of the Görgey Problem 1994, The Hungarian Revolution of 1848–49 and International Politics 1999. *Leisure interest:* gardening. *Address:* Institute of History, Hungarian Academy of Sciences, Uri u. 53, 1014 Budapest, Hungary. *Telephone:* (1) 356-9539. *Fax:* (1) 356-9539.

KOSCHNICK, Hans Karl-Heinrich; German politician; b. 2 April 1929, Bremen; m. Christel Risse; ed Mittelschule; Local Govt Official, Bremen 1945–51, 1954–63; Trade Union Sec. of the Union of Public Employees, Transport and Communications (ÖTV) 1951–54; mem. Social Democratic Party (SPD) 1950–, Fed. Exec. Council 1970–, Party Bd 1975–, Deputy Chair. SPD 1975–79; mem. Provincial Diet of Land Bremen (Landtag) and City Admin. 1955–63; Senator for the Interior 1963–67; Mayor of Bremen 1967–85; Pres. of the Senate, Bremen 1967–85; mem. Fed. Council (Bundesrat) 1965–, Pres. 1970–71, 1981–82; Nat. Vice-Chair. SPD 1975–79; Chair., German Union of Local Authorities (Deutscher Städtetag) 1971–77; mem. Bd Städtetag (Assoc. of German Municipalities) 1970–, Pres. 1971–77; mem. Exec. Cttee Int. Union of Local Authorities (IULA) 1972–77, 1980–85, Pres. 1981–85; MP 1987–94; EU Admin. in Mostar 1994–95; Govt Rep. for Bosnia 1998–; currently Chair. Steering Cttee. on Refugee Matters, Stability Pact for SE Europe; Dr. hc (Haifa Univ.) 1997, Hon. Citizen of Gdansk 1985, of Bremen 1999. *Leisure interest:* chess. *Address:* Rudolstädterweg 9, 28329 Bremen, Germany. *Telephone:* 4673733.

KOSHIBA, Masatoshi, PhD; Japanese physicist; b. 19 Sept. 1926, Toyohashi City, Aichi Pref.; ed Univ. of Tokyo, Univ. of Rochester, New York, USA; Prof., Dept of Physics, Univ. of Tokyo 1970–87, Prof. Emer. Int. Centre for Elementary Particle Physics 1987–; Prof. Tokai Univ. 1987–97; pioneer of neutrino-astronomy and cosmic-ray physics; led path-breaking experiments Kamiokande and Super-Kamiokande (massive detectors capturing neutrinos from the Sun and a distant supernova explosion 1987); Grosse Verdienstkreuz (Germany) 1985, Order of Culture 1988, Order of Cultural Merit 1997; Nishina Prize, Nishina Foundation 1987, Ashai Prize, Ashai Press 1988, 1999, Acad. Award, Acad. of Japan 1989, Fujuwara Science Foundation 1997, Wolf Prize, Govt of Israel 2000, Nobel Prize in Physics 2002. *Address:* International Centre for Elementary Particle Physics, University of Tokyo, 7-3-1 Hongo, Bunkyo-ku, Japan 113-0033, Japan (Office). *Telephone:* (3) 3815-8384 (Office). *Fax:* (3) 3814-8806 (Office). *E-mail:* hisho@icepp.s.u-tokyo.ac.jp (Office). *Website:* www.icepp.s.u-tokyo.ac.jp (Office).

KOSHIRO, Matsumoto, IX; Japanese actor; b. Teruaki Fujima, 1942; s. of the late Koshiro VIII; m.; one s.; debut in Kabuki (Japanese traditional theatre) when child; as child acted under name Kintaro, as young man Somegoro Ichikawa; became Koshiro IX 1980. *Plays include:* Kanjincho (and many other Kabuki plays), Man of La Mancha (included 10-week run on Broadway), The King and I (including 6-month run in West End), Half a Sixpence, Sweeney Todd, Fiddler on the Roof, Amadeus (Salieri). *Address:* c/o Kabukiza Theatre, No. 12–15 Ginza 4 chome, Chuo-ku, Tokyo 104, Japan.

KOSHLAND, Daniel E., Jr., BS, PhD; American professor of biochemistry; b. 30 March 1920, New York; s. of Daniel E. and Eleanor Haas Koshland; m. 1st Marian Elizabeth Elliott 1945 (died 1997); two s. three d.; m. 2nd Yvonne Cyr 2000; ed Univs of California and Chicago; Analytical Chemist, Shell Chemical Co. 1941–42; Research Assoc. and Group Leader, Manhattan

District, Univ. of Chicago and Oak Ridge Nat. Lab. 1941–46; Post-doctoral Fellow, Harvard Univ. 1949–51; Assoc. Biochemist, Biochemist, Sr Biochemist, Brookhaven Nat. Lab. 1951–65; Affiliate, Rockefeller Univ. 1958–65; Prof. of Biochem., Univ. of Calif., Berkeley 1965–97, Prof. of Molecular Biology 1997–, Chair. Dept Biochem. 1973–77; Visiting Prof. Cornell Univ. 1957–58; Pres. American Soc. of Biological Chemists 1973–74; Ed.-in-Chief, Science Magazine 1985–95; mem. NAS, American Acad. of Arts and Sciences, American Philosophical Soc.; Guggenheim Fellow 1972, Visiting Fellow, All Souls Coll., Oxford 1971–72; Fellow, American Asscn for Advancement of Science; Hon. mem. Japanese Biochem. Soc., Royal Swedish Acad. of Science; Hon. PhD (Weizmann Inst.) 1984, (Univ. of Massachusetts) 1992, (Ohio State Univ.) 1995, (Providence) 2000; Hon. ScD (Carnegie Mellon Univ.) 1985, Hon. LLD (Simon Fraser Univ.) 1986, (Univ. of Chicago) 1992; Hon. LHD (Mt. Sinai Univ.) 1991; J. Duckett Jones Award 1977, Pauling Award, American Chemical Soc. 1979, Edgar Fahs Smith Award, American Chemical Soc. 1979, Rosenstiel Award 1984, Waterford Prize 1984, Nat. Medal of Science 1990, Merck Award, American Soc. of Biochemistry and Molecular Biology 1991, Lasker Foundation Award 1998. *Publications:* 450 articles on enzymes in scientific journals; Bacterial Chemotaxis as a Model Behavioral System 1980. *Leisure interests:* tennis, golf, sailing. *Address:* c/o Department of Molecular and Cell Biology, University of California, 329 Stanley Hall, 3206, Berkeley, CA 94720 (Office); 3991 Happy Valley Road, Lafayette, CA 94549, USA (Home). *Telephone:* (510) 642-0416 (Office); (925) 284-9697 (Home). *Fax:* (510) 643-6386 (Office). *E-mail:* dek@vclink4.berkeley.edu (Office).

KOSHMAN, Col-Gen. Nikolai Pavlovich; Russian politician; b. 5 April 1944, Mironovka; s. of Pavel Pofirievich Koshman and Maria Fiedoseevna Koshman; m.; two s.; ed Mil. Acad. of Home Front and Transport; numerous posts from Commdr of team to Commdr of corps, railway armed forces 1973–91, Deputy Commdr 1991–95; mem. of Mission of Plenipotentiary Rep. of Russian Pres. to Chechen Repub.; Chair. Govt of Chechen Repub. 1996, Plenipotentiary Rep. of Russian Govt in Chechen Repub. with rank of Deputy Prime Minister 1999–2000; Deputy Minister of Transport, Russian Fed. 1997–; Head Fed. Service of Special Construction Rosspetsstroy 1997–98; Adviser to the Pres. of the Russian Fed. 2001–02; Deputy Minister of Communications Jan.–Oct. 2002; Chair. State Cttee of Construction 2002–. *Publication:* Restoration of the Economy and Social Sphere of the Chechen Republic 1999. *Leisure interests:* theatre, sports (football, tennis), hunting, travelling. *Address:* Gosstroi Rosii, Stroiteley str. 8, korp. 2, 117987 Moscow (Office); A. Zelynsky str. 6-37, 117534 Moscow, Russia (Home). *Telephone:* (095) 930-17-55 (Office); (095) 137-74-85 (Home). *Fax:* (095) 939-27-02 (Office).

KOSICE, Gyula; Argentine artist and poet; b. 26 April 1924, Košice, Czechoslovakia (now Slovakia); s. of Joseph F. Kosice and Eta Kosice (née Berger); m. Haydée Itaovit 1947; two d.; ed Acad. of Arts, Buenos Aires; co-f. Arturo magazine 1944, Concrete Art Invention 1945; f. Madí Art Movement 1946, f., Ed. Universal Madí Art magazine 1947; first use of neon gas in art 1946; introduction of water as essential component of his work 1948; creator Hydrospatial City (concept) 1948–; works include sculptures, hydrospatial courses, hydromurals; works in museums and pvt. collections in Argentina, Latin America, USA, Europe and Asia; Best Art Book, Asscn of Art Critics for Arte Madi 1982, Ordre des Arts et des Lettres 1989, Premio Trayectoria en el Arte, Nat. Arts Foundation 1994, Ciudadano Ilustre de la Ciudad de Buenos Aires 1997. *Exhibitions:* over 35 solo and 600 jt exhbns including Madí Art Exhbn Salon des Réalités Nouvelles, Paris 1948, 50-year retrospective Museum of Fine Arts, Buenos Aires 1991; Homenaje a Kosice, Museo Arte Moderno Buenos Aires 1994, anthology exhbn (120 works) Centro Recoleta, Buenos Aires 1999. *Publications:* Invención 1945, Madí Manifesto 1946, Golse-Se (poems) 1952, Peso y Medida de Alberto Hidalgo 1953, Antología Madí 1955, Geocultura de la Europa de Hoy 1959, Poème hydraulique 1960, Arte Hidrocinético 1968, La Ciudad Hidroespacial 1972, Arte y Arquitectura del Agua 1974, Arte Madí 1982, Obra Poética 1984, Entrevisiones 1984, Teoría sobre el Arte 1987, Arte y Filosofía Porvenirista 1996, Madí grafias 2001. *Leisure interests:* writing books on art, creating works of art. *Address:* Humahuaca 4662, Buenos Aires (Office); República de la India 3135 6° A, 1425 Buenos Aires, Argentina (Home). *Telephone:* (1) 867-1240 (Office); (1) 801-8615 (Home). *Fax:* (1) 807-0115 (Home). *E-mail:* gyulakosice@usa.net (Home). *Website:* www.kosice.com.ar (Office).

KOSOVAN, Col-Gen. Alexander Davydovich; Russian army officer and construction engineer; b. 26 Oct. 1941, Akhtyrskaya, Krasnodar Territory, Russia; m.; one s. one d.; ed Novosibirsk Inst. of Eng and Construction; head of construction group, chief engineer, Deputy Head Dept of Eng Construction, Ministry of Defence 1966–84; Chief Eng, Deputy Head Construction Dept Volga Mil. Command 1984–88; Deputy Commdr Caucasus Mil. Command on construction and quartering of forces 1988–92; First Deputy Head of Dept on Construction and Quartering of Forces, Russian Ministry of Defence 1992–97, Deputy Minister of Defence 1997–; Order for Service to Motherland in Armed Forces 1989, Order of Labour Red Banner 1990, other Govt decorations. *Publications:* numerous articles on problems of mil. construction, text-books and methodical manuals for univ. and mil. schools. *Leisure interest:* fishing. *Address:* Ministry of Defence, Znamenka str. 19, 103106 Moscow, Russia (Office). *Telephone:* (095) 293-30-28 (Office).

KOSSACK, Georg, FBA; German professor of pre- and early history; b. 25 June 1923, Neuruppin; s. of Fritz Kossack and Franziska (née v. Unruhe) Kossack; m. Ruth Kossack 1947; one s. one d.; Prof. Univ. of Kiel 1959–75,

Univ. of Munich 1975–, now Prof. Emer.; mem. German Archaeological Inst., Bayerische Akademie der Wissenschaften; Fellow British Acad., mem. Slovenian Acad. Ljubljana. *Publications:* Studien zum Symbolgut Urnenfelder und Hallstattzeit 1954, Südbayern während Hallstattzeit 1959, Graeberfelder Hallstattzeit 1979, Archsum auf Sylt I 1980, II 1987, Ed. Siedlungen im deutschen Küstengebiet 1984, Skythika 1987, Maoqinggou (with T. Höllmann) 1992, Towards Translating the Past. Selected Studies in Archaeology 1998, Religiöses Denken der Späthrouze – ū. frühen Eisenzeit 1999. *Leisure interest:* reading nineteenth-century history. *Address:* Pietzenkirchen 56A, 83083 Riedering, Germany. *Telephone:* 08036-7342.

KOSTABI, Kalev Marki; American artist and composer; b. 27 Nov. 1960, Los Angeles; ed Calif. State Univ., Fullerton; became involved in East Village art Movt, New York 1984; f. Kostabi World (studio, gallery, offices) 1988; retrospective exhbns. Mitsukoshi Museum, Tokyo 1992, Art Museum of Estonia, Tallinn 1998; represented in various perm. collections including Museum of Modern Art, New York, Metropolitan Museum of Art, New York, Guggenheim Museum, New York, Brooklyn Museum, Corcoran Gallery of Art, Washington, DC, Groninger Museum; has designed album covers including Guns 'n' Roses' Use Your Illusion, The Ramones' Adios Amigos; has also designed a Swatch watch, limited-edition vases, computer accessories; produces weekly cable TV show Inside Kostabi; lectures internationally. *Album:* I Did It Steinway 1998. *Publications include:* Sadness Because the Video Rental Store Was Closed, Kostabi: The Early Years, Conversations With Kostabi.

KOSTADINOVA, Stefka; Bulgarian high jumper (retd); b. 15 March 1965, Plovdiv; set world high jump record (2.09m.), Rome 1987; won silver medal, Olympic Games 1988, gold medal, Olympic Games 1996; five world indoor championship titles (to 1997); 1997 outdoor season curtailed due to foot injury requiring two operations, subsequently retd; Athlete of the Year in the Balkans 1996. *Address:* c/o Bulgarian Athletic Federation, bul. Vassil Levski 75, Sofia, Bulgaria (Office).

KOSTENKO, Lina Vasilievna; Ukrainian poet; b. 19 March 1930, Rzhischevo, Kiev Region; ed Maxim Gorky Inst. of Literature, Moscow; Ukrainian SSR State Prize 1987. *Publications:* Lights of the Earth 1957, The Winds 1958, Particles of the Heart 1961, Bank of the Eternal River 1977, Inimitability 1980, Marusya Churay (novel in verse) 1979–82, Scythian Woman 1981, Garden of Unmelting Snow 1987, Selected Poetry 1990, numerous publs in literary magazines. *Address:* Chkalova str. 52, Apt 8, 252054 Kiev, Ukraine (Home). *Telephone:* (44) 224-70-38 (Home).

KOSTIĆ, Branko; Serbia and Montenegro (Montenegrin) politician; b. 1939, Rvaši, Montenegro; joined CP 1957; Pres. of Presidency of Montenegro 1989–90; mem. Yugoslav Collective Presidency, Vice-Pres. 1991–92; Prof. of Law Univ. of Montenegro 1992–. *Address:* University of Montenegro, 81000 Podgorica, Cetinjski, put b.b., Serbia and Montenegro. *Telephone:* (81) 14484. *Fax:* (81) 11301.

KOSTIKOV, Vyacheslav Vasilyevich; Russian politician, journalist and diplomatist; b. 24 Aug. 1940, Moscow; m. Marina Smirnova, one d.; ed Moscow State Univ., All-Union Acad. of Foreign Trade, Sheffield Univ., UK; staff-mem.; ed. Div. of Information UNESCO Secr. in Paris 1972–78, 1982–88; political reviewer Press Agency Novosti 1978–82; Press Sec. of Pres. Boris Yeltsin 1992–94; plenipotentiary rep. of Russia in Vatican City and Amb. to Malta 1995–96; Pres. Finance Group Moskovsky Delovoy Mir (MDM) 1996–97; Deputy Dir-Gen. Media-Most Holding 1997–2001. *Publications:* numerous books including Romance with the President 1996; novels: The Heir, The Syzin's Dissonance, Bridges to the Left Bank; books on Russian emigration; numerous articles in dailies Izvestia, Ogonyok, reviews in Times of India. *Leisure interest:* classical music. *Address:* Most-Media, Maly Gnezdikovskiy per. 7, 103009 Moscow, Russia. *Telephone:* (095) 229-62-14.

KOSTIN, Andrei Leonidovich; Russian banking executive; b. 21 Sept. 1956, Moscow; m.; one s.; ed Moscow State Univ.; with Ministry of Foreign Affairs 1979–92, seconded to Russian Gen. Consulate, Australia 1979–82, Embassy in UK 1985–90; joined Investments and Finance Co. 1992; Deputy Head Dept of Foreign Investments, Imperial Bank 1993–95; First Deputy Chair., mem. Bd of Dirs, Nat. Reserve Bank 1994–96; Exec. Chair. Vnesheconombank 1996–2002, Chair. Bd of Dirs June 2002–; Order of Honour 1999. *Address:* Vneshconombank, Kuznetsky most 16, 103031 Moscow, Russia (Office). *Telephone:* (095) 258-46-01 (Office). *Fax:* (095) 258-49-04 (Office). *E-mail:* solo@vtb.ru (Office). *Website:* www.vtb.ru (Office).

KOSTIN, Ivan Mikhailovich; Russian engineer and business executive; b. 7 Oct. 1947, Barok, Tatarstan; m.; two s. one d.; ed Perm Polytech. Inst.; electrician Tetnefteprovod co. 1962–69; Master, then Head of shop at Perm plant of mine equipment 1969–74; Deputy head of shop at Kamsky Automobile plant (KAMAZ) 1974–81, Deputy Head of Dept 1982–86, Deputy Dir, then Dir on engine repair 1986–95, Dir of Research and Devt 1995–, Deputy Dir-Gen. 1995–96; First Vice-Pres. KAMAZ (jt stock co.) 1996–97, Dir-Gen. 1997–; Chair. Bd of Dirs KAMAZ (trade-financial co.) 1997–; Order, Sign of Hon.; Merited Machine-Constructor of Russian Fed. *Leisure interests:* sports, fishing. *Address:* Joint-Stock co. KAMAZ, Dzhalil prosp. 29, 423808 Naberezhnye Chelny, Tatarstan, Russia (Office). *Telephone:* (8552) 42-26-65 (Office). *Fax:* (8552) 42-26-65 (Office).

KOSTOV, Ivan; Bulgarian politician; fmr economist; Minister of Finance 1990–92; Chair. Union of Democratic Forces (SDS), now Pres.; Prime Minister of Bulgaria 1997–2001. *Address:* Sayuzna Demokratichni Sili, 1000, Sofia, Blvd. Rakovski 134, Bulgaria (Office). *Telephone:* (2) 88-25-01 (Office). *Fax:* (2) 981-05-22 (Office). *E-mail:* fortuna@infotel.bg (Office). *Website:* www.sds .bg (Office).

KOSTRZEWSKI, Jan Karol, MD, MPH; Polish scientist; b. 2 Dec. 1915, Cracow; s. of Jan Kostrzewski and Maria Sulikowska; m. Ewa Sobolewska 1948; one s. three d.; ed Jagiellonian Univ., Cracow and Harvard School of Public Health, Boston; Health Service Doctor 1939–51; Head of Epidemiology Dept, State Hygiene Inst., Warsaw 1951–78; Prof. of Epidemiology Warsaw Medical Acad. 1954–60; Under-Sec. of State, Ministry of Health and Social Welfare and Chief Sanitary Inspector 1961–68; Minister of Health and Social Welfare 1968–72; Scientist State Hygiene Inst. 1973–78; fmr Head of Epidemiology Dept; Prof. Emer. of Epidemiology, Nat. Inst. of Warsaw 1990–; Corresp. mem. Polish Acad. of Sciences (PAN) 1967–76, mem. 1976–, mem. Presidium 1971–89, Sec. Dept of Medical Sciences 1972–80, Vice-Pres. 1981–83, Pres. 1984–89; Chair. Cttee Nat. Health Protection Fund 1981–; Chair. Research Strengthening Group UNDP/World Bank/WHO Special Programme on Tropical Diseases Research; Vice-Chair. Nat. Council of Patriotic Movt for Nat. Rebirth 1983–89; Deputy to Sejm (Parl.) 1985–89; Chair. Presidium of Ecological Social Movt 1986–; fmr mem. Consultative Council attached to Chair. of Council of State; mem. Exec. Bd WHO 1973, Chair. 1975; mem. Council Int. Epidemiological Asscn 1974, Pres. 1977–81; Hon. mem. Mechnikov Soc. Microbiologists and Epidemiologists 1956–, later Pres.; Sec. Int. Comm. for Assessment of Smallpox Eradication in India, Nepal, Ethiopia, Horn of Africa and Bhutan 1977–79; Corresp. mem. Acad. Nat. de Médecine (Paris) 1979, Global Advisory Comm. for Medical Research 1980, Foreign mem. Acad. of Medical Sciences, USSR 1986, Foreign Fellow Indian Nat. Science Acad. 1986; Visiting Prof. of Centre Diseases Control, Atlanta, USA 1976; Heath Clark Lecturer Univ. of London 1986–87; mem. External Review Team for Human Reproduction Research Program 1988–89; Order of Banner of Labour 1st and 2nd Class, Commdr and Knight's Cross, Order of Polonia Restituta, Cross of Valour, Gold Cross of Merit, Warsaw Insurgent Cross and others; Dr hc (WAM, Łódź) 1979, (AM, Lublin) 1985. *Publications:* numerous works on epidemiology including Communicable Diseases and Their Control on the Territory of Poland in the XX Century (co-author and co-ed.). *Leisure interests:* sport, photography, skiing, fishing. *Address:* National Institute of Hygiene, ul. Chocimska 24, Warsaw (Office); Al. Róz 10M6, 00-556, Warsaw, Poland (Home). *Telephone:* (22) 8493104 (Office); (22) 6284988 (Home). *E-mail:* jan_kostrzewski@op.pl (Home).

KOŠTUNICA, Vojislav, LLB; Serbia and Montenegro (Serbian) politician and lawyer; b. 24 April 1944, Belgrade; s. of Jovan Kostunica and Radmila Arandjelovic; m. Radmila Radovic; ed Belgrade State Univ.; lecturer in law, Belgrade Univ. 1970–74; expelled for opposition to univ. admin. 1974; Sr researcher Inst. of Philosophy and Social Theories in Belgrade; took part in opposition Movt from 1980s; expelled from Inst., charges later lifted; founder mem. Democratic Party; left party in 1992 to form Democratic Party of Serbia (DPS), now Chair.; remained outside mainstream politics until nominated by opposition parties to stand as a cand. against Slobodan Milosevic (q.v.); Pres. of the Fed. Repub. of Yugoslavia (now Serbia and Montenegro) 2000–03. *Publications include:* Political System of Capitalism and Opposition 1978, Party Pluralism or Monism (jtly) 1983. *Address:* c/o Office of the President of Serbia and Montenegro, Andriecev venac 1, 11000 Belgrade, Serbia and Montenegro (Office).

KOSTYUK, Platon Grigorievich, DBiol; Ukrainian neurophysiologist, physician and biologist; b. 20 Aug. 1924, Kiev; s. of G. S. Kostyuk and M. F. Kostyuk; m. Liudmila V. Kostyuk 1950; two d.; ed Kiev State Univ. and Kiev Medical Inst.; mem. CPSU 1947–91; Head, Dept of Gen. Physiology of Nervous System, A.A. Bogomoletz Inst. of Physiology 1958–, Dir of Inst. 1966–; Head, Dept of Membrane Biophysics, Moscow Physico-Tech. Inst. 1982–; mem. Ukrainian Acad. of Sciences 1966– (Vice-Pres. 1993–98), Ukrainian Acad. of Medical Sciences 1994, Russian, Czechoslovak and Hungarian Acads., Akad. Leopoldina; mem. Exec. Cttee European Neurosciences Asscn (ENA); Chair. United Scientific Council for Problems of Human and Animal Physiology; Pavlov Prize 1960; Sechenov Prize 1977; State Prize 1983; A.A. Bogomoletz Prize 1987. *Publications:* Intracellular Perfusion of Excitable Cells 1984, Role of Calcium Ions in Nerve Cell Function 1991, Calcium Signalling in the Nervous System 1995, Plasticity in Nerve Cell Function 1998. *Leisure interests:* tennis, downhill skiing. *Address:* A. A. Bogomoletz Institute of Physiology, 4 Bogomoletz Street, 01601 Kiev 24, Ukraine. *Telephone:* (44) 253-2909 (Office); (44) 234-2071 (Home). *Fax:* (44) 253-64-58. *E-mail:* pkostyuk@serv.biph.kiev.ua (Office).

KOSUTH, Joseph; American artist; b. 31 Jan. 1945, Toledo, Ohio; Prof. School of Visual Arts, New York City 1967–, Hochschule für Bildende Kunst, Hamburg 1988–91, Kunstakademie, Stuttgart 1991–; Brandeis Univ. Creative Art Award 1991, Frederick R. Weisman Art Foundation Award 1991, Venice Biennale Menzione d'Onore 1; Chevalier des Arts et des Lettres. *Publication:* Art After Philosophy and After (collected writings) 1991. *Address:* 591 Broadway, New York, NY 10012, USA; Maagdestraat 6, 9000 Ghent, Belgium. *Telephone:* (212)-219-8984 (New York); (9) 233-48-49 (Ghent).

KOTAITE, Assad, LLD; Lebanese international aviation official and lawyer; b. 6 Nov. 1924, Hasbaya; s. of Adib Kotaite and Kamle Abousamra; m. Monique Ayoub 1983; ed French Univ., Beirut, Univ. of Paris and Acad. of Int. Law, The Hague; Head of Legal and Int. Affairs, Directorate of Civil Aviation, Lebanon 1953–56; Rep. of Lebanon, Council of ICAO 1956–70; Sec.-Gen. ICAO, 1970–76, Pres. Council 1976–; Pres. Int. Court of Aviation and Space Arbitration, Paris 1995–; many decorations from academic Insts. and states. *Address:* c/o International Civil Aviation Organization, 999 University Street, Suite 12.20, Montreal, Que., H3C 5H7 (Office); 5955 Wilderton Avenue, Apt. O4A, Montreal, Que., H3S 2V1, Canada (Home). *Telephone:* (514) 954-8011 (Office).

KOTCHEFF, Ted; Canadian film and stage director; b. 7 April 1931, Toronto; with CBC Television 1952–57; joined ABC-TV, London 1957. *Films include:* Life At The Top 1965, Two Gentlemen Sharing 1968, Wake In Fright 1971, The Apprenticeship of Duddy Kravitz (in Canada) 1973–74, Fun with Dick and Jane 1977, Who is Killing the Great Chefs of Europe? 1978, North Dallas Forty (Dir and wrote) 1979, First Blood, Split Image, 1982–83, Uncommon Valour 1984, Joshua, Then and Now 1985, Weekend at Bernie's 1989, Winter People (Dir) 1990, Folks! (actor) 1992, The Shooter 1996, The Populist, A Strange Affair 1996, Borrowed Hearts 1997, Crime in Connecticut 1999. *Plays include:* Play With A Tiger, Maggie May, The Au Pair Man, Have You Any Dirty Washing, Mother Dear? *Television plays include:* The Human Voice 1966, Of Mice And Men 1968, Edna The Inebriate Woman 1971.

KOTELKIN, Maj.-Gen. Aleksander Ivanovich; Russian politician; b. 19 Nov. 1954, Kiev; m.; one s.; ed Kiev Higher School of Eng and Aviation, Diplomatic Acad.; served in the army, engineer of aviation equipment Kiev Mil. command 1976–87; with USSR Mission in UN, New York 1988–90; on staff Ministry of External Econ. Relations 1991–94; Head Chief Dept on mil.-tech. co-operation 1993–94; Dir-Gen. State Co. Rosvooruzheniye 1994–97, Chief Adviser on Marketing 1997–; First Deputy Minister of Foreign Econ. Relations and Trade 1997–98; First Deputy Head Dept. of Municipal Property, Moscow Govt 1998–. *Address:* Karetny Ryad 2/1, 103006 Moscow, Russia. *Telephone:* (095) 299-55-37 (Office).

KOTELNIKOV, Vladimir Aleksandrovich; Russian radio and electronics engineer; b. 6 Sept. 1908, Kazan; s. of Alexander Petrovich Kotelnikov and Varvara Petrovna Kotelnikova; m. Anna Ivanova Bogatskaya 1990 (deceased); one s. two d.; ed Power Eng Inst., Moscow; Prof. and Dean, Radio Eng Faculty, Moscow Power Eng Inst. 1931–47, Head, Chair. of Radio Eng Principles, Moscow Power Eng Inst. 1944–80; Deputy Dir Inst. of Radio Eng and Electronics, USSR (now Russian) Acad. of Sciences 1953–54, Dir 1954–87, Hon. Dir 1987–; mem. USSR (now Russian) Acad. of Sciences 1953–, Vice-Pres. 1970–88, Acting Pres. May–Nov. 1975, Counsellor 1988–; Chair. 'Intercosmos' Council on Int. Co-operation in Space Research, USSR Acad. of Sciences 1980–93, Vice-Chair. 1993–; Chair. Supreme Soviet of RSFSR 1973–79; Vice-Pres. Int. Acad. of Astronautics 1983–95; Life Fellow Int. Inst. of Electrical and Electronics Engineers 1987–; Foreign mem. Polish Acad. of Sciences, Czechoslovak Acad. of Sciences, Mongolian Acad. of Sciences, Bulgarian Acad. of Sciences; State Prize 1943, 1946, Lenin Prize 1964, Hero of Socialist Labour (twice), Eduard Rhein Basic Research Award (Germany) 1999, Alexander Graham Bell Gold Medal, IEEE 2000; and other decorations. *Publications:* works on improvement of wireless communications, radio-location of planets. *Leisure interest:* books. *Address:* Russian Academy of Sciences, Leninsky Prospekt 14, 117901, GSP-I, Moscow, Russia. *Telephone:* (095) 954-38-28, 954-30-06. *Fax:* (095) 954-10-74.

KOTENKOV, Maj.-Gen. Aleksander Alekseyevich; Russian politician; b. 23 Sept. 1952, Krasnodar Territory; m.; one s.; ed Rostov-on-Don Inst. of Agric. Machine Construction, Mil.-Political Acad. by corresp.; engineer Rostov Don Factory Rubin 1974–75; army service 1975–90; People's Deputy Russian Fed. 1990–93; Deputy Chair. Cttee Supreme Soviet on Defence and Security 1991; Deputy Head, Head State Law Dept, Russian Presidency, 1992–93; Head Provincial Admin. Martial Law Zone N. Ossetia and Ingushetia 1993–95; Deputy Minister of Nat. Policy 1995–96; mem. State Duma (Parl.) 1993–96; Rep. of President in State Duma 1996–. *Address:* State Duma, Okhotny Ryad 1, 103265 Moscow, Russia (Office). *Telephone:* (095) 292-91-23 (Office).

KOTLYAKOV, Vladimir Mikhailovich, DrGeogSc; Russian geographer; b. 6 Nov. 1931, Lobnya, Moscow Region; m. Valentina Alexeevna Bazanova; two s.; ed Moscow State Univ.; jr researcher, sr researcher, Head of Glaciology Dept, Inst. of Geography USSR (now Russian) Acad. of Sciences 1954–86, Dir 1986–; corresp. mem., Russian Acad. of Sciences 1976, mem. 1991–; Vice-Pres. Russian Geographical Soc. 1980–2000, Hon. Pres. 2000–; People's Deputy of USSR 1989–91; mem. Acad. Europaea, Earth Council 1993–; Hon. mem. American, Mexican, Italian, Estonian and Georgian Geographical Socs., Int. Glaciological Soc.; Litke Gold Medal, Russian Geographical Soc. 1985, Przhevalsky Gold Medal, Russian Geographical Soc. 1995, State Prize of Russian Fed. 2002. *Publications include:* Snow Cover of Antarctica 1961, Snow Cover of the Earth and Glaciers 1968, Glaciology Dictionary 1984, Elsevier's Dictionary of Glaciology 1990, World of Snow and Ice 1994, Science, Society, Environment 1997, World Atlas of Snow and Ice Resources 1997; Collection of Selected Works: Glaciology of Antarctica (vol. 1) 2000, Geography in the Changing World (vol. 3) 2001, Ice, Love and Hypothesis (vol. 4) 2001. *Leisure interest:* travelling. *Address:* Institute of Geography, Russian Academy of Sciences, Staromonetny per. 29, 109017 Moscow (Office); Profsoyuznaya St 43-1-80, 117420 Moscow, Russia (Home). *Telephone:* (095) 959-00-32 (Office); (095) 331-32-63 (Home). *Fax:* (095) 959-00-33 (Office). *E-mail:* geograph@ online.ru (Office); igras@igras.geonet.ru (Office).

KOTTO, Yaphet Fredrick; American actor; b. 15 Nov. 1944, Harlem, New York; s. of Yaphet Mangobell Kotto and Gladys M. Kotto; m. Antoinette Pettyjohn 1975; six c. *Films include:* Nothing But a Man 1963, Liberation of Lord Byron Jones 1964, Across 110th Street 1973, Live and Let Die 1974, Report to the Commissioner 1974, Sharks Treasure 1974, Monkey Hustle 1975, Drum 1976, Blue Collar 1977, Alien 1978, Brubaker 1979, Hey Good Looking 1982, Fighting Back 1982, Star Chamber 1983, Eye of the Tiger, Prettykill, The Running Man, Midnight Run, Nightmare of the Devil (also Dir), Terminal Entry, Jigsaw, A Whisper to a Scream, Tripurie, Ministry of Vengeance, Hangfire, Freddy's Dead, Almost Blue 1992, Intent to Kill 1993, The Puppet Masters 1994, Two If By Sea 1996, The Defenders: Payback 1997, Stiletto Dance 2001. *Theatre includes:* Great White Hope, Blood Knot, Black Monday, In White America, A Good Place to Raise a Boy, Fences (London) 1990. *Television includes:* Raid on Entebbe 1977, Rage 1980, Women of San Quentin 1983, In Self Defense 1987, Badge of the Assassin, Harem, Desperado, Perry Mason, Prime Target, After the Shock, Chrome Soldiers, It's Nothing Personal, Extreme Justice, The American Clock, Deadline For Murder.

KOUANDÉTÉ, Lt-Col Maurice; Benin politician and army officer; b. 1939; ed Ecole de Guerre, Paris; Dir of Cabinet of Head of State 1967–69; Head of State and Head Provisional Govt Dec. 1967; Chief of Staff of Dahomey (now Benin) Army 1969–70; leader of coup which overthrew Pres. Zinsou Dec. 1969; mem. of Directory (three man body ruling Dahomey), Minister of the Economy, Finance and Co-operation 1969–70; arrested 1970; Deputy Sec. for Defence 1970–72; arrested Feb. 1972, sentenced to death May 1972, granted amnesty and released Dec. 1972; arrested Feb. 1996, detention overturned by constitutional court.

KOUCHNER, Bernard, DenM; French politician and doctor; b. 1 Nov. 1939, Avignon; two s. one d. by Evelyne Pisier; one s. by Christine Ockrent (q.v.); gastro-enterologist, Hôpital Cochin; Founder, Dir and Pres. Médecins sans Frontières 1971–79; Founder, Médecins du Monde 1980; has organized and undertaken numerous humanitarian missions around the world since 1968; Sec. of State, Ministry of Social Affairs and Employment May 1988; Sec. of State responsible for Humanitarian Action, Office of Prime Minister 1988–91, Ministry of Foreign Affairs 1991–92; Minister of Health and Humanitarian Action 1992–93, 1997–99, Minister Del. Ministry of Health 2001–02; MEP 1994–; UN Chief Admin., Kosovo 1999–2000; Founder Foundation for Humanitarian Action 1993–; radio broadcaster RTL 2 1995; Dag Hammarskjöld Prize 1979, Louis Weiss Prize (European Parl.) 1979, Athinai Prize (Alexander Onassis Foundation) 1981, Prix Europa 1984, Nobel Peace Prize (with Médecin sans Frontières) 1999. *Publications:* La France Sauvage, Les Voraces, L'Ile de Lumière, Charité Business, Le Devoir d'Ingérence (jtly) 1988, Les Nouvelles Solidarités 1989, Le Malheur des Autres 1991, Dieu et les Hommes (jtly) 1993, Vingt idées pour l'an 2000 1995, Ce que je crois 1995, La dictature medicale 1995, le Premier qui dit la Verité 2002; scripts for TV series under pseudonym Bernard Gridaine. *Address:* c/o Editions Robert Laffont, 24 avenue Marceau, 75008 Paris, France.

KOUDELKA, Josef; Czech photographer; b. 10 Jan. 1938, Boskovice; ed Univ. of Prague; aeronautical engineer, Prague and Bratislava 1961–67; specialized in photography 1967–; extensive travel throughout Europe documenting lives of gypsies; exhibited in Prague 1961, 1967, MOMA, New York 1975, Amsterdam 1978, Stockholm 1980, Hayward Gallery, London 1984 etc. mem. Magnum Photos Inc. 1971–; mem. Union of Czechoslovakian artists 1965–; Chevalier des Arts et des Lettres 1992; Prix Nadar 1978, Grand Prix Nat. de la Photographie (France) 1987, Hugo Erhurth Prize 1989, Prix Romanes 1989, Henri Cartier-Bresson Award 1991Century Medal of the Royal Photographic Soc., UK, Medal of Merit 2002, and others. *Solo exhibitions:* Museum of Modern Art, New York 1975, Hayward Gallery, London 1984, Nordisea Museum, Stockholm 1989, San Francisco Museum of Modern Art 1991, Palazzo delle Exposizione, Rome 1991, Museum de Arte de São Paulo 1995, Tokyo Metropolitan Museum of Photography 1997, retrospective exhbn, Prague 2002. *Publications:* Gypsies 1975, Exiles 1988, Reconnaissance: Wales 1998, Chaos 1999. *Address:* c/o Magnum Photos, 19 rue Hégesippe Moneau, 75018 Paris, France.

KOULOUMBIS, Evangelos; Greek politician and engineer; b. 1929, Athens; s. of Athanasios Kouloumbis and Anastasia Kouloumbis; m. Dimitra Lambrou; one s. one d.; ed Athens Polytechnic Univ.; founder mem. Civil Eng Asscn, mem. Gov. Council 1965–67, Pres. 1974–75; Pres. of Tech. Chamber 1974–81; Minister of Public Works in caretaker Govt 1974; Pres. Greek Cttee for Balkan Agreement and Co-operation 1975–; mem. Parl. 1981–89; Chair. Council of Energy Ministers of EEC 1983 and many Greek and int. conventions, Perm. Conf. of Engineers of SE Europe (COPISEE) 1978–80; hon. mem. League of Cypriot Engineers and Architects; mem. Greek Cttee UNESCO 1982–83; Minister without Portfolio 1981–82, for Energy and Nat. Resources 1982–84, of Physical Planning, Housing and Environment 1984, for Physical Planning, Housing, Public Works, Transport 1985–88, for the Environment, Physical Planning and Public Works 1985–88; Gov. Nat. Mortgage Bank of Greece 1993–95; Pres. Jt County Authorities of Athens and Piraeus 1995, Union of County Councils of Greece 1995. *Publications:* articles on economic, social and political matters. *Address:* 11 Kleomenous Street, 106 75 Athens, Greece. *Telephone:* (1) 7250333.

KOULOURIANOS, Dimitri, PhD; Greek economist; b. 4 Dec. 1930, Koroni; m.; one s. one d.; ed School of Econ. and Commercial Sciences, Athens and Univ. of Calif., Berkeley; Econ. Research Dept Bank of Greece 1957–67; World Bank (IBRD) 1968–81, participated in many missions to Africa, Asia and Latin America and was seconded as econ. adviser to Govt of Ethiopia; mem. European Parl. 1981; Gov. Hellenic Industrial Devt Bank; Minister of Finance 1982–83; fmr consultant to UNESCO; Perm. Rep. of Greece to OECD 1986–90; Alt. Dir EBRD 1991–. *Address:* c/o EBRD, 1 Exchange Square, 175 Bishopsgate, London, EC2A 2EH, England (Office).

KOUMAKOYE, Kassire Delwa, DenD; Chadian politician; b. Delwa Kassire Coumakoye, 31 Dec. 1949, Bongor; ed Ecole Nat. d'Admin., Chad, Inst. Int. d'Admin. Publique, Paris, Univ. de Paris I and II; Minister of Justice 1981–82, of Public Works, Housing and Town Planning 1987–88, of Justice 1988–89, of Posts and Telecommunications 1989–90, of Higher Educ. and Scientific Research 1989–90, of Communications and Liberties, Govt Spokesperson April–June 1993, of Justice June–Nov. 1993; Gen. Inspector of Admin. 1987–; Prime Minister of Chad 1993–95; mem. and Pres. Rassemblement nat. pour la démocratie et le progrès (RNDP) 1992–; also Leader Convention de l'opposition démocratique (alliance of opposition parties); champion of Cen. Africa in 3,000 m. steeple chase 1965 (record unbroken); sentenced to three months' imprisonment for possessing illegal weapons 1996; Chevalier Ordre de Mérite Centrafricain 1976, Commdr Ordre nat. du Tchad 1994. *Address:* B.P. 870, N'Djamena, Chad. *Telephone:* 29-09-59 (Home); 52-63-86. *Fax:* 51-63-86.

KOUMI, Margaret (Maggie); British journalist; b. 15 July 1942; d. of the late Yiasoumis Koumi and Melexidia Paraskeva; m. Ramon Sola 1980; ed Buckingham Gate, London; sec. Thomas Cook 1957–60; sub-ed., feature and fiction writer Visual Features Ltd 1960–66; sub-ed. TV World 1966–67; Production Ed. 19 Magazine 1967–69, Ed. 1969–86, concurrently Ed. Hair Magazine; Man. Ed. Practical Parenting, Practical Health, Practical Hair and Beauty 1986–87; Jt Ed. Hello! 1988–93, Ed. 1993–2001, freelance consultant 2001–; Ed. of the Year Award 1991. *Publication:* Beauty Care 1981. *Leisure interests:* work, reading. *Address:* Flat 8, 8 Mercer Street, London, WC2H 9QB, England. *Telephone:* (20) 7836-5989. *Fax:* (20) 7379-8295.

KOUYATÉ, Lansana; Guinean international official and diplomatist; fmr economist; fmr Special Rep. of UN Sec.-Gen., including missions to Somalia and Rwanda; Exec. Sec. Econ. Community of W African States (ECOWAS) 1997–2001. *Address:* c/o ECOWAS, Secretariat Building, 60 Yakubu Gowon Crescent, Asokoro, Abuja, Nigeria.

KOVÁČ, Michal; Slovak politician, economist and banker; b. 5 Aug. 1930, Lubiša, E Slovakia; m. Emília Kováčová; two s.; ed Commercial Acad., Bratislava Univ. of Econs; Asst Lecturer Bratislava Univ. of Econs 1954; joined staff State Bank of Czechoslovakia 1956; fmr financial adviser to Nat. Bank of Cuba; Deputy Dir Zivnostenska (trade bank), London 1967–69, recalled, expelled from CP and demoted to bank clerk 1969; researcher, lecturer 1970–78; elected to Fed. Ass. 1990; Minister of Finance, Slovak Repub. 1990, resgnd 1991; re-elected to Fed. Ass., Chair. Czech Fed. Ass. of Czech and Slovak Fed. Rep. June–Dec. 1992; Pres. of Slovak Repub. 1993–98; C-in-C the Armed Forces 1993–98; Chair. M. Kováč and V. Havel Foundation 1993–; fmr mem. Movt for a Democratic Slovakia, Deputy Chair. 1991–93; Grand Cross, Order of Merit (Poland) 1994, White Eagle Order (Poland) 1997, numerous Slovak decorations including White Double Cross Order, Lúdovít Štúr Order; CEELIA Award, American Bar Asscn 1995, Lions Club Award 1995. *Address:* c/o Office of the President, Hodžovo nám. 1, P.O. Box 128, 810 00 Bratislava, Slovakia.

KOVACEVICH, Richard M., MBA; American business executive; b. 1944; ed Stanford Univ.; Exec. Vice-Pres. Kenner Div., Gen. Mills Inc., Minneapolis 1967–72; Prin. Venture Capital 1972–75; Vice-Pres. Consumer Services Norwest Corpn, Minneapolis 1975, subsequently Sr Vice-Pres. New York banking group, Exec. Vice-Pres. Man. New York bank div., Exec. Vice-Pres., mem. policy Cttee, Vice-Chair., COO banking group, Pres., COO, Vice-Chair., Chair.and CEO 1996–; Pres., CEO Wells Fargo & Co. (merged with Norwest Corpn), San Francisco 1999–. *Leisure interest:* playing basketball. *Address:* Wells Fargo & Co., 420 Montgomery Street, San Francisco, CA 94104, USA (Office).

KOVACEVICH, Stephen; American pianist; b. 17 Oct. 1940, San Francisco; s. of Nicholas Kovacevich and Loreta Kovacevich (née Zuban); ed Berkeley High School, Calif.; studied under Lev Shorr and Dame Myra Hess; London début 1961; subsequently appeared at int. music festivals in Edin., Bath, Harrogate, Berlin, San Sebastián and Salzburg; a soloist at Henry Wood Promenade Concerts for fourteen seasons; tours frequently in Europe, America and Australasia; fmr Prin. Guest Conductor of Australian Chamber Orchestra; fmr Music Dir of Irish Chamber Orchestra; has conducted City of Birmingham Symphony, BBC Philharmonic, Bournemouth Symphony, Royal Liverpool Philharmonic orchestras, Chamber Orchestra of Europe, London Mozart Players, Nat. Youth Chamber Orchestra; numerous recordings; winner of Kimber Award, Calif. 1959, Mozart Prize, London 1962, Edison Award (for recording of Bartok's 2nd Piano Concerto), Gramophone Award 1993 (for recording of Brahms' 1st Piano Concerto). *Publication:* Schubert Anthology. *Leisure interests:* tennis, chess, cinema, Indian food. *Address:* c/o Van Walsum Management Ltd, 4 Addison Bridge Place, London, W14 8XP, England. *Telephone:* (20) 8371-4343. *Fax:* (20) 8371-4344. *E-mail:* vwm@vanwalsum.co.uk (Office). *Website:* www.vanwalsum.co.uk (Office).

KOVACIC, Ernst; Austrian violinist; b. 12 April 1943, Kapfenburg; m. Anna Maria Schuster 1968; four s.; ed Acad. of Music, Vienna; teacher Univ. of Music, Vienna 1975–; prizewinner, int. competitions, Geneva 1970, Barcelona 1971, Munich 1972; appears throughout Europe, UK and USA with leading orchestras and has appeared at many festivals including Salzburg, Berlin, Vienna, Bath, Edin. and Aldeburgh; gave Concerto by Thomas Wilson at London Proms 1993; repertoire includes maj. works of baroque, classical and romantic periods and contemporary works; Artistic Dir Vienna Chamber Orchestra 1996–98. *Address:* Im Muehlfeld 3, 2102, Bisamberg, Austria (Home).

KOVÁCS, András; Hungarian film director and script writer; b. 20 June 1925, Kide (now in Romania); m. Gabriella Pongrác; one s. one d.; ed Győrffy Coll. and Acad. of Dramatic and Cinematic Arts; Drama reader, Hungarian Film Studio 1950, Drama Dept Head 1951–57, Film Dir 1960–; Chair. Parl. Curatorium of Public Foundation for Hungarian TV 1996–98; Pres. Fed. of Hungarian Film and TV Artists 1981–86; Balázs B. Prize, Kossuth Prize 1970; named Eminent Artist. *Author:* Egy film forrásvidéke 1972. *TV films:* Menekülés Magyarországra (Flight to Hungary) 1980, György Lukács Portray 1986, Volt egyszer egy egyetem (Once Upon a University) 1995, Utak Vásárhelyröl (Roads from Vásárhely) 1996, Két Szólamban 2000, Reggeltól Hajnalig Válaszúton 2001, Film egy regényröl 2002, Egy borértő ember 2003. *Films:* Zápor (Summer Rain) 1960, Pesti háztetők (On the Roofs of Budapest) 1961, Isten őszi csillaga (Autumn Star) 1962, Nehéz emberek (Difficult People) 1964, Hideg napok (Cold Days) 1966, Falak (Walls) 1968, Ecstasy from 7 to 10 1969, Staféta (Relay Race) 1971, A magyar ugaron (Fallow Land) 1973, Bekötött szemmel (Blindfold) 1975, Labirintus (Labyrinth) 1976, A ménesgazda (The Stud Farm) 1978, Októberi vasárnap (A Sunday in October) 1979, Ideiglenes Paradicsom (Temporary Paradise) 1981, Szeretök (An Afternoon Affair) 1983, A vörös grófnö (The Red Countess) 1985, Valahol Magyarországon (Rearguard Struggle) 1987, Az álommenedzser (The Dream Manager) 1994. *Leisure interest:* gardening. *Address:* 1122 Budapest, Magyar Jakobinusok tere 2/3, Hungary. *Telephone:* (1) 356-7227.

KOVÁCS, Dénes; Hungarian violinist; b. 18 April 1930, Vác; s. of József Kovács and Margit Juhász; m.; one s. one d.; ed Budapest Acad. of Music under Ede Zathureczky; First Violinist, Budapest State Opera 1951–60; leading Violin Prof. at Budapest Music Acad. 1957–, Dir of Budapest Music Acad. 1967; Rector Ferenc Liszt Acad. of Music 1971–80, Dean of String Dept 1980–; concert tours all over Europe, in USA, USSR, Iran, India, China and Japan; mem. jury in int. competitions: Tchaikovsky, Moscow; Long-Thibaud, Paris; Jean Sibelius, Helsinki; Joseph Joachim, Vienna; Wieniawski, Warsaw; Tokyo; Kossuth Prize 1963, awarded Eminent Artist title 1970, Golden Medal of Labour 1974. *Address:* Music Academy, 1061 Budapest VI, Liszt Ferenc tér 8 (Office); Irányi utca 12, Budapest V, Hungary (Home). *Telephone:* (1) 141-4788 (Office).

KOVALEV, Col.-Gen. Nikolai Dmitriyevich; Russian security officer; b. 1949, Moscow; m.; one d.; ed Moscow Inst. of Electronic Machine Construction; on staff system of state security KGB 1974–; served for 2 years in Afghanistan; staff mem. Dept of Fed. Service of Counterespionage of Moscow and Moscow Region –1994; Deputy Dir Fed. Security Service (FSB) 1994–96; Acting Dir, then Dir 1996–98; mem. Security Council of Russia; mem. Comm. on Higher Mil. Titles and Posts, Council on Personnel Policy of Pres. of Russia; mem. to State Duma 1999–; mem. Otechestvo-All Russia faction; Chair. Comm. for Struggle Against Corruption 2000–. *Address:* State Duma, Okhotny Ryad 1, 103265 Moscow, Russia. *Telephone:* (095) 292-89-19 (Office). *Fax:* (095) 292-89-24 (Office).

KOVALEV, Sergey Adamovich, PhD; Russian politician; b. 2 March 1930, Seredina-Buda, Ukraine; s. of Adam Vasil'evich Kovalev and Valentina Vasilerna Kovaleva; m. 1st Elena Viktorovna Tokareva 1949; m. 2nd Luydmila Uyr'evna Boitsova 1967; one s. two d.; ed Moscow State Univ.; worked as researcher, Moscow Univ.; active participant in Movt for human rights since late 1960s; one of assocs. of Academician A. Sakharov, one of founders Initiative Group for Human Rights 1969; ed. Samizdat Bulletin Chronicles of Current Events, expelled from Moscow Univ. 1969; arrested on charge of anti-Soviet propaganda 1974, sentenced to seven years' imprisonment and three years in exile 1974; lived in Kalinin, returned to Moscow 1987; mem. Project Group for Human Rights of Int. Foundation for Survival and Devt of Humanity, Engineer Inst. of Problems of Data Transmission USSR Acad. of Sciences 1987–90; People's Deputy of Russian Fed. 1990–93; Chair. Cttee for Human Rights of Supreme Soviet of Russia 1990–93; Co-Chair. Soviet Del. on Moscow Conf. on Human Rights 1991; Chief of Russian Del. to UN Comm. on Human Rights 1992–95; one of founders and leaders of Vybor Rossii; mem. State Duma (Parl.) 1993–95, 1999–; Chair. Pres.'s Cttee on Human Rights 1994–96; Ombudsman of Russian Fed. 1994–95; Council of Europe Human Rights Prize 1995, Kt of Honour of Chkezia 1997. *Leisure interests:* hunting, fishing. *Address:* State Duma, Okhotny Ryad 1, 103009 Moscow, Russia. *Telephone:* (095) 292-93-43.

KOVALEVSKY, Jean, DèsSc; French astronomer; b. 18 May 1929, Neuilly-sur-Seine; s. of Jean Kovalevsky and Hélène Pavloff; m. Jeannine Reige 1956; two s. one d.; ed Univ. of Paris and Ecole Normale Supérieure; Research Asst Paris Observatory 1955–59, Yale Univ. 1957–58; Head of Computing and Celestial Mechanics Service, Bureau des Longitudes 1960–71; Exec. Dir Groupe de Recherches de Géodésie Spatiale 1971–78; Founder and first Dir Centre d'Etudes et de Recherches Géodynamiques et Astronomiques 1974–82, 1988–92; astronomer, Observatoire de la Côte d'Azur, Grasse 1986; Sec. Bureau Int. des Poids et Mesures 1991–97, Pres. 1997–; Pres. Bureau Nat. de Métrologie 1995–; mem. French Acad. of Sciences, Int. Acad. of Astronautics, Academia Europaea, Acad. of Sciences of Turin, French Acad. of Tech., Scientific Cttee European Space Agency 1979–81; Chevalier, Légion d'honneur, Commdr, Ordre du Mérite. *Publications:* Introduction to Celestial Mechanics 1967, Traité de Géodésie (with J. Levallois), Vol 4. 1971, Astrométrie moderne 1990, Modern Astronomy 1995; about 250 scientific papers. *Leisure interests:* gardening, stamp collection. *Address:* CERGA, Observatoire de la Côte d'Azur, avenue Copernic, 06130 Grasse (Office); Villa La Padovane, 8 rue St Michel, Saint-Antoine, 06130 Grasse, France (Home). *Telephone:* 4-93-40-53-87 (Office); 4-93-70-60-29 (Home). *Fax:* 4-93-40-53-33.

KOVANDA, Karel, MBA, PhD; Czech diplomatist; b. 5 Oct. 1944, Gilsland, UK; s. of Oldřich Kovanda and Ivy Norman; m. Noemi Berová 1993; one s. two d.; ed Prague School of Agric., Massachusetts Inst. of Tech. and Pepperdine Univ., USA; leadership, Czech Nat. Student Union 1968–69; emigrated to USA 1970; lecturer in political science and freelance journalist 1975–80; man. positions in U.S. pvt. sector 1980–90; returned to Czechoslovakia 1990; Czech Ministry of Foreign Affairs 1991–93, Political Dir 1993, Deputy Minister 1997–98; Perm. Rep. of Czech Repub. to UN 1993–97, to NATO 1998–; Pres. ECOSOC 1997. *Leisure interests:* literature, theatre, travel, stamp collecting. *Address:* Czech Delegation to NATO, NATO HQ, 1110 Brussels, Belgium. *Telephone:* (2) 707-17-27. *Fax:* (2) 707-17-03. *E-mail:* nato-brussels@embassy.mzv.cz.

KOWALCZYK, HE Archbishop Józef, DCL; Polish ecclesiastic and diplomatist; b. 28 Aug. 1938, Jadowniki Mokre; ed Hosianum Higher Ecclesiastic Seminary, Olsztyn, Catholic Univ. of Lublin, Pontifical Gregorian Univ., Rome, Roman Rota Studium; ordained Priest 1962; employee Roman Rota; employee Congregation for the Discipline of the Sacraments; organizer and head Polish Section, State Secr. 1978–89; titular Archbishop of Heraclea and Apostolic Nuncio in Poland 1989–; Hon. mem. Soc. of Polish Canon Lawyers; Dr hc (Agric. Acad., Cracow) 1999, (Cardinal S. Wyszyński Univ.) 2000, (Catholic Univ. of Lublin) 2001. *Publications:* Dojrzewanie czasu 1998, Na drodze konsekrowanej 1999, Służyć słowu 2000 and ed. of Karol Wojtyła's papers and Polish edition of papal teaching (14 Vols). *Address:* Nuncjatura Apostolska, al. J. Ch. Szucha 12, skr. poczt. 163, 00-582 Warsaw, Poland. *Telephone:* (22) 6288488. *Fax:* (22) 6284556.

KOYAMBOUNOU, Gabriel Jean Edouard; Central African Republic politician; b. Bangui; ed Univ. of Abidjan, École Nat. des Douanes, Françaises, Neuilly-sur-Seine, France; fmr civil servant; Prime Minister of Cen. African Repub. 1995–96; Minister of State in charge of Communication, Posts and Telecommunications, New Technologies and Francophone Affairs –2003; Second Vice-Pres. Mouvement pour la libération du peuple centrafricain (MLCP); Pres. Handball Fed.; Grand Officier, Ordre du Merite; Gold Medal in Sport. *Publication:* Mémoire sur le 'Droit Douanier'. *Leisure interest:* handball. *Address:* BP 42, Bangui, Central African Republic (Home).

KOZACHENKO, Leonid Petrovich; Ukrainian engineer, economist and politician; b. 14 May 1955, Veprik, Kiev region; m.; two d.; ed Ukrainian Acad. of Agric., All-Union Acad. of Foreign Trade; worked in agric. enterprises in Fastov region 1972–86; party functionary CP of Ukraine 1986–88; Deputy Head of Dept Ukrainian Ministry of Agric. 1991–2001; Dir Agroland Jan. 2001–; Prime Minister of Ukraine June–July 2001, Deputy Prime Minister 2002; f. Ukrainian League of Businessmen 1993; co-f. Ukrainian Asscn of Corn, Nat. Asscn of Stock Exchanges, Ukrainian Asscn for Ecology Protection; Founder and Pres. Ukrainian Agrarian Confed. 1998–, Co-Chair.; mem. Presidential Comm. on Agric., Presidium Ukrainian Union of Businessmen; mem. Co-ordination Council of Businessmen at Ministry of Agrarian Policy; Merited Worker of Agric. of Ukraine 1998. *Address:* c/o Cabinet of Ministers, Hrushevskogo 12/2, 252008 Kiev, Ukraine (Office).

KOZAK, Dmitry Nikolayevich; Russian politician and jurist; b. 7 Nov. 1958, Kirovograd Region, Ukraine; m.; two s.; ed Leningrad State Univ.; Asst to Prosecutor of Leningrad; on staff Asscn of Marine Trade Ports 1985–89; on staff Exec. Cttee Leningrad City Council 1990–91; Head of Law Dept Office, St Petersburg 1991–94; Chair. Law Cttee Admin., St Petersburg; mem. Govt of St Petersburg, mem. Comm. on Human Rights 1994–96; Vice-Gov. St Petersburg 1996–98; pvt. practice 1998–99; Deputy Head of Admin. of Russian Pres. on Legal Problems May–Aug. 1999; First Deputy Head of Govt of Russian Fed. 1999, Head 1999–2000; Deputy Head Admin. of Russian Pres. 2000–. *Address:* Administration of the President of the Russian Federation, Staraya pl. 4, entr. 1, Moscow, Russia (Office). *Telephone:* (095) 206-73-88 (Office).

KOZAKOV, Mikhail Mikhailovich; Russian actor and theatre director; b. 14 Oct. 1934, Leningrad; s. of Mikhail Kozakov; m. 1st; three c.; m. 3rd Anna Yampolskaya; one s. one d.; ed Moscow Art Theatre Studio School; actor Moscow Mayakovsky Theatre 1958–59, Sovremennik Theatre 1959–64, Moscow Art Theatre 1964–72; Theatre on Malaya Bronnaya 1972–81; worked in Israel as actor, Ghesher Theatre, Chamber Theatre Tel Aviv 1991–96; returned to Russia 1996; actor, Moscow Mayakovsky Theatre 1996–; f. own theatre co.; gives poetic concerts; debut in film Murder on Dante Street 1956; Peoples' Artist of Russia 1980, USSR and Russian State Prizes. *Films include:* The Year 1918, Nine Days of a Year, Eugénie Grandet, An Amphibian Man, A Straw Hat, A Comedy of Errors. *Films directed include:* Anonymous Star, Prokrovsky Gates, If to Believe Lopotukhin, Shadow, Faustus. *Publications:*

Third Call, Sketches in the Sand Actors' Book. *Address:* Mayakovsky Theatre, B. Nikitskaya str. 17, 103009 Moscow, Russia. *Telephone:* (095) 277-06-17 (Home).

KOŽENÁ, Magdalena; Czech singer (mezzo-soprano); b. 26 May 1973, Brno; ed Conservatoire, Brno, Acad. of Music and Dramatic Art, Bratislava; guest of Janáček's Opera, Brno 1991–; soloist Volksoper, Vienna 1996–97; has toured in Europe, USA, Japan, Venezuela, Taiwan, Hong Kong, S. Korea, Canada; charity concerts following floods in Czech Repub. 2002; debut at Salzburg Festival in Don Giovanni as Zerlina 2002; now working in early music; First Place in Int. Mozart Competition, Salzburg 1995; George Solti Prize (France), Echo Preis (Germany) 2000, Golden CD for Bach's Airs 2000, Gramophone Award (London) 2001. *Opera roles include:* Dorabella in Così Fan Tutte, Isabella in The Italian Girl in Algiers, Mercedes in Carmen, Annius in La Clemenza di Tito, lead in Orfo ed Eurydice (Gluck) 1999, Poppea in L'Incoronazione di Poppea (Monteverdi) 2000, Mélisande (Debussy) 2001. *Leisure interests:* philosophy, music, swimming, cycling. *Address:* c/o Agency Symfonieta, Beethovenova 4, 602 00 Brno (Office); Národní divadlo, Dvořákova 11, 600 00 Brno, Czech Republic (Home). *Telephone:* (5) 42215726 (Office). *E-mail:* obchodni.ndb@seznam. *Website:* www.ndbrno.cz.

KOZHIN, Vladimir Igorevich; Russian business executive; b. 28 Feb. 1959, Troitsk, Chelyabinsk Region; m. Alla Kozhina; one s.; ed Leningrad Electro-tech. Inst.; instructor, Head of Div., Petrograd Dist Comsomol Cttee; then on staff Research-Production Co. Azimuth, Dir-Gen. Russian-Polish Jt Co. Azimuth Int. Ltd 1991–93; Dir-Gen. St Petersburg Asscn of Jt Cos. 1993–94; Head N-W Cen. Fed. Dept of Currency and Export Control 1994–99, Head 1999–2000; Head Office of Russian Pres. 2000–. *Address:* Office of the President, Nikitnikov per. 2, entr. 5, Russia (Office). *Telephone:* (095) 206-82-88 (Office).

KOZHOKIN, Mikhail Mikhailovich, CandHist; Russian journalist; b. 23 Feb. 1962, Moscow; ed Moscow State Univ.; Jr researcher, researcher, Sr researcher Inst. of USA and Canada, USSR (now Russian) Acad. of Sciences 1988–92, Sr researcher Cen. of Econ. and Political Studies, worked with G. Yavlinsky 1992–93; Head Information Dept ONEXIMbank 1993–96; Deputy Chair. Exec. Cttee 1996–; Asst to First Deputy Chair. of Russian Govt, mem. Govt Comm. on Econ. Reform 1997–; Dir Holding Co. Interros on work with mass media and public relations; Chair. Bd of Dirs. Izvestia (newspaper) 1997–98, Ed.-in-Chief 1998–. *Leisure interests:* travelling, water tourism. *Address:* Izvestia, Tverskaya str. 18, korp. 1, 127994 Moscow, Russia (Office). *Telephone:* (095) 209-65-45 (Office). *E-mail:* izv@izvestia.ru (Office). *Website:* www.izvestia.ru (Office).

KOZHOKIN, Yevgeny Mikhailovich, DHist; Russian politologist; b. 9 April 1954, Moscow; m.; two d.; ed Moscow State Univ.; on staff Inst. of World History, USSR Acad. of Sciences 1984–90; People's Deputy of Russian Fed. 1990–93; Founder and Dir Russian Inst. for Strategic Studies (RISS) 1994. *Publications:* The French Workers: From the Great French Revolution to the Revolution of 1848 1985, The State and the People: From the Fronde to the Great French Revolution 1989 and more than 100 others. *Leisure interest:* swimming. *Address:* Russian Institute for Strategic Studies, Flotskaya str. 15, 125 413 Moscow, Russia (Office). *Telephone:* (095) 454-92-64 (Office). *Fax:* (095) 454-92-65 (Office). *E-mail:* prime@riss.ru (Office). *Website:* riss.netclub.ru (Office).

KOZLÍK, Sergej; Slovak politician; b. 27 July 1950, Bratislava; ed Univ. of Econs; clerk with Price Authority 1974–88; Head Dept of Industrial Prices, Ministry of Finance 1988–90; Dir Exec. Dept of Antimonopoly Office 1990–92; Sec. Movt for Democratic Slovakia (became political party 2000) 1992–; Vice-Premier, Govt of Slovakia 1993–94; Minister of Finance of Slovak Repub. 1994–97; Deputy to Nat. Council 1994–; Gov. World Bank 1994–98 Alt. Gov. IMF 1994–98. *Address:* National Council of the Slovak Republic, Mudroňova 1, 812 80 Bratislava, Slovakia. *Telephone:* (2) 5934-1111; (2) 5934-1238.

KOZLOV, Alexey Semenovich; Russian composer, saxophone player and band leader; b. 13 Oct. 1935, Moscow; m. 1st; one s.; m. 2nd Lyalya Adburakhmanovna Absalyamova; ed Moscow Inst. of Architecture, Moscow Music Coll.; researcher Inst. of Design 1963–76; started playing saxophone in youth clubs 1955; founder and leader of jazz quintet 1959, jazz band of café Molodezhnoye 1961–66; arranger and soloist orchestra VIO-66; teacher Moscow Experimental Studio of Jazz Music 1967–76; f. and music Dir jazz-rock ensemble Arsenal 1973–festivals and tours including Delhi and Bombay 1989, Woodstock 1990, Jazz Rally, Düsseldorf 1993, Carnegie Hall 1995, Bonn 1996, with Arsenal, Chamber Soloists of Moscow, the Shostakovich String Quartet, Ars Nova Trio; master classes in towns of Russia and Oklahoma City Univ. 1994; Gen.-Man. Jazz Div., Goskoncert 1995–97; mem. musical Cttee under Pres. of Russia 1997–; Art Dir Radio Jazz, Moscow 2001–; author of TV programmes, All That Jazz, Improvisation; composer of jazz, film and theatre music; Merited Artist of Russia; his ensemble Arsenal awarded Ovation Prize as the best jazz band in Russia 1995. *Publications:* Rock: Roots and Development 1989, Memoirs—My 20th Century, He-Goat on the Saxophone 2000; numerous articles in music journals. *Address:* Shchepkin str. 25, Apt. 28, 129090 Moscow, Russia. *Telephone:* (095) 288-31-56 (Home). *E-mail:* askozlov@mtu-net.ru (Home). *Website:* www.musiclab.ru (Home).

KOZLOV, Valery Vassilyevich, DrSc; Russian politician; b. 1 Jan. 1950, Kostyly, Ryazan Region; ed Moscow State Univ.; Sr Researcher Moscow State Univ. 1972, Deputy Dean, Chief Scientific Sec. –1998; Adviser to Ministry of

Gen. and Professional Educ. (later Ministry of Educ.) 1998–99, Deputy Minister 1999–; Corresp. mem. Russian Acad. of Sciences 1997–2000, mem. 2000–, Vice-Pres. 2002–; State Prize of the Russian Fed. 1994. *Address:* Russian Academy of Sceinces, Leninsky prosp. 14, GSP-I, 117910 Moscow, Russia (Office). *Telephone:* (095) 237-45-32 (Office); (095) 237-28-31 (Office). *Fax:* (095) 954-33-20 (Office). *Website:* www.pran.ru/structure.htm (Office).

KOZŁOWIECKI, HE Cardinal Adam; Zambian (b. Polish) ecclesiastic; b. 1 April 1911, Huta Komorowska; s. of Adam Kozłowiecki and Maria Janocha; ed Jesuit Faculty, Cracow, Jesuit Faculty, Lublin; entered Soc. of Jesus 1929; ordained priest 1937; arrested by Nazis 1939, in prison in Cracow and Wisnicz, then Auschwitz and Dachau Concentration Camps; Missionary, Kasisi Mission, Northern Rhodesia 1946–50; apptd. Apostolic Admin., Lusaka 1955, Titular Bishop of Lower Diospolis and Vicar Apostolic of Lusaka 1955; Archbishop of Lusaka 1959–69 (resgnd); Missionary in Zambia 1969–; cr. Cardinal Feb. 1998; Commdr, Order of Freedom, Zambia, Cross Commdr, Order of Merit, Poland. *Publications:* Chester-Beatty Papyrus p. 45, p. 46, p. 47 and the Greek Translation of the Gospel of St Luke by Fr. A. Merk, in Przegląd Biblijny 1938, Ucisk i Strapienie (memoirs of outbreak of war and life in the concentration camps) 1966, Moja Afryka–Moje Chingombe (Letters to Friends) 1997. *Leisure interests:* classical music, reading, especially history books, also P. G. Wodehouse. *Address:* Mpunde Mission, P.O. Box 80858, Kabwe, Zambia (Office).

KOZLOWSKI, L. Dennis, BS, MBA; American business executive; b. 16 Nov. 1946, Irvington, NJ; s. of Leo Kelly Kozlowski and Agnes Kozlowski (née Kozell); ed Seton Hall Univ., Rivier Coll.; Vice-Pres. Grinnell Fire Protection Systems Div., Providence 1976–81, Vice-Pres., Chief Financial Officer Ludlow Corpn, Tyco Labs., Needham, Mass. 1981–82, Pres., CEO Grinnell Corpn 1982–2002, Pres., COO Tyco Labs. Inc. 1989–92, CEO Tyco Int. 1992–2002, Chair. Bd Dirs. 1993–2002; indicted for conspiracy to avoid sales tax on artwork June 2002, charged with tampering with evidence 2002; charged with enterprise corruption Sept. 2002; Dir Raytheon, U.S. Office Products, Applied Powers; mem. Bd Regents, Seton Hall Univ. *Leisure interest:* flying helicopters. *Address:* Tyco International Ltd, 1 Tyco Park, Exeter, NH 03833, USA (Office).

KOZOL, Jonathan, BA; American author; b. 5 Sept. 1936, Boston; s. of Dr. Harry L. Kozol and Ruth Massell Kozol; ed Harvard Coll. and Magdalen Coll., Oxford; teacher in Boston area 1964–72; lecturer at numerous univs. 1973–85; Guggenheim Fellow 1972, 1984; Field Foundation Fellow 1973, 1974; Rockefeller Fellow 1978, Sr Fellow 1983; Rhodes Scholar 1958; Nat. Book Award 1968, Robert F. Kennedy Book Award 1989, New England Book Award 1992, Anisfield-Wolf Book Award 1996. *Publications:* Death At An Early Age 1967, Free Schools 1972, The Night Is Dark 1975, Children of the Revolution 1978, On Being a Teacher 1979, Prisoners of Silence 1980, Illiterate America 1985, Rachel and Her Children: Homeless Families in America 1988, Savage Inequalities: Children in America's Schools 1991, Amazing Grace 1995, Ordinary Resurrections 2000. *Address:* P.O. Box 145, Byfield, MA 01922, USA.

KOZYREV, Andrey Vladimirovich, CandHist; Russian politician; b. 27 March 1951, Brussels, Belgium; m. 2nd; one d.; ed Moscow State Inst. of Int. Relations; worker Kommunar factory, Moscow 1968–69; mem. staff USSR Ministry of Foreign Affairs, various posts, to Head of Sector 1974–86, Head of Dept of Int. Orgs 1986–90; Foreign Minister of Russian Fed. 1990–95; mem. State Duma (Parl.) 1995–99; mem. Bd Dirs, Dir E European Div. ICN Pharmaceuticals 1999–; Lecturer, Moscow Inst. of Int. Relations 1996–. *Publications:* Transfiguration 1995; numerous articles on foreign policy. *Address:* ICN Pharmaceuticals, Uscheva str. 24, 119048, Moscow, Russia. *Fax:* (095) 383-66-00, ext. 2101.

KPOTSRA, Roland Yao; Togolese politician, diplomatist and civil servant; b. 20 Feb. 1947, Lom; m.; two c.; joined Foreign Ministry as Desk Officer in Admin. Affairs Div. 1974, Dir Treaties and Legal Affairs Div. 1982–88, Dir Admin. and Personnel 1987–90; Sec. Perm. Mission to UN, New York 1976–79, Counsellor 1979–, Chargé d'affaires April–Aug. 1980, Perm. Rep. to UN 1996–2002; Chargé de Mission, Ministry of Foreign Affairs and Co-operation 1992–93, Sec.-Gen. 1993–96, Minister of Foreign Affairs and Co-operation 2002–; First Counsellor Embassy in Brazil 1980–82; Chargé d'aff-aires in Zimbabwe 1990–91; Leader of Del. to 63rd session of OAU Council of Ministers, 10th Ministerial Conf. of Movt of Non-Aligned Countries 1995; Deputy Head of Del. to OAU 50th Ass.; headed team at int. French-speaking conf. on conflict resolution from African perspective 1995; Lecturer in Diplo-matic History, École Nat. d'Admin, Togo; Chevalier, Nat. Order of Merit 1984, Officer, Order of Mono 1996. *Address:* Ministry of Foreign Affairs and Co-operation, place du Monument aux Morts, Lomé, Togo (Office). *Telephone:* 221-36–01 (Office). *Fax:* 221-39-79 (Office). *E-mail:* info@republicoftogo.com (Office). *Website:* www.republicoftogo.com.

KRABBE, Jeroen Aart; Netherlands actor, artist and director; b. 5 Dec. 1944; m. Herma van Geemert; three s.; ed Acad. of Fine Arts and Toneel Drama School, Amsterdam; acted in repertory theatre and formed own acting co. within the Netherlands; Best Actor Award, Madrid, Sorrento, Oxford 1984, Anne Frank Medal 1985, Golden Heart of Rotterdam 1986, Golden Calf Award 1996, film Left Luggage won award at Berlin Film Festival 1998, Commdr, Order of the Lion (Netherlands) 1999. *Exhibitions:* seven major exhbns. Francis Kyle Galleries, London 1993–99; many exhbns. in Holland, Curaçao and London. *Theatre includes:* The Diary of Anne Frank, Clouds,

Relatively Speaking, How the Other Half Lives, Cyrano de Bergerac, Danton's Death, Love's Labours Lost, Sleuth, A Day in the Death of Joe Egg, Sweet Bird of Youth, Love Letters. *TV appearances:* William of Orange (Netherlands), Miami Vice, Dynasty, One for the Dancer, Sweet Weapon, Only Love, Jesus, Stalin (all American TV); host talkshows; numerous roles in plays and series. *Films include:* Soldier of Orange 1977, A Flight of Rainbirds 1981, The Fourth Man 1984, The Shadow of Victory 1985, Turtle Diary, No Mercy 1987, The Living Daylights, A World Apart, Crossing Delancey, Melancholia 1989, The Prince of Tides 1991, Stalin 1991, Kafka 1991, King of the Hill 1991, The Fugitive 1993, Farinelli 1994, Immortal Beloved 1994, The Disappearance of García Lorca 1995, Business for Pleasure 1996, The Honest Courtesan 1996, Cinderella 1997, Left Luggage (directorial debut) 1997, Dangerous Beauty 1998, Discovery of Heaven (actor and Dir) 2001. *Publications:* The Economy Cookbook. *Address:* Van Eeghenstraat 107, 1071 EZ Amsterdam, Netherlands.

KRABBE, Katrin; German athlete; b. 1970, Neubrandenburg; m. Michael Zimmerman 1994; two s.; mem. Neubrandenburg team; winner of three gold medals in European Track and Field Championships 1990; 100m, 200m World Championships, Tokyo 1991; a failed drugs test in 1992 resulted in a ban from athletics and an end to her athletics career; ban reversed by Regional Court in Munich May 1995; accepted an out-of-court settlement from the IAAF following German court ruling in 2001 on dope case ($600,000 compensation ordered) 2002; now runs a sports shop in Neubrandenburg; German Sportswoman of the Year 1990, 1991.

KRAČUN, Davorin, PhD; Slovenian diplomatist, politician and professor of economics; b. 31 Oct. 1950, Maribor; m.; one s. one d.; ed Univs. of Maribor and Zagreb; teacher and researcher, School of Business and Econs, Univ. of Maribor 1974–, Prof. 1995–, Vice-Dean 1983–87; Minister of Planning 1992–93, Deputy Prime Minister and Minister of Econ. Relations and Devt 1993–95; Minister of Foreign Affairs 1996–97; Chair. Econ. Council of Govt 1995–97; Amb. to USA and Mexico 2000–; mem. Slovenian Nat. Bank Council 1986–91, Bd of Dirs. Slovenian Econ. Chamber 1988–92; co-f. Inst. for Econ. Diagnosis and Prognosis, Univ. of Maribor. *Publications:* over 300 publs. including scientific and professional papers and books, univ. textbooks, research reports, conf. proc. *Leisure interests:* skiing, tennis, golf. *Address:* Embassy of Slovenia, 1525 New Hampshire Avenue, NW, Washington, DC 20036, USA (Office). *Telephone:* (202) 667-5365 (Office). *Fax:* (202) 667-4563 (Office). *E-mail:* davorin.kracun@mzz-dkp.gov.si (Office). *Website:* www .embassy.org/slovenia (Office).

KRAFT, Christopher Columbus, Jr., BS; American space administrator; b. 28 Feb. 1924, Phoebus, Va; s. of Christopher Columbus and Vanda Olivia (Suddreth) Kraft; m. Elizabeth Anne Turnbull 1950; one s. one d.; ed Virginia Polytechnic Inst.; mem., Langley Aeronautical Lab., Nat. Advisory Cttee for Aeronautics 1945; selected to join Space Task Group on Project Mercury 1958; Flight Dir all Mercury Missions: Dir of Flight Operations, Manned Spacecraft Center 1963–69; elected mem. Nat. Acad. of Eng 1970; Deputy Dir Johnson Space Center 1970–72; Dir NASA Johnson Space Center 1972–82; Fellow, American Inst. of Aeronautics and Astronautics 1966; Fellow, American Astronautical Soc; Hon. DEng (Indiana Inst. of Tech.) 1966, (St Louis Univ., Ill.) 1967, (Villanova) 1979; Arthur S. Fleming Award 1963, NASA Outstanding Leadership Award 1963, Spirit of St Louis Medal, American Soc. of Mechanical Engineers 1967, NASA Distinguished Service Medal (twice) 1969, Chevalier, Légion d'honneur 1976, Nat. Civil Service League Career Service Award 1976, W. Randolph Lovelace Award (American Astronautical Soc.) 1977, Daniel and Florence Guggenheim Award (Int. Astronautics Fed.) 1978, AAIA von Karman Lectureship Award 1979, Goddard Memorial Trophy 1979, Roger W. Jones Award 1979, inducted into Virginia Aviation Hall of Fame 1979.

KRAFT, Robert Paul, PhD; American professor of astronomy and astrophysics; b. 16 June 1927, Seattle, Wash.; s. of Victor P. Kraft and Viola E. Ellis; m. Rosalie A. Reichmuth 1949; two s.; ed Univ. of Washington and Univ. of California at Berkeley; Instructor in mathematics and astronomy, Whittier Coll. 1949–51; Asst Prof. of Astronomy, Indiana Univ. 1956–58; Asst Prof. of Astronomy, Univ. of Chicago 1958–59; mem. staff, Mt Wilson and Palomar Observatories 1960–67; Astronomer and Prof., Lick Observatory 1967–92, Astronomer and Prof. Emer. 1992–, Acting Dir Lick Observatory 1968–70, 1971–73, Dir 1981–91; Dir Univ. of California Observatories 1988–91; Visiting Fellow, Joint Inst. of Laboratory Astrophysics, Univ. of Colo 1970; Pres. American Astronomical Soc. 1974–76; Vice-Pres. Int. Astronomical Union 1982–88, Pres. 1997–2000; mem. NAS, American Acad. of Arts and Sciences; Nat. Science Foundation Fellow 1953–55, Fairchild Scholar, California Inst. of Tech. 1980; Beatrice Tinsley Visiting Prof., Univ. of Texas 1991–92; Henry Norris Russell Lecturer 1995; Distinguished Alumnus Award, Univ. of Wash. 1995; DSc hc (Ind. Univ.) 1995; Warner Prize, American Astronomical Soc. 1962. *Publications:* articles in professional journals. *Leisure interests:* music (classical and rock), oenology, duplicate bridge. *Address:* Lick Observatory, University of California, Santa Cruz, CA 95064, USA. *Telephone:* (831) 459-3281. *Fax:* (831) 426-3115. *E-mail:* kraft@ucolick.org.

KRAFT, Vahur, BA; Estonian banker; b. b. 11 March 1961, Tartu; s. of Ülo Kraft and Aime Kraft; m. Anne Kraft 1990; one s.; ed Tartu Univ.; with Eesti Hoiupank (Estonian Savings Bank), rising to Head of Br. 1984–90; Vice-Chair. Bd of Dirs Eesti Sotsiaalpank (Estonian Social Bank) 1990–91; Deputy Gov. Eesti Pank (Bank of Estonia) 1991–95, Gov. 1995–; Vice-Gov. Estonia,

IMF 1992–95, Gov. 1995–; Chair. Bd of Trustees Tartu Univ. Foundation; Chair. Supervisory Bd Estonian Deposit Guarantee Fund; mem. Supervisory Council, Financial Supervision Authority, Council of the Stabilization Reserves, Bd Centre for Strategic Initiatives; Hon. mem. Tallinn Jr Chamber of Commerce; Order of White Star, Second Class. *Address:* Eesti Pank, Estonia Avenue 13, 15095 Tallinn, Estonia (Office). *Telephone:* (2) 668-0810 (Office). *Fax:* (2) 668-0836 (Office). *E-mail:* info@epbe.ee (Office). *Website:* www.bankofestonia.info (Office).

KRAGGERUD, Egil, DPhil; Norwegian professor of classical philology; b. 7 July 1939, S. Höland; s. of John Kraggerud and Borghild Westeren; m. Beate Sinding-Larsen 1963; three s. one d.; ed Oslo Katedralskole and Oslo Univ.; Research Fellow, Oslo Univ. 1965–67, Lecturer in Classics 1967–68, Prof. of Classical Philology 1969, now Prof. Emer.; Ed. Symbolae Osloenses 1972–94; mem. Norwegian Acad. of Science and Letters, Royal Norwegian Soc. of Sciences and Letters, Acad. Europaea; Thorleif Dahl's Literary Award 1992. *Publications:* Aeneisstudien 1968, Horaz und Actium 1984, Aeneiden (7 vols) 1983–89. *Leisure interests:* skiing, concerts. *Address:* Classical Department, University of Oslo, P.O. Box 1007, Blindern, 0316 Oslo (Office); Bygdöy allé 13, 0257 Oslo, Norway (Home). *Telephone:* 22-44-27-44 (Home). *Fax:* 22-85-44-42. *E-mail:* informasjon@uio.no (Office). *Website:* www.uio.no (Office).

KRAGULY, Radovan; British artist; b. 10 Sept. 1935, Prijedor, Yugoslavia; s. of Dragoja Kraguly and Mileva Kraguly; ed Acad. of Fine Arts, Belgrade, Cen. School of Arts and Crafts, London; lecturer Cambridge School of Art and Tech. –1965, Manchester Coll. of Art 1965–67, London Coll. of Printing and Design 1967–69, Ecole des Beaux Arts, Mons 1969–78, Parson School of Art and Design 1978–88; represented in perm. and major collections at Museum of Modern Art, Paris, British Museum, Victoria and Albert Museum, Museum of Modern Art, New York, Leicester Univ. Library, Library of Congress, Washington, City Art Gallery, Sarajevo, Art Council of Wales, Cardiff, Power Gallery, Sydney, Prenten Cabinet, Brussels, Nat. Museum and Gallery of Wales, Cardiff, Fond Nat. d'Art Contemporain, Paris, Manchester City Art Gallery, City Art Gallery, Banja Luka, Nat. Library of Wales, Aberystwyth, The Whitworth Art Gallery, Manchester, South London Art Gallery; numerous prizes and awards including Printmaking Prize (Jazu-Zagreb) 1962, Yugoslav Trienale Prize 1967, Grafika Creativa Prize (Helsinki) 1975, Int. Grand Prix Fondation Pierre Cornette de St Cyr (Paris) 1978, Int. Grand Prix, Drawing Biennial (Rijeka) 1980. *Exhibitions:* over 50 one-man shows and over 200 group shows in Europe and USA. *Publications include:* La Vache dans l'imaginaire 1989, The Imaginary Cow of Kraguly 1990, Kraguly–Gallery Vera Van Laer 1992, Hathor: Voies Lactées Kraguly 1995, Kraguly Hathor: VLK 1998. *Address:* Llwyngarth Fawr, Comin Coch, Builth Wells, Powys, LD2 3PP, Wales (Home); 22 rue Quincampoix, 75004 Paris, France. *Telephone:* (1597) 860340 (Wales) (Home); 1-42-74-70-47 (Paris). *Fax:* (1597) 860340 (Wales) (Home); 1-42-74-70-47 (Paris). *E-mail:* nenak@free.fr (Home).

KRAIJENHOFF, Jonkheer Gualtherus; Netherlands business executive; b. 11 July 1922; s. of Albertus Kraijenhoff and Gualthera Kraijenhoff; m. Yvonne Kessler; one s. two d.; ed Switzerland; Royal Air Force (UK) pilot 1943–47; joined NV Organon, Oss 1947, Man. Dir 1957; mem. Bd of Man. NV Kon. Zwanenberg-Organon 1959, Pres. 1963; mem. Bd of Man., Kon. Zout-Organon NV 1967, Pres. 1969; Vice-Pres. AKZO NV, Arnhem 1969, Pres. 1971–78, mem. Supervisory Council May 1978– (fmr Chair.); Dir S. G. Warburg and Co. 1978–; Dir APV Holdings 1983–; Pres. Netherlands Red Cross 1966–86, Chair. Cen. Laboratories for Blood Transfusion, Red Cross 1990–; KtStJ Netherlands Lion. *Address:* Zomerland, Louiseweg 15, Nijmegen, Netherlands (Home).

KRAINEV, Vladimir Vsevolodovich; Russian pianist; b. 1 April 1944, Krasnoyarsk; m. Tatyana Tarasova; ed Moscow State Conservatory with Heinrich Neuhaus and Stanislav Neuhaus; début with orchestra as child prodigy in Kharkov 1953, in Moscow 1963; prize winner of several int. competitions; soloist with maj. orchestras in many European cultural centres and festivals; played with Carlo Maria Giulini, Pierre Boulez, John Pritchard, Dmitry Kitayenko; teacher in Moscow Conservatory 1987–91, Hochschule für Musik in Hanover 1991–; People's Artist of Russia 1984, USSR State Prize 1986. *Repertoire includes:* most of classical concertos and all concertos by Mozart and Prokofiev. *Address:* Staatliche Hochschule für Musik und Theater, Walderseestrasse 100, Hanover, Germany. *Telephone:* (3212) 3641485 (Hanover); (095) 158-24-56 (Moscow).

KRAIVICHIEN, Thanin, LLB; Thai politician and jurist; b. 5 April 1927; m. Karen Andersen; five c.; ed Suan Kularp School, Thammasat Univ., Univ. of London, Gray's Inn; Sr Judge, Civil Court 1969; Sr Judge, Court of Appeal 1972; Judge, Supreme Court 1972–76, Sr Judge 1976; mem. Nat. Ass. 1973–76; Prime Minister 1976–77 (deposed in coup); Chair. Investment Bd of Thailand 1976–77; mem. of Privy Council. *Publications:* Democracy, Communist Ideology and Tactics, The Language of the Thai Law, The Use of Anti-Communist Law, Constitutional Monarchy, The Reform of the Legal and Judicial Systems during the Reign of King Chulalongkorn. *Address:* c/o Office of the Prime Minister, Government House, Bangkok, Thailand.

KRAJICEK, Richard; Netherlands tennis player; b. 6 Dec. 1972, Rotterdam; s. of Petr Krajicek and Ludmilla Krajicek; m. Daphne Dekkers 1999; one s. one d.; started playing tennis aged 3; turned professional 1989; reached semi-finals Australian Open 1992; Wimbledon Men's Singles Champion 1996;

won 20 titles to end of 2002. *Leisure interests:* US Pro Basketball Los Angeles Lakers, golf. *Address:* ATP Tour, 201 ATP Tour Boulevard, Ponte Vedra Beach, FL 32082, USA (Office).

KRALL, Hanna; Polish journalist and writer; b. 20 May 1937, Warsaw; m. Jerzy Szperkowicz; one d.; ed Univ. of Warsaw; reporter Życie Warszawy 1955–66, Polityka 1966–, corresp. in Moscow 1966–69; corresp. Tygodnik Powszechny, Gazeta Wyborcza; Prize of Minister of Culture and Art 1989, J. Shocken Literary Prize (Germany), Solidarity Cultural Prize 1995, Kulture Foundation Award 1999, Leipzig Book Fair Award 2000. *Publications include:* Na wschód od Arbatu (To the East of Arbat) 1972, Zdążyć przed Panem Bogiem (To Outwit God) 1976, Sześć odcieni bieli (Six shades of White) 1978, Sublokatorka (The Sub-tenant) 1983, Trudności ze wstawaniem (Difficulties Getting Up) 1988, Hipnoza (Hypnosis) 1989, Taniec na cudzym weselu (Dance at a Stranger's Wedding) 1993, Co się stało z naszą bajką (What's Happened to our Fairy Tale) 1994, Dowody na istnienie (Proofs of Existence) 1995, Tam już nie ma żadnej rzeki (There is No River Any More) 1998, To ty jesteś Daniel 2001 (books translated into over 10 languages). *Address:* Stowarzyszenie Pisarzy Polskich, ul. Krakowskie Przedmieście 87/89, 00-079 Warsaw, Poland (Office).

KRAMER, Larry, BA; American author; b. 25 June 1935, Bridgeport, Conn.; ed Yale Univ.; Production Exec. Columbia Pictures Corpn London 1961–65; Asst to Pres. United Artists, New York; producer-screenwriter, Women in Love 1970; co-founder, Gay Men's Health Crisis Inc. New York 1981; founder, ACT UP-AIDS Coalition to Unleash Power, New York 1988. *Publications:* Faggots 1978, The Normal Heart (play) 1985, Just Say No 1988, The Furniture of Home 1989, The Destiny of Me 1993.

KRAMER, Dame Leonie (Judith), AC, DBE, DPhil, FAHA, FACE; Australian emeritus professor of literature; b. 1 Oct. 1924; d. of the late A. L. Gibson and G. Gibson; m. Harold Kramer 1952 (deceased); two d.; ed Presbyterian Ladies Coll., Melbourne and Univs. of Melbourne and Oxford; Tutor, St Hugh's Coll., Oxford 1949–52; Assoc. Prof. Univ. of NSW 1963–68; Prof. of Australian Literature, Univ. of Sydney, 1968–89, Prof Emer. 1989–; Deputy Chancellor, Univ. of Sydney 1988–91, Chancellor 1991–2001; Vice-Pres. Australian Asscn for Teaching of English 1967–70; Vice-Pres. Australian Soc. of Authors 1969–71; mem. Nat. Literature Bd of Review 1970–73; mem. Council, Nat. Library of Australia 1975–81; Pres., then Vice-Pres. Australian Council for Educ. Standards 1973–; mem. Univs. Comm. 1974–86; Commr Australian Broadcasting Comm. (ABC) 1977–81, Chair. 1982–83, Dir Australia and NZ Banking Group 1983–94, Western Mining Corpn 1984–96, Quadrant Magazine Co. Ltd 1986–99 (Chair. 1988–99); mem. Council Nat. Roads and Motorists' Asscn 1984–95, Council Foundation for Young Australians 1989–, Asia Soc. 1991–2000; Nat. Pres. Australia-Britain Soc. 1984–93, Order of Australia Asscn 2001–; mem. Council Australian Nat. Univ. 1984–87; mem. Bd of Studies, NSW Dept. of Educ. 1990–2001; Chair. Bd of Dirs. Nat. Inst. of Dramatic Art (NIDA) 1987–91, Deputy Chair. 1991–95; Sr Fellow Inst. of Public Affairs (IPA) 1988–96; Commr Electricity Comm. (NSW) 1988–95; mem. World Book Encyclopaedia Advisory Bd 1989–99, Int. Advisory Cttee Encyclopaedia Britannica 1991–99, NSW Council of Australian Inst. of Co. Dirs. 1992–2001; Chair. Operation Rainbow Australia Ltd 1996–; Hon. Fellow St Hugh's Coll. Oxford 1994; Hon. Fellow St Andrew's Coll., Univ. of Sydney; Hon. DLitt (Tasmania), 1977 (Queensland) 1991, (NSW) 1992; Hon. LLD (Melbourne) 1983, (Australian Nat. Univ.) 1984; Hon. MA (Sydney) 1989; Britannica Award 1986. *Publications include:* (as L. J. Gibson): Henry Handel Richardson and Some of Her Sources 1954; (as Leonie Kramer): Australian Poetry 1961 (ed.) 1962, Companion to Australia Felix 1962, Myself When Laura 1966, A Guide to Language and Literature (with Robert D. Eagleson) 1977, A. D. Hope 1979, The Oxford History of Australian Literature (ed.) 1981, The Oxford Anthology of Australian Literature (Ed. with Adrian Mitchell) 1985, My Country: Australian Poetry and Short Stories–Two Hundred Years (2 Vols) 1985, James McAuley: Poetry, Essays etc. (Ed.) 1988, David Campbell: Collected Poems (Ed.) 1989, Collected Poems of James McAuley 1995. *Leisure interests:* gardening, music. *Address:* University of Sydney, Sydney, NSW, 2006 (Office); 12 Vaucluse Road, Vaucluse, NSW, 2030 Australia. *Telephone:* 93514164. *Fax:* 93514773 (Office). *E-mail:* L.Kramer@staff.unisyd.edu.au (Office).

KRAMNIK, Vladimir Borisovich; Russian chess player; b. 25 June 1975, Tuapse, Krasnodar Territory, Russia; m.; started playing chess at age of 4; cand. for Master title 1986; Grandmaster title 1991; World Champion among young people 16–18 years of age, winner World Chess Olympiads Manila 1992, Moscow 1994, Yerevan 1996; winner maj. int. tournaments and matches; since 1995 holds place among the 3 highest-rated players of the world; took part in World Championship 1993; ranked number one world player 1996; won match against Gary Kasparov for World Championship Oct. 2000; winner of Chess Oscar 2000, 2001; ranked world No. 2 Jan. 2003. *Publication:* Kramnik – My Life and Games (autobiog.) (with Takov Damsky). *Telephone:* (095) 495-32-72 (Moscow) (Home).

KRANTZ, Judith, BA; American author; b. 9 Jan. 1928, New York City; d. of Jack David Tarcher and Mary Brager; m. Stephen Krantz 1954; two s.; ed Wellesley Coll.; contrib. to Good Housekeeping 1948–54, McCalls 1954–59, Ladies Home Journal 1959–71; contributing ed. Cosmopolitan 1971–79. *Publications:* Scruples 1978, Princess Daisy 1980, Mistral's Daughter 1982,

I'll Take Manhattan 1986, Till We Meet Again 1988, Dazzle 1990, Scruples Two 1992, Lovers 1994, Spring Collection 1996, The Jewels of Teresa Kant 1998, Sex & Shopping: Confessions of a Nice Jewish Girl 2000.

KRĄPIEC, Mieczysław Albert; Polish ecclesiastic and professor of philosophy; b. 25 May 1921, Berezowica Mała n. Zbaraż (now Ukraine); ed Dominican Friars' College, Cracow, St Thomas Pontifical Univ., Rome, Catholic Univ. of Lublin; Dominican friar; ordained Priest 1945, Lecturer in Philosophy Dominican Friars' Coll., Cracow 1946–, teacher Catholic Univ. of Lublin 1951–, Prof. 1962, Dean Christian Philosophy Faculty 1959–62, 1969–70, Rector 1970–83, head Metaphysics Faculty; mem. Polish Acad. of Sciences 1994–; mem. Polish Acad. of Arts and Crafts, St Thomas Aquinas Pontifical Univ., Rome, European Acad. of Sciences and Arts, Salzburg; fmr Chair. and mem. Catholic Univ. of Lublin Scientific Soc.; Dr. hc (Pontifical Inst. of Medieval Studies, Toronto) 1989, (Catholic Univ. of Louvain, Belgium) 1991, (Tarnopol Univ. of Pedagogics, Ukraine) 1991, (Pedagogical Univ. of Tarnopol, Ukraine) 1993; Commdr.'s Order of Polonia Restituta, Grand Officer's Cross of Order of Leopold II (Belgium), Order of Academic Insignia of the French Acad. *Publications:* Theory of the Analogy of Existence of Metaphysical Methodology (jtly.) 1964, Metaphysics 1966, Aristotelian Concept of Substance 1966, I: a man 1974, A Man and Natural Law 1975, Language and Real World 1985, About Understanding Philosophy 1991, At the Foundations of Understanding Culture 1991, Introduction to Philosophy (jtly.) 1992, 1996, About Human Policy 1993, To Regain the Real World 1997, Considerations on the Nation 1998. *Leisure interests:* picking mushrooms, cooking. *Address:* ul. Złota 9, 20-112 Lublin, Poland. *Telephone:* (81) 5328727.

KRARUP, Thorleif, BSc, BComm; Danish banker and business executive; b. 1952; Chair. Man. Bd Nykredit 1987–91; Group CEO Tryg Nykredit Holding 1991–92; Group CEO Unidanmark 1992–2000; Chair. Exec. Bd Unibank 1992–2000; Deputy CEO Nordic Baltic Holding 2000; Group CEO Nordea 2000–02, Sr Vice-Pres. 2002–. *Address:* Nordea Bank Danmark, Christiansbro, Strandgade 3, PO Box 850, 0900, Copenhagen C, Denmark (Office). *Telephone:* (45) 33-33-33-33 (Office). *Fax:* (45) 33-33-10-56 (Office). *Website:* www.nordea.com (Office).

KRASHENINNIKOV, Pavel Vladimirovich, DJur; Russian lawyer; b. 21 June 1964, Polevskoye, Sverdlovsk Region; m.; one d.; ed Sverdlovsk Inst. of Law; teacher, Sverdlovsk Inst. of Law 1991–93; lecturer, Moscow State Univ. 1994–; Deputy Head, Chief Dept of Housing Policy, State Cttee on Construction of Russian Fed. 1993–; Head, Dept of Civil and Econ. Law, Ministry of Justice 1993–96; Deputy Chair. State Cttee on Antimonopoly Policy and Support of New Econ. Structures 1996–97; First Deputy Minister of Justice 1997–98, Acting Minister March 1998, Minister 1998–99; Co-ordinator, Pres., Comm. for Counteraction against Political Extremism in Russia 1998–99; mem. State Duma (Union of Right-Wing Forces faction) 1999, Chair. Legislative Cttee. *Publications:* over 70 articles on civil law. *Address:* State Duma, Okhotny Ryad, 103265 Moscow, Russia. *Telephone:* (095) 292-92-10 (Office). *Fax:* (095) 292-97-82 (Office).

KRASIKOV, Anatoly Andreyevich, DHist; Russian journalist and scholar; b. 3 Aug. 1931, Moscow; m.; one d.; ed Moscow Inst. of Int. Relations; on staff USSR Telegraph Agency TASS 1955–92; Deputy Dir-Gen. ITAR-TASS 1978–92; on staff of Pres. Yeltsin, Head of Press, Exec. Sec., Council on Interaction with Religious Orgs. of Russian Presidency 1992–96; Chair. Int. Christianity Cttee 1996; Head, Centre for Studies of Problems of Religion and Soc.; chief researcher, Inst. of Europe, Russian Acad. of Sciences 1996–; Pres. Russian Chapter, Int. Religious Liberty Asscn 1997–; Public Policy Scholar, Woodrow Wilson Center, Washington, DC 2000. *Publication:* Proselytism and Religious Liberty in Russia 1999. *Leisure interests:* music, archives, tourism. *Address:* Institute of Europe, Mokhovaya str.11, Bldg 3v, 103873 Moscow, Russia. *Telephone:* (095) 201-66-95 (Office). *Fax:* (095) 200-42-98 (Office). *E-mail:* ankras@online.ru (Office).

KRASIN, Yury Andreyevich, DSc; Russian politologist; b. 7 June 1929, Penza; one d.; ed Leningrad State Univ.; lecturer, asst prof., Leningrad State Pedagogical Inst. 1952–60; asst prof., Inst. of Professional Skill Improvement, Moscow State Univ. 1960–63; Sr Fellow, Inst. of Philosophy USSR (now Russian) Acad. of Sciences 1963; consultant, Int. Div. CP Cen. Cttee, Prof., Moscow Inst. of Professional Skill Improvement at Moscow State Univ. 1963–75; Prof., Head of Dept, Prorector,. Acad. of Social Sciences at CPSU Cent. Cttee 1975–87; Rector, Inst. of Social Sciences at CPSU Cen. Cttee 1987–91; Dir-Gen. Foundation of Social and Political Studies 1991–92; Dir Centre of Social Programmes, Int. Foundation of Social, Econ. and Politological Studies 1992–97; Adviser of Gorbachev Foundation 1997–; Head Centre for Analysis of Social and Political Processes, Inst. of Sociology Russian Acad. of Sciences 1993–; mem. Presidium Acad. of Political Science; Lomonosov Prize of Moscow State Univ. 1968; USSR State Prize 1980. *Publications:* 20 books including Dialectic of the Revolutionary Process 1972, Capitalism Today: Paradoxes of Development (jtly) 1989, Russia at the Crossroads: Authoritarianism or Democracy 1998, Russia: Quo Vadis? (with A. Galkin) 2003; articles on social movts., democratic reform in Russia, civil, social and political matters. *Leisure interests:* classical music, skiing. *Address:* Institute of Sociology, Krzhizhanovskogo str. 24/35, korp. 5, 117218 Moscow (Office); Malaya Philevskaya str. 44, Apt. 11, 121433 Moscow, Russia (Home). *Telephone:* (095) 719-09-40 (Office); (095) 144-29-83 (Home). *Fax:* (095) 945-74-01 (Office). *E-mail:* krasinyua@mtu-net.ru (Home).

KRASOVSKIY, Nikolay Nikolayevich, DrPhysMathSc; Russian mathematician and mechanician; b. 7 Sept. 1924, Sverdlovsk (now Ekaterinburg); ed Ural Polytechnic Inst.; teaching and scientific work, Ural Polytechnic Inst. 1949–55, 1957–59; mem. CPSU 1954–91; Research worker, Inst. of Mechanics, USSR (now Russian) Acad. of Sciences 1955–57, Prof. Ural Univ. 1959–70; scientific and admin. work, Inst. of Math. and Mechanics of Ural Scientific Centre, USSR (now Russian) Acad. of Sciences 1970–, Dir 1970–77, Chief Scientific Researcher 1977–; Corresp. mem. USSR (now Russian) Acad. of Sciences 1964–68, mem. 1968–; Hero of Socialist Labour 1974, Lenin Prize 1976, USSR State Prize 1984, Gold Medal of Liapunov, Russian Acad. of Sciences 1992, Great Gold Medal of Lomonosov, Russian Acad. of Sciences 1996, Order of Lenin, Order of the Red Banner, Order for Services to the Motherland (Third Class) and other decorations. *Publications:* works in field of stability of motion theory and theory of control systems, including Stability of Motion 1963, Game-Theoretical Control Problem (with A. I. Subbotin) 1988, Control under Lack of Information (with A. N. Krasovskiy) 1995. *Address:* c/o Institute of Mathematics and Mechanics, 620219 GSP-384, S. Kovalevskaya Str. 16, Ekaterinburg, Russia. *Telephone:* (3432) 74-40-13 (Office); (3432) 59-41-73 (Home). *Fax:* (3432) 74-25-81.

KRASTS, Guntars; Latvian politician and economist; b. 16 Oct. 1957, Riga, Latvia; m.; three s.; ed Latvian State Univ.; researcher Inst. of Agric. Econ. 1983–91; Chair. Exec. Bd RANG Ltd 1991–95; Minister of Econs 1995–97; Prime Minister of Latvia 1997–98; Vice-Prime Minister for EU Affairs 1998–99; Chair Saeima (Parl.) Foreign Affairs Cttee 1998–2002, European Affairs Cttee 2002–. *Publications:* numerous publs in Latvia and abroad on econ. and foreign policy issues. *Leisure interests:* swimming, skiing. *Address:* Parliament of Latvia, Jēkaba Street 10/12, Riga, 1811 Latvia (Office). *Telephone:* 708-73-24 (Office). *Fax:* 708-73-66 (Office). *E-mail:* guntars .krasts@saeima.lv (Office).

KRATOCHVÍLOVÁ, Jarmila; Czech athlete; b. 26 Jan. 1951, Golčův Jeníkov; ed gymnasium, Čáslav; accountant, Triola, Golčův Jeníkov 1970–71, mem. of the centre of top-level performance sports, Vysoké školy, Prague 1971–87 (retd); now coach; coach Czech Olympic team, Sydney 2000; int. achievements include gold medal, 400m track event, World Cup, Rome 1981; silver medal, Olympic Games, Moscow 1980; silver medal, 400m track event, European Championships, Athens 1982; gold medal, 400m and 800m track events, World Championships, Helsinki 1983; holds oldest-surviving women's world track records for indoor 400m (49.59s, Milan 1982) and outdoor 800m (1:53.28, Munich 1983) at end of 2002; Order of Labour (Czechoslovakia) 1983; UNESCO Fair Play Prize 1988. *Publication:* Waiting (with M. Krač, her coach). *Address:* TJ Slavoj Čáslav, TSM-Voaranty, 286 01 Čáslav (Office); Pod Vyšehradem 207, 582 82 Golčův Jeníkov, Czech Republic (Home).

KRAUCH, Carl Heinrich, Dr rer. nat; German business executive and chemist; b. 14 Sept. 1931, Heidelberg; s. of Carl Krauch and Maria (Lüders) Krauch; m. Ursula Kneller 1958; three s. one d.; ed Ruprecht-Karl Univ., Heidelberg, Georg-August Univ., Göttingen; Head of research group, radio-chemical Dept, Max-Planck Inst. für Kohlenforschung, Mülheim/Ruhr 1958–67; Lecturer, Univ. of Cologne 1965; Head of research group testing plastic materials, BASF, Ludwigshafen 1967; Prof. Johannes Gutenberg Univ., Mainz 1971; Head of Research and Devt, mem. Bd, Henkel & Cie GmbH., Düsseldorf 1971–80, Head, Chemical Products Div. 1975–80; mem. Bd, Hüls AG, Marl 1980, Chair. 1980–93; mem. Bd, VEBA AG, Düsseldorf July 1980–. *Publications:* over 40 in field of chemistry. *Leisure interests:* hunting and farming.

KRAUS, Andreas, DPhil; German historian; b. 5 March 1922, Erding; s. of Karl Kraus and Katharina Mayer; m. Maria Kastner 1947; one d.; ed Univ. of Munich; teacher 1949–61; Extraordinary Prof. of History, Philosophical and Theological Hochschule, Regensburg 1961–67; Prof. Univ. of Regensburg 1967–77; Prof. of Bavarian History Univ. of Munich 1977–, Prof. Emer. 1989–; mem. Bayerischen Akad. der Wissenschaften 1971; Bayerischer Verdienst-orden 1983, Bundesverdienstkreuz 1993, Komtur des St Gregorius Ordens mit Stern 1995, Bayerische Volksstiftung 1998. *Publications:* Die historische Forschung an der bayerischen Akademie der Wissenschaften 1959, Vernunft und Geschichte 1963, Das päpstliche Staatssekretariat 1964, Civitas Regia 1972, Regensburg 1979, Die naturwissenschaftliche Forschung an der bayer-ischen Akademie der Wissenschaften 1979, Geschichte Bayerns 1983, Hand-buch d. Bayerischen Geschichte Vol. II 1988, Maximilian I., Bayerns Grosser Kurfürst 1990, Handbuch d. Bayerischen Geschichte Vol. III 1-3, 1996–2001, Erding. Stadt mit vielen Gesichtern 1997, Das Gymnasium der Jesuiten in München (1558–1773) 2001, König Ludwig I, Handbuch d. Bayerischen Geschichte Vol. IV 2002. *Address:* Nederlingerstrasse 30a, 80638 Munich 19; Landsbergerstr. 74, 86938 Schondorf, Germany. *Telephone:* (89) 1575354 (Home); (81) 92407 (Schondorf).

KRAUSE, Günther; German politician; b. 1953, Halle; m.; fmr lecturer, Tech. Univ. Wismar; nat. service 1972–74; joined Christian Democratic Union (CDU) 1974; CDU Chair. Mecklenburg-Vorpommern 1989–90; State Sec. to fmr GDR Prime Minister Lothar de Maizière (q.v.) April 1990; Minister without Portfolio (responsible for structural changes to economy of fmr East Germany) 1990–91, of Transport 1991–93.

KRAUTHAMMER, Charles, MD; American journalist; b. 13 March 1950, New York; s. of Shulim Krauthammer and Thea Krauthammer; m. Robyn Trethewey; one s.; ed McGill Univ., Balliol Coll. Oxford and Harvard Univs., Medical School; Resident in Psychiatry, Mass. Gen. Hosp. Boston 1975–78;

Scientific Adviser, Dept of Health and Human Services, Washington, DC 1978–80; speech writer to Vice-Pres. Walter Mondale (q.v.), Washington, DC 1980–81; Sr Ed. The New Republic, Washington, DC 1981–88; essayist, Time Magazine 1983–; syndicated columnist, The Washington Post 1984–; mem. Bd of Advisers, The Nat. Interest, Public Interest; Nat. Magazine Award (for essays), American Soc. of Magazine Eds. 1984, Pulitzer Prize (for commentary) 1987. *Publications:* Cutting Edges 1985; contribs. to psychiatric journals. *Leisure interest:* chess. *Address:* c/o The Washington Post Writers Group, 1150 15th Street, NW, Washington, DC 20071, USA.

KRAUZE, Andrzej; Polish cartoonist; b. 1947, Warsaw; m. Małgosia Krauze; three s.; ed Acad. of Fine Art, Warsaw; during 1970s worked as cartoonist for periodicals Szpilki, Kultura, Solidarity Weekly; moved to London 1981; cartoonist for The Guardian, New Society, New Statesman and numerous other publs in the UK, France and the USA. *Art Exhibitions:* Three Decades: Drawings 1970–2000, Museum of Cartoon Art, Warsaw 2001. *Address:* c/o The Guardian, 119 Farringdon Road, London, EC1R 3ER, England (Office). *Telephone:* (20) 7278-2332 (Office).

KRAVCHENKO, Adm. Victor Andreyevich; Russian naval officer; b. 5 Dec. 1943, Bogdanovich, Sverdlovsk Region; m.; one d.; ed Higher Mil. Marine School, Mil. Marine Acad., Acad. of Gen. Staff; served as Sr Asst, submarine Commdr, Head of staff, submarine div. Commdr, First Deputy Head of Staff, Black Sea Fleet 1968–91; First Deputy Commdr, Baltic Fleet 1991–96; Commdr, Black Sea Fleet 1996–98; Head of Gen. Staff, First Deputy C-in-C Russian Navy 1998–; numerous awards and medals. *Address:* General Staff of the Russian Navy, B. Kozlovsky Per. 6, 103175 Moscow, Russia (Office). *Telephone:* (095) 204-38-62.

KRAVCHUK, Leonid Makarovich, Cand.Econ.Sc; Ukrainian politician; b. 10 Jan. 1934, Velykyi Zhytyn; s. of Makar Olexiyovich and Khima Ivanivna Kravchuk; m. Antonina Mikhailivna 1957; one s.; ed Kiev State Univ. and Acad. of Social Sciences, Moscow; teacher of Political Economy, Chernovitsky Tech. School; party work since 1960, on staff Ukrainian CP Cen. Cttee 1970–; Head Propaganda Dept 1980–88, Ideology Dept 1988–89, Sec. Cen. Cttee, Cand. mem. Politburo 1990; Chair. Ukrainian Supreme Soviet 1990–91; Pres. of Ukraine 1991–94; C-in-C Armed Forces of Ukraine 1991–94; mem. Ver-khovna Rada (Parl.) 1994–; People's Deputy of Ukraine 1998–; f. Mutual Understanding Movt 1994; mem. Social Democratic Party; Head All-Ukrai-nian Union of Democratic Forces Zlagoda 1999–; Chair. State Cttee for Admin. Reforms 1997–; Protector Kievo-Mogylianskaya Acad. Kiev 1991; Head Trusteeship Council, Children and Youth Activity Cen. of Ukraine 1992; Hon. Pres. East European Asscn of Businessmen; Hon. PhD (La Salle Univ., Philadelphia) 1992. *Leisure interests:* chess, books, cinema. *Address:* Ver-khovna Rada, M. Hrushevskoho 5, 252019 Kiev, Ukraine. *Telephone:* (44) 291-51-00.

KREBS, Edwin Gerhard, MD; American professor of biochemistry; b. 6 June 1918, Lansing, Iowa; s. of William Krebs and Louise Stegeman; m. Virginia French 1945; one s. two d.; ed Univ. of Illinois and Washington Univ. St Louis; intern, Barnes Hosp. St Louis 1944–45; Research Fellow, Washington Univ. St Louis 1946–48; Asst Prof. of Biochem. Univ. of Washington, Seattle 1948–52, Assoc. Prof. 1952–57, Prof. 1957–66; Prof. and Chair. Dept of Biological Chem., School of Medicine Univ. of Calif. Davis 1968–76; Prof. and Chair. Dept of Pharmacology, Univ. of Washington, Seattle 1977–83, Prof. of Biochem. and Pharmacology 1984–91; Sr Investigator, Howard Hughes Medical Inst. Seattle 1983–90, Sr Investigator Emer. 1991–; mem. NAS, American Soc. of Biological Chemists, American Acad. of Arts and Sciences; numerous professional appts; Nobel Prize for Medicine (with Edmond Fischer, q.v.) 1992; other awards and distinctions. *Address:* c/o Department of Pharmacology, University of Washington, Box 357750, Seattle, WA 98195, USA.

KREBS, Sir John Richard, Kt, MA, DPhil, FRS; British zoologist and scientific administrator; b. 11 April 1945, Sheffield; s. of Prof. Sir Hans Krebs and Margaret Fieldhouse; m. Katharine A. Fullerton 1968; two d.; ed City of Oxford High School and Pembroke Coll. Oxford; departmental demonstrator in Ornithology, Edward Grey Inst. and Oxford Lecturer in Zoology, Pembroke Coll. Oxford 1969–70; Asst Prof. Inst. of Resource Ecology, Univ. of BC Vancouver 1970–73; lecturer in Zoology, Univ. of Coll. of N Wales, Bangor 1973–74; SRC Research Officer, Animal Behaviour Research Group, Dept of Zoology, Oxford 1975–76; Lecturer in Zoology, Edward Grey Inst. of Field Ornithology, Oxford 1976–88, Fellow, Wolfson Coll. 1976–81, Fellow Pem-broke Coll. 1981–; E. P. Abraham Fellow in Zoology, Pembroke Coll. 1981–88, Fellow 1988–; Royal Soc. Research Prof. Univ. of Oxford 1988–; Chief Exec. Natural Environment Research Council 1994–2000; Chair. Food Standards Agency 2000–; Dir AFRC Unit of Ecology and Behaviour and NERC Unit of Behavioural Ecology 1989–94; Sr Scientific Consultant and Chair. Animals Research Cttee, Agricultural and Food Research Council 1991–94; External scientific mem. Max Planck Soc. 1985; Pres. Int. Soc. of Behavioural Ecology 1988–90, Asscn for Study of Animal Behaviour 1992–94; mem. Agricultural and Food Research Council 1988–94; mem. Academia Europaea; Foreign mem. American Philosophical Soc. 2000; Hon. mem. British Ecological Soc. 1999; Hon. Foreign mem. American Acad. of Arts and Sciences 2000; Hon. Fellow Cardiff Univ.1999; Hon. DSc (Sheffield) 1993, (Wales) 1997, (Bir-mingham) 1997, (Exeter) 1998, (Stirling) 2000, (Warwick) 2000, (Cranfield) 2001, (Kent) 2001, (Plymouth) 2001, (South Bank) 2001, (Heriot-Watt) 2002, (Queen's Univ., Belfast) 2002; Nuffield Foundation Science Fellowship 1981;

Scientific Medal, Zoological Soc. 1981, Bicentenary Medal, Linnaean Soc. 1983, Frink Medal, Zoological Soc. 1996, Elliott Coues Award, American Ornithologists' Union 1999, Asscn for Study of Animal Behaviour Award 2000, Benjamin Ward Richardson Gold Medal, Royal Soc. for Promotion of Health 2002. *Publications:* Behavioural Ecology: An Evolutionary Aproach (ed. with N. B. Davies) 1978, 1984, 1991, 1997, An Introduction to Behavioural Ecology (with N. B. Davies) 1981, 1986, 1993, Foraging Theory. Princeton Monographs in Behaviour and Ecology, No. 4 (with D. W. Stephens) 1987, Foraging Behaviour (ed. with A. Kamil and H. R. Pulliam) 1987, Behavioural and Neural Studies of Learning and Memory (ed. with G. Horn) 1991. *Leisure interests:* gardening, violin, running, walking. *Address:* Food Standards Agency, Aviation House, 125 Kingsway, London WC2B 6NH, England (Office). *Telephone:* (20) 7276-8625 (Office). *E-mail:* john.krebs@ foodstandards.gsi.gov.uk (Office).

KREBS, Robert Duncan, MBA; American transport executive; b. 2 May 1942, Sacramento; s. of Ward C. Krebs and Eleanor B. (née Duncan) Krebs; m. Anne Lindstrom 1971; two s. one d.; ed Stanford Univ., Harvard Univ.; Asst Gen. Man. S. Pacific Transportation Co., Houston 1974–75, Asst Regional Operations Man. 1975–76, Asst Vice-Pres. San Francisco 1967–77, Asst to Pres. 1977–79, Gen. Man. 1979, Vice-Pres. Transportation 1979-80, Operations 1980–82, Pres. 1982–83; Dir and Pres. Santa Fe S. Pacific Corpn (now Santa Fe Pacific Corpn) 1983–96, Pres., Chair. and CEO 1988–96, Pres., CEO Burlington Northern Santa Fe Corpn 1995–2000, Chair. 2000–; Dir Phelps Dodge Corpn, Fort Worth Symphony Orchestra, several other orgs. *Address:* Burlington Northern Santa Fe Corporation, P.O. Box 961052, Fort Worth, TX 76161, USA.

KREITZBERG, Peeter, DPhil; Estonian politician and academic; b. 14 Dec. 1948, Parnu; m. (divorced); one s. one d.; ed Tartu State Univ; Head of Students Bureau of Comprehensive Research, Tartu Univ. 1972–74, Lecturer, Sr Teacher, Asst Prof., then Prof. 1977–96; Prof. Tallinn Pedagogical Univ. 1977–; Minister of Culture and Educ. 1995; Deputy Mayor of Tallinn 1996–99; Mem. Riigikogu (Parl.) 1999–, Vice-Chair. 2001–; mem. British Soc. of Educ. Philosophy. *Publications include:* Principles of Classification and Concretising Targets in Education 1987, Legitimisation of Education Aims: Paradigms and Metaphors 1993. *Address:* Riigokogu, Tompea Castle, Lossi plats 1a, 0100 Tallinn, Estonia (Office). *Telephone:* (2) 631-63-11 (Office). *E-mail:* peeter.kreitzberg@riigokogu.ee (Office). *Website:* www.riigokogu.ee/ parliament.html (Office).

KREJČA, Otomar; Czech actor and director; b. 23 Nov. 1921, Skrýšov; s. of František Krejča and Ludmila Pechová; m. Marie Tomášová 1986; one s.; ed Charles Univ., Prague; mem. Prague Nat. Theatre 1951–69, Art Chief, Nat. Theatre Drama Section 1956–61; Founder and Artistic Dir of Divadlo za branou (Theatre Beyond the Gate) 1965–71, Dir 1971–72 (theatre shut 1972); Dir Theatre S.K.N. 1973–75; allowed to work only outside CSSR 1976–89; Artistic Dir Schauspielhaus Düsseldorf 1976–78, Atelier Théâtral de Louvain-la-Neuve 1979–81; Founder and Dir Divadlo za branou II, Prague 1990–94; Dir Prague Nat. Theatre 1997–98; Dr hc (Univ. of Prague) 2002, (AMU) 2002; State Prize 1951, 1968, Honoured Artist 1958, Kainz Medal (Austria) 1969, Int. Pirandello Prize (Italy) 1978, Distinction of Union of Soviet Asscns for Cultural Links and Friendship with Overseas 1991, Medal for Merit 1998; Ordre des Arts et des Lettres (France) 1978, 1991, K.I. Stanislavski Merit Award for World Theatre (Russia) 1999, Czech Literary Fund Prize 2000, Special Prize for Lifelong Mastery 2001, Artis Bohemiae Amicis Medal 2001, German Language Festival Prize 2002. *Plays directed include:* all Chekhov's plays, Romeo and Juliet, Hamlet, Measure for Measure (Shakespeare), Antigone (Sophocles), Life Is A Dream (Calderón), Waiting for Godot (Beckett), Faust (Goethe), Minetti (Bernard) and other classical and modern dramas; Guest Dir for productions in Havana, Brussels, Cologne, Salzburg, Vienna, Stockholm, Paris, Avignon, Genoa, Berlin. *Address:* Národní Divadlo, Ostrovní 1, Prague 1, Czech Republic (Office). *Telephone:* (2) 2491-0312 (Office). *Fax:* (2) 2490-1239 (Office).

KREMENYUK, Victor Aleksandrovich, DHist; Russian civil servant; b. 13 Dec. 1940, Odessa (now Ukraine); m. Lyudmila Agapova; one d.; ed Moscow Inst. of Int. Relations; army service 1963–68; with Mezdunarodnaya Zhizn magazine 1968–70; with Inst. of USA and Canada, USSR (now Russian) Acad. of Sciences 1970–; expert, Cttee on Int. Problems, USSR Supreme Soviet 1989–91; expert, State Duma 1993–; worked on project Process of Int. Negotiations in Int. Inst. of Applied System Analysis Austria, lectures and seminars in USA, Germany, Austria; Deputy Dir Inst. of USA and Canada 1989–; Chair. Expert Council of Political Sciences 1992–99; mem. Council on Higher Policy at Ministry of Foreign Affairs 1991–96; mem. Scientific Council, Russian Inst. of Strategic Studies 1995–; mem. Council of Social Sciences, Presidium of Russian Acad. of Sciences 1991–; mem. Nat. Geographical Soc., USA, Int. Asscn of Conflictology; mem. Consultative and Observation Councils Salzburg Seminar, Austria, Centre of Applied Studies on Negotiations, Switzerland; mem. Ed. Bds, magazines Econ., Politics and Ideology, Journal of Negotiations, USA 1990–2000, Journal of Peace Studies, USA; Nat. Prize for Science and Tech. (USSR) 1980, CPR Inst. for Dispute Resolution (New York) Bork Award 2002. *Publications:* over 100 articles and 12 scientific monographs; ed. over 50 scientific works in Russian and English. *Address:* Institute of USA and Canada, Khlebny per. 2/3, 121069 Moscow, Russia. *Telephone:* (095) 291-14-83 (Office); (095) 430-07-95 (Home). *Fax:* (095) 200-12-07 (Office). *E-mail:* vkremenyuk@yahoo.com (Office).

KREMER, Gidon; Russian/German violinist; b. 27 Feb. 1947, Riga, Latvia; ed Riga School of Music, Moscow Conservatory (with David Oistrakh); recitalist and orchestral soloist worldwide 1965–; has played in most major int. festivals including Berlin, Dubrovnik, Helsinki, London, Moscow, Prague, Salzburg, Tokyo and Zürich; has played with most major int. orchestras including Berlin Philharmonic, Boston Symphony, Concertgebouw, LA Philharmonic, New York Philharmonic, Philadelphia, San Francisco Symphony, Vienna Philharmonic, London Philharmonic, Royal Philharmonic, Philharmonia, NHK Symphony of Japan and all main Soviet orchestras; has worked with Bernstein, von Karajan, Giulini, Jochum, Previn, Abbado, Levine, Maazel, Muti, Harnoncourt, Mehta and Marriner; f. Lockenhaus Chamber Music Festival 1981; plays a Stradivarius; lives in Germany; prizewinner at Queen Elisabeth Competition, Brussels, Montreal Competition and Fourth Int. Tchaikovsky Competition (First Prize) 1970, Paganini Prize, Genoa; Grand Prix du Disque and Deutsche Schallplattenpreis. *Recordings:* has made more than 45 records. *Performances:* first performances include Henze, Stockhausen, Schnittke, Pärt, Astor Piazzola. *Address:* c/o ICM Artists, 40 West 57th Street, New York, NY 10023, USA.

KREMP, Herbert, DPhil; German journalist; b. 12 Aug. 1928, Munich; s. of Johann and Elisabeth Kremp; m. Brigitte Steffal 1956; two d. (one deceased); ed Munich Univ.; Reporter, Frankfurter Neue Presse 1956–57; Political Ed. Rheinische Post 1957–59; Dir Political Dept, Der Tag, Berlin 1959–61; Bonn Corresp. Rheinische Post 1961–63; Ed.-in-Chief, Rheinische Post 1963–68; Ed.-in-Chief, Die Welt 1969–77, Joint Ed. 1981–, Co-Publr 1984–87; Chief Corresp. in Beijing 1977–81, Ed.-in-Chief 1981–85, Chief Corresp. in Brussels 1987–, Jt Ed., Springer Group newspapers 1984–87; Konrad Adenauer Prize 1984, Bundesverdienstkreuz 1988. *Publications:* Am Ufer der Rubikon: Eine politische Anthropologie, Die Bambusbrücke: Ein asiatisches Tagebuch 1979, Wir brauchen unsere Geschichte 1988. *Address:* c/o Die Welt, Kochstrasse 50, 10969 Berlin, Germany.

KRENS, Thomas, MA; American museum director; b. 26 Dec. 1946, New York; ed Williams Coll., Southern Univ. of New York (SUNY), Albany and Yale Univ.; Asst Prof. of Art, Williams Coll., Williamstown, Mass. 1972–80, Asst Prof. of History of Art, grad. program. 1977–80, Adjunct. Prof. of Art History 1988–; Dir Williams Coll. Museum of Art 1980–88; consultant, Solomon R. Guggenheim Museum, New York 1986–88, Dir 1988–; Dir The Peggy Guggenheim Collection, Venice 1988–; Dir, Trustee Solomon R. Guggenheim Foundation 1988–; Hon. DHumLitt (State Univ. of NY). *Publications:* Jim Dine Prints: 1970–77 1977, The Prints of Helen Frankenthaler 1980, The Drawing of Robert Morris 1982, Robert Morris: The Mind/Body Problem 1994. *Address:* Solomon R. Guggenheim Museum, 1071 Fifth Avenue, New York, NY 10128, USA.

KRENZ, Egon; German politician; b. 1937; ed Teacher Training Inst. Putbus and Cen. Cttee of CPSU Party Univ. Moscow; joined Freie Deutsche Jugend (FDJ) 1953, Socialist Unity Party (SED) and Confed. of Free German Trade Unions 1955; various functions within FDJ and SED 1957–64; Sec. Ernst Thälmann Pioneer Org. 1967–74, Chair. 1971–74; First Sec. FDJ Cen. Council 1974–83; mem. Nat. Council of Nat. Front 1969–; cand. mem. Cen. Cttee of SED 1971–73, mem. 1973–90, Sec. 1989–90, cand. mem. Politburo 1976–83, mem. 1983–90, Gen. Sec. 1989–90; Deputy to Volkskammer 1971–90, mem. Presidium 1971–81, Chair. FDJ Faction 1971–76; mem. Council of State 1981–84, Deputy Chair. 1984–89, Chair. (Head of State) 1989–90; stripped of membership of CP (fmrly SED); now property developer, Berlin; faced charges of manslaughter for killings of persons fleeing over Berlin Wall and other borders 1994; on trial Aug. 1995; sentenced to six and a half years' imprisonment for the deaths of those trying to cross the Berlin Wall Aug. 1997; sentence upheld on appeal Nov. 1999; decorations include Karl Marx Orden, Banner der Arbeit, Verdienstmedaille der DDR.

KRENZ, Jan; Polish conductor and composer; b. 14 July 1926, Włocławek; s. of Otton Krenz and Eleonora Krenz; m. Alina Krenz 1958; one s.; ed Higher School of Music; conducting début, Łódź Philharmonic Orch. 1946; Chief Conductor, State Poznań Philharmonic Orchestra 1947–49; Chief Conductor Polish Nat. Radio Symphony Orchestra of Katowice 1953–67; Chief Conductor Danish Radio Orchestra, Copenhagen 1960s; Leader, Grand Opera House Orchestra (Teatr Wielki), Warsaw 1968–73; conducted Berlin Philharmonic, Staatskapelle Dresden, Leningrad Philharmonic and all the maj. London orchestras; Gen. Dir of Music, Bonn Orchestra 1979–82; frequent collaboration with Yomiuri Nippon Symphony Orchestra; performing only as guest conductor 1983–; Diploma of Ministry of Foreign Affairs 1980; Hon. mem. Asscn of Polish Composers; Hon. Conductor Polish Nat. Radio Symphony Orchestra of Katowice; State Prize 1955, 1972; Prize of Asscn of Polish Composers 1968; Grand Prix du Disque, France 1972; Prize of Polish Artists' and Musicians' Asscn (SPAM) Orfeusz 1974 decorations include Order of Banner of Labour (First Class) Commdr's Cross with Star of Polonia Restituta Order, State Prize (First Class) (twice). *Compositions include:* chamber, vocal and symphonic music, orchestral transcriptions of Polish classics, J. S. Bach and Szymanowski, film and stage music. *Leisure interest:* painting. *Address:* al. J. Ch. Szucha 16, 00-582 Warsaw, Poland.

KREPS, Juanita Morris, MA, PhD; American politician, economist and teacher; b. 11 Jan. 1921, Lynch, Ky; d. of the late Elmer and Cenia Blair Morris; m. Dr. Clifton H. Kreps, Jr 1944 (deceased); one s. two d. (one deceased); ed Berea Coll., Duke Univ.; Instructor in Econs, Denison Univ., Ohio 1945–46, Asst Prof. 1947–50; Lecturer, Hofstra Univ., NY, 1952–54,

Queens Coll., NY 1954–55; Visiting Asst Prof. Duke Univ., NC, Asst Prof. 1958–62, Assoc. Prof. 1963–68, Prof. 1968–72, Dean of Women's Coll., Asst Provost 1969–72, James B. Duke Prof. 1972–77, Vice-Pres. of Univ. 1973–77; US Sec. of Commerce 1977–79; Ford Faculty Research Fellow 1964–65; Dir NY Stock Exchange 1972–77, AT&T 1980–91, Armco Inc. 1980–91, UAL Inc. 1979–92, Eastman Kodak Co. 1975–77, 1979–91, J. C. Penney Co. 1972–77, 1979–91, Zurn Industries Inc. 1982–93, Deere & Co. 1982–92, Chrysler Corpn 1983–91, Citicorp 1979–89, RJR Nabisco 1975–77, 1979–89; Trustee, Coll. Retirement Equities Fund 1972–77, 1985–92, Berea Coll., Duke Endowment 1979–; Chair. Bd of Trustees, Educational Testing Service 1975–76; Pres. American Assen for Higher Educ. 1975–76; Pres. Bd of Overseers, Teachers Insurance and Annuity Assen and Coll. Retirement Equities Fund 1992–96; mem. Comm. on Future of Worker-Man. Relations to advise Secs of Commerce and Labor 1993–95; Trustee Berea Coll. 1972–78, 1980–98, Kenan Inst. of Pvt. Enterprise, Univ. of NC, Chapel Hill 1995–; Fellow American Acad. of Arts and Sciences 1988; 20 hon. degrees; NC Public Service Award 1976, Haskins Award 1984, Corp. Governance Award, Nat. Assen of Corp. Dirs (first recipient) 1987, Duke Univ. medal for Distinguished Meritorious service and many others. *Publications:* ed.: Employment, Income and Retirement Problems of the Aged 1963, Technology, Manpower and Retirement Policy 1966; ed. and contrib.: Lifetime Allocation of Work and Income 1971, Sex in the Marketplace: American Women at Work 1971; co-author: Principles of Economics (with C. E. Ferguson) 1962, 1965, Contemporary Labor Economics 1974, Sex, Age and Work 1975, Women and the American Economy, a Look to the 1980s 1976; over 60 papers on ageing, retirement and econs. *Leisure interests:* music, art. *Address:* 115 East Duke Building, Box 90768, Duke University, Durham, NC 27708; 29 Forest at Duke Drive, Durham, NC 27705, USA. *Telephone:* (919) 684-2616 (Office). *Fax:* (919) 684-8351.

KRESS, Victor Melkhiorovich; Russian politician; b. 16 Nov. 1948, Kostroma Region; m.; two c.; ed Novosibirsk Inst. of Agric., Russian Acad. of Man.; agronomist, agric. enterprises Tomsk Region; Deputy Chair., Agric.-Industrial complex Tomsk Region 1971–87; First Sec. Dist CP Cttee, Tomsk Region 1987–90; Chair. Tomsk Regional Soviet 1990–91; Head, Admin. of Tomsk Region 1991–96, Gov. 1996–; mem. Council of Russian Fed. 1993–2000; Chair. Interregional Assen Siberian Agreement. *Address:* Office of the Governor, Lenina Square 6, 634050 Tomsk, Russia. *Telephone:* (3822) 51-05-05 (Office); (3822) 51-06-86 (Office). *Fax:* (3822) 51-03-23 (Office); (3822) 51-07-30 (Office).

KRETZENBACHER, Leopold, DPhil; Austrian/German academic; b. 13 Nov. 1912, Leibnitz, Steiermark, Austria; s. of Michael Kretzenbacher and Franziska Kuder; m. Elfriede Jauker 1940; two s. four d.; ed Univ. of Graz; Univ. of Zagreb 1943–44; Prof. Univ. of Kiel 1961–66, Univ. of Munich 1966–78; Prof. Emer. Inst. für Deutsche und Vergleichende Volkskunde, Univ. of Munich 1978–; has undertaken extensive travels in Europe for purpose of ethnological research; mem. Acads. of Munich, Uppsala, Vienna, Slovenia, New York; DrIur hc (Graz); numerous awards. *Publications:* approx. 30 books and 400 studies. *Leisure interests:* mountain walking, cross-country skiing, swimming, listening to music. *Address:* Institut für Deutsche und Vergleichende Volkskunde, Ludwig-Maximilians-Universität, 80539 Munich, Geschwister-Scholl-Platz 1 (Office); Clemensstrasse 36/I, 80803 Munich, Germany (Home); 8403 Lebring, Stangorsdorf 20, Steiermark, Austria (Home). *Telephone:* (89) 396284 (Germany) (Home); (3182) 7665 (Austria) (Home).

KRIANGSAK CHOMANAN, Gen.; Thai politician and army officer; b. 1917; ed Thai Royal Mil. Acad. and U.S. Army Staff Coll.; served in Second World War and Korean War; Deputy Chief of Staff, Supreme Command Headquarters to 1974, Chief of Staff 1974–76; Deputy Supreme Commdr of Royal Thai Armed Forces 1976–77, Supreme Commdr 1978; participated in mil. coups Oct. 1976 and 1977; Gen. Sec. Nat. Admin. Reform Council Oct. 1976; Vice-Chair. Prime Minister's Advisory Council Oct. 1976–Oct. 1977; Sec.-Gen. Revolutionary Council, Nat. Dir of Peacekeeping Oct.–Nov. 1977; Sec.-Gen. Nat. Policy Council 1977–79; Prime Minister 1977–80, Minister of Finance 1979–80, of the Interior 1977–78, of Defence 1978–79, of Agric. 1979–80; MP for Muang Roi Et Aug. 1981; ordained as monk Jan. 1983; fmr Leader, Nat. Democratic Party; arrested Sept. 1985; granted bail Feb. 1986. *Address:* National Assembly, Bangkok, Thailand.

KRIEL, Hermanus Jacobus, BA, LLB; South African politician and lawyer; b. 14 Nov. 1941, Kakamas; s. of P. Kriel and Mrs. Kriel; one s. two d.; ed Hugenote Hoërskool, Univ. of Stellenbosch; conveyancer, notary 1968; Chair. Cape Div. Council 1976–77; mem. Cape Prov. Council 1977–84, Cape Exec. Cttee 1981–84; MP 1984–89; Minister of Planning, Prov. Affairs and Nat. Housing 1989–91, of Law and Order 1991–94; Premier of Western Cape Provincial Parl. 1994–97; F.C. Erasmus Award, Stella Officii Egregii. *Leisure interests:* golf, reading. *Address:* c/o Private Bag 9043, Cape Town 8000, South Africa.

KRIELE, Martin, DJur, LLM; German professor of law; b. 19 Jan. 1931, Opladen; s. of late Dr. Rudolf Kriele and of Konstanze Henckels; m. 1st Christel Grothues 1960; one s. one d.; m. 2nd Alexa Michalsen; ed Freiburg, Münster, Bonn and Yale Univs.; admitted to the Court 1961; Prof. of Philosophy of Law and Public Law, Univ. of Cologne 1967–; Dir Inst. for Political Philosophy and Problems of Legislation 1967; Judge, Constitutional Court of North Rhine–Westphalia 1976–88; Ed. Zeitschrift für Rechtspolitik 1968–. *Publications:* Kriterien der Gerechtigkeit 1963, Theorie der Rechtsge-

winnung 1967, Einführung in die Staatslehre 1975, Legitimitätsprobleme der Bundesrepublik 1977, Die Menschenrechte zwischen Ost und West 1977, Recht und praktische Vernunft 1979, Befreiung und politische Aufklärung 1980, Nicaragua, das blutende Herz Amerikas 1985, Die Demokratische Weltrevolution 1987, Recht, Vernunft, Wirklichkeit (essays) 1990. *Leisure interest:* music (piano). *Address:* University of Cologne, Seminar für Staatsphilosophie und Rechtspolitik, Albertus-Magnus-Platz 1, 50923 Cologne, Germany (Office); Dorf 11, 6900 Möggen, Austria (Home). *Telephone:* (221) 4702230 (Office); (5573) 3772 (Home). *Fax:* (221) 4705010 (Office); (5573) 3772 (Home).

KRIER, Léon; Luxembourg architect, urban planner and designer; b. 7 April 1946, Luxembourg; ed Univ. of Stuttgart; Asst to James Stirling London 1968–70, 1973–74; project partner with J. P. Kleihues, Berlin 1971–72; in pvt. practice in London 1974–; lecturer Architectural Assen School, London 1973–76, Royal Coll. of Art, London 1977, Princeton Univ. 1977; Jefferson Prof. of Architecture, Univ. Va Charlottesville 1982; E. Saarinen Prof., Yale Univ. 2001; architectural and urban design adviser to HRH The Prince of Wales; works include numerous city centre and housing redevt. plans, schools, univs., public bldgs. etc. in UK, Germany, Luxembourg, Spain, Italy, Greece, Sweden, U.S.A., Begium, St Lucia and France; City of Berlin Architecture Prize (with Rob Krier) 1975; Jefferson Medal for Architecture 1985, European Culture Prize 1995, Silver Medal Acad. Française 1997. *Exhibitions include:* Triennale, Milan 1973, Léon Krier and Rita Wolff, Inst. for Architecture & Urban Studies, New York 1978, City Segments, Walker Art Center, Minn. and elsewhere in USA 1980, Léon Krier: la ricostruzione della città europea, Verona 1980, Drawings by Léon Krier, Max Protech Gallery, New York 1981, Model Futures, ICA, London 1983, Léon Krier, Max Protech Gallery, New York 1984, Museum of Modern Art, New York 1985, Venice Biennale 1997. *Projects include:* masterplans for Poundbury 1988, Novoli, Florence 1993, Città Nuova, Alessandria, Italy 1997, Hardelot, France 2001; designs furniture for Giorgetti, Italy 1991–. *Publications include:* Buildings and Projects of James Stirling (ed.) 1974, The Reconstruction of the European City 1978, The City within the City (ed.) 1979, Architecture and Urban Design (ed. by Richard Economakis) 1967–92, Architecture: Choice or Fate 1997. *Address:* 8 rue des Chapeliers, 83830 Claviers, France.

KRIKALEV, Sergey Konstantinovich; Russian cosmonaut; b. 27 Aug. 1958, Leningrad; m.; one d.; ed Leningrad Mechanical Inst.; engineer Research Production Co. Energia 1981–85, took part in developing new samples of space tech.; Master of Sports in piloting; mem. Cosmonauts' team since 1985; took part in Jt space flights Soviet-French 1988–89, Soviet-British 1991, Discovery 1994, American Endeavor flight to new Int. Space Station Nov. 1998; spent 310 days in orbit on Soyuz TM-12 1991–92; third-rank cosmonaut; Hero of the Soviet Union 1989, Hero of the Russian Fed. 1992. *Address:* Yuriy Gagarin Centre for Cosmonauts Training, Zvezdny Gorodok, Moscow Region, Russia. *Telephone:* (095) 971-86-16.

KRIPKE, Saul Aaron, BA, LHD; American professor of philosophy; b. 13 Nov. 1940, Bay Shore, New York; s. of Myer Samuel Kripke and Dorothy Kripke; m. Margaret P. Gilbert 1976; ed Harvard Univ.; Soc. of Fellows, Harvard Univ. 1963–66, concurrently lecturer with rank of Asst Prof. Princeton Univ. 1964–66; lecturer Harvard Univ. 1966–68; Assoc. Prof. Rockefeller Univ. 1968–72, Prof. 1972–76; McCath Prof. of Philosophy, Princeton Univ. 1978–98; Fellow, American Acad. of Arts and Sciences; corresp. Fellow, British Acad.; Fulbright Fellow 1962–63; Guggenheim Fellow 1968–69, 1977–78; Visiting Fellow, All Souls Coll. Oxford 1977–78, 1989–90; Visiting Prof. The Hebrew Univ. 1989–; other visiting professorships etc.; Hon. DHumLitt (Univ. of Neb. at Omaha) 1977, (Johns Hopkins Univ.) 1997, (Univ. of Haifa) 1998. *Publications:* Naming and Necessity 1980, Wittgenstein on Rules and Private Language 1982; numerous papers in professional journals and anthologies. *Address:* Department of Philosophy, Princeton University, Princeton, NJ 08544, USA.

KRISHNAMURTY, G. V. G., BA, BSc, BL; Indian election commissioner (retd) and lawyer; b. 19 Nov. 1934, Chirala, Andhra Pradesh; s. of G. V. Subbarao and Mrs. G. Rajeswaramma; m. Mrs. G. Padma 1957; one s. one d.; ed Andhra Univ.; anti-British student activist and mem. Azad Hindu Fauz Youth League 1945–47; advocate, Andhra Pradesh High Court 1957; lecturer, Law Coll. Osmania Univ. 1958, 1962; Sr Research Officer, Indian Law Inst. 1962–63; advocate, Supreme Court; Deputy Legal Adviser, Comm. of Inquiry, Cabinet Secr. 1972–73; Additional Legal Adviser, Ministry of Law and ex-officio Govt Counsel, Delhi High Court 1973–76, 1978–79; Govt Arbitrator 1979–83; Jt Sec. and Legal Adviser 1983–87; Additional Sec. Govt of India 1987–88, Special Sec. 1988–89; Sec. Law Comm. of India 1989–92; Election Commr of India 1993–99; del. to various int. confs. etc.; numerous professional appts. and other distinctions; Hon. LLD (Jhansi Univ.) 1996. *Publications include:* Dynamics of Diplomacy 1968, Modern Diplomacy, Dialectics and Dimensions 1980; articles in legal journals. *Leisure interests:* reading, watching nature, cultural activities. *Address:* 1402 Kausumbhi, opp. Delhi Anand Vihar ISBT, Ghaziabad, Uttar Pradesh, India. *Telephone:* (120) 4778056 (Office); (120) 4778056 (Home). *Fax:* (120) 4778056 (Office); (120) 4778056 (Home).

KRISHNAN, Natarajan, B.A.ECONS.; Indian diplomatist; b. 6 Oct. 1928, Mayuram, Tamil Nadu; s. of the late V. Natarajan; m. Lalitha Krishnan; one s. two d.; ed Univ. of Madras; joined Indian Foreign Service 1951; Third Sec. later Second Sec., Bangkok 1955–56; Second Sec., Chargé d'Affaires, Phnom Penh 1956–57; Under Sec. Ministry of External Affairs 1957–58; First Sec.,

Chargé d'Affaires, Buenos Aires 1959–62; Deputy Sec., Dir Ministry of External Affairs 1962–67; Consul-Gen. and Perm. Rep. to UN Offices, Geneva 1967–71; Joint Sec. Ministry of External Affairs 1971–76; Amb. to Yugoslavia 1976–79; Additional Sec. Ministry of External Affairs 1979–81; Amb. and Perm. Rep. to UN 1981–87; Dean, School of Int. Studies, Pondicherry Univ. 1988–90; Prime Minister's Special Envoy for Africa 1987–89; mem. Exec. Bd UNESCO 1989–. *Address:* Flat 2C, King's Crest Apts., No. 8 Millers Road, Bangalore 560046, India.

KRISHNAN, Rappal Sangameswara, DSc, PhD; Indian physicist; b. 23 Sept. 1911, Chittur, Palghat Dist, Kerala; s. of R. P. Sangameswara Iyer and C. R. Ammini Ammal; m. Rajammal 1934; two s. three d. (one deceased); ed Univ. of Madras, St Joseph's Coll., Trichy, Indian Inst. of Science and Trinity Coll., Cambridge; Research Asst Indian Inst. of Science 1935–38; 1851 Exhbn Overseas Scholar, Univ. of Cambridge 1938–41; lecturer in Physics, Inst. of Science 1942–45, Asst Prof. 1945–48, Prof. and Head of Dept of Physics 1948–72, Prof. Emer. 1972–73; Vice-Chancellor Kerala Univ. 1973–77; Prin. Investigator, DST Project, Indian Inst. of Science, Bangalore 1977–82, Prof. Emer. 1983–87; Visiting Scientist and Investigator, CSIR Project, Nat. Aeronautical Lab., Bangalore 1987–90, CSIR Emer. Scientist 1990–; Fellow Inst. of Physics, London, American Physical Soc., Indian Acad. of Sciences, Indian Natural Sciences Acad.; Pres. Physics Section, Indian Science Congress 1949; Nat. Science Foundation Sr Foreign Scientist, Fellow, Dept of Physics, North Tex. State Univ. Denton, Tex. 1971–72; original contributions to colloid optics (Krishnan Effect), light-scattering, Raman effect, crystal physics, etc.; mem. Bd, Int. Bd, American Biographical Inst. Research Asscn; mem. Int. Biographical Asscn; recipient I.I.Sc. Golden Jubilee Distinguished Alumni Award 1986, Chandrasekhar Venkata Raman (Nobel Laureate) Centenary Medal 1988, MA of the Year, American Biographical Inst. Research Asscn. *Publications:* Progress in Crystal Physics, Vol. I 1958, Two Chapters in Raman Effect, Vol. I 1971, Thermal Expansion of Crystals 1979, Source Book on Raman Effect Vol. I (1928–1957) 1989, Vol II (1958–1970) 1991 and contribs. to other books. *Leisure interests:* tennis, walking, photography. *Address:* Material Science Division, National Aeronautical Laboratory, Bangalore 560017 (Office); 232, 18th Cross, Palace Upper Orchards, Sadasivanagar, Bangalore 560080, Karnataka, India (Home). *Telephone:* 570098 (Office); 3340703 (Home).

KRISTAN, Ivan, DJur; Slovenian politician and lawyer; b. 12 June 1930, Arnovo; ed Ljubljana Univ.; worked in trade unions 1956–67; teacher, Faculty of Law, Ljubljana Univ. 1967–77, Prof. 1977–87, Dean 1983–85, Rector 1985–87; mem. Cttee for Constitutional Reforms Slovenian Repub. 1970–74, 1987–90; mem. Constitutional Court of Yugoslavia 1987–91; Pres. Nat. Council of Slovenian Repub. 1992–98; author of over 200 books, articles and scientific papers on legal problems of human rights, federalism, self-determination and sovereignty of nations, including Constitutional Law of SFR Yugoslavia (co-author); Pres. of Supervising Cttee, Int. Asscn for Constitutional Law (IACL). *Address:* National Council, Subeceva 4, 61000 Ljubljana, Slovenia. *Telephone:* (61) 1261221. *Fax:* (61) 212251.

KRISTIANSEN, Erling (Engelbrecht); Danish diplomatist and government official; b. 31 Dec. 1912, Terndrup, Jutland; s. of the late Kristian E. Kristiansen and Andrea Kristiansen (née Madsen); m. 1st Annemarie Selinko 1938 (died 1986); m. 2nd Harriet Laursen (née Lund Jensen) 1996; ed Herning Gymnasium, Univs of Copenhagen and Geneva, Paris and London; Danish Civil Service, Ministry of Labour 1941, with Free Danish Legations Stockholm 1943, Washington 1944, London 1945; Commercial Sec. Danish Legation, London 1945–47; Head, Del. to OEEC 1948–50; Sec., Econ. Cttee of Cabinet 1950–51; Asst Under-Sec. of State, Ministry of Foreign Affairs 1951–53, Deputy Under-Sec. 1954–64; Amb. to UK 1964–77, (Doyen of the Diplomatic Corps 1973–77); concurrently to Ireland 1964–73; Chair. Danish Dels. to major econ. confs. 1954–63; Chair. Nordic Investment Bank 1978–80, mem. 1980–86; mem. Bd, The East Asiatic Co.; mem. Int. Advisory Bd S. G. Warburg & Co. (Mercury Int. Group); Dir several cos; co-f. and mem. Bd CARE Denmark; Hon. Pres. Anglo-Danish Soc.; Kt Grand Cross, Order of Dannebrog, Royal Victorian Order, Order of Falcon of Iceland, Grand Officier, Légion d'honneur and other decorations. *Publication:* Folkeforbundet (The League of Nations) 1938. *Leisure interests:* outdoor sports, languages. *Address:* Kratkrogen 8, 2920 Charlottenlund, Denmark.

KRISTOFFERSON, Kris, BA; American singer, song writer and actor; b. 22 June 1936, Brownsville, Texas; one s. one d. (by first marriage); m. 2nd Rita Coolidge 1973 (divorced 1980); one s.; m. 3rd Lisa Meyers 1983; four c.; ed Pomona Coll. and Oxford Univ.; Capt. in U.S. Army 1960–65; performed at Newport Folk Festival 1969; recording artist 1970–. *Singles include:* Help Me Make It Through the Night, Me and Bobby McGee, For the Good Times, When I Loved Her, Original Intent, Night of the Cyclone, Sandino, No Place to Hide, Cheating Hearts. *Albums include:* Kristofferson, The Silver-Tongued Devil and I, Border Lord, Jesus Was a Capricorn, Spooky Lady's Sideshow, Songs of Kristofferson, Who's to Bless and Who's to Blame, Easter Island, Shake Hands with the Devil (with Rita Coolidge) 1979, Third World War 1990, Highwayman II (with Highwaymen) 1990, Singer, Songwriter 1991. *Films include:* Cisco Pike 1972, Pat Garrett and Billy the Kid 1973, Blume in Love 1973, Bring Me the Head of Alfredo Garcia 1974, Alice Doesn't Live Here Anymore 1974, The Sailor Who Fell From Grace With The Sea 1976, A Star is Born 1976, Vigilante Force 1976, Semi-Tough 1977, Convoy 1978, Heaven's Gate 1981, Rollover 1981, Welcome Home 1989, Millennium 1989, A Soldier's Daughter Never Cries 1998, Come Dance with Me 1999. *Television appear-*

ances include: Freedom Road (TV film) 1979, Amerika (series) 1987, Rip 1989, Sandino, Christmas in Connecticut 1992, Tad 1995. *Address:* c/o One Way, 1 Prospect Avenue, P.O. Box 6429, Albany, NY 12206, USA.

KRISTOPANS, Vilis; Latvian politician; b. 13 June 1954; m.; ed Riga State Tech. Univ.; basketball player, Latvian team 1972–81; sports instructor Sports Cttee, Daugava Cen. Council 1977–83; coach, Head coach, basketball team VEF 1983–89; Chair. co-operative soc. Noster 1990; Dir-Gen. Jt Dardedze 1990–92; Vice-Pres. Interbaltija Ltd 1992–93; Minister of State Revenue 1993–94; Chair. Deutsche-Lettische Bank 1994–95; Minister of Transport Latvian Repub. 1995–98; Prime Minister of Latvia, also Minister of Agric. 1998–99; mem. Parl. (Seimas) 1993–98; mem. Bd Latvijas ceļš (Latvian Way) party; Pres. Latvian Basketball League 1992–97; mem. Ventspils Free Ports Bd 1994–. *Address:* Latvijas ceļš, Terbatas jela 4-9, 1011 Riga, Latvia (Office). *Telephone:* 708-7111 (Office).

KRIVINE, Alain; French journalist and politician; b. 10 July 1941, Paris; m. Michèle Martinet 1960; two d.; ed Lycée Condorcet and Faculté des Lettres de Paris; mem. Jeunesses communistes 1956, French Communist Party 1958; leader Union of Student Communists, Paris-Sorbonne Univ. 1964–65; f. Revolutionary Communist Youth 1966 (disbanded by the Govt 1968), Communist League 1969 (dissolved 1973); Cand. Presidential Elections 1969, 1974; Journalist Rouge 1969–; mem. Political Bureau of Ligue Communiste Révolutionnaire 1974–; MEP 1999–. *Publications:* La Farce électorale 1969, Questions sur la révolution 1973, Mais si, rebelles et repentis (with Daniel Bensaïd) 1988. *Address:* European Parliament, 97–113 rue Wiertz, 1047 Brussels, Belgium (Office); 2 rue Richard-Lenoir, 93100 Montreuil, France. *Telephone:* 1-48-70-42-30. *Fax:* 1-48-59-23-28. *E-mail:* akrivine@euro-parl.eu .int (Office).

KRIVINE, Emmanuel; French violinist and conductor; b. 7 May 1947, Grenoble; s. of Henri Krivine and Rejla Krivine (née Weisbrod); one d.; ed Conservatoire Nat. Supérieur de Musique et de Danse, Paris, Conservatoire Royal de Bruxelles; pupil of Henryk Szeryng and Yehudi Menuhin; solo violinist Paris 1964, Brussels 1965–68; Perm. Guest Conductor Radio-France 1976–83; Dir Lorraine-Metz Regional Orchestra 1981–83; Prin. Guest Conductor Orchestra of Lyon 1983; Artistic Dir French Nat. Youth Orchestra 1983–; Musical Dir Nat. Orchestra of Lyon 1987–2000; Conductor French Nat. Orchestra 2001–; Guest Conductor various int. orchestras including Berlin Philharmonic, Concertgebouw and Chamber Orchestra of Europe 1977–; Chevalier, Ordre nat. du Mérite, Officier des Arts et des Lettres; Ginette-Neveu Medal 1971 and numerous other awards. *Leisure interests:* literature, philosophy. *Address:* 2 rue Hotel de Ville, 1800 Vevey, Switzerland.

KRIWET, Heinz, Dr rer. pol; German business executive; b. 2 Nov. 1931, Bochum; ed Univs of Cologne and Freiburg; trainee, German Iron & Steel Fed. 1960–61; Personal Asst to Vice-Pres. Sales, Hüttenwerk Rheinhausen (Krupp) 1962–63, Man. Planning and Marketing Dept 1964–67; Gen. Man. Sales, Friedrich Krupp Hüttenwerke AG, Bochum 1968, mem. Exec. Bd in charge of Sales 1969–72; mem. Exec. Bd in charge of Sales, Thyssen AG, Düsseldorf 1973–83; Chair. Exec. Bd Thyssen Stahl AG, Duisburg 1983–91; Chair. Exec. Bd Thyssen AG, Düsseldorf March 1991–; Chair. Supervisory Bd Thyssen Industrie AG, Thyssen Handelsunion AG, Thyssen Edelstahlwerke AG, Thyssen Stahl AG, Thyssen Wohnbau GmbH, Rheinische Kalksteinwerke GmbH, Fried. Krupp AG Hoesch-Krupp; mem. Supervisory Bd Allianz Lebensversicherungs AG, Commerzbank AG, Mannesmann-Röhrenwerke AG, Pechiney Int. Paris, RWE Energie AG, Gerling Group, Hapag Lloyd, Leipziger Messe GmbH; mem. Bd of Dirs. The Budd Co. Troy, Mich., USA; mem. Man. Bd Inst. Int. du Fer et de l'Acier, Brussels; Chair. German Iron & Steel Fed. 1984–88. *Address:* Thyssen AG, August-Thyssen-Strasse 1, 40211 Düsseldorf, Germany.

KROEMER, Herbert, PhD; American physicist; b. 25 Aug. 1928, Weimar; ed Univ. of Göttingen; carried out pioneering work in semi-conductor research; Prof. of Electrical and Computer Eng, Univ. of Calif. 1985-; Nat. Lecturer IEEE Electron Devices Soc.; mem. Nat. Acad. of Eng, IEEE, American Physics Soc.–; Dr hc (Tech. Univ., Aachen) 1985, (Lund) 1998; J. Erbers Award 1973, Heinrich Welker Medal 1982, Jack Morton Award (IEEE) 1986, Alexander von Humboldt Research Award 1994, Nobel Prize for Physics (jt recipient) 2000. *Publications:* Quantum Mechanics: For Engineering, Materials Science and Applied Physics, Thermal Physics (jt author). *Address:* Electrical and Computer Engineering Department, Room 4107 Engineering I, University of California, Santa Barbara, CA 93106, USA (Office). *Telephone:* (805) 893-3078 (Office). *Fax:* (805) 893-8714 (Office). *E-mail:* kroemer@ece.ucsb.edu (Office).

KROGH, Desmond Charles, MA, EC. DRS., DPhil; South African banking and assurance executive; b. 19 July 1931, Windhoek, Namibia (SW Africa); s. of P. I. Krogh and B. Theron; m. Surine Groenewald 1956; two s.; ed Swakopmund High School, Univs of Cape Town, Amsterdam and Pretoria; lecturer in Econs, Univ. of Orange Free State 1956, Univ. of Pretoria 1957–61; Asst Econ. Adviser to Prime Minister 1961; Prof. of Econs, Univ. of South Africa 1962–69; Expert Witness to Int. Court of Justice on Econ. Devt of SW Africa 1966; mem. Prime Minister's Econ. Advisory Council 1967–73; Fulltime Adviser to Fiscal and Monetary Policy Comm. 1968–69; Exec. Dir of South African Federated Chamber of Industries 1969–73; Adviser to Govt negotiations with GATT 1971–72; Adviser to Reserve Bank of Zimbabwe (fmrly Rhodesia) 1973–74, Deputy Gov. 1974–76, Gov. 1976–83; Alt. Gov. IMF and World Bank 1980–83; Pres. Zimbabwe Inst. of Bankers 1981–82; Exec.

Deputy Chair. Lifegro Assurance Ltd 1983–86; Dir Devt Bank of Southern Africa; Special Adviser to Ministry of Finance 1986–89; Adviser to Reserve Bank of SA 1989–96; Council mem. Univ. of Pretoria 1986, SA Inst. of Int. Affairs 1988, Africa Inst. of SA 1988; Prof. Extraordinaire in Econs, Univ. of SA 1987; Medal and Prize of SA Econ. Soc. 1953, Netherlands-S. African Scholarship 1954–55, Ebden Prize 1957, USA Carnegie Study Grant 1960, Official Visitor to UK 1971; Commdr Order of Legion of Merit (Rhodesia) 1978. *Publications:* numerous articles on economic structure, development, inflation and finance in Southern Africa. *Leisure interests:* golf, history. *Address:* P.O. Box 11005, Maroelana 0161, South Africa.

KROGSGAARD-LARSEN, Povl, PhD, DSc; Danish professor of medicinal chemistry; b. 17 May 1941, Frøslev Mors; s. of Niels Saaby and Marie Saaby (née Krogsgaard) Larsen; m. Tove Krogsgaard-Larsen 1964; one s. one d.; Asst Prof. Royal Danish School of Pharmacy 1970–75, Assoc. Prof. 1975–86, Prof. 1986–, Rector 2001–; mem. Royal Danish Acad. of Sciences and Letters 1986, Danish Acad. of Natural Sciences 1987, Danish Acad. of Tech. Sciences 1987; mem. Bd Dirs Alfred Beuzon Foundation 1991–, Carlsberg Foundation 1993– (currently Chair.); Paul Ehrlich Prize 1989, Lundbeck Foundation Prize 1989, H. C. Ørsted Award 1967, Ole Rømer Award 1983, Astra Award 1991, W. Th. Nauta Award 1996. *Publications:* 330 scientific articles, 80 scientific reviews, 8 science books (ed.), 1 textbook (ed.). *Leisure interests:* history, sport. *Address:* Department of Medicinal Chemistry, The Royal Danish School of Pharmacy, 2 Universitetsparken, DK-2100 Copenhagen (Office); 25 Elmevej, Blovstrød, 3450 Allerød, Denmark (Home). *Telephone:* 35-30-65-11 (Office); 48-17-12-15 (Home). *Fax:* 35-30-60-40 (Office); 48-17-55-50 (Home). *E-mail:* ano@dfh.dk (Office).

KRÓL, Jan Władysław; Polish politician; b. 24 June 1950, Mielec; three c.; ed Higher School of Econs, Cracow, Jagiellonian Univ., Cracow; Worker PAX Soc. 1974–81, Inco-Veritas 1982–83, Remo and Rovan cos. 1983–89; mem. Solidarity Independent Self-governing Trade Union (NSZZ Solidarność) 1980–; assoc. Dziekania Political Thought Club 1984–88; deputy Govt Plenipotentiary for Local Govt Reform 1989–90; Deputy to the Sejm (Parl.) 1989–, Vice-Leader Trade and Services Comm. 1989–97, Sec. Democratic Union (UD) Parl. Caucus 1989–91, leader Extraordinary Cttee for consideration of bills within the State Enterprise Pact 1991–93, Vice-Marshal of Sejm 1997–2000; (Speaker) Co-Chair. Polish Ass. of Sejms of Poland and Lithuania 1997–2000; co.-f. and mem. ROAD (Democratic Campaign Citizens' Movt) 1990–91; Chair Polish-Canadian Econ. Council 1990; co.-f. and mem. Democratic Union 1991–94; mem. Nat. Polish Bd of the Friends of Lithuania Club 1992; mem. Freedom Union (UW) 1994– (also mem. Nat. Bd); Chair. Programme Bd Foundation for Econ. Educ. 1999–. *Publications:* Świadectwo (Evidence) 1989, Przodem do przodu (Face forward) 1993, Z notatnika posła (From Deputy Notebook) 1997, W dialogu (In Dialogue) 1999, Pułapki polskiej demokracji (Polish Democracy Traps) 2001; and numerous articles. *Leisure interests:* tourism, horses. *Address:* Fundacja Edukacji Ekonomicznej, Al. Jerozolimskie 30, 00-024 Warsaw, Poland (Office). *Telephone:* (22) 8280671 (Office). *Fax:* (22) 8280671 (Office). *E-mail:* fee@gdnet.pl (Office); secretariat@interklasa.pl (Office). *Website:* www.europa.edu.pl (Office).

KROL, John A., MSc; American business executive (retd); b. 16 Oct. 1936, Ware, Mass.; m. Janet Valley; two d.; ed Tufts Univ., Bettis Nuclear Reactor Eng School; commissioned in U.S. Navy 1959, worked as nuclear engineer Bureau of Ships Naval Reactors Br.; joined DuPont as chemist, Wilmington, Del. 1963; marketing and manufacturing positions with DuPont Fibers 1965–83, Vice-Pres. 1983, Sr Vice-Pres. 1990; Group Vice-Pres., Sr Vice-Pres. DuPont Agric. Products 1986; mem. Nat. Agricultural Chemists Asscn, Bd of Dirs. 1987–; Vice-Chair. DuPont 1992–97, Chair. 1997–98, Pres. 1995–97, CEO 1995–98; Dir Mead Corp., J. P. Morgan & Co., Nat. Asscn of Mfrs, Del. Art Museum, Wilmington 2000, Catalyst; Trustee Tufts Univ., Univ. of Del., Hagley Museum, U.S. Council for Int. Business; mem. American Chemical Soc. Corp. Liaison Bd, Business Roundtable, Business Council; mem. exec. Cttee Del. Business Roundtable, Business/Public Educ. Council. *Leisure interests:* golf, tennis, squash, skiing. *Address:* DuPont, 1007 North Market Street, Floor 2, Wilmington, DE 19801, USA. *E-mail:* jkrol01@aol.com.

KROLL, Alexander S., BA; American advertising executive; b. 1937; ed Rutgers Univ.; fmr player, NY Titans., American Football League; with Young & Rubicam, Inc., New York 1962–, copywriter 1962–68, Vice-Pres. 1968–69, Sr Vice-Pres. 1969–70, Exec. Vice-Pres. and Worldwide Creative Dir 1970–75, Pres. and COO 1982, CEO 1985, Chair. and CEO 1986–, also Dir; Man. Dir Young & Rubicam USA 1975–77, Pres. 1977; Kodak Life Achievement Award 1985, Nat. Coll. Athletic Asscn Silver Anniversary Award 1987. *Address:* Young & Rubicam Inc., 285 Madison Avenue, New York, NY 10017, USA.

KROLL, Lucien; Belgian architect and town-planner; b. 17 March 1927, Brussels; m. Simone Marti; two d.; ed Athénée Royal de Huy, Ecole Nat. Supérieure d'Architecture de la Cambre, Institut Supérieur d'Urbanisme de la Cambre, Institut Supérieur et International d'Urbanisme Appliqué, Brussels; numerous works in Belgium, France, Italy, Fed. Repub. of Germany, Italy and Rwanda 1953–; founder mem. Inst. d'Esthétique Industrielle 1956; own architectural practice 1952–; environmental research, Ecolonia, Netherlands; exhbns. of work in Brussels, Hanover, Utrecht, Aubervilliers, Copenhagen, Aarhus, Luxembourg, Boston; organized confs. including Habiter?, Brussels 1972; visiting prof. and lecturer many univs. throughout Europe, USA and Japan; mem. Acad. Française d'Architecture 1985–; Hon. mem.

Bund der Deutschen Architekten; Commdr des Arts et des Lettres; Médaille J.-F. Delarue (Acad. française d'Architecture) 1980. *Works:* houses, churches, schools, exhbns., industrial design, monasteries Ottignies and Rwanda; townplanning in Brussels and Kigali, Rwanda, Brussels (housing, with participation of future inhabitants) 1967, ministries and Pres.'s Palace, Rwanda, Medical Faculties Neighbourhood, Brussels 1970, Froidmont Dominican house 1970, housing, Cergy-Pontoise (with participation of future inhabitants) 1977, housing rehabilitation, Alençon 1978, Alma underground station, Brussels 1979, housing, Marne-la-Vallée 1980, Utrecht Acad., computeraided design and creation of 'Landscape' program 1981, housing, Laroche-Clermault, France, Bordeaux, St-Germain, France, Haarlem, Netherlands, Knokke, Pessac-Bordeaux, Bethoncourt, Montbéliard, St.-Dizier, etc.; schools Saint-Germain, Cinais en Touraine, Faenza (Italy); tech. lycée Belfort; Maison de 3e âge, Ostend; extension Univ. of St-Etienne; Maison de l'Environnement, Belfort; tech. lycée Caudry (High Environmental Quality). *Exhibition:* architecture exhbn 'Stabulations Libres', Brussels 2002. *Publications:* CAD-Architektur 1985, Architecture of Complexity 1986, Buildings and Projects (also in German and French) 1987, Componenten 1995, Bien vieillir chez soi 1995, Enfin chez soi 1996, Eco, Bio, Psycho about Urban Ecology 1996, Tutto e paesaggio (also in French 2001), Ecologie urbane 2002, Rassegna 'Lucien Kroll'; over 600 articles on industrial and urban architectural design and comparative architecture. *Address:* Atelier d'Urbanisme, d'Architecture et d'Informatique L. Kroll, Avenue Louis Berlaimont 20, Boîte 9, 1160 Brussels, Belgium. *Telephone:* (2) 673-35-39. *Fax:* (2) 673-89-27. *E-mail:* kroll@brutele.be (Office). *Website:* homeusers.brutele.be/kroll (Office).

KROON, Ciro Dominico; Netherlands Antilles politician; b. 31 Jan. 1916, Curaçao, Netherlands Antilles; s. of Eduard Bernardus Kroon and Catrijn Zimmerman; m. Edna Huis 1936; three s. one d.; ed Higher Grade School; in business until 1942; Admin., Social and Econ. Dept, Netherlands Antilles 1942–51; mem. Legis. Council of Netherlands Antilles 1949–51; Deputy for Social and Econ. Affairs and mem. Admin. Bd of island territory of Curaçao 1951–57; on various occasions Acting Gov. of Curaçao; Minister for Social and Econ. Affairs and Public Health, Netherlands Antilles 1957–68; Prime Minister of Netherlands Antilles Feb. 1968–May 1969; mem. Island Council of Curaçao 1971–73; Minister of Econ. Affairs 1973–75; Pres. Banco Mercantil Venezolano N.V. 1976– (Chair. Supervisory Bd 1994–); Commdr Order of Orange-Nassau, Knight Order of Netherlands Lion and Orders from Venezuela, Colombia and France. *Leisure interests:* sailing, fishing. *Address:* Banco Mercantil Venezolano N.V., Abraham de Veerstraat No. 1, P.O. Box 565, Willemstad, Curaçao, Netherlands Antilles.

KROPF, Susan, BA, MBA; American retail executive; ed St John's Univ., New York Univ.; joined Avon Products Inc. 1970, Vice-Pres. of Product Devt 1990–92, Sr Vice-Pres. of U.S. Marketing 1992–93, Sr Vice-Pres. of Global Product Man. 1993–94, Pres. New and Emerging Markets Div. 1994–97, Pres. Avon U.S. 1997–98, COO for N America 1999–2001, Co. Pres. and COO 2001–; mem. Bd of Dirs. Mead Corpn, Greenpoint Financial Corpn, The Fragrance Foundation; mem. Cosmetic Exec. Women, Fashion Group Int.; YWCA Acad. of Women Achievers Award 1997. *Address:* Avon Products, Inc. Headquarters, 1251 Avenue of the Americas, New York, NY 10020, USA (Office). *Telephone:* (800) 367-2866 (Office). *Website:* www.avoncompany.com (Office).

KROPIWNICKI, Jerzy Janusz, DEcon; Polish politician and economist; b. 5 July 1945, Częstochowa; m.; one s.; ed Warsaw School of Econs; scientific worker, Łódź Univ. 1968–81 (dismissed); mem. Solidarity Independent Self-governing Trade Union 1980–, Deputy Chair. Solidarity Łódź Region Br., mem. Solidarity Nat. Comm., co-organizer demonstration against martial law, arrested 13 Dec. 1981, sentenced to 6 years' imprisonment, released under amnesty July 1984; illegal activity 1984–90, co-organizer, Solidarity Regional Exec. Comm., Łódź 1984–86, co-organizer and activist, Working Group of Solidarity Nat. Comm. 1986–90; co-organizer and activist of Pastoral Care of Working People 1985–; lay worker, St Teresa's Roman Catholic Parish Church, Łódź 1986–89; scientific worker, Econ.-Sociological Faculty of Łódź Univ. 1989–; mem. Christian-Nat. Union (ZChN) 1989–, mem. Presidium of ZChN Gen. Bd 1989–93, Vice-Pres. 1991–93, 2000–; Deputy to Sejm (Parl.) 1991–93 and 1997–2001; Minister of Labour and Social Policy 1991–92; Minister-Head of Cen. Office of Planning 1992–93; Minister and Head of Governmental Centre for Strategic Studies 1997–2001; Minister of Regional Devt and Construction 2000–01. *Publications:* numerous articles on Econs and four books. *Leisure interests:* mountain hiking, reading (history and science-fiction). *Address:* Christian National Union, ul. Twarda 28, 00-853 Warsaw, Poland (Office). *Telephone:* (22) 6618649. *Fax:* (22) 6280804. *E-mail:* tombush@polbox.com (Office).

KROSS, Jaan; Estonian author and translator; b. 19 Feb. 1920, Tallinn; s. of Jaan Kross and Pauline Kross (née Uhlberg); m. Ellen Niit-Kross; ed Tartu Univ.; involved in nat. resistance under the Nazi occupation 1943–44; arrested by the Nazis Sept. 1944; Lecturer Tartu Univ. 1945–46; arrested by Soviet authorities in 1946 and imprisoned in Intalager (Gulag), Komi Autonomous Repub. 1946–50; deported to Krasnoyarsk region 1950–54; fully exonerated 1960; Sec. Estonian Writers' Union 1976–81, Deputy Chair. 1981–; published prose and poetry 1970–; mem. Riigikogu (Estonian Parl.) 1992–93; Dr hc (Tartu Univ.) 1989, (Helsinki Univ.) 1990; Amnesty Int. Literature Prize 1990, Baltic Ass. Literature Prize 1999. *Publications:* historical novels about Estonian history including The Czar's Madman, some travel books, literary and cultural reviews, opera librettos; works translated into more than 20 languages. *Address:* Harju Street 1, Apt. 6, 10146 Tallinn, Estonia (Home). *Telephone:* (2) 441-697 (Home).

KROTO, Sir Harold Walter, Kt, PhD, FRS; British professor of chemistry; b. 7 Oct. 1939; s. of Heinz Kroto and Edith Kroto; m. Margaret Henrietta Hunter 1963; two s.; ed Bolton School, Univ. of Sheffield; Postdoctoral Fellow Nat. Research Council, Canada 1964–66; Research Scientist Bell Telephone Labs., NJ, USA 1966–67; Tutorial Fellow Univ. of Sussex 1967–68, Lecturer 1968–77, Reader 1977–85, Prof. of Chem. 1985–91, Royal Soc. Research Prof. 1991–; Visiting Prof. Univ. of BC 1973, Univ. of S. Calif. 1981, Univ. of Calif. at LA 1988–92, Univ. of Calif., Santa Barbara, Distinguished Visiting Prof. 1996–; Chair. Bd Vega Science Trust 1995-, Exec. Producer Science Programmes for Network TV; fmr mem. Nat. Advisory Cttee on Cultural and Creative Educ.; Hon. Fellow Royal Soc. of Edin. 2000, Bolton Inst.; Tilden Lectureship, Royal Soc. of Chem. 1981; hon. degrees from Univs. of Brussels (Univ. Libre), Stockholm, Limburg, Sheffield, Kingston, Sussex, Helsinki, Nottingham, Yokohama City, Sheffield Hallam, Aberdeen, Leicester, Aveiro, Univ. Coll. London, Hull; shared Int. Prize for New Materials, American Physical Soc. 1992, Italgas Prize for Innovation in Chem. 1992, shared Hewlett Packard Europhysics Prize 1994, shared Nobel Prize for Chem. 1996; Longstaff Medal, Royal Soc. of Chem. 1993, shared Medal for Achievement in Carbon Science, American Carbon Soc. 1997, Ioannes Marcus Marei Medal, Prague 2000. *Publications:* Molecular Rotation Spectra 1975, 1983; 300 papers in chemistry, chemical physics and astronomy journals. *Leisure interests:* graphic design (winner Sunday Times Book Jacket Design Competition 1964, Möet Hennessy/Louis Vuitton Science pour l'Art Prize 1994), tennis. *Address:* School of Chemistry, Physics and Environmental Science, University of Sussex, Brighton, BN1 9QJ, England. *Telephone:* (1273) 678329.

KRUEGER, Anne O., PhD; American international official and economist; b. 12 Feb. 1934, Endicott, NY; d. of Leslie A. Osborn and Dora W. Osborn; m. James Henderson 1981; one d.; ed Oberlin Coll. and Univ. of Wisconsin; Asst Prof. of Econs, Univ. of Minn. 1959–63, Assoc. Prof. 1963–66, Prof. 1966–82; Research Assoc., Nat. Bureau of Econ. Research 1969–82; Vice-Pres. Econs and Research, IBRD Sept. 1982–86; Univ. Arts and Sciences Prof. of Econs, Duke Univ. 1987–92; Sr Fellow (non-resident) Brookings Inst. 1988–94; Herald L. and Caroline L. Ritch Prof. of Humanities and Sciences, Stanford Univ. 1993–, Dir Center for Research on Econ. Devt and Policy Reform 1996–2001; First Deputy Man. Dir IMF 2001–; visiting prof. at univs in USA, Denmark, Germany, France, Australia and Sweden; mem. editorial bds of several int. econ. journals; fmr Vice-Pres. American Econ. Asscn, Pres. 1996–97; Fellow, American Acad. of Arts and Sciences, Econometric Soc.; mem. NAS; Dr hc (Hacettepe Univ., Ankara) 1990; Hon. DHumLitt (Georgetown) 1993; Hon. DEcons (Monash Univ., Australia) 1995; Robertson Prize, Nat. Acad. of Science 1984, Bernhard-Harms Prize, Kiel Inst. 1990; Kenan Enterprise Award, Kenan Charitable Trust 1990, Frank E. Seidman Distinguished Award in Political Economy 1993. *Publications include:* Foreign Trade Regimes and Economic Development: Turkey 1974, The Benefits and Costs of Import Substitution in India: A Microeconomic Study 1975, Trade and Development in Korea (co-ed.) 1975, Growth, Distortions and Patterns of Trade Among Many Countries 1977, The Developmental Role of the Foreign Sector and Aid: Korea 1979, Trade and Employment in Developing Countries (co-ed.) 1981, Exchange Rate Determination 1983, The Political Economy of International Trade (co-ed.) 1989, Aid and Development (jtly) 1989, Perspectives on Trade and Development 1990, Political Economy of Policy Reform in Developing Countries 1993, American Trade Policy 1995, The WTO as an International Institution (ed.) 1998. *Address:* IMF, 700 19th Street, NW, Washington, DC 20431 (Office); Department of Economics, Stanford University, Stanford, CA 94305-6072; 41 Linaria Way, Portola Valley, CA 94028, USA (Home). *Telephone:* (202) 623-7300 (Office). *Fax:* (202) 623-6220 (Office). *Website:* www.imf.org.

KRUEGER, Hans-Joachim, DrIng, MBA; German business executive; b. 27 Feb. 1938, Berlin; mem. Exec. Bd Krupp Hoesch Stahl AG –1994; Chair. Eko Stahl GmbH 1994–

KRÜGER, Hardy; German actor and writer; b. 12 April 1928, Berlin; s. of Max and Auguste (née Meier) Krüger; m. 1st Renate Damrow; one d.; m. 2nd Francesca Marazzi; one s. one d.; m. 3rd Anita Park 1978; German repertory theatre 1945–56, entered films in 1943; several awards and prizes. *Films include:* Der Rest ist Schweigen 1959, Blind Date 1959, Taxi pour Tobrouk 1961, Hatari 1961, Les Dimanches de Ville d'Avray 1962, Les Quatre Verités 1962, Le Gros Coup 1963, Le Chant du Monde 1964, Flight of the Phoenix 1965, The Defector 1966, La Grande Sauterelle 1966, The Battle of Neretva 1968, The Secret of Santa Vittoria 1969, Death of A Stranger 1972, Le Solitaire 1973, Barry Lyndon 1974, Paper Tiger 1974, Potato Fritz (Best Actor Award, Cannes) 1975, A Bridge Too Far 1976, L'Autopsie d'un Monster 1976, The Wild Geese 1978. *Publications:* Ein Farm in Afrika 1970, Sawimbulu 1971, Wer stehend stirbt, lebt länger 1973, Der Schallmauer 1978, Die Frau der Griechen 1980, Junge Unrast 1983, Sibirienfahrt, Tagebuch einer Reise 1985, Frühstück mit Theodore 1990. *Address:* Maximilianstrasse 23, 80539 Munich, Germany.

KRÜGER, Manfred Paul, DPhil; German writer, professor and editor; b. 23 Feb. 1938, Köslin; s. of Paul Krüger and Hildegard Krüger; m. Christine Petersen 1962; three s. four d.; ed Oberrealschule Ansbach, Heidelberg Univ., Tübingen Univ.; Asst Prof., Erlangen Univ. 1966–73; lecturer at Inst. for

Spiritual Science and Arts, Nuremberg 1972–; Co-Ed. of the weekly Goetheanum 1984–96. *Publications:* Gérard de Nerval 1966, Wandlungen des Tragischen 1973, Nora Ruhtenberg 1976, Bilder und Gegenbilder 1978, Wortspuren 1980, Denkbilder 1981, Literatur und Geschichte 1982, Mondland 1982, Nah ist er 1983, Meditation 1983, Rosenroman 1985, Meditation und Karma 1988, Anthroposophie und Kunst 1988, Ästhetik der Freiheit 1992, Ichgeburt 1996, Das Ich und seine Masken 1997. *Address:* Ermreuther Strasse 25, 90411 Nuremberg, Germany. *Telephone:* (911) 5298491.

KRUGMAN, Paul Robin, PhD; American professor of economics; b. 28 Feb. 1953, Albany, New York; s. of David Krugman and Anita Krugman; m. Robin Leslie Bergman 1983; ed Yale Univ., Massachusetts Inst. of Tech.; Asst Prof., Yale Univ. 1977–79; Asst Prof. MIT 1979–80, Assoc. Prof. 1980–82, Prof. 1983–2000; Sr Staff Economist, Council of Econ. Advisers 1982–83; Columnist, New York Times 1999–; Prof. of Econs and Int. Affairs, Princeton Univ. 2000–; John Bates Clark Medal 1991. *Publications:* Market Structure and Foreign Trade (with E. Helpman) 1985, International Economics, Theory and Policy (with M. Obsfeld) 1988, The Age of Diminished Expectations 1990, Rethinking International Trade 1990, Geography and Trade 1991, Currencies and Crises 1992, Peddling Prosperity 1994. *Leisure interest:* music. *Address:* Princeton University, Princeton, NJ 08544, USA.

KRUMMACHER, Hans-Henrik, DPhil; German academic; b. 24 Aug. 1931, Essen-Werden; m. Eva Wentscher 1956; one s. four d.; ed Humboldt Univ. Berlin, Univs. of Heidelberg and Tübingen; Archivist, Schiller-Nationalmuseum, Marbach a.N. 1956–58; Asst Prof., Univ. of Cologne 1958–67; Prof. of German Literature, Univ. of Mainz 1967–99, Prof. Emer. 1999–; mem. Akademie der Wissenschaften und der Literatur zu Mainz 1984; Corresp. mem. Österreichische Akad. der Wissenschaften 1993. *Publications:* Das 'als ob' in der Lyrik 1965, Der junge Gryphius und die Tradition 1976; Ed. Eduard Mörike, Werke und Briefe 1967–, Neudrucke deutscher Literaturwerke 1975–. *Address:* Am Mainzer Weg 10, 55127 Mainz-Drais, Germany. *Telephone:* (6131) 477550.

KRUPP, Georg; German banker; b. 15 July 1936; fmr Deputy mem. Bd of Man. Dirs. Deutsche Bank; Chair. Supervisory Bd WMF Aktiengesellschaft, Geislingen, Kunz Holding GmbH & Co. KG, Gschwend; mem. Supervisory Bd IVECO Magirus AG, Ulm, Strabag AG, Cologne, Gerling-Konzern Versicherungs-Beteiligungs AG, Cologne, Rheinmetall AG, Düsseldorf, BHS Tabletop AG, Selb, Bizerba GmbH & Co. KG, Balingen, IVECO N.V., Amstelveen, Netherlands. *Address:* Deutsche Bank, Taunusanlage 12, 60325 Frankfurt am Main, Germany.

KRYLOV, Sergey Borisovich; Russian diplomatist; b. 26 Oct. 1949, Moscow; m.; two d.; ed Moscow State Inst. of Int. Relations, Diplomatic Acad. of Ministry of Foreign Relations; diplomatic service 1971–; translator, attaché Embassy, Zaire 1971–76; attaché, Third, Second Sec. Second Africa Dept, USSR Ministry of Foreign Affairs 1976–79; First Sec., Counsellor to Minister 1979–86, Asst to Deputy Minister 1986–89; Minister-Counsellor USSR Embassy, Portugal 1990–92; Dir of Dept, Exec. Sec. Ministry of Foreign Affairs of Russia 1992–93; Deputy Minister of Foreign Affairs, Russia 1993–96; Perm. Rep. to UN and other int. orgs, Geneva 1997–98; Amb. to Germany 1998–. *Address:* Russische Botschaft, Unter den Linden 63–65, 10117 Berlin, Germany. *Telephone:* (30) 2291420. *Fax:* (30) 2299397.

KRZAKLEWSKI, Marian, D.ING.; Polish politician and trade union activist; b. 23 Aug. 1950, Kolbuszowa; m.; two s.; ed Silesian Tech. Univ., Gliwice 1975; scientific worker Polish Acad. of Sciences (PAN) and Silesian Tech. Univ., Gliwice 1976–90; mem. Solidarity Trade Union (independent, self-governing union) 1980–; Chair. of Solidarity 1991–; mem. ICFTU 1991–; Co-founder and Leader Solidarity Election Action (AWS) 1996; Deputy to Sejm (Parl.) 1997–2001; Chair. Solidarity Election Action Parl. Club 1997–2001; main negotiator and jt architect of parl. and govt coalition Solidarity Election Action–Freedom Union; Co-founder and Chair. Social Movt of Solidarity Election Action (RS AWS) 1997–2000 (merged with three other parties to form Solidarity Electoral Action of the Right 2000); Hon. Chair. Social Movt of Solidarity Election Action (RS AWS) 1999; Man of the Year, Zycie newspaper 1996, Kisiel Prize 1997, Platinum Laurel of Skills 1998. *Leisure interests:* family life, tourism, sport, arts, literature. *Address:* Komisja Krajowa NSZ2 Solidarnose, ul. Wały Piastowska 24, 80-855, Gdańsk, Poland. *Telephone:* (58) 308 44 72. *Fax:* (58) 305 90 44.

KU CHEN-FU; Chinese civil servant; Dir Straits Communication Foundations; Adviser to Pres.; mem. Kuomintang (KMT) Cen. Standing Cttee 1994–. *Address:* c/o Office of the President, Chieshou Hall, 122 Chungking South Road, Sec. 1, Taipei 100, Taiwan. *Telephone:* (2) 3113731. *Fax:* (2) 3140746.

KUBAISI, Tarrad Al-; Iraqi journalist; b. 1937, Hit; m. Widdad Al-Jourani 1962; one s. two d.; ed Coll. of Literature, Univ. of Baghdad; Ed.-in-Chief, Al-Mawsu'a Al-Sagira (small encyclopaedia) 1976–77; Ed.-in-Chief, Al-Aqlam (magazine) 1978–81; Al-Maurid (magazine) 1984–87, 1989–90; Man. and Ed.-in-Chief, Afaq Arabia (magazine) 1991; Press Office and Iraq Cultural Centre, London 1982–84; Press Attaché, Morocco 1988–89; later Chair. Cultural Affairs Office. *Publications:* Introductions in Sumerian Sufi-African Poetry 1971, The New Iraqi Poetry 1972, The Stony Forest Trees 1975, The Forest and Seasons 1979, Al-Munzalat Book (Vol. I) 1992, (Vol. II) 1995, The Artistic Construction in Epic Literature 1994. *Leisure interests:* reading, swimming. *Address:* c/o P.O. Box 4032, Adhamiya, Baghdad, Iraq. *Telephone:* 4436044 (Office); 5544746 (Home).

KUBILIUS, Andrius; Lithuanian politician; b. 8 Dec. 1956; m. Rosa Kabiliene; two s.; ed Vilnius Univ.; fmr lab. technician, Vilnius Univ., then engineer, then scientific research Asst; joined Sajūdis Movt 1988, later Exec. Sec. Sajūdis Council; mem. Seimas 1992–, First Deputy Chair. 1996–; Prime Minister of Lithuania 1999–2000; mem. Homeland Union. *Address:* Gedimino pr. 53, 2039 Vilnius, Lithuania (Office). *Telephone:* (2) 615-872 (Office). *Fax:* (2) 225-071 (Office). *E-mail:* kasp@lrvk.lt (Office). *Website:* www.lrvk.lt (Office).

KUBILIUS, Jonas, DSc; Lithuanian mathematician; b. 27 July 1921, Fermos, Jurbarkas Dist; s. of Petras Kubilius and Petronélé Giedraitytė; m. Valerija Pilypaitė 1950; one s. one d.; ed Vilnius and Leningrad Univs. and Math. Inst. Moscow; Lab. Asst, Asst Prof. Vilnius Univ. 1945–48, Assoc. Prof., Prof. 1951–, Rector 1958–91; mem. Lithuanian Acad. of Sciences 1962–, mem. Presidium 1962–92; People's Deputy of USSR 1989–91; mem. Seimas (Parl.) of Lithuania 1992–96; Pres. Lithuanian Soc. of Math.; several orders; Dr hc (Greifswald, Prague, Salzburg and Latvian Univs); State Prize in Science 1958, 1980. *Publications:* Probability Methods in the Theory of Numbers 1959, Real Analysis 1970, Probability and Statistics 1980, Limit Theorems 1998; book of essays 1996; several hundred papers. *Leisure interests:* music, history, bibliophilism. *Address:* Vilniaus Universitetas, Universiteto 3, 2734 Vilnius (Office); Kuosų 14, 2055 Vilnius, Lithuania (Home). *Telephone:* (2) 332-228 (Office). *E-mail:* jonas.kubilius@maf.vu.lt (Office).

KUBIŠ, Ján; Slovak diplomatist; b. 12 Nov. 1952, Bratislava; m.; one d.; ed High School Jura Hronca, Bratislava; Moscow State Inst. for Int. Affairs 1971–76; Ministry of Foreign Affairs, Prague 1976–80, Second Sec. 1985–87, Head of Section, Security and Arms Control 1987–88, Dir.-Gen., Euro-Atlantic Section 1991–92; Attaché, Third Sec., Czechoslovak Embassy, Addis Ababa 1980–85; First Sec., Counsellor, Czechoslovak Embassy, Moscow 1989–90, Deputy Head 1990–91; Chair. OSCE Cttee of Sr Officials 1992; Amb. of Czechoslovakia to UN, GATT and other int. orgs., Geneva 1992, Amb. of the Slovak Repub. 1993–94; Special Ministerial Envoy and Slovak Chief Negotiator on the Pact for Stability in Europe, Paris 1994; Dir Conflict Prevention Centre, OSCE, Vienna 1994–98, Sec. Gen. 1999–; Special Rep. of UN Sec. Gen. for Tajikistan, Head of UN Mission of Observers, Dushanbe 1998–99; OSCE Medal 1998. *Address:* Office of the Secretary General, Organization for Security and Co-operation in Europe, Kärntner Ring 5–7, 1010 Vienna, Austria (Office). *Telephone:* (514) 36-240 (Office). *Fax:* (514) 36-99 (Office). *E-mail:* pm-sg@osce.org (Office).

KUBO, Ryogo; Japanese physicist and professor; b. 15 Feb. 1920, Tokyo; s. of Tokuji Kubo and Sei Terada; m. Chizuko Kamijo 1946, one s. two d.; ed Tokyo Imperial Univ. and Tokyo Univ.; Asst Prof., Dept of Physics, Tokyo Univ. 1948–54, Prof. 1954–80, Dean, Faculty of Science 1968–71; Prof., Research Inst. of Fundamental Physics, Kyoto Univ. 1980–81; Prof. Faculty of Science and Tech., Keio Univ. 1981; mem. American Acad. of Arts and Sciences 1973–; Foreign Assoc. NAS 1974–; Pres. Nishina Memorial Foundation 1979–; mem. Japan Acad. 1982–; Hon. DSc (Chicago Univ.) 1978; Hon. Imperial Award, Japan Acad. 1969, Order of Culture, Japan 1973, Boltzmann Medal 1977. *Publications:* several articles in scientific periodicals. *Leisure interest:* reading. *Address:* 1-6-5 Komagome Toshimaku, Tokyo 170, Japan (Home). *Telephone:* (3) 941-8748 (Home).

KUČAN, Milan; Slovenian politician and lawyer; b. 14 Jan. 1941, Krizevci, Slovenia; ed Ljubljana Univ.; joined Fed. of Communists of Slovenia 1958; mem. Cen. Cttee Fed. of Communists of Slovenia; Chair. Comm. on Educational Problems of Cen. Cttee, Youth Union of Slovenia 1963–65; Chair. Cen. Cttee 1968–69; mem. Cen. Cttee Communist Union of Slovenia 1973–78, Chair. 1986–89; Sec. Republican Conf. of Socialist Union of Slovenia 1973–78; Chair. Slovenian Skupščina (Parl.) 1978–86; Pres. of Slovenia 1990–2002. *Address:* c/o Office of the President, 1000 Ljubljana, Erjavčeva 17, Slovenia (Office).

KUCHMA, Leonid Danylovych, CTechSc; Ukrainian politician and manager; b. 9 Aug. 1938, Chaikine, Chernihiv Region; m. Ludmyla Mykolayovna Kuchma; one d.; ed Dnipropetrovsk Nat. Univ.; mem. CPSU 1960–91; eng., constructor, Chief Constructor Research-Production Pivdenny Machine-Building Plant 1960–75, Sec. Party Cttee 1975–82, Deputy Dir-Gen. 1982–86, Dir-Gen. 1986–92; mem. Cen. Cttee CP Ukraine 1981–91; People's Deputy of Ukraine 1991–94; Prime Minister of Ukraine 1992–93 (resgnd); Chair. Ukrainian Union of Industrialists and Entrepreneurs 1993–94; Pres. of Ukraine 1994–99, Nov. 1999–; Lenin Prize 1981, State Prize 1993, Order of St Volodimir (Gold) 1999. *Address:* Administration of the President of Ukraine, Bankova Str. 11, 01220 Kiev, Ukraine (Office). *Telephone:* (44) 255-73-33 (Office). *Fax:* (44) 255-61-61 (Office). *E-mail:* moderator@admin.gov.ua (Office). *Website:* www.president.gov.ua (Office).

KUDELKA, James Alexander; Canadian ballet company artistic director, choreographer and dancer; b. 10 Sept. 1955, Newmarket, Ont.; s. of John Kudelka and Kathleen Mary Kudelka (née Kellington); ed Nat. Ballet School of Canada; Dancer, Nat. Ballet of Canada 1972–81, Artist in Residence 1992–96, Artistic Dir 1996–; Prin. Dancer, Grand Ballets Canadiens 1981–84, Resident Choreographer 1984–90; Isadora Duncan Dance Award 1988, Dora Mavor Moore Award (for Fifteen Heterosexual Duets) 1991–92, (for The Nutcracker) 1995–96, Jean A. Chalmers Choreographic Award 1993, numerous Canada Council Grants. *Major works:* (for Nat. Ballet of Canada) Washington Square 1977, Pastorale 1990, Musings 1991, The Miraculous Mandarin 1993, Spring Awakening 1994, The Actress 1994, The Nutcracker

1995, The Four Seasons 1997, Swan Lake 1999, The Firebird 2000; (for Grand Ballets Canadiens) In Paradisum 1983, Désir 1991; (for Toronto Dance Theatre) Fifteen Heterosexual Duets 1991; (for Birmingham Royal Ballet, UK) Le Baiser de la fée 1996; (for American Ballet Theater) Cruel World 1994, States of Grace 1995; (for San Francisco Ballet) The Comfort Zone 1989, The End 1992, Terra Firma 1995, Some Women and Men 1998; (for Joffrey Ballet) The Heart of the Matter 1986. *Address:* The National Ballet of Canada, 470 Queens Quay West, Toronto, Ont., M5V 3K4, Canada. *Telephone:* (416) 345-9686. *Fax:* (416) 345-8323.

KUDLOW, Lawrence A., BA; American economist and government official; b. 20 Aug. 1947, Englewood, NJ; s. of Irving Howard and Ruth (née Grodnick) Kudlow; m. 1st Susan Cullman 1981, one d.; m. 2nd Judith Pond 1987; ed Univ. of Rochester, Woodrow Wilson School of Public and Int. Affairs, Princeton Univ.; Economist, Fed. Reserve Bank of New York 1973–75; Chief Economist and Corporate Vice-Pres. Paine, Webber, Jackson and Curtis, New York 1975–79; Chief Economist and Partner, Bear, Stearns and Co., New York 1979–81; Asst Dir for Econ. Policy, Office of Man. and Budget, Washington, DC 1981–82, Assoc. Dir for Econs and Planning 1982–83; Pres. and CEO Lawrence Kudlow and Assocs., Washington DC 1983–84; Pres. and CEO Rodman and Renshaw Economics Inc. 1984–86; Chief Economist and Man. Dir Rodman and Renshaw Capital Group Inc. 1984–86; Chief Economist, Bear, Stearns and Co. 1986–94. *Leisure interests:* tennis, golf. *Address:* c/o Bear, Stearns and Co. Inc., 245 Park Avenue, New York, NY 10041, USA.

KUDRIN, Aleksey Leonidovich, CandEcon; Russian politician; b. 12 Oct. 1960, Dobele, Latvia; m.; one d.; ed Leningrad State Univ., Inst. of Econs USSR Acad. of Sciences; on staff Inst. of Social-Econ. Problems Acad. of Sciences 1983–90; Deputy Chair. Cttee on Econ. Reform Leningrad City Exec. Bd 1990–91; Chair. Cttee on Finance St Petersburg Mayor's Office 1992–94; First Deputy Mayor of St Petersburg, Head Dept of Finance Mayor's Office, St Petersburg 1994–96; Deputy Head of Admin., Head Controlling Dept at Russian Presidency 1996–97; First Deputy Minister of Finance Russian Fed. 1997–99, concurrently Deputy Man. BRD 1997–99; First Deputy Chair. Unified Power Grids of Russia (state co.) 1999–2000; Deputy Prime Minister, Minister of Finance 2000–. *Leisure interests:* tennis, swimming. *Address:* House of Government, Council of Ministers, Krasnopresnenskaya nab. 2, 103274, Moscow (Office); Ministry of Finance, Ilyinka str. 9, 103097 Moscow, Russia (Office). *Telephone:* (095) 205-46-46 (Office).

KUDROW, Lisa, BSc; American actress; b. 30 July 1963, Encino, Calif.; m. Micheal Stern; one c.; ed Vassar Coll., Poughkeepsie, New York. *Television includes:* To the Moon Alice 1990, Mad About You 1992, Murder in High Places 1991, Bob 1992–, Friends 1994–, Armagedd'nsync 1999, Cheers, Coach, Flying Blind, Hope and Gloria. *Films include:* L.A. on $5 a Day 1989, Dance with Death 1991, The Unborn 1991, In the Heat of Passion 1992, The Crazysitter 1995, Mother 1996, Romy and Michelle's High School Reunion 1997, Clockwatchers 1997, The Opposite of Sex 1998, Hercules (voice) 1998, Analyze This 1999, Hanging Up 2000, Lucky Numbers 2000, Marci X 2001, All Over the Guy 2001, Dr. Dolittle 2 (voice) 2001, Analyze That 2002, Bark 2002. *Address:* POB 36849, Los Angeles, CA 90036-0849, USA (Office).

KUDRYAVTSEV, Vladimir Nikolaevich; Russian jurist; b. 10 April 1923, Moscow; m. Dodonova Yevgenia Nikolaevna 1945; two s.; ed Mil. Law. Acad.; on staff of Acad. 1950–56; teacher at Lenin Mil.-Political Acad. 1956–60; served in Soviet Army 1941–45; mem. CPSU 1945–91; on staff of Mil. Coll. of USSR Supreme Court 1960–63; Deputy Dir of All-Union Inst. for Crime Prevention 1963–69, Dir 1969–73; Dir of USSR Inst. of State and Law of Acad. of Sciences 1973–89, Hon. Dir 1989–; corresp. mem. of USSR (now Russian) Acad. of Sciences 1974–84, mem. 1984–, Vice-Pres. 1988–; Foreign mem. Bulgarian, Hungarian Acads. of Science; Vice-Pres. Int. Asscn of Democratic Lawyers 1984–90; People's Deputy of the USSR 1989–91; State Prize 1984. *Publications:* over 200 works on criminology and criminal law, including What Sort of State Are We Building? 1991, Social Deformations 1992, (ed.) The Manual of International Law (7 Vols) 1993–. *Leisure interests:* theatre, music, cinema, reading. *Address:* Russian Academy of Sciences, Leninski pr. 14, 17901 Moscow, Russia. *Telephone:* (095) 237-68-08. *Fax:* (095) 237-44-21.

KUFUOR, John Agyekum, MA; Ghanaian politician, lawyer and businessman; b. Ashanti; m. Theresa Kufuor; five c.; ed Prempeh Coll., Kumasi, Oxford Univ.; called to Bar, Lincoln's Inn 1961; Clerk of Kumasi City Council; Council Rep., Constituent Ass. 1968–69; MP; mem. of Progress Party (PP); a Deputy Foreign Minister; arrested after mil. coup and imprisoned for 15 months 1972–73; returned to law practice; presidential cand. New Patriotic Party (NPP) 1996; Pres. of Ghana 2001–. *Address:* Office of the President, P.O. Box 1627, Osu, Accra, Ghana (Office).

KUHLMANN, Kathleen Mary; American opera singer; b. 7 Dec. 1950, San Francisco; d. of Elvira L. and Hugo S. Kuhlmann; m. 1983 (divorced 1998); ed Mercy High School, San Francisco and Univ. of San Francisco; student Chicago Lyric Opera School 1976–79; Resident Mezzo-soprano, Cologne Opera 1980–82; freelance 1982–; int. débuts: Teatro alla Scala, Milan 1980, San Francisco Opera 1982, Royal Opera House, Covent Garden 1982, Teatro Regio Parma 1983, Glyndebourne Festival Opera 1983, Wiener Staatsoper 1983, Teatro Communale Pisa 1983, Chicago Lyric Opera 1984, Salzburger Festspiele 1985, Stuttgart Opera 1985, Hamburg State Opera 1985, Lausanne/Geneva 1986, Australian Opera 1986, Napoli 1987, Tel Aviv 1988, Capitôle de Toulouse 1988, Metropolitan Opera, New York 1989, Théâtre Châtelet, Paris 1989, Semperoper Dresden 1992, Bayerische Staatsoper,

Munich 1994, Staatsoper Unter den Linden, Berlin 1995, Deutsche Oper, Berlin 1995, Aix-en-Provence 1996, Opéra de Paris 1997, Opera di Roma 1998, Opéra de Bordeaux 1998; specializes in Rossini roles, also Monteverdi and Handel. *Address:* c/o IMG Paris (Vocal Division), 54 Avenue Marceau, 75008 Paris, France.

KUHN, Gustav, DPhil; Austrian conductor; b. 28 Aug. 1946, Salzburg; s. of Friedrich Kuhn and Hilde Kuhn; m. Andrea Kuhn 1971; one s. one d.; ed Acads. of Salzburg and Vienna and Univs. of Salzburg and Vienna; advanced conducting studies under Bruno Maderna and Herbert von Karajan; professional conductor in Istanbul (three years), Enschede (Netherlands), Dortmund (prin. conductor) and Vienna; début at Vienna State Opera (Elektra) 1977, Munich Nat. Theatre (Così fan tutte) 1978, Covent Garden, London 1979, Glyndebourne, Munich Opera Festival and Salzburg Festival 1980, Chicago (Fidelio) 1981, Paris Opéra 1982, La Scala, Milan 1984, Arena di Verona (Masked Ball) 1986, Rossini Opera Festival, Pesaro 1987; Gen. Music Dir in Berne, Bonn and Rome; production début in Trieste (Fliegender Holländer) 1986; other projects include Parsifal, Naples 1988, Salome, Rome 1988, Don Carlos (French version) and Don Carlo (Italian) for 250th anniversary Teatro Reggio, Turin 1990; Artistic Dir Macerata Festival, Italy (productions of Così fan tutte and Don Giovanni) 1990/91; Founder and Pres. Accademia di Montegal 1990, Tiroler Festspiele Erl festival, Austria 1997–; First Prize, Int. Conducting Contest of Austrian TV and Broadcasting Corpn (ORF) 1969; Lilly Lehmann Medal (Mozarteum Foundation); Max Reinhardt Medal (Salzburg); Senator of Honour Award 'Lorenzo il Magnifico' (Florence) 1988. *Publication:* Aus Liebe zur Musik 1993. *Leisure interest:* sailing. *Address:* Winkl 25, 6343 Erl, Austria (Office). *Telephone:* (5373) 8181.

KUHN, Michael, LLB; film company executive; ed Cambridge Univ.; solicitor Supreme Court 1974; lawyer Denton, Hall and Burgin, London; legal adviser Polygram UK, London 1974–78, Dir 1978–83; gen. counsel Polygram Int., London 1983–87, Sr Vice-Pres. 1987–93; Pres. Polygram Filmed Entertainment, Beverly Hills, Calif. 1991–93, Exec. Vice-Pres. Polygram Holding Inc., New York 1993–; mem. Man. Bd Polygram NV 1993–; Pres. and CEO Polygram Filmed Entertainment, Beverly Hills. *Address:* Polygram Filmed Entertainment, 9333 Wilshire Boulevard, Beverly Hills, CA 90210, USA (Office). *Website:* www.polygram.com (Office).

KÜHNE, Gunther Albert Hermann, DrIur, LLM; German professor of law; b. 25 Aug. 1939, Gelsenkirchen; s. of Friedrich and Gertrud Kühne (née Belgard); m. Elvira Schulz 1992; ed Univ. of Cologne and Columbia Univ., New York; part-time legal adviser to German mining cos 1963–68; Research Asst Bochum Univ. Law School 1967–70; Sr Govt official, Ministry of Econs, Bonn 1971–74; Sr official German del. OECD, Paris 1972–73; Sr Govt official, Ministry of Justice, Bonn 1974–78; Lecturer Private Law, Private Int. and Comparative Law, Bochum Univ. 1971–79; Prof. of Mining and Energy Law, Dir Inst. for German and Int. Mining and Energy Law, Tech. Univ. Clausthal 1978–; Visiting Prof. Bergakademie Freiberg 1992, Tel Aviv Univ. 1993–; Ordinary mem. Braunschweig Soc. of Sciences 1994; Hon. Prof. of Law, Univ. of Göttingen 1986–. *Publications:* numerous books and articles on aspects of law, including Die Parteiautonomie im internationalen Erbrecht 1973, IPR-Gesetz-Entwurf (Private Int. Law Reform Draft) 1980, Memorandum on the State and Reform of German International Family Law 1980, Wandel und Beharren im Bergrecht (jtly) 1992, Rechtsfragen der Aufsuchung und Gewinnung von in Steinkohleflözen beisitzendem Methangas 1994, Gegenwartsprobleme des Bergrechts (jtly) 1995, Wettbewerb, Bestandsschutz, Umweltschutz (jtly) 1997, Bestandsschutz alten Bergwerkseigentums unter besonderer Berücksichtigung des Art. 14 Grundgesetz 1998, Braunkohlenplanung und bergrechtliche Zulassungsverfahren 1999, Das deutsche Berg- und Energierecht auf dem Wege nach Europa (jtly) 2002, Das neue Energierecht in der Bewährung (co-ed.) 2002. *Address:* Arnold-Sommerfeld-Strasse 6, 38678 Clausthal-Zellerfeld, Germany. *Telephone:* (5323) 723025. *Fax:* (5323) 722507.

KÜHNL, Karel, DIur; Czech politician; b. 12 Sept. 1954, Prague; m.; one s. one d.; ed Charles Univ., Prague; freelance journalist in Australia 1978–87; ed. Radio Free Europe, Munich 1987–91; Chief Adviser to Premier; fmr Amb. to UK; MP for Freedom Union Party 1998–, Chair. 1999–2002; Minister for Industry and Trade 1998; Chair. of Freedom Union Club 1999–; mem. Coalition Freedom Union Party–DEU, KDU–ČSL, ODA (after merger of Freedom Union Party and DEU Dec. 2001). *Leisure interests:* cycling, tennis. *Address:* Parliament Buildings, Sněmovní 4, Prague 1, 118 26 Czech Republic (Office). *Telephone:* (2) 5717-1111 (Office). *Website:* www.psp.cz (Office); www.ikoalice.cz (Office).

KUHNT, Dietmar, PhD; German business executive; b. 16 Nov. 1937, Wrocław (Breslau); m. 1966; two c.; ed Univs. of Cologne and Freiburg; Perm. legal adviser, Rheinisch-Westfälisches Elektrizitätswerk AG 1968; mem. Bd Man. RWE Energie AG 1989, Chair. 1992–94; mem. Bd Man. RWE AG 1992–94, Chair. 1995–. *Address:* RWE AG, Opernplatz 1, 45128 Essen, Germany. *Telephone:* (201) 1200.

KUI FULIN, Gen.; Chinese army officer; b. Feb. 1938, Xinbin Co., Liaoning Prov.; joined CCP 1961; joined PLA Infantry School, Qiqihar 1956; served in combat units of Shenyang Mil. Region, successively promoted from platoon Commdr to div. chief-of-staff; studied PLA Mil. Acad. 1982; served as div. Commdr then corps chief-of-staff; Deputy Dir and Dir Operation Dept, PLA Gen. Staff HQ 1985, Asst to Chief of Gen. Staff 1992–95, Deputy Chief PLA

Gen. Staff 1995–; mem. 15th CCP Cen. Cttee 1997–; rank of Gen. 2000. *Address:* c/o Ministry of National Defence, Jingshanqian Jie, Beijing, People's Republic of China.

KUJAT, Gen. Harald; German army officer; b. 1 March 1942, Mielke; m. Sabine Kujat (née Becker); three c.; ed Kiel School, NATO Defence Coll.; Instructor in Non-commissioned Officer Training, Fed. Armed Forces, then Platoon Leader, Co. Exec. Officer and Personnel Officer 1959–72; with Fed. Ministry of Defence, positions included ADC to Minister 1972–75, Mil. Asst 1977–78, Armed Forces Staff Asst Br. Chief (Operational Doctrines, AF) 1978–80, Br. Chief (Nuclear and Global Arms Control) 1990–92, Deputy Chief of Staff (Mil. Police and Strategy) 1995, Dir Policy and Advisory Staff to Minister 1998–2000; 20th Gen. Staff Course (AF), Bundeswehr Command and Staff Coll. 1975–77; Section Chief (A3a), AF Support Command N 1977; Commdr Second Bn AF Training Regt 1985–88; Section Chief, Staff German Mil. Rep., NATO Mil. Cttee, Brussels 1988–90, Dir of Staff and Deputy Mil. Rep. 1992–95, Asst Dir Int. Mil. Staff (Plans and Policy) and Deputy Dir IMS, NATO 1996–98, Chair. NATO Mil. Cttee 2002–; Dir IFOR Co-ordination Centre (ICC), Supreme HQ Allied Powers in Europe (SHAPE), Belgium 1996; Chief of Staff, Fed. Armed Forces 2000–02; rank of Lt 1968, First Lt 1968, Capt. 1971, Maj. 1974, Lt-Col 1979, Col 1988, Brig.-Gen. 1992, Maj.-Gen. 1995, Lt-Gen. 1998, Gen. 2000; Gold Cross of Honour of the Bundeswehr, Cross of the Order of Merit of the FRG; Tidal Flood Memorial Medal 1962. *Leisure interests:* photography, horse riding. *Address:* International Military Staff, NATO Headquarters, Boulevard Leopold III, 1110 Brussels, Belgium (Office). *Telephone:* (322) 707-54-22 (Office). *Fax:* (322) 707-57-13 (Office). *Website:* www.nato.int/ims/home.htm (Office).

KUKAN, Eduard, LLD; Slovak politician and diplomatist; b. 26 Dec. 1939, Trnovec nad Váhom, W Slovakia; m.; one s. one d.; ed Moscow Inst. of Int. Relations, Charles Univ., Prague; joined Czechoslovakian Foreign Service 1964, mem. Africa Dept 1964–68, various posts at Embassy in Zambia 1968–73, mem. Secr. of Minister for Foreign Affairs 1973–77, Minister Counsellor, Embassy in USA 1977–81, Head Dept of Sub-Saharan Africa 1981–85, Amb. to Ethiopia 1985–88, Perm. Rep. of Czechoslovakia to UN, New York 1990–93, of Slovakia 1993–94; Deputy to Nat. Council of Slovak Repub. (Parl.) 1994–, Minister of Foreign Affairs March–Dec. 1994, mem. Foreign Relations Cttee 1994–; mem. Exec. Cttee Democratic Union of Slovakia 1994–, Chair. 1997–98; Vice-Chair. Slovak Democratic Coalition (SDK) 1998–; Minister of Foreign Affairs 1998–; UN Special Envoy for the Balkans 1999–2001; Vice-Chair. Slovak Democratic and Christian Union (SDKU) 2000–; Hon. LLD (Upsala Coll., NJ, USA) 1993. *Leisure interests:* tennis, theatre. *Address:* Ministry of Foreign Affairs, Hlboká cesta 2, 833 36 Bratislava, Slovakia. *Telephone:* (2) 5978-3001. *Fax:* (2) 5978-3009. *E-mail:* boris_gandel@foreign.gov.sk (Office). *Website:* www.foreign.gov.sk (Office).

KULAKOV, Anatoly Vasilyevich, DPhysMathSci; Russian scientist; b. 15 July 1938; m.; one s.; ed Leningrad Polytech. Inst.; researcher, Sr engineer., Deputy Dean, Leningrad Polytech. Inst. 1962–79; Scientific Sec., Deputy Chair., First Deputy Chair., Council on Science and Tech., USSR Council of Ministers 1979–90; Dir-Gen. Russian Industrialists and Entrepreneurs Union 1991–; Vice-Pres. Moscow Econ. Union 1997–; mem. Russian Bank of Reconstruction and Devt 1998–; Corresp. mem. USSR (now Russian) Acad. of Sciences 1984; main research in theory of electromagnetic interactions in systems of charged particles, plasma and solids. *Address:* Russian Academy of Sciences, Leninsky prosp. 32A, 117995 Moscow, Russia. *Telephone:* (095) 205-12-25 (Office).

KUŁAKOWSKI, Jan, DIur; Polish trade union leader and international official; b. 25 Aug. 1930, Myszków; s. of Konrad Kułakowski and Elodie Claessens; m. Zofia Kułakowska; three d.; ed Univ. of Leuven; left Poland for Belgium 1944; organized groups of young Polish workers in Belgium 1947–54; mem. Gen. Sec. Int. Fed. of Christian Trade Unions (IFCTU) 1954, Gen. Sec. European Org. of IFCTU 1962–74; Sec. European Trade Union Confed. 1974–76; Gen. Sec. World Confed. of Labour 1976–89; Amb. of Poland to the EU 1990–96; adviser to Polish Govt Plenipotentiary for European Integration and Foreign Assistance 1996; mem. Cttee for European Integration 1996; Sec. of State in the Chancellery of the Prime Minister 1998; Govt Plenipotentiary for Poland's negotiations on accession to the EU 1998–2001; Commdr's Cross with Star, Order of Polonia Restituta 1995, Cross, Grand Order of Leopold II (Belgium) 1999. *Address:* c/o Office of the Committee for European Integration, Al. Ujazdowskie 9, 00-918 Warsaw, Poland (Office).

KULCZYK, Jan, DJur; Polish business executive; b. 6 June 1950, Bydgoszcz; m.; two c.; ed Adam Mickiewicz Univ., Poznań, Acad. of Economy, Poznań; researcher Western Studies Inst., Polish Acad. of Sciences (PAN) 1974–; employee in family business Kulczyk Aussenhandelgesellschaft, Germany; Founder Interkulpol Co. and other cos. 1981–91, merged into Kulczyk Holding SA 1991, Pres. Supervisory Bd; also Pres. Supervisory Bd Telekomunikacja Polska SA, Towarzystwo Ubezpieczeń i Reasekuracji Warta SA, Autostrada Wielkopolska SA, Euro Agro Centrum SA, Kompania Piwowarska SA, Skoda Auto Polska SA; mem. Supervisory Bd Polenergia SA; Pres. Polish Council of Business 1995–97, Vice-Pres. 1997–; co-f. and Pres. Polish-German Chamber of Industry and Commerce 1995–98, Vice-Pres. 1998–2002, Pres. 2002–; Pres. Adam Mickiewicz Univ. Council, Poznań; mem. Nat. Museum Council, Church Commercial Council, Int. Govs. Council, Peres Centre for Peace 2000–; Order of Polonia Restituta, Order of Saint Stanisław, Order of Saint

Bridget, Golden Medal of Saint Paul Fathers; Kisiel Award. *Address:* Kulczyk Holding SA, ul. Krucza 24/26, 00-526 Warsaw, Poland (Office). *Telephone:* (22) 5223120 (Office).

KULHÁNEK, Vratislav, DipEng; Czech economist and engineer; b. 20 Nov. 1943, Plzeň; m. Marie Kulhánek 1944; two d.; ed Univs of Prague and Pardubice; Dir Motor Jirkov, České Budějovice 1991–92, Robert Bosch, České Budějovice; Chair. Bd Škoda Auto Mladá Boleslav 1998–; Pres. Asscn of Car Industry; Chair. ICC 2001–, CIOD; Prize of Czech–German Understanding, Germany 2000; Man. for the 21st Century 2000. *Leisure interests:* tennis, cars. *Address:* Škoda Auto A.S., Mladá Boleslav, 293 60 (Office); Srubec 346, 370 06 České Budějovice, Czech Republic (Home). *Telephone:* (326) 811-676 (Office); (38) 7200652 (Home). *Fax:* (326) 811-932 (Office). *E-mail:* vratislav.kulhanek@skoda-auto.cz (Office); kulhanek.cb@volny.cz (Home). *Website:* www.skoda-auto.cz (Office).

KULIEV, Avdy, CPhilSc; Turkmenistan politician; b. 1936, Ashkhabad; ed Turkmenistan State Univ., USSR Ministry of Foreign Affairs; researcher Inst. of Language and Literature Turkmenian Acad. of Sciences; mem. Inst. of Asian Peoples' Acad. of Sciences; Dir Russian language courses in Soviet Cultural Centre in Yemen 1960–71; diplomatic posts in USSR embassies in Arabic countries 1971–87, Acting Chargé d'Affaires Embassy in Qatar, Oman 1987–89, Counsellor Dept of Near East and North Africa USSR Ministry of Foreign Affairs 1989–90; Minister of Foreign Affairs of Turkmenistan 1990–92; fmr mem. Pres.'s Council; leader of opposition to Pres. Niyazov 1992–94; accused of subversive activity and declared enemy of the state by Pres. Niyazov; Pres. of Turkmenistan Fund; Publr of analytical bulletin Free Turkmenistan 1999–; lives in Prague and Moscow.

KULIK, Gennady Vasilyevich; Russian politician; b. 20 Jan. 1935, Zhekomskoye, Pskov region; m.; one s.; ed Leningrad State Univ.; researcher, Head of Dept, Siberian Div. of All-Union Inst. of Agricultural Econ. 1957–65; First Deputy Head, Novosibirsk Regional Dept of Agric. 1965; Deputy Head, Chief Dept of Planning and Econs, Ministry of Agric. RSFSR 1965–86; First Deputy Chair., RSFSR State Cttee of Agric. and Industry 1986–90; First Deputy Chair., RSFSR Council of Ministers, Minister of Agric. and Food 1990–91; USSR Peoples' Deputy 1990–92; adviser to Dir, Inex-Interexport (Moscow) 1993; mem. Exec. Bd Russian Agrarian Party, Deputy Chair. Russian Agrarian Union; mem. State Duma; Deputy Chair. Cttee on Budget, Taxes, Banks and Finance 1993–98; Deputy Chair. Govt of Russian Fed. 1998–99; mem. State Duma (Parl.) (Otechestvo-All Russia faction) 1999, mem. Cttee on Budget and Taxes; Merited Economist of Russia. *Address:* State Duma, Okhotny Ryad 1, 103265 Moscow, Russia. *Telephone:* (095) 292-62-23 (Office). *Fax:* (095) 292-69-66 (Office).

KULIKOV, Army Gen. Anatoly Sergeyevich, DEconSc; Russian politician and military officer; b. 4 Sept. 1946, Aigursky Apanasenkovsky, Stavropol Region; m.; two s. one d.; ed Vladikavkaz Mil. Command School, USSR Ministry of Internal Affairs, M. Frunze Mil. Acad., Mil. Acad. of Gen. Staff; served on Commdg posts from Commdr co. to highest posts Ministry of Internal Affairs of Russia 1966–92; Commdr of Internal Troops 1992–95; Head United Grouping of Fed. Troops in Chechen Repub. Jan.–July 1995; Minister of Internal Affairs of Russian Fed. 1995–98; Deputy Chair. of Russian Govt 1996–98; mem. Security Council of Russian Fed.1995–98; Chair. Cen. Council Ratniki Otechestva (Warriors of the Fatherland) Movt; Chair. Council on Econ. Security, Russian Acad. of Social Sciences; Sr Researcher, Inst. of Social and Political Studies (ISPIRAN), Acad. of Sciences 1998–; mem. State Duma (Parl.) 1999–, Chair. Subcttee. on Legislation Against Transnat. Crime and Terrorism 2000–; Chair. Bd World Anticriminal and Antiterrorism Forum –2001; Order for Services to the Fatherland (Third Degree), Order for Personal Courage, Order for Service to the Motherland in the Armed Forces of the USSR, 3rd Class, 'Golden Falcon' decoration. *Leisure interests:* hunting, fishing, shooting, woodworking. *Address:* 2/24 Bolshoy Rzhevsky Pereulok, 121069 Moscow (Office); Merzliakovsky per. 13, Apt. 59, 121069 Moscow (Home); ISPIRAN, Leninski prosp. 32A, 117334 Moscow, Russia. *Telephone:* (095) 202-15-65 (Office); (095) 290-46-28 (Office); (095) 290-15-66 (Office); (095) 239-68-00 (Home); (095) 938-19-10. *Fax:* (095) 202-15-65 (Office); (095) 290-46-28 (Office). *E-mail:* ratniki.ot@mtu-net.ru (Office); waaf@waaf.ru (Office). *Website:* www.waaf.ru (Office); www.ratnikeotechestva.ru (Home).

KULIKOV, Marshal Viktor Georgiyevich; Russian army officer (retd); b. 5 July 1921; ed Frunze Military Acad., Acad. of General Staff; joined Soviet Army 1938; Commdr of Platoon 1940, Chief of Staff tank battalion, Regt, brigade 1941–45; various command posts in tank detachments 1945–48; Frunze Mil. Acad. 1948–53; Commdr tank Regt, Chief of Staff tank div., Deputy Commdr of Army, Commdr of Army 1953–67; Commdr Kiev Mil. Area 1967–69; C-in-C Soviet Forces in Germany 1969–71; mem. CPSU 1942–; mem. Cen. Cttee of CPSU 1971–89; Chief of Gen. Staff and First Deputy Minister of Defence 1971–77; Marshal of the Soviet Union 1977; C-in-C of Armed Forces of Warsaw Pact 1977–89; Gen. Insp., Ministry of Defence Inspectorate 1989–91; State Mil. Adviser 1992; USSR People's Deputy 1989–91; mem. State Duma (Parl.) (Otechestvo-All Russia faction) 1999–, Chair. Cttee on War Veterans; Hero of the Soviet Union and other decorations. *Address:* State Duma, Okhotny Ryad 1, 103265 Moscow, Russia. *Telephone:* (095) 292-02-91. *Fax:* (095) 292-02-91.

KULIYEV, Eldar Gulam oglu; Azerbaijani diplomatist; b. 29 Aug. 1939, Baku; m.; two c.; ed Azerbaijan State Univ., Baku, Diplomatic Acad., Moscow; interpreter Project Aswan-Cairo, Egypt 1963–65; Second Sec., First Sec. Ministry of Foreign Affairs, Baku 1965–69; Vice-Consul, USSR Consulate, Aswan 1969–71, Consul 1971–73; First Sec. Soviet Embassy, Cairo 1973–76; Consul, USSR Consulate-Gen., Istanbul 1978–83; advanced studies at Diplomatic Acad., Moscow 1983–84; Counsellor Div. of Cultural Relations with Foreign Countries, Ministry of Foreign Affairs, Moscow 1983–85, Expert 1985–86; Expert Dept of Humanitarian and Cultural Relations, Ministry of Foreign Affairs, Moscow 1986–88; Minister-Counsellor USSR Embassy, Aden 1988–90; Deputy Consul-Gen. USSR Consulate-Gen., Aden 1990–91; Expert Legal Dept, Ministry of Foreign Affairs, Moscow 1991–92; Sr Counsellor Dept of Int. Orgs. and Global Affairs, Ministry of Foreign Affairs, Moscow; Sr Counsellor Analysis and Research Dept, Ministry of Foreign Affairs, Moscow 1993–94; Perm. Rep. to UN 1994–2001. *Address:* c/o Ministry of Foreign Affairs, Ghanjlar meydani 3, 370004 Baku, Azerbaijan.

KULKA, Konstanty Andrzej; Polish violinist; b. 5 March 1947, Gdańsk; m.; two d.; ed Higher State School of Music, Gdańsk; Prof. Acad. of Music, Warsaw 1994–; participant in 2 music competitions: Paganini Competition, Genoa 1964, Diploma and Special Prize; Music Competition, Munich 1966 (1st Prize); many gramophone, radio and TV recordings; soloist with Nat. Philharmonic Orchestra, Warsaw 1984–; Minister of Culture and Arts Prize 1969, 1973, Minister of Foreign Affairs Prize 1977, Pres. of Radio and TV Cttee Prize 1978, Prize Winner 33 Grand Prix du Disque Int. Sound Festival, Paris 1981; Gold Cross of Merit; Commdr's Cross, Order of Polonia Restituta. *Performances:* since 1967 has given c. 1,500 concerts all over the world and participates in many int. festivals including Lucerne, Prague, Bordeaux, Berlin, Granada, Barcelona, Brighton; concerts with Berlin Philharmonic Orchestra, Chicago Symphony Orchestra, Minneapolis Orchestra, London Symphony Orchestra, Konzertgebouw Amsterdam Orchestra, English Chamber Orchestra and others. *Leisure interests:* collecting gramophone records, bridge, collecting interesting kitchen recipes. *Address:* Filharmonia Narodowa, ul. Jasna 5, 00-950 Warsaw, Poland. *Telephone:* (605) 194753; (22) 5517203. *E-mail:* konstanty.kulka@wp.pl (Office).

KULONGOSKI, Ted; American state official and lawyer; b. 5 Nov. 1940, Mo.; m. Mary Kulongoski; three c.; enlisted in US Marine Corps; fmr truck driver and steelworker; f. law firm, Eugene; mem. House of Reps, Ore. 1974–78; mem. Senate, Ore. Legislature 1978–87, Insurance Commr 1987–92, Attorney-Gen. 1992–96; mem. Supreme Court, Ore. 1996–2001; Gov. of Ore. 2003–. *Address:* Office of the Governor, Capitol Building, Room 254, 99 Court Street, NE Salem, OR 97301, USA (Office).

KULUKUNDIS, Sir Eddie, Kt, OBE, FRSA; British business executive and theatre director; b. 20 April 1932; s. of late George Elias Kulukundis and of Eugenie Diacakis; m. Susan Hampshire (q.v.) 1981; ed Collegiate School, New York, Salisbury School, Conn. and Yale Univ.; mem. Baltic Exchange 1959–; mem. Lloyds 1964–95, mem. Council 1983–89; Dir Rethymnis & Kulukundis Ltd 1964–, London & Overseas Freighters 1980–85, 1989–; Chair. Knightsbridge Theatrical Productions Ltd 1970–; part-owner, Duke of York's Theatre, Ambassadors Theatre; Chair. Sports Aid Foundation 1988–93; mem. Council of Man. Royal Shakespeare Theatre, Royal Shakespeare Theatre Trust (Vice-Chair. 1983–); Gov. Raymond Mander and Joe Mitchenson Theatre Collection Ltd, Royal Shakespeare Theatre; Vice-Pres. Greenwich Theatre Ltd, Traverse Theatre Club.; Dir Hampstead Theatre Ltd; mem. Exec. Council, SWET. *London productions include:* (some jtly): Enemy 1969, The Happy Apple, Poor Horace, The Friends, How the Other Half Loves, Tea Party and the Basement (double bill), The Wild Duck 1970, After Haggerty, Hamlet, Charley's Aunt, Straight Up 1971, London Assurance, Journey's End 1972; Small Craft Warnings, A Private Matter, Dandy Dick 1973, The Waltz of the Toreadors, Life Class, Pygmalion, Play Mas, The Gentle Hook 1974, A Little Night Music, Entertaining Mr Sloane, The Gay Lord Quex, What the Butler Saw, Travesties, Lies, The Seagull, A Month in the Country, A Room with a View, Too True to be Good, The Bed Before Yesterday 1975, Dimetos, Banana Ridge, Wild Oats 1976, Candida, Man and Superman, Once a Catholic 1977, Privates on Parade, Gloo Joo 1978, Bent, Outside Edge, Last of the Red Hot Lovers 1979, Beecham, Born in the Gardens 1980, Tonight at 8.30, Steaming, Arms and the Man 1981, Steafel's Variations 1982, Messiah, Pack of Lies 1983, Of Mice and Men, The Secret Diary of Adrian Mole Aged 13³/₄ 1984, Camille 1985, The Cocktail Party 1986, Curtains 1987, Separation, South Pacific, Married Love, Over My Dead Body 1989, Never the Sinner 1990, The King and I, Carmen Jones 1991, Noel & Gertie, Slip of the Tongue, Shades, Annie Get Your Gun, Making it Better 1992, The Prime of Miss Jean Brodie 1994, Neville's Island 1994, The Killing of Sister George 1995. *New York productions include:* (jtly): How the Other Half Loves 1971, Sherlock Holmes, London Assurance 1974, Travesties 1975, The Merchant 1977, Players 1978, Once a Catholic 1979. *Address:* c/o Rethymnis & Kulukundis Ltd, 21 New Fetter Lane, London, EC4A 1JJ; c/o Knightsbridge Theatrical Productions Ltd, 21 New Fetter Lane, London, EC4A 1JJ, England. *Telephone:* (20) 7583-8687.

KUMA, Kengo; Japanese architect and university professor; b. 8 Aug. 1954, Kanagawa; s. of Hiroko Kuma and Toma Kuma; m.; one s.; ed Univ. of Tokyo; Visiting Scholar, Columbia Univ., USA 1985–86; f. Spatial Design Studio 1987; f. Kengo Kuma & Assocs. 1990; Visiting Prof. Keio Univ. 1998, Prof. 2001–; AIA Benedictus Award 1997, Architectural Inst. of Japan Award 1997, Int. Stone Architecture Award 2001. *Art Exhibitions:* Venice Biennale 1995, RIBA Gallery, London 2001. *Publications:* 10 Houses 1990, Introduction to Architecture – History and Ideology 1994, Catastrophe of Architectural

Desire 1994, Anti Object 2000. *Address:* Kengo Kuma and Associates, 2-12-12-9F, Minamiaoyama, Minato-ku, Tokyo 107-0062 (Office); 37-7-301 Yaraicho Shinjuku-ku, Tokyo 162-0805, Japan (Home). *Telephone:* (3) 3401-7721 (Office); (3) 3235-7784 (Home). *Fax:* (3) 3401-7778 (Office); (3) 3268-0928 (Home). *E-mail:* kuma@ba2.so-net.ne.jp (Office). *Website:* www02.so-net.ne.jp/~kuma (Office).

KUMAGAI, Hiroshi; Japanese politician; b. 25 June 1930, Shizuoka; m. Nobuko Kumagai; one s. one d.; ed Hitotsubashi Univ.; mem. House of Reps.; fmr Deputy Sec.-Gen. Japanese Renewal Party (Shinseito) (JRP), Democratic Party (DPJ) Oct. 1999–, currently Chair. Parl. Affairs Cttee; fmr mem. House of Councillors; Minister of Int. Trade and Industry 1993–94, Chief Cabinet Sec. May–June 1994. *Publications:* Reconstruction for Japan 1995, The Future of Japanese Politics 1981, New Centrism for Japan–Farewell to national rights politics 1999 (all in Japanese). *Leisure interests:* music (jazz etc), golf, reading (politics, economics, history, religion, etc). *Address:* Democratic Party of Japan, 1-11-1, Nagata-cho, Chiyoda-ku, Tokyo 100-0014 (Office); 227 Tomizuka-cho, Hamamatsu-city, Shizuoka 432, Japan (Home). *Telephone:* (3) 3595 9988 (Office). *E-mail:* democrat@smn.co.jp (Office). *Website:* www.dpj.or.jp/index-e.html/ (Office).

KUMALO, Dumisana Shadrack, MA; South African diplomatist and journalist; b. 16 Sept. 1947; m. (divorced); one s.; ed Univ. of South Africa, Indiana Univ., USA; reporter Golden City Post 1967–79; feature writer Drum magazine 1969–70; political reporter Sunday Times, Johannesburg 1970–76; Marketing Exec. Officer, Total Oil Co. 1976–77; went into exile 1977; Int. Educ. Program Co-ordinator, Phelps Stokes Fund, New York 1978–80; Projects Dir Africa Fund and the American Cttee on Africa 1980–97; Dir of U.S. Desk, Dept of Foreign Affairs 1997–99; Perm. Rep. to UN 1999–. *Address:* Permanent Mission of South Africa to the United Nations, 333 East 38th Street, 9th Floor, New York, NY 10016, USA (Office). *Telephone:* (212) 213-5583 (Office). *Fax:* (212) 692-2498 (Office). *E-mail:* southafrica@un.int (Office).

KUMARATUNGA, Chandrika Bandaranaike, PhD; Sri Lankan politician; b. 29 June 1945, Colombo; d. of late S.W.R.D. Bandaranaike (f. Sri Lanka Freedom Party (SLFP) and fmr Prime Minister 1956–59, assassinated 1959) and Sirima R.D. Bandaranaike (first elected woman Prime Minister in the world in 1960–65, 1970–77, 1994–2000, died 2000); m. Vijaya Kumaratunga 1978 (assassinated 1988); one s. one d.; ed St Bridget's Convent, Colombo, Univ. of Paris; mem. Exec. Cttee Women's League of SLFP 1974, Exec. Cttee and Working Cttee 1992, Cen. Cttee 1992, (Deputy Leader of SLFP); Chair., Man. Dir Dinakara Sinhala (daily newspaper) 1977–85; Vice-Pres. Sri Lanka Mahajana (People's) Party (SLMP) 1984, Pres. 1986; Leader SLMP and People's Alliance; Chief Minister, Minister of Law and Order, Finance and Planning, Educ., Employment and Cultural Affairs of the Western Prov. Council 1993–94; Prime Minister Aug.–Nov. 1994, also held posts of Minister of Finance and Planning, Ethnic Affairs and Nat. Integration, of Defence, of Buddha Sasana; Pres. of Sri Lanka Nov. 1994–; Additional Prin. Dir Land Reform Comm. 1972–75; Chair. Janawasa Comm. 1975–77; Expert Consultant, FAO 1977–80; Research Fellow, London Univ. 1988–91; Guest Univ. Lecturer, Bradford Univ., UK 1989, Jawaharlal Nehru Univ., India 1991. *Publications:* several research papers on land reform and food policies. *Leisure interests:* playing piano and guitar, tennis, swimming, Kandyan (nat.) dance, music, reading, art and sculpture, drama, cinema. *Address:* Presidential Secretariat, Republic Square, Colombo 1, Sri Lanka. *Telephone:* (1) 24801. *Website:* www.priu.gov.lk/execpres/presecretariat.html.

KUMBERNUSS, Astrid; German shot putter; b. 5 Feb. 1970, Grevesmuhlen; pnr. Dieter Kollark; one s.; gold medal, Olympic Games 1996, bronze medal, 2000; gold medal, World Championships 1995, 1997, 1999; gold medal, European Championships 1990, silver medal 1994; owns a sports shop in Neubrandenburg; Sportswoman of the Year 1997. *Leisure interests:* cinema. *Address:* Sportclub Neubrandenburg, Parkstraße 1, 17033 Neubrandenburg, Germany. *E-mail:* astrid-kumbernuss@scn.de (Office).

KUMIN, Maxine Winokur, MA; American writer and poet; b. 6 June 1925, Philadelphia; d. of Peter Winokur and Doll Simon; m. Victor M. Kumin 1946; one s. two d.; ed Radcliffe Coll; consultant in poetry, Library of Congress 1981–82; Fellow, Acad. of American Poets, Chancellor 1995–; Visiting Prof. MIT 1984, Univ. of Miami 1995, Pitzer Coll. 1996; McGee Prof. of Writing, Davidson Coll. 1997; Writer-in-Residence Fla Int. Univ. 1998; mem. Poetry Soc. of America, PEN America, Authors' Guild, Writers' Union; Pulitzer Prize for Poetry 1973, The Poets' Prize 1994, Aiken Taylor Poetry Prize 1995, Harvard Grad. School of Arts and Sciences Centennial Award 1996; Levinson Award, Poetry magazine 1987, American Acad. and Inst. of Arts Award 1989, Centennial Award, Harvard Grad. School of Arts & Sciences 1996. *Publications:* poetry: Halfway 1961, The Privilege 1965, The Nightmare Factory 1970, Up Country 1972, House, Bridge, Fountain, Gate 1975, The Retrieval System 1978, Our Ground Time Here Will Be Brief 1982, The Long Approach 1985, Nurture 1989, Looking for Luck 1992, Connecting the Dots 1996, Selected Poems 1960–1990 1997; novels: Through Dooms of Love 1965, The Passions of Uxport 1968, The Abduction 1971, The Designated Heir 1974; essays, short stories, children's books and poetry contribs. to nat. magazines. *Leisure interest:* breeding horses. *Address:* c/o Scott Waxman Agency Inc., 1650 Broadway, Suite 1011, New York, NY 10019, USA.

KUMMER, Wolfgang, DTech; Austrian professor of physics; b. 15 Oct. 1935, Krems; s. of Dr Friedrich Kummer and Maria Kummer; m. Dr Lore Pokorny 1960; ed Gymnasium Krems and Technical Univ. Vienna; Asst Tech. Univ. Vienna 1958–66; Dir Inst. of High Energy Physics, Austrian Acad. of Sciences 1966–71; Prof. of Theoretical Physics, Technical Univ. Vienna 1968–; Pres. CERN Council 1985–87; Chair. High Energy Particle Physics Bd, European Physical Soc. 1997–2000; Visiting Prof. Univ. of Philadelphia 1973, Princeton Univ. 1975, Brookhaven Nat. Lab. 1977, 1980 etc.; mem. Austrian Acad. of Sciences; Culture Award, Fed. Prov. of Lower Austria 1971, Innitzer Award 1981, E. Schrodinger Award (Austrian Acad. of Science) 1988. *Publications:* more than 160 scientific Publs on the theory of elementary particle physics and of gravity. *Leisure interests:* classical music, tennis, skiing. *Address:* Institut für Theoretische Physik, Technische Universität Wien, Wiedner Hauptstrasse 8-10, 1040 Vienna (Office); Liebhartstalstrasse 31, 1160 Vienna, Austria (Home). *Telephone:* (1) 58801/13620 (Office); (1) 9146790 (Home). *Fax:* (1) 58801/13699 (Office). *E-mail:* wkummer@tph.tuwien.ac.at (Office).

KUMP, Ernest Joseph, MA(Arch); American architect; b. 29 Dec. 1911, Bakersfield, Calif.; s. of Ernest J. Kump, Sr and Mary Petsche Kump; m. Josephine Miller Kump 1934; one s. one d.; ed Univ. of California (Berkeley) and Harvard Grad. School of Design; fmr Prof. of Architecture, Columbia Univ. and has lectured at numerous univs; founded own architectural firm 1934; Chair. Bd of Dirs Tekto Systems Research 1977–82; Sr Partner, KUMP, Architecture Research Assocs 1983; work has included college and univ. campuses, civic centres, performing arts centres and other public bldgs and new residential communities; consultant and panel or Cttee mem. for numerous orgs. including British Bldg Comm., Carnegie Foundation and US Govt; Consulting Architect to Ronald Reagan Pres. Library Foundation, Calif. 1987; mem. Task Force on Arts and Humanities 1981; mem. Berlin Akad. der Künste; Fellow American Inst. of Architects (Architectural Firm Award 1970), Life mem. RSA London; Hon. Fellow RIBA. *Publication:* A New Architecture for Man 1957. *Leisure interests:* inventing, philosophy, classical music, literature. *Address:* Villa Boecklin, Jupiterstrasse 15, 8032 Zürich, Switzerland.

KUNADZE, Georgy Fridrikhovich, CHisSc; Russian diplomatist and politologist; b. 21 Dec. 1948, Moscow; m.; one s.; ed Moscow Inst. of Oriental Languages; researcher Inst. of Oriental Studies USSR Acad. of Sciences 1971–83; diplomatic service 1983–, scientific attaché Embassy, Japan 1982–87, head of sector, Chief of Div. Inst. of World Econs and Int. Relations 1987–91; Deputy Minister of Foreign Affairs of Russia 1991–93; Amb. to Repub. of Korea 1993–96, Amb.-at-Large 1996–; Deputy Dir Inst. of USA and Canada, Russian Acad. of Sciences 1997–99; Chief Scientific Researcher Inst. of Int. Econ. and Int. Relations (IMEMO) 1999–. *Publications:* numerous articles. *Address:* IMEMO, Profsoyuznaya str. 23, 117859 Moscow, Russia. *Telephone:* (095) 128-81-09; (095) 128-25-18.

KÜNAST, Renate; German politician and lawyer; b. 15 Dec. 1955, Recklinghausen, North-Rhine/Westphalia; ed ed. FH Düsseldorf, JVA Berlin-Tegel Jura-Studium; social worker at penal inst. of Berlin-Tegel 1977–79; Co-Founder West Berlin Alternative List 1979; Parl. Leader Red-Green Coalition in Berlin; mem. Berlin Senate; Chair. Parl. Group Alliance 90/Greens –1993, then legal policy spokeswoman, Chair. Fed. Party Exec. 2000–; Fed. Minister for Consumer Protection, Food and Agric. 2001–. *Address:* Ministry of Consumer Protection, Food and Agriculture, Postfach 42, 10177 Berlin, Germany (Office). *Telephone:* (30) 20060. *Fax:* (30) 20064262. *E-mail:* renate.kuenast@gruene.de, internet@bml.bund.de (Office). *Website:* www.bml.de (Office).

KUNDERA, Milan; Czech/French writer; b. 1 April 1929, Brno; s. of Ludvik Kundera and Milada Kunderová-Janosikova; m. Věra Hrabánková 1967; ed Film Faculty, Acad. of Music and Dramatic Arts, Prague; Asst, later Asst Prof., Film Faculty, Acad. of Music and Dramatic Arts, Prague 1958–69; Prof., Univ. of Rennes 1975–80; Prof. Ecole des hautes études en sciences sociales, Paris 1980–; mem. Union of Czechoslovak Writers 1963–69; mem. Editorial Bd Literární noviny 1963–67, 1968; Union of Czechoslovak Writers' Prize (for The Joke) 1968, Czechoslovak Writers' Publishing House Prize (for Laughable Loves) 1969, Prix Médicis (for Life is Elsewhere) 1973, Premio letterario Mondello (for The Farewell Party) 1978, Commonwealth Award (for all his work) 1981, Prix Europa-Littérature 1982, Los Angeles Times Prize (for Unbearable Lightness of Being) 1984, Jerusalem Prize (for all his work) 1985, Nelly Sachs Preis (for all his work) 1987, Österreichische Staatspreis für Europäische Literatur 1988, The Independent (newspaper) Prize, London 1991, Aujourd'hui Prize (France) 1993, Medal of Merit (Czech Repub.) 1995, J. G. Herder Prize (Austria) 2000, Grand Prize, Acad. of France 2001. *Publications:* Drama: Jacques et son maître 1971–81; Short stories: Laughable Loves 1970; Novels: The Joke 1967, Life is Elsewhere 1973, La Valse aux adieux (The Farewell Waltz) 1976, Livre du rire et de l'oubli (The Book of Laughter and Forgetting) 1979, The Unbearable Lightness of Being 1984, The Art of the Novel 1987, Immortality 1990, Les Testaments trahis (Testaments Betrayed: An Essay in Nine Parts) 1993, Slowness 1995, L'Identità (Identity) 1997, La Ignorancia (Ignorance 2002) 2000. *Address:* c/o Gallimard, 5 rue Sébastien-Bottin, 75007 Paris, France.

KUNENE, Mazisi, MA; South African poet, political activist and lecturer; m. Mabowe Mathabo Kunene; four c.; ed Natal Univ., London Univ.; European and U.S. African Nat. Congress (ANC) Rep. 1959; co-f. Int. Anti-Apartheid Movt; lecturer Stanford Univ., Univ. of Calif., LA; named Africa's Poet

Laureate 1993. *Publications include:* Zulu Poems 1970, Emperor Shaka the Great (16,400 verses) 1979, Anthem of the Decades 1981, The Ancestor and the Sacred Mountain 1982.

KUNERT, Günter; German author; b. 6 March 1929, Berlin; s. of Adolf Kunert and Edith Warschauer; m. Marianne Todten 1951; Visiting Assoc. Prof. Univ. of Tex. (Austin) 1972; Writer-in-Residence Univ. of Warwick 1975; mem. Akad. der Künste, W Berlin, Akad. für Sprache und Dichtung, Darmstadt; Pres. Literaturgezellschaft, Schleswig-Holstein 1987–; Dr hc (Allegheny Coll., Penn.) 1988; Heinrich Mann Prize, Akad. der Künste (E Berlin) 1962, Becher Prize for Poetry 1973, Heinrich Heine Prize (City of Düsseldorf) 1985, Hölderlin Prize 1991, E.R. Curtius Prize 1991, Georg-Trakl-Preis (Austria), Erwachsenespiele (autobiog.), Bundesverdienstkreuz (First Class), etc. *Film:* Abschied and others. *Play:* The Time Machine (based on the novel by H. G. Wells). *TV screenplays include:* King Arthur 1990, An Obituary of the Wall 1991, Endstation: Harembar 1991 and 13 others. *Radio:* 10 radio plays. *Publications:* 55 volumes of poetry, prose, satire, essays, novels, short stories and lectures. *Leisure interests:* travel, collecting tin toys. *Address:* Schulstrasse 7, 25560 Kaisborstel, Germany. *Telephone:* (4892) 1414. *Fax:* (4892) 8403.

KÜNG, Hans, DTheol; Swiss theologian and academic; b. 19 March 1928, Sursee, Lucerne; ed Gregorian Univ., Rome, Inst. Catholique and Sorbonne, Paris; ordained priest 1954; mem. practical ministry, Lucerne Cathedral 1957–59; Scientific Asst for Dogmatic Catholic Theol., Univ. of Münster Westfalen 1959–60; Prof. Fundamental Theology, Univ. of Tübingen 1960–63; Prof. of Dogmatic and Ecumenical Theology and Dir, Inst. Ecumenical Research 1963–80, Prof. of Ecumenical Theology, Dir Inst. of Ecumenical Research (under direct responsibility of Pres. and Senate Univ. of Tübingen) 1980–96, Prof. Emer. 1996–; Guest Prof., Univ. of Chicago 1981, of Mich. 1983, of Toronto 1985, of Rice Univ., Houston 1987; numerous guest lectures at univs. worldwide; mem. PEN; Pres. Foundation Global Ethic, Germany 1995–, Switzerland 1997–; Co-Pres. World Conf. on Religion and Peace, New York; Founding mem. Int. Review of Theology, Concilium; Hon. DD (Univ. of Wales) 1998, numerous hon. degrees; Oskar Pfister Award, American Psychiatric Asscn 1986, Karl Barth Prize, Evangelische Kirche der Union, Berlin 1992, Hirt Prize, Zürich 1993, Silver Medal, Univ. of Tübingen 1996, Theodor Heuss Prize, Stuttgart 1998, Bundesverdienstkreuz (First Class), Göttingen Peace Award 2002. *Publications:* The Council: Reform and Reunion 1961, That the World May Believe 1963, The Council in Action 1963, Justification: The Doctrine of Karl Barth and a Catholic Reflection 1964, (with new introductory chapter and response of Karl Barth) 1981, Structures of the Church 1964, (with new preface) 1982, Freedom Today 1966, The Church 1967, Truthfulness 1968, Menschwerdung Gottes 1970, Infallible?–An Inquiry 1971, Why Priests? 1972, Fehlbar?–Eine Bilanz 1973, On being a Christian 1976, Signposts for the Future 1978, The Christian Challenge 1979, Freud and the Problem of God 1979, Does God Exist? 1980, The Church–Maintained in Truth 1980, Eternal Life? 1984, Christianity and the World Religions: Paths to Dialogue with Islam, Hinduism and Buddhism (with others) 1986, The Incarnation of God 1986, Church and Change: The Irish Experience 1986, Why I am still a Christian 1987, Theology for the Third Millennium: An Ecumenical View 1988, Christianity and Chinese Religions (with Julia Ching) 1989, Paradigm Change in Theology: A Symposium for the future 1989, Reforming the Church Today 1990, Global Responsibility: In Search of a New World Ethic 1991, Judaism 1992, Credo: The Apostles' Creed Explained for Today 1993, Great Christian Thinkers 1994, Christianity 1995, A Dignified Dying: a plea for personal responsibility (with Walter Jens) 1995, Yes to a Global Ethic (Ed.) 1996, A Global Ethic for Global Politics and Economics 1997, The Catholic Church: A Short History 2001; ed. Journal of Ecumenical Studies, Revue Internationale de Théologie Concilium, Theological Meditations, Ökumenische Theologie. *Leisure interests:* water sports, skiing, classical music. *Address:* 72076 Tübingen, Waldhäuserstrasse 23, Germany. *Telephone:* 62646. *Fax:* 610140.

KUNIN, Madeleine May, MA, MS; American politician and diplomatist; b. 28 Sept. 1933, Zürich, Switzerland; d. of Ferdinand May and Renee Bloch; m. Arthur S. Kunin 1959 (divorced 1995); three s. one d.; ed Univ. of Mass., Columbia Univ. and Univ. of Vermont; reporter, Burlington Free Press, Vermont 1957–58; Asst Producer, WCAX-TV, Burlington 1960–61; freelance writer and instructor in English, Trinity Coll. Burlington 1969–70; mem. Vermont House of Reps. 1973–78; Lt.-Gov. of Vermont 1979–82, Gov. 1985–91; Deputy Sec. of Educ. 1993–96; Fellow, Inst. of Politics, Kennedy School of Govt Harvard Univ. 1993–93; Amb. to Switzerland 1996–99; lecturer, Middlebury Coll., St Michael's Coll. 1984, now scholar in residence, Middlebury Coll.; Fellow, Bunting Inst., Radcliffe Coll., Cambridge, Mass. 1991–92; Democrat; several hon. degrees and other distinctions. *Publications:* The Big Green Book (with M. Stout) 1976, Living a Political Life 1994; articles in professional journals, magazines and newspapers. *Address:* Robert A. Jones House, Middlebury College, Middlebury, VT 05753 (Office); 60 Southwind Drive, Burlington, VT 05401, USA (Home). *E-mail:* mkunin@middlebury.edu (Office).

KUNITZ, Stanley J., MA; American writer and educator; b. 29 July 1905, Worcester, Mass.; s. of Solomon Z. Kunitz and Yetta Helen Jasspon; m. 1st Helen Pearce 1930; m. 2nd Eleanor Evans 1939; m. 3rd Elise Asher 1958; one d. from 2nd m.; ed Harvard Univ.; Ed. Wilson Library Bulletin 1928–42; service with U.S. Army, rising to rank of Staff Sergeant 1943–45; Prof. of Literature, Bennington Coll., Vt 1946–49; Dir of Seminar, Potsdam Summer

Workshop in Creative Arts 1949–53; Lecturer and Dir of Poetry Workshop, New School for Social Research, New York 1950–57; Dir Poetry Workshop, The Poetry Center, New York, 1958–62; Lecturer, Columbia Univ. 1963–66; Adjunct Prof. School of the Arts (Columbia) 1967–85; Founding mem., mem. Bd of Dirs. Fine Arts Work Center, Provincetown, Mass. 1968–; Sr Fellow in the Humanities (Princeton) 1978; Montgomery Fellow, Dartmouth Univ. 1991; Ed., Yale Series of Younger Poets, Yale Univ. Press 1969–77; Poetry Consultant of the Library of Congress 1974–76, Hon. Consultant in American Letters 1976–82; U.S. Poet Laureate 2000–; mem. American Acad. of Arts and Letters 1963, Nat. Inst. of Arts and Letters; Founding Pres. Poets House, New York 1985–90; Fellow, Yale Univ. 1969; Chancellor, Acad. of American Poets 1970–95; Hon. LittD (Clark Univ.) 1961, (Anna Maria College) 1977, (Worcester State Coll.) 1980, (St Mary's Coll., Md) 1994; Hon. D. Hum.Litt. (State Univ. of New York) 1987; awards include Garrison Medal for Poetry 1926, Blumenthal Prize 1941, Levinson Prize 1956, Harriet Monroe Award 1958, Pulitzer Prize for Poetry 1959, Brandeis Creative Arts Poetry Medal 1965, Fellowship Award, Acad. of American Poets 1968, Lenore Marshall Award for Poetry 1980, Bollingen Prize in Poetry 1987, designated New York State Poet, with Walt Whitman Citation of Merit 1987, Centennial Medal (Harvard Univ.) 1992, Nat. Medal of Arts 1993, Sr Fellowship Award, Nat. Endowment for the Arts 1984, named Walt Whitman Birthplace Poet 1989, Shelley Memorial Award 1995, Nat. Book Award 1995, Robert Frost Medal, Poetry Soc. of America 1998, Literary Arts Award, Nat. Council of Jewish Culture 2000. *Publications:* Intellectual Things 1930, Editions: Living Authors 1931, Authors Today and Yesterday 1933, Junior Book of Authors 1934, British Authors of the XIX Century 1936, American Authors 1600–1900 1938, XX Century Authors 1942, Passport to the War 1944, British Authors Before 1800 1952, XX Century Authors (First Supplement) 1955, Selected Poems 1958, Poems of John Keats 1964, European Authors 1000–1900 1967, The Testing-Tree (verse) 1971, Poems of Akhmatova (trans.) 1973, The Terrible Threshold (verse) 1974, Story under Full Sail (trans. of A. Voznesensky) 1974, The Coat Without a Seam (verse) 1974, A Kind of Order, a Kind of Folly 1975, Orchard Lamps (trans. of Ivan Drach) 1978, The Poems of Stanley Kunitz 1928–1978, 1979, The Wellfleet Whale and Companion Poems 1983, Next-to-Last Things: New Poems and Essays 1985, Ed. The Essential Blake 1987, Interviews and Encounters 1993, Passing Through: The Later Poems 1995, Ed. The Wild Card, Selected Poems Early and Late, of Karl Shapiro (with David Ignatow) 1998, The Collected Poems 2000. *Address:* 37 West 12th Street, New York, NY 10011, USA.

KUNITZSCH, Paul Horst Robert, DPhil; German professor of Arabic Studies (retd); b. 14 July 1930, Neu-Krüssow; ed Free Univ. of West Berlin; Lecturer in Arabic, Univ. of Göttingen 1956–57; taught German, Cairo 1957–60; lecturer, Goethe Inst., FRG 1960–63; Special Adviser, Radio Deutsche Welle, Cologne 1963–68; Research Fellow, Deutsche Forschungsgemeinschaft 1969–75; Lecturer in Arabic, Univ. of Munich 1975–77, Prof. of Arabic Studies 1977–95; mem. Bavarian Acad. of Sciences, Acad. Int. d'Histoire des Sciences, Paris; Corresp. mem. Acad. of Arabic Language, Cairo; Göttingen Acad. of Sciences Prize 1974. *Publications:* Arab. Sternnamen in Europa 1959, Der Almagest 1974, The Arabs and the Stars 1989; C. Ptolemäus, Der Sternkatalog (Ed.), 3 Vols 1986–91. *Address:* Davidstr. 17, 81927 Munich, Germany. *Telephone:* (89) 916280.

KUNTJORO-JAKTI, Dorodjatun, PhD; Indonesian politician and diplomatist; b. 1939, Rangkasbitung; ed Univ. of Indonesia and Univ. of California at Berkeley, USA; lecturer and fmr Dean of Econs, Univ. of Indonesia; Amb. to USA 2000–01; Co-ordinating Minister for the Economy, Finance and Industry 2001–. *Address:* Office of the Co-ordinating Minister for the Economy, Finance and Industry, Jalan Taman Suropati 2, Jakarta 10310, Indonesia.

KUNZE, Reiner; German author; b. 16 Aug. 1933, Oelsnitz/Erzgeb.; s. of Ernst Kunze and Martha Kunze (née Friedrich); m. Dr Elisabeth Mifka 1961; one s. one d.; ed Univ. of Leipzig; mem. Bavarian Acad. of Fine Arts, Acad. of Arts, West Berlin 1975–92, German Acad. for Languages and Literature, Darmstadt, Free Acad. of Arts Mannheim, Sächsische Akad. der Künste, Dresden; Hon. mem. Collegium Europaeum Jenense of Friedrich-Schiller-Universität Jena; Dr hc; numerous awards and prizes including Literary Prize of Bavarian Acad. of Fine Arts 1973, Georg Trakl Prize (Austria) 1977, Andreas Gryphius Prize 1977, Georg Büchner Prize 1977, Bavarian Film Prize 1979, Eichendorff Literature Prize 1984, Weilheimer Literaturpreis 1997, Europapreis für Poesie, Serbia 1998, Friedrich Hölderlin-Preis 1999; Hans Sahl Prize 2001; Bayerischer Verdienstorden 1988, Grosses Verdienstkreuz der BRD 1993; Bayerischer Maximiliansorden für Wissenschaft und Kunst 2001. *Publications:* Sensible Wege 1969, Der Löwe Leopold 1970, Zimmerlautstärke 1972, Brief mit blauem Siegel 1973, Die wunderbaren Jahre 1976, Auf eigene Hoffnung 1981, Eines jeden einziges Leben 1986, Das weisse Gedicht 1989, Deckname 'Lyrik' 1990, Wohin der Schlaf sich schlafen legt 1991, Mensch ohne Macht 1991, Am Sonnenhang 1993, Wo Freiheit ist... 1994, Steine und Lieder 1996, Der Dichter Jan Skácel 1996, Bindewort 'deutsch' 1997, Ein Tag auf dieser Erde 1998, Die Aura der Wörter 2002, Der Kuss der Koi 2002. *Address:* Am Sonnenhang 19, 94130 Obernzell, Germany.

KUO WAN-RONG; Chinese politician; ed Massachusetts Inst. of Tech.; fmrly Minister of Finance; mem. Kuomintang Cen. Standing Cttee 1994–. *Address:* c/o Ministry of Finance, 2 Ai Kuo West Road, Taipei, Taiwan.

KUO WEI-FAN, DR., M.ED.; Chinese politician and educationalist; b. 3 Sept. 1937, Tainan City; m. Mei-Ho L. Kuo 1969; one s. one d.; ed Provincial Taiwan Normal Univ. and Univ. of Paris; Assoc. Prof. Grad. Inst. of Educ., Nat. Taiwan Normal Univ. 1967–70, Prof. 1970–72, 1977–78, Dir 1978, Pres. Nat. Taiwan Normal Univ. 1978–84; Admin. Vice-Minister of Educ. 1972–77; Pres. Chinese Asscn of Special Educ. 1973–75, 1979–81, Chinese Asscn of Comparative Educ. 1981–82, 1993–; Minister of State 1984–88, 1993; Chair. Council of Cultural Planning and Devt 1988–93; Pres. Chinese Educ. Soc. 1985–87. *Leisure interests:* table tennis, tennis, music.

KUOK, Robert; Malaysian business executive; b. 6 Oct. 1923, Johore Bahru; m. twice; eight c.; ed Raffles Coll., Singapore; joined Mitsubishi, Johore Bahru 1941; worked for father's food distribution co. (supplying produce for Japanese POWs in British Malaya) 1945–48, f. (with other family mems.) Kuok Brothers co. 1948, moved business to Singapore and began sugar trade 1953, built first sugar refinery in Singapore, also trading in sugar futures, palm oil; built first of chain of Shangri-La hotels in Singapore early 1970s; acquired real estate in Malaysia, Singapore and China throughout the 1970s and 1980s; now Head Kerry Group (Hong Kong) with holdings in South-East Asia, People's Repub. of China, Australia and Canada; acquired holding in TV Broadcasts Ltd (Hong Kong) 1988, majority shareholding in Coca-Cola plant in China 1993, controlling share of South China Morning Post newspaper 1993 (Chair. South China Morning Post Publrs 1993–97); also owns significant shareholding in Citic Pacific, Chinese Govt's overseas conglomerate; est. several charitable foundations. *Address:* c/o Malayan Sugar Manufacturing Company, 18th Floor, Wisma Jerneh, 38 Jalan Sultan Ismail, 50250 Kuala Lumpur, Malaysia; c/o Kerry Group, 344 Bank of China Tower, 1st Garden Road, Hong Kong Special Administrative Region, People's Republic of China.

KURBI, Abu Bakr al-, BSc, MB, CH.B., FRCP; Yemeni politician and professor of medicine; b. 6 June 1942, Albiedha; three c.; ed Aden Coll. and Univs. of Edin. and London, UK; Dean Faculty of Science, San'a Univ. 1979–83, Faculty of Medicine 1982–87, Univ. Vice Rector 1982–93; Minister of Educ. 1993–94; mem. Consultative Council 1997–2001; Minister of Foreign Affairs 2001–; Chair. People's Charitable Soc. 1995–; has made several radio and TV programmes on educ., scientific research, non-governmental work, charity and medical topics; Yemen Unification Medal. *Publications:* over 40 publications on the biological effects of clinical chemistry, renal disease, gastrointestinal diseases and numerous papers on political and social issues. *Address:* Ministry of Foreign Affairs, San'a (Office); P.O. Box 11351, San'a, Yemen (Home). *Telephone:* (1) 276555 (Office). *Fax:* (1) 276613 (Office); (1) 402 (Home). *E-mail:* aqirbi@hotmail.com (Home).

KUREISHI, Hanif; British author; b. 1954, Bromley; three c.; ed King's Coll. London; worked as typist at Riverside Studios; writer-in-residence, Royal Court Theatre, London 1981; Chevalier des Arts et des Lettres 2002; Thames TV Playwright Award for first full-length play The Mother Country 1980, Evening Standard Best Film Award 1986 and New York Critics' Best Screenplay Award 1987 for My Beautiful Laundrette. *Stage plays include:* Birds of Passage (Hampstead), Outskirts (RSC), Borderline (Royal Court), adaptation of Brecht's Mother Courage (RSC), Sleep with Me (Nat. Theatre) 1999. *Screenplays:* My Beautiful Laundrette 1986, Sammy and Rosie Get Laid 1988, London Kills Me (also directed) 1991, My Son The Fanatic 1997, The Mother 2002. *TV film:* The Buddha of Suburbia (BBC) 1993. *Publications:* The Rainbow Sign (autobiography) 1986, The Buddha of Suburbia (novel) 1990, London Kills Me 1991, Eight Arms to Hold You (essay) 1991, The Black Album (novel) 1995, Love in a Blue Time (stories) 1997, My Son the Fanatic 1997, Intimacy (novel) 1998, Sleep with Me (play) 1998, Midnight All Day (stories) 1999, Gabriel's Gift (novel) 2001, Dreaming and Scheming (essays) 2002, The Body (novel) 2002; ed. (jtly) The Faber Book of Pop 1995; stories in Granta, Harpers (USA), London Review of Books and The Atlantic; regular contribs. to New Statesman and Society. *Leisure interests:* jazz, cricket. *Address:* c/o Rogers, Coleridge & White Ltd, 20 Powis Mews, London, W11 1JN, England.

KURIHARA, Harumi; Japanese business executive, cook, writer and broadcaster; b. Shimoda; m.; two s.; celebrity cook and homemaker; Head of publishing, design and retail business; author of several multi-million-selling cookbooks; designer of tableware, gardening tools and bedlinen; launched Harumi K range of luxury brands; owns Yutori no Kuukan restaurant, Tokyo. *Television:* numerous appearances on TV talk shows. *Address:* c/o Yutori no Kuukan, Sendagaya 3-16-5, Tokyo, Japan (Office). *Telephone:* (3) 5410-8845 (Office).

KŪRIS, Egidijus, DJur; Lithuanian judge and professor of law and international relations; b. 26 Oct. 1961, Vilnius; s. of Pranas Kūris and Vanda Kūrienė; m. Andronė Kūrienė; two s. one d.; ed Univ. of Vilnius, Moscow State Univ., Russia; Lecturer and Assoc. Prof., Faculty of Law, Univ. of Vilnius 1984–94, Assoc. Prof. then Prof., Inst. of Int. Relations and Political Science 1992–, Dir of Inst. 1992–99; Justice of Constitutional Court 1999–, Pres. 2002–. *Publications include:* Self-Government, Democracy and Law, (ed.) Lithuania's National Interest and Her Political System, (ed.) Democracy in Lithuania: Elite and Masses, (ed.) Lithuania and Her Neighbours, (ed.) Lithuanian Political Parties and Party System (Vol. 1-2), (ed.) Interest Groups, Power and Politics, (co-author) Lithuanian Constitutional Law. *Address:* Constitutional Court, Gedimino pr. 36, Vilnius 2600, Lithuania (Office). *Telephone:* (5) 2126398 (Office). *Fax:* (5) 2127975 (Office). *E-mail:* mailbox@lrkt.lt (Office). *Website:* www.lrkt.lt (Office).

KUROKAWA, Kisho, M.TECH.; Japanese architect; b. 8 April 1934, Aichi Prefecture; s. of Miki and Ineko Kurokawa; m. Ayako Wakao; one s. one d.; ed Kyoto and Tokyo Univs.; Pres. Kisho Kurokawa Architect & Assocs.; Chair. Urban Design Consultants Inc.; Adviser, Int. Design Conf. in Aspen, USA; Prin. Inst. of Social Eng; Adviser, Ministry of Construction, Prime Minister of Kazakhstan, municipal Govts. of Guangzhou and Shenzhen, People's Repub. of China; Analyst, Japan Broadcasting Corpn; mem. numerous Govt Cttees., Japan Inst. Architects, City Planning Inst. of Japan, Japan Architects' Asscn; Hon. mem. Union of Architects of Kazakhstan; Life Fellow, Royal Soc. of Arts; Hon. Fellow, AIA, RIBA; Hon. Prof., Univ. of Buenos Aires, Southeast Univ., People's Repub. of China; Visiting Prof. Tsinghua Univ., Beijing 1986; Academician, Japan Art Acad.; awarded The Madara, Bulgarian First Order 1979; Commdr Ordre de Lion de Finlande 1985; Gold Medal French Acad. of Architecture; Takamura Kotaro Design Prize and prizes in int. competitions in Peru, France, Fed. Repub. of Germany, Tanzania and Bulgaria, prize for conference city, Abu Dhabi, UAE 1976, for Univ. New Town, Al Ain, UAE; Chevalier de l'Ordre des Arts et Lettres, Ministry of Culture, France 1989, 1st Prize Osaka Pref. Govt HQ (Nat. Competition) 1989, Prize of Japan Art Acad. 1992; Grand Prix with Gold Medal for Hiroshima Museum at Sofia Biennale 1989 and numerous Japanese architectural awards. *Works include:* Nitto Food Co. 1963, Cen. Lodge in Nat. Childrens Land 1964, Hans Christian Andersen Memorial Lodge 1964, Sagae City Hall 1967, Odakyu Rest House 1969, Takara, Toshiba and Theme Pavilions, Expo 1970, Nakagin Capsule Tower 1972, Head Offices of Fukuoka Bank 1975, Sony Tower 1976, Sports Centre, Italy, Fujisawa New Town 1976, Ishikawa Cultural Centre 1977, Head Office, Japanese Red Cross Society 1977, Nat. Ethnology Museum 1977, Kumamoto Municipal Museum 1978, Daido Insurance Bldg, Tokyo 1978, Hotel Vitostia the New Otani, Sofia, Bulgaria 1979, Shoto Club, Tokyo 1980, Fukuoka Prefectural Governmental Headquarters 1981, Suginami Ward Cen. Library, Tokyo 1982, Saitama Pref. Museum of Modern Art 1982, Nat. Bunraku Theatre 1983, Kanagawa Citizens' Mutual Aid Asscn Bldg, Yokohama 1983, Wacoal Kojimachi Bldg, Tokyo, Roppongi Prince Hotel, Tokyo, Pavilions of IBM Japan, Toshiba, Mitsui, Foreign Reps., Electric Power 1984, Yasuda Fire Insurance Bldg, Automobile Mfrs.' Asscn at Tsukuba Int. Science Exposition 1985, Yoshiundo Bldg 1985, Koshi Kaikan Centre 1986, Nagoya City Art Museum 1987, Central Plaza 1 and 2, Brisbane 1988, Hiroshima City Museum of Contemporary Art 1988, Japanese-German Centre of Berlin 1988, Lotte World, Seoul 1989, Chinese-Japanese Youth Centre, Beijing 1990, Melbourne Centre, Australia 1991, Nara City Museum of Photography 1992, Pacific Tower, Paris La Défense 1992, Repub. Plaza, Singapore 1995, Kuala Lumpur Int. Airport, Malaysia 1998, New Wing, Van Gogh Museum 1999, Osaka Int. Convention Center, Japan 2000, Oita Stadium, Japan 2001. *Works in progress include:* Le Colisée, Nîmes, France, Osaka Pref. Govt HQ, Japan, Nat. Gallery, Japan, Planning New Capital, Kazakhstan, Pearl Riverside Area Concept Plan, Guangzhou, People's Repub. of China, Nat. Gallery, Tokyo. *Publications include:* Prefabricated House, Metabolism 1960 1960, Urban Design 1964, Action Architecture 1967, Homo-Movens 1969, Architectural Creation 1969, The Work of Kisho Kurokawa 1970, Creating Contemporary Architecture 1971, Conception of Metabolism, In the Realm of the Future 1972, The Archipelago of Information: The Future Japan 1972, Introduction to Urbanism 1973, Metabolism in Architecture, 1977, A Culture of Grays 1977, Concept of Space 1977, Concept of Cities 1977, Architecture and Design 1982, Thesis on Architecture 1982, A Cross Section of Japan 1983, Architecture of the Street 1983, Landscapes under the Road 1984, Prospective Dialogues for the 21st Century, Vols 1–3 1985, Philosophy of Symbiosis 1987, Rediscovering Japanese Space 1989, The Era of Nomad (Japanese) 1989, Intercultural Architecture 1991, Kisho Kurokawa–From Metabolism to Symbiosis 1992, The New Wave of Japanese Architecture 1993, Kuala Lumpur International Airport 1998, Millennium Kisho Kurokawa 2000. *Leisure interest:* photography. *Address:* Aoyama Bldg 11f., 1-2-3 Kita Aoyama, Minato-ku, Tokyo 107-0061, Japan. *Telephone:* (3) 3404-3481. *Fax:* (3) 3404-6222. *E-mail:* kurokawa@kisho.co.jp (Office).

KUROKAWA, Takeshi, BA; Japanese trade unionist; b. 1 April 1928, Gunma Pref.; one s. one d.; ed Chuo Univ.; Pres. Gen. Fed. of Pvt. Railway Workers' Union (Shitetsu Soren) 1980–88, Adviser 1988–; Vice-Pres. SOHYO (Gen. Council of Trade Unions of Japan) 1980–83, Pres. 1983–89, council became defunct following merger with RENGO to form Japan Trade Union (arfed. 1989). *Leisure interest:* reading. *Address:* 3-2-11 Kanda Surugadai, Chiyoda-ku, Tokyo, Japan. *Telephone:* (3) 251-0311.

KUROŃ, Jacek Jan, MA; Polish politician, historian and publicist; b. 3 March 1934, Lvov; m.; one s.; ed Warsaw Univ.; mem. Polish United Workers' Party (PZPR) March–Nov. 1953, 1956–64; mem. Chief Council of Polish Pathfinders' Union 1956; Assoc. workers' councils of Zerań and participant revival Movt at Warsaw Univ. 1956; teacher, Fine Arts Lycée, Warsaw 1957; Assoc. Na Przełaj (weekly) and Drużyna 1957–61; arrested 1964 and sentenced to three years' imprisonment for writing Open Letter to PZPR mems.; arrested March 1968 and sentenced to 3½ years imprisonment; co-f. illegal Cttee for Defence of Workers (KOR) 1976–81; lecturer, Scientific Courses Soc. 1978–89; mem. Solidarity Ind. Self-governing Trade Union 1980–91, adviser to Solidarity Interfactory Founding Cttee, Gdańsk, then to Nat. Understanding Comm. and Nat. Comm. of Solidarity Trade Union 1980–81; interned 1981–82, indicted on a charge of attempt of subverting a political system Sept. 1982, released under amnesty Aug. 1984; mem. Civic Cttee attached to Lech Wałęsa, Chair. of Solidarity Trade Union 1988–90; participant Round Table plenary debates, mem. group for political reforms Feb.–April 1989; Deputy to Sejm (Parl.) 1989–2001, Chair. Sejm Cttee for Nat. and Ethnic Minorities 1991–2001, Deputy Chair. Civic Parl. Caucus 1989–90, Democratic Union Parl. Caucus 1990–93, Freedom Union Parl. Caucus 1994–; Minister of Labour and Social Policy 1989–91, 1992–93; co-f. and mem. Democratic Union 1991–94, Freedom Union 1994–; Chair. SOS Foundation; Dr hc (Emory Univ., Atlanta) 1990; White Eagle Order 1998. *Publications:* Uwaga Zespół 1961, Polityka i odpowiedzialność (Politics and Responsibility) 1984, Zło, które czynię (The Evil I Do) 1984, Zdobyć milczącą większość (To Gain the Silent Majority) 1988, Wiara i wina (Faith and Fault, autobiography, part 1) 1990, Moja zupa (My Soup) 1991, Gwiezdny czas (Star Time) (autobiog., part 2) 1991.

KUROYANAGI, Tetsuko, BA; Japanese actress; b. 9 Aug. 1933, Tokyo; d. of Moritsuna Kuroyanagi and Cho Kuroyanagi; ed Tokyo Coll. of Music; theatrical training at Bungakuza Theatre, Tokyo and Mary Tarcai Studio, New York; TV debut with Japan Broadcasting Corpn (NHK) 1954; host, Tetsuko's Room (TV talk show), Asahi Nat. Broadcasting Co. 1976–; regular guest, Discover Wonders of the World (quiz show), Tokyo Broadcasting System 1987–; numerous stage appearances throughout Japan; founder and Pres. Totto Foundation (for training of deaf actors) 1981–; Councillor, World Wide Fund for Nature, Japan 1977–; UNICEF Goodwill Amb. 1984–; Dir Chihiro Iwasaki Art Museum of Picture Books 1995–; Minister of Foreign Affairs Award, etc. *Publications:* From New York With Love 1972, Totto-chan: The Little Girl at the Window 1981, Animal Theatre (photographic essay) 1983, Totto-channel 1984, My Friends 1986, Totto-chan's Children: A Goodwill Journey to the Children of the World. *Leisure interests:* travel, calligraphy, study of giant pandas. *Address:* Yoshida Naomi Office, No. 2 Tanizawa Building, 4th Floor, 3-2-11 Nishi-Azabu, Minato-ku, Tokyo 106-0031, Japan. *Telephone:* 3403-9296. *Fax:* 3403-5322.

KUROYEDOV, Adm. Vladimir Ivanovich; Russian naval officer; b. 5 Sept. 1944, Bamburovo, Primorsk Territory, Russia; m.; one s.; ed Pacific Higher S.O. Makarov Navy School, Navy Mil. Acad. of Gen. Staff; service in Pacific Ocean Fleet 1967–93; Head of Staff Pacific Fleet, Commdr 1996–97; First Deputy Commdr Baltic Fleet 1993–96; First Deputy Commdr Russian Navy 1997, Commdr Nov. 1997–; Corresp. mem. Russian Acad. of Rocket and Artillery; several decorations. *Publications:* numerous publications on mil. sciences and political problems. *Address:* General Staff of Russian Navy, Bolshoi Kozlovski per. 6, 103175 Moscow, Russia (Office). *Telephone:* (095) 204-38-82 (Office).

KURTÁG, György; Hungarian composer; b. 19 Feb. 1926, Lugos; ed Franz Liszt Music Acad., Budapest and in Paris; Prof. of Chamber Music, Franz Liszt Acad. of Music, Budapest 1967–86; Composer in residence Wissenschaftskolleg zu Berlin 1993–95, Wiener Konzerthaus, Vienna 1995–96; mem. Bayerische Akademie der Schönen Künste, Munich 1987, Akademie der Künste, Berlin 1987; Herder Prize, Hamburg 1993, Feltrinelli Prize, Accademia dei Lincei, Italy 1993, Austrian State Award for European Composers 1994, Denis de Rougemont Prize 1994; Officier des Arts et des Lettres. *Compositions include:* Viola Concerto 1954, String Quartet 1959, Wind Quintet 1959, The Sayings of Péter Bornemissza 1963–68, Hommage à Mihály András 1977, Bagatelles 1981, Scenes from a Novel 1981–82, Three Old Inscriptions 1967–86, Kafka-Fragmente 1985–87, Requiem for the Beloved 1982–87, Officium breve in memoriam Andreae Szervánszky 1988–89, Ligatura–Message to Frances-Marie 1989, Hommage à R. Sch. 1990, Transcriptions from Machaut to Bach 1974–91, Attila József Fragments 1981, Three in memoriam 1988–90, Games, two series, Beads 1994, Omaggio a Luigi Nono 1979, eight Choruses 1981–82, Songs of Despondency and Grief 1980–94, Inscriptions on a Grave in Cornwall 1994, Rückblick (Altes und Neues für vier Spieler, Hommage à Stockhausen) 1986, Three Songs to poems by János Pilinszky 1986, Mémoire de Laïka 1992, Curriculum Vitae 1992, Messages of the late Miss R. V. Troussova, Grabstein für Stephan, . . . quasi una fantasia . . ., Double Concerto, Samuel Beckett: What is the Word Stele. *Address:* Lihegő v.3, H-2621 Verőce; Liszt Ferenc tér 9.I.6, H-1061 Budapest, Hungary. *Telephone:* (1) 2735-0177; (91) 121-3994.

KURTZER, Daniel C., PhD; American diplomatist; ed Yeshiva Univ., Columbia Univ.; joined Foreign Service 1976; political officer, Bureau of Int. Organizational Affairs, Cairo and Tel Aviv Embassies; Deputy Dir, Office of Egyptian Affairs 1996; on Policy Planning Staff 1987; Deputy Asst Sec. for Near Eastern Affairs 1989; Prin. Deputy Asst Sec. for Intelligence and Research 1994, then Acting Asst Sec.; Amb. to Egypt 1997–2001, to Israel 2001–; Dir-Gen. of Foreign Service Award for Reporting. *Address:* American Embassy, P.O. Box 26180, 1 Ben Yahuda Street, Tel-Aviv, Israel (Office).

KUSAKABE, Etsuji; Japanese business executive; b. 31 Oct. 1923, Hyogo Pref.; s. of Yasutaro and Hisae Kusakabe; m. Masako Yoshikawa 1949; two s.; ed Kyoto Univ.; Dir The Furukawa Electric Co. Ltd 1972, Man. Dir 1975, Sr Man. Dir 1977, Vice-Pres. 1983–89, Chair. 1989–97. *Leisure interest:* golf. *Address:* c/o The Furukawa Electric Co. Ltd, 6-1, Marunouchi 2-chome, Chiyoda-ku, Tokyo 100, Japan.

KUSHAKOV, Andrei Anatolyevich; Russian diplomatist; b. 1952; ed Moscow State Inst. of Int. Relations; mem. staff Ministry of Foreign Affairs 1974–93; Adviser to Counsellor, Russian Embassy, South Africa 1993–97; Deputy Dir-Gen. Secr. of Ministry of Foreign Affairs, then Deputy Sec.-Gen. 1998–2000; Amb. to South Africa and Kingdom of Lesotho 2001–. *Address:*

Embassy of the Russian Federation, POB 6743, Pretoria 0001, South Africa (Office). *Telephone:* (12) 3631337 (Office); (12) 3631338 (Office). *E-mail:* ruspospr@mweb.co.za (Office).

KUSHNER, Aleksandr Semyonovich; Russian poet; b. 14 Sept. 1936, Leningrad; s. of Semyon Semyonovich Kushner and Asya Aleksandrovna Kushner; m. Elena Vsevolodovna Nevzglyadova 1981; one s.; ed Leningrad Pedagogical Inst.; lecturer in literature 1959–69. *Publications include:* First Impression 1962, Night Watch 1966, Omens 1969, Letter 1974, Direct Speech 1975, Voice 1978, Canvas 1981, The Tavrichesky Garden 1984, Daydreams 1986, Poems 1986 (Selected Poems), The Hedgerow 1988, A Night Melody 1991, Apollo in the Snow (selected essays on Russian literature of the nineteenth and twentieth centuries and personal memoirs) 1991, Apollo in the Snow (selected poems trans. into English) 1991, On the Gloomy Star (State Prize 1995) 1994, Selected Poetry 1997, The Fifth Element 1999; essays in literary journals. *Leisure interests:* reading, world painting. *Address:* Kaluzhsky pereulok No. 9, Apt 48, 193015 St Petersburg, Russia. *Telephone:* (812) 271-98-45.

KUSHNER, Eva, OC, PhD, FRSC; Canadian professor of French and comparative literature; b. 18 June 1929, Prague, Czechoslovakia; d. of late Josef Dubsky and Anna Dubsky-Cahill (née Kafka); m. Donn J. Kushner 1949; three s.; ed McGill Univ., Montreal; Prof. Carleton Univ. 1961–76; Prof. McGill Univ. 1976–87, Chair. French Dept 1976–80; Prof., Pres. Vic. Univ. 1987–94; Dir, Comparative Literature, Univ. of Toronto 1994–95; Vice-Pres. Int. Fed. for Modern Languages and Literatures 1987–93, Pres. 1996–99; Vice-Pres. RSC 1980–82; Visiting Prof. Princeton Univ. 2000; Mary Russell Jackman and Mary Coyne Rowell Prof., Victoria Univ. 2001; Hon. LitD (Acadia Univ.) 1988; Hon. DD (United Theological Coll., Montreal) 1992; Hon. DLitt (Univ. of St Michael's Coll.) 1993, (Univ. of Western Ont.) 1996; Dr hc (Szeged) 1997; Lifetime Achievement Award, Canadian Soc. for Renaissance Studies 2002. *Publications:* Patrice de la Tour du Pin 1961, Le Mythe d'Orphée dans la littérature française contemporaine 1961, Chants de Bohème 1963, Rina Lasnier 1967, Saint-Denys Garneau 1967, François Mauriac 1972, L'avènement de l'esprit nouveau 1400–80 (co-author) 1988, Théorie littéraire: problèmes et perspectives (co-author) 1989, Le problématique du sujet chez Montaigne (co-author) 1995, Histoire des poétiques (co-author) 1997, Crises et essors nouveaux 1560–1610 (co-author) 2000, Pontus de Tyard et son œuvre poétique 2001, The Living Prism: Itineraries in Comparative Literature 2001. *Leisure interests:* reading, swimming, travel, writing. *Address:* Victoria College, University of Toronto, 73 Queen's Park, Toronto, Ont., M5S 1K7 (Office); 63 Albany Avenue, Toronto, Ont. M5R 3C2, Canada (Home). *Telephone:* (416) 585-4592 (Office); (416) 538-0173 (Home). *Fax:* (416) 585-4459 (Office); (416) 538-8825 (Home). *E-mail:* eva.kushner@ utoronto.ca (Office); eva.kushner@utoronto.ca (Home).

KUSHNER, Robert Ellis, BA; American artist; b. 19 Aug. 1949, Pasadena, Calif.; s. of Joseph Kushner and Dorothy Browdy; m. Ellen Saltonstall 1978; two s. one d.; ed Univ. of Calif. San Diego; has participated in numerous group shows at Whitney Museum and Museum of Modern Art, New York etc.; Venice Biennale 1980, 1984; works represented in maj. permanent collections in USA, Tate Gallery, London etc. *Solo exhibitions include:* Holly Solomon Gallery, New York 1976, 1979, 1980, 1982, 1985, 1987, 1989, Michael Lord Gallery, Milwaukee 1988–90, 2000, Gallery Rudolf Swirner, Cologne 1982, 1986, Univ. of Colo Art Gallery, Boulder 1982, American Graffiti Gallery, Amsterdam 1982, Studio Marconi, Milan 1982, Castelli-Goodman-Solomon, East Hampton, New York, 1982, Whitney Museum 1985, ICA, Philadelphia 1987–88, J. B. Speed Art Museum, Louisville 1988, Aspen Art Museum, Colo 1988, Wichita Art Museum 1989, Staller Art Center, State Univ. of NY Stony Brook 1990, Irving Gallery, Palm Beach 1990, First Gallery, Moscow 1991, Sydney Art Museum 1992, Yoshiaki Inoue Gallery, Osaka 1992, 1994, 1996, David Floria Gallery, Aspen 1995, D. C. Moore Gallery, NY 1997, 1998, Hiroshima Prefectural Museum 1997, Gallery APA, Nagoya 1999, Takada Gallery, San Francisco 1999, Lizan-Tops Gallery, NY 1999, 2000, Brandta Klaedefabrik Odense, Denmark 2001. *Address:* D. C. Moore Gallery, 724 Fifth Avenue, New York, NY 10019, USA. *E-mail:* rzkushner@asan.com (Office).

KUSHNER, Tony; American playwright; b. New York; ed Columbia Univ., New York Univ.; Tony Award 1993, 1994, Critics' Circle Award, London Evening Standard Award, Pulitzer Prize for Angels in America (part one) 1993. *Publications:* Actors on Acting 1986, A Bright Room called Day 1990, Millennium Approaches (part one of Angels in America) 1992, Perestroika (part two) 1993, Slavs! 1994, Thinking about the Longstanding Problems of Virtue and Happiness 1995, Homebody/Kabul 2001. *Address:* c/o Joyce Ketay, The Joyce Ketay Agency, 1501 Broadway, Suite 1910, New York, NY 10036, USA.

KUSTURICA, Emir; Bosnia and Herzegovina film director; b. 24 Nov. 1954, Sarajevo; ed FAMU School, Prague; teacher Columbia Univ.; mem. rock and roll band No Smoking Orchestra 1986–; lives abroad. *Films:* Do You Remember Dolly Bell? (Golden Lion Award, Venice 1981), Time of the Gipsies (Best Dir, Cannes), When Father Was Away On Business (Palme d'Or, Cannes 1984), Arizona Dream (Special Jury Prize, Berlin 1993), Underground (Palme d'Or, Cannes 1995), White Cat Black Cat, La Veuve de Saint-Pierre 2000. *Albums;* (with No Smoking Orchestra) Greetings from Safari Land 1987, A Little Story of a Great Love 1989, Ja nisam odavle 1997, Unza Unza Time 1999. *E-mail:* marie-christine.malbert@libertysurf.fr (Office). *Website:* www.emirkusturica-nonsmoking.com (Office).

KUSUMAATMADJA, Mochtar, LLD; Indonesian politician; b. Feb. 1929, Jakarta; ed Univ. of Indonesia, Yale and Harvard Law Schools and Univ. of Chicago Law School; Minister of Justice 1974–77; Acting Foreign Minister 1977–78, then Minister of Foreign Affairs 1978–88, fmr Head of of UN Comm. responsible for the demarcation of the Iraq-Kuwait Border, resgnd 1992; Indonesian rep. at Law of the Sea Conference, Geneva and at Seabed Cttee sessions, New York; involvement in numerous int. orgs. *Address:* c/o Ministry of Foreign Affairs, Jalan Taman Pejambon 6, Jakarta, Indonesia.

KUSZNIEREWICZ, Mateusz; Polish yachtsman; b. 29 April 1975, Warsaw; s. of Zbigniew Kusznierewicz and Irena Kusznierewicz; ed Acad. of Physical Educ., Warsaw; Polish Youth Champion, OK-Dinghy Class 1989; European Champion, OK-Dinghy Class 1991; Olympic Champion, Finn Class 1996; World Champion, Finn Class 1998, 2000; European Champion, Finn Class 2000; Kt's Cross of Order of Polonia Restituta 1999; World Sailor of the Year (Int. Sailing Fed.) 1999. *Address:* No Limit Kusznierewicz Events, ul. Ostrobramska 75C, 04-175 Warsaw, Poland (Office). *Telephone:* (22) 6117272 (Office). *Fax:* (22) 6117273 (Office). *E-mail:* mkusznierewicz@akademia.org .pl (Office). *Website:* www.kusznierewicz.pl (Office).

KUTI, Femi Anikulapo; Nigerian musician; b. 1962, Lagos; s. of the late Fela Kuti; m. Funke; one s.; musician in his father's band, The Egypt 80, specializing in Afrobeat music; performed at the Hollywood Bowl (as substitute for his father) 1985; formed own group Positive Force 1987; signed to Motown 1995, to Barclay/Polygram 1997; numerous concerts, TV and radio appearances; est. New Shrine open-air nightclub 2000; current man. Wrasse Records; Kora Awards for Best Male Artist and Best West African Artist 1999, World Music Award for Best Selling African Artist 2000. *Albums include:* No Cause for Alarm? (with the Positive Force) 1989, M.Y.O.B. 1991, Femi Kuti 1995, Wonder Wonder 1995, Shoki Shoki 1998, Fight to Win 2001. *Publication:* AIDS in Africa (essay published by UNICEF in its Progress of Nations report) 2000. *Address:* c/o Wrasse Records, Wrasse House, The Drive, Tyrells Wood, Leatherhead, KT22 8QW, England. *Website:* www .wrasserecords.com.

KUTZ, Kazimierz; Polish film and theatrical director; b. 16 Feb. 1929, Szopienice nr. Katowice; m.; two s. two d.; ed Higher Film School, Łódź 1953; film and theatre dir 1959–; mem. Soc. of Authors (ZAIKS); Senator 1997–; Vice-Marshal of Senate 2001–; Dr hc (Univ. of Opole) 1997, State Prize (First Class) 1970, Golden Lion, Gdansk Film Festival for Paciorki jednego różańca 1981; Officer's Cross, Order of Polonia Restituta. *Films include:* Krzyż Walecznych 1959, Nikt nie woła 1960, Sól ziemi czarnej 1969, Perła w koronie 1970, Paciorki jednego różańca 1977, Linie 1975, Na straży swej stać będę 1983, Śmierć jak kromka chleba 1994, Zawrócony 1994, Pułkownik Kwiatkowski 1995. *Screenplays:* Sól ziemi czarnej, Perła koronie, Paciorki jednego różańca. *Plays:* Do piachu (Down to Sand), Kartoteka roznucona (The Card Index Scattered), Kartoteka (The Card Index), Na czworakach (On All Fours), Spaghetti i miecz (Spaghetti and the Sword), Damy i huzary (Ladies and Hussar) 2001. *Address:* ul. Marconich 5 m. 6, 02-954 Warsaw, Poland. *Telephone:* (22) 8589259.

KUWABARA, Takeo, BA; Japanese writer; b. 10 May 1904, Turuga; s. of Jitsuzo Kuwabara and Shin Uta; m. Tazu Tanaka 1933; one s. five d.; ed Kyoto Univ.; Lecturer Kyoto Univ. 1931–42; Asst Prof. Tohoku Univ. 1943–48; Prof. Kyoto Univ. 1948–68, Prof. Emer. 1968–; Dir Univ. Inst. of Humanistic Studies 1959–63; mem. Science Council of Japan 1951–71, Vice-Pres. 1960–71; Vice-Pres. Japan PEN Club 1974–75, 1981–85; mem. Japanese Acad. of Arts 1977; Man of Cultural Merits (Govt award) 1979. *Publications:* Fiction and Reality 1943, Reflections on Contemporary Japanese Culture 1947, Some Aspects of Contemporary French Literature 1949, Introduction to Literature 1950, Conquest of Mount Chogolisa 1959, Studies on J.-J. Rousseau 1951, Studies on the Encyclopédie 1954, Studies on the French Revolution 1959, Studies on Chomin Nakae 1966, European Civilization and Japan 1974, Selected Works (in 10 Vols) 1980-81. *Leisure interest:* mountaineering. *Address:* 421, Tonodan-Yabunosita, Kamikyo-ku, Kyoto, 602 Japan. *Telephone:* 231-0261.

KUWAIT, HH The Ruler of (see Sabah, Sheikh Jaber al-Ahmad as-).

KUWAIZ, Abdullah Ibrahim el, MA, MBA, PhD; Saudi Arabian banker, civil servant, politician and international official; b. 1939; two s. two d.; ed Pacific Lutheran Univ., USA, St Louis Univ., USA; Accountant, Pensions Dept 1959–67, Economist, Ministry of Finance and Nat. Economy 1967–81 (Adviser 1977–81); Exec. Dir Arab Monetary Fund, Abu Dhabi 1977–80; Co-Chair. Financial Co-operation Cttee, Euro-Arab Dialogue 1978–83; Asst Under-Sec. for Econ. Affairs 1981–87; Deputy Minister of Finance and Nat. Economy, Saudi Arabia 1987–; Dir-Gen. and Chair. of Bd Arab Monetary Fund, Abu Dhabi 1987–89; Chair. of Bd, Saudi-Kuwait Cement Co., Saudi Arabia 1991–93; Asst Sec.-Gen. for Econ. Affairs, Co-operation Council for the Arab States of the Gulf 1981–95; mem. of Bd and mem. Exec. Cttee, Gulf Int. Bank, Bahrain 1977–90; mem. of Bd Gulf Co-operation Council's Org. for Measures and Standards 1984–95, Oxford Energy Inst., Oxford, UK 1985–, Int. Maritime Bureau, London 1985–88, Econ. Forum, Cairo 1994–; Islamic Devt Bank, Jeddah 1997–, Arab Fund for Econ. Devt, Kuwait 1998–2000; Gen. Man. Gulf Int. Bank, Bahrain 1997–. *Publications:* numerous papers relating to banking, oil, finance and econ. Devt delivered at symposia in N America, Europe and the Middle East. *Address:* P.O. Box 10866, Riyadh 11462, Saudi Arabia (Office). *Telephone:* 4880882.

KUZMIN, Alexander Viktorovich; Russian architect; b. 12 July 1951, Moscow; s. of Victor Alexandrovich Kuzmin and Antonina Alexeevna Kuzmin; m. 1996; one s. one d.; ed Moscow Inst. of Architecture; researcher Research and Project Inst. of the Master Plan of Moscow, Dir 1987–; Deputy Head, Chief Moscow Dept of Architecture 1991, First Deputy Chair. Moscow Cttee of Architecture; elected Chief Architect of Moscow 1996, Chair. Architectural and City Planning Cttee., Moscow; mem. Russian Acad. of Architecture and Building Sciences 1998; chief architect of reconstruction of Moscow streets, cen. region of Moscow, building of Olympic village. *Leisure interest:* collecting old medals. *Address:* Moscow Committee of Architecture and City Planning, Triumphalnaya pl.1, 125047 Moscow, Russia (Office). *Telephone:* (095) 250-55-20 (Office). *Fax:* (095) 250-20-51 (Office).

KUZ'MUK, Col-Gen. Oleksander Ivanovich; Ukrainian military officer; b. 17 April 1954, Dyatilivka, Khmelnitsk Region, Ukraine; m.; two c.; ed Kharkov Guards' Higher Tank School, Moscow Mil. Acad. of Armoured Forces; Commdr tank platoon, Bn; deputy Commdr Regt, Group of Soviet Troops in Germany 1975–83; Commdg posts in Leningrad, Carpathian, Odessa Mil. commands 1983–95; Commdr Nat. Guards of Ukraine 1995–96; Minister of Defence 1996–2001. *Address:* c/o Ministry of Defence, Bankova str. 6, 252005 Kiev, Ukraine (Office).

KUZNETSOV, Anatoly Borisovich; Russian actor; b. 31 Dec. 1930, Moscow; s. of Boris Sergeevich Kuznetsov and Maria Davydovna Kuznetsova; ed Moscow Art Theatre School; mem. Union of Cinematographers, Union of Theatre Workers; People's Artist of Russia. *Films include:* Dangerous Routes 1954, A Guest from Kuban 1955, A Trip to Youth 1956, On War Roads 1958, Fortune 1959, Wait for the Letters 1960, My Friend Kolka 1961, Morning Trains 1963, Conscience 1965, Spring on Oder 1967, White Sun of the Desert 1969, Stolen Train 1971, Freedom 1971, Hot Snow 1972, The Single Road 1974, In the Zone of Particular Attention 1977, Incognito from Petersburg 1977, Kids Like Kids 1978, Second Spring 1979, His Holidays 1981, Copper Angel 1984, Battle for Moscow 1985, Without Sun 1987. *Address:* Glinishchevsky per. 5/7, Apt. 88, 103009 Moscow, Russia (Home). *Telephone:* (095) 200-58-47 (Home).

KUZNETSOV, Boris Avramovich; Russian barrister; b. 19 March 1944, Kirov; s. of Avram Mikhailovich Kuznetsov and Nina Aleksandrovna Khanova; m. 2nd Nadezhda Georgiyevna Chernaya; two c.; ed Moscow Juridical Acad., Research Inst. USSR Ministry of Internal Affairs; on staff Criminal Investigation Dept St Petersburg and Magadan Region 1962–82; mem. Magadan Regional Bd of Lawyers 1982–85, twice expelled for disagreement with party officials; Head of Lab. Inst. of Biology Problems of the N br. USSR Acad. of Sciences, Magadan 1985–89; adviser to mems Inter-regional people's deputy 1989–91; mem. St Petersburg Bd of Lawyers 1991–95; mem. Lawyers' Interrepub. Bd 1995–; Head Boris Kuznetsov and Partners Lawyer's Agency; Golden Sign for Defence of Russian-Speaking People and Intellectuals Outside Russia, 1998, Anatoli Koni's Medal 2001, Award Hanger from the Navy of the Russian Fed. *Leisure interests:* pre-Revolutionary juridical literature and literature on the navy, sailing models construction. *Address:* Boris Kuznetsov and Partners, Novy Arbat str. 19, Office 2205-2207, 103025 Moscow, Russia (Office); Frigate House, Koop 'Forest', Shoulgino Village, Moscow Region, Russia (Home). *Telephone:* (095) 203-43-40 (Office). *Fax:* (095) 203-44-71 (Office).

KUZNETSOV, Fedor Andreyevich; Russian chemist; b. 12 July 1932; m.; two c.; ed Leningrad State Univ.; army engineer 1955–58; researcher, head of lab., Deputy Dir, Inst. of Inorganic Chem., Siberian br. USSR (now Russian) Acad. of Sciences 1961–83, Dir 1983–; corresp. mem., USSR (now Russian) Acad. of Sciences 1984, mem. 1987–; main research in synthesis and studies of inorganic materials; Foreign mem. American Electro-Chemical Soc.; USSR State Prize 1981; N. Kurnakov Medal. *Address:* Institute of Inorganic Chemistry, Akademika Lavrentyev prosp. 3, 630090 Novosibirsk, Russia. *Telephone:* (3832) 135-59-50 (Office).

KUZNETSOV, Nikolai Aleksandrovich; Russian cybernetician; b. 9 March 1939; m.; two c.; ed Moscow Inst. of Physics and Tech.; Jr, Sr researcher, Deputy Dir Inst. of Problems of Man. 1965–88; Dir Gen. of Research Production Union Moskva 1988–89; Dir Inst. for Information Transmission Problems (IPPI) 1990–; Corresp. mem. USSR (now Russian) Acad. of Sciences 1987, mem. 1994; mem. IEEE; research in theory of automatic man. and informatics; USSR State Prize. *Publications include:* Management of Observations in Automatic Systems 1961, Synthesis of Algorithms at Variable Criterion of Optimality 1966, Methods of Study of Stability of Dissynchronized Pulse Systems 1991. *Leisure interests:* mountain skiing, singing. *Address:* Institute for Information Transmission Problems (IPPI), Russian Academy of Sciences, Bolshoi Karetny per. 19, 101447 Moscow, Russia. *Telephone:* (095) 209-42-25 (Office). *Fax:* (095) 209-05-79. *E-mail:* director@iitp.ru (Office).

KUZNETSOV, Nikolai Vasilyevich; Russian mathematician; b. 24 June 1939, Hachmas, Azerbaijan; s. of Vasilii Kuznetsov and Evdokia Gureutieva; m. Galina Pavlovna Kuznetsova 1975; two c.; ed Moscow Inst. of Physics and Tech.; Jr researcher Inst. of Math. USSR Acad. of Sciences 1965–69; Jr, Sr researcher Moscow V. Lenin Pedagogical Inst. 1969–70; head of div., head of Dept Cen. Research Inst. of Information and Tech.-Econ. Studies 1970–71; head of div. Research Inst. of Systems of Man. and Econs 1972–73; Sr researcher, head of lab. Khabarovsk Research Inst. of Complex Studies 1973–81; Deputy Dir Computer's Cen., Far E br. USSR Acad. of Sciences

1989–91; Deputy Dir Inst. of Applied Math. 1991–92; corresp. mem. USSR (now Russian) Acad. of Sciences 1987; research in spectral theory, theory of modular and automorphic functions in math. Physics. *Publications:* On Eigenfunctions of one Integral Equation 1970, Poincaré Series and Extended Lemer Hypothesis 1985; numerous articles in scientific journals. *Leisure interest:* chess. *Address:* Institute of Applied Mathematics, Far East Branch of Russian Academy of Sciences, Radio str. 7, 690041 Vladivostok, Russia (Office). *Telephone:* (4232) 31-19-07 (Vladivostok) (Office); (4212) 33-46-76 (Khabarovsk) (Office); (4212) 22-76-36 (Home).

KUZNETSOV, Oleg Leonidovich, DTech; Russian geophysicist; b. 1938; m.; two c.; ed Moscow S. Ordzhonikidze Inst. of Geological Research, Moscow State Univ.; researcher, Inst. of Oil, USSR (now Russian) Acad. of Sciences 1962–70; Head of lab., All-Union Inst. of Nuclear Geophysics and Geochemistry, USSR Ministry of Geology (now State Scientific Centre of All-Russian Inst. of Geosystems) 1970–79, Dir 1979–; Prof. Moscow State Univ. 1986–; Vice-Pres. Russian Acad. of Nat. Sciences 1990, Pres. 1994–; f. and Rector, Int. Univ. of Nature, Soc. and Man., Dubna 1994–; main research in geophysical processes, seismoacoustics, non-linear geophysics, geoinformatics and information tech.; mem. New York Acad. of Sciences 1994, Int. Acad. of Sciences on Nature and Soc. 1993, Int. Acad. of Higher Schooling 1995, Oriental Acad. of Oil and Gas 1994; Hon. mem. Hungarian Soc. of Geophysics, Euro-Asian Geophysical Soc.; USSR State Prize 1982, Prize of German Econ. Club 1996, A. Chizhevsky Prize 1997. *Publications:* over 280 scientific works including 11 monographs, 4 reference books, 67 inventions, over 60 patents. *Address:* Russian Academy of Natural Sciences, Varshavskoye shosse 8, 113105 Moscow, Russia. *Telephone:* (095) 954-53-50 (Office). *Fax:* (095) 958-37-11 (Office).

KVAMME, Floyd E., BS, M.S.E.; American computer scientist; ed Univ. of California at Berkeley and Syracuse Univ.; Founder mem. Nat. Semiconductor 1967, Gen. Man. Semiconductor Operations, Pres. Nat. Advanced Systems (subsidiary); Exec. Vice-Pres. of Sales and Marketing, Apple Computer 1982; partner Kleiner Perkins Caufield & Byers 1984–; Chair. Electronic Commerce Advisory Council for the State of Calif. 1998; currently Dir Office of Science and Tech. Policy, Washington, DC; Chair. Empower America; mem. Bds. Brio Tech., Gemfire, Harmonic, Nat. Semiconductor, Photon Dynamics, Power Integrations, Silicon Genesis, Markkula Center for Applied Ethics Advisory Bd, Santa Clara Univ., Nat. Venture Capital Asscn, Exec. Cttee of The Tech. Network; fmr mem. Finance Cttee, the Fong for Senate Campaign, High Tech. Advisory Cttee, Nat. Finance Cttee of the Bush for President Campaign. *Address:* Office of Science and Technology Policy, Eisenhower Executive Office Building, 17th Street and Pennsylvania Avenue, NW, Washington, DC 20502, USA (Office).

KVAPIL, Radoslav; Czech pianist; b. 15 March 1934, Brno; s. of Karel Kvapil and Marie Kvapilová; m. Eva Mašlaňová 1960 (died 1993); one s.; ed Gymnasium Dr. Kudely, Brno and Janáček Acad. of Musical Arts; first piano recital Brno 1954; 1st prize Janáček Competition 1958, Int. Competition, Czechoslovak Radio 1968; Prof. of Piano, Prague Conservatory 1963–73; concerts in countries throughout Europe, in USA and Japan 1963–; performed world premiere of Dvořák's Cypresses 1983; Dir South Bohemia Music Festival 1991–; Hon. Vice-Pres. Dvořák Soc., London; Pres. Yehudi Menuhin Soc., Prague 1990–, Dvořák Soc., Prague 1997–, Czech Soc. for Music and Arts 1990–; Chevalier des Arts et des Lettres 2002; Janáček Medal (Cultural Ministry). *Recordings include:* complete piano works of Dvořák and Martinů, complete piano and chamber music of Janáček, complete piano works of Jan Hugo Voříšek 1973–74, complete polka cycles of Smetana, Czech contemporary piano music, Piano Concerto by A. Rejcha (first ever recording), Anthology of Czech piano music (for Unicorn-Kanchana label), 8 vols, works of Dvořák performed on the composer's piano 1999. *Leisure interest:* chess. *Address:* Hradecká 5, 13000 Prague 3, Czech Republic. *Telephone:* (2) 67312430. *Fax:* (2) 67312430 (Home). *E-mail:* r.kvapil@ecn.cz (Office).

KVASHA, Igor Vladimirovich; Russian actor and stage director; b. 4 Feb. 1933, Moscow; m. Tatyana Semenovna Putiyevskaya; one s.; ed Moscow Art Theatre; with Moscow Art Theatre 1955–57; one of founders and leading actor Theatre Sovremennik 1956–; regularly appears on TV and radio, reciting prose and poems; People's Artist of Russia; Kumir Prize 1999; prizes of many film and theatre festivals for performing Russian repertoire including plays by A. Chekhov. *Films:* roles in over 80 films by dirs. Roshal, Room, Klimov, Bondarchuk, Daneliya and others 1960–. *Theatre:* (actor) theatre roles in classical and contemporary plays, including Cyrano de Bergerac (Cyrano de Bergerac by Rostand), Jimmy Porter (Look Back in Anger by Osborne), Luka (The Lower Depths by Gorky), Balalaikin (Balalaikin and Co. by Saltykov-Shchedrin), Gayev (Cherry Orchard by Chekhov), Chebutykin (Three Sisters by Chekhov), Dr. Stockman (Dr. Stockman by Ibsen), Lester (play by Schiller). *Theatre:* (director) staged productions include Days of the Turbins, The Hypocrites' Servitude by Bulgakov, The Average Downy Home Cat by Voinovich and G. Gorin, Cyrano de Bergerac (together with Yefremov), Molière by Bulgakov. *Radio:* many programmes including classical prose and poetry. *Television:* Wait For Me (Tefi Prize) 2001. *Leisure interest:* painting. *Address:* Chistoprudniy blv. 19, Moscow (Office); Glinishchevsky per. 5/7, Apt. 90, 103009 Moscow, Russia. *Telephone:* (095) 921-25-43 (Office); (095) 209-61-08 (Home). *Fax:* (095) 921-66-29 (Office).

KVASHNIN, Col-Gen. Anatoly Vassilyevich; Russian politician; b. 15 Aug. 1946, Ufa; ed Kurgan Machine Construction Inst., Acad. of Armoured Units, Acad. of Gen. Staff; army service, Commdr of regiment, div., army 1969–; Deputy, First Deputy Head Main Operation Dept 1993–95; Commdr Allied Group of armed forces in Chechnya 1994–95; Commdr Armed Forces of N Caucasian Command 1995–97; Acting Head, Head Gen. Staff of Armed Forces of Russian Fed. 1997–, concurrently First Deputy Minister of Defence, Russian Fed. May 1997–. *Leisure interests;* painting, sports. *Address:* Ministry of Defence, Znamenka str. 19, 103160 Moscow, Russia (Office). *Telephone:* (095) 293-20-47; (095) 923-28-23 (Office).

KVITSINSKY, Yuliy Aleksandrovich, CandJur; Russian diplomatist; b. 28 Sept. 1936, Rzev; s. of Aleksander Kvitsinsky and Maria Orlova; m. Inga Kuznetsova 1955; two d.; ed Moscow Inst. of Int. Relations; served in Embassy in GDR 1959–65, in FRG 1978–81; head of Soviet del., negotiations on medium-range nuclear weapons until latter broken off 1983; subsequently responsible for negotiations on Strategic Defence Initiative (SDI) Geneva talks 1985; Amb. to FRG 1986–90; Deputy Foreign Minister 1990–91, First Deputy Foreign Minister May–Sept. 1991; Chief Adviser, Dept of Planning 1991–92; Vice-Pres. Foreign Policy Asscn 1992–; Adviser to Pres., Council of Russian Fed. (Upper Chamber) 1996–97; Amb. to Norway 1997–; cand. mem. CPSU Cen. Cttee 1986–89, mem. 1989–91; Honoured Diplomat of Russian Fed. 2002; Order of Red Banner 1971, Order of Friendship Among People 1981, Order of October Revolution 1986. *Publications:* Vor dem Sturm 1993, Judas Ischariot 1996, General Vlassov 1997, Apostate 2002. *Leisure interest:* fishing. *Address:* Embassy of Russian Federation, Drammensveien 74, 0244 Oslo, Norway. *Telephone:* 22-55-32-78/79. *Fax:* 22-55-00-70. *E-mail:* rembassynor@mail.ru; consul@online.no. *Website:* www.norway.mid.ru.

KWAPONG, Alex. A., PhD; Ghanaian professor; b. 8 March 1927, Akropong, Akwapim; s. of E. A. and Theophilia Kwapong; m. Evelyn Teiko Caesar 1956; six d.; ed Achimota Coll. and King's Coll., Cambridge; Visiting Prof., Princeton Univ. 1962; fmr Pro Vice-Chancellor and Head of Classics Dept, Ghana Univ., Vice-Chancellor 1966–75; Vice-Rector for Institutional Planning and Resource Devt UN Univ. 1976–88; Lester B. Pearson Chair. in Devt Studies, Dalhousie Univ. 1988–91; Dir of African Programmes, Teacher Educ., Research and Evaluation, The Commonwealth of Learning 1991–93; mem. Political and Educ. Cttees., Nat. Liberation Council 1966; mem. Bd Aspen Inst. Berlin 1975–, Harold Macmillan Trust 1986–, Int. Council for Educ. Devt, Int. Foundation for Educ. and Self-help 1988–; Fellow, Ghana Acad. of Arts and Sciences; Hon. DLitt (Warwick, Ife, Ghana, Univ. of Ghana); Hon. LLD (Princeton); Order of Volta (Ghana). *Publications:* Higher Education and Development in Africa Today: A Reappraisal 1979; Under-development and the Challenges of the 1980s: The Role of Knowledge 1980, The Relevance of the African Universities to the Development Needs of Africa 1980, Medical Education and National Development 1987, Culture, Development and African Unity 1988, African Scientific and Technical Institution Building and the Role of International Co-operation 1988, The Challenge of Education in Africa 1988, Some Reflections on International Education in the 90s–in the Role of Service Learning in International Education 1989, Capacity Building and Human Resource Development in Africa (Ed. with B. Lesser) 1990, Meeting the Challenge, The African Capacity Building Initiative (Ed. with B. Lesser) 1992. *Leisure interests:* music, learning Japanese, tennis, billiards. *Address:* 19 Highfield Avenue, London, NW11 9EU, England. *Telephone:* (20) 8209-0878.

KWAŚNIEWSKA, Jolanta; Polish lawyer and campaigner; b. 3 June 1955, Gdansk; d. of Julian Konty and Anna Konty; m. Aleksander Kwaśniewski (q.v., Pres. of Poland 1995–) 1979; one d.; ed Gdansk Univ.; real estate agency owner 1991–95; f. Communication Without Barriers Foundation, Let's Open the World for Children programme 1997; co-f. (with Aleksander Kwaśniewski) Young Talent Help Fund; mem. UN Comit des Sages; Grand Ribbon of the Order of Leopold (Belgium) 1999, Grand Cross of the Order of Isabella the Catholic (Spain) 2001, Grand Cross of the Order of Merit (Germany) 2002, Grand Cross with the Ribbon of Terra Mariana (Estonia) 2002, Grand Ribbon of the Order of the Precious Crown (Japan) 2002, Order of Merit and Companion of Honour (Malta) 2002; Holy Brother Albert–Adam Chmielowski main prize 1997, Order of the Smile 1998, Doctor Henryk Jordan Medal 1999, Big Golden Heart Award, St Stanislaw Kostka Foundation 2000, For The Future of Children of Europe Award of Hungarian Asscn, Future of Europe Asscn 2002. *Leisure interests:* literature, theatre, music, fine arts, travel, skiing, tennis. *Address:* c/o Chancellery of the President of the Republic of Poland, Presidential Palace, ul. Krakowskie Przedmiescie 48/50, 00-071 Warsaw, Poland (Office).

KWAŚNIEWSKI, Aleksander; Polish politician; b. 15 Nov. 1954, Białogard, Koszalin Prov.; s. of Zdzisław Kwaśniewski and Aleksandra Kwaśniewska; m. Jolanta Konty 1979; one d.; ed Gdańsk Univ.; former active leader of youth Movt, including Chair. Univ. Council of Polish Socialist Students' Union (SZSP) at Gdańsk Univ., Head of Culture Dept of SZSP Gen. Bd 1979–80, mem. Exec. Cttee of SZSP Chief Council 1980–81; Ed.-in-Chief of students' weekly Itd, Warsaw 1981–84; Ed.-in-Chief of daily Sztandar Młodych (Banner of Youth), Warsaw 1984–85; mem. Council of Ministers 1985–89; Head Socio-Political Cttee 1988–89; Minister for Youth Affairs 1985–87; Chair. Cttee for Youth and Physical Culture 1987–90; mem. Polish United Workers' Party (PZPR) 1977–90; mem. Social Democracy of Repub. of Poland Party (SdRP) 1990–95, Chair. 1990–95; participant Round Table plenary debates, Co-Chair. team for trade union pluralism, mem. team for political reforms and group for Asscns. and territorial self-Govt 1989; co-f. Democratic Left Alliance 1991; Chair. Polish Olympic Cttee 1988–91; Deputy to Sejm (Parl.) 1991–95;

Chair Constitutional Cttee 1993–95; Supreme Commdr of Armed Forces 1995–; Pres. of Poland 1995–; Kt, Order of White Eagle and numerous int. honours and awards including Grand Croix, Légion d'honneur, Kt Grand Cross, Order of Bath, Kt Grand Cross, Order of St Michael and St George (GB), Grand Cross, Order of Merit (Italy) 1996, Order of Duke Gedyminas, First Class (Lithuania), Order of Leopold (Belgium), Golden Olympic Order, Int. Olympic Cttee 1998, Golden Order of Merit, Int. Amateur Athletic Fed. 1999, Order of Merit, European Olympic Cttee 2000, Order of the Repub. (Turkey) 2000, Great Order of King Tamislav with Ribbon and Great Star (Croatia) 2001, Order of Catholic Isabella with Chain (Spain) 2001, Nat. Order of Southern Cross (Brazil) 2002, Special Grand Cross of Merit (Peru) 2002, Grand Ribbon of the Great Order of Chrysanthemum (Japan) 2002. *Leisure interests:* sport, literature, films. *Address:* Pałac Prezydencki, ul. Krakowskie Przedmieście 48-50, 00-001 Warsaw, Poland (Office). *Telephone:* (22) 6951070 (Office). *Fax:* (22) 6951074 (Office). *Website:* www.prezydent.pl (Office).

KWIATKOWSKI, Marek; Polish professor of history of art; b. 25 April 1930, Caen, France; m.; ed Warsaw Univ.; curator Royal Łazienki palace and park for over 50 years, currently Dir, has organized numerous exhbns. and displays; mem. numerous asscns. including Friends of Animals Asscn; Homo Varsoviensis, Commdr's Cross, Order of Polonia Restituta; Klio Award. *Publications:* 22 books on art including Szymon Bogumił Zug 1971, Stanisław August – król architekt 1983, Architektura mieszkaniowa Warszawy XVII-XIX W 1986, Historia Warszawy XVI-XX wieku. Zabytki mówią 1999. *Leisure interests:* paintings, own museum in Sucha village. *Address:* Royal Łazienki, ul. Agrykoli 1, 00-460 Warsaw, Poland (Office). *Telephone:* (22) 6218212 (Office). *Fax:* (22) 6296945 (Office).

KWIATKOWSKI, Michal; Polish business executive; b. 1947; m.; one c.; ed Silesian Univ., Gliwice; engineer, promoted to Chief Engineer KWK Sosnica coalmine 1971–90; Deputy Dir Knurów Coalmine 1990–91, Dir 1991–93; Pres. Gliwice Coal Co. 1993–98, Weglokoks Co. 1998–2001, Polish Oil and Gas Co. (PGNiG) 2001–. *Address:* PGNiG S.A., ul. Krucza 6/14, 00-537 Warsaw, Poland (Office). *Telephone:* (22) 5835601 (Office). *Fax:* (22) 5835050 (Office). *E-mail:* zd.og@pgnig.pl (Office). *Website:* www.pgnig.pl (Office).

KWONG, Most Rev. Peter K. K., M.TH., DD; Hong Kong ecclesiastic; b. 28 Feb. 1936, Hong Kong; s. of Kwok-Kuen Kwong and Ching-lan Chan; m. Emily Ha; one s. two d.; ed Chung Chi Coll., Kenyon Coll. and Bexley Hall, Colgate Rochester; ordained priest, Anglican Church in Hong Kong 1966; Priest-in-charge, Crown of Thorns Church, Hong Kong 1965–66; Vicar, St James's Church, Hong Kong 1967–70; Curate, St Paul's Church, Hong Kong 1971–72; mem. teaching staff, Chinese Univ. of Hong Kong 1972–79; Diocesan Gen. Sec. Anglican Diocese of Hong Kong and Macao 1979–81; Bishop of Hong Kong and Macao 1981–98, Archbishop and Primate of Hong Kong Sheng Kung Hui 1998–, Bishop of Diocese of Hong Kong Island 1998–; Sr Adviser Community Chest of Hong Kong 1999–; mem. Exec. Cttee, Consultative Cttee for Basic Law of Hong Kong 1985–90, Chair. Finance Cttee 1987–90; Adviser on Hong Kong Affairs, State Dept of People's Repub. of China 1992–97; mem. Preparatory Cttee for Special Admin. Region 1996–97, Selection Cttee 1996–97, CPPCC 1998–; Hon. Treas. Council of the Church of East Asia 1981–83, Chair. 1999–; Hon. Dir Chinese Christian Churches Union 1981–; mem. Court, Hong Kong Univ. 1981–; Vice-Pres. Church Mission Soc. 1995–; numerous appts. in health, educ., social welfare, youth orgs. etc. *Address:* Bishop's House, 1 Lower Albert Road, Hong Kong Special Administrative Region, People's Republic of China (Office). *Telephone:* 25265355 (Office). *Fax:* 25212199 (Office). *E-mail:* office1@hkskh.org (Office).

KY, Air Vice-Marshal Nguyen Cao (see Nguyen Cao Ky, Air Vice-Marshal).

KYL, Jon Llewellyn, BA, LLB; American politician; b. 25 April 1942, Oakland, Neb.; s. of John H. Kyl and Arlene Griffith; m. Caryll Collins 1964; one s. one d.; ed Univ. of Arizona; practising lawyer, Jennings, Strouss & Salmon, Phoenix, Ariz.. 1966–86; legal counsel, Ariz. State Republican Party 1970–75; mem. U.S. House of Reps. 1986–94; Senator from Arizona Jan. 1994–. *Address:* U.S. Senate, 724 Senate Hart Building, Washington, DC 20515, USA.

KYNASTON, Nicolas; British organist; b. 10 Dec. 1941, Morebath, Devon; s. of the late Roger Tewkesbury Kynaston and of Jessie Dearn Caecilia Kynaston (née Parkes); m. 1st Judith Felicity Heron 1961 (divorced 1989); two s. two d.; m. 2nd Susan Harwood Styles 1989; ed Westminster Cathedral Choir School, Downside, Accademia Musicale Chigiana, Siena, Conservatorio Santa Cecilia, Rome, Royal Coll. of Music; Westminster Cathedral Organist 1961–71; début recital, Royal Festival Hall 1966; recording début 1968; concert career 1971–, travelling throughout Europe, N America, Asia and Africa; Artistic Dir J. W. Walker & Sons Ltd 1978–82, Consultant 1982–83; Organist Athens Concert Hall 1995–; Jury mem. Grand Prix de Chartres 1971, St Albans Int. Organ Festival 1975; Pres. Inc. Asscn of Organists 1983–85; Chair. Nat. Organ Teachers Encouragement Scheme 1993–96; mem. Westminster Abbey Fabric Comm. 2000–; consultant for various new organ projects; recordings include 6 nominated Critic's Choice, The Gramophone 1996 (also Ed.'s Choice); Hon. FRCO 1976; EMI/CFP Sales Award 1974; Deutscher Schallplattenpreis 1978. *Publication:* Transcriptions for Organ 1997. *Leisure interests:* walking, church architecture. *Address:* 28 High Park Road, Kew Gardens, Richmond-upon-Thames, Surrey, TW9 4BH, England. *Telephone:* (20) 8878-4455. *Fax:* (20) 8392-9314.

KYO, Machiko; Japanese actress; b. 1924; began her career as a dancer with the Shochiku Girls' Opera Co., Osaka; film début in Saigo ni Warau Otoko (Last Laughter) 1949; has appeared in over 80 films including Rashomon 1950, Ugetsu Monogatari 1953, Gate of Hell 1954, Story of Shunkin 1955, Akasen Chitai (Street of Shame), Teahouse of the August Moon 1956, Yoru no Cho (Night Butterflies) 1957, Odd Obsession 1959, Floating Weeds 1959, A Woman's Testament 1960, Ugetsu; Best Actress Award for Rashomon 1950; Jussie (Finland) Award 1957.

KYRIAKOU, Minos, BA; Greek shipowner and business executive; b. 1946, Athens; s. of Xenophon Kyriakou and Athina Revidies; m. (divorced); two s. one d.; ed in France and Switzerland and Columbia Univ. New York; owner Athenian Tankers Inc. 1965–; formed Bacoil Int. and Athenian Oil Trading Inc. (oil trading corpns.) 1978; founder and Pres. Aegean Foundation 1985–; org. Antenna FM (pvt. radio station) 1987; Chair. and CEO Antenna 1988–; started Antenna TV (TV network) 1989; through Antenna Satellite Inc. Antenna began broadcasting to whole American continent, Australia and Cyprus 1992; Hon. Consul-Gen. of Singapore in Greece 1988–; mem. Bd Govs. Singapore Port Authority 1988; Chair. of UN org. for civil, linguistic and religious rights of nat. minorities 1989; founder, Mediterranean Affairs Inc. (non-profit org.) publishing Mediterranean Quarterly, Washington, DC 1990–; Hon. Consul of Poland in Thessaloniki 1994–; Gold Medal, Legion of Honour of Poland; First Prize for book The Aegean Crisis 1987. *Publications:* The Aegean Crisis 1986, Siesta on a Volcano 1988. *Leisure interests:* reading (especially of history); collecting paintings and sculpture. *Address:* 10–12 Kifisias Avenue, 15125 Marousi, Greece.

KYRILL, Metropolitan of Smolensk and Kaliningrad, DTheol; Russian ecclesiastic; b. Vladimir Mikhailovich Gundyaev, 20 Nov. 1946, Leningrad; ed Leningrad Theological Acad.; took monastic vows, deacon, celibate priest 1969; personal sec. of Metropolitan of Leningrad 1970–71; ordained as archimandrite 1971; Rep. of Moscow Patriarchate to WCC, Switzerland 1971–74; mem. Cen. and Exec. Cttees., WCC 1975–79; Rector Leningrad Theological Acad. 1974–84; consecrated Bishop of Vyborg, Vicar of Leningrad Diocese 1976; Archbishop of Vyborg 1977–84, of Smolensk and Vyazma 1984–89, of Smolensk and Kaliningrad 1989–91; Metropolitan of Smolensk and Kaliningrad 1991–; Chair. Dept of External Church Relations of Moscow Patriarchate, mem. Holy Synod 1989–; Admin. Patriarchal parishes in Finland 1990–; TV broadcaster, Word of Pastor 1995–; Dr hc (Theological Acad., Budapest). *Address:* Moscow Patriarchate, Danilov Monastery, Danilovsky val. 22, 113191 Moscow, Russia. *Telephone:* (095) 230-22-50. *Fax:* (095) 230-26-19.

KYUNG-WHA CHUNG (see Chung, Kyung-Wha).

L

LA FOREST, Gerard V., BCL, MA, LLM, JSD, LLD, D.U., DCL, FRSC; Canadian lawyer; b. 1 April 1926, Grand Falls, NB; s. of J. Alfred La Forest and Philomene Lajoie; m. Marie Warner 1952; five d.; ed St Francis Xavier Univ., Univ. of New Brunswick, St John's Coll. Oxford, UK and Yale Univ., USA; called to Bar, New Brunswick 1949; QC 1968; practising lawyer, Grand Falls 1951–52; Advisory Counsel, Dept of Justice, Ottawa 1952–55; Legal Adviser, Irving Oil and assoc. cos 1955–56; Assoc. Prof. of Law, Univ. of New Brunswick 1956–63, Prof. 1963–68; Dean of Law, Univ. of Alberta 1968–70; Asst Deputy Attorney-Gen. of Canada (Research and Planning) 1970–74; Commr Law Reform Comm. of Canada 1974–79; Prof. and Dir Legis. Drafting Program, Faculty of Law (Common Law Section), Univ. of Ottawa 1979–81; Judge, Court of Appeal of New Brunswick 1981; Judge, Supreme Court of Canada 1985–97; Counsel, Stewart McKelvie Stirling Scales 1998–; Distinguished Legal Scholar in Residence, Univ. of NB 1998–; consultant to fed. and provincial govts; mem. numerous cttees, public bodies etc.; Fellow, World Acad. of Art and Science; numerous hon. degrees and other distinctions. *Publications:* Disallowance and Reservation of Provincial Legislation 1955, Extradition to and from Canada 1961, The Allocation of Taxing Power Under the Canadian Constitution 1967, Natural Resources and Public Property Under the Canadian Constitution 1969, Water Law in Canada 1973. *Address:* 320 University Avenue, Fredericton, NB, E3B 4J1, Canada.

LA PLANTE, Lynda; British television dramatist; m. Richard La Plante (divorced); ed Royal Coll. of Dramatic Art; fmr actress; appeared in The Gentle Touch, Out, Minder etc.; Founder and Chair. La Plante Productions 1994–. *Television includes:* Prime Suspect 1991, 1993, 1995, Civvies, Framed, Seekers, Widows (series), Comics (two-part drama) 1993, Cold Shoulder 2 1996, Cold Blood, Bella Mafia 1997, Trial and Retribution 1997–, Killer Net 1998, Mind Games 2000. *Publications include:* Entwined, Cold Shoulder, The Governor, She's Out, Cold Heart 1998, Sleeping Cruelty 2000. *Address:* La Plante Productions Ltd., Paramount House, 162–170 Wardour Street, London, W1V 3AT, England (Office).

LA RIVIÈRE, Jan Willem Maurits, PhD; Netherlands professor of environmental biology; b. 24 Dec. 1923, Rotterdam; m. Louise A. Kleijn 1958; one s. two d.; ed Erasmus Gymnasium, Rotterdam and Delft Univ. of Tech.; Postdoctoral Rockefeller Fellowship, Stanford Univ., USA; mem. scientific staff, Microbiology Dept, Delft Univ. of Tech. 1953–63; Prof. of Environmental Microbiology and Deputy Dir, Int. Inst. for Infrastructural, Hydraulic and Environmental Eng, Delft 1963–88, now Prof. Emer., Hon. Fellow 1996, Visiting Prof. Harvard Univ. 1967–68; Sec.-Gen. ICSU 1988–93; mem. numerous int. and nat. cttees, del. to UN confs, adviser, lecturer etc.; Hon. mem. Council, Int. Cell Research Org.; Fellow, World Acad. of Art and Science; Kt Order of Lion of Netherlands. *Publications:* Microbiology of Liquid Waste Treatment 1977, Biotechnology in Development Cooperation 1983, Water Quality: Present Status, Future Trends 1987, Threats to the World's Water 1989, Co-operation between Natural and Social Scientists in Global Change Research: Imperatives, Realities, Opportunities 1991, The Delft School of Microbiology in Historical Perspective 1996, some 80 publications in fields of microbiology, environment, water quality and int. scientific co-operation. *Leisure interests:* gardening, travel. *Address:* International Institute for Infrastructural, Hydraulic and Environmental Engineering, P.O. Box 3015, 2601 DA Delft (Office); 107 Veenweg, 2493 ZC The Hague, Netherlands (Home). *Telephone:* (70) 3205825 (Home). *E-mail:* lark@worldonline.nl (Home).

LA TOURETTE, John Ernest, PhD; American economist; b. 5 Nov. 1932, Perth Amboy, NJ; s. of John C. La Tourette and Charlotte R. Jones; m. Lillie (Lili) M. Drum 1957; one s. one d.; ed Rutgers Univ.; Service USAF, rank of Capt. 1955–58; Instructor in Econs Rutgers Univ. 1960–61; Asst Prof., Assoc. Prof., Prof. State Univ. of New York, Binghamton 1961–76, Chair. Dept of Econs 1967–75; Vice-Provost for Research and Dean, Grad. School, Bowling Green State Univ., Ohio 1976–79; Vice-Pres. and Provost, Northern Ill. Univ. 1979–86, Pres. 1986–2000; Prof. Emer. and Prof. of Econs, Northern Ill. Univ. 2000–; Ford Foundation Fellowship 1963; Brookings Inst. Research Professorship 1966–67; Univ. Research Fellowship, State Univ. of NY 1970. *Publications:* contributions to journals of econs. *Leisure interests:* fishing, collecting antiques. *Address:* Lowden Hall, Northern Illinois University, Dekalb, IL 60115 (Office); 218 S Deerview Circle, Prescott, AZ 86303, USA (Home). *Telephone:* (520) 443-1151 (Office).

LAAGE, Gerhart, DIPL.ING.; German architect and town planner; b. 19 April 1925, Hamburg; s. of Richard and Valerie (née Pitzner) Laage; m. Ursula Gebert 1959; one s. two d.; ed Technische Hochschule, Brunswick; freelance architect 1954–; Prof. of Theory of Architectural Planning, Univ. of Hanover 1963–92, Pro-Rector and Rector 1973–75, Dean 1983–84; Adviser to Fed. Govt on Planning for City of Bonn 1977–82; Pres. Fed. Architects Asscn 1990–92. *Publications:* Wohnungen von heute für Ansprüche von Morgen 1971, Planung und Mitbestimmung 1973, Planungstheorie für Architekten 1976, Wohnen beginnt auf der Strasse 1977, Handbuch für Architekturplanung 1978, Weder Traum noch Trauma 1978, Das Stadthaus–mehr als eine Bauform 1980, Kosten- und flächensparendes Bauen 1984, Warum wird nicht immer so gebaut 1985, Von Architecten, Bossen und Banausen 1989, Architektur ist Glücksache 1997. *Address:* Schulterblatt 36, 20357 Hamburg, Germany. *Telephone:* (40) 431950.

LAAR, Mart; Estonian politician and historian; b. 22 April 1960, Viljandi; s. of Tõnis Laar and Aime Laar; m. Katrin Kask 1982; one s. one d.; ed Tartu State Univ.; teacher schools of Tallinn 1983–85; Head of Dept Ministry of Culture of Estonia 1987–90; Deputy of Christian Democratic Party, Supreme Soviet of Estonia 1989–92; mem. Constitutional Ass. 1991–92, mem. Estonian Parl. (Riigikogu) 1992–; Founder and Chair. Pro Patria Union (Isamaaliit) Party 1992–95; Prime Minister of Estonia 1992–94, 1999–2002; apptd mem. of ISTAL by European Comm.; Estonian Order of the Nat. Coat of Arms (Second Class); Cavaliere di Gran Groce dei Santi Maurizio e Lazzaro; Das Grosskreuz des Verdienstorders des Bundesrepublic Deutschland; Nat. Order of Merit, Malta; Grand Cross, Ordre nat. du Mérite, France; Young Politician of the World (Jr Chamber Int.) 1993; European Tax Payer Asscn Year Prize 2001, European Bull, Davastoeconomic Forum, Global Link Award 2001, Adam Smith Award 2002. *Publications:* June 14 1941, Estonian History, War in the Woods, Little Country That Could, Back to the Future, Ten Years of Freedom in the CEE, and a number of scientific papers. *Leisure interests:* tennis, squash, history. *Address:* Estonian Parliament Riigikogu, Lossi plats 1A, Tallinn 15161, Estonia (Office). *Telephone:* 631-6612 (Office). *Fax:* 631-6604 (Office). *E-mail:* mart.laar@riigikogu.ee (Office). *Website:* www .riigikogu.ee (Office).

LABARDAKIS, Augoustinos; Greek ecclesiastic; b. 7 Feb. 1938, Voukoulies-Chania, Crete; s. of Emmanouil and Eurydike Labardakis; ed theological schools in Chalki, Turkey, Salzburg, Münster, West Berlin; ordained as priest, Greek Orthodox Church, FRG 1964; worked as priest, West Berlin 1964–72; ordained as Bishop 1972, as Greek Orthodox Metropolitan of the FRG and Exarch of Cen. Europe Nov. 1980–; Grosses Bundesverdienstkreuz, Verdienstorden des Landes Nordrhein-Westfalen, Höchste Stufe des Ehrenordens der Republik Griechenland. *Address:* Greek Orthodox Metropolis of Germany, Dietrich-Bonhoeffer-Strasse 2, 53227 Bonn; P.O. Box 300555, 53185 Bonn, Germany. *Telephone:* (228) 462041. *Fax:* (228) 464989.

LABARGE, Suzanne, BA, MBA; Canadian banking executive; b. 19 Sept. 1946, Ottawa; d. of Raymond Labarge and Margaret Labarge (née Wade); ed McMaster Univ., Harvard Univ., USA; joined Royal Bank of Canada 1971, Asst Gen. Man. for Loans, Int. Div. 1979–81, for Commercial Banking, Int. Div. 1981–82, Gen. Man. Royal Bank (Suisse) 1982–84, Exec. Vice-Pres. (Corp. Treasury) Royal Bank of Canada 1995–98, Vice-Chair and Chief Risk Officer 1998–; Asst Auditor-Gen. Office of the Auditor-Gen. of Canada 1985–87; Deputy Superintendent, Office of the Superintendent of Financial Insts. 1987–95; Chair. CLS Bank 2001–. *Address:* 8th Floor, South Tower, Royal Bank Plaza, 200 Bay Street, Toronto, Ont., M5J 2J5 (Office); Unit 10D, 66 Collier Street, Toronto, Ont., M4W 1L9, Canada (Home). *E-mail:* suzanne .labarge@royalbank.com (Office).

LABARRÈRE-PAULÉ, André, DèsSc; French politician and academic; b. 12 Jan. 1928, Pau; s. of Maximien Labarrère-Paulé and Catherine Bouilhat; ed Ecole Henri-IV, Collège Beau-Frêne, Pau, Univ. of Paris; Teacher, Digne Lycée 1956–58; scholarship to Arts Council of Canada 1958–59; Prof. Faculty of Arts and of Admin. Sciences, Laval Univ., Québec 1959–66; Prof. of History of Art, Ecole des Beaux-arts, Québec 1964–66; Deputy (Pyrénées-Atlantiques) to Nat. Ass. 1967–68, 1973, 1978, 1981, Vice-Pres. Nat. Ass. 1973–74; Gen. Councillor, Pau-Ouest 1967–73, Jurançon 1973–88; Teacher, Lycée Carnot, Paris 1968–70, Auch Lycée 1970; mem. Political Bureau and Steering Cttee, Parti Socialiste 1969–; Mayor of Pau 1971–; mem. Regional Council for Aquitaine 1974–, Pres. of Council 1979–81; Minister-Del. for Relations with Parl., attached to Prime Minister 1981–86. *Publications:* Pierre-Joseph-Olivier Chauveau 1962, Les instituteurs laïques au Canada français 1836–1900, Les laïques et la presse pédagogique au Canada français au XIXe siècle 1965, Les secrets de l'écriture 1965, Monseigneur Laflêche 1970, Pau 1973, Pau, ville jardin, Votre écriture, Messieurs! Les politiques dévoilés par leur écriture 1987, L'écriture des stars 1991, Le Bal des célibataires (novel) 1992, Le Baron rouge 1997. *Leisure interests:* geography, swimming, graphology, dogs, flowers, art history. *Address:* Assemblée Nationale, 75355 Paris (Office); Mairie de Pau, Place Royale, 64036 Pau Cedex (Office); 13 avenue de Béarn, 64000 Pau, France (Home). *Telephone:* 59-27-85-80 (Office). *Fax:* 59-27-26-18.

LABIS, Attilio; French ballet dancer, choreographer and writer; b. 5 Sept. 1936, Vincennes; s. of Umberto and Renée (née Cousin) Labis; m. Christiane Vlassi 1959; two s.; ed Ecole de danse académique de l'Opéra, Paris; mem. Corps de Ballet at the Paris Opera 1952, Premier Danseur 1959, Premier Danseur Etoile Chorégraphe1960–65, Maître de Ballet 1965–, Prof. of Dance; Prof. of Dance, Ecole de Danse; Prof. d'Adage et de Repertoire; Guest Dancer in London, Paris, Washington, Tokyo, Moscow, Kiev, Leningrad, Rome, Milan, Berlin, Munich, Stuttgart, Rio de Janeiro, Hong Kong, Singapore and Sydney; Chief Choreographer at the Paris Opera; World Amb. for l'Ecole Française; devised choreography for productions including Rencontre (TV) 1961, Arcades 1964, Iphigénie en Tauride 1965, Romeo and Juliet 1967, Spartacus 1973, Raymonda 1973; has created and interpreted numerous ballets including Giselle, Sleeping Beauty, Swan Lake, Don Quixote, Pièces Choréographiques (Peter Van Dijk), Pas de Dieux (Gene Kelly), Marines

(Georges Skibine), Icare (Serge Lifar), Symphonie Concertante, Sarracenia (Michel Descombey), Renart, Pas de danse (music by Gluck), Schéhérazade, Coppélia, Sarabande, Casse-Noisette, Etudes (Harold Lander), Spartacus, Arcades, Romeo et Juliette, Raymonda; Chevalier des Arts et des Lettres, Chevalier, Légion d'honneur 2002. *Address:* Opéra de Paris, 8 rue Scribe, 75009 Paris (Office); 13 Avenue Rubens, 78400 Chatou, France. *Telephone:* 1-30-53-48-07 (Paris). *Fax:* 1-30-53-57-80 (Paris) (Office).

LABUDA, Gerard, PhD; Polish historian; b. 28 Dec. 1916, Nowahuta, Kartuzy Dist; s. of Stanisław Labuda and Anastazja Baranowska; m. Countess Alberta Wielopolska 1943 (died 1999); four s. one d.; ed Clandestine Univ. of Western Lands, Warsaw; Docent 1945–50, Extraordinary Prof. 1950–56, Prof. 1956–; Rector, Adam Mickiewicz Univ., Poznan 1962–65; Sec.-Gen. Poznan Soc. of Friends of Learning 1961–72, Pres. 1972–75; Ed. Roczniki Historyczne (Annals of History) 1969–85; Corresp. mem. Polish Acad. of Sciences 1964–69, mem. 1969–, mem. Presidium 1972–94, Vice-Pres. 1984–86, 1987–89; mem. Consultative Council attached to Chair. of State Council 1986–89; Chair. Cttee for Research on Poles Living Abroad, Polish Acad. of Sciences 1973–80; fmr Chair. Poznan Br. of Polish Acad. of Sciences; Pres. Polish Acad. of Sciences and Letters, Cracow 1989–94; mem. European Soc. of Culture 1963–; Fellow Wissenschaftskoll. zu Berlin, Inst. for Advanced Studies 1981–82; mem. New York Acad. of Sciences 1995; Kt's Cross, Order of Polonia Restituta 1954, Officer's Cross 1960, Commdr's Cross 1976; Commdr's Cross with Star 1986, Great Cross 1996 and others; Dr hc (Gdańsk) 1986, (Toruń) 1993, (Jagiellon Univ. Cracow) 1995, (Warsaw) 1997, (Wrocław) 1999; State Prizes (3rd class) 1949, 1951, (2nd class) 1970; Palacki Medal (Czechoslovakia) 1968, Johannes Gottfried Herder Preis, Vienna 1991. *Publications:* Pierwsze państwo słowiańskie—państwo Samona (First Slavonic State–Samon's State) 1949, Fragmenty dziejów Słowiańszczyzny Zachodniej (Fragments of History of the West Slavs) Vols I–III 1960–74, Polska granica zachodnia: Tysiąc lat dziejów politycznych (The Western Frontier of Poland: A Thousand Years of Political History) 1971–1974, co-author, Słownik Starożytności Słowiańskich (Dictionary of Slavonic Antiquities), Historia Pomorza (History of Pomerania), Historia dyplomacji polskiej (Średniowiecze) (History of Polish Medieval Diplomacy) 1981, Dzieje Zakonu Krzyżackiego w Prusach (History of the Order of the Teutonic Knights in Prussia) 1986, Studia nad początkami państwa polskiego (Studies of the Origin of the Polish State Vols I and II) 1987–88, Mieszko II, King of Poland (1025–1034) 1992, Kashubian and their History 1995, Polsko-niemieckie rozmowy o przeszłości (Polish and German Talks About the Past) 1996, Kaszubskie, pomorskie i morskie (Kashubian, Pomeranian and Sea) 2000, Święty Wojciech, biskup-męczennik 2000, Mieszko I 2002. *Leisure interests:* sociology, linguistics. *Address:* ul. Kanclerska 8, 60-327 Poznan, Poland. *Telephone:* (61) 8673585. *Fax:* (61) 8687600 (Home).

LABUS, Miroljub, MSc, PhD; Serbia and Montenegro (Serbian) politician, lawyer and economist; b. 28 Feb. 1947, Mala Krsna; s. of Zdravko Labus and Draginja Labus (née Pavlovic); m. Olivera Labus (née Grabic); two d.; ed Belgrade Univ.; attorney-at-law, Belgrade 1970–71; Lecturer in Law Belgrade Univ. 1971, Prof. of Econs 1971–; Fulbright Lecturer, Cornell Univ., USA 1983, Visiting Asst. Prof. 1984; Sr Adviser, Fed. Statistics Office 1986–94; mem. Bd Ekonomska Misl i Ekonomske Analize journals; Fellow Econ. Inst. 1993–99; Deputy Prime Minister and Minister of Foreign Econ. Relations, Fed. Repub. of Yugoslavia 1987–91, Deputy Prime Minister, with responsibility for econ. relations with the int. community 2001–03; mem. Fed. Parl. and Cttee on Monetary Policy; Vice-Pres. Democratic Party 1994–97; mem. Standing Cttee on Econ. Affairs, UNDPM Sarajevo 1996; with UNDP 1996–97; joined IBRD 1997; Ed. The Economic Trends, Fed. Statistics Office, Belgrade, The Economic Barometer, Econ. Inst., Belgrade 2000–. *Publications:* Social and Collective Property Rights 1987, General Equilibrium Modelling (jtly) 1990, Contemporary Political Economy 1991, Foundations of Political Economy 1992, Foundations of Economics, 1995, other books and numerous articles on econ. problems. *Leisure interests:* woodwork, skiing. *Address:* Office of the Deputy Prime Minister, Palace of the Federation, Mihaila Pupina str. 2, 11070 Belgrade (Office); Gospodar Jevremova str. 13, Belgrade, Serbia and Montenegro (Home). *Telephone:* (11) 311-14-49 (Office). *Fax:* (11) 311-29-79 (Office). *E-mail:* cabinet@fmfer.sv.gov.yu (Office).

LACALLE HERRERA, Luis Alberto; Uruguayan politician, farmer and lawyer; b. 13 July 1941, Montevideo; s. of Carlos Lacalle and María Hortensia de Herrera Uriarte; m. María Julia Pou Brito del Pino 1970; two s. one d.; Deputy to Legis. Ass. 1971; elected Senator 1984; cand. for Pres. for Blanco Party 1989; Pres. of Uruguay 1990–95. *Address:* c/o Oficina del Presidente, Casa de Gobierno, Edif. Libertad, Avda Luis Alberto de Herrera 3350, Montevideo, Uruguay.

LACARTE-MURÓ, Julio; Uruguayan international civil servant and diplomat; b. 29 March 1918, Montevideo; s. of Antonio Lacarte and Julieta Muró de Lacarte; m. Ivy E O'Hara de Lacarte 1940; three c.; Deputy Exec. Sec. GATT 1947, Amb. to GATT, Chair. (Governing Council and the Contracting Parties), has participated in all eight GATT rounds 1947, 1949, 1951, 1956, 1960–61, 1964–67, 1973–79, 1986–93 (Uruguay round), as Chief Negotiator (for Uruguay); fmr Minister of Industry and Trade; fmr Amb. to numerous countries; mem. Appellate Body World Trade Org. 1995–; lecturer and int. consultant; decorations from Ecuador, Bolivia, Argentina and Germany.

Publications: The Globalisation of World Trade 1994 and other books on int. trade. *Leisure interests:* tennis, golf, chess, history. *Address:* c/o GATT, Centre William Rappard, 154 rue de Lausanne, 1211 Geneva 21, Switzerland.

LACAZE, Gen. Jeannou; French politician and army officer; b. 11 Feb. 1924, Hué, Viet Nam; s. of Jean Joseph and Andrée (née Momert) Lacaze; m. 2nd Geneviève Agostini 1997; one d. (and two s. two d. from fmr marriage); entered mil. acad., Saint-Cyr 1945; joined infantry; served Foreign Legion, Algeria, Tunisia and the Far East; Major 11th demi-brigade parachutiste de choc 1959–63; Commdr 2nd Foreign Parachute Regt (for a time in Chad) 1967; Dir of Intelligence, Service de documentation extérieure et de contre-espionage (SDECE) 1971–76; first mem. secret service to be made Gen.; Commdr 11th Parachute Div. 1976–79; Inspecteur de l'infanterie Aug. 1979; Lt-Gen. Feb. 1980; Commdr 1st mil. region and 3rd army corps, Commanding Officer, Paris Sept. 1980; Armed Forces Chief of Staff 1981–85; Special Counsellor, military relations with African continent countries 1985–89; mem. European Parl. 1989–94; Founder Union des Indépandants political party 1990; Pres. Asscn for the Devt of Relations between Europe and the Third World (Apretem); Pres. European Confed. of Former Fighters 1994–98; Founder Council Commerce et Industrie franco-irakien; Grand Officier Légion d'Honneur; Croix de guerre, Croix de la Valeur militaire. *Publication:* Le President et le champignon 1991. *Leisure interests:* riding, golf. *Address:* 1 bis quai aux Fleurs, 75004 Paris, France.

LACEY, Richard Westgarth, PhD, MD, FRCP; British professor of clinical microbiology; b. 11 Oct. 1940, London; s. of Jack Lacey and Sybil Lacey; m. Fionna Margaret Lacey 1972; two d.; ed Felsted School, Essex, Jesus Coll., Cambridge, London Hosp.; house officer, London Hosp. 1964–66, St Mary's Hosp., Eastbourne 1966; Sr House Officer, Registrar in Pathology, Bristol Royal Infirmary 1966–68; Lecturer, Reader in Clinical Microbiology, Univ. of Bristol 1968–74; Consultant in Chemical Pathology, Queen Elizabeth Hosp., King's Lynn 1975–83; Consultant in Infectious Diseases, East Anglian Regional Health Authority 1974–83, Leeds Health Authority 1983–98; Prof. of Medical Microbiology, Leeds Univ. 1983–98, Prof. Emer. 1998–; Consultant, WHO 1983–; Dick Memorial Lecture, Edin. Veterinary School 1990; Evian Health Award Winner 1989, Caroline Walker Award 1989, Campaign for Freedom of Information Award 1990. *Publications:* Safe Shopping, Safe Cooking, Safe Eating 1989, Unfit for Human Consumption 1991, Hard to Swallow 1994, Mad Cow Disease: the History of B.S.E. in Britain 1994, Poison on a Plate 1998 and over 200 papers and articles for journals. *Leisure interests:* gardening, painting, antique restoration (intermittently). *Address:* Department of Microbiology, University of Leeds, Leeds, LS2 9JT; Carlton Manor, Nr. Yeadon, Leeds, LS19 7BE, England (Home). *Telephone:* (113) 233 5596.

LACHAPELLE, David; American photographer; b. NC; ed Art Student's League, School of Visual Arts NC; began career by creating fine art images for Interview Magazine; photographer advertising campaigns for Keds, Estee Lauder, Prescriptives, Volvo, MasCosmetics, Diesel Jeans; widely published in fashion, music and entertainment magazines; photography prints and TV for clients including Jean Paul Gaultier, Giorgio Armani, MTV, Pepsi and Levis; fashion portraits of celebrities include Debbie Harry, Britney Spears, Madonna, David Bowie and Elton John; Best New Photographer of the Year, French Photo Magazine 1995, American Photo Magazine 1995; Photographer of the Year, VH1 Fashion Awards 1996; Infinity Award, Int. Centre of Photography 1997. *Exhibitions include:* LaChapelle: Fashion Photography, Barbican Gallery, London, UK 2002. *Publication:* LaChapelle Land (vol. of photographic images) 1997. *Address:* c/o Barbican Gallery, Barbican Centre, Silk Street, London, EC2Y 8DS, England (Office).

LACHMANN, Sir Peter Julius, Kt, ScD, FRS, FRCP, FRCPath, FMedSci; British immunologist; b. 23 Dec. 1931, Berlin, Germany; s. of Heinz Lachmann and Thea Heller; m. Sylvia Stephenson 1962; two s. one d.; ed Trinity Coll., Univ. of Cambridge and Univ. Coll. Hosp., London; Research Student, Dept of Pathology, Univ. of Cambridge 1958–60, Research Fellow, Empire Rheumatism Council 1962–64, Asst Dir of Research, Immunology Div. 1964–71; Prof. of Immunology, Royal Postgraduate Medical School, Univ. of London 1971–75; Hon. Consultant Pathologist, Hammersmith Hosp. 1971–75; Dir MRC Research Group on serum complement 1971–75; Sheila Joan Smith Prof. of Immunology, Univ. of Cambridge 1977–99, Prof. Emer. 1999–; Hon. Dir, MRC Molecular Immunopathology Unit 1980–97; Hon. Consultant Clinical Immunologist, Cambridge Health Dist 1976–99; Pres. Royal Coll. of Pathologists 1990–93, Acad. of Medical Sciences 1998–2002; Biological Sec. and Vice-Pres. The Royal Soc. 1993–98; Visiting Investigator Rockefeller Univ., New York 1960–61, Scripps Clinic and Research Foundation, La Jolla, Calif. 1966, 1975, 1980, 1986, Basel Inst. for Immunology 1971; Meyerhof Visiting Prof., Weizmann Inst., Rehovot 1989; Visiting Prof., Coll. de France 1993; Fellow, Christ's Coll., Univ. of Cambridge 1962–71, 1976–, Royal Postgraduate Medical School 1995, Imperial Coll. London 2001; Foreign Fellow Indian Nat. Acad. of Science 1997; mem. Medical Advisory Cttee, British Council 1983–97, Scientific Advisory Bd SmithKline Beecham 1995–2000; Chair. Science Cttee Asscn Medical Research Charities 1988–92; Chair. Medical Research Cttee Muscular Dystrophy Group 1986–90; Chair. Research Cttee, Digestive Disorders Foundation 2003–; Pres. Fed. of Nat. Academics of Medicine in the EU 2004–; Trustee Arthritis Research Campaign 2000–; Foundation Lecturer, Royal Coll. of Pathologists 1983; Langdon Brown Lecturer, Royal Coll. of Physicians 1986; Heberden Orator, British Soc. of Rheumatology 1986; Charnock Bradley Memorial Lecture 1992;

Plenary Lecture, Vienna 1993; Congress Lecture, BSI 1993, Frank May Lecture, Leicester 1994; Vanguard Medical Lecture, Univ. of Surrey 1998, Lloyd Roberts Lecture, Medical Soc. of London 1999, Jean Shanks Lecture, Acad. of Medical Sciences, London 2001; Gold Medal, European Complement Network 1997. *Publications:* Jt Ed. Clinical Aspects of Immunology, 1975, 1982, 1993. *Leisure interests:* keeping bees, walking in mountains. *Address:* Centre for Veterinary Science, Madingley Road, Cambridge, CB3 0ES (Office); 36 Conduit Head Road, Cambridge, CB3 0EY, England (Home). *Telephone:* (1223) 766242 (Office); (1223) 354433 (Home). *Fax:* (1223) 766244 (Office); (1223) 300169 (Home). *E-mail:* pjl1000@cam.ac.uk (Office); pjl1000@cam.ac.uk (Home).

LACHOUT, Karel, MusD; Czech composer, musicologist and writer; b. 30 April 1929, Prague; s. of Karel Lachout and Marie Lachoutová; m. (divorced); ed Charles Univ., Prague, Acad. of Musical Arts, Prague; teacher of music and English (approbation for grammar schools) 1952; Ed. Music Dept. Radio Prague 1953–79; freelance artist, composer and musicologist with specialization in Spanish and Latin American folk music. *Compositions include:* orchestral suite Such is Cuba 1962, Symphonietta for grand orchestra, orchestral suite America Latina with famous 'Mar del Plata', string quartets, piano pieces. *Radio:* scripts for music programmes on Radio Prague of authentic music from Latin America, Spain and other countries. *Publications:* The World Sings (Czech Music Fund Prize 1957) 1957, Music of Chile 1976, Music of Cuba (honoured by invitation from UNEAC to Music Festival, Havana 1986) 1979, Folk Music of Latin America (edn to commemorate 500th anniversary of discovery of Latin America, with 2 LP records and booklet) 1992. *Leisure interests:* languages (German, English, Spanish), travelling to explore origins of authentic folk music, relaxing at Roses (Costa Brava), philosophy of deeper sense of human life. *Address:* Viklefova 11, Prague 3, 130 00, Czech Republic (Home). *Telephone:* (2) 71770347 (Home).

LACINA, Ferdinand; Austrian politician; b. 31 Dec. 1942, Vienna; s. of Anna and Ferdinand Lacina; m. Monika Lacina 1966; one s. one d.; ed Hochschule für Welthandel, Vienna; various posts in Kammer für Arbeiter und Angestellte, Vienna 1964; Beirat für Wirtschafts- und Sozialfragen 1974; Dir Dept of Financial Planning, Österreichische Industrieverwaltungs A.G. 1978; Dir Pvt. Office of Fed. Chancellor Kreisky 1980; Sec. of State, Fed. Chancellery 1982; Fed. Minister of Transport Sept. 1984–Jan. 1985, of Public Economy and Transport 1985–86, of Finance 1986–95. *Publications:* Auslandskapital in Österreich (with O. Grünwald); articles in trade union newspapers and political and econ. journals. *Leisure interests:* literature, walking. *Address:* Stuberina, 5, 1010 Vienna, Austria (Office).

LACLOTTE, Michel René; French museum director; b. 27 Oct. 1929, Saint-Malo; s. of Pierre Laclotte and Huguette de Kermabon; ed Lycée Pasteur, Neuilly, Inst. d'art et d'archéologie de l'Univ. de Paris and Ecole du Louvre; Insp. Inspectorate of Provincial Museums 1955–66; Chief Curator of Paintings, Musée du Louvre 1966–87, of collection Musée d'Orsay 1978–86, Dir Musée du Louvre 1987–92, Pres. de l'Etablissement Public (Musée du Louvre) 1992–94; Pres. Mission de préfiguration, Institut Nat. d'Histoire de L'Art 1994–98; Commdr, Légion d'honneur, Ordre nat. du Mérite, des Arts et des Lettres; Grand prix nat. des Musées 1993; Hon. CBE 1994. *Publications:* various works on history of art, catalogues and articles in reviews mainly on Italian and French painting (14th to 15th centuries) and the Louvre Museum. *Address:* 10 bis rue du Pré-aux-Clercs, 75007 Paris, France (Home).

LACOSTE, Paul, OC, PhD; Canadian university administrator; b. 24 April 1923, Montréal; s. of Emile and Juliette (née Boucher) Lacoste; m. 1st Louise Mackay (divorced), 2nd Louise Marcil 1973 (died 1995); one s. two d.; ed Montréal, Chicago, Paris Univs; Vice-Pres., Montréal Univ. 1966–75; Prof. Dept of Philosophy, Montréal Univ. 1948–86; lawyer 1960–; Pres. Asscn des universités partiellement ou entièrement de langue française 1978–81, Fonds Int. de coopération universitaire 1978–81, Asscn of Univs and Colls of Canada 1978–79, Conf. of Rectors and Principals of Québec Univs 1977–80, mem. Bd Asscn of Commonwealth Univs 1977–80, Ecole polytechnique Montréal 1975–85, Clinical Research Inst. of Montréal 1975–, Ecole des hautes commerciales de Montréal 1982–85; Pres. Univ. of Montréal 1975–85; Chair. Comm. and Cttees of the Fed. Environmental Assessment Review to the Great-Whale Hydroelectric Project 1991–98; Hon. LLD (McGill Univ.) 1975, (Univ. of Toronto) 1978; Dr hc (Laval Univ.); Chevalier, Légion d'Honneur 1985. *Publications:* Justice et paix scolaire 1962, A Place of Liberty 1964, Le Canada au seuil du siècle de l'abondance 1969, Principes de gestion universitaire 1970, Education permanente et potentiel universitaire 1977. *Leisure interests:* reading, music, travel. *Address:* 2820 Willowdale Avenue, PQ, Montréal, H3T 1H5, Canada. *Telephone:* (514) 343-7727 (Office); (514) 342-6150 (Home).

LACROIX, Christian Marie Marc; French fashion designer; b. 16 May 1951, Arles; s. of Maxime Lacroix and Jeannette Bergier; m. Françoise Roesenstiehl 1989; ed Lycée Frédéric Mistral, Arles, Univ. Paul Valéry, Montpellier, Univ. Paris-Sorbonne and Ecole du Louvre; Asst Hermès 1978–79, Guy Paulin 1980–81; Artistic Dir Jean Patou 1981–87, Christian Lacroix Feb. 1987–, Emilio Pucci 2002–; design for Carmen, Nîmes, France 1988, for L'as-tu revue? 1991, for Les Caprices de Marianne 1994, for Phèdre, Comédie Française 1995; created costumes for Yoyaux, Opera Garnier 2000; decorated the TGV Méditerranée 2001; Chevalier, Arts et Lettres 1991; Dés d'or 1986, 1988, Council of fashion designers of America, Prix Balzac 1989, Goldene Spinnrad Award (Germany) 1990, Prix Molière (for costumes in

Phèdre) 1996. *Publication:* Pieces of a Pattern 1992, illustrations for albums Styles d'aujourd'hui 1995, Journal d'une collection 1996. *Address:* 73 rue du Faubourg Saint Honoré, 75008 Paris, France. *Telephone:* 1-42-65-79-08.

ŁĄCZKOWSKI, Paweł Julian, D.SOC.; Polish politician; b. 31 July 1942, Kielce; m. Maria Łączkowska; one s. three d.; ed Adam Mickiewicz Univ., Poznań; fmr scientific worker, Adam Mickiewicz Univ., Poznań 1966–90 1994–; mem. Solidarity Independent Self-governing Trade Union 1980–; Deputy to Sejm (Parl.) 1989–93, 1997–2001, Deputy Chair. Civic Parl. Club 1989–90, Chair. Sejm Circle of Christian Democrats 1990–91, Chair. Parl. Club of Christian Democrats' Party (PChD) 1991–93, Parl. Comm. for Regulations and Deputies 1997–2001, mem. Solidarity Election Action Parl. Caucus 1997–2001; co-founder Christian Democrats' Party (PChD) 1990, Leader 1992–99 merged with two other parties to form Alliance of Polish Christian Democrats 1999, currently Head of Political Council; Deputy Chair. Presidium Nat. Bd Solidarity Election Action 1999–2001; mem. Co-ordination Team Solidarity Election Action (AWS) 1996–99; Deputy Chair. Council of Ministers 1992–93. *Publications:* Circumstances for Stabilizing Worker Staff in Industrialized Districts 1977; numerous articles. *Leisure interest:* gardening. *Address:* Porozumienie Polskich Chrzescijanskich Demokratów, Sejm, ul. Wiejska 4/6, 00–902 Warsaw, Poland (Office). *Telephone:* (61) 8520120 (Home).

LADER, Malcolm Harold, OBE, PhD, MD, DSc, FRCPsych, FMedSci; British professor emeritus of clinical psychopharmacology; b. 27 Feb. 1936, Liverpool; s. of Abe Lader and Minnie Lader; m. Susan Packer 1961; three d.; ed Liverpool Inst. High School and Liverpool and London Univs; external mem. of scientific staff of MRC 1966–2001; Reader Univ. of London 1973–78, Prof. 1978, now Prof. Emer.; Consultant Psychiatrist, Bethlem Royal and Maudsley Hosps 1970–2001; mem. various UK Govt advisory bodies; Trustee Psychiatry Research Trust 2002–; Hon. Fellow American Coll. of Psychiatrists 1994, British Asscn for Psychopharmacology 1994, Soc. for the Study of Addiction 1998; Heinz Karger Memorial Foundation Prize 1974, Taylor Manor Award 1989. *Publications:* Psychiatry on Trial 1977, Biological Treatments in Psychiatry 1990, Anxiety Panic and Phobias 1997; numerous articles on psychopharmacology. *Leisure interests:* antiques, paintings. *Address:* Addiction Sciences Bldg, Institute of Psychiatry, De Crespigny Park, Denmark Hill, London, SE5 8AF, England. *Telephone:* (20) 7848-0372. *Fax:* (20) 7252-5437 (Office). *E-mail:* m.lader@iop.kcl.ac.uk (Office).

LADER, Philip, MA, JD; American diplomatist, government official, business executive and lawyer; b. 17 March 1946, Jackson Heights, NY; m. Linda LeSourd 1980; two d.; ed Duke Univ., Univ. of Michigan, Oxford and Harvard Univs; law clerk to circuit judge 1973; Pres. Sea Pines Co. 1979–83, Winthrop Univ., SC 1983–85, Bond Univ., Gold Coast, Australia 1991–93, Business Execs for Nat. Security, 1991; Exec. Vice-Pres. Sir James Goldsmith's US Holdings; Deputy Dir for Man., Office of Man. and Budget, Exec. Office of the Pres. 1993; Chair. Pres.'s Council for Integrity and Efficiency 1993, Pres.'s Man. Council, Policy Cttee, Nat. Performance Review 1993; Deputy Chief of Staff, White House 1993–94; Admin., US Small Business Admin. and Pres.'s Cabinet 1995–97; US Amb. to UK 1997–2001; Chair. WPP 2001–; Sr Adviser Morgan Stanley Int. 2001–; Dir AES, Marathon Oil and RAND Corpns; Chair. American Assocs of the Royal Acad. Trust; mem. Chief Execs Org., Prince of Wales' Trust Advisory Bd; Trustee British Museum, 21st Century Foundation, Windsor Leadership Trust, St Paul's Cathedral Foundation; 14 hon. doctorates; RSA Benjamin Franklin Medal 2001. *Leisure interests:* reading, tennis, walking. *Address:* 25 Cabot Square, Canary Wharf, London, England (Office); 41 East Battery, Charleston, SC 29401, USA (Home). *Telephone:* (20) 7425-6524 (Office).

LADOUCETTE, Philippe de, MA, DScS, DrSc ECON.; French government official; b. 15 March 1948, Paris; s. of Charles de Ladoucette; ed Ecole Nationale des Ponts et Chaussées; fmr civil engineer with Ministry of Equipment (responsible for state contracts with medium-sized towns) 1974–77; Commr for Industrialization, Ardennes 1977–83; responsible for industrial development, DATAR 1983–86; technical adviser, Ministry of Industry, Posts and Telecommunications and Tourism 1986–88; responsible for industrial matters, Secr.-Gen. of Channel Tunnel 1988–93; Asst Dir Office of Minister of Enterprise and Econ. Devt 1993–94; Pres. Houillères du Bassin du Centre et du Midi 1994–; Pres., Dir-Gen. Charbonnages de France 1996–; Chevalier, Légion d'honneur. *Leisure interest:* tennis. *Address:* Charbonnages de France, 100 avenue Albert 1er, B.P. 220, 92503 Rueil-Malmaison Cedex (Office); 40 avenue Marceau, 75008 Paris, France. *Telephone:* 1-47-52-37-00 (Office). *Fax:* 1-47-52-31-33 (Office). *E-mail:* www.groupecharbonnages.fr (Office).

LADREIT DE LACHARRIÈRE, Marc; French business executive; b. 6 Nov. 1940, Nice; s. of Pierre Ladreit de Lacharrière and Hélène Mora; m. Sibylle Lucet 1967; one s. three d.; ed Ecole Nat. d'Admin.; Asst Man. Banque de Suez et de l'Union des Mines 1970, Asst Dir 1971, Deputy Dir 1973; Vice-Pres. Masson Belfond Armand Colin 1974–95; Vice-Dir Banque de l'Indochine et de Suez 1975, Corporate Affairs Dir 1976; Financial Dir L'Oréal 1977, Man. Dir Admin. and Finance 1977, Vice-Pres. Man. Cttee 1978, mem. Strategic Cttee, Dir and Exec. Vice-Pres. 1984–91, Pres. of Finances 1987–91; Pres. La Revue des deux Mondes 1990–, Financière Marc de Lacharrière (Fimalac) 1991–; Council Banque de la Mutuelle industrielle 1988; Vice-Pres. Sofres 1992–97, fmr Vice-Pres. Centenaire Blanzy, Pres. 1994–98; Pres. Financière Sofres 1992–97, Lille Bonnières & Colombe et Alspi 1993–96, Comptoir Lyon

Allemand Louyot 1995–96; Chair. Geral, USA; Man. Dir Regefi and Holdilux, Luxembourg; Vice-Chair. L'Oréal (GB), Editions Masson; Dir Collection de l'Inst. de l'Entreprise, France Télécom 1995–98, Air France 1996–97, Canal+ 1998–, Flo Group 1998–; Louvre Museum 1999–; mem. Int. Council Renault Nissan 2000–; Lecturer, Inst. d'Etudes Politiques, Paris 1971, then Prof.; Adviser, Foreign Trade of France; numerous directorships; Officier, Légion d'honneur, Ordre Nat. du Mérite, Officier des Arts et des Lettres. *Leisure interests:* tennis, skiing. *Address:* Fimalac, 97 rue de Lille, 75007 Paris, France.

LAERMANN, Karl-Hans; German politician and university professor; b. 26 Dec. 1929, Kaulhausen; s. of Johann Laermann and Elisabeth Laermann; m. Hilde Woestemeyer 1955; three s. one d.; ed Rhenish-Westphalian Coll. of Advanced Tech., Aachen; Lecturer in Experimental Statics, Rhenish-Westphalian Coll. of Advanced Tech. 1966–74; Prof. of Statics, Bergische Univ. G.H. Wuppertal, Head Lab. for Experimental Stress Analysis and Measurement 1974–; mem. FDP 1968–, mem. Fed. Exec. Cttee 1980–90, N Rhine-Westphalian Exec. Cttee 1978–94, Chair. Fed. Cttee on Research and Tech. of FDP 1981–96; mem. Bundestag (Parl.) 1974–98; Deputy Chair. working group of FDP Parl. Group on Educ. and Science, Research and Tech. 1980–94; Fed. Minister of Educ. and Science Feb.–Nov. 1994; mem. Bd Trustees Volkswagen Foundation 1984–94, Friedrich Naumann Foundation 1984–, Anglo-German Foundation for the Study of Industrial Society 1989–99; mem. Admin. Bd Inter Nationes 1995–99; Extraordinary mem. Goethe Institut 1995–98; Hon. mem. VDI; Hon. CBE (UK) 1978, Commdr Order of Orange-Nassau (Netherlands) 1982, Great Cross with Star of Order of FRG 1996; Hon. Dr-Ing. (Magdeburg); Dr hc (Tech. Univ. Prague, Transilvania Univ. Braşov, Romania, Tech. Univ. Košice, Slovakia); Gold Medal of Honour, VDI 1999. *Publications:* Konstruktiver Ingenieurbau (Ed.) 1967, Experimentelle Plattenuntersuchungen-Theoretische Grundlagen 1971, Experimentelle Spannungsanalyse I, II 1972, 1977, Perspektiven – Ein Wissenschaftler in der Politik 1984, Optical Methods in Experimental Solid Mechanics (ed.) 2000 and about 230 publs on science and politics in int. journals. *Leisure interests:* painting, sailing. *Address:* Bergische Universität Wuppertal, FB11, Pauluskirche str. 7, 42285 Wuppertal (Office); Am Tannenberg 19, 41189 Mönchengladbach, Germany (Home). *Telephone:* (202) 4394077 (Office); (2166) 58164. *Fax:* (202) 4394078 (Office); (2166) 958077. *E-mail:* laermann@uni-wuppertal.de (Office); laermann.kh@vdi.de (Home).

LAFER, Celso; Brazilian politician and law professor; Prof. of Law, Univ. of São Paulo; Minister of Foreign Affairs 1992, 2001–; Amb. to World Trade Organization (WTO) and Head WTO Gen. Council and Dispute Settlement Comm. 1995–98; Minister of Industry and Commerce 1999. *Address:* Ministry of Foreign Affairs, Palácio do Itamaraty, Esplanada dos Ministérios, 70170-900 Brasília, DF, Brazil (Office). *Telephone:* (61) 411-6161 (Office). *Fax:* (61) 225-1272 (Office). *Website:* www.mre.gov.br (Office).

LAFFAN, Brigid, PhD; Irish professor of European politics; b. 6 Jan. 1955; d. of Con Burns and Aileen Burns; m. Michael Laffan 1979; one s. two d.; ed Univ. of Limerick, Coll. of Europe, Bruges, Trinity Coll. Dublin; researcher, European Cultural Foundation 1977–78; Lecturer, Coll. of Humanities, Univ. of Limerick 1979–86; Lecturer, Inst. of Public Admin. 1986–89; Newman Scholar, Univ. Coll. Dublin 1989–90, Lecturer, Dept of Politics 1990–91, Jean Monnet Prof. of European Politics 1991–; Visiting Prof., Coll. of Europe, Bruges 1992–. *Publications:* Ireland and South Africa 1988, Integration and Co-operation in Europe 1992, Constitution Building in the European Union (Ed.) 1996, The Finances of the European Union 1997, Europe's Experimental Union: Re-thinking Integration (jtly) 1999, numerous articles on Irish foreign policy, EC budgetary policy, insts, governance and political union. *Leisure interests:* theatre, reading, swimming. *Address:* Department of Politics, University College, Belfield, Dublin 4 (Office); 4 Willowbank, The Slopes, Monkstown, Co. Dublin, Ireland (Home). *Telephone:* (1) 706-8344 (Office); (1) 286-2617 (Home). *Fax:* (1) 706-1171 (Office); (1) 284-5331 (Home). *E-mail:* brigid.laffan@ucd.ie (Office).

LAFFITTE, Pierre Paul; French engineer and politician; b. 1 Jan. 1925, St Paul, Alpes Maritimes; s. of Jean Laffitte and Lucie Fink; m. 1st Sophie Glikman-Toumarkine (deceased); m. 2nd Anita Garcia; ed Lycée de Nice and Ecole Polytechnique; Dir Office of Geological, Geophysical and Mining Research 1953; Asst Dir-Gen. Office of Geological and Mining Research 1959–62, Deputy Dir 1963, Dir 1973–84; Gen. Engineer Mines 1973–; Pres. Conseil de Perfectionnement, Ecole Nat. Supérieure des Mines, Paris 1984–91; Founder Pres. Sophia-Antipolis 1969; Pres. Franco-German Asscn for Science and Tech., AFAST (German-French Asscn for Science and Tech.); Senator from Alpes Maritimes 1985–; Hon. PhD (Colorado School of Mines, USA) 1984, (Open Univ., England) 1990; De Gaulle-Adenauer Prize 1994; Officier, Légion d'Honneur; Officier, Ordre Nat. du Mérite; Commdr Order of Polar Star (Sweden); Commdr Order of Merit of Fed. Repub. of Germany. *Publications:* works on mining and geology, science parks, the information age, local development. *Leisure interest:* gardening. *Address:* Sophia Antipolis, place Sophie Laffitte, 06560 Valbonne (Office); Palais du Luxembourg, 75291 Paris Cedex 06; Ecole des Mines, 60 boulevard Saint Michel, 75006 Paris, France. *Telephone:* 4-92-96-78-00 (Sophia Antipolis) (Office); 1-40-51-90-30 (Ecole des Mines). *E-mail:* p.laffitte@senat.fr (Office). *Website:* www.sophia-antipolis.com.

LAFFONT, Jean-Jacques Marcel, PhD; French economist; b. 13 April 1947, Toulouse; s. of Jean Laffont and Emilienne Perry; m. Colette Sonntag 1968;

four d.; ed Lycée Pierre de Fermat, Toulouse, Univ. of Toulouse, Univ. of Paris, Harvard Univ.; researcher CNRS 1975–77; Prof., Univ. of Amiens 1977–78, Univ. of Toulouse 1978–; Sr Polytechnic Lecturer 1975–87; Dir of Studies Ecole des hautes études en sciences sociales 1980–; Fairschild Fellow, Calif. Inst. of Tech. 1987; Taussig Research Prof., Harvard Univ. 1988; mem. Inst. Universitaire de France 1991–; Fellow, then Pres. Econometric Soc. 1992; Hon. mem. American Econ. Asscn, French Asscn of Econ. Sciences; foreign mem. AAAS; Chevalier, Légion d'Honneur; Wells Prize, Harvard Univ., CNRS Silver Medal. *Publications:* Externalités et théorie économique 1977, Incentives in Public Decision-Making 1979, Fondements de l'économie publique 1982, Economie de l'information et de l'incertain 1985, A Theory of Incentives in Procurement and Regulation 1993, numerous articles in econ. Publs. *Leisure interests:* gardening, tennis, skiing. *Address:* Université des sciences sociales, place Anatole France, 31042 Toulouse (Office); 11 chemin des Tuileries, 31770 Colomiers, France (Home).

LAFFONT, Robert Raoul, LenD; French publishing executive; b. 30 Nov. 1916, Marseille; s. of Raymond Laffont and Nathalie Périer; m. Hélène Furterer 1987; three s. two d. (from previous marriages); ed Lycée Périer, Marseille and Ecole des Hautes Etudes Commerciales, Paris; Lt 94th Regt of Artillery, Montagne; f. Editions Robert Laffont, Marseille 1941, transferred to Paris 1945, Pres. 1959–86; Fondateur du Pont-Royal; Chevalier, Légion d'Honneur, Officier, Ordre Nat. du Mérite. *Publication:* Robert Laffont, éditeur 1974, Léger étonnement avant le saut 1995. *Leisure interest:* football. *Address:* Editions Robert Laffont, 24 avenue Marceau, 75008 Paris (Office); 11 rue Pierre Nicole, Paris 75005, France (Home). *Telephone:* 43-29-12-33 (Office); 43-26-02-41 (Home).

LAFLEY, Alan G., MBA; American business executive; b. 13 June 1947, Keene, NH; ed Harvard Business School; brand asst Joy, The Proctor & Gamble Co. 1977–78, sales training Denver Sales Dist 1978–80, Asst Brand Man. Tide 1978–80, Brand Man. Dawn & Ivory Snow 1980–81, Ivory Snow 1981–82, Cheer 1982–83, Assoc. Advertising Man. PS & D Div. 1983–86, Advertising Man. 1986–88, Gen. Man. Laundry Products PS & D Div. 1988–91, Vice-Pres. Laundry and Cleaning Products 1991–92, Group Vice-Pres., Pres. Laundry and Cleaning Products 1992–94, Group Vice-Pres. Far East Div. 1994–95, Exec. Vice-Pres., Pres. Asia Div. 1995–98, Exec. Vice-Pres. North American Div. 1998–99, Pres. Global Beauty Care and North America 1999–2000, Pres. and CEO The Proctor & Gamble Co. June 2000–; Trustee Hamilton Coll., Cincinnati Playhouse in the Park, Cincinnati Symphony Orchestra, Cincinnati Inst. of Fine Arts, Seven Hills School. *Address:* The Proctor & Gamble Co., 1 Proctor & Gamble Plaza, Cincinnati, OH 43202-3315, USA (Office). *Website:* www.pg.com (Office).

LAFONT, Bernadette Paule Anne; French actress; b. 28 Oct. 1938, Nîmes; d. of Roger Lafont and Simone Illaire; m. György Medveczky (divorced); one s. two d. (one deceased); ed Lycée de Nîmes; Pres. Assoc. Acas 1990–; Chevalier, Légion d'Honneur, Commdr des Arts et des Lettres; Triomphe du cinéma 1973, César for Best Supporting Actress 1985, Prix d'interpretation Lucarno 1993, Swann du coup de foudre de l'année, Festival of Romantic Film 1998, César d'honneur Life Achievement Award 2003. *Films include:* Les Mistons 1957, L'Eau à la bouche 1959, Les Bonnes femmes 1959, Compartiment tueurs 1965, Le Voleur 1966, La Fiancée du pirate 1969, Out One 1971, La Maman et la putain 1972, Une belle fille comme moi 1972, Zig-Zig 1974, Retour en force 1979, La Bête noire 1983, Le Pactole 1984, L'Effrontée 1985, Masques 1987, Prisonnières 1988, L'Air de rien 1990, Ville à vendre 1992, Personne ne m'aime 1994, Pourquoi partir? 1996, Rien sur Robert 1999, Recto! Verso 1999, Les Amants du Nil 2001, Les petites couleurs 2001, Super Ripoux 2003. *Plays include:* Bathory la Comtesse sanglante 1978, La Tour de la défense 1981, Désiré 1984, Barrio Chino 1987, Le Baladin du monde occidental 1988, Les Joyeuses et horrifiques farces du père Lalande 1989, La Frousse 1993, La Marguerite 1993, La Traversée 1996, L'Arlésienne 1997, Une table pour six 1998, Le faucon 1998, Monsieur Anédée 1999, Léo 2002, Monologues du vagin 2002–03, Un beau salaud 2002. *Radio:* Le feu au lac, Festival d'Avignon 1999, Les bonnes, France Culture 2000. *Television:* Les pigeons de Notre Dame 1964, Le malheur de Maloo 1982, Sautes de velours 1987, La tendresse de l'araignée. *Publications:* La Fiancée du cinéma 1978, Mes Enfants de la balle 1988, Le Roman de ma vie 1997 (autobiog.). *Address:* c/o Intertalent, 5 rue Clément Marot, 75008 Paris, France (Office).

LAFONTAINE, Oskar; German politician; b. 16 Sept. 1943, Saarlouis; m. Doris Vartan 1984; one step-d.; ed Univs of Bonn and Saarbrücken; Mayor of Saarbrücken 1976–85; mem. Saarland Landtag (Regional Parl.), Minister-Pres. 1985–98; Chair. SPD Regional Asscn, Saar 1977–96; mem. SPD Cen. Cttee; Vice-Chair. SPD 1987–96; Cand. for Chancellorship 1990; Leader SPD 1995–99 (resgnd); Minister of Finance 1998–99 (resgnd). *Publications:* Angst vor den Freunden 1983, Der andere Fortschritt 1985, Die Gesellschaft der Zukunft 1988, Das Lied vom Teilen 1989, Deutsche Wahrheiten 1990, Keine Angst vor der Globalisierung (jtly) 1998, Das Herz schlägt links (autobiog.) 2000. *Address:* c/o Ministry of Finance, Wilhelmstrasse 97, 10117 Berlin, Germany.

LAFORTE, Conrad, DèsSc, FRSC; Canadian university professor; b. 10 Nov. 1921, Kenogami, PQ; s. of Philippe Laforte and Marie-Mathilda Dallaire; m. Hélène Gauthier 1957; one d.; ed Montréal Univ. and Laval Univ.; librarian and archivist, Folklore Archives, Laval Univ. 1951–75; Instructor CELAT, Laval Univ. 1965–67, Asst Prof. 1967–73, Assoc. Prof. 1973–77, Prof. 1977–81, Titular Prof. Dept of History and CELAT 1981–88; mem. Royal Soc.

of Canada 1982; Fellow Emer. CELAT, Laval Univ. 1984; Distinguished Perm. mem. Folklore Studies Asscn of Canada 1988; Dr. hc (Sudbury, Ont.) 2000; Grand Prix, Soc. du patrimoine d'expression du Québec 1999; Médaille Luc Lacourcière 1981; Marius Barbeau Medal, Folklore Studies Asscn of Canada 1999 and other awards for folklore research. *Publications:* Le chanson folklorique et les écrivains du XIXe siècle 1973, Poétiques de la chanson traditionnelle française 1976, Catalogue de la chanson folklorique française (6 Vols) 1977–87, Menteries drôles et merveilleuses 1978, Survivances médiévales dans la chanson folklorique 1981, Chansons folkloriques à sujet religieux 1988, La chanson de tradition orale, une découverte des écrivains du XIXe siècle (en France et au Québec) 1995, Vision d'une société par les chansons de tradition orale à caractère épique et tragique 1997, Chansons de facture médiévale retrouvées dans la tradition orale (2 Vols) 1997. *Address:* 949 rue Gatineau, Ste.-Foy, PQ, G1V 3A2, Canada.

LAGARDE, Paul, DenD; French professor emeritus of law; b. 3 March 1934, Rennes; s. of Gaston Lagarde and Charlotte Béquignon; m. Bernadette Lamberts 1962; two s. one d.; ed Paris Univ.; Prof. Faculty of Law, Nancy 1961–69, Nanterre 1969–71; Prof. of Private Int. Law, Univ. of Paris I 1971–2001, now Prof. Emer.; Gen. Sec. Revue critique de droit international privé 1962, Ed.-in-Chief 1976, Dir 1990; Pres. Comité Français de droit int. privé 1987–90; Conseiller d'Etat en service extraordinaire 1996–2001; mem. Inst. of Int. Law; Gen. Sec. Comm. Int. de l'Etat Civil 2000–; Chevalier, Légion d'honneur; Dr hc (Freiburg i.Br.); Prize of Foundation Alexander von Humboldt 1992. *Publications:* Recherches sur l'ordre public en droit international privé 1959, La réciprocité en droit international privé 1977, Le principe de proximité dans le droit international privé contemporain 1987, Traité de droit international privé (with Henri Batiffol) 1993, La nationalité française 1997. *Address:* 2 Rue Henri Bocquillon, 75015 Paris, France. *Telephone:* 1-45-58-30-89. *Fax:* 1-44-26-00-84. *E-mail:* paul.lagarde@wanadoo.fr (Home).

LAGAYETTE, Philippe Ernest Georges; French government official and business executive; b. 16 June 1943, Tulle (Corrèze); s. of Elie Lagayette and Renée Portier; m. Marie-Louise Antoni 1979; two s. two d.; ed Ecole Polytechnique and Ecole Nat. d'Admin; Eng Génie Maritime 1965; Insp. des Finances 1970; Deputy Dir Treasury Man., Ministry of Economy, Finance and Budget 1980; Dir Cabinet of Minister of Economy, Finance and Budget 1981–84; Deputy Gov. Banque de France 1984, First Deputy Gov. 1990; Insp.-Gen. des Finances 1988–; Dir-Gen. Caisse des Dépôts et Consignations 1992–97; Pres. JP Morgan and Cie SA 1998–, Institut des Hautes Etudes Scientifiques; Officier, Légion d'honneur, Ordre nat. du Mérite. *Leisure interests:* hunting, tennis, skiing, cinema. *Address:* JP Morgan, 14 Place Vendôme, 75001 Paris (Office); 10 avenue d'Eylau, 75116 Paris, France (Home). *Telephone:* 1-40-15-49-88 (Office). *Fax:* 1-40-15-41-36 (Office). *E-mail:* lagayette_philippe@jpmorgan.com (Office). *Website:* www.jpmorgan.com (Office).

LAGERFELD, Karl-Otto; German fashion designer; b. 1938, Hamburg; ed privately and at art school, Hamburg; fashion apprentice with Balmain and Patou 1959; freelance designer associated with Fendi, Rome 1963–, Chloe, Paris 1964–83, Chanel, Paris 1982–, Isetan, Japan; designer Karl Lagerfeld's Women's Wear, Karl Lagerfeld France Inc. 1983–; first collection under his own name 1984; Hon. Teacher, Vienna 1983; costume design for film Comédie d'Amour 1989; awarded Golden Thimble 1986. *Publications:* Lagerfeld's Sketchbook (with Anna Piaggi), Helmut Newton 1990, Karl Lagerfeld Off the Record 1995. *Address:* Karl Lagerfeld France Inc., 75008 Paris, France (Office).

LAGERGREN, Gunnar Karl Andreas; Swedish judge; b. 23 Aug. 1912, Stockholm; m. Nina von Dardel 1943; one s. three d. (one d. Nane m. to Kofi Annan, UN Sec. Gen.); ed Stockholm Univ.; Arbitrator, Int. Chamber of Commerce (ICC), Paris 1949–81, Pres. Comm. on Int. Commercial Practice of ICC 1951–67; Judge, Stockholm Court of Appeal 1957–66; Pres. Court of Appeal for Western Sweden, Göteborg 1966–77; Judge, European Court of Human Rights, Strasbourg 1977–88; Pres. Supreme Restitution Court, Fed. Repub. of Germany 1964–90; Chair. Italian-Somali Arbitration Tribunal in Mogadishu 1964; Chair. Indo-Pakistan Western Boundary Tribunal, Geneva 1965–69; Vice-Pres. Arbitration Comm. on Property Rights and Interests in Germany, Koblenz 1956–69; mem. Int. Court, Tangier 1953–56; mem. Permanent Court of Arbitration, The Hague 1966–90; sole Arbitrator of the BP/Libya Concession Tribunal, Copenhagen 1972–75; Deputy Chair. Appeals Bd of the Council of Europe 1981–87, Chair. 1987–91 and 1994 (ad hoc); Pres. Iran-USA Claims Tribunal, The Hague 1981–84; Pres. Arbitral Tribunal for German External Debts, Koblenz 1982–; Pres. Egypt-Israel Taba Arbitration Tribunal, Geneva 1986–88; Pres. Raoul Wallenberg Inst. for Human Rights, Lund 1984–90; Marshal of the Realm (Excellency) 1976–82; Dr hc (Uppsala Univ.) 1965. *Address:* Dahlbergsvägen 22, 182 62 Djursholm, Sweden. *Telephone:* 87-55-58-26.

LAGHI, H.E. Cardinal Pio, STD, JCD; Italian ecclesiastic; b. 21 May 1922, Castiglione (Fiorlì); ed Pontifical Lateran Univ. Rome and Pontifical Ecclesiastical Acad.; Sec. Apostolic Nunciature, Managua 1952–54, Apostolic Del. Washington, DC 1954–61, Apostolic Nunciature, New Delhi 1961–64; served in Secr. of State of Vatican 1964–69; elevated to rank of Archbishop 1969; Apostolic Del. in Jerusalem and Palestine 1969–74, also assumed duties of Pro-Nuncio to Cyprus and Apostolic Visitor to Greece; Apostolic Nuncio, Argentina 1974–80; Apostolic Del. in USA 1980–84, Apostolic Pro-Nuncio 1984–90; Prefect, Congregation for Catholic Educ., Vatican 1990–98; cr.

Cardinal 1991; Pres. Pontifical Oratory of St Peter 1992; HE Cardinal Patron, Sovereign Mil. Order of Malta 1993. *Address:* c/o Congregation for Catholic Education, Palazzo delle Congregazioni, Piazza Pio XII 3, 00193 Rome, Vatican City.

LAGOS ESCOBAR, Ricardo, PhD; Chilean politician; b. 2 March 1938, Santiago; m. Luisa Durán; five c.; ed Univ. of Chile, Duke Univ., N Carolina; Prof. Univ. of Chile 1963–72, fmr Head School of Political and Admin. Sciences, fmr Dir Inst. of Econs, Gen. Sec. 1971; Visiting Prof. Univ. of N Carolina, Chapel Hill 1974–75; Chair. Alianza Democrática (AD) 1983–84; Chair. Partido por la Democracia (PPD) 1987–90; Minister of Educ. 1990–92, of Public Works 1994; Pres. of Chile March 2000–. *Publications:* Población, Pobreza y Mercado de Trabajo en América Latina 1997, numerous books and articles on econs and politics. *Address:* Office of the President, Palacio de la Moneda, Santiago, Chile (Office). *Telephone:* (2) 690-4000 (Office). *Fax:* (2) 698-4656.

LAGRAVENESE, Richard, BFA; American film screenplay writer, director and producer; b. 30 Oct. 1959, Brooklyn, New York; s. of Patrick LaGravenese and Lucille LaGravenese; m. Ann Weiss LaGravenese 1986; one d.; ed Lafayette High School, Emerson Coll. and New York Univ.; Independent Film Project Writer of the Year, Best Original Screenplay 2000, Erin Brockovich (co-writer) 2000. *Screenplays:* Rude Awakening, The Fisher King 1991, The Ref (also producer) 1994, A Little Princess 1995, The Bridges of Madison County 1995, The Horse Whisperer 1998, Living Out Loud (also dir) 1998, Unstrung Heroes, The Defective Detective 2002. *Leisure interests:* theatre, books, family. *Address:* c/o Kirsten Bonelli, 8383 Wilshire Boulevard, Suite 340, Beverly Hills, CA 90211, USA.

LAGU, Lt-Gen. Joseph; Sudanese politician, army officer and diplomatist; b. 21 Nov. 1931; s. of Yakobo Yanga and Marini Kaluma; ed Rumbek Secondary School, Mil. Acad. Omdurman; served in Sudanese Army 1960–63; joined South Sudan Liberation Movt 1963, Leader SSLM 1969; signed peace agreement with Govt of Sudan March 1972; Second Vice-Pres. of Sudan 1978–80, 1982–85; Pres. Supreme Exec. Council for the South 1978–80; fmr Perm. Rep. to UN; Order of the Two Niles 1972. *Publication:* The Anya-Nya–what we fight for 1972. *Address:* c/o Ministry of Foreign Affairs, Khartoum, Sudan.

LAGUMDZIJA, Zlatko, MSc, PhD; Bosnia and Herzegovina politician; b. 26 Dec. 1955, Sarajevo; m.; two c.; ed Univ. of Sarajevo, Harvard Univ., USA; Visiting Prof. Arizona Univ. 1988–89; Prof. of Econ. and Electrical Eng Univ. of Sarajevo 1989–, Dir Centre for Man. and Computer Tech. 1995; co-f. Social and Democratic Party SDP 1990, Chair. 1997–; mem. House of Reps of Parl. Ass. 1996–; Prime Minister, Minister of Foreign Affairs and Treasurer of the Insts of Bosnia and Herzegovina 2001; Minister of Foreign Affairs 2001–. *Address:* Ministry of Foreign Affairs, Musala 2, 71000 Sarajevo, Bosnia and Herzegovina (Office). *Telephone:* (33) 663813 (Office). *Fax:* (33) 472188 (Office). *E-mail:* info@mvp.gov.ba (Office). *Website:* www.mvp.gov.ba (Office).

LAHHAM, Duraid, BSc; Syrian actor and academic; b. 1934, Damascus; m. Hala Bitar; two s. one d.; ed Damascus Univ.; Lecturer, Univ. of Damascus 1955–60; stage roles 1960–; comedian; Pres. of the Syrian Assoc. of Artists 1967. *Films include:* The Pearl Necklace 1965, Dream Castle 1966, Love Affair in Istanbul 1967, As Saalik 1968, Khayyat As-Sayyidate 1969. *Publications:* author of several comedies. *Leisure interest:* accordionist. *Address:* Syrian Broadcasting Corporation, Omayya Square, Damascus, Syria.

LAHLAIDI, Abdelhafid, PhD; Moroccan professor of medicine; b. 20 May 1942; m.; three c.; ed Univ. of Paris, Univ. of Geneva; Prof. of Medicine, Mohammed V Univ. 1977–; Fellow Islamic Acad. of Sciences. *Publications:* Anatomie topographique, Applications, Anatom-Chirurgicles (5 Vols) 1986. *Address:* Université Mohammed V, BP 554, 3 rue Michlifen, Agdal, Rabat, Morocco (Office). *Telephone:* 67-13-18 (Office). *Fax:* 67-14-01 (Office). *Website:* www.emi.ac.ma.

LAHNSTEIN, Manfred; German politician and civil servant; b. 20 Dec. 1937, Rhineland; joined SPD 1959; at European Comm., Brussels, latterly as Chef de Cabinet to Commr Wilhelm Haferkamp 1967–73; econ. adviser, Chancellery 1973; moved to Finance Ministry 1974, successively Div. Head and State Sec. in charge of Financial and Monetary Policy 1974–80; Chancellor's Chief Civil Servant 1980–82; Minister of Finance April–Oct. 1982; Pres. Electronic Media Group; mem. Bd Dirs Bertelsmann AG 1983–, mem. Supervisory Bd 1994–. *Leisure interests:* music, smoking cigars. *Address:* Carl-Bertelsmannstrasse 270, 33335 Gütersloh, Germany.

LAHOUD, Gen. Emile; Lebanese politician and naval officer; b. 1936, Baabdat; s. of Gen. Jamil Lahoud and Adrenee Bajakian; m. Andrée Amadouni; two s. one d.; ed Brumana High School, also attended various courses at Naval Acads in UK and USA 1958–80; joined Mil. Acad. as cadet officer 1956, promoted to Ensign 1959, Sub.-Lt 1962, Lt 1968, Lt-Commdr 1974, Commdr 1976, Cap. 1980, Rear-Adm. 1985, Gen. 1989; Commdr of Second Fleet 1966–68, of First Fleet 1968–70; Staff of Army Fourth Bureau 1970–72; Chief of Personal Staff of Gen. Commdr of Armed Forces 1973–79; Dir of Personnel, Army HQ 1980–83; Pres. of Mil. Office, Ministry of Defence 1983–89; Gen. and Commdr of Armed Forces 1989–; Pres. of the Repub. of the Lebanon 1998–; Lebanese Medal of Merit Gold, Medal of Merit and Honour, Haiti 1974, War Medals 1991, 1992, Dawn of the South Medal 1993, Nat. Unity Medal 1993, Medal of Esteem 1994; Grand Cordon Order of the Cedar 1993, Commdr Légion d'Honneur 1993, Grand Cross of Argentina 1998, Order of Merit, Sr Officer Level (Italy) 1997, Order of Hussein ibn Ali (Jordan) 1999, Necklace of Independence (Qatar) 1999. *Publication:* Procedure and Modus Operandi 1998. *Leisure interests:* diving, swimming. *Address:* Presidential Palace, Baabda, Lebanon (Office). *Telephone:* (3) 777999 (Office). *Fax:* (5) 922400 (Office). *E-mail:* president_office@presidency .gov.lb (Office).

LAI, Jimmy; Hong Kong business executive, journalist and publisher; Propr Giordano (retail clothing chain) 1980–, Chair. 1980–94; Publr Next Magazine 1990–, Apple Daily 1995–. *Address:* Apple Daily, 6/F Garment Centre, 576–586 Castle Peak Road, Cheung Sha Wan; Next Magazine, Westlands Centre, 10/F, 20 Westlands Road, Quarry Bay, Hong Kong, Special Administrative Region, People's Republic of China. *Telephone:* 29908685 (Apple Daily); 28119686 (Next Magazine). *Fax:* 23708908 (Apple Daily); 28113862 (Next Magazine).

LAIDLAW, Sir Christophor Charles Fraser, Kt; British business executive; b. 9 Aug. 1922; s. of the late Hugh Alexander Lyon Laidlaw and Sarah Georgina Fraser; m. Nina Mary Prichard 1952; one s. three d.; ed Rugby School and St John's Coll. Cambridge; served War of 1939–45, Europe and Far East, Maj. on Gen. Staff; joined British Petroleum Co. Ltd (BP) 1948, BP rep. in Hamburg 1959–61, Gen. Man. Marketing Dept 1963–67, Dir BP Trading 1967, Pres. BP Belgium 1967–71, Dir (Operations) 1971–72, Chair. BP Germany 1972–83, Man. Dir BP Co. Ltd 1972–81, Deputy Chair. 1980–81; Chair. BP Oil 1977–81, BP Oil Int. 1981, ICL 1981–84; Pres. ICL France 1983; Dir Commercial Union Assurance Co. 1978–83, Barclays Bank Int. Ltd 1980–87, Barclays Bank 1981–88, Amerada Hess Corpn 1983–94, Dalgety 1984–92, Redland 1984–92, Barclays Merchant Bank 1984–87, Amerada Ltd 1985–98, Mercedes-Benz (UK) 1986–93, Daimler Benz (UK) Ltd 1994–99, Daimler Chrysler UK Holding 1999–2000; Chair. Boving & Co. 1984–85, Bridon PLC 1985–90; Dir INSEAD 1987–94 (Chair. UK Advisory Bd 1984–91); Master Tallow Chandlers Co. 1988–89; Pres. German Chamber of Industry and Commerce 1983–86; Vice-Pres. British-German Soc. 1996–; Hon. Fellow St John's Coll., Cambridge 1996. *Leisure interests:* fishing, shooting, opera. *Address:* 49 Chelsea Square, London, SW3 6LH, England. *Telephone:* (20) 7352-6942 (Home). *Fax:* (20) 7376-3182 (Home).

LAIDLER, David Ernest William, PhD, FRSC; Canadian/British economist; b. 12 Aug. 1938, Tynemouth, UK; s. of John Alphonse Laidler and Leonora Laidler (née Gosman); m. Antje Charlotte Breitwisch 1965; one d.; ed Tynemouth School, London School of Econs, Univs of Syracuse and Chicago, USA; Asst Lecturer, LSE 1961–62; Asst Prof., Univ. of Calif., Berkeley 1963–66; Lecturer, Univ. of Essex 1966–69; Prof., Univ. of Manchester 1969–75; Prof. of Econs, Univ. of Western Ont. 1975–, Bank of Montreal Prof. 2000–, Dept Chair. 1981–84; Special Advisor Bank of Canada 1998–99; Adjunct Scholar, CD Howe Inst., Toronto 1990–99, Canadian Bankers' Asscn Fellow 2000; Visiting Economist, Reserve Bank of Australia 1977; Assoc. Ed. Journal of Money, Credit and Banking 1979–; mem. Editorial Bd Pakistan Devt Review 1987–, European Journal of the History of Econ. Thought 1993–; fmr mem. editorial Bd several other journals; Co-Founder and mem. Exec. Cttee Money Study Group 1970–75; mem. Econs Cttee, CNAA, GB 1971–75, Econs Cttee, SSRC, GB 1972–75, Consortium on Macroeconomic Modelling and Forecasting, ESRC, GB 1981–88, Econ. Advisory Panel to Minister of Finance, Canada 1982–84; Co-ordinator Research Advisory Group on Econ. Ideas and Social Issues, Royal Comm. on the Econ. Union and Devt Prospects for Canada (Macdonald Comm.) 1984–85; Dir Philip Allan Publrs Ltd 1972–99; Pres. Canadian Econs Asscn 1987–88; BAAS Lister Lecturer 1972; Canadian Econs Asscn Douglas Purvis Prize 1994, Hellmuth Prize, Univ. of Western Ontario 1999. *Publications:* The Demand for Money 1969, Essays on Money and Inflation 1975, Monetarist Perspectives 1982, Taking Money Seriously 1990, The Golden Age of the Quantity Theory 1991, The Great Canadian Disinflation (with W. P. B. Robson) 1993, Money and Macroeconomics: Selected Essays 1998, Fabricating the Keynesian Revolution 1999. *Leisure interests:* going to concerts, opera and theatre. *Address:* Department of Economics, University of Western Ontario, London, Ont., N6A 5C2 (Office); 345 Grangeover Avenue, London, Ont., N6G 4K8, Canada (Home). *Telephone:* (519) 661-3400 (Office); (519) 438-0527 (Home). *Fax:* (519) 661-3666 (Office). *E-mail:* laidler@uwo.ca (Office).

LAINE, Dame Cleo (Mrs Clementina Dinah Dankworth), DBE; British singer; b. 28 Oct. 1927, Southall, Middx; m. 1st George Langridge 1947 (dissolved 1957), one s.; m. 2nd John Philip William Dankworth (q.v.) 1958, one s. one d.; joined Dankworth Orchestra 1953; lead role in Seven Deadly Sins, Edinburgh Festival and Sadler's Wells 1961; acting roles in Edinburgh Festival 1966, 1967; f. Wavendon Stables Performing Arts Centre (with John Dankworth) 1970; many appearances with symphony orchestras performing Façade (Walton) and other compositions; Julie in Show Boat, Adelphi Theatre 1971; title role in Colette, Comedy Theatre 1980; Desiree in A Little Night Music, Mich. Opera House, USA 1983; The Mystery of Edwin Drood, Broadway, NY 1986; Into the Woods (US Nat. Tour) 1989; frequent tours and TV appearances, Europe, Australia and USA; Freedom of Worshipful Co. of Musicians 2002; Hon. MA (Open Univ.) 1975; Hon. DMus (Berklee School of Music) 1982, (York) 1993; Hon. DA (Luton) 1994; Melody Maker and New Musical Express Top Girl Singer Awards 1956; Moscow Arts Theatre Award for acting role in Flesh to a Tiger 1958; top place in Int. Critics' Poll of American Jazz magazine Downbeat 1965; Woman of the Year (9th annual

Golden Feather Awards) 1973; Edison Award 1974; Variety Club of GB Show Business Personality Award (with John Dankworth) 1977; TV Times Viewers' Award for Most Exciting Female Singer on TV 1978; Grammy Award for Best Jazz Vocalist-Female 1985; Best Actress in a Musical (Edwin Drood) 1986; Theatre World Award for Edwin Drood 1986, Nat. Asscn of Recording Merchandisers (NARM) Presidential Lifetime Achievement Award 1990, Vocalist of the Year (British Jazz Awards) 1990, Lifetime Achievement Award (USA) 1991, ISPA Distinguished Artists Award 1999, Back Stage Bob Harrington Lifetime Achievement Award (with John Dankworth) 2001, BBC British Jazz Awards Lifetime Achievement Award (with John Dankworth) 2002. *Film:* Last of the Blonde Bombshells 2000. *Publications:* Cleo: An Autobiography 1994, You Can Sing If You Want To 1997. *Leisure interest:* painting. *Address:* The Old Rectory, Wavendon, Milton Keynes, MK17 8LT, England. *Fax:* (1908) 584414. *Website:* www.quarternotes.com (Office).

LAINE, Jermu Tapani; Finnish politician; b. 1931, Turku; Functionary, Ministry of Trade and Industry 1955–65; Lecturer in Commercial Studies, Valkeakoski 1965–69; Rector, Commercial Inst., Mänttä 1969–; municipal positions in Valkeakoski and Mänttä 1968–; Political Sec. to Prime Minister Sorsa 1972–73; Minister for Foreign Trade 1973–75; MP 1975–; Minister, Ministry of Finance 1982–83; Minister for Foreign Trade 1983–87; Chair. Supervisory Bd Valmet Og 1987–88; Dir-Gen. Finnish Customs Bd 1988–94; mem. Social Democratic Party. *Address:* Haapaniemenkatu 20D 60, 00530 Helsinki, Finland.

LAING, Jennifer Charlina Ellsworth; British advertising executive and management consultant; b. 1947, Southampton; d. of late James Ellsworth Laing and of Mary McKane (née Taylor); m. (divorced); joined Garland Compton 1969, firm subsequently taken over by Saatchi & Saatchi, Dir Saatchi & Saatchi Garland Compton 1977; Dir Leo Burnett 1978–80; rejoined Saatchi & Saatchi, Deputy Chair. 1981–87, Jt Chair. 1987–88, Chair. Saatchi & Saatchi Advertising 1995–96, Chief Exec. N American Operations, NY 1997–2000; Chair. CEO Aspect Hill Holliday 1988; formed Laing Henry Ltd 1990, merged with Saatchi & Saatchi 1995; Dir (non-exec.) Great Ormond Street Hosp. for Children NHS Trust 1994–96; fmr Dir Remploy; Fellow, Marketing Soc., Inst. of Practitioners in Advertising; mem. Exec. Bd Saatchi & Saatchi Advertising Worldwide 1996–2000; Fellow Marketing Soc.; Fellow Inst. of Practitioners in Advertising. *Leisure interests:* racing, ballet, opera, theatre, race-horse owner. *Address:* 20 Gloucester Crescent, London, NW1 7DS, England.

LAING, R(obert) Stanley, B.S.MECH.ENG., MBA; American business executive; b. 1 Nov. 1918, Seattle; s. of Robert Vardy Laing and Marie Laing (née Scott); m. 1st Janet Emmott Orr 1947 (died 1986), one s. four d.; m. 2nd Eva Nofke 1986 (died 1988); m. 3rd Mary Wilshire 1988; ed Univ. of Washington and Harvard Business School; with Nat. Cash Register Co., Dayton, Ohio 1947–72, Special Asst in Exec. Office 1947–49, Asst to Comptroller 1949, Gen. Auditor 1950–53, Asst Comptroller 1953–54, Comptroller 1954–60, Vice-Pres. (Finance) 1960–62, Exec. Vice-Pres. 1962–64, Pres. 1964–72; Dir and Chair. Business Equipment Mfg Asscn 1963–64; fmr Chair. Denison Univ. Bd of Trustees; fmr Dir Gen. Mills Inc., Mead Corpn, NCR Corpn, Cincinnati Milacron Inc., B. F. Goodrich Co., Armco Corpn, Amdahl Corpn, Sinclair Community Coll. Foundation; consultant to Fujitsu Ltd, Japan 1977–95; Order of Lateran Cross (Vatican). *Address:* 3430 South Dixie, Dayton, OH 45439 (Office); 650 West David Road, Dayton, OH 45429, USA (Home). *Telephone:* (513) 298-0884 (Office).

LAING, Stuart, MA; British diplomatist; b. 22 July 1948, Limpsfield, Surrey; s. of Denys Laing and Judy Dods; m. Sibella Dorman 1971; one s. two d.; ed Rugby School, Corpus Christi Coll. Cambridge; since joining HM Diplomatic Service has served in Jedda, Brussels, Cairo, Prague and Riyadh; High Commr in Brunei 1999–2002; Amb. to Oman April 2002–. *Leisure interests:* playing chamber music, hill-walking, desert travel. *Address:* Embassy of the United Kingdom, POB 185, Mina al-Fahal, Postal Code 116, Oman (Office). *Telephone:* 693977 (Office). *Fax:* 693087 (Office). *E-mail:* stuart.laing@fco.gov .uk (Office). *Website:* www.uk-gov.om (Office).

LAING OF DUNPHAIL, Baron (Life Peer), cr. 1991, of Dunphail in the District of Moray; **Hector Laing;** British company executive; b. 12 May 1923, Edinburgh; s. of Hector Laing and Margaret Norris Grant; m. Marian Clare Laurie 1950; three s.; ed Loretto School, Musselborough and Jesus Coll., Cambridge; joined McVitie & Price Ltd as a Dir 1947, Chair. 1963–64; Dir of United Biscuits Ltd 1953–64, Man. Dir 1964–85, Chair. United Biscuits (Holdings) PLC 1972–90; Council mem. Inst. of Dirs 1969–75; mem. Intervention Bd for Agric. Produce 1972–75; Dir Royal Insurance Co. 1970–78, Court of Bank of England 1973–91, Allied-Lyons 1979–82, Exxon Corpn (USA) 1984–94; Chair. Food & Drink Industries Council 1977–79, Scottish Business in the Community 1982–90, Business in the Community 1987–91; Pres. Inst. of Business Ethics 1991–94, Trident Trust 1992–94; mem. Advisory Council, London Enterprise Agency 1981; Jt Treas. Conservative Party 1988–93; Dr hc (Stirling) 1985, Hon. DLitt (Herriot Watt) 1986; Bronze Star (USA), Hambro Award 1979; Businessman of the Year 1979; Nat. Free Enterprise Award 1980. *Leisure interests:* gardening, walking. *Address:* High Meadows, Windsor Road, Gerrards Cross, Bucks., SL9 8ST, England. *Telephone:* (1753) 882437 (Home). *Fax:* (1753) 885106 (Home).

LAINSON, Ralph, OBE, DSc, FRS; British scientist (retd); b. 21 Feb. 1927, Upper Beeding, Sussex; s. of Charles Harry Lainson and Annie May Denyer;

m. 1st Ann Patricia Russell (divorced 1976), one s. two d.; m. 2nd Zéa Constante Lins 1978; ed Steyning Grammar School, Univ. of London; lecturer in Medical Protozoology London School of Hygiene and Tropical Medicine 1955–59, Attached Investigator, Dept of Medical Protozoology 1962–65; Officer-in-Charge Dermal Leishmaniasis Unit, Baking-Pot, Cayo Dist, Belize 1959–62; Dir Wellcome Parasitology Unit, Inst. Evandro Chagas, Fundação Serviços de Saúde Pública, Pará, Brazil 1965–92; Hon. Prof. Fed. Univ. of Pará 1982; Assoc. Fellow Third World Acad. of Sciences 1989; Hon. mem. British Soc. of Parasitology 1984, Soc. of Protozoologists; Hon. Fellow, London School of Hygiene and Tropical Medicine 1982, Royal Soc. of Tropical Medicine and Hygiene 1997; Chalmers Medal 1971, Manson Medal 1983 Royal Soc. of Tropical Medicine and Hygiene, Oswaldo Cruz Medal, Conselho Estadual de Cultura do Pará (Brazil) 1973, Medalha Comemorativa do 10° Aniversario da Instalação do Conselho Estadual de Saúde do Pará (Brazil) 1983. *Publications:* author or co-author of approx. 300 articles in scientific journals and textbooks. *Leisure interests:* fishing, collecting S. American Lepidoptera, music, philately. *Address:* Department of Parasitology, Institute Evandro Chagas, Avenida Almirante Barroso 492, 66090-000 Belém, Pará (Office); Avenida Visconde de Souza Franco 1237 (Edificio 'Visconti'), Apartamento 902, 66053-000 Belém, Pará, Brazil (Home). *Telephone:* (91) 211-4453 (Office); (91) 223-2382 (Home). *Fax:* (91) 226-1284 (Office); (91) 223-2382 (Home). *E-mail:* ralphlainson@iec.pa.gov.br (Office).

LAIRD, Sir Gavin Harry, Kt, CBE; British trade union official; b. 14 March 1933, Clydebank, Scotland; s. of James Laird and Frances Laird; m. Catherine Gillies Campbell 1956; one d.; shop stewards' convener, Singer, Clydebank for seven years; Regional Officer, Amalgamated Eng Union (fmrly Amalgamated Union of Eng Workers) 1972–75, Exec. Councillor for Scotland and NW England 1975–82, Gen. Sec. (AEU Section) 1992–95; Chair. Greater Manchester Buses North 1994–97; Chair. Murray Johnstone Venture Capital Trust 4 1999–; mem. Murray Johnston Private Acquisition Partnership Advisory Cttee 1999–; mem. Scottish TUC Gen. Council 1973–75; mem. TUC Gen. Council 1979–82; part-time Dir Highlands and Islands Devt Bd 1974–75; mem. Industrial Devt Advisory Bd 1979–86, Arts Council 1983–86, part-time Dir BNOC 1976–86; Chair. The Foundries EDC 1982–85; Dir Bank of England 1986–94; Dir (non-exec.) Scottish TV (Media Group) PLC 1986–99, Britannia Life 1988–2000, Britannia Investment Mans Ltd, Britannia Fund Mans (now Britannic Asset Mans) Ltd 1996–2000, GEC Scotland 1991–99, Edinburgh Investment Trust Ltd 1994–; Pres. Kent Active Retirement Asscn 1999–; Vice-Pres. Pre-Retirement Asscn of GB and NI 1999–; Trustee Anglo-German Foundation 1994–2000, John Smith Memorial Trust; mem. Editorial Bd European Business Journal; mem. Advisory Bd Know-How Fund for Poland 1990–95; mem. Armed Forces Pay Review Body 1995–98, Employment Appeal Tribunal 1996–; Fellow Paisley Coll. of Tech. 1991; Hon. DLitt (Keele Univ.) (Heriot Watt Univ.) 1994. *Leisure interests:* music, hill-walking, reading. *Address:* 9 Clevedon House, Holmbury Park, Bromley, BR1 2WG, England (Home). *Telephone:* (20) 8460-8998 (Home). *Fax:* (20) 8460-8998 (Home).

LAIRD, Melvin Robert, BA; American government official; b. 1 Sept. 1922, Omaha, Neb.; s. of Melvin and Helen Laird (née Connor); m. 1st Barbara Masters 1945 (died 1992); two s. one d.; m. 2nd Carole Fleischman 1993; ed Carleton Coll., Northfield, Minn.; served with Task Force 38 and 58, US Navy Pacific Fleet 1942–46; mem. Wisconsin Senate 1946–52, Chair. Wisconsin Legis. Council; mem. US House of Reps 1952–69, served on Appropriations Cttee, Chair. House of Republican Minority, mem. Republican Coordinating Council, Vice-Chair. Republican Nat. Platform Council 1960, Chair. 1964; US Sec. of Defense 1968–73; Counsellor to Pres. for Domestic Affairs 1973–74; Senior Counsellor for Nat. and Int. Affairs, Readers' Digest Asscn 1974–, now Vice-Pres.; Chair. COMSAT Corpn 1992–96; fmr mem. Bd the Kennedy Center, George Washington Univ., Airlie Foundation; mem. Bd Nat. Defense and Energy Projects of American Enterprise Inst., Thomas Jefferson Center Foundation of Univ. of Virginia, World Rehabilitation Fund; fmr Dir The Reader's Digest Asscn Inc., Metropolitan Life Insurance Co., Northwest Airlines, IDS Mutual Funds Group, Communications Satellite Corpn (Chair. 1992–96), Martin Marietta Corpn, Science Application Int. Corpn, Dir Public Oversight Bd; fmr Trustee, DeWitt and Lila Wallace-Reader's Digest Funds; Republican; over 300 awards and hon. degrees, including Albert Lasker Public Service Award, Statesman in Medicine Award (Airlie Foundation), The Harry S. Truman Award for distinguished service in defense; Presidential Medal of Freedom (USA), Order of Merit (1st Class) (Fed. Repub. of Germany), Commdr Légion d'honneur (France). *Publications include:* A House Divided: America's Strategy Gap 1962, The Conservative Papers (Ed.) 1964, Republican Papers (Ed.) 1968. *Address:* 1730 Rhode Island Avenue, NW, Suite 212, Washington, DC 20036, USA (Office).

LAKATANI, Sani; Niue politician; Prime Minister of Niue March 1999–2001; Minister for External Affairs, Finance, Customs and Revenue, Econ. and Planning Devt and Statistics, Business and Pvt. Sector Devt, Civil Aviation, Tourism, Int. Business Co. and Offshore Banking, Niue Devt Bank March 1999–2001; fmr Leader Niue People's Party (NPP); Chancellor Univ. of the South Pacific, Fiji 2000–(03); Deputy Premier and Minister for Planning, Econ. Devt and Statistics, the Niue Devt Bank, Post, Telecommunications and Information Computer Tech. Devt, Philatelic Bureau and Numismatics, Shipping, Investment and Trade, Civil Aviation and Police, Immigration and Disaster Man. 2002–. *Address:* c/o Office of the Prime Minister, Alofi, Niue (Office).

LAKE, N. Anthony, PhD; American public servant and academic; b. 1939, New York; m.; three c.; ed Harvard Univ., Cambridge Univ., UK, Woodrow Wilson School of Public and Int. Affairs, Princeton Univ.; joined Foreign Service 1962, Special Asst to Amb. Henry Cabot Lodge, Viet Nam; an aide to Sec. of State Henry Kissinger 1969–70; Head State Dept's policy planning operation –1981; Prof., Amherst Coll., Mass. 1981–84, Mount Holyoke Coll. 1984–92; co-f. journal Foreign Policy; a foreign policy adviser to fmr Pres. Clinton during presidential campaign 1992; Nat. Security Adviser 1993–96; nominated Dir CIA Dec. 1996, nomination withdrawn March 1997. *Publications:* The 'Tar Baby' Option: American Policy Toward Southern Rhodesia 1976, Third World Radical Regimes: U.S. Policy under Carter and Reagan 1985, Somoza Falling: A Case Study of Washington at Work 1990, Six Nightmares 2001. *Address:* c/o National Security Council, Executive Office Building, 1600 Pennsylvania Avenue, NW, Washington, DC 20500, USA.

LAKER, Sir Frederick Alfred, Kt; British business executive; b. 6 Aug. 1922; m. 4th Jacqueline Harvey; ed Simon Langton School, Canterbury; worked for Short Bros, Rochester 1938–40; Gen. Aircraft 1940–41; served with Air Transport Auxiliary 1941–46; with Aviation Traders 1946–60; British United Airways 1960–65; Chair. and Man. Dir Laker Airways Ltd 1966–82, Laker Airways (Bahamas) Ltd 1992–; Dir Skytrain Holidays 1982–83, Sir Freddie Laker Ltd 1982–, Northeastern Int. Airlines Inc. (USA) 1984–; mem. Jockey Club 1979–; Chair. Guild of Air Pilots and Navigators Benevolent Fund; Hon. Fellow UMIST 1978; Hon. DSc (City Univ.) 1979, (Cranfield Inst. of Tech.) 1980; Hon. LLD (Victoria Univ. of Manchester) 1981. *Leisure interests:* horse breeding, racing, sailing. *Address:* Princess Tower, West Sunrise, Box 40207, Freeport, Grand Bahama, Bahamas.

LAKHDAR, Zohra Ben, PhD; Tunisian academic; ed Univ. of Paris VI, Univ. of Tunis; fmr Head Spectroscopy Lab., Supervisor postgrad. students for Tunisian DEA Diploma, Co.-Chair. Molecular Spectroscopy Group for Master's Degree and PhD courses; Prof. of Physics, Univ. of Tunis 1992–; founder mem. Tunisian Physics Soc., Tunisian Astronomy Soc.; mem. Islamic Acad. of Sciences. *Address:* Université des Sciences des Techniques et de Médecine de Tunis, Campus Universitaire Manar II, 2092 Tunis, Tunisia (Office). *Telephone:* 873-366 (Office). *Fax:* 872-055 (Office).

LAKHOVA, Yekaterina Filippovna; Russian politician; b. 26 May 1948; m.; one d.; ed Sverdlovsk State Medical Inst.; pediatrician, Deputy Head of Div., Sverdlovsk (now Yekaterinburg) City Dept of Public Health, Deputy Head, Main Dept of Public Health, Sverdlovsk Regional Exec. Cttee 1972–90; RSFSR Peoples' Deputy, mem. Council of Repub. RSFSR Supreme Soviet, Chair. Cttee on Problems of Women, Motherhood and Childhood 1990–93; State Adviser on Problems of Family, Protection of Motherhood and Childhood 1992–; adviser to Russian Pres. on Problems of Family, Protection of Motherhood and Childhood 1992–94; Chair. Cttee on Problems of Women, Family and Demography of Russian Presidency 1992–; Founder and Chair. political Movt Women of Russia 1993; mem. State Duma 1993–; mem. Socialist Party of Russia 1996, Otechestvo (Homeland) political movt 1998. *Address:* State Duma, Okhotny Ryad 1, 103265 Moscow, Russia. *Telephone:* (095) 292-19-00 (Office).

LAL, Bansi, LLB; Indian politician; b. 26 Aug. 1927, Golagarh, Bhiwani District; s. of Chaudhary Mohar Singh; m. Smt. Vidya Devi 1945; two s. four d.; ed Punjab Univ. and Law Coll., Jullundur; started legal practice at Bhiwani 1956; Sec. Loharu Praja Mandal 1943–44; Gen. Sec. Tosham Mandal Congress Cttee 1955–58; Pres. Mandal Congress Cttee, Kural 1958–62; mem. Punjab PCC 1958–62, Rajya Sabha 1960–66, 1976–80, Haryana Assembly 1967; Chief Minister Haryana 1968–75, 1986–87, 1996–99; Minister without portfolio, Govt of India Dec. 1975, Minister of Defence 1975–77; Minister of Railways 1984–85; Minister of Transport 1985–86; mem. Lok Sabha; Chair. Cttee on Public Undertakings 1980–82, Cttee on Estimates 1982–84; Hon. LLD (Kurukshetra Univ., Haryana) 1972, Hon. DSc (Haryana Agric. Univ.) 1972. *Leisure interest:* reading. *Address:* Hansi Road, Bhiwani, Haryana State (Office); 9/5 Sarvapriya, New Delhi 16, India. *Telephone:* (1664) 42429 (Bhiwani) (Office); (11) 6852331 (New Delhi).

LAL, Deepak Kumar, MA, BPhil; British professor of political economy; b. 3 Jan. 1940, Lahore, India; s. of the late Nand Lal and of Shanti Devi; m. Barbara Ballis 1971; one s. one d.; ed Doon School, Dehra Dun, St Stephen's Coll., Delhi, India, Jesus Coll., Oxford; Indian Foreign Service 1963–65; Lecturer, Christ Church, Oxford 1966–68; Research Fellow, Nuffield Coll., Oxford 1968–70; Lecturer, Univ. Coll. London 1970–79, Reader 1979–84, Prof. of Political Economy, Univ. of London 1984–93, Prof. Emer. 1993–; James S. Coleman Prof. of Int. Devt Studies, Univ. of Calif. at Los Angeles 1991–; Consultant, Indian Planning Comm. 1973–74; Research Admin., World Bank, Washington, DC 1983–87; Dir Trade Policy Unit, Centre for Policy Studies 1993–96, Trade and Devt Unit, Inst. of Econ. Affairs 1997–; consultancy assignments ILO, UNCTAD, OECD, IBRD Ministry of Planning, Sri Lanka, Repub. of Korea 1970–. *Publications:* Wells and Welfare 1972, Methods of Project Analysis 1974, Appraising Foreign Investment in Developing Countries 1975, Unemployment and Wage Inflation in Industrial Economies 1977, Men or Machines 1978, Prices for Planning 1980, The Poverty of "Development Eonomics" 1983, Labour and Poverty in Kenya (with P. Collier) 1986, Stagflation, Savings and the State (Ed. with M. Wolf) 1986, The Hindu Equilibrium, 2 Vols 1988, 1989, Public Policy and Economic Development (Ed. with M. Scott) 1990, Development Economics, 4 Vols (Ed.) 1991, The Repressed Economy 1993, Against Dirigisme 1994, The Political

Economy of Poverty, Equity and Growth (with H. Myint) 1996, Unintended Consequences 1998, Unfinished Business 1999, Trade, Development and Political Economy (Ed. with R. Snape) 2001. *Leisure interests:* opera, theatre, tennis, bridge. *Address:* Department of Economics, 8369 Bunche Hall, University of California at Los Angeles, 405 Hilgard Avenue, Los Angeles, CA 90024, USA; A30 Nizamuddin West, New Delhi 110013, India; 2 Erskine Hill, London, NW11 6HB, England. *Telephone:* (310) 825-4521, (310) 206-2382 (Los Angeles); 462 9465 (New Delhi); (20) 8458-3713 (London).

LAL, Devendra, MSc, PhD, FRS; Indian scientist; b. 14 Feb. 1929, Varanasi (Banaras); s. of the late Dr Radhekrishna Lal and of Sita Devi; m. Aruna Damany 1955 (died 1993); ed Harish Chandra High School, Banaras Hindu Univ., Varanasi and Bombay Univ.; Assoc. Prof. Tata Inst. of Fundamental Research 1960–63, Prof. 1963–70, Sr Prof. 1970–72, Visiting Prof., Univ. of Calif. 1965–66; Prof., Scripps Inst. of Oceanography, Univ. of Calif. 1967–; Dir Physical Research Lab., Ahmedabad, 1972–83, Sr Prof. 1983–89, Fellow 1989–; Chair. working group on River Inputs to Ocean System 1977–81; Vice-Pres. Indian Acad. of Sciences, Bangalore 1978–82; Pres. Int. Asscn for Physical Sciences of the Ocean 1979–82, Int. Union of Geodesy and Geophysics 1983–87, Indian Geophysical Union 1980–82; Foreign Sec. Indian Nat. Science Acad., New Delhi 1981–84; mem. Scientific Advisory Cttee to the Cabinet 1979–83; mem. Jt Scientific Cttee of WMO 1979–83; mem. Group of Experts on Scientific Aspects of Marine Pollution, UNESCO, 1979–81; mem. Advisory Cttee on Environment, ICSU 1990–94; Foreign Assoc., NAS (USA); Fellow, Indian Acad. of Sciences, Bangalore, Indian Nat. Science Acad., New Delhi, Centre of the Earth Sciences Studies, Cochin 1983, Nat. Acad. Sciences, Allahabad 1988, Physical Research Laboratory, Ahmedabad 1990, Tata Inst. of Fundamental Research, Bombay 1996–, Geochemical Soc. (USA) 1997, AAAS 1997; Founding mem. Third World Acad. of Sciences, Italy 1983; Assoc. Royal Astronomical Soc. 1984; mem. Int. Acad. of Astronautics 1985; Hon. DSc (Banaras Univ., Varanasi) 1981; Krishnan Medal for Geochem. and Geophysics 1965; Shanti Swarup Bhatnagar Award for Physical Sciences, Council of Scientific and Industrial Research 1967; Repub. Day Nat. Award, Padma Shri 1971; Fed. of Indian Chambers of Commerce and Industry Award in Science and Tech. 1974; Jawaharlal Nehru Award for Science 1986; Goldschmidt Medal 1997. *Publications:* over 200 articles in scientific journals; Early Solar System Processes and the Present Solar System (Ed.), Biogeochemistry of the Arabian Sea (Ed.). *Leisure interests:* photography, painting, mathematical puzzles, chess. *Address:* Scripps Institution of Oceanography, GRD/0244, University of California, San Diego, La Jolla, CA 92093-0244 (Office); 4445 Via Precipicio, San Diego, CA 92122, USA (Home); No. 20, Jayantilal Park, Amli Bopal Road, Village Makarba, Ahmedabad 380009, India (Home). *Telephone:* (858) 534-2134 (Office); (858) 587-1535 (Home USA); 79-6741451 (India). *E-mail:* dlal@ucsd.edu (Office).

LAL, Jayawardena (L. R. U. Jayawardena), PhD; Sri Lankan economist; b. 27 May 1934, Colombo; s. of Neville Ubesinghe Jayawardena and the late Gertrude Mildred Jayawardena; m. Kumari de Zoysa 1958; one s.; ed Royal Coll., Colombo, King's Coll. Cambridge; Econs Affairs Officer, UN 1963–66; Econ. Adviser and Dir Perspective Planning Div., Ministry of Planning and Econ. Affairs 1963–71, Additional Sec. in Ministry 1971–75, Sec. to Treasury and Sec., Ministry of Finance and Planning 1975–78; Amb. to Belgium, Netherlands and Luxembourg and to the EC 1978–82; Dir-Gen. Econ. Affairs, Ministry of Foreign Affairs 1982–85; Asst Sec.-Gen. UN and Dir World Inst. for Devt Econs Research, Helsinki 1985–93; Econ. Adviser to Pres. of Sri Lanka 1994–99; Deputy Chair. Nat. Devt Council 1996–99; Deputy, Cttee of Twenty on Reform of Int. Monetary System 1972–74; elected successively Rapporteur, Vice-Chair. and Chair. Deputies, Group of 24 (G-24) 1971–75, successively 2nd Vice-Chair. and 1st Vice-Chair. Deputies 1997–99; mem. Group of Eminent Persons advising Brandt Comm. on Int. Devt Issues 1978–80; Hon. Fellow King's Coll. Cambridge 1989. *Publications:* author and co-author numerous publs on econs and finance. *Leisure interests:* reading, music. *Address:* 69 Gregory's Road, Colombo 7, Sri Lanka (Home). *Telephone:* (1) 692656 (Colombo) (Home).

LALIVE d'EPINAY, Pierre, BA, PhD, LIC.JUR., LIC.LITT.; Swiss lawyer; b. 8 Oct. 1923, La Chaux-de-Fonds; s. of Auguste Lalive and Mme Lalive; (brother of Jean-Flavien Lalive d'Epinay); m.; ed Geneva and Cambridge Univs; called to Geneva Bar; Prof. of Law, Geneva Univ. 1955, Dir Dept of Pvt. Law, Dean of Law School 1967–69; Prof. of Int. Business Law, Graduate Inst. of Int. Studies 1962–86, Hon. Prof. 1986–; Sr Partner Lalive and Partners; Pres. ICC Inst. of Int. Business Law and Practice, Swiss Arbitration Asscn; Visiting Prof. Columbia, Brussels and Cambridge Univs; Pres. Inst. of Int. Law, numerous Swiss Fed. comms and dels; Chair. of numerous int. arbitration tribunals; DJur (Lyon, Paris, Brussels, Rome); Balzan Prize 1990. *Publications:* more than 150 publs on int. law (public, pvt.), arbitration, contracts and family law. *Leisure interests:* tennis, music (opera), literature, book collecting. *Address:* Geneva University, Faculty of Law, 24 rue Général-Dufour, 1211 Geneva 4; c/o Lalive & Partners, 6 Athénée, 1205 Geneva (Office); Plateau de Champel 16, Geneva, Switzerland (Home). *Telephone:* (22) 3198700 (Office); (22) 7890312 (Home). *Fax:* (22) 3198760 (Office); (22) 3198762. *E-mail:* pr.lalive@lalive.ch (Office).

LALLA AICHA, HRH Princess; Moroccan diplomatist; eldest d. of the late King Mohammed V.; Amb. to UK 1965–69, to Italy 1969–73 (also accred to

Greece); Pres. Moroccan Red Crescent; Grand Cordon of Order of the Throne. *Address:* c/o Ministry of Foreign Affairs, avenue Franklin Roosevelt, Rabat, Morocco.

LALONDE, Brice; French politician and environmental consultant; b. 10 Feb. 1946, Neuilly; s. of Alain Lalonde and Fiona Forbes; m. Patricia Raynaud 1986; two s. (one deceased) two d.; one s. one d. from previous marriage; student leader 1968; Chair. Friends of the Earth 1972, French Branch 1978; Candidate for the Green Party, French Pres. Election 1981; Admin. European Environment Bureau 1983; Dir Paris Office Inst. for European Environmental Policy 1987; Sec. of State for the Environment 1988–89, for the Environment and the Prevention of Tech. and Natural Disasters 1989–90, Minister del. 1990–91, Minister of the Environment 1991–92; Pres. Génération Ecologie (Political Movt) 1990–; Mayor of Saint-Briac-sur-Mer 1995–; Chair. Cttee to Free Alexandr Nikitin 1996–; mem. Conseil Régional, Brittany 1998, Comité national de l'eau 1998–. *Publication:* L'écologie en bleu. *Address:* Génération Ecologie, 7 villa Virginie, 75014 Paris (Office); 65 blvd Arago, 75013 Paris (Home); Mairie, 18 rue de la Mairie, 35800 Saint-Briac-sur-Mer, France. *Telephone:* 1-56-53-53-73 (Office). *Fax:* 1-56-53-53-70 (Office). *E-mail:* generation.ecologie@wanadoo.fr (Office). *Website:* www .generation-ecologie.com (Office).

LALOR, Patrick Joseph; Irish politician; b. 21 July 1926, Dublin; s. of Joseph Lalor and Frances Lalor; m. Myra Murphy 1952; one s. three d.; ed in Abbeyleix and Knockbeg Coll., Carlow; fmr mem. Laois Co. Council and fmr exec. mem. Retail Grocery, Dairy and Allied Trades Asscn (RGDATA); mem. Dáil Eireann 1961–81; Parl. Sec. to Minister of Agric. and Fisheries 1965–66, to Minister for Transport, Power, Posts and Telegraphs 1966–69; Minister of Posts and Telegraphs 1969–70, for Industry and Commerce 1970–73; mem. Fianna Fáil, Chief Whip Parl. Party 1973–77; Parl. Sec. to the Taoiseach (Prime Minister) and to Minister of Defence Jan.–Dec. 1977, Minister of State at Depts of the Taoiseach and of Defence 1979 (resgnd); MEP 1979–94, Leader of Fianna Fail Party in European Parl. 1979, Vice-Pres. Group of European Progressive Democrats 1979–84; Quaestor 1979–82; Vice-Pres. of European Parl. 1982–87; Vice-Pres. European Renewal and Democratic Alliance Group 1986, European Democratic Alliance Group 1988; Quaestor of European Parl. 1989–94; mem. European Parl. Cttees on Transport and Tourism, Rules of Procedure, Political Affairs, Bureau and Enlarged Bureau 1989–94; Grand Officier du Ouissam Alaouite (Morocco) 1981. *Leisure interests:* hurling, Gaelic football, golf, drama. *Address:* Main Street, Abbeyleix, Portlaoise, Co. Laois, Ireland. *Telephone:* (502) 31206.

LALUMIÈRE, Catherine; French politician; b. 3 Aug. 1935, Rennes; m. Pierre Lalumière (deceased); specialist in public law; Lecturer, Univ. of Paris; mem. Steering Cttee, Parti Socialiste 1979; mem. Nat. Ass. for Gironde 1986–89; Adviser to Pres. on civil service; Sec. of State for the Civil Service and Admin. Reforms May–June 1981, Minister for Consumer Affairs 1981–83, Sec. of State 1983–84, Minister for European Affairs 1984–86; Sec.-Gen. Council of Europe 1989–94; Urban Community Councillor, Bordeaux 1989–; Municipal Councillor, Talence 1989–95; MEP 1994–, Vice-Pres. 2001–; Deputy Pres. Radical France 1996 (now Radical Socialist Party); Pres. European Radical Alliance 1994–; Hon. DCL (Durham) 1995. *Address:* European Parliament, 97–113 rue Wiertz, 1047 Brussels, Belgium.

LAMB, Allan Joseph; South African cricketer (retd); b. 20 June 1954, Langebaanweg, Cape Province; s. of Michael Lamb and Joan Lamb; m. Lindsay Lamb 1979; one s. one d.; ed Wynberg Boys' High School and Abbotts Coll.; middle-order right-hand batsman; teams: Western Province 1972–82 and 1992–93, OFS 1987–88, Northants. 1978–95 (Capt. 1989–95); qualified for England 1982 and played in 79 Tests 1982–92 (3 as Capt.), scoring 4,656 runs (average 36.0) including 14 hundreds; toured Australia 1982–83, 1986–87, 1990–91; scored 32,502 first-class runs (89 hundreds); 1,000 15 times; 122 limited-overs ints; Dir Lamb Assocs Event Man. Co., Grenada Sports Ltd; contrib. to Sky Sports Cricket; Wisden Cricketer of the year 1981. *Play:* Beef and Lamb in a stew (roadshow with Ian Botham) 1994–95. *Publication:* Silence of the Lamb (autobiog.) 1995. *Leisure interests:* tennis, golf, cycling, rugby, horse racing, fly-fishing, shooting. *Address:* Lamb Associates Ltd, First Floor, 4 St Giles Street, Northampton, NN1 1JB, England. *Telephone:* (1604) 231222 (Office). *Fax:* (1604) 239930 (Office).

LAMB, Willis Eugene, Jr, PhD, ScD, LHD; American physicist; b. 12 July 1913, Los Angeles, Calif.; s. of Willis Eugene and Marie Helen (Metcalf); m. 1st Ursula Schaefer 1939 (died 1996); m. 2nd Bruria Kaufman 1996; ed Univ. of California; Instructor, Columbia Univ. 1938, Prof. of Physics 1948–52; Loeb Lecturer, Harvard 1953–54; Prof. of Physics, Stanford Univ. 1951–56; Wykeham Prof. of Physics and Fellow, New Coll., Univ. of Oxford 1956–62; Henry Ford II Prof. of Physics, Yale Univ. 1962–72, J. Willard Gibbs Prof. of Physics, Yale Univ. 1972–74; Prof. of Physics and Optical Sciences, Univ. of Arizona 1974–, Regents Prof. 1990– Guggenheim Fellow 1960, Sr Alexander von Humboldt Fellow 1992–94; mem. NAS; Hon. mem. Optical Soc. of America; Hon. Fellow, Royal Soc. Edin.; Hon. ScD (Pennsylvania) 1953; Hon. LHD (Yeshiva) 1964; Hon. ScD (Gustavus Adolphus Coll.) 1975, (Columbia) 1990; Hon. Dr rer. nat (Ulm) 1997; awarded Rumford Premium (American Acad. of Arts and Sciences) 1953; Nobel Prize in Physics (shared with Prof. P. Kusch) 1955; Research Corpn Award 1955, Nat. Medal of Science 2000. *Address:* Optical Sciences Center, University of Arizona, Tucson, AZ 85721, USA. *E-mail:* willis@primus.optics.arizona.edu (Office).

LAMBECK, Kurt, FRS, FAA, D. PHIL., DSc; Australian professor of geophysics; b. 20 Sept. 1941, Loosdrecht, The Netherlands; s. of J. Lambeck and J. Weber; m. Bridget Marguerite Nicholls 1967; one s. one d.; ed Univ. of NSW, Tech. Univ. of Delft, Tech. Univ. of Athens and Oxford Univ.; Geodesist, Smithsonian Astrophysical Observatory 1967–70; Dir of Research, Paris Observatory 1970–73; Prof. of Geophysics, Univ. of Paris 1973–77, ANU 1977–, Dir Research School of Earth Sciences 1984–93; Sec. (Physical Sciences), Australian Acad. of Science 1996–; Chair. Antarctic Science Advisory Comm. 1999–; Foreign mem. Royal Netherlands Acad. of Arts and Sciences 1993, Norwegian Acad. of Science and Letters 1994, Academia Europaea 1999; Fellow American Geophysical Union 1976; Hon. mem. European Geophysics Soc. 1988–; Hon. DEng (Nat. Tech. Univ. of Greece); Macelwane Award, American Geophysical Union 1976, Whitten Medal 1993, Jaeger Medal, Australian Acad. of Science 1995, Alfred Wegener Medal, European Union of Geosciences 1996. *Publications:* The Earth's Variable Rotation 1980, Geophysical Geodesy 1988; numerous papers on geodesy and geophysics. *Address:* Research School of Earth Sciences, Australian National University, Canberra, ACT 0200; 31 Brand Street, Hughes, ACT 2605, Australia. *Telephone:* (2) 62495161.

LAMBERT, Christopher; American actor; b. 29 March 1957, New York; ed L'Ecole Roche, Int. School, Lycée d'Annemasse, Coll. Floriment, Geneva, Florent School, Paris and Paris Conservatoire; mil. service with Alpine Corps, Grenoble; trainee, Barclay's Bank, London 1976; professional debut in TV film Douchka 1977. *Films include:* Greystoke: the Story of Tarzan, Lord of the Apes 1983, Paroles et Musiques 1984, Subway 1985, Highlander 1986, I Love You 1986, The Sicilian, To Kill A Priest, Knight Moves 1992, Fortress 1994, Gunmen 1994, Roadflower, Mortal Kombat 1994, North Star (also exec. producer), Nirvana 1997, Fortress 2 2000, exec. producer When Saturday Comes, Highlander: Endgame 2000, Vercingétorix 2001, The Point Men 2001, The Piano Player 2002.

LAMBERT, Phyllis, CC, C.Q., O.A.L., M.S.ARCH., D.F.A.F.R.A.I.C., FRSC, RCA; Canadian architect; b. 24 Jan. 1927, Montréal, Québec; d. of Samuel and Saidye (Rosner) Bronfman; ed The Study, Montréal, Vassar Coll., New York, Illinois Inst. of Tech., Chicago; adjunct faculty mem., School of Architecture, McGill Univ.; Assoc. Prof., Faculty of Planning, Univ. of Montréal; Bd Chair. and Prin., Ridgway Ltd, Architects/Developers, Los Angeles 1972–84; Consulting Architect Centre Canadien d'Architecture (CCA), Montréal 1979–99, Founding Dir and Chair. Bd of Trustees 1979–; created Fonds d'investissement de Montréal, pvt. fund for revitalization of Montréal neighbourhoods 1997; est. IFCCA Prize for Design of Cities 1999; projects (as architect, consultant etc.) include: Seagram Bldg, New York (as Dir of Planning) 1954–58, Toronto-Dominion Centre 1962, Saidye Bronfman Centre, YM-YWHA, Montréal 1963–68, Les Promenades St-Bruno Shopping Centre, Québec 1974, Jane Tate House renovation, Montréal 1974–76, Biltmore Hotel renovation, Los Angeles 1976, renovation of housing units, St-Hubert St, Montréal 1979; instigated 700-unit co-operative housing renovation project, Milton Park, Montréal 1979–85; Dir restoration Ben Ezra synagogue, Cairo, Egypt 1981–94; jury mem. several cttees for architectural and urban design projects; numerous exhbns; mem. Bd of Trustees Inst. of Fine Arts, New York Univ., Visiting Cttee Princeton Univ., NJ, Visiting Cttee Harvard Univ.; Founding mem. Bd Int. Confed. of Architectural Museums (Pres. 1985–89) and several other bodies; frequent guest lecturer; mem. Bd of Overseers, Coll. of Architecture, Ill. Inst. of Tech., Advisory Council to School of Architecture, Princeton Univ.; Hon. FRIBA; numerous hon. degrees; numerous awards and prizes including American Inst. of Architects 25-Year Award of Excellence (Seagram Bldg), New York Landmarks Conservancy Award, Massey Medal, Royal Architectural Inst. of Canada (Saidye Bronfman Centre), Médaille de l'Académie d'Architecture, Paris 1988, Gabrielle Léger Medal, Heritage Canada Foundation 1988, Medal of Honour, Société Historique de Montréal 1990, Prix d'excellence en architecture, Ordre des Architectes du Québec 1990, Royal Architectural Inst. of Canada Gold Medal Award 1991, 1992 Honor Award (AIA), Lescarbot Award, Govt of Canada 1992, Prix Gérard-Morisset, Gov. of Québec 1994, Ordre de la Pléiade, Govt of Québec 1995, Hadrian Award, World Monuments Fund 1997, Int. Montblanc Arts Patronage Award 2001. *Publications:* Court House: A Photographic Document 1978, Photography and Architecture: 1839–1939, Opening the Gates of Eighteenth-Century Montréal (ed.) 1992, Fortifications and the Synagogue: The Fortress of Babylon and the Ben Ezra Synagogue, Cairo (ed.) 1994, Viewing Olmsted: Photographs by Robert Burley, Lee Friedlander and Geoffrey James (ed.) 1996, Mies in America (ed.) 2001. *Address:* c/o Centre Canadien d'Architecture, 1920 rue Baile, Montréal, Québec, H3H 2S6, Canada. *Telephone:* (514) 939-7000. *Fax:* (514) 939-7020.

LAMBERT, Richard Peter, BA; British journalist; b. 23 Sept. 1944; s. of Peter Lambert and Mary Lambert; m. Harriet Murray-Browne 1973; one s. one d.; ed Fettes Coll. and Balliol Coll. Oxford; mem. staff, Financial Times 1966–2001, Lex Column 1972, Financial Ed. 1978, New York Corresp. 1982, Deputy Ed. 1983, Ed. Financial Times 1991–2001; lecturer and contrib. to The Times 2001–; external mem. Bank of England Monetary Policy Cttee (MPC) June 2003–; Dir (non-exec.) London Int. Financial Futures Exchange (LIFFE), AXA Investment Mans, Int. Rescue Cttee UK; Chair. Visiting Arts; Gov. Royal Shakespeare Co.; UK Chair. Franco-British Colloque; mem. UK–India Round Table; mem. Int. Advisory Bd, British-American Business Inc.; Hon. DLitt (City Univ. London) 2000; Princess of Wales Amb. Award 2001; World Leadership Forum Business Journalist Decade of Excellence Award 2001. *Address:* c/o Bank of England, Threadneedle Street, London, EC2R 8AH, England.

LAMBERT, Yves Maurice; French international official and engineer; b. 4 June 1936, Nancy, Meurthe-et-Moselle; s. of André Arthur Lambert and Paulette Franck; m. Odile Revillon 1959; three s. one d.; ed Ecole Polytechnique, Paris, Nat. Civil Aviation School, Centre de Préparation à l'Admin. des Entreprises; Dir Org. de Gestion et de Sécurité de l'Algérie (OGSA), Algeria 1965–68; Tech. Adviser to Minister of Transport, France 1969–72; Rep. of France to ICAO Council 1972–76; Sec.-Gen. ICAO Aug. 1976–88, Dir of Air Navigation, Ministry of Equipment and Housing, Transport and the Sea 1989–93; Dir-Gen. Eurocontrol 1994–2001; Fellow Royal Aeronautical Soc. (UK); mem. Acad. Nat. de l'Air et de l'Espace; Officier, Légion d'honneur, Ordre nat. du Mérite, Médaille de l'Aéronautique, Glen Gilbert Award, Air Traffic Control Asscn 1997. *Address:* c/o Eurocontrol, 96 rue de la Fusée, 1130 Brussels, Belgium.

LAMBO, (Thomas) Adeoye, OBE, MB, ChB, MD, FRCPE, FRCPsy; Nigerian neuro-psychiatrist; b. 29 March 1923, Abeokuta; s. of the late Chief David Basil Lambo and Felicia Lambo; m. Dinah V. Adams 1945; three s.; ed Baptist Boys' High School, Abeokuta, Birmingham Univ., England, London Univ. Inst. of Psychiatry; Medical Officer, Nigerian Medical Services 1950–56; Govt Specialist-in-charge, Aro Hospital for Nervous Diseases; Consultant Physician, Univ. Coll. Ibadan 1956–63; Prof. and Head of Dept of Psychiatry and Neurology, Univ. of Ibadan 1963–71, Dean of Medical Faculty 1966–68; Vice-Chancellor, 1968–71; Asst Dir-Gen. WHO 1971–73, Deputy Dir-Gen. 1973–88; mem. Exec. Comm. World Fed. for Mental Health 1964–; Exec. Dir Lambo Foundation 1988–; Chair. Scientific Council for Africa, UN Advisory Cttee for Prevention of Crime and Treatment of Offenders, Co-ordinating Bd African Chairs of Tech. in Food Processing, Biotechnology, Nutrition and Health; Vice-Pres. World Asscn of Social Psychiatry; mem. of numerous asscns including Advisory Cttee for Mental Health, WHO, Exec. Cttee Council for Int. Org. for Medical Sciences, UNESCO, Expert Advisory Panel on Mental Health, WHO, Advisory Cttee for Health Research, WHO (Geneva), Royal Medico-Psychological Asscn, UK, Pontifical Acad. of Sciences Int. Epidemiological Asscn, Int. Hosp. Fed., Nigerian Medical Council; Founding mem. African Acad. of Sciences; Assoc. mem. Int. Asscn For Child Psychiatry and Allied Professions; Patron Asscn of Gen. and Pvt. Medical Practitioners of Nigeria 1999–; Hon. mem. Swiss Acad. of Medical Sciences, Third World Acad. of Sciences (Founding mem.); Commdr Order of the Niger 1979, Nigerian Nat. Order of Merit 1979; Hon. DSc (Ahmadu Bello Univ., Nigeria) 1967, (Long Island Univ., USA) 1975, (McGill Univ., Canada) 1978, (Univ. of Jos, Nigeria) 1979, (Univ. of Nigeria, Nskukka) 1979, (Hacettepe Univ., Turkey) 1980, (Hahnemann Univ. of Phila) 1984; Hon. LLD (Kent State Univ., USA) 1969, (Birmingham, UK) 1971, (Univ. of Pa) 1985; Dr hc (Univ. of Benin) 1973 (Univ. of Aix-Marseille, France) 1974, (Catholic Univ. of Louvain, Belgium) 1976, (Univ. of Debrecen, Hungary) 1987; Haile Selassie African Research Award 1970, Leader of Psychiatry Award, World Psychiatric Asscn 1999. *Publications:* Psychiatric Disorder among the Yorubas (co-author) 1963 and numerous articles in various medical journals. *Leisure interests:* collection of ethnographic material on Africa, of art of traditional and tribal religions, of ancient books on the history of medicine and on literature and philosophy. *Address:* Lambo Foundation, 11 Olatunbosun Street, Shonibare Estate, Maryland, P.O. Box 702, Ikeja, Lagos State, Nigeria (Office); 15 Olatunbosun Street, Shonibare Estate, Maryland, Ikeja, Lagos, Nigeria (Home). *Telephone:* (1) 4976110 (Office); (1) 4976110 (Home). *Fax:* (1) 4976110 (Office); (1) 4976110 (Home). *E-mail:* talambo@beta.linkserve.com (Office); talambo@beta.linkserve.com (Home).

LAMBRAKIS, Christos; Greek newspaper proprietor and journalist; b. 24 Feb. 1934; ed L.S.E; Publr and Ed. weekly Tachydromos (Courier) 1955–; succeeded father as Propr of dailies To Vima (Tribune), Ta Nea (News) and the weeklies Economicos Tachydromos (Economic Courier) 1957, Omada (The Team) 1958; Publr monthly Epoches 1963; Pres. Greek Section, Int. Press Inst.; imprisoned (Folegandros Prison Island) Nov. 1967. *Address:* c/o Lambrakis Press, Odos Christou Lada 3, 102 37 Athens, Greece. *Telephone:* 3230-221.

LAMBRON, Marc; French journalist and writer; b. 4 Feb. 1957, Lyon; s. of Paul Lambron and Jacqueline Lambron (née Denis); m. Sophie Missoffe 1983; one s. two d.; ed Ecole normale supérieure, Institut d'etudes politiques, Ecole nationale d'administration; columnist Point 1986–, Madame Figaro; mem. Conseil d'Etat 1985–; Prix des Deux Magots 1989, Prix Colette 1991, Prix Femina 1993; Chevalier des Arts et des Lettres. *Publications:* L'Impromptu de Madrid 1988, La nuit des masques 1990, Carnet de bal 1992, L'oeil du silence 1993, 1941 1997, Etrangers dans la nuit 2001, Carnet de bal II 2003. *Leisure interests:* music, cinema. *Address:* 17 rue Lagrange, 75005 Paris, France. *Telephone:* 1-40-51-02-12. *Fax:* 1-46-33-43-18.

LAMBSDORFF, Otto Graf Friedrich Wilhelm von der Wenge, DIur; German politician, government official and fmr company executive; b. 20 Dec. 1926, Aachen; ed Univs of Bonn and Cologne; Mil. service, prisoner of war, seriously wounded 1944–46; admitted to Bar at local and Dist courts of Düsseldorf 1960; activities in credit business, rising to power of attorney for a private bank 1955–71; mem. Bd of dirs. of an insurance co. 1971–77; mem. Bundestag 1972–; Fed. Minister of Econs 1977–84; Chair. Free Democratic Party (FDP) 1988–93, European Chair. Trilateral Comm. 1991–; Chair. Bd

Friedrich Naumann Foundation 1995–; Pres. Liberal Int. 1993–96; Rep. of Fed. Chancellor for the Foundation Initiative for German Industry 1999–2002; Dr hc 1980. *Publications:* Zielsetzungen-Aufgaben und Chancen der Marktwirtschaft 1978, Bewährung-Wirtschaftspolitik in Krisenzeiten 1980. *Address:* Strässchensweg 7, 53113 Bonn, Germany (Office). *Telephone:* (228) 236061 (Office). *Fax:* (228) 236069 (Office). *E-mail:* o.lambsdorff@t-online.de (Office).

LAMEDA, Guaicaipuro, MA; Venezuelan business executive, army officer and engineer; b. 6 Aug. 1954, Barquisimeto, Estada Lara; ed Mil. Acad. of Venezuela, Pacific Univ., USA, Inst. of Advanced Studies of Nat. Defense, Gen. Staff and Command School, USA; numerous managerial and educational posts in Venezuelan army and Govt, including Chief Planning Officer, Venezuelan Co. of Mil. Industries (CAVIM) 1992, Dir of Budget Office, Ministry of Defence 1996, Dir Govt Cen. Budget Office 1998; Chair Petróleos de Venezuela SA (PDVSA) 2000–02; Pres. of the Repub. Award, Nat. School for Advanced Defense Studies; 15 nat. and foreign distinctions; 3 mil. merit badges, 23 mil. honour awards. *Address:* c/o Edif. Petróleos de Venezuela, Torre Est, Avda Libertador, La Campina, Apdo 169, Caracas 1010-A, Venezuela.

LAMFALUSSY, Baron Alexandre, L. ÈS SC.ECON., DPhil; Belgian banker; b. 26 April 1929, Kapuvar, Hungary; m. Anne-Marie Cochard 1957; two s. two d.; ed Univ. of Louvain and Nuffield Coll. Oxford; economist, then econ. adviser, Banque de Bruxelles 1955–65; Visiting lecturer, Yale Univ. 1961–62; Exec. Dir and Chair. Exec. Bd Banque de Bruxelles 1965–75; Exec. Dir Banque Bruxelles Lambert 1975; Econ. Adviser, Head of Monetary and Econ. Dept BIS 1976–81, Asst Gen. Man. 1981–85, Gen. Man. 1985–93; Pres. of the European Monetary Inst. 1994–97. *Publications:* Investment and Growth in Mature Economies: The Case of Belgium 1961, The UK and the Six: An Essay on Growth in Western Europe 1963, Les marchés financiers en Europe 1968. *Address:* Postfach 102031, 60020 Frankfurt, Germany. *Telephone:* (69) 272270. *Fax:* (69) 27227227.

LAMINE LOUM, Mamadou; Senegalese politician; fmr Minister of Econ., Finance and Planning; Prime Minister of Senegal 1998–99; mem. Parti Socialiste (PS). *Address:* c/o Office of the Prime Minister, ave. Léopold Sedar Senghor, Dakar, Senegal. *Telephone:* 823-10-88. *Fax:* 822-55-78.

LAMIZANA, Lt-Gen. Aboubakar Sangoulé; Burkinabè politician and army officer; b. 1916, Dianra., Tougan; s. of Kafa and Diantoro Lamizana; m. Mouilo Kékélé Bintou 1947; six c.; served in French Army in Second World War and later in N Africa; joined Bataillon Autonome du Soudan Nigérien, Ségou 1947; with Centre d'Etudes Africaines et Asiatiques, Paris 1950; served in Indo-China; Jt Chief of Mil. Cabinet, Côte d'Ivoire 1956–59; Capt. 1957; served in N Africa 1959–60; Chief of Staff, Army of Upper Volta (now Burkina Faso) 1961, Lt-Col 1964, Brig.-Gen. 1967, Maj.-Gen. 1970, Lt-Gen. 1973; led coup d'état Jan. 1966; Pres. of Upper Volta 1966–80 (deposed in coup); Prime Minister 1966–71, 1974–78; Minister of Defence 1966–67, of Foreign Affairs 1966–67, of Information, Youth and Sports 1966–67, of Justice 1974–75; Grand Croix, Ordre nat. de Haute-Volta, Légion d'honneur, Croix de guerre, Croix de Valeur Militaire, other foreign decorations. *Leisure interest:* sport.

LAMJAV, Banzrachiin; Mongolian fmr politician; b. 1920; ed Higher School for Party Cadres, Ulaanbaatar and Higher Party School of the CPSU Cen. Cttee; Instructor at Prov. Cttee of the Mongolian Revolutionary Youth League; served in army as private, elected as Bureau secretary of the Youth League Cttee, worked as Asst and deputy chief of political Dept of Regt, then a brigade; Head of Section, Political Directorate, Mongolian People's Army (MPRP), then Deputy Chief of Dept; Deputy Chair. Party Cen. Cttee of MPRP Cen. Cttee 1954–56; First Sec. Party Cttee of Zavkhan Aimak (Prov.) 1956–58; Instructor at the MPRP Cen. Cttee 1958–62; Head of Personnel Dept MPRP Cen. Cttee 1962–86; concurrently First Deputy Chair. Party Control Cttee of MPRP Cen. Cttee 1979–86; Alt. mem. Political Bureau of MPRP Cen. Cttee 1986–87, mem. 1987–90 and Chair. Party Control Cttee MPRP Cen. Cttee 1986–90 (resgnd); fmr Deputy to the Great People's Hural; mem. of Presidium of Great People's Hural 1976–86.

LAMM, Donald Stephen, BA; American publisher; b. 31 May 1931, New York; s. of Lawrence W Lamm and Aleen A. Lassner; m. Jean S. Nicol 1958; two s. one d.; ed Fieldston School, Yale and Oxford Univs; Counter-intelligence Corps, US Army 1953–55; joined W. W. Norton & Co. Inc. 1956, college rep. 1956–59, Ed. 1959–2000, Dir 1964–2000, Vice-Pres. 1968–76, Chair. 1984–2000; Regents Lecturer, Univ. of Calif., Berkeley 1997–99; Pres. Yale Univ. Press; mem. Advisory Council Inst. of Early American History and Culture 1979–82; mem. Council on Foreign Relations 1978–; mem. Council, Woodrow Wilson Center, Int. Advisory Bd, Logos; Guest Fellow, Yale Univ. 1980, 1985, Trustee, The Roper Center 1984–; Fellow, Branford Coll. Yale Univ. 1985–2000, Center for Advanced Study in Behavioral Sciences 1998–99; Guest Fellow Woodrow Wilson Center 1996; Pres. Bd of Govs Yale Univ. 1986–; Ida H. Beam Distinguished Visiting Prof. Univ. of Iowa 1987–88. *Publications:* Economics and the Common Reader 1989, Beyond Literacy 1990, Book Publishing in the United States Today 1997, Perception, Cognition and Language 2000. *Leisure interests:* wilderness canoeing, skiing. *Address:* Carlisle & Co., 24 East 64th Street, New York, NY 10021 (Office); 741 Calle Picacho, Santa Fe, NM 87301, USA (Home).

LAMM, Richard D., LLB, CPA; American politician and lawyer; b. 8 Aug. 1935, Madison, Wis.; s. of A. E. Lamm; m. Dottie Lamm; one s. one d.; ed Univs

of Wisconsin and California; Certified Public Accountant, Ernst & Ernst, Denver 1961–62; lawyer, Colorado Anti-Discrimination Comm. 1962–63; Lawyer, Jones, Meiklejohn, Kilroy, Kehl & Lyons 1963–65; pvt. practice 1965–74; mem. Colorado House of Reps 1966–74; Assoc. Prof. of Law, Univ. of Denver 1969–74; Gov. of Colo 1975–87; Dir Center for Public Policy and Contemporary Issues, Univ. of Denver 1987–. *Publications:* The Angry West (with Michael McCarthy) 1982, 1988 (with Arnie Grossman) 1985, Megatraumas 1985, The Immigration Time Bomb 1985, A California Conspiracy (with Arnold Grossman) 1988. *Leisure interests:* mountain climbing, reading, bicycling. *Address:* Center for Public Policy and Contemporary Issues, University of Denver, 2050 East Iliff Avenue, Suite 224, Denver, CO 80208, USA. *Telephone:* (303) 871-3400. *Fax:* (303) 871-3066.

LAMM, Vanda Éva, PhD; Hungarian academic; b. 26 March 1945, Budapest; d. of Robert T. Lamm and Hedvig Lamm (née Vandel); ed Univ. of Budapest, Faculté int. pour l'enseignement du droit comparé, Strasbourg, France, Hague Acad. of Int. Law, Netherlands, Columbia Univ., USA; Research Fellow Inst. for Legal Studies, Hungarian Acad. of Sciences, Dir 1991–; Prof. of Int. Law Univ. of Miskolc 1998, Univ. of Budapest-Györ; mem. Perm. Court of Arbitration 1999–; Deputy mem. Court of Arbitration of OSCE; mem. UN CEDAW Cttee monitoring implementation of 1979 Convention on Elimination of Discrimination against Women; Pres. Int. Nuclear Law Asscn 2000–01; Sec.-Gen. Hungarian Br., Int. Law Asscn; Vice-Chair. Group of Governmental Experts on Third Party Liability, OECD-NEA; Assoc. mem. Inst. of Int. Law 2001–; Ed.-in-Chief Állam-és Jogtudomány; Ed. Acta Juridica Hungarica. *Publications:* numerous publs on nuclear law and int. law. *Address:* Institute for Legal Studies, Hungarian Academy of Sciences, 1250 Budapest, P.O. Box 25, I. Országház u. 30, Hungary (Office). *Telephone:* 355-7384 (Office). *Fax:* 375-7858 (Office). *E-mail:* lamm@jog.mta.hu.

LAMO DE ESPINOSA Y MICHELS DE CHAMPOURCÍN, Jaime; Spanish politician and agronomic engineer; b. 4 April 1941, Madrid; s. of Emilio Lamo de Espinosa and Maria Luisa Michels de Champourcin; m. Carmen Rocamora 1965; four d.; ed Colegio de Nuestra Señora del Pilar, Escuela Técnica Superior de Ingenieros Agrónomos, Univ. of Madrid; Asst Engineer, Study Group, Servicio Nacional de Concentración Parcelaria 1964–69; Tech. Dir Fondo de Ordenación y Regulación de Productos y Precios Agrarios (FORPPA) 1969–73; Sub-commissar for Devt Plan 1973; Dir of Tech. Cttee, Ministry of Agric. 1974; Dir-Gen. Food Industries 1974–76; Under-Sec. of Agric. 1976; Asst to Third Vice-Pres. of Govt 1977–78; Minister of Agric. and Fisheries 1978–81; Minister Asst to Pres. Council of Ministers 1981–82; mem. Congress of Deputies for Castellón 1979–; mem. Unión de Centro Democrático (UCD); Chief UCD spokesman in Congress 1981–82; Pres. 20th FAO World Conf. 1979–81; Pres. Conf. of OECD Ministers of Agric. 1980; Prof., Int. Centre for Advanced Mediterranean Agronomic Studies, Montpellier, France (OECD) 1980; Gran Cruz del Mérito Agrícola, Gran Cruz del Mérito Civil, Encomienda del Mérito Agrícola; Cross of Merit (Fed. Repub. of Germany); Croix du Mérite Civil (France). *Publications:* Agricultura a tiempo parcial y minifundios, Reflexiones sobre la política de precios y su armonización con la política general agraria, Los latifundios y el desarrollo agrario, Interrelación de las políticas de precio y de estructura en la agricultura, La agricultura en una sociedad democrática. *Leisure interests:* reading, music, painting. *Address:* José Abascal 46, Madrid, Spain. *Telephone:* 4413415.

LAMONICA, Roberto de; Brazilian artist; b. 27 Oct. 1933; ed Escola de Belas Artes de São Paulo and Museu de Arte Moderna, Rio de Janeiro; Prof. School of Fine Arts, Lima 1961–62, Univ. de Chile and Univ. Católica de Chile 1962–63, School of Fine Arts, Viña del Mar 1963–64; Prof. of Printmaking, Museum of Modern Art, Rio de Janeiro 1964–; has exhibited in Graphic Art exhbns all over the world; illustrations and covers for several books; numerous prizes. *Address:* Rua Aníbal de Mendonça 180, A.P. 202, Rio de Janeiro ZC-37, RJ, Brazil.

LAMONT, Most Rev. Donal, MA, STL; Irish ecclesiastic; b. Daniel Patrick Lamont, 27 July 1911, Ballycastle, Co. Antrim; s. of Daniel Lamont and Margaret Tumelty; ed Terenure Coll., Dublin, Univ. Coll., Dublin, Collegio Sant'Alberto, Rome; professed in Carmelite Order 1930; ordained priest, Rome 1937; Superior Carmelite Mission Rhodesia 1946; Prefect Apostolic, Umtali (now Mutare, Zimbabwe) 1953; Bishop of Umtali 1957–82; attended Second Vatican Council 1962–65; mem. Vatican Secr. for Promoting Christian Unity 1962–75; Pres. Rhodesia Catholic Bishop's Conf. 1970–72, Rep. at Roman Synods 1969, 1971, 1974; sentenced to prison for opposition to regime and deported from Rhodesia March 1977; returned to Umtali Diocese after independence 1980; resgnd as Bishop of Diocese 1982, now Emer. Bishop of Mutare; Hon. LLD (Univs of Notre Dame, Indiana, Seton Hall, NJ Mount St Mary's, Md, Marymount, NY); postage stamp issued in his honour by Govt of Kenya 1979; People of God Award, Washington Theological Union. *Publications:* Purchased People 1959, Speech from the Dock 1977. *Leisure interests:* reading, poetry, walking. *Address:* Terenure College, Dublin 6W, Ireland. *Telephone:* 4904621. *Fax:* 4902403.

LAMONT, Donald Alexander, MA; British diplomatist; b. 13 Jan. 1947; s. of Alexander Lamont and Alexa Lee Will; m. Lynda Margaret Campbell 1981; one s. one d.; ed Aberdeen Univ.; with British Leyland Motor Corpn 1970; Second Sec., then First Sec. FCO 1974; First Sec. UNIDO/IAEA, Vienna 1977; First Sec. (Commercial) Moscow 1980; First Sec. FCO 1982; Counsellor on secondment to Int. Inst. of Strategic Studies 1988; Political Adviser and Head of Chancery, British Mil. Govt, Berlin 1988–91; Amb. to Uruguay 1991–94;

Head of Repub. of Ireland Dept FCO 1994–97; Chief of Staff and Deputy High Rep., Sarajevo 1997–99; Gov. of Falkland Islands May 1999–; Commr for S. Georgia and S. Sandwich Islands May 1999–. *Address:* Office of the Governor, Government House, Port Stanley, Falkland Islands. *Telephone:* 27433 (Office). *Fax:* 27434 (Office). *E-mail:* gov.house@horizon.co.fk.

LAMONT OF LERWICK, Baron (Life Peer), cr. 1998, of Lerwick in the Shetland Islands; **Rt Hon Norman Stewart Hughson Lamont,** PC; British politician and writer; b. 8 May 1942, Lerwick, Shetland; s. of the late Daniel Lamont and of Helen Irene Hughson; m. Alice Rosemary White 1971; one s. one d.; ed Loretto School, Fitzwilliam Coll., Cambridge; personal Asst to Rt Hon Duncan Sandys MP 1965; mem. staff Conservative Research Dept 1966–68; MP for Kingston upon Thames 1972–97; Merchant Banker with NM Rothschild & Sons 1968–79, Dir Rothschild Asset Man.; Parl. Pvt. Sec. to Norman St John Stevas (Lord St John of Fawsley) 1974; Opposition Spokesman on Prices and Consumer Affairs 1975–76, on Industry 1976–79; Parl. Under-Sec. of State, Dept of Energy 1979–81; Minister of State, Dept of Trade and Industry 1981–85, of Defence Procurement 1985–86; Financial Sec. to Treasury 1986–89, Chief Sec. 1989–90; Chancellor of the Exchequer 1990–93; Chair. Conservatives Against a Fed. Europe 1998; Chair. Food Fund 1995–; Vice-Chair. Int. Nuclear Safety Comm., Bruges Group, East European Food Fund; mem. House of Lords Select Cttee on EU; Dir (non-exec.) N. M. Rothschild & Sons Ltd 1993–95; Dir Balli Group, Scottish Annuity & Life Holdings; Chair. Cambridge Univ. Conservative Asscn 1963; Pres. Cambridge Union 1964. *Publication:* Sovereign Britain 1995, In Office 1999. *Leisure interests:* ornithology, theatre, literature. *Address:* House of Lords, London, SW7A 0PW (Office); c/o Balli Group PLC, 5 Stanhope Gate, London, W1Y 5LA, England.

LAMRANI, Mohammed Karim (see Karim-Lamrani, Mohammed).

LAMY, Pascal Lucien Fernand; French civil servant; b. 8 April 1947, Levallois-Perret; s. of Jacques Lamy and Denise Dujardin; m. Geneviève Luchaire 1972; three s.; ed Lycée Carnot, Paris, Ecole des Hautes Etudes Commerciales, Paris, Inst. d'Etudes Politiques, Ecole Nationale d'Admin, Paris; served Inspection Générale des Finances 1975–79; Deputy Sec.-Gen., then Sec. Gen. Interministerial Cttee for the Remodelling of Industrial Structures (CIASI) Treasury Dept 1979–81; Tech. Advisor, then Deputy Dir Office of the Minister for Econ. and Financial Affairs 1981–82; Deputy Dir Office of the Prime Minister (Pierre Mauroy) 1983–84; Chef de Cabinet to Pres. of Comm. of EC (Jacques Delors) 1985–94; mem. Exec. Cttee Crédit Lyonnais 1994–99; Commr for Trade European Comm. July 1999–; Officier Légion d'honneur 1990, Kt Commdr's Cross (Badge and Star) of the Order of Merit (Germany), Commdr Order of Merit (Luxembourg); Dr hc (Louvain) 2003. *Publications:* L'Europe en première ligne 2002, L'Europe de nos volontés 2002; jt author report on welfare assistance for children. *Leisure interests:* tennis, jogging, marathon running. *Address:* Commission of the European Communities, 200 rue de la Loi, 1049 Brussels, Belgium (Office); Les Annonciades, le Boisgeloup, 27140 Gisors, Belgium (Home). *E-mail:* pascal.lamy@cec.eu.int (Office). *Website:* trade-info.cec.eu.int/europa/lamy/lamy.php (Office).

LANCASTER, (Christopher Ronald) Mark, BA; British artist; b. 14 May 1938, Holmfirth; s. of Charles Ronald Lancaster and Muriel Roebuck; ed Holme Valley Grammar School, Bootham School, York, Univ. of Newcastle-upon-Tyne; Asst to Andy Warhol, NY 1964; Lecturer Univ. of Newcastle 1965–66, Bath Acad. of Art 1966–68; Artist in Residence King's Coll., Cambridge 1968–70; Pvt. sec. to Jasper Johns, NY 1972–83; Prin. Designer and Artistic Adviser Merce Cunningham Dance Co., NY 1980–84; NY Dance and Performance Award 1989.

LANCE, James Waldo, AO, CBE, MD, FRCP, FRACP, FAA; Australian professor of neurology; b. 29 Oct. 1926, Wollongong, NSW; s. of Waldo Lance and Jessie Lance (née Stewart); m. Judith L. Logan 1957; one s. four d.; ed Geelong Grammar School, The King's School, Parramatta and Univ. of Sydney; Chair. Div. of Neurology, Prince Henry and Prince of Wales Hosps, Sydney 1961–91; Prof. of Neurology, Univ. of NSW 1975–91, Prof. Emer. 1992–; Pres. Australian Asscn of Neurologists 1978–81, Int. Headache Soc. 1987–89; Vice-Pres. Australian Acad. of Sciences 1984–85, World Fed. of Neurology 1991–93; Hon. DSc 1991; Harold G. Wolff Award of American Asscn for Study of Headache 1967, 1983. *Publications:* Headache 1975, The Golden Trout 1978, A Physiological Approach to Clinical Neurology (with J. G. McLeod 1981), Migraine and other Headaches 1986, Introductory Neurology (with J. G. McLeod) 1995, The Mechanism and Management of Headache with P. J. Goadsby 1998, Migraine and Other Headaches 2000. *Leisure interests:* swimming, trout fishing, travel. *Address:* Wales Medical Centre, 66 High Street, Randwick, NSW 2031 (Office); Medicolegal Opinions, 4th Floor, 135 Macquarie Street, Sydney, NSW 2000 (Office); 54 Queen Street, Woollahra, NSW 2025, Australia (Home). *Telephone:* (2) 9252-7788 (Office); (2) 9362-1876 (Home). *Fax:* (2) 9252-7799 (Office). *E-mail:* jimlance@bigpond.com (Home).

LANCELOT, Alain, DèsSc et ScHum; French university professor; b. 12 Jan. 1937, Chêne-Bougeries, Geneva, Switzerland; s. of Elisée Lancelot and Suzanne Perrin-Lancelot; m. Marie Thé Merlet 1958; one s. one d.; ed Inst. d'Etudes Politiques, Paris and Univ. of Paris-Sorbonne; Asst French Political Science Asscn 1959–62, Sec.-Gen. 1970–75; naval service 1962–63; Researcher, CNRS 1963–67; Prof. Inst. d'Etudes Politiques, Paris 1967–99, Prof. Emer. 1999–; Dir Centre for Study of French Political Life 1975–86; Dir

Inst. d'Etudes Politiques de Paris and Exec. Officer Fondation Nat. des Sciences Politiques 1987–96, mem. Bd 2001–; mem. Conseil Constitutionnel 1996–2001, Council for Democratic Elections, Bd Fondation Robert Schuman 2003–; substitute mem. Venice Comm. for Democracy Through Law 2002–; Commdr, Légion d'honneur, Officier Ordre Nat. du Mérite, des Arts et des Lettres, des Palmes Académiques; decorations from Germany and Italy. *Publications:* L'abstentionnisme électoral en France 1968, La vie politique en France depuis 1940 1975, Les élections sous la cinquième république 1983. *Leisure interest:* sailing. *Address:* Fondation Nationale des Sciences Politiques, 27 rue Saint-Guillaume, 75007 Paris (Office); 4 ter rue du Cherche-Midi, 75006 Paris, France (Home). *Telephone:* 1-45-49-50-50 (Office). *E-mail:* alain.lancelot@sciences-po.fr (Office).

LANCRY, Yehuda; Israeli diplomatist; b. 25 Sept. 1947, Bujad, Morocco; s. of Amram Lancry and Rouhama Lancry; m.; two s.; ed Univ. of Haifa, Univ. of Nice, France; Head Documentary and Film Publs Dept, Authority for Defence Tech. 1980–83; Mayor of Shlomi 1983–92; Guest Lecturer in French Literature, Haifa Univ. 1988–92; Head Public Council, Israel TV and Radio (Channel Two) 1991; Amb. to France 1992–95; mem. Knesset (Parl.) 1996–99; Perm. Rep. to UN, New York 1999–; Commdr, Légion d'honneur. *Publications:* Michel Butor ou la résistance 1994, Trêves et rêves (with Michel Butor and Henri Maccheroni) 1996. *Address:* Permanent Mission of Israel to the United Nations, 800 Second Avenue, New York, NY 10017, USA (Office). *Telephone:* (212) 499-5510 (Office). *Fax:* (212) 499-5516 (Office). *Website:* www.israel-un.org (Office).

LAND, Michael Francis, MA, PhD, FRS; British professor of biology; b. 12 April 1942, Dartmouth; s. of the late Prof. F. W. Land and of Mrs N. B. Land; m. 1st Judith Drinkwater 1966 (divorced 1980), one s.; m. 2nd Rosemary Roper 1980; two d.; ed Birkenhead School, Jesus Coll. Cambridge, Univ. Coll. London and Univ. of Calif., Berkeley (Miller Fellowship); Asst Prof. Univ. of Calif., Berkeley 1969–71; Lecturer, School of Biological Sciences, Univ. of Sussex 1971–77, Reader 1977–84, Prof. of Neurobiology 1984–; Foreign mem. Royal Physiographical Soc., Lund, Sweden 1995; Fellow Univ. Coll. London 1998; Visiting Prof. Univ. of Ore. 1980; Sr Visiting Fellow, ANU, Canberra 1982–84; Frank Smart Prize in Zoology, Cambridge 1963, ALCON Prize for Vision Research 1996, Rank Prize for Opto-electronics 1998; Frink Medal, Zoological Soc. of London 1994. *Publications:* Animal Eyes (with D. E. Nilsson) 2002, 130 articles and papers on aspects of vision in animals from visual optics to behaviour. *Leisure interests:* gardening, music. *Address:* School of Biological Sciences, University of Sussex, Brighton, BN1 9QG (Office); White House, Cuilfail, Lewes, Sussex, BN7 2BE, England (Home). *Telephone:* (1273) 678505 (Office); (1273) 476780 (Home). *E-mail:* m.f.land@sussex.ac.uk (Office).

LANDABURU ILLARRAMENDI, Eneko; Spanish international organization official; b. 11 March 1948, Paris; s. of Francisco Javier Nicolas Landaburu and Prudencia Francisca Constantina Illarramendi; m. Dominique Rambaud 1971; two s. one d.; ed Univ. of Paris, France; mem. staff Admin. and Financial Man. Dept, Société Labaz, Paris 1971–73, Asst to Man. Belgian subsidiary SA Labaz NV, Brussels 1973–75; Head of Study and Lecture Programmes, Centre Européen d'Etudes et d'Information sur les Sociétés Multinationales (CEEIM), Brussels 1975–79; PSOE Deputy, Spanish Basque Regional Parl. 1980–81; Adviser to Latin American Dept, Nestlé, Vevey, Switzerland 1981–82; Dir Institut de Recherche sur les Multinationales (IRM), Geneva, Switzerland 1983–86; Dir-Gen. for Regional Politics, EC Comm., Brussels 1986–2000, for Enlargement 2000–; Lecturer, Institut d'Etudes Européennes, Free Univ. of Brussels 1990–94; Alt. mem. Bd of Dirs of EIB 1993–; mem. Supervisory Bd European Investment Fund FEI-EIF 1994–; mem. Bd of Dirs Fondation 'Notre Europe' 1996–. *Address:* Office Char 4/116, 1049 Brussels (Office); Avenue Brugmann 125, 1190 Brussels, Belgium (Home). *Telephone:* (2) 295-19-68 (Office). *Fax:* (2) 296-84-90 (Office). *E-mail:* eneko.landaburu@cec.eu.int (Office).

LANDAIS, Hubert Léon; French museum administrator; b. 22 March 1921; s. of Pierre Landais and Odette Surmont; m. Madeleine Legris 1946; five s. one d.; ed Ecole Nat. des Chartes, Ecole du Louvre; staff mem. Louvre Museum 1946, Attendant 1946–48, Curator Middle Ages, Renaissance, Modern objets d'art 1948–62, Asst Curator to the Dir of Museums 1962–63, Chief Curator Nat. Museums 1963–65, Dir objets d'art Dept 1965–68, Inspector-Gen. of Museums 1968, Dir of the Museums 1977–87, Sec.-Gen. 1962–73, Pres. French Cttee 1973–; Pres. Réunion des musées nationaux 1977; Vice-Pres., Conseil d'admin. du musée de l'Armée 1962–87; mem. Int. Council of Museums 1974–77, Pres. 1977–83, Pres. professional ethics Cttee 1990–97; Co-Dir l'Univers des Formes 1977–91, numerous other appointments; Grand Officier, Légion d'honneur, Commdr Ordre nat. du Mérite et des Arts et des Lettres. *Publications:* Bronzes italiens de la Renaissance 1958, Histoire de Saumur 1997 and books and articles on objets d'art, especially medieval and porcelain. *Address:* 23 rue Bourdignon, 94100 St-Maur-des-Fossés, France (Home). *Telephone:* 1-48-83-25-82. *Fax:* 1-48-89-96-26 (Home).

LANDAU, Igor, MBA; French business executive; b. 13 July 1944, Saint-Flour, Cantal; ed Hautes Etudes Commerciales, INSEAD; Pres. La Compagnie du Roneo (German subsidiary), Frankfurt 1968–70; Consultant McKinsey Co., Paris 1971–75; Deputy to Pres. of Health Div., Rhône-Poulenc Inc. 1975, Exec. Vice-Pres. of Div. 1977–80, Chair. Health Sector 1987, mem. Exec. Cttee 1987, Group Pres. 1992, mem. Bd of Dirs 1998; mem. Man. Bd Aventis 1999–2002, Chair. Man. Bd 2000–, Chair. Supervisory Bd Aventis

Pharma AG 1999–2002; Pres. Supervisory Bd Centre Européen d'Educ. Perm.; mem. Inst. pour le Développement Industrial; mem. Bd Dirs Essilor. *Address:* Espace Européen de l'Enterprise, 16 avenue de l'Europe, 67300 Schiltigheim, France (Office). *Telephone:* 3-38-99-11-14 (Office). *Fax:* 3-88-99-11-13 (Office). *E-mail:* carsten.tilger@aventis.com (Office). *Website:* www .aventis.com (Office).

LANDAU, Jean-Pierre; French economist; b. 7 Nov. 1946, Paris; s. of André Landau and Andrée Pestre; m. Evelyne Dova 1979; ed Inst. d'études politiques de Paris, Ecole nat. d'admin; served in Ministry of Health and Social Security 1978–79; Asst Sec. for Trade Policy, Direction des Relations Économiques Extérieures 1986–89, various other positions in Ministry of Econ. and Finance; Exec. Dir IMF 1989–93; Dir Relations Economiques Extérieures (DREE) 1993–96; Dir-Gen. French Asscn of Banks 1999–2000; Financial Counsellor, French Embassy in UK 2001–; Dir EBRD 2001–; fmr Teacher of Econs, Inst. d'études politiques; fmr mem. of Bd, Renault. *Address:* French Embassy, 58 Knightsbridge, London, SW1X 7JT, England (Office); 13 rue de l'Odéon, 75006 Paris, France. *Telephone:* (20) 7201-1000 (Office). *Fax:* (20) 7201-1004 (Office).

LANDAU, Moshe, LLB; Israeli judge (retd); b. 29 April 1912, Danzig, Germany (now Gdańsk, Poland); s. of Dr Isaac Landau and Betty (née Eisenstädt); m. Leah Doukhan 1937; three d.; ed London Univ.; went to Israel 1933; called to Palestine Bar 1937; Magistrat of Haifa 1940, District Court Judge, Haifa 1948; Justice, Supreme Court, Jerusalem 1953–82, (Presiding Judge, Eichmann Trial), Deputy Pres. 1976–80, Pres. 1980–82; Israel Prize 1991. *Leisure interest:* piano. *Address:* 10 Alharizi Street, Jerusalem, Israel. *Telephone:* 2-5632757.

LANDAU, Peter, DJur; German professor of law; b. 26 Feb. 1935, Berlin; m. Angelika Linnemann 1971; one s. one d.; ed Univs of Berlin, Freiburg, Bonn and Yale Univ., USA; Prof. Univ. of Regensburg 1968–87; Prof. of Law, Univ. of Munich 1987–2003; mem. Bayerische Akad. der Wissenschaften; mem. Inst. for Advanced Study, Princeton, USA 1990–91; Pres. Inst. of Medieval Canon Law; mem. Medieval Acad. of America; Hon. DrIur (Basel) 1981; Dr hc (Munich) 1997, (Paris) 2001. *Publications:* Die Entstehung des kanonischen Infamiebegriffs von Gratian bis zur Glossa ordinaria 1966, Ius patronatus 1975, Strafrecht, Strafprozess und Rezeption (Jt Ed.) 1984, Officium und Libertas christiana 1991, Kanones und Dekretalen 1997. *Leisure interest:* art. *Address:* Leopold-Wenger-Institut für Rechtsgeschichte, Professor-Huber-Platz 2, 80539 Munich (Office); Sperberstr. 21c, 81827 Munich, Germany (Home). *Telephone:* (89) 21803263 (Office); (89) 4300121 (Home). *Fax:* (89) 21803081 (Office). *E-mail:* peter.landau@jura.uni-muenchen.de (Office).

LANDAU, Uzi, PhD; Israeli politician and systems analyst; b. 1943, Haifa; m.; three c.; ed Haifa Technion, Mass. Inst. of Tech., USA; served as a paratrooper officer during mil. service; mem. Knesset (Likud Party) 1984–, Chair. Foreign Affairs and Defense Cttee, State Control Cttee; Knesset Observer at the European Council; mem. Israeli Del. to Madrid Peace Conf.; Observer at the European Council; Minister of Public Security 2001–; Dir-Gen. Ministry of Transport; lecturer in the Technion, Israel Inst. of Tech., Haifa; mem. Bds El-Al Airlines, Israel Port Authority, Israel Airport Authority, Soc. for the Protection of Nature, Si'ah Vasig (Israel Debating Soc.). *Address:* Ministry of Public Security, P.O. Box 18182, Building No. 3, Kiryat Hamemshala (East), Jerusalem 91181, Israel (Office). *Telephone:* 2-5308003 (Office). *Fax:* 2-5847872 (Office). *E-mail:* mops@netvision.net.il (Office).

LANDER, Sir Stephen James, KCB, MA, PhD; British public servant; m. Felicity Lander 1972; one s. (died 2002) one d.; ed Bishop's Stortford Coll., Herts., Queens' Coll., Cambridge Univ.; with Inst. of Historical Research, London Univ.; joined Security Service 1975–, Dir 1992–96, Dir-Gen. 1996–2002; Ind. Commr (overseeing complaints against solicitors) The Law Soc. Nov. 2002–; fmrly with Foreign Office, Near E and N Africa Dept. *Address:* The Law Society, 113 Chancery Lane, London, WC2A 1PL, England. *Telephone:* (1926) 822057. *Fax:* (1926) 823140.

LANDES, David S., PhD; American professor of history; b. 29 April 1924, New York; s. of Harry and Sylvia Landes; m. Sonia Tarnopol 1943; one s. two d.; ed City Coll., New York, Harvard Univ.; Jr Fellow, Soc. of Fellows, Harvard Univ. 1950–53; Asst Prof. of Econs, Columbia Univ., New York 1952–55, Assoc. Prof. 1955–58; Fellow, Center for Advanced Study in Behavioral Sciences, Stanford, Calif. 1957–58; Prof. of History and Econs, Univ. of Calif., Berkeley 1958–64; Prof. of History, Harvard Univ. 1964–72, LeRoy B. Williams Prof. of History and Political Science 1972–75, Robert Walton Goelet Prof. of French History 1975–81, Prof. of Econs 1977–98, Coolidge Prof. of History 1981; Chair. Faculty Cttee on Social Studies 1981; Pres. Council on Research in Econ. History 1963–66; Dir Center for Middle Eastern Studies, Harvard Univ. 1966–68; Acting Dir Center for West European Studies, Harvard Univ. 1969–70; Pres. Econ. History Asscn 1976–77; Ellen McArthur Lecturer, Univ. of Cambridge 1964; Visiting Prof., Univ. of Paris IV 1972–73, Univ. of Zürich and Eidgenössische Technisch Hochschule, Zürich 1978; Richards Lectures, Univ. of Va 1978, Janeway Lectures, Princeton Univ. 1983; mem. Bd of Eds, various journals of history; Fellow, NAS, American Acad. of Arts and Sciences, American Philosophical Soc., British Acad., Royal Historical Soc.; Overseas Fellow, Churchill Coll., Cambridge 1968–69; Visiting Fellow, All Souls, Oxford 1985; mem. American Historical Asscn, Econ. History Asscn (also Trustee), Econ. History Soc., Soc. for French Historical Studies, Soc. d'Histoire Moderne and others; Assoc. mem. Fondation Royau-

mont pour le Progrès des Sciences de l'Homme; Dr hc (Lille) 1973. *Publications:* Bankers and Pashas 1958, The Unbound Prometheus 1968, Revolution in Time: Clocks and the Making of the Modern World 1983 and other books and articles on econ. and social history. *Leisure interests:* antiquarian horology, squash, tennis. *Address:* Department of Economics, Harvard University, Cambridge, MA 02138 (Office); 24 Highland Street, Cambridge, MA 02138, USA (Home). *Telephone:* (617) 495-4849 (Office); (617) 354-6308 (Home).

LANDON, Howard Chandler Robbins, BMus; American author and educator; b. 6 March 1926, Boston, Mass.; s. of William G. Landon and Dorothea LeB. Robbins; m. Else Radant 1957; ed Lenox School, Mass., Swarthmore Coll. and Boston Univ.; corresp. The Times 1958–61; Hon. Professorial Fellow, Univ. Coll. Cardiff 1971–78, John Bird Prof. of Music 1978–; Prof. of the Humanities, Middlebury Coll., Vt 1980–83; Verdienstkreuz für Kunst und Wissenschaft (Austria); Hon. DMus (Boston) 1969, (Belfast) 1974, (Bristol) 1982, (Toulouse) 1991. *Publications:* The Symphonies of Joseph Haydn 1955, Beethoven 1970, Joseph Haydn: Chronicle and Works (5 vols) 1976–80, Haydn: A Documentary Study 1982, Mozart & the Masons 1983, Handel and his World 1984, 1791: Mozart's Last Year 1987, Mozart: The Golden Years 1989, Mozart and Vienna 1991, Vivaldi 1992, Une journée particulière, 12 novembre 1791 1993, Horns in High C (memoirs) 1999, critical edns of many of works of Haydn, Mozart and 18th-century composers. *Leisure interests:* walking, swimming, cooking. *Address:* Château de Foncoussières, 81800 Rabastens (Tarn), France. *Telephone:* (5) 63-40-61-45.

LANDRY, Monique; Canadian fmr politician; b. 25 Dec. 1937, Montréal; d. of Auguste Landry and Antoinette Bourbeau (née Miquelon); m. Jean-Guy Landry 1958; three s. one d.; ed Univ. of Montréal; MP for Blainville-Deux-Montagnes 1984–; mem. of several inter-parl. asscns; Parl. Sec. to the Sec. of State 1984–85; Minister of Int. Trade; 1985–86; Minister of State for External Relations and Int. Devt 1986–92, for Indian and Northern Affairs 1991–92; Sec. of State of Canada Jan.–Nov. 1993; fmr mem. Standing Cttee on Communications and Culture, Jt Cttee on Official Languages Policy and Programs and the Standing Cttee on Finance, Trade and Econ. Affairs, Canada-Europe Parl. Asscn, Canada-France Inter-Parl. Asscn, Canada-NATO Parl. Asscn; Consultant Dessau Int. 1994–96, Pres. 1996–99; Pres. Dessau-Soprin Int. 1998–; Pres. Québec Arthritis Soc. Public Awareness Campaign 1988–; Woman of the year 1988, Salon de la Femme de Montréal 1988. *Leisure interests:* golf, tennis. *Address:* Dessau-Soprin International Inc., 1200 St Martin blvd, Suite 300, Lavar, Québec, H75 2E4, Canada.

LANDSBERGIS, Vytautas; Lithuanian politician and musicologist; b. 18 Oct. 1932, Kaunas; s. of Vytautas Landsbergis-Žemkalnis and Ona Jablonskyte-Landsbergienė; m. Gražina Ručyte; one s. two d.; ed J. Gruodis School of Music, Kaunas, Aušra Gymnasium, Kaunas, Lithuanian Acad. of Music; Teacher of Piano and Prof. of Musicology, Vilnius Conservatoire, Vilnius Pedagogical Inst.; fmr mem. Exec. Council and Secr. Composers' Union; Pres. M. K. Čiurlionis Soc.; mem. various arts and science bodies; elected to Initiative Group, Sajūdis Reform Movt, then to Sajūdis Seimas (Ass.) and Council 1988, Pres. Sajūdis Seimas Council 1988–90, Hon. Pres. Sajūdis Dec. 1991–; f. Lithuanian Conservative Party, Chair. 1993–; elected Deputy to USSR Congress of People's Deputies 1989–90; elected to Supreme Council of Lithuania Feb. 1990, Pres. Supreme Council 1990–92; mem. Seimas (Parl.) 1992–, Leader of Parl. Opposition 1992–96, Pres. Seimas 1996–2000; cand. for presidential elections 1997; Paul Harris Fellow (Rotary) 1991; gave concert at Moscow Conservatoire with Russian Nat. Acad. Symphonic Orchestra 1999; piano recitals in Calw, Hanover, Helsinki, Kwangjou, Moscow, New York, Paris, Tokyo, Trieste, Usedom, Vilnius, Warsaw, etc.; Hon. Fellow Cardiff Univ., UK 2000; Academician, Lithuanian Catholic Acad. 1997; Chevalier Légion d'Honneur 1997, Order of Grand Duke Vytautas, First Class (Lithuania) 1998, Grand Cross, Royal Norwegian Order of Merit 1998, Grand Cross Order of the Repub. (Poland) 1999, Order of Merit (Grand Cross), Order of Malta 1999, Grand-Croix Ordre Honneur (Greece) 1999, Pléiade Ordre de la Francophonie (France) 2000, Three Stars Order (Second Class) (Latvia) 2001, Order of the Cross of St Mary's Land (First Class) (Estonia) 2002; Hon. LLD (Loyola Univ., Chicago) 1991; Hon. PhD (Vytautas the Great Univ., Kaunas) 1992, (Klaipėda Univ., Lithuania) 1997; Hon. H.D. (Weber Univ., USA) 1992; Dr hc (Helsinki) 2000, (Sorbonne, Paris) 2001; Lithuanian State Award (for monograph on M. K. Čiurlionis) 1975; Norwegian People's Peace Prize (for role in restoration of Lithuanian independence; has used prize to est. Landsbergis Foundation to help disabled children and young musicians) 1991, Award of France Fund of Future 1991, Hermann-Ehlers Prize 1992, Catalan Ramon Llull IX Int. Prize 1994, Vibo Valentia Testimony Prize (Italy) 1998, Truman-Reagan Freedom Award (USA) 1999. *Recording:* Čiurlionis, Born of the Human Soul (works for solo piano) 1998. *Publications:* 23 books on musicology, art and music history (especially on artist and composer M. K. Čiurlionis) and politics including M. K. Čiurlionis – Time and Content 1992, Lithuania Independent Again 2000; numerous edns of scores (mostly of works by M. K. Čiurlionis); M. K. Čiurlionis – Thoughts, Pictures, Music (film script) 1965. *Leisure interests:* history, poetry. *Address:* Seimas of Lithuania, Prosp. Gedimino 53, Vilnius, Lithuania. *Telephone:* (52) 396663 (Office). *Fax:* (52) 396017 (Office). *E-mail:* vyland@lrs.lt (Office).

LANE, (Alan) Piers, BMus, ARCM; British/Australian pianist and broadcaster; b. 8 Jan. 1958, London; s. of Peter Alan Lane and Enid Muriel Hitchcock; ed Queensland Conservatorium of Music, Royal Coll. of Music,

London; broadcaster for BBC Radio 3; critic CD Review; has appeared with numerous orchestras including: London Philharmonic, Philharmonia, Royal Philharmonic, BBC Concert Orchestra, City of Birmingham Symphony, Halle, Australian Chamber Orchestra, New Zealand Symphony Orchestra, Auckland Philharmonic, Orchestra Ensemble Kanazawa (Japan), Orchestre National de France; has toured extensively in Australia, Africa, Europe, India, Japan, NZ, S. America, USA; has appeared at festivals including: Aldeburgh, BBC Promenade Concerts, Royal Albert Hall, Huntington, Husum Festival of Piano Rarities, Germany, Blair Atholl, Speedside, Toronto, Singapore Piano Festival, Newport Festival, Rhode Island, Duznicki Chopin Festival, Poland, Ruhr Piano Festival 2002, Bergen Festival, Bridgewater Piano Festival, Manchester Bagatelles Chopin Festival, Paris; Int. Adjudicator Tbilisi and Sydney Int. Piano Competitions; La Roque d'Anthéron Prof. RAM 2002–; Dir and Trustee The Hattori Foundation; Hon. mem. RAM 1994; Special Prize Bartok–Liszt Int. Competition, Budapest 1976, Best Australian Pianist, Sydney Int. Piano Competition 1977. Recordings include: Complete Etudes of Scriabin 1992, Piano Quintet by Brahms (New Budapest Quartet) 1992, Violin Virtuoso (with Tasmin Little) 1992, Sonatas by Shostakovich, Prokofiev, Schnittke and Rachmaninoff, d'Albert Concertos 1994, Vaughan-Williams and Delius Concertos plus Finzi Eclogue 1994, Elgar Piano Quintet (with Vellinger String Quartet) 1994, Delius Violin Sonatas (with Tasmin Little; Diapason d'Or) 1997, d'Albert Solo Piano Works 1997, Saint-Saëns Complete Etudes 1998 Kullak & Dreyschock Concertos (with Niklas Willen) 1999, Complete Scriabin Preludes 2000, Grainger Piano Transcriptions 2001, Bach Transcriptions 2002, Noscheles Etudes 2003. Address: Georgina Ivor Associates, 28 Old Devonshire Road, London, SW12 9RB, England (Office). Telephone: (20) 8673-7179 (Office). Fax: (20) 8675-8058 (Office). E-mail: info@giamanagement.com (Office). Website: www.giamanagement.com (Office).

LANE, Sir David Philip, Kt, PhD, FRS, FRSE, FRCPath, FRCSE, FMedSci; British professor of oncology; b. 1 July 1952; s. of John Wallace Lane and Cecelia Frances Evelyn Wright; m. Ellen Birgitte Muldal 1975; one s. one d.; ed Univ. Coll. London; Research Fellow Imperial Cancer Research Fund 1976–77, Staff Scientist 1985–90; lecturer Imperial Coll., London 1977–85; Prof. of Molecular Oncology, Univ. of Dundee 1990–, Dir Transformation Research Group, Cancer Research Campaign 1990–; Visiting Fellow Cold Spring Harbor Labs, NY 1978–80; Gibb Fellow Cancer Research UK; mem. European Molecular Biology Org. 1990; Co-Founder FMedSci 1998; Hon. DSc (Abertay, Dundee) 1999, (Stirling) 2000, (Aberdeen) 2002, (Birmingham) 2002; Charles Rodolphe Brubacher Foundation Prize 1993, Joseph Steiner Foundation Prize 1993, Yvette Mayent Prize, Inst. Curie 1994, Swedish Soc. of Oncology Medal 1994, Meyenberg Foundation Prize 1995, Silvanus Thompson Medal, British Inst. of Radiology 1996, Henry Dryerre Prize 1996, Paul Ehrlich Prize 1998, Tom Conors Prize 1998, Bruce Preller Prize 1998. Address: Cancer Research UK Laboratories, Department of Surgery and Medical Oncology, University of Dundee, Dundee, DD1 9SY, Scotland (Office). Telephone: (1382) 496362 (Office). Fax: (1382) 496363 (Office).

LANE, Baron (Life Peer), cr. 1979, of St Ippollitts in the County of Hertfordshire; **Geoffrey Dawson Lane,** PC, AFC; British judge; b. 17 July 1918, Derby; s. of the late Percy Albert Lane and Mary Lane (née Dawson); m. Jan Macdonald 1944; one s.; ed Shrewsbury, Trinity Coll. Cambridge; served in RAF 1939–45, Squadron Leader 1942; called to the Bar, Gray's Inn 1946, Bencher 1966; QC 1962; Deputy Chair. Bedfordshire Quarter Sessions 1960–66, Recorder of Bedford 1963–66; mem. Parole Bd 1970–72, Vice-Chair. 1972; a Judge, High Court of Justice, Queen's Bench Div. 1966–74; a Lord Justice of Appeal 1974–79; Lord of Appeal in Ordinary 1979; Lord Chief Justice of England 1980–92; Hon. Master of Bench, Inner Temple 1980; Hon. DCL (Cambridge) 1984. Address: Royal Courts of Justice, Strand, London, WC2A 2LL, England.

LANE, Neal Francis, MS, PhD, FAAS; American physicist; b. 22 Aug. 1938, Oklahoma; s. of Walter Lane and Harietta Hollander; m. Joni Williams 1960; one s. one d.; ed Univ. of Oklahoma; NSF Post-doctoral Fellow 1964–65; Asst Prof. of Physics, Rice Univ. Houston 1966–69, Assoc. Prof. 1969–72, Prof. 1972–84, 1986–93, Prof. of Space Physics and Astronomy 1972–84, Chair. Dept of Physics 1977–82, Provost 1986–93; Dir Div. of Physics, NSF, Washington, DC 1979–80; Dir NSF 1993–98; Chancellor, Univ. of Colo at Colorado Springs 1984–86; Asst to Pres. for Science and Tech., Dir Office of Science and Tech. Policy, Washington 1998–2001; Univ. Prof. and Sr Fellow James A. Baker III Inst. of Public Policy, Rice Univ. 2001–; Visiting Fellow, Jt Inst. for Lab. Astrophysics, Univ. of Colo at Boulder 1965–66, 1975–76, non-resident Fellow 1984–93; Distinguished Visiting Scientist, Ky Univ., Lexington 1980; mem. Comm. on Physics, Science, Math. and Applications, Nat. Research Council 1989–93, Bd Overseers Superconducting Super Collider (SSC), Univs Research Assn 1985–93, Advisory Cttee, Math. and Physical Sciences, NSF 1992–93; other professional appointments; Fellow, American Physics Soc., American Acad. of Arts and Sciences; mem. American Inst. of Physics; Alfred P. Sloan Foundation Fellow 1967–71; Hon. DHL (Okla, Marymount Univs 1995, (Ill. Inst. of Tech.) 1999; Hon. DSc (Univ. of Ala) 1994, (Mich. State Univ.) 1995, (Ohio State Univ.) 1996, (Washington Coll.) 1998, (Colorado) 1999, (Illinois Inst. of Tech.) 1999, (Queen's Univ. Belfast) 2000, (N Carolina State Univ.) 2001, (Mt Sinai School of Medicine, State Univ. of New York) 2002; Philip Hauge Abelson Award, American Asscn for the Advancement of Science 2000, William D. Carey Award, American Asscn for the Advancement of Science 2001. Publications: Quantum States of Atoms, Molecules and Solids, Understanding More Quantum Physics, articles in professional jour-

nals. Leisure interests: tennis, squash. Address: Department of Physics and Astronomy, Rice University, P.O. Box 1892, Houston, TX 77251, USA (Office). E-mail: neal@rice.edu (Office).

LANE FOX, Martha, BA; British business executive; b. 10 Feb. 1973; ed Oxford High School, Westminster School, Magdalen Coll. Oxford; business analyst, Spectrum Strategy Consultants 1994–96, Assoc. 1996–97; Business Devt Dir Carlton Communications 1997–98; co-founder (with Brent Hoberman, q.v. and COO lastminute.com 1998–. Address: lastminute.com PLC, Park House, 4th Floor, 116 Park Street, London, S1K 6NR, England (Office). Telephone: (20) 7802-4200 (Office). Fax: (20) 7659-4909 (Office). Website: www.lastminute.com (Office).

LANG, Andrew Richard, PhD, FInstP, FRS; British professor of physics; b. 9 Sept. 1924, St Annes-on-Sea, Lancs.; s. of late Ernest F. S. Lang and Susannah Lang (née Gueterbock); ed Univ. Coll. of South-West, Exeter and Univ. of Cambridge; Research Dept Lever Bros. Port Sunlight 1945–47; Research Asst Cavendish Lab. 1947–48; North American Philips, Irvington-on-Hudson, New York 1952–53; Instructor Harvard Univ. 1953–54, Asst Prof. 1954–59; Lecturer in Physics, Univ. of Bristol 1960–66, Reader 1966–79, Prof. 1979–87, Prof. Emer. 1987–, Sr Research Fellow 1995–; Foreign Assoc. Royal Soc. of SA; Charles Vernon Boys Prize, Inst. of Physics 1964, Hughes Medal, Royal Soc. 1997. Publications: contributions to learned journals. Address: 1B Elton Road, Bristol, BS8 1SJ, England. Telephone: (117) 973-9784.

LANG, Brian Andrew, MA, PhD; British university vice-chancellor; b. 2 Dec. 1945, Edinburgh; s. of Andrew Lang and Mary Lang; m. 1st 1975 (divorced 1982); m. 2nd 1983 (divorced 2001); two s. one d.; ed Royal High School, Edinburgh and Univ. of Edinburgh; social anthropological field research, Kenya 1969–70; Lecturer in Social Anthropology, Aarhus Univ. Denmark 1971–75; mem. scientific staff, Social Science Research Council 1976–79; Head, Historic Building Br., Scottish Office 1979–80; Dir Nat. Heritage Memorial Fund 1980–87; Dir of Public Affairs, Nat. Trust 1987–91; Chief Exec. and Deputy Chair. British Library 1991–2000; Prin. and Vice-Chancellor Univ. of St Andrews 2001; Visiting Prof. Napier Univ., Edin. 1999–; Visiting Scholar Getty Inst., Calif. 2000; mem. Council, Nat. Trust for Scotland 2001–, Council, St Leonard's School, St Andrews 2001–; Trustee Hopetown House Preservation Trust 2002–; Hon. Fellow, The Library Asscn 1997. Leisure interests: reading, music, museums, galleries, pottering. Address: Office of the Principal, College Gate, University of St Andrews, St Andrews, Fife KY16 9AJ, Scotland; 42 Grandison Road, London, SW11 6LW, England (Home); Hepburn Gardens, 96A Hepburn Gardens, St Andrews, Fife, KY16 9LP, Scotland (Home). Telephone: (1334) 462545 (Office); (20) 7228-0767 (London) (Home); (1334) 475595 (St Andrews) (Home). Fax: (1334) 462543 (Office). E-mail: principal@st-and.ac.uk (Office). Website: www.st-andrews.ac.uk (Office).

LANG, David, PhD; American composer; b. 1 Aug. 1957, LA; m.; three c.; ed Stanford Univ., Univ. of Iowa, Yale School of Music; studied with Jacob Druckman, Hans Werner Henze (q.v.) and Martin Bresnick; Jr Composer-in-Residence Horizons summer festival 1980s; commissioned by Boston Symphony Orchestra, Cleveland Orchestra, St Paul Chamber Orchestra, BBC Singers, American Composers Orchestra and Santa Fe Opera and Settembre Musica Festival, Turin; co-f. (with Michael Gordon and Julia Wolfe) New York annual music festival Bang on a Can 1987–; composed albums Cheating, Lying, Stealing 1996 and Brian Eno: Music for Airports 1998 for group Bang on a Can All-Stars; Rome Prize, American Acad., Rome; BMW Prize, Munich Biennale for New Music Theatre; Friedheim Award, Kennedy Center; Revson Fellowship with New York Philharmonic; grants from Guggenheim Foundation, New York Foundation of Arts and Nat. Endowment for the Arts. Compositions for orchestra include: Bonehead, Eating Living Monkeys, Int. Business Machine, for chamber groups include My Very Empty Mouth, My Evil Twin, Hunk of Burnin' Love, I Fought the Law, for solo instruments include The Anvil Chorus. Other works include: Illumination Rounds 1982, Frag 1985, Spud 1986, Are You Experienced? 1987–88. Operas include: Judith and Holofernes 1989, Modern Painters 1994 (for Santa Fe Opera) and The Carbon Copy Building (with Ben Katchor) 1999. Address: c/o Red Poppy Music, 66 Greene Street, Fifth Floor, New York, NY 10012, U.S.A. (Office).

LANG, Helmut; Austrian fashion designer; b. 10 March 1956, Vienna; est. own studio in Vienna 1977; made-to-measure shop opened in Vienna 1979; development of ready-to-wear collections 1984–86; presented Helmut Lang women's wear, Paris fashion week 1986–, menswear 1987–; began licence business 1988; Helmut Lang Underwear 1994; Helmut Lang Protective Eyewear 1995; Prof. of Masterclass of Fashion, Univ. of Applied Arts, Vienna 1993–; Council of American Fashion Designers of the Year Award 1996. Address: c/o Michele Montagne, 184 rue St Maur, 75010 Paris, France. Telephone: 1-42-03-91-00. Fax: 1-42-01-12-22.

LÁNG, István; Hungarian agrochemist; b. 26 Dec. 1931, Mohács; s. of József Láng and Anna Világi; m. Etelka Sorosinszki; one d.; ed Agricultural Univ. of Ivanovo, USSR; Fellow Research Inst. for Soil Sciences and Agricultural Chemistry, Budapest 1955–63; Exec. Sec. Section of Biological Sciences, Hungarian Acad. of Sciences 1963–70, Deputy Sec.-Gen. 1970–85, Sec.-Gen. 1985–93, Science Policy Adviser 1993–; Chair. Advisory Bd, Ministry of Environmental and Regional Policy 1994–96, Vice-Chair. 1998–; Chair. Hungarian Research Fund 1986–90; mem. World Comm. on Environment and Devt (Brundtland Comm.), Advisory Cttee on Environment, Int. Council for Science. *Leisure interests:* philately, bird watching. *Address:* c/o Hungarian Academy of Sciences, 1051 Budapest, Roosevelt tér 9, Hungary. *Telephone:* (1) 2692656. *Fax:* (1) 2692655. *E-mail:* ilang@office.mta.hu (Office).

LANG, Jack, DenD; French politician; b. 2 Sept. 1939, Mirecourt; s. of Roger Lang and Marie-Luce Bouchet; m. Monique Buczynski 1961; two d.; ed Lycée Henri-Poincaré, Nancy, Inst. of Political Studies, Paris; Founder and Dir World Festival of Univ. Theatre, Nancy 1963–77; Dir Théâtre du palais de Chaillot 1972–74; Prof. of Int. Law 1976–; Dir Educ. and Research Unit for econ. and legal sciences, Nancy 1977; Councillor, Paris 1977–81; Deputy Nat. Ass. 1986; Special Adviser to First Sec., Parti Socialiste (PS) 1978–81, PS Nat. Del. for Culture 1979–81; Minister of Culture and Communications 1981–83, 1984–86, May–June 1988, 1991–92, of Educ. and Culture 1992–93, also Minister for Major Public Works and Bicentenary 1988–89, of Educ. 2000–02; Govt spokesman 1991; Mayor of Blois 1989–2001; MEP 1994–97; Socialist Deputy from Loir-et-Cher March–Dec. 1993, 1997–; Pres. Foreign Affairs Cttee, Nat. Ass.; Hon. DLitt (Nottingham) 1990, Dr. hc (Royal Coll. of Art) 1993; Chevalier, Légion d'honneur; Prix Antonio de Sancha (Spain) 1997, Prix Wartburg (Germany) 1998. *Publications:* Lettre à Malraux 1996, Demain les femmes 1995, François Premier 1997. *Address:* c/o Assemblée nationale, 126 rue de l'Université, 75355 Paris 07 SP, France.

LANG, k.d. (Kathryn Dawn); Canadian popular singer and songwriter; b. 2 Nov. 1961, Consort, Alberta; d. of Adam Lang and Audrey L. Lang; began playing guitar aged 10; formed band The Reclines in early 1980s, played N American clubs 1982–87; performed at closing ceremony, Winter Olympics, Calgary 1988; performed with Sting, Bruce Springsteen, Peter Gabriel and Tracy Chapman in Amnesty Int. tour 1988; acting debut in film Salmonberries 1991; headline US tour 1992; played at Royal Albert Hall, London 1992; Eart Day benefit concert, Hollywood Bowl 1993; sang with Andy Bell, BRIT Awards 1993; TV appearances include Late Night With David Letterman, Wogan, The Arsenio Hall Show, The Tonight Show, Top of the Pops, Subject, South Bank Show documentary (ITV) 1995; Canadian CMA Awards for Best Entertainer of Year 1989, Best Album of Year 1990; Grammy Awards for Best Female Country Vocal Performance 1990, Best Pop Vocal 1993; Album of the Year, Ingénue 1993; American Music Awards, Favourite New Artist 1993, Songwriter of the Year (with Ben Mink) 1993; BRIT Award for Best Int. Female 1995. *Films include:* Salmonberries 1991, Teresa's Tattoo 1994, The Last Don 1997. *Singles include:* Friday Dance Promenade, Crying (duet with Roy Orbison) 1992, Mind of Love 1993, Miss Chatelaine 1993, Constant Craving 1993, Just Keep Me Moving 1993, If I Were You 1995. *Albums include:* A Truly Western Experience, Angel With A Lariat 1987, Shadowland 1988, Absolute Torch And Twang 1989, Ingenue 1992, Even Cowgirls Get The Blues (film soundtrack) 1993, All You Can Eat 1995, Drag 1997, Australian Tour 1997, Invincible Summer 2000, Live By Request 2001. *Address:* c/o WEA Records, The Warner Building, 28 Kensington Church Street, London, W8 4SP, England. *Website:* www.kdlang.com.

LANG, Hon. Otto, PC, OC, QC, BA, LLB, BCL, LLD; Canadian lawyer, politician, business executive and consultant; b. 14 May 1932, Handel, Sask.; s. of Otto T. Lang and Maria Theresa Merchant 1963 (divorced 1988); three s. four d.; m. 2nd Deborah J. McCawley 1989; one step-s. one step-d.; ed Univ. of Sask. and Oxford Univ., UK; admitted to Sask. Bar 1956, to Ont., Yukon and NWT Bars 1957, Manitoba Bar 1988; Asst Prof., Univ. of Saskatchewan, Faculty of Law 1956, Assoc. Prof. 1957, Prof. 1961, Dean of Law School 1961–68; MP for Saskatoon-Humboldt 1968–79; Minister without Portfolio 1968, with responsibility for Energy and Water Resources 1969, with responsibility for Canadian Wheat Bd 1969–79; Minister of Manpower & Immigration 1970–72, of Justice 1972–75, of Transport 1975–79, of Justice and Attorney-Gen. Aug.–Nov. 1978; Pres. Asscn of Canadian Law Teachers 1962–63; Vice-Pres. Sask. Liberal Asscn 1956–63; Fed. Campaign Chair. Liberal Party 1963–64; Past Pres. Saskatoon Social Planning Council; Exec. Vice-Pres. Pioneer Grain Co. Ltd 1979–88; mem. Bd of Dirs Investor Group Trust Co. 1985–; Chair. Transport Inst., Univ. of Manitoba 1988–93; Pres. and CEO Central Gas Manitoba Inc. 1993–99; consultant with GPC 2000–; Vice-Chair. of Bd, Winnipeg Airports Authority 1995–; Campaign Chair. Winnipeg United Way 1993; Chair. Royal Winnipeg Ballet Capital Campaign 1996–2000; Rhodes Scholar 1953; QC for Ont. 1972; for Sask. 1972; Hon. Consul-Gen. of Japan 1992–97. *Publication:* Contemporary Problems of Public Law in Canada (ed.) 1968. *Leisure interests:* curling, bridge, golf. *Address:* 6 Liss Road, St. Andrews, Man., R1A 2XZ (Office); Twin Oaks, 292 River Road, St Andrews, Man., R1A 2X2, Canada. *Telephone:* (204) 338-7242 (Office); (204) 334-9476 (Home). *Fax:* (204) 338-1524 (Office). *E-mail:* olang@mb.sympatico.ca (Office).

LANG OF MONKTON, Baron (Life Peer), cr. 1997, of Merrick and the Rhinns of Kells in Dumfries and Galloway; **Ian (Bruce) Lang;** British politician; b. 27 June 1940; s. of the late James F. Lang, DSC and of Maude Stewart; m. Sandra Montgomerie 1971; two d.; ed Lathallan School, Kincardineshire, Rugby School and Sidney Sussex Coll. Cambridge; MP for Galloway 1979–83, for Galloway and Upper Nithsdale 1983–97; Asst Govt Whip 1981–83; a Lord Commr of HM Treasury 1983–86; Parl. Under-Sec. of State, Dept of Employment 1986, Scottish Office 1986–87; Minister of State, Scottish Office 1987–90; Sec. of State for Scotland and Lord Keeper of the Great Seal of Scotland 1990–95; Pres. Bd of Trade 1995–97; mem. House of Lords Select Cttee on the Constitution 2001–; Chair. Murray tmt PLC 1998–;

Thistle Mining Inc. 1998–; Dir Marsh & McLennan Inc. 1997–, Second Scottish Nat. Trust PLC 1997–, European Telecom PLC 1997–, Lithgows Ltd 1997–, BFS US Special Opportunities Trust PLC; mem. Queen's Bodyguard for Scotland (Royal Co. of Archers) 1974–; DL Ayrshire and Arran 1998; mem. Conservative Party. *Publication:* Blue Remembered Years 2002. *Address:* House of Lords, London, SW1A 0PW, England.

LÅNGBACKA, Ralf Runar, MA; Finnish theatre director and professor of theatre science; b. 20 Nov. 1932, Närpes; s. of Runar Emanuel Långbacka and Hulda Emilia Långbacka (née Backlund); m. Runa Birgitta Danielsson 1961; two s. one d.; ed Åbo Akademi, Munich Univ. and Freie Univ., Berlin; Ed. Finnish Radio literary programmes 1955–56; Asst and Dir Lilla Teatern, Helsinki 1958–60; Man. and Artistic Dir Swedish Theatre, Turku 1960–63; Dir Finnish Nat. Theatre 1963–65; Artistic Dir Swedish Theatre, Helsinki 1965–67; freelance Dir in Finnish Nat. Opera, Helsinki, Municipal Theatre, Gothenburg, Sweden, Royal Dramatic Theatre, Stockholm, Sweden 1967–71 and in Denmark, Germany, Norway and Russia; mem. Finnish State Comm. of Dramatic Art 1967–70; Artistic Dir Municipal Theatre, Turku 1971–77; Head Finnish Dirs Asscn 1978–82; Artistic and Man. Dir Municipal Theatre, Helsinki 1983–87, Artistic Prof. 1979–83, 1988–93; Prof. of Theatre Science, Åbo Akademi, Turku 1994–97; Pres. Finnish Centre, Int. Theatre Inst. (ITI) 1983–96, mem. Bd (Excom) of ITI 1991–95; Corresp. mem. Akad. der Künste, Berlin 1979; The Critics Spurs 1963, Pro Finlandia 1973; Henrik-Steffens Award (Germany) 1994, Finland Prize, Swedish Acad., Sweden 1999, Finland Prize for Theatre 2001. *Film:* Puntila 1979. *Music:* directed operas: Wozzeck (Berg) 1967, 2001, Carmen (Bizet) 1969, Don Giovanni (Mozart) 1973, 1984, Macbeth (Verdi) 1980, 1993, Don Carlos (Verdi) 1995, Rigoletto (Verdi) 2000, 2001. *Plays:* directed over 100 performances of plays by Shakespeare, Chekhov, Brecht and Büchner. *Publications:* Teatterikirja (The Theatre Book) (with Kalle Holmberg) 1977, Bland annat om Brecht (On Brecht and Others) 1981, Möten med Tjechov (Meetings with Chekhov) 1986, Denna långa dag, detta korta liv (This long day, This short life: poems) 1988, Krocketspelaren (The Croquet Player, play) 1990, Olga, Irina och jag (Olga, Irina and I, play) 1991, Brecht og det realistiske teater (Brecht and the Realistic Theatre) 1998 and articles. *Leisure interests:* music, mushrooms, sailing. *Address:* Hope-asalmenranta 1B, 00570 Helsinki 57, Finland. *Telephone:* (9) 6849508 (Home); (40) 7323323. *Fax:* (9) 6849508 (Home). *E-mail:* ralf.langbacka@ kolumbus.fi (Home).

LANGBO, Arnold G.; Canadian business executive; b. 13 April 1937, Richmond, BC; s. of Osbjourn Langbo and Laura Marie Langbo (née Hauge); m. Martha M. Miller 1959; eight c.; ed Univ. of British Columbia, Vancouver; Sales Rep. Kellogg Canada Inc. 1956–67, Int. Div. 1967–69, Admin. Asst to Kellogg Co., Pres. 1969–70, Exec. Vice-Pres. 1970–71, Vice-Pres. of Kellogg Canada 1971–76, Salada Foods Ltd 1971–76, Pres., CEO Kellogg Salada Canada Ltd Inc. 1976–78, Pres. U.S. Food Products Div. of Kellogg Co. 1978–79, Corp. Vice-Pres. 1979–81, Exec. Vice-Pres. 1981–83, Group Exec. Vice-Pres. Kellogg Co. 1983–86, Pres. Kellogg Int. 1986–90, Pres., COO, Dir Kellogg Co. 1990–91, Chair., CEO 1992–98; Pres. Mrs Smith's Frozen Food Co. 1983–85, Chair., CEO 1985–; mem. Bd Dirs Johnson and Johnson, Grocery Mfrs of America, Advisory Bd J. L. Kellogg Grad. School of Man. at Northwestern Univ. *Address:* 7614 La Corniche Circle, Boca Raton, FL 33433, USA (Home). *E-mail:* pollylang@aol.com (Office).

LANGE, Rt Hon David Russell, CH, LLM, PC; New Zealand politician and fmr lawyer; b. 4 Aug. 1942, Otahuhu; s. of late Eric Roy Lange and Phoebe Fysh Lange; m. 1st Naomi Lange 1968 (divorced); three c.; m. 2nd Margaret Forsyth Pope 1992; one d.; ed Otahuhu Coll., Auckland Univ.; barrister and solicitor, sole practice at Kaikohe 1968, Auckland 1970–77; Labour Party MP for Mangere, Auckland 1977–96; Deputy Leader, Parl. Labour Party 1979–83, Leader 1983–89; fmr Opposition Spokesman on Foreign Affairs, Overseas Trade, Justice, Pacific Islands Affairs and Regional Devt; Prime Minister 1984–89; Minister in Charge of the Security Intelligence Service 1984–89, Minister of Foreign Affairs 1984–87, Minister of Educ. 1987–89; Attorney-Gen. 1989–90; Minister of State 1989–90; Minister in charge of SFO (Serious Fraud Office) 1989–90. *Publications:* Nuclear Free the New Zealand Way 1990, Broadsides 1992, Cuttings 1994. *Address:* P.O. Box 59-120, Mangere Bridge, Auckland, New Zealand (Home).

LANGE, Hartmut; German author; b. 31 March 1937, Berlin; s. of Johanna Lange and Karl Lange; m. Ulrike Ritter 1971; ed Babelsberg Film School; playwright at Deutsches Theater, Berlin 1961–65; freelance writer, W Berlin 1965–; Gerhart-Hauptmann-Preis 1968, Literatur Preis der Adenauer Stiftung 1998, Ehrengabe der Schiller-Stiftung von 1859 2000, Stato Svevo Preis 2003. *Publications:* Die Selbstverbrennung 1982, Deutsche Empfindungen 1983, Die Waldsteinsonate 1984, Das Konzert 1986, Die Ermüdung 1988, Vom Werden der Vernunft 1988, Gesammelte Theaterstücke (Collected Plays) 1988, Die Wattwanderung 1990, Die Reise nach Triest 1991, Die Stechpalme 1993, Schnitzlers Würgeengel 1995, Der Herr im Café 1996, Italienische Novellen 1998, Eine andere Form des Glücks 1999, Die Bildungsreise 2000, Das Streichquartett 2001, Irrtum als Erkenntnis 2002. *Leisure interest:* chess. *Address:* Hohenzollerndamm 197, 10717 Berlin, Germany; 06010 Niccone, Perugia, Italy.

LANGE, Hermann, DJur; German professor of law; b. 24 Jan. 1922, Dresden; s. of Arno Lange and Käthe (née Braun) Lange; m. Ulrike Moser 1960; one s. one d.; ed Kreuzgymnasium, Dresden and Univs on Leipzig, Munich and Freiburg/Breisgau; Asst Inst. of Legal History, Univ. of Freiburg/Breisgau

1949–53; Privatdozent, Freiburg/Breisgau 1953–55; Extraordinary Prof. Univ. of Innsbrück 1955–57; Prof. Univ. of Kiel 1957–62, Univ. of Mainz 1962–66, Univ. of Tübingen 1966– (now Emer.); mem. Akad. der Wissenschaften und Literatur, Mainz. *Publications:* Schadensersatz und Privatstrafe in der mittelalterlichen Rechtstheorie 1955, Familienrecht (Kommentar) 1962, Die Consilien des Baldus de Ubaldis 1974, Schadensersatzrecht 1979, Wandlungen des Schadenersatzrechts 1987, Die Anfänge der modernen Rechtswissenschaft 1993, Römisches Recht im Mittelalter 1997, 100 Jahre Bürgerliches Gesetzbuch 2001. *Address:* Ferdinand-Christian-Baur-Strasse 3, 72076 Tübingen, Germany. *Telephone:* (7071) 61216.

LANGE, Jessica; American actress; b. 20 April 1949, Cloquet, Minn.; d. of Al Lange and Dorothy Lange; m. Paco Grande 1970 (divorced 1982); one d. (with Mikhail Baryshnikov); one s. one d. (with Sam Shepard); ed Univ. of Minn.; student of mime with Etienne DeCroux, Paris; Dancer Opéra Comique, Paris; model, Wilhelmina Agency, NY; Star Showtime TV production Cat On A Hot Tin Roof 1984; in Summer stock production Angel On My Shoulder, NC 1980; play: A Streetcar Named Desire, London (Theatre World Award, Golden Globe (for TV performance) 1996) 1996. *Films include:* King Kong 1976, All That Jazz 1979, How to Beat the High Cost of Living 1980, The Postman Always Rings Twice 1981, Frances 1982, Tootsie 1982 (Acad. Award for Best Supporting Actress 1982), Country 1984, Sweet Dreams 1985, Crimes of the Heart 1986, Everybody's All American 1989, Far North 1989, Music Box 1989, Men Don't Leave 1989, Blue Sky 1990, Cape Fear 1991, Far North 1991, Night and the City 1993, Losing Isaiah, Rob Roy 1994, Blue Sky 1994 (Acad. Award for Best Actress 1995), A Thousand Acres 1997, Hush 1998, Cousin Bette 1998, Titus 1999. *Play:* Long Day's Journey into Night 2000. *Address:* c/o Toni Howard, ICM, 8942 Wilshire Boulevard, Beverly Hills, CA 90211, USA. *Website:* www.jessicalange.net (Office).

LANGE, Otto Ludwig, Dr rer. nat; German professor of botany (retd); b. 21 Aug. 1927, Dortmund; s. of Otto Lange and Marie (née Pralle) Lange; m. Rose Wilhelm 1959; two d.; ed Univs of Göttingen and Freiburg; Asst Prof. Univ. of Göttingen 1953–61; Dozent Technische Hochschule Darmstadt 1961–63; Prof. Forest Botany Univ. Göttingen 1963–67; Prof. Botany Univ. of Würzburg 1967–92, Emer. 1992–; Visiting Scientist Utah State Univ. 1973, 1985, Australian Nat. Univ., Canberra 1978–79; Dir Botanical Garden, Univ. of Würzburg 1967–92; co-ed. scientific journal Flora; mem. Deutsche Akad. der Naturforscher Leopoldina, Bayerische Akad. der Wissenschaften, Academia Europaea, Acad. Scientiarum et Artium Europaea; Corresp. mem. Akad. der Wissenschaften, Göttingen; Foreign Hon. mem. American Acad. of Arts and Sciences 1994; Bundesverdienstkreuz (1st Class) 1985; Dr hc (Bayreuth) 1995, (Tech. Univ., Lisbon) 1996, (Darmstadt) 2001; Antarctic Service Medal, US Govt 1974, Gottfried-Wilhem-Leibniz Prize, Deutsche Forschungsgemeinschaft 1986, Balzan Prize 1988, Adalbert Seifriz Prize 1990, Bayerische Maximiliansorden for Science and Art 1991, Acharius Medal, Int. Asscn of Lichenology 1992. *Publications:* Ed. (with others) 4 vols of Physiological Plant Ecology in Encyclopedia of Plant Physiology 1981–83; books on water and plant life, plant response to stress, forest decline, air pollution and biological soil crusts; book series Ecological Studies; 350 scientific papers. *Address:* Julius-von-Sachs-Institut für Biowissenschaften der Universität Würzburg, Julius-von-Sachs-Platz 3, 97082 Würzburg (Office); Leitengraben 37, 97084 Würzburg, Germany (Home). *Telephone:* (931) 888-6205 (Office); (931) 65249 (Home). *Fax:* (931) 6193178 (Home). *E-mail:* ollange@botanik.uni-wuerzburg.de (Office).

LANGER, Ivan, MD, MCL; Czech politician; b. 1 Jan. 1967, Olomouc; m. Markéta Vobořilová; one d.; ed Univ. of Olomouc, Charles Univ., Prague; Secr. Ministry for Justice of Czech Repub. 1993–96; mem. Council Olomouc 1994; mem. of Civic Democratic Party, Vice-Chair. 1998–; MP 1996–; Shadow Minister of the Interior 1999–2002; Vice-Chair. Chamber of Deputies (Parl.) 2002–; Hon. mem. Maltese Order of Help 1994–. *Publications:* Rational Antidrug Policy, After the Velvet Revolution. *Leisure interests:* tennis, music, theatre, film, golf. *Address:* Parliament Buildings, Sněmovní 4, Prague 1, 118 26 Czech Republic (Office). *Telephone:* (2) 57171111 (Office). *E-mail:* langer@psp.cz (Office). *Website:* www.psp.cz (Office).

LANGHOLM, Sivert; Norwegian professor of history; b. 19 May 1927, Haugesund; s. of Karl Johan Langholm and Anna Langholm; m. Eva Synnøve Bakkom 1959; one s. one d.; ed Univ. of Oslo; Lecturer in History, Univ. of Oslo 1961–71, research (project) leader 1971–74, Reader in History 1974–76, Prof. 1976–94, Dean, Faculty of Humanities 1985–90; mem. Det Norske Videnskaps Akademi; Hon. mem. Int. Comm. for the History of Univs. *Publications:* Stillingsretten 1966, Historisk Rekonstruksjon og Begrunnelse 1967, Elitenes Valg 1984. *Address:* Universitetet i Oslo, Avdeling for Historie, Postboks 1008, Blindern 0315, Oslo (Office); Parkgt. 12, 3513 Hønefoss, Norway (Home). *Telephone:* 22-85-68-09 (Office); 32-12-14-48 (Home).

LANGLANDS, Sir (Robert) Alan, Kt, SC, BSc, FCGI, CI, MGT; British university principal and healthcare administrator; b. 29 May 1952; s. of James Langlands and May (née Rankin) Langlands; m. Elizabeth McDonald 1977; one s. one d.; ed Allan Glen's School, Univ. of Glasgow; grad. trainee Nat. Health Service Scotland 1974–76; with Argyll and Clyde Health Bd 1976–78; with Simpson Memorial Maternity Pavilion, Elise Inglis Hosp. 1978–81; Unit Admin. Middx and Univ. Coll. Hosps and Hosp. for Women, Soho 1981–85; Dist Gen. Man. Harrow Health Authority 1985–89; Practice Leader Health Care, Towers Perrin 1989–91; Gen. Man. NW Thames Regional Health Authority 1991–92; Deputy Chief Exec. Nat. Health Service 1993–94, Chief

Exec. 1994–2000; mem. Central Research and Devt Cttee Nat. Health Service 1991–92; mem. Inst. of Health Services Man., Nat. Forum for Research and Devt 1994–2000; mem. Advisory Bd Centre for Corp. Strategy and Change, Univ. of Warwick 1995–2000; Prin. and Vice-Chancellor Univ. of Dundee 2000–; Hon. Prof. (Warwick Business School) 1996, Johns Hopkins Univ. 2000–; mem. Nat. Advisory Bd, Healthcare Advisory Bd of Institut Européen d'Admin des Affaires (INSEAD) 1998–; Hon. FFPHM 1994; Hon. FIA 1999; Hon. FCGI 2000; Hon. Fellow Royal Coll. of Gen. Practitioners 2001. *Leisure interests:* walking in Yorkshire and Scotland. *Address:* University of Dundee, Dundee, DD1 4HN, Scotland (Office).

LANGLANDS, Robert Phelan, MA, PhD, FRS; Canadian mathematician; b. 6 Oct. 1936, New Westminster; s. of Robert Langlands and Kathleen J. Phelan; m. Charlotte Cheverie 1956; two s. two d.; ed Univ. of British Columbia, Yale Univ., USA; Instructor, Assoc. Prof. Princeton Univ. 1960–67; Prof. Yale Univ. 1968–72; Prof. Inst. for Advanced Study, Princeton 1972–; mem. NAS, American Math. Soc.; several awards. *Publications:* Automorphic Forms on GL(2) (with H. Jacquet) 1970, Euler Products 1971, On the Functional Equations Satisfied by Eisenstein Series 1976, Base Change for GL (2) 1980, Les Débuts d'une Formule des Traces Stable 1983. *Leisure interests:* reading, travel. *Address:* School of Mathematics, Institute for Advanced Study, Olden Lane, Princeton, NJ 08540 (Office); 60 Battle Road, Princeton, NJ 08540, USA (Home). *Telephone:* (609) 734–8106 (Office); (609) 921-7222 (Home).

LANGSLET, Lars Roar, MA; Norwegian author; b. 5 March 1936, Nesbyen; s. of Knut Langslet and Alma Langslet; ed Univ. of Oslo; Assoc. Prof. 1969–89; MP 1969–89; Minister of Culture and Science 1981–86; writer Aftenposten newspaper 1990–97; Ed. Ordet 1997–; State Scholarship 1997–99; Pres. of Norwegian Acad. for Language and Literature 1995–; Commdr Order of St Olav, Dannebrog, Order of Gregory the Great, etc. *Publications:* Karl Marx 1963, Conservatism 1965, (biogs of) John Lyng 1989, King Olav V 1995, St Olav 1995, King Christian IV 1997, King Christian VIII 1998–99, Ludvig Holberg 2001. *Address:* Norske Akademi for Sprog og Litteratur, Inkognitogt, 24, 0256 Oslo 2 (Office); Rosenborggt. 5, 0356 Oslo, Norway. *Telephone:* 22-46-34-12. *Fax:* 22-55-37-43. *E-mail:* lars.roar.langslet@netcom.no (Office).

LANGUETIN, Pierre; Swiss diplomatist and central banker; b. 30 April 1923, Lausanne; m. Florentina Lobo 1951; one s. one d.; ed Univ. de Lausanne and LSE, UK; diplomatic career 1949–; in Div. of Exchange, OEEC, Paris; in Div. of Commerce, Fed. Dept of Public Economy 1955–76, Head of Secr. 1957–61, Chief of Section IA 1961–63; Chief of Subdiv. 1963; has been concerned with problems of European econ. co-operation; Asst Head of Bureau of Integration, Fed. Political Dept and Dept of Public Economy 1961; Swiss Del. to Trade Cttee, OECD, Paris 1961–76, Vice-Pres. 1963–76; mem. Swiss Del. to UNCTAD, Geneva 1964, New Delhi 1968; Swiss Rep. at various int. orgs 1965–66; Del. of Fed. Council for Trade Negotiations, title of Minister Plenipotentiary 1966–68; Head of Swiss Del. to EFTA Geneva 1967–76, title of Amb. 1968–76; Deputy Head of Swiss Negotiating Team with EEC 1970–72; Head of Swiss Del. to Exec. Cttee in special session OECD 1972–76; Head of Swiss Del. for accession negotiations to Int. Energy Agency 1974, Rep. for Switzerland to Governing Bd 1974–76; mem. Governing Bd of Swiss Nat. Bank 1976–81, Vice-Chair. 1981–84, Chair. 1985–88; mem. Bd of Dirs BIS 1985–88; Chair. Inst. for Public Admin. Studies, Lausanne 1988–97, Inst. for Bank and Financial Man., Lausanne 1990–96; Vice-Chair. Sandoz SA 1988–95; Chair. Rosbank (fmrly Unexim), Switzerland 1995–; mem. Bd of Dirs Ludwig Inst. 1987–, Swiss Reinsurance Co. 1988–93, Pargesa Holding SA 1988–2002, Paribas (Suisse) 1989–96 (Vice-Chair. 1992), Renault Finance 1989–99, Fin. Cpy Tradition 1995–; mem. Advisory Bd American Int. Group 1989–97, Arthur Andersen (Switzerland) 1991–97; mem. Bd of Dirs Chase Manhattan Pvt. Bank (Switzerland) 1991–2001, Prumerica Pvt. Bank (Switzerland) 2002–; mem. Int. Red Cross Cttee 1988–93; Dr hc (Lausanne) 1979. *Address:* 37 Muelinenstrasse, 3006 Bern, Switzerland. *Telephone:* (31) 3526613. *Fax:* (31) 3526613.

LANKESTER, Sir Timothy Patrick, KCB, MA; British government and university administrator; b. 15 April 1942, Cairo, Egypt; s. of the late Robin P. A. Lankester and of Jean D. Gilliat; m. Patricia Cockcroft 1968; three d.; ed Monkton Combe School, St John's Coll. Cambridge and Jonathan Edwards Coll., Yale; teacher St Michael's Coll., Belize 1960–61; Faraday Fellow, St John's Coll. Oxford 1965–66; Economist IBRD, Washington, DC 1966–69, New Delhi 1970–73; HM Treasury 1973–78, Under-Sec. 1983–85, Deputy Sec. 1988–89; Pvt. Sec. to Prime Minister Callaghan 1978–79, to Prime Minister Thatcher 1979–81; seconded to S. G. Warburg & Co. 1981–83; Econ. Minister, Washington, DC and UK Exec. Dir IMF and IBRD 1985–88; Perm. Sec. Overseas Devt Admin., FCO 1989–93, Dept for Educ. 1993–94; Dir SOAS, Univ. of London 1996–2000; Pres. Corpus Christi Coll. Oxford 2001–; Dir European Investment Bank 1988–89, Smith and Nephew 1996–, London Metal 1997–2001; Gov. Asia-Europe Foundation 1997–; Deputy Chair. British Council 1998–. *Address:* Corpus Christi College, Merton Street, Oxford OX1 4JF, England (Office). *Telephone:* (1865) 276740 (Office). *Fax:* (1865) 276769 (Office). *E-mail:* tim.lankester@ccc.ox.ac.uk (Office).

LANOVOY, Vasiliy Semenovich; Russian stage and film actor; b. 16 Jan. 1934, Moscow; s. of Semion Petrovich Lanovoy and Agafia Ivanovna Yakubenko; m. Irina Petrovna Kupchenko 1972; two s.; ed Shchukin Theatre School; actor with Vakhtangov Theatre 1957–; also works as narrator; Prof., Faculty of Artistic Speech, Schukin's Theatre School, Moscow 1995–; mem.

CPSU 1968–90; Lenin Prize 1980, People's Artist of USSR 1985. *Theatrical roles include:* Ognev in Korneichuk's Front, Prince Calaf in Gozzi's Princess Turandot, Caesar in Shaw's Antony and Cleopatra, Sagadeev in Abdullin's Thirteenth President, Don Juan in Pushkin's The Stone Guest, Trotsky in M. Shatrov's Peace of Brest, Oscar in La Bize's Murder at Lursin Street, Astrov in Uncle Vanya, J.B. Shaw in I. Kiltye's Dear Liar, King Henry in The Lion in Winter. *Films include:* War and Peace, Anna Karenina, The Strange Woman, Going in a Thunderstorm, The Picture, The Scarlet Sails, The Officers, Unknown War, The Colleges, Strategy for Victory, The Trifles of Life, Barin's Daughter. *Leisure interests:* volleyball, badminton, hunting, skiing, dogs. *Address:* Starokonyushenny per. 39, Apt. 18, 121002 Moscow, Russia. *Telephone:* (095) 203-94-03.

LANSBURY, Angela, CBE; British actress; b. 16 Oct. 1925, London; d. of Edgar Lansbury and of the late Moyna Macgill; m. 1st Richard Cromwell (divorced); m. 2nd Peter Shaw 1949; one s. one d. one step-s.; ed Webber Douglas School of Singing and Dramatic Art, Kensington, Feagin School of Drama and Radio, NY; film debut in Gaslight 1944; numerous appearances on London and New York stages and on TV; Hon. DHumLitt (Boston) 1990, Silver Mask for Lifetime Achievement BAFTA 1991; Lifetime Achievement Award, Screen Actors' Guild 1997, numerous other awards. *Films include:* Manchurian Candidate, In the Cool of the Day, Harlow, Moll Flanders, Bedknobs and Broomsticks, Death on the Nile, The Lady Vanishes 1980, The Mirror Cracked 1980, The Pirates of Penzance 1982, Company of Wolves 1983, Beauty and the Beast 1991. *Television includes:* Murder She Wrote 1984–96, The Shell Seekers 1989, South by Southwest 1997, A Story to Die For 2000. *Stage appearances include:* Hotel Paradiso 1957, Dear World 1969 (Tony Award), The King and I 1978, A Little Family Business 1983. *Publication:* Angela Lansbury's Positive Moves (with Mimi Avins) 1990. *Address:* Corymore Productions, Building 426, 100 Universal City Plaza, Universal City, CA 91608, USA; c/o William Morris, 31 Soho Square, London, W.1, England.

LANSING, Sherry, BS; American business executive; b. 31 July 1944, Chicago, Ill.; d. of Norton and Margot Lansing; m. 2nd William Friedkin (q.v.) 1991; ed Northwestern Univ., Evanston, Ill.; mathematics teacher, Public High Schools, LA, Calif. 1966–69; model, TV commercials, Max Factor Co. and Alberto-Culver 1969–70; appeared in films Loving and Rio Lobo 1970; Exec. Story Ed., Wagner Int. 1970–73; Vice-Pres. for Production, Heyday Productions 1973–75; Exec. Story Ed., then Vice-Pres. for Creative Affairs, MGM Studios 1975–77; Vice-Pres., then Sr Vice-Pres. for Production, Columbia Pictures 1977–80; Pres. 20th Century-Fox Productions 1980–83; Founder Jaffe-Lansing Productions, LA 1982–; Chair. Paramount Pictures 1992–. *Films produced include:* Racing with the Moon 1984, Firstborn 1984, Fatal Attraction 1987, The Accused 1989, Black Rain 1990, School Ties 1992, Indecent Proposal 1993. *Address:* Paramount Pictures Corporation, 5555 Melrose Avenue, Los Angeles, CA 90038, USA.

LANXADE, Adm. Jacques; French naval officer; b. 8 Sept. 1934, Toulon; m. Loïse Rostan d'Ancezune 1959; one s. three d.; ed Ecole Navale, Institut d'Admin des Affaires (Université Dauphiné); Commdr destroyers Le Champenois 1970–72, La Galissonnière 1976–77, frigate Duguay-Trouin 1980–81; rank of Rear-Adm. 1984; Commdr Indian Ocean maritime zone 1984–86; Commdr French fleet in the Indian Ocean 1986; rank of Vice-Adm. 1987; Chef du Cabinet Militaire to Minister of Defence 1988–89; Chief of Staff, Elysée Palace 1989; Chief of Staff of French Armed Forces 1991–95; Amb. to Tunisia 1995–99; mem. Atomic Energy Cttee 1991–95; Grand Officier Légion d'honneur, Officier, Ordre nat. du Mérite, Croix de la Valeur Militaire. *Publications:* Quand le monde a basculé 2001, Organizer la politique européenne et internationale de la France (report) 2002. *Leisure interests:* tennis, skiing. *Address:* 41 rue Saint-André des Arts, 75006 Paris, France (Home). *Telephone:* 1-43-25-60-15 (Office); 1-46-33-39-05 (Home). *Fax:* 1-43-25-60-15. *E-mail:* jacqueslanxade@noos.fr (Office).

LANYON, Lance Edward, CBE, PhD, DSc., FMedSci, MRCVS; British professor of veterinary anatomy and university administrator; b. 4 Jan. 1944; s. of the late Henry Lanyon and Heather Gordon (née Tyrrell); m. Mary Kear (divorced 1997); one s. one d.; ed Christ's Hosp., Univ. of Bristol; Lecturer Univ. of Bristol 1967, Reader in Veterinary Anatomy 1967–79; Assoc. Prof. Tufts School of Veterinary Medicine, Boston, USA 1980–83, Prof. 1983–84; Prof. of Veterinary Anatomy, Royal Veterinary Coll., Univ. of London 1984–89, personal title 1989–, Head Dept of Veterinary Anatomy 1984–87, of Veterinary Basic Sciences 1987–88; Prin. Royal Veterinary Coll. 1989–; Pro-Vice-Chancellor Univ. of London 1997–99. *Publications include:* numerous articles in professional journals; chapters in books on osteoporosis, orthopaedics and athletic training. *Leisure interests:* building, home improvements, sailing. *Address:* Royal Veterinary College, Royal College Street, London, NW1 0UT, England (Office). *Telephone:* (20) 7387-2898 (Office).

LAO CHONGPIN; Chinese artist; b. 3 Nov. 1936, Xinxing City., Guangdong; s. of Lao Xianguang and Chen Ermei; m. Luo Yuzing 1956; two s. one d.; ed Fine Arts Dept, Cen. China Teachers' Coll.; has painted more than one thousand landscapes and human figures in Japan, Canada, France, Egypt, Yugoslavia, Democratic People's Repub. of Korea, Pakistan, Burma, Jordan, Hungary, USSR, Albania 1973–; Dir Poetry Inst. 1987–; mem. staff Chinese Exhbn Agency, Ministry of Culture; mem. Chinese Artists' Assen, Advisory Cttee, Beijing Children's Fine Arts Research Acad., Chinese Poetry Assen, Int. Biographical Assen; Hon. Dir Hanlin Forest of Steles, Kaifeng, China

Shaolin Research Inst. of Painting and Calligraphy 1989. *Major works:* Harvest Time, Spring Ploughing, Harbour, Riverside, Arashiyama in Rain, Mosque in Lahore, Golden Pagoda of Rangoon, Pyramid and Sphinx, Autumn in Amman, Morning Glory on Seine River, Niagara Falls; group exhbns include Seven Star Cliff, Japan 1979, Scenery on Xinghu Lake, Mexico 1980, Drum Beaters, Hong Kong 1982, Panda, Wulongtang Waterfall, Belgium 1982, Scenery on Huangshan Mountain, Jordan 1983, Light Boats on the Yangtze River (Nat. Arts Museum) 1986, Scenes of Petra (Sact City Museum, Jordan) 1987, Waterfall of Lushan Mountain (Zacheta Art Museum, Poland) 1987; one-man exhbns in many Chinese cities and provs 1979–, Hong Kong 1988, Philippines 1989, Jordan 1990, Singapore 1995, India 1996; Sixth Asian Art Biennale, Bangladesh 1993. *Publication:* An Album of Sketches of Life in Foreign Countries 1986. *Leisure interests:* travel, music. *Address:* 1-301 Building No. 43, Xidahe Dongli, Chaoyang Qu, Beijing 100028, People's Republic of China. *Telephone:* (10) 64672946.

ŁAPICKI, Andrzej; Polish actor and director; b. 11 Nov. 1924, Riga, Latvia; s. of Borys Łapicki and Zofia Łapicka; m. Zofia Chrząszczewska 1947; one s. one d.; ed Underground Inst. of Theatrical Art, Warsaw; Actor in Łódź: Polish Army Theatre 1945–48, Kameralny (Chamber) Theatre 1948–49; in Warsaw: Współczesny (Contemporary) Theatre 1949–64, 1966–72, Dramatyczny (Dramatic) Theatre 1964–66, 1982–83, Narodowy (Nat.) Theatre 1972–81, Polski Theatre, Warsaw 1983–89; Artistic Dir Polski Theatre 1995–98; Lecturer Higher State School of Drama, Warsaw 1953–, Asst Prof. 1970–79, Extraordinary Prof. 1979–87, Ordinary Prof. 1987–, Dean Actors' Faculty 1971–81, Rector 1981–87, 1993–96; mem. SPATiF-ZASP (Assen of Polish Theatre and Film Actors) until 1982, 1989–96, Vice-Pres. 1976–79), Pres. 1989–96; mem. Int. Theatre Inst. (ITI) 1983–, mem. Gen. Bd 1983–91, Pres. 1989–96; Deputy to Sejm (Parl.) 1989–91 (Solidarity); Chair. Parl. Comm. of Culture and Mass Media 1989–91; Minister of Culture and Art Prize (1st Class), Pres. of Radio and TV Cttee Prize (five times), Commdr's Cross with Star, Order of Polonia Restituta, Gold Cross of Merit and other distinctions. *Stage appearances:* about 100 roles, including The Respectable Prostitute, The Night of the Iguana, L'Ecole des femmes, Ring Round the Moon, Biedermann und die Brandstifter, Way of Life. *Film appearances:* about 30 roles, including Dolle 1968, Everything for Sale 1969, Pilatus und Andere 1972, How Far from Here, How Near 1972, The Wedding 1973, Jealousy and Medicine 1973, Lava 1989; also some 50 TV roles; Dir of about 50 TV and 30 theatre plays. *Publication:* To Keep One's Distance 1999. *Address:* ul. Kartowicza 1/7 m. 50, 02-501 Warsaw, Poland.

LAPID, Joseph 'Tommy', LLB; Israeli politician and journalist; b. (Tomislav Lampel), 27 Dec. 1931, Novi Sad, Yugoslavia; s. of Béla Lampel and Katalin Lampel (née Bierman); m.; one s. one d.; ed Tel-Aviv Univ.; survivor of Holocaust, Budapest ghetto; emigrated from Yugoslavia to Israel 1948; Dir-Gen. Israel Broadcasting Authority 1979–84; editorial writer daily newspaper Maariv, Tel-Aviv 1985–99; mem. Knesset; Leader Shinui Party, Chair. Shinui Party in Knesset 1999–; Minister of Justice March 2003–; Chair. Israel Cable TV Assen 1989–94, Israel Chess Fed. 1996–99; Sokolov Prize for Radio Journalism. *Plays:* Black Man's Burden, Kameri Theatre, Tel-Aviv 1967, Catch the Thief, Habima Nat. Theatre, Tel-Aviv 1973. *Television:* Popolitica, Everything is Political. *Publications:* Very Important People 1963, Guide to Europe 1970, Coffee in Bed, A Man of My Age, My Week 1989, While I'm Speaking 1989, Lectures in Communications 2000, Something Has Gone Wrong 2001. *Address:* Shinui Party, P.O. Box 20533, 100 Ha' Hashmona'im St, Tel-Aviv 67133 (Office); Ministry of Justice, P.O. Box 1087, 29 Rehov Salahadin, Jerusalem 91010 (Office); 29 Lassalle Street, Tel-Aviv 63409, Israel (Home). *Telephone:* 2-6466666 (Office); 3-5272227 (Home). *Fax:* 2-6287757 (Office); 3-5228080 (Home). *E-mail:* pniot@justice.gov.il (Office); shinui@shinui.org.il (Office). *Website:* www.justice.gov.il (Office); www.shinui.org.il (Office).

LAPIDUS, Ted (Edmond); French fashion designer; b. 23 June 1929, Paris; s. of Robert Lapidus and Cécile Guitine; m. 2nd Ursula Mai 1970; two s. (one s. from previous marriage) one d.; ed Lycée Saint-Charles, Marseilles, Lycée Voltaire, Paris and medical studies at Univ. of Paris; mainly self-taught in fashion design; part-time fashion designer in Paris 1945–59; tailor, Club de Paris 1950; Founder-Man. Ted Lapidus Couture, Paris 1951–70, Pres.-Dir-Gen. 1970–; Admin. Ted Lapidus Int. SA.; est. boutiques in Paris, London, New York etc.; instructor in cutting and clothing design, Tokyo 1961; mem. Chambre Syndicale de la Couture Parisienne. *Address:* 66 boulevard Maurice-Barrès, 92200 Neuilly-sur-Seine, France.

LAPIERRE, Dominique; French journalist, author and philanthropist; b. 30 July 1931, Châtelaillon, Charente-Maritime; s. of Jean Lapierre and Luce Lapierre (née Andreotti); m. 2nd Dominique Conchon 1980; one d. (by first m.); ed Lycée Condorcet, Paris and LaFayette Univ., Easton, USA; Ed., Paris Match Magazine 1954–67; f. and Pres. Action Aid for Lepers' Children of Calcutta; Citizen of Honour of the City of Calcutta; Commdr Confrérie du Tastevin 1990; Grand Cross of the Order of Social Solidarity (Spain) 2002; Dr hc (Lafayette Univ.) 1982; Christopher Book Award 1986, Gold Medal of Calcutta, Int. Rainbow Prize, UN 2000, Vatican Prize for Peace 2000. *Publications:* Un dollar les mille kilomètres 1949, Honeymoon around the World 1953, En liberté sur les routes d'U.R.S.S. 1957, Russie portes ouvertes 1957, Les Caïds de New York 1958, Chessman m'a dit 1960, The City of Joy 1985, Beyond Love 1991, A Thousand Suns 1998, Five Past Midnight in Bhopal 2002; with Larry Collins: Is Paris Burning? 1964, ...Or I'll Dress You

In Mourning 1967, O Jerusalem 1971, Freedom at Midnight 1975, The Fifth Horseman 1980, A Thousand Suns 2000. *Leisure interests:* riding, tennis, collecting antiques. *Address:* 37 Rue Charles-Laffitte, 92200 Neuilly; Les Bignoles, val de Rian, 83350 Ramatuelle, France. *Telephone:* 1-46-37-34-34 (Neuilly); 4-94-97-17-31 (Ramatuelle). *Fax:* 4-94-97-38-05. *E-mail:* D .Lapierre@wandooo.fr (Home). *Website:* cityofjoy.org (Office).

LAPIS, Károly, DSc; Hungarian pathologist and clinical oncologist; b. 14 April 1926, Túrkeve; s. of Károly Lapis and Eszter Földesi; m. Ibolya Keresztes 1955; one s. one d.; ed Lóránd Eötvös Univ. Budapest; Scientific worker Oncopathological Research Inst. 1954–63; Prof. Postgraduate Medical School, Budapest 1963–68; Prof. 1st Inst. of Pathology and Experimental Cancer Research, Semmelweis Univ. of Budapest 1968–96, Prof. Emer.1998– (Dir 1968–93); Gordon Jacob Fellow Chester Beatty Research Inst., London 1959–60; Eleanor Roosevelt Fellow, Paris 1963–64; Visiting Prof. Duke Univ. Medical School, Durham, NC 1972; Fogarty Scholar, Nat. Cancer Inst., Bethesda 1984–85; Corresp. mem. Hungarian Acad. of Sciences 1970, mem. 1979–; Foreign mem. Medical Acad. of the USSR (now Acad. of Medical Sciences of Russia) 1987, Serbian Acad. of Sciences and Arts 1989; Pres. 14th Int. Cancer Congress of the UICC, Budapest 1986; Vice-Pres. European Assoc. for Cancer Research 1979–85; mem. Exec. Cttee European Soc. of Pathology 1989–93, French Electron Microscope Soc., German Soc. of Pathology, Int. Gastro-Surgical Club, Hungarian Cancer Soc. (Pres. 1974–84), Hungarian Soc. of Gastroenterology, Hungarian Soc. of Pathologists, Int. Acad. of Pathology (Hungarian section); Corresp. mem. American Asscn for Cancer Research; Dir Metastasis Research Soc. 1986–90; Chief Ed. Acta Morphologica Hungarica 1985–94; Hon. Citizen of Mezotur 1997; Labour Order of Merit 1978, 4th of April Order of Merit 1986; Genersich Prize 1994, Széchényi Prize 1996, George Weber Foundation Prize 1997; Krompecher Memorial Medal 1985, Semmelweis Memorial Medal 1987, Baló József Memorial Medal 1987, Hetényi Géza Memorial Medal 1990, 'Pro Optimo Merito in Gastroenterologia' Memorial Medal 1992. *Publications:* Lymphkno-tengeschwülste (co-author) 1966, The Liver 1979, Mediastinal Tumors and Pseudotumors (co-author) 1984, Co-ed. Liver carcinogenesis 1979, Ultra-structure of Tumours in Man 1981, Regulation and Control of Cell Pro-liferation 1984, Tumour Progression and Markers 1982, Models, Mechanisms and Etiology of Tumour Promotion 1984, Biochemistry and molecular genetics of cancer metastasis 1985, Lectures and Symposia of the 14th International Cancer Congress 1987, Morphological Diagnosis of Liver Dis-eases (in Russian) 1989, Pathology (Textbook in Hungarian) 1989, Sincerely About Cancer for Men and Women (in Hungarian) 2001. *Leisure interests:* tennis, gardening. *Address:* First Institute of Pathology and Experimental Cancer Research, Semmelweis University, Üllöi út 26, Budapest 1085 (Office); Lónyay u. 25, Budapest 1093, Hungary (Home). *Telephone:* (1) 266-1912 (Office); (1) 217-9699 (Home). *Fax:* (1) 317-1074 (Office). *E-mail:* klapis@korb1.sote.hu (Office).

LAPLI, Father Sir John Ini; Solomon Islands Anglican priest; s. of Christian Mekope and Ellen Lauai; m. Helen Lapli 1985; three s. one d.; ed Selwyn Coll., Guadalcanal, St John's Theological Coll., Auckland, New Zealand; tutor Theological Coll., Auckland 1982–83; teacher Catechist School, Rural Training Centre 1985; Parish Priest 1986; Bible Translator 1987–88; Premier of Temotu Prov. 1988–99; Gov.-Gen. of Solomon Is July 1999–. *Leisure interest:* gardening. *Address:* Government House, P.O. Box 252, Honiara, Solomon Islands. *Telephone:* 22222; 21777.

LAPPERT, Michael F., PhD, DSc, FRCS, FRS; British professor of chemistry; b. 31 Dec. 1928, Brno, Czechoslovakia; s. of Julius and Kornelie (née Beran) Lappert; m. Lorna McKenzie 1980; ed Wilson's Grammar School and Northern Polytechnic, London; Asst Lecturer, Northern Polytechnic, London 1952–53, Lecturer 1953–55, Sr Lecturer 1955–59; Lecturer, Univ. of Man-chester Inst. of Sciences and Tech. (UMIST) 1959–61, Sr Lecturer 1961–64; Reader, Univ. of Sussex 1964–69, Prof. of Chem. 1969–97, Research Prof. 1997–; Science and Eng Research Council Sr Research Fellow 1980–85; Pres. Dalton Div. (Royal Soc. of Chem.) 1989–91; Tilden Lecturer, Royal Soc. of Chem. 1972–73, Nyholm Lecturer 1994, Sir Edward Frankland Lecturer 1999; Hon. Dr rer. nat (Munich) 1989; Chem. Soc. Award in Main Group Metal Chem. 1970; Award in Organometallic Chem. 1978; ACS F. S. Kipping Award 1976. *Publications:* Metal and Metalloid Amides (jtly) 1980, Chemistry of Organo-Zirconum and -Hafnium Compounds (jtly) 1986 and more than 650 papers in scientific journals. *Leisure interests:* theatre, opera, art, travel, walking, tennis. *Address:* School of Chemistry, Physics and Environmental Science, University of Sussex, Brighton, E Sussex, BN1 9QJ (Office); 4 Varndean Gardens, Brighton, BN1 6WL (Home); John Dalton Cottage, Eaglesfield, Cockermouth, Cumbria, CA13 0SD, England. *Telephone:* (1273) 678316 (Office); (1273) 503661 (Brighton) (Home). *Fax:* (1273) 677196 (Brighton) (Office). *E-mail:* m.f.lappert@sussex.ac.uk (Office). *Website:* www .cpes.sussex.ac.uk/faculty/mfl (Office).

LAPSHIN, Mikhail Ivanovich, CEconSc; Russian politician; b. 1 Sept. 1934, Setovka, Altai Territory; m.; three s.; ed Moscow Timiryazev Agricultural Acad., Moscow Inst. of Foreign Languages; Dir Sovkhoz Zavety Ilyicha, Stupino, Moscow Region 1962–91; Pres. Jt-Stock Co. Zavety Ilyicha 1991–; People's Deputy of Russia 1990–93; mem. Agrarian Union; Leader Agrarian Party of Russia 1992–; mem. State Duma (Parl.) 1993–95, 1999–; initiated

split in Agrarian Party, joined pre-election block Otechestvo (Homeland) 1999. *Address:* Agrarian Party, Lesnaya str. 45A, Suite 401, Moscow, Russia. *Telephone:* (095) 978-88-84.

LAPTEV, Ivan Dmitrievich, DPhilSc; Russian editor and journalist; b. 15 Oct. 1934, Sladkoye, Omsk Dist; m. Tatyana Kareva 1966; one d.; ed Siberian Road Transport Inst., Acad. of Social Sciences; worked for CPSU Cen. Cttee; mem. CPSU 1960–91; worked at Omsk River Port 1952–60; teacher 1960–61; instructor, Soviet Army Sports Club 1961–64, literary collaborator and special corresp. Sovietskaya Rossiya 1964–67; Consultant for Kommunist (later named Free Thought) 1967–73; work with CPSU Cen. Cttee 1973–78; Section Ed. Pravda 1978–82, Deputy Ed. 1982–84; Chief Ed. Izvestia 1984–90; mem. USSR Supreme Soviet 1989–91; People's Deputy of the USSR 1989–91; Chair. Council of Union 1990–91; Gen. Man. Izvestia Publrs 1991–94; Deputy Chair. Fed. Press Cttee 1994–95, Chair. 1995–99; Head of Sector Professional Acad. of State Service to Russian Presidency 1995–; mem. Int. Acad. of Information 1993; Pres. Asscn of Chief Eds and Publrs 1993–. *Publications:* Ecological Problems 1978, The World of People in the World of Nature 1986; over 100 scientific articles on ecological problems. *Leisure interests:* reading, automobile engineering, cycle racing. *Address:* Academy of State Service, Vernadskogo prosp. 84, 117606 Moscow, Russia. *Telephone:* (095) 436-99-07.

LAPTEV, Vladimir Viktorovich, DJur; Russian jurist; b. 28 April 1924, Moscow; s. of V. I. Laptev and V. A. Lapteva; m. 1950; two s.; ed Law Dept, Moscow Inst. for Foreign Trade; mem. staff Inst. of State and Law, Russian Acad. of Sciences, Moscow 1955, Head Section, Econ. Law 1959, Head Centre of Entrepreneurial and Econ. Law 1992–97, Chief Scientific Research Officer 1997–; Head Chair of Entrepreneurial Law, Academic Law Univ., Moscow 1997; Visiting Prof. Emory Univ., Atlanta, Ga, USA 1992–93; Corresp. mem. USSR (now Russian) Acad. of Science 1979–87, mem. 1987–; Honoured Scientist of Russian Fed. 1977. *Publications:* more than 350 books and articles on econ. law, including Legal Status of Enterprises in Russia 1993, Intro-duction to Entrepreneurial Law 1994, Entrepreneurial Law: Notion and Subjects 1997, Joint Stock Company Law 1999. *Address:* Institute of State and Law, Znamenka Str. 10, 119841 GSP, Moscow G-19 (Office); Profsoyuz-naia str. 43-1-5, 117420 Moscow, Russia (Home). *Telephone:* (095) 291-86-03 (Office); (095) 331-32-24 (Home). *Fax:* (095) 291-85-74.

LAQUEUR, Walter; American historian and political commentator; b. 26 May 1921, Breslau, Germany (now Wrocław, Poland); s. of Fritz Laqueur and Else Berliner; m. 1st Barbara Koch 1941 (deceased); m. 2nd C. S. Wichmann; two d.; Ed. Survey 1955–65; Dir Inst. of Contemporary History and Wiener Library, London 1964–91; Ed. Journal of Contemporary History 1965–; Prof. of History Brandeis Univ. 1967–72; Prof. of History, Tel-Aviv Univ. 1970–87; Prof. of Govt Georgetown Univ. 1977–90; Chair. Int. Research Council, Center for Strategic and Int. Studies, Washington DC 1973–; Ed. Washington Papers 1973–, Washington Quarterly 1978–; Visiting Prof. of History, Harvard Univ. 1977; Rockefeller Fellow, Guggenheim Fellow; several hon. degrees. *Pub-lications:* Young Germany 1962, The Road to War 1967 1968, Europe Since Hitler 1970, A History of Zionism 1972, Confrontation 1974, Weimar 1974, Guerrilla 1976, Terrorism 1977, A Continent Astray: Europe 1970–78 1979, The Missing Years (novel) 1980, The Terrible Secret 1981, Farewell to Europe (novel) 1981, Germany Today 1985, A World of Secrets 1985, Breaking the Silence 1986, The Age of Terrorism 1987, The Long Road to Freedom 1989, Stalin 1990, Thursday's Child has Far to Go (autobiog.) 1993, Black Hundred 1993, The Dream That Failed 1994, Fascism 1997, Generation Exodus 2001, Yale Encyclopedia of the Holocaust (Ed.) 2001. *Leisure interest:* swimming. *Address:* c/o Journal of Contemporary History, 4 Devonshire Street, London, W1W 5BH, England.

LARA, Brian Charles; Trinidadian cricketer; b. 2 May 1969, Santa Cruz; s. of Banty Lara and Pearl Lara; ed San Juan Secondary, Fatima Coll., Port of Spain; started playing cricket aged 6; played football for Trinidad Under-14; played cricket for West Indies Under-19; captained a West Indies Youth XI against India, scoring 186; left-hand batsman; teams: Trinidad and Tobago 1987– (Capt. 1993–), Warwicks. 1994, 1998 (Capt.), making world record first-class score of 501 not out, including most runs in a day (390) and most boundaries in an innings (72) v. Durham, Edgbaston, 3 and 6 June 1994; 90 Tests for West Indies 1990–Dec. 2002 (18 as Capt.), scoring 7,572 runs (average 50.49) including 18 hundreds, highest score 375 (world record v. England, St John's, Antigua 16–18 April 1994); has scored 16,737 first-class runs (45 hundreds) to Dec. 2002, including 2,066 off 2,262 balls for Warwicks. 1994, with 6 hundreds in his first 7 innings; toured England 1991, 1995; 203 ODIs (One Day Ints) to end Dec. 2002, for 7,549 runs (average 42.65); Fed. of Int. Cricketers' Asscns Int. Cricketer of the Year 1999. *Publication:* Beating the Field (autobiog.) 1995. *Leisure interests:* golf, horse racing. *Address:* c/o West Indies Cricket Board, P.O. Box 616, St John's, Antigua.

LARA CASTRO, Jorge, MA; Paraguayan diplomatist and social scientist; b. 5 Aug. 1945, Asunción; s. of Mariano Lara Castro and Carmen Casco; m.; ed Catholic Univ., Asunción, Latin American Faculty of Social Sciences, Mexico City; human rights activist; Prof. Autonomous Nat. Univ. of Mexico 1979–81; Prof. Catholic Univ., Asunción 1974–75; Prof. Centre for Econ. Research and Teaching, Mexico City 1980–91; Prof. Faculty of Philosophy and Human Sciences, Catholic Univ. of Asunción, Paraguay 1992–98, Dir Dept of Soci-ology 1997–99; Pres. Inst. of San Martin, Paraguay; Perm. Rep. to UN 2000–01. *Publications:* numerous publs on capitalism in Brazil, the birth of the campesino movt, Latin American political systems and educ. and human rights in Paraguay. *Address:* c/o Ministry of Foreign Affairs, Juan E. O'Leary y Presidente Franco, Asunción, Paraguay (Office). *Telephone:* 687-3490 (Office). *Fax:* 818-1282 (Office).

LARAKI, Azeddine, PhD; Moroccan politician; b. 1929, Fez; ed Faculty of Medicine, Paris, France; Cabinet Dir, Ministry of Nat. Educ. 1958, of Public Health 1959; Dir Avicenne Hosp., Head of Respiratory Surgery and Pneumology 1960–, Prof. of Medicine 1967–; fmr mem. Exec. Cttee Istiqlal –1984; Minister of Nat. Educ. 1977–86; Prime Minister of Morocco 1986–92; Sec.-Gen. Org. of the Islamic Conf. 1996–2000; mem. Royal Acad. of Morocco. *Address:* c/o Organization of the Islamic Conference, Kilo 6, Mecca Road, P.O. Box 178, Jeddah 21411, Saudi Arabia.

LARAKI, Moulay Ahmed; Moroccan politician, physician and diplomatist; b. 15 Oct. 1931, Casablanca; ed Univ. de Paris, France; with Ministry of Foreign Affairs 1956–57; Perm. Rep. to UN 1957–59; Head of Hosp. Services, Casablanca 1956–61; Amb. to Spain 1962–65, to Switzerland 1965–66, to USA and concurrently Accred to Mexico, Canada and Venezuela 1966–67; Minister of Foreign Affairs 1967–69; Prime Minister 1969–71; Minister of Medical Affairs 1971–74; Minister of State for Foreign Affairs 1974–77. *Address:* c/o Office of the Prime Minister, Rabat, Morocco.

LARCO COX, Guillermo; Peruvian politician and engineer; b. 19 Feb. 1932; mem. Alianza Popular Revolucionaria Americana (APRA); Mayor of Trujillo 1964–66, 1967–68; civil engineer; Parl. Deputy for Dept of La Libertad 1980–85; Senator 1985; Prime Minister of Peru 1987–88, 1990; Minister for Presidency 1987–88; Prime Minister and Minister of Foreign Affairs 1989–90. *Address:* c/o Alianza Popular Revolucionaria Americana, Avda Alfonso Ugarte 1012, Lima 5, Peru. *Telephone:* 273860.

LARCOMBE, Brian, BCom; British business executive; b. 27 Aug. 1953; s. of John George Larcombe and Joyce Lucile Larcombe; m. Catherine Bullen 1983; ed Bromley Grammar School, Univ. of Birmingham; joined 3i Group PLC 1974, Local Dir 1982–88, Regional Dir 1988–92, Finance Dir and mem. Exec. Cttee 1992–, CEO 1997–; NXD Smith & Nephew PLC. *Address:* 3i Group, 91 Waterloo Road, London, SE1 8XP, England (Office). *Website:* www .3i.com (Office).

LARDY, Henry Arnold (Hal Derbauer), PhD, DSC; American professor of biochemistry; b. 19 Aug. 1917, S. Dakota; s. of Nick Lardy and Elizabeth Lardy; m. Annrita Dresselhuys 1943; three s. one d.; ed S Dakota State Univ. and Univs of Wis. and Toronto, Canada; Asst Prof., Univ. of Wis. 1945–47, Assoc. Prof. 1947–50, Prof. 1950–66, Co-Dir Inst. for Enzyme Research 1950–88, Vilas Prof. of Biological Sciences 1966–88, Prof. Emer. 1988–; Pres. Citizens vs. McCarthy 1952; mem. Nat. Acad. of Sciences, American Acad. of Arts and Sciences, American Philosophical Soc., American Soc. Biological Chemists (Pres. 1964), The Endocrine Soc., Harvey Soc.; Hon. mem. Japanese Biochemical Soc.; Hon. DSc (S Dakota State Univ.) 1978; ACS Paul Lewis Award in Enzyme Chem. 1949, Neuberg Medal, American Soc. of European Chemists 1956, Wolf Foundation Prize in Agric. 1981, Nat. Award for Agricultural Excellence 1981, Amory Award, American Acad. of Arts and Sciences 1984, Carl Hartman Award, Soc. for the Study of Reproduction 1984, W. C. Rose Award American Soc. of Biochem. and Molecular Biology 1988, Hilldale Award, Univ. of Wis. 1988. *Publications:* The Enzymes (co-ed.), 8 vols 1958–63 and research papers in biochemistry in scientific journals; two short stories. *Leisure interests:* tennis, riding, retriever field trials. *Address:* Institute for Enzyme Research, University of Wisconsin-Madison, 1710 University Avenue, Madison, WI 53705-4098 (Office); Thorstrand Road, Madison, WI 53705, USA (Home). *Telephone:* (608) 262-3372 (Office); (608) 233-1584 (Home). *Fax:* (608) 265-2904 (Office). *E-mail:* halardy@facstaff.wisc.edu (Office).

LARGE, Sir Andrew Mcleod Brooks, Kt, MA(Econ.), MBA; British banker; b. 7 Aug. 1942, Goudhurst, Kent; s. of the late Maj.-Gen. Stanley Large and of Janet Brooks; m. Susan Melville 1967; two s. one d.; ed Winchester Coll., Univ. of Cambridge and European Inst. of Business Admin. (INSEAD), Fontainebleau; British Petroleum 1964–71; Orion Bank Ltd 1971–79; Swiss Bank Corpn 1980–89, Man. Dir SBCI London 1980–83, Chief Exec. and Deputy Chair. SBCI London 1983–87, Group Chief Exec. SBCI London 1987–88, mem. Bd SBC 1988–90; Chair. Large, Smith & Walter 1990–92; Chair. Securities & Investments Bd (SIB) 1992–97; Deputy Chair. Barclays Bank 1998–2002, Dir 1998–2002; Chair. Euroclear 1998–2000; mem. Bd on Banking Supervision, Bank of England 1996–97, Deputy Gov. 2002–. *Leisure interests:* skiing, walking, gardening, apples, photography, music. *Address:* Bank of England, Threadneedle Street, London, EC2R 8AH, England (Office). *Telephone:* (20) 7601-4444. *Website:* www.bankofengland.co.uk.

LARGE, David Clay, PhD; American university professor and writer; b. 13 Aug. 1945, Scott Field, Ill.; s. of H. R. Large, Jr; m. 1st Jacque Hambly 1968 (divorced 1977); one s.; m. 2nd Margaret Wheeler 1980; ed Univ. of Washington, Univ. of California at Berkeley; taught Modern European History, Smith Coll. 1973–78, Yale Univ. 1978–83, Dean, Pierson Coll. 1981–83; Prof. of European History, Mont. State Univ. 1983–; Contrib. Ed. Mil. History Quarterly 1989; Woodrow Wilson Fellowship, Morse Fellowship (Yale), Nat. Endowment for the Humanities Fellowship, German Marshall Fund Fellowship. *Publications:* The Politics of Law and Order: A History of the Bavarian Einwohnerwehr 1980, Wagnerism in European Culture and Politics 1984, Between Two Fires: Europe's Path in the 1930s 1990, Contending with Hitler:

Varieties of German Resistance in the Third Reich 1991, Germans to the Front: West German Rearmament in the Adenauer Era 1996, Where Ghosts Walked: Munich's Road to the Third Reich 1997. *Leisure interests:* running, skiing, music, hiking. *Address:* 721 W Koch, Bozeman, MT 59715, USA (Home). *Telephone:* (406) 587-5079 (Home).

LARKIN, Anatoly Ivanovich; Russian physicist; b. 14 Oct. 1932; m.; two c.; ed Moscow Inst. of Physics and Eng; worked as engineer 1955–57; Jr researcher, Sr researcher, Inst. of Nuclear Energy 1957–65; Head of Sector, Landau Inst. of Theoretical Physics, Russian Acad. of Sciences 1965-; corresp. mem. USSR (now Russian) Acad. of Sciences 1979, mem. 1991–; mem. Ed. Bd Uspekhi Fizicheskikh Nauk, mem. Bd Scientific Council on Superlow-Temperature Physics; main research in superconductivity theory, phase transition theory. *Address:* L. D. Landau Institute for Theoretical Physics, Institutsky Prospect 12, Chernogolovka, Moscow Region, Noginsk District, 142432, Russia. *Telephone:* (095) 137-32-44; 702-93-17 (Office).

LARMORE, Jennifer May, BMus; American opera singer; b. 21 June 1958, Atlanta, Ga; d. of William C. Larmore and Eloise O. Larmore; m. William Powers 1980; ed Sprayberry High School, Marietta, Ga, Westminster Choir Coll., Princeton, NJ; operatic debut with L'Opéra de Nice, France 1985, debut with Metropolitan Opera, N.Y. 1995, Salzburg Festival debut 1994, Tanglewood Festival debut 1998; specialises in music of the Bel Canto and Baroque Periods; Spokesperson and Fundraiser, US Fund for UNICEF 1998–; William M. Sullivan Fellowship 1983; Maria Callas Vocal Competition, Barcelona 1984, McAllister Vocal Competition, Indianapolis 1986, Alumni Merit Award, Westminster Choir Coll. 1991, Gramophone Award for Best Baroque Album 1992, Richard Tucker Foundation Award, NY 1994. *Music:* over 40 recordings of operatic and solo repertoire; operatic appearances with most of the world's leading cos; recital appearances include Carnegie Hall, NY, Wigmore Hall, London, Musik Verein, Vienna, Concertgebauw, Amsterdam, Palais Garnier, Paris, L. G. Arts Center, Seoul, Teatro Colón, Buenos Aires, Teatro Liceo, Barcelona, Teatro Monnaie, Brussels, Arts Centre, Melbourne, etc. *Television:* appearances include Star Trek 30th Anniversary broadcast, live Christmas Eve service from St Patrick's Cathedral, numerous live broadcasts from the Metropolitan Opera, etc. *Achievements:* selected by the US Olympic Cttee to sing the Olympic Hymn for the closing of the Atlanta Olympic Summer Games 1996. *Leisure interests:* playing with pet dog, relaxing poolside, shopping. *Address:* c/o ICM Foster Division, 40 W. 57th Street, Floor 16 New York, NY 10019, U.S.A. (Office). *Telephone:* (212) 556-5633 (Office). *Fax:* (212) 556-6851 (Office). *E-mail:* jenniferlarmore@aol.com (Home).

LAROCCO, James A., MA; American diplomatist; b. Chicago, Ill.; ed Univ. of Portland, Johns Hopkins School of Advanced Int. Studies; entered Foreign Service 1973; staff Asst Office of Congressional Relations, State Dept; Commercial Attaché, Jeddah 1975–77; Econ. Officer, Cairo 1978–81; Econ. Section Chief Kuwait 1981–83; Deputy Dir, Office of Pakistan, Afghanistan and Bangladesh Affairs, Near East Asia Bureau 1984; Minister-Counsellor for Econ. Affairs, Beijing; Kuwait Task Force Co-ordinator, State Operations Center, Operation Desert Storm 1990; Deputy Dir American Inst. in Taiwan 1991; Deputy Chief of Mission, Tel-Aviv 1993; Amb. to Kuwait 1996–2001; currently Prin. Deputy Asst Sec. Bureau of Near Eastern Affairs, Dept of State; Congressional Fellowship 1983. *Address:* c/o Department of State, 2201 C Street, NW, Washington, DC 20520, USA (Office).

LAROQUE, Michèle; French actress; b. 15 June 1960, Nice; d. of Claude Laroque and Doïna Trandabur; m. Dominique Deschamps (divorced); one d.; ed Univ. of Nice; f. own production co. PBOF (Please Buy Our Films); Chevalier des Arts et des Lettres. *Films include:* The Hairdresser's Husband 1990, Pédale Douce 1995, Le Plus Beau Métier du Monde 1996, Ma Vie En Rose 1996, Serial Lover 1997, Doggy Bag 1999, Epouse-moi 2000, Le Placard 2001. *Theatre:* Silence en coulisses, Ornifle 1991, La Face cachée d'Orion, Une Folie 1993, Ils s'aiment 1996, Ils se sont aimés 2001. *Leisure interests:* tennis, skiing, riding, golf. *Address:* c/o Artmédia, Claire Blondel, 20 avenue Rapp, 75007 Paris, France (Office).

LAROSIÈRE DE CHAMPFEU, Jacques Martin Henri Marie de; French international civil servant; b. 12 Nov. 1929, Paris; s. of Robert de Larosière and Hugayte de Larosière (née de Champfeu); m. France du Bos 1960; one s. one d.; ed Lycée Louis-le-Grand, Paris Univ. and Ecole nat. d'Admin; Insp. adjoint 1958, Insp. des Finances 1960; Chargé de Mission in Inspectorate-Gen. of Finance 1961, External Finance Office 1963, Treasury 1965; Asst Dir Treasury 1967; Deputy Dir then Head of Dept, Ministry of Econs and Finance 1971; Prin. Pvt. Sec. to Valéry Giscard d'Estaing (then Minister of Econs and Finance) 1974; Under-Sec. of Treas. 1974–78; Pres. Group of Ten 1976–78; Dir-Gen. IMF 1978–87; Gov. Banque de France 1987–93, Hon. Gov. 1993–; Chair. Cttee of Govs, Group of Ten 1990–93; Pres. EBRD 1993–98; Sr Adviser BNP Paribas 1998–; Insp. Gen. des Finances 1981; Dir Renault 1971–74, Banque nat. de Paris 1973–78, Air France and Soc. nat. de chemins de fer français (SNCF) 1974–78, Soc. nat. industrielle aérospatiale 1976–78, Power Corpn 1998–; Alstom 1998–2001, France Télécom 1998–; Trustee Reuters 1999–; Censeur Banque de France 1974–93; Crédit nat. 1974–78, Comptoir des Entrepreneurs 1973–75, Crédit foncier de France 1975–78; Vice-Pres. Caisse nat. des Télécommunications 1974–78; mem. Acad. of Moral and Political Sciences 1993; Hon. mem. Soc. des Cincinnati de France; Commdr, Légion d'honneur, Chevalier, Ordre nat. du Mérite, Hon. KBE, numerous other awards. *Address:* BNP Paribas, 3 rue d'Antin, 75078 Paris cedex 02

(Office); 5 rue de Beaujolais, 75001 Paris, France (Home). *Telephone:* 1-42-98-24-28 (Office). *Fax:* 1-42-98-22-37 (Office). *E-mail:* jacques.delarosiere@bnpparibas (Office).

LARQUIÉ, André Olivier, LenD; French civil servant; b. 26 June 1938, Nay; s. of Henri Larquié and Simone Tauziède; ed Lycée Louis-le-Grand, Univ. of Paris and Ecole nat. d'Admin.; Deputy Dir Musique Art lyrique et Danse, Ministry of Culture and Communications 1978–79, Official Rep. 1981–83, 1987; Govt Commr Centre nat. d'art et de Culture Georges Pompidou 1981–84; Pres. Paris Opera 1983–87; Tech. Adviser to the Prime Minister May 1988–89; Pres. Théâtre Contemporain de la Danse, Asscn pour le Dialogue entre les Cultures 1985; Pres. Radio France Int. 1989–95; Pres. Cité de la Musique, Paris –2002, Ballet de Nancy et Lorraine, Théâtre du Chatelet, Paris; Departmental Head, Gen. Inspectorate, Ministry of Culture and Communication 2001; Commdr des Arts et Lettres 1983; Officier, Légion d'honneur 1996; Chevalier dans l'Ordre de la Pléïade 1997; Officier Ordre du Mérite agricole 1998; Commdr Ordre nat. du Mérite 2000; Commdr des Palmes académiques 2002–. *Publications:* official reports. *Leisure interests:* song and dance. *Address:* 3 place de Valois, 75001 Paris (Office); 15 rue de Saint-Simon, 75007 Paris, France (Home). *Telephone:* 1-40-15-77-52 (Office). *Fax:* 1-40-15-77-62 (Office); 1-45-48-48-30 (Home).

LARRABEE, Martin Glover, PhD; American professor of biophysics; b. 25 Jan. 1910, Boston, Mass.; s. of Ralph Clinton Larrabee and Ada Perkins Miller; m. 1st Sylvia Kimball 1932 (divorced 1944), one s. (died 1986); m. 2nd Barbara Belcher 1944 (deceased); one s.; m. 3rd Sarah Barnard Galloway 1998; ed Harvard Coll. and Univ. of Pennsylvania; Research Asst and Fellow, Univ. of Pa 1934–40, Assoc., Asst Prof., Assoc. Prof. 1941–49; Asst Prof. of Physiology, Cornell Medical Coll., New York City 1940–41; Assoc. Prof. of Biophysics, Johns Hopkins Univ. 1949–63, Prof. of Biophysics 1963–99, Prof. Emer. 1999–; mem. Nat. Acad. of Sciences, American Physiological Soc., Biophysical Soc., Int. Soc. for Neurochem., American Soc. for Neurochem., Soc. for Neuroscience; Foreign Assoc. Physiological Soc., England; Hon. MD (Lausanne) 1974. *Publications:* About 60 technical papers and 60 abstracts covering original research in the circulatory, respiratory and nervous systems of mammals, especially on synaptic and metabolic mechanisms in sympathetic ganglia. *Leisure interests:* hiking, trail construction and maintenance, skiing. *Address:* 11630 Glen Arm Road, Apt. U54, Glen Arm, MD 21057, USA (Home). *Telephone:* (410) 319-5187 (Home). *Fax:* (410) 592-6175 (Home).

LARRAIN, Juan, BA; Chilean diplomatist; b. 29 Aug. 1941, Santiago; m. Marial Cruchaga Belaunde; four c.; ed German School and Mil. Acad., Chile, Univ. of Chile, Diplomatic Acad., Ministry of Foreign Affairs; Asst Prof. School of Journalism, Catholic Univ. of Chile 1964–65; Prof. of Contemporary History Diplomatic Acad., Ministry of Foreign Affairs and Ed. Diplomacia (publ. of Acad.) 1978–79; Deputy Chief of Mission, OAS 1983–87, London 1988–90, Head First Commercial Mission to Ireland 1991, Deputy Dir Multilateral Econ. Affairs 1991–92, Consul-Gen. New York 1992–94, Deputy Perm. Rep. to UN 1994–99, Perm. Rep. 1999–2001, also Deputy Perm. Rep. to UN Security Council 1996–97; currently Head Monitoring Mechanism for Angola. *Address:* c/o Monitoring Mechanism for Angola, United Nations, New York, NY 10017, USA.

LARROCHA, Alicia de; Spanish concert pianist; b. 23 May 1923, Barcelona; d. of Eduardo de Larrocha and Teresa de Larrocha (née de la Calle); m. Juan Torra 1950; one s. one d.; first public recital, Barcelona 1928; first orchestral concert with Madrid Symphony Orchestra under Fernández Arbós, Madrid 1935; British debut Wigmore Hall 1953; concert tours in Europe, South America, USA, Canada, Japan, South Africa, NZ, Australia; Dir Academia Marshall, Barcelona 1959; recent appearances with City of Birmingham Symphony, London Symphony, London Symphony Orchestra; recitals at Barbican Hall 1989, Edin. Festival 1995, Barbican 1997; mem. Bd Dirs Musica en Compostela 1968; Hon. Pres. Int. Piano Archives, New York 1969; corresp. mem. Hispanic Soc. of America, New York 1972; Gold Medal, Academia Marshall 1943, Harriet Cohen Int. Music Award 1956, Grand Prix du Disque Acad. Charles Cros, Paris 1960, 1974, Paderewski Memorial Medal 1961, Orders of Civil Merit 1962, Isabel la Católica 1972, Edison Award, Amsterdam 1968, First Gold Medal, Mérito a la Vocación 1973, Grammy Award, USA 1974, 1975, Musician of the Year (Musical America Magazine) 1978, Edison Award, Amsterdam 1978, Gold Medal, Spanish Int. (USA) 1980, Medalla d'Oro of City of Barcelona 1982, Grand Prix du Disque 1991, Príncipe de Asturias Prize 1994. *Recordings:* Iberia 1974, 1989, Ravel Concertos 1975, Granados Goyescas 1991. *Address:* c/o Herbert H. Breslin Inc., 119 West 57th Street 1505, New York, NY 10019, USA (Office).

LARSEN, Kai, BA, MSc; Danish professor of botany; b. 15 Nov. 1926, Hillerød; s. of Axel G. Larsen and Elisabeth Hansen; m. Supee Saksuwan 1971; one s. three d.; ed Univ. of Copenhagen; Asst Scientist, Botany Dept Univ. of Copenhagen 1952–55; Asst Prof. Royal Danish School of Pharmacy 1955–62, Assoc. Prof. 1962–63; Prof. of Botany, Århus Univ. 1963–96, Prof. Emer. 1996–; Founder Botanical Inst. and Herbarium Jutlandicum, Århus; Ed.-in-Chief Nordic Journal of Botany and Opera Botanica; Ed. Flora of Thailand; Danish Ed. Flora Nordica; mem. Exec. Cttee Flora Malesiana Foundation (Leiden, Netherlands); adviser to Flora of China; led 13 botanical expeditions to Thailand 1958–95; Consultant, Queen Sirikit Botanical Gardens, Thailand 1996–; botanical consultant, Danish Nat. Encyclopedia; Visiting lecturer, Russian Acad. of Sciences, Acad. Sinica; Pres. Int. Asscn of Botanic Gardens 1981–87; mem. Royal Danish Acad. and Royal Norwegian Acad. of Science and Corresp. mem. of other int. socs; Kt Order of Dannebrog, First Class; Officer, Crown of Thailand; Hon. DSc (Prince of Songkla Univ., Thailand) 1994. *Publications:* about 250 scientific books and articles on tropical botany, nature conservation. *Leisure interests:* classical music (playing piano). *Address:* Botanical Institute, Nordlandsvej 68, 8240 Risskov (Office); Graastenvej 6, Søften, 8382 Hinnerup, Denmark (Home). *Telephone:* 89-42-47-08 (Office); 86-98-59-82 (Home). *Fax:* 89-42-47-47. *E-mail:* kai.larsen@biology.au.dk (Office).

LARSEN, Ralph Stanley, BA; American business executive; b. 19 Nov. 1938, Brooklyn, NY; s. of Andrew Larsen and Gurine (née Henningsen) Larsen; m. Dorothy M. Zeitfuss 1961; one s. two d.; ed Hofstra Univ.; served in USN 1956–58; manufacturing trainee, then supervisor of Production and Dir Marketing, Johnson & Johnson, New Brunswick, NJ 1962–77, Vice-Pres. Operations and Marketing, McNeil Consumer Products Co. Div. 1977–81, Pres. Chicopee Div. 1982–83, Co. Group Chair. 1985–86, Vice-Chair. Exec. Cttee, Bd of Dirs 1986–89, Chair. and CEO 1989–2002, also Pres.; Pres. Becton Dickenson Consumer Products, Paramus, NJ 1981–83; mem. Bd of Dirs AT&T, Xerox, NY Stock Exchange. *Leisure interests:* skiing, boating, art. *Address:* c/o Johnson & Johnson, 1 Johnson & Johnson Plaza, New Brunswick, NJ 08933, USA.

LARSEN, Terje Roed, PhD; Norwegian diplomatist and politician; b. 1947; f. and Exec. Dir Inst. Applied Social Sciences (FAFO) 1991; fmr Deputy Foreign Minister; facilitated negotiations between reps of Israel's Labour govt and Palestinian Liberation Org. (PLO) leading to signing of Declaration of Principles Sept. 1993; apptd UN Deputy Sec.-Gen. and Special Co-ordinator in the Occupied Territories May 1994–; currently Special Co-ordinator for the Middle East Peace Process and Personal Rep. of the UN Sec.-Gen. to the PLO and Palestinian Authority; also serves as Special Adviser to Ministry of Foreign Affairs. *Address:* UN Middle East Peace Process Mission, Department of Peace-keeping Operations, Room S-3727-B, United Nations, New York, NY 10017, USA (Office). *Telephone:* (212) 963-8079 (Office). *Fax:* (212) 963-9222 (Office). *Website:* www.un.org/depts/dpko (Office).

LARSON, Gary, BA; American cartoonist; b. 14 Aug. 1950, Tacoma, Wash.; s. of Vern Larson and Doris Larson; m. Toni Carmichael 1988; ed Washington State Univ.; performed in jazz duo 1972–75; worked in a music store; sold first cartoons to Pacific Search magazine; subsequently sold cartoons to Seattle Times, San Francisco Chronicle, Chronicle Features Syndicate; Exhibitions include: The Far Side of Science, Calif. Acad. of Sciences 1985, Smithsonian Nat. Museum of Nat. History, American Museum of Nat. History, New York, Los Angeles County Museum of Nat. History; Animated films: Gary Larson's Tales From The Far Side 1994 (Grand Prix, Annecy Film Festival 1995), Gary Larson's Tales From The Far Side II 1997; announced retirement Oct. 1994; Nat. Cartoonists Soc. Award for best syndicated panel of 1985; Outstanding Cartoonist of the Year Award 1991, 1994; Max and Moritz Prize for Best Int. Cartoon 1993; insect named after him: Strigiphilus garylarsoni (biting louse), also butterfly Serratoterga larsoni. *Films:* Gary Larson's Tales From The Far Side, Gary Larson's Tales From the Far Side II. *Publications:* The Far Side, Beyond The Far Side, In Search of The Far Side, Bride of The Far Side, Valley of The Far Side, It Came From The Far Side, Hound of The Far Side, The Far Side Observer, Night of the Crash-test Dummies, Wildlife Preserve, Wiener Dog Art, Unnatural Selections, Cows of Our Planet, The Chickens Are Restless, The Curse of Madame "C", Last Chapter and Worse 1996; Anthologies: The Far Side Gallery 1, 2, 3, 4 and 5, The PreHistory of The Far Side, There's A Hair in my Dirt! A Worm's Story 1998. *Leisure interests:* jazz guitar, pickup basketball. *Address:* c/o Andrews McMell Publishing, 4520 Main Street, Suite 700, Kansas City, MO 64111; Creators Syndicated International, 5777 West Century Boulevard, Suite 700, Los Angeles, CA 90045, USA (Office).

LARSSON, John, BD; Swedish Salvation Army Official; b. 2 April 1938; s. of Sture Larsson and Flora Larsson; m. Freda Turner 1969; two s.; ed Univ. of London, U.K.; commissioned as Officer, Upper Norwood Corps, The Salvation Army 1957; various appts in UK including Corps Officer, trainer, Territorial Youth Sec. for Scotland, British Territory Nat. Youth Sec.; apptd Chief. Sec., S. America W. 1980–84; Prin./William Booth Memorial Training Coll., London 1984–88; Asst Admin. Planning to Chief of Staff for UK 1988–90; Territorial Commdr of UK and Repub. of Ireland Territory 1990–93, of NZ and Fiji Territory 1993–96, of Sweden and Latvia Territory 1996–99; Chief of Staff 1999–2002; 17th Gen. of the Salvation Army Nov. 2002–. *Publications include:* Doctrine Without Tears 1974, Spiritual Breakthrough 1983, The Man Perfectly Filled with the Spirit 1986, How Your Corps Can Grow 1988. *Leisure interests:* music, walking. *Address:* The Salvation Army, International Headquarters, 101 Queen Victoria Street, London, EC4P 4EP, England (Office). *Telephone:* (20) 7332-0101 (Office). *Fax:* (20) 7332-8010 (Office). *E-mail:* the_general@salvationarmy.org (Office). *Website:* www.salvationarmy.org (Office).

LARSSON, Per; Swedish business executive; b. Feb. 1961, Harnosand; m.; three c.; ed Uppsala Univ.; fmrly broker, Föreningssparbanken; Chief Exec. OM 1985–; Global Leader for Tomorrow, World Econ. Forum 2001. *Leisure interests:* sport, spending time at second home in France, tennis. *Address:* OM, Norrlandsgatan 31, 105 78 Stockholm, Sweden (Office). *Telephone:* 84-05-60-00 (Office). *Website:* www.omgroup.com (Office).

LASICA, Milan, AM; Slovak actor, dramatist and scriptwriter; b. 3 Feb. 1940, Zvolen; s. of Vojtech Lasica and Edita Šmáliková; m. Magdalena Vašáryová; two d.; ed Univ. of Musical Arts, Bratislava; dramatist Slovak TV 1964–67; actor with theatres Divadlo na Korze 1967–71, Divaldo Večerní Brno 1971–72, Nová scéna 1972–89; f. Štúdio S-Bratislava 1989, Dir 1989–; co-operation as actor, dramatist and scriptwriter with Slovak and Czech TV, radio and theatres Semafor, Divadlo bez zábradlí and Labyrint. *Films include:* Vážení přatelé, Mimozemštané, Saturnin, Sladké hry minulého léta, Tři veteráni, Citová výchova dívek v Čechách, Srdečný pozdrav ze zeměkoule. *Plays include:* Cyrano, Don Juan, Mrtvé duše. *Achievements:* TV Prize Monte Carlo Festival. *Leisure interest:* golf. *Address:* Stúdio Lasica-Satinský, Nám 1 Mája 5, Bratislava, Slovakia (Office). *Telephone:* (2) 5292-1584 (Office). *Fax:* (2) 5292-5082 (Office).

LASKAWY, Philip A.; American management consultant (retd); b. 1941; m.; two s.; partner Ernst & Whinney 1978–81, Man. Partner 1981–85; Vice-Chair., Regional Man. Partner Ernst & Young (formed from merged cos. Ernst & Whinney and Arthur Young) 1985–93, Deputy Chair. 1993, Chair., CEO 1994–2001; Chair. Ernst & Young Int. 1997–2001; mem. Bd Dirs Cap Gemini, Ernst & Young, General Motors Corpn, Heidrick & Struggles Int'l., Inc., Henry Schein, Inc., Loews Corpn, The Progressive Corpn; mem. Bd Dance Theater Foundation (Alvin Ailey American Dance Theater), Educational Broadcasting Corpn (Thirteen WNET/New York), The Philharmonic Symphony Soc. of New York, Inc. *Address:* c/o Ernst & Young, 5 Times Square, New York, NY 10036, USA (Office).

LASKEY, Ronald Alfred, MA, DPhil., FRS, FMedSci; British professor of molecular biology and embryology; b. 26 Jan. 1945; s. of Thomas Leslie Laskey and Bessie Laskey; m. Margaret Anne Page 1971; one s. one d.; ed High Wycombe Royal Grammar School, Queen's Coll. Oxford; scientific staff mem. Imperial Cancer Research Fund 1970–73, Lab. of Molecular Biology, MRC 1973–83; Co-Dir Molecular Embryology Group, Cancer Research Campaign (CRC) 1983–91; Dir of CRC, Wellcome CRC Inst. 1991–; Charles Darwin Prof. of Animal Embryology, Darwin Coll. Cambridge 1983–, Fellow 1982–; Pres. British Soc. of Cell Biology 1996–99; mem. Academia Europaea 1989; Trustee Strangeways Research Lab. 1993–; Hon. Dir MRC Cancer Cell Unit 1999–; Coleworth Medal, Biochem. Soc. 1979, CIBA Medal, Biochem. Soc. 1997, Feldberg Foundation Prize 1998, Louis Jeantet Prize for Medicine, Jeantet Foundation, Geneva 1998. *Publications include:* Song for Cynical Scientists, More Songs for Cynical Scientists; articles on cell biology in professional journals. *Leisure interests:* music, mountains. *Address:* Wellcome Trust/ Cancer Research Campaign Institute for Cancer and Developmental Biology, Tennis Court Road, Cambridge, CB2 1QR, England (Office). *Telephone:* (1223) 334106 (Office).

LASKO, Peter Erik, CBE, BA, FBA, FRHistS; British professor emeritus, writer and lecturer (retd); b. 5 March 1924, Berlin, Germany; s. of Leo Lasko and Wally Lasko; m. Gwendoline Joan Norman 1948; three d.; ed St Martin's School of Art and Courtauld Inst. of Art, Univ. of London; Asst Keeper, Dept of British and Medieval Antiquities, British Museum 1950–65; Prof., School of Fine Arts, Univ. of E Anglia, Norwich 1965–74; Dir and Prof. Courtauld Inst. 1975–85; Trustee, British Museum 1980–95, Royal Armouries 1983–91; Commr, Cathedrals Advisory Comm. 1980–91, Royal Comm. on Historical Monuments of England 1984–90; Commr, Vice-Chair. Cathedrals Fabric Comm. for England 1991–96; Hon. DLitt (E Anglia). *Publications:* Ars Sacra 800–1200 1972, 1994, The Kingdom of the Franks 1971, Studies on Metalwork, Ivories and Stone 1994, Expressionist Roots of Modernism 2003. *Leisure interest:* walking. *Address:* 1 Hawke Lane, Bloxham, Oxon., OX15 4PY, England.

LASSALLE, Jacques Louis Bernard; French theatre director, actor and writer; b. 6 July 1936, Clermont-Ferrand; s. of Antoine Lassalle and Louise Lassalle (née Courbouleix); m. Françoise Marty 1958; three s.; ed Sorbonne, Paris, Conservatoire National Supérieur d'Art Dramatique de Paris; Asst Teacher, Institut d'Etudes Théâtrales 1969–77; f. Studio Théâtre de Vitry 1970; Teacher Conservatoire Nat. Supérieur de Paris 1981–83, 1994–2001; Dir-Gen. Théâtre Nat. de Strasbourg 1983–90; Administrateur Général, Comédie Française 1990–93; Dir Compagnie pour Mémoire; Officier, Légion d'honneur 1992; Commdr des Arts et des Lettres; Chevalier, Ordre nat. du Mérite; Grand prix nat. du théâtre. *Film:* Après 2002. *Plays:* Dir about 100 plays, particularly by Molière, Corneille, Racine, Euripides, Marivaux, Goldoni, Shakespeare, Labiche, Pirandello, Chekhov, Ibsen, Svevo, Lessing, Büchner, Hofmannsthal, Kundera, Sarraute, Brecht, Hare and Vinaver, also operas; recent productions include: La vie de Galilée 2000, Médée 2000, Le malin plaisir 2000, L'Ecole de danse 2000, Un jour d'été 2000, L'Ecole de femmes 2001, The Aspern Papers 2002, Don Juan 2002, Iphigénie en Tauride, La douleur, Platonov. *Television:* Ferveur Jacques Lassalle, Medée (Festival d'Avignon) 2000, Don Juan 2002. *Publications:* Jonathan des années 30, Un couple pour l'hiver, Pauses 1991, Conversations sur Don Juan 1994, L'amour d'Alceste 2000, Après 2002, Nathalie Sarraute ou l'obscur commencement de la parole 2002, numerous articles. *Leisure interests:* walking, swimming, reading, music, pre-1970 American films. *Address:* 47 boulevard Voltaire, 75011 Paris, France (Home). *Telephone:* 1-47-00-32-78 (Home). *Fax:* 1-47-00-32-78 (Home).

LASSERRE, Bruno Marie André, MPL; French public servant; b. 4 Jan. 1954, Talence, Gironde; s. of Jacques Lasserre and Marie Garrigou-Lagrange de David de Lastours; m. Marie-Laure Sergent 1988; two d.; ed Bordeaux Faculty of Law, Inst. of Political Studies, Bordeaux, Ecole Nat. d'Admin., Paris; mem. Conseil d'Etat 1978–, Maître des Requêtes 1983–; Chair.-Del. Comm. on right of reply on radio and TV 1980–82, Nat. Comm. on Freedom of Information 1982–86; Commissaire du gouvernement, Litigation Section of Conseil d'Etat 1984–86; Legal Counsel, France Telecom 1986–89; Head Regulatory Directorate for Posts and Telecommunications 1989–93; Dir-Gen. of Posts and Telecommunications 1993–97; consultant to Ministers for Industry and Foreign Affairs on Int. Telecommunications (1997–98); Pres. comité de sélection des inspecteurs des finances au tour extérieur 1998–2000; mem. Conseil de la concurrence 1998–; Supervisor of Privatisation of Société française de production (SFP) 2001; Chevalier, Légion d'Honneur; Officier Ordre nat. du Mérite. *Publication:* Open Government 1987. *Address:* Conseil d'Etat, place du Palais royal, 75100 Paris (Office); 14 avenue de Breteuil, 75007 Paris, France (Home).

LATASI, Kamuta; Tuvaluan politician; fmr Minister of Health, Educ. and Community Services; Prime Minister of Tuvalu 1993–97, Minister of Foreign Affairs and Econ. Planning 1993–97. *Address:* c/o Office of the Prime Minister, Vaiaku, Funafuti, Tuvalu.

LATERZA, Vito; Italian publisher; b. 11 Dec. 1926, Bari; s. of Giuseppe Laterza and Maria Lembo; m. Antonella Chiarini 1955; two c.; ed Univ. of Florence; joined family-owned publishing house Giuseppe Laterza & Figli S.p.A. 1949, Gen. Man. 1975–, now Hon. Pres.; Officier, Ordre des Arts et des Lettres 1988, Cavaliere del Lavoro 1990. *Leisure interest:* tennis. *Address:* Giuseppe Laterza & Figli SpA, Via di Villa Sacchetti 17, 00197 Rome (Office); Largo Elvezia 5, 00197 Rome, Italy (Home). *Telephone:* (06) 3218393 (Office); (06) 8080921 (Home). *Fax:* (06) 3223853 (Office). *E-mail:* laterza@laterza.it (Office).

LATOUR-ADRIEN, Hon. Sir (Jean François) Maurice, Kt, LLB; Mauritian judge; b. 4 March 1915, Vacoas; s. of the late Louis C. E. Adrien and Maria E. Latour; ed Royal Coll., Mauritius, Univ. Coll., London and Middle Temple, London; called to the Bar, Middle Temple 1940 and in Mauritius 1946; District Magistrate 1947–48; Crown Counsel 1948–60; Asst Attorney-Gen. 1960–61; Solicitor-Gen. 1961–64; Dir of Public Prosecutions 1964–66; Puisne Judge 1966–70; Chief Justice of the Supreme Court of Mauritius 1970–77; Acting Gov.-Gen. Feb. 1973, July–Aug. 1974, Jan.–Feb. 1975, June–Aug. 1975, July–Sept. 1976; Pres. Mauritius Red Cross 1978–; Vice-Pres. Mauritius Mental Health Asscn 1978–85, Pres. 1986–; Dir Mauritius Union Assurance Co. Ltd 1978–, Chair. 1982–; Dir Mauritius Commercial Bank Ltd 1980–83, 1984–87, 1988–91, 1992–95, 1996–99, 2000–02; Legal Consultant 1983–, Dir 1992–95, 1996–99, 2000–02, Vice-Pres. 1993, Pres. 1994, Vice-Pres. 1996–97; Legal Consultant, Fincorp Investment Ltd (fmrly Mauritius Commercial Bank Finance Corpn) 1991–, Caudan Devt Co. Ltd 1991–, Mauritius Commercial Bank Registry and Securities Ltd 1991–, Promotion and Devt Co. Ltd 1985–; Dir Union and Policy Investment Ltd 1998–, Union and Policy Offshore Ltd 1998–, MUA Leasing Ltd 1998–; Co-Ed. Mauritius Law Reports 1970–77; mem. War Memorial Bd of Trustees 1978–84, Vice-Pres. 1985–; mem. Institut de Droit d'Expression Française; Kt Order of St Lazarus of Jerusalem 1969. *Leisure interests:* music, reading. *Address:* c/o Mauritius Union Assurance Co. Ltd, 4 Léoville l'Homme Street, Port Louis (Office); Vacoas, Mauritius (Home). *Telephone:* 207-4185 (Office); 686-0389 (Home).

LATSIS, Otto Rudolfovich, DEconSc; Russian economist and journalist; b. 22 June 1934, Moscow; m.; one s. one d.; ed Moscow Univ.; mem. CPSU 1959; worked for newspapers, including Izvestiya 1956–71; joined staff of Problems of Peace and Socialism (journal), Prague 1971–75; worked on staff of Inst. of Econ. and World Socialist System, Moscow 1975–86; staff of journal Kommunist (renamed Free Thought 1991), Deputy Ed. 1986–91; mem. Cen. Cttee CPSU 1990–91; Political Observer, Izvestiya 1990–97, mem. Editorial Bd 1991–97; political observer, Noviye Izvestiya 1997–, Deputy Ed.-in-Chief 1998–; mem. Bd Social and Political Research Fund; Journalist of the Year Prize 1997, President's Prize 1997. *Publications:* ten books including Tireless Builder, What Happened to Us and What Will Happen 1995; numerous articles. *Address:* Dolgorukovskaya str. 19/8, 103006 Moscow, Russia. *Telephone:* (095) 795-31-57. *Fax:* 795-31-38/39.

LATTÈS, Robert; French business executive; b. 13 Dec. 1927, Paris; s. of Sadi Lattès and Renée Levi; m. Monique Lang 1949; two d.; ed Ecole Normale Supérieure; researcher in Pure Math., CNRS 1953–56; worked in math. physics and computers, French Atomic Energy Agency, Saclay 1956–59; joined Metra Group 1959, f. SIA (Société d'Informatique Appliquée) within Metra 1962, with SIA until 1974; Adviser to Chair. and Pres., then Exec. Vice-Pres. Paribas 1975–87; Pres. Pallas Venture 1988–95, Parindev 1988–95; Founding Chair., then Hon. Chair. Transgène 1980–87; Vice-Pres. Conseil supérieur du mercenat culturel; Dir Expand SA, European Venture Capital Asscn, Orchestre de Paris, Inst. des Vaisseaux et du Sang 1995–2000, Institut Pasteur, Lille 1995–2000; mem. Bd of Dirs L'Institut Lumière, mem. Conseil des applications de l'Acad. des Sciences 2000, Conseil nat. des incubateurs et capital d'amorçage 1999–; winner, World Bridge Championship 1956; Officier, Légion d'honneur, Comm., Ordre Nat. du Mérite. *Publications:* Méthode de Quasi-Réversibilité et Applications (with J.-L. Lions; trans. in English and other languages) 1967, Quelques problèmes aux limites de la Physique Mathématique 1967, Mille Milliards de dollars 1969, Matière grise année zero 1970, Pour une autre croissance 1973, La Fortune des Français 1977, L'Apprenti et le Sorcier (Les défis de l'innovation) 1988, Le Risque et le fortune 1990. *Leisure interests:* books, symphonic music, opera, art, cinema.

Address: Electra Fleming, 31 rue de Lisbonne, 75008 Paris (Office); 74 rue Raynouard, 75016 Paris, France (Home). *Telephone:* 1-53-83-79-10 (Office); 1-42-88-17-05 (Home). *Fax:* 1-53-83-79-20 (Office); 1-42-88-85-55 (Home).

LATTRE, André Marie Joseph de; French banker; b. 26 April 1923, Paris; m. Colette Petit 1947; three s. two d.; ed Univs de Paris à la Sorbonne and Grenoble and Ecole Libre des Sciences Politiques; Insp. of Finance 1946; with Ministry of Finance 1948–; Dept of External Finance 1949–54, Sub-Dir 1955–58; Alt. Exec. Dir IMF 1954; Prof. Inst. d'Etudes Politiques, Paris 1958–83; Financial Adviser to Pres. of the Repub. 1958–60; Perm. Sec. Ministry of Finance 1960–61; Dir of External Finance 1961; Censor, Bank of France 1962, Vice-Gov. 1966–74; Mission to India for Pres. IBRD 1965; Alt. Dir BIS 1973; Pres. Crédit National 1974–82; World Bank Special Rep. to IDA 1983; Man. Dir Inst. of Int. Finance, Washington 1983–86; Chair. Banque Française Standard-Chartered 1987–89; Chair. Banque Française de Service et de Crédit 1990–97; Commdr Légion d'honneur and foreign awards. *Publications:* Les Finances extérieures de la France 1959, Politique économique de la France depuis 1945 1967, Servir aux Finances 1999. *Leisure interests:* skiing, tennis. *Address:* 69 rue Perronet, 92200 Neuilly, France. *Telephone:* 1-46-24-79-00.

LATYPAW, Ural Ramdrakovich, LLD; Belarus (b. Bashkir) politician; b. 28 Feb. 1951, Katayevo, Bashkir ASSR; m.; one s. one d.; ed Kazan State Univ., State and Law Inst., USSR Acad. of Sciences, Higher KGB courses in Minsk; researcher for KGB, involvement in anti-terrorist measures, latterly Deputy Chief, Educational and Research Centre, Minsk 1974–98; retd from mil. (rank of Col) 1993; Jt Founder, Head, Deputy Head for Research and Science, Research Inst. for Devt and Security, Repub. of Belarus 1993–94; Asst to int. affairs to Belarus Pres. 1994–95, Chief Asst to Pres. 1995–98; Minister of Foreign Affairs 1998–99; Deputy Prime Minister and Minister of Foreign Affairs 1999–2000; State Sec. Feb.–Sept. 2001; Head of Presidential Admin Sept. 2001–; mem. Belarus and Russian Asscns of Int. Law. *Publications:* Legislative Problems in Combating Terrorism; articles on legislative, nat. and int. security issues. *Address:* Office of the President, vul. K. Marksa 38, Dom Urada, 220016 Minsk, Belarus. *Telephone:* (17) 222-60-06.

LATYSHEV, Col-Gen. Pyotr Mikhailovich; Russian politician and security officer; b. 30 Aug. 1948, Khmelnitsky, Ukraine; m.; two s.; ed Omsk Higher School of Ministry of Internal Affairs, Acad. of Ministry of Internal Affairs; inspector, then Head Perm Div. for Fight against Econ. Crime 1970–86; Head Dept of Internal Affairs Perm Oblast 1986–91; Head Dept of Internal Affairs, Krasnodar Territory 1991–94; Deputy Minister of Internal Affairs, Russian Fed. 1994–2000; Rep. of Pres. to Urals Fed. Dist 2000–; People's Deputy of Russian Fed. 1990–93; mem. Cttee of Supreme Soviet on Law and Fight against Crime 1993; State orders. *Address:* Office of the Plenipotentiary Representative of the President, Oktyabrskaya pl. 3, 620031 Yekaterinburg, Russia (Office). *Telephone:* (3432) 77-18-96 (Yekaterinburg), (095) 206-09-66 (Moscow) (Office).

LAU SIU-KAI, JP, PhD; Chinese academic and political adviser; b. 7 June 1947, Hong Kong; s. of Keng-por Lau and Wai-sin Fong; m. Sophie Lai-mui Kwok 1972; one s.; ed Univ. of Hong Kong, Univ. of Minnesota, USA; Assoc. Dir Hong Kong Inst. of Asia-Pacific Studies, Chinese Univ. of Hong Kong (CUKH) 1990, Chair. Dept of Sociology 1990–, Prof. of Sociology 1994–; mem., Preparatory Cttee for Hong Kong Special Admin. Region (SAR) 1996–97; political commentator on Hong Kong issues on TV, radio and in newspapers and magazines. *Publications:* Society and Politics in Hong Kong 1982, The Ethos of the Hong Kong Chinese 1988. *Leisure interests:* reading, walking. *Address:* Room 507, Esther Lee Building, Hong Kong Institute of Asia-Pacific Studies, Chinese University of Hong Hong Shatin, N.T., Hong Kong Special Administrative Region (Office); Flat B3, 8/F Cloudview Mansion, 8 Lok Fung Path, Fotan, N.T., Hong Kong Special Administrative Region, People's Republic of China (Home). *Telephone:* 26098778, 26096618 (Office); 26036438 (Home). *Fax:* 26035215, 26035213 (Office); 26036438 (Home). *E-mail:* siukailau@cuhk.edu. hk (Office). *Website:* www.cuhk.edu.hk/hkiaps, www .cuhk.edu.hk/soc/homepage.htm (Office).

LAUDA, Andreas-Nikolaus ("Niki"); Austrian racing driver; b. 22 Feb. 1949, Vienna; s. of Ernst Peter Lauda and Elisabeth Lauda; m. Marlene Knaus 1976; two s.; competed in hill climbs 1968, later in Formula 3, Formula 2 and sports car racing; winner 1972 John Player British Formula 2 Championship; started Formula 1 racing in 1971; World Champion 1975, 1977, 1984, runner-up 1976; retd 1979; returned to racing 1981, won US Formula 1 Grand Prix, British Grand Prix 1982, Dutch Grand Prix 1985; retd again 1985; f. Lauda Air 1979, Chair. –2000; CEO Ford's Premier Performance Div. 2001–02; Head Jaguar Racing Team 2001–02; winner of Victoria Sporting Club's Int. Award for Valour in 1977, following recovery from near-fatal crash in 1976 German Grand Prix at Nürburgring. *Grand Prix wins:* 1974 Spanish (Ferrari), 1974 Dutch (Ferrari), 1975 Monaco (Ferrari), 1975 Belgian (Ferrari), 1975 Swedish (Ferrari), 1975 French (Ferrari), 1975 United States (Ferrari), 1976 Brazilian (Ferrari), 1976 South African (Ferrari), 1976 Belgian (Ferrari), 1976 British (Ferrari), 1977 South African (Ferrari), 1977 German (Ferrari), 1977 Dutch (Ferrari), 1978 Swedish (Brabham-Alfa Romeo); 1978 Italian (Brabham-Alfa Romeo). *Leisure interests:* music, skiing. *Address:* Santa Eulalia, Ibiza, Spain; c/o Jaguar Racing, Bradbourne Drive, Tilbrook, Milton Keynes, MK7 8BJ, England (Office).

LAUDER, Estee; American business executive; b. New York; m. Joseph Lauder (deceased); two s.; Chair. Bd Estee Lauder Inc. (cosmetics co.) 1946–; Chevalier, Legion d'honneur; Hon. LLD (Univ. of Pa) 1986; recipient of numerous awards including Neiman-Marcus Fashion Award 1962, 1992, Albert Einstein Coll. of Medicine Spirit of Achievement Award 1968, Harpers Bazaar Top Ten Outstanding Women in Business 1970, Médaille de Vermeil de la Ville de Paris 1979, Athena Award 1985, Golda Meir 90th Anniversary Tribute Award 1988, Pres.'s Award (Cosmetic Exec. Women) 1989. *Publication:* Estee: A Success Story 1985. *Address:* Estee Lauder Inc., 767 Fifth Avenue, New York, NY 10153, USA.

LAUDER, Leonard Alan; American business executive; b. 19 March 1933, New York; s. of Joseph Lauder and Estee Lauder (née Mentzer); m. Evelyn Hausner 1959; two s.; ed Wharton School, Univ. of Pennsylvania; with Estee Lauder Inc. (cosmetics and fragrance co.) New York 1958–, Exec. Vice-Pres. 1962–72, Pres. 1972–82, Pres. and CEO 1982–, now Chair, CEO; Gov. Joseph H. Lauder Inst. of Man. and Int. Studies 1983–; Trustee Aspen Inst. for Humanistic Studies 1978–, Univ. of Pa 1977–; Pres. Whitney Museum of American Art 1977–. *Address:* Estee Lauder Inc., 767 Fifth Avenue, New York, NY 10153, USA.

LAUDER, Ronald Stephen, BS; American business executive and diplomatist; b. 26 Feb. 1944, New York; s. of Joseph Lauder and Estee Lauder (q.v.); m. Jo Carole Knopf 1967; two d.; ed Univ. of Pennsylvania, Univ. of Paris (Sorbonne), Univ. of Brussels; Estee Lauder N.V. Belgium 1965–67, Estee Lauder SA France 1967, Estee Lauder Sales Promotion Dir 1968–69, Vice-Pres. Sales Promotion, Clinique 1969–72, Exec. Vice-Pres., Gen. Man. Clinique, Inc. 1972–75, Exec. Vice-Pres. Estee Lauder Int. 1975–78, Exec. Vice-Pres. Estee Lauder Inc., Chair. Estee Lauder Int. 1978–83; Deputy Asst Sec. of Defense for European and NATO Policy 1983–86; Amb. to Austria 1986–87, pvt. investment man. New York 1987–, now E and Cen. Europe; Trustee, Museum of Modern Art 1975– (Chair. 1995–), Mt. Sinai Medical Center 1981–; Chair. and Pres. Lauder Investments; Chair. Cen. European Devt Corpn; Ordre du Mérite (France), Great Cross of the Order of Aeronautical Merit with White Ribbon (Spain), Dept of Defense Medal for Distinguished Public Service. *Address:* Lauder Investments Inc., 767 Fifth Avenue, Suite 4200, New York, NY 10153, USA.

LAUER, Reinhard, DPhil; German professor of Slavonic Philology; b. 15 March 1935, Bad Frankenhausen; s. of Erich Lauer and Rose Fischer; m. Stanka Ibler 1962; one d.; ed Univs of Marburg, Belgrade and Frankfurt and Freie Univ. Berlin; reader in German Language, Univ. of Zagreb 1960–62; Research Fellow, Univ. of Frankfurt 1962–69; Prof. of Slavonic Philology and Head of Dept of Slavonic Philology, Univ. of Göttingen 1969–; mem. Göttingen Acad., Serbian Acad., Croatian Acad., Austrian Acad.; Hon. mem. Bulgarian Philology Soc.; Valjavec Prize 1961, Yugoslav Flag with Golden Garland 1989. *Publications:* Heine in Serbien 1961, Gedichtform zwischen Schema und Verfall 1975, Europäischer Realismus (ed.) 1980, M. Krleža und der deutsche Expressionismus 1984, Sprachen und Literaturen Jugoslaviens (ed.) 1985, Poetika i ideologija 1987, Sprache, Literatur und Folklore bei Vuk St Karadžić (ed.) 1989, Kulturelle Traditionen in Bulgarien (co-ed.) 1989, Künstlerische Dialektik und Identitätssuche (ed.) 1990, Die Moderne in den Literaturen Südosteuropas (ed.) 1991, Höfische Kultur in Südosteuropa (co-ed.) 1994, Serbokroatische Autoren in deutscher Übersetzung (ed.) 1995, Slavica Gottingensia (ed.) 1995, Die Kultur Griechenlands in Mittelalter und Neuzeit (co-ed.) 1996, Die russische Seele 1997, Geschichte der russischen Literatur 2000, Deutsche und Slovakische Literatur (ed.) 2000, A. S. Puškins Werk und Wirkung (co-ed.) 2000, Philologie in Göttingen (ed.) 2001, Die literarische Avantgarde in Südosteuropa und ihr politische und gesellschaftliche Bedeutung (ed.) 2001. *Leisure interests:* music, painting, ornithology. *Address:* Seminar für Slavische Philologie der Universität, Humboldt-Allee 19, 3400 Göttingen (Office); Allensteiner Weg 32, 37120 Bovenden, Germany. *Telephone:* (551) 394701 (Office); (551) 81375 (Home).

LAUGERUD GARCÍA, Gen. Kjell Eugenio; Guatemalan politician and army officer; b. 24 Jan. 1930, Guatemala City; s. of Pedro E Laugerud and Catalina García; m. Helen Losi 1951; three s. two d.; Minister of Defence, Chief of Gen. Staff of Army 1970–74; Presidential Cand. of Movimiento de Liberación Nacional/Partido Institucional Democrático (MLN/PID) March 1974; Pres. of Guatemala 1974–78; numerous awards, including Legion of Merit (USA) 1971, Gran Collar Orden del Quetzal (Guatemala) 1974, Gran Cruz Brillantes Orden de El Sol (Peru), Orden del Mérito (Chile) 1978, etc. *Leisure interests:* horseback riding, collecting small arms, military history. *Address:* c/o Oficina del Presidente, Guatemala City, Guatemala.

LAUGHLIN, Robert B., PhD; American professor of applied physics; b. 1 Nov. 1950, Visalia, Calif.; m. Anita Rhona Perry 1979; two s.; ed Mass. Inst. of Tech., Cambridge; Postdoctoral Fellow Bell Telephone Lab. 1979–81, Lawrence Livermore Nat. Lab. 1981–82; Assoc. Prof. of Physics, Stanford Univ., Calif. 1985–89, Prof. of Physics 1989–, of Applied Physics 1993–; mem. AAAS, American Acad. of Arts and Sciences; Fellow American Physics Soc.; Franklin Inst. Medal 1998, Nobel Prize in Physics (for discovery of a new form of quantum fluid with fractionally charged excitations) 1998. *Publications:* numerous papers in scientific journals. *Address:* Department of Physics, Stanford University, Stanford, CA 94305, USA (Office). *Telephone:* (650) 723-4563 (Office). *Fax:* (650) 723-9389 (Office).

LAUGHTON, Sir Anthony Seymour, Kt, PhD, FRS; British oceanographic scientist; b. 29 April 1927; s. of Sydney T. Laughton and Dorothy (Chamberlain) Laughton; m. 1st Juliet A. Chapman 1957 (dissolved 1962), one s.; m. 2nd Barbara C. Bosanquet 1973, two d.; ed Marlborough Coll. and King's Coll. Cambridge; RNVR 1945–48; John Murray Student, Columbia Univ. New York 1954–55; Nat. Inst. of Oceanography, later Inst. of Oceanographic Sciences 1955–88, fmr Dir; mem. Jt IOC/IHO Guiding Cttee GEBCO (ocean charts) 1974–, Chair. 1986–; mem. Council, Univ. Coll. London 1983–93; mem. Co-ordinating Cttee for Marine Science and Tech. 1987–91; Pres. Challenger Soc. for Marine Science 1988–90; Trustee Natural History Museum 1990–95; Pres. Soc. Underwater Tech. 1995–97, Hydrographic Soc. 1997–99; mem. Governing Body Charterhouse School 1981–2000 (Chair. 1995–2000); Royal Soc. of Arts Silver Medal 1958; Prince Albert 1er Monaco Gold Medal 1980, Founders Medal, Royal Geographical Soc. 1987, Murchison Medal, Geological Soc. 1989. *Publications:* papers on marine geophysics. *Leisure interests:* music, gardening, sailing. *Address:* Okelands, Pickhurst Road, Chiddingfold, Surrey, GU8 4TS, England. *Telephone:* (1428) 683941.

LAUNDER, Brian Edward, DSc, DEng, FRS, FREng; British professor of engineering; b. 20 July 1939, London; s. of Harry Edward Launder and Elizabeth Ann Launder (née Ayers); m. Dagny Simonsen 1968; one s. one d.; ed Enfield Grammar School, Imperial Coll., London, MIT, Cambridge, USA; lecturer, then reader Mechanical Eng Dept, Imperial Coll., London 1964–76; Prof. of Mechanical Eng Univ. of Calif. at Davis 1976; Prof. of Mechanical Eng UMIST 1980–98, Head Mech. Eng Dept 1983–85, 1993–95, Research Prof. 1998–; Dir Environmental Strategy Group 1998–; Regional Dir Tyndall Centre for Climate Change Research 2001–; Ed.-in-Chief Int. Journal of Heat and Fluid Flow 1987–; assessor of French Research Labs CNRS, Paris, Grenoble, Toulouse 1992–; associate, Center for Turbulence Research, Stanford Univ., Calif. 1996–; Hon. Prof. (Nanjing Aerospace Inst.) 1993; Dr hc (Inst. Nat. Polytechnique, Toulouse) 1999; Busk Prize, Royal Aeronautical Soc. 1995, Computational Mechanics Award, Japan Soc. of Mechanical Engineers 1995, Daniel and Florence Guggenheim Award, Int. Council of Aeronautical Sciences 2000. *Publications include:* Mathematical Models of Turbulence 1972, Turbulent Shear Flows, Vols 1–9 (ed.) and over 200 papers on measurement and modelling of turbulent flow. *Leisure interests:* French culture and cuisine, bicycling and walking, photography. *Address:* Mechanical Engineering Department, University of Manchester Institute of Science and Technology, P.O. Box 88, Manchester, M60 1QD (Office); 4 Velvet House, 60 Sackville Street, Manchester, M1 3WE, England (Home). *Telephone:* (161) 200-3700 (Office). *Fax:* (161) 200-3723 (Office). *E-mail:* brian.launder@umist.ac.uk (Office).

LAURA, Ernesto Guido; Italian film festival director; b. 4 May 1932, Villafranca, Veronese; s. of the late Manuel Laura and of Pia Romei Laura; m. Anna Maria Vercellotti 1958; two s.; ed Dept of Law, Catholic Univ., Milan; Co-Nat. Sec. Centri Universitari Cinematografici 1953–54; Admin. Nat. Sec. Federazione Italiana Circoli del Cinema 1954–55; Chief Ed. Bianco e Nero 1956–58, Filmlexicon 1968; Film Critic, Il Veltro 1958–; mem. Editorial Bd Rivista del Cinematografo 1967–; Pres. Immagine, Centro Studi Iconografici 1968–; Dir Venice Film Festival 1969–; has directed various film documentaries including Diario di Una Dama Veneziana 1958, Riscoperta di un Maestro 1960, Alla Ricera di Franz Kafka 1964, Spielberg 1964, Don Minzoni (Special Award) 1967. *Publications:* Il Film Cecoslovacca 1960, La Censura Cinematografica 1961, Ladri di Biciclette 1969.

LAUREDO, Luis J., BA; American diplomatist, lawyer and businessman; m. Maria Regina Lauredo; two d.; ed Columbia Univ., Univ. of Madrid, Georgetown Univ.; Commr, Fla Public Service Comm. 1992–94; Exec. Dir Summit of the Americas 1994; Pres. Greenberg Taurig Consulting Inc.; Perm. Rep. to OAS 1999–2001; Sr Vice-Pres., Export-Import Bank of the United States; Trustee, Pan-American Devt Foundation; Chair. Miami Int. Press Center; mem. Bd, Hispanic Council on Foreign Affairs. *Address:* c/o Department of State, 2201 C Street, NW, Washington, DC 20520, USA.

LAUREL, Salvador Hidalgo, AB, LLD, LLB; Philippine politician; b. 18 Nov. 1928, Manila; s. of José P. Laurel; m. Celia Franco Diaz Laurel; eight c.; ed Univ. of the Philippines and Yale Univ., USA; Senator 1967–73 until imposition of martial law; Prof. of Law and Jurisprudence; f. Legal Aid Soc. of the Philippines; mem. interim Nat. Ass. 1978; active in opposition politics since 1982; Leader, United Nationalist Democratic Org. (UNIDO) 1981–91, Union for Nat. Action 1988–91; Vice-Pres. of Philippines 1986; Prime Minister Feb.–March 1986; Minister of Foreign Affairs 1986–87, Pres. Nacionalista Party 1989.

LAUREN, Ralph; American couturier; b. 14 Oct. 1939, Bronx, NY; s. of Frank Lifschitz and Frieda Lifschitz; m. Ricky L. Beer 1964; three s.; salesman, Bloomingdale's, New York, Brooks Bros. New York; Asst Buyer, Allied Stores, New York; Rep. Rivetz Necktie Mfrs New York; neckwear designer, Polo div. Beau Brummel, New York 1967–69; est. Polo Menswear Co., New York 1968–, Ralph Lauren's Women's Wear, New York 1971–, Polo Leathergoods 1978–, Polo Ralph Lauren Luggage 1982–, Ralph Lauren Home Collection 1983–; Chair. Polo Ralph Lauren Corpn (66 stores in USA, over 140 worldwide); recipient of many fashion awards inc. American Fashion Award 1975, Council of Fashion Designers of America Award 1981, CFDA Lifetime Achievement Award 1992. *Address:* Polo Ralph Lauren Corporation, 650 Madison Ave, New York, NY 10022, USA.

LAURÉN, Reidunn, DIur; Swedish lawyer and politician; m.; three c.; fmr Judge Admin. Court of Appeal, Stockholm; fmr Deputy Sec. Parl. Standing Cttee on Social Affairs; Legal Adviser Ministry of Labour; Perm. Under-Sec. Ministry of Housing and Physical Planning; Justice of the Supreme Admin. Court; Chair. Labour Court; Chair. Equal Opportunities Tribunal; Minister for Constitutional and Civil Law 1991–93; Pres. Admin. Court of Appeal 1994–97; Chair. Queen Sophia's Hosp. 1995–. *Publications:* Equal Opportunities at Work for Women and Men; numerous articles on legal matters. *Address:* Administrative Court of Appeal, Box 2302, 103 17 Stockholm, Sweden. *Telephone:* 700-3801.

LAURENS, André Antoine; French journalist; b. 7 Dec. 1934, Montpellier (Hérault); s. of André Laurens and Mme (née Raymonde Balle) Laurens; ed Lycée de Montpellier; journalist, L'Eclaireur Meridional (fortnightly), Montpellier 1953–54, Agence centrale de Presse, Paris 1958–62; mem. political staff, Le Monde 1963–69, Asst to head of political Dept 1969–82; Dir Le Monde 1982–84, Chief writer 1986–, Ombudsman 1994–; Vice-Pres. Société des Rédacteurs. *Publications:* Les nouveaux communistes 1972, D'une France à l'autre 1974, Le Métier politique ou la conquête du pouvoir 1980. *Address:* Le Monde, 21 bis rue Claude Bernard, 75242 Paris Cedex 05 (Office); 34 rue de Clichy, 75009 Paris, France (Home).

LAURENT, Jean, MSc, CE; French banking executive and administrator; b. 31 July 1944, Mazamet; m.; five c.; ed École Nat. Supérieure d'Aéronautique, Wichita State Univ., USA; Dir AMACAM Co. 1994–, Indocam 1996–, Indosuez Bank of Pvt. Man. 1998–, Crédit Lyonnais Oct. 1999–; Chair. Bd Segespar May 1999– (Dir 1994–), Union of Studies and Investments June 1999–, (Dir 1996–); CEO Crédit Agricole SA May 1999–; Vice-Pres. Banca Intesa and Bank Espirito Santo Sept. 1999–, Bd of Trustees Crédit Agricole Indosuez May 2000–; Pres. Fédération Bancaire Française, A.F.E.C.E.I. Jan. 2001–; Chevalier, Légion d'honneur, Officier, Ordre du Mérite agricole. *Address:* Crédit Agricole (CNCA) SA, 91–93 boulevard Pasteur, 75015 Paris, France (Office). *Telephone:* 1-43-23-52-02 (Office). *Fax:* 1-43-23-20-28 (Office). *Website:* www.credit-agricole.fr (Office).

LAURENT, Torvard Claude, MD; Swedish biochemist; b. 5 Dec. 1930, Stockholm; s. of Torbern Laurent and Bertha Svensson; m. Ulla B. G. Hellsing 1953; one s. two d.; ed Karolinska Inst., Stockholm; Instructor Karolinska Inst. 1949–52, 1954–58; Research Fellow and Research Assoc. Retina Foundation, Boston, USA 1953–54, 1959–61; Assoc. Prof. in Medical Chem. 1961–6 and Prof. of Medical and Physiological Chem. Univ. of Uppsala 1966–96; mem. Swedish Natural Science Research Council 1968–70, Swedish Medical Research Council 1970–77; Chair. Swedish Biochemical Soc. 1973–76; Visiting Prof. Monash Univ. 1979–80; Pres. Swedish Royal Acad. of Sciences 1991–94; mem. Nobel Cttee of Chem. 1992–2000; Science Sec., Wenner-Gren Foundation 1993–2002; Officier Ordre nat. du Mérite, France 2000; Hon. MD (Turku) 1993, (Bergen) 2000; Hon. PharmD (Bologna) 1994; Anders Jahre Prize (Univ. of Oslo) 1968, Pharmacia Award 1986, Eric Fernström Nordic Prize in Med. (Lund Univ.) 1989, Björkén Prize (Uppsala Univ.) 1990, King Carl XVI Gustaf's Gold Medal 1994. *Publications:* approximately 230 scientific papers. *Address:* Department of Medical Biochemistry and Microbiology, University of Uppsala BMC, Box 582, 751 23 Uppsala (Office); Hävelvägen 9, 756 47 Uppsala, Sweden (Home). *Telephone:* (18) 471-41-55 (Office); (18) 30-96-12 (Home). *Fax:* (18) 471-46-73. *E-mail:* torvard.laurent@imbim.uu.se (Office).

LAURENTS, Arthur; American playwright; b. 14 July 1917, New York; s. of Irving Laurents and Ada Robbins; ed Cornell Univ.; Radio Script-Writer 1939–40; mem. Screenwriters Guild, Acad. Motion Picture Arts and Sciences; Dir La Cage aux Folles (Tony Award) 1983, Sydney (Best Dir Award) 1985, London 1986, Birds of Paradise 1987; screenwriter, co-producer film The Turning Point 1977; writer and Dir of several Broadway plays including The Enclave 1973, Gypsy 1974, 1989; American Acad. of Arts and Letters Award (for play Home of the Brave) 1946; Writers Guild of America Award (for The Turning Point) 1977; Tony Award 1967, 1984; Drama Desk Award 1974, Screenwriters' Guild Award and Golden Globe Award (best screenplay) for The Turning Point. *Publications:* (novels) The Way We Were 1972, The Turning Point 1977; (memoir) Original Story by 2000; (screenplays): The Snake Pit 1948, Rope 1948, Caught 1948, Anna Lucasta 1949, Anastasia 1956, Bonjour Tristesse 1958, The Way We Were 1972, The Turning Point 1978; (plays) Home of the Brave 1946, The Bird Cage 1950, The Time of the Cuckoo 1952, A Clearing in the Woods 1956, Invitation to a March 1960, The Enclave 1973, Scream 1978, Jolson Sings Again 1995, The Radical Mystique 1995, My Good Name 1997, Big Potato 2000, Venecia (also dir) 2001, Claude Lazlo 2001; musical plays: West Side Story 1957, Gypsy 1959, Anyone Can Whistle 1964, Do I Hear a Waltz? 1964, Hallelulah Baby 1967, Nick and Nora 1991, Memoir, Original Story By 2000. *Address:* c/o William Morris Agency, 1325 Avenue of the Americas, New York, NY 10019, USA.

LAURIE, Hugh; British actor and comedian; b. 1959; s. of late (William George) Ranald (Mundell) Laurie; m. Jo Laurie 1989; two s. one d.; ed Eton, Cambridge Univ.; fmrly Pres. Footlights, Cambridge Univ. *Television appearances include:* (with Stephen Fry, q.v., A Bit of Fry and Laurie 1989–91, Jeeves and Wooster 1990–92. *Film appearances include:* Peter's Friends 1992, From A View to Death (Dir) 1995, Cousin Bette 1998, Maybe Baby 2000, Stuart Little 2000. *Publications:* Fry and Laurie 4 (with Stephen Fry) 1994, The Gun Seller 1996. *Address:* Hamilton Asper Ltd, Ground Floor, 24 Hanway Street, London, W1P 9DD, England. *Telephone:* (20) 7636-1221.

LAURIE, Robert Stephen, AM, BA; Australian diplomatist (retd); b. 5 Nov. 1936, Sydney; s. of the late W. R. Laurie; m. Diana V. M. Doyne 1969; one s. one d.; ed Knox Grammar School and Univ. of Sydney; joined Dept of External Affairs (now Dept of Foreign Affairs and Trade) 1958; served Colombo 1960, Moscow 1960–63; First Sec. Washington 1965–68; Counsellor, Hong Kong 1968–69; Deputy High Commr in India 1969–71; Amb. to Burma 1975–77, to Poland 1977–80; High Commr in Canada 1985–89, in New Zealand 1989–92; First Asst Sec., South Pacific, Middle East and Africa Divs, Dept of Foreign Affairs and Trade 1993–97; High Commr in India 1997–2001. *Leisure interests:* tennis, cricket, golf, music. *Address:* c/o Department of Foreign Affairs and Trade, Canberra, ACT 2600; 31 Arthur Circle, Manuka, ACT 2603, Australia.

LAURISTIN, Marju, PhD; Estonian politician and sociologist; b. 7 April 1940, Tallinn; d. of Johannes Lauristin (fmr Prime Minister of Estonia) and Olga Lauristin; m. Peeter Vihalemm 1978; two d.; ed Tartu Univ.; sociologist and Head of Dept of Journalism, Tartu Univ. –1989, Prof. 1993–; mem. CPSU –1990; f. Popular Front of Estonia 1988–92; mem. Governing Council 1988–; Chair. Estonia Social-Democratic Party 1990–94; USSR People's Deputy 1989–90; Deputy Speaker of Estonian Supreme Soviet (now Parl.) 1990–92; mem. Estonian Parl. 1992–95, 1999–; Minister of Social Affairs 1992–94; Order of Nat. Coat of Arms 1998, Democracy and Civil Soc. Award, USA and EU 1998. *Publication:* Return to the Western World: Cultural and Political Perspectives on the Estonian Post-Communist Transition (ed. with P. Vihalemm). *Leisure interest:* literature. *Address:* Ülikooli 18, Tartu 50090 (Office); Ropka str. 19, Apt. 12, Tartu 50111, Estonia (Home). *Telephone:* (7) 375-188 (Office); (7) 471-532. *Fax:* (7) 375-440. *E-mail:* marjulau@ut.ee (Home).

LAUTENBERG, Frank R., BS, DHL; American politician and business executive; b. 23 Jan. 1924, Paterson, NJ; s. of Samuel and Mollie Lautenberg; m.; one s. three d.; ed Columbia Univ.; f. Automatic Data Processing Inc., Clifton, NJ 1953, Exec. Vice-Pres. Admin. 1961–69, Pres. 1969–75, Chair. and CEO 1975–82; Senator from NJ 1982–2001, 2003–; Nat. Pres. American Friends of Hebrew Univ. 1973–74; Gen. Chair. and Pres. Nat. United Jewish Appeal 1975–77; Commr Port Authority, New York; mem. Int. Bd of Govs Hebrew Univ., Jerusalem; mem. Pres.'s Comm. on the Holocaust; f. Lautenberg Center for Gen. and Tumor Immunology, Medical School, Hebrew Univ., Jerusalem 1971; fmr Pres. Asscn of Data Processing Service Orgs; mem. Advisory Council, Columbia Univ. School of Business; mem. Bd Dirs eSpeed Inc. 2002; Hon. DHL (Hebrew Union Coll., Cincinnati and New York) 1977; Hon. PhD (Hebrew Univ., Jerusalem) 1978; Torch of Learning Award, American Friends of Hebrew Univ. 1971; Scopus Award 1975. *Address:* Office of the Senator from New Jersey, Hart Senate Office Building, Suite 825-A, Washington, DC 20510 (Office); 405 Route 3, Clifton, NJ 07015, USA (Home). *Telephone:* (202) 224-3224 (Office). *Fax:* (202) 228-4054 (Office). *Website:* lautenberg.senate.gov (Office).

LAUTI, Rt Hon Toaripi, PC; Tuvaluan politician; b. 28 Nov. 1928, Papua New Guinea; m.; three s. two d.; ed Queen Victoria School, Fiji, Wesley Coll., Paerata, NZ, St Andrew's Coll., Christchurch, Christchurch Teachers' Coll.; teacher in Tarawa, Gilbert Is (now Kiribati) 1953–62; Labour Relations and Training Officer for Nauru and Ocean Is Phosphate Comm. 1962–74; returned to Ellice Is (now Tuvalu) 1974; Chief Minister of Tuvalu 1975–78, Prime Minister 1978–81; Leader of the Opposition 1981–90; Gov. Gen. of Tuvalu 1990–95; also fmr Minister of Finance and Foreign Affairs. *Address:* P.O. Box 84, Funafuti, Tuvalu.

LAUTMANN, Rüdiger, DPhil, DJur; German professor of sociology; b. 22 Dec. 1935, Koblenz; s. of Kurt Lautmann and Sibylle Lautmann; Research Asst Univ. of Bielefeld and Dortmund 1968–71; Prof. of Sociology, Law School, Univ. of Bremen 1971–82, Dept of Sociology 1982–. *Publications:* Wert und Norm 1969, Die Funktion des Rechts in der modernen Gesellschaft (co-Ed.) 1970, Die Polizei (co-Ed.) 1971, Soziologie vor den Toren der Jurisprudenz 1971, Justiz–die stille Gewalt 1972, Seminar Gesellschaft und Homosexualität 1977, Rechtssoziologie–Examinatorium (co-Ed.) 1980, Der Zwang zur Tugend 1984, Die Gleichheit der Geschlechter und die Wirklichkeit des Rechts 1990, Das pornographische Begehren (co-author) 1990, Männerliebe im alten Deutschland (co-Ed.) 1992, Homosexualität (Ed.) 1993, Vom Guten, das noch stets das Böse schafft (co-Ed.) 1993, Die Lust am Kind 1994, Lexikon zur Soziologie (co-Ed.) 1994, Der Homosexuelle und sein Publikum 1997, Ausgrenzung macht krank (jtly.) 2000, Soziologie der Sexualität 2002, NS–Terror gegen Homosexuelle (co-Ed.) 2002. *Address:* 20099 Hamburg, Holzdamm 41, Germany. *Telephone:* (40) 2802503. *Fax:* (40) 2802509. *E-mail:* lautmannhh@aol.com (Home). *Website:* www.lautmann.de (Office).

LAUTNER, Georges Charles; French film director; b. 24 Jan. 1926, Nice; s. of Charles Lautner and Marie-Louise Vittoré; m. Caroline Ragon 1950; one s. one d.; ed Lycée Janson-de-Sailly, Ecole Montcel, Paris, Ecole Libre des Sciences Politiques and Faculté de Droit, Paris; Commdr des Arts et des Lettres, Chevalier, Légion d'honneur; Prix de l'Amicale des cadres de l'industrie cinématographique. *Films:* Marche ou crève 1959, Arrêtez les tambours 1960, Le Monocle noir, En plein cirage 1961, Le Septième Juré 1961, L'Oeil du Monocle 1962, Les Tontons Flingueurs 1963, Les Pissenlits par la racine 1963, Le Monocle rit jaune 1964, Les Barbouzes 1964, Les Bons Vivants 1965, Ne nous fâchons pas, Galia 1965, La Grande Sauterelle 1966, Fleur d'oseille 1967, Le Pacha 1967, La Route de Salina 1969, Laisse aller . . . c'est une valse 1970, Il était une fois un flic . . . 1971, Quelques Messieurs trop tranquilles 1972, La Valise 1973, Les Seins de glace 1974, Pas de problème 1975, On aura tout vu 1976, Mort d'un pourri 1977, Ils sont fous ces sorciers 1978, Flic ou voyou 1978, Le Guingolo 1979, Est-ce bien raisonnable? 1980, Le Professionnel 1981, Attention, une femme peut en cacher une autre 1983, Joyeuses Pâques 1984, Le Cowboy 1985, La Cage aux folles III 1985, La Vie dissolue de Gérard Floque 1986, La Maison assassinée 1987, L'Invitée surprise 1988, Présumé dangereux 1989, Triplex 1990, Room Service 1991, L'inconnu dans la maison 1992. *Television:* Les Redoubtables (series) 2001. *Address:* 1 boulevard Richard Wallace, 92200 Neuilly-sur-Seine (Home); 9 chemin des Basses Ribes, 06130 Grasse, France. *Telephone:* (4) 93-36-30-06. *Fax:* (4) 93-36-00-10.

LAUVERGEON, Anne Alice Marie; French government official; b. 2 Aug. 1959, Dijon; d. of Gérard Lauvergeon and Solange Martellière; m. Jean-Eric Molinard 1986; ed Lycées Lakanal, Sceaux, Lycée Voltaire, Orléans, Ecole Normale Supérieure and Ecole Nat. Supérieure des Mines, Paris; with Usinor 1983–84; Eng Inst. for Protection and Nuclear Safety, Centre d'Energie Atomique and Head of Div. Direction Régionale de l'Industrie et de la Recherche, Ile-de-France 1985–88; Asst to Head of Service of Conseil-Gén. des Mines 1988–89; Adviser on int. econ. and foreign trade, Presidency of Repub. 1990; Deputy Sec.-Gen. Presidency of Repub. 1990–95; Man. Lazard Frères & Cie. 1995–98; Pres. Dir-Gen. Compagnie générale des matières nucléaires (Cogema) 1999–; Deputy Dir-Gen. Alcatel Alsthom 1997–; Vice-Pres. Bd of Dirs Société d'applications générales d'électricité et de mécanique (Sagem) 2000–; mem. Strategy, Ethics and Environment Cttees, Suez Lyonnaise Group 2000; Dir Total Fina Elf 2000–; mem. Bd Pechiney 1996–, Framatome 1998. *Publication:* Sur les traces des dirigeants ou la vie du chef dans les grandes entreprises (co-author) 1988. *Address:* Cogema, 2 rue Paul Dautier, B.P. 4, 78141 Vélizy-Villacoublay Cedex (Office); Sagem, 6 avenue d'Iéna, 75116 Paris, France.

LAUZANNE, Bernard, LèsL; French journalist; b. 22 June 1916, Paris; s. of Gaston Lauzanne and Sylvia Scarognino; m. Lucie Gambini 1949; two d.; ed Lycée Condorcet and Univ. of Paris; war service and prisoner of war in Germany 1939–45; joined Radiodiffusion Française (R.T.F.) and worked on programme "Paris vous parle" 1945–59; Chief Sub-Ed., Le Monde 1945–59, News Ed. 1959–69, Asst Ed. 1969–74, Ed. 1974–78, Man. Ed. 1978–83; Directeur de Collection Éditions Denoël 1983–; Pres. France-Japan Asscn, Comité d'histoire de la radiodiffusion 1991–; Lauréat de l'Acad. française 1987; Chevalier, Légion d'honneur, Croix de guerre, Commdr of Sacred Treasure, Japan. *Leisure interests:* music, theatre, painting. *Address:* Éditions Denoël, 9 rue du Cherche-Midi, 75278 Paris Cedex 06 (Office); 5 rue Jean-Bart, 75006 Paris, France (Home). *Telephone:* 1-42-84-01-74.

LAVAGNA, Roberto; Argentine politician and economist; b. 24 March 1942, Buenos Aires; ed Univ. of Buenos Aires and Univ. of Brussels, Belgium; fmr mem. Radical Party; fmr Sec. of Industry and Foreign Trade –1987; mem. Justicialist Party; visiting researcher, Center for Int. Affairs, Harvard Univ., USA 1995; fmr Prof. Univ. of Buenos Aires; Dir Ecolatina consulting firm 1995; Amb. to EU 2000–02; Minister of Economy April 2002–. *Address:* Ministry of the Economy, Hipólito Yrigoyen 250, 1310 Buenos Aires, Argentina (Office). *Telephone:* (11) 4349-5000 (Office). *E-mail:* ministrosecpriv@mecon.gov.ar (Office). *Website:* www.mecon.gov.ar (Office).

LAVE, Lester B., PhD; American professor of economics; b. 5 Aug. 1939, Philadelphia, Pa; m. Judith Rice 1965; one s. one d.; ed Reed Coll., MIT and Harvard Univ.; Prof. of Econs Carnegie-Mellon Univ. 1963–, James Higgins Prof. of Econs 1984, 1992–; Sr Fellow, Brookings Inst. 1978–82; Visiting Asst Prof. Northwestern Univ. 1965–66; consultant, Gen. Motors Research Labs., U.S. Depts of Justice, Defense, Transportation, Health and Welfare, Environmental Protection Agency, Nuclear Regulatory Comm., Nat. Science Foundation, Office of Tech. Assessment; Pres. Soc. for Risk Analysis 1985–86. *Publications:* Technological Change 1966, Air Pollution and Human Health 1977, The Strategy of Social Regulation 1981, Scientific Basis of Health & Safety Regulation 1981, Clearing the Air 1981, Quantitative Risk Assessment 1982, Toxic Chemicals, Health and the Environment (with A. Upton) 1987; more than 200 scientific articles. *Leisure interests:* swimming, skiing. *Address:* Graduate School of Industrial Administration, Carnegie-Mellon University, 5000 Forbes Avenue, Pittsburgh, PA 15213, USA. *Telephone:* (412) 268-2000. *Fax:* (412) 268-7838. *Website:* www.emu.edu.

LAVELLI, Jorge; French theatre and opera director; b. Buenos Aires, Argentina; ed Ecole Charles Dullin et Jacques Lecoq, Paris, Université du Théâtre des Nations; Dir Théâtre Nat. de la Colline 1987–; Pres. Centre français de l'Inst. Int. du Théâtre (UNESCO) 1991–; Chevalier Légion d'honneur; Chevalier Ordre nat. du Mérite, Commdr Ordre des Arts et des Lettres, Cross of Commdr Order of Merit, Poland. *Plays include:* Le Mariage, Paris 1963, Berlin Festival 1964 (Grand Prix at Concours nat. des jeunes compagnies), Jeux de Massacre, Paris 1970 (Prix de la Critique), Le Roi se meurt, Paris 1976 (Prix Dominique de la mise en scène, Prix de la Critique), Doña Rosita La Soltera, Madrid, Jerusalem and Caracas Festivals and Paris 1980; at Théâtre Nat. de la Colline: Une Visite inopportune by Copi 1988 (Prix de la meilleure création française, Syndicat de la Critique), Réveille-toi Philadelphie 1988 (Prix de la meilleure création d'une pièce française, Syndicat de la Critique), La Veillée 1989, Greek 1990 (Molière Prize for best production), La Nonna 1990, Heldenplatz 1991, 1992. *Operas include:* The Trial (by Von Einem), Vienna State Opera 1970, Idomeneo, Angers 1975, Faust, Opéra de Paris 1975, L'Heure Espagnole and L'Enfant et les Sortilèges, La Scala Milan 1975, La Traviata, Aix-en-Provence Festival 1976,

Faust, Metropolitan Opera, New York, Kennedy Center, Washington 1976, Pelléas et Mélisande, Opéra de Paris 1977, Fidelio, Toulouse 1977, Madame Butterfly, La Scala, Milan and Opéra de Paris 1978, Alcina, Aix-en-Provence Festival 1978, Carmen, Strasbourg, Brussels 1978, Oedipus Rex, Opéra de Paris 1979, Le Nozze di Figaro, Aix-en-Provence Festival, Liège 1979, Dardanus (by Rameau), Opéra de Paris 1980, Les Arts Florissants (by Charpentier), Versailles 1982, Norma, Bonn 1983, Salome, Zürich 1986, La Clemenza di Tito, Hamburg 1986, The Makropoulos Affair, Buenos Aires 1986, Die Zauberflöte, Aix-en-Provence Festival 1989, Die Entführung aus dem Serail Aix-en-Provence Festival 1990; several opera productions for TV. *Address:* Théâtre National de la Colline, 15 rue Malte Brun, 75020 Paris, France. *Telephone:* 1-44-62-52-00. *Fax:* 1-44-62-52-90.

LAVENTHOL, David, MA; American publisher; b. 15 July 1933, Philadelphia; s. of Jesse Laventhol and Clare Horwald; m. Esther Coons 1958; one s. one d.; ed Yale Univ. and Univ. of Minnesota; Reporter, later News Ed., St Petersburg Times 1957–63; City Ed. New York Herald Tribune 1963–66; Asst Man. Ed. The Washington Post 1966–69; Assoc. Ed. Newsday 1969, Exec. Ed. 1969–70, Ed. 1970–78, Publr and CEO 1978–86, Chair. 1986–87; Group Vice-Pres. Times Mirror 1981–86, Sr Vice-Pres. 1986, Pres. 1987–93; CEO and Publr LA Times 1989–93; Ed.-at-large Times Mirror Co., LA 1994–98, Consultant Ed. 1998–99; Ed. and Publr Columbia Journalism Review 1999–; Chair. Pulitzer Prize Bd 1988–89; Vice-Chair. Int. Press Inst. 1985–92, Chair. 1992–95; Chair. Museum of Contemporary Art, LA 1993–97; Dir Newspaper Advertising Bureau, American Press Inst. 1988–, LA Times Washington Post/ News Service, Times Mirror Foundation, United Negro Coll. Fund; mem. Bd Dirs Assoc. Press 1993–96, Columbia Journalism School 1995–, Nat. Parkinson Foundation 1995–, Saratoga Performing Arts Center 1993–96; mem. American Soc. of Newspaper Eds. Writing Awards Bd, American Newspaper Publr Asscn, Century Asscn, Council on Foreign Relations. *Address:* Columbia Journalism Review, Columbia University, 2950 Broadway, New York, NY 10027, USA (Office). *E-mail:* malibunal@aol.com (Office).

LAVER, Rod(ney) George, MBE; Australian tennis player; b. 9 Aug. 1938, Rockhampton, Queensland; s. of R. S. Laver; m. Mary Benson 1966; one s.; ed Rockhampton Grammar and High Schools; turned professional player 1963; Australian Champion 1960, 1962, 1969; Wimbledon Champion 1961, 1962, 1968, 1969; USA Champion 1962, 1969; French Champion 1962, 1969; only player to win double Grand Slam 1962, 1969; played Davis Cup for Australia 1958, 1959, 1960, 1961, 1962 and 1973 (first open Davis Cup); in a 23-year career won 47 professional titles; Int. Tennis Hall of Fame 1981; Melbourne Park centre court renamed Rod Laver Arena in his honour 2000. *Publications:* How to Play Winning Tennis 1964, Education of a Tennis Player 1971. *Leisure interests:* golf, fishing, skiing. *Address:* c/o Tennis Australia, Private Bag 6060, Richmond South, Vic. 3121, Australia.

LAVER, William Graeme, PhD, FRS; Australian biochemist; b. 3 June 1929; s. of Lawrence Laver and Madge Laver; m. Judith Garrard Cahn 1954; one s. two d.; ed Univ. of Melbourne, Univ. of London; Tech. Asst Walter and Eliza Hall Inst. of Medical Research 1947–52; Research Asst Dept of Biochemistry, Univ. of Melbourne 1954–55; Research Fellow, John Curtin School of Medical Research, ANU 1958–62, Fellow 1962–64, Sr Fellow 1964–; Head Influenza Research Unit., ANU 1983–; Australia Prize (jtly) 1996. *Publications:* numerous papers on the structure of influenza viruses and on the origin and control of pandemic influenza. *Leisure interests:* climbing volcanoes, raising beef cattle, viticulture. *Address:* Barton Highway, Murrumbateman, NSW 2582, Australia. *Telephone:* (2) 6227-0061 (Office). *Fax:* (2) 6227-0062 (Office). *E-mail:* graeme.laver@bigpond.com (Office); wgraemelaver@hotmail.com (Home).

LAVEROV, Nikolai Pavlovich, DGeolMineralSc; Russian geologist; b. 12 Jan. 1930, Pozharishche, Archangel Region; m.; two d.; ed Moscow Inst. of Nonferrous Metals; mem. CPSU 1959–91; participated in geological expeditions, Jr researcher, scientific sec. on geological stations of Inst. of Geology, Ore Deposits, Mineralogy and Chemistry 1958–66; Deputy Chief Dept of research orgs., USSR Ministry of Geology 1966–68, Chief 1968–72; Scientific Leader on research of Resources of Urals Project 1972–87; Corresp. mem. USSR (now Russian) Acad. of Sciences 1979, mem. 1987; Vice-Pres. 1988–; Prof., Prorector, Head of Chair of Ecology and rational use of natural resources, Acad. of Nat. Econs, USSR Council of Ministers 1983–87; Pres. Acad. of Sciences of Kirghiz SSR 1987–89; Vice-Chair. USSR Council of Ministers, Chair. Cttee on Science and Tech. 1989–91; mem. Cen. CPSU Cttee 1990–91; Head of Comms of Acad. of Sciences investigating consequences of earthquake in Armenia 1988–; Chair. USSR Nat. Cttee of Geologists 1990–91; Pres. Lomonosov Fund 1992–; Head Comm. on problem of safe burial of radioactive waste; Ed.-in-Chief Geology of Ore Deposits. *Publications:* works on geology of uranium deposits, continental volcanism, econs of mineral products. *Address:* Presidium of Russian Academy of Sciences, Leninsky prospekt 12, 117901 Moscow, Russia. *Telephone:* (095) 954-29-68.

LAVIER, Bertrand; French artist; b. 14 June 1949, Châtillon-sur-Seine; s. of Jean Lavier and Geneviève Duteil; m. Gloria Friedmann 1989; ed Ecole Nat. Supérieure d' Horticulture; landscape artist and town planner, Marne Lavallée New Town 1971–72; at Centre de Recherches et d'Etudes sur le Paysage, Paris 1973–75; artist 1974–; First Prize (Sculpture), Biennale, Budapest 1984, Grand Prix Nat. de la Sculpture 1994. *Exhibitions include:* Centre Nat. d'Art contemporain, Paris 1975, Biennale, Venice 1976, 1997, Europa 79, Stuttgart 1979, Musée d'Art Moderne, Paris 1980, 1985, Galerie

Massimo Minini, Milan 1982, Dokumenta 7, Kassel 1982, Noveau Musée, Lyon Villeurbanne 1983, Lisson Gallery, London 1984, Galerie Durand–Dessert, Paris 1984, Kunsthalle, Bern 1984, Museum of Modern Art, New York 1984, Biennales, Paris, São Paulo 1985, I.C.A., London 1986, Museum of Modern Art, Tokyo 1986, Musée des Beaux-Arts, Dijon 1986, Gallery Buchmann, Basel 1986, Biennale of Sydney 1986, John Gibson Gallery, New York 1986, Museé des Beaux Arts, Grenoble 1986, Stedjelik van Abbemuseum, Eindhoven 1987, Galerie Durand-Dessert, Paris 1987, Dokumenta 8, Kassel 1987, Kröller-Müller Museum, Netherlands 1987, Univ. Art Museum, Berkeley, USA 1988, Nat. Museum of Modern Art, Vienna 1992, Museum of African and Oceanian Art, Paris 1995, Castello di Rivoli Museum of Contemporary Art, Turin 1996, Martin Gropius Museum, Berlin 1997. *Publication:* Bertrand Lavier présente la peinture des Martin de 1603 à 1984 1984. *Leisure interests:* hunting, motor-racing, tennis. *Address:* Galerie Durand-Dessert, 28 rue de Lappe, 75011 Paris (Office); rue La Demoiselle, 21510 Aignay-le-Duc, France (Home).

LAVÍN, Joaquín; Chilean politician and economist; b. 1955; m. María Estela León; seven c.; ed Pontificia Univ. Católica de Chile, Univ. of Chicago; econ. adviser to ODEPLAN (Ministry for Planning) 1975–77, Dean Faculty of Econ. and Admin. Sciences, Concepción Univ. 1979–81; Econ. Ed. El Mercurio 1986–88; fmr Sec.-Gen. UDI (Ind. Democratic Union); Dean Faculty of Econs and Business, Univ. del Desarrollo 1996–98; Mayor Las Condes 1992–96, 1996–2000; presidential candidate 2000; Mayor of Santiago 2000–; Founder La Vaca (NGO). *Publications:* Miguel Kast: Pasión de Vivir 1986, Chile Revolución Silenciosa 1987. *Address:* Partido Unión Demócrata Independiente, Suecia 286, Santiago, Chile (Office).

LAVRENTYEV, Mikhail Mikhailovich; Russian mathematician; b. 21 July 1932, Krasny Liman, Ukraine; m.; three c.; ed Moscow State Univ.; Jr, then Sr researcher, then head of lab. S.L. Sobolev Inst. of Math., Siberian Br. USSR Acad. of Sciences 1957–64, Dir 1986–, head of lab., then Deputy Dir Computation Centre 1964–86; mem. Russian Acad. of Sciences 1981; Lenin's Prize 1962, USSR State Prize 1987. *Address:* S.L. Sobolev Institute of Mathematics, Universitetsky prosp. 4, 630090 Novosibirsk, Russia (Office). *Telephone:* (3832) 35-44-50 (Office).

LAVROV, Kyrill Yuriyevich; Russian actor; b. 15 Sept. 1925, Kiev; army service 1943–50; actor Kiev Lesya Ukrainka Drama Theatre 1950–55; with Leningrad Big Drama Theatre 1955–, Artistic Dir 1989–; co-founder Memorial Fund; Chair. Exec. Bd USSR Union of Theatre Workers 1986–92; Pres. Int. Confed. of Theatre Unions 1992–; Deputy to USSR Supreme Soviet 1979–89; USSR People's Deputy 1989–91; acted in numerous classical and contemporary plays including Cabal and Lourc (Schiller), Macbeth, Wit Works Woe (Griboyedov), Three Sisters (Chekhov); Hero of Socialist Labour 1985, USSR People's Artist 1972, USSR State Prize 1978, 1982. *Films include:* Alive and Dead 1964, Retribution 1969, The Taming of the Fire 1974, The Brothers Karamasov 1970, Tchaikovsky 1970. *Address:* Michurinskaya 1, Apt. 36, 197046 St Petersburg, Russia (Home). *Telephone:* (812) 233-52-35 (Home).

LAVROV, Sergey Viktorovich; Russian diplomatist; b. 21 March 1950, Moscow; m.; one d.; ed Moscow Inst. of Int. Relations; diplomatic service 1972–; attaché USSR Embassy in Sri Lanka 1972–76, Sec. Dept of Int. Econ. Organizations Ministry of Foreign Affairs 1976–81, Sec., Counsellor USSR Mission, UN, New York 1981–88; Deputy Chief, then Chief Dept of Int. Econ. Relations Ministry of Foreign Affairs 1988–90; Dir Dept of Int. Organizations and Global Problems, Ministry of Foreign Affairs of Russia 1990–92, Deputy Minister 1992–94; Perm. Rep. to UN 1994–; Order of Honour 1996; Order of Service to the Nation 1997. *Leisure interest:* white-water rafting. *Address:* Permanent Mission of Russia to the United Nations, 136 East 67th Street, New York, NY 10021, USA. *Telephone:* (212) 861-4900 (Office). *Fax:* (212) 628-0252.

LAVROVSKY, Mikhail Leonidovich; Russian ballet dancer; b. 29 Oct. 1941, Tbilisi; s. of Yelena Chikvaidze and Leonid Lavrovsky; m. Dolores García Ordonyez 1986; one s.; ed Moscow Coll. of Choreography, Moscow State Inst. of Theatre Art; soloist Bolshoi Theatre 1963–88, coach Bolshoi Theatre 1992–; Prof. Moscow Coll. of Choreography 1988–94; f. and Head Choreographic School of M. Lavrovsky in Moscow 1993; prize winner Int. Competition in Varna, Bulgaria 1965, Lenin's Prize 1970, Nizhinsky Prize Paris Acad. of Dance 1972, USSR State Prize 1977, USSR People's Artist 1976. *Repertoire includes:* Giselle, Flames of Paris, Cinderella, Legend about Love, Don Quixote, Romeo and Juliet, Nutcracker, Angara, Paganini, Ivan the Terrible, Anyuta, Spartacus, Swan Lake, Bayadère. *Choreography:* Jazz Ballet (Porgy and Bess), Blues (Gershwin), Film Ballet Prometheus (Scriabin), Novella (Bach and Liszt), Plastic Ballet Revelations (Kikta), Fantasia Ballet Casanova (Mozart), Film Ballet on poem by Lermontov (First Prize New York Film Festival 1978), Bolshoi Theatre 1993. *Films include:* choreography and lead role Ali Baba and the Forty Thieves (Dir Kakhagadze), Fantasior (Dir Bunin). *Leisure interests:* sport, fencing, reading, cinema. *Address:* Bolshoi Theatre, Teatralnaya pl. 1, Moscow (Office); Voznesensky per. 16/4, Apt. 7, 103009 Moscow, Russia (Home). *Telephone:* 291-77-22 (Office); (095) 229-65-49, (095) 229-64-69 (Home). *Fax:* (095) 229-65-49 (Home).

LAW, HE Cardinal Bernard F., BA; American ecclesiastic; b. 4 Nov. 1931, Torreón; s. of Bernard A. Law and Helen Stubblefield; ed Harvard Univ.; ordained 1961; Bishop of Springfield-Cape Girardeau 1973; Archbishop of

Boston 1984–2002; cr. Cardinal by Pope John Paul II 1985. *Address:* c/o Cardinal's Residence, 2101 Commonwealth Avenue, Brighton, MA 02135, USA.

LAW, Bob; British artist; b. 22 Jan. 1934, Brentford, Middx; m. Georgina Cann 1965; one s. one d.; works include paintings and sculptures; exhibited in public collections including (in London) Tate Gallery, Victoria & Albert Museum, British Museum, Arts Council of GB, British Council; Southampton Art Gallery, City Art Gallery, Peterborough, Stedelijk Museum, Amsterdam, Museum of Modern Art, New York, Guggenheim Museum, New York, the Panza Collection, Milan, City Art Gallery, Johannesburg, Art Gallery of NSW, Sydney; French Govt Scholarship 1961–62; Arts Council of GB Award 1967, 1975, 1981. *Publication:* Art of the Fifties, Sixties and Seventies 1999. *Leisure interests:* architecture, prehistory. *Address:* The Warehouse, 18 Bread Street, Penzance, Cornwall, TR18 2EG, England. *Telephone:* (1736) 332495. *Fax:* (1736) 332495.

LAW, Jude; British actor; b. 29 Dec. 1972, London; s. of Peter Law and Maggie Law; m. Sadie Frost 1997; one step-s. two s. one d.; fmrly with Nat. Youth Music Theatre; co-f. Natural Nylon (production co.), Dir 2000–03. *Stage appearances include:* Joseph and the Amazing Technicolor Dreamcoat, Les Parents Terribles 1994, Ior 1995, Tis A Pity She's A Whore 1999, Doctor Faustus 2002. *Film appearances include:* Shopping 1994, I Love You I Love You Not 1996, Wilde 1997, Gattaca 1997, Midnight in the Garden of Good and Evil 1997, Bent, Music From Another Room 1998, Final Cut 1998, The Wisdom of Crocodiles 1998, eXistenZ 1999, The Talented Mr Ripley (BAFTA Award for Best Supporting Actor) 1999, Enemy at the Gates 2000, Love Honour and Obey 2000, AI: Artificial Intelligence 2001, Road to Perdition 2002. *Address:* c/o Julian Belfrage Associates, 46 Albemarle Street, London, W1S 4DF, England. *Website:* www.jude-law.net (Office).

LAW, Phillip Garth, AC, CBE, MSc, FTSE, FAA, FRSV, FAIP, FANZAAS, FRGS; Australian scientist, Antarctic explorer and educationist; b. 21 April 1912, Tallangatta, Vic.; s. of the late Arthur James Law and Lillie Law; m. Nel Allan 1941; ed Ballarat Teachers' Coll. and Univ. of Melbourne; Science master in secondary schools 1933–38; Tutor in Physics Newman Coll., Melbourne Univ. 1940–45 and Lecturer in Physics 1943–47; Research Physicist and Asst Sec. Scientific Instrument and Optical Panel, Ministry of Munitions 1940–45; Scientific Mission to New Guinea battle areas for the Australian Army 1944; Sr Scientific Officer Aust. Nat. Antarctic Research Expeditions 1947–48, Leader 1949–66; Dir Antarctic Div., Dept of External Affairs 1949–66; Australian Observer Norwegian-British-Swedish Antarctic Expedition 1950; led expeditions to establish first perm. Australian research station at Mawson, MacRobertson Land 1954, stations at Davis, Princess Elizabeth Land 1957 and at Casey 1965; exploration of coast of Australian Antarctica 1954–66; mem. gov. council Melbourne Univ. 1959–78, La Trobe Univ. 1964–74; Exec. Vice-Pres. Victoria Inst. of Colls 1966–77; Chair. Australian Nat. Cttee on Antarctic Research 1966–80, Royal Melbourne Inst. of Tech. Foundation 1994–99; mem. Council of Science Museum of Vic. 1968–83; Pres. Royal Soc. of Vic. 1967, 1968, Graduate Union, Univ. of Melbourne 1972–77, Victorian Inst. of Marine Sciences 1978–80, Australia and NZ Scientific Exploring Soc. 1976–81, Patron 1982–; Fellow Royal Soc. of Vic., Australian Acad. of Technological Sciences and Eng.; Hon. Fellow Royal Melbourne Inst. of Tech.; several hon. degrees including Hon. DAppSci (Melbourne), Hon. DSc (La Trobe), Hon. DEd (Vic. Inst. of Colls); Order of Merit Commonwealth Professional Officers Assoc. 1957, Clive Lord Memorial Medal Royal Soc. of Tasmania 1958, Founder's Medal Royal Geographical Soc. 1960, John Lewis Gold Medal Royal Geographical Soc. of Australia 1962, Vocational Service Award Melbourne Rotary Club 1970, James Cook Medal of the Royal Soc. of NSW 1988, Gold Medal Australian Geographic Soc. 1988, Pres.'s Award, Australian Scouts Assocn 1996, Clunies Ross Nat. Award for Lifetime Contribs to Science and Tech. 2001. *Publications:* ANARE (with Bechervaise) 1957, Antarctic Odyssey 1983, The Antarctic Voyage of H.M.A.S. Wyatt Earp 1995, You Have to be Lucky 1995, also numerous articles on Antarctic exploration and research and papers on cosmic rays, thermal conductivity, optics and education. *Leisure interests:* writing, music, tennis, skiing, swimming. *Address:* 16 Stanley Grove, Canterbury, Vic. 3126, Australia. *Telephone:* (3) 9882-5575.

LAWLER, James Ronald, MA, DUP; Australian academic; b. 15 Aug. 1929, Melbourne; m. Christiane Labossière 1954; one s. one d.; ed Univs of Melbourne and Paris, France; lecturer in French, Univ. of Queensland 1955–56; Sr Lecturer, Univ. of Melbourne 1956–62; Prof. of French, Head of Dept, Univ. of Western Australia 1963–71; Prof. of French, Chair., Univ. of Calif., Los Angeles 1971–74; McCulloch Prof. of French, Dalhousie Univ. 1974–79; Prof. of Romance Languages, Univ. of Chicago 1979–; Edward Carson Waller Distinguished Service Prof., Univ. of Chicago 1989–, Prof. Emer. 1998–; Visiting Prof. Collège de France 1985; Pres. Asscn Int. des Etudes Françaises 1998–; Carnegie Fellowship 1961–62; Commonwealth Interchange Visitor 1967; Guggenheim Fellowship 1974; Nat. Endowment of Humanities Fellowship 1984–85; Foundation Fellow, Australian Acad. of the Humanities; Prix Int. des Amitiés Françaises 1986, Prix du Rayonnement de la Langue Française, Acad. Française 1999; Officier, Ordre des Palmes académiques. *Publications:* Form and Meaning in Valéry's Le Cimetière Marin 1959, An Anthology of French Poetry 1960, Lecture de Valéry: Une Etude de Charmes 1963, The Language of French Symbolism 1969, The Poet as Analyst: Essays on Paul Valéry 1974, Paul Valéry: An Anthology 1976,

René Char: The Myth and the Poem 1978, Edgar Poe et les Poètes français 1989, Paul Valéry (ed.) 1991, Rimbaud's Theatre of the Self 1992, Poetry and Moral Dialectic: Baudelaire's Les Fleurs du Mal 1997; Founding Ed.: Essays in French Literature 1964, Dalhousie French Studies 1979. *Address:* Department of Romance Language and Literature, 1050 East 59th Street, Chicago, IL 60637, USA (Office). *Telephone:* (312) 702-8481.

LAWRENCE, Carmen Mary, PhD; Australian politician and fmr psychologist; b. 2 March 1948, Western Australia; d. of Ern Lawrence and Mary Lawrence; m. 1979; one s.; ed Santa Maria Coll., Perth; Sr Tutor, Dept of Psychiatry and Behavioural Science, Univ. of WA 1979, Lecturer and Course Controller in Behavioural Science applied to Medicine 1980–83; Research Psychologist in Research and Evaluation Unit, Psychiatric Services, Health Dept of WA 1983–86; mem. Western Australia State Ass. 1986–, apptd Minister for Educ. 1988, fmr Minister for Educ. and Aboriginal Affairs, Premier of WA 1990–93, also Treas., Minister for the Family and for Women's Interests; Leader of the Opposition, Shadow Treas., Shadow Minister for Employment, for Fed. Affairs 1993–94; Fed. Shadow Minister of Health 1994–96, on Status of Women and on Environment and the Arts 1996–97; mem. Fed. Parl. for Fremantle 1994–; Benjamin Rosenstamm Prize in Econs, British Psychological Soc. Prize for Psychology, Australian Psychological Soc. Prize for Psychology, H.I. Fowler Prize for Research in Psychology, J.A. Wood Memorial Prize and other awards and prizes. *Publications:* several academic papers on psychology. *Leisure interests:* reading, theatre, classical music, cooking. *Address:* Unit 7, Queensgate Mall, William Street, Fremantle WA 6160, Australia.

LAWRENCE, Peter Anthony, PhD, FRS; British biologist; b. 23 June 1941, Longridge; s. of Ivor D. Lawrence and Joy Liebert; m. Birgitta Haraldson 1971; ed Univ. of Cambridge; Commonwealth Fellowship, USA 1965–67; Dept of Genetics, Univ. of Cambridge 1967–69; Staff, MRC Lab. of Molecular Biology, Cambridge 1969–, Jt Head, Cell Biology Div. 1984–87; Foreign mem. Swedish Royal Acad. of Sciences 2001; Medal of Zoological Soc. of London 1977, Darwin Medal (Royal Soc.) 1994. *Publications:* The Making of a Fly 1992; numerous scientific papers. *Leisure interests:* garden, golf, trees, fungi, ascalaphidae, theatre. *Address:* 9 Temple End, Great Wilbraham, Cambridge, CB1 5JF, England. *Telephone:* (1223) 402282 (Office); (1223) 880505. *Fax:* (1223) 411582. *E-mail:* pal@ (Office). *Website:* www.mrc-lmb.cam.ac.uk/pal (Office).

LAWRENCE, Robert Swan; American physician; b. 6 Feb. 1938, Philadelphia; s. of Thomas George Lawrence and Catherine Swan Lawrence; m. Cynthia Starr Cole 1960; three s. two d.; ed Harvard Coll. and Medical School; Medical Epidemiologist, Center for Disease Control, US Public Health Service, Atlanta 1966–69; Asst to Assoc. Prof. of Medicine, Dir Div. of Community Medicine, NC Univ. School of Medicine 1970–74; Dir Div. of Primary Care, Asst to Assoc. Prof. of Medicine, Harvard Medical School 1974–91, Charles Davidson Assoc. Prof. of Medicine 1981–91; Assoc. Chief of Medicine, Cambridge Hosp. 1974–77, Chief of Medicine, Dir Dept of Medicine 1980–91; Dir Health Sciences, Rockefeller Foundation 1991–95; Adjunct Prof. of Medicine, New York Univ. 1991–95; Prof. of Health Policy, Assoc. Dean for Professional Educ. and Dir Center for a Livable Future, Bloomberg School of Public Health, Johns Hopkins Univ., 1995–, Prof. of Medicine, Johns Hopkins School of Medicine 1996–, Edyth Schoenrich Prof. of Preventive Medicine 2000–; Chair. US Preventive Services Task Force, Dept of Health and Human Services, US Govt 1984–89, mem. 1990–95; Ed. American Journal of Preventive Medicine 1990–92; mem. Inst. of Medicine, NAS 1978; Duncan Clark Lecture (Asscn of Teachers of Preventive Medicine) 1993; Pres. Physicians for Human Rights 1998–2002; Trustee Teachers' Coll. Columbia Univ. 1991–97; Maimonides Prize 1964, John Atkinson Ferrell Prize, UNC 1998; Special Recognition Award (American Coll. of Preventive Medicine) 1988; Leadership Award, Soc. Gen. Internal Medicine 1996, Albert Schweitzer Humanitarian Award 2002. *Publications:* Co-Ed. Preventing Disease: Beyond the Rhetoric 1990, Health Promotion and Disease Prevention in Clinical Practice 1996, International Perspectives on Environment, Development and Health 1997; 60 articles in scientific journals. *Address:* Johns Hopkins Bloomberg School of Public Health, 615 N Wolfe Street, Baltimore, MD 21205 (Office); Highfield House 1112, 4000 N Charles Street, Baltimore, MD 21218-1737, USA (Home). *Telephone:* (410) 614-4590 (Office); (410) 235-5474 (Home). *Fax:* (410) 614-8126 (Office).

LAWRENCE, Walter Nicholas Murray, MA; British underwriting agent; b. 8 Feb. 1935, London; s. of Henry Walter Neville Lawrence and Sarah Schuyler Lawrence (née Butler); m. Sally Louise O'Dwyer 1961; two d.; ed Winchester Coll., Trinity Coll. Oxford; with C. T. Bowring and Co. Ltd 1957–62, 1976–84, Treaty Dept 1957–62, Dir 1976–84; with Harvey Bowring and Others 1962–84, Asst Underwriter 1962–70, Underwriter 1970–84; Dir C. T. Bowring (Underwriting Agencies) Ltd 1973–84; Chair. Fairway Underwriting Agencies Ltd 1979–85; mem. Lloyd's Underwriter's Non-Marine Asscn, Deputy Chair. 1977, Chair. 1978; served Cttee of Lloyd's 1979–82, 1991, Deputy Chair. 1982, mem. Council of Lloyd's 1984–91, Deputy Chair. 1984–87, Chair. 1988–90; Dir, Chair. Murray Lawrence Holdings Ltd 1988–94, Murray Lawrence Mems. Agency Ltd 1988–92, Murray Lawrence & Partners Ltd 1989–93. *Leisure interests:* golf, opera, travel.

LAWRENSON, Peter John, DSc, FIEEE, FREng, FRS; British electrical engineer and business executive; b. 12 March 1933, Prescot; s. of John Lawrenson and Emily Houghton; m. Shirley H. Foster 1958; one s. three d.; ed Prescot

Grammar School and Manchester Univ.; research Eng General Electric Co., Ltd 1956–61; Lecturer, Univ. of Leeds 1961–65, Reader 1965–66, Prof. of Electrical Eng 1966–91, Head, Dept of Electrical and Electronic Eng 1974–84, Chair. Faculty of Science and Applied Science 1978–80; Chair. Switched Reluctance Drives Ltd 1981–97, Dir 1997–; Consultant Rolls-Royce; Pres. IEE 1992–93; James Alfred Ewing Medal 1983, Royal Soc. Esso Medal 1985, Faraday Medal (IEE) 1990, and other awards. *Publications:* The Analytical and Numerical Solution of Electromagnetic Field Problems 1992, other books and over 160 articles and patents in the field of electrical eng, particularly electromagnetics and electromechanics. *Leisure interests:* squash, lawn tennis, bridge, chess, jewellery making. *Address:* Hard Gap, Main Street, Linton, Wetherby, Yorks., LS22 4HT; Switched Reluctance Drives Ltd, East Park House, Otley Road, Harrogate, HG3 1PR, England (Office). *Telephone:* (1423) 845200 (Office). *Fax:* (1423) 845201 (Office).

LAWS, Richard Maitland, CBE, ScD, FRS, FIBiol; British scientist; b. 23 April 1926, Whitley Bay; s. of Percy Malcolm Laws and Florence May Heslop; m. Maureen Isobel Holmes 1954; three s.; ed Dame Allan's School, Newcastle and St Catharine's Coll., Cambridge; Biologist and Base Leader, Falkland Islands Dependencies Survey 1947–53; Whaling Insp., F/F Balaena 1953–54; Prin. Scientific Officer, Nat. Inst. of Oceanography, Godalming 1954–61; Dir, Nuffield Unit of Tropical Animal Ecology, Uganda 1961–67; Dir, Tsavo Research Project, Kenya 1967–68; Head, Life Sciences Div., British Antarctic Survey 1969–73; Dir, British Antarctic Survey, Cambridge 1973–87; Dir Sea Mammal Research Unit, Cambridge 1977–87; Master, St Edmund's Coll. Cambridge 1985–96; Sec. Zoological Soc. of London 1984–88; mem. Council of the Senate, Univ. of Cambridge 1989–92, Financial Bd 1988–91; Pres. Scientific Cttee for Antarctic Research 1990–94, Hon. mem. 1996; Foreign mem. Norwegian Acad. of Science and Letters 1998; 36th Annual Lecture, Ciba Foundation 1984, 2nd Cranbrook Memorial Lecture, Mammal Soc. 1987, 4th Annual Dice Lecture, Univ. of Kent 1997; Hon. mem. Soc. for Marine Mammalogy 1994; Hon. Warden, Uganda Nat. Parks 1996; Hon. Fellow St Catharine's Coll. 1982, St Edmund's Coll. 1996; Hon. DSc (Bath) 1991; Bruce Medal 1954, Scientific Medal, Zoological Soc., London 1965, Polar Medal 1976 and Second Clasp 2001. *Publications:* Elephants and Their Habitats (co-author) 1975, Scientific Research in Antarctica (ed.) 1977, Antarctic Ecology (ed.) 1984, Antarctic Nutrient Cycles and Food Webs (co-ed.) 1985, Antarctica: The Last Frontier 1989, Life at Low Temperatures (co-ed.) 1990, Antarctica and Environmental Change (co-ed.) 1992, Antarctic Seals: Research Methods and Techniques (ed.) 1993, Elephant Seals: Population Ecology, Behaviour and Physiology (co-ed.) 1994. *Leisure interests:* writing, gardening, photography, painting. *Address:* 3 The Footpath, Coton, Cambs., CB3 7PX, England. *Telephone:* (1954) 210567.

LAWSON, Hon. Dominic Ralph Campden, BA, FRSA; British journalist and editor; b. 17 Dec. 1956, London; s. of Nigel Lawson, now Lord Lawson of Blaby (q.v.) and the late Lady (Vanessa) Ayer; m. 1st Jane Fiona Wastell Whytehead 1982 (divorced 1991); m. 2nd Hon. Rosamond Monckton 1991; two d.; ed Westminster School, Christchurch, Oxford; mem. staff World Tonight and The Financial World Tonight, BBC 1979–81; mem. staff Financial Times (Energy Corresp. and Lex column) 1981–87; Deputy Ed. The Spectator 1987–90, Ed. 1990–95; Ed. The Sunday Telegraph 1995–; Columnist, Sunday Corresp. 1990, The Financial Times 1991–94, Daily Telegraph 1994–95; Harold Wincott Prize for Financial Journalism, Ed. of the Year, Soc. of Magazine Eds. 1990. *Publications:* Korchnoi, Kasparov 1983, Britain in the Eighties (jtly) 1989; ed. The Spectator Annual 1992, 1993, 1994, The Inner Game 1993. *Leisure interests:* chess, cricket. *Address:* The Sunday Telegraph, 1 Canada Square, Canary Wharf, London, E14 5DT, England.

LAWSON, Lesley (Twiggy); British model, singer and actress; b. 19 Sept. 1949, London; d. of William Hornby and Helen Hornby (née Reeman); m. 1st Michael Whitney Armstrong 1977 (died 1988); one d.; m. 2nd Leigh Lawson 1988; ed Brondesbury and Kilburn Grammar School; model 1966–70; Man. and Dir Twiggy Enterprises Ltd 1966–; f. Twiggy & Co. 1998–; launched Twiggy skin care range 2001; own British TV series; has made several LP records; two Golden Globe Awards 1970. *Films include:* The Boy Friend 1971, W, There Goes the Bride 1979, Blues Brothers 1981, The Doctor and the Devils 1986, Club Paradise 1986, Harem Hotel, Istanbul 1988, Young Charlie Chaplin (TV) 1989, Madame Sousatzka 1989, Woundings 1998. *Plays:* Cinderella 1976, Captain Beaky 1982, My One and Only 1983–84, Blithe Spirit, Chichester 1997, Noel and Gertie, USA 1998, If Love Were All, New York 1999, Blithe Spirit, New York 2002, Play What I Wrote 2002, Mrs Warren's Profession 2003. *Television:* own musical series 1975–76; has appeared in numerous TV dramas in UK and USA; chat shows: Twiggy's People 1998, Take Time with Twiggy 2001, This Morning 2001. *Publications:* Twiggy: An Autobiography 1975, An Open Look 1985, Twiggy in Black and White 1997. *Leisure interests:* music, design. *Address:* c/o Peters Fraser & Dunlop, Drury House, 34–43 Russell Street, London, WC2B 5HA, England. *Telephone:* (20) 7344-1010. *Fax:* (20) 7836-9544. *E-mail:* postmaster@pfd.co.uk (Office).

LAWSON, Sonia, MA, RA, RWS; British artist; b. 2 June 1934, Darlington; d. of late Frederick Lawson and Muriel Metcalfe; m. Charles William Congo 1969; one d.; ed Royal Coll. of Art, London; Visiting Lecturer, Royal Acad. Schools 1985–; works in collections including Imperial War Museum, London, Arts Council of England, Sheffield Graves, Belfast Art Gallery, Leeds Univ., Middlesbrough Art Gallery, Miny Works, Royal Acad. and Royal Coll. of Art Collections, Wakefield, Carlisle, Bolton and Rochdale Galleries, Univ. of Birmingham, St Peter's Oxford, Chatsworth House, The Vatican, Rome and pvt. collections in Europe, USA, Canada and Australia; works commissioned by Imperial War Museum, BAOR 1984, Lambeth Palace and The Vatican 1989, Univ. Centre Birmingham 1994, Barclays Capital Paris 1998; Rowney Drawing Prize 1984, Eastern Arts Drawing Prize 1984, 1989, Lorne Award 1987. *Exhibitions:* solo exhbns include London 1960, 1963, 1967, 1989, 1995, 1998, 2000, Leeds 1964, 2000, Billingham/Middlesbrough 1973, Harrogate 1979, retrospective touring exhbn 1982–83, Milton Keynes 1982, Sheffield 1982, Bradford 1982, 1989, Leicester and Hull 1983, 1987, Wakefield 1988, Birmingham 1994, Halifax (retrospective) 1996, Stafford 1999, Bristol 2000; numerous group exhbns; featured artist RWS London 2001, Carlow Arts Festival, Ireland 2001, Vertigo London 2002. *Publications:* drawings for Look at it This Way! (collection of poems) by James Kirkup 1993, New Year's Eve (short story) by Fay Weldon 1995. *Address:* c/o Royal Academy of Arts, Burlington House, Piccadilly, London, W1V 0DS, England. *Telephone:* (20) 7300-5680 (Academicians' Affairs Office, Royal Acad.). *Fax:* (20) 7300-5812. *E-mail:* art@sonialawson.co.uk (Home). *Website:* www.sonialawson.co.uk (Home).

LAWSON OF BLABY, Baron (Life Peer), cr. 1992, of Newnham in the County of Northamptonshire; **Nigel Lawson,** MA, PC; British politician; b. 11 March 1932, London; s. of Ralph Lawson and Joan Lawson (née Davis); m. 1st Vanessa Salmon (divorced 1980, died 1985); m. 2nd Thérèse Mary Maclear 1980; two s. four d. (one deceased); ed Westminster School and Christ Church, Oxford; Sub Lt, RDVR 1954–56; mem. editorial staff, Financial Times 1956–60; City Ed. Sunday Telegraph 1961–63; Special Asst to Prime Minister 1963–64; Financial Times columnist and BBC broadcaster 1965; Ed. The Spectator 1966–70; regular contributor to Sunday Times and Evening Standard 1970–71, The Times 1971–72; Fellow, Nuffield Coll. Oxford 1972–73; Special Political Adviser, Conservative Party HQ 1973–74; MP for Blaby, Leics. 1974–92; Opposition Whip 1976–77; Opposition spokesman on Treasury and Econ. Affairs 1977–79; Financial Sec. to the Treasury 1979–81; Sec. of State for Energy 1981–83, Chancellor of the Exchequer 1983–89; Dir (non-exec.) Barclays Bank 1990–98; Chair. Cen. Europe Trust 1990–, CAIB Emerging Russia Fund 1997–98; Adviser BZW 1990–91; Dir (non-exec.) and Consultant Guinness Peat Aviation (GPA) 1990–93; mem. Int. Advisory Bd Creditanstalt Bankverein 1991–99, TOTAL SA 1994–99, Advisory Council Prince's Youth Business Trust 1994–2001; mem. Governing Body Westminster School 1999–; Pres. British Inst. of Energy Econs 1995–; Hon. Student Christ Church, Oxford 1996; Finance Minister of the Year, Euromoney Magazine 1988. *Publications:* The Power Game (with Jock Bruce-Gardyne) 1976, The View from No. 11: Memoirs of a Tory Radical 1992, The Nigel Lawson Diet Book (with Thérèse Lawson) 1996 and various pamphlets. *Address:* House of Lords, London, SW1A 0PW, England.

LAWZI, Ahmed Abdel Kareem al–; Jordanian politician; b. 1925, Jubeiha, nr Amman; m.; ed Teachers' Training Coll., Baghdad, Iraq; Teacher, 1950–53; Asst to Chief of Royal Protocol 1953–56; Head of Ceremonies, Ministry of Foreign Affairs 1957; mem. Parl. 1961–62, 1962–63; Asst to Chief of Royal Court 1963–64; Minister of State, Prime Minister's Office 1964–65; mem. Senate 1965, 1967; Minister of the Interior for Municipal and Rural Affairs April–Oct. 1967; Minister of Finance 1970–71; Prime Minister 1971–73; Pres. Nat. Consultative Council 1978–79; various Jordanian and foreign decorations. *Address:* c/o Ministry of Foreign Affairs, P.O. Box 35217, Amman 11180, Jordan.

LAX, Melvin, PhD; American physicist; b. 8 March 1922, New York; s. of Morris Lax and Rose Hutterer; m. Judith Heckelman 1949; two s. two d.; ed New York Univ. and Mass. Inst. of Tech.; Research Physicist MIT 1942–45, Research Assoc. 1947; Prof. of Physics, Syracuse Univ. 1947–55; Consultant Naval Research Lab. 1951–55; Lecturer in Physics Princeton Univ. 1961, Oxford Univ. 1961–62; mem. Tech. Staff Bell Labs. 1955–72, Head Theoretical Physics Dept 1962–64, Consultant 1972–; Consultant Army Research Office 1972–, Los Alamos Science Lab. 1975–; Distinguished Prof. City Coll. of New York 1971–; Ed. Advanced Series in Applied Physics 1988–; mem. Publs Tech. Cttee of Optical Soc. of America 1992–94; Charles Hayden Scholar New York Univ.; Fellow American Physical Soc.; mem. NAS 1989–92, 1995–98; Wills Lamb Medal for Laser Science 1999. *Publications:* Scattering and Radiation from Circular Cylinders and Spheres (with M. Morse, A. N Lowan and H. Feshbach) 1946, Elementary Nuclear Theory (contrib.) 1947, Fluctuations and Coherence Phenomena in Classical and Quantum Physics (in Statistical Physics, Vol. 2) 1968, Symmetry Principles in Solid State and Molecular Physics 1974 and articles in journals. *Leisure interest:* tennis. *Address:* Department of Physics, City College, 138th Street and Convent Avenue, New York, NY 10031 (Office); 12 High Street, Summit, NJ 07901, USA (Home). *Telephone:* (212) 650-6864 (Office); (201) 273-6188 (Home). *Fax:* (212) 650-6940.

LAX, Peter D., PhD; American mathematician; b. 1 May 1926, Budapest, Hungary; s. of Henry Lax and Klara Kornfeld; m. Anneli Cahn 1948 (died 1999); two s.; ed New York Univ.; with Los Alamos Scientific Lab., Manhattan Project 1945–46; Asst Prof., New York Univ. 1951, Prof. 1957–99, Prof. Emer. 1999–; Dir AEC Computing and Applied Math. Center 1964–72, Courant Inst. of Math. Sciences 1972–80, Courant Math. and Computing Lab. 1980–; Fulbright Lecturer in Germany 1958; Visiting Lecturer, Oxford Univ. 1969; Pres. American Math. Soc. 1969–71, 1978–80; mem. American Acad. of Arts and Sciences, NAS, American Philosophical Soc.; Foreign Assoc. French Acad. of Sciences, Academia Sinica, Hungarian Acad. of Sciences; mem. Nat. Science Bd 1980–86; Foreign mem. Soviet (now Russian) Acad. of Sciences 1989; 8 hon. degrees; Chauvenet Prize, Math. Asscn of America 1974, Norbert Wiener Prize, American Math. Soc. and Soc. of Industrial and Applied Math. 1975, Nat. Medal of Science 1986, Wolf Prize 1987, Steele Prize, American Math. Soc. *Publications:* papers in learned journals. *Address:* Courant Institute of Mathematics, New York University, Room 912, 251 Mercer Street, New York, NY 10012, USA. *E-mail:* lax@cims.nyu.edu (Office).

LAY, Kenneth L., MA, PhD; American business executive; b. 15 April 1942, Missouri; s. of Omer Lay and Ruth Lay; m. Linda Phillips 1982; five c.; ed Univs of Missouri and Houston; corp. economist, Exxon Co. 1965; subsequent man. positions; Pres. Continental Resources Co. (fmrly Florida Gas Co.) and Exec. Vice-Pres. Continental Group 1974–79; Pres. and COO Transco Energy Co. 1981–84; Chair. and CEO Houston Natural Gas Corpn 1984–85; Chair., COO, and CEO Enron Corpn 1985–2000; Chair. and CEO 2000–02; Dir Eli Lilly & Co. –2002, Trust Co. West, Compaq Computer Corpn; mem. Bd Trustees The John Heinz III Center for Science, Econs and the Environment, The Business Council, American Enterprise Inst.; Guggenheim Fellow; Pvt. Sector Council Leadership Award 1997, Horatio Alger Award 1998. *Publications:* articles in books and journals. *Leisure interests:* skiing, running, golf.

LAYARD, Peter Richard Grenville Layard, Baron (Life Peer), cr. 2000, of Highgate in the London Borough of Haringey, BA, MSc; British economist; b. 15 March 1934, Welwyn Garden City; s. of John Willoughby Layard and Doris Layard; m. Molly Meacher 1991; ed Cambridge Univ., London School of Econs; school teacher, London County Council 1959–61; Sr Research Officer, Robbins Cttee on Higher Educ. 1961–64; Deputy Dir Higher Educ. Research Unit, LSE 1964–74, Lecturer, LSE 1968–75, Reader 1975–80, Prof. of Econ. 1980–99, Dir Centre for Econ. Performance 1990–, Head, Centre for Labour Econ. 1974–90; Consultant, Centre for European Policy Studies, Brussels 1982–86; mem. Univ. Grants Cttee 1985–89; Chair. Employment Inst. 1987–92; Co-Chair., World Economy Group of the World Inst. for Devt Econs Research 1989–93; Econ. Adviser to Russian Govt 1991–97; Fellow Econometric Soc. *Publications:* Cost Benefit Analysis 1973, Causes of Poverty (with D. Piachaud and M. Stewart) 1978, Microeconomic Theory (with A. A. Walters) 1978, More Jobs, Less Inflation 1982, The Causes of Unemployment (Ed. with C. Greenhalgh and A. Oswald) 1984, The Rise in Unemployment (Ed. with C. Bean and S. Nickell) 1986, How to Beat Unemployment 1986, Handbook of Labor Economics (Ed. with Orley C. Ashenfelter) 1987, The Performance of the British Economy (jtly) 1988, Unemployment: Macroeconomic Performance and the Labour Market (jtly) 1991, East-West Migration: the alternatives (jtly) 1992, Post-Communist Reform: Pain and Progress 1993 (jtly), Macroeconomics: a Text for Russia 1994, The Coming Russian Boom 1996 (jtly), What Labour Can Do 1997, Tackling Unemployment 1999, Tackling Inequality 1999, What the Future Holds (Ed. with R. Cooper). *Leisure interests:* walking, tennis. *Address:* Centre for Economic Performance, London School of Economics, Houghton Street, London, WC2A 2AE (Office); 45 Cholmeley Park, London, N6 5EL, England (Home). *Telephone:* (20) 7955-7281 (Office). *Fax:* (20) 7955-7595 (Office).

LAYNE, Kingsley, BA; Saint Vincent and the Grenadines civil servant and diplomatist; b. 1949; ed Univ. of the West Indies, Univ. of British Columbia, Inst. for Applied Behavioural Sciences; economist, Ministry of Trade, Agric. and Tourism 1973–74; Sr Official, Econ. Affairs Secr., Org. of Eastern Caribbean States, St John's, Antigua 1982–86; Perm. Sec., Ministry of Trade, Agric. and Industry 1986–87, Tourism, Aviation and Culture 1987–89, Trade and Tourism 1989–90; Perm. Rep. of Saint Vincent and the Grenadines to UN, New York 1990–94; Amb. to USA 1991–2000; Perm. Rep. to OAS, Vice-Chair. –1999. *Publications:* several pubs on staff devt and man. training. *Address:* c/o Ministry of Foreign Affairs, Kingstown, Saint Vincent and the Grenadines.

LAYNIE, Tamrat; Ethiopian politician; mem. Ethiopian People's Revolutionary Democratic Front (EPRDF); Prime Minister of Ethiopia 1991–95; sentenced to 18 years' imprisonment for corruption, embezzlement and abuse of office 2000. *Address:* c/o Office of the Prime Minister, P.O. Box 1013, Addis Ababa, Ethiopia.

LAZAR, Philippe; French scientist and administrator; b. 21 April 1936, Paris; s. of Maximilien Lazar and Françoise Lazar; m. Monique Lazar 1960; one s. one d.; ed Ecole Polytechnique, Paris; researcher, Nat. Inst. of Hygiene 1960, Dir of Research INSERM (French Nat. Inst. of Health and Medical Research) 1964, Dir Environmental Health Research Unit 1977, Chair. Scientific Council 1981, Dir-Gen. INSERM 1982–96; Chair. European Medical Research Councils (EMRC) 1994–96; Chair. Bd Research Inst. for Devt (IRD) 1997–2001; with Cour des Comptes 2001–; Visiting Prof. Harvard School of Public Health 1975; Commdr, Ordre nat. du Mérite; Officier, Légion d'honneur; Chevalier, Ordre des Arts et des Lettres. *Publications:* Eléments de probabilités et statistiques 1967, Méthodes statistiques en expérimentation biologique 1974, Les explorateurs de la santé 1989, L'éthique biomédicale en question 1995, La République a-t-elle besoin de savants? 1998. *Leisure interests:* arts, literature. *Address:* Cour des Comptes, 13 rue Cambon, 75100 Paris, 01 SP France. *Telephone:* 1-42-98-54-68 (Office). *Fax:* 1-42-98-59-71 (Office). *E-mail:* plazar@ccomptes.fr (Office); philippe.lazar@wanadoo.fr (Home).

LAZARENKO, Pavel Ivanovich, DEconSc; Ukrainian politician; b. 23 Jan. 1953, Karpivka, Dniepropetrovsk Region; m. Tamara Ivanivna Lazarenko; one s. two d.; ed Dniepropetrovsk Inst. of Agric.; worked as agronomist 1972–79, Chair. of Kolkhoz 1979–84, Head Dist Dept of Agric. Man.; First Deputy Chair. Dist Exec. Cttee; Chair. Council of Agro-Industrial Complex Dniepropetrovsk Region, First Deputy Chair. Regional Exec. Cttee; People's Deputy 1990–; Rep. Pres. of Ukraine in Dniepropetrovsk Region 1992–95; concurrently Chair. Dniepropetrovsk Regional State Admin.; First Vice-Prime Minister of Ukraine 1995–96; Prime Minister of Ukraine 1996–97; mem. Verkhovna Rada 1997–; Head Gromada (political movt); charged with corruption 1999, arrested in USA 2000, charges lifted by Parl. of Ukraine 2002.

LAZAREV, Alexander Nikolayevich; Russian conductor; b. 5 July 1945; m. Tamara Lazarev; one d.; ed Leningrad and Moscow Conservatoires; conducting debut at Bolshoi Theatre 1973, conducted numerous ballets and operas of the Bolshoi Theatre's European and Russian repertoires, founder and conductor Ensemble of Soloists of the Bolshoi Theatre 1978–89, Chief Conductor, Artistic Dir, Bolshoi Theatre 1987–95; Chief Conductor Duisburg Symphony Orchestra 1988–93; has conducted numerous orchestras including Berlin Philharmonic, Munich Philharmonic, Orchestra Sinfonica del Teatro alla Scala di Milano, Orchestre Nat. de France and others; UK debut with Royal Liverpool Philharmonic Orchestra 1987; subsequently performed with the City of Birmingham Symphony Orchestra, the Royal Scottish Nat. Orchestra, etc.; Prin. Guest Conductor BBC Symphony Orchestra, 1992–95; Royal Scottish Nat. Orchestra 1994–97, Prin. Conductor 1997–; First Prize USSR Nat. Competition 1971, First Prize and Gold Medal Karajan Competition (Berlin) 1972. *Address:* c/o Tennant Artists, Unit 2, 39 Tadema Road, London, SW10 0PZ, England. *Telephone:* (20) 7376-3758 (London); (095) 203-26-36 (Moscow). *Fax:* (20) 7351-0679 (Office). *E-mail:* info@tennantartists .demon.co.uk (Office).

LAZARUS, Shelly, MBA; American advertising executive; b. 1947, New York; m. George Lazarus; ed Smith Coll, Columbia Univ.; with Clairol 1970; with Ogilvy and Mather 1971–74, 1976–, Pres. N American Operations 1994–96, CEO 1996–, CEO Ogilvy and Mather Worldwide 1997–. *Address:* Ogilvy and Mather, 1 Soldiers Field Park, Apartment 413, Boston, MA 02163-1702, USA (Office).

LAZENBY, Alec, AO, ScD, FTSE, FIBiol, FAIAST; Australian agronomist and university administrator; b. 4 March 1927, UK; s. of G. Lazenby and E. Lazenby; m. Ann J. Hayward 1957; one s. two d.; ed Univ. Coll. of Wales and Univ. of Cambridge; Scientific Officer, Welsh Plant Breeding Station 1949–53; Demonstrator, Agricultural Botany, Univ. of Cambridge 1953–58, Lecturer in Agricultural Botany 1958–65, Fellow and Asst Tutor, Fitzwilliam Coll. 1962–65; Foundation Prof. of Agronomy, Univ. of New England, NSW 1965–70, Vice-Chancellor 1970–77; Dir Grassland Research Inst. 1977–82; Visiting Prof. Reading Univ. 1978–82; Hon. Professorial Fellow, Univ. of Wales 1979–82; Vice-Chancellor, Univ. of Tasmania 1982–91; consultant in higher educ. and agricultural research and man. 1991–; Hon. Prof. (Vic. Univ. of Tech.) 1992; Hon. DRurSci (New England) 1981; Hon. LLD (Univ. of Tasmania) 1992. *Publications:* Intensive Pasture Production (jt ed.) 1972, Australian Field Crops (jt ed.), Vol I 1975, Vol. II 1979, Australia's Plant Breeding Needs 1986, The Grass Crop (jt ed.) 1988, The Story of IDP 1999, Competition and Succession in Pastures (jt ed.) 2001; papers on pasture plant breeding, agronomy and weed ecology in various scientific journals. *Leisure interests:* golf, gardening and current affairs. *Address:* IDP Education Australia, 1-5 Geils Court, Deakin, ACT 2600, Australia.

LAZIO, Rick A., AB, JD; American politician and lawyer; b. 13 March 1958, Amityville, NY; s. of Anthony Lazio and Olive E (Christensen) Lazio; ed Vassar Coll., American Univ.; called to New York Bar 1984; Asst Dist Attorney Suffolk Co. Rackets Bureau, Hauppage, NY 1983–88, Exec. Asst Dist Attorney Suffolk Co. 1987–88, Village Attorney, Village of Lindenhurst, NY 1988–93; Man. Partner Glass, Lazio and Glass, Babylon, NY 1989–93; mem. Suffolk Co. Legis. from 11th Dist, NY 1989–93, mem. House of Reps., Deputy Majority Whip, then Asst. Majority Leader 1993–2000; Cand. for Senate New York State 2000; Pres., CEO Financial Services Forum 2001–; mem. Suffolk Co. Bar Asscn. *Leisure interests:* numismatics, guitar.

LAZORTHES, Guy Aman Félix, MD, DEsSc; French doctor and academic; b. 4 July 1910, Toulouse (Haute-Garonne); s. of Léonce Lazorthes; m. 1st Paulette Lazorthes (née Lahary); three s.; m. 2nd Annick Bouvy 1986; ed Lycée et Facultés de médecine et des sciences de Toulouse, Faculté des sciences de Paris; Prof. of Anatomy, Faculty of Medicine and Pharmacy of Toulouse 1948–63, Prof. of Clinical Neurosurgery 1963–79, Doyen of the Faculty 1958–70; Pres. Société de neurochirurgie de langue française 1958; Corresp. mem. Nat. Acad. of Medicine 1960, mem. 1970; Corresp. mem. Institut de France (Acad. des sciences) 1972, mem. 1975; participated in official missions to USA 1945–46, UK 1948, Latin America 1956, 1957, 1961, 1964, 1967, 1972, 1978, Denmark 1958, Turkey 1964, Far East 1967; Grand-croix, Légion d'honneur 2003, Grand-croix, Ordre nat. du Mérite, Commdr des Palmes académiques, Officier du Mérite agricole; Dr hc (Lima, Peru), (Santiago, Chile), (Bonn, Germany), (Barcelona, Spain). *Publications include:* Le Sympathique du membre inférieur 1938, Le Sympathique des membres 1941, Le Nerf terminal 1944, Le Système neurovasculaire (Prix Chaussier, Acad. des sciences 1951) 1949, Les Hémorragies intracraniennes 1952, Le Système nerveux périphérique (3rd edn) 1981, L'Hémorragie cérébrale vue par le neurochirurgien 1956, Vascularisation et Circulation cérébrales 1961, Le Système nerveux central (3rd edn) 1983, Vascularisation et Circulation de la moelle épinière 1973, Vascularisation et Circulation de l'encéphale, Vol. 1 1975, Vol. 2 1977, Le Cerveau et l'esprit 1982, L'Ouvrage des sens, fenêtres étroites sur le réel 1986, Le Cerveau et l'ordinateur 1988, Croyance et raison 1991, L'Homme, la médecine et le médecin 1992, L'Homme, la société et la médecine 1995, Sciences humaines et sociales 1996, Les Hallucinations (Prix La Bruyère, Acad. Française 1997) 1996, L'Imagination: source d'irrationnel et d'irréel, puissance créatrice 1999, L'Histoire du cerveau: genèse, organisation, devenir 1999, Carnets d'un médecin universitaire 2001, les Hallucinés célèbres 2001; numerous contribs to publs on neurosurgery and anatomy. *Address:* Institut de France, 23 quai Conti, 75006 Paris (Office); Résidence Garonne La Belle, 5 avenue Charles Malpel, bât. A – Appt. 19, 31500 Toulouse, France (Home).

LAZUTKIN, Valentin Valentinovich, CandPhil; Russian politician and journalist; b. 10 Jan. 1945, Kraskovo, Moscow Region; m.; one s. one d.; ed Moscow State Univ., Acad. of Social Sciences Cen. Cttee CPSU; Head Div. of Press and Information Cttee of Youth Orgs 1967–73; Deputy Head, Head Dept of Int. Relations, mem. Exec. Bd, Deputy Chair. USSR State Cttee on Radio and TV 1974–91; First Deputy Chair. 1991, Deputy Chair., Dir-Gen. of Int. Relations, Russian State TV-Radio Broadcasting Co. Ostankino 1991–93; First Deputy Chair. Feb.–Dec. 1993, First Deputy Head Russian Fed. Service on TV and Radio Broadcasting, concurrently Dir-Gen. Russian State TV-Radio Broadcasting Co. Ostankino 1993–95; Head Russian Fed. Service on TV and Radio Broadcasting 1995–98; Rector Humanitarian Inst. of TV and Radio 1998–; Chair. Interstate TV Service, Union of Russia and Belarus 1998–; Deputy Head Exec. Cttee Union of Russia and Belarus 2000–; Chair. Coordinating Bd Soyuz (Union) Media Group 2001–; mem. Russia Acad. of Natural Sciences; Officier des Arts et des Lettres, Peter the Great Prize and other decorations. *Leisure interests:* history, military heraldry. *Address:* Humanitarian Institute of TV and Radio Broadcasting, Brodnikov per. 3, 109180 Moscow, Russia (Office). *Telephone:* (095) 238-49-75 (Office).

LE BLANC, Bart, PhD; Netherlands banker; b. 4 Nov. 1946, Bois-le-Duc; s. of Christian Le Blanc and Johanna Bogaerts; m. Gérardine van Lanschot; one s. two d.; ed Leiden and Tilburg Univs; Special Adviser, Prime Minister's Office, Deputy Sec. to Cabinet 1973–79; Deputy Dir-Gen. for Civil Service at Home Office 1979–80; Dir-Gen. for Budget at Treasury 1980–83; Deputy Chair. Man. Bd F. van Lanschot Bankiers NV, 's-Hertogenbosch 1983–91; Sec.-Gen. EBRD, London 1991–94, Vice-Pres., Finance 1994–98; Dir Int. Finance, Caisse des Dépôts et Consignations, Paris 1998–; Prof. of Political Economy Univ. of Tilburg 1991–; Hon. Prof. Tilburg Univ. 1991–; Kt, Order of Netherlands Lion. *Publications:* books and contribs. on econ. and fiscal policy to nat. and int. journals. *Leisure interest:* farming in France. *Address:* University of Tilburg, Warandelaan 2, P.O. Box 90153, 5000 LE Tilburg, Netherlands.

LE BLANC, Matt; American actor; m. Melissa McKnight 2003; ed Newton N. High School; trained as a carpenter; appeared in TV commercials for Levi's 501 jeans, Coca-Cola, Doritos and Heinz Ketchup (winning Gold Lion Award, Cannes Film Festival 1987), New York 1987; began formal acting training 1988. *Television includes:* (series): TV 101 (as Chuck Bender) 1988, Top of the Heap 1991, Vinnie & Bobby 1992, Red Shoe Diaries, Rebel Highway, Friends (as Joey Tribbiani) 1994–, Married...With Children; (films): Anything to Survive 1990, Reform School Girl 1994. *Films include:* Lookin' Italian 1994, Ed 1996. *Leisure interest:* landscape photography. *Address:* c/o United Talent Agency, 9560 Wilshire Boulevard, Suite 500, Beverly Hills, CA 90212, USA (Office).

LE BRIS, Raymond-François; French professor of law and university administrator; b. 18 Sept. 1935, Gouesnou; s. of François Le Bris and Bernadette Le Bris (née Lunven); m. Jacqueline Pareau 1964; one s. two d.; ed Coll. Notre-Dame-de-Bon-Secours, Brest, Univ. of Rennes; Asst Lecturer law faculty, Univ. of Rennes 1958–63, Lecturer 1963–65; Prof. Univ. of Bordeaux 1965–68; Asst Dir Institut Henry-Vizioz des Antilles-Guyanne 1966; Prof. Univ. of Bretagne Occidentale 1969, 1976–77, Pres. 1971; Dir Institut de droit et des sciences économiques, Brest 1969; Deputy Dir for higher educ. and research, Ministry of Nat. Educ. 1972, Dir-Gen. 1972–74; Dir de Cabinet of Sec. of State for Univs 1974–76; Préfet, L'Ariège 1977–79, L'Ain 1979–81, Seine-Saint-Denis 1986–90; Prof. Univ. of Paris IX – Dauphiné 1981–86; Sec.-Gen. Conseil pour l'avenir de la France 1982–86; Dir-Gen. Chambre de commerce et d'industrie de Paris 1990–95; Dir Ecole Nat. d'Admin 1995–2000; expert consultant to Tekilec Airtronic, Sociovision CoFremca, NN France, Tilder Associates; mem. Bd MIT France, Bd of Trustees, Int. Council for Educational Devt; Préfet Honoraire; Officier, Légion d'Honneur; Commdr, Ordre Nat. du Mérite; Commdr des Palmes Académiques; Grand Officier, Ordre de Castello Branco (Brazil). *Publication:* Les universités à la loupe 1986. *Leisure interest:* cross-country and marathon running. *Address:* Tekilec Airtronic, 5 rue Carle Vernet, Sèvres 92 (Office); CoFremca, 16 rue d'Athènes, 75009, Paris (Office); Tilder Associates, 57 boulevard de Montmorency, 75026, Paris; 34 rue des Vignes, 75007 Paris, France (Home). *Telephone:* 1-46-90-23-50 (Office); 1-59-70-60-00 (Office); 1-45-25-14-32 (Home). *Fax:* 1-46-90-23-92 (Office). *E-mail:* raymond-francois .lebris@temex.fr (Office).

LE BROCQUY, Louis, DLitt, LLD, HRHA, FRSA, FSIAD; Irish artist; b. 10 Nov. 1916, Dublin; s. of the late Albert le Brocquy and Sybil de Lacy Staunton; m. 1st Jean Atkinson Stoney 1938; one d.; m. 2nd Anne Madden-Simpson 1958; two s.; ed St Gerard's School, Wicklow; founder mem., Irish Exhbn of Living Art 1943; Visiting Instructor, Cen. School of Arts and Crafts, London 1947–54; Visiting Tutor, RCA, London 1955–58; mem. Irish Council of Design 1963–65; Dir Kilkenny Design Workshops 1965–77; Dir Irish Museum of Modern Art 1989–94; works in Public Collections including Albright Knox Museum, Buffalo, Carnegie Inst., Pittsburgh, Detroit Inst., Hirshhorn Museum, Washington, Kunsthaus, Zürich, Guggenheim Museum, New York, Musée Picasso, Antibes, Uffizi Gallery, Florence, Columbus Museum, Ohio, San Diego Museum, Tate Gallery, London, Fondation Maeght, Saint Paul, Hugh Lane Municipal Gallery of Modern Art, Dublin, Irish Museum of Modern Art, Dublin, Ulster Museum, Belfast, Musée d'Art Moderne de la Ville de Paris, Nat. Gallery of Ireland, Dublin; Fellow Soc. of Industrial Artists 1960; Chevalier, Légion d'honneur 1975, Officier des Arts et des Lettres 1996, Officier, Ordre de la Couronne Belge 2001; Commdr du Bontemps de Médoc et des Graves 1969; Hon. DLitt (Dublin) 1962; Hon. LLD (Univ. Coll. Dublin) 1988; Hon. PhD (Dublin City Univ.) 1999; Hon. DUniv (Queen's Univ., Belfast) 2002; Premio Acquisto, Venice Biennale 1956, elected Saoi, Aosdána (Irish affiliation of distinguished artists) 1992, Glen Dimplex Prize 1998. *Exhibitions:* museum exhbns include: Municipal Gallery of Modern Art, Dublin 1966, Ulster Museum, Belfast 1967, Fondation Maeght, 1973, Arts Council, Belfast 1976, Musée d'Art Moderne de la Ville de Paris 1976, Crawford Municipal Gallery of Modern Art, Cork, 1976, Fundación Rodríguez-Acosta, Granada 1979, New York State Museum 1981, Boston Coll. 1982, Palais des Beaux Arts, Charleroi 1982, Arts Council, Dublin 1987, Ulster Museum 1987, aegis Nat. Gallery of Victoria, Melbourne, Festival Centre, Adelaide, Museum of Contemporary Art, Brisbane 1988, Musée Picasso, Antibes 1989, Museum of Modern Art, Kamakura 1991, City Museum of Art, Osaka 1991, City Museum of Contemporary Art, Hiroshima 1991, Irish Museum of Modern Art, Dublin 1996, Château Musée de Tours 1997, Municipal Gallery of Art, Ljubljana, Slovenia 1998, Museo de Arte Contemporaneo de Oaxaca 2000, Museo Gráficas de Oaxaca 2000, Irish Museum of Modern Art 2002. *Theatre design:* Scarecrow over the Corn, Gate Theatre, Dublin 1941, Amphitryon 38, Olympia Theatre, Dublin 1942, Waiting for Godot, Gate Theatre, Dublin 1988, Lincoln Center, New York 1996, Dublin 2003. *Illustrator:* Legends of Ireland (J. J. Campbell) 1955, The Tain (trans. Kinsella) 1969, The Playboy of the Western World (Synge) 1970, The Gododdin (trans. O'Grady) 1978, Ugolino (Seamus Heaney) 1979, Dubliners (Joyce) 1986, Stirrings Still (Samuel Beckett) 1988, An Anthology for Shakespeare (Ted Hughes) 1988, Poems 1930–1989 (Samuel Beckett) 2002. *Publications:* subject of four monographs and a biog. (Louis le Brocquy – A Painter Seeing His Way, Anne Madden le Brocquy) 1993. *Address:* c/o Gimpel Fils, 30 Davies Street, London, W1Y 1LG, England. *E-mail:* info@le-brocquy .com (Home). *Website:* www.lebrocquy.com (Home).

LE BRUN, Christopher Mark, MA, DFA, RA; British artist; b. 20 Dec. 1951, Portsmouth; s. of John Le Brun, BEM and Eileen B. Le Brun (née Miles); m. Charlotte Verity 1979; two s. one d.; ed Portsmouth Southern Grammar School, Slade School of Fine Art and Chelsea School of Art; Visiting Lecturer, Brighton Polytechnic 1975–82, Slade School of Fine Art 1978–83, Wimbledon School of Art 1981–83; Prof. of Drawing RA 2000–02; mem. Advisory Cttee, Prince of Wales's Drawing Studio 2000–; Chair. Educ. Cttee RA 2000–; work in numerous public collections including Tate Gallery, London and Museum of Modern Art, New York; Trustee Tate Gallery 1990–95, Nat. Gallery 1996–2003, Dulwich Picture Gallery 2000–; major comms include Liverpool Anglican Cathedral 1996; Gulbenkian Printmakers Award 1983, DAAD Award, W Berlin 1987–88 and other prizes. *Exhibitions:* one-man exhbns Nigel Greenwood Inc., London 1980, 1982, 1985, 1989, Gillespie-Laage-Salomon, Paris 1981, Sperone Westwater, New York 1983, 1986, 1988, Fruitmarket Gallery, Edin. 1985, Arnolfini Gallery, Bristol 1985, Kunsthalle Basel 1986, DAAD Gallery, Berlin 1988, Rudolf Zwirner, Cologne 1988, Marlborough Fine Art, London 1994, 1998, 2001, Astrup Fearnley Museum of Modern Art, Oslo 1995, Fitzwilliam Museum, Cambridge 1995, Art Center, Pasadena 1992; has participated in group exhbns in UK, Europe, Japan and USA including Venice Biennale 1982, 1984, Zeitgeist Berlin 1982, Encounters Nat. Gallery, London 2000. *Publication:* Christopher Le Brun 2001. *Address:* c/o Marlborough Fine Art, 6 Albemarle Street, London, W1X 4BY, England.

Le CARRÉ, John (see Cornwell, David John Moore).

Le CLÉZIO, Jean Marie Gustave; French/British writer; b. 13 April 1940, Nice; s. of Raoul Le Clézio and Simone le Clézio; m. 1st Rosalie Piquemal 1961; one d.; m. 2nd Jemia Jean 1975; ed Lycée and Univ. de Nice; travelled in Nigeria 1948, England (studied at Bristol and London Univs), USA 1965; Chevalier des Arts et des Lettres, Légion d'Honneur; Prix Renaudot 1963, Grand Prix Paul Morand (Acad. française) 1980, Grand Prix Jean Giono 1997, Prix Prince de Monaco 1998. *Publications:* Le procès-verbal (The Interrogation) 1963, La fièvre (Fever) (short stories) 1965, Le procès 1965, Le déluge 1966, L'extase matérielle (essay) 1967, Terra amata (novel) 1967, Le livre des fuites 1969, La guerre 1970, Haï 1971, Conversations 1971, Les géants 1973, Mydriase 1973, Voyages de l'autre côté 1975, Les prophéties du Chylam Balam 1976, Mondo et autres histoires, L'inconnu sur la terre 1978, Désert 1980, Trois villes saintes 1980, La ronde et autres faits divers 1982, Journal du chercheur d'or 1985, Voyage à Rodrigues 1986, Le rêve mexicain (essay) 1988, Printemps et autres saisons 1989, Sirandanes, Suivi de Petit lexique de la langue créole et des oiseaux (jtly) 1990, Onitsha 1991, Etoile errante 1992, Diego et Frida 1993, La Quarantaine 1995, Le Poisson d'or

1997, La Fête chantée 1997, Hasard et Angoli Mala 1999, Coeur brûlé et autres romances 2000. *Address:* c/o Editions Gallimard, 5 rue Sébastien-Bottin, 75007 Paris, France.

LE COZ, Martine; French novelist; b. Sept. 1955. *Publications include:* Léo, la nuit 1997, Le chagrin du zèbre 1998, Le nègre et la Méduse 1999, Céleste (Prix Renaudot) 2001. *Address:* c/o Editions du Rocher, 6 place St-Sulpice, 75279 Paris Cedex 06, France (Office).

LE DUC ANH, Gen.; Vietnamese politician and army officer; b. 1 Dec. 1920, Thua Thien-Hue; mem. Dang Cong Sang Viet Nam (CP); led Viet Cong combat units during Viet Nam War; mem. CP Politburo, Secr.; fmr Minister of Nat. Defence; Pres. of Viet Nam 1992–97. *Address:* c/o Office of the President, Hanoi, Viet Nam.

LE FLOCH-PRIGENT, Loïk; French business executive; b. 21 Sept. 1943, Brest; s. of Gérard Le Floch and Gabrielle Julienne; m.; one s. two d.; ed Inst. Nat. Polytechnique, Grenoble and Univ. of Missouri; scientific and tech. research, D.G.R.S.T. 1969–81; Dir of Cabinet of Industry Minister, Pierre Dreyfus 1981–82; Chair. and CEO Rhône-Poulenc 1982–86, Elf Aquitaine 1989–93, SNCF 1995–96; Chair. Gaz de France 1993–95, Asscn Europe et Entreprises 1994–, Club des présidents d'université et entreprise, Ecole Nat. Supérieure de Création Industrielle 1992–95; Dir Crédit Nat. 1985–97, Compagnie Gén. des Eaux 1990–96, Banco Cen. Hispano Americano 1990–94, Pallas 1991–, Pinault Printemps Redoute 1991–, Entrepose-Montalev 1994–; imprisoned for involvement in Elf Affair (financial scandal) May 2001; Officier, Légion d'honneur, Ordre nat. du Mérite.

LE GENDRE, Bertrand; French journalist; b. 25 Feb. 1948, Neuilly-sur-Seine; s. of Bernard Le Gendre and Catherine Chassaing de Borredon; m. 1st Jacqueline de Linares 1987 (divorced 1995); one s.; m. 2nd Nadia du Luc-Baccouche 1995; one s.; ed Collège Sainte-Croix-de-Neuilly, Univ. of Paris X, Inst. d'études politiques, Paris, Inst. des hautes études de défense nationale; joined Le Monde as journalist 1974, in charge of judicial desk 1983, Reporter 1987, Ed.-in-Chief 1993–; Visiting Assoc. Prof. Univ. de Paris II 2000–; Sub-Ed. Gallimard 1986–89; Prix de la Fondation Mumm pour la presse écrite 1986. *Address:* Le Monde, 21 bis rue Claude-Bernard, 75242 Paris Cédex 05 (Office); 16 rue de la Glacière, 75013 Paris, France (Home). *Telephone:* 1-42-17-26-14 (Office). *Fax:* 1-42-17-21-22 (Office). *E-mail:* legendre@lemonde.fr (Office).

LE GOFF, Jacques Louis; French professor of history; b. 1 Jan. 1924, Toulon; s. of Jean Le Goff and Germaine Ansaldi; m. Anna Dunin-Wasowicz 1962; one s. one d.; ed Lycées, Toulon, Marseilles and Louis-le-Grand, Paris, Ecole normale supérieure, Paris; history teacher 1950; Fellow of Lincoln Coll., Oxford 1951–52; mem. Ecole française de Rome 1953–54; Asst at Univ. of Lille 1954–59; Prof., then Dir of Studies, 6th Section, Ecole des hautes études (EHE) 1960, Pres. Ecole des hautes études en sciences sociales (fmr 6th Section of EHE) 1972–77; mem. Comité nat. de la recherche scientifique 1962–70, Comité des travaux historiques 1972, Conseil supérieur de la Recherche 1985–87; Co-Dir reviews Annales-Economies, sociétés, civilisations and Ethnologie Française 1972; Pres. Univ. Scientific Research Cttee 1993–; Grand Prix Nat. 1987, Gold Medal, CNRS 1991, Grand Prix Gobert 1996, Grand Prix d'Histoire 1997. *Publications:* Les Intellectuels au Moyen Age 1957, Le Moyen Age 1962, La Civilisation de l'occident médiéval 1964, Das Hochmittelalter 1965, Pour un autre Moyen Age 1978 (English trans. Time, Work and Culture in the Middle Ages 1980), La naissance du purgatoire 1981, L'apogée de la chrétienté 1982, L'imaginaire médiéval 1985, La bourse et la vie 1986, Histoire de la France religieuse (jtly) 1988, L'Homme médiéval 1989, L'Etat et les pouvoirs 1989, History and Memory 1993, St Louis 1996, Une vie pour l'histoire 1996, L'Europe racontée aux jeunes 1996, Un autre moyen âge 1999, Saint François d'Assise 1999, Dictionnaire raisonné de l'Occident médiéval 1999, La Vieille Europe et la nôtre 2000, Le Moyen Age en images 2001. *Leisure interests:* gastronomy and swimming. *Address:* c/o Editions Gallimard, 5 rue Sébastien Bottin, 75341 Paris Cedex 07 (Office); 11 rue Monticelli, 75014 Paris, France (Home).

Le GOY, Raymond Edgar Michel, MA; British civil servant; b. 1919, London; s. of J. Goy and May Callan; m. Silvia Ernestine Burnett 1960; two s.; ed William Ellis School, London, Gonville and Caius Coll. Cambridge; British Army 1940–46; entered Civil Service 1947, Road Transport and Establishments Divs, Ministry of Transport 1947–48; UK Shipping Adviser in Japan, Far East and SE Asia 1948–52; various posts in shipping and highway divs, Ministry of Transport and Civil Aviation 1952–57; Dir Goeland Co. 1953; Asst Sec. Railways and Inland Waterways Div., Ministry of Transport and Civil Aviation 1958; Asst Sec. Finance and Supply Ground Services and Aerodrome Management, Ministry of Aviation 1959–61, Dir of Admin. Navigational Services 1961–62; Asst Sec. Aviation Overseas Policy, Ministry of Aviation and Bd of Trade 1962–67; Under-Sec. of Civil Aviation 1968–73; Head Del. to European Civil Aviation Conf.; Dir-Gen. of Transport Comm. of EEC 1973–81, of Comm. of EU 1981–. *Publication:* The Victorian Burletta 1953. *Leisure interests:* theatre, music, race relations. *Address:* c/o Fortis Banque, Agence Schuman, Rond Point Schuman 10, 1040 Brussels, Belgium.

LE GREW, Daryl John, MArch; Australian university vice-chancellor and professor of architecture; b. 17 Sept. 1945, Melbourne; s. of A. J. Le Grew; m. Josephine Le Grew 1971; one s. two d.; ed Trinity Grammar School, Kew and Univ. of Melbourne; Lecturer Dept of Town and Regional Planning, Univ. of Melbourne 1969–73, Lecturer and Sr Lecturer Dept of Architecture and Building 1973–85; Prof. of Architecture, Deakin Univ. 1986–98, Dean Faculty of Design and Tech. 1992–93, Chair. Academic Bd 1992–98, Pro-Vice-Chancellor (Academic) 1993–94, Deputy Vice-Chancellor and Vice-Pres. (Academic) 1994–98; Vice-Chancellor Univ. of Canterbury, NZ 1998–; Visiting Fellow Bartlett School of Architecture and Planning, Univ. Coll., London Univ.; consultant UK Science Research Council Training Programme; architectural consultant and Adviser to Dir and Trustees of Nat. Gallery of Victoria, Melbourne for redevt of gallery site, to Dir and Council Museum of Victoria, Melbourne for its redevt, mem. Council; several sr appointments in business and higher educ.; Life Fellow Museum of Vic. 1997. *Leisure interests:* swimming, music, poetry, philosophy. *Address:* University of Canterbury, Private Bag 4800, Christchurch 1, New Zealand.

LE GUIN, Ursula Kroeber, MA; American writer; b. 1929, Berkeley, Calif.; d. of Alfred L. Kroeber and Theodora K. Kroeber; m. Charles A. Le Guin 1953; one s. two d.; ed Radcliffe Coll., Columbia Univ.; taught French, Mercer Univ., Univ. of Ida 1954-56; teacher, resident writer or visiting lecturer at numerous univs, including Univ. of Washington, Portland State Univ., Pacific Univ., Reading Univ., Univ. of Calif. at San Diego, Indiana Writers' Conf., Kenyon Coll., etc. 1971–; Mellon Prof. Tulane Univ. 1986; mem. Science Fiction Research Asscn, Authors' League, Writers' Guild W, PEN; Fellow Columbia Univ. 1952, Fulbright Fellow 1953; Hon. DLitt (Bucknell Univ., Lawrence Univ.); Hon. DHumLitt (Lewis and Clark Coll., Occidental Coll. Emory Univ.); Gandalf Award 1979, Harold Vursell Award, American Acad. and Inst. of Arts and Letters 1991, Bumbershoot Art Award 1998, Robert Kirsch Lifetime Achievement Award 2000 and over 30 awards for individual works including Hubbub annual poetry award 1995, Asimov's Reader's award 1995, Nebula Award 1996, James Tiptree Jr Retrospective Award 1995, 1997, Locus Readers Award 1995, 1996. *Publications include:* (novels) Rocannon's World 1966, Planet of Exile 1966, City of Illusion 1968, A Wizard of Earthsea 1968, The Left Hand of Darkness (Nebula Award, Hugo Award) 1969, The Tombs of Atuan 1970, The Lathe of Heaven 1971, The Farthest Shore (Nat. Book Award) 1972, The Dispossessed (Hugo Award) 1974, The Word for World is Forest 1976, Malafrena 1979, The Beginning Place 1980, The Eye of the Heron 1983, Always Coming Home (Kafka Award 1986) 1985, Tehanu 1990, The Telling 2000, The Other Wind 2001; (collections of stories) The Wind's Twelve Quarters 1975, Orsinian Tales 1977, The Compass Rose 1982, Buffalo Gals 1987, Searoad 1991, A Fisherman of the Inland Sea 1994, Four Ways to Forgiveness 1995, Unlocking the Air 1996, Tales from Earthsea 2001; (poetry and trans.) Wild Angels 1974, Hard Words 1981, In the Red Zone (with Henk Pander) 1983, Wild Oats and Fireweed 1988, The Twins, The Dream (with Diana Bellessi) 1997, Lao Tzu: Tao Te Ching: A Book about the Way and the Power of the Way 1997, Sixty Odd 1999; (criticism) Dancing at the Edge of the World 1989, The Language of the Night (review) 1992, Steering the Craft 1998; (for children) A Visit from Dr. Katz 1988, Solomon Leviathan 1988, Catwings 1988, Catwings Return 1989, Fire and Stone 1989, Fish Soup 1992, Wonderful Alexander and the Catwings 1994, Jane on her Own 1999, Tom Mouse 2001; (anthologies ed.) Nebula Award Stories XI 1977, Interfaces 1980, Edges 1980, The Norton Book of Science Fiction (with Brian Attebery and Karen Fowler) 1993; (screenplay) King Dog 1985. *Address:* c/o Virginia Kidd Agency, Box 278, Milford, PA 18337; c/o Bill Contardi, William Morris Agency, 1350 Avenue of the Americas, New York, NY 10019, USA. *Telephone:* (570) 296-6205 (Kidd Agency).

LE JINGYI; Chinese swimmer; b. March 1975, Shanghai; entered Chinese Women's Swimming Team 1991; fmr world record-holder at 50m and 100m freestyle; broke Olympic record for women's 100m freestyle and won gold medal at 26th Olympics, Atlanta 1996. *Address:* c/o State General Bureau for Physical Culture and Sports, 9 Tiyuguan Road, Chongwen District, Beijing, People's Republic of China.

LE KHA PHIEU, Gen.; Vietnamese army officer and politician; fmrly Chief of Army Political Dept; Sec.-Gen. CP of Viet Nam 1997–2001; mem. Politburo, Politburo Standing Bd. *Address:* Communist Party of Viet Nam, 1 Hoang Van Thu, Hanoi, Viet Nam.

LE PEN, Jean-Marie, LenD; French politician; b. 20 June 1928, La Trinité-sur-Mer, Morbihan; s. of Jean Le Pen and Anne-Marie Hervé; m. 1st Pierrette Lalanne, 1960 (divorced); three d.; m. 2nd Jeanne-Marie Paschos 1991; ed Coll. des Jésuites Saint-François-Xavier, Vannes, Lycée de Lorient, Univ. de Paris; Pres. Corpn des étudiants en droit de Paris 1949–51; Sub-Lt 1st foreign Bn of paratroopers, Indochina 1954–55; Political Ed. Caravelle 1955, Nat. Del. for Union de défense de la jeunesse française, then Deputy 1st Sector, La Seine; mem. Groupe d'union et de fraternité at Nat. Ass., independent Deputy for la Seine 1958–62; Gen. Sec. Front Nat. Combattant 1956, of Tixier Vignacour Cttee 1964–65; Dir Soc. d'études et relations publiques 1963–; Pres. Front Nat. 1972–, Front Nat. Provence-Alpes-Côte d'Azur 1992–2000; mem. Nat. Ass. 1986–88; MEP 1984–2000, Pres. groupe des droites européennes 1984–2000; Presidential cand. 1988, 2002; guilty of physical assault and banned from holding or seeking public office for 2 years, given 3 month suspended prison sentence April 1998; sentence on appeal: immunity removed by European Parl. Oct. 1998; Croix de la Valeur militaire. *Publications:* Les Français d'abord 1984, La France est de retour 1985, L'Espoir 1986, J'ai vu juste 1998. *Address:* Serp, 6 rue de Beaune, 75007 Paris (Office); 8 parc de Montretout, 92210 St-Cloud, France (Home).

LE PENSEC, Louis; French politician; b. 8 Jan. 1937, Mellac; s. of Jean Le Pensec and Marie-Anne Hervé; m. Colette Le Guilcher 1963; one s.; Personnel Officer, Société nationale d'étude et de construction de moteurs d'aviation 1963–66, Société anonyme de véhicules industriels et d'équipements mécaniques 1966–69; Teacher of Personnel Man., Legal Sciences Teaching and Research Unit, Univ. of Rennes 1970–73; Mayor of Mellac 1971–97; Deputy (Finistère) to Nat. Ass. 1973–81, 1983–88, 1993; Councillor for Finistère 1976–, Senator 1998–; mem. Steering Cttee, Parti Socialiste 1977, Exec. Bureau 1979; Minister for the Sea 1981–83, 1988, of Overseas Depts. and Territories 1988–93; Govt Spokesperson 1989–91; Vice-Pres. for Europe, Council of European Communities 1983–; Minister of Agric. and Fisheries 1997–98; Vice-Pres. County Council (Finistère) 1998–; Head ASEAN Mission for External Trade; mem. Senate Del. for EU 1999–; Commdr du Mérite maritime, du Mérite agricole, Order du Mérite (Côte d'Ivoire), Grand-croix du Royaume (Thailand). *Publication:* Ministre à Babord. *Leisure interest:* golf. *Address:* Hôtel du departement, 32 quai Dupleix, 29196 Quimper Cédex; Sénat, 75291 Paris (Office); Kerviguennou, 29300 Mellac, France (Home). *Telephone:* (2) 98-76-90-24 (Office); (2) 98-35-08-00 (Home). *Fax:* (2) 98-76-91-96 (Office); (2) 98-35-08-09 (Home). *E-mail:* louis.le-pensec@wanadoo.fr (Office).

LE PICHON, Xavier; French geologist; b. 18 June 1937, Quinhon, Viet Nam; s. of Jean-Louis Le Pichon and Hélène Tyl; m. Brigitte Barthélemy 1962; five c.; Research Asst Columbia Univ., New York 1963; Scientific Adviser, Centre Nat. pour l'Exploitation des Océans 1968, 1973; Head, Dept of Oceanography, Centre Océanologique de Bretagne, Brest 1969; Prof. Univ. P. & M. Curie, Paris 1978; Dir Dept of Geology, Ecole Normale Supérieure, Paris 1984–91, Dir Lab. of Geology 1984–2000; Prof. Collège de France (Chair. of Geodynamics) 1987–; Pres. Ifremer Scientific Council 1991–2000, Sr Jury Inst. Universitaire de France 1997; Visiting Prof. Oxford Univ. 1994, Univ. of Tokyo 1995, Rice Univ. Houston 2002; mem. Acad. des Sciences; Founder mem. Acad. Europaea 1988, NAS, USA 1995; Chevalier Légion d'Honneur, Commdr Ordre Nat. du Mérite; Dr hc (Dalhousie Univ.) 1989, (ETH, Zürich) 1992; Maurice Ewing Medal, American Geophysical Union 1984, Huntsman Award (Canada) 1987, Japan Prize 1990, Wollaston Medal (Geological Soc. of London) 1991, Baltzan Prize 2002. *Publications:* Plate Tectonics (with others) 1973, Expédition Famous, à 3000m sous l'Atlantique (with C. Riffaud) 1976, Kaiko, voyage aux extrémités de la mer 1986, Aux racines de l'homme, De la Mort à l'Amour 1997, La Mort, Desclée de Brouwer 1999. *Address:* Département de Géologie, Ecole Normale Supérieure, 24 rue Lhomond, 75005 Paris Cedex 05, France. *Telephone:* 1-44-32-22-50. *Fax:* 1-44-32-22-52. *E-mail:* lepichon@geologie.ens.fr. *Website:* www.geologie.ens.fr (Office).

LE PORS, Anicet; French politician, economist and jurist; b. 28 April 1931, Paris; s. of François Le Pors and Gabrielle Croguennec; m. Claudine Carteret 1959; one s. two d.; ed Collège Arago, Paris, Ecole de la Météorologie, Univ. of Paris, Centre d'étude des programmes économiques; Meteorological Eng, Marrakesh, Morocco 1953, Paris 1957–65; trade union official (CGT) 1955–77; Consultant, World Meteorological Org., Léopoldville, Congo (now Kinshasa, Democratic Repub. of Congo) 1960; Sec. Communist section of Met. Office 1962; Head of Dept, Ministry of Economy and Finance 1965; Sec. Cttee of Cen. Admin., Parti Communiste Français (PCF) 1976–77, Head of Nationalizations, Industrial Policy and Insts Dept, then of Int. Dept, PCF 1978, mem. Cen. Cttee 1979; Head of Interministerial Comm., Univ. of Paris XIII 1976–77 and Ecole supérieure des Sciences Economiques et Commerciales 1978; Senator (Hauts-de-Seine) 1977–81; Minister-Del. for the Civil Service and Admin. Reforms, attached to Prime Minister 1981–83; Sec. of State in charge of Public and Admin. Reform 1983–84; Sr mem. Council of State 1985–; mem. Higher Council for Integration; Councillor-Gen. from Hauts-de-Seine 1985–98; Vice-Pres. Nat. Council of Tourism 2000–; Chair. programme nouveaux services-emplois jeunes, Cttee de pilotage pour l'égal accès des femmes et des hommes, Comm. de parcours des réfugiés 2000–; Officier, Légion d'honneur; Officier, Ordre Nat. du Mérite. *Publications:* Les transferts Etats-industries en France et dans les pays occidentaux 1976, Les béquilles du capital 1977, Marianne à l'encan 1980, Contradictions 1984, L'état efficace 1985, Pendant la mue, le serpent est aveugle 1993, Le Nouvel Age de la citoyenneté 1997, La Citoyenneté 1999, Eloge de l'échec 2001. *Leisure interests:* swimming, sailing. *Address:* Conseil d'Etat, place du Palais-Royal, 75001 Paris (Office); 189 boulevard de la République, 92210 St-Cloud, France (Home). *E-mail:* anicetlp@club-internet.fr (Office).

LE PORTZ, Yves; French financial executive; b. 30 Aug. 1920, Hennebont; s. of Joseph Le Portz and Yvonne Le Doussal; m. Bernadette Champetier de Ribes 1946; five c.; ed Univ. de Paris à la Sorbonne, Ecole des Hautes Etudes Commerciales and Ecole Libre des Sciences Politiques; attached to Gen. Inspectorate of Finances 1943, Dir Adjoint du Cabinet, Président du Conseil 1948–49, Sous-Dir, Chef de Service, Ministry of Finance and Econ. Affairs 1951; Chief of Staff to Sec. of State for Finance and Econ. Affairs 1951–52; Chief of Staff to Minister for Posts, Telegraphs and Telephones 1952–55; Chief of Staff to Minister for Reconstruction and Housing 1955–57; French Del. to Econ. and Social Council of UN 1957–58; Dir-Gen. of Finance for Algeria 1958–62; Dir-Gen. Bank for Devt of Algeria 1959–62; Vice-Pres. and Vice-Chair. Bd Dirs European Investment Bank (EIB) 1962–70, Pres. and Chair. 1970–84, Hon. Pres. 1984; Pres. Supervisory Cttee, Bourse (Stock Exchange) Aug. 1984–88; Pres. Supervisory Cttee Investment Cos and Funds, Principality of Monaco 1988–; Insp.-Gen. of Finances 1971–84; Pres. Cttee de déontologie des commissaires aux comptes 1999–; Commdr, Légion d'honneur 1978, Grand Officier, Ordre nat. de Mérite. *Address:* 127 avenue de Wagram, 75017 Paris, France (Home). *Telephone:* 1-42-27-76-88.

LE RIVEREND, Julio; Cuban historian and philosopher; b. 4 Jan. 1959, Santiago de Cuba; s. of Ibis Le Riverend and Elíades Le Riverend; m. Marcia Medina Cruzata 1992; three c.; ed Rostov del Don Univ., Russia; fmr adviser Banco Nacional; Deputy Minister of Educ. and Amb. of Cuba to UNESCO 1973–76; fmr Vice-Pres. Acad. of Sciences and Pres. and Cultural Dir of Ateneo, Santiago de Cuba; fmr. Dir Biblioteca Nacional José Martí de Habana. *Publications:* works on Cuban economic history and the sugar cane industry, articles on cultural devt, problems of post modernity and social sciences: 1898–1998, Cien respuestas para un siglo de dudas 1998, El 98: La guerra que no cesa 1999. *Leisure interests:* literature, cinema. *Address:* Edificio Alamar No. 20, Apto. 19, Zona 1 Alamar, Havana, Cuba.

LE ROY LADURIE, Emmanuel, DèsSc; French historian; b. 19 July 1929, Les Moutiers en Cinglais; s. of Jacques Le Roy Ladurie and Léontine Dauger; m. Madeleine Pupponi 1956; one s. one d.; ed ed. Ecole Normale Supérieure; taught Lycée de Montpellier 1955–57; research attaché, CNRS 1957–60; Asst Faculté des Letters, Montpellier 1960–63; Asst lecturer, Dir of Studies Ecole des Hautes Etudes 1963; lecturer, the Sorbonne 1970–71, University of Paris VII 1971–73; Prof. of History of modern Civilization, Collège de France 1973–; Gen. Admin. Bibliothèque Nat. 1987–94, Pres. Scientific Council 1994–; mem. Conseil scientifique de l'Ecole Normale Supérieure 1998–; mem. Acad. des Sciences morales et politiques; Foreign Hon. mem. Acad. des Sciences américaines 1984; Commdr Légion d'honneur, Ordre des Arts et Lettres; 15 hon. degrees; Medal of Center for French Civilization and Culture, New York Univ. 1985. *Publications include:* Les paysans de Languedoc 1966, Histoire du climat depuis l'an mil 1967, Le territoire de l'historien Vol. I 1973, Vol. II 1978, Montaillou, village occitan de 1294 à 1324 1975, Le carnaval de Romans 1579–80 1980, L'argent, l'amour et la mort en pays d'oc 1980, Histoire de la France urbaine, Vol. III 1981, Paris-Montpellier PC-PSU 1945-1963 1982, La Sorcière de Jasmin 1983, Parmi les historiens 1983, The French Peasantry 1450–1680, Pierre Prion, scribe 1987, Monarchies 1987, L'Histoire de France de: L'Etat Royal 1460–1610 (jtly) 1987, L'Ancien Régime 1610–1770 (jtly) 1991, The Royal French State 1460–1610 1994, Le Siècle des Plaeter (1499–1628) 1995, The Ancien Régime: A History of France 1610–1774 1996, Mémoires 1902–1945 1997, L'Historien, le chiffre et le texte 1997, Saint-Simon, le système de la Cour 1997, Le Voyage de Thomas Plalter 2000, Histoire de France des Régions 2001, Histoire des paysans français de la Peste Noire à la Revolution 2002. *Leisure interests:* cycling, swimming. *Address:* Collège de France, 11 Place Marcelin-Berthelot, 75005 Paris; 88 rue d'Alleray, 75015 Paris, France (Home). *Telephone:* 1-44-27-10-38 (Office); 1-48-42-01-27. *Fax:* 1-44-27-12-40 (Office). *E-mail:* e.m.ladurie@wanadoo.fr (Home).

LEA, Ruth Jane, BA, MSc, FRSA, FSS; British economist; b. 22 Sept. 1947; d. of Thomas Lea and of the late Jane Lea (née Brown); ed Lymm Grammar School, Univs of York and Bristol; Asst statistician, Sr Econ. Asst HM Treasury 1970–73, statistician 1977–78; Lecturer in Econs Thames Polytechnic 1973–74; statistician Civil Service Coll. 1974–77, Cen. Statistics Office 1978–84; briefing and policy posts Dept of Trade and Industry 1984–88; with Mitsubishi Bank 1988–93, Chief Economist 1990–93; Chief UK Economist Lehman Brothers 1993–94; Econs Ed. Ind. TV News 1994–95; Head of Policy Unit Inst. of Dirs 1995–; mem. Retail Prices Advisory Cttee 1992–94, Nat. Consumer Council 1993–96, Rowntree Foundation Income and Wealth Inquiry Group 1993–94, Nurses' Pay Review Body 1994–98, Research Centres Bd ESRC 1996, Research Priorities Bd 1996–97, Statistics Advisory Cttee Office of Nat. Statistics 1996–97; Trustee, New Europe Research Trust 1999–; Council mem. Univ. of London 2001–; Hon. DBA (Greenwich) 1997. *Publications:* various publs for the Inst. of Dirs on business and econ. topics. *Leisure interests:* music (singing), philately, cat worship. *Address:* Policy Unit, The Institute of Directors, 116 Pall Mall, London, SW1Y 5ED (Office); 25 Redbourne Avenue, Finchley, London, N3 2BP, England (Home). *Telephone:* (20) 7451-3291 (Office); (20) 8346-3482 (Home). *Fax:* (20) 7839-2337 (Office); (20) 8346-0288 (Home).

LEACH, Adm. of the Fleet Sir Henry (Conyers), GCB, DL; British naval officer; b. 18 Nov. 1923; s. of Capt. John Catterall Leach and Evelyn Burrell Lee; m. Mary Jean McCall 1958 (died 1991); two d.; ed St Peter's Court, Broadstairs, Royal Naval Coll., Dartmouth; served cruiser Mauritius, S Atlantic and Indian Ocean 1941–42; battleship Duke of York (involved in Scharnhorst action) 1943–45, destroyers, Mediterranean 1945–46, gunnery 1947; gunnery appointments 1948–51; Gunnery Officer, cruiser Newcastle, Far East 1953–55; staff appointments 1955–59; commanded destroyer Dunkirk 1959–61; frigate Galatea (Capt. 27th Squadron and Mediterranean) 1965–67; Dir of Naval Plans 1968–70; commanded Commando Ship Albion 1970; Asst Chief of Naval Staff (Policy) 1971–73; Flag Officer First Flotilla 1974–75; Vice-Chief of Defence Staff 1976–77; C-in-C Fleet and Allied C-in-C, Channel and Eastern Atlantic 1977–79; Chief of Naval Staff and First Sea Lord 1979–82; First and Prin. Naval ADC to the Queen 1979–82; Pres. RN Benevolent Soc., Sea Cadet Asscn 1984–93; Pres. Royal Bath & West of England Soc. 1993, Vice-Pres. 1994–; Chair. St Dunstan's 1983–98, Hon. Vice-Pres. 1999–; Chair. Council, King Edward VII Hosp. 1987–98, Hon. Vice-Pres. 1998–; Gov. Cranleigh School 1983–93, St Catherine's 1987–93; Patron Meridian Trust Asscn, Hampshire Royal British Legion 1994–; Hon. Freeman Merchant Taylors, Shipwrights, City of London. *Publication:* Endure No

Makeshifts (autobiog.) 1993. *Leisure interests:* fishing, shooting, gardening, antique furniture repair. *Address:* Wonston Lea, Wonston, Winchester, Hants., SO21 3LS, England.

LEAF, Alexander, MD; American physician; b. 10 April 1920, Yokohama, Japan; s. of Dr Aaron L. Leaf and Dora Hural Leaf; m. Barbara L. Kincaid 1943; three d.; ed Univs of Washington and Michigan; Intern, Mass. Gen. Hosp. 1943–44, mem. staff 1949–, Physician-in-Chief 1966–81, Physician 1981–; Resident, Mayo Foundation, Rochester, Minn. 1944–45; Research Fellow, Univ. of Mich. 1947–49; mem. Faculty, Medical School, Harvard Univ. 1949–, Jackson Prof. of Clinical Medicine 1966–81, Ridley Watts Prof. of Preventive Medicine 1980–90, Jackson Prof. of Clinical Medicine Emer., 1990–; Visiting Fellow, Balliol Coll., Oxford 1971–72; Distinguished Physician, Brockton/West Roxbury Medical Center, Va 1992–97; mem. NAS, AAAS, American Acad. of Arts and Sciences, American Coll. of Physicians, The Biochemical Soc. (UK), Inst. of Medicine 1978 etc.; Kober Medal, Asscn of American Physicians 1995, A. M. Richards Award, Int. Soc. of Nephrology 1997. *Publications:* 300 articles in professional journals; Significance of the Body Fluids in Clinical Medicine, Youth in Old Age, Renal Pathophysiology. *Leisure interests:* music (flautist), jogging. *Address:* Massachusetts General Hospital, East 149, 13th Street, Charlestown, MA 02129 (Office); 5 Sussex Road, Winchester, MA 01890-3846, USA (Home). *Telephone:* (617) 726-5089 (Office); (781) 729-5852 (Home). *Fax:* (617) 726-6144 (Office). *E-mail:* aleaf@partners.org (Office).

LEAHY, Sir John H. G., KCMG, MA; British diplomatist (retd); b. 7 Feb. 1928, Worthing, Sussex; s. of the late William H. G. Leahy and Ethel Leahy; m. Elizabeth Anne Pitchford 1954; two s. two d.; ed Tonbridge School, Clare Coll. Cambridge, Yale Univ., USA; joined diplomatic service 1951, Third Sec., Singapore 1955–57; Second Sec., then First Sec., Paris 1958–62; First Sec., Tehran 1965–68; Counsellor, Paris 1973–75; attached to Northern Ireland Office, Belfast 1975–76; Amb. to South Africa 1979–82; Deputy Under-Sec. (Africa and the Middle East), FCO 1982–84; High Commr to Australia 1984–88; Dir Observer newspaper 1989–92; Dir (non-exec.) Lonrho PLC 1993–98, Chair. 1994–97; Master, Skinners' Co. 1993–94; Chair. Britain-Australia Soc. 1994–97; mem. Franco-British Council (Chair. 1989–93); Chair. Govs' Cttee Tonbridge School 1994–99; Pro-Chancellor City Univ. 1991–97; Hon. DCL (City Univ.) 1997; Officier, Légion d'honneur. *Address:* 16 Ripley Chase, The Goffs, Eastbourne, E Sussex, BN21 1HB, England. *Telephone:* (1323) 725368. *Fax:* (1323) 720437. *E-mail:* johnleahy@mistral.co.uk.

LEAHY, Patrick Joseph, JD; American politician and lawyer; b. 31 March 1940, Montpelier, Vt; s. of Howard Leahy and Alba Leahy (née Zambon); m. Marcelle Pomerleau 1962; two s. one d.; ed St Michael's Coll., Winooski, Vt and Georgetown Univ. Law Center, Washington, DC; admitted to practise law, State of Vermont 1964, US Supreme Court, Second Circuit Court of Appeals, New York, US Fed. Dist Court of Vt; Senator from Vermont 1975–; Vice-Chair. Senate Intelligence Cttee 1985–86; Chair. Judiciary Cttee 2001; mem. Vt Bar Asscn 1964–; Vice-Pres. Nat. Dist Attorneys' Asscn 1971–74; Distinguished Service Award of Nat. Dist Attorneys' Asscn 1974. *Leisure interests:* photography, reading, hiking, cross-country skiing. *Address:* US Senate, 433 Russell Senate Office Building, Washington, DC 20510, USA (Office).

LEAHY, Sir Terence Patrick, Kt, BSc; British business executive; b. 28 Feb. 1956, Liverpool; m. Alison Leahy; two s. one d.; ed St. Edward's Coll., Liverpool, Univ. of Manchester Inst. of Science and Tech.; Marketing Dir Tesco PLC 1992–95, Deputy Man. Dir 1995–97, Chief Exec. 1997–. *Leisure interests:* sport, reading, theatre, architecture. *Address:* Tesco PLC, Tesco House, P.O. Box 18, Delamare Road, Cheshunt, Herts., EN8 9SL, England (Office). *Telephone:* (1992) 632222 (Office). *Fax:* (1992) 644962 (Office). *E-mail:* terry.leahy@tesco.com (Office).

LEAKEY, Richard Erskine Frere, FRAI; Kenyan palaeontologist and conservationist; b. 19 Dec. 1944, Nairobi; s. of the late Louis Leakey and Mary Leakey ; m. Meave Gillian Epps 1970; three d.; ed the Duke of York School, Nairobi; trapper of primates for research 1961–65; co-leader of research expeditions to Lake Natron 1963–64, Omo River 1967; Dir Root & Leakey Safaris (tour co.) 1965–68; archaeological excavation, Lake Baringo 1966; Admin. Dir Nat. Museums of Kenya 1968–74, Dir and Chief Exec. 1974–89; research in Nakali/Suguta Valley 1978; leader of research projects, Koobi Fora 1979–81, W Turkana 1981–82, 1984–89, Buluk 1983; Dir Wildlife Conservation and Man. Dept 1989–90; Dir Kenya Wildlife Service 1990–94, 1998–99; Man. Dir Richard Leakey & Assocs Ltd 1994–98; nominated MP Nat. Ass. –1999; Perm. Sec., Sec. to the Cabinet, Head of the Public Service, Office of the Pres., Rep. of Kenya 1999–2001; numerous hon. positions including Chair. Wildlife Clubs of Kenya 1969–80 (Trustee 1980–), Foundation for Research into the Origins of Man (USA) 1971–85, Kenya Nat. Cttee of the United World Colls 1982–, E African Wildlife Soc. 1984–89, SAIDIA 1989–; Chair. Bd of Trustees, Nat. Museums of Kenya 1989–94; Co-Founder, Gen.-Sec. Safina Party 1995–98; Life Trustee L. S. B. Leakey Foundation; Trustee Nat. Fund for Disabled in Kenya 1980–95, Agricultural Research Foundation, Kenya 1986–; has given more than 750 public and scholarly Lectures; Foreign Hon. mem. American Acad. of Arts and Sciences 1998; Order of the Burning Spear, Kenya 1993; nine hon. degrees; numerous awards and honours including James Smithsonian Medal, USA 1990, Gold Medal, Royal Geographical Soc., UK 1990, World Ecology Medal, Int. Centre for Tropical Ecology, USA 1997. *Television documentaries:* Bones of Contention, Survival Anglia 1975, The Making of Mankind, BBC 1981, Earth Journal (presenter), NBC 1992. *Publications:* numerous articles on finds in the field of palaeontology in scientific journals, including Nature, Journal of World History, Science, American Journal of Physical Anthropology, etc.; contrib. to General History of Africa (Vol. I), Perspective on Human Evolution and Fossil Vertebrates of Africa; Origins (book, with R. Lewin) 1977, People of the Lake: Man, His Origins, Nature and Future (book, with R. Lewin) 1978, The Making of Mankind 1981, Human Origins 1982, One Life 1983, Origins Reconsidered (with R. Lewin) 1992, Origins of Humankind (with R. Lewin) 1995, The Sixth Extinction (with R. Lewin) 1995, Wildlife Wars (with V. Morrell) 2001. *Leisure interests:* sailing and cooking. *Address:* P.O. Box 24926, Nairobi, Kenya (Home). *Telephone:* (2) 710949 (Office). *Fax:* (2) 710955 (Office). *E-mail:* leakey@skyweb.co.ke (Home).

LEALOFI IV, Chief Tupua Tamasese; Samoan politician and doctor; b. 8 May 1922, Apia; m. Lita 1953; five c.; ed Fiji School of Medicine and postgraduate studies at Suva; medical practitioner 1945–69; succeeded to Paramount Chief (Tama-a-Aiga) of Tupua Tamasese 1965; mem. Council of Deputies 1968–69; mem. Legis. Ass. 1970; Prime Minister of Western Samoa 1970–73, 1975–76; Minister of Internal and External Dist Affairs, Labour and Audit, Police and Prisons 1975–76. *Leisure interests:* reading, golf. *Address:* Legislative Assembly, Apia, Samoa.

LEAR, Evelyn; American soprano; b. 8 Jan. 1926, Brooklyn, New York; d. of Nina Quartin; m. 2nd Thomas Stewart (q.v.); one s. one d. by previous marriage; ed New York Univ., Hunter Coll., Juilliard School, Lincoln Teachers Coll.; Fulbright Scholarship for study in Germany 1957; joined Berlin Opera, début in Ariadne auf Naxos 1959; début in UK in Four Last Songs with London Symphony Orchestra 1957; début at Metropolitan Opera in Mourning Becomes Electra 1967; début at La Scala, Milan, in Wozzeck 1971; regular performances with leading opera cos and orchestras in Europe and USA; guest appearances with Berlin Opera and Vienna State Opera; soloist with the leading American orchestras including New York Philharmonic, Chicago Symphony, Philadelphia Orchestra, Boston Symphony, San Francisco Symphony and Los Angeles Philharmonic; has given many recitals and orchestral concerts and operatic performances with Thomas Stewart; Concert Artists Guild Award 1955, Grammy Award for Best Operatic Performance 1965. *Film:* Buffalo Bill 1976. *Major roles include:* Marie in Wozzeck, Marschallin in Der Rosenkavalier, Countess in The Marriage of Figaro, Fiordiligi in Così fan tutte, Desdemona, Mimi, Dido in The Trojans, Donna Elvira in Don Giovanni, Marina in Boris Godunov, Tatiana in Eugene Onegin, Lavinia in Mourning Becomes Electra, title role in Lulu. *Recordings include:* Wozzeck, Lulu, The Flying Dutchman, The Magic Flute, Boris Godunov, Eugene Onegin, Bach's St John Passion, Pergolesi's Stabat Mater, Der Rosenkavalier. *Leisure interests:* reading, teaching, golf. *Address:* 414 Sailboat Circle, Lauderdale, FL 33326; 15101 Rosecroft Road, Rockville, MD 20853, USA (Home).

LEATHER, Sir Edwin Hartley Cameron, LLD, KCMG, KCVO; British/Canadian politician and administrator; b. 22 May 1919, Toronto, Canada; s. of Harold H. Leather and Grace C. Leather; m. Sheila A. A. Greenlees 1940 (died 1994); two d.; ed Trinity Coll. School, Royal Mil. Coll., Kingston, Canada; MP for N Somerset 1950–64; mem. Exec. Cttee British Commonwealth Producers' Asscn 1960–63, British Caribbean Asscn; Chair. Horder Centres for Arthritics 1962–65, Nat. Union of Conservative and Unionist Asscns 1970–71; Canadian Rep. Exec. Cttee, British Commonwealth Ex-servicemen's League 1954–63; Chair. Bath Festivals Soc. 1960–65; with Yehudi Menuhin School and Orchestra 1965–, mem. Bd of Dirs 1967–, Deputy Chair. 1967–73; Gov. of Bermuda 1973–77; Chair. United World Colls Cttee of Bermuda; Nat. Gov. Shaw Festival of Canada 1990–; Trustee Canadian Gurkha Welfare Asscn 1990–, Menuhin Foundation of Bermuda 1975–; Dir N. M. Rothschild (Bermuda) and other cos; founder Bermuda Festival; Past Grand Warden, Grand Lodge of England, Past Grand Registrar, Grand Lodge of Canada (Ont.); KStJ 1974; Hon. Fellow, Royal Soc. of Arts 1968; Hon. Bachelor of Mil. Science (Royal Mil. Coll. of Canada) 1974; Hon. LLD (Bath) 1975, (McMaster Univ., Canada); Nat. Inst. Social Sciences New York Gold Medal 1977. *Radio includes:* mem. BBC Any Questions team 1948–73. *Publications:* The Vienna Elephant, The Mozart Score, The Duveen Letter. *Leisure interests:* music, travel, reading. *Address:* 23 Inwood Drive, Paget, Bermuda. *Telephone:* (441) 236-0240. *Fax:* (441) 236-5534 (Home).

LÉAUD, Jean-Pierre; French actor; b. 5 May 1944, Paris; s. of Pierre Léaud and Jacqueline Pierreux; début as Antoine Doinel in Truffaut's The 400 Blows 1959, first of a series of Doinel films directed by Truffaut over 20 years. *Films include:* The 400 Blows 1959, La Chinoise, Weekend, Stolen Kisses, Le Gai Savoir, Last Tango in Paris, Masculin Féminin, Love on the Run 1978, Detective 1984, Virgin 1987, The Color of the Wind, Femme de Papier, Bunker Palace Hotel, I Hired a Contract Killer 1991, Paris at Dawn, The Birth of Love, Nobody Loves Me, The Seducer's Diary, A Hundred and One Nights, Irma Vep, Mon Homme, Pour Rire!, Elizabeth.

LEAVER, Sir Christopher, GBE, KStJ, JP; British business executive; b. 3 Nov. 1937, London; s. of Dr Robert Leaver and Audrey Kerpen; m. Helen Mireille Molyneux Benton 1975; one s. two d.; ed Eastbourne Coll.; commissioned Royal Army Ordnance Corps 1956–58; mem. Retail Food Trades Wages Council 1963–64; JP, Inner London 1970–83, City 1974–93; mem. Council, Royal Borough of Kensington and Chelsea 1970–73; Court of

Common Council (Ward of Dowgate), City of London 1973, Sheriff, City of London 1979–80; Lord Mayor of London 1981–82; Chair. London Tourist Bd Ltd 1983–89; Deputy Chair. Thames Water PLC 1989–93, Chair. 1993–94, Vice-Chair. 1994–2000; Bd of Brixton Prison 1975–78; Adviser to Sec. of State on Royal Parks 1993–96; Bd of Govs, City Univ. 1978–; Gov. Christ's Hospital School 1975, City of London Girls' School 1975–78; Chair. Young Musicians' Symphony Orchestra Trust 1979–81, Eastbourne Coll.; Trustee, London Symphony Orchestra 1983–91; Chancellor, City Univ. 1981–82; Vice-Pres. Nat. Playing Fields Asscn 1983–99; Church Commr 1982–93, 1996–99; Hon. Col 151 Regt RCT(V) 1983–89, Hon. Col Commdt RCT 1988–91; Dir (non-exec.) Unionamerica Holdings 1994–97; Trustee, Chichester Festival Theatre 1982–97; Chair. Pathfinder Properties PLC 1997; Hon. Liveryman, Farmers' Co. 1980, Water Conservators' Co. 2000; Hon. Liveryman Co. of Water Conservators; Freeman Co. of Watermen and Lightermen; Order of Oman. *Leisure interests:* gardening, music, travel.

LEAVER, Christopher John, CBE, MA, PhD, DIC, ARCS, FRS, FRSE; British professor of plant sciences; b. 31 May 1942, Bristol; s. of Douglas P. Leaver and Elizabeth C. Leaver; m. Anne Huggins 1971; one s. one d.; ed Imperial Coll. of Science, London; Fulbright Scholar, Purdue Univ., Ind., USA 1966–68; Scientific Officer, ARC Unit of Plant Physiology, Imperial Coll. London 1968–69; Lecturer, Univ. of Edinburgh 1969–80, Reader 1980–86, Science and Engineering Research Council Sr Research Fellow, 1985–89, Prof. of Plant Molecular Biology 1986–89; Sibthorpian Prof. of Plant Sciences 1990–, Head of Dept, Univ. of Oxford 1991–; Nuffield Commonwealth Bursary, Sr Visiting Fellowship (SERC), CSIRO Div. of Plant Industry, Canberra 1975; European Molecular Biology Org. Long-term Fellowship, Biozentrum, Basle 1980; mem. Governing Council, John Innes Centre, Norwich 1984–; Trustee, Nat. History Museum, London 1997–; mem. Council, Agric. and Food Research Council 1990–93; mem. Ministry of Agric., Fisheries and Food Priorities Bd 1990–93; mem. Royal Soc. Council 1992–94; mem. European Molecular Biology Org. (Council mem. 1992–97, Chair. 1996–97), Advisory Council on Science and Tech. 1992–93, Council Biochemical Soc. (Chair. NA & MB Group) (Vice-Chair. Exec. Cttee 2002–); Dir Isis Innovation Ltd, Univ. of Oxford 1996–2002; Del. Oxford Univ. Press 2002–; mem. Individual Merit Promotion Panel BBSRC 1996– (mem. Council 2000–), External Scientific Advisory Bd, Inst. of Molecular and Cell Biology, Univ. of Oporto, Scientific Advisory Bd, Inst. of Molecular and Cellular Biology, Singapore, ITQB Advisory Cttee, Univ. of Lisbon; mem. Academia Europaea; Fellow, St John's Coll. Oxford; Huxley Gold Medal, Imperial Coll. 1970; Tate & Lyle Award, Phytochemical Soc. of Europe 1984, Humboldt Prize 1997. *Publications:* ed several books; numerous papers in int. scientific journals. *Leisure interests:* walking and talking in Upper Coquetdale. *Address:* Department of Plant Sciences, University of Oxford, South Parks Road, Oxford, OX1 3RB, England. *Telephone:* (1865) 275143. *Fax:* (1865) 275144. *E-mail:* chris.leaver@ plants.ox.ac.uk (Office).

LEAVER, Peter Lawrence Oppenheim, QC; British lawyer; b. 28 Nov. 1944; s. of Marcus Isaac Leaver and Lena Leaver (née Oppenheim); m. Jane Rachel Pearl 1969; three s. one d.; ed Aldenham School, Elstree, Trinity Coll. Dublin; called to Bar Lincoln's Inn 1967, Recorder 1994–, Bencher 1995; Chief Exec. Football Asscn Premier League 1997–99; Chair. Bar Cttee 1989; Chair. Int. Practice Cttee 1990; mem. Cttee on Future of the Legal Profession 1986–88, Council of Legal Ed. 1986–91, Gen. Council of the Bar 1987–90; Dir Investment Man. Regulatory Org. 1994–2000; Deputy High Court Judge; mem. Chartered Inst. of Arbitrators; mem. Dispute Resolution Panel for Winter Olympics, Salt Lake City 2002. *Leisure interests:* sport, theatre, wine, opera. *Address:* 1 Essex Court, Temple, London, EC4Y 9AR (Office); 5 Hamilton Terrace, London, NW8 9RE, England (Home). *Telephone:* (20) 7583-2000 (Office); (20) 7286-0208 (Home). *Fax:* (20) 7583-0118 (Office). *E-mail:* clerks@oeclaw.co.uk (Office).

LEAVEY, Thomas Edward, MA, PhD; American international postal official; b. 10 Nov. 1934, Kansas City, Mo.; m. Anne Roland 1968; ed Josephinum Coll., Columbus, Ohio, Inst. Catholique, Paris and Princeton Univ.; Prof. Farleigh Dickinson Univ. Teaneck, NJ and George Washington Univ., Washington, DC 1968–70; various man. and exec. positions in US Postal Services, Los Angeles, Chicago and Washington DC 1970–87; Asst Postmaster-Gen. Int. Postal Affairs, USPS H.Q. 1987–94; Chair. Exec. Council, Universal Postal Union (UPU) 1989–94; Dir-Gen. Int. Bureau of UPU 1995–; John Wanamaker Award 1991, Heinrich von Stephan Medal. *Leisure interests:* golf, tennis. *Address:* Universal Postal Union, International Bureau, Postfach, 3000 Berne 15, Switzerland (Office).

LEAVITT, Michael Okerlund; American politician and insurance executive; b. 11 Feb. 1951, Cedar City, Utah; s. of Dixie Leavitt and Anne Okerlund; m. Jacalyn Smith; four s. one d.; ed S Utah Univ.; Sales Rep. Leavitt Group, Cedar City 1972–74, Account Exec. 1974–76; Man. Underwriting, Salt Lake City 1976–82, COO 1982–84, Pres. and CEO 1984–92; mem. Bd Dirs Pacificorp, Portland, Ore., Utah Power and Light Co., Salt Lake City, Great Western Thrift & Loan, Salt Lake City; mem. staff, Reagan–Bush '84; Gov. of Utah 1993–; Republican. *Leisure interest:* golf. *Address:* Office of the Governor, 210 State Capitol Building, Salt Lake City, UT 84114, USA.

LEBED, Aleksey Ivanovich; Russian politician; b. 14 April 1955, Novocherkassk, Rostov Region; m.; one s. one d.; ed Ryazan Higher School of Airborne Troops, Frunze Mil. Acad., St Petersburg State Univ.; mil. service in Afghanistan 1982; participated in mil. operations in different parts of

USSR 1980–92; Regt Commdr, 14th Army in Chişinău 1992, resgnd 1995; mem. State Duma 1995–96; Head of Govt Repub. of Khakassia 1996–; mem. Council of Fed. 1996–2001; mem. Congress of Russian Communities; Order of the Red Star; Dr hc (Khakassia Katanov State Univ.); Hon. Diploma (Supreme Council, Repub. of Khakassia); Medal for Courage, Peter the Great Prize 2001. *Publication:* article on regional econ. devt. *Leisure interests:* football, table tennis, billiards, downhill skiing. *Address:* House of Government, prosp. Lenina 67, 655019 Abakan, Republic of Khakassia, Russia. *Telephone:* (39022) 9-91-02 (Office). *Fax:* (39022) 6-50-96 (Office). *E-mail:* pressa@khakasnet.ru (Office). *Website:* www.gov.khakassia.ru.

LEBEDEV, Aleksander Aleksandrovich, CandHist; Russian diplomatist; b. 3 June 1938, Voronezh; m.; ed Moscow Inst. of Int. Relations; Head of sector USSR Cttee of Youth Orgs until 1964, First Deputy Chair. 1969–70; Rep., Vice-Pres. Int. Union of Students in Prague, Czechoslovakia 1964–69; Head of Div. Cen. Komsomol Cttee 1970–71; mem. Exec. Bd, Head of Dept All-Union Copyright Agency (VAAP) 1973–76; Rep. to World Peace Council, Helsinki, Finland 1976–79; Head of Div. World Econs and Int. Relations journal 1979–80, Deputy Ed.-in-Chief 1985–86; Head of Div. Int. Life journal 1980–85, New Time journal 1986–87; consultant, Head of Sector Cen. CPSU Cttee 1987–90, counsellor-envoy 1990–91; Amb. to Czechoslovakia 1991–93, to Czech Repub. 1993–97, of Special Missions, Ministry of Foreign Affairs 1998, to Turkey 1998–; Order, Sign of Hon. *Address:* Russian Embassy, Karyagdi Sok, 5 Cankaya, Ankara, Turkey (Office). *Telephone:* (312) 439-21-22 (Office). *Fax:* (312) 438-39-52 (Office).

LEBEDEV, Aleksander Yevgenyevich; Russian banker; b. 16 Dec. 1960; m.; one s.; ed Moscow Inst. of Int. Relations; staff mem. Inst. mem. of Econs of World Socialist System, USSR Acad. of Sciences 1982–83; staff mem. Ministry of Foreign Affairs 1983–; First, then Second Sec. Embassy to UK 1987–92; Rep. Swiss Bank in Russia 1992–93; Founder and Chair. of Bd Russian Investment Finance Co. 1993–; Chair. of Bd Nat. Reserve Bank 1995–; Chair. Nat. Investment Bd 1999–. *Address:* National Reserve Bank, N. Barmannaya str. 37A, 107066 Moscow, Russia (Office). *Telephone:* (095) 956-32-30 (Office). *Fax:* (095) 596-32-30 (Office).

LEBEDEV, Col-Gen. Sergey Nikolayevich; Russian security officer; b. 9 April 1948, Djizak, Uzbekistan; ed Kiev Polytech. Inst., Diplomatic Acad. of USSR Ministry of Foreign Affairs; staff mem. Chernigov br. Kiev Polytech. Inst. 1970; army service 1971–72; with state security bodies 1973–75, Foreign Intelligence Service 1975–78; Rep. of Foreign Intelligence Service to USA 1998–2000; Dir Fed. Foreign Intelligence Service Russian Fed. 2000–. *Address:* Federal Foreign Intelligence Service of Russia, Ostozhenka Str. 51/10, 119034 Moscow, Russia (Office). *Telephone:* (095) 429-30-09 (Office).

LEBEGUE, Daniel Simon Georges, BL; French banker; b. 4 May 1943, Lyon; s. of Robert Lebegue and Denise Lebegue (née Flachet); m. Chantal Biron 1970; one s. one d.; ed Univ. of Lyons, Inst. for Political Sciences and Nat. School for Admin., Paris; civil servant, Ministry of Economy and Finance 1969–73; Financial Adviser, Embassy in Japan 1974–76; Head of Balance of Payments Section, Treasury 1976–79, Head of Monetary Funds Section 1979–80; Deputy Dir of Savings and Financial Market 1980–81; Counsellor in charge of Economy and Finance, Prime Minister's Office 1981–83; Head of Dept of Financial and Monetary Affairs at Treasury 1983–84, Head of Treasury 1984–87; Pres. and COO Banque Nat. de Paris 1987–96, Vice-Chair. 1996–97; Pres. and CEO Caisse des dépôts et consignations (CDC) 1997–, Chair. CDC Ixis (formed after merger of CDC and CNCE) 2001–, Dir CDC Ixis Capital Markets; Dir Gaz de France, Thales, Areva; Chevalier Légion d'honneur, Chevalier Ordre nat. du Mérite. *Publications:* Le Trésor et la politique financière 1988, La fiscalité de l'épargne dans le marché unique européen 1988. *Leisure interests:* opera, cinema, hiking. *Address:* CDC Ixis, 56 rue de Lille, 75356 Paris (Office); 25 rue de Bourgogne, 75007 Paris, France (Home).

LEBLANC, Rt Hon Roméo A., PC, CC, CMM, CD; Canadian Governor-General; b. 18 Dec. 1927, L'Anse-aux-Cormier, Memramcook, NB; s. of Philias LeBlanc and Lucie LeBlanc; m. Diana Fowler; four c.; ed St-Joseph and Paris Univs; teacher, Drummond High School, NB 1951–53, NB Teachers' Coll., Fredericton 1955–59; corresp., Radio-Canada, Ottawa 1960–62, UK 1962–65, USA 1965–67; Press Sec. to Prime Minister Lester Pearson 1967–68, to Prime Minister Pierre Trudeau 1968–71; Asst to Pres. and Dir of Public Relations, Université de Moncton 1971–72; MP for Westmorland-Kent 1972–84; Minister of Fisheries 1974–76, of Fisheries and the Environment 1976–79, of Fisheries and Oceans 1980–82, of Public Works 1982–84; Senator, Beauséjour, NB 1984–95, Speaker 1993–95; Gov.-Gen. of Canada and C-in-C 1995–99; Visiting Scholar, Inst. of Canadian Studies, Carleton Univ., Ottawa 1985–86; Founding Pres. CBC/Radio-Canada Corresps' Asscn 1965; mem. Canada–France Parl. Asscn; 8 hon. degrees 1979–96. *Address:* PO Box 5254, Shediac, NB, E4P 8T9, Canada.

LEBLOND, Charles Philippe, CC, LèsSc, MD, PhD, DSc, FRSC, FRS; Canadian professor of anatomy; b. 5 Feb. 1910, Lille, France; s. of Oscar Leblond and Jeanne Desmarchelier; m. Gertrude Elinor Sternschuss 1936 (died 2000); three s. one d.; ed Univs of Lille, Paris, Montréal and the Sorbonne; Asst in Histology, Medical School, Univ. of Paris 1934–35; Rockefeller Fellow, School of Medicine, Yale Univ., USA 1936–37; Asst Laboratoire de Synthèse Atomique, Paris 1938–40; Lecturer in Histology and Embryology, McGill Univ. 1941–43, Asst Prof. of Anatomy 1943–46, Assoc. Prof. 1946–48, Prof. of Anatomy 1948–, Chair. Dept of Anatomy 1957–75; Fellow Royal Soc. of

Canada, Royal Soc. (London); Co-Founder Histochemical Soc., Journal of Histochemistry and Cytochemistry; mem. American Asscn of Anatomists, Canadian Asscn of Anatomists, American Soc. for Cell Biology, Histochemical Soc., Soc. for Experimental Biology and Medicine and others; Hon. DSc (Acadia, McGill, Montréal, York, Sherbrooke Univs); Prix Saintour, French Acad. 1935, Flavelle Medal, Royal Soc. of Canada 1961, Gairdner Fed. Award 1965, American Coll. of Physicians Award 1966, Province of Québec Biology Prize 1968, American Soc. for Cell Biology, E. B. Wilson Award 1982, Marie-Victorin Prize, Prov. of Québec 1992. *Achievements include:* pioneering work in cell biology by demonstrating migration of some cells and of molecules in all cells; co-discoverer of stem cell. *Publications:* The Use of Radioautography in Investigating Protein Synthesis (with K. B. Warren) 1965 and over 400 articles in scientific journals. *Leisure interests:* history, gardening. *Address:* Department of Anatomy and Cell Biology, McGill University, 3640 University Street, Montréal, Québec, H3A 2B2 (Office); 68 Chesterfield Avenue, Westmount, Montréal, Québec, H3Y 2M5, Canada. *Telephone:* (514) 398-6340 (Office); (514) 486-4837 (Home). *Fax:* (514) 398-5047 (Office). *E-mail:* cleblond@med.mcgill.ca (Office).

LEBOUDER, Jean-Pierre; Central African Republic politician; b. 1944; ed Ecole nationale supérieure agronomique, Toulouse, France; Dir Research Centre, Union cotonnière centrafricaine 1971–72, Dir-Gen. 1974–76; Minister of Rural Devt 1976, of Planning, Statistics and Int. Co-operation 1978–80; Prime Minister 1980–81. *Address:* c/o Office du Premier Ministre, Bangui, Central African Republic.

LEBOWITZ, Joel L., MS, PhD; American professor of mathematics and physics; b. 10 May 1930, Taceva, Czechoslovakia; m. 1st Estelle Mandelbaum 1953 (died 1996); 2nd Ann K. Beneduce 1999; ed Brooklyn Coll. and Syracuse Univ.; Nat. Science Foundation Postdoctoral Fellow, Yale Univ. 1956–57; Asst Prof. Stevens Inst. of Tech. 1957–59; Asst Prof. Belfer Grad. School of Science, Yeshiva Univ. 1959–60, Assoc. Prof. 1960–65, Prof. of Physics 1965–77, Chair. Dept of Physics 1968–76; Dir Center for Mathematical Sciences Research and Prof. of Math. and Physics, Rutgers Univ. 1977–; mem. NAS, AAAS, New York Acad. of Sciences, American Physical Soc.; Dr hc (Ecole Polytechnique Fédérale, Lausanne, Clark Univ.) 1999; Henri Poincaré Prize, IAMP 2000; Boltzmann Medal 1992, Max Planck Research Award 1993, Delmar S. Fahrney Medal, Franklin Inst. 1994, AAAS Scientific Freedom and Responsibility Award 1999 and other distinctions. *Publications:* 450 scientific papers. *Address:* Centre for Mathematical and Scientific Research, Busch Campus-Hill Center, Rutgers University, New Brunswick, NJ 08903, USA. *Telephone:* (732) 932-3117. *Fax:* (732) 445-4936. *E-mail:* lebowitz@sakharov .rutgers.edu (Office).

LEBRANCHU, Marylise; French university lecturer and politician; b. 25 April 1947, Loudéac (Côtes-d'Armor); d. of Adolphe Perrault Lebranchu and Marie Epert; m. Jean Lebranchu 1970; three c.; responsible for research, Nord-Finistère Semi-public Co. 1973–78; joined Parti Socialiste Unifié (PSU) 1972, Parti Socialiste (PS) 1977; Parl. Asst to Marie Jacq 1978–93; municipal councillor, Morlaix (Finistère) 1983, Mayor 1995–97; regional councillor 1986–; Nat. Ass. Deputy for Morlaix Constituency 1997–; Minister of State attached to Minister for the Economy, Finance and Industry, with responsibility for small and medium-sized enterprises, trade and artisan activities 1997–2000, Minister of Justice and Keeper of the Seals 2000–02; Jr Lecturer in Econs applied to town and country planning, Univ. of Brest 1990–; Trombinoscope Politician of the Year Award 2000. *Publication:* Etre Juste, Justement. *Leisure interest:* music. *Address:* 3 rampe Saint Nicolas, 29600 Morlaix (Office); Assemblée nationale, 126 rue de l'Université, 75355 Paris 07 SP, France. *Fax:* 1-40-63-77-65 (Office). *E-mail:* mlebranchu@ assemblee-nationale.fr.

LEBRAT, Jean Marcel Hubert; French engineer; b. 21 Jan. 1933, Levallois/Seine; s. of Marcel Lebrat and Simone Landré; m. Andrée Blaize 1956; two s.; ed Coll. de Mirecourt, Lycée Henri Poincaré, Nancy and Ecole spéciale des travaux publics; head of office of studies of navigation service of Saint-Quentin 1956–59; head of office of studies of construction service of canal from the North to Compiègne 1959–63; Eng Etablissement Public pour l'Aménagement de La Défense (Epad) 1963–68, asst to head of highway div. Epad 1968–70; divisional eng 1970; Asst Tech. Dir Soc. d'Aménagement des Halles (Semah) 1970–79, Tech. Dir 1979–83, Dir 1984–89; Pres. Etablissement public du Grand Louvre 1989–98; Engineer of bridges and roads 1995, Engineer-Gen. 1995–; Pres. Asscn Concordium Musée de la Fraternité 1998–; Hon. Pres. Cuba Co-operation; Admin. Musée des Arts Décoratifs; Chevalier, Légion d'honneur, Commdr, Ordre nat. du Mérite. *Leisure interests:* drawing, tennis, water sports. *Address:* 56 boulevard Saint-Denis, 92400 Courbevoie, France (Office). *Telephone:* 1-47-88-03-29 (Office). *E-mail:* lebrat.jean@ wanadoo.fr (Office).

LECAT, Jean-Philippe; French politician; b. 29 July 1935, Dijon; s. of Jean Lecat and Madeleine Bouchard; m. Nadine Irène Romm 1965; two d.; ed Ecole Nat. d'Admin.; mem. Council of State 1963–66, 1974, Auditor 1963–; Chargé de Mission, Prime Minister's Office 1966–68; Deputy to the Nat. Ass., Beaune 1968–72, 1973, 1978–81; Nat. Del. for Cultural Affairs, Union des Démocrates pour la République 1970–71, Asst Sec.-Gen. for Cultural Affairs and Information 1971–72; Spokesman of the Govt 1972–73; Sec. of State for Econ. 1973–74; Minister of Information 1973–74, of Culture and Communication 1978–81; mem. Bourgogne Regional Council 1973–; Del. to Natural Resources Conservation Conf. 1975; Chargé de Mission, Pres. of Repub. 1976–78 and

Spokesman of the Pres. 1976–81, Conseiller d'Etat 1988; Pres. Amis de Mozart Asscn 1987, Comm. du Château de Vincennes 1988–, Admin. Council Ecole Nat. du Patrimoine 1990–99, Admin. Council Acad. de France in Rome (Villa Medici) 1996; Special Adviser to Pres. Thomson Consumer Electronics 1991 (later Thomson Multimedia 1994–97); Pres. Acad. de France, Rome 1996–99; Chevalier, Légion d'honneur, Officier, Ordre nat. du Mérite, Commdr, Arts et Lettres; Grand Prix Nat. awarded by Minister of Culture 1996. *Publications:* Quand flamboyait la Toison d'or 1982, Beaune 1983, La Bourgogne 1985, Le siècle de la Toison d'or 1986, Bourgogne 1989, L'Ardeur et le tourment 1989. *Address:* Conseil d'Etat, 1 place du Palais-Royal, 75100 Paris (Office); 131 boulevard du Général Koenig, 92200 Neuilly-sur-Seine, France (Home).

LECERF, Olivier Maurice Marie; French industrialist; b. 2 Aug. 1929, Merville-Franceville; s. of Maurice Lecerf and Colette Lecerf (née Lainé); m. Annie Bazin de Jessey 1958; two s. two d.; ed Univ. of Paris, Centre d'Etudes Industrielles, Geneva; joined Ciments Lafarge 1956, marketing and man. responsibilities in Brazil and Canada 1956–65; Vice-Pres. Canada Cement Lafarge 1965–71; Vice-Chair. and Gen. Man. Ciments Lafarge 1973–74, Chair. and CEO 1974–82; Vice-Chair. and COO Lafarge SA 1983, Chair. and CEO 1984–89, Hon. Chair. 1989–; Dir L'Oréal; Officier, Légion d'honneur, Commandeur, Ordre nat. du Mérite. *Publication:* Au risque de gagner (jtly) 1991. *Leisure interest:* tennis. *Address:* 8 rue Guy de Maupassant, 75116 Paris, France (Home). *Telephone:* 1-45-04-78-49 (Home).

LECLANT, Jean, DèsSc; French professor of Egyptology; b. 8 Aug. 1920, Paris; s. of René Leclant and Laure Pannier; m. Marie-Françoise Alexandre-Hatvany 1988; ed Ecole Normale Supérieure, Paris and Inst. Français d'Archéologie Orientale, Cairo; Prof. Univ. of Strasbourg 1953–63, Sorbonne 1963–79, Coll. de France (Chair. of Egyptology) 1979–90 (Hon. Prof. 1990–); Dir of Studies, Ecole Pratique des Hautes Etudes (Vème Section) 1963–90; Perm. Sec. Acad. des Inscriptions et Belles Lettres (Inst. de France) 1983–; annual excavations Egypt, especially Karnak 1948–, Saqqarah 1963–; mem. Inst. Français in Cairo 1948–52; led archaeological expedition, Ethiopia 1952–56; Pres. Soc. Française d'Egyptologie, High Cttee of Nat. Celebrations 1998–; mem. Acad. des Sciences d'Outre-Mer, and many other learned socs in France and abroad; Grand Officier, Légion d'honneur; Commdr, Ordre du Mérite; Commdr, Ordre des Palmes Académiques; Commdr des Arts et Lettres; Chevalier, Mérite Militaire; Imperial Order of Menelik (Ethiopia); Grand Officier, Ordre de la Répub. d'Egypte; Dr hc (Leuven, Bologna); Prix Balsan, Prix Int. Cino del Duca. *Publications:* Karnak-Nord IV (jtly) 1954, Dans les Pas des Pharaons 1958, Montouemhat, Prince de la Ville 1963, Soleb I, Soleb II (jt ed.) 1966, 1971, Kition II (jtly) 1976, La culture des chasseurs du Nil et du Sahara, 2 vols (with P. Huard) 1980, Répertoire d'Epigraphique Méroïtique, 3 vols (jtly) 2000, Les Textes de la Pyramide de Pépy Ier 2001 and about 1,000 articles. *Address:* 23 quai Conti, 75006 Paris (Office); 25 quai Conti, 75006 Paris, France (Home). *Telephone:* 1-44-41-43-10. *Fax:* 1-44-41-43-11.

LECLERC, Edouard; French business executive; b. 20 Nov. 1926, Landerneau; s. of Eugène Leclerc and Marie Kerouanton; m. Hélène Diquélou 1950; one s. two d.; ed seminaries in Paris, Uriage-les-Bains and Saint-Cirgues; pioneer of Leclerc supermarket chain (first opened Landerneau) 1949–, more than 600 brs; Pres. Asscn nat. des centres Leclerc 1960–; Chevalier, Ordre nat. du Mérite. *Publications:* Ma vie pour un combat, la Part du bonheur 1976, Combat pour la distribution, Le soleil de l'Ouest. *Leisure interests:* archaeology, writing. *Address:* 11 rue Bélerit, 29800 Landerneau (Office); La Haye-Saint-Divy, P.O. Box 733, 29800 Landerneau, France (Home).

LECLERCQ, Patrick; French diplomatist; b. 2 Aug. 1938, Lille; m. 2nd Marie-Alice Berard; two s.; one s. from previous m.; ed Inst. d'Etudes Politiques, Paris, Ecole Nat. d'Admin.; joined Diplomatic Service 1966; Consul-Gen. Montréal, Canada 1982–85; Amb. to Jordan 1985–89, to Egypt 1991–96, to Spain 1996–99; Minister of State, Monaco 2000–; Officier, Légion d'honneur, Ordre nat. du Mérite; several foreign decorations including Orden del Merito and Isabel la Católica, Spain. *Address:* Office of the Minister of State, Ministry of State, Place de la Visitation, 98000 Monaco (Office). *Telephone:* 93-15-46-00 (Office). *Fax:* 93-15-80-12 (Office).

LECONTE, Patrice; French film director; b. Tours; ed Inst. des Hautes Etudes Cinématographiques; directing debut with Les Vécés Etaient Fermés de l'Intérieur; other films include: Monsieur Hire, Le Mari de la Coiffeuse 1990, Tango 1993, Ridicule 1996; also some 20 film advertisements a year including commercials for cos such as Peugeot and Carlsberg beer.

LECOURT, Robert, DenD; French politician and lawyer; b. 19 Sept. 1908, Pavilly; s. of Léon and Angèle (née Lépron) Lecourt; m. Marguerite Chabrerie 1932 (deceased); one d.; ed Coll. Saint-Jean-Baptiste-de-la-Salle, Rouen and Law Faculty, Caen; Lawyer, Court of Appeal, Rouen 1928–32, Paris 1932–73; mem. Comité directeur du mouvement Résistance 1942–45, L'Assemblée consultative provisoire 1944–45; mem. two Constituent Assemblies 1945–46, Nat. Ass. 1946–58; Minister of Justice 1948–49, 1957–58; concerned with Constitutional Reform 1957–58; Minister of State for Overseas Relations 1959–61; Judge, European Court of Justice 1962–76, Pres. 1967–76; mem. Constitutional Council 1979–89; Hon. Bencher, Gray's Inn; Commdr, Légion d'honneur, Croix de guerre, Grand Cross of Belgium, Luxembourg, FRG, Italy, Yugoslavia, Gabon, Madagascar and others; Dr hc (Exeter). *Pub-*

lications: Le juge devant le Marché commun 1970, L'Europe des juges 1976, Concorde sans concordat 1978. *Address:* 11 boulevard Suchet, 75016 Paris, France (Home).

LEDERBERG, Joshua, PhD, FAAS; American geneticist; b. 23 May 1925, Montclair, NJ; s. of Zwi H. Lederberg and Esther Lederberg; m. Marguerite Stein Kirsch 1968; one s. one d.; ed Columbia and Yale Univs; USN 1943–45; Research Fellow Yale Univ. 1946–47; Prof. of Genetics Univ. of Wis. 1947–59; Prof. of Genetics, Biology and Computer Science Stanford Univ. School of Medicine 1959–78; Pres. Rockefeller Univ., New York City 1978–90, Sackler F. Scholar 1990–, Prof. Emer. 1995; Chair. Advisory Bd Ellison Medical Foundation; Sr Fellow Center for Int. Security, Stanford Univ. 1998–; Visiting Prof. Univ. of Calif. at Berkeley 1950; Fulbright Visiting Prof. Univ. of Melbourne 1957; Trustee and mem. numerous bds and cttees; mem. Bd Council on Foreign Relations, New York City; scientific adviser to several cos especially in biotech.; mem. NAS; Hon. Life Gov. New York Acad. of Sciences; Foreign mem. Royal Soc., London; Fellow American Philosophical Soc., American Acad. of Arts and Sciences; Founder-mem. Acad. Univ. des Cultures; Hon. mem. AOA; Hon. Fellow New York Acad. of Medicine; Commdr des Arts et des Lettres; numerous hon. degrees; Nobel Prize in Medicine (for studies on org. of the genetic material in bacteria) (with Beadle and Tatum) 1958, US Nat. Medal of Science 1989, Benjamin Franklin Award, American Philosophical Soc. *Publications:* Emerging Infections 1992, Biological Weapons: containing the threat, (Ed.-in-Chief), Encyclopaedia of Microbiology, numerous papers and articles in various scientific and lay publs. *Address:* Rockefeller University, 1230 York Avenue, Suite 400, New York, NY 10021, USA. *Telephone:* (212) 327-7809.

LEDGER, Sir Philip Stevens, Kt, CBE, MA, DMus, LLD, FRCM, FRNCM, FRCO; British musician; b. 12 Dec. 1937, Bexhill-on-Sea, Sussex; s. of the late Walter Stephen and Winifred Kathleen Ledger (née Stevens); m. Mary Erryl Wells 1963; one s. one d.; ed Bexhill Grammar School, King's Coll. Cambridge; Master of the Music, Chelmsford Cathedral 1962–65; Dir of Music, Univ. of East Anglia 1965–73; Dean of School of Fine Arts and Music 1968–71; an Artistic Dir Aldeburgh Festival of Music and Arts 1968–89, Vice-Pres. 1989–; Conductor, Cambridge Univ. Musical Soc. 1973–82; Dir of Music and Organist, King's Coll. Cambridge 1974–82; Prin. Royal Scottish Acad. of Music and Drama 1982–2001; John Stewart of Rannoch Scholar in Sacred Music; Hon. mem. Royal Acad. of Music, Guildhall School of Music; Pres. Royal Coll. of Organists 1992–94; Pres. Inc. Soc. of Musicians 1994–95; Chair. Cttee of Prins of Conservatoires 1994–98; Hon. Prof. Univ. of Glasgow 1993–98; Silver Medal of Worshipful Company of Musicians, numerous hon. degrees. *Publications:* (ed.) Anthems for Choirs 2 and 3 1973, Oxford Book of English Madrigals 1978, editions of Byrd, Handel and Purcell and carol arrangements. *Leisure interests:* swimming, theatre, membership of Sette of Odd Volumes. *Address:* 2 Lancaster Drive, Upper Rissington, Cheltenham, Glos., GL54 2QZ, England (Home).

LEDINGHAM, John Gerard Garvin, MA, DM, FRCP; British professor of medicine; b. 19 Oct. 1929, London; s. of John Ledingham and Una C. Garvin; m. Dr Elaine Maliphant 1962; four d.; ed Rugby School, New Coll. Oxford and Middx Hosp. London; Registrar, Middx Hosp. 1960–62; Sr Registrar in Medicine, Westminster Hosp. 1962–64; Visiting Fellow, Col Univ. New York 1965–66; Consultant Physician, United Oxford Hosps 1966–74; May Reader in Medicine, Univ. of Oxford 1974–95, Prof. of Clinical Medicine 1989–95, Prof. Emer. 1995–, Dir of Clinical Studies 1977–81, 1990–95; Fellow, New Coll. Oxford 1974–95, Emer. Fellow 1995–, Hon. Fellow 2001–, Sub-Warden 1994–95; Hon. Clinical Dir Biochemical and Clinical NMR Unit, Medical Research Council 1988–95; mem. Nuffield Council on Bioethics; Trustee Nuffield Trust 1978–2002, Beit Trust; Osler Memorial Medal 2000. *Publications:* Oxford Textbook of Medicine (co-ed.) 1983, Concise Oxford Textbook of Medicine 2000; contribs to medical journals. *Leisure interests:* music, reading, golf. *Address:* 124 Oxford Road, Cumnor, Oxford, OX2 9PQ, England (Home). *Telephone:* (1865) 865806 (Home). *Fax:* (1865) 865806 (Home).

LEE, Allen Peng-Fei, OBE, BS, JP; Chinese business executive; b. 24 April 1940, Chefoo; m. Maria Choi Yuen Ha; two s. one d.; ed Univ. of Mich., USA; joined Lockheed Aircraft Ltd 1966, Test Eng Supervisor 1966–67, Test Eng Man. 1968–70; Eng Operations Man. Fabri-Teck Ltd 1967; Test Man. Ampex Ferrotec Ltd 1970–72, Man. Dir 1974–79; Gen. Man. Dataproducts Hong Kong Ltd 1972–74; Man. Dir Ampex World Operations SA 1979–83, Ampex Far East Operations 1983–; Dir, consultant Elec & Eltek Co. Ltd 1984; Chair. Hong Kong Productivity Council 1982, Hong Kong Liberal Party; mem. Industry Devt Bd 1983, Hong Kong Gen. Chamber of Commerce (Cttee and council mem.), Fed. of Hong Kong Industries, Broadcasting Review Bd 1984, Political Section of Preparatory Cttee for Hong Kong Special Admin. Region (S.A.R.); Outstanding Young Persons of Hong Kong Award 1977. *Leisure interests:* fishing, swimming, tennis. *Address:* Liberal Party, Shun Ho Tower, 2/F, 24–30 Ice House Street, Central Energy Plaza, Tsimshatsui East, Kowloon, Hong Kong Special Administrative Region, People's Republic of China. *Telephone:* 28696833. *Fax:* 28453671.

LEE, Christopher Frank Carandini, CBE; British actor, author and singer; b. 27 May 1922, London; s. of the late Lt-Col Geoffrey Trollope Lee and of Contessa Estelle Marie Carandini; m. Birgit Kroencke 1961; one d.; ed Summer Fields Preparatory School, Wellington Coll.; served RAF 1941–46; mentioned in despatches 1944; film industry 1947–; appeared in over 250 motion pictures and TV films; Officier des Arts, Sciences et des Lettres 1973;

Officier des Arts et Lettres 2002; Commdr St John of Jerusalem 1997; Life Achievement Award, Evening Standard Film Awards 2002, Life Achievement Award, Empire Magazine, World Award for Lifetime Achievement, Vienna 2002, German Video Award for Lifetime Achievement 2002. *Films include:* Moulin Rouge 1953, The Curse of Frankenstein 1956, Tale of Two Cities 1957, Dracula 1958, The Hound of the Baskervilles 1959, The Mummy 1959, Rasputin the Mad Monk 1965, The Wicker Man 1973, The Three Musketeers 1973, The Private Life of Sherlock Holmes 1973, The Four Musketeers 1975, The Man With the Golden Gun 1975, To the Devil a Daughter 1976, Airport 77 1977, Return from Witch Mountain, 1977, How the West Was Won 1977, Caravans 1977, The Silent Flute 1977, The Passage 1978, 1941 1978, Bear Island 1978, The Serial 1979, The Salamander 1980, An Eye for an Eye, Goliath Awaits, Charles and Diana, The Last Unicorn, The Far Pavilions, The House of the Long Shadows, The Return of Captain Invincible, The Howling Z, Behind the Mask, Roadstrip, Shaka Zulu, Mio my Mio, The Girl, Un Métier du Seigneur, Casanova, The Disputation, Murder Story, Round The World in 80 Days (TV), For Better, For Worse, Return of the Musketeers, Outlaws, Gremlins II 1989, Sherlock Holmes (US TV), Rainbow Thief, L'Avaro (Italy), Wahre Wunder (German TV) 1990, Young Indy (TV) 1991, Cybereden 1991, Death Train 1992, The Funny Man 1993, Police Academy–Mission to Moscow 1993, A Feast at Midnight 1994, The Stupids 1995, Moses (TV) 1995, Jinnah 1997, Sleepy Hollow 1999, The Lord of the Rings: The Fellowship of the Ring 2000, Star Wars: Episode II–Attack of the Clones 2000, The Lord of the Rings: The Two Towers 2002. *Music:* The King of Elfland's Daughter, Peter and the Wolf, The Soldier's Tale, The King and I, Wandering Star, It's Now or Never, Christopher Lee Sings Rogues, Devils, and Other Villains—From Broadway to Bayreuth. *Television appearances include:* Gormenghast 2000. *Publications:* Christopher Lee's Treasury of Terror, Christopher Lee's Archives of Evil 1975, Christopher Lee's The Great Villains 1977, Tall, Dark and Gruesome (autobiog.) 1977, (updated) 1997. *Leisure interests:* music, travel, golf. *Address:* c/o London Management, 2–4 Noel Street, London, W1V 3RB, England. *Website:* www.christopherleeweb .com.

LEE, David Morris, PhD; American professor of physics; b. 20 Jan. 1931, Rye, NY; s. of Marvin Lee and Annette Lee (née Franks); m. Dana Thorangkul 1960; two s.; ed Harvard Univ., Univ. of Connecticut, Yale Univ.; served U.S. Army 1952–54; Instructor of Physics, Cornell Univ., Ithaca, NY 1959–60, Asst Prof. 1960–63, Assoc. Prof. 1963–68, Prof. 1968–97; James Gilbert White Distinguished Prof. of Physical Sciences 1997–; Visiting Scientist Brookhaven Nat. Lab., Upton, NY 1966–67; Visiting Prof. Univ. of Fla, Gainesville 1974–75, 1994, Univ. of Calif. San Diego, La Jolla 1988; Visiting Lecturer, Peking Univ., Beijing, China 1981; Chair. Joseph Fourier Univ., Grenoble, France 1994; co-discoverer superfluid 3He, tricritical point of 3He-4He mixtures; co-observation of spin waves in spin polarized hydrogen gas; Fellow AAAS; mem. American Acad. of Arts and Sciences, NAS; John Simon Guggenheim Fellow 1966–67, 1974–75; Japan Soc. for Promotion of Sciences Fellow 1977; Sir Francis Simon Memorial Prize, British Inst. of Physics 1976, Oliver Buckley Prize, American Physical Soc. 1981, shared Nobel Prize for Physics 1996, Wilber Cross Medal, Yale Univ. 1998. *Address:* Physics Department, Cornell University, Clark Hall, Ithaca, NY 14853, USA.

LEE, David Tawei, PhD; Taiwanese government official; b. 15 Oct. 1949, Taipei; m.; one s. one d.; ed Nat. Taiwan Univ., Univ. of Virginia, U.S.A.; Man. Ed. Asia and the World Forum 1976–77; Staff Consultant Co-ordination Council for North American Affairs, Washington, DC 1982–88; Prin. Asst to Minister for Foreign Affairs 1988–89; Adjunct Assoc. Prof. of Int. Politics, Grad. School of Social Science, Nat. Taiwan Normal Univ. 1988–93; Deputy Dir Dept of Int. Information Services, Govt Information Office 1989–90; Deputy Dir Dept of N American Affairs, Ministry of Foreign Affairs 1990–93, Dir. 1996, Deputy Minister 1998–; Assoc. in Research, Fairbank Center for E Asian Research, Harvard Univ. 1993–96; Dir-Gen. Taipei Econ. and Cultural Office, Boston 1993–96; Deputy Dir-Gen. Govt Information Office, Exec. Yuan 1996–97; Dir-Gen. Govt Information Office, Exec. Yuan and Govt Spokesman 1997–2000. *Address:* Ministry of Foreign Affairs, 2 Chiehchou Road, Taipei, Taiwan.

LEE, Edward Graham, QC, LLM; Canadian diplomatist and lawyer; b. 21 Nov. 1931, Vancouver, BC; s. of William C. Lee and Dorothy F. Graham; m. Beverly J. Saul 1955; three d.; ed Univ. of British Columbia and Harvard Univ., U.S.A.; joined Canadian Dept of External Affairs 1956; Second Sec. Djakarta 1959–61; Counsellor, London 1965–69; Dir of Personnel, Dept of External Affairs 1969–72, Legal Adviser 1973–75; Amb. to Israel 1975–79, to S. Africa 1982–86; Asst Under-Sec. for USA Affairs 1979–82; Legal Adviser and Asst Deputy Minister for Legal, Consular and Immigration, Dept of External Affairs 1986–90; Amb. to Austria and Perm. Rep. to UN, Vienna 1990–93; Gov. IAEA 1990–93; Adjunct Prof. of Int. Law, Univ. of Ottawa 1993–; UN Observer, SA Elections 1994; Lecturer, SA Ministry of Foreign Affairs 1994; Pres. Canadian Council on Int. Law 1994–96. *Publications:* numerous articles in Canadian legal journals. *Leisure interests:* golf, walking, reading, gardening. *Address:* 703 Chapman Boulevard, Ottawa, Ont., K1G 1T5, Canada.

LEE, Hermione, MA, MPhil, FRSL, FBA; British academic; b. 29 Feb. 1948, Winchester; d. of Dr Benjamin Lee and Josephine Lee; m. John Barnard 1991; ed Univ. of Oxford; Instructor, Coll. of William and Mary, Williamsburg VA 1970–71; Lecturer, Dept of English, Univ. of Liverpool 1971–77; Lecturer

Dept of English, Univ. of York 1977–87, Sr Lecturer 1987–90, Reader 1990–93, Prof. 1993–98; Goldsmiths' Chair of English Literature and Fellow New Coll. Oxford 1998–; Presenter of Book Four on Channel Four TV 1982–86; reviewer, broadcaster; Hon. Fellow St Hilda's Coll. Oxford 1998, St Cross Coll. Oxford 1998; Hon. DLitt (Liverpool) 2002. *Publications:* The Novels of Virginia Woolf 1977, Elizabeth Bowen 1981 (2nd. ed. 1999), Philip Roth 1982, The Secret Self I 1985 and II 1987, The Mulberry Tree: Writings of Elizabeth Bowen 1986, Willa Cather: A Life Saved Up 1989, Virginia Woolf 1996, Virginia Woolf: Moments of Being (Ed.) 2002. *Leisure interests:* reading, music, countryside. *Address:* New College, Oxford, OX1 3BN, England. *Telephone:* (1865) 79555.

LEE, Gen. Honkon; South Korean diplomatist and army officer; b. 11 Dec. 1920, Kongjoo, Chungcheong Nan-do; s. of Kidong Lee and Jinsil Ahn; m. Kwiran Lee 1946; two s. four d.; ed Japanese Imperial Mil. Acad., Japanese Field Artillery School and U.S. Infantry School; Supt Korean Mil. Acad. 1946–48; Mil. Attaché, Washington 1949; Commdg Gen., Eighth Repub. of Korea Army Div. 1949–50, Third Army Corps 1950–51, First Army Corps 1952–54; UN Command Del. to Korean Armistice 1951–52; Chair. Jt Chiefs of Staff 1954–56, Chief of Staff 1956–58; Nat. Pres. Korean Veterans Asscn 1958–61; Amb. to Philippines 1961–62, to UK 1962–67 (also to Scandinavian countries, Iceland, Malta and African countries concurrently); Amb. at large 1967–69; Chair. President's Advisory Comm. on Govt Admin. 1969; Chair. Korea Anti-Communist League 1976–; Chair. Korea-British Soc. 1978–; decorations from Republic of Korea, USA, France, UK, Greece and Vatican. *Publications:* Nation's Destination 1950, Free Opinion (monthly publ.) 1976–. *Leisure interests:* horse riding, reading, music appreciation.

LEE, Hyung-Koo; South Korean banker; b. 30 Aug. 1940; m. 1969; ed Seoul Nat. Univ.; Deputy Dir Planning and Man. Office, Budget Bureau, Econ. Planning Bd (EPB) 1964; Sec. for Econ. Affairs, Presidential Secr. 1969–70; Dir and Dir-Gen. EPB 1971–81; Parvin Fellow, Woodrow Wilson School of Public Admin., Princeton Univ. 1978–79; Asst Minister, Ministry of Finance 1982; Vice-Minister, Ministry of Construction 1986, Ministry of Finance 1988, EPB 1988; Gov. Korea Devt Bank 1990–96. *Publications:* Economic Development in Korea, The Korean Economy, The Korean Economy Looks to the 21st Century. *Leisure interests:* golf, tennis. *Address:* 10-2, Gwancheol-dong, Jongno-gu, C.P.O. Box 28, Seoul, 110-111, Republic of Korea. *Telephone:* (2) 398-6114.

LEE, John Joseph, MRIA; Irish historian; b. 9 July 1942, Tralee; s. of Thomas P. Lee and Catherine Burke; m. Anne Marie Mitchell 1969; one s. two d.; ed Franciscan Coll. Gormanston, Univ. Coll. Dublin, Inst. for European History, Mainz, Peterhouse Coll. Cambridge; Admin. Officer, Dept of Finance, Dublin 1963; Asst in History, Univ. Coll. Dublin 1963–68; Research Fellow, Peterhouse Coll., Cambridge Univ. 1968–70; Official Fellow, Lecturer, Tutor 1970–74; Prof. of Modern History, Univ. Coll. Cork 1974–93, Prof. of History 1993–, Dean Faculty of Arts 1976–79, Vice-Pres. Univ. Coll. Cork 1982–85; Visiting Mellon Prof., Univ. of Pittsburgh, USA 1979, European Univ. Inst., Florence, Italy 1981; Guest Fellow, Austrian Acad. 1989; Eisenhower Fellow, USA 1989, Distinguished Visiting Prof. of World Peace, L.B.J. School, Univ. of Texas 1989–90; Visiting Sr Parnell Fellow, Magdalene Coll. Cambridge 1992–93, Visiting Arbuthnot Fellow, Univ. of Edin. 1997; Visiting Prof. Glucksman Ireland House, New York Univ. 1996; Columnist Sunday Tribune 1996–; Chair. Irish Scholarships Exchange Bd 1980–92, Irish Fulbright Comm. 1992–96; Visiting Glucksman Prof. of Irish Studies, New York Univ. 1999–2000; mem. Irish Senate 1993–97; mem. British-Irish Parl. Body 1993–97; Donnelly Prize, American Conf. for Irish Studies 1990, Irish Life/Sunday Independent Arts Award 1990, Aer Lingus/Irish Times Prize for Literature 1991. *Publications:* The Modernization of Irish Society 1848–1918 1973, 1989, Labour in German Industrialisation, in Cambridge Economic History of Europe, VII 1978, Ireland 1912–1985: Politics and Society 1989, Europe and America in the 1990s (Jt Ed.) 1991, The Shifting Balance of Power, Exploring the 20th Century 2000. *Leisure interests:* sport, reading. *Address:* Department of History, University College Cork, Western Road, Cork, Ireland. *Telephone:* (21) 902-685.

LEE, Kun-Hee, MBA; South Korean business executive; b. 9 Jan. 1942, Utryung, Gyeongnam; s. of Lee Byung-Chull and Park Doo-Eul; m. Ra Hee-ong 1967; four c.; ed Waseda Univ. Tokyo and George Washington Univ., USA; Exec. Dir Joong-Ang Daily News, Seoul 1968–78, Tong-Yang Broadcasting Corpn Seoul 1968–78; Vice-Chair. Samsung Group, Seoul 1978–87, Chair. 1987–; Vice-Chair. Korea-Japan Econ. Comm. Seoul 1981–, Fed. of Korean Industries 1987; Pres. Korean Amateur Wrestling Fed. 1982–; Dir Korean Youth Asscn 1982–; Vice-Pres. Korean Olympic Cttee 1993–; found guilty of bribery and sentenced to two years' imprisonment suspended for three years Aug. 1996; Hon. DBA (Seoul Nat. Univ.) 2000; Olympic Order, IOC 1996. *Publication:* Samsung New Management 1993. *Leisure interests:* horse-riding, golf, vintage car collection. *Address:* Samsung Group, 310, 2-ga Taepyeong-no, jung-gu, Seoul (Office); 740-10 Hannam-dong, Yongsan-gu, Seoul 100-102, Republic of Korea (Home). *Telephone:* (2) 28-4811 (Office). *Fax:* (2) 752-7926 (Office). *E-mail:* j-npr@samsung.co.kr (Office). *Website:* www .samsung.com (Office).

LEE, Martin Chu Ming, QC, JP, BA; Hong Kong politician and barrister; b. 8 June 1938, Hong Kong; m. Amelia Lee 1969; one s.; ed Univ. of Hong Kong; Chair. Hong Kong Bar Asscn 1980–83; mem. Hong Kong Legis. Council 1985–, Hong Kong Law Reform Comm. 1985–91, Basic Law Drafting Cttee 1985–90

(expelled for criticism of People's Repub. of China); Chair. Hong Kong Consumer Council 1988–91; formed United Democrats of Hong Kong, party opposed to Chinese mil. suppression of Tiananmen Square demonstrators in 1989, Leader 1990–94 (merged with Meeting Point party to become Democratic Party of Hong Kong, Chair. 1994–2002; Goodman Fellow, Univ. of Toronto 2000; Hon. LLD (Holy Cross Coll.) 1997, (Amherst Coll., USA) 1997; Prize for Freedom, Liberal Int. 1996, Int. Human Rights Award (American Bar Asscn) 1995, Democracy Award, Nat. Endowment for Democracy, USA 1997, Statesmanship Award, Claremont Inst., USA 1998, Schuman Medal, European Parl. 2000. *Publication:* The Basic Law: some basic flaws (with Szeto Wah) 1988. *Address:* Admiralty Centre, Room 704A, Tower I, 18 Harcourt Road, Hong Kong Special Administrative Region, People's Republic of China (Office); c/o Central Government Offices, Rooms 401-410, West Wing, 11 Ice House Street, Central, Hong Kong Special Administrative Region (Office). *Telephone:* 25290864 (Office). *Fax:* 28612829 (Office). *E-mail:* oml@ martinlee.org.hk (Office). *Website:* www.martinlee.org.hk (Office).

LEE, Shau-kee; Chinese business executive; b. 1929, Dailang, Pearl River Delta; s. of Lee Kai-po; m. Lau Wai-kuen 1966 (divorced 1981), two s. three d.; Founder and Chair, Henderson Investment Ltd; co-f. Sun Hung Kai Properties 1956 (now Vice-Chair.); Founder and Chair. Henderson Devt 1973, Henderson Land 1973, Henderson Investment Ltd 1988, Henderson China Holdings Ltd 1966 (now Exec. Dir); Henderson Cyber Ltd 2000 (Chair. and Man. Dir Henderson Group 1976–); Chair. Hong Kong and China Gas Co. Ltd; Dir Hong Kong Ferry (Holdings) Co. Ltd, Bank of E Asia, Miramar Hotel and Investment Co. Ltd. *Leisure interest:* golf. *Address:* Henderson Land Development Co. Ltd, 29/F, AIA Tower, 183 Electric Road, North Point, Hong Kong Special Administrative Region, People's Republic of China (Office). *Website:* www.hld.com (Office).

LEE, Spike (pseudonym of Shelton Jackson Lee); American film maker and actor; b. 20 March 1957, Atlanta, Ga; s. of Bill Lee and Jacquelyn Shelton; m. Tonya Lewis 1993; one d.; ed Morehouse Coll., Atlanta and New York Univ. Inst. of Film and Television; wrote scripts for Black Coll.: The Talented Tenth, Last Hustle in Brooklyn; produced, wrote, Dir Joe's Bed-Stuy Barbershop: We Cut Heads; has directed music videos, TV commercials and other short projects; Dr hc (New York Univ.) 1998; Commdr des Arts et des Lettres 2003; Cannes Film Festival Best New Dir 1986, LA Film Critics' Asscn Awards 1986, 1989, Chicago Film Festival Critics' Awards 1990, 1992, Golden Satellite Best Documentary 1997; inducted into Nat. Asscn for the Advancement of Colored People (NAACP) Hall of Fame 2003. *Films include:* She's Gotta Have It 1985 (Cannes Film Festival Prize for Best New Film), School Daze 1988, Do the Right Thing 1989, Love Supreme 1990, Mo' Better Blues 1990, Jungle Fever 1991, Malcolm X 1992, Crooklyn, Girl 6, Clockers 1995, Get on the Bus, He Got Game 1998, Summer of Sam 1999, Tales from the Hood 1995 (exec. producer), Bamboozled 2000, The Original Kings of Comedy 2000, Lisa Picard is Famous 2001, A Huey P. Newton Story 2001, The 25th Hour 2003. *Documentary:* Four Little Girls 1997. *Publications:* Spike Lee's Gotta Have It: Inside Guerilla Filmmaking 1987, Uplift the Race 1988, The Trials and Tribulations of the Making of Malcolm X 1992, Girl 6 1996, Get on the Bus 1996. *Leisure interest:* basketball. *Address:* Forty Acres and a Mule Filmworks, 124 De Kalb Avenue, Suite 2, Brooklyn, New York, NY 11217, USA.

LEE, Yeh Kwong Charles, LLM, F.C.C.A., ACIS; Chinese lawyer; b. 16 July 1936, Shanghai; m. Nancy Lee 1960; one s. one d.; ed London School of Econs; Audit Asst, Li Kwan Hung 1954–57, Peat Marwick Mitchell & Co., Hong Kong 1957–60; Asst Registrar, Registrar-Gen.'s Dept 1960–65; Articled Clerk, Nigel, Wallis & Apfel, Solicitors, UK 1965–68; Solicitor, Registrar-Gen.'s Dept 1968–70, Johnson Stokes & Master 1970–72, partner 1972–73; partner Charles Lee & Stephen Lo 1973, Woo Kwan Lee & Lo 1973–; mem. Council, Stock Exchange of Hong Kong Ltd 1988–, Chair. 1991; Dir several listed cos. *Leisure interests:* boating, scuba diving. *Address:* Woo Kwan Lee & Lo, 26/Fl. Jardine House, 1 Connaught Place, Hong Kong Special Administrative Region, People's Republic of China. *Telephone:* 8477823. *Fax:* 8450239.

LEE, Yuan-Tseh, PhD; Taiwanese professor of chemistry; b. 29 Nov. 1936, Hsinchu; s. of Tse Fan Lee and Pei Tasi; m. Bernice Wu 1963; two s. one d.; ed Nat. Taiwan Univ., Univ. of California, Berkeley, USA; Asst Prof. James Franck Inst. and Dept of Chem. Univ. of Chicago 1968–71, Assoc. Prof. 1971–72, Prof. of Chem. 1973–74; Prof. of Chem. Univ. of Calif., Berkeley 1974–94, Prof. Emer. 1994–, also Prin. Investigator, Lawrence Berkeley Lab. 1974–97; Pres. Academica Sinica 1994–; Sloan Fellow 1969; Guggenheim Fellow 1976; Miller Professorship 1981–82; mem. American Acad. of Arts and Sciences; Hon. Prof., Inst. of Chem., Chinese Acad. of Sciences, Beijing 1980–; shared Nobel Prize for Chem. 1986; E. O. Lawrence Award (US Dept of Energy), 1981 and many other awards and prizes. *Publications:* articles in professional journals. *Address:* Academia Sinica, 128 Academia Road, Section 2, Nanking, Taipei 11529, Taiwan (Office). *Telephone:* (2) 27822120 (Office). *Fax:* (2) 27853897 (Office). *Website:* www.sinica.edu.tw (Office).

LEE, Yung-San, MA, PhD; Taiwanese politician, economist and banking executive; b. 7 Dec. 1938; m.; three d.; ed Nat. Taiwan Univ., Univ. of Wisconsin, Madison, USA; joined as Asst, Inst. of Econs, Academia Sinica, served successively as Asst Research Fellow, Assoc. Research Fellow, Research Fellow 1962–70, Deputy Dir 1985–87, Dir 1988–90; Prof. of Econs Nat. Taiwan Univ. 1973–94; Visiting Scholar Harvard Univ., USA 1976–77; Dir Econ. Research Dept, Cen. Bank of China 1977–85; Pres. Chiao Tung

Bank 1990–94; Chair. Farmers Bank of China 1994–98, Int. Commercial Bank of China 1998–2002, Bankers Asscn of Taiwan 2000–02, Asian Bankers Asscn 2000–02; Minister of Finance 2002. *Address:* c/o Ministry of Finance, 2 I-Kuo West Road, Taipei, Taiwan (Office).

LEE HAN-DONG, BA; South Korean politician; b. 5 Dec. 1934, Gyeonggi-do; m. Nam Sook Cho; one s. ed Kyungbok High School, Seoul Nat. Univ.; Mil. Prosecutor, Rep. of Korea Army 1959, Staff Judge Advocate with 5th Corps 1961; Judge, Seoul Dist Court 1963, Prosecutor 1969, Prosecutor, Seoul High Prosecutor's Office and Deputy Dir of Legal Affairs Training, Ministry of Justice 1974; Sr Prosecutor, Daejeon Dist Prosecutor's Office 1975, Pusan Dist Prosecutor's Office 1977, Seoul Dist Prosecutor's Office 1980; mem. Nat. Ass. 1981–, Vice Speaker 1995; Deputy Floor Leader for Democratic Justice Party (DJP) 1981, Chief Sec. to Party Pres. 1982, DJP Sec. Gen. 1984, Floor Leader 1986, mem. Cen. Exec. Council 1990; Minister of Home Affairs 1988; Floor Leader for Democratic Liberal Party (DLP) 1993, Sr Adviser to Party Pres. 1996; Chief Exec., Chair. New Korea Party 1997, Grand Nat. Party 1997, Vice-Pres. 1998, Acting Pres. 1998; Acting Pres. United Liberal Democrats 2000, Pres. April 2000–; Prime Minister of Repub. of Korea 2000–02; Presidential Cand. 2002; Service Merit Medal 1976. *Address:* c/o Office of the Prime Minister, 77, Sejong-no, Jongno-gu, Seoul, Republic of Korea (Office).

LEE HOI-CHANG, BA; South Korean politician; b. 2 June 1935, Sohung, Hwanghae Prov.; m.; two s. one d.; ed Kyonggi High School, Seoul Nat. Univ., Harvard Univ., USA; service in AF, attained rank of Capt.; Judge, Incheon and Seoul Dist Court 1960–65; apptd Judge, Seoul High Court 1965, Sr Judge 1977; Prof., Judicial Research and Training Inst. 1971; Dir Planning and Co-ordination Office, Ministry of Court Admin 1980; Justice, Supreme Court 1981–86, 1988–93; practised law 1986–88, 1994–; Head of Nat. Election Comm. 1988–93; Head of Bd of Audit and Inspection 1993; Prime Minister of Repub. of Korea 1993; cand. of ruling New Korea Party in presidential elections 1997; Pres. Grand Nat. Party (GNP) 2000–02; cand. of GNP in presidential elections Dec. 2002. *Leisure interest:* listening to classical music. *Address:* 10-1401 Asia Seonsuchon Apt, Jamsil-7-dong, Songpa-gu, Seoul, Republic of Korea (Home). *Telephone:* (2) 3432-2030 (Home).

LEE HONG-KOO, PhD; South Korean politician and political scientist; b. 9 May 1934, Seoul; m.; one s. two d.; ed Seoul Nat. Univ., Emory and Yale Univs., USA; Asst Prof. Emory Univ. 1963–64, Case Western Reserve Univ. 1964–67; Asst Prof., Assoc. Prof., Prof. of Political Science, Seoul Nat. Univ. 1968–88, Dir Inst. of Social Sciences 1979–82; Fellow Woodrow Wilson Int. Center for Scholars, Smithsonian Inst. 1973–74, Harvard Law School 1974–75; Minister of Nat. Unification 1988–90; Special Asst to Pres. 1990–91; Amb. to UK 1991–93; Sr Vice-Chair. Advisory Council for Unification; Chair. Seoul 21st Century Cttee, The World Cup 2002 Bidding Cttee 1993–94; Deputy Prime Minister and Minister of Nat. Unification April–Dec. 1994, Prime Minister 1994–95; mem. Comm. on Global Governance 1991–95; Chair. New Korea Party May 1996; Amb. to USA 1998–2001. *Publications:* An Introduction to Political Science, One Hundred Years of Marxism, Modernization. *Address:* c/o Ministry of Foreign Affairs and Trade, 77 1-ga, Sejong-no, Jongno-gu, Seoul, Republic of Korea (Office).

LEE HSIEN LOONG, Brig.-Gen. "BG Lee"; Singaporean politician; b. 1952; s. of Lee Kuan Yew (q.v.) and Kwa Geok Choo; m. 1st (deceased 1982), one s. one d.; m. 2nd Ho Ching 1985; one s.; ed Catholic High School, Nat. Jr Coll., Cambridge, Harvard Univ.; nat. service 1971; Sr Army course at Fort Leavenworth, USA; Asst Chief of Gen. Staff (Operations) 1981–82, Chief of Staff (Gen. Staff) Singapore Army 1982–84; resgnd as Brig.-Gen. Aug. 1984, Nat. Reserves –2002; Political Sec. to Minister of Defence; MP for Teck Ghee Dec. 1984–; Chair. Comm. for Restructuring of the Economy 1985; Minister of State for Defence and for Trade and Industry 1985–86, for Trade and Industry 1986–93; Deputy Prime Minister 1990–, also Minister of Finance, Minister of Defence 1993–95, Second Minister of Defence (Services), Head Monetary Authority of Singapore; Second Asst Sec.-Gen. People's Action Party 1989–. *Leisure interests:* swimming, reading, jogging, computers. *Address:* Office of the Prime Minister, Orchard Road, Istana Annexe, Istana, Singapore 238823. *Telephone:* 2358577. *Fax:* 7324627. *Website:* www.pmo.gov .sg (Office).

LEE HUAN, MA; Taiwanese politician; b. 8 Feb. 1917, Hankow City; m.; two s. two d.; ed Nat. Chengchi Univ. and Columbia Univ.; Dir Shenyang Daily News 1946–48; Chief Sec., Deputy Dir-Gen. and Dir-Gen. China Youth Corps 1952–77; Prof. Nat. Chengchi Univ. 1962–79; Chair. Comm. for Youth Assistance and Guidance, Exec. Yuan 1967–72; Exec. Officer, Alumni Asscn of Nat. Chengchi Univ. 1977–80; Pres. Nat. Sun Yat-sen Univ. 1979–84; Minister of Educ. 1984–87; Prime Minister of Taiwan 1989–90; Sec.-Gen. Cen. Cttee Kuo-Min-Ta-Hui 1987–; Hon. PhD (Tan Kok) 1978; Hon. LLD (Sun Kyun Kwan) 1981.

LEE JONG-WOOK, MD; South Korean medical expert and international official; b. 12 April 1945, Seoul; ed Seoul Nat. Univ., Univ. of Hawaii, USA; joined World Health Org. (WHO) 1983, various tech., man. and policy positions including Dir Global Programme for Vaccines and Immunizations, Sr Policy Adviser, Dir Stop Tuberculosis Program 2000, Chief Tech. and Admin. Officer –2003, Dir-Gen. WHO July 2003–. *Address:* Office of the Director-General, WHO, Avenue Appia 20, 1211 Geneva 27, Switzerland (Office). *Telephone:* (22) 7912111 (Office). *Fax:* (22) 7913111 (Office). *E-mail:* info@who.int (Office). *Website:* www.who.int (Office).

LEE KI-TAEK, BSc; South Korean politician; b. 25 July 1937, Pohang; s. of the late Lee Dong-Sup and of Kim Nam-Chool; m. Lee Kyung-Ui 1968; one s. three d.; ed Korea Univ., Seoul, Univ. of Pennsylvania; involved in politics as student; mem. Korean Nat. Ass. 1967–; Chair. Special Cttee on Investigation of Political Corruption of the 5th Repub. 1988 and of Special Investigation Cttee of the 5th Repub. 1990; Chair. Pusan City Charter, New Democratic Party 1972, Sec. Gen. 1976, Vice-Pres. 1979; Chair. Inst. of Democratic Thoughts 1979; Vice-Pres. New Korea Democratic Party 1984, 1986; Vice-Pres. Reunification Democratic Party 1988–89, Floor Leader 1989; Chair. Democratic Party of Korea 1990, 1993, Co-Chair. 1991, Adviser 1995–96, Pres. 1995, 1996–98 (merged with New Korea Party to form Grand Nat. Party 1997); Hon. Prof. Yonbyun Univ., China 1995; Nat. Foundation Medal 1963. *Publications:* The Bridge of No Return 1978, History of Minority Parties in Korea 1987. *Leisure interest:* calligraphy. *Address:* 51-5, Yong Kang-dong, Mapo-gu, Seoul (Office); 187-12, Ahyun-dong, Seodaemun-gu, Seoul, Republic of Korea (Home). *Telephone:* (2) 711-3301 (Office); (2) 313-8551 (Home). *Fax:* (2) 711-3326 (Office); (2) 313-5219 (Home).

LEE KUAN YEW, MA; Singaporean politician and barrister; b. 16 Sept. 1923, Singapore; s. of the late Lee Chin Koon and Chua Jim Neo; m. Kwa Geok Choo 1950; two s. one d.; ed Raffles Coll., Singapore, Fitzwilliam Coll. Cambridge, UK; called to Bar, Middle Temple, London 1950, Hon. Bencher 1969; Advocate and Solicitor, Singapore 1951; a founder of People's Action Party 1954, Sec.-Gen. 1954–92; mem. Legis. Ass. 1955–; first Prime Minister Repub. of Singapore 1959, re-elected 1963, 1968, 1972, 1976, 1980, 1984, 1988; resgnd as Prime Minister Nov. 1990; Sr Minister in the Prime Minister's Office 1990–; mem. Singapore Internal Security Council 1959–; MP Fed. Parl. of Malaysia 1963–65; Chair. Singapore Investment Corpn 1981–; Fellow, Inst. of Politics, Harvard Univ. 1968; Hoyt Fellow, Berkeley Coll., Yale Univ. 1970; Hon. Fellow, Fitzwilliam Coll. Cambridge 1969, Royal Australasian Coll. of Surgeons 1973, RACP 1974; Hon. LLD (Royal Univ. of Cambodia) 1965, (Hong Kong) 1970, (Liverpool) 1971, (Sheffield) 1971; Hon. CH 1970; Hon. GCMG 1972; Bintang Republik Indonesia Adi Pradana 1973, Order of Sikatuna (Philippines) 1974, Most Hon. Order of Crown of Johore (First Class), 1984, Hon. Freeman, City of London 1982, numerous other distinctions. *Publications:* The Singapore Story – Memoirs of Lee Kuan Yew (Vol. 1), From Third World to First: The Singapore Story 1965–2000 (Vol. 2). *Leisure interests:* jogging, swimming, golf. *Address:* Prime Minister's Office, Istana Annexe, Singapore 238823, Republic of Singapore.

LEE KYUNG-SHIK; South Korean politician and banker; ed Korea Univ.; joined Bank of Korea; Econ. Planning Bd 1961–72; served in Office of Pres. 1972–74; later Vice-Minister of Communications and mem. Monetary Bd of Korea; Pres. Daewoo Motor Co. 1988–93, Korea Gas Corpn until 1993; Deputy Prime Minister and Minister of Econ. Planning 1993; Gov. Bank of Korea 1995–98. *Address:* c/o Bank of Korea, 110, 3-ga, Namdaemun-no, Jung-gu, Seoul 100-794, Republic of Korea.

LEE SOO-SUNG; South Korean politician and academic; fmr Pres. Seoul Nat. Univ.; Prime Minister of Repub. of Korea 1995–97. *Address:* c/o Office of the Prime Minister, 77 Sejong-no, Jongno-gu, Seoul, Republic of Korea.

LEE TENG-HUI, PhD; Taiwanese politician; b. 15 Jan. 1923, Taiwan; m. Tseng Wen-fui; two d.; ed Kyoto Imperial Univ., Japan, Nat. Taiwan Univ., Iowa State and Cornell Univs, USA; Asst Prof. Nat. Taiwan Univ. 1949–55, Assoc. Prof. 1956–58; Research Fellow, Taiwan Co-operative Bank 1953; Specialist and Econ. Analyst, Dept of Agric. and Forestry, Taiwan Prov. Govt 1954–57; Specialist, Joint Comm. on Rural Reconstruction (JCRR) 1957–61, Sr Specialist and Consultant 1961–70, Chief, Rural Economy Div. 1970–72; Prof. Nat. Chengchi Univ. 1958–78; Minister without Portfolio 1972–78; Mayor of Taipei City 1978–81; Gov. Taiwan Province 1981–84; Vice-Pres. of Repub. of China (Taiwan) 1984–88, Pres. 1988–2000; co-f. Taiwan Solidarity Union 2001; expelled from KMT (Kuomingtang) Party Sept. 2001; Hon. LLD (Southern Methodist Univ., USA) 1994; Int. Distinguished Achievement Citation, Iowa State Univ., USA and other awards. *Publications:* several works on agricultural development in Taiwan. *Leisure interests:* art, music and sport. *Address:* c/o Office of the President, 122 Chungking South Road, Sec. 1, Taipei 100, Taiwan.

LEE TSUNG-DAO, PhD; Chinese physicist; b. 25 Nov. 1926, Shanghai; s. of Tsing-Kong Lee and Ming-Chang Chang; m. Jeanette H. C. Chin 1950; two s.; ed Chekiang Univ., Nat. Southwest Univ., China and Univ. of Chicago, USA; Research Assoc. in Astronomy, Univ. of Chicago 1950; Research Assoc. and Lecturer in Physics, Univ. of California 1950–51; mem. Inst. for Advanced Study, Princeton, NJ 1951–53; Asst Prof. of Physics, Columbia Univ., New York 1953–55, Assoc. Prof. 1955–56, Prof. 1956–60, 1963; Enrico Fermi Prof. of Physics 1964–, Univ. Prof. 1984–; Prof. Princeton Inst. for Advanced Study 1960–63; mem. NAS; shared Nobel Prize for Physics 1957 with Prof. Yang Chen-ning for work on elementary particles; Albert Einstein Award in Science 1957. *Publications:* articles in physical journals. *Address:* Department of Physics, Columbia University, Building 538, Morningside Heights, W 120th Street, New York, NY 10027 (Office); 25 Claremont Avenue, New York, NY 10027, USA (Home). *Telephone:* (212) 854-1759 (Office). *Fax:* (212) 932-0418 (Office). *Website:* www.columbia.edu (Office).

LEE UFAN; South Korean painter; b. 1936, Gyeonsang Nam-do; ed Seoul Nat. Univ. and Nihon Univ., Tokyo; mem. Mono-Ha group (Japanese avant-garde art movt) late 1960s; Prof. Tama Art Univ., Tokyo 1973–93; Prof. Ecole

Nat. Supérieure des Beaux-Arts, Paris 1997–98; prize for critical writing 1969, Praemium Imperiale Award, Japan Art Asscn 2001; Cultural Decoration 1990, Chevalier des Arts et des Lettres 1991. *Solo art exhibitions include:* Tamura Gallery, Tokyo 1970, 1974, Tokyo Gallery 1973, 1977, 1980, 1983, 1986, 1989, 1993, 1996, 1999, Galerie Eric Fabre, Paris 1975, 1977, 1980, Galerie m, Bochum, Germany 1976, 1978, 1989, 1995, Hyondae Gallery, Seoul 1978, 1984, 1987, 1990, 1994, 1997, Galerie de Paris 1984, 1986, 1989, 1992, 1995, Kamakura Gallery, Tokyo 1985, 1990, 1993, 1999, Lisson Gallery, London 1996, Galerie Nat. du Jeu de Paume, Paris 1997, Lorenzelli Arte, Milan 1997, Städtisches Museum im Städel, Frankfurt 1998; has participated in numerous group exhbns 1968–. *Address:* c/o Ecole Nationale Supérieure des Beaux-Arts, 14 rue Bonaparte, 75006 Paris, France (Office).

LEE YOCK SUAN, BSc; Singaporean politician; b. 1946; m.; one s. one d.; ed Queenstown Secondary Technical School, Raffles Institution, Imperial Coll., Univ. of London, UK, Univ. of Singapore; Div. Dir (Projects), Econ. Devt Bd 1969–80; MP 1980–; Deputy Man. Dir Petrochemical Corpn of Singapore (Pte.) Ltd Jan.–Sept. 1981; Minister of State (Nat. Devt) 1981–83, (Finance) 1983–84, Sr Minister of State and Acting Minister for Labour 1985–86, Minister for Labour 1987–91, Second Minister of Educ. 1991–92, Minister of Educ. 1992–97, of Trade and Industry 1998–99, for Information and the Arts 1999–2001, of Environment 1999–2000, Minister in Prime Minister's Office and Second Minister of Foreign Affairs 2001–; Deputy Chair. People's Asscn 1984–91. *Leisure interest:* badminton. *Address:* Office of the Prime Minister, Orchard Road, Istana Annexe, Istana, Singapore 23882.

LEENHARDT, Jacques; French sociologist; b. 17 April 1942, Geneva, Switzerland; s. of Franz J. Leenhardt and Antoinette Chenevière; m. Françoise Warnod 1964 (divorced 1970); one s.; contrib. to Le Journal de Genève 1963–98, to Le Temps 1998–; Fellow Inst. for Advanced Study, Princeton Univ., NJ 1979–80; Visiting Prof. to Univs in Brazil, Chile, Germany, Mexico, Portugal, Puerto Rico, USA 1974–; now Dir of Studies, School of Advanced Studies in Social Sciences, Paris; Pres. French Art Critics Asscn 1981–90, Crestet Centre d'Art 1987–2002, Int. Art Critics Asscn 1990–96, Art in Nature 1991–; mem. European Acad. of Arts and Sciences 1992–; Chevalier des Arts et des Lettres 1983, Ordre nat. du Mérite 1987; Oficial Ordem Nacional do Cruzeiro do Sul (Brazil) 1998; Edra-Place Award 2000. *Publications include:* Lecture politique du roman 1973, Lire la lecture 1982, La force des mots 1982, Au Jardin des Malentendus 1990, Les Amériques latines en France 1992, Dans les jardins de Roberto Burle Marx 1994, Villette-Amazone 1996, Bienal do Mercosur 1998, Michel Corajoud, Paysagiste 2000, Erico Veríssimo. O romance da História 2001, Conscience du paysage: Le passant de Montreuil 2002. *Address:* École des Hautes Études en Sciences Sociales, 10 rue Monsieur le Prince, 75006 Paris, France. *Telephone:* 1-44-41-46-74. *Fax:* 1-44-41-46-76. *E-mail:* jacques.leenhardt@ehess.fr (Office). *Website:* www.ehess.fr/efisal (Office).

LEES, Sir David (Bryan), Kt, CBIM, FCA, FRSA; British business executive; b. 23 Nov. 1936, Aberdeen; s. of the late Rear-Admiral D. M. Lees, CB, DSO, and of C. D. M. Lees; m. Edith M. Bernard 1961; two s. one d.; ed Charterhouse; articled clerk, Binder Hamlyn & Co. (Chartered Accountants) 1957–62, Sr Audit Clerk 1962–63; Chief Accountant, Handley Page Ltd 1964–68; Financial Dir Handley Page Aircraft Ltd 1969; Chief Accountant, GKN Sankey Ltd 1970–72, Deputy Controller 1972–73, Dir, Sec., Controller 1973–76; Group Finance Exec. GKN Ltd 1976–77, Gen. Man. Finance 1977–82; Finance Dir GKN PLC 1982–87, Group Man. Dir 1987–88, CEO 1988–96, Chair. 1988–; Chair. Courtaulds 1996–98 (Dir 1991–98); Deputy Chair. Brambles Industries Ltd and Brambles Industries PLC 2001; Dir Bank of England 1991–99, Royal Opera House 1998–; Chair. Tate & Lyle PLC 1998–; Pres. Eng Employers' Fed. (EEF) 1990–92, Soc. of Business Economists 1994–99; mem. CBI Council 1988–, Chair. CBI Econ. Affairs Cttee 1988–94, mem. CBI Pres.'s Cttee 1988–96; Commr, Audit Comm. 1983–90; Gov. Shrewsbury School 1986–; mem. Listed Cos Advisory Cttee 1990–97, Nat. Defence Industries Council 1995–, European Round Table 1995–2002, Panel on Takeovers and Mergers 2001– and other bodies; Gov. Sutton's Hosp. in Charterhouse 1995–; Officer's Cross, Order of Merit (Germany) 1996; Founding Socs Centenary Award for Chartered Accountants 1999. *Leisure interests:* walking, golf, opera, music. *Address:* Tate & Lyle PLC, Sugar Quay, Lower Thames Street, London, EC3R 6DQ, England.

LEES, Martin; British engineer and international official; b. 1941; m.; four c.; ed Univ. of Cambridge, Coll. of Europe, Belgium; Rector and CEO UN Univ. for Peace Jan. 2001–. *Address:* United Nations University for Peace, P.O. Box 138, Ciudad Colón, Costa Rica (Office). *Telephone:* 249-1072 (Office). *Fax:* 249-1929 (Office). *E-mail:* info@upeace.org (Office). *Website:* www.upeace.org (Office).

LEEVES, Jane; British actress; b. 18 April 1963, E Grinstead, Sussex; d. of Colin Leeves and Ruth Leeves; m. Marshall Cohen 1996; one d.; co-f. (with Frasier co-star Peri Gilpin) Bristol Cities Production Co. 1998. *Films:* Monty Python's The Meaning of Life 1983, To Live and Die in LA 1985, The Hunger 1983, Mr Write 1994, Miracle on 34th Street 1994, James and the Giant Peach (voice) 1996, Hercules (voice) 1998, Don't Go Breaking My Heart 1998, Music of the Heart 1999, The Adventures of Tom Thumb and Thumbelina (voice) 2000. *Television:* The Benny Hill Show 1969, Double Trouble 1984, Throb 1986, Murphy Brown 1988, Seinfeld, Red Dwarf 1992, Just Deserts 1992, 1999, Frasier 1993–, Pandora's Clock 1996, The Great War and the Shaping of the 20th Century (voice) 1996. *Theatre:* Cabaret, Broadway 2002. *Leisure*

interests: reading, cooking, sports, dance classes. *Address:* Bristol Cities Productions, c/o Paramount Productions, 5555 Melrose Avenue, Los Angeles, CA 90038, USA (Office). *Telephone:* (323) 956-3513 (Office). *E-mail:* BrstlCty@aol.com (Office).

LEFRANÇOIS, Jacques Roger; Belgian accountant; b. 1 March 1929, Eu, Seine Maritime, France; s. of Roger Lefrançois and Simone Boussy; m. Rosa Van Laer Londerzeel 1952; one s. one d.; ed Coll. d'Eu, Inst. Nat. de Comptabilité; second accountant (Sogeco mar) 1948–52; Publicity Agent (Publi-Buro) 1952–68; confidential employee 1966–78; mem. Congress of European People (EFB-MFE) 1961–65; World Citizen for Peace through Human Rights 1965; proposed UN Day for World Peace and the Environment 1970; mem. Professional Union of Int. School of Detective Experts 1950–75, Belgium Comm. World Political Union, The Hague 1978–; First Sec. Universal Charter for Survival (UFOS) 1975; Pres. Group 'L'Homme Planétaire' 1970–98, f. and Sec. Gén. Conseil mondial de crise 1998–; mem. Flemish Asscn of Journalists of Periodical Press 1970–97; Ed. L'Indépandant Schaerbeek 1964–, Het Watervlietje 1975–2001; Sec. Flemish Regions, Parti Progressiste Belge 1989–93, Pres. 1985–89; Belgian Ombudsman/Médiateur Belge 1986–88; Pres. Flemish Progressive Party, European Flemish Programme 1989–92; Vice-Pres. European Progressive Party; Hon. Pres. and Public Relations Ombudsman Parti Mondial du Coeur 1993–97; Prize for Action to Promote European Federalism 1967. *Address:* 9 rue Leo Baekelandstr., 2030 Antwerp, Belgium. *Telephone:* (3) 542-04-58. *Fax:* (3) 542-04-58.

LEGGE-SCHWARZKOPF, Dame Elisabeth, DBE; Austrian/British (b. German) soprano; b. 9 Dec. 1915, Jarotschin/Poznań; d. of Friedrich Schwarzkopf and Elisabeth Schwarzkopf (née Fröhlich); m. Walter Legge 1953 (died 1979); ed Berlin Hochschule für Musik, studied with Prof. Lula Mysz-Gmeiner, Dr Heinrich Egenolf and Maria Ivogün-Raucheisen; debut at Deutsches Opernhaus, Berlin 1938; sang at inauguration of post-war Bayreuth Festival 1951; appeared at Vienna State Opera 1943–49, 1958–65, Royal Opera House, Covent Garden 1948–50, La Scala Milan 1948–63, San Francisco Opera 1955–79, Metropolitan Opera, New York 1964–66, Chicago Opera and others; guest singer, Salzburg Festival 1947–64, Reopening of Bayreuth Festival 1951; created Anne Trulove in Stravinsky's Rake's Progress; producer Der Rosenkavalier, Brussels 1981; Corresp. mem. Bayerische Akad. der Künste; Prof. (Baden-Württemberg) 1990; Hon. mem. Acad. di Santa Cecilia, Rome, Acad. of Arts and Letters, Stockholm, RAM, Vienna State Opera; Kammersängerin (Austria); Hon. Senator High School of Music Carl Maria von Weber, Dresden; Goldener Rathaus Mann, Vienna; Grosses Verdienstkreuz 1974; Order of Dannebrog (1st Class) (Denmark); mem. Ordre pour le Mérite (FRG) 1983; Commdr Ordre des Arts et des Lettres 1985; Grosses Bundesverdienstkreuz mit Stern 1995; Hon. DMus (Cambridge) 1976, American Univ. of Washington DC; Hon. DLit (Glasgow) 1990; Lilli Lehmann Medal, Salzburg 1950, Orfeo d'Oro, Mantua, Hugo Wolf Medal, Vienna, Litteris et Artibus Medal (Sweden), Diapason d'Or, Paris 1984, Premio Viotti 1991, Mozart Medal, Frankfurt, Vercelli, UNESCO Mozart Medal, Paris 1991, Gold Medal, Bundeshauptstadt Vienna. *Recordings include:* 16 complete operas, 6 complete operettas, songs, various symphonies, lieder and arias with orchestra, lieder with piano. *Principal roles include:* Rosina (Barber of Seville), Blondchen, Konstanze (Die Entführung aus dem Serail), Susanna, Contessa (Le Nozze di Figaro), Donna Elvira (Don Giovanni), Fiordiligi (Così fan Tutte), Pamina (Die Zauberflöte), Marzelline (Fidelio), Violeta (Traviata), Gilda (Rigoletto), Alice (Falstaff), Musetta, Mimi (La Bohème), Cio-Cio-San (Madame Butterfly), Liu (Turandot), Manon (Manon), Eva (Meistersinger), Elsa (Lohengrin), Hirtenknabe, Elisabeth (Tannhäuser), Mélisande (Pelléas et Mélisande), Iole (Herakles), Anne (Rake's Progress, world premiere), Margarethe (Faust), Marenka (Bartered Bride), Ännchen, Agatha (Freischütz), Nedda (Pagliacci), Zerbinetta (Ariadne), Sophie und Marschallin (Rosenkavalier), Madeleine (Capriccio), Orff (Trionfo d'Afrodite, world premiere); (concert performances): Leonore (Fidelio), Ilia (Idomeneo), Euridice (Orfeo ed Euridice), Cleopatra (Giulio Cesare). *Film:* Der Rosenkavalier (Salzburg Festival) 1961. *Publication:* On and Off the Record: A Memoir of Walter Legge (ed) 1982. *Leisure interests:* photography, mountain walking. *Address:* Kammersängerin, Rebhusstrasse 29, 8126 Zumikon, Switzerland.

LEGHARI, Farooq Ahmed Khan; Pakistani politician; b. 2 May 1940, Dera Ghazi Khan; s. of Nawabzada Sardar Mohammad Khan Leghari; m. 1965; two s. two d.; ed Punjab and Oxford Univs; joined Pakistan People's Party 1973; Chief Baluchi Leghari Tribe; Pakistan Civil Service 1964–73; elected to Senate 1975, to Nat. Ass. 1977; Minister for Production 1977; periods of imprisonment for opposition to Govt 1977–88; Sec. Gen. Pakistan People's Party and mem. Exec. Cttee 1978; elected mem. Nat. Ass. and Provincial Ass. 1988–, Leader of Opposition, Prov. Ass. 1988, Minister for Water and Power 1988–90, Deputy Leader of Opposition 1990–93, Minister of Finance 1993, Minister of Foreign Affairs Oct.–Nov. 1993; Pres. of Pakistan 1993–97; dismissed Govt of Benazir Bhutto 1996; Organizer and Founder Millat Party, currently Chair. *Leisure interests:* hunting, horseriding. *Address:* Village Choti, District Dera Ghazikhan, Punjab, Pakistan. *Telephone:* (42) 5729666.

LEGORRETA VILCHIS, Ricardo; Mexican architect; b. 7 May 1931, México, DF; s. of Luis Legorreta and Guadalupe Vilchis; m. María Luisa Hernández 1956; three s. three d.; ed Univ. of Mexico; Draughtsman and Chief Designer with José Villagran García 1948–55, Partner 1955–60; Prof. of Design, Univ. of Mexico 1959–62, Head of Experimental Group 1962–64; pvt.

practice 1961–63; f. Legorreta Arquitectos (LA) with Noe Castro and Carlos Vargas 1963, Dir 1963–; f. LA Diseños 1977, Pres. 1977–; main works: Camino Real Hotel, Mexico City, Hotel Regina, Cancun, Solana Project, Dallas, USA, Cathedral in Managua, Nicaragua; mem. Int. Cttee, Museum of Modern Art, New York 1970; mem. Bd of Judges, AIA 1977; Emer. Fellow, Colegio de Arquitectos de México 1978, mem. Bd of Judges 1980; mem. Pritzker Prize Jury 1984; mem. IAA (Sofia) 1989; Hon. mem. North American Inst. of Architects. *Publication:* Los muros de México (with Celanese Mexicana). *Leisure interests:* tennis, music. *Address:* Palacio de Versalles 285-A, Col Lomas Reforma, Código Postal 11020, México 10, DF (Office); Palacio de Versalles 285-A, Col Lomas Reforma, Código Postal 11020, México 10, DF, Mexico (Home). *Telephone:* 596-04-11 (Office); 596-21-88 (Home).

LEGQOG; Chinese politician; b. Oct. 1944, Gyangze, Tibet; joined CCP 1972; Sec. CCP Lhasa City Cttee 1991–98; Chair. Tibetan Autonomous Region 1998–; mem. CCP 15th Cen. Cttee 1997–. *Address:* c/o People's Government of Tibetan Autonomous Region, Lhasa, Tibet, People's Republic of China.

LEGRAS, Guy; French international organization official; b. 19 July 1938, Angers; s. of René Legras and Pauline Legras; m. Borka Oreb 1971; one s. one d.; ed Faculté de Droit, Paris, Inst. d'Etudes Politiques, Paris and Ecole Nat. d'Admin; joined Ministry of Foreign Affairs 1967; Cabinet of Sec. of State for Foreign Affairs 1968–71; Secr.-Gen. of Interministerial Cttee (SGCI) for European Affairs (Prime Minister) 1971–74; Cabinet of Sec.-Gen. of OECD 1974–77; Counsellor, Perm. Rep. of France at European Communities, Brussels 1977–80; Asst Sec.-Gen. SGCI 1980-82; Head, Dept of Econ. Affairs, Ministry of Foreign Affairs 1982–85; Dir-Gen. for Agric. Comm. of European Communities (now EC), Brussels 1985–99, for External Affairs 1999–; Minister Plenipotentiary 1988; Officier, Ordre nat. du Mérite, Chevalier, Légion d'honneur. *Leisure interest:* tennis. *Address:* Commission of the European Communities, 200 rue de la Loi, 1049 Brussels, Belgium (Office); 111 rue de Rennes, 75006 Paris, France.

LEGRIS, Manuel Christophe; French ballet dancer; b. 19 Oct. 1964, Paris; s. of Michel Legris and Raymonde Gazave; ed Paris Opera School of Dancing; mem. corps de ballet, Paris Opéra 1980, 'Danseur Etoile' 1986–; maj. roles at Paris Opéra include Arepo (Béjart) 1986, In the Middle Somewhat Elevated (Forsythe) 1987, Magnificat (Neumeier) 1987, Rules of the Game (Twyla Tharp) 1989, The Sleeping Beauty (Nureyev) 1989, Manon (MacMillan) 1990, Dances at the Gathering (Robbins) 1992; in Hamburg created Cinderella Story and Spring and Fall (Neumeier); has also appeared at Bolshoi Ballet, Moscow, La Scala, Milan, Royal Ballet, London, New York City Ballet, Tokyo Ballet, Stuttgart Ballet and others; Gold Medal, Osaka Competition 1984; Prix du Cercle Carpeaux 1986, Nijinsky Prize 1988, Benois de la danse Prize 1998; Officier des Arts et des Lettres 1998; Nijinsky Award 2000. *Film appearances include:* Romeo and Juliet, Le Spectre de la Rose, Notre Dame de Paris, L'Arlésienne, The Sleeping Beauty, Don Quixote. *Address:* Théâtre national de l'Opéra de Paris, 8 rue Scribe, 75009 Paris, France. *E-mail:* manuel.legris@wanadoo.fr (Office).

LEGWAILA, Legwaila Joseph, MA; Botswana diplomatist; b. 2 Feb. 1937, Mathathane; s. of Madume Legwaila and Morongwa Legwaila; m. Pholile Matsebula 1975; three d.; ed Bobonong School, Brussels School, SA, Serowe Teacher Training Coll., Univs of Calgary and Alberta, Canada; Asst Prin. External Affairs, Govt of Botswana 1973–74, Sr Pvt. Sec. to Pres. of Botswana 1974–80; Perm. Rep. to UN 1980–, High Commr in Guyana 1981, in Jamaica 1982, Amb. to Cuba 1983; Deputy Special Rep. of the UN Sec.-Gen. for Namibia 1989–90; Head of UN Mission in Ethiopia and Eritrea (UNMEE). *Publication:* Safari to Serowe (co-author) 1970. *Leisure interests:* music, cycling. *Address:* Botswana Mission to the United Nations, 103 East 37th Street, New York, NY 10016, USA (Office). *Telephone:* (212) 889-2277 (Office); (914) 636-4858 (Home). *Fax:* (212) 725-5061 (Office). *E-mail:* botswana@un.int (Office).

LEHMAN, Ronald Frank, II, PhD; American government official; b. 25 March 1946, Napa, Calif.; s. of Ronald Lehman and Esther Suhr; m. Susan Young 1979; ed Claremont Men's Coll. and Claremont Grad. School; army service, Vietnam 1969–71; Legis. Asst US Senate 1976–78; mem. professional staff, US Senate Armed Services Cttee 1978–82; Deputy Asst Sec. of Defense, Office of Int. Security Policy 1982–83; Sr Dir Defense Programs and Arms Control, Nat. Security Council 1983–86; Deputy US Negotiator for Strategic Nuclear Arms, Dept of State, Washington, DC 1985–86; Chief US Negotiator Geneva 1986–88; Deputy Asst to Pres. for Nat. Security Affairs 1986; Asst Sec. Dept of Defense 1988–89; Dir Arms Control and Disarmament Agency, Washington, DC 1989–93; Asst to Dir Lawrence Livermore Nat. Lab. 1993–, Dir Center for Global Security Research 1996–; mem. Presidential Advisory Bd on Arms Proliferation Policy 1995–96; Adjunct Prof. Georgetown Univ. 1982–89; mem. Bd Dirs US Inst. of Peace 1988–93, Keck Center for Int. and Strategic Studies (now Chair.), Claremont McKenna Coll.; mem. Int. Advisory Bd Inst. of Global Conflict and Cooperation, Univ. of Calif. San Diego 1994–; mem. IISS, Council on Foreign Relations, Atlantic Council. *Address:* Center for Global Security Research, Lawrence Livermore National Laboratory, P.O. Box 808, L-1, Livermore, CA 94551 (Office); 693 Encina Grande Drive, Palo Alto, CA 94306, USA (Home). *Telephone:* (925) 422-6141. *Fax:* (925) 422-5252. *E-mail:* lehman3@llnl.gov. *Website:* cgsr.llnl.gov.

LEHMANN, Erich Leo, PhD; American professor of statistics; b. 20 Nov. 1917, Strasbourg, France; s. of Julius Lehmann and Alma Schuster; m. Juliet

Popper Shaffer; one s. two d.; ed High School, Zurich, Switzerland, Univ. of Cambridge, Univ. of Calif., Berkeley; mem. Dept of Math. Univ. of Calif., Berkeley 1946–55, Dept of Statistics 1955–88, Prof. Emer. 1988–, Chair. Dept of Statistics 1973–76; Visiting Assoc. Prof. Columbia Univ. 1950, Stanford Univ. 1951–52, Visiting Lecturer Princeton Univ. 1951, Guggenheim Fellow 1955, 1966, 1979, Miller Research Prof. 1967, 1972; Sr Scholar, Educ. Testing Service 1995–; mem. NAS, American Acad. of Art and Sciences; fmr Pres. Inst. Math. Statistics; Dr hc (Leiden) 1985, (Chicago) 1991; American Statistical Asscn Samuel S. Wilks Memorial Award 1996. *Publications:* Testing Statistical Hypotheses 1959, Basic Concepts of Probability and Statistics (with J. L. Hodges, Jr) 1964, Nonparametrics: Statistical Methods based on Ranks 1975, Elements of Large Sample Theory 1998, Theory of Point Estimation (with George Casella) 1998, Ed. Annals of Mathematical Statistics 1953–55. *Leisure interests:* music, reading, hiking. *Address:* Department of Statistics, University of California, Berkeley, CA 94270, USA.

LEHMANN, HE Cardinal Karl, DPhil, DTheol; German ecclesiastic; b. 16 May 1936, Sigmaringen; s. of the late Karl Lehmann and of Margarete Lehmann; ed in Freiburg, Rome, Munich, Münster; ordained priest 1963; asst. to Karl Rahner, Munich and Münster 1964–67; consecrated Bishop of Mainz 1983; Pres. of Conf. of German Bishops 1987–; First Vice-Pres. Council of European Bishops Conferences (CCEE) 1993; cr. Cardinal 2001; Prof. of Theology Univ. of Mainz 1968–71; Prof. of Theology Univ. of Freiburg 1971–83; Hon. Dr hc (Innsbruck, Washington, Maynooth, Warsaw, Graz); Karl Barth Prize, Evangelical Union of Churches 1994, 'Golden Flower from Rheydt' of the town Mönchengladbach 1995, Bundesverdienstkreuz 2000; Hon. Citizen of Mainz 2001. *Publications:* Glauben bezeugen-Gesellschaft gestallen 1993; ed. of numerous religious journals. *Address:* Bischofsplatz 2a, 55116 Mainz, Germany (Office). *Telephone:* (6131) 253107 (Office). *Fax:* (6131) 229337 (Office). *E-mail:* bischof.lehmann@bistam-mainz.de (Office). *Website:* www.kath.de/bistam/mainz (Office).

LEHMBERG, Stanford Eugene, PhD; American professor of history; b. 23 Sept. 1931, McPherson, Kan.; s. of W.E. Lehmberg and Helen Lehmberg; m. Phyllis Barton 1962; one s.; ed Univ. of Kansas, Cambridge Univ., UK; mem. History Faculty, Univ. of Tex. at Austin 1956–69; Prof. of History, Univ. of Minn. 1967–98; Organist and Choirmaster, St Clement's Episcopal Church, St Paul, Minn. 1970–98; Fulbright Scholarship 1954–56; Guggenheim Fellow 1955–56, 1985–86, Fellow Royal Historical Soc., Soc. of Antiquaries; Hon. LittD (Cambridge) 1990. *Publications:* Sir Thomas Elyot, Tudor Humanist 1960, Sir Walter Mildmay and Tudor Government 1966, The Reformation Parliament, 1529–1536 1970, The Later Parliaments of Henry VIII 1977, The Reformation of Cathedrals 1988, The Peoples of the British Isles from Prehistoric Times to 1688 1991, Cathedrals Under Siege 1996, The University of Minnesota 1945–2001 2001; Ed. Sir Thomas Elyot, The Book Named the Governor 1962; articles, reviews. *Leisure interests:* music, the arts. *Address:* 1005 Calle Largo, Santa Fe, NM 87501, USA (Home). *Telephone:* (505) 986-5074. *Fax:* (505) 986-1724. *E-mail:* lehmberg@earthlink.net (Office).

LEHN, Jacques André, LèsL; French business executive; b. 15 July 1944, Lausanne, Switzerland; s. of François-Xavier Lehn and Geneviève Jaeger; ed lycées in Rabat (Morocco) and Sceaux, Sorbonne, Paris, Inst. d'Etudes Politiques, Paris and Ecole des Hautes Etudes Commerciales; Man. Consultant, Arthur Andersen 1969–76; Finance Dir Warner Lambert France 1976–79; Dir-Gen. Adams' France 1979–80; Dir Matra, Médias Br. 1980–81; Dir Hachette Group 1981–84, Deputy Dir-Gen. 1984–90, Dir-Gen. 1990; Dir-Gen. Matra-Hachette 1993–; Vice-Pres. Europe I Communication 1986–94, Deputy Pres. 1994–99; Pres., Dir-Gen. Europe développement int. 1996–; Pres. Supervisory Bd Europa Plus, France 1996–, Holpa 1996–; Chair. and CEO Go Mass Media, Go Outdoor Holdings Systems 1999–; Chair. of Supervisory Bd. Giraudy 1999–; numerous other business affiliations; Chevalier, Ordre Nat. du Mérite, Légion d'honneur. *Leisure interest:* yachting. *Address:* ORMA, 9 rue Royale, 75008 Paris (Office); 47 blvd Lannes, 75116 Paris, France (Home). *Telephone:* 1-53-30-86-07 (Office). *Fax:* 1-47-42-32-14 (Office).

LEHN, Jean-Marie Pierre, D. ÈS SC.; French professor of chemistry; b. 30 Sept. 1939, Rosheim, Bas-Rhin; s. of Pierre and Marie (née Salomon) Lehn; m. Sylvie Lederer 1965; two s.; ed Univ. of Strasbourg; various posts, CNRS 1960–66; post-doctoral research assoc. with Prof. R. B. Woodward, Harvard Univ., U.S.A. 1963–64; Asst Prof., Univ. of Strasbourg 1966–70, Assoc. Prof. 1970, Prof. 1970–79; Visiting Prof. of Chem., Harvard Univ. 1972, 1974, E.T.H., Zurich 1977, Cambridge Univ. 1984, Barcelona Univ. 1985; Prof Coll. de France, Paris 1979–; Pres. Scientific Council of Rhône-Poulenc 1992–, of Ministry of Nat. Educ., Youth and Sport 1989–93; mem. Research Strategy Cttee 1995, Inst. de France, Deutsche Akad. der Naturforscher Leopoldina, Accad. Nazionale dei Lincei; Foreign assoc. NAS; Foreign mem. Royal Netherlands Acad. of Arts and Sciences, Royal Soc. and many others; Foreign Hon. mem. American Acad. of Arts and Sciences; shared Nobel Prize in Chemistry 1987; Gold, Silver and Bronze Medals of CNRS; Gold Medal, Pontifical Acad. of Sciences 1981; Paracelsus Prize, Swiss Chem. Soc. 1982, von Humboldt Prize 1983, Karl Ziegler Prize (German Chem. Soc.) 1989, Davy Medal (Royal Soc.) 1997; Commdr Légion d'honneur, Officier Ordre nat. du Mérite; mem. Order "Pour le Mérite" 1990. *Publications:* about 500 scientific publications. *Leisure interest:* music. *Address:* Collège de France, 11 place Marcellin Berthelot, 75005 Paris (Office); 6 rue des Pontonniers, 67000 Strasbourg, France (Home); Université Louis-Pasteur, Institut Le Bel, 4 rue

Blaise Pascal, 67000 Strasbourg. *Telephone:* 1-44-27-13-60 (Office); (88) 37-06-42 (Home). *Fax:* 1-44-27-13-56 (Office). *E-mail:* lehn@chimie.u-strasbg.fi (Office).

LEHR, Ursula M., PhD; German politician and psychologist; b. 5 June 1930, Frankfurt am Main; d. of Georg-Josef Leipold and Gertrud Jendorff; m. 1st Helmut Lehr 1950 (died 1994); two s.; m. 2nd Hans Thomas 1998 (died 2001); Research Asst, Univ. of Bonn 1955–60, Research and Teaching Asst, Inst. of Psychology 1960–68, mem. perm. staff. 1968–69, Additional Prof. and Head Dept of Developmental Psychology 1969–72, Chair. Dept of Psychology and Dir Inst. of Psychology 1976–86, Hon. Prof. 1987–; Chair. of Pedagogics and Pedagogical Psychology, Albertus Magnus Univ., Cologne 1972; Dir Inst. of Gerontology, Ruprecht Karls Univ., Heidelberg 1986–88, 1991–96; Head German Centre for Research on Aging, Heidelberg 1996–; Fed. Minister of Youth, Families, Women and Health 1988–91; mem. Families Advisory Bd, Fed. Ministry of Youth, Families and Health 1972–80, WHO Expert Advisory Panel on Health of Elderly Persons 1983–87; mem. Parl. 1990–94; Vice-Pres. German Gerontological Soc. 1973–78, 1980–84, Pres. 1997–99; Founder mem. Acad. of Sciences, Berlin 1987–91; Corresp. mem. Acad. of Sciences, Austria 1994–, Sächsische Akad. der Wissenschaften 1998–; Hon. mem. Soc. of Gerontology of Switzerland, Spain, Mexico; Grosses Bundesverdienstkreuz 1996; Hon. PhD (Fribourg, Switzerland); Landesverdienstmedaillie Baden-Württemberg 1999. *Publications:* more than 700 scientific texts. *Leisure interests:* art (paintings of the Middle Ages), history of art. *Address:* Am Büchel 53B, 53173 Bonn, Germany (Home). *Telephone:* (228) 352849 (Home). *Fax:* (228) 352741 (Home). *E-mail:* ursula.lehr@t-online.de.

LEHTO, Olli Erkki, PhD; Finnish professor of mathematics; b. 30 May 1925, Helsinki; s. of P. V. Lauri Lehto and Hilma Autio; m. Eva G. Ekholm 1954; one s. two d.; ed Univ. of Helsinki; Docent, Univ. of Helsinki 1951–56, Assoc. Prof. 1956–61, Prof. of Math. 1961–88, Dean, Faculty of Science 1978–83, Rector 1983–88, Chancellor 1988–93; Pres. Finnish Math. Soc. 1962–85, Finnish Acads of Science and Letters 1979–98; Hon. Pres. Finnish Cultural Foundation 1998–; mem. Exec. Cttee Int. Math. Union 1975–90, Sec.-Gen. 1982–90; mem. Gen. Cttee Int. Council of Scientific Unions 1982–90; mem. Admin. Bd Int. Asscn of Univs 1985–95, Vice-Pres. 1990–95; Visiting Prof. at numerous univs in Europe, N America and Asia; Grand Cross, Order of the Finnish Lion 1989; Hon. PhD (Turku) 1980, (Moscow) 1989, (Åbo) 1993, (Bucharest) 1996, (Joensuu) 1999. *Publications:* History of the Int. Math. Union, Biog. of Rolf Nevanlinna, memoirs, four monographs and 60 papers in mathematical journals. *Leisure interest:* butterflies. *Address:* Yliopistonkatu 4, 00014 University of Helsinki, Helsinki (Office); Ritarikatu 3 A 7, 00170 Helsinki, Finland (Home). *Telephone:* (3589) 19122847 (Office); (3589) 662526 (Home). *Fax:* (3589) 19123213. *E-mail:* olli.lehto@helsinki.fi.

LEHTO, Sakari Tapani, BLL, BSc(Econ); Finnish business executive and writer; b. 26 Dec. 1923, Turku; s. of Reino Lehto and Hildi Lehto; m. Karin Hildén 1950; three d.; ed Helsinki School of Econs and Business Admin., Helsinki Univ. and MIT Sloan School; Chief Legal Counsellor and Dir Foreign Activities, United Paper Mills Ltd 1964–71; Man. Dir and Pres. Fed. of Finnish Industries 1964–71; Pres. and CEO Partek Corpn 1972–87, Vice-Chair. 1987–95; Chair. Insurance Ltd Sampo 1976–89, Insurance Co. Kaleva 1978–91, Tamfelt Oy Ab 1982–94, Keskus-Sato Oy 1984–91, Pensions Sampo 1985–90; Kuratorium Pro Baltica Forum 1993–98; Minister of Foreign Trade 1975–76; mem. Finland Defence Bd 1976–92; Fellow World Innovation Foundation; Hon. mem. Finnish Soc. for Futures Studies; Commdr Order of Liberty, First Class (Finland); Commdr Order of White Rose, First Class (Finland); Commdr Order of the Polar Star, First Class (Sweden); Commdr Order of the Lion of Finland; Hon. TechD; Hon. Econ.D. *Publications:* Managing Change – Strategies and Thoughts, Experiences Within Finnish Industry, With Luck? How Next? – Challenges to the Management; numerous articles in the areas of commercial law, trade and industrial policy. *Leisure interests:* golf, boating, skiing. *Address:* Puistokatu 9A5, 00140 Helsinki, Finland (Office/Home). *Telephone:* (9) 653447 (Office); (9) 660349 (Home). *Fax:* (9) 653447. *E-mail:* sakari.t.lehto@kolumbus.fi (Office).

LEI JIEQIONG, MA; Chinese politician and jurist; b. 1905, Guangzhou, Guangdong Prov.; d. of Lei Zichang and Li Peizhi; m. Yan Jingyao 1941; ed in USA; Yenching Univ., 1931–52; Vice-Dean Inst. of Politics and Law 1953–73; mem. Cttee for Implementation Campaign of Marriage Laws 1953; Deputy Dir, Bureau of Foreign Experts Admin. under State Council 1956–66, Prof. Beijing Univ. 1973–; Vice-Mayor of Beijing 1979–83; Chair. China Asscn for Promoting Democracy 1987–97; Hon. Pres. China Asscn of Women Judges, Asscn for Int. Understanding of China, Western Returned Students' Asscn, China Social Workers' Asscn; mem., Standing Cttee 5th CPPCC 1978–83; mem. Standing Cttee 6th NPC and Vice-Chair. of Law Cttee 1983–88; Vice-Chair. 6th NPC 1986–88; Vice-Chair. 7th NPC 1988–93; Vice-Chair. Standing Cttee 8th NPC 1994–98; numerous other appointments and hon. positions. *Address:* c/o 19 Xi Jiaomen Xiang, Xicheng District, Beijing, People's Republic of China.

LEI MINGQUI, Lt-Gen.; Chinese army officer; b. March 1942, Jiangjiaqiao, Qidong Co., Hengyang City, Hunan Prov.; ed Zhuzhou Aeronautical Acad. Hunan and PLA Political Acad.; entered armed services 1962; Dir Political Dept Guangzhou Mil. Region 1992–95; Deputy Political Commissar, Nanjing Mil. Region 1995–; mem. 14th and 15th CCP Cen. Cttees. *Address:* Office of the Deputy Political Commissar, Nanjing Military Region, People's Republic of China.

LEI ZHUHA; Chinese bank official; fmr Vice-Pres. Bank of China, Vice-Chair. Bd of Dirs 1993–; Pres. Import and Export Bank of China 1994–99; Sr. Adviser Dayue Consulting. *Address:* c/o Import and Export Bank of China, 1 Dingandongli, Yongdingmenwai, Beijing, People's Republic of China.

LEIBINGER, Berthold; German business executive; joined TRUMPF as engineer 1950, now owner and Chief Exec.; mem. Advisory Bd Deutsche Bank, BASF. *Address:* TRUMPF GmbH & Co. KG, Johann-Maus-Strasse 2, 71254 Ditzingen, Germany. *Telephone:* (7156) 303230. *E-mail:* berthold.leibinger@de.trumpf.com (Office). *Website:* www.trumpf.com.

LEIBLER, Kenneth Robert, BA; American business executive; b. 21 Feb. 1949, New York; s. of Max Leibler and Martha (née Dales) Leibler; m. Marcia Kate Reiss 1973; one s. one d.; ed Syracuse Univ. and Univ. of Pennsylvania; Options Man. Lehman Bros. 1972–75; Vice-Pres. Options American Stock Exchange, NY 1975–79, Sr Vice-Pres. Admin. and Finance 1979–81, Exec. Vice-Pres. Admin. and Finance 1981–85, Sr Exec. Vice-Pres. 1985–86, Pres. 1986–90; Pres. Liberty Financial Cos. 1990–; Instructor NY Inst. of Finance; Dir Securities Industry Automation Corpn; mem. Finance Execs Inst. of Securities Industry Asscn American Stock Exchange Clearing Corpn. *Publication:* (contrib.) Handbook of Financial Markets: Securities, Options, Futures 1981. *Address:* Liberty Financial Companies, 600 Atlanta Avenue, Boston, MA 02110, USA.

LEIBOVITZ, Annie; American photographer; b. 2 Oct. 1949, Conn.; ed San Francisco Art Inst.; photographed rock 'n' roll stars and other celebrities for Rolling Stone magazine in 1970s; chief photographer, Vanity Fair 1983–; proprietor Annie Leibovitz Studio, New York; celebrity portraits include John Lennon, Mick Jagger, Bette Midler, Louis Armstrong, Ella Fitzgerald, Jessye Norman, Mikhail Baryshnikov, Arnold Schwarzenegger and Tom Wolfe; retrospective exhbn Smithsonian Nat. Portrait Gallery, Washington, DC 1991; Innovation in Photography Award (American Soc. of Magazine Photographers) 1987. *Publication:* Photographs 1970–90 1992, Women (with Susan Sontag) 2000. *Address:* Annie Leibovitz Studio, 547 West 26th Street, New York, NY 10001; c/o Jim Moffat, Art and Commerce, 755 Washington Street, New York, NY 10014, USA. *E-mail:* als@leibovitzstudio.com (Office).

LEIFERKUS, Sergey Petrovich; Russian baritone; b. 4 April 1946, Leningrad; ed Leningrad Conservatory; stage debut in Leningrad Theatre of Musical Comedy 1972; soloist Maly Theatre of Opera and Ballet 1972–78; Kirov (now Mariinsky) Theatre of Opera and Ballet 1978–85; winner of int. competitions Belgrade 1973, Zwickau 1974, Paris 1976, Ostend 1979; sings in various opera houses of Europe and America; repertoire includes leading parts in Don Giovanni, Eugene Onegin, Queen of Spades, Otello (Verdi), Carmen, Lohengrin, Faust, Traviata, Aida, Die Königskinder (Humperdinck), The Pearl Fishers (Bizet), War and Peace, The Flaming Angel (Prokofiev), Dead Souls (R. Shchedrin), etc.; wide concert repertoire includes oratorios and cycles by Bach, Handel, Mozart, Schumann, Mahler, Mussorgsky. *Address:* 5 The Paddocks, Abberbury Road, Iffley, Oxford, OX4 4ET, England.

LEIFLAND, Leif, LLB; Swedish diplomatist; b. 30 Dec. 1925, Stockholm; s. of Sigfrid Leifland and Elna Leifland; m. Karin Abard 1954 (died 1999); one s. two d.; ed Univ. of Lund; joined Ministry of Foreign Affairs 1952; served Athens 1953, Bonn 1955, Washington 1961, 1970; Sec. Foreign Relations Cttee, Swedish Parl. 1966–70; Under-Sec. for Political Affairs 1975–77; Perm. Under-Sec. of State for Foreign Affairs 1977–82; Amb. to UK 1982–91; Chair. Bd, Swedish Inst. of Int. Affairs 1991–2002; Hon. GCVO. *Publications:* The Blacklisting of Axel Wenner-Gren 1989, General Böhme's Choice 1992, The Year of the Frost 1997; various articles on foreign policy and national security questions. *Address:* Nybrogatan 77, 114 40 Stockholm, Sweden. *Telephone:* 86-61-46-12.

LEIGH, Irene May, BSc, MBBS, MD, DSc(Med), FRCP, FMedSci; British dermatologist and cell biologist; b. 25 April 1947, Liverpool; d. of A. Allen and M. L. Allen; m. 1st Nigel Leigh 1969 (divorced 1999); one s. three d.; m. 2nd J. E. Kernthaler 2000; two step-s. one step-d.; ed Merchant Taylors' Girls' School, London Hosp. Medical Coll.; Dir Cancer Research UK (fmrly Imperial Cancer Research Fund) Skin Tumour Lab. 1989–98; Prof. of Dermatology, Barts and London School of Medicine and Dentistry (BLSMD) 1992–98, Research Dean 1996–2001, Prof. of Cellular and Molecular Medicine 1998–; Jt Research Dir Barts and London NHS Trust and BLSMD 2002–. *Publications:* peer-reviewed publs in biomedical literature. *Leisure interests:* baroque music, opera, theatre, cinema, children, grandchildren. *Address:* Cancer Research UK Skin Tumour Laboratory, Centre for Cutaneous Research, Barts and the London, Queen Mary's School of Medicine and Dentistry, 2 Newark Street, London, E1 2AT (Office); 14 Oakeshott Avenue, London, N6 6NS, England (Home). *Telephone:* (20) 7882-7170 (Office); (20) 8340-4761 (Home). *Fax:* (20) 7882-7171 (Office). *E-mail:* i.leigh@cancer.org.uk (Office); jkernthaler@iee.org (Home). *Website:* www.qmul.ac.uk (Office).

LEIGH, Jennifer Jason; American actress; b. 5 Feb. 1962, Los Angeles, Calif.; d. of late Vic Morrow and of Barbara Turner; ed Palisades High School; appeared in Walt Disney TV movie The Young Runaways aged 15; other TV films include The Killing of Randy Webster 1981, The Best Little Girl in the World 1981. *Films include:* Eyes of a Stranger 1981, Fast Times at Ridgemont High 1982, Grandview, USA 1984, Flesh and Blood 1985, The Hitcher 1986, The Men's Club 1986, Heart of Midnight 1989, The Big Picture 1989, Miami Blues 1990, Last Exit to Brooklyn 1990, Crooked Hearts 1991, Backdraft

1991, Rush 1992, Single White Female 1992, Short Cuts 1993, The Hudsucker Proxy 1994, Mrs Parker and the Vicious Circle 1994, Georgia 1995, Kansas City 1996, Washington Square 1997, eXistenZ 1999, The King is Alive 2000, The Anniversary Party 2001, Crossed Over 2002. *Stage appearances include:* Sunshine, Off-Broadway 1989. *Address:* c/o Tracey Jacobs, 8942 Wilshire Boulevard, Beverly Hills, CA 90211 (Office); c/o Elaine Rich, 2400 Whitman Place, Los Angeles, CA 90068, USA.

LEIGH, Mike, OBE; British dramatist and film and theatre director; b. 20 Feb. 1943, Salford, Lancs.; s. of the late A. A. Leigh and of P. P. Leigh (née Cousin); m. Alison Steadman (q.v.) 1973 (divorced 2001); two s.; ed Royal Acad. of Dramatic Art, Camberwell School of Arts and Crafts, Cen. School of Art and Design, London Film School; Chair. Govs London Film School 2001–; Officier des Arts et des Lettres; Hon. MA (Salford) 1991, (Northampton) 2000; Hon. DLitt (Staffs.) 2000, (Essex) 2002. *Plays:* The Box Play 1965, My Parents Have Gone to Carlisle, The Last Crusade of the Five Little Nuns 1966, Nenaa 1967, Individual Fruit Pies, Down Here and Up There, Big Basil 1968, Epilogue, Glum Victoria and the Lad with Specs 1969, Bleak Moments 1970, A Rancid Pong 1971, Wholesome Glory, The Jaws of Death, Dick Whittington and His Cat 1973, Babies Grow Old, The Silent Majority 1974, Abigail's Party 1977 (also TV play), Ecstasy 1979, Goose-Pimples (London Evening Standard and London Drama Critics' Choice Best Comedy Awards 1981) 1981, Smelling A Rat 1988, Greek Tragedy 1989 (in Australia), 1990 (in UK), It's a Great Big Shame! 1993. *Television films:* A Mug's Game 1972, Hard Labour 1973, The Permissive Society, The Birth of the 2001 F.A. Cup Final Goalie, Old Chums, Probation, A Light Snack, Afternoon 1975, Nuts in May, Knock for Knock 1976, The Kiss of Death 1977, Abigail's Party 1977, Who's Who 1978, Grown Ups 1980, Home Sweet Home 1981, Meantime 1983, Four Days in July 1984, The Short and Curlies 1987. *Feature films:* Bleak Moments (Golden Leopard, Locarno Film Festival, Golden Hugo, Chicago Film Festival 1972) 1971, High Hopes (Int. Critics' Prize, Venice Film Festival 1989, London Evening Standard Peter Sellers Best Comedy Film Award 1990) 1989, Life is Sweet 1991, Naked (Best Dir Cannes Film Festival 1993) 1993, Secrets and Lies (winner Palme d'Or) 1996, (Alexander Korda Award, BAFTA 1997), Career Girls 1997, Topsy-Turvy 1999 (London Evening Standard Best Film 1999, Los Angeles Film Critics' Circle Best Film 1999, New York Film Critics' Circle Best Film 1999), All or Nothing 2002. *Radio play:* Too Much of a Good Thing 1979. *Publications:* Abigail's Party and Goose-Pimples 1982, Ecstasy and Smelling a Rat 1989, Naked and other Screenplays 1995, Secrets and Lies 1997, Career Girls 1997, Topsy-Turvy 1999, All or Nothing 2002. *Address:* c/o Peters, Fraser & Dunlop, Drury House, 34–43 Russell Street, London, WC2B 5HA, England. *Telephone:* (20) 7344-1000.

LEIGH-PEMBERTON, Rt Hon Robert (Robin) (see Kingsdown, Baron).

LEIGHTON, Allan Leslie; British business executive; b. 12 April 1953; m.; two s. one d.; ed Magdalen Coll. School, North Oxon. Polytechnic, A.M.P. Harvard; with Mars Confectionary 1974–91, rising to Business Sector Man. UK Grocery Div.; Sales Dir Pedigree Petfoods 1991–92; joined ASDA Stores Ltd as Group Marketing Dir 1992, then successively Retail Dir, Deputy Chief Exec.; Chief Exec. 1996; Pres. and CEO Wal-Mart Europe 1999–2000; Dir (non-exec.) Wilson Connolly Holdings PLC 1995 (Deputy Chair. 2000, interim CEO 2001–02); Dir (non-exec.) BSkyB PLC 1999, Dyson Ltd, Scottish Power PLC 2001, George Weston Ltd 2001, Consignia PLC 2001; Chair. (non-exec.) lastminute.com 2000, Cannons Group Ltd 2001; Chair. Race for Opportunity 2000, BHS Ltd 2000; Deputy Chair. (non-exec.) Leeds Sporting PLC 1998. *Address:* lastminute.com, 116 Park Street, Park House, London, W1N 6NR, England (Office). *Telephone:* (20) 7802-4200. *Fax:* (20) 7659-4948 (Office). *Website:* www.lastminute.co.uk (Office).

LEIGHTON, John; British art historian and museum director; b. 1959; trained as art historian; Curator for 19th Century Paintings, Nat. Gallery, London 1987–97; Dir Van Gogh Museum, Amsterdam 1997–, organised exhbn 'Van Gogh and Gauguin' in conjunction with Chicago Art Inst. 1997–2002. *Address:* Van Gogh Museum, POB 75366, 1070 AJ Amsterdam, The Netherlands (Office).

LEIJONHUFVUD, Baron Axel Stig Bengt, PhD; Swedish professor of economics; b. 9 June 1933, Stockholm; s. of Erik G. Leijonhufvud and Helene A. Neovius; m. 1st Marta E. Ising 1955 (divorced 1977), 2nd Earlene J. Craver 1977; one s. two d.; ed Univs of Lund, Pittsburgh and Northwestern Univ.; Acting Asst Prof. of Econs, Univ. of Calif. at Los Angeles (UCLA) 1964–67, Assoc. Prof. 1967–71, Prof. of Econs 1971–94, Chair. Dept of Econs 1980–83, 1990–92, Dir Center for Computable Econs 1991–97; Prof. of Monetary Econs, Univ. of Trento 1995–; Dir Computable and Experimental Econs Lab. 1996–; Visiting Prof. Stockholm School of Econ. and Commerce 1979–80, 1986, 1987, 1996, Inst. for Advanced Studies, Vienna 1976, 1987, Inst. for Advanced Studies, Jerusalem 1987, Nihon Univ. Tokyo 1980, European Univ. Inst., Florence 1982, 1986–87, 1989, Istituto Torcuato di Tella, Buenos Aires 1989, 1995; Ständiger Gastprof. Univ. of Konstanz 1982–85; mem. Econ. Export Cttee of Pres. of Kazakhstan 1991; other professional appts., Cttee memberships etc.; Brookings Inst. Fellow 1963–64; Marshall Lecturer, Univ. of Cambridge 1974; Overseas Fellow, Churchill Coll. Cambridge 1974; Inst. for Advanced Study Fellow 1983–84; Dr hc (Lund) 1983, (Nice, Sophia Antipolis) 1995. *Publications:* On Keynesian Economics and the Economics of Keynes: A Study in Monetary Theory 1968, Keynes and the Classics: Two Lectures 1969, Information and Coordination: Essays in Macroeconomic Theory 1981, High Inflation (jtly) 1995, Macroeconomic Instability and Coordination 2000,

Monetary Theory as a Basis for Monetary Policy (ed.) 2001, Monetary Theory and Policy Experience (ed.) 2001; contribs to professional journals. *Address:* Department of Economics, University of Trento, Via Inama 5, 38100 Trento, Italy. *Telephone:* (0461) 882279. *E-mail:* axel@ucla.edu (Office). *Website:* www .ceel.economia.unitn.it.

LEINONEN, Tatu Einari, MSc, DTech; Finnish professor of machine design; b. 21 Sept. 1938, Kajaani; s. of Aate Leinonen and Aili Leinonen (née Nieminen); m. Tuula Tuovinen 1968; one s. two d.; lecturer, Tech. Inst. of Helsinki 1963; researcher, Tech. Research Centre of Finland 1965; Design Engineer State Railway Co. 1966; Prof. of Machine Design, Univ. of Oulu 1968–; Visiting Prof. Univ. of Vt, USA 1976, Mich. Tech. Univ., USA 1977, 1981–82, 1991, Univ. of Fla, USA 1991, Lakehead Univ., Canada 1991, 2000, Toin Univ. of Yokohama, Japan 1994, Yanshan Univ., China 2000. *Publications:* more than 300 papers and books 1966–. *Leisure interests:* cross-country skiing, golf. *Address:* Matemaatikoutie 6, 90570 Oulu, Finland (Home); Department of Mechanical Engineering, P.O. Box 4900, 9014 University of Oulu. *Telephone:* (8) 5532050. *Fax:* (8) 5532026. *E-mail:* tatu@me .oulu.fi (Office). *Website:* www.oulu.fi (Office).

LEIPOLD, Gerd, PhD; German environmentalist; b. 1 Jan. 1951, Rot an der Rot; two c.; ed Max-Planck Inst. for Meteorology, Hamburg; trained as scientist; joined Greenpeace Germany as volunteer 1980, joined full-time 1983, later mem. Exec. Cttee and Trustee, Int. Co-ordinator Nuclear Free Seas Campaign 1987, fmr Chair. Bd Green Peace Nordic, mem. Bd Greenpeace USSR, Dir Greenpeace Nuclear Disarmament Campaign, London, Acting Int. Exec. Dir Greenpeace Int. Feb.–June 2001, Int. Exec. Dir June 2001–; set up own consultancy to advice NGOs on strategy and communications 1993. *Address:* Greenpeace International, Keizersgracht 176, Amsterdam 1016 DW, Netherlands (Office); c/o Im Hebsack 4, 88430 Rot, Germany (Home). *Telephone:* (20) 5236282 (Office). *Fax:* (20) 5236246 (Office). *E-mail:* gleipold@mail.nli.gl3 (Office). *Website:* www.greenpeace.org (Office).

LEIRNER, Sheila; Brazilian art critic and curator; b. 25 Sept. 1948, São Paulo; d. of Abraham L. Klinger and Giselda Leirner Klinger; m. 1st Décio Tozzi 1970 (divorced 1972); m. 2nd Gustavo Halbreich 1974 (divorced 1988); two s.; ed Univ. of Vincennes and Ecole Pratique des Hautes Etudes, Sorbonne, Paris; production asst to Luis S. Person and film critic 1970; visual arts columnist, Ultima Hora, São Paulo 1971–74; art critic, O Estado de São Paulo 1975–90, now independent curator and art critic; mem. Brazilian Asscn of Art Critics 1976; mem. Cen. Advisory Bd Fantastic Art in Latin America, Indianapolis Museum 1984; Exec. Dir Latin American Asscn of Visual Arts, Buenos Aires 1984; corresp. Colombia magazine and D'Ars, Milan 1984–90; mem. arts and culture comm. São Paulo Biennial Foundation 1982–87; Gen. Curator, 18th and 19th São Paulo Biennial 1984–88; Curator, Painterly/ Pictorico, Los Angeles Municipal Art Gallery and Museu de Arte de São Paulo 1989–90; other professional memberships, appointments and honours. *Publications:* selected works of art criticism. *Leisure interests:* literature, music, collecting dolls houses.

LEITH, Prudence Margaret (Prue), OBE, FRSA; British caterer and author; b. 18 Feb. 1940, Cape Town, South Africa; d. of late Stewart Leith and of Margaret Inglis; m. Rayne Kruger (died 2002); one s. one d.; ed Haywards Heath, Sussex, St Mary's, Johannesburg, Cape Town Univ., Sorbonne, Paris and Cordon Bleu School, London; started Leith's Good Food (commercial catering co.) 1965, Leith's restaurant 1969; cookery corresp. Daily Mail 1969–73; Man. Dir Prudence Leith Ltd 1972–94, Chair. Leith's Ltd 1994–96; opened Leith's School of Food and Wine 1975; added Leith's Farm 1976; cookery corresp. Daily Express 1976–80; Cookery Ed. The Guardian 1980–85, columnist 1986–90; subject of TV documentaries by BBC and Channel 4; presented series Tricks of the Trade, BBC 1; Vice-Pres. Restaurateurs' Asscn of GB; Gov. Nat. Inst. of Econ. and Social Research; Vice-Patron Women in Finance and Banking; Chair. UK Cttee New Era Schools' Trust 1994–2000, Royal Soc. of Arts 1995–97 (Deputy Chair. 1997–2000), The British Food Heritage Trust 1997–, Forum for the Future 2000; Dir (non-exec.) Halifax PLC 1992–99, Whitbread PLC 1995–, Argyll Group 1989–96, Woolworths 2001–; Hon. Fellow Univ. Salford 1992; Visiting Prof., Univ. of N London 1993–; mem. Nat. Council for Vocational Qualifications and UK Skills, Stamp Cttee 1997–; Gov. Kingsmead City Tech. Coll., Ashridge Man. Coll.; Reader for Queen's Anniversary Prizes; Patron Prue Leith Coll. of Food and Wine, Johannesburg 1997–; Chair. 3E's Enterprises 1998–, King's Coll. 1998; Trustee Forum for the Future 1998–; Training for Life 1999–, Places for People 1999–; Freeman City of London 1994; DL Greater London 1998; Fellow Salford Univ.; Dr hc (Open Univ.) 1997, (Oxford Brookes) 2000; Business Woman of the Year 1990. *Publications include:* Leith's All-Party Cook Book 1969, Parkinson's Pie 1972, Cooking for Friends 1978, The Best of Prue Leith 1979, Leith's Cookery Course (with J. B. Reynaud) 1979–80, The Cook's Handbook 1981, Prue Leith's Pocket Book of Dinner Parties 1983, Dinner Parties 1984, Leith's Cookery School (with C. Waldegrave) 1985, Entertaining with Style (with P. Tyrer) 1986, Confident Cooking (part-work) 1989–90, Leith's Cookery Bible 1991, Leith's Complete Christmas 1992, Leith's Book of Baking 1993, Leith's Vegetarian Cookery 1993, Leith's Step by Step Cookery 1993, Leaving Patrick (novel) 1999, Sisters (novel) 2001. *Leisure interests:* walking, fishing, gardening, tennis, old cookbooks, kitchen antiques, Trollope. *Address:* 94 Kensington Park Road, London, W11 2PN, England. *Telephone:* (20) 7221-5282. *Fax:* (20) 7221-1846. *E-mail:* pmleith@ dial.pipex.com (Office).

LEJEUNE, Michael L.; American international finance official; b. 22 March 1918, Manchester, England; s. of F. Arnold Lejeune and Gladys Lejeune (née Brown); m. Margaret Werden Wilson 1947; two s. one d.; ed Cate School, Carpinteria, Calif., Yale Univ. and Yale Univ. Graduate School; Teacher St Paul's School, Concord, New Hampshire 1941; Volunteer in King's Royal Rifle Corps in British Army 1942–46; joined staff of IBRD (World Bank) 1946, Personnel Officer 1948–50, Asst to Loan Dir and Sec. Staff Loan Cttee, Loan Dept 1950–52, Chief of Div., Europe, Africa and Australasia Dept 1952–57, Asst Dir of Operations, Europe, Africa and Australasia 1957–63, Asst Dir of Operations, Far East 1963–64; Dir of Admin., IBRD, IDA and IFC 1964–67, Dir Middle East and North Africa Dept 1967–68, Dir Europe, Middle East and North Africa Dept 1968–69, Dir Eastern Africa Dept 1970–74, Exec. Sec. Consultative Group on Int. Agric. Research 1974–83, Sr Adviser to Vice-Pres. Operations Policy 1983; Consultant 1983–; Trustee, Santa Barbara Foundation 1991–99, Vice-Pres. 1999. *Publication:* Partners Against Hunger: The Consultative Group on International Agricultural Research (with Warren C. Baum) 1986. *Address:* 80 Conejo Road, Santa Barbara, CA 93103, USA. *Telephone:* (805) 963-6598.

LEKHANYA, Maj.-Gen. Justin; Lesotho politician and army officer; Commdr of Lesotho Army; Head Mil. Council and Council of Ministers 1986–91, Minister of Defence and Internal Security 1986–91, also Minister of Public Service, Youth and Women's Affairs, Food Man. Units and Cabinet Office; ousted in coup; now Leader Basotho Nat. Party (BNP). *Address:* Basotho National Party (BNP), P.O. Box 124, Maseru 100, Lesotho.

LEKISHVILI, Niko Mikhailovich; Georgian politician; b. 20 April 1947, Tbilisi; m.; two d.; ed Tbilisi Polytech. Inst., Moscow Acad. of Nat. Econ.; Sr Lab. Asst Georgian Polytech. Inst. 1971–72; Komsomol functionary 1972–77; Second Sec., Chair. Dist Exec. Cttee, First Sec. Pervomay Dist CP Cttee, Tbilisi 1977–89; Second Sec., First Sec. Tbilisi City CP Cttee 1989–90; Chair. Tbilisi City Soviet 1990; Deputy Supreme Soviet Georgian SSR 1990–91; Chief State Counsellor Georgian Cabinet of Ministers Jan.–Nov. 1992; mem. Parl. Repub. of Georgia 1992–95, 1999–; Deputy Prime Minister Sept.–Oct. 1993; Mayor Tbilisi 1993–95; State Minister of Georgia 1995–98; Chair. Union of Tax-Payers. *Address:* Ingorokva str. 7, 380034, Tbilisi, Georgia. *Telephone:* (32) 93-62-40.

LEKOTA, Mosiuoa Patrick (Terror); South African politician; b. 13 Aug. 1948, Senekal, Orange Free State; s. of the late Mapiloko Lekota and Mamosiuoa Lekota; m. Cynthia Lekota 1975; two s. two d. (deceased); ed Univ. of the North (Turfloop); perm. organizer, South African Students' Org. (SASO) 1972–74; charged under Terrorism Act 1974; tried and imprisoned on Robben Island 1976–82; Nat. Publicity Sec. United Democratic Front (UDF) 1983–91; fmrly with ANC org. in Natal; Organiser for ANC in Northern Free States 1990; mem. ANC Working Cttee 1991–, Nat. Chair. ANC Nat. Exec. Cttee 1991–, Chair. Southern OFS of Nat. Exec. Comm. 1991, Sec. Elections Comm. 1992–94; Nat. Chair. ANC 1997–, detained 1983, 1984, 1985; on trial with 21 others charged with treason and murder in Delmas case 1986, convicted 1988, sentenced to 12 years' imprisonment after being held in custody for 4 years; conviction overturned by Appeal Court 1989; in exile, returned to S Africa 1990; Premier Free State Prov. Legislature 1994; Chair. Nat. Council of Provinces 1997–; Minister of Defence June 1999–. *Leisure interests:* cycling, reading, soccer, rugby and studying wildlife. *Address:* Ministry of Defence, Armscor Building, Block 5, Nossob Street, Erasmusrand 0181, South Africa (Office). *Telephone:* (12) 3556119 (Office). *Fax:* (12) 3470118 (Office). *E-mail:* webmaster@mil.za (Office).

LELONG, Pierre; Haitian diplomatist and engineer; b. 5 Jan. 1936, Jeremie; m.; two c.; ed Nat. Autonomous Univ. of Mexico; joined Ministry of the Navy, Mexico, Officer-in-Charge of Structural Studies, Directorate-Gen. of Maritime Projects 1962–72, Asst Dir.-Gen. for Computer Science 1972–82, Dir of works and structural safety, Fed. Dist 1989; Amb. to Mexico 1991–96; fmr del. to many regional orgs., del. to Second Int. Conf. of New or Restored Democracies, Managua 1994, Conf. on the Situation of Haitian Refugees, Tegucigalpa 1994 and Conf. of OAS, Managua 1994; Perm. Rep. to UN 1996–2001; Chair. Sixth Cttee (Legal), UN Gen. Ass. 2001–; Lecturer Faculty of Eng, Nat. Autonomous Univ. of Mexico 1975–90. *Address:* United Nations General Assembly, New York, NY 10017, USA (Office).

LELONG, Pierre Alexandre; French administrative official; b. 22 May 1931, Paris; s. of Prof. Marcel Lelong; m. Catherine Demargne 1958; four s. one d.; ed Coll. Stanislas, Paris, Univ. of Paris and Ecole Nat. d'Admin.; Ministry of Finance and Econ. Affairs 1958–62; Econ. Adviser to Prime Minister Pompidou 1962–67; Gen. Man. Fonds d'Orientation et de Régularisation des Marchés Agricoles (FORMA) 1967–68; MP for Finistère 1968–74; Sec. of State for Posts and Telecommunications 1974–75; Judge, Court of Accounts 1975–77; mem. European Court of Auditors 1977–, Pres. 1981–84; Pres. of Section (Defence) at Court of Accounts 1990–94, Pres. of Chamber (European Affairs) 1994–; Pres. Interministerial Cttee for Mil., Aeronautic and Mechanical State Procurements 1997–; Pres. Consultative Cttee on Secret Defence Affairs 1999–; Commdr, Légion d'Honneur, Officier, Ordre du Mérite; Grand Cross, Ordre de la Couronne de Chêne (Luxembourg). *Leisure interests:* sea fishing, hunting. *Address:* 35 rue Saint-Dominique, 75007 Paris (Office); 130 rue de Rennes, 75006 Paris (Home); Keremma, 29430 Tréflez, Finistère (Home); 880 route des Serres, Saint Paul 06570, France (Home). *Telephone:* 1-42-75-75-00 (Office); 1-45-44-12-49 (Home); 2-98-61-41-94

(Home); 4-93-32-12-15 (Home). *Fax:* 1-42-75-75-97 (Office); 1-45-44-12-49 (Home); 2-98-61-41-94 (Home). *E-mail:* pierre.lelong@dial.oleane.com (Office); lelongdemargne@aol.com.

LELONG, Pierre Jacques, D. ÈS SC.; French academic; b. 14 March 1912, Paris; s. of Charles Lelong and Marguerite Lelong (née Bronner); m. 1st Jacqueline Ferrand 1947, two s. m. 2nd France Fages 1976; ed Ecole Normale Supérieure and Ecole des Sciences Politiques; Prof. Science Faculty, Grenoble 1942–44; Prof. Science Faculty, Lille 1944–54, Université de Paris VI 1954–81, Prof. Emer.; Research Counsellor for Pres. De Gaulle 1959–62; Pres. du Comité Consultatif de la Recherche et de la Comm. du Plan 1961–63; Pres. Comm. mathématique CNRS 1962–66; mem. Section (Plan), Conseil Economique et Social 1992–96; mem. Acad. des Sciences 1986–; Officier Légion d'Honneur, Commdr du Soleil (Peru), Commdr de l'Etoile Noire. *Publications:* Fonctions plurisousharmoniques 1942, Integration and Positivity in Complex Analysis 1958, Entire functions of several complex variables 1986, numerous research papers on complex analysis and articles on politics, the economy and scientific research. *Address:* 9 place de Rungis, 75013 Paris, France. *Telephone:* 1-45-81-51-45 (Home).

LELOUCH, Claude; French film director; b. 30 Oct. 1937, Paris; s. of Simon Lelouch and Charlotte Abeilard; m. Christine Cochet 1968 (divorced); m. 2nd Marie-Sophie Pochat; four c., three c. from previous relationships; m. 3rd Alessandra Martines 1995; Pres. and Dir-Gen. Société Les Films 13, 1966–; Chevalier, Ordre nat. du Mérite, Officier des Arts et des Lettres, Grand Prix Nationaux 1993; Dr hc (UMIST) 1996; Golden Globe, Ephèbe d'or (for Les Misérables) 1996. *Films include:* L'amour des si..., La femme-spectacle, Une fille et des fusils, Les grands moments, Pour un maillot jaune, Un homme et une femme; (Palme d'or, Cannes 1966, Acad. Award 1966), Vivre pour vivre, Treize jours en France, La vie, l'amour, la mort, Un homme qui me plaît, Le Voyou, Smic, Smac, Smoc, co-dir Visions of Eight 1973, L'Aventure c'est l'aventure, La bonne année 1973, (producer, dir, author) Toute une vie 1974, Mariage 1974, Le chat et la souris 1975, Le bon et les méchants 1975, Rendezvous 1976, Si c'était à refaire 1976, Un autre homme, une autre chance 1977, Robert et Robert 1978, A nous deux 1979, Les uns et les autres 1981, Edith et Marcel 1983, Viva la vie 1984, Partir, revenir 1985, Un homme et une femme... 20 ans après 1986, Attention bandits 1987, Itinéraire d'un enfant gâté 1988, Il y a des jours... et de lunes 1990, La Belle Histoire 1992, Tout Ça Pour Ça 1993, Hommes, Femmes, Mode d'Emploi 1995, Les Misérables 1995, Hasards ou coïncidences 1998, Une pour toutes 2000. *Publication:* Itinéraire d'un enfant très gâté (autobiog.) 2000. *Address:* 15 avenue Hoche, 75008 Paris, France. *Telephone:* 42-25-00-89.

LELYVELD, Joseph Salem; American journalist; b. 5 April 1937, Cincinnati; s. of Arthur Joseph Lelyveld and Toby Bookholz; m. Carolyn Fox 1958; two d.; ed Columbia Univ., New York; Reporter, Ed. New York Times 1963–, Foreign Corresp. Johannesburg, New Delhi, Hong Kong, London 1965–86, columnist, staff writer 1977, 1984–85, Foreign Ed. 1987–89, Deputy Man. Ed. 1989–90, Man. Ed. 1990–94, Exec. Ed. April 1994–2001; George Polk Memorial Award 1972, 1984. *Publication:* Move Your Shadow (Pulitzer Prize) 1985. *Address:* c/o New York Times, 229 W 43rd Street, New York, NY 10036, USA.

LEM, Stanisław; Polish writer and essayist; b. 12 Sept. 1921, Lvov; s. of Samuel Lem and Sabina Lem; m. Barbara Leśniak 1953; one s.; ed Lvov Med. Inst., Jagiellonian Univ., Cracow; literary début with novel Człowiek z Marsa (Man from Mars) in weekly Nowy Świat Przygód, Katowice 1946; mem. Poland 2000 Comm. of Polish Acad. of Sciences 1972–, Polish Acad. of Arts and Sciences 1994; mem. Science Fiction Writers of America 1973–76, Polish PEN Club 1978–, Asscn of Polish Authors 1989–; Dr hc (Jagiellonian Univ., Cracow) 1998; several literary awards. *Major works:* science-fiction novels include Astronauci (The Astronauts) 1951, Obłok Magellana (Magellan's Cloud) 1955, Eden 1959, Śledztwo (The Investigation, detective story) 1959, Powrót z gwiazd (Return from the Stars) 1961, Solaris 1961, Pamiętnik znaleziony w wannie (Memoirs Founded in a Bathtub) 1963, Niezwyciężony (The Invincible) 1964, Głos Pana (Master's Voice) 1968, Doskonała próżnia (A Perfect Vacuum) 1971, Bezsenność. Opowiadania 1971, Transfer 1975, Katar (The Chain of Chance, thriller) 1976, Maska (The Mask) 1976, Wizja lokalna 1982, Kongres futurologiczny (Futurological Congress) 1983, Prowokacja 1984. *Science fiction stories include:* Dzienniki gwiazdowe (The Star Diaries) 1957, Księga robotów (Book of Robots) 1961, Bajki robotów (Robots' Fairy-Tales) 1964, Cyberiada (Cyberiad) 1965, Opowieści o pilocie Pirxie (The Tales of Pirx the Pilot) 1967, Fiasko 1987. *Essays include:* Dialogi (The Dialogues) 1957, Summa technologiae 1964, 1967, 1974, 1984, Prowokacja (Provocation) 1989, Tajemnica chińskiego pokoju (Secret of the Chinese Room) 1996, Bomba Megabitowa 1999, Okamgnienie 2000; Fantastyka i futurologia 1970, 1972, 1984, Golem XIV 1981, series of novels; Czas nieutracony Part I–III 1955, autobiographical novel: Wysoki zamek (High Castle) 1966; books translated into 36 languages. *Address:* ul. Narwik 66, 30-437 Cracow, Poland. *Telephone:* (12) 262-03-42. *Fax:* (12) 262-00-32. *E-mail:* lem@pro.onet.pl (Office). *Website:* www.lem.pl (Office).

LEMAN, Alexander B., FRAIC, FRSA; Canadian urban analyst and planner; b. 5 May 1926, Belgrade, Yugoslavia; s. of Boris E. Leman and Nataly Leman; m. 1st Catherine B. Leman 1950 (deceased); m. 2nd N. Bella Leman 1968; two s. two d.; ed Univ. of Belgrade; Prin. Partner, The Leman Partnership, Architects 1956–; Pres. Leman Group Inc., Consultants on Human Settlements and Devt 1971–; Chair. and CEO Urbanitas, Inc., Planners and Builders of Urban Communities; Chair. of Bd Royal Architectural Inst. of

Canada Research Corpn 1982–86; Co-Chair. UNESCO Int. Conf. on Culture and Devt 1985; Chair. World Congress on Conservation of Natural and Built Environments 1989; Dir Devt of Bangkok Regional Plan 1992–95; Advisor to Ont. Ministry of Housing on New Town Devt 1994–95; Founding mem. and Dir Shelter for the Homeless Foundation; Progressive Architecture Award 1973, UN Habitat Award 1990. *Publications:* Great Lakes Megalopolis: From Civilization to Ecumenization 1976 and articles on human settlements, environment and urban planning and analysis in professional journals. *Leisure interests:* writing, travel, community activities. *Address:* Leman Group Inc., The Hudson's Bay Centre, 2 Bloor Street East, 28th Floor, Toronto, Ont., M4W 1A8 (Office); 44 Charles Street W, Suite 4203, Toronto, Ont., M4Y 1R8, Canada (Home). *Telephone:* (416) 964-1865 (Office). *Fax:* (416) 964-6065 (Office). *E-mail:* lemanab@aol.com (Office).

LEMIERRE, Jean; French international civil servant; b. 1951; fmrly Dir Ministry of Finance, Paris, Chair. Econ. and Finance Cttee, EU; Pres. EBRD 2000–. *Address:* European Bank for Reconstruction and Development, 1 Exchange Square, 175 Bishopsgate, London, EC2A 2EH, England (Office). *Telephone:* (20) 7338-6000 (Office). *Fax:* (20) 7338-6100 (Office). *Website:* www .ebrd.com (Office).

LEMIEUX, Joseph Henry, BS; American business executive; b. 2 March 1931, Providence, RI; s. of Joseph C. Lemieux and Mildred L. Lemieux; m. Frances J. Schmidt 1956; three s. two d.; ed Stonehill Coll., Univ. of Rhode Island, Bryant Coll., Providence; joined Glass Container Div., Owens-Ill. as trainee 1957, numerous posts include Plant Comptroller 1961, Admin. Man. 1964, Plant Man. 1965–72, Vice-Pres. 1972–78, Group Vice-Pres. 1979–84, Exec. Vice-Pres. and Pres. Packaging Operations 1984–86, Pres and COO 1986–90, Pres., CEO 1990–91, Chair., CEO 1991, Chair. Bd of Dirs Health Care and Retirement Corpn of America 1986; Dr hc Business Admin. (Bryant Coll.) 1994; Outstanding Young Man of America, US Jr Chamber of Commerce 1965, Ellis Island Medal of Honor 2001. *Leisure interests:* golf, tennis. *Address:* Owens-Illinois Inc., One Sea Gate, Toledo, OH 43666, USA. *Telephone:* (419) 247 5800.

LEMOND, Greg; American cyclist and motor racing driver; b. 26 June 1961, Los Angeles; m. Kathy LeMond; two s. one d.; began professional competitive cycling career 1980; won Coors Classic stage race 1981, 1985; won Tour de France 1986, 1989, 1990; three World Champion titles; retd from cycling due to injury 1994; currently designer of bicycles; also leads cycling tours; now engaged in auto racing, professional series debut 1997 (with U.S. F2000); Sports Illustrated Sportsman of the Year 1989, ABC Wide World of Sports Athlete of the Year 1989, 1990, Jesse Owens Int. Trophy Awards—World's Most Outstanding Athlete 1991. *Address:* c/o Trek Travel, 801 West Madison, Waterloo, WI 53594, USA. *Website:* www.lemondbikes.com (Office).

LEMOS, Nikolas Spyridon; Greek business executive; b. 8 Sept. 1933, Oinoussai, Chios; s. of Spyros A. Lemos and Irene N Pateras; m. Irini Doxiadis 1976; three s. three d.; ed Univ. School of Navigation, Southampton, Edinburgh Univ.; officer, Capt. on various types of merchant ships; port capt. several shipyards in numerous countries; Man. Dir Lemos & Pateras 1966–83; Founder and Chair. NS Lemos & Co. Ltd (Shipbrokers) 1983–99; Pres. Maritime Museum Oinoussai; mem. Council Det Norske Veritas; Trustee Thyateira and St Nicholas Trust; Actuarius of Ecumenical Patriarche Constantinopoleos. *Leisure interests:* fishing, sailing, scuba diving, skiing, swimming. *Address:* c/o 116 Kolokotroni Street, GR 185 35 Piraeus, Greece (Office). *Telephone:* (1) 4181601 (Office). *Fax:* (1) 4582809 (Office).

LEMOS SIMMONDS, Carlos, DrIur; Colombian politician; b. Popayán, Cauca; m. Martha Blanco Guake; four c.; ed Lycée of Cauca Univ. and Cauca Univ.; Prof. of Colombian Political History, Universidad Javeriana; Prof. of Colombian Econ. History, Free Univ. of Colombia; Dir of Consigna magazine 1982–87; mem. of Bogotá Council 1972–74, 1986–88; mem. House of Reps 1974–78; Gov. of Cauca Prov. 1976–77; Sec.-Gen. of the Presidency 1978–79; Senator 1978–81; Minister of Foreign Affairs 1981–82; Amb. to the OAS 1987–89; Minister of Communications Feb.–Oct. 1989; Minister of Government (Interior) 1989–90; Del. to Nat. Constitutional Ass. 1990–91; Chair of Bogotá Council 1992; cand. for Pres. of Colombia 1992; Amb. to Austria 1995, to UK 1995; Vice-Pres. of Colombia 1996–98; Orders of Boyacá, San Carlos, Civil Merit (Spain), Independence (Equatorial Guinea), Merit (Italy, Chile and Ecuador), Sol (Peru) and Balboa (Panama), Commdr Order of Isabel la Católica. *Publications include:* Francisco de Paula Santander, An Iconography, The Pre-Columbian Economy. *Address:* Palacio de Nariño, Carrera 8A, 7–26, Santafé de Bogotá, DC, Colombia.

LEMPER, Ute; German singer, dancer and actress; b. 4 July 1963, Münster; one s. one d.; ed Dance Acad., Cologne, Max Reinhardt Seminar on Dramatic Art, Vienna; leading role in Viennese production of Cats 1983; appeared in Peter Pan, Berlin, Cabaret, Düsseldorf and Paris (recipient of Molière Award 1987), Chicago (Laurence Olivier Award) 1997–99 (London and New York), Life's a Swindle tour 1999, Punishing Kiss tour 2000; French Culture Prize 1993. *Albums include:* Ute Lemper Sings Kurt Weill 1988, (Vol. 2) 1993, Threepenny Opera 1988, Mahagonny Songspiel 1989, Illusions 1992, Espace Indécent 1993, City of Strangers 1995, Berlin Cabaret Songs 1996, All that Jazz/The Best of Ute Lemper 1998, Punishing Kiss 2000. *Television appearances include:* L'Affaire Dreyfus (Arte), Tales from the Crypt (HBO), Illusions (Granada) and The Look of Love (Gillian Lynn). *Film appearances include:* L'Autrichienne 1989, Moscou Parade 1992, Coupable d'Innocence 1993, Prêt

à Porter 1995, Bogus 1996, Combat de Fauves, A River Made to Drown In, Appetite 1997. *Address:* c/o Oliver Gluzman, 40 rue de la Folie Régnault, 75011 Paris, France. *Telephone:* 1-44-93-02-02. *Fax:* 1-44-93-04-40. *E-mail:* info@visiteursdusoir.com (Office). *Website:* www.visiteursdusoir.com (Office).

LENAERTS, Koenraad, LLM, MPA, PhD; Belgian judge; b. 20 Dec. 1954, Mortsel; m. Kris Grimonprez; six d.; ed Univs of Namur and Leuven and Harvard Univ., USA; Asst Prof. Leuven Univ. 1979–82, Assoc. Prof. 1982–83, Prof. of EC Law 1983–; Prof. of European Insts, Coll. of Europe, Bruges 1984–89; law clerk to Judge R. Joliet, Court of Justice of European Communities 1984–85; mem. Brussels Bar 1986–89; Judge, Court of First Instance of the European Community, Luxembourg 1989–; Visiting Prof. Univ. of Burundi 1983, 1986, Univ. of Strasbourg 1986–89, Harvard Univ. 1988–89; various academic distinctions, fellowships and prizes. *Publications:* 'The Negative Implications' of the Commerce Clause and 'Preemption' Doctrines as Federalism Related Limitations on State Power: a Historical Review 1978, Constitutie en rechter 1983, International privaatrecht (with G. Van Hecke) 1986, Le juge et la constitution aux Etats-Unis d'Amérique et dans l'ordre juridique européen 1988, Two Hundred Years of U.S. Constitution and Thirty Years of EEC Treaty: Outlook for a Comparison 1988, Constitutional Law of the European Union (with P. Van Nuffel) 1999, Procedural Law of the European Union (with D. Arts) 1999, articles and contribs. to reviews etc. *Address:* Court of the First Instance of the European Communities, blvd. Konrad Adenauer, 2925 Luxembourg. *Telephone:* 4303-1. *Fax:* 4303-2100. *Website:* ww.curia.eu.int (Office).

LENDL, Ivan; American (born Czech) tennis player; b. 7 March 1960, Ostrava; s. of Jiri Lendl and Olga Lendlova; m. Samantha Frankel 1989; five d.; Davis Cup player 1978–85, winner 1980; winner, Italian Jr Singles 1978, French Jr Singles 1978, Wimbledon Jr Singles 1978, Spanish Open Singles 1980, 1981, S. American Open Singles 1981, Canadian Open Singles 1980, 1981, WCT Tournament of Champion Singles 1982, WCT Masters Singles 1982, WCT Finals Singles 1982, Masters Champion 1985, 1986, French Open Champion 1984, 1986, 1987, US Open Champion 1985, 1986, 1987, US Clay Court Champion 1985, Italian Open Champion 1986, Australian Open Champion 1989, 1990; finalist Wimbledon 1986; held world No. 1 ranking for a record 270 weeks; won 94 singles titles and six doubles; named World Champion (Int. Tennis Fed.) 1985, 1986, 1990; retd Dec. 1994; granted American citizenship 1992; ATP Player of the Year 1985, 1986, 1987, inducted Int. Tennis Hall of Fame 2001, mem. Laureus World Sports Acad. *Publication:* Ivan Lendl's Power Tennis. *Leisure interests:* golf, collecting art. *Address:* c/o Laureus World Sports Academy, 15 Hill Street, London, W1 5QT, England. *Telephone:* (20) 7514-2700.

LENGSAVAD, Somsavat; Laotian politician; b. 15 June 1945, Luang-phrabang; m. Bounkongmany Lengsavad; one s. two d.; ed Nat. Org. for the Study of Policy and Admin.; Head of the Secr., Cabinet of the Lao People's Revolutionary Party (LPRP) Cen. Cttee. 1975–82; Deputy Chief, Council of Ministers; Deputy Minister; First Vice-Chair. LPRP History Research Comm. 1982–88, Chief of the Cabinet of LPRP and Cabinet of Ministers 1991–93; Amb. to Bulgaria 1989–91; Minister of Foreign Affairs 1993–; Deputy Prime Minister 1998–; Medal of Liberty Issara, Medal of Labour, Anti-Imperialist Cross, Revolutionary Medal People's Repub. of Korea, Medal of Friendship Govts of Cuba and Bulgaria; Dr rer. pol Ramkhamheang Univ., Thailand 2000. *Leisure interests:* reading, golf, singing. *Address:* Ministry of Foreign Affairs, rue That Luang, Ban Phonxay, Vientiane, Laos (Office). *Telephone:* (21) 414001 (Office); (21) 414049 (Home). *Fax:* (21) 414007 (Office). *E-mail:* cabmofa@pan-laos.net.la (Office).

LENK, Hans Albert Paul, PhD; German professor of philosophy; b. 23 March 1935, Berlin; s. of Albert Lenk and Annemarie Lenk; m. Ulrike Reincke; two s. one d.; ed Lauenburgische Gelehrtenschule, Ratzeburg, Freiburg and Kiel Univs, Tech. Univ. of Berlin; Asst Prof. Tech. Univ. of Berlin 1962, Assoc. Prof. 1966, Prof. (Wissenschaftlicher Rat und Prof.) 1969; Chair. and Prof. of Philosophy, Karlsruhe Univ. 1969–, Dean, Coll. of Humanities and Social Sciences 1973–75; Dean and Prof. Philosophy of Social Sciences and Theory of Planning, European Faculty of Land Use and Devt, Strasbourg 1983–; Visiting Prof. numerous foreign univs; Hon. Prof. Tech. Univ., Budapest 1992; Green Honors Chair. Tex. Christian Univ., Fort Worth 1987; Pres. Int. Philosophic Soc. for Study of Sport 1980–81, Int. Olympic Union 1980–90, European Forum, Baden 1980–; Vice-Pres. European Acad. of Sciences and Philosophy of Law 1986–; Pres. Gen. Soc. for Philosophy in Germany 1991–93; Pres. Argentine-German Soc. of Philosophy 1992–, German-Hungarian Soc. of Philosophy 1993, Chilean-German Soc. of Philosophy 1995–, German-Romanian Soc. of Philosophy 2001–; Vice-Pres. Féd. Int. des Sociétés de Philosophie 1998–; mem. American Acad. of Kinesiology and Physical Educ., Nat. Olympic Cttee for Germany –1992, German UNESCO Comm. –1992, Inst. Int. de Philosophie 1994 (mem. Bd 1996–2000), Int. Acad. of Philosophy of Science 1995–; Amateur Coach World Champion Eight Oar Crew 1966; Hon. mem. Int. Olympic Acad., Romanian Acad. of Science, Dept of Philosophy 2001; Dr hc (Deutsche Sporthochschule, Cologne) 1986, (Córdoba) 1992, (Tech. Univ. Budapest) 1993, (Univ. Pécs) 1994, Moscow (Univ. of Humanistic Studies) 1995, (Int. Ind. Univ. for Ecology and Politology) 2001; four German, two European and one Olympic title for rowing, Silver Leaf of Fed. Pres. 1959, 1960, Scientific Diem Plaque 1962, Sievert Award (Olympian Int.) 1973, Noel Baker Prize (UNESCO) 1978, Outstanding Academic Book Award 1979, Outstanding Intellectual and Outstanding Scholar of the 20th Century (IBC),

Man of the Year 2000 (ABI). *Publications:* more than 100 books, including Kritik der logischen Konstanten 1968, Team Dynamics 1977, Pragmatische Vernunft 1979, Social Philosophy of Athletics 1979, Zur Sozialphilosophie der Technik 1982, Zwischen Wissenschaftstheorie und Sozialwissenschaft 1985, Zwischen Sozialpsychologie und Sozialphilosophie 1987, Kritik der kleinen Vernunft 1987, Das Prinzip Fairness 1989, Tagebuch einer Rückreise 1991, Prometheisches Philosophieren zwischen Praxis und Paradox 1991, Zwischen Wissenschaft und Ethik 1992, Philosophie und Interpretation 1993, Interpretationskonstrukte 1993, Macht und Machtbarkeit der Technik 1994, Schemaspiele 1995, Interpretation und Realität 1995, Einführung in die angewandte Ethik 1997, Einführung in die Erkenntnistheorie 1998, Konkrete Humanität 1998, Praxisnahes Philosophieren 1999, Erfassung der Wirklichkeit 2000, Kreative Aufstiege 2000, Advances and Problems in the Philosophy of Technology (ed.) 2001, Das Denken und sein Gehalt 2001, Kleine Philosophie des Gehirns 2001; more than 1,200 articles. *Address:* Universität (TH) Karlsruhe, Institut für Philosophie, Kollegium am Schloss, Bau 2, 76128 Karlsruhe (Office); Neubrunnenschlag 15, 76337 Waldbronn, Germany (Home). *Telephone:* (721) 6082149 (Office); (7243) 67971 (Home). *Fax:* (721) 6083084 (Office); (7243) 67971 (Home). *E-mail:* ed05@rz.uni-karlsruhe.de (Office).

LENK, Thomas; German sculptor and graphic artist; b. 15 June 1933, Berlin; s. of Franz Lenk and Anneliese Lenk (née Hoernecke); m. Maria Bendig 1959; two d.; Guest Prof., Heluwan Univ., Cairo 1978; mem. Humboldt-Gesellschaft 1992; Hon. Life mem., Art Gallery of Ont., Toronto 1988; Carnegie Int. Purchase Award 1967, Third Prize, Socha Piestanskych Parkov, Bratislava 1969, Prize of 2nd Norwegian Graphics Biennale 1974, Verleihung des Professorentitels 1989. *Exhibitions:* one-man shows in Wiesbaden 1958, Stuttgart 1962, 1965, 1968, 1970, 1974, 1977, 1981, Wuppertal 1963, 1994, Ulm 1964, 1970, Zürich 1966, 1969, Kassel 1966, New York, London, Milan 1967, Münster 1968, 1980, Darmstadt 1968, Detroit 1969, Bochum 1971, Essen 1971, 1973, Düsseldorf 1971, 1974, 1980, Saarbrücken 1971, 1982, Cologne 1976, Alexandria 1978, Tübingen 1980, Nürnberg, Munich 1983, Mannheim, Leverkusen, Linz 1985, Staatsgaleri, Stuttgart 1986, Cottbus, Dessau, Ingoldstadt, Munich 1995, Badisches Landesmuseum, Karlsruhe 1998 Goethe Inst., Budapest 2000, Galerie Geiger, Konstanz 2001; has participated in numerous group exhbn in Europe, Canada, USA and Japan; exhibited at XXXV Venice Biennale 1970, IV Documenta, Kassel 1968. *Address:* Gemeinde Braunsbach, 74542 Schloss Tierberg, Germany. *Telephone:* (7905) 362. *Fax:* (7905) 362.

LENNINGS, Manfred, DrIng; German industrialist; b. 23 Feb. 1934, Oberhausen; s. of Wilhelm Lennings and Amanda Albert; m. Renate Stelbrink 1961; one s. one d.; ed Gymnasium Geislingen/Steige, Univ. of Munich and Bergakademie Clausthal; Chair. German Student Org. 1959–60; Asst of Man. Bd, Gutehoffnungshütte (GHH) Aktienverein 1964–67, Deputy mem. 1969, Chair. 1975–83; mem. Man. Bd, Deutsche Werft AG 1968–69; Chair. Man. Bd Howaldtwerke-Deutsche Werft AG 1970–74; Consultant Westdeutsche Landesbank 1984–99; Consultant 1999–; Chair. Supervisory Bd Gildemeister AG, Heitkamp-Deilmann-Haniel GmbH; mem. Supervisory Bd Deutsche Post AG, IVG Immobilien AG. *Leisure interests:* modern painting and literature, swimming. *Address:* Schmachtenbergstr. 142, 45219 Essen, Germany. *Telephone:* (2054) 12020. *Fax:* (2054) 120222.

LENNKH, Georg, LLD; Austrian diplomatist; b. 8 Dec. 1939, Graz; s. of Friedrich Lennkh and Elisabeth Lennkh; m. Annie Lechevalier 1966; one s. one d.; ed Univ. of Graz, Johns Hopkins School of Advanced Informational Studies, Bologna and Univ. of Chapel Hill, NC, USA; entered Fed. Ministry for Foreign Affairs 1965; served Tokyo 1968–72, Austrian Mission to UN, New York 1972–76, Dept for Int. Orgs, Ministry of Foreign Affairs 1976–78; served Cabinet Office of Fed. Chancellor Kreisky, with responsibility for foreign relations 1978–82; Perm. Rep. to OECD 1982–93; Dir Gen. Dept for Devt Cooperation, Fed. Ministry of Foreign Affairs 1993–. *Leisure interest:* skiing. *Address:* Ministry for Foreign Affairs, Ballhausplatz 2, 1014 Vienna, Austria. *Telephone:* (1) 531-15-0. *Fax:* (1) 535-45-30. *E-mail:* georg.lennkh@bmaa.gv.at (Office). *Website:* www.bmaa.gv.at (Office).

LENNOX, Annie, ARAM; British rock singer; b. 25 Dec. 1954, Aberdeen; d. of late Thomas A. Lennox and of Dorothy Lennox (née Ferguson); m. Uri Fruchtmann 1988; two d.; ed Aberdeen High School for Girls, Royal Acad. of Music; Founder mem. (with Dave Stewart, q.v.) The Tourists 1979–80, Eurythmics 1980; Eurythmics tours UK, Europe, USA, 1983, 1984, world tours 1986–87, 1989–90, world-wide 'Peacetour' 1999, tours in USA and Europe 2000; numerous singles and album sales awards; other awards include Best UK Video (for Love is a Stranger) 1982, Grammy Awards for Best Video Album and for Best Female Performance (for Sweet Dreams), Ivor Novello Award for Best Pop Song (Sweet Dreams), American Soc. of Composers Award, BPI Award for Best Female Vocalist 1982/83, 1987/88, 1989/90, 1992/93, BPI for Best Album (for Diva) 1992/93, Ivor Novello Award for Best Song (for Why) 1992, Brit Award for Best Female Solo Artist 1996, Grammy Award for Best Female Pop Vocals (for No More I Love You's) 1996, Brit Award for Outstanding Contrib. to Music 1999, Tartan Cleff Award 2001. *Albums:* (Eurythmics) Touch 1984, Be Yourself Tonight 1985, Revenge 1986, We Too Are One 1989, Greatest Hits 1991, Peace 1999; (solo) Diva 1992, Medusa 1995, Bare 2003. *Address:* c/o Tara Goldsmid, 19 Management Ltd, 33, Ransomes Dock, 35–37 Parkgate Road, London, SW11 4NP, England. *Telephone:* (20) 7801-1919. *Fax:* (20) 7801-1920.

LENNOX-BOYD, Simon Ronald Rupert (see Boyd of Merton, 2nd Viscount).

LENZ, Carl Otto, DJur; German lawyer; b. 5 June 1930, Berlin; s. of the late Dr Otto Lenz and of Marieliese Pohl; m. Ursula Heinrich 1960; two s. three d.; ed schools in Germany and Switzerland, and Harvard and Cornell Univs, USA; Sec.-Gen. Christian Democratic Group, European Parl. 1956–66; mem. Bundestag 1965–84; Advocate-Gen. European Court of Justice 1984–97; Hon. Prof. of European Law, Saarland Univ. 1990–; Grosses Bundesverdienstkreuz 1976, Grosskreuz des Verdienstordens (Grand Duchy of Luxembourg) 1998 and numerous other honours. *Publications:* Die Notverstandsverfassung des GG 1971, EG Handbuch Recht im Binnenmarkt 1994, EG-Vortrag Kommentar 1994. *Address:* Rodensteinstrasse 22, 64625 Bensheim, Germany.

LENZ, Guy; Luxembourg army officer; b. 28 Jan. 1946, Pétange; s. of Louis Lenz and Hélène Ludovicy; m. Liliane Wetz; two d.; ed Belgian Infantry School, Armed Forces Staff Coll., Norfolk, Va; rank of Lt 1973, Capt. 1976, Maj. 1982, Lt-Col 1986, Col 1998; Chief of Staff of the Luxembourg Army 1998–; served as Head of Operations and Training, Deputy Commdr of the Mil. Training Centre; Head of GIVO at HQ, Mil. Councillor at NATO; Mil. Rep. at SHAPE; Perm. Rep. to NATO Mil. Cttee; Mil. Del. WEU Perm. Council; Commdr Ordre de Mérite, Cross for 25 years service, Kt Order of Civilian and Mil. 'Mérite de Adolphe de Nassau', Meritorious Service Medal (USA), Commdr Ordre de la Couronne de Chêne (Belgium), Kt Ordre d'Orange de Nassau (Netherlands). *Address:* Headquarters of the Armed Forces, 38–44 rue Goethe, B.P. 873, 1018 Luxembourg (Office); 50 rue um Böchel, 9017 Ettelbruck, Luxembourg (Home). *Telephone:* 488836 (Office); 819680 (Home). *Fax:* 402605 (Office); 819680 (Home). *E-mail:* burcema@pt.lu (Office).

LENZ, Siegfried; German writer; b. 17 March 1926, Lyck, East Prussia; m. Liselotte Lenz; ed High School, Samter and Univ. of Hamburg; Cultural Ed. Die Welt 1949–51; freelance writer 1952–; Gerhart Hauptmann Prize 1961, Bremer Literaturpreis 1962, German Freemasons' Literary Prize 1970, Kulturpreis, Goslar 1978, Bayern Literary Prize 1995, Goethe Prize 1999; Hon. Citizen of Hamburg 2001–. *Publications:* include novels: Es waren Habichte in der Luft 1951, Duell mit dem Schatten 1953, Der Mann im Strom 1957, 1958, Brot und Spiele 1959, Stadtgespräche 1963, Deutschstunde 1968, Das Vorbild 1973, Heimatmuseum 1978, Der Verlust 1981, Ein Kriegsende 1984, Die Auflehnung 1994; stories: So zärtlich war Suleyken 1955, Jäger des Spotts 1958, Das Feuerschiff 1960, Der Spielverderber 1965, Einstein überquert die Elbe bei Hamburg 1975; plays: Zeit der Schuldlosen 1961, Das Gesicht 1963, Haussuchung (radio plays) 1967. *Address:* Preusserstrasse 4, 22605 Hamburg, Germany. *Telephone:* 880-83-09.

LEÓN PORTILLA, Miguel, PhD; Mexican anthropologist and historian; b. 22 Feb. 1926, Mexico City; s. of Miguel León Ortiz and Luisa Portilla Nájera; m. Ascensión Hernández Triviño 1965; one d.; ed Loyola Univ. of Los Angeles and Nat. Univ. of Mexico; Sec.-Gen. Inter-American Indian Inst. 1955–59, Asst Dir 1959–60, Dir 1960–66; Asst Dir Seminar for Náhuatl Culture, Nat. Univ. of Mexico 1956, Dir Inst. of Historical Research 1963–78, Prof. Emer. 1988–; Dir América Indígena 1960; Adviser, Int. Inst. of Different Civilisations 1960; Perm. Rep. of Mexico to UNESCO, Paris 1987; mem. Bd Govs Nat. Univ. Mexico 1976; mem. American Anthropological Assen 1960–, Mexican Acad. of Language 1962–, Société des Américanistes de Paris 1966–, Mexican Acad. of History 1969–, Nat. Coll. of Mexico 1971–; Corresp. mem. Royal Spanish Acad. of History 1969–; Guggenheim Fellow 1969; American Anthropological Assen Fifth Distinguished Lecturer 1974; Fellow Portuguese Acad. of History, Lisbon 1995, Nat. Acad. of Sciences, USA 1995; Hon. mem. American Historical Assen 1991, NAS 1995; Hon. Prof. (Southern Methodist Univ., Dallas, Tex.) 1980, (California) 1986, (Tel Aviv) 1987, (Toulouse) 1990, (Colima) 1993, (San Andrés, Bolivia) 1994, (Brown Univ.) 1996, Carolina Univ. Prague 2000; Commendatore Repub. Italiana 1977, Serra Award 1978, Nat. Prize in the Social Sciences (Mexico) 1981, Manuel Gamio Anthropological Award 1983, Nat. Univ. of Mexico Prize 1994, Belisario Domínguez Medal (Mexico) 1997, Great Cross of Alfonso X el sabio (Spain) 1998, Ordre des Palmes Académiques (France) 2000, Bartolomé de las Casas Prize (Spain) 2001. *Publications:* La Filosofía Náhuatl 1956, Visión de los Vencidos 1959, Los Antiguos Mexicanos 1961, The Broken Spears, Aztec Account of the Conquest of Mexico 1962, Rückkehr der Götter 1962, Aztec Thought and Culture 1963, Literaturas Precolombinas de México 1964, Imagen del México Antiguo 1964, Le Crépuscule des Aztèques 1965, Trece Poetas del Mundo Azteca 1967, Pre-Columbian Literatures of Mexico 1969, Tiempo y Realidad en el Pensamiento Maya 1968, Testimonios Sudcalifornianos 1970, De Teotihuacan a los Aztecas 1971, The Norteño Variety of Mexican Culture 1972, The Voyages of Francisco de Ortega to California 1632–1636 1972, Time and Reality in the Thought of the Maya 1973, Historia Natural y Crónica de la Antigua California 1973, Il Rovescio della Conquista, Testimonianze Asteche, Maya e Inca 1974, Aztecs and Navajos 1975, Endangered Cultures: The Indian in Latin America 1975, Indian Place Names of Baja California 1977, L'Envers de la conquête 1977, Los Manifestos en Náhuatl de Emiliano Zapata 1978, Toltecayotl, Aspectos de la Cultura Náhuatl 1980, Mesoamerican Spirituality 1980, Middle America 1981, Literaturas de Anahuac y del Imcario 1982, Mesoamerica before 1519 1984, Codex Fejérváry-Mayer, a Book of the Merchants, 1985, La Pensée Aztèque 1985, Libro de los Coloquios 1986, Das Alte Mexiko: Religion 1986, Huehuehtlahtolli, Testimonies of the Ancient

Word 1988, Mesoamerica in 1492 and on the eve of 1992, 1988, Poésie Náhuatl d'amour et d'amitié 1991, Fifteen Poets of the Aztec World 1992, The Aztec Image of Self and Society 1992, Raíces indígenas, presencia hispánica 1993, La flecha en el blanco 1995, Bernardino de Sahagún: Pionero de la antropología 1999, Tonantzin Guadalupe 2000. *Leisure interests:* scouting and gardening. *Address:* Instituto de Investigaciones Históriens, Ciudad Universitaria, UNAM, 04510 México, DF; Calle de Alberto Zamora 131, Coyoacán, 04000 México, DF, Mexico. *Telephone:* (5) 665-4417 (Office); (5) 554-0802. *Fax:* (5) 665-0070. *E-mail:* portilla@servidor.unam.mx (Office).

LEONARD, Brian Edmund, PhD, DSc, MRIA; Irish professor of pharmacology; b. 30 May 1936, Winchester; s. of Harold E. Leonard and Dorothy Coley; m. Helga F. Mühlpfordt 1959; two d.; ed Univ. of Birmingham; Dept of Medical Biochem. Univ. of Birmingham 1956–62; Lecturer in Pharmacology, Univ. of Nottingham 1962–68; Tech. Officer, CNS Research, ICI Pharmaceuticals Div. Alderley Park, Cheshire 1968–71; Group Leader, CNS Pharmacology, Organon International BV, Oss, Netherlands 1971–74; Prof. of Pharmacology, Univ. Coll. Galway 1974–, Prof. Emer. 1999–; Councillor CINP 1996–2000, Treas. 1992–96, Pres. Elect 2002–04; Visiting Prof. Brain and Behaviour Research Inst., Maastricht Univ.; Pres. British Asscn Psychopharmacology 1988–90; Pres. Int. Soc. for the Investigation of Stress; Assoc. mem. Royal Coll. of Psychiatrists; Foreign Corresp. mem. American Coll. Neuropsychopharmacology; Visiting Fellow Magdalen Coll. Oxford 1990–91; Hon. Prof. Faculty of Medicine, Queen's Univ. Belfast, NI; Silver Medal, Royal Irish Acad. 1996. *Publications:* Fundamentals of Psychopharmacology 1992, Fundamentals of Psychoimmunology 2000; over 400 articles in int. scientific journals. *Leisure interests:* entomology, classical music, political science. *Address:* Pharmacology Department, National University of Ireland, Galway (Office); Currabhaitia, Tullykyne, Moycullen, Co. Galway, Ireland (Home). *Telephone:* (91) 524411 (Ext. 3837) (Office); (91) 555292. *Fax:* (91) 525700 (Office). *E-mail:* belucg@iol.ie (Home).

LEONARD, Elmore, PhB; American novelist and screenwriter; b. 11 Oct. 1925, New Orleans; s. of Elmore John and Flora Amelia Leonard (née Rivé); m. 1st Beverly Claire Cline 1949 (divorced 1977), three s. two d.; m. 2nd Joan Leanne Lancaster 1979 (died 1993); m. 3rd Christine Kent 1993; ed Univ. of Detroit; mem. Writers' Guild of America, Authors' Guild, Mystery Writers of America, Western Writers of America. *Publications:* 31 novels including: Hombre 1961, City Primeval 1980, Split Images 1982, Cat Chaser 1982, La Brava 1983, Stick 1983, Glitz 1985, Bandits 1987, Touch 1987, Freaky Deaky 1988, Killshot 1989, Get Shorty 1990, Maximum Bob 1991, Rum Punch 1992, Pronto 1993, Riding the Rap 1995, Out of Sight 1996; screenplays: Cuba Libre 1998, Be Cool 1999. *Address:* c/o Random House Inc., 201 East 50th Street, New York, NY 10022 (Office); c/o Michael Siegel, 9150 Wilshire Blvd, Suite 350, Beverly Hills, CA 90212, USA.

LEONARD, Rt Rev Monsignor and Rt Hon Graham Douglas, KCVO, PC, MA, DD, STD; British ecclesiastic; b. 8 May 1921, Greenwich; s. of the late Rev. Douglas Leonard; m. Vivien Priscilla Swann 1943; two s.; ed Monkton Combe School, Balliol Coll. Oxford, Westcott House, Cambridge; Capt. Oxon. and Bucks. Light Infantry 1941–45, Army Operational Research Group 1944–45; ordained Deacon 1947, Priest 1948; Curacies 1948–52; Vicar of Ardleigh 1952–55; Dir Religious Educ., Diocese of St Albans, Canon, St Albans Cathedral 1955–58; Gen. Sec. Nat. Soc. and Gen. Sec. Church of England Schools Council 1958–62; Archdeacon of Hampstead, Rector of St Andrew Undershaft and St Mary Axe 1962–64; Bishop of Willesden 1964–73, of Truro 1973–81, of London 1981–91; received into Roman Catholic Church and ordained conditionally as a priest April 1994; mem. Anglican/Orthodox Joint Doctrinal Comm. 1974–81; Superior Gen. Soc. of Mary 1973–94 (Vice-Pres. 1994–); Chair. Church of England Bd for Social Responsibility 1976–83, Churches Main Cttee 1981–91, BBC and IBA Cen. Religious Advisory Cttee 1984–89, Bd of Educ. 1983–88; Pres. Path to Rome Int. Convention 1998–2001; mem. Polytechnics and Colls Funding Council 1989–93; Dean of HM Chapels Royal 1981–91, Prelate of Order of British Empire 1981–91, Prelate Imperial Soc. of Kts Bachelor 1986–91; Episcopal Canon of Jerusalem 1981–91; John Findlay Green Foundation Lecture, Fulton 1987; Hensley Henson Lecturer, Oxford Univ. 1991–92; Hon. Fellow Balliol Coll. Oxford 1986; Hon. Bencher, Middle Temple 1981; Prelate of Honour of His Holiness 2000; Hon. DD (Episcopal Theological Seminary, Kentucky) 1974; Hon. DCnL (Nashotah House) 1983; Hon. STD (Siena Coll.) 1994; Hon. LLD (Simon Greenleaf School of Law) 1987; Hon. DD (Westminster Coll. Fulton) 1987; Hon. DLitt (CNAA) 1989. *Publications:* The Gospel is for Everyone 1971, God Alive: Priorities in Pastoral Theology 1981, Firmly I Believe and Truly 1985, Life in Christ 1986, Path to Rome (contrib.) 1999; contribs to several theological works. *Leisure interests:* music, reading. *Address:* 25 Woodlands Road, Witney, Oxon., OX28 2DR, England.

LEONARD, Hugh (John Keyes Byrne); Irish playwright; b. John Joseph Byrne, 9 Nov. 1926, Dublin; m. Paule Jacquet 1955 (died 2000); one d.; ed Presentation Coll., Dún Laoghaire; worked as Civil Servant 1945–49; Script Ed. Granada TV, England 1961–63; Literary Ed., Abbey Theatre, Dublin 1976–77; Programme Dir, Dublin Theatre Festival 1978–; Hon. DHL (RI); Hon. DLitt (Trinity Coll. Dublin); Writers' Guild Award 1966, Tony Award, Critics Circle Award, Drama Desk Award, Outer Critics Award 1978. *Stage plays include:* The Big Birthday 1957, A Leap in the Dark 1957, Madigan's Lock 1958, A Walk on the Water 1960, The Passion of Peter Ginty 1961, Stephen D 1962, The Poker Session 1963, Dublin 1 1963, The Saints Go

Cycling In 1965, Mick and Mick 1966, The Quick and the Dead 1967, The Au Pair Man 1968, The Barracks 1969, The Patrick Pearse Motel 1971, Da 1973, Thieves 1973, Summer 1974, Times of Wolves and Tigers 1974, Irishmen 1975, Time Was 1976, A Life 1977, Moving Days 1981, The Mask of Moriarty 1984, Moving 1991, Senna for Sonny 1994, The Lily Lally Show 1994, Chamber Music (2 plays) 1994, Magic 1997, Love in the Title 1998. *Writing for television includes:* Silent Song 1967, Nicholas Nickleby 1977, London Belongs to Me 1977, The Last Campaign 1978, The Ring and the Rose 1978, Strumpet City 1979, The Little World of Don Camillo 1980, Kill 1982, Good Behaviour 1982, O'Neill 1983, Beyond the Pale 1984, The Irish RM 1985, A Life 1986, Troubles 1987, Parnell and the Englishwoman 1988, A Wild People 2001. *Films:* Herself Surprised 1977, Da 1984, Widows' Peak 1984, Troubles 1984, Banjaxed 1995. *Adaptations:* Great Expectations 1995, A Tale of Two Cities 1996. *Publications:* Home Before Night (autobiog.) 1979, Out After Dark (autobiog.) 1988, Parnell and the Englishwoman 1989, I, Orla! 1990, Rover and other Cats (a memoir) 1992, The Off-Shore Island (novel) 1993, The Mogs (for children) 1995, Magic 1997, Fillums 2003. *Leisure interests:* river cruising, conversation, travel, gastronomy, vintage movies, travel in France. *Address:* 6 Rossaun, Pilot View, Dalkey, Co. Dublin, Ireland. *Telephone:* (1) 280-9590. *E-mail:* panache@indigo.ie (Office).

LEONARD, Hugh Terence; New Zealand broadcasting executive; b. 20 July 1938, Greymouth; s. of Michael James Leonard and Elizabeth Leonard (née Storey); m. Pauline Lobendahn 1965; one s. two d.; joined NZ Broadcasting Service 1956, Fiji Broadcasting Comm. 1960, Gen. Man. 1973–85; Sec.-Gen. Asia-Pacific Broadcasting Union (ABU) 1985–; Fiji Independence Medal 1970. *Leisure interests:* classic motorcycles, remote-controlled model aircraft, computers. *Address:* Asia-Pacific Broadcasting Union, P.O. Box 1164, 59700 Kuala Lumpur, Malaysia (Office). *Telephone:* (3) 22823592 (Office). *Fax:* (3) 22825292 (Office). *E-mail:* sg@abu.org.my (Office). *Website:* www.abu.org.my (Office).

LEONARD, Nelson Jordan, BS, DSc, PhD; American professor of chemistry; b. 1 Sept. 1916, Newark, NJ; s. of Harvey Nelson Leonard and Olga Pauline Jordan; m. 1st Louise Cornelie Vermey 1947 (died 1987); three s. one d.; m. 2nd Peggy Phelps 1992; ed Lehigh, Oxford and Columbia Univs; Research Asst, Univ. of Ill. 1942–43, Instructor 1943–44, Assoc. 1944–45, 1946–47, Asst Prof. 1947–49, Assoc. Prof. 1949–52, Prof. of Chem. 1952–, Head of Div. of Organic Chem. 1954–63 and Prof. of Biochem. 1973–86; mem. Center for Advanced Study, Univ. of Ill. 1968–86, Reynold C. Fuson Prof. of Chem. 1981–86, RC Fuson Prof., Emer. 1986–; Fogarty Scholar-in-Residence, NIH, Bethesda 1989–90; Sherman Fairchild Distinguished Scholar, Calif. Inst. of Tech. 1991, Faculty Assoc. 1992–; Scientific Consultant and Special Investigator, Field Intelligence Agency Technical, US Army and US Dept of Commerce, European Theater 1945–46; Ed. Organic Syntheses 1951–58, mem. Advisory Bd 1959–, Bd of Dirs. 1969–, Vice-Pres. 1976–80, Pres. 1980–88; mem. Exec. Cttee Journal of Organic Chemistry 1951–54, mem. Editorial Bd 1957–61; mem. Editorial Bd Journal of ACS 1960–72; mem. Advisory Bd Biochemistry 1973–78; Sec., Div. of Organic Chem., ACS 1949–54, Chair. 1956; mem. Advisory Panel for Chem. of Nat. Science Foundation 1958–61, Program Cttee in the Basic Physical Sciences of Alfred P. Sloan Foundation 1961–66, Study Section in Medicinal Chem. of NIH 1963–67, Educational Advisory Bd of John Simon Guggenheim Memorial Foundation 1969–88, Cttee of Selection 1977–88, Advisory Cttee, Searle Scholars Program, Chicago Community Trust 1982–85; Visiting Prof. Univ. of Calif. at Los Angeles 1953; mem. NAS 1955–; titular mem. Organic Chem. Div., Int. Union of Pure and Applied Chem. 1981–85, co-opted mem. 1985–87, Sec. 1987–89, Vice-Pres. 1989–91, Pres. 1991–93; Fellow, American Acad. of Arts and Sciences 1961– (Vice-Pres. 1990–93), American Philosophical Soc. 1996–; Foreign mem. Polish Acad. of Sciences; Swiss American Foundation Lecturer 1953, 1970, Julius Stieglitz Memorial Lecturer (ACS) 1962, Backer Lecturer, Univ. of Groningen 1972, and other lectureships; Hon. ScD (Lehigh, Ill., Adam Mickiewicz Univ., Poland); ACS Award for Creative Work in Synthetic Organic Chem. 1963, Synthetic Organic Chemical Mfrs Asscn Medal 1970, Edgar Fahs Smith Award, ACS and Univ. of Pa 1975, Roger Adams Award in Organic Chemistry, ACS 1981, Wheland Award, Univ. of Chicago 1991, Creativity Award (Univ. of Oregon) 1994, Paul G. Gassman Distinguished Service Award (ACS) 1994, Arthur C. Cope Scholar Award (ACS) 1995. *Publications:* numerous research articles in scientific journals. *Address:* Division of Chemistry and Chemical Engineering, Mail Code 164-30, Pasadena, CA 91125; 389 California Terrace, Pasadena, CA 91105, USA. *Telephone:* (626) 395-6541; (626) 792-7745. *Fax:* (626) 568-3749.

LEONARD, Ray Charles ("Sugar Ray"); American boxer (retd); b. 17 May 1956, Wilmington, NC; s. of Cicero Leonard and Getha Leonard; m. 1st Juanita Wilkinson 1980 (divorced 1990); two s.; m. 2nd Bernadette Robi 1993; one s. one d.; ed Palmer Park High School, Md; amateur boxer 1970–77; won 140 of 145 amateur fights; world amateur champion 1974, US Amateur Athletic Union champion 1974, Pan-American Games gold medallist 1975, Olympic gold medallist 1976; guaranteed record purse of $25,000 for first professional fight Feb. 1977; won North American welterweight title from Pete Ranzany August 1979; won World Boxing Council version of world welterweight title from Wilfred Benitez Nov. 1979; retained title against Dave Green March 1980, lost it to Roberto Durán (q.v.), Montréal, June 1980; regained it from Durán, New Orleans, Nov. 1980; world jr middleweight title, World Boxing Asscn (WBA) June 1981; won WBA world welterweight title from Tommy Hearns to become undisputed world champion Sept. 1981, drew rematch June 1989; 36 professional fights, 33 wins, lost 2, drawn 1; retd from boxing Nov. 1982; returned to the ring April 1987; won World middleweight title, lost to Terry Norris 1991, retd from boxing 1991; returned to ring March 1997; lost Int. Boxing Council middleweight title fight to Hector Camacho 1997; boxing promoter (Sugar Ray Leonard Boxing); commentator for Home Box Office TV Co.; motivational speaker; Ring magazine's Fighter of the Decade for the 1980s. *Address:* Suite 206-B, 4401 East West Highway, Bethesda, MD 20814, USA. *Telephone:* (310) 471-3100 (Office). *Website:* www .srlboxing.com (Office).

LEONG, Lampo, MFA; American (born Chinese) artist and educator; b. 3 July 1961, Guangzhou; ed Guangzhou Fine Arts Inst., California Coll. of Arts & Crafts, Oakland, USA; Instructor, Calif. Coll. of Arts and Crafts 1986–87; Lecturer, San Francisco State Univ., Calif. 1988–96, Asst Prof. 1996–2001; Asst Prof. Univ. of Missouri-Columbia 2001–; Instructor, Univ. of Calif., Berkeley 1989, Art Studio 1990–; Instructor Chabot Coll., Hayward, Calif. 1989–94, Diablo Valley Coll., Pleasant Hill, Calif. 1998–; Art Instructor Mission Coll., Santa Clara, Calif. 1999–2001; Guest Speaker Asian Art Museum of San Francisco 1985, 1990, 1992, 1994, 1996–2001, Univ. of Calif. at Berkeley, Dept of Art History 1997, 1998, 2001, Stanford Univ. Inst. for Int. Studies 1999, 2000; 40 solo exhbns and 140 group exhbns Japan, China, Macao, Hong Kong, Taiwan, Canada, USA, England, France, Spain 1981–; works in many collections world-wide (including Japan, China, Hong Kong, Macao, Taiwan, Indonesia, Canada, USA, Germany; Vice-Pres. Oriental Art Asscn, USA; Co-Founder, Dir Chinese–American Culture Exchange Asscn, USA; mem. Nat. Modern Meticulous Painting Soc., China, Macao Soc. of Social Sciences; Gold Medal Award, 15th Macao Painting Exhbn 1998, Macao, Bronze Award, 20th Century Asian Pacific Art Competition, Asian Pacific Art Inst., Washington DC, Winner Tulane Review Art Contest 2002, Juror's Award, 39th Annual and 1st Virtual Exhbn, Sumi-e Soc. of America 2002 . *Exhibitions include:* From Chinese Ink to Abstraction, Chinese Culture Center, San Francisco 2000, Chinese American Artists, Art in Embassies, US Dept of State, Washington DC 2001, New Arrivals Univ. of Missouri-Columbia 2001, Nat. Small Print Exhbn Univ. of Wisconsin-Parkside, Kemosha 2002, Marking Time Nat. Exhbn Fredericksburg Center for the Creative Arts 2002, George E. Ohr Nat. Art Challenge, The Ohr–O'Keefe Museum of Art, Biloxi, Miss. 2002, Contemporary IV Int. Juried Exhbn, Period Gallery Ints, Omaha, Neb. 2002, Plain Arts IV Int. Juried Exhbn, Pittsburg State Univ., Pittsburg, Kan. 2002, 29th Annual Nat. Juried Competition, Masur Museum of Art, Monroe, La 2002, Lyrical Brush: East Asian Calligraphy, State Univ. of New York-Stony Brook 2002, 25th Int. Exhbn, Watercolor Art Soc.-Houston, Two Allen Center, Tex. 2002, Marking Time, Current Work 2002: A National Competition, Rosenthal Gallery, Fayetteville State Univ., NC 2002. *Leisure interests:* photography, film, travel, ballroom dancing. *Address:* Department of Art, A126 Fine Arts, University of Missouri-Columbia, Columbia, MO 65211, USA (Office). *Telephone:* (573) 882-9446 (Office); (573) 474-7543 (Home). *Fax:* (573) 884-6807 (Office). *E-mail:* leongl@missouri.edu (Office); L@LampoLeong.com. *Website:* www.LampoLeong.com (Home).

LEONHARD, Kurt Ernst Albert; German author, translator and editor; b. 5 Feb. 1910, Berlin; s. of Paul Leonhard and Erna Leonhard; m. Ilse Bliedner 1943; two d.; ed Reformrealgymnasium, Berlin-Karlshorst and Univ. of Berlin; bookseller, author, art critic and publisher's reader 1937–41; mil. service 1941–46; freelance author, trans. and lecturer 1946–; publisher's reader, Esslingen 1950–59; Prof. hc 1976; Hon. mem. Stuttgart Acad. 1985; Verdienstmedaille, Baden-Württemberg 1984. *Publications:* Die heilige Fläche 1947, Augenschein und Inbegriff 1953, Gegenwelt (poems) 1956, Cézanne (monograph) 1966, Picasso, Graphik 1966, Dante Alighieri (monograph) 1970, Wort wider Wort (poems) 1974, Das zehnte Loch (poems) 1983, Gegenbilder (poetry and prose) 1986, Zirkelschlüsse 1988, Texte aus sechs Jahrzehnten 1995. *Leisure interests:* travel, art, nature. *Address:* Auchtweg 24, 73734 Esslingen, Germany. *Telephone:* (711) 384688.

LEONHARDT, Rudolf Walter, DPhil; German journalist and author; b. 9 Feb. 1921, Altenburg; s. of Rudolf Leonhardt and Paula (née Zeiger) Leonhardt; m. Ulrike Zoerb; two s. one d.; ed Berlin, Leipzig, Bonn, Cambridge and London; Lecturer in German, Cambridge Univ. 1948–50; Foreign Corresp. Die Zeit, London 1953–55, Cultural Ed. Die Zeit, Hamburg 1957–73, Deputy Ed.-in-Chief 1974–87; author 1987–. *Publications:* The Structure of a Novel 1950, Notes on German Literature 1955, 77 x England 1957 (trans. into Spanish 1964), Der Sündenfall der deutschen Germanistik 1959, Leben ohne Literatur? 1961, x-mal Deutschland 1961 (trans. into English, Italian, Spanish 1964), Zeitnotizen 1963, Junge deutsche Dichter für Anfänger 1964, Reise in ein fernes Land (with Marion Gräfin Dönhoff and Theo Sommer) 1964 (trans. into Japanese 1965), Kästner für Erwachsene 1966, Wer wirft den ersten Stein? 1969, Sylt für Anfänger 1969, Haschisch-Report 1970, Drei Wochen und drei Tage–Japan-Tagebuch 1970, Deutschland 1972, Argumente Pro und Contra 1974, Das Weib, das ich geliebet hab–Heines Mädchen und Frauen 1975, Journalismus und Wahrheit 1976, Lieder aus dem Krieg 1979, Sylt 1870–1920 1980, Hamburg 1985, Deutschland 1990. *Leisure interest:* people. *Address:* Leuchtturmweg 42A, 22559 Hamburg, Germany. *Telephone:* (40) 817757.

LEONI, Téa; American actress; b. 25 Feb. 1966; m. David Duchovny (q.v.). 1997. *Films:* Switch 1991, A League of Their Own 1992, Wyatt Earp 1994, Bad Boys 1995, Flirting with Disaster 1996, Deep Impact 1998, There's No Fish Food in Heaven 1999. *TV:* (sitcoms) Naked Truth, Flying Blind 1995. *Address:* c/o ICM, 8942 Wilshire Boulevard, Beverly Hills, CA 90211, USA.

LEONOV, Maj.-Gen. Aleksey Arkhipovich; Russian cosmonaut; b. 30 May 1934, Kamerovo Region; s. of Arkhip Leonov and Yevdokia Leonov; m. Svetlana Leonova; two d.; ed Chuguevsky Air Force School for Pilots and Zhukovsky Air Force Engineering Academy; Pilot 1956–59; mem. CPSU 1957–91; cosmonaut training 1960; first man to walk in space 1965: took part in flight of space-ship Voskhod 2 and moved 5 metres into space outside space-ship; Pilot-Cosmonaut of USSR; Deputy Commdr Gagarin Cosmonauts Training Centre 1971; took part in joint flight Soyuz 19–Apollo 1975; Maj.-Gen. 1975; Chair. Council of Founders of Novosti Press Agency 1969–90; Deputy Head, Centre of Cosmonaut Training 1975–92; Dir Cheteck-Cosmos Co. 1992–; Pres. Investment Fund Alfa-Capital 1991–; Vice-Pres. Alpha Bank 2000; Co-Chair. Bd Int. Asscn of Cosmonauts; mem. Int. Acad. of Astronauts; Hon. DrScEng; Hero of the Soviet Union 1965, 1975, Yuri Gagarin Gold Medal, Hero of Bulgaria, Hero of Vietnam, Order of Lenin (twice), USSR State Prize 1981; hon. citizen of cities in Russia and USA. *Publications:* numerous books, papers and articles, notably on the psychological activity of cosmonauts. *Leisure interests:* painting, shooting movies. *Address:* Alfa-Capital, Mashi Poryvayevoy str. 9, 107078 Moscow, Russia. *Telephone:* (095) 786-29-29.

LÉONTIEFF, Alexandre, D. EN SC. ECON.; French Polynesian politician; b. 20 Oct. 1948, Teahupoo, Tahiti; s. of Maxime Léontieff and Louise Teahu; m. Demecia Jurd 1972; two s.; mem. of Territorial Ass. French Polynesia 1977–; Vice-Pres. Govt of Polynesia 1984–86; Minister of Economy, of the Sea and Tourism 1986–87; Pres. Govt of Polynesia 1987–91; Deputy to French Nat. Ass. 1986. *Address:* Résidence Taina, B.P. No. 2737, Papeete, French Polynesia.

LEONTYEV, Leopold Igorevich, DrTechSci; Russian metallurgist; b. 1 Dec. 1934, Sverdlovsk (now Yekaterinburg); m.; two s.; ed Urals Polytech. Inst.; researcher, Head of Lab., then Deputy Dir Inst. of Metallurgy, Ural br. of USSR (now Russian) Acad. of Sciences 1957–93, Deputy Chair. 1993, currently mem. Presidium, also mem. Russian Acad. of Sciences 1997, mem. Presidium 2000; First Deputy Minister of Science and Tech. 1993–96, 1997–2000; First Deputy Chair. State Cttee on Science and Tech. 1996–97. *Publications:* numerous scientific publs on the devt of physical and chem. fundamentals and processes of complex use of metallurgic raw materials. *Address:* Presidium of Ural Branch of Russian Academy of Sciences, Yekaterinburg, Pervomayskaya str. 91, 620219 Yekaterinburg, Russia (Office). *Telephone:* (095) 237-39-31 (Moscow) (Office); (3432) 74-53-85 (Yekaterinburg) (Office).

LEONTYEV, Mikhail Vladimirovich; Russian journalist; b. 12 Oct. 1958, Moscow; m.; two c.; ed Moscow Plekhanov Inst. of Nat. Econs; political reviewer Kommersant (newspaper) 1987–90; on staff newspaper Atmoda (Riga) and Experimental Creative Cen. in Moscow 1989–91; Ed. Div. of Politics Nezavisimaya Gazeta (newspaper) 1990–92; First Deputy Ed.-in-Chief daily Business MN 1992–93; First Deputy Ed.-in-Chief Segodnya (newspaper) 1993–97; political reviewer TV-Cen. Channel 1997–98, ORT Channel 1999–; Ed.-in-Chief journal Fas 2000–. *Address:* Obshchestvennoye Rossiyskoe Televideniye (ORT), Akademika Koroleva str. 12, 127000 Moscow, Russia (Office). *Telephone:* (095) 217 94-72, (095) 217-94-73 (Office).

LEOPHAIRATANA, Prachai, M.S.EE.; Thai business executive; b. 28 Aug. 1944; s. of Phorn Leophairatana and Boonsri Leophairatana; m. Orapin Leophairatana 1974; ed Canterbury Univ., New Zealand, Univ. of Calif., Berkeley; CEO Thai Petrochemical Industry PCL 1988–, TPI Polene PCL, TPI Group of Cos 1988–; Man. Dir Hong Yiah Seng Co. Ltd 1986–; mem. Senate; Chair. Bd of Dirs United Grain Industry Co. Ltd 1986–, Bangkok Union Insurance PCL 1986–, Thai Industrial Estate Corp. Ltd 1988–, Exec. Bd Thai Caprolactam PCL 1989–, Uhde (Thailand) Co. Ltd 1990–, Thai Int. Tankers Co. Ltd 1994–; Vice-Chair. Bd of Dirs Thai Alliance Textile Co. Ltd 1986–; Dir Rice Export Asscns, Thai–Chinese Friendship Asscn, Thai–Chinese Promotion of Investment and Trade Asscn, Bd of Trade of Thailand; Sec.-Gen. Environment for Better Life Foundation; Kt Grand Cross Most Noble Order of the Crown of Thailand; Kt Grand Cross (1st Class) Exalted Order of the White Elephant; Kt Grand Cordon (Special Class) Most Noble Order of the Crown of Thailand; Companion (4th Class) Most Admirable Order of the Direkgunabhom. *Address:* Thai Petrochemical Industry PCL, TPI Tower, 26/56 Thanen Chan Tat Mai, Thungmahamek Sathorn, Bangkok 10210, Thailand. *Telephone:* (2) 6785000. *Fax:* (2) 6785001. *E-mail:* tpiadmin@tpigroup.co .th (Office). *Website:* www.tpigroup.co.th (Office).

LEOPOLD, Luna Bergere, PhD; American geologist and engineer; b. 8 Oct. 1915, New Mexico; s. of Aldo Leopold and Estella Bergere; m. 1st Carolyn Clugston 1940; m. 2nd Barbara Beck Nelson 1973; one s. one d.; ed Harvard Univ. and Univs of California and Wisconsin; U.S. Army 1941–46; Head Meteorologist, Pineapple Research Inst. of Hawaii 1946–50; Hydraulic Engineer, U.S. Geological Survey, Washington, DC 1950–66, Chief Hydrologist 1956–66, Sr Research Hydrologist 1966–71; Prof. of Geology, Univ. of Calif. 1973–; mem. NAS; Hon. DSc (St Andrews) 1981, (Murcia) 1984; Kirk Bryan Award, Geological Soc. of America, Cullum Geographical Medal, American Geographical Soc., Distinguished Service Award, U.S. Dept of Interior, Veth Medal, Royal Netherlands Geographical Soc., Rockefeller Public Service

Award, Warren Prize, NAS, Busk Medal, Royal Geographical Soc., R. K. Linsley Award, American Inst. of Hydrology, Nat. Medal of Science and other awards. *Publications:* The Flood Control Controversy (with Thomas Maddock, Jr) 1954, Fluvial Processes in Geomorphology 1964, Water 1974, Water in Environmental Planning (with Thomas Dunne) 1978, A View of the River 1994, Water, Rivers and Creeks 1997 and over 100 scientific papers on water, hydrology and rivers. *Address:* Department of Geology, University of California, Berkeley, CA 94720; P.O. Box 1040, Pinedale, WY 82941, USA (Home).

LÉOTARD, François Gérard Marie; French politician; b. 26 March 1942, Cannes; s. of André Léotard and Antoinette Tomasi; m. 1st France Reynier 1976; m. 2nd Ysabel Duret 1992; one s. one d.; ed Lycées Charlemagne and Henri IV, Paris, Faculté de Droit and Inst. d'Etudes Politiques, Paris and Ecole Nat. d'Admin; Sec. of Chancellery, Ministry of Foreign Affairs 1968–71; Admin. Town Planning 1973–75; Sous-préfet 1974–77; Mayor of Fréjus 1977–92, 1993–97, Municipal Councillor 1992; Deputy to Nat. Ass. (UDF-PR) 1978–86, 1988–92; Conseiller-Gen., Var 1980–88; Sec.-Gen. Parti Républicain 1982–88, Pres. 1988–90, 1995–97, Hon. Pres. 1990–95; Vice-Pres. Union pour la Démocratie Française (UDF) 1983–84, Pres. 1996–98; Minister of Culture and Communications 1986–88, of Nat. Defence (oversaw peace-keeping operations in Bosnia) 1993–95; Deputy for Var 1988–92, 1995–97, 1997–2002; with EU Special Envoy to Macedonia 2001–; Insp. Gen. des Finances pour l'extérieur Dec. 2001–; Chevalier, Ordre nat. du Mérite. *Publications:* A Mots Decouverts 1987, Culture: Les Chemins de Printemps 1988, La Ville aimée: mes chemins de Fréjus 1989, Pendant la Crise, le spectacle continue 1989, Adresse au Président des Républiques françaises 1991, Place de la République 1992, Ma Liberté 1995, Pour l'honneur 1997, Je vous hais tous avec douceur 2000, Paroles d'immortels 2001. *Leisure interests:* running, tennis, parachuting. *Address:* c/o Assemblée Nationale, 75355 Paris, France.

LEPAGE, Corinne Dominique Marguerite; French politician and lawyer; b. 11 May 1951, Boulogne-Billancourt; d. of Philippe Lepage and Jacqueline Schulmann; m. 1st Christian Jessua, one d.; m. 2nd Christian Huglo, one s.; ed Lycée Molière, Univ. of Paris II and Inst. d'Etudes Politiques, Paris; in legal partnership 1971–76; barrister, Paris 1978–; Dir of Studies, Univ. of Paris II 1974–77; Dir of Educ. Univ. of Metz 1978–80; Mayor of Cabourg 1978–2001; Maître de conférences, Inst. d'Etudes Politiques, Paris 1979–87; Course Dir Univ. of Paris II 1982–86, Univ. of Paris XII 1984–94; mem. Bar Council 1987–89; Vice-Pres., Pres. Asscn of Admin. Law Advocates 1989–95; Minister of the Environment 1995–97; Pres. Asscn nationale des docteurs en droit 1998–; Vice-Pres. Environnement sans frontières 1998–, Asscn européenne des Générations emploi mondialisation 1999–; Pres. Comité de Recherche Indépendante et d'Information sur le Génie Génétique (CRII-GEN); Leader CAP 21-Citoyenneté Action Participation pour le 21è siècle, Presidential cand. 2002. *Publications:* Code annoté des procédures administratives contentieuses 1990, Les audits de l'environnement 1992, On ne peut rien faire, Madame le ministre 1998, Bien gérer l'environnement, une chance pour l'entreprise 1999, La Politique de Précaution 2001; numerous articles in La Gazette du Palais. *Leisure interests:* cinema, reading, tennis, skiing, swimming. *Address:* CAP 21, 40 rue de Monceau, 75008 Paris (Office); Jérôme, 1 avenue du Casino Ouest, 14390 Villa Cabourg, France (Home).

LEPAGE, Robert; French-Canadian actor and theatre and film director; b. 1957, Québec City; ed Conservatoire d'Art Dramatique Québec, Canada; Artistic Dir Nat. Arts Centre Ottawa, Canada 1990–92; Hon. PhD (Laval) 1994; Hon. DLitt (Toronto, McGill) 1997; Hon. LLD (Concordia) 1999; Evening Standard Award for Best Play 2001 and various other awards. *Films:* (scriptwriter, dir) The Confessional 1995, The Polygraph 1996, Nô 1998, Possible Worlds 2000. *Operas:* (dir) Bluebeard's Castle 1992, Erwartung 1992, The Damnation of Faust 1999. *Productions include:* Dragon's Trilogy (co-writer, dir and actor) 1984, Vinci (writer, dir and actor) 1986, Tectonic Plates (co-writer, dir and actor) 1988, A Midsummer Night's Dream (dir) 1992, The Geometry of Miracles (co-writer, dir) 1998, The Far Side of the Moon (writer, dir and actor) 2000. *Address:* 103 Dalhousie, Québec City, PQ, G1K 4B9, Canada. *Telephone:* (418) 692-0055. *Fax:* (418) 692-5400 (Office). *E-mail:* roleinc@attglobal.net (Office).

LEPPARD, Raymond John, CBE, MA; British conductor and composer; b. 11 Aug. 1927, London; s. of A. V. Leppard and B. M. Beck; ed Trinity Coll. Cambridge; Fellow of Trinity Coll., Univ. Lecturer in Music 1958–68; Music Dir, BBC Philharmonic (fmrly BBC Northern Symphony) Orchestra 1973–80; Prin. Guest Conductor, St Louis Symphony Orchestra 1984–93; Music Dir Indianapolis Symphony Orchestra 1987–; has conducted New York Philharmonic, Chicago Symphony, Philadelphia and Pittsburgh Symphony Orchestras and Royal Opera, Covent Garden, English Nat. Opera, Metropolitan Opera, New York, New York City Opera and San Francisco Opera; realizations of Monteverdi's L'Incoronazione di Poppea, Il Ritorno d'Ulisse and L'Orfeo and Cavalli's L'Ormindo, L'Egisto, La Calisto and L'Orione. *Publication:* Authenticity in Music 1989. *Leisure interests:* friends, theatre, reading. *Address:* Orchard House, 5040 Buttonwood Crescent, Indianapolis, IN 46228; Indianapolis Symphony Orchestra, 45 Monument Circus, Indianapolis, IN 46204, USA. *Telephone:* (317) 259-9020 (Home). *Fax:* (317) 259-0916.

LEPPER, Andrzej; Polish politician and trade union official; b. 13 June 1954, Stowiecino; s. of Jan Lepper and Anna Lepper; m. Irena Lepper; one s. two d.; ed Agric. Tech. School; worked in public and co-operative sector 1976–80; farmer 1980–; Founder and Pres. Trade Union of Farmers 1991–92; mem. Nat. Council of Agric. Chambers 1998–; councillor Local Parl. of the Western Pomeranian Voivodship 1998–2001; Deputy to Sejm (Parl.) 2001–, Vice-Marshal of Sejm 2001–02; Chair. Self Defence Party of the Repub. of Poland (Partia Samoobrona Rzeczypospolitej Polskiej) 2001–; Medal of Hope of Pope John Paul II 1995, Medal of Albert Schweitzer 2001. *Publications include:* Samoobrona—dlaczego, przed czym? (Self Defence—Why and Against What?) 1993, Kazdy kij ma dwa konce (Every Stick Has Two Ends) 2001, Lista Leppera (The List of Lepper) 2002. *Leisure interests:* horse riding, swimming, boxing. *Address:* Partia Samoobrona Rzeczypospolitej Polskiej, Aleje Jerozolimskie 30, 00-204 Warsaw, Poland (Office). *Telephone:* (22) 6250472 (Office). *Fax:* (22) 6250477 (Office). *E-mail:* samoobrona@samoobrona.org.pl (Office). *Website:* www.samoobrona.org.pl (Office).

LEPPING, Sir George, GCMG, MBE; Solomon Islands politician and government official; b. 22 Nov. 1947; s. of Chief Dionisio Tanutanu and Regina Suluki; m. Margaret Kwalea Teioli 1972; two s. five d.; ed King George VI Secondary School, Agric. Coll., Vudal, Reading Univ.; Field Officer, Dept of Agric. and Rural Econ. 1968, Pres. Solomon Is. Amateur Athletics Union 1970–73, 1981–82; Sr Field Officer then Under-Sec. (Agric.), Ministry of Agric. 1979–80; Perm. Sec. Ministry of Home Affairs and Nat. Devt 1981–84; Project Dir Rural Services Project 1984–87; Minister of Finance 1988; Gov.-Gen. 1988–94; Leader, then Pres. People's Alliance Party 1996–; fmr mem., Dir or Chair., various Govt bodies. *Leisure interests:* reading, swimming, lawn tennis, snooker, snorkelling, high-speed boat driving, fishing; first Solomon Islands athlete to win int. sports medals; KStJ 1991. *Address:* P.O. Box 1431, Honiara; People's Alliance Party, P.O. Box 722, Honiara, Solomon Islands.

LERACH, Wiliam S.; American lawyer; m. (divorced) three times; three c.; partner Michelle Ciccarelli; Partner, Milberg Weiss Bershad Hynes & Lerach LLP; frequent commentator and lecturer on securities and corp. law, class and derivative actions, accountants' liability and attorneys' fees; mem. ABA's Litigation Section's Cttee on Class Actions and Derivative Skills, American Law Inst. Faculty on Fed. and State Class Action Litigation; Master American Inns of Court; fmr Pres. Nat. Asscn of Securities and Commercial Lawyers; mem. Editorial Bd Class Action Reports; Guest Lecturer at Stanford Univ., UCLA, Univ. of Calif. at San Diego, San Diego State Univ., Univ. of Pittsburgh, Council of Institutional Investors, Int. Corp. Governance Network; mem. United States Holocaust Memorial Council. *Address:* Milberg Weiss Bershad Hynes & Lerach LLP, Attention: Confidential Inquiries, 401 B Street, Suite 1700, San Diego, CA 92101, USA (Office). *Telephone:* (619) 231-1058 (Office). *Fax:* (619) 231-7423 (Office). *E-mail:* wsl@mwbhl.com (Office). *Website:* www.milberg.com (Office).

LERCHE, Peter Fritz Franz, DJur; German professor of law; b. 12 Jan. 1928, Leitmeritz; s. of Dr Fritz Lerche and Karoline Lerche (née Artmann); m. Dr Ilse Lerche (née Peschek) 1955; two s.; ed Univ. of Munich; Prof. Freie Universität Berlin 1960; Prof. of Public Law, Univ. of Munich 1965; mem. Bavarian Acad. of Sciences; fmr mem. Council of Science; First Pres. Union of German Lecturers in Public Law 1982; fmr mem. numerous govt comms and attorney in governmental lawsuits, etc.; Bavarian Order of Merit, Maximiliansorden; Hon. DJur; numerous other awards. *Publications:* Ordentlicher Rechtsweg und Verwaltungsrechtsweg 1953, Übermass und Verfassungsrecht 1961, Werbung und Verfassung 1967, Rundfunkmonopol 1970, Verfassungsrechtliche Fragen zur Pressekonzentration 1971, Verfassungsrechtliche Aspekte der 'inneren Pressefreiheit' 1974, Kernkraft und rechtlicher Wandel 1981, Städte und Kabelkommunikation 1982, Mitarbeit an Maunz/Dürig, Kommentar zum Grundgesetz, Verfassungsgerichtsbarkeit in besonderen Situationen 2001. *Leisure interest:* study of the hippopotamus. *Address:* Junkerstrasse 13, 82131 Gauting, Germany. *Telephone:* (89) 8502088.

LESCHLY, Jan; Danish business executive; m. Lotte Enngelbred 1963; four s.; ed Coll. of Pharmacy, School of Econ. and Business Administration Copenhagen, Princeton Univ., USA; Novo Industries A/S 1972–1979; Vice-Pres. Commercial Devt, Squibb Corpn 1979, US Pres. 1981, Group Vice-Pres. and Dir 1984, Exec. Vice-Pres. 1986; Pres. and COO 1988; Chair. SmithKline Beecham Pharmaceuticals 1990, CEO 1994–2000; Chair. and CEO Care Capital LLC 2000–; mem. pharmaceutical assocs and educational bodies. *Address:* Care Capital LLC, Princeton Overlook I, 100 Overlook Center and Route 1, Princeton, NJ 08540, USA.

LESCURE, Pierre François Amar; French business executive; b. 2 July 1945, Paris; s. of François Lescure and Paulette Baudoin; m. Frédérique Fayles-Bernstein 1996; ed Lycée Turgot, Paris, Centre de formation des journalistes; reporter and newsreader Radio Télé Luxembourg 1965–68; with Radio Caroline and Radio Monte Carlo 1968–72; newsreader and presenter Office de radiodiffusion télévision française (ORTF) 1973–77, Deputy Ed., weekend programmes 1977–80; Dir Programmes Europe 1 1980–81; Ed.-in-Chief Antenne 2 1982–84; Head of Programmes 1984–86; Dir-Gen. Canal+ 1986–94, Chair. and Man. Dir 1994–2000, Chair. Bd of Dirs 2000–02; Chair. Canal Jimmy 1991–2002; Chair. and Man. Dir Paris Saint-Germain Football SA 1991–, Le Studio Canal+ 1991–2002, Le Monde Presse 1994–; Chair. UGCDA (audiovisual rights co.) 1997–, CanalPro 1997–2002, Multithématiques 2001–; Deputy Exec. Cttee Havas 1997–; Dir and mem. Strategic Cttee Havas Group 1993–; mem. Advisory Bd Lagardère Group 2000–; Homme de la décennie de la télévision, CB News 1996, Man. de l'année, le

Nouvel économiste 1996 and other awards; Chevalier Ordre Nat. du Mérite, Officier des Arts et des Lettres. *Publications:* A nous la radio. *Address:* c/o Paris Saint-Germain Football, 30 avenue du Parc des Princes, 75016 Paris, France.

LESIN, Mikhail Yuryevich; Russian politician and journalist; b. 11 July 1958; m.; one s.; ed Moscow Inst. of Eng and Construction; fmr eng constructor; f. Igrotechnika (later Intelleks) Co-operative 1989–91; Founder and Chair. Bd of Dirs Videoint. (advertising co.) 1991–; mem. of staff RIA Novosti, Dir-Gen. Novosti-TV Co. 1993–96; Head of Dept of Public Relations, Russian Presidency 1996–97 (resgnd); First Deputy Chair. All-Russian State TV Co. 1997–99; Minister of Press, TV, Broadcasting and Telecommunications (subsequently the Press, Broadcasting and Mass Media) 1999–. *Address:* Ministry of the Press, Broadcasting and Mass Media, Strastnoy blvd 5, 101409 GSP-4 Moscow, Russia (Office). *Telephone:* (095) 209-63-52, (095) 209-77-61 (Office). *E-mail:* lesin@mptr.ru (Office).

LESLIE, Sir Peter Evelyn, Kt, MA, FIB, FLS; British banker; b. 24 March 1931, Oxford; s. of late Patrick Holt Leslie and Evelyn de Berry; m. Charlotte Chapman-Andrews 1975; two step-s. two step-d.; ed Stowe School and New Coll. Oxford; joined Barclays Bank DCO 1955, served in Sudan, Algeria, Zaire, Kenya and the Bahamas; Gen. Man. Barclays Bank Ltd 1973–76, Dir 1979–91; Sr Gen. Man. Barclays Bank Int. 1980–83; Chief Gen. Man. Barclays Bank PLC 1985–87, Man. Dir 1987–88, Deputy Chair. 1987–91; Deputy Chair. Midland Group 1991–92; Chair. British Bankers' Asscn Exec. Cttee 1978–79, mem. Export Guarantees Advisory Council 1978–81, Chair. 1987–92; Chair. Cttee London and Scottish Clearing Bankers 1986–88; mem. Bd of Banking Supervision, Bank of England 1989–94; Chair. NCM UK 1995–98, mem. Supervisory Bd NCM Holding NV Amsterdam 1995–2000; Chair. Overseas Devt Inst. 1988–95, Commonwealth Devt Corpn 1989–95; Gov. Stowe School 1983–2001 (Chair. 1994–2001); mem. Council for Ind. and Higher Educ. 1987–91; Chair. Queen's Coll., London 1989–94; Oxford Univ. Audit Cttee 1992–2001; Curator Univ. Chest, Oxford 1990–95; mem. Council, Ranfurly Library Service 1991–94, Royal Inst. of Int. Affairs, Chatham House 1991–97; mem. Bd Int. Inst. for Environment and Devt 1992–95. *Leisure interests:* natural history, historical research. *Address:* 153 Sutherland Avenue, London, W9 1ES, England. *Telephone:* (20) 7289-4920.

LESOTHO, King of (see Letsie III).

LESOURNE, Jacques François; French newspaper editor and academic; b. 26 Dec. 1928, La Rochelle; s. of André Lesourne and Simone Lesourne (née Guille); m. Odile Melin, 1961; one s. two d.; ed Lycée Montaigne, Bordeaux, École Polytechnique, École Nationale Supérieure des Mines de Paris; Head Econ. Service of French Collieries 1954–57; Dir Gen., later Pres. METRA Int. and SEMA 1958–75; Prof. of Econs École des Mines de Saint-Étienne 1958–61; Prof. of Industrial Econs École Nationale Supérieure de la Statistique 1960–63; Pres. Asscn Française d'Informatique et de Recherche Operationnelle 1966–67; mem. Council Int. Inst. of Applied Systems Analysis, Vienna 1973–79, Inst. of Man. Science 1976–79; Prof. Conservatoire Nat. des Arts et Métiers 1974–; Dir Projet Interfuturs OECD 1976–79; Dir of Studies, Inst. Auguste Comte 1979–81; Pres. Comm. on Employment and Social Relations of 8th Plan 1979–81; mem. Comm. du Bilan 1981, Council European Econ. Asscn 1984–89; Pres. Asscn Française de Science Économique 1981–83, Int. Federation of Operational Research Socs 1986–89; Dir and Man. Ed. Le Monde 1991–94; Pres. Futuribles Int. 1993–, Centre for Study and Research on Qualifications 1996–; mem. Acad. des Technologies; Officier, Légion d'honneur, Commdr, Ordre nat. du Mérite, Officier des Palmes Académiques. *Publications:* Economic Technique and Industrial Management 1958, Du bon usage de l'étude économique dans l'entreprise 1966, Les systèmes du destin 1976, L'entreprise et ses futurs 1985, Éducation et société, L'après-Communisme, de l'Atlantique à l'Oural 1990, The Economics of Order and Disorder 1991, Vérités et mensonges sur le chômage 1995, Le Modèle français: Grandeur et Décadence 1998, Un Homme de notre Siècle 2000, Ces Avenirs qui n'ont pas eu lieu 2001, Leçons de Microéconomie évolutionniste (with A. Orléan and B. Wallises) 2002. *Leisure interest:* piano. *Address:* 52 rue de Vaugirard, 75006 Paris, France (Home). *Telephone:* 1-43-25-66-05 (Home). *Fax:* 1-56-24-47-98. *E-mail:* jolesourne@wanadoo.fr (Home).

LESSARD, Claude; Canadian business executive; b. 29 July 1949, Notre Dame du Portage; s. of Carmen Cerat and Jean-Luc Lessard; m. Marie Lortie 1971; three s.; ed Univ. Laval, Québec; Pres. and CEO Cossette Communication-Marketing 1980–; Dir Canam-Manac, Inst. de Cardiologie de Québec, Opéra de Québec, Fac. des Sciences de l'Admin., Univ. Laval, Fondation Communautaire du Grand Québec, DiagnoCure Inc.; Co-Chair. Canadian Congress of Advertising 1995; Hermes Prize (Univ. of Laval) 1984, Dimensions Prize 1987, 'Spiess' Bessies Award 1993, ACA Gold Medal 1994. *Leisure interests:* golf, skiing, riding. *Address:* Cossette Communication-Marketing, 437 Grande-Allée Est, Québec, PQ, G1R 2J5, Canada. *Telephone:* (418) 647-2727. *Fax:* (418) 523 1689.

LESSELS, Norman, CBE, CA; British chartered accountant; b. 2 Sept. 1938, Edinburgh; s. of John Clark Lessels and Gertrude Margaret Ellen Lessels (née Jack); m. 1st Gillian Durward Clark 1960 (died 1979); one s. (and one s. one d. deceased); m. 2nd Christine Stevenson Hitchman 1981; ed Melville Coll., Edin., Edin. Acad.; apprentice with Graham Smart & Annan, Edin. 1955–60, with Thomson McLintock & Co., London 1960–61; partner, Wallace & Somerville, Edin., subsequently merged with Whinney Murray & Co.,

latterly Ernst & Whinney 1962–80; partner, Chiene & Tait, CA 1980–93, Sr Partner 1993–98; Dir (non-exec.) The Standard Life Assurance Co. 1978–2002 (Chair. 1988–98), Cairn Energy PLC 1988–, Bank of Scotland 1988–97, General Surety & Guarantee Co. Ltd 1988–97, Havelock Europa PLC –1998 (Chair. 1993–98), NWS Bank PLC 1989–97, Robert Wiseman Dairies PLC 1994–, Martin Currie Portfolio Investment Trust PLC 1999–2001; Pres. Inst. of Chartered Accountants of Scotland 1987–88; Chair. Tilney & Co. 1993–98. *Leisure interests:* golf, bridge, music. *Address:* 50 Lothian Road, Edinburgh, EH3 9BY (Office); 11 Forres Street, Edinburgh, EH3 6BJ, Scotland (Home). *Telephone:* (131) 475-3000 (Office); (131) 225-5596 (Home). *Fax:* (131) 475-3030 (Office). *E-mail:* nlessels@cairn-energy.plc.uk (Office).

LESSING, Doris May, CH; British writer; b. 22 Oct. 1919, Kermanshah, Persia; d. of Alfred Cook Taylor and Emily Maude Taylor (née McVeagh); m. 1st F. A. C. Wisdom 1939–43; m. 2nd Gottfried Anton Nicolai Lessing 1944–49; two s. (one deceased) one d.; ed Roman Catholic Convent and Girls' High School, Salisbury, Southern Rhodesia; Assoc. mem. American Acad. of Arts and Letters 1974; Nat. Inst. of Arts and Letters 1974; mem. Inst. for Cultural Research 1974; Pres. Book Trust 1996–; Hon. Fellow MLA (US) 1974; D.Fellow in Literature (East Anglia) 1991; Hon. DLitt (Princeton) 1989, Durham (1990), (Warwick) 1994, (Bard Coll. New York State) 1994, (Harvard) 1995, (Oxford) 1996; five Somerset Maugham Awards, Soc. of Authors 1954–, Austrian State Prize for European Literature 1981, Shakespeare Prize, Hamburg 1982, Grinzane Cavour Award, Italy 1989, Woman of the Year, Norway 1995, Premi Internacional Catalunya, Spain 1999, David Cohen Literary Prize 2001, Príncipe de Asturias, Spain 2001, PEN Award 2002. *Publications:* (novels) The Grass is Singing 1950 (made into film), Children of Violence (Martha Quest 1952, A Proper Marriage 1954, A Ripple from the Storm 1965, The Four-Gated City 1969), Retreat to Innocence 1956, The Golden Notebook 1962 (Prix Médicis for French trans.), Carnet d'Or 1976), Briefing for a Descent into Hell 1971 (shortlisted for Booker Prize 1971), The Summer Before the Dark 1973, The Memoirs of a Survivor 1974 (made into film), Canopus in Argos series (Re: Colonised Planet 5, Shikasta 1979, The Marriages between Zones Three, Four and Five 1980, The Sirian Experiments 1981, The Making of the Representative for Planet 8 1982, The Sentimental Agents in the Volyen Empire 1983), The Diary of a Good Neighbour (under pseudonym Jane Somers) 1983, If the Old Could (under pseudonym Jane Somers) 1984, The Diaries of Jane Somers 1984, The Good Terrorist 1985 (W. H. Smith Literary Award 1986, Palermo Prize and Premio Internazionale Mondello 1987), The Fifth Child 1988, Love, Again 1996, Mara and Dann 1999, Ben, in the World 2000, The Old Age of El Magnifico 2000, The Sweetest Dream 2001; (short stories) Collected African Stories: Vol. 1, This Was the Old Chief's Country 1951, Vol. 2, The Sun Between Their Feet 1973, Five 1953, The Habit of Loving 1957, A Man and Two Women 1963, African Stories 1964, Winter in July 1966, The Black Madonna 1966, The Story of a Non-Marrying Man and Other Stories 1972, A Sunrise on the Veld 1975, A Mild Attack of the Locusts 1977, Collected Stories: Vol. 1, To Room Nineteen 1978, Vol. 2, The Temptation of Jack Orkney 1978, London Observed: Stories and Sketches 1992; (non-fiction includes): Going Home 1957 (revised edn 1968), Particularly Cats 1967, Particularly Cats and More Cats 1989, African Laughter: Four Visits to Zimbabwe 1992, Under My Skin 1994 (Los Angeles Times Book Prize 1995, James Tait Memorial Prize 1995), Walking in the Shade 1997; (plays) Each His Own Wilderness 1958, Play with a Tiger 1962, The Singing Door 1973; (other publs include): Fourteen Poems 1959, A Small Personal Voice 1974, Doris Lessing Reader 1990. *Address:* c/o Jonathan Clowes Ltd, 10 Iron Bridge House, Bridge Approach, London, NW1 8BD, England.

LESTER, Adrian (Anthony); British actor; b. 14 Aug. 1968, Birmingham; ed Royal Acad. of Dramatic Art; mem. Amnesty Int., Greenpeace, RADA Council, Artistic Bd, Royal Nat. Theatre; Time Out Award 1992, Olivier Award 1996, Carlton Theatre Award 2001. *Theatre appearances include:* Cory in Fences, Garrick 1990, Paul Poitier in Six Degrees of Separation (Time Out Award), Royal Court and Comedy Theatre 1992, Anthony Hope in Sweeney Todd, Royal Nat. Theatre 1994, Rosalind in As You Like It (Time Out Award), Albery and Bouffes du Nord 1995, Company (Olivier Award), Albery and Donmar 1996, Hamlet, Bouffes du Nord and Young Vic 2001, Henry V, Royal Nat. Theatre. *Television films include:* For the Greater Good, In the Dark. *Films include:* Up on the Roof 1997, Primary Colors 1997, Storm Damage, Love's Labour's Lost 1999, Dust 2001, Final Curtain 2001, Tomorrow 2002. *Leisure interests:* martial arts, music, scuba diving, dance. *Address:* c/o Artists Rights Group (ARG), 4 Great Portland Street, London, W1W 8PA, England. *Telephone:* (20) 7436-6400. *Fax:* (20) 7436-6700. *E-mail:* latimer@org.com (Office).

LESTER, Richard; American film director; b. 19 Jan. 1932, Philadelphia; s. of Elliott Lester and Ella Young; m. Deirdre V. Smith 1956; one s. one d.; ed William Penn Charter School, Univ. of Pennsylvania; TV Dir, CBS 1952–54, ITV 1955–59; Composer 1954–57; Film Dir 1959–; Acad. Award Nomination 1960; Grand Prix, Cannes Festival 1965; Best Dir Rio de Janeiro Festival 1966; Gandhi Peace Prize, Berlin Festival 1969; Best Dir Tehran Festival 1974. *Films directed:* The Running, Jumping and Standing Still Film 1959, It's Trad, Dad 1962, The Mouse on the Moon 1963, A Hard Day's Night 1963 (re-release 2000), The Knack 1965, Help! 1965, A Funny Thing Happened on the Way to the Forum 1966, How I Won the War 1967, Petulia 1968, The Bed Sitting Room 1969, The Three Musketeers 1973, Juggernaut 1974, The Four Musketeers 1974, Royal Flash 1975, Robin and Marian 1976, The Ritz 1976,

Butch and Sundance: The Early Days 1979, Cuba 1979, Superman II 1980, Superman III 1983, Finders Keepers 1984, The Return of the Musketeers 1989, Get Back 1990. *Leisure interests:* tennis, music. *Address:* c/o Creative Artists Agency, 9830 Wilshire Boulevard, Beverly Hills, CA 90212, USA.

LESTER OF HERNE HILL, Baron (Life Peer), cr. 1993, of Herne Hill in the London Borough of Southwark; **Anthony Paul Lester,** QC, BA, LLM; British lawyer; b. 3 July 1936, London; s. of Harry Lester and Kate Lester; m. Catherine Elizabeth Debora Wassey 1971; one s. one d.; ed City of London School, Trinity Coll. Cambridge, Harvard Law School; called to Bar, Lincoln's Inn 1963, Bencher 1985; Special Adviser to Home Sec. 1974–76; QC 1975; Special Adviser to Northern Ireland Standing Advisory Comm. on Human Rights 1975–77; Recorder, South-Eastern Circuit 1987–93; Hon. Visiting Prof., Univ. Coll. London 1983–; mem. Bd of Dirs Salzburg Seminar 1996–2000; mem. Bd of Overseers, Univ. of Pa Law School 1977–90, Council of Justice; mem. Court of Govs, LSE 1980–94; Pres. Interights 1983–; UK legal expert EEC Comm. Network Cttee on Equal Pay and Sex Discrimination 1983–93; mem. House of Lords Select Cttee on European Communities Subcttee E (Law and Insts.), Subcttee on 1996 Inter-Governmental Conf., Subcttee F (Social Affairs, Educ. and Home Affairs) 1996–2000; Co-Chair. of Bd European Roma Rights Centre, Budapest 1999–2001; Gov. British Inst. of Human Rights; Chair. Bd of Govs, James Allen's Girls' School 1987–93; Chair. Runnymede Trust 1990–93; mem. Advisory Cttee Centre for Public Law, Univ. of Cambridge 1999–, Int. Advisory Bd, Open Soc. Inst. 2000–, Parl. Jt Human Rights Comm. 2001–; Foreign Hon. mem. American Acad. of Arts and Sciences 2002; hon. degrees/fellowships from Open Univ., Univ. Coll., London Univ., Ulster Univ., South Bank Univ.; Liberty Human Rights Lawyer of the Year 1997. *Publications:* Justice in the American South (Amnesty Int.) 1964, Race and Law (co-author) 1972; Ed.-in-Chief Butterworths Human Rights Cases; Consultant Ed. and Contrib. Halsbury's Laws of England Title Constitutional Law and Human Rights (4th Edn 1996), Human Rights Law and Practice (co-ed.) 1999 and articles on race relations, public affairs and int. law. *Address:* Blackstone Chambers, Blackstone House, Temple, London, EC4Y 9BW, England. *Telephone:* (20) 7583-1770.

L'ESTRANGE, Michael, MA; Australian diplomatist and civil servant; b. 12 Oct. 1952, Sydney; s. of James Michael L'Estrange and Iris Corrigan; m. Jane Allen 1982; five s.; ed St Aloysius Coll. (Milson's Point), Sydney Univ., Oxford Univ.; mem. staff Dept of Prime Minister and Cabinet 1981–87; Visiting Fellow Georgetown Univ. 1987–88, Univ. of Calif. at Berkeley, USA 1988–89; Sr Policy Adviser Office of Fed. Leader of Opposition 1989–94; Exec. Dir Menzies Research Centre 1995–96; Sec. to Cabinet and Head of Cabinet Policy Unit, Canberra 1996–2000; High Commr in UK 2000–; Harkness Fellowship 1986, Rhodes Scholar, Oxford Univ. 1975. *Leisure interests:* cricket, rugby, golf. *Address:* Australian High Commission, Australia House, Strand, London, WC2B 4LA, England (Office). *Telephone:* (20) 7887-5220 (Office).

LETOKHOV, Vladilen Stepanovich, PhD, DSc; Russian physicist; b. 10 Nov. 1939, Irkutsk; s. of Stepan G. Letokhov and Anna V. (née Sevastianova) Letokhova; m. 1st Maria Letokhova 1965 (divorced 1973); m. 2nd Tina Karu 1979; one d.; ed Moscow Physical Tech. Inst., P.N. Lebedev Physical Inst.; researcher, P. N. Lebedev Physical Inst. 1966–70; Head Laser Spectroscopy Dept, Inst. of Spectroscopy, USSR (now Russian) Acad. of Sciences 1970–, Vice-Dir for Research 1970–89; Prof., Moscow Physical-Tech. Inst. 1973–; Dir Laser Lab., Soviet (now Russian) Branch of World Lab. 1990–; Fellow American Optical Soc.; mem. New York Acad. of Sciences, Max Planck Soc., Germany, European Acad. of Arts and Sciences; Lenin Prize for Science and Tech. 1978, Jubilee Medal of 600th Anniversary of Heidelberg Union 1985, European Physics Soc. Prize for Quantum Electronics 1998. *Publications:* Nonlinear Laser Spectroscopy 1977, Nonlinear Laser Chemistry 1987, Photoionization Laser Spectroscopy 1987, 10 other scientific books and about 780 publs in scientific journals. *Leisure interests:* music, swimming, house design. *Address:* Institute of Spectroscopy, Troitsk, 142190 Moscow (Office); Puchkovo-66, Troitsk, Moscow Region, Russia (Home). *Telephone:* (095) 334-05-78 (Office); (095) 334-02-30 (Home). *Fax:* (095) 334-08-86.

ŁĘTOWSKA, Ewa Anna, LLD; Polish lawyer; b. 22 March 1940, Warsaw; m. Janusz Łętowski (deceased); ed Warsaw Univ.; scientific worker Inst. of Legal Science Polish Acad. of Sciences, Warsaw 1962–; lecturer Dept of Law Warsaw Univ. 1963–83; Commr for Civil Rights Protection 1987–92; lecturer and author of educational material Helsinki Foundation for Human Rights, Warsaw 1992–99; lawyer Supreme Administrative Court 1999–; Judge, Polish Constitutional Tribunal 2002–; Corresp. mem. Polish Acad. of Arts and Sciences, Cracow and Acad. of Comparative Law, Paris; mem. Helsinki Cttee.; recipient of many scientific awards; Kt's Cross, Order of Polonia Restituta; Friedrich Ebert Stiftung Award. *Publications:* 19 books on civil law, consumer protection and constitutional law; co-author of three books about music; introductions to theatre programmes, concerts and opera reviews; over 30 articles. *Leisure interests:* classical music, vocalism. *Address:* Biuro Trybunału Konstytucyjnego, ul. J. Ch. Szucha 12A, 00-918 Warsaw (Office); Instytut Nauk Prawnych PAN, ul. Nowy Świat 72, 00-330 Warsaw, Poland (Office). *Telephone:* (22) 8267853 (Institute) (Office). *Website:* www.trybunal .gov.pl (Office).

LETSIE III, King of Lesotho, BLL; b. 17 July 1963, Morija; s. of the late King Moshoeshoe II and Queen Mamohato Berenc Seeiso; ed Nat. Univ. of Lesotho, Univs of Bristol, Cambridge and London; Prin. Chief of Matsieng 1989;

installed as King Nov. 1990, abdicated Jan. 1995, reinstated following his father's death Feb. 1996–; Patron of Prince Mohato Award (Khau Ea Khosana Mohato). *Leisure interests:* classical and traditional music, horse riding, rugby, squash, tennis. *Address:* Royal Palace, Maseru, Lesotho.

LETTE, Kathy; Australian author; b. 11 Nov. 1958, Sydney; d. of Mervyn Lette and Val Lette; m. Geoffrey Robertson (q.v.) 1990; one s. one d.; ed autodidact. *Plays:* Wet Dreams 1985, Perfect Mismatch 1985, Grommitts 1988, I'm So Sorry for You, I Really Am 1994. *Radio:* I'm So Happy For You, I Really Am. *Publications:* Puberty Blues (with G. Carey) 1979, HIT and MS 1984, Girls' Night Out 1987, The Llama Parlour 1991, Foetal Attraction 1993, Mad Cows 1996; (essays) She Done Him Wrong, The Constant Sinner in Introduction to Mae West 1995, Altar Ego 1998, Nip 'n Tuck 2001. *Leisure interests:* scuba diving, opera, theatre, 'girl talk', flirting, drinking champagne, feminism. *Address:* c/o Ed Victor, 6 Bayley Street, London, WC1B 3HB, England. *Telephone:* (20) 7304-4100. *Fax:* (20) 7304-4111.

LETTERMAN, David; American broadcaster; b. 12 April 1947, Indianapolis; s. of Joseph Letterman and Dorothy Letterman; m. Michelle Cook 1969 (divorced 1977); ed Ball State Univ.; radio and TV announcer, Indianapolis; performer, The Comedy Store, LA 1975–; TV appearances include: Rock Concert, Gong Show; frequent guest host, The Tonight Show; host, David Letterman Show 1980, Late Night with David Letterman 1982; The Late Show with David Letterman, (also writer) CBS 1993–; TV scriptwriter including Bob Hope Special, Good Times, Paul Lynde Comedy Hour, John Denver Special; recipient of six Emmy Awards. *Publications include:* David Letterman's Book of Top Ten Lists 1996. *Leisure interests:* baseball, basketball, running. *Address:* Late Show with David Letterman, Ed Sullivan Theater, 1697 Broadway, New York, NY 10019, USA.

LEUENBERGER, Moritz; Swiss politician and lawyer; b. 21 Sept. 1946, Biel/Bienne; s. of Robert Leuenberger and Ruth Leuenberger; two s.; ed Univ. of Zürich; pvt. practice as lawyer 1972–91; joined Social Democratic Party (SP) 1969, Leader Zürich SP 1972–80; mem. Zürich City Council 1974–83; Pres. Swiss Tenants' Asscn 1986–91; elected to Nat. Council 1979; elected to Zürich Cantonal Council 1991, Dir of Justice and Internal Affairs 1991–95; Fed. Councillor 1995–; Minister, Fed. Dept of Transport, Communications and Energy 1995–, Head Fed. Dept of Environment, Transport, Energy and Communications (subsequently Transport, Energy and Communications) 2001–; Vice-Pres. of the Swiss Confed. 2000, Pres. 2001. *Address:* Federal Department of Transport, Energy and Communications, Bundeshaus-Nord, 3003 Berne, Switzerland. *Telephone:* (31) 3225511. *Fax:* (31) 3119576.

LEUNG, Oi Sie (Elsie), LLM, JP; Chinese legal official; b. 24 April 1939, Hong Kong; ed Univ. of Hong Kong; admitted as solicitor of Hong Kong 1968, as overseas solicitor, UK Supreme Court 1976; Notary Public 1978; admitted as solicitor and barrister of Victoria, Australia 1982; founding mem. Hong Kong Fed. of Women Lawyers 1975, Hong Kong Fed. of Women 1993; Pres. Int. Fed. of Women Lawyers 1994; del. 7th People's Congress of Guangdong Prov. 1989–93, 8th Nat. People's Congress 1993–97, People's Repub. of China; Sec. for Justice of Hong Kong Special Admin. Region 1997–; Fellow Int. Acad. of Matrimonial Lawyers 1994; Grand Bauhinia Medal (Hong Kong) 2002. *Address:* Department of Justice, Secretary for Justice's Office, 4th Floor, High Block, Queensway Government Offices, 66 Queensway, Hong Kong Special Administrative Region, People's Republic of China (Office). *Telephone:* (852) 28692001 (Office). *Fax:* (852) 28773978 (Office). *E-mail:* sjo@doj.gov.hk (Office). *Website:* www.info.gov.hk/justice (Office).

LEUNG CHUN-YING; Chinese civil servant; b. 1954, Hong Kong; m. Regina Tong Ching Yee; three c.; ed Bristol Polytechnic, King's Coll. London; fmr Sec. Gen. Basic Law Consultative Cttee; Vice-Chair. Preparatory Cttee, Hong Kong Special Admin. Region; Convenor Exec. Council; Hon. DBA; Gold Bauhinia Star. *Address:* 10th Floor, Jardine House, Central, Hong Kong Special Administrative Region, People's Republic of China (Office). *Telephone:* (852) 25070503 (Office). *Fax:* (852) 25301555 (Office). *E-mail:* leungcy@dtz.com.hk (Office).

LEUNG KAM CHUNG, Antony, BSc; Hong Kong banker and official; b. 29 Jan. 1952, Hong Kong; m. 1st Sophie Leung; m. 2nd Fu Mingxia 2002; ed Univ. of Hong Kong, Harvard Business School, USA; Man. Dir and Regional Man. for Greater China and the Philippines, Chase Manhattan Bank; Chair. Univ. Grants Cttee 1993–98; Dir Hong Kong Futures Exchange 1987–90, Hong Kong Policy Research Inst. 1996–; Trustee Queen Mary Hosp. Charitable Trust 1993–, Hong Kong Centre for Econ. Research 1995–98; Hong Kong Affairs Adviser 1994–97; Arbitrator China Int. Econ. and Trade Arbitration Comm. 1994–; mem. Industrial Devt Bd 1985, Univ. and Polytechnic Grants Cttee 1990–93, Bd Provisional Airport Authority 1990–95, Bd Airport Authority 1995–99, Cen. Policy Unit 1992–93, Bd Hong Kong Community Chest 1992–94, Educ. Comm. 1993–98 (Chair. 1998), Standing Council Chinese Soc. of Macroeconomics, State Planning Comm. 1994–, Exchange Fund Advisory Cttee 1993–, Prep. Cttee of Hong Kong Special Admin. Region 1996–97, Exec. Council Hong Kong Special Admin. Region July 1997–; Financial Sec. Exec. Council 2001–. *Leisure interest:* golf. *Address:* Office of the Financial Secretary, 12th Floor, West Wing, Central Government Offices, Lower Albert Road, Central, Hong Kong Special Administrative Region, People's Republic of China. *Telephone:* 2810-2589. *Fax:* 2840-0569. *E-mail:* fso@fso.gov.hk. *Website:* www.info.gov.hk/fso.

LEUTHEUSSER-SCHNARRENBERGER, Sabine; German politician; b. 26 July 1951, Minden, Westphalia; m. E. Schnarrenberger; ed Univs of Göttingen and Bielefeld; with German Patent Office 1979–90; Head Admin., Personnel and Budget Dept 1990; Fed. Minister of Justice 1992–96; mem. Free Democratic Party (FDP), Chair (Dist Asscn, Starnberg) 1984–2000, Chair. (Dist Asscn Bayern) 2000–; mem. Bundestag 1990–, mem. FDP Nat. Exec. 1991–96, of numerous cttees. *Leisure interests:* mountaineering, skiing. *Address:* Platz der Republik, 11011 Berlin (Office); Freie Demokratische Partei, Reinhardstrasse 14, 10117 Berlin, Germany. *Telephone:* (30) 2849580. *Fax:* (30) 28495822. *E-mail:* tdh@fdp.de (Office). *Website:* www.fdp.de (Office).

LEVEAUX, David; British theatre director; b. 13 Dec. 1957; s. of Michael Leveaux and Eve Powell; ed Univ. of Manchester; Assoc. Dir Riverside Studios 1981–85; Artistic Dir Theatre Project Tokyo 1993– has directed productions for Nat. Theatre, RSC, ENO. *Productions include:* A Moon for the Misbegotten 1984, No Man's Land 1992, Anna Christie (Tony Award 1993), Moonlight, The Turn of the Screw, Salome, The Real Thing, Nine 1996, Electra 1998. *Address:* c/o Simpson Fox Associates Ltd, 52 Shaftesbury Avenue, London, W1V, 7DE, England (Office). *Telephone:* (20) 7434-9167 (Office). *Fax:* (20) 7494-2887. *E-mail:* cary@simpson-fox.demon.co.uk.

LEVELT, Willem J. M., PhD; Netherlands psychologist and psycholinguist; b. 17 May 1938, Amsterdam; s. of Dr W. H. Levelt and J. Levelt-Berger; m. Elisabeth C. M. Jacobs 1963; two s. one d.; ed Leiden Univ.; staff. mem. Inst. for Perception, Soesterberg 1962–65; Research Fellow Center for Cognitive Studies, Harvard Univ. 1965–66; Visiting Asst Prof. Univ. of Illinois 1966–67; Prof. of Experimental Psychology, Groningen Univ. 1967–70, Nijmegen Univ. 1971–79, Hon. Prof. of Psycholinguistics 1980–; Leader Max-Planck Project Group for Psycholinguistics, Nijmegen 1976–79; Dir Max-Planck-Inst. for Psycholinguistics, Nijmegen 1980–; Visiting Prof. Louvain Univ. 1967–70; mem. Inst. for Advanced Study, Princeton 1971–72; mem. Royal Netherlands Acad. of Sciences, Academia Europaea. *Publications:* On binocular rivalry 1968, Formal grammars in linguistics and psycholinguistics, 3 Vols 1974, Speaking: From intention to articulation 1989. *Leisure interest:* playing the traverso. *Address:* Max-Planck-Institute for Psycholinguistics, Wundtlaan 1, 6525 XD Nijmegen, Netherlands. *Telephone:* (24) 3521-911. *Fax:* (24) 3521-213.

LEVENE, Ben, RA; British artist; b. 23 Dec. 1938, London; s. of Charlotte Levene (née Leapman) and Mark Levene; m. Susan Margaret Williams 1978; one s. two d.; ed Slade School of Fine Art; as Visiting Lecturer taught painting and drawing at Camberwell School of Art 1963–89; Visiting Tutor RA Schools 1980–95, City and Guilds 1990–95; Curator Royal Acad. Schools 1995–98; elected Assoc. of Royal Acad. 1975. *Solo exhibitions include:* Thackeray Gallery, Kensington 1973, 1975, 1978, 1981, Browse & Darby, Cork Street 1988, 1993, 2001, New Ashgate Gallery, Farnham 1994. *Invited exhibitions include:* British Painting 1952–77, Royal Acad., Hill Samuel's Exhbns, London, Arthur Young Exhbns, London. *Open shows include:* Bradford City Art Gallery, Chichester Arts Festival, GLC Spirit of London, Festival Hall (prize-winner), Whitechapel Open, Laing Landscape Competition. *Leisure interest:* gardening. *Address:* c/o Annie Wiess, The Royal Academy of Arts, Piccadilly, London, W1V 0DS; c/o Browse & Darby, 19 Cork Street, London, W1X 2LP, England. *Telephone:* (20) 7734-7984 (Gallery); (20) 7439-7438 (Royal Academy).

LEVENE OF PORTSOKEN, Baron (Life Peer), cr. 1997, of Portsoken in the City of London; **Peter Keith Levene,** KBE, BA, JP, FCIT, CIMgt; British business executive; b. 8 Dec. 1941, Pinner, Middx; s. of the late Maurice Levene and Rose Levene; m. Wendy Ann Levene 1966; two s. one d.; ed City of London School and Univ. of Manchester; joined United Scientific Holdings 1963, Man. Dir 1968, Chair. 1982; Personal Adviser to Sec. of State for Defence 1984; Chief of Defence Procurement, Ministry of Defence 1985–91; mem. SE Asia Trade Advisory Group 1979–83, Council, Defence Mfrs Asscn 1982–85, Vice-Chair. 1983–84, Chair. 1984–85; Chair. European NATO Nat. Armaments Dirs. 1990–91, Docklands Light Railway Ltd 1991–94; Special Adviser to Sec. of State for the Environment 1991–92; Adviser to Prime Minister on Efficiency 1992–97; Special Adviser to Pres. of the Bd of Trade 1992–95; Chair. Public Competition and Purchasing Unit, HM Treasury 1991–92; Deputy Chair. Wasserstein Perella & Co. Ltd 1991–94; Chair. and CEO Canary Wharf Ltd 1993–96; Sr Adviser Morgan Stanley & Co. Ltd 1996–98; Chair. Bankers Trust Int. 1998–99; Chair. Investment Banking Europe, Deutsche Bank AG 1999–2001, General Dynamics UK Ltd 2001–; Vice-Chair. Deutsche Bank UK 2001–02; Chair. Lloyds of London 2002–; Dir Haymarket Group Ltd 1997–, J. Sainsbury PLC 2001–; Alderman, City of London 1984–; Sheriff 1995–96, Lord Mayor of London 1998–99; Hon. Col Commdt Royal Corps of Transport 1991–93, Royal Logistics Corps 1993–; Master Worshipful Co. of Carmen 1992–93; Fellow Queen Mary and Westfield Coll., London Univ. 1995; KStJ; Commdr Order Nat. du Mérite 1996, Kt Commdr Order of Merit (Germany) 1998, Middle Cross Order of Merit (Hungary) 1999; Hon. DSc (City Univ.) 1998. *Leisure interests:* skiing, travel, watching Association football. *Address:* Lloyds of London, 1 Lime Street, London, EC3M 7HA, England (Office). *Telephone:* (20) 7327-6556 (Office). *Fax:* (20) 7327-5926 (Office). *E-mail:* peter.levene@lloyds.com (Office). *Website:* www.lloyds.com.

LEVENTAL, Valery Yakovlevich; Russian artist and stage designer; b. 17 Aug. 1942, Moscow; ed All-Union State Cinematography Inst.; with Bolshoi Theatre 1965–95, Chief designer 1988–95; Chief designer Moscow A. P. Chekhov Arts Theatre 2001–; corresp. mem. USSR (now Russian) Acad. of Arts 1988; People's Artist of the USSR 1989; designs and sets for Cinderella, Romeo and Juliet, Anna Karenina, Khovanshchina, Prince Igor (Vilnius and Sofia), Tosca, Così fan tutte, Madame Butterfly, Otello, Till Eulenspiegel, Icarus, décor for experimental ballets of Maiya Plisetskaya (q.v.) and Vladimir V. Vasiliyev; also for Love for Three Oranges (Berlin), War and Peace, Dead Souls (Bolshoi). *Theatrical designs:* Woe from Wit, The Bedbug, The Wedding (Gogol), The Marriage of Figaro, The Duenna, Macbeth (1979), The Seagull (1979), Boris Godunov. *Film designs:* Romeo and Juliet, Phèdre. *Address:* Sadovaya-Spasskaya Street 19, Apartment 88, 107078 Moscow, Russia. *Telephone:* (095) 975-14-94.

LÉVÊQUE, Jean André Eugène; French aeronautical engineer; b. 30 April 1929, Béthune; s. of André and Elise (Forêt) Lévêque; m. Geneviève Cauwet 1953; two s.; ed Ecole Polytechnique, Paris; with Air Navigation Directorate of Ministry of Public Works and Transport 1954–60, Eng in Air Traffic Bureau 1954, Head of Airports Bureau 1956–60; Civil Aviation Tech. Adviser to Minister of Public Works and Transport 1960–63; Head of Div. in European Org. for the Safety of Air Navigation (EUROCONTROL), Brussels 1964–67; with Secretariat-General for Civil Aviation, Paris 1968–78, Tech. Adviser to Sec.-Gen. 1968–70, Acting Sec.-Gen., then Dir of Air Navigation 1971–78; Dir-Gen. EUROCONTROL 1978–83, now mem.; Head of Gen. Inspection for Civil Aviation 1983; Chair. Conseil Supérieur Infrastructure and Air Navigation 1989–94; Pres. Admin. Council Ecole Nationale de l'Aviation Civile 1990–97; Vice-Pres. Admin. Bd Météo-France; Officier, Légion d'honneur, Commdr de l'Ordre nat. du Mérite, Médaille de l'Aéronautique. *Leisure interests:* skiing, table tennis. *Address:* 13 rue Gambetta, 92100 Boulogne-Billancourt, France (Home). *Telephone:* 1-48-25-50-66. *E-mail:* leveque.jean@libertysuf.fr (Office).

LÉVÊQUE, Jean-Maxime; French banker; b. 9 Sept. 1923, Paris; s. of Pierre Lévêque and Marthe Tisserand; m. Anne Charles-Laurent 1947; one s. two d. (one d. deceased); ed Lycée Buffon, Faculté de Droit, Paris, Ecole libre des sciences politiques and Ecole Nat. d'Admin; Inspector of Finances 1950; external finance official 1950–56; temporary appointment, IMF and IBRD 1956–58; Dir European Investment Bank 1958–60; Adviser, Sec.-Gen. of Presidency of Repub. 1960–64; Sec.-Gen. Conseil Nat. du Crédit 1960–64; Dir-Gen. Crédit Commercial de France 1964, Chief Exec. 1966, Vice-Pres. 1971, Pres. 1976, then Hon. Pres.; Pres. Union des Banques pour l'Equipement 1965, Vice-Pres. 1976–82; Pres., Dir-Gen. Crédit Lyonnais 1986–88, Hon. Pres. 1988; Pres. Banque de l'Union Maritime et Financière 1989–97, Euro-Clinvest 1988–94, Financière Galliéra 1990–94; numerous other director-ships and professional appointments; Officier, Légion d'honneur, Commdr Ordre nat. du Mérite, Croix de guerre; Prix Renaissance 1983. *Publications:* Dénationalisations: mode d'emploi 1985, En première ligne 1986. *Address:* 16 rue de Bièvre, 75005 Paris, France.

LÉVÊQUE, Michel, LenD; French diplomatist; b. 19 July 1933, Algiers, Algeria; s. of Raymond Lévêque and Suzanne (née Lucchini) Lévêque; m. Georgette Vandekerchove 1956; one s. two d.; ed Lycée Henri-IV, Faculté de Droit, Paris Univ.; Adviser to Minister of Finance and Planning, Abidjan 1960–63; Adviser on Atomic Affairs Ministry of Foreign Affairs, Paris 1963–64, First. Sec. American Section 1968–69, Second Adviser Personnel Dept 1972–73, Asst Dir of African and Malagasy Affairs 1982–85, Dir 1989–91; First Embassy Sec. Moscow 1965–67, Second Adviser Sofia 1970–71, Cultural and Co-operation Adviser Tunis 1974–78; Political Adviser NATO Int. Secr. 1978–82; Amb. to Libya 1985–89, to Morocco 1991–93, to Brazil 1993–94, to Algeria 1995–97, Minister of State for the Principality of Monaco 1997–2000; Commdr Légion d'Honneur, Officier Ordre Nat. du Mérite, Croix de la Valeur Militaire. *Address:* 57 rue de l'Université, 75007 Paris, France.

LEVER, Sir Jeremy Frederick, Kt, KCMG, MA, QC, FRSA; British lawyer; b. 23 June 1933, London; s. of the late Arnold Lever and of Elizabeth Cramer (née Nathan); ed Bradfield Coll., Berks., University Coll. Oxford, Nuffield Coll. Oxford; Fellow All Souls Coll. Oxford 1957, Sub-Warden 1982–84, Sr Dean 1988–; QC (England and Wales) 1972, (Northern Ireland) 1988; Bencher, Gray's Inn 1986–; Dir (non-exec.) Dunlop Holdings Ltd 1973–80, The Wellcome Foundation 1983–94; mem. arbitral tribunal, U.S./UK Arbi-tration concerning Heathrow Airport user charges 1989–94, Univ. of Ports-mouth Ind. Inquiry 1995; Chair. Oftel Advisory Body on Fair Trading in Telecommunications 1996–2000, Performing Rights Soc. Appeals Panel 1997–2001; Visiting Prof. Wissenschaftszentrum, Berlin, für Sozialforschung Jan.–March 1999; Pres. Oxford Union Soc. 1957; mem. Council British Inst. of Int. and Comparative Law 1987–; Africa Gen. Service Medal. *Publications:* The Law of Restrictive Trading Agreements 1964, (with W. van Gerven) Comparative Law Casebook, Torts and other legal works. *Leisure interests:* porcelain, music. *Address:* 26 John Street, London, WC1N 2BW; All Souls College, Oxford, OX1 4AL; Monckton Chambers, 4 Raymond Buildings, Gray's Inn, London, WC1R 5BP, England (Office). *Telephone:* (20) 7831-0351 (London); (1865) 279379 (Oxford); (20) 7405-7211 (Office). *Fax:* (20) 7405-1675 (London); (1865) 279299 (Oxford); (20) 7405-2084 (Office). *E-mail:* chambers@monckton.co.uk (Office). *Website:* www.monckton.co.uk (Office).

LEVER, Sir Paul, KCMG, MA; British diplomatist; b. 31 March 1944; s. of John Morrison Lever and Doris Grace Lever (née Battey); m. Patricia Anne Ramsay 1990; ed St Paul's School, Queen's Coll., Oxford; Third Sec. FCO 1966–67; Third then Second Sec., Embassy Helsinki 1967–71; Second then

First Sec., UK Del. to NATO 1971–73; with FCO, London 1973–81; Asst Pvt. Sec. to Sec. of State for Foreign and Commonwealth Affairs 1978–81; Chef de Cabinet to Vice-Pres. of EEC 1981–85; Head UN Dept, FCO 1985–86, Head Defence Dept 1986–87, Security Policy Dept 1987–90; Amb. and Head UK Del. to Conventional Arms Control Negotiations, Vienna 1990–92; Asst Under-Sec. of State, FCO 1992–94, Deputy Sec. Cabinet Office and Chair. Jt Intelligence Cttee 1994–96; Deputy Under-Sec. of State (Dir for EU and Econ. Affairs), FCO 1996–97; Amb. to Germany 1998–2003; Hon. LLD (Birmingham) 2001. *Leisure interests:* walking, art deco pottery. *Address:* c/o Foreign and Commonwealth Office, Whitehall, London, SW1A 2AH, England.

LEVETE, Amanda; British architect; b. 17 Nov. 1955, Bridgend; d. of Michael Levete and Gina Levete (née Seagrim); m. Jan Kaplicky 1991; one s.; ed St Paul's Girls' School, London, Hammersmith School of Art, Architectural Asscn, London; worked with Alsop & Lyall 1980–81, YRM Architects 1982–84, Powis & Levete 1983–86, Richard Rogers & Partners 1984–89; Dir Future Systems 1989–; mem. Bd ARB 1997–2000, Architecture Foundation 1997–, Artangel 2000–; Outstanding Retail Experience Award, Selfridges Kids 2002. *Work includes:* Space Station Wardroom Table (NASA Certificate of Recognition 1989), MOMI Tent (British Construction Industry Award 1992), Hauer/King House (1st Prize, Aluminium Imagination Award 1995, Civic Trust Award 1996) 1992, Stonehenge Visitor Centre (1st Prize, AJ/Bovis Royal Acad. Award 1993), West India Quay Bridge (RIBA Award 1998, Civic Trust Award 1998, British Construction Industry Award 1998) 1994, House in Wales 1996, Floating Bridge, W India Quay, London 1997 (RIBA Award 1998), Wild At Heart (RIBA Award 1998), Comme des Garçons New York Tunnel 1998, Media Centre at Lord's Cricket Ground (Stirling Prize 1999, BCIA 1999) 1999, NatWest Media Centre (World Architecture Awards 2001, Civic Trust Award 2000, RIBA Stirling Prize 1999, British Construction Industry Award 1999, 1st Prize, Aluminium Imagination Award 1999) 1999, Selfridges Birmingham Bridge 2003, Selfridges Dept Store, Birmingham 2003,. *Exhibitions:* RIBA '40 Under Forty' 1989, RA Summer Show, London 1990, 1993, 1994, 1995, 1996, 2001, 2002, Future Systems, RIBA, London 1991, Storefront, New York 1992, Inst. of Contemporary Arts, London 1998, Future Systems Originals, Faggionato Fine Arts Gallery, London 2001, Venice Biennale 2002. *Address:* Future Systems, The Warehouse, 20 Victoria Gardens, London, W11 3PE, England (Office). *Telephone:* (20) 7243-7670 (Office). *Fax:* (20) 7243-7690 (Office). *E-mail:* email@future-systems.com (Office). *Website:* www.future-systems.com (Office).

LEVETT, Michael John (Mike), BComm, FIA, FFA; South African insurance executive; b. 6 June 1939, Cape Town; m. Mary Gillian Aston 1966; two s. one d.; ed Christian Brothers Coll., Cape Town, Univ. of Cape Town; joined Old Mutual Life Assurance Soc. 1959, Gen. Man. 1981–85, Man. Dir 1985–, Chair. 1990–, CEO–2001; Deputy Chair. Mutual & Federal; Dir Barlows, Cen. Africa Bldg Soc., S. African Breweries 1984–, Nedcor; Hon. DEconSc. *Leisure interests:* skiing, tennis. *Address:* Old Mutual PLC, 3rd Floor, Lansdowne House, 57 Berkeley Square, London, W1J 6ER, England. *Telephone:* (20) 7569-0100 (Office). *Fax:* (20) 7569-0200 (Office). *E-mail:* michael.levett@omg.co.uk (Office).

LEVEY, Sir Michael (Vincent), Kt, LVO, FBA, FRSL; British art historian; b. 8 June 1927, London; s. of the late O L. H. Levey and Gladys Mary Milestone; m. Brigid Brophy 1954 (died 1995); one d.; ed Oratory School and Exeter Coll., Oxford; officer, British Army 1945–48; Asst Keeper Nat. Gallery 1951–66, Deputy Keeper 1966–68, Keeper 1968–73, Deputy Dir 1970–73, Dir 1973–86; Slade Prof. of Art Cambridge Univ. and Fellow of King's Coll. Cambridge 1963–64; Slade Prof. of Art, Oxford Univ. 1994–95; fmr Chair. Nat. Dirs Conf.; Foreign mem. Ateneo Veneto, Italy; Hon. Fellow, Exeter Coll., Oxford; Hon. LittD (Manchester). *Publications:* Edited Nat. Gallery Catalogues: 18th Cent. Italian Schools 1956, The German School 1959, Painting in XVIIIth Century Venice 1959; From Giotto to Cézanne 1962, Later Italian Pictures in the Royal Collection 1964, Dürer 1964, A Room-to-room Guide to the National Gallery 1964, Rococo to Revolution 1966, Fifty Works of English and American Literature We Could do Without (with Brigid Brophy and Charles Osborne) 1967, Bronzino 1967, Early Renaissance 1967 (awarded Hawthornden Prize 1968), A History of Western Art 1968, Holbein's Christina of Denmark, Duchess of Milan 1968, 17th and 18th Cent. Italian Schools (Nat. Gallery Catalogue) 1971, Painting at Court 1971, The Life and Death of Mozart 1971, Art and Architecture in 18th Cent. France (co-author) 1972, High Renaissance 1975, The World of Ottoman Art 1976, The Case of Walter Pater 1978, Sir Thomas Lawrence (Exhbn catalogue) 1979, The Painter Depicted (Neurath Lecture) 1982, Tempting Fate (fiction) 1982, An Affair on the Appian Way (fiction) 1984, Giambattista Tiepolo 1986 (Banister Fletcher Prize), The National Gallery Collection 1987, Men At Work (fiction) 1989, The Soul of the Eye (anthology) 1990, Painting and Sculpture in France 1700–1789 1993, Florence: A Portrait 1996, The Chapel is on Fire (memoir) 2000, The Burlington Magazine (anthology) 2003. *Address:* 36 Little Lane, Louth, Lincs., LN11 9DU, England.

LEVI, Arrigo, PhD; Italian journalist and political writer; b. 17 July 1926, Modena; s. of Enzo Levi and Ida Levi (née Donati); m. Carmela Lenci 1952; one d.; ed Univs of Buenos Aires and Bologna; refugee in Argentina 1942–46; Negev Brigade, Israeli Army 1948–49; BBC European Services 1951–53; London Coresp. Gazzetta del Popolo and Corriere d'Informazione 1952–59; Moscow Coresp. Corriere della Sera 1960–62; news anchor man on Italian State Television 1966–68; special coresp. La Stampa 1969–73, Ed. in Chief

1973–78, special coresp. 1978–; columnist on int. affairs, The Times 1979–83; Leader Writer C. Della Sera 1988–; Premio Marconi, Premio St Vincent. *Publications:* Il potere in Russia 1965, Journey among the Economists 1972. *Address:* c/o Piazza S. Carlo 206, 10121 Turin, Italy.

LEVI, Isaac, PhD; American professor of philosophy; b. 30 June 1930, New York; s. of Eliezer Asher Levi and Eva Lunenfeld; m. Judith R. Levi 1951; two s.; ed New York and Columbia Univs; Asst Prof. of Philosophy, Case Western Reserve Univ. 1957–62, The City Coll. of New York 1962–64; Assoc. Prof. then Full Prof. of Philosophy, Case Western Reserve Univ. 1964–67, Chair. Dept 1968–70; Prof. of Philosophy, Columbia Univ. 1970–, Chair. Dept 1973–76, 1989–91, John Dewey Prof. of Philosophy 1992–; Visiting Fellow Corpus Christi Coll. Cambridge, UK 1973, Darwin Coll. 1989, All Souls Coll. Oxford 1988, Inst. of Advanced Study, Hebrew Univ. of Jerusalem 1994, Wolfson Coll. Cambridge 1997; Guggenheim Fellow, Fulbright Scholar and other awards; mem. American Acad. of Arts and Sciences; Dr hc (Lund) 1988; Univ. of Helsinki Medal. *Publications:* For the Sake of the Argument 1966, Gambling with Truth 1967, Enterprise of Knowledge 1980, Decisions and Revisions 1984, Hard Choices 1986, The Fixation of Belief and its Undoing 1991, For the Sake of the Argument 1996, The Covenant of Reason 1997. *Address:* 718 Philosophy Hall, Columbia University, New York, NY 10027 (Office); 25 Claremont Avenue, New York, NY 10027, USA (Home). *Telephone:* (212) 854-6946; 854-5197 (Office); (212) 864-3615 (Home). *Fax:* (212) 864-3615 (Home). *E-mail:* levi@columbia.edu (Office).

LEVI, Noel, CBE, BA; Papua New Guinea politician and diplomatist; b. Wasangula Noel Levi, 6 Feb. 1942, Nonopai, Kavieng; m. Josepha Muna Levi; two s. two d.; ed Scots Coll., Queensland, Papua New Guinea Admin. Coll., Cromwell Coll. Univ. of Queensland and Univ. of Papua New Guinea; patrol officer Dept of Dist Admin., Papua New Guinea 1967, later Asst Dist Commr; Asst Sec. Dept of Chief Minister 1973; Sec. Dept of Defence 1974; Minister of Foreign Affairs 1980; Amb. to People's Repub. of China 1987; High Commr in UK (also accred to Israel, Zimbabwe and Egypt) 1991; Sec. Dept of the Prime Minister and Nat. Exec. Council 1995; Sec.-Gen. Pacific Islands Forum Secr. 1998–. *Leisure interests:* reading, walking, watching rugby. *Address:* Pacific Islands Forum Secretariat, Private Mail Bag, Suva (Office); House No. 4, Forum Secretariat Compound, Ratu Sukuna Road, Suva, Fiji (Home). *Telephone:* (679) 3312600 (Office); (679) 3306535 (Home). *Fax:* (679) 3302204 (Office). *E-mail:* noell@forumsec.org.fj (Office). *Website:* www.forumsec.org.fj (Office).

LEVI, Yoel, MA; Romanian/American conductor; b. 16 Aug. 1950, Romania; m.; ed Tel-Aviv and Jerusalem Acads of Music, Guildhall School of Music, London; studied under Mendi Rodan, Franco Ferrara, Kiril Kondrashin; won First Prize Conductors' Int. Competition Besançon, France 1978; Asst to Lorin Maazel Cleveland Orchestra for six years, Resident Conductor 1980–84; Music Dir Atlanta Symphony Orchestra (ASO) 1988–, extensive European tour 1991; frequent guest conductor of orchestras throughout N America, Europe and the Far East; conducted Stockholm Philharmonic at Nobel Prize Ceremony 1991; performed at Opening Ceremonies of Centennial Olympic Games 1996; apptd first Music Adviser to Israel Festival for 1997/98 seasons; opera conducting debut La Fanciulla del West at Teatro Comunale, Florence 1997; Distinguished Visiting Prof., Univ. of Ga School of Music; Hon. DFA (Oglethorpe Univ., Atlanta) 1997; Best Orchestra of the Year (awarded to ASO), Int. Classical Music Awards 1991–92. *Address:* Askonas Holt Ltd, Lonsdale Chambers, 27 Chancery Lane, London, WC2A 1PF, England. *Telephone:* (20) 7400-1700. *Fax:* (20) 7400-1799.

LEVI-MONTALCINI, Rita; Italian research scientist; b. 22 April 1909, Turin; d. of Adamo Levi and Adele Montalcini; ed Turin Univ. Medical School; engaged in neurological research in Turin and Brussels 1936–41, in a country-cottage in Piemonte 1941–43; in hiding in Florence during German occupation 1943–44; medical doctor working among war refugees in Florence 1944–45; resumed academic positions at Univ. of Turin 1945; worked in St Louis, USA with Prof. Viktor Hamburger from 1947, Assoc. Prof. 1956, Prof. 1958–77; Dir Inst. of Cell Biology of Italian Nat. Council of Research, Rome 1969–78, Guest Prof. 1979–89, Guest Prof. Inst. of Neurobiology 1989–; Pres. Inst. della Enciclopedia Italiana Treccani; Nobel Prize for Medicine 1986 (with Stanley Cohen for work on chemical growth factors which control growth and Devt in humans and animals; nominated Senator for Life. *Publication:* In Praise of Imperfection: My Life and Work 1988. *Address:* Institute of Neurobiology, C.N.R., Viale Marx 15, 00137, Rome, Italy. *Telephone:* (6) 86090510 (Office). *Fax:* (6) 86090269 (Office).

LÉVI-STRAUSS, Claude; French anthropologist, university professor and writer; b. 28 Nov. 1908, Brussels, Belgium; s. of Raymond Lévi-Strauss and Emma Lévy; m. 1st Dina Dreyfus 1932; m. 2nd Rose Marie Ullmo 1946, one s.; m. 3rd Monique Roman 1954; one s.; ed Lycée Janson de Sailly, Paris and Univ. de Paris à la Sorbonne; Prof. Univ. of São Paulo, Brazil 1935–39; Visiting Prof. New School for Social Research, New York 1942–45; Cultural Counsellor, French Embassy to USA 1946–47; Assoc. Dir Musée de l'Homme, Paris 1949–50; Dir of Studies, Ecole Pratique des Hautes Etudes, Paris 1950–74; Prof. Collège de France 1959–82, Hon. Prof. 1983–; mem. Acad. Française; Foreign mem. Royal Acad. of the Netherlands, Norwegian Acad. of Sciences and Letters, American Acad. of Arts and Sciences, American Acad. and Inst. of Arts and Letters, British Acad.; Foreign Assoc. US NAS; Hon. mem. Royal Anthropological Inst., American Philosophical Soc. and London School of Oriental and African Studies; Grand-Croix, Légion d'Honneur,

Commdr Ordre Nat. du Mérite, des Palmes académiques, des Arts et des Lettres; Dr hc (Brussels, Harvard, Yale, Chicago, Columbia, Oxford, Stirling, Zaire, Mexico, Uppsala, Johns Hopkins, Montréal, Québec, Visva-Bharati Univ., India); Prix Paul Pelliot 1949; Huxley Memorial Medal 1965, Viking Fund Gold Medal 1966, Gold Medal CNRS 1967; Erasmus Prize 1973, Aby M. Warburg Prize 1996. *Publications:* La vie familiale et sociale des indiens Nambikwara 1948, Les structures élémentaires de la parenté 1949, Tristes tropiques 1955, Anthropologie structurale 1958, Le totémisme aujourd'hui 1962, La pensée sauvage 1962, Le cru et le cuit 1964, Du miel aux cendres 1967, L'origine des manières de table 1968, L'homme nu 1971, Anthropologie structurale deux 1973, La voie des masques 1975, 1979, Le regard éloigné 1983, Paroles données 1984, La potière jalouse 1985, De près et de loin (with Didier Eribon) 1988, Histoire de Lynx 1991, Regarder, écouter, lire 1993, Saudades do Brasil 1994. *Leisure interest:* country life. *Address:* Laboratoire d'Anthropologie Sociale, Collège de France, 52 rue du Cardinal Lemoine, 75005 Paris (Office); 2 rue des Marronniers, 75016 Paris, France (Home). *Telephone:* 1-44-27-17-31 (Office); 1-42-88-34-71 (Home). *Fax:* 1-44-27-17-66 (Office).

LEVIE, Simon Hijman; Netherlands art historian (retd); b. 17 Jan. 1925, Rheden; m. Mary Levie-Lion 1935; one s. two d.; ed Univ. of Basel, Switzerland; Keeper, Central Museum, Utrecht; Dir, Historical Museum, Amsterdam; Dir-Gen. Rijksmuseum Amsterdam; Dir Simart Art Consultancy, Amsterdam 1990–. *Address:* Minervalaan 70 II, 1077 PG Amsterdam, Netherlands. *Telephone:* (20) 6718895. *Fax:* (20) 6738088.

LEVIN, Bernard (see Levin, Henry Bernard).

LEVIN, Carl, JD; American politician; b. 28 June 1934, Detroit, Mich.; s. of Saul R. Levin and Bess (née Levinson) Levin; m. Barbara Halpern 1961; three d.; ed Central High School, Detroit, Swarthmore Coll., Pa and Harvard Law School; Asst Mich. Attorney Gen. and Gen. Counsel for Mich. Civil Rights Comm. 1964–67; Special Asst Attorney Gen. and Chief Appellate Attorney for Defender's Office of Legal Aid and Defender Assoc. of Detroit 1968–69; elected to Detroit City Council 1969, re-elected as City Council Pres. 1973; U.S. Senator from Michigan 1979–; Chair. Armed Services Cttee 2001–; mem. Governmental Affairs Cttee; Democrat. *Address:* U.S. Senate, 269 Russell Senate Office Building, Washington, DC 20510, USA. *Telephone:* (202) 224-6221.

LEVIN, Gerald Manuel, BA, LLB; American publishing executive; b. 6 May 1939, Philadelphia; s. of David Levin and Pauline Schantzer; m. 1st Carol S. Needlemam 1959 (divorced 1970), two s. (one s. deceased), one d.; m. 2nd Barbara Riley 1970, one s. one d.; ed Haverford Coll. and Univ. of Pa; Assoc. Simpson, Thatcher & Bartlett, New York 1963–67; Gen. Man., COO Devt and Resources Corpn New York 1967–71; Rep. Int. Basic Economy Corpn Tehran 1971–72; Vice-Pres. Programming, Home Box Office, New York 1972–73, Pres., CEO 1973–76, Chair., CEO 1976–79; Group Vice-Pres. (Video), Time Inc. New York 1979–84, Exec. Vice-Pres. 1984–88, Vice-Chair., Dir 1988–90; Vice-Chair., Dir Time-Warner Inc. (to merge with Turner Broadcasting Systems) New York 1990–92, COO 1991, Chair. 1990–95; Pres. 1992–95, Jt CEO 1992–93, CEO and Chair. 1992–2001, CEO AOL Time Warner 2001–02 (created after merger of Time Warner and American Online 2000); Dir NY Stock Exchange; Treas. NY Philharmonic Orchestra; mem. Bd of Dirs Whittle Communications Partnership, New York, Ronald H. Brown Foundation, Living Memorial to the Holocaust (Museum of Jewish Heritage); Hon. LLD (Texas Coll.) 1985, (Middlebury Coll.) 1994, Hon. LHD (Univ. of Denver) 1995; Media Person of the Year Award, Cannes Lions Int. Advertising Festival 2001. *Leisure interests:* reading, jogging. *Address:* c/o AOL Time Warner, 75 Rockfeller Plaza, # 2919, New York, NY 10019, U.S.A.

LEVIN, (Henry) Bernard, CBE, BSc(Econ); British journalist and author; b. 19 Aug. 1928; s. of late Phillip Levin and Rose Levin (née Racklin); ed Christ's Hosp., LSE, Univ. of London; writer, regular and occasional, many newspapers and magazines, UK and abroad, including The Times, London, Sunday Times, Observer, Manchester Guardian, Truth, Spectator, Daily Express, Daily Mail, Newsweek, Int. Herald Tribune 1953–; writer and broadcaster for radio and TV 1952–; Pres. English Asscn 1984–85, Vice-Pres. 1985–88; numerous awards for journalism; Hon. Fellow (LSE) 1977–; mem. Order of Polonia Restituta (by Polish Govt-in-Exile) 1976, Chairman's Award, British Press Awards 1997. *Publications:* The Pendulum Years 1971, Taking Sides 1979, The Conducted Tour 1981, Speaking Up 1982, Enthusiasms 1983, The Way We Live Now 1984, Hannibal's Footsteps 1985, In These Times 1986, To the End of the Rhine 1987, All Things Considered 1988, A Walk up Fifth Avenue 1989, Now Read On 1990, If You Want My Opinion 1992, A World Elsewhere 1994, I Should Say So 1995, Enough Said 1998. *Address:* c/o The Times, 1 Pennington Street, London, E1 9XN, England. *Telephone:* (20) 7782-5859. *Fax:* (20) 7782-5229.

LEVIN, Ira, AB; American writer; b. 27 Aug. 1929, New York; s. of Charles Levin and Beatrice Levin (née Schlansky); m. 1st Gabrielle Aronsohn 1960 (divorced 1968); three s.; m. 2nd Phyllis Finkel 1979 (divorced 1982); ed Horace Mann School, Drake Univ., Iowa, New York Univ.; U.S. Army 1953–55, wrote training films for the troops and a service comedy No Time for Sergeants (film version released 1958); mem. Authors' Guild, American Soc. of Composers, Authors and Publishers, Dramatists Guild (mem. Council 1980–); Edgar Allen Poe Award 1953, 1980. *Plays include:* Interlock 1958, Critic's Choice 1960, General Seeger 1962, Drat! The Cat! 1965, Doctor Cook's Garden 1967, Veronica's Room 1973, Deathtrap 1978, Cantorial 1982, Sliver 1991. *Novels include:* A Kiss Before Dying 1953, Rosemary's Baby 1967, This Perfect Day 1970, The Stepford Wives 1972, Boys from Brazil 1976, Sliver 1991, Son of Rosemary 1997. *Address:* c/o Harold Ober Associates, 425 Madison Avenue, New York, NY 10017, USA.

LEVIN, Richard Charles, PhD; American professor of economics; b. 7 April 1947, San Francisco; s. of Derek Levin and Phylys Goldstein; m. Jane Aries 1968; two s. two d.; ed Stanford and Yale Univs and Merton Coll. Oxford; Asst Prof. of Econs Yale Univ. 1974–79, Assoc. Prof. 1979–82, Prof. of Econs and Man. 1982–92, Dir Grad. Studies in Econs 1984–86, Chair. Dept of Econs 1987–92, Frederick William Beinecke Prof. of Econs 1992–, Dean, Grad. School 1992–93, Pres. Yale Univ. 1993–; Trustee Hewlett Foundation, Univs Research Assn 1994–99; Fellow Merton Coll. Oxford 1996; Fellow American Acad. of Arts and Sciences; mem. Yale-New Haven Hosp. Bd of Trustees 1993–, Yale-New Haven Health Services Corpn Inc. 1993–; mem. American Econ. Asscn, Econometric Soc.; numerous professional and consulting activities; Hon. LLD (Princeton) 1993, (Harvard) 1994; Hon. DCL (Oxford) 1998. *Publication:* The Work of the University 2003. *Address:* Office of the President, Yale University, 105 Wall Street, New Haven, CT 06511, USA. *Telephone:* (203) 432-1333. *Website:* www.yale.edu (Office).

LEVINE, Alan J., JD; American entertainment company executive; b. 8 March 1947, Los Angeles; s. of Phil Levine and Shirley Lauber; m. Judy Birnbaum 1973; two c.; ed Univ. of Southern Calif.; called to Bar, Calif. 1972, U.S. Dist Court (South Dist), Calif. 1972; partner, Pacht, Ross, Warne, Bernhard & Sears, LA 1971–78, Schiff, Hirsch & Schreiber, Beverly Hills, Calif. 1978–80, Armstrong, Hirsch & Levine, LA 1980–89; Pres., COO SONY Pictures Entertainment Inc., Culver, Calif. 1989–96, Chair. 1994–96, entertainment and media consultant 1996–99; Counsel to Ziffren, Brittenham, Branca & Fischer, L.A. 1999–. *Address:* 1801 Century Park West, Los Angeles, CA 90067, USA. *Telephone:* (310) 275-2611. *Fax:* (310) 275-7305.

LEVINE, David, BFA, BS; American artist; b. 20 Dec. 1926, Brooklyn; s. of Harry Levine and Lena Levine; m. Kathy Hayes Levine; one s. one d.; ed Temple Univ. and Hans Hoffman School of Painting; served U.S. Army 1945–46; mem. American Acad. of Arts and Letters; Guggenheim Fellow 1967; Gold Medal for Graphic Art, American Acad. of Arts and Letters, Tiffany, Polk Award and other awards. *Exhibitions:* one-man shows Forum Gallery, New York 1966–, Georgia Museum of Art 1968, Calif. Palace Legion of Honor 1968–69, 1971–72, 1983, Wesleyan Univ. 1970, Brooklyn Museum 1971, Princeton Univ. 1972, Galerie Yves Lambert, Paris 1972, Yale Univ. 1973, Hirshhorn Museum and Sculpture Garden, Washington 1976, Galerie Claude Bernard 1979, Philips Gallery 1980, Pierpont Morgan Library 1981, Santa Fe East Gallery 1983, Meredith Long, Houston 1984, Ashmolean Museum 1987–88. *Publication:* Aesop (The Fables of) 1975, The Arts of David Levine 1978. *Leisure interest:* tennis. *Address:* 161 Henry Street, New York, NY 11201 (Home); c/o Forum Gallery, 745 5th Avenue, New York, NY 10151, USA; c/o Galerie Claude Bernard, 9 rue des Beaux-Arts, Paris 6ème, France. *Telephone:* (718) 522-1808 (Office).

LEVINE, Jack; American artist; b. 3 Jan. 1915, Boston, Mass.; s. of Samuel Levine and Mary Levine (née Grinker); m. Ruth Gikow 1946 (died 1982); one d.; studied with Dr Denman W. Ross and H. K. Zimmerman; one-man exhibition Downtown Gallery, New York 1938; Artists 1942 Exhbn, Museum of Modern Art, New York 1943; exhibited at Jeu de Paume, Paris 1938; Carnegie Int. Exhbn 1938, 1939, 1940; Retrospective Exhbns Inst. of Contemporary Art, Boston 1953, Whitney Museum of American Art, New York 1955, Palacio de Bellas Artes, Mexico 1960, Brooklyn Museum 1999; Dunn Int. Exhbn, Tate Gallery, London 1963; one-man Exhbn The Jewish Museum, New York 1978–79; pictures in Museum of Modern Art, William Hayes Fogg Museum (Harvard), Addison Gallery, Andover, Mass., Vatican Museum, etc.; mem., fmr Pres., fmr Chancellor American Acad. of Arts and Letter; fmr Pres. Inst. of Arts and Letters; Hon. DFA (Colby Coll., Maine). *Publication:* Jack Levine by Jack Levine 1989. *Address:* c/o DC Moore Gallery, 724 Fifth Avenue, 8th Floor, New York, NY 10019, USA. *Telephone:* (212) 247-2111 (Office). *Fax:* (212) 247-2119 (Office). *E-mail:* dcmooregal@earthlink.net (Office). *Website:* www.artnet.com/dcmoore.html (Office).

LEVINET, James; American musician, conductor and pianist; b. 23 June 1943, Cincinnati, Ohio; s. of Lawrence M. Levine and Helen Levine (née Goldstein); ed Walnut Hills High School, Cincinnati, The Juilliard School, New York; Asst Conductor, Cleveland Orchestra 1964–70; Prin. Conductor, Metropolitan Opera, New York 1973–, Music Dir 1976–, Artistic Dir 1986–; Music Dir Ravinia Festival 1973–93, Cincinnati May Festival 1974–78; Chief Conductor, Munich Philharmonic 1999–2004; Music Dir UBS Verbier Festival Youth Orchestra 2000–; Music Dir Boston Symphony Orchestra 2004–; regular appearances as conductor and pianist in Europe and the USA with orchestras including Vienna Philharmonic, Berlin Philharmonic, Chicago Symphony, Philadelphia Orchestra, Philharmonia, Dresden Staatskapelle, Boston Symphony, New York Philharmonic, Israel Philharmonic, Salzburg and Bayreuth Festivals; conducted Metropolitan Opera premieres of I Vespri Siciliani, Stiffelio, I Lombardi (Verdi), The Rise and Fall of the City of Mahagonny (Weill), Lulu (Berg), Porgy and Bess (Gershwin), Oedipus Rex (Stravinsky), Idomeneo, La Clemenza di Tito (Mozart), Erwartung, Moses und Aron (Schönberg), La Cenerentola (Rossini), The Ghosts of Versailles (Corigliano) (world premiere) The Great Gatsby (Harbison) (world premiere); conductor Salzburg Festival premieres of Offenbach's Les contes d'Hoffmann

1980 and Schönberg's Moses und Aron 1987; Dr hc (Univ. of Cincinnati, New England Conservatory, Northwestern Univ., State Univ. of New York, The Juilliard School); Grammy Awards for recordings of Orff's Carmina Burana, Mahler's Symphony No. 7, Brahms' A German Requiem, Verdi's La Traviata, Wagner's Das Rheingold, Die Walküre, Götterdämmerung, Strauss' Ariadne auf Naxos; Cultural Award of New York City 1980, Smetana Medal 1987, Gold Medal, Nat. Inst. of Social Sciences 1996, Nat. Medal of Arts 1997, Anton Seidl Award 1997, Lotus Award 1997, Kennedy Center Honors 2002, World Econs Forum Crystal Award 2003. *Address:* Metropolitan Opera, Lincoln Center, New York, NY 10023, USA. *Website:* www.metopera.org (Office); www .muenchnerphilharmoniker.org (Office); www.verbierorchestra.com (Office).

LEVINE, Seymour, PhD; American university professor; b. 23 Jan. 1925, Brooklyn, New York; s. of Joseph Levine and Rose Reines; m. Barbara Lou McWilliams 1950; one s. two d.; ed Univ. of Denver, New York Univ.; Asst Prof., Div. of Research, Boston Univ. 1952–53; Postdoctoral Fellow, Michael Reese Hosp., Chicago 1953–55, Research Assoc. 1955–56; Asst Prof., Dept of Psychiatry, Ohio State Univ. 1956–60; Postdoctoral Fellow, Maudsley Hosp., London, England 1960–62; Assoc. Prof., Dept of Psychiatry, Stanford Univ. 1962–69, Prof. 1969–96, Dir Stanford Primate Facility 1976–; Dir Biological Sciences Research Training Program 1971–; Consultant, Foundation of Human Devt, Univ. Coll. Dublin, Ireland 1973–; Pres. Int. Soc. of Developmental Psychobiology 1975–76; Pres. Int. Soc. of Psychoneuroendocrinology; Hoffheimer Research Award 1961, Research Career Devt Award 1962, Research Scientist Award 1967. *Publications:* (Co-author) Stress, arousal and the pituitary-adrenal system 1979, chapters and articles on stress in animals and humans. *Leisure interests:* music, art, sports. *Address:* c/o Stanford Primate Facility, Stanford University, Stanford, CA 94305, USA. *Telephone:* (650) 723-2300 (Office). *Website:* www.stanford.edu (Office).

LEVINGSTON, Gen. Roberto Marcelo; Argentine politician and army officer; b. 10 Jan. 1920, San Luis; s. of Guillermo Levingston and Carmen Laborda; m. Betty Nelly Andrés 1943; two s. (one deceased) one d.; ed Pius IX Coll., Nat. Mil. Coll., Army Intelligence School, Escuela Superior de Guerra and Center for High Mil. Studies; entered army as cadet, Nat. Mil. Coll. 1938, Sub-Lt 1941, Brig.-Gen. 1966; Army Information Officer 1947–50; mem. Gen. Staff 1951–57; Prof., Escuela Superior de Guerra 1958–62; Head of Army Information Services 1963–64; Dir-Gen. Lemos School of Logistics 1965–66; Head of Intelligence of Jt Chiefs of Staff 1967–68; Mil. Attaché Army Del. to Interamerican Defense Bd and Pres. Special Comm. on Acquisitions in USA 1969–70; Pres. and Prime Minister of Argentina 1970–71; Pres. Circle of Studies of Nat. Argentine Movt. *Publications:* political and military works. *Leisure interests:* reading of all kinds, particularly on politics, economics and military subjects, music and sport. *Address:* 11 de Septiembre 1735-17 A, Buenos Aires, Argentina. *Telephone:* 782-4433 (Home).

LEVINSON, Barry; American screenwriter, director and producer; b. 6 April 1942, Baltimore, Md; m. Diana Levinson; ed American Univ.; fmrly wrote and acted on TV comedy show in LA; later worked on network TV; wrote and appeared, The Carol Burnett Show; worked on film scripts for Silent Movie and High Anxiety (with Mel Brooks). *Television includes:* writer for Tim Conway Comedy Hour, The Marty Feldman Comedy Machine, The Carol Burnett Show (Emmy Awards 1974, 1975); exec. producer, Harry, 30 Minutes of Investigative Ticking, Diner, Homicide: Life on the Street (several Peabody Awards), Oz, The Beat 2000. *Films directed:* Diner, The Natural, Young Sherlock Holmes, Tin Men, Good Morning Vietnam, Rain Man (Acad. Award 1988), Disclosure 1995; directed and produced Avalon, Bugsy, Toys; Jimmy Hollywood (dir, writer) 1994, Sleepers 1996, Wag the Dog 1997, Sphere 1998, Liberty Heights 2000, An Everlasting Piece 2001, Bandits 2001. *Writer:* Diner, Tin Men, Avalon; co-wrote screenplays with Valerie Curtin for And Justice for All, Inside Moves, Best Friends, Unfaithfully Yours, Toys, Liberty Heights. *Actor:* Quiz Show 1994, Rain Man 1988, High Anxiety. *Address:* c/o Baltimore/Spring Creek Pictures, Building 133-208, 4000 Warner Boulevard, Burbank, CA 91522, USA. *Website:* www.levinson.com (Office).

LEVITIN, Mikhail Zakharovich; Russian stage director and writer; b. 27 Dec. 1945, Odessa, Ukraine; m.; one d. one s.; ed Moscow Inst. of Theatre Arts; Founder and Artistic Dir Moscow Theatre Hermitage 1981–. *Stage productions include:* Wanderings of Pilgrim Billy, Faryatyev's Fantasies in Moscow Theatre of Soviet Army, Alice Behind the Mirror, Moscow Theatre of Young Spectators, Harm! Harms! Shardam! or Clowns' School 1981, Pauper or Zanda's Death 1986, Evening in a Lunatic Asylum 1991, Maria, Moscow Theatre Hermitage 1996, New Year Tree at Ivanovs', Omsk Drama Theatre 1996. *Publications:* Other Man's Spectacle, My Friend Believes, Bolero, Sheer Indecency, Plutodrama, Dog's Shit. *Address:* Moscow Theatre Hermitage, Karentny Ryad 3, 103006 Moscow, Russia (Office). *Telephone:* (095) 209-20-76 (Office).

LEVITIS, Yefim Zavelyevich; Russian religious leader; b. 29 Nov. 1930; m.; one s.; ed Moscow Inst. of Aviation, Jewish seminary at Moscow Choral Synagogue, Higher Rabbis' School, Budapest; Scientific Sec. Moscow Jewish community 1975–80; Rabbi, St Petersburg 1980–91; Chief Rabbi, Great Choral Synagogue 1991–; Deputy Chief Rabbi of Russia responsible for co-operation with non-Jewish orgs; mem. Jewish Conf. of Rabbis; mem. Working Group, Consultative Council of Confession Heads, St Petersburg. *Address:* Great Choral Synagogue, 2nd Lermontovsky pr., St Petersburg, Russia. *Telephone:* (812) 114-00-78 (Office).

LEVITT, Arthur, Jr.; American business executive; b. 3 Feb. 1931, Brooklyn; s. of Arthur Levitt and Dorothy Wolff; m. Marylin Blauner 1955; one s. one d.; ed Williams Coll.; Asst Promotion Dir Time Inc. New York 1954–59; Exec. Vice-Pres., Dir Oppenheimer Industries Inc. Kansas City 1959–62; with Shearson Hayden Stone Inc. (now Shearson Lehman Bros. Inc.), New York 1962–78, Pres. 1969–78; Chair., CEO, Dir American Stock Exchange, New York 1978–89; Chair. Levitt Media Co. New York 1989–93, New York City Econ. Devt Corpn 1990–93; Chair. Securities and Exchange Comm. 1993–2001; various directorships and other business and public appts.; Hon. LLD (Williams Coll.) 1980, (Pace) 1980, (Hamilton Coll.) 1981, (Long Island) 1984, (Hofstra) 1985. *Address:* c/o Securities and Exchange Commission, 450 Fifth Street, NW, Washington, DC 20001, USA.

LEVITTE, Jean-David, LLB; French diplomatist and civil servant; b. 14 June 1946, Moissac; m. Marie-Cécile Levitte; two d.; ed Inst. of Political Science, Nat. School of Oriental Languages; joined Ministry of Foreign Affairs 1970, positions included Man. Econ. Affairs 1974–75, Asst Dir Dept for W Africa 1984–86, Adjunct Dir of Cabinet 1986–88, Dir Dept for Asia and Oceania 1990–93, Dir-Gen. of Cultural, Scientific and Tech. Relations 1993–95; Vice-Consul in Hong Kong 1971; Third Sec. Embassy in Beijing, People's Repub. of China 1972–74; Counsellor Perm. Mission to UN, New York 1981–84, Perm. Rep. to UN, Geneva 1988–90, New York 2000–02; Diplomatic Adviser to Pres. 1995–2000; Amb. to USA 2002–; Chargé de Mission, Secr.-Gen. of Presidency 1975–81; Officier, Légion d'honneur. *Address:* Embassy of France, 4101 Reservoir Road, NW, Washington, DC 20007, USA (Office). *Telephone:* (202) 944-6000 (Office). *Fax:* (202) 944-6166 (Office). *E-mail:* info-washington@diplomatie.gouv.fr (Office). *Website:* www .ambafrance-us.org (Office).

LEVY, Alain M., MBA; record company executive; b. 19 Dec. 1946, France; ed Ecole des Mines, France, Univ. of Pennsylvania; Asst to the Pres. CBS Int., New York 1972–73, Vice-Pres. Marketing for Europe, Paris 1973, Vice-Pres. of Creative Operations for Europe also Man. CBS Italy 1978; Man. Dir CBS Disques, France 1979, CEO PolyGram France 1984, Exec. Vice-Pres. PolyGram Group, France and Fed. Repub. of Germany 1988, Man. U.S. Operations PolyGram Group 1990–98, Pres., CEO, mem. Bd Man. PolyGram USA 1991–98; mem. Group Man. Cttee Philips Electronics, majority shareholder PolyGram USA 1991–98; Chair. Bd EMI Group PLC 2001–, Chair. and CEO EMI Recorded Music 2001–. *Address:* EMI Group PLC, 4 Tenterden Street, Hanover Square, London, W1A 2AY (Office); 8 St James's Square, London, SW1Y 4JU, England. *Telephone:* (20) 7355-4848 (Office). *Fax:* (20) 7495-1307 (Office). *Website:* www.emigroup.com (Office).

LEVY, Bernard-Henri; French writer; b. 5 Nov. 1948, Beni-Saf, Algeria; s. of André Levy and Ginette Levy; m. 1st Sylvie Bouscasse 1980; one s. one d.; m. 2nd Arielle Sonnery 1993; ed Ecole Normale Supérieure (rue d'Ulm), Paris; War Corresp. for Combat 1971–72; Lecturer in Epistemology, Univ. of Strasbourg, in Philosophy, Ecole Normale Supérieure 1973; mem. François Mitterrand's Group of Experts 1973–76; joined Editions Grasset as Ed. 'nouvelle philosophie' series 1973; Ed. Idées section, Quotidien de Paris; Contrib. to Nouvel Observateur and Temps Modernes 1974; Co-Founder Action Int. contre la Faim 1980, Radio Free Kabul 1981, SOS Racisme; f. and Dir Règle du jeu 1990–; Pres. Supervisory Council Sept-Arte 1993–; seconded by French Govt to Kabul, Afghanistan 2002. *Film directed:* Le Jour la Nuit 1997. *Publications:* Les Indes Rouges 1973, La Barbarie à Visage Humain 1977, Le Testament de Dieu 1979, L'Idéologie Française 1981, Questions de Principe 1983, Le Diable en tête (Prix Médicis) 1984, Impressions d'Asie 1985, Questions de Principe Deux 1986, Eloge des Intellectuels 1987, Les Derniers jours de Charles Baudelaire (Prix Interallié) 1988, Questions de Principe Trois 1990, Les Années 80 "de stella" 1990, Les Bronzes de César 1991, Les Aventures de la Liberté 1991, Piet Mondrian 1992, Piero Della Francesca 1992, Le Jugement Dernier (play) 1992, Questions de principe IV 1992, Les Hommes et les Femmes (jtly) 1993, Un Jour dans la mort de Sarajevo (screenplay, jtly) 1993, Bosna! (screenplay, jtly) 1994, La pureté dangereuse 1995, Questions de principe V 1995, Le lys et la cendre 1996, Comédie 1997, Le siècle de Sartre 2000, Réflexion sur la Guerre, Le mal et la fin de l'histoire 2001, Mémoire vive 2001, Qui a tué Daniel Pearl? 2003. *Leisure interests:* skiing, judo, water-skiing. *Address:* Editions Grasset et Fasquelle, 61 rue des Saint-Pères, 75006 Paris, France. *Telephone:* 1-44-39-22-00. *Fax:* 1-42-22-64-18.

LEVY, David; Israeli politician; b. 1938, Morocco; emigrated to Israel 1957; construction worker; joined Histadrut; elected to Knesset (Parl.), representing Herut (Freedom) group of Gahal 1969– (subsequently of Likud Bloc); Likud cand. for Sec.-Gen. of Histadrut 1977, 1981; Minister of Immigrant Absorption 1977–78, of Construction and Housing 1978–90, of Foreign Affairs 1990–92, 1996–97, 1999–2000, Deputy Prime Minister 1981–84, 1988–92, Minister without portfolio –2002; f. Gesher Party 1996, currently Leader. *Address:* c/o Gesher, Jerusalem, Israel. *Website:* www.gesher.org.il.

LEVY, Itzhak; politician and rabbi; b. 1947, Morocco; m.; five c.; ed Kerem B'Yavne and Yeshivat Hakotel; emigrated to Israel in 1957; ordained rabbi; served in Israeli Defence Forces, to rank of Maj.; Nat. Religious Party mem. Knesset (Parl.) 1988–, mem. Knesset House Cttee, Cttees on Finance, on Constitution, Law and Justice, on Labour and Social Welfare 1988–92, on Knesset House Cttee and Cttee on Constitution, Law and Justice 1992–96; Minister of Transport 1996–98, later of Housing, currently Minister without

Portfolio; mem. Bnei Akiva Exec. and World Secr.; Leader Nat. Religious Party; Chair. Israel–Argentina Parl. Friendship League. *Address:* National Religious Party, Jerusalem, Israel. *Telephone:* 2-377277. *Fax:* 2-377757.

LÉVY, Jacques Bernard, DèsSc; French metallurgist; b. Jan. 1937, Constantine, Algeria; s. of Gilbert Lévy and Renée Cassin; m. Marianne Neuburger 1964; two s. one d.; ed Ecole Polytechnique, Ecole des Mines de Paris, Univ. de Paris VI; Prof. of Metallurgy, Ecole des Mines de St-Etienne 1962, Dir Dept of Metallurgy 1974; Post-doctoral Fellow, Univ. of Waterloo, Ont., Canada 1968; Scientific Dir Ecole des Mines de Paris 1976, Dir 1984–2001; mem. Conseil Général des Mines; Ingénieur général du corps des mines 1983; Chair. (Research Comm.) Conf. des Grandes Ecoles 1984; mem. Royal Swedish Acad. of Eng Sciences 1989; Pres. Conf. of European Schools for Advanced Eng Educ. and Research 1990; Pres. Conf. des Grandes Ecoles 1993; mem. Conseil pour les Applications de l'Académie des Sciences 1999, Acad. des Technologies 2000–; Officier, Légion d'honneur, Commdr, Ordre nat. du mérite, Commdr, Ordre des Palmes académiques; Dr hc (Catholic Univ. of Louvain) 1996; Prix Jean Rist (Soc. Française de Métallurgie) 1972. *Publications:* about 30 publs on physical metallurgy (grain boundaries and interfaces, structure and properties of metals and alloys), official reports on materials science and eng higher educ. *Leisure interests:* skiing, tennis. *Address:* Ecole Nationale Supérieure des Mines, 60 boulevard Saint-Michel, 75272 Paris Cedex 06, France. *Telephone:* 1-40-51-90-18. *Fax:* 1-40-51-90-25. *E-mail:* levy@dg.ensmp.fr (Office). *Website:* www.ensmp.fr (Office).

LEVY, Michael Abraham, Baron (Life Peer), cr. 1997, of Mill Hill in the London Borough of Barnet, FCA, CA; British business executive, consultant and foundation administrator; b. 11 July 1944; s. of Samuel Levy and Annie Levy; m. Gilda Levy (née Altbach) 1967; one s. one d.; ed Hackney Downs Grammar School; chartered accountant Lubbock Fine 1961–66; Prin. M. Levy & Co. 1966–69; Partner Wagner, Prager, Levy & Partners 1969–73; Chair. Magnet Group of Cos 1973–88, D & J Securities Ltd 1988–92, M & G Records 1992–97; Vice-Chair. Phonographic Performance Ltd 1979–84, British Phonographic Industry Ltd 1984–87; Chair. British Music Industry Awards Cttee 1992–95, Patron 1995–; Nat. Campaign Chair. United Jt Israel Appeal 1982–85, Hon. Vice-Pres. 1994–2000, Hon. Pres. 2000–; currently Special Envoy of Prime Minister to Middle East; Chair. Jewish Care 1991–97, Pres. 1998–, Chair. Jewish Care Community Foundation 1995–; Vice-Chair. Cen. Council for Jewish Community Services 1994–, Chief Rabbinate Awards for Excellence 1992–, Foundation for Educ. 1993–; mem. Jewish Agency World Bd of Govs 1990–95, World Chair. Youth Aliyah Cttee 1991–95; mem. Keren Hayesod World Bd of Trustees 1991–95, World Comm. on Israel–Diaspora Relations 1995–, Int. Bd Govs Peres Centre for Peace 1997–, Advisory Council Foreign Policy Centre 1997–, FCO Panel 2000, 1998–2000, Nat. Council Voluntary Orgs. Advisory Cttee 1998–, Community Legal Service Champions Panel 1999–, Hon. Cttee Israel, Britain and the Commonwealth Asscn 2000–; Pres. CSV 1998–; Trustee Holocaust Educ. Trust 1997–, Policy Network Foundation 2000–; Patron Ben Guri Art Soc. 1997–2000, Save a Child's Heart Foundation 2000–; Gov. Jewish Free School 1990–95, Hon. Pres. 1995–; Chair. Wireart Ltd and Chase Music Ltd (fmrly M & G Music Ltd) 1992–; Hon. PhD (Middlesex Univ.) 1999, B'nai B'rith First Lodge Award 1994, Scopus Award Hebrew Univ. of Jerusalem 1998. *Leisure interest:* tennis. *Address:* House of Lords, Westminster, London, SW1A 0PW, England (Office).

LEWANDOWSKI, Janusz Antoni, PhD; Polish politician and economist; b. 13 June 1951, Lublin; s. of Karol Lewandowski and Halina Lewandowska; m. Lidia Talewska Lewandowska 1997; one d.; ed Gdańsk Univ.; mem. staff Gdańsk Univ. 1974–84 (dismissed); econ. adviser Solidarity Trade Union, Gdańsk 1980–81; lecturer Harvard Univ., USA; with Polish Ocean Lines, then consulting firm 1984–85; assoc. journal Przegląd Polityczny (pen-name Jędrzej Branecki) 1984–89; co-founder pvt. Gdańsk Inst. of Market Econs 1989–, Chair. Programme Bd 1993–94; Minister of Proprietary Transformations 1991–93; co-founder and Pres. Liberal-Democratic Congress 1990–94; Deputy to Sejm (Parl.) 1991–93, 1997–, Vice-Chair. Parl. Cttee for Treasury, Affranchisement and Privatization 1997–; mem. Freedom Union (UW) 1994–2001, Civil Platform 2001–. *Publication:* Samorząd w dobie 'Solidarności' 1984, Neoliberałowie wobec współczesności 1989, Strategia rozwoju województwa gdańskiego (jtly.) 1997. *Leisure interests:* sport, mountain hiking. *Address:* Biuro Poselskie, ul. Świętojańska 130/2, 81–381 Gdynia, Poland. *Telephone:* (58) 7816354 (Office). *Fax:* (58) 6200787 (Office). *E-mail:* janusz.lewandowski@hoga.pl (Office). *Website:* www.januszlewandowski.pl (Office).

LEWINTON, Sir Christopher, Kt, CEng, FEng, FIMechE, FRAeS; British/American business executive; b. 6 Jan. 1932, London; s. of Joseph Lewinton and Elizabeth Lewinton; m. 1st Jennifer Alcock (divorced); two s.; m. 2nd Louise Head 1979; two step-s.; ed Acton Tech. Coll.; commissioned army service in REME; Pres. Wilkinson Sword, N America 1960–70, CEO Wilkinson Sword Group 1970–85; Pres. Int. Group, Allegheny Int. 1976–85; Chief Exec. TI Group 1986–99, Chair. and CEO 1989–2000; Chair. Dowty Group PLC 1992–2000; Dir Reed Elsevier 1993–99, Y&R/WPP 1999–2003; mem. Supervisory Bd Mannesmann AG 1996–99; Chair. J. F. Lehman Europe 2000–; Adviser to Booz Allen Hamilton Inc. 2000–, to Morgan Stanley Capital Partners 2000–; Hon. DTech (Brunel) 1977. *Leisure interests:* golf, tennis, travel, reading. *Address:* J. F. Lehman & Co., 63 Curzon Street, London, W1J 8PD, England (Office); 450 Park Avenue, New York, NY 10022, USA (Office). *Telephone:* (20) 7758-8090 (London) (Office); (212) 634-1156 (New York) (Office). *Fax:* (20) 7491-7065 (London) (Office); (212) 634-1155 (New York) (Office). *E-mail:* clewinton@cl-partners.co.uk (Office). *Website:* www.jflpartners.com (Office).

LEWIS, Anthony Robert (Tony), CBE, MA; British cricketer, commentator and journalist; b. 6 July 1938, Swansea, Wales; s. of Wilfred Lewis and Florence Lewis (née Flower); m. Joan Pritchard 1962; two d.; ed Neath Grammar School, Christ's Coll. Cambridge; right-hand batsman; teams: Glamorgan, Cambridge Univ.; double blue and debut at int. level; led Glamorgan to their first Co. Championship title 1969; played in 9 Tests (8 as Capt.) scoring 457 runs (average 32.64); 20,495 first-class runs (average 32.4) including 30 hundreds; retd 1974; became cricket commentator and journalist; Pres. Marylebone Cricket Club (MCC) 1998–2000, secured admission of women into MCC Club; fmr Chair. (now Pres.) Glamorgan Co. Cricket Club (CCC); Chair. Welsh Tourist Bd; led Welsh campaign to host 2010 Ryder Cup; Hon. Fellow (St David's Univ. Coll., Lampeter) 1993, (Glamorgan Univ.) 1995, (Univ. of Wales, Swansea) 1996, (Cardiff Univ.) 1999. *Publications:* A Summer of Cricket 1976, Playing Days 1985, Double Century 1987, Cricket in Many Lands 1991, MCC Masterclass 1994. *Leisure interests:* classical music, golf. *Address:* Castellan, Near Llantrisant, Mid Glamorgan, CF72 8LP, Wales (Home).

LEWIS, Bernard, BA, PhD, FBA, FRHistS; American (naturalized 1982) university professor; b. 31 May 1916, London, England; m. Ruth Hélène Oppenhejm 1947 (divorced 1974); one s. one d.; ed Univs of London and Paris; Lecturer in Islamic History, School of Oriental Studies, Univ. of London 1938; served in RAC and Intelligence Corps 1940–41; attached to Foreign Office 1941–45; Prof. of History of the Near and Middle East, Univ. of London 1949–74; Cleveland E. Dodge Prof. of Near Eastern Studies, Princeton Univ. 1974–86, Prof. Emer. 1986–; Dir Annenberg Research Inst., Philadelphia 1986–90; Visiting Prof. of History, Univ. of Calif. at LA 1955–56, Columbia Univ. 1960, Ind. Univ. 1963, Princeton Univ. 1964, Univ. of Calif. at Berkeley 1965, Coll. de France 1980, École des Hautes Études en Sciences Sociales, Paris 1983, 1988, Univ. of Chicago 1985; Visiting mem. Inst. for Advanced Study, Princeton Univ. 1969, mem. 1974–86; A. D. White Prof.-at-Large, Cornell Univ. 1984–90; mem. Bd of Dirs Institut für die Wissenschaften von Menschen, Vienna 1988; Jefferson Lecturer in the Humanities, US Nat. Endowment for the Humanities 1990; Tanner Lecturer, Brasenose Coll., Oxford 1990; Henry M. Jackson Memorial Lecturer (Seattle) 1992; mem. British Acad., American Philosophical Soc. 1973, American Acad. of Arts and Sciences 1983; Corresp. mem. Inst. d'Egypte, Cairo 1969–, Inst. de France 1994–; Fellow Univ. Coll., London 1976; Hon. mem. Turkish Historical Soc., Société Asiatique, Paris, Ataturk Acad. of History, Language and Culture, Ankara, Turkish Acad. of Sciences; Hon. Fellow SOAS, London 1986; Dr hc (Hebrew Univ., Jerusalem) 1974, (Tel Aviv) 1979, (State Univ. of NY Binghamton, Univ. of Penn., Hebrew Union Coll., Cincinnati) 1987, (Univ. of Haifa, Yeshiva Univ., New York) 1991, (Bar-Ilan Univ.) 1992, (Brandeis) 1993, (Ben-Gurion, Ankara) 1996; Harvey Prize 1978, Ataturk Peace Prize 1998. *Publications:* The Origins of Ismā'ilism 1940, Turkey Today 1940, British Contributions to Arabic Studies 1941, Handbook of Diplomatic and Political Arabic 1947, 1956, Land of Enchanters (ed.) 1948, The Arabs in History 1950, 1993, Notes and Documents from the Turkish Archives 1952, The Emergence of Modern Turkey 1961, 1968, 2001, The Kingly Crown 1961, Historians of the Middle East (co-ed. with P. M. Holt) 1962, Istanbul and the Civilization of the Ottoman Empire 1963, The Middle East and the West 1964, The Assassins 1967, Race and Colour in Islam 1971, Islam in History 1973, Islamic Civilization (ed.) 1974, Islam from the Prophet Muhammad to the Capture of Constantinople (2 vols) 1974, History–Remembered, Recovered, Invented 1975, The World of Islam (ed.) 1976, Population and Revenue in the Towns of Palestine in the Sixteenth Century (with Amnon Cohen) 1978, The Muslim Discovery of Europe 1982, The Jews of Islam 1984, Semites and Anti-Semites 1986, As Others See Us (co-ed.) 1986, The Political Language of Islam 1988, 1999, Race and Slavery in the Middle East 1990, Islam and the West 1993, The Shaping of the Modern Middle East 1994, Cultures in Conflict: Christians, Muslims and Jews in the Age of Discovery 1995, The Middle East: Two Thousand Years of History from the Rise of Christianity to the Present Day 1995, The Future of the Middle East 1997, The Multiple Identities of the Middle East 1998, Uno squardo dal Medio Oriente 1999, A Middle East Mosaic: Fragments of life, letters and history 2000, Music of a Distant Drum, Classical Arabic, Persian, Turkish and Hebrew Poems 2001, What Went Wrong? Western Impact and Middle Eastern Response 2002. *Address:* Department of Near Eastern Studies, Princeton University, Princeton, NJ 08544, USA. *Telephone:* (609) 258-4280.

LEWIS, Carl (Frederick Carlton); American athlete; b. 1 July 1961, Birmingham, Ala; s. of the late William Lewis and of Evelyn Lawler Lewis; ed Univ. of Houston; won World Cup competition 1981, first World Championships (with 8.55m); achieved world record 8.79m jump 1983; gold medals at Olympic Games 1984 for 100m, 200 m., long jump and 4×100m; athlete in fields of sprints and long jump; silver medal for 200m, gold medal for 100m, Olympic Games 1988; jumped 8.64m New York 1991; world record for 100m 9.86 seconds Aug. 1991 (surpassed 1994); gold medal, long jump Olympic Games 1992; gold medal for long jump (8.50m), Olympic Games 1996; retd 1997; has won a total of nine Olympic gold medals; f. Carl Lewis Fund to help disadvantaged youths; appeared in several TV and film projects produced by the Carl Lewis Entertainment Group; Hon. Chair. Negro Coll. Fund; Track and Field News Athlete of the Decade 1980–89, World Athlete of the Year

1982, 1983, 1984, IAAF Athlete of the Century 1999. *Address:* c/o Carl Lewis International Fan Club, P.O. Box 57, Houston, TX 77257-1990, USA. *Website:* www.lewis.com (Office).

LEWIS, Charles Edwin; American professor of medicine; b. 28 Dec. 1928, Kansas City, Mo.; s. of Claude Herbert Lewis and Maudie Friels (née Holaday); m. Mary Ann Gurera 1963; three s. one d.; ed Univs of Kansas and Cincinatti and Harvard Medical School; USAF 1955–56; Fellow, The Kettering Lab. 1956–59; Asst Prof. Epidemiology, Baylor Univ. 1959–61; Assoc. Prof. of Medicine, Univ. of Kansas 1962–64, Prof. and Chair. Dept of Community Medicine 1964–69; Prof. and Head of Div. of Health Services and Prof. of Medicine, UCLA 1970–72, Chief, Div. of Gen. Internal Medicine 1972–90, Prof. of Nursing, School of Nursing 1973–, Dir UCLA Center for Health Promotion and Disease Prevention 1991–, Head Div. of Preventive and Occupational Medicine 1991–93, Dir Health Services Research Center 1991–93, Chair. Academic Senate 1995–96; Regent, ACP 1989; Master American Coll. of Physicians; mem. Inst. of Medicine (NAS); Ginsberg Prize, Univ. of Kan., Rosenthal Award (ACP) 1980. *Publications:* more than 120 research publs in journals and 15 chapters in books. *Leisure interests:* music, travel. *Address:* 221 Burlingame Avenue, Los Angeles, CA 90049, USA (Home); UCLA Center for Health Promotion & Disease Prevention, Los Angeles, CA 90095 (Office). *Telephone:* (310) 825-6709 (Office). *Fax:* (310) 209-5717 (Office); (310) 394-8929 (Home); (310) 206-5717. *E-mail:* lewis@admin .ph.ucla.edu (Office).

LEWIS, Dan, PhD, DSc, FRS; British geneticist; b. 30 Dec. 1910, Stoke on Trent; s. of Ernest Albert Lewis and Edith Jane Lewis; m. Mary P. E Burry 1933; one d.; ed High School, Newcastle under Lyme and Univs of Reading and London; student gardener 1929–31; plant breeder, John Innes Inst. 1935, Head Dept of Genetics 1947; Rockefeller Fellowship Calif. Inst. of Tech. 1955–56; Quain Prof. of Botany, Univ. Coll. London 1957–78, Prof. Emer. 1978–; Hon. Research Fellow, Univ. Coll. London 1978–; Visiting Prof. of Genetics, Univ. of Calif., Berkeley 1961, Delhi 1965, Singapore 1970; Visiting Prof., Queen Mary Coll., London 1978–; Pres. Genetical Soc. 1968–71; mem. Univ. Grants Cttee 1968–74; Freedom Chelsea Physic Garden 1977; Hon. Life mem. City Univ. 1999. *Publications:* Sexual Incompatibility in Plants and articles on genetics; Ed. Science Progress. *Leisure interests:* swimming, music, gardening. *Address:* Flat 2, 56/57 Myddelton Square, London, EC1R 1YA, England. *Telephone:* (20) 7278-6948.

LEWIS, Denise, OBE; British athlete; b. 27 Aug. 1972, W Bromwich; d. of Joan Lewis; partner Patrick Stevens; one d.; specializes in heptathlon; club: Birchfield Harriers; Commonwealth heptathlon record-holder (6,736 points) 1997; fifth European Jr Championships 1991; gold medal Commonwealth Games 1994; gold medal European Cup 1995; bronze medal Olympic Games 1996; silver medal World Championships 1997; gold medal European Championships 1998; gold medal Commonwealth Championships 1998; silver medal World Championships 1999; new Commonwealth Record (6,831 points) 2000; gold medal, Olympic Games 2000; British Athletics Writers Female Athlete of the Year 1998, 2000, Sports Writers Assn Sportswoman of the year 2000. *Publication:* Denise Lewis: Faster, Higher, Stronger (autobiog.) 2001. *Address:* c/o MTC (UK) Ltd, 20 York Street, London, W1U 6PU, England. *Telephone:* (20) 7935-8000. *Fax:* (20) 7935-8066. *E-mail:* info.mtc-uk.com (Office). *Website:* www.mtc-uk.com (Office).

LEWIS, Douglas Grinslade, PC, LLB, FCA, QC; Canadian politician; b. 17 April 1938, Toronto, Ont.; s. of Horace Grinslade and Brenda Hazeldine Lewis (née Reynolds); m. Linda Diane Haggans 1962; two s. three d.; ed Univ. of Toronto, Osgoode Hall Law School; Progressive Conservative MP for Simcoe N 1979–93; Parl. Sec. to Minister of Supply and Services 1979; Deputy Opposition House Leader 1981, Opposition House Leader 1983; Parl. Sec. to Pres. of Treasury Bd 1984, to Pres. of Privy Council 1985, to Deputy Prime Minister and Pres. of Queen's Privy Council for Canada 1986–87; Minister of State (Deputy House Leader) and Minister of State (Treasury Bd) 1987–88; Acting Pres. Treasury Bd 1988; Minister of Justice, Attorney-Gen. and Govt House Leader 1989–90; Minister of Transport 1990–91; Solicitor-Gen. 1991–93. *Address:* Box 535, Orillia, Ont., L3V 6K2, Canada.

LEWIS, Edward B., PhD; American professor of biology; b. 20 May 1918, Wilkes-Barre; s. of Edward B. Lewis and Laura Histed Lewis; m. Pamela Harrah 1946; three s. (one deceased); ed Minnesota Univ. and Calif. Inst. of Tech.; Instructor, Calif. Inst. of Tech. 1946–48, Asst Prof. 1948–49, Assoc. Prof. 1949–56, Prof. 1956–88, Thomas Hunt Morgan Prof. of Biology Emer. 1988–; Rockefeller Foundation Fellow, Cambridge Univ. 1947–48; Sec. Genetics Soc. of America 1962–64, Vice-Pres. 1966–67, Pres. 1967; Guest Prof., Inst. of Genetics, Copenhagen Univ. 1975–76; mem. NAS, American Acad. of Arts and Sciences, Genetics Soc. of America, American Philosophical Soc.; Foreign mem. Royal Soc. 1989; Hon. mem. Genetical Soc. of Great Britain 1990; Hon. PhD (Umeå, Sweden) 1981; Hon. DSc (Minn. Univ.) 1993; Thomas Hunt Morgan Medal, Gairdner Foundation Int. Award 1987, Wolf Prize for Medicine (jtly with John B. Gurdon, q.v., 1989), Rosenstiel Medical Research Award 1990, Nat. Medal of Science (USA) 1990, Albert Lasker Basic Medical Research Award (jtly) 1991, Louisa Gross Horwitz Prize 1992, shared Nobel Prize for Medicine 1995. *Leisure interest:* playing the flute. *Address:* Biology Division 156–29, California Institute of Technology, 1201 E California Boulevard, Pasadena, CA 91125; 805 Winthrop Road, San Marino, CA 91108, USA. *Telephone:* (626) 395-4941. *Fax:* (626) 564-9685.

LEWIS, Geoffrey David, MA, FSA; British museologist; b. 13 April 1933, Brighton, Sussex; s. of David Lewis and Esther Lewis; m. Frances May Wilderspin 1956; three d.; ed Varndean Grammar School, Brighton, Univ. of Liverpool; Asst Curator, Worthing Museum and Art Gallery 1950–60; Deputy Dir (and Keeper of Antiquities) Sheffield City Museum 1960–65; Dir Sheffield City Museums 1966–72, Liverpool City Museums 1972–74, Merseyside Co. Museums 1974–77; Dir of Museum Studies, Univ. of Leicester 1977–89, Assoc. Teacher 1989–92; Hon. Lecturer in British Prehistory, Univ. of Sheffield 1965–72; Fellow Museums Asscn London 1966, Pres. 1980–81, Pres. Int. Council of Museums 1983–89, Chair. Advisory Cttee 1974–80, Chair. Ethics Cttee 1996–; mem. Bd of Trustees Royal Armouries 1990–99, Chair. Design Cttee 1995–99; Chair. Printing Matters (Bude) Ltd 1991–96; Deputy Chair. The Genesis Agendum 1996–; Gov. Wolvey School 1993–, Chair. of Govs 1998–2003; Hon. Fellow Museums Asscn 1989. *Publications:* The South Yorkshire Glass Industry 1964, Prehistoric and Roman Times in the Sheffield Area (Co-author) 1968, For Instruction and Recreation 1989, Manual of Curatorship (Co-Ed.) 1992; contrib. to Encyclopaedia Britannica and Britannica Online; many articles relating to archaeology and museums. *Leisure interests:* walking, computing. *Address:* 4 Orchard Close, Wolvey, Hinckley, Leics., LE10 3LR, England. *Telephone:* (1455) 220708. *Fax:* (1455) 220708. *E-mail:* mail@geoffreylewis.co.uk (Office); Geoffrey_Lewis@btinternet.com (Home). *Website:* www.geoffreylewis.co.uk (Office).

LEWIS, Baron (Life Peer), cr. 1989, of Newnham; **Jack Lewis,** Kt, PhD, FRSC, FRS; British professor of chemistry; b. 13 Feb. 1928, Barrow; m. Elfreida M. Lamb 1951; one s. one d.; ed Barrow Grammar School and Univs of London and Nottingham; Lecturer, Univ. of Sheffield 1954–56, Imperial Coll. London 1956–57; Lecturer-Reader, Univ. Coll. London 1957–61; Prof. of Chem. Univ. of Manchester 1961–67, Univ. Coll. London 1967–70, Univ. of Cambridge 1970–95; Warden, Robinson Coll. Cambridge 1975–2001; mem. numerous cttees etc.; Foreign Assoc. NAS; Foreign mem. American Philosophical Soc. 1994, Accad. Naz. dei Lincei 1995; Hon. FRSC; Hon. Fellow Sidney Sussex Coll. Cambridge (Fellow 1970–77); Chevalier, Ordre des Palmes Académiques, Commdr Cross of the Order of Merit (Poland) and other distinctions; 21 hon. degrees; Davy Medal, Royal Soc. 1985 and other awards. *Publications:* papers in scientific journals. *Address:* Robinson College, Grange Road, Cambridge, CB3 9AN, England (Office).

LEWIS, Jerry (Joseph Levitch); American comedian, writer, director, producer and actor; b. 16 March 1926, Newark, NJ; s. of Danny and Rachael Lewis; m. 1st Patti Palmer 1944 (divorced); five s.; m. 2nd SanDee Pitnick 1983; one d.; performed in nightclubs as a comedian before teaming with Dean Martin in 1946 at the 500 Club, Atlantic City, NJ; Nat. Chair. Muscular Dystrophy Asscn of America 1951–; Prof. of Cinema at Univ. of Southern Calif.; mem. Screen Directors Guild; Hon. DHumLitt (Mercy Coll. Westchester, N.Y) 1987, (Emerson Coll., Boston, Mass.) 1993; N. Neal Pike Prize for Service to the Handicapped, Boston Univ. School of Law 1984; numerous awards and honours including Best Dir of the Year Award (8 times), Lifetime Achievement Award, American Medical Asscn 1996, Golden Lion Award, Venice Int. Film 1999; Chevalier, Légion d'honneur 1984, Commdr des Arts et Lettres 1984. *Films:* made film début with Dean Martin in My Friend Irma 1949; other films (many also as producer and/or Dir) include: My Friend Irma Goes West 1950, That's My Boy 1951, The Caddy 1952, Sailor Beware 1952, Jumping Jacks 1953, The Stooge 1953, Scared Stiff 1953, Living it Up 1954, Three Ring Circus 1954, You're Never Too Young 1955, Partners 1956, Hollywood or Bust 1956, The Delicate Delinquent 1957, The Sad Sack 1958, Rock a Bye Baby 1958, The Geisha Boy 1958, Visit to a Small Planet 1959, The Bellboy 1960, Cinderfella 1960, It's Only Money 1961, The Errand Boy 1962, The Patsy 1964, The Disorderly Orderly 1964, The Family Jewels 1965, Boeing-Boeing 1965, Three On a Couch 1965, Way Way Out 1966, The Big Mouth 1967, Don't Raise the Bridge, Lower the River 1968, One More Time 1969, Hook, Line and Sinker 1969, Which Way to the Front? 1970, The Day the Clown Cried 1972, Hardly Working 1979, King of Comedy 1981, Slapstick of Another Kind 1982, Smorgasbord 1983, How Did You Get In? 1985, Mr Saturday Night 1992, Funny Bones 1995. *Play:* Damn Yankees 1995, on tour 1995–97. *Television appearances include:* Startime, The Ed Sullivan Show and the Jazz Singer. *Publications:* The Total Film-Maker 1971, Jerry Lewis in Person 1982. *Leisure interests:* golf, sailing. *Address:* Jerry Lewis Films Inc., 3160 W Sahara Avenue, C-16, Las Vegas, NV 89102; c/o William Morris Agency Inc., 151 South El Comino Drive, Beverly Hills, CA 90212, USA. *Website:* www.jerrylewiscomedy.com (Office).

LEWIS, Jerry Lee; American rock musician; b. 29 Sept. 1935, Ferriday, La; m. six times; one s. (deceased); one d.; ed ed. Waxahachie Bible Inst., Texas; inducted into Rock and Roll Hall of Fame 1986. *Singles include:* Crazy Arms, Whole Lotta Shakin' Goin' On, Great Balls of Fire, Breathless, What'd I Say, There Must Be More To Love Than This, Would You Take Another Chance on Me?, Chantilly Lace. *Albums include:* The Greatest Live Show on Earth, The Session, Back to Back 1996, By Invitation Only 2000. *Films include:* Jamboree, High School Confidential. *Theatre includes:* Iago in Catch My Soul. *Address:* Warner Bros Records, 75 Rockefeller Plaza, New York, NY 10019, USA (Office).

LEWIS, Joseph C. (Joe); British business executive; b. London; s. of late Charles Lewis; m.; one d.; joined father's small catering business; with father ran Hanover Grand chain of banqueting suites, London 1970s; moved to New Providence, Bahamas 1979; founder and owner Tavistock Group of financial services, property and retail businesses; shareholder Rapallo Ltd, London, English Nat. Investment Corpn (ENIC), Tamarind Int., Hong Kong, auction house Christie's, London. *Address:* P.O. Box N7776, Lyford Cay, New Providence, Bahamas.

LEWIS, Juliette; American film actress; b. 21 June 1973, Fernando Valley, Calif.; d. of Geoffrey Lewis and Glenis Batley Lewis; m. Steve Berra 1999; Chicago Film Critics' Asscn Most Promising Actress 1991, NATO/ShoNest Female Star of Tomorrow 1993, Venice Film Festival Pasinetti Prize 1994. *Films include:* My Stepmother is an Alien 1988, Meet the Hollowheads 1989, National Lampoons Christmas Vacation 1989, Cape Fear 1991, Crooked Hearts 1991, Husbands and Wives 1992, Kalifornia 1993, One Hot Summer, That Night 1993, What's Eating Gilbert Grape 1993, Romeo is Bleeding 1994, Natural Born Killers 1994, Mixed Nuts 1994, The Basketball Diaries 1995, Strange Days 1995, From Dusk Till Dawn 1996, The Evening Star 1996, The Audition, Full Tilt Boogie 1997, The Other Sister 1999, The 4th Floor 1999, Way of the Gun 2000, My Louisiana Sky 2001. *Television appearances include:* Homefires (mini-series), I Married Dora 1988, Too Young To Die (movie) 1989, A Family For Joe 1990. *Address:* c/o Norman Brokaw, William Morris Agency, 151 South El Camino Boulevard, Beverly Hills, CA 90212, USA.

LEWIS, Kenneth D., BA; American banking executive; b. 9 April 1947, Meridian, Miss.; ed Georgia State Univ., Stanford Univ.; Credit Analyst NCNB, Charlotte NC 1969–77, Man. NCNB Int. Banking Corpn, NY 1977–79, Sr Vice-Pres. and Man. U.S. Dept 1979–83, Middle Market Group Exec. (following creation of Bank of America group) 1983–86, Pres. Fla Div. 1986–88, Pres. Tex. Div. 1988–90, Pres. Consumer and Commercial Banking 1990–99, Pres. and COO Bank of America Corpn 1999–2001, Chair., Pres. and CEO 2001–; mem. Bd of Dirs Health Man. Assocs Inc., Homeownership Educ. and Counseling Inst., Lowe's Cos. Inc., Presbyterian Hosp. Foundation (fmr Chair.); Chair. Bd of Trustees, Nat. Urban League. *Address:* Bank of America Corporate Center, 100 North Tryon Street, Charlotte, NC 28255, USA (Office). *Telephone:* (888) 279-3457 (Office). *Website:* www.bofa.com (Office).

LEWIS, Lennox, CBE; British heavyweight boxer; b. 2 Sept. 1965, London; s. of Violet Blake; defeated Jean Chanet to win European heavyweight title, Crystal Palace 1990; defeated Gary Mason to win British heavyweight title, Wembley 1991; Commonwealth heavyweight; WBC heavyweight 1992; defeated Frank Bruno 1993; WBC world champion 1993–94, 1997–; defended WBC title and challenged for World Boxing Asscn (WBA) and Int. Boxing Fed. (IBF) titles, against Evander Holyfield (q.v.) March 1999, bout declared a draw; undisputed world heavyweight champion 1999–2001 (lost WBC and IBF titles when defeated by Hasim Rahman April 2001); regained title of world heavyweight champion from Hasim Rahman Nov. 2001; retained title of undisputed world heavyweight champion June 2002– (after beating Mike Tyson, q.v.); 40 professional wins (20 losses, 1 draw, 31 knock-outs); f. Lennox Lewis Coll., Hackney 1994; Dr hc (Univ. of London) 1999. *Film:* Ocean's Eleven 2002. *Publications:* Lennox Lewis (autobiog.) 1993, Lennox 2002. *Leisure interests:* action movie watching, urban music, cross training, golf, chess. *Address:* Office of Lennox Lewis, Suite 206, Gainsborough House, 81 Oxford Street, London, W1D 2EU, England (Office). *Telephone:* (20) 7903-5074 (Office). *Fax:* (20) 7903-5075 (Office). *E-mail:* rose@lennoxlewis .com, roseobianwu@lennoxlewis.com (Office). *Website:* www.lennoxlewis.com (Office).

LEWIS, Neville Brice, MP; Jamaican politician; b. 19 May 1936, Middle Quarters, St Elizabeth; s. of Neville C. and Marie Lewis; m. Jasmin Lewis; one s. one d.; ed Munro Coll., St Elizabeth and Lincoln's Inn, London; accounting clerk, McCaulay's Motor Service, Kingston 1959–61; legal studies in London 1961; later worked in property man. in London; returned to Jamaica 1976; MP for NW St Elizabeth 1976–; Minister of Social Security 1980–83, of Local Govt 1983–89; mem. Jamaica Labour Party (Deputy Leader 1983). *Address:* c/o Jamaica Labour Party, 20 Belmont Road, Kingston 5, Jamaica.

LEWIS, Norman; British writer; b. 28 June 1908, Enfield, London; m. Lesley Lewis; one s. two d.; ed Enfield Grammar School; owned chain of photography shops; served Army Intelligence Corps 1939–45. *Publications:* (fiction) Samara 1949, A Single Pilgrim 1953, The Day of the Fox 1955, The Volcanoes Above Us 1957, A Small War Made to Order 1966, The Sicilian Specialist 1974, The German Company 1979, A Suitable Case for Corruption 1984; (travel) Sand and Sea in Arabia 1938, A Dragon Apparent 1951, Golden Earth 1952, The Changing Sky 1959, The Honoured Society 1964, Naples '44 1978, Cuban Passage 1982, Voices of the Old Sea 1984, The Missionaries 1988, An Empire of the East 1993, In Sicily 2000, (autobiog.) The Jackdaw Cake, Voyage by Dhow 2001. *Leisure interest:* exploring remote areas of Latin America and the Far East. *Address:* The Old Parsonage, Finchingfield, Essex, CM7 4LB, England (Home). *Telephone:* (1371) 810278 (Home).

LEWIS, Patrick Albert, PhD; Antigua and Barbuda diplomatist and historian; b. 27 Nov. 1938, St John's; m.; two c.; ed Hampton Inst. and Univ. of Cincinnati; Asst Prof. Univ. of Cincinnati 1971–73, Asst Prof., Assoc. Prof., Prof. of History, Hampton Univ. 1973–84; Adviser to Deputy Prime Minister of Antigua and Barbuda 1984–87, Minister-Counsellor, Perm. Mission to the UN 1987–91, Amb. to UN 1995–, to Brazil 1999–. *Leisure interests:* cricket, movies, theatre, music. *Address:* Permanent Mission of Antigua and Barbuda

to the United Nations, 610 Fifth Avenue, Suite 311, New York, NY 10020, USA (Office). *Telephone:* (212) 541-4117 (Office). *Fax:* (212) 757-1607 (Office). *E-mail:* atgun@undp.org.

LEWIS, Roger Charles, BMus, FRSA; British broadcasting executive; b. 24 Aug. 1954; s. of the late Griffith Charles Job Lewis and Dorothy Lewis (née Russ); m. Christine Trollope 1980; two s.; ed Cynffig Comprehensive School, Bridgend, Univ. of Nottingham; freelance musician 1976–80; Music Officer Darlington Arts Centre 1980–82; presenter Radio Tees 1981–84; producer Capital Radio 1984–85; BBC Radio 1 1985–87, Head of Music Radio 1 1987–90; Dir Classical Div. EMI Records 1990–95, Man. Dir 1995, Man. Dir EMI Premier 1995–97; Pres. Decca Record Co. 1997–98; Man. Dir and Programme Controller Classic FM 1998–; Dir GWR PLC 1998–, The Radio Corpn Ltd 1999–; Chair. Music and Dance Scheme Advisory Group, Dept for Educ. and Science 2000–, Barchester Group 2001–; Trustee Masterprize (Int. Composers' Competition) 1995–, Masterclass Charitable Trust 2000–; Chair. Trustees Ogmore Centre 1996–; Pres. Bromley Youth Music Trust 2000–; mem. WNO Devt Circle 2001–; Sony Radio Award 1987, 1988, 1989, Grand Award Winner and Gold Medal, New York Radio Festival 1987, One World Broadcasting Trust Award 1989, NTL Commercial Radio Programmer of the Year 2002. *Leisure interests:* rugby, wine, walking, skiing. *Address:* Classic FM House, 7 Swallow Place, London, W1B 2AG, England (Office). *Telephone:* (20) 7344-2781 (Office). *Fax:* (20) 7344-2783 (Office).

LEWIS, Russell T.; American newspaper executive; b. 1948; Pres., Gen. Man. The New York Times, New York 1993–97, Pres., CEO 1997–. *Leisure interests:* fitness, running, golf. *Address:* The New York Times, 229 West 43rd Street, New York, NY 10036, U.S.A. (Office).

LEWIS, Samuel Winfield, MA; American diplomatist; b. 1 Oct. 1930, Houston; s. of Samuel W Lewis and Sue Roselle Hurley Lewis; m. Sallie S. Smoot 1953; one s. one d.; ed Yale and Johns Hopkins Univs; Exec. Asst American Trucking Asscn, Washington 1953–54; entered Foreign Service 1954; with Consulate, Naples 1954–55; Consul, Florence 1955–59; Officer-in-Charge Italian Affairs, Dept of State 1959–61; Special Asst to Under-Sec. of State 1961–63; Deputy Asst Dir US AID Mission to Brazil 1964–66; Deputy Dir Office for Brazil Affairs, Dept of State 1967–68; senior staff mem. for Latin American Affairs, Nat. Security Council, White House 1968–69; Special Asst for Policy Planning, Bureau of Inter-American Affairs 1969, to Dir-Gen. Foreign Service 1969–71; Deputy Chief of Mission and Counsellor, US Embassy, Kabul 1971–74; Deputy Dir Policy Planning Staff, Dept of State 1974–75, Asst Sec. of State for Int. Organization 1975–77; Amb. to Israel 1977–85; Pres. US Inst. of Peace 1987–93; Dir Policy Planning Staff, Dept of State 1993–94; Visiting Fellow, Princeton Univ. 1963–64; Diplomat-in-Residence, Johns Hopkins Foreign Policy Inst. 1985–87; Guest Scholar, The Brookings Inst., Washington, DC 1987; Visiting Prof., Hamilton Coll. 1995, 1997; Counselor, Washington Inst. for Near East Policy 1995–98; Adjunct Prof. Georgetown Univ. 1996; mem. Council on Foreign Relations, Vice-Chair. Center for Preventive Action 1995–97; Vice-Chair. American Acad. of Diplomacy 1995–99; mem. The Middle East Inst., Cousteau Soc.; mem. Bd of Dirs Inst. for the Study of Diplomacy, Georgetown Univ. 1994–, Inst. of World Affairs 1996–; mem. Bd Asscn for Diplomatic Studies and Training 1994–; Sr Adviser Israel Policy Forum 1998–; Chair. Bd of Overseers, Harry S. Truman Inst. for Advancement of Peace, Hebrew Univ. of Jerusalem 1986–91; Sr Int. Fellow, Dayan Centre for Middle Eastern and African Affairs, Tel Aviv Univ. 1986–87; Hon. PhD; Hon. DHumLitt; William A. Jump Award 1967, Meritorious Honor Award (Dept of State) 1967, Presidential Man. Improvement Award 1970, Distinguished Honor Awards 1977, 1985, Wilbur J. Carr Award 1985. *Publications:* Soviet and American Attitudes toward the Arab-Israeli Peace Process, in Super Power Rivalry in the Middle East 1987, The United States and Israel 1977–1988, in The Middle East: Ten Years after Camp David 1988, Making Peace among Arabs and Israelis 1991, The United States and Israel: Evolution of an Unwritten Alliance 1999; numerous articles. *Leisure interests:* golf, tennis, scuba diving, nature photography, travel, painting. *Address:* 6232 Nelway Drive, McLean, VA 22101, USA. *Telephone:* (703) 448-1997 (Home). *E-mail:* sixtymeter@aol.com (Home).

LEWIS, Stephen; Canadian international civil servant, politician and lecturer; b. 11 Nov. 1937, Ottawa; s. of David and Sophie Lewis; m. Michele Landsberg 1963; three c.; ed Univ. of Toronto, Univ. of British Columbia; spent two years teaching and travelling in Africa; fmr Dir of Org., New Democratic Party (NDP), Prov. Leader 1970–77; MP for Scarborough W, Ont. Legis. 1963–78; Amb. and Perm Rep. of Canadian Mission to UN 1984–88; Special Adviser to UN Sec.-Gen. on African Econ. Recovery 1986–91; Special Rep. to UNICEF 1990–95, Deputy Exec. Dir 1995–99; apptd UN Special Envoy on AIDS in Africa 2001–; mem. Int. Panel of Eminent Persons 1999–; Hon. LLD from 12 univs; Gordon Sinclair ACTRA Award 1982; B'nai B'rith Human Rights Award 1983. *Publication:* Art Out of Agony 1983. *Address:* 6 Montclair Avenue, Toronto, Ont., M4V 1W1, Canada; Special Envoy on AIDS in Africa, United Nations, New York, NY 10017, USA.

LEWIS, Vaughan Allen, PhD, CBE; Saint Lucia politician and academic; b. 17 May 1940; m. Shirley May Lewis; two d.; ed Univ. of Manchester, UK; temporary Asst Lecturer, Dept of Political Theory, Univ. Coll. Swansea, Wales 1963–64; Asst Lecturer, Dept of Politics, Univ. of Liverpool 1964–66; Research Fellow Dept of Govt, Univ. of Manchester 1966–68; Lecturer, Dept of Govt, Univ. of the West Indies, Mona, Jamaica 1968–72, Part-time Lecturer, Inst. of Int. Relations, Univ. of the West Indies, St Augustine,

Trinidad 1974–80, Acting Dir Inst. of Social and Econ. Research, Univ. of the West Indies 1974, Dir (rank of Full Prof.) 1977–82; Dir-Gen. Org. of Eastern Caribbean States, Castries, St Lucia 1982–95; Prime Minister of Saint Lucia 1996–97; Prof. of Int. Relations, Inst. of Int. Relations, Univ. of the West Indies 1999–; Visiting Prof. Fla Int. Univ. 1980, Ford Foundation Visiting Fellow Yale Univ. 1981. *Publications:* numerous books, papers and articles on int. relations, particularly concerning the Caribbean. *Address:* Institute of International Relations, University of the West Indies, St Augustine Campus, St Augustine, Trinidad and Tobago. *E-mail:* lewisv@diplomacy.edu (Office); lewisv@candw.lc (Home).

LEWITT, Sol, BFA; American artist; b. 1928, Hartford, Conn.; ed Syracuse Univ.; Instructor Museum of Modern Art School 1964–67, Cooper Union 1967, School of Visual Arts, NY 1969–70, New York Univ. 1970; numerous retrospective exhbns including retrospective travelling exhbn 1990–95; also represented in a number of perm. collections. *Solo exhibitions include:* Guggenheim Museum 1971, Museum of Modern Art, NY 1971, Walker Art Center 1972, Museum of Modern Art, Oxford 1973, Stedelijk Museum, Amsterdam 1974, Visual Arts Museum, NY 1976, San Francisco Museum of Art 1975, Wadsworth Atheneum, Hartford 1981, Musée d'Art Contemporain, Bordeaux 1983, Stedelijk Museum, Amsterdam 1984, Stedelijk Van Abbemuseum, Eindhoven 1984, Tate Gallery 1986, Hirshhorn Museum 1987, Walker Art Center, Minn. 1988, Kunsthalle, Berne 1989, Touko Museum of Contemporary Art 1990, San Francisco Museum of Modern Art 2000, Museum of Contemporary Art, Chicago, Whitney Museum of American Art, New York. *Group exhibitions include:* Sculpture Annual, Whitney Museum of American Art, NY 1967, Minimal Art, The Hague 1968, Städtische Kunsthalle, Düsseldorf 1969, La Jolla Museum of Contemporary Art 1970, Tokyo Biennale 1970, Guggenheim Int., NY 1971, Whitney Biennial NY 1979, Hayward Gallery, London 1980, Int. Sculpture Exhbn Basle 1980, Musée Nat. d'Art Moderne, Paris 1981, Art Inst. Chicago 1982, Museum of Modern Art, NY 1983, Museum of Contemporary Art, LA 1986, Venice Biennale 1988. *Publications:* numerous articles for specialist magazines on sculpture, drawing and conceptual art. *Address:* c/o Susanna Singer, 50 Riverside Drive, New York, NY 10024, USA.

LEYE, Jean-Marie; Ni-Vanuatu politician; Pres. of Vanuatu 1994–99. *Address:* c/o Office of the President, Port Vila, Vanuatu.

L'HEUREUX-DUBÉ, The Hon. Madame Justice Claire, BA, LLL; Canadian judge; b. 7 Sept. 1927, Québec City; d. of Paul L'Heureux and Marguerite Dion; m. Dr Arthur Dubé 1957 (died 1978); one s. (died 1994) one d.; ed Monastère des Ursulines, Rimouski, Coll. Notre-Dame de Bellevue, Québec, Laval Univ.; called to Québec Bar 1952; practised with Bard, L'Heureux & Philippon (known as L'Heureux, Philippon, Garneau, Tourigny, St Arnaud & Assocs. from 1969) 1952–73; Counsellor of the Québec Bar 1968–70, Del. at Gen. Council 1968–70; QC 1969; Lecturer in Family Law, Cours de formation professionnelle du Barreau du Québec 1970–73; Royal Comm. of Inquiries in matters relating to the Dept of Manpower and Immigration 1973–76; Judge, Superior Court of Québec 1973, Québec Court of Appeal 1979; Judge, Supreme Court of Canada 1987–2002; Vice-Pres. Canadian Consumers' Council 1970–73, Vanier Inst. of the Family 1972–73, Int. Soc. on Family Law 1982–88; mem. Canadian Bar Assocn, Canadian Inst. for Admin. of Justice; Pres. Family Law Cttee and Family Court Cttee, Québec Civil Code Revision Office 1972–76, Int. Comm. of Jurists (Canadian Section) 1981–83, Vice-Pres. 1992–98, Pres. 1998–2002; mem. Nat. Council, Canadian Human Rights Foundation 1980–84, Québec Assocn of Comparative Law (Pres. 1984–90); Chair. Editorial Bd The Canadian Bar Review 1985; Assoc. mem. Int. Acad. of Comparative Law 1992–; mem. American Law Inst. 1995–; numerous other professional appointments and affiliations; Hon. Lt Col Helicopter Squadron 430 1994 (retd 1996); Hon. mem. American Coll. of Trial Lawyers 1995; Hon.LLD (Dalhousie) 1981, (Montréal) 1983, (Laval) 1984, (Ottawa) 1988, (Québec à Rimouski) 1989, (Toronto) 1994, (Queen's) 1995, (Gonzaga) 1996, (Windsor) 2000, (York) 2001, (Concordia) 2001, (Law Soc. of Upper Canada) 2002; Medal of Québec Bar 1987, 1995, Montréal Bar 1994; Int. Year of the Family Medal (Québec) 1994, Canadian Award, Canadian Hadassah-WIZO 1996, Prix de la Justice, Canadian Inst. for the Administration of Justice 1997, Margaret Brent Women Lawyers of Achievement Award, ABA 1998, Int. Acad. of Law and Mental Health Yves Pélicier Award 2002. *Address:* Université Laval, rue des Sciences Humaines, Pavillon de Koninck, Bureau #3107, Québec City, G1K 7P4, Canada (Office).

LHO SHIN-YONG; South Korean politician and diplomatist; b. 28 Feb. 1930, S. Pyongyang Prov.; ed Law Coll. of Seoul Nat. Univ., Kentucky State Univ.; joined diplomatic service 1956, Dir Planning and Man. Office, Ministry of Foreign Affairs 1967; Consul-Gen., LA, USA 1969–72; Amb. to India 1973, to Geneva 1976; Vice-Foreign Minister 1974, Foreign Minister 1980–82, Prime Minister 1985–87; Head, Agency of Nat. Security Planning 1982–85; mem. Democratic Justice Party (later New Korea Party to be merged with Democratic Party to form Grand Nat. Party).

LI, Andrew K. N., QC, LLM; Chinese chief justice; b. (Li Kwok Nang Andrew), 12 Dec. 1948, Hong Kong; s. of Li Fook Kow and the late Edith Kwong Li; m. Judy Woo Mo Ying; two d.; ed St Paul's Co-Educational Coll., Hong Kong, Cambridge Univ., UK; called to Bar, Middle Temple 1970, Hong Kong 1973; practised at Hong Kong Bar 1973–97; Chief Justice, Court of Final Appeal of Hong Kong 1997–; Hon. Bencher Middle Temple 1997; Hon. Fellow Fitzwilliam Coll. Cambridge 1999; hon. degrees (Hong Kong Univ. of Science and

Tech.) 1993, (Baptist Univ.) 1994, (Open Univ. of Hong Kong) 1997, (Univ. of Hong Kong), (The Griffith Univ.) 2001, (Univ. of NSW) 2002. *Leisure interests:* reading, tennis, hiking, horse racing. *Address:* Court of Final Appeal, No. 1 Battery Path, Central, Hong Kong Special Administrative Region (Office); Chief Justice's House, 18 Gough Hill Road, The Peak, Hong Kong Special Administrative Region, People's Republic of China (Home). *Telephone:* 21230011 (Office); 28497169 (Home). *Fax:* 21210310 (Office); 28492191 (Home). *E-mail:* andrewknli@judiciary.gov.hk (Office). *Website:* www.info .gov.hk/jud (Office).

LI, Arthur K. C., G.B.S., BChir, MA, MD; British surgeon and academic; b. b. 23 June 1945, Hong Kong; ed King's Coll., Middlesex Hosp. Medical School; house physician, Addenbrooke's Hosp., Cambridge 1969–70, Rotational Sr House Officer 1970–71; house surgeon, Middx Hosp., London 1970; Rotational Surgical Registrar, Queen Elisabeth II Hosp. 1971-71, Hillingdon Hosp., Uxbridge 1972–73; Surgical Registrar, St. Mary's Hosp., London 1973–75; Lecturer in Surgery and Sr Surgical Registrar, Royal Free Hosp., London 1975–77; Chair. Div. of Jr Hosp. Doctors, Royal Free Hosp. London 1975–77; Consultant Surgeon and Sr Lecturer in Surgery 1980–82; Stanley Thomas Johnson Foundation Research Fellow, Harvard Medical School, Mass. Gen. Hosp. and Shriners Burns Inst., Boston 1977–78, Clinical and Research Fellow 1978–79, Surgical Staff and Instructor in Surgery 1979–80; Foundation Prof. of Surgery and Chair. of Surgical Services, Chinese Univ. of Hong Kong and the Prince of Wales Hosp. 1982–95, Assoc. Dean, Faculty of Medicine 1986–92, Dean 1992–96, Prof. of Surgery 1995, Vice-Chancellor (Pres.) and mem. of Univ. Council 1996–; Chair. Hosp. Gov. Cttee United Christian Hosp. 1987–97; mem. Bd United Christian Medical Services 1987–; Visiting Prof. Yale Univ. 1989; Pearce Gould Visiting Prof. in Surgery Univ. Coll. London and Middx School of Medicine 1993; Edward Tooth Prof., Royal Brisbane Hosp. 1995; mem. Int. Advisory Panel Ministry of Health, UAE 1993–; Edward Hallaran Bennett Lecturer, Trinity Coll. Dublin 1995; Sir Edward Dunlop Memorial Lecturer, Royal Australian Coll. of Surgeons 2000; Visiting Prof. RACS 1984, 1986, Nat. Univ. of Singapore 1986; Hon. Prof. of Surgery Sun Yat-sen Univ. of Medical Sciences, Guangzhou 1986; Hon. Prof. of Surgery, People's Hosp., Beijing Medical Univ. 1987; Hon. Prof. of Surgery, Mil. Postgrad. Medical School and Chinese PLA Gen. Hosp., Beijing 1994; Hon. Fellow Philippines Coll. of Surgeons 1994; Hon. FRCS (Glasgow) 1995; Hon. Prof. Peking Union Medical Coll. 1996; Hon. Fellow Sidney Sussex Coll. Cambridge; Hon. Prof. Shanghai Medical Univ.; Hon. FRSM 1997; Hon. FRCS (Ireland); Hon. FACS 2000; Hon. Fellow Assocn of Surgeons of Great Britain and Ireland 1998; Hon. DSc Hull Univ. 1999; Hon. DLitt Hong Kong Univ. of Science and Tech. 1999; Dr hc Soka Univ., Tokyo 1999; European Soc. for Surgical Research Prize 1980, Moynihan Medal 1982, Royal Coll. of Surgeons Gordon Watson Medal 1987, Stanford Cade Memorial Medal 1988, Royal Marsden Surgical Soc. Ernest Miles Memorial Medal 1990, Pres.'s Gold Medal Royal Coll. of Surgeons of Edin. 1996, Gold Bauhinia Star, Govt of Hong Kong Special Admin. Region 2000. *Publications:* numerous research papers in learned journals. *Leisure interests:* reading, skiing, scuba diving. *Address:* The Chinese University of Hong Kong, Shatin, New Territories, Hong Kong Special Administrative Region, People's Republic of China (Office). *Telephone:* (852) 26098600 (Office). *Fax:* (852) 26036197 (Office). *Website:* www .cuhk.edu.hk (Office).

LI, Richard; Hong Kong computer engineer and business executive; b. 1966; s. of Li Ka-shing; ed Stanford Univ., USA; cr. Star TV (first satellite cable TV network in Asia) 1992; Founder, Chair. and CEO Pacific Century Group (PCG—internet co.) 1993–, Pacific Century CyberWorks (PCCW) Ltd 1999– (PCCW merged with Cable & Wireless HKT 2000), PCWW Japan 2000–; Chair. Pacific Century Regional Devts Ltd; cr. Network of the World (NOW—internet and digital TV content service) 2000, NOW Japan 2001. *Address:* Pacific Century CyberWorks Ltd., Floor 39, PCCW Tower, Taikoo Place, 979 Kings Road, Quarry Bay 070, Hong Kong Special Administrative Region, People's Republic of China (Office). *Telephone:* 28882888 (Office). *Fax:* 28778877 (Office). *Website:* www.pccw.com (Office).

LI, Simon Fook-sean, LLB; Chinese judge (retd); b. 19 April 1922, Hong Kong; m. Maria Veronica Lillian; four s. one d.; ed King's Coll., Hong Kong, Univ. of Hong Kong, Nat. Kwangsi Univ., Univ. Coll. London, Lincoln's Inn, London; Crown Counsel, Attorney-Gen.'s Chambers 1953–65, Hong Kong Govt Dist Judge 1966–71, High Court Judge 1971–80, Justice of Appeal 1980–84, Vice-Pres. Court of Appeal 1984–87; Hong Kong Affairs Adviser, People's Repub. of China 1992–97; Deputy Dir Preparatory Cttee for Hong Kong Special Admin. Region (HKSAR) 1995–97; Dir Bank of E Asia, Hong Kong 1987–; Fellow Univ. Coll. London 1991; Hon. Fellow Chinese Univ. of Hong Kong 2002; Hon. LLD (Chinese Univ. of Hong Kong) 1986; Grand Bauhinia Medal, HKSAR 1997. *Address:* 3/F Shun Pont Commercial Building, 5–11 Thomson Road, Hong Kong Special Administrative Region, People's Republic of China (Office). *Telephone:* 2866 8680 (Office). *Fax:* 25202016 (Office); 25776490 (Home).

LI BAOTIAN; Chinese actor; b. Dec. 1946, Xuzhou, Jiangsu Prov.; ed Cen. Acad. of Drama; teacher Cen. Acad. of Drama 1981–; acted in Judou, Shanghai Triad, Prime Minister Hunchback Liu (TV series). *Address:* Central Academy of Drama, Beijing, People's Republic of China.

LI BOYONG; Chinese state official and engineer; b. 1932, Tianjin City; ed Air Force Inst. of Mil. Eng., fmr USSR; Vice-Minister, Labour and Personnel 1986–93; mem. 14th CCP Cen. Cttee 1992–97; Minister of Labour 1993–98;

Vice-Chair. Legal Affairs Cttee of 9th NPC 1998–. *Address:* c/o Standing Committee of National People's Congress, Beijing 100716, People's Republic of China.

LI CHANG'AN; Chinese party and state official; b. 1935, Tai'an Co., Liaoning Prov.; ed Shandong Tech. Coll.; joined CCP 1961; alt. mem. 12th CCP Cen. Cttee 1982, mem. 1985; Deputy Sec. CCP Cttee, Shandong Prov. 1983–88; Gov. of Shandong 1985–88; Deputy Sec.-Gen. CCP State Council 1987; Deputy Head State Flood Control Headquarters 1988, Cen. Forest Fire Prevention 1987; Deputy Head Leading Group for Comprehensive Agricultural Devt 1990–; Vice-Chair. State Tourism Cttee 1988. *Address:* State Council, Zhong Nan Hai, Beijing, People's Republic of China.

LI CHANGCHUN; Chinese party and government official; b. 1944, Jilin City; m. Zhang Shurong; ed Harbin Polytechnic Univ.; joined CCP 1965; Mayor, Shenyang Municipality 1983–86; Sec. Shenyang Mun. CCP Cttee 1985; Deputy Sec. Liaoning Prov. CCP Cttee 1985–86; Dir Foreign Affairs Office 1988–; Gov. of Liaoning Prov. 1986–90; Gov. of Henan Prov. 1991–93; Sec. CCP 5th Henan Prov. Cttee 1992–98; Chair. Standing Cttee Henan Provincial People's Congress 1993–98; alt. mem. 12th CCP Cen. Cttee 1985; Dir Foreign Affairs Office 1988–; mem. 13th CCP Cen. Cttee 1987–92, 14th CCP Cen. Cttee 1992–97, 15th CCP Cen. Cttee 1997–2002, CCP Politburo 1997–2002, 16th CCP Cen. Cttee 2002–, Standing Cttee CCP Politburo 2002–, Sec. CCP Guangdong Prov. Cttee 1998–. *Address:* Chinese Communist Party Guangdong Provincial Committee, Guangzhou, People's Republic of China.

LI CHUNTING; Chinese provincial governor; b. Oct. 1936, Luotang village, Zhaili, Qixia Co., Shandong Prov.; joined CCP 1958; worked as farmer; assumed leading posts at village, township, co., prefectural and city level; fmr Deputy Sec. CCP Qixia Co. Cttee, Deputy Sec. CCP Yantai Prefectural Cttee, Head Prov. Metallurgical Dept; Vice-Gov. Shandong Prov. 1988–95, Gov. 1995–2001; Deputy Sec. CCP Shandong Prov. Cttee 1992–2001; Vice-Chair. NPC Agric. and Rural Affairs Cttee 2001–. *Address:* National People's Congress, Tiananmen, Beijing, People's Republic of China.

LI DADONG; Chinese engineer; b. 24 Feb. 1938, Beijing; ed Peking Univ.; Fellow Chinese Acad. of Eng; Chair. Standing Cttee of Chemical Eng, Metallurgy and Material Eng Dept, Chinese Acad. of Eng; Sr Engineer and Dir Petrochemical Science Research Inst., China Petro-Chemical; developed 11 series of 16 varieties of hydrogenated catalytic agents; many nat., provincial and ministerial prizes. *Publications:* published 70 research papers. *Address:* Petrochemical Science Research Institute, 18 Xueyuan Road, Beijing 100083, People's Republic of China (Office). *Telephone:* (10) 62310757 (Office). *Fax:* (10) 62311290 (Office). *E-mail:* ripp@mimi.cnc.ac.cn (Office).

LI DAOYU; Chinese diplomatist; b. 7 Aug. 1932, Shanghai; m. Ye Zhao Lie 1956; two s.; ed Univ. of Shanghai; joined Foreign Service 1952; held various posts Dept of Int. Orgs and Confs; Deputy Perm. Rep. to UN at Geneva 1983–84; Dir Dept of Int. Orgs, Foreign Ministry 1984–88; Asst Foreign Minister 1988–90; Perm. Rep. to UN, New York 1990–93, Amb. to USA 1993–98; led Chinese Del. to ESCAP session 1989; fmr Vice-Chair. Chinese Nat. Comm., UNESCO, Nat. Cttee for Pacific Econ. Co-operation, Preparatory Cttee of China for Int. Space Year 1992, Nat. Cttee for Int. Decade for Natural Disaster Reduction; fmr rep. of China on Comm. on Human Rights, ECOSOC and UNCTAD; Vice-Chair. Overseas Chinese Affairs Cttee of 9th NPC 1998; mem. Standing Cttee NPC 1998–; Chair. Chinese Assen of Int. Public Relations 1999–, Chinese Assen of Arms Control and Disarmament 2001–. *Address:* c/o Ministry of Foreign Affairs, 225 Chaoyangmennei Dajie, Dongsi, Beijing 100701, People's Republic of China.

LI DESHENG, Gen.; Chinese army officer (retd); b. 1916, Xinxian Co., Henan Prov.; joined Red Army 1930, CCP 1932; Commdr, Red 4th Front Army on Long March 1934–36; Div. Commdr 2nd Field Army, People's Liberation Army 1949; Maj.-Gen. PLA 1955, Gen. 1988; Commdr Anhui Mil. Dist, PLA 1967; Chair. Anhui Revolutionary Cttee 1968; Alt. mem. Politburo, 9th Cen. Cttee of CCP 1969; Dir, Gen. Political Dept, PLA 1969–74; First Sec. CCP Anhui 1971–73; mem. Standing Cttee of Politburo and Vice-Chair. 10th Cen. Cttee of CCP 1973–75; mem. Politburo 11th Cen. Cttee of CCP 1977; mem. Politburo 12th Cen. Cttee of CCP 1982–85; Commdr Shenyang Mil. Region, PLA 1974–85, Head, Leading Group for the Prevention and Treatment of Endemic Disease in N China, Cen. Cttee 1977; First Sec. CCP Cttee, PLA Shenyang Mil. Region 1978–85; mem. Standing Cttee, Cen. Advisory Comm. 1985–92; Political Commissar, Leading Group of All-Army Financial and Econ. Discipline Inspection 1985–, PLA Nat. Defence Univ.; mem. Standing Comm. CCP Cen. Advisory Comm. 1985, 1987; Hon. Pres. Beijing Inst. of Modernization Admin Aug. 1986–; Sr Adviser China Soc. of Mil. Sciences 1991–; Pres. Chinese Patriotic Programs Fed. 1995–; Hon. Pres. Wushi (Martial Arts) Assen 1988–; mem. Presidium 14th CCP Nat. Congress Oct. 1992. *Address:* c/o Shenyang Military Region, People's Republic of China.

LI DEZHU; Chinese party and government official; b. 1943, Wangqing Co., Jilin Prov.; ed Yanbian Univ.; joined CCP 1965; Vice-Gov. of Jilin Prov. 1988–93; Deputy Head United Front Work Dept 1992–; Pres. Chinese Assen of Ethnic Minorities for External Exchanges 1992–; Minister State Comm. of Ethnic Affairs 1998–; mem. 14th CCP Cen. Cttee 1992–97, 15th CCP Cen. Cttee 1997–2002, 16th CCP Cen. Cttee 2002–. *Address:* State Ethnic Affairs Commision, 252 Teipingqiao Street, Beijing 100800, People's Republic of China. *Telephone:* (1) 66032288. *E-mail:* webmaster@mail.seac.gov.cn (Office). *Website:* www.seac.gov.cn.

LI FANG, BA, LLB; Chinese political scientist; b. 7 March 1925, Changde City, Hunan Prov.; s. of Li Xin Zhai and Wang Fu Ying; m. Zhang Cun Li 1954; one s. one d.; ed Nanjing Univ. and Beijing Foreign Studies Univ.; Prof. and Research Fellow, Beijing Inst. of Political Science, Chinese Acad. of Social Sciences 1980–; Dir Research Dept of Public Admin, Inst. of Political Science; Prof. Beijing Univ., Nanjing Univ., Lanzhou Univ.; Perm. Council mem. Chinese Soc. of Public Admin; council mem. Assen for Political Reform of China; Visiting Scolar and Research Fellow Erasmus Univ. (Holland), Newcastle Univ. (GB), Tokyo Univ., City Coll. of New York, Columbia Univ.; Murdoch Univ. (WA), Albert Einstein Inst. (USA); Deputy Ed.-in-Chief The Volume of Public Administration of the Encyclopaedia of China; Fellowship Ford Foundation 1989–90, Albert Einstein Inst. 1993–94; mem. Assen of Political Science of America, American Soc. of Public Admin. *Publications:* Selections from Chinese literature (2 vols) 1980, Outline of Public Administration, 1985, Elements of Public Administration 1989, Nonviolent Struggle 1997; numerous articles on science and literature. *Leisure interests:* carpentry, Chinese opera. *Address:* 9th Building, 905 Furongli, Wanquanhelu, Haidian, Beijing 100080; c/o Political Science Institute, Shatan Bei Jie, Beijing, 100720, People's Republic of China. *Telephone:* 2569305. *Fax:* 2562721. *E-mail:* bj-hd-lifang@263.net (Home).

LI FURONG; Chinese sports administrator; b. 1942, Shanghai City; Deputy, 5th NPC 1978–83; Deputy Dir Training Bureau under the Comm. for Physical Culture and Sports 1983, Dir 1986–; Vice-Chair. Youth Fed. 1983; Vice-Minister of the Physical Culture and Sports Comm. 1987; Sec.-Gen. Chinese Olympic Team, Seoul 1988; Vice-Pres. Chinese Olympic Cttee 1989–; apptd Vice-Minister in charge of State Gen. Admin for Sports 1999. *Address:* 9 Tiyuguan Road, Beijing 100763, People's Republic of China.

LI FUSHAN; Chinese artist and engraver; b. June 1940, Quinhuangdao, Hebei; s. of Li Yinchang and Wang Lihui; m. Lei Suoxia 1961; one s. two d.; worked at Quinhuangdao Cultural Centre 1959–62, at Shanhaiguan Cultural Centre 1962–, deputy researcher 1994–; his works are in pvt. collections in Canada, USA, Italy, NZ and countries in SE Asia; Dir Quinhuangdao Arts Asscn; mem. Hebei br. China Arts Asscn, Hebei Prov. Research Asscn of Etched Plates. *Leisure interests:* classical literature, photography. *Address:* Shanhaiguan Cultural Centre, Quinhuangdao, Hebei Province, People's Republic of China. *Telephone:* 5051418; 3069987.

LI GENSHEN; Chinese party official and engineer; b. 1 July 1930, Huzhou City, Zhejiang Prov.; s. of Li Xin-pei and Zhang Zhu-bao; m. Xu Ying; one s. two d.; ed Jiaotong Univ., Shanghai and in USSR; Dir and Chief Engineer, No. 3 Research Inst., No. 7 Research Acad., China Shipbuilding Industrial Corpn; Chair. Bd Harbin Power Equipment Co. 1993–97, Dir (non-exec.) 1997–; mem. Standing Cttee Heilongjiang Prov. CCP Cttee 1983–92, Sec.-Gen. 1984, Deputy Sec. 1985–86; Vice-Chair. Heilongjiang Prov. 8th People's Congress 1993–96; Sec. Harbin Mun. CCP Cttee 1985, Chair. 1983–; Standing Cttee CCP Heilongjiang Prov. Cttee 1988; mem. CCP Cen. Cttee 1987; mem. Standing Cttee 1988. *Publication:* Principles, Design and Testing of Marine Steam and Gas Turbines. *Leisure interest:* reading. *Address:* 1 Guomin Street, Nangang District, Harbin 150001, Heilongjiang Province, People's Republic of China. *Telephone:* (451) 3624054. *Fax:* (451) 2135700.

LI GUI RONG; Chinese brewery executive; fmr Deputy Dir, then Dir Qingdao Municipal Planning Comm.; Chair. Tsingtao Brewery Co. Ltd 1996–. *Address:* Tsingtao Beer Tower, May Fourth Square, Hong Kong Road, Central Qingdao, Shandong 266071, People's Republic of China (Office). *Telephone:* (532) 5711119 (Office). *Fax:* (532) 5714719 (Office). *Website:* www.tsingtaobeer.com.cn (Office).

LI GUIXIAN; Chinese party official; b. 1938, Gaixian Co., Liaoning Prov.; ed Mendeleyev Chemical Tech. Inst., Moscow; joined CCP 1962; Deputy Dir, Chief Engineer Jinzhou City Bureau of Electronics Industry 1977; Deputy Dir Liaoning Provincial Bureau of Electronics Industry 1979; Vice-Gov., Liaoning 1982–83; Sec. CCP Cttee, Liaoning Prov. 1985–86; Sec. CCP Cttee, Anhui Prov. 1986–88; Gov. PRC Cen. Bank 1988–93 (resgnd); mem. 14th CCP Cen. Cttee 1992–97; State Councillor 1993–98; Pres. State Administrative Coll. 1994–98; Head State Council Leading Group on Boundary Delimitation 1995–; mem. 15th CCP Cen. Cttee 1997–2002; Vice-Chair. Nat. Cttee of 9th CPPCC 1998; Pres. Chinese Assen for Int. Understanding 1999–; fmr Dir China Cttee of Int. Decade for Natural Disaster Reduction. *Address:* National Committee of Chinese People's Political Consultative Conference, 23 Taipingqiao Street, Beijing, People's Republic of China.

LI GUOGUANG; Chinese judge; Vice-Pres., mem. judicial Cttee Supreme People's Court 1995–. *Address:* Supreme People's Court, Beijing, People's Republic of China.

LI GUOHAO, EngD; Chinese bridge engineer; b. 13 April 1913, Meixian Co., Guangdong Prov.; ed Shanghai Tongji Univ., Darmstadt Polytech. Inst., Germany; Chair. Nanjing Changjiang River Bridge Tech. Advisory Cttee 1958–66; council mem. Shanghai People's Govt 1955–; Vice-Pres. Shanghai Tongji Univ. 1962–66; in disgrace during Cultural Revolution 1966–76; Pres. Shanghai Tongji Univ. 1979–84, Hon. Pres. 1984–; Vice-Pres. Soc. of Civil Eng of China 1984; Chair. Shanghai CPPCC 1983–88; Sr Fellow Chinese Acad. of Sciences, Chinese Acad. of Eng 1998–; Goethe Medal (Fed. Repub. of Germany) 1982. *Publications:* The Torsion Theory of Truss Girders-Torsion, Stability and Vibration of Truss Bridges 1977, Analysis of Box Girder and

Truss Bridges 1987 and 7 other monographs and 50 papers. *Address:* c/o Chinese Academy of Sciences, 52 San Li He Road, Beijing 100864, People's Republic of China. *Telephone:* 337833.

LI HAO; Chinese politician; b. Dec. 1926, Dianbai Co., Guangdong Prov.; s. of Li Hansan and Cheng Li; m. Cheng Huizheng 1943; one s. two d.; ed Zhongshan Univ., Guangzhou; joined CCP 1949; Deputy Sec.-Gen. of State Council, Beijing 1983–85; Vice-Gov. Guangdong Prov. 1985–88; Mayor, Shenzhen City, Sec. of CCP Shenzhen Cttee 1985–93; mem. and Vice-Chair. Financial and Econ. Cttee 8th NPC 1993–; part-time Prof. Beijing Univ. and People's Univ. of China. *Address:* Shenzhen People's Government, Guangdong, People's Republic of China. *Telephone:* (755) 2239440.

LI HONGZHI; Chinese spiritual leader; b. 7 July 1952, Jilin Prov.; m.; one d.; fmr stud farm worker, trumpeter in police band and grain clerk; leader Falun Gong spiritual movt 1992–; lives in exile in New York, USA. *Publication:* Zhuan Falun (Law of the Wheel) 1996. *Address:* c/o The Universe Publishing, P.O. Box 193, Gillette, NJ 07933, USA (Office). *Telephone:* (888) 353-2288 (Office). *Fax:* (888) 214-2172 (Office).

LI HUAJI; Chinese artist; b. 16 Feb. 1931, Beijing; s. of Li Jue-Tian and Zhang Yun-Zheng; m. Quan Zhenghuan 1959; two d.; mem. Acad. Cttee and Dir Mural Painting Dept, Cen. Acad. of Fine Arts; Vice-Dir Mural Painting Cttee, Artists' Asscn of China; mem. Oil Painting Research Asscn 1988–; important murals include Hunting (Harbin Swan Hotel), 5,000 Years of Culture (Beijing Nat. Library). *Leisure interests:* classical music, Beijing opera. *Address:* 6/F Hongmiao Beili, 100025 Beijing 3-601, People's Republic of China. *Telephone:* (1) 552213.

LI JIANGUO; Chinese politician; b. April 1946, Juanchen Co., Shandong Prov.; ed Shandong Univ., joined CCP 1971; Dir Gen. Office of CCP Tianjin Mun. Party Cttee 1983; Vice-Sec.-Gen., Dir Gen. Office of CCP Tianjin Mun. Party Cttee 1988, Sec.-Gen. 1989, Sec. CCP Heping Dist Cttee 1991; Vice-Sec. CCP Tianjin Mun. Cttee 1992; alt. mem. 14th CCP Cen. Cttee 1992; Sec. CCP Shaanxi Provincial Cttee 1997–2002, fmr Chair. Standing Cttee of People's Congress; mem. 15th CCP Cen. Cttee 1997–2002. *Address:* Chinese Communist Party Shaanxi Provincial Committee, Xian City, Shaanxi Province, People's Republic of China.

LI JIATING; Chinese politician; b. April 1944, Shiping, Yunnan Prov.; ed Tsinghua Univ.; joined CCP 1964; cadre CCP Heilongjiang Prov. Cttee; Vice-Dir Office of Heilongjiang Prov. Econ. Cttee; Comm. then Vice-Dir of Comm.; Vice-Mayor then Mayor of Harbin; Asst Gov. of Heilongjiang Prov. 1968–93; Vice-Gov. Yunnan Prov. 1993–98, Gov. 1998–2001; alt. mem. CCP 14th and 15th Cen. Cttees. 1992–2001; arrested and detained pending trial on corruption charges 2002. *Address:* c/o Yunnan Provincial People's Government, Kunming, People's Republic of China.

LI JI'NAI; Chinese military official; b. July 1942, Tengzhou City, Shandong Prov.; ed Harbin Acad. of Mil. Eng; joined CCP 1965; joined PLA 1967; various posts 2nd Artillery; Dir Cadre Dept PLA Gen. Political Dept 1987–90, Deputy Dir 1990–92; Deputy Political Commissar, State Comm. of Science, Tech. and Industry for Nat. Defence 1992–95, Political Commissar 1995, PLA Gen. Equipment Dept 1998–; rank of Maj.-Gen. 1988, Lt-Gen. 1993, Gen. 2000; alt. mem. 14th CCP Cen. Cttee; mem. 15th CCP Cen. Cttee 1997–2002. *Address:* State Commission of Science, Technology and Industry for National Defence, Jingshanqian Jie, Beijing, People's Republic of China. *Telephone:* (1) 6370000.

LI JING, Gen.; Chinese army officer and party official; b. 1930; ed Air Force Aviation Acad. of China; joined PLA 1946, CCP 1949; Deputy Chief PLA Navy Staff 1973–80; Deputy Commdr Naval Air Force 1980–82; Deputy Commdr PLA Navy 1982–92 and concurrently Commdr Naval Air Force 1985–90; Deputy Chief of PLA Gen. Staff HQ 1992–95; rank of Vice-Adm. 1988, Gen. 1994; mem. 7th NPC 1987–92; mem. 14th CCP Cen. Cttee 1992–97; mem. Standing Cttee, Vice-Chair. Foreign Affairs Cttee, 9th Nat. Cttee of CPPCC 1998–; Sr Adviser Int. Strategy Soc. 1998–. *Address:* c/o National Committee of Chinese People's Political Consultative Conference, 23 Taipingqiao Street, Beijing, People's Republic of China.

LI JINHUA; Chinese politician; b. 1943, Rudong Co., Jiangsu Prov.; ed Cen. Inst. of Finance and Banking; joined CCP 1965; Dir Econ. and Trade Dept of Shaanxi Prov. 1985; Deputy Auditor Gen. Nat. Audit Office 1985–98, Auditor Gen. 1998–; mem. 14th CCP Cen. Cttee for Discipline Inspection 1992; mem. 15th CCP Cen. Cttee 1997–2002, 16th CCP Cen. Cttee 2002–; Chair. Environmental Auditing Cttee (and mem. Governing Bd), Asian Org. of Supreme Audit Insts; Hon. Prof. Peking Univ., Nankai Univ., Cen. Univ. of Finance and Banking, Nanjing Audit Inst. *Leisure interests:* calligraphy, bridge, swimming, climbing. *Address:* National Audit Office, 1 Bei Lu Yuan, Zhanlan Road, Xicheng District, Beijing 100830, People's Republic of China. *Telephone:* (10) 68301502 (Office). *Fax:* (10) 68330958. *Website:* www.audit.gov.cn (Office).

LI JIULONG, Gen.; Chinese army officer; b. 1929, Fengrun Co., Hebei Prov.; joined Red Army and CCP 1945; took part in Jinzheng Campaign of Korean War 1953; Commdr, 160th Div., 54th Army 1972; Commdr, 54th Army 1980; Commdr Jinan Mil. Region, PLA 1985, Chengdu Mil. Region 1991–94; Vice-Chair. Internal Affairs and Judicial Cttee of 9th NPC 1998–; mem. 12th CCP Cen. Cttee 1985–87, 13th CCP Cen. Cttee 1987–92, 14th CCP Cen. Cttee 1992–97; rank of Lt-Gen. 1988, Gen. 1994. *Address:* Jinan Military Region Headquarters, Jinan, Shandong, People's Republic of China.

LI KA-SHING, CBE, JP; Chinese entrepreneur; b. 1928, Chaozhou; m. Chong Yuet-ming (deceased); two s.; moved with family from mainland to Hong Kong 1940; worked in watch-strap co. 1943; salesman, later Man. then Gen. Man., for toy mfg co. 1945–50; est. Cheung Kong Plastics Factory 1950; first real estate venture 1958; est. Cheung Kong Real Estate Co. Ltd 1971; Chair. Cheung Kong (Holdings) Ltd 1971–; acquired Hutchison Whampoa Ltd trading and industrial conglomerate 1979, Chair. 1981–; acquired Hong Kong Electric Holdings Ltd 1985; has investments in numerous countries; mem. Drafting Cttee for Basic Law of Hong Kong Special Admin. Region (HKSAR) 1985–90; Hong Kong Affairs Adviser for People's Repub. of China 1992–97; mem. Preliminary Working Cttee of the Preparatory Cttee for the HKSAR 1993–95, mem. Preparatory Cttee 1995–97; mem. Selection Cttee for the first Govt of the HKSAR Nov. 1996; f. Li Ka Shing Foundation Ltd 1980; f. Shantou Univ. 1981; Hon. citizen of eight cities in People's Repub. of China; Hon. KBE; Grand Officer of the Order Vasco Nunez de Balboa (Panama) 1982, Commdr Order of the Crown (Belgium) 1986, Commdr Order of Leopold (Belgium) 2000; Hon. LLD (Hong Kong) 1986, (Calgary, Canada) 1992, (Chinese Univ. of Hong Kong) 1997, (Cambridge, UK) 1999; Hon. DScS (Hong Kong Univ. of Science and Tech.) 1995, (City Univ. of Hong Kong) 1998, (Open Univ. of Hong Kong) 1999; Dr hc (Beijing) 1992; Adjudicator, Entrepreneur of the Millennium Award, The Times newspaper and Ernst & Young, UK 1999, Grand Bauhinia Medal 2001. *Address:* 70/F, Cheung Kong Center, 2 Queen's Road, Central, Hong Kong Special Administrative Region, People's Republic of China (Office). *Telephone:* (852) 21288888 (Office). *Fax:* (852) 28684491 (Office). *Website:* www.ckh.com.hk (Office).

LI KEQIANG; Chinese politician; b. 1955, Dingyuan Co., Anhui Prov.; ed Peking Univ.; joined CCP 1976; Sec. Communist Youth League, Beijing Univ. Cttee; Vice-Dir Dept of Schools and Colls of Communist Youth League Cen. Cttee; Sec. Secr. of Communist Youth League Cen. Cttee 1982–93, First Sec. Communist Youth League 1993–98; fmr Acting Gov. Henan Prov., Deputy Gov. 1998–99, Gov. 1999–2003, Chair. Standing Cttee People's Congress, He'nan Prov. 2003–; mem. 15th CCP Cen. Cttee 1997–2002. *Address:* c/o People's Government, Zhengzhou, Henan Province, People's Republic of China. *Website:* www.henan.gov.cn.

LI KEYU; Chinese fashion and costume designer; b. 15 May 1929, Shanghai; m. Yuan Mao 1955; ed Cen. Acad. of Fine Arts; Chief Costume Designer of Cen. Ballet; Deputy Dir Chinese Soc. of Stage Design; mem. Bd All-China Artists' Asscn, Chinese Dancers' Asscn; Deputy Dir China Export Garments Research Centre; Sr consultant, Beijing Inst. of Fashion Tech.; has designed costumes for many works, including Swan Lake, Le Corsaire, The Maid of the Sea, The Fountain of Bakhchisarai, La Esmeralda, The Red Detachment of Women, The East is Red, The New Year Sacrifice (Ministry of Culture costume design prize), Zigeunerweisen (Ministry of Culture costume design prize), Othello (for Peking Opera, Beijing's costume design prize), Tang Music and Dance, Zheng Ban Qiao (Houston Ballet), Fu (Hongkong Ballet), La Péri (Houston Ballet); winner sole costume design prize, 4th Japan World Ballet Competition, Osaka 1984. *Publications:* two vols of sketches. *Address:* 21 Gong-jian Hutong, Di An-Men, Beijing 100009, People's Republic of China. *Telephone:* 4035474.

LI LAIZHU, Gen.; Chinese army officer and party official; b. 1932, Shen Co., Shandong Prov.; ed PLA Mil. and Political Acad.; joined PLA 1947, CCP 1948; Deputy Commdr of Beijing Mil. Area Command 1985; rank of Lt-Gen. PLA 1988; Commdr Beijing Mil. Region 1994–97; Gen. mem. 14th CCP Cen. Cttee 1992–97; rank of Gen. 1994. *Address:* Beijing Military Area Command, People's Liberation Army, Beijing, People's Republic of China.

LI LANQING; Chinese government and party official; b. May 1932, Zhenjiang Co., Jiangsu Prov.; ed Shanghai Fudan Univ.; joined CCP 1952; Vice-Mayor Tianjin 1983–85; Vice-Minister Foreign Econ. Relations and Trade 1986–90, Minister 1990–93; mem. 8th NPC 1993–98; alt. mem. 13th CCP Cen. Cttee 1987–92; mem. 14th CCP Cen. Cttee 1992–97, 15th CCP Cen. Cttee 1997–2002; mem. CCP Politburo 1992–, Standing Cttee, CCP Politburo 1997–2002; Vice-Premier 1993–2002; Head Nat. Leading Group for Foreign Investments (State Council) 1994–; Chair. Academic Degrees Cttee 1995–; Deputy Head Cen. Leading Group for Party Bldg Work 1994–. *Address:* c/o Zhongguo Gongchan Dang (Chinese Communist Party), Zhongnanhai, Beijing, People's Republic of China.

LI LIGONG; Chinese party official; b. 20 Feb. 1925, Jiaocheng, Shanxi; s. of Li Zhengliang and Li Shi; m. Xie Bin; two s. three d.; Sec. CCP County Cttee, Sec. CCP Pref. Cttee, Sec. Communist Youth League of Shanxi Prov., mem. Cen. Cttee Communist Youth League 1953–65; Sec. Communist Youth League, Beijing Municipal Cttee 1966; Vice-Dir Beijing Municipal Revolutionary Cttee 1977; Sec. CCP Beijing Municipal Cttee 1978–81; Exec. Sec. CCP Shanxi Prov. Cttee 1981–83, Sec. 1983–91; Dir CCP Shanxi Advisory Cttee 1991–92; mem. CCP Cen. Comm. for Inspecting Discipline 1979–82; mem. 12th Cen. Cttee CCP 1982, 13th Cen. Cttee 1987; mem. Standing Cttee 8th NPC 1992–98; mem. 9th NPC 1998–. *Publication:* Shanxi in Contemporary China (Chief Ed.). *Leisure interests:* swimming, fencing, tennis, hiking. *Address:* General Office of the Chinese Communist Party Shanxi Provincial Committee, 369 Yingze Street, Taiyuan, Shanxi, People's Republic of China. *Telephone:* 4045093.

LI LIN; Chinese physicist; b. 31 Oct. 1923, Beijing; d. of J.S. Lee and Lin Hsu; m. C. L. Tsou 1949; one d.; ed Birmingham Univ., Cambridge Univ., UK;

returned to China 1951; researcher, Mechanics Lab., Academia Sinica 1951–57; Research Fellow, Beijing Atomic Energy Inst. 1958–; Research Fellow, Inst. of Physics, Academia Sinica 1978–; mem. Dept of Math. and Physics, Academia Sinica 1980–; mem. Chinese Acad. of Sciences; First Prize Nat. Science and Tech. Awards; winner of several collective prizes. *Leisure interest:* music. *Address:* Institute of Physics, Chinese Acad. of Sciences, P.O. Box 603, Beijing 100080, People's Republic of China. *Telephone:* (10) 82649175 (Office); (10) 68422342 (Home). *Fax:* (10) 82649531 (Office). *E-mail:* lilin@aphy.iphy.ac.cn (Office); annalee@yeah.com (Home).

LI LING; Chinese musician; b. 28 Dec. 1913, Taishan Co., Guangdong Prov.; s. of Li Daoxi and Wu Lianzhu; m. Chen Yunfeng; one s. three d.; ed Yan'an Lu Xun Art Coll.; joined CCP 1941; Art Dir, Cen. Song and Dance Ensemble 1952–56; Dir Cen. Philharmonic Soc. 1956–66; in disgrace during Cultural Revolution 1966–77; Vice-Chair. Chinese Musicians' Asscn 1979–; Sec. Fed. Literary and Art Circles of China 1981–; Dir China Musical Coll. 1980–86; Vice-Chair. Standing Cttee, 8th Guizhou Provincial Peoples' Congress 1994–. *Leisure interest:* painting. *Address:* Chinese Musicians Association, Beijing, People's Republic of China. *Telephone:* (1) 5029308.

LI LINGWEI; Chinese badminton player; b. 1964; won women's singles title at 3rd World Badminton Championships, Copenhagen 1982; elected 7th in list of ten best Chinese athletes 1984; won women's singles and women's doubles (co-player Wu Dixi) at 5th ALBA World Cup, Jakarta 1985; won women's singles, at World Badminton Grand Prix finals, Tokyo 1985, at Dunhill China Open Badminton Championships, Nanjing 1987, at Malaysian Badminton Open, Kuala Lumpur 1987, at World Grand Prix, Hong Kong 1988, at China Badminton Open 1988, at Danish Badminton Open, Odense 1988, at All-England Badminton Championships 1989, at 6th World Badminton Championships, Jakarta; coached Chinese women's singles players; mem. Int. Badminton Fed. (IBF) Events and Devt Cttee; IBF Hall of Fame 1998. *Address:* China Sports Federation, Beijing, People's Republic of China.

LI LUYE; Chinese diplomatist; b. 1925, Beijing; Dir Dept of Int. Orgs of Foreign Ministry 1980–; Pres. of Chinese People's Asscn for Friendship with Foreign Countries 1990–, Dir Chinese Int. Studies Centre 1990–, Vice-Chair. Foreign Affairs Cttee; Pres. China Nat. Cttee for Pacific Econ. Co-operation 1991; mem. Standing Cttee of 8th NPC 1993–98. *Address:* Chinese People's Association for Friendship with Foreign Countries, Taijichang, Beijing 100002, People's Republic of China.

LI MORAN; Chinese actor; b. 28 Nov. 1927, Shangzhi, Heilongjiang Prov.; joined Qingwen Drama Soc. 1945; joined the Arts Troupe affiliated to Northeast Arts Workers' Asscn in Harbin 1947; actor, Vice-Pres., Pres. Liaoning People's Arts Theatre 1954–; Chair. Chinese Dramatists' Asscn. *Address:* 52 Dongsi Ba Tiao, Beijing 100007, People's Republic of China (Office). *Telephone:* (10) 64042457 (Office).

LI PENG; Chinese politician; b. Oct. 1928, Shanghai City; s. of the late Li Shuoxun and of Zhao Juntao; m. Zhu Lin 1958; two s. one d.; ed Moscow Power Inst.; Vice-Minister of Electric Power Industry 1980–81, Minister 1981–82; Vice-Minister of Water Conservancy and Electric Power 1982–83; Vice-Premier of State Council 1983–87; Minister in Charge of State Educ. Comm. 1985–86; Acting Premier 1987–88; Premier of People's Repub. of China 1988–98; Chair. Standing Cttee 9th NPC 1998–2003; mem. 12th Cen. Cttee of CCP 1982–87, 13th CCP Cen. Cttee 1987–92, 14th CCP Cen. Cttee 1992–97, 15th CCP Cen. Cttee 1997–2002; mem. Political Bureau 1985–2002, Standing Cttee 1987–2002; mem. Secr. CCP Cen. Cttee 1985–87; announced retirement 2003. *Address:* c/o Zhongguo Gongchan Dang (Chinese Communist Party), Zhongnanhai, Beijing, People's Republic of China.

LI QI; Chinese artist; b. Sept. 1928, Pingyao, Shanxi Prov.; ed North China United Univ.; Lecturer then Prof. of Chinese Painting, Cen. Acad. of Fine Art 1950–; several portraits of Chinese leaders. *Publication:* Portraits by Li Qui. *Address:* Central Academy of Fine Art, 5 Xiaowei Hutong, East District, Beijing 100730, People's Republic of China.

LI QIANYUAN, Maj.-Gen.; Chinese army officer; b. March 1942, Linxian, Henan Prov.; ed Zhengzhou Textile Machinery Inst., PLA Mil. Acad.; joined PLA 1961; joined CCP May 1963; divisional chief of staff, army group Commdr 1982–90; Deputy Chief of Staff, Guangzhou Mil. Command 1990–94; Chief of Staff, Lanzhou Mil. Command 1994–99, Commdr 1999–; mem. 13th CCP Cen. Cttee 1987–92; alt. mem. 15th CCP Cen. Cttee 1997–2002. *Address:* Headquarters, Lanzhou Military Command, Lanzhou, Gansu Province, People's Republic of China (Office).

LI QINGKUI, PhD; Chinese biologist and administrator; b. 1912, Ningpo Co., Zhejiang Prov.; ed Univ. of Illinois, USA; Chair. Soc. of Pedology 1962; Deputy Dir Nanjing Inst. of Pedology 1965; Pres. Soc. of Pedology 1978; Vice-Chair. Jiangsu Prov. CP 1983; mem. Dept of Biology, Academia Sinica 1985–. *Address:* Nanjing Institute of Pedology, Nanjing City, Jiangsu Province, People's Republic of China.

LI RENCHEN; Chinese journalist; b. Oct. 1941, Changyi County, Shandong Prov.; ed Fudan Univ.; mem. CCP 1975–; Features and Photos Service, Comm. for Cultural Relations with Foreign Countries 1964–66; Ed. Huizhou Bao, Anhui Prov.; Ed. People's Daily and Deputy Dir Commentary Dept People's Daily 1983–86; Deputy Ed.-in-Chief, Renmin Ribao (People's Daily)

1986–; writes under pen name Chen Ping. *Address:* Renmin Ribao, 2 Jin Tai Xi Lu, Choo Yong Men Nai, Beijing100733, People's Republic of China. *Telephone:* (1) 65092121. *Fax:* (1) 65091982.

LI RONGRONG; Chinese economist and state official; b. Dec. 1944, Suzhou, Jiangsu Prov.; ed Tianjin Univ.; workshop chief Wuxi Oil Pump and Oil Throttle Factory, Deputy Man., then Man. 1968–86; Vice-Chair. Wuxi Econ. Comm., Dir Wuxi Bureau of Light Industry, Chair. Wuxi Planning Comm.; Deputy Dir State Council Production Office; Vice-Chair. Jiangsu Prov. Planning and Econ. Comm. 1986–91, State Council Econ. and Trade Office, State Devt Planning Comm.; Sec.-Gen. State Econ. and Trade Comm., Deputy Dir 1992–95, Vice-Chair. 1996–2001, Chair. 2001–; joined CCP 1983. *Address:* 26 Xuanwumen West Street, Beijing 100053, People's Republic of China (Office). *Telephone:* (10) 63192154 (Office). *E-mail:* webmaster@setc .gov.cn (Office). *Website:* www.setc.gov.cn (Office).

LI RUI; Chinese party official; b. 1917, Pingjiang Co., Hunan Prov.; ed Wuhan Univ.; joined CCP 1937; cadre in Hunan 1950; Asst Minister of Water Conservancy and Electrical Power 1955–58; in political disgrace 1967–79; Vice-Minister, 4th Ministry of Machine Building 1979–82; Vice-Minister, Power Industry 1979–82; Dir State Bureau of Computers 1980–; mem. 12th Cen. Cttee CCP 1982–85; mem. Cen. Advisory Comm. 1987–; Deputy Dir State Bureau of Tech. Supervision 1991–; Deputy Head Org. Dept CCP 1983. *Publications:* The Early Revolutionary Activities of Comrade Mao Zedong, Some Fundamental Problems Concerning the Total Utilization Plan for the Yellow River. *Address:* Central Committee of the Chinese Communist Party, Beijing, People's Republic of China.

LI RUIHUAN; Chinese party and government official; b. Sept. 1934, Baodi Co., Tianjing; Vice-Chair. Beijing Trade Union 1973; Dir-Gen. Work Site for Mao Zedong Memorial Hall, Beijing 1977; Deputy for Beijing, 5th NPC 1978; Sec. Communist Youth League 1979–81; mem. Standing Cttee, 5th NPC 1978–83; Deputy Mayor Tianjin 1981, Acting Mayor 1982, Mayor Tianjin 1982–89; Sec. CCP Cttee, Tianjin 1982–89; Vice-Pres. All-China Youth Fed. 1980; mem. 12th CCP Cen. Cttee 1982–87, 13th CCP Cen. Cttee 1987–92, 14th CCP Cen. Cttee 1992–97, 15th CCP Cen. Cttee 1997–2002; mem. Politburo 1987–2002, Standing Cttee Politburo 1989, Perm. mem. Politburo 1992–2002; Chair. 8th Nat. Cttee CPPCC 1993–98; Chair. 9th Nat. Cttee CPPCC 1998–2002; named Nat. Model Worker 1979; Hon. Pres. Chinese Fed. for the Disabled 1993–; Hon Pres. Chinese Table Tennis Asscn 1990–. *Address:* Zhongguo Gongchan Dang (Chinese Communist Party), Zhongnanhai, Beijing, People's Republic of China.

LI SANLI, DSc; Chinese computer scientist; b. 1935, Shanghai; ed Tsinghua Univ., Acad. of Sciences, USSR; Co-Chair. Accreditation Cttee Computer Discipline of State Academic Comm. of the State Council; Deputy Chief Ed. China Computer Encyclopaedia; Exec. Dir of China Computer Fed.; Pres. IEEE in China; Dir of EUROMICRO in Europe; Dir Research Inst. of Computer Sciences and Eng, Qinghua Univ., Jt Dean Coll. of Computer Eng and Science, Shanghai Univ. *Publications:* 11 books including RISC–Single and Multiple Issue Architecture and more than 100 research papers. *Address:* Research Institute of Computer Sciences and Engineering, Qinghua University, 1 Qinghuayuan,Beijing 100084, People's Republic of China (Office). *Telephone:* 62561144 (Office). *Fax:* 62562768 (Office).

LI SHENGLIN; Chinese politician; b. Nov. 1946, Nantong Co., Jiangsu Prov.; ed Zhejiang Coll. of Agricultural Machinery 1970; joined CCP 1973; Vice-Mayor of Tianjin 1991–93, Mayor 1993–; Vice-Sec. CCP Tianjin Mun. Cttee 1993–; mem. 15th CCP Cen. Cttee 1997–2002. *Address:* Chinese Communist Party Tianjin Municipal Committee, Tianjin, People's Republic of China.

LI SHENZHI; Chinese international affairs scholar; b. 1923, Wuxi, Nanjing Prov.; ed Chengdu Yanjing Univ.; joined CCP 1948; section head, Vice-Dir Int. Affairs Dept, Xinhua News Agency 1949–57; branded a "rightist" and exiled 1957–79; Dir Inst. of American Studies, Chinese Acad. of Social Sciences; Vice-Pres. Chinese Acad. of Social Sciences 1979–. *Address:* Chinese Academy of Social Sciences, 5 Jianguomen Nei Dajie, Beijing 100732, People's Republic of China (Office).

LI SHIJI; Chinese opera singer; b. May 1933, Suzhou Co., Jiangsu Prov.; Head First Troupe, Beijing Opera Theatre 1989–; mem. 7th CPPCC 1988–93, 8th 1993–98; Vice-Chair. China Fed. of Literary and Art Circles 2001. *Beijing Operas include:* Wenji's Return to the Hans, Concubine Mei, A Green Jade Hairpin, Wedding on the Execution Ground. *Address:* Beijing Opera Theatre, 11 Hufang Road, Xuanwu District, Beijing 100052, People's Republic of China.

LI TIEYING; Chinese state official; b. Sept. 1936, Yan'an, Shaanxi Prov.; s. of late Li Weihan; m. Qin Xinhua; ed Charles Univ., Czechoslovakia; fmr deputy Dir of an electronics research inst.; Sec. CCP Cttee, Shenyang Municipality 1981–85; alt. mem. 12th CCP Cen. Cttee 1982, mem. 1985; mem. 13th CCP Cen. Cttee 1987–92, 14th CCP Cen. Cttee 1992–97, 15th CCP Cen. Cttee 1997–2002; Sec. CCP Cttee, Liaoning Prov. 1983–86; Minister of Electronics Industry 1985–88; Minister in charge of State Educ. Comm. 1988–93, of State Comm. for Econ. Reconstruction 1987–88; Chair. Cen. Patriotic Public Health Campaign Cttee; State Councillor 1988–98; Minister of State Ed. Comm. 1988–93, of State Comm. for Econ. Restructuring 1993–; Head Leading Group for the Reform of the Housing System 1993–; Deputy Head Nat. Leading Group for Anti-Disaster and Relief Work 1991–; Pres.

Chinese Acad. of Social Sciences 1998–; mem. Politburo of CCP 1992–; Del., World Conf. on Educ., Bangkok 1990, visited India, Laos 1992; Hon. Pres. Athletics Asscn, Soc. of Nat. Conditions. *Address:* Politburo, Zhongguo Gongchan Dang, Beijing (Office); Chinese Academy of Social Sciences, 5 Jianguomen Nei Da Jie, Beijing 100732, People's Republic of China. *Telephone:* 65137744 (Office).

LI WEIKANG; Chinese opera singer; b. Feb. 1947, Beijing; ed China Acad. of Traditional Operas; Dir Troupe No. 2, China Peking Opera Co., performer Beijing Peking Opera Co. 1987–; Plum Blossom Award 1984; Gold Album Award, for Lead Role at Nat. Theatrical Performance Ass.; Gold Prize at Nat. Mei Lanfang Grand Competition; Gold Eagle Award for Best Actress. *Address:* Beijing Opera Company, Beijing, People's Republic of China (Office).

LI XIMING; Chinese party and government official; b. 1926, Shulu Co., Hebei Prov.; ed Qinghua Univ.; Sec. CCP Cttee, Shijingshan Power Plant; identified as Govt cadre 1975; Vice-Minister of Water Conservancy and Electric Power 1976–79; Vice-Minister of Electric Power Industry 1979–82; Minister of Urban and Rural Construction and Environmental Protection 1982–84; mem. 12th Cen. Cttee, CCP 1982–87; mem. Politburo 13th Cen. Cttee CCP 1987–92; First Political Commissar PLA Garrison, Beijing 1984–92; CCP First Sec. Beijing 1984–92; mem. Political Bureau CCP; Vice-Chair. Cen. Patriotic Public Health Campaign Cttee, CCP Cen. Cttee 1983; Vice-Chair. Environmental Protection Cttee, State Council 1984; Pres. Urban Devt Scientific Research Soc. 1984; Vice-Chair. Cen. Greening Cttee 1983; Vice-Chair. Standing Cttee of 8th NPC 1993–98. *Address:* Standing Committee of National People's Congress, Beijing, People's Republic of China.

LI XINLIANG, Gen.; Chinese army officer and party official; b. 1936, Laiyang Co., Shandong Prov.; joined PLA 1953, CCP 1956; Commdr Autonomous Region Mil. Dist, Guangxi Prov. 1983–88; Party Cttee Sec. PLA Guangxi Mil. Area Command 1986–89; mem. 13th CCP Cen. Cttee 1987–92; Deputy Commdr Guangzhou Mil. Region 1989–94; Political Commissar Shenyang Mil. Region 1994–95, Commdr Shenyang Mil. Area Command 1995–97; rank of Lt-Gen. 1993; Commdr Beijing Mil. Area Command 1997; rank of Gen. 1998; mem. 15th CCP Cen. Cttee 1997–2002. *Address:* Commander's Office, Beijing Military Area Command, Beijing, People's Republic of China.

LI XU'E; Chinese state and aerospace official; b. 1928, Hanyang, Hubei Prov.; ed Qinghua Univ.; joined CCP 1955; Vice-Minister of Space Industry 1982–85; Minister of Astronautics (Space) Industry 1985–88; Vice-Minister State Science and Tech. Comm. 1988–93; Chair. Bd of Dirs China Science and Tech. Consultant Corpn 1983–; Vice-Chair. Environmental Protection Cttee 1988–; a Deputy Head Co-ordination Group for Weather Change 1990–; a Vice-Chair. China Cttee of Int. Decade for Nat. Disaster Reduction 1991–; Pres. Soc. of Social Devt Science 1992–, of China Soc. of Geographic Information System 1994–; mem. 12th CCP Cen. Cttee 1982–87, 8th NPC 1993–98, 9th NPC 1998–; Vice-Chair. Educ., Science, Culture and Public Health Cttee; Head Dels to Poland, Finland, India. *Address:* Standing Committee of National People's Congress, Beijing, People's Republic of China.

LI YAN, (Zhuang bei); Chinese painter; b. Nov. 1943, Beijing; s. of Li Ku Chan and Li Hui Wen; m. Sun Yan Hua 1972; one d.; Prof. Cen. Inst. of Arts and Crafts and of Shandong; fmr Vice-Pres. Li Ku Chan Museum; mem. Chinese Artists' Asscn; Assoc. Prof. Cen. Acad. of Art and Design; Deputy Dir of Li Kuchan Memorial; Vice-Pres. Int. Soc. Yi Jing, Research Fellow Research Soc. Yi Jing; Specialist, Appraising Cttee of Chinese Arts of Calligraphy and Painting; specializes in painting figures, animals and mountains and water scenes and in calligraphy; over 10,000 sketches and paintings from life, 3,000 exercises in Chinese painting 1956–; mem. 9th CPPCC 1998–; mem. Beijing PCCC; works have been exhibited in Sweden, USA, Canada, Japan, Singapore, Philippines, Hong Kong, Tanzania; gave lectures at Hong Kong Univ. 1980; held lectures and exhbn in India 1989, in Malaysia 1991, in Indonesia 1993; subject of TV films by Shen Zhen TV 1986 and Swedish TV 1986, presenter of CCTV's The Wind of China 1995; important works include Chinese Emperor, Zhou Wen Emperor, Lao Zi, Confucian Worry about Taoism, Lao Zi and Einstein, Five-Colour Earth, Start Sailing, A Swarm of Monkeys, Cat and Chrysanthemum, Tiger Cub. *Publications:* Yi Jing Album 1993; several magazine articles on art. *Leisure interests:* writing poetry, Qigong, The Book of Changes. *Address:* No. 2-1, Building 15, Nan sha Go, San Li He, Xi Cheng District, Beijing, People's Republic of China. *Telephone:* 68523844.

LI YINING; Chinese economist; b. Nov. 1930, Yizheng Co., Jiangsu Prov.; ed Peking Univ.; Prof., Dean Economy Admin. Dept, Peking Univ.; joined CCP 1984; Vice-Chair. 8th Chinese Democratic League Cen. Cttee 1997–; mem. Standing Cttee 7th NPC, 8th NPC; Vice-Chair. Finance and Econ. Cttee of 9th NPC 1998–; now Dean Guanhua School of Man. *Address:* Guanhua School of Management, Peking University, 5 Yiheyuan Road, Hai Diau, Beijing 100871, People's Republic of China. *Telephone:* 62752114 (Office). *Fax:* 627517207 (Office). *Website:* www.pku.edu.cn (Office).

LI YIYI; Chinese metallurgist; b. 20 Oct. 1933, Suzhou, Jiangsu Prov.; ed Beijing Univ. of Iron and Steel Tech.; China's first female workshop chief in charge of a blast furnace in 1950s; researcher Metal Research Inst., Chinese Acad. of Sciences 1962–, Vice-Dir 1986, Dir 1990–98; mem. 4th Presidium, Chinese Acad. of Sciences 2000–; Fellow Chinese Acad. of Sciences; Vice-Pres. Chinese Soc. for Metals and Chinese Materials Research Society; developed

five series of hydrogen-resistant steels; Nat. Science and Tech. Advancement Award (twice); Chinese Acad. of Sciences Award for Advancement in Science and Tech. (three times). *Publications:* more than 150 research papers. *Address:* Metal Research Institute, Chinese Academy of Sciences, 72 Wenhua Road, Shenyang 110015, People's Republic of China (Office). *Telephone:* (24) 3843531 (Office). *Fax:* (24) 3891320 (Office). *E-mail:* yyli@imr.ac.cn (Office).

LI YUANCHAO; Chinese politician; b. 1950, Lianshui Co., Jiangsu Prov.; ed Shanghai Fudan Univ.; joined CCP 1978; Sec. Communist Youth League 1983; Sec. Shanghai Branch of the Communist Youth League 1983; Dir Nat. Cttee for Young Pioneers' work under the Communist Youth League 1984; Vice-Chair. Youth Fed. 1986–96; Deputy Dir First Bureau, Information Office 1993–, Cen. Office for Overseas Publicity 1994–2000; Vice-Minister of Information Office, State Council 1993–96, of Culture 1996–2000; Vice-Sec. CCP Jiangsu Prov. Cttee 2000–; Vice-Chair. Women and Youth Cttee; mem. CPPCC 7th Nat. Cttee 1988–93. *Address:* Chinese Communist Party, Jiangsu Provincial Committee, Nanjing, People's Republic of China.

LI ZEHOU; Chinese philosopher; b. 1930, Changsha, Hunan Prov.; ed Hu'an No. 1 Prov. Normal School, Peking Univ.; Asst Research Fellow, Assoc. Research Fellow then Research Fellow Philosophy Inst., Chinese Acad. of Sciences 1955–; Vice-Chair. Aesthetics Soc. of China; mem. Exec. Council Chinese Writers Asscn and Soc. of Sun Yat-sen Studies. *Publications:* Critique of Critical Philosophy, The Course of Beauty, History of Chinese Aesthetics, Essays on China's Ancient Intellectual History. *Address:* Institute of Philosophy, Chinese Academy of Social Sciences, Beijing, People's Republic of China (Office).

LI ZEMIN; Chinese party official; b. 1934, Cangxi Co., Sichuan Prov.; Deputy Sec. Shenyang Mun. CCP Cttee Liaoning Prov. 1985; Deputy Sec. Liaoning Prov. CCP Cttee 1985–86; mem. 13th CCP Cen. Cttee 1987–92; Sec. CCP Zhejiang Prov. Cttee 1988–98; Chair. Standing Cttee of People's Congress 1993–; mem. 15th CCP Cen. Cttee 1997–2002. *Address:* Standing Committee of Zhejiang Provincial People's Congress, Hangzhou, Zhejiang Province, People's Republic of China.

LI ZHAOXING, MA; Chinese politician and diplomatist; b. Oct. 1940, Jiaonan, Shandong Prov.; m.; one s.; ed Peking Univ., Beijing Foreign Languages Inst.; joined CCP Dec. 1965; clerk Soc. of Diplomacy 1967–70; attaché Embassy, Kenya 1970–77; clerk Information Dept, Ministry of Foreign Affairs 1977–83; First Sec. Embassy, Lesotho 1983–85; Vice-Dir then Dir Information Dept, Ministry of Foreign Affairs 1985–90; Asst to Minister of Foreign Affairs 1990–92; Chinese Rep. and Amb. to UN 1992–95; Vice-Minister of Foreign Affairs 1995–98; Amb. to USA 1998–2000; Vice-Minister of Foreign Affairs 2000–03, Minister of Foreign Affairs 2003–; alt. mem. 15th CCP Cen. Cttee 1997–2002, 16th CCP Cen. Cttee 2002–. *Address:* Ministry of Foreign Affairs, 225 Chaoyang-mennei Dajie, Dongsi, Beijing 100701, People's Republic of China (Office). *Telephone:* (10) 65961114 (Office). *Fax:* (10) 65962146 (Office). *E-mail:* webmaster@fmprc.gov.cn (Office). *Website:* www.fmprc.gov.cn (Office).

LI ZHAOZHUO; Chinese politician; b. Sept. 1944, Pingguo, Guangxi; ed Guangxi Univ., Nanning; joined CCP 1974; technician Debao Co. Hydroelectric Power Bureau, Guangxi 1975; Sec. Nanning Municipal Cttee –1997; Vice-Sec. Guangxi Zhuang Autonomous Region Cttee 1997–98; Chair. People's Govt of Guangxi Zhuang Autonomous Region 1998–; mem. 15th CCP Cen. Cttee 1997–2002. *Address:* People's Government of Guangxi Zhuang Autonomous Region, 1 Minle Road, Nanning 530012, Guangxi, People's Republic of China (Office). *Telephone:* (771) 284114 (Office). *E-mail:* gov@gxi .gov.cn. *Website:* www.gxi.gov.cn (Office).

LI ZHENGWU; Chinese academic; Pres. Soc. of Nuclear Fusion and Plasma 1980–; mem. Nat. Cttee 7th CPPCC 1988–93. *Address:* Chinese Academy of Sciences, 52 San Li He Road, Beijing 100864, People's Republic of China.

LI ZHENSHENG; Chinese geneticist; b. 1931, Zibo, Shandong Prov.; ed Shandong Agricultural Coll.; Dir Northwest Botanical Research Inst.; Fellow Chinese Acad. of Sciences, now Vice-Pres.; Vice-Chair. China Science and Tech. Asscn; mem. 4th Presidium, Chinese Acad. of Sciences 2000–; bred super wheat varieties Xiaoyan Nos. 4, 5 and 6; created the blue-grained wheat monosomic system (BGM); pioneered 'the nullisomic backcrossing method' for fast breeding alien substitution lines of wheat and laid a foundation for wheat chromosome eng breeding; awarded title of Nat. Model Worker 1980. *Publications:* Outline of Distant Hybridisation of Plants, Distant Hybridisation of Wheat. *Address:* Chinese Academy of Sciences, 52 Sanlihe Road, Beijing 100864, People's Republic of China (Office).

LIAN, Hans Jacob Biörn; Norwegian diplomatist; b. 31 March 1942, Oslo; ed Univ. of Neuchâtel, Switzerland; Political Dir 1992–94, Amb. and Perm. Rep. to UN, NY 1994–98, to NATO 1998–. *Address:* North Atlantic Treaty Organization, blvd Léopold III, 1110 Brussels (Office); 2, clos Henri Vaes, Brussels, Belgium (Home). *Telephone:* (2) 707-41-11 (Office); (2) 731-86-62 (Home). *Fax:* (2) 707-45-79 (Office). *E-mail:* hjbl@mfa.no, natodoc@hq.nato .int (Office). *Website:* www.nato.into (Office).

LIANG, Dong-Cai, PhD; Chinese molecular biophysicist and protein crystallographer; b. 29 May 1932, Guangzhou; ed Zhong-Shan Univ., Inst. of Organo-Element Compounds, USSR Acad. of Sciences, Royal Inst., UK, Oxford Univ., UK; Prof., Inst. of Biophysics, Chinese Acad. of Sciences (Dir

1983–86); mem. Chinese Acad. of Sciences 1980–, Dir Biology Div.; Fellow Third World Acad. of Sciences 1985–; Vice-Chair. Nat. Natural Science Foundation of China 1986–95, adviser 1995–98, Chair. Inspection Cttee 1998–2001; mem. Cttee on Biomacromolecule Crystallography of Int. Soc. of Crystallography 1981–84; mem. Council of Int. Soc. of Biophysics 1993–99, 4th Presidium of Depts., Chinese Acad. of Science 2000–; Pres. Chinese Biophysics Soc. 1983–86, 1991–98; Vice-Pres. Chinese Biochemistry Soc. 1987–90; Chinese Nat. Scientific Prize (2nd Rank) 1982, 1989, Scientific Prize (2nd Rank), Chinese Acad. of Sciences 1986, 1992, Scientific Prize (1st Rank), Chinese Acad. of Sciences 1987. *Publications:* more than 110 papers in scientific journals. *Address:* Institute of Biophysics, Chinese Academy of Sciences, Beijing 100101, People's Republic of China. *Telephone:* (10) 64888506. *Fax:* (10) 64889867.

LIANG GUANGLIE, Gen.; Chinese army officer; b. Dec. 1940, Santai Co., Sichuan Prov.; ed Xinyang Infantry Acad. 1963, PLA Mil. Acad. 1982; joined PLA 1958; joined CCP 1959; Vice-Div. Commdr and then Div. Commdr 1979–82; Vice-Army Commdr then Army Commdr, Vice-Commdr PLA Beijing Mil. Area Command 1983–97; alt. mem. 13th CCP Cen. Cttee 1987, 14th CCP Cen. Cttee 1992; Commdr PLA Shenyang Mil. Area Command 1997–2000; Commdr PLA Nanjing Mil. Area Command 2000–03; mem. 15th CCP Cen. Cttee 1997–2002; Chief of Gen. Staff, PLA 2003–. *Address:* People's Liberation Army, c/o Ministry of National Defence, 20 Jingshanqian Jie, Beijing, People's Republic of China.

LIANG SHOUPAN, MS; Chinese rocket engineer; b. 13 April 1916, Fujien; s. of Ching Tung Liang and Yun Jiao Lin; m. He Fu 1942; one s.; ed Tsinghua Univ., Mass. Inst. of Tech., USA; Deputy Dir Rocket Research Inst. 1965–81; Deputy Dir of Science and Tech., Ministry of Astronautics 1982–88; Sr Technical Adviser, Ministry of Aeronautics and Astronautics Industry 1999–; Chief designer 'Silkworm' and other anti-ship missile projects; mem. Dept of Tech. Sciences, Academia Sinica 1981–; Sr Tech. Adviser, China Aerospace Science and Tech. Corpn 1999–, China Aerospace Machinery and Electronics Corpn 1999–; Hon. Special Prize of Nat. Tech. 1988. *Leisure interests:* Chinese history, novels, Chinese chess. *Address:* Ministry of Aeronautics and Astronautics Industry, P.O. Box 849, Beijing, People's Republic of China. *Telephone:* 68371539. *Fax:* 68370849.

LIANG XIAOSHENG; Chinese writer; b. Sept. 1949, Harbin; worker on land reclamation project; local newspaper reporter; Chinese language student, Fudan Univ. 1975; mem. Chinese Writers' Asscn, Chinese Film-makers' Asscn; mem. and official of Chinese Film Script-writers' Asscn; Film Script Ed., Beijing Film Studio. *Publications:* four anthologies of short stories, an anthology of medium-length novels and two novels, most of which have been adapted as films or TV plays; works include: This is a Strange Land, Literary Accomplishments, Blizzard at Midnight (all of which have won All-China Short Novel Prizes), For the Harvest, TV play based on Blizzard at Midnight (awarded All-China TV Playscript Grand Prize). *Address:* Editorial Department, "Creative Cinema", 19 Bei-huan Xilu Street, Beijing, People's Republic of China.

LIAO BINGXIONG; Chinese cartoonist; b. 21 Oct. 1915, Canton; one s. three d.; Vice-Chair. Guangdong br., Chinese Artists' Asscn. *Exhibitions include:* Spring and Autumn in Cats' Kingdom 1945, A 50 Years' Retrospective 1982. *Publication:* Bingxiong's Cartoons 1932–82. *Address:* Room 302, Block 2, 871 Renmin Road, Guangzhou 510180, People's Republic of China. *Telephone:* 6661480.

LIAO HANSHENG, Lt-Gen.; Chinese government official; b. 1911, Sangzhi Co., Hunan Prov.; Political Commissar 6th Div., 2nd Front Army 1934; Political Commissar, Div. 2nd Front, Red Army 1936; Political Comm. 716 Regiment, 120th Div., 8th Route Army; Political Commissar 1st Column, NW Liberation Army 1947; Political Commissar 2nd Army Group, CCP Red Army 1949; Chair. Qinghai Mil. & Admin. Cttee 1949; Political Commissar, Qinghai Mil. Area 1949; Vice-Chair., Qinghai People's Provincial Govt 1949–56; Deputy Commdr Qinghai Mil. Area 1950; mem. NW Mil. and Admin. Cttee 1950; mem. NW Admin. Cttee 1953; Deputy Political Commissar NW Mil. Area 1954; Deputy for PLA to 1st NPC 1954; mem. Nat. Defence Council 1954; rank of Lt-Gen. 1955; alt. mem. CCP 8th Cen. Cttee 1956; Pres. Mil. Acad. of PLA 1957; responsible person PLA Units, Nanjing 1957, Beijing 1962; Deputy for Beijing PLA Units to 3rd NPC 1964; mem. Presidium 3rd NPC 1964; Sec. CCP N China Bureau 1965; detained in Beijing Garrison HQ, 1967; Branded a 3-Anti Element 1967; resumed activities 1972; Vice-Pres. Acad. of Mil. Science 1974; First Political Commissar PLA Nanjing Mil. Region 1978–80, PLA Shenyang Units 1980–85; mem. 12th CCP Cen. Cttee 1982–85; Vice-Chair. Standing Cttee 6th Nat. People's Congress 1983–87, 7th 1988–93; Chair. Cen. Patriotic Public Health Campaign Cttee 1983–; Chair. Foreign Affairs Cttee 1988; mem. Presidium 6th NPC 1986, 7th NPC 1988; Vice-Chair. 7th NPC 1988; Chair. Credentials Cttee, NPC 1986–; Hon. Pres. Sports Aviation Asscn 1988–; Adviser Soc. for the Promotion of Chinese Cultural Exchanges and Co-operation 1992–. *Address:* c/o Standing Committee, National People's Congress, Tiananmen Square, Beijing, People's Republic of China.

LIAO HUI; Chinese government official; b. 1941, Huiyang Co., Guangdong Prov.; s. of late Liao Chengzhi and Jing Puchum; joined CCP 1965; mem. 12th CCP Cen. Cttee 1985, 13th CCP Cen. Cttee 1987–92, 14th CCP Cen. Cttee 1992–97, 15th CCP Cen. Cttee 1997–2002; Dir Overseas Chinese Affairs

Office, State Council 1984–; Dir Hong Kong and Macao Affairs Office 1997–; mem. 21st Century Comm. for China-Japan Friendship 1985–; Hon. Vice-Chair. Zhonghai Inst. of Agricultural Tech. 1987–. *Address:* c/o State Council, Zhong Nan Hai, Beijing, People's Republic of China.

LIAO SHANTAO, PhD; Chinese professor of mathematics; b. 4 Jan. 1920, Hunan Prov.; m. Wang Hongyi 1943; three s.; ed South-West United Univ., Univ. of Chicago; Prof. of Math., Beijing Univ. 1961–; Nat. Scientific Prize of China 1982; TWAS Award in Math. 1986. *Address:* Department of Mathematics, Beijing University, Xinyiekouwai Street 19, Beijing100875, People's Republic of China.

LIAO XILONG, Gen.; Chinese army officer; b. June 1940, Sinan Co., Guizhou Prov.; joined PLA 1959, CCP 1963; served as Platoon Commdr 1966–67, Co. Commdr 1969–71, Deputy Chief of a regt combat training section 1971–73, Deputy Chief of a div. mil. affairs section 1973–78, Deputy Regt Commdr 1978–79, Regt Commdr 1979–80, Deputy Div. Commdr 1981–83, Div. Commdr 1983, Corps Commdr 1984–85, Deputy Commdr Chengdu Mil. Region 1985–95, Commdr 1995–2003; Dir-Gen. Logistics Dept, PLA 2003–; rank of Gen. 2000. *Address:* People's Liberation Army, c/o Ministry of National Defence, 20 Jingshanqian Jie, Beijing 100009, People's Republic of China.

LIBAI, David, LLD; Israeli politician and lawyer; b. 1934, Tel Aviv; ed Chicago Univ., USA; Head Israel Bar Asscn; Deputy Attorney-Gen.; Dir Inst. of Criminology and Criminal Law, Tel Aviv Univ., Dean of Students; Chair. Labour Party Constitution Cttee; Chair. Israel-Britain Parl. Friendship Asscn; Chair. Public Audit (Control) Cttee 1984–92; Spokesman Ministry of Justice, Minister of Justice 1992–96; fmr mem. Nat. Comm. of Inquiry on Prison Conditions, Press Council, Knesset (Parl.) 1984–, served on various cttees.; mem. Israel Labour Party. *Publications:* numerous articles on legal issues. *Address:* Israel Labour Party, P.O. Box 62033, Tel-Aviv, 61620 (Office); Knesset, Jerusalem, Israel. *Telephone:* (3) 6899444 (Office). *Fax:* (3) 6899420 (Office). *E-mail:* avoda@inter.net.il (Office).

LIBANIO CHRISTO, Carlos Alberto (Frei Betto); Brazilian Dominican brother and writer; b. 25 Aug. 1944, Belo Horizonte; s. of Antônio Carlos Vieira Christo and Maria Stella Libanio Christo; ed Univ. of Brazil, Escola Dominicana de Teologia and Seminário São Leopoldo; Nat. leader, Catholic Young Students 1962–64; political prisoner 1964; newspaper and magazine ed. 1966–69; political prisoner 1969–73; organizer of basic Church communities 1973–79; teacher, popular educ. 1977–; writer and teacher with Workers' Pastoral 1979–; Dir América Libre (magazine) 1993–2003; mem. Council Swedish Foundation for Human Rights 1991–96; Consultant, Movimento dos Trabalhadores Rurais Sem Terra (MST); mem. and consultant Inst. Itaú Cultural, Inst. Cidadania –2003; Special Assessor of the Presidency of the Repub. 2003–; Intellectual of the Year Prize, Brazilian Writers' Union 1986, Human Rights Prize, Bruno Kreisky Foundation, Vienna 1987, Crea de Meio Ambiente Prize, Conselho Regional de Engenharia e Arquitetura, Rio de Janeiro; Paolo E. Borsellino Award (Italy) for work in human rights 1998, Friendship Medal (Cuba) 2000, Chico Mendes de Resistência Medal, Grupo Tortura Nunca Mais, Rio de Janeiro. *Publications include:* 48 books including Batismo de Sangue (Jabuti Prize, Brazilian Book Asscn, 1985); Oração na Ação, Letters from a Prisoner of Conscience, Les Frères de Tito, Against Principalities and Powers, Fidel and Religion, Fome de Pão e de Beleza 1990, A Menina e o Elefante 1990, Uala, o Amor 1991, Alucinado Som de Tuba 1992, O Paraíso Perdido-Nos bastidores do socialismo 1993, A Obra do Artista-Uma Visão Holística do Universo 1995, Comer como um frade... 1996, O Vencedor 1996, Entre todos os homens 1997, Cotidiano e Mistério, Talita abre a porta dos Evangelhos 1998, A noite em que Jesus nasceu (Best Young Readers' Book, Art Critics Asscn of S. Paulo 1998), Hotel Brasil (detective story), O Doisiemão 2001, A mulbrer samantana 2001, A mula de Balaão 2001, Alpasetto 2002, Lula-um operário na presidência 2003. *Leisure interests:* cooking, swimming. *Address:* Rua Atibaia 420, 01235-010 São Paulo, S.P., Brazil. *Telephone:* (11) 864-0844; (11) 38651473. *Fax:* (11) 38656941.

LIBERADZKI, Bogusław Marian; Polish politician and economist; b. 12 Sept. 1948, Sochaczew; m.; two s.; ed Main School of Planning and Statistics, Warsaw and Univ. of Illinois, USA; Scientist, Main School of Planning and Statistics (now Warsaw School of Econs) Warsaw 1971–; Dir Transport Econs Research Centre, Warsaw 1986–89; Deputy Minister of Transport 1989–93; mem. Transport Comm., Polish Acad. of Science 1988–96, European Rail Congress Council, Brussels; Chair. Supervisory Bd Polish LOT Airways –1993; Minister of Transport and Maritime Economy 1993–97; Deputy to Sejm (Parl.) 1997–; mem. Democratic Left Alliance (SLD) Parl. Club; Chair. Maritime Univ. Szczecin 1998–, Warsaw School of Econs 1999– (Chair. Dept of Transport); Golden Medal of Merit 1978; Fulbright Scholarship 1986. *Publications:* Economics of Railways 1980, Supply of Railroad Services 1981, Transport: Demand, Supply, Equilibrium 1999. *Leisure interests:* biographies, gardening. *Address:* Sejm, 00-902 Warsaw, ul. Wiejska 4/6 (Office); Biuro Poselskie, ul. Garncarska 5, 70-402 Szczecin, Poland. *Telephone:* (22) 285927 (Office); (91) 4341918. *Fax:* (22) 6293375 (Office). *Website:* www.sejm.gov.pl (Office).

LIBERAKI, Margarita; Greek novelist and dramatist; b. 1919, Athens; d. of Themistuclis and Sapho Liberaki; m. Georges Karapanos 1941 (divorced); one d.; ed Athens Univ.; lives in Paris and Greece, writes in Greek and French; plays performed at Festival d'Avignon, Festival of Athens, Nat. Theatre,

Athens. *Publications:* The Trees 1947, The Straw Hats 1950, Trois étés 1950, The Other Alexander 1952, The Mystery 1976; plays: Kandaules' Wife 1955, The Danaids 1956, L'autre Alexandre 1957, Le saint prince 1959, La lune a faim 1961, Sparagmos 1965, Le bain de mer 1967, Erotica 1970, Zoe 1985; film scripts: Magic City 1953, Phaedra 1961, Three Summers (TV series) 1996, Diaspora 1999. *Leisure interest:* painting. *Address:* 7 rue de L'Eperon, 75006 Paris, France; 2 Strat. Sindesmou, 106 73 Athens, Greece. *Telephone:* 1-46-33-05-92 (Paris).

LIBERIA-PETERS, Maria; Netherlands Antilles politician; m.; Leader Nat. Volkspartij (Nat. People's Party); Prime Minister of Netherlands Antilles 1984–85, 1988–93. *Address:* c/o Partido Nashonal di Pueblo, Willemstad, Curaçao, Netherlands Antilles.

LIBESKIND, Daniel, BArch, MA; American architect; b. 1946, Poland; s. of Nachman Libeskind and Dora Blaustein; m. Nina Lewis 1969; two s. one d.; ed Cooper Union for the Advancement of Science and Art, New York, Univ. of Essex, England; fmr Head Dept of Architecture Cranbrook Acad. of Art; fmr Sr Scholar John Paul Getty Centre; fmr Visiting Prof. Harvard Univ.; fmr Bannister Fletcher Prof. Univ. of London; fmr holder Davenport Chair Yale Univ.; architectural practice Berlin 1989–; Prof. Hochschule für Gestaltung, Karlsruhe; holder of Creative Chair, Univ. of Pa, USA; mem. Akad. der Kunst 1990–, European Acad. of Arts and Letters; Dr hc (Humboldt Univ.) 1997, (Univ. of Essex) 1999; Berlin Cultural Prize 1996, Hiroshima Art Prize 2001; Award for Achitecture, American Acad. of Arts and Letters 1996, Goethe Medallion 2000. *Projects include:* (architectural) Felix-Nussbaum-Haus, Osnabrück, Germany 1998, Jewish Museum (German Architecture Prize 1999), Berlin 1999, Imperial War Museum – North Manchester 2001, Weil Gallery, Majorca 2001, Jewish Museum, Copenhagen 2002, CUBE Bar and Resturant, Manchester 2002; projects in progress include: The Spiral: Extension to Vic. and Albert Museum, London, Maurice Wohl Convention Centre, Tel Aviv, Extension to Denver Art Museum, USA, Jewish Museum, San Francisco, new faculty for JVC Univ. Guadalajara, Mexico, Postgrad. Centre, Univ. of N London; (urban and landscape) Osaka Folly, Japan 1987, Marking the City Boundries, Groningen, Netherlands 1989-90, Polderland Garden, Almere, Netherlands 1997, Uozu Mountain Pavilion, Japan 1997. *Publications:* Radix—Matrix: Architecture and Writings 1997, The Space of Encounter 2001. *Leisure interests:* Listening to music, meditation. *Address:* Architectural Studio Libeskind, Windscheidstrasse 18, 10627 Berlin, Germany (Office). *Telephone:* (30) 3277820 (Office). *Fax:* (30) 32778299 (Office). *E-mail:* info@daniel-lieeskind.com (Office). *Website:* www.daniel-libeskind.com.

LICHFIELD, 5th Earl of, cr. 1831; **Thomas Patrick John Anson,** FRPS; British photographer; b. 25 April 1939; s. of the late Viscount Anson and Princess Anne of Denmark; m. Lady Leonora Grosvenor 1975 (divorced 1986); one s. two d.; ed Harrow School, Sandhurst; army service, Grenadier Guards 1957–62; now works as photographer; numerous exhbns worldwide; Fellow British Inst. of Professional Photographers; Hon. DL (Stafford) 1996. *Publications:* The Most Beautiful Women 1981, Lichfield on Photography 1981, A Royal Album 1982, Patrick Lichfield's Unipart Calendar Book 1982, Patrick Lichfield Creating the Unipart Calendar 1983, Hot Foot to Zabriskie Point 1985, Lichfield on Travel Photography 1986, Not the Whole Truth (autobiog.) 1986, Lichfield in Retrospect 1988, Queen Mother: the Lichfield Selection 1990, Elizabeth R.: a Photographic Celebration of 40 years 1991. *Leisure interests:* country pursuits, arboriculture, gardening. *Address:* Shugborough Hall, Stafford; Lichfield Studios, 133 Oxford Gardens, London, W10 6NE, England (Studio). *Telephone:* (1889) 881454 (Stafford); (20) 8969-6161 (London). *Fax:* (20) 8960-6494 (London). *E-mail:* lichfield@lichfieldstudios.co.uk.

LICK, Dale Wesley, PhD; American professor of educational leadership; b. 7 Jan. 1938, Marlette, Mich.; s. of John R. Lick and Florence May Lick (née Baxter); m. Marilyn Kay Foster 1956; one s. three d.; ed Michigan State Univ., Univ. of California, Riverside; Instructor and Chair. Dept of Math., Port Huron Jr Coll. (later St Clair Co. Community Coll.), Port Huron, Mich. 1959–60; Asst to Comptroller, Line and Staff Man., Michigan Bell Telephone Co., Detroit, Mich. 1961; Instructor of Math., Univ. of Redlands, Calif. 1961–63; Teaching Asst in Math., Univ. of Calif., Riverside, Calif., 1964–65; Asst Prof. of Math., Univ. of Tenn. 1965–67, Assoc. Prof. 1968–69; textbook and manuscript reviewer for several publrs 1966–; Visiting Research Mathematician, Applied Math. Dept, Brookhaven Nat. Lab., Upton, New York 1967–68; Consultant, Computing Tech. Center, Union Carbide Corpn, Oak Ridge, Tenn., under auspices of US Atomic Energy Comm. 1966–71; Adjunct Assoc. Prof., Dept of Pharmacology (Biomathematics), Temple Medical School, Temple Univ. 1969–72; Head and Assoc. Prof., Dept of Math., Drexel Univ., Philadelphia, Pa 1969–72; Vice-Pres. for Academic Affairs, Russell Sage Coll., Troy, New York 1972–74; Dean, School of Sciences and Health Professions and Prof. of Math. and Computing Sciences, Old Dominion Univ., Norfolk, Va 1974–78; Pres. and Prof. of Math. and Computer Sciences, Georgia Southern Coll., Statesboro, Ga 1978–86; Pres. and Prof. of Math., Univ. of Maine 1986–91, Fla State Univ., Tallahassee 1991–93; Univ. Prof., Fla State Univ. 1993–; mem. American Asscn of Univ. Admins, American Asscn of Univ. Profs, American Math. Soc., Math. Asscn of America, Asscn Study of Higher Educ. *Publications:* Fundamentals of Algebra 1970, Whole-Faculty Study Groups: A Powerful Way to Change School and Enhance Learning (jtly) 1998, New Directions in Mentoring: Creating a Culture of Synergy (jtly) 1999, Whole-Faculty Study Groups: Creating Student-Based Professional Development (jtly) 2001, numerous book chapters, papers and articles in learned journals and 285 newspaper columns. *Leisure interests:* sports, reading, writing, the arts, church work. *Address:* University Center C-4600, Florida State University, Tallahassee, FL 32306-2540 (Office); 348 Remington Run Loop, Tallahassee, FL 32312-1402, USA (Home). *Telephone:* (850) 644-0013 (Office); (850) 553-4080 (Home). *Fax:* (850) 553-4081 (Office); (850) 553-4081 (Home). *E-mail:* dlick@lsi.fsu.edu (Office); dlick@lsi.fsu.edu (Home). *Website:* www.fsu.edu/~edleadr/lick.html.

LIDDELL, Rt. Hon. Helen, PC; British politician; b. 6 Dec. 1950; d. of Hugh Reilly and the late Bridget Lawrie Reilly; m. Alistair Henderson Liddell 1972; one s. one d.; ed St Patrick's High School, Coatbridge and Strathclyde Univ.; Head Econ. Dept Scottish TUC 1971–75, Asst Sec. 1975–76; Econ. Corresp. BBC Scotland 1976–77; Scottish Sec. Labour Party 1977–88; Dir Personnel and Public Affairs, Scottish Daily Record and Sunday Mail Ltd 1988–92; Chief Exec. Business Venture Programme 1993–94; MP for Monklands E 1994–97, for Airdrie and Shotts 1997–, Opposition spokeswoman on Scotland 1995–97; Econ. Sec. HM Treasury 1997–98, Minister of State Scottish Office 1998–99; Minister of Transport 1999–2001; Sec. of State for Scotland 2001–. *Publication:* Elite 1990. *Leisure interests:* cooking, hill-walking, music, writing. *Address:* House of Commons, London SW1A 0AA, England (Office). *Telephone:* (20) 7219-3000 (Office).

LIDMAN, Sara; Swedish writer; b. 30 Dec. 1923; d. of Andreas and Jenny Lidman (née Lundman); ed Uppsala Univ.; first four books deal with life in sparsely populated N Sweden; in S. Africa 1960, in Kenya 1962–64, in N Viet Nam 1965. *Publications include:* Tjärdalen 1953, Hjortronlandet 1955, Aina 1956, Regnspiran 1958, Bära mistel 1960, Jag o min son 1961, Med fem diamanter 1964, Samtal i Hanoi 1966, Gruva 1968, Vänner o uvänner 1969, Marta, Marta 1970, Fåglarna i Nam Dinh 1973, Libretto till två baletter, Inga träd skall väcka dig 1974, Balansen 1975, Din tjänare hör 1977.

LIEBENBERG, Christo Ferro, MPA, P.M.D.; South African politician and retd banker; b. 2 Oct. 1934, Touwsriver; s. of Christiaan Liebenberg and Helene Griessel; m. Elly Liebenberg 1959; two s.; ed Worcester Boys' High School, Harvard Univ., INSEAD and Cranfield; joined Nedbank, Cape Town 1952; Man. Dir Nedbank, Johannesburg 1988–90; CEO Nedcor 1990–94; fmr Chair. Credit Guarantee Insurance Corpn of Africa Ltd, Syfrets Ltd, Cape Town; fmr Deputy Chair. NedPerm Bank; Pres. Inst. of Bankers in S. Africa 1991; Minister of Finance 1994–96; Dir various financial insts. *Leisure interests:* music, photography, theatre, ballet, reading, golf. *Address:* c/o Ministry of Finance, 240 Vermeulen Street, Pretoria 0002, South Africa.

LIEBERMAN, Avigdor, BA; Israeli politician; b. 5 June 1958, USSR; m.; three c.; ed Hebrew Univ.; rank of corporal during mil. service; mem. Knesset (Parl.) 1999– (Israel B'Aitainu Party, Ihud Leumi-Israel B'Aitainu Party), mem. Foreign Affairs & Defence Cttee; Minister of Nat. Infrastructure 2001–02, of Transport 2003–; Sec. Nat. Workers' Union; Chair. Bd of Dirs of Information Industries; Dir of Econ. Corpn of Jerusalem 1983–88; Dir Likud Movt 1993–96; Dir Prime Minister's Office 1996–97; f. Zionist Forum; Founder and Leader Israel B'Aitainu Party. *Leisure interests:* football, tennis. *Address:* Ministry of Transport, Klal Building, 97 Jaffa Street, Jerusalem 91000, Israel (Office). *Telephone:* 2-6228211. *Fax:* 2-6228693. *E-mail:* aliebarman@knesset.gov.il (Office). *Website:* www.mot.gov.il.

LIEBERMAN, Joseph I., BA, JD; American politician; b. 24 Feb. 1942, Stamford, Conn.; s. of Henry and Marcia (née Manger) Lieberman; m. Hadassah Freilich 1983; two s. two d.; ed Yale Univ.; called to Bar, Conn. 1967; mem. Conn. Senate 1971–81, Senate Majority Leader 1975–81; Partner Lieberman, Segaloff & Wolfson, New Haven 1972–83; Attorney Gen. State of Conn., Hartford 1983–88, Senator for Conn. 1989–; Chair. Democratic Leadership Council 1995–; Vice-Pres. Cand. for Democratic Party 2000; mem. Governmental Affairs Cttee, Small Business Cttee, Trustee Wadsworth Atheneum, Univ. of Bridgeport; Democrat. *Publications:* The Power Broker 1966, The Scorpion and the Tarantula 1970, The Legacy 1981, Child Support in America 1986. *Address:* U.S. Senate, 706 Hart Senate Office Building, Washington, DC 20510, USA.

LIEBERMAN, Seymour, PhD; American professor of biochemistry; b. 1 Dec. 1916, New York; s. of Samuel D. Lieberman and Sadie Levin; m. Sandra Spar 1944; one s.; ed Brooklyn Coll., New York, Univ. of Illinois and Stanford Univ., Calif.; Prof. of Biochem., Coll. of Physicians and Surgeons, Columbia Univ. 1962–87, Prof. Emer. 1987–, Assoc. Dean 1984–90, Vice-Provost 1988–89, Assoc. Dir Office of Science and Tech. 1991–99; Program Officer The Ford Foundation 1974–75; Pres. St Luke's-Roosevelt Inst. for Health Sciences 1981–97; mem. NAS 1977–; Ciba Award 1952, Koch Award 1970, Roussel Prize (France) 1984, Dale Medal 1986, Dist Service Award (Columbia Univ.) 1991. *Publications:* A Heuristic Proposal for Understanding Steroidogenic Processes 1984, Detection in Bovine Brain of Sulfate Esters of Cholesterol and Sitosterol 1986 and more than 150 other publs. *Leisure interest:* tennis. *Address:* 432 W. 58th Street, New York, NY 10019; 515 E 72nd Street, New York, NY 10021, USA. *E-mail:* sl22@columbia.edu (Office).

LIEM SIOE LIONG; Indonesian business executive; b. 1917, Fuqing District, Fujan, S. China; m.; three s. one d.; emigrated to Central Java 1938; began own coffee powder business during World War II, establishing himself as provisions supplier for rebel army fighting for independence from the Dutch; began to build own business empire in late 1940s, now has substantial shareholdings in 192 cos involved in trade, finance, food, chemicals, pharmaceuticals, textiles; majority shareholder in First Pacific Group (Hong Kong-based banking, trading and property co.); major shareholdings in Bank of Cen. Asia (Indonesia's largest pvt. bank), Indocement and Bogasari Flour Mills. *Address:* PT Perkasa Indonesia Cement Enterprise, Level 13, Wisma Indocement Kav. 70–71, Jalan Jenderal Sudirman, Jakarta, Indonesia.

LIEN CHAN, MSc, PhD; Taiwanese politician; b. 27 Aug. 1936, Sian, Shansi; s. of Chen Tung Lien and Chao Lan-Kun Lien; m. Yui Fang; two s. two d.; ed Nat. Taiwan Univ. and Univ. of Chicago, USA; Assoc. Prof. Nat. Taiwan Univ. 1968–69, Prof. and Chair. Dept of Political Science and Dir Graduate Inst. of Political Science 1969–75; Amb. to El Salvador 1975–76; Dir Dept of Youth Affairs, Cen. Cttee Kuomintang 1976–78; Deputy Sec.-Gen. Cen. Cttee Kuomintang 1978, mem. Cen. Standing Cttee 1983–, Chair. 2000–; Chair. Nat. Youth Comm., Exec. Yuan 1978–81; Minister of Communications 1981–87; Vice-Premier 1987–88; Minister of Foreign Affairs 1989–90; Gov. Taiwan Provincial Govt 1990–93; Premier of Taiwan 1993–97; Vice-Pres. of Taiwan 1997–2000; Presidential Cand. 2000; Pres. Chinese Asscn of Political Science 1979–82. *Publications:* The Foundation of Democracy, Taiwan in China's External Relations, Western Political Thought. *Leisure interests:* golf, swimming, music. *Address:* Kuomintang, 11 Chung Shan South Road, Taipei 100, Taiwan (Office). *Telephone:* (2) 23121472 (Office). *Fax:* (2) 2343524 (Office). *Website:* www.kmt.org.tw (Office).

LIENDO, Maj.-Gen. Horacio Tomás; Argentine politician and army officer; b. 17 Dec. 1924, Córdoba; ed Mil. Coll.; first post with 4th Bn, Communications; with 6th Motorized Bn, Communications; as Capt., entered Army War Coll. 1954, later Gen. Staff Officer; served in Communications Inspection, Army Gen. Staff, and, as Second-in-Command, 4th Bn, Communications; rank of Maj. 1959; 61st Communications Command; under orders of Mil. Attaché, USA 1962; rank of Lt-Col 1965, Col 1970, Gen. 1980; Minister of Labour 1976–79; Chief of Staff, Armed Forces 1979–81; Minister of the Interior March–Nov. 1981; Pres. of Argentina (a.i.) Nov.–Dec. 1981.

LIEPA, Andris; Russian/Latvian ballet dancer and choreographer; b. 6 Jan. 1962, Moscow; s. of the late Marius Liepa and of Margarita Zhigunova; brother of Ilze Liepa (q.v.); m. Yekaterina Liepa; one d.; ed Moscow Choreographic School of Bolshoi Theatre; with Bolshoi Ballet 1980–87; prize-winner int. competitions Moscow 1985, Jackson, USA (Grand Prix) 1986; lived in the West 1987–; appeared with New York City Ballet, subsequently with American Ballet Theater; danced in Raymonda Variations, Swan Lake (Baryshnikov), Romeo and Juliet (Macmillan), Violin Concerto (Balanchine); worked with Nina Ananiashvili, Carla Fracci and other partners; choreographer 1993–; has adapted Fokine ballets for film, including Return to the Firebird; guest artist with Kirov (now Mariinsky) Ballet, London tour 1990; works in USA, Russia and Latvia. *Address:* Bryusov per. 17, Apt. 13, 103009 Moscow, Russia. *Telephone:* (095) 241-81-37.

LIEPA, Ilze; Russian/Latvian ballerina; b. 22 Nov. 1963; d. of the late Maris Liepa and of Margarita Zhigunova; sister of Andris Liepa (q.v.); m. 1st Sergey Stadler (divorced); m. 2nd Vladislovas A. Paulius; ed Moscow Choreographic School of Bolshoi Theatre; with Bolshoi ballet 1982–; danced on various stages of Europe and America performing parts of classic repertoire, including Legend about Love, Romeo and Juliet, Firebird, Don Quixote, Corsair, Raimonda, Prince Igor; début in England concert Stars of World Ballet, Covent Garden (Firebird), tours with Bolshoi Theatre in most countries of Europe and America, independently toured in Argentina, Greece, Taiwan, Japan; Artistic Dir Golden Age Asscn 1994–98; f. Maris Liepa Foundation; Prize of Russian Trade Unions, Hon. Artist of Russian Fed. *Films include:* The Shining World 1983, Bambi's Childhood 1984, Lermontov 1985, Lomononov 1987, Return of the Firebird 1994. *Plays include:* Your Sister and Captive 1999, The Empress's Dream 2000. *Publication:* Circle of the Sun (play) 2000. *Address:* Bryusov per. 17, Apt. 12, 103009 Moscow, Russia. *Telephone:* (095) 229-23-88. *Fax:* (095) 229-23-88. *E-mail:* vpaulius@stk.mmtel.ru.

LIESEN, Klaus, DJur; German business executive; b. 15 April 1931; fmr Chair. Exec. Bd Ruhrgas AG, Chair. Supervisory Bd 1996–; Chair. Supervisory Bd Volkswagen AG; fmr Chair. Supervisory Bd AllianzHolding AG; other directorships in steel, energy, banking and insurance cos; Dr rer. pol hc. *Address:* Ruhrgas AG, Huttropstrasse 60, 45117 Essen, Germany. *Telephone:* 20118400.

LIESLER, Josef; Czech artist; b. 19 Sept. 1912, Vidolice, Kadan; m. Blažena Málková; two s.; ed Charles Univ., Prague; Prof. of Drawing and Architecture Charles Univ., Prague 1945–49; has designed over 100 books cover designs and over 100 postage stamps; has exhibited paintings, graphic art and postage stamps in numerous galleries including Czech National Gallery, Prague and Uffizi Gallery, Florence, Italy; mem. "Sedm v Října" (Seven in October group) 1938, SVU Mánes 1942, SČUG Hollar 1945, Section "58" 1958, Belgian Royal Acad. 1969; Hon. mem. Florence Acad. 1964, Czech Bibliophiles 1977–; UNESCO prize for finest postage stamp worldwide 1975 (Hydrologie). *Exhibitions include:* 'Sedm v řijnu' 1939, SVU Mánes Prague 1945, 1948, 1988, Václav Špala Gallery Prague 1959, Sofia, Plovdiv, Burgas, Varna, Stara Zagora 1961, Oslo 1964, Frankfurt, Hamburg 1965, Cortina d'Ampezzo, Baghdad, Kahira, Rabat 1966, Berlin 1969, Vienna, Amsterdam 1972, Mestska Gallery Bratislava 1977, Bochum 1984, Gallery Fronta Prague 1985, Dortmund 1989, Castle Kadan 1993, Portheimka Gallery Prague 1996. *Publications include:* numerous articles on painting and graphic arts. *Leisure*

interests: painting, writing. *Address:* c/o Akademie výtvarných umění—AVU, ul. Akademie 4, 17000 Prague 7 (Office); Xaverova 17, 15000 Prague 5, Czech Republic (Home). *Telephone:* (2) 51562525 (Home).

LIFVON GUO; Taiwanese singer; m.; cowherd aged ten; performs folk songs and folk chants mixed with modern dance beats; with wife and some 30 indigenous singers toured Switzerland, France, Germany, Netherlands and Italy 1987. *Albums include:* Return to Innocence (more than 5 million copies sold), Cross of Changes.

LIGACHEV, Yegor Kuzmich; Russian politician; b. 29 Sept. 1920; m.; one s.; ed Moscow Inst. of Aviation and CPSU Higher Party School; Engineer 1943–49; joined CPSU 1944; Party and Local Govt Official Novosibirsk 1949–55; Vice-Chair. Novosibirsk Regional Soviet of Working People's Deputies 1955–58; Sec. Novosibirsk Regional Cttee CPSU 1959–61, mem. Cen. Cttee CPSU 1961–65; First Sec. Tomsk Regional Cttee CPSU 1965–83; Cand. mem. Cen. Cttee CPSU 1966–76, mem. 1976–90, mem. Politburo 1985–90; Deputy to Supreme Soviet 1966–89; Sec. Cen. Cttee in Charge of Personnel and Ideology 1983–88; in Charge of Agric. 1988–90; People's Deputy of the USSR 1989–91; active in Russian nat. and communist movt; Vice-Chair. Union of Communist Parties of fmr USSR 1995–; mem. State Duma (Parl.) 1999–. *Publication:* Inside Gorbachev's Kremlin 1993. *Address:* Communist Party of Russian Federation, Bolshoy Zlatoustinsky per. 8/7, 101000 Moscow, Russia; State Duma, Okhotny Ryad 1, 103265 Moscow. *Telephone:* 206-87-89 (Communist Party).

LIGETI, György Sándor; Austrian composer; b. 28 May 1923, Romania; s. of Dr Sándor Ligeti and Dr Ilona Somogyi; m. Vera Spitz 1957; one s.; ed Budapest Acad. of Music (studied with Ferenc Farkas and Sándor Veress); taught Budapest Acad. of Music 1950–56; left Hungary 1956; Guest Prof., Stockholm Acad. of Music 1961–71; Composer-in-Residence, Stanford Univ., Calif. 1972; worked in Electronic Studios, Cologne, Fed. Repub. of Germany; active in music composition, Cologne, Vienna, Stockholm, Berlin and Darmstadt; Prof. of Composition, Hamburg Music Acad. 1973–89; mem. Swedish Royal Acad. of Music 1964, Acad. of Arts, Berlin 1968, Free Acad. of Arts, Hamburg 1972, Bavarian Acad. of Fine Arts, Munich 1978, American Acad. and Inst. of Arts and Letters 1984; Orden pour le Mérite, Bonn 1975, Grawemeyer Award 1986; Commdr, Ordre Nat. des Arts et Lettres, France 1988; Praemium Imperiale Prize (Japan) 1991, Balzan Award 1991; shared Wolf Prize 1996. *Works include:* Artikulation (tape piece) 1958, Apparitions (orchestral) 1958–59, Atmosphères (orchestral) 1960, Volumina (organ) 1961–62, Poème Symphonique for 100 metronomes 1962, Aventures for three singers and seven instrumentalists 1962, Requiem for soprano, mezzo-soprano, two choirs and orchestra 1963–65, Lux Aeterna for 16-part chorus 1966, Concerto for cello and orchestra 1966, Lontano (orchestral) 1967, Continuum (harpsichord), Ten pieces for wind quintet 1968, Ramifications for string orchestra or 12 solo strings 1968–69, String Quartet No. 2 1968, Melodien (orchestral) 1971, Monument, Selfportrait, Movement (for two pianos) 1976, Le Grand Macabre (opera) 1974–77, Trio (violin, horn, piano) 1982, 3 Phantasien nach Hölderlin (chorus) 1982, Hungarian Etudes (chorus) 1983, 9 Piano Etudes 1985–89, Piano Concerto 1985–88, Nonsense Madrigals for 6 Singers 1988, Violin Concerto 1991, Viola Sonata 1996. *Address:* Himmelhofgasse 34, 1130 Vienna, Austria; Mövenstrasse 3, 2000 Hamburg 60, Germany.

LIIKANEN, Erkki Antero, M.POL.SC.; Finnish politician; b. 19 Sept. 1950, Mikkeli; m. Hanna-Liisa Issakainen 1971; mem. Parl. 1972–; Minister of Finance 1987–90; mem. Social Democratic Party (SDP) Cttee 1978–, Gen. Sec. 1981–87; Amb. to EU 1990–95; EC Commr for Budget, Personnel and Admin 1995–99, for Industry and Information (subsequently Enterprise, Competitiveness, Innovation and the Information Society) July 1999–. *Address:* European Commission, 200 rue de la Loi, 1049 Brussels, Belgium. *Telephone:* (2) 299-11-11. *Fax:* (2) 295-01-38. *Website:* europa.eu.int/comm/index_en.htm (Office).

LIJN, Liliane; American artist; b. 22 Dec. 1939, New York; d. of Herman Segall and Helena Kustanowicz; m. Takis Vassilakis 1961; one s.; partner Stephen Weiss 1969; one s. one d. *Exhibitions include:* London, Paris, Nice, Barcelona, Venice (1986 Biennale), Nagoya, Montréal, etc.; public comms include: White Koan, Univ. of Warwick, Coventry 1972, Circle of Light, Milton Keynes 1979, Carbon Black, Nat. Chemical Labs, Teddington 1988, Argo, N.M. Schroder HQ, Poole 1988, Inner Light, Prudential Insurance HQ, Reading 1993, Dragon's Dance, Marks & Spencer, Cardiff 1993, Earth Sea Light Koan, St Mary's Hosp., Isle of Wight 1997; work in public collections includes: Tate Gallery, London, Musée de la Ville de Paris, Museum of Modern Art, New York, Chicago Inst., Victoria & Albert Museum, London, Bibliothèque Nat., Paris, Museum of Fine Arts, Berne, Glasgow Museum, Museum of NSW, Australia, City Art Gallery, Manchester, Henry Moore Foundation, Leeds. *Films:* What is the Sound of One Hand Clapping? 1975, Look, a Doll! My Mother's Story 1999. *Publications:* Crossing Map 1982, Six Throws of the Oracular Keys 1982, Her Mother's Voice 1996, Light and Memory 2002. *Leisure interests:* cooking, walking, gardening, travelling. *Address:* 99 Camden Mews, London, NW1 9BU, England (Office). *Telephone:* (20) 7485-8524 (Office). *Fax:* (20) 7485-8524 (Office). *E-mail:* lijn@lineone.net (Office). *Website:* www.dada.it/dadart/lijn (Office); www.lijn.net (Home).

LIKHACHEV, Vasily Nikolayevich, DJur; Russian politician; b. 5 Jan. 1952, Gorky; s. of Nina F. Likhacheva; m. Nailya Imatovna Taktasheva; two d.; ed Kazan State Univ.; Asst, then docent Chair of State Law, Kazan State Univ. 1978–82, 1983–87; teacher Nat. School of Law Guinea-Bissau 1982–83; Prof. Univ. of Madagascar 1987–88; Head Div. of State Law Tatar Regional CPSU Cttee 1988–90; Chair. Cttee of Constitutional Control Tatar SSR 1990–91; elected Vice-Pres. Repub. of Tatarstan 1991–95, Chair. State Council of Tatarstan 1995–; Deputy Chair. Council of Fed. of Russian Parl. 1996–98; Amb. and Perm. Rep. of Russian Fed. to EU 1998–. *Publications:* five books; more than 100 articles on questions of int. and state law. *Leisure interests:* music, art, sailing. *Address:* 31–33, boulevard du Régent, 1000 Brussels, Belgium. *Telephone:* (32) 512-36-10. *Fax:* (32) 513-76-49. *E-mail:* misrusce@scypro.be (Office).

LILIĆ, Zoran; Serbia and Montenegro (Serbian) politician; b. 27 Aug. 1953, Brza Palanka, Serbia; s. of Sokol Lilić and Dobrila Lilić; m. Ljubica Brković-Lilić 1980; one s.; ed Belgrade Univ.; several posts as grad. engineer, then man., with state-owned Rekord enterprise, Belgrade; fmr Pres. Exec. Bd Yugoslav Tyre Makers Business Asscn, mem. Presidency of Belgrade Chamber of Economy, Pres. Man. Bd of Belgrade Airport, mem. Council of Faculty of Tech.; mem. Serbian League of Communists, subsequently Socialist Party of Serbia (SPS); Deputy to Nat. Ass. of Repub. of Serbia 1990, Chair. Cttee on Industry, Energy, Mining and Construction, Chief of Group of SPS Deputies; re-elected Deputy and also Pres. of Nat. Ass. 1992; Pres. of Fed. Repub. of Yugoslavia 1993–97; Vice-Prime Minister of Yugoslavia 1997–2000; Vice-Pres. Socialist Party of Serbia (SPS) 1995–; testified against successor Slobodan Milosevic at Int. Criminal Tribunal for fmr Yugoslavia, The Hague, Netherlands July 2002. *Leisure interests:* fishing, football, chess. *Address:* Socijalistička partija Srbije, 11000 Belgrade, bul. Lenjina 6, Serbia and Montenegro. *Telephone:* (11) 634291. *Fax:* (11) 628642. *Website:* www.sps .org.yu (Office).

LILL, John Richard, OBE, FRCM; British pianist; b. 17 March 1944, London; s. of George Lill and the late Margery (née Young) Lill; ed Leyton County High School and Royal Coll. of Music; London début at Royal Festival Hall 1963; plays regularly in European capitals, the USA and the Far East, as recitalist and as soloist with most prin. orchestras; recognized as leading interpreter of Beethoven; Prof., Royal Coll. of Music; Fellow, Trinity Coll. of Music, London, London Coll. of Music; Hon. DSc (Univ. of Aston), Hon. DMus (Exeter Univ.); numerous prizes include First Prize, Int. Tchaikovsky Competition, Moscow 1970. *Recordings include:* complete Beethoven piano sonatas and concertos, complete piano music of Rachmaninov, Brahms piano concertos and Prokofiev sonatas. *Leisure interests:* chess, amateur radio, walking. *Address:* c/o Askonas Holt Ltd, Lonsdale Chambers, 27 Chancery Lane, London, WC2A 1PF, England. *Telephone:* (20) 7400-1700.

LILLEE, Dennis Keith, MBE; Australian cricketer; b. 18 July 1949, Perth; s. of K. Lillee; m. Helen Lillee 1970; two s.; ed Belmay State School, Belmont High School; right-arm fast bowler, lower-order right-hand batsman; played for WA 1969–84, Tasmania 1987–88, Northants 1988; 70 Tests for Australia 1970–84, taking then world record 355 wickets (average 23.9), including record 167 wickets in 29 Tests against England; toured England 1972, 1975, 1980, 1981, 1983 (World Cup), took 882 first-class wickets (average 23.5); Coach Western Australian Cricket Asscn 2000; coaching fast bowlers, MRF Pace Foundation, Chennai, India 2001, Dennis Lillee Fast Bowling Acad. (est. June 2002) 2002–; continued playing cricket, bowling for the Australian Cricket Bd Chair.'s XI –2000; Wisden Cricketer of the Year 1973, named mem. of Australia's Team of the Century. *Publications:* Back to the Mark 1974, The Art of Fast Bowling 1977, Dennis Lillee's Book of Family Fitness 1980, My Life in Cricket 1982, Over and Out 1984. *Leisure Interests:* music, philately. *Address:* c/o Swan Sport, P.O. Box 158, Byron Bay, NSW 2481, Australia.

LILLEY, James Roderick, MA; American diplomat, scholar and intelligence officer; b. 15 Jan. 1928, Tsingtao, China; s. of late Frank W Lilley and Inez Bush; m. Sally Booth 1954; three s.; ed Phillips Exeter Acad., Yale Univ. and George Washington Univ.; Adjunct Prof. School of Advanced Int. Studies, Johns Hopkins Univ. 1978–80; Consultant, Hunt Oil, Dallas, Tex. 1979–81; East Asian Dir Nat. Security Council, White House, Washington, DC Jan.–Nov. 1981; Dir American Inst. in Taiwan, Taipei 1982–84; Consultant, Otis Elevator Co., Farmington, Conn. 1984–85; Deputy Asst Sec. of State, East Asian and Pacific Affairs, Dept of State 1985–86; Amb. to Republic of Korea 1986–89, to China 1989–91; Asst Sec. Defense Dept, Wash. 1991–93; Resident Fellow American Enterprise Inst., Washington 1993–; Distinguished Intelligence Medal, Kang Hwa Medal, Rep. of Korea. *Publications:* Beyond MFN 1994, Chinese Military Modernization 1996, Crisis in the Taiwan Strait 1997, China's Military Faces the Future 1999. *Leisure interests:* swimming, bicycling, reading history. *Address:* American Enterprise Institute, 11th Floor, 1150 17th Street, NW, Washington, DC 20036 (Office); 7301 Maple Avenue, Bethesda, MD 20815, USA (Home). *Telephone:* (202) 862-5949 (Office); (301) 652-5278 (Home). *Fax:* (202) 862-5808 (Office); (301) 951-9492 (Home). *E-mail:* jlilley@aei.org (Office).

LILLEY, Rt Hon Peter Bruce, PC, MA; British politician; b. 23 Aug. 1943, Kent; s. of S. Arnold Lilley and Lilian Lilley (née Elliott); m. Gail Ansell 1979; ed Dulwich Coll., Clare Coll. Cambridge; Chair. Bow Group 1973; MP for St Albans 1983–97, for Hitchin and Harpenden 1997–; Econ. Sec. to Treasury 1987–89, Financial Sec. 1989–90; Sec. of State for Trade and Industry 1990–92, for Social Security 1992–97; Opposition Front Bench Spokesman for Treasury 1997–98; Deputy Leader of the Opposition 1998–99; fmr Dir Greenwell Montague (Oil Analyst). *Publications:* The Delusion of Incomes

Policy (with Samuel Brittan) 1977, The End of the Keynesian Era 1980, Thatcherism: The Next Generation 1990, Winning the Welfare Debate 1996, Patient Power 2000, Common Sense on Cannabis 2001, Taking Liberties 2002. *Leisure interest:* France (and most things French). *Address:* House of Commons, London, SW1A 0AA, England.

LILOV, Alexander Vassilev, PhD; Bulgarian politician and scientist; b. 31 Aug. 1933, Granichak, Vidin; s. of Vassil Lilov and Kamenka Petrovski; m. Anna Lilova 1962; one s. two d.; ed Sofia Univ.; leading mem. Young Communist League (YCL) 1951–63; Deputy Head Propaganda Dept, Head Arts and Culture Dept, BCP Cen. Cttee; mem. BCP Cen. Cttee 1971–, Sec. 1972–83, 1989–, mem. Politburo 1974–83, 1989–; Dir Inst. for Contemporary Sciences 1983–90; Chair. Higher Council Bulgarian Socialist Party 1990–91, mem. 1991–; Dir Inst. for Strategic Investigations 1991–; fmr mem. State Council; MP Nat. Ass. 1990–; corresp. mem. Bulgarian Acad. of Sciences. *Publications:* The Nature of Works of Art 1979, Imagination and Creative Work 1986, Europe: To Be or Not to Be 1988 (co-author), Europe: Dialogue and Co-operation 1989. *Leisure interests:* art, skiing. *Address:* Higher Council of the Bulgarian Socialist Party, P.O. Box 382, 20 Positano Street, Sofia (Office); 12 Veliko Tirnovo Str., 1504 Sofia, Bulgaria (Home). *Telephone:* 87-34-64 (Office); 44-60-33 (Home).

LIM CHWEN JENG; British architect and academic; b. 1964, Ipoh, Malaysia; s. of Kar Sun Lim and Yoke Kheng Leong; ed St Michael's Inst., Ipoh, Malaysia, Ashville Coll., Harrogate, Architectural Asscn School of Architecture, London; tutor, Architectural Asscn (AA), London 1989–90; lecturer Bartlett School of Architecture, Univ. Coll. London 1990–91, Sr Lecturer 1993–, Dir Bartlett Architecture Research Lab. 1999–; Sr Lecturer Univ. of E London 1990–93, Univ. of N London 1991–99; Dir Studio 8 Architects, London 1994–; Visiting Prof. Curtin Univ., Perth, Australia 1996, Stadelschule, Frankfurt 1997–98, 2000–01, Technological Univ., Lund, Sweden 2001, MacKintosh School of Architecture, Glasgow 2001, School of Architecture, Århus, Denmark 2002; RIBA External Examiner 2000–; RIBA Pres.'s Medals for Academic Contrib. in Architecture 1997, 1998, 1999; several prizes for architectural research projects including 1st Prize Bldg Centre Trust Competition 'Housing: a demonstration project' 1987, Univ. Coll. London Cultural Centre Int. Competition 1996, Cen. Glass Int. Competition Japan: Glasshouse 2001, 2nd Prize Japanese/NCE Competition: an image of the bridge of the future 1987, Concept House 2000 (Int.) Ideal Home Exhbn 1999; numerous exhbns Europe, Japan, Canada, USA, Australia. *Publications:* 441/10... We'll Reconfigure the Space When You're Ready 1996, Sins + Other Spatial Relatives 2000, Realms of Impossibility: Water 2002, Realms of Impossibility: Ground 2002, Realms of Impossibility: Air 2002, How Green is Your Garden? 2003. *Address:* Bartlett School of Architecture, 22 Gordon Street, London, WC1H 0QB (Office); Flat 8, 95 Greencroft Gardens, London, NW6 3PG, England (Home). *Telephone:* (20) 7679-4842 (Office). *E-mail:* mail@cjlim-studio8.com (Office). *Website:* www.cjlim-studio8.com (Office).

LIM DONG-WON; South Korean politician and diplomatist; b. 25 July 1934; ed Korea Mil. Acad., Seoul Nat. Univ.; Asst Prof. Korean Mil. Acad. 1964–69; with Armed Forces, attained rank of Maj.-Gen. 1980, now retd; apptd Amb. to Nigeria 1981, to Australia 1984; Chancellor Inst. of Foreign Affairs and Nat. Security, Ministry of Foreign Affairs 1988–92; Chair. Presidential Comm. on Arms Control 1990; Del. South–North High-Level Talks 1990–92; apptd Chair. Asscn for Nat. Unification of Korea 1993; mem. Unification Policy Evaluation Cttee 1993; Sec.-Gen. Kim Dae Jung Peace Foundation for the Asia-Pacific 1995; Sr Sec. for Nat. Security and Foreign Affairs, Pres. Sec. 1998; Minister for Unification (involved in reconciliatory Sunshine Policy towards North Korea) 1999–2001; Dir-Gen. Nat. Intelligence Service 1999–2001; Special Envoy to North Korea April 2002; fmr staff mem. Sejong Inst. *Address:* c/o Ministry of Unification, 77-6, Sejong-no, Jongno-gu, Seoul 110-760, Republic of Korea (Office).

LIM KENG YAIK, Dato' Seri, MB, BCh; Malaysian politician; b. 8 April 1939, Tapah, Perak; m. Wong Yoon Chuan; three c.; ed Queen's Univ., Belfast; Senator 1972–78; Minister with Special Functions 1972–73, of Primary Industries 1986–; mem. State Exec. Council, Perak 1978–86; mem. Parl. 1986–; Pres. Gerakan 1980–. *Address:* Ministry of Primary Industries, 6th–8th Floors, Menara Daya Bumi, Jalan Sultan Hishamuddin, 50654 Kuala Lumpur, Malaysia. *Telephone:* (3) 22747511 (Office). *Fax:* (3) 22745014 (Office). *E-mail:* webeditor@kpu.gov.my (Office). *Website:* www.kpu.gov.my (Office).

LIM KIM SAN; Singaporean politician; b. 30 Nov. 1916, Singapore; s. of Choon Huat and Wee Geok Khuan Lim; m. Pang Gek Kim 1939; two s. four d.; ed Anglo-Chinese School, Raffles Coll., Singapore; Dir United Chinese Bank Ltd, Chair. Batu Pahat Bank Ltd and Pacific Bank Ltd 1940–; mem. and Deputy Chair. Public Service Comm., Singapore 1959–63; Chair. Housing Devt Bd 1960–63; Deputy Chair. Econ. Devt Bd 1961–63; Minister for Nat. Devt 1963–65, for Finance 1965–67, for the Interior and Defence 1967–70, for Educ. 1970–72, for the Environment 1972–75, 1979–81, for Nat. Devt 1975–79, for Communications 1975–78; Acting Pres. March 1989; Chair. Council of Presidential Advisers 1992–; Chair. Port of Singapore Authority 1979–94; Chair. Public Utilities Bd 1971–78, Bd Trustees, Consumers' Co-operative Ltd 1973; Man. Dir Monetary Authority of Singapore 1981–82; mem. of Dewan Ra'ayat; Chair. Singapore Press Holdings Ltd 1988–; Chair. Times Publication Ltd; Darjah Utama Temasek (Order of Temasek) 1962,

Ramon Magsaysay Award for Community Leadership 1965 and others. *Leisure interest:* golf. *Address:* Singapore Press Holdings Ltd, News Centre, 82 Genting Lane, Singapore 349567 (Office). *Telephone:* 7438800 (Office). *Fax:* 7484919 (Office). *Website:* www.sph.com.sg (Office).

LIM PIN, MA, MD, FRCP, FRCPE, FRACP, FACP; Singaporean professor of medicine and endocrinologist; b. 12 Jan. 1936, Penang, Malaysia; m. Shirley Loo Ngai Seong 1964; two s. one d.; ed Raffles Inst., Singapore and Cambridge Univ.; Registrar, King's Coll. Hosp., London 1965; Medical Officer, Ministry of Health, Singapore 1965–66; Lecturer in Medicine, Nat. Univ. of Singapore 1966–70, Sr Lecturer 1971–73, Assoc. Prof. of Medicine 1974–77, Prof. and Head of Dept 1978–81, Deputy Vice-Chancellor 1979–81, Vice-Chancellor 1981–2000; Prof. of Medicine Nat. Univ. of Singapore 2000–, Prof. of Medicine and Sr Consultant Endocrinologist, Nat. Univ. Hosp. 2000–; Commonwealth Medical Fellow, The Royal Infirmary, Edin. 1970; Chair. Nat. Wages Council, Bio-ethics Advisory Cttee, Tropical Marine Science Inst.; Dir United Overseas Bank; mem. Dupont ASEAN Advisory Council; mem. Chinese Heritage Council 1995–; mem. Bd of Advisers, Mendaki, Bd of Dirs S*Bio Pte Ltd, Bd of Dirs Blue Dot Capital Pte Ltd; Corp. Adviser, Singapore Techs Pte Ltd; Patron Mensa Singapore Eisenhower Fellow 1982; Hon. Fellow, Coll. of General Practitioners, Singapore 1982, Royal Australian Coll. of Obstetricians and Gynaecologists 1992, Royal Coll. of Physicians and Surgeons of Glasgow 1997, Royal Coll. of Surgeons of Edin. 1997, Int. Coll. of Dentists, USA 1999 (Dental Surgery), Royal Coll. of Surgeons of Edin. 1999; Officier, Ordre des Palmes académiques 1988, Singapore Distinguished Service Order 2000; Hon. DSc (Univ. of Hull) 1999; Rep. of Singapore Public Admin. Medal (Gold) 1984, Meritorious Service Medal 1990, Friend of Labour Award, NTUC 1995, Gordon Arthur Ransome Orator 2000, Lee Foundation–NHG Lifetime Achievement Award 2002. *Publications:* numerous articles in medical journals. *Leisure Interest:* swimming. *Address:* Department of Medicine, National University of Singapore/National University Hospital, 5 Lower Kent Ridge Road, 119074 Singapore. *Telephone:* 67724976 (Office). *Fax:* 67735627 (Office). *Website:* www.nus.edu.sg (Office).

LIMBACH, Jutta; German judge and professor of law; b. 27 March 1934, Berlin; m.; three c.; ed Freie Universität Berlin and Freiburg Univ.; Prof. of Civil Law and Legal Sociology, Freie Universität Berlin 1971–; Senator of Justice, Berlin 1989–94; Pres. Fed. Constitutional Court 1994–; Dr hc (Basle) 1999; Justice in the World Award, Madrid 2000; Grosses Goldene Ehrenzeichen der Republik Österreich 1998. *Publications:* Theorie und Wirklichkeit der GmbH 1966, Der verständige Rechtsgenosse 1977, Die gemeinsame Sorge geschiedener Eltern in der Rechtspraxis 1988, "In Namen des Volkes" – Macht und Verantwortung der Richter 1999, Das Bundesverfassungsgericht 2001. *Address:* Goethe Institut InterNationes e.V., Helene-Weber-Allee 1, 80637 Munich, Germany (Office). *Telephone:* (89) 159210 (Office). *Fax:* (89) 15921450 (Office). *E-mail:* zv@goethe.de (Office). *Website:* www.goethe.de (Office).

LIMONOV, Eduard (pseudonym of Eduard Veniaminovich Savenko); Russian poet and writer; b. 22 Feb. 1943, Dzerzhinsk, Gorky Dist; m. 1st Yelena Limonova Shchapova 1971 (divorced); m. 2nd Natalia Medvedeva (divorced); first wrote poetry at age of 15; in Kharkov 1965–67, moved to Moscow in 1967, worked as a tailor; left USSR 1974; settled in New York 1975; participant in Russian nationalist movt 1990–; returned to Russia 1991; Chair. Nat. Radical Party 1992–93; Chair. Nat. Bolshevik Party 1994–; arrested on terrorism and conspiracy charges 2002, sentenced by Saratov Oblast Court to four years' imprisonment for illegal acquisition and possession of arms April 2003. *Publications include:* verse and prose in Kontinent, Ekho, Kovcheg, Apollon –1977 (in trans. in England, USA, Austria and Switzerland), It's Me – Eddie (novel) 1979 and Russian (Russkoye) (verse) 1979, Diary of a Failure 1982, Teenager Savenko 1983, The Young Scoundrel 1986, The Death of Contemporary Heroes 1993, The Murder of the Sentry 1993, Selected Works (3 vols) 1999; articles in Russian Communist and Nationalist newspapers 1989–.

LIN, Chia-Chiao, MA, PhD, LLD; American applied mathematician; b. 7 July 1916, Fukien, China; s. of Kai and Y. T. Lin; m. Shou-Ying Liang 1946; one d.; ed Nat. Tsing Hua Univ., Univ. of Toronto, Calif. Inst. of Technology; Asst Prof. of Applied Math., Brown Univ. 1945–46, Assoc. Prof. 1946–47; Assoc. Prof. of Math., MIT 1947–53, Prof. 1953–66, Inst. Prof. of Applied Math., 1966–87; Prof. Emer. of Math., 1987–; Guggenheim Fellow 1954–55, 1960; Pres. Soc. for Industrial and Applied Math. 1973; mem. NAS; John von Neumann Lecturer, Soc. for Industrial and Applied Math. 1967. *Publications:* The Theory of Hydrodynamic Stability 1955, Turbulent Flow, Theoretical Aspects 1963. *Leisure interest:* astronomy. *Address:* c/o Department of Mathematics, Massachusetts Institute of Technology, Cambridge, MA 02139, USA.

LIN, Cho-Liang, BMus; American concert violinist; b. 29 Jan. 1960, Taiwan; s. of Kuo-Jing Lin and Kuo-Ling Yu; m. Deborah Lin; ed Juilliard School, New York, Sydney Conservatoire; concert tours worldwide; over 100 performances a year; soloist with leading orchestras including London Symphony Orchestra, Philharmonia, Concertgebouw, Orchestre de Paris, Chicago Symphony Orchestra, Philadelphia Orchestra and Boston Symphony Orchestra; played Tchaikovsky's Concerto at London Proms 1999; 20 solo albums; Founder, Dir Taipei Int. Music Festival; mem. Faculty Juilliard School 1991–; Gramophone Record Award 1989, Musical American's Instrumentalist of the

Year 2000. *Leisure interests:* tennis, wine. *Address:* c/o ICM Artists (London) Ltd, Oxford House, 76 Oxford Street, London, W1N 0AX, England (Office); Juilliard School, 60 Lincoln Center Plaza, New York, NY 10023, USA.

LIN, Hsin-i, BSc; Taiwanese politician and business executive; b. 2 Dec. 1946; m.; three c.; ed Nat. Cheng Kung Univ.; engineer China Motor Corpn, later Deputy Man. Eng Div. 1972–76, Deputy Man. Marketing Div. 1976–79, Man. Yangmei Plant 1980–82, Vice-Pres. 1982–87, Exec. Vice-Pres. 1987–90, Pres. 1991–96, Vice-Chair. 1997–2000; Chair. Sino Diamond Motors Ltd 1993–2000, Automotive Research and Testing Centre 1996–2000, Newa Insurance Co. Ltd 1999–2000; Minister of Econ. Affairs 2000–02; Vice-Premier and Chair. Council of Econ. Planning and Devt 2002–. *Address:* Council for Economic Planning and Development, 9th Floor, 87 Nanking East Road, Section 2, Taipei, Taiwan (Office). *Telephone:* (2) 2522-5300 (Office). *Fax:* (2) 2551-9011 (Office). *Website:* www.cepd.gov.tw (Office).

LIN, See-Yan, MA, MPA, PhD, FIB, F.I.S.; Malaysian banker; b. 3 Nov. 1939, Ipoh; ed Univ. of Malaya in Singapore, Harvard Univ., USA; Tutor in Econs, Univ. of Malaya 1961–63, Harvard Univ. 1970–72, 1976–77; Statistician, Dept of Statistics 1961–63; Econ. Adviser, Minister of Finance 1966–69; Dir Malaysian Rubber Exchange and Licensing Bd (MRELB) 1974–85; mem. Council on Malaysian Invisible Trade (COMIT) 1981–85, Econ. Panel of the Prime Minister 1982–87, Capital Issues Cttee (CIC) 1985–86; Chief Economist, Bank Negara Malaysia (Cen. Bank of Malaysia) 1973–77, Econ. Adviser 1977–80, Deputy Gov. 1980; Chair. Credit Guarantee Corpn Malaysia Berhad (CGC), Malaysian Insurance Inst. (MII); Deputy Chair. Industrial Bank of Malaysia Berhad (Bank Industri); Dir Malaysia Export Credit Insurance Berhad (MECIB), Govt Officers Housing Corpn, Seacen Research and Training Centre, Malaysian Wildlife Conservation Foundation; mem. Malaysia Program Advisory Council, US-ASIAN Centre for Tech. Exchange, Commonwealth Group of Experts on the Debt Crisis 1984, IMF Working Party on Statistical Discrepancy in World Currency Imbalances 1985–87, IMF Cttee of Balance of Payments Compilers 1987; Pres. Malaysian Econ. Asscn; Eisenhower Fellow 1986. *Publications:* numerous articles in academic, banking and business journals. *Address:* Bank Negara Malaysia, Jalan Kuching, P.O. Box 10922, 50929 Kuala Lumpur, Malaysia.

LIN CHIN-SHENG, BL; Taiwanese government official; b. 4 Aug. 1916; ed Law Coll., Tokyo Imperial Univ.; Magistrate, Chiayi Co. Govt 1951–54; Chair. Yunlin Co. HQ, Kuomintang (Nationalist Party of China) 1954–57; Magistrate, Yunlin Co. Govt 1957–64; Dir Cheng-Ching Lake Industrial Waterworks 1964–67; Commr Taiwan Prov. Govt 1966–70; Sec.-Gen. Taiwan Provincial HQ, Kuomintang 1967–68, Chair. Taipei Municipal HQ 1969–70, Deputy Sec.-Gen. Cen. Cttee 1970–72, mem. Standing Cttee of Cen. Cttee 1976–; Minister of the Interior 1972–76, of Communications 1976–81, without Portfolio 1981–84; Vice-Pres. Examination Yuan 1984–93; Sr Adviser to Pres. of Taiwan 1993; mem. Standing Cttee of Kuomintang Cen. Cttee 1976–; Order of the Brilliant Star. *Address:* c/o Kuomintang, 11 Chung Shan South Road, Taipei 100, Taiwan.

LIN CHING-HSIA; Taiwanese film actress; b. 1955, Taiwan; lived in Calif. 1979–81; now lives mainly in Hong Kong; has appeared in 82 films including: Outside the Window, Dream Lovers, Police Story, Starry, Starry Night. *Address:* c/o Taiwan Cinema and Drama Association, 10/F, 196 Chunghua Road, Sec. 1, Taipei, Taiwan.

LIN CHUAN, PhD; Taiwanese politician; b. 13 Dec. 1951; m.; two d.; ed Fu Jen Catholic Univ., Nat. Chengchi Univ., Univ. of Ill., USA; Assoc. Research Fellow Chung Hua Inst. for Econ. Research 1994–89; Assoc. Prof. Dept of Public Finance, Nat. Chengchi Univ. 1989–90, Prof. 1990–95, 1998–2000; Dir Bureau of Finance, Taipei City Govt 1995–98; Dir-Gen. Directorate-Gen. of Budget, Accounting and Statistics 2000–02; Minister of Finance Nov. 2002–. *Address:* Ministry of Finance, 2 Ai Kuo West Road, Taipei, Taiwan (Office). *Telephone:* (2) 2322-8000 (Office). *Fax:* (2) 2322-8000 (Office). *Website:* www .mof.gov.tw (Office).

LIN LANYING, PhD; Chinese scientist; b. 7 Feb. 1918, Putian Co., Fujian Prov.; ed Fujian Xiehe Univ., Pennsylvania Univ., USA; returned to China 1957; Research Fellow, Semiconductors Inst. Academia Sinica 1957–; Vice-Chair., Youth Fed. of China 1962–66; mem. Standing Cttee 3rd NPC 1964–66; Deputy, 4th NPC 1974–78; Deputy Dir, Semiconductors Inst. 1977; Vice-Chair. Nat. Cttee China Science and Tech Asscn 1980–; mem. Standing Cttee 5th NPC 1978–83, 6th NPC 1983–88, 7th NPC 1988–93; mem. Dept of Tech. Sciences, Academia Sinica 1985–; mem. Presidium, 5th, 6th, 7th NPC; Vice-Pres. Asscn for Science and Tech. 1980–; mem. 7th NPC 1988–93; mem. Educ., Science, Culture and Public Health Cttee 7th NPC 1988–93; mem. Standing Cttee 8th NPC 1993, mem. Educ., Science, Culture and Public Health Cttee; numerous prizes. *Publications:* CZ-Silicon and FZ Silicon Crystal Growth and its Property Studies 1957–78, Vapour and Liquid Phase Epitaxy Growth of the High Purity GaAs and its Property Studies 1978–1982, A Study on New Donors in CZ-Si 1984–1988, GaAs Grown in Space 1986, High Electron Mobility Materials MBE Growth and Property Studies 1993. *Address:* Room 401, Building 809, Haidian Huang Zhuang, Beijing 100080, People's Republic of China. *Telephone:* (861) 2554942. *Fax:* (861) 2562389.

LIN LIN; Chinese writer; b. 27 Sept. 1910, Zhao'an Co., Fujian Prov.; s. of the late Lin Hede and of Zhen Yilian; m. 1st Wu Lanjiao 1930 (deceased); m. 2nd Chen Ling 1950; two s. two d.; ed Zhao'an middle school, Chinese Univ., Beijing, Waseda Univ. Tokyo, Japan; joined Left-Wing Movt in Literature,

1934–36; returned to Shanghai 1936; Ed., Jiuwang Daily, Shanghai 1937, Guangzhou 1938, Guilin 1939–41; Chief Ed. of Huaqiao Guide, Manila, Philippines 1941–47; Prof., Dept of Chinese Literature, Dade Coll., Hong Kong 1947–49; Cultural Counsellor, Embassy, New Delhi, India 1955–58; Vice-Pres. of the China-Japan Friendship Assen 1965–; Vice-Pres. Chinese People's Asscn for Friendship with Foreign Countries 1973–86; Pres. China Soc. for Study of Japanese Literature 1980–94, Hon. Pres. 1994–; mem. 5th, 6th and 7th Nat. Cttees Chinese People's Political Consultative Conf. 1978–93; Hon. mem. Nat. Cttee, Adviser, Chinese Writers' Asscn 2002–; Yakushi Inoue Cultural Exchange Award 1996. *Publications:* Poems of India 1958, Essays about Japan 1982, A Selection of Japanese Classical Haiku 1983, The Sea and the Ship (essays) 1987, A Selection of Japanese Modern Haiku 1990, Amaranthus (poems) 1991, Cutting Clouds (Chinese haiku) 1994, Continued Essays About Japan 1994, Memoirs of My First 88 Years 2002. *Address:* Room 402, Building 22, Congwenmen Dongdajie Street, Beijing 100062, People's Republic of China.

LIN LIYUN; Chinese state official; b. 1933, Taizhong, Taiwan; ed Kobe, Japan, Beijing Univ.; council mem. Sino-Japanese Friendship Asscn 1973–; mem. 10th CCP Cen. Cttee 1973; mem. Standing Cttee 4th NPC 1975; Deputy for Taiwan to 5th NPC 1978, 6th NPC 1983; Vice-Pres. Women's Fed. 1978–, mem. Exec. Council 1988–; Pres. Fed. of Taiwan Compatriots 1981–; mem. 12th CCP Cen. Cttee 1982–87; mem. Presidium 6th NPC 1986–88; Standing Cttee NPC 1984–88; mem. Credentials Cttee NPC 1984–88; mem. Overseas Chinese Cttee NPC 1986– (now Vice-Chair.); mem. 13th CCP Cen. Cttee 1987–92, 14th CCP Cen. Cttee 1992–97, 15th CCP Cen. Cttee 1997–2002; Vice-Chair. 14th NPC Overseas Chinese Affairs Cttee; adviser Asscn for the Promotion of the Peaceful Reunification of China 1988–; mem. Working Group for Unification of the Motherland 1984–; Vice-Pres. China Int. Cultural Exchange Centre 1984–; Vice-Pres. All China Fed. of Returned Overseas Chinese 1994–; Vice-Pres. All-China Sports Fed. 1979–; Adviser Asscn for Relations Across the Taiwan Straits. *Address:* Chinese Communist Party Central Committee, Beijing, People's Republic of China.

LIN RUO; Chinese party official; b. 1924, Chaoan, Guangdong Prov.; ed Zhonshan Univ.; joined CCP 1945; First Deputy Sec. Zhanjiang Pref. 1966–, Deputy Dir Nanfang Daily 1971–; Sec. CCP Cttee Zhanjiang Pref. 1977–; Dir Nanfang Ribao 1980; mem. 12th CCP Cen. Cttee 1982–87; Sec. CCP Cttee, Guangdong Prov. 1983–93; mem. 13th CCP Cen. Cttee 1987–92; Del. 7th NPCC 1988–92; Chair. People's Congress of Guangdong Prov. 1990–96. *Address:* c/o Guangdong Provincial Chinese Communist Party, Guangzhou, Guangdong, People's Republic of China.

LIN YANG-KANG, BA; Taiwanese politician; b. 10 June 1927, Nantou Co.; s. of Lin Chih-Chang and Lin Chen Ruan; m. Chen Ho 1945; one s. three d.; ed Nat. Taiwan Univ.; Chair. Yunlin Co. HQ, Kuomintang 1964–67; Magistrate, Nantou Co. 1967–72; Commr Dept of Reconstruction, Taiwan Provincial Govt 1972–76; Mayor of Taipei 1976–78; Gov. Taiwan Prov. 1978–81; Minister of Interior 1981–84; Vice-Premier of Taiwan 1984–87; Pres. Judicial Yuan 1987–94; Sr Advisor to Pres. 1994–95 (party membership suspended 1995); stood as ind. Presidential cand. March 1996. *Leisure interests:* hiking, reading and studying, music, films. *Address:* 124 Chungking South Road, Section 1, Taipei, Taiwan.

LIN ZHAOHUA; Chinese theatre director; b. 1 July 1936, Tianjin; s. of Lin Baogui and Zhang Shuzhen; m. Binzhu He 1964; one s. one d.; Vice-Pres. and Dir Beijing People's Art Theatre 1984–; mem. Standing Cttee, China Theatre Asscn 1984–; Chair. Art Cttee Beijing People's Art Theatre 1984–. *Productions include:* The Red Heart 1978, Just Opinion 1980, Warning Signal 1982, Bus Stop 1983, Marriage and Funerals 1984, Wild Man 1985, Amadeus Schweyk in the Second World War; A Grandfather's Nirvana 1986, Peace Lake 1988, Farmland is Greenspread Again 1989, Chinese Orphan 1989, Hamlet 1989, Countryside Anecdote 1990, A Report from Hu-tuo River 1991, Mountain Flower (Beijing Opera) 1991, Bird and Man, Romulus the Great 1993, Ruan Lingyu 1994, Faust 1994, Chess and Man 1996, Fisherman 1997, Three Sisters Waiting For Godot (adapted from Chekhov's Three Sisters and Beckett's Waiting for Godot) 1998, The Teahouse 1999, Li Yu: His Romance and his Theatrical Troupe 1999, Prime Minister Liu The Hunchback (Beijing Opera) 2000, Richard III 2001, Lu Xun: Adaptation of Ancient Mythologies 2001, Cai Wen Ji (Anhui Opera) 2001. *Publications:* Stage Art of Warning Signal (ed.) 1985, Stage Art of Marriages and Funerals, On Theatrical Directing. *Leisure interests:* Chinese yoga, swimming, music, playing the erhu. *Address:* Beijing People's Art Theatre, 22 Wangfujing Street, Beijing; 3-7-503, East Block, Ditan Beili, Heping li, Beijing, People's Republic of China (Home). *Telephone:* (10) 65135801 (Office); (10) 64214081 (Home). *Fax:* (10) 65139770 (Office).

LINACRE, Sir (John) Gordon (Seymour), Kt, CBE, AFC, DFM, CBIM, FRSA; British newspaper executive; b. 23 Sept. 1920, Sheffield; s. of John J. Linacre and Beatrice B. Linacre; m. Irene A. Gordon 1943; two d.; ed Firth Park Grammar School, Sheffield; served RAF, rank of Squadron Leader 1939–46; journalistic appointments Sheffield Telegraph/Star 1937–47; Kemsley News Service 1947–50; Deputy Ed. Newcastle Journal 1950–56, Newcastle Evening Chronicle 1956–57; Ed. Sheffield Star 1958–61; Asst Gen. Man. Sheffield Newspapers Ltd 1961–63; Exec. Dir Thomson Regional Newspapers Ltd, London 1963–65; Man. Dir Yorkshire Post Newspapers Ltd 1965–83, Deputy Chair. 1981–83, Chair. 1983–90, Pres. 1990–; Dir United Newspapers PLC 1969–91, Deputy Chair. 1981–91, Chief Exec. 1983–88; Deputy Chair.

Express Newspapers PLC 1985–88; also fmr Chair. United Provincial Newspapers Ltd, Sheffield Newspapers Ltd, Lancashire Evening Post Ltd, Northampton Mercury Co. Ltd, East Yorkshire Printers Ltd etc.; Dir Yorkshire TV 1969–90; Chair. Leeds Univ. Foundation 1989–2000; Chair. Chameleon TV Ltd 1994–; Chair. Opera North Ltd 1978–98, Pres. 1998–; many other professional and public appointments; Grand Ufficiale, Ordine al Merito della Repubblica Italiana; Hon. LLD (Leeds) 1991. *Leisure interests:* fly-fishing, hill-walking, golf, music, theatre. *Address:* White Windows, Staircase Lane, Bramhope, Leeds, LS16 9JD, England. *Telephone:* (113) 284-2751.

LINAKER, Lawrence Edward (Paddy); British business executive; b. 22 July 1934, Hants.; s. of late Lawrence Wignall and Rose Linaker; m. Elizabeth Susan Elam 1963; one s.; ed Malvern Coll.; with Esso Petroleum 1957–63; joined M & G Group 1963, Deputy Chair. and Chief Exec. 1987–94; Chair. M & G Investment Man. 1987–94; Dir Securities Inst. 1992–94; Chair. Fleming Geared Growth Investment Trust PLC 1997–, Fleming Geared Income and Investment Trust PLC 1997–2001; fmr Chair. Marling Industries PLC, Fisons; mem. Bd Lloyds TSB Group PLC, Fleming Mercantile Investment Trust 1994–, Wolverhampton & Dudley Breweries PLC 1996–; mem. Council, Royal Postgrad. Medical School 1977–88, Gov. Body, Soc. for the Promotion of Christian Knowledge 1976–94, Council, Malvern Coll. 1989–; Chair. Institutional Fund Man.'s Asscn 1992–94, YMCA Nat. Coll. 1992–2000; Trustee TSB Foundation for England and Wales. *Leisure interests:* music, wine, gardening. *Address:* Swyre Farm, Aldsworth, Nr Cheltenham, Glos., England.

LINCOLN, Blanche Lambert, BA; American politician; b. 30 Sept. 1960, Helena, Ark.; ed Randolph-Macon Woman's Coll.; mem. of US House of Reps from Ark. 1992–96; Senator from Arkansas Jan. 1999–; Democrat. *Address:* US Senate, 825 Hart Senate Building, Washington, DC 20510, USA. *Telephone:* (202) 224-4843.

LINDAHL, George, BSc; American petroleum executive; ed Univ. of Alabama, Tulane Univ., Harvard Univ.; began career as geologist and Man. Amoco Production Co.; Exec. Vice-Pres., Dir and Partner Walker Energy Partners of Houston –1987; joined Union Pacific Resources (UPR) Group, Inc. Jan. 1987, Pres. and COO 1996–99, Chair., Pres. and CEO 1999–2001; Dir Anadarko Petroleum Corpn, Vice-Chair. –2001; mem. Pres.'s Council, Univ. of Ala; mem. visiting Cttee Petroleum and Geosystems Engineering Dept, Univ. of Tex. at Austin; mem. Texas Hall of Fame Foundation; fmr Pres. Fort Worth Petroleum Club; mem. All-American Wildcatters 1999. *Address:* c/o Anadarko Petroleum Corporation, 17001 Northchase Drive, Houston, TX 77060, USA (Office). *Website:* www.anadarko.com (Office).

LINDAHL, Tomas, MD, FRS; Swedish scientist; b. 28 Jan. 1938, Stockholm; ed Karolinska Inst., Stockholm; Deputy Dir of Research, Cancer Research UK London Research Inst. *Address:* Cancer Research UK London Research Institute, Clare Hall Laboratories, South Mimms, Herts., EN6 3LD, England (Office). *Telephone:* (20) 7269-3993 (Office). *Fax:* (20) 7269-3803 (Office). *E-mail:* t.lindahl@cancer.org.uk (Office).

LINDBECK, Assar, PhD; Swedish professor of international economics; b. 26 Jan. 1930, Umeå; s. of Karl Lindbeck and Eugenia Lindbeck (née Sundelin); m. Dorothy Nordlund 1953; one s. one d.; ed Univs of Uppsala and Stockholm; Asst Prof., Univ. of Mich., USA 1958; with Swedish Treasury 1958–62; Asst Prof. of Econs, Univ. of Stockholm 1962–63, Prof. 1964–71, Prof. of Int. Econs, Dir Inst. of Int. Econs 1971–94; Visiting Prof. Columbia Univ., USA 1968–69, Univ. of Calif. at Berkeley 1969, Nat. Univ. Australia 1970, Yale Univ. 1976, Stanford Univ. 1977; Consultant World Bank 1986–87; mem. Nobel Prize Cttee on Econs 1969–94 (Chair. 1980–94); several prizes. *Publications:* A Study in Monetary Analysis, Swedish Economic Policy, Economics of the Agricultural Sector, The Political Economy of the New Left, The Insider-Outsider Theory (with Dennis Snower), Unemployment and Macroeconomics. *Leisure interest:* painting. *Address:* Institute for International Economic Studies, Stockholm University, 10691 Stockholm (Office); 50 Östermalmsgatan, 11426 Stockholm, Sweden (Home). *Telephone:* (8) 16-30-78 (Office); (8) 21-23-37 (Home). *Fax:* (8) 16-29-46 (Office); (8) 21-23-37 (Home). *E-mail:* assar@iies.su.se (Office). *Website:* www.iies.su.se.

LINDBLOM, Seppo Olavi, LIC.POL.SC.; Finnish bank executive and politician; b. 9 Aug. 1935, Helsinki; s. of Olavi and Aura (née Sammal) Lindblom; m. Anneli Johanson 1958; four d.; ed Univ. of Helsinki; Man. br. office, Finnish Workers' Savings Bank 1958–60; Economist, Bank of Finland 1960–68; Sec. to Prime Minister 1968–70; Head, Labour Inst. for Econ. Research 1970–72; Minister in Ministry of Trade and Industry 1972; Head, Dept of Nat. Econ. Ministry of Finance 1973–74; Nat. Conciliator for Incomes Policy 1973–74; Dir Bank of Finland 1974–82, mem. Bd of Man. 1982–87; Minister of Trade and Industry 1983–87; Chair. and Chief Exec. Postipankki Ltd 1988–96. *Leisure interests:* music, chess.

LINDEGAARD, Jørgen; Danish airline executive; b. 1948; worked as exec. in telecommunications eng; fmr Pres. Fyns Telefon A/S, Københavns Telefon A/S; fmr mem. Exec. Bd Tele Danmark; Pres. and CEO GN Store Nord 1997–; Pres. and CEO SAS Group 2001–. *Address:* SAS AB, Frösundaviks Allé 1, Solna, 195 87 Stockholm, Sweden (Office). *Telephone:* (8) 797-00-00 (Office). *Fax:* (8) 797-12-10 (Office). *Website:* www.scandinavian.net (Office).

LINDEMAN, Fredrik Otto, DPhil; Norwegian professor of linguistics; b. 3 March 1936, Oslo; s. of Carl Fredrik Lindeman and Agnes Augusta Lindeman;

m. Bente Konow Taranger 1960; one s. one d.; ed Univ. of Oslo; Prof. of Indo-European Linguistics, Univ. of Copenhagen 1970, Univ. of Oslo 1976–; Dals Prize for Outstanding Achievement, Univ. of Oslo 1997. *Publications:* Les Origines Indo-Européennes de la 'Verschärfung' Germanique 1964, Einfüh-rung in die Laryngaltheorie 1970, The Triple Representation of Schwa in Greek and some related problems of Indo-European Phonology 1982, Studies in Comparative Indo-European Linguistics 1996, Introduction to the 'Lar-yngeal Theory' 1997, Våre Arveord Etymologisk Ordbok (with Harald Bjor-vand) 2000. *Leisure interest:* music. *Address:* P.O. Box 1102, Blindern, 0317 Oslo (Office); Abbedikollen 13, 0280 Oslo 2, Norway (Home). *Telephone:* 22-85-67-87 (Office); 22-50-92-78 (Home).

LINDENSTRAUSS, Joram, PhD; Israeli professor of mathematics; b. 28 Oct. 1936, Tel Aviv; m. Naomi Salinger 1962; one s. three d.; ed Hebrew Univ., Jerusalem; Sr Lecturer in Math., Hebrew Univ. 1965, Assoc. Prof. 1967, Prof. 1970–; Visiting Prof. Univs Yale, Washington, California, Texas, Inst. Mittag Leffler, Inst. for Advanced Study, Princeton; mem. Israel Acad. of Science and Humanities; Israeli Prize in Math. 1981. *Publications:* Classical Banach Spaces, Vols I–II, 1977, 1979, Geometric Non Linear Functional Analysis, Vol. I (jtly) 2000, Handbook of the Geometry of Banach Spaces, Vol. I (co-ed.) 2001. *Address:* Hebrew University of Jerusalem, Mount Scopus, 91 905 Jerusalem; 36 Habanai Str., Jerusalem, Israel. *Telephone:* 2-522762.

LINDERBERG, Jan Erik, FD; Danish professor of theoretical chemistry; b. 27 Oct. 1934, Karlskoga, Sweden; s. of David Linderberg and Sara Bäckström; m. Gunnel Björstam 1957; two s.; ed Uppsala Univ.; Docent, Uppsala Univ. 1964–68; Prof. of Theoretical Chem. Århus Univ. 1968–; Adjunct Prof. of Chem., Univ. Fla Gainesville, Univ. Utah; mem. Royal Danish Soc. of Sciences and Letters, Int. Acad. of Quantum Molecular Science, Royal Soc. of Science (Uppsala). *Publications:* Role of Correlation in Electronic Systems 1964, Propagators in Quantum Chemistry (co-author), Quantum Science (with others) 1976. *Leisure interest:* orienteering. *Address:* Århus University, Department of Chemistry, Langelandsgade 140, 8000 Århus C; Janus la Cours gade 20, 8000 Århus C, Denmark. *Telephone:* 89-42-38-29 (Office); 86-12-02-41 (Home). *Fax:* 86-19-61-99 (Office). *E-mail:* jan@chem.au.dk (Office). *Website:* www.chem.au.dk/staff (Office).

LINDH, (Ylva) Anna Maria, BL; Swedish politician; b. 19 June 1957, Stockholm; d. of Staffan Lindh and Nancy Lindh; m. Bo Holmberg 1991; two s.; ed Sanobro School, Enkoping, Univ. of Uppsala; Pres. of the Nat Council of Swedish Youth 1981–83; MP and mem. Standing Cttee on Taxation 1982–85; Pres. of the Social Democratic Youth League 1984–90; Pres. Govt Council of Alcohol and Drug Politics 1986–90; Vice-Pres. Int. Union of Socialist Youth 1987–89; mem. Exec. Cttee Social Democratic Party 1991–; Pres. Cttee for Home Affairs, Party of European Socialists 1992–94; Minister of the Environment 1994–98; MP 1998–; Minister of Foreign Affairs 1998–; mem. Stockholm City Council; Vice-Mayor, Stockholm 1991–94, mem. Cen-tral (Exec.) Cttee, Pres. Culture Cttee, Leisure Cttee; Pres. Bd Stockholm City Theatre. *Leisure interests:* theatre, music, novels. *Address:* Ministry of For-eign Affairs, Gustav Adolfstorg 1, 10339 Stockholm, Sweden. *Telephone:* (8) 405-10-00. *Fax:* (8) 723-11-76. *Website:* www.ud.se (Office).

LINDNER, Carl Henry; American business executive; b. 22 April 1919, Dayton, Ohio; s. of Carl Henry Lindner and Clara Lindner (née Serrer); m. Edith Bailey 1953; three s.; Co-Founder United Dairy Farmers 1940; Pres. American Finance Corpn, Cincinnati 1959–84, Chair. 1959–, CEO 1984–; Chair., CEO, Chair. Exec. Cttee United Brands Co. (now Chiquita Brands Int. Inc.), NY 1984–; Chair. Penn Cen. Corpn (now American Premier Under-writers), Greenwich, Conn. 1983–, CEO 1987–94; Chair. and CEO Great American Communications Co. 1987–; now Chair. and CEO American Finance Group, Cincinnati; mem. Bd of Dirs Mission Inst., Bd of Advisers Business Admin. Coll., Univ. of Cincinnati; owner, CEO Cincinnati Reds (baseball team) 1999–.

LINDSAY, Most Rev. and Hon. Orland Ugham, OJ, BD; Jamaican/Antiguan ecclesiastic (retd); b. 24 March 1928, Jamaica; s. of Hubert Lindsay and Ida Lindsay; m. Olga Daphne Wright 1959; three s.; ed Mayfield Govt School, Southfield, Jamaica, Culham Coll. Oxford, England, St Peter's Theo-logical Coll., Jamaica, Montréal Diocesan Theological Coll. at McGill Univ., Canada; served in RAF 1944–49; teacher Franklin Town Govt School 1949–52; Asst Master Kingston Coll. 1952–53, 1958–63; ordained Deacon, Jamaica 1956; Asst Curate St Peter's Vere Cure 1956–57; ordained Priest 1957; Chaplain Kingston Coll. 1958–63; Asst Curate in charge of Manchioneal Cure 1960–63; Sec. Jamaica Diocesan Synod 1962–70; Chaplain Jamaica Defence Force 1963–67; Prin. Church Teachers' Coll., Mandeville, Jamaica 1967–70; Bishop of Antigua, latterly of NE Caribbean and Aruba 1970–98; Archbishop of the West Indies 1986–98; Order of Distinction (Antigua) 1996, Order of Jamaica 1997; Hon. DD (Berkeley Divinity School, Yale Univ.) 1978, (St Paul's Coll., S. Va) 1998; Hon. STD (Diocesan Theological Coll., Montréal) 1997. *Leisure interests:* swimming, listening to music, reading, photography. *Address:* Crosbies, P.O. Box 3456, Antigua. *Telephone:* 560-1724. *Fax:* 462-2090. *E-mail:* orland@candw.ag (Home).

LINDSAY, Robert; British actor; b. 12 Dec. 1949, Ilkeston, Derbyshire; m. Cheryl Hall (divorced); one d. by actress Diana Weston; ed Royal Acad. of Dramatic Art (RADA); stage career commenced at Manchester Royal Exchange; appeared in Me and My Girl, London, Broadway and LA 1985–87 (recipient Olivier, Tony and Fred Astaire awards); appeared as Henry II in

Anouilh's Beckett, London 1991, Cyrano de Bergerac, London 1992. *Films:* Bert Rigby, You're a Fool, Loser Takes All, Strike It Rich, Fierce Creatures 1996. *Television appearances include:* Edmund in King Lear (Granada), Wolfie in comedy series Citizen Smith, Michael Murray in serial GBH (Channel 4) 1991; Genghis Cohn, Jake's Progress, Goodbye My Love 1996, Oliver (Olivier Award for Best Actor in a Musical), Richard III 1998, Fagin in Oliver Twist 1999.

LINDSEY, Lawrence B., PhD; American economist; b. 18 July 1954, Peeks-kill, NY; s. of Merritt Lindsey and Helen Hissam; m. Susan Lindsey 1982; three c.; ed Bowdoin Coll., Harvard Univ.; on staff of Pres. Reagan's Council of Econ. Advisers; Special Asst for Policy Devt to Pres. Bush; fmr Prof. of Econs, Harvard Univ.; mem. Bd of Govs Fed. Reserve System 1991–97; Man. Dir Econ. Strategies Inc. 1997–2001; Econ. Adviser to Pres. 2001–02; Dir Nat. Econ. Council 2001–02; Chair. Bd Neighborhood Reinvestment Corpn 1993–97; Resident Scholar and holder Arthur C. Burns Chair., American Enterprise Inst. 1997–2001; Hon. JuD (Bowdoin Coll.) 1993; Distinguished Public Service Award, Boston Bar Asscn 1994. *Publications:* The Growth Experiment: How the New Tax Policy is Transforming the US Economy 1990, Econ. Puppetmasters: Lessons From the Halls of Power 1999; numerous articles in professional pubs. *Address:* c/o National Economic Council, The White House, 1600 Pennsylvania Avenue, NW, Washington, DC 20502, USA (Office).

LINDSKOG, Martin; Swedish broadcasting executive; b. 5 April 1953, Stockholm; s. of Bjorn Lindskog and Britt-Marie Lindskog; m. Joan Estes; one s.; ed Stockholm School of Econs; with Esselte Group 1977–90; CEO Filmnet Int. Holdings 1990–93; joined SBS 1993, Pres. 1996–. *Address:* SBS Broad-casting S.A., P.O. Box 26205, 10041 Stockholm, Sweden (Office). *Telephone:* (8) 54-51-22-00 (Office). *Fax:* (8) 23-25-05 (Office). *Website:* sbsbroadcasting.se (Office).

LINDSLEY, Donald Benjamin, AB, MA, PhD; American professor of psy-chology and physiology; b. 23 Dec. 1907, Brownhelm, Ohio; s. of Benjamin Kent Lindsley and Martha Elizabeth Jenne; m. Ellen Ford 1933; two s. two d.; ed Wittenberg Univ. and Univ. of Iowa; Instructor in Psychology, Univ. of Ill. 1932–33; Nat. Research Council Fellow, Harvard Medical School 1933–35; Research Assoc., W Reserve Univ. Medical School 1935–38; Asst Prof. Brown Univ. and Dir Psychology and Neurophysiology Lab., Bradley Hosp. 1938–46; Dir Radar Research Project, Office of Scientific Research and Devt, Yale Univ., Camp Murphy and Boca Raton Air Force Base, Fla 1943–46; Prof. of Psychology, Northwestern Univ. 1946–51; Prof. of Psychology, Physiology and Psychiatry, Univ. of Calif., Los Angeles 1951–77, Prof. Emer. 1977–, mem. Brain Research Inst., Univ. of Calif., Los Angeles 1961–, Chair. Dept of Psychology 1959–62; Phillips Visiting Lecturer, Haverford Coll. 1961; Pillsbury Visiting Lecturer, Cornell Univ. 1963; Special Visiting Lecturer, Mich. State Univ. 1964; mem. Amazon Neurobiological Expedition on Research Vessel Alpha Helix 1967; Visiting Lecturer, Univ. of Sydney, Australia 1972 and 10 South African univs 1969; Lashley Lecturer, Queens Coll., NY 1979; mem. NAS, American Acad. of Arts and Sciences, Soc. of Experimental Psychologists, Int. Brain Research Org., American Physio-logical Soc., Soc. for Neuroscience (Annual Donald B. Lindsley Prize in Behavioral Neuroscience est. in his name 1978); Foreign mem. Finnish Acad. of Science and Letters 1987; William James Lecturer, Harvard 1958; Gug-genheim Fellow 1959; Hon. mem. American Electroencephalography Soc. 1980; Hon. mem. of Great Distinction, Western Electroencephalography Soc.; Hon. Fellow Univ. of Calif. at Los Angeles School of Medicine 1986; Hon. DSc (Brown Univ.) 1958, (Wittenberg Univ.) 1959, (Trinity Coll.) 1965, (Loyola Univ.) 1969; Hon. PhD (Johannes Gutenberg Univ., Mainz) 1977; Presi-dential Certificate of Merit for Second World War Research Work, Dis-tinguished Scientific Contribution Award, American Psychological Asscn, Distinguished Scientific Achievement Award, Soc. Psychophysiological Research 1984, Ralph Gerard Prize (jtly), Soc. for Neuroscience 1988, Amer-ican Psychological Foundation Gold Award 1989, Herbert Jasper Award (American Electro-encephalographic Soc.) 1994, Wilder Penfield Award (Western Electroencephalographic Soc.) 1996, Century Award, Int. Org. of Psychophysiology 1998. *Publications:* 250 publs, including scientific works in journals and 40 chapters in books; subjects: emotion, electro-encephalog-raphy, neurophysiology, perception, attention, brain function, developmental neurology, autonomic function, sleep and wakefulness, conditioning and learning, etc. *Leisure interests:* music, photography, gardening, golf, travel. *Address:* 471 23rd Street, Santa Monica, CA 90402-3125, USA (Home). *Telephone:* (310) 395-8026 (Home).

LINDSTEN, Jan Eric, PhD, MD; Swedish professor of clinical genetics; b. 23 Jan. 1935, Stockholm; s. of Carl-Eric Lindsten and Lisa M. Hallberg; m. Marianne E. Östling 1960; two s. one d.; ed Uppsala Univ. and Karolinska Inst. Stockholm; Prof. of Human Genetics, Aarhus 1968–70; Prof. of Medical Genetics, Karolinska Inst. 1969–2000, Prof. Emer. 2000–, Head, Dept of Clinical Genetics 1970–90; Chief Medical Officer, Karolinska Hosp. 1987–90, Man. Dir 1990–94; Man. Dir Nat. Univ. Hosp. Copenhagen 1994–96; Dean Medical Faculty, Karolinska Inst. 1996–98; Sec. Nobel Ass. and Medical Nobel Cttee Karolinska Inst. 1979–90; mem. Royal Swedish Acad. of Sciences. *Publications:* 300 publs in the field of medical genetics, especially clinical genetics. *Address:* CMM, Karolinska Hospital, 17176 Stockholm, Sweden (Office). *Telephone:* (8) 51-77-63-53 (Office). *Fax:* (8) 51-77-64-80 (Office). *E-mail:* jan.lindsten@cmm.ki.se (Office).

LINEKER, Gary Winston, OBE; British footballer and television presenter; b. 30 Nov. 1960, Leicester; s. of Barry Lineker and Margaret Patricia Morris Lineker (née Abbs); m. Michelle Denise Cockayne 1986; four s.; ed City of Leicester Boys' Grammar School; debut as professional footballer, Leicester City 1978; transferred to Everton 1985; mem. England team 1984–92, rep. England 1986 World Cup, Mexico, 1990 World Cup, Italy, Capt. of England 1990–92; FC Barcelona 1986–89; transferred to Tottenham Hotspur 1989–92; 80 caps, 48 goals June 1992; with Grampus Eight Team, Japan 1994; never booked in a 16-year career; Freeman City of Leicester 1995; Hon. MA (Leicester) 1992, (Loughborough) 1992; Football Writers' Asscn Player of the Year 1986, 1992, Professional Footballers' Asscn Footballer of the Year 1986, FIFA Fair Play Award 1990; only English player to win Golden Boot Award for scoring most goals in a World Cup 1986. *Television includes:* sports commentator; presenter, Match of the Day, BBC TV 1995–; team capt., They Think It's All Over (quiz show) 1995–. *Leisure interests:* cricket, golf, snooker. *Address:* c/o SFX Sports Group, 35/36 Grosvenor Street, London, W1K 4QX, England. *Telephone:* (20) 7529-4300 (Office). *Fax:* (20) 7529-4347 (Office).

LING, Sergei Stepanovich; Belarus politician, diplomatist and agronomist; b. 7 May 1937; m.; three c.; ed Belarus Agricultural Acad., Higher CPSU School, CPSU Cen. Cttee; agronomist sovkhoz, Lesnoye Kopylsk Dist, chief agronomist sovkhoz, Krynitsa Kopylsk Dist, chief agronomist, Deputy Dir Lyuban Production Co., Chief Soligorsk Production Agric. Admin; Deputy Chair. then Chair. Slutsk Dist Exec. Cttee, Sec. Smolevichi Dist CPSU Cttee 1960–72; Chief Agric. Div., Sec. Minsk Regional Belarus CP Cttee 1972–82; First Deputy Chair. then Chair. Exec. Cttee Minsk Regional Soviet 1982–86; Chair. Belarus State Cttee on Prices, Deputy Chair. State Planning Cttee 1986–90; Head Agric. Div., Sec. Cen. Cttee Belarus CP 1990–91; Deputy Chair. Belarus Council of Ministers; Chair. State Cttee on Econs and Planning 1991–; Deputy Prime Minister of Belarus 1994–96, Acting Prime Minister 1996–97, Prime Minister 1997–2000; Perm. Rep. to UN 2000–. *Address:* Permanent Mission of Belarus, 136 East 67th Street, New York, NY 10021, USA. *Telephone:* (212) 535-3420 (Office). *Fax:* (212) 734-4810 (Office). *E-mail:* belarus@un.int (Office). *Website:* www.un.int/belarus.

LING JIEFANG (pseudonym of Er Yuehe); Chinese writer; b. Oct. 1945, Xiyang, Shanxi Prov.; Chair. Nanyang Literary and Art Circles 1985–; Vice-Chair. He'nan Prov. Asscn of Writers 1996–; Nat. Achievement by Self-Study Medal 1996, Nat. Wuyi Labour Medal 1998. *Publications:* The Great Emperor Kangwi (4 vols), Emperor Yongzheng (3 vols, Nat. Excellent Novel 1997), Emperor Qianlong (6 vols). *Leisure interests:* chess, card games. *Address:* 13 South Square Street, Nanyang, He'nan Province, 473000 (Office); Literary and Art Circles of Wolong District, Nanyang, He'nan Province, 473000, People's Republic of China (Home). *Telephone:* (377) 3161798 (Office); (377) 3219098 (Home). *Fax:* (377) 3219098 (Home).

LING LIONG SIK, Dato' Seri, MB, BS; Malaysian politician; b. 18 Sept. 1943, Kuala Kangsar, Perak; m. Datin Ee Nah Ong 1968; two c.; ed King Edward VII School, Royal Mil. Coll. and Univ. of Singapore; Parl. Sec. Ministry of Local Govt and Fed. Territory 1976–77; Deputy Minister of Information 1978–82, of Finance 1982–84, of Educ. 1985–86; Minister of Transport 1986–; Deputy Pres. Malaysian Chinese Asscn 1985–87, Pres. 1987–. *Leisure interests:* reading, golf. *Address:* Ministry of Transport, Wisma Perdana, Level 5–7, Block D5, Parcel D, Federal Government Administrative Centre 62502, Putrajaya, Malaysia (Office). *Telephone:* (3) 88866000 (Office). *Fax:* (3) 88892537 (Office). *E-mail:* LeeLC@mot.gov.my (Office). *Website:* www.mot.gov.my (Office).

LINGHU AN; Chinese politician; b. Oct. 1946, Pinglu Co., Shanxi Prov.; ed Beijing Eng Inst.; joined CCP 1965; Exec. Vice-Mayor Dalian City 1988; Vice-Minister of Labour 1989; Vice-Sec. CCP Yunnan Provincial Cttee 1993, Sec. 1997–2001; mem. 15th CCP Cen. Cttee 1997–2002, 16th CCP Cen. Cttee 2002–; Chair. Yunnan Prov. People's Political Consultative Conf. 1998–2001; Vice-Auditor-Gen. Nat. Audit Office 2001–. *Address:* 1 Beiluyuan, Zhanlan Road, Beijing, 100830 People's Republic of China. *Telephone:* 68301520 (Office). *E-mail:* master@audit.gov.cn (Office).

LINGLE, Linda; American state official; b. 1953, St. Louis, Mo.; ed Birmingham High, Calif., Calif. State Univ.; fmr public information officer Hawaii Teamsters and Hotel Workers' Union; f. Moloka'i Free Press; mem. Maui Co. Council 1980–90; Mayor of Maui Co. 1990–98; adviser to Guam and Pohnpei on performance-based budgeting; Leader Republican Party, Hawaii 1998–; Gov. of Hawaii 2002–; mem. Bd Girl Scout Council. *Address:* Office of the Governor, State Capitol, Honolulu, HI 96813, USA (Office). *Telephone:* (808) 586-0034 (Office). *Fax:* (808) 586-0006 (Office). *Website:* gov.state.hi.us (Office).

LINK, Christoph, DJur; German/Austrian professor of law; b. 13 June 1933, Dresden; s. of late Hellmuth Link and of Gerda Link; m. 1st Eva Link 1957; m. 2nd Sibylle Obermayer 1991; two s. one d.; ed Kreuzschule, Dresden and Univs of Marburg, Cologne and Munich; Prof. Vienna 1971–77, Salzburg 1977–79, Hon. Prof. 1979–; Göttingen 1979–86; Prof. of State Admin and Church Law, Univ. of Erlangen 1986, now Prof. Emer.; Dir Hans-Liermann-Inst. für Kirchenrecht 1986–2001; mem. Akad. der Wissenschaften, Göttingen. *Publications:* Die Grundlagen der Kirchenverfassung im lutherischen Konfessionalismus des 19ten Jahrhunderts 1966, Herrschaftsordnung und bürgerliche Freiheit 1979, Hugo Grotius als Staatsdenker 1983, Kirchen und privater Rundfunk (with A. Pahlke) 1985, Staat und Kirche in der neuer-endeutschen Geschichte 2000. *Address:* Hans-Liermann-Institut für Kirchenrecht, 91054 Erlangen, Hindenburgstrasse 34 (Office); Ruehlstrasse 35, 91054 Erlangen, Germany (Home). *Telephone:* (9131) 8522242 (Office); (9131) 209335 (Home). *Fax:* (9131) 8524064 (Office); (9131) 534566 (Home). *E-mail:* hli@jura.uni-erlangen.de (Office); linkerta@aol.com (Home). *Website:* www.jura.uni-erlangen.de (Office).

LINKEVIČIUS, Linas Antanas; Lithuanian politician and diplomatist; b. 6 Jan. 1961, Vilnius; m. 1982; two d.; ed Kaunas Polytechnical Inst.; worked in technical insts 1983–92; reviewer newspaper Tiesa 1992–93; mem. Democratic Labour Party 1990–95; elected to Seimas (Parl.) 1992; Chair. Parl. delegation to N Atlantic Ass. 1992–93; Deputy Chair. Parl. Comm. on Foreign Affairs 1992–93; Minister of Nat. Defence 1993–96, 2000–; Amb. to NATO and to WEU 1997–99. *Address:* Ministry of National Defence, Totorju 25/3, Vilnius 2001, Lithuania (Office). *Telephone:* (526) 24821. *Fax:* (526) 26082 (Office). *E-mail:* vis@kam.lt. *Website:* www.kam.lt.

LINKLATER, Richard; American film director; b. 1967; f. own film co. Detour Films, Austin, Tex.; Founder, Artistic Dir Austin Film Soc.; Silver Bear, Berlin Film Festival 1995 for Before Sunrise. *Films:* Slacker 1991, Dazed and Confused 1993, Before Sunrise 1995, Suburbia 1997, The Newton Boys 1998, Waking Life 2001.

LINNANE, Anthony William, AM, DSc, PhD, FRS, FAA, FTSE; Australian biochemist; b. 17 July 1930, Sydney; s. of late W P. Linnane; m. 1st Judith Neil 1956 (dissolved 1979); one s. one d.; m. 2nd Daryl Woods 1980; one s. one d.; ed Sydney Univ., Univ. of Wisconsin, USA; Postdoctoral Fellow, Univ. of Wis. 1956–58; Lecturer, then Sr Lecturer, Sydney Univ. 1958–62; Reader, Monash Univ. 1962–65, Prof. of Biochem. 1965–94, Emer. Prof. 1996–; Dir Centre for Molecular Biology and Medicine 1984–, Man. Dir 1996–; Ed.-in-Chief Biochemistry and Molecular Biology Int. 1980–98; Visiting Prof., Univ. of Wis. 1967–68; Hon. Prof., Melbourne Univ. 1996–; Pres. Australian Biochemical Soc. 1974–76, Fed. of Asian and Oceanic Biochemical Socs 1975–77, 12th Int. Congress of Biochem., Perth 1982; Foundation Pres. Australian Soc. for Cellular and Molecular Gerontology 2000; Treas., Int. Union of Biochemistry and Molecular Biology 1988–97; Distinguished Service Award, Int. Union of Biochem. and Molecular Biology 2000. *Publications:* over 300 scientific publs. *Leisure interests:* golf, reading, horseracing. *Address:* 24 Myrtle Road, Canterbury, Vic. 3126, Australia (Home); Centre for Molecular Biology and Medicine, 185–187 Hoddle Street, Richmond, Vic. 3121 (Office). *Telephone:* (3) 9888-6526 (Home); (3) 9426-4200 (Office). *Fax:* (3) 9830-5415 (Home); (3) 9426-4201 (Office). *E-mail:* tlinnane@cmbm.com.au (Office). *Website:* www.cmbm.com.au (Office).

LINNER, Carl Sture, MA, PhD; Swedish international civil servant; b. 15 June 1917, Stockholm; s. of Carl W. Linner and Hanna Hellstedt; m. Clio Tambakopoulou 1944; two s.; ed Stockholm and Uppsala Univs; Assoc. Prof. of Greek, Uppsala Univ. 1943; Del. to Int. Red Cross, Greece 1943–45; Dir AB Electrolux, Stockholm 1945–50; Dir Swedish Employers' Confed. 1950–51; Exec. Vice-Pres. AB Bahco, Stockholm 1951–57; Pres. Swedish Lamco Syndicate 1957; Exec. Vice.-Pres. and Gen. Man. Liberian-American-Swedish Minerals Co., Monrovia 1958–60; Chief UN Civilian Operations, later UN Mission, in the Congo 1960–61; Special Rep. of UN Sec.-Gen. in Brussels and London 1962; UN Rep. in Greece, Israel and Cyprus 1962–65, in London 1965–68, in Tunis 1968–71, UNDP, New York 1971–73; Resident Rep. UNDP in Egypt 1973–77; Sr Consultant, FAO 1977–87; mem. Royal Swedish Acad. of Letters, History and Antiquities, Royal Acad. of Arts and Sciences, Uppsala, Societas Litterarum Humaniorum Regiae Upsaliensis; Hon. Prof. (Uppsala) 1992; Star of Africa, Commdr Order of Phoenix, Commdr Order of Honour (Greece); Hon. DPhil(Cyprus) 1998; Prince Carl Medal, Royal Award, Swedish Acad., Letterstedts Award, Royal Acad. of Science, Cultural Award, Natur & Kultur, Bonniers Award, City of Athens Award. *Publications:* Syntaktische und lexikalische Studien zur Historia Lausiaca des Palladios 1943, Giorgos Seferis 1963, Roms Konungahävder 1964, Fredrika Bremer i Grekland 1965, W. H. Humphreys' First Journal of the Greek War of Independence 1967, Thucydides 1978, Min odyssé 1982, Bysantinska porträtt 1984, Homeros 1985, Bistånd till Afrika 1985, Disaster Relief for Development 1986, Hellenika 1986, En värld utan gränser 1988, Den gyllene lyran: Archilochos, Sapfo, Pindaros 1989, Europas födelse 1991, Lans och bage: Aischylos Perserna 1992, Anna Komnenas värld 1993, Bysantinsk Kulturhistoria 1994, Ensamhet och gemenskap 1995, Mulåsnan på Akropolis 1996, Pol Pot och Kambodja 1997, Ökenfäderna 1998, Hellenskt och romerskt 1998, Sicilien 1999, Tidevarv komma, tidevarv försvinna 2000, Europas ungtid 2002. *Leisure interests:* poetry, sports. *Address:* 24 Phokylidou, 10673 Athens, Greece. *Telephone:* (1) 3611780.

LINOWITZ, Sol Myron, LLB; American diplomatist and lawyer; b. 7 Dec. 1913, Trenton, NJ; s. of Joseph Linowitz and Rose Linowitz (née Oglenskye); m. Evelyn Zimmerman 1939; four d.; ed Hamilton Coll. and Cornell Univ. Law School; Asst Gen. Counsel, Office of Price Admin, Washington 1942–44; Officer, Office of Gen. Counsel, Navy Dept 1944–46; fmr Partner, Harris, Beach, Wilcox, Dale & Linowitz; Gen. Counsel, Chair. Bd and Chair. Exec. Cttee Xerox Corpn 1958–66; Chair. Bd Xerox Int. 1966; Chair. Nat. Urban Coalition 1970–75; Pres. Fed. City Council 1974–78; Pres. NY State, American Asscn for UN; mem. Council on Foreign Relations, American Jewish Cttee, American Bar Asscn, NY Bar Asscn, American Asscn UN; US Amb. to OAS and US Rep. on the Inter-American Cttee of the Alliance for Progress 1966–69; Sr Partner Coudert Brothers (Int. Law firm) 1969–84, Sr Counsel

1984–94; co-negotiator, Panama Canal Treaties 1977; personal Amb. of Pres. Carter to Middle East negotiations 1979–81; Chair. Presidential Cttee on World Hunger 1978–79; Head of Comm. for US–Latin American Relations; Co-Chair. Inter-American Dialogue 1981–92; Fellow, American Acad. of Arts and Sciences; Chair. American Acad. of Diplomacy 1984–89; Hon. Chair. Acad. for Educ. Devt 1986–; Trustee, Cornell Univ., Hamilton Coll., Johns Hopkins Univ., American Assembly; hon. degrees (LLD and LHD) from more than 40 colls and univs; Presidential Medal of Freedom 1998. *Publications:* This Troubled Urban World 1974, The Making of a Public Man (a memoir) 1985, The Betrayed Profession: Lawyering in the Twentieth Century 1994. *Leisure interest:* violin. *Address:* Academy for Educational Development, 1875 Connecticut Avenue, Washington, DC 20009 (Office); 2230 California Street, Apt. 4BE, NW, Washington, DC 20008, USA. *Telephone:* (202) 884-8156. *Fax:* (202) 884-8401 (Office). *E-mail:* bflint@aed.org.

LINSKENS, Hansferdinand (Ingenrieth), DPhil; German professor of botany; b. 22 May 1921, Lahr; s. of late Albert W. Linskens and Maria E. Bayer; m. Ingrid M. Rast 1954; two s. two d.; ed Univs of Berlin, Cologne and Bonn, Eidgenössische Tech. Hochschule, Zürich; Battelle Memorial Fellow, ETH, Zürich 1952–53; Privat Dozent, Univ. of Cologne 1954–56; Prof. of Botany, Univ. of Nijmegen, Netherlands 1957–86, Dean, Faculty of Science 1980–85; Prof. of Geobotany, Univ. of Eichstätt 1986–; Adjunct Prof. Univ. of Mass. 1988–; Prof. a Contratto, Univ. of Siena 1987–; mem. Royal Dutch Acad., Deutsche Akad. der Naturforscher Leopoldina, Linnean Soc. of London, Royal Belgian Acad., New York Acad. of Science, Accad. dei Fisiocritici Siena; NATO stipendiary, Lisbon 1960; Visiting Prof. Marine Biological Lab., Woods Hole, Mass. 1966, 1968; Man. Ed. Sexual Plant Reproduction 1988–93, Theoretical and Applied Genetics 1975–85; Hon. mem. Royal Dutch Botanical Soc. 1980; Dr. hc (Lille) 1982, (Siena) 1985; K. Heyer Prize for Allergy Research 1984. *Publications:* Papierchromatographie im der Botanik 1958, Pollen Physiology and Fertilization 1964, Fertilization in Higher Plants 1974, Pollen Biology Biochemistry 1974, Cellular Interaction (with J. Heslop-Harrison) 1985; Modern Methods in Plant Analysis (series) 1966–99, Monographs in Theoretical and Applied Genetics (series) 1975–, Sexual Plant Reproduction 1988–. *Leisure interests:* history of science, collecting autographs. *Address:* Oosterbergweg 5, 6573 EE Beek, Netherlands; Goldberglein 7, 91056 Erlangen, Germany. *Telephone:* 246841652 (Beek); 9131440517 (Erlangen). *Fax:* 24652409 (Nijmegen). *E-mail:* joseb@sci.kun.nl (Office); ProfhfLinskens@aol.com.

LIONAES, Aase; Norwegian politician; b. 10 April 1907, Oslo; d. of Erling Lionaes and Anna Lionaes; m. Kurt Jonas 1938; one d.; ed Univ. of Oslo and LSE; mem. Storting (Parl.) 1953; Vice-Pres. of the Lagting (Upper House) 1965–69, of the Odelsting (Lower House) 1969–77; mem. Govt del. to UN 1946–65; mem. Nobel Peace Prize Cttee 1948, Pres. 1968–79; mem. Norwegian Labour Party; Hon. LLD (Oxford Coll., Ohio). *Address:* c/o Det norske Arbeiderparti, Youngstorget ZA, P.O. Box 8743, 0028 Oslo (Office); Pans Vei nr 8, Ulvøya, N Oslo, Norway. *Telephone:* (2) 282408.

LIOTTA, Ray, BFA; American actor; b. 18 Dec. 1955, Newark, NJ; s. of Alfred Liotta and Mary Liotta; m. Michelle Grace 1997; one d.; ed Univ. of Miami. *Films:* The Lonely Lady 1983, Something Wild 1986, Arena Brains 1987, Dominick and Eugene 1988, Field of Dreams 1989, Goodfellas 1990, Article 99 1992, Unlawful Entry 1992, No Escape 1994, Corrina, Corrina 1994, Operation Dumbo Drop 1995, Unforgettable 1996, Turbulence 1997, Phoenix 1997, Copland 1997, The Rat Pack 1998, Forever Mine 1999, Muppets From Space 1999, Blow 2001, Heartbreakers 2001, Hannibal 2001, John Q. 2002, A Rumor of Angels 2002, Narc 2002. *Television appearances include:* Another World, NBC 1978–80, Hardhat & Legs (CBS movie) 1980, Crazy Times (ABC pilot) 1981, Casablanca, NBC 1983, Our Family Honour, NBC 1985–86, Women & Men 2–In Love There Are No Rules 1991, The Rat Pack 1998, Point of Origin 2002. *Address:* c/o Endeavor Talent Agency, 9701 Wilshire Boulevard, 10th Floor, Beverly Hills, CA 90212, USA.

LIPKIN, Semen Izrailevich; Russian writer, poet and translator; b. 19 Sept. 1911, Odessa; s. of Israel Lipkin and Rosalia Lipkin; m. Inna Lvovna Lisnyanskaya (q.v.) 1967; two s. three d.; ed Moscow Econ. Inst.; served in Soviet Army 1941–45; resgnd from Union of Writers 1980 (membership restored 1989); Rudaki State Prize 1967, People's Poet of Kalmyk ASSR 1968, Tukai Prize 1991, Sakharov Prize, Pushkin Prize (Germany) 1995. *Translations include:* Dzangar (Kalmyk epic) 1940, Geser (Buryat epic) 1968, Mahabharata (Indian epic) 1969, also from classical Tadzhik, Uzbek and Kirghiz writers. *Poetry:* Eyewitness 1967, A Notebook of Being 1977, Freewill 1981, A Nomadic Flame 1984, Lire 1989. *Novels:* Ten-day Period 1983, Life and Destiny of Vasilii Grossman 1990, The Flaming Coal 1991, The Characters 1991, Moonlight 1991, The Notes of the Lodger 1992, April 1993, Before the Sunset 1995, The Second Road (memoirs) 1995, Quadriga (memoirs) 1997. *Address:* Usievicha Street 8, Apt. 4b, 125315 Moscow, Russia. *Telephone:* (095) 155-75-98.

LIPOVSEK, Marjana; Slovenian singer; b. 3 Dec. 1946, Ljubljana; ed in Ljubljana and Graz Music Acad., Austria; joined Vienna State Opera, then Hamburg State Opera, Fed. Repub. of Germany; operatic roles include Oktavian, Dorabella, Ulrica, Mistress Quickly, Orfeo, Azucena, Amneris, Brangäne, Fricka, Marfa (in Khovanshchina) and Marie (in Wozzeck); has sung in the leading European opera houses including Berlin, Madrid, Frankfurt, La Scala, Vienna State Opera and Bavarian State Opera, Munich; int. debut as recitalist, Salzburg Festival 1985; Grand Prix du Disque for Frank

Martin's Cornet, Prix Spécial du Jury Nouvelle Académie du Disque Français; Gustav Mahler Gold Medal (Bavaria) 1993, (Vienna) 1996. *Recordings include:* the Bach Passions, Gluck's Orfeo, Handel's Messiah, Beethoven's Choral Symphony, Wagner's Das Rheingold, Johann Strauss's Die Fledermaus and Frank Martin's Cornet. *Television includes:* various concerts and recitals, Carmen, Samson and Delila, Der Ring des Nibelungen, Die Frau ohne Schatten, Tristan und Isolde. *Address:* c/o Askonas Holt Ltd, Lonsdale Chambers, 27 Chancery Lane, London, WC2A 1PF, England (Office); c/o Artists Management Zürich, Rütistr. 52, 8044 Zürich Gockhausen, Switzerland. *Telephone:* (1) 8218957 (Office). *Fax:* (1) 8210127 (Office). *E-mail:* schuetz@artistsman.com.

LIPPONEN, Paavo Tapio; Finnish politician; b. 23 April 1941, Turtola (now Pello); m. Päivi Lipponen 1998; three d.; ed Univ. of Helsinki, Dartmouth Coll., USA; journalist 1963–67; Research and Int. Affairs Sec. and Head Political Section Finnish Social Democratic Party (SDP) 1967–79; Pvt. Sec. (Special Political Adviser) to Prime Minister 1979–82; Political Sec. to Minister of Labour 1983; Man. Dir Viestintä Teema Oy 1988–95; Head Finnish Inst. of Int. Affairs 1989–91; Chair. Supervisory Bd Outokumpu Oy 1989–90; mem. Helsinki City Council 1985–95; MP 1983–87, 1991–; mem. SDP Party Cttee 1987–90, Chair. SDP Helsinki Dist 1985–92, Chair. of SDP 1993–; Speaker of Parl. March–April 1995; Prime Minister of Finland 1995–2003; Dr hc (Dartmouth Coll., USA) 1997, (Finlandia Univ.) 2000. *Publications:* Muutoksen suunta 1986, Kohti Eurooppaa 2001. *Leisure interests:* architecture, swimming. *Address:* Suomen Sosialidemokraattinen Puolue—SDP, Saariniemenkatu 6, 00530 Helsinki, Finland (Office). *Telephone:* (9) 478988 (Office). *Fax:* (9) 712752 (Office). *E-mail:* palaute@sdp.fi. *Website:* www.sdp.fi (Office).

LIPSET, Seymour Martin, PhD; American professor of political science and sociology; b. 18 March 1922, New York; s. of Max Lipset and Lena Lippman; m. 1st Elsie Braun 1944 (died 1987); two s. one d.; m. 2nd Sydnee Guyer 1990; ed City Coll. of New York and Columbia Univ.; Asst Prof. Univ. of Calif. at Berkeley 1948–50; Asst then Assoc. Prof. and Asst Dir Bureau of Applied Social Research, Columbia Univ. 1950–56; Prof. of Sociology, Univ. of Calif. at Berkeley 1956–66; George D. Markham Prof. of Govt and Sociology, Harvard Univ. 1966–75; Sr Fellow, The Hoover Inst., Stanford Univ. 1975–, Caroline S.G. Munro Prof. of Political Science and Sociology 1975–92; Hazel Prof. of Public Policy, George Mason Univ., Fairfax, Va 1990–; Pres. American Political Science Assen 1981–82, American Sociological Assen 1992–93; Fellow, NAS, American Acad. of Arts and Sciences; Dir Aurora Foundation 1985–95, U.S. Inst. of Peace 1996–; Fellow Guggenheim Foundation 1971–72; Rawson Award 1986; MacIver Award 1962; Gunnar Myrdal Award 1970; numerous hon. degrees. *Publications:* Agrarian Socialism 1950, Political Man: The Social Bases of Politics 1960, The First New Nation 1963, Revolution and Counterrevolution 1968, Rebellion in the University (with W. Schneider) 1972, The Confidence Gap: Business, Labor and Government in the Public Eye 1983, Unions in Transition (ed.) 1986, Consensus and Conflict 1987, Continental Divide: The Institutions and Values of the United States and Canada 1990, The Educational Background of American Jews 1994, Jews and the New American Scene 1995 (with Earl Raab), American Exceptionalism 1996, Who's Who in Democracy 1997, Democracy in Asia and Africa 1998, Democracy in Europe and the Americas 1998, It Didn't Happen Here: Why Socialism Failed in the United States (with Gary Marks) 2000. *Leisure interests:* swimming, reading, walking, politics. *Address:* School of Public Policy, George Mason University, 3401 N Fairfax Drive, Arlington, VA 22201; 213 Hoover Memorial Building, Stanford University, Stanford, CA 94305, USA. *Telephone:* (703) 993-2283.

LIPSKA, Ewa; Polish poet; b. 8 Oct. 1945, Cracow; ed Acad. of Fine Arts, Cracow; Co-Ed. Pismo 1981–83; mem. editorial Bd Dekada Literacka 1990–92; First Sec. Polish Embassy, Vienna 1991–95, Adviser 1995–97; Deputy Dir Polish Inst., Vienna 1991–95, Dir 1995–97; mem. Assen of Polish Writers, Polish and Austrian PEN Club; Koscielscy Foundation Award (Switzerland) 1973, Robert Graves PEN Club Award 1979, Ind. Foundation of Supporting of Polish Culture—Polcul Foundation Award 1990, PEN Club Award 1993, Alfred Jurzykowski Foundation Award (USA) 1993, City of Cracow Award 1995, Andrzej Bursa Award 1997, Literary Laurel 2002. *Publications include:* Wiersze (Poems) 1967, Drugi zbiór wierszy (Second Vol. of Poems) 1970, Trzeci zbiór wierszy (Third Vol. of Poems) 1972, Czwarty zbiór wierszy (Fourth Vol. of Poems) 1974, Piaty zbiór wierszy (Fifth Vol. of Poems) 1978, Zywa smierc (Living Death) 1979, Dom Spokojnej Mlodosci (House of the Quiet Youth) 1979, Nie o smierc tutaj chodzi, lecz o bialy kordonek 1982, Utwory wybrane (Selected Poems) 1986, Przechowalnia ciemnosci 1985, Strefa ograniczonego postoju 1990, Wakacje Mizantropa (Misantrope's Holidays) 1993, Stypendysci czasu 1994, Wspólnicy zielonego wiatraczka 1996, Ludzie dla poczatkujacych (People for Beginners) 1997, Zycie zastepcze (Substitute Life) (Polish-German edition 1998), Godziny poza godzinami (After-hours Hours) 1999, Biale truskawki (White Strawberries) 2000, Sklepy zoologiczne (Pet Shops) 2001, Uwaga stopien 2002; selections of poems translated include Versei (Hungary) 1979, Vernisaz (Czechoslovakia) 1979, Such Times (Canada) 1981, Huis voor een vredige jeugd 1982, Auf den Dächern der Mausoleen (Germany) 1983, En misantrops ferie (Denmark) 1990, Meine Zeit. Mein Leib. Mein Leben (Austria) 1990, Poet? Criminal? Madman? (UK) 1991, Wakancitie na mizantropa (Bulgaria) 1994, Zon (Sweden) 1997, Stipiendisti Wremiena (Yugoslavia) 1998, Mennesker for Begyndere (Denmark) 1999, Mesohu me vdekjen (Albania) 2000, Menseen voor beginners (Netherlands) 2000, Sedemnast cervenych vevericiek (Slovakia) 2001, Selection of Poems (Israel) 2001, Fresas Blancas (Spain) 2001, Pet Shops (UK) 2002. *Address:* ul. Zbrojów 10 m. 13, 30-042 Cracow, Poland (Home). *Website:* ewa_lipska@hotmail.com (Home).

LIPTON, Sir Stuart Anthony, Kt; British property developer; b. 9 Nov. 1942; s. of Bertram Green and Jeanette Lipton; m. Ruth Marks 1966; two s. one d.; ed Berkhamsted School; Dir Sterling Land Co. 1971–73, First Palace Securities Ltd 1973–76; Man. Dir Greycoat PLC 1976–83; Chief Exec. Stanhope Properties PLC 1983–95, Stanhope PLC 1995–; Chair. Comm. for Architecture and the Built Environment 1999–; Adviser new Glyndebourne Opera House 1988–94; Dir Nat. Gallery Trust Foundation 1998–; Trustee Whitechapel Art Gallery 1987–94; mem. Bd Royal Nat. Theatre 1988–98, Royal Opera House 1998–; mem. Governing Body Imperial Coll. 1987–, Royal Fine Art Comm. 1988–99, LSE 2000–; Hon. mem. RIBA; Hon. Fellow Imperial Coll.

LIPWORTH, Sir (Maurice) Sydney, Kt, BCom, LLB; British barrister and businessman; b. 13 May 1931, Johannesburg, South Africa; s. of Isidore Lipworth and Rae Lipworth; m. Rosa Liwarek 1957; two s.; ed King Edward VII School, Johannesburg, Univ. of Witwatersrand; practising barrister, Johannesburg 1956–64; Dir (non-exec.) Liberty Life Assc̈n of Africa Ltd 1956–64; Exec. Pvt. Trading Cos. 1964–67; Exec. Dir Abbey Life Assurance PLC 1968–70; Vice-Pres. and Dir Abbey Int. Corpn Inc. 1968–70; one of co-founders and Dir Allied Dunbar Assurance PLC 1970–88, Deputy Man. Dir 1977–79, Jt Man. Dir 1979–84, Deputy Chair. 1984–88; Dir J. Rothschild Holdings PLC 1984–87, BAT Industries PLC 1985–88; Deputy Chair., Dir (non-exec.) Nat. Westminster Bank 1993–2000; Chair., Dir (non-exec.) Zeneca Group PLC 1995–99 (Dir 1994–99); Dir (non-exec.) Carlton Communications PLC 1993–, Centrica PLC 1999–; Chair. Monopolies and Mergers Comm. 1988–92, Bar Assc̈n for Commerce, Finance and Industry 1991–92, Financial Reporting Council 1993–2001; mem. Sr Salaries Review Body 1994–; Deputy Chair. of Trustees Philharmonia Orchestra 1986–93, Chair. 1993–; Trustee South Bank Ltd 1996–; Int. Accounting Cttee Foundation 2000–; mem. European Policy Forum; Hon. QC 1993. *Leisure interests:* music, theatre, tennis. *Address:* 41 Lothbury, London, EC2P 2BP (Office); International Accounting Standards Board, 30 Cannon Street, EC4M 6XH, England. *Telephone:* (20) 7726-1000. *Fax:* (20) 7726-1038.

LISITSYN, Aleksander Petrovich; Russian marine geologist and geophysicist; b. 3 July 1923; m.; two c.; ed Moscow Geological Prospecting Inst.; Jr, Sr Researcher, head of lab., head of div. Inst. of Oceanology USSR Acad. of Sciences 1953–81, Head of Dept 1981–; Corresp. mem. USSR (now Russian) Acad. of Sciences 1974, mem. 1994; research in geochem. of seas and oceans; USSR State Prize, F. Shepard Award. *Publications include:* Sedimentation in the World Ocean 1972, Geological History of Oceans, 1980, Biogeochemistry of Oceans 1983, Marine Glacial and Marine Ice Sedimentation 1994, Oceanic Sedimentation, Lithography and Geochemistry 1996. *Address:* Institute of Oceanology, Russian Academy of Sciences, Krasikova str. 23, 117218 Moscow, Russia. *Telephone:* (095) 124-85-28 (Office).

LISITSYN, Anatoly Ivanovich; Russian politician; b. 26 June 1947, Bolshiye Smenki, Kalinin Region; m.; one c.; ed Leningrad Acad. of Forest Tech.; Rybinsk furniture factory 1987, also Chair., Rybinsk City Dist Exec. Cttee 1987–90; Chair. Rybinsk City Exec. Cttee 1990–91; Deputy Head, Head, Yaroslavl Regional Admin 1991–92; mem. Council of Fed. 1993–; mem. Movt Our Home is Russia (resgnd); mem. People's Democratic Party 1995; Gov. of Yaroslavl Region 1995–; Chair. Interregional Assc̈n Cen. Russia; mem. Council of Russian Fed. 1996–2000; mem. Bd Union of Russian Govs. *Address:* Office of the Governor, Sovetskaya pl. 3, 150000 Yaroslavl, Russia. *Telephone:* (852) 72-81-28 (Office). *Fax:* (852) 32-84-14 (Office). *E-mail:* gubern@adm.yar.ru (Office).

LISNYANSKAYA, Inna Lvovna; Russian writer; b. 24 June 1928, Baku; m. Semen I. Lipkin (q.v.); first works published 1949; resgnd from Union of Writers 1980 (membership restored 1989). *Publications include:* This Happened to Me 1957, Faithfulness 1958, Not Simply Love 1963, The Light of Grape 1978; contributed to the literary almanac Metropole 1979; Verse 1970–83, 1984, On the Edge of Sleep 1984, The Circle 1985, Airy Layer 1990, Poetry 1991, About Music of the Poem without Hero by Akhmatova 1991, After All 1994, The Lonely Gift 1995, The Box with a Triple Bottom (Study on Akhmatova's Poem Without the Hero) 1995, Selected Poetry 2000. *Address:* Usievicha Street 8, Apt. 16, 125315 Moscow, Russia. *Telephone:* (095) 155-75-98.

LISOV, Yevgeny Kuzmich; Russian politician and lawyer; b. 1940, Ivanovo Region; ed Saratov State Univ.; investigator, Dist Prosecutor's Office, Kursk Region, Sr Investigator, Head of Div., Deputy Head, Investigation Dept, RSFSR Prosecutor's Office; Deputy Gen. Prosecutor of Russian Fed. 1991–93; investigated coup d'état 1991; Deputy Prosecutor of Moscow 1993–95; attorney, Moscow Regional Coll. of Barristers; expert, magazine Ogonyok 1995–98; Deputy Head, Admin of Russian Presidency, Head, Main Control Dept, Admin of Russian Presidency 1998–. *Publications:* Kremlin Conspiracy (with V. G. Stepankov, q.v.); articles in magazines and newspapers. *Address:* Administration of the President, Staraya pl. 4, 103132 Moscow, Russia. *Telephone:* (095) 206-48-51 (Office). *Fax:* (095) 206-51-65.

LISSAKERS, Karin Margareta, MA; American international civil servant; b. 16 Aug. 1944; m.; two c.; ed Ohio State Univ. and Johns Hopkins Univ.; mem. staff, Cttee on Foreign Relations, U.S. Senate, Washington, DC 1972–78; Deputy Dir Econ. Policy Planning Staff, U.S. Dept of State 1978–80; Sr Assoc. Carnegie Endowment for Int. Peace, New York 1981–83; Lecturer in int. banking, Dir int. business and banking programme, School of Int. Public Affairs, Columbia Univ. New York 1985–93; U.S. Exec. Dir IMF 1993–2001; Mem. Council on Foreign Relations. *Publications:* Banks, Borrowers and the Establishment 1991; articles in professional journals. *Address:* c/o Council on Foreign Relations, The Harold Pratt House, 58 East 68th Street, New York, NY 10021, USA. *Telephone:* (212) 434-9400. *Fax:* (212) 861-1789.

LISSNER, Stéphane Michel; French theatre director; b. 23 Jan. 1953, Paris; s. of Georges Lissner and Elisabeth Landenbaum; two s. one d.; ed Coll. Stanislas and Lycée Henri IV, Paris; Sec.-Gen. Centre dramatique, Aubervilliers 1977–78; Co-Dir Centre dramatique, Nice 1978–83; Dir-Gen. Orchestre de Paris 1994–96; Artistic Dir Teatro Real de Paris 1996–97; Dir Aix-en-Provence Festival 1996–; Co-Dir Théâtre des Bouffes du Nord 1998–. *Publication:* Métro Chapelle 2000.

LISSOUBA, Pascal, D. ÈS SC.; Republic of Congo politician; b. 15 Nov. 1931, Tsinguidi, Congo (Brazzaville); s. of Albert Lissouba and Marie Bouanga; m. 2nd Jocelyne Pierrot 1967; one s. six d.; ed secondary education in Nice, France and Ecole Supérieure d'Agriculture, Tunis, Tunisia; fmr agricultural specialist; Prime Minister of Congo (Brazzaville) 1963–66, concurrently Minister of Trade and Industry and Agric.; Prof. of Genetics, Brazzaville 1966–71, concurrently Minister of Planning 1968, Minister of Agric., Waterways and Forests 1969; Dir Ecole Supérieure des Sciences, Brazzaville 1970; sentenced to life imprisonment for complicity in assassination of Pres. Ngouabi 1977, subsequently released and exiled; Dir African Bureau for Science and Tech., Nairobi 1981–; Leader Union panafricaine pour la Démocratie sociale (UPADS); Pres. of Congo People's Repub. 1992–97; in exile, Burkina Faso. *Leisure interests:* geology, music.

LIST, Roland, DrScNat, FRSC; Canadian international official and physicist; b. 21 Feb. 1929, Frauenfeld, Thurgau, Switzerland; s. of August Joseph List and Anna Kaufmann; m. Gertrud K. Egli 1956 (died 1996); two c.; ed Swiss Fed. Inst. of Tech., Zürich; Head, Hail Section, Swiss Fed. Inst. for Snow and Avalanche Research, Davos 1952–63; Prof. of Physics (Meteorology), Dept of Physics, Univ. of Toronto 1963–82, 1984–94, Prof. Emer. 1994–, Assoc. Chair. Dept of Physics 1969–73; Deputy Sec.-Gen. WMO 1982–84; Chair. Exec. Cttee Panel of Experts on Weather Modification, WMO, Geneva 1969–82; Dir Univ. Corpn for Atmospheric Research, Boulder, Colo 1974–77; mem. Science Council, Space Shuttle Program (NASA) 1978–80; Chair. Italian Scientific Cttee for Rain Enhancement 1990–98; Sec.-Gen. Int. Assc̈n of Meteorology and Atmospheric Sciences 1995–; Rep. of Int. Union for Geodesy and Geophysics with WMO and World Climate Research Program 1995–; mem. and Chair. Planned and Inadvertent Weather Modification Cttee, American Meteorological Soc. 1996–2003; mem. or chair. many int., Canadian, US and Swiss cttees; consultant to UN, UNEP, World Bank, Inco and many other orgs; Visiting Prof. Swiss Fed. Inst. of Tech., Zürich 1974, 1998; Pres. Rotary Club of Toronto–Don Mills 1995–96; mem. Canadian and Swiss Acads of Sciences, Canadian Meteorological and Oceanic Soc., American Meteorological Soc., Canadian Geophysical Union, Royal Meteorological Soc., American and Swiss Physical Socs, etc.; Sesquicentennial Medal, Univ. of Leningrad 1970; Patterson Medal, Canadian Meteorological Service; Plaque of Recognition, Thailand. *Publications:* over 220 papers and many reports in the field of cloud physics, weather modification, classical physics, heat and mass transfer and aerodynamics. *Address:* Department of Physics, University of Toronto, Toronto, Ont., M5S 1A7 (Office); Ph-8, 1555 Finch Avenue E, North York, Ont., M2J 4X9, Canada (Home). *Telephone:* (416) 978-2982 (Office); (416) 494-3621 (Home). *Fax:* (416) 978-8905. *E-mail:* listr@attcanada.ca (Office).

LISULO, Daniel Muchiwa, SC, BA, LLB; Zambian politician and lawyer; b. 6 Dec. 1930, Mongu; s. of Musialela Lisulo and Wamusheke Lisulo; m. Mary Mambo 1968 (died 1976); three s. two d.; ed Loyola Coll. of Madras Univ., Law Faculty of Delhi Univ., India; active in independence struggle 1953–63; with Anglo-American Corpn (Cen. Africa) 1963–64; Asst Solicitor, Ellis & Co., Lusaka 1964–67; Sr Partner Lisulo & Co. 1968–; Dir Bank of Zambia 1964–77; mem. and Chair. Local Govt Service Comm. 1964–72; mem. Nat. Comm. on One Party System in Zambia; Dir various cos; mem. Cen. Cttee United Nat. Independence Party (UNIP) 1972–88, Legal Counsel of UNIP 1974–76; mem. Nat. Assembly 1977–83; Minister of Legal Affairs and Attorney-Gen. 1977–78, Prime Minister of Zambia 1978–81; Vice-Pres. Nat. Party (NP) 1995; Chair. Social and Cultural Sub-Cttee, UNIP 1981–82, Appointments and Disciplinary Cttee, UNIP 1982–83, Political and Legal Cttee of UNIP 1983–88; Chair. ZIMCO (Zambia Industrial and Mining Corpn Ltd) 1979–81; Vice-Pres. World Peace Council 1986–89; mem. Inter-Action Council 1988–. *Leisure interests:* swimming, hunting, boating, soccer. *Address:* Lisulo and Co., 6th Floor, Kulima Tower, Katunjila Road, P.O. Box 32259, Lusaka 10101, Zambia. *Telephone:* 228627/28. *Fax:* 225777.

LITAVRIN, Gennady Grigoryevich; Russian historian; b. 6 Oct. 1925; m.; two c.; ed Moscow State Univ.; Teacher Moscow State Univ. 1954–55; Sr Ed. Ministry of Public Educ. 1955; Jr, Sr Researcher Inst. of History USSR Acad. of Sciences 1955–68; Sr, Leading Researcher Inst. of Slavonic Studies USSR Acad. of Sciences 1968–87, Head of Div. 1987–; corresp. mem. USSR (now Russian) Acad. of Sciences 1987, mem. 1994; research in history of Bulgaria, processes of formation of feudal regime, agrarian relations and social struggle in Byzantium, of Russian-Byzantine relations, problems of Balkan ethnogenesis; mem. Comm. on Studies and Promotion of Slavic Cultures, on Studies of Treasures of Aphone Monasteries. *Publications include:* Byzantine Society and State in the X–XI Centuries 1977. *Address:* Institute of Slavonic Studies, Russian Academy of Sciences, Leninsky pr. 32, 117334 Moscow, Russia. *Telephone:* (095) 938-57-85, 938-17-80 (Office); (095) 211-88-87 (Home).

LITHERLAND, Albert Edward, PhD, FRS, FRSC; Canadian professor of physics; b. 12 March 1928, Wallasey, England; s. of Albert Litherland and Ethel Clement; m. Anne Allen 1956; two d.; ed Wallasey Grammar School and Liverpool Univ.; Scientific Officer, Atomic Energy of Canada 1955–66; Prof. of Physics, Toronto Univ. 1966–79, Univ. Prof. 1979–93, Univ. Prof. Emer. 1993–, Dir Isotrace Lab. 1982–; Guggenheim Fellow 1986; Hon. DSc (Toronto) 1998; Gold Medal, Canadian Assen of Physicists 1971, Rutherford Medal and Prize, Inst. of Physics 1974, Henry Marshall Tory Gold Medal, Royal Soc. of Canada 1993. *Publications:* numerous scientific papers. *Leisure interests:* reading, travel. *Address:* Apartment 801, 120 Rosedale Valley Road, Toronto, Ont., M4W 1P8, Canada. *Telephone:* (416) 923-5616. *Fax:* (416) 923-4711 (Office).

LITTEL, Robert; American writer; b. 1935; fmr journalist; writer of Cold War espionage fiction. *Publications include:* If Israel Lost the War (co-author with Richard Z. Cheznoff and Edward Klein) 1969, The Czech Black Book 1969, The Defection of A. J. Lewinter 1973, Sweet Reason 1974, The October Circle 1976, Mother Russia 1978, The Debriefing 1979, The Amateur 1981, The Sisters 1985, The Revolutionist: The Visiting Professor 1994, Walking Back the Cat 1996, The Company 2002. *Address:* c/o Simon and Schuster, 1230 Sixth Avenue, New York, NY 10020, USA (Office).

LITTLE, Ian Malcolm David, AFC, CBE, DPhil, FBA; British economist; b. 18 Dec. 1918, Rugby; s. of Brig.-Gen. M. O. Little and Iris H. Little (née Brassey); m. 1st Doreen Hennessey 1946 (died 1984); one s. one d.; m. 2nd Lydia Segrave 1991; ed Eton Coll. and New Coll. Oxford; RAF Officer 1939–46; Fellow, All Souls Coll. Oxford 1948–50, Trinity Coll. Oxford 1950–52, Nuffield Coll. Oxford 1952–76, Prof. Econs of Underdeveloped Countries 1971–76, Fellow Emer. 1976–; Deputy Dir Econ. Section, HM Treasury 1953–55; mem. MIT Center for Int. Studies, India 1958–59, 1965; Vice-Pres. OECD Devt Centre, Paris 1965–67; mem. Bd British Airports Authority 1969–74; Special Adviser, IBRD, Washington, DC 1976–78, Consultant 1984–85; Project Dir Twentieth Century Fund, New York 1978–81; Hon. DSc (Edin.). *Publications:* A Critique of Welfare Economics 1950, The Price of Fuel 1952, Aid to Africa 1964, Economic Development, Theory, Policy and International Relations 1982, Collection and Recollections 1999, Ethics, Economics, and Politics 2002; jt author of several other books. *Address:* Nuffield College, Oxford, OX1 1NF (Office); Hedgerows, Pyrton, Watlington, 0X49 5AP, England (Home). *Telephone:* (1865) 278539 (Office); (1491) 613703. *Fax:* (1865) 278621 (Office).

LITTLE, Robert Alastair, MA; British restaurateur and chef; b. 25 June 1950, Colne, Lancs.; s. of R. G. Little and M. I. Little; m. 1st Kirsten Pedersen 1981; one s. one d.; m. 2nd Sharon Jacob 2000; ed Downing Coll. Cambridge; Chef Old Compton Wine Bar 1974–77, L'Escargot 1981–82, 192 Kensington Park Road 1982–83; Chef, Propr Le Routier 1977–79, Simpsons 1979–81, Alastair Little 1985–; food columnist Daily Mail 1993–. *Publications:* Keep it Simple 1993, Mediterranean Redefined (with Richard Whittington) 1995, Alastair Little's Italian Kitchen 1996, Soho Cooking 2000. *Leisure interests:* jigsaws, trashy novels, travel, wine. *Address:* 49 Frith Street, London, W1V 5TE, England. *Telephone:* (20) 7434-5183.

LITTLE, Tasmin E., ARCM, FGSM; British concert violinist; b. 13 May 1965, London; d. of George Little and Gillian Little; m. Michael Hatch 1993; one d.; ed Yehudi Menuhin School, Guildhall School of Music; studied privately with Lorand Fenyves in Canada; performed with New York Philharmonic, Leipzig Gewandhaus, Berlin Symphony, London Symphony, Philharmonia, Royal Philharmonic, Royal Liverpool Philharmonic, European Community Chamber, Royal Danish and Stavanger Symphony orchestras; has played in orchestras conducted by Kurt Masur, Vladimir Ashkenazy, Leonard Slatkin, Tadaaki Otaka, Sir Charles Groves, Andrew Davis, Jerzy Maksymiuk, Vernon Handley, Yan Pascal Tortelier, Sir Edward Downes, Yehudi Menuhin and Sir Simon Rattle; played at the Proms since 1990; concerto and recital performances in UK, Europe, Scandinavia, South America, Hong Kong, Oman, Zimbabwe, Australia, NZ, USA and Japan; numerous TV appearances including BBC Last Night of the Proms 1995, 1998; Hon. DLitt (Bradford) 1996; Hon. DMus (Leicester) 2002. *Recordings include:* concertos of Bruch, Dvořák, Brahms, Sibelius, Delius, Rubbra, Saxton, George Lloyd, Ravel, Debussy, Poulenc, Delius, Elgar, Bax, Finzi; Dohnanyi violin sonatas, Bruch Scottish Fantasy, Lalo Symphonie Espagnole, Pärt Spiegel im Spiegel and Fratres. *Publication:* paper on Delius' violin concerto. *Leisure interests:* theatre, cinema, swimming, languages. *Address:* c/o Askonas Holt Ltd., 27 Chancery Lane, London, WC2A 1PF, England. *Telephone:* (20) 7400-1700.

LITTLE RICHARD; American rock singer and songwriter; b. Richard Wayne Penniman, 5 Dec. 1932, Macon, Ga; adopted s. of Enotris Johnson and Ann Johnson; R&B singer in various bands, including own band The Upsetters; gospel singer 1960–62; world-wide tours and concerts include: Star Club, Hamburg, Germany (with Beatles) 1962, European tour (with Beatles and Rolling Stones) 1963, British tour (with Everly Brothers) 1963, Rock 'n' Roll Revival Concert, Toronto (with Chuck Berry, Fats Domino, Jerry Lee Lewis,

Gene Vincent, Bo Diddley) 1969, Toronto Pop Festival 1970, Randall Island Rock Festival (with Jimi Hendrix, Jethro Tull) 1970, Rock 'n' Roll Spectaculars, Madison Square Garden 1972–, Muhammad Ali's 50th Birthday Celebration, Benefit For Lupus Foundation, Universal City 1992, Westbury Music Fair 1992, Giants of Rock 'n' Roll, Wembley Arena 1992, US tour 2002; announced retirement 2002; Grammy Lifetime Achievement Award 1993. *Singles include:* Ain't That Good News, Tutti Frutti 1956, Long Tall Sally 1956, Rip It Up, Ready Teddy, The Girl Can't Help It 1957, She's Got It 1957, Lucille 1957, Keep A Knockin' 1957, Jenny Jenny 1957, Good Golly Miss Molly 1958, Baby Face 1959, Bama Lama Bama Loo 1964, I Don't Know What You've Got But It's Got Me, Without Love, Poor Dog, Hurry Sundown, Get Down With It, Great Gosh A Mighty, Operator. *Albums:* Cast A Long Shadow 1956, Little Richard Vol. 1 1957, Little Richard Vol. 2 1957, Little Richard Vol. 3 1957, Here's Little Richard 1957, The Fabulous Little Richard 1959, Clap Your Hands 1960, Pray Along With Little Richard Vol. 1 1960, Pray Along With Little Richard Vol. 2 1960, King Of The Gospel Singers 1962, Sings Spirituals 1963, Sings the Gospel 1964, Little Richard Is Back 1965, The Wild and Frantic Little Richard 1965, The Explosive Little Richard 1967, Rock 'n' Roll Forever 1967, Good Golly Miss Molly 1969, Little Richard 1969, Right Now 1970, Rock Hard Rock Heavy 1970, Little Richard 1970, Well Alright! 1970, Mr Big 1971, The Rill Thing 1971, The Second Coming 1971, Dollars 1972, The Original 1972, You Can't Keep A Good Man Down 1972, Rip It Up 1973, Talkin' 'Bout Soul 1974, Recorded Live 1974, Keep A Knockin' 1975, Sings 1976, Little Richard Live 1976, Now 1977, Lucille 1988, Shake It All About 1992, Shag On Down By The Union Hall 1996. *Films include:* Don't Knock the Rock 1956, Mr Rock 'n' Roll 1957, The Girl Can't Help It 1957, Keep On Rockin' 1970, Down and Out in Beverly Hills 1986, Mother Goose Rock 'n' Rhyme (Disney Channel) 1989. *Address:* c/o Richard de la Font Agency Inc., 4845 South Sheridan Rd, Suite 505, Tulsa, OK 74145-5719, USA.

LITTLECHILD, Stephen Charles, PhD; British economist and public servant; b. 27 Aug. 1943, Wisbech; s. of Sidney F. Littlechild and Joyce M. Littlechild; m. Kate Crombie 1974 (died 1982); two s. one d.; ed Wisbech Grammar School, Univ. of Birmingham, Univ. of Texas, USA; Harkness Fellow 1965–67; Sr Research Lecturer in Econs, Graduate Centre for Man. Studies, Univ. of Birmingham 1970–72; Prof. of Applied Econs and Head of Econs, Econometrics, Statistics and Marketing Subject Group, Aston Man. Centre, Birmingham 1972–75; Prof. of Commerce, Head Dept of Industrial Econs and Business Studies 1975–89; Visiting Scholar, Dept of Econs, Univ. of Calif., LA, USA 1975; Visiting Prof., New York, Stanford and Chicago Univs and Va Polytechnic 1979–80; mem. Monopolies and Mergers Comm. 1983–89, Sec. of State for Energy's Advisory Council on Research and Devt 1987–89; Dir-Gen. of Electricity Supply 1989–98; Hon. Prof. Univ. of Birmingham Business School 1995–; Prin. Research Fellow Judge Inst. of Man. Studies, Univ. of Cambridge 2000–; Hon. DSc (Birmingham) 2001. *Publications:* Operational Research for Managers 1977, (with M. F. Shutler) 1991, The Fallacy of the Mixed Economy 1978, 1986, Elements of Telecommunications Economics 1979, Energy Strategies for the UK (with K. G. Vaidya) 1982, Regulation of British Telecommunications' Profitability 1983, Economic Regulation of Privatised Water Authorities 1986. *Leisure interest:* family history. *Address:* White House, The Green, Tanworth-in-Arden, Solihull, West Midlands, B94 5AL, England (Home). *E-mail:* sclittlechild@tanworth .mercianet.co.uk (Office).

LITTMAN, Mark, QC; British barrister-at-law and business executive; b. 4 Sept. 1920, London; s. of Jack Littman and Lilian Littman; m. Marguerite Lamkin 1965; ed Owen's School, LSE and Queens Coll. Oxford; Lt RDVR 1941–46; called to Bar, Middle Temple 1947; Dir Rio Tinto-Zinc Corpn 1968–91; Pres. Bar Assen for Commerce, Finance and Industry 1974–80; mem. Bar Council 1973–75, mem. of Senate of the Inns of Court and the Bar 1974–75; Deputy Chair. British Steel Corpn 1970–79; Dir Commercial Union Assurance Co. Ltd 1970–81, Granada Group Ltd 1977–93, British Enkalon Ltd 1972–80, Amerada Hess Corpn 1973–86, Envirotech Corpn 1974–78, Burton Group PLC 1983–93; Treas. Middle Temple 1988; Bencher of the Middle Temple 1970; mem. Royal Comm. on Legal Services 1976; mem. Int. Council for Commercial Arbitration 1978–; mem. Court of Govs, LSE 1980–; Vice-Chair. London Int. Arbitration Trust 1980–. *Address:* 79 Chester Square, London, SW1W 9DU, England. *Telephone:* (20) 7730-2973.

LITTON, Andrew, MM; American orchestral conductor and pianist; b. 16 May 1959, New York; ed Fieldston High School, Mozarteum, Juilliard School; Asst Conductor, La Scala, Milan 1980–81; Exxon/Arts Endowment Asst Conductor, then Assoc. Conductor, Nat. Symphony Orchestra, Washington, DC 1982–86; Prin. Guest Conductor, Bournemouth Symphony Orchestra 1986–88, Prin. Conductor and Artistic Adviser 1988–94, Conductor Laureate 1994–; Prin. Conductor Dallas Symphony Orchestra 1994–; guest conductor many leading orchestras world-wide, including Chicago Symphony, Philadelphia, Los Angeles Philharmonic, Pittsburgh Symphony, Toronto Symphony, Montréal Symphony, Vancouver Symphony, London Philharmonic, Royal Philharmonic, London Symphony, English Chamber, Leipzig Gewandhaus, Moscow State Symphony, Stockholm Philharmonic, RSO Berlin, RAI Milan, Orchestre Nat. de France, Suisse Romande, Tokyo Philharmonic, Melbourne Symphony and Sydney Symphony orchestras; début at Metropolitan Opera, New York with Eugen Onegin 1989; conducted Leoncavallo, La Bohème and Falstaff, St Louis Opera, Hansel and Gretel, LA Opera 1992, Porgy and Bess, Royal Opera House, Covent Garden 1992, Salome, English Nat. Opera 1996; music consultant to film The Chosen; Hon. DMus (Bournemouth) 1992; winner William Kapell Memorial U.S. Nat. Piano Competition 1978; winner Bruno Walter Conducting Fellowship 1981, BBC/Rupert Foundation Int. Conductors Competition 1982. *Recordings include:* Mahler Symphony No. 1 and Songs of a Wayfarer, Elgar Enigma Variations, complete Tchaikovsky symphony cycle, complete Rachmaninov symphony cycle, Shostakovich Symphony No. 10, Gershwin Rhapsody in Blue, Concerto in F and Ravel Concerto in G (as piano soloist and conductor), Bernstein Symphony No. 2, Brahms Symphony No. 1. *Address:* c/o IMG Artists, 616 Chiswick High Road, London, W4 5RX, England. *Telephone:* (20) 8233-5800. *Fax:* (20) 8233-5801.

LITVAK KING, Jaime, MA, PhD; Mexican archaeologist; b. 10 Dec. 1933, Mexico City; s. of Abraham Litvak and Eugenia King; m. 1st Elena Kaminski 1954 (divorced 1968); one d.; m. 2nd Carmen Aguilera 1972 (divorced 1978); ed Univ. Nacional Autónoma de México; Asst Dept of Prehistory, Inst. Nacional de Antropología e Historia 1960–63, Researcher 1963–66; Lecturer Escuela Nacional de Antropología e Historia 1963–74; Head Sección de Máquinas Electrónicas, Museo Nacional de Antropología 1966–68; Asst Research Fellow, Anthropological Section, Univ. Nacional Autónoma de México 1968–72, Full Research Fellow 1972–74, Head of Section 1973; Dir Inst. for Anthropological Research, Univ. Nacional Autónoma de México 1973–85, Dir-Gen. for Academic Projects 1985–86; Chair. Anthropology, Univ. of the Americas 1987–89; Joint Chair. Archaeology, Escuela Nacional de Antropología 1966–67, Chair. 1969–71; Co-Ed. Antropología Matemática 1968–74; Research Ed. American Antiquity 1971–74; Advisory Ed. Mesoamerican Archaeology, Abstracts in Anthropology 1973–74; Visiting Prof., Univ. of Minn. 1981, Univ. of New Mexico 1985–86; Mellon Prof. of Humanities, Tulane Univ. 1988; Prof. Emer., Univ. of Mexico 1998–, Nat. Researcher System 1998–; Coordinator Library of the Inst. of Anthropological Research 1993–; Gen. Sec. Mexican Anthropological Soc. 1970–76, 1981–83; mem. Mexican Scientific Research Acad. 1972–, Nat. Researcher, Class III, Mexico; mem. Bd of Dirs Museum Computer Network 1982–88; Fray Bernardino de Sahagún (Mexican Nat. Award for Anthropology) 1970, Nat. Researcher, Mexican Scientific Research Acad. 1984; Prize in Humanities Research, Univ. of Mexico 1996. *Radio:* Espacio Universitario, Radio UNAM 1985–2001; La Musica en la vida, Radio Unam 1996–. *Television:* Introducción a la Universidad 1977–79; Videocosmos, Antropología e Informática 1987–88. *Publications:* El Valle de Xochicalco 1970, Cihuatlán y Tepecoacuilco 1971, Xochicalco: Un Asentamiento Urbano Prehispánico 1974, Ancient Mexico 1985, Todas las piedras tienen 2000 años 1985, and others. *Address:* Instituto de Investigaciones Antropológicas, Universidad Nacional Autónoma de México, Ciudad Universitaria, 04510 México, DF (Office); Tervel 402, Pedredal 2, Contreras, México, DF C.P. 10720, Mexico (Home). *Telephone:* (5) 622-9659 (Office), (5) 568-6176 (Home). *Fax:* (5) 622-9660 (Office). *E-mail:* phuman@servidor.unam.mx (Office); litvak@servidor.unam.mx (Home). *Website:* biblioweb.dgsca.unam.mx/humanidades (Office).

LITVINOV, Boris Vasilyevich; Russian physicist and engineer; b. 12 Nov. 1929; m.; three c.; ed Moscow Inst. of Mech.; lab. engineer, Sr engineer, Sr researcher, Deputy Head of Div., Research Inst. of Experimental Physics 1952–61; Chief constructor, All-Union Inst. of Tech. Physics, USSR (now Russian) Ministry of Medium Machine Bldg (now Ministry of Atomic Energy) 1961–77; First Deputy Scientific Dir 1978–97, Deputy Scientific Dir 1997–; corresp. mem. USSR (now Russian) Acad. of Sciences 1991, mem. 1997–; main research in applied physics, Devt of new constructions of exploding devices; Labour Banner 1956, Order of Lenin 1962, 1977, 1981, Lenin Prize 1966, Order of October Revolution 1971, Hero of Socialist Labour 1981, Merit to Motherland (3rd Class) 1995. *Publications:* Metals and Minerals Research in Spherical Shockwaves, Power Engineering of Deuterium Explosion, Basic Engineering Activity. *Leisure interest:* carving. *Address:* Institute of Technical Physics, P.O. Box 245, 456770 Chelyabinsk, Russia. *E-mail:* lit@kbone .ch70.chel.su (Office); litvinov@snezhinsk.zu (Home).

LITVINOVA, Renata Muratovna; Russian actress and scriptwriter; b. 11 Jan. 1968, Moscow; d. of Murat Vergazov and Alissa Litvinova; m. Mikhail Dobrovsky; ed All-Union State Inst. of Cinematography; mem. Union of Theatre Workers. *Films include:* Passions, Two Arrows, Three Stories, The Border–Taiga Romance. *Scriptwriter for films:* Leningrad, November, Non-Love, Tractorists 2, Men's Confessions, Principal and Compassionate Eye, Three Stories, There is No Death for Me (Dir). *Publications:* Prize of Film Festival Centaurs for Passions. *Leisure interests:* antiques, cats. *Address:* Menzhinskogo str. 38. korp. 1, Apt. 104, Moscow, Russia (Home). *Telephone:* (095) 470-35-52 (Home).

LIU, Ts'un-yan, AO, PhD, DLit; Australian professor of Chinese; b. 11 Aug. 1917, Peking, China; s. of the late Tsung-ch'üan Liu and of Huang Yü-shu Liu; m. Chiang Szuyung 1940; one s. one d.; ed Univs of Peking, London and Hong Kong; Chair. Chinese Panel, Queen's Coll., Hong Kong 1952–59; lecturer Northcote Training Coll., Hong Kong 1959–62; Sr Lecturer Govt Evening School, Hong Kong 1959–62; Sr Lecturer, Reader in Chinese, ANU 1962–66, Prof. and Head of Dept of Chinese 1966–82, Dean Faculty of Asian Studies 1970–72, 1973–75, Prof. Emer. 1983–, Univ. Fellow 1983–; Visiting Prof. Columbia Univ. 1966, Harvard-Yenching Inst. 1969, Hawaii Univ. 1969, Univ. of Paris (Vincennes) 1973, Univ. of Malaya 1976, Chinese Univ. of Hong Kong 1976–77, Waseda Univ. 1981, Nat. Univ. of Singapore 1984–85; Fellow, Royal Asiatic Soc. 1957; Foundation Fellow, Australian Acad. of the Humanities 1969; Hon. D. Litt. (Yeungnam Univ., South Korea) 1972, (Hong Kong)

1988, (Murdoch) 1989, (ANU) 1997. *Publications:* Buddhist and Taoist Influences on Chinese Novels 1962, Chinese Popular Fiction in Two London Libraries 1967, Selected Papers from the Hall of Harmonious Wind 1976, Chinese Middlebrow Fiction from the Ch'ing and Early Republican Era 1984, New Excursions from the Hall of Harmonious Wind 1984, Hofengtang Wenji (selected papers in Chinese) 1992, Ta Tu, The Grand Capital 1996, Hofentang Xinwenji 1997, Daojia yii daoshu 2000. *Leisure interests:* singing, Beijing opera. *Address:* China & Korea Centre, Australian National University, Canberra, ACT 2601, Australia.

LIU BINGSEN; Chinese calligrapher; b. Aug. 1937, Shanghai; ed Beijing Acad. of Arts; Asst technician, Asst Research Fellow, Assoc. Research Fellow, Research Fellow Beijing Palace Museum 1962–86; mem. Standing Cttee, 8th and 9th CPPCC; Vice-Chair. Chinese Calligraphers Asscn; Vice-Chair. China Fed. of Literary and Art Circles 2001. *Publications:* Travel Notes of Past Dynasties; Purple Wall and Autumn Grass. *Address:* Palace Museum, Beijing, People's Republic of China (Office).

LIU BINYAN; Chinese writer and journalist; b. 7 Feb. 1925, Changchun City, Jilin Prov.; journalist, Renmin Ribao, Beijing 1980–88; Vice-Pres. Writer's Union of China 1985–87; charged with "bourgeois liberalization" and expelled from CCP 1987; visiting Prof. in USA 1988–. *Publications:* On Literature and Life 1985, Selected Works of Liu Binyan 1988. *Address:* Room 204, Gate 7, Building Min 20, Jintai Xi Road, Beijing, People's Republic of China.

LIU BOSU; Chinese professor of fine art; b. Nov. 1935, Nanchang City, Jiangxi Prov.; ed Cen. Inst. of Fine Arts 1955; Assoc. Prof. 1981–83, Prof. 1983–, Vice Dir Cen. Inst. of Fine Arts 1986–; Dir Chinese Painting Acad. 1993–; mem. 7th CPPCC 1988–93, 8th 1993–98. *Address:* 5 Jiaowei Hutong Lane, Dongcheng District, Beijing 100005, People's Republic of China.

LIU CHUANZHI; Chinese computer scientist and business executive; b. 29 April 1944, Zhenjiang, Jiangsu Prov.; ed Xi'an Mil. Telecommunications Inst.; researcher, Research Inst. No. 10 of State Science and Tech. Comm., Chengdu 1967–70; researcher, Computational Science Research Inst. of Chinese Acad. of Sciences 1970–83; f. Computational Science Research Inst. Inc. 1984; f. the Legend Group Inc. 1989 (largest computer co. in China); elected one of China's Top Ten Econ. Figures 2000. *Address:* 10 Kexueyuan Nan Lu, Beijing 100080, People's Republic of China (Office). *Telephone:* (10) 62572078 (Office).

LIU DANZHAI; Chinese traditional artist; b. 4 March 1931, Wenzhou, Zhejiang; s. of Liu Xiuqing and Liu Chenshi; m. Wang Weilis 1953; one s. one d.; also known as Liu Xiaosu, Liu Hun and Hai Yun Sheng; noted for "ren wu hua" (figure painting); teacher Wenzhou Westlake Elementary School 1949–51; Painter, Shanghai Books Publs 1951–56; Art Ed. Shanghai Educational Publishing House 1956–72; Painter, Shanghai People's Fine Arts Publishing House 1972–83; Prof. Shanghai Teachers' Univ. 1985–; Visiting Prof. Wenzhou Univ. 1985–; Artist, Shanghai Acad. of Chinese Arts 1956–; Art Counsellor, Shanghai Jiaotong Univ. 1981–; Head of Fine Arts Faculty, Shanghai Teacher's Univ. 1987–; mem. Chinese Artists' Asscn 1953–, mem. Bd of Dirs, Shanghai Br. 1953–; Nat. First Award for Prints 1981; First Award for Chinese Prints (Japan) 1981; Hon. Prize for Chinese Sport Art (Chinese Olympic Cttee) 1985. *Exhibitions include:* (Liu Xiaosu) Wenzhou 1941, 1946, (Liu Danzhai) Shanghai 1979, Hongzhou 1984, Ishimaki, Japan 1985, Hong Kong 1988, Taiwan 1989, 1991, South-east Asia 1993, Taiwan 1996, Hong Kong 1996, travelling exhbn Paris, Rome, Amsterdam, Heidelberg 1996; Jt Exhbn, Four Contemporary Chinese Ink Painting Masters from Shanghai, Taiwan 1994; works in Nat. Museum of Fine Arts, Nat. Museum of History, Beijing and in many pvt. collections in Asia, Europe and N America. *Publications:* Images of a Dream of Red Mansions 1979, The 12 Beauties of Jinling from A Dream of Red Mansions (prints) 1981, Album of Chinese Poets 1983, Liu Danzhai: One Hundred Illustrations for 'Strange Studio' 1985, A Dream of Red Mansions 1985, Liu Danzhai (monograph) 1987, Liu Danzhai: Selections from Picture-Story Book 1987, Album of Liu Danzhai's Paintings 1988, Calendar of Paintings 1993; monographs on paintings and calligraphy by Liu Danzhai Shanghai, Hong Kong, Taiwan 1996. *Leisure interests:* poetry, travel, stone collecting. *Address:* 43 An Ting Road, Apt. 6, Shanghai, 200031, People's Republic of China. *Telephone:* 64720332.

LIU DEHAI; Chinese musician and university professor; b. May 1937, Cangxian Co., Hebei Prov.; ed Centre Music Inst.; Prof. Centre Music Inst. 1984–; mem. 7th CPPCC 1988–93, 8th 1993–98.

LIU FANGREN; Chinese party official; b. 1936, Wugong, Shaanxi; joined CCP 1954; Deputy Sec. Jiangxi Prov. CCP Cttee 1985; alt. mem. CCP Cen. Cttee 1987–92; Sec. CCP 7th Guizhou Prov. Cttee 1993–2001; Chair. Standing Cttee Guizhou Prov. People's Congress 1998–; mem. 15th CCP Cen. Cttee 1997–2002. *Address:* Standing Committee of Guizhou Provincial People's Congress, Guiyang, Guizhou Province, People's Republic of China.

LIU GANG; Chinese dissident; leader of Tiananmen Square pro-democracy demonstrations 1989; imprisoned 1989–95; fled China; granted temporary asylum in USA 1996.

LIU GUOGUANG; Chinese party official and economist; b. 16 Oct. 1923, Nanjing; s. of Liu Zhihe and Zhiang Shulang; m. Liu Guoshiang 1948; two s. one d.; ed South-West Univ., Kunming and Moscow, USSR; joined CCP 1961; Vice-Pres. Chinese Acad. of Social Sciences 1982–93, Special Adviser 1993–; Prof. Beijing Univ.; Alt. mem. 12th Cen. Cttee, CCP 1982–87, 13th Cen. Cttee

1987–92; mem. 8th N.P.C. Standing Cttee 1993–98, mem. Financial and Econ. Cttee; mem. State Academic Degree Comm. 1988–95; mem. State Council Project Review Cttee for Three Gorges Project 1990–93. *Publications include:* The Problem Concerning the Reform of the Management System of the National Economy, Problems Concerning China's Strategy of Economic Readjustment, Economic Reform and Economic Readjustment, Developing Marxist Theory in the Practice of Reform, Reform, Stability and Development: Macroeconomic Management under the Dual-Track System, New Stage of China's Economic Reform and Development. *Leisure interest:* music. *Address:* Chinese Academy of Social Sciences, Beijing, People's Republic of China. *Telephone:* 65137435. *Fax:* 65138154.

LIU HANZHANG; Chinese business executive; b. 1936, Gongxian, Henan Prov.; ed Taiyuan School of Metallurgical Industry; worker Anshan Iron and Steel Co. 1956–58; technician, workshop Dir, subsidiary factory Dir, gen. factory Dir, then Chair. and Gen. Man., Handan Iron and Steel Co. 1958–. *Address:* Handan Iron and Steel Company, Handan, Henan, People's Republic of China (Office).

LIU HONGLIANG; Chinese scientist; b. 20 June 1932, Dalian, Liaoning Prov.; ed Tsinghua Univ.; Fellow Chinese Acad. of Eng; Pres. and Prof. Chinese Environmental Science Research Inst. 1982–; Chair. Agric., Textile and Environment Eng Div., Chinese Acad. of Eng. *Publications:* over 20 research papers and a number of monographs. *Address:* Chinese Environmental Science Research Institute, Dayangfang, Beiyuan, Andingmen Wai, Beijing 100012, People's Republic of China (Office). *Telephone:* (10) 64232542 (Office). *Fax:* (10) 64232542 (Office). *E-mail:* engach@mail.cae.ac.cn (Office).

LIU HONGRU; Chinese banker; b. 1930, Yushu, Jilin; ed Northeast Mil. Coll., Chinese People's Univ., Moscow Univ., Moscow Financial Coll., USSR; joined CCP 1948; Vice-Gov. Agricultural Bank of China 1979–80; Vice-Gov. People's Bank of China 1981–89, Vice-Pres. Council People's Bank of China 1980; Vice-Minister State Comm. for Restructuring the Economy 1988–93; Vice-Gov. People's Bank of China 1981–89; Vice-Chair. Securities Comm. of the State Council 1992–95; Part-time Prof., Beijing, Qinghua and Nankai Univs; Pres. Financial and Banking Inst. of China, China Monetary Coll. 1989–, China Finance and Economics Univ.; Deputy Head Leading Group for the Reform of the Housing System 1991–; Chair. China Securities Regulatory Comm. 1992–95; alt. mem. 13th CCP Cen. Cttee 1987–92; Vice-Chair. Econ. Cttee, 8th and 9th Nat. Cttees. of CPPCC; Hon. Pres. Securities and Futures Coll., Univ. of Hanzhou 1995–. *Publications include:* Questions on Socialist China's Currency and Banking, Questions on Socialist Credit. *Address:* National Committee of Chinese People's Political Consultative Conference, 23 Taipingqiao Street, Beijing, People's Republic of China.

LIU HUAN; Chinese singer; b. Aug. 1963, Tianjin; ed Beijing Int. Relations Inst.; numerous albums; songs include theme from The Water Margin (TV). *Address:* Department of French, Beijing International Relations Institute, Beijing, People's Republic of China.

LIU HUANZHANG; Chinese sculptor; b. 30 Dec. 1930, Balihan, Inner Mongolia; m. Shen Chaohui 1968; one d.; ed Beijing Yuying Pvt. School, Beijing Cen. Acad. of Fine Arts; Assoc. Prof., Sculpture Studio, Beijing Cen. Acad. of Fine Arts 1956–; works at Tangshan No. 1 Middle School, Chen Jinlun Middle School, Beijing, Meixian, Guangdong Prov., Lanzhou Inst., Gansu Prov. *Exhibitions include:* China Art Gallery 1958, 1961, 1981, 1989, Paris Salon (France) 1981, West Africa 1981, Hong Kong 1985, USA, Hungary. *Publications:* Liu Huanzhang Carre Works Selection 1984, Sculpture Works Selection 1985, Seals Selection 1988. *Leisure interests:* sports, growing flowers. *Address:* Building No. 3, 1-102, Hong Miao Beili Chao Yang, Beijing, People's Republic of China.

LIU HUAQING, Gen.; Chinese naval officer; b. Oct. 1916, Dawu Co., Hubei Prov.; m. Xu Hongxin; joined Red Army 1931, CCP 1935; Head, Political Dept, 11th Corps, 2nd Field Army 1949; transferred to Navy 1950; Maj.-Gen. PLA 1955; Rear-Admiral, PLA, Luda (Port Arthur and Dairen) 1958; Vice-Chair. Scientific and Technological Comm. for Nat. Defence 1967, First Vice-Chair. 1968; mem. Cultural Revolution Group, PLA 1967; disappeared during Cultural Revolution; Vice-Minister, State Scientific and Technological Comm., State Council 1978–80; Asst to Chief of PLA Gen. Staff 1979–80; Deputy Chief of Staff, PLA 1980–88, Commdr PLA Navy 1982–88; Vice-Chair. CCP Cen. Mil. Comm. 1990–97; mem. 12th CCP Cen. Cttee 1982–85, 14th CCP Cen. Cttee 1992–97; mem. Cen. Advisory Cttee 1985–92; Gen., PLA 1988–; Vice-Chair. Cen. Mil. Comm. 1989–97; standing mem. CCP Politburo 1992–97; Vice-Chair. Cen. Mil. Comm. of PRC 1994; Hon. Pres. Chinese Soc. of Mil. Sciences 1991–, Yachting Asscn. *Address:* c/o People's Liberation Army, Central Military Commission of the People's Republic of China, Beijing, People's Republic of China.

LIU HUAQIU; Chinese diplomatist; b. Nov. 1939, Wuchuan Co., Guangdong Prov.; ed Foreign Affairs Inst.; joined CCP 1965; Second Sec. Embassy, Ghana 1973; Clerk Gen. Office of State Council 1981; Counsellor then Minister Embassy, Australia 1984; Dir Dept of Affairs of the Americas and Oceania, Ministry of Foreign Affairs 1986; Asst to Minister of Foreign Affairs 1988; Vice-Minister of Foreign Affairs 1989; alt. mem. 14th CCP Cen. Cttee 1992; Dir Foreign Affairs Office, State Council 1995–; mem. 15th CCP Cen. Cttee 1997–. *Address:* Foreign Affairs Office, State Council, Beijing, People's Republic of China.

LIU JIANFENG; Chinese provincial administrator and politician; b. 1936, Ninghe Co., Hebei Prov.; ed in USSR; joined CCP 1956; Vice-Minister of Electronics Industry 1984–88; Deputy Sec. Hainan Prov. 1988; Gov. Hainan Prov. 1989–93; mem. 14th CCP Cen. Cttee 1992–97, 15th CCP Cen. Cttee 1997–2002, 16th CCP Cen. Cttee 2002–; Vice-Minister of Electronics Industry 1993–98; Vice-Minister of Information Industry 1998; Minister for Gen. Admin. of Civil Aviation of China 1998–. *Address:* Ministry for The General Administration of Civil Aviation of China, Beijing, People's Republic of China.

LIU JIANG; Chinese government official; b. 1940, Beijing; m.; two d.; ed Shihezi Agricultural Coll.; joined CCP 1978; Vice-Minister of Agric., Animal Husbandry and Fishery 1986–90; Vice-Chair. State Planning Comm. 1990–93; Minister of Agric. 1993–98; Vice-Chair. State Devt Planning Comm. 1998–; Deputy Head State Working Group for Comprehensive Agricultural Devt; mem. 15th CCP Cen. Cttee 1997–. *Address:* State Development Planning Commission, 38 Yuetan Nan Jie, Xicheng Qu, Beijing, People's Republic of China.

LIU JIBIN; Chinese politician; b. Dec. 1938, Longkou, Shandong Prov.; ed Beijing Aeronautics Inst.; joined CCP 1966; engineer, Section Dir then Vice-Man. Shenyang Songling Machinery Factory, Vice-Chief Engineer Ministry of Aeronautics Industry then Vice Minister, Dir State Admin. for State-Owned Assets 1962–88; Vice-Minister of Finance 1988–98; Minister in Charge of Commission of Science, Tech. and Industry for Nat. Defence 1998–2003. *Address:* c/o Zhongguo Gongchan Dang (Chinese Communist Party), 1 Zhongnanhai, Beijing, People's Republic of China (Office).

LIU JIE; Chinese business executive; b. Nov. 1943, Shucheng, Anhui Prov.; ed Wuhan Iron and Steel Inst., E.M. Beijing Iron and Steel Inst.; technician, Wuhan Iron and Steel Co. 1968; Chair. and Gen. Man., Anshan Iron and Steel Group Inc. 1994–; Fellow, Chinese Acad. of Eng 1996–. *Address:* Anshan Iron and Steel Group Inc., Huangang hu, Tiexi Qu, Anshan 114021, People's Republic of China (Office). *Telephone:* (412) 6723090 (Office). *Fax:* (412) 6723090 (Office).

LIU JINGSONG, Gen.; Chinese army officer; b. 1933, Shishou, Hubei; ed Mil. Coll., PLA; joined CCP 1954; Commdr, Shenyang Mil. Region, PLA 1985—; mem. 12th CCP Cen. Cttee 1985–87, 13th CCP Cen. Cttee 1987–92, 14th CCP Cen. Cttee 1992–97, 15th CCP Cen. Cttee 1997–2002; rank of Lt-Gen., PLA 1988, Gen. 1994; Commdr Lanzhou Mil. Region 1992–; Pres. Acad. of Mil. Sciences 1997–. *Address:* Office of the President, PLA Academy of Military Sciences, Beijing, People's Republic of China.

LIU JIYUAN; Chinese aeronautical engineer; b. 1933, Xing Co., Shanxi Prov.; ed higher industrial inst. Moscow, USSR; joined CCP 1952–; technician, No. 5 Research Acad. Ministry of Nat. Defence 1960–64; Dir and Sr Engineer No. 12 Research Inst. of No. 1 Research Acad. under 7th Ministry of Machine-Bldg Industry 1980–83; Deputy Dir No. 1 Research Acad. under Ministry of Astronautics Industry 1983–84; Vice-Minister of Astronautics Industry 1984; Vice-Minister, Ministry of Aeronautics and Astronautics Industry 1988–93; Pres. China Aerospace Industry Corpn (State Aerospace Bureau) 1993–; mem. 14th CCP Cen. Cttee 1992–97, 15th CCP Cen. Cttee 1997–2002. *Address:* China Aerospace Industry Corporation, Beijing, People's Republic of China.

LIU LIYING; Chinese civil servant; b. 1932, Dongping, Shandong Prov.; ed Harbin Public Security Bureau Cadre School; joined CCP 1949; fmrly Vice-Chief and then Chief Cadre Section, Dir Political Dept, Vice-Chief Constable of Shenyang Public Security Bureau; Vice-Dir Discipline Inspection Dept, Discipline Inspection Cttee of CCP Cen. Cttee, mem. Standing Cttee 1983–; Vice-Sec. Discipline Inspection Cttee of CCP Cen. Cttee 1997–; headed the investigation into several maj. corruption cases. *Address:* Discipline Inspection Committee of Chinese Communist Party Central Committee, Beijing, People's Republic of China.

LIU MINGZU; Chinese political official; Chair. Guangxi Regional People's Congress 1993–94; Deputy Sec., Standing Cttee and mem. CCP Guangxi Regional Cttee –1994; mem., Standing Cttee, mem. and Sec. CCP Inner Mongolia Autonomous Region Cttee 1994–2001; Chair. Inner Mongolia Regional People's Congress 1997–; mem. 15th CCP Cen. Cttee 1997–2002. *Address:* Inner Mongolia Regional Committee of the CCP, Hohhot, Nei Monggol, People's Republic of China.

LIU NIANQU; Chinese composer; b. 24 Nov. 1945, Shanghai; s. of Liu Jin Chuang and Wang Yun Cong; m. Cai Lu 1973; one d.; Art Inspector Gen. Shanghai Int. Arts Festival 1987; Art Dir Shanghai Creation Centre; Vice Sec.-Gen. Org. Cttee 1990, Shanghai Art Festival; Vice-Chair. Exec. Cttee 1991, Shanghai Spring Arts Festival; Vice-Chair. Shanghai Musicians Asscn; Councillor China Musicians Asscn. *Compositions include:* Phoenix Singing at Qi San Mountain (dance drama) 1983, 1989, Spring of Life and Universe (oratorio) 1989 (1st Prize Shanghai Art Festival). *Leisure interests:* table tennis, football. *Address:* Shanghai Municipal Bureau of Culture, 709 Ju Lu Road, Shanghai, People's Republic of China.

LIU QI; Chinese government official; b. 1936; joined CCP 1960; alt. mem. CCP Cen. Cttee 1992–97; Minister of Metallurgical Industry 1993–98; mem. 15th CCP Cen. Cttee 1997–2002; Vice-Sec. CCP Beijing Municipal Cttee and Vice-Mayor of Beijing 1998–99, Mayor of Beijing 1999–. *Address:* Beijing Municipal People's Government, Beijing, People's Republic of China.

LIU SHAHE; Chinese poet; b. 11 Nov. 1931, Chengdu, Sichuan Prov.; m. 1st 1966; one s. one d.; m. 2nd 1992; ed Sichuan Univ.; mem. editorial staff The Stars (poetry magazine) –1957 and 1979–; satirical poem Verses of Plants (1957) led to condemnation as 'bourgeois rightist'; in labour camp during Cultural Revolution 1966–77, rehabilitated 1979. *Publications include:* Night on the Farm 1956, Farewell to Mars 1957, Liu Shahe Poetic Works 1982, Travelling Trace 1983, Farewell to my Home 1983, Sing Alone 1989, Selected Poems of Seven Chinese Poets 1993, Random Notes by Liu Shahe 1995, River of Quicksand (poetry) 1995, River of Quicksand (short texts) 2001. *Leisure interest:* UFOs. *Address:* 30 Dacisi Road, Chengdu City, Sichuan Province, People's Republic of China. *Telephone:* (28) 6781738 (Home).

LIU SHAOHUI; Chinese artist; b. 27 Aug. 1940, Szechuan; s. of Liu Veizheng and Xiong Wenying; m. Yang Yijing 1968; one s. one d.; ed Cen. Inst. of Applied Arts, Beijing; fmr Dir Art Layout Office, Yunnan People's Publishing House; Assoc. Prof. Pedagogical Inst., Guilin Pref.; mem. Chinese Artists Asscn; Assoc. Pres. Guilin Chinese Painting Acad. 1995–; engaged in design and research; exhbns in USA, Japan, Bulgaria, Hong Kong, Italy, Taiwan; works at Guilin Arts Garden; main designer for film Fire Boy (1st Prize, Int. Animated Film Festival, Japan 1984); Prize of Nat. Art Works of Excellence 1981 and 1983; Japanese Int. Fine Arts Exhbn Prize of the Highest Honour. *Works include:* Zhaoshutun – Legend of a Dai Prince, An Elementary Theory on Binding and Layout of Books, The Candlewick Fairy 1985, Cowrie and a Little Girl 1986, Fine Arts Collection 1989. *Publications:* Yunnan School – A Renaissance in Chinese Painting 1988, Selected Paintings by Liu Shaohui 1989, The Third Sister Liu 1993, Selected Paintings of Guilin Chinese Painting Academy 1995. *Leisure interests:* music, travel, table-tennis. *Address:* Pedagogical Institute, Guilin Prefecture, 45 Xing Yi Road, Guilin, People's Republic of China.

LIU SHUNYAO, Gen.; Chinese air force officer; ed PLA Nat. Defence Univ.; fmrly Deputy Commdr, then Commdr Air Force, Lanzhou Mil. Region; Deputy Commdr of Air Force, rank of Lt-Gen. 1994, Commdr 1996–, Gen. 2000–; mem. 15th CCP Cen. Cttee 1997–2002. *Address:* c/o Ministry of National Defence, Jingshangian Jie, Beijing, People's Republic of China. *Telephone:* (10) 66370000.

LIU SHUTIAN, Lt-Gen.; Chinese army officer; b. 1940, Tengzhou Co., Shandong Prov.; joined PLA 1958; joined CCP 1960; Dir Army Political Dept 1986, Army Political Commissar, Deputy Political Commissar Guangzhou Mil. Area Command; mem. 15th CCP Cen. Cttee 1997–2002. *Address:* Guangzhou Military Area Command Headquarters, Guangzhou, People's Republic of China.

LIU XIAOQING; Chinese actress; b. 30 Oct. 1955, Chengdu City, Sichuan Prov.; d. of Ran Changru and Liu Huihua; m. Chen Guojun (divorced 1991); ed Sichuan Music School; 10th Hundred Flowers Best Actress Award for Furong Zhen (Lotus Town) 1986; 7th Golden Cock Best Actress Award for Furong Zhen 1986; 11th Hundred Flowers Best Actress Award for Yuanye 1988, 12th Hundred Flowers Best Actress Award for Chuntao 1989. *Publication:* My Way, My Eight Years, From a Movie Star to Billionaire. *Address:* P.O. Box 38, Asia Sport Village, Beijing, People's Republic of China. *Telephone:* (10) 4915988. *Fax:* (10) 4915899.

LIU XINWU; Chinese writer; b. 4 June 1942, Chengdu, Sichuan Prov.; s. of Liu Tianyan and Wang Yuntao; m. Lu Xiaoge 1970; one s.; ed Beijing Teachers' Coll.; school teacher 1961–76; with Beijing Publishing House 1976–80; lived in Beijing 1950–; Ed.-in-Chief People's Literature 1987–89; professional writer 1980–; mem. Standing Cttee, China All Nation Youth Fed. –1992; mem. Council, Chinese Writers' Asscn. *Publications:* short stories: Class Counsellor (Nationwide Short Story Prize 1977), The Position of Love 1978, I Love Every Piece of Green Leaves (Nationwide Short Story Prize 1979), Black Walls 1982, A Scanning over the May 19th Accident 1985; novels: Ruyi (As You Wish) 1980, Overpass 1981; novel: Drum Tower (Mao Dun Literature Prize 1984); Liu Xinwu Collected Works (8 Vols) 1993. *Leisure interests:* reading, travelling, painting, stamp collecting, music, gardening. *Address:* 8 Building No. 1404, Anding Menwai Dongheyan, Beijing 100011, People's Republic of China. *Telephone:* 4213965 (Home).

LIU YANDONG; Chinese politician; b. 1944, Nantong City, Jiangsu Prov.; joined CCP 1964; Sec. of Secr. of Cen. Cttee of Communist Youth League of China 1982–; mem Standing Cttee CPPCC 8th Nat Cttee; Deputy Head United Front Work Dept 1991–; alt. mem. 15th CCP Cen. Cttee 1997–99. *Address:* All-China Youth Federation, Bldg 10, Qianmen Dong Dajie Street, Beijing 100051, People's Republic of China.

LIU YUAN; Chinese government official; b. 1951, Beijing; s. of the late Liu Shaoqi; fmr Chair. of PRC and Wang Guangmei; joined CCP 1982; Vice-Mayor of Zhengzhou City 1988; Second Political Commissar PRC Police Force 1993–. *Address:* Headquarters of Chinese People's Armed Police Force, Beijing, People's Republic of China.

LIU YUNSHAN; Chinese politician; b. July 1947, Tumed, Inner Mongolia; ed Jining Normal School, Inner Mongolia 1968; joined CCP 1971; Vice-Sec. Communist Youth League Inner Mongolia Autonomous Regional Cttee, Dir Propaganda Dept, then Vice-Sec. CCP, Sec. CCP Chifeng City Cttee; Sec. CCP Inner Mongolia Autonomous Regional Cttee; Vice-Dir Propaganda Dept of

CCP Cen. Cttee 1993–; alt. mem. 12th, 14th CCP Cen. Cttees., mem. 15th CCP Cen. Cttee 1997–2002. *Address:* Propaganda Department of Chinese Communist Party Central Committee, Beijing, People's Republic of China.

LIU ZHENGWEI; Chinese party official; b. 1930, Xinzheng, Henan; joined CCP 1952; mem. 12th CCP Cen. Cttee 1982; Sec. CCP Cttee, Nanyang Pref., Henan 1982–83; Sec. CCP Cttee, Henan Prov. 1983, Deputy Sec. 1983; Deputy Sec. CCP Guizhou Provincial Cttee 1987, Sec. 1988–93; mem. 13th CCP Cen. Cttee 1987–92, 14th CCP Cen. Cttee 1992–97; Chair. Standing Cttee of People's Congress, Guizhou 1993; Deputy Sec. Work Cttee for Cen. Govt Organs 1993–94, Sec. 1994–. *Address:* c/o Guizhou Provincial Chinese Communist Party, Guiyang, Guizhou, People's Republic of China.

LIU ZHENWU, Maj.-Gen.; Chinese army officer; Commdr PLA Hong Kong Garrison 1997; alt. mem. 15th CCP Cen. Cttee 1997–2002. *Address:* Ministry of National Defence, Jingshanqian Jie, Beijing, People's Republic of China.

LIU ZHONGDE; Chinese administrator; b. 1933, Ji'an Co., Jilin Prov.; Deputy Sec.-Gen. of State Council 1988–92; Deputy Head Propaganda Dept 1990–; mem. Cen. Group for Propaganda and Thought; Vice-Minister of Culture 1992–93, Minister 1993–98; Chair. Science, Educational Culture, Public Health and Physical Culture Cttee, 9th Nat. Cttee of CPPCC 1998–; Pres. Asscn for Artists of Ministry of Culture 1993–; Vice-Pres. Party Bldg Research Soc.; mem. 14th CCP Cen. Cttee 1992–97, 15th CCP Cen. Cttee 1997–. *Address:* A 83 Beiheyan Street, Beijing 100722, People's Republic of China.

LIU ZHONGLI; Chinese state official; b. 1934, Ningbo City, Zhejiang Prov.; joined CCP 1954; Deputy Div. Chief, Vice-Chair., Chair. Heilongjiang Prov. Planning Comm. 1973–84, Chair. Planning and Econ. Comm. 1984–95; Vice-Gov. Heilongjiang Prov. 1985–88; Vice-Chair. State Cttee for Enterprise Man. 1988; Vice-Minister of Finance 1988–93, Minister 1993–98; Dir State Gen. Admin. of Taxation 1994–98; Dir Econ. System Reform Office of State Council 1998–2000; Deputy Head Cen. Financial and Econ. Leading Group; mem. 14th CCP Cen. Cttee 1992–97, mem. 15th CCP Cen. Cttee 1997–2002. *Address:* Chinese Communist Party, Beijing, People's Republic of China.

LIU ZHONGYI; Chinese administrator; b. 1930, Wuchang City, Hubei Prov.; joined CCP 1954; Vice-Minister State Planning Comm. 1985–89; Minister of Agric. 1990–93; mem. 14th CCP Cen. Cttee 1992–97; Deputy Dir-Gen. Devt Research Centre 1993–; State Leading Group for Comprehensive Agricultural Devt 1990–; Vice-Chair. Agric. and Rural Affairs Cttee, 9th NPC 1998–. *Address:* c/o Standing Committee of National People's Congress, Beijing, People's Republic of China.

LIVADIOTTI, Massimo; Italian painter; b. 20 Nov. 1959, Zavia, Libya; s. of Mario Livadiotti and Giovanna Mattera; ed Accad. di Belle Arti, Rome; maj. shows Rome 1987, 1989, 1994, 2000, Milan 1990, 1992, Bologna 1994; retrospectives Petöfi Museum, Budapest 1997, Sociedade Nacional de Belas Artes, Lisbon 2000; numerous group exhbns; work inspired by San Filippo Neri acquired by the Vatican 1995. *Exhibitions include:* Kalós Gallery, Parma 2001, Museum of Modern Art, Ostend 2001. *Publications:* Monograph 1987, Anthology Monographs to accompany exhbns at Centro Ausoni, Rome, Petöfi Museum, Budapest, Sociedade Nacional de Belas Artes, Lisbon 2001, Kalós Arte Contemporanea 2001. *Leisure interests:* gardening and light exercise. *Address:* Piazza Vittorio Emanuele II, N 31, 00185 Rome, Italy. *Telephone:* (06) 4468302. *Fax:* (06) 7726 1541.

LIVELY, Penelope Margaret, CBE, FRSL; British author; b. 17 March 1933, Cairo, Egypt; d. of Roger Low and Vera Greer; m. Jack Lively 1957; one s. one d.; ed St Anne's Coll. Oxford; mem. Bd British Library 1993–99, Bd British Council 1998–; mem. Soc. of Authors, PEN; Hon. Fellow Swansea Univ. 2002; Hon. DLitt (Tufts Univ.) 1993, (Warwick) 1998. *Publications:* Astercote 1970, The Whispering Knights 1971, The Wild Hunt of Hagworthy 1971, The Driftway 1972, The Ghost of Thomas Kempe 1973 (Carnegie Medal), The House in Norham Gardens 1974, Going Back 1975, Boy Without a Name 1975, A Stitch in Time 1976 (Whitbread Award), The Stained Glass Window 1976, Fanny's Sister 1976, The Presence of the Past (non-fiction) 1976, The Road to Lichfield 1977, The Voyage of QV66 1978, Nothing Missing but the Samovar and other stories 1978 (Southern Arts Literature Prize), Treasures of Time 1979 (Nat. Book Award), Fanny and the Monsters 1979, Judgement Day 1980, Fanny and the Battle of Potter's Piece 1980, The Revenge of Samuel Stokes 1981, Next to Nature, Art 1982, Perfect Happiness 1983, Corruption 1984, According to Mark 1984, Uninvited Ghosts and other stories 1984, Pack of Cards (short stories) 1986, Debbie and the Little Devil 1987, A House Inside Out 1987, Moon Tiger 1987 (Booker-McConnell Prize), Passing On 1989, Going Back 1991, City of the Mind 1991, Cleopatra's Sister 1993, The Cat, The Crow and the Banyan Tree 1994, Oleander, Jacaranda (autobiog.) 1994, Heatwave 1996, Beyond the Blue Mountains 1997, Spiderweb 1998, A House Unlocked 2001, In Search of a Homeland: The Story of the Aeneid 2001, The Photograph 2003; television and radio scripts. *Leisure interests:* gardening, landscape history, talking, listening. *Address:* c/o David Higham Associates, 5–8 Lower John Street, Golden Square, London, W1F 4HA, England. *Telephone:* (20) 7434-5900. *Fax:* (20) 7437-1072.

LIVINGSTONE, Ken(neth) Robert; British politician; b. 17 June 1945, London; s. of Robert Moffat Livingstone and Ethel Ada Kennard; m. Christine Pamela Chapman 1973 (divorced 1982); ed Tulse Hill Comprehensive School, Phillipa Fawcett Coll. of Educ.; Technician, Cancer Research Unit, Royal

Marsden Hospital 1962–70; Councillor, Borough of Lambeth 1971–78, of Camden 1978–82, of Greater London Council 1973–86 (Leader 1981–86); MP for Brent East 1987–2001; Mayor of London 2000–; joined Labour Party 1969, mem. Regional Exec. 1974–86, Nat. Exec. Council 1987–89, 1997–, Northern Ireland Select Cttee 1997–99; mem. Council, Zoological Soc. of London 1994– (Vice-Pres. 1996–98). *Publications:* If Voting Changed Anything They'd Abolish It 1987, Livingstone's Labour 1989. *Leisure interests:* science fiction, cinema, natural history. *Address:* Greater London Authority, City Hall, Queen's Walk, London, SE1 2AA, England. *Telephone:* (20) 7983-4000 (Office). *Fax:* (20) 7983-4008 (Office). *E-mail:* mayor@london.gov.uk (Office). *Website:* www.london.gov.uk (Office).

LIVINGSTONE, Marco Eduardo, MA; American art historian; b. 17 March 1952, Detroit; s. of Leon Livingstone and Alicia Arce Fernández; ed Univ. of Toronto, Courtauld Inst. of Fine Art, Univ. of London; Asst Keeper of British Art, Walker Art Gallery, Liverpool 1976–82; Deputy Dir Museum of Modern Art, Oxford 1982–86; Area Ed. for 20th Century The Dictionary of Art 1986–91, Deputy Ed. for 19th and 20th Centuries 1987–91; UK adviser to Art Life, Tokyo 1989–98; freelance writer and exhbn organizer 1991–. *Publications include:* Sheer Magic by Allen Jones 1979, Allen Jones Retrospective 1979, David Hockney 1981, Patrick Caulfield 1981, Peter Phillips Retrovision 1982, Duane Michals 1984, Stephen Buckley: Many Angles 1985, Arthur Tress: Talisman 1986, Stephen Farthing: Mute Accomplices 1987, David Hockney: Faces 1987, Michael Sandle 1988, Pop Art: A Continuing History 1990, Tim Head 1992, Tom Wesselmann 1993, Duane Hanson 1994, David Hockney in California 1994, Jim Dine: Flowers and Plants 1994, Allen Jones Prints 1995, Jim Dine: The Body and its Metaphors 1996, George Segal 1997, The Pop '60s: Transatlantic Crossing 1997, The Essential Duane Michals 1997, R. B. Kitaj: An American in Europe 1998, Jim Dine: The Alchemy of Images 1998, David Hockney: Space and Line 1999, Signature Pieces: Contemporary British Prints and Multiples 1999, Patrick Caulfield 1999, Photographics 2000, Jim Dine: Subjects 2000, Encounters: New Art from Old (contrib.) 2000, Kienholz Tableau Drawings 2001, Callum Innes: Exposed Paintings 2001, Langlands & Bell: The Language of Places 2002, David Hockney: Egyptian Journeys 2002, Clive Barker Sculpture (with Ann Fermon) 2002, Maurice Cockrill (with Nicholas Alfrey) 2002, Blast to Freeze (contrib.) 2002. *Leisure interests:* music, languages, travel, collecting art. *Address:* 36 St George's Avenue, London, N7 0HD, England; 27 rue des Ecouffes, 75004 Paris, France. *Telephone:* (20) 7607-0282 (London); 1-48-87-60-65 (Paris). *Fax:* (20) 7607-8694 (London). *E-mail:* marcolivingstone@aol.com (Office).

LIVNAT, Limor, BA; Israeli politician; b. 1950, Haifa; m.; two c.; ed Tel Aviv Univ.; worked in advertising and public relations; mem. Knesset (Parl.) 1992–, mem. Knesset Educ. and Culture Cttee, Labour and Social Affairs Cttee 1991–96, Chair. Knesset Cttee for Advancement of Status of Women 1993–94, Sub-Cttee on Women's Representation, Parl. Comm. of Inquiry into domestic violence 1995; Chair. of Likud and of Benjamin Netanyahu's election campaign 1996; Minister of Communications 1996–99, of Educ. 2001–; fmr Vice-Chair. World Likud Movt, fmr mem. Educ. and Cultural Cttee, Labour and Social Affairs Cttee, Comm. for Commercial TV. *Address:* Ministry of Education, P.O. Box 292, 34 Shivtei Israel Street, Jerusalem 91999, Israel (Office). *Telephone:* 2-5602222 (Office). *Fax:* 2-5602752 (Office). *E-mail:* info@education.gov.il (Office). *Website:* www.education.gov.il (Office).

LIVSHITZ, Aleksander Yakovlevich, DEcon; Russian economist; b. 6 Sept. 1946, Berlin, Germany; s. of Yakov Livshitz and Liya Livshitz; m. Galina Markina 1966; two d.; ed G. Plekhanov Inst. of Nat. Econ.; teacher, Chair. Prof. Moscow Machine Tool Instrumentation Inst. 1974–; Deputy Chief Analytical Centre, Admin. of Pres. 1992–94; Head of Pres.'s Advisers 1994; Asst to Pres. on problems of economy 1994–96; Deputy Prime Minister and Minister of Finance 1996–97; Deputy Head of Pres. Admin. March 1997–98; Head Econ. Policy Fund 1998–; Rep. for relations with G7 countries 1999; Adviser to Prime Minister 2000–; Deputy Dir-Gen. Russian Aluminium Co. 2001–; mem. UN Comm. on Financing of Devt 2001. *Publications:* Introduction to Market Economy 1991, Economic Reform in Russia and its Price 1994, more than 150 works on econ. problems of Russia, econ. situation in USA in 1980s. *Address:* Russkiy Aluminiy, Nikoloyamskaya str. 13, Bldg 1, 109240 Moscow, Russia. *Telephone:* (095) 720-51-70.

LJUNGGREN, Olof, LLB; Swedish publisher and business executive; b. 5 Jan. 1933, Eskilstuna; s. of Lars Ljunggren and Elisabeth Ljunggren; m. 1st Lena Carlsöö; m. 2nd Margreth Bäcklund; three s.; ed Univ. of Stockholm; Sec. Tidningarnas Arbetsgivareförening (Swedish Newspaper Employers' Asscn) 1959–62, Pres. and CEO 1962–66; Deputy Pres. and CEO Allers Förlag AB 1967–72, Pres. and CEO 1972–74; Pres. and CEO Svenska Dagbladet 1974–78; Pres. and CEO Svenska Arbetsgivareföreningen (Swedish Employers' Confed.) 1978–89; Chair. of Bd Askild & Kärnekull Förlag AB 1971–74, Nord Artel AB 1971–78, Centralförbundet Folk och Försvar (Vice-Chair. 1978–83) 1983–86, Richard Hägglöf Fondkommission AB 1984–87, Svenska Dagbladet 1989–91, Liber AB 1990–98 (Vice-Chair. 1998–), Intentia AB 1994–, AMF 1995–, AFA 1995–2001, Addum AB 1996–99, Consolis AB Oy 1997–; mem. Bd, SPP 1978–93, Investor 1989–92, Providentia 1989–92, Alfa Laval 1989–92, Trygg Hansa 1990–95, and numerous other bds; Kt Commdr Order of the White Rose of Finland 1982, The King's Medal of the 12th Dimension with the Ribbon of the Order of the Seraphim 1987, Kommendörskorset av Den Kgl. Norske Fortjenstorden; Hon. MD. *Leisure interests:*

shooting, golf, classical music, playing the piano. *Address:* Skeppargatan 7, 114 52 Stockholm, Sweden. *Telephone:* (708) 928563 (Office); (8) 6678785 (Home). *Fax:* (8) 6678785 (Home). *E-mail:* olof.ljunggren2@telia.com (Home).

LJUNGQVIST, Bengt, BA; Swedish business executive and lawyer; b. 13 Aug. 1937, Stockholm; s. of Gunnar Ljungqvist and Solveig Ljungqvist; m. 1st Sylvia Elmstedt 1961 (divorced 1977); m. 2nd Christina (née Hedén) Ljungqvist 1978; two s. two d.; ed Stockholm Univ.; joined Malmström and Malmenfelt Advokatbyrå, Stockholm 1967, partner 1971–; Solicitor-Royal 1995–; Pres. Bd of City Planning, Danderyd 1976–85, Chair. City Council, Danderyd 1986–; mem. Council, Swedish Bar Asscn 1983–, Vice-Pres. 1985–; Pres. Swedish Bar Asscn 1989–92; mem. Council Int. Bar Asscn 1984–90; Pres. JP-Bank Stockholm, Swedish Real Property Owners Asscn 1991–96; Vice-Pres. Union Int. de la Propriété Immobilière 1993–96; mem. Bd, Länsförsäkringar-Stockholm 1993–, Pres. 1995–. *Address:* Midgårdsvägen 1, 182 61 Djursholm, Sweden (Home). *Telephone:* (8) 679-69-50 (Office); (8) 755-31-96 (Home).

LLESHI, Maj.-Gen. Haxhi; Albanian politician; b. 1913; fought with Resistance against Italian and German occupations 1939–45; mem. provisional Govt 1944; Minister of the Interior 1944–46; Maj.-Gen. Albanian Army; Pres. Presidium of the People's Ass. (Head of State) 1953–82; mem. Cen. Cttee Albanian Workers' Party 1953. *Address:* Abdyl Frasheri Str., Tirana, Albania.

LLEWELLYN, John; American scientist; b. 22 April 1933, Cardiff, UK; s. of John Llewellyn and Morella (née Roberts); m. Valerie Davies-Jones; one s. two d.; ed Univ. Coll., Cardiff, Wales; Research Fellow, Nat. Research Council of Canada 1958–60; Assoc. Prof. School of Eng Science, Florida State Univ. 1964–72; selected by NASA as scientist-astronaut 1967; Dean, School of Eng Science, Florida State Univ. 1970–72; Prof. Depts of Chemical and Mechanical Eng, Coll. of Eng, Univ. of South Fla, Tampa 1973–, Dir Eng Computing 1986–, Dir Academic Computing 1993–; Co-ordinator, Scientist in the Sea Project 1973; aquanaut Nat. Oceanographic Atmospheric Admin; Scientific consultant on marine environment, energy and industrial computer applications; Pres. J. Vector Inc., K. Vector Inc.; mem. Royal Inst. of Chem., AIAA, Radiation Research Soc. *Publications:* Principles and Applications of Digital Devices 1983, Basic Elements of Digital Systems 1983. *Leisure interests:* sailing, underwater exploration. *Address:* Academic Computing, University of South Florida, 4202 E Fowler Avenue, L1B 618, Tampa, FL 33620 (Office); 3010 St Charles Drive, Tampa, FL 33618, USA (Home). *Telephone:* (813) 974-1780 (Office). *Fax:* (813) 974-1799.

LLEWELLYN SMITH, Sir Chris(topher) Hubert, Kt, DPhil, FRS; British theoretical physicist; b. 19 Nov. 1942; s. of the late John Clare Llewellyn Smith and of Margaret Emily Frances Crawford; m. Virginia Grey 1966; one s. one d.; ed Wellington Coll. and New Coll. Oxford; Royal Soc. Exchange Fellow, Lebedev Inst., Moscow 1967–68; Fellow, Centre Européen pour la Recherche Nucléaire (CERN), Geneva 1968–70, Staff mem. 1972–74, Chair. Scientific Policy Cttee 1990–92, Dir-Gen. CERN European Lab. for Particle Physics 1994–98; Research Assoc., Stanford Linear Accelerator Center (SLAC), Calif., USA 1970–72; Univ. Lecturer in Theoretical Physics, Univ. of Oxford and Fellow St John's Coll. 1974–98, Reader in Theoretical Physics 1980–87, Prof. 1987–98 (on leave of absence 1994–98), Chair. of Physics 1987–92, Sr Research Fellow in Theoretical Physics 2002–; Pres. and Provost Univ. Coll. London 1999–2002; mem. various advisory bodies for SLAC, CERN, DESY (Deutsches Elektronen-Synchrotron, Hamburg) and SERC (Science and Eng Research Council) 1972–92; mem. Advisory Council on Science and Tech. 1989–92; Fellow American Physical Soc.; Foreign Fellow Indian Nat. Science Acad.; mem. Academia Europaea; Hon. Fellow Univ. of Wales 1998; Hon. DSc (Bristol, Shandong, Granada); Maxwell Medal 1979, US Dept of Energy Distinguished Assoc. Award 1998, US NSF Distinguished Service Award 1998, Medal of Japanese Assoc. of Medical Sciences 1997, Gold Medal, Slovak Acad. of Science 1998, Glazebrook Medal, Inst. of Physics 1999. *Publications:* numerous articles in scientific journals including Nuclear Physics, Physics Letters, Physics Review. *Leisure interests:* books, travel, opera. *Address:* Theoretical Physics, Department of Physics, 1 Keble Road, Oxford, OX1 3NP, England. *Telephone:* (1865) 273999 (Office). *Fax:* (1865) 273947 (Office). *E-mail:* c.llewellyn-smith@physics.ox.ac.uk (Office).

LLEWELLYN SMITH, Elizabeth, CB, MA; British college principal (retd); b. 17 Aug. 1934, Upshire; d. of the late John Clare Llewellyn Smith and of Margaret Emily Frances Crawford; sister of Sir Michael John Llewellyn Smith (q.v.) and Sir Chris Llewellyn Smith; ed Christ's Hospital, Univ. of Cambridge and Royal Coll. of Defence Studies; fmr civil servant; Deputy Dir-Gen. of Fair Trading 1982–87; Deputy Sec. Dept of Trade and Industry 1987–90; Dir European Investment Bank 1987–90; Prin. St Hilda's Coll. Oxford 1990–2001; mem. Business Appointments Panel, DTI 1996–2002, Ind. Disciplinary Bd Accountancy Foundation 2001–, Research Ethics Cttee Health and Safety Exec., Council Consumers' Asscn 2002–; Hon. Fellow Girton Coll., Cambridge 1994, St Mary's Coll., Univ. of Durham 1999, St Hilda's Coll., Oxford 2001. *Leisure interests:* travel, books, entertaining. *Address:* Brook Cottage, Taston, nr Charlbury, Oxon., OX7 3JL, England (Home). *Telephone:* (1608) 811874 (Home). *E-mail:* e.llewellynsmith@btopenworld.com (Home).

LLEWELLYN SMITH, Sir Michael John, KCVO, CMG, DPhil; British diplomatist (retd); b. 25 April 1939; s. of the late John Clare Llewellyn Smith and of Margaret Emily Frances Crawford; brother of Elizabeth Llewellyn Smith (q.v.) and Sir Chris Llewellyn Smith; m. Colette Gaulier 1967; one s. one d.; ed New Coll. Oxford, St Antony's Coll. Oxford; at Embassy, Moscow 1973–75, at Embassy, Paris 1976–78; at Royal Coll. of Defence Studies 1979; at Embassy, Athens 1980–83; Head W European Dept FCO 1984–85, Head Soviet Dept 1985–88; Minister Embassy, Paris 1988–91; British Amb. to Poland 1991–96, to Greece 1996–99; Vice-Chair. Cathedrals Fabric Comm. for England 1999–; Chair. British Inst. in Paris 2000–; Dir (non-exec.) Coca-Cola HBC SA 2000–; John D. Criticos Prize 1999. *Publications:* The Great Island: A Study of Crete 1965, Ionian Vision: Greece in Asia Minor 1919–22 1973, The British Embassy Athens 1998. *Leisure Interests:* music, wine, walking in Greek mountains. *Address:* Middle House, Frouds Close, Childrey, Wantage, Oxon., OX12 9NT, England; c/o United Oxford and Cambridge University Club, 71 Pall Mall, London, SW1Y 5HD. *E-mail:* michael@mjls.demon.co.uk (Home).

LLOWARCH, Martin Edge, CBIM, FCA, F.I.C.A.; British business executive; b. 28 Dec. 1935; s. of Wilfred Llowarch and Olga Llowarch; m. Ann Marion Buchanan 1965; one s. two d.; ed Stowe School; with Buckingham, Coopers & Lybrand 1962–68; with British Steel PLC (fmrly British Steel Corpn) 1968–, Head of Special Projects 1968, Man. Dir (SA) 1971, Dir Finance and Admin. (Int.) 1973, Finance Dir Tubes Div. 1975, Financial Controller Strip Products Group 1980, Man. Dir for Finance 1983, Dir 1984–91, Deputy CEO 1986, CEO 1986–91; Chair. (part-time) Transport Devt Group PLC 1992–2000; Deputy Chair. (non-exec.) Firth Rixson (fmrly Johnson and Firth Brown PLC) 1992–93, Chair. 1993–2001; Dir (non-exec.) Abbey Nat. PLC 1989– (Deputy Chair. 1994–99), Hickson Int. PLC 1992–99; mem. Accounting Standards Cttee 1985–87. *Leisure interests:* sport, music, gardening, reading. *Address:* c/o Abbey National PLC, 215 Baker Street, London, N.W.1, England.

LLOYD, Chris(tine) Marie Evert (see Evert, Chris(tine) Marie).

LLOYD, Christopher; American actor; b. 22 Oct. 1938, Stamford, Conn.; m. Jane Walker Wood 1991; ed Neighborhood Playhouse, New York; film debut One Flew over the Cuckoo's Nest 1975. *Films include:* Butch and Sundance: The Early Days, The Onion Field, The Black Marble, The Legend of the Lone Ranger, Mr Mom, To Be or Not To Be, Star Trek III: The Search for Spock, Adventures of Buckaroo Banzai, Back to the Future, Clue, Who Framed Roger Rabbit?, Track 29, Walk Like a Man, Eight Men Out, The Dream Team, Why Me?, Anastasia, The Real Blonde, Back to the Future, Part II, Back to the Future, Part III, The Addams Family, Twenty Bucks (Independent Spirit Award for Best Dramatic Actor), Dennis the Menace, Addams Family Values, Angels in the Endzone, The Pagemaster, Camp Nowhere, The Radioland Murders, Things To Do in Denver When You're Dead 1995, Cadillac Ranch 1996, Changing Habits 1996, Dinner at Fred's, Baby Geniuses, My Favorite Martian 1999, Man on the Moon 1999, Chasing Destiny 2000, When Good Ghouls Go Bad 2001, Wit 2001, Wish You Were Dead, Interstate 60 2003. *Plays:* Red White & Madox, Possessed, Midsummer Night's Dream, Kaspar (Drama Desk and Obie Awards 1973), Unexpected Man 2002, Mornings at 7 (Broadway) 2002, Twelfth Night (Shakespeare in the Park) 2002. *Television includes:* Barney Miller, Cheers, Taxi (two Emmy Awards including Best Supporting Actor), Best of the West, The Dictator, Tales from Hollywood Hills: Pat Hobby – Teamed with Genius, September Gun, Road to Avonlea (Emmy Award for Best Supporting Actor), Alice in Wonderland, Right to Remain Silent, The Edge, Quicksilver Highway, Spin City, Cyberchase, Tremors, Malcolm in the Middle. *Address:* c/o The Gersh Agency, 252 North Canon Drive, Beverly Hills, CA 90210; c/o Andy Freedman, 20 Ironsides Street #18, Marina Del Ray, CA 90292, USA.

LLOYD, Clive Hubert, AO CBE; Guyanese cricketer; b. 31 Aug. 1944, Georgetown, British Guiana (now Guyana); s. of the late Arthur Christopher Lloyd and Sylvia Thelma Lloyd; cousin of Lance Gibbs; m. Waveney Benjamin 1971; one s. two d.; ed Chatham High School, Georgetown; left-hand batsman, right-arm medium-paced bowler; played for British Guiana/Guyana 1963–83, Lancashire 1968–86 (Capt. 1981–83, 1986); 110 Tests for W Indies 1966–1985, record 74 as Capt., scoring 7,515 runs (average 46.6) including 19 hundreds; toured England 1969, 1973, 1975 (World Cup), 1976, 1979 (World Cup), 1980, 1983 (World Cup), 1984; scored 31,232 first-class runs including 79 hundreds; W Indies Team Man. 1988–89 and 1996–99; Int. Cricket Council Referee 1992–95; Exec. Promotions Officer, Project Fullemploy 1987–; Dir Red Rose Radio PLC 1981; Patron Nat. Lottery Charities Bd; Hon. Fellow Manchester Polytechnic, Lancs. Polytechnic 1986; Hon. MA (Manchester, Hull); Hon. DLitt (Univ. of W Indies, Jamaica); Golden Arrow of Achievement (Guyana) 1975, Wisden Cricketer of the Year 1971. *Publications:* Living for Cricket (with Tony Cozier) 1980, Winning Captaincy (with Mihir Bose) 1985. *Address:* c/o Harefield, Harefield Drive, Wilmslow, Cheshire, SK9 1NJ, England.

LLOYD, David Robert, MA, PhD, FInstP; British professor of chemistry; b. 19 May 1937, Derby; s. of George Lloyd and Effie Lloyd; m. Heidi Hoffman 1964; one s. one d.; ed Halesowen Grammar School, Worcs. and Selwyn Coll. Cambridge; temporary lecturer, Chem. Dept, Northwestern Univ., Evanston, USA 1963–65; Lecturer in Chem., Univ. of Birmingham 1965–78; Prof. of Chem., Trinity Coll., Dublin, Ireland 1978–2000, Head Chem. Dept 1978–85, 1992–94; A. von Humboldt Fellowship 1962–63; mem. Royal Irish Acad.; Fellow, Trinity Coll. Dublin. *Publications:* approx. 110 papers on aspects of chemistry and physics. *Leisure interests:* music, hill walking, domestic chores, theology. *Address:* Trinity College, Dublin 2, Ireland.

LLOYD, Sir Geoffrey Ernest Richard, Kt, PhD, FBA; British professor of philosophy; b. 25 Jan. 1933, London; s. of William Ernest Lloyd and Olive Irene Neville Lloyd; m. Janet Elizabeth Lloyd 1956; three s.; ed Charterhouse and King's Coll. Cambridge; Asst Lecturer in Classics, Cambridge Univ. 1965–67, Lecturer 1967–74, Reader in Ancient Philosophy and Science 1974–83, Prof. 1983–2000; Master, Darwin Coll., Cambridge 1989–2000, Hon. Fellow 2000–; Fellow King's Coll. 1957–89, Hon. Fellow 1990–; A. D. White Prof.-at-Large, Cornell Univ. 1990–96; Chair. East Asian History of Science Trust 1992–2002; mem. Japan Soc. for the Promotion of Science, Int. Acad. of the History of Science; Zhu Kezhen Visiting Prof., Inst. for the History of Natural Science, Beijing 2002; Foreign Hon. mem. American Acad. of Arts and Sciences 1995; Sarton Medal 1987. *Publications:* Polarity and Analogy 1966, Aristotle, the Growth and Structure of his Thought 1968, Early Greek Science: Thales to Aristotle 1970, Greek Science after Aristotle 1973, Hippocratic Writings (Ed.) 1978, Aristotle on Mind and the Senses (Ed.) 1978, Magic, Reason and Experience 1979, Science, Folklore and Ideology 1983, Science and Morality in Greco-Roman Antiquity 1985, The Revolutions of Wisdom 1987, Demystifying Mentalities 1990, Methods and Problems in Greek Science 1991, Adversaries and Authorities 1996, Aristotelian Explorations 1996, Greek Thought (Ed.) 2000, The Ambitions of Curiosity 2002, The Way and The Word (with N. Sivin) 2002, In the Grip of Disease, Studies in the Greek Imagination 2003. *Leisure interest:* travel. *Address:* 2 Prospect Row, Cambridge, CB1 1DU, England. *Telephone:* (1223) 355970.

LLOYD, John Nicol Fortune, MA; British journalist; b. 15 April 1946; s. of Christopher Lloyd and Joan A. Fortune; m. 1st Judith Ferguson 1974 (divorced 1979); m. 2nd Marcia Levy 1983 (divorced 1997); one s.; ed Waid Comprehensive School and Univ. of Edinburgh; Ed. Time Out 1972–73; reporter, London Programme 1974–76; Producer, Weekend World 1976–77; industrial reporter, labour corresp., industrial and labour ed. Financial Times 1977–86; Ed. New Statesman 1986–87, Assoc. Ed. 1996–; with Financial Times 1987– (Moscow Corresp. 1991–95); freelance journalist 1996–; Dir East-West Trust, NY 1997–, Foreign Policy Centre 1999–; Journalist of the Year, Granada Awards 1984, Specialist Writer of the Year, IPC Awards 1985; Rio Tinto David Watt Memorial Prize 1997. *Publications:* The Politics of Industrial Change (with Ian Benson) 1982, The Miners' Strike: Loss without Limit (with Martin Adeney) 1986, In Search of Work (with Charles Leadbeater) 1987, Counterblasts (contrib.) 1989, Rebirth of a Nation: an Anatomy of Russia 1998, Re-engaging Russia 2000, The Protest Ethic 2001. *Leisure interests:* opera, hill walking, squash. *Address:* New Statesman, Victoria Station House, 7th Floor, 191 Victoria Street, London, SW1E 5NE, England (Office). *Telephone:* (20) 7828-1232 (Office). *Fax:* (20) 7828-1881 (Office). *E-mail:* info@newstatesman.co.uk (Office).

LLOYD, Robert Andrew, CBE; British opera singer; b. 2 March 1940, Southend; s. of William Edward Lloyd and May Lloyd (née Waples); m. 1st Sandra D. Watkins 1964 (divorced 1990); one s. three d.; m. 2nd Lynda A. Hazell (née Powell) 1992; ed Southend High School for Boys, Keble Coll. Oxford, London Opera Centre; served as Lt in Royal Navy 1963–66; Lecturer, Bramshill Police Coll. 1966–68; Prin. Bass, Sadlers Wells Opera 1969–72, Royal Opera House 1972–83; freelance singer with all maj. opera houses and orchestras world-wide, frequent broadcasts as presenter, BBC radio and TV 1983–; film appearances: Parsifal, Bluebeard's Castle; performed title role in Tarkovsky production of Boris Godunov at Kirov Opera, Leningrad 1990; created role of Tyrone in Tower by Alun Hoddinott; Visiting Prof. Royal Coll. of Music, London 1996–; Pres. British Youth Opera 1988–94, Southend Choral Soc. 1996–; mem. Exec. Cttee Musicians' Benevolent Fund 1989–92; mem. Conservatoires Advisory Group 1993–99; Hon. Fellow Keble Coll. 1990; Patron Carl Rosa Trust 1994–; Artist of the Year, Teatro Colón, Buenos Aires 1996, Charles Santley Award 1997, Chaliapin Commemoration Medal (St Petersburg) 1998. *Radio:* regular presenter for BBC Radio 3. *Television:* wrote and presented documentary Six Foot Cinderella 1990, subject of BBC documentary Bob the Bass. *Publications:* numerous contribs to magazines. *Leisure interests:* sailing, hill walking, history. *Address:* Askonas Holt Ltd, Lonsdale Chambers, 27 Chancery Lane, London, WC2A 1PF, England. *Telephone:* (20) 7400-1713 (Office); (20) 8883-0664.

LLOYD-JONES, David Mathias, BA; Welsh musician; b. 19 Nov. 1934, London; s. of the late Sir Vincent Lloyd-Jones and Margaret Alwena Mathias; m. Anne Carolyn Whitehead 1964; two s. one d.; ed Westminster School, Magdalen Coll. Oxford; Repetiteur, Royal Opera 1959–61; Chorus Master, New Opera Co. 1961–64; conducted at Bath Festival 1966, City of London Festival 1966, Wexford Festival 1967–70, Scottish Opera 1968, Welsh Nat. Opera 1968, Royal Opera, Covent Garden 1971, Sadler's Wells Opera Co. (now ENO) 1969; Asst Music Dir ENO 1972–78; Artistic Dir Opera North 1978–90; also conductor for TV operas (Eugene Onegin, The Flying Dutchman, Hansel and Gretel) and has appeared with most British symphony orchestras and conducted worldwide; Chair. Delius Trust 1997–, Gen. Ed. William Walton Edn 1996–; Hon. DMus (Leeds) 1986. *Music:* many acclaimed recordings of British and Russian music; has edited works by composers, including Mussorgsky, Bizet, Walton, Berlioz, Elgar and Sullivan. *Publications:* Boris Godunov–Translation, Vocal Score, Eugene Onegin–Translation, Vocal Score, Boris Godunov–Critical Edition of Original Full Score, numerous contribs to publs including Grove's Dictionary of Music and Musicians, Musik in Geschichte und Gegenwart, Music and Letters, The Listener. *Leisure* *interests:* theatre, French cuisine, rose growing. *Address:* 94 Whitelands House, Cheltenham Terrace, London, SW3 4RA, England (Home). *Telephone:* (20) 7730-8695. *Fax:* (20) 7730-8695.

LLOYD-JONES, Sir (Peter) Hugh (Jefferd), Kt, MA, FBA; British classical scholar; b. 21 Sept. 1922, St Peter Port, Guernsey; s. of Brevet-Major W. Lloyd-Jones, DSO and Norah Leila Jefferd; m. 1st Frances Elisabeth Hedley 1953 (divorced 1981); two s. one d.; m. 2nd Mary R. Lefkowitz 1982; ed Lycée Français du Royaume-Uni (London), Westminster School and Christ Church, Oxford; served in Indian Intelligence Corps 1942–46; Fellow, Jesus Coll. Cambridge 1948–54; Fellow and E.P. Warren Praelector in Classics, Corpus Christi Coll. Oxford 1954–60; Regius Prof. of Greek and Student of Christ Church 1960–89, Prof. Emer. 1989–; J. H. Gray Lecturer, Cambridge 1961; Visiting Prof. Yale Univ. 1964–65, 1967–68; Sather Prof. of Classical Literature, Univ. of Calif. at Berkeley 1969–70; Alexander White Visiting Prof. Univ. of Chicago 1972; Visiting Prof., Harvard Univ. 1976–77; mem. Acad. of Athens; Corresp. mem. American Acad. of Arts and Sciences, Nordrhein-Westfälische Akad. der Wissenschaften, Accad. di Archeologia, Lettere e belle Arti di Napoli, Bayerische Akad. der Wissenschaften, American Philosophical Soc.; Hon. DHumLitt (Chicago) 1970; Hon. DPhil (Tel Aviv) 1984; Hon. PhD (Thessaloniki) 1999, (Göttingen) 2002; Chancellor's Prize for Latin Prose, Ireland and Craven Scholarships 1947. *Publications:* Appendix to Aeschylus (Loeb Classical Library) 1957, Menandri Dyscolus (Oxford Classical Texts) 1960; The Justice of Zeus 1971, (ed.) Maurice Bowra: a Celebration 1974, Females of the Species 1975, Myths of the Zodiac 1978, Mythical Beasts 1980, Blood for the Ghosts 1982, Classical Survivals 1982, Supplementum Hellenisticum (with P. J. Parsons) 1983; translated Paul Maas, Greek Metre 1962, Aeschylus Agamemnon, The Libation-Bearers and The Eumenides 1970, Sophoclea (with N. G. Wilson) 1990, Academic Papers (2 Vols) 1990, Sophoclis Fabulae (with N. G. Wilson) 1990, Greek in a Cold Climate 1991, Sophocles (Loeb Classical Library, 3 Vols) 1994–96, Sophocles: Second Thoughts (with N. G. Wilson) 1997; edited The Greeks 1962, Tacitus 1964; articles and reviews in periodicals. *Leisure interests:* cats, remembering old cricket. *Address:* 15 West Riding, Wellesley, MA 02482, USA. *Telephone:* (781) 237-2212. *Fax:* (781) 237-2246. *E-mail:* mlefkowitz@wellesley.educ (Home).

LLOYD WEBBER, Baron (Life Peer), cr. 1997, of Sydmonton in the County of Hampshire; **Andrew Lloyd Webber,** Kt, FRCM; British composer; b. 22 March 1948; s. of the late William Southcombe Lloyd Webber, CBE, DMUS, FRCM, FRCO and Jean Hermione Johnstone; brother of Julian Lloyd Webber (q.v.); m. 1st Sarah Jane Tudor (née Hugill) 1971 (divorced 1983); one s. one d.; m. 2nd Sarah Brightman 1984 (divorced 1990); m. 3rd Madeleine Astrid Gurdon 1991; two s. one d.; ed Westminster School, Magdalen Coll. Oxford, Royal Coll. of Music; Chair. The Really Useful Group Ltd; awards include 7 Tony Awards, 4 Drama Desk Awards, 6 Laurence Olivier Awards, Triple Play Awards, 1996 ASCAP 1988, Praemium Imperiale Award 1995, 3 Grammy Awards, Golden Globe Award, Golden Globe, Academy Award 1996, Richard Rodgers Award 1996, London Critics' Circle Best Musical 2000. *Works:* (musicals): Joseph and the Amazing Technicolor Dreamcoat (lyrics by Tim Rice) 1968 (revised 1973, 1991), Jesus Christ Superstar (lyrics by Tim Rice) 1970 (revised 1996), Jeeves (lyrics by Alan Ayckbourn) 1975, Evita (lyrics by Tim Rice) 1976 (stage version 1978), Variations 1977 (symphonic version 1986), Tell me on a Sunday (lyrics by Don Black) 1980, Cats (based on T. S. Eliot's Old Possum's Book of Practical Cats) (Tony Awards for Best Score and Best Musical 1983) 1981, Song and Dance (lyrics by Don Black) 1982, Starlight Express (lyrics by Richard Stilgoe) 1984, The Phantom of the Opera (Tony Award for Best Musical 1988) (lyrics by Richard Stilgoe and Charles Hart) 1986, Aspects of Love (lyrics by Don Black and Charles Hart) 1989, Sunset Boulevard (Tony Awards for Best Score and Best Musical 1995) (lyrics by Christopher Hampton and Don Black) 1993, By Jeeves 1996 (lyrics by Alan Ayckbourn), Whistle Down the Wind (lyrics by Jim Steinman) 1996, The Beautiful Game (book and lyrics by Ben Elton) 2000; (other compositions): Requiem Mass 1985, Amigos Para Siempre (official theme for 1992 Olympic Games); (film scores): Gumshoe 1971, The Odessa File 1974, Jesus Christ Superstar 1974. *Producer:* Jeeves Takes Charge 1975, Cats 1981, Song and Dance 1982, Daisy Pulls It Off 1983, The Hired Man 1984, Starlight Express 1984, On Your Toes 1984, The Phantom of the Opera 1986, Cafe Puccini 1986, The Resistable Rise of Arturo Ui 1987, Lend Me a Tenor 1988, Aspects of Love 1989, Shirley Valentine (Broadway) 1989, Joseph and the Amazing Technicolor Dreamcoat 1973, 1974, 1978, 1980, 1991, La Bête 1992, Sunset Boulevard 1993, By Jeeves 1996, Whistle Down the Wind 1996, 1998, Jesus Christ Superstar 1996, 1998, The Beautiful Game 2000, Bombay Dreams 2002, and others. *Publications:* Evita (with Tim Rice) 1978, Cats: the book of the musical 1981, Joseph and the Amazing Technicolor Dreamcoat (with Tim Rice) 1982, The Complete Phantom of the Opera 1987, The Complete Aspects of Love 1989, Sunset Boulevard: from movie to musical 1993; food critic Daily Telegraph 1996–99. *Leisure interests:* architecture, art. *Address:* The Really Useful Group Ltd, 22 Tower Street, London, WC2H 9NS, England. *Telephone:* (20) 7240-0880 (Office). *Fax:* (20) 7240-1204 (Office). *Website:* www.reallyuseful.com (Office).

LLOYD WEBBER, Julian, FRCM; British cellist; b. 14 April 1951, London; s. of the late William Southcombe Lloyd Webber CBE, DMUS, FRCM, FRCO and of Jean Hermione Johnstone; brother of Lord Lloyd Webber; m. 1st Celia M. Ballantyne 1974 (divorced 1989); m. 2nd Zohra Mahmoud Ghazi 1989 (divorced 1999); one s.; m. 3rd Kheira Bourahla 2001; ed Univ. Coll. School and Royal Coll. of Music; debut at Queen Elizabeth Hall 1972; debut with

Berlin Philharmonic Orchestra 1984; appears at major int. concert halls and has undertaken concert tours throughout Europe, N and S America, S Africa, Australasia, Singapore, Japan, China, Hong Kong and Korea; numerous television appearances and broadcasts in UK, Netherlands, Africa, Germany, Scandinavia, France, Belgium, Spain, Australasia and USA; British Phonographic Industry Award for Best Classical Recording 1986, Crystal Award, World Economic Forum (Switzerland) 1998. *Music:* Recordings include world premieres of Britten's 3rd Suite for Solo Cello, Bridge's Oration, Rodrigo's Cello Concerto, Holst's Invocation, Gavin Bryar's Cello Concerto, James MacMillan's Kiss on Wood, Michael Nyman's Cello and Saxophone Concerto, Sullivan's Cello Concerto, Vaughan Williams' Fantasia on Sussex Folk Tunes, Andrew Lloyd Webber's Variations, Elgar's Cello Concerto, Dvořák Concerto, Saint-Saëns Concerto, Lalo Concerto, Walton Concerto, Britten Cello Symphony; premiered Philip Glass Concerto, Beijing 2001. *Publications:* Frank Bridge, Six Pieces 1982, Young Cellist's Repertoire (3 Vols) 1984, Travels with my Cello 1984, Song of the Birds 1985, Recital Repertoire for Cellists 1986, Short Sharp Shocks 1990, The Great Cello Solos 1992, The Essential Cello 1997, Cello Moods 1999. *Leisure interests:* topography (especially British), football (Leyton Orient). *Address:* c/o IMG Artists Europe, Lovell House, 616 Chiswick High Road, London, W4 5RX, England. *Telephone:* (20) 8233-5800. *Fax:* (20) 8233-5801. *E-mail:* vcorley-smith@imgworld.com (Office). *Website:* www.julianlloydwebber.com (Office).

LÔ, Ismaël; Senegalese musician; b. Aug. 1956; m.; ed Institut des arts de Dakar; singer and composer of African folk songs in Wolof and French. *Recordings:* 21 albums including Iso 1995, Jammu Africa 1996, Dabah 2001. *Leisure interests:* painting, farming. *Address:* Syllart Productions, c/o Next Music, 52 rue Paul Lescop, 92000 Nanterre, France (Office).

LO, K. S.; Chinese business executive; b. 1909, Guangdong Prov., China; m.; ed Univ. of Hong Kong; lived in Malaysia aged 10 to 20; set up Vitasoy soy milk factory in Causeway Bay Dist of Hong Kong 1940–42; resumed business after World War II; Vitasoy (now run by his son Winston Lo) listed on Hong Kong Stock Exchange 1994; maj. benefactor of Hong Kong Museum of Tea Ware. *Leisure interest:* collecting teapots. *Address:* c/o Vitasoy, Whole Building 1, Kinwong Street, Tuen Mun, New Territory, Hong Kong Special Administrative Region, People's Republic of China. *Telephone:* 24660333. *Fax:* 24563441.

LO, Vincent Hong Sui; Chinese business executive; b. 18 April 1948, Hong Kong; m. Jean Lo 1981; one s. one d.; ed Univ. of New South Wales, Australia; f. Shui On Group 1971, now Chair. and Chief. Exec.; Chair. Hong Kong Gen. Chamber of Commerce 1991–92; mem. Exec. Cttee Basic Law Consultative Cttee 1985–90; mem. Bd Land Devt Corpn 1988–90; mem. Hong Kong Trade Devt Council 1991–92, Hong Kong Baptist Coll. 1987–89; mem. Standing Cttee on Judicial Salaries & Conditions of Service 1988–94, Standing Cttee on Directorate Salaries & Conditions of Service 1988–94; mem. Council, Exec. Cttee Hong Kong Man. Asscn 1984–94; Pres. Business and Professionals Fed. of Hong Kong; mem. Preparatory Cttee for the Hong Kong Special Admin. Region 1996–97; Hong Kong Affairs Adviser, PRC State Council's Office of Hong Kong & Macao Affairs/Xinhua News Agency, Hong Kong Br. 1994–97; Adviser China Soc. of Macroecons., Peking Univ. China Centre for Econ. Research; mem. Gov.'s Business Council 1992–97, Airport Authority 1990–99, Hong Kong/United States Econ. Co-operation Cttee; Dir The Real Estate Developers Asscn of Hong Kong, The Community Chest of Hong Kong 1990–95, Great Eagle Holdings Ltd.; Dir (non. exec.) Hang Seng Bank Ltd, New World China Land Ltd; Chair. Council Hong Kong Univ. of Science and Tech.; JP 1999; DBA hc (Hong Kong Univ. of Science and Tech.) 1996, Advisory Professorship (Shanghai Tongji Univ.) 1996, (Shanghai Univ.) 1998; Hon. Citizen of Shanghai 1998; Gold Bauhinia Star 1998. *Address:* 34/F Shui On Centre, 6–8 Harbour Road, Hong Kong Special Administrative Region, People's Republic of China.

LOACH, Kenneth, BA; British film director; b. 17 June 1936, Nuneaton; s. of the late John Loach and of Vivien Loach (née Hamlin); m. Lesley Ashton 1962; three s. (one deceased) two d.; ed King Edward VI School, Nuneaton, St Peter's Hall (now Coll.), Oxford; BBC trainee, Drama Dept 1963; freelance film Dir 1963–; Hon. DLitt (St Andrews) (Staffs. Univ., Bristol); Dr. hc (Royal Coll. of Art) 1998; Hon. Fellow, St Peter's Coll. Oxford. *Films:* Poor Cow 1967, Kes 1969, In Black and White 1970, Family Life 1971, Black Jack 1979, Looks and Smiles 1981, Fatherland 1986, Hidden Agenda 1990, Riff-Raff 1991, Raining Stones 1993, Ladybird, Ladybird 1994, Land and Freedom 1995, Carla's Song 1996, My Name is Joe 1998, Bread and Roses 2001, The Navigators 2001, Sweet Sixteen 2002, 11.09.01 UK Segment 2002. *Television:* Diary of a Young Man 1964, Three Clear Sundays 1965, The End of Arthur's Marriage 1965, Up the Junction 1965, Coming Out Party 1965, Cathy Come Home 1966, In Two Minds 1966, The Golden Vision 1969, The Big Flame 1970, After a Lifetime 1971, The Rank and File 1972, Days of Hope (four films) 1975, The Price of Coal 1977, The Gamekeeper 1979, Auditions 1980, A Question of Leadership 1980, The Red and the Blue 1983, Questions of Leadership 1983, Which Side are You on? 1984, The View from the Woodpile 1988, Time to Go 1989, Dispatches: Arthur Scargill 1991, The Flickering Flame 1996, Another City 1998. *Address:* c/o Sixteen Films, 2nd Floor, 187 Wardour Street, London, W1F 8ZB, England.

LOADER, Danyon Joseph, ONZ; New Zealand swimmer; b. 21 April 1975, Timaru; s. of Peter Loader and Daphne Loader; ed Berkeley Univ., San Francisco, USA; world short-course record in 200m butterfly 1991; silver medallist Olympic Games 1992; gold, silver (three times) and bronze medallist Commonwealth Games 1994; gold medallist 200m and 400m freestyle Olympic Games 1996; est. over 40 NZ records; retd 2000; motivational speaker with Speakers New Zealand; NZ Sportsman of the Decade (1990s), Lonsdale Cup, NZ Olympic Cttee. *Leisure interests:* reading, films, surfing, scuba diving, socializing. *Address:* 9 Prince Albert Road, St Kilda, Dunedin, New Zealand (Home). *Telephone:* (3) 455-2486 (Home).

LOBASHEV, Vladimir Mikhailovich; Russian nuclear physicist; b. 29 July 1934, Leningrad; s. of Mikhail Yefimovich Lobashev and Nina Vladimirovna Yevropeitseva; m. Muza Romanovna Lobasheva; two s. two d.; ed Leningrad Univ.; mem. CPSU 1970–91; mem. of staff of Physical-Tech. Inst. 1957–72; Scientific Leader, Moscow Meson Factory Programme; Head, Experimental Physics Div. of Inst. for Nuclear Research at USSR (now Russian) Acad. of Sciences 1972–; Leader, Lab. for Weak Interaction Study, Leningrad (now St Petersburg) Inst. for Nuclear Physics 1972–; Corresp. mem. USSR (now Russian) Acad. of Sciences 1970–. *Leisure interest:* tennis. *Address:* Institute for Nuclear Research, Academy of Sciences, Prospect 60 Let Oktyabrya 7A, 117312 Troitsk, Moscow Region, Russia. *Telephone:* (095) 334-01-90 (Office); (095) 334-03-18 (Home).

LOBKOWICZ, Michal; Czech politician; b. 20 July 1964, Prague; m.; one s.; ed Charles Univ., Prague; MP for ODS/Civic Democratic Party 1996–98; mem. Freedom Union (FU) 1998–; fmr Head of Foreign Minister's Office; Minister of Defence Jan.–July 1998; mem. Cttee for European Integration 1998–2002, Cttee for Defence and Security 1998–2002; left parl. functions following elections in 2002; now works in pvt. sector. *Address:* c/o Parliament of the Czech Republic, Sněmovní 4, 118 26 Prague 1, Czech Republic.

LOBKOWICZ, Nicholas, DPhil; American political philosopher; b. 9 July 1931, Prague, Czechoslovakia (now Czech Repub.); s. of Prince Jan Lobkowicz and Countess Marie Czernin; m. 1st Countess Josephine Waldburg-Zeil 1953; three s. two d.; m. 2nd Aleksandra N. Cieślińska 1999; ed Collegium Maria Hilf, Switzerland, Univs of Erlangen and Fribourg; Assoc. Prof. of Philosophy, Univ. of Notre Dame, Ind. 1960–67; Prof. of Political Theory and Philosophy, Univ. of Munich 1967–90, Dean School of Arts and Letters 1970–71, Rector Magnificus 1971–76, Pres. Univ. of Munich 1976–82; Pres. Catholic Univ. of Eichstätt 1984–96, Dir Inst. of Cen. and Eastern European Studies 1994–; mem. Bd of Dirs Fed. Inst. of Int. and E European Studies, Cologne 1972–75, Senate, West German Rectors' Conf. 1976–82, Perm. Cttee European Rectors' Conf. 1979–84, Council Int. Fed. of Catholic Univs. 1984–91; founding mem. Int. Metaphysical Asscn; mem. Cen. Cttee of German Catholics 1980–84; mem. Ukrainian Acad. of Arts and Science (USA) 1979–; mem. W Europe Advisory Cttee to Radio Free Europe/Radio Liberty 1980–2002, Chair. 1994–2002; Founder mem., Vice-Pres. European Acad. of Sciences and Arts 1990–; Pres. Freier Deutscher Autorenverband 1985–91; mem. Pontifical Council for Culture 1982–93; Pres. Czechoslovak Christian Acad. in Rome 1983–90; ; Hon. Citizen Dallas, Tex.; Hon. DHL (Wayne State Univ.); Hon. DLL (Univ. of Notre Dame); Hon. DrPhil (Seoul and Ukrainian Univ., Munich, Catholic Univ. of America); Hon. DTheol (Charles Univ., Prague). *Publications:* Theory and Practice 1967, Ende aller Religion? 1976, Marxismus und Machtergreifung 1978, Wortmeldung zu Staat, Kirche, Universität 1981, Irrwege der Angst 1983, Das europäische Erbe 1984, Das Konzil 1986, Zeitwende 1993, Czas przelomu 1996, Rationalität und Innerlichkeit 1997, Duše Evropy 2001. *Address:* Am Kirchberg 6, 91804 Mörnsheim, Germany (Home); Katholische Universität, 85071 Eichstätt. *Telephone:* (8421) 931717 (Office); (9094) 749 (Home). *Fax:* (8421) 931780 (Office); (9094) 1357 (Home). *E-mail:* nikolaus.lobkowicz@nexgo.de (Home).

LOBO, José Carlos; Mozambican politician and fmr teacher; b. 14 Sept. 1942, Quelimane; s. of Carlos Lobo Chibaia and Catarina Carlos Ernesto; m. Iveth Venichand Lobo 1978; two c.; ed California State Univ., USA; joined Mozambique Liberation Front (FRELIMO) in Tanzania 1964; Teacher and Dean of Students at Mozambique Inst., Dar es Salaam 1964–66; studied at Calif. State Univ., USA until 1973; Headmaster, FRELIMO Secondary School, Bagamoyo, Tanzania 1974–75; Headmaster, FRELIMO Secondary School, Ribaue, Mozambique 1975; Dir of Int. Orgs and Confs Dept, Ministry of Foreign Affairs 1975–76; Perm. Rep. to UN 1976–83; mem. Cen. Cttee FRELIMO 1983–; Minister of Mineral Resources 1983–84; mem. of People's Ass. 1983–; Vice-Minister of Foreign Affairs 1984–; FRELIMO 20th Anniversary Medallion. *Address:* c/o Ministry of Foreign Affairs and Co-operation, Avda Julius Nyerere 4, Maputo, Mozambique.

LOBO ANTUNES, António, MD; Portuguese novelist; b. 1 Sept. 1942, Lisbon; three d.; higher educ. in Portugal; fmr doctor and psychiatrist; now full-time writer (his experience of the Portuguese colonial war in Africa being a maj. influence); French Culture Prize, Prix du Meilleur Livre Etranger and other awards for novels. *Publications:* thirteen novels. *Address:* Avenida Afonso III 23, 3°c, 1900 Lisbon, Portugal. *Telephone:* 8155566.

LØCHEN, Yngvar Formo, DPhil; Norwegian professor of sociology; b. 31 May 1931, Oslo; s. of Arne and Valgjerd Løchen; m. Vivi Poulsen 1956; ed Univ. of Oslo; Researcher, Norwegian Research Council 1956–60; Research Fellow, Univ. of Oslo 1960–65, Assoc. Prof., Inst. of Social Medicine 1965–71; Prof. of Sociology, Univ. of Tromsø 1971–, Chair. Cen. Cttee of Research 1975–77, Rector Univ. of Tromsø 1977–81; Chair. Social Science, Norwegian Research Council 1986–89; mem. Norwegian Acad. of Science. *Publications:* Ideals and Realities in a Mental Hospital 1965, The Dilemma of the Sociol-

ogist 1970, The Treatment Society 1971, Rely on Your Own Forces 1976, A Common Purpose and Communality (Ed.) 1990, Commitment and Imagination 1993. *Leisure interest:* music.

LOCHHEAD, Liz; British poet, playwright, screenwriter and teacher; b. 26 Dec. 1947, Motherwell; fmr art school teacher, Glasgow and Bristol; Lecturer Univ. of Glasgow; BBC Scotland Prize 1971, Scottish Arts Council Award 1972. *Television includes:* Damages (BBC). *Publications include:* Poetry: Memo for Spring 1972, The Grimm Sisters 1981, Dreaming of Frankenstein and Collected Poems 1984, True Confessions and True Clichés 1985, Bagpipe Muzak 1991, Cuba/Dog House (with Gina Moxley) 2000; Plays: Blood and Ice 1982, Silver Service 1984, Dracula (adaptation) 1989, Mary Queen of Scots Got Her Head Chopped Off 1989, Molière's Tartuffe (Scots trans. in rhyming couplets), Perfect Days 1998, Medea (adaptation) 2000, Misery Guts (adaptation) 2002; Screenplay: Now and Then 1972; Anthology Contributions: Penguin Modern Poets Vols 3 and 4, Shouting It Out 1995. *Address:* 11 Kersland Street, Glasgow, G12 8BW, Scotland (Office).

LOCK, Thomas Graham, CBIM, BSc, FIM, CEng; British business executive; b. 19 Oct. 1931, Cardiff; s. of Robert H. Lock and Morfydd Lock (née Thomas); m. Janice O B. Jones 1954 (divorced 1992, died 1995); two d.; ed Whitchurch Grammar School, Univ. Coll. of S. Wales, Monmouthshire Coll. of Advanced Tech. (Aston) and Harvard Business School, USA; Instructor Lt RN 1953–56; joined Lucas Industries Ltd 1956; Production Foreman, Lucas Electrical Ltd 1957–59, Factory Man. 1959–61; Dir Girling Bremsen GmbH 1961–66; Overseas Operations Dir Girling Ltd 1966–73; Gen. Man. and Dir Lucas Service Overseas Ltd 1973–79; Man. Dir Industrial Div. Amalgamated Metal Corpn PLC 1979–83, Chief Exec. 1983–91; Dir (non-exec.) Evode Group PLC 1985–91, Marshalls Universal PLC 1983–86; Liveryman Co. of Gold and Silver Wyre Drawers 1988–; Freeman, City of London. *Leisure interests:* sailing, music, skiing. *Address:* Parolas Villa, 4520 Pareklisia, nr Limassol, Cyprus. *Telephone:* (25) 634965. *E-mail:* brython@cytanet.com.cy.

LOCKE, Edwin Allen, Jr, AB; American business executive; b. 8 June 1910, Boston, Mass.; s. of Edwin A. Locke and Elizabeth Ferguson Locke; m. 1st Dorothy Q. Clark 1934 (divorced); two s. one d.; m. 2nd Karin Marsh 1952; one s.; ed Harvard Univ.; with Paris Br., Chase Nat. Bank, NY 1933–35, London Br. 1935–36, New York 1936–40; served in Office of Co-ordinator of Purchases, Advisory Comm. to Council of Nat. Defense 1940–41; Asst Deputy Dir Priorities Div., Office of Production Man. 1941; Deputy Chief Staff Officer Supply Priorities and Allocation Bd 1941–42; Asst to Chair. War Production Bd 1942–44; Exec. Asst to Personal Rep. of the Pres. 1944–45; Personal Rep. of the Pres., Washington and China 1945–46, Special Asst to the Pres. March–Dec. 1946; Vice-Pres. of the Chase Nat. Bank, New York 1947–51; Trustee, China Medical Bd Inc. 1947–80; apptd Special Rep. of Sec. of State, with personal rank of Amb. to co-ordinate econ. and tech. assistance programmes in the Near East 1951–53; Pres. and Dir Union Tank Car Co. 1953–63; Dir Harris Trust and Savings Bank 1955–63; Dir Federal Home Loan Bank of Chicago 1956–63, Chair. 1961–63; mem. special Presidential mission to Liberia and Tunisia; Pres. and Dir Modern Homes Construction Co. 1963–67, Coastal Products Corpn 1963–67; Dir Manpower Inc. 1961–75, Warner Nat. Corpn 1969–77, Nat. American Life Insurance Co. of Pa 1968–85, Bankers Nat. Life Insurance Co. 1982–85, Nat. American Insurance Co. of New York 1981–85; financial consultant and investment banker 1985–; Pres. and CEO American Paper Inst. 1968–77; Dir Alusit Holdings L.P. 1993–; Pres. Econ. Club of New York 1977–85. *Address:* 935 N Halifax Avenue, Apt. 1009, Daytona Beach, FL 32118, USA.

LOCKE, Gary, BA, JD; American state official; b. 21 Jan. 1950; s. of James Locke and Julie Locke; m. Mona Lee Locke 1994; ed Yale Univ., Boston Univ.; Deputy Prosecuting Attorney, State of Washington, King Co.; mem. House of Reps 1982–93; Gov. of Washington 1996–; apptd Chief Exec. King Co. 1993. *Address:* Office of the Governor, POB 40002, Olympia, WA 98504-0002, USA (Office).

LOCKHART, James, BMus, FRCM, FRCO(CHM); British conductor and music director; b. 16 Oct. 1930, Edinburgh; s. of Archibald C. Lockhart and Mary B. Lawrence; m. Sheila Grogan 1954; two s. one d.; ed George Watson's Coll., Edin., Univ. of Edin. and Royal Coll. of Music; Asst Conductor, Yorkshire Symphony Orchestra 1954–55; Repetiteur and Asst Conductor, Städtische Bühnen Münster 1955–56, Bayerische Staatsoper, Munich 1956–57, Glyndebourne Festival Opera 1957–59; Dir Opera Workshop, Univ. of Texas 1957–59; Repetiteur and Asst Conductor, Royal Opera House, Covent Garden 1959–60, Conductor 1962–68; Asst Conductor, BBC Scottish Orchestra 1960–61; Conductor, Sadler's Wells Opera 1961–62; Prof. Royal Coll. of Music 1962–72; Musical Dir Welsh Nat. Opera 1968–73; Generalmusikdirektor, Staatstheater Kassel 1972–80, Koblenz and Theater der Stadt, Koblenz 1981–88, Rheinische Philharmonie 1981–91; Prin. Guest Conductor, BBC Concert Orchestra 1982–87; Dir of Opera, Royal Coll. of Music 1986–92, London Royal Schools' Vocal Faculty 1992–96, Opera Consultant 1996–98; Guest Prof. of Conducting, Tokyo Nat. Univ. of Fine Arts and Music (Tokyo Geidai) 1998–2001, Prof. Emer. 2001–; freelance conductor 2001–; Hon. RAM. *Leisure interests:* travel, swimming, hill-walking. *Address:* 105 Woodcock Hill, Harrow, Middx, HA3 0JJ, England (Home). *Telephone:* (20) 8907-2112 (Home). *Fax:* (20) 8907-2112 (Home). *E-mail:* Lockgrog@aol.com (Home).

LOCKWOOD, David, CBE, PhD, FBA, FRSA; British university professor; b. 9 April 1929, Holmfirth, Yorks.; s. of Herbert Lockwood and Edith Annie

Lockwood (née Lockwood); m. Leonore Davidoff 1954; three s.; ed Honley Grammar School, LSE; Trainee, Victoria Textiles, Honley, Yorks. 1944–47; Nat. Service, Intelligence Corps, Austria 1947–49; Univ. of London Postgraduate Studentship in Econs 1952–53; Asst Lecturer and Lecturer in Sociology, LSE 1953–60; Rockefeller Fellow, Univ. of Calif. (Berkeley), USA 1958–59; Univ. Lecturer, Faculty of Econs and Fellow of St John's Coll. Cambridge 1960–68; Visiting Prof., Dept of Sociology, Columbia Univ., USA 1966–67; Prof., Dept of Sociology, Univ. of Essex 1968–2001, Prof. Emer. 2001–, Pro-Vice-Chancellor 1989–92; Visiting Prof., Delhi School of Econs 1975, Stockholm Univ. 1989; Visiting Fellow, RSSS ANU 1993; mem. Social Science Research Council (Chair. Sociology and Social Admin. Cttee 1973–76), Academia Europaea 1990; Chair. Econ. and Social Research Council Review of Govt Social Classifications1994–98; Hon. DUniv (Essex) 2001. *Publications:* The Affluent Worker in the Class Structure, 3 vols (jtly) 1968–69, The Blackcoated Worker 1989, Solidarity and Schism 1992; numerous articles in journals and symposia. *Address:* 82 High Street, Wivenhoe, CO7 9AB, Essex, England. *Telephone:* (1206) 823530 (Home). *E-mail:* lockd@essex.ac.uk (Office).

LODDER, Celsius Antônio, MSc; Brazilian international administrator and economist; b. 28 May 1944, Nova Lima, Minas Gerais; s. of Ary Lodder and Maria van Krimpen Lodder; three d.; ed Fed. Univ. of Minas Gerais, Belo Horizonte, Getúlio Vargas Foundation, Rio de Janeiro and Inst. of Social Studies, The Hague; researcher, Applied Econs Research Inst. Ministry of Econ., Finance and Planning 1970–80; subsequently held appointments with State of Minas Gerais and Fed. Govt of Brazil; Sec. for Commercial Policy, Ministry of Finance, later at Ministry of Industry, Commerce and Tourism; Supt Nat. Supply Authority, Ministry of Finance; Chief Adviser, State Bank of Minas Gerais 1983–84; Co-ordinator, Intergovernmental Relations Office, Civil Cabinet of Pres. of Brazil; Lecturer in Econs at various Brazilian univs; Exec. Dir Int. Coffee Org. 1994–2002. *Publications:* books and reports on matters related to regional planning and Devt. *Leisure interests:* reading, walking. *Address:* c/o International Coffee Organization, 22 Berners Street, London, W1P 4DD, England.

LODGE, David John, CBE, PhD, FRSL; British novelist and professor of modern English literature; b. 28 Jan. 1935; s. of William F. Lodge and Rosalie M. (née Murphy) Lodge; m. Mary F. Jacob 1959; two s. one d.; ed St Joseph's Acad., Blackheath and Univ. Coll., London; British Council, London 1959–60; Asst Lecturer in English, Univ. of Birmingham 1960–62, Lecturer 1963–71, Sr Lecturer 1971–73, Reader 1973–76, Prof. of Modern English Literature 1976–87, Hon. Prof. 1987-2000, Emer. Prof. 2001–; Chair. Booker Prize Cttee 1989; Harkness Commonwealth Fellow, 1964–65; Visiting Assoc. Prof. Univ. of Calif. at Berkeley 1969; Henfield Writing Fellow, Univ. of E Anglia 1977; Fellow, Univ. Coll. London 1982, Goldsmith's Coll. 1992; Yorkshire Post Fiction Prize 1975; Hawthornden Prize 1976; Chevalier des Arts et des Lettres 1997. *Publications:* The Picturegoers 1960, Ginger, You're Barmy 1962, The British Museum is Falling Down 1965, Out of the Shelter 1970, Changing Places 1975, How Far Can You Go? 1980 (Whitbread Book of Year Award), Small World 1984, Nice Work 1988 (Sunday Express Book of the Year Award), The Writing Game (play) 1991, Paradise News 1991, Therapy 1995, Home Truths (play and novella) 1999, Thinks... (novel) 2001, Consciousness and the Novel 2002; eight vols of criticism. *Leisure interests:* tennis, television, cinema. *Address:* c/o Department of English, University of Birmingham, Birmingham, B15 2TT, England.

LODHI, Maleeha, PhD; Pakistani diplomatist and journalist; m. (divorced); one s.; ed London School of Econs; Lecturer in Politics and Sociology, LSE 1980–85; fmr lecturer, Dept of Public Admin. Quaid-i-Azam Univ., Islamabad; Ed. The Muslim; Ed. and Co-founder The News (daily newspaper) 1985–93, 1997–2000; Amb. to USA 1993–97, (with rank of Minister of State) 2000–02; Fellow Pakistan Inst. of Devt Econs; award from All Pakistan Newspaper Soc. 1994. *Publications:* Pakistan's Encounter with Democracy, The External Dimension 1994; numerous contribs to int. journals. *Address:* 7-A, Street 17, F-6/2, Islamabad, Pakistan.

LOEHNIS, Anthony David, CMG, MA; British banker; b. 12 March 1936, London; s. of Sir Clive Loehnis and Rosemary Loehnis (née Ryder); m. Jennifer Forsyth Anderson 1965; three s.; ed Eton Coll., New Coll. Oxford, Harvard School of Public Admin; in Diplomatic Service 1960–66; with J. Henry Schroder Wagg and Co. Ltd 1967–80 (seconded to Bank of England 1977–79); Assoc. Dir Bank of England 1980–81, Exec. Dir (Overseas Affairs) 1981–89; Group Exec. Dir, Vice-Chair. S. G. Warburg and Co. 1989–92; Exec. Dir UK–Japan 21st Century Group 1999–2002; Dir (non-exec.) St James's Place UK PLC 1993–, St James's Place Capital PLC 1993–, St James's Place Int. PLC 1995–, Alpha Bank London PLC 1994–, Tokyo-Mitsubishi Int. PLC 1996–, AGCO Corpn (USA) 1997–; Chair. Public Works Loan Bd 1997–. *Address:* 2nd Floor, 14–16 Regent Street, London, SW1Y 4PH; 11 Cranleigh, 139 Ladbroke Road, London, W11 3PX, England. *Telephone:* (20) 7925-1144 (Office). *Fax:* (20) 7930-0931 (Office).

LÖFGREN, Lars, PhD; Swedish theatre, film and television director, playwright and poet; b. 6 Sept. 1935, The Arctic Circle; m. Anna-Karin Gillberg 1963; one s. two d.; ed Gustavus Adolphus Coll., USA, Stanford Univ., USA, Sorbonne, France, Uppsala Univ., Sweden; Dir Royal Dramatic Theatre of Sweden 1985–97, Nordic Museum 1997–; Royal Prize of Swedish Acad. 1996. *Publications:* various plays, filmscripts, TV scripts, poetry, novels. *Address:* Lagman Linds Vag 14, 18275 Stocksund, Sweden.

LOGAN, Malcolm Ian, AC, DipEd, PhD; Australian university vice-chancellor; b. 3 June 1931, Inverell, NSW; s. of the late A. J. Logan; m. Antoinette Lalich 1954; one d.; ed Tamworth High School, New England Univ. Coll., Sydney Teachers' Coll., Sydney Univ.; Lecturer in Geography, Sydney Teachers' Coll. 1956–58, Univ. of Sydney 1959–64, Sr Lecturer 1965–67; Prof. of Geography and Urban and Regional Planning, Univ. of Wis., Madison, USA 1967–71; Prof. of Geography, Monash Univ. 1971–86, Pro-Vice-Chancellor 1982–85, Deputy Vice-Chancellor 1986, Vice-Chancellor 1987–96, also fmr Pres.; Deputy Chair. Int. Devt Program of Australian Univs 1991–93; Chair. Australian Centre for Contemporary Art 1990, Open Learning Agency of Australia 1993–96, Monash Int. Pty Ltd 1994–96 TENTAS Pty Ltd 1998–, Australia Educ. Gateway Pty Ltd 1998–; Dir Australia Communications Computing Inst. 1998–, Job Scene Pty Ltd 2000–; Chair. and Dir Pinnacle Pty Ltd 2000–; mem. Comm. for the Future 1995–; Visiting Prof. Univ. of Ibadan, Nigeria 1970–71, LSE, London, UK 1973; Nanyang Univ., Singapore 1979. *Publications:* (co-author) Studies in Australian Geography 1968, New Viewpoints in Urban and Industrial Geography 1971, Urban and Regional Australia 1975, Urbanisation, The Australian Experience 1980, The Brittle Rim 1989, Reconstructing Asia: The Economic Miracle That Never Was, The Future That Is (jtly) 1998. *Leisure interests:* golf, reading. *Address:* 1/50 Bourke Street, Melbourne, Vic. 3000; c/o Monash University, Wellington Road, Clayton, Vic. 3168, Australia.

LOGUE, Christopher John; British writer; b. 23 Nov. 1926, Southsea; s. of John Logue and Molly Logue (née Chapman); m. Rosemary Hill 1985; ed Prior Park Coll., Bath and Portsmouth Grammar School; First Wilfred Owen Award for Poetry 1998, Civil List Pension for Services to Literature 2002. *Screenplays:* Savage Messiah (Dir Ken Russell 1972), Crusoe (based on Defoe's novel, with Walon Green) 1989. *Recordings:* Red Bird (poetry and jazz, with Tony Kinsey and Bill Le Sage) 1960, Songs from the Establishment 1962, The Death of Patroclus 1963, Audiologue (recordings 1958-98) 2001. *Film roles:* Swinburne in Ken Russell's Dante's Inferno 1966, John Ball in John Irvin's The Peasant's Revolt 1969, Cardinal Richelieu in Ken Russell's The Devils 1970; also TV and stage roles. *Publications:* (verse) Wand & Quadrant 1953, Devil, Maggot & Son 1956, Songs 1959, Patrocleia 1962, Pax 1967, New Numbers 1969, War Music 1981, Ode to the Dodo 1981, Kings 1991, The Husbands 1995, Selected Poems 1996; Prince Charming: A Memoir 1999, All Day Permanent Red 2003; (plays) The Trial of Cob & Leach 1959, The Lilywhite Boys (with Harry Cookson) 1959, trans. Brecht and Weill, The Seven Deadly Sins 1986; (anthologies) The Children's Book of Comic Verse 1979, London in Verse 1982, Sweet and Sour 1983, The Oxford Book of Pseuds 1983, The Children's Book of Children's Rhymes 1986; contrib. Private Eye, The Times, Sunday Times. *Address:* 41 Camberwell Grove, London, SE5 8JA, England.

LOGUNOV, Anatoly Alekseyevich; Russian theoretical physicist; b. 30 Dec. 1926, Obsharovka, Samara Region; s. of Aleksei Ivanovich Logunov and Agrippina Kuzminichna Logunova; m. Anna Nikolayevna Eshliman 1951 (died 1997); one s. (deceased) one d.; ed Moscow State Univ.; mem. CPSU 1960–91; mem. faculty staff Moscow State Univ. 1951–56; Deputy Dir for Research, Theoretical Physics Lab., Jt Inst. for Nuclear Research, Dubna 1956–63, Prof. 1961; Dir of Serpukhov Inst. for High Energy Physics (IHEP), Protvino, Moscow 1963–74, IHEP Research Leader 1974–, Dir State Research Centre IHEP 1993–; Rector Moscow State Univ. 1977–92; mem. USSR (now Russian) Acad. of Sciences 1972–, Vice-Pres. 1974–91; Head, State Scientific-Tech. Programme of High Energy Physics 1987–91; mem. Acad. of Creative Endeavours 1992–; Full Prof. Inst. of Fundamental Research, Molise, Italy; mem. Editorial Bd Asia-Pacific Peace Forum 1995–; Chief Ed. annual publ. Science and Humankind 1977–91, journal Theoretical and Math. Physics 1989–; main research on quantum field theory, elementary particle physics, gravitation and relativity theory; Cand. mem. Cen. Cttee CPSU 1981–86, mem. 1986–90; Deputy, USSR Supreme Soviet 1978–89; Hon. Prof. Tokai Daygaku and Vasada Univs, Japan; four Orders of Lenin, Order of Honour, Order of Pole Star (Mongolia), Order of Yugoslavian Banner with Ribbon, Commdr Cross of Order of Merit (Poland), Order of Merit III Degree 1995, II Degree 2002; numerous hon. degrees; Lenin Prize 1970, USSR State Prizes 1973, 1984, Lyapunov Medal, Gibbs Medal, Hero of Socialist Labour 1980, Gold Medal Czech Acad. of Sciences. *Publications include:* Lectures on Relativity and Gravitation Theory, The Updated Analysis of the Problem 1987, On Henri Poincaret's work On the Dynamics of the Electron 1988, The Third Irisated Bridge 1988, Relativistic Theory of Gravitation 1989, Principles of Quantum Field Theory 1990, Gravitational Field Theory 2000, The Theory of Gravity 2001; more than 350 contribs to scientific journals on high energy and elementary particle physics and on latest ideas about space-time and gravitation. *Address:* State Research Centre Institute for High Energy Physics, 142281 Protvino, Moscow Region, Russia. *Telephone:* (0967) 74-25-79. *Fax:* (0967) 74-49-37. *E-mail:* logunov@mx.ihep.su (Office).

LOHSE, Eduard, DTheol; German ecclesiastic; b. 19 Feb. 1924, Hamburg; s. of Dr Walther Lohse and Dr Wilhelmine Lohse (née Barrelet); m. Roswitha Flitner 1952; two s. one d.; ed Bethel/Bielefeld and Göttingen; Pastor, Hamburg 1952; Privatdozent, Faculty of Protestant Theology, Mainz 1953; Prof. of New Testament, Kiel 1956, Göttingen 1964; Bishop of Hanover 1971–88; Pres. of the Council of the Evangelical Church in Germany 1979–85; mem. Göttingen Akad. der Wissenschaften; Hon. DTheol (Mainz) 1961, (Glasgow) 1983. *Publications:* Märtyrer und Gottesknecht 1955, Die Offenbarung des Johannes 1960, Die Texte aus Qumran 1964, Die Geschichte des

Leidens und Sterbens Jesu Christi 1964, Die Briefe an die Kolosser und an Philemon 1968, Umwelt des Neuen Testaments 1971, Entstehung des Neuen Testaments 1972, Die Einheit des Neuen Testaments 1973, Grundriss der neutestamentlichen Theologie 1974, Die Urkunde der Christen 1979, Die Vielfalt des Neuen Testaments 1982, Die Ethik der Bergpredigt 1984, Kleine Evangelische Pastoralethik 1985, Theologische Ethik des Neuen Testaments 1988, Erneuern und Bewahren Evangelische Kirche 1970–90 1993, Paulus – eine Biographie 1996. *Leisure interest:* music. *Address:* Ernst-Curtius-Weg 7, 37075 Göttingen, Germany. *Telephone:* (551) 42424.

LOKOLOKO, Sir Tore, GCMG, OBE; Papua New Guinea politician; b. 21 Sept. 1930, Iokea, Gulf Province; s. of Paramount Chief Lokoloko Tore and Kevau-Sarufa; m. Lalahaia Meakoro 1950; four s. six d.; elected to House of Ass. (now Nat. Parl.) as Opposition mem. for Kerema (Gulf Prov.); Gov.-Gen. of Papua New Guinea 1977–83; Chair. Indosuez Niugine Bank 1983–89; KStJ. *Leisure interests:* golf, fishing. *Address:* P.O. Box 5622, Boroko, NCD, Papua New Guinea.

LOLLOBRIGIDA, Gina; Italian actress; b. 4 July 1927, Sibiaco; d. of Giovanni Mercuri and Giuseppina Mercuri; m. Milko Skofic 1949; one s.; ed Liceo Artistico, Rome; fmr model; first screen role in Pagliacci 1947. *Films include:* Campane a Martello 1948, Cuori senza Frontiere 1949, Achtung, Banditi! 1951, Enrico Caruso 1951, Fanfan la Tulipe 1951, Altri Tempi 1952, The Wayward Wife 1952, Les belles de la nuit 1952, Pane, amore e fantasia 1953, La Provinciale 1953, Pane, amore e gelosia, La Romana 1954, Il Grande Gioco 1954, La Donna più bella del Mondo 1955, Trapeze 1956, Notre Dame de Paris 1956, Solomon and Sheba 1959, Never So Few 1960, Go Naked in the World 1961, She Got What She Asked For 1963, Woman of Straw 1964, Le Bambole 1965, Hotel Paradiso 1966, Les Sultans 1966, Le Piacevoli Notti 1966, Cervantes 1966, La Morte Fatto L'uovo (A Curious Way to Love) and (Death Laid an Egg) 1967, Stuntman 1968, Buona Sera Mrs Campbell 1968, Un Bellissimo Novembre (That Splendid November) 1968, The Private Navy of Sgt O'Farrell 1968, Peccato Mortale (The Lonely Woman) and (Roses and Green Peppers) 1972, King, Queen, Knave 1972, Le Avventure Di Pinocchio 1972, Bad Man's River 1972, Falcon Crest TV Series 1984, Deceptions 1985, (TV film) 1985, The Bocce Showdown 1990, Les Cent et Une Nuits (A Hundred and One Nights) 1995, Plucked, XXL 1997. *Publications:* Italia Mia (photography) 1974, The Philippines. *Leisure interest:* photography. *Address:* Via Appia Antica 223, 00178 Rome, Italy.

LOM, Herbert; British actor; b. 11 Sept. 1917, Prague, Czechoslovakia; s. of Charles Lom and Olga Lom; m. (divorced); two s. one d.; ed Prague Univ., Old Vic., Westminster School; theatre work in Prague before coming to England in 1939; joined the Old Vic theatre school; entered films 1940; worked with BBC European Section 1940–46. *Films include:* Tomorrow We Live 1941, The Young Mr Pitt 1942, The Dark Tower 1943, Night Boat to Dublin 1945, Appointment With Crime 1946, Good Time Girl 1947, Cage of Gold 1950, Star of India 1953, The Ladykillers 1955, War and Peace 1955, Passport to Shame 1958, North-West Frontier 1959, El Cid 1961, The Phantom of the Opera 1962, A Shot in the Dark 1963, Marrakesh 1965, Gambit 1966, Doppelganger 1968, The Picture of Dorian Gray 1970, Return of the Pink Panther 1974, The Pink Panther Strikes Again 1976, Charleston 1976, Revenge of the Pink Panther 1977, Trail of the Pink Panther 1981, Curse of the Pink Panther 1983, Dead Zone 1984, Memed My Hawk 1984, King Solomon's Mines 1985, Whoops Apocalypse, Going Bananas 1986, Scoop 1987, Coast of Skeletons, Master of Dragonard Hill 1987, Ten Little Indians 1989, The Masque of the Red Death 1990, The Pope Must Die 1991, The Sect 1991, Son of the Pink Panther 1992. *Television appearances include:* The Human Jungle 1963, Hawaii Five-O 1971, The Acts of Peter and Paul 1980, Lace 1985. *Plays include:* The King and I, Theatre Royal, London 1951-53. *Publications:* Enter a Spy, the Double Life of Christopher Marlowe 1978, Dr Guillotine 1992. *Leisure interest:* books. *Address:* c/o London Management, 2–4 Noel Street, London, W1V 3RB, England.

LOMAX, (Janis) Rachel, MA, MSc; British civil servant and economist; b. 15 July 1945; d. of William Salmon and Dilys Salmon; m. Michael Acworth Lomax 1967 (divorced 1990); two s.; ed Cheltenham Lady's Coll., Girton Coll. Cambridge, LSE; Econ. Asst HM Treasury 1968, Econ. Adviser 1972, Sr Econ. Adviser 1978, Prin. Pvt. Sec. to Chancellor of the Exchequer 1985–86, Under-Sec. 1986–90, Deputy Chief Econ. Adviser 1990–92, Deputy Sec. Financial Insts and Markets 1992–94, Deputy Sec. Cabinet Office 1994–95; Vice-Pres. and Chief of Staff IBRD 1995–96; Perm. Sec. Welsh Office 1996–99, Dept of Social Security, then Dept for Work and Pensions 1999–2002; Perm. Sec. Dept for Transport 2002–; Deputy Gov. Bank of England July 2003–; Chair. UK Selection Cttee, Harkness Fellowships 1995–97; mem. Council Royal Econ. Soc 1989–94; Gov. De Montfort Univ. 1997–, Henley Coll. of Man. 2000–. *Address:* Bank of England, Threadneedle Street, London, EC2R 8AH, England (Office). *Telephone:* (20) 7601-4444 (Office). *Fax:* (20) 7601-3047 (Office). *Website:* www.bankofengland.co.uk (Office).

LOMU, Jonah; New Zealand rugby football player and athlete; b. 12 May 1975, Auckland; m. Tanya Rutter 1996 (divorced); pnr Teina Stace; ed Wesley Coll., Auckland; bank officer ASB Bank of NZ; youngest ever capped All Black (at 19 years and 45 days); wing; int. debut NZ versus France 1994; semi-finalist at World Cup, S. Africa 1995; out of action for a year with a rare kidney disorder, returned to int. side for All Blacks' UK tour end of 1997; gold medal rugby sevens, Kuala Lumpur Commonwealth Games 1998; 63 caps (185 Test points including 37 tries) by end of 2002; ran 100m in 10.8 seconds. *Website:* www.jonahlomu.com (Office).

LONDOÑO PAREDES, Julio; Colombian politician; b. 10 June 1938, Bogotá; ed San Isidro Hermanos Maristas School, El Carmen Inst. and Mil. Cadet School, Bogotá; Prof. of Int. Politics at Univ. of Jorge Tadeo Lozano, Bogotá; Prof. of Int. Public Law at Univ. of El Rosario, Bogotá; served in Army, retd 1981 with rank of Lt-Col; Head of Frontier Div. at Ministry of Foreign Affairs 1968–79, Sec.-Gen. 1979–82, Vice-Minister 1982–83, Minister 1986–90; Amb. to Panama 1983–86; Perm. Rep. to U.N. 1994–99; currently Amb. to Cuba. *Publications:* History of the Colombo-Peruvian Conflict of 1932, Colombian Territorial Law, Colombian Border Issues. *Address:* Embassy of Colombia, Calle 14, No 515, entre 5 y 7, Miramar, Havana, Cuba. *Telephone:* (7) 24-1246. *Fax:* (7) 24-1249.

LONG, Malcolm William, LLB; Australian broadcasting executive; b. 13 April 1948, Fremantle, WA; s. of William Long and Dorothy Long; m. Helen Maxwell 1973; two d.; ed Univ. of Western Australia; Dir Radio Talks and Documentaries, ABC 1978–82; Man. (Radio) Victorian ABC 1982–84; Dir ABC Radio 1985–92; Deputy Man. Dir Australian Broadcasting Corpn 1992–93; Dir PANT Ltd 1996–; Man. Dir SBS Corpn 1993–97; Man. Dir Malcolm Long Assocs Pty Ltd 1997–; Pres. Australian Museum Trust 1995–2000; Dir Macquarie Communications Infrastructure Group 2001–, Australian Film Television and Radio School 2003–; EMR Chair. Exec. Cttee Int. Inst. of Communications; mem. Australian Broadcasting Authority 2000. *Publications:* Marx & Beyond 1973, Beyond the Mechanical Mind (with P. Fry) 1977; numerous articles on broadcasting policy and culture. *Leisure interests:* music, reading, running. *Address:* Australian Film Television and Radio School, PO Box 126, North Ride, NSW 1670, Australia. *Telephone:* (2) 9805-6611 (Office). *Fax:* (2) 9887-1030 (Office).

LONG, Marceau, LèsL, LenD; French civil servant; b. 22 April 1926, Aix-en-Provence, Bouches-du-Rhône; s. of Lucien Long and Marcelle Seymard; m. Josette Niel 1949; two s. three d.; ed Lycée Mignet, Univ. of Aix-en-Provence, École nat. d'admin; Lecturer, Ecole nat. d'admin 1953–56, Inst. d'Etudes politiques 1953–56; seminars Ecole nat. d'admin 1963–68; at Council of State 1952–57, 1975–, Vice-Pres. 1987–95, apptd auditor 1952, master of petitions 1957, Sec.-Gen. to Govt 1975–82, Counsellor of State on long-term secondment 1976; apptd to Govt Comm. 1957, Tech. Counsellor to Cabinet, Sec. of State on Tunisian and Moroccan Affairs, then Foreign Affairs, then Judicial Counsellor to French Embassy, Morocco 1958, Dir-Gen. Admin. and Public Offices 1961–67, Sec. Gen. Admin, Ministry of Armies 1967–73, mem. Atomic Energy Cttee 1975–82; Chair. Organisation de la radio et de la télévision françaises (ORTF) 1973–74; Chair. Cie Air-Inter 1982–84; Chair. Cie Air France 1984–87; Chair. Cttee Inquiry on Law of Nationality 1987, Council of Admin. Tribunals and Courts of Appeal 1988–95; Lecturer Inst. d'études politiques de Paris, Ecole nat. d'admin 1963–68 (Chair. Bd of Govs 1987); Dir Crédit industriel et commercial bank 1982–87, Soc. de Gestion de participations aéronautiques 1985; apptd Pres. Admin. Council, Ecole nat. d'admin, Institut int. d'admin publique 1987, Inst. français des relations int. 1998–; Pres. Franco-American Foundation 1989–92, Hon. Pres. 1993–; Pres. Haut conseil à l'intégration 1989–93, 1994–95, Inst. des hautes études de la justice 1995–97, Inst. de la gestion déléguée 1996–2001; mem. Court of Arbitration, The Hague 1991–; mem. numerous admin. councils and cttees; Grand Officier, Légion d'honneur, Commdr Ordre nat. du Mérite, Officier des Palmes académiques. *Publications:* L'Economie de la Fonction Publique 1967, Les Services de Premier Ministre 1981, Les Grands Arrêts de la Jurisprudence Administrative (co-author) 1984, Etre Français aujourd'hui et demain, Rapport de la Commission de la Nationalité 1988, L'Esprit de justice: Portalis 1997 and numerous contribs to magazines and books on public office and law. *Address:* Institut français des relations internationales, 27 rue de la Procession, 75015 Paris (Office).

LONG, Richard, RA; British artist; b. 2 June 1945, Bristol; s. of Maurice Long and Frances Carpenter; m. Denise Johnston 1969 (divorced 1999); two d.; ed West of England Coll. of Art, Bristol and St Martin's School of Art, London; has exhibited widely since mid-1960s; work exhibited Städtisches Museum, Mönchengladbach 1970, Museum of Modern Art, New York 1972, Stedelijk Museum, Amsterdam 1973, Scottish Museum of Modern Art, Edin. 1974, Kunsthalle, Berne 1977, Nat. Gallery of Canada, Ottawa 1982, Solomon R. Guggenheim Museum, New York 1986, Tate Gallery 1990, Hayward Gallery, London (retrospective) 1991, ARC, Paris 1993, Palazzo delle Esposizioni, Rome 1994, São Paulo Bienal 1994, Nat. Modern Art Museum of Kyoto 1996, Kunstverein Hanover 1999, Guggenheim, Bilbao 2000, Museum Kurhaus Kleve 2001, Tate St Ives 2002; Chevalier des Arts et des Lettres 1990; Hon. DLit (Bristol) 1995; Turner Prize 1989, Wilhelm Lembruck Prize 1995. *Publications include:* South America 1972, River Avon Book 1979, Twelve Works 1981, Countless Stones 1983, Stone Water Miles 1987, Old World New World 1988, Nile 1990, Walking in Circles 1991, Mountains and Waters 1992, River to River 1993, Mirage 1997, A Walk Across Across England 1997, From Time to time 1997, Every Grain of Sand 1999, Midday 2001, A Moving World 2002, Walking the Line 2002. *Address:* c/o Haunch of Venison, 6 Haunch of Venison Yard, London, W1K 5ES, England.

LONGO, Jeannie Michèle Alice; French cyclist; b. 31 Oct. 1958, Annecy; d. of Jean Longo and Yvette Longo; m. Patrice Ciprelli 1985; ed Inst. d'Etudes Commerciales (Grenoble) and Univ. of Limoges; French cycling champion

1979–86; winner of 13 world titles including world champion (road) 1985, 1987, world champion 1988, 1989, world champion (against the clock) Spain 1997; winner Tour of Colorado 1986, 1987, Tour of Colombia 1987, 1988, Tour of Norway 1987, Tour de France 1987; silver medal World Track Race 1987; holder of several world records including world record for 3 km, Covered Track, Grenoble 1992; winner French Cycle Racing Championship 1992; silver medallist Olympic Games, Barcelona 1992, gold medallist Road Race, Olympic Games, Atlanta 1996; still competing in 2002 having amassed over 700 career wins, more than any other cyclist in history, setting 37 world records; Consultant France Télévision 1999–; Médaille d'Or, La Jeunesse et les Sports, Médaille d'Or, Acad. des Sports. *Address:* Fédération Française de Cyclisme, 5 rue de Rome, 93561 Rosny-sous-Bois, France. *Website:* www.jeannielongo.com (Home).

LONGRIGG, Anthony James, CMG; British diplomatist; b. 21 April 1944; m. Jane Rosa Cowlin 1968; three d.; joined FCO 1972, with Research Unit 1973; First Sec. Chancery, Moscow 1975–78; with E African Dept FCO 1978–80, Conf. for Security and Co-operation in Europe, FCO 1980–81; First Sec., Brasilia 1981–85; with Soviet Dept FCO 1985–87; Counsellor, Moscow 1987–91; Counsellor Econ./EU Affairs, Madrid 1991–95; Head S. Atlantic/Antarctic Dept FCO 1995–97; Minister and Deputy Head of Mission, Moscow 1997–2000; Gov. of Montserrat 2001–. *Address:* Office of the Governor, McChesney's Estate, Olveston, Plymouth, Montserrat (Office).

LONGUET, Gérard Edmond Jacques; French politician; b. 24 Feb. 1946, Neuilly-sur-Seine; s. of Jacques Longuet and Marie-Antoinette Laurent; m. Brigitte Fossorier 1967; four d.; ed Paris Univ.; Pvt. Sec. to Prefect of Eure's Office 1973–74, to Prefect of Somme's Office 1974–76, to Sec. of State (attached to Prime Minister's Office) 1977–78; Deputy of Meuse 1978–81, 1988–93, Vice-Pres. Gen. Councillor's Office 1982–92; Gen. Councillor Seuil d'Argonne 1979–92, Town Councillor 1983; mem. European Parl. 1984–86; Sec. of State March–Aug. 1986, then Minister at Ministry of Industry 1986–88, Minister of Industry, Posts and Telecommunications and Foreign Trade 1993–94; Sec.-Gen. Union pour la Démocratie Française (UDF) 1989; Pres. Republican Party 1990–95, Regional Council of Lorraine 1992–; Senateur de la Meuse 2001–; Collection Dir France Empire publrs; Pres. Sokrates Group. *Publications:* L'Epreuve de vérité 1995, L'Espoir industriel 1995. *Leisure interest:* skiing. *Address:* Conseil Regional de Lorraine, Place Gabriel Hocquard, B.P. 1004, 57036 Metz cedex 1; Palais du Luxembourg, 15 rue de Vaugirard, 75006, Paris; Sokrates Group, 119 rue de Paris, 92 100 Boulogne-Billancourt, France (Office). *Telephone:* 3-87-33-60-01 (Metz); 1-42-34-39-71 (Senate). *Fax:* 3-87-33-61-01 (Metz); 1-42-34-43-14 (Senate). *E-mail:* glonguet@c-lorraine.fr (Office); g.longuet@senate.fr (Office).

LONGUET-HIGGINS, Hugh Christopher, MA, DPhil, FRS, FRSE; British university professor; b. 11 April 1923, Lenham, Kent; s. of the late Henry H. L. Longuet-Higgins and Albinia Cecil Bazeley; brother of Michael Selwyn Longuet-Higgins (q.v.); ed Winchester Coll., Balliol Coll. Oxford; Research Fellow Balliol Coll. 1947–48; Research Assoc. Univ. of Chicago 1948–49; Lecturer and Reader in Theoretical Chem., Victoria Univ. of Manchester 1949–52; Prof. of Theoretical Physics King's Coll. London 1952–54; Fellow, Corpus Christi Coll. and Prof. of Theoretical Chem., Univ. of Cambridge 1954–67; Royal Soc. Research Prof., Univ. of Edin. 1968–74, Univ. of Sussex 1974–89, Prof. Emer. 1989–, Harrison Memorial Prize 1950; Gov. of BBC 1979–84; Foreign mem. American Acad. of Arts and Sciences 1961; Foreign Assoc. NAS 1968–; Life Fellow, Corpus Christi Coll. Cambridge; Hon. Fellow, Balliol Coll. Oxford 1969, Wolfson Coll. Cambridge 1977; Dr hc (York) 1973, (Essex) 1981, (Bristol) 1983, (Sussex) 1989, (Sheffield) 1995. *Publications include:* The Nature of Mind (Gifford Lectures) 1972, Mental Processes 1987 and about 200 papers in scientific journals. *Leisure interest:* music. *Address:* Centre for Research on Perception and Cognition, Laboratory of Experimental Psychology, University of Sussex, Falmer, Brighton, BN1 9QG, England. *Telephone:* (1273) 678341.

LONGUET-HIGGINS, Michael Selwyn, MA, PhD, FRS; British research scientist; b. 8 Dec. 1925, Lenham, Kent; s. of the late Henry H. L. Longuet-Higgins and Albinia Cecil Bazeley; brother of Hugh Christopher Longuet-Higgins (q.v.); m. Joan R. Tattersall 1958; two s. two d.; ed Winchester Coll., Trinity Coll., Cambridge Univ.; Research Fellow, Trinity Coll. Cambridge 1951–55, Commonwealth Fund Fellow, Scripps Inst., La Jolla, 1951–52; Research Scientist, Nat. Inst. of Oceanography 1954–67; Visiting Prof. MIT 1958; Visiting Prof. Inst. of Geophysics, Univ. of Calif. 1961–62; Visiting Prof. Univ. of Adelaide 1963–64; Prof. of Oceanography, Oregon State Univ., Corvallis 1967–69; Royal Soc. Research Prof., Cambridge Univ. (jt appointment with Inst. of Oceanographic Sciences) 1969–89; Sr Research Physicist, La Jolla Inst. 1989–; Fellow Trinity Coll. Cambridge 1969–; Foreign Assoc. NAS 1979; Fellow, Royal Soc. 1963; Hon. LLD (Glasgow) 1979; Hon. DTech (Tech. Univ. of Denmark) 1979; Sverdrup Gold Medal of American Meteorological Soc. 1983; Int. Coastal Eng Award, American Soc. of Civil Engineers 1984. *Publications:* contribs to scientific journals on physics and math. of the sea, especially ocean waves and currents. *Leisure interests:* music, gardening, mathematical toys. *Address:* Gage Farm, Comberton, Cambridge, CB3 7DH, England (Home); Institute for Non-Linear Sciences, University of California San Diego, La Jolla, CA 92093 U.S.A. (Office). *Telephone:* (858) 534-3936 (USA); (1223) 262346 (Home). *E-mail:* mlonguet@ucsd.edu (Office).

LØNNING, Inge Johan, DTheol; Norwegian politician and theologian; b. 20 Feb. 1938, Bergen; s. of the late Per Lønning and of Anna (née Strømø) Lønning; m. Kari Andersen 1962; two s. two d.; ed Univs of Bergen and Oslo and Pastoral Seminary of Church of Norway; Naval Chaplain 1964–65; Asst Prof. Univ. of Oslo 1965–70; Research Fellow, Univ. of Tübingen 1967; Prof. of Systematic Theology, Univ. of Oslo 1971–, Dean, Faculty of Theology 1977–81, Rector, Univ. of Oslo 1985–92; ed. journal Kirke og Kultur 1968–; mem. Oslo City Council 1972–76; Chair. Bd Norwegian Research Council for Science and Humanities 1980–84; Pres. Norsemen's Fed. 1989–2000, Nat. Rectors' Conf. 1989–92; Leader, European Movt in Norway 1993–95; mem. Parl. 1997–, Vice-Pres. Stortinget (Parl.) 2001; Vice-Pres. Høyre 1997–2002; Pres. Nordic Council 2003–; mem. Norwegian Acad. of Science and Letters, Royal Norwegian Soc., Royal Soc. of Letters, Sweden; Commdr Royal Norwegian Order of St Olav; Commdr with Star, Order of Merit of FRG; Hon. DD (Luther Coll. Decorah USA, Åbo Acad., Finland). *Publications:* Kanon im Kanon. Zum Dogmatischen Grundlagenproblem des Neutestamentlichen Kanons 1972, Martin Luther: Selected Writings (6 vols, ed.) 1978–83, Fellesskap og frihet. Tid for idepolitikk 1997. *Leisure interests:* fishing, skiing. *Address:* Stortinget, Karl Johans Gate, 0026 Oslo; Skullerudstubben 22, 1188 Oslo, Norway (Home). *Telephone:* 23-31-30-03 (Office); 22-28-95-12 (Home). *Fax:* 23-31-38-38 (Office); 22-85-03-01 (Home).

LONSDALE, Anne M., BALitHum; British university administrator; b. 16 Feb. 1941, Huddersfield, Yorks.; d. of A. C. G. Menzies and Molly Menzies; m. 1st Geoffrey Griffin 1962 (died 1962); m. 2nd Roger Lonsdale 1964 (divorced 1994); one s. one d.; ed St Anne's Coll. Oxford; Lecturer in Classical Chinese, St Anne's Coll. Oxford 1965–73; Univ. Admin. 1973–86; Dir External Relations Office, Univ. of Oxford 1986–93; Sec.-Gen. Cen. European Univ. 1993–96; Pres. New Hall, Cambridge Univ. 1996–, Pro-Vice-Chancellor Cambridge Univ. 1998–; Council of Senate, Cambridge Univ. 1997–; mem. Commonwealth Scholarship Comm. 1996–; mem. Governing Body of the GB Assoc. for Cen. and Eastern Europe; Trustee, Moscow School of Social and Econ. Sciences, LEAD Int. UK, Newton Trust; Cavaliere Ordine al Merito della Repubblica Italiana 1992, Officier des Palmes académiques; Dr hc (Tashkent Oriental Studies Univ. Uzbekistan) 2001. *Publications:* publs on Chinese literature and univ. admin. *Leisure interests:* travel, film, contemporary art. *Address:* New Hall, Cambridge, CB3 0DF, England. *Telephone:* (1223) 762201. *Fax:* (1223) 762217.

LOOMIS, Henry, AB; American broadcasting executive and fmr government official; b. 19 April 1919, Tuxedo Park, NY; s. of Alfred Lee Loomis and Ellen Holman Farnsworth Loomis; m. 1st Mary Paul Macleod 1946 (divorced 1974); two s. two d.; m. 2nd Jacqueline C. Williams 1974; four step-s.; ed Harvard Univ. and Univ. of California; U.S. Navy 1940–45; Asst to the Pres., MIT 1947–50; Asst to Chair. of Research and Devt Bd, Dept of Defense, Washington, DC 1950–51; Consultant, Psychological Strategy Bd, Washington, DC 1951–52; mem. Staff, Pres. Cttee on Int. Information 1953; Chief, Office of Research and Intelligence, U.S. Information Agency, Washington, DC 1954–57; Staff Dir to Special Asst to Pres. for Science and Tech., White House 1957–58; Dir Broadcasting Service (Voice of America), U.S. Information Agency, Washington, DC 1958–65; Deputy U.S. Commr of Educ., Dept of Health, Educ. and Welfare, Washington, DC 1965–66; Partner, St Vincent's Island Co., New York 1966–69; Deputy Dir U.S. Information Agency, Washington, DC 1969–72; Pres. Corpn for Public Broadcasting 1972–78; mem. Bd of Trustees, Mitre Corpn 1979–91, Bd, Nat. History Museum 1990– (Vice-Chair. 1991–92), Bd, Jacksonville Zoological Soc. 1991–96; Trustee Museum of Science and History Jacksonville 1991–96; Rockefeller Public Service Award in Foreign Affairs 1963; Distinguished Service Award, U.S. Information Agency 1963. *Leisure interests:* sailing, hunting, fishing, skiing. *Address:* 4661 Ortega Island Drive, Jacksonville, FL 32210, USA (Home).

LOONE, Eero; Estonian philosopher; b. 26 May 1935, Tartu; s. of Nikolai Loone and Leida Loone (née Rebane); m. 1st Halliki Uibo 1965; m. 2nd Leiki Sikk 1971; two d.; ed Moscow Univ. and Acad. of Sciences, Moscow; mem. CPSU 1965–90; Teacher, Univ. Tartu 1963–, Prof. 1985–, Head Dept of Philosophy 1986–89, 1993–94, Head Dept of Philosophy and Political Science 1989–93; Visiting Prof. British Acad. 1993, Ashby Lecturer 1994; Founding mem. independent Estonian Union of Scientists 1989–, Estonia Foreign Policy Inst. 1991, Estonian Political Science Asscn 1993–; mem. Int. Political Science Asscn 1994–; NATO Democratic Insts Fellow 1993–94; Life mem. Clare Hall (Cambridge) 1990–; Fulbright Scholar, Columbia Univ. 1997; Head Dept of Philosophy, Univ. of Tartu 1998–2000. *Publications include:* Contemporary Philosophy of History 1980 (in English trans. as Soviet Marxism and Analytical Philosophies of History 1990). *Leisure interest:* science fiction. *Address:* Department of Philosophy, University of Tartu, Ulikooli, 18, 50090 Tartu (Office); Kaunase pst. 16-40, 50704 Tartu, Estonia (Home). *Telephone:* (7) 375314 (Office); (7) 484554 (Home). *Fax:* (7) 375317 (Office); (7) 465345. *E-mail:* eloone@ut.ee (Office).

LOPARDO, Frank; American opera singer; b. 23 Dec. 1957, New York; m. Carolyn J. Montalbano 1982; two s.; ed Queen's Coll. New York and Juilliard School of Music; studied with Dr Robert White Jr; professional debut as Tamino in The Magic Flute, St Louis 1984; debut at La Scala, Milan 1987, Glyndebourne Festival 1987, Metropolitan Opera as Almaviva in Il Barbiere di Siviglia 1989–90; now appears regularly at leading opera houses and music festivals around the world; roles include Alfredo in La Traviata, Lensky in Eugene Onegin, Edgardo in Lucia di Lammermoor, The Duke in Rigoletto, Ferrando in Così fan tutte, Don Giovanni; also appears as soloist with leading orchestras and in recordings of such works as Mozart's Requiem, Carl Orff's

Carmina Burana, Mozart's Don Giovanni and Così fan tutte, Verdi's Falstaff and La Traviata, as well as Rossini's Il Barbiere di Siviglia, Semiramide and L'Italiana in Algeri; Hon. DMus (Aaron Copland School of Music). *Leisure interest:* golf. *Address:* c/o Royal Opera House, Covent Garden, London, WC2E 9DD, England; 167 Shaw Avenue, Valley Stream, New York, NY 11580; Metropolitan Opera, Lincoln Center, New York, NY 10023, USA. *Telephone:* (516) 568-0355. *Fax:* (516) 568-0355.

LOPATKIN, Nikolai Alekseyevich, DMed; Russian urologist; b. 18 Feb. 1924; ed Second Moscow Medical Inst.; intern, docent Second Moscow Medical Inst. 1950–62; Prof., Head of Chair of Urology and Operative Nephrology 1963; Main Urologist of USSR Ministry of Public Health 1978–83; Dir, Prof. Research Inst. of Urology 1983–; Chair. All-Union Soc. of Urologists 1972–91; mem. Russian Acad. of Medical Sciences 1974; Chair. Scientific Council on Urology and Operative Nephrology, Russian Acad. of Sciences 1991; Ed.-in-Chief Urology and Nephrology; USSR State Prize (three times), Hero of Socialist Labour and other decorations. *Publications:* more than 250 works on urology, diagnostics and treatment of kidney insufficiency and kidney transplantation. *Address:* Research Institute of Urology, 3 Parkovaya ul. 51, 105483 Moscow, Russia. *Telephone:* (095) 164-66-20.

LOPATKINA, Ulyana Vyacheslavovna; Russian ballerina; b. 23 Oct. 1973, Kerch; ed Vaganova Acad. of Russian Ballet; soloist Mariinsky Theatre 1991–; State Prize of Russian Fed. 1998. *Repertoire includes:* leading roles in Giselle, Sleeping Beauty, Anna Karenina, Fountain of Bakhchisarai, Raimonda, Scheherazade, Swan Lake, Bayadera, (Corsair), performs in Goya-Divertissement; tours with Mariinsky Theatre in Europe, N and S. America. *Address:* Mariinsky Theatre, Teatralnaya pl. 1, St Petersburg, Russia (Office). *Telephone:* (812) 315-57-24 (Office).

LOPES, António Simões, PhD; Portuguese university professor; b. 3 Feb. 1934, Colmeal, Góis; s. of António Lopes de Oliveira and Emília Simões; m. Maria Helena Simões 1960; ed Instituto Superior de Ciências Económicas e Financeiras, Universidade Técnica de Lisboa, Brasenose Coll., Oxford Univ., UK; Asst Prof. 1962–68; researcher, Gulbenkian Inst. for Science 1964–72; Consultant, Gulbenkian Foundation 1972–74; Prof., Tech. Univ. of Lisbon 1973, Vice-Rector 1982–85, Acting Rector 1985–87, Rector 1987; mem. Bd, Univ. of Evora 1974–77; Prof., Portuguese Catholic Univ. 1979–81; mem. Scientific Bd, Faculty of Econs, Univ. of Coimbra 1979–; Chair. Portuguese Council of Rectors 1985–87, Portuguese Asscn for Regional Devt 1985–90, Asscn of Univs of Portuguese-Speaking Countries 1986–89; Hon. Prof. Univ. of Maranhão, Brazil; Hon. DCL (Kent) 1992; Chevalier, Ordre Nat. du Mérite, France, Grã-Cruz, Ordem da Instrucção Pública, Portugal. *Publications:* Estrutura da População Activa Portuguesa 1967, As Funções Económicas dos Pequenos Centros 1971, Desenvolvimento Regional (3rd Edn) 1989 and other books; various articles. *Address:* R. Abade Baçal 21, Mercês, 2725 Mem Martins; Alameda St.o António Capuchos 1, 1100 Lisbon, Portugal. *Telephone:* 521061; 521227.

LOPES, Henri; Republic of the Congo author and politician; b. 12 Sept. 1937, Léopoldville, Belgian Congo (now Kinshasa, Democratic Republic of the Congo); s. of Jean-Marie Lopes and Micheline Vulturi; m. Nirva Pasbeau 1961; one s. three d.; ed France; Minister of Nat. Educ. 1968–71, of Foreign Affairs 1971–73; mem. Political Bureau, Congolese Labour Party 1973; Prime Minister and Minister of Planning 1973–75, of Finance 1977–80; UNESCO Asst Dir-Gen. for Programme Support 1982–86, UNESCO Asst Dir-Gen. for Culture and Communication 1986–90, for Culture 1990–94, for Foreign Affairs 1994–95, Deputy Dir-Gen. 1996–98; Amb. to France (with responsibility for Portugal, Spain, the U.K. and the Vatican City) 1998–; mem. Haut Conseil de la Francophonie; Chevalier, Légion d'Honneur, Commdr du Mérite Congolais, etc.; Prix littéraire de l'Afrique noire 1972, Prix SIMBA de littérature 1978, Prix de littérature du Président (Congo), Prix de l'Acad. de Bretagne et des Pays de la Loire 1990, Grand Prix de la Francophonie de l'Académie Française 1993. *Publications:* Tribaliques (short stories), La Nouvelle Romance (novel), Learning to be (with others), Sans tam-tam (novel) 1977, Le Pleurer Rire (novel) 1982, Le Chercheur d'Afriques (novel) 1990, Sur l'autre Rive (novel) 1992, Le Lys et le flamboyant (novel) 1997. *Address:* Embassy of the Republic of the Congo, 37 bis rue Paul Valéry, 75116 Paris, France (Office). *Telephone:* 1-45-00-34-26. *Fax:* 1-45-00-34-26.

LOPEZ, Jennifer; American actress and singer; b. 24 July 1970, Bronx, NY; m. Chris Judd 2001 (divorced 2002); Golden Globe 1998, MTV Movie Award 1999. *Albums:* On the 6 1999, J. Lo 2001, This is Me...Then 2002. *Films include:* My Little Girl 1986, My Family – Mi Familia 1995, Money Train 1995, Jack 1996, Blood and Wine 1997, Selena 1997, Anaconda 1997, Selena 1997, U Turn 1997, Out of Sight 1998, Antz (voice) 1998, Thieves 1999, Pluto Nash 1999, The Cell 2000, The Wedding Planner 2001, Angel Eyes 2001, Enough 2002, Maid in Manhattan 2002. *Television appearances include:* In Living Color 1990, Second Chances 1993, South Central 1994, Hotel Malibu 1994. *Address:* International Creative Management, 8942 Wilshire Boulevard, Beverly Hills, CA 90211, USA. *Website:* www.jenniferlopez.com.

LÓPEZ ARELLANO, Gen. Oswaldo; Honduran politician and air force officer; b. 30 June 1921; ed School of Mil. Aviation and Flight Training, USA; joined armed forces 1939, Lt 1947, Col 1958; Chief of Armed Forces 1956–75; mem. Mil. Junta, Chief of Mil. Govt of Honduras, Minister of Nat. Defence,

Minister of Public Security 1963–66; Pres. of Honduras 1966–71, 1972–75; now Pres. Servicio Aéreo de Honduras; several decorations. *Address:* Servicio Aéreo de Honduras, Apdo 129, Tegucigalpa, DC, Honduras.

LÓPEZ-COBOS, Jesús, DPhil; Spanish orchestral conductor; b. 25 Feb. 1940, Toro; s. of Lorenzo López and Gregoria Cobos; ed Madrid Univ. (philosophy), Madrid Conservatory (composition) and Vienna Acad. (conducting); worked with major orchestras including London Symphony, Royal Philharmonic, Philharmonia, Concertgebouw, Vienna Philharmonic, Vienna Symphony, Berlin Philharmonic, Hamburg NDR, Munich Philharmonic, Cleveland, Chicago Symphony, New York Philharmonic, Philadelphia, Pittsburgh Symphony; conducted new opera productions at La Scala, Milan, Covent Garden, London and Metropolitan Opera, New York; Gen. Musikdirektor, Deutsche Oper, Berlin 1981–90; Prin. Guest Conductor London Philharmonic Orchestra 1981–86; Prin. Conductor and Artistic Dir, Spanish Nat. Orchestra 1984–89; Music Dir, Cincinnati Symphony Orchestra 1986–2001 (now Music Dir Emer.), Music Dir Lausanne Chamber Orchestra 1990–2000, Orchestre Français des Jeunes 1998–2001; Cross of Merit (1st Class) (FRG) 1989; Officier des Arts et des Lettres 2001; Dr hc (Arts Univ. Cincinatti); First Prize, Besançon Int. Conductors' Competition 1969, Prince of Asturias Award (Spanish Govt) 1981, Founders Award, American Soc. of Composers, Authors and Publrs 1988, Fine Arts Medal (Spain) 2001. *Recordings include:* Bruckner symphonies, Haydn symphonies, Donizetti's Lucia di Lammermoor, Rossini's Otello and recital discs with José Carreras, works by Mahler, Respighi, Franck, de Falla, Villa-Lobos and Richard Strauss and Rossini's Il Barbiere di Siviglia and L'Italiana in Algeri. *Address:* 8 Chemin de Bellerive, 1007 Lausanne, Switzerland. *Fax:* (24) 6010852.

LÓPEZ GARCÍA, Antonio; Spanish artist; b. 6 Jan. 1936, Tomelloso; m. María Moreno 1961; two d.; ed Escuela de Bellas Artes de San Fernando, Madrid; solo exhbns in Ateneo de Madrid and Galería Biosca, Madrid 1957, 1961, Staempfli Gallery, New York 1965, 1968–69, Galleria Galatea, Turin 1972, Galerie Claude Bernard, Paris 1972, Museo de Albacete 1985, Musée d'Art Moderne, Brussels 1985, Marlborough Galleries, New York and London 1986, Museo Nacional Centro de Arte Reina Sofía, Madrid 1993, 2001, Fundación FOCUS, Seville 1994, Centro Cultural Isabel de Farnesio, Aranjuez 2000, Centro Cultural Palacio de la Audiencia, Soria 2000; group exhbns including Arco 2000, Madrid and New York 2000, Memoria y Modernidad, Centro Cultural San Marcos, Toledo 2001, Arco 2001, Madrid and New York 2001, Cinquante ans de sculpture espagnole, Palais Royal, Paris 2001, Nuovo Realismo Spagnolo, Galleria Marieschi, Milan, Italy and Galería Mario Sequeira, Braga, Portugal 2002, Arco 2002, Madrid and New York 2002, Escultura Española, Marlborough Gallery, Monte Carlo 2002; Prize of Diputación de Jaén 1957, Prize of Fundación Rodríguez Acosta 1958, Molino de Oro Prize of Exposición Regional de Valdepeñas 1959, Darmstadt Prize 1974, Medalla de Oro, Castilla-La Mancha 1986, Medalla de Oro, Comunidad de Madrid 1990. *Film:* El Sol del Membrillo (The Quince Tree Sun) 1992. *Address:* c/o Galería Marlborough SA, Orfila 5, 28010 Madrid (Office); Poniente 3, 28036 Madrid, Spain (Home). *Telephone:* (91) 3191414 (Office). *Fax:* (91) 3084345 (Office). *E-mail:* info@galeriamarlborough.com (Office). *Website:* www.galeriamarlborough.com (Office).

LÓPEZ-IBOR, Juan José, MD; Spanish professor of psychiatry; b. 17 Dec. 1941, Madrid; s. of Juan J. López-Ibor Sr and Socorro Alino; m. Cristina Alcocer 1967; four c.; ed Madrid and Frankfurt Univs and St Bartholomew's Hosp., London; Asst Prof. of Psychiatry, Madrid Univ. 1962–72; Head Prof. of Psychiatry, Oviedo Univ. 1972–73, Salamanca Univ. 1973–74, Alcalá de Henares Univ. 1982–; Head, Psychiatric Unit, Ramón y Cajal Hosp. 1977–; Pres. Spanish Psychiatry Soc. 1978–80; Pres. Int. Coll. of Psychosomatic Medicine 1985; Temporary Adviser WHO 1984; Hon. mem. World Psychiatric Asscn. *Publications:* Los Equivalentes Depresivos 1972, 1978, El Cuerpo y la Corporalidad 1974, Las Depresiones 1976, Tratado de Psiquiatría 1982, 1984. *Leisure interests:* skiing, water skiing. *Address:* Avenida Nueva Zelanda 44, 28035 Madrid, Spain. *Telephone:* (91) 3739199.

LÓPEZ MICHELSEN, Alfonso; Colombian politician and lawyer (retd); b. 30 June 1913, Bogotá; s. of Alfonso López Pumarejo (Pres. of Colombia 1934–38, 1942–45) and María Michelsen; m. Cecilia Caballero de López; ed London, Brussels, Colegio Mayor de Nuestra Señora del Rosario, Bogotá, Santiago (Chile) and Georgetown Univ., Washington, DC, USA; fmr teacher at Univ. Nacional de Colombia, Univ. Libre de Bogotá and Colegio Mayor de Nuestra Señora del Rosario; legal practice; spent seven years as emigré in Mexico 1952–58; later an Ed. of El Liberal (weekly); mem. Chamber of Deputies 1960–62, 1962–66; Founder, Leader of moderate wing of Movimiento Revolucionario Liberal 1958–67; joined Partido Liberal 1967, Leader 1982; Gov. of César Dept 1967–68; Minister of Foreign Affairs 1968–70; Pres. of Colombia 1974–78. *Publications:* Introduction to the Study of the Colombian Constitution 1942, Benjamin Constant or the Father of Bourgeois Liberalism 1946, Colombian Inquiries, The Chosen Ones (novel). *Leisure interest:* golf. *Address:* Carrera 8 No. 87-49, Piso 8, Bogotá (Office); Carrera 8 No. 87-49, Piso 7, Bogotá, Colombia (Home). *Telephone:* (1) 6100181 (Office); (1) 6101147 (Home). *Fax:* (1) 6101750 (Office); (1) 6101750 (Home).

LÓPEZ-PORTILLO Y PACHECO, José; Mexican politician and lawyer; b. 16 June 1920, Mexico City; s. of José López-Portillo y Weber; m. Carmen Romano; one s. two d.; ed Law Nat. Faculty, Univ. Nacional Autónoma de México, Univ. de Chile; Prof. of Gen. Theory on the State, Univ. Nacional Autónoma de México 1954, Assoc. Prof. of Political Sciences 1956–58; Founder

Prof. in Admin. Sciences Doctorate, Comm. School of the Nat. Polytechnical Inst. 1961; with Partido Revolucionario Institucional (PRI) 1959–64; Technical Assoc., Head Office of Ministry of Patrimony 1960; Co-ordinator Border Urban Devt Cttee 1962; mem. Intersecretarial Comm. for Nat. Devt 1966; Under-Sec. of the Presidency 1968; Under-Sec. Ministry of Patrimony 1970; Gen. Dir Electricity Fed. Comm. 1972–73; Sec. for Finances and Public Credit 1973–75; Pres. of Mexico 1976–82; fmr Gov. for Mexico, IMF; Ordem Nacional do Cruzeiro do Sul (Brazil) 1978. *Publications:* Valoración de la Estatal, Génesis y Teoría del Estado Moderno, Quetzalcoatl, Don Q. *Address:* c/o Palacio de Gobierno, México, DF, Mexico.

LÓPEZ TRUJILLO, HE Cardinal Alfonso; Colombian ecclesiastic; b. 8 Nov. 1935, Villahermosa, Ibagué; ordained priest 1960; Titular Bishop of Boseta with personal title of Archbishop 1971–; Archbishop of Medellín 1979–90; Pres. Pontifical Council for the Family 1990–; Pres. Latin American Conf. of Bishops; Pontifical Comm. for Latin America (CELAM) 1979–83; mem. Sacred Congregation for the Doctrine of the Faith, Congregation for Bishops, for Evangelisation of Peoples, Secr. for Non-believers; cr. Cardinal 1983. *Address:* Piazza San Calisto 16, Vatican City, Rome, Italy. *Telephone:* 317980.

LORAN, Oleg Borisovich, DrMed; Russian surgeon and urologist; b. 24 June 1943, Moscow; s. of Boris Yulievich Loran and Irina Donatovna Loran; m. Irina Petrovna Grebennikova; one s. two d.; ed Moscow Sechenov Inst. of Medicine; surgeon Salda City Hosp. Sverdlovsk Region 1966–69; intern, urologist Moscow Botkin Hosp. of Urgent Medicine 1969–72; Asst, Head Div. of Urology, Prof. Moscow Medical Inst. of Stomatology (now Moscow State Medical and Stomatological Univ.) 1972–; Chief Urologist Ministry of Public Health of Russian Fed.; Chief Scientific Sec. Russian Soc. of Urologists 1978; mem. European Asscn of Urologists 1992; mem. Exec. Bd E European Soc. of Urologists; mem. Editorial Bd journals Urology and Nephrology, Annals of Surgery; mem. Higher Attestation Comm. of Russian Fed.; Diplomas of American Asscn of Urologists and American Urological Foundation. *Publications:* over 230 scientific works including 9 books on problems of urology, 10 patents. *Leisure interests:* music, theatre. *Address:* Moscow State Medical Stomatological Institute, Delegatskaya str. 20/1, 103473 Moscow, Russia (Office). *Telephone:* (095) 281-65-13 (Office).

LORD, Winston, BA; American civil servant and diplomatist; b. 14 Aug. 1937, New York; s. of Oswald Bates Lord and Mary Lord (née Pillsbury); m. Bette Bao 1963; one s. one d.; ed Yale Univ., Fletcher School of Law and Diplomacy; mem. Staff Congressional Relations, Politico-mil. and Econ. Affairs, US Dept of State, Washington 1961–65, Geneva 1965–67; mem. staff Int. Affairs, US Dept of Defense, Washington 1967–69; mem. staff Nat. Security Council, Washington 1969–73, Special Asst to Asst to Pres. on Security Affairs 1970–73; Dir Policy Planning Staff, US Dept of State, Washington 1973–77; Pres. Council on Foreign Relations 1977–85; Amb. to People's Repub. of China 1985–89; freelance lecturer, writer New York 1989–93; Asst Sec. of State for East Asian and Pacific Affairs 1993; Chair. Carnegie Endowment Nat. Comm. on America and the New World 1991–92, Nat. Endowment for Democracy 1992–93; Vice-Chair. Int. Rescue Cttee 1991–93; fmr mem. Bd of Dirs Fletcher School of Law and Diplomacy, Int. Rescue Cttee, Nat. Cttee on US–China Relations, Nat. Endowment for Democracy, US–Japan Foundation; several hon. degrees. *Leisure interests:* sports, literature, arts. *Address:* Bureau of East Asian and Pacific Affairs, Department of State, Room 6205, Washington, DC 20520, USA. *Telephone:* (202) 647-9596.

LORDKIPANIDZE, Vazha Giorgevich, DEcon; Georgian politician, sociologist and demographer; b. 29 Nov. 1949, Tbilisi; m. Irina Khomeriki; two d.; ed Tbilisi State Univ., Moscow Acad. of Social Sciences; Teacher Tbilisi State Univ. 1975–, Head Demography Dept 2000–; Sec., Second, First Secr. Cen. Comsomol Cttee of Georgia 1980–86; First Sec. Tbilisi Dist CP Cttee 1986–88; Head Dept of Culture and Ideology Cen. Cttee, CP of Georgia 1988–90; Sr Researcher Inst. of Demography and Sociology, Georgian Acad. of Sciences 1991–92; Chief State Counsellor State Council of Georgia 1992; Head of Personnel Eduard Shevardnadze Admin. 1992–95; Amb. to Russia 1995–98; Minister of State 1998–2000; mem. Parl. 2000–; Pres. Demographers' Asscn of Georgia 2000–; Vice-Pres. Int. Research Centre for East–West Relationships 2000–; mem. Georgian Acad. of Econs 1996–, UN Int. Acad. of Informatics. *Address:* Tbilisi State University, 1 Chavchavadze Avenue, 380079 Tbilisi (Office); 5 Larsi Street, Flat 9, Tbilisi, Georgia (Home). *Telephone:* (32) 25-12-38 (Office); (32) 23-20-70 (Home). *Fax:* (32) 25-12-39 (Office); (32) 99-05-13 (Home). *E-mail:* ikhomeriki@hotmail.com.

LOREN, Sophia; Italian-born French actress; b. 20 Sept. 1934, Rome; d. of Riccardo Scicolone and Romilda Villani; m. Carlo Ponti (q.v.) 1957 (marriage annulled 1962; m. 1966); two s.; ed Scuole Magistrali Superiori; first screen appearance as an extra in Quo Vadis; has appeared in many Italian and other films including E Arrivato l'Accordatore 1951, Africa sotto i Mari (first leading role), La Tratta delle Bianche, La Favorita 1952, Aida 1953, Il Paese dei Campanelli, Miseria e Nobiltà, Il Segno di Venere 1953, Tempi Nostri 1953, Carosello Napoletano 1953, L'Oro di Napoli 1954, Attila 1954, Peccato che sia una canaglia, La Bella Mugnaia, La Donna del Fiume 1955, Boccaccio 1970, Matrimonio All'Italiana; and in the following American films: The Pride and the Passion 1955, Boy on a Dolphin, Legend of the Lost 1956, Desire Under the Elms 1957, That Kind of Woman 1958, Houseboat 1958, The Key 1958, The Black Orchid (Venice Festival Award 1958) 1958, It Started in Naples,

Heller in Pink Tights 1960, The Millionairess 1961, Two Women (Cannes Film Festival Award for Best Actress 1961) 1961, El Cid 1961, Madame Sans Gêne 1962, Yesterday, Today and Tomorrow 1963, The Fall of the Roman Empire 1964, Lady L 1965, Operation Crossbow 1965, Judith 1965, A Countess from Hong Kong 1965, Arabesque 1966, More than a Miracle 1967, The Priest's Wife 1970, Sunflower 1970, Hot Autumn 1971, Man of La Mancha 1972, Brief Encounter (TV) 1974, The Verdict 1974, The Voyage 1974, The Cassandra Crossing 1977, A Special Day 1977, Firepower 1978, Brass Target 1979, Blood Feud 1981, Mother Courage 1986, Two Women 1989, Prêt à Porter 1995, Grumpier Old Men, Between Strangers 2002; Chair. Nat. Alliance for Prevention and Treatment of Child Abuse and Maltreatment; Goodwill Amb. for Refugees 1992; Chevalier Légion d'honneur; Hon. Acad. Award 1991. *Publications:* Eat with Me 1972, Sophia Loren on Women and Beauty 1984. *Address:* Case Postale 430, 1211 Geneva 12, Switzerland.

LORENTZ, Francis; French business executive; b. 22 May 1942, Mulhouse; s. of Paul Lorentz and Lucienne Lorentz (née Biechy); m. Laure Doumenc; three c.; ed Lycée Kléber, Strasbourg, Ecole des Hautes Etudes Commerciales, Ecole Nat. d'Admin; with Ministry of Economy 1970–78; Exec. Vice-Pres. Société Lyonnaise des Eaux 1978–80; joined Honeywell-Bull 1982, Chair. and CEO Groupe Bull SA 1987–92; Chair. Dir-Gen. Régie autonome des transports parisiens (RATP) 1992–94; Prof., Univ. of Paris-Dauphine 1994–2000; Chair. Etablissement public de financement et de restructuration (EPFR) 1996–2000, Institut de l'audiovisual et des télécommunications en Europe 2000–; Dir Gen. Laser (groupe Galeries Lafayette) 2000–; Pres. e-LaSer and LaSer Informatique 2000–; Pres. French Nat. e-Business Task Force. *Publications:* several publs on devt admin, state-owned cos, industrial policy and e-business. *Leisure interests:* skiing, mountaineering, contemporary art, diving. *Address:* e-LaSer, 66 rue des Archives, 75003 Paris, France. *Telephone:* 1-44-83-16-68 (Office). *Fax:* 1-44-83-17-13 (Office). *E-mail:* florentz@laser.fr (Office).

LORENZ, Hans-Walter, Dr rer. pol; German economist; b. 3 Aug. 1951, Bielefeld; s. of Walter Lorenz and Lieselotte Lorenz; m. Karin Hottmann 1987; ed Univ. of Göttingen; Research Asst Univ. of Göttingen 1977–82, Asst Prof. 1984–91, Privatdozent 1991–94; Prof., of Econs Univ. of Jena 1994–; Visiting Scholar, Univ. of Calif. at Berkeley 1982–83; Visiting Prof. Univ. of Tech., Sydney, Australia 1999. *Publications:* Business Cycle Theory (with G. Gabisch) 1987, Nonlinear Dynamical Economics and Chaotic Motion 1989, Determinismus, nicht-lineare Dynamik und wirtschafliche Evolution 1991. *Address:* Wirtschaftswissenschaftliche Fakultät, Friedrich-Schiller-Universität, 07740 Jena; Hermann-Föge-Weg 1a, 37073 Göttingen, Germany. *Telephone:* (3641) 943210 (Office); (551) 44317 (Home). *Fax:* (3641) 943212; (551) 44974 (Home). *E-mail:* H.W.Lorenz@wiwi.uni-jena.de (Office).

LORIMER, George Huntly, PhD, FRS; British scientist; b. 14 Oct. 1942; s. of the late Gordon Lorimer and of Ellen Lorimer; m. Freia Schulz-Baldes 1970; one s. one d.; ed George Watson's Coll. Edinburgh and Univ. of St Andrews, Univ. of Illinois, Michigan State Univ.; scientist, Max-Planck Society, Berlin, 1972–74; Research Fellow, Inst. for Advanced Studies, Canberra 1974–77; Prin. Investigator, then Research Leader Cen. Research Dept, E.I. Du Pont de Nemours & Co. 1978–91, Dupont Fellow 1991–97; scientist, Soc. for Environmental Research, Munich 1977; mem. NAS 1997, Editorial Bd Journal of Biological Chem. 1998; Research Award, Alexander von Humboldt Foundation 1997. *Leisure interests:* philately, music. *Address:* 7705 Lake Glen Drive, Glen Dale, MD 20769, USA.

LORING, John Robbins, BA; American artist; b. 23 Nov. 1939, Chicago; s. of Edward D'Arcy and China Robbins Loring (née Logeman) ed Yale Univ., Ecole des Beaux Arts, Paris; Distinguished Visiting Prof., Univ. of Calif. at Davis 1977; Bureau Chief Architectural Digest magazine, New York 1977–78; Design Dir Tiffany and Co., New York 1979–, Exec. Vice-Pres., 1981–84, Sr Vice-Pres. Design and Merchandising 1984–; mem. acquisitions comm. Dept of prints and illustrated books, Museum of Modern Art, New York 1990–; Contributing Ed. Arts magazine 1973–; work in perm. collections Museum of Modern Art, New York, Whitney Museum of American Art, Chicago Art Inst., Boston Museum of Fine Arts, RI School of Design, Baltimore Museum of Art, Yale Univ. Art Gallery, NY Historical Soc.; works commissioned by US Customhouse, New York, Prudential Insurance Co., Woodbridge, NJ, City of Scranton, Pa; Hon. DrArts (Pratt Inst.) 1996; Edith Wharton Award, Design and Art Soc. 1988. *Solo exhibitions include:* Baltimore, New York, Long Beach, San Francisco 1964–76, Paris, Vienna, Venice. *Group exhibitions include:* Phila, New York, Chicago, Ljubljana, Cracow 1971–76. *Publications:* The New Tiffany Table Settings 1981, Tiffany Taste 1986, Tiffany's 150 Years 1987, The Tiffany Wedding 1988, Tiffany Parties 1989, The Tiffany Gourmet 1992, A Tiffany Christmas 1996, Tiffany's 20th Century 1997, Tiffany Jewels 1999, Paulding Farnham, Tiffany's Last Genius 2000, Magnificent Tiffany Silver 2001, Louis Comfort Tiffany at Tiffany & Co. 2002. *Leisure interests:* collecting 20th-century decorative arts, writing on design and lifestyle. *Address:* Tiffany & Co., 727 Fifth Avenue, New York, NY 10022 (Office); 403 West 46th Street, New York, NY 10036, USA (Home). *Telephone:* (212) 230-5339 (Office).

LORIOD, Yvonne; French pianist; b. 20 Jan. 1924, Houilles; d. of Gaston Loriod and Simone Loriod (née Bilhaut); m. Olivier Messiaen 1961 (died 1992); Prof. of Piano, Conservatoire National de Musique, Paris; specializes in interpretation of complete works including Bach's Well-Tempered Klavier, Beethoven sonatas, Mozart piano concertos, works of Chopin and Debussy and complete works of Olivier Messiaen; first performances in Paris of Bartok's 1st and 2nd concertos, Schoenberg concerto and works by Messiaen, Jolivet, Boulez and other contemporary composers; 7 Grand Prix du Disque, Grand Prix de la Sacem 1986; Commdr Légion d'honneur, Officier des Arts et Lettres, Grand Officier du Mérite. *Address:* c/o Bureau de Concerts Maurice Werner, 17 rue du 4 Septembre, 75002 Paris, France.

LORSCHEIDER, HE Cardinal Aloisio; Brazilian ecclesiastic; b. 8 Oct. 1924, Linha Geraldo, Porto Alegre; ordained priest 1948; Bishop of Santo Angelo 1962–73; Archbishop of Fortaleza 1973–95, of Aparecida July 1995–; cr. Cardinal 1976; mem. Sacred Congregation for the Clergy, for Religious Orders and Secular Insts, Secr. for Non-Christians; entitled S. Pietro in Montorio. *Address:* Gúna Metropolitana, CP 05, Tone de Basilica 48 andar, 12570-000 Aparecida, SP, Brazil. *Telephone:* (125) 362418.

LÖSCHNAK, Franz, DJur; Austrian politician; b. 4 March 1940, Vienna; m.; one s.; ed Univ. of Vienna; employed with Vienna City Council 1959–77, Dir of Personnel Affairs and Admin. Org. 1977; Under-Sec. Fed. Chancellery 1977; Minister, Fed. Chancellery 1985–87; Minister of Health and the Civil Service 1987–89; Minister of the Interior 1989–95.

LOSHAK, Victor Grigoryevich; Russian journalist; b. 20 April 1952, Zaporozhye, Ukraine; s. of Grigory Abramovich Loshak and Anna Davydovna Loshak; m. Marina Devovna Loshak; one d.; ed Odessa State Univ.; corresp. for various Odessa newspapers 1973–83; special corresp. Izvestia 1983–86; political observer Moskovskye Novosti 1986–91, First Deputy Ed. 1991–92, Ed.-in-Chief 1992–; Pres. Jt Stock Co. Moskiye Novosti; broadcaster for Kultura (TV channel); mem. Int. Inst. of Press (Vice-Pres. Russian br.); Prize of Journalists' Union of Moscow, Order of Honour. *Address:* Moskovskye Novosti, Tverskaya str. 16/2, 125009 Moscow, Russia (Office). *Telephone:* (095) 209-19-84 (Office). *Fax:* (095) 209-17-28 (Office). *E-mail:* info@mm.ru (Office). *Website:* www.mn.ru (Office).

LOSHCHININ, Valery Vassilyevich; Russian diplomatist; b. 11 Sept. 1940; m.; two c.; ed Belarus State Univ., Diplomatic Acad. of USSR Ministry of Foreign Affairs; with Ministry of Foreign Affairs Belarus SSR, then USSR Ministry of Foreign Affairs 1965–77; with Perm. Mission to Russia 1977–89; Deputy Perm. Rep. to int. orgs in Geneva 1989–95; Dir Second European Dept, Russian Ministry of Foreign Affairs 1995–96; Amb. to Belarus 1996–99; Perm. Rep. to int. orgs in Vienna 1999–2001; Deputy Minister of Foreign Affairs (responsible for relations with CIS countries) 2001–. *Address:* Ministry of Foreign Affairs, Smolenskaya-Sennaya 32/34, 121200 Moscow, Russia (Office). *Telephone:* (095) 244-15-09 (Office). *Fax:* (095) 253-90-80 (Office). *E-mail:* vl@mid.ru (Office).

LOSYUKOV, Aleksander Prokhovich; Russian diplomatist; b. 15 Nov. 1943; m.; two c.; ed Moscow State Inst. of Int. Relations; Attaché, USSR Embassy, Afghanistan 1968–72; Attaché, Third Sec., then Second Sec. Secr. of the First Deputy Minister of Foreign Affairs 1972–78; Second Sec., then First Sec. USSR Embassy, USA 1978–81; First Sec., Gen. Secr., Ministry of Foreign Affairs 1981–82; Asst to Deputy Minister of Foreign Affairs 1982–85; Counsellor-Envoy, USSR Embassy, The Philippines 1985–90; Deputy Head, Dept of Pacific Ocean countries and SE Asia, Ministry of Foreign Affairs 1990, Head, Dept of Gen. Problems of Asian-Pacific Ocean region 1990–92; Head, Dept of Asia-Pacific Ocean region, Ministry of Foreign Affairs 1992; Amb. to New Zealand (concurrently Kingdom of Tonga, Western Samoa and Cook Islands) 1992–94, to Australia (concurrently Fiji, Vanuatu and Nauru) 1997; Dir Second Dept of Asia 1997–99, Ministry of Foreign Affairs, Dir Dept of Gen. Secr. then Sec.-Gen. 1999–2000, Deputy Minister of Foreign Affairs 2000–. *Address:* Ministry of Foreign Affairs, Smolenskaya-Sennaya 32/34, 121200 Moscow, Russia (Office). *Telephone:* (095) 244-92-21 (Office). *Fax:* (095) 253-90-77 (Office). *E-mail:* alosyukov@mid.ru (Office).

LOTHE, Jens, DPhil; Norwegian professor of physics; b. 25 Nov. 1931, Oslo; s. of Jakob Lothe and Borghild Lothe; m. Solveig E. Seeberg 1960; two s. one d.; ed Univ. of Oslo; lecturer, Univ. of Oslo 1959–63, Assoc. Prof. 1963–72, Prof. of Physics 1972–; mem. Norwegian Acad. of Science and Letters. *Publications:* The Theory of Dislocations (with J. P. Hirth) 1967; numerous papers on elastic waves. *Address:* Nedre Ringvolls 5, 1339 Voyenenga, Norway. *Telephone:* 67133076.

LOTON, Brian Thorley, AC, B.MET.E.; Australian business executive; b. 17 May 1929, Perth; s. of the late Sir Thorley Loton; m. Joan Kemelfield 1956; two s. two d.; ed Hale School, Perth, Trinity Coll., Melbourne Univ.; started as Cadet, Broken Hill Pty Co. Ltd 1954, Tech. Asst to Production Superintendent 1959, Asst Chief Engineer 1961, Gen. Man. Planning and Devt 1969, Man. Dir 1982–91, CEO 1985–91, Deputy Chair. 1991–92, Chair. 1992–97; Gen. Man., Newcastle Steelworks 1970, Exec. Gen. Man. Steel Div. 1973, Dir 1976, Chief Gen. Man. 1977; Chair. Business Council of Australia 1989–90, Pres. 1990–92; Pres. Australian Mining Industry Council 1983–84; Chair. Int. Iron and Steel Inst. 1991–92; Jt Vice-Chair. Nat. Australia Bank 1992–99 (Dir 1988–99); Dir Amcor 1992–99; Chair. Atlas Copco Australia Pty Ltd 1996–2001; mem. Faculty of Eng, Melbourne Univ. 1980–83; Int. Counsellor, The Conf. Bd 1984–96, Int. Counsellor Emer. 1996–; Dept of Immigration and Ethnic Affairs Advisory Cttee 1980–82; Australasian Inst. of Mining and Metallurgy, Australian Science and Tech. Council 1977–80; Fellow, Australian Inst. of Co. Dirs, Australian Acad. of Tech. Sciences and Eng,

Trinity Coll. (Univ. of Melbourne) 1990; Hon. Fellow, Inst. of Engineers Australia. *Address:* P.O. Box 86A, Melbourne, Vic. 3001, Australia. *Telephone:* (3) 9932-7904. *Fax:* (3) 9620-7714.

LOTT, (Chester) Trent, BPA, JD; American politician; b. 9 Oct. 1941, Grenada, Miss.; s. of Chester P. Lott and Iona (née Watson) Lott; m. Patricia E. Thompson 1964; one s. one d.; ed Univ. of Mississippi; called to Miss. Bar 1967; Assoc. Bryan & Gordon, Pascagoula, Miss. 1967; Admin. Asst to Congressman Colmer 1968–73; mem. 93rd–100th Congresses from 5th Dist Miss., Repub. Whip 97th and 98th Congresses; Senator from Miss. 1989–2002; Senate Majority Leader 1996–2001, Nov.–Dec. 2002, Minority Leader 2001–02; named as observer from House to Geneva Arms Control talks; mem. Senate Republican Policy Cttee; mem. American Bar Asscn; Republican; Golden Bulldog Award, Guardian of Small Business Award. *Address:* c/o US Senate, 487 Russell Senate Building, Washington, DC 20510, USA.

LOTT, Dame Felicity Ann Emwhyla, DBE, BA, FRAM; British singer; b. 8 May 1947, Cheltenham; d. of John A. Lott and Whyla Lott (née Williams); m. 1st Robin Golding 1973 (divorced); m. 2nd Gabriel Woolf 1984; one d.; ed Pate's Grammar School for Girls, Cheltenham, Royal Holloway Coll., Univ. of London and Royal Acad. of Music; début English Nat. Opera 1975, Glyndebourne 1977; has sung prin. roles Covent Garden, Glyndebourne, English Nat. Opera, Metropolitan Opera, New York, Vienna, La Scala, Milan, Paris Opera, Brussels, Hamburg, Munich, Chicago; wide recital repertoire; founder mem. Songmakers' Almanac; many recordings; Hon. Fellow Royal Holloway Coll.; Officier des Arts et des Lettres 2000, Chevalier Légion d'honneur 2001; Dr hc (Sussex) 1990; Hon. DLitt (Loughborough) 1996; Hon. DMus (London) 1997, (Royal Scottish Acad. of Music and Drama) 1998, (Oxford) 2001; Kammersängerin, Bayerische Staatsoper, Munich 2003. *Leisure interests:* reading, gardening. *Address:* c/o Askonas Holt Ltd, Lonsdale Chambers, 27 Chancery Lane, London, WC2A 1PF, England. *Telephone:* (20) 7400-1700. *Fax:* (20) 7400-0799. *E-mail:* info@askonasholt.co.uk (Office). *Website:* www .askonasholt.co.uk (Office); www.felicitylott.de.

LOUCKS, Vernon R., Jr, MBA; American business executive (retd); b. 24 Oct. 1934, Evanston, Ill.; s. of Vernon Reece Loucks and Sue Burton; m. Linda Olson; six c.; ed Yale Univ. and Harvard Graduate School of Business Admin.; served as First Lt US Marine Corps; fmr Sr man. consultant, George Fry & Assocs; joined Baxter Int. Inc. 1966, mem. Bd of Dirs. 1975, Pres. and COO 1976, CEO 1987–98, Chair. 1987; Dir The Dun & Bradstreet Corpn, Emerson Electric Co., Inc., Quaker Oats Co., Anheuser-Busch Cos; numerous civic and educational appointments; Yale Medal 1997; several awards including Chicago Inst. of Medicine Citizen Fellowship Award 1982. *Address:* c/o Baxter Healthcare Corporation, 1450 Waukegan Road, Waukegan, IL 60085, USA.

LOUDON, Aarnout Alexander, LLM; Netherlands business executive; b. 10 Dec. 1936, The Hague; m. Talitha Adine Charlotte Boon 1962; two s.; ed Univ. of Utrecht; joined Bank Mees & Hope 1964, Head, New Issues Dept 1967; joined Akzo Group 1969, Dir Financial Affairs Azco, Arnhem 1971; Finance Dir Akzo Coatings, France 1972; Pres. Akzo, Brazil 1975–77; mem. Man. Bd Akzo NV 1977, Deputy Chair. 1978, Chair. Bd 1982–94; Chair. Supervisory Bd Akzo Nobel NV 1995–; Chair. Supervisory Bd ABN AMRO Holding NV 1996–, HBG 1999–; mem. Supervisory Bd Royal Dutch Petroleum Co. 1997–; Dir (non-exec.) Corus Group PLC; mem. Int. Advisory Bd Allianz AG, Munich; mem. Senate, Dutch Parl. 1995–99. *Leisure interest:* horseback riding. *Address:* Velperweg 76, 6800 BS Arnhem (Office); Rembrandt kaan 16, 6881 CS Velp, Netherlands (Home). *Telephone:* (26) 3663651 (Office); (26) 3646606 (Home). *Fax:* (26) 3665030 (Office); (26) 3649528 (Home).

LOUDON, Rodney, DPhil, FRS; British theoretical physicist; b. 25 July 1934, Manchester; s. of Albert Loudon and Doris Helen Loudon (née Blane); m. Mary A. Philips 1960; one s. one d.; ed Bury Grammar School, Oxford Univ., Univ. of California at Berkeley, USA; Scientific Civil Servant, RRE, Malvern 1960–65; mem. Tech. Staff, Bell Laboratories, Murray Hill, NJ, USA 1965–66, 1970, RCA, Zürich, Switzerland 1975, British Telecom Research Labs 1984, 1989–95; Prof. of Physics, Essex Univ. 1967–; Visiting Prof. Yale 1975, Univ. of Calif. Irvine 1980, Ecole Polytechnique, Lausanne 1985, Univ. of Rome 1987, 1996; Fellow Optical Soc. of America 1994; Thomas Young Medal and Prize (Inst. of Physics) 1987, Max Born Award (Optical Soc. of America) 1992, Humboldt Award 1998. *Publications:* The Quantum Theory of Light 1973, 1983, 2000, Scattering of Light by Crystals (with W. Hayes) 1978, Surface Excitations (Ed. with V.M. Agranovich) 1984, An Introduction to the Properties of Condensed Matter (with D. Barber) 1989. *Leisure interest:* classical music. *Address:* 3 Gaston Street, East Bergholt, Colchester, Essex, CO7 6SD, England. *Telephone:* (1206) 298550.

LOUEKOSKI, Matti Kalevi; Finnish politician, business executive and lawyer; b. 14 April 1941, Oulu; m. Pirjo Hiltunen 1969; one s. one d.; Sec.-Gen. Union of Finnish Student Corpns 1967–69; official at Ministry of Finance and Ministry of Interior 1969–70; Counsellor of Higher Educ. 1970–72; Special Adviser, Office of the Council of State 1975–76; established own law firm 1978; Dir Finnish Workers' Savings Bank 1979–83; mem. Parl. 1976–79, 1983–96; Minister of Educ. 1971–72; Minister without Portfolio Feb.–Sept. 1972; Minister of Justice 1972–75, of Justice and Nordic Co-operation 1987–90, of Finance 1990–91; Vice-Speaker of Parl. 1985–87, 1995–96; mem.

Bd Bank of Finland 1996–2000, Deputy Gov. 2001–; mem. Social Democratic Party. *Address:* Bank of Finland, P.O. Box 160, 00101 Helsinki, Finland. *Telephone:* 1831. *Fax:* 661676. *E-mail:* info@bof.fi. *Website:* www.bof.fi.

LOUËT, Philippe Marie Alexandre Gabriel, LenD; French diplomatist; b. 7 July 1933, Paris; s. of Michel Louet and Marguerite Louet (née Perrin); m. 1st Hélène Delorme; one s.; m. 2nd Penelope Wilkinson 1974; two s. one step-s.; ed Coll. Saint-Martin, Pontoise, Lycée Janson-de-Sailly, Inst. d'études politiques de Paris, Ecole nat. d'admin; with Dept of Political Affairs, Ministry of Foreign Affairs 1962–66; second, later First Sec. to Perm. Rep. of France to the EEC 1966–71; Tech. Adviser, Ministry of Industrial and Scientific Devt 1971–74, Ministry of Foreign Affairs 1974, Deputy Dir for Scientific Affairs and Dir for Spatial and Atomic Matters 1976–81; Deputy Perm. Rep. to the UN 1981–86; Amb. to Turkey 1986–88; Perm. Rep. to the EEC, Brussels 1988–89; Amb. to Sweden 1989–92; Diplomatic Adviser to the Govt 1992–; Officier, Légion d'honneur, Officier, Ordre nat. du Mérite, Grand Officier, Ordre de l'Etoile Polaire (Sweden). *Leisure interest:* sailing. *Address:* Conseiller diplomatique du gouvernement, 19 ave Kléber, 75116 Paris (Office); 2 avenue de Camoëns, 75116 Paris, France (Home). *Telephone:* 1-43-17-77-66 (Office). *Fax:* 1-43-17-77-73.

LOUGHRAN, James, FRNCM, FRSAMD; British conductor; b. 30 June 1931, Glasgow; s. of James Loughran and Agnes (née Fox) Loughran; m. 1st Nancy Coggon 1961 (divorced 1983, died 1996); two s.; m. 2nd Ludmila Navratil 1985; ed Glasgow, Bonn, Amsterdam and Milan; Assoc. Conductor, Bournemouth Symphony Orchestra 1962–65; debut Royal Opera House, Covent Garden 1964; Prin. Conductor BBC Scottish Symphony Orchestra 1965–71; Prin. Conductor and Musical Adviser, Hallé Orchestra 1971–83, Conductor Laureate 1983–91; debut New York Philharmonic with Westminster Choir 1972; Prin. Conductor Bamberg Symphony Orchestra 1979–83; Chief Guest Conductor BBC Welsh Symphony Orchestra 1987–90; Guest Conductor of prin. orchestras of Europe, America, Australia and Japan, Guest Perm. Conductor, Japan Philharmonic Symphony Orchestra 1993; Chief Conductor Århus Symphony Orchestra, Denmark 1996–; BBC Proms 1965–89 including The Last Night 5 times 1977–85; recorded complete Beethoven Symphonies with London Symphony Orchestra as contribution to European Broadcasting Union Beethoven Bicentenary Celebrations 1969–70; recordings with Hallé, London Philharmonic, Philharmonia, BBC Symphony, Århus Symphony and Scottish Chamber Orchestras; Liveryman, Worshipful Co. of Musicians 1992; Hon. DMus (Sheffield) 1983; First Prize, Philharmonia Orchestra Conducting Competition 1961, Gold Disc EMI 1983. *Leisure interest:* unwinding. *Address:* 34 Cleveden Drive, Glasgow G12 0RX, Scotland. *Telephone:* (141) 337-2091 (Home). *Fax:* (141) 357-0643 (Home).

LOUIS, Jean-Victor, DenD; Belgian lawyer and university professor; b. 10 Jan. 1938, Uccle; m. Maria Rosa Moya Benavent 1963; three s.; ed Univ. Libre de Bruxelles; Sec. Inst. d'Etudes Européennes, Univ. Libre de Bruxelles 1967–71, Dir 1971–72, Dir of Research 1977–80, Pres. 1980–92; Lecturer, Univ. Libre de Bruxelles 1970–73, Prof. 1973–; Prof. European Univ. Inst. 1998-2002; Adviser, Nat. Bank of Belgium 1972–80, Head, Legal Dept 1980–97, Adviser to Bd of Dirs 1990–97; Pres. Belgian Asscn for European Law 1983–85; legal expert, Institutional Cttee European Parl. 1992–94; Pres. Initiative Cttee 96, European Movt 1995–98; Chair. Groupe d'Etudes Politiques Européennes (TEPSA), Monetary Cttee of Int. Law Asscn; Dir Cahiers de Droit Européen 1977–; Exec. Dir Philippe Wiener-Maurice Ansbach Foundation 1971–2002, Pres. 2002–; Dr hc (Univ. Paris 2) 2001, Emile Bernheim Prize 1969; P. H. Spaak Prize 1979; Commdr Order of Belgian Crown. *Publications:* Les règlements de la Communauté économique européenne 1969, Le Droit de la Communauté économique européenne (dir and co-author), 15 vols 1970–, The European Community Legal Order 1979, Implementing the Tokyo Round (with J. Jackson and M. Matsushita) 1984, Vers un Système européen de banques centrales (ed.) 1989, From the EMS to the Monetary Union 1990, Banking Supervision in the EC (ed.) 1995, L'Union européenne et l'avenir de ses institutions 1996, The Euro and European Integration (ed.) 1999; many articles on EC law, especially in field of monetary cooperation and integration. *Address:* 524 avenue Louise, Boîte 9, 1050 Brussels, Belgium (Home). *E-mail:* louis@ive.it (Office).

LOUIS-DREYFUS, Robert Louis Maurice, MBA; French business executive; b. 14 June 1946, Paris; s. of Jean Louis-Dreyfus and Jeanne Depierre; m. 1st Sarah Oberholzer; m. 2nd Margarita Bogdanova; three s.; ed Lycée Marcel Roby, Saint-Germain-en-Laye and Harvard Business School, USA; Dir Louis-Dreyfus, SA 1973–81, Sr Exec. Vice-Pres. and COO 1982–83; Pres. and CEO IMS Int. 1984–89; Gen. Man. Saatchi & Saatchi 1989–93, CEO 1990–93, Dir (non-exec.) 1993; Pres. Adidas (now Adidas-Salomon) AG 1993–, Pres. L'Olympique de Marseille 1996–, Louis Dreyfus Communication 2000–; Chair. Bd Dirs Tag Heuer à Mariu 1997–99. *Address:* Louis Dreyfus Communications, 1 Square Chaptal, 92309 Levallois Cedex, France; Ortstrasse 4, 7270 Davos-platz, Switzerland (Home). *Telephone:* 1-58-63-10-00 (Office). *Fax:* 1-58-63-15-64 (Office).

LOUISY, Rt Hon Allan (Fitzgerald Laurent), PC, CBE; Saint Lucia politician; fmr Judge Supreme Court of Grenada; Leader of St Lucia Labour Party 1974–82; Prime Minister of Saint Lucia, Minister of Finance, Home Affairs, Information and Tourism 1979–81, Minister without Portfolio 1981–82, Minister of Legal Affairs Jan.–May 1982.

LOUISY, Dame Calliopa Pearlette, GCMG PhD; Saint Lucia politician and educator; b. 8 June 1946, Laborie, Saint Lucia; d. of Rita Louisy; ed St Joseph's Convent Secondary School, Univ. of the West Indies, Université Laval, Québec, Univ. of Bristol, UK; grad. teacher St Joseph's Convent 1969–72, 1975–76; tutor Saint Lucia 'A' Level Coll. 1976–1981, Prin. 1981–86; Dean Sir Arthur Lewis Community Coll. 1986–94, Vice-Prin. 1994–95, Prin. 1996–97; Gov.-Gen. of Saint Lucia 1997–; Commonwealth Scholar 1972; Hon. LLD (Bristol) 1999; Int. Woman of the Year 1998; Grand Cross Order of St Lucia 1997. *Publications:* A Guide to the Writing of Creole 1981, The Changing Role of the Small State in Higher Education 1994, Dilemmas of Insider Research in a Small Country Setting 1997. *Leisure interests:* the performing arts, culture, gardening. *Address:* Government House, Morne Fortune, Castries, Saint Lucia, West Indies. *Telephone:* (758) 452-2481 (Office). *Fax:* (758) 453-2731. *E-mail:* govgenslu@candw.lc (Home).

LOULY, Lt-Col Mohamed Mahmoud Ould Ahmed; Mauritanian politician and army officer; Minister for Control and Investigation July 1978–Jan. 1979, in charge of the Perm. Secr. of the Mil. Cttee for Nat. Recovery (CMRN) Jan.–March 1979, for the Civil Service and Higher, Tech. and Vocational Training March–May 1979; Pres. of Mauritania 1979–80. *Address:* c/o Office du Président, Comité de Redressement National, Nouackchott, Mauritania.

LOUNASMAA, Olli Viktor, MS, DPhil; Finnish physicist; b. 20 Aug. 1930, Turku; s. of Aarno Lounasmaa and Inki Lounasmaa (née von Hellens); m. Inkeri Kupiainen 1951; two d.; ed Univs of Helsinki, Oxford and Turku; Resident Research Assoc., Argonne Nat. Lab., Chicago 1960–65; Prof. of Tech. Physics, Helsinki Univ. of Technology 1965–70; Prof., Acad. of Finland 1970–95; Dir Low Temperature Lab., Helsinki Univ. of Tech. 1968–95; Visiting Prof. in USA, Japan, India, Germany; Chair. Ministry of Educ. Working Groups on basic research 1980, 1984; Assessor of Math. Sciences for Ministry of Educ. 1995; fmr Pres. Comm. on Cryophysics, Int. Inst. of Refrigeration; fmr Chair. Very Low Temperature Physics Comm., Int. Union of Pure and Applied Physics; fmr mem. Int Cryogenic Engineering Comm., Exec. Cttee European Physical Soc.; mem. Finnish Acad. of Tech. Sciences 1965, Finnish Acad. of Sciences and Letters 1969 (Pres. 1992); Academician (Finland) 1997; Fellow American Physical Soc. 1986; Foreign mem. Royal Swedish Acad. of Sciences 1974, Societas Scientiarum Fennica 1976, Academia Europaea 1990, NAS 1998; Hon. mem. Finnish Physical Soc. (Chair. 1967); Commdr, First Class, Order of White Rose of Finland; Commdr Order of the Lion of Finland; Dr hc (Helsinki) 1990, (Tampere Univ. of Tech.) 1992, (Helsinki Univ. of Tech.) 1998; Hon. MD (Helsinki) 2000; Homén Prize 1969, Emil Aaltonen Foundation Prize 1973, Finnish Cultural Foundation Prize 1978, Fritz London Memorial Award (USA) 1984, Körber-Stiftung Prize for the Advancement of European Science (Germany) 1987, Finnish Govt Inventor's Prize 1990, Prof. of the Year Award 1991, Forschungspreise of the Alexander von Humboldt Stiftung (Germany), Wihuri Int. Prize (Finland) 1994, P. L. Kapitza Gold Medal (Russia) 1995, Italgas Prize for Physics (Italy) 1995, Mendelssohn Prize and Gold Medal (UK) 1996. *Publications:* Experimental Principles and Methods Below 1K; 220 scientific papers. *Leisure interests:* gardening, travelling. *Address:* Low Temperature Laboratory, Box 2200, Helsinki University of Technology, 02015 Hut Espoo (Office); Ritokalliontie 21 B, 00330 Helsinki, Finland (Home). *Telephone:* (9) 4512952 (Office); (9) 2215178; (9) 481541 (Home). *Fax:* (9) 4512969 (Office); (9) 2215178 (Home). *E-mail:* olli.lounasmaa@hut.fi (Office). *Website:* boojum.hut.fi/personnel/lounasmaa/ (Office).

LOURDUSAMY, HE Cardinal Simon; Indian ecclesiastic; b. 5 Feb. 1924, Kalleri, Pondicherry; ordained 1951; consecrated Bishop (Titular Church of Sozusa, Libya) 1962; Titular Archbishop of Philippi 1964; Archbishop of Bangalore 1968–71; cr. Cardinal 1985; Sec. Congregation for the Evangelization of Peoples 1973–85; Pres. Pontifical Missionary Work. *Address:* Congregation for the Eastern Churches, Palazzo dei Convertendi, Via della Conciliazione 34, 00193 Rome (Office); Palazzo dei Convertendi, Via dei Corridori 64, 00193 Rome, Italy (Home).

LOUTFY, Aly, PhD; Egyptian fmr politician and professor of economics; b. 6 Oct. 1935, Cairo; s. of Mahmoud Loutfy; m. Eglal Mabrouk 1966; one s.; ed Ain Shams and Louzan Univs; joined staff, Faculty of Commerce Ain Shams Univ. 1957, Prof. and Chair. Dept of Econs 1980; Prof. High Inst. of Co-operative and Admin. Studies; Part-time Prof. Inst. of Arab Research and Studies, Cairo; mem. Bd of Dirs Bank of Alexandria 1977–78, Bank of Commerce and Devt (Cairo) 1981–; mem. Legis., Political Science and Econ. Asscn 1977, Delta Sugar Co. 1978, Bank of Commerce and Devt 1980; Minister of Finance 1978–80; Prime Minister of Egypt 1985–86; Speaker of the Shoura Council 1985–89; Ideal Prof. Award, Egyptian Univs 1974, Gold Mercury Int. Award 1979. *Publications:* Economic Evolution, Economic Development, Economic Planning, Studies on Mathematical Economics and Econometrics, Financing Problems in Developing Countries, Industrialization Problems in Under-Developed Countries; 30 research papers in economics in Arabic, French and English. *Leisure interests:* tennis, reading, travel. *Address:* 29 Ahmed Heshmat Street, Zamalek, Cairo, Egypt (Home). *Telephone:* 7366068.

LOUVIER, Alain; French composer and conductor; b. 13 Sept. 1945, Paris, France; s. of René Louvier and Marthe Louvier (née Fournier); one s. one d.; ed Centre Nat. de Télé-Enseignement, Conservatoire Nat. Supérieur de Musique, Paris; Dir Conservatoire Nat. de Région, Boulogne-Billancourt 1972–86; Dir Conservatoire Nat. Supérieur de Musique, Paris 1986–91, Prof. of Musical Analysis 1991–; Prix de Rome 1968, Arthur Honegger Award 1975,

Paul Gilson Award 1981. *Works include:* Chant des limbes (for orchestra) 1969, 3 Atmosphères (for clarinet and orchestra) 1974, Le Clavecin non tempéré 1978, Messe des Apôtres 1978, Casta Diva (with Maurice Béjart) 1980, Poèmes de Ronsard (for voice ensemble and chamber orchestra) 1984, Envol d'écailles (for flute, viola and harp) 1986, Chant des aires (for 25 flutes) 1988, L'Isola dei Numeri 1992, Itinéraires d'outre-rêve 1994, Un gamelan à Paris 1995, Concerto for alto 1996, Météores (for two pianos and orchestra) 1998, String Quartet 1999, Eclipse (for flute and string trio) 2000, Une cloche de feu rose dans les nuages (for piano and 11 voices) 2000, Nuit de feu, Rumeur d'espace 2001. *Publications:* L'Orchestre 1997, Les claviers de lumière 2002. *Leisure interests:* botany and entomology. *Address:* CNSMDP, 209 avenue Jean Jaurès, 75019 Paris (Office); 53 avenue Victor Hugo, 92100 Boulogne-Billancourt, France (Home). *Telephone:* 1-48-25-14-68 (Home). *Fax:* 1-48-25-10-92 (Home). *E-mail:* alainlouvier@minitel.net (Home).

LOUW, Eugene, BA, LLB; South African politician and lawyer; b. 15 July 1931, Cape Town; s. of Anath Louw and Johanna de Jager; m. Hantie Phyfer 1964; three s. one d.; ed Bellville High School and Univ. of Stellenbosch; Chair. Students' Council, Univ. of Stellenbosch 1957; attorney, pvt. practice, Durbanville 1964–79, 1993–; Mayor of Durbanville 1967–72; mem. Parl. for Durbanville 1974–79, Malmesbury 1972–74, Paarl 1989–94; Admin. of Cape Prov. 1979–89; Minister of Home Affairs 1989–92, of Defence and Public Works 1992–93; Chair. and Sr Partner Louw and Coetzee 1994–; Chair. Nat. Huguenot Tercentenary Festival Cttee 1988, Capab 1982–88, Nat. Dias Quincentenary Festival Cttee 1988, Constitutional Investigation Cttee into Regional Local Govt; Patron, W Prov. Rugby Union 1979–89; Abe Bailey Travel Bursary Holder; Alumnus of the Year Award (Stellenbosch Univ.) 1993; recipient of 7 hon. citizenships; four public buildings named after him. *Address:* Louw and Coetzee, 35 Main Road, 7550 Durbanville (Office); 10 Watsonia Close, Plattekloof, 7500 Parow (Home); P.O. Box 15432, Panorama 7506, South Africa. *Telephone:* (21) 9763180 (Office); (21) 9305624 (Home); (21) 9305620. *Fax:* (21) 9764288 (Office); (21) 9305621 (Home). *E-mail:* louwcoet@mweb.co.za.

LOUW, Michael James Minnaar, BA; South African civil servant; b. 9 Nov. 1939; m.; three c.; ed Orange Free State Univ.; with Dept of Labour; with Directorate for Mil. Intelligence, South African Defence Force (SADF) 1964–69; joined Bureau for State Security (became Nat. Intelligence Service) 1969, Special Adviser to Dir-Gen., Deputy Dir-Gen. 1988–92, Dir-Gen. 1992–94, Chief 1994–. *Address:* Private Bag X3, Hatfield 0028, South Africa.

LOUW, Raymond; South African publisher and editor; b. 13 Oct. 1926, Cape Town; s. of George K. E. Louw and Helen K. Louw (née Finlay); m. Jean Ramsay Byres 1950; two s. one d.; ed Parktown High School, Johannesburg; reporter on Rand Daily Mail 1946–50, Worthing Herald 1951–52, North-Western Evening Mail 1953–54, Westminster Press Provincial Newspapers (London) 1955–56; Night News Ed. Rand Daily Mail 1958–59, News Ed. 1960–65, Ed. 1966–77; News Ed. Sunday Times 1959–60; Chair. SA Morning Newspaper Group 1975–77; Gen. Man. SA Associated Newspapers 1977–82; Ed. and Publr Southern Africa Report 1982–; Chair. Media Defence Fund 1989–94, Campaign for Open Media 1985–94 (now merged as Freedom of Expression Inst., Chair. 1994–96); New Era Schools Trust; mem. Task Group on Govt Communications 1996; mem. Exec. Bd, Int. Press Inst., London, 1979–87, Fellow 1994; mem. Independent Media Comm. 1994; chosen by Int. Press Inst. to travel to Cameroon to make plea for release from jail of Pius Njawe (Ed. of Le Messager) 1998; Pringle Medal for services to journalism 1976, 1992. *Publications:* Four Days in Lusaka – Whites from 'Home' in talks with the ANC 1989, Report on the media situation in South Africa (for UNESCO) 1994; narrative for Nelson Mandela Pictorial Biography by Peter Magubane; numerous papers and articles on the media and press freedom. *Leisure interests:* sailing, walking, travel, wildlife. *Address:* Southern Africa Report, P.O. Box 261579, Excom, Johannesburg 2023; 23 Duncombe Road, Forest Town, Johannesburg 2193, South Africa (Home). *Telephone:* (11) 646-8790 (Office); (11) 646-8790 (Home). *Fax:* (11) 646-2596 (Office); (11) 646-2596 (Home). *E-mail:* rlouw@sn.apc.org (Office). *Website:* www.sareport.co.za (Office).

LOVE, Courtney; American rock musician; b. 1967; m. Kurt Cobain (deceased); one d. one s.; mem. rock band Hole (f. in LA 1989). *Films:* The People vs. Larry Flynt 1996, Basquiat 1996, Life 1997, Man on the Moon 1999. *Recordings include:* Retard Girl 1990, Pretty on the Inside 1991, Beautiful Son (single) 1993, Live Through This 1994. *Address:* c/o David Geffen Co., 9130 W Sunset Boulevard, Los Angeles, CA 90069, USA. *Website:* www.holemusic.com.

LØVEID, Cecilie Meyer; Norwegian playwright and poet; b. 21 Aug. 1951, Mysen; d. of Erik Løveid and Ingrid Meyer; m. Bjørn H. Ianke 1978; one s. two d.; ed arts and crafts school in Bergen and studies in graphic design, theatre history and drama; mem. editorial staff, Profil (magazine) 1969; Sec. Norsk Forfattersentrum, Vestlandsardelingen 1974; Teacher, Writing Arts Centre, Bergen 1986; mem. Literary Council, Den norske Fordatterforening 1987; Prix Italia 1982; Aschehons Prize; Donblans Prize. *Publications:* Most (novel) 1972, Sug (novel) 1979, Måkespisere (radio play) 1982, Balansedame (play) 1986, Maria Q. (play) 1991, Rhindøtrene (play) 1996. *Leisure interests:* old wooden toys, walking in the mountains, swimming. *Address:* Huitfeldtsgt. 36, 0253 Oslo, Norway. *Telephone:* 22-83-05-63. *Fax:* 22-83-43-73.

LOVELL, Sir (Alfred Charles) Bernard, Kt, OBE, PhD, MSc, FRS; British radio astronomer; b. 31 Aug. 1913, Oldland Common, Glos.; s. of Gilbert Lovell and Emily Laura Lovell (née Adams); m. Mary Joyce Chesterman 1937 (died 1993); two s. three d.; ed Bristol Univ.; Asst Lecturer in Physics, Univ. of Manchester 1936–39, Lecturer 1945–47, Sr Lecturer 1947–49, Reader 1949–51, Prof. of Radio Astronomy 1951–81, Emer. Prof. 1981–; with Telecommunications Research Est. 1939–45; Founder and Dir Nuffield Radio Astronomy Labs, Jodrell Bank 1945–81; Fellow, Royal Soc. 1955; Pres. Royal Astronomical Soc. 1969–71, British Asscn 1974–75; Vice-Pres. Int. Astronomical Union 1970–76; mem. Aeronautical Research Council 1955–58, Science Research Council 1965–70; Pres. Guild of Church Musicians 1976–89; Master Worshipful Co. of Musicians 1986–87; Hon. Foreign mem. American Acad. of Arts and Sciences 1955; Hon. mem. New York Acad. of Sciences 1960, Royal Northern Coll. of Music; Hon. Fellow Royal Swedish Acad. 1962, Inst. of Electrical Engineers 1967, Inst. of Physics 1975; Hon. Freeman City of Manchester 1977; Ordre du Mérite pour la Recherche et l'Invention 1962; Polish Order of Merit 1975; Hon. LLD (Edin.) 1961, (Calgary) 1966, (Liverpool) 1999; Hon. DSc (Leicester) 1961, (Leeds) 1966, (Bath, London) 1967, (Bristol) 1970; Hon. DUniv (Stirling) 1974, (Surrey) 1975; Royal Medal of Royal Soc. 1960, Daniel and Florence Guggenheim Int. Astronautics Award 1961. Maitland Silver Medal, Inst. of Structural Engineers 1964, Churchill Gold Medal, Soc. of Engineers 1964, Benjamin Franklin Medal, Royal Soc. of Arts 1980, Gold Medal, Royal Astronomical Soc. 1981. *Publications:* Science and Civilisation 1939, World Power Resources and Social Development 1945, Radio Astronomy 1952, Meteor Astronomy 1954, The Exploration of Space by Radio 1957, The Individual and the Universe (The Reith Lectures 1958), The Exploration of Outer Space 1962, Discovering the Universe 1963, Our Present Knowledge of the Universe 1967, Ed. (with Tom Margerison) The Explosion of Science: The Physical Universe 1967, The Story of Jodrell Bank 1968, The Origins and International Economics of Space Exploration 1973, Out of the Zenith: Jodrell Bank 1957–1970 1973, Man's Relation to the Universe 1975, P. M. S. Blackett – A Biographical Memoir 1976, In the Centre of Immensities 1978, Emerging Cosmology 1981, The Jodrell Bank Telescopes 1985, Voice of the Universe 1987, Pathways to the Universe (with Sir Francis Graham-Smith) 1988, Astronomer by Chance 1990, Echoes of War 1991. *Leisure interests:* music, gardening, cricket. *Address:* The Quinta, Swettenham, nr Congleton, Cheshire, England (Home). *Telephone:* (1477) 571254. *Fax:* (1477) 571954.

LOVELOCK, James Ephraim, CH, CBE, PhD, DSc, FRS; British scientist; b. 26 July 1919; s. of Tom Arthur Lovelock and Nellie Ann Elizabeth Lovelock (née March); m. 1st Helen Mary Hyslop 1942 (died 1989); two s. two d.; m. 2nd Sandra Jean Orchard 1991; ed Manchester Univ., London Univ.; staff scientist, Nat. Inst. for Medical Research 1941–61; Prof. of Chem. Baylor Univ. Coll. of Medicine, Tex., USA 1961–64; independent scientist 1964–; Fellow Harvard Univ. 1954–55, Yale Univ. 1958–59; Visiting Prof., Reading Univ. 1967–90; Pres. Marine Biology Asscn 1986–90; Hon. Visiting Fellow Green Coll. Oxford 1994–; Norbert Gerbier Prize of the World Meteorological Asscn 1988, Amsterdam Environment Prize 1990, Volvo Environment Prize 1996, Nonino Prize 1996, The Blue Planet Prize 1997. *Publications:* Gaia 1979, The Great Extinction (co-author) 1983, The Greening of Mars (co-author) 1984; The Ages of Gaia 1988, Gaia: The Practical Science of Planetary Medicine 1991, Homage to Gaia: The Life of an Independent Scientist 2000. *Leisure interests:* walking, reading novels, music. *Address:* Coombe Mill, St Giles on the Heath, Launceston, Cornwall, PL15 9RY, England.

LOWE, Douglas Ackley, AM; Australian fmr politician and administrator; b. 15 May 1942, Hobart; s. of Ackley Reginald and Dulcie Mary Lowe; m. Pamela June Grant 1963; two s. two d.; ed St Virgil's Coll.; worked as electrical fitter, Electrolytic Co.; State Sec. Tasmanian Section, Australian Labour Party 1965–69, State Pres. 1974–75; mem. Tasmania House of Ass. for Franklin 1969–81, Independent 1981–86; Minister for Housing 1972–74; Chief Sec. 1974–76; Deputy Premier 1975–77; Minister for Planning and Reorganization 1975–76, for Industrial Relations 1976–79, for Planning and Environment 1976, for Health 1976–77; Premier of Tasmania 1977–81; Minister for Manpower Planning 1977–79, for Econ. Planning and Devt 1979–80, for Energy 1979, Treas. 1980–81; mem. Tasmanian Legis. Council 1986–92; Deputy Govt Leader Tasmanian Legis. Council 1989–92; Exec. Officer, Tasmanian Br., Australian Medical Asscn 1992–; Del. to Australian Constitutional Convention; Queen's Silver Jubilee Medal 1977; State Pres., Tasmanian Swimming Inc. 1991–98, Life mem. 2000–; Australian Sports Medal 2000, Centenary Medal 2000. *Publication:* The Price of Power 1984. *Leisure interests:* swimming, tennis, fishing, football. *Address:* Australian Medical Association (Tasmanian Branch), 2 Gore Street, South Hobart, Tasmania 7004 (Office); 1 Michele Court, Berriedale, Tasmania 7010, Australia (Home). *Telephone:* (362) 232-047 (Office). *Fax:* (362) 236-469.

LOWE, Sir Frank Budge, Kt; British business executive; b. 23 Aug. 1941; s. of Stephen Lowe and Marion Lowe; m. Dawn Lowe 1991; two s. one d.; ed Westminster School; Man. Dir Collett Dickenson Pearce 1972–79; Founder and Chair. Lowe Group 1981; Founder and Chair. Octagon 1997; Dir Interpublic 1990–; Visiting Prof. Univ. Coll. London 1990–. *Leisure interests:* tennis, skiing, shooting. *Address:* The Lowe Group, 4 Eaton Gate, London, SW1W 9BJ, England.

LOWRY, Bates, PhB, MA, PhD; American art historian and museum director; b. 21 June 1923, Cincinnati, Ohio; s. of Bates Lowry and Eleanor Meyer; m.

Isabel Barrett 1946; two d.; ed Univ. of Chicago; Asst Prof. Univ. of Calif. 1954–57; Asst Prof. New York Univ., Inst. of Fine Arts 1957–59; Prof., Chair. Art Dept Pomona Coll. 1959–63, Prof. Brown Univ. 1963–68, Chair. Dept of Art 1965–68; Dir Museum of Modern Art, New York 1968–69; mem. Inst. for Advanced Study 1971; Prof., Chair. Art Dept, Univ. of Mass., Boston 1971–80; Dir Nat. Bldg Museum, Washington, DC 1980–87; mem. Bds of Dirs Soc. of Architectural Historians 1959–61, 1963–65, College Art Asscn 1962–65; Ed.-in-Chief, Art Bulletin 1965–67; Ed. College Art Asscn Monographs Series 1957–59, 1965–68; mem. Bd of Consultants, NEH 1975–81; mem. Editorial Bd Smithsonian Inst. Press 1981–87; Consultant, Getty Museum (Calif.) 1992; Chair. Nat. Exec. Cttee, Cttee to Rescue Italian Art (CRIA) 1966–76; Pres. The Dunlap Soc. 1974–92; Distinguished Visiting Prof., Univ. of Delaware 1988–89; Trustee, American Fed. of Arts; Guggenheim Fellowship 1972; Hon. mem. Accademia del Disegno (Florence); Grand Officer Star of Solidarity of Italy 1968; Gov.'s Award for Fine Arts, Rhode Island 1967. *Publications*: The Visual Experience 1961, Renaissance Architecture 1962, Muse or Ego 1963, The Architecture of Washington, DC 1977–80, Building a National Image 1985, Looking for Leonardo 1993, The Silver Canvas: Daguerreotype Masterpieces from the J. Paul Getty Museum 1998. *Address*: 255 Massachusetts Avenue, Boston, MA 02115, USA.

LOWRY, Glenn David, MA, PhD; American museum director; b. New York; s. of Warren Lowry and Laure Lowry (née Lynn); m. Susan Chambers 1974; three s.; ed Williams Coll., Harvard Univ.; Asst Curator Fogg Art Museum, Harvard Univ. 1978–80; research Asst in archaeological survey, Amalfi, Italy 1980; Curator (Oriental art) Museum of Art, Providence, RI 1981–82; Dir Joseph and Margaret Muscarelle Museum of Art, Williamsburg, Va 1982–84; Curator (Near Eastern Art) Freer Gallery, Smithsonian Inst., Washington 1984–90, Curatorial Co-ordinator 1987–89; Dir Art Gallery of Ont., Toronto 1990–95; Dir Museum of Modern Art, New York 1995–. *Publications include*: Fatehpur-Sikri: A Source Book 1985, From Concept to Context: Approaches to Asian and Islamic Calligraphy 1986, A Jeweler's Eye 1988, Timur and the Princely Vision: Persian Art and Culture in the Fifteenth Century 1989, Europe and the Arts of Islam: The Politics of Taste 1991. *Address*: Museum of Modern Art, 11 West 53rd Street, New York, NY 10019-5498, U.S.A. (Office).

LOZOYA-SOLIS, Jesús; Mexican paediatric surgeon; b. 3 March 1910, Parral, Chihuahua; s. of the late Leodegario Lozoya and Josefa Solis; m. 1st Susana Thalmann 1937 (divorced 1958); m. 2nd Margarita Prieto de Lozoya 1959; four s. one d.; ed Mil. Medical School of Mexico, Western Reserve Univ. Hosp., Cleveland, Ohio, Harvard Univ. Children's Hosp.; founder of paediatric surgery in Mexico 1940–52; Hosp. Infantil of Mexico 1940–52; Asst Prof. Pediatrics and Surgical Pediatrics 1940; Pres. Mexican Soc. of Pediatrics 1948–50; Pres. Mexican br. American Acad. of Pediatrics 1944–46; Pres. Laboratorios Infan of Mexico 1949–; Pres. Mexican Soc. Pediatric Surgery 1958–60; Founder and first Pres. Pan-American Pediatric Surgery Asscn 1966–68, World Symposium Pediatric Surgery 1965–68, World Fed. Pediatric Surgeons 1974; Founder of Dept of Pediatrics of Armed Forces of Mexico 1940 (Prof. Emer. Mexico Mil. Medical School), Nat. Inst. for the Protection of Children 1958; Senator of the Repub. 1952–55; Gov. of Chihuahua 1955–56; Gen. of Mexican Army 1949 (retd 1977); Guest Prof. of Pediatric Surgery at numerous univs; mem. American Acad. of Pediatrics 1944, American Coll. of Surgeons 1945, American Mil. Surgeons Asscn, Mediterranean Acad.; Pres. organizing Cttee World Fed. of Pediatric Surgery Asscns 1972–74; Pediatric Surgery Adviser to Int. Pediatric Asscn 1980–83; Hon. mem. American Pediatric Surgical Asscn, Pacific; Asscn of Pediatric Surgeons and many other pediatric surgery asscns awards; Chevalier, Hospitalare of Malta 1976, Medical Benefactor 1976. *Publications*: Paediatría Quirúrgica 1959, México ayer y hoy, visto por un pediátra mexicano 1965, La escuela médico militar de México 1977 and numerous articles. *Leisure interests*: history, philosophy, anthropology, writing, lecturing, gardening, travelling, riding. *Address*: Calzada Tlalpan 4515, México 22, DF, Mexico. *Telephone*: 5730094.

LU, (Hsiu-lien) Annette; Taiwanese politician; b. 7 June 1944, Taoyuan; ed Taiwan Prov. Taipei First Girls' High School, Nat. Taiwan Univ., Univ. of Illinois and Harvard Univ., USA; fmr Sr Specialist, Section Chief Exec. Law and Regulations Cttee of Exec. Yuan; participated in street demonstrations; sentenced to twelve years imprisonment 1979, released after 5 years and 4 months on medical parole; f. N American Taiwanese Women's Asscn, Clean Election Coalition 1985–90; organized and led Alliance for the Promotion of UN Membership for Taiwan 1991; Democratic Progressive Party (DPP) mem. Legis. Yuan for Taoyuan, mem. Foreign Affairs Cttee 1992–95; Nat. Policy Adviser to Pres. 1996; Magistrate for Taoyuan Co. 1996–99; Vice-Pres. of Taiwan 2000–; Chair. Third Global Summit of Women, Taiwan 1994; f. Centre for Women's and Children's Safety; World Peace Prize 2001. *Publications*: (novels) These Three Women, Empathy; (non-fiction) New Feminism, I Love Taiwan, Viewing Taiwan from Abroad, Retrying the Formosa Case. *Address*: Office of the President, Chiehshou Hall, 122 Chunking, South Road, Sec. 1, Taipei 100, Taiwan (Office). *Telephone*: (2) 23718889 (Office). *Fax*: (2) 23611604 (Office). *E-mail*: public@mail.oop.gov.tw (Office). *Website*: www.oop .gov.tw (Office).

LU DAOPEI; Chinese medical scientist; b. Oct. 1931, Shanghai; ed Tongji Medical Coll.; doctor, doctor-in-charge, Chief Doctor, Prof. Dir of Internal Medicine, People's Hosp. of Beijing Medical Coll.1955–; Fellow, Chinese Acad.

of Eng 1996–; Vice-Chair. Chinese Medical Soc.; initiator of bone-marrow transplants in China. *Address*: 42 Bei Lishi Lu, Beijing 100044, People's Republic of China (Office). *Telephone*: (10) 68314422 (Office).

LU GONGXUN; Chinese party official; b. 1933, Shuoxian Co., Shanxi Prov.; joined CCP 1950; alt. mem. 12th CCP Cen. Cttee 1982, 13th Cen. Cttee 1987; Sec. CCP Cttee, Zuoyun Co., Shanxi Prov. 1982–83, Chair. Standing Cttee of People's Congress, Shanxi Prov. 1993; alt. mem. Cen. Cttee 1987; mem. CCP Cttee, Shanxi 1983–, Deputy Sec. 1988–. *Address*: Shanxi Provincial Chinese Communist Party, Taiyuan, Shanxi, People's Republic of China.

LU GUANQIU; Chinese business executive; b. Dec. 1944, Xiaoshan, Zhejiang Prov.; Founder and Pres. Hangzhou Wanxiang Group (producer and exporter of cardan joints). *Address*: Wanxiang Group, Hangzhou, Zhejiang Province, People's Republic of China (Office).

LU HAO; Chinese politician; b. April 1947, Changli, Hebei Prov.; ed Shenyang School of Chemical Eng, Dalian Eng Coll., Lanzhou Univ.; joined CCP 1981; technician PLA 1968–75; teaching asst, political tutor, Lanzhou Univ. 1982; Vice-Dir then Dir-Gen. Office of CCP Gansu Prov. Cttee 1982–85; Vice-Dir then Dir Org. Dept of CCP Gansu Prov. 1985–96; Sec CCP Lanzhou City Cttee 1996–2000; Acting Gov. Gansu Prov. 2001. *Address*: Office of the Governor, Gansu Provincial People's Government, Lanzhou, Gansu Province, People's Republic of China (Office).

LU JIANXUN; Chinese telecommunications engineer; b. 11 Sept. 1929, Beijing; ed Tsinghua Univ.; fmrly Pres. China Ships Research Inst.; Chair. Standing Cttee Information and Electronic Eng Dept, Chinese Acad. of Eng; Fellow Chinese Acad. of Eng; Vice-Chair. China Shipbuilding Eng Soc.; presided over research and devt of communications system on submarines, pioneered research on long-wave communications and developed a range of communications equipment and systems for testing intercontinental ballistic missiles. *Address*: 2A Shuangquanbao, Deshengmen Wai, Beijing 100085, People's Republic of China (Office). *Telephone*: (10) 64876644 (Office). *Fax*: (10) 64881612 (Office). *E-mail*: ljx@public.bta.net.cn (Office).

LU LIANGSHU; Chinese agronomist; b. 3 Nov. 1924, Shanghai; s. of Lu Zezhi and Hu Lian; m. Yin Xueli 1950; three s.; deputy to 3rd NPC 1965, 5th NPC 1978; Deputy to 13th CCP 1988; Deputy Dir Science and Tech. Committee, Ministry of Agric. 1983; Pres. Chinese Acad. of Agricultural Sciences 1982–87; Pres. of Chinese Asscn of Agricultural Science Socs 1982–92; a Vice-Pres. Chinese Acad. of Eng (CAE) 1994–. *Publications*: Food Composition and Development Strategy in China, Compilation on China's Agricultural Devt Strategy and the Progress of Science and Tech. *Leisure interests*: swimming, music. *Address*: Chinese Academy of Agricultural Sciences, 30 Baishiqiao Road, Beijing 100081, People's Republic of China. *Telephone*: (10) 68975516 (Office). *Fax*: (10) 62174142 (Office). *E-mail*: xujm@mail.caas.net.cn (Office).

LU PING; Chinese civil servant; b. 7 Oct. 1927, Shanghai; m. Xi Liang 1949; one s. one d.; ed St John's Univ., Shanghai; Deputy Dir of Hong Kong and Macao Affairs Office, State Council 1987–90, Dir 1990–97; mem. 14th CCP Cen. Cttee 1992–97; Vice-Chair. Preparatory Working Cttee for the Hong Kong Special Admin. Region 1993–95, Sec.-Gen. 1995–; Dir Hong Kong Govt Admin. Dept 1994–97. *Address*: State Council, Zhong Nan Hai, Beijing, People's Republic of China.

LU QIHUI; Chinese sculptor; b. 8 April 1936, Shanghai; d. of Ren Jin; m. Fang Zen-Xian 1960; one s. one d.; ed Sculpture Dept, Cen. Art Acad., E China Branch 1955–61; teacher, Shanghai Art College 1961–65; professional sculptor, Shanghai Oil Painting and Sculpture Inst. 1965–, Prof. 1988–; mem. Chinese Artists' Asscn. *Works include*: Transplanting rice seedlings, workers group statues, Nat. Industrial Exhibition 1960, Statue of Child Labourers 1974, Sculpture for Chairman Mao Memorial Hall 1977, Statue of Lu Xun 1979, Angrily seeking Verses against Reign of Terror 1980, Plateau in the Morning Sun 1986, Bada, an ancient Chinese Artist 1987 (exhibited New York in Contemporary Oil Painting from the PRC), The Emotion at Plateau 1989, Zhang Zhong-Jingi a Pioneer of Chinese Medical Science 1990 (bronze), Song Jie-Cai Rang of a Tibetan 1990 (stone), Hawk-dancing 1991 (statue), Wang Ge-Ji memorial (bronze) 1992, Magic painter Mar-Lang (bronze) 1993, Wu Chan-Shu memorial (bronze), one for Shanghai Memorial Hall 1994, one for Japanese Fakuoka 1995, Xia-Qiu-Son (bronze) 1995, Balzac Memorial (bronze), Garden of Famous People, Shanghai 1996, Sampan (bronze), for Shanghai Stadium 1997, Wu Fu-Zhi memorial (bronze) 1998, The Sound of Spring (forging) 2001. *Leisure interests*: Chinese painting, sport. *Address*: 100-301, 398 Xin-Pei Road, Xin-Zuan, Shanghai, People's Republic of China. *Telephone*: (21) 64987283.

LU QIKENG; Chinese mathematician; b. 17 May 1927, Fushan City, Guangdong Prov.; m. Mulan Zhang 1962; one s. one d.; ed Zhongshan Univ.; research fellow, Math. Inst. Academia Sinica 1978–; Deputy Dir of Math. Inst. 1981–83; Research Prof. Shantou Univ. 1994–; mem. Dept Math. and Physics, Academia Sinica 1980–92, Chinese Math. Soc. 1952–, Chinese Acad. of Sciences 1980–, American Math Soc. 1992–, AAAS (USA) 1996–, New York Acad. of Sciences 1997–; Hua Loo Keng Prize 1992. *Publications*: The Classical Manifolds and Classical Domains 1994, New Results of Classical Manifolds and Classical Domains 1997. *Leisure interest*: classical music. *Address*: Institute of Mathematics, Shantou University, Beijing 515043, People's Republic of China. *Telephone*: (10) 6254-1841 (Office); (10) 6255-5142 (Home). *Fax*: (10) 6256-8356.

LU RONGJING; Chinese administrator; b. 1933, Lujiang Co., Anhui Prov.; joined CCP 1954; Gov. Anhui Prov. 1987–93; Sec. CCP Anhui Prov. Cttee 1988–98; mem. CPPCC Standing Cttee 1999–; mem. 14th CCP Cen. Cttee 1992–97, 15th CCP Cen. Cttee 1997–2002. *Address:* c/o Anhui Provincial Government, 1 Changjang Road, Hefei City, Anhui Province, People's Republic of China.

LU RUIHUA, MA; Chinese politician; b. Nov. 1938, Chaozhou City, Guangdong Prov.; ed Zhongshan Univ.; joined CCP 1972; fmrly engineer, Deputy Dir, Dir Foshan Analytical Instrument Factory; fmrly Mayor of Foshan, Vice-Chair. Foshan City Econ. Cttee, mem. Standing Cttee CCP Guangdong Prov. Cttee, mem. then Deputy Sec. Standing Cttee CCP Foshan City Cttee, Deputy 7th NPC 1988, 8th NPC 1996; Vice-Gov. Guangdong Prov. 1991–96, Gov. 1996–; alt. mem. 14th CCP Cen. Cttee 1992–97, mem. 15th CCP Cen. Cttee 1997–2002. *Address:* People's Government of Guangdong, Guangzhou, Guangdong Province, People's Republic of China.

LU SHENGRONG; Chinese sports official; b. 1940, Beijing; ed Beijing Foreign Languages Inst.; Vice-Pres. Int. Badminton Fed. 1984–93, Pres. 1993–2001; mem. IOC 1996–. *Address:* c/o State General Bureau for Physical Culture and Sports, 9 Tiyuguan Road, Chongwen District, Beijing, People's Republic of China.

LU SHENGZHONG, MA; Chinese artist; b. 4 Jan. 1952, Pingdu Co., Shandong Prov.; s. of Lu Wanjin and Jiang Yongzhen; m. Liu Guangjun 1980; one s.; ed Cen. Acad. of Fine Arts; specializes in Chinese folk arts; Instructor at Cen. Acad. of Fine Arts; Deputy Sec.-Gen. Chinese Asscn of Fine Artists. *Exhibitions include:* China Avant Garde, Asia and Pacific Museum, USA, Paper Cut Art: Exhibition of Calling the Souls. *Works include:* When Heaven and Earth are in Harmony, All Living Things, Thrive, Life, Solitary Walking, Magic and Acrobatics. *Publications include:* Chinese Folk Papercut, Chinese Folk New Year Paintings, Arts from My Mother, Solitary Walk on the Holy Road, Outline of Chinese Folk Woodcut Print, Words of Calling the Souls. *Address:* Central Academy of Fine Arts, 5 Xiaowei Hutong, Beijing, People's Republic of China.

LU SHIH-PENG, BA; Taiwanese professor of history; b. 16 Sept. 1928, Kaoyu, Chiang Su; s. of the late Lu Chun-tai and Lu Chia Chu-yin; m. Julia Weichun; one s. one d.; ed Nat. Taiwan Univ., Taipei, Harvard Univ., USA; Teaching Asst, Nat. Taiwan Univ., Taipei 1953–55; Research Asst, Academica Sinica, Taipei 1955–58; Lecturer, Tunghai Univ., Taichung 1958–63, Assoc. Prof. 1963–67, Prof. of History 1967–, Dir Evening School 1972–81, Chair. Dept of History 1981–87, Dean Coll. of Arts 1988–94; Visiting Scholar, Harvard Univ. 1961–63; Outstanding Youth, China Youth Corps 1952; Outstanding Prof., Ministry of Educ. 1992. *Publications:* Vietnam during the period of Chinese Rule 1964, The Modern History of China 1979, The Contemporary History of China 1992. *Address:* Tunghai University, 181 Tunghai harbour Road, Sec. 3, Taichung, Taiwan (Office). *Telephone:* (4) 3590121 (Office). *Fax:* (4) 3590361 (Office). *E-mail:* kpwang@mail.thu.edu.tw (Office).

LU WENFU; Chinese writer; b. 1928, Taixing Co., Jiangsu Prov.; ed Huazhong Univ.; Vice-Chair. of Chinese Writers' Asscn 1985–; joined Int. PEN in New York 1986. *Publications:* Hidden Deep in the Lane, Dedication (Nat. Prize 1978), The Pedlar's Family (Nat. Prize 1980), Fence (Nat. Prize 1983), The Gourmet (Nat. Prize 1984). *Address:* Suzhou Branch of the Federation of Literary and Art Circles, Suzhou City, Jiangsu Province, People's Republic of China.

LU XUEYI; Chinese economist; b. 1933, Wuxi, Jiangsu Prov.; ed Beijing Univ. Inst. of Philosophy, Chinese Acad. of Social Sciences; Vice-Dir Rural Devt Research Inst., Vice-Dir then Dir Inst. of Sociology, Chinese Acad. of Social Sciences 1985–. *Publications:* A Golden Time for Agricultural Development, Contemporary Chinese Countryside, Contemporary Chinese Peasants. *Address:* Institute of Sociology, Chinese Academy of Social Sciences, Beijing, People's Republic of China.

LU YANSHAO; Chinese artist; b. 26 June 1909, Jiading Cty., Shanghai, Subei Yancheng; s. of Lu Yunbo and Zhu Xuan; m. Zhu Yanyin 1929; three s. two d.; Prof. Zhejiang Acad. of Fine Arts 1982–; Deputy 6th NPC 1983–; Bd Dir All-China Artists' Asscn; Pres. Zhejiang Landscape Soc.; mem. NPC. *Publications:* Some Opinions on Landscape Painting 1980, Manual of Lu Yanshao's Studio Drawings 1985, Lu Yanshao's Autobiography 1985.

LU YONGXIANG; Chinese university professor and government official; b. 28 April 1942, Ningbo City, Zhejiang Prov.; s. of Lu Zhau and Lee Feng; m. Diao Linlin 1966; one s. one d.; ed Zhejiang Univ., Tech. Univ. of Aachen, Germany; Asst Lecturer, Dept of Mechanical Eng, Zhejiang Univ. 1964–79, Assoc. Prof. 1981–83, Full Prof., Dir Inst. of Fluid Power Transmission and Control 1983–, Vice-Pres. Univ. 1985–88, Pres. 1988–; Pres. Zhejiang Univ. 1989–95; Vice-Pres. Chinese Acad. of Sciences 1993–97, Pres. 1997–, Academician 1991; Vice-Chair. China Asscn for Science and Tech. 1986–96; mem. Chinese Acad. of Eng 1993, Academic Degrees Comm. of State Council 1986–; TWAS 1990; Vice-Pres. Third World Acad. of Sciences 1999–; Del. NPC 1983–91; alt. mem. 14th CCP Cen. Cttee, mem. 15th CCP Cen. Cttee 1997–2002; mem. 4th Presidium of Depts, Chinese Acad. of Sciences 2000–; Second Prize for Nat. Invention 1988, Third Prize 1989, Higher Eng Educ. Prize of Nation 1989, Gao Hua Super Prize 1993, Rudolf Diesel Gold Medal (Germany) 1997 and many other awards and prizes. *Publications:* Electro-

hydraulic Proportional Technique 1988; more than 160 published papers and over 20 patents. *Leisure interests:* model aeroplanes, playing football. *Address:* China Academy of Sciences, 52 Sanlihe Road, Beijing 100864, People's Republic of China. *Telephone:* (10) 68597289. *Fax:* (10) 68512458. *E-mail:* engach@mail.cae.ac.cn (Office).

LU YOUMEI; Chinese engineer; b. 1934, Taicang Co., Jiangsu Prov.; ed Dept of River Structure and Hydropower Station Construction of E China Inst. of Water Conservancy; mem. CCP 1956–; engineer Bureau for Construction of Liujia Gorge Hydropower Station of Yellow River until 1970; posts in various bureaux of Ministry of Water Conservancy and Electric Power 1978–84; Vice-Minister of Water Conservancy and Electric Power 1984–88; Vice-Minister, Ministry of Energy Resources 1988–93; Pres. China Yangtze Three Gorges Project Construction; Vice Chair. Three Gorges Project Construction Cttee 1993–.

LUBBERS, Ruud (Rudolphus) Frans Marie; Netherlands politician; b. 7 May 1939, Rotterdam; s. of Paulus J. Lubbers and Wilhelmine K. Van Laack; m. Maria E J. Hoogeweegen 1962; two s. one d.; ed Erasmus Univ., Rotterdam; Sec. to Man. Bd, Lubbers Hollandia Eng Works 1963–65, Co-Dir 1965; mem. Bd Netherlands Christian Employers' Fed., Fed. of Mechanical and Electrical Eng Industries; mem. Programmes Advisory Council of Catholic Broadcasting Asscn; Minister of Econ. Affairs 1973–77; mem. Christian Democratic Appeal 1977, Parl. Leader 1978; mem. Second Chamber of States-Gen. (Parl.) 1977–2000; Prime Minister of the Netherlands 1982–94; Hon. Minister of State; UN High Commr for Refugees Oct. 2000–. *Address:* United Nations High Commissioner for Refugees, CP 2500, 1211 Geneva 2 dépôt, Switzerland (Office). *Telephone:* (22) 7398502 (Office). *Fax:* (22) 7397312 (Office). *E-mail:* hqpi00@unhcr.ch (Office). *Website:* www.unhcr.ch (Office).

LUBICH, Chiara; Italian religious movement leader; b. 22 Jan. 1920, Trento; d. of Luigi Lubich and Luigia Lubich; ed Teachers' Training Inst. and Faculty of Philosophy, Univ. of Venice; Founder and Pres. Focolare Movt, a worldwide spiritual movt based on the Gospels, currently active in 184 countries 1943–; participated in extraordinary Synod of Bishops 1985–99, Synod on the Vocation and Mission of the Laity 1987; Facilitator of inter-religious dialogue in Tokyo 1981, Thailand 1997, New York 1998, Washington 2000, India 2001; addressed Unity of Peoples UN Symposium, New York 1997, Switzerland 1998, Rome 2000; consultant, Pontifical Council for the Laity; Hon. Pres. World Conf. on Religion and Peace; Cross of Order of St Augustine of Canterbury 1981; Byzantine Cross, Phanar, Istanbul 1984; Cross of the South (Brazil) 1997; German Cross of Merit 2002 and other decorations; numerous hon. doctorates; Templeton Prize for Progress in Religion and Peace 1977, Plaque of St Catherine of Siena 1987, Ecumenical Augustan Peace Prize, Augsburg, Germany 1988, First Int. Prize Franciscan Int. Centre of Studies for Dialogue among Peoples 1993, Ardent Eagle of St Wenceslaus, Seal of City of Trent 1995, UNESCO Prize for Peace Educ. 1996, Human Rights Prize, Council of Europe 1998, Defender of Peace Award, India 2001. *Publications include:* 4 Vols of Spiritual Writings, Diary 1964/65 1967, It's a Whole new Scene 1969, Conversations with the Gen 1974, To the Gen 3, I 1974, II 1976, Why Have You Forsaken Me, the Key to Unity 1984, Encounters with the Orient 1986, On the Holy Journey 1987, From Scripture to Life 1991, Into the Light 1996, Journey to Heaven 1997, And Christmas Comes Back 1997, Where Life Lights Up 1998, Love Wins 1998, Christian Living Today 1998, Here and now 1999, United in His Name 2000, Heaven on Earth 2000, The Cry 2001. *Address:* 306 via di Frascati, 00040 Rocca di Papa, RM, Italy. *Telephone:* (06) 947989. *Fax:* (06) 94749320. *E-mail:* sif@focolare.org (Office). *Website:* www.focolare.org (Office).

LUBIMOV, Alexey Borisovich; Russian pianist; b. 16 Sept. 1944, Moscow; m. Aza Lubimova; one d.; ed Moscow State Conservatory; winner int. competitions in Rio de Janeiro 1965 (1st prize) and Montréal 1968; soloist, chamber musician, pianist, harpsichordist, organist; organizer and artistic dir of chamber ensembles and festivals of experimental character; well-known performer on historical keyboard instruments 1980–; teacher Moscow Conservatory 1968–75, Prof. 1997–; Prof. Univ. Mozarteum, Salzburg 1999–. *Address:* Klimentovskiy per. 9, Apt. 12, Moscow, Russia (Home). *Telephone:* (095) 951-62-51. *Fax:* (095) 152-28-29.

LUBIN, Steven, BA, MS, PhD; American pianist; b. 22 Feb. 1942, New York; s. of Jack Lubin and Sophie Lubin; m. Wendy Lubin 1974; two s.; ed Harvard Univ., Juilliard School, New York Univ.; piano studies with Lisa Grad, Nadia Reisenberg, Seymour Lipkin, Rosina Lhevinne, Beveridge Webster; recital and concert tours in USA, Canada, Mexico, England, France, The Netherlands, Spain, Italy, Germany, Austria, Finland and Ukraine; f. The Mozartean Players 1978–; mem. Faculty Juilliard School 1964–65, Aspen Music School 1967, Cornell Univ. 1971–75, Vassar Coll. 1971–75; Adjunct. Prof., School of the Arts, State Univ. of New York (SUNY) Purchase, NY 1975–; Martha Baird Rockefeller Grant 1968, Stereo Review Recording of the Year Award 1988, Kempner Distinguished Professor Award, State Univ. of New York, Purchase, NY 1999–2001. *Recordings:* complete Beethoven Piano Concertos, Mozart and Schubert Trios, Six Mozart Concertos as soloist and conductor and other solo and chamber music. *Publications:* articles in The New York Times, Keynote, Ovation, Keyboard Classics and Historical Performance, Brahms Soc. Newsletter 1999; contrib. to The Complete Schwanengesang 2000. *Leisure interests:* reading about relativity and quantum mechanics. *Address:* Conservatory of Music, School of the Arts, State University of New York, Purchase, NY 10577, USA.

LUBIS, Mochtar; Indonesian journalist; b. 7 March 1922, Padang, Sumatra; s. of Raja Pandapotan and Siti Madinah; m. Siti Halimah 1945; two s. one d.; joined Indonesian Antara News Agency 1945; Publr Indonesian Raya (daily) 1949–61, Ed. 1956–51, 1966; published and edited The Times of Indonesia 1952; now Dir-Gen. Press Foundation of Asia, Manila, Philippines; Chair. The Jakarta Acad.; Chair. Yayasan Obor Indonesia (books); Asst Ed. Worldpaper, Boston, USA; Chair. Editorial Bd, Solidarity Magazine, Manila; Pres. Magsaysay Award for the Press 1958, returned award 1995; mem. Bd Int. Press Inst.; mem. UNESCO Comm. for Communication Problems; Chair. Obor Indonesia Foundation; Nat. Literary Award 1953; Golden Pen of Freedom, Int. Fed. of Publrs 1967, Press Foundation of Asia. *Publications:* Pers and Wartawan, Tak Ada Esok, Si Djamal (short stories), Djalan Tak Ada Udjung, Korean Notebook, Perkenalan Di Asia Tenggara, Melawat Ke Amerika, Stories from Europe, Indonesia Dimata Dunia, Stories from China, A Road with No End (novel) 1952, Twilight in Djakarta 1963, Tiger! Tiger!, Subversive Notes, Love and Death 1976, Indonesia, Land under the Rainbow (history), Land under the Sun (a report on Indonesia Today) 1983, Bromocorah (short stories) 1987, Termites. *Leisure interests:* gardening, sailing, nature study. *Address:* Press Foundation of Asia, S & L Building, 3rd Floor, 1500 Roxas Boulevard, P.O. Box 1843, Metro Manila, Philippines (Office); Jalan Bonang No. 17, Jakarta 10320, Indonesia. *Telephone:* (2) 5253265 (Office); 331128; (2) 5224365. *E-mail:* pfa@pressasia.org (Office). *Website:* www.pressasia.org (Office).

LUBOVITCH, Lar; American choreographer; b. 9 April 1943, Chicago, Ill.; ed Univ. of Iowa, Juilliard School; danced in numerous modern, ballet and jazz cos; Founder and Artistic Dir Lar Lubovitch Dance Co. 1968–; has choreographed more than 60 dances for the co.; his works are included in repertoires of several major int. dance cos including New York City Ballet, American Ballet Theater, Paris Opera Ballet, Royal Danish Ballet, Stuttgart Ballet, White Oak Dance Project and Netherlands Dance Theatre; has created dances for ice-skaters including John Curry; Guggenheim Fellowship 1971. *Dances created include:* Whirligogs (music by Luciano Berio) 1969, The Time Before the Time After (After the Time Before) (Stravinsky) 1971, Les Noces (Stravinsky) 1976, Marimba (Steve Reich) 1976, Exultate, Jubilate (Mozart) 1977, Scriabin Dances (Scriabin) 1977, North Star (Philip Glass) 1978, Cavalcade (Reich) 1980, Beau Danube (Strauss) 1981, Big Shoulders (no music) 1983, A Brahms Symphony 1985, Concerto Six Twenty-Two (Mozart) 1986, Sleeping Beauty (Tchaikovsky; full-length televised ice-dancing version starring Robin Cousins and Rosalynn Sumners) 1987, Into the Woods (Sondheim) 1987, Musette (Poulenc) 1988, Rhapsody in Blue (Gershwin) 1988, Fandango (Ravel) 1989, Waiting for the Sunrise (Les Paul and Mary Ford) 1991, American Gesture (Charles Ives) 1992, The Red Shoes (Jule Styne; Astaire Award, Theater Devt Fund 1994) 1993, The Planets (Holst) 1994, Oklahoma! (Rodgers and Hammerstein) 1994, The King and I (Rodgers and Hammerstein) 1996, Adagio (Bach) 1996, Othello (Goldenthal) 1997, Meadow (Schubert, etc.) 1999, The Hunchback of Notre Dame (Menken) 1999, Men's Stories (Marshall) 2000, My Funny Valentine (Rodgers) 2001, Smile With My Heart (Laird) 2002. *Television:* The Sleeping Beauty 1987, Concerto Six Twenty-Two and North Star/Dancemaker 1988, Fandango/Pictures From the Edge 1989, The Planets 1995, Othello 2003. *Address:* Lar Lubovitch Dance Company, 229 West 42nd Street, 8th Floor, New York, NY 10036, USA. *Telephone:* (212) 221-7909. *Fax:* (212) 221-7938. *E-mail:* lubovitch@aol.com (Office).

LUBRANI, Uri; Israeli diplomatist; b. 7 Oct. 1926, Haifa; s. of Ahron Lubrani and Rose Lubrani; m. Sarah Levi 1953; four d.; ed Univ. of London; fmr Head of Chancery, Office of Foreign Minister, Office of Prime Minister, Adviser to Prime Minister on Arab Affairs; later Amb. to Uganda, Rwanda, Burundi, Ethiopia and Iran; now Govt Co-ordinator for Lebanese Affairs; in charge of airlift of 18,000 Ethiopian Jews (Falashas) to Israel 1991; head Israeli team, negotiations on release of Israeli hostages in Lebanon and Shia Muslim prisoners in Israel; head Israeli del. to bilateral peace talks with Lebanon, Washington, DC 1992; now Adviser to the Minister of Defence; DPhil hc (Ben-Gurion Univ.) 1991, (Beer) 1991; Jabotinsky Annual Award for Services to the Jewish People 1991, David Ben-Gurion Award. *Address:* Office of the Adviser to the Minister of Defence, Ministry of Defence, Hakirya, Tel Aviv, Israel. *Telephone:* 3-6975157. *Fax:* 3-6977358. *E-mail:* liban@mod.gov.il (Office).

LUCAS, Sir Colin Renshaw, Kt, MA, DPhil, FRHistS; British academic; b. 25 Aug. 1940; s. of the late Frank Renshaw Lucas and of Janine Charpentier; m. 1st Christiane Berchon de Fontaine Goubert 1964 (divorced 1975); one s.; m. 2nd Mary Louise Hume 1990; ed Sherborne School, Lincoln Coll. Oxford; Asst Lecturer, then Lecturer Sheffield Univ. 1965–69; Visiting Asst Prof. Indiana Univ., USA 1969–70; Lecturer Manchester Univ. 1970–73; Fellow Balliol Coll. Oxford, Lecturer in Modern History, Oxford Univ. 1973–90; Prof. Chicago Univ., USA 1990–94, Dean Div. of Social Sciences 1993–94; Master Balliol Coll. 1994–2001; Pro-Vice-Chancellor Oxford Univ. 1995–97, Vice-Chancellor 1997–2004; Officier des Arts et des Lettres; Chevalier, Ordre du Mérite (France), Légion d'honneur (France) 1998; Hon. DLitt (Lyon) 1989, (Sheffield) 2000, (Univ. of WA) 2000, (Glasgow) 2001, (Princeton) 2002, (Beijing) 2002. *Publications:* The Structure of the Terror 1973, Beyond the Terror (with G. Lewis) 1983, The Political Culture of the French Revolution (ed.) 1988; contribs to academic journals. *Address:* University Offices, Wellington Square, Oxford, OX1 2JD, England. *Telephone:* (1865) 270243 (Office). *Fax:* (1865) 270085 (Office). *E-mail:* vice-chancellor@admin.ox.ac.uk (Office).

LUCAS, Cornel, FRPS, FBIPP; British photographer; b. 12 Sept. 1923, London; s. of the late John Thomas Lucas and of Mary Elizabeth Lucas; m. Jennifer Susan Linden Travers 1960; three s. one d.; ed Westminster Univ.; RAF Photographic School 1941–46; mem. staff Two Cities Films, Denham, Pinewood Studios, Columbia Pictures, Universal Int. Films 1947–59; opened own studios No. 2, Chelsea Manor Studios, London 1959, Man. Dir 1959–; work in perm. collections of Nat. Portrait Gallery, Nat. Museum of Photography, Museum of Photography, Bradford, Royal Photographic Soc., Bath, Jersey Museum of Photography; Hon. mem. BAFTA; BAFTA Award for outstanding contrib. to British Film Industry. *Publication:* Heads and Tales 1988. *Leisure interests:* painting, music, gardening, golf. *Address:* 57 Addison Road, London, W14 8JJ, England. *Telephone:* (20) 7602-3219.

LUCAS, Craig, BFA; American playwright and screenwriter; b. 30 April 1951, Atlanta, Ga; s. of Charles Samuel Lucas and Eleanore Alltmont Lucas; ed Boston Univ.; Rockefeller and Guggenheim Fellowships; mem. Dramatists' Guild, PEN, Writers' Guild of America; Sundance Audience Award, Obie and Outer Critics' Award, Los Angeles Drama Critics' Award. *Plays:* Missing Persons 1980, Reckless 1983, Blue Window 1984, Prelude to a Kiss 1987 and The Scare 1989, God's Heart 1994, The Dying Gaul 1996, Savage Light (with David Schulner) 1996. *Musicals:* Marry Me a Little (anthology of songs by Stephen Sondheim) 1981, Three Postcards (music and lyrics by Craig Carnelia) 1987. *Films:* Blue Window 1987, Longtime Companion 1990, Prelude to a Kiss 1991, Reckless 1995. *Publications:* Anti-Naturalism 1989, Reckless and Blue Window 1989, Prelude to a Kiss 1991; several plays. *Address:* c/o Peter Franklin, William Morris Agency, 151 South El Camino Drive, Beverly Hills, CA 90212, USA.

LUCAS, George, BA; American film director; b. 14 May 1944, Modesto, Calif.; ed Univ. Southern Calif.; with Warner Bros. Studio; asst to Francis Ford Coppola on The Rain People, also dir documentary on making of that film; f. Lucasfilm Ltd; dir, co-author screenplay films THX-1138 1970, American Graffiti 1973; dir, author screenplay Star Wars 1977, also novel of same title 1977; Exec. Producer More American Graffiti 1979, The Empire Strikes Back 1980, Raiders of the Lost Ark 1981, Return of the Jedi 1982, Indiana Jones and the Temple of Doom 1984, Howard the Duck 1986, Labyrinth 1988, Willow 1988, Tucker: The Man and His Dream 1988, Mishima (co-exec. producer) 1985, Indiana Jones and the Last Crusade 1989, The Young Indiana Jones Chronicles (TV Series) 1992–93, Radioland Murders 1994; dir, author Star Wars Episode I: The Phantom Menace 1999, Star Wars Episode II: Attack of the Clones 2002; Dr hc (Univ. of Southern Calif.) 1994; Irving Thalberg Award 1992. *Address:* Lucasfilm Ltd, P.O. Box 2009, San Rafael, CA 94912, USA.

LUCAS, Robert Emerson; American economist; b. 1937, Yakima, Wash.; Prof. Univ. of Chicago 1975–80, John Dewey Distinguished Service Prof. 1980–; Fellow AAAS; mem. NAS; Assoc. Ed. Journal of Monetary Econs 1977–; Nobel Prize for Econs 1995. *Address:* Department of Economics, University of Chicago, 1126 E 59th Street, Chicago, IL 60637, USA.

LUCAS, Sarah, BA; British artist; b. 1962, London; d. of Irene Lucas; ed London Coll. of Printing, Goldsmiths Coll., London; works with variety of materials and media, including photographs, sculpture and installations. *Art exhibitions:* Penis Nailed to a Board, City Racing, London 1992, Sarah Lucas, Museum Boymans-van Beuningen, Rotterdam 1996, The Law, London 1997, Car Park, Ludwig Museum, Cologne 1997, The Fag Show, Sadie Coles HQ, London 2000, Sarah Lucas – Beyond the Pleasure Principle, The Freud Museum, London 2000, Sarah Lucas, Installation at Tate Modern, London 2002. *Dance:* Before and After: The Fall, The Michael Clark Co. (set design for a new work performed on tour) 2001. *Television:* Two Melons and a Stinking Fish (Illuminations for BBC TV/Arts Council) 1996, This Is Modern Art (Channel 4 six-part series) 1999, The History of Britart (BBC) 2001. *Publications:* subject of three biogs: Sarah Lucas (by Chris Dercon and Jan van Adrichem) 1996, Sarah Lucas – Self-Portraits and More Sex (by Victoria Combalia and Angus Cook) 2000, Sarah Lucas (by Matthew Collings) 2002. *Address:* c/o Sadie Coles HQ, 35 Heddon Street, London, W1B 4BP, England (Office). *Telephone:* (20) 7434-2227 (Office). *Fax:* (20) 7434-2228 (Office). *E-mail:* press@sadiecoles.com (Office). *Website:* www.sadiecoles.com (Office).

LUCAS GARCÍA, Gen. Fernando Romeo; Guatemalan politician; Minister of Nat. Defence 1975–76; Pres. of Guatemala 1978–82; Cand. for Partido Revolucionario and Partido Institucional Democrático.

LUCE, Charles F., LLB; American lawyer and business executive; b. 29 Aug. 1917, Platteville, Wis.; s. of James O. Luce and Wilma Grindell; m. Helen G. Oden 1942; two s. two d.; ed Univ. of Wisconsin Law School and Yale Law School; admitted to Wis. Bar 1941, Ore. Bar 1945, Wash. Bar 1946, New York Bar 1981; Law clerk to late Mr Justice Hugo Black, Supreme Court 1943–44; Attorney, Bonneville Power Admin., Portland, Ore. 1944–46; in pvt. law practice, Walla Walla, Wash. 1946–61; Bonneville Power Administrator 1961–66; Under-Sec. of the Interior 1966–67; Chair. Bd of Trustees, Consolidated Edison Co. of New York Inc. 1967–82, CEO 1967–81, Chair. Emer. 1982–; partner Preston, Ellis and Holman, Portland 1982–86; Special Counsel Metropolitan Life Insurance Co. 1987–94; Dir Emer. Metropolitan Life Insurance Co.; Trustee Henry M. Jackson Foundation; Trustee Emer. Columbia Univ.; mem. various advisory cttees, etc. *Address:* Consol Edison, 4 Irving Place, New York, NY 10003, USA.

LUCE, Henry, III, BA; American publisher, journalist and foundation administrator; b. 28 April 1925, New York; s. of Henry R. Luce and Lila Hotz Tyng; m. 1st Patricia Potter 1947 (divorced 1954); one s. one d.; m. 2nd Claire McGill 1960 (died 1971); three step-s.; m. 3rd Nancy Bryan Cassiday 1975 (died 1987); two step-s. (one deceased); m. 4th Leila Eliott Burton Hadley 1990; two step-s. two step-d.; ed Brooks School and Yale Univ.; served USNR 1943–46; Commdr's Asst, Hoover Comm. on Org. Exec. Branch of Govt 1948–49; Reporter, Cleveland Press 1949–51; Washington Corresp. Time Inc. 1951–53, Time writer 1953–55, Head New Bldg Dept 1956–60, Asst to Publr 1960–61, Circulation Dir Fortune and Architectural Forum 1961–64, House and Home 1962–64, Vice-Pres. 1964–80, Chief London Bureau 1966–68, Publr Fortune 1968–69, Publr Time 1969–72; Vice-Pres. for Corporate Planning and Dir Time Inc. 1967–89; Dir Time Warner Inc. 1989–96; Pres. and CEO Henry Luce Foundation 1958–90, Chair. and CEO 1990–2002, Chair. Emer. 2002–; Pres. Asscn of American Corresps in London 1968; Pres. The New Museum of Contemporary Art 1977–98; Chair. American Security Systems Inc.; mem. American Council for UN Univ., Foreign Policy Asscn (Gov., Medal 1997), Trustee, Eisenhower Exchange Fellowships, Princeton Theological Seminary, Center of Theological Inquiry, Coll. of Wooster, China Inst. in America, A Christian Ministry in the Nat. Parks, New York Historical Soc.; Pres. The Pilgrims; Chair. American Russian Youth Orchestra; Dir Nat. Cttee on US–China Relations, Fishers Island Devt Co.; Hon. LHD (St Michael's Coll., Long Island Univ., Pratt Inst.); Hon. LLD (Coll. of Wooster); Hon. DLitt (Cen. Philippine Univ.); Dr hc (Mapuce Inst. of Tech.); American Asscn of Museums Medal for Distinguished Philanthropy 1994, Cen. Park Conservancy Frederick Law Olmstead Award 1996, St Nicholas Soc. Medal 1998, Augustine Graham Medal, Brooklyn Museum of Art 2000, Conrado Benitez Medal, Philippine Univ. for Women 2000. *Leisure interest:* art collecting. *Address:* Suite 1500, 720 Fifth Avenue, New York, NY 10019 (Office); Mill Hill Road, Mill Neck, NY 11765, USA (Home); 4 Sutton Place, New York, NY 10022. *Telephone:* (212) 582-5531 (Office); (516) 922-0356 (Home); (212) 759-8640. *Fax:* (212) 246-1867 (Office); (212) 759-6831 (Home). *E-mail:* hl@hluce.org (Office).

LUCE, Baron (Life Peer), cr. 2000, of Adur in the County of West Sussex; **Richard Napier Luce,** Kt, PC, GCVO, DL; British politician (retd); b. 14 Oct. 1936, London; s. of the late Sir William Luce, GBE, KCMG and of Lady Luce (née Margaret Napier); m. Rose Helen Nicholson 1961; two s.; ed Wellington Coll. and Christ's Coll. Cambridge, Wadham Coll. Oxford; Subaltern, Wilts. Regiment, Nat. Service 1955–57; Dist Officer, Kenya 1961–63; Marketing Man. Gallaher Ltd 1963–65; Marketing Man. Spirella Co. of GB 1965–67; Dir Nat. Innovation Centre 1967–71; mem. European Advisory Bd Corning Glass Int. 1976–79; Dir (non-exec.) Booker Tate 1991–96, Meridian Broadcasting 1991–97; MP for Arundel and Shoreham 1971–74, for Shoreham 1974–92; Opposition Whip 1974–75; Opposition Spokesman, Foreign and Commonwealth Affairs 1977–79; Parl. Under-Sec. of State 1979–81; Minister of State, FCO 1981–82, 1983–85; Minister of State (Minister for the Arts) and Minister of State for Civil Service, Privy Council Office 1985–90; Gov. and C-in-C Gibraltar 1997–2000; Lord Chamberlain 2000–; Vice-Chancellor Univ. of Buckingham 1992–96; Chair. Atlantic Council of UK 1991–96, Commonwealth Foundation 1992–96; mem. Royal Mint Advisory Cttee, Bd Trustees, Royal Collection Trust, Advisory Bd Next Century Foundation; Pres. Voluntary Arts Network, Royal Overseas League; Vice-Pres. Friends of the Commonwealth Foundation; Gov. Ditchley Foundation; Trustee Geographers' Map Trustees Ltd (A–Z), Nicholson Charity; Trustee Emer. Royal Acad. of Arts; Vice-Patron Harambee and Langalanga Trusts; mem. Conservative Party; Hon. Vice-Pres. Overseas Pensioners' Asscn; Hon. Fellow Atlantic Council of the UK; KStJ. *Leisure interests:* walking, swimming, painting, reading, piano. *Address:* Lord Chamberlain's Office, Buckingham Palace, London, SW1 (Office); c/o House of Lords, Westminster, London, SW1A 0PW, England. *Telephone:* (20) 7930-4832 (Office); (20) 7024-4262 (Office).

LUCE, R(obert) Duncan, PhD; American mathematical psychologist; b. 16 May 1925, Scranton, Pa; s. of Robert R. Luce and Ruth Downer Luce; m. 1st Gay Gaer 1950; m. 2nd Cynthia Newby 1967; one d.; m. 3rd Carolyn A. Scheer 1988; ed Massachusetts Inst. of Tech.; mem. staff, Research Lab. of Electronics MIT 1950–53; Asst Prof. of Sociology and Mathematical Statistics, Columbia Univ. 1954–57; Fellow Center for Advanced Study in the Behavioral Sciences 1954–55, 1966–67, 1987–88; Lecturer in Social Relations, Harvard Univ. 1957–59, Prof. of Psychology 1976–83, Victor S. Thomas Prof. of Psychology 1984–88, Emer. 1988–; Distinguished Prof. of Cognitive Sciences 1988–94, Dir Irvine Research Unit in Math. Behavioral Science, Univ. of Calif. at Irvine 1988–92, Dir Inst. for Math. Behavioral Sciences 1992–98, Distinguished Research Prof. of Cognitive Sciences and Research Prof. of Econs 1994–; Prof. of Psychology, Univ. of Pa 1959–68, Benjamin Franklin Prof. 1968–69; Visiting Prof. Inst. for Advanced Study, Princeton, NJ 1969–72; Prof. of Social Science, Univ. of Calif., Irvine 1972–75; mem. NAS, American Acad. of Arts and Sciences, American Philosophical Soc., Soc. of Experimental Psychologists; American Psychological Asscn Distinguished Scientific Contrib. Award 1972, American Psychological Foundation Gold Medal for Life Achievement 2001, Univ. of Calif. Irvine Award 2001. *Publications:* Games and Decisions (with H. Raiffa), Individual Choice Behavior, Handbook of Mathematical Psychology (Jt Ed.), Contemporary Developments in Mathematical Psychology (jt ed.), Foundations of Measurement Vols I, II, III (with D. H. Krantz, P. Suppes and A. Tversky) 1971–90, Response Times, Stevens' Handbook of Experimental Psychology (jt ed.), Sound & Hearing,

Utility of Gains and Losses: Measurement – Theoretical and Experimental Approaches 2000; and over 190 articles in scientific journals. *Address:* Social Science Plaza, University of California at Irvine, Irvine, CA 92697-5100; 20 Whitman Court, Irvine, CA 92612-4057, USA (Home). *Telephone:* (949) 824-6239 (Office); (949) 854 8203 (Home). *Fax:* (949) 824-3733 (Office).

LUCHKO, Klara Stepanovna; Russian cinema and stage actress; b. 1 July 1925, Poltava, Ukraine; m. 1st Sergey Lukianov 1959 (died 1963); m. 2nd Dmitriy Mamleev; one d.; ed VGIK; actress, Cinema Actors' Theatre-Studio 1948–; mem. Nika Cinema Acad., Russian Acad. of Cinema 2000–; People's Artist of USSR, Badge of Honour; Cinema Actors Guild's Prize for Outstanding Contrib. to Profession 1999, Order For Services to Motherland 2000. *Roles include:* Dasha Shelest in Cossacks by Kuban (USSR State Prize 1951), Viola and Sebastian in Twelfth Night, Lisa in Big Family (Prize at Cannes Film Festival 1955), Jadwiga in Red Lives 1958, Natasha in Under the Seven Winds 1962, Claudia Pushlakova in The Gypsies (TV serial), Madlen in Cascet, Mother in Another's Child 1982, Nuikina in We, the Undersigned (TV) 1982, Dgozephina in Carnival 1983, Golovina in The Alarming Sunday 1983, Claudia in Budulai's Return 1986, Marianna in Play in Death 1991, Doctor in Eyes 1993, Nastya in Parable 1995, Blessed in Legend 1997, Miller in The Sun Strike 2003; narrator in weekly TV programme Films of our Memory 1993–96 and Movie Star 1997–2000. *Publications:* Am I Guilty? (screenplay and book), Faith, Thank You for All! (book) 2002. *Leisure interests:* travelling, music, the arts. *Address:* Kotelnicheskaya Nab. 1/15, Korp. B, Apt. 308, 109240 Moscow, Russia. *Telephone:* (095) 915-43-67.

LUCIE-SMITH, (John) Edward (McKenzie), MA, FRSL; British art critic and poet; b. 27 Feb. 1933, Kingston, Jamaica; s. of John Dudley Lucie-Smith and Mary Lushington; ed King's School, Canterbury, Merton Coll. Oxford; officer RAF 1954–56; fmrly worked in advertising and as freelance journalist and broadcaster; contributes to The Times, Sunday Times, Independent, Mail-on-Sunday, Spectator, New Statesman, Evening Standard, Encounter, London Magazine, Illustrated London News; mem. Acad. de Poésie Européenne. *Exhibitions:* photographs: Art Kiosk (Brussels) 1999, Galena Toni Benin (Barcelona) 2000, Rosenfeld Gallery (Tel Aviv) 2001. *Publications as sole author include:* A Tropical Childhood and Other Poems 1961, Confessions and Histories 1964, What is a Painting? 1966, Thinking About Art 1968, Towards Silence 1968, Movements in Art Since 1945 1969, Art in Britain 69–70 1970, A Concise History of French Painting 1971, Symbolist Art 1972, Eroticism in Western Art 1972, The First London Catalogue 1974, The Well Wishers 1974, The Burnt Child (autobiog.) 1975, The Invented Eye (early photography) 1975, World of the Makers 1975, Joan of Arc 1976, Fantin-Latour 1977, The Dark Pageant (novel) 1977, Art Today 1977, A Concise History of Furniture 1979, Super Realism 1979, Cultural Calendar of the Twentieth Century 1979, Art in the Seventies 1980, The Story of Craft 1981, The Body 1981, A History of Industrial Design 1983, Art Terms: An Illustrated Dictionary 1984, Art in the Thirties 1985, American Art Now 1985, Lives of the Great Twentieth Century Artists 1986, Sculpture Since 1945 1987, Art in the Eighties 1990, Art Deco Painting 1990, Fletcher Benton 1990, Jean Rustin 1991, Harry Holland 1992, Art and Civilisation 1992, Andres Nagel 1992, Wendy Taylor 1992, Alexander 1992, British Art Now 1993, Race, Sex and Gender: Issues in Contemporary Art 1994, American Realism 1994, Art Today 1995, Visual Arts in the Twentieth Century 1996, Arts Erotica: an Arousing History of Erotic Art 1997, Adam 1998, Stone 1998, Zoo 1998, Judy Chicago: an American Vision 2000, Flesh and Photographs 2000, Changing Shape (poems) 2002; has edited numerous anthologies. *Leisure interest:* the Internet. *Address:* c/o Rogers, Coleridge and White, 20 Powis Mews, London, W11 1JN, England.

LUCINSCHI, Petru, CandPhilSc; Moldovan politician; b. 27 Jan. 1940, Floresti; s. of Chiril Lucinschi and Parascovia Lucinschi; m. Antonina Georgievna Lucinschi 1965; two s.; ed Kishinev Univ. and CPSU Cen. Cttee Higher Party School; served in Soviet Army 1962–63; Komsomol work for Cen. Cttee of Moldavian CP 1963–71; mem. CPSU 1964–91; First Sec. of Bălti City Komsomol Cttee 1964–65; Head of Section, Second Sec., First Sec. of Cen. Cttee of Moldavian Komsomol 1965–71; Sec. of Cen. Cttee of Moldavian CP 1971–76, First Sec. Nov. 1989–91; First Sec. of Kishinev City Cttee 1976–78; Deputy Head, Propaganda Dept of CPSU Cen. Cttee 1978–86; Second Sec. of Cen. Cttee of Tadzhik CP 1986–89; Cand. mem. of CPSU Cen. Cttee 1986–89, mem. 1989–91, Sec. 1990–91; Deputy to USSR Supreme Soviet 1986–89; USSR People's Deputy 1989–91; mem. CPSU Politburo, 1990–91; Moldovan Amb. to Russia 1992–93; fmr. Leader Agrarian Democratic Party; Chair. Moldovan Parl. 1993–2001; Pres. of Moldova 1996–2000; Head Fund for Strategic Studies and Devt of Int. Relations 2001–; Chevalier, Légion d'honneur 1998; numerous awards. *Leisure interests:* sports, travelling, reading, theatre. *Address:* c/o Office of the President, 23 Nicolae Jorga str., 277033 Chişinău, Moldova.

LUCIUS, Wulf D. von, Dr rer. pol; German scientific publisher; b. 29 Nov. 1938, Jena; s. of the late Tankred R. von Lucius and of Annelise Fischer; m. Akka Achelis 1967; three s.; ed Heidelberg, Berlin and Freiburg; mil. service 1958–60; Asst Inst. of Econometrics, Freiburg 1965–66; worked in several publishing houses and as public accountant 1966–69; partner and Man. Dir Gustav Fischer Verlag 1969–95; mem. Bd of Exec. Officers, German Publrs. Asscn (Börsenverein) 1976–86; mem. Bd C. Hanser Verlag 1984–; Publr and Pres. Lucius & Lucius Verlag, Stuttgart 1996–; Chair. Int. Publishers Copyright Council 1995–98, Asscn of Scientific Publrs in Germany

1994–2001; mem. Exec. Cttee Int. Publrs Asscn Geneva 1996–; Friedrich-Perthes-Medaille 1999, Antiquaria Preis 2001. *Publications:* Bücherlust-Vom Sammeln 2000; numerous articles on publishing, copyright and book history. *Leisure interests:* collecting fine prints and artists' books. *Address:* Gerokstr. 51, 70184 Stuttgart (Office); Ameisenbergstrasse 22, 7000 Stuttgart 1, Germany. *Telephone:* (711) 242060 (Office); (711) 264386 (Home). *Fax:* (711) 242088 (Office). *E-mail:* lucius@luciusverlag.com (Office). *Website:* luciusverlag.com (Office).

ŁUCZAK, Aleksander Piotr, PhD; Polish politician and historian; b. 10 Sept. 1943, Legionowo; m. Janina Zakrzewska; one d.; ed Warsaw Univ. and Adam Mickiewicz Univ., Poznań; mem. United Peasants' Party (ZLS) 1966–91; mem. Polish Peasants' Party (PSL) 1991–; lecturer, Dept of History of the Peasant Movt Cen. Cttee ZSL until 1976; mem. Faculty, Univ. of Warsaw 1976–, Asst Prof. 1983–91, Prof. 1991; Adviser to Pres. of Cen. Cttee ZSL 1976–79; Head, Dept of Ideology, Press and Propaganda, Cen. Cttee PSL 1986, Vice-Chair., Head Council PSL 1991–97; Deputy Minister of Nat. Educ. 1986–87; Head, Office of Council of Ministers June–Oct. 1992; Deputy Prime Minister and Minister of Educ. 1993–94; Deputy Prime Minister, Minister and Head of Scientific Research Cttee 1994–96; Minister and Head of Scientific Research Cttee 1996–97; Deputy to Sejm (Parl.) 1989–2001; Chair. Polish Asscn of Adult Educ. 1995–2001; Pres. World Scout Parl. Union 1997–2000; mem. Nat. Broadcasting Council 2001–. *Publications:* more than 30 publs on recent history of Poland and the peasant movt. *Leisure interest:* tennis. *Address:* National Broadcasting Council, ul. Sobieskiego 101, 00-763 Warsaw, Poland (Office). *Telephone:* (22) 8402379 (Office). *E-mail:* luczak@krrit.gov.pl (Office).

LUDER, Owen (Harold), CBE, FRSA; British architect, planner, environmentalist and writer; b. 7 Aug. 1928, London; s. of late Edward Charles Luder and of Ellen Clara Luder; m. 1st Rose Dorothy (Doris) Broadstock 1951 (dissolved 1988); one s. (deceased) four d.; m. 2nd Jacqueline Ollerton 1989; ed Brixton School of Building, Regent St Polytechnic Evening School of Architecture (now Univ. of Westminster), Brixton School of Architecture; f. Owen Luder Partnership 1957, Sr Partner until 1978 (when partnership became an unlimited co.), Chair. and Man. Dir 1978–87; f. Owen Luder Consultancy Communication in Construction 1988; Dir (non-exec.) Jarvis PLC 1995–; Council mem. RIBA 1967–97, Hon. Treas. 1975–78, Pres. 1981–83, Sr Vice-Pres. 1994–95, Pres. 1995–97, Architect mem. Architects' Registration Bd and Vice-Chair. 1997–2002, Chair. 2002–03; Pres. Norwood Soc. 1982–92; Sec.-Treas. Commonwealth Asscn of Architects 1985–87; Pres. UIA Congress 1986; Vice-Pres. Membership Communications 1989–90; Dir Communication in Construction Ltd 1990; Consultant to Nat. Coal Bd for environmental, architectural and planning issues on Vale of Belvoir Coal Mining Project, UK 1975–87; Architect/Planner for Revitalisation schemes for British Rail Eng Works at Shildon Co. Durham and Swindon; Consultant for many commercial devt schemes; mem. Acad. of Experts 1992–, Vice-Chair. 1997–98; RIBA Architecture Bronze Medal 1963, Town Planning and Housing Council Silver Jubilee Award 'Housing in the 80s' and various other architectural, design and civic trust awards and commendations. *Publications:* Promotion and Marketing for Building Professionals 1988, Sports Stadia After Hillsborough 1990, Keeping Out of Trouble 1999, frequent contributions to nat. and tech. publications. *Leisure interests:* photography, writing, Arsenal Football Club, swimming. *Address:* Communication in Construction Ltd, 2 Smith Square, London, SW1P 3HS, England. *Telephone:* (20) 7222-4737. *E-mail:* owenluder@dial.pipex.com.

LUDEWIG, Johannes, PhD; German civil servant and business executive; b. 6 July 1945, Hamburg; m.; three c.; ed Univ. of Hamburg, Stanford Univ., USA, Ecole Nat. d'Admin., Paris; worked on energy, econ. and business policy Fed. Ministry of Econs 1975–83; joined Office of the Fed. Chancellor 1983, Ministerial Dir Dept of Econ. and Financial Policy 1991–94; fmr State Sec. Fed. Ministry of Econs; fmr Commr of Fed. Govt for New German Fed. States; mem. Exec. Bd Deutsche Bahn AG 1997–99, Chair. 1997–99. *Address:* c/o Deutsche Bahn AG, Stephensonstrasse 1, 60326 Frankfurt am Main, Germany.

LUDWIG, Christa; Austrian mezzo-soprano; b. 16 March 1928, Berlin, Germany; d. of Anton Ludwig and Eugenie Besalla-Ludwig; m. 1st Walter Berry 1957 (divorced 1970); one s.; m. 2nd Paul-Emile Deiber 1972; opera debut at 18, guest appearance at the Athens Festival in Epidauros 1965; joined Vienna State Opera 1955, Hon. mem. 1981; appearances at Festivals in Salzburg, Bayreuth, Lucerne, Holland, Prague, Saratoga, Stockholm; guest appearances in season in Vienna, New York, Chicago, Buenos Aires, Milan, Berlin, Munich; numerous recitals and soloist in concerts; Hon. mem. Vienna Konzerthaus, Vienna Philharmonic; Hon. Prof.; Commdr des Arts et des Lettres 1989; Chevalier, Légion d'honneur 1989; Grosses Ehrenzeichen 1994; Commdr, Ordre pour le Mérite (France) 1997; winner of Bach-Concours, record award for Fricka in Walküre and Des Knaben Wunderhorn, awarded title of Kammersängerin by Austrian Govt 1962, Prix des Affaires Culturelles for recording of Venus in Tannhäuser, Paris 1972, Silver Rose (Vienna Philharmonic) 1980, Golden Ring (Staatsoper, Vienna) 1980, Golden Gustav Mahler Medal 1980, Hugo Wolf Medal 1980, Gold Medal (City of Vienna) 1988. *Recordings include:* Lieder and complete operas including Norma (with Maria Callas), Lohengrin, Così fan tutte, Der Rosenkavalier, Carmen, Götterdämmerung, Die Walküre, Bluebeard's Castle, Don Giovanni, Die Zauberflöte, Le Nozze di Figaro, Capriccio, Fidelio. *Publication:* In My Own Voice

(biog.) 1994. *Leisure interests:* music, archaeology, reading, home movie making, cooking, sewing, fashion, shopping, weaving, rug knitting and travelling. *Address:* 1458 Ter, Chemin des Colles, 06740 Châteauneuf de Grasse, France; c/o Heidrun Artmüller, Goethegasse 1, 1010 Vienna, Austria. *Telephone:* (4) 97010531 (Home). *Fax:* (4) 97010529 (Home).

LUEDERITZ, Alexander, DrIur; German professor of law; b. 19 March 1932, Göttingen; s. of Heinrich Luederitz and Gertrud Luederitz; m. Renate (née Wessling) Luederitz 1960; one s. one d.; ed Cologne and Lausanne Schools of Law; mem. of the Bar 1961–65; Prof. of Law, Frankfurt Univ. 1966–70, Dean, Faculty of Law 1969–70; Prof. of Law and Dir Inst. for Int. and Foreign Pvt. Law, Univ. of Cologne 1971–, Dean, Faculty of Law 1979–80; Visiting Prof. Univ. of Calif., Berkeley 1982, Univ. d'Auvergne 1989, 1991, Univ. of Ill., Urbana 1995, Univ. of Toulouse 1995, 1996; Fellow, American Council of Learned Socs. *Publications:* Auslegung von Rechtsgeschäften 1966, International Sales 1991, International Privatrecht 1992, Commentary on German Conflicts Law (Corporation, Agency, Torts) 1996, Family Law 1997; articles in learned journals. *Leisure interests:* hiking, stamp collecting. *Address:* Kellerhardtsweg 12, 51503 Roesrath, Germany. *Telephone:* (221) 470-2288; (2205) 3124. *Fax:* (221) 470 5129; (2205) 3124.

LUERS, William Henry, MA, FAAS; American diplomatist and art museum president; b. 15 May 1929, Springfield, Ill.; s. of Carl U. Luers and Ann L. Luers; m. Wendy Woods Turnbull 1979; three s. one d. by previous marriage and two step-d.; ed Hamilton Coll., Columbia and Northwestern Univs; Foreign Service Officer Dept of State 1957; Vice-Consul, Naples, Italy 1957–60; Second Sec. Embassy, Moscow 1963–65; Political Counsellor, Caracas, Venezuela 1969–73; Deputy Exec. Sec., Dept of State 1973–75; Deputy Asst Sec. for Inter-American Affairs, Washington 1975–77, Deputy Asst Sec. for Europe 1977–78; Amb. to Venezuela 1978–82, to Czechoslovakia 1983–86; Pres. Metropolitan Museum of Art, New York 1986–99; Pres. and CEO UN Asscn of USA 1999–; mem. Bd Rockefeller Brothers Fund, IDEX Corpn, AOL-Latin America, Scudder Funds, Wickes Corpn; mem. Council on Foreign Relations. *Address:* UNA-USA, 801 Second Avenue, New York, NY 10017, USA.

LUGAR, Richard Green, MA; American politician; b. 4 April 1932, Indianapolis, Ind.; s. of Marvin L. Lugar and Bertha Green Lugar; m. Charlene Smeltzer 1956; four s.; ed Shortridge High School, Denison Univ., Ohio, Pembroke Coll., Oxford Univ.; Rhodes Scholar, Pembroke Coll. Oxford 1956; served USN 1957–60; Vice-Pres. and Treas. Thomas Green & Co. Inc. 1960–67, Sec.-Treas. 1968; Treas. Lugar Stock Farms Inc. 1960; mem. Bd of Trustees, Denison Univ. 1966, Advisory Bd. Univ., Purdue Univ. at Indianapolis 1969–75, Bd of Trustees of Ind. Cen. Univ. 1970; Vice-Chair. 1975, Visiting Prof. of Political Science, Dir of Public Affairs 1975–76; mem. Visiting Cttee of Harvard–MIT Jt Centre for Urban Studies 1973; mem. Bd of Dirs, Indianapolis Centre for Advanced Research 1973–76; mem. Indianapolis Bd of School Commrs 1964–67, Vice-Pres. 1965; Mayor of Indianapolis 1968–75; del. and keynote speaker, Ind. Republican Convention 1968, del. 1972; del. mem. Platform Cttee, Repub. Nat. Convention 1968, del., keynote speaker and mem. Platform Cttee 1972; Candidate for US Senate 1974, Senator from Indiana 1977–; mem. Advisory Comm. on Intergovernmental Relations 1969–75, Vice-Chair. 1970–75; mem. Advisory Bd of US Conf. of Mayors 1969–75; mem. Pres. Model Cities Advisory Task Force 1969–70, State and Local Govt Advisory Cttee of Office of Econ. Opportunity 1969–73, Nat. Advisory Comm. on Criminal Justice Standards and Goals 1971–73; Pres. of Advisory Council, Nat. League of Cities 1971, mem. Council 1972–75; Chair. Nat. Republican Senatorial Cttee 1983–84; Chair. Foreign Relations Cttee 1985–87, 2003–, Cttee on Agric. 1995–2001; mem. Bd of Dirs. of Westview Osteopathic Hosp. 1969–76, Indianapolis Symphony Orch., Nat. Endowment for Democracy; mem. Nat. Acad. of Public Admin., Rotary Club of Indianapolis and other civic orgs; Trustee Denison Univ., Indianapolis Univ.; Hon. Doctorates from 20 colls and univs in USA 1970–78; Exceptional Service Award, Office of Econ. Opportunity 1972, Fiorello La Guardia Award, New School of Social Research 1975. *Publication:* Letters to the Next President 1988. *Leisure interests:* music, reading, running, golf, tennis. *Address:* US Senate, 306 Hart Senate Office Building, Washington, DC 20510, USA. *Telephone:* (202) 224-4814.

LUHRMANN, Baz(mark) Anthony; Australian film and theatre director; b. 17 Sept. 1962, NSW; m. Catherine Martin 1997; ed Narrabeen High School, Sydney; theatre work with Peter Brook; owns Bazmark production co., Sydney; acting roles in films The Winter of Our Dreams 1982, The Dark Room 1984. *Films:* Strictly Ballroom 1992, La Bohème (TV) 1993, Romeo and Juliet 1996, Moulin Rouge 2001. *Plays:* Strictly Ballroom, Haircut. *Operas directed:* La Bohème, Sydney 1990, New York 2002, San Francisco 2002, A Midsummer Night's Dream, Sydney 1993. *Address:* c/o Hilary Linstead and Associates Pty Ltd, Level 18, Plaza II, 500 Oxford Street, Bondi Junction, NSW 2022, Australia (Office).

LUI, Frank Fakaotimanava; Niuean politician; Premier of Niue 1993–99, also Minister for External Relations, Niueans Overseas, Police and Immigration, Civil Aviation and Public Service Comm. *Address:* c/o Office of the Premier, Alofi, Niue.

LUIK, Juri; Estonian diplomatist, politician and journalist; b. 17 Aug. 1966, Tallinn; m.; ed Tartu Univ.; Political Ed. Vikerkaar (weekly) 1988–90; specialist on Anglo-Saxon Countries Estonian Inst. 1989–91; Head Political

Dept, Ministry of Foreign Affairs 1991–92; mem. Riigikogu (Parl.) 1992–95; Minister without portfolio responsible for Estonian-Russian Negotiations 1992–93; Minister of Defence 1993–94; Minister of Foreign Affairs 1994–95; Sr Research Fellow, Carnegie Foundation 1995–96; apptd Amb. to NATO and Benelux States, Brussels 1996; mem. Pro Patria (Isamaaliit) Party 1989–; Minister of Defence 1999–2001. *Leisure interests:* theatre, films, tennis. *Address:* Ministry of Defence, Pikkstr. 57, Tallinn, Estonia. *Telephone:* (2) 6406000 (Office). *Fax:* (2) 6399165 (Office).

LUKA, Faimalaga; Tuvaluan politician; fmr Minister for Internal Affairs and Rural and Urban Devt; fmr Minister for Natural Resources and Environment; Prime Minister of Tuvalu, Minister of Foreign Affairs, Finance and Econ. Planning and Trade and Commerce Feb.–Dec. 2001. *Address:* c/o Office of the Prime Minister, PMB, Vaiaku, Funafuti, Tuvalu (Office).

LUKAS, D. Wayne, EdM; American racehorse trainer; b. 2 Sept. 1935, Antigo, Wis.; s. of Ted Lukas and Bea Lukas; m. Laura Lukas; one s.; ed Univ. of Wisconsin; began career as Asst Basketball Coach, Univ. of Wisconsin, then Head Basketball Coach, LaCrosse High School; later spent more than ten years training quarter horses, with a record 150 wins; switched to training thoroughbreds 1978; six consecutive Triple Crown race wins: Tabasco Cat–Preakness 1994, Belmont 1994, Thunder Gulch–Derby 1995, Belmont 1995, Timber Country–Preakness 1995, Grindstone–Kentucky Derby 1996; total of 13 Breeder's Cup wins; all-time leading money winner (over $200 million); now makes guest appearances as motivational speaker; four-time Eclipse Award winner–Trainer of the Year, Nat. Museum of Racing's Hall of Fame 1999. *Address:* c/o Program Resources Professional Speakers Bureau, P.O. Box 22307, Louisville, KY 40252, USA (Office).

LUKASHENKA, Alyaksandr Ryhoravich; Belarus politician and economist; b. 30 Aug. 1954, Kopys, Belarus; m. Galina Rodionovna Lukashenko; two s.; ed Mogilev Pedagogical Inst., Belarus Agric. Acad.; Sec. Komsomol Cttee, Shklov, instructor Political Div. Komsomol Cttee W Border Dist 1975–77; Sec. Komsomol Cttee Mogilev City Food Dept; instructor regional Exec. Cttee 1977–80; Deputy Commdr of Co. 1980–82; Deputy Chair. Udarnik collective farm 1982–83; Deputy Dir Enterprise of Construction Materials 1983–85; Sec. CP Cttee Collective Farm of V. I. Lenin, Shklov Dist 1985–87; Dir Gorodets state farm 1987–94; elected Deputy of Supreme Council of Belarus SSR 1990–94; Chair. Parl. Comm. on Struggle against Corruption 1993–94; elected Pres. of Belarus 1994–; Chair. Higher Council of Belarus and Russia Union 1997–; Chair. Supreme State Council of the Union State of Belarus and Russia 2000–; Hon. Academician of the Russian Acad. of Sciences 1995; Order of the Holy Cross of the Knights of the Holy Sepulchre 2000; M. Sholokhov Int. Award 1997. *Address:* Office of the President, Karl Marx Street 38, 220016 Minsk, Belarus. *Telephone:* (172) 22-28-72 (Office). *Fax:* (172) 26-06-10 (Office). *E-mail:* contact@president.gov.by (Office); www .president.gov.by (Office).

LUKE, Hon. Justice Desmond Edgar Fashole, BL, MA; Sierra Leonean lawyer, diplomatist and politician; b. 6 Oct. 1935, Freetown; s. of Sir Emile Fashole-Luke and Lady Christina Fashole-Luke; one s. one d.; ed Prince of Wales School, Freetown, Kings Coll., Taunton, UK, Keble Coll. Oxford, UK, Magdalene Coll. Cambridge, UK, Georgetown Univ., Washington, USA; admitted to Bar of England and Wales 1962, of Sierra Leone 1963; in pvt practice, barrister and solicitor 1963–69; Legal Adviser to Mobil Oil, British Petrol, Bata Shoe Co., Barclays Bank, Diamond Corpn, Allen & Elliot (SL) Ltd, Singer Sewing Machine Co. Ltd, Trade Marks Owners Asscn, Adams and Adams Patent Attorneys and other industrial and commercial cos 1963–69; UN Human Rights Fellow, India 1964; Amb. to FRG (concurrently accred. to Netherlands, Belgium and Luxembourg 1970–73) 1969–73, to France, Italy and Perm. Rep. to EEC 1971–73; Deputy Leader Del. to Heads of State Summit OAU, Addis Ababa, Non-Aligned Summit, Algeria 1969, Commonwealth Prime Minister's Conf., Ottawa 1973, Abidjan Peace Talks 1996, ECOWAS Conf., Abuja 1997, UN Gen. Ass., NY 1997; Leader Del. to IAEA Conf., Vienna 1970, to African Econ. Conf., Milan 1971, to Council of Ministers OAU, Addis Ababa 1973–75, to UN Gen. Ass., NY 1973–74; Minister of Foreign Affairs 1973–75 (resgnd), of Health 1977–78; Man. Dir Africa Int. Ltd 1975; Chair. Comm. for Consolidation of Peace (CCP) 1996–97; Chief Justice of Sierra Leone 1998–2002 (retd); Special Envoy of Pres. Kabbah to Pres. Kuffour of Ghana 2002; Grand Cross Order of Merit (FRG) 1973, Grand Cordon of Order of Menelik II (Ethiopia) 1973; Oxford Blues Athletic Awards 1955–58, Finalist (long jump) Commonwealth Games, Cardiff 1958, Oxford and Cambridge Freshman's Champion and Record Holder (high jump) 1954; Men in Action Certificate of Merit for Contrib. to Restoration of Democracy in Sierra Leone 1999, Jarwlee Lewis Meritorious Award for Services to State 2001. *Publications include:* Republican Constitution: What Form? *Leisure interests:* sports, art, music. *Address:* c/o Office of the Chief Justice, Supreme Court, Freetown (Office); Luke House, POB 214, Freetown, Sierra Leone (Home). *Telephone:* (22) 231863 (Office). *Fax:* (22) 225670 (Office). *E-mail:* fasholeluke@yahoo.com (Home).

LUKEŠ, Milan, PhD; Czech academic; b. 14 Dec. 1933, Prague; s. of Miloš Lukeš and Bohumila Topičová; m. Ilona Milatová; one d.; ed Acad. of Performing Arts; Ed. Orbis Publishing House, Prague 1956–60; Ed. then Ed.-in-Chief, Theatre (journal) 1960–69; Reader, then Lecturer, Prof. Faculty of Arts, Charles Univ., Prague 1969–; Dir Nat. Theatre, Prague 1985–89, Chair. Council 1994–2000; Co-Ed. Svět a divadlo (World and Theatre journal) 1996–; Chair. Int. Theatre Festival, Pilsen 1996–2001; Minister of Culture, Czech Repub. 1989–90; Vice-Premier, Govt of Czech Repub. 1990–92; Deputy to Czech Nat. Council (Parl.) 1990–92. *Publications:* Eugene O'Neill, Principles of Shakespearean Text Theory, The Art of Drama; critical reviews and essays, translations of dramas. *Address:* Svět a divadlo, Celetná 17, Prague 1, 11000, Czech Republic. *Telephone:* 224817180. *Fax:* 224818184. *E-mail:* svet@ divadlo.cz (Office).

LUKIANENKO, Levko (Hryhorovych); Ukrainian politician; b. 24 Aug. 1928, Chrypivka, Chernigiv Region; s. of Hryzko Lukianenko and Natalka Lukianenko; m. Nadia Oleyandrivna Lukianenko; two d.; ed Moscow M. V. Lomonosov State Univ.; mem. CPSU 1953–61; served in Soviet Army 1944–53; legal adviser, Lvov CPSU Regional Cttee 1958–59; barrister 1959–61; sentenced to death 1961 for formation of Ukrainian Workers' and Peasants' League, but sentence commuted to 15 years' imprisonment, released 1976; Co-Founder, on release, of Ukrainian Helsinki Group 1976, again arrested, sentenced to 10 years' imprisonment and 5 years' exile, returned to Ukraine 1989; mem. Verkhovna Rada (Parl.) 1990–92, 1994–98, 2002–; Chair. Ukrainian Republican Party 1990–92, Hon. Chair. 1992–; Presidential Cand. Ukrainian elections 1991; Amb. to Canada 1992–93; Chair. Ukrainian Asscn of Researchers into Famine in Ukraine; Hon. LLD (Alberta); Merit of Honour of Ukrainian Pres. *Publications:* Confession from the Condemned Cell 1991, For Ukraine 1991, I Believe in God and Ukraine 1991, The Birth of a New Era 1997, In the Land of the Maple Leaf 1998. *Leisure interests:* music, gardening. *Address:* 20 Sadova Street, v. khotiv, Kyivo-Sviatosh District, 08171 Kiev, Ukraine. *Telephone:* (44) 489-0527. *Fax:* (44) 489-0527.

LUKIN, Vladimir Petrovich, DHist; Russian politician and diplomatist; b. 13 July 1937, Omsk; m.; two s.; ed Moscow State Pedagogical Inst.; researcher, Museum of Revolution, Inst. of World Econs and Int. Relations, USSR Acad. of Sciences 1959–65; on staff of journal Problems of Peace and Socialism, Prague until Aug. 1968 after Soviet invasion; staff mem. of the Inst. of USA, Canada 1968–87; deputy Dir Dept of Assessment and Planning of the USSR Ministry of Foreign Affairs 1987–90; People's Deputy of RSFSR (now Russia) 1990–93; Chair. Foreign Affairs Cttee of the Russian Supreme Soviet 1990–92; Amb. to USA 1992–94; leader of pre-election bloc (later political movt) Yabloko (with G. Javlinsky), Deputy Chair.; mem. State Duma (Parl.) 1993–, Chair. Cttee for Foreign Affairs 1994–99; Deputy Chair. State Duma 2000–02. *Publications include:* Centres of Power: conceptions and reality, China's Place in US Global Policy, With Concern and Hope: Russia and the West. *Leisure interests:* Russian literature, soccer. *Address:* State Duma, Okhotny Ryad 1, 103009 Moscow, Russia. *Telephone:* (095) 292-88-68. *Fax:* (095) 292-67-83.

LUKINOV, Ivan Illarionovich, DEconSc; Ukrainian economist; b. 5 Oct. 1927, Belgorod Region; s. of Illarion Ivanovich Lukinov and Praskovya Olexiyevna Lukinova; m. Tatyana Borisovna Kozminskaya 1956; one s. one d.; ed Kharkov Agric. Inst.; mem. CPSU 1953–91; worked for Ukrainian Acad. of Sciences Inst. of Econ. 1951–56; head of a section of Cen. Cttee of Ukrainian CP 1956–67; head of section at Ukrainian Inst. of Econs 1965–67; Dir of Schlichter Ukrainian Inst. of Econ. and Org. of Agric. Production 1967–76, Prof. 1968; Dir Inst. of Econs, Ukrainian Acad. of Sciences 1976–, Academic Sec. 1993–99; Vice-Pres. Ukrainian Nat. Acad. of Sciences 1979–93; mem. of USSR (now Russian) Acad. of Sciences 1984–, Lenin All-Union (now Russian) Acad. of Agric. Science 1973–, European Asscn of Agric. Economists (EAAE) 1977–; Vice-Pres. EAAE 1990–93; Hon. mem. Royal Swedish Acad. of Agric. and Forestry 1975; Médaille d'Or SPI N 0099116, Paris 1999, Nikolai D. Kondratieff Gold Medal, Moscow 2001, Gold Medal 'Leader of European Community in XXI Century', Luxembourg 2001, American Medal of Honor of ABI 2002. *Publications:* author of over 530 research works on econ. theory, price policy and reproduction, cooperation and integration in agro-industrial complexes, econ. transformations. *Leisure interests:* gardening, sport. *Address:* Institute of Economics, National Academy of Sciences, Volodimirskaya 54, 01601 Kiev 30 (Office); 2-4/7, Pushkinskaya str., apt. 89, 01034 Kiev 34, Ukraine. *Telephone:* (44) 235-13-61, 290-84-44 (Office); (44) 229-64-50 (Home). *Fax:* (44) 290-86-63 (Office). *E-mail:* Lukinov@instecon-base.kiev.ua.

LUKMAN, Rilwanu, BSc, CEng; Nigerian international civil servant, business executive and engineer; b. 26 Aug. 1938, Zaria, Kaduna State; s. of Qadi Lukman and Hajia Ramatu Lukman; m. 1966; two s. one d.; ed Govt Coll. Zaria (now Barewa), Nigerian Coll. of Arts, Science and Tech. (now Ahmadu Bello Univ.), Royal School of Mines, Imperial Coll. of Science and Tech., Univ. of London, Inst. of Prospecting and Mineral Deposits, Univ. of Mining and Metallurgy, Leoben, Austria, McGill Univ., Montreal, Canada; Asst Mining Engineer, A.G. Statagruvor, Sweden 1962–64; Inspector of Mines and Sr Inspector of Mines, Ministry of Mines and Power, Jos 1964–67, Acting Asst Chief Inspector of Mines 1968–70; Gen. Man. Cement Co. of Northern Nigeria Ltd, Sokoto 1970–74; Gen. Man. and Chief Exec. Nigerian Mining Corpn, Jos 1974–84; Fed. Minister of Mines, Power and Steel, Lagos 1984–85, of Petroleum Resources, Lagos 1986–89, of Foreign Affairs 1989–90; Pres. OPEC Conf. 1986–89, Sec.-Gen. OPEC 1995–2000, Head Del. from Nigeria 2001, Alt. Pres. 2001–02; Fellow and Hon. Fellow Inst. of Mining and Metallurgy; Fellow Imperial Coll. London, Nigerian Mining and Geoscience Soc.; Past Vice-Pres. Asscn of Geoscientists for Int. Devt; mem. Soc. of Mining Engineers of AIME; Hon. KBE 1989; Officier Légion d'honneur 1990; Order of Liberator, First Class, Venezuela 1990; Hon. PhD (Bologna) 1988; Hon. DSc

(Maiduguri) 1989, (Ahmadu Bello) 1991; Dr hc (Moore House Coll. Atlanta) 1989. *Leisure interests:* reading, walking. *Address:* c/o OPEC, Obere Donaustrasse 93, 1020 Vienna, Austria.

LUKOJI, Mulumba; Democratic Republic of the Congo politician and university professor; First State Commr March–July 1991.

LUKYANOV, Anatoliy Ivanovich, DJurSc; Russian politician and poet; b. 7 May 1930; m.; one d.; ed Moscow Univ.; mem. CPSU 1955–91; mem. CP of Russian Fed. 1992–; Chief Consultant on Legal Comm. of USSR Council of Ministers 1956–61; Deputy Head of Dept of Presidium of USSR Supreme Soviet 1969–76, Head of Secr. 1977–83; mem. of editorial staff of Sovietskoe Gosudarstvo i Pravo 1978; mem. Cen. Auditing Comm. CPSU 1981–86, 1986–89; Deputy of RSFSR Supreme Soviet 1984–91; Head of Gen. Dept of Cen. Cttee CPSU 1985–87, Sec. of Cen. Cttee 1987–88; Cand. mem. Political Bureau 1988–90; First Vice-Chair. of Presidium, USSR Supreme Soviet 1988–90, Chair. 1990–91; Chief Adviser on Legal Reform in USSR 1986–89; mem. Cen. Cttee CPSU 1986–91; People's Deputy of USSR 1989–91; arrested 1991 following failed coup d'état; charged with conspiracy Jan. 1992; released on bail Dec. 1992, on trial 1993–94; mem. State Duma (Parl.) 1993–, mem. Cttee for legis. and judicial reform 1994, Chair. 1996–99; Chair. Cttee for State Org. 2000–; mem. Presidium, Cen. Exec. Cttee CP of Russian Fed. *Publications include:* many articles and books on Soviet legal system and Soviet constitution, three vols of poetry (under pseudonym A. Osenev). *Address:* State Duma, Okhotny Ryad 1, 103265 Moscow, Russia. *Telephone:* (095) 292-32-65. *Fax:* (095) 292-05-99.

LULA DA SILVA, Luis Inácio; Brazilian politician and trade unionist; b. 27 Oct. 1945, Garanhuns, Pernambuco; s. of Aristides Inácio da Silva and Eurídice Ferreira de Mello; m. Marisa Leticia 1974; qualified as mechanic; started working at Indústrias Villares steelworks 1966; Assoc. mem. Exec. Cttee, São Bernardo do Campo and Diadema Metalworkers' Union 1969–72, First Sec. (responsible for social security) 1972–75, Pres. 1975–80; led steelworkers' strikes 1978, 1979; Pres. Partido dos Trabalhadores (Labour Party) 1980–87, 1993; a leader of the 'Elections Now' campaign for direct presidential elections 1984; a leader of campaign to impeach Pres. Collor de Mello 1992; Fed. Deputy 1986–; Presidential Cand. 1989, 1994, 2002; f. a 'Parallel Govt' (to prepare an alternative set of policies for the country) 1990; Pres. of Brazil 2003–. *Address:* Office of the President, Palácio do Planalto, 4° andar, 70150-900 Brasília, DF, Brazil (Office). *Telephone:* (61) 411-1573 (Office). *Fax:* (61) 323–1461 (Office). *E-mail:* casacivil@planalto.gov.br (Office). *Website:* www.presidencia.gov.br (Office).

LUMET, Sidney; American film director; b. 25 June 1924, Philadelphia; s. of Baruch Lumet and Eugenia Wemus; m. 1st Rita Gam (divorced); m. 2nd Gloria Vanderbilt 1956 (divorced 1963); m. 3rd Gail Jones 1963 (divorced 1978); m. 4th Mary Gimbel 1980; two d.; ed Columbia Univ.; started as a child actor, later theatrical dir and teacher; Assoc. Dir CBS 1950, Dir 1951–57; Hon. Life mem. Directors Guild of America; D. W. Griffith Lifetime Achievement Award 1993. *Films include:* Twelve Angry Men 1957, Stage Struck 1958, That Kind of Woman 1959, The Fugitive Kind 1960, A View from the Bridge 1961, A Long Day's Journey into Night 1962, The Pawnbroker 1965, Fail Safe 1964, The Hill 1965, The Group 1965, The Deadly Affair 1966, Bye, Bye Braverman 1968, The Seagull 1968, The Appointment 1969, Blood Kin 1969, The Offence, The Anderson Tapes 1972, Child's Play 1973, Serpico 1973, Lovin' Molly 1974, Murder on the Orient Express 1974, Dog Day Afternoon 1975, Network 1976, Equus 1977, The Wiz 1978, Just Tell Me What You Want 1980, Prince of the City 1981, Deathtrap 1982, The Verdict 1982, Daniel 1983, Garbo Talks 1984, Power 1986, The Morning After 1986, Running on Empty 1988, Family Business 1989, Close to Eden 1992, A Stranger Among Us 1992, Guilty as Sin 1993, Night Falls on Manhattan 1997, Critical Care 1997, Q & A 1998, Gloria 1998, Whistle 2000, The Beautiful Mrs Selderman 2000. *Play:* Caligula 1960. *Publication:* Making Movies 1995. *Address:* c/o ICM, 8942 Wilshire Boulevard, Suite 219, Beverly Hills, CA 90211, USA.

LUMLEY, Joanna Lamond, OBE, FRGS; British actress; b. 1 May 1946, Kashmir; d. of James Rutherford Lumley and Thyra Beatrice Rose Lumley; m. 1st Jeremy Lloyd (divorced); m. 2nd Stephen Barlow 1986; one s.; ed Army School, Kuala Lumpur, Mickledene Kent, St Mary's St Leonards on Sea; Hon. DLitt (Kent) 1994; Hon. DUniv (Oxford Brookes) 2000; BAFTA Award 1992, 1994, Special BAFTA 2000. *Films include:* Some Girls Do, Tam Lin, The Breaking of Bumbo, Games That Lovers Play, Don't Just Lie There Say Something, The Plank, On Her Majesty's Secret Service, Trail of the Pink Panther, Curse of the Pink Panther, Satanic Rites of Dracula 1978, Shirley Valentine, Innocent Lies 1995, James and the Giant Peach 1996, Cold Comfort Farm 1996, Prince Valiant 1997, Parting Shots 1998, The Tale of Sweeney Todd 1998, Mad Cows 1999, Maybe Baby 1999, The Cat's Meow 2000, Ella Enchanted 2002. *Stage appearances include:* Noël Coward's Blithe Spirit 1986, Vanilla 1990, Revengers Comedies 1991, The Letter 1995, Hedda Gabler, The Cherry Orchard, Private Lives, An Ideal Husband. *Television appearances include:* Release, Mark II Wife, Comedy Playhouse, It's Awfully Bad for Your Eyes Darling, Coronation Street, The Protectors, General Hospital 1974–75, The New Avengers 1976–77, Steptoe & Son, Are You Being Served?, The Cuckoo Waltz, Up The Workers, That was Tori, Sapphire and Steel 1978, Absolutely Fabulous (TV series) 1992–94, Class Act 1994, Girl Friday (documentary) 1994, White Rajahs of Sarawak (documentary), Joanna Lumley in the Kingdom of the Thunder Dragon (documentary) 1997, Coming Home 1998, A Rather English Marriage 1998, Nancherrow, Dr Willoughby,

MD, Mirrorball 1999, Absolutely Fabulous (series 4) 2001, Giraffes on the Move (documentary) 2001, Up in Town 2002, Absolutely Fabulous Special 2002; co-producer The Cazalets (BBC1) 2001. *Publications:* Stare Back and Smile (memoirs) 1989, Forces' Sweethearts 1993, Girl Friday 1994, Joanna Lumley in the Kingdom of the Thunder Dragon 1997. *Leisure interests:* walking, gardening, collecting things, painting, music, travelling. *Address:* c/o Conway van Gelder, 3rd Floor, 18–21 Jermyn Street, London, SW1 6HP, England.

LUMSDEN, Andrew Gino Sita, PhD, FRS; British professor of neurobiology; b. 22 Jan. 1947, Beaconsfield; m. (divorced); ed Kingswood School, Bath, St Catharine's Coll. Cambridge, Yale Univ., USA, London Univ.; Lecturer in Anatomy, Sr Lecturer, then Reader, Guy's Hosp. Medical School; Prof. of Developmental Neurobiology, King's Coll., London 1989–; Visiting Prof., Univ. of Calif. at Berkeley 1994; Howard Hughes Int. Research Scholar 1993–98; Fulbright Scholar. *Publications:* The Developing Brain (jtly) 2001, more than 100 scientific publs. *Leisure interests:* mechanical eng, natural history. *Address:* Medical Research Council Centre for Developmental Neurobiology, King's College London, New Hunts House, Guy's Campus, London, SE1 1UL (Office); 16 Elephant Lane, London, SE16 4JD, England (Home). *Telephone:* (20) 7848-6520 (Office); (20) 7640-0187 (Home). *Fax:* (20) 7848-6550 (Office); (20) 7640-0189 (Home). *E-mail:* andrew.lumsden@kcl.ac.uk (Office).

LUMSDEN, Sir David (James), Kt, MusB, MA, DPhil, FRSCM; British musician; b. 19 March 1928, Newcastle-upon-Tyne; s. of Albert Lumsden and Vera May Lumsden (née Tate); m. Sheila Daniels 1951; two s. two d.; ed Dame Allan's School, Newcastle-upon-Tyne, Selwyn Coll. Cambridge (organ scholar); Asst Organist, St John's Coll. Cambridge 1951–53; Organist and Choirmaster St Mary's, Nottingham and Univ. Organist 1954–56; Founder and Conductor Nottingham Bach Soc. 1954–59; Rector Chori Southwell Minster 1956–59; Dir of Music, Keele 1958–59; Prof. of Harmony, RAM 1959–61; Fellow and Organist New Coll. Oxford and Lecturer, Faculty of Music, Oxford Univ. 1959–76; Prin. Royal Scottish Acad. of Music and Drama, Glasgow 1976–82; Prin. RAM 1982–93; Conductor Oxford Harmonic Soc. 1961–63; Organist Sheldonian Theatre 1964–76; Harpsichordist to the London Virtuosi 1972–75; Pres. Inc. Asscn of Organists 1966–68; Visiting Prof. Yale Univ., USA 1974–75; Conductor Oxford Sinfonia 1967–70; Choragus Oxford Univ. 1968–72; Pres. Inc. Soc. of Musicians 1984–85, Royal Coll. of Organists 1986–88; Chair. Nat. Youth Orchestra 1985–94, Nat. Early Music Asscn 1986–89; mem. Bd Scottish Opera 1978–83, ENO 1984–89; Hon. Fellow, Selwyn Coll. Cambridge, New Coll. Oxford, King's Coll., London; Hon. RAM; Hon. FRCO; Hon. GSMD; Hon. FRCM; Hon. FRSAMD; Hon. FRNCM; Hon. FTCL; Hon. FLCM; Hon. DLitt (Reading) 1989. *Publications:* An Anthology of English Lute Music 1954, Thomas Robinson's Schoole of Musicke 1603 1971, Music for the Lute (Gen. Ed.) 1965–82. *Leisure interests:* reading, walking, theatre, photography, travel. *Address:* Melton House, Soham, Cambridgeshire, CB7 5DB, England. *Telephone:* (1353) 720100. *Fax:* (1353) 720918. *E-mail:* davidlumsden@compuserve.com (Home).

LUMSDEN, Lynne Ann; American publishing executive; b. 30 July 1947, Battle Creek, Mich.; d. of Arthur Lumsden and Ruth Pandy; m. Jon Harden 1986; one d.; ed Univ. of Paris, Sarah Lawrence Coll., City Grad. Center and New York Univ.; copy ed., Harcourt, Brace, Jovanovich, New York 1970–71; ed., Appleton-Century Crofts, New York 1971–73; Coll. Div. Prentice Hall 1974–78, Sr Ed. Coll. Div. 1978–81; Asst Vice-Pres. and Ed.-in-Chief, Spectrum Books 1981–82, Vice-Pres. and Editorial Dir, Gen. Publishing Div. 1982–85; Exec. Vice-Pres., Publr and Co-owner, Dodd, Mead & Co., Inc. New York 1985–89; Owner, Chair. JBH Communications Inc. Hartford, Conn. 1989–; Publr Hartford News and Southside Media 1989–. *Address:* 11 Hammer Street, Hartford, CT 06114, USA (Office).

LUNA, Bigas; Spanish film director; m. *Films:* Jamón, Jamón, Huevos de Oro (Golden Balls) 1994, The Tit and the Moon 1994, Bambola 1996, La Femme de Chambre du Titanic 1997, Volvérunt 1999, Son de Mar 2001. *Website:* www.bigasluna.com.

LUNA, Ricardo V., AB, MIA; Peruvian diplomatist; b. 19 Nov. 1940, Lima; s. of Ricardo Luna and Victoria Mendoza de Luna; m. Margarita Proaño 1969; one d.; ed Princeton Univ., NJ and Columbia Univ., USA, Diplomatic Acad. of Peru; joined Diplomatic Service 1967, posts held include Third Sec., Div. of Econ. Affairs, Foreign Ministry 1967, Third Sec., Embassy in UK 1968–70, Second Sec., Embassy in Israel 1970–71, First Sec., Perm. Mission of Peru to UN Office at Geneva; Head UN Dept, Foreign Ministry 1975–77; Counsellor, Embassy in USA 1978; Chef du Cabinet of Minister for Foreign Affairs 1979; Minister Counsellor, Mission of Peru to UNESCO 1980, Embassy in Ecuador 1987; Fellow Center for Int. Affairs, Harvard Univ., USA 1980–81; Minister, Perm. Mission to UN 1984; Under-Sec. for Multilateral Policy, Ministry of Foreign Affairs 1987–89; Perm. Rep. of Peru to UN 1989–92; Amb. to USA 1992–99; Lecturer Woodrow Wilson School of Public and Int. Affairs, Princeton Univ.; Founding mem. Peruvian Centre for Int. Studies; mem. Peruvian Soc. of Int. Law. *Leisure interests:* art, art history, jazz, cinema, mountain climbing, hiking. *Address:* Woodrow Wilson School of Public and International Affairs, Princeton University, Princeton, NJ 08544, USA. *Telephone:* (202) 833-9860. *Fax:* (202) 659-8124.

LUND, Henning, DPhil; Danish professor emeritus of chemistry; b. 15 Sept. 1929, Copenhagen; s. of Prof. Hakon Lund and Bergljot I. G. Lund (née Dahl);

m. Else Margrethe Thorup 1953; one s. three d.; ed Århus Katedralskole and Tech. Univ. of Copenhagen; Research Chemist Leo Pharmaceutical Products 1952–60; Research Fellow Harvard Univ. 1954–55; Asst Prof. of Chem. 1960, Prof. 1964–99, Prof. Emer. 1999–; Visiting Prof. Japan 1976, France 1981; Chair. UNESCO workshop for European Co-operation in Organic Electrochem. 1976–81; Section Co-Chair. Int. Soc. of Electrochem. 1973–78, 1986–90, Nat. Sec. 1986–90; Pres. Learned Soc., Univ. of Århus 1973–79; mem. Danish Research Council for Tech. Sciences 1977–82, Vice-Chair. 1980–82; mem. Royal Danish Acad. of Sciences and Letters 1979; Dr hc (Rennes) 1998; Bjerrums Gold Medal 1969, M. M. Baizer Award (Electrochemical Soc.) 1996. *Publications:* Elektrodereaktioner i Organisk Polarografi og Voltammetri 1961, Encyclopaedia of Electrochemistry of the Elements, Vols 11–15 (co-ed.) 1978–84, Organic Electrochemistry (ed.) 1983, 1991, 2000. *Leisure interests:* music, literature, jogging. *Address:* Department of Chemistry, University of Århus, 8000 Århus; Vinkelvej 8A, 8240 Risskov, Denmark (Home). *Telephone:* (45) 89-42-39-05 (Univ.); (45) 86-17-90-27 (Home). *Fax:* (45) 86-19-61-99 (Office). *E-mail:* hlund@chem.au (Office).

LUND, Peter Anthony; American broadcasting executive; b. 12 Jan. 1941, Minneapolis; s. of Arthur H. Lund and Elizabeth Rohan; m. Theresa M. Kessel 1960; two s.; ed St Thomas Coll.; announcer, sales rep. Station KCCR, Pierce, S. Dak. 1961–62; sales rep. Station KELO TV, Sioux Falls, S. Dak. 1962–64; sales rep., sales man. Station WTTC, Minneapolis 1964–66; Gen. Sales Man. Westinghouse Broadcasting Co. 1966–71; Vice-Pres., Man. Station KSDO, San Diego, Calif. 1972–75, Station WTOP, Washington, DC 1976–77; Vice-Pres. CBS-owned AM Stations, New York 1977–80; Vice-Pres., Gen. Man. WBBM-TV, Chicago 1980–83, WCBS-TV, New York 1983–84; Exec. Vice-Pres. CBS Sports, New York 1984–85, Pres. 1985–87; Pres. Multimedia Entertainment 1987–90; Exec. Vice-Pres., Pres. Marketing, CBS 1990–94; Broadcast Group Pres. CBS Pres. 1995–97, Exec. Vice-Pres. CBS TV Network 1994–95, CEO CBS 1995–97, Pres. CEO CBS TV and Cable 1997–. *Address:* CBS, 51 W 52nd Street, New York, NY 10019, USA.

LUNDBERG, Bo Klas Oskar, FRAeS; Swedish aeronautical scientist; b. 1 Dec. 1907, Karlskoga; s. of Ehrenfried Lundberg and Fanny Lundberg; m. Svea Maria Johansson 1935; two s. two d.; ed Hudiksvalls Läroverk and Royal Inst. of Tech., Stockholm; Dr in Aeronautics; Designer Test Pilot, AB Svenska Järnvägsverkstäderna, Aeroplanavdelningen, Linköping 1931–35, Sparmanns flygplanverkstad, Stockholm 1935–37; Asst Insp. at the Bd of Civil Aviation, Stockholm 1937–38; Chief, Aeronautical Dept, Götaverken, Gothenburg 1939; Chief Designer J-22 Fighter, Royal Air Bd 1940–44; Chief, Structures Dept, Aeronautical Research Inst. of Sweden 1944–47, Dir-Gen. 1947–67, Aviation Consultant 1967–; Fellow Royal Swedish Acad. of Eng Sciences, Canadian Aeronautics and Space Inst., Socio Onorario, Istituto Internazionale delle Comunicazioni; mem. AAAS; Hon. Fellow AIAA; Thulin Medal, Silver 1948, Gold 1955, Flight Safety Foundation Air Safety Award 1960, Sherman Fairchild Certificate of Merit 1963, Monsanto Aviation Safety Award 1963, Carl August Wicander Gold Medal 1966. *Publications include:* Fatigue Life of Airplane Structures (18th Wright Brothers Lecture) 1954, Should Supersonic Airliners be Permitted? 1961, Some Special Problems Connected with Supersonic Transport 1961, Speed and Safety in Civil Aviation (3rd Daniel and Florence Guggenheim Memorial Lecture) 1962, The Allotment of Probability Shares (APS) Method, A Guidance for Flight Safety Measures 1966, Economic and Social Aspects of Commercial Aviation at Supersonic Speeds 1972, Why the SST Should Be Stopped Once and For All 1973; numerous articles and papers mainly on the problems of aircraft safety and supersonic transport. *Leisure interests:* golf, tennis.

LUNDGREEN-NIELSEN, Flemming Torkild Jacob, DPhil; Danish university professor; b. 24 Jan. 1937, Hellerup; s. of Otto Nielsen and Edith Mortensen; ed Frederiksborg Statsskole and Univ. of Copenhagen; teaching posts at Univ. of Copenhagen 1965–, Lecturer 1972–88, Prof. DIS Study Div. 1970–90, Docent 1988–; mem. Danish Soc. of Language and Literature, Royal Acad. of Sciences and Letters. *Publications:* Grundtvig. Skaebne og forsyn 1965, Den nordiske fortaelling i det 18. årh. 1968, Det handlende om I-II 1980, CC Lyschanders digtning I-II 1989, Jens Bielke: Relation om Grønland 1990, Grundtvig og danskhed, in Dansk identitetshistorie 3 1992, På sporet af dansk identitet 1992, København laest og påskrevet 1997, Svøbt i mår. Dansk Folkevisekultur 1550–1700 I–IV (Ed. and Contrib.) 1999–2002; articles on Danish and Scandinavian literary subjects. *Address:* Institute of Nordic Philology, University of Copenhagen, Njalsgade 80, 2300 Copenhagen S (Office); Upsalagade 22, 2100 Copenhagen Ø, Denmark (Home). *Telephone:* 35-32-83-11; 35-32-83-37 (Office); 35-43-46-68 (Home). *Fax:* 35-32-83-77. *E-mail:* flemnil@hum.ku.dk.

LUNDGREN, Dolph, MA; American actor; b. 3 Nov. 1959, Stockholm, Sweden; ed Washington State Univ., Mass. Inst. of Tech. and Royal Inst. of Tech. Stockholm; fmr doorman at Limelight disco, New York. *Films include:* A View to a Kill, Rocky IV, Masters of the Universe, Red Scorpion, The Punisher, I Come in Peace, The Eleventh Station, Dark Angel, Showdown in Little Tokyo, Universal Soldier, The Joshua Tree, Meltdown, Army of One, Johnny Mnemonic, The Shooter, The Algonquin Goodbye, The Peacekeeper 1997, The Minion, Sweepers 1999, Storm Catcher 1999, Bridge of Dragons 1999, The Last Patrol 2000, The Last Warrior 2000, Agent Red 2001.

LUNDY, Victor Alfred, MArch, FAIA; American architect; b. 1 Feb. 1923, New York; s. of Alfred Henry Lundy and Rachel Lundy; m. 1st Shirley Corwin 1947 (divorced 1959); one s. one d.; m. 2nd Anstis Manton Burwell 1960; one s.; ed New York Univ. Coll. of Architecture, Harvard Univ.; mil. service 1943–46; pvt. practice, Sarasota, Fla 1951–59, New York 1960–75, projects include US Tax Court Bldg and Plaza, Washington, DC, US Embassy in Colombo, Sri Lanka, Recreation Shelters for Smithsonian Inst., travelling air-supported Exhbn Bldg and exhibit for US Atomic Energy Comm. and commercial, religious and govt bldgs throughout the USA and overseas; pvt. practice, Houston, Tex. 1976–87, Design Prin. and Vice-Pres. HKS Inc., Dallas, Tex. 1984–90, visiting professorships and lectureships, Harvard, Yale, Columbia, Calif. (Berkeley) and Houston Univs and Rome Univ., Italy; work included in many exhbns including São Paulo Int. Biennial Exhbn of Architecture 1957, America Builds, Berlin 1957, Fifth Congress Union Internationale des Architectes, Moscow 1958, Expo '70, Osaka, Japan 1970; Fellow AIA; numerous prizes and awards including Purple Heart Medal and US Combat Infantry Badge. *Projects include:* GTE Telephone Operations World HQ, Irving, Tex., Greyhound Corp. (now Dial Corp.) Center, Phoenix, Ariz., Mack Center II, Tampa, Fla, Walnut Glen Tower (now Dr Pepper Bldg), Dallas, Tex. Austin Centre-Radisson Hotel and One Congress Plaza, Austin, Tex. *Address:* HKS Inc., 1111 Plaza of the Americas North, Suite LB 307, Dallas, TX 75201 (Office); 701 Mulberry Lane, Bellaire, TX 77401, USA (Home). *Telephone:* (214) 969-3396.

LUNENFELD, Bruno, MD, FRCOG; Israeli endocrinologist; b. 11 Feb. 1927, Vienna, Austria; s. of David Lunenfeld and Ernestine Lunenfeld; m. Pnina Buyanover 1996; two s.; ed British Inst. of Eng Tech., Medical School, Univ. of Geneva, Switzerland; Acting Chief, Endocrine Research and Devt, Tel-Hashomer 1962–64; Scientist, Weizman Inst. of Science 1961–66; Assoc. Prof. and Head Dept of Biology, Bar-Ilan Univ. 1964–69, Prof. Ordinarius and Head Dept of Life Sciences 1969–71, Prof. of Life Sciences 1971; Dir Inst. of Endocrinology, Sheba Medical Centre 1964–92, Chair. Div. of Labs 1977–81, Chair. Research and Ethical Cttee 1977–81; mem. Expert Cttee on Biological Standardization, WHO 1967–87; Counsellor External Relations to Minister of Health and Head Dept of Int. Relations, Ministry of Health 1981–85; Acting Chief Scientist, Ministry of Health 1984–86; mem. Nat. Council for Research and Devt 1985–87; Visiting Prof., Yale School of Medicine, USA 1986–87; mem. Nat. Council for Health and Social Affairs 1985–87; Pres. Israel Fertility Asscn 1979–83, Israel Endocrine Soc. 1992–95; Pres. Int. Soc. for the Study of the Aging Male 1997–; Medical Dir Int. Fertility Inst., Ranana 1996–99; Vice-Pres. Scientific Council of Israel Medical Asscn; mem. Exec. Bd Scientific Council, Exec. Council of Int. Cttee for Research in Reproduction, Exec. Council Medical Examination Bd, Exec. Council of Int. Andrology Soc., Exec. Council of Int. Soc. of Gynaecological Endocrinology (and Treas. 1992–96); Ed.-in-Chief The Aging Male 1997–; Hon. Fellow American Coll. of Obstetricians and Gynaecologists; Pliskin Prize, Israel Trade Union Sick Fund 1962, Yaffeh Prize, Ministry of Health 1963, US Public Health Service Special Recognition Award 1983, Jacob Henle Medal (Georg Augustus Univ., Göttingen) 1993, Verdienstkreuz First Class (Germany) 1995. *Achievement:* discovered the clinical use of Human Menopausal Gonadotropin for the treatment of female and male infertility. *Publications:* 21 books including, Infertility, Diagnosis and Treatment of Functional Infertility 1978, Ovulation Induction 1982, Diagnosis and Management of Male Infertility 1984, Ovulation Induction and In Vitro Fertilization 1986, Infertility in Male and Female 1986, 1993, Textbook of Men's Health 2002; 25 chapters in books; 495 papers in scientific journals; 120 published lectures and abstracts. *Leisure interest:* sailing, walking. *Address:* 7 Rav Ashi Street, 69395 Tel-Aviv, Israel (Home). *Telephone:* 3-6425434 (Home). *Fax:* 3-6424454 (Home). *E-mail:* blunert@attglobal.net (Office).

LUNGIN, Pavel Semenovich; Russian scriptwriter and director; b. 12 July 1949, Moscow; m. Yelena Lungina; ed Moscow State Univ.; debut as script writer 1976, film dir 1990; Special Prize, Cannes Film Festival. *Films include:* The Problem is Brother 1976, The End of Taiga Emperor 1978, Invincible 1983, Fellow Traveller 1987, Oriental Romance 1992; Dir: Taxi-Blues 1990, Luna Park 1992, Line of Life 1996, Wedding 1999, Oligarch 2001. *Address:* Novy Arbat str. 31, apt 8, 121009 Moscow, Russia (Home). *Telephone:* (095) 205-04-32 (Home).

LUO GAN, DipEng; Chinese state and party official; b. 14 July 1935, Jinan, Shandong; m. He Zuozhi 1965; one s. one d.; ed Leipzig Univ.; joined CCP 1960; metallurgical and casting engineer; Vice-Gov. Henan Prov. 1981–83; alt. mem. 12th CCP Cen. Cttee 1982–87, mem. 13th Cen. Cttee 1987–92, 14th Cen. Cttee 1992–97, 15th CCP Cen. Cttee 1997–2002, 16th CCP Cen. Cttee 2002–; Sec. CCP Cttee, Henan 1983–85; mem. CCP Politburo, Sec. Secr. CCP Cen. Cttee 1997–2002; mem. Standing Cttee, Sec. Secr. CCP Cen. Cttee 1997–2002; mem. Standing Cttee 2002–; Vice-Pres. All-China Fed. of Trade Unions 1983–88; Sec.-Gen. of State Council 1988–98; State Councillor 1993–; Sec. Work Cttee for Cen. Govt Organs 1989–; Vice-Premier of State Council 1998–2003. *Address:* State Council, Zhong Nan Hai, Beijing, People's Republic of China.

LUO HAOCAI; Chinese judge and politician; b. March 1934, Anxi Co., Fujian Prov.; ed Beijing Univ.; teaching Asst, Lecturer, Assoc. Prof., Prof. Dept of Law, Beijing Univ. 1960–86; Vice-Pres. Beijing Univ. 1986–95; Chair. Beijing Fed. of Returned Overseas Chinese; Vice-Chair. China Law Soc.; mem. Standing Cttee China Admin. Man. Asscn; Vice-Pres. and mem. Judicial Cttee Supreme People's Court 1995–98; Vice-Chair. China Zhi Gong Dang (Party for Public Interests) 1992–97, Chair. 1997–; mem. Standing Cttee and Deputy Sec.-Gen. CPPCC 8th Nat. Cttee 1993–98, Vice-Chair. 9th Nat. Cttee

1998–. *Address:* National Committee of Chinese People's Political Consultative Conference, 23 Taipingqiao Street, Beijing, People's Republic of China. *E-mail:* zhigong@public2.east.net.cn (Office).

LUO PINGAN; Chinese artist; b. 12 April 1945, Xian; s. of Luo Deyu and Tian Cuilan; m. Qi Juyan 1969; two s.; ed Xian Acad. of Fine Arts; mem. China Artists' Asscn, Shaanxi br.; Artist of Shaanxi Imperial Art Gallery (traditional Chinese painting); Vice-Pres. Changan Imperial Art Acad.; 2nd Exhbn of paintings, sponsored by China Art Gallery and Research Inst. of Traditional Chinese Painting, Beijing, Feb. 1988; third Exhbn Hubei Prov. 1991; 4th Exhbn Tabei City, Taiwan; numerous exhbns subsequently; Dir Artistic Cttee of China Artistic Asscn, Shaanxi br.; Excellent Works Prize, Beijing 1988, Copper Medal of 7th Nat. Artistic Works-Exhbn 1989. *Publications:* The Collection of Luo Pingan's Painting, Collected Landscapes by Luo Pingan. *Leisure interests:* literature, folk art, countryside and music. *Address:* 32 North Street, Xian, Shaanxi Province, People's Republic of China. *Telephone:* 25333; 7251984 (Home).

LUO YUANZHENG, PhD; Chinese university professor; b. 14 Feb. 1924, Chengdu, Sichuan Prov.; s. of Zhungi Luo and Suqing You; m. Lida Feng 1947; one s. one d.; ed West Union Univ. Chengdu, Univ. of Calif., St Olife Coll., USA and Univ. of Leningrad, Russia; Sec. Econ. Dept Scientific Planning Cttee State Council 1956–57; Dir Co-ordination Office for Econ. Affairs, State Planning Comm. 1978–80; Deputy Dir and Research Fellow, Inst. of World Econs and Politics, Chinese Acad. of Social Sciences 1978–83; mem. Econ. Research Centre, State Council 1980–84; Exec. Chair. Sec. and Founder, All-China Union of Asscns for Econ. Studies 1981–84; Visiting Prof. Australian Nat. Univ. 1981; Prof. Beijing Univ. (and a dozen other Chinese univs) 1981–; Sr adviser to several provs and municipalities 1981–; Pres. Chinese Correspondence Univ. of Econ. Sciences 1984–88; Prof. European Man. School, Paris 1988; other professional appointments, editorships etc.; Vice-Pres. Int. Econ. Asscn 1989–92; Pres. China Int. Cultural Educ. Inst. 1992–; Chair. Econ. Forum of Hong Kong 1992; mem. Academic Advisory Bd Int. Centre for Econ. Growth (ICEG) 1992–; mem. CPPCC 1986–, mem. Econ. Cttee 1986–; Gen. Adviser to China Chamber of Commerce; Dir Asia Pacific Bd of Lucas; recipient of awards of State Council, Ministry of Higher Educ. etc. *Publications include:* On an Economic Community in the Pacific Region 1981, Impact of Socio-Economic Model on Education, Science and Culture 1983, Internationalization of Economic Life and China's Policy of Opening to the Outside World 1984, World Economy and China, On the Developmental Strategy Problems of an Economic Society 1986, Structural Reform and Economic Development in China 1989, Selected Works of Luo Yuangheng, The New Phase of China's Economic Development and Prospects for the New Century; papers on China's economy, world econ. devt etc. *Leisure interests:* music, Chinese classical poetry and verse. *Address:* 10-7-41 Xibianmenwai Dajei, 100045, Beijing, People's Republic of China. *Telephone:* 8523152 (Office); 8312308 (Home). *Fax:* 8534865 (Office); 8312308 (Home).

LUPERTZ, Markus; German artist and professor; b. 25 April 1941, Liberec, Bohemia; ed Werkkunstschule, Krefeld, Kunstakademie, Düsseldorf, Villa Romana, Florence; Prof. State Acad. of Fine Arts, Karlsruhe 1976, Prof. and Dir Acad. of Art, Düsseldorf 1986–; numerous exhbns; Villa Romana Prize 1970, Prize of Deutschen Kritikerverband, Esslingen Artists' Guild 1990. *Publications:* Selected Poems 1961–83. *Address:* c/o Galerie Michael Werner, Gertrudenstrasse 24-28, 5000 Cologne 1, Germany. *Telephone:* (221) 925462.

LUPOLIANSKI, Uri; Israeli politician; s. of Jacob Lupolianski and of the late Sarah Lupolianski; m.; twelve c.; school teacher, Jerusalem 1970s; Founder and Chair. Yad Sarah (charitable foundation) 1976–; Deputy Mayor of Jerusalem –2003, Acting Mayor 2003–; mem. United Torah Judaism; The Israel Prize 1994. *Address:* Yad Sarah, 124 Herzl Boulevard, 96187 Jerusalem, Israel (Office). *Telephone:* 2-2644429 (Office). *E-mail:* info@yadsarah .org.il (Office). *Website:* www.yadsarah.org.il (Office).

LUPU, Radu, MA; Romanian pianist; b. 30 Nov. 1945, Galaţi; s. of Meyer Lupu and Ana Gabor; ed High School, Braşov, Moscow Conservatoire, USSR; first piano lessons 1951; won scholarship to Moscow 1961; entered Moscow Conservatoire 1963, graduated 1969; First Prize, Van Cliburn Competition 1966; First Prize, Enescu Int. Competition, Bucharest 1967; First Prize, Leeds Int. Competition 1969; a leading interpreter of the German classical composers; appears frequently with all the major orchestras; has toured Eastern Europe with London Symphony Orchestra; American debut 1972; gave world première of André Tchaikowsky Piano Concerto, London 1975; Grammy Award for Best Instrumental Record of Year (for Schubert record) 1995, Edison Award for Best Instrumental Record of Year (for Schumann record) 1995. *Recordings include:* complete Beethoven cycle (with Israel Philharmonic and Zubin Mehta), complete Mozart sonatas for violin and piano with Szymon Goldberg), Brahms piano concerto No. 1 (with Edo de Waart and London Philharmonic Orchestra), Mozart piano concerto K467 (with Uri Segal and English Chamber Orchestra), various Beethoven and Schubert sonatas, Mozart and Beethoven wind quintets in E flat, Mozart concerto for 2 pianos and concerto for 3 pianos transcribed for 2 pianos (with Murray Perahia and English Chamber Orchestra), Schubert Fantasie in F minor and Mozart sonata in D for 2 pianos (with Murray Perahia), Schubert Lieder (with Barbara Hendricks), Schubert Piano Duets (with Daniel Barenboim). *Leisure interests:* history, chess, bridge. *Address:* c/o Terry Harrison Artists, The

Orchard, Market Street, Charlbury, Oxon., OX7 3PJ, England. *Telephone:* (1608) 810330. *Fax:* (1608) 811331. *E-mail:* artists@terryharrison.force9.co .uk (Office). *Website:* www.terryharrison.force9.co.uk (Office).

LURIE, Alison, AB; American novelist; b. 3 Sept. 1926, Chicago; d. of Harry Lawrence and Bernice Stewart Lurie; m. 1st Jonathon Peale Bishop 1948 (divorced 1985); three s.; m. 2nd Edward Hower 1996; ed Radcliffe Coll.; Lecturer in English, Cornell Univ. 1969–73, Adjunct Assoc. Prof. 1973–76, Assoc. Prof. 1976–79, Prof. 1979–; Yaddo Foundation Fellow 1963, 1964, 1966, 1984, Guggenheim Fellow 1965, Rockefeller Foundation Fellow 1967; Literature Award, American Acad. of Arts and Letters 1978, Pulitzer Prize in Fiction 1985. *Publications:* V. R. Lang: a Memoir 1959, Love and Friendship 1962, The Nowhere City 1965, Imaginary Friends 1967, Real People 1969, The War Between the Tates 1974, Only Children 1979, The Language of Clothes 1981, Foreign Affairs 1985, The Man with a Shattered World 1987, The Truth about Lorin Jones 1988, Don't Tell the Grown Ups, Subversive Children's Literature (essays) 1990, Women and Ghosts 1994, The Last Resort 1998, Familiar Spirits 2001. *Address:* Department of English, Cornell University, Ithaca, New York, NY 14853, USA. *E-mail:* al28@cornell.edu (Office).

LURIE, Ranan Raymond; American political cartoonist; b. 26 May 1932, Port Said, Egypt; s. of Joseph Lurie and Rose Lurie (née Sam) (parents Israeli citizens); m. Tamar Fletcher 1958; two s. two d.; ed Herzelia Coll., Tel Aviv and Jerusalem Art Coll.; Corresp. Maariv Daily 1950–52; Features Ed. Hador Daily 1953–54; Ed.-in-Chief Tavel (weekly magazine) 1954–55; staff political cartoonist Yedioth Aharonot Daily 1955–66, Honolulu Advertiser 1979; went to USA (invited by Life Magazine) 1968, naturalized 1974; political cartoonist, Life Magazine, New York 1968–73; political cartoonist interviewer Die Welt, Bonn 1980–81; Contrib. New York Times 1970–; Contrib. Ed. and political cartoonist, Newsweek Int. 1974–76; Ed., political cartoonist, Vision Magazine of S America 1974–76; syndicated United Features Syndicate 1971–73; syndicated nationally by Los Angeles Times and internationally by New York Times to over 260 newspapers 1973–75; syndicated nationally by King Features Syndicate, internationally by Editors Press Syndicate (345 newspapers) 1975–83, in USA by Universal Press Syndicate 1982–86; Lecturer, Univ. of Hawaii, American Program Bureau, Boston; political cartoonist, The Times, London 1981–83; Sr Political Analyst and cartoonist, The Asahi Shimbun, Tokyo 1983–84; Sr Analyst and political cartoonist, US News and World Report, Washington 1984–85; political cartoonist Time Magazine 1994–97; Ed.-in-Chief Cartoon News 1996–; Chief Editorial Dir Editors' Press Service 1985; inventor of first animated electronic television news cartoon; joined MacNeil/Lehrer News Hour as daily political cartoonist/analyst, appearing on 275 TV stations; Nightline (ABC TV network programme) and ZDF (German nat. TV); launched TV cartoon nationally; creator of Taiwan's official new nat. cartoon symbol 'Cousin Lee'; cr. Japan's nat. cartoon symbol 'Taro San'; TV Cartoon launched by ABC (USA) and ZDF (Germany); fine arts shows in Israel, Canada, USA 1960–75, including Expo 1967, Canada, Dominion Gallery, Montréal, Canada, Lim Gallery, Tel-Aviv 1965, Overseas Press Club, New York 1962, 1964, 1975, US Senate, Washington 1973, Honolulu Acad. Fine Arts 1979; exhibited in numerous group shows including Smithsonian Inst. 1972; trained as Parachute Officer, French Foreign Legion 1955, British Paratroopers 1956, US 101 Airborn Div. 1962, served as Combat Paratroop Maj., Israeli Army Reserve 1950–67; Sr Adjunct Fellow with The Center for Strategic and Int. Studies, Washington, DC; mem. Asscn of Editorial Cartoonists, Nat. Cartoonists' Soc. of America; mem. MENSA; Nat. Fed. of Hispanic-owned Papers est. Ranan R. Lurie Political Cartoon Award 1994; syndicated internationally to 1,098 papers in 104 countries; listed in Guinness Book of World Records as most widely syndicated political cartoonist in the world (Certificate of Merit for 20 years as consecutive title holder); Chief Judge Seoul Int. Cartoon Competition 1996; the UN established an Annual Int. Award in his honour (LurieUNaward.com) 1999; Hon. Assoc. mem. Asahi Shimbun; recipient highest Israeli journalism award 1954; U.S. Headliners Award 1972; named Outstanding Editorial Cartoonist of Nat. Cartoonist Soc. 1972–78; Salon Award, Montréal Cartoon 1971; New York Front Page Award 1972, 1974, 1977, Certificate of Merit of US Publication Designers 1974, Hon. Mention, Overseas Press Club 1979, winner of John Fischetti Political Cartoon Award 1982, Toastmasters' Int. and Leadership Award 1985, UN Soc. of Writers Award for Excellence 1995, Hubert H. Humphrey First Amendment Freedoms Prize 1996, Cartoon Award, UN 2000. *Publications:* Among the Suns 1952, Lurie's Best Cartoons (Israel) 1961, Nixon Rated Cartoons (New York Times) 1973, Pardon Me, Mr President (New York Times) 1974, Lurie's Worlds (USA) 1980, So sieht es Lurie (Germany) 1981, Lurie's Almanac (UK) 1982, (USA) 1983, Taro's International Politics, Taro-San No Kokusai Seijigaku (Japan) 1984, Lurie's Middle East 1986, Lurie's Mideast Almanac (Israel) 1986, Lurie's Far East Views (China) 1987; creator The Expandable Painting 1969. *Leisure interests:* Tamar (wife), Rod, Barak (sons), Daphne, Danielle (daughters). *Address:* Cartoonews International, 375 Park Avenue, Suite 1301, New York, NY 10152, USA. *Telephone:* (212) 980-0855 (Office). *Fax:* (212) 980-1664 (Office). *Website:* cartoonews.com.

LUSCOMBE, David Edward, LittD, FBA, FSA, FRHistS; British historian; b. 22 July 1938, London; s. of Edward Dominic Luscombe and Nora Luscombe; m. Megan Phillips 1960; three s. one d.; ed St Michael's Convent School, Finchley Catholic Grammar School, London and King's Coll. Cambridge; Fellow, King's Coll. 1962–64, Churchill Coll. Cambridge 1964–72; Prof. of

Medieval History, Univ. of Sheffield 1972–95, Leverhulme Personal Research Prof. of Medieval History 1995–, Research Prof. of Medieval History 2000–, Dean of Faculty of Arts 1985–87, Pro-Vice-Chancellor 1990–94, Chair. Humanities Research Inst. 1992–, Dir for Research in the Humanities Div. of Grad. School 1994–; mem. Governing Body, later the Asscn of St Edmund's House, Cambridge 1971–84; Dir Historical Asscn Summer School 1976, 1992; Visiting Prof. Royal Soc. of Canada 1991, Univ. of Conn. at Storrs 1993; Visiting Fellow All Souls Coll. Oxford 1994; Raleigh Lecturer, at British Acad. 1988; British Acad. Exchange Visitor to Japan Acad. 1996; mem. Council, British Acad. 1989–97, Publs Sec. 1990–97, Chair. Medieval Texts Editorial Cttee 1991–; mem. Publs Cttee 1989-97 (Chair. 1990–97), mem. Humanities Research Bd 1994–96; mem. Cttee, Soc. for Study of Medieval Languages and Literature 1991–96, Council, Royal Historical Soc. 1981–85, Cttee, Ecclesiastical History Soc. 1976–79, Supervisory Cttee British Acad./Oxford Univ. Press for New Dictionary of Nat. Biography 1992–99, Assoc. Ed. 1993–; Vice-Pres. Société int. pour l'étude de la philosophie médiévale 1987–97, Pres. 1997–; mem. Commonwealth Scholarships Comm. in UK 1994–2000; Auditor, Higher Educ. Quality Council, Div. of Quality Audit 1994–97; mem. Council Worksop Coll. and Ranby House School 1996–; Fellow of the Woodward Corpn 2000–; Hon. Sec. Cambridge Univ. Catholic Asscn 1968–70. *Publications:* The School of Peter Abelard, Peter Abelard's Ethics, Church and Government in the Middle Ages (jt ed.) 1976, Petrus Abaelardus (1079–1142): Person, Werk, und Wirkung (jt ed.) 1980, The Evolution of Medieval Thought by David Knowles (ed. revised edn with C. Brooke) 1988, David Knowles Remembered (co-author) 1991, Anselm, Aosta, Bec and Canterbury (jt ed.) 1996, Medieval Thought 1997; Cambridge Studies in Medieval Life and Thought, 4th series (Advisory Ed.) 1983–88, (Gen. Ed.) 1988–; articles in learned journals. *Leisure interests:* swimming, walking a spaniel, using libraries. *Address:* Department of History, Sheffield University, Sheffield, S10 2TN; 4 Caxton Road, Sheffield, S10 3DE, England (Home). *Telephone:* (114) 222-2555 (Office); (114) 268-6355 (Home). *Fax:* (114) 278-8304 (Office). *E-mail:* D.Luscombe@sheffield.ac.uk.

LUSINCHI, Jaime; Venezuelan politician and paediatrician; b. 27 May 1924, Clarines, Anzoátegui; m. Gladys Castillo (divorced 1988); five c.; ed Univ. del Oriente, Univ. Central; active mem. Acción Democrática (AD) Party 1941–; Pres. Legis. Ass. for Anzoátegui and regional Gen. Sec. 1948–52; arrested during presidency of Gen. Marcos Pérez Jiménez; in exile in Argentina, Chile and USA 1952–58; returned to Venezuela 1958; mem Rómulo Betancourt's electoral comm. 1958, mem. Nat. Exec. Cttee of AD 1958, Dir Int. Affairs 1958–61, Deputy for Anzoátegui 1959–67, Pres. Parl. Group 1968–78, Senator for Anzoátegui 1979–83, Presidential Cand. 1977, Sec.-Gen. AD 1980–83, Party Leader 1980–84; Pres. of Venezuela 1984–89; Senator 1989; sought refuge in Costa Rica from legal proceedings 1995; Paediatrician, Lincoln Hosp., Bellevue Medical Centre, New York 1958; mem. American Acad. of Pediatrics.

LÜST, Reimar, Dr rer. nat; German physicist; b. 25 March 1923, Barmen; s. of Hero Lüst and Grete Lüst (née Strunck); m. 1st Dr Rhea Kulka 1953; two s.; 2nd Nina Grunenberg 1986; ed Univs of Frankfurt am Main and Göttingen; Research Physicist, Max Planck Insts Göttingen and Munich 1950–60, Enrico Fermi Inst., Univ. of Chicago 1955–56, Princeton Univ. 1956; Head, Dept for Extraterrestrial Physics, Max Planck Inst. for Physics and Astrophysics 1960, Dir Inst. of Extraterrestrial Physics 1963–72; Visiting Prof., Univ. of New York 1959, MIT 1961, Calif. Inst. of Tech. 1962, 1966; Chair. German Research Council 1969–72, Deutsche Gesellschaft für Luft- und Raumfahrt 1968–72; Pres. Max-Planck-Gesellschaft 1972–84; Dir-Gen. European Space Agency 1984–90; Prof. Univ. of Hamburg 1992–; Pres. Alexander von Humboldt Foundation 1989–99, Hon. Pres. 1999; Chair. Bd Int. Univ. Bremen 1999; mem. Int. Acad. of Astronautics, Royal Astronomical Soc., Bavarian Acad. Sciences; Corresp. mem. Real Acad. de Ciencias Exactas, Físicas y Naturales de Madrid; Fellow Imperial Coll. of Science and Tech., London; Hon. Prof. Inst. for Theoretical Physics, Chinese Acad. of Sciences, Beijing 1997, Beijing Univ. 1997; Hon. Foreign mem. American Acad. of Arts and Sciences, Austrian Acad. of Sciences; Hon. mem. Heidelberg Acad. of Sciences, Senat Max-Planck-Gesellschaft, Deutsche Gesellschaft für Luft- und Raumfahrt; Officier, Ordre des Palmes Académiques; Officier, Légion d'honneur; Bayerischer Maximiliansorden für Wissenschaft und Kunst; Grosses Verdienstkreuz mit Stern und Schulterband; Distinguished Service Cross (Poland) 1997; Dr hc (Sofia) 1991, (Birmingham) 1993, (Slovak Acad. of Sciences) 1995 and several other hon. degrees from int. univs; Planet 4386 named Lüst 1991; Daniel and Florence Guggenheim Int. Astronautics Award, Personality of the Year 1986, Tsiolkowsky Medal (USSR Fed. of Cosmonauts) 1987, Harnack Medal of Max Planck Soc. 1993; and numerous other awards; shared Adenauer-de Gaulle Prize 1994. *Publications:* articles on space research, astrophysics and plasmaphysics. *Leisure interests:* history, tennis, skiing. *Address:* Max-Planck-Institut für Meteorologie, Bundesstr. 55, 20146 Hamburg (Office); Bellevue 49, 22301 Hamburg, Germany. *Telephone:* (40) 41173300. *Fax:* (40) 41173390; (40) 41173390 (Office).

LUSTIG, Arnošt; Czech writer and academic; b. 21 Dec. 1926, Prague; s. of Emil Lustig and Terezie Lustig (née Löwy); m. Věra Weislitz 1949; one s. one d.; ed Coll. of Political and Social Sciences, Prague; in concentration camps at Terezín, Auschwitz and Buchenwald, Second World War; Radio Prague corresp. in Arab-Israeli war 1948, 1949; Radio Prague reporter 1948–58; Ed. Mladý svět (weekly) 1958–59, screenplay writer for Studio Barandov 1960–68, for Jadran-Film Yugoslavia 1969–70; naturalized American citizen 1979; mem. Cen. Cttee Union of Czechoslovak Writers 1963–69, mem. Presidium 1963–69; mem. Int. Writing Program 1970–71; Visiting Lecturer Univ. of Iowa 1971–72; Visiting Prof. Drake Univ., Iowa 1972–73; Prof. of Literature, American Univ., Washington, DC 1973–; lecturer J. Škvorecký Literary Acad. 2000–; Hon. Pres. Franz Kafka Soc., Prague 1990–; Hon. mem. Club of Czech Writers 1999–; Hon. DHL (Spertus Coll. of Judaica, Chicago) 1986; Klement Gottwald State Prize 1967, B'nai B'rith Prize 1974, Nat. Jewish Book Award 1980, 1986, Emmy Award, The Nat. Acad. of Television Arts and Sciences 1986, Publr's Weekly Literary Prize, USA 1991, Karel Čapek Literary Prize, Prague PEN Club Int. 1996, Medal of Merit, Czech Repub. 2000. *Screenplays:* Names for which there are no people (Prague) 1960, Theresienstadt (Prague) 1965, Stolen Childhood (Italy) 1966, Triumph of Memory (PBS) 1984, Previous Legacy (USA) 1984, Fighter (USA) 2000, Tamge (Prague) 2002. *Films:* Europa (co-author; autobiographical documentary) 1998, Fighter (autobiographical documentary) 2000. *Publications:* Démanty noci (Diamonds of the Night, short stories, two of which were filmed 1961, 1964) 1958, Blue Day (story, filmed for TV) 1960, remade 1995, Night and Hope (short stories) 1958, filmed as Transport z ráje (Transport from Paradise) 1962, Modlitba za Kateřinu Horovitzovou (A Prayer for Katerina Horovitzova–novel, filmed for TV) 1965, Dita Saxova (novel) 1962 (filmed 1968, republished 1994), The Street of Lost Brothers (short stories) 1962, Prague Crossroads 1964, The Man the Size of a Stamp 1965 (radio plays), Nobody will be Humiliated (long stories) 1965, The White Birches in Autumn (novel) 1966, Bitter Smell of Almonds (novel) 1968, Darling (novel) 1969, Darkness Casts No Shadow (novel) 1976, Children of the Holocaust (3 vols, collected stories) 1977–78, 1986, 1995, 1996, The Holocaust and the Film Arts (essay with Josef Lustig) 1980, The Precious Legacy (screenplay for documentary) 1984, The Unloved (from the diary of 17-year-old Pearl Sch., novel) 1985, 1996, Indecent Dreams (collection of short novels) 1988, Street of Lost Brothers (collection of stories) 1990, Colette, Girl from Antwerp (novel, in Czech) 1993, Tanga, Girl from Hamburg (novel, in Czech) 1993, Porges (novel, in Czech) 1995, Friends (novel, in Czech) 1995, House of the Echo Returned (novel) 1995, Chasm (novel, in Czech) 1996, Beautiful Green Eyes (in Czech), (in English) 2002, in Jewish Yearbook 1997–1998, Fire on the Water (3 novellas) 1998, Initiation 2001, Bitter Smell of Almonds (3 vols of collected stories) 2001, Collected Works (8 vols) 1992–2002, Lustig ist Gott, Gott ist Lustig 2001, House of Returned Echo 2002; text for symphonic poem Night and Hope (with Otmar Macha) 1963, The Beadle of Prague (text for a cantata) 1983; Answers (2 interviews) 2002, Essays 2002, Zasvěcení (interviews) 2002. *Leisure interests:* swimming, travelling, skiing, soccer. *Address:* 4000 Tunlaw Road, NW, Apartment 825, Washington, DC 20007, USA. *Telephone:* (202) 885-2984 (Office); (202) 338-5357 (Home). *Fax:* (202) 885-2938 (Office).

LUSTIGER, HE Cardinal Jean-Marie, MPh, Lic en Theol; French ecclesiastic; b. 17 Sept. 1926, Paris; s. of Charles and Gisèle Lustiger; ed Carmelite Seminary, Inst. Catholique de Paris and Université de Paris (Sorbonne); ordained priest 1954; Chaplain to the students, Sorbonne 1954–69; Dir Centre Richelieu, Paris 1959–69; Pastor, Sainte-Jeanne-de-Chantal parish, Paris 1969–79; Bishop of Orléans 1979–81; Archbishop of Paris Jan. 1981–; cr. Cardinal Feb. 1983; mem. Acad. Française. *Publications:* Sermons d'un curé de Paris 1978, Pain de vie, Peuple de Dieu 1981, Osez croire, Osez vivre 1985, Premiers pas dans la prière 1986, Six sermons aux élus de la Nation 1986, Le choix de Dieu 1987, The Lord's Prayer 1988, La Messe 1988, Le Sacrement de l'Onction des malades 1990, Dieu merci, les droits de l'homme 1990, Nons avons rendez-vous avec l'Europe 1991, Petites paroles de nuit de Noël 1992, Devenez dignes de la condition humaine 1995, Le Baptême de votre enfant 1997, Soyez heureux 1997, Pour l'Europe, un nouvel art de vivre 1999, Les Prêtres que Dieu donne 2000, Comme Dieu vous aime 2001, La promesse 2002. *Address:* Maison diocésaine, 7 rue Saint Vincent, 75018 Paris, France.

LUSZTIG, George, MA, PhD, FRS; American professor of mathematics; b. 20 May 1946, Timişoara, Romania; m. Michal-Nina Abraham 1972 (divorced 2000); two d.; ed Univ. of Bucharest and Princeton Univ.; Visiting mem. Inst. for Advanced Study, Princeton, NJ 1969–71; Research Fellow, Dept of Math., Univ. of Warwick 1971–72, Lecturer 1972-74, Prof. 1974-78; Prof. of Math. MIT 1978–; mem. NAS; Guggenheim Fellowship 1982; Cole Prize in Algebra (American Math. Soc.) 1985, Brouwer Medal (Dutch Math. Soc.) 1999. *Publications:* The Discrete Series of GLn over a Finite Field, 1974, Characters of Reductive Groups over a Finite Field 1984, Introduction to Quantum Groups 1993. *Leisure interest:* yoga. *Address:* Department of Mathematics, Massachusetts Institute of Technology, Room 2-276, 77 Massachusetts Avenue, Cambridge, MA 02139 (Office); 106 Grant Avenue, Newton, MA 02459, USA.

LUTON, Jean-Marie; French engineer; b. 4 Aug. 1942, Chamalières; s. of Pierre Luton and Marie Luton; m. Cécile Robine 1967; three s.; ed Lycée Blaise Pascal, Clermont-Ferrand, Lycée St Louis, Paris, Faculté des Sciences, Paris and Ecole Polytechnique; Centre Nat. de la Recherche Scientifique (CNRS) 1964–71; Ministry of Industrial and Scientific Devt 1971–73; Head of Research, Centre Nat. d'Etudes Spatiales (CNES) 1974–75, Head of Planning 1975–78, Dir of Programmes and Planning 1978–84, Deputy Dir-Gen. 1984–87; Dir of Space Programmes, Aérospatiale 1987–89; Dir-Gen. CNES 1989–90; Dir-Gen. European Space Agency 1990–97; Pres., Dir-Gen., then Chair. Arianespace 1997–; Chevalier, Légion d'honneur, Officier, Ordre nat. du Mérite; Prix de l'Astronautique; Prix de l'Innovateur industriel, Society of Satellite Professionals (USA) 1998. *Leisure interests:* tennis, sailing. *Address:* Arianespace, boulevard de l'Europe, B.P. 177, 91006 Evry Cédex, France.

LUTTER, Marcus Michael, PhD; German professor of law; b. 11 Dec. 1930, Munich; s. of Michael Lutter; m. Rebecca Garbe 1957; one s. two d.; ed Univs of Munich, Paris and Freiburg; notary, Rockenhausen 1957–60; research scholarship, Deutsche Forschungsgesellschaft, Brussels, Strasbourg, Paris, Rome, Utrecht 1961–63; notary, Rockenhausen and external lecturer, Univ. of Mainz 1964–65; Prof. Inst. for Civil Law, German and European Trade and Econ. Law, Univ. of Bochum 1966–79; fmr Prof. and Dir Inst. for Trade and Econ. Law, Univ. of Bonn, now Prof. Emer. and Dean of the Centre for European Econ. Law; Visiting Prof. Univ. of Calif. at Berkeley 1972, Tschno Univ., Tokyo 1982, Oxford Univ. 1997; Pres. German Lawyers' Asscn 1982–88; Hon. PhD (Vienna), (Warsaw). *Publications:* The Letter of Intent 1983, Information and Confidentiality in the Supervisory Board 1984, Duties and Rights of Board Members 1993, European Company Law 1996; various monographs and treatises especially on participation, jt stock cos and supervisory bds; Publr Zeitschrift für Unternehmens-und Gesellschaftsrecht. *Address:* Zentrum für Europäisches Wirtschaftsrecht der Universität Bonn, Adenauerallee 24-42, 53113 Bonn (Office); Auf der Steige 6, 53129 Bonn, Germany (Home). *Telephone:* (228) 739559 (Office); (228) 231722 (Home). *Fax:* (228) 737078 (Office). *E-mail:* marcus.lutter@jura.uni-bonn.de (Office).

LUTTWAK, Edward Nicolae, PhD; American academic, international consultant and writer; b. 4 Nov. 1942, Arad, Romania; s. of Joseph Luttwak and Clara Baruch; m. Dalya Iaari 1970; one s. one d.; ed elementary schools in Palermo and Milan, Carmel Coll., Wallingford, UK, London School of Econs and John Hopkins Univ.; Lecturer, Univ. of Bath, UK 1965–67; Consultant, Walter J. Levy SA (London) 1967–68; Visiting Prof. Johns Hopkins Univ. 1974–76; Sr Fellow, Georgetown Univ. Center for Strategic and Int. Studies 1977–87, Burke Chair. of Strategy 1987–92, Sr Fellow 1992–; Consultant to Office of Sec. of Defense 1975, to Policy Planning Council, Dept of State 1981, Nat. Security Council 1987, Dept of Defense 1987, to Govts of Italy, Korea, Spain; Prin., Edward N. Luttwak Inc. Int. Consultants 1981–; Int. Assoc. Inst. of Fiscal and Monetary Policy, Japan Ministry of Finance (Okurasho); mem. editorial Bd of The American Scholar, Journal of Strategic Studies, The National Interest, Géopolitique, The Washington Quarterly, Orbis; Nimitz Lectureship, Univ. of Calif. 1987, Tanner Lecturer, Yale Univ. 1989, Rosonstiel Lecturer, Grinner Coll. 1992. *Publications:* Coup d'Etat 1968, Dictionary of Modern War 1972, The Israeli Army 1975, The Political Uses of Sea Power 1976, The Grand Strategy of the Roman Empire 1978, Strategy and Politics: Collected Essays 1979, The Grand Strategy of the Soviet Union 1983, The Pentagon and the Art of War 1985, Strategy and History: collected essays 1985, International Security Yearbook 1984/85 (with Barry M. Brechman) 1985, On the Meaning of Victory 1986, Strategy: The Logic of War and Peace 1987, The Dictionary of Modern War (with Stuart Koehl) 1991, The Endangered American Dream 1993, Il Fantasma della Povertà (co-author) 1996, Cose è davvero la Democrazia 1996, La Renaissance de la puissance aérienne stratégique 1998, Turbo-Capitalism 1999, Il Libro della Libertà 2000; his books have been translated into 14 languages. *Leisure interest:* ranching in the Amazon. *Address:* Center for Strategic and International Studies, 1800 K Street, NW, Washington, DC 20006, USA. *Telephone:* (202) 775-3145. *Fax:* (202) 775-3199.

LUTZ, Robert A., MBA; American business executive; b. 12 Feb. 1932, Zürich, Switzerland; s. of Robert H. Lutz and Marguerite Lutz; m. 1st Betty D. Lutz 1956 (divorced 1979); m. 2nd Heide-Marie Schmid 1980 (divorced 1993); m. 3rd Denise Ford 1994; four d. from 1st marriage; ed Univ. of Calif. at Berkeley; Capt. U.S. Marine Corps 1954–59; Research Assoc. IMEDE, Lausanne 1962–63; Senior Analyst, Forward Planning, Gen. Motors, New York 1963–65; Staff Asst, Man. Dir.'s Staff, Adam Opel AG (GM) 1965–66; various man. positions, GM (France) 1966–69; Asst Domestic Gen. Sales Man., Merchandising, Adam Opel AG 1969, Dir of Sales and mem. Management Bd 1969–70; Vice-Pres. (Sales) and mem. Management Bd, BMW AG 1970–74; Gen. Man. Ford of Germany 1974–76; Vice-Pres. (Truck Operations), Ford of Europe 1976–77; Pres. Ford of Europe 1977–79; Vice-Pres. Ford Motor Co. and Chair. of Bd, Ford of Europe 1979–82; Exec. Vice-Pres. Ford Int. Automotive Operations 1982–86, Exec. Vice-Pres. N American Truck Operations 1986; Head, Int. Operations Chrysler 1986–91, Chrysler Corpn 1991–96, Corpn Vice-Chair. 1997, Exec. Vice-Pres. 1986–88, Pres., Chrysler Motors Corpn 1988–96, also COO; Chair., CEO, Pres. Exide Corpn 1998–2001, Chair. 2001–; Vice-Chair. of Product Devt, Gen. Motors (GM) 2001–, Chair. GM N America 2001–; Bd Divs Silicon Graphics, ASCOM, Switzerland. *Publication:* Guts. *Address:* Exide Corporation, 645 Pennsylvania Street, Reading, PA 19601, USA (Office).

LUXEMBOURG, Grand Duke of (see Henri).

LUXON, Benjamin Matthew, CBE, FGSM; British musician; b. 24 March 1937, Redruth, Cornwall; s. of Maxwell Luxon and Lucille Grigg; m. Sheila Amit 1969; two s. one d.; ed Truro School, Westminster Training Coll., Guildhall School of Music and Drama; always a freelance artist; sang with English Opera Group 1963–70; has sung with Royal Opera House, Covent Garden and Glyndebourne Festival Opera 1971–96, Boston Symphony Orchestra 1975–96, Netherlands Opera 1976–96, Frankfurt Opera House 1977–96; performs as recitalist with piano accompanist David Willison; folksinging partnership with Bill Grofut 1976–96; has recorded for all major record cos; retd from professional singing due to severe hearing loss 1996; Hon. mem. RAM; Hon. DMus (Exeter Univ.), (RSA of Music and Drama) 1996, (Canterbury Christ Church Coll.) 1997; Bard of Cornish Gorseth. *Leisure interests:* most sports, English watercolours of 18th and 19th centuries. *Address:* The Mazet, Relubbus Lane, St Hilary, Penzance, Cornwall, TR20 9DS, England.

LUXTON, John, BAgrSc; New Zealand politician; m.; three c.; ed Massey Univ.; Nat. Party MP for Matamata 1987–96, for Karapiro 1996–99; Minister of Housing and Energy, Assoc. Minister of Educ. 1990–93, Assoc. Minister of Maori Affairs. 1991–97; Minister of Maori Affairs, Police and Assoc. Minister of Educ. 1993–97, Minister of Commerce, Fisheries, Lands and Biosecurity, for Industry and Assoc. Minister for Agric. 1997–98; Minister of Food, Fibre, Biosecurity and Border Control, Assoc. Minister of Immigration and Assoc. Minister for Int. Trade 1998–99; Nat. Party Spokesperson on Int. Trade Negotiations and Inward Investment and Regional Devt, Assoc. Foreign Affairs 2000–01; Nat. Party Spokesman for Tourism, Communications, Inward Investment 2001–; fmr Chair. Tatua Industry Co-operative Dairy Co. Ltd, Deputy Chair. Wallford Meats Ltd; Dir Wallace Corpn Ltd, Tatua Co-operative Dairy Co., Asia 2000 Foundation; int. agric. consultant and farmer; AC Cameron Memorial Award 1987. *Address:* Parliament Buildings, Wellington, New Zealand. *Telephone:* (4) 471-9509 (Office). *Fax:* (4) 473-0469 (Office). *E-mail:* john.luxton@parliament.govt.nz (Office).

LUZHKOV, Yuri Mikhailovich; Russian politician; b. 21 Sept. 1936, Moscow; m. 1st; two s.; m. 2nd Yelena Baturina; two d.; ed Gubkin Inst. of Oil and Gas, Moscow; researcher, Research Inst. of Plastic Materials 1958–64; Head of Div. Ministry of Chemical Industry 1964–87; First Deputy Chair. Exec. Cttee, Moscow City Council and Chair. Moscow Agric. Industry Dept 1987–90; Chair. Exec. Cttee, Moscow City Council 1990–91; Vice-Mayor of Moscow and Premier Moscow City Govt 1991–92, Mayor and Head of City Govt 1992–, re-elected 1996, 1999; mem. Russian Council of Fed. 1996–2001; Founder, Co-Chair. Otechestvo (Fatherland) Movt 1998–; Co-Chair. Organising Cttee of United Party Yedinstro-Otechestvo; Chair. Int. Fund Assistance to Free Enterprise; Hon. Prof. Acad. of Labour and Social Relations; Golden Mask Prize for support of the arts. *Publications:* 72 Hours of Agony 1991, The Quietist Negotiations 1994, We Are Your Children, Moscow 1996. *Leisure interests:* football, fishing, bee-keeping. *Address:* Government of Moscow, Tverskaya str. 13, 103032 Moscow, Russia. *Telephone:* (095) 292-04-78, 229-32-97. *Fax:* (095) 234-32-97; (095) 234-32-95. *E-mail:* mayor@mos.ru.

LUZÓN LÓPEZ, Francisco; Spanish banker; b. 1 Jan. 1948, Cañavate (Cuenca); trainee, Banco de Vizcaya 1972, Regional Man. Seville 1974, Man. of Planning and Man. Control, Bilbao 1975–78, Int. Div. Madrid 1978–80, Man. London 1980–81; mem. Bd and Gen. Man. Banco de Crédito Comercial 1981–82; mem. Bd and Gen. Man. Banco Occidental 1982–85; Gen. Man. Commercial Banking Network 1985–87; mem. Bd and Gen. Man. Banco de Vizcaya 1987–88, Banco Bilbao-Vizcaya 1988; Chair. Banco Exterior de España 1988–99; Vice-Pres. Banco Atlántico and mem. Bd Teneo 1991–94; Chair. Argentaria 1991, Caja Postal SA 1991–, Banco de Crédito Local 1994–99, Banco Hipotecario de España 1994–, Corporación Bancaria de España SA. *Address:* Paseo de Recoletos 10, 28001 Madrid, Spain. *Telephone:* (91) 5377000. *Fax:* (91) 5378034.

LUZZATTO, Lucio, FRCPath, FRCP; Italian geneticist and haematologist; b. 28 Sept. 1936, Genoa; s. of the late Aldo Luzzatto and of Anna Luzzatto Gabrielli; m. Paola Caboara 1963; one s. one d.; ed Liceo D'Oria, Genoa, Univ. of Genoa Medical School, Univ. of Pavia; Sr Lecturer in charge of Sub-Dept of Haematology, Univ. of Ibadan, Nigeria 1967–68, Prof. of Haematology 1968–74, Consultant Haematologist, Univ. Coll. Hosp. Ibadan, Nigeria 1967–68; Dir Int. Inst. of Genetics and Biophysics, CNR, Naples 1974–81; Prof. of Haematology (Univ. of London) and Dir of Haematology Dept Royal Postgrad. Medical School, Consultant Haematologist Hammersmith Hosp., London, UK 1981–94, Hon. Dir MRC/LRF Leukaemia Unit, London 1987–93; Chair. Dept of Human Genetics, Courtney Steel Chair., Attending Physician in Genetics and Haematology, mem. Cell Biology Program, Memorial Sloan-Kettering Cancer Center, New York, Prof. of Medicine and Human Genetics, Cornell Univ. Medical Coll., New York 1994–2000; Scientific Dir Nat. Inst. of Cancer Research (IST), Genoa, Italy 2000–; Hon. DSc (Ibadan) 1998; Dr hc of Pharmacy (Urbino) 1990; Pius XI Medal 1967, Sanremo Int. Prize for Human Genetics 1982, Int. Chiron Award for Biomedical Research 1995, Premio Napoli 1995. *Publications:* 330 articles in scientific journals and scientific and medical textbooks. *Address:* Istituto Nazionale Ricerca sul Cancro (IST), Largo R. Benzi 10, Genoa, Italy. *Telephone:* (10) 352776 (Office). *Fax:* (10) 355573 (Office). *E-mail:* lucio.luzzatto@istge.it (Office).

LVOV, Dmitry Semenovich, DEconSc; Russian economist; b. 2 Feb. 1930, Moscow; m.; two c.; ed Moscow S. Ordzhonikidze Inst. of Eng and Econ.; Sr Researcher, Head of Lab., Head of Div., Prof. Moscow Inst. of Eng and Econ., later Inst. of Econ. USSR Acad. of Sciences; Deputy Dir Cen. Inst. of Math. and Econ.; corresp. mem. USSR (now Russian) Acad. of Sciences 1987, mem. 1994, Deputy Chair. Council on Econ. Man. 1995–, Acad.-Sec. Dept of Econs 1996–2002; author of alternative econ. reform project Oct. 1998–; Pres. Int. Cen. for studies of econ. reforms; Ed.-in-Chief Econ. Science of Contemporary Russia. *Publications include:* 14 books including Effective Management of Technical Development 1990; over 250 works on econ. efficiency of capital investments and new tech., pricing, prognosis of tech. processes. *Leisure interest:* poetry. *Address:* Central Institute of Mathematics and Economics, Krasikov str. 32, 117418 Moscow, Russia. *Telephone:* (095) 129-08-22; (095) 129-16-44 (Office).

LYAKHOV, Vladimir Afanasyevich; Russian cosmonaut (retd); b. 20 July 1941, Antratsit; m.; two c.; ed Kharkov Aviation School for Pilots, Gagarin Mil. Acad.; mem. CPSU 1963–91; served in fmr Soviet Air Force 1964–; mem. Cosmonaut team 1967–95; Commdr of space-ship Soyuz-32 1979 and Soyuz T-9 which connected up with orbital station Salyut-7; Commdr Soyuz TM5-6 1988; space-walked 1983; worked in Yuri Gagarin Centre 1995–99; Hero of Soviet Union (twice); K. Tsiolkovski Gold Medal. *Address:* Yuri Gagarin Centre, Zvezdny Gorodok, Moscow Region, Russia. *Telephone:* (095) 971-86-16.

LYAKISHEV, Nikolai Pavlovich; Russian metallurgist; b. 5 Oct. 1929; m.; two d.; ed Moscow Inst. of Steel and Alloys; Researcher, then Head of Lab., Deputy Dir, Dir Bardin Cen. Research Inst. of Black Metals; Dir Baikov Inst. of Metallurgy and Material Science, USSR (now Russian) Acad. of Sciences; Corresp. mem. USSR (now Russian) Acad. of Sciences 1981, mem. 1987, mem. Presidium 1991–2001; Lenin Prize, USSR State Prize. *Publications include:* main works in the field of steelmaking and ferroalloys, structural materials, including Niobium in Steel and Alloys 1971, Metallurgy of Chromium 1977, Aluminothermics 1978, Theory and Practice of Ferroalloys Production 1999, Metallic Single Crystals 2002. *Leisure interest:* chess. *Address:* Baikov Institute of Metallurgy and Material Science, Leninsky Prospect 49, 119911 Moscow, Russia (Office). *Telephone:* (095) 135-20-60 (Office). *Fax:* (095) 135-86-80 (Office).

LYALL, John Adrian, RIBA, FRSA; British architect; b. 12 Dec. 1949, Daws Heath, Essex; s. of Keith Lyall and Phyllis Lyall (née Sharps); m. Sallie Jean Davies 1991; one s. one d.; ed Southend High School for Boys, Essex, Architectural Asscn School of Architecture; worked for Cedric Price, Piano & Rogers, Bahr, Vermeer & Haecker, Rock Townsend 1966–79; Founder Multimatch Design Group 1970–73; in practice with Will Alsop as Alsop & Lyall, later Alsop, Lyall & Störmer 1980–91; Man. Dir John Lyall Architects 1991–; RIBA Vice-Pres. of Cultural Affairs 1997, of Future Studies 1999–2000, Chair. of Validation Task Force, RIBA 2001; Bannister Fletcher Prof. Univ. Coll. London 1998; design teaching and lecturing at Architectural Asscn and Bartlett Schools, London and univs in USA, UK, Russia, Chile, Colombia and Ecuador; design adviser to Cardiff Bay Devt Corpn and English Partnerships; apptd as enabler for CABE 2001 and Chair. of RIBA's Validation Task Force 2001–02; numerous awards including: RIBA Nat. Awards 1991, 1999; Leeds Award for Architecture 1990, 1992; Ironbridge Award, British Archaeological Soc. 1990, 1992, 1998; RIBA White Rose Award 1991, Civic Trust 1991, Design Week Award 1991, Royal Inst. of Chartered Surveyors Urban Renewal Award 1995. *Television:* contrib. to Masterclass – Denys Lasdun; panel mem. BBC Knowledge 2000–01. *Dance:* design collaborator with Rosemary Butcher Dance Co. on various performances 1990–96. *Music:* production designer for Opera 80 travelling opera 1980–83. *Achievements:* award-winning bldgs include: The Corn Exchange, Leeds, White Cloth Hall, Leeds, Tottenham Hale Station, London, North Greenwich Jubilee Line Station, London, Crystal Palace Park, London, Regeneration of Cranfield Mills, Ipswich (in progress). *Publications:* John Lyall: Contexts and Catalysts; contrib. to Context – New Buildings in Historic Settings. *Leisure interest:* choral singing. *Address:* John Lyall Architects, 13–19 Curtain Road, London, EC2A 3LT (Office); Newlands, Gandish Road, East Bergholt, Suffolk, CO7 6TP, England (Home). *Telephone:* (20) 7375-3324 (Office); (1206) 298368 (Home). *Fax:* (20) 7375-3325 (Office). *E-mail:* john@johnlyallarchitects.com (Office); john.lyall4@virgin.net (Home). *Website:* www.johnlyallarchitects.com (Office).

LYELL, Sir Nicholas (Walter), Kt, PC, QC; British politician; b. 6 Dec. 1938; s. of the late Sir Maurice Legat Lyell and of Veronica Mary Lyell; m. Susanna Mary Fletcher 1967; two s. two d.; ed Stowe School, Christ Church, Oxford; nat. service RA 1957–59; Walter Runciman & Co. 1962–64; called to the Bar, Inner Temple 1965, Bencher 1986; pvt. practice London (Commercial, Industrial and Public Law) 1965–86, 1997–, a Recorder 1985–2001; Jt Sec. Constitutional Cttee 1979; MP for Hemel Hempstead 1979–83, for Mid Bedfordshire 1983–97, for Bedfordshire North East 1997–2001; Parl. Pvt. Sec. to Attorney-Gen. 1979–86; Parl. Under-Sec. of State (Social Security) DHSS 1986–87; Solicitor-Gen. 1987–92, Attorney-Gen. 1992–97; Shadow Attorney-Gen. 1997–99; Chair. Soc. of Conservative Lawyers; Vice-Chair. British Field Sports Soc. 1983–86; Gov. Stowe School 1990–, Chair. 2001–. *Leisure interests:* gardening, shooting, drawing. *Address:* Monckton Chambers, 4 Raymond Buildings, Grays Inn, London, WC1R 5BP, England. *Telephone:* (20) 7405-7211.

LYGO, Adm. Sir Raymond Derek, KCB, FRAeS, FRSA, CBIM; British business executive; b. 15 March 1924, Ilford, Essex; s. of the late Edwin and of Ada E Lygo; m. Pepper van Osten 1950; two s. one d.; ed Ilford County High School and Clarkes Coll., Bromley; The Times 1940; naval airman, Royal Navy 1942; served V.S.N. 1949–51; CO 759 Squadron 1951–53, 800 Squadron 1954–56, HMS Lowestoft 1959–61, HMS Juno 1967–69, CO HMS Ark Royal 1969–71; Vice-Chief of Naval Staff 1975–77, Chief of Naval Staff 1977–78; joined British Aerospace 1978, Man. Dir Hatfield/Lostock Div. 1978–80, Chair. and Chief Exec. Dynamics Group 1980–82; Man. Dir British Aerospace PLC 1983–86, mem. Bd 1980–89, Chief Exec. 1985–89; Chair. British Aerospace Enterprises Ltd, British Aerospace (space systems) Ltd and British Aerospace Holdings Inc. 1988–89, Rutland Trust PLC 1992–99, TNT Express (UK) 1992–97, TNT Europe Ltd 1992–97, River and Mercantile First UK Investment Trust (now Liontrust) 1997–; Dir James Capel Corporate Finance 1990–92; Chair. Royal Ordnance PLC 1987; Pres. Soc. of British Aerospace

Cos. 1984–85, Vice-Pres. 1985–; Patron Youth Sports Trust 1996–; Liveryman Coachmakers; Freeman City of London. *Leisure interests:* building, gardening, joinery. *Address:* c/o Barclays Premier Banking, 54 Lombard Street, London, EC3 9EX, England.

LYKKETOFT, Mogens; Danish politician; b. 9 Jan. 1946, Copenhagen; m. Jytte Hilden 1982; two d.; ed Univ. of Copenhagen; worked at Econ. Council of the Labour Movt 1966–81, Head of Dept 1975–81; mem. Folketing (Parl.) 1981–, Political Spokesman for Social Democratic Party 1991–93, 2001–02, Leader 2002–; Minister for Inland Revenue 1981; Minister of Finance 1993–2000, of Foreign Affairs 2000–01. *Publications:* ed. of several books and numerous articles in magazines, periodicals and newspapers. *Address:* Folketinget, Christiansberg, 1240 Copenhagen; Odensegade 17, 1, 2100 Copenhagen, Denmark (Home). *Telephone:* 33-37-55-00 (Office); 35-38-00-89 (Home). *Fax:* 33-12-55-02 (Office); 35-42-91-96. *E-mail:* smoly@ft.dk (Office). *Website:* www.socialdemokratiet.dk (Office).

LYMAN, Princeton, PhD; American diplomatist; b. 20 Nov. 1935, San Francisco; s. of Arthur Lyman and Gertrude Lyman; m. Helen Ermann 1957; three d.; ed Univ. of Calif. at Berkeley and Harvard Univ.; joined US Govt service 1961; Agency for Int. Devt 1961–80; Dir USAID, Addis Ababa 1976–78; Dept of State 1980–; Deputy Asst Sec. for Africa 1981–86; Amb. to Nigeria 1986–89, to South Africa 1992–95; Dir Bureau of Refugee Programs 1989–92; Asst Sec. of State for Int. Org. Affairs 1997–; Bd Divs American Foreign Service Asscn; Dept of State Superior Honor Award; Pres.'s Distinguished Service Award. *Publications:* Korean Development: The Interplay of Politics and Economics 1971. *Leisure interests:* tennis, photography, piano. *Address:* Bureau of International Organizations, 2201 C Street, NW, Washington, DC 20520, USA.

LYMPANY, Dame Moura, DBE, FRAM; British concert pianist; b. 18 Aug. 1916, Saltash, Cornwall; d. of John Johnstone and Beatrice Lympany; m. 1st Colin Defries 1944 (divorced 1950); m. 2nd Bennet H. Korn 1951 (divorced 1961); one s. (deceased); ed Belgium, Austria, England; first performance, Harrogate 1929; has played in USA, Canada, South America, Australia, New Zealand, India and most European countries including the fmr USSR; started Festival de la Musique et du Vin, (Rasiguères France) 1981, Le Festival des Sept Chapelles (Brittany), 1986; Medal of Cultural Merit (Portugal) 1989, Charles Heidsieck Prize (Royal Philharmonic Soc.) 1989; Commdr Order of Crown (Belgium) 1980, Chevalier des Arts et des Lettres (France) 1992, Order of Prince Henry the Navigator (Portugal) 1996. *Publication:* Autobiography 1991. *Leisure interests:* gardening, reading, tapestry. *Address:* c/o Transart, 8 Bristol Gardens, London, W9 2JG, England.

LYNAM, Desmond Michael, ACII; British sports broadcaster; b. 17 Sept. 1942, Ennis, Repub. of Ireland; s. of Edward Lynam and Gertrude Veronica Malone; m. Susan Eleanor Skinner (divorced 1974); one s.; ed Varndean Grammar School, Brighton, Brighton Business Coll.; career in insurance –1967; freelance journalist and reporter local radio 1967–69; reporter, presenter and commentator BBC Radio 1969–78; presenter and commentator BBC TV Sport 1978–99 (including Grandstand, Sportsnight, Match of the Day, Commonwealth and Olympic Games and World Cup coverage); presenter Holiday (BBC) 1988–89, How Do They Do That? (BBC) 1994–96; presenter, The Des Lynam Show (BBC Radio) 1998–99, ITV Sport 1999–, BAFTA TV Awards (ITV) 2000, The Premiership (ITV) 2001–; TV Sports Presenter of the Year, TRIC 1985, 1987, 1988, 1993, 1997, Radio Times Male TV Personality 1989, RTS Sports Presenter of the Year 1994, 1998, Richard Dimbleby Award, BAFTA 1994, Variety Club of GB Media Award 1997. *Publications:* Guide to the Commonwealth Games 1986, The 1988 Olympics 1988, The 1992 Olympics 1992, Sport Crazy 1998. *Leisure interests:* golf, tennis, Brighton and Hove Albion, reading, theatre. *Address:* c/o Jane Morgan Management Ltd, Cafe Royal, 68 Regent Street, London, W1B 5EL, England. *Telephone:* (20) 7287-6045 (Office). *Fax:* (20) 7494-4093 (Office). *E-mail:* enquiries@janemorganmgt.com (Office).

LYNCH, David; American film director; b. 20 Jan. 1946, Missoula, Mont.; m. 1st Peggy Reavey 1967 (divorced); one d.; m. 2nd Mary Fisk 1977 (divorced); one s.; ed Hammond High School, Alexandria, Corcoran School of Art, Washington, DC, School of Museum of Fine Arts, Boston and Pennsylvania Acad. of Fine Arts, Philadelphia; Fellow, Center for Advanced Film Studies, American Film Inst., LA 1970; Dr hc (Royal Coll. of Art) 1991. *Films include:* The Grandmother 1970, Eraserhead 1977, The Elephant Man 1980, Dune 1984, Blue Velvet 1986 (Golden Palm, Cannes), Wild at Heart 1990 (Golden Palm, Cannes 1990), Storyville 1991, Twin Peaks: Fire Walk With Me 1992, Lost Highway 1997, Crumb (presenter), The Straight Stay 1999, Mullholland Drive (Best Dir, Cannes Film Festival) 2000. *Television includes:* Twin Peaks 1990, Mulholland Drive 2000. *Address:* c/o Endeavor Talent Agency, 9701 Wilshire Boulevard, 10th Floor, Beverly Hills, CA 90212, USA (Office).

LYNCH, Michael Francis, AM; Australian arts administrator; b. 6 Dec. 1950, Sydney; s. of Wilfred Brian Lynch and Joan Margaret Lynch; m. 1st Jane Scott 1967 (divorced 1987); one d.; m. 2nd Irene Hannan; two step s.; m. 3rd Christine Josephine Lynch; ed Marcellin Coll., Randwick, Univ. of Sydney; fmr Gen. Man. King O'Malley Theatre Co., Australian Theatre for Young People; Admin. Australian Nat. Playwrights Conf.; Gen. Man. Nimrod Theatre 1976–78; Casting Dir and Man. Partner Forecast Pty Ltd 1981–89; Gen. Man. Sydney Theatre Co. 1989–94, Australia Council 1994–98; Chief Exec. Sydney Opera House 1998–2002; Chief Exec. South Bank Centre,

London 2002–. *Leisure interests:* film, theatre, racing, beach. *Address:* South Bank Centre, South Bank, London, SE1 8XX, England (Office). *Website:* www .sbc.org.uk (Office).

LYNCH, Peter; American stock investor; b. 1944; m. Carolyn Lynch; three d.; Man. Fidelity Magellan Fund, Boston 1977–90; Trustee Fidelity Investments 1990–. *Publication:* One Up on Wall Street. *Address:* 27 State Street, Boston, MA 02109, USA.

LYNCH, Philip; business executive; fmr Man. Dir Lehman Brothers; fmr Chair. Int. Petroleum Exchange; Chief Exec. Exchange Clearing House (ECHO) 1996–.

LYNDEN-BELL, Donald, CBE, MA, PhD, FRS; British professor of astrophysics; b. 5 April 1935, Dover; s. of the late Lt-Col L. A. Lynden-Bell and of M. R. Lynden-Bell; m. Ruth M. Truscott 1961; one s. one d.; ed Marlborough Coll. and Clare Coll. Cambridge; Harkness Fellow, Calif. Inst. of Tech. and Hale Observatories 1960–62, Visiting Assoc. 1969–70, Research Fellow, then Fellow and Dir of Studies in Math., Clare Coll. Cambridge 1960–65; Asst Lecturer in Applied Math. Univ. of Cambridge 1962–65; Prin. Scientific Officer, later Sr Prin. Scientific Officer, Royal Greenwich Observatory, Herstmonceux 1965–72; Prof. of Astrophysics, Univ. of Cambridge 1972–2001; Dir Inst. of Astronomy, Cambridge 1972–77, 1982–87, 1992–94; Visiting Professorial Fellow, Queen's Univ. Belfast 1996–; Pres. Royal Astronomical Soc. 1985–87; Foreign Assoc., NAS 1993; Hon. mem. American Astronomical Soc. 2001; Hon. DSc (Sussex) 1987; Eddington Medal 1984, Gold Medal (Royal Astronomical Soc.) 1993, (Royal Soc. of SA), Catherine Wolf Bruce Medal of the Astronomical Soc. of the Pacific 1998, J. J. Carty Award, NAS 2000, Russell Lecturer, American Astronomical Soc. 2000. *Publications:* article in journal Nature 1969 gave the theory of quasars predicting giant black holes in galactic nuclei (found 1995); contribs to Monthly Notices of Royal Astronomical Soc. *Leisure interest:* hill-walking. *Address:* Institute of Astronomy, The Observatories, Madingley Road, Cambridge, CB3 0HA, England. *Telephone:* (1223) 337526.

LYNE, Adrian; British film director; b. Peterborough; m. Samantha Lyne; one d.; ed Highgate School; joined J. Walter Thompson (advertising agency) in post room, later became asst producer of commercials; with two partners set up own co. Jennie & Lyne 1971; Dir commercials including advertisements for Calvin Klein clothes and Pepsi Cola; Palme d'Or, Cannes Commercial Film Festival 1976, 1978. *Films include:* Foxes, Flashdance 1983, 9½ Weeks 1986, Fatal Attraction 1991, Jacob's Ladder (also co-writer)1990, Indecent Proposal 1993, Lolita 1997 and two short films: The Table, Mr Smith.

LYNE, Sir Roderic Michael John, BA, KBE, CMG; British diplomatist; b. 31 March 1948; s. of the late Air Vice-Marshal Michael Lyne and of Avril Joy Buckley; m. Amanda Mary Smith 1969; two s. one d.; ed Eton Coll., Univ. of Leeds; joined Diplomatic Service 1970, British Embassy, Moscow 1972–74, British Embassy, Senegal 1974–76; Eastern Europe and Soviet Dept, FCO 1976–78, Rhodesia Dept 1979, Asst Pvt. Sec. to Foreign and Commonwealth Sec. 1979–82; Perm. Mission to UN, New York 1982–86; Visiting Research Fellow, Royal Inst. of Int. Affairs 1986–87; Head of Chancery and Political Section, Embassy, Moscow 1987–90; Head of Soviet Dept, FCO 1990–91, of Eastern Dept 1992–93; Pvt. Sec. to Prime Minister 1993–96; Dir of Policy Devt for CIS, Middle East and Africa British Gas PLC 1996; Perm. Rep. to UN, Geneva 1997–2000; Amb. to Russia 2000–; Hon. Prof., Moscow Higher School of Social and Econ. Studies 2001; Hon. PhD (Leeds) 2002. *Leisure interest:* sport. *Address:* British Embassy, 121099 Moscow, Smolenskaya Naberezhnaya 10, Russia (Office). *Telephone:* (095) 956-72-00 (Office). *Fax:* (095) 956-72-01 (Office). *E-mail:* moscow@britishembassy.ru (Office). *Website:* www.britemb.msk.ru (Office).

LYNN, Dame Vera, DBE; British singer; b. 20 March 1917; d. of Bertram Welch and Ann Welch; m. Harry Lewis 1941; one d.; ed Brampton Road School, East Ham; joined singing troupe 1928; ran dancing school 1932; broadcast with Joe Loss and joined Charlie Kunz band 1935; singer with Ambrose Orchestra 1937–40, then went solo; voted most popular singer in Daily Express competition 1939; own radio show Sincerely Yours 1941–47; sang to troops abroad during Second World War, named 'Forces' Sweetheart'; appeared in Applesauce, London 1941; post-war radio and TV shows and numerous appearances abroad including Denmark, Canada, South Africa and Australia; most successful record Auf Wiederseh'n; Pres. Printers' Charitable Corpn 1980; Hon. Citizen Winnipeg 1975; Freedom of City of London 1978, Commdr Order of Orange-Nassau (Holland), Burma Star Medal and War Medal 1985, Variety Club Int. Humanitarian Award, European Woman of Achievement Award 1994. *Publications:* Vocal Refrain (autobiog.) 1975, We'll Meet Again (with Robin Cross) 1989, The Woman Who Won the War (with Robin Cross and Jenny de Gex) 1990, Unsung Heroines 1990. *Leisure interests:* gardening, painting, sewing, swimming.

LYNNE, Gillian, CBE; British director, choreographer, dancer and actress; d. of the late Leslie Pyrke and of Barbara Pyrke (née Hart); m. Peter Land 1980; ed Baston School, Bromley, Kent, Arts Educational School; leading soloist, Sadler's Wells Ballet 1944–51; star dancer, London Palladium 1951–53; role in film Master of Ballantrae 1952; lead dancer in Can-Can, Coliseum, London 1954–55; numerous roles as dancer, actress and revue artist; conceived, directed, choreographed and starred in Collages, Edin. Festival 1963; choreography for numerous TV shows; Trustee The Arts Educational School, London; Gov. Sadler's Wells Foundation; Patron Ind.

Dancers' Resettlement Trust, Liverpool Inst. for Performing Arts, Language of Dance Centre, Holland Park, British Asscn of Choreographers, Adventures in Motion Pictures Ltd. *Choreography includes:* The Owl and the Pussy Cat (first ballet) 1962, Queen of the Cats 1962–63, Wonderful Life (first film) 1963–64, Every Day's a Holiday, Three Hats for Lisa (musical film) 1964, The Roar of the Greasepaint, and Pickwick, Broadway 1965, The Flying Dutchman, Covent Garden 1966, Half a Sixpence (film) 1966–67, How Now Dow Jones, Broadway 1967, Midsummer Marriage, Covent Garden 1968, The Trojans, Covent Garden, 1969, 1977, Breakaway (ballet), Scottish Theatre Ballet 1969, Phil the Fluter, Palace 1969, Ambassador, Her Majesty's 1971, Man of La Mancha (film) 1972, The Card, Queen's Theatre 1973, Hans Christian Andersen, London Palladium 1975, The Way of the World, Aldwych 1978, My Fair Lady, nat. tour and Adelphi 1979, Parsifal, Covent Garden 1979, Cats (also Assoc. Dir), New London Theatre (Olivier Award) 1981 and subsequently Broadway 1982, nat. and world tour (Molière Award for Best Musical, Paris 1989), Café Soir (ballet), Houston Ballet Co. 1985, Cabaret, Strand 1986, The Phantom of the Opera, Her Majesty's 1986 (world tour 1989–93), A Simple Man (ballet), Sadler's Wells 1988, The Brontës, Northern Ballet Theatre 1995 (also Dir), The Secret Garden (also musical staging), RSC Stratford 2000 and London 2001, Chitty Chitty Bang Bang (also musical staging), London 2002. *Director and choreographer:* The Match Girls, Globe 1966, Bluebeard, Sadler's Wells Opera 1966 and new production Sadler's Wells Opera, Coliseum 1969, Love on the Dole (musical), Nottingham Playhouse 1970, Liberty Ranch, Greenwich 1972, Once Upon a Time, Duke of York's, London 1972, Jasperina, Amsterdam 1978, Cats, Vienna (Silver Order of Merit, Austria 1984) 1983, Paris 1989, Valentine's Day, Chichester 1991, Globe 1992, Dancing in the Dark 1991, What the World Needs, Old Blobe, San Diego 1997–98, Gigi, Vienna 1999, Richard Whittington, Sadler's Wells 1999. *Directed:* Round Leicester Square (review), Prince Charles 1963, Tonight at Eight, Hampstead 1970 and Fortune 1971, Little White Lies, Nottingham 1971, A Midsummer Night's Dream (Co-Dir), Stratford 1977, Tomfoolery, Criterion 1980, To Those Born Later, New End 1981, La Ronde RSC Aldwych 1982, That's What Friends are For!, Mayfair 1996, Avow, USA 1996. *Directed and appeared in:* Alone Plus One, Newcastle 1982, The Rehearsal, Yvonne Arnaud, Guildford and tour 1983, Cabaret, Strand 1986. *Staged:* England Our England (revue), Prince's 1961, 200 Motels (pop-opera film) 1971, musical numbers in Quilp (film) 1974, A Comedy of Errors, Stratford 1976 (TV musical 1977), musical version of As You Like It, Stratford 1977, Songbook, Globe 1979, Once in a Lifetime, Aldwych 1979, new stage act for Tommy Steele 1979, wedding sequence in Yentl (film) 1982, European Vacation II (film) 1985, Pirelli Calendar 1988, Pickwick, Chichester and Sadler's Wells 1993. *Choreographed for television:* Peter and the Wolf (narrated and mimed all nine parts) 1958, At the Hawk's Well (ballet) 1975, There Was a Girl 1975, The Fool on the Hill (first colour special for Australian Broadcasting Corpn with the Australian Ballet and Sydney Symphony Orchestra in Sydney Opera House) 1975, Muppet Show series 1976–80, Alice in Wonderland (musical staging) 1985; shows and specials for Val Doonican, Perry Como, Petula Clark, Nana Mouskouri, John Curry, Harry Secombe, Ray Charles and Mike Burstein; also produced and devised Noel Coward and Cleo Laine specials. *Directed for television:* The Various Ends of Mrs F's Friends 1981, Easy Money 1982, (also devised) Le Morte d'Arthur (Samuel G. Engel Award, USA) 1983, A Simple Man (BAFTA Award for Direction and Choreography)1987, The Look of Love 1989. *Publications:* (contrib.) Cats, The Book of the Musical; articles in Dancing Times. *Address:* Lean Two Productions Ltd, 18 Rutland Street, London, SW7 1EF, England (Office). *Telephone:* (20) 7584-9342 (Office). *Fax:* (20) 7225-3651 (Office).

LYNTON, Michael, MBA; American publisher; b. 1 Jan. 1960, London, UK; s. of Mark O L. Lynton and Marion Sonnenberg; m. Elizabeth Jane Alter; two d.; ed Harvard Coll., Harvard Business School; Assoc., The First Boston Corpn 1982–85; Sr Vice-Pres. Disney Publishing Group 1987–93, Pres. Hollywood Pictures, The Walt Disney Co. 1993–96; Chair. and CEO The Penguin Group 1996–2000; Pres. AOL Int. 2000–, also Pres. for Int. Efforts and Exec. Vice-Pres. AOL Time Warner Inc. 2002–. *Address:* AOL International, 7th Floor, 45 West 18th Street, New York, NY 10014, USA. *Website:* www .aoltimewarner.com.

LYON, Mary Frances, BA, PhD, ScD, FRS, FIBiol; British geneticist; b. 15 May 1925, Norwich; d. of Clifford James Lyon and Louise Frances Lyon (née Kirby); ed Woking Grammar School, Girton Coll. Cambridge; on Medical Research Council (MRC) Scientific Staff, Inst. of Animal Genetics Edin. 1950–55; Scientific Staff MRC Radiobiology Unit, Harwell 1955–90, Head of Genetics Section 1962–87; Clothworkers Visiting Research Fellow, Girton Coll. Cambridge 1970–71; Foreign Assoc. Nat. Acad. of Sciences 1979; Foreign Hon. mem. American Acad. of Arts and Sciences 1980; Francis Amory Prize, American Acad. of Arts and Sciences 1977, Royal Medal, Royal Soc. 1984, San Remo Int. Prize for Genetics 1985, Gairdner Int. Award 1985, William Allan Award, American Soc. of Human Genetics 1986, Wolf Prize in Medicine 1997. *Publications:* papers on genetics in scientific journals. *Address:* Medical Research Council Mammalian Genetics Unit, Harwell, Didcot, Oxon., OX11 0RD, England. *Telephone:* (1235) 834393. *Fax:* (1235) 834776. *E-mail:* m .lyon@har.mrc.ac.uk (Office).

LYONS, Sir John, Kt, LittD, PhD, FBA; British professor of linguistics; b. 23 May 1932, Manchester; s. of Michael Austin Lyons and Mary Bridget O'Sullivan; m. Danielle Jacqueline Simonet 1959; two d.; ed St Bede's Coll. Manchester and Christ's Coll. Cambridge; Lecturer in Comparative Linguistics, SOAS, Univ. of London 1957–61; Lecturer in Linguistics and Fellow of Christ's Coll., Univ. of Cambridge 1961; Prof. of Gen. Linguistics, Univ. of Edin. 1964–76; Prof. of Linguistics, Univ. of Sussex 1976–84, Dean, School of Social Sciences 1979–81, Pro-Vice-Chancellor 1981–84, Visiting Prof. of Linguistics 1984–; Master of Trinity Hall, Cambridge 1984–2000; Hon. Fellow Christ's Coll. Cambridge 1985; Hon. mem. Linguistic Soc. of America; Dr hc (Univ. Catholique, Louvain) 1980; Hon. DLitt (Reading) 1986, (Edin.) 1988, (Sussex) 1990, (Antwerp) 1992. *Publications:* Structural Semantics 1963, Introduction to Theoretical Linguistics 1968, Chomsky 1970, 1977, 1991, New Horizons in Linguistics 1970, Semantics 1 and 2 1977, Language and Linguistics 1980, Language, Meaning and Context 1981, Natural Language and Universal Grammar 1991, Linguistic Semantics 1995. *Address:* Master's Lodge, Trinity Hall, Cambridge, CB2 1TJ, England. *Telephone:* (1223) 332540. *Fax:* (1223) 462116.

LYSSARIDES, Vassos, MD; Cypriot politician; b. 13 May 1920, Lefkara; s. of Michael Lyssarides and Eleni Lyssanides; m. Barbara Cornwall 1963; ed Univ. of Athens; mem. House of Reps 1960–, Pres. 1985–91; Pres. Socialist Party of Cyprus (EDEK) (now Movt of Social Democrats (KISOS)) 1969–2002, Hon. Pres. 2002–; Sec.-Gen. Int. Cttee of Solidarity with the Struggle of the Peoples of Southern Africa; Vice-Pres. Presidium, Afro-Asian Peoples' Solidarity Org.; Hon. Pres. Nicosia Medical Asscn Hippocrates. *Exhibitions:* two in Cyprus, one in Greece. *Leisure interests:* poetry, painting. *Address:* P.O. Box 21064, 1096 Nicosia, Cyprus. *Telephone:* 22666763. *Fax:* 22666762. *E-mail:* info@kisos.org (Office). *Website:* www.kisos.org (Office).

LYTH, Ragnar Vilhelm, BA; Swedish theatre director; b. 2 April 1944, Karlstad; s. of Arne Lyth and Reidunn Eleonore; m. 1st Karin Falk 1967; m. 2nd Kerstin Österlin 1996; two s.; ed Nat. Film School, Swedish Dramatic Inst.; theatre and TV director in Sweden, Norway and Denmark; represented Sweden at int. TV festival 'INPUT', Philadelphia, Banff, Montréal 1985, 1989, 1993; Head of Stage Dirs Swedish Dramatic Inst. 1984–86; Chair. Swedish Dirs' Union; Head Vestmanlands Theatre; Prof. of Theatre Direction; recipient of Sweden Art Award. *Plays directed include:* The Wild Duck 1997, Hedda Gabler 1998, Faust (I and II) 1999, Temperance 2000, The General Inspector 2001. *Television:* Death Dance 1981, Hamlet 1985, Don Juan 1988, Maclean 1991. *Leisure interest:* nature. *Address:* Sjöbjörnsvägen 25, 11767 Stockholm, Sweden. *Telephone:* (8) 19-88-93. *E-mail:* lyth@spray.se (Home).

LYTTELTON, Humphrey Richard Adeane; British bandleader and journalist; b. 23 May 1921, Eton, Bucks.; s. of the late Hon. George William Lyttelton; m. 1st Patricia Mary Braithwaite 1948 (divorced 1952); one d.; m. 2nd Elizabeth Jill Richardson 1952; two s. one d.; ed Sunningdale School, Eton Coll.; Grenadier Guards 1941–46; Camberwell Art School 1947–48; formed own band 1948; cartoonist for London Daily Mail 1949–53; freelance journalist and leader of Humphrey Lyttelton's Band 1953–; recorded Parlophone 1950–60, Columbia 1960–63, Black Lion 1973–83, Calligraph Records (own label) 1984–, contrib. Melody Maker 1954–2001, Reynolds News 1955–62, Sunday Citizen 1962–67, Harpers and Queen (Restaurant column) 1968–76, Punch; Compère BBC jazz programmes: Jazz Scene, Jazz Club, Jazz 625 (TV); frequent TV appearances; Chair. "I'm Sorry I Haven't a Clue" BBC Radio 4 1972–; Pres. Soc. for Italic Handwriting 1990–; Hon. Prof. of Music, Keele Univ. 1993; Hon. DLitt (Warwick) 1987, (Loughborough) 1988, Hon. DMus (Durham) 1994, (Keele) 1992. *Publications:* I Play as I Please 1954, Second Chorus 1958, Take it from the Top 1975, The Best of Jazz–Basin Street to Harlem 1978, Humphrey Lyttelton's Jazz and Big Band Quiz 1979, The Best of Jazz 2–Enter the Giants 1981, Why No Beethoven? The diary of a vagrant musician 1984, The Best of Jazz 1998. *Leisure interests:* birdwatching, calligraphy. *Address:* BBC, Broadcasting House, Portland Place, London, W1A 4WW; Alyn Close, Barnet Road, Arkley, Herts., EN5 3LS, England (Home). *Telephone:* (20) 7580-4468 (London).

LYUBIMOV, Yuriy Petrovich; Hungarian/Russian/Israeli actor and theatrical director; b. 30 Sept. 1917, Yaroslavl'; m. 7th Katalin Lyubimov; one s.; ed Vakhtangov Theatre Studio; served in Soviet Army 1939–47; mem. CPSU 1947–83; Teacher and Producer Shukin Drama School (Vakhtangov Theatre) 1953–64; Dir Moscow Theatre of Drama and Comedy (Taganka) 1964–84, 1989–; left the Soviet Union 1984, acquired Israeli citizenship 1987, returned 1988, citizenship restored 1989, acquired Hungarian citizenship 1999; awards include State Prizes 1952, 1997, People's Artist of Russia 1991, Order of the Great Patriotic War 1996, Services to the Motherland, 1st Class 1997, Triumph Premium 1998. *Roles include:* Oleg Koshevoy (The Young Guard by Fadeyev), Shubin (On the Eve by Turgenev), Chris (All My Sons by Arthur Miller), Benedict (Much Ado About Nothing), Mozart (The Little Tragedies by Pushkin); prominent in Soviet films 1947–, including Busy Stock, Robinson Crusoe, Cuban Cossacks. *Theatre productions include:* The Good Woman of Szechuan 1963, Ten Days that Shook the World 1965, Mother (Gorky) 1969, Hamlet 1972, Crime and Punishment (London) 1983, The Devils (London, Paris) 1985, Boris Godunov (Moscow) 1987, Hamlet (London) 1989, Self-Murderer (Moscow) 1990, Electra (Moscow) 1992, Zhivago (Vienna) 1993, The Seagull (Athens) 1993, Creditors (Athens) 1994, Medea (Athens) 1995, The Brothers Karamazov (Moscow) 1997, Marat-Sade (Moscow) 1998, Chronicles (Moscow) 2000, Eugene Onegin (Moscow) 2000 and others (total of 90). *Opera productions include:* Al gran sole carico d'amore (La Scala) 1975, Boris Godunov (La Scala) 1981, Eugene Onegin (Bonn) 1987, The Queen of Spades (Karlsruhe), 1990, Lady Macbeth of Mtsensk (Hamburg) 1990, Nabucco (Bonn) 1997, Love for Three Oranges (Munich) 1991. *Leisure interests:* music, cinema, gardening. *Address:* Taganka Theatre, Zemlanoy val 76, Moscow 109004 (Office); M. Nikitskaya str. 16–21, Moscow 121069, Russia (Home). *Telephone:* (095) 915-10-37 (Office); (095) 290-19-34 (Home). *Fax:* (095) 274-00-33 (Office); (095) 290-19-34 (Home). *E-mail:* taganka-theatre@mtu-net.ru (Office). *Website:* www.taganka.org (Office).

LYUBSHIN, Stanislav Andreyevich; Russian actor; b. 6 April 1933; m.; two s.; ed Shchepkin Theatre School; worked with various Moscow theatres: Sovremennik, Taganka, Yermolova, Malaya Bronnaya 1959–80; one of prin. actors with Moscow Arts Theatre 1980–, Anton Chekhov Arts Theatre 1987–; film debut 1959; RSFSR People's Artist 1981. *Roles in:* No Sackings Today 1959, I am Twenty Today 1965, Sword and Shield 1968, Red Square 1970, Defence Counsel 1977, Call Me into the Faraway 1978, Five Evenings 1979, Three Years 1980 (dir with D. A. Dolinin), Encounter 1981, Tartuffe 1984, Phantoms among us 1985, Ivanov 1989 and many other film and stage roles. *Address:* Vernadskogo prosp. 123, Apt. 171, 117571 Moscow, Russia. *Telephone:* (095) 433-35-14.

LŽICAR, Josef, DIur; Czech lawyer; b. 6 June 1944, Švábenice; s. of Josef Lžicar and Anna Lžicar; m. Zdenka; one s.; ed Charles Univ., Prague; lawyer and advocate 1967–; Chief of Office of Pres. of Czechoslovak Repub. 1989–1990; mem. Czech Chamber of Advocates 1990–, Helsinki Cttee 1990–. *Leisure interest:* ornithology. *Address:* Sokolovska 24–37, 18600 Prague 8, Czech Republic (Office). *Telephone:* (2) 22325334 (Office).

NOTE: All names beginning Mc and Mac are treated as if they began Mac.

MA, Yo Yo, BA; American cellist; b. 7 Oct. 1955, Paris; of Chinese parentage; m. Jill A. Hornor 1978; one s. one d.; ed Harvard Univ. and cello studies with his father, with Leonard Rose and at Juilliard School of Music, New York; first public recital at age of five; winner Avery Fisher Prize 1978 since when he has performed under many distinguished conductors with all the maj. orchestras of the world including Berlin Philharmonic, Boston Symphony, Chicago Symphony, Israel Philharmonic, London Symphony Orchestra and New York Philharmonic; regularly participates in festivals of Tanglewood, Ravinia, Blossom, Salzburg and Edin.; also appears in chamber music ensembles with artists such as Emanuel Ax, Leonard Rose, Pinchas Zukerman, Gidon Kremer and fmrly Yehudi Menuhin; records for Sony Classical Masterworks; established The Silk Road Project to promote study of cultural, artistic and intellectual traditions of the route; Dr hc (Northeastern) 1985 and from 11 other colls or univs including Harvard, Yale, Tufts and Juilliard, Chinese Univ. of Hong Kong; Glenn Gould Prize 1999; 14 Grammy Awards including one for his recording of the six Bach Suites for Unaccompanied Cello 1984, two Emmy Awards, 19 Canadian Gemini Awards. *Address:* c/o I.C.M. Artists, 40 W 57th Street, New York, NY 10019, USA.

MA CHUNG-CH'EN (see Ma Zhongchen).

MA FENG, (MA SHUMING); Chinese writer; b. 1922, Xiaoyi Co., Shanxi Prov.; ed Lu Xun Acad. of Literature and Art, Yan'an; joined 8th Route Army and CCP 1938; first short story (First Reconnaissance) published 1942; mem. China-Britain Friendship Asscn 1983–; Vice-Chair. CPPCC Provincial Cttee, Shanxi 1986–; Pres. Soc. of Chinese Folk Literature 1987–; Exec. Vice-Chair. Nat. Cttee China Fed. of Literary and Art Circles 1988–; Vice-Chair. Chinese Writers' Asscn 1990–; mem. Foreign Affairs Cttee. *Publications include:* Heroes of Lüliang (with Xi Rong), Liu Hulan (novel), The Young People of One Village (film script) and numerous short stories, including The Marriage Ceremony (Nat. Short Story Award Winner 1980). *Address:* China Federation of Literary and Art Circles, 10 Nong Zhan Guan Nanli, Beijing 100026, People's Republic of China. *Telephone:* 5005588.

MA HONG; Chinese economist; b. 1920, Dingxiang Co., Shanxi Prov.; ed Marxism-Leninism Coll., Yan'an; joined CCP 1937; Vice-Pres. Chinese Acad. of Social Sciences 1979–82, Pres. 1982–85; Adviser to State Planning Comm. and State Comm. for Restructuring Econ. System 1982–85; Deputy Sec.-Gen. State Council, Dir-Gen. Research Centre for Econ., Tech. and Social Devt of State Council 1982–85, Pres. Devt Research Centre, State Council 1985, Hon. Dir-Gen. Devt Research Centre 1993–; Pres. China Comprehensive Devt Research Inst. 1991–; Pres. China Scientific Research Soc. for Policy Study 1994–; mem. NPC Standing Cttee; Chief Ed. Contemporary China Series, China in the Year 2000 Series. *Address:* Development Research Centre of the State Council, 22 Xianmen Street, Beijing, People's Republic of China. *Telephone:* 6013530.

MA QIZHI; Chinese politician; b. Nov. 1943, Jingyuan, Ningxia; ed Cen. Inst. of Nationalities; joined CCP 1972; high school teacher in Anshan and Yinchuan; cadre of Communist Youth League Ningxia Hui Autonomous Region Cttee; Vice-Sec. CCP Guyuan Pref. Cttee; CtteeVice-Sec., now Dir-Gen.CCP Yinnan Pref.; Dir Propaganda Dept of CCP Ningxia Hui Autonomous Region Cttee 1969–93, Vice-Sec. 1993–98; Chair. Ningxia Hui Autonomous Region 1998–; alt. mem. CCP 14th and 15th Cen. Cttee 1992–2002; mem. CCP 16th Cen. Cttee 2002–. *Address:* c/o People's Government of Ningxia Hui Autonomous Region, Yinchuan, Ningxia, People's Republic of China.

MA WANFAN, (MAYI); Chinese business executive; b. 1930, Longkou Co., Shandong Prov.; Chair. China Nat. Chemicals Corpn 1989–; mem. 7th CPPCC 1987–92, 8th 1993–, 9th 1998. *Address:* China National Chemicals Corporation, 16 Hepingli 7 District, Beijing 100013, People's Republic of China.

MA WANQI; Chinese politician; b. 1919, Nanhai Co., Guandong Prov.; mem. 5th Nat. Cttee CPPCC 1978–82; Perm. mem. 6th Nat. Cttee CPPCC 1983–88; mem. 6th Standing Cttee NPC 1986–88; 7th Standing Cttee NPC 1988–92; Vice-Chair. 8th Nat. Cttee CPPCC 1993–98, 9th Nat. Cttee 1998–; Vice-Pres. All-China Sports Fed. *Address:* National Committee of Chinese People's Political Consultative Conference, 23 Taiping Qiao Street, Beijing, People's Republic of China.

MA YING-JEOU; Taiwanese politician and professor of law; b. 13 July 1950, Hong Kong; s. of Ma He-Ling; m.; two d.; ed Taiwan Nat. Univ., New York and Harvard Univs, USA; Prof. of Law Taiwan 1981; mem. Kuomintang—KMT party, Deputy Sec.-Gen. 1981–88; fmr Head Mainland Affairs Council; Minister of Justice 1993–96, removed from office and demoted after he denounced corruption within KMT 1996; resgnd from cabinet 1997; elected Mayor of Taipei 1998–. *Address:* Office of the Mayor of Taipei, c/o Kuomintang—KMT, 11 Chung Shan South Road, Taipei 100, Taiwan (Office). *E-mail:* mayor@mail.tcg.gov.tw (Office). *Website:* www.taipei.gov.tw (Office).

MA YONGWEI; Chinese banker; b. 1942; ed Qinghua Univ.; joined CCP 1965; Chair., Pres. People's Insurance Co. of China, now China Insurance Group; fmr Pres. Agric. Bank of China. *Address:* China Insurance Group, 410 Fu Cheng Men Nei Dajie, Beijing, People's Republic of China. *Telephone:* (10) 66016688. *Fax:* (10) 66011689.

MA YUAN; Chinese judge; b. 30 June 1930, Xinmin Co., Liaoning Prov.; two s.; ed Chinese People's Univ., Beijing; joined CCP 1953; teacher Dept of Law, Beijing Univ. and part-time lawyer 1955–62, part-time Prof. 1990–; Asst Judge, Judge Supreme People's Court 1963–82, Deputy Dir Civil Dept 1982–85, Vice-Pres. Supreme People's Court 1985–; mem. Standing Cttee All China Women's Fed.; Vice-Pres. China Marriage and Family Research Inst. 1983–; Pres. Chinese Asscn of Women Judges 1994–; Asst Sec.-Gen. Civil and Econ. Law Cttee, China Law Soc. 1983–. *Address:* Supreme People's Court, 27 Dong Jiaomin Xiang, Beijing 1000745, People's Republic of China. *Telephone:* (10) 65136195.

MA YUZHEN; Chinese diplomatist; b. 26 Sept. 1934, Beijing; s. of Ma Zhiqiang and Li Jinhui; m. Zou Jichun 1961; one s. one d.; ed Beijing Inst. of Foreign Languages; served in Information Dept of the Ministry of Foreign Affairs 1954–63, Deputy Div. Chief, then Div. Chief 1969–80, Dir 1984–88; Attaché, Third Sec. Embassy, Burma 1963–69, First Sec., Counsellor Embassy, Ghana 1980–84, Consul-Gen. (ambassadorial rank) LA 1988–91, Amb. to UK 1991–95; Deputy Dir State Council's Information Office 1995–97; Foreign Ministry Commr for China, Hong Kong 1997–2001; mem. Nat. Cttee Chinese People's Political Consultative Conf. 1998–. *Leisure interests:* reading, music, Beijing Opera. *Address:* c/o Ministry of Foreign Affairs, Beijing 100701 (Office); Room 501, No. 30, Dongjiaominxiang, Beijing 100006, People's Republic of China (Home).

MA ZHENGANG; Chinese diplomatist; b. 9 Nov. 1940, Shandong; m. Chen Xiaodong; one s.; ed Beijing Foreign Languages Univ., Ealing Tech. Coll., London, LSE; staff mem., Attaché, Embassy in Yugoslavia 1970–74; Attaché N American and Oceanic Affairs Dept, Ministry of Foreign Affairs, Beijing 1974–81, Deputy Dir, Dir N. American and Oceanic Affairs Dept 1985–90, Deputy Dir-Gen., Dir-Gen. N. American and Oceanic Affairs Dept 1991–95; Vice-Consul, Consul Consulate-Gen., Vancouver 1981–85; Counsellor, Embassy in Washington, DC 1990–91; Vice-Minister of Foreign Affairs 1995–97; Amb. to UK 1997–. *Leisure interests:* literature, bridge, table tennis. *Address:* Embassy of the People's Republic of China, 49–51 Portland Place, London, W1B 1JL, England. *Telephone:* (20) 7299-4035 (Office). *Fax:* (20) 7636-2981. *Website:* www.chinese-embassy.org.uk.

MA ZHONGCHEN; Chinese party official; b. 1936, Tai'an, Shandong; joined CCP 1956; alt. mem. 12th CCP Cen. Cttee 1982, 13th Cen. Cttee 1987; Sec. CCP Cttee, Tai'an Municipality, Shandong Prov. 1982–88; Vice-Gov. Shandong 1988–89; Deputy Sec. Shandong Prov. CP 1988–92, Henan Prov. CCP Cttee; NPC Deputy; alt. mem. 14th Cen. Cttee CCP 1992–97, mem. 15th CCP Cen. Cttee 1997–; Gov. Henan Prov. 1993–98; Sec. Henan Prov. CCP Cttee 1993–2000. *Address:* c/o Office of the Governor, Zhengzhou City, Henan Province, People's Republic of China.

MAATHAI, Wangari, PhD; Kenyan ecologist and biologist; b. 1 April 1940, Nyeri; d. of Muta Njugi and Wanjiru Kibicho; m. Mwangi Maathai 1969 (divorced 1980); two s. one d.; fmr Head, Veterinary Anatomy, Nairobi Univ.; f. Kenya Green Belt Movt 1977; fmr mem. Forum for Restoration of Democracy; arrested 1992; shared Hunger Project Prize 1991; Right Livelihood Award 1984, Edin. Medal 1993, Goldman Environment Prize 1994 and others. *Leisure interests:* swimming, reading. *Address:* Green Belt Movement, P.O. Box 67545, Nairobi, Kenya. *Telephone:* 504264. *Fax:* 504264.

MAAZEL, Lorin, FRCM; American conductor and musician; b. 6 March 1930, Neuilly, France; s. of Lincoln and Marie Varencove Maazel; m. 1st Israela Margalit; four c.; m. 2nd Dietlinde Turban 1986; one s.; ed under Vladimir Bakaleinikoff and at Univ. of Pittsburgh; début as conductor 1938; Conductor, American Symphony Orchestras 1938–; violin recitalist; European début 1953; festivals include Bayreuth, Salzburg, Edin.; tours include S. America, Australia, USSR and Japan; Artistic Dir, Deutsche Oper Berlin 1965–71; Musical Dir Radio Symphony Orchestra, Berlin 1965–75; Assoc. Prin. Conductor, New Philharmonia Orchestra, London 1970–72; Dir Cleveland Orchestra 1971–82, Conductor Emer. 1982–86; Prin. Guest Conductor London Philharmonia 1976–80; Dir Vienna State Opera 1982–84, Music Dir Pittsburgh Symphony Orchestra 1988–96; Music Dir Bavarian Radio Symphony Orchestra 1993–2001, NY Philharmonic 2002–; Music Dir Orchestre Nat. de France 1988–90; Hon. DMus (Pittsburgh) 1968, (Royal Coll. of Music) 1984; DHumLitt (Beaver Coll.) 1973; Hon. DCL (Univ. of South Sewanee) 1988; Hon. Dr. (Ind.) 1988; Officier, Légion d'honneur 1981, Finnish Commdr of the Lion, Portuguese Commdr, Bundesverdienstkreuz (Germany). *Leisure interests:* swimming, tennis, reading. *Address:* New York Philharmonic, Avery Fisher Hall, 10 Lincoln Center Plaza, New York, NY 10023, USA (Office); c/o Z des Aubris, Tal 15 5th Floor, 80331, Munich, Germany. *Website:* www.nyphilharmonic.org (Office).

MABILANGAN, Felipe H., MA; Philippine diplomatist; m. Ada Kalaw Ledesma; three c.; ed Univs. of Oxford and Geneva; various positions, Dept of Foreign Affairs 1971–79, Dir-Gen. for European Affairs 1988; Amb. to

France (also Accred to Portugal) 1979–87, to China (also Accred to Mongolia) 1989–95; Perm. Rep. to UN 1995–2001; mem. UN Advisory Cttee on Admin. and Budgetary Questions; del. to numerous int. confs.; Nat. Order of Merit. *Address:* c/o Department of Foreign Affairs, DFA Building, 2330 Pasay City, Metro Manila, Philippines (Office).

MABUS, Raymond Edwin, Jr, MA, JD; American politician and lawyer; b. 11 Oct. 1948, Starkville, Miss.; s. of Raymond Edwin Mabus, Sr and Lucille C. Mabus; m. (divorced); two d.; ed Univ. of Mississippi, Johns Hopkins Univ., Harvard Univ.; called to Texas Bar 1976, Washington, DC 1978; Mississippi 1982; Law Clerk US Circuit Court of Appeals, Montgomery, Ala 1976–77; Legal Counsel to House of Reps., DC 1977–78; Assoc. Fried, Frank et al., Washington, DC 1979–80; Gov.'s Legislative Aide, State of Miss., Jackson 1980–83; State Auditor, State of Miss. 1984–88; Gov. of Miss. 1988–92; Amb. to Saudi Arabia 1994–96; Counsel, Baker Donaldson Bearman & Caldwell 1996–; Chair. Southern Govs'. Asscn, Southern Regional Educ. Bd; Woodrow Wilson Scholarship, Johns Hopkins Univ. 1969; King Abdul Aziz Award, Saudi Arabia 1996, Distinguished Public Service Award, US Dept of Defense; Democrat. *Leisure interests:* spectator sports, walking, reading, photography, scuba diving. *Address:* 121 Little Creek Road, Ridgelands, MS 39157 (Office); 121 Little Creek Road, Ridgelands, MS 39157, USA (Home). *Telephone:* (601) 605-9400 (Office); (601) 605-7400 (Home). *Fax:* (601) 607-7104 (Office); (601) 607-7104 (Home).

McALEESE, Mary Patricia, FRSA, MRIA, LLB, MA, MIL.; Irish head of state; b. 27 June 1951, Belfast, Northern Ireland; d. of Patrick J. Leneghan and Claire McManus; m. Martin McAleese 1976; one s. two d.; ed Queen's Univ. Belfast, Inn of Court of N Ireland, King's Inns, Dublin and Trinity Coll., Dublin; Reid Prof. Trinity Coll., Dublin 1975–79, 1981–87; current affairs journalist and presenter, RTE 1979–85; Dir Inst. of Professional Legal Studies 1987–97; Pro-Vice-Chancellor, Queen's Univ., Belfast 1994–97; Pres. of Ireland 1997–; Dir (non-exec.) N Ireland Electricity 1992–97, Channel 4 TV 1993–97, fmr Dir Royal Group of Hosps Trust; Hon. Fellow Trinity Coll. Dublin, Inst. of Engineers of Ireland, Royal Coll. of Surgeons, Coll. of Anaesthetists, Liverpool John Moore's Univ., Royal Coll. of Physicians and Surgeons, Glasgow; Hon. Bencher, King's Inns, Inn of Court of N Ireland; Hon. LLD (Nat. Univ. of Ireland, Vic. Univ. of Tech., Australia, Saint Mary's Univ., Canada, Loyola Law School, LA, Univ. of Aberdeen, Univ. of Surrey, Queen's, Belfast), (Nottingham) 1998, (Trinity Coll. Dublin), (Metropolitan Univ. Manchester, Univ. of Delaware, Univ. of Bristol); Hon. DHumLitt (Rochester Inst. of Tech., NY, USA); Hon. DLitt (Univ. of Ulster); Silver Jubilee Commemoration Medal, Charles Univ., Prague. *Publications:* The Irish Martyrs 1995, Reconciled Being 1997. *Leisure interests:* hillwalking, theology. *Address:* Áras an Uachtaráin, Phoenix Park, Dublin 8, Ireland (Office). *Telephone:* (1) 617-1000. *Fax:* (1) 617-1001. *E-mail:* webmaster@aras.irlgov.ie (Office). *Website:* www.irlgov.ie/aras (Office).

MCALLISTER, Ian, CBE, BSc; British transport executive; b. 17 Aug. 1943, Glasgow; m. Susan McAllister; three s. one d.; ed Thornleigh Salesian Coll., Bolton, Univ. Coll. London; grad. economist Ford Motor Co. Ltd 1964, joined Depts of Marketing and Sales 1968, held various positions within Parts Operations 1968–78, Gen. Field Man. Eastern Dist, Ford of Britain 1978, responsible for German Operations 1980s, Man. Dir Ford of Britain 1991, Chair. 1992–2002; Chair. (non-exec.) Network Rail 2002–; Dir (non-exec.) Scottish & Newcastle; Deputy Chair. Qualifications and Curriculum Authority; involved with numerous public orgs. *Leisure interests:* Manchester United football club, 'trash' novels. *Address:* Network Rail, Floor 4, Maple House, 149 Tottenham Court Road, London, W1T 7NF, England (Office).

MACAN, Tom, BEcons; British diplomatist; b. 14 Nov. 1946, Manchester; s. of Dr Thomas Townley Macan and Zaida Bindloss Macan (née Boddington); one s. one d.; ed Shrewsbury School, Univ. of Sussex; joined HM Diplomatic Service 1969, served in Bonn, Brasília and FCO; Press Sec. Embassy in Bonn 1981; Head Commonwealth Co-ordination Dept, FCO 1986–88, Head Training Dept 1988–90; Deputy Head of Mission to Lisbon 1990–95; Amb. to Lithuania 1995–98; seconded to BOE Group 1998–99; Minister in New Delhi 1999–2002; Gov. of the Virgin Islands 2002–; mem. Inst. of Linguistics. *Leisure interests:* sailing, steamboats, church architecture. *Address:* Office of the Governor, POB 702, Road Town, Tortola, British Virgin Islands (Office). *Telephone:* 494-2345 (Office). *Fax:* 494-5790 (Office).

MACAPAGAL ARROYO, Gloria, PhD; Philippine politician, economist, educator and journalist; b. 4 May 1948, Lubao, Pampanga; d. of late Diosdado Macapagal and Evangelina Macaraeg Macapagal; two s. one d.; ed Assumption Coll., Georgetown Univ., Ateneo de Manila Univ., Univ. of the Philippines; Under-Sec. Dept of Trade and Industry 1986–92; Senator 1992–98; Sec. Dept of Social Welfare and Devt, Vice-Pres. of Repub. 1998–2001; Pres. of the Philippines 2001–; named Outstanding Senator by Asiaweek, Woman of the Year by Catholic Educ. Asscn of the Philippines. *Address:* Office of the President, New Executive Building, Malacañang Palace Compound, J.P. Laurel Street, San Miguel, Metro Manila, Philippines. *Telephone:* (2) 7356047. *Fax:* (2) 7358006. *E-mail:* gma@easy.net.ph (Office).

MACARA, Sir Alexander Wiseman, Kt, DPH, DSc, FRCP (UK), FRCPE (E), FRCGP, FFPHM, FFOM, FMedSci; British physician; b. 4 May 1932, Irvine, Scotland; s. of the Rev. Alexander Macara and Marion Macara; m. Sylvia May Williams 1964; one s. one d.; ed Irvine Royal Acad., Univ. of Glasgow, London School of Hygiene and Tropical Medicine; lecturer, then consultant Sr lecturer in Social Medicine, Univ. of Bristol 1964–97; Sec.-Gen. Asscn of Schools of

Public Health in Europe 1975–89, World Fed. for Educ. and Research in Public Health 1988–97; Dir WHO Collaborating Centre in Environmental Health 1988–97; Chair. BMA 1993–98; Visiting Prof. of Health Studies, Univ. of York 1998–2002; Chair. Nat. Heart Forum (UK) 1998–; Hecht Prize, London School of Hygiene and Tropical Medicine; Gold Medal, Italian Soc. of Hygiene and Preventive Medicine 1991, Médaille d'Or, Ordre de Médecine Français 1997, Gold Medal, British Medical Asscn 1999, Andrija Stampar Medal 2002. *Publications:* has published extensively on public health, ethics in medicine, health care and epidemiology. *Leisure interests:* music, gardening, human rights activities. *Address:* Elgon, 10 Cheyne Road, Stoke Bishop, Bristol, BS9 2DH, England. *Telephone:* (117) 968-2838. *Fax:* (117) 968-4602.

MACARRÓN JAIME, Ricardo; Spanish painter; b. 9 April 1926, Madrid; m. Alicia Macarrón Jaime 1951; two d.; ed Escuela Superior de Bellas Artes de San Fernando, Madrid and scholarship in Paris; Prof. of Drawing and Painting, Escuela Superior de Bellas Artes, Madrid; has painted many portraits of royalty and nobility; mem. Royal Soc. of Portrait Painters 1962; numerous one-man exhbns. in Spain and abroad including two in London and one in New York; represented at Museo de Arte Contemporáneo, Madrid, Univ. of Oslo and Fundación Güell, Barcelona, portraits at the Royal Soc. of Portrait Painters; numerous awards. *Leisure interests:* walking in the country, hunting, playing chess. *Address:* Agustín de Bethencourt No. 7, Madrid 3, Spain.

McASLAN, John Renwick, MA, RIBA, FRSA; British architect; b. 16 Feb. 1954, Glasgow, Scotland; s. of Prof. T. Crawford and Jean Renwick McAslan; m. Dava Sagenkahn 1981; one s. two d.; ed Dunoon Grammar School, Dollar Acad., Edin. Univ.; with Cambridge Seven Assocs, Cambridge, Mass. 1978–80; Richard Rogers Partnership, London 1980–84; Dir Troughton McAslan 1984–96; Chair. John McAslan + Partners 1996–; extensive int. teaching experience at architectural schools including London, Edin., Mexico City, Sydney, Helsinki, Seoul, Tokyo 1990–; Chair. of numerous architectural award juries in the UK 1990–; Prof., Univ. of Wales 1998–2001; Foundation Trustee, Whitechapel Art Gallery 1989–97; Founder, John McAslan Family Trust, London 1999, Volubilis Foundation, Morocco 2001; Assoc. int. mem. AIA; Architect of the Year Award, Civic Trust Award, RIBA Award for Architecture, Int. Brunel Award, Structural Steel Design Award, Royal Acad. of Arts Award, European Heritage Award, Architectural Inst. of Japan Award. *Art Exhibitions:* Royal Acad. of Arts, Art Inst. of Chicago, Museum of Contemporary Art LA, RIBA. *Publications:* numerous int. publs on architectural work, including monographs and profiles. *Leisure interests:* travel, sport, opera, spending time with family. *Address:* John McAslan + Partners, 202 Kensington Church Street, London, W8 4DP, England (Office). *Telephone:* (20) 7727-2663 (Office). *Fax:* (20) 7721-8835 (Office). *E-mail:* j.mcaslan@mcaslan.co.uk (Office). *Website:* www.mcaslan.co.uk (Office).

MCAULIFFE, Terry, JD; American politician and lawyer; b. Syracuse, New York; m. Dorothy Swann; five c.; ed Catholic Univ. of America, Georgetown Law Center; joined Carter-Mondale Re-election Cttee; mem. Democratic Party, served in various positions including Finance Dir Democratic Nat. Cttee (DNC), Finance Dir Democratic Congressional Campaign Cttee, Nat. Finance Chair. Presidential Campaign of Dick Gephardt 1988, Nat. Co-Chair. Presidential Campaign Clinton-Gore 1996, Co-Chair. Presidential Inaugural Cttee 1997, Chair. DNC Convention, LA 2000, Chair. DNC Feb. 2001–, cr. Hispanic Project, Women's Vote Center, Voting Rights Inst.; est. many cos in fields of banking, insurance, marketing and real estate; practising attorney. *Address:* Democratic National Committee, 430 South Capitol Street, SE, Washington, DC 20003, USA (Office). *Telephone:* (202) 863-8000 (Office). *Fax:* (202) 863-8174 (Office). *Website:* www.democrats.org (Office).

McBAIN, Ed (see Hunter, Evan).

McBRIDE, Christian; American jazz bass player; b. 31 May 1972, Philadelphia; s. of Lee Smith; ed High School for Creative and Performing Arts, Philadelphia, Juilliard School, New York; Scholarship to Juilliard School. *Films include:* Café Society 1995, Kansas City 1996. *Recordings include:* Ray Brown's Super Bass 1989, Roy Hargrove's Public Eye 1990, Kenny Kirkland album 1991, Joshua Redman 1993, Introducing Joshua Redman 1999, Bobby Hutcherson's Skyline 1999, Don Braden's Fire Within 1999; played with Bobby Watson, Freddie Hubbard and Benny Green; f. own groups, solo albums include Gettin' To It 1994, Number Two Express 1995, Fingerpainting: The Music of Herbie Hancock 1997, A Family Affair 1998. *Address:* c/o Verve Records/Universal, 555 W 57th Street, 10th Floor, New York, NY 10019, USA (Office).

McBRIDE, William Griffith, AO, CBE, MD, FRCOG, FRACOG, FRSM, MACT; Australian molecular biologist and medical practitioner; b. 25 May 1927, Sydney; s. of John McBride and Myrine Griffith; m. Patricia Glover 1957; two s. two d.; ed Canterbury Boys' High School, Sydney, Conservatorium of Music, Sydney, Univ. of London, Univ. of Sydney; Medical Officer, St George Hosp. 1950, Consultant Obstetrician and Gynaecologist 1958; Medical Officer, Launceston Gen. Hosp. 1951; Medical Officer, Women's Hosp., Sydney 1952–53, Medical Supt 1955–57, Consultant Obstetrician 1966–83; Consultant Gynaecologist, Bankstown Hosp., Sydney 1957–66; Consultant Obstetrician and Gynaecologist, Royal Hosp. for Women 1983–88; Consultant, L.B. Johnson Tropical Medicine Center, American Samoa 1998–, Govt of Solomon Islands Medical Services (for AUSAID) 1999–; examiner in Obstetrics and Gynaecology Univs of Sydney and NSW; Fellow of the Senate

Univ. of Sydney 1974–90; mem. Faculty of Medicine Univ. of Sydney 1966–90; mem. WHO Cttee on Safety of Contraceptives 1971; Dir, Foundation 41 Research Lab. 1972–93; discovered that thalidomide caused birth defects (Lancet 1961), that thalidomide is a mutagen (B.M.J. 1994); showed that radioactive labelled thalidomide binds with DNA in rats 1997; Dir Australian Opera 1979–82; mem. Australian Opera Council 1984–; Hereford cattle judge, W. Midlands Show 1988; mem. AAAS American Coll. of Toxicologists, Soc. for Risk Analysis, New York Acad. of Sciences; Gold Medal and B.P. Prize (L'Institut de la Vie) 1971. *Publications:* Killing the Messenger 1994, Pharmacology & Toxicology 1999; over 100 papers in medical and scientific journals. *Leisure interests:* surfing, tennis, riding, golf, breeder of Hereford cattle. *Address:* 11 Waratah Street, Mona Vale 2103 (Home); 95 Elizabeth Bay Road, Elizabeth Bay, NSW 2011, Australia. *Telephone:* (2) 9368-7808. *Fax:* (2) 9368-7807.

McBRIDE, William James (Willie-John), MBE; Irish rugby football player and business executive (retd); b. 6 June 1940, Toomebridge, Northern Ireland; s. of William James McBride and Irene Patterson; m. Penny Michael 1966; one s. one d.; ed Ballymena Acad.; first played rugby for Ireland against England 1962; six Lions tours, S. Africa 1962, NZ 1966, S. Africa 1968, NZ 1971, S. Africa 1974, Capt. unbeaten Lions 1974, Man. Lions 1983 NZ; holder of 63 int. caps; 17 Test appearances for Lions (record); toured Australia 1967 and Argentina 1970 for Ireland; fmr Asst Bank Man.; Pres. Ballymena RFC; Vice-Pres. Northern Ireland Riding for Disabled; Freeman Borough of Newtownabbey, Int. Rugby Hall of Fame 1997. *Leisure interests:* golf, gardening, after-dinner speaking. *Address:* Gorse Lodge, 105 Ballycorr Road, Ballyclare, Co. Antrim, BT39 9DE, Northern Ireland. *Telephone:* (28) 9335-2710. *Fax:* (28) 9335-2710.

McBRIEN, Rev. Richard Peter, MA, STD; American professor of theology and ecclesiastic; b. 19 Aug. 1936, Hartford, Conn.; s. of late Thomas H. McBrien and Catherine Botticelli; ed St Thomas Seminary, Bloomfield, Conn., St John Seminary, Brighton, Mass. and Pontifical Gregorian Univ., Rome; Prof. of Theology and Dean of Studies Pope John XXIII Nat. Seminary, Weston, Mass. 1965–70; Prof. Boston Coll., Newton, Mass. 1970–80; Chair. Dept of Theology, Univ. of Notre Dame, Ind. 1980–91, Prof. 1980–; John Courtney Murray Award, Catholic Theology Soc. of America 1976, Christopher Award for Catholicism (book) 1981. *Publications:* Do We Need the Church? 1969, Church: The Continuing Quest 1970, The Remaking of the Church 1973, Catholicism (2 Vols) 1980, Caesar's Coin: Religion and Politics in America 1987, Report on the Church: Catholicism since Vatican II 1992, Catholicism (new Edn) 1994, The HarperCollins Encyclopedia of Catholicism (Gen. Ed.) 1995, Responses to 101 Questions on the Church 1996, Lives of the Popes: The Pontiffs from St Peter to John Paul II 1997, Lives of the Saints: From Mary and St Francis of Assisi to John XXIII and Mother Teresa 2001. *Leisure interests:* reading, films. *Address:* Department of Theology, University of Notre Dame, 327 O'Shaughnessy Hall, Notre Dame, IN 46556, USA. *Telephone:* (219) 631-5151.

McCABE, Eamonn Patrick; British photographer; b. 28 July 1948; s. of James McCabe and Celia McCabe; m. 1st Ruth Calvert 1972 (divorced 1993); one s.; m. 2nd Rebecca Smithers 1997; one d.; ed Challoner School, Finchley and San Francisco State Coll.; fmr freelance photographer for local papers and The Guardian for one year; staff photographer, The Observer 1977–86, 1987–88; Official Photographer, Pope's Visit to Britain 1982; Picture Ed. Sportsweek 1986–87, The Guardian 1988–2001; Dir Newscast 2001–; Fellow in Photography, Nat. Museum of Photography and TV, Bradford 1988; Hon. Prof. Thames Valley Univ. 1994; Sports Photographer of the Year, Royal Photographic Soc. and Sports Council 1978, 1979, 1981, 1984, News Photographer of the Year, British Press Awards 1985, Picture Ed. of the Year (Nikon Press Awards) 1992, 1993, 1995, 1997. *Publications:* Sports Photographer 1981, Eamonn McCabe, Photographer 1987, Emerald Gems of Ireland 2001. *Leisure interests:* playing tennis, squash, cinema. *Address:* c/o The Guardian, 119 Farringdon Road, London EC1R 3ER, England. *Telephone:* (20) 7278-2332.

McCABE, John, CBE, MUS.B., F.R.M.C.M., F.L.C.M., FRCM, RAM, F.T.C.L.; British musician; b. 21 April 1939, Huyton, Lancs. (now Merseyside); s. of Frank McCabe and Elisabeth (Herlitzius) McCabe; m. 1st Hilary Tann 1968 (divorced 1974); m. 2nd Monica Smith 1974; ed Liverpool Inst. High School for Boys, Manchester Univ., Royal Manchester Coll. of Music, Staatliche Hochschule für Musik, Munich; Pianist-in-residence, University Coll., Cardiff 1965–68; Pres. Inc. Soc. of Musicians 1983–84; Dir London Coll. of Music 1983–90; Chair. Asscn of Professional Composers 1985–86; travels worldwide as pianist-composer; Hon. D. Phil. (T.V.U.) 2001; Royal Manchester Inst. Medal 1962, Royal Philharmonic Prize 1962, Special Citation, Koussevitsky Recording Foundation 1974, Award for service to British music, Composers Guild 1975. *Compositions include:* The Chagall Windows, Variations on a theme of Hartmann, Notturni ed Alba, Concerto for Orchestra, Cloudcatcher Fells, Fire at Durilgai, Canyons, Edward II (ballet), Arthur, Part I: Arthur Pendragon, Arthur, Part II: Le Mort d'Arthur (ballets), plus other stage works, symphonies, concertos, much orchestral and chamber music, vocal works and keyboard music; numerous piano recordings including complete piano works of Haydn and Nielsen. *Publications:* Rachmaninov, Bartok's Orchestral Music, Haydn's Piano Sonatas, Alan Rawsthorne: Portrait of a Composer and numerous articles on music. *Leisure interests:* books, films,

cricket, snooker. *Address:* 86 Albany Road, Sittingbourne, Kent, ME10 1EL, England (Home); c/o Novello and Co. Ltd, Music Sales, 8/9 Frith Street, London, W1V 5TZ.

McCABE, Patrick; Irish writer; b. 1955, Co. Monaghan; m.; two d.; fmr teacher of disabled children; has written plays for BBC Radio and stage play Frank Pig Says Hello, based on novel The Butcher Boy; awards include Hennessy Award, Sunday Independent Arts Award. *Film:* The Butcher Boy (co-writer). *Publications:* Music on Clinton Street 1986, Carn 1989, The Butcher Boy 1992 (Irish Times/Aer Lingus Fiction Prize 1992, shortlisted for Booker Prize 1992), The Dead School 1996, Breakfast on Pluto 1997, Mondo Desperado 1998, Emerald Gems of Ireland 2000. *Leisure interests:* cinema, music. *Address:* c/o Picador, Macmillan General Books, 25 Eccleston Place, London, SW1W 9NF, England. *Telephone:* (20) 7881-8000. *Fax:* (20) 7881-8001.

McCAFFREY, Gen. Barry R., MA; American government administrator, consultant and fmr army officer; b. 17 Nov. 1942, Taunton, Mass., s. of William Joseph McCaffrey and Mary Veronica Curtin; m. Jill Ann Faulkner 1964; one s. two d.; ed US Military Acad., American Univ., Command and General Staff Coll., Army War Coll.; commissioned into US Army 1964, Co. Commdr 1st Cavalry Div., Viet Nam 1968–69, Asst Prof. of Social Sciences, Dept of Social Sciences, US Mil. Acad. 1972–75; Bn Commdr 3rd Infantry Div., Germany 1979–83; Div. Chief of Staff, Brigade Commdr 9th Infantry Div. 1983–86; Asst Commandant US Army Infantry School 1986–88; US Deputy Military Rep. to NATO 1988–89; Prin. Staff Asst to Chair. of Jt Chiefs of Staff, Chief of Strategic Planning 1989–90; Div. Commdr 24th Infantry Div. 1990–95; led. div. into Iraq in Operation Desert Storm 1991; fmr Commdr-in-Chief US Armed Forces Southern Command; at retirement youngest four-star Gen. in Army; Dir White House Office of Nat. Drug Control Policy 1996–2001; fmr mem. prin. negotiation team START II Nuclear Arms Control Treaty; mem. Nat. Security Council, Council on Foreign Relations, Nat. Asscn for Advancement of Colored People; most highly decorated combat officer on retirement; Pres. B. R. McCaffrey Assocs; currently an NBC News analyst; Distinguished Service Cross (twice), Silver Star (twice), Distinguished Service Medal, Combat Infantry Badge. *Television:* as ONDCP Dir, appeared in over 4,000 television news stories and over 12,000 newspaper articles; media coverage includes Meet the Press, This Week, Fox Sunday News, Nightline, Today, Good Morning America, One to One and C-Span Washington Journal. *Publications:* Proceedings of the Twenty-Fifth Student Conference on United States Affairs 1973, We Are Soldiers All: An Analysis of Possible Roles for Women in the Army 1973, numerous articles on mil. subjects, drugs law enforcement and money laundering. *Leisure interests:* hunting, reading mil. history. *Address:* BR McCaffrey Associates LLC, 1800 Diagonal Road, Suite 600, Alexandria, VA 22314, USA. *Telephone:* (703) 684-4414 (Office). *Fax:* (703) 684-1806 (Office). *E-mail:* brm.associates@att.net (Office).

McCAIN, John Sidney III, DFC; American politician; b. 29 Aug. 1936, Panama Canal Zone, Panama; s. of John Sidney McCain and Roberta Wright; m. Cindy Hensley 1980; five s. one d.; ed U.S. Naval Acad. and Nat. War Coll.; Ensign, U.S. Navy 1958, Capt. 1977; Dir Navy Senate Liaison Office, Washington 1977–81; Bd Dirs. Community Assistance League, Phoenix 1981–82; mem. 99th Congress from 1st Ariz. Dist; Senator from Arizona 1986–; cand. for Republican nomination for Presidency; mem. Armed Services Cttee, Science and Transport Cttee, Indian Affairs Cttee; Republican; various decorations including Legion of Merit, Silver Star, Purple Heart Vietnamese Legion of Honour. *Publication:* Faith of My Fathers 1999. *Address:* U.S. Senate, 241 Russell Senate Office Building, Washington, DC 20510, USA.

McCALLUM, Martin, FRSA; British theatre producer; b. 6 April 1950, Blackpool; s. of Raymond McCallum and Jessie McCallum; m. 1st Lesley Nunnerley 1971 (divorced); one s. one d.; m. 2nd Julie Edmest (divorced); one d.; m. 3rd Mary Ann Rolfe; two s.; ed Barfield School Surrey, Frensham Heights School Surrey; began career as student Asst Stage Man. Castle Theatre, Farnham Surrey 1967; worked as actor, stage man., lighting and sound technician; Production Man. Nat. Theatre at Old Vic (with Laurence Olivier) 1971–75, productions included Filumena, Evita, Sweeney Todd, CATS; Consultant to Glyndebourne Festival Opera, Arts Council's Regional Theatre Scheme; Man. Dir Cameron Mackintosh Ltd 1981–2000, Vice-Chair. 2000–03; Dir Donmar Warehouse Theatre 1992–, Chair. 1996–; initiated Wyndham Report 1998; est. New Writing Symposium 1999; Pres. Soc. of London Theatre 1999–2002; initiated inaugural jt Theatre Conf. of SOLT/TMA/ITC "Theatre 2001 Future Directions"; mem. League of American Theatres and Producers 1988–, Drama Panel, Arts Council of England 1999–, Cultural Strategy Group London 2000–; mem. V&A Theatre Museum Cttee; consultant on design projects including Old Fire Station Theatre, Oxford (new build), Prince Edward Theatre (restoration) 1993, Musical Hall, Stuttgart (new build) 1994, Capital Theatre, Sydney (restoration) 1995, Musical Theatre, Duisberg (new build) 1996, Theatre Royal, Sydney (restoration) 1998, Wales Millennium Centre, Lyric Theatre (new build) 1998, Auditorium Theatre, Chicago (restoration) 2001, Schaumburg Village Theatre, Illinois (new build) 2003, Fine Arts Building Theatre, Chicago (restoration study) 2003, Prince of Wales Theatre, London (restoration) 2003; Fellow, Royal Society of Arts 1995. *Leisure interests:* performing arts, music, art, gardens. *Address:* 110 Elgin Street, London, W11 2JL, England (Home). *Telephone:* (20) 7229-1732 (Home). *Fax:* (20) 7727-7501 (Home). *E-mail:* maremail@compuserve.com (Home).

McCANDLESS, Bruce, II; American astronaut (retd) and manager; b. Byron Willis McCandless, 8 June 1937, Boston, Mass.; s. of late Rear-Adm. Bruce McCandless and Sue W.B. McCandless Inman; m. Alfreda Bernice Doyle 1960; one s. one d.; ed US Naval Acad., Stanford Univ. and Univ. of Houston; flight training, Pensacola, Fla and Kingsville, Tex.; weapons system and carrier landing training, Key West, Fla 1960; carrier duty, Fighter Squadron 102 1960–64; instrument flight instructor, Attack Squadron 43, Naval Air Station, Apollo Soucek Field, Oceana, Va; graduate studies in electrical Eng, Stanford Univ. until 1966; selected by NASA as astronaut April 1966; Co-investigator Astronaut Manoeuvring Unit Experiment on Skylab 1968–74; back-up crew for first Skylab Mission 1973; Mission Specialist on STS-11, first flight of manned manoeuvring unit; Mission Specialist on STS-31, Hubble Space Telescope deployment; retd from Navy as Capt. Aug. 1990; Man. Payload Systems and Tech., Lockheed Martin Astronautics Group and Vice-Pres. Lockheed Martin Overseas Corpn 1990–; Prin. Staff Engineer Lockheed Martin Astronautics 1990–97; Chief. Scientist Reusable Space Transportation Systems 1997–; V. A. Prather Award, American Astronautical Soc. 1975, 1985, NASA Space Flight Medal 1984, 1991, Nat. Air and Space Museum Trophy 1985, Nat. Aeronautical Asscn Collier Trophy 1985, NASA Exceptional Eng Achievement Medal 1985, Defense Distinguished Service Medal 1985, Legion of Merit 1988. *Leisure interests:* electronics, scuba diving, sailing, photography. *Address:* Mail Stop DC 3005, Lockheed Martin Astronautics, P.O. Box 179, Denver, CO 80201 (Office); 21852 Pleasant Park Road, Conifer, CO 80433-6802, USA (Home). *Telephone:* (303) 971-6308 (Office). *Fax:* (303) 971-7698 (Office). *E-mail:* bruce.mccandless@lmco.com (Office); brucemcc@logcabin.com (Home).

McCANN, Norman, ARAM, FRSA, FID; British concert agent; b. 24 April 1920, London; s. of Bert McCann and Violetta McCann; m. Lucille Graham 1945; one s.; ed Royal Acad. of Music; has appeared in opera, concerts, musical shows, Shakespearean productions and on radio and TV; lecturer at the Comenius Univ. and Trinity Coll. of Music; Admin. and Artistic Dir British Opera Co.; Curator, Int. Music Museum; Dir of Production, Hintlesham Festival; Artistic Adviser, Battle Festival; Exec. Dir Children's Opera Group; Concerts Organizer, Int. Eisteddfod; Concert Man. Goldsmith's Choral Union; Chair. Minerva Ballet Trust; Concerts Man. and Artistic Adviser, S. and N. Wales Asscn of Choirs; Pres. and Chair. English Singers and Speakers Asscn of GB; Past Pres. British Asscn of Concert Agents; Pres. Lewisham Chamber of Commerce; Chair. Lewisham Conservative Asscn; manager and business adviser to many distinguished artists; Hon. Assoc. Royal Acad. of Music; mem. British Inst. of Man.; Order of Kyril & Methodius (Bulgaria). *Leisure interests:* gardening, music, food.

McCARRICK, HE Cardinal Theodore Edgar; American ecclesiastic; b. 7 July 1930, New York; ordained priest 1958; Auxiliary Bishop of New York 1977; Bishop of Metuchen 1981; Archbishop of Newark 1986–2000; Archbishop of Washington 2001–; cr. Cardinal 2001; Pres. Papal Foundation 1997–; mem. US Sec. of State's Advisory Cttee on Religious Freedom Abroad 1996–99, US Comm. for Int. Religious Freedom 1999–2001; Order of Cedars of Lebanon 2000, Eleanor Roosevelt Award for Human Rights 2000. *Address:* Archdiocesan Pastoral Center, 5001 Eastern Avenue, PO Box 29260, Washington, DC 20017, USA (Office). *Telephone:* (301) 853-4540 (Office). *Fax:* (301) 853-5346 (Office).

McCARTHY, Callum, PhD; British civil servant, economist and banker; b. 29 Feb. 1944, Brentwood, Essex; s. of Ralph McCarthy and Agnes Graham; m. Penelope Ann Gee 1966; two s. one d.; ed Univs of Oxford and Stirling, Business School, Stanford Univ.; econ. and operations researcher ICI 1965; Prin. Pvt. Sec. to Roy Hattersley (q.v.) and Norman Tebbit (q.v.), Dept of Trade and Industry 1972–85, also Under-Sec.; Dir of Corp. Finance, Kleinwort Benson 1985–89; Man. Dir, Head of Corp. Finance, BZW 1989–93; CEO Barclays Bank Group Japan and N America 1993–98; Dir-Gen. of UK Gas Supply 1998–2003; Dir-Gen. of UK Electricity Supply 1999–2003; Chair. Gas and Electricity Markets Authority 2000–; Chief Exec. Ofgem 2000–03; Chair. Financial Services Authority (FSA) 2003–. *Publication:* Introduction to Technological Economics (with D. S. Davies) 1967. *Leisure interests:* walking, reading, bee-keeping. *Address:* The Financial Services Authority, 25 The North Colonnade, Canary Wharf, London, E14 5HS, England. *Telephone:* (20) 7676-1000 (Office). *E-mail:* www.fsa.gov.uk (Office).

McCARTHY, Cormac; American author; b. 1933, Rhode Island; s. of Charles Joseph McCarthy and Gladys McGrail; m. 1st Lee Holleman 1961 (divorced); one s.; m. 2nd Annie DeLisle (divorced); m. 3rd Jennifer Winkley 1998; ed Univ. of Tennessee; USAF 1953–57; MacArthur Fellowship 1981; Guggenheim Fellowship; Rockefeller Fellowship. *Publications:* novels: The Orchard Keeper 1965, Outer Dark 1968, Child of God 1973, Suttree 1979, Blood Meridian 1985, All the Pretty Horses (Vol. 1 of The Bouden Trilogy) 1992, The Crossing (Vol. 2 of The Bouden Trilogy) 1994, Cities of the Plain (Vol. 3 of The Bouden Trilogy) 1998; play: The Stonemason 1994. *Address:* 1011 N Mesa Street, El Paso, TX 79902, USA.

McCARTHY, Eugene Joseph, MA; American politician and writer; b. 29 March 1916, Watkins, Minn.; s. of late Michael J. McCarthy and Anna Baden McCarthy; m. Abigail Quigley 1945 (died 2001); one s. three d. (one deceased); ed St John's Univ., Collegeville, Minn. and Minnesota Univ.; successively Prof. of Econs and Educ., St John's Univ., Collegeville, Minn.; Civilian Tech. Asst, War Dept Mil. Intelligence Division; Acting Chair. Sociology Dept, St Thomas Coll., St Paul, Minn.; mem. U.S. House of Reps. (Fourth Minn.

district) 1949–58; Senator from Minnesota 1959–70; Liberal Independent cand. for Presidency 1976; Adlai Stevenson Prof. of Political Science, New School for Social Research 1973–74; syndicated columnist 1977–; Dir Harcourt Brace Jovanovich Inc.; Hon. LLD (St Louis) 1955, (Swathmore), (Washington) ; HE Cardinal Newman Award 1955. *Publications:* Frontiers in American Democracy 1960, Dictionary of American Politics 1962, A Liberal Answer to the Conservative Challenge 1964, The Limits of Power: America's Role in the World 1967, The Year of the People 1969, Other Things and the Aardvark (poems) 1970, The Hard Years 1975, Mr. Raccoon and his friends (children's stories) 1977, America Revisited 1978, Ground Fog and Night (poetry) 1979, A Political Bestiary (co-author) 1979, The Ultimate Tyranny 1979, Gene McCarthy's Minnesota 1982, The View from Rappahanock 1984, Up 'Til Now: A Memoir of the Decline of American Politics 1987, The View from Rappahannock II 1989, Required Reading–Book of Essays (jtly.) 1989, Colony of the World 1993, Selected Poems 1997, No Fault Politics 1998, American Bestiary. *Address:* 271 Hawlin Road, Woodville, VA 22749; 2512 Queens, Washington, DC 20007, USA. *Telephone:* (202) 339-8884.

McCARTHY, John Philip, AO, MA, LLB; Australian diplomatist; b. 29 Nov. 1942, Washington, USA; s. of Edwin McCarthy and Marjorie McCarthy; two d.; ed Cambridge Univ.; barrister 1964; joined Dept of Foreign Affairs 1968; Second Sec. Vientiane 1969–72; First Sec. Washington 1973–75; Chargé d'affaires, Damascus 1977–78; Sr pvt. sec. to Minister for Foreign Affairs 1979–80; Amb. to Democratic Repub. of Viet Nam 1981–83, to Mexico 1985–87, to Thailand 1992–94, to U.S.A. 1995–97, to Indonesia 1997–2000, to Japan 2001–; Head, Public Affairs Br., Dept of Foreign Affairs 1983–84; First Asst Sec. Public Affairs Div., Canberra, Minister (Congressional Liaison) Washington; First Asst Sec. Int. Orgs and Legal Div., Dept of Foreign Affairs and Trade –1992; Deputy Sec. Dept of Foreign Affairs and Trade, Canberra 1994–95. *Leisure interests:* drama, skiing, Asian art, walking, travel. *Address:* Embassy of Australia, 2-1-14, Mita, Minato-ku, Tokyo 108-8361, Japan (Office). *Telephone:* (3) 5232-4111 (Office). *Fax:* (3) 5232-4157 (Office). *Website:* www.australia.or.jp (Office).

McCARTNEY, Rt Hon. Ian; British politician; b. 25 April 1951; s. of Hugh McCartney; m. 1st (divorced); two d. one s. (deceased); m. 2nd Ann Parkes ; joined Labour Party 1966, Labour Party Organiser 1973–87; Councillor for Wigan Borough 1982–87; MP (Labour) for Makerfield 1987–; Opposition Spokesperson on NHS (Nat. Health Service) 1992–94, on Employment 1994–96, Chief Spokesperson on Employment 1996–97; Minister of State Dept of Trade and Industry 1997–99, Cabinet Office 1999–2001; Minister for Pensions Dept for Work and Pensions 2001–03; Chair. Labour Party 2003–. *Leisure interests:* Rugby League (supports Wigan Warriors). *Address:* Labour Party Headquarters, Millbank Tower, Millbank, London, SW1P 4GT, England (Office). *Telephone:* (8705) 900200 (Office). *Fax:* (20) 7802-1234 (Office). *Website:* www.labour.org.uk (Office).

McCARTNEY, Sir (James) Paul, Kt, MBE, FRCM; British songwriter and performer; b. 18 June 1942, Liverpool; s. of James McCartney and Mary McCartney; m. 1st Linda Eastman 1969 (died 1998); one s. two d. one step-d.; m. 2nd Heather Mills 2002; ed Stockton Wood Road Primary School, Speke, Joseph Williams Primary School, Gateacre and Liverpool Inst.; plays guitar, piano and organ; taught himself to play trumpet at age of 13; wrote first song 1956, wrote numerous songs with John Lennon; joined pop group The Quarrymen 1956; appeared under various titles until formation of The Beatles 1960; appeared with The Beatles in the following activities: performances in Hamburg 1960, 1961, 1962, The Cavern, Liverpool 1960, 1961; worldwide tours 1963–66; attended Transcendental Meditation Course at Maharishi's Acad., Rishikesh, India Feb. 1968; formed Apple Ltd, parent org. of The Beatles Group of Cos. 1968; left The Beatles after collapse of Apple Corpn Ltd 1970; formed MPL group of cos. 1970; first solo album McCartney 1970; formed own pop group Wings 1971 (disbanded 1981); tours of Britain and Europe 1972–73, UK and Australia 1975, Europe and USA 1976, UK 1979, World Tour 1989–90; albums with the Beatles: Please Please Me 1963, With the Beatles 1963, A Hard Day's Night 1964, Beatles for Sale 1965, Help! 1965, Rubber Soul 1966, Revolver 1966, Sgt. Pepper's Lonely Hearts Club Band 1967, Magical Mystery Tour 1967, The Beatles (White Album) 1968, Yellow Submarine 1969, Abbey Road 1969, Let it Be 1970, Anthology I 1995, Anthology II 1996; other albums: Ram 1971, Wildlife 1971, Red Rose Speedway 1973, Band on the Run 1973, Venus and Mars 1975, Wings at the Speed of Sound 1976, Wings Over America 1976, London Town 1978, Wings Greatest 1978, Back to the Egg 1979, McCartney II 1980, Tug of War 1982, Pipes of Peace 1983, Give My Regards to Broad Street 1984, Press to Play 1986, All the Best 1987, Flowers in the Dirt 1989, Jet 1989, Tripping the Live Fantastic 1990, Unplugged: The Official Bootleg 1991, Paul McCartney's Liverpool Oratorio 1991, Off the Ground 1993, Flaming Pie 1997, Wingspan 2001, Driving Rain 2001; composed Liverpool Oratorio (with Carl Davis, q.v.) 1991; Symphony: Standing Stone 1997, Run, Devil Run 1999; composed soundtrack music for The Family Way 1966, James Paul McCartney 1973, Live and Let Die 1973, The Zoo Gang (TV series) 1973; Films by The Beatles: A Hard Day's Night 1964, Help! 1965, Yellow Submarine (animated colour cartoon film) 1968, Let it Be 1970; TV film Magical Mystery Tour 1967; Wings over the World (TV) 1979, Rockshow 1981; Give My Regards to Broad Street (wrote and Dir) 1984, Rupert and the Frog Song (wrote and produced) 1985 (BAFTA Award Best Animated Film), Press to Play 1986; concert film Get Back 1991; Hon. Fellow (Liverpool John Moores Univ.) 1998; Hon. Dr. (Sussex) 1988; two Grammy Awards for Band on the Run (including Best Pop

Vocal Performance) 1975, Ivor Novello Award for Best Selling British Record 1977–78 for single Mull of Kintyre, for Int. Hit of the Year 1982 for single Ebony and Ivory, for Outstanding Services to British Music 1989; Guinness Book of Records "Triple Superlative Award" (43 songs each selling more than 1 million copies, holder of 60 gold discs, estimated sales of 100 million albums and 100 million singles) 1979; Lifetime Achievement Award 1990; Freeman of Liverpool 1984; Lifetime Achievement Award People for the Ethical Treatment of Animals (with Linda McCartney) 1996, Polar Music Prize 1992; Fellowship British Acad. of Composers and Songwriters 2000. *Radio:* (series) Routes of Rock (BBC) 1999. *Publications:* Paintings 2000, The Beatles Anthology (with George Harrison and Ringo Starr) 2000, Sun Prints (with Linda McCartney) 2001, Many Years From Now (autobiog.) 2001, Blackbird Singing: Poems and Lyrics 1965–1999 2001. *Address:* c/o MPL Communications Ltd, 1 Soho Square, London, W1V 6BQ, England.

McCARTNEY, Stella, BA; British fashion designer; b. 13 Sept. 1971; d. of Sir Paul McCartney (q.v.) and the late Linda McCartney; ed Cen. St Martin's Coll. of Art and Design; work with Christian Lacroix at age 15 and later with Betty Jackson; work experience in Fashion Dept, Vogue magazine; after graduating set up own design co. in London; fmr Chief Designer for Chloe, Paris; designed collection for Gucci 2001; VH1/Vogue Fashion and Music Designer of the Year 2000. *Address:* Gucci Group, via Don Lorenzo Perosi, 6 Casellina di Scandici, 50018 Florence, Italy (Office). *Website:* www.gucci.con, www.stellamccartney .com (Office).

McCARTY, Maclyn, AB, MD; American medical research scientist; b. 9 June 1911, South Bend. Ind.; s. of Earl Hauser and Hazel Beagle McCarty; m. 1st Anita Davies 1934 (divorced 1966), 2nd Marjorie Steiner 1966; three s. one d.; ed Kenosha High School, Wis., Stanford and Johns Hopkins Univs.; Intern and Asst Resident in Pediatrics, Johns Hopkins Hosp. 1937–40; Fellow in Medicine, New York Univ. 1940–41; Fellow in Medical Sciences of Nat. Research Council (with O. T. Avery), Rockefeller Inst. for Medical Research (now Rockefeller Univ.) 1941–42, Active Duty (USNR) Naval Research Unit 1942–46, Assoc. and Assoc. Physician 1946–48, Assoc. mem. and Assoc. Physician 1948–50, mem. (Prof.) 1950–81, Physician in Chief to the Hosp. 1960–74, Vice-Pres. 1965–78, John D. Rockefeller, Jr Prof. 1977–81, Prof. Emer. 1981–; Vice-Pres. Helen Hay Whitney Foundation, Chair. Scientific Advisory Cttee 1963–96; Ed. Journal of Experimental Medicine 1963–; 1st Waterford Biomedical Award 1977; Robert Koch Gold Medal (Fed. Repub. of Germany) 1981, Kovalenko Medal, NAS 1988, Wolf Prize, Israel 1990, Albert Lasker Special Public Health Award 1994; Order of Repub., First Degree (Egypt) 1982; Commdr.'s Cross of the Order of Merit (Fed. Repub. of Germany) 1984. *Publications:* The Transforming Principle: Discovering that Genes are made of DNA 1985; numerous scientific papers, mainly in Journal of Experimental Medicine. *Leisure interests:* travel, reading. *Address:* The Rockefeller University, 66th Street and York Avenue, New York, NY 10021, USA. *Telephone:* (212) 327-8158. *Fax:* (212) 327-8960.

McCOLGAN, Elizabeth (Liz), MBE; British athlete; b. 24 May 1964, Dundee, Scotland; d. of Martin Lynch and Elizabeth Fearn; m. Peter McColgan 1987; four c.; ed Univ. of Alabama; coached by Grete Waitz; gold medal Commonwealth Games 10,000m 1986, 1990; silver medal World Cross Country Championships 1987, bronze medal 1991; silver medal Olympic Games 10,000m 1988; silver medal World Indoor Championships 3,000m 1989; bronze medal Commonwealth Games 3,000m 1990; gold medal World Championships 10,000m 1991; gold medal World Half-Marathon Championships 1992; first in New York City Marathon 1991; first in Tokyo Marathon 1992, third in 1996; third in London Marathon 1993, fifth in 1995, first in 1996, second in 1997, 1998; retd 2001; runs her own fitness centre and coaches young athletes in Dundee; BBC Sports Personality of the Year 1991. *Leisure interests:* cooking, cinema, crosswords. *Address:* c/o Marquee UK, 6 George Street, Nottingham, NG1 3BE, England. *Telephone:* (115) 948-3206. *Fax:* (115) 952-7203.

McCOLL OF DULWICH, Baron (Life Peer), cr. 1989, of Bermondsey in the London Borough of Southwark; **Ian McColl,** CBE, MS, FRCS, FRCSE, FACS; British professor of surgery; b. 6 Jan. 1933; s. of the late Frederick George McColl and Winifred Edith McColl; m. Jean Lennox McNair 1960; one s. two d.; ed Hutchesons' Grammar School, Glasgow, St Paul's School, London, Guy's Hosp. Medical School, Univ. of London; Moynihan Fellowship, Asscn of Surgeons 1967; Reader in Surgery, St Bartholomew's Hosp., London 1967–71, Sub-Dean, St Bartholomew's Hosp. Medical Coll. 1969–71; Prof. of Surgery, Guy's Hosp., London 1971–98 Consultant Surgeon 1971–98, Dir of Surgery 1985–98; Chair. Dept of Surgery, United Medical and Dental Schools, St Thomas' Hosps 1985–92; Hon. Consultant to British Army 1976 –98; Parl. Pvt. Sec. (Lords) to Prime Minister 1994–97; Deputy Speaker House of Lords 1994–2002; Chair. Bd of Govs Mildmay Mission Hosp. 1984–; Vice-Chair. Disablement Services Authority for England 1987–91; Chair. Bd Dirs, Vice-Chair. Int. Bd Mercy Ships 1998–; mem. Council, Royal Coll. of Surgeons 1986–94, Council, Imperial Cancer Research Fund 1986–94; Pres. Nat. Asscn of Limbless Disabled, Soc. of Minimally Invasive Surgery, Leprosy Mission; Vice-Pres. John Grooms Asscn for the Disabled; mem. Bd of Govs American Coll. of Surgeons 1982–88; Fellow King's Coll. London 2001; George and Thomas Hutcheson's Award 2000, Nat. Maritime Historical Soc. Award 2002, Great Scot Award 2002. *Eponymous lectures:* Arris and Gale (2), Erasmus Wilson, Haig Gudenian Memorial, Colles, Letsomian, Lord Cohen Memorial. *Publications:* Intestinal Absorption in Man 1976, NHS Data Book 1984, Govt Report on supply of artificial legs and wheelchairs for England; articles on colonic diseases, medical audit and amputations. *Leisure interest:* forestry. *Address:* House of Lords, London, SW1A 0PW, England. *Telephone:* (20) 7219-5141 (Office). *Fax:* (20) 7407-6615 (Office). *E-mail:* mccolli@parliament.uk (Office).

McCOMB, Leonard William Joseph, DIPL. FINE ART; British artist; b. 3 Aug. 1930, Glasgow; s. of Archibald McComb and Delia McComb; m. 1st Elizabeth Henstock 1955 (marriage dissolved 1963); m. 2nd Joan Allwork 1966 (died 1967); m. 3rd Barbara Gittel 1973; ed Manchester Art School, Slade School of Fine Art, Univ. of London; teacher at art schools in Bristol, Oxford and London (RA schools, Slade, Goldsmiths', Sir John Cass) 1960–; Keeper of the RA 1995–98; Hon. mem. Royal Watercolour Soc. 1996, Royal Soc. of Printmakers 1996; selected as artist representing England to design Millennium Medal for the Vatican 2000; Jubilee Prize, RA 1986, Korn Ferry Award 1990, Times Watercolour Competition Prize 1992, 1993, Nordstern Printmaking Prize, RA 1992, Royal Watercolour Soc. Prize 1998. *Commissions include:* ceramic and tapestry design, Boots, Nottingham, series of three oil paintings painted on site at Bingham Canyon Copper Mines, USA for RTZ London, commemorative bronze gold leaf portrait of John Brooks of Brooks Univ., Oxford, painting of site in Cornwall where first transatlantic cable was laid between England and America, Cable & Wireless, portrait of Doris Lessing, Nat. Portrait Gallery, London. *One-man Exhibitions include:* Blossoms and Flowers, Coracle Press Gallery, London 1979, Drawings, Paintings and Sculpture, Serpentine Gallery, London and tour, 1983, Paintings from the South, Gillian Jason Gallery, London 1989, Drawings and Paintings, Darby Gallery, London 1993, Portraits, NY Studio Gallery. *Group Exhibitions include:* Art Council 1976, 1980, 1982, 1987, RA 1977, 1989, Venice 1980, Tate Gallery 1984, Hirshhorn Gallery, Washington 1986, Raab Gallery, Berlin 1986, Museum of Modern Art, Brussels 1987, Dublin 1997, Flowers East Gallery, London 1998. *Works on display in public collections include:* Arts Council, British Council, I.C.A., Cambridge Univ., Tate Gallery, Victoria & Albert Museum, Ulster Museum, etc. *Radio:* Kaleidoscope (BBC Radio Four) 1984, Life's Little Luxuries (BBC Radio Four) 2001. *Television:* The South Bank Show – Royal Acad. Chat 1999. *Leisure interests:* travelling, walking. *Address:* 4 Blenheim Studios, 29 Blenheim Gardens, London, SW2 5EU, England (Home). *Telephone:* (20) 8671-5510 (Home).

McCONAUGHEY, Matthew; American actor; b. 4 Nov. 1969, Ulvade, Tex.; ed Univ. of Texas at Austin. *Film appearances include:* Dazed and Confused, The Return of the Texas Chainsaw Massacre, Boys on the Side, My Boyfriend's Back 1993, Angels in the Outfield 1994, Scorpion Spring, Submission 1995, Glory Daze, Lone Star, A Time to Kill 1996, Larger Than Life 1997, Amistad, Contact, Making Sandwiches, Last Flight of the Raven, Newton Boys, South Beach, EdTV 1999, U-571 2000, The Wedding Planner 2001. *Address:* c/o Warner Brothers Incorporated, 4000 Warner Boulevard, Suite 1101, Burbank, CA 91522, USA.

MCCONNELL, Addison Mitchell (Mitch), Jr, BA, JD; American politician and lawyer; b. 20 Feb. 1942, Tuscumbia, Ala; s. of Addison Charles McConnell and Julia McConnell (née Shockley); m. Elaine Chao 1993; three c.; ed Univs of Louisville and Ky; admitted to Bar, Ky 1967; Chief Legis. Asst to Senator Marlow Cook, Washington 1968–70; est. legal practice, Louisville 1970; Deputy Asst US Attorney-Gen. 1974–75; Judge Jefferson Co., Louisville 1978–85; Senator from Ky 1985–; Chair. Nat. Republican Senatorial Cttee, Rules and Admin Cttee, mem. Agric., Nutrition and Forestry Cttee, Appropriations Cttee, Chair. Jefferson Co. Republican Cttee 1973–74; Co-Chair. Nat. Child Tragedies Coalition 1981; Founding Chair. Ky Task Force on Exploited and Missing Children 1982; mem. Pres.'s Partnership on Child Safety; mem. Ky Asscn of County Judge Execs (Pres. 1982), Nat. Inst. of Justice (mem. Advisory Bd 1982–84); Commendation, Nat. Trust in Historical Preservation in the US 1982; Conservationist of the Year Award, League of Ky. Sportsmen 1983; Certificate of Appreciation, American Correctional Asscn. 1985. *Leisure interests:* cooking, fishing. *Address:* Office of the Senator from Kentucky, US Senate, Senate Buildings, Washington, DC 20510, USA (Office).

McCONNELL, David John, PhD, MRIA; Irish professor of molecular genetics; b. 15 May 1944, Dublin; s. of John J. McConnell and Joan Warwick; m. Janet Overend 1966; two s.; ed Zion Nat. Schools, Rathgar, Dublin, Sandford Park School, Ranelagh, Dublin, Trinity Coll. Dublin and Calif. Inst. of Tech.; Lecturer in Genetics, Trinity Coll. Dublin 1970–85, Fellow 1978, Assoc. Prof. of Genetics 1985–90, Head, Dept of Genetics 1987–, Prof. of Genetics 1990–; Eleanor Roosevelt Fellow, Int. Union Against Cancer, Lab. of Prof. Wally Gilbert, Dept of Biochem. and Molecular Biology Harvard Univ. 1976–77; Visiting Prof. Univ. of Calif. (Davis) 1979; consultant in genetic eng and biotech. UNIDO 1982–; UNDP Star consultant, Beijing Agric. Univ. 1987; Chair. Adelaide Hosp. 1988–94, Pres. 1995–2001; Pres. Royal Zoological Soc. of Ireland 1992–96, Fellow; other professional appts.; mem. European Molecular Biological Org. (EMBO); Vice-Provost for Quatercentenary Affairs, Trinity Coll. Dublin 1991–92; Vice-Provost Trinity Coll. Dublin 1999–2001; Chair. Irish Times Trust 2001–; mem. Irish Council for Science, Tech. and Innovation 1997–. *Publications:* more than 100 papers in scientific journals. *Leisure interests:* windsurfing, Kerry, gardening. *Address:* Department of Genetics, Smurfit Institute of Genetics, Trinity College, Dublin 2, Ireland. *Telephone:* (1) 702-2008, 702-1140. *Fax:* (1) 671-4968. *E-mail:* david .mcconnell@tcd.ie.

McCONNELL, Harden M., PhD; American professor emeritus of chemistry; b. 18 July 1927, Richmond, Va; s. of Harry R. McConnell and Frances McConnell (née Coffee); m. Sofia Glogovac 1956; two s. one d.; ed George Washington Univ., California Inst. of Tech. and Univ. of Chicago; with Dept of Physics, Univ. of Chicago, Nat. Research Fellow 1950–52; Shell Devt Co., Emeryville, Calif. 1952–56; Asst Prof. of Chem., Calif. Inst. of Tech. 1956–58, Assoc. Prof. of Chem. 1958–59, Prof. of Chem. 1959–63, Prof. of Chem. and Physics 1963–64; Prof. of Chem. Stanford Univ. 1964–79, Robert Eckles Swain Prof. of Chemistry 1979–, Chair. Dept of Chem. 1989–92; mem. several bds, Neuroscience Research Program, MIT; f. Molecular Devices Corpn 1983; Pres. Foundation for Basic Research in Chemistry 1990–96; Fellow, American Physical Soc., Biophysical Soc. 1999, American Soc. of Biological Chemists, American Assen for the Advancement of Science 1982; mem. ACS, NAS, Int. Acad. of Quantum Molecular Science, AAAS; Foreign mem. Serbian Acad. of Sciences and Arts; Harkins Lecturer, Univ. of Chicago 1967, Falk-Plaut Lecturer, Columbia Univ. 1967, Renaud Foundation Lecturer 1971, Peter Debye Lecturer, Cornell Univ. 1973, Harvey Lecturer, Rockefeller Univ. 1977, A. L. Patterson Lecturer, Inst. for Cancer Research, Phil. 1978, Pauling Lecturer, Stanford Univ. 1981, Remsen Memorial Lecturer, Maryland Section ACS 1982, Prof. du Collège de France 1986, Le Bel Lecturer, Strasbourg 1986, Swift Lecturer, Calif. Inst. of Tech. 1986, Venable Lecturer, Univ. of N. Carolina 1987, Linus Pauling Distinguished Lecturer, Oregon State Univ. 1987, Davis Lecturer, Univ. of New Orleans 1990; Fellow Biophysical Soc. 1999; Calif. Section Award of ACS 1961, Nat. ACS Award in Pure Chem. 1962, Harrison Howe Award 1968, Irving Langmuir Award in Chemical Physics 1971, Alumni Achievement Award (George Washington Univ.) 1971, Dickson Prize for Science (Carnegie-Mellon Univ.) 1982, Distinguished Alumni Award (Calif. Inst. of Tech.) 1982, Wolf Prize in Chemistry 1983–84, ISCO Award 1984, Pauling Medal, Puget Sound and Oregon ACS Sections 1987, Wheland Medal, Univ. of Chicago 1988, NAS Award in Chemical Sciences 1988, Sherman Fairchild Distinguished Scholar, Calif. Inst. of Tech. 1988, Nat. Medal of Science 1989, Peter Debeye Award, Physical Chemistry, American Chemistry Society 1990, Bruker Prize, Royal Soc. of Chem. 1995, ACS Award in Surface Science 1997, Gold Medal of Int. ESR Soc. 1997, Zavoisky Award 2000, Welch Award 2002. *Publications:* over 400 scientific publns in the field of chem., chemical physics, biophysics and immunology. *Leisure interest:* mathematics. *Address:* Department of Chemistry, Stanford University, Stanford, CA 94305, USA (Office). *Telephone:* (415) 723-4571.

McCONNELL, Rt Hon Jack Wilson, BSc, DipEd; British politician; b. 30 June 1960, Irvine, Ayrshire; s. of William Wilson McConnell and Elizabeth McEwan McConnell; m. Bridget Mary McLuckie 1990; one s. one d.; ed Arran High School, Isle of Arran, Stirling Univ.; math. teacher, Alloa 1983–92; Labour mem. Stirling Dist Council 1984–92, Treas. 1988–92, Leader 1990–92; Gen. Sec. Scottish Labour Party (SLP) 1992–98; co-ordinated Labour's Yes Yes Referendum Campaign 1997; mem. Scottish Constitutional Convention 1989–98; MSP for Motherwell and Wishaw; Minister for Finance, Scottish Exec. 1999–2000, for Educ. and External Affairs 2000–01; First Minister of Scotland 2001–; mem. Convention of Scottish Local Authorities (COSLA) 1988–92; mem. GMB, Amnesty Int. *Leisure interests:* golf, swimming, music, watching football. *Address:* Scottish Executive, St Andrew's House, Regent Road, Edinburgh, EH1 3DG, Scotland (Office). *Telephone:* (131) 348-5831 (Office). *Fax:* (131) 348-5993 (Office). *E-mail:* jack.mcconnell .msp@scottish.parliament.uk (Office). *Website:* www.scottish.parliament.uk (Office).

McCORKINDALE, Douglas H.; American business executive; b. 14 Jan 1939, New York; ed Columbia Coll. and Law School; Harlan Fiske Stone Scholar, Columbia Law School; joined Gannett as gen. counsel in 1971, Sr Vice-Pres. Finance and Law and mem. Bd Dirs 1977, Chief Financial and Admin. Officer 1983–97, Vice-Chair. 1985–2001, Pres. 1997–, CEO 2001–, Chair. 2001–; Dir Continental Airlines Inc.; dir or trustee of numerous mutual funds in Prudential Group. *Address:* Gannett Co. Inc., 7950 Jones Branch Drive, McLean, VA 22107, USA (Office). *Telephone:* (703) 854-6000 (Office). *E-mail:* gcishare@info.gannett.com (Office). *Website:* www.gannett.com (Office).

MacCORMAC, Sir Richard Cornelius, Kt, CBE, P.P.R.I.B.A., FRSA, RA; British architect; b. 3 Sept. 1938; s. of Henry MacCormac and Marion Maud Broomhall; m. Susan Karin Landen 1964; two s. (one deceased); ed Westminster School, Trinity Coll. Cambridge, Univ. Coll. London; served RN 1957–59; Project Architect, London Borough of Merton 1967–69; est. pvt. practice 1969; partner MacCormac, Jamieson, Prichard Architects 1972–, Chair. 2002–; taught in Dept of Architecture, Cambridge Univ. 1969–75, 1979–81, Univ. Lecturer 1976–79; Studio Tutor, LSE City Policy and Eng 1998; Pres. RIBA 1991–93; London Forum of Amenity and Civic Socs. 1997–; Dir Spitalfields Workspace 1981–; mem. Royal Fine Art Comm. 1983–93, mem. Architecture Cttee, Royal Acad. 1998–, Exhbns. Cttee 1999–; Visiting Prof. Univ. of Edin. 1982–85, Univ. of Hull 1998–99; Adviser British Council 1993–; Trustee Greenwich Foundation 1997–2002. *Major works include:* Cable & Wireles Coll., Coventry (Royal Fine Art Comm./Sunday Times Bldg of the Year Award 1994); Garden Quadrangle, St John's Coll., Oxford (Independent on Sunday Bldg of the Year Award 1994); Bowra Bldg, Wadham Coll., Oxford; Burrell's Fields, Trinity Coll., Cambridge; Ruskin Library, Lancaster Univ. (Independent on Sunday Bldg of the Year Award 1996); Southwark Station, Jubilee Line extension, London; Wellcome Wing, Science Museum, London. *Leisure interests:* sailing, music, reading. *Address:* 9 Heneage Street, London, E1 5LJ, England. *Telephone:* (20) 7377-9262. *Fax:* (20) 7247-7854. *E-mail:* mjp@mjparchitects.co.uk (Office).

MacCORMICK, Sir (Donald) Neil, MA, LLD, FBA, FRSE; British professor of law; b. 27 May 1941, Glasgow; s. of John MacDonald MacCormick and Margaret Isobel Miller; m. 1st Caroline Rona Barr 1965 (divorced 1991); three d.; m. 2nd Flora Margaret Britain (née Milne) 1992; ed High School of Glasgow, Univ. of Glasgow, Balliol Coll., Oxford; Lecturer in Jurisprudence, Queen's Coll., Dundee, St Andrews Univ. 1965–67; Fellow and Tutor in Jurisprudence, Balliol Coll., Oxford 1967–72; Regius Prof. of Public Law and the Law of Nature and Nations, Univ. of Edin. 1972– (on leave of absence 1999–), Dean of the Faculty of Law 1973–76, 1985–88; Vice-Prin. (Int.) Univ. of Edin. 1997–99, Leverhulme Personal Research Prof. 1997–99; Pres. Soc. of Public Teachers of Law 1983–84; mem. Nat. Council of Scottish Nat. Party 1978–84, 1985–86, 1989–, Vice-Pres. 1999–; Foreign mem. Finnish Acad. of Sciences and Letters 1994; MEP (SNP) 1999–; Hon. LLD (Uppsala Univ.) 1986, (Queen's Univ., Kingston, Ont.) 1996, (Glasgow) 1999. *Publications:* Legal Reasoning and Legal Theory 1978, H. L. A. Hart 1981, Legal Right and Social Democracy 1982, An Institutional Theory of Law 1986, The Scottish Debate (ed.) 1970, The Legal Mind (ed.) 1986, Enlightenment Rights and Revolution (ed.) 1989, Interpreting Statutes (ed.) 1991, Essays on Legal Reasoning (2 Vols) 1991, Controversies About the Ontology of Law (ed.) 1991, Interpreting Precedents 1997, Questioning Sovereignty 1999. *Leisure interests:* gardening, hill-walking, dinghy sailing, politics (Scottish Nat. Party), piping. *Address:* European Parliament, 60 rue Wiertz, 1047 Brussels, Belgium (Office); 19 Pentland Terrace, Edinburgh, EH10 6HA, Scotland (Home). *Telephone:* (131) 447-7945 (Home).

MCCORMICK, Steven J., BS, JD; American conservationist and lawyer; ed Univ. of Calif. at Berkeley, Univ. of Calif. Hastings Coll., Stanford Univ.; Western Regional Rep. The Nature Conservancy (TNC) 1977–80, Calif. Field Rep. 1980–94, Exec. Dir TNC Calif. 1984–2000, Western Div. Rep. 1998–2000, Pres. and CEO TNC 2001–; Partner Resources Law Group LLP 2000–01; Silver Award, Dept of the Interior 1986, Conservation Award 1989, Edmund G. Pat Brown Award 1999. *Address:* The Nature Conservancy, 4245 North Fairfax Drive, Suite 100, Arlington, VA 22203-1606, USA (Office). *Telephone:* (800) 628-6860 (Office). *Website:* www.tnc.org (Office).

McCOURT, Frank; Irish author; b. 1931, New York, USA; s. of Malachy McCourt and Angela McCourt; moved to Ireland in 1935; taught in New York City public schools for 27 years; with brother Malachy performed a two-person musical review based on their life as young men in Ireland. *Publications:* Angela's Ashes (Pulitzer Prize 1997, Nat. Book Critics' Circle Award 1997, Los Angeles Times Book Award 1997, film 2000) 1996, 'Tis: A Memoir 1999. *Address:* c/o Author Mail, 7th Floor, HarperCollins Publishers Inc., 10 East 53rd Street, New York, NY 10022, USA (Office).

McCOWEN, Alec, CBE; British actor; b. 26 May 1925, Tunbridge Wells; s. of Duncan McCowen and Mary Walkden; ed Skinners School, Tunbridge Wells and Royal Acad. of Dramatic Art; mem. Nat. Theatre; Variety Club Stage Actor 1970; Old Vic Theatre: played Touchstone, Ford, Richard II, Mercutio, Malvolio, Oberon 1959–60; with RSC: played Fool in King Lear 1964; Hadrian VII 1968, The Philanthropist 1970, The Misanthrope 1972, Dr Dysart in Equus 1972, Henry Higgins in Pygmalion 1974, Ben in The Family Dance 1976; with Prospect Co.: Antony in Antony and Cleopatra 1977; solo performance of St Mark's Gospel 1978, 1981; Frank in Tishoo 1979; Malvolio in Twelfth Night (TV) 1980; with Nat. Theatre: Crocker-Harris in The Browning Version, Arthur in Harlequinade; Capt. Corcoran in HMS Pinafore 1981, Adolf Hitler in The Portage to San Cristobal of AH 1982, solo performance in Kipling 1983, Reilly in The Cocktail Party 1986, Nicolai in Fathers and Sons 1987, Vladimir in Waiting for Godot 1987, Modern Love 1988, Dr Scoper in The Heiress 1989, Harry in Exclusive 1989, George in A Single Man 1990, Father Jack in Dancing at Lughnasa 1990, Caesar in Caesar and Cleopatra, Michael in Someone Who'll Watch Over Me 1992, Prospero in The Tempest 1993, Elgar in Elgar's Rondo, Gaev in The Cherry Orchard 1995, Clem in Tom and Clem 1997, Narrator in Peter Pan 1998; Dir: Definitely the Bahamas 1987; Evening Standard (now The Standard) Best Actor 1969, 1972, 1982. *Films:* Frenzy 1971, Travels with my Aunt 1973, Stevie 1978, The Assam Garden 1985, Personal Services 1986, Henry V 1989, Age of Innocence 1992, Gangs of New York 2000. *Television:* Private Lives 1976, Mr. Palfrey of Westminster 1984, Hunted Down 1989. *Publications:* Young Gemini 1979, Double Bill 1980 and Personal Mark 1984. *Leisure interests:* music and gardening. *Address:* c/o Jeremy Conway, Eagle House, 18–21 Jermyn Street, London, SW1Y 6HP, England.

MCCOY, Tony; Irish jockey; b. 4 May 1974, Co. Antrim, NI; s. of Peadar McCoy; apprentice to Jim Bolger 1989; won first race Legal Steps at Thurles 1992; Champion Hurdle Winner, Make a Stand 1997; Cheltenham Gold Cup Winner, Mr Mulligan 1997; 1000th winner Majadou, Cheltenham 1999; 1500th winner Celtic Nave, Exeter 2001; champion jump jockey for seven successive seasons 1995–2002; greatest no. of career winners by any jockey 2002; greatest no. of winners in any season by any jockey (289) 2001–02 (broke 55-year old record). *Publication:* McCoy: The Autobiography 2002. *Address:* c/o Midas Public Relations, 7-8 Kendrick Mews, London, SW7 3HG, England (Office).

McCREDIE, Andrew Dalgarno, AM, MA, DPhil, FAHA; Australian professor of musicology; b. 3 Sept. 1930, Sydney; s. of Harold A. McCredie and Marjorie

C. (née Dalgarno) McCredie; m. Xenia Rosner 1965; one d.; ed Univ. of Sydney, Royal Acad. of Music, London, Univs. of Copenhagen, Stockholm, Hamburg; Sr Research Fellow, Univ. of Adelaide 1965–69, Sr Lecturer in Musicology 1970–73, Reader in Musicology 1974–77, Prof. 1978–94, Prof. Emer. 1994–; Adjunct Prof. Monash Univ. 1997–; Hon. Visiting Prof. Univ. of Queensland (Brisbane) 1997–; Visiting Lecturer Univs. of Amsterdam, Utrecht 1964, Western Australia 1970, City Univ. of New York 1974, Yale, Pennsylvania 1977, Ljubljana, Bologna, Marburg, Frankfurt, Cracow, Warsaw 1978, Copenhagen, Belfast (Queen's Univ.), Hamburg, Munich, Zentral Inst. für Musikforschung (Berlin), Berne, Basle, Zurich 1983, Melbourne, Stockholm, Tübingen 1986, Heidelberg, Saarbrücken, Queen's Univ., Kingston, Ont., Brandeis (Boston), City Univ. of New York 1987, NSW (Sydney) 1987, Munich, Braunschweig 1988, Wolfenbüttel, Mainz, Edmonton, Calgary, Saskatoon, London (Ont.), Toronto 1989, Cardiff 1992, Cologne 1994, Zagreb 1994, Dresden (1994, 1996), Cologne Weimar (2001), Louvain (2002); mem. Council Int. Musicological Soc. 1977–87; Mem. Inst. for Advanced Musical Studies, King's Coll. Univ., London 1993; Adviser Musica Antiqua Europae Orientalis 1977–; advisory, corresp.; appts. Int. Review of Aesthetics and Sociology of Music 1981–, Current Musicology 1987–, Studies in Music 1980; Edward J. Dent Medal 1974, Paderewski Medal-Bydgoszcz Philharmonia 1982, Australian Centennial Medal (2004). *Publications:* Musical Composition in Australia (3 Vols) 1969, Karl Amadeus Hartmann: Catalogue of all his works with biography 1981 (trans. German), Miscellanea Musicologica, Adelaide (Ed.) 1966–94, Paperbacks on Musicology (Gen. Ed.) 1978–, From Colonel Light into the Footlights: The Performing Arts in South Australia from 1836 to the Present 1988, Clemens von Franckenstein 1991, Ludwig Thuille 1993, Karl Amadeus Hartmann 1995, Werner Egle 1997. *Leisure interests:* travel, books, art, antiques, walking. *Address:* Tintorettostrasse 1, 80638 Munich, Germany; 13/18 Lansell Road, Toorak, Vic. 3142, Australia (Home). *Telephone:* (89) 178-2325 (Germany); (3) 9826-6348 (Australia) (Home).

McCREEVY, Charlie, BComm, FCA; Irish politician; b. Sept. 1949, Sallins, Co. Kildare; m. (separated); three s. three d.; ed Univ. Coll. Dublin; partner, Tynan Dillon & Co. (chartered accountants), Dublin, Naas and Ballyhaunis; mem. Kildare Co. Council 1979–85; mem. Dáil 1977–; Minister for Social Welfare 1992–93, for Tourism and Trade 1993–94, for Finance 1997–; fmr Fianna Fáil Spokesperson on Finance. *Address:* Department of Finance, Government Buildings, Upper Merrion Street, Dublin 2; Hillview House, Kilcullen Ross, Naas, Co. Kildare, Ireland. *Telephone:* (1) 6767571 (Office). *Fax:* (1) 6789936 (Office). *E-mail:* minister@finance.irlgov.ie (Office). *Website:* www.gov.ie/finance (Office).

McCRUM, (John) Robert, MA; British writer and newspaper editor; b. 7 July 1953; s. of Michael William McCrum (q.v.) and Christine Mary Kathleen fforde; m. 1st Olivia Timbs (divorced 1984); m. 2nd Sarah Lyall 1995; two d.; ed Sherborne School, Corpus Christi Coll., Cambridge and Univ. of Pennsylvania; house reader Chatto & Windus 1977–79; Editorial Dir Faber and Faber Ltd 1979–89, Ed.-in-Chief 1990–96; Literary Ed. Observer newspaper 1996–; scriptwriter and co-producer The Story of English TV series 1980–86; Tony Godwin Prize 1979, Peabody Award 1986, Emmy Award 1987. *Publications:* In the Secret State 1980, A Loss of Heart 1982, The Fabulous Englishman 1984, The Story of English 1986, The World is a Banana 1988, Mainland 1991, The Psychological Moment 1993, Suspicion 1996, My Year Off 1998. *Leisure interest:* the works of P. G. Wodehouse. *Address:* The Observer, 119 Farringdon Road, London, EC1R 3ER, England.

McCRUM, Michael William, CBE, MA; British university administrator and headmaster; b. 23 May 1924, Alverstoke, Gosport, Hants.; s. of late Capt. C. R. McCrum, RN and Ivy H. C. McCrum (née Nicholson); m. Christine M. K. fforde 1952; three s. one d.; ed Sherborne School and Corpus Christi Coll., Cambridge; Asst Master, Rugby School 1948–50; Fellow, Corpus Christi Coll. Cambridge 1949–80, Second Tutor 1950–51, Tutor 1951–62, Master 1980–94; Headmaster of Tonbridge School 1962–70; Head Master of Eton Coll. 1970–80; Gov. Sherborne School 1980–94, King's School, Canterbury 1980–94, Rugby School 1982–94; Vice-Chancellor Cambridge Univ. 1987–89; Pres. Cambridge Soc. 1989–96, Chair. Faculty Bd of Educ.1981–86, 1990–93; Chair. Cathedrals Fabric Comm. for England 1991–99, Governing Bodies Asscn 1989–94, Independent Schools Jt Council 1992–94; Trustee Henry Fund 1994–95; Hon. Freeman, Skinners Co. 1980; Hon. Fellow Corpus Christi Coll. 1994–; Hon. D.Ed. (Univ. of Vic.); Comendador de la Orden de Isabel la Católica (Spain) 1988. *Publications:* Select Documents of the Principates of the Flavian Emperors AD 68-96 1961, Thomas Arnold, Head Master 1989, The Man Jesus 2000. *Address:* 32 Clarendon Street, Cambridge, CB1 1JX, England. *Telephone:* (1223) 353303.

McCULLAGH, Peter, PhD, FRS; British statistician; b. 8 Jan. 1952, Plumbridge, Northern Ireland; s. of John A. McCullagh and Margaret B. McCullagh; m. Rosa Bogues 1977; one s. three d.; ed Univ. of Birmingham, Imperial Coll. London; Asst Prof., Univ. of Chicago 1977–79, Prof. 1985–; lecturer Imperial Coll. London 1979–85; Guy Medal (Bronze), Royal Statistical Soc. 1983, COPSS Award 1990. *Publications:* Tensor Methods 1987, Generalized Linear Models (jtly.) 1989. *Address:* Department of Statistics, University of Chicago, 5734 University Avenue, Chicago, IL 60637 (Office); 5039 Ellis Avenue, Chicago, IL 60615, USA (Home). *Telephone:* (773) 702-8340 (Office). *Fax:* (773) 702-9810 (Office). *E-mail:* pmcc@galton.uchicago.edu (Office). *Website:* www.stat.uchicago.edu/~pmcc (Office).

McCULLIN, Donald, CBE; British photographer; b. 9 Oct. 1935, London; s. of Frederick and Jessica McCullin; m. 1st Christine Dent 1959 (divorced 1987); two s. one d. and one s. by Laraine Ashton; m. 2nd Marilyn Bridges 1995 (divorced 2001); m. 3rd Catherine Fairweather 2002; one s.; ed Tollington Park Secondary Modern, Hammersmith Art and Crafts School; RAF Nat. Service; photographer with Observer for four years; photographer with Sunday Times, London for eighteen years; freelance 1980–; has covered eight wars–Viet Nam, Cambodia, Biafra, Congo, Israel, Cyprus, Chad, Lebanon–and many famine areas; has travelled to 64 countries; World Press Photographer 1964, Warsaw Gold Medal 1964, Granada TV Award 1967, 1969, Two Gold, One Silver Art Director Awards, UK. *Art Exhibitions:* Retrospective Maison Européenne de la Photographie Paris 2001, Retrospective Foam Museum Amsterdam 2002. *Publications:* The Destruction Business 1971, The Concerned Photographer II 1972, Is Anyone Taking Notice? 1973, Hearts of Darkness 1980, Battle Beirut–A City in Crisis 1983, Perspectives 1987, Skulduggery 1987, Open Skies 1989, Unreasonable Behaviour (autobiog.) 1990, Sleeping with Ghosts 1995; A Life's Work in Photography 1995, India 1999, Don McCullin A Retrospective 2001. *Leisure interests:* walking in countries, collecting Victorian children's books, looking at things and people. *Address:* c/o Hamiltons Gallery, 13 Carlos Place, London, W1X 2EU, England. *Telephone:* (20) 7499-9494 (Office). *E-mail:* info@hamiltonsgallery.com (Office). *Website:* www.hamiltonsgallery.com (Office).

McCULLOUGH, Colleen; Australian author; b. 1 June 1937, Wellington, NSW; m. Ric Robinson 1984; ed Holy Cross Coll., Woollahra, Sydney Univ., Inst. of Child Health, London Univ.; career as neurophysiologist in Sydney, London and at Yale Univ. Medical School, USA; moved to Norfolk Island, S. Pacific 1979; Hon. DLitt (Macquarie) 1993. *Publications:* novels: Tim 1974, The Thorn Birds 1977, An Indecent Obsession 1981, A Creed for the Third Millennium 1985, The Ladies of Missalonghi 1987, The First Man in Rome 1990, The Grass Crown 1991, Fortune's Favorites 1993, Caesar's Women 1996, Caesar 1997, The Song of Troy 1998; Cooking with Colleen McCullough and Jean Easthope 1982; Roden Cutler, VC The Biography 1998; Morgan's Run 2000. *Address:* "Out Yenna", Norfolk Island, Oceania (via Australia). *Fax:* (6723) 23313.

McDAID, James, MB, B.CH., BAO; Irish politician and medical doctor; b. 3 Oct. 1949, Termon, Co. Donegal; m. Marguerite McLoughlin (separated); three s. one d.; ed St Eunan's Coll., Letterkenny, Nat. Univ. of Ireland, Galway; Sr Surgical House Officer, Letterkenny Gen. Hosp. 1974–79; Gen. Practitioner, Letterkenny 1979; f., Pres. Donegal Hospice Movt 1988; mem. Dáil Éireann for Donegal NE 1989; Minister (desig.) for Defence 1991 (resgnd); mem. Dáil Cttee on Women's Rights 1992, Cttee of Public Accounts 1993, Cttee on Foreign Affairs and NI Sub-Cttee 1995; Spokesperson on North/South Devts. 1995, for Equality and Law Reform 1996–97; Minister for Tourism, Sport and Recreation 1997–. *Leisure interests:* football, horse racing, golf. *Address:* Department of Tourism, Sport and Recreation, Kildare Street, Dublin 2 (Office); Pearse Road, Letterkenny, Co. Donegal, Ireland (Home). *Telephone:* (1) 6313800 (Office); (74) 25132 (Home). *Fax:* (1) 6611201 (Office). *E-mail:* dtsr@iol.ie (Office). *Website:* www.irlgov.ie/tourism-sport (Office).

MACDIARMID, Alan G., PhD; American scientist; b. 14 April 1927, New Zealand; m. 1954; four c.; ed Univ. of Wisconsin, Cambridge Univ., Univ. of New Zealand; pioneered work on conductive polymers; with Univ. of Pennsylvania 1955–; now Blanchard Prof. of Chemistry; American Chemical Soc. Award 1999, Nobel Prize for Chemistry (Jt recipient) 2000. *Address:* University of Pennsylvania, 231 South 34th Street, Philadelphia, PA 19104, USA (Office). *Telephone:* (215) 898-8307 (Office). *Fax:* (215) 898-8378 (Office). *E-mail:* macdiarm@sas.upenn.edu (Office).

McDIARMID, Ian, MA; British actor and artistic director; b. 11 Aug. 1944, Carnoustie, Scotland; s. of the late Frederick McDiarmid and Hilda Emslie; ed Univ. of St Andrews, Royal Scottish Acad. of Music and Dramatic Art, Glasgow; Actor; Assoc. Dir Royal Exchange, Manchester; Jt Artistic Dir (with Jonathan Kent) Almeida Theatre 1990–2002; Gold Medal Royal Scottish Acad. of Music and Dramatic Art 1968, Olivier Award for Best Actor, Critics Circle Award for Best Actor 2001. *Films include:* The Awakening 1980, Dragonslayer 1981, Gorky Park 1983, Return of the Jedi 1983, Dirty Rotten Scoundrels 1988, Restoration 1995, Little Orphan Annie 1995, Star Wars: Episode I–The Phantom Menace 1999, Sleepy Hollow 2000, Star Wars Episode II: Attack of the Clones. *Plays include:* Almeida Theatre: Ivanov, Tartuffe, School for Wives, Creditors, Kurt Weill Concerts, Government Inspector, The Jew of Malta, The Tempest 2000, Faith Healer; RSC: Henry V, The Merchant of Venice, The Party, Crimes in Hot Countries, The Castle; Royal Court: Hated Nightfall, Love of a Good Man, Insignificance; Barbican: The Soldier's Tale; Royal Exchange, Manchester: Edward II, The Country Wife; Aldwych: The Black Prince; Oxford Playhouse: Peer Gynt, Mephisto. *Plays directed include:* Almeida Theatre: Scenes from an Execution, Venice Preserved, Siren Song, A Hard Heart, Lulu, The Possibilities, The Rehearsal. Royal Exchange: Don Juan. *Television includes:* Richard's Things 1981, Chernobyl: The Final Warning 1991, Heart of Darkness 1994, Hillsborough 1996, Rebecca, Karaoke, Creditors, The Nation's Health, The Professionals, Great Expectations 1999, All the King's Men 1999, Crime and Punishment 2001. *Address:* c/o ICM, Oxford House, London, W1, England.

McDONAGH, Enda; Irish professor of moral theology; b. 27 June 1930, Co. Mayo; s. of Patrick McDonagh and Mary Kelly; ed St Jarlath's Coll., Tuam,

St Patrick's Coll., Maynooth, Gregorian Univ., Rome and Univ. of Munich; Prof. of Moral Theology (and Canon Law), St Patrick's Coll. 1958–, Dir Postgraduate Studies in Theology 1970–76, Dean of Faculty of Theology 1973–79; Lecturer in Irish School of Ecumenics, Dublin 1970–; Husking Prof. of Theology, Univ. of Notre Dame, USA 1979–81; McKeever Prof. of Theology, New York 1990–92; Chair. Governing Body, Univ. Coll. Cork 1999–; Ferguson Lecturer, Univ. of Manchester March 1978; Leverhulme Research Fellow, Univ. of Cambridge 1978; Hon. LLD (Nat. Univ. of Ireland) 2000, Hon. DD (Trinity Coll. Dublin) 2001. *Publications:* Roman Catholics and Unity 1963, Religious Freedom 1967, Invitation and Response 1972, Gift and Call 1975, Social Ethics and the Christian 1979, Doing the Truth 1979, Church and Politics: The Case History of Zimbabwe 1980, The Making of Disciples 1982, Between Chaos and New Creation 1987; ed. and contrib. The Meaning of Christian Marriage 1963, Moral Theology Renewed 1965, Truth and Life 1968, Faith and the Hungry Grass 1989, The Gracing of Society 1990, Salvation or Survival 1993, Faith in Fragments 1995, The Risk of God 2000. *Leisure interests:* poetry and music. *Address:* St Patrick's College, Maynooth, Co. Kildare, Ireland. *Telephone:* (1) 285222.

McDONALD, Donald Benjamin, AO, BCom; Australian business executive; b. 1 Sept. 1938, Sydney; s. of Benjamin McDonald and Maida Hands; m. Janet Isabel McDonald 1964; one s. one d.; ed Univ. of New S. Wales; Finance Dir Vogue Publs 1965–68; with Australian Opera 1968–72 (Gen. Man. 1987–96), Musica Viva Australia 1972–78; Gen. Man. Sydney Theatre Co. 1980–86; Dir Australian Tourist Comm. 1993–96; Chair. Australian Broadcasting Corpn 1996–; Dir Festival, Perth 1998–, Univ. of NSW Foundation 1998–, Focus Publishing Pty Ltd 1999–2000; mem. Bd Welsh Nat. Opera, Cardiff, Wales 1997–2000; Visiting Fellow Univ. of Edin. 1992; Fellow Senate Univ., Sydney 1994–97. *Leisure interests:* reading, swimming. *Address:* Australian Broadcasting Corporation, 700 Harris Street, Ultimo, N.S.W. 2007, Australia (Office). *Telephone:* (2) 9333-1500 (Radio) (Office). *Fax:* (2) 9333-2603 (Radio) (Office). *Website:* www.abc.net.au (Office).

MACDONALD, Hon. Donald Stovel, PC, CC, BA, LLM; Canadian politician and lawyer; b. 1 March 1932, Ottawa, Ont.; s. of Donald A. Macdonald and Marjorie I. Stovel; m. 1st Ruth Hutchison 1961 (died 1987); four d.; m. 2nd Adrian Merchant Lang 1988; three step-s. three step-d.; ed Ottawa public schools, Ashbury Coll., Ottawa, Univs. of Toronto and Cambridge and Osgoode Hall and Harvard Law Schools; with McCarthy and McCarthy, Barristers, Toronto 1957–62; MP 1962–78; Parl. Sec. to Minister of Justice 1963–65, to Minister of Finance 1965, to Sec. of State for External Affairs 1966–68, to Minister of Industry 1968; Minister without Portfolio 1968; Pres. Privy Council and Govt House Leader 1968; Minister of Nat. Defence 1970–72, of Energy, Mines and Resources 1972–75, of Finance 1975–77; partner, firm McCarthy & McCarthy, Toronto 1977–88; Counsel, McCarthy Tétrault, Toronto 1991–2000; High Commr in the UK 1988–91; Chair. Royal Comm. on the Econ. Union and Devt Prospects for Canada 1982–85, Inst. for Research and Public Policy, Montreal 1991–97; Chair. and Dir Siemens Canada Ltd, Dir Aber Diamond Corpn, Alberta Energy Co. Ltd, Sun Life Assurance Co. of Canada, Trans-Canada Pipelines Ltd, Boise Cascade Corpn 1996–, Chair. Atlantic Council of Canada, Special Advisory Cttee on competition in Ont.'s electricity system 1995–96, Design Exchange, Toronto 1993–96, Canadian Friends of Cambridge Univ. 1995–97; Sr Adviser UBS Bunting Warburg, Toronto 2000; Rowell Fellowship, Canadian Inst. of Int. Affairs 1956; Freeman City of London; Hon. Fellow Trinity Hall, Cambridge Univ. 1994; Hon. LLD (St Lawrence Univ., Univ. of New Brunswick), (Univ. of Toronto) 2000; Hon. DEng (Colo School of Mines). *Leisure interests:* cross-country skiing, tennis. *Address:* 27 Marlborough Avenue, Toronto, Ont., M5R 1X5, Canada (Home). *Telephone:* (416) 964-6757 (Home). *Fax:* (416) 964-8901 (Home). *E-mail:* London@merchantmac.com.

McDONALD, Edward Lawson, MA, MD, FRCP, FACC, FAHA; British cardiologist; b. 8 Feb. 1918; s. of Charles S. McDonald and Mabel D. McDonald; m. (divorced); one s.; ed Felsted School, Clare Coll. Cambridge, Middlesex Hosp., Univ. of London and Harvard Univ.; served in HMS Glasgow, World War II, Temporary Surgeon-Lt RNVR 1943–46; Consultant Cardiologist, Nat. Heart Hosp., London 1961–83 (Hon. Consultant 1983–), King Edward VII Hosp. for Officers, London 1968–83, King Edward VII Hosp. Midhurst 1970–92, Consultant Emer. 1992–; Asst Dir Inst. of Cardiology 1955–61; mem. Scientific Council Revista Portuguesa de Cardiologia; mem. Cardiology Cttee Royal Coll. of Physicians 1963–76; Chair. Jt Advisory Cttee Royal Coll. of Physicians and British Cardiac Soc. 1973–75; mem. Bd of Govs Nat. Heart and Chest Hosps 1975–82, Council, British Heart Foundation 1975–83; Adviser to Malaysian Govt; visiting lecturer univs and cardiac socs Europe, N. and S. America, China and fmr USSR; Emer. Fellow American Heart Asscn; Int. Fellow Council on Clinical Cardiology; Fellow Emer. American Coll. of Cardiology; Hon. Fellow Turkish Medical Soc.; mem. British Cardiac Soc. (mem. Council 1967–71, Chair. 1979), Asscn of Physicians of GB and Ireland, Italian Soc. of Cardiology, Pakistan Cardiac Soc. and other medical socs in S. America; mem. Most Hon. Order of Crown of Johore 1980. *Publications:* Medical and Surgical Cardiology 1969, Very Early Recognition of Coronary Heart Disease (Ed.) 1978; contrib. to learned journals. *Leisure interests:* art, skiing, mountain walking, sailing. *Address:* 9 Bentinck Mansions, Bentinck Street, London, W1U 2ER, England. *Telephone:* (20) 7935-7101. *Fax:* (20) 7467-4312 (Office).

MACDONALD, Hon. Flora Isabel, CC, PC; Canadian politician and consultant; b. 3 June 1926, North Sydney, NS; d. of George Frederick and Mary Isabel (née Royle) MacDonald; ed North Sydney High School, Empire Business Coll. and National Defence Coll., Kingston; Exec. Dir Progressive Conservative Headquarters 1957–66; admin. officer and tutor Dept of Political Studies Queen's Univ. 1966–72; Nat. Sec. Progressive Conservative Asscn of Canada 1966–69; MP for Kingston and the Islands, Ont. 1972–88; Sec. of State for External Affairs 1979–80; Minister of Employment and Immigration 1984–86, of Communications 1986–88; Host, weekly TV series North/South 1990–94; Chair. Int. Devt Research Centre 1992–97, Shastri Indo-Canada Advisory Council, HelpAge Int., London, UK 1997–2001; Co-Chair. Canadian Co-ordinating Cttee UN Year of Older Persons 1999; Patron, Commonwealth Human Rights Initiative; Dir Care Canada; Pres.Future Generations, Franklin, W.V., Partnership Africa-Canada, C.O.D.E.; mem. Carnegie Comm. on Preventing Deadly Conflict 1994–99; Hon. Patron for Canada of Nat. Museums of Scotland; Visiting Fellow, Centre for Canadian Studies, Edin. Univ. Sept.–Dec. 1989, Pres. Asscn. of Canadian Clubs 1999–, World Federalists of Canada 2001–; Progressive Conservative; 12 hon. degrees; Companion Order of Ont. 1995, UN Asscn Pearson Peace Medal 2000, UNIFEM Canada Award 2002. *Leisure interests:* travel, reading, speed-skating. *Address:* 1103, 350 Queen Elizabeth Driveway, Ottawa, Ont., K1S 3N1, Canada (Home). *Telephone:* (613) 238-1098. *Fax:* (613) 238-6330. *E-mail:* flora@intranet.ca (Home).

McDONALD, Forrest, PhD; American professor of history; b. 7 Jan. 1927, Orange, Tex.; s. of John Forrest and Myra M. McGill; m. Ellen Shapiro 1963; five c.; ed Orange High School and Univ. of Tex. (Austin); State Historical Soc. of Wis. 1953–58; Assoc. Prof. Brown Univ. 1959–64, Prof. 1964–67; Prof. Wayne State Univ. 1967–76; Prof. Univ. of Ala 1976–87, Distinguished Research Prof. 1976, 1987–; JP Harrison Visiting Prof. Coll. of William and Mary 1986–87; Guggenheim Fellow 1962–63; George Washington Medal (Freedom's Foundation) 1980, Frances Tavern Book Award 1980, American Revolution Round Table Book Award 1986, 16th Jefferson Lecturer in the Humanities (Nat. Endowment for the Humanities) 1987, Ingersoll Prize, Richard M. Weaver Award 1990, Salvatori Award for Academic Excellence 1992. *Publications:* We The People: The Economic Origins of the Constitution 1958, Insull 1962, E Pluribus Unum: The Formation of the American Republic 1965, Presidency of George Washington 1974, Presidency of Thomas Jefferson 1976, Alexander Hamilton: A Biography 1980, A Constitutional History of the United States 1982, Novus Ordo Seclorum: The Intellectual Origins of the Constitution 1985, Requiem: Variations on Eighteenth-Century Themes 1988, The American Presidency: An Intellectual History 1994, States' Rights and the Union 2000. *Leisure interests:* gardening, tennis. *Address:* P.O. Box 155, Coker, AL 35452, USA. *Telephone:* (205) 339-0317.

McDONALD, Gabrielle Kirk, LLB; American judge; b. 12 April 1942, St Paul; d. of James G. Kirk and Frances R. Kirk; m. Mark T. McDonald; one s. one d.; ed Howard Univ.; fmr law professor; fed. judge, Houston, Tex. 1979–88; partner Matthews Branscomb, Austin, Tex. 1988–; serving on UN int. tribunal on war crimes in fmr Yugoslavia, The Hague 1993–, Pres. 1997–2001; mem. ABA, Nat. Bar Asscn. *Address:* United Nations International Criminal Tribunal for Former Yugoslavia, Public Information Unit, P.O. Box 13888, Churchillplein, The Hague 2501, Netherlands. *Telephone:* (70) 512-5233. *Fax:* (70) 512-5355. *Website:* www.un.org/icty (Office).

MACDONALD, (Hugh) Ian, OC, BCom, BPhil, MA; Canadian university professor and economist; b. 27 June 1929, Toronto; five c.; ed Univ. of Toronto, Oxford Univ., UK; Chief Economist, Govt of Ont. 1965–67, Deputy Treas. 1967–68, Deputy Minister of Treasury and Econs 1968–72, Deputy Minister of Econs and Intergovernmental Affairs 1972–74; Pres. York Univ., Toronto 1974–84, Pres. Emer. 1984–, Dir York Int. 1984–94, Prof. of Public Policy and Econs 1984–, Dir Master of Public Admin. Program 1984; Chair. Commonwealth of Learning, Vancouver 1994–; Hon. Life mem. Canadian Olympic Asscn 1997–; Hon. LLD (Toronto) 1974, DUniv (Open Univ., UK) 1998, Hon. DLitt (Open Univ., Sri Lanka) 1999, (The B.R. Ambedkar Open Univ., Hyderabad, India) 2002; Gov.-Gen.'s Medal 1952, Centennial Medal 1967, Queen's Silver Jubilee Medal 1977, Award of Merit, Canadian Bureau for Int. Educ. 1994, Vanier Medal 2000, Queen's Golden Jubilee Medal 2002; Kt of Grace, Order of St Lazarus of Jerusalem 1978. *Publications:* numerous articles, essays and contribs to books. *Leisure interests:* ice hockey and tennis. *Address:* York University, Room 226R, Schulich School of Business, 4700 Keele Street, Toronto, Ont., M3J 1P3 (Office); Commonwealth of Learning, 1285 West Broadway, Suite 600, Vancouver, BC V6H 3X8, Canada (Office). *Telephone:* (416) 736-5632 (Toronto) (Office). *Fax:* (416) 736-5643 (Toronto) (Office). *E-mail:* yorkmpa@yorku.ca (Office).

McDONALD, John W., AB, JD; American diplomatist, international official and lawyer; b. 18 Feb. 1922, Koblenz, Germany; s. of John Warlick McDonald and Ethel Mae Raynor; m. 1st Barbara Jane Stewart 1943 (divorced); one s. three d.; m. 2nd Christel Meyer 1970; ed Univ. of Illinois, Nat. War Coll., Washington, DC; admitted to Ill. Supreme Court Bar 1946, to US Supreme Court 1951; Legal Div., US Office of Mil. Govt, Berlin 1947; Asst District Attorney, US Mil. Govt Courts, Frankfurt 1947–50; Sec. Law Cttee, Allied High Comm. 1950–52; mem. Mission to NATO and OECD, Paris 1952–54; Office of Exec. Sec. Dept of State 1954–55; Exec. Sec. to Dir of Int. Co-operation Admin. 1955–59; US Econ. Co-ordinator for CENTO Affairs, Ankara 1959–63; Chief, Econ. and Commercial Sections, Cairo 1963–66; Deputy Dir Office of Econ. and Social Affairs, Dept of State 1967–68, Dir 1968–71; Co-ordinator, UN Multilateral Devt Programmes, Dept of State 1971–74, Acting Deputy Asst Sec. for Econ. and Social Affairs 1971, 1973;

Deputy Dir-Gen. Int. Labour Org. (ILO) 1974–78; Pres. Int. Telecommunications Satellite Org. (INTELSAT) Conf. on Privileges and Immunities 1978; Amb. to UN Conf. on TCDC 1978; Sec.-Gen. 27th Colombo Plan Ministerial Meeting 1978; US Co-ordinator for UN Decade on Drinking Water and Sanitation 1979; rep. to UN Confs. with rank of Amb. 1978–; Amb. to UNIDO III 1979–80; Chair. Fed. Cttee for UN Int. Year of Disabled Persons; Amb. to UN World Assembly on Ageing 1981–82; Co-ordinator for Multilateral Affairs, Center for the Study of Foreign Affairs, US Dept of State 1983–87; Pres. Iowa Peace Inst. 1988–92, People-to-People Cttee for the Handicapped, Countdown 2001, World Cttee: UN Decade of Disabled Persons; del. to many int. confs; Bd of Dirs Global Water; Chair. American Asscn for Int. Ageing 1983–; Professorial Lecturer in Law, The George Washington Univ. Nat. Law Center 1987–89; Adjunct Prof. Political Science, Grinnell Coll. 1989–92; Distinguished Visiting Prof., George Mason Univ., Fairfax, Va 1992–93; Adjunct Prof. Union Inst. 1995–98, George Mason Univ. 1998–2000; Chair. and CEO Inst. for Multi-Track Diplomacy, Washington 1992–; mem. Cosmos Club, American Foreign Service Asscn, US Asscn for the Club of Rome, DKE; Hon. PhD (Mt. Mercy Coll.) 1989, (Teiko Mary Crest Univ.) 1991, (Salisbury State Univ.) 1993; Superior Honour Award, Dept of State 1972, Presidential Meritorial Service Award 1984. *Publications:* The North-South Dialogue and the United Nations 1982, How To Be a Delegate 1984, International Negotiations 1985, Perspectives on Negotiation: Four Case Studies 1986, Conflict Resolution: Track Two Diplomacy 1987, US-Soviet Summitry 1987, US Base Rights Negotiations 1989, Multi-Track Diplomacy 1991, Defining a US Negotiating Style 1996. *Leisure interests:* reading, tennis, fencing, skiing. *Address:* IMTD, 1925 N Lynn Street, 12th Floor, Washington, DC 20006 (Office); 3800 North Fairfax Drive, 1001 Washington, VA 22209, USA (Home). *Telephone:* (703) 528-3863 (Office); (703) 525-9755 (Home). *Fax:* (703) 528-5776 (Office). *E-mail:* jmcdonald@imtd.org (Office). *Website:* www.imtd.org (Office).

MACDONALD, Julien, MA; Welsh fashion designer; b. 19 March 1972, Merthyr, Tydfyl; ed Royal Coll. of Art; worked for Alexander McQueen and Koji Tatsuno as a student; knitwear designer for Chanel Ready-to-Wear, Chanel Couture and Karl Lagerfeld; has had four shows in his own right; Art Dir Max Factor Spring/Summer 1999 advertising campaign (including TV commercial); Chief Designer Givenchy 2001–; consultant Boots PLC 2001–; London Fashion Award for Glamour. *Address:* Givenchy, 3 avenue Georges V, 75008 Paris, France (Office); First Floor Studio, 135–139 Curtain Road, London, EC2A 3BX; 20th Century Theatre, 291 Westbourne Grove, London, W11 2CA, England. *Telephone:* 44-31-50-00 (Office). *Fax:* 47-23-04-67 (Office).

McDONALD, Sir Trevor, Kt, OBE; British broadcasting journalist; b. 16 Aug. 1939, Trinidad; m.; two s. one d.; worked on newspapers, radio and TV, Trinidad 1960–69; Producer BBC Caribbean Service and World Service, London 1969–73; reporter Ind. TV News 1973–78, sports corresp. 1978–80, diplomatic corresp. 1980–87, newscaster 1982–87, Diplomatic Ed. Channel Four News 1987–89, newscaster News at 5.40 1989–90, News at Ten 1990–99, ITV Evening News 1999–2000, ITV News at Ten 2001–; Chair. Better English Campaign 1995–97, Nuffield Language Inquiry 1998–2000; Gov. English-Speaking Union of the Commonwealth 2000–; Pres. European Year of Languages 2000; Chancellor South Bank Univ. 1999–; Hon. Fellow Liverpool John Moores Univ. 1998; ; Hon. D. Litt. (South Bank) 1994, (Plymouth) 1995, (Southampton Inst.) 1997, (Nottingham) 1997; Dr. hc (Surrey) 1997, (Open Univ.) 1997; Hon. LLD (Univ. of West Indies) 1996; Newscaster of the Year TV and Radio Industries Club 1993, 1997, 1999; Gold Medal, Royal TV Soc. 1998, Richard Dimbleby Award for outstanding contrib. to TV, BAFTA 1999. *Publications:* Clive Lloyd: a biography 1985, Vivian Richards: a biography 1987, Queen and Commonwealth 1989, Fortunate Circumstances (autobiog.) 1993, Favourite Poems 1997, World of Poetry 1999. *Leisure interests:* tennis, golf, cricket. *Address:* c/o ITN, 200 Gray's Inn Road, London, WC1X 8XZ, England. *Telephone:* (20) 7833-3000 (Office).

McDONNELL, Sanford N., MS; American business executive; b. 12 Oct. 1922, Little Rock, Ark.; s. of William A. and Carolyn C. McDonnell; nephew of James S. McDonnell; m. Priscilla Robb 1946; one s. one d.; ed Princeton Univ., Univ. of Colorado and Washington Univ.; joined McDonnell Aircraft Co. 1948, Vice-Pres. (Project Man.) 1959, F4H Vice-Pres. and Gen. Man. 1961, mem. Bd of Dirs. 1962–67, mem. Finance Cttee 1962, Exec. Cttee 1963; Vice-Pres. Aircraft Gen. Man. 1965, Pres. 1966; Dir McDonnell Douglas Corpn 1967, Vice-Pres. March 1971; Exec. Vice-Pres. McDonnell Aircraft Co. March 1971; Pres. McDonnell Douglas Corpn 1971–72, Pres. 1972–80, CEO 1972–88, Chair. 1980–88, Chair. Emer. 1988–; mem. Bd of Govs. Aerospace Industries Asscn Nov. 1974–; Fellow, American Inst. of Aeronautics and Astronautics and mem. many other professional orgs.; mem. Bd of Dirs. First Union Bankcorpn. in St Louis; mem. Nat. Exec. Bd, Boy Scouts of America. *Address:* McDonnell Douglas Corporation, P.O. Box 516, St Louis, MO 63166, USA.

McDONOUGH, William J., BS, MA; American banker; b. 21 April 1934, Chicago, Ill.; m. Suzanne Clarke 1985; three s. three d.; ed Holy Cross Coll., Worcester, Mass. and Georgetown Univ.; US Navy 1956–61; US State Dept 1961–67; First Nat. Bank of Chicago 1967–89, Vice-Chair. Bd and Dir holding co. 1986–89; subsequently served as adviser to IBRD and IFC; special adviser to Pres. of IDB; Chair. Ill. Comm. on Future of Public Service; Exec. Vice-Pres. and Head, Markets Group, Fed. Reserve Bank of New York and Man. Open Market Operations for Fed. Open Market Cttee 1992–93; Vice-Chair. Fed. Open Market Cttee; Pres. and CEO Fed. Reserve Bank of New York

1993–2003; mem. Trilateral Comm. Group of Thirty; mem. Bd of Dirs B.I.S. and Chair. Basle Cttee on Banking Supervision; mem. Bd of Dirs Council on Foreign Relations, Foreign Policy Asscn., New York Philharmonic Orchestra, Inst. for Int. Econs; Yale Distinguished Leadership in Global Capital Markets Award 2001. *Address:* c/o Federal Reserve Bank of New York, 33 Liberty Street, New York, NY 10045, USA (Office).

McDORMAND, Frances; American actress; b. 23 June 1957, Chicago, Ill.; d. of Veron McDormand and Noreen McDormand; m. Joel Coen 1994; one s.; ed Yale Univ. School of Drama; Screen Actors' Guild Award 1996, London Film (Critics' Circle Award 1996, Ind. Spirit Award 1996, American Comedy Award 1997, LA Film Critics Award 2000. *Films include:* Blood Simple 1984, Raising Arizona 1987, Mississippi Burning 1988, Chattahoochee 1990, Darkman 1990, Miller's Crossing 1990, Hidden Agenda 1990, The Butcher's Wife 1991, Passed Away 1992, Short Cuts 1993, Beyond Rangoon 1995, Fargo 1996 (Acad. Award for Best Actress), Primal Fear 1996, Lone Star 1996, Paradise Road 1997, Johnny Skidmarks 1997, Madeline 1998, Talk of Angels 1998, Wonder Boys 1999, Almost Famous 2000, The Man Who Wasn't There 2001, Upheaval 2001, Laurel Canyon 2002, City By the Sea 2003; has appeared in several TV series. *Stage appearances include:* Awake and Sing 1984, Painting Churches 1984, The Three Sisters 1985, All My Sons 1986, A Streetcar Named Desire 1988, Moon for the Misbegotten 1992, Sisters Rosensweig 1993, The Swan 1993.

MacDOUGALL, Sir (George) Donald (Alastair), CBE, FBA; British economist; b. 26 Oct. 1912, Glasgow, Scotland; s. of the late Daniel MacDougall and the late Beatrice Miller; m. 1st Bridget Christabel Bartrum 1937 (divorced 1977); one s. one d.; m. 2nd Laura Margaret, Lady Hall 1977 (died 1995); ed Kelvinside Acad., Glasgow, Shrewsbury School, Balliol Coll., Oxford; Asst Lecturer, Leeds Univ. 1936–39; mem. Sir Winston Churchill's Statistical Branch 1939–45 and 1951–53; Fellow Wadham Coll., Oxford 1945–50, Nuffield Coll. 1947–64; Reader in Int. Econs, Oxford 1951–52; Econ. Dir OEEC, Paris 1948–49; Econ. Dir Nat. Econ. Devt Office 1962–64; Dir-Gen. Dept of Econ. Affairs 1964–68; Head of Govt Econ. Service and Chief Econ. Adviser to Treasury 1969–73; Chief Econ. Adviser CBI 1973–84; Pres. Royal Econ. Soc. 1972–74; Chair. Council Nat. Inst. of Econ. and Social Research 1974–87; Chair. EEC Study Group on Role of Public Finance in European Integration 1975–77; Pres. Soc. for Strategic Planning 1977–85; Vice-Pres. Soc. of Business Economists 1978–; Hon. Fellow, Wadham Coll. 1964–, Nuffield Coll. 1967–, Balliol Coll. 1992–; Dr hc Leeds, Strathclyde, Aston. *Publications:* The World Dollar Problem 1957, Studies in Political Economy (2 Vols) 1975, Don and Mandarin: Memoirs of an Economist 1987 and other books and articles on economic matters. *Leisure interest:* fishing. *Address:* Flat K, 19 Warwick Square, London, SW1V 2AB, England. *Telephone:* (20) 7821-1998. *E-mail:* donald.mac@virgin.net.

MacDOWELL, Andie; American film actress; b. 21 April 1958, S. Carolina; d. of Marion MacDowell and the late Pauline MacDowell; m. 1st Paul Qualley; two d. one s.; m. 2nd Rhett DeCamp Hartzog 2001. *Television appearances include:* Women and Men 2, In Love There Are No Rules 1991, Sahara's Secret. *Films include:* Greystoke 1984, St Elmo's Fire 1985, Sex, Lies and Videotape 1989, Green Card 1990, Hudson Hawk 1991, The Object of Beauty 1991, The Player 1992, Ruby 1992, Groundhog Day 1993, Short Cuts 1993, Bad Girls 1994, Four Weddings and a Funeral 1994, Unstrung Heroes 1995, My Life and Me 1996, Multiplicity 1996, The End of Violence 1997, Town and Country 1998, Shadrack 1998, The Scalper 1998, Just the Ticket 1998, Muppets From Space 1999, The Music 2000, Town and Country 2001, Harrison's Flowers 2002. *Address:* c/o I.C.M., 8942 Wilshire Blvd., Beverly Hills, CA 90211, USA.

McDOWELL, David Keith, MA; New Zealand diplomatist and conservationist; b. 30 April 1937, Palmerston North; s. of Keith McDowell and Gwen McDowell; m. Jan Ingram 1960; one s. three d.; ed Victoria Univ. of Wellington; joined Ministry of Foreign Affairs 1959, Head, UN and African and Middle East Divs. 1973, Dir of External Aid 1973–76, Head, Econ. Div. 1980–81, Special Asst to Sec. Gen., Commonwealth Secr., London 1969–72; High Commr in Fiji 1977–80, in India, Nepal and Bangladesh 1983–85; Asst Sec. of Foreign Affairs for Asia, Australia and the Americas 1981–85; First Sec., Perm. Mission to UN 1964–68, Perm. Rep. 1985–88; Dir-Gen. Dept of Conservation 1988–89; CEO Dept of Prime Minister and Cabinet 1989–91; Amb. to Japan 1992–94; Dir-Gen. World Conservation Union, Switzerland 1994–99; pvt. consultant 1999–. *Leisure interests:* fishing, boating, tennis, conservation, gardening, music. *Address:* 86 Waerenga Road, Otaki, New Zealand. *Telephone:* (6) 364-6296 (Office). *Fax:* (6) 364-6205 (Office). *E-mail:* jan.david.mcdowell@xtra.co.nz (Office).

McDOWELL, John Henry, MA, FBA, F.A.A.A.S.; British professor of philosophy; b. 7 March 1942, Boksburg, South Africa; s. of Sir Henry McDowell and Norah (née Douthwaite) McDowell; m. Andrea Lehrke 1977; ed St John's Coll. Johannesburg, Univ. Coll. of Rhodesia and Nyasaland, New Coll. Oxford; Fellow, Praelector in Philosophy, Univ. Coll. Oxford 1966–86; Prof. of Philosophy, Univ. of Pittsburgh 1986–88, Univ. Prof. 1988–. *Publications:* Ed. (with Gareth Evans) Truth and Meaning, Ed. (with Philip Pettit) Subject, Thought and Context, Mind and World, Mind, Value and Reality, Meaning, Knowledge and Reality; trans. of Plato, Theaetetus. *Leisure interests:* gardening, reading. *Address:* Department of Philosophy, University of Pittsburgh, Pittsburgh, PA 15260, USA. *Telephone:* (412) 624-5792.

McDOWELL, Malcolm (Malcolm Taylor); British actor; b. 13 June 1943, Leeds; m. 1st Mary Steenburgen 1980; one s. one d.; m. 2nd Kelley Kuhr 1992; began career with the RSC at Stratford 1965–66; early television appearances in such series as Dixon of Dock Green, Z Cars. *Stage appearances:* RSC, Stratford 1965–66, Entertaining Mr. Sloane, Royal Court 1975, Look Back in Anger, New York 1980, In Celebration, New York 1984, Holiday Old Vic 1987, Another Time, Old Vic 1993. *Films include:* If. . . . 1969, Figures in a Landscape 1970, The Raging Moon 1971, A Clockwork Orange 1971, O Lucky Man 1973, Royal Flash 1975, Aces High 1976, Voyage of the Damned 1977, Caligula 1977, The Passage 1978, Time After Time 1979, Cat People 1981, Blue Thunder 1983, Get Crazy 1983, Britannia Hospital 1984, Gulag 1985, The Caller 1987, Sunset 1987, Sunrise 1988, Class of 1999, Il Maestro 1989, Moon 44, Double Game, Class of 1999, Snake Eyes, Schweitzer, Assassin of the Tsar 1991, The Player, Chain of Desire, East Wind, Night Train to Venice, Star Trek: Generations 1995, Tank Girl 1995, Kids of the Round Table, Where Truth Lies, Mr Magoo 1998, Gangster No 1 2000. *Television includes:* Our Friends in the North. *Address:* c/o Markham and Froggatt, 4 Windmill Street, London, W1P 1HF, England.

MacEACHEN, Hon. Allan J., PC, MA; Canadian politician; b. 6 July 1921, Inverness, NS; s. of Angus MacEachen and Annie Gillies; ed St Francis Xavier Univ., Univs. of Toronto and Chicago and MIT; Prof. of Econs, St Francis Xavier Univ. 1946–48, later Head, Dept of Econs and Social Sciences; mem. House of Commons 1953–58, 1962–84; MP for Cape Breton Highlands-Cans., NS 1953–84; Special Asst and Consultant on Econ. Affairs to Lester Pearson 1958; Minister of Labour 1963–65; Minister of Nat. Health and Welfare 1965–68, of Manpower and Immigration 1968–70, of Finance 1980–82; Pres. Privy Council and Govt House Leader 1970–74; Sec. of State for External Affairs 1974–76; Pres. Privy Council 1976–77 and Deputy Prime Minister 1977–79; Deputy Leader of Opposition and Opposition House Leader 1979; Deputy Prime Minister and Minister of Finance 1980–82; Deputy Prime Minister and Sec. of State for External Affairs 1982–84; mem. Senate 1984–96, Leader of Govt in Senate June–Oct. 1984, Leader of Opposition in Senate 1984–91; Chair. Int. IMF Group of Ten 1980–81, Interim Cttee of IMF, Conf. on Int. Econ. Co-operation, 1982 Ministerial Meeting of the GATT, Int. Advisory Council of Bank of Montreal 1986–91; Canadian Chair. Atlantik-Brücke Annual Symposium (Canada-Germany Conf.) 1984–; Chair. Advisory Council Int. Ocean Inst. 1996–; Bd Dirs. North-South Inst. 1996–; Trustee Royal Ottawa Health Care Group 1987–95; mem. Bd of Govs. St Francis Xavier Univ.; Order of Merit, Germany. *Address:* R.R.1, Whycocomagh, B0E 3M0, Nova Scotia, Canada (Home).

McENERY, Peter Robert; British actor; b. 21 Feb. 1940; s. of the late Charles McEnery and of Ada Mary Brinson; m. 1978; one d.; founder mem. and assoc. artist with the RSC. *Theatre roles include:* Eugene in Look Homeward Angel 1962, Rudge in Next Time I'll Sing to You 1963, Konstantin in The Seagull 1964, Edward Gover in Made in Bangkok 1986, Trigorin in The Seagull 1975, Fredrick in A Little Night Music 1990, Torvald in A Doll's House 1994, Hector in Heartbreak House 1997, Claudius in Hamlet (R.N.T.) 2000–01, Laertes, Clarence, Tybalt, Silvius, Patroclus, Bassanio, Orlando, Pericles, Brutus, Antipholus, Albie Sachs, Lorenzaccio (with RSC). *Plays directed:* Richard III 1971, The Wound 1972. *TV:* Clayhanger 1976, The Aphrodite Inheritance 1979, The Jail Diary of Albie Sachs 1980, Japanese Style 1982, The Collectors 1986, The Mistress 1986, Witchcraft 1991, Reach for the Moon 2000. *Films:* Tunes of Glory 1961, Victim 1961, The Moon-spinners 1963, Entertaining Mr Sloane 1970, La Curée, J'ai tué Raspoutine, Le Mur d'Atlantique, Le Montreur de Boxe. *Leisure interests:* steam railway preservation, skiing, American football. *Address:* Richard Stone Partnership, 2 Henrietta Street, London, C2E 8PS, England. *Telephone:* (20) 4497-0849. *Fax:* (20) 7323-0101.

McENROE, John Patrick; American tennis player; b. 16 Feb. 1959, Wiesbaden, then Fed. Repub. of Germany; s. of John P. McEnroe I and Katy McEnroe; m. 1st Tatum O'Neal (q.v.) 1986; two s. one d.; 2nd Patty Smyth; two c.; one step-d.; ed Trinity High School, NJ and Stanford Univ., Calif.; amateur player 1976–78, professional 1978–93; USA Singles Champion 1979, 1980, 1981, 1984; USA Doubles Champion 1979, 1981, 1989; Wimbledon Champion (doubles) 1979, 1981, 1983, 1984, 1992, (singles) 1981, 1983, 1984; WCT Champion 1979, 1981, 1983, 1984, 1989; Grand Prix Champion 1979, 1983, 1984; played Davis Cup for USA 1978, 1979, 1980, 1981, 1982, 1983, 1984, 1985; only player to have reached the Wimbledon semi-finals (1977) as pre-tournament qualifier, semi-finalist 1989; won 154 tournaments; Capt. US Davis Cup team 1999–2000; tennis sportscaster USA Network 1993; mem. Men's Sr's Tours Circuits 1994; winner Quality Challenge, Worldwide Sr Tennis Circuit 1999; owner John McEnroe Gallery; Int. Tennis Hall of Fame 1999. *Television:* presenter The Chair (game show) 2002–. *Publications:* You Cannot Be Serious (autobiog. with James Kaplan) 2002. *Leisure interest:* music. *Address:* The John McEnroe Gallery, 41 Greene Street, New York, NY 10013, USA.

McENTEE, Andrew, BA, LLB; British lawyer; b. 2 July 1957, Glasgow, Scotland; s. of Shaun McEntee and Margaret McEntee (née O'Neill); ed Univ. of Stirling, Univ. of Wolverhampton, Univ. of N. London; case worker, Citizens' Advice Bureau 1982–83, Scottish Council for Civil Liberties (now Scottish Human Rights Centre) 1983–84; community care worker, Strathclyde Social Work Dept 1985–86; Gen. Sec. Chile Cttee for Human Rights/South American Human Rights Coordination 1986–91; Gen. Sec. Cen. America Human Rights Cttee 1993–96; UK apptd. Chair. Amnesty Int.

Lawyers Network 1994, Chair. Amnesty Int. UK 1998; Sr Consultant Atlantic Celtic Films Co. 1996–; UK Chair. Coalition for an Int. Criminal Court 1997–; adviser to Spanish and Chilean lawyers and victims and coordinator of Amnesty Int. case during extradition proceedings against Gen. Augusto Pinochet 1998–2000; writer and lecturer on human rights. *Leisure interests:* gardening, walking, 20th-century arts. *Address:* c/o Amnesty International, 99 Rosebery Avenue, London, EC1R 4RE, England (Office).

McEWAN, Angus David, BE, M.ENG.SC., PhD, FAA, F.T.S.E.; Australian oceanographer; b. 20 July 1937, Alloa, Scotland; s. of David R. McEwan and Anne Marion McEwan; m. Juliana R. Britten 1961; two d.; ed Melbourne High School, Caulfield Tech. Coll., Melbourne Univ., Cambridge Univ.; engineer, Aeronautical Research Labs., Melbourne 1956–58, Research Scientist 1961–62, 1966–69; Research Scientist, Program Leader, Chief Research Scientist, Div. of Atmospheric Research, CSIRO, Aspendale, Vic. 1972–81, Foundation Chief, Div. of Oceanography, Hobart 1981–95; Sr Scientific Adviser (Oceanographer) to CSIRO and Bureau of Meteorology 1995–; Hon. Research Prof. Univ. of Tasmania 1988–; Chief Australian Nat. Del., Inter-governmental Oceanographic Comm. (IOC) 1995–; Chair. Inter-governmental Cttee for the Global Ocean Observing System 1997–2001; Nat. Del. Oceanic Research (SCOR); mem. numerous other nat. bodies and cttees. concerning marine science; Queen Elizabeth Fellow 1969–71; Rossby Fellow (Woods Hole Oceanographic Inst.) 1975; Australian Centenary Medal 2003. *Publications:* scientific articles on geophysical fluid dynamics. *Leisure interests:* sailing, sketching, woodwork. *Address:* Bureau of Meteorology, Box 727, Hobart, Tasmania 7001 (Office); 300 Sandy Bay Road, Sandy Bay, Tasmania 7005, Australia (Home). *Telephone:* (3) 6221-2090. *Fax:* (3) 6221-2089. *E-mail:* amcewan@bom.gov.au (Office); oceans@iprimus.com.au (Home).

McEWAN, Geraldine; British actress; b. 9 May 1932, Old Windsor, Berks.; d. of Donald McKeown and Norah McKeown; m. Hugh Cruttwell 1953; one s. one d.; ed Windsor County Girls' School. *Television:* The Prime of Miss Jean Brodie (TV Critics Best Actress Award) 1978, L'Elégance 1982, The Barchester Chronicles 1982, Come Into the Garden, Maude 1982, Mapp and Lucia 1985–86, Oranges Are Not The Only Fruit 1990 (BAFTA Best Actress Award), Mulberry 1992–93, The Red Dwarf 1999, Thin Ice 2000, Victoria Wood's Christmas Special 2000, Carrie's War 2003. *Films:* The Adventures of Tom Jones 1975, Escape from the Dark 1978, Foreign Body 1986, Henry V 1989, Robin Hood: Prince of Thieves 1991, Moses 1995, The Love Letter 1999, Titus 2000, Love's Labours Lost 2000, The Contaminated Man 2000, The Magdalene Sisters 2002, Food for Love 2002, Pure 2002. *Stage appearances:* first engagement with Theatre Royal, Windsor 1949; London appearances in Who Goes There? 1951, Sweet Madness, For Better, For Worse, Summertime; Shakespeare Memorial Theatre, Stratford on Avon 1956, 1958, 1961 playing Princess of France (Love's Labours Lost), Olivia (Twelfth Night), Ophelia (Hamlet), Marina (Pericles), Beatrice (Much Ado about Nothing); played in School for Scandal, USA 1962, The Private Ear and The Public Eye, USA 1963; appearances as mem. Nat. Theatre 1965–71: Armstrong's Last Goodnight, Love for Love, A Flea in Her Ear, The Dance of Death, Edward II, Home and Beauty, Rites, The Way of the World, The White Devil, Amphitryon 38; other theatre appearances include: Dear Love 1973, Chez Nous 1974, The Little Hut 1974, Oh Coward! (musical) 1975, On Approval 1975, Look After Lulu 1978; with Nat. Theatre: The Browning Version 1980, Harlequinade 1980, The Provoked Wife 1980–81, The Rivals (Evening Standard Drama Award for Best Actress), You Can't Take It With You 1983–84; A Lie of the Mind (Royal Court) 1987, Lettice and Lovage (Globe Theatre) 1988–89, Hamlet (Riverside Studios) 1992, The Bird Sanctuary (Abbey Theatre) 1994, The Way of the World (Nat. Theatre; Evening Standard Drama Award for Best Actress) 1995, Grace Note (Old Vic) 1997, The Chairs (Royal Court) 1997, (Golden Theatre, New York) 1998, Hay Fever (Savoy) 1999. *Radio:* Arrived 2002. *Directed:* As You Like It 1988, Treats 1989, Waiting for Sir Larry 1990, Four Door Saloon 1991, Keyboard Skills 1993. *Address:* c/o ICM Oxford House, 76 Oxford Street, London, W1D 1BS, England.

McEWAN, Ian (Russell), CBE, MA; British author; b. 21 June 1948, Aldershot, Hants.; s. of the late David McEwan and of Rose Moore; m. 1st Penny Allen 1982 (divorced 1995); two s. and two step-d.; m. 2nd Annalena McAfee 1997; ed Woolverstone Hall, Univs of Sussex and E Anglia; Hon. mem. American Acad. of Arts and Sciences 1997, Hon. DPhil (Sussex) 1989, (E Anglia) 1993, (London) 1998; Primo Letterario, Prato 1982; Prix Femina 1993; Shakespeare Prize 1999. *Publications:* First Love, Last Rites (Somerset Maugham Prize) 1975, In Between the Sheets 1978, The Cement Garden 1978, The Imitation Game 1980, The Comfort of Strangers 1981, Or Shall we Die? (libretto) 1983, The Ploughman's Lunch (film script) 1983, The Child in Time (Whitbread Novel of the Year Award) 1987, Soursweet (screenplay) 1987, A Move Abroad 1989, The Innocent 1990, Black Dogs 1992, The Daydreamer 1994, The Short Stories 1995, Enduring Love 1997, Amsterdam (Booker Prize) 1998, Atonement (Nat. Book Critics Circle Award 2003) 2001. *Leisure interest:* hiking. *Address:* c/o Jonathan Cape, Random Century House, 20 Vauxhall Bridge Road, London, SW1V 2SA, England. *Website:* www.ianmcewan.ws.

McFADDEN, Daniel L., PhD; American economist; b. 29 July 1937, Raleigh, NC; ed Univ. of Minnesota; mem. Dept of Econs, Univ. of Calif. at Berkeley; Nobel Prize for Econs 2000 (Jt recipient). *Publications include:* Lectures on Longitudinal Analysis (Underground Classics in Economics) (Jt author).

Address: Department of Economics, University of California, Berkeley, CA 94720, USA (Office). *Telephone:* (510) 643-8428 (Office). *Fax:* (510) 642-0638 (Office). *E-mail:* mcfadden@econ.berkeley.edu (Office).

McFADDEN, Mary; American fashion designer; b. 1 Oct. 1938, New York; d. of Alexander Bloomfield McFadden and Mary Josephine Cutting; m. 1st Philip Harari 1964 (divorced); one d.; m. 2nd Frank McEwen 1968 (divorced); m. 3rd Armin Schmidt (divorced); m. 4th Kohle Yohannan (divorced); m. 5th Vasilios Calitsis 1996 (divorced); ed École Lubec, Paris, Sorbonne, Paris, Traphagen School of Design, New York and Columbia Univ., New York and New School for Social Research, New York; Dir of Public Relations, Christian Dior, New York 1962–64; merchandising ed. Vogue, SA 1964–65; political and travel columnist, Rand Daily Mail, SA 1965–68; founder Vukutu Sculpture Workshop, Rhodesia 1968–70; freelance ed. My Fair Lady, Cape Town and French Vogue 1968–70; Special Projects Ed. American Vogue 1970–73; fashion and jewellery designer (noted for tunics made from African and Chinese silks), New York 1973–; Chair. Mary McFadden Inc. 1976–; partner MMcF Collection by Mary McFadden 1991–; adviser Nat. Endowment for Arts; numerous awards include Neiman Marcus Award 1979, Best Dressed List Hall of Fame 1979, Coty American Fashion Critics' Hall of Fame Award 1979, Woman of the Year, Police Athletic League 1990, New York Landmarks Conservancy 1994, Designer of the Decade and Beyond, Fashion Group Int. and Phila Breast Health Inst. 1997, Legends Award, Pratt Inst. *Films:* Zooni – The Last Chak Empress, Sufism in India. *Television:* QVC, Worldly Accessories. *Publications:* contribs. to Vogue and House & Garden. *Leisure interests:* tennis, squash, travelling the world, lecturing. *Address:* Mary McFadden Inc., 240 West 35th Street, Floor 17, New York, NY 10001 (Office); 525 East 72nd Street, Apt. 2A, New York, NY 10021, USA (Home). *Telephone:* (212) 736-4078 (Office); (212) 772-1125 (Home). *Fax:* (212) 239-7259 (Office); (212) 239-7259. *E-mail:* mcfconture@aol.com (Office). *Website:* www .marymcfadden.conture.com (Office).

MACFADYEN, Air Marshal Ian David, C.B., OBE, FRAeS; British government official and retd air force officer; b. 19 Feb. 1942, Maidenhead, Berks.; s. of Air Marshal Sir Douglas Macfadyen and Lady Macfadyen (now Rowan); m. Sally Harvey 1967; one s.; one d.; ed Marlborough Coll., RAF Coll. Cranwell; joined RAF 1960, Cranwell cadet 1960–63, 19 Squadron 1965–68, HQ, RAF Strike Command 1969; Flying Instructor RAF Coll. Cranwell 1970–73, RAF Staff Coll. 1973, 111 Squadron 1974–75; Flight Commdr 43 Squadron 1976, HQ 2ATAF RAF Germany 1976–79, Command 29 Squadron 1980–83, 23 Squadron 1983; with Ministry of Defence 1983–85, 1989–90; with Command RAF Leuchars, Fife 1985–87, Royal Coll. of Defence Studies 1988; Chief of Staff then Commdr HQ British Forces Middle East, Riyadh 1990–91, Asst Chief of Defence Staff, Operational Requirements (Air Systems) 1991–94; Dir-Gen. Saudi Arabia Armed Forces Project 1994–98; retd 1999; Lt-Gov. Isle of Man 2000–; Trustee RAF Museum 1999–; Liveryman Guild of Air Pilots and Navigators (GAPAN) 1999–; Sword of Honour, Cranwell 1963; Queen's Commendation for Valuable Service in the Air (QCVSA) 1973; Officer, Order of St John of Jerusalem 2001. *Publication:* Gulf War contrib. to Imperial War Museum Book of Modern Warfare 1945–2000 2002. *Leisure interests:* golf, shooting, watercolour painting, gliding, history. *Address:* Government House, Onchan, Isle of Man, IM3 1RR. *Telephone:* (1624) 620147 (Office). *Fax:* (1624) 663707 (Office). *E-mail:* christopher.tummon@chiefsecs .gov.im (Office). *Website:* iom.gov.co.uk (Office).

McFADYEN, Jock, MA; British artist; b. 18 Sept. 1950, Paisley, Scotland; s. of James Lachlan McFadyen and Margaret McFadyen; m. 1st Carol Hambleton 1972 (divorced 1987); one s.; m. 2nd Susie Honeyman 1991; one s. one d.; ed Chelsea School of Art; has made works about London, New York, Belfast, Berlin, Orkney and France; represented in 30 public collections and in numerous pvt. and corp. collections; artist in residence Nat. Gallery, London 1981; tutor Slade School of Fine Art 1985–; designed sets and costumes for The Judas Tree, Royal Opera House, Covent Garden 1992; Arts Council Major Award 1979; Prize-winner John Moores Liverpool Exhbn 1991. *Exhibitions:* has held 36 solo exhbns. including Nat. Gallery 1982, Camden Arts Centre 1988, Imperial War Museum 1991, Talbot Rice Gallery, Edin. 1998, The Pier Arts Centre, St. Magnus Festival, Orkney 1999, Agnew's, London 2001; has also exhibited in numerous maj. mixed exhbns. and int. touring shows. *Leisure interests:* cycling, motorcycling, walking, swimming, children. *Address:* 15 Victoria Park Square, London, E2 9PB, England; 73 Montgomery Street, Edinburgh, Scotland; Orthe, St. Martin de Connée, France. *Telephone:* (20) 8983-3825 (London).

MACFARLANE, Alan Donald James, DPhil, PhD, MA, FBA; British academic; b. 20 Dec. 1941, Assam, India; s. of Donald Macfarlane and Iris Macfarlane; m. 1st Gillian Ions 1965; m. 2nd Sarah Harrison 1981; one d.; ed Sedbergh School, Worcester Coll., Oxford, London School of Econs and School of Oriental & African Studies, London Univ.; Sr Research Fellow in History, King's Coll. Cambridge 1971–75; Lecturer in Social Anthropology, Univ. of Cambridge 1975–81, Reader in Historical Anthropology 1981–91; Prof. of Anthropological Science 1991–; Fellow, King's Coll., Cambridge 1981–; Radcliffe-Brown Memorial Lecture (British Acad.) 1992; Rivers Memorial Medal 1984. *TV series:* The Day the World Took Off (adviser and participant), Channel 4 2000. *Publications:* Witchcraft in Tudor and Stuart England 1970, Family Life of Ralph Josselin 1970, The Diary of Ralph Josselin (Ed.) 1976, Resources and Population 1976, The Origins of English Individualism 1977, The Justice and the Mare's Ale 1981, Marriage and Love in England 1986, The Culture of Capitalism 1987, The Nagas: Hill Peoples of North India (co-

author) 1990, The Cambridge Database System Manual 1990, The Savage Wars of Peace 1997, The Riddle of the Modern World: Of Liberty, Wealth and Equality 2000; Ed. and trans. (with Sarah Harrison) of Bernard Pignède, The Gurungs of Nepal 1993, The Making of the Modern World: Visions from West and East 2002, The Glass Bathyscaphe: How Glass Changed the World (with Gerry Martin) 2002, Green Gold: The Empire of Tea (with Iris Macfarlane) 2003. *Leisure interests:* gardening, walking, music. *Address:* King's College, Cambridge, CB2 1ST; 25 Lode Road, Lode, nr Cambridge, CB5 9ER, England. *Telephone:* (1223) 811976.

MacFARLANE, Alistair George James, Kt, CBE, DSc, PhD, ScD, FRS, FEng, FRSE; British professor of engineering and vice-chancellor (retd.); b. 9 May 1931, Edin.; s. of George R. MacFarlane and Mary MacFarlane; m. Nora Williams 1954; one s.; ed Hamilton Acad., Univ. of Glasgow, Univ. of London, Univ. of Manchester; with Metropolitan-Vickers, Manchester 1953–58; Lecturer Queen Mary Coll., Univ. of London 1959–65, Reader 1965–66; Reader in Control Eng UMIST 1966–69, Prof. 1969–74; Prof. of Eng Univ. of Cambridge 1974–89; Fellow Selwyn Coll., Cambridge 1974–89, Vice-Master 1980–88; Prin. and Vice-Chancellor Heriot-Watt Univ., Edin. 1989–96, Emer. Research Fellow 1997–99; Chair. Cambridge Control Ltd 1985–89; mem. Council SERC 1981–85, Computer Bd 1983–88; Chair. Scottish Council for Research in Educ. 1992–98, Scottish Library and Information Council 1994–98, Advisory Body on High Performance Computing 1994–98, BT Advisory Forum 1997–; Academic Advisor Univ. of Highlands and Islands Project 1997–; Trustee Scottish Library and Information System Council 1994–98; mem. Royal Soc. Council 1997–99, Chair. Educ. Cttee 2000–; Hon. Fellow, Selwyn Coll. 1989–; Hon. DEng (Glasgow) 1995; Hon. DUniv (Heriot-Watt) 1997, (Paisley) 1997; Hon. DSc (Abertay Dundee) 1998; Hon. DLitt (Lincolnshire and Humberside) 1999. *Publications:* Engineering Systems Analysis 1964, Dynamical System Models 1970, (with I. Postlethwaite) A Complex Variable Approach to the Analysis of Linear Multivariable Feedback Systems 1979, (Ed.) Frequency-Response Methods in Control Systems 1979, (Ed.) Complex Variable Methods for Linear Multivariable Feedback Systems 1980, (with S. Hung) Multivariable Feedback: a quasi-classical approach 1982, (with G. K. H. Pang) An Expert Systems Approach to Computer-Aided Design of Multivariable Systems 1987. *Address:* 2 Rookwood Gardens, Rothbury Road, Longframlington, Northumberland, NE65 8HX, England (Home). *Telephone:* (1665) 570784 (Home). *E-mail:* alistair.macfarlane@btinternet .com (Home).

MACFARLANE, Ian J.; Australian central banker; b. 22 June 1946, Sydney; ed Monash Univ.; taught at Monash Univ.; with Inst. of Econs and Statistics, Oxford Univ., then in economic forecasting and surveys at OECD, Paris 1973–78; joined Reserve Bank of Australia (Research Dept) 1979, Head of Research 1988, Asst Gov. (Econ.) 1990–92, Deputy Gov. 1992–96, Gov. 1996–. *Address:* Reserve Bank of Australia, GPOB 3947, Sydney, NSW 2001, Australia. *Telephone:* (2) 9551-8111. *Fax:* (2) 9551-8030.

McFARLANE, John, OBE, MA, MBA; British banking executive; b. 1947, Dumfries; ed Dumfries Acad., Univ. of Edinburgh, Cranfield School of Man., London Business School; with Ford Motor Co., UK 1969–74; various exec. positions with Citibank, later becoming UK CEO 1974–93; Group Exec. Dir Standard Chartered Bank 1993–97; CEO Australia and New Zealand Banking Group Ltd (ANZ) Oct. 1997–; Deputy Chair. Axiss Australia; mem. Bd The Business Council of Australia, Australian Grad. School of Man., Financial Markets Foundation for Children; mem. Council, Australian Bankers Assocn; fmr Dir London Stock Exchange, Capital Radio PLC, The Securities Assocn, The Auditing Practices Bd, Cranfield School of Man., Financial Law Panel. *Leisure interests:* personal computing, keeping fit, acoustic guitar, painting and sculpture. *Address:* Australia and New Zealand Banking Group Ltd, 100 Queen Street, Melbourne 3000, Australia (Office). *Website:* www.anz.com.au (Office).

MCFARLANE, Robert Carl, MS; American government official; b. 12 July 1937, Washington, DC; s. of William McFarlane and Alma Carl; m. Jonda Riley 1959; one s. two d.; ed US Naval Acad. and Inst. des Hautes Etudes, Geneva; US Marine Corps, Second Lt rising to Lt-Col 1959–79; White House Fellow, Exec. Asst Council to Pres. for Legis. Affairs 1971–72; Mil. Asst to Henry Kissinger (q.v.) 1973–75; Exec. Asst to Asst to Pres. for Nat. Security Affairs 1975–76; Special Asst to Pres. 1976–77; Research Fellow Nat. Defence Univ., Washington, DC 1977–78; mem. Professional Staff Senate Comm. on Armed Services 1979–81; Counsellor Dept of State 1981–82; Deputy Asst to Pres., Nat. Security Affairs 1982–83; Personal Rep. of US Pres. in Middle East July–Oct. 1983; Asst to Pres. for Nat. Security Affairs 1983–85; Chair. and CEO McFarlane Assocn 1986–; lobbyist for Macedonia 1992; Distinguished Service Medal and other medals and awards. *Publications:* At Sea Where We Belong 1971, Crisis Resolution (co-author) 1978, The Political Potential of Parity 1979.

MACFARLANE OF BEARSDEN, Baron (Life Peer), cr. 1991, in the District of Bearsden and Milngavie; **Norman Somerville Macfarlane,** KT, FRSE; British business executive; b. 5 March 1926; s. of Daniel Robertson Macfarlane and Jessie Lindsay Somerville; m. Marguerite Mary Campbell 1953; one s. four d.; ed Glasgow High School; f. N. S. Macfarlane and Co. Ltd 1949, Chair. Macfarlane Group (Clansman) PLC 1973–98, Man. Dir 1973–90; Chair. Scottish Industrialists Council 1975–; Dir Glasgow Chamber of Commerce 1976–79; Chair. The Fine Art Soc. PLC 1976–98 (Hon. Pres. 1998); Underwriting mem. of Lloyds 1978–97; Dir American Trust PLC 1980–97, Chair.

1984–97; Dir Clydesdale Bank PLC 1980–96, Deputy Chair. 1993–96; Dir Edin. Fund Mans PLC 1980–98; Dir Gen. Accident Fire and Life Assurance Corpn PLC 1984–96; Chair. Guinness Co. 1987–89, Jt Deputy Chair. 1989–92; Chair. United Distillers PLC 1987–96, Hon. Life Pres. 1996–; Chair. Arthur Bell Distillers 1989; mem. Council CBI Scotland 1975–81; mem. Bd Scottish Devt Agency 1979–87; Chair. Glasgow Devt Agency 1985–92; Vice-Chair. Scottish Ballet 1983–87, (Dir 1975–87), Pres. 2001–; Pres. Stationers' Asscn of GB and Ireland 1965, Co. of Stationers of Glasgow 1968–70, Glasgow High School Club 1970–72, Royal Glasgow Inst. of the Fine Arts 1976–87; Hon. Pres. Charles Rennie Mackintosh Soc. 1988–; Regent Royal Coll. of Surgeons, Edin. 1997–; Dir Scottish Nat. Orchestra 1977–82, Third Eye Centre 1978–81; Gov. Glasgow School of Art 1976–87; Scottish Patron, Nat. Art Collection Fund 1978–; Patron Scottish Licensed Trade Asscn 1992–; Chair. Govs, High School of Glasgow 1979–92, Hon. Pres. 1992–; mem. Royal Fine Art Comm. for Scotland 1980–82; Lord High Commr Gen. Ass., Church of Scotland 1992, 1993, 1997; mem. Court, Glasgow Univ. 1979–87; Trustee, Nat. Heritage Memorial Fund 1984–97, Nat. Galleries of Scotland 1986–97; D. L. Dunbartonshire 1993; Hon. Patron Queen's Park Football Club; Vice-Pres. Professional Golfers Asscn; Hon. F.R.I.A.S., F. Scotvec., F.R.C.P.S. Glas.; Hon. Fellow Glasgow School of Art 1993; Hon. LLD (Strathclyde) 1986, (Glasgow) 1988, (Glasgow Caledonian) 1993, (Aberdeen) 1995; DUniv (Stirling) 1992; Dr hc (Edin.) 1992. *Leisure interests:* golf, cricket, theatre, art. *Address:* Macfarlane Group PLC, Clansman House, 21 Newton Place, Glasgow, G3 7PY (Office); 50 Manse Road, Bearsden, Glasgow, G61 3PN, Scotland. *Telephone:* (141) 333-9666 (Office). *Fax:* (141) 333-1988 (Office).

McGAHERN, John; Irish writer; b. 12 Nov. 1934, Dublin; s. of Francis McGahern and Susan McManus; m. Madeline Green 1973; ed Presentation Coll., Carrick-on-Shannon, St Patrick's Coll. and Univ. Coll. Dublin; primary school teacher 1955–64; Research Fellow, Univ. of Reading, England 1968–71; Northern Arts Fellow, Univs. of Durham and Newcastle-upon-Tyne, England 1974–76; Visiting Prof., Colgate Univ., New York, USA 1969, 1972, 1977, 1980, 1983, 1991, 1996; Literary Fellow, Trinity Coll., Dublin 1988; mem. Irish Acad. of Letters; Fellow Royal Literary Soc.; mem. Aosdana; Soc. of Authors Travelling Fellowship; Hon. DLitt (Trinity Coll. Dublin) 1992, (Galway) 1994; AE Memorial Award; Macauley Fellowship, Arts Council of GB Award; American Irish Award; Irish Times–Aer Lingus Literature Prize 1990, GPA Award 1992, Prix Etrangère Ecureuil 1994; Chevalier Ordre des Arts et des Lettres 1989. *Publications:* The Barracks 1963, The Dark 1965, Nightlines 1970, The Leavetaking 1975, Getting Through 1978, The Pornographer 1979, High Ground 1985, The Rockingham Shoot 1987, Amongst Women 1990, The Power of Darkness 1991, The Collected Stories 1992, That They May Face the Rising Sun 2002. *Address:* c/o Faber & Faber, 3 Queen Square, London, WC1N 3AU, England.

McGHEE, George C., DPhil; American government official and business executive; b. 10 March 1912, Waco, Tex.; s. of George Summers McGhee and Magnolia Spruce; m. Cecilia DeGolyer 1938; two s. four d.; ed Southern Methodist Univ., Dallas, Univ. of Oklahoma, Oxford Univ. and Univ. of London; Subsurface Geologist, The Atlantic Refining Co. 1930–31; Geophysicist, Continental Oil Co. 1933–34; Vice-Pres. Nat. Geophysical Co., Dallas 1937–39; Partner DeGolyer, MacNaughton and McGhee 1940–41; independent explorer for and producer of oil 1940–; Sr Liaison Officer OPM and WPB 1941–43; U.S. Deputy Exec. Sec. Combined Raw Materials Bd 1942–43; Special Asst to the Under-Sec. of State for Econ. Affairs 1946–47; Co-ordinator for Aid to Greece and Turkey, Dept of State 1947–49; Special Rep. of Sec. of State to Near East on Palestine Refugee problem with personal rank of Minister 1949; Special Asst to Sec. of State 1949; Asst Sec. Near East, South Asian and African Affairs 1949–51; Amb. to Turkey 1951–53; Adviser NATO Council, Ottawa 1951; Dir Inst. of Inter-American Affairs, Inter-American Educ. Foundation 1946–51; Dir U.S. Commercial Co. 1946; Dir Foreign Service Educ. Foundation 1947–; Consultant, Nat. Security Council 1958–59; Counsellor, Dept of State and Chair. Policy Planning Council Jan.–Nov. 1961; Under-Sec. of State for Political Affairs 1961–63; Amb. to Fed. Repub. of Germany 1963–68; Amb.-at-Large 1968–69; Dir Panama Canal Co. 1962–63, Mobil Oil Co. 1969–82, Procter & Gamble Co. 1969–82, American Security & Trust Co. 1969–82, Trans World Airlines 1976–82; Chair. of Bd Saturday Review/World 1973–76; Chair. Smithsonian Assocs. 1976–78; Owner McGhee Production Co.; Dir of Trustees, Robert Coll., Istanbul 1953–61, Brookings Inst. 1954–61, Cttee for Econ. Devt 1957–, Aspen Inst. Humanistic Studies 1958–, Vassar Coll. 1959–61, Duke Univ. 1962–78; Chair. Business Council for Int. Understanding 1969–74; Chair. English Speaking Union, USA 1970–74, Deputy Chair. Int. Council of the English Speaking Union 1974; Chair. Nat. Trust for Historic Preservation 1971–75, Int. Man. and Devt Inst. 1972–, Fed. City Housing Corpn 1972–, Piedmont Environmental Council; Trustee, George C. Marshall Research Foundation, American Council on Germany, The American Univ., The Asia Foundation 1974–; Dir Atlantic Council 1975–, Atlantic Inst. for Int. Affairs 1977–, Cordier Fellow, Advisory Council, Columbia Univ. 1977–; Pres. Fed. City Council 1970–74, etc.; mem. Bd Nat. Civil Service League 1967–71, Salzburg Seminar 1969–71; mem. Japan-U.S. Econ. Advisory Council 1970–74, American Petroleum Inst., American Asscn Petroleum Geologists, Soc. of Exploring Geophysicists, American Inst. Mining and Metallurgical Engineers, Council on Foreign Relations (New York), American Foreign Service Asscn, Acad. of Political Science, Washington Inst. of Foreign Affairs, Dept of Conservation and Econ. Devt, Club of Rome, American Philosophical Soc.; mem. Bd of Trustees, American Univ. 1981–, Council of American Ambs. 1984–, Visiting Cttee for Arthur M. Sackler Gallery at Smithsonian Inst. 1986–; Vice-Chair. Bd of Dirs. Inst. for the Study of Diplomacy, Georgetown Univ.; served in USNR 1943–46; Lt-Col USAF Reserve 1949–; Hon. Fellow, Queen's Coll., Oxford 1968; Hon. LLD (Tulane Univ.) 1957, (Maryland Univ.) 1965; Hon. DCL (Southern Methodist Univ.) 1953; Hon. DSc (Univ. of Tampa) 1969; Legion of Merit; Asiatic Ribbon with three battle stars; mem. Order Hospital St John of Jerusalem 1972–, numerous other awards. *Publications:* Envoy to the Middle World 1983, At the Creation of a New Germany 1989, The US-Turkish-NATO Middle East Connection 1990, Ed. Diplomacy for the Future 1987, Ed. National Interest and Global Goals 1989, Life in Alanya: Turkish Delight 1992, International Community, A Goal for a New World Order 1992, On the Frontline in the Cold War 1997, The Ambassador 2001, I Did It This Way 2001. *Address:* Farmer's Delight, 36276 Mountville Road, Middleburg, VA 20117, USA. *Telephone:* (540) 687-3451. *Fax:* (540) 687-3451.

MacGIBBON, Ross; British film director and fmr. ballet dancer; ed Royal Ballet School; dancer with Royal Ballet 1973–86; started working in TV 1986. *Films:* dance film White Man Sleeps (Channel 4), Wyoming (1st Prize, IMZ DanceScreen competition) 1989; Dir The Far End of The Garden 1991, Should Accidentally Fall (Special Jury Prize, 1994 Video-Dance Grand Prix, Vancouver), Echo 1996 (Special Jury Prize). *Television:* Dir and produced Swinger (BBC2) 1996, Peter and the Wolf (BBC1), The Judas Tree (Channel 4), film on closure of the Royal Opera House (BBC2).

McGILLIS, Kelly; American actress; b. 9 July 1957, Newport Beach, Calif.; m. Fred Tillman 1988; three c.; ed Pacific School of Performing Arts and Juilliard School of Music, New York. *Films include:* Witness, Reuben, Reuben, Private Sessions, Top Gun1986, The Accused 1988, The House on Carroll Street, Dreamers, Made in Heaven, Promised Land, Winter People, Lie Down With Lions, Cat Chaser, Before and After Death, Grand Isle, The Babe, North, Painted Angels, Ground Control, Morgan's Ferry 1999, At First Sight 1999; several TV movies and stage appearances.

McGINN, Colin, MA, BPhil; British professor of philosophy; b. 10 March 1950; s. of Joseph McGinn and June McGinn; one s.; ed Manchester and Oxford Univs.; lecturer, Univ. Coll. London 1974–85; Wilde Reader in Mental Philosophy, Oxford Univ. 1985–90; Prof., Rutgers Univ., USA 1990–; John Locke Prize 1973. *Publications:* The Character of Mind 1981, The Subjective View 1982, Wittgenstein on Meaning 1984, Mental Content 1989, The Problem of Consciousness 1991, The Space Trap 1992, Moral Literacy 1992, Problems in Philosophy 1993. *Leisure interest:* fitness. *Address:* Rutgers University, P.O. Box 2101, New Brunswick, NY 08903 (Office); 270 West End Avenue, Apt. 9E, New York, NY 10023, USA. *Telephone:* (908) 932-1766 (Office).

McGINN, Richard A., BA; American business executive; b. 1947; m.; one d.; ed Grinnell Coll., Iowa; with Ill. Bell 1969; exec. positions int. and computer systems groups AT&T 1978, CEO network systems; CEO, Pres. Lucent Techs. 1997–, Chair., CEO –2000; mem. Bd Dirs. Lucent Techs., Oracle Corpn, American Express Co. Business Council. *Leisure interests:* adventure sports, deep-sea fishing. *Address:* c/o Lucent Technologies, 600 Mountain Avenue, Murray Hill, NJ 07974, USA (Office).

McGOUGH, Roger, OBE, MA; British poet; b. 9 Nov. 1937, Liverpool; s. of Roger McGough and Mary McGarry; m. 1st Thelma Monaghan 1970 (divorced 1980); m. 2nd Hilary Clough 1986; three s. one d.; ed St Mary's Coll., Liverpool, Hull Univ.; Poetry Fellow Univ. of Loughborough 1973–75; writer-in-residence Western Australia Coll. of Educ., Perth 1986, Univ. of Hamburg 1994; Vice-Pres. The Poetry Society 1996– (mem. Exec. Council 1989–93); Trustee Chelsea Arts Club 1987–, fmr Chair.; Hon. Prof. Thames Valley Univ.; Fellow John Moores Univ. 1999; Freeman City of Liverpool 2001; Hon. MA (Nene Coll.) 1998; Signal Award 1984, 1998, BAFTA Award 1984, 1992, Cholmondeley Award 1998. *Music:* wrote and performed Top Twenty hits Lily the Pink and Thank U Very Much 1968–69. *Plays include:* The Sound Collector and My Dad's a Fire-eater (for children); wrote lyrics for Broadway production of The Wind in the Willows 1984. *Plays for radio include:* Summer with Monika, FX, Walking the Dog. *Publications:* Watchwords 1969, After the Merrymaking 1971, Out of Sequence 1972, Gig 1972, Sporting Relations 1974, In the Glassroom 1976, Summer with Monika 1978, Holiday on Death Row 1979, Unlucky for Some 1981, Waving at Trains 1982, Melting into the Foreground 1986, Blazing Fruit: Selected Poems 1967–1987 1989, You at the Back 1991, Defying Gravity 1992, The Spotted Unicorn 1998, The Way Things Are 1999, Everyday Eclipses 2002, Collected Poems of Roger McGough 2003; for children: Mr Noselighter 1977, The Great Smile Robbery 1982, Sky in the Pie 1983, The Stowaways 1986, Noah's Ark 1986, Nailing the Shadow 1987, An Imaginary Menagerie 1988, Helen Highwater 1989, Counting by Numbers 1989, Pillow Talk 1990, The Lighthouse That Ran Away 1991, My Dad's a Fire-eater 1992, Another Custard Pie 1993, Lucky 1993, Stinkers Ahoy! 1995, The Magic Fountain 1995, The Kite and Caitlin 1996, Bad Bad Cats 1997, Until I Met Dudley 1998, Good Enough to Eat 2002, Moonthief 2002, What On Earth Can It Be? 2003; ed: Strictly Private 1981, The Kingfisher Book of Comic Verse 1986, The Kingfisher Books of Poems About Love 1997, The Ring of Words (anthology) 1998, Wicked Poems 2002. *Address:* c/o Peters Fraser and Dunlop, Drury House, 34–43 Russell Street, London, WC2B 5HA, England. *Telephone:* (20) 7344-1000. *Fax:* (20) 7836-9539. *E-mail:* personal@rogermcgough.org.uk (Office). *Website:* www.rogermcgough.org.uk (Office).

McGOVERN, George Stanley, PhD; American politician; b. 19 July 1922, Avon, S. Dakota; s. of Rev. J. C. McGovern and Frances McLean McGovern;

m. Eleanor Faye Stegeberg 1943; one s. four d.; ed Dakota Wesleyan Univ. and Northwestern Univ.; served USAF, Second World War; Teacher, Northwestern Univ. 1948–50; Prof. of History and Political Science, Dakota Wesleyan Univ. 1950–53; Exec. Sec. S. Dak. Democratic Party 1953–56; mem. U.S. House of Reps. 1957–61, served Agricultural Cttee; Dir "Food for Peace" Programme 1961–62; Senator from South Dakota 1963–81; partner John Kornmeier Assocs., Washington 1981; lecturer, North-Western Univ., Chicago 1981; Democratic cand. for U.S. Presidency 1972, 1984; Chair. Americans for Common Sense 1981–82; Perm. Rep. FAO, Rome 1998–; fmr Pres. Middle East Policy Council; fmr Jt owner roadside inn, Stratford, Conn.; Presidential Medal of Freedom 2000, Food for Life Award, World Food Program 2000. *Publications:* The Colorado Coal Strike 1913–14 1953, War Against Want 1964, Agricultural Thought in the Twentieth Century 1967, A Time of War, a Time of Peace 1968, The Great Coalfield War (with Leonard Guttridge) 1972, An American Journey 1974, Grassroots (autobiog.) 1978, Terry My Daughter's Life-and-Death Struggle with Alcoholism 1996. *Address:* FAO, Viale delle Terme di Caracalla, 00100 Rome, Italy (Office); P.O. Box 5591, Friendship Station, Washington, DC 20016, USA (Home). *E-mail:* jedelhoff@usaid.gov (Office).

McGRATH, John Brian, BSc; British business executive; b. 20 June 1938; m. Sandy Watson 1964; one s. one d.; ed Brunel Univ.; worked at UKAEA 1962–65; with NCB 1965–67; with Ford Motor Co. 1967–71; with Jaguar Cars 1971–75; with Stone-Platt 1976–82; Man. Dir Construction and Mining Div. and Chief Exec. Compair 1982–83; joined Grand Metropolitan PLC 1985, Group Dir Watney Mann & Truman Brewers Ltd 1985, Chair. and Man. Dir Grand Metropolitan Brewing 1986–88, Jt Man. Dir Int. Distillers & Vintners 1988–91, Man. Dir and COO 1991–92, Chief Exec. 1992–93, Chair. and Chief Exec. 1993–96, Group Chief Exec. Grand Metropolitan PLC 1996–97; Dir (non-exec.) Cookson Group 1993–; Chair. Scotch Whisky Assen 1995–2000; Chair. Guinness Ltd (now Diageo PLC) 1997–2000, CEO 1997–2000; Chair. Boots Co. PLC 2000–03 (Dir 1998–2003). *Address:* c/o The Boots Company PLC, Nightingale House, 65 Curzon Street, London, W1Y 7PE, England (Office).

McGRATH, Judith, BA; American television executive; b. 1952, Scranton; ed Cedar Crest Coll., Allentown, Pa; fmrly Copy Chief, Glamour Magazine, Sr Writer Mademoiselle Magazine, copywriter, Nat. Advertising, Phila; copywriter Warner Amex Satellite Entertainment Co. (later MTV Networks) 1981, subsequently Editorial Dir MTV, Exec. Vice-Pres., Creative Dir, then Co-Pres. and Creative Dir; Pres. Networks, New York City Ballet, Rock the Vote. *Address:* MTV, 1515 Broadway, New York, NY 10036, USA (Office).

McGRAW, Harold Whittlesey (Terry), III, BA, MBA; American business executive; b. 30 Aug. 1948, Summit, NJ; s. of Harold W. McGraw, Jr; m. Nancy Goodrich 1973; one s. one d.; ed Tufts Univ., Univ. of Pennsylvania; fmr mem. financial man. staff GTE, GTE Man. Corp.; Asst Vice-Pres. Pension Investment McGraw-Hill Inc., New York 1980–83, Dir Corp. Planning Systems 1983–84, Vice-Pres. Corp. Planning, mem. Bd Dirs. 1984–85; Group Vice-Pres. Public Transport Group, McGraw-Hill Publs Co., New York 1985–86, Group Vice-Pres. Public Transport, Aerospace and Defense Group 1986–98, Pres. 1987–88; Pres. McGraw-Hill Financial Services Co., New York 1988–89; mem. Bd Dirs. The McGraw Hill Cos. 1987–, Pres., COO 1993–98, Pres., CEO 1998–99, Chair., Pres., CEO 1998–; mem. Bd Dirs. Bestfoods, Hartley House, New York 1983–, Nat. Actors Theater, Nat. Acad. Foundation; Co-Chair. Carnegie Hall's Corp. Fund; mem. The Business Council, Business Roundtable. *Address:* The McGraw Hill Companies, Suite C3A, Floor 49, 1221 Avenue of the Americas, New York, NY 10020, USA (Office).

MCGREEVEY, James E., BA; American state official; b. 6 Aug. 1957, Jersey City; s. of John McGreevey and Veronica McGreevey; m. Dina Matos; two d.; ed St Joseph's High School, Columbia Univ., Georgetown Univ., Harvard Univ.; fmrly man. with Merck & Co.; fmr Asst Prosecutor for Middlesex Co., Exec. Dir of State Parole Bd; mem. State Ass., New Jersey 1990–91, State Senate 1994–97; Mayor of Woodbridge 1992–2002; Gov. of New Jersey 2002–. *Address:* Office of the Governor, POB 001, Trenton, NJ 08625, USA (Office). *Telephone:* (609) 292-6000 (Office). *Fax:* (609) 292-3454 (Office). *Website:* www .state.nj.us.

McGREGOR, Ewan; British actor; b. 31 March 1971, Perth; s. of James McGregor and Carol McGregor; ed Guildhall School of Music and Drama; began career with Perth Repertory Theatre; Hon. DLitt (Ulster Univ.). *Theatre includes:* What the Butler Saw, Little Malcolm and his Struggle against the Eunuchs (Hampstead Theatre Club) 1999 and Comedy Theatre, London. *Television includes:* Lipstick on Your Collar, Scarlet and Black, Kavanagh QC, Doggin' Around, Tales From the Crypt, ER. *Films include:* Being Human, Family Style, Shallow Grave (Best Actor Dinard Film Festival 1994), Blue Juice, The Pillow Book, Trainspotting, Emma, Brassed Off, Nightwatch, The Serpent's Kiss, A Life Less Ordinary, Velvet Goldmine, Star Wars Episode I: The Phantom Menace, Little Voice, Rogue Trader, Eye of the Beholder, Nora, Moulin Rouge (Best Actor, Berlin Film Festival, Empire Award, Variety Club Awards, Film Critics' Awards) 2001, Black Hawk Down 2002, Star Wars Episode II: Attack of the Clones 2002, Down with Love 2003, Young Adam 2003. *Leisure interest:* motor bikes. *Address:* c/o Peters, Fraser and Dunlop, Drury House, 34-43 Russell Street, London, WC2B 5HA, England. *Telephone:* (20) 7344-1010. *Fax:* (20) 7352-8135.

McGREGOR, Harvey, QC, MA, DCL, SJD; British barrister and academic lawyer; b. 25 Feb. 1926, Aberdeen; s. of late William G. R. McGregor and

Agnes Reid; ed Inverurie Acad., Scarborough Boys' High School, Queen's Coll. Oxford and Harvard Univ.; Bigelow Teaching Fellow, Univ. of Chicago 1950–51; called to the Bar, Inner Temple, London 1955, Bencher 1985; Fellow, New Coll. Oxford 1972–85, Warden 1985–96, Hon. Fellow 1996; Privilegiate, St Hilda's Coll. Oxford; consultant to Law Comm. 1966–73; Deputy Ind. Chair. London and Provincial Theatre Councils 1971–92, Ind. Chair. 1992–; Visiting Prof. New York Univ. and Rutgers Univ. 1963–69; Fellow, Winchester Coll. 1985–96; mem. Editorial Bd Modern Law Review 1986–; mem. Acad. of European Pvt. Lawyers 1994–; Trustee Oxford Union 1977– (Chair. 1994–); Hon. Prof. Univ. of Edin.; Trustee Migraine Trust 1999–; Assoc. mem. Soc. of Writers to the Signet 2002–; Founding Fellow Inst. of Contemporary Scotland 2002. *Publication:* A Contract Code 1993, McGregor on Damages (17th edn) 2003. *Leisure interests:* music, theatre, travel. *Address:* 4 Paper Buildings, Temple, London, EC4Y 7EX (Chambers) (Office); 29 Howard Place, Edinburgh, EH3 5JY, Scotland (Residence) (Home). *Telephone:* (20) 7353-3366 (Chambers) (Office); (131) 556-8680 (Residence) (Home). *Fax:* (20) 7353-5778 (Office); (131) 556-8686 (Home). *E-mail:* harvey.mcgregor@ 4paperbuildings.com (Office); harvey.mcgregor@4paperbuildings.com (Home).

McGREGOR, Sir Ian Alexander, Kt, CBE, FRCP, DTM&H, FRS, FRSE; British medical scientist; b. 26 Aug. 1922, Cambuslang, Lanarks.; s. of John McGregor and Isabella Taylor; m. Nancy J. Small 1954; one s. one d.; ed Rutherglen Acad. and St Mungo's Coll., Glasgow; mem. scientific staff, MRC Human Nutrition Unit 1949–53; Dir MRC Labs., The Gambia 1954–74, 1978–80; Head, Lab. of Tropical Community Studies, Nat. Inst. for Medical Research (MRC), Mill Hill, London 1974–77; Liverpool Univ. Professorial Fellow, Liverpool School of Tropical Medicine 1981–87, Visiting Prof. 1981–94; mem. scientific staff MRC at Liverpool School of Tropical Medicine 1981–84; Pres. Royal Soc. of Tropical Medicine and Hygiene 1983–85; mem. various advisory cttees. etc. including WHO Advisory Panel on Malaria 1961; Chair. WHO Expert Cttee on Malaria 1985–89; Hon. mem. American Soc. of Tropical Medicine and Hygiene 1984; Hon. Fellow Royal Soc. of Tropical Medicine and Hygiene 1995; Hon. F.R.C.P.S., Glasgow 1984; Hon. LLD (Aberdeen) 1983; Hon. DSc (Glasgow) 1984; Stewart Prize in Epidemiology, British Medical Assen 1971, Darling Foundation Medal and Prize, World Health Org. 1974, Glaxo Prize for Medical Writing 1989; several medals including Mary Kingsley Medal, Liverpool School of Tropical Medicine 1989. *Publications:* Ed. (with W H. Wernsdorfer) Malaria, 2 Vols 1988; some 170 papers on malaria and other aspects of health in the tropics. *Leisure interests:* ornithology, fishing, gardening. *Address:* Greenlooms House, Homington, Salisbury, Wilts., SP5 4NL, England. *Telephone:* (1722) 718452.

MacGREGOR, Joanna Clare, BA, FRAM; British concert pianist; b. 16 July 1959, London; d. of Angela MacGregor and Alfred MacGregor; m. Richard Williams 1986; one d. (deceased); ed South Hampstead High School for Girls, New Hall Coll. Cambridge, Royal Acad. of Music; Young Concert Artists Trust concerts and recitals, UK 1985–88; performances of classical, jazz and contemporary music in over 40 countries; has performed with Rotterdam, Oslo and Netherlands Radio Philharmonic Orchestras, Sydney, Berlin, Chicago and London Symphony Orchestras, New York Philharmonic; has worked with Sir Harrison Birtwistle, Pierre Boulez, John Adams, Lou Harrison and jazz artists Django Bates and Andy Sheppard; numerous radio and TV appearances including Last Night of the Proms 1997; established own record label Sound Circus 1998; conducting debut on UK tour with Britten Sinfonia, Assoc. Artistic Dir 2002–; mem. Arts Council of England 1998–; Hon. Fellow Royal Acad. of Music, Trinity Coll. of Music, RSA; European Encouragement Prize for Music 1995, South Bank Show Award for Classical Music 2000. *Publications:* Music Tuition Book, Joanna MacGregor's Piano World (5 vols) 2001. *Address:* c/o Ingpen and Williams, 26 Wadham Road, London, SW15 2LR, England. *Telephone:* (20) 8874-3222.

MacGREGOR, Baron (Life Peer), cr. 2001, of Pulham Market in the County of Norfolk; **John Roddick Russell MacGregor,** OBE, PC, MA, LLB; British politician and businessman; b. 14 Feb. 1937; s. of the late Dr. N S. R. MacGregor; m. Jean Mary Elizabeth Dungey 1962; one s. two d.; ed Merchiston Castle School, Edin., St Andrews Univ., King's Coll., London; Univ. Admin. 1961–62; Editorial Staff, New Society 1962–63; Special Asst to Prime Minister, Sir Alec Douglas-Home 1963–64; Conservative Research Dept 1964–65; Head of Pvt. Office of Rt Hon Edward Heath (Leader of Opposition) 1965–68; Conservative MP for South Norfolk 1974–2001; an Opposition Whip 1977–79; a Lord Commr of HM Treasury 1979–81, Parl. Under-Sec. of State, Dept of Industry 1981–83; Minister of State, Minister of Agric., Fisheries and Food 1983–85, 1987–89; Chief Sec. to HM Treasury 1985–87; Sec. of State for Educ. and Science 1989–90; Lord Pres. of the Council and Leader of the House of Commons 1990–92; Sec. of State for Transport 1992–94; with Hill Samuel & Co. Ltd 1968–79, Dir 1973–79, Deputy Chair. Hill Samuel Bank 1994–96, also Dir; Dir Slough Estates 1995–, Associated British Foods 1994–, Unigate (now Uniq) 1996–99, London and Manchester Group 1997–98, Friends Provident 1998–, Supervisory Bd Daf Trucks N.V. 2000–; Vice-Pres. Local Govt Assen (1997–99); mem. Neill Cttee now Wicks Cttee on Standards in Public Life) 1994–; Chair. Fed. of Univ. Conservative and Unionist Assens. 1959, Bow Group 1963–64; First Pres. Conservative and Christian Democratic Youth Community 1963–65; mem. Magic Circle 1989, Inner Magic Circle 1999; mem. Council King's Coll. London 1996–2002, Inst. of Dirs 1996–,

Norwich Cathedral 2002–; Hon. Fellow King's Coll. London 1990; Hon. LLD (Westminster) 1995. *Leisure interests:* music, reading, travelling, gardening, conjuring. *Address:* c/o House of Lords, London, SW1A 0PW, England.

MacGREGOR, (Robert) Neil; British editor and gallery director; b. 16 June 1946; s. of Alexander and Anna MacGregor (née Neil); ed Glasgow Acad., New Coll., Oxford, Ecole Normale Supérieure, Paris, Univ. of Edinburgh, Courtauld Inst. of Art; lecturer, Univ. of Reading 1976; Ed. The Burlington Magazine 1981–86; Dir Nat. Gallery 1987–2002; Dir British Museum 2002–; Trustee Pilgrim Trust 1990–; Chair. Conf. of UK Nat. Museum Dirs. 1991–97; Curator Cen. Inst. for Art History, Munich 1992–; mem. Supervisory Bd Rijksmuseum, Amsterdam 1995–; mem. Faculty of Advocates, Edin. 1972; Dr. hc (York) 1992, (Edin.) 1994, (Reading) 1997, (Leicester) 1997, (Glasgow) 1998, (Strathclyde) 1998, (Oxford) 1998, (Exeter) 1998, (London) 1999. *Radio:* contributor to numerous radio programmes. *Television:* has presented two major series on art. *Publications:* A Victim of Anonymity 1994, Seeing Salvation 2000; numerous articles in Apollo, The Burlington Magazine, Connoisseur, etc. *Address:* British Museum, Great Russell Street, London, WC1B 3DG, England. *Telephone:* (20) 7323-8299. *Website:* www .thebritishmuseum.ac.uk (Office).

MacGREGOR, Susan (Sue) Katriona, CBE; British broadcaster and journalist; b. 30 Aug. 1941, Oxford; d. of late Dr James MacGregor and Margaret MacGregor; ed Herschel School, Cape, SA; announcer/producer South African Broadcasting Corpn 1962–67; BBC Radio reporter World at One, World This Weekend, PM 1967–72; Presenter (BBC Radio 4) Woman's Hour 1972–87, Tuesday Call, Conversation Piece, Today 1984–2002, (BBC TV) Around Westminster, Dateline London; Visiting Prof. of Journalism Nottingham Trent Univ. 1995–; mem. Royal Coll. of Physicians Cttee on Ethical Issues in Medicine 1985–2000; mem. Bd Royal Nat. Theatre 1998–2002; Hon. MRCP 1995; Hon. DLitt (Nottingham) 1996, Hon. LLD (Dundee) 1997, Hon. DLitt (Nottingham Trent) 2000, (Staffordshire) 2001, (N London) 2002. *Publication:* Woman of Today 2002. *Leisure interests:* theatre, cinema, skiing. *Address:* c/o Felicity Bryan, 2a North Parade, Oxford, OX2 6LX, England. *Telephone:* (1865) 513816.

McGUFFIN, Peter, MB, CH.B, PhD, FRCP, F.R.C.PSYCH.; British psychiatrist and geneticist; b. 4 Feb. 1949, Belfast; s. of Capt. William McGuffin and Melba M. Burnison; m. Prof. Anne Farmer 1972; one s. two d.; ed Univs. of Leeds and London; MRC Fellow and Lecturer, Inst. of Psychiatry, London 1979–81; Visiting MRC Fellow, Washington Univ. Medical School, St Louis, Mo. 1981–82; MRC Sr Fellow, Hon. Consultant and Sr Lecturer, Inst. of Psychiatry, King's Coll. Hosp. London 1982–86; Prof. of Psychological Medicine, Univ. of Wales Coll. of Medicine 1987–98; Prof. of Psychiatric Genetics and Dir Social, Genetic and Developmental Psychiatry Research Centre, Inst. of Psychiatry, King's Coll. London 1998–; Foundation Fellow Acad. of Medical Sciences (UK) 1998; Fattorini Prize, Leeds Univ. 1972. *Publications include:* Scientific Principles of Psychopathology, The New Genetics of Mental Illness, Seminars on Psychiatric Genetics, Essentials of Postgraduate Psychiatry, Behavioural Genetics (4th Edn), Measuring Psychopathology; many scientific papers and articles. *Leisure interests:* music (especially classical guitar), horse riding, running with my dogs. *Address:* Institute of Psychiatry, de Crespigny Park, London, SE5 8AF, England (Office). *Telephone:* (20) 7848-0871 (Office). *Fax:* (20) 7848-0866 (Office). *E-mail:* p.mcguffin@iop.kcl.ac.uk (Office).

McGUINNESS, Frank, M.PHIL.; Irish playwright and university lecturer; b. 29 July 1953, Buncrana, Donegal; s. of Patrick McGuinness and Celine McGuinness; ed University Coll. Dublin; Lecturer in English, Univ. of Ulster, Coleraine 1977–79, Univ. Coll. Dublin 1979–80, St Patrick's Coll., Maynooth 1984–97, Univ. Coll. Dublin 1997–; Dir Abbey Theatre, Dublin 1992–96; Hon. DLitt (Ulster) 2000; Harvey's Award, Evening Standard Drama Award, Ewart-Biggs Peace Prize, Cheltenham Literary Prize, Fringe First, Irish American Literary Prize 1992, Independent on Sunday Best Play 1992, New York Drama Critics' Award 1993, Writers' Guild Award 1993, Tony Award for Best Revival 1997; Officier des Arts et des Lettres. *Publications:* The Factory Girls 1982, Observe the Sons of Ulster Marching towards the Somme 1985, Baglady 1985, Innocence 1986, Rosmersholm, A Version 1987, Scout 1987, Yerma: A Version 1987, Carthaginians 1988, The Hen House 1989, Peer Gynt, A Version 1989, Mary and Lizzie 1989, Three Sisters, A Version 1990, The Bread Man 1990, The Threepenny Opera, A Version 1991, Someone Who'll Watch Over Me 1992, The Bird Sanctuary 1994, Hedda Gabler, A Version 1994, Uncle Vanya, A Version 1995, Booterstown: Poems 1995, Selected Plays: Vol. I 1996, The Dazzling Dark: Introduction 1996, A Doll's House: A Version 1996, The Caucasian Chalk Circle: A Version 1997, Electra: A Version 1997, Mutabilitie 1997, Dancing at Lughnasa: A Screenplay 1998, The Storm: A Version 1998, Dolly West's Kitchen 1999, The Sea With No Ships: Poems 1999, Miss Julie: A Version 2000, The Barbaric Comedies 2000. *Leisure interests:* walking, painting, botany. *Address:* Department of Anglo-Irish Literature, University College Dublin, Belfield, Dublin 4 (Office); 32 Booterstown Avenue, Dublin, Ireland.

McGUINNESS, Martin; Irish politician; b. 23 May 1950, Derry; m.; four c.; took part in secret London talks between Sec. of State for Northern Ireland and Irish Republican Army (IRA) July 1972; imprisoned for six months during 1973 in Irish Repub. after conviction for IRA membership; elected to Northern Ireland Ass., refused seat; stood against John Hume (q.v.) in gen. elections of 1982, 1987, 1992; MP for Mid-Ulster, House of Commons 1997–; mem. Ulster-Mid, N Ireland Ass. 1998–2000 (Ass. suspended Feb. 2000), 2000–02 (Ass.

suspended Oct. 2002); Minister of Educ. 1999–2002; spokesman for Sinn Féin, also mem. Nat. Exec.; involved in peace negotiations with British Govt. *Leisure interest:* fly-fishing. *Address:* Sinn Féin, 51–55 Falls Road, Belfast, BT12 4PD, Northern Ireland (Office). *Telephone:* (28) 9022-3000. *E-mail:* sinnfein@iol.ie (Office). *Website:* www.irlnet.com/sinnfein (Office).

McGWIRE, Mark David; American professional baseball player; b. 1 Oct. 1963, Pomona, Calif.; s. of John McGwire and Ginger McGwire; brother of Dan McGwire, former pro baseball player; m. Kathy McGwire (divorced); one s.; ed Univ. of South California; with Oaklands Athletics 1984–97; St Louis Cardinals 1997–; mem U.S. Olympic baseball team 1984; player World Series 1988–90; on All-Star team 1987–92, 1995–96, 1999; scored record 70 home runs during 1997–98 season; f. Mark McGwire Foundation for Children 1987; American League Rookie of the Year, Baseball Writers' Asscn of America 1987; Golden Glove Award 1990; Silver Slugger Award 1992; Sportsman of the Year (jtly. with Sammy Sosa), Sports Illustrated 1998, Player of the Month 1999, Player of the Year, Assoc. Press 1999. *Publications:* Mark McGwire: Home Run Hero (biog.) by Rob Rains 1999. *Address:* c/o St Louis Cardinals, Busch Stadium, 250 Stadium Plaza, St Louis, MO 63120, USA.

MACH, David Stefan, MA, RA; British sculptor; b. 18 March 1956, Methil, Fife; s. of Joseph Mach and Martha Cassidy; m. Lesley June White 1979; ed Buckhaven High School, Duncan of Jordanstone and Royal Colls. of Art; full-time sculptor 1982–; also occasional visiting lecturer; Visiting Prof. Edin. Coll. of Art 1999–; Prof. of Sculpture Royal Acad. 2000–; sculptures exhibited at galleries in England, Scotland, NY, São Paulo Biennale, Venice Biennale; City of Glasgow Lord Provost Prize 1992. *Leisure interests:* gardening, tennis, travelling, driving, films, television. *Address:* 64 Canonbie Road, Forest Hill, London, SE23 3AG, England. *Telephone:* (20) 8649-7947 (Office); (20) 8699-1668. *Fax:* (20) 8699-1211 (Home). *E-mail:* davidmach@davidmach.com (Office). *Website:* www.davidmach.com (Office).

MACHARSKI, HE Cardinal Franciszek, DTheol; Polish ecclesiastic; b. 20 May 1927, Cracow; ed Jagiellonian Univ., Cracow, Fribourg Univ., Switzerland; ordained priest 1950; engaged in pastoral work 1950–56; taught pastoral theology Pontifical Faculty of Theology, Cracow 1962–68; Rector, Cracow Seminary 1970–78; Archbishop Metropolitan of Cracow, 1979–; High Chancellor, Pontifical Acad. of Theology, Cracow; cr. HE Cardinal 1979, entitled S. Giovanni a Porta Latina; mem. Sacred Congregation for the Clergy 1979–, Sacred Congregation for Catholic Educ. 1979–, Sacred Congregation for Bishops 1983–, Council for Public Affairs 1984–88; mem. Council of Cardinals and Bishops 1988–; mem. Secr. for Non-Believers 1981–86, Congregatation for the Clergy 1999–, Congregation for the Evangelization of Peoples 1999–; Vice-Pres. Episcopate of Poland, Conf. 1979–94; mem. Main Council Episcopate of Poland 1996–, Episcopate Cttee for Gen. Ministry 1989–; Vice-Chair. Scientific Council of Episcopate of Poland, 1984–89, Episcopate Cttee for Ministry of Working People 1981; Chair. Episcopate Cttee for Laity 1979–91, Episcopate Cttee for Catholic Science 1981–94; mem. Episcopate Cttee for Ministry of Priesthood 1996–, Perm. Council of Episcopate of Poland 1996–2002; Chair. Second Ass. of Synod of Bishops of Europe 1999; Papal Legate to Int. Marian and Mariological Congress Kevelaer 1987, Nat. Eucharistic Congress, Bratislava 2000; Dr. hc (Fu Jen Catholic Univ., Taipei, Adamson Univ., Manila) 1989, (Acad. of Catholic Theology, Warsaw) 1992, (Pontifical Acad. of Theology, Cracow) 2000, (Jagiellonian Univ., Cracow) 2000; Order of Smile 1998; hon. citizen of many Polish cities and towns. *Publications:* Collections: Sermons at the Calvary Shrine 1994, To Serve with Wisdom 1994, From the See of St Stanislaus 1995; more than 250 articles, sermons, speeches and pastoral letters. *Address:* ul. Franciszkańska 3, 31-004 Cracow, Poland. *Telephone:* (12) 4294340, 6288110. *Fax:* (12) 4294405.

McHENRY, Donald F., MSc; American diplomatist; b. 13 Oct. 1936, St Louis, Mo.; m. Mary Williamson (divorced 1978); one s. two d.; ed Illinois State Univ., Southern Illinois and Georgetown Univs.; taught Howard Univ., Washington 1959–62; joined Dept of State 1963, Head Dependent Areas Section, Office of UN Political Affairs 1965–68; Asst to US Sec. of State 1969; Special Asst to Dept Counsellor 1969–71; lecturer, School of Foreign Service, Georgetown Univ., Guest Scholar, The Brookings Inst. and Int. Affairs Fellow, Council on Foreign Relations (on leave from State Dept) 1971–73; resgnd from State Dept 1973; Project Dir Humanitarian Policy Studies, Carnegie Endowment for Int. Peace, Washington 1973–76; served Pres. Carter's transition team 1976–77; Amb. and Deputy Perm. Rep. to UN 1977–79, Perm. Rep. 1979–81; Distinguished Prof. in the Practice of Diplomacy, School of Foreign Service, Georgetown Univ. 1981–; Dir Int. Paper Co., Coca Cola Co., Fleet Nat. Bank, Boston Financial Corpn, Inst. for Int. Econs, The American Ditchley Foundation, AT&T, GlaxoSmithKline PLC, mem. Council on Foreign Relations (fmr Dir); mem. Editorial Bd Foreign Policy Magazine; fmr Trustee The Brookings Inst., fmr Trustee Johnson Foundation, Ford Foundation; fmr Chair. Bd Africare; fmr Gov. Mayo Foundation; American Stock Exchange; Fellow American Acad. of Arts and Sciences; Superior Honor Award, Dept of State 1966. *Publication:* Micronesia: Trust Betrayed 1975. *Address:* c/o School of Foreign Service, Georgetown University, ICC 301, Washington, DC 20057, USA.

MACHI, Sueo, PhD; Japanese atomic energy scientist; b. 15 Jan. 1934; s. of Yosaku Machi and Kichi Machi; m. 1964; one s. one d.; ed Univs. of Shizuoka and Kyoto; employed in Japanese petrochemical industry 1959–63; joined

Takasaki Radiation Chem. Research Establishment (TRCRE) of Japan Atomic Energy Research Inst. (JAERI) 1963; Gen. Man. Process Lab. II, TRCRE 1972–78; Gen. Man. Radiation Eng Section, TRCRE 1978–80; Section Head, Industrial Applications and Chem. Section and Co-ordinator of Regional Co-operative Agreement for Asia and Pacific, IAEA; Deputy Dir Office of Planning, JAERI, Tokyo; Dir Dept of Research, TRCRE 1986, later Dir Dept of Devt; Dir-Gen. 1989–91; apptd. Deputy Dir-Gen. and Head of Dept of Research and Isotopes, IAEA 1991, later Deputy Dir.-Gen. Dept. of Nuclear Sciences; currently Sr. Man. Dir. Japan Atomic Industrial Forum, Nat. Co-ordinator Forum for Nuclear Co-operation in Asia; Dr. hc (Bucharest) 1995; Japan Chemical Soc. Prize 1969, The Iwatani Prize 1990, Minister of Science and Tech. Prize 1990. *Address:* Japan Atomic Industrial Forum, Toshin Building, 6th floor, 1-13, 1-chome Shimbashi, Minato-ku, Tokyo, 105-8605, Japan. *Telephone:* (3) 3508-2411. *Fax:* (3) 3508-2094.

MACHULSKI, Juliusz; Polish film director, screenwriter and producer; b. 10 March 1955, Olsztyn; s. of Jan Machulski and Halina Machulski; m. 1995; two c.; ed Film School Łódź, California Inst. of Arts, Valencia, USA; CEO Studio Filmowe Zebra; producer of about 25 films; numerous Polish and foreign film awards. *Films:* Direct Connection (TV) 1979, Vabank 1981, Sexmission 1983, Vabank II 1984, Kingsajz 1987, Déjà vu 1989, V.I.P. 1991, Squadron 199, Girl Guide 1995, Mothers, Wives and Mistresses (TV series) 1995–98, Kiler 1997, Two Kilers 1998, Money Isn't Everything 2001, The Blockbuster Movie 2003. *Television play:* The Jury 1995, Meridian 19 2003. *Publications:* Vabank 1 and 2 (scripts) 1986, V.I.P. (script) 1990, Kiler (script) 1998, Kiler 2 1999, Sexmission 2001. *Leisure interest:* reading. *Address:* Studio Filmowe Zebra, ul. Puławska 61, 02-595 Warsaw, Poland (Office). *Telephone:* (22) 845 54 84 (Office).

MACHUNGO, Mário Fernandes da Graça; Mozambican politician; b. 1 Dec. 1940, Chicuque-Maxixe, Inhambane Prov.; m. Maria Eugénia Paiva Cruz; two d.; ed Inst. for Higher Learning in Econ. and Financial Sciences (ISCEF), Portugal; became underground mem. Mozambique Liberation Front (FRELIMO) 1962; Pres. Students' Union, ISCEF 1964–65; subsequently expelled from ISCEF; completed studies 1969; returned to Mozambique, worked as economist with Nat. Devt Bank; apptd. Minister for Econ. Co-operation in transitional Govt 1974; Minister for Trade and Industry 1975–76, for Industry and Energy 1976–78, for Agric. 1978–80, for Agric. and Planning 1980–83, for Planning 1983–94, Prime Minister of Mozambique 1986–94; elected to Cen. Cttee and Political Bureau of FRELIMO Party 1977, re-elected 1983, elected to Secr. and fmr Sec. for Econ. Policy 1986; Chair. Banco Internacional de Moçambique 1995–. *Address:* Banco International de Moçambique, Avda Zedequias Mananhela 478, CP 2657, Maputo, Mozambique (Office). *Telephone:* (1) 429390 (Office). *Fax:* (1) 429389 (Office).

McINERNEY, Jay; American writer; m. 1st Linda Rossiter; m. 2nd Merry Raymond; m. 3rd Helen Bransford 1991; one s. one d.; ed Williams Univ. *Publications include:* Bright Lights, Big City 1984, Ransom 1986, Story of My Life 1988, Brightness Falls 1992, The Last of the Savages 1996, Model Behavior 1998, How It Ended 2000.

MACINNIS, Joseph Beverley, CM, MD; Canadian marine research scientist; b. 2 March 1937, Barrie, Ont.; s. of Allistair MacInnis and Beverly Saunders; m. Deborah J. Ferris 1971; one s. three d.; ed Univs. of Toronto and Pennsylvania; Pres. Undersea Research Ltd and has held consulting contracts for U.S. Navy, Smithsonian Inst., IBM, Canadian Ministry of State for Science and Tech. and Canadian Dept of Environment; est. SUBLIMNOS, Canada's first underwater manned station programme 1969; led 14 scientific expeditions into Arctic 1970–79 and during third expedition, SUB-IGLOO, world's first polar dive station established under ice; co-ordinated diving programme for ICE Station LOREX 1979; led team which discovered remains of English barque Breadalbane, sunk in 1853, 700 miles north of Arctic Circle in 340 feet of water; host, The New Wave (CBC television series) 1975–76, The Newfoundlanders: Voices from the Sea 1978; scientific consultant, Mysteries of the Sea (ABC) 1979; co-ordinator, Shot Point 260 (Texaco Canada film), Breakthrough (Dome Petroleum film) 1979; consultant Titanic Project 1985; first Canadian to dive to the Titanic 1987; Co-leader IMAX-Titanic Expedition 1991; has lectured and shown his films in all parts of world including Israel, Germany, Australia, the Philippines, USSR and Singapore; Pres. Undersea Research Ltd; mem. Canadian Environmental Advisory Council, Canadian Council of Fitness and Health; Fellow, Royal Canadian Geographical Soc.; Hon. FRCP; Hon. LLD; Dr. hc (Queen's) 1990. *Publications:* Underwater Images 1971, Underwater Man 1974, Coastline Canada 1982, Shipwreck Shores 1982, The Land that Devours Ships 1984, Titanic: In a New Light 1992, Saving the Oceans 1992 (Gen. Ed.), more than 30 scientific papers and articles in Scientific American, National Geographic Magazine etc. *Address:* 14 Dale Avenue, Toronto, Ont. M4W 1K4, Canada.

McINTOSH OF HUDNALL, Baroness (Life Peer), cr. 1999, of Hampstead in the London Borough of Camden; **Genista Mary McIntosh,** BA, FRSA; British theatrical administrator; b. 23 Sept. 1946, London; d. of Geoffrey Tandy and Maire Tandy; m. Neil S. W. McIntosh 1971 (divorced); one s. one d.; ed Hemel Hempstead Grammar School, Univ. of York; Casting Dir, RSC 1972–77, Planning Controller 1977–84, Sr Admin. 1986–90, Assoc. Producer 1990; Exec. Dir Royal Nat. Theatre 1990–96, 1997–2002; Chief Exec. Royal Opera House Jan.–May 1997; Principal, The Guildhall School of Music and Drama 2002–; Dir Marmont Man. Ltd 1984–86; Dr hc (York) 1998. *Leisure interests:* music, gardening, reading. *Address:* The Guildhall School of Music and Drama, London, EC2Y 8DT, England.

McINTYRE, Sir Donald Conroy, Kt, CBE, OBE; British bass opera singer; b. 22 Oct. 1934, Auckland, NZ; s. of George Douglas and Hermyn McIntyre; m. Jill Redington 1961; three d.; ed Mt. Albert Grammar School, Auckland, Auckland Teachers' Training Coll. and Guildhall School of Music, London; Prin. Bass, Sadler's Wells Opera 1960–67; with Royal Opera House, Covent Garden 1967–; annual appearances at Bayreuth Festival 1967–81; frequent int. guest appearances; Hon. DMus (Auckland) 1992; Fidelio Medal A.I.D.O. 1989, NZ Award for outstanding contribs., Festival of the Arts 1990. *Roles include:* Wotan and Wanderer (Der Ring), Dutchman (Der Fliegende Holländer), Telramund (Lohengrin), Barak (Die Frau ohne Schatten), Pizzaro (Fidelio), Golaud (Pelléas et Mélisande), Kurwenal and King Marke (Tristan and Isolde), Gurnemanz, Klingsor and Amfortas (Parsifal), Heyst (Victory), Jochanaan (Salome), Macbeth, Scarpia (Tosca), the Count (Marriage of Figaro), Nick Shadow (The Rake's Progress), Hans Sachs (Die Meistersinger), Dr. Schöne (Woyzeck), Cardillac (Cardillac Hindemith), Rocco (Fidelio), The Doctor (Der Freischütz), Prospero (Un Re In Asloto), Sarastro (Magic Flute), Balstrode (Peter Grimes), Telramund (Lohengrin), Prus (The Makropoulos Case), Rheingold, The Ring (video); recordings include Pelléas et Mélisande, Oedipus Rex, Il Trovatore, etc. *Leisure interests:* farm, tennis, walking. *Address:* c/o Ingpen & Williams, 26 Wadham Road, London, SW15 2LR (Agent); Fox Hill Farm, Jackass Lane, Keston, Bromley, Kent, BR2 6AN, England (Home). *Telephone:* (1689) 855368 (Home). *Fax:* (1689) 860724 (Home).

MacINTYRE, Iain, MB, CH.B., PhD, DSc, F.R.C.PATH., FRCP, FMedSci, FRS; British professor of chemical pathology; b. 30 Aug. 1924, Glasgow; s. of John MacIntyre and Margaret Fraser Shaw; m. Mabel Wilson Jamieson 1947; one d.; ed Jordanhill Coll. School, Univs. of Glasgow and London; Asst Clinical Pathologist, United Sheffield Hosps. and Hon. Demonstrator in Biochemistry, Univ. of Sheffield 1948–52; Registrar in Chemical Pathology, Royal Postgraduate Medical School, Hammersmith Hosp., London 1952–54, Sir Jack Drummond Memorial Fellow 1954–56, Asst Lecturer in Chemical Pathology 1956–59, Lecturer 1959–63, Reader 1963–67, Prof. of Endocrine Chem. 1967–82, Dir Endocrine Unit 1967–89, Chair. Academic Bd 1986–89; Prof. of Chemical Pathology, Univ. of London 1982–89, now Research Dir William Harvey Research Inst., St Bartholomew's and the Royal London School of Medicine and Dentistry, Queen Mary Coll., London; Visiting Scientist, NIH, Bethesda, Md, USA 1960–61; Visiting Prof. of Medicine, Univ. of Calif., San Francisco 1964, Univ. of Melbourne 1980; Visiting Lecturer, USSR Acad. of Sciences, Moscow 1978; Visiting Prof. St George's Hosp. Medical School 1989–; A. J. S. McFadzean Lecture, Univ. of Hong Kong 1981; Transatlantic Lecture, American Endocrine Soc. 1987; Per Edman Memorial Lecturer, Melbourne 1990; Vice-Pres. English Chess Assen 1989–; Founder Fellow Acad. of Medical Sciences 1998; Hon. mem. Asscn of American Physicians 1998; Hon. MD (Turin), (Sheffield) 2002; Gairdner Int. Award, Toronto 1967, Elsevier Int. Award 1992, Paget Foundation John B. Johnson Award 1995. *Publications:* numerous articles on endocrinology. *Leisure interests:* tennis, chess, music. *Address:* William Harvey Research Institute, Charterhouse Square, London, EC1M 6BQ (Office); Great Broadhurst Farm, Broad Oak, Heathfield, E. Sussex, TN21 8UX, England (Home). *Telephone:* (20) 7882-6168 (Office); (1435) 883515 (Home). *Fax:* (20) 7882-6162 (Office); (1435) 883611 (Home). *E-mail:* i.macintyre@qmul.ac.uk (Office); calc@broadoak .demon.co.uk (Home).

McINTYRE, Very Rev. John, CVO, MA, BD, DLitt, DD, DHL, FRSE; British ecclesiastic and university professor; b. 20 May 1916, Glasgow; s. of John C. McIntyre and Annie Summers; m. Jessie B. Buick 1945; two s. one d.; ed Bathgate Acad. and Univ. of Edinburgh; Minister, Church of Scotland, Fenwick Parish Church 1943–45; Hunter Baillie Prof. of Theology St Andrew's Coll. Univ. of Sydney 1946–56, Prin. 1950–56; Prof. of Divinity, Univ. of Edin. 1956–86, Dean Faculty of Divinity and Prin. New Coll. 1968–74, Acting Prin. and Vice-Chancellor 1973–74, 1979; Chaplain to HM The Queen in Scotland 1974–86, Chaplain Extraordinary 1974, 1986–; Dean, Order of the Thistle 1974–89; Moderator, Gen. Ass. of Church of Scotland 1982; Vice-Pres. Royal Soc. of Edin. 1983–86; Fulbright Visiting Prof. Union Theological Seminary, New York 1953; Warfield Lecturer, Princeton Theol. Seminary 1966; Laidlaw Lecturer, Knox Coll. Toronto 1987; Sprunt Lecturer, Union Theological Seminary, Richmond, Va 1988; Hon. Fellow St Andrew's Coll., Univ. of Sydney 1991–; Dr hc (Edin.) 1987. *Publications:* St Anselm and his Critics 1954, The Christian Doctrine of History 1957, On the Love of God 1962, The Shape of Christology 1966, Faith, Theology and Imagination 1987, The Shape of Soteriology 1992, Theology After the Storm (Ed. and Introduction by G. D. Badcock) 1997, The Shape of Pneumatology 1997. *Address:* 317 Mayfield Court, 27 West Savile Terrace, Edinburgh, EH9 3DT, Scotland. *Telephone:* (131) 667-1203.

MACK, Connie (Cornelius McGillicuddy), III; American politician; b. 29 Oct. 1940, Philadelphia; s. of Cornelius M. and Susan (née Sheppard) McGillicuddy; m. Ludie Priscilla 1960; one s. one d.; ed Univ. of Florida, Sun Bank, Ft Myers, Fla; Vice-Pres. Business Devt First Nat. Bank, Ft Myers 1968–71; Sr Vice-Pres., Dir Sun Bank, Cape Coral, Fla 1971–75; Pres., Dir Florida Nat. Bank, Cape Coral 1972–82; mem. US House of Reps from Fla 1983–89, Senator from Florida 1989–2000; Republican Conf. Chair. 105th Congress 1996; Dir Fed. Reserve Bd, Miami 1981–82; Sr Policy Adviser, Shaw

Pittman 2001–; mem. Bd of Dirs, Chair. Palmer Drug Abuse Program, Cape Coral, Subcttee on Econ. Policy 1999–; mem. Bd of Dirs Cape Coral Hosp.; Republican. *Address:* c/o Shaw Pittman, 2300 North Street, NW, Washington, DC 200375, USA (Office).

MACK SMITH, Denis, CBE, FBA, MA; British author and fmr professor of history; b. 3 March 1920, London; s. of Wilfrid Mack Smith and Altiora Gauntlett; m. Catharine Stevenson; two d.; ed St Paul's Cathedral Choir School, Haileybury Coll., Peterhouse, Cambridge; Fellow, Tutor, Peterhouse, Cambridge 1947, now Hon. Fellow; Sr Research Fellow, All Souls Coll., Oxford 1962, Emer. Fellow 1987–; Extraordinary Fellow, Wolfson Coll. 1987–2000, Hon. Fellow 2000–; Chair. Asscn for the Study of Modern Italy 1988–; Grande Ufficiale, Italian Order of Merit, Hon. Citizen of Santa Margherita Ligure. *Publications:* Cavour and Garibaldi in 1860 1954, Garibaldi 1957, Medieval and Modern Sicily 1968, The Making of Italy 1796–1866 1968, Italy: a modern history 1969, Victor Emanuel, Cavour and the Risorgimento 1971, Mussolini's Roman Empire 1976, Cento Anni di Vita Italiana attraverso il Corriere della Sera 1978, Mussolini 1981, Cavour 1985, Italy and its Monarchy 1989, Mazzini 1993, Modern Italy 1997, La Storia Manipolata 1998. *Leisure interests:* music, travel. *Address:* White Lodge, Osler Road, Headington, Oxford, OX3 9BJ, England. *Telephone:* (1865) 762878.

McKANE, William, MA, PhD, DLitt, DD, FBA, FRSE; British academic; b. 18 Feb. 1921, Dundee; s. of Thomas and Jemima S. McKane; m. Agnes M. Howie 1952; three s. two d.; ed Univs. of St Andrews and Glasgow; RAF 1941–45; Lecturer in Hebrew, Univ. of Glasgow 1953, Sr Lecturer 1956; Prof. of Hebrew and Oriental Languages, Univ. of St Andrews 1968–90, Emer. Prof. 1990–, Dean, Faculty of Divinity 1973–77; Prin. St Mary's Coll., St Andrews 1982–86; Fellow Nat. Humanities Centre, NC, USA 1987–88; Corresp. mem. Akademie der Wissenschaften in Göttingen; Hon. DD (Edin.) 1984; Burkitt Medal (British Acad.) 1985. *Publications:* Prophets and Wise Men 1965, Proverbs, A New Approach 1970, Studies in the Patriarchal Narratives 1979, Jeremiah 1–25 (introduction and critical commentary) 1986, Selected Christian Hebraists 1989, A Late Harvest 1995, Jeremiah 26–52 (introduction and critical commentary) 1996, Micah: Introduction and commentary 1998; articles in British and European journals. *Leisure interest:* walking. *Address:* 51 Irvine Crescent, St Andrews, Fife, KY16 8LG, Scotland. *Telephone:* (1334) 473797.

MACKAY, Charles Dorsey, MA, MBA; British businessman; b. 14 April 1940, Congleton; s. of late Brig. Kenneth Mackay and Evelyn Ingram; m. Annmarie Joder-Pfeiffer 1964; two s. (one deceased) one d.; ed Cheltenham Coll., Queens' Coll. Cambridge and European Inst. of Business Admin. (INSEAD), Fontainebleau; with BP Co. 1957–69, McKinsey & Co. 1969–76, Pakhoed Holding N.V. Rotterdam 1976–81; Dir Chloride Group PLC 1981–86, Chair. Overseas Div. 1981–85, Power Electronics Div. 1985–86; Inchcape Dir PLC 1986–96; Chair. and Chief Exec. Inchcape Pacific Ltd 1986–91, Chief Exec. 1991–96, Deputy Chair. 1995–96; Dir (non-exec.) Hongkong and Shanghai Banking Corpn Ltd 1986–92, HSBC Holdings 1992–98, Midland Bank 1992–93, British Airways 1993–96, Gucci Group NV 1997–2001, Johnson Matthey PLC 1999–, Eurotunnel Group 1997– (Deputy Chair. 1999–2001, Chair. 2001–); Deputy Chair. Thistle Hotels PLC 1996–; Chair. TDG PLC 2000–; mem. Bd INSEAD 2000–. *Leisure interests:* travel, tennis, skiing, classical music, opera, chess. *Address:* Eurotunnel Group, Golden Cross House, 8 Duncannon Street, London, WC2N 4JF, England (Office). *Telephone:* (20) 7484-5684 (Office). *Fax:* (20) 7484-5155 (Office). *E-mail:* charles.mackay@eurotunnel.com (Office). *Website:* www .eurotunnel.co.uk (Office).

MacKAY, Sir Donald Iain, Kt, MA, FRSE, FRSGS; British economist; b. 27 Feb. 1937, Kobe, Japan; s. of William MacKay and Rhona MacKay; m. Diana Marjory Raffan 1961; one s. two d.; ed Dollar Acad., Aberdeen Univ.; with English Electric Co. 1959–62; Lecturer Aberdeen Univ. 1962–65, Prof. 1971–76; Lecturer Glasgow Univ. 1965–68, Sr Lecturer 1968–71; Consultant to Sec. of State for Scotland 1971–; Chair. Pieda PLC 1974–97; lecturer BAAS 1974; Lister Prof. Heriot-Watt Univ. 1976–82, Hon. Prof. 1990–; Chair. Scottish Enterprise 1993–97, Chair. DTZ Pieda Consulting 1997–, Scottish Science Trust 1997–99, Edin. Business School 1997–; Dir Grampian Holdings 1987–99, Chair. 1999–; mem. Scottish Econ. Council 1985–; Dr. hc (Stirling) 1994; Hon. DLitt (Aberdeen) 1994. *Publications:* Geographical Mobility and the Brain Drain 1969, Local Labour Markets and Wage Structures 1970, Labour Markets under Different Employment Conditions 1971, The Political Economy of North Sea Oil 1975, The Economics of Self-Government 1977; numerous articles in econ. and political journals. *Leisure interests:* bridge, golf, tennis. *Address:* Newfield, 14 Gamekeeper's Road, Edinburgh, EH4 6LU, Scotland. *Telephone:* (131) 336-1936.

MACKAY OF CLASHFERN, Baron (Life Peer), cr. 1979, of Eddrachillis in the District of Sutherland; **James Peter Hymers Mackay,** KT, PC, QC, MA, LLB, FRSE; British advocate; b. 2 July 1927, Scotland; s. of James Mackay and Janet Hymers; m. Elizabeth Gunn Hymers 1958; one s. two d.; ed George Heriot's School, Edin., Univ. of Edin., Trinity Coll. Cambridge; Lecturer in Math., Univ. of St Andrews 1948–50; Major Scholar, Trinity Coll., Cambridge 1947, Sr Scholar 1951; admitted to Faculty of Advocates 1955; QC 1965; Vice-Dean Faculty of Advocates 1973–76, Dean 1976–79, Lord Advocate 1979–84; Sheriff Prin., Renfrew and Argyll 1972–74; Commr Northern Lighthouses 1972–84; Dir Stenhouse Holdings Ltd 1976–78; Senator of Coll. of Justice in Scotland 1984–85; Lord of Appeal in Ordinary 1985–87; Lord Chancellor 1987–97; Chancellor Heriot-Watt Univ. 1991–; Ed.-in-Chief Halsbury's Laws of England 1998–; Part-time mem. Scottish Law Comm. 1976–79; mem.

Insurance Brokers' Registration Council 1978–79; Fellow, Inst. of Taxation, American Coll. of Trial Lawyers, Int. Acad. of Trial Lawyers; Hon. Fellow, Inst. of Civil Engineers, Trinity Coll., Cambridge, Girton Coll., Cambridge; Hon. FRCPE; Hon. F.R.C.S.(E), Hon. FRCOG; Hon. LLD (Edin., Dundee, Strathclyde, Aberdeen, St Andrews, Birmingham, Newcastle, Bath, Leicester, De Montfort, Glasgow, Cambridge Robert Gordon Nat. Law School of Indiana); Hon. DCL (Newcastle), (Oxford) 1998. *Publication:* Armour on Valuation for Rating (Sr Ed.) 1961, 1971. *Leisure interests:* walking, travel, country pursuits. *Address:* House of Lords, Westminster, London, SW1A 0PW, England.

McKECHNIE, Dame Sheila, DBE; British civil servant; b. 3 May 1948, Falkirk; ed Falkirk High School, Edinburgh and Warwick Univs.; Research Asst Oxford Univ. 1971–72; Asst Gen. Sec. Wall Paper Workers Union Staff Section 1972–74; Workers' Educ. Assoc. Tutor Manchester 1974–76; Health and Safety Officer ASTMS 1976–85; Dir Shelter 1985–94, Consumers' Assoc. 1995–; (Dir non-exec.) Bank of England 1998–; Hon. DUniv (Open) 1994; Hon. DSc (Edin.) 1994. *Address:* Consumers' Association, 2 Marylebone Road, London, NW1 4DF, England (Office). *E-mail:* do@which.co.uk (Office).

McKEE, John Angus; Canadian business executive; b. 31 Aug. 1935, Toronto, Ont.; s. of John W McKee and Margaret E Phippen; m. Susan E Harley 1970; one s. one d.; ed Trinity Coll. School, Port Hope, Ont. and Univ. of Toronto; joined the Patiño Mining Corpn 1962, Asst to Pres. 1963, Vice-Pres. (Corporate Devt) 1966; Man. Dir Consolidated Tin Smelters Ltd 1968–71; owner J. A. McKee and Assocs. Ltd 1971–83; Pres. and CEO Canadian Occidental Petroleum Ltd 1983–93; Chair., Pres., CEO Gulfstream Resources Canada 1993–2001; Dir Stone and Webster Canada Ltd, Stone and Webster Inc. (USA), Teradyne Canada Ltd, CVI Ltd and others; mem. Bd of Govs., Trinity Coll. School, Port Hope. *Leisure interests:* skiing, shooting.

MacKELLAR, Hon. Michael John Randal, B.SCI.AGR., MA; Australian agricultural scientist, politician and business executive; b. 27 Oct. 1938, Sydney; s. of Geoffrey Neil and Colleen Randal MacKellar; m. Robin Morey Smith 1969; two s. one d.; ed Sydney Church of England Grammar School, Sydney Univ., Balliol Coll., Oxford; New South Wales Dept of Agric. 1961–69; mem. for Warringah, NSW, House of Reps. 1969–94; Parl. Sec. to Leader of Opposition 1973–74; Shadow Minister for Immigration 1974–75; Minister for Immigration and Ethnic Affairs 1975–79, Minister Assisting the Treas. 1978–79, Minister for Health 1979–82, Minister Assisting the Prime Minister 1979–80, Minister for Home Affairs and Environment Feb.–March 1981; Shadow Minister for Foreign Affairs 1983–84, for Science and Special Minister of State 1984–85; Deputy Opposition Leader of the House 1985; Opposition Whip 1989; mem. numerous House of Reps. Cttees. 1970–90; Chair. House of Reps. Standing Cttee on Environment and Conservation 1982–83; mem. first Australian Parl. del. to People's Repub. of China 1973, Leader del. to UN Habitat Conf. 1976; mem. NSW Advisory Cttee for Australian Broadcasting Comm. 1973–75, Advisory Council of CSIRO 1984, Council of Australian Nat. Univ. 1970–76; CEO Plastics and Chemicals Industries Asscn 1994–97; COO Baker Medical Research Inst. 1997–; Bd mem. Sydney Paralympic Games Organizing Cttee 1997–2000; Chair. Australia/N.Z. Food Authority 1998–, Franchising Policy Council of Australia 1998–, FAO Centre for Excellence, Monash Univ. 1999–; Liberal Party. *Leisure interests:* tennis, cricket, golf, reading, photography. *Address:* 19/158-160 Wattletree Road Malvern, Vic. 3144, Australia.

McKELLEN, Sir Ian Murray, Kt, CBE, BA; British actor; b. 25 May 1939, Burnley, Lancs.; s. of Denis Murray McKellen and Margery (Sutcliffe) McKellen; ed Bolton School, St Catharine's Coll., Cambridge; council mem. British Actors' Equity 1970–71; Cameron Mackintosh Prof. of Contemporary Theatre, Oxford Univ. 1991; Hon. DLitt (Nottingham) 1989, (Oxford) 1991; Clarence Derwent Award 1964; Variety and Plays and Players awards 1966; Actor of the Year (Plays and Players) 1976; Soc. of W End Theatres Award for Best Actor in Revival 1977, for Best Comedy Performance 1978, for Best Actor in a New Play 1979, Tony Award 1981, Drama Desk 1981, Outer Critics Circle Award 1981; Royal TV Soc. Performer of the Year 1983; Laurence Olivier Award 1984, 1991; Evening Standard Best Actor Award 1984, 1989, Screen Actor's Guild Award for best supporting Actor 2000. *Films include:* Alfred the Great 1969, The Promise 1969, A Touch of Love 1969, Priest of Love 1981, The Keep 1982, Plenty, Zina 1985, Scandal 1988, The Ballad of Little Jo 1992, I'll Do Anything 1992, Last Action Hero 1993, Six Degrees of Separation 1993, The Shadow 1994, Jack and Sarah 1994, Restoration 1994, Richard III 1995, Bent 1996, Swept from the Sea 1996, Apt Pupil 1997, Gods and Monsters 1998, X-Men 1999, Lord of the Rings: The Fellowship of the Ring 2001, Lord of the Rings: The Two Towers 2002, X-Men 2 2003, Emile 2003, Lord of the Rings: The Return of the King 2003. *Stage appearances:* first stage appearance as Roper (A Man for All Seasons), Belgrade Theatre, Coventry 1961; numerous other parts include title-roles in Henry V, Luther, Ipswich 1962–63; Aufidius (Coriolanus), Arthur Seaton (Saturday Night and Sunday Morning), title-role in Sir Thomas More, Nottingham Playhouse 1963–64; London début as Godfrey (A Scent of Flowers), Duke of York's Theatre 1964; Claudio (Much Ado About Nothing), Protestant Evangelist (Last Goodnight), Capt. de Foenix (Trelawny of the Wells), Nat. Theatre Co. 1965; Alvin (A Lily in Little India), Hampstead and St Martin's 1965–66; Andrew Cobham (Their Very Own and Golden City), Royal Court 1966; title-part in O'Flaherty, VC and Bonaparte (The Man of Destiny), Mermaid 1966; Leonidik (The Promise), Oxford Playhouse, Fortune and Henry Miller (Broadway début) 1966–67; Tom (The White Liars), Harold Gorringe (Black Comedy), Lyric 1968; Richard

II (Edin. Festival 1969), Edward II, Hamlet, Prospect Theatre Co. 1968–71, British tour, Mermaid and Piccadilly Theatres; Darkly (Billy's Last Stand), Theatre Upstairs 1970; Capt. Plume (The Recruiting Officer), Corporal Hill (Chips With Everything), Cambridge Theatre Co. 1970; Svetlovidov (Swan Song), Crucible, Sheffield 1971; founder-mem. Actors' Co., Edin. Festival 1972 and touring as Giovanni ('Tis Pity She's A Whore), Page-Boy (Ruling the Roost), Prince Yoremitsu (The Three Arrows), title-role in Michael, the Wood Demon, Footman (The Way of The World), then Knots, Shaw Theatre, Edgar (King Lear), Brooklyn Acad. and Giovanni, Wimbledon 1973–74; début with RSC as Dr. Faustus (Edin. Festival) 1974; title-role in The Marquis of Keith, Philip the Bastard (King John), Aldwych 1974–75; Colin (Ashes), Young Vic. 1975; Aubrey Bagot (Too True to Be Good), also at Globe, Romeo, Macbeth, Bernick (Pillars of the Community), Face (The Alchemist) Stratford season 1976; Langevin (Days of the Commune) 1976–78; organized RSC British tour of Twelfth Night (Toby Belch) and Three Sisters (Andrei); Max (Bent), Royal Court and Criterion 1979, Amadeus (New York) 1980, Short List (Hampstead Theatre Club), Cowardice (Ambassadors) 1983; int. tour of one-man show Acting Shakespeare (LA and Ritz Theatre, New York) 1984, (London) 1987; Assoc. Dir Nat. Theatre of Great Britain (also actor) 1984–86; Venice Preserv'd (Pierre), Coriolanus; Wild Honey (Platonov); McKellen/Petherbridge Nat. Theatre Group: Duchess of Malfi (Bosola), Real Inspector Hound (Hound), The Critic (Mr Puff), The Cherry Orchard (Lopakhin); Wild Honey (Va Theatre, New York), USA Shakespeare tour 1987; Henceforward (Vaudeville Theatre) 1988–89; Othello (Iago) RSC 1989; Royal Nat. Theatre: Bent (Max), King Lear (Kent), Richard III 1990–92 (World Tour then U.S. Tour), Napoli Milionaria 1991, Uncle Vanya 1992, An Enemy of the People 1997, Peter Pan 1997; The Seagull, Present Laughter, The Tempest (W Yorks. Playhouse) 1998–99, Dance of Death (Broadhurst Theatre, NY) 2001. *TV appearances include:* David Copperfield 1965, Ross 1969, Richard II, Edward II and Hamlet 1970, Hedda Gabler 1974, Macbeth, Every Good Boy Deserves Favour, Dying Day 1979, Acting Shakespeare 1981, Walter, The Scarlet Pimpernel 1982, Walter and June 1983, Countdown to War 1989, Othello 1990, Tales of the City 1993, Cold Comfort Farm 1995, Rasputin 1996. *Publication:* William Shakespeare's Richard III (jtly.) 1996. *Address:* c/o ICM, 76 Oxford Street, London, W1N 0AX, England. *Telephone:* (20) 7636-6565. *Fax:* (20) 7323-0101. *Website:* www.mckellen.com.

McKENNA, Frank Joseph, LLB, PC, QC; Canadian politician and lawyer; b. 19 Jan. 1948, Apohaqui, Kings Co., NB; s. of Joseph McKenna and Olive Moody; m. Julie Friel 1972; two s. one d.; ed St Francis Xavier Univ., Queen's Univ. and Univ. of NB; Special Asst to Pres., Privy Council 1971; Research Asst Constitutional Law Unit, PMO 1973; partner, Martin, Lordon, McKenna, Martin & Bowes; Counsel, McInnes, Cooper 1998–; mem. NB Bar Asscn, Canadian Bar Asscn; mem. Legis. Ass. 1982–97; Leader, NB Liberal Party 1985–97; Premier, Prov. of NB 1987–97; Dir numerous prov., nat. and internet corpns; Hon. LLD (Univ. of NB) 1988, (Mount Allison) 1991, (St Francis Xavier) 1994, (St Thomas) 1996, (Ryerson Polytechnic) 1999, (Royal Mil. Coll.) 2000; Vanier Award 1988, Econ. Developer of the Year, Econ. Developers' Asscn of Canada 1993, Distinction Award, Canadian Advanced Tech. Asscn 1996. *Leisure interests:* reading, sports and current affairs. *Address:* 655 Main Street, P.O. Box 1368, Moncton, NB, E1C 8T6, Canada (Office). *Telephone:* (506) 857-8970 (Office). *Fax:* (506) 857-4095 (Office). *E-mail:* frank.mckenna@mcinnescooper.com (Office).

McKENNA, Stephen Francis, DFA; British/Irish painter; b. 20 March 1939, Ashford, Middx; s. of the late Maj. James McKenna and Violet (née Kinnear) McKenna; one s.; ed HE Cardinal Vaughan Memorial School, London, De La Salle Coll., Hong Kong, Andover Grammar School, St Illtyd's Coll., Cardiff, Welbeck Coll., Royal Mil. Acad., Sandhurst, Slade School of Fine Art; Sr Lecturer in Painting, Canterbury Coll. of Art 1965–68; Visiting Lecturer, Goldsmiths Coll., Univ. of London 1968–72; lived in Bonn 1971–79, Brussels 1979–84; invited to Berlin by Kunstler Programm DAAD 1984; in London, Donegal and Umbria 1985–; Guest Prof. of Painting, Hochschule für Bildende Künste, Braunschweig, Germany, 1995–. *Solo exhibitions include:* Barry Barker Gallery, London, 1978, 1979, Edward Totah Gallery, London 1985, 1986, 1988, Gallery Seno, Milan, Kunsthalle, Düsseldorf 1986, Raab Gallery, Berlin, ICA, London, Sander Gallery, NY 1985, Van Abbemuseum Eindhoven, Gallery Springer, Berlin 1984, Museum of Modern Art, Oxford, Gallery Isy Brachot, Brussels, Gallery Swajcer, Antwerp 1983, Orchard Gallery, Derry 1981, 1988, Kerlin Gallery, Dublin 1988–90, 1993, 1995, Galeria Manuela Boscolo, Busto Arsizio 1990, Galería Estampa, Madrid 1990, 1992, Galeria Inge Baecker, Cologne 1990, Sala Uno, Rome 1991, Casa Masaccio, Valdarno 1991, Kerlin Gallery, Dublin 1992, Galerie des Beaux Arts, Brussels 1992, Galerie Nikolaus Fischer, Frankfurt Main 1993, Irish Museum of Modern Art, Dublin 1993, Fruitmarket Gallery, Edin. 1994, Arts Council Gallery, Belfast 1994, Reeds Wharf Gallery, London 1995; works in numerous public collections. *Publications:* numerous catalogues; texts: 'On Landscape' 1984, Parables of Painting 1980. *Leisure interest:* conversation. *Address:* Crocknafeola, Killybegs, County Donegal, Ireland.

McKENNA, Thomas Patrick (T.P.); Irish actor; b. 7 Sept. 1931, Cavan; s. of Ralph McKenna and Mary McKenna; m. May White 1956; four s. one d.; joined Abbey Theatre Co., Dublin 1954, Hon. Life Mem. 1966. *Films include:* Siege of Sidney Street, Girl with Green Eyes, Ferry Cross the Mersey, Young Cassidy, Ulysses, Charge of the Light Brigade, Anne of the Thousand Days, Perfect Friday, Villain, Straw Dogs, Portrait of the Artist as a Young Man, A Child's Voice, Exposure, The Outsider, Silver Dream Racer, The Scarlet and the Black, To the Lighthouse, Mehmed my Hawk, Doctor and the Devils, Honour, Profit and Pleasure, Cat's Eyes, Anything Legal Considered, O.S.S., Strong Medicine, Pascali's Island, Red Scorpion, Valmont, Monarch, Kings in Grass Castles, The American 1998, Longitude 2000, The Great Céile War 2002. *Television includes:* Jack the Ripper, Dr. Who, Miss Marple, Shoot to Kill (TV film), Parnell and the Englishwoman, The Chief (series 2, 3, 4), Rumpole of the Bailey, Events at Drimaghleen (TV film), The Law Lords (TV film), Lovejoy, Casualty, Heartbeat, Stendhal's Scarlet and Black, Kavanagh QC, The Ambassador, Morse, Ballykissangel, Anytime Now, The Bill, Rockface. *Stage:* Molly Sweeney by Brian Friel, world premiere, Gate Theatre, Dublin 1994 and Almeida Theatre, London, Hirst in No Man's Land, Pinter Festival at Gate Theatre 1997, Brian Friel's version of Uncle Vanya, world premiere, Gate Theatre 1998 and Lincoln Center Festival, New York 1999. *Radio:* more than 100 radio plays for BBC. *Leisure interests:* reading, sport, music. *Address:* 28 Claverley Grove, London, N3 2DH, England (Home). *Telephone:* (20) 8346-4118 (Home). *Fax:* (20) 8346-4118 (Home).

McKENNA, Virginia; British actress and conservationist; b. 7 June 1931, London; d. of Terence McKenna and Anne Marie Dennis; m. Bill Travers (died 1994); three s. one d.; ed Herons Ghyll, Horsham, Sussex, Herschel, Cape Town, S. Africa, Cen. School of Speech and Drama, London; f. Zoo Check Charitable Trust (now The Born Free Foundation) 1984; film debut in The Second Mrs Tanqueray. *TV appearances include:* Romeo and Juliet 1955 (Best Actress Award), Lovejoy 1991, The Camomile Lawn, Ruth Rendell Mysteries 1992, September (mini-series) 1995 and documentary The Lion at World's End 1971, The Scold's Bridle 1998, The Deep Blue Sea, A Passage to India, Cheap in August, Puccini, Girls in Uniform, Peter Pan, Waters of the Moon, The Whistleblower. *Films include:* Father's Doing Fine, The Cruel Sea, Simba, The Ship that Died of Shame, A Town Like Alice (BAFTA Best Actress Award), The Smallest Show on Earth, The Barretts of Wimpole Street, Carve Her Name With Pride 1957 (Prix Femina, Belgium), The Passionate Summer, Wreck of the Mary Deare, Two Living, One Dead, Born Free1965 (Best Actress Award, Variety Club), Ring of Bright Water, An Elephant Called Slowly, Waterloo, Swallows and Amazons, The Disappearance, Holocaust-2000, Staggered, Sliding Doors. *Stage appearances include:* The King And I 1979 (Swet Award), Hamlet (RSC) 1985, Winnie 1988, A Little Night Music, The Devils (RSC), The Beggar's Opera (RSC), A Winter's Tale, As You Like It, The River Line, Penny for a Song, I Capture the Castle, A Personal Affair, The Bad Samaritan. *Radio:* The Devils, The Flame Trees of Thika, A Town Like Alice. *Publications:* On Playing with Lions (with Bill Travers), Some Of My Friends Have Tails, Into the Blue 1992, Journey to Freedom 1997; Co-Ed. and Contrib. Beyond the Bars, Headlines from the Jungle (verse) 1990, Back to the Blue 1997. *Leisure interests:* classical music, poetry, walking in the countryside, gardening. *Address:* c/o Derek Webster, A.I.M., 5 Denmark Street, London, W.C.1B 3NH, England; Born Free Foundation, 3 Grove House, Foundry Lane, Horsham, West Sussex, RH13 5PL (Office). *Telephone:* (1403) 240170 (Office). *Fax:* (1403) 327838 (Office). *E-mail:* bffdorking@btopenworld.com (Office).

McKENNON, Keith Robert, BS; American business executive; b. 25 Dec. 1933, Condon, Ore.; s. of Russell McKennon and Lois Edgerton; m. Patricia Dragon 1961; three s.; ed Pendleton High School, Golden Gate Coll. and Oregon State Univ.; joined Dow Chemical USA 1955; Dir Public Affairs, The Dow Chemical Co. 1978, Vice-Pres. 1980, Vice-Pres. Agricultural Products 1982; Vice-Pres. Product Dept Man. Dow Chemical USA Jan. 1983; Group Vice-Pres. Global Agricultural Products, Legal, Employee Relations and Public Affairs, The Dow Chemical Co. April 1983; mem. Bd of Dirs. The Dow Chemical Co. 1983–, Group Vice-Pres. and Dir of Research and Devt 1985, Exec. Vice-Pres. 1987–92; Pres. Dow Chemical USA 1987–90; Chair., CEO Dow Corning Corpn 1992–94; Chair. Pacific Corpn 1994–99; Deputy Chair. Scottish Power PLC 1999–2001; Dir Chemical Bank and Trust Co., Chemical Financial Corpn, Dowell Schlumberger Inc., Dow Corning Corpn, Marion Merrill Dow, Pacific Corpn, Nat. Legal Center for the Public Interests etc; Gold Medal, Soc. of Chemical Industry 1994. *Leisure interests:* tennis, fishing, reading. *Address:* c/o Pacific Corporation, 825 N E Multnomah Street, Suite 2000, Portland, OR 97232 (Office); 6079 N. Paradise View Drive, Paradise Valley, AZ 85253, USA. *Telephone:* (602) 553-0141 (Home); (503) 226-0225 (summer). *Fax:* (602) 553-0182 (Home). *E-mail:* kmck96@aol.com (Home).

McKENZIE, Dan Peter, MA, PhD, FRS; British geologist; b. 21 Feb. 1942, Cheltenham; s. of W. S. and N. M. (née Fairbrother) McKenzie; m. Indira M. Misra 1971; one s.; ed Westminster School and King's Coll., Cambridge; Fellow, King's Coll. 1965–73, 1977–, Sr Asst in Research, Dept of Earth Sciences, Univ. of Cambridge 1969–73, Asst Dir of Research 1973–79, Reader in Tectonics 1979–85, Prof. of Earth Sciences 1985–96, Royal Soc. Research Prof. 1996–; Foreign Assoc. NAS; Balzan Prize 1981, Japan Prize 1990, Crafoord Prize 2002. *Publications:* papers in professional journals. *Leisure interest:* gardening. *Address:* Bullard Laboratories, Madingley Rise, Madingley Road, Cambridge, CB3 0EZ, England.

MACKENZIE, Gen. Sir Jeremy John George, GCB, OBE; British army officer; b. 11 Feb. 1941, Nairobi, Kenya; s. of late Lt-Col John William Elliot Mackenzie and of Valerie Mackenzie (née Dawes); m. Elizabeth Lyon (née Wertenbaker) 1969; one s. one d.; ed Duke of York School, Nairobi, Kenya, Staff Coll.; commissioned Queen's Own Highlanders 1961; Canadian Forces Staff Coll. 1974; Brigade Maj. 24 Airportable Brigade 1975–76; CO 1 Queen's Own Highlanders, N Ireland and Hong Kong 1979–82; Instructor Staff Coll. 1982–83; Col Army Staff Duties 2 1983–84; Commdr 12th Armoured Brigade 1984–86; Service Fellowship King's Coll., Univ. of London 1987; Deputy

Commdt 1987–89; Commdt 1989, Staff Coll.; GOC 4th Armoured Div. BAOR 1989–91; Col Commdt WRAC 1990–92, AG Corps 1992–98, APTC 1997–; Col Highlanders 1994–2001; Commdr 1st (British) Corps 1991–92, NATO's ACE Rapid Reaction Corps (ARRC) 1992–94, Deputy Supreme Allied Commdr, Europe 1994–98, now consultant to NATO aspirant cos.; ADC (Gen.) 1997–99; Gov. Royal Hosp. Chelsea 1999–; Brig. Queen's Bodyguard of Scotland (RCA); Commdr US Legion of Merit 1997 (second award 1999); Hungarian Presidential Order of Merit (1st Class) 1998, Czech Defence Minister's Order of Merit (1st Class) 1998, Bulgarian Order of the Madara Horseman (1st Class) 1999, Slovenian Gold Medal of the Armed Forces 2003. *Publication:* The British Army and the Operational Level of War 1989. *Leisure interests:* shooting, fishing, painting. *Address:* Royal Hospital, Chelsea, London, SW3 4SR, England.

MacKENZIE, Kelvin; British journalist; b. 22 Oct. 1946; m. Jacqueline M. Holland 1969; two s. one d.; joined The Sun as sub-editor 1972, subsequently Night Ed.; apptd Man. Ed. New York Post 1978; rejoined The Sun as Night Ed. 1980; Night Ed. Daily Express Feb. 1981; rejoined The Sun, Ed. 1981–94; Man. Dir BSkyB Jan.–Oct. 1994 (resgnd); Dir Mirror Group PLC 1994–98, Deputy Chief Exec. and Group Man. Dir 1997–98; Chair., CEO Talk Radio UK 1998–2000; now Chair., CEO The Wireless Group. *Address:* The Wireless Group, 18 Hatfields, London, SE1 8DJ, England (Office).

McKENZIE, Kevin; American ballet dancer, choreographer and director; b. 29 April 1954, Burlington, Vt; s. of Raymond James McKenzie and Ruth Davison; ed Acad. of Washington School of Ballet; Soloist with Nat. Ballet of Washington 1972–74; Prin. dancer, Joffrey Ballet 1974–78; Prin. dancer, American Ballet Theater 1979–91, Artistic Dir 1992–; Perm. guest artist, Washington Ballet 1990–91, Artistic Assoc. 1991–92; Assoc. Dir New Amsterdam Ballet 1984–; Hon. PhD (St Michael's Coll.); Silver Medal Varna Int. Ballet Competition 1972. *Directed* (with Susan Jones): Don Quixote (A.B.T.) 1995, Swan Lake (A.B.T.) 2000. *Address:* American Ballet Theater, 890 Broadway, New York, NY 10003, USA. *Telephone:* (212) 477-3030. *Fax:* (212) 254-5938.

McKENZIE SMITH, Ian, OBE, PRSA; British artist; b. 3 Aug. 1935, Montrose, Angus; s. of James McKenzie Smith and Mary Benzie; m. Mary Rodge Fotheringham 1963; two s. one d.; ed Robert Gordon's Coll., Aberdeen, Gray's School of Art, Aberdeen, Hospitalfield Coll. of Art, Arbroath, Aberdeen Coll. of Educ.; teacher of art, Fife 1960–63; educ. officer, Council of Industrial Design, Scottish Cttee 1963–68; Dir Aberdeen Art Gallery and Museums 1968–89; City Arts and Recreation Officer, Aberdeen 1989–96, Sec. Aberdeen Highland Games 1989–96; Deputy Pres. and Treas. RSA 1990–91, Sec. 1991–98, Pres. 1998–; Trustee Nat. Galleries of Scotland 1999–; mem. Scottish Arts Council 1970–77 (Chair. Art Cttee 1975–77), Scottish Museums Council 1980–87 (Chair. Industrial Cttee 1985–87); mem. Advisory Council on Export of Works of Art 1991–, Museums and Galleries Comm. 1997–2000; mem. Bd Friends of RSA 1972–, RSA Enterprises 1972–; Hon. RA 1999; trustee of numerous funds; Hon. LLD (Aberdeen) 1991; Hon. D.Art (The Robert Gordon Univ., Aberdeen) 2000; RSA Guthrie Award 1971, RSA Gillies Award 1980, R.S.W. May Marshall Brown Award 1980. *Work in many perm. collections including:* Scottish Nat. Gallery of Modern Art, Scottish Arts Council, Arts Council of NI, Aberdeen Art Gallery and Museums, Glasgow Art Gallery and Museums, Nuffield Foundation, Carnegie Trust, RSA, Robert Fleming Holdings, IBM, Deutsche Morgan Grenfell, Grampian Hosps. Art Trust, The Lord Chancellor, City Art Collection Edinburgh, Perth Art Gallery, Hunterian Gallery Glasgow. *Address:* Royal Scottish Academy, The Mound, Edinburgh, EH2 2EL (Office); 70 Hamilton Place, Aberdeen, AB15 5BA, Scotland (Home). *Telephone:* (131) 558-7097 (Office); (1224) 644531 (Home). *Fax:* (131) 557-6417 (Office); (1224) 626253 (Home). *E-mail:* info@royalscottishacademy.org (Office); imckenziesmith@supanet.com (Home). *Website:* www.royalscottishacademy.org (Office).

MACKERRAS, Sir Charles, Kt, AC, CBE; British conductor; b. 17 Nov. 1925, Schenectady, USA of Australian parentage; s. of Alan and Catherine Mackerras; m. Judith Wilkins 1947; two d.; ed Sydney Grammar School, NSW Conservatoire and Prague Acad. of Music; Prin. Oboist Sydney Symphony Orchestra 1943–46; Staff Conductor Sadler's Wells Opera 1948–53; Prin. Conductor BBC Concert Orchestra 1954–56; guest opera conductor at Covent Garden, English Nat. Opera, Berlin State Opera, Hamburg State Opera, Vienna State Opera, etc. 1956–66; First Conductor, Hamburg State Opera 1966–69; Musical Dir, Sadler's Wells Opera, later English Nat. Opera 1970–77, Chief Guest Conductor, BBC Symphony Orchestra 1976–79; Chief Conductor Sydney Symphony Orchestra 1982–85; Prin. Guest Conductor Royal Liverpool Philharmonic Orchestra 1986–88; Musical Dir Welsh Nat. Opera 1987–92, Conductor Emer. 1993–; Prin. Guest Conductor Scottish Chamber Orchestra 1992–95, Conductor Laureate 1995–; Prin. Guest Conductor San Francisco Opera 1993–96 (Conductor Emer. 1996–), Royal Philharmonic Orchestra 1993–96, Czech Philharmonic Orchestra 1997–, Philharmonia Orchestra 2002–; Music Dir Orchestra of St Luke's 1998–2001; Pres. Trinity Coll. of Music 2000–; guest conductor in Europe, USA, Canada and Australia; Hon. RAM 1969, FRCM 1987, FRNCM, FTCL; Hon. Fellow St. Peter's Coll. Oxford 1999; Hon. DMus (Hull) 1990, (Nottingham) 1991, (York, Masaryk, Czech Repub. and Griffith, Australia) 1994, (Oxford) 1997, (Prague Acad. of Music) 1999, (Napier) 2000; Prix Caecilia 1999, Preis der Deutschen Schallplattenkritik 1999, Chopin Prize and Lifetime Achievement Award, Midem, Cannes 2000; Evening Standard Award for Most Outstanding Achievement in Opera 1977, Janáček Medal 1978, Gramophone Record of the

Year 1977, 1980, 1999, Gramophone Best Opera Recording 1983, 1984, 1994, 1999, Grammy Award for Best Opera 1981; Medal of Merit, Czech Repub. 1996, Asscn of British Orchestras Award 2001. *Arrangements:* Ballets: Pineapple Poll 1951, Lady and the Fool 1954, Melbourne Cup 1965; Arthur Sullivan's Lost Cello Concerto 1986. *Recordings:* numerous, notably Janáček, Handel, Mozart operas and symphonies, Brahms and Beethoven symphonies. *Publications:* musical articles in various magazines. *Leisure interests:* languages, yachting. *Address:* 10 Hamilton Terrace, London, NW8 9UG, England. *Telephone:* 020 7286-4047. *Fax:* 020 7289-5893.

MACKEY, James Patrick, BA, LPh, BD, STL, DD, PhD; Irish professor of theology; b. 9 Feb. 1934, Ireland; s. of Peter Mackey and Esther Morrissey; m. Noelle Quinlan 1973; one s. one d.; ed Mount St Joseph Coll., Nat. Univ. of Ireland, Pontifical Univ., Maynooth and Queen's Univ., Belfast; ordained priest 1958; lecturer in Philosophy Queen's Univ. 1960–66, Philosophy and Theology St John's Coll., Waterford 1966–69; Assoc. Prof. of Philosophical and Systematic Theology Univ. of San Francisco 1969–73, Prof. 1973–79; Visiting Prof. Univ. of Calif. Berkeley 1974–75; Thomas Chalmers Prof. of Theology Univ. of Edin. 1979–99, Dean of Faculty of Divinity 1984–88, Dir Grad. School and Assoc. Dean 1995–98, Prof. Emer. 1999–, Fellow Faculty of Divinity 1999–2002; Visiting Prof. Univ. of Dublin Trinity Coll. 2000–; curricular consultant Univ. Coll., Cork 2000–; Visiting Prof. Dartmouth Coll., NH 1989, Univ. of San Francisco 1990; British Acad. Research Scholarship 1964–65; scripted and presented TV series The Hall of Mirrors 1984, The Gods of War 1986, Dir Derry City Int. Conf. on the Cultures of Europe 1992; Ed. Studies in World Christianity 1995–. *Publications:* Life and Grace 1966, Morals, Law and Authority (Ed.) 1969, The Problems of Religious Faith 1974, Jesus, The Man and the Myth 1979, The Christian Experience of God as Trinity 1983, Religious Imagination (Ed.) 1986, Modern Theology 1987, An Introduction to Celtic Christianity 1989, Power and Christian Ethics 1994, The Cultures of Europe (Ed.) 1994, The Critique of Theological Reason 2000, Religion and Politics in Ireland at the Turn of the Millennium (Ed.) 2003. *Leisure interest:* sailing. *Address:* School of Hebrew, Biblical and Theological Studies, Trinity College, Dublin 2 (Office); 15 Glenville Park, Dunmore Road, Waterford, Ireland (Home). *Telephone:* (1) 6081297 (Office); (51) 844624 (Home). *E-mail:* jpmackey_ie@yahoo.co.uk (Home).

MACKIE, Robert Gordon; American costume and fashion designer; b. 24 March 1940, Monterey Park, Calif.; s. of Charles Robert Smith and Mildred Agnes (Smith) Mackie; m. Marianne Wolford 1960 (divorced); one s.; ed Chouinard Art Inst.; mem. staff Edith Head 1962–63; designed costumes for film Divorce, American Style 1966; Co-Designer for films Lady Sings the Blues 1972, Funny Lady 1975; designer for numerous TV shows including: Brigadoon 1966, Alice Through the Looking Glass 1967, Carousel 1967, Kismet 1967, Fred Astaire Show 1968, Diana Ross and The Supremes 1969, Carol Burnett Show 1967–77, Sonny and Cher Comedy Hour 1971, Cher 1976, Sonny and Cher Show 1976–77, Diahann Carroll Summer Show 1976; Co-Designer theatrical productions On The Town 1971, Lorelei 1972, The Best Little Whorehouse Goes Public 1994; Emmy Award (co-recipient) 1967, Emmy Award 1969, 1976, 1983, Costume Designers' Guild Award 1968. *Publication:* Dressing for Glamour 1969. *Address:* Bob Mackie Ltd, 530 7th Avenue, New York, NY 10018, USA.

McKILLOP, Thomas Fulton Wilson, PhD; British business executive and scientist; b. 19 March 1943; s. of Hugh McKillop and Annie McKillop (née Wilson); m. Elizabeth Kettle 1966; one s. two d.; ed Irvine Royal Acad., Univ. of Glasgow, Centre de Mécanique Ondulatoire Appliquée Paris; research scientist, ICI Corp. Laboratory 1969–75; Head of Natural Products Research, ICI Pharmaceuticals Ltd 1975–78, Dir of Research, France 1978–80, Chem. Man. 1980–84, Gen. Man. of Research 1984–85, Gen. Man. Devt 1985–89, Tech. Dir 1989–94; Dir (non-exec.) Amersham Int. PLC 1992–97, Nycomed Amersham PLC 1997–2000, Lloyds TSB PLC 1999–; CEO Astra Zeneca 1994– (fmrly Zeneca), Dir 1996–; Pro-Chancellor, Univ. of Leicester 1998–; mem. Soc. for Drug Research, ACS, Royal Inst., Trustee Darwin Trust of Edin. 1995–; Hon. LLD (Manchester) 1999, Hon. DSc (Glasgow) 2000, (Leicester) 2000, (Huddersfield) 2000. *Leisure interests:* carpentry, music, reading, walking. *Address:* c/o AstraZeneca Group PLC, 15 Stanhope Gate, London, W1Y 6LN, England (Office). *Telephone:* (20) 7304-5000 (Office). *Fax:* (20) 7304-5192 (Office).

MACKIN, Martin, MA; Irish politician; b. 23 Dec. 1963, Drogheda, Co. Louth; s. of Thomas Mackin and Josephine Mackin; ed Univ. Coll. Dublin, Coll. of Commerce, Dublin, Nat. Univ. of Ireland; press officer, Fianna Fáil 1992–95, Dir Fianna Fáil European Office 1995–98, Gen. Sec. Fianna Fáil 1998–. *Leisure interests:* music, current affairs, reading. *Address:* c/o Áras De Valera, 65–66 Lower Mount Street, Dublin 2, Ireland (Office). *Telephone:* (1) 676-1551. *Fax:* (1) 678-5960. *E-mail:* martin@fiannafail.ie (Office). *Website:* www.fiannafail.ie (Office).

McKINLEY, Brunson; American diplomatist; b. 8 Feb. 1943, Fla USA; s. of Kenneth William McKinley and Lois Rebecca McKinley; m. Nancy McKinley (née Padlon); one s. one d.; ed Univ. of Chicago, Harvard Univ.; US Army 1965–70, with service in Viet Nam; diplomatic service of the US with posts in Italy, China, Vietnam, UK, Germany; Amb. to Haiti 1986–89, specialized in refugee and migration issues 1990–94, helped defuse Haitian-Cuban boat crisis 1994, developed trans-Atlantic dialogue on migration, successfully directed US participation in comprehensive action plan for Indo-Chinese refugees; US Bosnia Humanitarian Coordinator 1995–98; prin. compiler of refugee annex of Dayton Accords; Dir-Gen. Int. Org. for Migration 1998–; Bronze Star, Air Medal, Award for Valor. *Address:* International Organization for Migration, 17 route des Morillons, CP 71, 1211 Geneva 19 (Office); 15 Grande Rue, CH-1260 Nyon, Switzerland (Home). *Telephone:* (22) 717-9383 (Office). *Fax:* (22) 717-9440 (Office). *E-mail:* bmckinley@iom.int (Office).

MCKINNELL, Henry A. (Hank), BA, MBA, PhD; American pharmaceutical company executive; ed Univ. of BC, Canada, Stanford Univ. Grad. School of Business; joined Pfizer Inc., Tokyo 1971, served in various exec. positions including Pres. Pfizer Asia, Hong Kong, Pres. Medical Technology Group, Chief Financial Officer, Pres. Pharmaceutical Group 1997, Pres. and COO 1999–2000, Pres. and CEO 2000–01, Chair. and CEO 2001–; Dir Chamber of Commerce, Business Council, Royal Shakespeare Co. America, Japan Soc.; mem. Bd Dirs Moody's Corpn, ExxonMobil Corpn, John Wiley & Sons Inc., Business Roundtable (BRT), Business-Higher Educ. Forum (B-HEF); Chair. Advisory Council, Stanford Univ. Grad. School of Business; mem. Presidential Advisory Council on HIV/AIDS (PACHA); Fellow NYC Public Library, NYC Police Foundation, Channel Thirteen/WNET, J.F. Kennedy Center for the Performing Arts. *Address:* Pfizer Inc., 235 East 42nd Street, New York, NY 10017-5755, USA (Office). *Website:* www.pfizer.com (Office).

MCKINNON, Rt Hon. Donald Charles, PC; New Zealand politician; b. 27 Feb. 1939; s. of Maj.-Gen. Walter McKinnon and Anna McKinnon (née Plimmer); m. 1st Patricia Maude Moore 1964 (divorced 1995); three s. one d.; m. 2nd Clare de Lore 1995; one s.; fmr estate agent and farm man. consultant; Nat. Party MP for Albany 1978–; fmr Jr and Sr Govt Whip, Opposition Spokesperson for Defence and Health; Sr Opposition Whip 1984–87; Deputy Prime Minister 1990–96; Leader of the House 1993–96; Minister of Foreign Affairs and Trade, of Pacific Island Affairs, 1990–99, for Disarmament and Arms Control 1996–99; Sec.-Gen. of the Commonwealth 2000–; DComm (Lincoln, NZ), Dr hc (four Univs of Manchester) 2002. *Leisure interests:* rugby, cricket, jogging, tennis, reading, riding. *Address:* Commonwealth Secretariat, Marlborough House, Pall Mall, London, SW1Y 5HX, England. *Telephone:* (20) 7747-6103 (Office). *Fax:* (20) 7930-2299 (Office). *E-mail:* secretary-general@commonwealth.int (Office). *Website:* www.thecommonwealth.org (Office).

MCKINNON, Sir James, Kt, CA, FCMA; British public servant; b. 1929; ed Camphill School; Co. Sec. Macfarlane Lang & Co. Ltd, Glasgow 1955–65; Business Consultant, McLintock, Moores & Murray, Glasgow 1965–67; Finance Dir Imperial Group PLC, London 1967–86; Dir-Gen. Office of Gas Supply 1986–93; Chair. Ionica 1993–98; Chair. (non-exec.) Cowie Group 1994–; Pres. Inst. of Chartered Accountants of Scotland 1985–86. *Publications:* articles in professional publs. *Leisure interest:* skiing. *Address:* c/o Ionica PLC, Cowley Road, Cambridge, CB4 4AS, England.

MACKINTOSH, Sir Cameron Anthony, Kt; British theatre producer; b. 17 Oct. 1946, Enfield; s. of late Ian Mackintosh and of Diana Mackintosh; ed Prior Park Coll. Bath; stage hand then Asst Stage Man. Theatre Royal, Drury Lane; worked with Emile Littler 1966, with Robin Alexander 1967; producer 1969–; Chair. Cameron Mackintosh 1981–; Dir Delfont Mackintosh 1991–, My Fair Lady 2001; Hon. Fellow St Catherine's Coll. Oxford; Observer Award for Outstanding Achievement, Laurence Olivier Award 1991. *Productions:* Little Women 1967, Anything Goes 1969, Trelawney 1972, The Card 1973, Winnie the Pooh 1974, Owl and the Pussycat Went to See 1975, Godspell 1975, Side by Side by Sondheim 1976, Oliver! 1977, Diary of a Madam 1977, After Shave 1977, Gingerbread Man 1978, Out on a Limb 1978, My Fair Lady 1979, Oklahoma! 1980, Tomfoolery 1980, Jeeves Takes Charge 1981, Cats 1981, Song and Dance 1982, Blondel 1983, Little Shop of Horrors 1983, Abbacadabra 1983, The Boyfriend 1984, Les Misérables 1985, Café Puccini 1985, Phantom of the Opera 1986, Follies 1987, Miss Saigon 1989, Just So 1990, Five Guys Named Moe 1990, Moby Dick 1992, Putting it Together 1992, The Card 1992, Carousel 1993, Oliver! 1994, Martin Guerre 1996, The Fix 1997, Oklahoma! 1999, The Witches of Eastwick 2000, My Fair Lady 2001. *Leisure interests:* cooking, taking holidays. *Address:* Cameron Mackintosh Ltd, 1 Bedford Square, London, WC1B 3RA, England. *Telephone:* (20) 7637-8866. *Fax:* (20) 7436-2683.

MACKINTOSH, Nicholas John, DPhil, FRS; British professor of experimental psychology; b. 9 July 1935; s. of Dr. Ian Mackintosh and Daphne Mackintosh; m. 1st Janet Ann Scott 1960 (divorced 1978); one s. one d.; m. 2nd Bundy Wilson 1978 (divorced 1989); two s.; m. 3rd Leonora Caroline Brosan 1992; one s.; ed Winchester and Magdalen Coll., Oxford; lecturer, Univ. of Oxford 1964–67; Resident Prof., Dalhousie Univ. 1967–73; Prof., Univ. of Sussex 1973–81; Prof. of Experimental Psychology and Professorial Fellow of King's Coll., Cambridge 1981–2002; Resident Fellow, Lincoln Coll., Oxford 1966–67; Visiting Prof., Univ. of Pennsylvania 1965–66, Univ. of Hawaii 1972–73, Bryn Mawr Coll. 1977; Ed. Quality Journal of Experimental Psychology 1977–84. *Publications:* Fundamental Issues in Associative Learning (ed. with W. K. Honig) 1969, Mechanisms of Animal Discrimination Learning (with N. S. Sutherland) 1971, the Psychology of Animal Learning 1974, Conditioning and Associative Learning 1983, Animal Learning and Cognition 1994, Cyril Burt: fraud or framed? 1995, IQ and Human Intelligence 1998, papers in psychological journals. *Address:* C/o King's College, Cambridge, CB2 1ST, England. *Telephone:* (1223) 351386.

MCKNIGHT, Hon. William Hunter; Canadian politician; b. 12 July 1940, Elrose, Sask.; m. Beverley Ogden; two s.; ed Wartime and Elrose, Sask.; fmr farmer and business exec.; MP 1979–93, fmr Chair. House Standing Cttee on Agric., fmr mem. Transport Cttee, Man. and mem.'s Services Cttee, Finance,

Trade and Econ. Affairs Cttee, fmr Progressive Conservative Party spokesperson on Canadian Wheat Bd, on Int. Trade, fmr Deputy Opposition House Leader; Progressive Conservative Party Minister of Labour 1984–86, of Indian Affairs and Northern Devt 1986–89, of Defence 1989–91, of Agric. 1991–93, of Energy, Mines and Resources 1993; Chair. NAFTA Trade Consultants Inc. 1993; f. Dir, Chair., Anvil Range Mining Corpn 1994–; Dir Gamblers Restaurant Inc. 1995–, Marvas Devts. Ltd 1995–, Mid-North Resources Ltd 1995–, R.E.S. Int. Inc. 1995, Sci-Tec Instruments Inc. 1995–; Hon. Consul, Ecuador 1995. *Address:* c/o Progressive Conservative Party of Canada, 275 Slater Street, Suite 501, Ottawa, Ont. K1P 5H9, Canada.

McKUEN, Rod; American author and composer; b. 29 April 1933, Oakland, Calif.; has appeared in numerous films, concerts and on TV, composer of film scores and background music for TV shows; composer-lyricist of many songs; Pres. of numerous record and book cos.; mem. Bd of Dirs. American Nat. Theater of Ballet, Animal Concern; mem. Bd of Govs. Nat. Acad. of Recording Arts and Sciences; mem. A.S.C.A.P., Writers Guild, A.F.T.R.A., MPA, NARAS; Pres. of American Guild of Variety Artists (AGVA); mem. Bd of Dirs. Calif. Music Theater; Grand Prix du Disque 1966, 1974, 1975, 1982, Golden Globe 1969, Motion Picture Daily Award 1969; LA Shrine Club Award 1975, Freedoms Foundation 1975, Horatio Alger Award 1976; Brandeis Univ. Literary Trust Award 1981, Freedoms Foundation Patriot Medal 1981, Salvation Army Man of the Year 1983, Rose d'Or, Cannes 1986, Myasthenia Gravis Community Service Award 1986. *Works include:* Symphony Number One, Concerto for Guitar and Orchestra, Concerto for Four Harpsichords, Seascapes for Piano and Orchestra, Adagio for Harp and Strings, Piano Variations, Concerto Number Three for Piano and Orchestra 1972, The Plains of My Country (ballet) 1972, The City (orchestral suite) 1973, Ballad of Distances (orchestral suite) 1973, Bicentennial Ballet 1975, Symphony Number Three 1975, over 200 record albums. *Film scores:* Joanna 1968, The Prime of Miss Jean Brodie 1969, Me, Natalie 1969, A Boy Named Charlie Brown 1970, Come to Your Senses 1971, Scandalous John 1971, Wildflowers 1971, The Borrowers 1973, Lisa Bright and Dark 1973, Awareness of Emily 1976, The Unknown War 1979, Man to Himself 1980, Portrait of Rod McKuen 1982, Death Rides this Trail 1983, The Living End 1983, The Beach 1984. *Publications:* And Autumn Came 1954, Stanyan Street and Other Sorrows 1966, Listen to the Warm 1967, Twelve Years of Christmas 1968, In Someone's Shadow 1969, With Love 1970, Caught in the Quiet 1970, Fields of Wonder 1971, The Carols of Christmas 1971, And to Each Season 1972, Beyond the Boardwalk 1972, Come to Me in Silence 1973, America–An Affirmation 1974, Seasons in the Sun 1974, Alone, Moment to Moment 1974, The McKuen Omnibus 1975, Celebrations of the Heart 1975, My Country 200 1975, I'm Strong but I Like Roses, Sleep Warm, Beyond the Boardwalk 1976, The Sea Around Me ... The Hills Above 1976, Finding My Father (biographical) 1977, Coming Close to Earth 1977, Hand in Hand . . . 1977, Love's Been Good to Me 1979, We Touch the Sky 1979, Looking for a Friend 1980, An Outstretched Hand 1980, The Power Bright and Shining 1980, Too Many Midnights 1981, Rod McKuen's Book of Days 1981, The Beautiful Strangers 1981, The Works of Rod McKuen, Vol. 1, Poetry 1982, Watch for the Wind . . . 1982, Rod McKuen—1984 Book of Days 1983, The Sound of Solitude 1983, Suspension Bridge 1984, Another Beautiful Day 1985, Valentines 1985, Intervals 1986. *Address:* P.O. Box 2783, Los Angeles, CA 90028, USA.

MacLACHLAN, Kyle, BFA; American film actor; b. 22 Feb. 1959, Yakima, Wash.; ed Univ. of Washington, Seattle; stage appearances in regional Shakespeare productions and off-Broadway in Palace of Amateurs. *Films include:* Dune 1984, Blue Velvet 1986, The Hidden 1988, Don't Tell Her It's Me 1990, The Doors 1991, Where the Day Takes You 1992, The Trial 1993, Twin Peaks: Fire Walk With Me 1992, Rich in Love 1993, Against the Wall 1994, The Flintstones 1994, Roswell 1994, Showgirls 1995, Trigger Effect 1996, Mad Dog Time 1996, One Night Stand 1997, X-Change 2000, Hamlet 2000, Timecode 2000, Perfume 2001, Me Without You 2001, Miranda 2002. *Plays:* Palace of Amateurs, Minetta Lane Theatre (off Broadway), New York, On An Average Day, Comedy Theatre, London 2002. *Television includes:* Northwest Passage, The O'Conners, Twin Peaks 1990–91, Sex and the City 2000–. *Address:* U.T.A., 9560 Wilshire Boulevard, 5th Floor, Beverly Hills, CA 90212, USA; c/o Kathryn Fleming, PFD, Drury House 34–43 Russell Street, London, WC2B 5HA, England.

McLACHLIN, Beverley, MPh; Canadian judge; b. 7 Sept. 1943, Pincher Creek, Alberta; d. of Ernest Gletz and Eleanora Kruschell; m. 1st Rory McLachlin (died 1988); one s.; m. 2nd Frank McArdle 1992; ed Univ. of Alberta, Edmonton; practised law with Wood, Moir, Hyde & Ross (Edmonton) 1968–71; called to the Bar of BC; practised law with Bull, Housser and Tupper (Vancouver) 1972–75; Assoc. Prof. Univ. of BC 1975–81; named to Co. Court of Vancouver 1981, Supreme Court of BC, BC Court of Appeal 1986–88; Chief Justice of the Supreme Court of BC 1988–89; sworn in as a Justice of the Supreme Court of Canada 1989; Chief Justice of Canada Jan. 2000–; Hon. LL.D (Toronto) 1995, (York) 1999, (Law Soc. Upper Canada) 2000, (Ottawa) 2000, (Calgary) 2000, (Brock Univ.) 2000, (Simon Fraser Univ.) 2000, (Victoria) 2000, (Alberta) 2000, (Lethbridge) 2001, (Bridgewater State Coll.) 2001, (Mount St Vincent Univ. 2002, (PEI) 2002. *Leisure interests:* hiking, swimming, cross-country skiing. *Address:* Supreme Court of Canada, Supreme Court Building, 301 Wellington Street, Ottawa, Ont., K1A 0J1, Canada (Office). *Telephone:* (613) 992-6940 (Office). *Fax:* (613) 952-3192 (Office).

McLAGLEN, Andrew V.; British film director; b. 28 July 1920, London; s. of Victor McLaglen; ed Univ. of Va. *Television includes:* Gunsmoke, Have

Gun–Will Travel, Perry Mason, Rawhide, The Lineup, The Lieutenant, The Dirty Dozen, The Next Mission, On Wings of Eagles, The Blue and the Gray, The Shadow Riders, Travis McGee. *Films include:* Gun the Man Down 1956, Man in the Vault 1956, The Abductors 1957, Freckles 1960, The Little Shepherd of Kingdom Come 1961, McLintock 1963, Shenandoah 1965, The Rare Breed 1966, Monkeys, Go Home! 1967, The Way West 1967, The Ballad of Josie 1968, The Devil's Brigade 1968, Bandoleroi 1968, Hellfighters 1969, The Undefeated 1969, Chisum 1970, One More Train to Rob 1971, Fool's Parade 1971, Something Big 1971, Cahill, U.S. Marshal 1973, Mitchell 1975, The Log of the Black Pearl 1975, Stowaway to the Moon 1975, Banjo Hackett: Roamin' Free 1976, The Last Hard Men 1976, Murder at the World Series 1977, Breakthrough Sergeant Steiner 1978, The Wild Geese 1979, North Sea Hijack 1980, The Sea Wolves 1981, Deprisa, Deprisa 1981, Sweet Hours 1982, Antonieta 1982, The Shadow Riders 1982, The Blue and the Gray 1982, Carmen 1983, Travis McGee 1983, Sahara 1983, Return to the River Kwai, Eye of the Widow 1989.

MacLAINE, Shirley; American film actress, writer and film director; b. 24 April 1934, Richmond, Va; d. of Ira Beaty and Kathlyn MacLean; sister of Warren Bull Beatty; m. Steve Parker 1954; one d.; ed grammar school and Lee High School, Washington; fmr chorus girl and dancer; Star of the Year Award (Theater Owners of America) 1967; Best Actress Award for role in Desperate Characters, Berlin Film Festival 1971; Lifetime Achievement Award, Berlin Film Festival 1999, Life Achievement Award, Malibu Film Festival 2001. *Films include:* The Trouble With Harry, Artists and Models, Around The World in 80 Days, Hot Spell, The Matchmaker, Can-Can, Career, The Apartment, Two For The Seesaw, The Children's Hour, Irma La Douce, What A Way To Go, The Yellow Rolls-Royce, Gambit, Woman Times Seven, The Bliss of Mrs. Blossom, Sweet Charity, Two Mules For Sister Sara, Desperate Characters, The Possessions of Joel Delaney, The Turning Point 1977, Being There 1979, Loving Couples 1980, The Change of Seasons 1981, Slapstick 1981, Terms of Endearment (Acad. Award for Best Actress) 1984, Out on a Limb 1987, Madame Sousatzka (Golden Globe Award for Best Actress) 1989, Steel Magnolias 1989, Waiting for the Light 1990, Postcards from the Edge 1990, Used People 1993, Wrestling Ernest Hemingway 1994, Guarding Tess 1994, Mrs Westbourne 1995, The Evening Star 1995, Mrs. Winterbourne 1996, The Celluloid Closet, Evening Star, Looking for Lulu, Bet Bruce, Bruno (also Dir). *Revues:* If My Friends Could See Me Now 1974, To London With Love 1976, London 1982, Out There Tonight 1990. *Television films:* The West Side Waltz 1994, Joan of Arc, These Old Broads 2001. *Video:* Shirley MacLaine's Inner Workout 1989. *Produced and Co-directed:* The Other Half of the Sky–A China Memoir 1973. *Publications:* Don't Fall Off the Mountain 1971, The New Celebrity Cookbook 1973, You Can Get There From Here 1975 (Vols 1 and 2 of autobiog.), Out on a Limb (Vol. 3) 1983, Dancing in the Light 1985 (Vol. 4), It's All in the Playing (Vol. 5) 1987, Going Within (Vol. 6) 1989, Dance While You Can (Vol. 7) 1991, My Lucky Stars (Vol. 8) 1995, The Camino 2000. *Address:* MacLaine Enterprises Inc., 25200 Malibu Road, Suite 4, Malibu, CA 90265, USA (Office). *Telephone:* (310) 317-8500. *Fax:* (310) 317-8504. *Website:* shirleymaclaine.com.

MacLANE, Saunders, PhD; American mathematician; b. 4 Aug. 1909, Norwich, Conn.; s. of Donald B. MacLane and Winifred A. Saunders; m. 1st Dorothy M. Jones 1933 (died 1985); two d.; m. 2nd Osa Segal 1986; ed Yale Coll., Univ. of Chicago, Göttingen Univ.; Benjamin Peirce Instructor in Math., Harvard Univ. 1934–36; Instructor Cornell Univ. 1936–37, Chicago Univ. 1937–38; Asst Prof., Harvard Univ. 1938–41, Assoc. Prof. 1941–46, Prof. 1946–47; Prof. Univ. of Chicago 1947–62, Max Mason Distinguished Service Prof. in Math., Univ. of Chicago 1963–82, Prof. Emer. 1982–; mem. Nat. Acad. of Sciences, Vice-Pres. 1973–81; Vice-Pres. American Philosophical Soc. 1968–71; mem. Nat. Science Bd 1974–80; Pres. American Math. Soc. 1973–74; Hon. ScD, Hon. LLD; Nat. Medal of Science 1989. *Publications:* Survey of Modern Algebra (with G. Birkhoff) 1941, Homology 1963, Algebra (with G. Birkhoff) 1967, Categories for the Working Mathematician 1972, Mathematics: Form and Function 1985, Sheaves in Geometry and Logic, A First Introduction to Topos Theory (with Ieke Moerdijk) 1992. *Leisure interests:* sailing, skiing, photography, hiking. *Address:* Department of Mathematics, The University of Chicago, 5734 University Avenue, Chicago, IL 60637 (Office); 5712 South Dorchester Avenue, Chicago, IL 60637, USA (Home). *Telephone:* (773) 702-7330 (Office); (773) 363-0099 (Home). *Fax:* (773) 702-9787.

McLAREN, Dame Anne, DBE, MA, DPhil, FRS, FRCOG; British biologist; b. 26 April 1927; d. of 2nd Baron Aberconway; m. Donald Michie (divorced); one s. two d.; ed Univ. of Oxford; mem. scientific staff of Agric. Research Council's Unit of Animal Genetics, Edin. 1959–74; Dir MRC's Mammalian Devt Unit, London 1974–92; Prin. Research Assoc., Wellcome/Cancer Research Campaign Inst. 1992–; Foreign Sec. Royal Soc. 1991–96, Vice-Pres. 1992–96; Pres. BAAS 1993–94; Research Fellow, King's Coll., Cambridge 1992–96, Hon. Fellow 1996–; Chair. Governing Body, Lister Inst. of Preventive Medicine 1994– Trustee Nat. History Museum 1994–; author of many scientific publications; Hon. Fellow Univ. Coll. London 1993; Gold Medal (Royal Soc.). *Address:* Wellcome/CRC Institute, Tennis Court Road, Cambridge, CB2 1QR; 40 Ainger Road, London, NW3 3AT, England.

McLAREN, Digby Johns, OC, MA, PhD, FRS, FRSC; Canadian geologist; b. 11 Dec. 1919, N Ireland; s. of James and Louie (née Kinsey) McLaren; m. Phyllis Matkin 1942; two s. one d.; ed Sedbergh School, Yorks., Queens' Coll., Cambridge and Univ. of Michigan; Capt. Royal Artillery 1940–46; geologist,

Geol. Survey of Canada 1948–80, Dir-Gen. 1973–80; Dir Inst. of Sedimentary and Petroleum Geology 1967–73; Asst Deputy Minister, Science and Tech., Dept of Energy, Mines and Resources 1980–81, Sr Scientific Adviser 1980–84; Prof. Dept of Geology, Univ. of Ottawa 1981–88; Chair. Int. Geological Correlation Prog., UNESCO/IUGS 1976–80, adviser in earth science to Dir-Gen. of UNESCO 1980; Chair. and Organizer of two Dahlem Confs. (Berlin) on Resources and World Devt 1986; Pres. Geological Soc. of America 1982, Royal Soc. of Canada 1987–90; Foreign Assoc., U.S. Nat. Acad. of Sciences; Corresp. mem. Société géologique de France; Foreign mem. American Philosophical Soc.; Foreign Hon. Fellow European Union of Geoscientists; Hon.D.Sc. (Ottawa) 1980, (Carleton) 1993, (Waterloo) 1996; Gold Medal (Science), Professional Inst. 1979, Leopold von Buch Medal, Geological Soc. of Germany 1983, Edward Coke Medal, Geological Soc. of London 1985, Logan Medal, Geological Assocn of Canada 1987, Hollis Hedberg Award in Energy, Southern Methodist Univ. 1994. *Publications:* Resources and World Development (ed.) 1987, Planet Under Stress (ed.) 1990; papers, bulletins, memoirs and maps on regional geology, western and Arctic Canada, palæontology, time, historical geology, evolution, extinction, global change, population etc. *Leisure interests:* skiing, music, gardening. *Address:* No. 607, 420 Mackay Street, Ottawa, Ont. K1M 2C4, Canada. *Telephone:* (613) 742-3067.

MacLAREN, Hon. Roy, PC; Canadian politician and businessman; b. 26 Oct. 1934, Vancouver; s. of Wilbur MacLaren and Anne Bailey MacLaren; m. Alethea Mitchell 1959; two s. one d.; ed Univ. of British Columbia, Cambridge Univ., UK, Harvard Univ., USA, Univ. of Toronto; joined Dept of External Affairs 1957; served in Hanoi, Prague, Geneva, Ottawa, New York; Dir Public Affairs, Massey Ferguson Ltd 1969–73; Pres. Ogilvy and Mather (Canada) Ltd 1974–76; Chair. CB Media Ltd 1977–83, 1984–93; Dir Deutsche Bank (Canada), Royal LePage Ltd, London Insurance Group Inc.; elected Liberal MP for Etobicoke North 1979–96; Parl. Sec. to Minister of Energy, Mines & Resources 1980–82; Minister of State (Finance) 1983, Minister of Nat. Revenue 1984, for Int. Trade 1993–96; High Commr in UK 1996–2000; Dir (non-exec.) Standard Life, Canadian Tire, Brascan, Patheon, Broadview Press, Pacific Safety Products, Amec N American Advisory Bd 2001–; Dir Canadian Opera Co.; Chair. Canada-India Business Council, Canadian Inst. of Int. Affairs, Canada-Europe Round Table; Hon. Col 7th Toronto Rgt. Royal Canadian Artillery; Dr Sacred Letters hc (Toronto), Hon. Dr Civil Letters (Univ. of N Alabama), Hon. LLD (Univ. of New Brunswick). *Publications:* Canadians in Russia, 1918–1919 1976, Canadians on the Nile, 1882–1898 1978, Canadians Behind Enemy Lines, 1939–1945 1981, Honourable Mentions 1986, African Exploits: The Diaries of William Grant Stairs 1997. *Leisure interests:* skiing, cross-country walking. *Address:* 425 Russell Hill Road, Toronto, Ont. M5P 2S4, Canada (Office).

McLARTY, Thomas F. "Mack"; American politician and businessman; b. 1946; m. Donna K. Cochran 1969; two s.; ed Univ. of Arkansas; worked in family automobile and transport business; elected to Ark. House of Reps. 1969; apptd. mem. Bd Arkla Inc., La., subsequently joined staff, apptd. Chair. 1985; fmr Chair. and Treasurer Ark. Democratic Party; Chief of Staff to Pres.-elect Bill Clinton 1993–94, Presidential Counselor 1994–2001.

McLAUGHLIN, Hon. Audrey, PC; Canadian politician; b. 7 Nov. 1936, Dutton, Ont.; d. of William Brown and Margaret Brown; one s. one d.; ed Univ. of Western Ont., Univ. of Toronto; ran small business and consulting business, Whitehorse; fmr Exec. Dir Metro Toronto Br. of Canadian Mental Asscn, caseworker with Children's Aid Soc. of Toronto; taught at Adisadel Coll., Ghana; MP for Yukon 1987–97; Fed. Leader New Democratic Party 1989–; Special Rep. Govt of Yukon on Circumpolar Affairs 1997–2000; mem. Advisory Cttee Northern Research Inst. Yukon Coll. 1998–, Bd Univ. of the Arctic 2000–; Paul Harris Fellow Rotary Int. 1998; Dr. hc (Toronto); Hon. Sr Fellow, Renison Coll., Univ. of Waterloo; Chevalier des. Nat. des Parlementaries de Langue Française 1991. *Publication:* A Woman's Place: My Life and Politics 1992. *Leisure interests:* skiing, reading, travel. *Address:* 410 Hoge Street, Whitehorse, Yukon, Y1A 1W2, Canada (Home). *Telephone:* (867) 668-3321 (Office). *E-mail:* andreymc@internorth.com (Office).

MacLAURIN OF KNEBWORTH, Baron (Life Peer), cr. 1996, of Knebworth in the County of Hertfordshire; **Ian Charter MacLaurin,** Kt, DL, FRSA; British company executive; b. 30 March 1937, Blackheath; s. of Arthur and Evelina MacLaurin; m. 1st Ann Margaret Collar 1962 (died 1999) ; one s. two d.; m. 2nd Paula Elizabeth Brooke 2001; ed Malvern Coll., Worcs.; joined Tesco as a Trainee Man. 1959; Dir Tesco Stores (Holdings) Ltd 1970, Man. Dir 1974–83, Deputy Chair. 1983–85, Chair. 1985–97; Chancellor, Univ. of Herts. 1996–; Chair. England and Wales Cricket Bd 1996–2002; non-exec. Dir Enterprise Oil 1984–91, Gleneagles Hotels PLC 1992–, Guinness PLC 1986–95, Nat. Westminster Bank PLC 1990–97, Vodafone 1997– (Chair. 1998–99, Deputy Chair. 1999–2000, Chair. 2000–), Whitbread PLC 1997–2001 (Deputy Chair. 1999–), Health Clinic 2001–02; Pres. Inst. of Grocery Distribution 1989–92; Fellow Inst. of Marketing 1987; Freeman of City of London 1981; Chair. Malvern Coll. Council 2003–; mem. MCC; mem. Lords Taverners and Worshipful Co. of Carmen; Hon. Fellow (Wales Cardiff) 1996;Hon. DUniv (Stirling) 1986, Dr hc (Hertfordshire). *Publication:* Tiger by the Tail (memoirs) 1999. *Leisure interests:* cricket, golf. *Address:* 14 Great College Street, London, SW1P 3RX (Office); House of Lords, London, SW1A 0PW, England. *Telephone:* (20) 7233-2203 (Office). *Fax:* (20) 7233-0438 (Office). *E-mail:* sally.hennessy@vodaphone.com (Office).

MacLAVERTY, Bernard, BA; Irish writer; b. 14 Sept. 1942, Belfast; s. of John MacLaverty and Mary MacLaverty; m. Madeline McGuckin 1967; four c.; fmrly medical lab. technician, English teacher; fmr writer-in-residence Univ. of Aberdeen; mem. Aosdána; has received numerous awards. *Films:* screenplays for Cal 1984, Lamb 1985. *Publications:* novels: Lamb, Cal, Grace Notes, The Anatomy School; short stories: Secrets and Other Stories, A Time to Dance and Other Stories, The Great Profundo and Other Stories, Walking the Dog and Other Stories. *Address:* 26 Roxburgh Street, Glasgow, G12 9AP, Scotland.

McLAY, James Kenneth, QSO, LLB; New Zealand politician, lawyer and business consultant; b. 21 Feb. 1945, Auckland; s. of late Robert McLay and Joyce Evelyn Dee; m. Marcy Farden 1983; one s.; ed King's Coll. and Univ. of Auckland; Officer, Territorial Force 1967–70; barrister 1968–; Man. Ed. Recent Law 1969–70; mem. Parl. for Birkenhead 1975–87; Attorney-Gen. and Minister of Justice 1978–84; Deputy Prime Minister 1984; Leader of Opposition 1984–86; Man. Dir J. K. McLay Ltd 1987–; Deputy Chair. TrustBank Auckland Ltd 1988–93; Chair. Macquarie New Zealand Ltd (Subsidiary of Macquarie Bank, Australia) 1994–; Chair. Unichem Chemist Ltd 1999–; mem. 1990 Comm. 1988–91; mem. Ministerial Working Party on Accident Compensation 1991; Chair. Review of Defence Funding and Man. 1991, Wholesale Electricity Market Study 1991–92, Wholesale Electricity Market Devt Group 1993–94; NZ Commr to Int. Whaling Comm. 1993–; Chair. Roading Advisory Group 1997, Project Marukav Audit Group 1998–; mem. Bd Evergreen Forests Ltd 1995–, MotorRace NZ Ltd 1996–99, Neurouz Ltd 2001–; Mem. Advisory Bd Westfield New Zealand Ltd 1998–; Adviser to Building Industry Authority on revision to earthquake codes 1997; Trustee Auckland Medical School Foundation 1993–99; Nat. Party; NZ Suffrage Centennial Model. *Publications:* numerous papers, articles, etc. on political, commercial and environmental issues. *Leisure interest:* trout fishing. *Address:* P.O. Box 8885, Auckland 1, New Zealand. *Telephone:* 377-0633. *Fax:* 309-6220. *E-mail:* jmclay@mclay.co.nz.

McLEAN, Don; American singer, instrumentalist and composer; b. 2 Oct. 1945, New Rochelle, NY; s. of Donald McLean and Elizabeth Bucci; m. Patrisha Shnier 1987; one s. one d.; ed Villanova Univ. and Iona Coll.; Pres. Benny Bird Corpn, Inc.; mem. Hudson River Sloop Singers 1969; solo concert tours throughout USA, Canada, Australia, Europe, Far East etc.; numerous TV appearances; composer of film scores for Fraternity Row, Flight of Dragons; composer of over 200 songs including Prime Time, American Pie, Tapestry, Vincent (Starry, Starry Night), And I Love You So, Castles In the Air, etc.; recipient of many gold discs in USA, Australia, UK and Ireland; Israel Cultural Award 1981. *Recordings include:* Tapestry 1970, American Pie 1971, Don McLean 1972, Playin' Favorites 1973, Homeless Brother 1974, Solo 1976, Prime Time 1977, Chain Lightning 1979, Believers 1982, For the Memories Vol. I and II 1986, Love Tracks 1988, Headroom 1991, Don McLean Christmas 1992, Favourites and Rarities (Box Set) 1993, The River of Love 1995, numerous compilation packages, etc. *Publications:* Songs of Don McLean 1972, The Songs of Don McLean (Vol. II) 1974. *Leisure interests:* antique furniture, film history, western horsemanship (trail riding). *Address:* C/o Atlantic Records, 1790 Avenue of the Americas, New York, NY 10104 (Office); Benny Bird Co., 1838 Black Rock Turnpike, Fairfield, CT 06432, USA.

McLEAN, Hon. Rev. Walter Franklin, PC, LLD, MDiv; Canadian politician, clergyman and international consultant; b. 26 April 1936, Leamington, Ont.; s. of J. L. W. McLean; m. Barbara Scott 1961; four s.; ed Victoria Coll., Univ. of British Columbia, Knox Coll., Univ. of Toronto, Univ. of Edinburgh; co-founder CUSO (fmrly first Nigerian Co-ordinator); fmr Exec. Dir Man. Centennial Corpn; fmr Minister of Knox Presbyterian Church, Waterloo; Alderman for City of Waterloo 1976–79; MP 1979–93; fmr mem. Standing Cttee on Communications and Culture, on External Affairs, on Nat. Defence; fmr mem. Special Sub-Cttee on Latin America and Caribbean; Sec. of State of Canada 1984–85, Minister of State (Immigration) and Minister Responsible for the Status of Women 1984–86; mem. Canadian Del. to UN 1986–93; Special Rep. to UN on Southern Africa and Commonwealth Affairs 1989–93; Canadian Rep. at Southern Africa Devt Co-ordination Conf. (SADCC) 1987–93; at Commonwealth Foreign Ministers' Confs. 1987, 1988, 1989, 1991; Chair. Parl. Sub-Cttee on Devt and Human Rights, 1990–93; Pres. Franklin Consulting Services Ltd 1994–; Prin. Osborne Group 2000–; fmr Pres. Int. Council of Parliamentarians for Global Action; Hon. Consul of Namibia; Chair. Canadian UNA Human Rights Cttee, Criminal Compensation Bd of Ontario 2000–; Convenor Millennium Celebration, Presbyterian Church in Canada; Progressive Conservative Party; Dr. hc (Wilfrid Laurier) 1995, Hon. DD (Knox Coll. Toronto); Canadian Bureau for Int. Educ. Award of Merit 1994; Queen's 50th Anniversary Medal 2002, Distinguished Alumni Award (Univ. of Victoria) 2002. *Leisure interests:* golf, curling, music. *Address:* 122 Avondale Avenue, S, Waterloo, Ont., N2L 2C3, Canada. *Telephone:* (519) 578-5932 (Office). *Fax:* (519) 578-7799. *E-mail:* franklin@sympatico.ca (Office); bmclean@presbyterian.ca (Office).

McLEISH, Henry; British politician; b. Methil, Fife; m. 1st (died 1995); one s. one d.; m. 2nd Julie McLeish 1998; ed Buckhaven High School, Methil, Heriot-Watt Univ.; began career as local govt research officer and planning officer; lecturer in Social Sciences, Heriot-Watt Univ. 1973–87; mem. Kirkcaldy Dist Council 1974–77; mem. Fife Regional Council 1978–87, Leader 1982–87; MSP for Fife Cen. 1999–; Opposition Spokesman on Social Security 1996–97; Minister for Enterprise and Lifelong Learning 1997–2000; First

Minister of Scotland 2000–01. *Leisure interests:* reading, history, life and work of Robert Burns. *Address:* Scottish Parliament, George IV Bridge, Edinburgh, EH99 1SP (Office); 12 Little Carron Gardens, St Andrews, Fife, KY16 8QL, Scotland.

MACLENNAN OF ROGART, Baron (Life peer), cr. 2001, of Rogart Sutherland; **Rt Hon Robert Adam Ross Maclennan,** PC, MA, LLB; British politician and barrister-at-law; b. 26 June 1936, Glasgow; s. of Sir Hector Maclennan and Lady Maclennan; m. Helen Cutter Noyes 1968; one s. one d. one step-s.; ed Glasgow Academy, Balliol Coll., Oxford, Trinity Coll., Cambridge, Columbia Univ., New York; MP for Caithness and Sutherland 1966–97, Caithness, Sutherland and Easter Ross 1997–2001; Parl. Pvt. Sec. to Sec. of State for Commonwealth Affairs and Minister without portfolio 1967–70, Parl. Under-Sec. of State for Prices and Consumer Protection 1974–79; Opposition Spokesman on Scottish Affairs 1970–71, on Defence 1971–72, on Foreign Affairs 1980–81; resigned from Labour Party 1981; founder mem. SDP 1981; SDP Spokesman on Agriculture 1981–87, on Home and Legal Affairs 1983–87, on Econ. Affairs 1987; Leader SDP 1987–88; Jt Leader SLD 1988; Liberal Democrat convenor on Home Affairs 1988–94, Legal Affairs 1988–94, Nat. Heritage 1992–94; mem. Public Accounts Cttee 1979–2001; Liberal Democrat 1994–98, Spokesperson on Constitutional Affairs, Culture and Media 1994–2001; mem. Convention on Future of Europe 2002–. *Music:* wrote librettos of operas The Lie 1992 and Friend of the People 1999. *Leisure interests:* music, theatre and visual arts. *Address:* House of Lords, London, SW1A 0PW, England (Office). *Telephone:* (20) 7219-4133 (Office). *E-mail:* maclennanr@parliament.uk (Office).

MACLEOD, Hugh Angus MacIntosh, BSc, DTech; American (b. British) professor of optical sciences; b. 20 June 1933, Glasgow; s. of Dr John Macleod and Agnes Donaldson Macleod; m. Ann Turner 1957; four s. one d.; ed Lenzie Acad., Univ. of Glasgow; engineer Sperry Gyroscope Co. Ltd 1954–60; Chief Engineer Williamson Mfg Co. Ltd 1960–62; Sr Physicist Mervyn Instruments Ltd 1963; Tech. Man. Sir Howard Grubb, Parsons and Co. Ltd 1963–70; Reader in Thin Film Physics, Newcastle upon Tyne Polytechnic 1971–79; Assoc. Prof. Univ. of Aix-Marseille III 1976, 1979; Prof. of Optical Sciences, Univ. of Arizona, USA 1979–95; Dir-at-large, Optical Soc. of America 1987–89; Pres. Thin Film Center Inc. 1992–; Fellow SPIE, Optical Soc. of America, Inst. of Physics (London); Dr hc (Aix-Marseille); Gold Medal SPIE 1987, Esther Hoffman Beller Medal, Optical Soc. of America 1997, John Matteuci Award 2000, Nathaniel H. Sugerman Award 2002. *Publications:* Thin-Film Optical Filters 1969 (3rd edn 2001); over 200 articles, papers and book chapters on optics of thin films. *Leisure interests:* piano, computing. *Address:* 2745 E via Rotonda, Tucson, AZ 85716, USA (Home); 18 Black Swan Close, Pease Pottage, RH11 9BB, England. *Telephone:* (520) 322-6171 (Office); (520) 795-5019 (Home); (1293) 518788 (England). *Fax:* (520) 325-8721 (Office). *E-mail:* angus@thinfilmcenter.com (Office). *Website:* www.thinfilmcenter .com (Office).

McLEOD, James Graham, AO, MB, DPhil, DSc, FRACP, FRCP, FAA, F.T.S.E.; Australian professor of neurology and medicine; b. 18 Jan. 1932, Sydney; s. of Hector R. McLeod and Dorothy S. McLeod (née Craig); m. Robyn E. Rule 1962; two s. two d.; ed Univ. of Sydney, Oxford Univ., Univ. of London, Harvard Univ.; Sr Lecturer, Univ. of Sydney 1967–69, Assoc. Prof. 1970–72, Bosch Prof. of Medicine 1972–97, Bushell Prof. of Neurology 1978–97, Prof. Emer. 1997–; Visiting Medical Officer, Royal Prince Alfred Hosp., Sydney 1965–, Head, Dept of Neurology 1978–94; mem. Bd of Dirs Royal North Shore Hosp., Sydney (Vice-Chair.) 1978–86; Pres. Australian Asscn of Neurologists 1980–83; Rhodes Scholar 1953–56; Nuffield Travelling Fellow 1964–65; Sir Arthur Sims Travelling Prof. 1983–84; Commonwealth Sr Medical Fellowship 1989; mem. Australian Science and Tech. Council 1987–93; Fellow Australian Acad. of Tech. Science and Eng, Australian Acad. of Science (Vice-Pres. 1987–88, Treas. 1993–97); Dr hc (Aix-Marseille) 1992. *Publications:* A Physiological Approach to Clinical Neurology (with J. W. Lance, q.v.,), Introductory Neurology (with J. W. Lance, q.v.) 1989, Peripheral Neuropathy in Childhood (with R. A. Ouvrier and J. D. Pollard) 1999, Inflammatory Neuropathies (Ed.) 1994. *Leisure interests:* swimming, boating. *Address:* Department of Medicine, University of Sydney, Sydney, NSW 2006 (Office); 2 James Street, Woollahra, NSW 2025, Australia (Home). *Telephone:* (2) 9351-3385 (Office); (2) 9362-8362 (Home). *Fax:* (2) 9351-4018 (Office); (2) 9362-8348 (Home).

MACLEOD, Sir (Nathaniel William) Hamish, KBE, MA; British civil servant (retd); b. 6 Jan. 1940; s. of George Henry Torquil Macleod and Ruth Natalie Wade; m. Fionna Mary Campbell 1970; one s. one d.; ed Strathallan School, Perthshire, St Andrews Univ., Univ. of Bristol; commercial trainee Stewarts and Lloyds, Birmingham 1958–62; Admin. Officer Hong Kong Govt 1966, Dir of Trade and Chief Trade Negotiator 1983–87, Sec. for Trade and Industry 1987–89, Sec. for the Treasury 1989–91, Financial Sec. 1991–95; JP (Hong Kong) 1979–95; mem. Bd of Dirs Fleming Asian Trust (Chair.), Scottish Community Foundation, Scottish Oriental Smaller Cos. Trust 1995–. *Leisure interests:* walking, golf. *Address:* 20 York Road, Edinburgh, EH5 3EH, Scotland. *Telephone:* (131) 552-5058. *E-mail:* macleodhamish@hotmail.com.

McMAHON, Sir Christopher William "Kit", Kt, MA; British fmr banker; b. 10 July 1927, Melbourne, Australia; s. of late Dr J. J. and Margaret McMahon; m. 1st Marion E. Kelso 1956; two s.; m. 2nd Alison Braimbridge 1982; ed Melbourne Grammar School, Univ. of Melbourne and Magdalen Coll., Oxford; Econ. Asst, HM Treasury 1953–57; Econ. Adviser, British

Embassy, Washington, DC 1957–60; Fellow and Tutor in Econs, Magdalen Coll., Oxford 1960–64; Adviser, Bank of England 1964–66, Adviser to Govs. 1966–70, Exec. Dir 1970–80, Deputy Gov. March 1980–85; Deputy Chair. and Chair. (desig.) Midland Bank PLC 1986–87, Dir 1986–91, Chair. 1987–91; Dir Eurotunnel 1987–91, Midland Montagu Holdings 1987–91, Hong Kong and Shanghai Banking Corpn 1987–91,Thomas Cook 1989–91, Pentos 1991–95, Taylor Woodrow PLC 1991–2000, Angela Flowers 1992–, Aegis 1993–99, FI Group 1994–2000; Chair. Japan Festival Fund 1992; Chair. (non-exec.) Coutts Consulting Group PLC 1992–96; Deputy Chair. Taylor Woodrow 1997–2000; mem. Steering Cttee, Consultative Group on Int. Econ. and Monetary Affairs (Group of Thirty) 1978–84; mem. Court London Univ. 1984–86; Trustee, Whitechapel Art Gallery 1984–90; Trustee Royal Opera House Trust 1984–86, Bd Royal Opera House 1989–97; Gov. Birkbeck Coll. 1991–; Chevalier, Légion d'honneur. *Publications:* Sterling in the Sixties 1964, Techniques of Economic Forecasting 1965. *Leisure interests:* gardening, walking. *Address:* The Old House, Burleigh, Stroud, Glos., GL5 2PQ, England.

McMANNERS, John, CBE, DLitt, FBA; British professor of ecclesiastical history; b. 25 Dec. 1916, Ferryhill, Co. Durham; s. of Rev. Canon Joseph McManners and Ann McManners; m. Sarah Carruthers Errington 1951; two s. two d.; ed Oxford and Durham Univs.; mil. service in Royal Northumberland Fusiliers (rank of Maj.) 1939–45; Fellow St Edmund Hall, Oxford 1948–56, Hon. Fellow 1983; Prof. of History, Univ. of Tasmania 1956–59, Univ. of Sydney, Australia 1959–66, Univ. of Leicester 1967–72; Regius Prof. of Ecclesiastical History, Univ. of Oxford 1972–84; Fellow and Chaplain, All Souls Coll., Oxford 1981–; Dir d'études associé, Ecole Pratique des Hautes Etudes, Sec. IV, Paris 1980–81; Trustee Nat. Portrait Gallery 1970–78; mem. Doctrine Comm. Church of England 1978–81; Fellow Australian Acad. of the Humanities 1970; Hon. DLitt (Durham) 1984; Wolfson Literary Award 1982; Officer of the Order of King George I of The Hellenes 1945, Commdr, Ordre des Palmes Académiques 1990, Commdr Ordre du Mérite Nat. 2001. *Publications:* French Ecclesiastical Society under the Ancien Régime–Angers 1960, Men, Machines and Freedom 1966, The French Revolution and the Church 1969, Church and State in France 1870–1914 1972, Death and the Enlightenment 1981, Church and Society in 18th-Century France (2 Vols) 1998; contrib. to New Cambridge Modern History Vols VI and VIII, Ed. Oxford Illustrated History of Christianity 1990, All Souls and the Shipley Case 1808–1810 2001, Fusilier–Recollections and Reflections 1939–1945. *Address:* All Souls College, Oxford, OX1 4AL; 71 Cunliffe Close, Oxford, OX1 4AL, England (Home). *Telephone:* (1865) 557589 (Home).

McMASTER, Sir Brian John, Kt, CBE, LLB; British arts administrator; b. 9 May 1943; ed Wellington Coll., Bristol Univ.; with Int. Artists' Dept, EMI Ltd 1968–73; Controller of Opera Planning, English Nat. Opera 1973–76; Gen. Admin., subsequently Man. Dir Welsh Nat. Opera 1976–91; Festival Dir and Chief Exec. Edin. Int. Festival 1991–; Artistic Dir Vancouver Opera 1984–89. *Address:* The Hub, Edinburgh's Festival Centre, Castlehill, Royal Mile, Edinburgh, EH1 2NE, Scotland. *Telephone:* (131) 473-2032 (Office). *Fax:* (131) 473-2002 (Office). *E-mail:* eif@eif.co.uk (Office). *Website:* www.eif.co.uk (Office).

MACMILLAN, Jake, PhD, DScFRS; British professor of organic chemistry; b. 13 Sept. 1924, Scotland; s. of John MacMillan and Barbara Lindsay; m. Anne Levy 1952; one s. two d.; ed Lanark Grammar School and Glasgow Univ.; Assoc. Research Man., ICI 1962–63; Lecturer in Organic Chem., Bristol Univ. 1963–68, Reader 1968–78, Personal Chair. 1978–83, Head of Dept and Alfred Capper Pass Prof. of Organic Chem. 1983–90, Prof. Emer. 1990–, Sr Resident Fellow 1990–; Foreign Assoc. NAS (USA) 1991–; Flintoff Medal 1978 and Hugo Muller Medal 1989, Royal Soc. of Chem., Research Medal, Int. Plant Growth Substance Asscn 1982, Charles Reid Barnes Award, American Soc. of Plant Physiology 1988, Pergamon Phytochem. Prize 1995. *Publications:* over 290 papers and 3 books on organic chemistry and plant hormones. *Leisure interests:* gardening, theatre, golf. *Address:* School of Chemistry, University of Bristol, Bristol, BS8 1TS (Office); 1 Rylestone Grove, Bristol, BS9 3UT, England (Home). *Telephone:* (117) 925-1295 (Office); (117) 9620535 (Home). *Fax:* (117) 925-1295 (Office). *E-mail:* jake.macmillan@bris.ac.uk (Office).

McMURTRY, Larry; American writer; b. 3 June 1936, Wichita Falls, Tex.; s. of William Jefferson McMurtry and Hazel McIver; m. Josephine Ballard 1959 (divorced 1966); one s.; co-writer and co-producer with Diana Ossana of CBS mini-series Streets of Laredo and ABC mini-series Dead Man's Walk 1996. *Publications:* Horseman Pass By (published in UK as Hud) 1961, Leaving Cheyenne 1963, The Last Picture Show 1966 (screenplay with Peter Bogdanovich 1971), In a Narrow Grave (essays) 1968, Moving On 1970, All My Friends Are Going to be Strangers 1972, It's Always We Rambled (essay) 1974, Terms of Endearment 1975, Somebody's Darling 1978, Cadillac Jack 1982, The Desert Rose 1983, Lonesome Dove 1985, Texasville 1987, Film Flam: Essay on Hollywood 1987, Anything for Billy 1988, Some Can Whistle 1989, Buffalo Girls 1990, The Evening Star 1992, Streets of Laredo 1993, Pretty Boy Floyd (with Diana Ossana) 1993, The Late Child 1995, Dead Man's Walk 1995, Zeke and Ned (novel, with Diana Ossana) 1996, Comanche Moon 1997, Duane Depressed 1998. *Leisure interest:* antiquarian bookselling. *Address:* Simon & Schuster, 1230 6th Avenue, New York, NY 10020; c/o Saria Co. Inc., 2509 North Campbell Avenue, Suite 95, Tucson, AZ 85719, USA. *Fax:* (520) 690-1454.

McNALLY, Derek, PhD; British astronomer (retd); b. 28 Oct. 1934, Belfast; s. of David McNally and Sarah McNally (née Long); m. Shirley Allen 1959; one s. one d.; ed Royal Belfast Acad. Inst., Queen's Univ., Belfast and Royal Holloway Coll., London; Sec. Royal Astronomical Soc. 1966–72, Vice-Pres. 1972–73, Treas. 1996–2001; Asst Dir Univ. of London Observatory 1966–88, Dir 1988–97; Sr Lecturer in Astronomy, Univ. Coll., London 1970–99; Asst Gen. Sec. Int. Astronomical Union 1985–88, Gen. Sec. 1988–91; Chair. ICSU Working Group on Adverse Environmental Impacts on Astronomy 1993–96; Hon. Visting Fellow, Univ. of Herts. 1999– (2003). *Publications:* Positional Astronomy 1974, The Vanishing Universe (Ed.) 1994, New Trends in Astronomy Teaching (Ed.) 1998; numerous articles in astronomical journals. *Leisure interests:* natural history, music, travel. *E-mail:* dmn@star.herts.ac .uk (Office).

McNAMARA, Pamela; American business executive; b. 1958; consultant Arthur D. Little, Inc. 1980, Head North America Man. Consulting, Leader Global Health Care Practice, mem. Bd of Dirs 1998–, Acting CEO Feb.–Aug. 2001, CEO Aug. 2001–. *Address:* Arthur D. Little, Inc., Acorn Park, Cambridge, MA 02140, USA (Office). *Telephone:* (617) 498-5000 (Office).

McNAMARA, Robert Strange, LLD; American politician, international civil servant and business executive; b. 9 June 1916, San Francisco; s. of Robert James McNamara and Clara Nell Strange; m. Margaret Craig McNamara 1940 (died 1981); one s. two d.; ed Univ. of California and Harvard Univ.; Asst Prof. in Business Admin., Harvard Univ. 1940–43; served Army Air Force 1943–46; Exec. Ford Motor Co. 1946–61, Vice-Pres. 1955–60, Pres. 1960–61; U.S. Sec. of Defense 1961–68; Pres. IBRD (World Bank) 1968–81; Dir Royal Dutch Shell 1981; Dir The Washington Post Co. 1981, Bank of America 1981, Corning Glass Works 1981, TWA 1981, Caspian Holdings 1995–; Chair. Overseas Devt Council 1982; Adviser Robeco Group 1982; mem. Steering Cttee on IBRD Reorganization 1987; mem. Ford Foundation, Brookings Inst., Calif. Inst. of Tech., Urban Inst.; mem. American Acad. of Arts and Sciences, Advisory Council, Int. Reporting Systems 1981–83, Barbara Ward Fund 1982; Hon. LLD (St Andrews) 1981; Hon. DCL (Oxford) 1987, (Harvard) 1997; U.S. Medal of Freedom (with distinction) 1968, Albert Einstein Peace Prize 1983, Franklin D. Roosevelt Freedom Medal 1983, Onassis Award 1988; Legion of Merit. *Publications:* The Essence of Security: Reflections in Office 1968, One Hundred Countries–Two Billion People 1973, The McNamara Years at the World Bank 1981, Blundering into Disaster, Out of the Cold: New Thinking for American Foreign and Defence Policy in the 21st Century 1990, In Retrospect: The Tragedy and Lessons of Vietnam 1995, Argument Without End: The Search for Answers to the Vietnam Tragedy 1999, Wilson's Ghost 2001. *Address:* 1350 I Street, NW, Suite 500, Washington, DC, 20005, USA. *Telephone:* (202) 682-3132. *Fax:* (202) 682-3130.

MACNAUGHTON, Sir Malcolm Campbell, Kt, MD, L.L.D., FRCOG, FRCP, FRSE, F.F.F.P.; British professor of obstetrics and gynaecology; b. 4 April 1925, Glasgow; s. of James Hay Macnaughton and Mary Robieson Hogarth; m. Margaret-Ann Galt 1955; two s. three d.; ed Glasgow Acad. and Glasgow Univ.; Sr Lecturer, Obstetrics and Gynaecology, Dundee and St Andrews Univs. 1961–70; Muirhead Prof. of Obstetrics and Gynaecology, Glasgow Univ. 1970–90; British Emer. Prof. of Obstetrics and Gynaecology; Pres. Royal Coll. of Obstetricians and Gynaecologists, London 1984–87; Chair. Working Party on Accident and Emergency Services in Scotland (Scotmeg); Vice-Pres. Royal Coll. of Midwives 1992–; mem. Academic Bd St George's Univ. Medical School, Grenada, W.I.; Hon. Fellow Sri Lanka Coll. of Obstetricians and Gynaecologists, Royal Australian Coll. of Obstetricians and Gynaecologists, American Coll. of Obstetricians and Gynaecologists, Royal Coll. of Anaesthetists. *Publications:* Combined Textbook of Obstetrics and Gynaecology 1976, The Ovary 1976, Medical Gynaecology 1985. *Leisure interests:* walking, fishing, curling, golf. *Address:* Beechwood, 15 Boclair Road, Bearsden, Glasgow, G61 2AF, Scotland. *Telephone:* (141) 942-1909.

McNEALY, Scott, BA, MBA; American computer company executive; b. 1954; ed Harvard and Stanford Univs.; Sales Engineer Rockwell Int. Corpn, Troy, Mich. 1976–78; Staff Engineer FMC Corpn, Chicago 1980–81; Dir Operations, Onyx Systems, San José, Calif. 1981–82; joined Sun Microsystems Inc., Mountain View, Calif. 1982–, now Chair., Pres. CEO and Dir. *Address:* Sun Microsystems Inc., 901 San Antonio Road, Palo Alto, CA 94303, USA.

McNEE, Sir David Blackstock, Kt, FBIM, FRSA; British fmr police officer; b. 23 March 1925, Glasgow; s. of John McNee and late Mary McNee (née Blackstock); m. Isabella Clayton Hopkins 1952 (died 1997); one d.; ed Woodside Sr Secondary School, Glasgow; Deputy Chief Constable, Dunbartonshire Constabulary 1968–71; Chief Constable, City of Glasgow Police 1971–75; Chief Constable, Strathclyde Police 1975–77; Commr, Metropolitan Police 1977–82; Dir Fleet Holdings 1983–86; Chair. (non-exec.) Scottish Express Newspapers 1983; Orr Pollock & Co. Ltd (Greenock Telegraph), Craig M. Jeffrey Ltd (Helensburgh Advertiser), Integrated Security Services Ltd; Adviser Bd British Airways 1982–87; Dir (non-exec.) Clydesdale Bank PLC; Pres. Royal Life Saving Soc. 1982–90, Nat. Bible Soc. of Scotland 1983–96, Glasgow City Cttee, Cancer Relief 1987–93; CBIM 1980; Order of St John 1974, Commdr 1977; Hon. Col 32 (Scottish) Signal Regt (Volunteers) 1988–92; Freeman, City of London 1977; Queen's Police Medal 1975. *Publication:* McNee's Law 1983. *Leisure interests:* fishing, golf, music.

MacNEIL, Cornell Hill; American opera singer; b. 24 Sept. 1922, Minneapolis, Minn.; s. of Walter Hill and Harriette Belle (Cornell) MacNeil; m. 1st Margaret Gavan 1947 (divorced 1972); two s. three d.; m. 2nd Tania Rudensky

1972; ed Julius Hartt School of Music, Univ. of Hartford, West Hartford, Conn.; appeared on Broadway in Sweethearts 1947, Where's Charley 1949; operatic début as John Sorel in world premiere of The Consul (Menotti) 1950; début with New York City Opera as Germont in La Traviata 1953, at La Scala, Milan, as Charles V in Ernani 1959, at Metropolitan Opera, New York in title-role of Rigoletto 1959; has appeared in leading opera houses of Europe, USA, S. America; Pres. American Guild of Musical Artists 1971–77, mem.1971–; Alumnus of Year, Hartt School of Music 1976; Grammy Award for best opera recording (La Traviata) 1984; Medal of Achievement, Acad. of Vocal Arts 1985. *Leisure interests:* cooking, woodwork, gardening. *Address:* c/o Columbia Artists Management Ltd, 165 West 57th Street, New York, NY 10019, USA (Office).

McNICOL, Donald, PhD, FRSA; Australian university vice-chancellor; b. 18 April 1939, Adelaide; s. of Ian Robertson McNicol and Sadie Isabelle Williams; m. Kathleen Margaret Wells 1963; one s. two d.; ed Unley High School, Univ. of Adelaide, Cambridge Univ.; lecturer in Psychology, Univ. of Adelaide 1967–71; Sr Lecturer in Psychology, Univ. of NSW 1971–74, Assoc. Prof. 1975–81; Prof. of Psychology, Univ. of Tasmania 1981–86; Commr for Univs. and Chair. Univs. Advisory Council of Commonwealth Tertiary Educ. Comm. 1986–88; Vice-Chancellor Univ. of New England 1988–90, Univ. of Sydney 1990–96, Univ. of Tasmania 1996–; Deputy Pres. Australian Vice-Chancellors' Cttee 1993–94, Pres. 1994–96; Pres. Asscn of Univs. of S. Asia and the Pacific (AUAP) 1998–99; Pres. Australian Higher Educ. Industrial Asscn 2000–; Fellow Australian Psychological Soc. *Publication:* A Primer of Signal Detection Theory 1972. *Leisure interests:* walking, music, reading. *Address:* Office of the Vice-Chancellor, University of Tasmania, G.P.O. Box 252–51, Hobart, Tasmania, 2001, Australia. *Telephone:* (3) 6226-2002. *Fax:* (3) 6226-2001. *E-mail:* vice.chancellor@utas.edu.au (Office). *Website:* www.utas.edu.au (Office).

McNULTY, Sir (Robert William) Roy, Kt, CBE; British civil aviation executive; b. 7 Nov. 1937; s. of Jack McNulty and Nancy McNulty; m. Ismay Ratcliffe Rome 1963; one s. two d.; ed Portora Royal School, Enniskillen and Trinity Coll. Dublin; Audit Man. Peat Marwick Mitchell & Co., Glasgow 1963–66, Sr Man. Consultant, Belfast 1977–78; Accounting Methods Man. Chrysler UK, Linwood 1966–68; Man. Accountant Harland & Wolff, Belfast 1968–72, Computer Services Man. 1972–74, Man. Services Man. 1975–76; Exec. Dir Finance and Admin., Shorts Brothers PLC 1978–85, Deputy Man. Dir 1986–88, Man. Dir and CEO 1988–92, Pres. 1992–96, Chair. 1996–99; Chair. Nat. Air Traffic Services Ltd 1999–2001; Chair. Civil Aviation Authority Sept. 2001– (mem. Bd 1999–); Chair. NI Growth Challenge 1993–98, Tech. Foresight Defence and Aerospace Panel 1994–95, Dept of Trade and Industry Aviation Cttee 1995–98, The Odyssey Trust Co. Ltd 1997–99; Pres. Soc. of British Aerospace Cos. 1993–94; Dir (non-exec.) Norbrook Laboratories Ltd 1990–, Ulster Bank 1996–; mem. Council Soc. of British Aerospace Cos. 1988 (Pres. 1993–94, Treas. 1995–99); mem. IDB for NI 1992–98, Steering Group for UK Foresight Programme 1997; Hon. FRAeS, CIMgt; Hon. DSc (Queen's Univ. of Belfast) 1999. *Address:* Civil Aviation Authority, CAA House, 45–59 Kingsway, London, WC2B 6TE, England (Office). *Telephone:* (20) 7453-6002 (Office). *Website:* www.caa.co.uk (Office).

McPEAK, Merrill Anthony, DSM, DFC, MS; American air force officer (retd) and business executive; b. 9 Jan. 1936, Santa Rosa, Calif.; s. of Merrill Addison McPeak and Winifred Alice (Stewart) McPeak Bendall; m. Elynor Fay Moskowitz 1956; two s.; ed San Diego State Coll., Calif., George Washington Univ., Washington; commissioned officer USAF 1957, progressed through ranks to Gen. 1988; Commdr-in-Chief Pacific Air Forces, Hickam, Hawaii 1988–90; Chief of Staff USAF 1990–94, consultant 1994–; Chair. ECC Int. Corpn 1997–. *Address:* 17360 SW Grandview, Lake Oswego, OR 97034, USA. *E-mail:* tmcpeak@earthlink.net (Office).

McPHEE, Jonathan; American music director and conductor; b. Philadelphia; ed Royal Acad. of Music, London and Juilliard School of Music; affiliate Martha Graham Dance Co., New York 1979–89, Joffrey Ballet, Chicago 1980–86, Dance Theater of Harlem 1980–86; now Music Dir and Prin. Conductor Boston Ballet; has conducted for numerous dance cos. including American Ballet Theater and New York City Ballet; has also conducted dance music, musical theatre, operetta and grand opera. *Radio:* Kids Classical Hour (Gabriel Award 1998), WCRB radio station. *Recordings include:* The Nutcracker, The Sleeping Beauty 2000 (both with Boston Ballet Orchestra). *Address:* c/o Boston Ballet, 19 Clarendon Street, Boston, MA 02116-6100, USA (Office). *Telephone:* (617) 695-6950 (Office). *Website:* www.bostonballet.org (Office).

MACPHERSON, Elle; Australian fashion model and business executive; b. 29 March 1963, Killara, Sydney; d. of Peter Gow and Frances Macpherson; m. Gilles Bensimon (divorced 1989); one s. by Arpad Busson; Chief Exec. Elle Macpherson Inc.; designs and promotes own lingerie for Brendon; promotes Elle Macpherson sportswear; co-owner Fashion Cafe, New York. *Films:* Sirens 1994, Jane Eyre 1994, If Lucy Fell 1996, Beautopia 1998, With Friends Like These 1998; video: Stretch and Strengthen, The Body Workout 1995. *Address:* Artist Management, Penn House, B414 East 52nd Street, New York, NY 10022, USA.

McPHERSON, Harry Cummings, Jr., BA, LLB; American government official and lawyer; b. 22 Aug. 1929, Tyler, Tex.; s. of Harry Cummings and Nan (née Hight) McPherson; m. 1st Clayton Read 1952 (divorced 1981); two s.; m. 2nd Patricia DeGroot 1981; one s.; ed Tyler High School, Texas,

Southern Methodist Univ., Dallas, Univ. of the South, Tennessee, Columbia Univ. and Univ. of Texas Law School; U.S. Air Force 1950–53; admitted to Texas Bar 1955; Asst Gen. Counsel, Dem. Policy Cttee, U.S. Senate 1956–59, Assoc. Counsel 1959–61, Gen. Counsel 1961–63; Deputy Under Sec. for Int. Affairs, Dept of Army 1963–64; Asst Sec. of State for Educational and Cultural Affairs 1964–65; Special Asst and Counsel to Pres. Johnson 1965–69; Special Counsel to the Pres. 1966–69; Vice-Chair. John F. Kennedy Center for Performing Arts 1969–76, Gen. Counsel 1977–91; pvt. law practice, Washington, DC 1969–; Chair. Task Force on Domestic Policy, Democratic Advisory Council of Elected Officials 1974; mem. Pres.'s Comm. on the Accident at Three Mile Island 1979; Pres. Federal City Council, Washington, DC 1983–88; Vice-Chair. U.S. Int. Cultural and Trade Center Comm. 1988–93; Pres. Econ. Club of Washington 1992–99; mem. Defense Base Closure and Realignment Comm. 1993. *Publication:* A Political Education 1972. *Address:* 901 15th Street, NW, Washington, DC 20005 (Office); 10213 Montgomery Avenue, Kensington, MD 20895, USA (Home). *E-mail:* hcmcpherson@verner.com.

McPHERSON, James M., PhD; American historian; b. 11 Oct. 1936, Valley City, ND; s. of James M. McPherson and Miriam O. McPherson; m. Patricia Rasche 1958; one d.; ed Gustavus Adolphus Coll. and Johns Hopkins Univ.; Instructor Princeton Univ. 1962–65, Asst Prof. 1965–66, Assoc. Prof. 1966–72, Prof. of History 1972–82, Edwards Prof. of American History 1982–91, George Henry Davis Prof. of American History 1991; Pres. Soc. of American Historians 2000–; Guggenheim Fellow 1967–68; Huntington Seaver Fellow 1987–88; Jefferson Lecture 2000; Pres. American Historical Asscn 2003; Anisfield-Wolf Prize in Race Relations 1965; Pulitzer Prize in History 1989, Lincoln Prize 1998, Theodore and Franklin D. Roosevelt Prize in Naval History 1998. *Publications:* The Struggle for Equality: Abolitionists and the Negro in the Civil War and Reconstruction 1964, The Negro's Civil War 1965, The Abolitionist Legacy 1975, Ordeal by Fire: The Civil War and Reconstruction 1982, Battle Cry of Freedom: The Civil War Era 1988, Abraham Lincoln and the Second American Revolution 1991, Images of the Civil War 1992, Gettysburg 1993, What They Fought For 1861–1865 1994, The Atlas of the Civil War 1994, Drawn With the Sword: Reflections on the American Civil War 1996, For Cause and Comrades: Why Men Fought in the Civil War 1997, Lamson of the Gettysburg: The Civil War Letters of Lt Roswell H. Lamson, US Navy 1997, Is Blood Thicker Than Water? Crises of Nationalism in the Modern World 1998, Crossroads of Freedom: Antietam, The Battle That Changed the Course of the Civil War 2002, Hallowed Ground: A Walk at Gettysburg 2003. *Leisure interests:* tennis, bicycling, sailing. *Address:* 15 Randall Road, Princeton, NJ 08540, USA (Home). *Telephone:* (609) 924-9226 (Home).

McPHERSON, Melville Peter, BA, MBA, JD; American government official and lawyer; b. 27 Oct. 1940, Lowell, Mich.; s. of Donald McPherson and Ellura E (Frost) McPherson; m. Joanne Paddock McPherson 1989; four c.; Peace Corps volunteer, Peru 1964–65; with Internal Revenue Service, Washington 1969–75; Special Asst to Pres. and Deputy Dir Presidential Personnel White House, Washington 1975–77; partner Vorys, Sater, Seymour & Pease, Washington 1977–80; Acting Counsel to Pres., White House 1980–81; Admin. Agency for Int. Devt, Washington 1981–87; Deputy Sec., Dept of Treasury 1987–89; Group Exec. Vice-Pres. Bank of America 1989–93; Pres. Mich. State Univ. 1993–; Exec. Vice-Pres. Bank of America 1989–93; mem. Bd for Int. Food and Agric. Devt 1977–80; mem. Michigan and DC Bar Asscn. *Address:* Office of the President, Michigan State University, 450 Administration Bldg, E Lansing, MI 48824–1046; 1 Abbot Road, E Lansing, MI 48824, USA (Home). *Telephone:* (517) 355-6560 (Office). *Fax:* (517) 432-0200 (Office). *E-mail:* mcpher20@msu.edu (Office).

MACQUARRIE, Rev. John, TD, PhD, DLitt, DD, FBA; British fmr professor of theology and priest; b. 27 June 1919, Renfrew, Scotland; s. of John Macquarrie and Robina Macquarrie (née McInnes); m. Jenny Fallow Welsh 1949; two s. one d.; ed Renfrew High School, Paisley Grammar School and Univ. of Glasgow; British Army Chaplain 1945–48; Incumbent, St Ninian's Church, Brechin 1948–53; Lecturer in Systematic Theology, Univ. of Glasgow 1953–62; Prof. of Systematic Theology, Union Theological Seminary, New York, USA 1962–70; Hon. Curate, St Mary's, Manhattanville, New York 1965–70; Lady Margaret Prof. of Divinity, Oxford Univ. and Canon of Christ Church Oxford 1970–86; Gifford Lecturer, Univ. of St Andrews 1983–84; Consultant, Lambeth Confs. 1968, 1978; HarperCollins Religious Book Award 1991. *Publications:* An Existentialist Theology 1955, Twentieth Century Religious Thought 1963, Principles of Christian Theology 1966, God-Talk 1967, Existentialism 1972, In Search of Humanity 1982, In Search of Deity 1984, Theology, Church and Ministry 1986, Jesus Christ in Modern Thought 1990, Mary for All Christians 1991, Heidegger and Christianity 1994, Invitation to Faith 1995, The Mediators 1995, A Guide to the Sacraments 1997, Christology Revisited 1998, On Being a Theologian 1999, Stubborn Theological Questions 2003. *Leisure interests:* hill walking, the language and literature of Scottish Gaelic. *Address:* 206 Headley Way, Oxford, OX3 7TA, England. *Telephone:* (1865) 761889.

McQUEEN, Alexander, MA; British fashion designer; b. London; ed St Martin's School of Art, London; left school aged 16, worked for London tailors Anderson & Shepherd, Gieves & Hawkes and theatrical costumiers Bermans & Nathans, designer Koji Tatsuno and Romeo Gigli in Rome; his final collection at St Martin's 1992 est. his reputation; subsequent shows include The Birds, Highland Rape, The Hunger, Dante, La Poupée, It's a Jungle Out

There, Untitled; acquired Italian Mfg co. Onward Kashiyama; Chief Designer, Givenchy, Paris 1996–2000, of Gucci Dec. 2000–; Designer of the Year, London Fashion Awards 1996, 2000, Jt winner (with John Galliano, q.v., 1997, Special Achievement Award, London Fashion Awards 1998. *Address:* c/o Gucci Group N.V. Rembrandt Tower, 1 Amstelplein, 1096 MA Amsterdam, The Netherlands; 1st Floor, 10 Amwell Street, London, EC1R 1UQ, England. *Telephone:* (20) 7278-4333. *Fax:* (20) 7278-3828. *Website:* www.gucci.com (Office).

McQUEEN, Steve; British artist; b. 1969, London; ed Chelsea School of Art, Goldsmith's Coll., Tish School of Arts, New York Univ.; has exhibited widely in Europe and USA; maj. solo exhbn ICA, London; works primarily in corp. film, photography and sculpture; ICA Futures Award 1996, DAAD artist's scholarship 1998, winner Turner Prize 1999. *Works include:* Bear 1993, Five Easy Pieces 1995, Stage 1996, Just Above My Head 1996, Deadpan 1997, Drumroll 1998. *Address:* c/o The Tate Gallery, Millbank, London, S.W.1, England. *Telephone:* (20) 7887-8000.

McRAE, Colin, MBE; British racing car driver; b. 5 Aug. 1968, Lanark, Scotland; s. of Jimmy McRae; m.; one d.; made debut 1986; mem. 555 Subaru World Rally Team 1991–98, Ford Martini World Rally Team 1999–2000; British Rally Champion 1991, 1992, 1998; World Rally Champion (youngest ever) 1995; winner numerous rallies including NZ 1993, 1994, 1995, Malaysia 1993, Australia 1994, 1997, Indonesia 1995, Thailand 1996, San Remo 1996, 1997, Safari 1997, RAC 1997, Kenya 1999, Portugal 1999, Spain 2000, 2001, Greece 2000, 2001, 2002, Argentina 2001, Kenya 2001. *Leisure interests:* water skiing, motorcross, mountain-biking. *Address:* c/o M Sport Ltd, Dovenby Hall, Dovenby, Cockermouth, Cumbria, CA13 0PN, England. *Website:* www.colinmcrae.com (Office).

MACSHANE, Denis, MA, PhD; British politician; b. 21 May 1948; s. of the late Jan Matyjaszec and of Isobel MacShane; m. Nathalie Pham 1987; one s. four d.; ed Merton Coll. Oxford, Birkbeck Coll. London; reporter BBC 1969–77; Pres. Nat. Union of Journalists 1978–79; Policy Dir Int. Metalworkers Fed. 1980–92; Dir European Policy Inst. 1992–94; MP for Rotherham (Labour Party) May 1994–; Parl. Pvt Sec. to Ministers of Foreign Affairs 1997–2001; Parl. Under-Sec. of State, FCO 2001–02; Minister for Europe Oct. 2002–; Visiting Fellow St Antony's Coll. Oxford 1998–99; mem. Council RIIA 1999–. *Publications include:* Solidarity: Poland's Independent Trade Union 1981, François Mitterrand: A Political Odyssey 1982, Black Workers, Unions and the Struggle for Democracy in South Africa 1984, International Labour and the Origins of the Cold War 1992, Britain's Steel Industry in the 21st Century 1996. *Address:* House of Commons, London, SW1A 0AA, England (Office).

McSHARRY, Deirdre Mary; Irish journalist, editor and curator; b. 4 April 1932, London, England; d. of the late Dr John McSharry and Mary O'Brien; ed Dominican Convent, Wicklow, Trinity Coll., Dublin Univ.; actress at Gate Theatre, Dublin 1953–55; freelance with The Irish Times 1953; mem. staff Evening Herald, Dublin 1955–56; with bookshop Metropolitan Museum of Art, New York 1956; Reporter Women's Wear Daily, New York 1956–58; mem. staff Woman's Own 1959–62; Fashion Ed. Evening News 1962; Woman's Ed. Daily Express 1963–66; Fashion Ed. The Sun 1967–71; Fashion Ed. Cosmopolitan 1972, Ed. 1973–85; Ed.-in-Chief Country Living 1986–89; Consultant Nat. Magazine Co. and Magazine Div. The Hearst Corpn 1990–92; Ed. Countryside magazine 1991–92; Chair. Bath Friends of The American Museum in Britain, Bath; mem. Council of the American Museum, Council of the Bath Festivals Trust 2002; Trustee The American Museum (in Britain) 2002; Ed. of the Year (Periodical Publrs Assocn) 1981, 1987, Mark Boxer Award: Editor's Ed. 1991. *Art Exhibitions (as curator):* Inspirations – The Textile Tradition (The American Museum) 2001, Quilt Bonanza (The American Museum) 2003. *Publication:* Inspirations: The Textile Tradition Then and Now (American Museum Catalogue) 2001. *Leisure interests:* architecture, textiles, decorative arts, theatre, literature. *Address:* Southfield House, 16 High Street, Rode, BA3 6NZ, England. *Telephone:* (1373) 831263 (Home). *Fax:* (1373) 831263 (Home).

MacSHARRY, Ray; Irish politician; b. 29 April 1938, Sligo; s. of Patrick McSharry and Annie Clarke; m. Elaine Neilan 1960; three s. three d.; ed Summerhill Coll., Sligo; fmr haulier, auctioneer, farm-owner; joined Sligo Jr Chamber of Commerce 1966 (past Pres.); mem. Sligo County Council, Sligo Borough Council and Sligo Town Vocational Educ. Cttee 1967–78; mem. Dáil 1969–89; Minister of State, Dept of Finance and Public Service 1977–79; Minister for Agriculture 1979–81; Tanaiste and Minister for Finance March–Nov. 1982; MEP for Connaught/Ulster 1984–87; Minister for Finance 1987–88; EC Commr with responsibility for Agric. and Rural Devt 1989–93; pvt. business 1993–; Chair. London City Airport, Irish Equine Centre 1995; Dir Ryanair; Dir Bank of Ireland Group 1993–; Gov. E.I.B. 1982; Freeman Borough of Sligo 1993; Fianna Fáil; Hon. D.Econ.Sci. (Limerick) 1994, Hon. LLD (Nat. Univ. of Ireland) 1994; Grand-Croix, Order of Leopold II 1993; Business and Finance Man. of the Year 1988, Marcora Prize, Italy 1991, European of the Year 1992. *Leisure interest:* sport. *Address:* Alcantara, Pearse Road, Sligo, Ireland. *Telephone:* (71) 69902. *Fax:* (71) 69902.

McTEER, Janet; British actress; b. 5 Aug. 1961; d. of Alan McTeer and Jean McTeer; ed Royal Acad. of Dramatic Arts, London; Olivier Award, Evening Standard Award, Tony Award; Bancroft Gold Medal 1983. *Films:* Tumbleweeds 1999, The King is Alive 2000, Songcatcher 2001, The Intended (also co-writer) 2001. *Theatre includes:* Much Ado About Nothing, Uncle Vanya, Simpatico, Vivat! Vivat Regina, London 1995, A Doll's House, London, NY,

1996–97. *Television appearances include:* The Governor, A Masculine Ending, Don't Leave Me This Way, A Portrait of a Marriage, Precious Bane. *Leisure interests:* cooking, gardens. *Address:* c/o Michael Foster, ARG, 46 Maddox Street, London, W1S 1QA, England. *Telephone:* (20) 7436-6400.

McTIERNAN, John; American film director; b. 8 Jan. 1951, New York; m. Donna Dubrow; ed Juilliard School of Drama, State Univ. of New York, Old Westbury Filmmaking Coll. *Films:* Nomads (also screenplay), Predator, Die Hard, The Hunt for Red October, Medicine Man, Last Action Hero (also co-producer), Die Hard with a Vengeance 1995, The Thomas Crown Affair 1999, The 13th Warrior 1999, Rollerball 2002.

McVIE, John Gordon, MD, DSc, FRCP, F.R.C.P.S., FRCPE, F.R.C.S.E., FMedSci; British doctor and cancer specialist; b. 13 Jan. 1945, Glasgow; s. of John McVie and Lindsaye Mair; m. 1st Evelyn Strang 1966 (divorced 1996); three s.; m. 2nd Claudia Joan Burke; one step-s. one step-d.; ed Royal High School, Edin. and Univ. of Edin.; MRC Fellow, Univ. of Edin. 1970–71, lecturer in Therapeutics 1971–76; Sr lecturer in Clinical Oncology, Univ. of Glasgow 1976–80; Head, Clinical Research Unit, Netherlands Cancer Inst. Amsterdam 1980–84, Clinical Research Dir 1984–89; Scientific Dir Cancer Research Campaign 1989–96; Dir Gen. Cancer Research UK 1996–2002; Visiting Prof. British Postgrad. Medical Fed. Univ. of London 1990–96; Pres. European Org. for Research and Treatment of Cancer 1994; European Ed. Journal of Nat. Cancer Inst. 1995–2001; Dir Cancer Intelligence 2002–; mem. numerous advisory cttees. etc. *Publications:* Cancer Assessment and Monitoring 1979, Autologous Bone Marrow Transplantation and Solid Tumours 1984, Microspheres and Drug Therapy 1984, Clinical and Experimental Pathology and Biology of Lung Cancer 1985; 35 chapters in books; 159 articles in books and journals. *Leisure interests:* opera, theatre, cooking, Italian wine-tasting. *Address:* 4 Stanley Road, Bristol, BS6 6NW, England (Office). *Telephone:* (7785) 325558 (Office); (1179) 244527 (Home). *Fax:* (1179) 232699 (Office). *E-mail:* gordonmcvie@doctors.org.uk (Office).

McWHERTER, Ned R.; American politician; b. 15 Oct. 1930, Palmersville, Tenn.; s. of Harmon R. McWherter and Lucille Smith; m. Bette Jean Beck (deceased); one s. one d.; mem. Tenn. House of Reps. 1968–87, Speaker 1973–87; Gov. of Tennessee 1987–95; Chair. Bd Eagle Distributors Inc., Volunteer Distribution Co., Weakley Co. Bank; Dir Coca-Cola Bottling Co., Consolidated, Piedmont Natural Gas Co., American Battle Monument Comm.; Gov. U.S. Postal Service, Washington 1996–; Democrat. *Address:* P.O. Box 30, Dresden, TN 38225, USA.

McWHIRTER, Norris Dewar, CBE, MA; British publisher, broadcaster and writer; b. 12 Aug. 1925, London; s. of William Allan McWhirter and Margaret Williamson; m. 1st Carole Eckert 1957 (died 1987); one s. one d.; m. 2nd Tessa Mary Pocock 1991; ed Marlborough Coll. and Trinity Coll., Oxford; Sub-Lt RNVR 1943–46; Dir McWhirter Twins Ltd (facts and figures agency) 1950–; Chair. William McWhirter & Son Ltd (electrical eng) 1955–86; Athletics Corresp. The Star 1951–60, The Observer 1951–67, Ed., Athletics World 1952–56; Dir Guinness Publs (fmrly Guinness Superlatives) Ltd 1954–96, Man. Dir 1954–76; BBC TV commentator Olympic Games 1960–72; contested gen. elections, Orpington, Kent (Conservative) 1964, 1966; co-founder, Chair. Redwood Press Ltd 1966–72; mem. Sports Council 1970–73; Dir Gieves Group Ltd 1972–95; Presenter BBC TV series "The Record Breakers" 1972–88; co-founder and Vice-Chair. The Freedom Asscn 1975–83, Chair. 1983–2000. *Publications:* Get To Your Marks 1951, Guinness Book of World Records (Ed. and Compiler of 420 editions in 38 languages to 2000) 1955–86; Dunlop Book of Facts 1964, 1966, Guinness Book of Answers, 10th Edn 1996, Ross, Story of a Shared Life 1976, Treason at Maastricht (jtly) 1994, Time and Space 1999, Millennium Book of Records 1999. *Leisure interests:* family tennis, exploring islands. *Address:* c/o Room 222, Southbank House, Black Prince Road, London, SE1 7SJ, England.

McWILLIAM, Candia Frances Juliet, BA; British writer; b. 1 July 1955, Edin.; d. of Colin McWilliam and Margaret McWilliam; m. 1st Quentin Gerard Carew Wallop (now Earl of Portsmouth) 1981; one s. one d.; m. 2nd Fram Dinshaw; one s.; ed Sherborne School, Dorset and Girton Coll., Cambridge. *Publications:* (novels) A Cast of Knives 1988, A Little Stranger 1989, Debatable Land 1994; (short stories) Wait till I Tell You 1997. *Address:* 21 Beaumont Buildings, Oxford, OX1 2LL, England. *Telephone:* (1865) 511931.

McWILLIAMS, Sir Francis, GBE, BSc, FEng, FCGI; British arbitrator and civil engineer; b. 8 Feb. 1926, Edin.; s. of John McWilliams and Mary McWilliams; m. Winifred Segger 1950; two s.; ed Holy Cross Acad., Edin., Edin. Univ.; engineer with various local authorities and contractors in UK 1945–53; Town Engineer, Petaling Jaya Devt Corpn, Malaysia 1954–64; Consulting Civil and Structural Engineer, F. McWilliams & Assocs., Kuala Lumpur 1964–76; full-time student 1976–78; called to English bar at Lincoln's Inn 1978; pupil barrister 1978–79; Int. Arbitrator 1979–; magistrate City of London Bench 1980–96; Chair. Centre for Econs and Business Research 1992–2002; Vice-Pres. and Chair. British/Malaysian Soc. 1994–2001; mem. Panel of Arbitrators of Inst. of Civil Engineers and other bodies; Sheriff City of London 1988–89; Lord Mayor of London 1992–93; Bencher of Lincoln's Inn 1993; fmr mem. Court of Aldermen, City of London; Fellow City and Guilds Inst.; Master Worshipful Co. of Engineers 1990–91; Hon. Fellow Inst. of Civil Engineers; KStJ; Master Worshipful Co. of Lorimers 1995; Hon. DCL (City Univ.) 1992, Hon. DEng (Kingston), Dr hc (Edin.) and several other honours. *Publication:* Urban Regeneration and Environmental Challenge, Pray Silence for 'Jock' Whittinton (From Building Sewers to Suing Builders). *Leisure interests:* golf, skiing. *Address:* Flat 7, Whittingehame House, Whittingehame, E. Lothian, EH41 4QA, Scotland (Home). *Telephone:* (1368) 850619 (Home). *Fax:* (1368) 850619 (Home).

MACY, William H.; American actor; b. 13 March 1950, Miami, Fla; ed Goddard Coll., Vermont; co-f. St Nicholas Theater Co., Atlantic Theater Co. *Stage appearances include:* The Man in 605 1980, Twelfth Night, Bureaucrat, A Call From the East, The Dining Room, Speakeasy, Wild Life, Flirtations, Baby With the Bathwater, The Nice and the Nasty, Bodies Rest and Motion, Oh Hell!, Prairie du Chien, The Shawl, An Evening With Dorothy Parker, The Dining Room, A Call From the Sea, The Beaver Coat, Life During Wartime, Mr Gogol and Mr Preen, Oleanna, Our Town. *Play directed:* Boy's Life. *Film appearances include:* Without a Trace, The Last Dragon, Radio Days, Somewhere in Time, Hello Again, House of Games, Things Change, Homicide, Shadows and Fog, Benny and Joon, Searching for Bobby Fischer, The Client, Oleanna, The Silence of the Lambs, Murder in the First, Mr Holland's Opus, Down Periscope, Fargo, Ghosts of Mississippi, Air Force One, Wag the Dog, Pleasantville 1998, A Civil Action, Psycho 1998, Magnolia 1999, State and Maine 2000, Panic 2000, Focus 2001, Jurassic Park III 2001, Welcome to Collinwood 2002, The Cooler 2003, Stealing Sinatra 2003, Out of Order 2003. *Film directed:* Lip Service. *Television appearances include:* Chicago Hope (series), The Murder of Mary Phagan (mini-series), Texan, A Murderous Affair, The Water Engine, Heart of Justice, A Private Matter, The Con, A Slight Case of Murder.

MADDEN, John; British film director; b. 8 April 1949, Portsmouth. *Television includes:* Inspector Morse (episodes), Prime Suspect IV, Ethan Frome. *Films:* Mrs. Brown 1997, Shakespeare in Love (Acad. Award for Best Film, BAFTA Award for Best Film) 1998, Captain Corelli's Mandolin 2001.

MADDOX, Sir John (Royden), Kt; British writer and publishing editor; b. 27 Nov. 1925; s. of A. J. Maddox and M. E. Maddox; m. 1st Nancy Fanning (died 1960); one s. one d.; m. 2nd Brenda Power Murphy 1960; one s. one d.; ed Christ Church, Oxford, King's Coll., London; asst lecturer, then lecturer in Theoretical Physics, Manchester Univ. 1949–55; science corresp. The Guardian 1955–64; Affiliate, Rockefeller Inst., New York 1962–63; Asst Dir Nuffield Foundation and Co-ordinator Nuffield Foundation Science Teaching Project 1964–66; Man. Dir Macmillan Journals Ltd 1970–72; Dir Macmillan & Co. Ltd 1968–73; Chair. Maddox Editorial Ltd 1972–74; Dir Nuffield Foundation 1975–80; Ed. Nature 1966–73, 1980–96; mem. Crickadarn and Gwendwr Community Council 1981–; Hon. Fellow Royal Soc. 2000; Hon. DTech (Surrey) 1982, Hon. DSc (Univ. of E Anglia) 1992, (Liverpool) 1994. *Publications:* The Spread of Nuclear Weapons (jtly) 1962, Revolution in Biology 1964, The Doomsday Syndrome 1972, Beyond the Energy Crisis 1975, What Remains to be Discovered 1987. *Address:* 9 Pitt Street, London, W8 4NX, England (Home). *Telephone:* (20) 7937-9750 (Home).

MADDY, Penelope Jo, PhD; American professor of logic and philosophy of science and professor of mathematics; b. 4 July 1950, Tulsa, Okla; ed Univ. of California, Berkeley, Princeton Univ.; lecturer then Asst Prof. of Philosophy, Univ. of Notre Dame 1978–83; Assoc. Prof. of Philosophy, Univ. of Ill. at Chicago 1983–87; Assoc. Prof. of Philosophy and Math., Univ., of Calif. at Irvine 1987–89, Prof. 1989–, Chair. Philosophy Dept 1991–95, Prof. of Logic and Phiosophy of Science 1998–, Chair. Logic and Philosophy of Science 1998–2001; Westinghouse Science Scholarship 1968–72, Marshall Fellowship 1972–73, AAUW Fellowship 1982–83, NSF Fellowships 1986, 1988–89, 1990–91, 1994–95; mem. American Acad. of Arts and Sciences 1998–. *Publications:* Realism in Mathematics 1990, Naturalism in Mathematics 1997 (Lakatos Prize 2002). *Address:* Department of Logic and Philosophy of Science, School of Social Sciences, University of California at Irvine, Irvine, CA 92697, USA. *Telephone:* (949) 824-4133.

MADE, Joseph; Zimbabwean politician; mem. ZANU-PLF; Minister for Lands, Agric. and Rural Devt; mem. Pres. Robert Mugabe's 'Gang of Four' politicians. *Address:* Ministry of Lands, Agriculture and Rural Development, Ngungunyana Building, 1 Borrowdale Road, Private Bag 7701, Causeway, Harare, Zimbabwe (Office). *Telephone:* (4) 742223 (Office). *Fax:* (4) 734646 (Office).

MADELIN, Alain, LenD; French politician and lawyer; b. 26 March 1946, Paris; three c.; lawyer, Paris office, Fed. Nat. des Républicains Indépendants (FNRI) 1968–; mem. Nat. Secr. FNRI 1977; elected Deputy to Nat. Ass. (UDF-PR) 1978–86; co-organizer UDF 1989–93; Vice-Pres. UDF 1991–96; Minister of Industry, Posts and Telecommunications and Tourism 1986–88, of Enterprise and Econ. Devt 1993–95, of Econ. and Finance May–Aug. 1995; Sec.-Gen. Republican Party 1988–89, Vice-Pres. 1989–96; Pres. France-Corée Asscn 1991–93; Vice-Pres. Regional Council of Brittany 1992–98; Mayor of Redon 1995–2000; mem. European Parl. 1989–; Pres. Inst. Euro 92 1988–97, f., Pres. Idées Action 1993–97; Leader Démocratie libérale 1997–; Presidential cand. 2002. *Publications:* Pour libérer l'école 1984, Chers compatriotes 1994, Quand les autruches relèveront la tête 1995, Aux Sources du modèle libéral français 1997, Le Droit du plus faible 1999. *Address:* Démocratie libérale, 113 rue de l'Université, 75007 Paris; Assemblée nationale, 75355 Paris, France; European Parliament, 97-113 rue Wiertz, 1047 Brussels, Belgium.

MADFAI, Husham H. Fahmi al-, BSc; Iraqi engineering consultant and government official; b. 28 Oct. 1928, Baghdad; s. of Hassan Fahmi Al-Madfai and Wajiha Nouri Al-Madfai; m. 1st Suad A. Mohloom (died 1984); one s. one

d.; m. 2nd Suha M. A. Bakri 1993; ed Cen. High School, Baghdad, Eng Coll., Univ. of Baghdad, Hammersmith School of Art & Design, London, Inst. of Structural Engineers, London; civil engineer, Basrah Petroleum Co. 1953–55; with Dept of Housing and Tourism Design and Policies, Devt Bd 1957–63; Head. Tech. Dept, Municipality of Baghdad 1963–68; own consulting firm (architects, planners and designers) 1968–80; Deputy Mayor (responsible for planning and man.), City of Baghdad 1980–88; own consulting firm (studies and eng) 1988–; Regional Consultant (feasibility, studies and design), Amman, Jordan 1994–; mem. Iraqi Asscn of Philosophers and Scientists 1994. *Publications include:* Health Aspects in Town Planning 1968, Low-cost Prefabricated Housing 1975, Housing Programme for Iraq until the year 2000 1976, Environmental Problems in Arab Cities 1995. *Leisure interests:* archaeology, studying ancient cities, music, paintings, reading biographies, swimming, long walks. *Address:* P.O. Box 941021, Shmesan 1, Amman 11194, Jordan; Maghrib Street, Adhamiya 22/14/302, Baghdad, Iraq. *Telephone:* (6) 5688470 (Jordan); (1) 4225021/2 (Iraq). *Fax:* (6) 5688498 (Jordan).

MADFAI, Kahtan al, BArch, PhD; Iraqi architect, town planner and author; b. 15 April 1926, Baghdad; s. of late Hassan Fahmi al Madfai and of Wajiha Shaikh Noori Shirwai; m. Lily Vassiliki Vorré 1957; one d.; ed Univ. of Wales Inst. of Science and Tech., Cardiff, UK; practised as architect in public housing sector 1957, planning and design 1961; co-f. Architectural School of Baghdad 1961; lecturer on theory of design 1955–69; f. architectural firm Dar al Imara 1954–79; Asst Man. Gen. Housing Iraq Project 1973–2000; designer and consultant architect; Chair. Pan-Arab Jury for awarding prizes for Arab Town Projects 1985–87; delivered papers and seminars Istanbul 1985, Oxford 1986, Tunis 1987, 1989, Bahrain 1994, Baghdad 1994, Univ. of S. Ga, USA 1996, AIA, Atlanta, USA 1996, Amman 1996; co-f. Soc. of Iraqi Artists; mem. S.P. Group of Artists, Baghdad; works in Baghdad include Ministry of Finance 1968, Bunniyd Mosque 1972, Museum of Natural History 1973, Burj Rubaya apartment building Abu Dhabi 1990, Fatiha Halls project 2003; several first prizes in architectural competitions including Rohoon Bank Bldg, Baghdad 1955, Baghdad Cen. Commercial Zone 1970, Cen. P.O. 1975, Mohammedia Touristic Project, Basra 1977, Great Mosque Competition 1984. *Art Exhibition:* Art of K. Madfai (Baghdad) 2002. *Publications:* several books on architecture and town planning including Development of the Iraqi House 1956, Criteria for Baghdad's New Master Plan 1965, A Manifesto for Arabic Architecture 1986, Architecture and Language 1987, Allah and the Architect 1997; poetry: Fulool 1965, Zem Zem Zeman 1972, Reconstruction of the Sumerian God Abu 1990. *Leisure interests:* modern art, modern poetry, modern philosophy. *Address:* 22 Vassileos Constantinou, 11635 Athens, Greece. *Telephone:* (210) 723-2836 (Office); (210) 751-4120 (Home). *Fax:* (210) 724-9920.

MADI, Hamada ('Boléro'); Comoran politician; b. 1965, Moheli Island; obtained degree in constitutional law in Ukraine; fmr high school head teacher; fmr adviser to Pres., Sec.-Gen. Comoros Republican Party; Sec.-Gen. Presidency, responsible for Defence 1999–2000, Prime Minister of the Comoros 2000–. *Address:* Office of the Prime Minister, Moroni, Comoros (Office). *Telephone:* 74-44-00 (Office). *Fax:* 74-44-32 (Office). *Website:* www .primature-rficomores.com.

MADKOUR, Al-Sharif Mohamed Abdel-Khalek, PhD; Egyptian business executive, university professor and consultant; b. 8 Jan. 1948, Giza; s. of Ibrahim Bayoumi Madkour and Bahia Abdel-Khalek Madkour; m. Afkar el Kharadly 1970; two d.; ed Ecole des Hautes Etudes en Sciences Sociales, Univ. de la Sorbonne, Paris and Univ. of Cairo; Attaché, Industrial Devt Center for Arab States, League of Arab States, Cairo 1969–78; Dir-Gen. Al-Ahram Org. 1978–85; mem. Bd Al-Ahram Investment Co. 1981–85; Sr Research Scientist, School of Information and Computer Sciences, Ga Inst. of Tech. Atlanta, Ga, USA 1980–83; Dir Egyptian Nat. Scientific and Tech. Information Network 1980–82; Prof. Faculty of Mass Communications, Univ. of Cairo 1982; Pres. Phoenix Int.-Madkour Assocs. Inc., McLean, Va, USA 1986; Chair. and CEO Egyptian Co. for Tourism and Services, Cairo 1987; Chair. Cairo-Systems, S.A.R.L., Cairo 1990–, Multinat. Multimedia Computing Inc. Cairo 1992–; Chair. and CEO Marketing Via Internet, Cairo 1997–. *Publications:* Information Services of Egypt 1981, Towards a National Information Policy for Egypt 1982, Information Systems in Egypt: New Trends, Latent Challenges 1984. *Leisure interests:* bridge, snooker, tennis, soccer. *Address:* 4 Gamal el Din Abu el Mahassen Square, Garden City, Cairo (Office); 8 Nile Street, Giza, Cairo, Egypt (Home). *Telephone:* (2) 7960581 (Office); (2) 7962407 (Home). *Fax:* (2) 7962407 (Office); (2) 5703014 (Home). *E-mail:* mvi-egypt@bigfoot.com (Office); madkour@intouch.com (Home). *Website:* shopegypt.com (Office).

MADKOUR, Nazli, MA; Egyptian artist; b. 25 Feb. 1949, Cairo; d. of Mokhtar Madkour and Malak Salem; m. Mohamed Salmawy 1970; one s. one d.; ed Cairo Univ., American Univ., Cairo; fmrly econ. expert for Industrial Devt Centre for Arab States; professional artist 1981–; numerous solo and collective exhbns.; represented in public and pvt. collections in Egypt and internationally. *Publication:* Egyptian Women and Artistic Creativity 1989. *Leisure interests:* travel, reading, music. *Address:* 9 Street 216 Digla, Maadi, Cairo 11435, Egypt. *Telephone:* (2) 5197047 (Office); (2) 5199752 (Home). *Fax:* (2) 5197047.

MÁDL, Ferenc, PhD; Hungarian politician and lawyer; b. 29 Jan. 1931, Bánd Co. Veszprém; s. of A. Mádl. m. 1955; one s.; ed Univ. of Pécs and Eötvös Loránd Univ., Budapest; mem. Hungarian Acad. of Sciences, inst. for legal sciences and state admin. 1973; Dir Inst. of Civil Law Disciplines, Eötvös

Univ., Budapest 1978; head Dept of the Law of Conflicts and Int. Economic Relations 1985; mem. Hungarian Acad. of Sciences 1987–; mem. Governing Council UNIDROIT 1989–; mem. European Acad. of Sciences and Art 1989–, European Acad., of Sciences 1990–, Int. Acad. of Commercial Law, Inst. of Int. Law 1991–; Minister without Portfolio 1990–92, of Culture and Educ. 1992–94; Presidential cand. 1995; Pres. of Hungary 2000–. *Publications:* author of 20 books on law of int. econ. relations, int. investment law, EEC law, etc and about 200 law review articles. *Address:* 1364 Budapest, Egyetem tér 1-3, Hungary. *Telephone:* 36 (1) 266-6486.

MADONNA, (Madonna Louise Veronica Ciccone); American singer and actress; b. 16 Aug. 1958, Detroit; d. of Sylvio Ciccone and Madonna Ciccone; m. 1st Sean Penn 1985 (divorced 1989); one d. by Carlos Leon; m. 2nd Guy Ritchie 2000; one s.; ed Alvin Ailey Dance School; has sold over 55 million records worldwide (20 million albums, 35 million singles); toured UK 1983, 1987, France 1987, Fed. Germany 1987; Commercial for Pepsi Cola 1989; Vice-Pres. ICA, London; face of Max Factor. *Albums:* Madonna–the First Album, Like a Virgin, True Blue, You Can Dance, I'm Breathless 1990, The Immaculate Collection 1990, Erotica 1992, Bedtime Stories 1994, Something to Remember 1995, Ray of Light (Grammy Award for Best Pop Album) 1999, Music 2000, American Life 2003. *Singles include:* Everybody, Burning Up, Holiday, Borderline, Like a Virgin, Material Girl, Into the Groove, Dress You Up, Crazy for You, Papa Don't Preach, La Isla Bonita, Who's That Girl?, True Blue, Like a Prayer, Justify My Love 1990, Erotica 1992, Bedtime Stories 1994, Frozen 1998, Beautiful Stranger 1999, American Pie 2000, Music 2000, Don't Tell Me 2000, What It Feels Like for a Girl 2001, Die Another Day 2002, American Life 2003. *Films include:* Desperately Seeking Susan, Shanghai Surprise, Who's That Girl?, Bloodhounds of Broadway, Dick Tracy 1989, Soap-dish 1990, Shadows and Fog 1991, A League of Their Own, In Bed with Madonna 1991, Body of Evidence 1992, Snake Eyes 1994, The Girlie Show 1994, Dangerous Game 1994, Evita 1996, Four Rooms 1996, The Next Best Thing 2000, Swept Away 2002, Die Another Day 2002. *Plays:* Speed-the-Plow 1988, Up for Grabs (Wyndhams Theatre) 2002. *Publication:* Sex 1992. *Address:* 8491 West Sunset Boulevard, Suite 485, West Hollywood, CA 90069; Maverick Recording Company, 9348 Civic Centre Drive, Suite 100, Beverly Hills, CA 90210, USA.

MADRAZO PINTADO, Roberto, LLB; Mexican politician and lawyer; b. 30 July 1952; s. of Carlos Madrazo Becerra y la Profra and Graciela Pintado Jiménez; m. Isabel de la Parra Trillo; two s. three d.; ed Universidad Nacional Autónoma, Mexico; entered civil service 1971; legal Asst to Alvaro Obregón 1971–72; worked in office of Chief Justice 1972, adviser on social affairs 1979–81; Deputy Sec.-Gen. for Youth, Partido Revolucionario Institucional (PRI) 1975, Sec.-Gen. Nat. Movt of Revolutionary Youth 1977, Sec. of Public Relations and Man. 1984–87, Sec. of Org. 1988–, Pres. PRI March 2002–; elected Fed. Deputy, State of Tabasco 1976, State Gov. 1988–91; mem. 55th legislature, Fed. Govt 1991–93; Founder and Pres. Escuela Nacional de Cuadros; apptd. Sec. of the Great Comm., Palace of San Lazaro. *Publications:* Urbanism, Services and Public Security; numerous articles on social affairs, int. relations and Devt. *Address:* Partido Revolucionario Institucional (PRI), Insurgentes Norte 59, Edif. 2, subsótano, Col Buenavista, 06359 México, DF, Mexico (Office). *Telephone:* (5) 591-1595 (Office). *Fax:* (5) 546-3552 (Office). *Website:* www.pri.org.mx (Office).

MADRID HURTADO, Miguel de la (see De La Madrid Hurtado, Miguel).

MADSEN, Ib Henning, PhD; Danish professor of mathematics; b. 12 April 1942, Copenhagen; s. of Henning Madsen and Gudrun Madsen (née Davids-Thomsen); m. 1st Benedicte Rechnitzer 1963 (divorced 1982); m. 2nd Ulla Lykke Jorgensen 1984; two s.; ed Univ. of Copenhagen and Univ. of Chicago; Research Stipend Aarhus Univ. 1965–70; Research Instructor Univ. of Chicago 1971–72; Assoc. Prof. Aarhus Univ. 1971–83, Prof. of Math. 1983–; ed Acta Mathematica 1988–; mem. Royal Danish Acad. of Sciences 1978, Inst. for Advanced Study, Princeton 1986–87, Royal Swedish Acad. of Sciences 1998, Royal Norwegian Acad. 2002; Rigmor and Carl Holst-Knudsen Science Prize 1982, Humboldt Research Award 1992. *Publications:* The Classifying Spaces for Surgery and Cobordism of Manifolds (with R. J. Milgram) 1979, From Calculus to Cohomology (with J. Tornehave) 1997. *Address:* Department of Mathematics, Aarhus University, 8000 Aarhus C (Office); Vestervang 2, 222, 8000 Aarhus C, Denmark (Home). *Telephone:* 89-42-34-51 (Office). *Fax:* 86-13-17-69 (Office). *E-mail:* imadsen@imf.au.dk (Office).

MADSEN, Mette; Danish fmr politician and writer; b. 3 July 1924, Pandrup, North Jutland; d. of Holger Fruensgaard; a professional writer, including collections of poetry; Liberal MP 1971–87; mem. of Presidium Folketing 1981–84; Minister for Ecclesiastical Affairs 1984–88; Chair. Supervisory Cttee Royal Theatre 1978–84, Cttee for Culture and Information, N Atlantic Council 1982–84. *Publications:* Og så er der Kaffe (political memoirs) 1992, I Anledning Af. (songs and poetry) 1994, Husk Nu at Neje (memoirs) 1997, Tiden der Fulgte: 20 Top-Chefers Farvel til Magten (Goodbye to Power) 1998. *Address:* Blegdalsparken 53, 9000 Ålborg, Denmark.

MADSEN, Michael; American actor; b. 25 Sept. 1958, Chicago, Ill.; m. Jeannine Bisignano; one s.; began acting career at Steppenwolf Theatre, Chicago, appearing in plays including Of Mice and Men, A Streetcar Named Desire; appeared in Broadway production of A Streetcar Named Desire 1992. *Films:* Wargames (debut) 1983, The Natural, Racing with the Moon 1984, The Killing Time 1987, Shadows in the Storm, Iguana 1988, Blood Red 1989, Kill Me Again 1990, The Doors 1991, The End of Innocence 1991, Thelma and Louise 1991, Fatal Instinct 1992, Inside Edge 1992, Reservoir Dogs 1992, Straight Talk 1992, Almost Blue 1992, Free Willy 1993, A House in the Hills 1993, Money for Nothing 1993, Trouble Bound 1993, Wyatt Earp 1993, The Getaway 1994, Dead Connection 1994, Species, Free Willy II: The Adventure Home 1995, The Winner 1996, Red Line 1996, Mulholland Falls 1996, Man With A Gun 1996, The Last Days of Frankie the Fly 1996, Rough Draft 1997, The Maker 1997, Donnie Brasco 1997, Catherine's Grove 1997, Papertrail 1997, The Girl Gets Moe 1997, Executive Target 1997, The Thief and the Stripper 1998, Supreme Sanction 1998, The Florentine 1998, Species II 1998, Detour 1999, Code of the Dragon 2000, The Ghost 2000, High Noon 2000, L.A.P.D. Conspiracy 2001, L.A.P.D. To Protect and Serve 2001. *Television includes:* (series) Our Family Honor 1985–86; (films) Special Bulletin 1983, War and Remembrance 1988, Montana 1990, Baby Snatcher 1992, Beyond the Law 1994. *Address:* c/o Michael Manchal, 9830 Wilshire Boulevard, Beverly Hills, CA 90212, USA. *E-mail:* www.michaelmadsen.com.

MADUNA, Penuell Mpapa, LLD; South African politician and lawyer; b. 29 Dec. 1952; m. Nompumelelo Cheryl Maduna; three c.; ed Univ. of Zimbabwe, Univ. of Witwatersrand; worked in underground structures of ANC in 1970s, twice incarcerated and prosecuted; left SA 1980; fmr Regional Admin. Sec. Tanzania, Office of Treasurer-Gen. of ANC; fmr staff mem. and Legal Adviser, ANC HQ Lusaka, est. Dept of Legal and Constitutional Affairs 1985, founder mem. Constitutional Cttee, participated in meetings with SA Govt and officials in 1980s and early 1990s leading to est. of Convention for a Democratic South Africa, mem. Negotiating Comm., now mem. Nat. Exec. Cttee; MP Nat. Ass.; Minister of Mineral and Energy Affairs 1996–99, of Justice and Constitutional Devt 1999–; Bd mem. Faculty of Law, Univ. of Witwatersrand 1996–. *Publication:* Fundamental Rights in the New Constitution 1994 (co-author). *Leisure interests:* soccer, reading, debating. *Address:* Ministry of Justice and Constitutional Development, Presidia Building, 8th Floor, corner Pretorius and Paul Kruger Streets, Pretoria 0002, South Africa (Office). *Telephone:* (12) 3238581 (Office). *Fax:* (12) 3111708 (Office); (11) 4632030 (Home). *E-mail:* mdemka@justice.gov.za (Office). *Website:* www.doj.gov.za (Office).

MADURO, Ricardo, BA; Honduran politician and central banker; b. Panamá, Panama; m. Miriam Andreu; one s. (deceased) three d.; ed Stanford Univ., USA; mem. Partido Nacional (Nationalist Party), currently Chair. Cen. Cttee; Dir Rafael Callejas's election campaigns 1985, 1989; apptd. Chair. Banco Cen. de Honduras 1990; fmr Co-ordinator of the Econ. Office; Pres. of Honduras 2002–. *Address:* Office of the President, Palacio José Cecilio del Valle, Boulevard Juan Pablo II, Tegucigalpa, Honduras (Office). *Telephone:* 232-6282 (Office). *Fax:* 231-0097 (Office).

MAE, Vanessa; British violinist; b. 27 Oct. 1978, Singapore; ed Cen. Conservatoire, Beijing, People's Repub. of China, Royal Coll. of Music, London, UK; studied with Lin Yao Ji and Felix Andrievsky; concerto debut (age 10), Philharmonic Orchestra 1989; first Nat. Tour of UK with Tchaikovsky Concerto 1990; first Int. Tour with London Mozart Players 1990; released three classical recordings with orchestra (youngest artist to record both Tchaikovsky and Beethoven Violin Concertos) 1990–92; over 400 live performances in the Middle East, South Africa, China, South East Asia, Russia, Europe, Baltic States, Cen. Asia, USA, Cen. and S. America; The Classical Tour 1997, Int. Red Hot Tour 1995, Storm on World Tour 1998; performed at Hong Kong to China Reunification Ceremony 1996, exclusively for HM The Queen, Buckingham Palace 1998, at 50th Anniversary of Geneva Conventions 1999; opened Classical Brit Awards, Royal Albert Hall 2000; collaborated on soundtrack for Walt Disney film Mulan; catwalk debut with Jean-Paul Gaultier; frequent TV appearances and participant in 'crossover' concerts; involved in work with ICRC, participated in TV Campaign Even Wars Have Limits; BAMBI Top Int. Classical Artist Award, ECHO Klassik Award for Bestselling Album of the Year 1995, World Music Award for Best Selling Classical Artist 1996. *Recordings include:* Tchaikovsky and Beethoven Concertos 1990, The Violin Player (quadruple platinum) 1994, The Classical Album I 1996, China Girl: The Classical Album II 1997, Storm 1998, The Original Four Seasons 2000, Vanessa May: The Classical Collection Part I 2000. *Film:* Arabian Nights 2000. *Leisure interests:* snow skiing, dining out, academic studies, waterskiing, reading. *Address:* c/o Trittico Ltd., 34 Philimore Walk, London, W8 7SA, England (Office). *Website:* www.vanessamae .com (Office).

MAEDA, Terunobu, LLB; Japanese business executive; b. 2 Jan. 1945; ed Univ. of Tokyo; joined Fuji Bank Ltd 1968, becoming Dir and Gen. Man. of Credit Planning Div., Dir and Gen. of Man. Corp. Planning Div., Man. Dir and Head of Public and Financial Inst. Group, Chief Financial Officer, Deputy Pres.; Pres. and CEO Mizuho Holdings Inc. 2002–. *Address:* Mizuho Holdings Inc., 6-1 Marunouchi, 1-chome, Chiyoda-ku, Tokyo, Japan (Office). *Telephone:* (3) 5224-1111 (Office). *Website:* www.mizuho-fg.co.jp (Office).

MAEGAARD, Jan Carl Christian, DR.PHIL; Danish musicologist and composer; b. 14 April 1926, Copenhagen; s. of late Johannes H. Maegaard and Gerda Glahnson; m. Kirsten Offer Andersen 1973 (divorced 1989); two d.; ed Royal Danish Conservatory and Univ. of Copenhagen; freelance musician 1949–56; music critic for various newspapers 1952–60; teacher of theory and music history, Royal Danish Conservatory 1953–58; Asst Prof. Univ. of Copenhagen 1959, Assoc. Prof. 1961–71, Prof. 1971–96; Visiting Prof. State Univ. of New York at Stony Brook 1974; Prof. of Music. UCLA 1978–81; consultant to music Dept Danish State Radio 1962–78, Chief Consultant

1982–; Chair. Music Cttee State Endowment for the Arts 1968–71; mem. Bd Danish State Radio and Television 1970–74; mem. Danish and Norwegian Acads.; Kt of Dannebrog I (First Class). *Compositions include:* Elegy of Equinox (for voice, cello and organ), Five Preludes (solo violin), Trio Serenade (piano trio), Chamber Concerto No. 2, Due tempi (for orchestra), Musica riservata I (string quartet), Musica riservata II (for reed quartet), Musica riservata III (for flute, oboe, cello and cembalo), Canon for three flutes, Labirinto I (for viola), Labirinto II (for guitar), Triptykon (for violin, string orchestra), Jeu mosaïque (for harp and chamber orchestra), Partita (for organ), Concerto for cello and orchestra, Partita for cello, Orchestration of Arnold Shoenberg's Variations on a Recitative for organ, Completion of J. S. Bach's Die Kunst der Fuge (for organ), Duo-Phantasy (for two guitars), Pierrot in the Ballroom (for two guitars), Kinderblicke (for two guitars), Progressive Variations (for violin and cello), Die Engel (bass, organ), Intermezzo (organ), Die Verlassenen Liebhaber (bass, organ), Elegia (viola, string orchestra). *Publications:* Musikalsk Modernisme 1964, Studien zur Entwicklung des dodekaphonen Statzes bei Arnold Schönberg I–III 1972, Praeludier til Musik af Schönberg 1976, Indføring i Romantisk Harmonik I-II 1980, 1986, Kuhlaus Kanons (with Gorm Busk) 1996; numerous articles. *Leisure interest:* playing the double bass. *Address:* Duevej 14, 6, 2000 Frederiksberg, Denmark. *Telephone:* 38-88-07-80.

MAEHLER, Herwig Gustav Theodor, PhD, FBA; German papyrologist; b. 29 April 1935, Berlin; s. of Ludwig Maehler and Lisa Maehler; m. Margaret Anderson 1963; two d.; ed Katharineum, Lübeck and Univs of Hamburg, Tübingen and Basle; British Council Scholarship, Oxford 1961–62; Research Asst Dept of Classics, Univ. of Hamburg 1962–63, Dept of Manuscripts, Hamburg Univ. Library 1963–64; Keeper of Greek Papyri, Egyptian Museum, West Berlin 1964–79; Lecturer in Classics, Freie Universität Berlin 1975–79; Reader in Papyrology, Univ. Coll. London 1979–81, Prof. 1981–2000, Prof. Emer. 2000–; Visiting Fellow, Inst. for Advanced Studies in the Humanities, Edin. 1977; Visiting Prof., Univs. of Urbino 1984, Bologna 1986, Bari 1988, Basle 1990, Budapest 1998; corresp. mem. German Archaeological Inst.; Fellow Accademia Nazionale dei Lincei, Rome; Dr hc (Helsinki) 2000, (Budapest) 2001, (Rome II Tor Vergata) 2003. *Publications:* Die Auffassung des Dichterberufs im frühen Griechentum bis zur Zeit Pindars 1963, Die Handschriften der S. Jacobi-Kirche Hamburg 1967, Urkunden römischer Zeit 1968, Papyri aus Hermupolis 1974, Die Lieder des Bakchylides (2 Vols) 1982, 1997; Greek Bookhands of the Early Byzantine Period (with G. Cavallo) 1987; editions of Bacchylides and Pindar. *Leisure interests:* chamber music (viola), horse riding (dressage). *Address:* 11 Oak Avenue, Priory Park, London, N8 8LJ, England. *Telephone:* (20) 8348-1375 (Home). *Fax:* (20) 7209-2324. *E-mail:* hgt.maehler@virgin.net (Home).

MAFATLAL, Arvind N.; Indian industrialist; b. 27 Oct. 1923, Ahmedabad; s. of late Navinchandra Mafatlal and of Vijayalaxmi N. Mafatlal; m. Sushila A. Mafatlal; two s. one d.; ed St Xavier's High School and Sydenham Coll. of Commerce and Econs, Mumbai; joined Mafatlal Group of Cos. 1941, Chair. 1955–; Dir Tata Eng and Locomotive Co. Ltd and others; Chair. Nat. Organic Chem. Industries Ltd, Shri Sadguru Seva Sangh Trust; Trustee Bharatiya Agro-Industries Foundation, Uruli Kanchan, Employers' Del. to 43rd Session, ILO Conf.; Durga Prasad Khaitan Memorial Gold Medal 1966, Business Leadership Award (Madras Man. Asscn) 1971, Sir Jehangir Ghandy Medal for Industrial Peace (Xavier Labour Relations Inst.) 1979. *Leisure interest:* golf. *Address:* Mafatlal House, Backbay Reclamation, Mumbai 400 020 (Office); 10 Altamount Road, Mumbai 400 026, India (Home); Mafatlal Centre, Nariman Point, Mumbai 400021. *Telephone:* (22) 202-6944 (Office); (22) 386-8350 (Home). *Fax:* (22) 202-7750.

MAGAÑA BORJA, Alvaro Alfredo; Salvadorean politician and economist; b. 8 Oct. 1925, Ahuachapán; m. Concha Marina Granados; six c.; ed Univs of El Salvador and Chicago, Università degli Studi di Roma; worked abroad for OAS; Sec. of State for Housing 1960–61; Dir El Salvador Mortgage Bank 1961–65, Cen. Reserve Bank of El Salvador; Pres. of El Salvador 1982–84. *Publications:* Derecho Constitucional Tributario–El Principio de Legalidad 1993, Derecho Constitucional Presupuestario Salvadoreño 1996, Derechos Fundamentales y Constitución 1997, La Constitucionalización del Principio de Reserva de Ley Tributaria en El Salvador 1997; and various articles on constitutional law, fiscal law and public finances.

MAGARIÑOS, Carlos Alfredo, MBA; Argentine international civil servant; b. 16 Aug. 1962, Buenos Aires; ed Nat. Univ. of Buenos Aires, Int. Devt Law Inst., Italy, Wharton School, Univ. of Pennsylvania; analyst, Office of Strategic Planning and Foreign Trade, Banco Ciudad de Buenos Aires 1984–86; joined Ministry of Economy 1992, Under-Sec. of State for Industry 1992–93, Sec. of State for Mining and Industry 1993–96; Econ. and Trade Rep. of Argentina, Washington, DC, USA 1996–97; rank of Amb. 1996; Dir-Gen. UNIDO 1997–2001, 2001–; Dr. hc (Lomonosov, Moscow) 1999, (Econ. Sciences and Public Admin., Budapest) 2000, (Solid and Business Sciences, Buenos Aires) 2001; Trophée des performances de l'année 2000, Inst. Supérieur de Gestion, Paris 2000. *Publications:* El Rol del Estado en la Política Industrial de los 90; articles on econ. and industrial issues including, Reforming the UN System: UNIDO's Need-Driven Model, Gearing Up for a New Development Agenda. *Address:* United Nations Industrial Development Organization, Vienna International Centre, P.O. Box 300, 1400 Vienna, Austria (Office). *Telephone:* (1) 260260 ext. 3001 (Office). *Fax:* (1) 2692669 (Office). *E-mail:* unido@unido.org (Office). *Website:* www.unido.org (Office).

MAGAZINER, Henry Jonas, FAIA; American historical architect and architectural historian; b. 13 Sept. 1911, Philadelphia; s. of Louis Magaziner and Selma Magaziner; m. Reba Henken 1938 (died 1997); one s. one d.; ed Univ. of Pennsylvania, Stevens Inst. of Tech.; fmrly Day and Zimmermann Inc., Albert Kahn, Wright Aeronautical Corpn, Louis Magaziner; has worked on own account for numerous public, institutional and commercial orgs.; Nat. Park Service Regional Historical Architect 1972–87; pvt. practice 1956–72, 1987–; mem. AIA Coll. of Fellows and Comm. on Historic Resources; Founder, Past Pres. Ebenezer Maxwell Mansion (Victorian Museum); mem. Editorial Bd Soc. of Architectural Historians 55-vol. Buildings of the United States; Presidential Award for Good Design for the Govt, Biddle Award for Historical Preservation Projects 1999, Harbeson Award for Contribs. to the Architectural Profession 2000, Germantown Hall of Fame for Community Service. *Achievements:* responsible for historic buildings presentation clauses in the standard Bldg codes. *Publication:* The Golden Age of Ironwork 2000. *Address:* 1504 South Street, Philadelphia, PA 19146 (Office); 2 Franklin Town Boulevard (#2404), Philadelphia, PA 19103, USA (Home). *Telephone:* (215) 545-1076 (Office); (215) 575-9360 (Home). *Fax:* (215) 545-8397 (Office).

MAGEE, Bryan, MA; British author and broadcaster; b. 12 April 1930, London; s. of Frederick Magee and Sheila Lynch; m. Ingrid Söderlund 1954 (deceased); one d.; ed Christ's Hosp., Lycée Hôche, Versailles, Keble Coll. Oxford and Yale Univ.; lecturer in Philosophy, Balliol Coll. Oxford 1970–71; Visiting Fellow, All Souls Coll. Oxford 1973–74; MP for Leyton 1974–83; Pres. Critics Circle of GB 1983–84; Hon. Sr Research Fellow, King's Coll. London 1984–94, Visiting Prof. 1994–2000; Hon. Fellow, Queen Mary Coll. London 1988–; Fellow, Queen Mary and Westfield Coll. London 1989–; Visiting Fellow Wolfson Coll. Oxford 1991–94, New Coll. Oxford 1995, Merton Coll. Oxford 1998, St. Catherine's Coll. Oxford 2000, Peterhouse Cambridge 2001; mem. Arts Council of GB and Chair. Music Panel 1993–94; Hon. Fellow Keble Coll. Oxford 1994–; Silver Medal, Royal TV Soc. *Publications:* The New Radicalism 1962, The Democratic Revolution 1964, Aspects of Wagner 1968 (revised Edn 1988), Modern British Philosophy 1971 (re-issued as Talking Philosophy 2001), Popper 1973, Facing Death 1977, Men of Ideas 1978, The Philosophy of Schopenhauer 1983, 1997, The Great Philosophers 1987, On Blindness 1995 (re-issued as Sight Unseen 1998), Confessions of a Philosopher 1997, The Story of Philosophy 1998, Wagner and Philosophy 2000, Clouds of Glory 2003. *Leisure interests:* music, theatre. *Address:* Wolfson College, Oxford, OX2 6UD, England.

MAGISTRETTI, Vico; Italian architect, industrial designer and interior decorator; b. 6 Oct. 1920, Milan; s. of Piergiulio Magistretti and Luisa Tosi Magistretti; one s. one d.; ed Ginnasio Liceo Parini and Politecnico di Milano; industrial design for Artemide, Cassina SpA, Habitat-Conran, Knoll Int., Fritz Hansen, Azucena, La Rinascente, De Padova I.C.F., Montina Fratelli, Oca Brazil, Asko Finlandia, Poggi, Carrara & Matta, Spalding (USA), Rosenthal-Selb (GDR), Fiat Auto SpA etc.; lectures at Venice architectural school, Barcelona Coll. of Architecture, Vienna, Toronto, Frankfurt, London, Belfast etc.; Hon. Prof. Royal Coll. of Art, London 1990; Hon. Royal Design for Industry, Royal Soc. of Arts, London 1992; Hon. Sr Fellow Royal Coll. of Art, London 1996; Gold Medal, Soc. of Industrial Artists and Designers 1985. *Exhibitions:* Museum of Modern Art, New York, Metropolitan Museum of Art, New York, Victoria and Albert Museum, London, Philadelphia Museum of Art, Conran Museum, London, Design Museum, London, Museum Kunst Gewerbe, Hamburg, Museum für Angewandte Kunst, Cologne, Kunst Museum, Düsseldorf, Kunst Industrie Museum, Copenhagen, Kunst Gewerbe Museum, Zürich. *Publications:* L'Eleganza della Ragione Vibasca; articles in journals, magazines and newspapers. *Leisure interest:* golf. *Address:* Via Conservatorio 20, Milan, Italy. *Telephone:* (02) 76002964. *Fax:* (02) 781538. *E-mail:* fido@infuturo.it (Office).

MAGNÉLI, Arne, FIL.DR.; Swedish chemist; b. 6 Dec. 1914, Stockholm; s. of Agge and Valborg (née Hultman) Magnéli; m. Barbro Wigh 1946 (died 1989); two s. one d.; ed Univs. of Stockholm and Uppsala; Research Asst, Univ. of Uppsala 1941–50; Docent in Chemistry 1950–53; Assoc. Prof. of Inorganic and Physical Chemistry 1953–61, Univ. of Stockholm, Prof. of Inorganic Chemistry 1961–80, Prof. Emer. 1981–; mem. Exec. Cttee, Int. Union of Crystallography 1972–81, Pres. 1975–78; Sec. Nobel Cttee for Physics 1966–73, for Chemistry 1966–86, mem. Swedish Natural Science Research Council 1965–71; mem. Bd of Dirs., Nobel Foundation 1973–85; Chair. Swedish Nat. Cttee for Chemistry 1984–95; mem. Royal Swedish Acad. of Sciences, Royal Soc. of Sciences, Uppsala (Pres. 1990–91); Foreign mem. French Acad. of Sciences 1989; Dr. hc (Univ. Pierre et Marie Curie, Paris) 1988; Bergstedt Prize 1947, Bjurzon Prize 1950, Norblad-Ekstrand Medal 1954, Bror Holmberg Medal 1980, Gregori Aminoff Prize 1989, Gold Medal of French Soc. for High Temperature and Ceramics Research (Soc. des Hautes Températures et des Réfractaires) 1990, co-recipient 1992 Ettore Majorana-Erice Science for Peace Prize 1994; Commdr Ordre nat. du Mérite; Officier des Palmes Académiques. *Publications:* research articles in chemical crystallography and solid state inorganic chemistry. *Address:* Arrhenius Laboratory, University of Stockholm, 106 91 Stockholm; Royal Academy of Sciences, 104 05 Stockholm; Öregrundsgatan 14, 115 28 Sweden (Home). *Telephone:* (8) 16-12-55; 673-95-00 (Univ.); (18) 51-86-50 (Home). *Fax:* (8) 15-26-99.

MAGNUSSON, Magnus, MA, FRSE, FRSA, FSA; Icelandic writer and broadcaster; b. 12 Oct. 1929; s. of the late Sigursteinn Magnusson and Ingibjorg Sigurdardóttir; m. Mamie Baird 1954; one s. three d. (and one s. deceased); ed Edin. Acad. and Jesus Coll., Oxford; Asst Ed. Scottish Daily Express then

The Scotsman; presenter various TV and radio programmes including: Chronicle, Mastermind, Pebble Mill at One, BC, The Archaeology of the Bible Lands, Tonight, Cause for Concern, All Things Considered, Living Legends, Vikings!, Birds for All Seasons; Ed. The Bodley Head Archaeologies, Popular Archaeology 1979–80; Chair. Ancient Monuments Bd for Scotland 1981–89, Cairngorms Working Party 1991–93, N.C.C. for Scotland 1991–92, Scottish Nat. Heritage 1992–99, Paths for All 1996–; Rector Edin. Univ. 1975–78; mem. UK Cttee for European Year of the Environment 1987, Bd of Trustees Nat. Museums of Scotland 1985–89; Pres. R.S.P.B. 1985–90; Hon. Vice-Pres. Age Concern Scotland, R.S.S.P.C.C.; FSA Scot. 1974; Hon. Fellow Jesus Coll. Oxford 1990: Hon. F.R.I.A.S. 1987; F.R.S.G.S. 1991; Dr. hc (Edin.) 1978; Hon. DUniv (York) 1981, (Paisley) 1993, Hon. DLitt (Strathclyde) 1993, (Napier) 1994, (Glasgow) 2001, (Glasgow Caledonian) 2001; Iceland Media Award 1985, Silver Jubilee Medal 1977, Medlicott Medal 1989; Kt of Order of the Falcon (Iceland) 1975, Commdr 1986; Hon. KBE 1989. *Translations:* Icelandic sagas (with Hermann Pálsson) 1999, 2002 and works by Halldor Laxness and Samivel; contribs. to various historical and novelty books; introductions to numerous books on historical, geographical and cultural themes. *Edited* Echoes in Stone 1983, Reader's Digest Book of Facts 1985, Chambers Biographical Dictionary 1990, The Nature of Scotland 1991. *Publications:* Introducing Archaeology 1972, Viking Expansion Westwards 1973, The Clacken and the Slate 1974, Hammer of the North (Norse mythology) 1976, BC, The Archaeology of the Bible Lands 1977, Landlord or Tenant?: A View of Irish History 1978, Iceland 1979, Vikings! Magnus on the Move 1980, Treasures of Scotland 1981, Lindisfarne: The Cradle Island 1984, Iceland Saga 1987, I've Started, So I'll Finish 1997, Rum: Nature's Island 1997, Magnus Magnusson's Quiz Book 2000, Scotland: The Story of a Nation 2000. *Leisure interests:* digging and delving. *Address:* Blairskaith House, Balmore-Torrance, Glasgow, G64 4AX, Scotland. *Telephone:* (1360) 620226.

MAGNUSSON, Thor Eyfeld; Icelandic state antiquary; b. 18 Nov. 1937, Hvammstangi; s. of Magnus Richardson and Sigridur Thordardóttir; m. Maria V. Heiddal 1964; two s. one d.; ed Univ. of Uppsala; Asst Curator, Nat. Museum 1964, State Antiquary 1968–. *Address:* National Museum, Sudurgata 41, 101 Reykjavik (Office); Bauganes 26, 101 Reykjavik, Iceland (Home). *Telephone:* 5302200. *Fax:* 5302201.

MAGOMEDOV, Magomedali Magomedovich; Russian/Dagestan politician; b. 15 June 1930, Levashi, Dagestan Autonomous Repub.; m.; six c.; ed Dagestan State Pedagogical Inst., Dagestan Inst. of Agric.; teacher, Dir Levashi secondary school, then Head Levashi Dept of Nat. Educ. 1949–57; Chair. Levashi Kolkhoz 1957–66; Head Agric. Production unit Levashi Dist 1966–69; Chair. Levashi Dist Exec. Cttee 1969–70; First Sec. Levashi Dist CP Cttee 1970–75; Head Div. of Agric. Dagestan Regional CP Cttee 1975–79; Deputy Chair., Chair. Council of Ministers Dagestan Autonomous Repub. 1979–87; Chair. Presidium Supreme Soviet Dagestan Autonomous Repub. 1987–94; Chair. State Council (Head Repub. of Dagestan) 1994–; mem. Russian Council of Fed. 1993–2001. *Address:* House of Government, Lenina pl., 167005 Makhachkala, Dagestan, Russia (Office). *Telephone:* (8722) 67-30-59 (Office); (8722) 67-30-60. *Fax:* (8722) 705-92-89.

MAGOWAN, Peter Alden, MA; American business executive; b. 5 April 1942, New York; s. of Robert Anderson and Doris Merrill Magowan; m. 1st Jill Tarlau (divorced 1982); m. 2nd Deborah Johnston 1982; three d. from 1st marriage; ed Stanford Univ., Oxford Univ., Johns Hopkins School of Advanced Int. Studies; Store Man., Washington, DC, Safeway Stores, 1968–70, Dist Man., Houston, Tex. 1970, Retail Operations Man., Phoenix, Ariz. 1971–72, Div. Man., Tulsa, Okla 1973–76, Man., Int. Div., Toronto, Canada 1976–78, Western Regional Man., San Francisco, Calif. 1978–79, Dir, Safeway Stores, Inc. 1979, Chair. of the Bd 1980–98, CEO 1980–93, Pres. and COO 1988, also Chair. Exec. Cttee; Pres., Man. Gen. Partner, San Francisco Giants Baseball Team 1993–; fmr Dir of U.S. Chamber of Commerce, The Hudson Inst., Pacific Gas and Electric Co., Food Marketing Inst.; Dir Caterpillar, Chrysler Corpn; mem. Advisory Council, Johns Hopkins School of Advanced Int. Studies; Trustee, Johns Hopkins Univ.; Exec. of the year 2000, Sports Business Journal. *Address:* San Francisco Giants, 24 Willie Mays Plaza, San Francisco, CA 94124; Safeway Stores Inc., 201 4th Street, Oakland, CA 94660, USA. *Telephone:* (415) 972-1950 (Office). *Fax:* (415) 947-3399.

MAGRIS, Claudio; Italian journalist, writer and university professor; b. 10 April 1939, Trieste; s. of Duilio Magris and Pia de Grisogono Magris; m. Marisa Madieri 1964; two s.; ed Univ. of Turin; lecturer in German Language and Literature, Univ. of Trieste 1968–70, Turin 1970–78, Trieste 1978–; mem. Deutsche Akademie für Sprache und Dichtung (Darmstadt), Österreichische Akademie der Wissenschaften, Accademia delle Scienze di Torino, Ateneo Veneto, Akademie der Wissenschaften (Göttingen); prizes and awards include: Debenedetti 1972, Val di Comino 1978, Goethe Medaille 1980, Aquileia 1983, Premiolino 1983, San Giusto d'Oro 1984, Musil Medaille der Stadt Klagenfurt 1984, Bagutta 1987, Accademia dei Lincei 1987, Marotta 1987, Città di Modena 1987, Antico Fattore 1988, Juan Carlos I 1989, Premio Strega 1997, Premio Chiara alla Carriera 1999, Premio Würth per la Cultura Europea 1999, Premio Grinzane Piemonte 1999, Medaglia d'Oro della Cultura della Scuola e dell' Arte 1999, Premio Sikken 2000, Premio Nietsche 2000, Premium Erasmianum 2001, Leipziger Buchpreis zur Europäischen Verständigung 2001; Österreichisches Ehrenkreuz für Wissenschaft und Kunst (First Class). *Publications:* Il Mito absburgico nella letteratura austriaca moderna 1963, 1988, Wilhelm Heinse 1968, Lontano da dove. Joseph

Roth e la tradizione ebraico-orientale 1971, Dietro le parole 1978, Itaca e oltre 1982, Trieste. Un'identità di frontiera 1982, 1987, L'anello di Clarisse 1984, Illazioni su una sciabola 1984, Danubio 1986 (trans. in numerous languages), Stadelmann 1988, Microcosmi 1997, Utopia e disincanto 1999; numerous essays and book reviews in Corriere della Sera and other European newspapers and periodicals; trans. Ibsen, Kleist, Schnitzler, Büchner. *Address:* Università degli Studi Trieste, Piazzale Europa 1, 34127 Trieste; Via Carpaccio 2, Trieste, Italy. *Telephone:* (040) 6767111 (Office); (040) 305428. *Fax:* (040) 6763093 (Office); (040) 314455.

MAGUIRE, Adrian Edward, BPhil, MA, FSA; Irish jockey; b. 29 April 1971; s. of Joseph Maguire and of the late Philomena Maguire; m. Sabrina Maguire 1995; one d.; ed Kilmessan Nat. School, Trim Vocational School; champion pony race rider 1986, champion point-to-point rider 1990–91, champion conditional jockey 1991–92; wins include Cheltenham Gold Cup, Irish Grand Nat. (youngest ever winning jockey), Galway Plate, Imperial Cup, Greenalls Gold Cup, Queen Mother Champion Chase, King George VI Chase, Triumph Hurdle, Cathcart Chase 1994, Scottish National 1998, Whitbread Gold Cup 1998; holds records for most point-to-point winners in a season, most winners in a season for a conditional jockey (71) 1991–92; retd 2002 following neck injury, having won over 1,000 races. *Leisure interests:* squash, watching television. *Address:* c/o The Jockey Club (Jockey Section), 42 Portman Square, London, W1H 0EM; 17 Willes Close, Faringdon, Oxon. SN7 7DU, England (Home).

MAGUIRE, Tobey; American actor; b. 27 June 1975, Santa Monica, Calif.; s. of Vincent Maguire and Wendy Maguire; began career acting in commercials. *Television includes:* (sitcoms): Blossom 1991, Roseanne 1991, Jake and the Fatman, Great Scott! 1992, This Boy's Life 1993; (films): Spoils of War 1994, A Child's Cry for Help 1994. *Films include:* S.F.W. 1994, Revenge of the Red Baron 1994, Duke of Groove 1995, Seduced by Madness 1996, Joyride 1996, Deconstructing Harry 1997, The Ice Storm 1997, Pleasantville 1998, Fear and Loathing in Las Vegas 1998, Don's Plum 1998, Ride With the Devil 1999, The Cider House Rules 1999, Wonderboys 2000, Spiderman 2002. *Leisure interests:* boardgames, basketball, backgammon, yoga. *Address:* c/o The Gersh Agency, POB 5617, Beverly Hills, CA 90210, USA (Office).

MAGYAR, Balint, PhD; Hungarian sociologist and politician; b. 1952, Budapest; m. Róza Hodosán; one d.; ed Eötvös Loránd Univ. of Budapest; Research Fellow Inst. of World Econ., Hungarian Acad. of Sciences, Financial Research Ltd 1988–90; involved in dissident political activities from 1979; founding mem. Alliance of Free Democrats (SZDSZ), Pres. 1998–2000, mem. Exec. Bd 2001–; MP 1990–, mem. Parl. Cttee on Local Govt Issues 1990–92, on European Integration Issues 1992–, Vice-Chair. Parl. Cttee on Nat. Security 1994–; Minister of Culture and Educ., then of Educ. 1996–; Dir Hungarian Stories (documentary film); Ferenc Erdei Prize 1988 (for Dunaapát), Special Prize, Critics' Prize Budapest Film Festival 1988 (for Hungarian Stories). *Publication:* Dunaapát 1944–58 (sociography of a Hungarian village). *Address:* SZDSZ, 1143 Budapest, Gizella u. 36, Hungary. *Telephone:* (1) 441-5824. *Fax:* (1) 441-5952. *E-mail:* balint.magyar@szdsz.hu (Office). *Website:* www.szdsz.hu (Office).

MAHANTA, Prafulla Kumar, BSc, LLB; Indian politician; b. 23 Dec. 1952, Rupnarayan Satra; s. of Deva Kanta and Lakshmi Prava; m. Joyasree Goswami; one s. one d.; f. Asom Gana Parishad (regional political party) 1985; Chief Minister of Assam 1985–90, 1996–2001. *Address:* Rupnarayan Satra, Kallabor, Nagaon District, Assam, India (Home). *Telephone:* (361) 562222 (Office); (361) 561291. *Fax:* (361) 562069 (Office).

MAHARAJ, Mac (Sathyandranath Ragunanan), B.ADMIN.; South African politician; b. 22 April 1935, Newcastle; s. of N.R. Maharaj; m. Zarina Maharaj; two c.; ed St Oswald's High School; Ed. New Age 1956; lived in UK 1957–61, founding mem. British Anti-Apartheid Movement; mem. Umkhonto Wesizwe (ANC's armed wing) 1961, underwent mil. training in GDR 1961–62; returned to SA 1962; sentenced to 12 years' imprisonment Dec. 1964, served prison sentence on Robben Island 1965–76; left SA 1976; with ANC H.Q., Lusaka, Zambia, Sec. Underground Section 1977; mem. Revolutionary Council 1978, Politico-Mil. Council 1985; mem. ANC Negotiation Cttee, Political Cttee 1984, Nat. Exec. Council 1985–90, 1991–, Nat. Working Cttee; Commdr Operation Vula, SA 1988–90; mem. Political Bureau and Cen. Cttee 1990; with Codesa Secr.; Jt Sec. Transitional Exec. Council 1994; Minister of Transport, Govt of Nat. Unity 1994–99. *Address:* c/o Private Bag X193 Pretoria 0001, South Africa.

MAHAREY, Steve, MA; New Zealand politician and academic; m. Liz Mackay; two step-s.; taught business admin., Sr Lecturer in Sociology Massey Univ.; mem. Palmerston North City Council 1986–89, Chair. Palmerston North Labour Electorate Cttee, mem. Policy Council; Labour MP for Palmerston North 1990–; Opposition Spokesperson on Social Welfare and Employment, Broadcasting and Communications and Labour Relations 1994–97; Assoc. Spokesperson on Educ. with specific responsibility for Tertiary Educ., Educ. and Employment 1990–93, served on the Social Services, Educ. and Science, Commerce, Justice and Law Reform and Broadcasting Parl. Select Cttees.; Minister of Social Services and Employment, Minister of Broadcasting, Assoc. Minister of Educ. (Tertiary Educ.), Community and Voluntary Sector 1999–, Chair. Cabinet Social Equity Cttee; mem. of Cabinet Cttees. for Policy, Educ. and Health, Appointments and Honours, Econ. Devt, Legislation. *Publications:* numerous articles on media and cultural studies and social change. *Leisure interests:* mountain biking, swimming, music, social and political theory, travel, spectator sports. *Address:* Parliament Buildings, Wellington, New Zealand (Office). *Telephone:* (4) 470-6552 (Office). *Fax:* (4) 495-8443 (Office). *E-mail:* smaharey@ministers.govt.nz (Office). *Website:* www.beehive.govt.nz/maharey/ (Office).

MAHAT, Ram Sharan, MA, PhD; Nepalese politician; b. 1 Jan. 1951, Nuwakot; s. of Tol Kumari Mahat; m. Roshana Mahat; one s. one d.; ed Tribhuban Univ., Gokhale Inst. of Politics and Econs, Poona, India, School of Int. Service, American Univ.; Asst Resident Rep. UNDP, Islamabad 1989–90; econ. adviser to Prime Minister of Nepal 1991–92; Vice-Chair. Nat. Planning Comm. 1991–94; MP from Nuwakot Dist 1994–; Minister of Finance 1995–99, 2001. *Publications:* Industrial Financing in Nepal, numerous articles on nat. and int. econ. issues. *Leisure interests:* social service, reading books. *Address:* Bansbari, Kathmandu, Nepal (Home). *Telephone:* (1) 373132 (Home). *Fax:* (1) 372356 (Home).

MAHATHIR BIN MOHAMAD; Malaysian politician; b. 20 Dec. 1925, Alur Setar, Kedah; m. Dr. Siti Hasmah binti Haji Mohd Ali 1956; three s. two d.; ed Sultan Abdul Hamid Coll. and Univ. of Malaya in Singapore; Medical Officer, Kedah, Langkawi and Perlis 1953–57; private practice 1957–64; mem. UMNO (now Umno Baru) Supreme Council 1965–69, 1972– (Pres. 1981–), mem. Supreme Council 1972–; mem. House of Reps. for Kota Setar Selatan 1964–69, for Kubang Pasu 1974–; mem. Senate 1973; Chair. Food Industries of Malaysia Sdn. Bhd. 1973; Minister of Educ. 1974–77, of Trade and Industry 1977–81, of Defence 1981–86, of Home Affairs 1986–99, of Justice 1987, of Natural and Rural Devt; Deputy Prime Minister 1976–81, Prime Minister of Malaysia 1981–(2003). *Publication:* The Malay Dilemma 1969, The Way Forward 1998. *Address:* c/o Prime Minister's Department, Blok Utama, Tingkat 1-5, Pusat Pentadbiran Kerajaan Persekutuan, 62502 Putrajaya, Malaysia (Office). *Telephone:* (3) 88888000 (Office). *Fax:* (3) 88883424 (Office). *E-mail:* ppm@smpke.jpm.my. *Website:* www.smpke.jpm .my (Office).

MAHAVIR, Bhai, PhD, LLB; Indian politician; b. 30 Oct. 1922, Lahore, Pakistan; s. of Bhai Parmanand and Bhagya Sudhi; m. Krishna Bhai Mahavir; two d.; lecturer in Econs, D.A.V. Coll., Lahore 1944; fmr Man. Dir Akashvani Prakashan Ltd; founder mem. and first Gen. Sec. Bharatiya Jana Sangh; Pres. Delhi Pradesh Jana Sangh 1968–69; mem. Rajya Sabha 1968–74, 1978–84; Chair. Cttee on Subordinate Legislation of Rajya Sabha 1982–84; detained during Emergency Period; Chair. Governing Body, Rajdhani Coll., New Delhi; Dir Bhai Parmanand Vidya Mandir; Sec. Bhai Parmanand Smarak Samiti; mem. Nat. Exec. Bharatiya Janata Party; Gov. of Madhya Pradesh 1998–. *Address:* Raj Bhavan, Bhopal (Office); 389 D/S, New Rajendra Nagar, New Delhi 60, India (Home). *Telephone:* (755) 551300 (Office); (11) 5763550 (Home).

MAHAYNI, Mohammad Khaled al-, PhD; Syrian politician and economist; b. 30 May 1943, Damascus; s. of Salim al-Mahayni and Weedad Araman; m. Falak Sakkal 1966; two s. two d.; ed Damascus Univ.; various public financial and econ. appts. 1961–70; auditor 1970–77; Dir of Debt Fund and Information, Ministry of Finance 1979–80, of Public Enterprises 1981–84; Deputy Minister of Finance 1984–87, Minister 1987–2001; Gov. IBRD 1987–2001, Arab Bank for Econ. Devt in Africa 1989–; Prof. Damascus Univ. 2001–. *Publications:* Methodology of the General Budget of the State in the Syrian Arab Republic 1984, Supplementary Policies for Financial Planning 1995, Government Accounting 1996, Public Finance and Tax Legislation 1999. *Leisure interests:* reading and computing. *Address:* c/o Ministry of Finance, P.O. Box 13136, Jule Jamal Street, Damascus, Syria.

MAHBUBANI, Kishore; Singaporean diplomatist; b. 24 Oct. 1948, Singapore; s. of Mohandas Mahbubani; m. Anne King Markey 1985; two s. one d.; ed Univ. of Singapore and Dalhousie Univ., Canada; joined Ministry of Foreign Affairs 1971, Deputy Dir 1979–82, Deputy Sec. 1989–93, Perm. Sec. 1993–; Chargé d'affaires to Cambodia 1973–74; Counsellor at Singapore Embassy in Malaysia 1976–79; mem. of Singapore dels. to several sessions of UN Gen. Ass. and int. confs. 1979–83; Deputy Chief at Washington, DC Embassy 1982–84; Perm. Rep. of Singapore to UN, New York (concurrently High Commr in Canada and Amb. to Mexico) 1984–89; Dean, Civil Service Coll. 1993–96; Perm. Rep. to UN 1998–. *Leisure interests:* golf, jogging. *Address:* Permanent Mission of Singapore to the United Nations, 231 East 51st Street, New York, NY 10022, USA (Office). *Telephone:* (212) 826-0840 (Office). *Fax:* (212) 826-2964 (Office). *E-mail:* singapore@un.int (Office). *Website:* www.mfa.gov.sg/newyork.

MAHDI, Sadiq Al (since 1978 known as Sadiq Abdul Rahman); Sudanese politician; b. 1936; great grandson of Imam Abdul-Rahman El Mahdi, s. of late Siddik El Mahdi; ed Comboni Coll., Khartoum and St John's Coll., Oxford; Leader, Umma Mahdist (now New Nat. Umma) Party 1961; Prime Minister 1966–67, 1986–89; overthrown in coup June 1989, arrested July 1989, released and put under house arrest Nov. 1989; Minister of Defence 1986–89; arrested on a charge of high treason 1969; exiled April 1970; returned to Sudan and arrested Feb. 1974; released April 1974; exiled 1974–77; led unsuccessful coup against fmr Pres. Nimeri July 1976, returned to Sudan Sept 1977; reconciliation with Pres. Nimeri 1977; mem. Cttee Sudanese Socialist Union (SSU) 1978–79; mem. Nat. Ass. 1986–89; led mediation mission in U.S. hostages in Iran Crisis Jan. 1980; Visiting Fellow St Antony's Coll., Oxford 1983; returned to prison Sept. 1983, released Dec. 1984; granted amnesty May 1991; arrested on charges of conspiring against mil. Govt June

1994; rearrested May 1995; escaped from house arrest Dec. 1996; in Eritrea 1996–2000, returned to Sudan Nov. 2000. *Publication:* Problems of the South Sudan.

MAHDI, Salah el-, PhD; Tunisian flautist and composer; b. 9 Feb. 1925, Tunis; ed Rashidia Inst., Zituna Univ., Inst. of Admin. Tunis and Univ. of Poitiers; teacher of music, Rashidia Inst. 1943; Dir Rashidia Inst. 1949; Judge, Law Courts of Tunis 1951; fmr Dir Dept of Fine Arts, Ministry of Educ.; participated in setting-up of Nat. Acad. of Music, Dance and Dramatic Art; Head of Direction of Music and Folk Art, Ministry of Culture 1961; later Pres. Nat. Cultural Cttee and Pres. Nat. Cttee of Music; f. Nat. Troupe of Popular Arts 1962; set up Tunisian Symphony Orchestra 1962, Nat. Soc. for Preservation of Koran, Nat. School of Koranic Intoned Psalms; participant at numerous UNESCO and other int. congresses; founding mem. Int. Inst. of Comparative Music, Berlin; Pres. World Org. of Folk Arts and Traditions, Vienna; has held many other int. musical and cultural appts.; mem. Soc. des Auteurs, Compositeurs et Editions de Musique (SACEM), now Hon. mem.; more than 600 compositions including classical and folk songs, oriental and Western instrumental music, four nubas, several muwashahs, bashrafs, symphonic poems, chamber music and pieces for piano, flute, violin and harp. *Publications:* many musical, historical and literary works on Arab music including a compilation of Tunisian musical heritage; radio and stage plays. *Address:* 22 rue Brasil, Tunis, Tunisia.

MAHDI AL TAJIR, Mohamed; Bahraini diplomatist and administrator; b. 26 Dec. 1931, Bahrain; m. Zohra Al-Tajir 1956; five s. one d.; ed Bahrain Govt School and Preston Grammar School, Lancs., England; Department of Port and Customs, Govt of Bahrain, Dir 1955–63; Dir Dept of His Highness the Ruler's Affairs and Petroleum Affairs March 1963–; Dir Nat. Bank of Dubai Ltd 1963–; Dir Dubai Petroleum Co. April 1963–; Dir Dubai Nat. Air Travel Agency Jan. 1966–; Dir Qatar-Dubai Currency Bd Oct 1965–73; Chair. South Eastern Dubai Drilling Co. April 1968–; Dir Dubai Dry Dock Co. 1973–; Amb. of the United Arab Emirates to UK 1972–82, 1983–86, also Accred to France 1972–77; Hon. Citizen of State of Texas, USA 1963. *Address:* P.O. Box 207, Dubai, United Arab Emirates.

MAHELE BOKOUNGO LIEKO, Gen.; Democratic Republic of the Congo army officer; joined Zairean army, involved in numerous conflicts in Zaire, also in Zairean action in Rwanda 1990; fmr Chief of Staff, Zaire Armed Forces (F.A.Z.), reappointed Dec. 1996; removed when Mobutu Govt overthrown May 1997.

MAHER, Terence Anthony; British bookseller and publisher; b. 5 Dec. 1935, Manchester; s. of late Herbert Maher and Lillian Maher; m. Barbara Grunbaum 1960; three s.; ed Xaverian Coll., Manchester; Controller, Carborundum Co. Ltd 1961–69; Dir Corp. Finance, First Nat. Finance Corpn 1969–72; f. Pentos PLC 1972, Chair., CEO –1993; Chair. and CEO Dillons Bookstores 1977–93; Athena Int. 1980–93, Ryman 1987–93; Chair. The Chalford Publishing Co. Ltd 1994–98, Maher Booksellers Ltd 1995–, Race Dynamics Ltd 1998–; Founder Trustee of Liberal Democrats 1988; mem. Advisory Council on Libraries 1997–98; Fellow of the Chartered Asscn of Certified Accountants. *Publications:* (jtly.) Counterblast 1965, Effective Politics 1966, Against My Better Judgement (autobiog.) 1994, Unfinished Business (fiction) 2003. *Leisure interests:* skiing, tennis, walking, reading, bridge. *Address:* 33 Clarence Terrace, Regent's Park, London, NW1 4RD; The Old House, Whichford, nr Shipston on Stour, Warwicks., CV36 5PG, England. *Telephone:* (20) 7723-4254 (London); (1608) 684-614 (Whichford).

MAHER ALI, Abdel Moneim, PhD; Egyptian biologist and business executive; b. 9 March 1922, Dammanhour; s. of Ali Elsayed Shehata and Nagia M. Manaā; m. Fardous Abbas Abdelal 1948; two s.; ed Cairo Univ., Univ. Coll. London, Ein Shams Univ.; Founder, Gen. Sec. Egyptian Youth Hostel Assoc. 1955–1970; Dir Cen. Agric. Pesticide Lab. UNDP Project 1963–69; Head Plant Protection Dept Assiut Univ. 1970, now Emer. Prof.; Gen. Sec. Egyptian Zoological Soc., Egyptian Asscn for Conservation of Nature and Natural Resources, Egyptian Asscn for Environment Care, Egyptian Asscn for Medicinal Plants 1975–; Founder then Consultant, Wady Elassiuty Protected Area 1980–94; Pres. ARADIS Co. SAE, Arab. Co. Environment Disinfection SAE Co. 1983–; now Chief Ed. Egyptian Journal for Natural Resources and Wildlife; Conservation Merit Award, World Wildlife Fund, Science and Arts 1st Class, Order of the Repub. 5th, 3rd and 2nd and other awards. *Publications include:* textbook on pest control, articles in scientific periodicals. *Leisure interests:* travel, sightseeing, archaeological tours. *Address:* 45 Jule Gamal Street, Agouza, Gizah (Office); 50 Wizaret El Ziraā Street, 12th Floor, Dokki, Gizah (Home); P.O. Box 318, Dokki Gizah, Egypt. *Telephone:* (2) 346-2029 (Office); (2) 337-3988. *Fax:* (2) 346-2029. *E-mail:* medplantus@yahoo .com (Office).

MAHER ES-SAYED, Ahmad, LLB; Egyptian politician; b. 14 Sept. 1935, Cairo; m.; ed Cairo Univ.; served in embassies in Cairo, Kinshasa, Paris, Zürich 1959–77; Amb. to Portugal 1980–82, to Belgium 1982–84, to USSR 1988–92, to USA 1992–99; Dir Arab Fund for Tech. Assistance to African States, League of Arab States 2000–01; Minister of Foreign Affairs 2001–; Order of the Repub. First Class (Egypt), Order of Merit Commdr Class (France), Order of the Great Cross (Portugal). *Address:* Ministry of Foreign Affairs, Corniche en-Nil, Cairo, Egypt (Office). *Telephone:* (2) 5749523 (Office). *Fax:* (2) 5749533 (Office). *E-mail:* ForMin@idsc.gov.eg (Office). *Website:* www.mfa.gov.eg (Office).

MAHFOUZ, Naguib; Egyptian author; b. 11 Dec. 1911, Gamaliya, Cairo; s. of Abdel Aziz Ibrahim and Fatima Mostapha Mahfouz; m. Attiyat Allah 1954; two d.; ed Univ. of Cairo; civil servant 1934; successively with Univ. of Cairo, Ministry of Waqfs, Dept of Arts and Censorship Bd 1936–59; Dir Foundation for Support of Cinema, State Cinema Org. 1959–69; contrib. to Al Ahram; Hon. mem. American Acad. of Arts and Letters, American Acad. of Arts and Sciences 2002; Nat. Prize for Letters 1970; Nobel Prize for Literature 1988; Collar of the Repub. 1972, Order of the Repub. *Films based on his works include:* The Beginning and the End, Midaq Alley, Respected Sir; numerous films in Arabic. *Television based on his works includes:* Palace Walk, Palace of Desire; numerous others in Arabic. *Publications in English include:* fiction: Midaq Alley 1966, Mirrors 1977, Miramar 1978, Children of Gebelawi 1981 (retitled Children of our Alley 1996), The Thief and the Dogs 1984, Wedding Song 1984, The Beginning and the End 1985, Autumn Quail 1985, The Beggar 1986, Respected Sir 1986, The Search 1987, God's World 1988, Fountain and Tomb 1988, Palace Walk 1989 (Egyptian State Prize 1956 for Arabic Edn), Palace of Desire 1991, Sugar Street 1992, The Journey of Ibn Fattouma 1992, Adrift on the Nile 1993, The Harafish 1994, Arabian Nights and Days 1995, The Day The Leader was Killed 1997, Echoes of an Autobiography 1997, Akhenaton: Dweller in Truth 1998, The Cairo Trilogy 2000; Naguib Mahfouz at Sidi Gabere: Conversations with the Nobel Laureate 2001, The Complete Naguib Mahfouz Library: The Twenty Fiction Vols of the Nobel Laureate in English 2001; Voices from the Other World: Ancient Egyptian Tales 2002; publications in Arabic include: over 40 novels and short stories. *Address:* American University in Cairo Press, 113 Sharia Kasr El Aini, Cairo, Egypt (Office). *Telephone:* (2) 797-6398 (Office). *Fax:* (2) 794-1440 (Office). *E-mail:* aleya@aucegypt.edu (Office). *Website:* www.aucpress.com (Office).

MAHGOUB, Mohammed Ahmed; Sudanese politician and lawyer; b. 1908; ed Gordon Coll. and Khartoum School of Law; practising lawyer; fmr mem. Legis. Assembly; accompanied Umma Party Del. to UN 1947; mem. Constitution Amendment Comm.; non-party candidate in Gen. Election 1954; Leader of the Opposition 1954–56; Minister of Foreign Affairs 1956–58, 1964–65; Prime Minister of Sudan 1965–66, 1967–69; practising solicitor 1958–64. *Publications:* Democracy on Trial 1974 and several Vols of poetry (in Arabic). *Address:* 60c Prince's Gate, Exhibition Road, London, S.W.7, England.

MAHINDRA, Keshub, BSc, CIMgt; Indian business executive; b. 9 Oct. 1923, Simla; s. of late Kailash Chandra Mahindra and Savitri Mahindra; m. Sudha Y. Varde 1956; three d.; ed Univ. of Pennsylvania, USA; Chair. Mahindra and Mahindra Ltd, Bd of Govs. Mahindra United World Coll. of India; Dir Bombay Dyeing and Mfg Co. Ltd, Bombay Burmah Trading Corpn Ltd, Tata Iron and Steel Co. Ltd, Tata Chemicals Ltd, Housing Devt Finance Corpn Ltd (now Vice-Chair.), United World Coll. Int. Ltd, UK, Mahindra Ugine Steel Co. Ltd (now Chair.), Infrastructure Leasing & Financial Services Ltd, etc.; Pres. Asscn of Indian Automobile Mfrs 1964–65, Bombay Chamber of Commerce and Industry 1966–67, Assoc. Chamber of Commerce and Industry 1969–70, Employers' Fed. of India 1985–97, Indo-American Soc. 1991–92; mem. Apex Advisory Council of Assoc. Chambers of Commerce and Industry of India, Int. Council Asia Soc. New York 1983–97; Vice-Pres. Nat. Soc. for Clean Cities; numerous other appointments; Hon. Fellow All India Man. Asscn 1990; Modi Enterprises Man of the Year Award 1980, Giants Int. Business Leadership Award 1972–82, Madras Man. Asscn Business Leadership Award 1983, Indian Businessman of the Year 1989, Rotary Award 1992, Rashtra Bhushan Award 1993, Sri Gandhi Medal for Industrial Peace 1994, Rotary Vocational Excellence Award in the Field of Industry 1996, IMC Diamond Jubilee Endowment Trust Award 1997, Motorindia Automan Award 2000, Dadabhai Naoroji Int. Award for Excellence and Lifetime Achievement 2000; Chevalier Légion d'honneur 1987. *Leisure interests:* golf, tennis, photography, reading. *Address:* Mahindra & Mahindra Ltd, Gateway Building, Apollo Bunder, Mumbai 400 001 (Office); St Helen's Court, Pedder Road, Mumbai 400 026, India (Home). *Telephone:* (22) 2875488 (Office); (22) 3804106 (Home). *Fax:* (22) 2875489.

MAHMOUD, Mohamed Kamel, DSc; Egyptian professor of chemistry and research administrator; b. 5 Sept. 1926; ed Univ. of Cairo; demonstrator Chem. Dept, Faculty of Sciences, Cairo Univ. 1948–54, lecturer 1954–57; mem. Nat. Research Centre mission to Switzerland 1957–60; Asst Research Prof., Nat. Research Centre 1960–64, Research Prof. and Head, Textile Research Div. 1964–74, Pres. Nat. Research Centre 1974–84; Pres. Acad. of Scientific Research and Tech. 1984–86; Research Prof. Nat. Research Centre 1986–; mem. Inst. of Egypt, Scientific Council of Africa, Egyptian Chem. Soc., Bd Acad. of Scientific Research and Tech.; Fellow Islamic Acad. of Sciences, Vice-Pres. 1986–94; State Prize of Chem. 1965, Order of Merit, First Grade with Star (Germany) 1979; Order of Science and Art, First Grade 1981. *Address:* National Research Centre, Al-Tahrir Street, Dokki, Cairo, Egypt (Office). *Telephone:* (2) 701010 (Office). *Fax:* (2) 700931 (Office).

MAHMUD, ZAKIR, BE, MBA; Pakistani banker; b. Hyderabad, India; s. of Naziruddin Mahmud; m. Butool Mahmud 1978; two d. one s.; ed Matric Cantt Public School, Nat. Coll., Adamjee Science Coll., NED Eng Coll., Univ. of Calif., USA; with Bank of America, Ireland 1972–78, Karachi 1978–81, Lahore 1981–85, Bahrain 1985–91; with Credit Agricole Indosuez Bank 1991–2002, Man. for Pakistan 1995–2002; Pres. Habib Bank Ltd 2002–. *Leisure interests:* listening to music, old Indian films. *Address:* Habib Bank Ltd., Habib Bank Plaza, I.I. Chundrigar Road, Karachi, Pakistan (Office). *Website:* www.habibbank.com.

MAHON, Sir (John) Denis, Kt, CH, CBE, MA, FBA; British art historian; b. 8 Nov. 1910; s. of the late John FitzGerald Mahon and Lady Alice Evelyn Browne; ed Eton and Christ Church, Oxford; Trustee of the Nat. Gallery 1957–64, 1966–73; mem. Advisory Panel, Nat. Art Collections Fund 1975–; specialist in 17th Century Italian paintings and has notable collection, exhibited Nat. Gallery London 1997; mem. Cttee of the Biennial Exhbns., Bologna, Italy; Corresp. Fellow Accad. Raffaello, Urbino 1968, Ateneo Veneto 1987; Hon. DLitt (Newcastle) 1969, (Oxford) 1994, (La Sapienza, Rome) 1998, (Bologna) 2002; Medal for Benemeriti della Cultura for services to criticism and history of Italian art 1957, Archiginnasio d'Oro, City of Bologna 1968, Serena Medal for Italian Studies, British Acad. 1972, Hon. Citizen, Cento 1982. *Publications:* Studies in Seicento Art and Theory 1947, Poussiniana 1962, The Drawings of Guercino in the collection of HM The Queen at Windsor Castle (with N. Turner) 1989; various contribs. to catalogues of art exhbns. and numerous articles in Publs on history of art. *Address:* 33 Cadogan Square, London, SW1X 0HU, England. *Telephone:* (20) 7235-7311, (20) 7235-2530.

MAHONEY, Rev. John Aloysius (Jack), SJ, MA, DTheol, CCMI; British university professor; b. 14 Jan. 1931, Coatbridge, Scotland; s. of Patrick Mahoney and Margaret Doris; ed Our Lady's High School, Motherwell, St Aloysius Coll. Glasgow, Univ. of Glasgow and Gregorian Univ. Rome; lecturer in Moral and Pastoral Theology, Heythrop Coll. Oxon. 1967–70; lecturer in Moral and Pastoral Theology, Heythrop Coll. Univ. of London 1970–86, Prin. 1976–81; F. D. Maurice Prof. of Moral and Social Theology, King's Coll. London 1986–93 Prof. Emer. 1999–; Founding Dir King's Coll. Business Ethics Research Centre 1987–93; Mercers' School Memorial Prof. of Commerce, Gresham Coll. City of London 1987–93; Dixons Prof. of Business Ethics and Social Responsibility, London Business School 1993–98; Founding Dir Lauriston Centre for Contemporary Belief and Action, Edin.; Hon. Fellow Faculty of Divinity, Edin. Univ. 1998–, Gresham Coll., London 1999–, St Mary's Univ. Coll. 1999–, Heythrop Coll. Univ. of London 2000–. *Publications:* Seeking the Spirit: Essays in Moral and Pastoral Theology 1981, Bioethics and Belief: Religion and Medicine in Dialogue 1984, The Making of Moral Theology: A Study of the Roman Catholic Tradition 1987, Teaching Business Ethics in the UK, Europe and the USA 1990, Business Ethics in a New Europe (ed.) 1992. *Leisure interests:* piano, sketching, unrequited golf. *Address:* 28 Lauriston Street, Edinburgh, EH3 9DJ, Scotland. *Telephone:* (131) 228-6621. *E-mail:* jmlaur@aol.com (Home).

MAHONY, HE Cardinal Roger Michael, BA, STB; American ecclesiastic; b. 27 Feb. 1936, Hollywood, Calif.; s. of late Victor James Mahony and Loretta Marie Baron; ed St John's Seminary Coll., St John's Theologate, California, Catholic Univ. of America, Washington, DC; ordained RC Priest, Fresno, Calif. 1962; Bishop, Fresno, Calif. 1975; Bishop of Stockton, Calif. 1980; Archbishop of LA 1985; cr. Cardinal Priest 1991; Archbishop of LA 1985–; mem. numerous cttees. of Nat. Confs. of Catholic Bishops, USA 1976–; several Pontifical Councils, Vatican 1984–; Dr hc (Loyola Marymount, LA) 1986, (Portland, Ore.) 1988, (Notre Dame, Ind.) 1989, (St Patrick's Coll., Ireland) 1991, (S California) 2002. *Address:* 3424 Wilshire Boulevard, Los Angeles, CA 90010, USA (Office). *Telephone:* (213) 637-7288 (Office). *Fax:* (213) 637-6510 (Office).

MAHUAD WITTS, Jamil, PhD; Ecuadorean politician and lawyer; b. 29 July 1949, Loja; s. of Jorge Antonio Mahuad Chalela and Rosa Witt García; m. Tatiana Calderón (divorced); one d.; ed Pontificia Universidad Católica del Ecuador, John F. Kennedy School of Govt, Harvard Univ., USA; legal assessor and Dir of pvt. credit banks 1973–78; Pres. Federación de Estudiantes Universitarios Católicos del Ecuador 1974–75; Regional Sec. Federación de Estudiantes de las Universidades Católicas de América Latina 1975–81; mem. Democracia Popular 1981; Dir Empresa Nacional de Productos Vitales 1981–83; Minister of Labour 1981–83; Pres. Democracia Popular 1987–88, 1991–93; Vice-Pres. Demócrata Cristiano de América (ODCA), Andina Region 1991–97; Mayor of Quito 1992–98; Pres. of Ecuador 1998–2000 (deposed by armed forces). *Address:* C/o Democracia Popular, Calle Luis Saá 153 y Hnos Pazmiño, Casilla 17-01-2300, Quito, Ecuador.

MAIDEN, Sir Colin James, Kt, ME (NZ), DPhil; New Zealand university vice-chancellor (retd) and company director; b. 5 May 1933, Auckland; s. of Henry A. Maiden and Lorna Richardson; m. Jenefor Mary Rowe 1957; one s. three d.; ed Univs. of Auckland and Oxford; Head, Hypersonic Physics Section, Canadian Armament Research and Devt Establishment, Québec City, Canada 1958–60; Sr lecturer in Mechanical Eng Univ. of Auckland 1960–61; Head, Material Sciences Lab. Gen. Motors Corpn Defence Research Labs. Santa Barbara, Calif. 1961–66; Man. of Process Eng Gen. Motors Corpn Tech. Centre, Warren, Mich. 1966–70; Vice-Chancellor, Univ. of Auckland 1971–94; Chair. NZ Energy Research and Devt Cttee 1974–81, NZ Vice-Chancellor's Cttee 1977–78, 1991, Liquid Fuels Trust Bd 1978–86, NZ Synthetic Fuels Corpn Ltd 1980–90, Tower Insurance Co. Ltd 1988–, Fisher & Paykel Ltd 1978–2001, Independent Newspapers Ltd 1989–2001(now Dir); Dir Mason Industries Ltd 1971–78, Farmers Trading Co. Ltd, 1973–86, Winstone Ltd 1978–88, Wilkins & Davies Ltd 1986–89, New Zealand Steel Ltd 1988–92, ANZ Banking Group (NZ) Ltd 1990–93, The NZ Refining Co. Ltd 1991–, Progressive Enterprises Ltd 1992–2000, DB Group Ltd 1994–, Sedgwick (NZ) Ltd 1994–98 (now Chair.), Transpower New Zealand Ltd 1994– (now Chair.), Tower Ltd 1995–2003, Foodland Associated Ltd 2000–, Fisher and Paykel Healthcare Corpn Ltd 2001–; various professional appts.; Hon. Treas. Asscn of Commonwealth Univs. 1988–98; Hon. LLD (Auckland); Queen Elizabeth Silver Jubilee Medal 1977, Medal of Univ. of Bonn 1983, Thomson Medal,

Royal Soc. of NZ 1986, Symons Award, Asscn of Commonwealth Univs. 1999. *Publications:* numerous scientific and tech. papers. *Leisure interest:* tennis. *Address:* 7 Chatfield Place, Remuera, Auckland 5, New Zealand. *Telephone:* (9) 529-0380. *Fax:* (9) 522-4374.

MAIJ-WEGGEN, Hanja; Netherlands politician; b. 29 Dec. 1943; trained as nurse; subsequently became lecturer in health care; mem. European Parl. 1979–, Vice-Chair. European People's Party (Christian Democratic Group) 1987; Minister of Transport 1989–94, also of Public Works and Water Man.; mem. Christian Democratic Appeal. *Address:* European Parliament, 97-113 rue Wiertz, 1047 Brussels, Belgium (Office); Parliament, Brussels, Belgium. *Telephone:* (2) 284-78-67.

MAILER, Norman Kingsley, BS; American writer; b. 31 Jan. 1923, Long Branch, NJ; s. of Isaac Barnett Mailer and Fanny Schneider; m. 1st Beatrice Silverman 1944 (divorced 1952); one d.; m. 2nd Adele Morales 1954 (divorced 1962); two d.; m. 3rd Lady Jeanne Campbell 1962 (divorced 1963); one d.; m. 4th Beverly Rentz Bentley 1963 (divorced 1980); two s. one d.; m. 5th Carol Stevens (divorced); one d.; m. 6th Norris Church 1980; one s.; ed Harvard Univ.; served in US Army 1944–46; Co-f. New York weekly Village Voice 1955; mem. Editorial Bd of Dissent magazine 1953–69, American Acad. of Arts and Letters 1984–; Pres. of PEN (US Chapter) 1984–86; Dir films: Wild 90 1967, Beyond the Law 1967, Maidstone 1968, Tough Guys Don't Dance 1987; acted in film Ragtime 1981; Nat. Book Award for Arts and Letters 1969; Pulitzer Prize for Non-Fiction 1969, for Fiction 1980; 14th Annual Award for outstanding service to the arts, McDowell Colony 1973. *Publications:* The Naked and The Dead 1948, Barbary Shore 1951, The Deer Park 1955 (dramatized 1967), Advertisements for Myself 1959, Deaths for the Ladies (poems) 1962, The Presidential Papers 1963, An American Dream 1964, Cannibals and Christians 1966, Why are we in Vietnam?: A Novel 1967, The Armies of the Night 1968, Miami and the Siege of Chicago 1968, Moonshot 1969, A Fire on the Moon 1970, The Prisoner of Sex 1971, Existential Errands 1972, St George and the Godfather 1972, Marilyn 1973, The Faith of Graffiti 1974, The Fight 1975, Some Honourable Men 1976, Genius and Lust–A Journey Through the Writings of Henry Miller 1976, A Transit to Narcissus 1978, The Executioner's Song 1979, Of Women and Their Elegance 1980, The Essential Mailer (selections) 1982, Pieces and Pontifications 1982, Ancient Evenings (novel) 1983, Tough Guys Don't Dance (novel) 1984, Harlot's Ghost (novel) 1991, Oswald's Tale 1995, Portrait of Picasso as a Young Man 1995, The Gospel According to the Son 1997, The Time of Our Time 1998, The Spooky Art: Thoughts on Writing 2003, Why Are We At War? 2003; contribs. to numerous magazines. *Address:* c/o American Academy of Arts and Letters, 633 West 155th Street, New York, NY 10032, USA (Office).

MAINI, Sir Ravinder Nath, Kt, BA, MB, BChir, FRCP, FRCPE, FMedSci; British rheumatologist; b. 17 Nov. 1937; s. of Sir Amar (Nath) Maini and Saheli Maini (née Mehra); m. 1st Marianne Gorm 1963 (divorced 1986); one s. one d. (and one s. deceased); m. 2nd Geraldine Room 1987; two s.; ed Univ. of Cambridge; jr medical appointments at Guy's, Brompton and Charing Cross Hosps 1962–70; Consultant Physician St. Stephen's Hosp., London 1970–76, Rheumatology Dept, Charing Cross Hosp. 1970; Prof. of Immunology of Rheumatic Diseases, Charing Cross and Westminster Medical School 1981–89; Dir Kennedy Inst. of Rheumatology 1990–2000 (Head Clinical Immunology Div. 1979); Prof. of Rheumatology 1989–, Head Kennedy Inst. of Rheumatology Div., Imperial Coll. School of Medicine at Charing Cross Hosp. Campus (fmrly Charing Cross and Westminster Medical School), Univ. of London 2000–; Pres. British Soc. for Rheumatology 1989–90 (Heberden Orator 1988), British League Against Rheumatism 1985–89; Chair. Research Subcttee 1980–85 and mem. Scientific Coordinating Cttee, Arthritis and Rheumatism Council 1980–95; Chair. Standing Cttee for Investigative Rheumatology, European League Against Rheumatism 1990–97; mem. Exec. Cttee, Asscn of Physicians of GB and Ireland 1989–91; Chair. Rheumatology Cttee, Royal Coll. of Physicians 1992–96 (Croonian Lecturer 1995, Lumleian Lecturer 1999); mem. European Union of Medical Specialists 1994– (Pres. Section of Rheumatology 1996–99, Chair. European Bd of Rheumatology 1996–99); Samuel Hyde Lecturer, Royal Soc. of Medicine 1998; Hon. Consultant, Charing Cross Hosp., Hammersmith Hosps. NHS Trust; Dr hc (Univ. René Descartes, Paris) 1994; Hon. mem. Australian Rheumatism Asscn 1977, Norwegian Soc. for Rheumatology 1988, American Coll. of Rheumatology 1988, Hellenic Rheumatology Soc. 1989, Hungarian Rheumatology Soc. 1990, Scandinavian Soc. for Immunology 1996, Mexican Soc. for Rheumatology 1996; Carol Nachman Prize for Rheumatology (jt recipient), City of Wiesbaden 1999, Distinguished Investigator Award, American Coll. of Rheumatology 1999, Crafoord Prize (jt recipient), Royal Swedish Acad. of Sciences 2000, Courtin-Clarins Prize (jt recipient), Asscn de Recherche sur la Polyarthrite 2000. *Publications include:* Immunology of Rheumatic Diseases 1977, Modulation of Autoimmune Disease (Ed.) 1981, Textbook of the Rheumatic Diseases, 6th edn. (contrib.) 1986, T-Cell Activation in Health and Disease (Ed.) 1989, Rheumatoid Arthritis (Ed.) 1992, Oxford Textbook of Rheumatology (contrib.) 1993, Rheumatology (Section Ed.) 1993, Manual of Biological Markers of Disease (Co-Ed.: Section A, Methods of Autoantibody Detection 1993, Section B, Autoantigens 1994, Section C, Clinical Significance of Autoantibodies 1996), Oxford Textbook of Medicine (contrib.) 2001; numerous articles in scientific journals. *Leisure interests:* music appreciation, walking. *Address:* Kennedy Institute of Rheumatology, 1 Aspenlea Road, London, W6 8LH, England (Office). *Telephone:* (20) 8383-4444 (Office).

MAIORESCU, Mircea, PhD; Romanian professor of medicine and politician; b. 23 May 1926, Bucharest; s. of Octav Maiorescu and Elena Maiorescu; m. Zoe Maiorescuh; one s. one d.; ed Paediatrics Coll. of Bucharest; teacher Carol Davila Univ., Bucharest 1956–, Prof. 1974–; Dir Mother and Child Protection Inst. 1978–84; Prof., Marie Curie Paediatrics Clinic Bucharest Univ. of Medicine; mem. European Asscn of Pediatric Cardiology 1983, Acad. of Medical Sciences of Romania 1991, New York Acad. of Sciences 1992; Minister of Health 1991–92; Vice-Pres. WHO Gen. Ass. 1992; mem. Cttee Romanian Soc. of Pediatrics, Romanian Soc. of Pediatric Cardiology; Visiting Prof. Louisville Univ., Ky, USA 1995; Award for Int. Medical Cooperation, Baylor Health Care Systems (Dallas, Tex.) and Humana Foundation (Louisville, Ky), USA 1999. *Publications:* over 300 works. *Leisure interests:* classical music, essays., philosophy, poetry. *Address:* Marie Curie University Hospital for Children, Bulevard Brâncoveanu 20, 75544 Bucharest (Office); Str. Nicolae Filimon 31, 77728 Bucharest, Romania (Home).

MAIRE, Edmond; French trades union official; b. 24 Jan. 1931, Epinay-sur-Seine; s. of Julien Maire and Marie-Thérèse Conchou; m. Raymonde Le Goff 1954; three c.; ed Conservatoire Nat. des Arts et Métiers; technician, chemical industry; Perm. Sec. Fed. of Chemical Industries of Conféd. Française Démocratique du Travail (C.F.D.T.) 1958–70; mem. Exec. Cttee of C.F.D.T., in charge of professional and social action; Sec.-Gen. of C.F.D.T. 1971–88; Pres. Villages-Vacances-Familles (VVF) 1989–99; Pres. de la Section Affaires Sociales du Conseil Nat. du Tourisme 1989–99; Pres. Société d'investissement France Active 1999–; mem. Conseil Economique et Social 1969–74. *Publications:* Demain l'autogestion 1976, Nouvelles frontières pour le syndicalisme 1987, L'Esprit libre 1999. *Address:* 37 rue Bergère, 75009 Paris (Office); 145 rue Pelleport, 75020 Paris, France (Home). *Telephone:* 1-53-24-26-26 (Office). *Fax:* 1-53-24-26-63 (Office). *E-mail:* edmondm@franceactive.org.

MAISENBERG, Oleg; Austrian pianist; b. 29 April 1945, Odessa, USSR (now Ukraine); s. of Adel and Josef Maisenberg; two c.; ed Moscow Gnessin Inst. of Music (pupil of A. Yokheles); winner Franz Schubert Competition in Vienna 1967, 20th Century Music Competition, Vienna 1967; performed Rachmaninov's 1st Piano Concert with Nat. Orchestra of Moldavia; emigrated to Austria 1981; concert performances worldwide as soloist and chamber musician; recordings of Schubert, Schuman, Liszt, Scriabin, Berg, Stravinsky, R. Strauss, Dvořák, Milhaud, Weber, Schönberg, Bartok, Rachmaninov and Prokofiev; Prof. Stuttgart Conservatory and Vienna Acad. of Music, Hon. mem. Konzerthaus Gesellschaft, Vienna. *Address:* c/o Concerto Winderstein, Leopoldstrasse 25, 80802 Munich; In Der Gugl 7-9, Klosterneuburg 3400, Austria; Agentur Dr Raab/Dr Böhm, Plankengasse 7, 1010 Vienna, Austria. *Telephone:* (22) 432-64-85. *Fax:* (22) 432-64-85.

MAISKY, Mischa (Michael); Belgian (b. USSR) concert cellist; b. 10 Jan. 1948, Riga, Latvia; m. Maryanne Kay Lipman 1983; one s. one d.; ed Moscow Conservatory (with Mstislav Rostropovich), Univ. of Southern California; début with Leningrad Philharmonic Orchestra 1965; emigrated to Israel 1972; début with Pittsburgh Symphony Orchestra at Carnegie Hall 1973; début at Royal Festival Hall 1976; début at Berlin Philharmonic Hall 1978; numerous TV, film and video appearances all over the world; played Walton Concerto, London Festival Hall 1993, Shostakovich Concerto, London Proms; All-Soviet prize-winner 1965, Int. Tchaikovsky Competition 1966; also winner of Cassada Competition, Florence 1973 and Rostropovich Competition, Paris 1981; Grand Prix du Disque, Paris 1985; Record Acad. Prize, Tokyo 1985. *Recordings include:* Six Suites for Solo Cello (Bach), Three Sonatas for Cello and Piano (Bach), Concerto in A minor Op. 102 for Violin, Cello and Orchestra (Brahms), Concerto for Cello and Orchestra in A Minor (Schumann). *Leisure interests:* music, chess, computing. *Address:* 138 Meerlaan, 1900 Overijse, Belgium.

MAISONROUGE, Jacques (Gaston); French business executive and electronics engineer; b. 20 Sept. 1924, Cachan; s. of Paul Maisonrouge and Suzanne Maisonrouge (née Cazas); m. Françoise Féron 1948; one s. four d.; ed Lycée Saint-Louis, Paris, Ecole Centrale des Arts et Manufactures; joined IBM France as engineer 1948, Asst Sales Dir 1954, mem. Bd dirs. 1965–; Marketing Man. IBM World Trade Europe Corpn 1956, Regional Man. 1958, Asst Gen. Man. 1959, Vice-Pres. 1962, Pres. and CEO 1964; Pres. IBM World Trade Corpn 1967–81, Sr Vice-Pres. IBM Corpn 1972–84, Chair. IBM World Trade Europe-Africa 1974–81, IBM World Trade Corpn 1976–84, mem. Bd dirs. IBM Corpn 1984, IBM Europe-Africa-Middle East 1988–95; Vice-Chair. Bd dirs. Liquid Air Corpn 1984–86 (mem. Bd dirs. 1971–94); Dir.-Gen. for Industry, Ministry of Industry and Tourism 1986–87; Pres. Saint-Honoré Europe 1989–92; Chair. Bd dirs. Ecole Centrale des Arts et Manufactures 1977–87, Centre Français du Commerce Extérieur 1987–89, Image de la France Comm. 1989–90; Chair. Bd of Govs. American Hosp., Paris 1993–96 (Gov. 1990–), Asscn France-Etats-Unis 1994–2000; Chancellor Int. Acad. of Man. 1988–93; mem. Atomic Energy Cttee 1986–87; Grand Officier Légion d'honneur, Commdr Ordre Nat. du Mérite et des Palmes Académiques, Officier des Arts et Lettres and decorations from Austria, Malta, Italy, Belgium, Sweden and Vatican City. *Publication:* International Manager 1985. *Leisure interests:* walking in the mountains, spending time with his 10 grandchildren. *Address:* 3 boulevard Flandrin, 75116 Paris, France (Home). *Telephone:* 1-40-72-76-96. *Fax:* 1-40-72-71-38 (Home).

MAITLAND, Sir Donald James Dundas, GCMG, OBE, MA, FRSA; British diplomatist and civil servant (retd); b. 16 Aug. 1922, Edin.; s. of Thomas D.

Maitland and Wilhelmina S. Dundas; m. Jean Marie Young 1950; one s. one d.; ed George Watson's Coll. and Edin. Univ.; Army Service 1941–47; joined Diplomatic Service 1947; Consul, Amara 1950; British Embassy, Baghdad 1950–53; Private Sec. to Minister of State, Foreign Office 1954–56; Dir Middle East Centre for Arab Studies, Lebanon 1956–60; Foreign Office 1960–63; Counsellor, British Embassy, Cairo 1963–65; Head, News Dept, Foreign Office 1965–67; Prin. Private Sec. to Foreign and Commonwealth Sec. 1967–69; Amb. to Libya 1969–70; Chief Press Sec. to Prime Minister 1970–73; Perm. Rep. to UN 1973–74; Deputy Under-Sec., FCO 1974–75; mem. British Overseas Trade Bd 1974–75; UK mem. Commonwealth Group on Trade, Aid and Devt 1975; UK Perm. Rep. to European Communities 1975–79; Deputy Perm. Under-Sec. FCO 1979–80; Perm. Under-Sec. of State, Dept of Energy 1980–82; Chair. UK Cttee World Communications Year 1983; Chair. Ind. Comm. World-wide Telecommunications Devt (Maitland Comm.) 1983–85; Govt Dir Britoil 1983–85; Dir Slough Estates 1983–92, Northern Eng Industries 1986–89; Adviser, British Telecom 1985–86; Deputy Chair. Independent Broadcasting Authority (IBA) 1986–89; Chair. Health Educ. Authority 1989–94; Pro-Chancellor, Bath Univ. 1996–2000, Visiting Prof. 2000–; mem. Commonwealth War Graves Comm. 1983–87; Chair. Christians for Europe (later Charlemagne Inst.) 1984–93; Pres. Federal Trust for Educ. and Research 1987–; Chair. Govs Westminster Coll., Oxford 1994–97; Chair. Thinknet Comm. 1989–95; Dir Project Hope UK 1996–; Hon. Fellow Bath Spa Univ. Coll. 2000; Hon. LLD (Bath) 1995; Hon. DLitt (Univ. of West of England) 2000. *Publications:* Diverse Times, Sundry Places (autobiog.) 1996, Spring Blossom, Autumn Leaves (miscellany) 1998, The Boot and Other Stories 1999, The Running Tide 2000, Edinburgh – Seat of Learning 2002. *Leisure interests:* music, hill-walking. *Address:* 2 Rosemary Walk, Church Street, Bradford on Avon, BA15 1BP, England. *Telephone:* (1225) 863063. *Fax:* (1225) 723157.

MAITLAND SMITH, Geoffrey, FCA; British business executive and accountant; b. 27 Feb. 1933, London; s. of late Philip John Maitland Smith and of Kathleen (née Goff) Maitland Smith; m. 3rd Lucinda Enid Whyte 1986; four s. two d.; ed Univ. Coll. School, London; Partner, Thornton Baker & Co., Chartered Accountants 1960–70; Dir Sears PLC (fmrly Sears Holdings PLC) 1971–95, Chief Exec. 1978–88, Jt Chair. 1984–85, Chair. 1985–95; Chair. British Shoe Corpn 1984–92, Mallet PLC 1986–89, Selfridges Ltd 1985–93, Garrard & Co. 1985–90, Mappin & Webb Ltd 1985–90, Hammerson PLC 1993–99 (Dir 1990–99), W and F. C. Bonham and Sons Ltd 1996–2000, Fiske PLC (non-exec.) 2000–; Pres. Intercontinental Group of Dept Stores 1990–95; Deputy Chair. Midland Bank 1992–96 (Dir 1986–96); Dir Asprey PLC 1980–93, Cen. Ind. Television 1983–85, Courtaulds PLC 1983–90, Imperial Group PLC 1984–86, HSBC Holdings PLC 1992–96; Hon. Vice-Pres. Inst. of Marketing 1987–94; mem. Bd Financial Reporting Council 1990–98; Chair. Council, Univ. Coll. School 1987–96. *Leisure interest:* opera. *Address:* Fiske PLC, Salisbury House, London Wall, London, EC2M 5QS, England (Office); Manor Barn, Fifield, Oxon., OX7 6HF. *Telephone:* (20) 7448-4700 (Office); (1993) 832441. *Fax:* (20) 7256-5365 (Office); (1993) 832442 (Home).

MAITLIS, Peter M., PhD, FRS, FRSC, FCIC; British professor of chemistry; b. 15 Jan. 1933, Berlin; s. of Jacob Maitlis and Judith Maitlis; m. Marion Basco 1959; three d.; ed Univ. of Birmingham and Univ. of London; Asst Lecturer, Univ. of London 1956–60; Fulbright Fellow and Research Assoc., Harvard and Cornell Univs., USA, 1960–62; Asst Prof., Assoc. Prof. and Prof., McMaster Univ., Canada 1962–72; Prof. of Inorganic Chem., Sheffield Univ. 1972–94, Research Prof. 1994–2002, Research Prof. Emeritus 2003–; Chair. Science and Eng Research Council, Chem. Cttee 1985–88; Pres. Dalton Div., Royal Soc. of Chem. 1985–87, Ludwig Mond Lecturer 1997; mem. Council The Royal Soc. 1991–93; Foreign mem. Accad. dei Lincei, Italy 1999; Sir Edward Frankland Lecturer, Royal Soc. of Chem. 1985; Tilden Lecturer 1979; David Craig Lecturer, Australian Nat. Univ. 2000; Stone Lecturer Bristol Univ. 2001; Paolo Chini Lecturer Italian Chemical Soc. 2001; Fellow, Alfred P. Sloan Foundation 1967–69; Steacie Prize in Natural Sciences 1970, Royal Soc. of Chem. Medal 1981, Kurnakov Medal of Russian Acad. of Sciences 1998. *Publications:* The Organic Chemistry of Palladium, 2 Vols 1971; numerous research Publs in scientific journals. *Leisure interests:* music, travel, reading. *Address:* Department of Chemistry, The University, Sheffield, S3 7HF, England. *Telephone:* (114) 222-9320.

MAITRE, Jean-Philippe; Swiss lawyer and politician; b. 18 June 1949, Geneva; ed Univ. of Geneva; barrister 1973–85; Nat. Councillor, Swiss Fed. Parl. 1983–; Minister of the Economy 1985–97; Pres. of Govt of Geneva 1992–97. *Address:* 3 place Claparède, 1205 Geneva, Switzerland (Office). *Telephone:* (22) 7034750 (Office). *Fax:* (22) 7034751 (Office). *E-mail:* jpmgeneve@nomea.ch (Office).

MAJALI, Abdel Salam al-, MD, D.L.C., FACS, DH.C.; Jordanian university president; b. 18 Feb. 1925, Karak; s. of Attallah Majali and Khadeejeh Serougi; m. Joan M. Lachlan 1956; two s. one d.; ed Medical Coll., Syrian Univ., Damascus; Dir-Gen. and Ear, Nose and Throat Consultant, The Royal Medical Services, Jordanian Armed Forces, Amman 1960–69; Minister of Health 1969–71; Pres. Univ. of Jordan, Amman 1971–76, 1980–90; Minister of Educ. and Minister of State for Prime Ministry Affairs 1976–79; Prime Minister of Jordan 1993–95, 1997–99, Minister of Defence and Foreign Affairs 1993–95, Minister of Defence 1997–99; Chair. and mem. UN Univ. Council, Tokyo 1977–83; Fellow, American Coll. of Surgeons; Dr. hc (Hacettepe Univ.), Ankara) 1974; Jordan Independence Medal; Medal of St John of Jerusalem and other decorations.

MAJEKODUNMI, Chief the Hon. Moses Adekoyejo, Chief Otun of Egbaland, Chief Maiyegun of Lagos, Chief Bashegun of Ede, Chief Agba-Akin of Oshogbo, Chief Kaiyero of Akure, Chief Maiyegun of Iwo, Chief Asipa of Iragbiji, CMG, CFR, LLD, MA, MD, FRCPI, F.M.C.O.G., FRCOG, M.A.O., D.C.H., LM; Nigerian administrator and physician; b. 17 Aug. 1916, Abeokuta; s. of Chief J. B. Majekodun, Chief Otun of Egbaland and Alice Oladunni (Soetan); m. 1st Nola C. Maclaughlin 1943 (divorced 1963); five s. three d.; m. 2nd Katsina Saratu Atta 1964; ed Abeokuta Grammar School, St Gregory's Coll., Lagos, Trinity Coll., Dublin; House Physician, Nat. Children's Hosp., Dublin 1941–43; Medical Officer, Nigeria 1943–49; Consulting Obstetrician, Massey Street Maternity Hosp., General Hosp. and Creek Hosp., Lagos 1949–60; Sr Specialist Obstetrician, Nigerian Federal Gov. Medical Services 1949–60; Senator and Leader of Senate 1960; Minister of State for the Army 1960–61, Fed. Minister of Health 1961–66; Fed. Minister of Health and Information 1965; Admin. for W Nigeria 1962; Pres. 16th World Health Assembly 1963; Int. Vice-Pres., 3rd World Conf. on Medical Educ., New Delhi 1966; Chancellor Ogun State Univ. 1986–; Chair. Merchant Banking Corpn Nigeria Ltd, Westminster Dredging (Nigeria) Ltd 1990–; mem. Bd of Govs., St Gregory's Coll., Lagos; Chair. Bd of Govs., St Nicholas Hosp., Lagos 1967–; Chair. Bd Dirs. Lion Bldgs. Ltd; Dir Abbott Labs. (Nigeria) Ltd, Swiss Nigeria Chemical Co., Johnson and Johnson (Nigeria) Ltd; Trustee, J. K. Randle Memorial Hall, Lagos; mem. Soc. Gynaecology and Obstetrics, Nigeria; Hon. LLD (Trinity Coll., Dublin), Hon. DSc (Lagos), (Ogun State Univ.). *Publications:* Premature Infants: Management and Prognosis 1943, Behold the Key (play) 1944, Partial Atresia of the Cervix Complicating Pregnancy 1946, Sub-Acute Intussusception in Adolescents 1948, Thiopentone Sodium in Operative Obstetrics 1954, Rupture of the Uterus involving the Bladder 1955, Effects of Malnutrition in Pregnancy and Lactation 1957, Medical Education and the Health Services: A Critical Review of Priorities in a Developing Country 1966. *Leisure interests:* riding, squash, swimming. *Address:* Ogun State University, PMB 2002, Ago-Iwoye, Ogun State (Office); 3 Kingsway, Ikoyi, Lagos, Nigeria (Home). *Telephone:* (37) 390149 (Office); 681660 (Home).

MAJKO, Pandeli Sotir, LLB; Albanian politician; b. 15 Nov. 1967; m.; two c.; ed Univ. of Tirana; Rep. Dec. 1990 Movt; co-f. Democratic Party 1990, left party 1991; joined Socialist Party of Albania 1991, Sec.-Gen. of Public Relations 1996–97, Sec. 1997–99, also leader of Parl. Group, head of del. to Org. for Security and Co-operation in Europe; Prime Minister of Albania 1998–99, Feb.–July 2002; Minister of Defence 2002–; f. Forum of Euro-Socialist Youth 1991; Chair. Euro-Socialist Forum 1992–95; MP 1992–; Torch of Democracy Award 1993. *Address:* Ministria e Mbrojtjes, Bulevardi Dëmorët e Kombit, Tirana; Council of Ministers, Këshilli i Ministrave, Tirana, Albania. *Telephone:* (42) 22103. *Fax:* (42) 28325. *E-mail:* info@mod.gov.al. *Website:* www.mod.gov.al.

MAJOR, Clarence, PhD; American novelist, poet and painter; b. 31 Dec. 1936, Atlanta, Ga; s. of Clarence Major and Inez Huff; m. Pamela Ritter 1980; ed Union Graduate School, Yellow Springs and Cincinnati, Ohio, Univ. of the State of New York, Albany; Prof., Dept of English, Univ. of California, Davis 1989–; has given lectures in USA, Europe and in N and W Africa; Western States Book Award for Fiction (for My Amputations); The Pushcart Prize; Fulbright Fellowship; Nat. Council on the Arts Award, Finalist Nat. Book Award 1999; Int. Writers Hall of Fame, Wendolyn Brooks Foundation Award, Chicago. State Univ. *Exhibitions include:* Knesgie Art Museum, East Lansing, Mich. Natsoulas Art Gallery, Davis, Calif., Gayles Art Gallery Chicago, Sarah Lawrence Coll., NY, First Nat. Bank, Boulder, Colo, Schacknow Museum of Art, Plantation Florida, Exploding Head Gallery, Sacramento, CA. *Publications:* (novels) All-Night Visitors 1969, NO 1973, Reflex and Bone Structure 1975, Emergency Exit 1979, My Amputations 1986, Such was the Season 1987, Painted Turtle: Woman with Guitar 1988; (short stories) Fun and Games 1990, Calling the Wind: Twentieth Century African-American Short Stories 1993, Dirty Bird Blues 1996, All-Night Visitors (new version) 1998; (poetry) Swallow the Lake 1970, Symptoms and Madness 1971, Private Line 1971, The Cotton Club 1972, The Syncopated Cakewalk 1974, Inside Diameter: The France Poems 1985, Surfaces and Masks 1987, Some Observations of a Stranger at Zuni in the Latter Part of the Century 1989, The Garden Thrives, Twentieth Century African-American Poetry 1995, Configurations: New and Selected Poems 1958–98, 1998, Waiting for Sweet Baby 2002; (non-fiction) Dictionary of Afro-American Slang 1970, The Dark and Feeling: Black American Writers and their Work 1974, Juba to Jive: A Dictionary of African-American Slang 1994, Necessary Distance: Essays and Criticism 2001, Come by Here: My Mother's Life 2002; Conversations with Clarence Major; numerous works in anthologies and periodicals. *Address:* Department of English, 281 Voorhies Hall, University of California, Davis, CA 95616, USA. *Telephone:* (916) 752-5677.

MAJOR, Jean-Louis, LPh, MA, PhD, FRSC; Canadian author and academic; b. 16 July 1937, Cornwall, Canada; s. of Joseph Major and Noella Daoust; m. Bibiane Landry 1960; one d.; ed Univ. of Ottawa and Ecole Pratique des Hautes Etudes; Lecturer, Dept of Philosophy, Univ. of Ottawa 1961–65, Prof. Dept des Lettres Françaises 1965, Titular Prof. 1971–99, Assoc. Dean (Research), Faculty of Arts 1991–97, Prof. Emer. 1999–; Visiting Prof. Dept of French, Univ. of Toronto 1970–71; Dir Corpus d'éditions critiques and Bibliothèque du nouveau monde 1981–; Chair. Academic Advisory Cttee of Ont. Council on Univ. Affairs 1991–93; mem. Acad. des Lettres et Sciences Humaines 1976; Lorne Pierce Medal, Royal Soc. of Canada 2000. *Publications include:* Saint-Exupéry, l'écriture et la pensée 1968, Anne Hébert et le miracle de la parole 1976, Le jeu en étoile 1978, Entre l'écriture et la parole 1984, a critical Edn of Cocteau's Léone, Journal d'Henriette Dessaules 1989, Trente arpent de Ringuet 1991, Mailles à l'envers 1999, Québec Literature: From Collective Identity to Modernity and Back 1999, Contes par-ci par-là 2001, Antifables 2002. *Address:* Département des Lettres Françaises, University of Ottawa, Ottawa, Ont., K1N 6N5 (Office); PO Box 357, St Isidore, Ont., K0C 2B0, Canada (Home). *Telephone:* (613) 562-5798. *Fax:* (613) 562-5207. *E-mail:* corpus@uottawa.ca (Office). *Website:* www.uottawa.ca/publications/bnm (Office).

MAJOR, Rt Hon John, CH, PC, AIB, FIB; British politician and banker; b. 29 March 1943, Merton; s. of late Thomas Major and Gwendolyn Major; m. Norma Christina Elizabeth Johnson 1970; one s. one d.; ed Rutlish Grammar School, Merton; mem. Lambeth Borough Council 1968–71; Sr exec. Standard Chartered Bank PLC 1965–79; MP for Huntingdon 1983–2001 (Huntingdonshire 1979–83); Parl. Pvt. Sec. to Home Office Minister 1981–83; Asst Govt Whip 1983–84; Lord Commr of Treasury 1984–85; Under-Sec. of State for Social Security 1985–86; Minister for Social Security and the Disabled 1986–87; Chief Sec. to Treasury 1987–89; Sec. of State for Foreign and Commonwealth Affairs July–Oct. 1989; Chancellor of the Exchequer 1989–90; Prime Minister, First Lord of the Treasury and Minister for the Civil Service 1990–97; Leader of the Conservative Party 1990–97; Parl. Consultant to Guild of Glass Engravers 1979–83; Pres. Eastern Area Young Conservatives 1983–85, Nat. Asthma Campaign 1998–, Surrey Co. Cricket Club 2000–02; Chair. Carlyle Group (European Bd) 2001–, Ditchley Council 2000–; Sr Adviser Credit Suisse First Boston (CSFB) 2001–; Dir (non-exec.) Mayflower Corpn 2000–03; mem. Main Cttee MCC 2001–; Patron Child of Achievement Award, Consortium for Street Children, 2002–, Deafblind UK 2002–, 21st Century Trust 2002–; Hon. Master of the Bench of the Middle Temple 1992, Hon. Freeman Merchant Taylors' Co. 2002–. *Publication:* The Autobiography 1999. *Leisure interests:* football, cricket, opera, theatre, reading, travel. *Address:* PO Box 38506, London, SW1P 1ZW, England.

MAJOR, Dame Malvina Lorraine, DBE; New Zealand operatic soprano; b. 28 Jan. 1943, Hamilton; d. of Vincent Major and Eva Major; m. Winston William Richard Fleming 1965 (died 1990); one s. two d.; ed Hamilton Tech. Coll. and London Opera Centre; debut as Rosina in The Barber of Seville, Salzburg Festival 1968; performances in Europe, UK, USA, Australia, Japan, Jordan, Egypt and NZ; concerts, opera and recording with NZ Symphony Orchestra, Auckland Philharmonia and Southern Symphony Orchestra; Founder Dame Malvina Major Foundation (for excellence in the performing arts) 1991; Amb. for the NZ Year of the Family 1994; Prof. of Singing, Canterbury Univ.; Hon. life mem. NZ Horticultural Soc.; Patron Christchurch City Choir, Canterbury Opera, Nelson School of Music, Waikato Multiple Sclerosis; NZ winner Mobil Song Quest 1963, Kathleen Ferrier Competition winner 1966, Outstanding Achievements in Music Award 1988, NZ Medal 1990, Entertainer and Int. Performer of the Year 1992, NZ Music Award–Classical Disc 1993, 1994 and numerous other awards for services to music. *Leisure interests:* family, golf, sewing. *Address:* P.O. Box 11-175, Manners Street, Wellington, New Zealand. *Telephone:* (4) 495-7483.

MAKANIN, Vladimir Semenovich; Russian writer; b. 13 March 1937, Orsk, Orenburg Region; ed Moscow Univ., Higher Workshop for Scenario Writers and Film Dirs.; started writing 1965; Russian Booker Prize 1993, Pushkin Prize 1998, Penne Prize, Italy 1999, Russian State Prize 2000. *Publications include:* Straight Line 1965, Air-Vent, Portrait and Around (novel) 1976, Story about an Old Settlement (collection of short stories) 1974, Voices 1982, River with a Fast Current 1983, Where the Skies Meet the Hills 1987, One and One 1987, Subject of Averaging 1992, The Loss: A Novella and Two Stories (Writings from an Unbound Europe), Baize-Covered Table with Decanter 1993, Quasi 1993, Captives 1996, Escape Hatch and The Long Road Ahead: Two Novellas 1998, Underground, or a Hero of Our Time 1998, Letter "A" 2000, A Good Love Story 2000. *Address:* Novinski Boulevard 16, Apartment 14, 121069 Moscow, Russia. *Telephone:* (095) 291-92-53. *Fax:* (095) 781-01-82. *E-mail:* vmakanin@hotmail.com.

MAKARCZYK, Jerzy, LLD; Polish judge and professor of law; b. 24 July 1938; s. of Zbigniew Makarczyk and Hanna Olszowska; ed Warsaw Univ. and Inst. of Legal Sciences, Polish Acad. of Sciences; Assoc. Prof. of Int. Public Law 1975, Prof. 1988; Deputy Dir Inst. of Legal Sciences, Polish Acad. of Sciences 1981–88, Prof. 1992–; Deputy Minister of Foreign Affairs 1989–90; Sec. of State, Ministry of Foreign Affairs 1990–92; in charge of negotiations with USSR and then Russia on withdrawal of troops from Polish Territory 1990–92; Judge, European Court of Human Rights 1992–; mem. ILO High Level Team to Myanmar 2000–1; Adviser to Pres. of Repub. of Poland 2002–; Pres. Int. Law Asscn 1988–90; mem. Inst. de Droit Int. 1993; Manfred Lachs Foundation Award 1998; Commdr Légion d'honneur. *Publications:* Financing of Economic Development in the United Nations System 1974, Principles of a New International Economic Order 1988; ed. Collection of Essays in Honour of Judge Manfred Lachs 1984, Theory of International Law at the Threshold of the XXIst Century (ed.) 1996. *Leisure interests:* tennis, sailing. *Address:* ul. Bernardyńska 30 m. 5, 02-904 Warsaw, Poland. *Telephone:* (22) 6429540. *Fax:* (22) 6429540. *E-mail:* mjakarczyk@prezydent.pl.

MAKAREVICH, Andrei Vadimovich; Russian composer, singer and artist; b. 11 Dec. 1954, Moscow; one s.; ed Moscow Inst. of Architecture; founder, artistic dir, soloist Machine of Time (first professional rock group in Russia) 1969–; creator, presenter Smak (TV programme); drawings have been exhibited in Moscow, St Petersburg, Riga, Caserta (Italy); merited artist RSFSR. *Leisure interest:* underwater hunting. *Address:* ORT (Russian Public TV), Smak, Akademika Koroleva str. 12, 127000 Moscow, Russia. *Telephone:* (095) 217-79-88; (095) 367-63-09. *Website:* www.mashina.ru (Office).

MAKAROV, Andrey Mikhailovich, C.JUR.; Russian barrister; b. 22 July 1954, Moscow; ed Moscow State Univ.; worked in Research Inst., USSR Ministry of Internal Affairs 1976–83; mem. Moscow City Bd of Lawyers 1983–, acted as the defence lawyer in numerous maj. trials, including trial of fmr Deputy Minister of Internal Affairs V. Churbanov; Chief of Dept supervising activities of Comm. of Security Council in struggle against crime and corruption July–Oct. 1993; mem. State Duma (Parl.) 1993–99; Exec. Dir Russian br. of SOROS Foundation; Pres. Chess Fed. of Russia 1994–97; mem. Exec. Cttee Int. Chess Fed. (FIDE); Head Barristers co. A. Makarov and A. Tobak 1998–; Chair. Council of Experts on Improving Tax System, State Duma 2000–. *Address:* Andrey Makarov and Aleksandr Tobak Barristers Bureau, Leningradsky Prospect 39A, 125167 Moscow, Russia. *Telephone:* (095) 213-86-94.

MAKAROV, Igor Mikhailovich, DSc; Russian scientist; b. 22 Oct. 1927, Saratov; s. of Mikhail Ilyich Makarov and Yelena Ivanovna Makarova; m. Praskovia Alexandrovna Makarova 1953; one s.; ed S. Ordzhonikidze Moscow Aviation Inst.; scientific worker and chief of lab. 1949–72; Instructor, Deputy Chief, Dept of Science and Educ., C.P.S.U. 1962–75; Deputy Minister for Higher and Specialized Secondary Educ. of USSR 1975–88; Corresp. mem. USSR (now Russian) Acad. of Sciences 1974–87, mem. 1987–; Chief Scientific Sec. Presidium of USSR (now Russian) Acad. of Sciences 1988–92, Chief Scientific Sec. Russian Acad. of Sciences 1992–96, Adviser to Pres. 1996–; Chair. Dept of Cybernetics, Moscow Inst. of Radio-electronics and Automation 1978–; Russian Rep. to Int. Council of Scientific Unions; Chair. Scientific Council on Robotics and Flexible Mfg, Russian Acad. of Sciences; Deputy Chief Ed. Automatic Control; mem. Editorial Bd Future of Science, Science and Humanity; Chief Ed. Herald of the Russian Acad. of Sciences; Chief Ed. Series Cybernetics; Deputy Chief Ed. Automation and Telemechanics; USSR State Prize 1984, Russian State Prize 1995; Order of Red Banner of Labour. *Publications:* Linear Automatic Systems 1975, Theory of Automatic Control (2 Vols) 1977, Objective-oriented Complex Programs 1980, Theory of Choice and Decision-making 1982, Cybernetics Today: Achievements, Challenges, Prospects 1984, Cybernetics and Informatics 1986, Informatics and Progress in Science and Technology 1987, Time-Impulse Automatic Control System 1998, Logistical Differential Models of Technological Transfer 1999; numerous scientific papers on man. and control, artificial intelligence, robotics, mfg tech., educ. *Leisure interests:* tennis, skiing, hunting. *Address:* Presidium of the Russian Academy of Sciences, 32A Leninsky Prospect, 119991 Moscow GSP-1, Russia. *Telephone:* (095) 938-19-06. *Fax:* (095) 938-53-68.

MAKAROV, Valery Leonidovich, PhD; Russian economist; b. 25 May 1937, Novosibirsk; s. of Leonid Makarov and Dina Yershov; m. Irena Nikolaev 1961; one s. one d.; ed Moscow Econ. Inst.; scientific worker, Inst. of Math., Siberian Div. USSR Acad. of Sciences 1961–67, Lab. Chief 1967–73, Deputy Dir 1973–80, Gen. Sec. Siberian Div. 1980–83; Prof. of Mathematical Econs Novosibirsk Univ. 1970–83; Dir Nat. Inst. of Industrial Man., Moscow 1983–85; Dir Central Econs and Math. Inst. 1985–; Prof. at Moscow Univ.; Founder and Rector, New Econ. School, Moscow 1992–; Ed.-in-Chief, Journal of Math. and Econ. Methods.; mem. Ed. Bd Econs of Planning, Econs of Transition, Econ. Systems Research; mem. Exec. Cttee, Int. Econ. Asscn 1995–; mem. several Govt comms.; Corresp. mem. USSR (now Russian) Acad. of Science 1979, mem. 1990; Fellow Econometric Soc.; Kantorovich Award (for contrib. to econ. theory) 1995. *Publications:* Mathematical Theory of Economic Dynamics and Equilibria (with A. Rubinov) 1977, Models and Computers in Economics 1979, Computer Simulation in Analysis of Regional Problems 1987, Mathematical Economic Theory: Pure and Mixed Types of Economic Mechanisms (with A. Rubinov and M. Levin) 1994. *Leisure interests:* tennis, skiing. *Address:* Central Economics and Mathematics Institute, Russian Academy of Sciences, Nakhimouski Prospect 47, 117418 Moscow, Russia. *Telephone:* (095) 129-10-11 (Office); (095) 229-01-50 (Home). *Fax:* (095) 310-70-15.

MAKAROVA, Inna Vladimirovna; Russian actress; b. 28 July 1926, Taiga, Kemerovo district; d. of Vladimir Makarov and Anna German; m. 1st S. Bondarchuk 1947; m. 2nd M. Perelman; one d.; ed All-Union Film Inst.; USSR State Prize 1949; Order of Red Banner of Labour, People's Artist of USSR 1985, Order of Merit RSFSR 1967. *Roles include:* Luba Shevtsova (Young Guard) 1948, Katya (Vysota) 1957, Varya (My Dear Man) 1958, Nadya (Girls) 1962, Dusya (Women) 1966, Nonna (The Rumyantsev Affair) 1956, Anfisa (Balsaminov's Wedding) 1965, Maria (Russian Field) 1972, Anna Pavlovna (Poshechonsk Old Times) 1977, Larissa (The Meek Love) 1980, The Governess (Dead Souls) 1983, Netla (Childhood and Youth of Bembi) 1988, Actress (A Loan for Marriage) 1990. *Leisure interest:* gardening. *Address:* Ukrainian Blvd. 11, Apt. 14, 121059 Moscow, Russia. *Telephone:* (095) 243-00-93.

MAKAROVA, Natalia Romanovna; Russian ballerina; b. 1940, Leningrad; m. 3rd Edward Karkar 1976; one s.; ed Vagonova Ballet School, Leningrad; mem. Kirov Ballet 1959–70; sought political asylum, London 1970; Prin. Dancer, American Ballet Theatre 1970–92; appeared with Kirov Co. in London 1988, USSR 1989; f. Makarova and Co. 1980; Guest Artist, Royal Ballet 1972; Guest Artist, London Festival Ballet 1984; retd from dancing

1992; Dir Sleeping Beauty, Royal Ballet 2003; Honoured Artist of RSFSR. *Television:* In a Class of Her Own, Assoluta, Natasha 1985, Makarova Returns 1989, Great Railway Journeys: St Petersburg to Tashkent 1994. *Plays:* On Your Toes (musical), Broadway, New York (Tony Award for Best Actress in a Musical), West End, London (Laurence Olivier Award) 1984, Tovarich, Chichester Festival then West End, London 1991, Two for the Seesaw, Moscow 1992. *Publications:* A Dance Autobiography 1979, On Your Toes 1984. *Address:* c/o The Royal Ballet, Royal Opera House, Covent Garden, London, WC2E 9DD, England.

MAKEBA, Miriam (Zenzile); South African singer; b. 4 March 1932, Prospect Township, Johannesburg; m. 1st James Kubay 1950 (divorced 1952); one d. (deceased 1985); m. 2nd Sonny Pillay 1959; m. 3rd Hugh Masekela 1964 (divorced 1966); m. 4th Stokely Carmichael 1968 (divorced 1978); m. 5th Bageot Bah 1980; ed Methodist Training School, Pretoria; Amb. to FAO 1999–; Polar Prize, Royal Swedish Acad. of Music 2002. *Albums include:* Miriam Makeba 1960, The World of Miriam Makeba 1962, The Click Song 1965, Sangoma 1988, Welela 1989, Eyes on Tomorrow 1991, Miriam Makeba and the Skylarks 1991, The Best of Miriam Makeba and the Skylarks 1998, Live from Paris and Conakry 1998, Homeland 2000, The Best of the Early Years 2002. *Publication:* Makeba: My Story 1988 (autobiog.). *Address:* c/o Food and Agricultural Organization, UN Agency Building, North Maxwell Road, PO Box 1628, Accra, Ghana.

MAKHALINA, Yulia Victorovna; Russian ballet dancer; b. 23 June 1968, St Petersburg; ed Vaganova Acad. of Russian Ballet; ballet dancer Mariinsky Theatre 1985–89, prima ballerina 1989–; Winner Int. Ballet Competition in Paris 1990 (Gold Medal and Grand Prix), Merited Artist of Russia. *Roles include:* Aurora and Lilac Fairy (Sleeping Beauty), Giselle and Myrtha (Giselle), Kitri (Don Quixote), Medora (Le Corsaire), Odette/Odile (Swan Lake), Nikiya and Gamzatti (La Bayadère), Mekhmene and Banu (Legend of Love), Maria (Fountain of Bakhchisarai), Zobeide (Sheherezade), Fire Bird (Firebird), Maria Taglioni (Pas de Quatre), Anna (Anna Karenina), Cinderella (Cinderella), Carmen (Carmen), Duchess of Alba (Goya Divertissement). *Address:* Mariinsky Theatre, Teatralnaya pl. 1, St Petersburg, Russia (Office). *Telephone:* (812) 315-57-12 (Office).

MAKHDOOM, Syed Faisal Hayat, MA; Pakistani politician; m.; one s. one d.; ed Aichitson Coll., FC Govt Coll., Lahore, King's Coll. London, UK; elected to Nat. Ass. 1977–; Sr mem. Cen. Exec. Cttee, Pakistan People's Party 1987–; fmr Sr Minister for Home and Services and Gen. Admin., Punjab Cabinet; Minister for Commerce, Industries and Local Govt –2002; Minister of the Interior, Narcotics Div., Control and Capital Admin. and Devt Divs. 2002–. *Leisure interests:* squash, cricket, riding. *Address:* Ministry of the Interior and Narcotics Control, Block R, Pakistan Secretariat, Islamabad, Pakistan (Office). *Telephone:* (51) 9212026 (Office). *Fax:* (51) 9202642 (Office).

MAKHMALBAF, Mohsen; Iranian film director and novelist; b. 1957, Tehran; Ecumenical Jury Prize (for Kandahar), Cannes Int. Film Festival 2001. *Films:* Nasooh Repentance 1982, Two Sightless Eyes 1983, Seeking Sanctuary 1984, The Boycott 1985, The Pedlar 1987, The Cyclist 1988, Marriage of the Blessed 1989, Time of Love 1991, Nights of Zayandeh Rude 1991, Once Upon a Time...the Cinema 1992, The Actor 1993, A Selection of Images in Ghajar Dynasty 1993, Stone and Glass 1994, Salam Cinema 1994, Gabbeh 1996, A Moment of Innocence 1996, The Apple 1998, The Silence 1998, Kandahar 2001. *Address:* Green Film House, 98 Mirdamad Boulevard, P.O. Box 19395/4866, Tehran, Iran (Office); c/o MK2 Diffusion, 55 rue Traversière, 75012 Paris, France (Office). *Telephone:* (21) 2225960 (Iran) (Office); 1-43-07-92-74 (France) (Office). *Fax:* (21) 2270970 (Iran) (Office); 1-43-41-32-30 (France) (Office). *Website:* www.makhmalbaf.com (Office).

MAKHULU, Most Rev. Walter Paul Khotso, CMG; British ecclesiastic; b. 2 July 1935, Johannesburg, SA; s. of Paul Makhulu; m. Rosemary Makhulu 1966; one s. one d.; ed Pimville Govt School, Johannesburg, Khaiso Secondary School, Coll. of the Resurrection and St Peter, SA, St Andrew's Coll., Birmingham; Area Sec. for Eastern Africa and African Refugees, Comm. on Inter-Church Aid Refugee and World Service, World Council of Churches 1975–79; Bishop of Botswana 1979–2000; Archbishop of Cen. Africa 1980–2000, Archbishop Emer. 2000–; Pres. All Africa Conf. of Churches 1981–86; Pres. World Council of Churches 1983–91; Hon. Curate Holy Trinity, Geneva; Presidential Order of Honour (Botswana) 2002; Hon. DD (Kent) 1988, (Gen. Theol. Seminary, New York) 1990; Officier, l'Ordre des Palmes Académiques 1981. *Leisure interests:* music, international affairs. *Address:* Cheyne House, 10 Crondace Road, Fulham, London, SW6 4BB, England. *Telephone:* (20) 7371-9419 (Office). *E-mail:* bishmak@makhulu .fsnet.co.uk (Office).

MAKI, Fumihiko, MArch; Japanese architect; b. 6 Sept. 1928, Tokyo; m. Misao 1960; two d.; ed Univ. of Tokyo, Cranbrook School of Art, Michigan and Harvard Univ.; Assoc. Prof. Washington Univ. 1956–62, Harvard Univ. 1962–66; lecturer, Dept of Urban Eng, Univ. of Tokyo 1964–, Prof. of Architecture 1979; Prin. Partner, Maki and Assocs. 1964–; mem. of Trilateral Comm. 1975–; Hon. Fellow, American Inst. of Architects 1980, RIBA, German Inst. of Architects, French Acad. of Architecture; Hon. Dr of Art and Architecture (Washington, USA); Wolf Prize, Pritzker Architecture Prize, Prince of Wales Prize in Urban Design, Arnold Brunner Memorial Prize in Architecture, Praemium Imperiale 1999; Reynolds Memorial Award (for Spiral) 1987, Thomas Jefferson Medal for Architecture 1990, Gold Medal, Int. Union of Architects (U.I.A.), Officier Ordre des Arts et des Lettres 1998. *Exhibitions include:* Venice Biennale 1991, Light Construction, Museum of Modern Art, New York 1995, Architecture in Japan–Tradition in the Future, Acad. of Fine Arts, Vienna, From the Sublime to the Meticulous, Taipei, Taiwan 1997, Pritzker Architecture Prize 1979–1999, Art Inst. of Chicago 1999. *Major works include:* Toyoda Memorial Hall, Nagoya Univ. 1960, Nat. Aquarium, Okinawa 1975, Hillside Terrace Housing Complex 1978–98, Iwasaki Art Museum 1979, Keio Univ. Library, Mita Campus 1981, Spiral 1985, Tepia 1989, Nippon Convention Centre (Makuhari Messe) Stage 1 1989, Stage 2 1998, Tokyo Metropolitan Gymnasium 1990, YKK Research and Devt Centre 1993, Center for Arts Yerba Buena Gardens 1993, Isar Buropark 1995. *Publications:* Investigations in Collective Form 1964, Movement Systems in the City 1965, Metabolism 1960, Structure in Art and Science (contrib.) 1965. *Leisure interests:* reading, chess. *Address:* 13-4, Hachiyama-cho, Shibuya-ku, Tokyo 150-0035 (Office); 16-22, 5-chome Higashi-Gotanda, Shinagawa-ku, Tokyo 141-0022, Japan. *Telephone:* (3) 3780-3880 (Office); (3) 3441-8038 (Home). *Fax:* (3) 3780-3881 (Office). *Website:* www.maki-and-associates.co.jp (Office).

MAKIHARA, Minoru, BA; Japanese business executive; b. 12 Jan.1930, Hampstead, England; m. Kikuko Makihara; ed in England, Japan, Harvard Univ.; joined Mitsubishi Corpn Marine Products Dept 1956–59, London Br. 1959–70, Rep. Mitsubishi Int. Seattle and Washington 1970–80, Gen. Man. Marine Products Dept, Tokyo 1980–87, Pres. Mitsubishi Int. New York 1987–90, Sr Man. Dir Mitsubishi Corpn, also Chair. Mitsubishi Int. 1990–92, Pres. Mitsubishi Corpn 1992–98, Pres., Chair. 1998–; mem. Chair. Council Daimler Chrysler 2001–. *Address:* Office of the Chairman, Mitsubishi Corporation, 2-6-3 Marunouchi, Chiyoda-ku, Tokyo 100-8086, Japan.

MAKIN, Andre (Andrei); French/Russian writer; b. 1957; s. of Maria Stepanovna Dolina; worked as teacher of literature in Novgorod; emigrated from USSR to France 1987, wrote in French; Goncourt Prix and Medici Prize for The French Testament 1995. *Publications include:* (novel) Daughter of the Hero of the Soviet Union, Time of the River of Amur, The French Testament, The Crime of Olga Arbyelina 1999; lives in Paris.

MÄKINEN, Tommi; Finnish racing driver; b. 26 June 1964, Puuppola, Jyväskylä; s. of Jukka Mäkinen; pnr. Eliisa Järvelä; one s.; first competed on farm tractors, won Jr Finnish nat. ploughing title 1982, 1985, Sr title 1992; began rally car racing career in Finnish Championships 1985; Group N Finnish Champion 1988; won Arctic Rally 1989, Rally Thailand World Rally Champion 1996, 1997, 1998, 1999; set record for most world championship rally race wins (24 victories 1994–2002); record four consecutive wins at the Monte Carlo Rally (to 2002). *Leisure interests:* skiing, cycling, trial biking, hunting. *Address:* c/o Federation internationale de l'automobile, 8 Place de la Concorde, 75008 Paris, France. *Website:* www.tommimakinen.net (Office).

MAKINO, Takamori; Japanese politician; mem. of House of Reps.; fmr Dir LDP Foreign Affairs Div.; fmr Deputy Chief Cabinet Sec.; fmr Parl. Vice-Minister for Foreign Affairs; Minister for Labour 1999–2000. *Address:* c/o Ministry of Labour, 1-2-2, Kasumigaseki, Chiyoda-ku, Tokyo 100-0013, Japan (Office).

MAKK, Károly; Hungarian film director; b. 22 Dec. 1925; s. of Kálmán Makk and Emma Szmolka; m. Andrea Zsiga-Kiss (separated); one s. one d.; ed Budapest Univ. of Sciences, Univ. of Dramatic and Cinematic Arts; Asst lecturer 1953, lecturer 1959–; mem. Univ. Council; worked as assistant Dir MAFILM Studio 1946–53, Dir 1954–; Guest lecturer Istituto Centro Sperimentale per Film, Rome 1976 and German Film Acad., Munich 1973–74; mem. Hungarian Acad. of Art 1992–; Merited Artist and Eminent Artist titles, Balázs Béla Prize 1959, Kossuth Prize 1973, Outstanding Artist Prize 1982, Lifetime Achievement Award, Figueira da Foz, Portugal 1986, Life Achievement Award, Hungarian Film Festival 1994. *Films directed include:* Liliomfi (Cannes selection) 1954, Ház a sziklák alatt (House under the Rocks) 1957 (San Francisco Grand Prix 1959), 39-es dandár (The Brigade No. 39) 1959, Megszállottak (The Fanatics) 1962, Elveszett paradicsom (The Lost Paradise) 1963, Az utolsó előtti ember (The Last but One) 1963, Isten és ember előtti (Before God and Man) 1968, Szerelem (Love) 1970 (1971 International Journalist Fed. Award and Jury's Special Award of Cannes), Macskajáték (Catsplay, nominated for Acad. Award) 1974, Egy erkölcsös éjszaka (A very moral night) 1977, Két történet a félmúltból (Two stories from the Recent Past), A téglafal mögött (Behind the Brick Wall), Philemon and Baucis, 1981, Egymásra nézve (Another Way) 1981 (1982 Int. Critiques Award and Best Female Performance of Cannes), Játszani kell (Playing for Keeps) 1984, Az utolsó kézirat (The Last Manuscript) 1987, Magyar rekviem (Hungarian Requiem) 1990, Magyar Pizza 1995, Játékos (The Gambler) 1997 (1998 Best Film, Pescara). *Plays directed:* Enigma Variations 1998, Rebecaa 1999, WIT 2001. *Address:* 1022 Budapest, Hankóczy Jenő utca 15, Hungary. *Telephone:* (1) 326-9314. *Fax:* (1) 326-9314 (Home). *E-mail:* ggaleria@axelero.hu (Office).

MAKKAWI, Khalil, PhD; Lebanese diplomatist; b. 15 Jan. 1930, Beirut; s. of Abdel Basset Makkawi and Rosa Makkawi; m. Zahira Sibaei 1958; one s. one d.; ed American Univ. of Beirut, Cairo Univ., Columbia Univ., New York; joined Foreign Ministry 1957, served in UN Section 1957–59, Deputy Perm. Rep. to UN, New York 1961–64, First Sec., Embassy in Washington 1964–67, Chief of Int. Relations Dept, Foreign Ministry, Beirut 1967–70, Counsellor, Embassy in London 1970–71, Minister Plenipotentiary, London 1971–73, Amb. to GDR 1973–78, to UK and Repub. of Ireland 1978–83; Dir Political Dept, Foreign Ministry, Beirut, Chair. Preparatory Cttee of Lebanese Nat. Dialogue, mem. Lebanese Security Arrangement Cttee for South of Lebanon

1983–85, Amb. to Italy and Perm. Rep. to FAO 1985–90, Perm. Rep. to UN, New York 1990–94; Vice-Chair. Exec. Bd UNICEF 1993–95, Pres. 1995; Co-Chair. Int. Support Group for mine clearance in Lebanon (representing Ministry of Nat. Defence) 2002. *Address:* c/o Ministry of National Defence, Yarze, Beirut, Lebanon.

MAKKI, Mohammed Hassan, DEcon; Yemeni politician and diplomatist; b. 22 Dec. 1933; ed Univs. of Bologna and Rome; Adviser, Ministry of Econ. 1960–62, Deputy Minister 1962, Minister 1963–64; Minister of Foreign Affairs April–Sept. 1966, 1967–68; Amb. to Italy 1968–70, 1977–79, to Fed. Repub. of Germany 1970–72; Deputy Prime Minister 1972–74; Prime Minister March–June 1974; Deputy Prime Minister for Econ. Affairs June–Oct. 1974, 1980–84; Deputy Prime Minister of Yemen Arab Repub. 1985–90; First Deputy Prime Minister of Republic of Yemen 1990–93; Perm. Rep. to UN 1974–76, Amb. to USA (also Accred to Canada) 1975–76.

MAKOGON, Yuri Feodorovich, D.TECH.SC.; Russian physicist and engineer; b. 15 May 1930; s. of Feodor Ivanovich Makogon and Efrosinia Shevchenko; m. Inna Aleksandrovna Makogon 1961; one s. one d.; ed Krasnodar Petroleum Inst., Moscow Gubkin Petroleum Inst.; worked at Shebelinka Gas Field 1956–58; Asst then Asst Prof. Moscow Petroleum Inst. 1961–74; Head of Lab. All-Union Gas Research Inst. 1974–88; Head of Lab. Oil and Gas Research Inst. 1988–; Head Natural Gas Hydrates Lab., Russian Sciences Acad.; Dir Hydrocarbons and Environment Inst., Russian Acad. of Natural Sciences 1991–97; Head of Lab., Texas A-M Univ. 1994–; Deputy Chair. Earth Sciences Section, Natural Sciences of Russia Acad.; mem. U.S. Soc. of Petroleum Engineers (SPE), Chair. SPE Moscow section, Chair. Oil and Gas Scientific Council, Presidium of Russian Acad. of Natural Sciences, mem. Russian Oil and Gas Industry, Scientific-Tech. Soc., mem. Earth Sciences Section Bureau; Gubkin State Prize 1989. *Publications:* more than 200 Publs; author of 8 monographs, 217 papers, 33 patents. *Address:* Vernadskogo prosp. 9, Apt. 509, Moscow 117311, Russia; Offshore Technology Research Center, 1200 Mariner Drive, Texas A-M University, College Station, TX 77845, USA. *Telephone:* (095) 131-02-09 (Russia); (409) 847-90-11 (Office); (409) 846-4608 (USA) (Home).

MAKONI, Simba Herbert Stanley, BSc, PhD; Zimbabwean politician; b. 22 March 1950, Makoni; s. of Basil Kamunda and Clara Kamunda (née Matimba); m. Chipo Makoni (née Ususu) 1975; three s.; ed Univ. of Leeds and Leicester Polytechnic, UK; joined Zimbabwe African Nat. Union-Patriotic Front (ZANU-PF); ZANU Chief Rep. to W Europe 1977–80; MP, Nat. Ass. of Zimbabwe 1980–84; Deputy Minister of Agric. 1980; Minister of Industry and Energy Devt 1981–83, of Youth, Sport and Culture 1984, of Finance and Econ. Devt 2000–02; Exec. Sec., Southern African Devt Community (SADC) 1984–93; Chief Exec. and Man. Dir Zimbabwe Newspapers Ltd, Zimpapers 1994–; Man. Partner Makonsult Ltd; mem. UN Panel of Advisers on African Devt 1992–94, Inst. of Dirs., Zimbabwe 1994–, Zimbabwe Inst. of Man. 1994–, Council of Reps., South Centre 1994–, Nat. Blood Transfusion Service 1995–; mem. Nat. Council, Conf. of Zimbabwe Industries (CZI) 1996–, Chair. Econ. Affairs Cttee 1996–; mem. Nat. Econ. Consultative Forum 1998; Patron Nat. Council of Disabled Persons of Zimbabwe 1982–, Zimbabwe Inst. of Motor Industry 1995–. *Leisure interests:* gardening, reading, squash, health and fitness. *Address:* c/o Ministry of Finance and Economic Development, 2nd Floor, Munhumutapa Building, Samora Machel Avenue, Private Bag 7705, Causeway, Harare, Zimbabwe (Office).

MAKOVECZ, Imre; Hungarian architect; b. 20 Nov. 1935, Budapest; m. Marianne Szabó; two s. one d.; ed Budapest Tech. Univ.; with Buváti (architectural planning inst.) 1959–62; held various positions at planning and architectural insts. Szövterv 1963–71, Váti 1971–81; planning architect Pilis Forest Park State Farm 1981–86, 1986–; projects include Hungarian Pavilion, Int. Fair, Seville 1992, hotel and cultural bldgs. in Hungary, churches at Paks 1987, Siófok 1989, Százhalombatta; Head MAKONA (architectural planning co-operative); Prof. Applied Arts School; mem. Int. Architectural Acad. 1992–; Hon. Fellowship American, German and Scottish Architectural Asscns., RIBA; Dr. hc (Dundee); Ybl Miklós Prize 1969, Kossuth Prize (Middle Cross with Star) 1990; Grand Gold Medal of French Architectural Acad. 1997. *Address:* MAKONA, 1034 Budapest, Kecske u. 25, Hungary. *Telephone:* (1) 388-1701; (1) 388-1702.

MAKOVETSKY, Sergey Vasilievich; Russian actor; b. 13 June 1958, Kiev; ed Moscow Shchukin Theatre School; with Moscow Vakhtangov Theatre 1980–; with Roman Viktyuk Theatre 1990–; Moscow Theatre Spring Prize 1989 (for Zoya's Apartment), Golden Aries Prize (Actor of the Year) 1993, Nika Acad. of Cinema Award 1993. *Films include:* Aleksander Proletkin (To Take Alive), Chumak (Crew of a Fighting Machine), Semen Kotko (I am a Son of the Working People), Makarov, Russian Riot, Brother-1, Brother-2. *Plays acted in include:* The Master's Lessons, Madame Butterfly, Loika's Flat. *Address:* Vakhtangov Theatre, Arbat str. 26, 121007 Moscow, Russia (Office). *Telephone:* (095) 241-01-28 (Office).

MAKSAKOVA, Ludmila Vasilyevna; Russian actress; b. 26 Sept. 1941, Moscow; d. of Maria Maksakova; m.; one s. one d.; ed Moscow Shchukin Theatre School; leading actress Moscow Vakhtangov Theatre 1961–; numerous film roles; RSFSR Merited Artist 1971, RSFSR People's Artist 1980, State Prize of Russian Fed. (for Guilty without Guilt) 1995, Order for Service to Motherland. *Theatre includes:* Princess Turandot in Adelma, Masha in Living Corpse, Nicol in The Prodigious Snob, Nastasha Filipovna in The Idiot, Anna Karenina, Duchess of Marlborough in Glass of Water,

Korzinkina in Guilty without Guilt, the Countess in The Queen of Spades. *Address:* Bryusov per. 7, Apt. 70, 103009 Moscow, Russia. *Telephone:* (095) 229-94-98.

MAKSIMOVA, Yekaterina Sergeyevna; Russian ballet dancer, balletmaster and dance teacher; b. 1 Feb. 1939, Moscow; d. of Sergey Maksimov and Tatiana Maksimova; m. Vladimir Vasilyev; ed Bolshoi Theatre Ballet School, State Inst. of Theatrical Arts; with Bolshoi Theatre Ballet Co. 1958–88, coach 1998–; toured widely; coach, Kremlin Ballet 1995–; Gold Medal, Varna (int. competition) 1964, Pavlova Prize of Paris Acad. of Dance 1969; Marius Petipa Prize, Paris Acad. of Dance 1972; People's Artist of USSR 1973; Prize for Best Female Role, Prague Int. TV Film Festival 1979; USSR State Prize 1981; Jino Tagni Int. Prize, Rome 1989; Russian State Order of Merit 1999. *Main roles:* Masha (Nutcracker), Katerina (Stone Flower), Seventh Waltz, Prelude (Chopiniana), Maria (Fountain of Bakhchisarai), Giselle (Giselle), Mavka (Song of the Forest by Zhukovsky), Jeanne (Flames of Paris), Anyuta (Anyuta), the Muse (Paganini by Rachmaninov), Lizzie (The Path of Thunder by Karayev), Cinderella (Cinderella), Aurora (Sleeping Beauty), Kitri (Don Quixote), Frigia (Spartacus by Khachaturyan), leading role in Hussars' Ballad by Khrennikov, Juliet (Romeo and Juliet by Béjart), Natalie (Natalie, or The Swiss Milkmaid), Rose (Blue Angel), Romola (Nijinsky), Glove Maker (Gaité Parisienne), Tatiana (Onegin), Odette/Odile (Swan Lake), Eola (Icarus), Ballerina (Petrushka), Eva (Creation of the World). *Films:* Galatea, The Old Tango, Anyuta, Fouette, Traviata, Adam and Eva, Dame of Class, Chapliniana, Crystal Shoe, These Charming Sounds, Fragments of One's Biography, Trapezium. *TV documentaries:* Creation of Dance, Road to Big Ballet, World of Dance, Pages of Modern Dance, Katya and Volodya, Yekaterina Maksimova, Duet, ... And There Is Always Something Unsaid. *Leisure interests:* reading, sewing. *Address:* c/o State Academic Bolshoi Theatre, Teatralnaya pl. 1, Moscow (Office). Smolenskaya Naberezhnaya 5/13-62, 121009 Moscow, Russia (Home). *Telephone:* (095) 292-06-55 (Office); (095) 244-02-27 (Home). *Fax:* (095) 254-73-68 (Office); (095) 244-02-27 (Home). *E-mail:* panart@mail.com (Office); info@vasiliev.com (Home). *Website:* www.bolshoi.ru (Office); www.maximova.bolshoi.ru (Home).

MAKSYMIUK, Jerzy; Polish conductor, composer and pianist; b. 9 April 1936, Grodno, Byelorussia; s. of Roman Maksymiuk and Bronisława Maksymiuk; m. Irena Kirjacka; ed Acad. of Music, Warsaw ; Conductor, Great Theatre, Warsaw 1970–72; f. Polish Chamber Orchestra 1972–84; Conductor, Polish Nat. Radio Symphony Orchestra, Katowice; Prin. Conductor BBC Scottish Symphony Orchestra, Glasgow 1983–93; (tours of Greece, Canada and Fed. Repub. of Germany); guest conductor Calgary Symphony, Nat. Arts Centre (Ottawa), English Chamber, Scottish Chamber, City of Birmingham Symphony, London Symphony, London Philharmonic, Tokyo Metropolitan Symphony, Staatskapelle, Sinfonia Varsovia and other orchestras; has toured Europe, USA, Canada, Japan, Israel and Australia with Polish Chamber Orchestra; collaborated with English Nat. Opera (Mozart's Don Giovanni) 1990, (Johann Strauss' Die Fledermaus) 1993. *Address:* Gdańska 2 m. 14, 01-633 Warsaw, Poland. *Telephone:* (22) 8323021.

MAKTOUM, HH Sheikh Maktoum bin Rashid al-, Ruler of Dubai; b. 1941; s. of the late Rashid bin Said al-Maktoum; m. 1971; succeeded his father Sheikh Rashid bin Said al-Maktoum as 5th Sheikh 1990; Prime Minister of the UAE 1971–79, 1991–; Deputy Prime Minister 1979–90; concurrently Vice-Pres. 1990–. *Address:* Office of the Prime Minister, PO Box 12848, Dubai; Ruler's Palace, Dubai, United Arab Emirates. *Telephone:* (4) 3534550 (Office). *Fax:* (4) 3530111 (Office).

MAKTOUM, Sheikh Muhammad bin Rashid al-, Crown Prince of Dubai; b. 1948; s. of late Sheikh Rashid al-Maktoum; trained in British army and RAF; currently Minister of Defence of the UAE; with brothers Sheikh Maktoum al-Maktoum, Sheikh Hamdan al-Maktoum and Sheikh Ahmed al-Maktoum has had racing interests in UK 1976–; first winner, Hatta, Goodwood 1977; with brothers now owns studs, stables, country houses and sporting estates in Newmarket and elsewhere in UK; worldwide racing interests based at Dalham Hall Stud, Newmarket; horses trained in England, Ireland and France; Dir Godolphin Racing, Dubai; f. Racing Post (daily) 1986; owner, Balanchine, winner, Irish Derby 1994; winner, numerous classic races; leading owner 1985–89, 1991–93. *Address:* Ministry of Defence, PO Box 2838, Dubai, United Arab Emirates (Office); c/o Warren Towers, Newmarket, Suffolk, England. *Telephone:* (4) 532330 (Office). *Fax:* (4) 531974 (Office). *Website:* www.sheikhmohammed.co.ae.

MAKUZA, Bernard; Rwandan politician; mem. Mouvement démocratique républicain; Prime Minister of Rwanda March 2000–. *Address:* Office of the Prime Minister, Kigali, Rwanda (Office).

MAKWETU, Clarence Mlamli; South African politician; b. 6 Dec. 1928, Cofimvaba, Transkei; s. of Minah Makwetu and late Gqongo Makwetu; ed Hoyita Primary School, Keilands Mission School, Nkwanca Sr Secondary School and Lovedale School; joined ANC Youth League 1954; instrumental in formation of ANC 1959; detained several times 1960–63; then served five years on Robben Island; subsequently returned to Transkei, working in construction and insurance; detained again 1977, 1979; banished by Chief Kaiser Matanzima (q.v.) to Libido Dist 1979–84; returned home and continued farming 1984; detained 1986; First Pres. Pan Africanist Movt 1989–90; Deputy Pres. Pan Africanist Congress of Azania (PAC) March–Dec. 1990; Pres. PAC 1990; MP Nat. Ass. 1994–. *Address:* c/o P.A.C., P.O. Box 25245, Ferreirastown 2048, South Africa.

MALABO, Capt. Cristino Seriche Bioke (see Bioke Malabo, Capt. Cristino Seriche).

MAŁACHOWSKI, Aleksander; Polish politician, journalist and writer; b. 23 Nov. 1924, Lvov; m.; three s.; ed Wrocław Univ.; imprisoned during Soviet occupation 1940; during Nazi occupation mem. of Resistance 1942–44; sent to labour camp in Russia 1944; Asst, Wrocław Univ. 1946; journalist on many periodicals and Polish Radio and TV 1953–88; Deputy to Sejm (Parl.) 1989–97; mem. Cttee Mass Media and Cttee Econ. Politics and Finance; mem. Labour Union Parl. Caucus; Vice-Marshal of Sejm 1995–97; mem. Polish del. to Parl. Ass., Council of Europe; mem. Solidarity Trade Union (NSZZ Solidarność) 1980–91; co-f. and mem. Labour Union 1992–; Pres. Polish Red Cross 1998–; Grand Cross, Order of Poland's Rebirth 1999. *Television:* numerous TV films and documentaries. *Publications:* Rzeczniepospolita 1964, Diaspora 1967, Iliada półinteligentów 1972, Nawijki o ćwiartowaniu Smoka 1991, Żytem szczęśliwie 1993, Zapiski z Domu pod Ptakami 1999; numerous press articles. *Address:* Polski Czerwony Krzyż, ul. Mokotowska 14, 00-561 Warsaw, Poland. *Telephone:* (22) 628-55-75. *Fax:* (22) 628-41-68 (Office). *E-mail:* zarzad.glowny@pck.org.pl (Office); head.office@pck.org.pl (Office).

MALAN, Gen. Magnus André de Merindol, BSc; South African politician and fmr army officer; b. 30 Jan. 1930, Pretoria; m. Magrietha Johanna Van der Walt 1962; two s. one d.; ed Univ. of Pretoria; rank of Gen., S. African Defence Force; Chief of the Army 1973–76; Chief of Defence Staff 1976–80; Minister of Defence 1980–91, of Housing and Works, Water Affairs and Forestry 1991–93; Chair. Ministers Council House of Ass. 1991–93; arrested, charged with murder Nov. 1995, acquitted Oct. 1996; medals include Star of South Africa 1975, Southern Cross Decoration 1977, Pro Patria Medal 1977.

MALAN, Pedro, PhD; Brazilian economist; b. 19 Feb. 1943, Rio de Janeiro; s. of Elysio S. Malan and Regina S. Malan; m. 1st Ana María Toledo Piza Rudge; m. 2nd Catarina Gontijo Souza Lima 1980; two s. one d.; ed St Ignatius School, Rio de Janeiro, Polytechnic School of Catholic Univ. of Rio de Janeiro, School of Econs and Univ. of California, Berkeley; with Inst. of Applied Research, Brazilian Ministry of Planning 1966–69, 1973–83; Faculty of Econs, Catholic Univ. of Rio de Janeiro Jan.–Dec. 1979; Head Int. Trade and Finance Section, Inst. of Applied Econ. Research 1980–83; Dir Policy Analysis and Research Div. Centre of Transnat. Corpns, UN, New York 1983–84; Dept of Int. Econs and Social Affairs 1985–86; Exec. Dir World Bank, Washington, DC 1986–90; Exec. Dir Inter-American Devt Bank 1990–92; Pres. Cen. Bank of Brazil 1993–94; Minister of Finance 1994–2002; Fed. of São Paulo Industries Prize for book External Economic Policy and Industrialization in Brazil 1980, Légion d'honneur 1996, Order of Mil. Merit 1998, Order of Naval Merit 1998. *Publications:* The Structure of Protection in Brazil (with J. Bergsman) 1971, The Brazilian Economy in the 1970s: Old and New Developments (with R. Bonelli) 1977, Brazilian External Debt and its Implications 1978, Structural Models of Inflation and Balance of Payments Disequilibria in Semi-Industrialized Economies (with John R. Wells) 1984, Financial Integration with the World Economy, The Brazilian Case 1983, Relações Econômicas Internacionais do Brasil no Período 1945–64 1984, Debt, Trade and Development: the crucial years ahead 1985. *Leisure interests:* literature, classical music, diplomatic and financial history, swimming, tennis. *Address:* c/o Ministry of Finance, Esplanada dos Ministérios, Bloco P, 5 andar, 70048 Brasília, DF, Brazil (Office).

MALAN, Wynand Charl, L.L.B.; South African politician, attorney and consultant; b. 25 May 1943, Port Elizabeth; s. of Dawid Johannes Malan and Annie (née de Swardt) Malan; m. Judith Rousseau 1967; two s. one d.; ed Linden Hoerskool, Johannesburg and Univ. of Pretoria; attorney and partner, van Wyk de Vries, Malan & Steyn, Johannesburg 1966–67, Leader Nat. Jeugbond, Transvaal 1972–74; mem. Rapportraad 1971–73, Nat. Chair. 1974–76; Randburg Town Councillor and Chair. Man. Cttee 1977; Nat. Party MP for Randburg 1977–87, Independent MP for Randburg 1987–88, Democratic Party MP for Randburg 1989–90; fmr Leader Nat. Democratic Movt; fmr Co-Leader Democratic Party; mem. The Truth and Reconciliation Comm. 1995–; Eisenhower Fellowship 1980; ASPU Newsmaker of the Year Award 1987. *Leisure interests:* golf, chess, numismatics. *Address:* P.O. Box 2075, Randburg 2125, South Africa.

MALASHENKO, Igor Yevgenyevich, CAND.PHIL.SC.; Russian journalist; b. 2 Oct. 1954, Moscow; m. Yelena Pivovarova; two d.; ed Moscow State Univ.; Jr, sr researcher Inst. of USA and Canada USSR Acad. of Sciences 1980–89, research in problems of the concept of nuclear deterrence and public opinion; staff-mem. Int. Div. Cen. Cttee CPSU, admin. of Pres. Gorbachev March–Dec. 1991; political Dir TV & Radio Co. Ostankino 1992–93; Pres. and Dir-Gen. Ind. TV Co. NTV 1993–, Pres. NTV-Telemost Holding 1998; First Deputy Chair. Bd of Dirs Media-Most Co. 1998–2001; adviser to Pres. of Russia on public relations problems, mem. election campaign staff of B. Yeltsin 1996; Prize of Russian Union of Journalists 1994. *Leisure interests:* golf, photography. *Address:* NTV-Telemost, Academica Koroleva str. 19, 127427 Moscow, Russia. *Telephone:* (095) 215-15-88 (Office).

MALATESTA, Lamberto; Italian chemist; b. 20 June 1912, Milan; s. of Dr. Giuseppe Malatesta and Clara Tombolan Fava; m. Rachele Pizzotti 1947; one s. two d.; ed Milan Univ.; Asst to the Chair of Industrial Chem., Milan Univ. 1937, Reader 1940, Lecturer 1942, Chair. Prof. of Analytical Chem. 1948–51, of Gen. and Inorganic Chem. 1951–87, Dir Istituto di Chimica Generale 1951–82, Dir Dept Inorganic Chem. 1982–87, Prof. Emer. 1987– (retd); Dir of

a Centre of Consiglio Nazionale delle Ricerche 1970–82; Dir Gazzetta Chimica Italiana 1971–84; Pres. Società Chimica Italiana 1971–73, 1981–83; Pres. of Div. of Inorganic Chem., IUPAC 1975–77, Pres. Chemical Sciences Cttee, Nat. Research Council (CNR) 1976–81; Fellow, Accad. Nazionale dei Lincei, Istituto Lombardo Accad. di Scienze e Lettere; Hon. Fellow, Chemical Soc. (London); Prize of the Pres. of Italian Repub. 1963; Gold Medal for Educ., Culture and Art 1974, Gold Medal for Lifetime Achievement 1998, Gold Medal Federchimica 1999. *Publications:* General Chemistry (in Italian) 1965, Inorganic Chemistry (in Italian) 1968; co-author: Isocyanide Compounds of Metals 1968, Zerovalent Compounds of Metals 1974; about 140 original papers in scientific journals. *Leisure interests:* swimming, playing bridge. *Address:* Via Carpaccio 2, 20133 Milan, Italy. *Telephone:* (02) 2360350.

MALAUD, Philippe, LenD; French politician and diplomatist; b. 2 Oct. 1925, Paris; s. of Jacques Malaud and Odette Malaud (née Desruol du Tronçay); m. Chantal de Gorguette d'Argoeuves 1951; one d.; ed Lycée Lamartine, Mâcon, Lycée Janson-de-Sailly, Paris Univ., Ecole Libre des Sciences Politiques; joined cen. admin. of Foreign Office 1947; Embassy Attaché, Warsaw 1949; 2nd Sec., Cairo 1952; studied Ecole Nat. d'Admin. 1954–56; Personnel Dept Foreign Office 1957; Deputy Chief 1958–61, then Chief of Cabinet of Foreign Ministry under Couve de Murville 1961–67; Dir Cabinet A. Bettencourt, Sec. of State for Foreign Affairs 1967–68; elected Deputy for Saône-et-Loire, Nat. Ass. 1968, 1973, 1978; Sec. of State for the Civil Service and Information 1968–73; Minister of Information 1973, of Civil Service 1973–74; Ministre Plenipotentiaire, Foreign Office 1975; Mayor of Dompierre-les-Ormes 1965, 1971, 1972, 1978; Gen. Councillor for Canton of Matour 1967, 1973, 1979, 1985; Pres. of Gen. Council of Saône-et-Loire 1970–79; European Pres. World Fed. of Twin Towns 1973–; Political Dir Nouveaux Jours 1975; Pres. of Nat. Centre of the Self-Employed and Agricultural Workers 1980–87 (Hon. Pres. 1992–), Pres. Nat. Fed. of the Self-Employed 1988–; Vice-Pres. RDE Group, European Parl., Strasbourg; mem. European Parl. 1984–89, Pres. Confed. of European Conservative Movts 1989–, Union for Enterprise in Europe (UEE); Officer, Légion d'honneur, Ordre du Mérite; Commdr, American Legion. *Publications:* La Révolution Libérale 1976, La Renaissance Conservatrice 1992. *Leisure interest:* history. *Address:* 8 rue du Commandant Schloesing, 75116 Paris; Bois du Lin, 71970 Dompierre-les-Ormes, France. *Telephone:* (6) 80-33-35-15.

MALAURIE, Jean, PhD; French anthropogeographer and writer; b. 22 Dec. 1922, Mainz, Germany; s. of Albert Malaurie and Isabelle (Regnault) Malaurie; m. Monique Laporte 1951; one s. one d.; ed Lycée Condorcet, Faculté des Lettres de Paris, Inst. of Geography Univ. of Paris; Attaché then Research Fellow CNRS 1948–56; mem. Nat. Comm. on Geography 1955–67, 1980–82; Prof. of Arctic Geomorphology and Anthropogeography, Ecole des Hautes Etudes en Sciences Sociales (E.H.E.S.S.), Paris 1957–; Founder and Dir Centre for Arctic Studies, CNRS-E.H.E.S.S. 1957–; Dir Arctic Research, CNRS 1979–91, Dir Emer. 1992–; Pres. Fondation Française d'études nordiques 1964–75, Société Arctique Française 1981–90; Hon. Pres. Fonds Polaire Jean Malaurie, Bibliothèque centrale, Nat. Museum of Natural History, Paris 1992–; Hon. Dean Northern People's State Univ. Herzen, St Petersburg 1992 (and Gold Medal); Founder and Dir Terre Humaine anthropological book series 1955–; Founder, Dir Inter-Nord int. journal of Arctic studies 1961 (20 vols); Chair. and organizer 14 int. Arctic confs. and seminars; has made 9 documentary films on the Inuit, including The Last Kings of Thule 1970, Inuit, from Siberia to Greenland 1980, Hainak-Inuit 1993; has led 31 Arctic scientific expeditions; the first French explorer to reach North geomagnetic pole by dog-sledge 29 May 1951; Hon. Pres. State Polar Acad. St Petersburg 1994–; Chair. Cttee for the Defence of Arctic Minorities in Russia; Foundation for Culture, Moscow 1990–; mem. Acad. of Human Sciences of Russia 1997–; Dr. hc (St Petersburg) 2001; Award of Acad. française 1968, Polar Medal, Société de Géographie, Paris 1953, 1961, Académie des sciences Award 1967, Gold Medal Société arctique française 1990, CNRS Medal 1992, Gold Medal, Société de Géographie Paris 1996, Grand Prix de la Ville de Paris 1999 Grand Prix Jules Verne 2000; Officier Légion d'honneur, Commdr Ordre nat. du mérite, Commdr Ordre des Arts et Lettres. *Films:* Les Derniers Rois de Thulé 1969, 2002, Inuit (7 films) 1980, Haïnak Inuit 1993. *Publications include:* Hoggar 1954, Les Derniers Rois de Thulé (trans. into 22 languages) 1955, Thèmes de recherche géomorphologique dans le nord-ouest du Groenland 1968, Ultima Thulé 1990 (2nd edn), Hummocks 1999, L'appel du nord 2001, Anthropogéographie arctique 2002, Un Homme Sans Influence 2003. *Address:* Centre d'études arctiques (E.H.E.S.S.), 105 boulevard Raspail, 75006 Paris, France. *Telephone:* 1-45-49-76-45. *Fax:* 1-45-49-76-01. *E-mail:* jeanmalaurie@ehess.fr (Office).

MALAVOLTA, Euripedes, DSc; Brazilian agricultural biochemist; b. 13 Aug. 1926, Araraquara, São Paulo; s. of Antônio Malavolta and Lucia Canassa Malavolta; m. Leila M. B. Malavolta 1953 (divorced 1988); two s. three d.; ed Escola Superior de Agricultura, Luiz de Queiroz (Univ. de São Paulo) and Univ. of California (Berkeley), USA; Instructor in Agricultural Chem., Univ. de São Paulo 1949, Private Docent 1951, Prof. of Agricultural Biochem. 1958–84; Research Assoc. Univ. of Calif. 1952–53, Visiting Prof. 1959–60; Dean, Escola Superior de Agricultura, Luiz de Queiroz, Univ. de São Paulo 1964–70, Dean Inst. of Physics and Chem. (São Carlos) 1972–76; State Council of Educ. 1980–84; mem. Brazilian Acad. of Sciences, São Paulo Acad. of Sciences, Int. Cttee of Plant Analysis and Fertilizer Problems, Int. Cttee of Plant Nutrition, Int. Soc. Soil Science, Third World Acad. of Sciences; Fellow Rockefeller Foundation, USA; Hon. mem. Brazilian Soil Science Soc., Colombian Soil Science Soc.; Moinho Santista Prize (Agric. Sciences) 1982, Fernando Costa Medal 1991, Prudente de Moraes Medal 1991; Commdr. Nat. Order of Scientific Merit 1998. *Achievement:* pioneer work on the use of nuclear energy in agricultural research in Latin America. *Publications:* Elements of Agricultural Chemistry 1954, Manual of Agricultural Chemistry 1959, On the Mineral Nutrition of Some Tropical Crops 1962, Manual of Agricultural Chemistry-Soil Fertility and Plant Nutrition 1976, ABC of Fertilization 1954, Elements of Plant Nutrition 1981, Evaluation of the Nutritional Status of Plants 1989, Nutritional Disorders in Cerrado Soils 1985, Nutrition and Fertilization of Citrus 1990, Nutrition and Fertilization of Coffee 1992, Fertilizers and Their Impact on the Environment: Myths and Facts 1994, Nutrient and Fertilizer Management in Sugarcane 1994, History of Coffee in Brazil 2000. *Leisure interests:* reading, music, stamp-collecting. *Address:* Centro de Energia Nuclear na Agricultura, Universidade de São Paulo, Piracicaba, 13416-000 São Paulo, SP (Office); Travessa Portugal, 146 Piracicaba, 13416-470 São Paulo, SP, Brazil (Home). *Telephone:* (19) 3429-4695 (Office); (19) 3422-3948 (Home). *Fax:* (19) 3429-4610. *E-mail:* mala@cena.usp.br (Office).

MALCOMSON, James Martin, PhD, FBA; British professor of economics and academic economist; b. 23 June 1946, Staunton-on-Wye; s. of E. Watlock Malcomson and Madeline (Stuart) Malcomson; m. Sally Claire Richards 1979; one d. (deceased); ed Gonville and Caius Coll., Univ. of Cambridge, Harvard Univ., USA; Research Fellow, lecturer, Sr Lecturer, Univ. of York 1971–85; Prof. of Econs Univ. of Southampton 1985–98; Prof. of Econs Univ. of Oxford 1999–; Fellow All Souls Coll. Oxford 1999–. *Publications:* numerous articles in scientific journals. *Leisure interests:* walking, music, film, theatre. *Address:* All Souls College, Oxford, OX1 4AL, England. *Telephone:* (1865) 279379. *Fax:* (1865) 279299.

MALECELA, Cigwiyemisi John Samwel; Tanzanian politician and diplomatist; b. 1934, Dodoma; m. Ezerina Mwaipopo; one s. three d.; ed Bombay Univ. and Cambridge Univ.; Admin. Officer, Civil Service 1960–61; Consul in USA and Third Sec. to the UN 1962; Regional Commr, Mwanza Region 1963; Perm. Rep. to the UN 1964–68; Amb. to Ethiopia 1968; E African Minister for Communications, Research and Social Services, E African Community 1969–72; Minister of Foreign Affairs 1972–75, of Agric. 1975–80, of Mines 1980–81, of Transport and Communications 1982–85; Regional Commr, Iringa 1987–89; High Commr in UK 1989–90; Prime Minister and First Vice-Pres. of Tanzania 1990–95; Minister without Portfolio 1995; Vice-Chair. Chama Cha Mapinduzi Party 1992–95; Vice-Chair. Desert Locust Control Org. for East Africa; mem. Commonwealth Group on S. Africa 1985; Order of Merit of First Degree, Egypt; First Order of Independence, Equatorial Guinea. *Leisure interests:* reading, sports. *Address:* P.O. Box 2324, Dodoma, Tanzania.

MALEK, Redha; Algerian politician and diplomatist; b. 1931, Batna; s. of Malek Ahmed and Ladjouze Zoulikha; m. Rafida Cheriet 1963; two s. one d.; ed in Algiers and Paris; Ed.-in-Chief El-Moudjahid (weekly newspaper of F.L.N.); mem. Algerian delegation to negotiations of Evian 1961–62, Drafting Cttee of Program of Tripoli setting out F.L.N. political programme 1962, mem. Central Cttee FLN 1979–; Drafting Cttee of Nat. Charter 1976; Amb. to Yugoslavia 1963–65, to France 1965–70, to USSR 1970–77, to USA 1979–82, to UK 1982–84; Minister of Information and Culture 1978–79; Pres. Conseil Nat. Consultatif 1992; Minister of Foreign Affairs 1992–93; mem. High Council of State 1992–94; Prime Minister of Algeria 1993–94; Pres. Alliance Nat. Républicaine (A.N.R.) 1995; involved in negotiations for release of 52 American hostages in Iran 1980–81; Harold Weill Medal (New York Univ.). *Publications:* Tradition et Révolution 1993, L'Algérie à Evian 1995. *Address:* 2 Rue Ahmed Bey, Algiers, Algeria.

MALENCHENKO, Col Yuri Ivanovich; Russian/Ukrainian cosmonaut; b. 22 Dec. 1961, Svetlovodsk, Ukraine; m.; one s.; ed Kharkov Higher Mil. Aviation School, Zhukovsky Mil. Aviation Eng Acad.; army service 1979–; mil. pilot of 3rd class, flew more than 800 hours in fighters; mem. staff Y. Gagarin Cosmonauts' Training Centre 1987–, cosmonaut-explorer 1995–; participant of flight to space station Mir Aug.–Sept. 1994; achieved manual docking with the cargo spaceship Progress after two failures of automatic docking. *Address:* Yuri Gagarin Cosmonauts' Training Centre, Zvezdny gorodok, Moscow Region, Russia.

MALER, Leopoldo Mario, LLB; Argentine artist and art foundation executive; b. 2 April 1937, Buenos Aires; s. of Abraham Maler and Esther Kraiselburd; m. 1st Silvia Oclander 1967; m. 2nd Joyce Pieck 1973; m. 3rd María Rosa Baquero 1988; one s.; ed Univ. of Buenos Aires; journalist, BBC World Service (Latin American Service) 1961–64, 1967–74, UN Radio, New York 1980–82; Dean Parsons School of Design, Dominican Repub. 1983–85; Dir Napa Contemporary Arts Foundation 1988–91; Examiner Prof., Leeds Polytechnic and Middlesex Polytechnic Depts. of Art, UK 1976–78; one-man show Otros Diluvios, Centro Cultural, Buenos Aires 1987; monuments at Olympic Park, Korea, Parque de las Naciones, Madrid, Lamentin, Guadaloupe (Madonna and Child); Ed. NACA Journal 1992–; Guggenheim Fellow 1977; First Grand Prix, 14th Int. Biennale, São Paulo 1977, Gen. Motors Prize, Biennale of Sports in the Arts, Montevideo 1982, Gandhi Prize for Social Communication, Buenos Aires 1984, City of Madrid Medal for Artistic Merit 1991. *Group exhibitions include:* Silence, Camden Arts Centre, London 1972, Mortal Issues, Whitechapel Gallery 1975, Hayward Gallery, London 1978, Venice Biennale 1981, 1985, Int. Sculpture Conf., Washington, DC

1990. *Film:* Man in Silence 1964 (Best Short Film, London Film Festival 1964). *Ballet:* X IT, The Place, London 1969. *Leisure interests:* scuba-diving, psychology, sailing, music. *Address:* Apdo. Postal 25320, Santo Domingo, Dominican Republic. *Telephone:* (809) 696-0072.

MALERBA, Luigi; Italian author and scriptwriter; b. 11 Nov. 1927, Berceto (Parma); s. of Pietro and Maria Olari; m. Anna Lapenna 1962; two s.; ed Liceo Classico Romagnosi di Parma and Faculty of Law, Univ. of Parma; Dir of review Sequenze 1948–51; Advertising Man. of review Discoteca 1956–60, Ed. 1960–65; Premio Selezione Campiello for Il Serpente 1966; Golden Nymph Award for best TV film, Int. TV Festival, Monte Carlo for Ai poeti non si spara; Premio Sila for Salto mortale 1969; Prix Médicis (France) for best non-French novel for Salto mortale 1970. *Publications:* La scoperta dell'alfabeto 1963, Il serpente 1966, Salto mortale 1968, Storie dell'Anno Mille (with Tonino Guerra, illustrations by Adriano Zannino) 1969–71, Il protagonista 1973, Le rose imperiali 1974, Mozziconi 1975, Storiette 1977, Le parole abbandonate 1977, Pinocchio con gli stivali 1977, Il pataffio 1978, C'era una volta la città di Luni 1978, La storia e la gloria 1979, Dopo il pescecane 1979, Le galline pensierose 1980, Diario di un sognatore 1981, Storiette tascabili 1984, Cina Cina 1985, Il pianeta azzurro 1986, Testa d'argento 1988, Il fuoco greco 1990, Le pietre volanti 1992, Il cavaliere e la sua ombra 1992, Il viaggiatore sedentario 1993, Le maschere 1995, Che vergogna scrivere 1996, Interviste impossibili 1997, Avventure 1997, La Superficie di Eliane 1999. *Leisure interests:* agriculture and protection of nature. *Address:* Via Tor Millina 31, 00186 Rome, Italy.

MALEWEZI, Rt Hon Justin Chimera, BA; Malawi teacher, educational administrator and politician; b. 23 Dec. 1944, Ntchisi; s. of the late Canon John Julius Malewezi and of Bartlet Rachel Malewezi; m. Felicity Rozina Chizalema 1970; two s. two d.; ed Columbia Univ., New York; secondary school teacher 1967–69, headmaster 1969–74, educ. admin. 1974–78; Deputy Sec., Ministry of Finance and Prin. Sec. in various ministries 1978–89; Head of Civil Service 1989–91; Vice-Pres. of Malawi 1994–99, 1999–. *Leisure interests:* tennis, football. *Address:* Office of the Vice-President, PO Box 30399, Capital City, Lilongwe 3 (Office); PO Box 30086, Linongwe 3, Malawi (Home). *Telephone:* 780218 (Office). *Fax:* 780521 (Office); 624662 (Office). *E-mail:* vicepres@sdnp.org.mw (Office).

MALFITANO, Catherine; American opera singer (soprano); b. 18 April 1948, New York City; d. of Maria Maslova and Joseph Malfitano; one d.; ed Manhattan School of Music; has appeared at Lyric Opera, Chicago, Metropolitan Opera, NY, La Scala, Milan, Deutsche Opera, Berlin, Salzburg Festival, Royal Opera House, Covent Garden, London, Paris, Geneva, Vienna, Rome, Marseilles, LA, Florence, Hamburg, Barcelona, Israel; Hon. PhD (De Paul Univ.); received Emmy Award for Tosca. *Operas:* 60 roles in operas including: Madame Butterfly 1995, 1997, Il Trittico, Salome 1995, Wozzeck 1997, Eugene Onegin, Tosca, Don Giovanni, Fidelio, McTeague (world première), Antony and Cleopatra, The Makropulos Case, Mahagonny 1998, Bolcom 1999, Macbeth 1999. *Address:* c/o CAMT, 165 N 57th Street, New York, NY 10019, USA (Office); c/o Rita Schütz, Artists Management, Rütistrasse 52, 8044 Zürich-Gockhausen, Switzerland.

MALHOUTRA, Manmohan, MA; Indian international official and consultant; b. 15 Sept. 1937, Izatnagar; s. of Col Gopal Das Malhoutra and Shukla Malhoutra; m. Leela Nath 1963; two d.; ed Delhi Univ., Balliol Coll., Oxford; entered Indian Admin. Service 1961; mem. Prime Minister's Secr. 1966–73; joined Commonwealth Secr. 1974; Dir Sec.-Gen.'s Office and Int. Affairs Div. 1977–82, Asst Commonwealth Sec.-Gen. 1982–93; Conf. Sec. to Commonwealth Heads of Govt Meetings, London 1977, Lusaka 1979, Melbourne 1981, also at Asia-Pacific Regional Heads of Govt Meetings; led Commonwealth Secr. team in Observer Group at pre-independence elections in Zimbabwe 1980; elections in Uganda 1980; Sec. Commonwealth Southern Africa Cttee; Head of Secr. of Commonwealth Group of Eminent Persons on South Africa 1986; Chef de Cabinet, Commonwealth Sec.-Gen.'s Office 1982–90, Head Commonwealth Secr. Human Resource Devt Group 1983–93; mem. Bd of Dirs. Int. Inst. for Democracy and Electoral Assistance, Stockholm 1996–; Sec.-Gen. Rajiv Gandhi Foundation, New Delhi 2001–; Rhodes Scholar 1958. *Leisure interests:* reading, music, tennis. *Address:* 118 Golf Links, New Delhi 110 003, India; 10 Oakeshott Avenue, Highgate, London, N6 6NS, England. *Telephone:* (11) 24633475 (India); (20) 8340-3189 (England). *Fax:* (11) 24643630 (India). *E-mail:* monimal@del6.vsnl.net.in (Home).

MALICK, Terrence; American film director; b. 30 Nov. 1943, Waco, Texas; ed Centre for Advanced Film Studies, American Film Inst.; Golden Berlin Bear Award 1999, Chicago Film Critics Asscn Award 1999, Golden Satellite Award 1999 (all for The Thin Red Line). *Films:* Badlands, Days of Heaven 1978 (New York Film Critics Award, Nat. Soc. of Film Critics Award, Cannes Film Festival Award), The Thin Red Line 1998, The Moviegoer. *Address:* c/o DGA, 7920 Sunset Boulevard, Los Angeles, CA 90046, USA (Office); c/o Harley Williams, 1900 Avenue of the Stars, Floor 17, Los Angeles, CA 90067.

MALIELEGAOI, Tuila'epa Sailele; Samoan politician; fmr Deputy Prime Minister and Minister of Finance, Trade, Industry and Commerce and Tourism; Prime Minister of Samoa 1998–; mem. Human Rights Protection Party (HRPP). *Address:* Prime Minister's Department, P.O. Box L 1861, Apia, Samoa. *Telephone:* 63122. *Fax:* 21339. *E-mail:* pmdept@ipasifika.net (Office).

MALIETOA TANUMAFILI II, HH, CBE; Samoan head of state; b. 4 Jan. 1913; ed Wesley Coll., Auckland, New Zealand; Adviser, Samoan Govt 1940;

mem. NZ del. to UN 1958; fmr mem. Council of State; Joint Head of State of Western Samoa (now Samoa) 1962–63, Sole Head (O le Ao o le Malo) April 1963–; Fautua of Maliena. *Address:* Government House, Vailima, Apia, Samoa.

MALIK, Art; British actor; m.; two d. *Television:* The Jewel in the Crown, Chessgame, The Far Pavilions, The Black Tower, Death is Part of the Process, After the War, Shadow of the Cobra, Stolen. *Films:* Richard's Things, A Passage to India, Underworld, Living Daylights, Side Streets, City of Joy 1992, Wimbledon Poisoner 1994, The Lies 1994, A Kid in King Arthur's Court 1995, Path to Paradise 1997, Booty Call 1997, Cleopatra 1999. *Theatre:* Othello (RSC), Cymbeline and Great Expectations (Royal Exchange, Manchester).

MALIK, Gunwantsingh Jaswantsingh, MA; Indian diplomatist; b. 29 May 1921, Karachi; s. of late Jaswant Singh Malik and Balwant Kaur (Bhagat) Malik; m. Gurkirat Kaur 1948 (dissolved 1982); two s.; RAF 1943–46; Indian Foreign Service 1947–79, Second Sec., Indian Embassy, Brussels 1948–50, Addis Ababa 1950; Under-Sec. Ministry of External Affairs 1950–52; First Sec. and Chargé d'affaires Argentina 1952–56; in Japan 1956–59; Counsellor (Commercial) and Asst Commr Singapore 1959–63; Dir Ministry of Commerce 1963–64; Jt-Sec. Ministry of External Affairs 1964–65; Amb. to Philippines 1965–68, to Senegal, concurrently to Côte d'Ivoire, Mauritania, The Gambia and Upper Volta 1968–70, to Chile (also Accred to Peru, Ecuador and Colombia) 1970–74, to Thailand 1974–77, to Spain 1977–79; Leader trade del. to S. America 1964; mem. del. to ECAFE 1965, to Group of 77 in Lima 1971, to Gov. Body of UNDP 1971, to UNCTAD III 1972, to ESCAP 1975; Chair. Tech. and Drafting Cttee, ESCAP 1976; Deputy Chair. Cttee of the Whole 1977; Dir Indian Shaving Products 1986–88; Sec. Asscn Indian Diplomats 1983–84, 1989–91, Vice-Pres. 1985–86, Pres. 1986–87; Vice-Chair. Delhi Chapter Soc. for Int. Devt 1985–89; Chair. Ahluwalia Baradi Trusts 1988–93; Vice-Pres. Alliance Française de Delhi 1990–98, Pres. 2000–02; Chair. Maharani Voyages Pvt. Ltd 1995–. *Publications:* numerous literary, political and economic articles. *Leisure interests:* photography, writing, touring. *Address:* C224 Defence Colony, New Delhi 110 024, India. *Telephone:* (11) 4619785. *Fax:* (11) 4645819 (Home).

MALIK, Iftikhar Ali, BA; Pakistani industrialist and trade union official; b. 30 Dec. 1944, Lahore; employee with Auto Spare Parts, AutoFilter; fmr Chair. Exec. Cttee Pakistan Automobile Spare Parts Importers and Dealers Asscn (PASPIDA); mem. Exec. Cttee Lahore Chambers of Commerce and Industry 1980s; fmr Vice-Pres. and Zonal Chair. The Fed. of Pakistan Chambers of Commerce and Industry (FPCCI) 1994–, currently Pres. and Life mem.; also Life mem. SAARC Chamber of Commerce and Industry, Pak-Indo Chambers of Commerce and Industry, ECO Chambers of Commerce and Industry. *Address:* Federation of Pakistan Chambers of Commerce and Industry, Federation House, Main Clifton, P.O.B. 13875, Karachi 75600, Pakistan (Office). *Telephone:* (42) 772561618 (Office). *Fax:* (42) 7722627 (Office). *E-mail:* guard@brain.net.pk (Office). *Website:* www.fpcci.com.

MALINVAUD, Edmond, LenD; French economist; b. 25 April 1923, Limoges; s. of Auguste Malinvaud and Andrée Ballet; m. Elizabeth Compagnon 1952; two d.; ed Lycée Gay-Lussac, Limoges, Lycée du Parc, Lyon, Univ. of Paris, Ecole polytechnique; with Inst. nat. de statistique et des études économiques 1948–66, Insp. Gen. 1966–74, Man. Dir 1974–87; Prof. Collège de France 1987–93, Hon. Prof. 1993–; Researcher, Cowles Foundation for Research in Econs, Chicago 1951; Prof., Ecole pratique des hautes études 1957–93; Prof., Univ. of Calif. at Berkeley 1961, 1967; Dir Ecole nat. de la statistique et de l'admin. économique 1962–66; Chair. Int. Econometric Soc. 1963: Assoc. Prof., Law Faculty, Univ. of Paris 1969–71; Vice-Chair. Soc. de Statistique de Paris 1971–73, Chair. 1974; Dir of Econ. Projections, Ministry of Econ. and Finance 1972–74; mem. Bd Banque de France 1972–88; Dir Banque nat. de Paris 1973–81; Vice-Pres. Asscn française des sciences économiques 1985–87; Chair. Int. Econ. Asscn 1974–77; Chair. Int. Statistical Inst. 1979–81; Admin. Groupe des assurances nationales 1981–89;Pres. l'Academie pontificale des sciences sociales 1994–; Dr. hc (Univs. of Basle, Louvain, Helsinki, Geneva, Lausanne, Montreal, Rome, Frankfurt, Milan, Lisbon, Athens, Santiago de Compostela, Bonn, Bielefeld); Médaille d'argent, CNRS, Paolo Baffi Prize for Economics, Recktenwald Prize for Econs; Commdr, Légion d'honneur, Commdr, Palmes academiques Grand Croix, Ordre nat. du mérite. *Publications:* Initiation à la compatibilité nationale 1957, Méthodes statistiques de l'économétrie 1964, Leçons de théorie micro-économique 1968, La croissance française 1972, Réexamen de la théorie du chômage 1980, Théorie macroéconomique 1981, Essais sur la théorie du chômage 1983, Voies de la recherche macroéconomique 1991, Equilibre général dans les économies de marché 1993, Diagnosing Unemployment 1994, Macroeconomic Theory, Vols A and B 1998 Vol. C 2000. *Address:* 42 avenue de Saxe, 75007 Paris, France (Home).

MALJERS, Floris; Netherlands business executive; b. 12 Aug. 1933, Middelburg; m. J. H. de Jongh 1958; two s. one d. (deceased); ed Univ. of Amsterdam; joined Unilever 1959; Man. Dir Unilever, Colombia 1964, Unilever, Turkey 1966; Man. Dir Vdberg & Jurgens, Netherlands 1970; mem. Parent Bd of Unilever and Head of Man. Edible Fats Group 1974; Chair. Unilever N.V. 1984–94, Vice-Chair. Unilever PLC 1984; Chair. Supervisory Bd Philips, Electronics NV, 1994; Dir Amoco 1994–98, ABN/Amro Bank, KLM, Royal Dutch Airlines 1991–, Philips Electronics, Guinness 1994–98;

Gov. European Policy Forum 1993–; Chair. Bd of Trustees Utrecht Univ. Hosp. 1994–, Rotterdam School of Man., Erasmus Univ. 1999–; Hon. KBE 1992. *Address:* P.O.Box 11550, 2502 AN The Hague, Netherlands.

MÄLK, Raul; Estonian diplomatist and fmr journalist; b. 14 May 1952, Parnu, Estonia; ed Tartu Univ., Leningrad Inst. of Political Studies; economist and researcher Inst. of Econs, Estonian Acad. of Sciences 1975–77; Sr editor, Deputy Ed.-in-Chief, Ed.-in-Chief Estonian Radio 1977–90; Deputy Head Office of Chair. Supreme Soviet of Estonia 1990–92; adviser to Minister of Foreign Affairs 1992–93; Head Office of Minister of Foreign Affairs 1993–94; Deputy Perm. Under-Sec. Ministry of Foreign Affairs 1994–96; Amb. to UK (also Accred to Ireland) 1996–2001, to Portugal 2000; Minister of Foreign Affairs 1998–99; Head Estonian dels. for negotiations with Russia, Finland, Latvia 1994–96; Dir-Gen. Policy Planning Dept, MFA 2001–; Estonian Journalists' Union Award 1990. *Leisure interests:* theatre, attending sports events. *Address:* Ministry of Foreign Affairs, Islandi square 1, 15049 Tallinn SW7 5DG, Estonia (Office). *Telephone:* 631-7000 (Tallinn) (Office). *Fax:* 631-7099 (Tallinn) (Office).

MALKOVICH, John; American actor; b. 9 Dec. 1953, Christopher, Ill.; s. of Dan Malkovich and Joe Anne Malkovich; m. Glenne Headley 1982 (divorced 1988); m. 2nd Nicoletta Peyran; one s. one d.; ed Eastern Illinois and Illinois State Univs.; co-f. Steppenwolf Theatre, Chicago 1976; mem. Creative Bd of Dirs Artists Ind. Network. *Theatre appearances include:* True West 1982, Death of a Salesman 1984, Burn This 1987; Dir Balm in Gilead 1984–85, Arms and the Man 1985, Coyote Ugly 1985, The Caretaker 1986, Burn This 1990, A Slip of the Tongue 1992, Libra 1994, Steppenwolf 1994. *Films include:* Places in the Heart 1984, The Killing Fields 1984, Eleni 1985, Making Mr. Right 1987, The Glass Menagerie 1987, Empire of the Sun 1987, Miles from Home 1988, Dangerous Liaisons 1989, Jane, La Putaine du roi 1989, Queen's Logic 1989, The Sheltering Sky 1989, The Object of Beauty 1991, Shadows and Fog 1992, Of Mice and Men 1992, Jennifer Eight, Alive, In the Line of Fire, Mary Reilly 1994, The Ogre 1995, Mulholland Falls 1996, Portrait of a Lady 1996, Con Air, The Man in the Iron Mask 1997, Rounders 1998, Time Regained 1998, Being John Malkovich 1999, The Libertine 1999 (also Dir), Ladies Room 1999, Joan of Arc 1999, Shadow of the Vampire 2000, Les Âmes fortes 2001, Je Rentre à la Maison 2001, Hotel 2001, Knockaround Guys 2001, The Dancer Upstairs (Dir and Producer) 2002, Ripley's Game 2003, Johnny English 2003; Exec. Prod. The Accidental Tourist. *Address:* c/o Artists Independent Network, 32 Tavistock Street, London, WC2E 7PB, England (Office). *E-mail:* mail@artistindependent.com (Office). *Website:* www .artistsindependent.com (Office).

MALLABY, Sir Christopher Leslie George, GCMG, GCVO, BA; British diplomatist and business executive; b. 7 July 1936, Camberley, Surrey; s. of Brig. A. W S. Mallaby and M. C. Mallaby (née Jones); m. Pascale Thierry-Mieg 1961; one s. three d.; ed Eton Coll., King's Coll., Cambridge; diplomatic postings in Moscow 1961–63, Berlin 1966–69, New York 1970–74, Moscow 1974–77, Bonn 1982–85; Head of Arms Control, Soviet and E European and Planning Depts., FCO 1977–82; Deputy Sec. to Cabinet 1985–88; Amb. to Fed. Repub. of Germany (now Germany) 1988–92, to France 1993–96; Man. Dir UBS Warburg 1998–; Chair. Primary Immunodeficiency Asscn 1996–2002, Advisory Bd Gt. Britain Centre, Humboldt Univ. Berlin 1998–, Advisory Bd German Studies Inst., Birmingham Univ. 1998–; European Org. for Research and Treatment of Cancer 2000–; Dir Charter European Investment 1996–, Sun Life and Provincial Holdings PLC 1996–2000, EDF Trading 1999–; Adviser to RMC 1996–2000, Herbert Smith 1997–2001; Trustee Tate Gallery 1996–2002, Reuters 1998–; Founder, Trustee Entente Cordiale Scholarships 1996– (Chair. 2001–); Chair. Somerset House Trustees 2002–; Grand Cross, Order of Merit, (Germany), Grand Officier, Légion d'honneur. *Leisure interests:* grandchildren. *Address:* c/o UBS Warburg, 2 Finsbury Avenue, London, EC2M 2PP, England.

MALLET, Robert Albert Marie Georges, DèsSc, D. EN D.; French university rector and author; b. 15 March 1915, Paris; s. of Georges Mallet and Valentine Monnet; m. 1st Francine Leullier 1944 (divorced); two s.; m. 2nd Yvonne Noviant 1985; ed Faculté des Lettres and Faculté de Droit, Paris; Dir, Ecole Nat. des Lettres, Antananarivo, Malagasy Repub. 1959, subsequently Dean, Faculty of Letters, Madagascar; Rector, Acad. d'Amiens 1964–68, Univ. of Paris 1969–80; Pres. Asscn des universités partiellement ou entièrement de langue française 1972–75, Hon. Pres. 1975–; Pres. Comité perm. des mondialistes de France 1978–; Pres. Jury du Prix Apollinaire; mem. Universal Movement for Scientific Responsibility (Pres. 1974), Acad. royale de Belgique; Silver Medal, City of Paris 1952; Prix de la Critique 1955; Grand prix de poésie, Acad. française 1977, Prix des libraires 1987, Grand Prix de la Société des poètes français 1989, Prix mondial Cino del Duca 1993; Grand Officier, Légion d'honneur, Commdr des Arts et Lettres, Croix de guerre, Commdr, Palmes académiques, Ordre nat. Malagasy. *Publications:* poems: Le poème du sablier, La rose en ses remous, Quand le miroir s'étonne, Silex éclaté, L'Espace d'une fenêtre 1978, L'Ombre chaude 1984, Presqu'îles, presqu'amours 1986, Cette plume qui tournoie 1988, Semer l'arbre 1991; plays: Le filandier, Satire en trois temps cinq mouvements, Le train de nuit, L'équipage au complet; novels: Région inhabitée, Ellynn, Les rives incertaines; numerous other publications. *Address:* 18 rue de la Glacière, 75013 Paris, France.

MALLET, W. George, G.C.S.L., GCMG, CBE; Saint Lucia politician (retd); b. 24 July 1923, Colón, Panama; m. Beryl Bernadine Leonce; ed RC Boys' School,

Castries Intermediate Secondary School; marketing man. of a Castries commercial firm; mem. Castries City Council 1952–64; elected to Legis. Council 1958; Minister for Trade, Industry, Agric. and Tourism 1964–79; mem. Opposition 1979–82; Deputy Prime Minister and Minister for Trade, Industry and Tourism 1982–92; Deputy Prime Minister and Minister for Foreign Affairs, Trade and Industry 1992–96; Gov.-Gen. of Saint Lucia 1996–97. *Address:* P.O. Box 216, Castries (Office); The Morne, Castries, Saint Lucia (Home). *Telephone:* 452-2318 (Office); 453-7252 (Home). *Fax:* 452-4677 (Office).

MALLINCKRODT, Georg Wilhelm von; German banker; b. 19 Aug. 1930, Eichholz; s. of Arnold von Mallinckrodt and Valentine von Mallinckrodt (née von Joest); m. Charmaine Brenda Schroder 1958; two s. two d.; ed Schule Schloss Salem; with Afga AG, Munich 1948–51; with Munchmeyer & Co., 1951–53; with Kleinwort & Co., London 1953–54; with J. Henry Schroder Bank Corp., NY 1954–55, 1957–, with J. Henry Schroder & Co. Ltd 1960, Dir Schroders PLC 1977, Chair. 1984–97, Pres. 1995–; Chair. J. Henry Schroder Bank AG, Zurich 1984–, Schroder Inc., NY 1984–; Dir Schroders Australia Holdings Ltd, Sydney 1984–2001, Schroder & Co. Inc., NY 1986–2000, Schroder Int. Merchant Bankers Ltd, Singapore 1988–2000, Siemens PLC 1989–2001; with Union Bank of Switzerland, Geneva 1956–57; Hon. DCL (Bishop's Univ., Québec) 1994; Cross of the Order of Merit (Fed. Repub. of Germany) 1990; Hon. KBE 1997; Commdr.'s Cross of Order of Merit 2001. *Leisure interests:* opera, shooting. *Address:* Schroders PLC, 31 Gresham Street, London, EC2V 7QA, England. *Telephone:* (20) 7658-6370. *Fax:* (20) 7658-2211.

MALLOCH BROWN, Mark, MA; British international organization official; m.; three c.; ed Univ. of Cambridge, Univ. of Michigan, USA; worked for UNHCR first in Thailand in charge of field operations for Cambodian refugees, then in Geneva as Deputy Chief of Emergency Unit 1979–83; Political Corresp. Economist 1977–79; founder, Economist Devt Report, 1983–86; lead int. partner Sawyer Miller Group (communications management firm), advising govts. political leaders and corpns. 1986–94; mem. Soros Advisory Cttee on Bosnia and Herzegovina 1993–94; Dir of External Affairs, IBRD 1994–96, Vice-Pres. for External Affairs 1996–99, for UN Affairs 1996–99; Admin. UN Devt Programme (UNDP) July 1999–; Vice-Chair. Bd of Refugees Int., Washington, DC, USA. *Address:* UNDP, 1 United Nations Plaza, New York, NY 10017, USA (Office). *Telephone:* (212) 906-5791 (Office). *Fax:* (212) 906-5778 (Office). *E-mail:* mark.malloch.brown@undp.org (Office).

MALLON, Séamus; Northern Irish politician, teacher and playwright; b. 17 Aug. 1936, Markethill, Co. Armagh, Northern Ireland; m.; one d.; ed Christian Bros.; Grammar School, Newry, St Joseph's Coll. of Educ., Belfast; Chair. Social Democratic and Labour Party (SDLP) 1973–74, Deputy Leader 1979–2001; mem. Nat. Ass. 1973–74, Armagh Dist Councillor 1973–86; mem. Nat. Convention 1974–75; elected to Nat. Ass. 1982 but disqualified; mem. Irish Senate 1982, New Ireland Forum 1983–84, Forum for Peace and Reconciliation 1994–95, Nat. Forum and Talks 1996–98, British-Irish Inter-Parl. Body; MP, House of Commons for Newry and Armagh 1986–; mem. NI Ass. for Newry and Armagh 1998–2000; (Ass. suspended 11 Feb. 2000); Deputy First Minister (desig.) 1998–99, Deputy First Minister 1999–2000; Hon. LLD (Queen's Belfast) 1999, (NCEA) 2000, (Nat. Univ. Ireland) 2002. *Leisure interests:* golf, fishing, literature. *Address:* 2 Bridge Street, Newry, Co. Down, BT35 8AE (Office); 5 Castleview, Markethill, Armagh, BT60 1QP, Northern Ireland (Home). *Telephone:* (28) 3026-7933 (Office); (28) 3755-1411 (Home). *Fax:* (28) 3026-7828 (Office).

MALLOUM, Brig.-Gen. Félix; Chadian army officer; b. 1932, Fort-Archambault (now Sarh); ed Mil. Schools, Brazzaville, Fréjus, Saint-Maixent; served in French Army, Indo-China 1953–55, Algeria; joined Chad Nat. Army; Lt-Col 1961, Capt. 1962, Col 1968; fmr Head of Mil. Corps at the Presidency; Chief of Staff of the Army Dec. 1972–Sept. 1973; C-in-C of the Armed Forces 1972–73; under house arrest June 1973, released April 1975 after coup deposed Pres. Tombalbaye; Head of State, Chair. Supreme Mil. Council 1975–79, Pres. Council of Ministers, Minister of Defence and Ex-Servicemen 1975–79; resigned March 1979 after signing Kano Peace Agreement with Front Nat. du Tchad.

MALOFEEV, Anatoly Aleksandrovich; Belarus politician; b. 14 May 1933, Gomel; one d.; ed Gomel Railway Coll., Belarus State Inst. of Nat. Econ., Higher Party School; worked as locksmith, Minsk, then Gomel and Minsk carriage repair plants 1949–62; mil. service; mem. CPSU 1954–91; various posts on CP cttees. Gomel, at Dept of Chemical and Light Industries of Cen. Cttee of CP of Belarus, Chair. Gomel Regional Exec. Cttee of CP of Belarus, mem. Cen. CPSU Cttee 1986–91, Politburo 1990–91; USSR People's Deputy 1989–91; Deputy Supreme Soviet of Belorussia 1982–92; First Sec. Cen. Cttee of CP of Belorussia 1990–93; mem. Chamber of Reps 1996–2000, 2000–, Chair. 1997–2000; Chair. Parl. Comm. for Econ. Policies and Reforms 1996, Cttee on Int. Affairs and Ties with the CIS 2000–; Order Red Banner of Labour (twice), Award of the Fatherland (3rd degree) 1999. *Address:* Sovetskaya Str. 11, 220010 Minsk, Belarus (Office). *Telephone:* (17) 222-6398 (Office). *Fax:* (17) 222-6461 (Office). *E-mail:* mizhn@belarus.minsk.bs (Office).

MALONE, John C.; American telecommunications executive; b. 1941; m. Leslie Malone; ed Yale, Johns Hopkins Univs.; fmr Pres. Jerrold Electronics Corpn; Pres., CEO Tele-Communications Inc. Denver, then Chair., CEO 1996–99; Chair., Dir Liberty Media Corpn Denver 1999–. *Address:* c/o Tele-Comm Inc., 9197 South Peoria Street, Englewood, CO 80111, USA.

MALONE, Thomas Francis, ScD; American geophysicist; b. 3 May 1917, Sioux City, Iowa; s. of John and Mary (Hourigan) Malone; m. Rosalie A. Doran 1942; five s. one d.; ed S. Dakota State School of Mines and Tech. and MIT; mem. of Staff MIT 1941–43, Asst Prof. 1943–51, Assoc. Prof. 1951–54; Dir Travelers Weather Service and Travelers Weather Research Center for Travelers Insurance Co., Hartford, Conn. 1954–56, Dir of Research 1956–69, Second Vice-Pres. 1964–66, Vice-Pres. 1966–68, Sr Vice-Pres. 1968–70; Dean of Graduate School, Univ. of Connecticut 1970–73; Dir Holcomb Research Inst., Butler Univ. 1973–83, Dir Emer. 1983–; Sec.-Gen. Scientific Cttee on Problems of Environment 1970–72; Pres. American Meteorological Soc. 1960–62, American Geophysical Union 1961–64, Inst. of Ecology 1978–81, Vice-Pres. Int. Council of Scientific Unions 1970–72, Treas. 1978–84; Foreign Sec. Nat. Acad. of Sciences 1978–82, Chair. Bd on Atmospheric Sciences and Climate 1981–84; Scholar in Residence St Joseph Coll., Conn. 1983; Distinguished Scholar, NC State Univ. 1990–98; mem. Scientific Advisory Cttee on Climate Impact Assessment and Response, UNEP 1992– Advisory Cttee on Accreditation, Conn. Dept of Higher Educ. 2000–(2002); Fellow Royal Irish Acad. 1982–, Nat. Sciences Resources for the Future 1983–84, American Acad. of Arts and Sciences 1999–; Exec. Scientist, Connecticut Acad. of Science and Eng 1987–91; mem. NAS, AAAS, American Geophysical Union; Univ.'s Distinguished Scholar Emer., NC State Univ. 1999–; Hon. DEng; Hon. LHD; Hon. ScD (Bates Coll.) 1988; Losey Award, Inst. of Aerospace Sciences 1960; Charles Franklin Brooks Award 1964 and Cleveland Abbe Award 1968 (American Meteorological Soc.), Int. Meteorological Soc. Prize 1984, World Meteorological Org. Gold Medal 1984, St Francis of Assisi Prize for Environment 1991, AAAS Award for Int. Scientific Co-operation, Irving Award American Distance Learning Consortium 1997. *Publications:* numerous articles in scientific journals. *Address:* 5 Bishop Road, Apt. 203, West Hartford, CT 06119, USA. *Telephone:* (860) 236-2426 (Home). *Fax:* (860) 527-2161 (Office); (860) 233-6250 (Home). *E-mail:* tfmalone@aol.com (Office). tfmalone@aol.com (Home).

MALOUF, David George Joseph, AO, BA; Australian writer; b. 20 March 1934, Brisbane; s. of G.Malouf; ed Brisbane Grammar School and Univ. of Queensland; Hon. Fellow, Australian Acad. of the Humanities; Gold Medal, Australian Literature Soc. 1962, 1974, Age Book of the Year, NSW Premier's Award for Fiction, Vance Palmer Award, Pascal Prize, Commonwealth Writers' Prize and Prix Femina Etranger, for The Great World 1991, inaugural IMPAC Dublin Literary Award 1993; named Neustadt Int. Prize for Literature, Oklahoma Univ. 2000, many other awards. *Publications include:* poetry: Bicycle and other poems 1970, Neighbours in a Thicket 1974, First Things Last 1981, Selected Poems 1991, Poems 1959–89 1992; novels: Johnno 1975, An Imaginary Life 1978, Child's Play 1982, Fly Away Peter 1982, Harland's Half Acre 1984, Antipodes (stories), 12 Edmonstone Street 1985, The Great World 1990, Remembering Babylon 1993, The Conversations at Curlow Creek 1996, Dream Stuff 2000; play, Blood Relations 1987; opera librettos: Voss 1986, Mer de Glace 1991, Baa Baa Black Sheep 1993. *Address:* c/o Barbara Mobbs, 35A Sutherland Crescent, Darling Point, Sydney, NSW 2027, Australia.

MALPAS, Sir Robert, Kt, CBE, BSc, FEng, FIMechE, FIChemE; British business executive; b. 9 Aug. 1927; s. of the late Cheshyre Malpas and of Louise Marie Marcelle Boni; m. Josephine Dickenson 1956; ed Taunton School, St George's Coll., Buenos Aires, Argentina, Durham Univ.; joined ICI Ltd 1948; CEO ICI Europa Ltd 1973; Dir ICI 1975; Pres. Halcon Int. Inc., New York 1978–82; Chair. Power Gen PLC 1988–90, Cookson Group PLC 1991–97; Man. Dir British Petroleum (BP) 1983–89; Dir (non-exec.) Bd BOC Group 1981–96, Eurotunnel 1987–2000 (Chair. 1996–98), Barings PLC 1989–95, Repsol SA (Spain) 1989–; mem. Eng Council 1983–88; (Vice-Chair. 1984–88); Sr Vice-Pres. Royal Acad. of Eng 1989–92; Chair. LINK 1987–93; Chair. Natural Environment Research Council 1993–96, Ferghana Partners 1997–; Dir (non-exec.) Evolution PLC; Hon. Fellow Royal Soc. of Chem.; Hon. degrees from Loughborough, Newcastle, Surrey, Bath, Durham, Sheffield Hallam, Westminster Univs.; Order of Civil Merit, Spain 1968. *Leisure interests:* theatre, opera, reading, music, sports. *Address:* 2 Spencer Park, London, SW18 2SX, England. *Telephone:* (20) 8877-4250 (Home). *Fax:* (20) 8877-1197 (Office). *E-mail:* bobmalpas@aol.com (Home).

MALTBY, Per Eugen, DPhil; Norwegian astrophysicist; b. 3 Nov. 1933, Oslo; s. of Olaf K. Maltby and Else M. (née Raastad) Maltby; m. Elisabet Ruud 1956; two c.; ed Univ. of Oslo; Research Asst, Univ. of Oslo 1955–60, lecturer 1963–66, Assoc. Prof. 1967–82, Prof. 1983–, Chair., Astronomy Dept 1975–77; Research Fellow, Calif. Inst. of Tech. 1960–61, Sr Research Fellow 1964–65; amanuensis Univ. of Bergen 1961–63; Visiting Scientist CSIRO, Sydney 1974–75; Chair. Norwegian Council for Natural Science Research 1978–80; mem. Norwegian Acad. of Sciences and Letters, Int. Astronomical Union, American Astronomical Soc., European Physics Soc., Norwegian Physics Soc. *Address:* Postboks 1029, Blindern, 0315 Oslo 3 (Office); Vaekerøvn 126A, 0383 Oslo, Norway (Home).

MAŁYSZ, Adam; Polish skier; b. 4 Dec. 1977, Wisła; m.; one d.; ed Technical School, Ustronie; world champion Great Ski-Jump 2001, runner-up Middle Ski-Jump 2001; winner World Cup in ski jumping 2001, Four Ski-Jumps competition 2001; winner Polish Championships 2002. *Address:* ul. Kopydło 59, 43-374 Wisła, Poland (Office).

MAMATSASHVILI, Teimuraz; Georgian diplomatist, engineer and economist; b. 10 Nov. 1942, Tbilisi; s. of David Mamatsashvili and Maria

Robakidze; m. Irina Arkhangelskaya 1967; two d.; ed Georgian Ploytech. Inst., Tbilisi, Acad. of Foreign Trade, Moscow; Sr Engineer, Inst. of Metrology, Tbilisi 1965–70; Sr Engineer, Trade Representation of USSR in Australia 1973–77; Sr Engineer, Deputy Dir, Dir Licensmash co. (part of Licensintorg Corpn), Moscow 1977–89; Trade Rep. to Tokyo, Japan 1989–92; Minister of Foreign Econ. Relations 1992–93; Amb. Extraordinary and Plenipotentiary to UK 1995–, to Ireland 1998–; Perm. Rep. to Int. Maritime Org. 1995–; Gov. EBRD 1996–; two state Orders of USSR 1979, 1989. *Leisure interests:* hunting, video filming, gardening. *Address:* Embassy of Georgia, 4 Russell Gardens, London, W14 8EZ (Office); 11 Queen's Gate Terrace, London, SW7 5PR, England (Home); 4 Uznadze St., Appt. 31, Tbilisi, Georgia (Home). *Telephone:* (20) 7603-7799 (Office); (20) 7225-0949 (London) (Home). *Fax:* (20) 7603-6682 (Office). *E-mail:* geoemb@dircon.co.uk (Office).

MAMBA, Clifford Sibusio, BSc; Swazi diplomatist; b. 5 May 1963; m.; ed Middlesex Univ., UK; Amb. to Repub. of Korea then the EU 1991–96; Amb. to Malaysia 1996–2000; Perm. Rep. to UN 2000–; fmr Chair. African, Caribbean and Pacific Group of States Cttee of Ambs., ACP Ambassadorial Sub-Cttee for Sugar. *Leisure interests:* sports, reading, travel. *Address:* Permanent Mission of Swaziland to the United Nations, 408 East 50th Street, New York, NY 10022, USA (Office). *Telephone:* (212) 371-8910 (Office). *Fax:* (212) 754-2755 (Office). *E-mail:* swaziland@un.int (Office).

MAMEDOV, Georgy Enverovich, C.HIS.SC.; Russian diplomatist; b. 9 Sept. 1947, Moscow; m.; one s. one d.; ed Moscow Inst. of Int. Relations; researcher Inst. of USA and Canada 1970–77, mem. staff USSR Embassy in USA 1977–81, Sec., Counsellor, Deputy Chief, then Chief Dept of USA and Canada, USSR Ministry of Foreign Affairs 1981–91, Deputy Minister of Foreign Affairs of Russia 1991–; mem. State Cttee. on Defence Industry 1996–98. *Address:* Ministry of Foreign Affairs, Smolenskaya-Sennaya 32/34, Moscow, Russia. *Telephone:* (095) 244-92-55. *Fax:* (095) 253-90-78. *E-mail:* gmamedov@mid.ru (Office).

MAMERT, Jean Albert; French public servant; b. 26 March 1928; s. of Paul Mamert and Marthe Maynadier; m. Monique Petit 1966; one s. one d.; ed Lycée et Faculté de Droit, Montpellier, Inst. d'Études Politiques, Paris, Ecole Nat. d'Admin., Paris; Auditor 1955, later Master of Requests, Council of State 1962–; Tech. Counsellor of Govt for Constitutional Problems, 1958–59, Sec.-Gen. Constitutional Consultative Cttee 1958; Chief of Prime Minister's Office Jan.–July 1959; Sec.-Gen. Econ. and Social Council 1959–72; Dir-Gen. Cino del Duca 1978; mem. EEC Econ. and Social Cttee 1970–74; with Michelin Group 1972–78, Pres. Pneumatiques Michelin SA, Spain 1974–78; Dir-Gen. Editions Mondiales 1978–80; Pres. Société Lorraine de matériel minier et métallurgique (S.L.M.M.) 1980; Dir France-Soir 1983–84; Dir Avenir-Publicité 1984–89; Gen. Del. Asscn Nat. des Sociétés par Action 1986–89, Pres. 1989–97; Vice Prin. SICOVAM 1986–; Dir 1996–; mem. Operations Comm. of the Bourse (Paris Stock Exchange) 1996–; Hon. Pres., Dir Nat. Asscn of Jt Stock Cos. (ANSA) 1997–; Chevalier Légion d'honneur. *Address:* 15 place du Général Catroux, 75017 Paris (Office); 89 rue de l'Assomption, 75016 Paris, France.

MAMET, David Alan, BA; American playwright and director; b. 30 Nov. 1947, Chicago; s. of Bernard Morris Mamet and Lenore June (née Silver) Mamet; m. 1st Lindsay Crouse 1977 (divorced); m. 2nd Rebecca Pidgeon 1991; ed Goddard Coll., Plainfield, Vermont; Artist-in-residence Goddard Coll. 1971–73; Artistic Dir, St Nicholas Theatre Co., Chicago 1973–75; Guest Lecturer, Univ. of Chicago 1975, 1979, NY Univ. 1981; Assoc. Artistic Dir Goodman Theatre, Chicago 1978; Assoc. Prof. of Film, Columbia Univ. 1988; Dir (films) House of Games 1986, Things Change 1987, Homicide 1991; (play) A Life in the Theatre 1989; Hon.D.Litt. (Dartmouth Coll.) 1996; recipient Outer Critics Circle Award for contrib. to American theatre 1978. *Publications:* The Duck Variations 1971, Sexual Perversity in Chicago 1973 (Village Voice Obie Award 1976), The Reunion 1973, Squirrels 1974, American Buffalo (Village Voice Obie Award 1976) 1976, (NY Drama Critics Circle Award 1977), A Life in the Theatre 1976, The Water Engine 1976, The Woods 1977, Lone Canoe 1978, Prairie du Chien 1978, Lakeboat 1980, Donny March 1981, Edmond 1982 (Village Voice Obie Award 1983), The Disappearance of the Jews 1983, The Shawl 1985, Glengarry Glen Ross (Pulitzer prize for Drama, NY Drama Critics Circle award) 1984, Speed-the-Plow 1987, Bobby, Gould in Hell 1989, The Old Neighborhood 1991, Oleanna 1992, Ricky Jay and his 52 Assistants 1994, Death Defying Acts 1996, Boston Marriage 1999; (screenplays) The Postman Always Rings Twice 1979, The Verdict 1980, The Untouchables 1986, House of Games 1986, Things Change (with Shel Silverstein) 1987, We're No Angels 1987, Oh Hell! 1991, Homicide 1991, Hoffa 1991, Glengarry Glen Ross 1992, The Rising Sun 1992, Oleanna 1994, The Edge 1996, The Spanish Prisoner 1996, Wag the Dog 1997, Boston Marriage 2001, Meist 2001; (children's books) Mr. Warm and Cold 1985, The Owl (with Lindsay Crouse) 1987, The Winslow Boy 1999; (essays) Writing in Restaurants 1986, Some Freaks 1989, On Directing Film 1990, The Hero Pony 1990, The Cabin 1992, A Whore's Profession 1993 (also screenplay adaptation), The Cryptogram 1994, The Village (novel) 1994, Passover 1995, Make-Believe Town: Essays and Remembrances 1996, Plays 1996, Plays 2 1996, The Duck and the Goat 1996, The Old Religion 1996, True and False 1996, The Old Neighborhood 1998, Jafsie and John Henry 2000, State and Main (writer, Dir) 2000. *Address:* c/o Howard Rosenstone, Rosenstone/Wender Agency, 38 East 29th Street, 10th Floor, New York, NY 10016, U.S.A.

MAMLIN, Gennadiy Semenovich; Russian author; b. 7 Nov. 1925, Simferopol; m. Diana Karakhanova; studied piano; worked as accompanist, wrote music, served in Soviet Army 1942–44, was wounded; first works published 1950. *Plays include:* Nikita Snegiryov 1956, But with Alyoshka We Are Friends 1961, Miracle at Noon 1964, Fireworks 1965, Hey there, Hello! 1970, Let's speak about the Strangeness of Love 1975, Salute to Dinosaurs 1979, The Bells 1985, Two Steps from the End of the World 1988, Life 1989, Magic Shoes 1992, On the Last Turn 1997, The Diamond Grief 1998. *Address:* Krasnoarmeiskaya Str. 27, Apt. 104, 125319 Moscow, Russia. *Telephone:* (095) 151-88-20.

MAMO, Sir Anthony Joseph, OBE, QC, LLD, BA, K.U.O.M., S.G.; Maltese former Head of State and judge; b. 8 Jan. 1909, Birkirkara; s. of late Joseph and Carla (née Brincat) Mamo; m. Margaret Agius 1939; one s. two d.; ed Archbishop's Seminary, Malta and Royal Univ. of Malta; mem. Statute Law Revision Comm. 1936–42; Crown Counsel 1942–51; Prof. of Criminal Law, Royal Univ. of Malta 1943–57; Deputy Attorney-Gen. 1952–54; Attorney-Gen. 1955; Chief Justice and Pres. of HM Court of Appeal 1957; Pres. HM Constitutional Court 1964; Pres. HM Court of Criminal Appeal 1967; Gov.-Gen. of Malta 1971–74; Pres. of the Repub. 1974–76; Hon. LLD (Libya) 1971; Hon. DLitt (Malta) 1969; Companion of Honour, Nat. Order of Merit of Malta 1990, Xirka Gieh ir-Repubblika 1992, KStJ, Gieh Birkirkara 1996. *Publications:* lectures on criminal law and criminal procedure delivered at the Royal Univ. of Malta. *Leisure interest:* reading. *Address:* c/o Casa Arkati, Constitution Street, Mosta, Malta. *Telephone:* 434342. *Fax:* 431817.

MAMUT, Alexander Leonidovich; Russian business executive and lawyer; b. 29 Jan. 1960, Russia; s. of Leonid Mamut; ed Moscow State Univ.; lawyer 1985–; f. and Head ALM Consulting Co. 1990–; business activities 1989–; f. and mem. Bd of Dirs Bank Imperial 1990–; founder and Chair. Exec. Bd Co. on Project Financing 1993–; later Jt Stock Interbanking Credit Org. Co. for Project Financing (COPF) 1996–2000; mem. Bd MDM Bank 2000–; mem. Council on Industrial Policy and Business of Russian Govt 1994–; adviser to Head of Admin. Russian Presidency 1998–; mem. Bd of Dirs Sobinbank 1999–; mem. Observation Council Bank Moskovsky Delovoy Mir MDM-Bank 1999–, now Chair. *Address:* MDM Bank, Sadovnicheskaya str.3, 113035 Moscow, Russia (Office). *Telephone:* (095) 797 95 00 (Office).

MANABE, Syukuro, DSc; American (b. Japanese) meteorologist; b. 21 Sept. 1931; s. of Seiichi Manabe and Sueko (Akashi) Manabe; m. Nobuko Nakamura 1962; two d.; ed Tokyo Univ.; research meteorologist, Gen. Circulation Research Section, US Weather Bureau, Washington, DC 1958–63; Sr Research Meteorologist, Geophysical Fluid Dynamics Lab., Environmental Science Services Admin., Washington, DC 1963–68, Nat. Oceanic and Atmospheric Admin., Princeton, NJ 1968–97, mem. Sr Exec. Service, USA 1979–96, Sr Scientist 1996–97; Dir Global Warming Research Program, Frontier Research System for Global Change 1997–2001; lecturer with rank of Prof., Atmospheric and Oceanic Sciences Program, Princeton Univ. 1968–1997; Visiting Research Collaborator, Atmospheric and Oceanic Science Program, Princeton Univ. 2002–; mem. US Nat. Research Council Comm. on Geosciences, Environment and Resources 1990–93; mem. NAS; Foreign mem. Academia Europaea, Royal Soc. of Canada; Fellow American Geophysical Union (AGU), American Asscn for the Advancement of Science; Hon. mem. American Meteorological Soc. (AMS); Rossby Research Medal (AMS) 1992, Blue Planet Prize (Asahi Glass Foundation) 1992, Revelle Medal (AGU) 1993, Asahi Prize (Asahi Shimbun Foundation), Volvo Environmental Prize (Volvo Foundation) 1997, Milankovitch Medal (European Geophysical Soc.) 1998 and many other awards. *Publications:* more than 140 papers in scientific journals. *Leisure interests:* swimming, running. *Address:* Program in Atmospheric and Oceanic Sciences, Princeton University, PO Box CN710, Sayre Hall, Forrestal Campus, Princeton, NJ 08544-0710, USA (Office). *Telephone:* (609) 258-2790 (Office); (609) 924-0734 (Home). *Fax:* (609) 258-2850 (Office); (609) 924-6360 (Home). *E-mail:* manabe@splash.princeton.edu (Office).

MANAGADZE, Nodar Shotayevich; Georgian film director and scriptwriter; b. 19 March 1943, Tbilisi, Georgia; s. of Shota Managadze and Gabilaia Ketevan; m. Janelidze Manana 1966; one s.; ed Rustaveli Theatre Inst., Tbilisi; Dir Georgian Films 1988–; mem. Supervisory Council Kartuli Pilmi JSC 1994–; Lecturer Faculty of Cinema Tbilisi Ivane Javakhishvili State Univ. 1996–. *Films include:* Expectation 1970, The Warmth of Your Hands 1972 (1st Prize Tbilisi Film Festival 1972, A Common Wall 1973, The Silver Siren 1973 (1st Prize Naples Film Festival 1973), How the Fine Fellow was Married 1974, Living Legends 1979 (participant of Cannes Film Festival, Best Film, Sitges Film Festival 1988), The Dam in the Mountains 1980, Spring is on the Wane 1984, Eh! Maestro 1987 (Special Prize, San Remo Film Festival 1988, First Prize, Baku Film Festival 1988), Noah 1990, Epiphany 1994 (Grand Prix, Tbilisi Film Festival 1994, Special Prize, Sochi Int. Film Festival 1994), The Migration of the Angel 2001 (Best Dir, Tambov Orthodox Christian Countries Film Festival 2001). *Leisure interests:* mountains, music, sports. *Address:* Bakradze Str. 11, 380009, Tbilisi, Georgia. *Telephone:* (32) 93-27-17; (32) 99-99-71. *Fax:* (32) 51-09-10. *E-mail:* nmanagadze@yahoo.com (Home).

MANASSEH, Leonard Sulla, OBE, RA, FRIBA, FCSD; British architect; b. 21 May 1916; s. of the late Alan Manasseh and Esther Manasseh (née Elias); m. 1st 1947 (divorced 1956); two s.; m. 2nd Sarah Delaforce 1957; two s. one d. (deceased); ed Cheltenham Coll., The Architectural Asscn School of Architecture; Asst Architect, CREN London and Guy Morgan & Partners; teaching staff, Architectural Assen and Kingston School of Art 1941–43; served Fleet Air Arm 1943–46; Asst Architect, Herts. County Council 1946–48; Sr Architect, Stevenage New Town Devt Corpn 1948–50; partner, Leonard Manasseh Partnership 1950–; teaching staff, Architectural Assen 1951–59; opened office in Singapore and Malaysia with James Cubitt & Partners 1953–54; mem. Council, Architectural Assen 1959–66, Pres. 1964–65, Council of Industrial Design 1965–68, Council RIBA 1968–70, 1976–82 (Hon. Sec. 1979–81), Council, Nat. Trust 1977–91, Ancient Monuments Bd 1978–84, Bd, Chatham Historic Dockyard Trust 1984–97; Pres. Franco-British Union of Architects 1978–79; RA Rep. Bd of Govs. Dulwich Schools Foundation 1987–95; Surveyor to Dulwich Picture Gallery 1987–94, Chair. 1988–93; Pres. Royal West of England Acad. 1989–94. *Work includes:* houses, housing and schools, industrial work, power stations, research centres, municipal offices, conservation plan for Beaulieu Estate, Nat. Motor Museum, Beaulieu, Wellington Country Park, Stratfield Saye, Pumping Station, Weymouth, British Museum refurbishment, additions to Old Royal Observatory, Greenwich, Service Yard, Hampstead Heath, for City of London 1992. *Publications:* Office Buildings (with 3rd Baron Cunliffe) 1962, Snowdon Summit Report (Countryside Comm.) 1974, Eastbourne Harbour Study (Trustees, Chatsworth Settlement) 1976; planning reports and studies. *Leisure interests:* photography, travel, painting, watching aeroplanes, being optimistic. *Address:* 6 Bacon's Lane, Highgate, London, N6 6BL, England. *Telephone:* (20) 8340-5528. *Fax:* (20) 8347-6313.

MANCEL, Jean-François; French politician; b. 1948; s. of Michel Mancel and Renée Baque; six c.; ed Faculté de droit et Inst. d'études politiques, Paris; Pres. Conseil Général, Oise; Pres. Oise Departmental Ass. 1985–; Deputy to Nat. Ass. 1978–; Conseiller Général 1979; Sec.-Gen. Rassemblement pour la République (RPR) 1995–97. *Leisure interests:* skiing, tennis. *Address:* Conseil Général de l'Oise, 1 rue Cambry, BP 941, 60024 Beauvais; Rassemblement pour la République, 123 rue de Lille, 75007 Paris, France.

MANCHAM, Sir James Richard Marie, Kt, FRSA; British politician, lawyer and int. consultant; b. 11 Aug. 1939, Victoria, Mahé, Seychelles; s. of the late Richard and Evelyne (née Tirant) Mancham; m. 1st Heather Jean Evans 1963 (divorced 1974); one s. one d.; m. 2nd Catherine Olsen 1985; one s.; ed Univ. of Paris and Middle Temple, London; Called to the Bar, Middle Temple 1961; mem. Legis. Council of the Seychelles 1961; mem. Govt Council 1967; founder and leader, Social Dem. Party 1964, revived 1992–; mem. Legis. Ass. 1970–76, of Nat. Ass. 1976–77; Chief Minister 1970–75, Prime Minister 1975–76; Pres. of the Republic of Seychelles 1976–77 (deposed by coup); int. trade consultant 1981–; Chair. Mahé Publications Ltd 1984–, Airominor Ltd 1987–; Pres. Berlin-European Airways 1988–90; Founder and Chair. Crusade for the Restoration of Democracy in Seychelles 1990–; Leader of the Opposition, Pres. Democratic Party 1992–; lecturer in Geopolitics of the Indian Ocean, Int. Univ. of Japan 1996; Hon. KBE 1976; Officier, Légion d'honneur, Grand Chevalier La Chaire de Rotisseur and numerous medals and decorations. *Publications:* Reflections and Echoes from the Seychelles, Paradise Raped 1983, Galloo: The Undiscovered Paradise 1984, New York's Robin Island 1985, Peace of Mind 1989, Adages of An Exile 1991, Oh, Mighty America 1998. *Leisure interests:* travel, water sports, tennis, writing. *Address:* P.O. Box 29, Mahé, Seychelles.

MANCHESTER, William, BA, AM; American writer; b. 1 April 1922, Attleboro, Mass.; s. of William Raymond Manchester and Sallie Thompson Manchester; m. Julia Brown Marshall 1948 (died 1998); one s. two d.; ed Univ. of Massachusetts, Dartmouth Coll. and Univ. of Missouri; Reporter Daily Oklahoman 1945–46; Reporter, Foreign Corresp., War Corresp. Baltimore Sun 1947–55; Man. Ed. Wesleyan Univ. Publs 1955–64; Fellow, Wesleyan Univ. Center for Advanced Studies 1959–60, Wesleyan Univ. E Coll. 1968–86; mem. faculty, Wesleyan Univ. 1968–69, Writer-in-Residence 1975–, Adjunct Prof. of History 1979–92, Prof. Emer. 1992–; Fellow Pierson Coll., Yale Univ. 1991–; Pres. Bd of Trustees, Univ. of Mass. Library 1970–72; mem. Bd dirs. Winston Churchill Travelling Fellowship 1990–2000; mem. PEN, Soc. of American Historians, American History Assen; Hon. Fellow Yale Univ. 1988; Hon. LHD (Univ. of Mass.) 1965, (Univ. of New Haven) 1979, (Russell Sage Coll.) 1990; Hon.Litt.D. (Skidmore Coll.) 1987, (Univ. of Richmond) 1988, (Wesleyan Univ.) 2000; Purple Heart 1945; Guggenheim Fellow 1959; Dag Hammarskjöld Int. Prize in Literature 1967, Overseas Press Club Award 1968, Univ. of Missouri Award 1969, President's Cabinet Award (Univ. of Detroit) 1980, McConaughty Award (Wesleyan Univ.) 1980, Troy Medal (Univ. of Mass.) 1980, Lincoln Literary Award 1983, Distinguished Public Service Award, Conn. Bar Assen 1985, Blenheim Award 1986, Washington Irving Award 1988, Sarah Josepha Hale Award 1994, Helmerich Distinguished Author Award 2000, Nat. Humanities Medal 2001. *Publications:* Disturber of the Peace 1951, The City of Anger 1953, Shadow of the Monsoon 1956, Beard the Lion 1958, A Rockefeller Family Portrait 1959, The Long Gainer 1961, Portrait of a President 1962, The Death of a President 1967, The Arms of Krupp 1968, The Glory and the Dream 1974, Controversy and Other Essays in Journalism 1976, American Caesar 1978, Goodbye Darkness 1980, The Last Lion: Winston Spencer Churchill 1874–1932 (vol. 1), Visions of Glory (vol. 2), Alone 1983, One Brief Shining Moment 1983, In Our Time 1989, A World Lit Only by Fire: The Medieval Mind and the Renaissance, Portrait of an Age 1992. *Address:* 316 Pine Street, Middletown, CT 06457, USA. *Telephone:* (860) 346-4789.

MANCINI, Giuseppe Federico, LLD; Italian professor of law and advocate; b. 23 Dec. 1927, Perugia; s. of Ettore Mancini and Fulvia Lina Valigi; m.

Vittoria Ghigi 1956; two d.; ed Bologna, Bordeaux, Paris and Chicago Univs.; Lecturer (Libero docente) in Labour Law 1956; Lecturer Univ. of Urbino 1956–62; Visiting Prof. of Italian Politics, Johns Hopkins Bologna Center 1957–76; Supply Lecturer in Labour Law, Univ. of Bologna 1962; taught a course at Univ. of N Carolina and gave seminars in Dept of Govt Harvard Univ. 1965, 1990; Prof. of Labour Law Univ. of Bologna 1965–79; Prof. Faculty of Pol. Science, Rome Univ. 1979–82; Prof. of Pvt. Comparative Law, Univ. of Bologna 1982; mem. Consiglio Superiore della Magistratura (Gen. Council of the Judiciary) 1976–81; Advocate-Gen., Court of Justice of the European Communities, Luxembourg 1982, First Advocate-Gen. 1985–86, Judge 1988–99, Pres. 6th Chamber 1990–93; Dr. hc (Univ. of Córdoba, Spain) 1984. *Publications:* La responsabilità contrattuale del prestatore di lavoro 1958, Il recesso unilaterale e i rapporti di lavoro 1962, Giuffrè (Vol. I) 1962, (Vol. II) 1965, Lo Statuto dei diritti dei lavoratori, Commentario (with G. Ghezzi, L. Montuschi and U. Romagnoli), Costituzione e movimento operaio 1976, Terroristi e riformisti 1981. *Leisure interests:* swimming, science fiction.

MANCINO, Nicola; Italian politician and lawyer; b. 15 Oct. 1931, Montefalcione, Avellino; fmr communal, prov. and regional councillor, Chair. Campania Regional Exec. Council (twice), Christian Democrat (DC) Prov. Sec., Avellino, Regional Sec. Campania; elected Senator from Avellino 1976, 1979, 1983, 1987; Chair. DC Parl. Group 1984; Minister of Interior 1992–94, Pres. of Senate 1996–2001. *Address:* c/o The Senate, Rome, Italy.

MANCUSO, Frank G.; American film industry executive; b. 25 July 1933, Buffalo; m. Fay Mancuso; one s. one d.; ed State Univ., NY; joined Paramount Pictures Corpn, Buffalo, NY 1962; Vice-Pres. and Gen. Sales Man. Paramount Pictures Corpn of Canada Ltd, Toronto 1970–72, Pres. and subsequently head of Paramount's Western Div., LA, USA 1972-76; Vice-Pres., Gen. Sales Man. Paramount's Motion Picture Div., New York 1976–78, Sr Vice-Pres. 1978–79, Exec. Vice-Pres. in charge of Distribution and Marketing 1979–80; Pres. Paramount Distribution 1980–83; Pres. Motion Picture Group of Paramount Pictures Corpn 1983–84; Chair. and CEO Paramount Pictures Corpn 1984–91; Chair., CEO MGM 1993–99; Consultant Santa Monica, Calif. 1999–; Vice-Pres. Variety Clubs Int. and of Motion Picture Pioneers; Chair. of Bd of Will Rogers Memorial Fund; Dir Will Rogers Memorial Fund, NY-Cornell Medical Center, Burke Rehabilitation Center, UCLA Medical Center, Museum of Broadcasting, Acad. of Motion Picture Arts and Sciences, Motion Picture Assen and other orgs.; Sherrill G. Corwin Human Relations Award, American Jewish Cttee 1985. *Address:* Metro-Goldwyn-Mayer Inc., Suite B-201, 2500 Broadway, Santa Monica, CA 90404, USA.

MANDABA, Jean-Luc; Central African Republic politician and medical practitioner; Minister of Health 1981; imprisoned for political opinions 1982, case against him subsequently dismissed; Vice-Chair. Mouvement de Libération du Peuple Centrafricain (MPLC); Prime Minister of Cen. African Repub. 1993–95. *Address:* c/o Office of the Prime Minister, Bangui, Central African Republic.

MANDELA, Nelson Rolihlahla; South African politician and lawyer; b. 1918, Umtata, Transkei; s. of Chief of Tembu tribe; m. 1st Evelyn Mandela 1944 (divorced 1957); four c. (two deceased); m. 2nd Winnie Mandela (q.v.) 1958 (divorced 1996); two d.; m. 3rd Graca Machel (widow of the late Pres. Machel of Mozambique) 1998; ed Univ. Coll. of Fort Hare, Univ. of the Witwatersrand; legal practice, Johannesburg 1952; Nat. organizer African Nat. Congress (ANC); on trial for treason 1956–61 (acquitted 1961); arrested 1962, sentenced to five years' imprisonment Nov. 1962; on trial for further charges 1963–64, sentenced to life imprisonment June 1964; released Feb. 1990; Deputy Pres. ANC 1990–91, Pres. 1991–97, mem. Nat. Exec. Cttee 1991–; Pres. of South Africa 1994–99; Chancellor Univ. of the North 1992–; Jt Pres. United World Colls. 1995–; Hon. LLD (Nat. Univ. of Lesotho) 1979, (City Coll. of City Univ. of New York) 1983, (Lancaster) 1984, (Strathclyde) 1985, (Calcutta) 1986, (Harare) 1987, (Kent) 1992, Hon. DLitt (Texas Southern Univ.) 1991; Dr. hc (Complutense) 1991; Hon. DCL (Oxford) 1996, Cambridge (1996), Hon. LLD (London) 1996, Bristol (1996), (Nottingham) 1996, (Warwick) 1996, (De Montfort) 1996, (Glasgow Caledonian) 1996; Hon. Fellow Magdalene Coll., Cambridge 2001; Hon. Freeman of London; Jawaharlal Nehru Award (India) 1979, Bruno Kreisky Prize for Human Rights 1981, Freedom of City of Glasgow 1981, Hon. Citizen of Rome 1983, Simon Bolivar Int. Prize (UNESCO) 1983; Third World Prize 1985, Sakharov Prize 1988, Gaddafi Human Rights Prize 1989, Freeman of Dublin 1988, Bharat Ratna (India) 1990, Order of the Niger 1990, Jt winner Houphouët Prize (UNESCO) 1991, Nishan-e-Pakistan 1992, Asturias Prize 1992, Liberty Medal (USA) 1993; shared Nobel Prize for Peace 1993; Mandela-Fulbright Prize 1993; Hon. Bencher Lincoln's Inn 1994; Tun Abdul Razak Award 1994; Anne Frank Medal 1994, Int. Freedom Award 2000, Hon. QC 2000. *Publications:* No Easy Walk to Freedom 1965, How Far We Slaves Have Come: South Africa and Cuba in Today's World (with Fidel Castro) 1991, Nelson Mandela Speaks: Forging a Non-Racial Democratic South Africa 1993, Long Walk to Freedom 1994. *Address:* c/o ANC, 51 Plein Street, Johannesburg 2001, South Africa (Office). *Telephone:* (11) 3307000 (Office). *Fax:* (11) 3360302 (Office). *E-mail:* info@anc.org.za (Office).

MANDELA, (Nomzano) Winnie; South African politician; b. Nomzano Winnie Madikizela, 1934, Bizana, Pondoland, Transkei; m. Nelson Mandela (q.v.) 1958 (divorced 1996); two d.; active mem. of African Nat. Congress (ANC) until its banning in 1960; campaigned constantly on behalf of her husband gaoled for life for political activities 1964–90; held in solitary confinement 1969–70; named a 'banned person' by S African authorities 1976; Head ANC Social Welfare Operations 1990–92; sentenced to six years' imprisonment on four counts of kidnapping and of being an accessory to assault May 1991; sentence upheld on appeal, except charge of being an accessory to assault; prison term waived to suspended two-year term, fine imposed June 1993; suspended from ANC Women's League 1993, Head 1997; mem. ANC Nat. Exec. Cttee 1994, Deputy Minister for Arts, Culture, Science and Tech., Govt of Nat. Unity 1994–95; charged with fraud Oct. 2001, convicted of fraud and sentenced to five years' imprisonment with one year suspended April 2003; Third World Prize 1985. *Publication:* Part of My Soul Went with Him 1985.

MANDELBROT, Benoit B., PhD; French/American mathematician, physicist and university professor; b. 20 Nov. 1924, Warsaw, Poland; s. of Charles M. Mandelbrot and Belle Lurie Mandelbrot; m. Aliette Kagan 1955; two s.; ed Ecole Polytechnique, Paris, California Inst. of Technology, Pasadena, Faculté des Sciences, Paris; Jr mem. and Rockefeller Scholar Inst. for Advanced Study, Princeton, NJ 1953–54; Jr Prof. of Maths. Univ. Geneva 1955–57, Univ. Lille and Ecole Polytechnique, Paris 1957–58; Research Staff mem. IBM Thomas J. Watson Research Center, New York 1958–74, IBM Fellow 1974–93, Fellow Emer.; Abraham Robinson Adjunct Prof. of Math. Sciences, Yale Univ. 1987–99, Sterling Prof. 1999–; Prof. Acad. of Sciences of Paris 1995; Visiting Prof. Harvard Univ. 1962–64, 1979–80, 1984–87; Einstein Coll. of Medicine 1970; Visitor MIT 1953, Univ. Paris 1966, Coll. de France 1973, etc.; Fellow American Acad. of Arts and Sciences, American Physical Soc., American Geophysical Union, Inst. of Math. Statistics, Econometric Soc., AAAS; Foreign Assoc. Norwegian Acad. of Sciences; mem. NAS European Acad. of Arts, Sciences and Humanities (Paris), Int. Statistical Inst., Société Mathématique de France, American Math. Soc.; Chevalier, Légion d'honneur; Hon. DSc (Syracuse) 1986, (Laurentian) 1986, (Boston) 1987, (State Univ. of NY) 1988, (Bremen) 1988, (Guelph) 1989, (Dallas) 1992, (Union) 1993, (Buenos Aires) 1993, (Tel Aviv) 1995, (Open Univ.) 1998, (Athens) 1998, (St. Andrews) 1999, (Emory) 2002; Hon. DHL (Pace) 1989; Humboldt Prize 1988, Wolf Prize for Physics 1993, John Scott Award 1999, L. F. Richardson Medal for Geophysics 2000, Procter Prize of Sigma Xi 2002, Japan Prize for Science and Tech. 2002; and numerous other awards. *Publications include:* Les objets fractals: forme, hasard et dimension 1975, 1984, 1989, 1995, Fractals: Form, Chance and Dimension 1977, The Fractal Geometry of Nature 1982 2002, Fractals and Scaling in Finance: Discontinuity, Concentration, Risk 1997, Fractales, hasard et finance 1997, Multifractals and Low-Frequency Noise: Wild Self-Affinity in Physics 1998, Gaussian Self-Affinity and Fractals 2000, Nel mondo dei frattali 2001, Globality, The Earth, Low-frequency Noise and R/S 2002, Fractals, Graphics and Mathematical Education (with M.L. Frame) 2002, Fractals in Chaos and Statistical Physics 2003. *Leisure interest:* music. *Address:* Mathematics Department, Yale University, New Haven, CT 06520 (Office); 21 Overhill Road, Scarsdale, NY 10583, USA (Home). *Telephone:* (203) 432-6471 (Yale) (Office); (914) 945-1712. *Fax:* (203) 432-7316 (Office); (914) 472-9016 (Home); (914) 945-4149.

MANDELSON, Rt Hon Peter Benjamin, PC; British politician; b. 21 Oct. 1953; s. of the late George Mandelson and of Mary (née Morrison) Mandelson; ed St Catherine's Coll., Oxford; joined TUC, with Econ. Dept 1977–78; Chair. British Youth Council 1978–80; producer London Weekend TV 1982–85; Dir of Campaigns and Communications, Labour Party 1985–90; MP for Hartlepool 1992–; an Opposition Whip 1994–97, Shadow Frontbench Spokesman on Civil Service 1995–96, on Election Planning 1996–97; Chair. Gen. Election Planning Group 1995–97; Minister without Portfolio 1997–98; Sec. of State for Trade and Industry July–Dec. 1998 (resgnd.), for Northern Ireland 1999–2001 (resgnd.); Vice-Chair. British Council 1999–; Chair. UK-Japan 21st Century Group 2001–; mem. council London Borough of Lambeth 1979–82; industrial consultant SRU Group 1990–92; mem. Int. Advisory Cttee Centre for European Policy Studies 1993–; Trustee Whitechapel Art Gallery 1994–; mem. Panel 2000 1998–. *Publications:* Youth Unemployment: causes and cures 1977, Broadcasting and Youth 1980, The Blair Revolution: Can New Labour Deliver? 1996. *Leisure interests:* country walking, swimming, reading. *Address:* House of Commons, London, SW1A 0AA (Office); 30 Hutton Avenue, Hartlepool, Cleveland, TS26 9PN, England. *Telephone:* (20) 7219-4607 (Office); (1429) 866173 (constituency). *Fax:* (20) 7219-4525 (Office).

MANDELSTAM, Stanley, PhD, FRS; British professor of physics; b. 12 Dec. 1928, Johannesburg, S. Africa; s. of Boris Mandelstam and Beatrice (née Liknaitzky) Mandelstam; ed Univs. of Witwatersrand, Cambridge and Birmingham; Boese Postdoctoral Fellow, Columbia Univ., USA 1957–58; Asst Research Physicist, Univ. of Calif. (Berkeley) 1958–60; Prof. of Math. Physics, Univ. of Birmingham 1960–63; Prof. of Physics, Univ. of Calif. (Berkeley) 1963–94, Prof. Emer. 1994–; Prof. Associé. Univ. de Paris Sud 1979–80, 1984–85. *Publications:* papers on theoretical particle physics. *Leisure interests:* reading, music. *Address:* Department of Physics, University of California, Berkeley, CA 94720 (Office); 1800 Spruce Street, Berkeley, CA 94720, USA (Home). *Telephone:* (415) 642-5237 (Office); (415) 540-5318 (Home).

MANDIL, Claude; French administrative official, engineer and business executive; b. 9 Jan. 1942, Lyon; s. of Léon Mandil and Renée (née Mizraki) Mandil; m. Annick Goubelle 1966; four s. one d.; ed Lycée Pasteur de Neuilly and Ecole Polytechnique; Mining Engineer, Metz 1967–71, Rennes 1971–74; Délégation à l'Aménagement du Territoire et à l'Action régionale (DATAR) 1974–77; Inter-Dept Dir and Regional Del. Agence nat. de Valorisation de la Recherche, Anvar 1978–81; Tech. Adviser to Prime Minister 1981–82; Dir-Gen. Inst. of Industrial Devt (IDI) 1983, Pres. 1984–88; Dir-Gen. Bureau des recherches géologiques et minières (BRGM) 1988; Dir-Gen. Energies et Matières Premières, Ministry of Industry and Land Devt 1990–98; Deputy Man. Dir Gaz de France 1998–2000; Pres. Institut français du pétrole (IFP) 2000–03; Exec. Dir Int. Energy Agency 2003–; Officier, Ordre nat. du Mérite, Officier, Légion d'honneur, awards from Germany and Norway. *Leisure interest:* music. *Address:* International Energy Agency, 9 rue de la Fédération, 75739 Paris cedex 15 (Office); 6 rue du Plateau Saint Antoine, 78150 Le Chesnay, France (Home). *E-mail:* claude.mandil@iea.org (Office). *Website:* www.iea.org (Office).

MANEKSHAW, Field Marshal Sam Hormuzji Framji Jamshedji, MC; Indian army officer; b. 3 April 1914, Amritsar; s. of Dr H. F. J. Manekshaw and Mrs. H. F. J. Manekshaw; m. Silloo Manekshaw 1939; two d.; ed Sherwood Coll., Nainital, Indian Mil. Acad., Dehra Dun; commissioned 1934; active service in Waziristan, NW Frontier Provs 1940–41; World War II Burma 1942 wounded in action, awarded immediate Mil. Cross; graduated Staff Coll., Quetta 1943; served as Brigade Maj. Razmak Brigade, Waziristan 1943–44; Instructor Staff Coll., Quetta 1944; active service in Burma and French Indo-China 1945–46; Gen. Staff Officer Grade I, Mil. Operations Directorate, Army H.Q. 1946–47, Brig. 1947; Dir Mil. Operations 1948–52; Commdr 167 Infantry Brigade 1952–54; Col 8th Gurkha Rifles 1953–; Dir Mil. Training 1954–55; Commdt Infantry School, Mhow 1955–56; attended Imperial Defence Coll., London 1957; promoted Maj.-Gen. and appointed GOC 26 Infantry Div. in Jammu and Kashmir 1957; Commdt Defence Services Staff Coll., Wellington 1958–62; GOC IV Corps. 1962–63; GOC-in-C Western Command 1963–64, Eastern Command 1964–69; Chief of the Army Staff 1969–73; promoted Field Marshal 1973; Gen. of Nepalese Army 1970; Chair. of six cos; Dir of ten cos; awarded Padma Bhushan 1967, Padma Vibhushan 1971, US Order of Merit 1970. *Leisure interests:* fishing, gardening, music. *Address:* Stavka, Springfield, Conoor, The Nilgiris, South India.

MANESSIS, Aristovoulos; Greek professor of law; b. 23 March 1922, Argostoli; s. of Ioannis Manessis and Eustathia Vlysma; m. Mary Manoledaki 1961; ed Univs. of Thessaloniki, Paris and Heidelberg; lecturer in Constitutional Law, Univ. of Thessaloniki 1957, Prof. 1961–68 (dismissed by mil. regime); Prof. of Public Law, Univ. of Amiens 1970–74; Prof. and Dean, Faculty of Law, Univ. of Thessaloniki 1974–80; mem. Special Supreme Court 1976–77, 1987–88; Prof. of Constitutional Law, Univ. of Athens 1980, Dean, Faculty of Law 1982–83, 1987–88, Prof. Emer. 1988–; Pres. Union of Greek Constitutionalists 1984–89; Pres. Council of Studies of Greek Parl. 1987–; mem. Acad. of Athens 1992–; Dr. hc (Amiens) 1980, (Thrace) 1990. *Publications:* The Law of Necessity 1953, The Guarantees of the Observance of the Constitution (Vol. 1) 1956, (Vol. 2) 1965, The Legal and Political Status of the President of the Republic 1975, Constitutional Law 1980, Constitutional Theory and Practice 1980, Civil Liberties 1982, Law, Politics, Constitution 1984, The Constitutional Revision of 1986 1989, The Constitution in the 21st Century 1993, Problems Regarding the Protection of Human Rights 1995; in French: Deux Etats nés en 1830, Ressemblances et dissemblances constitutionnelles entre la Belgique et la Grèce 1959, L'évolution des institutions politiques de la Grèce 1986, La protection constitutionnelle des droits de l'homme en Grèce et dans les autres Etats membres de l'Union Européenne 1993. *Leisure interest:* listening to classical music. *Address:* 14A, J. Gennadiou Street, 11521 Athens, Greece. *Telephone:* (1) 7210644. *Fax:* (1) 3234064.

MANFREDI, Valerio Massimo; Italian archaeologist and author; b. 1943; specialist in topography of the ancient world; has taken part in many archaeological excavations in Italy and abroad; has taught at Università Cattolica, Milan, Venice Univ., Loyola Univ., Chicago and Ecole Pratique des Hautes Etudes, Paris; corresp. on antiquities for Publs Panorama and Il Messaggero. *Publications include:* Xenophon's Anabasis (translator), Lo Scudo di Talos, Palladion, Il Faraone delle Sabbie, L'Oracolo, Le Paludi di Hesperia, La Torre della Solitudine, Alexandros: Child of a Dream, Alexander: The Sands of Amon, Alexander: The Ends of the Earth. *Address:* c/o Macmillan Books, 20 New Wharf Road, London, N1 9RR, England (Office). *Telephone:* (20) 7014-6000 (Office). *Fax:* (20) 7014-6001 (Office). *Website:* www .panmacmillan.com (Office).

MANGANYI, Noel Chabani, DLitt, DPhil; South African civil servant and psychologist; b. 13 March 1940; s. of Frans Manganyi and Sophie Manganyi; m. 1st Esmé Kakana (divorced); m. 2nd Dr. Peggy Sekele 1990; two d.; Post Doctoral Fellow School of Medicine, Yale Univ. 1973–75; Prof. of Psychology Univ. of Transkei 1976–80; Prof., Sr Research Fellow Witwatersrand Univ. 1981–90; in active forensic practice of psychology as expert witness for defence of anti-apartheid activists at Supreme Court, S.A. –1991; Vice-Chancellor Univ. of the N, Pietersburg 1991–92; Exec. Dir PSI Jt Educ. Trust 1993–94; Dir-Gen. of Nat. Educ. 1994–; Founder, Violence and Health Resources Project, Witwatersrand Univ. 1986; mem. several psychology orgs. *Publications:* Treachery and Innocence: Psychology and Racial Difference in South Africa 1991, A Black Man Called Sekoto; 7 other books and 12 articles in scientific and professional journals. *Address:* Private Bag X212, Pretoria 0001, South Africa.

MANGLA, P. B.; Indian professor of library and information science; b. 5 July 1936, India; s. of Radha Krishan; m. Raj Mangla 1961; one s. one d.; ed Univ. of Punjab, Univ. of Delhi, Columbia Univ., New York, London; Prof. and Head of Dept of Library Sciences, Univ. of Tabriz, Iran 1970–72, Visiting Prof. 1974–75; UNESCO expert, Guyana 1978–79; Prof. and Head of Dept of

Library and Information Sciences, Univ. of Delhi 1972–, Dean Faculty of Arts 1976–78, 1984–88, Chair. Bd of Research Studies 1979–85; Library Consultant, Reserve Bank of India, Bombay 1992–93; Library Adviser, YMCA New Delhi 1992–; various other admin. posts in Delhi and numerous other univs 1972–; Chair. Manpower Devt Cttee of Nat. Information System in Science and Tech. 1977–; Sr Vice-Pres. and founder-mem. Indian Asscn of Academic Librarians 1981–83; mem. Bd Int. Fed. of Library Asscns and Insts 1983– (Vice-Pres. 1987–89, 1989–91), Inst. of Information Scientists; Nat. Prof. of the U.G.C. 1984–86; Chair. Bd of Eds Univ. of Delhi Annual Reports 1989–; mem. Ed. Bd Third World Libraries (USA) 1989–, Journal of Library and Information Science, Education for Information, Amsterdam 1982–, Review in Library and Information Science, USA, LIBRI (Copenhagen), Third World Libraries (Chicago), Int. Journal of Information and Library Research (UK) 1989–; Special Adviser IFLA Regional Section for Asia and Oceania 1991–; Chair. Programme Implementation Cttee, Nat. Service Scheme, Delhi Univ. 1989–, Gov. Body Deshbandhu Coll. (Delhi Univ.) 1990–95, Univ. Grants Cttee (UGC) Panel of Library and Information Science 1992–, Prof. Mangla Research Foundation 2001, Dyal Singh Coll. (Delhi Univ.) 2001–; mem. Steering Cttee Inflibnet (UGC) 1990–; mem. Planning Comm. (Govt of India) Working Group on Modernization of Libraries and Informatics for 7th, 8th and 9th Five-Year Plans; mem. Research Cttee INSDOC New Delhi 2000–02, Nat. Inst. of Science Communication and Information Resources 2002–; mem. Nat. Advisory Cttee Nat. Library 2002–, Expert Cttee Asiatic Soc. 2002–; Hon. Fellow Indian Library Asscn; several memorial lectures; Rockefeller Foundation (New York) Merit Scholarship 1961–62; received British Council sponsorship 1979, 1980, 1987, 1989, IDRC (Canada) sponsorship 1983, 1991; Int. Library Movt Award (India) 1984, Shiromani Award for Human Excellence 1991, IFLA Gold Medal 1991. *Publications:* author/ed. of numerous books and specialist reviews in India and overseas. *Leisure interests:* travel, reading. *Address:* EB-210 Maya Enclave, New Delhi 110064, India. *Telephone:* (11) 2512-0458; (11) 2512-0331 (Home).

MANGOAELA, Percy Metsing, BSc, BEd, LLB; Lesotho diplomatist and international civil servant; b. 26 Aug. 1942, Berea; m.; two d.; ed Memorial Univ. of Newfoundland, Dalhousie Univ., Canada, Makerere Univ., Kampala and Harvard Univ.; radio news reporter Dept of Information and Broadcasting 1966–68; joined Lesotho civil service 1968, Asst Sec., Ministry of Foreign Affairs, then Desk Officer, Int. Orgs. and N America –1970; Dir of Civil Aviation 1973–76, Prin. Sec., Ministry of Transport and Communications 1976–79, 1990; Deputy Co-ordinator UN Transport and Communications Decade for Africa, UN Econ. Comm. for Africa 1979–89; Prin. Sec., Depts. of Trade and Industry and Consumer Affairs 1991–92; Dir Southern Africa Transport and Communications Comm., Maputo 1994–95; Perm. Rep. to the UN 1995–2001. *Address:* c/o Ministry of Foreign Affairs, P.O. Box 1387, Maseru 100, Lesotho.

MANGOLD, Klaus; German business executive; b. 6 June 1943, Pforzheim; m.; two c.; ed Univ. of Munich, Univ. of Heidelberg, Univ. of Geneva; Asst Man. German-Mexican Chamber of Commerce, Mexico City 1972–73; Section Jr Barrister Thyssen 1973–75; Man. Union of German Textile Industry, Stuttgart 1976; mem. Bd Dirs Rhodia AG (Rhone Poulenc Group) 1983–90; Chair. Bd Quelle-Schickedanz AG, Fürth 1991–94; mem. Bd Dirs Daimler-Benz AG and Chair. Bd Daimler-Benz InterServices AG 1995–; mem. Bd Dirs Daimler-Chrysler Services AG, Berlin 1997–, Chair. 1998–; mem. of numerous supervisory and advisory bds including Dresdner Kleinwort Benson N America, Deutsche Bank AG Berlin, Lahmeyer Int., Chubb Corpn, USA; Chair. Bd Friends of the German Inst. for Econ. Research, Berlin; mem. supervisory cttee of numerous DaimlerChrysler Services AG-affiliated cos; Chevalier, Légion d'honneur. *Publications:* Die Zukunft der Dienstleistung (Ed.) 1997, Die Welt der Dienstleistung (Ed.) 1998. *Address:* DaimlerChrysler AG, 70546 Stuttgart; Eichhornstr. 3, 10875 Berlin, Germany.

MANGOLD, Robert Peter, MFA; American artist; b. 12 Oct. 1937, N Tonawanda, NY; ed Cleveland Inst. of Art and Yale Univ.; Instructor School of Visual Arts, New York 1963–, Hunter Coll. 1964–65, Cornell Univ. Skowhegan Summer Art School 1968; one-man exhbns Daniel Weinberg Gallery, LA 1984, Akron Art Museum 1984, Pace Gallery 1992, Le Consortium Dijon, France 1992; retrospective Exhbn Stedelijk Museum, Amsterdam 1982; has participated in numerous exhbns notably at Whitney Museum, New York 1968, 1973, 1979, 1983, Solomon R. Guggenheim Museum, New York 1971, Documenta, Kassel, W. Germany 1972, 1977, 1982, Museum of Contemporary Art, Chicago 1974, Ritter Klagenfurt, Austria 1992–93; work represented in numerous public collections in USA, UK and Europe including Whitney Museum, Solomon R. Guggenheim Museum, Museum of Fine Arts, Houston, Tate Gallery, London, Kunsthaus Zürich and Stedelijk Museum Amsterdam; Guggenheim Grant 1969; Nat. Council on Arts Award 1966.

MANGOPE, Chief Lucas Manyane; South African politician and tribal chief; b. 27 Dec. 1923, Motswedi, Zeerust; s. of Manyane and Semakaleng Mangope; m. Leah Tscholofelo Dolo 1951; four s. three d.; ed St Peter's Coll. and Bethel Coll.; worked in the Dept of Bantu Admin. and Devt, later taught at Motswedi; succeeded his father as Chief of the Bahurutshe-Boo-Manyane 1959; Vice-Chair. Tswana Territorial Authority 1961–68, Chief Councillor, Exec. Council 1968–72; Chief Minister of Bophuthatswana Homeland 1972–77; fmr Prime Minister, Minister of Finance, Minister of Law and

Order; Pres. 1977–94; mem. North-West Prov. legislature. *Leisure interests:* soccer, tennis, choral music. *Address:* PO Box 245, Buhrmannsdrif 2867, South Africa. *Telephone:* (18) 3814044 (Office). *Fax:* (18) 3185979.

MANHIRE, William (Bill), M.PHIL.; New Zealand poet and academic; b. 27 Dec. 1946, Invercargill; s. of Jack Manhire and Madeline Mary Manhire; m. Barbara Marion McLeod 1970; one s. one d.; ed S. Otago Dist High School, Otago Boys' High School, Univ. of Otago, Univ. Coll., London; Lecturer in English, Vic. Univ., Wellington 1973, f. influential creative writing programme 1976, Prof. of Creative Writing and English Literature 1997–; Dir Int. Inst. of Modern Letters 2001–; Fiction Ed. Victoria Univ. Press 1976–96; Fulbright Visiting Prof. in NZ Studies, Georgetown Univ., USA Jan.–June 1999; inaugural Poet Laureate of NZ 1997–99; Nuffield Fellowship 1981; NZ Book Award 1977, 1984, 1992, 1996; Montana Book Award 1994. *Publications:* The Elaboration 1972, How to Take Off Your Clothes at the Picnic 1977, Good Looks 1982, Some Other Country (ed.) 1984, Zoetropes 1984, Maurice Gee 1986, Six By Six (ed.) 1989, Milky Way Bar 1991, Soho Square (ed.) 1991, South Pacific 1994, 100 New Zealand Poems 1994 (ed.), Sheet Music 1996, My Sunshine 1996, Mutes and Earthquakes 1997, What to Call Your Child 1999, Doubtful Sounds 2000, Spectacular Babies (ed.) 2001, Collected Poems 2001. *Leisure interest:* swimming. *Address:* Creative Writing Programme, Victoria University, P.O. Box 600, Wellington, New Zealand. *Telephone:* (4) 463-6808. *Fax:* (4) 463-6865 (Office). *E-mail:* bill.manhire@vuw.ac.nz (Office).

MANIATOPOULOS, Constantinos S.; Greek European Union official and business executive; b. 1941; m. Theodora Hiou; one s.; ed Athens and Paris; fmrly employed in energy and industry sectors; Chair. and Man. Dir EKO Petroleum Co., Greece; Special Adviser to Minister of Energy; mem. Bd various nat. advisory bodies; Gen. Sec. Tech. Chamber of Greece; Dir-Gen. for Energy, EC (now EU) Comm. 1986–95. *Address:* 13 Makedonias Street, Kifissia, Athens, Greece; 10 Akti Miaouli, 18538 Piraeus (Office).

MANIGAT, Leslie; Haitian politician and academic; b. 16 Aug. 1930, Port-au-Prince; m. 2nd Mirlande Manigat 1970; f. School of Int. Studies at Univ. of Haiti, first Dir; fmr Research Assoc. Johns Hopkins Univ., Washington; fmr Prof. Inst. of Political Studies, Paris; then with Univ. of West Indies, Trinidad and Tobago; with Simón Bolívar Univ., Caracas 1978; returned from 23 years in exile 1986; Pres. of Haiti Jan. 1988, overthrown June 1988.

MANILOV, Col-Gen. Valery Leonidovich, PhD; Russian civil servant and army officer; b. 10 Jan. 1939, Tulchin, Ukraine; m.; one d.; ed Odessa Higher Infantry School, Mil.-Political Acad., Gen. Staff Mil. Acad.; service in Odessa, Baikal mil. commands, S. Group of armed forces, service in Afghanistan; on staff USSR Ministry of Defence 1988–; Head Information Service of Jt Armed Forces of CIS 1992–93; Asst to Sec. Russian Security Council July–Oct. 1993, Deputy Sec. 1993–96; First Deputy Head of Gen. Staff. 1998–2000; mem. Acad. of Mil. Sciences, Russian Acad. of Natural Sciences, Int. Acad. of Informatization; mem. Council of Fed., Rep. Primorsky Territory 2001–. *Address:* Council of Federation, B. Dmitrovka 26, 103426 Moscow, Russia. *Telephone:* (095) 252-89-77.

MANILOW, Barry; American singer and composer; b. 17 June 1946, New York; s. of Harold Manilow and Edna Manilow; ed New York Coll. Music; worked in mailroom, CBS; film ed. WCBS-TV; Dir Music Ed Sullivan's Pilots; Dir Music, Conductor and Producer for Bette Midler; appeared in TV film Copacabana 1985; Broadway production, Barry Manilow at the Gershwin 1989; Amb. for Prince's Trust 1996; Producer of Year 1975; Ruby Award, After Dark magazine 1976; Photoplay Gold Medal Award 1976; Tony Award (Jt) 1977, named Humanitarian of the Year (Starlight Foundation) 1991. *Songs include:* Mandy, I Write the Songs, At the Copa, Looks Like We Made It, Can't Smile Without You, Even Now, Could it be Magic and others. *Publication:* Sweet Life: Adventures on the Way to Paradise 1987. *Address:* Arista Records, 6 West 57th Street, New York, NY 10019, USA.

MANIN, Yuri Ivanovich, BSc, PhD; Russian mathematician; b. 16 Feb. 1937, Simferopol; s. of Ivan Manin and Rebecca Miller; m. Xenia Semenova; one s.; ed Moscow State Univ.; Researcher Steklov Math. Inst. Moscow 1960–, now Prin. Researcher; Prof. of Math. Moscow State Univ. 1965–91; Visiting Prof. several univs. including Harvard Univ., MIT, Columbia Univ. 1991–93; Scientific mem. Max Planck Inst. for Math., Bonn 1993–, Dir, Man. Dir 1995–; Corresp. mem. Russian Acad. of Sciences 1990, Göttingen Acad. of Sciences; Foreign mem. Royal Netherlands Acad. of Arts and Sciences; mem. Academia Europaea; mem. Pontifical Acad. of Science, Vatican; mem. Acad. Leopoldina Germany; numerous hon. doctorates and awards including Lenin Prize 1967, Brouwer Gold Medal 1987, Frederic Esser Nemmers Prize 1994, Rolf Schock Math. Prize (Royal Swedish Acad. of Sciences) 1999, King Faisal Prize for Science 2002, Georg Cantor Medal of German Math. Soc. 2002. *Publications:* Frobenius Manifolds, Quantum Cohomology and Moduli Spaces 1999; author, co-author of 11 monographs and about 200 scientific papers. *Address:* Max Planck Institute for Mathematics, Vivatsgasse 7, 53111 Bonn, Germany (Office). *Telephone:* (228) 402271 (Office). *Fax:* (228) 402277 (Office). *E-mail:* manin@mpim-bonn.mpg.de (Office).

MANKIEWICZ, Frank, MS, AB, LLB; American public affairs executive; b. 16 May 1924, New York; s. of Herman J. and Sara Mankiewicz; m. Holly Jolley 1952 (divorced); two s.; m. 2nd Patricia O'Brien 1988; ed Columbia Univ., Univ. of Calif., Berkeley and Los Angeles; mem. Calif. and DC Bars; practised as lawyer, Los Angeles 1955–61; served with Peace Corps as Country Dir,

Lima, Peru and later as Regional Dir for Latin America; Press Sec. to late Senator Robert F. Kennedy 1966–68; syndicated columnist (with Tom Braden), Washington and co-presenter, nightly newscast on CBS television affiliate 1968–71; Campaign Dir presidential campaign of George McGovern 1972; Pres. Nat. Public Radio 1977–83; Vice-Chair. Gray and Co. (now Hill and Knowlton) 1983–; Hon. DHL (Lincoln Univ.); Univ. of Calif. (LA) Public Service Award. *Publications:* Perfectly Clear: Nixon from Whittier to Watergate 1973, U.S. *v.* Richard Nixon: The Final Crisis 1975, With Fidel: A Portrait of Castro and Cuba 1975, Remote Control: Television and the Manipulation of American Life 1977. *Leisure interests:* baseball, literature, U.S. political history. *Address:* Hill and Knowlton, 600 New Hampshire Avenue, NW, Washington, DC 20037, USA. *Telephone:* (202) 944-5104 (Office); (202) 333-7400. *Fax:* (202) 944-1961 (Office). *E-mail:* fmankiew@hillandknowlton.com (Office).

MANLEY, Albert Leslie; South African diplomatist; b. 1945, Cape Town; s. of Albert George Rowan Manley and Mary Leslie Manley; m. Charlene Manley 1988; three s. one d.; ed Univ. of Free State; entered Dept of Foreign Affairs 1969, Desk Officer for Middle E 1974–76, Planning Section of Ministry, Pretoria and Cape Town 1981–82, other posts 1982–86; Vice-Consul in Lourenço Marques (now Maputo) 1970–74; Counsellor for Political Affairs at Embassy, London 1977–81; Perm. Rep. to UN, New York 1987–88, Geneva 1988–92; Head Int. Econs, Foreign Ministry 1992–94, Head Int. Devt and Econ. Affairs 1995–98; Minister at South African Embassy and Mission to the EU, Brussels 1998–; Fellow Center for Int. Affairs, Harvard Univ. 1994–95. *Leisure interests:* golf, music, books. *Address:* South African Embassy and Mission to European Union, 26 rue de la Loi, 1040 Brussels (Office); 157 avenue de Tervuren, Woluwe-St Pierre, 1150 Brussels, Belgium (Home). *Telephone:* (2) 285-4404 (Office); (2) 733-3866 (Home). *Fax:* (2) 285-4487 (Office). *E-mail:* manley_saembassy@hotmail.com (Office).

MANLEY, John, LLB; Canadian politician and lawyer; b. 5 Jan. 1950, Ottawa; s. of John Joseph Manley and Mildred Charlotte Scharf; m. Judith Manley; one s. two d.; ed Carleton Univ., Univ. of Ottawa; fmrly practitioner in business and income tax law, Ottawa; law clerk to Chief Justice of Canada 1976–77; Chair. Ottawa-Carleton Bd. Trade 1985–86; mem. Parl. 1988–; Minister of Industry 1993–2000, also Minister responsible for Atlantic Canada Opportunities Agency, Canada Econ. Devt and Western Econ. Diversification 1996–97; Minister of Foreign Affairs 2000–02; Chair. Ad Hoc Cabinet Cttee on Public Security and Anti-terrorism; Deputy Prime Minister of Canada and Minister of Infastructure and Crown Corpn 2002–; Minister of Finance 2002–; Political Minister for Ont. 2002–; Chair. Cabinet Cttees. on Econ. Union and on Social Union 2002–; held responsibility for numerous Govt agencies including Canadian Space Agency, Nat. Research Council, Business Devt Bank of Canada, Canadian Tourism Comm.; Dr. hc (Ottawa) 1998; Internet Person of the Year 2000, Newsmaker of the Year, Time Canada 2001. *Leisure interest:* marathon runner. *Address:* House of Commons, Room 209–S, Centre Block, Ottawa, Ont. KIA, OA6, Canada (Office). *Telephone:* (613) 952-4900. *Website:* www.johnmanley.com (Office).

MANN, Emily Betsy, BA, MFA; American writer, theatre director and playwright; b. 12 April 1952, Boston, Mass.; d. of Arthur Mann and Sylvia Mann (née Blut); m. Gary Mailman; one s. from previous m.; ed Harvard Univ., Univ. of Minn.; Resident Dir Guthrie Theatre, Minneapolis 1976–79; Dir Brooklyn Acad. of Music (BAM) Theatre Co., Brooklyn, NY 1980–81; freelance writer and dir, New York 1981–90; Artistic Dir McCarter Theatre, Princeton, NJ 1990–; mem. Soc. of Stage Dirs and Choreographers, Theatre Communications Group, New Dramatists, PEN, Writer's Guild; mem. Exec. Bd Dramatists' Guild; Alumnae Recognition Award, Harvard Univ. 1999; BUSH Fellowship 1975–76; Rosamond Gilder Award, New Drama Forum Asscn 1983; NEA Asscns Grant 1984; Tony Award for Outstanding Regional Theatre 1984; Guggenheim Fellowship 1985; McKnight Fellowship 1985; CAPS Award 1985; NEA Playwrights Fellowship 1986; Women of Achievement Award, Brandeis Univ. 1995; Woman of Achievement Award, Douglass Coll. of NJ 1996; Outstanding Achievement in the Theatre, Rosamond Gilder Award 1999. *Plays directed include:* Suddenly Last Summer, Loeb Drama Center 1971; The Bull Gets the Matador Once in a Lifetime, Agassiz Theatre 1972; Macbeth, Loeb Drama Center 1973; Matrix, Guthrie Theater 1975; The Birthday Party, Guthrie Theatre 1975; Cold, Guthrie Theatre 1976; Ashes, Guthrie 2 Theater 1977, Cincinnati Playhouse 1980; Annulla, Guthrie Theatre 1977, New Theater of Brooklyn 1989; Dark Pony and Reunion, Guthrie Theater 1978; The Farm, Actors Theatre of St Paul 1978; On Mount Chimborazo, Guthrie 2 Theater, 1978; Surprise Surprise, Guthrie 2 Theater 1978; The Roads in Germany, Theatre in the Round 1978; The Glass Menagerie, Guthrie Theater 1979, McCarter Theatre 1990; He and She, Brooklyn Acad. of Music 1980; Still Life (Obie Award), Goodman Theatre 1980, American Place Theatre 1981; Dwarfman Master of a Million Shapes, Goodman Theatre 1981; A Doll House, Oregon Contemporary Theater 1982, Hartford Stage Co. 1986; Through the Leaves, Empty Space Theatre 1983; A Weekend Near Madison, Astor Place Theater 1983; The Value of Names, Hartford Stage Co. 1984; Execution of Justice, Guthrie Theater 1985, Virginia Theatre (Broadway) 1986; Hedda Gabbler, La Jolla Playhouse 1987; Betsey Brown, American Music Theater Festival 1989, McCarter Theatre 1991; Miss Julie, McCarter Theater 1992; Three Sisters, McCarter Theatre 1992; Cat on a Hot Tin Roof, McCarter Theatre 1992; Twilight: Los Angeles 1992 (L.A. NAACP Award for Best Dir.), Mark Taper Forum/McCarter Theatre 1993; The Perfectionist, McCarter Theatre 1993; The Matchmaker, McCarter Theatre 1994; Having our Say, McCarter Theatre 1995, Booth Theatre (Broadway) 1995; The Mai, McCarter Theatre 1996; Betrayal, McCarter Theatre 1997; The House of Bernarda Alba, McCarter Theatre 1997; Safe as Houses, McCarter Theatre 1998; Meshugah, McCarter Theatre 1998; Fool for Love, McCarter Theatre 1999; The Cherry Orchard, McCarter Theatre 2000; Romeo and Juliet, McCarter Theatre 2001; Because He Can, McCarter Theatre 2001; All Over, McCarter Theatre and Roundabout Theatre Co. 2002; The Tempest, McCarter Theatre 2003. *Plays translated and adapted include:* Nights and Days (Les nuits et les jours, Pierre Laville) 1985, Miss Julie 1992, The House of Bernarda Alba 1997, Meshugah 1998, Uncle Vanya 2003. *Plays included in publications:* New Plays USA 1, New Plays 3, Coming to Terms: American Plays and the Vietnam War 1985, The Ten Best Plays of 1986, Out Front 1988, Testimonies: Four Plays by Emily Mann (Theatre Communications Group Inc.) 1997. *Publications include:* (plays): Annulla Allen: The Autobiography of a Survivor 1977, Still Life (six Obie Awards 1981, Fringe First Award 1985) 1982, Execution of Justice (Helen Hayes Award, Bay Area Theatre Critics Circle Award, HBO/USA Award, Playwriting Award Women's Cttee. Dramatists Guild for Dramatizing Issues of Conscience) 1986, Having Our Say: The Delaney Sisters' First 100 Years (LA Nat. Asscn for the Advancement of Colored People–NAACP Award for Best Play) 1994, Greensboro: A Requiem 1996; (musicals): Betsey Brown: A Rhythm and Blues Musical (co-author with Ntozake Shange); (screenplays): Fanny Kelly (unproduced) 1981, You Strike a Woman, You Strike a Rock: The Story of Winnie Mandela (unproduced mini-series) 1988, The Greensboro Massacre (unproduced) 1992, Having Our Say (Christopher Award, Peabody Award) 1999; Political Stages (co-ed.) 2002. *Address:* McCarter Theatre, 91 University Place, Princeton, NJ 08540-5121, USA (Office). *Telephone:* (609) 258-6502 (Office). *Fax:* (609) 497-0369 (Office). *E-mail:* emann@mccarter.org (Office). *Website:* www.mccarter.org.

MANN, Michael K.; American producer, director and writer; b. Chicago; ed Univ. of Wisconsin, London Film School; Exec. Producer (TV) Miami Vice, Crime Story, Drug Wars: Camarena Story, Drug Wars: Cocaine Cartel, Police Story, Starsky and Hutch; mem. Writers Guild, Dirs. Guild; Best Dir Award (for The Jericho Mile), Dirs. Guild; two Emmy Awards. *Films directed include:* The Jericho Mile (TV film, also scriptwriter, 1979), Thief (also exec. producer and scriptwriter) 1981, The Keep (also scriptwriter) 1981, Manhunter (also scriptwriter) 1986, Last of the Mohicans (also co-producer, scriptwriter) 1992, Heat (also co-producer, scriptwriter) 1995, The Insider (also producer) 1999. *Address:* c/o Creative Artists Agency, 9830 Wilshire Boulevard, Beverly Hills, CA 90212, USA.

MANN, Robert Wellesley, SB, SM, ScD; American professor of engineering design and biomedical research; b. 6 Oct. 1924, Brooklyn, New York; s. of Arthur Wellesley Mann and Helen Rieger Mann; m. Margaret Florencourt Mann 1950 (died 2002); one s. one d.; ed M.I.T; Draftsman Bell Telephone Labs. 1942–43, 1946–47; Technician (3rd) U.S. Army Signal Corps 1943–46; Research Engineer and Supervisor Design Div. Dynamic Analysis and Control Lab., MIT 1951–56, Asst Prof. of Mechanical Eng 1953–58, Head Eng Design Div. Dept of Mechanical Eng 1957–66, 1982–83, Assoc. Prof. of Mechanical Eng 1958–63, Prof. 1963–70, Germeshausen Prof. 1970–72, Prof. of Eng 1972–74, Whitaker Prof. of Biomedical Eng 1974–92, Whitaker Prof. Emer. 1992–; Prof. Harvard-MIT Div. of Health Sciences and Tech. 1973–; Pres. Carroll Center for the Blind 1968-74, Nat. Braille Press 1990–94; Dir Newman Lab. for Biomechanics and Human Rehabilitation 1975–92; Dir Bioeng. Programmes, Whitaker Coll., MIT 1986–89; Dir Harvard-MIT Rehabilitation Eng Center 1988–92; mem. NAS, Nat. Acad. of Eng, Inst. of Medicine; Fellow American Acad. of Arts and Sciences, Inst. of Electrical and Electronics Engineers, American Soc. of Mechanical Engineers, AAAS, American Inst. of Medical and Biological Engineers; Chair. Flannery O'Connor-Andalusia Foundation 2002–; Co-trustee Mary Flannery O'Connor Charitable Trust 2002–; Gold Medal, American Soc. of Mechanical Engineers, Lissner Award for Outstanding Bioeng., New England Award, Goldenson Award for Outstanding Scientific Research for the Physically Handicapped, James R. Killian Jr Faculty Achievement Award, MIT, Inaugural Recipient, Dr. Martin Luther King, Jr Leadership Award, MIT. *Publications:* over 400 professional publs and four patents on missile research, eng design, computer-aided design, biomedical eng, human rehabilitation, synovial joint biomechanics and the etiology of osteoarthritis. *Leisure interests:* family, gardening, crafts, sailing. *Address:* Massachusetts Institute of Technology, Room 3-137D, 77 Massachusetts Avenue, Cambridge, MA 02139 (Office); 5 Pelham Road, Lexington, MA 02421, USA (Home). *Telephone:* (617) 253-2220 (Office); (781) 862-6953 (Home). *Fax:* (781) 862 6953 (Home). *E-mail:* rwmann@mit.edu (Office); rwmann@mit.edu (Home). *Website:* me.mit.edu/people/rwmann.html (Office); me.mit.edu/people/rwmann.html (Home).

MANN, Yuri Vladimirovich, D.PHIL.SC.; Russian literary scholar and historian; b. 9 June 1929, Moscow; s. of Vladimir Mann and Sonja Mann; m. Galina Mann 1956; two s.; ed Moscow Univ.; school teacher, Moscow 1952–56; Prof. of Russian Literature, Gorky Inst. of World Literature –1992; Prof. Russian State Humanitarian Univ. 1992–; Chief Ed. Complete Academic Works of N. V. Gogol (23 vols); mem. CPSU 1952–90, Russian PEN Centre 1995, Acad. of Natural Sciences 1996; Visiting Prof. Chicago Univ. 1991. *Publications include:* The Grotesque in Literature 1966, Russian Philosophical Aesthetics 1820s–1830s 1969, The Poetics of Russian Romanticism 1976, The Poetics of Gogol 1978, In Search of a Live Soul–Gogol's Dead Souls 1984, The Dialectics of Image 1987, The Aksakov Family 1992, Beyond the Mask of Laughter: The Life of Nikolai Gogol 1994, The Dynamics of Russian

Romanticism 1995, The Poetics of Gogol: Variations on the Theme 1996; Russian Literature XIX century. Romanticism 2001. *Address:* Russian State Humanitarian University, Ul. Chayanov 15, Moscow 125267 (Office); 3 Tverskaya - Yamskaya 44, Apt. 5, Moscow 129010, Russia (Home). *Telephone:* (095) 250-66-92 (Office); (095) 250-52-97 (Home). *E-mail:* ymann@si.ru (Home).

MANNAI, Jassim Abdullah al-, PhD; Bahraini finance official; b. 1948; ed Univ. of the Sorbonne, Paris, France and Harvard Business School; Exec. Vice-Pres. Gulf Investment Corpn, Kuwait 1987–94; CEO and Chair. Arab Trade Financing Program, Abu Dhabi 1994–; Dir-Gen. and Chair. Arab Monetary Fund, Abu Dhabi 1994–; Chair. Inter Arab Rating Co. EC (mem. Fitch IBCA Group) 1995–2001. *Publications:* numerous articles on economic and financial issues in various publications. *Address:* Office of the Director General, Arab Monetary Fund, P.O. Box 2818, Abu Dhabi, United Arab Emirates (Office). *Telephone:* (2) 6345354 (Office). *Fax:* (2) 6332089 (Office). *E-mail:* dg@amfad.org.ae (Office). *Website:* www.amf.org.ae (Office).

MANNING, Sir David Geoffrey, Kt, KCMG, BA; British diplomatist; b. 5 Dec. 1949, Portsmouth; s. of John Robert Manning and Joan Barbara Manning; m. Catherine Marjory Parkinson 1973; ed Ardingly Coll., Oriel Coll. Oxford, Johns Hopkins Univ., USA; Third Sec., FCO (Mexico, Cen. America Dept) 1972; Third, later Second Sec., Warsaw 1974–76; Second, later First Sec., New Delhi 1977–80; E European and Soviet Dept FCO 1980–82; Policy Planning Staff, FCO 1982–84; First Sec. (Political Internal), Paris 1984–88; Counsellor on loan to Cabinet Office 1988–90; Counsellor, Head of Political Section, Moscow 1990–93; Head, Eastern Dept (fmrly Soviet Dept), FCO 1993–94; British mem. of ICFY Contact Group on Bosnia April–Nov. 1994; Head of Planning Staff 1994–95; Amb. to Israel 1995–98; Deputy Under-Sec. of State, FCO 1998–2000; Perm. Rep. to NATO Jan.–Aug. 2001; Foreign Policy Adviser to Prime Minister 2001–03; Head of Cabinet Office Defence and Overseas Secr. 2001–03; Amb. to USA 2003–. *Address:* British Embassy, 3100 Massachusetts Avenue, Washington, DC, 20008, USA (Office). *Telephone:* (202) 588-7800 (Office). *E-mail:* ppa@washington.mail.fco.gov.uk (Office). *Website:* www.britainusa.com (Office).

MANNING, Jane, OBE, FRAM, FRCM, GRSM; British concert and opera singer; b. 20 Sept. 1938, Norwich; d. of the late Gerald Manning and Lily Thompson; m. Anthony Payne 1966; ed Norwich High School for Girls, RAM, London and Scuola di Canto, Cureglia, Switzerland; London début concert 1964; since then active world-wide as freelance soprano soloist with special expertise in contemporary music; more than 350 BBC broadcasts; regular tours of USA since 1981 and of Australia since 1978; appearances at all leading European festivals and concert halls; New York début 1983; more than 300 world premières including several operas; Founder/Artistic Dir Jane's Minstrels (ensemble) 1988; many recordings including complete vocal works of Messiaen and Satie; Vice-Pres. Soc. for Promotion of New Music 1996–; Visiting Prof., Mills Coll., Oakland, Calif. 1981, 1982, 1983, 1986, Royal Coll. of Music 1995–; Hon. Prof. Keele Univ. 1996–2002; visiting lecturer, univs. in UK, USA, Canada, Australia, NZ and Scandinavia; mem. Exec. Cttee Musicians' Benevolent Fund; Hon. DUniv (York) 1988; Special Award for Services to British Music, Composers' Guild of GB 1973. *Publications:* New Vocal Repertory (Vol. I) 1986, (Vol. II) 1998, A Messiaen Companion 1995. *Leisure interests:* cooking, ornithology, cinema, philosophy, reading. *Address:* 2 Wilton Square, London, N.1, England. *Telephone:* (20) 7359-1593. *Fax:* (20) 7226-4369. *E-mail:* jane@wiltonsq.demon.co.uk (Home). *Website:* www .classical-artists/janemanning (Home).

MANNING, Patrick Augustus Mervyn, BSc; Trinidad and Tobago politician; b. 17 Aug. 1946, San Fernando, Trinidad; s. of Arnold Manning and Elaine Manning; m. Hazel Anne-Marie Kinsale 1972; two s.; ed Presentation Coll., San Fernando and Univ. of the West Indies; refinery operator Texaco, Trinidad 1965–66; Parl. Sec. 1971–78, Minister 1978–86; Minister of Information and of Industry and Commerce 1981, of Energy 1981–86; Leader of the Opposition 1986–90; Prime Minister 1991–95, 2001–; also Minister of Finance; fmr Minister of Nat. Security; Leader People's Nat. Movt (PNM) 1987–. *Leisure interests:* table tennis, chess, reading. *Address:* Office of the Prime Minister, Whitehall, Maraval Road, Port of Spain; People's National Movement, 1 Tranquillity Street, Port of Spain, Trinidad. *Telephone:* 622-1625 (Office); 625-1533. *Fax:* 622-0055 (Office). *E-mail:* opm@trinidad.net; opm@ttgov.gov.tt (Office). *Website:* www.opm.gov.tt.

MANNING, Robert Joseph; American journalist; b. 25 Dec. 1919, Binghamton, NY; s. of Joseph James Manning and Agnes Pauline Brown; m. 1st Margaret Marinda Raymond 1944 (died 1984); three s.; m. 2nd Theresa Slomkowski 1987; US Army service 1942–43; Nieman Fellow, Harvard Univ. 1945–46; State Dept and White House Corresp. United Press. 1944–46, Chief UN Corresp. United Press. 1946–49; Writer, Time magazine 1949–55, Senior Ed. 1955–58, Chief, London Bureau, Time, Life, Fortune, Sports Illustrated magazines 1958–61; Sunday Ed., New York Herald Tribune 1961–62; Asst Sec. of State for Public Affairs, US Dept of State 1962–64; Exec. Ed. Atlantic Monthly 1964–66, Ed.-in-Chief 1966–80; Vice-Pres. Atlantic Monthly Co. 1966–80; Ed.-in-Chief Boston Publishing Co. 1981–87; Pres., Ed.-in-Chief Bobcat Books Inc., Boston 1987–; Fellow, Kennedy Inst. of Politics, Harvard Univ. 1980; mem. AAAS. *Publications include:* Who We Are 1976, The Swamp Root Chronicle 1992, The Vietnam Experience (25 Vols). *Address:* 1200 Washington Street, Apt 507, Boston, MA 02118, USA (Office and Home). *E-mail:* bobcat1225@rcn.com (Office).

MANNINGHAM-BULLER, Eliza(beth) Lydia; British government official; b. 14 July 1948; d. of Sir Reginald Manningham-Buller and Lady Mary Lilian Lindsay; m. 1991; ed Northampton High School, Benenden School, Kent and Lady Margaret Hall, Oxford Univ.; fmr English teacher; joined MI5 Security Service 1974, worked on case of KGB defector Oleg Gordievsky and Lockerbie disaster, served as MI5 liaison officer at British Embassy in Washington DC, Dir for Surveillance and Tech. Operations 1993, Dir of Irish Counter-terrorism, Dir of Finance and Information Tech., Deputy Dir-Gen. 1997–2002, Dir-Gen. Oct. 2002–. *Address:* MI5 Security Service, PO Box 3255, London, SW1P 1AE, England (Office). *Telephone:* (20) 7930-9000 (Office). *Website:* www.mi5.gov.uk (Office).

MANOLIČ, Josip (Joža); Croatian politician and lawyer; b. 22 March 1920, Kalinovac; m. Marija Manolić (née Eker); three d.; ed Zagreb Univ.; youth orgs. and trade union activist 1938–; mem. anti-fascist movt; Sec. Dist Cttee League of Communist Youth of Croatia; Chief Dept of Nat. Security in Bjelovar 1945–46 (dismissed); worked in Ministry of Internal Affairs of Croatia 1948–60; Interior Affairs Secr. in Zagreb 1960–65; mem. of Parl. Repub. of Croatia, Pres. Legis. Body of Constitutional Comm. 1965–71; mandate suspended because of nationalist activities; co-founder Croatian Democratic Union (HDZ) first Chair. Exec. Cttee 1989, Vice-Pres. 1990–; mem. of Croatian Parl. 1990–; Pres. Croatian Govt 1990–91, Vice-Pres. Presidency of Repub. Croatia –1999; 1990–91; Pres. House of Counties of Croatian Parl. 1992–94; Pres. Emergency Bd of Croatia; Dir Bureau for the Protection of Constitutional Order 1991–93; founder of Croatian Independent Democrats (HND), Pres. of HND; an organizer of Croatian army; certificate for participation in anti-Fascist struggle 1941–45, certificate for participation in the defence of the homeland 1991–92. *Publication:* Manolić 1989–95 (collection of interviews). *Leisure interest:* chess. *Address:* Nazorova str. 57, 41000 Zagreb, Croatia (Office). *Telephone:* (1) 4848476 (Office).

MANSELL, Nigel, OBE; British racing driver; b. 8 Aug. 1953, Upton-on-Severn; s. of Eric Marshall and Joyce Marshall; m. Rosanne Perry; two s. one d.; ed Matthew Bolton Polytechnic, Sollihall Tech. Coll.; began racing in karts; won 11 regional Championships 1969–76; Formula Ford and Formula Three 1976–79; Formula Two, later Formula One 1980; Lotus team 1981–84; Williams-Honda team 1985–87; Williams-Judd team 1988; Ferrari team 1989–90; Williams-Renault team 1991–92 and 1994 (part-time); McLaren team 1995; first competed in a Grand Prix, Austria 1980; won 31 Grand Prix 1980–94, record since beaten by Michael Schumacher; Formula One World Drivers Champion 1992; American Newman-Haas Indy Car Team 1993; Indy Car Champion 1993; special constable; owner of Woodbury Park Golf and Country Club 1993–; Hon. DEng (Birmingham) 1993; BBC Sports Personality of the Year 1986, 1992. *Publications:* Mansell and Williams (with Derick Allsop) 1992, Nigel Mansell's IndyCar Racing (with Jeremy Shaw) 1993, My Autobiography (with James Allen) 1995, Driven to Win (with Derick Allsop). *Leisure interests:* golf, fishing, flying. *Address:* c/o Nicki Dance, Woodbury Park Golf and Country Club, Woodbury Castle, Woodbury, Exeter, Devon, EX5 1JJ, England. *Telephone:* (1395) 233382 (Office). *Fax:* (1395) 232978 (Office). *E-mail:* nickidance@woodburypark.co.uk.

MANSER, Michael John, CBE, RA, DIPL. ARCH., PRIBA; British architect; b. 23 March 1929, London; s. of the late Edmund G. and Augusta M. Manser; m. Dolores Josephine Bernini 1953; one s. one d.; ed School of Architecture, The Polytechnic of Cen. London; Chair. The Manser Practice (architects) 1961–; architectural corresp. The Observer 1964–66; engaged on wide variety of architectural projects including pvt. housing, industrial buildings, research labs., schools, swimming pools, commercial and domestic renovation and refurbishment, hotels, offices, air ferry terminals, London Underground stations, health bldgs.; Pres. RIBA 1983–85; Academician Royal Acad. 1994; RIBA Rep. RSA 1987–93 (Chair. Art for Architecture Award Scheme 1990–); mem. Council Nat. Trust 1991–93; Assessor Art in the Workplace Awards 1988–; Chair. Art and Work Awards 1996–; mem. Royal Acad. Council 1998–Architectural Cttee 1998–, City of Westminster Public Art Panel 1999–, Works Cttee. 1999–, Remuneration Cttee. 2000–, Audit Cttee. 2000–; Royal W of England Academician 1993–; Hon. FRAIC; Civic Trust Award 1967, Civic Trust Commendation 1973, European Architectural Heritage Award 1975, Dept of Environment Good Design in Housing Award 1975, Structural Steel Design Award 1976, 1995, RIBA Award Commendation 1977; RIBA Award, RIBA Regional Award 1991, Royal Fine Art Comm. and Sunday Times Bldg of the Year Finalist 1991, Quarternario Int. Award for Innovative Tech. in Architecture Finalist 1993, Civic Trust Award 1993, RIBA Award and Regional Award 1995. *Publications:* Planning Your Kitchen (co-author); contributions to nat. and tech. press. *Leisure interests:* architecture, music, gardening, boats, books. *Address:* The Manser Practice, Bridge Studios, Hammersmith Bridge, London, W6 9DA; Morton House, Chiswick Mall, London, W4 2PS, England. *Telephone:* (20) 8741-4381 (Office).

MANSFIELD, Eric Harold, MA, ScD, F.I.M.A., F.R.ENG., FRAeS, FRS; British structural research scientist; b. 24 May 1923, Croydon, Surrey; s. of Harold G. and Grace Pfundt Mansfield; m. 1st 1947 (divorced 1973); m. 2nd Eunice Shuttleworth-Parker 1974; two s. one d.; ed St Lawrence Coll., Ramsgate, Trinity Hall, Cambridge; various grades, Structures Dept, Royal Aircraft Est., Farnborough 1943–83, Chief Scientific Officer 1980–83; Visiting Prof. Univ. of Surrey 1984–90; mem. British Nat. Cttee for Theoretical and Applied Mechanics 1973–79, Gen. Ass. Int. Union of Theoretical and Applied Mechanics 1976–80; originator of Neutral Hole Theory, The Inextensional Theory for thin plates, Wrinkled Membrane Theory (modern version), Theory of Gravity-induced Wrinkles in Vertical Membranes, Theory for Objects Supported by Surface Tension, Theory for the Collapse of Rigid-Plastic Plates; Bronze Medal, Royal Aeronautical Soc. 1967, James Alfred Ewing Gold Medal for Eng Research 1991, Royal Medal, Royal Soc. 1994. *Publications:* Bending and Stretching of Plates 1964, 1989, Bridge: the Ultimate Limits 1986; articles in professional journals. *Leisure interests:* bridge, palaeontology, snorkelling, walking the dog. *Address:* Primrose Cottage, Alresford Road, Cheriton, Hants., SO24 0QJ, England. *Telephone:* (1962) 771280.

MANSFIELD, Michael, QC, BA; British barrister; b. 12 Oct. 1941, London; s. of Frank Mansfield and Marjorie Sayers; m. 1st Melian Mansfield 1967 (divorced 1992); three s. two d.; m. 2nd Yvette Mansfield 1992; one s.; ed Highgate School and Keele Univ.; began practising 1967; est. Tooks Court chambers 1984; specialist in civil liberties work; Prof. of Law, Westminster Univ. 1997–; films for BBC TV: Inside Story 1991, Presumed Guilty; Patron Acre Lane Neighbourhood Chambers, Brixton 1997–; Hon. Fellow, Kent Univ.; Hon. LLD (South Bank Univ.) 1994, (Univ. of Herts.) 1995, (Keele Univ.) 1995. *Publication:* Presumed Guilty 1994. *Leisure interests:* my children, drumming. *Address:* Tooks Court Chambers, 14 Tooks Court, Cursitor Street, London, EC4Y 1JY, England. *Telephone:* (20) 7405-8828. *Fax:* (20) 7405-6680.

MANSFIELD, Sir Peter, Kt, PhD, FRS; British professor of physics; b. 9 Oct. 1933, London; s. of late S. G. Mansfield and R. L. Mansfield; m. Jean M. Kibble 1962; two d.; ed William Penn School, Peckham and Queen Mary Coll., London; Research Assoc. Dept of Physics, Univ. of Ill. 1962; lecturer, Univ. of Nottingham 1964, Sr Lecturer 1967, Reader 1970, Prof. of Physics 1979–94, Prof. Emer. in Residence 1995–; MRC Professorial Fellow 1983–88; Sr Visitor, Max Planck Inst. for Medical Research, Heidelberg 1972–73; Fellow, Queen Mary Coll. 1985; Pres. Soc. of Magnetic Resonance in Medicine 1987–88; Hon. mem. British Inst. of Radiology (BIR) 1993; Hon. FRCR 1992; Hon. Fellow Inst. of Physics 1996; Hon. Dr. Med. (Strasbourg) 1995; Hon. DSc (Univ. of Kent at Canterbury) 1996; Royal Soc. Wellcome Foundation Gold Medal and Prize 1985, Duddell Medal, Inst. of Physics 1988, Royal Soc. Mullard Medal 1990, ISMAR Prize 1992, Barclay Medal, BJR 1993, Gold Medal, European Asscn of Radiology 1995, Garmisch-Partenkirchen Prize for MRI 1995, Rank Prize 1997 and other awards. *Publications:* NMR Imaging in Biomedicine 1982, NMR Imaging (co-ed.) 1990, MRI in Medicine 1995; some 200 scientific Publs in learned journals. *Leisure interests:* reading, languages, flying. *Address:* Magnetic Resonance Centre, Department of Physics, University of Nottingham, NG7 2RD, England. *Telephone:* (115) 9514740. *Fax:* (115) 9515166.

MANSFIELD, Terence Arthur, PhD, FRS; British professor of biology; b. 18 Jan. 1937, Ashby-de-la-Zouch; s. of Sydney W. Mansfield and Rose Mansfield (née Sinfield); m. Margaret M. James 1963; two s.; ed Univ. of Nottingham, Univ. of Reading; Research Fellow Reading Univ. 1961–65; lecturer and Prof. Univ. of Lancaster 1965–87, Dir Inst. of Environmental and Biological Sciences 1987–94, Provost of Science and Eng 1994–97, Research Prof. 1996–2001, Emer. Prof. 2001–; mem. Agric. and Food Research Council 1989–93. *Publications:* Physiology of Stomata (co-author) 1968, Stomatal Physiology (co-Ed.) 1981, Plant Adaptation to Environmental Stress (co-Ed.) 1993, Disturbance of the Nitrogen Cycle (co-Ed.) 1998; numerous chapters and journal articles on aspects of botanical science. *Leisure interests:* cricket, hill-walking. *Address:* Institute of Environmental and Biological Sciences, University of Lancaster, Bailrigg, Lancaster, LA1 4YQ, England. *Telephone:* (1524) 593779 (Office). *Fax:* (1524) 843854. *E-mail:* t.mansfield@lancaster.ac.uk (Office); mm-mansfield@beeb.net (Home).

MANSHARD, Walther, Dr rer. nat; German international civil servant and university professor; b. 17 Nov. 1923, Hamburg; s. of Otto and Ida Manshard; m. Helga Koch 1951; one d.; ed Univ. of Hamburg; Asst lecturer, Univ. of Southampton, UK 1950–52; lecturer, Univ. of Ghana 1952–60; Dozent, Univ. of Cologne 1960–63; Prof. Univ. of Giessen 1963–70; Prin. Dir UNESCO Dept of Environmental Sciences 1970–73; Prof., Head of Dept Univ. of Freiburg 1973–77, 1980–; Vice-Rector, UN Univ., Tokyo 1977–80; Sec.-Gen. and Treas. Int. Geographical Union 1976–84; Sr Adviser UN Univ. 1990–93; Hon. DLitt 1991. *Publications:* Die geographischen Grundlagen der Wirtschaft Ghanas 1961, Tropisches Afrika 1963, Agrargeographie der Tropen 1968, Afrika–Südlich der Sahara 1970, Tropical Agriculture 1974, Die Städte des tropischen Afrika 1977, Renewable Natural Resources and the Environment 1981, Entwicklungprobleme in Agrarräumen Tropen-Afrikas 1988, Umwelt v. Entwicklung in den Tropen 1995. *Address:* Geographisches Institut, University of Freiburg, Werderring 4, 79085 Freiburg i. Br.; Schwarzwald-strasse 24, 79189 Bad Krozingen, Germany. *Telephone:* (761) 2033571 (Office); (7633) 3488 (Home). *Fax:* (761) 2033575 (Office); (7633) 101253 (Home). *E-mail:* waltermanshard@geographie.uni-freiburg.de (Office).

MANSINGH, Lalit, MA; Indian diplomatist; b. 29 April 1941, Cuttack; s. of the late Mayadhar Mansingh and of Hemalata (Behura) Mansingh; m. Indira Singh 1976; one s. one d.; ed Stewart and C. S. Zila Schools, Utkal Univ., Indian School of Int. Studies, New Delhi; lecturer in political science 1961–63; joined diplomatic service 1963, Deputy Chief of Mission to Kabul 1971–74, to Brussels 1976–80, to Washington 1989–92, Amb. to UAE 1980–83; High Commr to Nigeria 1993–95, to London 1998–99; Jt Sec. Dept of Econ. Affairs, Ministry of Finance 1984–85; Dir Gen. Indian Council for Cultural Relations 1985–89; Dean Foreign Service Inst., New Delhi 1995–96; Perm. Sec. Ministry of External Affairs 1997–98; Amb. to USA 2001–. *Publication:* Indian

Foreign Policy: Agenda for the 21st Century (Ed.-in-Chief) 1998. *Leisure interests:* classical music, dance, fine arts, theatre. *Address:* Indian Embassy, 2107 Massachusetts Avenue, NW, Washington, DC 20008, USA. *Telephone:* (202) 939-7000. *Fax:* (202) 265-4351. *Website:* www.indianembassy.org (Office).

MANSUROV, Tair Aimukhametovich, DR. POLIT. SC.; Kazakhstan diplomatist; b. 1 Jan. 1948, Sarkand, Taldykorgan Region, Kazakhstan; s. of Aymukhamet Mansurov and Maken Tursynbekova; m. Saule Bakirova; three c.; ed Kazakh Polytech. Inst., Higher CP School at Cen. CPSU Cttee; worked in construction orgs. Alma-Ata, chief engineer Almaatacentrostroi 1965–73; leading post in CP 1973–88; Second Sec. Karaganda Region CP Cttee, Head of Sector Cen. CPSU Cttee 1989–91; deputy to Kazakhstan Supreme Soviet, co-ordinator Interparl. Comm. of Russia and Kazakhstan 1990–93; Pres. Foundation of Devt Kazakhstan (Moscow) 1991–94; rank of Amb.; Amb. to Russian Fed. 1994–2002, concurrently Amb. to Finland 1996–2002; mem. Acad. of Creativity, Int. Acad. of High School, Acad. of Social Sciences; Kurmet Order 1996. *Publications:* Faces of Sovereignty: Sovereignty in Terms of Social History, Kazakhstan and Russia: Sovereignization, Integration, Experience of Strategic Partnership. *Leisure interests:* literature, philosophy, history, memoirs. *Address:* c/o Ministry of Foreign Affairs, 473000 Astana, Kazakhstan.

MANTEL, Hilary Mary, B.JUR., FRSL; British writer; b. 6 July 1952, Hadfield, Derbyshire; d. of Henry Thompson and Margaret Mary Thompson; m. Gerald McEwen 1973; ed Harrytown Convent, Cheshire, London School of Econs, Sheffield Univ.; Assoc. London Coll. of Music. *Radio:* The Giant (drama) 2002. *Publications:* Every Day is Mother's Day 1985, Vacant Possession 1986, Eight Months on Ghazzah Street 1988, Fludd 1989 (Winifred Holtby Memorial Award, Southern Arts Literature Prize, Cheltenham Festival Prize), A Place of Greater Safety 1992 (Sunday Express Book of the Year Award 1993), A Change of Climate 1994, An Experiment in Love 1995 (Hawthornden Prize 1996), The Giant, O'Brien 1998, Giving up the Ghost 2003, Learning to Talk 2003. *Address:* c/o A. M. Heath & Co., 79 St Martin's Lane, London, WC2N 4AA, England.

MANUEL, Trevor Andrew; South African politician; b. 31 Jan. 1956, Cape Town; s. of Abraham J. Manuel and Philma van Söhnen; m. Lynn Matthews; three s.; ed Harold Cressy High School; mem. Labour Party Youth 1969–71, Policy Man. on Devt 1989–; construction technician 1974–81; Sec. Kensington Civic Asscn 1977–82; founding mem. W Cape United Democratic Front (UDF) 1980s, Sec. Regional Exec. UDF 1983–90, mem. UDF Nat. Exec. Cttee 1983–86, 1989–90; Organizer CAHAC 1981–82; field worker Educational Resource and Information Centre 1982–84; in detention 1985, 1987–88, 1989, restricted 1985–86, 1986–90 (when not in detention); Publicity Sec. ANC W Cape; mem. ANC Nat. Exec. Cttee 1991–; Minister of Trade and Industry, Govt of Nat. Unity 1994–96; Minister of Finance 1996–2001. *Address:* c/o Private Bag X115, Pretoria 0001, South Africa.

MANUELLA, Sir Tulaga, GCMG, MBE; Tuvaluan fmr Governor-General and accountant; b. 26 Aug. 1936; s. of Teuhu Manuella and Malesa Moevasa; m. Milikini Uinifaleti; two s. three d.; sub-accountant and ledger keeper 1953–55; clerical officer 1955–57; Sr Asst, then Asst Accountant Treasury 1957–75; Asst Accountant, Tuvalu Govt; Accountant, then Acting Financial Sec., Ministry of Finance 1976–84; Financial Sec. Financial Div. Church of Tuvalu 1984–86; Pacific Conf. of Churches, Suva, Fiji 1987–91; Co-ordinator of Finance and Admin. Ekalesia Kelisiano 1992–94; Gov.-Gen. of Tuvalu 1994–1998; Chancellor Univ. of the S. Pacific 1997–2000; Patron Pacific Islands Soc. in Britain and Ireland 1995. *Address:* c/o Office of the Governor-General, P.O. Box 50, Vaiaku, Funafuti, Tuvalu (Office).

MANUKYAN, Vazgen Mikayelovich; Armenian politician and mathematician; b. 13 Feb. 1946, Leninakan (now Kuimayri); s. of Mikael Manukyan and Astkhik Manukyan; m. Vardui Rafaelovna Ishkhanyan; three d.; ed Yerevan State Univ.; Jr researcher Computation Cen. Armenian Acad. of Sciences 1969–72; teacher, Sr researcher Yerevan State Univ. 1972–90; political activities since 1960s, one of founders and leaders Club of Armenian Culture 1967, mem. and co-ordinator Cttee Karabakh 1988–; mem. of Bd, co-ordinator Armenian Pan-Nat. Movt 1989–90, leader Nat. Democratic Union 1991–; deputy Armenian Supreme Soviet 1990–91; Chair. Armenian Council of Ministers 1990–91; State Minister of Armenia Sept.–Oct. 1992; mem. Council of Nat. Security at Pres. 1992–93; Minister of Defence 1992–93; Chair. Cttee on Econ. Reform, State Comm. on Land Reform and Privatization; mem. Parl. 1991–; one of leaders of opposition; Cand. for Presidency 1996. *Publications:* It is Time to Jump off the Train 1990. *Address:* National Assembly, Marshal Bagramian Prosp. 26, 375016 Yerevan, Armenia.

MANYIKA, Elliott T.; Zimbabwean politician; fmr diplomatist; mem. ZANU-PF; currently Minister of Youth; mem. of Pres. Robert Mugabe's 'Gang of Four' politicians; Head of Youth Militia. *Address:* Ministry of Youth Development, Gender and Employment Creation, ZANU-PF Building, Private Bag 7762, Causeway, Harare, Zimbabwe (Office). *Telephone:* (4) 734641 (Office). *Fax:* (4) 732709 (Office).

MANZ, Wolfgang; German pianist; b. 6 Aug. 1960, Düsseldorf; m. Julia Goldstein 1985; two s. one d.; studied with Drahomir Toman, Prague and Karlheinz Kämmerling, Hanover; teacher, High School of Music, Karlsruhe 1994–98; concert tours UK, Germany, Belgium and Japan; performed Promenade Concerts, London 1984, Gilels Memorial Concert, Düsseldorf 1986,

Karajan Foundation, Paris 1987; First Prize Mendelssohn Competition, Berlin 1981, Second Prize, Leeds Piano Competition 1981, Second Prize Brussels Queen Elizabeth Competition 1983, Van Cliburn Int. Piano Competition Award, Texas 1989. *Recordings include:* Chopin Studies, Beethoven Triple Concerto, with English Chamber Orchestra, solo recital Liszt, Schumann and Debussy, Dohnanyi Piano Quintet. *Leisure interests:* composing, swimming, gardening. *Address:* Pasteurallee 55, 30655 Hanover, Germany. *Telephone:* (511) 5476025. *Fax:* (511) 5497432.

MANZONI, Giacomo, MusM; Italian composer; b. 26 Sept. 1932, Milan; m. Eugenia Tretti 1960; one s.; ed Bocconi Univ., Milan, Univ. of Tübingen and Conservatorio Verdi, Milan; Ed. Il Diapason (music review) 1956; music critic, l'Unità 1958–66; music ed. Prisma 1968; mem. editorial staff, Musica/Realtà 1980–; Prof. Conservatorio Verdi 1962–64, 1974–91, Conservatorio Martini, Bologna 1965–68, 1969–74, Scuola di Musica Fiesole 1988–, Accademia Musicale Pescarese 1993–96; mem. Accad. Nazionale di Santa Cecilia, Rome 1994–; has given master courses in composition in Buenos Aires, Granada, Tokyo, Santiago, Beijing, etc.; Dr hc (Udine); Premio Abbiati 1989. *Compositions include:* La Sentenza 1960, Atomtod 1965, 'Insiemi' 1967, Ombre (alla memoria di Che Guevara) for chorus and orchestra 1968, Per M. Robespierre 1975, Parole da Beckett 1971, Masse: omaggio a E. Varèse 1977, Ode 1982, Scene Sinfoniche per il Dr. Faustus 1984, Dedica (su testi di Maderna) 1985, Dr. Faustus: Scene dal romanzo di T. Mann 1989, 10 versi di E. Dickinson 1989, Malinamusik 1991, Finale e aria (I. Bachmann) 1991, Il deserto cresce (F. Nietzsche) 1992, Moi, Antonin A. (Artaud) 1997, Trame d'Ombre (da Zeami) 1998, O Europa! (A. József) 1999; Musica notturna 1966, Oltre la soglia, for voice and string quartet 2000 and other chamber music; Una voce chiama, for voice, viola and live electronics (F. Fortini) 1994, Quanto oscura selva trovai (Dante), for trombone, chorus and live electronics 1995; film and incidental music. *Publications:* A. Schoenberg 1975, Scritti 1991, Tradizione e Utopia 1994; translations of Adorno and Schönberg. *Address:* Viale Papiniano 31, 20123 Milan, Italy. *Telephone:* (02) 4817955. *E-mail:* gmanz-@libero .it (Home).

MAO RUBO; Chinese politician; b. 1938, Yangzhou City, Jiangsu Prov.; ed Nanjing Univ.; joined CCP 1959; Vice-Dir then Dir Meteorological Office of Tibet; Vice-Sec. CCP Tibet Autonomous Regional Cttee, Vice-Chair. Tibet Autonomous Region; Sec. CCP Ningxia Hui Autonomous Regional Cttee; mem. 15th CCP Cen. Cttee 1997–2002; Chair. People's Congress of Ningxia Hui Autonomous Region 1998. *Address:* Standing Committee, People's Congress of Ningxia Hui Autonomous Region, Yinchuan City, Ningxia Hui Autonomous Region, People's Republic of China.

MAO ZHIYONG; Chinese party official; b. 1929, Yueyang Co., Hunan Prov.; joined CCP 1952; Sec. CCP Yueyang Co. Cttee 1964–66; Deputy CCP Sec. of Yueyang Pref. and Deputy CCP Sec. of Changde Pref., Hunan 1966–71; Deputy Sec.-Gen. CCP Hunan Prov. Cttee 1972–73, First Sec., Sec. 1977–88; mem. 11th CCP Cen. Cttee 1977–82; mem. 5th NPC 1978–80; mem. 12th CCP Cen. Cttee 1982–87, 13th CCP Cen. Cttee 1987–92; Sec. CCP Jiangxi Prov. Cttee 1988–95; mem. 14th CCP Cen. Cttee 1992–97; Chair. Standing Cttee Jiangxi Prov. People's Congress 1993–98; mem. 8th NPC 1993–98; Vice-Chair. 9th CPPCC Nat. Cttee 1998. *Address:* National Committee of Chinese People's Political Consultative Committee, 23 Taipingqiao Street, Beijing, People's Republic of China.

MAOATE, Terepai, PhD; Cook Islands politician; Prime Minister and Minister of Finance 2000–02, numerous other portfolios; fmr Gov. Asian Devt Bank; currently Leader Democratic Alliance Party and Leader of the Opposition. *Address:* Democratic Alliance Party, P.O. Box 73, Rarotonga, Cook Islands (Office). *Telephone:* 21224 (Office).

MAOR, Galia, MBA; Israeli banker; m.; three c.; joined Bank of Israel 1963, supervisor of banks 1982–89; private consultancy 1989–91; joined Bank Leumi as Deputy Gen. Man. 1991, Pres. and CEO 1995–; mem. various cttees. *Address:* Bank Leumi le-Israel BM, PO Box 2, 24-32 Yehuda Halevi Street, Tel-Aviv 65546, Israel (Office). *Telephone:* 3-5148111 (Office). *Fax:* 3-5661872 (Office). *Website:* www.bankleumi.co.il (Office).

MAPFUMO, Thomas Tafirenyika Mukanya; Zimbabwean musician; b. 2 July 1945, Marondera. *Music:* f. The Hallelujah Chicken Run Band 1973, Black Spirits 1976, Blacks Unlimited, performed with The Pied Pipers, Acid Band. *Solo albums include:* Hokoto 1979, Mbira Music of Zimba 1980, Gwindingwi 1981, Ndangariro 1983, Corruption 1984, Mr. Music 1985, Chimurenga For Justice 1986, Zimbabwe-Mozambique 1987, Nyamaropa Nhimutimu 1989, Chimurenga Masterpis 1991, Chimurenga Singles 1991, Shumba 1992, Hondo 1993, Chimurenga Int'l 1993.

MAPONYA, Richard John; South African business executive; b. 24 Dec. 1926, Pietersburg; s. of late Godfrey Kgabane Maponya and Mary Machichane (née Mogashoa) Maponya; m. Marina Nompinti Sondlo (died 1992); two s. four d.; ed Kagiso Teacher's Training Coll., Pietersburg; proprietor Maponya's Supply Stores 1952–; Dir Maponya's Bus Services 1965, Maponya's Funeral Parlour (Pty) Ltd 1976, Afro Shopping Construction Enterprises (Pty) Ltd, Maponya's Discount Supermarket 1983–, Maponya's Bottle Store, Maponya's Motors (Pty) Ltd, Maponya Motors Property Holdings (Pty) Ltd, Maponya's Orlando Restaurant (Pty) Ltd, Maponya's Stud Farm, Lebowa Devt Corpn, numerous other cos.; Man. Dir MA Africa (Pty) Ltd, Mountain Motors, Soweto 1978–; Propr BMW Agency, Soweto; race horse owner; f. and Pres. NAFCOC 1965; Chair. Trade and Transport Cttee, Soweto Council; mem. Urban Bantu

Council 1965–76; Pres. Black Proprietors Garage Owners' Asscn. *Leisure interests:* racing, music. *Address:* P.O. Box 783045, Sandton 2146, South Africa.

MAPURANGA, Machivenyika Tobias, PhD; Zimbabwean diplomatist; b. 22 March 1947; m.; five c.; ed London, Oxford and Edin. Univs.; fmr High Commr. in Zambia; Deputy Sec., Political and Econ. Affairs, Ministry of Foreign Affairs 1986–87; Special Rep. of OAU Sec.-Gen. to Rwanda 1992–95, Head OAU Del. Arusha Peace Talks, Asst Sec.-Gen. in several depts. of the OAU; Deputy Perm. Sec., Political and Econ. Affairs, Ministry of Foreign Affairs, Zimbabwe 1995–96; Perm. Rep. to the UN 1996–99, Chair. Fourth Cttee (Special Political and Decolonization), UN Gen. Ass. 1997. *Address:* c/o Ministry of Foreign Affairs, Manhumutapa Building, Samora Machel Avenue, P.O. Box 4240, Causeway, Harare, Zimbabwe (Office).

MAQUEDA, Juan Carlos; Argentine politician, lawyer and university teacher; b. 29 Dec. 1949, Río Tercero; ed La Salle Coll. and Catholic Univ. of Córdoba; Prof. of Law, Catholic Univ. of Córdoba 1977–80, Adjunct Prof. of Natural Law 1980, Prof. of History of Political Insts of Argentina 1981, Asst Prof. of Natural Law 1981–82, 1983–84, Prof. 1984–85, Adjunct Prof. of Constitutional Law 1985, Prof. of Political Theory 1986; Tech. Sec. Faculty of Law and Social Sciences, Univ. of Córdoba 1980–86; mem. Justicialista party; Provincial Deputy, Córdoba 1986–91; Deputy to Nat. Ass. 1991–99; Minister of Educ., Prov. of Córdoba 1999–2001; Pres. Constitutional Convention of Prov. of Córdoba Aug. 2001; Senator from Córdoba 2001–03, Vice-Pres. Nat. Senate 2001, Pres. 2002; mem. Fed. Council of Nat. Culture and Educ. 1999–2001; Vice-Pres. Argentine Group, Parliamentarians for Global Action. *Publications include:* El Pensamiento Político Español del Siglo XVI 1980, Los Partidos Políticos: Ordenamiento Legal 1985, Sistemas Electorales y los Sistemas de Partidos 1985, La Nueva Constitución de Córdoba: Labor Constituyente y Debates 1987, Labor Parlamentaria en la Cámera de Diputados de la Provincia de Códoba y Debates 1988, 1989. *Address:* c/o Senado, Hipólito Yrigoyen 1849, 3° Piso, 1310 Buenos Aires, Argentina (Office). *E-mail:* juan.maqueda@senado.gov.ar (Office). *Website:* www.senado.gov.ar (Office).

MARA, Rt. Hon. Ratu Sir Kamisese Kapaiwai Tuimacilai, GCMG, KBE, C.F., M.S.D., MA; Fijian politician; b. 13 May 1920; s. of the late Tui Nayau and Adi Lusiana Qolikoro; m. Adi Lady Lala Mara 1951; three s. (one deceased) five d.; ed Queen Victoria School and Cen. Medical School, Suva, Fiji, Sacred Heart Coll., Otago Univ., Wadham Coll. Oxford and London School of Econs; joined British Colonial Service 1950; Admin. Officer, Dist Officer and Commr, Fiji 1951–61; mem. Legis. Council, Fiji 1953–89; mem. Exec. Council, Fiji 1959–61; mem. for Natural Resources 1964–66; f. Alliance Party 1960; Leader, Fiji Del. Constitutional Conf., London 1965; Chief Minister 1967–70; Prime Minister 1970–87, Prime Minister and Minister of Foreign Affairs 1977–87, 1987–92 and of Foreign Affairs and the Public Service 1987–89, of Foreign Affairs and Home Affairs 1989; Leader of Opposition April–May 1987; Pres. and Commdr-in-Chief of Fiji 1994–98, of the Repub. of the Fiji Islands 1998–2000; Adviser on Foreign Affairs Gov. Gen.'s Interim Govt May–Sept. 1987; KStJ; Hon. Fellow Wadham Coll. Oxford 1971, LSE 1986; Hon. LLD (Guam, Otago, New Delhi, Papua New Guinea); Hon. Dr. Political Science (Yonsei Univ., Korea) 1978; Hon. DUniv (Univ. of S. Pacific) 1980; Pacific Man of the Year 1984; Grand Master, Order of the National Lion (Senegal) 1975, Order of Diplomatic Service Merit (Repub. of Korea) 1978, Chancellor of Order of Fiji 1995, Kt. Grand Cross Pian Order with Star 1995, Pacific Man of the Century 2000. *Publications:* The Pacific Way: A Memoir. *Leisure interests:* fishing, golf. *Address:* c/o Office of the President, Government Buildings, P.O. Box 2513, Suva, Fiji.

MARADONA, Diego Armando; Argentine footballer; b. 30 Oct. 1960, Lanús, Buenos Aires; s. of Diego Maradona and Dalma Salvadora Franco; m. Claudia Villafane; two d.; with Boca Juniors, Argentina 1981–82, Barcelona Football Club 1982–84; with Naples Football Club 1984–91, Sevilla (Spain) 1992–93, Boca Jrs. 1997, Badajoz 1998–; won Youth World Cup with Argentina nat. team 1979, won World Cup with Argentina nat. team 1986; founded Maradona Produccione; fmr Amb. for UNICEF; banned from football for 15 months after drugs test; convicted by Naples Court on charges of possession of cocaine, 14-month suspended sentence and fine of 4 million lire, Sept. 1991; Fed. Court in Buenos Aires ruled he had complied with the treatment; suspended for 15 months for taking performance-enhancing drugs in World Cup Finals June 1994; indicted for shooting an air rifle at journalists Aug. 1994; resgnd as coach of Deporto Mandiyu 1994; Capt. of Argentina 1993; Pres. Int. Asscn of Professional Footballers 1995–; South American Player of the Year 1979, World Football of the Year 1986, Footballer of the Century Award, Féd. Int. de Football Asscn (France) 2000.

MARAFINO, Vincent Norman, MBA; American business executive; b. 8 June 1930, Boston; m. Doris M. Vernall 1958; three d.; ed San Jose State Coll. and Santa Clara Univ.; served with USAF 1953–55; Chief Accountant, American Standard Advance Tech. Lab., Mountain View, Calif. 1956–59; with Lockheed Missiles & Space Co., Sunnyvale, Calif. 1959–70; Asst Controller, Lockheed Corpn Burbank, Calif. 1970–71, Vice Pres., Controller 1971–77, Sr Vice-Pres. Finance 1977–83, Exec. Vice-Pres., Chief Financial and Admin. Officer 1983–88, Vice-Chair. of Bd and Chief Financial and Admin. Officer 1988–; mem. Bd of Dirs. Lockheed Missiles and Space Co., Inc.; Chair. Bd of Dirs. Lockheed Finance Corpn; mem. Bd of Trustees Holy Cross Medical

Center, Mission Hills; mem. Financial Execs. Inst., American Inst. of CPAS. *Address:* Lockheed Corporation, 6801 Rockledge Drive, Bethesda, MD 20817, USA.

MARAGALL, Pasqual, OBEPhD; Spanish civil servant and academic; b. 13 Jan. 1941, Barcelona; m.; three c.; ed Barcelona Univ., New School for Social Research, New York; lecturer in Econs Barcelona Univ.; Mayor of Barcelona 1982–, organizer of 1992 Olympic Games in Barcelona; Insignia Order of the Légion d'honneur 1993; Hon. DLitt (Winchester Art School UK), Dr hc (Johns Hopkins USA) 1997, Laurea hc (Reggio Calabria Italy) 1998; Medal of the Council of Europe 1984, Olympic Golden Award 1992, Golden Medal Award Spanish Inst. New York 1993. *Address:* Catalan Socialist Party, Nicaragua 75, E-08029 Barcelona, Spain. *Telephone:* (934) 955400 (Office). *Fax:* (934) 955430 (Office). *E-mail:* pmaragall@psc.es (Office). *Website:* www.psc.es (Office).

MARAINI, Dacia; Italian author; b. 13 Nov. 1936; d. of Fosco Maraini and Alliata Topazia; ed Collegio S.S. Annunziata, Florence and Rome; Prix Formentor for L'Età del Malessere (The Age of Discontent) 1962. *Publications:* La Vacanza 1962, L'Età del Malessere 1962, Crudeltà All' Aria Aperta (poems) 1966, A Memoria (novel) 1967, La famiglia normale (one-act play) 1967, Il ricatto a teatro (play) 1968, Memoirs of a Female Thief 1973, Donna in Guerra (novel) 1975, Mangiami Pure (poems) 1980, I Sogni di Clitennestra (5 plays) 1981, Lettere a Marina (novel) 1981, Lezioni d'Amore (6 plays) 1982, Dimenticato di Dimenticare (poems) 1983, Isolina (novel) 1985, Devour me too (short stories) 1987, La Bionda, la bruna e l'asino (essays) 1987, La Lunga Vita di Marianna Ucria (novel) 1990, Bagheria (novel) 1993, Voci (novel) 1994, Buio (short stories) 1999, Fare Teatro (play) 2000. *Address:* Via Beccaria 18, 00196 Rome, Italy. *Telephone:* 3611795.

MARANDA, Pierre Jean, MA, LPh, PhD, FRSC; Canadian professor of anthropology; b. 27 March 1930, Québec; s. of Lucien Maranda and Marie-Alma Rochette; m. Elli-Kaija Köngäs 1962 (deceased); two s.; ed Laval Univ., Québec, Univ. of Montreal and Harvard Univ.; Asst Prof. of Classics, Univ. Laval 1955–58; Research Fellow, Harvard Univ. 1966–70; Dir of Research Ecole Pratique des Hautes Etudes, Paris 1968–69; Assoc. Prof. of Anthropology Univ. of BC 1969–71, Prof. 1971–75; Prof. Collège de France, Paris 1975; Research Prof. Laval Univ. 1976–96, Prof. Emer. 1996–; Pres. Steering Cttee of Cultural Hypermedia Encyclopedia of Oceania 1996–; Visiting Prof., Fed. Univ. of Rio de Janeiro 1983, Univ. of Toronto, ISISSS 1985, 1987, Univ. of BC 1986, Université Omar Bongo, Libreville, Gabon 1991, 1992, Ecole des hautes études en sciences sociales, Paris 1994; Dr. hc (Memorial Univ., Newfoundland) 1985; Médaille du Collège de France 1975, Canada Council Molson Prize in the Social Sciences and Humanities 1997. *Films:* Behind the Masks (with Claude Lévi-Strauss), Nat. Film Bd of Canada 1974, The Lau of Malaita, Solomon Islands (with Leslie Woodhead), Granada TV 1987. *Publications:* Structural Models in Folklore and Transformational Essays (with E. K. Köngäs) 1963, French Kinship: Structure and History 1974, Mythology 1974, Soviet Structural Folkloristics 1974, Dialogue conjugal 1985, DISCAN: A Computer Programme for Discourse Analysis 1989, L'unité dans la diversité culturelle: Une geste bantu, Vol. 1: Le sens des symboles fang, mbede, eshira 1993, The Double Twist: From Ethnography to Morphodynamics (ed.) 2001; plus over 60 articles in scientific journals. *Leisure interests:* skiing, swimming, tennis, bridge, music, art. *Address:* Département d'Anthropologie, Université Laval, Québec, G1K 7P4, Canada (Office). *Telephone:* (418) 656-5867 (Office); (418) 999-8570 (Home); (418) 656-2131. *Fax:* (418) 656-2831 (Office). *E-mail:* pierre.maranda@ant.ulaval.ca (Office); pmaranda@videotron.ca (Home). *Website:* www.oceanie.org (Office).

MARBER, Patrick; British writer and director; b. 19 Sept. 1964, London; s. of Brian Marber and Angela Benjamin; m. Debra Gillett; one s.; ed Wadham Coll., Oxford; Evening Standard Award for Best Comedy 1995, Writers' Guild Award for Best West End Play 1995 (both for Dealer's Choice), Evening Standard Best Comedy Award 1997, Critics' Circle Award for Best Play 1997, Olivier Award 1998, New York Drama Critics' Award 1999 (all four for Closer). *Plays directed and/or written include:* Dealer's Choice 1995, Blue Remembered Hills 1996, '1953' 1996, Closer 1997, The Old Neighbourhood 1998, The Caretaker 2000, Howard Katz 2001. *Television work includes:* The Day Today, Paul Calf Video Diary, Knowing Me Knowing You, 3 Fights 2 Weddings and a Funeral, The Curator, After Miss Julie. *Publications include:* Dealer's Choice 1995, After Miss Julie 1996, Closer 1997, Howard Katz 2001. *Address:* c/o Judy Daish Associates Ltd, 2 St Charles Place, London, W10 6EG, England. *Telephone:* (20) 8964-8811. *Fax:* (20) 8964-8966.

MARCANO, Luis Herrera, DIur; Venezuelan diplomatist and professor of law; b. 13 Dec. 1931, Caracas; m. Maria Sardi de Herrera; staff mem. Ministry of Foreign Affairs 1950–55, adviser 1956–57, Dir Int. Orgs. 1958, Dir Office of the Commrs for Guyana 1965–67, Dir Int. Policy 1968, Adviser to the Minister 1969–72, 1978, mem. Foreign Relations Advisory Comm. 1979–84, Amb. and mem. Comm. for Maritime Delimitation with Colombia 1980, mem. Council of Legal Advisers 1984–, legal adviser 1990–91, Co-ordinator of Pro Tempore Secr. of Rio Group 1990, external adviser 1992–99, adviser to Ministers of Interior and Justice 1999; Amb. and Deputy Perm. Rep. to UN, New York 2000; Amb. and Deputy Chief of Mission in Washington, DC 2001, Chargé d'affaires (acting) 2002–03; Prof. of Public Int. Law, Universidad Cen. de Venezuela 1963–89, Dir School of Law 1978–81, Dean Faculty of Legal and Political Sciences 1981–84; Exec. Sec. Organizing Comm., Universidad Simon Rodríguez 1972–76; mem. Interamerican Juridical Cttee, OAS 1982–, Pres.

1990–92; legal adviser Latin American Econ. System 1986–90; adviser to UN Truth Comm. for El Salvador 1992–93, mem. UN Comm. of Inquiry for Burundi 1995–96; adviser to Petroleos de Venezuela 1985–86. *Address:* c/o Ministry of Foreign Affairs, Torre MRE, esq. de Carmelitas, Avda Urdaneta, Caracas, 1010, Venezuela (Office).

MARCEAU, Félicien (pseudonym of Louis Carette); French writer; b. 16 Sept. 1913, Cortenberg, Belgium; s. of Louis Carette and Marie Lefèvre; m. 2nd Bianca Licenziati 1953; ed Coll. de la Sainte Trinité à Louvain and Univ. de Louvain; mem. Acad. Française 1975; Prix Interallié for Les élans du coeur 1955, Prix Goncourt for Creezy 1969, Prix Prince Pierre de Monaco 1974; Grand Prix du Théâtre 1975; Officier Légion d'honneur, Ordre nat. du Mérite, Commdr des Arts et des Lettres. *Publications:* Novels: Chasseneuil 1948, L'Homme du Roi 1952, Bergère Légère 1953, Creezy 1969, Le corps de mon ennemi 1975, Appelez-moi Mademoiselle 1984, La Carriole du Père Juniet 1985, Les passions partagées 1987, Un Oiseau dans le Ciel 1989, Les ingénus 1992, La Terrasse de Lucrezia 1993, Le Voyage de noces de Figaro 1994, La grande fille 1997, La Fille du Pharaon 1998, L'affiche 2000; plays: L'oeuf 1956, La bonne soupe 1958, La preuve par quatre 1965, Un jour j'ai rencontré la vérité 1967, Le babour 1969, L'ouvre-boîte 1972, L'homme en question 1973, A nous de jouer 1979; essays: Balzac et son monde 1955, Le roman en liberté 1977, Une insolente liberté: Les aventures de Casanova 1983, L'Imagination est une science exacte 1998; memoirs: Les années courtes 1968. *Leisure interest:* painting. *Address:* c/o Les Editions Gallimard, 5 rue Sébastien-Bottin, 75007 Paris; Academie Française, 23 quai de Conti, 75006 Paris, France. *Telephone:* 1-49-54-42-00; 1-44-41-43-06.

MARCEAU, Marcel; French mime; b. Marcel Mangel, 22 March 1923, Strasbourg; s. of Charles and Anne (née Werzberg) Mangel; m. 1st Huguette Mallet (divorced); two s.; m. 2nd Ella Jaroszewicz 1966 (divorced); m. 3rd Anne Sicco 1975 (divorced); two d.; ed Lille and Strasbourg Lycées; Dir Compagnie de Mime Marcel Marceau 1948–64, Int. School of Mime, Paris 1978–; annual world tours and numerous television appearances throughout the world; created Don Juan (mime drama) 1964, Candide (ballet), Hamburg 1971; creator of the character "Bip"; Dir Ecole de Mimodrame Marcel Marceau 1978–; mem. Académie des Beaux Arts, Inst. de France 1991, Berlin Acad. of Arts; Hon. degrees (Univ. of Michigan) 1986, (Princeton and Oregon Univs.) 1987; Officier, Légion d'honneur, Commdr des Arts et Lettres 1973, Grand Officier du Mérite 1998. *Exhibitions include:* New York, Ann Arbor (Mich.), Germany, Tokyo, Paris. *Films include:* Mic-Mac 1949, Le Manteau 1951, Pantomimes de Bip 1957, La belle et l'empereur 1959, Barbarella 1967, Scrooge/A Christmas Carol 1973, Shanks 1973, Silent Movie 1976. *Mimes include:* Exercices de style (filmed), Mort avant l'aube, Le joueur de flûte, Moriana et Galvau, Pierrot de Montmartre, Les trois perruques, etc.; other films: Pantomime, Un jardin public, Le fabricant de masques, Paris qui rit, Paris qui pleure. *Publications:* Les sept péchés capitaux, Les rêveries de Bip, Alphabet Book, Counting Book, L'histoire de Bip, The Third Eye, Pimporelló 1987. *Leisure interests:* painting, poetry, fencing, chess. *Address:* Compagnie de Mime Marcel Marceau, 32 rue de Londres, 75009 Paris, France (Office); Institut de France, 23 quai Conti, 75006 Paris. *Telephone:* 1-42-80-48-32 (Office); 2-37-82-08-47 (Home). *Fax:* 1-48-74-91-87 (Office); 2-37-65-91-59 (Home).

MARCEAU, Sophie (pseudonym of Sophie Danièle Sylvie Maupu); French actress; b. 17 Nov. 1966, Paris; d. of Benoît Maupu and Simone Morisset; one s.; Meilleur Espoir Féminin (for César) 1982, (for Molière) 1991 and several foreign prizes. *Films:* La Boum 1981, La Boum 2 1982, Fort Saganne 1984, Joyeuses Pâques 1985, L'Amour Braque 1985, Police 1985, Descente aux Enfers 1986, Chouans! 1987, L'Etudiante 1988, Mes Nuits Sont Plus Belles Que Vos Jours 1989, Pacific Palisades 1989, Pour Sacha 1991, La Note Bleue 1991, Fanfan 1993, La Fille de D'Artagnan 1994, Braveheart 1995, Beyond the Clouds 1995, Firelight 1995, Anna Karenine 1996, Marquise 1997, The World is not Enough 1998, La Fidelité 1999, Belphégor 2001. *Stage appearances include:* Eurydice 1991, Pygmalion 1993. *Publication:* Menteuse 1996. *Leisure interests:* countryside, music, reading, travel. *Address:* c/o Artmédia, 20 avenue Rapp, 75007 Paris, France (Office). *Telephone:* 1-44-31-22-00.

MARCHAND, Philippe, LenD; French politician and lawyer; b. 1 Sept. 1939, Angoulême, Charente; s. of Guy Marchand and Madeleine Bonat; m. Marie-Odile Filliau 1965; three s.; ed Collège de Parthenay, Univ. of Poitiers; lawyer at Saintes bar 1965–92; local councillor, Charente-Maritime 1976–, Saintes 1982–; Socialist Deputy for Charente-Maritime 1978–90, Vice-Pres. Assemblée Nationale 1985–86; Vice-Pres. Socialist Group in Parl. 1990–91; Titular Judge, High Court 1987; mem. Nat Comm. on Information Tech. and Freedom 1982–86, 1988–; Minister-del. in Ministry of the Interior 1990–91, Minister of the Interior 1991–92; regional councillor, Poitou-Charentes 1992–; Officier Légion d'honneur, Grand Cross of the Orden Isabel la Católica (Spain). *Address:* Conseil d'Etat, Palais Royal, 75100 Paris (Office); 45 chemin des Genêts, 17690 Angoulins, France (Home).

MARCHENKO, Grigori Alexandrovich; Kazakhstan banker; b. 26 Dec. 1959, Almaty; m.; ed Moscow State Inst. of Int. Relations, Georgetown Univ., USA; engineer-designer and acting Deputy Head, Dept. of Sr. Mans. Ministry of Non-Ferrous Metals, Kazakh S.S.R. 1984–85; Trans., Ed. and Leader Marketing Information Group, Kazakh Scientific Research Inst. 1986–88; acting head Design Bureau of Semiconductor Machine Building, Chair. Scientific Production Co-operative Centre 1988–90; Asst to Vice-Pres. of Kazakhstan 1992–93; Deputy Gov. Nat. Bank of Kazakhstan 1994–96, Gov.

1999–; Chair. Nat. Securities Comm. of Kazakhstan 1996–98; Pres. DB Securities of Kazakhstan 1998–99; Pew Fellow Georgetown Univ. 1994. *Address:* National Bank of Kazakhstan, 21 Koktem-3, Almaty 480090, Kazakhstan (Office). *Telephone:* (3272) 59-68-00 (Office). *Fax:* (3272) 63-73-42 (Office). *E-mail:* hq@nationalbank.kz (Office). *Website:* www.nationalbank .kz (Office).

MARCHUK, Guriy Ivanovich; Russian mathematician; b. 8 June 1925, Petro-Khersonets Village, Orenburg Region; m.; three c.; ed Leningrad State Univ.; Sr Research Assoc., Head of Dept, Inst. of Physics and Energetics, Obninsk 1953–62; Inst. of Maths. of Siberian Br. of USSR Acad. of Sciences 1962–64; Prof., Novosibirsk Univ. 1962–80; Deputy Chair., Chair. of Presidium, Siberian Br. of USSR Acad. of Sciences 1964–79; Dir Computing Centre of Siberian Br. of USSR Acad. of Sciences 1964–79; Deputy Chair. USSR Council of Ministers and Chair. State Cttee for Science and Tech. 1980–86; Dir Dept of Computing Math. (now Inst.), Acad. of Sciences 1980–, Adviser to Dir 1999–; Corresp. mem. USSR (now Russian) Acad. of Sciences 1962–68, mem. 1968–, Vice-Pres. 1975–78, Pres. 1986–91, Chair. Scientific Council on Medicine 1987–91; Deputy to USSR Supreme Soviet 1979–89; Lenin Prize 1961, A. Karpinski Prize, Hamburg 1988; Order of Lenin (four times), Keldysh Gold Medal 1981, Chebyshev Gold Medal 1996 and other decorations. *Publications:* works on problems of computational math. and physics of atmosphere. *Address:* Institute of Numerical Mathematics, Gubkin Str. 8, 117333, Moscow, Russia. *Telephone:* (095) 938-17-69. *Fax:* (095) 938-18-21.

MARCHUK, Gen. Yevgen Kirilovich, C.JUR.; Ukrainian politician; b. 28 Jan. 1941, Dolinivka, Kirovograd Region; m.; two s.; ed Kirovograd Pedagogical Inst.; worked as school teacher of Ukrainian and German Languages; with Ukrainian KGB (State Security Cttee) 1963–91, Deputy Chair. 1990–91; Chair. Nat. Security Service of Ukraine 1991; State Minister of Defence, Nat. Security and Emergencies 1991–94; Deputy Prime Minister July 1994, First Deputy Prime Minister 1994–95; Prime Minister of Ukraine 1995–96; mem. Verkhovna Rada (United Social Democratic Party faction) 1996–; Head Cttee of Social Policy and Labour 1998–; Pres. Ukrainian Transport Union 1998; presidential cand. 1999; Sec. Ukrainian Nat. Security and Defence Council 2000–. *Address:* National Security and Defence Council of Ukraine, Domandarma Kameneva Str. 8, 01133, Kiev, Ukraine. *Telephone:* (44) 291-60-27 (Office). *Fax:* (44) 226-29-36 (Office).

MARCINKEVIČIUS, Justinas; Lithuanian poet, playwright and translator; b. 10 March 1930, Vazhatkiemis, Lithuania; s. of Motiejus Marcinkevičius and Ieva Marcinkevičius; m. Genovaitė Kalvaitytė 1955; two d.; ed Univ. of Vilnius; began literary career 1953; mem. CPSU 1957–90; USSR People's Deputy 1989–91; mem. Lithuanian Acad. of Science 1990, Lithuanian Council of Culture and Art 1991; awards include State Prizes (twice), People's Poet of Lithuania, J. G. Horder Award 1997, Polish PEN Centre Award 1997, Santarvé Award 1999; Grand Duke Gediminas Order. *Publications include:* I Ask to Speak 1955, The Twentieth Spring 1955, The Pine that Laughed 1961, Blood and Ashes 1961, Hands that Share out the Bread 1963, The Wall 1965, Mindaugas 1968, The Cathedral 1971, Mazhvidas 1977, The Tender Touch of Life 1978, The Only Land 1984, For the Living and the Dead 1988, Lullaby to the Homeland and the Mother 1992, By the Rye and by the Hearth 1993, Poems from the Diary 1993, The Harmony of the Flowing River 1995. *Address:* Mildos gve. 33, Apt. 6, 2055 Vilnius, Lithuania. *Telephone:* (2) 740162.

MARCINKUS, Most Rev. Paul Casimir; American ecclesiastic; b. 15 Jan. 1922; ordained as a Roman Catholic priest 1947; Asst Pastor, St Cristina's Parish, Chicago 1947–52; joined Vatican State Secr. 1952; served as papal diplomatist in Canada and Bolivia; Gen. Man. Istituto per le Opere di Religione (Vatican Bank) 1969–71, Chair. 1971–89; Pro-Pres. Pontifical Comm. for the Vatican City State 1981–90; Titular Archbishop of Orta 1981–.

MARCKER, Kjeld Adrian, PhD; Danish molecular biologist; b. 27 Dec. 1932, Nyborg; s. of Kjeld A. C. Marcker and Minna C. Callesen; m. Anne Birgit Hansen 1964; three d.; ed Nyborg Gymnasium and Univ. of Copenhagen; Dept of Physical Chem., Univ. of Copenhagen 1958; Carlsberg-Wellcome Fellow, MRC Lab. of Molecular Biol., Cambridge 1962, mem. staff 1964; Fellow, King's Coll. Cambridge 1968; Prof. in Molecular Biology, Aarhus Univ. 1970–; mem. Royal Danish Acad., Danish Acad. of Tech. Science, Academiae Europaeae; Novo Medical Prize 1971; Anders Jahre Medical Prize 1973. *Publications:* articles in scientific journals. *Leisure interests:* soccer, birdwatching, history. *Address:* Laboratory of Gene Expression, Department of Molecular Biology, University of Aarhus, Gustav Wieds Vej 10, 8000 Aarhus C; Tjoernehegnet 32, DK-8541 Skoedstrup, Denmark (Home). *Telephone:* 89-42-50-17. *Fax:* 86-20-12-22.

MARCOS, Imelda Romualdez; Philippine politician and social leader; b. *c.* 1930; m. Ferdinand E Marcos (died 1989); one s. two d.; Gov. of Metro Manila 1975–86; Roving Amb.; visited Beijing 1976; took part in negotiations in Libya over self-govt for southern provinces 1977; leader Kilusan Bagong Lipunan (New Society Movt) 1978–81; mem. Batasang Pambansa (Interim Legis. Ass.) 1978–83; Minister of Human Settlements 1978–79, 1984–86, of Human Settlements and Ecology 1979–83; mem. Cabinet Exec. Cttee 1982–84; Chair. Southern Philippines Devt Authority 1980–86; indicted for embezzlement 1988, acquitted 1990; returned to Philippines Nov. 1991; sentenced to 18 to 24 years' imprisonment for criminal graft Sept. 1993; convicted of two charges of corruption, sentenced to 9–12 years on each Sept. 1993; sentenced on appeal

to Supreme Court; faced four charges of graft Sept. 1995; Presidential Cand. 1992; mem. Senate 1995–. *Records include:* Imelda Papin featuring songs with Mrs Imelda Romualdez Marcos 1989.

MARCUS, Claude, DEcon; French advertising executive; b. 28 Aug. 1924, Paris; s. of Jack Marcus and Louise Bleustein; m. Claudine Pohl 1948; one s. three d.; ed Faculté des Lettres, Aix and Faculté de Droit, Paris; Vice-Chair. Supervisory Bd, Man. Dir Publicis, Chair. Publicis Int.; Chair. Perm. Comm. Advertising Profession/Consumer Unions; Chevalier Légion d'honneur; Officier, Ordre nat. du Mérite, Médaille des Evadés, Chevalier, Ordre des Palmes académiques et de l'Economie nationale. *Leisure interests:* antiques, tennis. *Address:* 133 avenue des Champs-Elysées, 75008 Paris, France. *Telephone:* 1-44-43-70-02. *Fax:* 1-45-20-18-01 (Home). *E-mail:* claudius6@ wanadoo.fr (Home).

MARCUS, Rudolph Arthur; American professor of chemistry; b. 21 July 1923, Montreal, Canada; s. of Myer and Esther Marcus; m. Laura Hearne 1949; three s.; ed McGill Univ.; worked for Nat. Research Council of Canada 1946–49; Univ. of N Carolina 1949–51; Asst Prof. Polytech. Inst. of Brooklyn 1951–54, Assoc. Prof. 1954–58, Prof. 1958–64; Prof. Univ. of Ill. 1964–68; Arthur Amos Noyes Prof. of Chem., Calif. Inst. of Tech. 1978–; Visiting Prof. of Theoretical Chem., Oxford Univ. 1975–76; Visiting Linnett Prof. of Chem., Univ. of Cambridge 1996; Hon. Prof. Fudan Univ., Shanghai 1994–; Hon. Prof. Inst. of Chem., Chinese Acad. of Sciences, Beijing 1995–; mem. Courant Inst. of Mathematical Sciences, New York Univ. 1960–61, Council, Gordon Research Confs. 1965–68, Chair. Bd of Trustees and mem. Bd 1966–69; Chair. Div. of Physical Chem., American Chemical Soc. 1964–65; mem. Exec. Cttee American Physical Soc. Div. of Chemical Physics 1970–72, Advisory Bd American Chemical Soc. Petroleum Research Fund 1970–72, Review Cttee Argonne Nat. Laboratory Chem. Dept 1966–72 (Chair. 1968–69), Brookhaven Nat. Lab. 1971–73, Radiation Lab., Univ. of Notre Dame 1976–78, External Advisory Bd, NSF Center for Photoinduced Charge Transfer 1990–, Nat. Research Council/N.A.S., Cttee on Climatic Impact; Chair. Cttee on Kinetics of Chemical Reactions 1975–77, Panel on Atmospheric Chem. 1975–78, Cttee on Chemical Sciences 1977–79, Cttee Survey Opportunities in Chem. 1982–86, Math. Panel, Int. Benchmarking of U.S. Research Fields 1996–98, Advisory Cttee for Chem. Nat. Science Foundation 1977–80, Review Cttee Chem. Depts. Princeton Univ. 1972–78, Polytech. Inst. of NY 1977–80, Calif. Inst. of Tech. 1977–78, Cttee for Accountability of Federally Funded Research, COSEPUP 2000–01; Adviser, State Key Lab. for Structural Chem. of Unstable and Stable Species, Beijing 1995, Center for Molecular Sciences, Chinese Acad. of Sciences, Beijing 1995–; mem. editorial bds., Laser Chem. 1982–, Advances in Chemical Physics 1984–, World Scientific Publishing 1987–, Int. Reviews in Physical Chem. 1988–, Progress in Physics, Chem. and Mechanics (China) 1989–, Journal of the Chemical Soc. Perkin Transactions 2 1992–, Chemical Physics Research (India) 1992–, Trends in Chemical Physical Research (India) 1992–; Hon. Ed. Int. Journal of Quantum Chem. 1996–; mem. NAS, American Philosophical Soc. (mem. Council 1999–); Fellow, American Acad. of Arts and Sciences, Co-Chair. Exec. Cttee Western Section; Foreign mem. Royal Society, London; Foreign Fellow, Royal Soc. of Canada; Foreign mem. Chinese Acad. of Sciences; mem. Int. Acad. Quantum Molecular Science; Assoc. mem. Center for Advanced Studies, Univ. of Ill. 1968–69; numerous lectureships; Nat. Science Foundation Sr Post-Doctoral Fellowship 1960–61; Alfred P. Sloan Fellowship 1960–63; Fulbright-Hays Sr Scholar 1971–72; Hon. Fellow Royal Soc. of Chem., Univ. Coll. Oxford 1995–; Hon. Visitor Nat. Science Council, Taiwan 1999; Hon. mem. Int. Soc. of Electrochem., Korean Chem. Soc., Int. Soc. for Theoretical Chemical Physics; Hon. DSc (Chicago) 1983, (Polytechnic Univ.) 1986, (Gothenburg) 1987, (McGill) 1988, (New Brunswick) 1993, (Queen's) 1993, (Oxford) 1995, (Yokohama Nat. Univ.) 1996, (Univ. of NC) 1996, (Univ. of Ill.) 1997, (Technion–Israel Inst. of Tech.) 1998, (Univ. Politécnica de Valencia, Spain) 1999, (Northwestern Univ.) 2000; Anne Molson Prize for Chem. 1943; Alexander von Humboldt Foundation Sr U.S. Scientist Award 1976, Irving Langmuir Award in Chem. Physics (American Chemical Soc.) 1978, R. A. Robinson Medal, Faraday Div., Royal Soc. of Chem. 1982, C. F. Chandler Medal (Univ. of Columbia) 1983, Wolf Prize 1985, Peter Debye Award in Physical Chem. (American Chemical Soc.) 1988, Willard Gibbs Medal (American Chemical Soc.) 1988, Centenary Medal, Faraday Div., Royal Soc. Chem. 1988, Nat. Medal of Science 1989, Theodore William Richards Medal (American Chem. Soc.) 1990, Evans Award (Ohio State Univ.) 1990, Edgar Fahs Smith Award, Remsen Award, Pauling Medal (all American Chemical Soc.) 1991, Nobel Prize for Chem. 1992, Hirschfelder Prize in Theoretical Chem. (Univ. of Wisconsin) 1993, American Acad. of Achievement Golden Plate Award 1993, Lavoisier Medal (Soc. Française de Chimie) 1994, Hon. Citizen of Winnipeg 1995, Auburn-Kosolapoff Award (American Chem. Soc.) 1996, Award in Theoretical Chem., Oesper Award (both American Chem. Soc.) 1997, Top 75 Award, Chemical and Eng News, American Chemical Soc. 1998, Key to City of Taipei, Taiwan 1999. *Publications:* numerous articles in scientific journals, especially Journal of Chemical Physics and Journal of Physical Chem. *Leisure interests:* music, history, tennis and skiing. *Address:* 331 South Hill Avenue, Pasadena, CA 91106, USA (Home); Noyes Laboratory, 127-72, California Institute of Technology, Pasadena, CA 91125. *Telephone:* (626) 395-6566 (Office). *Fax:* (626) 792-8485. *E-mail:* ram@caltech.edu (Office).

MARCUS, Ruth Barcan, PhD; American professor of philosophy; b. 2 Aug. 1921, New York; d. of Samuel Barcan and Rose Post; m. Jules A. Marcus 1942 (divorced 1976); two s. two d.; ed New York and Yale Univs.; Research Assoc. Inst. for Human Relations, Yale Univ. 1945–47; Assoc. Prof. Roosevelt Univ. 1959–64; Prof. and Chair. Dept of Philosophy, Univ. of Ill. 1964–70; Prof. Northwestern Univ. 1970–73; Reuben Post Halleck Prof. of Philosophy, Yale Univ. 1973–93, Sr Research Scholar 1994–; Visiting Distinguished Prof., Univ. of Calif., Irvine 1994—99; Adviser, Oxford Univ. Press New York 1980–90; Guggenheim Fellow 1953–54; NSF Fellow 1963–64; Fellow, Center for Advanced Studies, Stanford Univ. 1979, Inst. for Advanced Study in the Humanities, Univ. of Edin. 1983, Wolfson Coll. Oxford 1985, 1986, Clare Hall, Cambridge 1988 (Perm. mem. Common Room); Fellow, American Acad. of Arts and Sciences; mem. and Pres. Inst. int. de Philosophie, Paris 1990–93, Hon. Pres. 1993–; Chair. Nat. Bd of Officers, American Philosophical Asscn 1977–83; Pres. Asscn for Symbolic Logic 1983–86; Pres. Elizabethan Club 1988–90; mem. Council on Philosophical Studies (Pres. 1988–), Steering Cttee, Fed. Int. Soc. de Philosophie 1985–99 (Pres. 1990–93, Hon. Pres. 1994–); mem. numerous editorial bds.; Hon. DHumLitt (Ill.) 1995; Medal, Coll. de France 1986, Wilbur Cross Medal, Yale Univ. 2000. *Publications:* The Logical Enterprise (ed. with A. Anderson and R. Martin) 1975, Logic Methodology and Philosophy of Science (ed.) 1986, Modalities 1993, 1995; articles in professional journals. *Address:* Department of Philosophy, Box 208306, Yale University, New Haven, CT 06520, USA (Office). *Telephone:* (203) 432-1665 (Office). *Fax:* (203) 432-7950.

MÅRDH, Per-Anders, MD, PhD; Swedish university professor and physician; b. 9 April 1941, Stockholm; s. of Gustav-Adolf Mårdh and Inga-Greta (née Bodin) Mårdh; m. 1st Ingrid Ekstrand 1967; one s. one d.; m. 2nd Nina Ulvelius 1997; ed Univ. of Lund; Assoc. Prof. Univ. of Lund 1973; Dir WHO Collaboration Centre for Sexually Transmitted Diseases, Univ. of Lund 1980–85, then Uppsala Univ. 1985–; Prof. Clinical Bacteriology, Univ. of Uppsala 1984–; founder Scandinavian Asscn for Travel Medicine and Health 1990; mem. Bd Int. Tourist Health Org.; Fernström's Award for young prominent research workers 1982. *Publications:* as Ed.: Genital Infections and Their Complications 1975, Chlamydia trachomatis in Genital and Related Infections 1982, Chlamydial Infections 1982, International Perspectives on Neglected Sexually Transmitted Diseases 1983, Gas Chromatography/Mass Spectrometry in Applications in Microbiology 1984, Sexually Transmitted Diseases 1984, Bacterial Vaginosis 1984, Coagulase–negative Staphylococci 1986, Infections in Primary Health Care 1986, Genital Candida-infection 1990, Vaginitis/Vaginosis 1991, Travel and Migration Medicine 1997; Author: Chlamydia 1988, Swedish Red Houses 1991, Travel Well Travel Healthy 1992, Travel Medicine 1994. *Leisure interests:* art, skiing. *Address:* Centre for STD Research, Uppsala, University Box 552, 751 22 Uppsala, Sweden. *Telephone:* (18) 471-00-00.

MAREE, John B., BComm, AMP; South African business executive; b. 13 Aug. 1924, Middelburg, Cape; s. of Dr John Maree; m. Joy du Plessis 1950; one s.; ed Univ. of the Witwatersrand and Harvard Business School; Chair. Eskom Electricity Council 1985–97, Nedcor Group of Cos. 1990–97, Denel Ltd 1992–95, Powertech Ltd 1997; Dir Devt Bank of SA, Old Mutual; Fellow Inst. of Marketing Man. 1991–; Hon. DCom; Star of SA 1985; Order for Meritorious Service (Gold) 1989; one of top 5 Businessmen of the Year 1981; Chevalier, Légion d'honneur; Order of Cloud and Banner, People's Repub. of China. *Leisure interests:* golf, gardening. *Address:* 52 4th Road, Hyde Park, Sandton 2196, South Africa (Home). *Telephone:* (11) 881-4363 (Office); (11) 788-8812 (Home). *Fax:* (11) 881-4799.

MARES, Petr, PhD; Czech politician and academic; b. 15 Jan. 1953; m.; one d.; ed Charles Univ., Prague, Warsaw Univ., Poland; engineer Strojinvestav Eng Co. 1989–81; researcher Inst. of Czechoslovak History 1981–84; record keeper Dept of Archives, Gen. Trade Union 1987–88; researcher Dept of History and Theory of Film-Making, Czechoslovak Films Inst. 1988–90; Sec. Chair. of Political Sciences, Faculty of Social Sciences, Charles Univ. 1990, Vice-Dean for Study Affairs, Head Dept of American Studies Inst. of Int. Studies –1996; Fellow Univ. of Calgary, Canada 1996; Chair. Cttee for Science, Educ., Culture and Youth, Chamber of Deputies 1998–2002; Deputy Prime Minister of the Czech Repub. 2002–. *Publications include:* History of the Lands of the Czech Crown: Part II (co-author) 1992, United States Presidents 1994, History and NATO (co-author) 1997; many articles in professional journals. *Address:* Office of the Government, nábř. E. Beneše 4, 118 01 Prague 1, Czech Republic (Office).

MARGELOV, Mikhail Vitalyevich; Russian politician; b. 22 Dec. 1964, Moscow; m.; one s.; trans. Int. Dept, CPSU Cen. Cttee 1984–86; Arabic teacher Higher KGB School 1986–89; Chief Ed. Arab Dept, ITAR-TASS 1989–90; with consulting cos World Resources, Boston Consulting Group, Ban & Co. 1990–95; with Video Int. 1995–; co-ordinator Boris Yeltsin Presidential election campaign; First Deputy Head Dept of Man., Russian Presidium 1996–97, Head of Dept of Public Relations 1997–98; Head of Advisory Group to the Chair., State Customs Cttee 1998; Head of Political Advisory Group, Novosti Information Agency 1999; Head of Russian Information Centre 1999–2000; Rep. for Pskov region, Russian Fed. Ass. 2000–, mem. Council of Feds, Chair. Int. Affairs Cttee 2001–. *Address:* Nekrasov str. 23, Office 241, 180001 Pskov (Office); Council of Federations, Bolshaya Dmitrovka str. 26, Moscow, Russia (Office). *Telephone:* (88112) 16-08-31 (Office); (095) 292-13-58 (Office).

MARGÉOT, HE Cardinal Jean, PhL, STL; Mauritian ecclesiastic; b. 3 Feb. 1916, Quatre-Bornes; s. of Joseph Margéot and Marie Harel; ed Séminaire Français, Rome, Pontifical Gregorian Univ.; ordained 1938, elected Bishop of Port-Louis 1969, consecrated 1969; cr. HE Cardinal 1988; Grand Officer Order of the Star and Key 1997. *Address:* Bonne Terre, Vacoas, Mauritius. *Telephone:* 424-5716. *Fax:* 426-5190. *E-mail:* jmargeot@bow.intnet.mu (Office).

MARGOLIASH, Emanuel, MD; American biochemist; b. 10 Feb. 1920, Cairo, Egypt; s. of Wolf Margoliash and Bertha Margoliash (née Kotler); m. Sima Beshkin 1944; two s.; ed Mission Laïque Française, Cairo, American Univ. of Beirut, Lebanon; Research Fellow, Dept of Experimental Pathology, Hebrew Univ., Jerusalem 1945–48; served as Medical Officer in the Israel Army 1948–49; Sr Asst in Experimental Pathology, Cancer Research Labs., Hadassah Medical School, Hebrew Univ., Jerusalem 1951; worked under Prof. D. Keilin, Molteno Inst., Univ. of Cambridge, England 1951–53; Acting Head, Cancer Research Labs., Hadassah Medical School, Hebrew Univ., Jerusalem 1954–58, Lecturer in Experimental Pathology, 1955; worked at Nobel Inst., Dept of Biochem. under a fellowship of the Dazian Foundation for Medical Research 1958; Research Assoc., Dept of Biochem., Univ. of Utah Coll. of Medicine, Salt Lake City, Utah, USA 1958–60; Research Assoc., McGill-Montreal Gen. Hospital Research Inst., Montreal, Canada 1960–62; Research Fellow and Head, Protein Section, Dept of Molecular Biology, Abbott Labs., North Chicago, Ill. 1962–71; Professorial Lecturer, Dept of Biochem., Univ. of Chicago, Ill. 1964–71; Prof. of Biochem. and Molecular Biology, Northwestern Univ., Evanston, Ill. 1971–90, Chair. Dept of Biochem., Molecular Biology and Cell Biology 1979–82, Owen L. Coon Prof. of Molecular Biology 1988–90, Prof. Emer. 1990–; Prof., Lab. of Molecular Biology, Dept of Biological Sciences, Univ. of Ill., at Chicago 1989–, Co-ordinator 1989–93; mem. Nat. Acad. of Sciences and numerous scientific socs.; Fellow, American Acad. of Arts and Sciences, American Acad. of Microbiology; mem. Editorial Bd of Journal of Biological Chem. 1966–72, Biochemical Genetics 1966–80, Journal of Molecular Evolution 1971–82, Biochem. and Molecular Biology Int. 1981–99; mem. Int. Union of Biochem. Cttee on Nomenclature 1962–, Advisory Cttee, Mich. State Univ. Atomic Energy Comm. Plant Research Lab. 1967–72; Co-Chair. Gordon Research Conf. on Proteins 1967; Keilin Memorial Lectureship of the Biochemical Soc. 1970; Harvey Soc. Lectureship 1970–71; mem. Publs Cttee, American Soc. of Biological Chemists Inc. 1973–76; mem. of Exec. Cttee of U.S. Bioenergetics Group of the Biophysical Soc. 1980–; Rudi Lemberg Fellow, Australian Acad. of Science 1981; Guggenheim Fellow 1983. *Publications:* more than 275 scientific papers and volumes. *Address:* Department of Biological Sciences, (M/C 066), The University of Illinois at Chicago, 845 W Taylor Street, Chicago, IL 60607-7060, USA. *Telephone:* (312) 996-8268. *Fax:* (312) 996-2805.

MARGRAVE, John, BS, PhD; American professor of chemistry; b. 13 April 1924, Kansas City; s. of Orville Frank Margrave and Bernice J. Hamilton Margrave; m. Mary Lou Davis 1950; one s. one d.; ed Univ. of Kansas, Lawrence; AEC Postdoctoral Fellow, Univ. of Calif., Berkeley 1951–52; Instructor, Assoc. Prof. then Prof. of Chem., Univ. of Wis. 1952–63; Prof. of Chem., Rice Univ. 1963–, Chair. Dept of Chem. 1967–72, E. D. Butcher Prof. 1986–, Dean of Advanced Studies and Research, Rice Univ. 1972–80, Vice-Pres. 1980–86; consultant to Govt agencies and pvt. industry; Pres. MarChem Inc. 1970–, High Temperature Science Inc. 1976–; Vice-Pres. for Research, Houston Area Research Center (HARC) 1986–89, Chief Scientific Officer 1989–2002; Dir Materials Science Research Center 1986–94; Chair. Cttee on Chemical Processes in Severe Nuclear Accidents, Nat. Research Council 1987–88; Chair. Cttee on Remediation of Molten Salt Reactor, Nat. Research Council 1996–97; Lecturer Ohio Areospace Inst. 1999; Dir Woodlands Science and Art Center 1999–; Fellow AAAS, American Physical Soc.; mem. Chemical Soc. (UK) and other socs.; Fellow American Inst. of Chemists; mem. NAS; Alfred P. Sloan Research Fellow 1956–57, 1957–58; Guggenheim Research Fellow 1961; mem. numerous advisory cttees. and editorial bds.; numerous awards include American Chemical Soc. Award in Inorganic Chem. 1967, Award in Fluorine Chem. 1980, Distinguished Alumnus Award 1981, two IR-100 Awards, Chemical Pioneer Award American Inst. of Chemists 2002. *Publications:* over 700 scientific pubs, including 4 books and 19 patents; in 2000–02 over 20 publs on nanotechnology. *Leisure interests:* stamp collecting, music, gardening. *Address:* Rice University, PO Box 1892, 6100 South Main, Houston, TX 77005 (Office); 4511 Verone, Bellaire, TX 77401, USA, USA (Home). *Telephone:* (713) 348-4813 (Office); (713) 667-9887 (Home). *Fax:* (713) 523-8236 (Office). *E-mail:* margrav@rice.edu (Office).

MARGRETHE II, HM, Queen of Denmark; b. 16 April 1940; d. of the late King Frederik IX and Queen Ingrid; m. Count Henri de Laborde de Monpezat (now Prince Henrik of Denmark) 1967; two s.; ed Univs of Copenhagen, Aarhus and Cambridge, Sorbonne, Paris and London School of Econs; succeeded to the throne 14 Jan. 1972; has undertaken many official visits abroad with her husband, travelling extensively in Europe, the Far East, North and South America; Hon. KG 1979, Hon. Freedom of City of London 2000, Hon. Bencher of the Middle Temple 1992; Hon. Fellow Lucy Cavendish Coll. Cambridge 1989, Girton Coll. Cambridge 1992; Hon. LLD (Cambridge) 1975; Dr hc (London) 1980, (Univ. of Iceland) 1986, (Oxford) 1992, (Edin.) 2000; Medal of the Headmastership, Univ. of Paris 1987. *Achievements (miscellaneous):* illustrated J. R. R. Tolkien's Lord of the Rings (1977), Historierne om Regnar Lodbrog, Norse Legends as told by Jorgen Stegelmann (1979), Bjarkemaal (1982), Poul Oerum's Comedy in Florens (1990) and Cantabile poems by HRH the Prince Consort (2000), designed costumes for TV Theatre's The Shepherdess and the Chimney-sweep (1987), scenography and costumes for the ballet A Folk Tale, Royal Theatre (1991), découpages for TV film about the Hans Christian Andersen fairy tale Snedronningen (1999–2000), scenography and costumes for Tivoli pantomime ballet Kaerlighed i Skarnkassen (2001), illustrations for Karen Blixen's Seven Gothic Tales (2002). *Art exhibitions include:* Exhbn of sketches and finished works at Køge Art Gallery Sketch Collection (1988), The Glass Museum, Ebeltoft (1988), Millesgården, Stockholm (1989), Blåfarveværket, Norway (1991), Baron Boltens Gård, Copenhagen (1991), Gammel Holtegaard (1993), Herning Art Gallery (1993), Exhbns paintings and church textiles in Aarhus Museum of Art, in Marienlyst Palace and The Danish Library in Flensburg, Germany, of church textiles in Reykjavik, Iceland (1998) of paintings and lithographs in Gallery J.M.S., Oslo (1999), of paintings at Sofiero Sweden (2002), of découpages used as illustrations in new edn of Seven Gothic Tales at Karen Blixen Museum Rungstedlund (2002), of paintings and ecclesiastical textiles at Didrichsen Art Museum Helsinki 2002. *Publications:* (Trans.) All Men are Mortal (with HRH the Prince Consort) 1981, The Valley 1988, The Fields 1989, The Forest (trans.) 1989. *Address:* Amalienborg, 1257 Copenhagen K; PO Box 2143, DK-1015 Copenhagen K, Denmark. *E-mail:* hofmarskallatet@kongehuset.dk (Office). *Website:* www.kongehuset.dk (Office).

MARGULIS, Lynn, PhD; American biologist; b. 5 March 1938, Chicago; d. of Morris and Leone Wise Alexander; m. 1st Carl Sagan 1957; m. 2nd T. N. Margulis 1967; three s. one d.; ed Univs of Chicago, Wisconsin and Calif. at Berkeley; Research Assoc. Dept of Biology, Brandeis Univ. 1963–64, Lecturer 1963–65, Biology Co-ordinator, Peace Corps, Colombia Project 1965–66; Consultant and Staff mem. The Elementary Science Study, Educational Services 1963–67; Adjunct Asst Prof. Dept of Biology, Boston Univ. 1966–67, Asst Prof. 1967–71, Assoc. Prof. 1971–77, Prof. 1977–88, Univ. Prof. 1986–88; Distinguished Prof. Univ. of Mass., Amherst 1988–99; Visiting Prof. Dept of Marine Biology, Scripps Inst. of Oceanography Jan.–March 1980, Dept of Geology and Planetary Science Calif. Inst. of Tech. 1980, Dept of Microbiology, Universidad Autónoma de Barcelona, Spain 1986; NASA-Ames Planetary Biology and Microbial Ecology Summer Research Programme 1980, 1982, 1984; Guggenheim Foundation Fellow 1979; Sherman Fairchild Distinguished Scholar, Calif. Inst. of Tech. 1977; mem. NAS; Fellow AAAS; NASA Public Service Award 1981, Nat. Medal of Service 1999. *Publications:* Origin of Eukaryotic Cells 1970, Origins of Life I (Ed.) 1970, Origins of Life II (Ed.) 1971, Origins of Life: Planetary Astronomy (Ed.) 1973, Origins of Life: Chemistry and Radioastronomy (Ed.) 1973, Limits of Life (Ed. with C. Ponnamperuma) 1980, Symbiosis in Cell Evolution 1981, Early Life 1982, Five Kingdoms: An Illustrated Guide to the Phyla of Life on Earth (with K. V. Schwartz) 1982, Origins of Sex (with D. Sagan) 1986, Microcosmos: Four billion years of evolution from our bacterial ancestors (with D. Sagan) 1986, 1991, Garden of Microbial Delights 1988, Biospheres From Earth to Space (with D. Sagan) 1988, Global Ecology (with René Fester) 1989, Handbook Protoctista (Ed.) 1990, Mystery Dance (with D. Sagan) 1991, Symbiosis as a Source of Evolutionary Innovation: Speciation and Morphogenesis (Ed. with R. Fester) 1991, Environmental Evolution: the Effect of the Origin and Evolution of Life on Planet Earth (Ed. with L. Olendzenski) 1992, Concepts of Symbiogenesis (Ed.) 1992, Diversity of Life: The Five Kingdoms 1992, Symbiosis in Cell Evolution: Microbial Communities in the Archean and Proterozoic Eons 1993, Illustrated Glossary of the Protoctista (with H. McKhann and L. Olendzenski) 1993, The Illustrated Five Kingdoms. A Guide to the Diversity of Life on Earth (with K. V. Schwartz and M. Dolan) 1993, What is Life? (with D. Sagan) 1995, Slanted Truths (with D. Sagan) 1997, What Is Sex? (with D. Sagan) 1998. *Leisure interests:* fiction, Spain, pre-Columbian Mexican culture. *Address:* Department of Geosciences, Morrill Science Center, University of Massachusetts, Amherst, MA 01003, USA. *Telephone:* (413) 545-3244. *Fax:* (413) 545-1200.

MARIAM, Lt-Col Mengistu Haile; Ethiopian politician and army officer; b. 26 May 1937, Addis Ababa; m. Wubanchi Bishaw 1968; one s. two d.; ed Holeta Mil. Acad.; served in Army's Third Div., attaining rank of Maj.; mem. Armed Forces Co-ordinating Cttee (Derg) June 1974–; took leading part in overthrow of Emperor Haile Selassie Sept. 1974, Head of Derg Exec. Cttee Nov. 1974; First Vice-Chair. Provisional Mil. Admin. Council (PMAC) 1974–77, Chair. (Head of State) 1977–91; Pres. of Democratic Repub. of Ethiopia 1987–91 (overthrown in coup); Chair. PMAC Standing Cttee; Chair. Council of Ministers 1976–91, OAU 1983–84; Sec.-Gen. Workers' Party of Ethiopia 1984–91; accused of genocide in absentia; now living in Zimbabwe as political refugee. *Leisure interests:* swimming, tennis, chess, reading, watching films. *Address:* PO Box 1536, Gunhill Enclave, Harare, Zimbabwe. *Telephone:* 745254.

MARIANI, Carlo Maria; Italian artist; b. 25 July 1935, Rome; s. of Anastasio Mariani and Anita de Angelis; m. 1st B. Brantsen 1959 (divorced 1983); m. 2nd Carol Lane 1990; one s. one d.; ed Acad. of Fine Arts, Rome; lives and works in Rome and New York; participated in Documenta 7, Kassel 1982, Venice Biennale 1982, 1984, 1990, Sydney Biennial 1986 and numerous other group exhbns. in USA, Canada, UK, USSR, Europe and S. America; Fetrinelli Prize, Accademia dei Lincei 1998. *Solo exhibitions include:* Galerie Paul Maenz, Cologne 1977, Sperone Westwater Fischer, New York 1981, Sperone Westwater, New York 1984, 1987, Galerie Séroussi, Paris 1985, Galerie Tanit, Munich 1986, Michael Kohn Gallery, LA 1988, 1992, Studio d'Arte Cannaviello, Milan 1988, Drammen Kunstforening, Norway 1990, Hirschl & Adler Modern, New York 1990, 1993, Mathildenhöhe, Darmstadt 1991–92, LA Co.

Museum of Art 1992, Premio Marche, Ancona, Frye Museum 1999, Rupertinum, Salzburg 2000, Katonah Museum, New York, Ostend Museum of Modern Art 2001.

MARIÁTEGUI CHIAPPE, Sandro; Peruvian politician; b. 5 Dec. 1922; s. of José Carlos Mariátegui; m. Matilde de Zela; one d.; Deputy for Lima 1963–68; Minister of Finance and Trade 1965–67; Founder Acción Popular (AP) Party, Sec.-Gen. 1985–87; Senator 1980–; Pres. of Senate 1982–83; Prime Minister and Minister of Foreign Affairs April–Oct. 1984. *Address:* Av. Ramírez Gaston 375, Miraflores, Lima, Peru.

MARIE, Aurelius John Baptiste Lamothe, MBE; Dominican politician and lawyer; b. 23 Dec. 1904, Portsmouth, Dominica; s. of Bright Percival Marie and Lily Marie; m. Bernadette Dubois 1964; fmr magistrate; Pres. of Dominica 1980–83. *Leisure interests:* gardening, reading, hiking. *Address:* Zicack, Portsmouth, Dominica.

MARIN, Maguy; French choreographer and artistic director; b. 2 June 1951, Toulouse; s. of Antonio Marin and Luisa Calle; ed Conservatoire de Toulouse; joined Maurice Béjart's Ballet du XXème siècle; joined Ballet Théâtre de l'Arche (subsequently Compagnie Maguy Marin) 1979; Grand Prix Nat. de la chorégraphie 1983; Chevalier, Ordre des Arts et des Lettres. *Choreographic works include:* May B 1981, Babel Babel 1982, Jaleo 1983, Hymen 1984, Calambre 1985, Cinderella 1985, Eden 1986, Leçons de Ténèbres 1987, Coups d'états 1988, Groosland 1989, Cortex 1991, Made in France 1992, Ay Dios 1993, Waterzooï 1993, Ramdam 1995, Aujourd'hui peut-être 1996, Pour ainsi dire 1999, Quoi qu'il en soit 1999. *Address:* Compagnie Maguy Marin, Centre Chorégraphique National de Rillieux-la-Pape, 10 boulevard de Lattre de Tassigny, B.P 106, 69143 Rillieux-la-Pape Cedex, France . *Telephone:* (4) 72-01-12-30. *Fax:* (4) 72-01-12-31. *E-mail:* compagnie-maguy@marin.fr (Office). *Website:* www.compagnie-maguymarin.fr (Office).

MARIN GONZALEZ, Manuel, MA; Spanish international official; b. 21 Oct. 1949, Ciudad Real; m. Carmen Ortiz; two c.; ed Madrid Univ., Coll. of Europe, Bruges and Univ. of Nancy; joined Spanish Socialist Party 1975; MP for Ciudad Real, La Mancha 1977–; Sec. of State for Relations with the EEC 1982–85; EEC (now European Commission) Commr for Social Affairs, Employment, Educ. and Training 1986–89, for Co-operation and Devt 1989–94, for External Relations with the Mediterranean (South), Near and Middle East, Latin America and Asia (except Japan, People's Repub. of China, Repub. of Korea, Hong Kong, Macao, Taiwan) 1995–99, Vice-Pres. of Comm. 1993–99; Pres. (acting) 1999; Spokesman, Foreign Affairs Cttee., Congress 2001–; Grand Cross, Order of Isabel la Católica.

MARININA, Col. Aleksandra Borisovna (pseudonym of Marina Anatolyevna Alekseyeva), PhD; Russian writer and fmr criminologist; b. 16 June 1957, Lviv, Ukraine; m. Col Sergey Zatochny; ed Moscow State Univ.; fmr mem. of staff Acad. of Internal Affairs; began writing detective stories 1991–; mem. of staff Moscow Inst. of Justice, Ministry of Internal Affairs 1994–97. *Films for TV:* Kamenskaya (48 episodes). *Publications:* Death and Some Love, Ghost of Music, Stolen Dream, I Died Yesterday, Men's Game, Forced Murderer, Black List, Requiem, When Gods Laugh, He who knows (Vols 1-2) and numerous others. *Address:* COP Literary Agency, Zhukovskogo str. 4, Apt. 29, 103062 Moscow (Office); Verhnaya Krasnoselskaya str. 9, Apt. 44, 107140 Moscow, Russia (Home). *Telephone:* (095) 928-84-56 (Office); (095) 975-45-35 (Home). *Fax:* (095) 928-84-56 (Office). *E-mail:* alexandra@marinina.ru (Office). *Website:* marinina.ru (Home).

MARINO, Dan; American football player; b. 15 Sept. 1961, Pittsburgh; s. of Daniel Marino and Veronica Marino; m. Claire Marino; three s. two d. (one adopted); ed Cen. Catholic High School, Univ. of Pittsburgh; quarter-back for the Miami Dolphins (Nat. Football League–NFL) 1983–1999; retd 2000; career totals include 420 touchdown passes, 4,967 completed passes; records include most yards gained through passing in a career (61,631), in a season (5,084 in 1984); f. Dan Marino Foundation; business enterprises include Dan Marino's Town Tavern restaurant; Dir Business Devt, Dreams Inc. 2000–; host on HBO's weekly football programme 'Inside the NFL'; 16-time winner of AFC Offensive Player of the Week; NFL Man of the Year award 1998; College Football Hall of Fame 2002. *Publication:* Marino–On the Record. *Address:* 1304 SW 160th Avenue, Suite 113, Sunrise, FL 33326, USA. *Website:* www.danmarino.com (Office).

MARINOS, Yannis, BA; Greek journalist; b. 20 July 1930, Hermoupolis; ed Univ. of Athens; journalist, To Vima (daily) 1953–65; journalist, Economicos Tachydromos, Ed.-in-Chief 1956, Ed. and Dir 1964–96, consultant/columnist 1996–; political commentator in Ta Nea (daily) 1972–75; columnist, To Vima (daily political journal) 1992–; commentator for many radio and TV stations in Greece; mem. European Parl. 1999–; Deputy Nea Democratia and European Popular Party 1999–; mem. Bd Lambrakis Research Foundation, Org. of Music Hall of Athens; Hon. PhD (Aristotelian Univ. Salonika) 1999; more than 30 awards including Best European Journalist of 1989 (EC Comm. and Asscn of European Journalists) and awards from UN and Athens Acad. *Publications:* The Palestinian Problem and Cyprus 1975, For a Change Towards Better 1983, Greece in Crisis 1987, Common Sense 1993. *Leisure interests:* literature, history, classical music, fishing. *Address:* 9 Merlin Street, Athens 106 71 (Office); 2 Kontziadon Street, Piraeus 185 37, Greece (Home). *Telephone:* (210) 3641828 (Office); (210) 4526823 (Home). *Fax:* (210) 3641839. *E-mail:* jmarinos@dolnet.gr (Office).

MARIO, Ernest, PhD; American company director and pharmacist; b. 12 June 1938, Clifton, NJ; s. of Jerry Mario and Edith Mario; m. Mildred Martha Daume 1961; three s.; ed Rutgers Coll. of Pharmacy, New Brunswick, NJ, Univ. of Rhode Island; Vice-Pres. Mfg Operations, Smith Kline 1974–77; joined E. R. Squibb & Sons 1977, Vice Pres. Mfg for U.S. Pharmaceuticals Div. 1977–79, Vice-Pres. Gen. Man., Chemical Div. 1979–81, Pres. Chemical Eng Div. and Sr Vice-Pres. 1981–83, Pres. and CEO Squibb Medical Products 1983–86, mem. Bd 1984–85; Pres. Glaxo Inc. 1986–89, Chair. 1989–91, apptd. to Bd of Glaxo Holdings PLC 1988, Chief Exec. 1989–93, Deputy Chair. 1992–93; Co-Chair. CEO ALZA Corpn 1993–97, Chair., CEO 1997–2001; Chair. American Foundation for Pharmaceutical Educ.; Trustee Duke Univ., Rockefeller Univ., Univ. of RI Foundation. *Leisure interests:* golf, swimming. *Address:* 25 Haslet Avenue, Princeton, NJ 08540, USA (Home).

MARION, Jean-Luc; French professor of metaphysics; b. 3 July 1946, Meudon; s. of late Jean E. Marion and of Suzanne Roussey; m. Corinne Nicolas 1970; two s.; ed Lycée Int. de Sèvres, Ecole Normale Supérieure, Ulm and Univ. of Paris, Sorbonne; Asst Prof., Univ. of Paris, Sorbonne 1973–81, Prof. 1995–; Dir Ecole Doctorale V 1998–; Prof. Univ. of Poitiers 1981–88; Prof. Univ. of Paris X (Nanterre) 1988–95; Ed.-in-Chief, Communio (review), Paris 1975–85; Dir Epiméthée, Presses Universitaires de France, Paris 1981–; John Nureen Prof. Univ. of Chicago 1992–; Titular, HE Cardinal Mercier Chair. Catholic Univ., Leuven 1987; Prix Charles Lambert, Acad. des Sciences Morales et Politiques 1978; Grand Prix de Philosophie, Acad. Française 1992. *Publications:* Sur l'ontologie grise de Descartes 1975, L'idole et la distance 1977, Sur la théologie blanche de Descartes 1981, Dieu sans l'être 1982, Sur le prisme métaphysique de Descartes 1986, Réduction et Donation 1989, La croisée du visible 1991, Questions cartésiennes 1991, Questions cartésiennes II 1996, Hergé. Tintin le terrible 1996, Etant donné 1997, De surcroît 2001, Le phénomène érotique 2003. *Address:* Université de Paris Sorbonne, I rue Victor Cousin, 75005 Paris, France (Office); University of Chicago, 5801 South Ellis Avenue, Chicago, IL 60637, USA. *Telephone:* 1-40-46-26-83.

MARJANOVIĆ, Mirko; Serbia and Montenegro (Serbian) politician and economist; b. 27 July 1937, Knin, Croatia; s. of Disan Marjanović and Marija Marjanović; m. Borjana Marjanović, one s. one d.; ed Belgrade Univ.; Man., Deputy Gen. Dir TVIK 1970–72; Dir Rep. in Moscow 1973–77; Dir Chelik Co. 1977–79; Gen. Dir, Foreign Trade Co. Progres 1979–94; Prime Minister of Repub. of Serbia 1993–2001. *Address:* c/o Vlada Republike Srbije, Nemanjiná 11, 11000 Belgrade, Serbia and Montenegro.

MARJORIBANKS, Kevin, BSc, MA, PhD, F.A.S.S.A., FACE, FRSS; Australian academic; b. 25 July 1940, Sydney; s. of Hugh Marjoribanks and Irene Marjoribanks; m. Janice Lily 1962; one s. one d.; ed Univ. of NSW, Univ. of New England, Harvard Univ., USA, Univ. of Toronto, Canada; Teaching Fellow Harvard Univ. 1967–69; Asst Prof. Univ. of Toronto 1969–70; lecturer in Sociology, Univ. of Oxford 1970–75; Prof. of Educ. Univ. of Adelaide 1974–, Pro-Vice-Chancellor 1986–87, Vice-Chancellor 1987–93, Head Grad. School of Educ. 1996–; Visiting Prof., Oxford Univ. 1994–95. *Publications:* Environments for Learning 1974, Families and Their Learning Environments 1979, Ethnic Families and Children's Achievements 1980, The Foundations of Students' Learning 1991, Families, Schools and Children's Learning 1994, Australian Education 1999, Family and School Capital 2002. *Leisure interests:* writing, music, reading. *Address:* University of Adelaide, Adelaide (Office); 81 Molesworth Street, North Adelaide, SA 5006, Australia (Home). *Telephone:* (8) 8303-3784 (Office); (8) 8267-5613 (Home). *Fax:* (8) 8303-3604 (Office). *E-mail:* kevin.marjoribanks@adelaide.edu.au (Office).

MARK, Alan Francis, DCNZM, CBE, PhD, FRSNZ; New Zealand professor of botany; b. 19 June 1932, Dunedin; s. of Cyril L. Mark and Frances E. Marshall; m. Patricia K. Davie 1957; two s. two d.; ed Mosgiel District High School, Univ. of Otago and Duke Univ., N. Carolina; Otago Catchment Bd, Dunedin 1959–61; Sr Research Fellow, Hellaby Indigenous Grasslands Research Trust 1961–65, Adviser in Research 1965–2000; Chair. Bd. of Govs 2000–; Lecturer, Univ. of Otago 1960, Sr Lecturer 1966, Assoc. Prof. 1969, Prof. of Botany 1975–98, Prof. Emer. 1998–; Visiting Asst Prof. Duke Univ. 1966; Fulbright Travel Award 1955; James B. Duke Fellowship 1957; Hon. mem. NZ Alpine Club 2002; Loder Cup 1975, NZ 1990 Commemoration Medal, The Inaugural Awards of NZ (Conservation/Environment) 1994, Hutton Medal (Botanical/Conservation Research), Royal Soc. of NZ 1997. *Publications:* New Zealand Alpine Plants (with N. M. Adams) 1973; about 150 scientific papers. *Leisure interests:* nature conservation, enjoying the outdoors. *Address:* Department of Botany, University of Otago, Box 56, Dunedin (Office); 205 Wakari Road, Helensburgh, Dunedin, New Zealand (Home). *Telephone:* (3) 479-75-73 (Office); (3) 476-32-29 (Home). *Fax:* (3) 479-75-83. *E-mail:* amark@otago.ac.nz (Office).

MARK, Reuben, AB, MBA; American business executive; b. 21 Jan. 1939, Jersey City, NJ; s. of Edward Mark and Libbie (née Berman) Mark; m. Arlene Slobzian 1964; two s. one d.; ed Middlebury Coll. and Harvard Univ.; with Colgate-Palmolive Co., New York 1963–, Pres., Gen. Man. Venezuela 1972–73, Canada 1973–74, Vice-Pres., Gen. Man. Far East Div. 1974–75, Household Products Div. 1975–79, Group Vice-Pres. Domestic Operations 1979–81, Exec. Vice-Pres. 1981–83, COO 1983–84, Pres. 1983–86, CEO 1984–, Chair. 1986–; lecturer in Business Admin., Univ. of Conn. 1977; mem. Bd of Dirs. Soap and Detergent Asscn. *Address:* Colgate-Palmolive Co., 300 Park Avenue, New York, NY 10022, USA.

MARK, Sir Robert, Kt, GBE, MA; British fmr police official; b. 13 March 1917, Manchester; s. of the late John and Louisa Hobson Mark; m. Kathleen Mary Leahy 1941 (died 1997); one s. one d.; ed William Hulme's Grammar School, Manchester; Constable to Chief Supt. Manchester Police 1937–42, 1947–56; Chief Constable of Leicester 1957–67; Asst Commr, Metropolitan Police (London) 1967–68, Deputy Commr 1968–72, Commr 1972–77; Royal Armoured Corps 1942–47, Lt Phantom (GHQ Liaison Regt) NW Europe 1944–45, Maj. Control Comm. for Germany 1945–47; mem. Standing Advisory Council on Penal System 1966; Assessor to Lord Mountbatten's Inquiry into Prison Security 1966; mem. Advisory Cttee on Police in N Ireland 1969; Dir Automobile Asscn 1977–87, Control Risks Ltd 1981–87; Visiting Fellow Nuffield Coll., Oxford 1970–78; Lecture tour of N America for World Affairs Council and FCO Oct. 1971; Dimbleby Memorial Lecturer, BBC TV 1973; KStJ; Hon. Freeman City of Westminster 1977; Hon. LLM (Leicester) 1966, Hon. DLitt (Loughborough) 1976, Hon. LLD (Liverpool) 1978, (Manchester) 1978; Queen's Police Medal 1965. *Publications:* numerous articles in the national press and in legal and police journals; Edwin Stevens Lecture to the Laity at the Royal Society of Medicine 1972, Policing a Perplexed Society 1977, In the Office of Constable (autobiog.) 1978. *Address:* Esher, Surrey, KT10 8LU, England.

MARKARYAN, Andranik Naapetovich; Armenian politician and cybernetician; b. 12 June 1951, Yerevan; m.; three c.; ed Yerevan State Polytechnic Inst.; engineer research inst. of Yerevan –1990; political activities 1965–; mem. underground Nat. United Party 1968; imprisoned for 2 years for political activities 1974; mem. Repub. Party of Armenia 1992–, Chair. 1999–; Deputy Nat. Ass. of Armenia 1995– (Head Parl. block Yedinstvo); Prime Minister of Armenia 2000–. *Address:* Office of the Prime Minister, Government House, Parliament Square 1, 375010 Yerevan, Armenia (Office). *Telephone:* (2) 52-02-04 (Office). *Fax:* (2) 52-03-60 (Office).

MARKHAM, Kenneth Ronald, PhD, FRSNZ, F.N.Z.I.C.; New Zealand research chemist; b. 19 June 1937, Christchurch; s. of Harold W. Markham and Alicia B. Markham; m. E. P. Eddy 1966; two d.; ed Victoria Univ. of Wellington, Melbourne Univ.; Tech. Trainee, Dominion Lab., Wellington 1955–62; Scientist Chem. Div., DSIR, Lower Hutt 1962–65; Post-Doctoral Fellow, Botany Dept, Univ. of Texas 1965–66, Asst Prof. 1967; Scientist, Organic Chem. Section, Chem. Div., DSIR 1968–75, Section Leader, Natural Products Section 1976–92, Group Leader Chem. Div. 1980–87; Plant Chem. Team Man. Distinguished Scientist, Industrial Research Ltd 1992–; Monsanto Chemicals Research Fellow 1960; Sr Research Fellow (Chem. Div. DSIR) 1987; Hon. Research Assoc., Biological Sciences, Vic. Univ. of Wellington 1998–; mem. Ed. Advisory Bd int. journal Phytochemical Analysis 1990–, Int. Journal of Flavonoid Research 1998–; Int. Corresp., Groupe Polyphenols 1992–; Easterfield Award (Royal Inst. of Chem.) 1971, NZ Govt Ministerial Award for Excellence in Science 1990, Science and Tech. Medal, Royal Soc. of NZ 1997, Pergamon Phytochemistry Prize 1999. *Publications:* The Systematic Identification of Flavonoids (with Mabry and Thomas) 1970, Techniques of Flavonoid Chemistry 1982; 17 invited chapters on flavonoids and spectroscopy, 237 scientific papers on phytochem. and its interpretation in int. journals 1960–; one patent on UV screens. *Leisure interests:* philately, swimming, stock market, photography, table tennis, world news, petanque. *Address:* Industrial Research Ltd (IRL), PO Box 31310, Lower Hutt (Office); 160 Raumati Road, Paraparaumu, New Zealand (Home). *Telephone:* 569-0577 (Office); 905-5285 (Home). *Fax:* (4) 569-0055 (Office). *E-mail:* k.markham@irl.cri.nz (Office); k.markham@xtra.co.nz (Home).

MARKHAM, Richard J.; American business executive; b. 26 Sept. 1950, Hornell, New York; ed Purdue Univ. School of Pharmacy; Dist Man. Merck Sharp & Dohme Div., Merck & Co. Inc., served successively as Product Man., Sr Product Man., Dir of Market Planning 1973–86, Exec. Dir of Marketing Planning 1986–87, Vice-Pres. of Marketing 1987–89, Vice-Pres. Merck Sharp & Dohme Int. 1989–91, Sr Vice-Pres. Merck & Co. 1993; mem. Bd Dirs Marion Merrell Dow Inc. 1993, Pres. and COO 1993–95; COO Hoechst Marion Roussel 1995–97, CEO 1997–99; CEO Aventis Pharma 1999–2002, Chair. Man. Bd Aventis Pharma AG 1999–2002, Vice-Chair. 2002–, COO 2002–; mem. Bd Dirs Pharmaceutical Research and Mfrs Asscn; mem. Bd Trustees Health Care Inst., NJ. *Address:* Espace Européen de l'Entreprise, 16 avenue de l'Europe, 67300 Schiltigheim, France (Office). *Telephone:* 3-88-99-11-14 (Office). *Fax:* 3-88-99-11-13 (Office). *E-mail:* carsten.tilger@aventis.com (Office). *Website:* www.aventis.com (Office).

MARKOPOULOS, Christos, DSc; Greek politician and nuclear chemist; b. 25 Dec. 1925, Athens; s. of Antony Markopoulos and Paraskevi Vergopoulou; m. 1st Sapfo Mazaraki 1954 (divorced 1960); one s.; m. 2nd Kleopatra Papadopoulou 1974; two s.; ed Varvakios High School, Teachers' Acad., Athens, Univ. of Athens, Leicester Coll. of Tech., UK; Nat. State Chem. Lab. 1956–59; Group Leader, Greek Atomic Energy Comm. 1962–69, Dir Radioimmunochem. 1977–81; Asst Prof., Nat. Tech. Univ. of Athens 1965; Sr Researcher, Imperial Coll., London 1968; Visiting Scientist, Tech. Hochschule, Darmstadt, FRG; Visiting Prof., Univ. of Bologna 1973; Pres. Hellenic Nuclear Soc. 1975–81; mem. Steering Cttee, European Nuclear Soc. 1979–81; mem. Cen. Cttee, Panhellenic Socialistic Movement (PASOK) 1975–93; mem. European Parl. 1981–84 (mem. Energy, Research and Tech. Comm.); Amb.-at-Large for West European Countries 1984–85; mem. Nat. Parl. of Greece 1985–89 (Pres. Foreign Affairs Cttee 1986–87); Head of Greek Parl. Del. in Council of Europe 1986–88 (Vice-Pres. Parl. Ass. 1987–88); Minister in charge of Int. Orgs. 1988–89; Pres. Panhellenic Movt for Nat. Independence, World

Peace and Disarmament 1981–90; Founder Int. Peace Olympiad Bureau, Co-ordinator First Peace Olympiad 1989; Founder and Pres. Movt for Peace, Human Rights and Nat. Independence 1991–2001 (Hon. Pres. 2001–), Fed. of Balkan Non-Governmental Orgs. for Peace and Co-operation 1993–; Pres. Int. Organizing Cttee, 2nd European Conf. on Peace, Democracy and Co-operation in Balkans 1996; Pro Merito Medal, Parl. Ass. Council of Europe 1986, Model of Council of Europe 1988, Medal of Civilization, UNESCO 1989, Diploma and Medal for Contrib. to Peace and Welfare of Humanity, Int. Peace Bureau 1992, Honour Award for Contrib. to Progress of Science of Chem., Asscn of Greek Chemists 1997, Honour Prize for Participation in Nat. Resistance against German occupation 1999. *Publications:* Organic Chemistry (2 Vols) 1963 and 1971, Inorganic Chemistry (2 Vols) 1968 and 1971, Introduction to Modern Chemistry 1973, The Dominance of Prota and the Theory of Enforced Randomness 1991, Order and Anarchy 1996, Chance and Order 1997, Alexandre and Diogenes 1999, Conjectures and Arpisms 1999; and numerous articles on nuclear disarmament, peace, int. affairs, European relations and human rights. *Leisure interests:* swimming, classical music. *Address:* 8 Diochrous Street, 11528 Athens (Office); 34 Eratous Street, 15561 Holargos, Athens, Greece (Home). *Telephone:* (1) 7211929 (Office); (1) 6524687 (Home). *Fax:* (1) 7211035 (Office); (1) 6526847. *E-mail:* febang@otenet.gr (Office); ch_marko@otenet.gr (Home).

MARKOV, Sergey Aleksandrovich; Russian politician and academic; b. 18 April 1958, Dubna, Moscow Region; s. of Aleksander Nikolayevich Markov and Anna Dmitriyevna Markova; m. Nina Leonidovna Markova; one d.; ed Moscow State Univ.; teacher Moscow Inst. of Radio Electronics and Automatics, Moscow Inst. of Political Sciences; consultant Security Council, Russian Fed.; visiting scholar Univ. of Wisconsin-Madison; sr consultant Nat. Democratic Inst. of Int. Relations 1997–; Dir Inst. of Political Studies 1997–; consulting expert numerous nat. and int. orgs including Security Council at Russian Presidium, State Duma, Nat. Democratic Inst. of Int. Relations, Chase Manhattan Bank, ING Baring, Renaissance Capital 1990–; Exec. Dir Asscn of Consulting Centres, Russian Asscn of Political Sciences 1991–; Ed.-in-Chief, internet publr for strana.ru; Prof. Moscow State Univ.; Prof. Higher School of Econs 2000–; Co-Chair. Moscow Carnegie Centre 1994–97; Chair. Org. Cttee Civil Forum 2001; Co-ordinator Nat. Civil Council on Foreign Policy Dec. 2002–. *Leisure interests:* tennis, swimming, cycling. *Address:* Institute of Political Studies, Zubovsky blvd 4, entrance 8, 119021 Moscow Russia (Office). *Telephone:* (095) 201-80-50 (Office). *Fax:* (095) 201-81-70 (Office). *E-mail:* markov@fep.ru (Office).

MARKOVA, Dame Alicia (Lilian Alicia Marks), DBE; British prima ballerina; b. 1 Dec. 1910, London; d. of Arthur Tristman Marks and Eileen Barry; ed privately; first appeared in Dick Whittington at the Kennington Theatre 1920; studied under Astafieva and appeared with Legat Ballet Group 1923; taken into Russian Ballet by Serge Diaghilev 1924, studied under Enrico Cecchetti and toured with the co. until Diaghilev's death in 1929 (Song of a Nightingale created for her); Prima Ballerina, Rambert Club 1931–34; first Prima Ballerina of Vic-Wells (now the Royal Ballet) 1933–35; formed Markova-Dolin Ballet Co 1935 and toured UK till 1938; with Ballet Russe de Monte Carlo 1938–41; and Ballet Theatre 1941–44; toured North and Cen. America with Markova-Dolin group 1944–45; many guest appearances 1946–47; concerts with Dolin in USA, Far East and South Africa 1947–49; formed Festival Ballet company with Dolin 1950–52; guest artist with Teatro Colón in Buenos Aires 1952, Sadler's Wells, Ballet Theatre, Marquis de Cuevas Ballet and Metropolitan Opera 1953; Royal Winnipeg Ballet 1953; with de Cuevas Ballet in London 1954; with Royal Danish Ballet 1955; Scala Milan, Municipal Theatre Rio de Janeiro 1956; Royal Ballet Covent Garden 1957; Italian Opera Season, Drury Lane, Festival Ballet Tour 1958 and Season 1959; appearances with Royal Ballet and Festival Ballet 1960; with the Metropolitan Opera Co. 1954–58; British Prima Ballerina Assoluta; Dir Metropolitan Opera Ballet of New York 1963–69; Distinguished Lecturer on Ballet at Cincinnati Univ. 1970, Prof. of Ballet and Performing Arts 1970–; produced Les Sylphides, Australian Ballet 1976, London Festival Ballet 1977, Northern Ballet Theatre 1978, Royal Ballet School 1978, Royal Winnipeg Ballet 1979; "Masterclass" BBC TV series 1980; Pres. London Ballet Circle 1981–, All England Dance Competition 1983–, Arts Educational Trust Schools 1984–, London Festival Ballet 1986–, English Nat. Ballet 1989–; A.N.C.E.C. (Italy) 1990–; Vice-Pres. Royal Acad. of Dancing 1958–; Guest Prof., Royal Ballet School 1972–; Gov. Royal Ballet 1973–; Prof. Yorkshire Ballet Seminars 1973–; int. consultant 1990–; London Studio Centre consultant 1990–; Guest Prof. de Danse, Paris Opera Ballet 1975; Guest Prof., Australian Ballet 1976; Pres. Int. Dance Competition, Paris 1986; Patron Abingdon Ballet Seminars 1990–; Hon. Dr. Music (Leicester) 1966, Hon. Mus.D. (E Anglia Univ.) 1982. *Publications:* Giselle and I 1960, Markova Remembers 1986. *Leisure interest:* music. *Address:* c/o Royal Ballet School, Talgarth Road, London, W14 9DE, England.

MARKOVÍC, Ante; Croatian politician (retd); b. 25 Nov. 1924, Konjic; ed Zagreb Univ.; Sec. League of Communist Youth; Engineer, Designer and Head Test Dept, Rade Koncar factory, Dir-Gen. 1961–86; Pres. Exec. Council of Croatia 1982–86; Pres. Presidency of Croatia 1986–88; Pres. Fed. Exec. Council 1989–91.

MARKOWITZ, Harry M., PhD; American professor of finance; b. 24 Aug. 1927, Chicago; s. of Morris Markowitz and Mildred Gruber; m. Barbara Gay; research staff, Rand Corpn Santa Monica, Calif. 1952–60, 1961–63; Tech. Dir Consolidated Analysis Centers, Ltd, Santa Monica 1963–68; Prof. Univ. of

Calif. at LA 1968–69; Pres. Arbitrage Man. Co., New York 1969–72; in pvt. practice as consultant, New York 1972–74; research staff, T. J. Watson Research Center, IBM, Yorktown Hills, NY 1974–83; Speiser Prof. of Finance, Baruch Coll. City Univ. of New York 1982–90, Vice-Pres. Inst. of Man. Science 1960–62; Pres. Harry Markowitz Co. 1984–; Dir Research Daiwa Securities Trust Co. 1990–2000; Fellow, Econometric Soc., American Acad. of Arts and Sciences; Pres. American Finance Asscn 1982; Nobel Prize in Econs (with W. F. Sharpe and M. H. Miller), 1990. *Publications:* Portfolio Selection: Efficient Diversification of Investments 1959, Mean-Variance Analysis in Portfolio Choice 1987; co-author, SIMSCRIPT Simulation Programming Language 1963; co-ed. Process Analysis of Economic Capabilities 1963. *Address:* 1010 Turquoise Street, Suite 245, San Diego, CA 92109, USA.

MARKS, David Joseph, MBE, RIBA; British architect; b. 15 Dec. 1952, Stockholm, Sweden; s. of Melville Marks and Gunilla Marta Loven; m. Julia Barfield; one s. two d.; ed Int. School of Geneva, Switzerland, Kingston Polytech. School of Architecture, Architectural Asscn School of Architecture, London; fmrly with Tetra Ltd, Richard Rogers Partnership; co-f. Marks Barfield Architects with Julia Barfield 1989, London Eye Co. 1994, as Man. Dir raised the finance for Devt of the London Eye; lectures include The Prince's Foundation Urban Villages Forum 2000, Royal Inst. 2001, RIBA 2000, Royal Acad. of Arts 2000, 2001, British European Group Conf., Rome 2001, Berlin 2001; Royal Inst. of Chartered Surveyors Award, RIBA Award for Architecture 2000, London Tourism Awards 2000, London First Millennium Award, American Inst. of Architects Design Award 2000, European Award for Steel Structures 2001, Blueprint Award 2001, Prince Philip Designers Prize, Special Commendation 2001, Faculty of Bldg, Barbara Miller Trophy 2001, Pride of Britain Award for Innovation 2001, Design Week Special Award 2001, D&AD Awards, Silver and Gold 2001 and several other awards. *Exhibitions:* Royal Acad. of Arts 1997, 1998, 1999, 2000, 2001, UKwithNY exhbn 2001, Materials Gallery, Science Museum, London (perm. exhbn). *Leisure interests:* family pursuits. *Address:* Marks Barfield Architects, 50 Bromells Road, London, SW4 0BG (Office); 63 Priory Grove, London, SW8 2PD, England (Home). *Telephone:* (20) 7501-0180 (Office). *Fax:* (20) 7498-7103 (Office). *E-mail:* dmarks@marksbarfield.com (Office). *Website:* www.marksbarfield.com (Office).

MARKS, Dennis Michael, BA; British music and arts executive and programme maker; b. 2 July 1948, London; s. of Samuel Marks and Kitty Ostrovsky; m. 1st Deborah Cranston 1972; one s. one d.; m. 2nd Sally Groves 1992; ed Haberdashers Askes School, Elstree, Trinity Coll., Cambridge; Dir and Producer BBC TV Music and Arts 1972–78; co-f. Bristol Arts Unit 1978–81; f. Third Eye Productions 1981–85; Ed. Music Features BBC TV 1985–88, Asst Head of Music and Arts 1988–91, Head of Music BBC TV 1991–93; Gen. Dir English Nat. Opera 1993–97; Pres. Int. Music Centre, Vienna 1989–92; Italia Prize 1989, Royal Philharmonic Soc. Award 1990. *Publications:* Great Railway Journeys 1981, Repercussions (Afro-American Music) 1985. *Leisure interests:* cookery, travel. *Address:* 12 Camden Square, London, NW1 9UY, England.

MARKS, Michael, CBE; British business executive; b. 28 Dec. 1941, London; one s. two d.; ed St Paul's School, London; joined Smith Bros. 1958, Dir 1975, Chief Exec. 1987, Chief Exec. and Exec. Chair. Smith New Court 1995; Co-Head Global Equities Group, Merrill Lynch 1995–98, Exec. Chair. Merrill Lynch Europe, Middle East & Africa 1998–2003, Exec. Vice-Pres. Merrill Lynch & Co. 2001–03, Chair. Merrill Lynch Investment Mans. (MLIM) 2001–03, mem. Exec. Man. Cttee Merrill Lynch; mem. Int. Markets Advisory Bd, Nat. Asscn of Securities Dealers 1991–, Bd, London Stock Exchange 1994–; Chair. London Investment Banking Asscn 1998–. *Address:* c/o Merrill Lynch, 25 Ropemaker Street, London, EC2Y 9LY, England (Office).

MARKS, Paul Alan, MD; American oncologist and cell biologist; b. 16 Aug. 1926, New York; s. of Robert R. Marks and Sarah (Bohorad) Marks; m. Joan Harriet Rosen 1953; two s. one d.; ed Columbia Coll. and Columbia Univ.; Fellow, Columbia Coll. of Physicians and Surgeons 1952–53, Assoc. 1955–56, mem. of Faculty 1956–82, Dir Haematology Training 1961–74, Prof. of Medicine 1967–82, Dean Faculty of Medicine and Vice-Pres. Medical Affairs 1970–73, Dir Comprehensive Cancer Center 1972–80, Vice-Pres. Health Sciences 1973–80, Prof. of Human Genetics and Devt 1969–82, Frode Jensen Prof. of Medicine 1974–80; Prof. of Medicine and Genetics, Cornell Univ. Coll. of Medicine, New York 1982–; Prof. Cornell Univ. Grad. School in Medical Sciences 1983–; Attending Physician Presbyterian Hosp., New York 1967–83; Pres. and CEO Memorial Sloan-Kettering Cancer Center 1980–99, Pres. Emer. 2000; Attending Physician Memorial Hosp. for Cancer and Allied Diseases 1980–; mem. Sloan-Kettering Inst. for Cancer Research 1980–; Adjunct Prof. Rockefeller Univ. 1980–; Visiting Physician, Rockefeller Univ. Hosp. 1980–; Trustee Hadassah Medical Centre, Jerusalem 1996–2000; mem. Advisory Cttee to Dir, NIH 1993–96, NIH External Advisory Cttee-Intramural Research Program Review 1993–94; mem. editorial bds. of several scientific journals; Gov. Weizmann Inst. 1976–96; Dir Revson Foundation 1976–91; Master American Coll. of Physicians; mem. Inst. of Medicine, NAS; Fellow Royal Soc. of Medicine, London; research focus is on histone deacetylase inhibitors, mechanism of action and potential as anti-cancer agents; Dr. hc (Urbino) 1982, (Tel Aviv) 1992, (Columbia Univ., NY) 2000; Hon. PhD (Hebrew Univ., Jerusalem) 1987; Recognition for Acad. Accomplishments, Chinese Acad. of Medical Sciences 1982, Centenary Medal, Institut Pasteur 1987, Pres.'s Nat. Medal of Science 1991, Gold Medal for Distinguished Academic Accomplishments, Coll. of Physicians and Surgeons of Columbia

Univ., New York, Japan Foundation for Cancer Research Award 1995, John Jay Award for Distinguished Professional Achievement, Columbia Coll. 1996, Lifetime Achievement Award Greater NY Hosp. Asscn 1997, Humanitarian Award, Breast Cancer Foundation 2000, The John Stearns Award for Lifetime Achievement in Medicine, NY Acad. of Medicine 2002; and other awards. *Publications:* over 400 articles in scientific journals. *leisure interest:* tennis. *Address:* Memorial Sloan-Kettering Cancer Center, 1275 York Avenue, New York, NY 10021 (Office); P.O. Box 1485, Washington, CT 06793, USA (Home). *Telephone:* (212) 639-6568 (Office). *Fax:* (212) 639-2861 (Office). *E-mail:* paula_marks@mskcc.org (Office).

MARKWORT, Helmut; German journalist, publisher, editor and presenter; b. 8 Dec. 1936, Darmstadt; s. of August Markwort and Else Markwort (née Volz); started in journalism 1956, various posts in local media –1966; founder Ed.-in-Chief of several magazines and radio stations; Presenter live talk show Markwort 19.10h 1990–; Ed.-in-Chief and CEO Focus Magazine 1993–; Man. Focus TV 1996–; Publr Focus Money 2000–; Head of Bd Tomorrow Focus AG 2001–, Playboy Publishing Deutschland AG 2002–; Horizont 'Mann der Medien' Award 1983, 1993, Advertising Age 'Marketing Superstar' 1994, Hildegard von Bingen Award for Journalism, BDS Mittelstandspreis Award, Bavarian's Merit Medal 1996, Nat. Merit Cross (1st Class) 1999. *Leisure interests:* football, theatre. *Address:* Focus Magazine, Arabella str. 23, 81925, Munich, Germany (Office). *Fax:* (89) 92502026 (Office). *Website:* www.focus-online.de (Office).

MARMOT, Sir Michael Gideon, Kt, M.B.B.S., M.F.C.M., PhD, FFPHM, FRCP; British professor of cardiovascular epidemiology and director of health research; b. 26 Jan. 1945; s. of Nathan Marmot and Alice Marmot (née Weiner); m. Alexandra Naomi Ferster 1971; two s. one d.; ed Univ. of Sydney and Univ. of California at Berkeley; Resident Medical Officer Royal Prince Alfred Hosp. 1969–70; Fellowship in Thoracic Medicine 1970–71; Resident Fellow and Lecturer Univ. of Calif. at Berkeley 1971–76 (fellowships from Berkeley and American Heart Asscn); lecturer then Sr Lecturer in Epidemiology London School of Hygiene and Tropical Medicine 1976–85, Prof. of Epidemiology and Public Health Medicine 1985–; Dir Int. Centre for Health and Society, Univ. Coll. London 1994–; Hon. Consultant in Public Health Medicine, Bloomsbury and Islington Dist Health Authority 1985–; Visiting Prof. Royal Soc. of Medicine 1987; M.R.C. Research Professorship 1995. *Publications:* numerous articles in learned journals. *Leisure interests:* viola, tennis. *Address:* University College London, Department of Epidemiology and Public Health, 1–19 Torrington Place, London, WC1E 6BT; Wildwood Cottage, 17 North End, London, NW3 7HK, England (Home). *Telephone:* (20) 8458-2125 (Home); (20) 7679-1717. *Fax:* (20) 7813-0242. *E-mail:* m.marmot@ucl.ac.uk (Office).

MARONI, Roberto; Italian politician; b. 15 March 1955, Varese; m.; two s.; graduated in law; worked in banks for ten years, then head of legal office of a U.S. multinational for eight years; entered politics 1979; co-f. Lega Lombarda party (subsequently Lega Nord); elected Councillor, Varese; apptd. mem. Lega Lombarda Nat. Council; Deputy 1992–; became Leader of party in Chamber of Deputies; elected Lega Nord Deputy in Gen. Elections March 1994; Minister for the Interior 1994–95, of Labour and Welfare 2001–. *Leisure interests:* football, playing saxophone. *Address:* Ministry of Labour and Welfare, Via Flavia 6, 00187 Rome, Italy. *Telephone:* (06) 46831. *Fax:* (06) 47887174. *E-mail:* capo.gabinetto@minwelfare.it. *Website:* www.minwelfare.it.

MAROSI, Ernö, PhD; Hungarian art historian; b. 18 April 1940, Miskolc; s. of Ferenc Marosi and Magdolna Kecskés; m. Julia Szabó; ed Budapest University of Arts and Sciences; lecturer at the Dept of Art History (Budapest Acad. of Arts and Sciences) 1963, Prof. 1991; mem. Research Group Hungarian Acad. of Sciences, then Dir of Research Inst. 1974–91, Head of Dept 1974–91, Dir 1991–; mem. Int. Cttee of UNESCO on the History of Art 1991–; Sec. of TMB (Nat. Postgrad. Degree Granting Board), Special Cttee on the History of Art, Architecture and Archaeology; corresp. mem. of Hungarian Acad. of Sciences 1993–. *Publications:* A középkori müvészet világa (The World of Arts of the Middle Ages) 1969, A román kor müvészete (The Arts of the Romanesque Age) 1972, Bevezetés a müvészettörténetbe (Introduction to the History of Arts) 1973, Magyar falusi templomok (Village Churches in Hungary) 1975, Emlék márványból vagy homokkököl (Relics from Marble or Sandstone) 1976, Die Änfange der Gotik in Ungarn 1984, Magyarországi müvészet 1300–1470 körül (Arts in Hungary 1300–1470) 1984, A budavári szoborlelet (jtly.) 1989. *Address:* MTA, Müvészettörténeti Intézete, 1014 Budapest, Úri utca 49, Hungary. *Telephone:* (1) 175-9011.

MAROVIĆ, Svetozor; Serbia and Montenegro (Montenegrin) politician; b. 21 March 1955, Kotor, Montenegro; s. of Jovo Marović and Ivana Marović; m. Djina Marović; two c.; ed Univ. of Montenegro; Dir Municipal Public Accounting Dept in Budva; mem. Presidency of Cen. Cttee of League of Communists of Montenegro; Sec.-Gen. of Democratic Socialist Party of Montenegro, currently Deputy Chair.; mem. Parl. of Montenegro, Speaker 1998–2002; mem. Chamber of Citizens Parl. of Yugoslavia 1997; November's Award, Budva. *Leisure Interests:* Volleyball. *Address:* c/o Nemanjina Obala 5, 81000 Podgorica, Montenegro, Serbia and Montenegro (Office).

MARQUAND, David Ian, FBA, FRHistS, FRSA; British professor of politics; b. 20 Sept. 1934, Cardiff; s. of Rt Hon Hilary Marquand and Rachel Marquand; m. Judith M. Reed 1959; one s. one d.; ed Emanuel School, Magdalen Coll. Oxford; Sr scholar, St Antony's Coll. Oxford 1957–58; teaching Asst Univ. of

Calif. 1958–59; editorial writer, The Guardian 1959–61; Research Fellow, St Antony's Coll. Oxford 1962–64; lecturer in politics, Univ. of Sussex 1964–66; mem. Parl. (Labour) for Ashfield, Notts. 1966–77; del. to Council of Europe and W.E.U. assemblies 1970–73; Opposition spokesman on treasury affairs 1971–72; Chief Adviser, Sec.-Gen. European Comm. 1977–78; Prof. of Contemporary History and Politics, Salford Univ. 1978–91; Prof. of Politics, Univ. of Sheffield 1991–96, Dir Political Economy Research Centre 1993–96, Hon. Prof. 1997–; Prin. Mansfield Coll., Univ. of Oxford 1996–; Jt Ed. The Political Quarterly 1987–96; George Orwell Memorial Prize 1979. *Publications:* Ramsay Macdonald 1973, Parliament for Europe 1979, The Unprincipled Society 1988, The Progressive Dilemma 1991, The New Reckoning 1997, Religion and Democracy 2000. *Leisure interest:* walking. *Address:* Mansfield College, Oxford, OX1 3TF, England. *Telephone:* (1865) 270980.

MARQUARDT, Klaus Max, Dr rer. pol; German business executive; b. 18 Dec. 1926, Berlin; s. of Dr. Arno Marquardt and Ruth Marquardt; m. Brigitte Weber; three d.; ed Realgymnasium Berlin, Univ. Berlin and Tech. Univ. Berlin; mem. Bd ARAL AG –1971, Chair. 1971–86; Pres. Petroleum Econ. Asscn 1979–86; Chair. Supervisory Bd, Westfalenbank AG, Bochum; mem. Supervisory Bd Energieversorgung Sachsen Ost AG, Dresden; Grosses Bundesverdienstkreuz. *Address:* Roggenkamp 14, 44797 Bochum, Germany (Office). *Telephone:* (234) 791091 (Office). *Fax:* (234) 791091.

MÁRQUEZ, Gabriel García (see García Márquez, Gabriel (Gabo)).

MÁRQUEZ DE LA PLATA IRARRAZAVAL, Alfonso; Chilean politician; b. 19 July 1933, Santiago; s. of Fernando Márquez de la Plata Echenique and Rosa Yrarrazaval Fernández; m. María de la Luz Cortes Heyermann 1957; one s. one d.; ed Universidad Católica de Chile; Vice-Chair. Sociedad Nacional de Agricultura 1969–73, Chair. 1973–77; Chair. Banco de Santiago 1977–78; Minister of Agric. 1978–80; mem. Govt Legislative Comm. 1981–83; Dir A.F.P. Provida 1981–83, Compañía de Cervecerías Unidas 1981–83, Banco de Crédito e Inversiones 1981–83; Co-Proprietor and Admin. Sociedad Agrícola Caren Ltda; Govt Minister-Sec.-Gen. 1983–84, Minister of Labour and Social Security 1984–88; Chair. Nat. TV Council 1989–92; Espiga de Oro, Colegio Ingenieros Agrónomos 1998. *Publications:* El Salto al Futuro 1992, El Gobierno Ideal 1993, Mirando al Futuro 1998, Una Persecución Vergonzosa 2001, El Peligro Totalitario 2002. *Address:* Av. Presidente Kennedy 4150, Dp. 901, Santiago, Chile. *Telephone:* (2) 2084229. *Fax:* (2) 2061731.

MARR, Andrew William Stevenson, BA; British journalist; b. 31 July 1959, Glasgow; s. of Donald Marr and Valerie Marr; m. Jackie Ashley 1987; one s. two d.; ed Dundee High School, Craigflower School, Loretto School, Trinity Hall, Cambridge; gen. reporter, business reporter The Scotsman 1982–84, Parliamentary Corresp. 1984–86, Political Ed. 1988; Political Ed. The Economist 1988–92; Political Corresp. The Independent 1986–88, Chief Commentator 1992–96, Ed. 1996–98, Ed.-in-Chief 1998; Political Ed. BBC 2000–; presenter Start the Week, BBC Radio 4 2002–; columnist The Observer and The Express 1998–; Chair. Jury Bd Samuel Johnson Prize for Non-Fiction; Commentator of the Year 1995. *Publications:* The Battle for Scotland 1992, Ruling Britannia 1995, The Day Britain Died 2000. *Leisure interests:* reading, wining and dining, painting. *Address:* c/o BBC Westminster, 4 Millbank, London, SW1P 3JA, England.

MARRAKCHI, Ahmad, PhD; Tunisian university administrator; b. 9 Feb. 1935, Sfax; m.; four c.; ed Toulouse Univ., France; Assoc. Prof., then Prof. Univ. of Tunis; Dir Tunis Nat. School of Eng (ENIT) 1975–85; est. Faculty of Tech. at Univ. of Qatar, Dean of Faculty and adviser to Pres. of Univ. 1990–99; mem. French Soc. of Electricians, European Soc. for Eng Training, founding mem. and Pres. Tunisian Soc. of Electronics Specialists; Fellow Islamic Acad. of Sciences. *Address:* Islamic Academy of Sciences, P.O. Box 830036, Amman, Jordan (Office). *Telephone:* 5522104 (Office). *Fax:* 5511803 (Office).

MARRINER, Sir Neville, Kt, CBE, FRCM, FRAM; British music director and conductor; b. 15 April 1924, Lincoln; s. of Herbert H. Marriner and Ethel M. Marriner; m. Elizabeth M. Sims 1955; one s. one d.; ed Lincoln School, Royal Coll. of Music; f. and Dir Acad. of St Martin in the Fields 1956–; Musical Dir LA Chamber Orchestra 1969–78; Dir S. Bank Festival of Music 1975–78, Dir Meadowbrook Festival Detroit 1979; Music Dir Minn. Orchestra 1979–86, Stuttgart Radio Symphony Orchestra 1984–89, Barbican Summer Festival 1985–87; Fellow Trinity Coll. of Music, Hong Kong Acad. for Performing Arts; Hon. DMus (Hull) 1998, (Royal Scottish Acad.) 1999; Tagore Gold Medal, six Edison Awards (Netherlands), two Mozart Gemeinde Awards (Austria), Grand Prix du Disque (France) (three times); Kt of the Polar Star 1984, Officier, Ordre des Arts et des Lettres 1995. *Address:* c/o Academy of St Martin-in-the-Fields, Raine House, Raine Street, London, E1 9RG, England.

MARRON, Donald Baird; American banker; b. 21 July 1934, Goshen, NY; m. Catherine D. Calligar; ed Baruch School of Business; investment analyst New York Trust Co. 1951–56, Lionel D. Edie Co. 1956–58; Man. Research Dept George O'Neill & Co. 1958–59; Pres. D. B. Marron & Co. Inc. 1959–65, Mitchell Hutchins & Co. Inc. (merger with D. B. Marron & Co. Inc.) 1965–69, Pres., CEO 1969–77; Pres. PaineWebber Inc. (merger with Mitchell Hutchins & Co. Inc.) 1977–88, CEO 1980–, Chair. Bd 1981–; Co-founder, fmr Chair. Data Resources Inc.; fmr Dir New York Stock Exchange; Vice-Chair. Bd Trustees Museum of Modern Art; mem. Council on Foreign Relations Inc., Pres.'s Cttee on The Arts and the Humanities Inc. *Address:* Paine Webber

Group Inc., 14th Floor, 1285 Avenue of the Americas, New York, NY 10019 (Office); Museum of Modern Art, 11 West 53rd Street, New York, NY 10019, USA (Office).

MARS, Forrest Edward, Jr; American business executive; b. 1931; s. of the late Forrest Mars, Sr; brother of John Franklin Mars (q.v.); m. Virginia Cretella 1955 (divorced 1990); four d.; ed Yale Univ.; CEO Mars, Inc. –2000, also Chair., Co-Pres. *Address:* Mars, Inc., 6885 Elm Street, McLean, VA 22101-3810, USA (Office).

MARS, John Franklin; American business executive; b. 1935; s. of the late Forrest Mars, Sr; brother of Forrest Mars, Jr (q.v.); m.; two c.; ed Yale Univ.; Chair. Kal Kan Foods, Inc.; Co-Pres. Mars, Inc. 1973–, CEO 2000–. *Address:* Mars, Inc., 6885 Elm Street, McLean, VA 22101-3810, USA (Office).

MARS-JONES, Adam; British author; b. 1954; s. of the late Sir William Mars-Jones; ed Westminster School, Trinity Hall, Cambridge and Univ. of Va; film critic, The Independent 1989–97; film critic, The Times 1999–2001; Somerset Maugham Award 1982. *Publications:* Lantern Lecture (short stories) 1981, Mae West is Dead 1983, The Darker Proof (with Edmund White) 1987, Monopolies of Loss 1992, The Waters of Thirst (novel) 1993, Blind Bitter Happiness (essays) 1997. *Address:* 42B Calabria Road, Highbury, London, N5 1HU, England.

MARSALIS, Wynton; American trumpeter and music administrator; b. 18 Oct. 1961, New Orleans; s. of Ellis Marsalis and Dolores Marsalis; three c.; ed Berks. Music Center, Tanglewood, Juilliard School, New York; joined Art Blakey's big band 1980; in addition to regular appearances in many countries with his own jazz quintet, he follows a classical career and has performed with the world's top orchestras; Artistic Dir Lincoln Centre Jazz Dept 1990–; numerous int. awards, including the Grand Prix du Disque and Grammy Award in both jazz and classical categories in 1983; Pulitzer Prize for Music 1997, Algur H. Meadows Award, Southern Methodist Univ. 1997. *Albums include:* The Majesty of the Blues 1989, Crescent City Christmas Card 1989, Tune in Tomorrow 1991, Baroque Duet 1992, Blue Interlude 1992, Citi Movement 1993, In This House, On This Morning 1994, Wynton Marsalis 1995, The All-American Hero 1996 (jtly.) Live at Bubba's 1996, Jump Start and jazz 1997, One By One 1998, Gold Collection 1998. *Publications:* Sweet Swing Blues on the Road 1994, Marsalis on Music 1995, Requiem 1999. *Address:* Agency for the Performing Arts, 9200 Sunset Boulevard, Suite 1200, West Hollywood, CA 90069, USA.

MARSH, Baron (Life Peer), cr. 1981, of Mannington in the County of Wiltshire; **Richard William Marsh,** Kt, PC; British public servant and politician; b. 14 March 1928; s. of William Marsh; m. 1st Evelyn Mary Andrews 1950 (divorced 1973); two s.; m. 2nd Caroline Dutton 1973 (died 1975); m. 3rd Felicity McFadzean 1979; ed Jennings School, Swindon, Woolwich Polytechnic and Ruskin Coll., Oxford; Health Services Officer, Nat. Union of Public Employees 1951–59; mem. Clerical and Admin. Whitley Council for Health Service 1953–59; MP for Greenwich 1959–71; Parl. Sec. Ministry of Labour 1964–65; Jt Parl. Sec. Ministry of Tech. 1965–66; Minister of Power 1966–68, of Transport 1968–69; Dir Michael Saunders Man. Services 1970–71, Nat. Carbonizing Ltd 1970–71, Concord Rotaflex 1970–71; Chair. British Railways Bd 1971–76, Newspaper Publishers Asscn Ltd 1976–89, Allied Investments Ltd 1977–82, British Iron & Steel Consumers' Council 1977–82, Lee Cooper Licensing Services 1980–83, Dual Fuel Systems 1981, Lee Cooper Group 1983, TV-am 1983–84 (Deputy Chair. 1981–83), Lopex PLC 1986–97, Laurentian Financial Group PLC 1986–; Dir Imperial Life of Canada UK 1983–90; Chair. British Industry Cttee on SA Ltd 1989–, Mannington Man. Services 1989–; Chair. and Chief Exec. Laurentian Holdings Co. 1989; Chair. China and Eastern Investments Trust, Hong Kong 1990–98 (Dir 1987–98); Adviser Nissan Motor Co. 1981–, Fujitec 1982–. *Publication:* Off the Rails (memoirs) 1978. *Address:* House of Lords, London, SW1A 0PW, England.

MARSH, Rodney William, MBE; Australian cricketer; b. 4 Nov. 1947, Armadale, Western Australia; m.; three s.; ed Univ. of Western Australia; Australian Test cricketer (wicket-keeper) 1970–84; Test career 96 matches, 355 dismissals (343 caught, 12 stumped), batting average 26.51 (three centuries); One-day international career 92 matches, 124 dismissals (120 caught, four stumped), batting average 20.08; Head Coach Commonwealth Bank Cricket Acad. 1991–2001; Dir England and Wales Cricket Board Nat. Acad. 2001–; Wisden Cricketer of the Year 1982. *Publication:* (with Jack Pollard) The Glovemen 1994. *Leisure interests:* golf, watching Aussie rules football. *Address:* ECB National Academy, c/o Andrew Walpole, Media Relations Manager, Lord's Cricket Ground, London, NW8 8QZ, England (Office); 4 Briar Avenue, Medindie, South Australia 5081, Australia (Home). *E-mail:* rodney.marsh@ecb.co.uk (Office); rmarsh@bettanet.net.au (Home).

MARSHALL, Alexander Badenoch, MA; British business executive; b. 31 Dec. 1924, Dunfermline, Fife, Scotland; s. of David Marshall; m. Mona K. D. Kirk 1961; two s. one d.; ed Glenalmond and Worcester Coll., Oxford; served RNVR 1943–46; with the P & O Group 1947–79, CEO 1972–79; Chair. Bestobell PLC 1979–85; Dir Commercial Union Assurance Co. PLC 1970–90, Chair. 1983–90; Dir The Maersk Co. Ltd 1980–95, Vice-Chair. 1983–87, Chair. 1987–93; Dir Royal Bank of Canada 1985–95; Chair. RBC (UK) Holdings Ltd 1988–95; Vice-Chair. The Boots Co. PLC 1985–91; Chair. UK-S Africa Trade Asscn 1982–85; Co-Chair. British N American Cttee 1985–90; Pres. UK Chamber of Shipping 1994–95; Dir Seascope Shipping Holdings

PLC 1997–99. *Publication:* Taking the Adventure 1999. *Leisure interests:* gardening, hill-walking, sheep. *Address:* Crest House, Woldingham, Surrey, CR3 7DH, England.

MARSHALL, Barry J., FRS, FAA; Australian gastroenterologist; ed Univ. of Western Australia; physician, Royal Perth Hosp. 1974–83; Research Fellow, gastroenterologist, Prof. of Medicine, Univ. of Va, USA 1986–96; Hon. Research Fellow, Helicobacter pylori Research Lab., Sir Charles Gairdner Hosp., Perth; Albert Lasker Award 1995, Dr. A. H. Heineken Prize for Medicine 1998, Australian Achiever Award 1998, Florey Medal 1998, Buchanan Medal, Royal Soc. of Medicine, London 1998, Benjamin Franklin Award for Life Sciences 1999, Poppy Award, Australian Inst. of Political Sciences 2000. *Research:* collaborated with Robin Warren on research leading to culture of Helicobacter pylori 1982 and recognition of asscn between H.pylori, gastritis, peptic ulcer and gastric cancer. *Leisure interests:* computers, electronics, photography. *Address:* H.pylori Research Laboratory, Sir Charles Gairdner Hospital, Verdun Street, Nedlands, WA 6009, Australia (Office).

MARSHALL, (C.) Penny; American actress and director; b. 15 Oct. 1943, New York; d. of Anthony Marshall and Marjorie Ward; m. 1st Michael Henry (divorced), one d.; m. 2nd Robert Reiner 1971 (divorced 1979); ed Univ. of New Mexico. *Films:* appeared in: How Sweet It Is 1967, The Savage Seven 1968, The Grasshopper 1979, '1941' 1979, Movers and Shakers 1985, She's Having a Baby 1988, The Hard Way 1991, Hocus Pocus 1993, Get Shorty 1995; directed: Jumpin' Jack Flash 1986, Big 1988, Awakenings 1990, A League of their Own 1992, Renaissance Man 1994, The Preacher's Wife 1996, The Time Tunnel: The Movie 1999, Jackie's Back 1999; produced: Getting Away With Murder 1995, With Friends Like These 1998, Saving Grace 1998, Live from Baghdad. *Television includes:* The Odd Couple 1972–74, Friends and Lovers 1974, Let's Switch 1974, Chico and the Man 1975, Mary Tyler Moore 1975, Heaven Help Us 1975, Saturday Night Live 1975–77, Battle of Network Stars 1976, Barry Manilow Special 1976, The Tonight Show 1976–77, Mike Douglas Show 1975–77, Merv Griffin Show 1976–77, $20,000 Pyramid 1976–77, Laverne and Shirley 1976–83, More Than Friends (TV film) 1978, Love Thy Neighbor (TV film) 1984. *Address:* Parkway Productions, 10202 Washington Blvd., Culver City, CA 90232, USA.

MARSHALL, (Cedric) Russell, C.N.Z.M., BA; New Zealand diplomat; b. 15 Feb. 1936, Nelson; s. of Cedric Thomas Marshall and Gladys Margaret (née Hopley) Marshall; m. Barbara May Watson 1961; two s. one d.; ed Nelson Coll., Christchurch Teachers' Coll., Trinity Theological Coll., Auckland, Victoria Univ.; teacher at various schools 1955–56; Methodist Minister in Christchurch 1960–66, Masterton 1967–71; MP for Wanganui 1972–90; Minister of Educ. and for the Environment 1984–86, of Educ. and of Conservation 1986–87, of Foreign Affairs 1987–90, Disarmament and Arms Control 1987–89, Pacific Island Affairs 1989–90; Sr Opposition Whip 1978–79; Chancellor, Vic. Univ. of Wellington 2000–02; High Commr to UK and Nigeria, Amb. to Ireland 2002–; Chair. NZ Comm. for UNESCO 1990–99, Africa Information Centre Trustees 1991–95, Commonwealth Observer Group, Seychelles 1993, Commonwealth Observer Mission to S. Africa 1994, Cambodia Trust (Aotearoa-NZ) 1994–2001, Polytechnics Int. NZ 1994–2001, Educ. NZ 1998–2001, Tertiary Educ. Advisory Comm. 2000–01, Cambodia Trust (UK) 2002–; mem. Commonwealth Observer Group, Lesotho 1993, Victoria Univ. (Wellington) Council 1994–2002, UNESCO Exec. Bd 1995–99 (Chair. Finance and Admin. Comm. 1997–99) Nelson Mandela Trustees 1995–; Labour. *Leisure interests:* classical music, genealogy. *Address:* New Zealand High Commission, New Zealand House, 80 The Haymarket, London, SW1Y 4TQ, England (Office). *Telephone:* (20) 7930-8422 (Office). *Fax:* (20) 7839-4580 (Office). *E-mail:* russell.marshall@mfat.govt.nz (Office).

MARSHALL, Geoffrey, PhD, FBA; British academic; b. 22 April 1929, Chesterfield; s. of Leonard William and Kate Marshall; m. Patricia Anne Woodcock 1957; two s.; ed Arnold School, Blackpool, Univs. of Manchester and Glasgow; Research Fellow, Nuffield Coll., Oxford 1955–57; Fellow and Praelector in Politics, Queen's Coll. Oxford 1957–93, Provost 1993–99; Visiting Prof.-at-large, Cornell Univ. 1985–91; mem. Oxford City Council 1964–74; Sheriff of City of Oxford 1970; del. Oxford Univ. Press 1987–92. *Publications:* Parliamentary Sovereignty and the Commonwealth 1957, Some Problems of the Constitution (with G. C. Moodie) 1959, Police and Government 1965, Constitutional Theory 1971, Constitutional Conventions 1984, Ministerial Responsibility 1989. *Address:* Queens College, Oxford, OX1 4AW, England. *Telephone:* (1865) 516114.

MARSHALL, Margaret Anne, OBE; British concert and opera singer; b. 4 Jan. 1949, Stirling; d. of Robert and Margaret Marshall; m. Dr Graeme G. K. Davidson 1970; two d.; ed High School of Stirling and Royal Scottish Acad. of Music and Drama; first opera appearance in Orfeo ed Euridice, Florence 1977; has since sung at La Scala, Covent Garden, Glyndebourne, Scottish Opera, Barcelona, Hamburg, Cologne and Salzburg; concert performances in maj. European and US cities and festivals with maj. orchestras; numerous recordings; First Prize, Munich Int. Competition 1974; James Gulliver Award for Performing Arts in Scotland. *Leisure interests:* squash, golf, cooking. *Address:* Woodside, Main Street, Gargunnock, Stirling, FK8 3BP, Scotland.

MARSHALL, Sir Peter, KCMG; British diplomatist; b. 30 July 1924, Reading; s. of late R. H. Marshall and Winifred Marshall; m. 1st Patricia R. Stoddart 1957 (died 1981); one s. one d.; m. 2nd Judith (née Miller) Tomlin 1989; ed Tonbridge School and Corpus Christi Coll., Cambridge; RAFVR

1943–46; served HM Foreign (later Diplomatic) Service 1949–83; Aide to British Amb., Washington, DC 1952–56; Head of Chancery, Baghdad 1961, Bangkok 1962–64, Paris 1969–71; Deputy Dir Treasury Centre for Admin. Studies 1965–66; Counsellor, UK Mission, Geneva 1966–69; Head, Financial Relations Dept, FCO 1971–73, Asst Under-Sec. of State 1973–75; Minister, UK Mission to UN, New York 1975–79; Perm. Rep. UK Mission, Geneva 1979–83; Commonwealth Deputy Sec.-Gen. (Econ.) 1983–88; Chair. Royal Commonwealth Soc. 1988–92, Commonwealth Trust 1989–92; Chair. Jt Commonwealth Socs. Council 1993–; Pres. Queen Elizabeth House, Oxford 1990–94; Visiting Lecturer, Diplomatic Acad. of London 1989–2001; Hon. Fellow, Corpus Christi Coll., Cambridge 1989, Univ. of Westminster 1992. *Publications:* The Dynamics of Diplomacy 1989, The United Kingdom–the United Nations (contrib.) 1990, Diplomacy Beyond 2000 (ed.) 1996, Positive Diplomacy 1997, Are Diplomats Really Necessary? (ed.) 1999, The Information Explosion (ed.) 1999. *Leisure interests:* music, golf. *Address:* 26 Queensdale Road, London, W11 4QB, England. *Telephone:* (20) 7229-1921. *Fax:* (20) 7229-1921 (Home).

MARSHALL, Ray, PhD; American economist and government official; b. 22 Aug. 1928, Oak Grove, La.; m. Patricia Williams 1946; one s. three d.; ed Millsaps Coll., Miss., Louisiana State Univ., Univ. of Calif. at Berkeley; Fulbright Research Scholar, Finland; post-doctoral research, Harvard Univ.; Instructor San Francisco State Coll.; Assoc. Prof. and Prof. Univs. of Miss., Ky, La.; Prof. of Econs, Texas Univ. 1962–67, Prof. of Econs 1969 and fmrly Dir Center for Study of Human Resources, Chair. Dept 1970–72, Prof. of Econs and Public Affairs, Lyndon B. Johnson School of Public Affairs 1981; Rapoport Prof. Econs and Public Affairs, Univ. of Tex. at Austin; Co-Chair. Comm. on the Skills of the American Workforce; Trustee German Marshall Fund and Carnegie Corpn of NY 1982–90; mem. Comm. on Future of Labor/Man. Relations; US Sec. of Labor 1977–81; Hon. degrees (Maryland, Cleveland State, Millaaps Coll., Bates Coll., Rutgers, Ind., Tulane, Utah State, St Edward's); Lifetime Achievement Award, Industrial Relations Research Asscn 2001. *Publications:* The Negro Worker 1967, The Negro and Apprenticeship 1967, Cooperatives and Rural Poverty in the South 1971, Human Resources and Labor Markets 1972, Anthology of Labor Economics 1972, Human Resources and Labor Markets 1975, Labor Economics: Wages, Employment and Trade Unionism 1976, The Role of Unions in the American Economy 1976, An Economic Strategy for the 1980s 1981, Work and Women in the Eighties 1983, Unheard Voices: Labor and Economic Policy in a Competitive World 1987, Economics of Education 1988, Losing Direction: Families, Human Resource Development and Economic Performance 1991, Thinking for a Living (with Marc Tucker) 1992, Back to Shared Prosperity (ed.) 2000. *Address:* c/o University of Texas at Austin, L.B.J. School of Public Affairs, Drawer Y, University Station, Austin, TX 78713, USA. *Telephone:* (512) 471-6242 (Office); (512) 345-1828 (Home). *Fax:* (512) 345-8491 (Home).

MARSHALL, Robin, PhD, FRS; British professor of physics; b. 5 Jan. 1940, Skipton, Yorks.; s. of late Robert Marshall and Grace Eileen Marshall; m. 1963; two s. one d.; ed Ermysted's Grammar School, Skipton; research scientist, DESY, MIT, Daresbury Lab., Rutherford Appleton Lab. 1965–92; Sr Prin. Scientific Officer (Individual Merit) Rutherford Appleton Lab. 1985–92; Prof. of Experimental Physics, Univ. of Manchester 1992–; Dir and Co. Sec. Frontiers Science and TV Ltd; Max Born Medal and Prize, German Physical Soc. 1997. *Publications:* over 200 scientific papers. *Leisure interests:* painting and drawing, movies. *Address:* Department of Physics and Astronomy, University of Manchester, Manchester, M13 9PL, England (Office). *Telephone:* (161) 275-4170 (Office). *Fax:* (161) 275-4246 (Office).

MARSHALL OF KNIGHTSBRIDGE, Baron (Life Peer), cr. 1998, of Knightsbridge in the City of Westminster; **Colin (Marsh) Marshall,** Kt; British airline executive; b. 16 Nov. 1933, Edgware, Middlesex; s. of Marsh Marshall and Florence M. Marshall; m. Janet Cracknell 1958; one d.; ed Univ. Coll. School, Hampstead; cadet purser, later Deputy Purser, Orient Steam Navigation Co. 1958–64; with Hertz Corpn 1958–64; with Avis Inc. 1964–79, Exec. Vice-Pres. and COO New York 1971–75, Pres. and COO, New York 1975–76, Pres. and CEO, New York 1976–79; Exec. Vice-Pres. and Sector Exec. Norton Simon Inc., 1979–81; Dir and Deputy Chief. Exec. Dir Sears Holdings PLC 1981–83; Chief Exec. British Airways 1983–95, Deputy Chair. 1989–93, Exec. Chair. 1993–95, Chair. (non-exec.) 1996–(2003); Chair. Inchcape 1996–2000, Siebe PLC (now Invensys PLC) 1996–(2003); Deputy Chair. British Telecommunications 1996–2001; Deputy Pres. CBI 1995–96, Pres. 1996–98; Dir Grand Metropolitan PLC 1988–95, Midland Group 1989–, HSBC Holdings 1992–, US Air 1993–96, Qantas 1993–96, 2000–01, British Telecommunications 1995–2001; Chair. Int. Advisory Bd British American Business Council 1994– ; Pres. Commonwealth Youth Exchange Council 1998–; Deputy Pres. CBI 1998– (Pres. 1996–98); Chair. Britain in Europe 1998–, Chatham House 1999–, CBI Int. Advisory Bd 2002–, Royal Inst. of Int. Affairs –2003; mem. Bd IBM UK Ltd 1990–1995, Panel 2000 1998–99; Hon. DLitt (Suffolk, USA) 1984, (Westminster) 1999, Hon. LLD (Bath) 1989, (American Univ. London) 1993, (Lancaster) 1997, Hon. DSc (Buckingham) 1990, (Cranfield) 1997, Dr of Business (London Guildhall) 2000. *Leisure interests:* tennis, skiing. *Address:* c/o British Airways PLC, Waterside (HBB3), PO Box 365, Harmondsworth, Middlesex, UP7 0GB, England. *Telephone:* (20) 8738-5107 (Office). *Fax:* (20) 8738-9801 (Office). *E-mail:* anne.p.hensman@ britishairways.com (Office). *Website:* www.ba.com (Office).

MARTEL, Yann; Canadian author; b. 1963, Spain; ed Trent Univ.; grew up in Alaska, BC, Costa Rica, France, Ont. and Mexico; fmr tree planter,

dishwasher, security guard; became professional writer 1990; works have been published internationally. *Publications include:* Facts Behind the Helsinki Roccamatios (Journey Prize) 1993, Self 1996, Life of Pi (Hugh MacLennan Prize for Fiction, Man Booker Prize 2002) 2002. *Leisure interests:* yoga, writing, volunteer in a palliative care unit. *Address:* c/o Knopf Canada, Random House of Canada Ltd., One Toronto Street, Unit 300, Toronto, Ont. M5C 2VC, Canada (Office). *Telephone:* (416) 364-4449 (Office). *Fax:* (416) 364-6863 (Office). *Website:* www.randomhouse.ca (Office).

MARTELLI, Claudio; Italian politician; b. 24 Sept. 1943, Milan; m.; four c.; mem. Italian Socialist Party (PSI) 1967–93, mem. Secr. 1973–75, Leader PSI Group, Milan Municipal Council 1975–79; elected Deputy 1979, 1983, 1987, 1992; Deputy Prime Minister 1989–92, Minister of Justice 1991–93; elected MEP for Italian Democratic Socialists (SDI) 1999, mem. Cttee on Foreign Affairs, Human Rights, Common Security and Defence Policy, mem. Interparliamentary Del. for Relations with South-East Europe; Spokesman League of Socialists 2000–; Ed.-in-Chief La Sinistra Sociale socialist review. *Address:* European Parliament, Centre Européen, Plateau du Kirchberg, B.P. 1601, 2929 Luxembourg.

MARTENS, Wilfried, DenD; Belgian politician; b. 19 April 1936, Sleidinge; ed Louvain Univ.; lawyer Court of Appeal, Ghent 1960; fmr Leader Vlaamse Volksbeweging; Adviser to Harmel Cabinet 1965, to Vanden Boeynants Cabinet 1966; Head of Mission to Tindemans Cabinet (Community Affairs) 1968; Pres. Christelijke Volkspartij-Jongeren (CVP Youth Org. 1967–71), Pres. CVP 1972–79; mem. Parl. for Ghent-Eeklo 1974–91, mem. Senate for Brussels-Halle-Vilvoorde 1991–94; co-founder European People's Party (EPP) 1976, Pres. Working Cttee on Policy 1976–77, Pres. 1990–, Pres. EPP Group, European Parl. 1994–99; Prime Minister 1979–81, 1981–92; Minister of State 1992–; Pres. European Union of Christian Democrats 1993–96; Pres. Christian Democratic Int. 2000–01; Charles V Prize (for contrib. to EU) 1998; numerous Belgian and int. awards. *Address:* European People's Party, 67 rue d'Arlon, 1040 Brussels, Belgium (Office). *Telephone:* (2) 285-41-59 (Office). *Fax:* (2) 285-41-55 (Office). *E-mail:* presid@evppe.be (Office). *Website:* www .eppe.org (Office).

MÅRTENSON, Jan; Swedish diplomatist; b. 14 Feb. 1933, Uppsala; m.; two s. two d.; ed Univ. of Uppsala; held various Foreign Ministry and diplomatic posts until 1966; Head Section UN Dept Ministry for Foreign Affairs, Stockholm 1966–67, Head Information Dept 1973–75; Deputy Dir Stockholm Int. Peace Research Inst. 1968–69; Sec.-Gen. Swedish Prep. Cttee for UN Conf. on Human Environment 1970–72; Chef de Cabinet for King of Sweden 1975–79; Asst Sec.-Gen. Centre for Disarmament UN Dept of Political and Security Council Affairs 1979–82, Under-Sec.-Gen. for Disarmament Affairs 1983–87; Chair. UN Appointments and Promotions Bd 1984–86; Sec.-Gen. Int. Conf. on Relationship between Disarmament and devt 1987; Dir-Gen. UN Office, Geneva 1987–92, Under-Sec.-Gen. and Head UN Centre for Human Rights, Geneva 1987–92, Co-ordinator UN Second Decade Against Racism 1987; Amb. to Switzerland and Liechtenstein 1993–95; Amb.-at-Large, Ministry of Foreign Affairs 1996–98; Marshal of the Diplomatic Corps 1999–; Chair. Int. Club, Stockholm, Travellers' Club, Stockholm. *Publications:* some 40 books; articles on disarmament and human rights. *Leisure interests:* gardening, fishing. *Address:* Karlaplan 14, 115 20 Stockholm, Sweden. *Telephone:* (8) 660-98-39.

MÅRTENSSON, Arne, MBA; Swedish banker; b. 10 Oct. 1951, Vänersborg; s. of Aldo Mårtensson and Ingrid Mårtensson; m. 2nd Heléne Melin-Mårtensson 1996; ed Stockholm School of Econs, Harvard Business School, USA; Industrial Devt Dept, Svenska Handelsbanken 1972–75, Vice-Pres. and Head Credit Dept, Regional Unit, Western Sweden 1975–77, Sr Vice-Pres. Admin., Cen. Sweden 1977–80, Sr Vice-Pres. and Area Man. Stockholm City 1980–84, Exec. Vice-Pres. and Gen. Man., Western Sweden, 1984–89, Pres. Stockholm 1989–90, Group Chief Exec. 1991–2001, Chair. 2001–; mem. (non-exec.) Bd Holmen AB, Industrivärden AB, Swedish Industry and Stock Exchange Cttee., Sandvik AB, Skanska AB, ICC Sweden, V & S Vin & Spirit AB, Stockholm School of Econs. Advisory Bd. (Chair.), Högskoleföreningen mem. Int. Business Council of the World Econ. Forum, Industrial Council, Royal Swedish Acad. of Eng Sciences. *Leisure interests:* sailing, jogging, skiing. *Address:* Svenska Handelsbanken, 106 70 Stockholm (Office); Stenbocksvägen 3, 182 62 Djursholm, Sweden (Home). *Telephone:* (8) 22-92-20 (Office). *Fax:* (8) 701-11-95 (Office). *Website:* www.handelsbanken.se/ireng (Office).

MARTIN, Agnes, B. S., M. F. A.; American artist; b. 22 March 1912, Maklin, Sask., Canada; d. of Malcolm I. Martin and Margaret Kinnon; ed Columbia Univ.; first showing in Betty Parsons Gallery, New York 1958; retrospective exhbns. ICA Philadelphia 1955, Pasadena 1956, Hayward Gallery, London 1977, Stedelijk Museum, Amsterdam 1977, 1990, Whitney Museum, New York 1991; represented in perm. collections Museum of Modern Art, New York, Albright-Knox Gallery, Solomon R. Guggenheim Museum, Tate Gallery, London and many others. *Address:* Pace Wildenstein, 32 E 57th Street, New York, NY 10022; 414 Placitas Road, 37 Taos, NM 87571, USA. *Telephone:* (212) 421-3292.

MARTIN, Sir Clive Haydn, Kt, OBE, TD, DL, FCMA, FCIS; British business executive; b. 20 March 1935, s. of Thomas Stanley Martin and Dorothy Gladys Martin; m. Linda Constance Basil Penn 1959; one s. three d.; ed St Alban's School, Haileybury and Imperial Service Coll., London School of Printing and Graphic Arts; nat. service in Germany 1956–58; Man. Dir Staples Printers Ltd (now MPG Ltd) 1972–85, Chair. 1978–; ADC to The Queen 1982–86;

Alderman, City of London 1985–, Sheriff 1996–97, Lord Mayor of London 1999–2000; Master, Stationers' and Newspaper Makers' Co. 1997–98; Commanding Officer Hon. Artillery Co. 1978–80, Regimental Col 1981–83, Master Gunner, Tower of London 1981–83; Fellow Inst. of Printing; Hon. DCL (City Univ.), Dr. h.c. (London Inst.) 2001. *Leisure interests:* ocean racing, walking, cycling. *Address:* MPG Ltd., The Gresham Press, Old Woking, Surrey, GU22 9LH, England (Office). *Telephone:* (1483) 757501 (Office). *Fax:* (1483) 724629 (Office).

MARTIN, G. Steven, PhD, FRS; American/British biochemist and biologist; b. 19 Sept. 1943, Oxford, England; s. of Kurt Martin and Hanna Martin; m. Gail Zuckman 1969; one s.; ed Manchester Grammar School, Univ. of Cambridge; Postdoctoral Fellow, Virus Lab., Univ. of Calif. at Berkeley 1968–71; mem. of staff Imperial Cancer Research Fund, London 1971–75; Asst Prof. Dept of Zoology, Univ. of Calif. at Berkeley 1975–79, Assoc. Prof. 1979–83, Prof. 1983–89, also Asst Research Virologist Cancer Research Lab. 1975–79, Assoc. Research Virologist 1979–83, Research Virologist 1983–, Prof. Dept of Molecular and Cell Biology 1989–, Head, Div. of Cell and Developmental Biology 1999–; John Simon Guggenheim Memorial Foundation Fellowship 1991–92; Fellow Royal Soc. 1998–; American Cancer Soc. Scholar Award in Cancer Research 1991–92. *Publications:* articles in various learned journals including Nature, Science, Cell. *Leisure interests:* hiking, bicycling, reading. *Address:* University of California at Berkeley, 401 Barker Hall #3204, Berkeley, CA 94720, USA. *Telephone:* (510) 642-1508. *Fax:* (510) 643-1729.

MARTIN, Sir George (Henry), Kt, CBE; British music industry executive, producer and composer (retd); b. 3 Jan. 1926; s. of Henry Martin and Bertha Beatrice Martin; m. 1st Sheena Rose Chisholm 1948; one s. one d.; m. 2nd Judy Lockhart Smith 1966; one s. one d.; ed Bromley Co. School, Kent, Guildhall School of Music and Drama; Sub-Lt RDVR 1944–47; worked at BBC 1950; with EMI Records Ltd 1950–65, produced all records featuring The Beatles and numerous other artists; formed AIR Group of cos. 1965, Chair. 1965–; built AIR Studios 1969; built AIR Studios, Montserrat 1979; completed new AIR Studios, Lyndhurst Hall, Hampstead 1992; co. merged with Chrysalis Group 1974, Dir 1978–; Chair. Heart of London Radio 1994–; scored the music for 15 films; Hon. Fellow Guildhall School of Music; Hon. mem. Royal Acad. of Music; Hon. DMus (Berklee Coll. of Music, Boston) 1989, MA (Salford) 1992; Grammy Awards 1964, 1967 (two), 1973, 1993, 1996; Ivor Novello Awards 1963, 1979. *Publications:* All You Need Is Ears 1979, Making Music 1983, Summer of Love 1994. *Leisure interests:* boats, sculpture, tennis, snooker. *Address:* c/o AIR Studios, Lyndhurst Hall, Hampstead, London, NW3 5NG, England. *Telephone:* (20) 7794-0660 (Office). *Fax:* (20) 7794-8518 (Office).

MARTIN, Henri-Jean, DèsSc; French professor of bibliographic studies; b. 16 Jan. 1924, Paris; s. of Gabriel Martin and Louise Desbazeille; m. Odile Lorber 1955; one s. three d.; ed Sorbonne, Ecole Nationale des Chartes; librarian, then Conservator, Bibliothèque Nationale 1947–58; seconded to CNRS 1958–62; Chief Conservator City Libraries, Lyon 1962–70; Dir of Studies, Ecole Pratique des Hautes Etudes 1960–; Emer. Prof., Ecole Nationale des Chartes; Visiting Fellow All Souls Coll. 1993; Corresp. Fellow British Acad.; Médaille d'Argent (CNRS) 1970, Grand Prix d'Histoire de la Ville de Paris 1985, Prix Louise Weiss (Bibliothèque Nationale), 1st Grand Prix Gobert (Académie Française) 1989, Gutenberg-Preis 1998; Chevalier Légion d'honneur. *Publications:* L'Apparition du livre (with Lucien Febvre) 1958, Livre, pouvoirs et société à Paris au XVIIe siècle (2 Vols) 1969, Histoire et pouvoirs de l'écrit 1988; Histoire de l'édition française (with Roger Chartier) (4 Vols) 1983–86; La Naissance du livre moderne 2000. *Leisure interest:* travelling. *Address:* Ecole Nationale des Chartes, 19 rue de la Sorbonne, 75005 Paris, France. *Telephone:* 1-55-42-75-00.

MARTIN, James Grubbs, PhD; American politician; b. 11 Dec. 1935, Savannah, Ga; s. of Arthur M. and Mary J. (Grubbs) Martin; m. Dorothy A. McAulay 1957; two s. one d.; ed Davidson (NC) Coll. and Princeton Univ.; Assoc. Prof. of Chem. Davidson Coll. 1960–72; mem. 93rd–98th Congresses from NC; Gov. of North Carolina 1985–93; Vice-Pres. Carolinas Medical Center 1993–2000; Dir James G. Cannon Medical Research Center 1993–, J. A. Jones Construction 1993–, Duke Energy Co. 1994–, Family Dollar Stores Inc. 1997–; Trustee Davidson Coll. 1998–; Republican; Charles Lathrop Parsons Award, American Chemical Soc. 1983. *Leisure interests:* golf, sailing, music. *Address:* Carolinas Medical Center, P.O. Box 32861, Charlotte, NC 28232, USA. *Telephone:* (704) 355-5314. *Fax:* (704) 355-0300 (Office). *E-mail:* jgmartin@carolinas.org (Office).

MARTIN, John Joseph Charles; British public relations executive; b. 25 Nov. 1940, Hove, Sussex; s. of Benjamin Martin and Lucille Martin; m. Frances Oster 1979; one s. one d.; ed Latymer Upper School; Dir Welbeck Public Relations 1972, Chief Exec. 1984, Chair. Welbeck Golin/Harris Communications Ltd 1988–; Founder John Martin Communications 1997. *Leisure interests:* painting, tennis. *Address:* Welbeck Golin/Harris Communications, 43 King Street, Covent Garden, London, WC2E 8RJ (Office); 53 Hampstead Way, Hampstead Garden Suburb, London, N.W.11, England (Home). *Telephone:* (20) 7836-6677 (Office); (20) 8455-8482 (Home). *Fax:* (20) 7836-5820 (Office).

MARTIN, Sir Laurence Woodward, Kt, MA, PhD, DL; British professor; b. 30 July 1928, St Austell; s. of Leonard Martin and Florence Mary Woodward; m. Betty Parnall 1951; one s. one d.; ed St Austell Grammar School, Christ's

Coll., Cambridge, Yale Univ.; RAF Flying Officer 1948–51; Asst Prof. MIT 1956–61; Assoc. Prof. Johns Hopkins Univ. 1961–64; Prof. Univ. of Wales 1964–68; King's Coll. London 1968–78; Vice-Chancellor Univ. of Newcastle 1978–90, Emer. Prof. 1991–; Arleigh Burke Chair in Strategy Center for Strategic and Int. Studies, Washington, D. C. 1998–2000; Visiting Prof. Univ. of Wales 1985–90; Dir Royal Inst. of Int. Affairs 1991–96; Fellow, King's Coll., London; Lees Knowles Lecturer, Cambridge; Reith Lecturer BBC; Hon. DCL (Newcastle) 1991. *Radio:* Reith Lectures 1981. *Publications:* Peace Without Victory 1958, The Sea in Modern Strategy 1967, Arms and Strategy 1973, The Two Edged Sword 1982, The Changing Face of Nuclear War 1987, British Foreign Policy (jtly) 1997. *Leisure interests:* travel, walking, fishing. *Address:* Center for Statistics and International Studies, 1800 K Street, N.W., Washington, DC 20001, USA (Office); 35, Witley Court, Coram Street, London, WC1N 1HP, England (Home). *E-mail:* lmartin@csis.org (Office).

MARTIN, Lynn; American politician; b. 26 Dec. 1939, Chicago, Ill.; m. Harry Leinenweber; two d.; ed Univ. of Ill.; mem. Winnebago Co. Bd 1972–76; mem. Ill. House of Reps. 1977–79, Senate 1979–81; mem. House of Reps. 1981–91; Sec. of Labor 1991–93; Vice-Chair. House Repub. Conf. 1982–86; Co-Chair. Bi-partisan Ethics Task Force; mem. House Rules Cttee, House Budget Cttee, Cttee on Public Works and Transportation, Cttee on Dist of Columbia; Prof. of Govt, Harvard Univ. 1993–. *Address:* Department of Government, Harvard University, Cambridge, MA 02138, USA.

MARTIN, Rt. Hon. Michael John; British politician; b. 3 July 1945; s. of Michael Martin and Mary Martin; m. Mary McLay 1966; one s. one d.; ed St Patrick's Boys' School, Glasgow; fmr sheet metal worker; AUEW Shop Steward, Rolls Royce, Hillington 1970–74, TU Organizer 1976–79; Councillor for Fairfield Ward, Glasgow Corpn 1973–74, for Balornock Ward, Glasgow Dist Council 1974–79; MP for Glasgow, Springburn 1979–; Parl. Pvt. Sec. to Rt. Hon. Denis Healey 1981–83; mem. Select Cttee for Trade and Industry 1983–86; Chair. Scottish Grand Cttee 1987–97; mem. Speaker's Panel of Chair. 1987–2000; Dep. Speaker of House of Commons 1997–2000, Speaker 2000–; mem. Coll. of Piping 1989–. *Leisure interests:* hill walking, local history, piping. *Address:* House of Commons, London, SW1A 0AA, England (Office). *Telephone:* (20) 7219-3000 (Office).

MARTIN, Micheál, MA; Irish politician; b. 16 Aug. 1960, Cork; s. of Paddy Martin; m. Mary O'Shea; one s.; ed Colaiste Chriost Rí, Univ. Coll., Cork; fmr secondary school teacher; elected to Cork Corpn 1985, Alderman 1991; former. Chair. Arts Cttee; Lord Mayor of Cork 1992–93; mem. Dáil Éireann 1989–; fmr Chair. Oireachtas All Party Cttee on the Irish Language; fmr mem. Dail Cttee on Crime, Dail Cttee on Finance and Gen. Affairs; Minister for Educ. 1997–2000, for Health and Children 2000–; Nat. Chair. Fianna Fail Nat. Exec. 1988–; Nat. Chair. Ogra Fianna Fail; mem. Bd Cork Opera House, Graffiti Theatre Co., Nat. Sculpture Factory, Everyman Palace Theatre, Crawford Gallery, College of Commerce and several school bds.; fmr mem. Governing Body Univ. Coll., Cork; won Cork Examiner Political Speaker of the Year Award 1987. *Address:* Department of Health and Children, Hawkins House, Hawkins Street, Dublin 2, Ireland (Office); 16 Silver Manor, Ballinlough, Cork, Ireland (Home). *Telephone:* (1) 6354000 (Office); (1) 295218 (Home). *Fax:* (1) 6354001 (Office). *E-mail:* queries@health.irlgov.ie (Office). *Website:* www.doh.ie (Office).

MARTIN, Hon. Paul, PC, BPhil; Canadian politician; b. 1938, Windsor, Ont.; m. Sheila Cowan; three s.; ed Univs. of Ottawa and Toronto; worked in legal branch of ECSC; called to Bar, Ontario 1966; with Power Corpn of Canada, Montreal; Chair. and CEO Canada Steamship Lines; Dir of seven maj. Canadian cos.; mem. Parl. 1988–; cand. for leadership of Liberal Party 1990; Co-Chair. Nat. Platform Cttee, Liberal Party of Canada 1993; Minister of Finance 1993–2002, also Minister Responsible for Fed. Office of Regional Devt 1993–95; Chair. G-20 (int. group) 1999–2002. *Publication:* Creating opportunity: The Liberal Plan for Canada (jtly.). *Address:* Parliament of Canada, Parliament Hill, Ottawa, Ont., Canada.

MARTIN, Ricky; Puerto Rican pop singer and actor; b. 24 Dec. 1971, San José; mem. Menudo (Latin pop band) 1984–89; worked as actor and singer in Mexico; played Miguel in General Hospital (TV series, USA), Marius in Les Misérables, Broadway; TV Spokesperson for Puerto Rican Tourism; has sold over 15 million records world-wide; Grammy Award for Best Latin Pop Album 1998. *Albums include:* Ricky Martin 1991, Me Amarás, A Medio Vivir 1995, Vuelve 1998, Ricky Martin 1999. *Singles include:* La Copa de la Vida (official song of World Cup, France '98), Vuelve, Un Dos Tres, Livin' La Vida Loca, Shake Your Bon-Bon, Story (with Christina Aguilera). *Address:* c/o Sony Music Latin, 550 Madison Avenue, New York, NY 10022, USA.

MARTIN, Steve; American actor and comedian; b. 1945, Waco, Texas; s. of Glenn Martin and Mary Lee Martin; m. Victoria Tennant 1986 (divorced 1994); ed Long Beach State Coll., Univ. of California, Los Angeles; TV writer for several shows; nightclub comedian; TV special Steve Martin: a Wild and Crazy Guy 1978; Georgie Award, American Guild of Variety Artists 1977, 1978. *Recordings:* Let's Get Small 1977 (Grammy Award), A Wild and Crazy Guy 1978 (Grammy Award), Comedy is not Pretty 1979, The Steve Martin Bros. *Film appearances include:* The Absent Minded Waiter, Sgt. Pepper's Lonely Hearts Club Band 1978, The Muppet Movie 1979, The Jerk 1979 (also screenwriter), Pennies from Heaven 1981, Dead Men Don't Wear Plaid 1982, The Man With Two Brains 1983, The Lonely Guy 1984, All of Me 1984 (Nat. Soc. of Film Critics Actor's Award), Three Amigos 1986, Little Shop of Horrors 1986, Roxanne 1987 (also screenwriter and Exec. Producer), Planes, Trains and Automobiles 1987, Parenthood 1989, My Blue Heaven, LA Story, Grand Canyon, Father of the Bride, Housesitter 1992, Leap of Faith 1992, Twist of Fate 1994, Mixed Nuts 1994, Father of the Bride 2, Sgt. Bilko 1995, The Spanish Prisoner, The Out of Towners, Bowfinger 1999, Joe Gould's Secret 2000, Novocaine 2001. *Address:* c/o Michelle Bega, Rogers & Cowan, 1888 Century Park East, Suite 500, Los Angeles, CA 90067 (Office); ICM, 8942 Wilshire Blvd, Beverly Hills, CA 90211, USA.

MARTIN, Todd; American tennis player; b. 8 July 1970, Hinsdale, Ill.; s. of Dale Martin and Lynn Martin; ed Northwestern Coll.; winner, New Haven Challenger 1989; turned professional 1990; semi-finalist Stella Artois Grass Court Championships, London 1993, Champion 1994, Champion (doubles with Pete Sampras, q.v.) 1995; finalist, Australian Open 1994, Grand Slam Cup, Munich 1995; semi-finalist, US Open 1994, Wimbledon 1994, 1996, Paris Open 1998; Champion, Scania Stockholm Open 1998; winner of 13 pro titles by end of 2002; mem. US Davis Cup Team 1994–99; Pres. ATP Players' Council 1996–97; Adidas/ATP Tour Sportsmanship Award 1993, 1994, ATP Tour Most Improved Player 1993. *Address:* c/o Advantage International, 1751 Pinnacle Drive, Suite 1500, McLean, VA 22102, USA.

MARTIN DELGADO, José María, D. EN. D.; Spanish university rector; b. 26 June 1947, Málaga; s. of Rafael Martín Delgado and María Jesús Martín Delgado; m. Irene Martín Delgado 1973; one s. two d.; ed Univs. of Granada and Bologna; Prof. of Fiscal and Tax Law, Univ. of Granada, Univ. Autónoma de Madrid, Univ. Autónoma de Barcelona, Univ. La Laguna and Univ. of Málaga (fmr Dean Faculty of Law) 1969–; Rector, Univ. of Málaga 1984–; mem. Spanish Asscn of Fiscal Law, Int. Fiscal Asscn; Dr. hc (Dickinson Coll., Pa). *Publications:* Análisis Jurídico del Fondo de Previsiones para Inversiones, Ordenamiento Tributario Español 1977, Sistema Democrático y Derecho Tributario. *Leisure interests:* reading, music, fishing, tennis. *Address:* Plaza El Ejido, s/n. Edificio Rectorado, 29071 Málaga (Office); C/. Mariano de Cavia, No. 9, 29016, Málaga, Spain (Home). *Telephone:* 253200 (Office); 296063 (Home).

MARTÍN FERNÁNDEZ, Miguel; Spanish banker; b. 9 Nov. 1943, Jerez de la Frontera; m. Anne Catherine Cleary 1972; one s. two d.; ed Univ. Complutense, Madrid; Head Budget and Finance Sections, Ministry of Finance 1969–72, Deputy Dir 1972–76; Economist, World Bank, Latin American Region 1976–77, Alt. Exec. Dir for Spain, Italy and Portugal, World Bank 1977–78; Dir-Gen. Treasury, Ministry of Finance 1978–79; Under-Sec. for Budget and Public Expenditure 1979–81; Pres. Inst. for Official Credit 1982; Head Annual Accounts Centre, Banco de España 1983–84; Under-Sec. Economy and Finance 1984–86; Dir-Gen. Banco de España 1986–92, Deputy Gov. 1992–2000, Head Internal Audit Office 2000–; Gran Placa de la Orden del Mérito Postal, Encomienda del Mérito Agrícola. *Address:* Banco de España, Calle Alcalá 50, 28014 Madrid, Spain.

MARTIN-LÖF, Per Erik Rutger, PhD; Swedish mathematician and philosopher; b. 8 May 1942, Stockholm; s. of Sverker Emil Bernhard Martin-Löf and Gertrud Cecilia Benedicks; m. Kerstin Maria Birgitta Forsell; one s. two d.; ed Stockholm Univ.; Asst, Math. Statistics, Stockholm Univ. 1961–64, Doctoral Scholar, Faculty of Science 1965–66, 1967–68, Docent, Math. Statistics 1969–70, Prof. of Logic 1994–; State Scholar of Swedish Inst., Moscow Univ. 1964–65; Amanuensis, Math. Inst., Aarhus Univ., Denmark 1966–67; Asst Prof., Dept of Math., Univ. of Ill., Chicago, USA 1968–69; researcher in Math. Logic, Swedish Natural Science Research Council 1970–81, in Logic 1981–83, Prof. of Logic 1983–94; mem. Academia Europaea, Royal Swedish Acad. of Sciences. *Publications:* Notes on Constructive Mathematics 1970, Intuitionistic Type Theory 1984. *Leisure interest:* ornithology. *Address:* Department of Mathematics, Stockholm University, 106 91 Stockholm (Office); Barnhusgatan 4, 111 23 Stockholm, Sweden (Home). *Telephone:* (8) 16-45-32 (Office); (8) 20-05-83 (Home). *Fax:* (8) 612-67-17 (Office). *E-mail:* pml@math.su.se (Office).

MARTIN MATEO, Ramón; Spanish professor of administrative law; b. 31 Aug. 1928, Valladolid; s. of Andrés Martín Mateo and Julia Martín Mateo; m. Clara Abad Lobejón 1966; four c.; Prof. of Admin. Law, Univs. of País Vasco, Madrid, Valladolid and Alicante; Rector Univ. of Alicante 1986; Order Mérito Civil; Order of Andrés Bello (Venezuela). *Publications:* D°- Administrativo Económico 1974, Manual de Derecho Administrativo, Bioética y Derecho 1987, Liberalización de la Economía: Más Estado, menos Administración, La eficacia social de la jurisdicción contencioso-administrativa 1989, Tratado de Derecho Ambiental (3 Vols) 1991–97. *Leisure interests:* mountaineering, music. *Address:* c/o Universidad de Alicante, Carretera de S. Vicente del Raspeig, 03690 Alicante, Spain.

MARTÍN VILLA, Rodolfo; Spanish politician and business executive; b. 3 Oct. 1934, Santa María del Páramo, León; m. María Pilar Pena Medina; two c.; ed Escuela Superior de Ingenieros Industriales, Madrid; Leader of Madrid Section, Sindicato Español Universitario, Nat. Leader 1962–64; Sec.-Gen. Syndical Org. 1969–74; mem. Council of the Realm; Nat. Econ. Adviser, Nat. Inst. of Industry; Nat. Econ. Adviser, Banco de Crédito Industrial, later Pres.; Civil Gov. of Barcelona and Prov. Head of Falangist Movement 1974–75; Minister for Relations with Trade Unions 1975–76, of the Interior 1976–79, of Territorial Admin. 1980–82; mem. Parl. (for Unión de Centro Democrático) 1977–83; First Deputy Prime Minister 1981–82; mem. Parl. (for Partido Popular) 1989–; mem. Exec. Cttee, Partido Popular 1989–; Chair. Endesa (Co.) 2000–02; mem. Sr Corps of Inspectors of State Finance; fmr mem. special

group of industrial engineers assisting Treasury. *Address:* c/o Endesa, Príncipe de Vergara 187, 28002 Madrid, Spain. *Telephone:* (91) 2131000 (Office). *Website:* www.endesa.es (Office).

MARTINA, Dominico (Don) F.; Netherlands Antilles politician; fmr finance officer, Govt of Curaçao; head, Govt social affairs Dept; f. Movimentu Antiyas Nobo 1979, Leader 1979–; MP 1979–; Prime Minister of Netherlands Antilles 1979–84, 1985–88. *Address:* Movimentu Antiyas Nobo, Landhuis Morgenster, Willemstad, Curaçao, Netherlands Antilles. *Telephone:* (9) 468-4781.

MARTINEAU, Rt Hon Paul, PC, QC; Canadian lawyer, judge and politician; b. 10 April 1921, Bryson, Québec; s. of Alphonse Martineau and Lucienne Lemieux; m. 1st Hélène Neclaw 1946 (died 2000); two d.; m. 2nd Jolanta Bak; legal practice at Campbells Bay, Que. 1950–, at Hull, Québec 1966–; fmr Crown Attorney for District of Pontiac, Québec; MP 1958–65; Parl. Asst to Prime Minister 1959–61; Deputy Speaker of House of Commons 1961–62; Minister of Mines and Tech. Surveys 1962–63; mem. Royal Comm. on Admin. of Justice 1967–70; Puisne Judge Superior Court Prov. of Québec 1980–96; Progressive Conservative. *Leisure interests:* painting, travelling. *Address:* 1204 Mountain Road, Aylmer, Québec J9H 5E1, Canada (Home). *Telephone:* (819) 827-2065 (Home). *Fax:* (819) 827-9169.

MARTINEZ, Arthur C., MBA; American business executive; b. 25 Sept. 1939, NY; s. of Arthur F. Martinez and Agnes (Caulfield) Martinez; m. Elizabeth Rusch 1966; two c.; ed Polytechnic Univ., Harvard Univ.; joined Exxon Chemical Co. 1960; Int. Paper Co. 1967–69; Talley Industries 1969–70; exec. positions in int. finance, RCA Corpn New York 1970–80; Sr Vice-Pres. and Chief Financial Officer, Saks 1980–84, Exec. Vice-Pres. for Admin. 1984-87; Sr Vice-Pres. and Group Chief Exec. Retail Div. BATUS Inc. 1987–90; Chair. and CEO Sears Merchandise Group, Sears, Roebuck & Co. 1992–95; fmr Vice-Chair. and mem Bd Dirs Saks Fifth Avenue, New York; Chair., CEO and mem. Bd Dirs Sears, Roebuck & Co., 1995–2000, CEO, Pres. 2000–; Chair. Bd Dirs Nat. Retail Fed.; fmrly Dir Ameritech Corpn and Amoco Corpn; mem. Bd Dirs. Fed. Reserve Bank of Chicago, Pepsi Co. Inc., Liz Claiborne Inc., Int. Flavors and Fragrances Inc., Martha Stewart Omni Media Inc.; Trustee Chicago Symphony Orchestra. *Leisure interests:* gardening, golf, tennis. *Address:* Sears Tower Suite 9800, P.O. Box 061079, Chicago, IL 40606, USA.

MARTINEZ, Conchita; Spanish tennis player; b. 16 April 1972, Monzón; d. of Cecilio Martínez and Conchita Martínez; turned professional 1988; reached last 16 French Open 1988, quarter-finals French Open 1989, 1990, 1991, 1992, 1993, semi-finals Italian Open 1991, French Open 1994, Australian, French and US Opens and Wimbledon 1995, French and US Opens 1996, quarter-finals Olympic Games 1992; with Arantxa Sanchez-Vicario (q.v.) won Olympic Doubles silver medal 1992 and bronze medal 1996; won Italian Open 1993, Hilton Head (SC), Italian Open, Stratton (Vt) 1994, Wimbledon Singles Champion 1994 (first Spanish woman to win title); by end of 2002 had won 42 WTA tour titles; Spanish Fed. Cup Team 1988–96, 1998, 2000–01; WTA Tour Most Impressive Newcomer 1989, Most Improved Player, Tennis Magazine 1994, ITF Award of Excellence 2001, Int. Tennis Hall of Fame 2001. *Leisure interests:* golf, horse riding, music, soccer, cinema, beach volleyball, skiing.

MARTINEZ, Mel; American politician and lawyer; b. 1947; m. Kitty Martinez; three c.; ed Florida State Univ. Coll. of Law; lawyer, Orlando 1973–98; Chair. Orange Co., Fla 1998–, CEO Govt providing urban services to residents; Sec. of Housing and Urban Devt 2001–; Chair. of Gov. Jeb Bush's Growth Man. Study Comm., of Bd Greater Orlando Aviation Authority, of Bd Orlando/Orange Co. Expressway Authority. *Address:* Department of Housing and Urban Development, 451 7th Street, SW, Washington, DC 20410, USA (Office). *Telephone:* (202) 708-0980 (Office). *Fax:* (202) 708-0299 (Office). *Website:* www.hud.gov (Office).

MARTINEZ, Victor Hipolito; Argentine politician, lawyer and law professor; b. 24 Nov. 1924, Córdoba; m. Fanny Munte; three s.; ed Univ. of Córdoba; Rep. to the Prov. Ass. of Córdoba 1967; Mayor of Córdoba 1963–66; Dir of newspaper Los Principios 1970–72; Vice-Pres. of Argentina 1983–89. *Address:* Senado de la Nación Argentina, Hipolito Yrigoyen 1849, C.P. 1089, Buenos Aires, Argentina.

MARTÍNEZ DE PERÓN, María Estela (Isabelita); Argentine politician and fmr dancer; b. 6 Feb. 1931, La Rioja Province; m. Gen. Juan Domingo Perón (Pres. of Argentina 1946–55, 1973–74) 1961 (died 1974); joined troupe of travelling folk dancers; danced in cabaret in several S American countries; lived in Spain 1960–73; returned to Argentina with Juan Perón, became Vice-Pres. of Argentina 1973–74, Pres. 1974–76 (deposed by mil. coup); Chair. Peronist Party 1974–85; detained 1976–81; settled in Madrid, Spain 1985.

MARTÍNEZ SOMALO, HE Cardinal Eduardo; Spanish ecclesiastic; b. 31 March 1927, Baños de Río Tobía; ordained 1950; elected Bishop of Tagora 1975, consecrated 1975, then Archbishop; cr. Cardinal 1988; mem., fmr Prefect of the Congregation for Divine Worship and the Discipline of the Sacraments; Prefect of Congregation for Insts. of Consecrated Life and for Socs. of Apostolic Life 1992–; Chamberlain of the Holy Roman Soc.; mem. Pontifical Comm. for Latin America, Congregations for Evangelization of Peoples, for the Clergy, for Catholic Educ. *Address:* Palazzo delle Congregazioni, Piazza Pio XII 3, 00193 Rome, Italy.

MARTINI, HE Cardinal Carlo Maria; Italian ecclesiastic; b. 15 Feb. 1927, Turin; ordained priest 1952; Archbishop of Milan 1980–2002; Consultant to Sacred Congregations for the Bishops, Doctrine of Faith, Religions and Catholic Educ.; mem. Pontifical Council for Culture; cr. Cardinal 1983; Pres. CCEE (Consilium Conferentiarum Episcopalium Europae) 1987–2002. *Address:* c/o Palazzo Arcivescovile, Piazza Fontana 2, 20122 Milan, Italy.

MARTINO, Antonio; Italian politician and university lecturer; b. 22 Dec. 1944, Messina, Sicily; s. of Gaetano Martino; lecturer in Monetary History and Politics, Chair. Faculty of Political Science, mem. Bd of Dirs. Libera Università Internazionale degli Studi Sociali (LUISS), Rome; fmr mem. Liberal Party (PLI); joined Forza Italia party Jan. 1994; Parl. Deputy March 1994–; Minister for Foreign Affairs 1994–95, of Defence 2001–. *Address:* Ministry of Defence, Via XX Settembre 8, 00187 Rome, Italy (Office). *Telephone:* (06) 4882126 (Office). *Fax:* (06) 4747775 (Office).

MARTINO, Juan José Bremer, BL; Mexican diplomatist; b. 1944, Mexico City; ed Nat. Autonomous Univ.; Pvt Sec. to Pres. of Mexico 1972–75, Deputy Sec. Ministry of the Presidency 1975–76; Head Nat. Fine Arts Inst. 1976–82; Deputy Sec. for Cultural Affairs, Ministry of Educ. 1982; Amb. to Sweden 1982, to USSR 1988–90, to Germany 1990–98, to Spain 1998–2000, to USA 2000–; Pres. Foreign Affairs Cttee of Chamber of Deputies 1985–88 (Co-Chair. Mexican Dels. to XXVI and XXVII Mexico–US Interparl. Comm. meetings Colorado Springs 1986, New Orleans 1988); mem. Ford Foundation Comm. to Study the Future of Mexican–American Relations 1986; Pres. Cervantino Int. Festival 1983; guest lecturer at several US, Mexican and European univs. *Address:* Embassy of Mexico, 1911 Pennsylvania Avenue, NW, Washington, DC 20006, USA (Office). *Telephone:* (202) 728-1600 (Office). *Fax:* (202) 728-1698 (Office). *E-mail:* mexembusa@aol.com (Office). *Website:* www.embassyofmexico.org (Office).

MARTINO, Archbishop Renato, DCnL; Italian ecclesiastic; b. 1933, Salerno; served in Diplomatic Service of the Holy See 1962–; fmr Apostolic Del. to Singapore, Malaysia, Laos and Brunei; fmr Apostolic Pro-nuncio to Thailand and Singapore; Perm. Observer of the Holy See to the UN 1986–2002, participated in Conf. of Sustainable Devt, Rio de Janeiro, Brazil 1992, Conf. on Population Devt, Cairo, Egypt 1994, Summit on Women, Beijing, China 1995, Conf. on Sustainable Devt, Johannesburg, SA 2001; Pres. Pontifical Council for Justice and Peace 2002–; decorations from govts of Italy, Portugal, Thailand, Argentina, Venezuela, Lebanon; four hon. doctorates. *Address:* Pontifical Council for Justice and Peace, Piazza S. Calisto 16, 00153 Rome, Italy (Office). *Telephone:* (06) 69879911 (Office). *Fax:* (06) 69887205 (Office). *E-mail:* pcjustpax@justpeace.va (Office).

MARTINS, António Gentil da Silva; Portuguese paediatric and plastic surgeon; b. 10 July 1930, Lisbon; s. of António Augusto da Silva Martins and Maria Madalena Gentil da Silva Martins; m. Maria Guilhermina Ivens Ferraz Jardim da Silva Martins 1963; three s. five d.; ed Univ. of Lisbon; Medical Faculty, Univ. of Lisbon 1953–; intern, Hospitais Civis, Lisbon; Registrar, Alder Hey Children's Hosp., Liverpool; founder and Head, Paediatric Dept Instituto Português de Oncologia de F. Gentil 1960–87, consultant paediatric surgeon 1987–; paediatric surgeon, Hosp. D. Estefania (Children's Hosp.), Lisbon 1965, Dir of Paediatric Surgery 1987–; Assoc. Prof. of Paediatric Surgery, Faculty of Medical Sciences, Lisbon 1984–2002; Temporary Consultant Paediatric Cancer, WHO 1977, EEC 1991; Pres. Portuguese Soc. of Plastic and Reconstructive Surgery 1968–74, Ordem dos Médicos (Portuguese Medical Asscn) 1978–86, Portuguese Asscn of Paediatric Surgeons 1975–84, 1991–94, World Medical Asscn 1981–83, Southern Branch Portuguese League Against Cancer 1988–94; Pres. Portuguese League Against Cancer 1995–97; mem. Exec. Council World Fed. of Asscns. of Paediatric Surgeons 1983–89; Council, Int. Conf. of Childhood Cancer Parent Asscns. 1994–95; mem. numerous other professional socs. etc.; awarded Silver Plate for film on separation of Siamese twins; Grande Oficial da Ordem do Infante D. Henrique (1980) and other awards. *Achievements include:* separation of six pairs of Siamese twins with nine survivors. *Publications:* textbook on Plastic Surgery of the Ibero-Latin-American Foundation of Plastic Surgery (co-author) 1986, textbook on Intersexual States (co-author), Le Médecin et les droits de l'homme (co-author) 1982. *Leisure interests:* target-shooting, volleyball, tennis, collecting stamps and coins, music, photography. *Address:* Av. Almirante Reis 62-5 Dto, 1050 Lisbon (Office); Rua D. Francisco Manuel de Melo 1 3°, Lisbon 1070-085, Portugal (Home). *Telephone:* (1) 218126663 (Office); (1) 213851436 (Home). *Fax:* (1) 213851436 (Home).

MARTINS, Peter; American ballet director, choreographer and former dancer; b. 27 Oct. 1946, Copenhagen, Denmark; m. 1st Lise la Cour (divorced 1973); one c.; m. 2nd Darci Kistler (q.v.) 1991; one d.; pupil of Vera Volkova and Stanley Williams with Royal Danish Ballet; Dir NY City Ballet; Teacher, School of American Ballet 1975, NY Ballet 1975, Ballet Master 1981–83, Co-Ballet Master-in-Chief 1983–89, Master-in-Chief 1989; Artistic Adviser, Pa Ballet 1982–; mem. Royal Danish Ballet 1965–67, Prin. Dancer (including Bournonville repertory) 1967; Guest Artist, NY Ballet 1967–70, Prin. Dancer 1970–83; Guest Artist Regional Ballet Cos. US, also Nat. Ballet, Canada, Royal Ballet, London, Grand Theatre, Geneva, Paris Opera, Vienna State Opera, Munich State Opera, London Festival Ballet, Ballet Int., Royal Danish Ballet; Dance magazine award 1977; Cue's Golden Apple award 1977, Award of Merit, Phila Art Alliance 1985. *Choreographed Broadway musicals include:* Dream of the Twins (co-choreographer) 1982, On your Toes 1982, Song and Dance 1985. *Choreographed works include:* Calcium Light Night 1977, Tricolore (Pas de Basque Section) 1978, Rossini Pas de Deux 1978, Tango-Tango (ice ballet) 1978, Dido and Aeneas 1979, Sonate di Scarlatti 1979, Eight Easy Pieces 1980, Lille Suite 1980, Suite from Histoire de Soldat 1981, Capriccio Italien 1981, The Magic Flute 1981, Symphony No. 1 1981, Délibes Divertissement 1982, Piano-Rag-Music 1982, Concerto for Two Solo Pianos 1982, Waltzes 1983, Rossini Quartets 1983, Tango 1983, A Schubertiad 1984, Mozart Violin Concerto 1984, Poulenc Sonata 1985, La Sylphide 1985, Valse Triste 1985, Eight More 1985, We Are the World 1985, Eight Miniatures 1985, Ecstatic Orange, Tanzspiel 1988, Jazz 1993, Symphonic Dances 1994, Barber Violin Concerto 1994, Mozart Piano Concerto (No. 17) 1994, X-Ray 1995. *Publication:* Far From Denmark (autobiog.) 1982. *Address:* New York City Ballet, New York State Theater, 20 Lincoln Center Plaza, New York, NY 10023, USA.

MARTINS, Rudolf, LLD; Austrian diplomatist (retd); b. 9 Feb. 1915, Zürich; s. of Martin Martins and Carola Martins (née Dobolschek); ed Humanistisches Gymnasium (Vienna XIII) and Univ. of Vienna; with Fed. Chamber of Commerce, Vienna 1946–47; Austrian Trade Commr for Switzerland and Liechtenstein and Sec. of Austrian Chamber of Commerce for Switzerland, Zürich 1947–49; with Fed. Chamber of Commerce, Vienna 1949–59; Counsellor, Adviser on Multilateral Trade and Commerce, Ministry of Foreign Affairs 1959–63; Counsellor, Head of Dept for Multilateral Trade and Commerce Questions, Ministry of Trade and Reconstruction 1963–65; Amb. and Perm. Austrian Rep. to Office of UN and UN Specialized Agencies, Geneva and Leader of Austrian Del. to European Free Trade Asscn (EFTA) 1965–68, 1972–76; Envoy Extraordinary and Minister Plenipotentiary, Head of Dept for Multilateral Trade and Commerce Questions, Ministry of Foreign Affairs 1968–72; Office of the Sec.-Gen. Ministry of Foreign Affairs 1977; Consul-Gen. of Austria at Zagreb 1978–80; Hon. Amb. for Life 1980; Goldenes Ehrenzeichen für Verdienste um die Republik Österreich. *Publications:* Statesmanship in Civil War (Spain's President Azaña) 1982, Medieval Bosnia 1987, Von der Souveränität zur Globalisierung im Erlebnis eines Diplomaten 1998; numerous articles; Ed. Der Arlberg und seine Strasse 1992. *Leisure interests:* music, linguistics. *Address:* Schloss Schönbrunn 39, 1130 Vienna, Austria (Home).

MARTINSON, Ida Marie, PhD; American professor of nursing; b. 8 Nov. 1936, Mentor, Minn.; m. Paul Martinson 1962; one s. one d.; ed St Luke's Hosp. School of Nursing, Duluth, Minn. and Univs of Minnesota and Illinois; Instructor in Tuberculosis Nursing, St Luke's Hosp., Duluth 1957–58; Instructor in Nursing, Thornton Jr Coll., Harvey, Ill. 1967–69; Asst Prof. and Chair. of Research, Univ. of Minn. School of Nursing 1972–74, Assoc. Prof. and Dir of Research 1974–77, Prof. and Dir of Research 1977–82; Prof. Dept of Family Health Care Nursing, Univ. of Calif., San Francisco 1982–, Chair. 1982–89; Carl Walter and Margaret Davis Walter Visiting Prof. at Payne Bolton School of Nursing, Case Western Reserve Univ., Cleveland, Ohio 1994–96; Chair., Prof., Dept of Health Sciences, Hong Kong Polytechnic Univ. 1996–2000; Fellow American Acad. of Nursing; mem. Inst. of Medicine, NAS 1981–, mem. Governing Council 1984–86; Pres. Children's Hospice Int. 1986–88; Co-founder of Children's Cancer Foundation, Taiwan; f. East Asia Forum of Nursing Schools (EAFONS); Sigma Theta Tau Int. Soc. of Nursing 1999. *Publications:* Home Care: A manual for implementation of home care for children dying of cancer 1978, Home Care: A manual for parents (with D. Moldow) 1979, Family Nursing 1989, Home Care Health Nursing 1989; more than 100 articles in journals, 56 book chapters (1994) and one film; ed. of several books on home and family nursing. *Leisure interests:* skiing, walking, reading. *Address:* 2 Koret Way, Room N411Y, Department of Family Health Care Nursing, University of California, San Francisco, CA 94143, USA. *Telephone:* (415) 476-4694. *Fax:* (415) 753-2161 (Office). *E-mail:* ida .martinson@nursing.ucsf.edu (Office).

MARTIROSSIAN, Radick Martirosovich, PhD; Armenian scientist; b. 1 May 1936, Madagis, Nagorno Karabakh; s. of Martiros A. Martirossian and Astkhik G. Harutunian; m. Rena A. Kasparova 1965, two s.; ed Yerevan State Univ. and Lebedev Physics Inst. of Acad. of Sciences, Moscow; Dir Inst. of Radiophysics and Electronics, Nat. Acad. of Sciences of Armenia 1980–; Rector, Yerevan State Univ. Oct. 1993–; mem. Armenian Acad. of Sciences, 'Intercosmos' and 'Radioastronomy' scientific councils; research areas: microwave quantum amplifiers, remote sensing, microwave telecommunications, radioastronomy; Armenian State Prize in Science and Eng 1988, Ukrainian State Prize 1989; Gagarin Medal for Space Research. *Leisure interest:* chess. *Address:* Yerevan State University, 1 Alex Manoogian Street, 375049 Yerevan, Armenia. *Telephone:* (2) 55-46-29. *Fax:* (2) 15-10-87.

MARTO, Michel, MA, PhD; Jordanian economist and politician; b. 21 Aug. 1940, Jerusalem; s. of Issa Marto; m. Lucy Peridakis 1970; one s. two d.; ed Middle East Tech. Univ., Ankara, Univ. of S Calif., LA; Dir Econ. Research, Central Bank of Jordan 1969–70, Deputy Gov. 1989–97; Dir Econ. Research, Royal Scientific Soc. 1970–75; economist, World Bank, Washington DC 1975–77; Deputy Gen. Man. Jordan Fertilizer Industry 1977–79; Deputy Gen. Man. Bank of Jordan 1979–86, Man. Dir 1986–89; Chair. Jordanian Securities Comm. 1997–98; Minister of Finance 1998–; Al-Hussein Distinguished Service Medal, Jordanian Star Medal (1st Class), Jordanian Independence Medal (1st Class), Chevalier, Ordre du mérite national, France; Commdr Légion d'honneur; Omicron Delta Epsilon (Honor Soc. in Econs), USA, Phi Kappa Phi (Top Univ. Grad.), USA. *Publications:* various articles on economic topics in specialist journals. *Leisure interests:* reading, music, theatre. *Address:* Ministry of Finance, PO Box 85, Amman 11118 (Office); PO Box

2927, Amman 11181, Jordan. *Telephone:* (6) 4643313 (Office); (6) 5926745 (Home). *Fax:* (6) 4643121 (Office); (6) 5930718 (Home). *E-mail:* michelmarto@hotmail.com.

MARTONYI, János, PhD; Hungarian politician and lawyer; b. 5 April 1944, Kolozsvár (now Cluj-Napoca, Romania); m.; one s. one d.; ed József Attila Univ., Szeged, City of London Coll., Hague Acad. of Int. Law; Trade Sec., Brussels 1979–84; Head of Dept, Ministry of Foreign Trade 1984–89; Commr for Privatization 1989–90; State Sec. Ministry of Int. Econ. Relations 1990–91, Ministry of Foreign Affairs 1991–94, Minister of Foreign Affairs 1998–; Prof. Loránd Eötvös Univ., Budapest 1990; Head Inst. of Private Int. Law, József Attila Univ., Szeged 1997; Visiting Prof. Colls. of Europe, Bruges, Belgium and Natolin, Poland; man. partner Martonyi és Kajtár, Baker and McKenzie (law firm), Budapest office 1994–98; Commdr Légion d'honneur, Grosses Goldenes Ehrenzeichen (Austria) 2000. *Publications:* numerous papers in various languages. *Address:* Ministry of Foreign Affairs, 1027 Budapest, Bem rkp. 47, Hungary. *Telephone:* (1) 458-1000. *Fax:* (1) 212-5918. *E-mail:* titkarsag.min@kum.hu (Office). *Website:* www.mfa.gov.hu (Office).

MARTRE, Henri Jean François; French telecommunications and space engineer; b. 6 Feb. 1928, Bélesta; s. of Marius Martre and Paule Maugard; m. Odette Coppier 1953; three d.; ed Ecole Polytechnique; telecommunications Eeng 1952–59; Deputy Head of telecommunications service in the production of armaments 1961–64, Head of Bureau Département Electronique, then Head Industrial Bureau of the Cen. Service of Telecommunications to the Ministerial Del. for Armaments 1964–66, Deputy Dir Industrial Affairs 1966, Dir of Programmes and Industrial Aspects of Armaments 1971–74, Gen. Eng First Class for Armaments 1974, Gen. Del. for Armaments 1977–83, State Admin. Société Nat. Industrielle Aérospatiale 1974–77, also SNECMA, Société Française d'Equipements pour la Navigation Aérienne; mem. Atomic Energy Cttee 1977–83; Pres. and Dir-Gen. Société Aérospatiale 1983–92; Vice-Pres. Surveillance Council for the Airbus Industry 1986–92; Pres. Club d'information et de reflexion sur l'économie mondiale (Cirem) 1987–98, Asscn européenne des constructeurs de matériel aérospatial 1988 (Hon. Pres. 1988), Groupement des industries françaises aéronautiques et spatiales (Gifas) 1990–93, France-Japan Cttee 1991–, Edifrance 1992–94, Asscn Française de Normalisation (AFNOR) 1993–2002, Supervisory Bd ESL Network 1996–; mem. Bd of Dirs Siemens-France 1994–99, Renault 1996–, France Telecom 2003–; Vice-Pres. Conseil de Surveillance de Bertin & Cie 1996, Pres. 1997–99; mem. Conseil supérieur de l'aviation marchande 1998–; Trustee Sogepa-Advisory Council Banque de France, Andersen; Grand-Croix Légion d'honneur, Commdr, Ordre nat. du Mérite, Médaille de l'Aéronautique, Grand Officer Order of Merit (Germany), Order of the Crown (Belgium), Order of the Pole Star (Sweden), Commdr Legion of Merit (USA), Commdr White Rose (Finland), Order of Mil. Merit (Brazil), Order of the Sacred Treasure (Japan). *Leisure interests:* skiing, sailing. *Address:* 13 rue du Clos Fenquières, 75015 Paris, France (Home). *Telephone:* 1-45-33-08-82 (Home). *E-mail:* henrimartre@noos.fr (Office).

MARTY, Martin E., MDiv, PhD, STM; American professor of religious history and ecclesiastic; b. 5 Feb. 1928, West Point, Neb.; s. of Emil A. Marty and Anne Louise Wuerdemann Marty; m. 1st Elsa Schumacher 1952 (died 1981); seven c.; m. 2nd Harriet Lindemann 1982; ed Concordia Seminary, St Louis, Lutheran School of Theology, Chicago and Univ. of Chicago; Lutheran Minister 1952–63; Prof. of History of Modern Christianity Univ. of Chicago 1963–, Fairfax M. Cone Distinguished Service Prof. 1978–98; Assoc. Ed. The Christian Century 1956–85, Sr Ed. 1985–98; Sr Scholar in Residence, Park Ridge Center 1985, Pres. 1985–89; Pres. American Soc. of Church History 1971, American Catholic History Asscn 1981, American Acad. of Religion 1988; Dir Fundamentalism project American Acad. of Arts and Sciences 1988–, The Public Religion Project 1996–99; Fellow AAAS, Soc. of American Historians; over 70 hon. degrees; Nat. Book Award for Righteous Empire 1972; Nat. Medal Humanities 1997. *Publications:* many books and numerous articles on religious history, theology and cultural criticism. *Leisure interests:* good eating, baroque music, calligraphy. *Address:* 239 Scottswood Road, Riverside, IL 60546, USA (Home). *E-mail:* memarty@aol.com (Home).

MARTYNOV, Vladlen Arkadyevich, D.ECON.SC.; Russian economist; b. 14 Dec. 1929, Saratov; s. of Arkady Martynov and Evdokiya Martynova; m. Liya Romanova 1955; m.; one s.; ed Leningrad Univ.; mem. CPSU 1952–91; lecturer, Leningrad Eng Inst. 1955–57; Sr researcher, Head of Sector, Deputy Dir Inst. of World Economy and Int. Relations (IMEMO) 1957–89, Dir 1989–; Corresp. mem. USSR (now Russian) Acad. of Sciences 1987–94, mem. 1994–; mem. CPSU Cen. Cttee 1990–91; USSR State Prize 1977. *Publications:* articles on agriculture of industrially developed countries and capitalist economies. *Leisure interests:* classical music, swimming. *Address:* Institute of World Economy and International Relations (IMEMO), Profsoyuznaya Str. 23, GSP-7, 117859 Moscow, Russia. *Telephone:* (095) 120-43-32 (Office); (095) 429-66-41 (Home). *Fax:* (095) 310-7027 (Office). *E-mail:* imemoran@glas.apc.org (Office).

MARTZ, Judy Helen; American state official; b. 28 July 1943, Big Timber, Mont.; m. Harry Martz 1965; one s. one d.; propr. Martz Disposal Services, 1971–; mem. U.S. World Speed Skating Team, Japan, 1963, U.S. Olympic Team, Innsbruck, Austria 1964; Exec. Dir. U.S. High Altitude Speed Skating Center, Butte, Mont, 1985–89; field rep., Senator Conrad Burns, 1989–96; Gov. State of Mont. 1996–; coach, Mont. Amateur Speed Skating Asscn; Pres. Advisory Bd., U.S. Int. Speed Skating Asscn; mem. Bd. Dirs. Youth Hockey Asscn, St James Community Hospital, Oasis HUD Housing Project; Miss Rodeo Mont. 1963, Butte Sports Hall of Fame 1987. *Address:* Office of the Governor, State Capitol, Helena, MT 59620-0801, U.S.A. (Office).

MARUF, Taha Mohi ed-Din, LLB; Iraqi politician and diplomatist; b. 1924, Sulaimaniyah; s. of Muhyiddin and Fatima Marouf; ed Coll. of Law, Univ. of Baghdad; worked as lawyer; joined Diplomatic Service 1949; Minister of State 1968–70; Minister of Works and Housing 1968; Amb. to Italy, concurrently non-resident Amb. to Malta and Albania 1970–74; Vice-Pres. of Iraq 1974–2003; mem. Higher Cttee of Nat. Progressive Front 1975–2003; Chair. African Affairs Bureau of Revolutionary Command Council 1976–2003.

MARUSIN, Yury Mikhailovich; Russian tenor; b. 8 Dec. 1945, Kizel, Perm Region; ed Leningrad State Conservatory; soloist Maly Opera and Ballet Theatre Leningrad 1972–80; soloist Mariinsky Theatre 1980–90; guest soloist Wiener Staatsoper 1986–91; USSR State Prize 1985; Best Foreign Singer Diploma (Italy) 1982, People's Artist of USSR 1983. *Repertoire includes:* over 50 parts in operas. *Address:* IMC Artists Management Inc., 51 MacDougal Street, Suite 300, New York, NY 10012, USA. *Telephone:* (800) 353-6494 (Office). *E-mail:* imcartist@onebox.com (Office).

MARUSTE, Rait; Estonian judge; b. 27 Sept. 1953, Pärnu; s. of Albert Maruste and Mare Maruste; m. Mare Maruste (née Nurk) 1976; one s. one d.; ed Pärnu Jaagupi Secondary School, Tartu Univ.; lecturer, Tartu Univ. 1977–85, Sr Lecturer 1985–87, Asst Prof. 1987–, Head of Dept of Criminal Law and Procedure 1991; cand. for doctorate 1991–93; fmr. Chief Justice of Supreme Court. *Publications:* Human Rights and Principles of Fair Trial 1993. *Leisure interests:* sailing, skiing. *Address:* Lossi str. 17, EE 2400 Tartu, Estonia; Pikk str. 94, Apt. 27, EE 2400 Tartu (Home). *Telephone:* 441411; (7) 436696 (Home). *Fax:* (7) 441433.

MARX, György, PhD; Hungarian physicist; b. 25 May 1927, Budapest; s. of Dr István Marx and Julia László; m. Edit Koczkás 1952; two s. one d.; ed Eötvös Univ., Budapest; started as staff member, Univ. Inst. for Theoretical Physics, Eötvös Univ., Univ. Prof. 1964–; Prof., Dept of Atomic Physics 1970–97, Prof. Emer. 1997–; Pres. Hungarian Physical Soc. 1996–99; Fellow Hungarian Acad. of Sciences 1970–, Int. Astronautical Acad., Paris 1976–, Academia Europaea, London 1988–, American Physical Soc. 1998–, Inst. of Physics, London 1998–; Hon. mem. Group for Int. Research in Educ. of Physics 1998–; Hon. Prof. Univ. of Vienna 1970–; fmr Vice-Pres. Int. Union for Pure and Applied Physics, Int. Astronautical Fed.; fmr Chair. High Energy Div. of European Physical Soc., Bioastronomy Comm. of Int. Astronomical Union; Hon. Pres. Roland Eötvös Physical Soc.; Visiting Prof. Univs of Stanford 1965–66, Mexico 1965, Vienna 1970, Lahore 1973, Nanjing 1987, Kyoto 1988; initiator Int. Neutrino Conf. series 1972, Chair. Int. Neutrino Cttee; principal fields: particle, nuclear and astrophysics; discoverer of lepton charge conservation; Kossuth Prize 1956; Labour Order of Merit Golden Degree 1968; Golden Comenius Medal, Bratislava 1996, Medal of Simón Bolívar Univ., Caracas 1996, Medal of IUPAP's Int. Comm. on Physics Educ. 1997, Bragg Medal, Inst. of Physics, London 2001. *Publications:* Életrevaló atomok (Atoms in Action) 1978, Jövőidőben (Future Tense) 1979, Atomközelben (Atom at Close Range) 1981, Atommag-közelben (Nuclears at Close Range) 1996, The Voice of the Martians 1997 (in Hungarian, English and Japanese) and other books; 500 papers in Hungarian and 250 in foreign scientific journals. *Leisure interests:* school education, space, archaeology. *Address:* Department of Atomic Physics, Eötvös University, Pázmány sétány 1A, 1117 Budapest (Office); Fehérvári út 119, 1119 Budapest, Hungary (Home). *Telephone:* (1) 372-2751 (Office); (1) 205-5139 (Home). *Fax:* (1) 372-2753. *E-mail:* marx@lauder.hu.

MAS, Artur; Spanish politician; ed Liceu Francès de Barcelona, L'Escola Aula, Faculties of Law and Econs., Univ. of Barcelona; joined Dept of Trade and Tourism, Generalitat, Barcelona 1982; est. Partnership for Commercial Promotion of Catalonia (COPCA); mem. list Convergència i Unió, Barcelona 1987, selected for municipal elections 1991, elected Deputy to Parl. of Catalonia 1995, Spokesperson for Generalitat 2000, Regional Minister 2001; Leader Convergència i Unió (CiU) Coalition 2000–; Pres. Convergència Democràtica de Catalunya (CDC) 1997–, Sec.-Gen. 2000–; Dir Investment Co., Catalan Industrial Group 1988–; mem. Admin Bd Caixa d'Estalvis de Catalunya. *Leisure interest:* French literature. *Address:* Convergència Democràtica de Catalunya (CDC), Córcega 331-333, 08037 Barcelona, Spain (Office).

MASÁR, Vladimír; Slovak banker; b. 2 May 1958, Partizánske; s. of Vladimír Masár and Jolana Masárová; m. Dagmar Glasová 1983; one s. one d.; ed Univ. of Econs Bratislava; State Bank of Czechoslovakia 1981–90; Deputy Dir City Br., Gen. Credit Bank 1990–91; Dir Credit Dept Tatra Bank-Slovakia 1992; State Sec. Ministry of Finance of Slovakia 1992; Gov. Nat. Bank of Slovakia 1993–99; Chair., Partner Deloitte & Touche 2000–. *Leisure interests:* swimming, tennis. *Address:* Deloitte & Touche, BBC, Prievozká 12, 821 09 Bratislava, Slovakia. *Telephone:* (7) 5824-9133 (Office). *Fax:* (7) 5824-9222 (Office). *E-mail:* vladimir.masar@deloitte.sk (Office). *Website:* www.deloittece.com (Office).

MASARSKY, Mark Veniaminovich, CAND. PHIL. SC.; Russian business executive and journalist; b. 19 June 1940, Muryinskoye, Novgorod Region; m. Olga Yevgen'yevna Fedosova; one s. one d.; ed Rostov Univ.; teacher, Taganrog Radio-Tech. Inst. 1965–67, Rostov Univ. 1967–70, Khabarovsk Polytechnical Inst. 1970–75; Corresp. Young Communist 1977–82; f. and mem. Gold-diggers of Petchora co-operative 1982–87; f. and Chair. Volkhov Jt-stock co. 1987–, Russian Gold co.; one of founders of Moscow Commodity Exchange; Pres. Int. Asscn of Factory Leaders 1992–2001; Chair. Entrepreneurs Council, Moscow Govt 1996–; mem. Bd of Dirs. Russian Bank of Reconstruction and Devt, Novobank Volkhov-Presnaya Investment Co., ITAR-TASS Co.; mem. Expert-Analytical Council to Pres. Yeltsin; mem. Conciliatory Comm. on Public Accord Agreement; mem. Bd Public Chamber, Pres.'s Admin. *Publications:* The Convincing, Time of Orders and Times of Troubles. *Address:* Entrepreneurs Council, Moscow Government, Novy Arbat 36, Moscow, Russia. *Telephone:* (095) 290-87-04.

MASCARENHAS GOMEZ MONTEIRO, António Manuel; Cape Verde politician and lawyer; m. Maria Monteiro 1967; one s. two d.; ed Univ. of Lisbon, Univ. of Coimbra, Catholic Univ. Louvain, Belgium; Asst and researcher, Inter-university Centre Public Law, Belgium 1974–77; Sec.-Gen. Nat. Ass. 1977–80; Judge of Supreme Court 1980–90; Pres. of Cape Verde 1991–2001; f. Asscns. of Magistrates of Cape Verde 1977; Pres. Third Conference on Regional System of Human Rights Protection in Africa, America and Europe, Strasbourg 1992; mem. OAU Mission to Angola 1992; Pres. Colloquium on Constitutional Transition in Africa at Catholic Univ. Louvain 1993; Presidential Medal of Freedom 1991. *Publications:* Reflexions sur compétence d'un gouvernement démissionnaire 1977, La notion de l'expédition des affaires courantes 1977, La Charte Africaine des Droits de l'Homme et des Peuples 1991. *Address:* c/o Presidência da República, C.P. 100, Praia, Santiago, Cape Verde.

MASCHLER, Thomas Michael; British publisher; b. 16 Aug. 1933; s. of Kurt Leo Maschler and Rita Masseron; m. 1st Fay Coventry 1970 (divorced 1987); one s. two d.; m. 2nd Regina Kulinicz 1988; ed Leighton Park School; Production Asst, André Deutsch 1955–56; Editor, MacGibbon and Kee 1956–58; Fiction Editor, Penguin Books 1958–60; Editorial Dir, Jonathan Cape Ltd 1960–70, Dir 1960–, Chair. 1970–91, Publr 1991–; Dir Random House 1987; Assoc. Producer The French Lieutenant's Woman (film) 1981. *Publications:* Ed. Declarations 1957, New English Dramatists Series 1959–63. *Address:* c/o Random Century House, 20 Vauxhall Bridge Road, London, SW1V 2SA, England.

MASEFIELD, John Thorold, CMG, MA; British diplomatist; b. 1 Oct 1939, Kampala, Uganda; s. of Dr Geoffrey Bussell Masefield and Mildred Joy Thorold Rogers; m. Jennifer Mary Trowell MBE1962; two s. one d. (and one d. deceased); ed Repton School, Derbyshire, St John's Coll. Cambridge; joined Commonwealth Relations Office 1962, Pvt. Sec. to Perm. Under-Sec. 1963–64, Second Sec. Kuala Lumpur 1964–65, Warsaw 1966–67, FCO 1967–69, First Sec. UK Del. to Disarmament Conf., Geneva 1970–74, Deputy Head Planning Staff. FCO 1974–77, Far Eastern Dept 1977–79, Counsellor, Head of Chancery, Consul-Gen. Islamabad 1979–82, Head Personnel Services Dept FCO 1982–85, Head Far Eastern Dept 1985–87, Fellow Center for Int. Affairs, Harvard Univ. 1987–88, mem. Civil Service Selection Bd 1988–89; High Commr in Tanzania 1989–92; Asst Under-Sec. of State for S and SE Asia and the Pacific, FCO 1992–94; High Commr in Nigeria 1994–97 (also Accred to Benin and Chad); Gov. and C-in-C of Bermuda 1997–2001; KStJ. *Leisure interests:* fruit and vegetables. *Address:* c/o Foreign and Commonwealth Office, Whitehall, London, SW1A 2AH, England.

MASEFIELD, Sir Peter Gordon, Kt, MA, CEng, FRAeS, F.C.INST.T., FBIM, C.I.MECH.E.; British administrator and engineer; b. 19 March 1914, Trentham, Staffordshire; s. of late Dr. W Gordon Masefield, CBE, MRCS, LRCP and Marian Ada Lloyd-Owen; m. Patricia Doreen Rooney 1936; three s. one d.; ed Westminster School, Chillon Coll., Switzerland and Jesus Coll., Cambridge; on Design Staff, Fairey Aviation Co. Ltd 1935–37; Asst Tech. Ed. The Aeroplane 1937–39, Tech. Ed. 1939–43; war corresp. and air corresp. The Sunday Times 1940–43; Personal Adviser on Civil Air Transport to Lord Privy Seal and Sec. of Civil Aviation Cttee of War Cabinet 1943–45; British Civil Air Attaché, British Embassy, Washington, DC 1945–46; Dir-Gen. of Long-Term Planning and Projects, Ministry of Civil Aviation 1947–48; Chief Exec. and mem. of Bd British European Airways 1949–56; Man. Dir Bristol Aircraft Ltd 1956–60, British Executive and General Aviation Ltd, Beagle Aircraft Ltd 1960–67 (Chair. 1968–70); Chair. London Transport Exec. 1980–82; Dir Pressed Steel Co. Ltd 1960–67; Pres. Inst. of Transport 1955–56; mem. Aeronautical Research Council 1956–60, Pres. Royal Aeronautical Soc. 1959–60; Chair. Air Transport Section, London Chamber of Commerce 1962–65; Chair. British Airports Authority 1965–71; Chair. Royal Aero Club of the UK 1964–70; Vice-Chair. United Service and Royal Aero Club 1970–71; Chair. Imperial War Museum 1977–78; Chair. British Asscn of Aviation Consultants 1972–84 (Patron 1984–), Project Man. Ltd 1972–88; Pres. Nigerian-British Chamber of Commerce 1977–81; Chair., CEO London Transport 1980–82; Dir Nationwide Building Soc. 1973–86, London Transport Exec. 1973–82, Worldwide Estates Ltd 1972–88, Worldwide Properties Ltd; Deputy Chair. Caledonian Airways Ltd 1978–87; Chair. Royal Soc. of Arts 1977–79, Vice-Pres. 1980; Chair. Brooklands Museum Trust 1987–93, Pres. 1993–; mem. CAA Flight Time Limitations Bd, Bd of London Transport Exec.; Hon. Fellow, Inst. Aeronautics and Astronautics (USA), Canadian Aeronautical and Space Inst.; Hon. DSc (Cranfield), DTech (Loughborough). *Publication:* To Ride the Storm 1982. *Leisure interests:* reading, writing, gardening, photography, flying. *Address:* Rosehill, Doods Way, Reigate, Surrey, RH2 0JT, England. *Telephone:* (1737) 242396.

MASEKELA, Hugh; South African trumpeter; b. 1939, nr Johannesburg; fmrly in voluntary exile since early 1960s, in UK, USA, Ghana, Nigeria, Guinea and Botswana; f. Botswana Int. School of Music 1986. *Recordings include:* Home is Where the Music Is (with Dudu Pukwana, in London) 1972, I Am Not Afraid (with Hedzoleh Soundz) Technobush 1985, Beatin' Aroun De Bush 1992; wrote Broadway musical Sarafina; Musical Dir Graceland.

MASERA, Rainer Stefano, DPhil; Italian banker; b. 6 May 1944, Como; s. of Francesco Masera; m. Giovanna Aveta; two c.; ed La Sapienza Univ., Rome, Oxford Univ., UK; Economist, Bank for Int. Settlements, Basle 1971–75; mem. staff, then Head Int. Dept, Research Dept, Bank of Italy 1975–77, Head Research Dept 1982–84, Cen. Dir for Econs Research 1985–88; Alt. mem. EEC Monetary Cttee 1977–81; Dir-Gen. Istituto Mobiliare Italiano (IMI) 1988–; Chair. Sanpaolo IMI SpA 1998–; fmr Minister of the Budget. *Publications:* L'Unificazione Monetaria e lo SME 1980, A European Central Bank 1989, International Monetary and Financial Integration 1988, Prospects for the European Monetary System 1990, Intermediari, Mercati e Finanza d'Impresa 1991. *Leisure interests:* tennis, skiing. *Address:* Istituto Mobiliare Italiano, Viale dell'Arte 25, 00144 Rome, Italy (Office).

MASERI, Attilio, MD, FRCP; Italian cardiologist; b. 12 Nov. 1935; s. of Adriano Maseri and Antonietta Albini; m. Countess Francesca Maseri Florio di Santo Stefano 1960 (died 2000); one s.; ed Classical Lycée Cividale, Padua Univ. Medical School; Research Fellow Univ. of Pisa 1960–65, Columbia Univ., New York, USA 1965–66, Johns Hopkins Univ., Baltimore, USA 1966–67; Asst Prof., Univ. of Pisa 1967–70, Prof. of Internal Medicine 1970, Prof. of Cardiovascular Pathophysiology, Prof. of Medicine (Locum) 1972–79, Sir John McMichael Prof. of Cardiovascular Medicine, Royal Postgraduate Medical School, Hammersmith Hosp., Univ. of London 1979–91; Prof. of Cardiology and Dir Inst. of Cardiology, Catholic Univ. of Rome 1991–; Fellow American Coll. of Cardiology; Life mem. Johns Hopkins Soc. of Scholars; King Faisal Int. Prize 1992; Distinguished Scientist Award, American Coll. of Cardiology 1996; Kt of Malta. *Publications:* Myocardial Blood Flow in Man 1972, Primary and Secondary Angina 1977, Perspectives on Coronary Care 1979, Ischemic Heart Disease 1995; articles in major int. cardiological and medical journals. *Leisure interests:* skiing, tennis, sailing. *Address:* Via Zandonai 9-11, 00194 Rome, Italy.

MASHEKE, Gen. Malimba; Zambian politician and army officer; fmr Army Commdr; Minister of Defence 1985–88, of Home Affairs 1988–89; Prime Minister of Zambia 1989–91. *Address:* c/o Office of the Prime Minister, P.O. Box 30208, Lusaka, Zambia.

MASHELKAR, Raghunath Anant, BChemEng, PhD; Indian research scientist; b. 1 Jan. 1943, Mashel, Goa; ed Univ. of Bombay; Dir-Gen. Council of Scientific and Industrial Research and Sec., Govt of India Dept of Scientific and Industrial Research July 1995–; Pres. Physical Science, Nat. Acad. of Sciences 1991; Gen. Pres. Indian Science Congress 1999–2000; Chancellor, Assam Univ. 2000–; Fellow, Indian Acad. of Sciences 1983, Indian Nat. Science Acad. 1984, Nat. Acad. of Eng 1987, Third World Acad. of Sciences 1991; numerous awards and prizes including Shanti Swarup Bhatnagar Prize 1982, 2001, UDCT Outstanding Alumni Medal 1985, Fed. of Indian Chambers of Commerce and Industry Award 1987, Padmashri 1991, GD Birla Award for Scientific Research 1993, Goyal Prize 1996, JRD Tata Corporate Leadership Award 1998, Padma Bhushan 2000, numerous honorary degrees including DSc (hc) from Univs. of Salford, UK 1993, Kanpur 1995, Indian School of Mines 1997, Bundelkhand Univ. 2000, Guwahati Univ. 2000, Anna Univ. 2000, Univ. of London 2001. *Publications:* numerous research papers on macromolecules in books and learned journals. *Address:* Council of Scientific and Industrial Research, Anusandhan Bhavan, 2 Rafi Marg, New Delhi 110 001 (Office); CSIR/Science Centre, Lodi Garden's Gate No. 2, Lodi Estate, New Delhi 110 003, India (Home). *Telephone:* (11) 3710472, 3717053 (Office); (11) 4618851, 4649359 (Home). *Fax:* (11) 3710618 (Office). *E-mail:* dgcsir@csir .res.in (Office). *Website:* www.csir.res.in (Office).

MASHKOV, Vladimir Lvovich; Russian actor; b. 27 Nov. 1963, Tula; s. of Lev Petrovich Mashkov and Natalya Ivanovna Nikiforova; m. 1st Tatyana Lvovna Mashkova; one d.; 2nd Ksenia Borisovna Mashkova; ed Moscow Art Theatre School; actor and stage Dir Oleg Tabakov Theatre-Studio 1988–; main roles in most productions; staged 5 productions; various film roles; numerous awards including K. Stanislavsky Prize for Best Direction 1994, Crystal Turandot Prize for Best Play 1995, Baltic Pearl for fast career growth 1997; various awards for best actor in film and theatre. *Film roles include:* Moscow Nights, Limita 1994, American Daughter 1995, Thief 1997, Sympathy Seeker 1997, Three Suns 1998, 15 Minutes 1999, American Rhapsody 1999, Dancing at the Blue Iguana 2000, Two Moons 2000, The Quickie 2000, Behind Enemy Lines 2001. *Plays (as stage director):* Star House by Local Time, Passions for Bumbarash, The Death-Defying Act, The Threepenny Opera, Number 13 (2001). *Address:* Oleg Tabakov Theatre-Studio, Chaplygina str. 12A, Moscow, Russia. *Telephone:* (095) 916-21-21 (Theatre); (095) 925-73-44 (Yelena Chukhrai Art Agency). *E-mail:* grtagent@mtu-net.ru (Office). *E-mail:* v_mashkoff@mtu-net.ru (Home).

MASIRE, Quett Ketumile Joni, LLD, JP; Botswana politician; b. 23 July 1925, Kanye; s. of Joni Masire and Gabaipone Masire; m. Gladys Olebile Molefi 1957; three s. three d.; ed Kanye and Tiger Kloof; founded Seepapitso Secondary School 1950; reporter, later Dir, African Echo 1958; mem. Bangwaketse Tribal Council, Legis. Council; fmr mem. Exec. Council; founder mem. Botswana Democratic Party (BDP); mem. Legis. (now Nat.) Ass. March 1965;

Deputy Prime Minister 1965–66; attended Independence Conf., London Feb. 1966; Vice-Pres. and Minister of Finance 1966–80 and of Devt Planning 1967–80, Pres. of Botswana 1980–98; Chair. Southern African Devt. Community 1999, Congo Facilitator 1999–; Hon. LLD (Williams Coll.) 1980, (Sussex) 1986, (St John); Naledi Ya Botswana (Star of the Nation) 1986; Hon. GCMG. *Leisure interest:* watching football. *Address:* P.O. Box 70, Gaborone, Botswana (Home). *Telephone:* 353391 (Home).

MASKHADOV (MASKADOV), Gen. Khalid 'Aslan' A.; Russian (Chechen) politician and army officer; b. 21 Sept. 1951, Kazakhstan; m.; one s. one d.; ed Tbilisi Higher Artillery School, M. Kalinin Moscow Higher Artillery Acad; returned to Chechnya 1957; army service since 1969; Commdr platoon Far E, Cen. Group of Troops (Hungary), Commdr artillery Regt, Head of staff rocket forces and artillery of Vilnius Garrison, took part in attack on Vilnius TV Jan. 1991; Commdr div. Baltic Mil. Command 1969–91; retd as Col 1992; rank of Gen. Nov. 1992–; Head of Counterespionage, Head of Staff of Armed Forces 1993–, concurrently Minister of Defence Chechen Repub. Ichkeria 1995–96; took part in negotiations with Russian authorities, signed peace agreement with Gen. A. Lebed 1996; Prime Minister and Minister of Defence Coalition Govt Chechen Repub. of Ichkeria (Chechnya) 1996–97; elected Pres. of Chechnya Jan. 1997; fighting against Russian troops 1999–.

MASLYUKOV, Yuri Dmitriyevich; Russian politician; b. 30 Sept. 1937, Leninabad, Tadjik SSR; m. Svetlanana Ivanov Maslyukova; one s.; ed Leningrad Inst. of Mechanics, Higher Mil. Artillery School; Sr engineer, Deputy Head of Dept, Izhevsk Research Inst. of Tech. of Ministry of Defence Industry 1962–70; chief engineer, Deputy Dir Izhevsk Machine Construction Factory 1970–74; Head, Main Dept of Tech., Ministry of Defence Industry 1974–79; Deputy Minister of Defence Industry 1974–82; First Deputy Chair. USSR State Planning Cttee 1982–85; Deputy Chair., First Deputy Chair., USSR Council of Ministers 1985; Chair. State Comm. on Mil. and Industrial Problems 1985; Chair. USSR State Planning Cttee 1985–91; Deputy Chair. USSR Council of Ministers, Chair. State Mil. Industrial Comm. 1991; leading expert, Voronezh Co. SOKOL 1993–94; Dir.-Gen. Yugtrustinvest 1994–95; mem. CPSU Cen. Cttee 1986–91, Cand. mem. of Politburo 1988, mem. 1989; Deputy USSR Supreme Soviet 1990–91; mem. USSR Presidential Council 1991; mem. State Duma 1993–98, 1999–; Chair. Cttee on Econ. Policy 1995–98; Minister of Industry and Trade of Russian Fed. July–Sept. 1998; First Deputy Chair. of Govt Sept. 1998–; mem. Cen. Cttee CP of Russian Fed. 1997; Chair. Cttee on Industry, Construction and Scientific Tech. 1998–99, 2000–; Adviser to V. Semenikhin Inst. of Automation 1999–2000; mem. Co-ordination Council, Movt of People's Patriotic Union of Russia. *Address:* State Duma, Okhotny Ryad 1, 103265 Moscow, Russia (Office). *Telephone:* (095) 292-04-98, 292-03-15 (Office). *Fax:* (095) 292-37-63 (Office).

MASOL, Vitaliy Andreyevich, PhD; Ukrainian politician; b. 14 Nov. 1928, Olshivka, Chernigov Region; s. of Andrei Dmitrievich Masol and Lidiya Grigorievna Masol; m. Nina Vasilievna Masol 1978; one s.; ed Kiev Polytechnic Inst., Inst. of Econ. Man.; foreman, shop foreman, deputy chief engineer, Novokramatorsk machine-construction plant 1951–63, Dir 1963–71; mem. CPSU 1956–91; General Dir of production unit of heavy machine-construction factories in Kramatorsk (Ukraine) 1971–72; First Deputy Chair. of Gosplan for Ukrainian SSR 1972–79; Deputy Chair. Ukrainian Council of Ministers 1979–87, Chair. (Prime Minister) 1987–90 (resigned following mass student demonstrations), reapptd. 1994–95; mem. of CPSU Cen. Auditing Cttee 1981–86; Chair. Planning and Budget Comm., USSR Supreme Soviet 1982–87; mem. Cen. Cttee CPSU 1989–91; Deputy to USSR Supreme Soviet 1979–89, USSR People's Deputy 1989–91; mem. Parl. of Ukraine 1990–98, Higher Council of Pres. of Ukraine 1997–; adviser to Rostok bank; numerous orders and awards including Order of Lenin (twice), Order of Count Yaroslav Mudry 1998. *Leisure interest:* tourism. *Address:* Desyatinnaya str. 8, Apt. 8, Kiev 252025, Ukraine.

MASON, Sir (Basil) John, Kt, C.B., DSc, FRS; British meteorologist; b. 18 Aug. 1923, Docking, Norfolk; s. of the late John Robert and Olive Mason; m. Doreen Sheila Jones 1948; two s.; ed Fakenham Grammar School and Univ. Coll., Nottingham; commissioned, Radar Branch, RAF 1944–46; Shirley Research Fellow, Univ. of Nottingham 1947; Asst lecturer in Meteorology, Imperial Coll., London 1948–49, lecturer 1949; Warren Research Fellow, Royal Soc. 1957; Visiting Prof. of Meteorology, Univ. of Calif. 1959–60; Prof. of Cloud Physics, Imperial Coll. of Science and Tech., Univ. of London 1961–65; Dir-Gen. Meteorological Office 1965–83, Pres. Royal Meteorological Soc. 1968–70; mem. Exec. Cttee World Meteorological Org. 1965–75, 1977–83; Chair. Council, Univ. of Surrey 1971–75; Pro-Chancellor Univ. of Surrey 1979–85; Pres. Inst. of Physics 1976–78; Treas. and Sr Vice-Pres. Royal Soc. 1976–86; Dir Fulmer Research Inst. 1976–78; Pres. BAAS 1982–83; Dir Royal Soc. Project on Acidification of Surface Waters 1983–90; mem. Advisory Bd Research Councils 1983–86; Pres. UMIST 1986–94, Chancellor 1994–96; Chair. Grad. School for Environment, Imperial Coll., London 1995–98; Chair. ICSU/WMO Scientific Cttee for World Climate Research Prog., Co-ordinating Cttee for Marine Science and Tech. 1987–89; Pres. Nat. Soc. for Clean Air 1989–91, Asscn for Science Educ. 1992–93, Nat. Soc. of Environmental Eng 1999–; Foreign mem. Norwegian Acad. of Science 1993; Bakerian Lecture, Royal Soc. 1971; Halley Lecture, Oxford Univ. 1977; Lecturer, Linacre Coll., Oxford 1990; Rutherford Lecture, Royal Soc. 1990; Hon. Fellow Imperial Coll. of Science and Tech. 1974, UMIST 1979; Hon. DSc (Nottingham) 1966, (Durham) 1970, (Strathclyde) 1975, (City Univ.) 1980, (Sussex) 1983, (E Anglia) 1988, (Plymouth Polytechnic) 1990, (Heriot-Watt) 1991, (UMIST)

1994, (Reading) 1998; Hugh Robert Mill Medal, Royal Meteorological Soc. 1959, Charles Chree Medal and Prize, Physical Soc. 1965, Rumford Medal, Royal Soc. 1972, Glazebrook Medal and Prize, Inst. of Physics 1974, Symons Memorial Gold Medal, Royal Meteorological Soc. 1975, Naylor Prize and Lectureship, London Math. Soc. 1979, Royal Medal, Royal Soc. 1991. *Publications:* The Physics of Clouds 1957, Clouds, Rain and Rain-making 1962, Acid Rain 1992. *Leisure interests:* music, foreign travel. *Address:* Department of Environmental Science, Imperial College, London, SW7 (Office); 64 Christchurch Road, East Sheen, London, SW14, England (Home). *Telephone:* (20) 7594-9287 (Office); (20) 8876-2557 (Home). *Fax:* (20) 7581-0245 (Office).

MASON, Sir John (see Mason, Sir (Basil) John).

MASON, Sir John (Charles Moir), KCMG, MA; British/Australian fmr diplomatist and business executive; b. 13 May 1927, Manchester; s. of late Charles M. Mason and Madeline Mason; m. Margaret Newton 1954; one s. one d.; ed Manchester Grammar School and Peterhouse, Cambridge; army service 1944–48, Korea 1950–51; joined diplomatic service 1952; Second Sec., Rome 1954–56, Warsaw 1956–59; Foreign Office 1959–61; First Sec. (Commercial), Damascus 1961–65; Foreign Office 1965–68; Dir of Trade Devt and Deputy Consul-Gen., New York 1968–71; Head, European Integration Dept, FCO 1971–72; seconded as Under-Sec. Export Credits Guarantee Dept 1972–75; Asst Under-Sec. of State, FCO 1975–76; Amb. to Israel 1976–80; High Commr in Australia 1980–84; Chair. Lloyds Bank NZA Ltd, Sydney 1985–90, Lloyds Int. Ltd 1987–90, Thorn-EMI (Australia) Ltd 1985–94, Vickers Shipbuilders (Australia) Ltd 1985–91, Multicon Ltd 1987–90, Prudential (Australia) Ltd 1987–92, Prudential Finance Ltd 1987–90, Prudential Funds Man. Ltd 1987–92, Bequests Cttee, RACP 1992–95; Bd of Advisers Spencer Stuart and Assocs., Sydney 1985–96; Pres. Heart Foundation N Shore Hosp., Sydney 1985–92; Dir Wellcome (Australia) Ltd 1985–90, Nat. Bank of New Zealand 1985–90; Fluor (Australia) Ltd, Melbourne 1985–92; Deputy Chair. Churchill Memorial Trust 1985–2001, Chair. Pirelli Cables Australia Ltd 1993–99, Cttee Magna Carta Park, Canberra 1996–2001; Public mem. Australian Press Council 1992–99; lay mem. Professional Conduct Cttees., Bar Council and Law Soc. of NSW 1992–99; mem. Cambridge Commonwealth Trust 1993–, Duke of Edinburgh's Award Scheme in Australia 1996–99. *Publication:* Diplomatic Despatches, From a Son to His Mother 1998. *Address:* 147 Dover Road, Dover Heights, Sydney, NSW 2030, Australia; c/o Lloyds TSB Bank PLC, Cox's & King's Branch, P.O. Box 1190, London, SW1Y 5NA, England. *Telephone:* (2) 9371-7863 (Sydney). *Fax:* (2) 9371-7863 (Sydney). *E-mail:* jcmmason@ozemail.com.au (Home).

MASON, Monica, OBE; British (b. South African) ballet company artistic director; b. 6 Sept. 1941, Johannesburg, SA; d. of Richard Mason and E. Fabian; m. Austin Bennett 1968; ed Johannesburg, SA, Nesta Brooking School of Ballet, England and Royal Ballet School, London; joined Royal Ballet in Corps de Ballet 1958, Soloist 1963, Prin. 1968, Sr Prin. –1989; selected by Kenneth Macmillan to create role of Chosen Maiden in Rite of Spring 1962; other roles created for her include: Diversions, Calliope Rag in Elite Syncopations, Electra, Mistress in Manon, Romeo and Juliet, Midwife in Rituals, Adieu 1980, Nursey in Isadora, Summer in The Four Seasons, The Ropes of Time; appeared in mime roles including Carbosse in The Sleeping Beauty and Lady Capulet in MacMillan's Romeo and Juliet; recently created role of Mrs. Grose in William Tuckett's The Turn of the Screw; Répétiteur and Asst to Prin. Choreographer, Royal Ballet 1980–84, Prin. Répétiteur 1984–91, Asst Dir Royal Ballet 1991–2002, Dir Dec. 2002–; Hon. DUniv (Surrey) 1996. *Repertory includes:* Odette/Odile in Swan Lake, Princess Aurora in The Sleeping Beauty, title role in Giselle, Prelude and Mazurka in Les Sylphides, leading role in Raymonda Act III, dramatic parts including Hostess in Les Biches and the Black Queen in Checkmate; other major roles include: leading role in MacMillan's Song of the Earth, Nijinska's Les Noces and Nureyev's Kingdom of the Shades scene from La Bayadère; appeared in first performances by Royal Ballet of Hans van Manen's Adagio Hammerklavier, Jerome Robbins' Dances at a Gathering and In the Night, Balanchine's Liebeslieder Walzer and Tudor's Dark Elegies; other roles include: the Lilac Fairy in The Sleeping Beauty, Empress Elisabeth and Mitzi Caspar in MacMillan's Meyerling, title role in The Firebird, Variation I in Frederick Ashton's Birthday Offering, the Fairy Godmother and Winter Fairy in Cinderella, Lady Elgar in Enigma Variations, Queen of Denmark in Helpmann's Hamlet. *Address:* Royal Opera House, Covent Garden, London, WC2E 9DD England (Office). *Website:* www.royalopera.org/ballet (Office).

MASON, Paul James, CB, PhD, FRS; British meteorologist; b. 16 March 1946, Southampton; s. of Charles Ernest Edward Mason and Phyllis Mary Mason (née Swan); m. Elizabeth Mary Slaney 1968; one s. one d.; ed Univs. of Nottingham and Reading; scientific officer then Prin. Scientific Officer, Meteorological Office 1967–79, Head Meteorological Research Unit, Cardington 1979–85, Asst Dir Boundary Layer Br., Meteorological Office 1985–89, Deputy Dir Physical Research, Meteorological Office 1989–91, Chief Scientist 1991–2003; Dir UWERN Univ. of Reading 2003–; mem. Council Royal Meteorological Soc. 1989–90, Pres. 1992–94; mem. Editorial Bd Boundary Layer Meteorology 1988–; Fellow Royal Soc. 1995; mem. Academia Europaea 1998; L. G. Groves Prize for Meteorology 1980, Buchan Prize (Royal Meteorological Soc.) 1986. *Publications:* scientific papers in meteorology and fluid dynamics journals. *Leisure interests:* walking and exploring the countryside. *Address:* Dept of Meteorology, University of Reading, Whiteknights, Reading, Berks., RG66 6BB, England (Office).

MASON, Sir Ronald, KCB, FRS, FRSC, CChem, D.SC, CEng, FIM; British professor of chemical physics (retd), industrialist and civil servant; b. 22 July 1930, Wales; s. of David John Mason and Olwen Mason (née James); m. 1st E. Pauline Pattinson 1953; m. 2nd E. Rosemary Grey-Edwards 1979; three d.; ed Quaker's Yard Grammar School and Univs of Wales and London; Research Assoc., Univ. Coll. London 1953–60; Lecturer, Imperial Coll. London 1960–63; Prof., Univ. of Sheffield 1963–70; Prof., Univ. of Sussex 1970–88; Chief Scientific Adviser, Ministry of Defence 1977–83; Pro-Vice-Chancellor, Univ. of Sussex 1977–78; many visiting professorships in Australia, Canada, France, Israel, New Zealand and USA 1965–83, Int. Relations, Univ. Coll. of Wales; Chair. Hunting Ltd 1986–87, British Ceramics Research Ltd 1990–98, Univ. Coll. London Hosps. Nat. Health Service Trust 1993–2001, Science Applications Int. Corpn (UK) Ltd 1993–96; Pres. British Hydromechanics Research Asscn 1986–95, Inst. of Materials 1995–96; Chair. Council for Arms Control, London 1986–91; mem. UN Disarmament Studies Comm. 1983–91; Fellow Univ. Coll., London 1995; Hon. Fellow Polytechnic of Wales 1987, Hon. FIMechE 1993; Hon. DSc (Wales) 1986, (Keele) 1993; medals of various learned socs. *Publications:* many scientific research pubs on structural chem. and chemical physics of surfaces, author/ed. of 10 monographs, papers on defence policies and tech. *Leisure interests:* gardening, travelling, music, opera. *Address:* Chestnuts Farm, Weedon, Bucks, HP22 4NH, England. *Telephone:* (1296) 641353 (Home). *Fax:* (1296) 641353 (Home). *E-mail:* masons@chestnuts100.freeserve.co.uk.

MASON OF BARNSLEY, Baron (Life Peer), cr. 1987, of Barnsley in South Yorkshire; **Roy Mason,** PC, DL; British politician; b. 18 April 1924, Barnsley, Yorks; s. of Joseph and Mary Mason; m. Marjorie Sowden 1945; two d.; ed Carlton Junior School, Royston Sr School and London School of Econs (T.U.C. Course); mine worker 1938–53; branch official, Nat. Union of Mineworkers 1947–53; mem. Yorkshire Miners' Council 1949–53; MP for Barnsley (now Barnsley Cen.) 1953–87; Minister of State (Shipping), Bd of Trade 1964–67; Minister of Defence (Equipment) 1967–68; Postmaster-Gen. April–June 1968; Minister of Power 1968–69; Pres. Bd of Trade 1969–70; Sec. of State for Defence 1974–76, for Northern Ireland 1976–79; Opposition Spokesman for Agric., Fisheries and Food 1979–81; Labour. *Publication:* Paying the Price. *Address:* House of Lords, Westminster, London, SW1A 0PW (Office); 12 Victoria Avenue, Barnsley, S. Yorks., S70 2BH, England (Home).

MASOUD, Ahmad Wali, MA; Afghanistan diplomatist; b. 1 Nov. 1964, Kabul; brother of the late Ahmed Shah Masoud, leader of Northern Alliance military forces in Afghanistan; m.; three d.; ed Muslim Public School Peshawar-Pakistan, Mid-Cornwall Coll. of Further Educ., Polytechnic of Central London, Westminster Univ.; Foreign News Reporter Times Newspaper 1989; Ed. Ariana News Bulletin 1989–1992; Rep. Jamiat Islami Afghanistan, main political faction in Afghanistan, fighting Russian Occupation 1989–92; Second Sec. Embassy of Afghanistan, London 1992, First Sec. and Chargé d'affaires, 1993, Minister Counsellor and Chargé d'affaires 1993–. *Address:* Embassy of Afghanistan, 31 Prince's Gate, London, SW7 1QQ, England (Office). *Telephone:* (20) 7589-8891 (Office). *Fax:* (20) 7584-4801 (Office). *E-mail:* afghanembassy@btinternet.com (Office).

MASRI, Taher Nashat, B.B.A.; Jordanian diplomatist; b. 5 March 1942, Nablus; s. of Nashat Masri and Hadiyah Solh; m. Samar Bitar 1968; one s. one d.; ed Al-Najah Nat. Coll., Nablus and North Texas State Univ.; with Cen. Bank of Jordan 1965–73; MP 1973–74, 1984–88, 89–97; Minister of State for Occupied Territories Affairs 1973–74; Amb. to Spain 1975–78, to France 1978–83, also Accred to Belgium 1979–80, Rep. to E.E.C. 1978–80; Perm. Del. to UNESCO 1978–83; Amb. to UK 1983–84; Minister of Foreign Affairs 1984–88, Jan.–June 1991; Deputy Prime Minister, Minister of State for Econ. Affairs April–Sept. 1989; Chair. Foreign Relations Cttee 1989–91, 1992–93; Prime Minister and Minister of Defence June–Nov. 1991; Speaker Nat. Ass. 1993–94; Senator 1998–2001; Rapporteur Royal Comm. for Drafting of the Nat. Charter 1990; Chair. Bd Princess Haya Cultural Center for Children 1992–; Pres. Nat. Soc. for the Enhancement of Freedom and Democracy (JUND) 1993–97, Jordanian-Spanish Friendship Asscn 1998–; Pres. Bd of Trustees Science and Tech. Univ., Irbid; Commr for Civic Socs. with Arab League, Cairo; numerous decorations and awards, including Grand Cordon, Jewelled Al-Nahda (Jordan), Order of Al-Kawkab (Jordan) 1974, Gran Cruz de Mérito Civil (Spain) 1977, Order of Isabel la Católica (Spain) 1978, Commdr, Légion d'honneur 1981, Grand Officier, Order Nat. du Mérite, Order of Merit (FRG, Grand Cross, First Class), Knight Grand Cross (Italy); Hon. G.B.E. *Address:* PO Box 5550, Amman 11183, Jordan. *Telephone:* (6) 4642227 (Office); (6) 5920600 (Home). *Fax:* (6) 4642226. *E-mail:* t.n.masri@index.com .jo (Office).

MASSAD, Carlos, MA, PhD; Chilean banker and economist; b. 29 Aug. 1932, Santiago; m.; five c.; ed Univ. of Chile, Chicago Univ.; Dir of Dept of Econs, Univ. of Chile 1959–64; Vice-Pres. Cen. Bank of Chile 1964–67, Pres. 1967–70, Gov. 1996–; Exec. Dir of IMF 1970–74; mem. of Advisory Cttee, World Bank 1978–81; various posts, Econ. Comm. for Latin America (CEPAL) 1970–92; Exec. Pres., Eduardo Frei Montalva Foundation 1993–94; Minister of Health 1994–96; Euromoney Best Cen. Banker of Latin America 1997, The Banker Cen. Bank Gov. for the Americas Region of the Year 2001. *Publications:* Macroeconomics 1979, Rudiments of Economics 1980, Adjustment With Growth 1984; Economic Analysis: An Introduction to Microeconomics 1986, Internal Debt and Financial Stability (Vol. 1) 1987, (Vol. 2) 1988, The Financial System and Resource Distribution: Study based on Latin America and the Caribbean 1990, Elements of Economics: An Introduction to Economic

Analysis 1993, On Public Health and Other Topics 1995, Macroeconomía en un mundo interdependiente (with Guillermo Patillo) 2000; and numerous articles. *Address:* Central Bank of Chile, Agustinas 1180, Castilla 967, Santiago, Chile (Office). *Telephone:* (56) 2670-2300 (Office). *Fax:* (56) 2697-2271 (Office). *Website:* www.bcentral.cl (Office).

MASSÉ, Hon. Marcel, PC, MP, OC, QC, BA, LLB, BPhilEcon; Canadian politician and civil servant; b. 23 June 1940, Montreal; m. Josée M'Baye 1965; three s. one d.; ed Univ. of Montreal, McGill Univ., Montreal, Univ. of Warsaw, Poland, Oxford Univ., England; called to Bar, Québec 1963; Admin. and Econs Div., World Bank, Washington, DC 1967–71; Econ. Adviser, Privy Council Office, Ottawa 1971–72; Deputy Minister of Finance, Prov. of NB 1973–74, Chair. Cabinet Secr. 1974–77; Deputy Sec. Cabinet for Fed. Prov. Relations, Ottawa 1977–79, Deputy Sec. Cabinet (Operations), Privy Council Office 1979, Sec. to the Cabinet and Clerk of the Privy Council Office 1979–80; Pres. Canadian Int. Devt Agency, Ottawa 1980–82; Under-Sec. of State for External Affairs, Ottawa 1982–85; Canadian Exec. Dir IMF, Washington 1985–89; Pres. Canadian Int. Devt Agency (CIDA) 1989–93; Sec. to Cabinet for Intergovernmental Affairs March–June 1993; MP for Hull-Aylmer 1993–99; Pres. of the Privy Council and Minister of Intergovernmental Affairs and responsible for Public Service Renewal 1993–96; Pres. of Treasury Bd Jan. 1996–99, Exec. Dir Inter-American Devt Bank 1999–2002; Exec. Dir World Bank 2002–; Hon. DCL (Acadia Univ.) 1983; Hon. LLD (New Brunswick) 1984; Dr. hc (Univ. du Québec) 1992, (Ottawa Univ.) 1996. *Address:* 1818 H Street, NW, Washington, DC 20433, USA (Office).

MASSE, Hon. Marcel; Canadian politician; b. 27 May 1936, Saint-Jean-De-Matha, Québec; s. of Rosaire Masse and Angeline Clermont; m. Cecile Martin 1960; one s. one d.; ed Ecole normale Jacques-Cartier, Univ. of Montreal, Sorbonne, City of London Coll., European Inst. of Business Admin.; fmr teacher of Ancient History, Lanaudière Regional School Bd; Dir Lavalin (Eng Co.) 1974–84 (also Project Dir for UNDP, Vice-Pres., Vice-Pres. of Marketing and Commercial Devt); mem. Québec Nat. Ass. 1966–73 (held portfolios of Minister of State for Educ., Minister Responsible for Public Service, for Inter-Governmental Affairs, Minister of Planning and Devt); Minister of Communications 1984–85, 1985–86, of Energy, Mines and Resources 1986–89, of Communications 1989–90, responsible for La Francophonie 1990, of Defence 1991–93; Chief Consultant CFC 1994–95; Del.–Gen. of Québec to France 1996–97; Pres. Comm. franco-québécoise sur les lieux de mémoire communs 1996, Comm. des biens culturels du Québec 1997–2000; fmr Pres. Wilfrid Pelletier Foundation; Dir numerous orgs. including Montreal Symphony Orchestra, Canadian Writers' Foundation, Canadian Refugee Foundation, Lanaudière Summer Festival, Club de Dakar, Jeunesses Musicales du Canada; Progressive Conservative; Officier, Légion d'honneur, Ordre du Québec. *Leisure interests:* reading, music, fishing, skiing. *Address:* 576, route 329-C.P. 1030, Saint-Donat, Quebec, J0T 2C0, Canada.

MASSENGALE, Martin Andrew, MS, PhD; American university administrator and agronomist; b. 25 Oct. 1933, Monticello, Ky; s. of late Elbert G. Massengale and Orpha Massengale; m. Ruth A. Klingelhofer 1959; one s. one d.; ed W Kentucky Univ. and Univ. of Wis.; Asst Agronomist and Asst Prof. Univ. of Ariz., Tucson 1958–62, Assoc. Agronomist and Assoc. Prof. 1962–65, Agronomist and Prof. 1965–66, Agronomist, Prof. and Head of Dept 1966–74, Assoc. Dean, Coll. of Agric. and Assoc. Dir Agricultural Experiment Station 1974–76; Vice-Chancellor for Agric. and Natural Resources, Univ. of Neb., Lincoln 1976–81, Chancellor 1981–91, Interim Pres. 1989–91, Pres. 1991–94, Pres. Emer., Dir Center for Grassland Studies and Foundation Distinguished Prof. 1994–; Pres. Crop Science Soc. of America 1973–74, Grazing Lands Forum 1997–98; Chair. Agronomic Science Foundation; Fellow, AAAS, American Soc. of Agronomy, Crop Science Soc. of America and other professional socs.; mem. numerous cttees., nat. panels, advisory bds., etc. including Exec. Comm. and Advisory Bd to US Sec. of Agric.; Hon. Lifetime Trustee Neb. Council on Econ. Educ. 1999; Dr hc (Neb. Wesleyan Univ., Senshu Univ., Tokyo); Distinguished Alumni (Western Kentucky) 2002; many other honours and awards including Triumph of Agri Award 1999, Nebraska Agriculture Relations Co. Honoree 2000, Nebraska LEAD Alumni Asscn 'Friend of LEAD' Award 2001, Outstanding President's Award All-American Football Foundation 2001. *Publication:* Renewable Resource Management for Forestry and Agriculture (co-ed.) 1978. *Leisure interests:* reading, travel, golf, photography. *Address:* 220 Keim Hall, University of Nebraska, Lincoln, NE 68583-0953 (Office); 3436 West Cape Charles Road, Lincoln, NE 68516, USA (Home). *Telephone:* (402) 472-4101 (Office), (402) 420-5350 (Home). *Fax:* (402) 472-4104. *E-mail:* mmassengale1@unl.edu (Office). *Website:* www.grassland.unl .edu (Office).

MASSERET, Jean-Pierre; French politician; b. 23 Aug. 1944, Cusset (Alliers); s. of Lucien Masseret and Claudia Rollet; m. Marie-Hélène Roddier 1967; three c.; ed Inst. des Hautes Etudes de Défense Nat.; fmr Chief Insp., Inland Revenue; mem. staff of Minister for War Veterans 1981–86; Senator for Moselle 1983–, Vice-Chair. Senate Finance Cttee; Minister of State attached to Minister of Defence, with responsibility for War Veterans 1997–2001; Mayor of Hayange (Moselle); Lorraine regional councillor; mem. Parti Socialiste political Cttee; mem. Parl. Ass. of WEU, of Council of Europe, Socialist Party Nat. Office; fmr Chair. Lorraine Athletics League; fmr regional champion runner. *Address:* Palais du Luxembourg, 75291 Paris; Hôtel de Ville, place de la Résistance et de la Déportation, 57700 Hayange, France.

MASSEVITCH, Alla Genrikhovna, DSc; Russian astrophysicist; b. 9 Oct. 1918, Tbilisi; d. of Genrik Massevitch and Natalie Zhgenti; m. Joseph Friedlander 1942; one d.; ed Moscow Industrial Pedagogical Inst., Moscow Univ.; Assistant Prof. of Astrophysics Moscow Univ. 1946–48, Prof. 1948–, Prof. Emer.; Vice-Pres. Astronomical Council, USSR (now Russian) Acad. of Sciences 1952–88, Chief Scientific Researcher Astronomical Inst. 1988–2002; in charge of optical (visual, photographic and laser ranging) tracking of Soviet (now Russian) space vehicles 1958–89; mem. Nat. Cttee for the Int. Space Year 1989–93; Chair. Working Group I, Cttee for Space Research (COSPAR) 1961–66; Vice-Pres. Comm. 44 JAU (Extraterrestrial Astronomy) 1961–67; Pres. Comm. 35 JAU (Internal Structure of Stars) 1967–70; Deputy Sec.-Gen. UNISPACE –1982, Pres. of Section Satellite Tracking for Geodesy, Inter-Cosmos Co-operation 1968–89; Assoc. Ed. Astrophysics and Space Science 1986–94; mem. Editorial Bd Astrophysica 1987–; Vice-Pres. Inst. for Soviet-American (now Russian-American) Relations 1967; Vice-Pres. Bd Soviet Peace Cttee 1967–92; Foreign mem. Royal Astronomical Soc. 1963, Indian Nat. Acad. of Sciences 1980, Austrian Acad. of Sciences 1985; mem. Int. Acad. of Astronautics 1964; Hon. mem. Russian Acad. of Cosmonautics 1997; Int. Astronautics Prize (Galaber Prize) 1965, USSR State Prize 1975, Honoured Scientist of Russia 1980 and decorations from Russia, Bulgaria, Mongolia and Poland. *Publications:* three books on stellar evolution, one on satellite geodesy, several popular books on astronomy; 168 papers on internal structure of stars, stellar evolution and optical tracking of satellites, mainly in Astronomical Journal of the USSR, Publications of the Sternberg Astronomical Inst. and Scientific Information of the Astronomical Council 1945–. *Leisure interests:* collecting coffee machines and cookery books. *Address:* Astronomical Institute of the Russian Acad. of Sciences, 48 Piatnitskaya Street, Moscow 109017 (Office); 6 Pushkurev per., Apt. 4, Moscow 103045, Russia. *Telephone:* (095) 208-93-33 (Home). *Fax:* (095) 230-20-81.

MASSEY, Anna; British actress; b. Sussex; d. of Raymond Massey and Adrienne Allen; m. 1st Jeremy Huggins 1958 (divorced 1963); one s.; m. 2nd Prof. Uri Andres 1988; ed in London, New York, France, Switzerland and Italy; Best Supporting Actress Award, Soc. of West End Theatre for The Importance of Being Earnest 1983, Best Actress, Locarno Film Festival for Journey into the Shadows 1984, Royal TV Soc. Award for Sacred Heart and Hotel du Lac 1986, Best Supporting Actress, British Theatre Asscn for The Importance of Being Earnest and A Kind of Alaska 1986; BAFTA Award for Best Actress for role in TV film Hotel du Lac 1987, The Respectable Trade 1998. *Films include:* Frenzy, David Copperfield, The Looking Glass War, The Corn is Green, Sweet William, Another Country, Five Days One Summer, Sakharov, The Chain, Mountains of the Moon, Killing Dad, Journey into the Shadows, Season's Greetings, The Day After the Fair, The Christmas Tree, Sunchild, A Tale of Two Cities, Haunted 1995, The Grotesque 1995, The Slab Boys 1997, Déjà Vu 1997, Captain Jack 1998, Mad Cows 1998, Room to Rent 2001, Possession 2001, The Importance of Being Earnest 2002. *Theatre roles:* debut in The Reluctant Debutante aged 17; subsequent appearances in School for Scandal, The Doctor's Dilemma, The Right Honourable Gentleman, The Miracle Worker, The Glass Menagerie, The Prime of Miss Jean Brodie; appeared with Nat. Theatre in 1970s and 1980s in Heartbreak House, Close of Play, Summer, The Importance of Being Earnest, Alaska, Family Voices, King Lear, Mary Stuart; also appeared at The Royal Court in Spoiled, The Seagull. *Radio:* many radio plays and narration of This Sceptred Isle BBC Radio 1999. *Television includes:* Mrs Danvers in Rebecca, Lady Nelson in I Remember Nelson, The Cherry Orchard, Mansfield Park, Journey into the Shadows: Portrait of Owen John 1983, Hotel du Lac 1986, The Sleeper 2001. *Address:* c/o Markham and Froggatt Ltd, 4 Windmill Street, London, W1P 1HF, England.

MASSON, Jacques, LenD; French banker; b. 17 April 1924, Paris; s. of Georges Masson and Yvonne (née Poutot) Masson; m. Annie Bedhet 1946; one s. two d. (one deceased); ed Faculté de Droit, Paris, Ecole Nat. d'Organisation Economique et Sociale and Centre de Perfectionnement dans l'Administration des Affaires; joined Banque Nat. de Paris (BNP) 1950, Asst Dir 1963, Dir in charge of Paris branches 1964, Dir 1972, Asst Dir-Gen. 1978, Dir-Gen. 1982–87, Hon. Dir-Gen. 1987; Prof. Inst. Technique de banque du Conservatoire nat. des arts et métiers 1971–; Dir Basaltes 1988–; mem. Banking Comm.; Pres. BNP Bail; Chair. Bd of Dirs. Groupement des Cartes Bancaires CB 1988–93; Dir SILEC, Nouvelles Galeries, Devanlay, Soc. Nouvelle des Basaltes, Econoler France, Soc. Cheddito France SA; mem. Supervisory Bd, SOVAC; Chevalier, Légion d'honneur, Officier, Ordre Nat. du Mérite. *Address:* 34 rue du Docteur Blanche, 75016 Paris, France (Home).

MASSONDE, Majidine Ben Said; Comoran politician; Prime Minister 1996–97; Interim Pres. of the Comoros 1998–99, Pres. Feb.–May 1999; mem. Parti Udzima. *Address:* c/o Office of the President, Moroni, Comoros.

MASTER, Simon Harcourt; British publisher; b. 10 April 1944, Caterham; s. of Humphrey R. Master and Rachel B. Plumbly; m. Georgina M. C. Batsford 1969; two s.; ed Ardingly Coll. Sussex; Publishing Dir Pan Books Ltd 1973–80, Man. Dir 1980–87; Chief Exec. Random House UK and Exec. Vice-Pres. Random House Int. Group 1987–89, Group Man. Dir Random Century Group 1989–90, Group Deputy Chair. 1989–, Chair., CEO Gen. Books Div., Random House UK 1992–; Chair., Arrow Books 1990–92; Dir (non-exec.) H.M.S.O. 1990–95; mem. Council Publrs. Asscn 1989–95 (Vice-Pres. 1995–96, 2000–2001, Pres. 1996–97, 2001–02). *Leisure interests:* gardening, golf, classic cars, scuba diving. *Address:* Flat 1, St George's Mansions, Causton Street, London, SW1P 4RZ, England (Home). *Telephone:* (20) 7630-7121 (Home).

MASTERKOVA, Svetlana Aleksandrovna; Russian track and field athlete; b. 17 Jan. 1968, Achinsk; m. Assiat Saitov; one d.; worked with coaches Yakov Yelyanov and Svetlana Styrkina; Atlanta Olympic Games Champion (800m and 1,500m) 1996, gold medal World Championships Seville 1999; severe Achilles tendon problems curtailed her competitive career thereafter; set world records 1,000m and one mile in Aug. 1996 (still stands as at end 2002); retd 2000 after Sydney Olympic Games; Best Woman Athlete of the Year, Monte Carlo 1996; Merited Master of Sports; Best Woman Athlete of Russia 1996, 1997; Order For Service to Motherland. *Address:* All-Russian Athletic Federation, Luzhnetskaya nab. 8, 119871 Moscow, Russia (Office). *Telephone:* (095) 201-01-50 (Office).

MASTERSON, Patrick, PhD, MRIA; Irish university professor; b. 19 Oct. 1936, Dublin; s. of Laurence Masterson and Violet Masterson; m. Frances Lenehan; one s. three d.; ed Belvedere Coll., Castlenock Coll., Univ. Coll., Dublin, Univ. of Louvain; mem. staff Dept of Metaphysics, Univ. Coll., Dublin 1963–72, Prof. Faculties of Arts, Philosophy and Sociology 1977–80, Dean of the Faculty of Philosophy and Sociology 1980–83, Registrar 1983–86, Pres. 1986–93; Pres. European Univ. Inst., Florence 1994–; Vice-Chancellor Nat. Univ. of Ireland 1987, 1988, 1993; Dr. hc (Caen), (Trinity Coll. Dublin), (New York); Grande Oficial, Ordem do Mérito da República Portuguesa, Grande Ufficiale della Repubblica Italiana. *Publications:* Atheism and Alienation: A Study of the Philosophical Sources of Contemporary Atheism 1971, Images of Man in Ancient and Medieval Thought: (Studia Gerardo Verbeke ab amicis et collegis dictata) 1976. *Leisure interests:* modern art, reading, theatre, fishing. *Address:* Office of the President, European University Institute, Badia Fiesolana, Via dei Roccettini 9, 50016 San Domenico di Fiesole (FI), Italy. *Telephone:* (055) 4685310. *Fax:* (055) 4685312.

MASTERSON, Valerie, CBE; British opera and concert singer; b. Birkenhead; d. of Edward Masterson and Rita McGrath; m. Andrew March; one s. one d.; Prof. of Singing, Royal Acad. of Music, London 1992–; Pres. British Youth Opera 1994–99, Vice-Pres. 2000–; has sung with D'Oyly Carte Opera, Glyndebourne, Royal Opera House, Covent Garden and English Nat. Opera and on TV and radio; also in major opera houses abroad including Paris, Aix-en-Provence, Toulouse, Munich, Geneva, San Francisco and Chicago; Hon. FRCM 1992, RAM 1993; Hon. DLitt (South Bank Univ.) 1999; Award for Outstanding Individual Performance of the Year in a New Opera, Soc. of West End Theatre 1983. *Opera roles include:* La Traviata, Manon, Semele, Merry Widow, Louise, Lucia di Lammermoor, Mireille; other leading roles in Faust, Alcina, Die Entführung aus dem Serail, Le Nozze di Figaro, Così fan Tutte, La Bohème, Magic Flute, Julius Caesar, Rigoletto, Orlando, Der Rosenkavalier, Xerxes, The Pearl Fishers, Die Fledermaus etc. *Recordings include:* Julius Caesar, La Traviata, Elisabetta Regina d'Inghilterra, Bitter Sweet, Ring Cycle, recitals and various Gilbert and Sullivan discs. *Leisure interests:* tennis, swimming. *Address:* c/o Music International, 13 Ardilaun Road, London, N5 2QR, England.

MASUI, Yoshio, PhD, FRS; Canadian (b. Japanese) biologist; b. 1931, Kyoto; s. of Fusa-Jiro Masui and Toyoko Masui; m. Yuriko Masui 1959; one s. one d.; ed Kyoto Univ.; teacher of biology, Konan High School, Kobe; Research Asst, Biology Dept, Konan Univ. 1955–61, Lecturer 1961–65, Asst Prof. 1965–68, Prof. Emer. 1999–; lecturer, Biology Dept, Yale Univ. 1969; Assoc. Prof. Zoology Dept, Univ. of Toronto 1969–78, Prof. 1978–97, Prof. Emer. 1997–; Visiting Prof. Tokyo Univ. 1999, Hiroshima Univ. 2000; discovered Maturation Promoting Factor (MPF), cytostatic factor (CSF) proteins in the cytoplasm of cells that controls cell div.; Manning Award 1991, Gairdner Int. Award 1992, Albert Lasker Medical Research Award 1998. *Publications:* numerous scientific papers. *Address:* Department of Zoology, University of Toronto, 25 Harbord Street, Toronto, Ont. M5S 3G5 (Office); 32 Overton Cr., Don Mills, North York, Toronto, Ont. M3B 2V2, Canada (Home). *Telephone:* (416) 978-3493 (Office); (416) 444-6972 (Home). *Fax:* (416) 978-8532 (Office). *E-mail:* masui@zoo.utoronto.ca (Office); masui@zoo.utoronto.ca (Home).

MASUR, Kurt; German conductor; b. 18 July 1927, Brieg, Silesia, Poland; ed Hochschule für Musik, Leipzig; theatre conductor in Erfurt and Leipzig 1948–55, conductor, Dresden Philharmonic 1955–58, Chief Conductor 1967–72; Gen. Musical Dir, Mecklenburg State Theatre 1958–60; Prin. Musical Dir, Komische Oper in East Berlin 1960–64; Conductor, Leipzig Gewandhaus Orchestra 1970, Music Dir 1970–96; Music Dir Conductor New York Philharmonic 1991–2002; Prin. Conductor London Philharmonic Orchestra 1991–; Music Dir Orchestre nat. de France 2001–; has toured extensively in Europe and the USA; début in USA with Cleveland Orchestra 1974; Freeman of City of Leipzig; Hon. Pres. Kulturstiftung, Leipzig; Hon. degrees from seven American univs. and Univ. of Leipzig; Prin. Conductor London Philharmonic Orchestra 2000–; Officier, Légion d'honneur, Bundesverdienstkreuz, Hon. Citizen of Brieg (Poland), Commdr Cross of Merit (Poland) 1999. *Address:* Masur Music International Inc., Ansonia PO Box 231478, New York, NY 10023, USA (Office). *Telephone:* (646) 623-5803 (Office). *Fax:* (212) 414-8276 (Office). *E-mail:* stefana@muasurmusic.com (Office). *Website:* www.kurtmasur.com (Office).

MASUREL, Jean-Louis Antoine Nicolas, MBA; French industrialist and vineyard owner; b. 18 Sept. 1940, Cannes; s. of Antoine and Anne-Marie (née Gallant) Masurel; m. 1st 1964; two d.; m. 2nd Martine Fabrega 1987; ed

Hautes Etudes Commerciales, Graduate School of Business Admin., Harvard Univ.; with Morgan Guaranty Trust Co., New York, last position Sr Vice-Pres. New York 1964–80; Sr Exec. Vice-Pres. Banque de Paris & des Pays Bas 1980–82; Deputy Pres. Banque Paribas 1982–83; Man. Dir Moët-Hennessy 1983–89, Vice-Chair. 1987; Man. Dir LVMH Moët-Hennessy Louis Vuitton 1987–89; Pres. Arcos Investissement SA 1989–, Hediard SA 1991–95; Hon. Pres. Harvard Business School Club de France 1993–96; Dir Peugeot SA 1987, Soc. des Bains de Mer (SBM), Monaco 1994–; Sr Int. Adviser, BBL Investment Banking 1997–99, ING Barings 1999–2001; Dir Banque du Gothard SAM, Monaco 1998–, Oudart SA 1999–; Gov. American Hosp. in Paris; wine producer in Neoules (Domaine de Trians-Var); Chevalier des Arts et des Lettres 1996; Chevalier Légion d'honneur 2001. *Leisure interests:* hunting, skiing. *Address:* Arcos Investissement, 10a rue de la Paix, 75002 Paris; Domaine de Trians, 83136 Néoules, France (Home). *Telephone:* 1-42-96-01-96. *Fax:* 1-42-96-01-70. *E-mail:* jlmasurel@wanadoo.fr (Office). *Website:* www .trians.com (Home).

MATANE, Sir Paulias Nguna, Kt, CMG, OBE; Papua New Guinea diplomatist; b. 21 Sept. 1931, Viviran, Rabaul; s. of Ilias and Elta (Toto) Matane; m. Kaludia Peril 1957; two s. two d.; senior positions in Dept of Educ. 1957–69; mem. Public Service Bd 1969; Head, Dept of Lands, Surveys and Mines 1969, of Business Devt 1970–75; Amb. to USA and Mexico 1975–80, Perm. Rep. to UN 1975–81, High Commr in Canada 1977–81; Sec., Dept of Foreign Affairs and Trade 1980–85; Chair. Cttee on the Philosophy of Educ. for Papua New Guinea 1986–88, Cocoa Industry Investigating Cttee of Cocoa Quality in Papua New Guinea 1986–88, Ocean Trading Co. Pty Ltd 1989–91, Newton Pacific (PNG) Pty Ltd 1989–; Censorship Bd of PNG 1990–93; Dir Triad Pacific (PNG) Pty Ltd 1987–96 (Chair. 1987–91); Presenter weekly radio programme Insait Long Komuniti 1998–, weekly programme on EMTV 1990–; Columnist The Time Traveller, in The National Newspaper 1999–; Dir Nat. Museum and Art Gallery (Bd of Trustees) 1995–99, Pres. 1999–; Dir Nat. Library and Archives 1996–; mem. Nat. Investment and Devt Authority, Nat. Tourism Authority, Nat. Citizenship Advisory Cttee, Univ. of Papua New Guinea Council; Hon. DTech (Papua New Guinea) 1985; Hon. DPhil (Papua New Guinea) 1985; 10th Independence Anniversary Medal 1985, UN 40th Anniversary Medal, Silver Jubilee Medal 2001. *Publications:* My Childhood in New Guinea, A New Guinean Travels through Africa, Two New Guineans Travel through South East Asia, What Good is Business?, Aimbe the Magician, Aimbe the Challenger, Aimbe the School Dropout, Aimbe the Pastor, Kum Tumun of Minj, Two Papua New Guineans Discover the Bible Lands (later retitled Travels Through the Bible Lands) 1987, To Serve with Love 1989, Chit-Chats 1991, East to West–The Longest Train Trip in the World 1991, Let's Do It PNG, Trekking through the New Worlds, Voyage to Antarctica 1996, Laughter Made in PNG 1996, Amazing Discoveries in 40 Years of Marriage 1996, The Word Power 1998, The Other Side of Port Moresby . . . In Pictures 1998, A Trip of a Lifetime 1998, Waliling Community United Church Then and Now 1998, Coach Adventures Down Under 1999, Some Answers to our Management Problems in the Public and Private Sectors 1999, More Answers to Our Management Problems 1999, Chit-Chats (vol. 3) 2000, Management for Excellence 2001, Exploring the Holy Lands 2001, Travels Through South-East Asia (Vols 1 and 2) 2001, Humour: The Papua New Guinean Way, Ripples in the South Pacific Ocean. *Leisure interests:* reading, squash, writing, travel. *Address:* Paulias Matane Foundation Inc., P.O. Box 680, Rabaul, ENBP, Papua New Guinea. *Telephone:* 9829153. *Fax:* 9829151. *E-mail:* newtonp@global.net.pg (Office).

MATANZIMA, Chief Kaiser; South African politician and lawyer; b. 1915, St Mark's Dist; s. of the late Mhlobo Matanzima; m. Nozuko Jayinja 1954; four s. five d.; ed Lovedale Missionary Institution and Fort Hare Univ. Coll.; Chief, Amahale Clan of Tembus, St Mark's District 1940; mem. United Transkeian Gen. Council 1942–56; Perm. Head Emigrant Tembuland Regional Authority and mem. Exec. Cttee Transkeian Territorial Authority 1956–58; Regional Chief of Emigrant Tembuland 1958–61; Presiding Chief Transkeian Territorial Authority 1961–63; Chief Minister of Transkei 1963–76, Prime Minister 1976–79; Pres. Repub. of Transkei 1979–85; Leader, Transkei Nat. Party 1987–88; Chancellor, Univ. of Transkei 1977–88; Freeman of Umtata 1982; Hon. LLD (Fort Hare). *Publications:* Independence My Way 1977. *Address:* Qamata, Bizana District, Transkei, South Africa.

MATEŠA, Zlatko; Croatian politician; b. 7 June 1949, Zagreb; m.; two c.; ed Zagreb Univ., Henley Man. College, UK; Asst Judge, Judge Zagreb Mun. Court 1978–; Asst Man., Man. Legal Dept INA-Trade (Industrija Nafte Asscn) 1978–82, Dir Legal and Personnel Dept 1982–85, Dir Joint Admin. Services 1985–89, mem. Man. Bd, Vice-Pres. 1989–90; Asst to Gen.-Man. INA-HQ 1990–92; mem. Croatian Democratic Union (HDZ); Dir Agency for Reconstruction and Devt of Govt of Croatia 1992–93; Minister without Portfolio 1993–95; Minister of Econ. Sept.–Nov. 1995; Prime Minister of Croatia 1995–2000. *Address:* c/o Office of the Prime Minister, Radićev trg 7, 41000 Zagreb, Croatia.

MATHÉ, Georges, MD; French professor of medicine; b. 9 July 1922, Sermages; s. of Adrien and Francine (née Doridot) Mathé; m. Marie-Louise Servier 1954; one d.; ed Lycée Banville, Moulins and Univ. de Paris; Head of Clinic, Medical Faculty, Paris Univ. 1952–53, Assoc. Prof. of Cancer Research Fac. Medicine, Paris 1956–67; Head, Dept of Haematology, Inst. Gustave-Roussy 1961; Tech. Counsellor, Ministry of Health 1964–66; Dir Inst. de Cancérologie et d'Immunogénétique 1965; Prof. of Experimental Cancerology, Faculté de Médecine, Univ. de Paris-Sud, Villejuif 1966; Ed.-in-Chief Biomedicine and Pharmacotherapy; Co-ed. Medical Oncology & Tumor Pharmacotherapy; consultant Swiss Hospital of Paris –1991, Hosp. of Oncology, Sofia; mem. Cen. Cttee Rassemblement pour la Répub.; Prés. Comité Consultatif de la Recherche Scientifique et Tech. 1972–75, Medical Oncology Soc., Comité cancer, European Hospital of Rome; mem. Royal Soc. of Medicine, New York Acad. of Sciences; Médaille d'or des hôpitaux de Paris; Commdr, Légion d'honneur, Grand Officier; Ordre nat. du Mérite, Commendatore dell'Ordine al Merito della Repub. Italiana; Grand Prix Humanitaire de France, Medawar Laureate Transplantation Soc. 2002; numerous foreign and international scientific awards. *Publications:* Le métabolisme de l'eau (with J. Hamburger) 1952, La greffe (with J. L. Amiel) 1962, Aspects histologiques et cytologiques des leucémies et hématosarcomes (with G. Séman) 1963, L'aplasie myélolymphoide de l'irradiation totale (with J. L. Amiel) 1965, Sémiologie médicale (with G. Richet) 1965 (3rd Edn 1977), La chimiothérapie des cancers 1966 (3rd Edn 1974), Le cancer 1967, Bone Marrow Transplantation and White Cells Transfusions (with J. L. Amiel and L. Schwarzenberg) 1971, La santé: est-elle au dessus de nos moyens? (with Catherine Mathé) 1970, Natural History and Modern Treatment of Hodgkin's Disease (with M. Tubianan) 1973, Histocytological typing of the neoplastic diseases of the haematopoietic and lymphoid tissues (with H. Rappaport) 1973, Cancérologie générale et clinique (with A. Cattan) 1974, Le temps d'y penser 1974, Immunothérapie active des cancers: immunoprévention et immunorestauration 1976, Cancer Active Immunotherapy; Immunoporphylaxis and Immunorestoration: An Introduction 1976, Cancer Chemotherapy: Its Role in the Treatment Strategy of Hematologic Malignancies and Solid Tumors (with A. Clarysse and Y. Kenis) 1976, Dossier Cancer 1977, L'homme qui voulait être guéri 1985 (novel), Nagasaki (play), Le Sexe des Dieux et des Diables 1992 (play), Le Sida sidère la science, le sexe et les sceaux 1995. *Leisure interests:* novel writing, theatre. *Address:* ICI, 6 rue Minard, BP 60, 92133 Issy-les-Moulineaux (Office); Hôpital Suisse de Paris, 10 rue Minard, 92130 Issy-les-Moulineaux; Le Fonbois, 10 Rue du Bon Puits, Arpajon, 91290 La Norville, France (Home). *Telephone:* 64-90-03-58 (Home).

MATHER, Graham Christopher Spencer, MA; British politician, solicitor and administrator; b. 23 Oct. 1954, Preston, Lancs.; s. of Thomas Mather and Doreen Mather; m. 1st Fiona Marion McMillan Bell 1981 (divorced 1995); two s.; m. 2nd Geneviève Elizabeth Fairhurst 1997; ed Hutton Grammar School, New Coll., Oxford (Burnet Law Scholar); Asst to Dir-Gen. Inst. of Dirs 1980, est. Policy Unit 1983, Head of Policy Unit 1983–86; Deputy Dir Inst. of Econ. Affairs 1987, Gen. Dir 1987–92; Pres. European Policy Forum 1992–, European Media Forum 1997–, European Financial Forum 1999–; MEP for Hampshire North and Oxford 1994–; Visiting Fellow, Nuffield Coll. Oxford 1992–99; mem. Competition Comm. Appeals Tribunal 2000; mem. Monopolies and Mergers Comm. 1989–94, Westminster City Council 1982–86; Conservative parl. cand. for Blackburn 1983; Vice-Pres. Strategic Planning Soc. 1993–, Asscn of Dist Councils 1994–97; mem. Public Policy Advisory Bd Queen Mary and Westfield Coll. London 1993–; Consultant Tudor Investment Corpn, Medley Global Advisers; Patron Govt Affairs Group, Inst. of Public Relations 1996–. *Publications:* Striking out Strikes (with C. G. Hanson) 1988; Europe's Constitutional Future (contrib.) 1990, Making Decisions in Britain 2000; papers and contribs. to journals. *Address:* 125 Pall Mall, London, SW1Y 5EA, England. *Telephone:* (20) 7839-7557. *Fax:* (20) 7839-7339. *E-mail:* graham.mather@epfltd.org (Office). *Website:* www.epfltd.org.

MATHER, Richard Martin, BArch; British architect; b. 30 May 1937; s. of the late Richard John Mather and Opal Martin; ed School of Architecture and Allied Arts, Univ. of Oregon; Assoc. Teacher Univ. Coll. London, Univ. of Westminster, Harvard Grad. School of Design 1967–88; Prin. Rick Mather Architects 1973–; RIBA External Examiner to Univs and Colls in England and Scotland 1986–; consultant Architect Architectural Asscn 1978–92 (mem. Council 1992–96), Univ. of E. Anglia 1988–92, Univ. of Southampton 1996; Trustee, Victoria & Albert Museum 2000–. *Major works include:* Times Headquarters Bldg, London (RIBA Award 1992), All Glass Structure, London (RIBA Award 1994), Arco Bldg, Keble Coll., Oxford (RIBA Award 1996, Civic Trust Award 1997), Sloan Robinson Bldg 2002, ISMA Centre, Univ. of Reading 1998 (RIBA Award 1999), Neptune Court, Nat. Maritime Museum (Civic Trust Award 2000), Wallace Collection 2000, Dulwich Picture Gallery (RIBA Crown Estates Conservation Award 2001, AIA Business Week/Architectural Record Award 2001, Civic Trust Award 2002), London S. Bank Centre Masterplan 2000–, Greenwich World Heritage Site Masterplan 2002–, Ashmolean Museum Masterplan 2002–, Natural History Museum Masterplan 2003–. *Publications:* Zen Restaurants: Rick Mather 1992, Rick Mather: Urban Approches 1992. *Leisure interests:* food, gardens, skiing. *Address:* Rick Mather Architects, 123 Camden High Street, London, NW1 7JR, England (Office). *Telephone:* (20) 7284-1727 (Office). *Fax:* (20) 7267-7826 (Office). *E-mail:* info@rickmather.com (Office).

MATHEWS, (Forrest) David, PhD; American educationalist and foundation executive; b. 6 Dec. 1935, Grove Hill, Ala; s. of Forrest Lee and Doris Mathews; m. Mary Chapman 1960; two d.; ed Univ. of Alabama and Columbia Univ.; Infantry Officer U.S. Army Reserves 1959–67; Pres. Univ. of Ala 1969–80, Lecturer and Prof. of History 1969–80; Sec. of Health, Educ. and Welfare 1975–77; Chair. Nat. Council for Public Policy Educ. 1980–; Dir Acad. Educ. Devt 1975–; mem. Bd Dirs. Nat. Civic League 1996–; mem. numerous advisory bds., etc.; Trustee Nat. March of Dimes 1977–85, John F. Kennedy Center for Performing Arts 1975–77, Woodrow Wilson Int. Center for Scholars 1975–77, Miles Coll. 1978–, Teachers Coll., Columbia Univ. 1977–95, Gerald R. Ford Foundation 1988–; Pres. and CEO Charles F.

Kettering Foundation 1981–; numerous awards and hon. degrees. *Publications:* works on history of Southern USA, higher educ. in public policy, including The Changing Agenda for American Higher Education, The Promise of Democracy, Is There a Public for Public Schools? 1996, Politics for People: Finding a Responsible Voice 1999. *Leisure interest:* gardening. *Address:* 200 Commons Road, Dayton, OH 45459; 6050 Mad River Road, Dayton, OH 45459, USA. *Telephone:* (937) 434-7300 (Office). *Fax:* (937) 428-5353 (Office). *E-mail:* jenkyn@kettering.org (Office).

MATHIAS, Charles McCurdy; American politician and lawyer; b. 24 July 1922, Frederick, Md; s. of Charles McC. Mathias, Sr and Theresa Trail Mathias; m. Ann Hickling Bradford 1958; two s.; ed public schools, Frederick, Md, Haverford Coll., Yale Univ. and Univ. of Maryland; apprentice seaman 1942, commissioned Ensign 1944, sea duty, Pacific 1944–46; Capt. U.S. Naval Reserve retd; admitted to Maryland Bar 1949, to U.S. Supreme Court Bar 1954; Asst Attorney-Gen. of Maryland 1953, 1954; City Attorney, Frederick, Md 1954–59; mem. Md House of Dels. 1958; mem. U.S. House of Reps. 1960–68; U.S. Senator from Maryland 1969–87; Milton S. Eisenhower Distinguished Professor in Public Policy, Johns Hopkins School for Advanced Int. Studies 1987–; Chair. Senate Rules and Admin. Cttee 1981–87; Chair. of Bd First American Bankshares 1993–; Republican; Légion d'honneur (France), Order of Orange-Nassau (Netherlands), Order of Merit (FRG), Hon. KBE (UK). *Address:* 51 Louisiana Avenue, NW, Washington, DC 20001 (Office); 3808 Leland Street, Chevy Chase, MD 20815, USA (Home).

MATHIAS, Peter, CBE, MA, DLitt, LittD, FBA, FRHistS; British professor of economic history (retd); b. 10 Jan. 1928, Somerset; s. of John Samuel Mathias and Marian Helen Love; m. Elizabeth Ann Blackmore 1958; two s. one d.; ed Colstons Hosp., Bristol, Jesus Coll. Cambridge and Harvard Univ., USA; Research Fellow, Jesus Coll. 1953–55; Lecturer, History Faculty, Cambridge Univ. 1955–68, Tutor and Dir of Studies, Queens' Coll., Sr Proctor, Cambridge Univ. 1965–66; Chichele Prof. of Econ. History, Oxford Univ. and Fellow of All Souls Coll. 1969–87; Master of Downing Coll., Cambridge 1987–95; Pres. Int. Econ. History Asscn 1974–78, Hon. Pres. 1978–; Pres. Business Archive Council 1984–95, Vice-Pres. 1995–; Chair. British Library Advisory Council 1994–99; Vice-Pres. Royal Historical Soc. 1975–80 (Hon. Vice-Pres. 2001–), Int. Inst. of Econ. History Francesco Datini Prato 1987–99; Hon. Treas. British Acad. 1979–88, Econ. History Soc. 1967–88 (Pres. 1989–92, Vice-Pres. 1992–); mem. Advisory Bd of the Research Councils 1983–88; Chair. History of Medicine Panel, Wellcome Trust 1980–88; Syndic Fitzwilliam Museum 1987–98; Chair. Fitzwilliam Museum Enterprises Ltd 1990–99, Friends of Kettle's Yard 1989–95, Bd of Continuing Educ., Cambridge Univ. 1991–95; Curator Bodleian Library, Oxford 1972–87; mem. Academia Europaea 1989, Beirat Wissenschaftskolleg, Berlin 1992–98, Russian Acad. of Sciences 2002; Foreign mem. Royal Danish Acad., Royal Belgian Acad.; Trustee GB-Sasakawa Foundation 1994–, Chair. 1997–; Hon. Fellow Jesus Coll., Queens' Coll., Downing Coll. Cambridge; Hon. LittD (Buckingham, Birmingham, Hull, Warwick, de Montfort, East Anglia); Maria Theresa Medal Univ. of Pavia 2002. *Publications:* Brewing Industry in England 1700–1830 1959, Retailing Revolution 1967, Tradesmen's Tokens 1962, The First Industrial Nation 1969, 1983, The Transformation of England 1979, L'economia britannica dal 1815 al 1914 1994; Gen. Ed. Cambridge Economic History of Europe 1968–90. *Leisure interests:* travel, New Hall porcelain. *Address:* Bassingbourn Mill, Mill Lane, Bassingbourn, Royston, Herts., SG8 5PP, England. *Telephone:* (1763) 248708 (Home). *Fax:* (1763) 248708 (Office).

MATHIESEN, Matthias (Árnason), CAND. JURIS; Icelandic politician and lawyer; b. 6 Aug. 1931, Hafnarfjörður; s. of Árni M. and Svava E Mathiesen; m. Sigrún Thorgilsdóttir 1956; two s. one d.; ed Univ. of Iceland; Chief Exec. Hafnarfjörður Savings Bank 1958–67, Chair. 1967; Advocate, Supreme Court 1967–74; mem. Althing (Parl.) 1959–, Speaker Lower Chamber 1970–71; Rep. of Althing to Nordic Council 1965–74, mem. Presidium 1970–71, 1973–74, Pres. 1970–71, 1980–81; Del. North Atlantic Ass., NATO 1963–69, 1972, Chair. Icelandic Del. 1964–67, Pres. of Ass. 1967–68; mem. Bd E Thorgilsson & Co. Ltd, Hafnarfjörður 1973–, Chair. 1982–; Dir Nat. Bank of Iceland 1961–74, 1980–83; Icelandic mem. of Bd of Govs. World Bank Group (IBRD, IDA, IFC) 1983–85; Minister of Finance 1974–78, Minister of Commerce (including Banking) and of Nordic Co-operation 1983–85, for Foreign Affairs 1985–87, of Communications 1987–88; mem. Cen. Cttee, Independence Party 1965–. *Address:* Hringbraut 59, Hafnarfjörður, Iceland (Home). *Telephone:* (91) 5-02-76 (Home).

MATHIEU, Georges Victor Adolphe, LèsL; French artist; b. 27 Jan. 1921, Boulogne; s. of Adolphe Mathieu d'Escaudoeuvres and Madeleine Dupré d'Ausque; ed Facultés de droit et des lettres, Lille; Teacher of English; Public Relations Man., United States Lines; exhibited at Paris 1950, New York 1952, Japan 1957, Scandinavia 1958, England, Spain, Italy, Switzerland, Germany, Austria and S. America 1959, Middle East 1961–62, Canada 1963; special exhbn of work held at Musée Municipal d'Art Moderne, Paris 1963; exhbn of 100 paintings, Galerie Charpentier, Paris 1965; designed gardens and bldgs for BC transformer factory, Fontenay-le-comte 1966; 16 posters for Air France exhibited at Musée Nat. d'Art Moderne, Paris 1967; exhbn of 10 tapestries at Musée de la Manufacture Nat. des Gobelins 1969; designed 18 medals for Paris Mint 1971, new 10F coin 1974; works exhibited in numerous countries including shows in Antibes 1976, Ostend 1977, Grand Palais, Paris 1978, Wildenstein Gallery, New York, Dominion Gallery, Montreal 1979, Musée de la Poste, Paris 1980, Galerie Kasper, Morges, Switzerland 1983, Théâtre municipal de Brives 1984; retrospective show, Palais des Papes, Avignon

1985; Galerie Calvin, Geneva 1985, Wally Findlay Galleries 1986, Galerie Schindler, Berne 1986, Galerie du Luxembourg 1986, Galerie Protée, Paris, Stockholm 1990, Boulogne sur Mer 1992, Museum of Modern Art, Toulouse 1995; creator of "Tachisme"; mem. Acad. of Fine Arts; Officier, Légion d'honneur, des Arts et des Lettres; Ordre de la Couronne de Belgique. *Principal works:* Hommage à la Mort 1950, Hommage au Maréchal de Turenne 1952, Les Capétiens Partout 1954, La Victoire de Denain 1963, Hommage à Jean Cocteau 1963, Paris, Capitale des Arts 1965, Hommages aux Frères Boisserée 1967, Hommage à Condillac 1968, La prise de Bergen op Zoom 1969, Election de Charles Quint 1971, Matta-Salums 1978, La Libération de Paris 1980, La Libération d'Orléans par Jeanne d'Arc 1982, Monumental sculpture in Neuilly 1982, in Charenton 1982, Ceiling-painting in Boulogne-Billancourt town hall 1983, Massacre des 269 1985, Le Paradis des orages 1988, L'Immortalité ruinée 1989, La Complainte silencieuse des enfants de Bogotá 1989, Rumeur de paradis 1991. *Publications:* Au-delà du Tachisme, Le privilège d'Etre, De la Révolte à la Renaissance, La Réponse de l'Abstraction lyrique, L'abstraction prophétique, Le massacre de la sensibilité 1996, Désormais seul en face de Dieu 1998. *Address:* Institut de France, 23 quai Conti, 75006 Paris, France (Office).

MATHIEU, Michel, LenD; French politician; b. 25 July 1944, Montpellier (Hérault); ed Univ. of Paris, Ecole Nat. d'Admin; currently High Commr of French Polynesia; Officier Légion d'honneur, Ordre nat. du Mérite, du Merite agricole; Chevalier du Mérite de la FDR. *Address:* Office of the High Commissioner of the Republic, Bureau du Haut Commissaire, avenue Bruat, BP 115, 98713 Papeete, French Polynesia (Office). *Telephone:* 46-86-86 (Office). *Fax:* 46-85-09 (Office). *E-mail:* m.mathieu@haut-commissariat.pf (Office).

MATHIS, Edith; Swiss soprano; b. 11 Feb. 1938, Lucerne; m. Bernhard Klee; ed Lucerne Conservatoire; début Lucerne (in The Magic Flute) 1956; sang with Cologne Opera 1959–62; appeared Salzburg Festival 1960, Deutsche Oper, W Berlin 1963; début Glyndebourne (Cherubino in Nozze di Figaro) 1962, Covent Garden (Susanna in Nozze di Figaro) 1970, Metropolitan Opera House, New York (Pamina in The Magic Flute) 1970, Berne City Opera 1990; sang to Mendelssohn, Brahms and Schubert, Wigmore Hall, London 1997; mem. Hamburg State Opera 1960–75. *Address:* c/o Ingpen & William Ltd, 26 Wadham Road, London, SW15 2LR, England (Office); c/o Bueker-Management, Postfach 1169, Hanover, Germany. *Telephone:* (20) 8874-3222 (Office).

MATHIS-EDDY, Darlene, PhD; American poet and professor of English; b. 19 March 1937, Elkhart, Ind.; d. of the late William Eugene Mathis and Fern Roose Paulmer Mathis; m. Spencer Livingston Eddy, Jr 1964 (died 1971); ed Goshen Coll. and Rutgers Univ.; Instructor in English, Douglass Coll. 1962–64; Instructor in English, Rutgers Univ. 1964, 1965, Rutgers Univ. Coll. (Adult Educ.) 1967; Asst Prof. in English, Ball State Univ. 1967–71, Assoc. Prof. 1971–75, Prof. 1975–, Poet-in-Residence 1989–93; Consulting Ed. Blue Unicorn 1995–; Founding Ed. The Hedge Row Press 1995–; mem. Comm. on Women for the Nat. Council of Teachers of English 1976–79; Poetry Ed. BSU Forum; Woodrow Wilson Nat. Fellow 1959–62, Notable Woodrow Nat. Fellow 1991 and numerous other fellowships. *Publications:* Leaf Threads, Wind Rhymes 1986, The Worlds of King Lear 1971, Weathering 1992, Reflections: Studies in Light 1993; Contributing Ed. Snowy Egret 1988–90; numerous poems in literary reviews; articles in American Literature, English Language Notes, etc. *Leisure interests:* gardening, music, antiques, reading, sketching, photography, bird watching, cooking. *Address:* Department of English, Robert Bell Building, Office No. 248, Ball State University, Muncie, IN 47306; 1409 West HE Cardinal Street, Muncie, IN 47303, USA (Home). *Telephone:* (317) 285-8580 (Home).

MATHUR, Murari Lal, PhD; Indian professor of mechanical engineering; b. 10 July 1931, Masuda; s. of late Dr. S. D. Mathur and Lalti Devi; m. Vimla Mathur 1961; one s. three d.; ed Govt Coll., Ajmer, Birla Engineering Coll., Pilani, Glasgow Univ., UK; Asst Prof., MBM Eng Coll., Govt of Rajasthan 1952–57; Deputy Dir of Tech. Educ. and Sec. Bd of Tech. Educ., Govt of Rajasthan 1957–58; Prof. and Head Mechanical Eng Dept, Univ. of Jodhpur 1963–85, Prof., Dean Faculty of Eng 1966–68, 1974, 1977–80, Vice-Chancellor 1985–90; Prof. Emer. 1991–; Chair. Automotive Prime-Movers Sectional Cttee, Indian Bureau of Standards; Co-ordinator Solar Passive House Project; design consultant heat exchanger and heat recovery equipment; consultant Cen. Silk Bd and other industries; Fellow Inst. of Engineers (India); Sri Chandra Prakash Memorial Gold Medal, Pres. of India's Prize, Inst. of Engineers Award. *Films:* has produced two educational films. *Publications:* books on thermal eng, internal combustion engines, gas turbines and jet propulsion, thermodynamics, fluid mechanics and machines, machine drawing and heat transfer; over 80 research papers. *Leisure interests:* reading, writing, lecturing on educational topics and topics concerning energy and environment, social service. *Address:* Alok Villa, 17-A, Shastri Nagar, Jodhpur 342 003, Rajasthan, India (Home). *Telephone:* 433207 (Home).

MATIBA, Kenneth; Kenyan politician; Chair. Kenya Breweries 1968–79; founder, Kenya Football League; fmr Chair. Kenya Football Fed.; entered Parl. 1979; resigned from Govt over election-rigging 1988; imprisoned for 10 months for leading multi-party democracy movt July 1990; Chair. FORD-Asili Party; contested presidential election Dec. 1992. *Leisure interest:* mountain climbing. *Address:* Ford-Asili Party, Nairobi, Kenya.

MATIN, Abdul, MA, PhD; Pakistani economist; b. 1 March 1932, Sawabi; s. of Dur Jamil Khan; m. Azra Matin 1959; three s.; ed Univs. of Peshawar and Bonn; Chair. Dept of Econs, Univ. of Peshawar and Dir Bd of Econs, North-

West Frontier Prov. (NWFP) 1959–70; Chief Economist, Govt of NWFP 1970–72; Minister and Deputy Perm. Rep., Pakistan Mission at UN, New York 1973–76; Exec. Dir ADBP, Islamabad 1977–85; Vice-Chancellor, Univ. of Peshawar 1987–89; Vice-Pres. and mem. of Cen. Cttee, Pakistan Tehrik-i-Insaaf (Movement for Justice) 1996–; Chair. of Task Forces to Regulate Pvt. Educational Insts in NWFP 1999–, to Reform Higher Secondary Govt Schools in NWFP 2000–; mem. Nat. Comm. on Manpower, Govt of Pakistan; mem. Educ. Inquiry Cttee NWFP; Chair. Govt Working Group on Transport Policy 1991–92, Universities Services Reforms and Man. Cttee, Govt of NWFP 1998; mem. Quaid-e-Azam Mazar Man. Bd 2000–; engaged in research project: "Revival and Reconstruction of Muslim World"; mem. Bd of Man. Pakistan Bait-ul-Mal (PBM); prepared policy draft for Nat. Centre for Rehabilitation of Child Labour (NCRCL) 2001; mem. Higher Educ. Comm. of Pakistan 2003–; Hamdard Foundation Award for Outstanding Services 1992. *Publications:* Industrialization of NWFP 1970; 80 articles on the problems, policies and pattern of econ. devt in professional journals. *Leisure interests:* extension lectures, public speeches. *Address:* House No. 27, Street No. 9, Sector D-3, Phase I, Hayat-ABAD, Peshawar, N.W.F.P., Pakistan. *Telephone:* 817144.

MATIN, M. A., FRCS; Bangladeshi politician; b. 1 Dec. 1937, Pabna; ed Dhaka Medical Coll.; worked in Royal Eye Hosp. and King's Coll. Hosp., London 1964–67; Assoc. Prof. of Ophthalmology, Inst. of Postgraduate Medicine and Research, Dhaka 1967–72, Prof., then Head of Dept 1972–; Hon. Col and Consultant Ophthalmologist, Combined Mil. Hosp., Dhaka 1976; MP 1979–, re-elected BNP MP 2001–; Minister of Civil Aviation and Tourism 1979, Minister of Youth Devt and of Health and Population Control 1981, Minister of Home Affairs 1981–82, Minister of Commerce 1984, Minister of Works 1985, Deputy Prime Minister in charge of Ministry of Home Affairs 1986–88; Deputy Prime Minister 1988–89; Minister of Health and Family Planning 1988, 1989, of Home Affairs 1988–89; fmr Sec.-Gen. and Pres. Bangladesh Ophthalmological Soc. and Pres. Bangladesh Medical Services Asscn; Vice-Chair. Bangladesh Medical Research Council and Vice-Pres. Bangladesh Coll. of Physicians and Surgeons; Alim Memorial Gold Medal; Int. Award, Asian Pacific Acad. of Ophthalmology 1981. *Address:* c/o Ministry of Health and Family Planning, 3rd Floor, Bangladesh Secretariat, Dhaka; Shantinagar, Dhaka, Bangladesh (Home).

MATLOCK, Jack Foust Jr., MA; American diplomatist; b. 1 Oct. 1929, Greensboro; s. of Jack Foust Matlock and Nellie McSwain; m. Rebecca Burrum 1949; four s. one d.; ed Duke and Columbia Univs. and Russian Inst.; Instructor, Dartmouth 1953–56; joined foreign service, State Dept 1956, Official in Washington 1956–58, Embassy Official, Vienna 1958–60, Consul Gen., Munich 1960–61, Embassy Official, Moscow 1961–63, Accra, Ghana 1963–66, Zanzibar 1967–69, Dar es Salaam 1969–70, Country Dir for USSR, State Dept 1971–74, Deputy Chief of Mission, Embassy in Moscow 1974–78, Diplomat-in-Residence, Vanderbilt Univ. 1978–79, Deputy Dir, Foreign Service Inst., Washington 1979–80, Amb. to Czechoslovakia 1981–83, to USSR, 1987–91; Special Asst to Pres. and Sr Dir European and Soviet Affairs, Nat. Security Council 1983–87; Sr Research Fellow Columbia Univ. 1991–93; Kathryn and Shelby Collum Davis Prof. 1993–96; George F. Kennan Prof., Inst. for Advanced Study, Princeton, NJ 1996–2001; Visiting Prof. Princeton Univ. 2001–; mem. American Acad. of Diplomacy, Council on Foreign Relations, American Philosophical Soc.; Dickey Fellow Dartmouth Coll. 1992; Hon. LLD (Greensboro Coll.) 1989, Albright Coll. (1992), Connecticut Coll. (1993); Superior Honor Award, US State Dept, Presidential Meritorious Service Award, McIver Award for Distinguished Public Service 1994 and many others. *Publications:* Ed. Index to J. V. Stalin's Works 1971, Autopsy on an Empire: The American Ambassador's Account of the Collapse of the Soviet Union 1995. *Address:* 940 Princeton-Kingston Road, Princeton, NJ 08540, USA. *Telephone:* (609) 252-1953 (Home). *Fax:* (609) 252-9373 (Home). *E-mail:* jfmatlo@attglobal.net (Home).

MATOKA, Peter Wilfred, PhD; Zambian politician, international civil servant and diplomatist; b. 8 April 1930, Mwinilunga, NW Prov.; m. Grace J. Mukahlera 1957; two s. one d.; ed Rhodes Univ., S. Africa, American Univ., Washington, DC, Univ. of Zambia, Univ. of Warwick, England; civil servant, N Rhodesia Govt 1954–64; mem. of Parl. of Zambia 1964–78; Minister of Information and Postal Services 1964–65, of Health 1965–66, of Works and Housing 1967, of Power, Transport and Works 1968; mem. Cen. Cttee, United Nat. Independence Party (UNIP) 1967, 1971–78; Minister for Luapula Prov. 1969; High Commr of Zambia in UK 1969–70, concurrently accredited to the Vatican; Minister for the S. Prov. 1970, of Health 1971–72, of Local Govt and Housing 1972–77, of Devt Planning 1977, of Econ. and Tech. Co-operation 1977–78; Chief Whip, Nat. Ass. 1973–78; Sr Regional Adviser UN Econ. Comm. for Africa, Addis Ababa 1979–83; High Commr in Zimbabwe 1984–88; Chair. Social and Cultural Sub-Cttee of Cen. Cttee of UNIP 1988–90, of Science and Tech. Sub-Cttee 1990–91; Sr Lecturer, Social Devt Studies Dept, Univ. of Zambia 1995–; Chair. WHO Africa Region 1966; Pres. Africa, Caribbean and Pacific Group of States 1977; Chair. Nat. Inst. of Scientific Research 1977; Chair. Zambia-Kenya and Zambia-Yugoslavia Perm. Comms. 1977; Chair. Lusaka MULPOC 1977; Chair. and Man. Dir FilZam Projects and Investments Services Centre Ltd 1992–; Vice-Chair. Nat. Tender Bd 1977; Life mem. CPA; mem. Perm. Human Rights Comm. of Zambia 1997–; Nat. Consultant on Child Labour Issues 1997–; Kt of St Gregory (Vatican) 1964; Kt, Egypt and Ethiopia. *Leisure interests:* gardening, television,

walking. *Address:* University of Zambia, P.O. Box 32379, Lusaka (Office); Ibex Hill, P.O. Box 50101, Lusaka, Zambia (Home). *Telephone:* (1) 291777 (Office); (1) 260221 (Home). *Fax:* (1) 253952. *E-mail:* registra@unza.zm (Office).

MATOLCSY, György; Hungarian politician and economist; b. 1955, Budapest; m.; two c.; ed Budapest Univ. of Economic Sciences; Jr official Industrial Org. Inst. 1977–78; mem. staff Ministry of Finance 1978–81, mem. Secr. 1981–85; Fellow Finance Research Inst. 1985–90; Political State Sec. Prime Minister's Office 1990–91; Dir Privatization Research Inst. 1991; Dir EBRD, London 1991–94; Dir Property Foundation, Inst. for Privatization Studies 1995–99; Minister of Econ. Affairs 2000–02. *Address:* c/o Ministry of Economic Affairs, Honvéd u. 13–15, 1055 Budapest, Hungary (Office).

MATOMÄKI, Tauno, M.SC.(ENG.); Finnish business executive; b. 14 April 1937, Nakkila; s. of Niilo Matomäki and Martta Matomäki; m. Leena (née Nilsson) Matomäki 1963; one s. three d.; ed Tech. Univ., Helsinki; joined Rauma-Repola 1967, various positions, Pres. and CEO 1987–, Pres. and CEO Repola Ltd 1991–; Chair. Bd of Dirs. Rauma Ltd, United Paper Mills Ltd, Pohjolan Voima Ltd, Finnyards Ltd, Confed. of Finnish Industries, Finnish Employers' Confed.; mem. Bd of Dirs. Effjohn AB; mem. Supervisory Bd Teollisuuden Voima Oy (Chair.), Kansallis-Osake-Pankki, Pohjola Insurance Co., Ilmarinen Pension Insurance Co., Polar Rakennusosakeyhtiö, Uusi Suomi Oy; Kt, Order of the White Rose of Finland (First Class).

MATORIN, Vladimir Anatolievich; Russian singer (bass); b. 2 May 1948, Moscow; s. of Anatoly Ivanovich Matorin and Maria Tarasovna Matorina; m. Svetlana Sergeyevna Matorina; one s.; ed Gnessin Pedagogical Inst. (now Acad.) of Music; soloist Moscow Stanislavsky and Nemirovich-Danchenko Music Theatre 1974–92, Bolshoi Theatre 1991–; winner All-Union Glinka Competition of vocalists and Int. Competition of singers in Geneva; numerous int. tours; Merited Artist of Russia, People's Artist of Russia. *Opera roles include:* Boris Godunov, Ivan Susanin, King Rene (Iolanthe), Gremin (Eugene Onegin), Dosifei (Khovanshchina), Count Galitsky (Prince Igor), Don Basilio (Barber of Seville), Count (Invisible City of Kitezh) and others. *Leisure interests:* poetry, sacred music, travelling by car. *Address:* Bolshoi Theatre of Russia, Teatralnaya pl. 1, 103009 Moscow (Office); Ulansky per. 21, korp. 1 Apt. 53, 103045 Moscow, Russia (Home). *Telephone:* (095) 292-38-86 (Bolshoi Opera); (095) 280-44-17 (Home).

MATSEPE-CASABURRI, Ivy F., PhD; South African politician and civil servant; d. of late Dorrington Matsepe and Violet Matsepe; m. (divorced); ed Rutgers Univ., NJ and Fort Hare Univ.; Academic Registrar and Sr lecturer, UN Inst. for Namibia, Lusaka, Zambia 1985–90; Exec. Dir Educ. Devt Trust 1990–93; Chair. S.A.B.C. 1993; Minister of Posts, Telecommunications and Broadcasting (later of Communications) 1999–; Pres. Asscn of African Women for Research and Devt 1988–. *Publications:* articles in African Journal of Political Economy. *Leisure interests:* music, reading, sports. *Address:* Ministry of Communications, Nkululeko House, Iparioli Office Park, 339 Duncan Street, 0083 Hatfield, Pretoria; P.O. Box 91123, Auckland Park 2006, South Africa. *Telephone:* (12) 4278111 (Office); (11) 714 3900. *Fax:* (12) 3626915 (Office); (11) 714 3569. *E-mail:* nowjoan@doc.org.za. *Website:* www.doc.gov.za/index.html (Office).

MATSUMOTO, Ken, MA; Japanese business executive; b. 2 Feb. 1935, Shanghai, China; s. of Shigeharu and Hanako Matsumoto; m. Junko Masuda 1969; one s.; ed Gakushuin High School, Swarthmore Coll., USA, Univ. of Tokyo; mem. Bd of Dirs., Auburn Steel Co. Inc., Auburn, NY 1973–77; Sr Man. Export Dept-I, Nippon Steel Corpn 1977–84; Dir Research Div., The Fair Trade Center 1984–90, Man. Dir 1990–; awarded Bancroft Scholarship. *Leisure interests:* tennis, skiing. *Address:* 5-11-38, Miyazaki, Miyamae-ku, Kawasaki-shi, Kanagawa-ken, 216 Japan. *Telephone:* (44) 854-0693.

MATSUO, Minoru, DEng; Japanese university administrator and professor of engineering; b. 4 July 1936, Kyoto; ed Kyoto Univ.; Asst Prof. School of Eng, Kyoto Univ. 1964–65, Assoc. Prof. 1965–72; Assoc. Prof. School of Eng., Nagoya Univ. 1972–78, Prof. 1978–98, Univ. Senator 1987–89, Dean 1989–92, Dir Center for Integrated Research in Science and Eng 1995–97, Pres. of Nagoya Univ. 1998–. *Publications include:* Reliability in Geotechnical Design 1984. *Address:* Nagoya University, Furo-cho, Chikusa-ku, Nagoya, 464–8601, Japan (Office). *Telephone:* (52) 789-2000 (Office). *Fax:* (52) 789-2005 (Office). *Website:* www.nagoya-u.ac.jp (Office).

MATSUSHITA, Masaharu, B.IUR.; Japanese business executive; b. 17 Sept. 1912, Tokyo; s. of Eiji Matsushita and Shizuko Hirata; m. Sachiko Matsushita; two s. one d.; ed Tokyo Imperial Univ.; Mitsui Bank 1935–40; Matsushita Electric Industrial Co. Ltd 1940–, Auditor 1944–47, Dir, mem. Bd, 1947–49, Exec. Vice-Pres. 1949–61, Pres. 1961–77, Chair. Bd 1977–; Dir Matsushita Electronics Corpn 1952–72, 1985–, Chair. 1972–85; Auditor, Matsushita Real Estate Co. Ltd 1952–68, Dir 1968–; Dir Matsushita Communication Industrial Co. Ltd 1958–70, Chair. 1970–86; Dir Matsushita Seiko Co. Ltd 1956–87, Kyushu Matsushita Electric Co. Ltd 1955–87, Matsushita Reiki Co. Ltd (formerly Nakagawa Electric Inc.) 1961–87, Matsushita Electric Corpn of America 1959–74 (Chair. 1974–); Pres. Electronics Industries Asscn of Japan 1968–70; Rep. Dir, Kansai Cttee for Econ. Devt 1962–, Dir 1975–; mem. Standing Cttee, Osaka Chamber of Commerce 1966–; Standing Dir, Kansai Econ. Fed. 1970–, Vice-Pres. 1977–; Blue Ribbon Medal 1972; Commdr of Order of Orange-Nassau (Netherlands) 1975. *Address:* Matsushita Electric Industrial Co. Ltd, 1006 Ouza Kadoma, Kadoma-shi Osaka 571-8501, Japan. *Telephone:* (6) 6908-1121. *Fax:* (6) 6908-2351. *Website:* www .panasonic.co.jp/global (Office).

MATSUSHITA, Yasuo; Japanese banker; b. 1 Jan. 1926; Admin. Vice-Minister of Finance 1982; Pres. Taiyo Kobe Bank 1987; Chair. Mitsui Taiyo Kobe Bank 1990–92, renamed Sakura Bank 1992–94; Gov. Bank of Japan 1994–98. *Leisure interests:* reading, tennis. *Address:* c/o Bank of Japan, 2-1-1, Chuo-ku, Tokyo 108-8660, Japan.

MATSUURA, Koichiro; Japanese international organization official and diplomatist; b. 1937, Tokyo; ed Univ. of Tokyo, Haverford Coll., Pa; began diplomatic career 1959; Dir.-Gen. Econ. Co-operation Bureau, Ministry of Foreign Affairs 1988, Dir.-Gen. N American Affairs Bureau 1990; Deputy Minister for Foreign Affairs; Amb. to France 1994–98; Chair. UNESCO's World Heritage Cttee 1998–99; Dir.-Gen. UNESCO 1999–. *Address:* UNESCO, 7 place de Fontenoy, 75352 Paris, France (Office). *Telephone:* 1-45-68-10-00 (Office). *Fax:* 1-45-67-16-90 (Office). *Website:* www.unesco.org.

MATSUYAMA, Yoshinori, LLD; Japanese professor of psychology; b. 5 Dec. 1923, Kyoto; m. Michiko Kinugasa 1949; one s. two d.; ed Doshisha and Osaka Univs.; Prof. of Psychology, Doshisha Univ. 1959–93, Pres. 1973–79, 1980–83, Chancellor 1985– (Chair. Bd of Trustees 1985–93); Hon. LLD (Wesleyan Univ., Conn. and Amherst Coll., Mass.). *Publications:* A Study on Behaviour Disorders 1957, A Study on Anxiety 1961, Psychology of Motivation 1967, Human Motivation 1981. *Address:* Doshisha University, Karasuma Imadegawa, Kamigyo-ku, Kyoto 602-80 (Office); 90 Matsubaracho Ichijoji Sakyoku, Kyoto 606, Japan. *Telephone:* (75) 251-3110 (Office); (75) 701-8625. *Fax:* (75) 251-3075 (Office). *E-mail:* ji-shomu@mail.doshisha.ac.jp (Office). *Website:* www.doshisha.ac.jp (Office).

MATSUYEV, Denis Leonidovich; Russian pianist; b. 11 June 1975, Irkutsk; s. of Leonid Matsuyev and Irina Gomelskaya; ed Moscow State Conservatory (pupil of Prof. S. Dozensky); concerts 1993–; soloist Moscow State Academic Philharmonic Soc. 1995–; recitals in Paris, New York, Munich, Hamburg, Athens, Salzburg, Tokyo, Moscow and St Petersburg; played with State Symphony Orchestra of Russian Fed., Hon. Ensemble of Russia (St Petersburg), Tokyo Symphony, Budapest Philharmonic, Seoul Philharmonic; debut in London at Andrew Lloyd Webber Festival 1996; numerous tours in USA; Grand Prix Int. Piano Contest in SA 1993, 1st Prize 11th Int. Tchaikovsky Competition, Moscow 1998. *Address:* Marshal Zhukov prosp. 13, Apt 4, 123308 Moscow, Russia (Home). *Telephone:* (095) 290-17-04 (Home).

MATTARELLA, Sergio; Italian politician and lecturer in law; b. 23 July 1941, Palermo; m.; three c.; ed Palermo Univ.; fmr mem. Nat. Council and Cen. Leadership Christian Democrat Party, Deputy Political Sec. 1990–92; now mem. Italian Popular Party; Deputy for Palermo-Trapani-Agrigento-Caltanissetta 1983–, for Sicilia 1 1994–; fmr Minister for Relations with Parl., Minister for Educ. –1990, Deputy Prime Minister 1998–2001, Minister for Defence 1999–2001; fmr Deputy Chair. Bicamerale; fmr Vice-Pres. Parl. Cttee on Terrorism; fmr mem. Parl. Inquiry Cttee on Mafia; mem. Third Standing Comm. on Foreign and EC Affairs; Political Ed. Il Popolo 1992–94; Prof. of Parl. Law Palermo Univ. *Address:* c/o Camera dei Deputati, Piazza di Monte Citorio 1, 00186 Rome, Italy (Office).

MATTHÄUS, Lothar ('Loddar'); German professional football manager and player; b. 21 March 1961, Erlangen; professional debut with Borussia Mönchengladbach 1979; with Bayern Munich 1984–88, 1992–2000 (won UEFA Cup 1996); with Inter Milan 1988–92 (won Italian Championship 1989, won UEFA Cup 1991); with New York Metro Stars Mar.–Nov. 2000; Sports Dir Rapid Vienna 2001–02; with German nat. team 1980–96, 1998–2000 (captain 1990, won World Cup 1990), played in 25 World Cup matches, played for nat. team 150 times; World Sportsman of the Year 1990, World Footballer of the Year 1990, 1991, European Footballer of the Year 1990. *Address:* c/o Rapid Vienna Football Club, Vienna, Austria (Office).

MATTHÄUS-MAIER, Ingrid; German politician; b. 9 Sept. 1945, Werlte; d. of Heinz-Günther Matthäus and Helmtraud (née von Hagen) Matthäus; m. Robert Maier 1974; one s. one d.; Academic Asst Higher Admin. Court, later Judge, Admin. Court, Münster; mem. Bundestag (Free Democratic Party) 1976–82, Chair. Finance Cttee 1979–82; mem. Bundestag (Social Democratic Party) 1983–99; Deputy Chair. and Financial Policy Spokeswoman of SPD Parl. Group 1988–99; mem. Bd Dirs Kreditanstalt für Wiederaufbau (KfW) 1999–. *Address:* Palmengartenstr. 5–9, 60325 Frankfurt am Main, Germany (Home). *Telephone:* (69) 74314466 (Office). *Fax:* (69) 74314141 (Office). *E-mail:* ingrid.matthaeus-maier@kfw.de (Office).

MATTHES, Ulrich; German actor; b. 9 May 1959, Berlin; s. of Günter Matthes and Else Matthes; with Düsseldorfer Schauspielhaus 1986–87, Bayerisches Staatstheater, Munich 1987–89, Kammerspiele, Munich 1989–92, Schaubühne, Berlin 1992–98, Deutsches Theater, Berlin; Förderpreis, Kunstpreis Berlin 1991, O.E. Hasse-Preis 1992, Bayerischer Filmpreis 1999. *Address:* Bleibtreustr. 8, 10623 Berlin, Germany.

MATTHEWS, Peter Hugoe, LittD, FBA; British professor of linguistics; b. 10 March 1934, Oswestry; s. of John Hugo Matthews and Cecily Eileen Elmsley Hagarty; m. Lucienne Marie Jeanne Schleich 1984; one step-s. one step-d.; ed Montpellier School, Paignton, Clifton Coll., St John's Coll., Cambridge; lecturer, Univ. Coll. of N Wales, Bangor 1960–65, at Ind. Univ., Bloomington

1963–64; Lecturer, Reader and Prof., Univ. of Reading 1965–80; Visiting Prof. Deccan Coll., Poona 1969–70; Sr Research Fellow King's Coll., Cambridge 1970–71; Fellow, Nias Wassenaar, Holland 1977–78; Prof. and Head of Dept of Linguistics, Univ. of Cambridge 1980–2001 and Fellow of St John's Coll. 1980–, Praelector 1987–2001, Prof. Emer. 2001–; Pres. Philological Soc. 1992–96, Vice-Pres. 1996–; Hon. mem. Linguistics Soc. of America 1994–. *Publications:* Inflectional Morphology 1972, Morphology 1974, Generative Grammar and Linguistic Competence 1979, Syntax 1981, Grammatical Theory in the United States from Bloomfield to Chomsky 1993, The Concise Oxford Dictionary of Linguistics 1997, A Short History of Structural Linguistics 2001, Linguistics: A Very Short Introduction 2003. *Leisure interests:* cycling, gardening. *Address:* St John's College, Cambridge, CB2 1TP (Office); 10 Fendon Close, Cambridge, CB1 7RU, England (Home); 22 Rue Nina et Julien Lefevre, 1952 Luxembourg. *Telephone:* (1223) 338768 (Office); (1223) 247553 (Home).

MATTHEWS, Robert Charles Oliver, CBE, MA, FBA; British economist; b. 16 June 1927, Edin.; s. of Oliver Harwood Matthews and Ida Finlay; m. Joyce Lloyds 1948; one d.; ed Edin. Acad. and Corpus Christi and Nuffield Colls., Oxford; Asst Univ. Lecturer, then Lecturer, Cambridge 1949–65; Drummond Prof. of Political Economy 1965–75, All Souls Coll., Oxford; Master of Clare Coll., Cambridge 1975–93; Fellow 1993–; Prof. of Political Economy, Cambridge 1980–91, now Prof. Emer.; Chair. Social Science Research Council 1972–75; Fellow, St John's Coll., Cambridge 1950–65, All Souls Coll., Oxford 1965–75; Hon. Fellow, Corpus Christi Coll., Oxford; Hon. DLitt (Warwick Univ.) 1981, (Abertay) 1996. *Publications:* A Study in Trade Cycle History 1954, The Trade Cycle 1958, Economic Growth: A Survey (with F. H. Hahn) 1964, Economic Growth: Trends and Factors (ed.) 1981, British Economic Growth 1856–1973 (with C. H. Feinstein and J. Odling-Smee) 1982, Slower Growth in the Western World (ed.) 1982, Contemporary Problems of Economic Policy (ed., with J. R. Sargent) 1983, Economy and Democracy (ed.) 1985, Mostly Three-Movers; collected chess problems 1995 and articles in learned journals. *Leisure interest:* chess problems. *Address:* Clare College, Cambridge, CB2 1TL, England. *Telephone:* (1223) 333200.

MATTHIAS, Stefanos; Greek judge (retd); b. 27 May 1935, Athens; m.; one d.; ed Univ. of Athens, Univ. of Poitiers, France; judge 1961–; Pres. Supreme Civil and Penal Court 1996–2002; Dir Nat. School for Judges 1994–96. *Publications:* more than 30 studies and articles on pvt. law and on European Convention on Human Rights. *Leisure interest:* painting. *Address:* Areios Pagos – Supreme Civil and Penal Court, Leoforos Alexandras 121, 115 22 Athens (Office); 26 Niriidon Str., Paleon Faliron, 17561, Greece (Home). *Telephone:* (1) 06411506 (Office); (1) 09827466 (Home). *Fax:* (1) 06433799 (Office). *E-mail:* areios@otenet.gr (Office).

MATTHIESSEN, Peter, BA; American writer; b. 22 May 1927, New York; s. of Erard A. Matthiessen and Elizabeth (née Carey) Matthiessen; m. 1st Patricia Southgate 1951 (divorced); m. 2nd Deborah Love 1963 (deceased); three s. one d.; m. 3rd Maria Eckhart 1980; ed The Sorbonne, Paris, Yale Univ.; f. Paris Review (with Patricia Southgate); ordained a Zen Monk 1981; fmr correspondent, New Yorker; Trustee New York Zoological Soc. 1965–78; mem. Nat. Inst. of Arts and Letters. *Publications:* Race Rock 1954, Partisans 1955, Raditzer 1960, Wildlife in America 1959, The Cloud Forest 1961, Under the Mountain Wall 1963, At Play in the Fields of the Lord 1965, The Shore Birds of North America 1967, Oomingmak: The Expedition to the Musk Ox Island in the Bering Sea 1967, Sal si puedes 1969, Blue Meridian 1971, The Tree Where Man Was Born 1972, The Wind Birds 1973, Far Tortuga 1975, The Snow Leopard 1978, Sand Rivers 1981, In the Spirit of the Crazy Horse 1983, Indian Country 1984, Midnight Turning Grey 1984, Nine-Headed Dragon River 1986, Men's Lives 1986, Partisans 1987, On the River Styx 1989, Killing Mr Watson 1990, African Silences 1991, Baikal 1992, African Silences 1992, Shadows of Africa 1992, East of Lo Monthang: In the Land of Mustang 1995, Tigers in the Snow 2000.

MATTHIESSEN, Poul Christian, MA, D.SC.(ECON.); Danish professor of demography; b. 1 Feb. 1933, Odense; s. of Jens P. E. Matthiessen and Laura C. Nielsen; m. Ulla Bay 1986; two d.; research Asst Copenhagen Telephone Co. 1958–63; lecturer in Statistics and Demography, Univ. of Copenhagen 1963–70, Prof. of Demography 1971–95; Pres. Carlsberg Foundation 1993–2002; Chair. Carlsberg's Bequest in Memory of Brewer J. C. Jacobsen 1993–2003; mem. Bd of Dirs Museum of Nat. History at Frederiksborg Castle 1993–2002; mem. European Population Cttee 1972, Royal Danish Acad. of Science and Letters 1982, Academia Europaea 1988; mem. Supervisory Bd Carlsberg A/S 1989–2003, Chair. Supervisory Bd Carlsberg A/S 1993–2003; mem. Supervisory Bd Royal Scandinavia 1993–2001, Fredericia Bryggeri 1993–97, Falcon Bryggerier AB 1998–2001; mem. Bd dirs. Den Berlingske Fond 1999. *Publications:* Infant Mortality in Denmark 1931–60 1964, Growth of Population: Causes and Implications 1965, Demographic Methods (Vol. I–III) 1970, Some Aspects of the Demographic Transition in Denmark 1970, The Limitation of Family Size in Denmark (Vol. I–II) 1985, Population and Society 2002. *Leisure interests:* literature, history, architecture. *Address:* Collstrops Fond, H. C. Andersens Boulevard 37, 1553 Copenhagen V (Office); Prs. Alexandrines Allé 14, 2920 Charlottenlund, Denmark (Home). *Telephone:* 33-43-27-34 (Office). *Fax:* 33-32-30-86. *E-mail:* pcm@post.tele.dk (Office).

MATTHÖFER, Hans; German politician; b. 25 Sept. 1925, Bochum; m. Traute Mecklenburg 1951; ed Univs. of Frankfurt Main and Madison, Wis.,

USA; Mem. of Social Democratic Party (SPD) 1950–; mem. Econ. Dept IG Metall 1953, Head of Educ. and Training Dept 1961; mem. OECD Washington and Paris 1957–61; mem. Bundestag (Parl.) 1961–87; mem. Bundestag Cttees. for Econ., Econ. Co-operation, Law, Foreign Affairs; Parl. Sec. of State, Ministry of Econ. Co-operation 1972–74; mem. Exec. Cttee SPD 1973–85, mem. Presidency and Treas. 1985–87; Minister for Research and Tech. 1974–78, of Finance 1978–82, of Posts and Telecommunications April–Oct. 1982; Chair. BG-AG Holding Co. 1987–97; Adviser to Bulgarian Govt 1997–2000; Vice-Pres. Latin America Parliamentarians' Group 1961, 1983; mem. hon. Presidium of German Section, Amnesty Int. 1961; Pres. Deutsche Stiftung für Entwicklungsländer (Foundation for Overseas Devt) 1971–73; Vice-Chair. Enquiry Comm. on Tech. Assessment of Bundestag 1984–86; Publisher of Vorwärts 1985–88; Pres. German Supporting Cttee for ORT 1989–; Gran Cruz del Mérito Civil (Spain) 1989, Gran Maestre de la Orden del Mayo al Mérito (Argentina) 1985, Gran Cruz de la Orden de Bernardo O'Higgins (Chile) 1992. *Publications: Der Unterschied zwischen den Tariflöhnen und den Effektivverdiensten in der Metallindustrie der Bundesrepublik 1956, Technological Change in the Metal Industries 1961/62, Der Beitrag politischer Bildung zur Emanzipation der Arbeitnehmer–Materialien zur Frage des Bildungsurlaubs 1970, Streiks und streikähnliche Formen des Kampfes der Arbeitnehmer im Kapitalismus 1971, Für eine menschliche Zukunft—Sozialdemokratische Forschungs- und Technologiepolitik 1976, Humanisierung der Arbeit und Produktivität in der Industriegesellschaft 1977, 1978, 1980, Agenda 2000-Vorschläge zur Wirtschafts- und Gesellschaftspolitik 1993; numerous articles on trades unions, research, technology, development, politics, economics and finance. *Leisure interests:* chess, reading. *Address:* Schreyerstrasse 38, 61476 Kronberg Taunus, Germany. *Telephone:* (6173) 79334 (Kronberg).

MATTHUS, Siegfried; German composer; b. 13 April 1934, Mallenuppen, E Prussia; s. of late Franz Matthus and of Luise Perrey; m. Helga Spitzer 1958; one s.; ed Hochschule für Musik, Berlin, Acad. of Arts and Music, Berlin (masterclass with Hanns Eisler); composer and consultant, Komische Oper, Berlin 1964–; Prof. 1985–; Artistic Dir Chamber Opera Festival, Rheinsberg; mem. Acad. of Arts of GDR, Acad. of Arts of W Berlin, Acad. of Arts, Munich; Nat. Prize 1972, 1984, Bundesverdienstkreuz (First Class) 2000. *Compositions include:* ten operas, one oratorio, concertos, orchestral and chamber music, etc. *Leisure interests:* swimming, jogging, carpentry. *Address:* Elisabethweg 10, 13187 Berlin; Seepromenade 15, 16348 Stolzenhagen, Germany. *Telephone:* (30) 4857362 (Berlin); (33397) 21736 (Stolzenhagen). *Fax:* (30) 48096604 (Berlin); (33397) 71400 (Stolzenhagen). *E-mail:* smatthus@aol .com (Home).

MATTILA, Karita Marjatta; Finnish opera singer; b. 5 Sept. 1960, Somero; d. of Arja Mattila and Erkki Mattila (née Somerikko); m. Tapio Kuneinen 1992; ed Sibelius Acad., Finland and teachers Liisa Linko-Malmio, and Vera Rozsa in London; operatic début at Finnish Nat. Opera as the Countess (Marriage of Figaro) 1983; appeared with Brussels Opera as Countess, Eva, Rosalinde 1984–85; début at Royal Opera House, Covent Garden as Fiordiligi 1986, subsequent appearances as Pamina, Countess and Agathe 1986–89, Donna Elvira 1992, Musetta 1994, Elisabeth de Valois 1996, Elsa 1997, Chrysothemis 1997; appeared at Barenboim-Ponnelle Festival, Paris 1986, Tel Aviv 1987, 1990; début at Metropolitan Opera as Donna Elvira 1990, Eva (Meistersinger) 1993, Lisa 1995, Musetta 1996, Elsa (Lohengrin) 1998, Amelia (Simon Boccanegra) 1999, Fidelio 2000, Chrysothemis 2002, Jenufa 2003; début at Opéra Nat. de Paris as Elsa 1996, Hanna Glawari 1997, Lisa 2001; Théâtre du Châtelet: Elisabeth de Valois 1996, Desdemona 2001, Arabella 2002; appearances at Salzburg Festival: Donna Anna 1999, Fiordiligi 2000, Jenufa 2001; has also appeared in Washington, Houston, Chicago and San Francisco; recitals throughout Europe; has worked under maj. conductors including Sir Colin Davis, Claudio Abbado, von Dohnanyi, Giulini, Sinopoli, Solti, Haitink, Maazel, Levine; First Prize, Finnish Nat. Singing Competition 1981, First Prize, BBC Singer of the World, Cardiff 1983; Evening Standard Award 1997, Acad. du Disque Lyrique Award 1997, Grammy Award for Best Opera 1998, Pro Finlandia 2001. *Recordings:* over 50 solo and opera recordings for major labels. *Leisure interests:* sport, yoga, golf, sailing. *Address:* c/o IMG Artists Europe, 616 Chiswick High Road, London, W4 5RX, England. *Telephone:* (20) 8233-5800 (Office). *E-mail:* tapio .kuneinen@pp.inet.fi (Home).

MATTINGLY, Mack Francis, BS; American government official and business executive; b. 7 Jan. 1931, Anderson, Ind.; s. of Joseph Hilbert and Beatrice Wayts Mattingly; m. 1st Carolyn Longcamp 1957 (deceased); two d.; m. 2nd Leslie Ann Davisson 1998; ed Indiana Univ.; served USAF 1951–55; Account Supervisor, Arvin Industries, Ind. 1957–59; Marketing Man. IBM Corpn Ga 1959–79; owner M/s, Inc. 1975–80; Republican U.S. Senator from Georgia 1981–87; Asst Sec.-Gen. for Defence Support, NATO, Brussels 1987–90; speaker and author on defence and foreign policy matters 1990–92, U.S. Amb. to Seychelles 1992–93; Chair. Southeastern Legal Foundation; mem. Bd of Dirs. Marshall Legacy Inst., Cumberland Preservation Soc., Novecon Tech., CompuCredit, etc.; Sec. of Defense Distinguished Service Medal for Outstanding Public Service 1988 and other awards. *Publications:* numerous articles, speeches and book chapters. *Address:* 4315 10th Street, East Beach, St Simons Island, GA 31522, USA (Home). *Telephone:* (912) 638-5430.

MATUBRAIMOV, Almambet Matubraimovich; Kyrgyzstan politician; b. 1952, Osh Region, Kyrgyzstan; ed Tashkent Inst. of Light and Textile Industry; worker in sovkhoz Kursheb Osh Region; master, Sr master textile factory KKSK 1977–80; army service 1980–82; head of workshop, head of production textile factory KKSK (later Bishkek) 1982–84, Dir 1984–90; Chair. Exec. Cttee Sverdlov Region, Frunze (later Bishkek) 1990–91; First Deputy Minister of Industry Repub. of Kyrgyzstan 1991–93; First Deputy Prime Minister 1991–93; Chair. People's Council of Repub. of Kyrgyzstan (Uluk Kenesh) 1995–99; in opposition to Pres. Akayev 1999. *Address:* Uluk Kenesh, 720003 Bishkek, Kyrgyzstan.

MATUSCHKA, Mario, Graf von, DJur; German diplomatist; b. 27 Feb. 1931, Oppeln, Silesia; s. of Michael, Graf von Matuschka and Pia, Gräfin Stillfried-Rattonitz; m. Eleonore, Gräfin von Waldburg-Wolfegg 1962; two s. two d.; ed St Matthias Gymnasium, Breslau, Domgymnasium, Fulda and Univs. of Fribourg, Paris and Munich; entered foreign service 1961; Attaché, German Observer's Mission at UN, New York 1961–62; Vice-Consul, Consul, Salzburg 1963–66; Second Sec. Islamabad 1966–68; First Sec. Tokyo 1968–71; Foreign Office, Bonn 1971–75, 1978–80, 1982–88, 1990–93; Economic Counsellor, London 1975–78; Deputy Chief of Protocol, UN, New York 1980–82; State Sec., Chief of Protocol, Land Berlin 1988–90; Amb. and Perm. Rep. of Germany to OECD 1993–96; Diplomatic Adviser to Commr Gen., Expo 2000, Hanover 1996–97; Dir Holy See's Pavilion June–Oct. 2000; Sec. Gen. Internationaler Club La Redoute e.V. 1997–2000, mem. Bd 2000–02; Head of Del. St Hedwig 2002–; Order of Merit (Germany); decorations from Holy See, Japan, Portugal and Sovereign Mil. Order of Malta. *Address:* Kurfürstenallee 1, 53177 Bonn (Office); Drachenfelsstr. 45, 53757 St Augustin, Germany (Home). *Telephone:* (2241) 337707 (Office). *Fax:* (2241) 337707 (Office). *E-mail:* grafmatuschka@aol.com (Home).

MATUTE AUSEJO, Ana María; Spanish writer; b. 26 July 1925, Barcelona; d. of Facundo Matute and Mary Ausejo; m. 1952 (dissolved 1963); one s.; ed "Damas Negras" French Nuns Coll.; collaborated on literary magazine Destino; Visiting lecturer, Indiana Univ. 1965–66, Oklahoma Univ. 1969–; Writer-in-Residence, Univ. of Virginia 1978–79; mem. Hispanic Soc. of America; "Highly Commended Author", Hans Christian Andersen Jury, Lisbon 1972. *Children's books:* El País de la Pizarra 1956, Paulina 1961, El Sal Tamontes Verde 1961, Caballito Loco 1961, El Aprendiz 1961, Carnavalito 1961, El Polizón del "Ulises" (Lazarillo Prize) 1965. *Publications:* Los Abel 1947, Fiesta Al Noroeste (Café Gijón Prize) 1952, Pequeño Teatro (Planeta Prize) 1954, Los Niños Tontos 1956, Los Hijos Muertos (Nat. Literary Prize and Critics Prize) 1959, Primera Memoria (Nadal Prize) 1959, Tres y un sueño 1961, Historias de la Artamila 1961, El Río 1963, El Tiempo 1963, Los Soldados lloran de noche 1964 (Fastenrath Prize 1969), El Arrepentido y otras Narraciones 1967, Algunos Muchachos 1968, La Trampa 1969, La Torre Vigia 1971, Olvidado Rey Gudu 1974. *Leisure interests:* painting, drawing, the cinema.

MATUTES JUAN, Abel; Spanish international organizational official and politician; b. 31 Oct. 1941, Ibiza; s. of Antonio and Carmen Matutes; m. Nieves Prats; one s. three d.; ed Univ. of Barcelona; studies in law and economics; fmr entrepreneur in tourism and property in island of Ibiza; fmr lecturer in Econs and Public Finance, Univ. of Barcelona; Deputy Chair. Ibiza & Formentera Tourist Bd 1964–69; Deputy Alianza Popular 1982–85; Deputy Nat. Chair. Alianza Popular; Mayor of Ibiza 1970–71; EC Commr for Credits and Investments, Small and Medium Sized Enterprises and Financial Eng 1986–89, for American Policy, Latin American Relations 1989–93, for Energy and Euratom Supply Agency, Transport 1993–95; Nat. Vice-Pres., then mem. Exec. Cttee. political party Partido Popular (fmrly Alianza Popular) 1979–; mem. European Parl. 1994–96; Minister of Foreign Affairs 1996–2000. *Leisure interests:* tennis, sailing. *Address:* P.O. Box 416, Ibiza, Spain (Office).

MATVEYEVA, Novella Nikolaevna; Russian poet and chansonnier; b. 7 Oct. 1934, Pushkin, nr Leningrad; d. of Nikolai Nikolaevich Matveye-Bodryi and Nadejda Timofeevna Matveyeva (Orleneva); m. Ivan Semjonovich Kiuru 1963. *Recordings:* A Gipsy Girl 1966, What a Strong Wind! 1966, Poems and Songs 1973, A Princess on a Peascod 1980, A Trail is my Home 1982, (with Ivan Kiuru) The Music of Light 1984, My Small Raven 1985, Ballads 1985, A Red-haired Girl 1986, The Unseverable Circle 1991, (with I. Kiuru) The Poetic Dialogue 1993, (with I. Kiuru) Hosanna to Skhodnya 1993, Sonnets to Dashkova 1994, Minuet 1994. *Publications:* Lirika 1961, Little Ship 1963, Selected Lyrics 1964, The Soul of Things 1966, Reflection of a Sunbeam 1966, School for Swallows 1973, River 1978, The Song's Law 1983, The Land of the Surf 1983, Rabbit's Village 1984, Selected Works 1986, Praising the Labour 1987, An Unseverable Circle 1988, Poems 1988; (play) The Foretelling of an Eagle (in Theatre magazine) 1988. *Leisure interests:* listening to the radio (plays, classical music), reading. *Address:* Kammergerski per. 2, Apt. 42, 103009 Moscow, Russia. *Telephone:* (095) 292-33-61.

MATVIYENKO, Valentina Ivanovna; Russian politician; b. 7 April 1949, Shepetovka, USSR (now Ukraine); m. Vladimir Vasilyevich Matviyenko; one s.; ed Leningrad Inst. of Chem. and Pharmaceuticals, Acad. of Social Sciences at CPSU Cen. Cttee; Komsomol work 1972–84; First Sec. Krasnogvardeysk Dist CP Cttee, Leningrad 1984–86; Deputy Chair. Exec. Cttee Leningrad City Soviet on Problems of Culture and Educ. 1988–89; USSR Peoples' Deputy, mem. Supreme Soviet 1989–92; mem. of Presidium, Chair. Cttee on Problems of Family, Motherhood and Childhood Protection 1989–91; Russian Amb. to Malta 1991–95, to Greece 1997–98; rank of Amb. Extraordinary and Plenipotentiary; Dir Dept on Relations with Subjects of Russian Fed., Parl. and Public Orgs. Ministry of Foreign Affairs 1995–97, Deputy Prime Minister of

Russian Fed. 1998–2003, Chair. Comms on Int. Humanitarian Aid and Religious Orgs; Presidential Rep. in the North-West Fed. Okrug 2003–. *Address:* House of Government, Krasnopresnenskaya nab. 2, 103274 Moscow, Russia. *Telephone:* (095) 205-51-43, 205-89-77 (Office). *Fax:* (095) 205-45-44 (Office).

MATYUKHIN, Col-Gen. Vladimir Georgyevich, CAND.TECH.SCI.; Russian business executive and government official; b. 4 Feb. 1945, Moscow; ed Higher KGB School, Moscow Inst. of Energy, Moscow State Univ.; mem. staff Moscow Pedagogical Inst. 1962–64; engineer Construction Bureau, Moscow Inst. of Energy 1964–73; service in state security organs 1969–; Deputy Dir-Gen. Fed. Agency of Govt Telecommunications and Information 1993–99, Dir-Gen. 1999–; corresp. mem. Acad. of Cryptography. *Address:* Federal Agency of Governmental Telecommunications and Information, Office of the President, B. Kiselny per. 4, 103031 Moscow, Russia (Office). *Telephone:* (095) 224-37-37 (Office).

MAU, Vladimir Alexandrovich, DR.ECON.; Russian politician and economist; b. 1959, Moscow; ed Moscow Plekhanov Inst. of Nat. Econs; with Inst. of Econs USSR Acad. of Sciences –1991, Inst. of Econ. Problems of Transitional Period (worked as Asst to Yegor Gaidar, q.v.), mem. Party Demokraticheskiy Vybor Rossii 1990–99; Head Operating Cen. of Econ. Reforms Govt of Russian Fed. 1999–2002, Rector Acad. of Nat. Economy 2002–. *Publications:* articles and monographs on econ. problems. *Address:* Academy of National Economy, Vernadskogo Prospekt 82, 125468 Moscow, Russia (Office). *Telephone:* (095) 434-83-89 (Office).

MAUCHER, Helmut; German business executive; b. 9 Dec. 1927, Eisenharz/ Allgäu; joined Nestlé AG 1948; Various man. positions within the Nestlé Co. in Germany 1964–80, Pres. and CEO Nestlé-Gruppe Deutschland, Frankfurt 1975, Exec. Vice-Pres. Nestlé SA, Vevey, Switzerland 1980–81, CEO 1981, Chair. Bd 1990–2000 and CEO 1990–97, Hon. Chair. 2000–; Fortune Magazine Gold Medal 1984; Grosses Bundesverdienstkreuz, Grosses Goldenes Ehrenzeichen mit dem Stern für Verdienste um die Republik Oesterreich. *Address:* Nestlé AG, Avenue Nestlé 55, 1800 Vevey, Switzerland.

MAUD, Hon. Sir Humphrey John Hamilton, KCMG, MA; British diplomatist (retd); b. 17 April 1934, Oxford; s. of Lord and Lady Redcliffe-Maud; m. Maria Eugenia Gazitua 1963; three s.; ed Eton Coll., King's Coll., Cambridge, Nuffield Coll., Oxford; Instructor in Classics, Univ. of Minn., USA 1958–59; joined Diplomatic Service 1959, Third Sec. Madrid 1961–63, Third, later Second Sec. Havana 1963–65, at FCO 1966–68, Cabinet Office 1968–69, First Sec. Paris 1970–74, Sabbatical at Nuffield Coll., Oxford (Econs) 1974–75, Head Financial Relations Dept, FCO 1975–79, Minister, Madrid 1979–82, Amb. to Luxembourg 1982–84; Asst Under-Sec. of State (Econ. and Commercial) 1985–88; High Commr in Cyprus 1988–89; Amb. to Argentina 1990–93 (reopened diplomatic relations between Britain and Argentina 1990 after the Falklands War); Commonwealth Deputy Sec.-Gen. 1993–99; Chair. Commonwealth Disaster Man. Agency Ltd, Emerging Markets Partnership-Financial Advisers; mem. Nat. Youth Orchestra 1949–52. *Leisure interests:* music, golf, bird-watching. *Address:* 31 Queen Anne's Grove, London, W4 1HW, England (Home). *Telephone:* (20) 8994-2808 (Home). *Fax:* (20) 8995-1165 (Home). *E-mail:* hmaud@aol.com (Home).

MAUDE, Rt Hon Francis (Anthony Aylmer), PC, MA; British politician; b. 4 July 1953; s. of Baron Maude of Stratford-upon-Avon; m. Christina Jane Hadfield 1984; two s. three d.; ed Abingdon School, Corpus Christi Coll., Cambridge; called to Bar 1977 (Forster Boulton Prize); Councillor Westminster City Council 1978–84; MP for Warwicks. N 1983–92, for Horsham 1997–; Parl. Pvt. Sec. to Minister of State for Employment 1984–85; an Asst Govt Whip 1985–87; Parl. Under-Sec. of State Dept of Trade and Industry 1987–89; Minister of State, FCO 1989–90; Financial Sec. to HM Treasury 1990–92; Chair. Govt.'s Deregulation Task Force 1994–97; Shadow Chancellor 1998–2000, Shadow Foreign Sec. 2000–01; Dir Salomon Brothers 1992–93, Asda Group 1992–99; Advisory Dir Morgan Stanley and Co.; Conservative. *Leisure interests:* skiing, cricket, reading, music. *Address:* House of Commons, London, SW1A 0AA, England.

MAULDE, Bruno Guy André Jean de, LenD; French banker; b. 27 March 1934, Toulouse; s. of Guy de Maulde and Suzanne Mazars; m. Dominique Le Henaff 1958; three d.; ed Inst. of Political Studies, Toulouse, Nat. Coll. of Admin.; Insp. des Finances 1962; Adviser, External Econ. Relations Dept, Finance Ministry 1967–68; Alt. Exec. Dir IMF for France 1968–70; Financial attaché, Embassy, USA 1968–70, in New York 1970–71; French Treasury Adviser 1971–74, Asst Dir 1974–77, Deputy Dir 1977–78; Deputy Man. Dir Caisse Nat. de Crédit Agricole 1979–81; Financial Minister, Embassy of France and Exec. Dir IMF and IBRD, Washington 1981–85; Chair. and CEO Crédit du Nord 1986–93; Chair. Conseil des Bourses de Valeurs (CBV) 1990–94; Dir Compagnie Financière de Paribas 1993–94; Dir of various other corpns. and public insts.; mem. Council of Monetary Policy, Banque de France 1994–97; Chevalier, Légion d'honneur, Ordre nat. du Mérite, Croix de la Valeur militaire, Officier du Mérite agricole. *Leisure interest:* yachting. *Address:* Rozaven, 29930 Pont-Aven, France.

MAUNG MAUNG KHA, U; Myanmar politician; mem. Cen. Exec. Cttee Burma Socialist Programme Party (BSPP); Minister for Industry and Labour 1973–74, for Industry 1974–75, for Mines 1975–77, Prime Minister of Burma (now Myanmar) 1977–88; mem. State Council 1977–88. *Address:* c/o Office of the Prime Minister, Yangon, Myanmar.

MAUPIN, Armistead Jones, Jr.; American writer; b. 13 May 1944; s. of Armistead Jones Maupin and the late Diana Jane (Barton) Maupin; ed Univ. of North Carolina; reporter News and Courier, Charleston, SC 1970–71; AP, San Francisco 1971–72; Account Exec. Lowry Russom and Leeper Public Relations 1973; columnist Pacific Sun Magazine 1974; publicist San Francisco Opera 1975; serialist San Francisco Chronicle 1976–77, 1981, 1983; Commentator K.R.O.N.-TV San Francisco 1979; serialist San Francisco Examiner 1986; Exec. Producer Armistead Maupin's Tales of the City 1993; contrib. to New York Times, Los Angeles Times and others; numerous awards, including: Freedom Leadership Award, Freedoms Foundation 1972, Communications Award, Metropolitan Elections Comm., LA 1989, Exceptional Achievement Award, American Libraries Asscn 1990, Outstanding Miniseries Award, Gay and Lesbian Alliance Against Defamation 1994. *Publications:* Tales of the City 1978, More Tales of the City 1980, Further Tales of the City 1982, Babycakes 1984, Significant Others 1987, Sure of You 1989, 28 Barbary Lane 1990, Back to Barbary Lane 1991, Maybe the Moon 1992, The Essential Clive Baker (co-author) 1999, The Night Listener 2000; Librettist: Heart's Desire 1990. *Address:* c/o Literary Bent, P.O. Box 4109990, Suite 528, San Francisco, CA 94141 (Office); c/o Amanda Urban, 40 West 57th Street. Floor 16, New York, NY 10019, USA. *E-mail:* inquiries@literarybent .cor (Office).

MAURA, Carmen, BA; Spanish film actress; b. 15 Sept. 1945, Madrid; d. of Antonio Maura; worked as a cabaret singer and translator; has appeared in numerous films including many of Pedro Almodóvar's works; Best Actress, European Film Awards for roles in Pedro Almodóvar's Women on the Verge of a Nervous Breakdown 1989 and Carlos Saura's Ay, Carmela! 1991. *Other films include:* Law of Desire, Dark Habits, Le Saut Périlleux, Be Unfaithful and Don't Look With Whom, Matador, In Heaven as on Earth, The Anonymous Queen, How to be a Woman and Not Die in the Attempt, Shadows in a Conflict, Louis the Child King, How to be Miserable and Enjoy It, The Flower of My Secret, Una Pareja de Tres, El Palomo cojo, Happiness in the Field, Tortilla y cinema, Alliance cherche doigt, Elles.

MAUROY, Pierre; French politician; b. 5 July 1928, Cartignies; s. of Henri Mauroy and Adrienne Bronne; m. Gilberte Deboudt 1951; one s.; ed Lycée de Cambrai, Ecole normale nationale d'apprentissage, Cachan; Nat. Sec. Jeunesses socialistes 1950–58; Tech. Teacher, Colombes 1952; Sec.-Gen. Syndicat des collèges d'enseignement tech. section, Féd. de l'Educ. Nat. 1955–59; Fed. Sec. for the North, Section Française de l'Internationale Ouvrière 1961, mem. Political Bureau 1963, Deputy Sec.-Gen. 1966; mem. Exec. Cttee, Féd. de la gauche démocratique et socialiste 1965–68; Gen. Councillor, Cateau 1967–73; Vice-Pres. Gen. Council, Nord Département 1967–73; Municipal Councillor, Lille 1971, First Deputy Mayor 1971, Mayor 1973–2001; First Sec. and Nat. Co-ordinating Sec., Northern Fed., Parti Socialiste 1971–79; Deputy (Nord) to Nat. Ass. 1973–81, 1986, Senator 1992–; First Sec. Parti Socialiste 1989–92; Pres. Socialist Int. 1992–99, Regional Council, Nord-Pas-de-Calais 1974; Pres. Nat. Fed. Léo Lagrange youth centres 1972–81, Hon. Pres. 1981–84; mem. European Parl. 1979–81, Vice-Pres. Political Cttee; Political Dir Action socialiste Hebdo newspaper 1979–81; Prime Minister of France 1981–84; Pres. World Fed. of Twinned Towns 1983–92; Pres. Communauté urbaine de Lille 1989–, Comm. pour la décentralisation 1999–; founder, Pres. Jean Jaurès Foundation 1992–; Grand cordon de l'ordre de la Répub. de Tunisie, Grand-croix, Ordre nat. du Mérite. *Publications:* Héritiers de l'avenir 1977, C'est ici le chemin 1982, A gauche 1985, Parole de Lillois 1994, Léo Lagrange (biog.) 1997, Mémoires: vous mettrez du bleu au ciel 2003. *Address:* Sénat, 75291 Paris Cedex 06 (Office); 17–19 rue Voltaire, 59000 Lille, France (Home). *E-mail:* p.mauroy@senat.fr (Office).

MAURSTAD, Toralv (St Olav); Norwegian actor and theatre director; b. 24 Nov. 1926, Oslo; s. of Alfred and Tordis Maurstad; m. Beate Eriksen; ed Universitet i Uppsala and Royal Acad. of Dramatic Art, London; trained as concert pianist; début in Trondheim 1947; Oslo Nye Teater 1951; Oslo Nat. Theatre 1954; Man. Dir Oslo Nye Teater (Oslo Municipal Theatre) 1967–78; Man. Dir Nat. Theatre 1978–86, Actor/Dir Nat. Theatre 1987–; Norwegian Sr Golf Champion 1992; Oslo Critics Award, Ibsen Prize, Amanda, Aamot Statuette, Kt First Class, Order of St Olav (Norway), Order of Oranian (Netherlands). *Plays acted in or directed include:* Young Woodley 1949, Pal Joey 1952, Peer Gynt 1954, Long Day's Journey 1962, Teenage Love 1963, Hamlet 1964, Arturo Ui (in Bremen, Germany) 1965, Brand (Ibsen) 1966, Of Love Remembered (New York) 1967, Cabaret 1968, Scapino 1975, Two Gentlemen of Verona 1976, The Moon of the Misbegotten 1976, Same Time Next Year 1977, Twigs 1977 (also TV production), Sly Fox 1978, Whose Life is it Anyway? 1979, Masquerade 1980, Amadeus 1980, Much Ado about Nothing 1981, Kennen Sie die Milchstrasse? 1982, Duet for One 1982, Hamlet 1983, Private Lives (with Liv Ullman) 1993, Dear Liar 1996, The Pretenders 1998, Copenhagen 2000, Enigma Variation 2001. *Films:* Line 1960, Kalde Spor 1962, Song of Norway 1970, After Rubicon 1987, Chasing the Kidney Stone 1996, Gurin 1998. *Radio plays:* Doll's House, Peer Gynt, Masquerade. *Television:* Last Place on Earth, Hotel Cesar, Song of Norway. *Publication:* Du Store Min (autobiog.). *Leisure interests:* skiing, hunting, fishing, golf, tennis. *Address:* Nationaltheatret, Stortingsgt. 15, Oslo 1 (Office); Box 58, Holmenkollen, 0712, Norway (Home); Thorleif, Hangsvei 20, Voksenkollen 0712, Oslo, Norway. *Telephone:* 22-14-18-84 (Home). *Fax:* 22-14-18-84 (Home). *E-mail:* toralv@powertech.no, toralv@totto.no (Home).

MAVROMMATIS, Andreas V.; Cypriot diplomatist and barrister; b. 9 June 1932, Larnaca; s. of Vladimiros and Marthe (Andreou) Mavrommatis; m.

Mary Cahalane 1955; one s. three d.; ed Greek Gymnasium, Limassol, Lincoln's Inn, London; practising advocate 1954–58; Magistrate 1958–60; Dist Judge 1960–70; Minister of Labour and Social Insurance 1970–72; Special Adviser on Foreign and Legal Affairs to Pres. of Cyprus 1972–75; Perm. Rep. to UN Office at Geneva 1975–78, to UN, New York 1979–82; Greek Cypriot Interlocutor in Intercommunal Talks 1982–89; Perm. Rep. to UN, New York 1989–92; Adviser to the Pres. of the Republic, mem. of Working Group on the Cyprus Question July–Dec. 1992; Govt Spokesman Dec. 1992–; Chair. UN Cttee on Human Rights; fmr Pres. ECOSOC; Chair. UN Cttee on Relations with the Host Country. *Publication:* Treaties in Force in Cyprus. *Leisure interests:* reading, walking. *Address:* 10 Platon Street, Engomi, Nicosia, Cyprus. *Telephone:* 351878. *Fax:* 357111.

MAWER, Philip John Courtney, MA, DPA, FRSA; British church official and civil servant; b. 30 July 1947; s. of Eric Douglas Mawer and Thora Constance Mawer; m. Mary Ann Moxon 1972; one s. two d.; ed Hull Grammar School, Univ. of Edin., Univ. of London; Sr Pres. Student Rep. Council 1969–70; joined Home Office 1971; Pvt Sec. to Minister of State 1974–76; Nuffield and Leverhulme Travelling Fellowship 1978–79; Sec. Lord Scarman Inquiry into Brixton Riots 1981; Asst Sec. Head of Industrial Relations, Prison Dept 1984–87; Prin. Pvt Sec. to Home Sec. Douglas Hurd 1987–89; Under-Sec. Cabinet Office 1989–90; Gen.-Sec. Church of England Synod 1990–; Sec.-Gen. Archbishop's Council 1997–; Parl. Commr for Standards March 2002–; Dir (non-exec.) Ecclesiastical Insurance Group 1996–; Trustee All Churches Trust 1992–; mem. Governing Body SPCK 1994–; Patron Church Housing Trust 1996–. *Leisure interests:* family, friends. *Address:* Office of the Parliamentary Commissioner for Standards, House of Commons, London, SW1A 0AA, England (Office). *Telephone:* (20) 7219-0311 (Office). *Fax:* (20) 7219-0490 (Office). *E-mail:* pcs@parliament.uk (Office).

MAWHINNEY, Rt. Hon. Sir Brian Stanley, Kt, PC, PhD; British politician; b. 26 July 1940; s. of Frederick Stanley Arnot Mawhinney and Coralie Jean Mawhinney; m. Betty Louise Oja 1965; two s. one d.; ed Royal Belfast Academical Inst., Queen's Univ. Belfast, Univ. of Michigan, USA, Univ. of London; Asst Prof. of Radiation Research, Univ. of Iowa, USA 1968–70; lecturer, subsequently Sr Lecturer, Royal Free Hosp. School of Medicine 1970–84; mem. MRC 1980–83; MP for Peterborough 1979–97, for Cambridgeshire NW 1997–; Parl. Under-Sec. of State for Northern Ireland 1986–90; Minister of State, Northern Ireland Office 1990–92, Dept of Health 1992–94; Sec. of State for Transport 1994–95; Chair. Conservative Party 1995–97; Opposition Front Bench Spokesman on Home Affairs 1997–98; Pres. Conservative Trade Unionists 1987–90; mem. Gen. Synod of Church of England 1985–90; Chair. Football League 2003–. *Publication:* Conflict and Christianity in Northern Ireland (co-author) 1976, In the Firing Line—Faith, Power, Politics, Forgiveness 1999. *Leisure interests:* sport, reading. *Address:* House of Commons, London, SW1A 0AA, England.

MAXWELL, Hamish; British business executive; marketing and int. man. Philip Morris Cos. Inc., Chair. and CEO 1984–91; mem. Bd WPP Group PLC 1996–, Chair. 1996–; Dir (non-exec.) Bankers Trust, Sola Int. *Address:* WPP Group PLC, 27 Farm Street, London, W1X 6RD, England (Office). *Telephone:* (20) 7408-2204 (Office). *Fax:* (20) 7493-6819 (Office). *E-mail:* enquiries@wpp.com (Office). *Website:* www.wpp.com (Office).

MAXWELL, Ian, MA; British/French publisher; b. 15 June 1956, Maisons-Laffitte, France; s. of the late (Ian) Robert Maxwell and of Elisabeth Meynard; brother of Kevin Maxwell (q.v.); m.1st Laura Plumb 1991 (divorced 1998); m. 2nd Tara Dudley Smith 1999; ed Marlborough Coll. and Balliol Coll., Oxford; Man. Dir Pergamon Press France 1980–81; Jt Man. Dir Pergamon Pres. GmbH 1980; Marketing Dir Pergamon Press Inc. 1982–83; Dir Sales Devt BPCC PLC 1985–86; Dir Group Marketing BPCC PLC (now Maxwell Communication Corpn PLC) 1986; Chair. Agence Centrale de Presse, Paris 1986–89; Dir TFI TV station, Paris 1987–89; CEO Maxwell Pergamon Publrs 1988–89; Jt Man. Dir Maxwell Communication Corpn 1988–91; Acting Chair. Mirror Group Newspapers 1991; Dir New York Daily News –1991, Telemonde Holdings 1997–; publishing consultant Westbourne Communications Ltd 1993; Publr Maximov Publs Ltd. 1995–; Chair. Derby Co. Football Club 1984–87, Vice-Chair. 1987–91; mem. Nat. Theatre Devt Council 1986; Pres. Club d'Investissement Media 1988. *Leisure interests:* skiing, water skiing, watching football.

MAXWELL, Kevin Francis Herbert, MA; British businessman; b. 20 Feb. 1959, Maisons-Laffitte, France; s. of the late (Ian) Robert Maxwell and of Elisabeth Maxwell; brother of Ian Maxwell (q.v.); m. Pandora Deborah Karen Warnford-Davis 1984; two s. four d.; ed Marlborough Coll., Balliol Coll. Oxford; Chair. Oxford United Football Club 1987–92; Vice-Chair. Macmillan Inc. 1988–91; Jt Man. Dir Maxwell Communication Corpn 1988–91, Chair. 1991; Publr and Chair. New York Daily News –1991; Chief Exec. Equitel Communications 1998–; Dir Telemonde Holdings 1997–, Telemonde Inc. 1999– (Chair. 1999); Trustee New School NY 1988–92. *Leisure interests:* football, watercolour painting. *Address:* Moulsford Manor, Moulsford, Oxon. OX10 9HO, England.

MAXWELL DAVIES, Sir Peter, Kt, CBE, MUS.B., FRCM, FRSAMD; British composer; b. 8 Sept. 1934, Manchester; s. of Thomas Davies and Hilda (née Howard) Davies; ed Leigh Grammar School, Royal Manchester Coll. of Music, Manchester Univ.; studied with Goffredo Petrassi, Rome 1957 and with Roger Sessions, Milton Babbitt, Earl Kim, Princeton Univ., NJ, USA (Harkness Fellow) 1962–64; Dir of Music, Cirencester Grammar School 1959–62; lecture

tours in Europe, Australia, USA, Canada, Brazil; Visiting Composer, Univ. of Adelaide 1966; Prof. of Composition, Royal Northern Coll. of Music, Manchester 1965–80 (Fellow 1978); Pres. Schools Music Asscn 1983–, Composers' Guild of GB 1986–, Nat. Fed. of Music Socs 1989–, Cheltenham Arts Festival 1994–96, Soc. for Promotion of New Music 1995–; Visiting Fromm Prof. of Composition, Harvard Univ. 1985; f. and Co-Dir (with Harrison Birtwistle) Pierrot Players 1967–71; f. and Artistic Dir The Fires of London 1971–87; f. and Artistic Dir St Magnus Festival, Orkney Islands 1977–86, Pres. 1986–; Artistic Dir Dartington Summer School of Music 1979–84; Assoc. Conductor and Composer Scottish Chamber Orchestra 1985–94, Composer Laureate 1994–; Conductor/Composer, BBC Philharmonic Orchestra (Manchester) 1992–2001; Assoc. Conductor/Composer Royal Philharmonic Orchestra 1992–2001; mem. Accademia Filarmonia Romana 1979, Royal Swedish Acad. of Music 1993, Bayerische Akad. der Schönen Künste 1998; Hon. mem. Royal Acad. of Music 1979, Guildhall School of Music and Drama 1981, Royal Philharmonic Soc. 1987, Royal Scottish Acad. 2001; Hon. Fellow Royal Incorporation of Architects in Scotland 1994; several hon. degrees including Hon. DMus (Edin.) 1979, (Manchester) 1981, (Bristol) 1984, (Open Univ.) 1986, (Glasgow) 1993, (Durham) 1994, (Hull) 2001; Hon. DLitt (Warwick) 1986, (Salford) 1999; Hon. DUniv (Heriot Watt) 2002; Olivetti Prize 1959; Koussevitsky Award 1964, Koussevitsky Recording Award 1966, Cobbett Medal for services to chamber music 1989, First Award of Asscn of British Orchestras, for contribs to orchestras and orchestral life in UK 1991, Gulliver Award for Performing Arts in Scotland 1991, Nat. Fed. of Music Socs Charles Groves Award for outstanding contrib. to British Music 1995, Royal Philharmonic Soc. Award for Large-scale Composition (for Symphony No. 5) 1995; Officier des Arts et des Lettres 1988. *Compositions include:* Sonata for trumpet and piano 1955, Alma redemptoris mater for ensemble 1957, St Michael sonata for 17 wind instruments 1957, Prolation for orchestra 1958, Five Motets for soli, chorus and ensemble 1959, O Magnum Mysterium for chorus, instruments and organ 1960, String Quartet 1961, Leopardi Fragments for soprano, contralto and chamber ensemble 1962, First Fantasia on John Taverner's In Nomine for orchestra 1962, Veni Sancte Spiritus for soli, chorus and orchestra 1963, Second Fantasia on John Taverner's In Nomine 1964, Ecce Manus Tradentis for mixed chorus and instruments 1964, Shepherd's Calendar for young singers and instrumentalists 1965, Revelation and Fall for soprano and instrumental ensemble 1966, Antechrist for chamber ensemble 1967, Missa super L'Homme Armé for speaker and ensemble 1968, revised 1971, Stedman Caters for instruments 1968, St Thomas Wake-Foxtrot for orchestra 1969, Worldes Blis 1969, Eram quasi Agnus (instrumental motet) 1969, Eight Songs for a Mad King for male singer and ensemble 1969, Vesalii Icones for dancer and ensemble 1969, Taverner (opera) 1970, From Stone to Thorn for mezzo-soprano and instrumental ensemble 1971, Blind Man's Buff (masque) 1972, Hymn to Saint Magnus for chamber ensemble and mezzo-soprano 1972, Stone Litany for mezzo-soprano and orchestra 1973, Miss Donnithorne's Maggot for mezzo-soprano and chamber ensemble 1974, Ave Maris Stella for chamber ensemble 1975, Three Studies for Percussion 1975, The Blind Fiddler for soprano and chamber ensemble 1975, Stevie's Ferry to Hoy (beginner's piano solo) 1975, Five Klee Pictures for percussion, piano and strings, revised 1976, Three Organ Voluntaries 1976, Kinloche His Fantassie (Kinloch/Davies) 1976, Anakreontika (Greek songs for mezzo-soprano) 1976, Orchestral Symphony No. 1 1976, The Martyrdom of St Magnus (chamber opera) 1976, Westerlings (unaccompanied part songs) 1977, A Mirror of Whitening Light for chamber ensemble 1977, Le Jongleur de Notre Dame (Masque) 1978, The Two Fiddlers 1978, Salome (ballet) 1978, Black Pentecost (for voices and orchestra) 1979, Solstice of Light (for Tenor, Chorus and Organ) 1979, The Lighthouse (chamber opera) 1979, Cinderella (pantomime opera for young performers) 1979, A Welcome to Orkney (chamber ensemble) 1980, Orchestral Symphony No. 2 1980, Little Quartet (string quartet) 1980, The Yellow Cake Revue (for voice and piano) 1980, Piano Sonata 1981, Little Quartet No. 2 (for string quartet) 1981, Lullabye for Lucy 1981, Salome 1981, Brass Quintet 1981, Songs of Hoy (Masque for children's voices and instruments) 1981, Sea Eagle (for horn solo) 1982, Image, Reflection, Shadow (for chamber ensemble) 1982, Sinfonia Concertante (for chamber orchestra) 1982, Into the Labyrinth (tenor and chamber orchestra) 1983, Sinfonietta Accademica (chamber orchestra) 1983, Guitar Sonata 1984, The No. 11 Bus 1984, One Star, At Last (carol) 1984, Symphony No. 3 (for orchestra) 1984, Violin Concerto 1985, An Orkney Wedding, with Sunrise 1985, Oboe Concerto 1986, Resurrection (opera in one act with prologue) 1987, Cello Concerto 1988, Mishkenot (chamber ensemble) 1988, Trumpet Concerto 1988, The Great Bank Robbery 1989, Symphony No. 4 1989, Concerto No. 3 for horn and trumpet 1989, No. 4 for clarinet 1990, Caroline Mathilde (ballet) 1990, Tractus 1990, Dangerous Errand (for tenor soli and chorus) 1990, The Spiders' Revenge 1991, First Grace of Light 1991, Strathclyde Concerto No. 5 for violin and viola, No. 6 for flute 1991, Ojai Festival Overture 1991, A Selkie Tale (music-theatre work for performance by children) 1992, The Turn of the Tide (for orchestra and children's chorus and instrumental groups) 1992, Strathclyde Concerto No. 7 (for double bass) 1992, Sir Charles his Pavan 1992, Strathclyde Concerto No. 8 (for bassoon) 1993, A Spell for Green Corn: The MacDonald Dances 1993, Symphony No. 5 1994, Cross Lane Fair (for orchestra) 1994, Strathclyde Concerto No. 9 (for six woodwind instruments) 1994, The Three Kings (for chorus, orchestra and soloists) 1995, The Beltane Fire (choreographic poem) 1995, The Doctor of Myddfai (opera) 1995, Symphony No. 6 1996, Strathclyde Concerto No. 10 (for orchestra) 1996, Piccolo Concerto 1996, Job (oratorio for chorus, orchestra and soloists) 1997, Mavis in Las Vegas—Theme and Variations 1997, Orkney Saga

I: Fifteen keels laid in Norway for Jerusalem-farers 1997, The Jacobite Rising (for chorus, orchestra and soloists) 1997, Piano Concerto 1997, Orkney Saga II: In Kirkwall, the first red Saint Magnus stones 1997, A Reel of Seven Fishermen 1998, Sea Elegy (for chorus, orchestra and soloists) 1998, Roma Amor Labyrinthus 1998, Maxwell's Reel with Northern Lights 1998, Swinton Jig 1998, Temenos with Mermaids and Angels (for flute and orchestra) 1998, Sails in Orkney Saga III: An Orkney Wintering (for alto saxophone and orchestra) 1999, Trumpet quintet (for string quartet and trumpet) 1999, Mr Emmet Takes a Walk 1999, Horn Concerto 1999, Orkney Saga IV: Westerly Gale in Biscay, Salt in the Bread Broken 2000, Symphony No. 7 2000, Antarctic Symphony (Symphony No. 8) 2000, Canticum Canticorum 2001, De Assumtione Beatae Mariae Virginis 2001, Crossing Kings Reach 2001, Mass 2002, Naxos Quartet No. 1 2002, Piano Trio 2002, Naxos Quartet No. 2 2003; has written music for films: The Devils, The Boyfriend and many piano pieces, works for choir, instrumental works and realizations of fifteenth and sixteenth century composers. *Address:* c/o Judy Arnold, 50 Hogarth Road, London, SW5 0PU, England. *Telephone:* (20) 7370-2328. *Fax:* (20) 7373-6730. *E-mail:* j.arnold@maxopus.com. *Website:* www.maxopus.com.

MAY, Elaine; American actress, film director and entertainer; b. 21 April 1932, Philadelphia; d. of Jack Berlin; m. 1st Marvin May (divorced); one d.; m. 2nd Sheldon Harnick 1962 (divorced 1963); appeared on radio and stage as child; performed Playwright's Theater, Chicago; appeared in student production Miss Julie, Univ. of Chicago; with Mike Nichols (q.v.) and others in improvisatory theatre group, The Compass (nightclub), Chicago 1954–57; improvised nightclub double-act with Mike Nichols, appeared New York Town Hall 1959; An Evening with Mike Nichols and Elaine May, Golden Theatre, New York 1960–61; numerous TV and radio appearances; weekly appearance NBC radio show Nightline. *Films:* Luv 1967, A New Leaf (also Dir) 1972, The Heartbreak Kid (Dir) 1973, Mikey and Nicky (Dir) 1976 (writer, Dir remake 1985), California Suite 1978, Heaven Can Wait (co-author screenplay) 1978, In The Spirit 1990, The Birdcage 1996 (co-author screenplay), Primary Colors (co-author screenplay). *Publications:* Better Part of Valour (play) 1983, Hotline 1983, Mr. Gogol and Mr. Preen 1991, Death Defying Acts 1995. *Address:* c/o Julian Schlossberg, Castle Hill Productions, Suite 1502, 1414 Avenue of the Americas, New York, NY 10019, USA.

MAY OF OXFORD, Baron (Life Peer), cr. 2001, of Oxford in the County of Oxfordshire; **Robert McCredie May,** Kt, AC, PhD, FRS, FAAS; Australian professor of biology; b. 1 Aug. 1936, Sydney; s. of Henry W. May and Kathleen M. McCredie; m. Judith Feiner 1962; one d.; ed Sydney Boys' High School, Univ. of Sydney; Gordon MacKay Lecturer in Applied Math., Harvard Univ. 1959–61; at Univ. of Sydney 1962–73; Sr Lecturer in Theoretical Physics 1962–64, Reader 1964–69, Personal Chair 1969–73; Class of 1877 Prof. of Biology, Princeton Univ. 1973–88, Chair. Univ. Research Bd 1977–88; Royal Soc. Research Prof., Dept of Zoology, Oxford Univ. and Imperial Coll., London 1988–; Chief Scientific Adviser to UK Govt and Head, Office of Science and Tech. 1995–2000; Pres. Royal Soc. 2000–; mem. Australian Acad. of Sciences 1991–, Academia Europaea 1994–; Fellow, Merton Coll., Oxford 1988–; Foreign mem. NAS 1992–; Trustee British Museum 1989–, Royal Botanic Gardens, Kew 1991–95, WWF (UK) 1990–94, Nuffield Foundation 1993–; Croonian Lecturer, Hitchcock Lecturer, John M. Prather Lecturer; numerous hon. degrees; Crafoord Prize, Royal Swedish Acad. 1996, Balzan Prize 1998; MacArthur Award, Weldon Memorial Prize, Edgeworth David Medal. *Publications:* Stability and Complexity in Model Ecosystems 1973, Exploitation of Marine Communities (ed.) 1974, Theoretical Ecology: Principles and Applications (ed.) 1976, Population Biology of Infectious Diseases (ed.) 1982, Exploitation of Marine Ecosystems (ed.) 1984, Perspectives in Ecological Theory (ed.) 1989, Population Regulation and Dynamics (ed.) 1990, Infectious Diseases of Humans: Transmission and Control (with R. M. Anderson) 1991, Large Scale Ecology and Conservation Biology 1994, Extinction Rates 1995, Evolution of Biological Diversity 1999, Virus Dynamics: the Mathematical Foundations of Immunology and Virology (with Martin Nowak) 2000. *Leisure interests:* tennis, running, hiking. *Address:* Royal Society, 6 Carlton House Terrace, London, SW1Y 5AG, England. *Telephone:* (20) 7451-2507 (Office). *Fax:* (20) 7451-2691 (Office). *E-mail:* robert.may@royalsoc.ac.uk (Office). *Website:* www.royalsoc.ac.uk (Office).

MAY, Theresa Mary, MA; British politician; b. 1 Oct. 1956; d. of Rev. Hubert Brasier and Zaidee Brasier (née Barnes); m. Philip John May 1980; ed St. Hugh's Coll., Oxford; worked for Bank of England 1977–83; with Inter-Bank Research Org. 1983–85; with Asscn for Payment Clearing Services 1985–97 (Head of European Affairs Unit 1989–96); mem. (Conservative Party) Merton London Borough Council 1986–94; contested (Conservative Party) Durham NW 1992, Barking June 1994; MP (Conservative) for Maidenhead 1997–; Opposition Frontbench Spokeswoman on Educ. and Employment 1998–99; Shadow Sec. of State for Educ. and Employment 1999–2001; Shadow Sec. for Transport, Local Govt and the Regions 2001–02; Chair. Conservative Party 2002–. *Leisure interests:* walking, cooking. *Address:* House of Commons, Westminster, London, SW1A 0AA, England (Office).

MAYAKI, Ibrahim Assane; Niger politician; b. 24 Sept. 1951, Niamey; s. of Assane Adamou Mayaki and Marie Mosconi; m. Marly Perez Marin 1976; one s. one d.; fmr Minister of Foreign Affairs and Co-operation; Prime Minister of Niger 1997–99. *Leisure interest:* taekwondo. *Address:* c/o B.P. 353, Niamey, Niger.

MAYALL, Richard Michael (Rik); British comedian, actor and writer; b. 7 March 1958; s. of John Mayall and Gillian Mayall; m. Barbara Robbin; one s. two d.; ed Univ. of Manchester; f. 20th Century Coyote theatre co. *Theatre includes:* The Common Pursuit 1988, Waiting for Godot 1991–92, The Government Inspector, Cell Mates 1995, A Family Affair 2000. *Television includes:* The Young Ones (also creator and co-writer, two series, BBC) 1982, 1984, The Comic Strip Presents (Channel Four) 1983–84, 1992, George's Marvellous Medicine (five episodes, Jackanory, BBC) 1985, The New Statesman (four series, YTV) 1987–88, 1990, 1994 (Int. Emmy Award 1989, BAFTA Best New Comedy 1990, Special Craft Gold Medal Best Performer/ Narrator), Grim Tales (two series 1990), Bottom (three series, BBC) 1990, 1992, 1994 (British Comedy Awards Best New Comedy 1992), Rik Mayall Presents (two trilogies of films, Granada TV) 1992–94 (British Comedy Awards Best Comedy Actor 1993), Wham Bham Strawberry Jam! (BBC) 1995, The Alan B'Stard Interview with Brian Walden 1995, In the Red 1998, The Bill 1999, Jonathan Creek 1999, The Knock 2000, Murder Rooms 2000, Tales of Uplift and Moral Improvement 2000. *Films include:* Whoops Apocalypse 1982, Drop Dead Fred 1990, Horse Opera 1992, Remember Me 1996, Bring Me the Head of Mavis Davis 1996 (Best Actor, San Remo Film Festival 1997), Guest House Paradiso 1999, Merlin–The Return 1999, Kevin of the North 2000, Jesus Christ, Super Star 2000; provided voices for animations including Tom Thumb in The World of Peter Rabbit and Friends–The Tale of Two Bad Mice 1994, Toad in Willows in Winter 1995 (Emmy Award 1997), The Robber King in The Snow Queen 1995, Prince Froglip in The Princess and the Goblin, Hero Baby in How to be a Little Sod 1995, Young William Tell in Oscar's Orchestra 1996. *Live Stand Up includes:* Comic Strip 1982, Kevin Turvey and Bastard Squad 1983, Rik Mayall, Ben Elton, Andy De La Tour (UK tour & Edin. Fringe) 1983, Rik Mayall and Ben Elton 1984–85, (Australian tour) 1986, 1992, Rik Mayall and Andy De La Tour 1989–90, Rik Mayall and Adrian Edmondson (UK tours) 1993, 1995, 1997, 2001. *Radio includes:* The Sound of Trumpets (Radio 4) 1999, A Higher Education (Radio 4) 2000. *Address:* c/o Aude Powell, The Brunskill Management Limited, Suite 8A, 169 Queen's Gate, London, SW7 5HE, England. *Telephone:* (20) 7581-3388 (London) (Office); (1768) 881430. *Fax:* (20) 7589-9460 (London) (Office); (1768) 881850.

MAYER, Christian (pseudonym Carl Amery); German author; b. 9 April 1922, Munich; s. of Dr. Anton Mayer and Anna Mayer (née Schneller); m. Marijane Gerth 1950; three s. two d.; ed Humanistisches Gymnasium, Freising and Passau, Univ. of Munich and Catholic Univ. of America, Washington, DC; freelance author 1949–; Dir of City Libraries, Munich 1967–71; mem., fmr Chair. Bavarian Acad. of the Arts; co-founder German Literary Fund 1980; Chair. E F. Schumachergesellschaft 1980; Pres. PEN Centre of Fed. Repub. of Germany 1989–90; Literary Prize, City of Munich 1991, Fed. Cross of Merit, First Class. *Publications:* novels: Der Wettbewerb 1954, Die Grosse Deutsche Tour 1958, Das Königsprojekt 1974, Der Untergang der Stadt Passau 1975, An den Feuern der Leyermark 1979, Die Wallfahrer 1986, Das Geheimnis der Krypta 1990; essays: Die Kapitulation 1963, Fragen an Welt und Kirche 1967, Das Ende der Vorsehung 1972, Natur als Politik 1976, Leb Wohl Geliebtes Volk der Bayern 1980, G. K. Chesterton oder Der Kampf gegen die Kälte 1981, Die Botschaft des Jahrtausends 1994, Hitler als Vorläufer 1998, Global Exit 2002; various radio essays, radio plays, translations, etc. *Leisure interests:* cooking, walking. *Address:* Drächslstrasse 7, 81541 Munich, Germany. *Telephone:* (89) 486134. *Fax:* (89) 4801997 (Home).

MAYER, Colin, MA, DPhil; British academic; b. 12 May 1953, London; s. of the late Harold Charles Mayer and of Anne Louise Mayer; m. Annette Patricia Haynes 1979; two d.; ed St. Paul's School, Oriel Coll., Oxford, Wolfson Coll., Oxford, Harvard Univ.; HM Treasury, London 1976–78; Harkness Fellow, Harvard Univ. 1979–80; Fellow in Econs, St. Anne's Coll., Oxford 1980–86; Price Waterhouse Prof. of Corp. Finance, City Univ. Business School 1987–92; Prof. of Econs and Finance, Univ. of Warwick 1992–94; Peter Moores Prof. of Man. Studies, Saïd Business School, Oxford 1994–; Chair. OXERA Ltd 1987–; Dir Oxford Financial Research Centre 1994–; del. Oxford Univ. Press 1996–; Assoc. Ed. Journal of Int. Financial Man., European Financial Man. Journal, Fiscal Studies, Scottish Journal of Political Economy, Oxford Review of Econ. Policy; mem. Exec. Cttee Royal Econ. Soc. 2002–(06); Fellow of Wadham Coll., Oxford 1994–; Gov. St Paul's School London 2002–(06); Hon. Fellow St Anne's Coll., Oxford Univ. 1993. *Publications:* Economic Analysis of Accounting Profitability (jtly.) 1986, Risk, Regulation and Investor Protection (jtly.) 1989, European Financial Integration (jtly) 1991, Capital Markets and Financial Intermediation (jtly) 1993, Hostile Takeovers (jtly) 1994, Asset Management and Investor Protection (jtly) 2002. *Leisure interests:* piano, jogging, reading philosophy and science. *Address:* Saïd Business School, University of Oxford, Park End Street, Oxford, OX1 1HP, England (Office); Wadham College, Oxford, OX1 3PN. *Telephone:* (1865) 288919 (Office). *Fax:* (1865) 288805 (Office).

MAYER, HE Cardinal Paul Augustin, OSB; German ecclesiastic; b. 23 May 1911, Altoetting; ordained 1935; consecrated Bishop (Titular See of Satrianum) 1972, then Archbishop; cr. Cardinal 1985. *Address:* Città del Vaticano, Rome; via Rusticucci 13, 00193 Rome, Italy (Home).

MAYER, Peter, MA; American publisher; b. Hampstead, London; ed Columbia Univ., Christ Church, Oxford; graduate Fellow, Indiana Univ.; Fulbright Fellow, Freie Universität Berlin 1959; worked with Orion Press before joining Avon books for 14 years; Publr and Pres. Pocketbooks 1976–78; Chief. Exec. Penguin Books Ltd, London 1978–96, laterChair. Penguin USA;

exec. positions with The Overlook Press (co–f. with his father 1970) 1996–, acquired Duckworth publrs 2003; Fellow Ind. Univ. *Publication:* The Pacifist Conscience (ed) 1966. *Address:* c/o Penguin USA, 375 Hudson Street, New York, NY 10014, USA.

MAYER, Thomas; German conductor; ed State Acad. of Music, Berlin; worked in opera houses of Beuthen, Leipzig, Teplitz and Aussig, subsequently Asst to Erich Kleiber, Fritz Busch and Arturo Toscanini, Teatro Colón, Buenos Aires; directed German opera season, Santiago, Chile and State Symphony Orchestra of Montevideo, Uruguay; conducted at Metropolitan Opera, New York 1974, subsequently Dir Venezuelan Symphony Orchestra, Halifax and Ottawa orchestras, Canada; guest conductor with many orchestras in Europe, N America and Australia; a regular conductor of Sinfonie Orchestra Berlin (West) and Berlin Symphony Orchestra (East) 1974–.

MAYER-KUCKUK, Theo, Dr rer. nat; German nuclear physicist; b. 10 May 1927, Rastatt; m. Irmgard Meyer 1965; two s.; ed Univ. of Heidelberg; Research Fellow, Max Planck Institut für Kernphysik, Heidelberg 1953–59, Scientific mem. 1964; Research Fellow, Calif. Inst. of Tech., Pasadena 1960–61; Dozent, Univ. of Heidelberg 1962, Tech. Univ. Munich 1963; Prof. of Physics, Univ. of Bonn 1965–92, Dir Inst. of Nuclear and Radiation Physics 1965–92; Vice-Pres. Int. Union of Pure and Applied Physics (IUPAP) 1984–90; Pres. German Physical Soc. 1990–92, Vice-Pres. 1992–96; Scientific Dir Magnus-Haus Berlin 1994–; mem. Acad. of Sciences of Nordrhein-Westfalen 1982; Röntgenpreis, Univ. of Giessen 1964. *Publications:* Kernphysik, Atomphysik, Der gebrochene Spiegel 1989; research papers and review articles in physics journals. *Leisure interest:* sailing. *Address:* Institut für Strahlen- und Kernphysik der Universität Bonn, Nussallee 14, 53113 Bonn (Office); Dreiserstr.26, 12587 Berlin, Germany (Home). *Telephone:* (228) 732201 (Office); (30) 6409-5993 (Home). *Fax:* (30) 6495-8134 (Home). *E-mail:* emka@iskp.uni-bonn.de (Office); temka@web.de (Home).

MAYFIELD, Rt Rev Christopher John, MA; British ecclesiastic; b. 18 Dec. 1935; s. of Dr. Roger Mayfield and Muriel Mayfield; m. Caroline Roberts 1962; two s. one d.; ed Sedbergh School, Gonville & Caius Coll. Cambridge and Linacre House, Oxford; ordained deacon 1963, priest 1964; curate, St Martin-in-the-Bull Ring, Birmingham 1963–67; lecturer, St Martin's, Birmingham 1967–71; Vicar of Luton 1971–80; Archdeacon of Bedford 1979–85; Bishop Suffragan of Wolverhampton 1985–93; Bishop of Manchester 1993–; Lord Bishop of Manchester, House of Lords 1998; Hon. MSc (Cranfield) 1984. *Leisure interests:* marriage, evangelism, walking, watching cricket. *Address:* Bishopscourt, Bury New Road, Manchester, M7 4LE, England. *Telephone:* (161) 792-2096. *Fax:* (161) 792-6826. *E-mail:* bishop@bishopscourtman.free-online.co.uk (Office).

MAYHEW, Judith, LLM; New Zealand politician, lawyer and academic; b. 18 Oct. 1948, Dunedin; m. 1976 (divorced 1986); ed Otago Girls' High School, Univ. of Otago, NZ; barrister and solicitor, NZ 1973, solicitor, England and Wales 1993; lecturer in Law, Univ. of Otago 1970–73; lecturer in Law and Sub Dean, Univ. of Southampton, UK 1973–76, King's Coll. London 1976–89; Dir Anglo-French law degree, Sorbonne, Paris 1976–79; Dir of Training and Employment Law, Titmuss Sainer Dechert 1989–94; Dir of Educ. and Training, Wilde Sapte 1994–99; City and Business Adviser to Mayor of London 2000–; mem. of Court of Common Council Corpn of London 1986–, Chair Policy and Resources Cttee 1997–2002; Special Adviser to Chair. of Clifford Chance 2000–; Dir Gresham Coll. 1990–, London First Centre 1996–, Int. Financial Services London (fmrly British Invisibles) 1996–, London First 1997–, 4Ps 1997–, London Devt Agency 2000, Cross River Partnership; Trustee Natural History Museum 1998–; Gov. Birkbeck Coll. London 1993–; Chair. Royal Opera House, London 2003–; Hon. LLD (Otago) 1998, (City Univ. London) 1999. *Leisure interests:* opera, theatre, old English roses, tennis. *Address:* Royal Opera House, Covent Garden, London, WC2E 9DD, England (Office). *Telephone:* (20) 7240-1200 (Office). *Website:* www.royalopera.org.

MAYHEW OF TWYSDEN, Baron (Life Peer), cr. 1997, of Kilndown in the County of Kent; **Patrick Barnabas Burke Mayhew,** Kt, PC, QC; British politician and barrister; b. 11 Sept. 1929, Cookham, Berks.; s. of the late A. G. H. Mayhew and Sheila M. B. Roche; m. Jean Elizabeth Gurney 1963; four s.; ed Tonbridge School and Balliol Coll., Oxford; Pres. Oxford Union Soc. 1952; called to Bar (Middle Temple) 1955; apptd. QC 1972; MP (Conservative) for Tunbridge Wells (now Royal Tunbridge Wells) 1974–97; Parl. Sec., Dept of Employment 1979–81; Minister of State, Home Office 1981–83; Solicitor-Gen. 1983–87; Attorney-Gen. 1987–92; Sec. of State for Northern Ireland 1992–97; Dir (non-exec.) Western Provident Asscn 1998–, Vice-Chair. 2000–; Chair. Prime Minister's Advisory Cttee on Business Appointments 1999–. *Leisure interests:* country pursuits, sailing. *Address:* House of Lords, Westminster, London, SW1A 0PW, England. *Telephone:* (20) 7219-3000.

MAYNARD SMITH, John, BA, BSc, FRS; British professor; b. 6 Jan. 1920, London; s. of Sidney Maynard Smith and Isobel Mary Pitman; m. Sheila Matthew 1941; two s. one d.; ed Eton Coll., Trinity Coll., Cambridge, Univ. Coll., London; aircraft engineer 1941–47; lecturer in Zoology, Univ. Coll. London 1952–65; School of Biological Sciences, Univ. of Sussex, (Dean 1965–72), Prof. of Biology 1965–85, Prof. Emer. 1985–; Foreign Assoc. NAS; Hon. DSc (Kent, Sussex, Simon Fraser, Oxford, Chicago); Darwin Medal, Royal Soc. 1986, Royal Medal 1997, Balzan Prize 1991, shared Crafoord Prize 1999, Copley Medal 1999, Kyoto Prize 2001. *Publications:* The Theory of Evolution 1958, The Evolution of Sex 1978, Evolution and the Theory of Games 1983, Evolutionary Genetics 1989, The Major Transitions in Evolution

(with E Szathmáry) 1995, The Origins of Life 1999. *Leisure interests:* gardening, talking. *Address:* 5 Mountfield House, Mountfield Road, Lewes, Sussex, BN7 2XA, England (Home). *Telephone:* (1273) 474659.

MAYNE, David Quinn, PhD, DSc, FRS, F.R.ENG.; British university professor; b. 23 April 1930, Germiston, South Africa; s. of Leslie Harper Mayne and Jane Quin; m. Josephine Mary Hess 1954; three d.; ed Christian Brothers' Coll., Boksburg, Univ. of The Witwatersrand, South Africa; lecturer, Univ. of The Witwatersrand 1951–54, 1957–59; Research Engineer, British Thomson Houston Co. 1955–56; lecturer, Imperial Coll. of Science, Tech. and Medicine 1959–66, Reader 1967–70, Prof. 1970–89; Prof. of Electrical and Computer Eng., Univ. of Calif., Davis 1989–96, Prof. Emer. 1997–, Head Dept of Electrical Eng 1984–88, Sr Research Fellow Science Research Council 1979; Sr Research Fellow Dept of Electrical and Electronic Eng, Imperial Coll., Univ. of London 1996–; Visiting Research Fellow, Harvard Univ., USA 1970; Visiting Prof. Univ. of Calif., Berkeley, Univ. of Newcastle, Australia, IIT, Delhi, Academia Sinica, China, Univ. of Calif., Santa Barbara; Fellow IEEE 1976, IEE 1980, Imperial Coll. 2000; Hon. DTech (Lund); Heaviside Premium 1979, 1984, Harold Hartley Medal 1984. *Publications:* Differential Dynamic Programming 1970; 250 papers in professional journals on optimization, optimal control, adaptive control and optimization-based design. *Leisure interests:* walking, cross-country skiing, music. *Address:* 123 Elgin Crescent, London, W11 2JH, England.

MAYNE, (David) Roger, BA; British photographer and artist; b. 5 May 1929, Cambridge; s. of A. B. Mayne and D. Mayne (née Watson); m. Ann Jellicoe 1962; one d. one s.; ed Rugby School, Balliol Coll., Oxford; self-taught in photography; photographs of London and other city street scenes 1955–61; taught at Bath Acad. of Art, Corsham 1966–69; works in Museum of Modern Art, New York, Metropolitan Museum of Art, New York, Art Inst. of Chicago, Bibliothèque Nationale, Paris, Nat. Gallery of Australia, Canberra, V & A Museum, London, Arts Council of GB. *Exhibitions:* main solo exhbns: ICA, London 1956, AIA Gallery, London 1959, Portraits, Royal Court Foyer 1960, Arnolfini Gallery, Bristol 1965, Daughter and Son, Half Moon, London 1972, then Arnolfini 1974 and Diaframma, Milan 1977, Landscape Photographs, ICA 1978, Retrospective, V & A Museum, London 1986, Parco, Tokyo 1986, Prakapas Gallery, New York 1989, Street Photographs 1956–61, South Bank Centre Tour 1987–91, Zelda Cheatle Gallery, London 1992, 1999, St Ives Painters, Tate St Ives 2001; mixed exhbns. include: Art for Society, Whitechapel Art Gallery, London 1978, Objects the V & A Collects, V & A 1978, Personal Choice, V & A 1983, Subjective Fotografie, Folkwang Museum, Essen and tour 1984–85, Through the Looking Glass, British Photography 1945–89, Barbican Art Gallery, London and Manchester City Art Gallery 1989, The Sixties London Art Scene, Barbican Art Gallery, London 1993, Three Masters, Laurence Miller Gallery, New York 1993, Young Meteors, British Photojournalism 1957–65, Nat. Museum of Photography, Film and TV, Bradford 1998, Transition–The London Art Scene in the Fifties, Barbican Art Gallery 2002. *Publications:* Things Being Various (with others) 1967, The Shell Guide to Devon (with Ann Jellicoe) 1975, The Street Photographs of Roger Mayne 1986, 1993, Roger Mayne Photographs 2001. *Leisure interests:* listening to music, looking at art exhbns., watching sport. *Address:* Colway Manor, Colway Lane, Lyme Regis, Dorset, DT7 3HD, England. *Telephone:* (1297) 442821.

MAYOR ZARAGOZA, Federico, DR.PHAR.; Spanish politician, biologist and university official; b. 27 Jan. 1934, Barcelona; s. of Federico Mayor and Juana Zaragoza; m. María Angeles Menéndez 1956; two s. one d.; ed Univ. Complutense of Madrid; Prof. of Biochem., Faculty of Pharmacy, Granada Univ. 1963–73; Rector, Granada Univ. 1968–72; Prof. of Biochem., Autonomous Univ., Madrid 1973, Chair. Severo Ochoa Molecular Biology Centre (Higher Council of Scientific Research) 1974–78; Under-Sec. Ministry of Educ. and Science 1974–75; mem. Cortes (Parl.) for Granada 1977–78; Chair. Advisory Cttee for Scientific and Tech. Research 1974–78; Deputy Dir-Gen. UNESCO 1978–81, Dir-Gen. 1987–99; Minister for Educ. and Science 1981–82; Dir Inst. of the Sciences of Man, Madrid 1983–87; mem. European Parl. 1987; Pres. Scientific Council, Ramón Areces Foundation, Madrid 1989–, Culture and Peace Foundation 2000–, First Mark Communications 2000–; mem. Club of Rome 1981–; Academician, Royal Acad. of Pharmacy; mem. European Acad. of Arts, Sciences and Humanities, Int. Cell Research Org. (ICRO), AAAS, The Biochemical Soc. (UK), French Soc. of Biological Chem., American Chemical Soc., Academia de Bellas Artes and numerous other orgs.; Dr. hc (Westminster) 1995; Grand Cross, Alfonso X El Sabio, Orden Civil de la Sanidad, Carlos III, Caro y Cuervo (Colombia); Commdr Placa del Libertador (Venezuela); Grand Officier, Ordre Nat. du Mérite (France). *Publications:* A contraviento (poems) 1987, Mañana siempre es tarde 1987 (English version: Tomorrow Is Always Too Late 1992), Aguafuertes (poems) 1991 (English version: Patterns 1994), La nueva página 1994, La mémoire de l'avenir 1994, Terral (poems) 1998 (English version: Land Wind 1998), Un monde nouveau 1999, Los nudos gordianos 2000; numerous specialized works, trans., articles. *Leisure interests:* reading, writing, music. *Address:* Fundación Cultura de Paz, Velázquez 14, 3° D, 28001 Madrid (Office); Mar Caribe 15, Interland, Majadahonda, 28220 Madrid, Spain (Home). *Telephone:* (91) 4261555 (Office); (91) 6382345 (Home). *Fax:* (91) 4316387 (Office). *E-mail:* info.culturadepaz@pangea.org (Office).

MAYORSKY, Boris Grigoryevich; Russian diplomatist; b. 19 May 1937, Odessa, Ukraine; m.; two d.; ed Moscow Inst. of Int. Relations, UNO Translation Courses; with Africa Div. USSR Ministry of Foreign Affairs 1961;

on staff USSR Enbassy, Ghana 1961–64; attaché 1964–65; with UN European Secr., Geneva 1966–69, World Health Org., Geneva 1969–70; First Sec., Head of Sector Law Div. USSR Ministry of Foreign Affairs 1970–73; adviser, Comm. on Law Problems of Space, USSR Ministry of Foreign Affairs 1973–89; First Deputy Head, Head Dept on Int. Scientific and Tech. Co-operation 1989–92; Amb. to Kenya 1992–2000, to Spain 2000–02. *Address:* Ministry of Foreign Affairs, 121200 Smolenskaya-Sennaya 32/34, Moscow, Russia (Office). *Telephone:* (91) 4112524 (Office). *Fax:* (91) 5629712 (Office).

MAYOUX, Jacques Georges Maurice Sylvain; French banker and businessman; b. 18 July 1924, Paris; s. of Georges Mayoux and Madeleine de Busscher; one s. one d.; ed Ecole des Hautes Etudes Commerciales, Ecole Libre des Sciences Politiques, Faculté de Droit et des Lettres de Paris; studied at Ecole Nat. d'Admin. 1949–51; Personal adviser to Minister of Finance 1958, Asst Gen. Sec. Comité Interministeriel pour les Questions de Coopération Economique Européenne 1958–63; mem. Gen. Council, Banque de France 1963–73; Gen. Man. Caisse Nat. de Crédit Agricole 1963–75; Prof., Inst. d'Etudes Politiques 1964–72; Chair., Gen. Man. Agritel 1972–75, SACILOR (Aciéries et laminoirs de Lorraine) 1978–82, SOLLAC (Soc. Lorraine de laminage continu) 1980–82; Pres. SOLMER 1980–81, Soc. Générale SA 1982–86 (Hon. Pres. 1986, Hon. Chair.), Cen. Cttee for Rural Renovation 1971, Fondation H.E.C. 1978–90; Pres. French-Canadian Chamber of Commerce 1986–90; Vice-Chair. Goldman Sachs Europe 1989; Insp. Général des Finances 1976–87; Vice-Pres. Admin. Council Euris 1990–; mem. Supervisory Bd Harpener Gesellschaft 1980–86, Conseil Ordre de la Légion d'honneur 1993–; Commdr, Légion d'honneur, Commdr, Ordre nat. du Mérite, Officier des Arts et des Lettres; Commdr, Phoenix (Greece). *Address:* Société Générale, 38 rue de Bassano, 75008 Paris (Office); Goldman Sachs (Europe), 2 rue de Thann, 75017 Paris, France (Office); 65 avenue Foch, 75115 Paris, France (Home). *Telephone:* 1-42-12-11-30 (Office). *Fax:* 1-42-12-11-99 (Office). *E-mail:* jacques.mayoux@gs.com (Office).

MAYR, Ernst, PhD; American professor emeritus of biology; b. 5 July 1904, Kempten, Germany; s. of Otto Mayr and Helene Pusinelli; m. Margarete Simon 1935 (deceased); two d.; ed Univs. of Greifswald and Berlin; Asst Curator, Univ. of Berlin 1926–32; Assoc. Curator, Whitney-Rothschild Collection of American Museum of Natural History 1932–44, Curator 1944–53; Alexander Agassiz Prof. of Zoology, Harvard Univ. 1953–75, Emer. 1975–; Dir Museum of Comparative Zoology 1961–70; Visiting Prof., Univ. of Minn. 1949, 1974, Univs. of Pavia and Wash. 1951–52; lecturer, Columbia Univ. 1941, 1950, Philadelphia Acad. of Sciences 1947, Univ. of Calif. at Davis 1967; expeditions to Dutch New Guinea, Mandated Territory of New Guinea and Solomon Islands 1928–30; Fellow, American Acad. of Arts and Sciences; mem. NAS, American Philosophical Soc.; Corresp. Fellow, Zoological Soc. of India; Foreign mem. Royal Soc., Acad. des Sciences 1989; Hon. Foreign and Corresp. mem. of 26 foreign socs.; 17 U.S. and foreign Hon. doctorates; numerous awards including Leidy Medal of Acad. of Natural Sciences, Philadelphia 1946, Wallace Darwin Medal of Linnean Soc., London 1958, Daniel Giraud Eliot Medal of NAS 1967, Centennial Medal of American Museum of Natural History 1969, Nat. Medal of Science 1970, Linnean Medal 1977, Balzan Prize 1983, Darwin Medal, Royal Soc. 1984, Sarton Medal 1986, Japan Prize 1994, Benjamin Franklin Medal 1995, Lewis Thomas Prize 1998, Crafoord Prize 1999. *Publications:* List of New Guinea Birds 1941, Systematics and the Origin of Species 1942, Birds of the Southwest Pacific 1945, Birds of the Philippines 1946, Methods and Principles of Systematic Zoology 1953, The Species Problem (Editor, American Asscn for the Advancement of Science Publication No. 50) 1957, Animal Species and Evolution 1963, Principles of Systematic Zoology 1969, 1991, Populations, Species and Evolution 1970, Evolution and the Diversity of Life 1976, The Evolutionary Synthesis (ed.) 1980, The Growth of Biological Thought 1982, Toward a New Philosophy of Biology 1988, One Long Argument 1991, This Is Biology 1997, What Evolution Is 2001, The Birds of Northern Melanesia 2001; and 700 articles in journals. *Leisure interests:* natural history, history of biology. *Address:* 207 Badger Terrace, Bedford, MA 01730, USA (Home). *Telephone:* (617) 495-2476 (Office); (781) 275-9777 (Home).

MAYS, Willie; American baseball player; b. 6 May 1931, Westfield; s. of William Howard Mays and Ann Mays; Nat. League Rookie of the Year 1951; played for the New York Giants, San Francisco Giants and New York Mets; career statistics include 3,283 hits and 660 home runs; two-time Most Valuable Player; 12 Gold Gloves; played in a record-tying 24 All-Star games; participated in four World Series; retd, signed ten-year contract as goodwill amb. and part-time coach for the New York Mets; Special Asst to Team Pres., San Francisco Giants 1986–; Associated Press Athlete of the Year Award 1954, elected to the Baseball Hall of Fame 1979. *Address:* San Francisco Giants, Pacific Bell Park, 24 Willie Mays Plaza, San Francisco, CA 94107 USA (Office). *Telephone:* (415) 972-2000 (Office). *Website:* www.sfgiants.com (Office).

MAYSTADT, Philippe, MA, PhD; Belgian politician and international finance executive; b. 14 March 1948, Petit-Rechain; m.; three c.; ed Claremont Grad. School, Los Angeles and Catholic Univ. of Louvain; Asst Prof. Catholic Univ. of Louvain 1970–77, Prof. 1989–; Adviser, Office of Minister for Regional Affairs 1974; Deputy for Charleroi 1977–91; Sec. of State for Regional Economy and Urban Planning 1979–80; Minister of Civil Service and Scientific Policy 1980–81, for the Budget, Scientific Policy and Planning 1981–85, of Econ. Affairs 1985–88; Deputy Prime Minister 1986–88; Minister of Finance 1988–98, of Foreign Trade 1995–98; Deputy Prime Minister

1995–98; Pres. Parti Social Chrétien June 1998–Dec. 1999; mem. Senate June 1999–Dec. 1999; Pres. European Investment Bank 2000–; Chair. IMF Interim Cttee 1993–98; Finance Minister of the Year, Euromoney magazine 1990. *Publications:* Listen and then Decide 1988, Market and State in a Globalized Economy 1998. *Address:* European Investment Bank, 100 Boulevard Konrad Adenauer, 2950 Luxembourg (Office). *Telephone:* 4379-4464 (Office). *Fax:* 4379-4474 (Office). *E-mail:* p.maystadt@eib.org (Office). *Website:* www.eib.org (Office).

MAZANKOWSKI, Rt Hon Donald Frank, PC, OC; Canadian politician and business consultant; b. 27 July 1935, Viking, Alta.; s. of the late Frank Mazankowski and Dora Lonowski; m. Lorraine E. Poleschuk 1958; three s.; ed High School; mem. Parl. 1968–93; Minister of Transport and Minister responsible for Canadian Wheat Board 1979; Minister of Transport 1984–86; Pres. Treasury Bd 1987–88; Minister responsible for Privatization, Regulatory Affairs and Operations 1988, of Agric. 1989–91, of Finance 1991–93; Deputy Prime Minister 1989–93, Pres. of the Queen's Privy Council for Canada 1989–91; business consultant 1993–; Chair. Inst. of Health Econs., Canadian Genetics Diseases Network, Alberta Premier's Advisory Council on Health; Gov. Univ. of Alberta; Dir. numerous cos.; Progressive Conservative Party; Hon. DEng (Tech. Univ. of Nova Scotia) 1987, Hon. LLD (Univ. of Alberta) 1993; Paul Harris Fellow Rotary Int. *Leisure interests:* fishing, golf. *Address:* PO Box 1350, Vegreville, Alta., T9C 1S5, Canada (Office and Home). *Telephone:* (780) 632-2258 (Office). *Fax:* (780) 632-4737 (Office). *E-mail:* maz1@agt.net (Office).

MAZEAUD, Pierre; French politician; b. 24 Aug. 1929, Lyon; m. 1st Marie Prohom 1953 (divorced 1960); two d.; m. 2nd Sophie Hamel 1967; one s. one d.; Judge of Tribunal of Instance, Lamentin, Martinique 1961; in charge of Conf., Faculty of Law, Paris 1955; Tech. Adviser to Prime Minister 1961; Judge of Tribunal of Great Instance, Versailles 1962; Tech. Adviser to Minister of Justice 1962; Tech. Adviser to Minister of Youth and Sports 1967–68; Deputy for Hauts-de-Seine 1968–73, for Haute-Savoie 1988–98, Vice-Pres. Nat. Ass. 1992–93, 1997–98, Vice-Pres. Groupe des députés sportifs 1968; Minister responsible for Youth and Sport 1973–76; Councillor of State 1976; Pres. Law Comm. of Assemblée Nationale 1987–88, 1993–98; Titular Judge, High Court 1987–97; Mayor, Saint-Julien-en-Genevois 1979–89; regional councillor, Rhône-Alpes 1992–98; mem. Constitutional Council 1998–; climbed Everest 1978 (oldest man to climb Everest); Officier, Légion d'honneur. *Publications:* Montagne pour un homme nu 1971, Everest 1978, Sport et Liberté 1980, Nanga Parbat–montagne cruelle 1982, Des cailloux et des mouches ou l'échec à l'Himalaya 1985, Rappel au Règlement 1995. *Address:* Conseil constitutionnel, 2 rue de Montpensier, 75001 Paris (Office); 8 rue Charlemagne, 75004 Paris, France (Home). *Telephone:* 40-15-30-16 (Office).

MAZOWIECKI, Tadeusz; Polish politician and journalist; b. 18 April 1927, Płock; s. of Bronisław Mazowiecki and Jadwiga Mazowiecka; widower; three s.; Chair. Acad. Publishing Co-operative, Warsaw 1947–48; mem. Catholic Asscn PAX; contrib. to daily and weekly PAX Publs, dismissed 1955; co-f., mem. of Bd, Vice-Pres. Warsaw Catholic Intelligentsia Club (KIK) 1956; co-f. and Chief Ed. Catholic monthly Więź (Bond) 1958–81; Deputy to Sejm (Parl.) (Catholic Group "ZNAK") PRL (Polish People's Repub.) 1961–72; mem. of various opposition groups and protest movts. 1968–89; co-f. and mem. Council Soc. for Acad. Courses (Flying Univ.) 1977–89; Head, Team of Experts, Lenin Shipyard, Gdańsk 1980; co-Ed. Solidarity Trades Union Statutes; adviser to Solidarity Nat. Consultative Comm.; organizer and First Chief Ed. of Solidarity weekly 1981–89; interned 1981–82; participant Round Table plenary debates, Co-Chair. group for union pluralism, mem. group for political reforms, team for mass-media, co-ordinator negotiation teams from opposition 1989; Prime Minister of Poland 1989–90; Deputy to Sejm (Parl.) 1991–2001; Chair. Democratic Union 1990–94; Chair. (merged with Liberal Democratic Congress to form Freedom Union) Freedom Union 1994–95; Chair. Parl. Comm. for European Integration 1997–2001; UN Special Rapporteur of Comm. on Human Rights investigating human rights situation in fmr Yugoslavia 1992–95; mem. PEN Club; Dr. hc (Louvain) 1990, (Genoa) 1991, (Giessen) 1993, (Poitiers) 1994, (Exeter) 1998, (Acad. of Econs, Katowice) 1999; Peace Prize (Anglican Church, New York) 1990, Premio Napoli 1992; Hon. LLD (Exeter) 1997; Andrzej Strug Award 1990, Freedom Award (American Jewish Congress) 1990, Giorgio La Pira Award of Peace and Culture 1991, Polish-German Award 1994, St Adalbert Award 1995, Order of White Eagle 1995, European Human Rights Award 1996, Officier Légion d'honneur 1998. *Publications include:* Cross-roads and Values 1971, The Second Face of Europe 1979, Internment 1984. *Address:* Biuro Tadeusza Mazowieckiego, Polska Fundacja im. Roberta Schumana, Al. Ujazdowskie 37, 00-540 Warsaw, Poland. *Telephone:* (22) 6212161, 6217555 (Office). *Fax:* (22) 6297214 (Office). *E-mail:* t.mazowiecki@schuman.org.pl (Office).

MAZRUI, Ali A., MA, DPhil; Kenyan professor of political science; b. 24 Feb. 1933, Mombasa; s. of Al'Amin Ali Mazrui and Safia Suleiman Mazrui; m. 1st Molly Vickerman 1962 (divorced 1982); three s.; m. 2nd Pauline Ejima Uti-Mazrui 1991; two s.; ed Columbia Univ., New York, Univs. of Manchester and Oxford; Lecturer in Political Science, Makerere Univ., Uganda 1963–65, Prof. of Political Science 1965–72, Dean of Social Sciences 1967–69; Assoc. Ed. Transition Magazine 1964–73, Co-Ed. Mawazo Journal 1967–73; Visiting Prof. Univ. of Chicago 1965; Research Assoc. Harvard Univ. 1965–66; Dir African Section, World Order Models Project 1968–73; Visiting Prof. Northwestern Univ., USA 1969, McGill and Denver Univs. 1969, London and

Manchester Univs. 1971, Dyason Lecture Tour of Australia 1972; Vice-Pres. Int. Political Science Asscn 1970–73, Int. Congress of Africanists 1967–73, Int. Congress of African Studies 1978–85, Int. African Inst. 1987–, World Congress of Black Intellectuals 1988–; Fellow, Center for Advanced Study in the Behavioral Sciences, Stanford 1972–73; Prof. of Political Science, Univ. of Michigan 1973–91; Sr Visiting Fellow, Hoover Inst. on War, Revolution and Peace, Stanford 1973–74; Dir Centre for Afro-American and African Studies 1979–81; Research Prof. Univ. of Jos, Nigeria 1981–86; Andrew D. White Prof.-at-Large, Cornell Univ. 1986–92; Albert Schweitzer Prof. in the Humanities, State Univ. of New York, Binghamton 1989–; Ibn Khaldun Prof.-at-Large School of Islamic and Social Sciences, Leesbury, Va 1997–; Walter Rodney Distinguished Prof. Univ. of Guyana, Georgetown 1997–98; Reith Lecturer 1979; Presenter BBC TV series The Africans 1986; mem. World Bank's Council of African Advisers; Int. Org. Essay Prize 1964, Northwestern Univ. Book Prize 1969. *Publications:* Towards a Pax Africana 1967, On Heroes and Uhuru-Worship 1967, The Anglo-African Commonwealth 1967, Violence and Thought 1969, Co-Ed. Protest and Power in Black Africa 1970, The Trial of Christopher Okigbo 1971, Cultural Engineering and Nation Building in East Africa 1972, (Co-Ed.) Africa in World Affairs: The Next Thirty Years 1973, A World Federation of Cultures: An African Perspective 1976, Political Values and the Educated Class in Africa 1978, Africa's International Relations 1978, The African Condition (Reith Lectures) 1980, Nationalism and New States in Africa (Co-author) 1984, The Africans: A Triple Heritage 1986, Cultural Forces in World Politics 1989, Ed. Africa Since 1935 (Vol. VIII of UNESCO General History of Africa) 1993, The Power of Babel: Language and Governance in Africa's Experience 1998. *Leisure interests:* travel, dining out, swimming, reading thrillers and mystery novels. *Address:* State University of New York, Institute of Global Culture Studies, Office of Schweitzer Chair., P.O. Box 6000, Binghampton, NY 13902 (Office); 313 Murray Hill Road, Vestal, NY 13850, U.S.A. (Home). *Telephone:* (607) 7774494.

MAZUROK, Yuri Antonovich; Ukrainian opera singer (baritone); b. 18 July 1931, Krasnik, Poland (now Ukraine); one s.; ed Lvov Inst. and Moscow Conservatoire; awards include Prague Spring Vocal Competition 1960, Int. Enesco Singing Competition, Bucharest, 1961, First Prize at World Fair, Montreal, 1967; début with Bolshoi Opera 1963, Prin. of the co. 1964–2001; has performed world-wide; retd from opera stage 2001; USSR People's Artist 1976. *roles include:* Eugene (Eugene Onegin), Prince Yeletsky (The Queen of Spades), Andrei (War and Peace), Figaro (The Barber of Seville), Scarpia (Tosca) and Escamillo (Carmen) and especially Verdi repertoire, including René (Un Ballo in Maschera), Rodrigo (Don Carlos), Germont (La Traviata). *Address:* Teatralnaya Pl. 1, Bolshoi Theatre, 103009 Moscow, Russia. *Telephone:* (095) 201-24-85 (Home).

MAZURSKY, Paul, BA; American film writer, director and actor; b. Irwin Mazursky, 25 April 1930, Brooklyn, NY; s. of David Mazursky and Jean Gerson; m. Betsy Purdy 1953; two d.; ed Brooklyn Coll.; stage, TV and film actor 1951–; night club comedian 1954–60; writer, Danny Kaye Show 1963–67; co-writer, I Love You, Alice B. Toklas (film) 1968; Dr hc (Brooklyn Coll.). *Films include:* as writer and Dir, Bob & Carol & Ted & Alice 1969, Alex in Wonderland 1970, Blume in Love 1972, Harry & Tonto 1973, Next Stop, Greenwich Village 1976, An Unmarried Woman 1977–78, Willie & Phil 1979–80, Tempest 1982, Moscow on the Hudson 1984; as writer, producer and Dir, Down and Out in Beverly Hills 1986, Moon Over Parador 1988, Enemies A Love Story, Scenes From a Mall, The Pickle 1992, Faithful 1995, Winchell 1998; as actor films include: A Star is Born, Scenes from the Class Struggle in Beverly Hills, Man Trouble, Deathwatch, Miami Rhapsody, Two Days in the Valley, Touch, Coast to Coast (actor/dir) 2003. *Television:* Once and Again, The Sopranos. *Publications:* Show Me the Magic (autobiog.). *Address:* c/o Ken Kamins, 8942 Wilshire Boulevard, Beverly Hills, CA 92011, USA.

MAZZARELLA, David; American newspaper editor; b. 1938; with Assoc. Press, Lisbon, New York, Rome 1962–70; with Daily American, Rome 1971–75, Gannett News, Washington, DC 1976–77, The Bridgewater, Bridgewater, NJ 1977–83; Ed., Sr Vice-Pres. USA Today –1999; Ombudsman Stars and Stripes newspaper 2000–01, Ed. Dir 2001–. *Address:* Stars and Stripes, 529 14th Street N.W., Suite 350, Washington DC 20450, USA. *Telephone:* (202) 761-0900. *Fax:* (202) 761-089. *Website:* www.stripes.com.

MAZZONI DELLA STELLA, Vittorio; Italian banker; b. 21 May 1941, Siena; ed Univ. of Florence; joined Monte dei Paschi di Siena bank, Naples 1966, worked in Rome, then Siena brs, then in Market and Econ. Research Dept, apptd Man. 1976, mem. Bd of Dirs 1990, Deputy Chair. 1991–, Deputy Chair. Monte dei Paschi Banque, Paris 1991; mem. Bd of Dirs Sindibank, Barcelona 1991; Chair. ICLE (MPS banking group), Rome 1991; mem. Bd of Dirs Centro Finanziaria SpA, Rome 1987–; mem. Bd of Dirs and Exec. Cttee Deposit Protection Fund, Rome 1991–; mem. Bd Asscn of Italian Bankers (ABI) 1991–; elected Prov. Councillor, Siena 1980, Deputy Chair. Prov. Council 1980–82, Mayor 1983–90; Chair. Chigiana Foundation (music acad.), Siena 1991–. *Address:* Monte dei Paschi di Siena, Siena, Italy.

MBA-ABESSOLE, Paul, PhD, DTheol; Gabonese ecclesiastic and teacher; b. 9 Oct. 1939, Ngnung-Ako, Kango; ed Univ. de Paris, Inst. Catholique de Paris; teacher of French 1964–65; religious instructor 1965–73; curate 1973–76; political refugee in France 1983–89; typesetter 1984, 1986–87; returned to Gabon 1989; Founder and Leader Morena-bûcheron 1990, renamed Rassemblement nat. des bûcherons 1991, then Rassemblement pour le Gabon 2000; Presidential cand. 1993, 1998; Mayor of Libreville 1996–; Pres. of World Conf. of Mayors 1999; Minister of State for Human Rights and Missions 2002–. *Leisure interest:* reading. *Address:* P.O. Box 44, Libreville, Gabon (Office). *Telephone:* 76-31-22 (Office); 74-76-04 (Home). *Fax:* 74-58-51 (Office).

MBASOGO, Lt-Col Teodoro Obiang Nguema; Equatorial Guinean politician and army officer; ed in Spain; fmr Deputy Minister of Defence; overthrew fmr Pres. Macias Nguema in coup; Pres. of Equatorial Guinea Aug. 1979–; Supreme Commdr of the Armed Forces 1979–; Minister of Defence 1986. *Address:* Oficina del Presidente, Malabo, Equatorial Guinea.

M'BAYE, Kéba; Senegalese judge; b. 5 Aug. 1924, Kaolack; s. of Abdoul M'baye and Coura M'bengue; m. Mariette Diarra 1951; three s. five d.; ed Ecole Nat. de la France d'Outre-mer; Judge of Appeal, Supreme Court of Senegal, First Pres. 1964; fmr Chair. Int. Comm. of Jurists, Chair. Comm. on Codification of Law of Civil and Commercial Liabilities; Vice-Chair. Exec. Cttee, Int. Inst. of Human Rights (René Cassin Foundation); mem. Supreme Council of Magistrature, Int. Penal Law Asscn (and Admin. Council), Int. Criminology Asscn, Société de Législation comparée, Int. Olympic Cttee (mem. Exec. Bd); Judge, Int. Court of Justice, The Hague 1982–91 (Vice-Pres. 1987–91); fmr mem. various UN bodies, fmr mem. or Chair. Comm. on Human Rights and other such cttees. and in various symposia organized by Int. Asscn of Legal Sciences, Red Cross, Unidroit and UNESCO; fmr Pres. and mem. Int. Cttee on Comparative Law, Int. African Law Asscn, Int. Cttee for Social Science Documentation; Hon. Pres. World Fed. of UN Asscns. *Publications:* numerous Publs on Senegalese law, the law of Black Africa and human rights. *Leisure interest:* golf. *Address:* Rue "G" angle rue Léon Gontran Damas, B.P. 5865, Dakar, Senegal. *Telephone:* (221) 25-55-01.

MBEKI, Thabo Mvuyelwa, MA; South African politician; b. 18 June 1942, Idutywa; s. of the late Govan Mbeki and of Epainette Mbeki; m. Zanele Dlamini 1974; ed Lovedale, Alice, St John's Umtata, Univ. of London and Sussex Univ.; Leader African Students Org. 1961; Youth Organizer for African Nat. Congress (ANC), Johannesburg 1961–62; 6 weeks detention, Byo 1962; left SA 1962; official, ANC offices, London, England 1967–70; mil. training, USSR 1970; Asst Sec. ANC Revolutionary Council 1971–72; Acting ANC Rep., Swaziland 1975–76; ANC Rep., Nigeria 1976–78; mem. ANC, N.E.C. 1975, re-elected 1985; Dir Information and Publicity, ANC 1984–89, Head, Dept of Int. Affairs 1989–93, Chair. ANC 1993; First Deputy Pres. of SA 1994–99; Pres. of South Africa 1999–; mem. Nat. Exec. Cttee, Del. on Talks about Talks, with SA Govt 1990; mem. Bd IOC 1993–; Pres. African Union 2002–; Hon. KCMG. *Address:* Office of the President, Private Bag X1000, Pretoria 0001, South Africa (Office). *Telephone:* (12) 3191500 (Office). *Fax:* (12) 3238246 (Office). *E-mail:* president@po.gov.za (Office). *Website:* www.gov.za/president (Office).

M'BOW, Amadou-Mahtar, LèsL; Senegalese educationist; b. 20 March 1921, Dakar; m. Raymonde Sylvain 1951; one s. two d.; ed Faculté des Lettres, Univ. de Paris; Prof., Coll. de Rosso, Mauritania 1951–53; Dir Service of Fundamental Educ. 1953–57; Minister of Educ. and Culture 1957–58; Prof. Lycée Faidherbe, St Louis 1958–64; Ecole Normale Supérieure, Dakar 1964–66; Minister of Educ. 1966–68; Minister of Culture, Youth and Sports 1968–70; Asst Dir-Gen. for Educ., UNESCO 1970–74; Dir-Gen. UNESCO 1974–87; Hon. Prof., Faculty of Humanities, Ind. Univ. of Santo Domingo (Dominican Repub.), Ecole Normale Supérieure, Dakar 1979, Nat. Independent Univ. of Mexico 1979, Escuela Superior de Administración y Dirección de Empresas, Barcelona 1984; mem. Acad. du Royaume du Maroc; Assoc. mem. Acad. of Athens; 46 hon. doctorates, 35 decorations, freedom of 11 cities (1987) including Dr. hc (Univ. of the Andes, State Univ. of Mongolia, State Univ. of Haiti, Khartoum, Sri Lanka, Tribhuvan Univ. Nepal, Pontifical Catholic Univ. of Peru, Buenos Aires, Granada, Sherbrooke, W Indies, Open Univ. UK, Belfast, Sofia, Nairobi, Philippines, Malaya, Venice, Uppsala, Moscow, Paris); Grand Cross of the Order of the Liberator (Venezuela), Grand Cross of the Order of the Sun (Peru), Commdr and Grand Officier Ordre National (Ivory Coast), Commdr des Palmes académiques (France), Officier, Ordre du Mérite (Senegal), Commdr de l'Ordre national de Haute Volta, Bintang Jasa Utama (Order of Merit, Indonesia), Kawkab Star (Jordan), Order of Merit (Syria) and numerous other decorations; Prix "Terre des Hommes", Canada. *Publications:* numerous monographs, articles in educational journals, textbooks, etc. *Address:* B.P. 5276, Dakar-Fann, Senegal; B.P. 434, Rabat, Morocco.

MBOWENI, Tito, MA; South African politician and banker; b. 16 March 1959, Tzaneem, Nothern Prov.; ed Nat. Univ. of Lesotho and Univ. of E Anglia; mem. ANC 1980 (ANC, Zambia 1988), fmr Deputy Head Dept of Econ. Planning, Co-ordinator for Trade and Industry; Minister of Labour, Govt of Nat. Unity 1994–99; Gov. SA Reserve Bank 1999–; Hon. Prof. of Econs Univ. of S Africa 2002–03; Hon. DComm (Univ. of Natal) 2001. *Leisure interests:* fly-fishing, soccer. *Address:* South African Reserve Bank, 370 Church Street, PO Box 427, Pretoria 0001, South Africa (Office). *Telephone:* (12) 3133911, 3133052 (Office). *Fax:* (12) 3134181 (Office). *E-mail:* maxine.hlaba@resbank.co.za (Office). *Website:* www.resbank.co.za (Office).

MDLALOSE, Frank Themba, BSc, UED, MB, CH.B.; South African politician and diplomatist; b. 29 Nov. 1931, Nqutu Dist KwaZulu; s. of Jaconiah Zwelabo Mdlalose and Thabitha Mthembu; m. Eunice Nokuthula 1956; three s. two d.; ed Univ. of Fort Hare, Rhodes Univ. and Univ. of Natal; Intern, King Edward VII Hosp. Durban 1959; pvt. medical practice, Pretoria 1960–62, Steadville, Ladysmith, Natal, Atteridgeville 1962–70; medical practitioner, Madadeni 1970–78; Nat. Chair. Inkatha 1977; Minister of Health, KwaZulu 1983–90,

Acting Minister of Educ. 1990, Minister without Portfolio 1991–94; Premier, KwaZulu-Natal 1994; Amb. to Egypt –2002. *Address:* PO Box 14110, Madadeni 2951, South Africa.

MEACHER, Rt Hon Michael Hugh, PC, MP; British politician; b. 4 Nov. 1939, Hemel Hempstead, Herts.; s. of late George H. and Doris M. (née Foxell) Meacher; m. 1st Molly C. (née Reid) 1962 (divorced 1985); two s. two d.; m. 2nd Lucianne Craven 1988; ed Berkhamsted School, New Coll., Oxford and London School of Econs; Lecturer in Social Admin., Univ. of York and LSE 1966–70; MP for Oldham West 1970–97, for Oldham West and Royton 1997–; Jr Minister, Dept of Industry 1974–75, Dept of Health and Social Security 1975–76, Dept of Trade 1976–79; mem. Nat. Exec. Cttee of Labour Party 1983–88, Shadow Cabinet 1983–97, Shadow Spokesman for Health and Social Security 1983–87, for Employment 1987–89, for Social Security 1989–92, for Overseas Devt 1992–93, for Citizens' Rights 1993–94, for Transport 1994–95, for Employment 1995–96, for Environmental Protection 1996–97; Minister of State for the Environment May 1997–; mem. Treasury Select Cttee 1980–83; cand. for deputy leadership of Labour Party 1983; mem. Child Poverty Action Group and other voluntary orgs. *Publications:* Taken for a Ride: Special Residential Homes for the Elderly Mentally Infirm: A Study of Separatism in Social Policy 1972, Socialism with a Human Face 1982, Diffusing Power 1992; over 1,000 articles on econ., industrial and social policy, regional devt, defence issues, the Welfare State, media reform, civil service reform, the police, etc. *Leisure interests:* sport, music, reading. *Address:* House of Commons, Westminster, London, SW1A 0AA (Office); 34 Kingscliffe Gardens, London, SW19, England (Home).

MEADOWS, Bernard William; British sculptor; b. 19 Feb. 1915, Norwich; s. of W. A. F. Meadows and E. M. Meadows; m. Marjorie Winifred Payne 1939; two d.; ed City of Norwich School, Norwich School of Art and Royal Coll. of Art; exhibited Venice Biennale 1952, 1964, British Council exhbns, N. and S. America, Germany, Canada, New Zealand, Australia, Scandinavia, Finland and France; open-air exhbns of Sculpture, Battersea Park, London 1952, 1960, 1963, 1966, Paris 1956, Holland Park 1957, Antwerp 1953, 1959, Arnhem 1958, British Pavilion, Brussels 1958, São Paulo Bienal 1958, Carnegie Inst., Pittsburgh 1959–61; one-man exhbns London and New York 1957–; works in Tate Gallery, Victoria and Albert Museum and collections in Europe, America and Australia; mem. Royal Fine Art Comm. 1971–76; Prof. of Sculpture, Royal Coll. of Art, London 1960–80. *Publication:* 34 etchings and box (for Molloy by Samuel Beckett) 1967. *Address:* 34 Belsize Grove, London, NW3 4TR, England. *Telephone:* (20) 7722-0772.

MÉBIAME, Léon; Gabonese politician; b. 1 Sept. 1934, Libreville; ed Coll. Moderne, Libreville, Centre de Préparation aux Carrières Administratives, Brazzaville, Ecole Fédérale de Police, Ecole Nat. de Police, Lyon, France; posted to Chad 1957–59; Police Supt 1960; further studies at Sûreté Nat. Française, Paris; Deputy Dir Sûreté Nat., Gabon 1962–63, Dir 1963–67; successively Under-Sec. of State for the Interior, Minister Del. for the Interior and Minister of State in charge of Labour, Social Affairs and the Nat. Org. of Gabonese Women 1967; Vice-Pres. of the Govt, Keeper of the Seals and Minister of Justice Jan.–July 1968; Vice-Pres. of the Govt in charge of Co-ordination 1968–75, Pres. Nat. Consultative Council 1972; Prime Minister 1975–90; Minister of Co-ordination, Housing and Town Planning 1975–76, of Land Registry 1976–78, of Co-ordination, Agric., Rural Devt, Waters and Forests 1978–79, in Charge of State Corpns. 1980–82, for Merchant Marine and Civil Service 1982–83, of Transport and Civil and Commercial Aviation 1989–90; Presidential Cand. Dec. 1993; Commdr Etoile Equatoriale; Grand Officier, Order nat. de Côte d'Ivoire, du Mérite Centrafricain; Chevalier, Etoile Noire du Bénin. *Address:* c/o Office du Premier Ministre, B.P. 546, Libreville, Gabon.

MECHANIC, David, MA, PhD; American professor of behavioural sciences; b. 21 Feb. 1936, New York; s. of Louis Mechanic and Tillie (Penn) Mechanic; m. Kate Mechanic; two s.; ed City Coll. of NY and Stanford Univ.; mem. Faculty, Univ. of Wis. 1960–79, Prof. of Sociology 1965–73, John Bascom Prof. 1973–79, Dir Center for Medical Sociology and Health Services Research 1971–79, Chair. Dept of Sociology 1968–70; Prof. of Social Work and Sociology, Rutgers Univ. 1979–, Univ. Prof. and Dean Faculty of Arts and Sciences 1981–84, Univ. Prof. and Rene Dubos Prof. of Behavioral Sciences 1984–, Dir Inst. for Health, Health Care Policy and Aging Research 1985–; mem. various advisory panels etc.; mem. NAS; mem. Inst. of Medicine of NAS, American Acad. of Arts and Sciences; Guggenheim Fellowship 1977–78; numerous awards. *Publications:* author of twelve books and about 400 papers and chapters and ed. of eleven books on sociological and health care subjects. *Address:* Institute for Health, Health Care Policy and Aging Research, Rutgers University, 30 College Avenue, New Brunswick, NJ 08901, USA (Office). *Telephone:* (732) 932-8415. *Fax:* (732) 932-1253. *E-mail:* mechanic@rci.rutgers.edu (Office). *Website:* www.ihhcpar.rutgers.edu (Office).

MECHANIC, William M. (Bill), PhD; American business executive; b. Detroit, Mich.; ed Michigan State Univ., Univ. of Southern California; Dir of Programming SelecTV 1978–80, Vice-Pres. Programming 1980–82; Vice-Pres. Pay TV, Paramount Pictures Corpn 1982–84; Vice-Pres. Pay TV Sales, Walt Disney Pictures and TV 1984–85, Sr Vice-Pres. Video 1985–87, Pres. Int. Theatrical Distribution and Worldwide Video 1987–93; Pres. and COO 20th Century Fox Film Entertainment 1993–96, Chair. and CEO 1996–; Pres. Fox Inc., Beverly Hills, Calif. *Address:* Fox Inc., 10201 W. Pico Boulevard, Los Angeles, CA 90035, USA (Office). *Telephone:* (310) 369-1000 (Office).

MEČIAR, Vladimír, DrIur; Slovak politician; b. 26 July 1942, Zvolen; s. of Jozef Mečiar and Anna (née Tomková) Mečiarová; m. Margita Mečiarová (née Bencková); two s. two d.; ed Komenský Univ., Bratislava; clerk 1959–69; various posts in Czechoslovak Union of Youth 1967–68; expelled from all posts and CP; employed as manual worker because of his attitude to Soviet occupation of CSSR, Heavy Eng Works, Dubnica nad Váhom 1970–73; clerk, later commercial lawyer for Skloobal Nemšová 1973–90; politically active again after collapse of communist system 1989; Minister of Interior and Environment, Govt of Slovak (Fed.) Repub. 1990, Deputy to House of Nations, Fed. Ass. 1990–92; Chair. Movt for Democratic Slovakia (HZDS) 1991–; Premier, Govt of Slovak Repub. 1990–91, 1992, of Slovakia 1993–98; Opposition MP 2002–; Dr. hc (Lomonosov Univ., Moscow) 1995, (Brača Karič Univ., Yugoslavia) 1996; Order of Maltese Cross 1995, Peutinger Award (Germany) 1995. *Publications:* Slovakia, Be Self-Confident!, Slovak Taboo. *Leisure interests:* sport, music, literature, hiking. *Address:* Movement for Democratic Slovakia, Tomášikova 32/a, Bratislava, Slovakia. *Telephone:* (2) 43331769. *Fax:* (2) 43424213 (Office). *E-mail:* predseda@hzds.sk (Office). *Website:* www.hzds.sk (Office).

MECKSEPER, Friedrich; German painter and printmaker; b. 8 June 1936, Bremen; s. of Gustav Meckseper and Lily Ringel-Debatin; m. Barbara Müller 1962; one s. two d.; ed State Art Acad., Stuttgart, State Univ. for the Visual Arts, Berlin; numerous one-man and group exhbns in Europe, USA, Australia and Japan; represented in many major museums of contemporary art and at print biennials world-wide; Prof. of Art, Int. Summer Acad., Salzburg 1977–79; Guest lecturer, London 1968; German-Rome Prize 1963, Prize of the 7th Biennale, Tokyo 1970, of the 6th Biennale, Fredrikstad 1982, of the 1st Kochi Int. Print Triennial, Japan 1990. *Publications:* Friedrich Meckseper, Etchings 1956–1994; catalogue raisonné of the graphic work 1994. *Leisure interests:* locomotives, steamboats, ballooning, paintings, etchings, books. *Address:* Landhausstrasse 13, 10717 Berlin, Germany.

MEDAK, Peter; British film director; b. 23 Dec. 1940, Budapest, Hungary; m. Julia Migenes 1989; two s. four d.; worked with AB-Pathe, London 1956–63; Dir Universal Pictures 1963–, Paramount Pictures 1967–; has directed several operas, plays and series for U.S. TV. *Films directed include:* Negatives 1968, A Day in the Death of Joe Egg 1970, The Ruling Class 1973, Third Girl From the Left 1973, Ghost in the Noonday Sun 1975, The Odd Job 1978, The Changeling 1979, Zorro, Zorro, The Gay Blade 1981, Breaking Through 1984, The Men's Club, The Krays 1990, The Love You Make 1991, Let Him Have It 1991, Romeo is Bleeding 1994, Pontiac Moon 1994, Hunchback of Notre Dame 1996, Species 2 1997, David Copperfield 1998, Feast of All Saints 2000. *Address:* Armstrong and Hirsch, 1885 Century Park East, Suite 1888, Century City, CA 90067 (Office); Scott J. Feinstein, 16255 Ventura Boulevard, Suite 625, Encino, CA 91436, USA.

MEDGYESSY, Péter, PhD; Hungarian politician and economist; b. 1942, Budapest; ed Univ. of Budapest; held several positions in Ministry of Finance, Dept of Finance, Dept of Prices, Dept of Int. Finances; fmr Dir-Gen. Dept of State Budget; Minister of Finance 1987–88; Deputy Prime Minister in interim Govt of Miklós Németh (q.v.) 1988–89; Pres., Chief Exec. Magyar Paribas 1990–94; Pres., Chief Exec. Hungarian Bank for Investment and Devt Ltd 1994–96; Minister of Finance 1996–98; Pres. Inter-Europa Bank 1998–; Prime Minister of Hungary 2002–; Prof. Coll. of Finance and Accounting, Budapest; Pres. Hungarian Econ. Soc.; Dir Int. Inst. of Public Finance, Saarbrücken; mem. Presidium Hungarian Bank Asscn 1996–, Council of World Econ. Forum; Chevalier Légion d'honneur, Medium Cross with Star, Order of Hungarian Repub. 2000. *Publications:* several articles on budgetary and exchange rate policies and monetary system in financial and econ. Publs. *Address:* Office of the Prime Minister, Kossuth Lajos tér 1–3, 1055 Budapest; Inter-Europa Bank, 1054 Budapest, Szabadság tér 15, Hungary. *Telephone:* (1) 441-4000; (1) 373-6208 (Office). *Fax:* (1) 268–3050; (1) 373-6230 (Office). *Website:* www.kancellaria.gov.hu.

MEDICI, Giuseppe; Italian politician and agricultural economist; b. 24 Oct. 1907; ed Univs. of Milan and Bologna; Prof. of Agricultural Econs, Univ. of Perugia 1935, of Turin 1936–47; Pres. Istituto Nazionale di Economia Agraria, Rome 1947–62; mem. Italian dels. to ECA international confs.; Pres. Ente Maremma (Land Reform Agency) 1951–53; Prof. Univ. of Naples 1952, Univ. of Rome 1960; mem. of the Senate (Christian Democrat); Minister of Agric. 1954–55, of the Treasury 1956–58, of the Budget 1958–59, of Educ. 1959–60; Minister without Portfolio (with responsibilities for Admin. Reform) 1962–63, Minister of the Budget June–Nov. 1963, Minister of Industry and Commerce 1963–65; Minister of Foreign Affairs June–Dec. 1968, 1972–73; Chair. Montedison 1977; Gov. EIB 1958; Pres. Senate Comm. for Foreign Affairs 1960–62; Pres. World Food Conf., Rome 1974. *Publications include:* Principii di Estimo 1948 (abridged edn in English Principles of Appraisal 1953), Italy: Agricultural Aspects 1949, I Tipi d'Impresa dell' Agricoltura 1951, Agricoltura e Disoccupazione Vol. I 1952, Land Property and Land Tenure in Italy 1952, Lezioni di Politica Economica 1967.

MEDINA ESTÉVEZ, HE Cardinal Jorge Arturo; Chilean ecclesiastic; b. 23 Dec. 1926, Santiago de Chile; ordained priest 1954; Bishop 1985, of Rancagua 1987, of Valparaíso 1993; Archbishop Emer., See of Valparaíso and Pro-Prefect Congregation for Divine Worship and the Discipline of the Sacraments 1996–2002; cr. Cardinal Feb. 1998. *Address:* c/o Congregation for Divine Worship and the Discipline of the Sacraments, Piazza Pio XII 10, 00193 Rome, Italy.

MEDVEDEV, Armen Nikolayevich, CAND. OF ARTS; Russian journalist and civil servant; b. 28 May 1938, Moscow; m.; one d.; ed ed. All-Union Inst. of Cinematography; mem. of staff Bureau of Propaganda of Soviet Cinema, USSR (now Russian) State Cttee on Cinematography 1959–, mem. Bd of Dirs 1984–87, First Deputy Chair. 1987–89, Chair. 1992–; Ed.-in-Chief Soviet Film (magazine) 1966–72; Deputy Ed.-in-Chief Iskusstvo Kino (magazine) 1972–75, 1976–82, Ed.-in-Chief 1982–84; Ed.-in-Chief All-Union Co. Soyuzinformkino 1975–76; Head Dept of Culture and Public Educ., USSR Council of Ministers 1989–91; fmr consultant Govt of USSR 1991; Pres. R. Bykov Int. Fund of Devt of Cinema and TV for Children and Youth 1999–; Order for Service to Motherland. *Address:* Koshtoyanz str. 6, Apt. 225, 117454 Moscow, Russia. *Telephone:* (095) 133-12-19.

MEDVEDEV, Nikolai Pavlovich; Russian politician; b. 26 Nov. 1952, Anayevo, Mordovia; m.; one s. one d.; ed Mordovian State Pedagogical Inst., Higher Comsomol School, Central Comsomol Cttee; with Saransk Professional Tech. School; worked in Comsomol orgs. 1975–83; instructor, Saransk City CP Cttee, Sec. CP Cttee Saransk Machine-construction Factory 1983–90; Deputy Chair. Saransk City Soviet 1990–; RSFSR Peoples' Deputy; mem. Presidium, Supreme Soviet; mem. Comm. on Int. Relations at Soviet of Nationalities 1990–93; Head of Dept, Admin. of Russian Presidency 1993–94; Dir Inst. of Regional Policy 1995–97; Deputy Minister on Co-operation with CIS countries 1994–95; mem. State Duma (Yabloko group) 1996–99; Dir Moscow Inst. of Regional Policy 2000–. *Publications:* several books including Establishment of Federalism in Russia, National Policy in Russia: From Unitarism to Federalism, International Conflicts and Political Stability. *Address:* Moscow Institute of Regional Policy, Moscow, Russia.

MEDVEDEV, Roy Aleksandrovich, PhD; Russian historian and sociologist; b. 14 Nov. 1925, Tbilisi; s. of Aleksandr Romanovich Medvedev and Yulia Medvedeva; twin brother of Zhores Medvedev (q.v.); m. Galina A. Gaidina 1956; one s.; ed Leningrad State Univ., Acad. of Pedagogical Sciences of USSR; mem. CPSU –1969, 1989–91; worker at mil. factory 1943–46; teacher of history, Ural Secondary School 1951–53; Dir of Secondary School in Leningrad region 1954–56; Deputy to Ed.-in-Chief of Publishing House of Pedagogical Literature, Moscow 1957–59; Head of Dept, Research Inst. of Vocational Educ., Acad. of Pedagogical Sciences of USSR 1960–70, Senior Scientist 1970–71; freelance author 1972–; People's Deputy of USSR, mem. Supreme Soviet of USSR 1989–91; mem. Cen. Cttee CPSU 1990–91; Co-Chair. Socialist Party of Labour 1991–. *Publications:* Vocational Education in Secondary School 1960, Faut-il réhabiliter Staline? 1969, A Question of Madness (with Zhores Medvedev) 1971, Let History Judge 1972, On Socialist Democracy 1975, Qui a écrit le "Don Paisible"? 1975, La Révolution d'octobre était-elle inéluctable? 1975, Solschenizyn und die Sowjetische Linke 1976, Khrushchev–The Years in Power (with Zhores Medvedev) 1976, Political Essays 1976, Problems in the Literary Biography of Mikhail Sholokhov 1977, Samizdat Register 1978, Philip Mironov and the Russian Civil War (with S. Starikov) 1978, The October Revolution 1979, On Stalin and Stalinism 1979, On Soviet Dissent 1980, Nikolai Bukharin–The Last Years 1980, Leninism and Western Socialism 1981, An End to Silence 1982, Khrushchev 1983, All Stalin's Men 1984, China and Superpowers 1986, L'URSS che cambia (with G. Chiesa) 1987, Time of Change (with G. Chiesa) 1990, Brezhnev: A Political Biography 1991, Gensek s Lybianki: A Political Portrait of Andropov 1993, 1917. The Russian Revolution 1997, Capitalism in Russia? 1998, The Unknown Andropov 1998, Post-Soviet Russia 2000, The Unknown Stalin (with Zhores Medvedev) 2001, Putin 2002; and over 400 professional and general articles. *Leisure interest:* allotment gardening. *Address:* c/o Z. A. Medvedev, 4 Osborn Gardens, London, NW7 1DY, England; Abonnement Post Box 258, 125475 Moscow A-475, Russia. *Telephone:* (095) 451-12-84 (Home). *Fax:* (095) 455-83-77 (Home).

MEDVEDEV, Zhores Aleksandrovich, PhD; British/Russian biologist; b. 14 Nov. 1925, Tbilisi, USSR; s. of Aleksandr Romanovich Medvedev and Yulia Medvedeva; twin brother of Roy Medvedev (q.v.); m. Margarita Nikolayevna Buzina 1951; two s.; ed Timiriazev Acad. of Agricultural Sciences, Moscow, Inst. of Plant Physiology, USSR Acad. of Sciences; joined Soviet Army 1943, served at front as a pvt.; Scientist, later Sr Scientist, Dept of Agrochemistry and Biochemistry, Timiriazev Acad. 1951–62; Head of Lab., Molecular Radiobiology, Inst. of Medical Radiology, Obninsk 1963–69; Sr Scientist All-Union Scientific Research Inst. of Physiology and Biochemistry of Farm Animals, Borovsk 1970–72; Sr Scientist, Nat. Inst. for Medical Research, London 1973–92; mem. New York Acad. of Sciences, American Gerontological Soc., Biochemical Soc., Genetic Soc.; Soviet citizenship restored 1990; Book award of the Moscow Naturalist Soc. 1965, Aging Research Award of US Aging Asscn 1984, René Schubert Preis in Gerontology 1985. *Publications:* Protein Biosynthesis and Problems of Heredity, Development and Ageing 1963, Molecular-Genetic Mechanisms of Development 1968, The Rise and Fall of T. D. Lysenko 1969, The Medvedev Papers 1970, A Question of Madness (with Roy Medvedev) 1971, Ten Years After 1973, Khrushchev–The Years in Power (with Roy Medvedev) 1976, Soviet Science 1978, The Nuclear Disaster in the Urals 1979, Andropov 1983, Gorbachev 1986, Soviet Agriculture 1987, The Legacy of Chernobyl 1990, The Unknown Stalin (with Roy Medvedev) 2001; Stalin and the Jewish Problem 2003; and over 400 papers and articles on gerontology, genetics, biochemistry, environment, history and other topics. *Leisure interests:* social research and writing, gardening. *Address:* 4 Osborn Gardens, London, NW7 1DY, England. *Telephone:* (20) 8346-4158.

MEEK, Paul Derald, BS; American business executive; b. 15 Aug. 1930, McAllen, Tex.; s. of William Van Meek and Martha Mary (née Sharp) Meek; m. Betty Catherine Robertson 1954; four d.; ed Univ. of Texas, Austin; with Tech. Dept Humble Oil & Refining Co., Baytown, Tex. 1953–55; Cosden Oil & Chem. Co. 1955–76, Pres. 1968–76; Dir American Petrofina Inc. (now FINA), Dallas 1968–, Vice-Pres., COO 1976–83, Pres., CEO 1983–86, Chair. Bd, Pres., CEO 1984–86, Chair. Bd 1986–98; mem. Advisory Council Coll. Eng Foundation, Univ. of Texas 1979–; Co-Chair. Industrial Div. United Way of Metropolitan Dallas 1981–82; Chair. Public Utilities Comm. of Tex. 1989–92; Trustee Southwest Research Inst.; mem. American Petroleum Inst., Dallas Wildcat Comm. (Chair. 1987–88). *Publication:* (contrib.) Advances in Petroleum Chemistry and Refining 1957. *Address:* c/o FINA Inc., P.O. Box 2159, 8350 N Central Expressway, Dallas, TX 75221, USA.

MEESE, Edwin III, LLB; American government official, lawyer and academic; b. 1931; s. of Edwin Meese Jr and Leone Meese; m. Ursula Meese; one s. one d.; ed Yale Univ. and Univ. of Calif. at Berkeley; taught law, Univ. of San Diego Law School, Dir Center for Criminal Justice Policy and Man.; Sr position under Gov. Reagan, State House, Sacramento, Calif.; Reagan's Campaign Chief of Staff, presidential elections 1980, Dir Transition Org. 1980–81; Counsellor to Pres. Reagan and Man. Nat. Security Council, Domestic Policy and Cabinet Staffs 1981–85; Attorney Gen. of USA 1985–88; Distinguished Fellow, Heritage Foundation, Washington 1988–; Distinguished Visiting Fellow, Hoover Inst., Stanford Univ., Calif. 1988–; Distinguished Sr Fellow, Inst. for United States Studies, Univ. of London 1996–; Harvard Univ. John F. Kennedy School of Govt Medal 1986. *Publication:* With Reagan: The Inside Story 1992. *Leisure interest:* collecting models of police patrol cars. *Address:* The Heritage Foundation, 214 Massachusetts Avenue, NE, Washington, DC 20002, USA. *Telephone:* (202) 546-4400. *Fax:* (202) 546-8328.

MEGARRY, Rt. Hon. Sir Robert (Edgar), Kt, MA, LLD, FBA; British judge (retd); b. 1 June 1910, Croydon, Surrey; s. of the late Robert Lindsay Megarry and Irene Clark; m. Iris Davies 1936 (died 2001); three d.; ed Lancing Coll., Trinity Hall, Cambridge; Solicitor 1935–41, certificate of honour and called to the Bar, Lincoln's Inn 1944, in practice 1946–67, QC 1956–67, Asst Reader in Equity in the Inns of Court 1946–51, Reader 1951–71, judge, Chancery Div. of High Court 1967–76, Vice-Chancellor 1976–82, Vice-Chancellor of the Supreme Court 1982–85; Prin., Ministry of Supply 1940–44, Asst Sec. 1944–46; Bencher, Lincoln's Inn 1962, Treas. 1981; Dir of Law Soc.'s Refresher Courses 1944–47; Book Review Ed. and Asst Ed., Law Quarterly Review 1944–67; Visiting Prof. New York Univ. School of Law 1960–61, Osgoode Hall Law School, Toronto 1964; Regents' Prof., U.C.L.A. 1983; mem. Gen. Council of the Bar 1948–52, Lord Chancellor's Law Reform Cttee 1952–73, Senate of the Inns of Court and the Bar 1966–70, 1980–82, Advisory Council on Public Records 1980–85; Chair. Notting Hill Housing Trust 1967–68, Friends of Lancing Chapel 1969–93, Inc. Council of Law Reporting 1972–87; Pres. Soc. of Public Teachers of Law 1965–66, Selden Soc. 1976–79, Lancing Club 1974–98; Hon. Life mem., Canadian Bar Asscn, American Law Inst.; the Visitor, Essex Univ. 1983–90, Clare Hall, Cambridge 1984–88; Hon. Fellow Trinity Hall, Cambridge 1973; Hon. LLD (Hull) 1963, (Nottingham) 1979, (Law Soc. of Upper Canada) 1982, (London) 1988; Hon. D.U. (Essex) 1991. *Publications:* The Rent Acts 1939, A Manual of the Law of Real Property 1946, Miscellany-at-Law 1955, The Law of Real Property (with Prof. H. W R. Wade) 1957, Lawyer and Litigant in England 1962, Arabinesque-at-Law 1969, A Second Miscellany-at-Law 1973. *Leisure interests:* heterogeneous. *Address:* Institute of Advanced Legal Studies, 17 Russell Square, London, WC1B 5DR (Office); 5 Stone Buildings, Lincoln's Inn, London, WC2A 3XT, England (Home). *Telephone:* (20) 7862-5800 (Russell Square) (Office); (20) 7242-8607 (Lincoln's Inn) (Home).

MEGAWATI SUKARNOPUTRI; Indonesian politician; b. 23 Jan. 1947, Jogjakarta; d. of the late Achmed Sukarno (fmr Pres. of Indonesia) and Fatmawati; m. 1st Surendro (deceased); m. 2nd Hassan Gamal Ahmad Hassan; m. 3rd Taufik Kiemas; three c.; mem. House of Reps. (Partai Demokrasi Indonesia–PDI) 1987; Leader PDI 1993–96 (deposed); Chair. Partai Demokrasi Indonesia Perjuangan (PDI-P) 1996–; Vice-Pres. of Indonesia 1999–2001, Pres. 2001–. *Address:* Office of the President, Istana Merdeka, Jakarta, Indonesia (Office); Partai Demokrasi Indonesia Perguangan (PDI-P), c/o Dewan Perwakilan Rakyat, Jalan Gatot Subroto 16, Jakarta. *Telephone:* (21) 3840946 (Office).

MEGRET, Bruno André Alexandre, MSc; French politician and engineer; b. 4 April 1949, Paris; s. of Jacques Megret and Colette Constantinides; m. Catherine Rascovsky 1992; two s.; ed Lycée Louis-le-Grand, Paris, Univ. of California at Berkeley, École Polytechnique; Head of Dept Nat. Devt Programme 1975–76; Dist Engineer, Eng Dept, Essonne Département 1977–79; Tech. Adviser Office of Minister for Overseas Service 1979–81; Deputy Dir Infrastructure and Transport Ile-de-France Region 1981–86; Deputy Front nat. d'Isère 1986–88, Vice-Pres. Front nat. parl. group 1987–98, expelled from Front nat. Dec. 1998; Founder and Leader Mouvement nationale républicaine (MNR) 1999–; MEP 1989–99; Regional Councillor Provence-Côte d'Azur 1992–, Special Adviser to Mayor of Vitrolles 1997; mem. and Hon. Pres. Comités d'action républicaine. *Publications:* Demain le chêne 1982, L'Impératif du renouveau 1986, La Flamme 1990, L'Alternative nationale 1996, La Troisième voie 1997, La Nouvelle Europe 1998, Le Chagrin et l'espérance 1999, Pour que vive la France 2000, La France à l'endroit 2001. *Address:* MNR, 15 rue Cronstadt, 75015 Paris, France (Office).

MÉHAIGNERIE, Pierre; French politician and engineer; b. 4 May 1939, Balazé, Ille et Vilaine; s. of Alexis and Pauline (Boursier) Méhaignerie; m. Julie Harding 1965; one s. one d.; ed Lycée Saint-Louis, Paris, Ecole nationale supérieure agronomique, Rennes, Ecole supérieure de sciences agronomiques appliquées, Paris; engineer, Génie Rural des Eaux et Forêts, Dept of Agric. 1965–67; technical counsellor, Ministry of Agric. 1969–71, Ministry of Cultural Affairs 1971–73; mem. Nat. Ass. for Ille-et-Vilaine 1973–76, 1981–86, 1988–93, 1995–; County Councillor for Vitré-Est 1976–2001, elected Mayor of Vitré April 1977–; Sec. of State to Minister of Agric. 1976–77; Minister of Agric. 1977–81, of Housing, Transport and Urban Affairs 1986–88, of Justice 1993–95; Pres. Finance Comm., Nat. Ass. 1995–97; Pres. Finance Comm. Nat. Ass. 2002–; mem. European Parl. 1979; Vice-Pres. Union pour la démocratie française 1988–2002; Pres. Conseil Gen. d'Ille et Vilaine 1982–2001, Pres. Centre des démocrates sociaux 1982–94; Commdr du Mérite agricole. *Publications:* Aux Français qui ne veulent plus être gouvernés de haut 1995. *Address:* 76 rue du Rachapt, 35500 Vitré, France (Home); Assemblée Nationale, 75355 Paris. *Telephone:* 1-40-63-66-12 (Office). *E-mail:* pmehaign@club-internet.fr (Office). *Website:* www .pierre-mehaignerie.org (Office).

MEHROTRA, Ram Charan, DPhil, DSc, PhD; Indian professor of chemistry; b. 16 Feb. 1922, Kanpur, Uttar Pradesh; s. of the late R. B. Mehrotra and Mrs. Chameli Mehrotra; m. Suman Mehrotra 1944; one s. two d.; ed Allahabad Univ., London Univ.; lecturer Allahabad Univ. 1944–54; Reader Lucknow Univ. 1954–58; Prof. Gorakhpur Univ. 1958–62, Dean Faculty of Science 1959–62; Prof. Rajasthan Univ. 1962–82, Prof. Emer. 1982–, Dean Faculty of Science 1962–65, Vice-Chancellor 1968–69, 1972, 1973, Dir, Special Assistance Programme 1979; Vice-Chancellor Delhi Univ. 1974–79; Vice-Chancellor Allahabad Univ. 1991–; Pres. Chem. Section, Indian Science Congress 1967, Indian Chemical Soc. 1976–77, Indian Science Congress Asscn 1979, Vigyan Parishad, Allahabad 1979–83; Vice-Pres. Indian Nat. Science Acad. 1977–78; mem. Bd and Governing Body CSIR 1963–66, 1976–80, Chem. Advisory Cttee Atomic Energy Establishment 1963–67, Univ. Grants Review Cttee 1974–77, Inorganic Chem. Div., Int. Union of Pure and Applied Chem. 1977–81, Univ. Grants Comm. 1982–85, Comm. on Status of Teachers 1983–84; Inorg. Nomenclature Comm. 1981–; Fellow Nat. Acad. of Sciences, Allahabad, Royal Inst. of Chem., UK, Indian Nat. Science Acad., Indian Acad. of Sciences; DSc hc (Meerut Univ.); E G. Hill Memorial Prize, Allahabad Univ. 1949, Sir S. S. Bhatnagar Award 1965, Fed. of FICCI Award for Science and Tech. 1975, Seshadri Award of Indian Nat. Science Acad. 1976, P. C. Ray Memorial Award, Indian Chemical Soc. 1977, J. C. Ghosh Medal, Indian Chemical Soc. 1986, 1st Fed. of Asian Chemical Soc. Award 1987, Platinum Jubilee Award of the Indian Science Congress by the Prime Minister of India 1988, Atma Ram Award for popularization of Science (Silver Jubilee of Cen. Hindi Org.), N R. Dhar Memorial Award (Diamond Jubilee Nat. Acad. Sciences) 1991, G. P. Chatterjee Award of ISCA 1991 and numerous other awards and distinctions. *Publications:* (Jt) Bombay to Mumbai 1998; over 700 textbooks, research papers and three treatises in chemistry. *Leisure interests:* photography and writing popular articles on science and technology. *Address:* Allahabad University, Allahabad 211002, India. *Telephone:* 50668.

MEHTA, A. D. "Sonny"; publishing company executive; b. 1943, India; ed Univ. of Cambridge; fmrly with Pan and Picador Publs, UK; Pres. Alfred A. Knopf Div. of Random House, New York 1987–, now also Ed.-in-Chief; Pres., Ed.-in-Chief Knopf Publishing Group. *Address:* Alfred A. Knopf Inc., 299 Park Avenue, New York, NY 10171, USA.

MEHTA, Aman, B.ECON.; Indian banker; b. 1946, India; m.; two c.; ed Delhi Univ.; with Mercantile Bank Ltd 1967–69; joined Hongkong and Shanghai Banking Corpn Ltd (HSBC) 1969, roles in various Depts. including Operations, Credit, Br. and Area Man., Merchant Banking, Man. Corp. Planning 1985, Chair. and Chief Exec. HSBC USA Inc. 1993–95, Deputy Chair. HSBC Bank Middle East 1995–98, Gen. Man. Int. and later Exec. Dir Int. HSBC 1998, CEO 1999–; Chair. HSBC Bank Malaysia Berhad 1999–, Dir HSBC Bank Australia, HSBC Investment Bank Asia Holdings Ltd, HSBC Holdings BV Netherlands; Man. Dir The Saudi British Bank 1988–91, Group Gen. Man. 1991–92. *Address:* Hongkong and Shanghai Banking Corporation Limited, Level 34, HSBC Main Building, 1 Queen's Road Central, Hong Kong Special Administrative Region, People's Republic of China (Office). *Telephone:* 28221111 (Office). *Fax:* 28101112 (Office). *Website:* www.asiapacific .hsbc.com (Office).

MEHTA, Ved Parkash, M.A.; American writer and academic; b. 21 March 1934, Lahore, Pakistan; s. of Amolak Ram and Shanti Ram; m. Linn Cary 1983; two d.; ed Arkansas School for the Blind, Pomona Coll., Calif., Balliol Coll., Oxford, England, Harvard Univ.; staff writer New Yorker magazine 1961–94; Visiting Fellow Balliol Coll., Oxford 1988–89; Rosenkranz Chair in Writing, Yale Univ. 1990–93; Visiting Prof. of English and History, Vassar Coll., NY 1994–96; Sr Fellow, Columbia Univ. 1996–97; Fellow, Stanford Univ. 1997–98. *Publications:* Face to Face 1957, Walking the Indian Streets 1960, Fly and the Fly Bottle 1963, The New Theologian 1966, John Is Easy to Please 1970, Daddyji 1972, Delinquent Chacha (novel) 1976, Mahatma Gandhi and His Apostles 1977, Mamaji 1979, Vedi 1982, The Ledge Between the Streams 1984, Sound Shadows of the New World 1986, The Stolen Light 1989, Up at Oxford 1993, Remembering Mr Shawn's New Yorker 1998, All for Love 2001. *Address:* c/o Granta, 1755 Broadway, 5th Floor, New York, NY 10019, USA (Office). *Telephone:* (212) 246-1313 (Office). *Fax:* (212) 586-8003 (Office).

MEHTA, Zarin, FCA; Indian music administrator; b. 28 Oct. 1938, Bombay; s. of the late Mehli Mehta and of Tehmina Daruvala Mehta; brother of Zubin Mehta (q.v.) ; m. Carmen Lasky 1966; two c.; CA, London 1957, accountant Frederic B. Smart & Co., London 1957–62, Coopers & Lybrand, Montreal 1962–81; Dir Orchestre Symphonique de Montréal 1973–81, Man. Dir 1981–90; Exec. Dir and COO Ravinia Festival, Ill. 1990–99, CEO 1999–2000; Exec. Dir New York Philharmonic 2000–; mem. Ordre de Comptables Agréés du Québec. *Address:* New York Philharmonic, Administrative Offices, Avery Fisher Hall, 10 Lincoln Center Plaza, New York, NY 10023, USA (Office). *Telephone:* (212) 875-5000 (Office). *Website:* www.newyorkphilharmonic.org (Office).

MEHTA, Zubin; Indian conductor; b. 29 April 1936, Bombay; s. of the late Mehli Mehta and of Tehmina Daruvala Mehta; m. 1st Carmen Lasky 1958 (divorced); one s. one d.; m. 2nd Nancy Diane Kovack 1969; ed Vienna Acad. of Music, studied under Hans Swarowsky; first professional conducting in Belgium, Yugoslavia and UK (Liverpool); Music Dir Montreal Symphony 1961–67, Los Angeles Philharmonic Orchestra 1962–78; Music Dir New York Philharmonic Orchestra 1978–91; Music Dir Israel Philharmonic 1969–, appointed Dir for Life 1981; Dir Bavarian State Opera 1998–; conductor at festivals of Holland, Prague, Vienna, Salzburg and Spoleto; debut at La Scala, Milan 1969; conducts regularly with the Vienna and Berlin Orchestras; winner of Liverpool Int. Conductors' Competition 1958; Music Dir Maggio Musicale, Florence 1969, 1986–; Dr. hc Tel Aviv Univ., Weizmann Inst. of Science, The Hebrew Univ. of Jerusalem, Jewish Theological Seminary, Westminster Choir Coll., Princeton, Brooklyn Coll., Colgate Univ.; shared Wolf Prize 1996; Commendatore (Italy), Médaille d'Or Vermeil (City of Paris), Commdr des Arts et des Lettres (France), Great Silver Medal of Service (Austria) 1997, Padma Vibhushan (India) 2001. *Leisure interest:* cricket. *Address:* Israel Philharmonic Orchestra, 1 Huberman Street, Box 11292, 61112 Tel Aviv, Israel; Orchestra Maggio Musicale, Teatro Communale, Via Solferino 15, I-50123 Florence, Italy.

MEI BAOJIU; Chinese opera singer; b. Feb. 1934, Beijing; s. of Mei Lanfang; actor Mei Lanfang Peking Opera Company 1951–62, actor (1st Class) Beijing Peking Opera Troupe 1962–; played lead roles in plays of the Mei school of Peking opera. *Plays:* Phoenix Returning to Its Nest, The Imperial Concubine Getting Drunk, Xiang Yu Bidding Farewell to Yu Ji, Yuzhoufeng. *Address:* Beijing Peking Opera Troupe, Beijing, People's Republic of China (Office).

MEIER, Richard Alan, BArch; American architect; b. 12 Oct. 1934, Newark, NJ; s. of Jerome Meier and Carolyn (née Kaltenbacher) Meier; m. Katherine Gormley 1978 (divorced); one s. one d.; ed Cornell Univ.; with Frank Grad & Sons, NJ 1957, Davis, Brody & Wisniewski, New York 1958–59, Skidmore, Owings & Merrill 1959–60, Marcel Breuer & Assocs 1960–63; Prof. Architectural Design Cooper Union 1962–73; Prin. Architect, Richard Meier & Assocs, New York 1963–80, Richard Meier & Partners 1980–; Visiting Critic Pratt Inst. 1960–62, 1965, Princeton 1963, Syracuse Univ. 1964; Architect American Acad. in Rome 1973–74; Visiting Prof. of Architecture Yale Univ. 1975, 1977, Harvard 1977; Eliot Noyes Visiting Critic in Architecture 1980–81; mem. Advisory Council Cornell Univ.; mem. Jerusalem Comm.; Fellow American Acad. of Arts and Sciences; AIA Awards: 1968–71, 1974, 1976, 1977, 1983, 1984, 1989, 1993, 1998, 1999, Pritzker Architect Prize 1984, RIBA Gold Medal 1988, Progressive Architecture Gold Medal 1997, AIA Gold Medal 1997, Praemium Imperiale 1997; Commdr des Arts et Lettres (France) 1984. *Exhibitions:* XV Triennale, Italy 1973, Princeton Univ., Biennale Italy 1976, Cooper Union, Cooper Hewitt Museum, New York 1976–77, Leo Castelli Gallery, New York 1977, Museum of Modern Art, New York 1981, Jeu de Paume, Paris 1999, Architecture Inst., Rotterdam 2001. *Major works:* Smith House, Darien, Conn. 1967, Bronx Devt Center 1977, Renault Head., France 1981, High Museum of Art, Atlanta, Ga 1983, Museum für Kunsthandwerk, Germany 1984, Museum of Contemporary Art, Barcelona 1995, City Hall and Cen. Library, The Hague 1995, J. Paul Getty Center 1997 and others. *Publication:* Building the Getty. *Address:* Richard Meier & Partners, 475 10th Avenue, Floor 6, New York, NY 10018, USA.

MEINER, Richard; German publisher; b. 8 April 1918, Dresden; s. of Felix Meiner and Elisabeth Meiner (née Gensel); m. Ursula Ehlert 1947; one s. one d.; mil. service 1937–45; f. Richard Meiner Verlages, Hamburg 1948–64; Dir Verlage Felix Meiner 1964–81, Felix Meiner Verlag GmbH, Hamburg 1981–98; Mil. Medal; Gold Medal of Union of German Booksellers 1983; Medal of Honour of German Bücherei Leipzig 1987, Hon. Fellow German Soc. for Philosophy in Germany 1988, Bundesverdienstkreuz I. Klasse 1989. *Publications:* Verlegerische Betreuung der Philosophischen Bibliothek, Corpus Philosophorum Teutonicarum Medii Aevi, G.W.F. Hegel, Gesammelte Werke. Krit. Ausgabe, G.W.F. Hegel, Vorlesungen, Kant-Forschungen, Nicolai de Cusa Opera omnia. Krit. Ausgabe, Handbuch PRAGMATIK, Studien zum achtzehnten Jahrhundert und weitere philosophische Reihen und Einzelmonographien. *Leisure interests:* tennis, skiing. *Address:* c/o Felix Meiner Verlag GmbH, Richardstrasse 47, 22081 Hamburg, Germany.

MEINWALD, Jerrold, MA, PhD, FAAS; American professor of chemistry; b. 16 Jan. 1927, New York, NY; s. of Dr Herman Meinwald and Sophie Baskind; m. 1st Dr Yvonne Chu 1955 (divorced 1979); two d.; m. 2nd Dr Charlotte Greenspan 1980; one d.; ed Brooklyn and Queen's Colls, Univ. of Chicago and Harvard Univ.; Instructor in Chem. Cornell Univ. 1952–54, Asst Prof. 1954–58, Assoc. Prof. 1958–61, Prof. 1961–72, Acting Chair. of Chem. 1968; Prof. of Chem. Univ. of Calif., San Diego 1972–73; Prof. of Chem. Cornell Univ.

1973–80, Goldwin Smith Prof. of Chem. 1980–, Andrew Mellon Foundation Prof. 1993–95; Visiting Prof. Harvard Medical School 1997; Pres. Int. Soc. of Chemical Ecology 1988–89; Chemical Consultant, Schering-Plough Corpn 1957–2000, Procter & Gamble Pharmaceuticals 1958–96, Cambridge Neuroscience Research Inc. 1987–93; Consultant on Chemical Ecology, Max-Planck Soc. 1995–97; mem. of Visiting Cttee for Chem., Brookhaven Nat. Lab. 1969–73; numerous lectureships USA, Canada, UK, Australia, NZ, France, Czechoslovakia, Switzerland, Belgium, China, Taiwan, Brazil, Japan; mem. Medicinal Chem. Study Section "A" of Nat. Insts. of Health 1964–66, Chair. 1966–68; Editorial Bd of Organic Reactions 1967–78, Journal of Chemical Ecology 1974–, Insect Science and its Application 1979–91; Chair. Div. of Organic Chem., ACS 1968; Alfred P. Sloan Foundation Fellow 1958–62, Guggenheim Fellow 1960–61, 1976–77, Nat. Insts. of Health Special Postdoctoral Fellow 1967–68, Fogarty Int. Scholar 1983–84; Distinguished Scholar-in-Residence, Hope Coll., Holland, Mich. 1984; NAS Exchange Scholar to Czechoslovakia 1987; Fellow, Center for Advanced Study in the Behavioral Sciences (Stanford) 1990–91; Research Dir Int. Centre of Insect Physiology and Ecology, Nairobi 1970–77; Advisory Bd, Petroleum Research Fund 1970–73, Advisory Bd, Research Corpn 1978–83, Advisory Council Dept of Chem. Princeton Univ. 1978–82, Advisory Bd Chem. Section, NSF 1979–82, Scientific Advisory Bd, Native Plants Inc. 1987–93; Organizing Chair. Sino-American Symposium on the Chemistry of Natural Products, Shanghai 1980, UNESCO's Working Group on Co-operation in the Field of Natural Products Chem. 1982–87, Chem. Program Cttee, Alfred P. Sloan Foundation 1985–91; mem. Bd of Dirs. Xerces Soc. 1994–, Scientific Cttee Probem/Amazonia 1996–; mem. NAS, American Philosophical Soc.; Fellow, American Acad. of Arts and Sciences, Japan Soc. for the Promotion of Science; Hon. PhD (Göteborg) 1989; Edgar Fah Smith Award, ACS 1977, E. Guenther Award, ACS 1984, Distinguished Scientist-Lecturer Award, Kalamazoo Section of ACS 1985, A. C. Cope Scholar Award, ACS 1989, Tyler Prize in Environmental Science 1990, Gustavus John Esselen Award for Chem. in the Public Interest, ACS 1991, Silver Medal (Int. Soc. of Chemical Ecology) 1991, J. Heyrovsky Medal (Czech Acad. of Sciences) 1996. *Publications:* Advances in Alicyclic Chemistry Vol. I (co-author) 1966, Explorations in Chemical Ecology (co-ed.) 1987, Pheromone Biochemistry (co-author) 1987, Chemical Ecology: The Chemistry of Biotic Interaction (co-ed.) 1995; over 400 research articles in major chem. journals. *Leisure interests:* playing flute, baroque flute and recorder. *Address:* Department of Chemistry and Chemical Biology, Cornell University, Ithaca, NY 14853 (Office); 429 Warren Road, Ithaca, NY 14850, USA (Home). *Telephone:* (607) 255-3301 (Office); (607) 257-0035 (Home). *Fax:* (607) 255-3407 (Office). *E-mail:* circe@cornell.edu (Office). *Website:* www.chem.cornell.edu/department/faculty/meinwald/meinwald.html (Office).

MEIRELLES, Fernando; Brazilian film director; b. 11 Sept. 1955, São Paulo; ed Universidade de São Paulo; trained as architect; created experimental video productions at univ.; producer of TV programmes including Crig Rá, O Mundo no Ar, Ernesto Varella, TV Mix, Comédia da Vida Privada, Cidade dos Homens 1980s; Dir Rá-Tim-Bum (children's series, TV Cultura) 1989–90; co-Founder 02 Filmes Co. (largest commercial production co. in Brazil) 1990s; debut as feature film dir 1997; several awards for Rá-Tim-Bum including New York Film and TV Festival Gold Medal, Cannes Film Festival Lion and Clio Awards; over 20 other prizes. *Films include:* O Menino Maloquinho (Crazy Kid) 1997, A no Meio Passa um Trem (short film) 1998, Domesticas (Maids) 2000, Cidade de Deus (City of God) 2001, Palace II (short film) 2001. *Address:* c/o Levinefilm, Rua Antonina 207, Sumare, São Paulo, SP 01255-010, Brazil (Office).

MEIRELLES, Henrique de Campos, BCE, MBA; Brazilian central banker; ed Univ. of São Paulo, Fed. Univ. of Rio de Janeiro and Harvard Business School; Man. Dir BankBoston Leasing 1974, Vice-Pres., São Paulo 1978, Head Commercial Bank in Brazil 1980, Deputy Country Man. 1981, Pres. and Regional Man. in Brazil 1984, Pres. and COO BankBoston Corpn 1996, Pres. FleetBoston's Global and Wholesale Bank and mem. Bd Dirs, also Office of the Chair. FleetBoston Financial 1999–2002; Gov. Cen. Bank of Brazil 2002–; mem. Bd Dirs Raytheon Corpn, New York, New England Conservatory, Inst. of Contemporary Art, Accion Int.; mem. Advisory Council Sloan School of Man., MIT, Harvard Business School Initiative on Global Corp. Governance, Boston Coll. Carroll School of Man., Center for Latin American Issues of the George Washington Univ., Brazilian-American Chamber of Commerce, New York, Adolfo Ibañez Univ., Santiago, Chile; Founding Pres. Latin American Leasing Fed.; Chair. Emer. Brazilian Asscn of Int. Banks; Chair. Soc. for the Revitalization of the City of São Paulo, Travessia Foundation; mem. Exec. Cttee US Brazilian Business Council, American Chamber of Commerce, São Paulo. *Address:* Banco Central do Brasil, SBS, Q.03, Bloco B, CP 04-0170, 70074-900 Brasília, DF, Brazil (Office). *Telephone:* (61) 414-1000 (Office). *Fax:* (61) 223-1033 (Office). *Website:* www.bcb.gov.br (Office).

MEIRING, Gen. Georg Lodewyk, MSc; South African army officer; b. 18 Oct. 1939, Ladybrand; m. Anna Maria G. Brink; three s. two d.; ed Univ. of Orange Free State; Officer Commdg Witswatersrand Command, Johannesburg 1981–82; Chief of Army Staff, Logistics, SA Defence Force (SADF), Pretoria 1982–83; Gen. Officer Commdg SW Africa Territory Defence Forces, Windhoek 1987–89; Gen. Officer Commdg Far North, Pietersburg 1989–90; Deputy Chief, SA Army, SADF, Pretoria 1983–87, 1990–93, Chief 1993–94; Chief S. African Nat. Defence Force (SANDF) 1994–98; several mil. decorations. *Leisure interests:* hunting, gardening, reading, walking. *Address:* Private Bag X414, Pretoria 0001, South Africa.

MEISER, Richard Johannes, MD; German professor of internal medicine; b. 10 Aug. 1931, Cottbus; s. of Richard W Meiser and Hasmig Bunyadian; ed gymnasium and studies in philosophy and medicine; Univ. Prof. in Internal Medicine (Haematology), Univ. of Saarland 1971–; Pres. Univ. of Saarland 1983–97; Vice-Pres. for Int. Affairs, West German Rectors' Conf. (WRK) 1987; Officier, Ordre Nat. du Mérite (France); Officier, Ordre de Mérite (Luxembourg). *Publications:* studies on macroglobulinemia in tropical splenomegaly (1966/67), on the metabolism of mycloma cells (1970), on tropical parasites, on combination chemotherapy (1981); Aktuelle Probleme und Perspektiven des Arztrechts (co-ed.) 1989. *Leisure interests:* literature, souvenirs. *Address:* Domagkstrasse 2, 6650 Homburg-Saar, Germany (Home). *Telephone:* (6841) 5868 (Home).

MEISNER, HE Cardinal Joachim; German ecclesiastic; b. 25 Dec. 1933, Breslau; s. of Walter Meisner and Hedwig Meisner; ed Univ. of Erfurt, Pastoral Seminary at Neuzelle; ordained priest 1962, Chaplain of St Ägidien, Heiligenstadt 1963–66, St Crucis, Erfurt 1966, Rector of the Diocese of Erfurt 1966–75, Suffragan Bishop, Erfurt 1975–80, Bishop of Berlin 1980–89; cr. Cardinal 1983; Archbishop of Cologne and Primate of Germany 1988–; Hon. PhD (Jesuit Univ., Manila) 1990; Hon. Citizen of Miguel Pereira, Brazil 1992. *Publications:* Das Auditorium Coelicum am Dom zu Erfurt 1960, Nachreformatorische katholische Frömmigkeitsformen in Erfurt 1971, various articles in magazines. *Leisure interest:* Christian art. *Address:* Kardinal-Frings-Str. 10, 50668 Cologne, Germany. *Telephone:* 16421.

MEJDANI, Rexhep, PhD; Albanian politician; fmr Sec.-Gen. Socialist Party of Albania; Pres. of Albania 1997–2002. *Address:* c/o Council of Ministers, Këshilli i Ministrave, Tirana, Albania.

MEJÍA, HE Cardinal Jorge María; Argentine ecclesiastic; b. 31 Jan. 1923, Buenos Aires; ordained priest 1945; Bishop 1986; Archbishop 1994; Titular Archbishop of Apollonia; Archivist and Librarian, Holy Roman Church; cr. Cardinal 2001. *Address:* Palazzo Apostolico Vaticano, 00120 Città del Vaticano, Italy (Office).

MEJÍA DOMÍNGUEZ, Rafael Hipólito; Dominican Republic politician; Pres. of the Dominican Repub. Aug. 2000–. *Address:* Administrative Secretariat of the Presidency, Palacio Nacional, Avda México, esq. Dr. Delgado, Santo Domingo, D.N., Dominican Republic (Office). *Telephone:* 686-4771 (Office). *Fax:* 688-2100 (Office). *Website:* www.presidencia.gov.do.

MEKSI, Aleksandr; Albanian politician and engineer; fmr construction engineer and restorer of medieval architecture; mem. Democratic Party (DP); Prime Minister of Albania 1992–97. *Address:* c/o Council of Ministers, Tirana, Albania.

MELAMID, Aleksandr; Russian artist; b. 14 July 1945, Moscow; initial artistic training at Moscow Art School; originator (with Vitaliy Komar) of 'Sots-art'; mem. of USSR Union of Artists, expelled for "distortion of Soviet reality and non-conformity with the principles of Socialist realism" 1972; emigrated to USA 1979. *Exhibitions:* some work shown at Ronald Feldman Gallery, New York 1976; two-man exhbn (with Vitaliy Komar) at same gallery 1985 and at museums in USA, Australia, Europe. *Principal works include:* Young Marx 1976, Colour Writing 1972, Quotation 1972, Post Art 1973, Factory for Producing Blue Smoke 1975, Poster Series 1980.

MELANDRI, Giovanna, BEcons; Italian politician; b. 28 Jan. 1962, New York, USA; Co-ordinator Industrial and Tech. Policy Unit, Montedison 1983–87; Head Int. Office Legambiente (Environmental League) and Chair. Scientific Cttee 1988–94; mem. Italian Del. to Conf. on Sustainable Devt, Bergen 1990, to UN Conf. on Environment and Devt, Rio de Janeiro 1992; mem. Exec. Cttee Legambiente 1982–89, Nat. Secr. 1989–; mem. Nat. Exec. Cttee Partito Democratico Socialista (PDS) 1991–, Democratici di Sinistra 1998–; mem. Exec. with responsibility for Communications Policy 1996–; mem. Camera dei Deputati 1994–; Minister of Culture 1998–2001; fmr mem. Progressisti-federativo Group, in charge of work on bioethics and assisted reproduction, External Cttee to Special Comm. on Child Welfare, fmr Pres. Cttee on Human Rights, fmr mem. Comm. on Culture and Comm.; del. to first UN World Forum on TV 1997; Pres. Madre Provetta 1995–99; f. Italian Emily's List 1998; mem. Editorial Cttee Madre Provetta News 1997–, Tomorrow and La Nuova Ecologia environmental periodicals 1986–91. *Publications:* (Ed.): Ambiente Italia (annual environmental report of Legambiente) 1989–94, Italian World Watch Magazine 1986–91, Digitalia, l'ultima rivoluzione 1998. *Address:* c/o Democratici di Sinistra (DS), Via delle Botteghe Oscure 4, 00186 Rome, Italy (Office).

MELCHETT, Peter Robert Henry Mond, 4th Baron, cr. 1928, LLB, MA; British organic farmer, environmentalist and fmr politician; b. 24 Feb. 1948, Norfolk; s. of Lord Julian Melchett (died 1973) and Sonia Melchett; one s. one d.; ed Eton Coll., Univ. of Cambridge, Keele Univ., Staffs.; mem. Labour Party; House of Lords Peer 1973–99; Govt Minister, Depts of Environment and Industry 1975–77; Minister of State, NI Office 1977–79; joined Greenpeace UK 1985, Chair. and Exec. Dir (arrested and imprisoned two days for destroying six acres of GM maize at farm in Lyng, cleared of causing criminal damage Norfolk Crown Court 2000) 1995–2000; Chair. Greenpeace Japan 1995–2000; resgnd from Bd Greenpeace Int. 2002; adviser on environmental and social issues to Iceland Ltd (food retailer) 2001; Consultant, Corp. Responsibility Dept, Burson-Marsteller UK (public relations co.) Jan. 2002–; Policy Dir Soil Asscn (organic foods certification body) 2002–. *Address:* Soil Association Bristol House, 40–56 Victoria Street, Bristol, BS1 6BY (Office);

Burson-Marsteller, 24–28 Bloomsbury Way, London, WC1A 2PX, England (Office). *Telephone:* :(117) 929-0661 F: 0117 925 2504 (Office); (20) 7831-6262 (Office). *Fax:* (117) 925-2504 (Office); (20) 7430-1033 (Office). *E-mail:* pmelchett@soilassociation.org (Office); peter_melchett@bm.com (Office). *Website:* www.soilassociation.org (Office); www.bm.com (Office).

MELEŞCANU, Teodor Viorel, PhD; Romanian jurist and politician; b. 10 March 1941, Brad, Hunedoara Co.; m.; one d.; ed Bucharest Univ., Univ. Inst. for Higher Int. Studies, Geneva; with Ministry of Foreign Affairs 1966; mem. numerous dels. to UNO confs.; First Sec. UN, Geneva; Secretary, Ministry of Foreign Affairs; Minister of Foreign Affairs 1992–96, also Deputy Prime Minister; Senator (for Prahova constituency) 1996–2000; Assoc. Prof. of Int. Law, Univ. of Bucharest 1996–; researcher, Romanian Inst. for Int. Studies 1996–; Founder and Pres. Alliance for Romania (socio-democratic party) 1997–2001, merged into Nat. Liberal Party 2001, First Vice-Pres. 2001–; presidential cand. 2000; mem. Asscn of Int. Law and Int. Relations (ADIRI), Int. Law Comm. (UN). *Publications:* Responsibility of States for the Peaceful Use of Nuclear Energy 1973, International Labour Organization Functioning and Activity, numerous studies and articles. *Address:* National Liberal Party, Bd. Nicolae Balcescu 21, 70112 Bucharest, Romania.

MELETINSKY, Eleazar Moiseyevich, DLit; Russian philologist; b. 22 Oct. 1918, Kharkov, Ukraine; s. of Moise Meletinsky and Raisa Margolis; m. Elena Andreyevna Kumpan; ed Moscow Inst. of History, Philosophy and Literature; army service World War II 1941–46; Head of Chair. Petrozavodsk Univ. 1946–49; arrested, imprisoned in Gulag 1949–54; Sr Researcher Inst. of World Literature USSR Acad. of Sciences 1956–92; Dir Inst. of Higher Humanitarian Studies 1992–; Prize Pitré 1971, USSR State Prize 1990; Order of the Patriotic War (Second Class). *Publications:* The Hero of Fairy Tales 1958, The Origin of the Heroic Epos 1963, Edda and the First Epic Form 1968, Poetics of Myth 1976, Paleosifirian Epic Mythology 1979, The Medieval Novel 1983, Introduction to Historic Poetics or Epics and the Novel 1986, Historical Poetics of the Novella 1990, On Literary Archetypes 1994, From Myth to Literature 2000, Notes of Work of Dostoevsky 2001; and works on problems of semiotics, history of folklore, mythology. *Address:* Institute of Higher Humanitarian Studies, Miusskaya str. 6, 125267 Moscow (Office); Udalicova 12, Apt. 36, 117415 Moscow, Russia (Home). *Telephone:* (095) 250-66-68 (Office); (095) 133-15-98 (Home). *Fax:* (095) 252-51-09 (Office).

MELIKISHVILI, Giorgi Aleksandrovich; Georgian historian; b. 30 Dec. 1918, Tbilisi; s. of Aleksandre Ekaterine Melikishvili and Yekaterina Melikishvili; m. Elene Dochanashvili 1942; one s. two d.; ed Tbilisi Univ.; works deal with the ancient history of the Near East and Transcaucasia; Prof. Tbilisi Univ.; Dir of Historical Inst. of Georgian Acad. of Sciences 1965–; mem. Acad. of Sciences of Georgia 1960–; Lenin Prize 1957. *Publications:* Nairi-Urartu 1954, Urartian Inscriptions in Cuneiform Characters 1960, History of Ancient Georgia 1959, The Most Ancient Settlers of the Caucasus and Near East 1965, Die urartäische Sprache 1971, Sketches of Georgian History, Vol. I (ed.) 1989, Studies of Ancient History of Georgia, Caucasus and Near East 1999. *Address:* Taktakishvili str. 3/43 Apt. 37, Tbilisi 380079, Georgia. *Telephone:* (32) 22-10-06.

MELKERT, Ad, MA; Netherlands politician; b. 12 Feb. 1956, Gouda; m. Adrianus Melkert; two c.; ed Univ. of Amsterdam; Pres., Council of European Nat. Youth Cttees 1979–81; Sec.-Gen. Youth Forum of the EC 1981–84; Pres. Nat. Cttee, UN Int. Youth Year 1984–85; Asst to Gen. Sec., Dir Internal Affairs, Netherlands Org. for Int. Devt Co-operation 1984–86; mem. Parl. 1986–; Minister of Social Affairs and Employment 1994–98; Parliamentary Leader Partij van de Arbeid (PvdA – Labour Party) 1998–2002, Party Leader 2001–02 (resgnd after 2002 election defeat); Exec. Dir World Bank (IBRD) 2002–. *Address:* PvdA, Herengracht 54, PO Box 1310, 1000 BH Amsterdam, Netherlands (Office); Office of the Executive Director (Netherlands) IBRD, 1818 H Street, NW, Washington, DC 20433, USA (Office). *Telephone:* (20) 5512155 (Netherlands); (202) 458-2052 (USA). *Fax:* (20) 5512330 (Netherlands); (202) 522-1572 (USA). *E-mail:* pvda@pvda.nl; amelkert@worldbank.org. *Website:* www.pvda.nl.

MELLERS, Wilfrid Howard, OBE, MA, DMus, DPhil; British composer, author and university professor emeritus; b. 26 April 1914, Leamington; s. of Percy Wilfrid Mellers and Hilda Maria Lawrence; m. 1st Vera Hobbs 1940; m. 2nd Peggy Pauline Lewis 1950 (divorced 1975); two d.; m. 3rd Robin Hildyard 1987; ed Leamington Coll. and Downing Coll. Cambridge; Supervisor in English Studies and Lecturer in Music, Downing Coll. 1945–48; Staff Tutor in Music, Extramural Dept, Univ. of Birmingham 1948–60; Distinguished Andrew Mellon Visiting Prof. of Music, Univ. of Pittsburgh, USA 1960–63; Prof. and Head of Dept of Music, Univ. of York 1964–81, now Emer.; Part-time Prof., Guildhall School of Music, London, City Univ., London and Keele Univ. 1981–; many compositions and books published; Hon. DPhil (City Univ.) 1981. *Publications:* François Couperin and the French Classical Tradition 1950, Man and His Music 1957, Music in a New Found Land (themes and developments in American music) 1964, Harmonious Meeting 1964, Twilight of the Gods: The Beatles in Retrospect 1973, Bach and the Dance of God 1981, Beethoven and the Voice of God 1984, A Darker Shade of Pale: A Backdrop to Bob Dylan 1984, Angels of the Night: Women Jazz and Pop Singers in the Twentieth Century 1986, The Masks of Orpheus 1986, Vaughan Williams and the Vision of Albion 1988, Le Jardin Retrouvé: Homage to Federico Mompou 1989, The Music of Percy Grainger 1992, The Music of Francis Poulenc 1993,

Between Old Worlds and New 1997, Singing in the Wilderness 2001, Celestial Music 2002. *Address:* Oliver Sheldon House, 17 Aldwark, York, YO1 7BX, England (Office). *Telephone:* (1904) 638686.

MELLES, Carl; Austrian conductor; b. 15 July 1926, Budapest; s. of György Melles and Maria Lazar; m. Gertrude Dertnig 1963; one s. one d.; ed Gymnasium and Acad. of Music, Budapest; conducts all the maj. orchestras of Europe including Vienna and Berlin Philharmonic, New Philharmonia London, Scala Milan; guest appearances at Flanders, Salzburg and Bayreuth Festivals and Vienna State Opera; concert tours in Europe, Japan, S. Africa; Hon. Conductor Brunswick State Orchestra 1996–; Hon. mem. Vienna Singakademie 1978; Franz Liszt Prize, Budapest 1954, Prize of Italian Record Critic Asscn for Dallapiccola's Il Prigioniero 1974; Brahms Medal, Vienna Singverein 1983, Hon. Gold Medal, City of Vienna 1986, Great Silver Badge of Honour, Austria. *Recordings:* Classical Excellence, Hollywood, Florida with the Austrian Broadcast Symphony Orchestra, Beethoven symphonies I–IX. *Leisure interest:* literature. *Address:* Grünbergstrasse 4, 1130 Vienna, Austria. *Telephone:* (1) 813-52-06. *Fax:* (1) 813-52-06.

MELLINK, Machteld Johanna, PhD; Netherlands archaeologist; b. 26 Oct. 1917, Amsterdam; d. of Johan Mellink and Machteld Kruyff; ed Amsterdam and Utrecht Univs; Field Asst Tarsus excavations 1947–49; Asst Prof. of Classical Archaeology Bryn Mawr Coll. 1949–53, Assoc. Prof., Chair. Dept of Classical and Near Eastern Archaeology 1953–62, Prof. 1962–88, Prof. Emer. 1988–; staff mem. Gordion excavations organized by Pennsylvania Univ. Museum 1950, during which the putative tomb of King Midas was discovered 1957; Field Dir excavations at Karataş-Semayük in Lycia 1963–; excavator archaic and Graeco-Persian painted tombs near Elmali 1969–; advisory staff mem., Troy excavations, Univs. of Tübingen and Cincinnati 1988–; Pres. Archaeological Inst. of America 1981–84; Vice-Pres. American Research Inst. in Turkey 1980–, Pres. 1988–92; Hon. LLD (Pennsylvania) 1987; Hon. DHist (Eskişehir, Turkey) 1990; L. Wharton Drexel Medal 1994, Gold Medal, Archaeological Inst. of America 1991. *Publications:* Hyakinthos 1943, A Hittite Cemetery at Gordion 1956, Kizilbel: an archaic painted tomb chamber in northern Lycia 1998; Archaeology in Anatolia (reports in American Journal of Archaeology) 1955–93; co-author Frühe Stufen der Kunst 1974; ed. Dark Ages and Nomads 1964, ed. Troy and the Trojan War 1986, ed. series Elmali-Karataş, Vol. I 1992, Vol. II 1994. *Address:* Department of Classical and Near Eastern Archaeology, Bryn Mawr College, Bryn Mawr, PA 19010 (Office); 264 Montgomery Avenue, Haverford, PA 19041, USA (Home). *Telephone:* (610) 526-5339 (Office); (610) 642-3896 (Home). *Fax:* (610) 526-7479 (Office).

MELLOR, Rt Hon David, PC, QC, FZS; British politician and journalist; b. 12 March 1949; s. of Douglas H. Mellor; m. Judith Hall 1974 (divorced 1996); two s.; ed Swanage Grammar School, Christ's Coll. Cambridge; called to Bar (Inner Temple) 1972; apptd. QC 1987; Chair. Cambridge Univ. Conservative Asscn 1970; fmr Vice-Chair. Chelsea Conservative Asscn; MP for Putney 1979–97; Parl. Under-Sec. of State, Dept of Energy 1981–83, Home Office 1983–86, Minister of State, Home Office 1986–87, FCO 1987–88; Minister for Health 1988–89; Minister of State, Home Office 1989–90; Minister for the Arts July–Nov. 1990; Chief Sec. to Treasury 1990–92; Sec. of State for Nat. Heritage April–Sept. 1992; Consultant Middle East Broadcasting Centre, Middle East Economic Digest, Abela Holdings, RACAL Tacticom, British Aerospace, Ernst & Young, G.K.N.; mem. Bd ENO 1993–95; Chair. Sports Aid Foundation 1993–97, Football Task Force 1997–99; Deputy Chair. Trustees London Philharmonic Orchestra 1989–; presenter 6.06 BBC Radio 5 1993–99, The Midnight Hour, BBC 2 1997–99, Across the Threshold (series) 1998–, Classic FM 1998–; sports columnist, Evening Standard 1997–; music critic, Mail on Sunday 2000–; fmr mem. Council Nat. Youth Orchestra; Special Trustee Westminster Hosp. 1979–86; elected Hon. Assoc. British Veterinary Asscn for work for animal welfare 1986; Variety Club Award for BBC Radio Personality of the Year 1994. *Leisure interests:* classical music, football, reading. *Address:* c/o House of Commons, London, SW1A 0AA, England.

MELLOR, David Hugh, MA, MEng, MS, PhD, ScD, FBA; British professor of philosophy; b. 10 July 1938, London; s. of S. D. Mellor and E. N. (née Hughes) Mellor; ed Newcastle Royal Grammar School, Manchester Grammar School and Pembroke Coll., Cambridge; Harkness Fellowship in Chem. Eng, Univ. of Minnesota 1960–62, MIT School of Chem. Eng Practise 1962; Tech. Officer, Imperial Chemical Industries (ICI) 1962–63; research student in philosophy 1963–68; Fellow, Pembroke Coll., Cambridge 1964–70; Fellow, Darwin Coll., Cambridge 1971–, Vice-Master 1983–87; Asst Lecturer in Philosophy, Univ. of Cambridge 1965–70, Lecturer 1970–83, Reader in Metaphysics 1983–86, Prof. of Philosophy 1986–99, Prof. Emer. 1999–, Pro-Vice-Chancellor 2000–01; Hon. Prof. of Philosophy, Keele Univ. 1989–92; Visiting Fellow in Philosophy, ANU 1975; Radcliffe Fellow in Philosophy 1978–80, Visiting Prof. Auckland Univ. 1985; Pres. British Soc. for the Philosophy of Science 1985–87, Pres. Aristotelian Soc. 1992–93; Hon. PhD (Lund Univ.) 1997. *Publications:* The Matter of Chance 1971, Real Time 1981, Matters of Metaphysics 1991, The Facts of Causation 1995, Real Time II 1998; numerous articles on philosophy of science, metaphysics and philosophy of mind. *Leisure interest:* theatre. *Address:* 25 Orchard Street, Cambridge, CB1 1JS, England. *Telephone:* (1223) 740017. *Fax:* (1223) 740017. *E-mail:* d.h.mellor@phil.cam.ac.uk (Home). *Website:* www.dar.cam.ac.uk/~dhm11 (Home).

MELLY, (Alan) George (Heywood); British jazz musician; b. 17 Aug. 1926; s. of Francis Heywood and Edith Maud Melly; m. 1st Victoria Vaughan 1955 (divorced 1962); m. 2nd Diane Margaret Campion Dawson 1963; one s. one step-d.; ed Stowe School; able seaman R.N. 1944–47; Asst London Gallery 1948–50; sang with Mick Mulligan's Jazz Band 1949–61; performer with John Chilton's Feetwarmers 1974–; wrote Flook strip cartoon balloons 1956–71; pop music critic, The Observer 1965–67, TV critic 1967–71, film critic 1971–73; scriptwriter for films Smashing Time 1968, Take a Girl Like You 1970; Critic of the Year IPC Nat. Press Awards 1970. *Publications:* I Flook 1962, Owning Up 1965, Revolt into Style 1970, Flook by Trog 1970, Rum Bum and Concertina 1977, The Media Mob (jtly.) 1980, Tribe of One: Great Naive and Primitive Painters of the British Isles 1981, Great Lovers (jtly.) 1991, Mellymobile 1982, Scouse Mouse 1984, It's All Writ Out for You: The Life and Work of Scottie Wilson 1986, Paris and Surrealists (jtly.) 1991, Don't Tell Sybil: An Intimate Memoir of E. L. T. Mesens 1997. *Leisure interests:* collecting modern paintings, singing and listening to 1920s' blues, trout fishing. *Address:* 81 Frithville Gardens, Shepherds Bush, London, W12 7JQ, England (Home).

MELMON, Kenneth L.; American professor of medicine and pharmacology; b. 20 July 1934, San Francisco; s. of Abe Melmon and Jean Kahn; m. Elyce Ester Edelman 1957; one s. one d.; ed Stanford Univ. and California Medical School, San Francisco, NIH Heart Inst.; Clinical Assoc., Nat. Heart and Lung Inst. 1961–64; Chief Resident in Medicine, Washington Univ. 1964–65; Chief of Section of Clinical Pharmacology, Calif. Univ. (San Francisco) 1965–68, Chief of Div. 1968–78; Chair., Dept of Medicine, Stanford Univ. 1978–84, Prof. of Medicine and Molecular Pharmacology 1978–2000; Chair. Academic Senate, School of Medicine 1996–2000, Steering Cttee Academic Senate 1996–98; Dir Technical Transfer Program, Stanford Univ. Hosp. 1986–93, Assoc. Dean for Postgrad. Medical Educ. 1994–2000, Prof. Emer. 2000–; f. Center for Molecular and Genetic Medicine, Center for Molecular and Clinical Immunology, Stanford Community Physicians; helped to est. Hewlett Award for Scientific and Sensitive Medicine; mem. Nat. Bd of Medical Examiners 1987–97; Burroughs Wellcome Clinical Pharmacology Scholar; Special Fellow NIH 1970; Guggenheim Fellow 1971; Burrough Wellcome Clinical Pharmacology Award, Guggenheim Award, Hunter Award for Clinical Therapeutics 1998. *Publications:* Ed. Cardiovascular Therapeutics 1974, Clinical Pharmacology 1978, 1983, 1992, 2000; Assoc. Ed. The Pharmacological Basis of Therapeutics 1980; devised Stanford Health Information Network for Educ.; over 300 scientific papers. *Leisure interests:* backpacking, swimming, business, photography, bicycling, woodworking, fishing. *Address:* 51 Cragmont Way, Woodside, CA 94062, USA (Home). *Telephone:* (650) 367-9395 (Home). *E-mail:* KMelmon@Skolar.com (Office).

MELNIKOV, Vitaly Vyacheslavovich; Russian film director; b. 1 May 1928; m. Tamara Aleksandrovna Melnikova; ed All-Union State Inst. of Cinema (VGIK) under S. I. Yutkevich and M. I. Romm; series of documentary films 1953–64; Artistic Dir Golos studio 1989–; Sec. St Petersburg Union of Cinematographers; People's Artist of Russia 1986, Venice Film Festival Prize 1981. *Films include:* Barbos Visits Bobik, 1965, Chukotka's Boss 1967, Mum's Got Married 1970, Hello and Goodbye! 1973, Xenia, Fyodor's Favourite Wife 1974, The Elder Son 1975, Wedding 1978, September Holiday 1979, Two Lines in Small Print 1981, Unicum 1984, First Meeting—Last Meeting 1986, To Marry a Captain 1987, The Tsar's Hunting 1989, Chicha 1991, The Vareny's Last Case 1994, Tsarevich Alexey 1998, Night Lights 2000. *Address:* Svetlanovsky proyezd 105, Apt. 20, 195269 St Petersburg, Russia. *Telephone:* (812) 532-51-88.

MELNIZKY, Walter, DJur; Austrian judge; b. 1 Nov. 1928, Vienna; s. of Ernst Melnizky and Maria Melnizky; m. Gertrude Melnizky 1953; one s.; ed Univ. of Vienna; Judge 1954–57, 1962–69; Public Prosecutor 1957–62; Gen. Prosecutor 1969–86; Pres. Supreme Court 1987–93; Chair. Court of Arbitration Gen. Medical Council of Vienna 1995–; Pres. Automobilclub Austria (ÖAMTC) 1980–; consultant Syndicus Asscn of Public Experts 1988–; Komturkreuz des Landes Niederösterreich und Burgenlandes, Grosses Goldenes Ehrenzeichen am Bande (Austria), Grosses Verdienstkreuz mit Stern und Schulterband (Germany). *Publications:* numerous juridical essays, especially on traffic law and criminal law. *Leisure interests:* classical music, opera. *Address:* ÖAMTC, 1010 Vienna, Schubertring 1–3 (Office); 1190 Vienna, Hannplatz 4/14, Austria (Home). *Telephone:* (1) 711-99-702 (Office); (1) 368-73-74 (Home). *Fax:* (1) 711-99-1565 (Office); (1) 368-73-74 (Home).

MELROSE, Donald Blair, D. PHIL., FAA; Australian professor of physics; b. 13 Sept. 1940, Hobart, Tasmania; s. of the late Andrew B. Melrose and of Isla L. Luff; m. Sara C. Knabe 1969; one s. one d.; ed N Sydney Boys' High School, John Curtin High School, Fremantle and Univs. of W Australia, Tasmania and Oxford; Research Fellow, Univ. of Sussex 1965–66; Research Assoc. Belfer Grad. School of Science, Yeshiva Univ., New York 1966–68; Research Fellow, Center for Theoretical Physics, Univ. of Md 1968–69; Sr Lecturer in Theoretical Physics, ANU 1969–72, Reader 1972–79; Prof. of Theoretical Physics, Univ. of Sydney 1979–, Dir Research Centre for Theoretical Astrophysics 1991–, Univ. Prof. 2000–; Rhodes Scholar 1962; Pawsey Medal (Australian Acad. of Science) 1974, Walter Boas Medal (Australian Inst. of Physics) 1986, Thomas Ranken Lyle Medal (Australian Acad. of Science) 1987, Harrie Massey Medal and Prize (Inst. of Physics) 1998. *Publications:* Plasma Physics (2 Vols) 1980, Instabilities in Space and Laboratory Plasmas 1986, Electromagnetic Processes in Dispersive Media (with R. C. McPhedran) 1991, Plasma Astrophysics (with J. G. Kirk and E. R. Priest) 1994; over 200 papers in scientific Publs. *Leisure interests:* rugby union, surfing, jogging, squash. *Address:* School of Physics, University of Sydney, Sydney, NSW 2006

(Office); 10 Balfour Street, Wollstonecraft, NSW 2065, Australia (Home). *Telephone:* (2) 9351-2537 (Office); (2) 9438-3635 (Home). *Fax:* (2) 9351-7726. (Office).

MELVILLE-ROSS, Timothy David, FCIS, F.I.O.B., FRSA, CIMgt; British business executive; b. 3 Oct. 1944, Westward Ho, Devon; s. of the late Antony Melville-Ross and Anne Fane; m. Camilla Probert 1967; two s. one d.; ed Uppingham School and Portsmouth Coll. of Tech.; BP 1963–73; Rowe Swann & Co. (stockbrokers) 1973–74; Nationwide Bldg Soc. 1974, Dir and Chief Exec. 1985–94; Dir Monument Oil & Gas PLC 1992–99; Dir-Gen. Inst. of Dirs. 1994–99; Chair. Collectable Cards Ltd 1998–2001; Deputy Chair. Monument Oil and Gas PLC 1997–99; Dir Bovis Homes Ltd 1997–, DTZ Holdings PLC (Chair. 2000–); Chair. Investors in People UK 1999–, NewsCast Ltd, Bank Insinger de Beaufort N.V.; Dir Katalyst Ltd, Royal London Mutual Insurance, Manganese Bronze PLC. *Leisure interests:* reading, music, bridge, sport, the countryside. *Address:* DTZ Holdings PLC, 1 Curzon Street, London, W1A 5PZ; Little Bevills, Bures, Suffolk, CO8 5JN, England (Home). *Telephone:* (1787) 229188 (Office); (1787) 227424 (Home). *Fax:* (1787) 228596 (Home). *E-mail:* tim.melville-ross@dtz.com (Office); tim@littlebevills.freeserve.co.uk (Home).

MEMMI, Albert; French writer; b. 15 Dec. 1920, Tunis; s. of François Memmi and Marguerite née Sarfati; m. Germaine Dubach 1946; three c.; ed Lycée Carnot, Tunis, Univ. of Algiers and Univ. de Paris à la Sorbonne; Teacher of Philosophy, Tunis 1955; Dir Psychological Centre, Tunis 1956; Researcher, CNRS, Paris 1959–; Asst Prof. Ecole pratique des hautes études 1959–66, Prof. 1966–70; Prof., Inst. de Psychanalise, Paris 1968–; Prof. Univ. of Paris 1970–, Dir Social Sciences Dept 1973–76, Dir Anthropological Lab.; mem. Acad. des Sciences d'Outre-mer; Vice-Pres. Pen Club 1977-80, Comité nat. Laïcité-République 1991; Dr. hc (Ben Gurion) 1999; Officier Légion d'honneur; Commdr Ordre de Nichan Iftikhar; Officier Palmes académiques, Officier Arts et Lettres, Officier Ordre République Tunisienne, Prix de Carthage 1953, Prix Fénéon 1953, Prix Simba 1993, Prix de l'Union Rationaliste, Grand Prix Littéraire de l'Afrique du Nord, Grand Prix de la ville de Bari, Chevalier des affaires culturelles du Burkina Faso. *Publications include:* The Pillar of Salt 1953, Strangers 1955, Colonized, Colonizer 1957, Portrait of a Jew 1962, Anthologie des écrivains nord-africains 1965, Les français et le racisme 1965, The Liberation of the Jew 1966, Dominated Man 1968, Decolonisation 1970, The Scorpion 1970, Jews and Arabs 1974, Entretien 1975, La terre intérieure 1976, Le désert 1977, The Dependence 1979, Le racisme 1982, Ce que je crois 1985, L'Écriture colorée 1986, Les écrivains francophones du Maghreb 1987, Le Pharaon 1988, Le Mirliton du Ciel 1990, Bonheurs 1992, A contre-courants 1993, Ah, quel bonheur 1995, Le Juif et l'autre 1995, Le Buveur et l'amoureux 1998, Le nomade immobile 2000, Dictionnaire à l'usage des incrédules. *Leisure interest:* writing. *Address:* 5 rue Saint Merri, 75004 Paris, France. *Telephone:* 1-40-29-08-31. *Fax:* 1-42-74-25-22.

MEN, Mikhail Aleksandrovich; Russian politician; b. 12 Nov. 1960, Semkhoz, Moscow Region; s. of Aleksander Men; m.; one d.; ed Moscow Gubkin Inst. of Gas and Oil, Moscow State Inst. of Culture; Russian Acad. of State Service; fmr stage dir amateur theatre and clubs of Moscow; mem. Moscow region Duma 1993–95; mem. State Duma (Parl.) 1995–99; Deputy Chair. Cttee on Culture 1995–; Chair. All-Union Christian Union 1996–; Chair. Aleksander Men Foundation; elected Vice-Gov. Moscow region 2000–02, resgd; Deputy Mayor of Moscow Nov. 2002–. *Publication:* Culture and Religion 2001. *Address:* Government of Moscow, Tverskaya str.13, 103032 Moscow, Russia (Office). *Telephone:* (095) 777-77-77 (Office); (095) 292-16-37 (Office).

MÉNAGE, Gilles Marie Marcel; French government official; b. 5 July 1943, Bourg-la-Reine (Hauts-de-Seine); s. of Georges Ménage and Jeanne Paillotet; m. 1st Marie-France Beaussire (divorced); two d.; m. 2nd Doris Lenz; one s. one d.; ed Lycée Lakanal, Sceaux, Lycée Berthollet, Annecy, Inst. d'Études Politiques, Paris and Ecole Nat. d'Admin; civil admin., Ministry of Interior 1969; Deputy Prefect, Head of Staff for Prefect of Tarn-et-Garonne 1969–70, then for Prefect of Haute-Vienne and Limousin 1970–74; Tech. Adviser to Sec. of State for Posts and Telecommunications (PTT) 1974; Head of Staff for Pierre Lelong, Sec. for PTT 1974–76; Deputy Prefect and Special Adviser to Prefect of Paris 1976–77; Head of Staff for Prefect/Sec.-Gen. of Préfecture de Paris 1977–81; Sr Lecturer, Inst. d'Etudes Politiques, Paris 1976–77, Inst. Int. d'Admin. Publique 1980–81; Tech. Adviser, then Deputy Head of Staff for Pres. of France 1982–88, Chief of Staff 1988–92; Chair. Electricité de France 1992–95; working on energy project for Ministry of Industry 1996–97; Prefect 1997–; Chair. Int. Consortiums Consultants 1998–; Pres. 'Les florilèges du Château fiodal de Madaillon'; Chevalier, Ordre Nat. du Mérite, Chevalier, Légion d'honneur. *Publications:* La France face aux dangers de guerre 1981, L'oeil du pouvoir: les Affaires de l'État (1981–1986) 1999, L'oeil du pouvoir: Face aut terrorismes (1981–1986) 2000, L'oeil du pouvoir: Face au terrorisme moyen oriental (1981–86) 2001. *Leisure interests:* skiing, music, organizing concerts for talented young musicians. *Address:* EDF, 38 rue Jacques Ibert, 92300 Levallois-Perret (Office); International Consortiums, 18–20 rue Fourcroy, 75017 Paris (Office); 18-20 rue Fourcroy, 75017 Paris, France (Home). *Telephone:* 1-40-42-82-85 (Office); 1-43-80-47-37 (Home). *E-mail:* gilles.menage@libertysurf.fr (Office).

MENAGHARISHVILI, Irakli Afinogenovich; Georgian politician; b. 18 May 1951, Tbilisi; s. of Afinogen Menagarishvili and Ekaterine Jorbenadze; m. Manana Mikaberidze 1975; two s.; ed Tbilisi State Inst. of Medicine; leader

Comsomol Orgs. 1976–80; head of City Public Health Dept 1980–82; First Deputy Minister of Public Health 1982–86, Minister 1986–91, 1992–93; Dir Georgian Cen. of Strategic Studies; Co-ordinator of Humanitarian Aid of State Council of Georgia 1991–92; Deputy Prime Minister 1993–95; Minister of Foreign Affairs, 1995–. *Address:* Ministry of Foreign Affairs, 4 Chitadze Street, 380008 Tbilisi, Georgia. *Telephone:* (32) 98-93-77. *Fax:* (32) 98-93-80.

MENCHÚ TUM, Rigoberta; Guatemalan human rights activist; b. 9 Jan. 1959, San Miguel Uspantán; d. of the late Vicente Menchu and Juana Menchu; m. Angel Canil 1995; two c.; began campaigning for rights of Indians as a teenager; fled to Mexico after parents and brother were murdered by security forces 1980; co-ordinated protests in San Marcos against 500th anniversary of arrival of Columbus in Americas 1992; f. Rigoberta Menchú Tum Foundation, Guatemala City; Int. Goodwill Amb. UNESCO 1996–; Pres. UN Indigenous Initiative for Peace 1999; awarded Nobel Peace Prize 1992. *Publications:* I, Rigoberta (trans. into 12 languages) 1983 Rigobeta: Grandson of the Mayas (co-author) 1998. *Address:* c/o Vicente Menchú Foundation, P.O. Box 5274, Berkeley, CA 94705, USA.

MENDES, Sam, CBE; British theatre director; b. 1 Aug. 1965; s. of Valerie Mendes and Peter Mendes; ed Magdalen Coll. School, Oxford and Peterhouse, Cambridge; fmr artistic Dir Minerva Studio Theatre, Chichester; Artistic Dir Donmar Warehouse 1992–2002; Critics' Circle Award 1989, 1993, 1996, Olivier Award for Best Dir 1996, Tony Award 1998, LA Critics' Award, Broadcast Critcs' Award, Toronto People's Choice Award, Golden Globe Award (all 1999), Shakespeare Prize, Acad. Award for Best Dir (also Best Film) for American Beauty 2000. *Films:* American Beauty 1999, Road to Perdition 2002. *Plays directed include:* London Assurance (Chichester), The Cherry Orchard (London), Kean (Old Vic, London), The Plough and the Stars (Young Vic, London) 1991, Troilus and Cressida (RSC) 1991, The Alchemist (RSC) 1991, Richard III (RSC) 1992, The Tempest (RSC) 1993; Nat. Theatre debut with The Sea 1991, The Rise and Fall of Little Voice (Nat. and Aldwych) 1992, The Birthday Party 1994, Othello (also world tour); Assassins, Translations, Cabaret, Glengarry Glen Ross, The Glass Menagerie, Company, Habeas Corpus, The Front Page, The Blue Room, To the Green Fields Beyond (all at Donmar Warehouse) 1992–2000; Uncle Vanya and Twelfth Night (Donmar Warehouse, Olivier Award for Best Dir 2003, Olivier Special Award 2003) 2002, Oliver! (London Palladium), Cabaret, The Blue Room (Broadway, NY). *Leisure interest:* cricket. *Address:* c/o Donmar Warehouse, 41 Earlham Street, London, WC2H 9LD, England.

MENDOZA, June, AO, RP; British portrait painter; b. Melbourne; d. of John Morton and Dot Mendoza; m. Keith Mackrell; one s. three d.; ed Lauriston School for Girls, Melbourne, St Martin's School of Art, London; portraits include HM Queen Elizabeth II, HM Queen Elizabeth, the Queen Mother, HRH The Prince of Wales, Diana, Princess of Wales, Baroness Thatcher, Prime Ministers of Fiji, Australia, Philippines, Singapore, Pres. of Iceland, Philippines and many other Govt, academic, industrial, regimental, theatrical and sporting personalities, series of internationally known musicians, large boardroom and family groups; large canvas for the House of Commons (440 portraits) of the House in session, for Australian House of Reps. (170 portraits) for Parl., Canberra; has made numerous TV appearances and lectures regularly in UK and overseas; mem. Royal Soc. of Portrait Painters, Royal Inst. of Oil Painters; Hon. mem. Soc. of Women Artists; Hon. D.Litt (Bath, Loughborough); Freeman of City of London 1997. *Exhibition:* solo Exhbn Mall Galleries, London 1999. *Leisure interests:* classical and jazz music, theatre. *Address:* 34 Inner Park Road, London, SW19 6DD, England. *Telephone:* (20) 8788-7826 (Home). *Fax:* (20) 8780-0728 (Home).

MENEM, Carlos Saul, DJur; Argentine politician; b. 2 July 1935, Anillaco, La Rioja; s. of Saul Menem and Muhibe Akil; m. 1st Zulema Fátima Yoma 1966 (divorced); one s. (deceased) one d.; m. 2nd Cecilia Bolocco 2001; ed Córdoba Univ.; f. Juventud Peronista (Peron Youth Group), La Rioja Prov. 1955; defended political prisoners following Sept. 1955 coup; Legal Adviser, Confederación General del Trabajo, La Rioja Prov. 1955–70; cand. Prov. Deputy 1958; Pres. Partido Justicialista, La Rioja Prov. 1963–; elected Gov. La Rioja 1973, re-elected 1983, 1987; imprisoned following mil. coup 1976–81; cand. for Pres. Argentine Repub. for Partido Justicialista 1989; Pres. of Argentina 1989–99; Vice-Pres. Conf. of Latin American Popular Parties (COPPAL) 1990–; arrested for alleged involvement in illegal arms sales during his presidency June 2001, charged July 2001, placed under house arrest for five months; Presidential Cand. 2003. *Publications:* Argentine, Now or Never, Argentina Year 2000, The Productive Revolution (with Eduardo Duhalde). *Leisure interests:* flying, tennis. *Address:* Partido Justicialista, Buenos Aires, Argentina.

MENEZES, Fradique Bandeira Melo de; São Tomé e Príncipe politician and business executive; b. 1942; m. (wife deceased); ed Instituto Superior de Psicologia Aplicada, Lisbon, Univ. of Brussels; fmr Minister for Foreign Trade; fmr Amb. to Belgium and Netherlands; mem. Acção Democrática Independente (ADI) party; Pres. of São Tomé e Príncipe 2001–, also C-in-C of Armed Forces. *Address:* Office of the President, São Tomé, São Tomé e Príncipe (Office).

MENG JIANZHU; Chinese politician; b. July 1947, Wu Co., Jiangsu Prov.; joined CCP 1971; Deputy Sec.-Gen. Shanghai Municipal Govt 1992; Deputy Mayor and Chair. Shanghai Econ. Restructuring Cttee 1993; Deputy Sec. Shanghai Municipal Cttee 1996; Sec. Jiangxi Prov. Cttee, Chair. Standing Cttee Jiangxi People's Congress 2001; alt. mem. 15th CCP Cen. Cttee

1997–2002. *Address:* Chinese Communist Party Jiangxi Provincial Committee, 5 Beijing West Road, Nanchang 330046, People's Republic of China (Office).

MENG XUENONG; Chinese politician; b. 1949; mem. Communist Youth League 1980s, worked under Hu Jintao, Pres. of People's Repub. of China; Mayor of Beijing Jan.–April 2003–. *Address:* Office of the Mayor, Beijing Municipal People's Government, Beijing, People's Republic of China (Office).

MENGES, Chris; British cinematographer and film director; b. 15 Sept. 1940, Kingston; m. 2nd Judy Freeman 1978; five c. from 1st marriage; TV cameraman on documentaries filmed in Africa, Asia, S. America. *Films include:* cinematographer: Kes, The Empire Strikes Back, Local Hero, Comfort and Joy, The Killing Fields (Acad. Award 1984), Marie, The Mission (Acad. Award 1986), Singing the Blues in Red, Shy People, High Season, Michael Collins (LA Film Critics Award 1997); Dir: A World Apart, Crisscross, The Life and Death of Chico Mendes, Second Best.

MENGISTU HAILE MARIAM (see Mariam, Mengistu Haile).

MENKEN, Alan; American composer; b. 22 July 1949, New York; ed New York Univ.; began composing and performing Lehman Engel Musical Theatre Workshop, BMI. *Theatre music includes:* God Bless You Mr Rosewater 1979 (Off-Broadway debut), Little Shop of Horrors (with Howard Ashman), Kicks, The Apprenticeship of Duddy Kravitz, Diamonds, Personals, Let Freedom Sing, Weird Romance, Beauty and the Beast, A Christmas Carol. *Film music includes:* Little Shop of Horrors 1986, The Little Mermaid 1988 (two Acad. Awards 1989), Beauty and the Beast 1990 (two Acad. Awards 1991), Lincoln 1992, Newsies 1992, Aladdin 1992 (two Acad. Awards 1993), Life with Mikey 1993, Pocahontas (with Stephen Schwartz) 1995 (Golden Globe Award 1996, two Acad. Awards 1996). *Address:* The Shukat Company, 340 West 55th Street, Apt. 1A, New York, NY 10019, USA. *Telephone:* (212) 582-7614 (Office).

MENKERIOS, Haile, MA; Eritrean diplomatist and economist; b. 1 Oct. 1946, Adi Felesti; s. of Drar Menkerios and Negusse Giorgis; m. Tesfamariam Ghennet 1979; one s. one d.; ed Addis Ababa, Brandeis and Harvard Univs.; teaching Asst Harvard Univ. 1971–73; combatant in Eritrean People's Liberation Army (EPLA) 1973–74; Head of Tigrigna Section, Dept of Information and Propaganda, Eritrean People's Liberation Front (EPLF) 1974–75, mem. Foreign Relations Cttee 1976–77, mem. Cen. Council 1977–, Asst to Head of Dept of Foreign Relations 1977–79, Head of African Relations 1977–79, Research Div., Dept of Conscientization, Educ. and Culture 1979–86, Research and Information Centre of Eritrea 1986–87, Research and Policy Div., Dept of Foreign Relations 1987–90, Gov. of East and South Zone 1990–91; mem. Eritrean Nat. Council 1991–; Rep. of Provisional Govt of Eritrea to Ethiopia 1991–93; Special Envoy of Pres. to Somalia 1991–96, to the Greater Lakes Region 1996–97; mem. High Level Horn of Africa Cttee on Somalia 1993–95; Amb. of State of Eritrea to Ethiopia and OAU 1993–96; Amb., Perm. Rep. of State of Eritrea to UN 1997–2001; has also worked in different mediation efforts in conflicts within Horn of Africa and been Special Envoy of Pres. of Eritrea to numerous African countries and forums 1992–97. *Publications:* various articles on African politics. *Leisure interests:* reading, sports. *Address:* 241 Ardsley Road, Scardale, NY 10583, USA (Home). *E-mail:* hmenkerios@aol.com (Office).

MENON, Mambillikalathil Govind Kumar, MSc, PhD, FRS; Indian physicist; b. 28 Aug. 1928, Mangalore; s. of Kizhekepat Sankara Menon and Mambillikalathil Narayaniamma; m. Indumati Patel 1955; one s. one d.; ed Jaswant Coll., Jodhpur, Royal Inst. of Science, Bombay, Univ. of Bristol; Research Assoc., Univ. of Bristol 1952–53; Sr Award of Royal Comm. for Exhbn of 1851, Univ. of Bristol 1953–55; Reader, Tata Inst. of Fundamental Research, Bombay 1955–58; Assoc. Prof. 1958–60, Prof. and Dean of Physics Faculty 1960–64, Sr Prof. and Deputy Dir (Physics) 1964–66, Dir Tata Inst. of Fundamental Research 1966–75; Chair. Electronics Comm. and Sec. to Govt of India Dept of Electronics 1971–78; Scientific Adviser to Minister of Defence, Dir-Gen. Defence Research and Devt Org. and Sec. for Defence Research 1974–78; Dir-Gen. Council of Scientific and Industrial Research 1978–81; Sec. to Govt of India, Dept of Science and Tech. 1978–82, Dept of Environment 1981–82; Chair. Comm. for Additional Sources of Energy; Chair. Science Advisory Cttee to Cabinet 1982–85; CV Raman Prof., Indian Nat. Science Acad. 1986–91; Scientific Adviser to P.M. 1986–89 and mem. Govt Planning Comm. (with rank of Minister of State) 1982–89; Minister of State for Science and Tech. and for Educ. 1989–90; MP 1990–96; Chair. Cosmic Ray Comm. ICSU/IUPAP 1973–75, Bharat Electronics Ltd, Bharat Dynamics Ltd (Missiles); Pres. Asia Electronics Union 1973–75, Indian Science Congress Asscn 1981–82, India Int. Centre, New Delhi 1983–88, Int. Council of Scientific Unions 1988–93, Indian Statistical Inst. 1990–; mem. Bd Dirs. Escorts Ltd Indfos Industries Ltd; Vice-Pres. Int. Union of Pure & Applied Physics (IUPAP), Third World Acad. of Sciences 1983–88; Dr. Vikram Sarabhai Distinguished Prof. Indian Space Research Org. 1999–; mem. Pontifical Acad. of Sciences, Rome, Bd Inst. for Advanced Studies, (UNV), Tokyo ; Fellow, Indian Acad. of Sciences (Pres. 1974–76), Indian Nat. Science Acad. (Pres. 1981–82); M.N. Saha Distinguished Fellow 1994–99; Hon. Fellow Nat. Acad. of Sciences, India (Pres. 1987–88), Tata Inst. of Fundamental Research, Inst. of Electronics and Telecommunications Eng of India, Indian Inst. of Science, Bangalore, Nat. Inst. of Educ., Inst. of Physics (UK) 1997; Hon. mem. Inst. of Electrical and Electronic Engineers Inc.; Foreign Hon. mem. American Acad. of Arts and Sciences, Russian Acad. of Sciences; Hon. Pres. Asia Electronic Union; Hon. DEng (Stevens Inst. of Tech., USA); Hon.

DSc (Jodhpur, Delhi, Sardar Patel, Roorkee, Banaras Hindu, Jadavpur, Sri Venkateswara, Allahabad, Andhra, Utkal, North Bengal, Aligarh Muslim, Guru Nanak Dev and Bristol Univs. and I.I.T., Madras and Kharagpur); Shanti Swarup Bhatnagar Award for Physical Sciences, Council of Scientific and Industrial Research 1960; Repub. Day (Nat.) Awards, Govt of India: Padma Shri 1961, Padma Bhushan 1968, Padma Vibhushan 1985; Khaitan Medal, Royal Asiatic Soc. 1973; Cecil Powell Medal, European Physical Soc. 1978, G. P. Chatterjee Award of Indian Science Congress Asscn 1984, Award for Professional Excellence 1984, Pandit Jawaharlal Nehru Award for Sciences 1983, Om Prakash Bhasin Award for Science and Tech. 1985, C. V. Raman Medal of Indian Nat. Science Acad. 1985, Fourth J. C. Bose Triennial Gold Medal of Bose Inst. 1984; Sri Ashutosh Mukherjee Award of Indian Science Congress Asscn 1988; Abdus Salam Medal, Third World Acad. of Sciences 1997. *Publications:* 140 papers on cosmic ray and elementary particle physics. *Leisure interests:* bird-watching, photography. *Address:* C-63, Tarang Apts., 19 I. P. Ext., Mother Dairy Road, Patparganj, Delhi 110092, India. *Telephone:* (11) 2725010. *Fax:* (11) 2732243. *E-mail:* mgkmenon@ren02 .nic.in.

MENOTTI, Gian Carlo; Italian composer; b. 7 July 1911, Cadegliano; one s.; ed Curtis Inst. of Music, Philadelphia, Pa; went to USA 1928; mem. teaching staff Curtis Inst. of Music 1941–45; Hon. Assoc. Nat. Inst. of Arts and Letters 1953; Founder and Pres. Festival of Two Worlds, Spoleto, Italy; Hon. BM (Curtis Inst. of Music); Guggenheim Award 1946, 1947; Pulitzer Prize 1950, 1955; Kennedy Center Award 1984. *Compositions include:* operas: Amelia Goes to the Ball, The Old Maid and the Thief, The Island God, The Telephone, The Medium, The Consul, Amahl and the Night Visitors, The Labyrinth (own libretti), The Saint of Bleecker Street 1954, The Last Savage 1963, Martin's Lie 1964, Help, Help, The Glotolinks (space opera for children) 1968, The Most Important Man in the World 1971, Tamu Tamu 1973, Arrival 1973, La Loca 1979, St Teresa 1982, The Boy Who Grew Too Fast 1982, Goya 1986, Giorno di Nozze 1988; Song of Hope (cantata) 1980; ballet: Sebastian; film: The Medium (producer); Vanessa (libretto) 1958, The Unicorn, The Gorgon and the Manticore—a Madrigal Fable, Maria Golovin 1959, The Last Superman 1961, The Death of a Bishop of Brindisi (cantata) 1963; chamber music, songs, etc. *Address:* ASCAP Building, 1 Lincoln Plaza, New York, NY 10023, USA; Yester House, Gifford, E Lothian, EH41 4JF, Scotland.

MENSAH, Joseph Henry, MSc; Ghanaian politician; b. 31 Oct. 1928; ed Achimota Coll., Univ. Coll. of Gold Coast (now Univ. of Ghana), London School of Econs and Stanford Univ.; Asst Insp. of Taxes 1953; Research Fellow, Univ. Coll. of Gold Coast 1953–57; Lecturer in Econs, Univ. of Ghana 1957–58; Economist, UN H.Q., New York 1958–61; Chief Economist, Prin. Sec. and Exec. Sec. of Nat. Planning Comm. Ghana 1961–65; Economist, UN Dir, Div. of Trade and Econ. Co-operation and Econ. Comm. for Africa (ECA) 1965–69; Commr of Finance April–July 1969; MP for Sunyani (Progress Party) 1969–72; Minister of Finance 1969–72 and of Econ. Planning 1969–71; arrested Jan. 1972, released July 1973; re-arrested 1975; sentenced to eight years' imprisonment with hard labour Oct. 1975, released June 1978, in exile in London 1982; returned to Ghana Feb. 1995; MP for Sunyani East (New Patriotic Party) 1996–2000, Minority Leader in Parl. 1997–2000; re-elected MP for Sunyani East 2000, Majority Leader in Parl.; Minister in Charge of Govt Business, Minister for Parl. Affairs; Chair. Nat. Plan. Comm. *Address:* Office of Majority Leader, Parliament, Accra, Ghana (Office). *Telephone:* (21) 663399 (Office).

MENSHIKOV, Oleg Yevgenyevich; Russian actor; b. 8 Nov. 1960, Serpukhov, Moscow Region; ed Shchepkin Higher School of Theatre Art, Maly Theatre; Laurence Olivier Prize for Yesenin 1991, Film Critics Prize for Best Actor of 1994, prizes for best men's role at Festivals Kinotaurus 1996, Baltic Pearl 1996, other awards. *Major roles in films:* Kinsfolk, Flights in Dreams and When Awake, Kiss, Pokrovskye Gates, M. Lomonosov, Staircase, Moozund, Duba-Duba, Burnt by the Sun, Caucasian Prisoner, My Favourite Clown, Barber of Siberia, East-West, Envy of Gods, The Stop at Demand; in films of dirs N. Mikhalkov, A. Proshkin, A. Muratov, D. Khvan, S. Bodrov, R. Balayan, V. Kozakov, A. Sakharov. *Theatre roles include:* Ganya Ivolgin (Idiot after Dostoyevsky) 1981, Sergey (Sports Scenes of 1981) 1986, Caligula (Caligula) 1989, Yesenin (When She Danced) London 1991, Ikharev (Gamblers) London 1992, Nizhinsky (N. Nizhinsky) 1993. *Address:* Maly Kozykhinsky per. 8/18, Apt. 3, Moscow, Russia. *Telephone:* (095) 299-02-17 (Home).

MENSHOV, Vladimir Valentinovich; Russian film director and actor; b. 17 Sept. 1939, Baku; m. Vera Alentova 1963; one d.; ed Moscow Arts Theatre Studio School, All-Union State Inst. of Cinema (VGIK) 1970; RSFSR State Prize 1978, Acad. Award for Moscow Does Not Believe in Tears 1980, USSR State Prize 1981, RSFSR Artist of Merit 1984, Prize of American Guild of Cinema Owners. *Leading roles in:* A Man in His Place 1973, Last Meeting 1974, Personal Opinions 1977, Time for Reflection 1983, The Intercept 1986, Where is Nofelet? 1987, The Town Zero 1988, Red Mob 1993, Russian Ragtime 1993. *Films include:* Loss (Rozygrysh) 1977, Moscow Does Not Believe in Tears 1980, Love and Doves 1984, Shirly-Myrly 1995. *Address:* 3-d Tverskaya-Yamskaya 52, Apt. 29, 125047 Moscow, Russia. *Telephone:* (095) 250-85-43.

MENTER, Sir James Woodham, Kt, MA, PhD, ScD, FRS; British physicist, fmr university principal and company director (retd); b. 22 Aug. 1921; s. of the late Horace Menter and Jane Anne Lackenby; m. Marjorie Jean Whyte-Smith 1947; two s. one d.; ed Dover Grammar School and Peterhouse, Cambridge;

Experimental Officer, Admiralty 1942–45; Researcher, Univ. of Cambridge 1946–54; Tube Investments Research Labs., Dir of Research and Devt 1965–76; Dir Tube Investments Research Labs. 1961–68, Tube Investments PLC 1965–86, Round Oak Steelworks Ltd 1967–76, British Petroleum PLC 1976–87, Steetley PLC 1981–85; mem. SRC 1967–72; Vice-Pres. Royal Soc. 1971–76, Treas. 1972–76; Deputy Chair. Advisory Council Applied Research and Devt 1976–79; mem. Cttee of Inquiry into Eng Profession 1977–80; Man. Royal Inst. 1981–84, Vice-Pres. 1983–85, Chair. Council 1984–85; Fellow, Churchill Coll., Cambridge 1966–86; Pres. Inst. of Physics 1970–72, Metals Soc. 1976; Prin. Queen Mary Coll., Univ. of London 1976–86, Fellow 1986–; mem. Court Univ. of Stirling 1988–94; Hon. FRSE 1992; Hon. D. Tech. (Brunel) 1974; Hon. DUniv (Stirling) 1996; Bessemer Medal, Iron and Steel Inst. 1973, Glazebrook Medal and Prize, Inst. of Physics 1977. *Publications:* scientific papers in Proceedings of Royal Society, Advances in Physics, Inst. Iron and Steel and others. *Leisure interest:* fishing. *Address:* Strathlea, Taybridge Terrace, Aberfeldy, Perthshire, Scotland.

MENTRÉ, Paul; French civil servant and diplomatist; b. 28 June 1935, Nancy; s. of Paul Mentré and Cécile de Loye; m. 1st Sabine Brundsaux 1958 (divorced 1975); two d.; m. 2nd Gaëlle Bretillot 1975; two s.; m. 3rd Jehanne Collard 1992; ed Ecole Polytechnique, Ecole Nat. d'Admin; Insp. of Finance 1960; Special Asst, French Treas. 1965–70; Deputy Dir of the Cabinet of the Minister of Finance (V. Giscard d'Estaing) 1971–73; Under-Sec. Ministry of Economy and Finance 1971–72; Dir Crédit National 1973–75, Crédit Lyonnais 1973–75; Gen. Del. for Energy 1975–78; Financial Minister, French Embassy in Washington, DC 1978–82; Exec. Dir IMF and World Bank 1978–81; Insp.-Gen. of Finance 1981; Man. Dir Banque Nationale de Paris 1986–87, Dir-Gen. 1987–90; Pres. Dir-Gen. Crédit Nat. 1987–90; Pres. Crédit sucrier 1990, technopole de Caen Synergia 1991–94, Valréal 1992–, Trouville-Deauville Dist 1995–; mem. Supervisory Council Crédit local de France 1987–90; Dir European Investment Bank 1987–91; Chevalier, Ordre nat. du Mérite, des Arts et des Lettres; Saudi Royal Order. *Publications:* Imaginer l'avenir, Gulliver enchaîné 1982, L'Amerique et nous, L'insoutenable légèreté du fort 1989, articles on economic issues in Le Figaro, Le Monde and Les Echos. *Leisure interests:* tennis, skiing. *Address:* 18 rue de Bourgogne, 75007 Paris, France (Home).

MENZEL, Jiří; Czech film and theatre director and actor; b. 23 Feb. 1938; s. of Josef Menzel and Božena Jindřichová; ed Film Acad. of Performing Arts, specialized in film directing, 1957–61; film Dir and actor 1962–89; Head of Dept of Film Directing, Film Acad. of Performing Arts, Prague 1990–92; Producer of Studio 89 1991–; Dir Vinohradské divadlo (theatre) 1997, 1998–, Artistic Dir 2000; mem. Supervisory Bd O.P.S., Prague, European City of Culture 2000 1999; Oscar Prize, Santa Monica 1968 for Closely Observed Trains, Akira Kurosawa Prize for Lifelong Merits in Cinematography, San Francisco 1990, Ennio Flaiano, Prize for Lifetime Achievement in Cinematography, Pescara, Italy 1989; Officier, Ordre des Arts et des Lettres (France) 1990, Medal of Merit 1996, Czech Lion Prize, Czech Film and TV Acad. (for lifetime career) 1997, Golden Seal Prize (Yugoslavia) 1997. *Films directed include:* Closely Observed Trains, Skylarks on the String, Oh, My Village, End of the Old Times, Grand Prize of the Int. Film Producers' Meeting, Cannes 1990, The Beggar's Opera 1991, The Life and Extraordinary Adventures of Private Ivan Chonkin 1994. *Opera directed:* Dalibor by Smetana Cagliari 1999. *Plays directed:* Pré by J. Suchys, Prague 1999, A Midsummer Night's Dream, Český Krumlov 2000. *Publication:* Tak nevím (novel) 1998. *Leisure interest:* literature. *Address:* Studio 89, Krátký film Praha a.s., Jindřišská 34, 112 07 Prague 1 (Office); Divadlo na Vinchradech, Náměstí míru 7, 12000 Prague 2, Czech Republic (Home). *Telephone:* (2) 22520452 (Office). *Fax:* (2) 22520452. *E-mail:* dnv@anet.cz.

MER, Francis Paul, LèsLECON.; French business executive; b. 25 May 1939, Pau, Basses Pyrénées; s. of René Mer and Yvonne Casalta; m. Catherine Bonfils 1964; three d.; ed Lycée Montesquieu, Bordeaux, Ecole Nationale Supérieure des Mines, Paris and Ecole Polytechnique; mining engineer, Ministry of Industry 1966; tech. adviser, Abidjan 1967–68; Chair. Interministerial Cttee on European Econ. Co-operation 1969–70; Head of Planning, Saint-Gobain Industries 1971; Dir of Planning, Compagnie Saint-Gobain-Pont-à-Mousson 1973; Dir of Planning, later Dir-Gen. Saint-Gobain Industries 1973; Dir Société des Maisons Phénix 1976–78; Asst Dir-Gen. Saint-Gobain-Pont-à-Mousson 1978–82, Pres.-Dir-Gen. de Pont-à-Mousson SA 1982–86; Pres.-Dir-Gen. Usinor-Sacilor 1986–2002, Chair. Usinor Group 2001–02; Pres. Chambre syndicale de la sidérurgie française 1988–, Conservatoire Nat. des Arts et Métiers 1989–, Eurofer 1990–, Asscn nat. de Recherche Technique 1991–, Centre d'études prospectives et d'informations internationales 1995–2000; Pres. Int. Iron and Steel Inst. (INSI) 1997–; Dir Crédit Lyonnais 1997–, Electricité de France 1997–, Air France 1997–; Minister of the Economy, Finance and Industry May 2002–; Officier, Légion d'honneur, Ordre nat. du Mérite. *Address:* Ministry of the Economy, Finance and Industry, 139 rue de Bercy, 75007 Paris (Office); 9 rue Bobierre-de-Vallière, 92340 Bourg-la-Reine, France (Home). *Telephone:* 1-40-04-04-04. *Fax:* 1-43-43-75-97. *Website:* www.finances.gouv.fr.

MERCADO JARRIN, Gen. Luis Edgardo; Peruvian politician and army officer; b. 19 Sept. 1919, Barranco, Lima; s. of Dr. Alejandro Mercado Ballón and Florinda Jarrín de Mercado; m. Gladys Neumann Terán de Mercado 1951; one s. four d.; ed primary and secondary school, Colegio la Libertad de Moquegua, Escuela Militar de Chorrillos; commissioned 1940, Gen. of Div. 1970–; Prof. Escuela Militar, Escuela de Artillería, Escuela Superior de

Guerra, Centro de Altos Estudios Militares, etc.; Dir of Army Intelligence; del. of Peruvian Army to several inter-American army confs.; guest lecturer to U.S. Army, Fort Holabird and Fort Bragg; Commdt-Gen. Centro de Instrucción Militar del Perú 1968; Minister of Foreign Affairs 1968–71; Army Chief of Staff Jan.–Dec. 1972; Prime Minister and Minister of War 1973–75; awards include Grand Cross of Orden Militar de Ayacucho and Orden al Mérito Militar, Orden del Sol and orders from Colombia, Portugal, Argentina, Bolivia, Brazil and Venezuela. *Publications:* La Política y la Estrategia Militar en la Guerra Contrasubversiva en América Latina, El Ejército de Hoy en Nuestra Sociedad en Período de Transición y en el Campo Internacional, El Ejército y la Empresa; contributor to magazine of Interamerican Defence Coll., USA, Revista Militar del Perú, Brazilian Military Journal. *Leisure interests:* tennis, riding, classical music, reading (contemporary mil. philosophy, sociology and econ.). *Address:* Avenida Velasco Astete 1140, Chacarrilla del Estanque, Lima, Peru. *Telephone:* 256823.

MERCADO RAMOS, Fernando, BA, JD; Puerto Rican politician and lawyer; b. 18 June 1957, Lares; s. of Tomas Mercado-Estremere and Luz M. Ramos-Valez; m. Michelle Waters; two s.; ed Univ. of Puerto Rico, Univ. of Madrid, Spain; teacher of psychology and sociology Colegio Nuestra Señora del Carmen Rió Piedras 1979–1981; legal counsel Culture Comm., House of Reps. 1982–84; Exec. Dir Comm. of the Govt 1985–88, Sec.-Gen. 1989–92; judge Court of the First Instance 1992, Sec.-Gen. 1999; Sec.-Gen. Partido Popular Democrático 1999–2000; Sec. of State 2001–; mem. American Acad. of Judicial Educ. 1996–, American Judicature Soc., American Bar Assscn Judicial Admin. Div., American Judges' Asscn, Colegio de Abogados de Puerto Rico 1981–. *Publications include:* Grito a la Intimidad 1976, Un Pensamiento en Viaje 1990, Un Nuevo Lider: Esperanza de una Nueva Generación 1991. *Leisure interests:* reading, swimming, writing. *Address:* Office of the Secretary of the State, Department of State, P.O.B. 3271, San Juan, PR 00902-3271, Puerto Rico (Office). *Telephone:* (787) 723-4343 (Office). *Fax:* (787) 725-7303 (Office). *E-mail:* fmercado@estado.gobierno.pr (Office). *Website:* www.estado.gobierno.pr (Office).

MERCHANT, Ismail, BA, MBA; Indian film producer and film director; b. 25 Dec. 1936, Bombay; s. of Noormohamed Haji Abdul Rehman and Hazra Memon; ed St Xavier's Coll., Bombay, New York Univ.; f. Merchant Ivory Productions (with James Ivory, q.v.) 1961; Commdr des Arts et des Lettres; BAFTA Fellowship 2002. *Films:* (as producer) The Creation of Woman 1960, The Householder 1963, Shakespeare Wallah 1965, The Guru 1969, Bombay Talkie 1970, Adventures of a Brown Man in Search of Civilization 1971, Savages 1972, Helen, Queen of the Nautch Girls 1973, Autobiography of a Princess 1975, The Wild Party 1975, Sweet Sounds 1976, Roseland 1977, Hullabaloo Over Georgie and Bonnie's Pictures 1978, The Europeans 1979, Jane Austen in Manhattan 1980, Quartet 1981, Heat and Dust 1982, The Bostonians 1984, A Room with a View 1986, Maurice 1987, The Deceivers 1988, Slaves of New York 1989, Mr and Mrs Bridge 1990, The Ballad of the Sad Cafe 1991, Howards End 1992, The Remains of the Day 1993, Jefferson in Paris 1994, Feast of July 1995, Surviving Picasso 1996, A Soldier's Daughter Never Cries 1997, The Golden Bowl 2000, Refuge 2002, Le Divorce 2003; (as dir) Mahatma and the Mad Boy 1973, The Courtesans of Bombay 1983, In Custody 1994, The Proprietor 1996, Cotton Mary 1999, The Mystic Masseur 2001. *Publications:* Ismail Merchant's Indian Cuisine 1986, Hullaballoo in Old Jaypoore 1988, Ismail Merchant's Vegetarian Cooking 1992, Ismail Merchant's Florence 1994, Ismail Merchant's Passionate Meals 1994, Once Upon a Time, The Proprietor 1996, Ismail Merchant's Paris: Filming and Feasting in France 1999, My Passage from India: A Filmmaker's Journey from Bombay to Hollywood and Beyond. *Leisure interests:* cooking, music, cycling. *Address:* 250 West 57th Street, Suite 1825, New York, NY 10107 (Office); 400 East 52nd Street, New York, NY 10022, USA (Home). *Telephone:* (212) 582-8049 (Office). *E-mail:* imerchant@merchantivory.com (Office). *Website:* www.merchantivory.com (Office).

MERCIECA, Mgr Joseph, BA, S.TH.D., JUD; Maltese ecclesiastic; b. 11 Nov. 1928, Victoria, Gozo; s. of Saverio Mercieca and Giovanna Vassallo; ed Gozo Seminary, Gregorian Univ. and Lateran Univ., Rome; ordained priest 1952; Rector Gozo Seminary 1952–69; Judge of Roman Rota 1969–74; ordained Titular Bishop of Gemelle in Numidia, apptd. Auxiliary Bishop of Malta 1974; Vicar-Gen. 1975–76; Consultor, Congregation of the Sacraments and Congregation for the Doctrine of Faith, Vatican City 1976; Archbishop of Malta, Pres. Maltese Episcopal Conf. 1976–; mem. Apostolic Segnatura, Rome 1991. *Address:* Archbishop's Curia, Floriana (Office); Archbishop's Palace, Mdina, Malta (Home). *Telephone:* 21234317 (Office). *Fax:* 21223307 (Office).

MERCKX, Eddy; Belgian cyclist; b. 17 June 1945, Meen, Brussels sel-Kiezegem; m. Claudine Merckx; one s. one d.; world amateur champion 1963, first professional race 1964, winner World Road Championships 1967, 1971, 1974, Tours of Italy 1968, 1970, 1972, 1973, 1974, Tours de France 1969, 1970, 1971, 1972, 1974 (shares record for most wins, holds record (34) for most stage wins), Tours of Belgium 1970, 1971, Tour of Spain 1973, Tour of Switzerland 1974, thirty-two major classics; broke the then world hour record, Mexico City 1972; retd 1978 with 525 wins in 1,800 races; involved with manufacture of bicycles which bear his name 1980–; Belgian Sportsman of the Year 1969–74 (record), Belgian Athlete of the Century. *Website:* www.eddymerckx.be.

MEREDITH, William (Morris Meredith), AB; American poet and educationalist; b. 9 Jan. 1919, New York; s. of William Morris and Nelley (née Keyser) Meredith; ed Princeton Univ.; reporter New York Times 1940–41;

Instructor in English and Creative Writing Princeton Univ. 1946–50; Asst Prof. in English Univ. of Hawaii 1950–51; mem. Faculty Conn. Coll. 1955, Prof. of English 1965–83; Dir Conn. Coll. Humanities-Upward Bound Program 1964–68; Poetry Conservator Library of Congress 1978–80; Chancellor Acad. of American Poets 1964; mem. Nat. Inst. of Arts and Letters; Air Medal with Oak Leaf Cluster; awarded Loines Prize Nat. Inst. of Arts and Letters 1966, Van Wyck Brooks Award 1971, Int. Nicola Vaptsarov Prize in Literature, Sofia 1979, Pulitzer Prize for Poetry 1988, Nat. Book Award 1997. *Publications include:* poems: Love Letter from an Impossible Land 1944, Ships and Other Figures 1948, The Open Sea and Other Poems 1958, Shelley 1962, The Wreck of the Thresher and Other Poems 1964, Winter Verse 1964, Alcools (trans.) 1964, Earth Walk: New and Selected Poems 1970, Hazard, The Painter 1975, The Cheer 1980, Partial Accounts: New and Selected Poems 1987, Effort at Speech 1997. *Address:* 337 Kitemaug Road, Uncasville, CT 06382, USA (Office).

MEREZHKO, Viktor Ivanovich; Russian scriptwriter; b. 28 July 1937, Olginfeld, Rostov-on-Don Region; m. (wife deceased); one s. one d.; ed Ukrainian Inst. of Polygraphy, Lvov, All-Union Inst. of Cinematography; engineer Molot Publrs, Rostov-on-Don 1961–64; freelance 1968–; TV broadcaster and Head of History Programming; Vice-Pres. TV-6 Ind. TV; Chair. Kinoshock Festival, Nika Prize Cttee; State Prize 1986; Fipressi Prize, Venice Festival for Under the Blue Sky 1987. *Films:* over 45 film scripts including Hello and Goodbye 1971, The Quagmire 1979, The Kin 1981, Dream and Walking Flights 1983, Under the Blue Sky, Ryba: My Chicken 1993, The Two from Big Road 1996, Caucasus Roulette 1998. *Plays include:* I'm a Woman, Cry, Caucasian Roulette. *Leisure interest:* collecting side-arms. *Address:* Usiyevicha str 8, Apt. 133, 125319 Moscow, Russia (Home). *Telephone:* (095) 217-57-58; (095) 155-74-59 (Home).

MERI, Lennart; Estonian politician; b. 29 March 1929, Tallinn; s. of Georg-Peter Meri and Alice-Brigitta Meri; m. Helle Pihlak; two s. one d.; ed Tartu Univ.; deported to Siberia with family 1941–46; forbidden to practise history, took part in scientific expeditions to Middle Asia; Head of Manuscript Section Vanemuine Theatre; worked for Estonian Radio; Scriptwriter and Dir Tallinnfilm; Sec. Estonian Writers' Asscn; Founder, Dir Estonian Inst. 1989–90; active in Movt for Independence 1980s; Minister of Foreign Affairs 1990–92; Amb. to Finland April–Oct. 1992; Pres. of Estonia 1992–2001; Dr. hc (Helsinki Univ.) 1976; several decorations including from Mexico, Sweden, Finland, Denmark, Jordan, Latvia. *Publications:* numerous travel stories, literary essays, translations; several films depicting the history of Finno-Ugric people and the nations living by the Baltic Sea. *Leisure interests:* history, literature, maps. *Address:* Pilviku str. 3, Tallin, Estonia.

MERIDOR, Dan; Israeli politician and lawyer; b. 1947, Jerusalem; m.; four c.; ed Hebrew Univ.; fmr mem. Likud Party; Sec. of Govt 1982–84; mem. Knesset 1984–; Minister of Justice 1988–92, of Finance 1996–97; Leader Centre Party 2001–. *Address:* c/o Ministry of Finance, P.O. Box 883, 1 Rehov Kaplan, Kiryat Ben-Gurion, Jerusalem 91008, Israel.

MERIKAS, George, MD; Greek politician and professor of medicine; b. 5 May 1911, Agios Andreas; s. of Emmanuel Merikas and Helen (née Kritikou) Merikas; m. Irene (née Koutsogianni) Merikas 1945 (died 1971); two s. one d.; ed Medical School, Univ. of Athens; Assoc. Prof. of Medicine, Univ. of Athens 1953, Prof. 1970–78; Dir Dept of Medicine, Evangelismos Hosp., Athens 1960–70; Fulbright Grant, Univ. of Cincinnati Medical School 1964–65; mem. Acad of Athens 1978–, Pres. 1988–89; Minister of Health, Welfare and Social Services 1989–90; Pres. Nat. Aids Cttee in Greece 1988–; mem. Accad. Tiberina, New York Acad. of Sciences, Asscn for the Advancement of Sciences. *Publications:* Hepatitis Associated Antigen in Chronic Liver Disease 1970, Australia Antigen in the Liver 1972, Hepatitis B Core Antigen and Antibody in Primary Liver Cancer 1975, Internal Medicine, 2 Vols 1976, Cholesterol Gall-Stone Dissolution by CDC 1976. *Leisure interests:* literature, history. *Address:* 6 Vasileos Irakliou Str., 10682 Athens, Greece. *Telephone:* (1) 8210719.

MERINO CASTRO, Adm. José Toribio; Chilean naval officer; b. 14 Dec. 1915; m. Gabriela Margarita Riofrío Bustos 1952; three d.; ed Naval Acad.; specialized as Gunnery Officer, Naval Acad.; naval service on Maipo 1936, Rancagua 1939; Instructor Blanco Encalada 1940; Div. Officer Almirante Latorre 1943; Asst F.C. Officer USS Raleigh, Pacific Theater 1944; Artillery Officer, Serrano 1945; Commdr of Corvette Papudo 1952; Staff Coll. Course 1954; Tech. Adviser of Armaments 1955; Commdr of Destroyer Williams 1962, Riveros 1963; Vice-Chief of Gen. Staff 1964; C-in-C of the Fleet 1970–71; C-in-C of First Naval Zone 1972–73; C-in-C of the Navy 1973; mem. of the Govt Junta 1973–90; Armed Forces Medal III, II, I, Grand Star of Merit, Cross for Naval Merit, Decoration of Pres. of Repub. (Chile).

MERKEL, Angela, Dr rer. nat; German politician; b. 17 July 1954, Hamburg; ed Univ. of Leipzig; Research Assoc. Zentralinstitut für physikalische Chemie, East Berlin 1978–90; joined Demokratischer Aufruch (DA) 1989, Press Officer 1990; Deputy Spokesman for Govt of Lothar de la Maizière March–Oct. 1990; joined Christian Democratic Union (CDU) 1990, Deputy Fed. Chair. 1991–98, Gen. Sec. 1998–2000, Chair. March 2000–; mem. Bundestag 1990–; Minister for Women and Young People 1991–94, for Environment, Nature Conservation and Nuclear Safety 1994–98. *Address:* CDU, Konrad-Adenauer-Haus, Friedrich-Ebert-Allee 73–75 53113 Bonn, Germany (Office). *Telephone:* (228) 5440 (Office). *Fax:* (228) 544216 (Office). *E-mail:* organisation@cdu.de (Office). *Website:* www.cdu.de (Office).

MERKELBACH, Reinhold, DPhil; German professor of classics; b. 7 June 1918, Grenzhausen; s. of Paul Merkelbach and Gertrud Stade; m. Lotte Dorn 1941; one s. two d.; ed Schondorf Gymnasium, Univs of Munich and Hamburg; Asst at Classics Inst. Univ. of Cologne 1950–57, Prof. 1961–83, Prof. Emer. 1983–; Prof. Erlangen Univ. 1957–61; mem. Rheinisch-Westfälisch Akad. der Wissenschaften 1979–; Corresp. mem. British Acad. 1986–; Dr. hc Besançon 1978. *Publications:* Untersuchungen zur Odyssee 1951, Die Quellen des griechischen Alexanderromans 1954, Roman und Mysterium im Altertum 1961, Isisfeste 1962, (with M. West) Fragmenta Hesiodea 1968, (with F. Solmsen and M. West) Hesiodi Opera 1970, 1989, Mithras 1984, Die Hirten des Dionysos 1988, Platons Menon 1988, (with M. Totti) Abrasax I–IV 1990–96, Die Bedeutung des Geldes für die Geschichte der griechisch-römischen Welt 1992, Isis regina—Zeus Sarapis 1995, Hestia und Erigone 1996, Philologica 1997, (with J. Stauber) Steinepigramme aus dem griechischen Osten 1998–2001; many edns of Greek inscriptions, Ed. of Zeitschrift für Papyrologie und Epigraphik, Epigraphica anatolica, Beiträge zur klassischen Philologie. *Address:* Im Haferkamp 17, 51427 Bergisch-Gladbach, Germany. *Telephone:* (2204) 60727. *Fax:* (2204) 60727.

MERLINI, Cesare; Italian international affairs scholar and fmr professor of nuclear technologies; b. 29 April 1933, Rome; m.; two s. two d.; lecturer in Nuclear Technologies 1967–76; Prof. of Nuclear Technologies, Turin Polytechnic 1976–85; Dir Istituto Affari Internazionali, Rome 1970–79, Pres. 1979–2000; Pres. Exec. Cttee Council for USA and Italy 1983–92; mem. Bd of Dirs. and Exec. Cttee Unione Tipografico-Editrice Torinese publrs SpA, Turin, Chair. 1999–; mem. Trilateral Comm. 1973–2001, Council, Int. Inst. for Strategic Studies, London 1993–99, Gen. Council, Aspen Inst. Italia, Rome; mem. Bd of Dirs, Asscn Jean Monnet, Paris, ISPI, Milan. *Publications:* Fine dell'atomo? Passato e futuro delle applicazioni civili e militari dell'energia nucleare 1987, L'Europa degli Anni Novanta; Scenari per un futuro imprevisto (Co-author and Ed.) 1991; co-author and ed. of numerous books on nuclear energy and int. strategy, author of numerous articles on European and int. affairs and of scientific publs on nuclear reactors and related technological and eng problems. *Address:* Unione Tipografico-Editrice Torinese, Corsso Raffaello 28, 10125 Turin, Italy.

MERLONI, Vittorio; Italian industrialist; b. 30 April 1933, Fabriano, Ancona; m. Franca Carloni; four c.; ed Univ. of Perugia; Pres. Merloni Elettrodomestici SpA 1970–; mem. Confederazione Generale dell'Industria Italiana (Confindustra) 1976–, Pres. 1980–84; Dir Harvard Business School 1981; mem. two dels. to China; mem. Consiglio Nazionale dell'Economia e del Lavoro (Nat. Council of Economy and Labour); Cavaliere di Gran Croce al merito della Repubblica. *Leisure interests:* racing cars, boats. *Address:* Merloni Elettrodomestici SpA, Via Aristide Merloni 45, 60044 Fabriano, Ancona, Italy (Office).

MERLYN-REES, Baron (Life Peer), cr. 1992, of Morley and South Leeds in the County of West Yorkshire and of Cilfynydd in the County of Mid-Glamorgan; **Merlyn Merlyn-Rees,** PC, M.SC.(ECON.); British politician and lecturer; b. 18 Dec. 1920, Cilfynydd; s. of the late Levi Daniel Rees and Edith May Rees; name changed to Merlyn-Rees by deed poll 1992; m. Colleen Faith Cleveley 1949; three s.; ed Harrow Weald Grammar School, Goldsmiths Coll., London and London School of Econs; served RAF 1941–46, rank of Squadron Leader; Teacher, Harrow Weald Grammar School 1949–60; Labour Party Head Office 1960–62; Lecturer Luton Coll. of Tech. 1962–63; MP for Leeds S. 1963–83, for Morley and Leeds S. 1983–92; Parl. Pvt. Sec. to Chancellor of Exchequer 1964–65; Under-Sec. Ministry of Defence 1965–68, Home Office 1968–70; Opposition Spokesman for NI 1970–74; mem. Departmental Cttee Investigating Official Secrets Act; Sec. of State for NI 1974–76; Home Sec. 1976–79, Opposition Spokesman for Home Affairs 1979–80, for Energy 1980–83, Co-ordinator of Econ. Planning; mem. Cttee of Inquiry into events leading to Argentine invasion of the Falklands 1982; Pres. South Leeds Groundwork Trust 2001–; Pres. Video Standards Council 1990; Hon. Fellow, Goldsmiths' Coll., London; Hon. LLD (Wales) 1987, (Leeds) 1992. *Publications:* The Public Sector in the Mixed Economy 1973, Northern Ireland: A Personal Perspective 1985. *Leisure interest:* reading. *Address:* House of Lords, London, SW1A 0PW, England. *Telephone:* (20) 7219-3000.

MERMAZ, Louis; French politician and professor of history; b. 20 Aug. 1931, Paris; m. Annie d'Arbigny; 3 c.; teacher Lycée le Mans, Lycée Lakanal, Sceaux; Jr Lecturer in Contemporary History, Univ. of Clermont-Ferrand; Sec.-Gen. Convention des institutions républicaines 1965–69; mem. Socialist Party Nat. Secr. 1974–79, 1987–; mem. Nat. Ass. for Isère 1967–68, 1973–90, 1997–; Mayor of Vienne 1971–2001; Conseiller Gén. Canton of Vienne-Nord 1973–79, Vienne-Sud 1979–88; Pres. Conseil gén. of Isère 1976–85; Chair. Socialist Party Exec. Cttee 1979; Minister of Transport May–June 1981, of Equipment and Transport May–June 1988, of Agric. and Forests 1990–92, for Relations with Parl. and Govt Spokesman 1992–93; Pres. Nat. Ass. 1981–86, Socialist Group in Nat. Ass. 1988–90, Asscn Mer du Nord-Méditerranée 1989–94; mem. Senate for Isère 2001–; Chevalier Légion d'honneur. *Publications:* Madame Sabatier, Les Hohenzollern, L'autre volonté 1984, Madame de Maintenon 1985, Les Geôles de la République 2001. *Address:* Sénat, Palais du Luxembourg, 15 rue du Vaugirard, 75005 Paris (Office); Permanence Parlementaire, 2 rue des Célestes, 38200 Vienne, France. *Telephone:* 1-42-34-28-58 (Office); 4-74-85-47-58.

MERO, Muhammad Mustafa, PhD; Syrian politician; b. 1940, Tal-Mineen, Damascus; m.; two s. three d.; ed Damascus Univ.; Mayor of Daraa 1980–86,

of Al-Hasaka 1986–93; Gov. of Aleppo 1993–2000; Prime Minister of Syria March 2000–. *Address:* Office of the Prime Minister, rue Chahbandar, Damascus, Syria (Office). *Telephone:* (11) 2226000 (Office).

MERRIFIELD, (Robert) Bruce; American biochemist; b. 15 July 1921, Texas; s. of George Merrifield and Lorene Merrifield; m. Elizabeth Furlong 1949; one s. five d.; ed Univ. of California, Los Angeles (U.C.L.A.); Chemist, Park Research Foundation 1943–44; Teaching Asst, Chem. Dept U.C.L.A. 1944–47, Research Asst, Medical School 1948–49; Asst to Assoc. Prof. Rockefeller Inst. 1949–66, Prof. of Biochem. 1966–92, John D. Rockefeller Jr Prof. 1984–92, Prof. Emer. 1992–; developed solid phase peptide synthesis; mem. NAS; Nobel Guest Prof. 1968; Lasker Award 1969, Gairdner Award 1970, Intra-Science Award 1970, ACS Award 1972, Nichols Award 1973, Pierce Award 1979, Nobel Prize for Chem. 1984 for Devt of method of synthesising peptides and proteins, U.C.L.A. Distinguished Service Medal 1986, Rudiger Award, European Peptide Soc. 1990, RSC Medal 1990, Chemistry Pioneer Award, American Inst. of Chemists 1993; Glenn T. Seaborg Medal 1993, Order of San Carlos (Columbia). *Publications:* 150 articles in various scientific journals. *Leisure interests:* tennis, camping, hiking. *Address:* Rockefeller University, 1230 York Avenue, New York, NY 10021 (Office); 43 Merrifield Way, Cresskill, NJ 07626, USA (Home). *Telephone:* (212) 327-8244 (Office); (201) 567-0329 (Home). *Fax:* (212) 327-8245 (Office).

MERRILL, Robert; American baritone; b. 4 June 1919, Brooklyn, New York; s. of Abraham Miller and Lillian (née Balaban) Merrill; m. Marion Machno 1954; one s. one d.; debut at Metropolitan Opera as Germont (La Traviata) 1945; has since appeared throughout USA and Europe in most of the baritone repertoire including: Gérard (André Chénier), Renato (A Masked Ball), Figaro (The Barber of Seville), Rodrigo (Don Carlos), Scarpia (Tosca), Amonasro (Aida) and Rigoletto; singer with NBC 1946–; many concert and TV appearances; frequent recordings; Nat. Medal of Arts 1993, Medal of Honor, Ellis Island 1999 and numerous other awards. *Publications:* Once More from the Beginning 1965, Between Acts 1976, The Divas 1978. *Leisure interests:* art and golf.

MERSCH, Yves; Luxembourg central banker; b. 1 Oct. 1949; one s. one d.; called to the Bar, Luxembourg 1974; Public Law Asst, Univ. Paris–South 1974; Budget Asst, Ministry of Finance 1975; mem. staff IMF, Washington, DC, USA 1976–77; Minister of Finance, Fiscal Affairs and Structural Policies 1977–80; Adviser, Ministry of Finance, Monetary Affairs and Int. Financial Relations 1981; Govt Commr Luxembourg Stock Exchange 1985; Dir Treasury 1989; Pres. Luxembourg Cen. Bank 1998–; mem. Governing Council, European Cen. Bank. *Address:* Banque Centrale du Luxembourg, 2 boulevard Royal, 2983 Luxembourg, Luxembourg (Office). *Telephone:* 47-74-1 (Office). *Fax:* 47-74-49-01 (Office). *E-mail:* direction@bcl.lu (Office). *Website:* www.bcl.lu (Office).

MERSON, Michael; American international civil servant; b. 7 June 1945, New York; ed Amherst Coll., State of New York Health Science Center, Johns Hopkins Univ.; joined Center for Disease Control, Atlanta 1972; worked in several countries including Brazil and Bangladesh; joined WHO 1978, Medical Officer DirWHO Diarrhoeal Diseases Control Prog. 1978–87, Dir Acute Respiratory Infections Control Programme 1987–90; Exec. Dir Global Programme on AIDS 1990–95; Dean and Chair Dept of Epidemiology and Public Health, Yale Univ. School of Medicine 1995–, Lauder Prof. of Public Health 2001–; Surgeon Gen. Exemplary Service Medal, S. Flemming Award, Frank Bobbott Alumni Award, Award for Outstanding Contribution to the Campaign Against HIV/AIDS (Russia). *Publications:* International Health: Diseases, Programs, Systems and Policies (co-ed.); over 150 articles on subjects from food-borne diseases to effectiveness of HIV interventions and numerous book chapters (jtly).

MERTIN, Klaus, Dr rer. pol; German banker; b. 9 March 1922; Chair. of Supervisory Bd Deutsche Bank Berlin AG, Berlin, Dierig Holding AG, Augsburg; Deputy Chair. of Supervisory Bd Deutsche Centralbodenkredit AG, Berlin, Cologne; mem. of Supervisory Bd AG für Industrie und Verkehrswesen, Frankfurt, Badenwerk AG, Karlsruhe, Daimler-Benz AG, Stuttgart, Gerling-Konzern-Versicherungs-Beteiligungs AG, Cologne, Heidelberger Druckmaschinen AG, Heidelberg, Karstadt AG, Essen, Rheinmetall Berlin AG, Düsseldorf, Salamander AG, Kornwestheim, Schindler Aufzügefabrik GmbH, Berlin; mem. of Advisory Bd Barmenia Versicherungen, Wuppertal; mem. of Admin. Council Deutsche Bank Compagnie Financière Luxembourg, Luxembourg; mem. of Exec. Council Schott Glaswerke, Mainz. *Address:* Deutsche Bank AG, Taunusanlage 12, 60325 Frankfurt am Main, Germany.

MERTLÍK, Pavel; Czech politician and economist; b. 7 May 1961, Havlíčkův Brod; m. Dana Mertlík; two s.; ed School of Econs, Prague, Charles Univ., Prague; Prof. of Econs, Charles Univ. –1998; mem. Czech Social Democratic Party 1995–; Minister of Finance and Deputy Prime Minister 1998–2001; with Centre for Czech Integration to European Economy 1998–2001; Chief Economist Raiffeisen Bank, Prague 2001–. *Publications:* numerous articles on privatization of Czech industry. *Leisure interests:* cycling, fishing, skiing. *Address:* Raiffeisenbank, Václavské nám.č.11, 12000 Prague 2, Czech Republic (Office). *Telephone:* (2) 21421811 (Office). *Fax:* (2) 21421811 (Office). *E-mail:* praha@raiffleas.cz (Office). *Website:* www.rb.cz (Office).

MERTON, John Ralph, M.B.E.(MIL.); British artist; b. 7 May 1913, London; s. of Sir Thomas Ralph Merton, KBE and Violet Margery Harcourt Sawyer; m.

Viola Penelope von Bernd 1938; three d. (one deceased); ed Eton. Coll., Balliol Coll., Oxford; served World War II, Lt Col Air Photo Reconnaissance Research Unit 1944; Legion of Merit, USA 1944. *Portraits include:* Jane Dalkeith (now Duchess of Buccleuch) (Royal Acad. 'A' Award) 1958, Triple Portrait of HRH The Princess of Wales 1988, drawing of HM The Queen as Head of the Order of Merit 1989, James Meade (winner Nobel Prize for Economics) 1987, Paul Nitze 1991, Lord and Lady Romsey With a Mirror Reflecting Broadlands 1997. *Publication:* A Journey Through an Artist's Life (limited Edn) 1994. *Leisure interests:* music, making things, underwater photography. *Address:* Pound House, Pound Lane, Oare, Nr. Marlborough, Wiltshire, SN8 4JA, England. *Telephone:* (1672) 563539.

MERTON, Robert C., PhD; American economist; b. 31 July 1944, New York; s. of Robert K. Merton and Suzanne Merton; m. June Rose 1966 (separated 1996); two s. one d.; ed Columbia Univ., Calif. Inst. of Tech., Mass. Inst. of Tech.; Instructor in Econs MIT 1969–70; Asst Prof. of Finance Alfred P. Sloan School of Man. 1970–73, Assoc. Prof. 1973–74, Prof. 1974–80, J.C. Penney Prof. of Man. 1980–88; Visiting Prof. of Finance, Harvard Univ. 1987–88, George Fisher Baker Prof. of Business Admin. 1988–98; John and Natty McArthur Univ. Prof. 1998–; Research Assoc. Nat. Bureau of Econ. Research 1979–; Sr Adviser Office of Chair., Salomon Inc. 1988–93; Prin., Co-Founder Long-Term Capital Man. Greenwich, Conn. 1993–99; Sr Adviser, JP Morgan & Co. 1999–2001; Co-Founder Integrated Finance Ltd 2002–; Sr Fellow Int. Asscn of Financial Engineers; Fellow Econometric Soc., American Acad. of Arts and Sciences, Financial Man. Asscn 2000; mem. NAS, American Finance Asscn (Dir 1982–84, Pres. 1986, Fellow 2000); numerous editorial bds.; Hon. Prof. H.E.C. School of Man., Paris 1995–; Hon. MA (Harvard) 1989; Hon. LLD (Chicago) 1991; Hon. DEcon Sc. (Lausanne) 1996; Dr. hc (Paris-Dauphine) 1997; Hon. Dr. Man. Sc. (Nat. Sun Yat-sen Univ., Taiwan) 1998; awarded Leo Melamed Prize, Univ. of Chicago Business School 1983, Financial Engineer of the Year Award, Int. Asscn of Financial Engineers 1993, shared Nobel Prize for Econs 1997 for devising Black-Scholes Model for determining value of derivatives, Michael Pupin Medal for Service to the Nation, Columbia Univ. 1998, Distinguished Alumni Award, Calif. Inst. of Tech. 1999, numerous other awards. *Publications:* The Collected Scientific Papers of Paul A. Samuelson, Vol. III (Ed.) 1972, Continuous-Time Finance 1990, Casebook in Financial Engineering: Applied Studies in Financial Innovation (jtly.) 1995, The Global Financial System: A Functional Perspective (jtly.) 1995, Finance (jtly.) 2000, numerous articles in professional journals. *Address:* Graduate School of Business, Harvard University, 397 Morgan, Soldiers Field, Boston, MA 02163, USA. *Telephone:* (617) 495-6678 (Office). *Fax:* (617) 495-8863 (Office). *E-mail:* rmerton@hbs.edu (Office). *Website:* www.people.hbs.edu/rmerton (Home).

MERZ, Friedrich; German politician and lawyer; b. 11 Nov. 1955, Brilon; m. Charlotte Gass; one s. two d.; judge Saarbrücken Dist Court 1985–86; lawyer 1986–, Asscn of Chemical Industry 1986–89, Regional Court of Appeal, Cologne 1992–; MEP 1989–94; Parliamentary Leader Christian Democratic Union (CDU) 2000–; mem. Bundestag 1994–. *Address:* Bundeshaus, Platz der Republik, 11011 Berlin, Germany (Office); CDU, Konrad-Adenauer-Haus, Klingelhöferstrasse 8, 10785 Berlin. *Telephone:* (30) 220700. *Fax:* (30) 22070111. *E-mail:* post@cdu.de (Office). *Website:* www.cdu.de (Home).

MESELSON, Matthew Stanley, PhB, PhD, FAAS; American professor of molecular biology; b. 24 May 1930, Denver, Colo; s. of Hymen Avram and Ann Swedlow Meselson; m. 1st Katherine Kaynis 1960; m. 2nd Sarah Leah Page 1969; two d.; m. 3rd Jeanne Guillemin 1986; ed Univ. of Chicago, Univ. of California (Berkeley) and California Inst. of Tech.; Research Fellow, Calif. Inst. of Tech. 1957–58, Asst Prof. of Physical Chem. 1958–59, Sr Research Fellow in Chemical Biology 1959–60; Assoc. Prof. of Biology, Harvard Univ. 1960–64, Prof. of Biology 1964–76, Thomas Dudley Cabot Prof. of Nat. Sciences 1976–; Chair. Fed. of American Scientists 1986–88; mem. Inst. of Medicine, NAS, American Acad. of Arts and Sciences, Acad. Santa Chiara, American Philosophical Soc., Council on Foreign Relations; Foreign mem. Royal Soc., Acad. des Sciences, Russian Acad. of Sciences; Hon. DSc (Oakland Coll.) 1966, (Columbia) 1971, (Chicago) 1975; Hon. ScD (Yale) 1987; Dr. hc (Princeton) 1988; Prize for Molecular Biology, NAS 1963, Eli Lilly Award in Microbiology and Immunology 1964; Public Service Award, Fed. of American Scientists 1972 Alumni Medal, Univ. of Chicago Alumni Asscn 1971, Alumni Distinguished Service Award, Calif. Inst. of Tech. 1975, Lehman Award of NY Acad. of Sciences 1975, Leo Szilard Award, American Physical Soc. 1978, Presidential Award of NY Acad. of Sciences 1983, MacArthur Fellow 1984–89, Scientific Freedom and Responsibility Award, AAAS 1990, Thomas Hunt Morgan Medal (Genetics Soc. of America) 1995. *Publications:* numerous papers on the biochem. and molecular biology of nucleic acids and on arms control of biological and chemical weapons, in various numbers of Proceedings of NAS and of Scientific American, etc. *Address:* Sherman Fairchild Building, 7 Divinity Avenue, Harvard University, Cambridge, MA 02138, USA. *Telephone:* (617) 495-2264. *Website:* mcb.harvard.edu/meselson/ (Office).

MESGUICH, Daniel Elie Emile; French actor and theatre and opera director; b. 15 July 1952, Algiers; s. of William Mesguich and Jacqueline Boukabza; m. Danielle Barthélémy 1971; one s. three d.; ed Lycée Thiers, Marseilles, Sorbonne, Paris and Conservatoire Nat. Supérieur d'Art Dramatique; actor 1969–; stage dir 1972–; f. Théâtre du Miroir 1974; Prof. Conservatoire Nat. Supérieur d'Art Dramatique 1983–; Dir Théâtre Gérard Philippe, Saint-Denis 1986–88, Théâtre de la Métaphore, Lille 1991–98; numerous appearances on stage, film and TV and dir of numerous stage plays and operas; Chevalier, Ordre Nat. du Mérite, Officier des Arts et des Lettres. *Films:* Molière 1977, La Fille de Prague avec un sac très lourd 1978, Dossier 51 1978, L'Amour en fuite 1978, Clair de femme 1979, La Banquière 1980, Allon-z'enfants 1981, La Chanson du mal-aimé 1981, Les Iles 1982, La Belle captive 1982, L'Araignée de satin 1982, Contes clandestins 1983, Les Mots pour le dire 1983, Paris vu par 20 ans après 1984, Le Radeau de la Méduse 1988, 1998, L'Autrichienne 1989, Toussaint Louverture 1989, La Femme fardée 1990, Jefferson in Paris 1994, Tiré à part 1997. *Publication:* L'Eternel éphémère 1991. *Address:* Agence A, Monita Derriuex, 34 rue Vivienne, 75002 Paris, France.

MESHKOV, Aleksi Yuryevich; Russian diplomatist and politician; b. 29 Aug. 1959, Moscow; m. Galina Ivanovna Meshkova; two s. two d.; ed Moscow State Inst. of Int. Relations; with diplomatic service 1981–; referent, attaché then Third Sec. USSR Embassy, Spain 1981–86, First Sec., Counsellor then Sr Counsellor (Russian Embassy) 1992–97; Third, Second, First Sec. then Head of Div., Dept of Co-operation in Science and Tech., Ministry of Foreign Affairs 1986–92, Deputy Head, Dept of European Co-operation 1997–98, Head, Dept of Foreign Policy Planning 1999–2001, mem. Collegiate Ministry of Foreign Affairs 2000–, Deputy Minister of Foreign Affairs 2001–; Order of Friendship. *Address:* Ministry of Foreign Affairs, Smolenskaya-Sennaya 32–34, 121200 Moscow, Russia (Office). *Telephone:* (095) 244-16-94 (Office). *Fax:* (095) 244-37-38 (Office). *E-mail:* meshkov@mid.ru (Office).

MESIĆ, Stipe; Croatian politician; b. 24 Dec. 1934, Orahovica; m.; two d.; ed Univ. of Zagreb; active in student politics; MP of Socialist Repub. of Croatia, mid 1960s; served one-year prison sentence for participation in Croatian Spring Movt, early 1970s; Sec. Croatian Democratic Union (HDZ), later Chair. Exec. Council; Prime Minister first govt of Repub. of Croatia 1990; mem. Presidency of Socialist Fed. Repub. of Yugoslavia, subsequently Pres. until resgnd 1991; Speaker Croatian Parl. 1992–94; f. Croatian Independent Democrats 1994; joined Croatian People's Party (HNS) 1997; Pres. Repub. of Croatia 2000–; Hon. mem. Int. Foundation of Raoul Wallenberg 2002; State Order of the Star of Romania 2000, Grand Star of the Decoration of Honour for Merit (Austria) 2001, Golden Order Gjergj Kastrioti Skënderbeu (Albania) 2001, Grand Cross of the Order of Saviour (Greece) 2001, Order of St Michael and St George (Great Britain); Charles Univ. Medal (Czech Repub.) 2001, Crans Montana Forum Award 2002, American Bar Asscn Award 2002. *Publications:* The Break-up of Yugoslavia: Political Memoirs 1992, 1994. *Leisure interests:* nanbudo, swimming. *Address:* Office of the President, Pantovčak 241, 10000 Zagreb, Croatia (Office). *Telephone:* (1) 4565191 (Office). *Fax:* (1) 4565299 (Office). *E-mail:* office@president.hr (Office). *Website:* www.predsjednik.hr (Office).

MESKILL, Thomas Joseph, BS; American politician and lawyer; b. 30 Jan. 1928, New Britain, Conn.; s. of the late Thomas Joseph Meskill and of Laura Warren Meskill; m. Mary T. Grady; three s. two d.; ed New Britain Senior High School, Trinity Coll., Hartford, Univ. of Connecticut Law School and New York Univ. School of Law; Asst Corpn Counsel, New Britain 1960–62; Mayor of New Britain 1962–64; Corpn Counsel 1965–66; elected to Congress 1966, 1968; Gov. of Connecticut 1970–75; Judge US Circuit Court 1975–, Chief Judge 1992–93; mem. American Bar Asscn; Republican. *Address:* US Court of Appeals, Old Post Office Plaza, Suite 204, 114 W Main Street, New Britain, CT 06051, USA (Office). *Telephone:* (860) 828-1301 (Home).

MESKÓ, Attila, DSc; Hungarian professor of geophysics; b. 23 April 1940, Budapest; s. of Illés Meskó and Ida Tóth; m.; two d.; ed Lóránd Eötvös Univ.; Asst and research worker Lóránd Eötvös Geophysical Inst., Hungarian Acad. of Sciences, Seismological Observatory and Dept of Sciences, Observatory and Dept of Geophysics 1958–59, 1964–73; consultant with seismic prospecting co. 1966–83; Assoc. Prof. in Geophysics 1973–80; Head of Research Group for Environmental Physics and Geophysics 1985–93; Deputy Sec.-Gen. Hungarian Acad. of Sciences 1999–; Pres. Geophysical Cttee Hungarian Acad. of Sciences 1979–92, Earth Sciences Dept, Lóránd Eötvös Univ. 1994–, Asscn of Hungarian Geophysicists 1998–; mem. Hungarian Acad. of Sciences; State Prize 1978. *Publications:* numerous books and papers in scientific journals. *Leisure interest:* music. *Address:* 1126 Budapest, Böszörményi u. 19/c, Hungary. *Telephone:* (1) 3127069 (Office); (1) 3559546. *Fax:* (1) 3113868 (Office). *E-mail:* mesko@office.mta.hu (Office).

MESSAGER, Annette; French artist; b. 30 Nov. 1943, Berck-sur-Mer; d. of André and Marie L. (née Chalessin) Messager; ed Ecole Nationale Supérieure des Arts Décoratifs; Prix National de Sculpture 1996; Chevalier, Ordre des Arts et des Lettres. *Solo exhibitions include:* Munich and Grenoble 1973, Musée d'Art Moderne, Paris 1974, 1984, Rheinisches Landesmuseum, Bonn 1976, 1978, Galerie Seriaal, Amsterdam 1977, Holly Solomon Gallery, New York 1978, Galerie Gillespie-Laage, Paris 1979, 1980, Fine Arts Gallery, Univ. of Calif. and Irvine, San Francisco Museum of Modern Art 1981, PS 1, New York, Galerie Hans Mayer, Düsseldorf 1981, Artist's Space, New York 1982, Musée des Beaux-Arts, Calais, Galérie Gillespie-Laage-Salomon, Paris 1983, Vienna and Zurich 1984, Riverside Studio, London 1985, Galerie Gillespie-Laage-Salomon, Sydney 1985, Galerie Laage Salomon, Paris 1988, Consortium Dijon 1988, Centre d'Art Contemporain, Castres 1988, Musée de Grenoble 1989, Musée de la Roche sur Yon, Musée de Rochechouart, Bonner Kunstverein, Düsseldorf Kunstverein, Galerie Crousel-Robelin, Paris 1990, Galerie Elisabette Kaufmann, Basle, Mercer Union, Cold City Gallery, Toronto 1991, Arnolfini, Bristol, Douglas Hyde Gallery, Dublin, Camden Arts Centre, London, Univ. of Iowa Museum of Art 1992, Josh Baer Gallery, New

York 1993, Monika Sprüth Gallery, Cologne 1994, Musée d'Art Moderne, Paris, Los Angeles Co. Museum of Art, Pace Roberts Foundation, San Antonio, USA, Museum of Modern Art, New York 1995, Art Inst. of Chicago 1996, Larry Gagosian Gallery, New York 1997, Musée des Arts d'Afrique et d'Océanie, Paris 1998, Museo Nacional Centro de Arte Reina Sofía, Madrid 1999, Galerie Marian Goodman, Paris 2000, Monika Sprüth Gallery Cologne 2000, Musée des Beaux-Arts Nantes 2002, Palazzo delle Papesse Centro de Arte Contemporanea Siena 2002, Documenta XI Kassell 2002. *Address:* c/o Marian Goodman, 79 rue du Temple, 75003 Paris (Office); 146 boulevard Camelinat, 92240 Malakoff, France. *Telephone:* 1-42-53-45-77.

MESSAS, David, LPh; rabbi; b. 15 July 1934, Meknès, Morocco; s. of Shalom Messas; Dir Edmond-Fleg Univ. Centre, Ecole Maimonde de Boulogne-billancourt 1968, Tout Familial (student's forum) 1973; Rabbi for Algerons community, Synagogue du Brith Shalom 1984; Chief Rabbi of Geneva 1989–94, of Paris 1995; Chevalier Légion d'honneur, Chevalier Ordre des Palmes Académiques, Prix de Jérusalem. *Address:* c/o Consistoire Israélite de Paris, 17 rue Saint Georges, 75009 Paris, France.

MESSER, Thomas Maria, MA; American museum director; b. 9 Feb. 1920, Bratislava, Czechoslovakia; s. of Richard Messer and Agatha (Albrecht) Messer; m. Remedios García Villa 1948; ed Thiel Coll. (Greenville, Pa), Boston, Paris and Harvard Univs; Dir, Roswell Museum, New Mexico 1949–52; Directorships American Fed. of Arts 1952–56, Trustee and First Vice-Pres. 1972–75; Dir, Boston Inst. of Contemporary Art 1956–61; Dir Solomon R. Guggenheim Museum, New York 1961–88; Pres. Asscn of Art Museum Dirs. 1974–75 (Hon. mem. 1988–); Chair. Int. Cttee for Museums and Collections of Modern Art, Int. Council of Museums 1974–77, Hon. Chair. 1977–; Chair. Int. Exhbns Cttee 1976–78, US/ICOM (Nat. Cttee of Int. Council of Museums) 1979–81; Adjunct Prof. of Art History, Harvard Univ. 1960; Barnard Coll. 1965, 1971; Sr Fellow, Center for Advanced Studies, Wesleyan Univ. 1966; Trustee Center for Inter-American Relations (now Americas Soc.) 1974–, Exec. Council Int. Council of Museums 1983–85; Vice-Chair. US Int. Council of Museums Cttee of American Asscn of Museums, Washington, DC 1979–81; Pres. MacDowell Colony Inc. 1977–80; Dir Solomon R. Guggenheim Foundation 1980–88, Trustee 1985–90, Dir Emer. 1990–; mem. Advisory Bd, Palazzo Grassi Venice 1986–97; Trustee Fontana Foundation, Milan 1988–; Chair. Arts Int., Inst. of Int. Educ. 1988–90; Trustee, Inst. of Int. Educ. 1991–99, Hon. Trustee 1999–, Fontana Foundation 1996–; Curatorships Schirn Kunsthalle, Frankfurt 1988–99, Sr Adviser La Caixa Foundation, Barcelona 1990–94; Visiting Prof. Frankfurt Goethe Univ. 1991–; fmr mem. Museum Advisory Panel of Nat. Endowment for the Arts, Art Advisory Panel to Commr of Internal Revenue Service 1974–77; mem. Council Nat. Gallery of the Czech Repub. 1994–99; Trustee Isamo Noguchi Foundation, New York and Tokyo 1998–; Hon. mem. Inst. of Int. Educ. 1999–; Dr Fine Arts hc (Univ. of Mass.), (Thisk Coll. Greenville USA), (Univ. of Arts, Philadelphia); Kt, Royal Order of St Olav (Norway); Officer's Cross of Order of Merit (FRG) 1975; Officer of Order of Leopold II (Belgium) 1978, Officier Légion d'honneur 1989, Austrian Cross of Honour for Science and Art 1981, Goethe Medal 1990. *Major retrospective exhibitions at the Guggenheim Museum include:* Edvard Munch, Vasily Kandinsky, Egon Schiele, Paul Klee and Alberto Giacometti. *Publications:* The Emergent Decade: Latin American Painters and Paintings in the 1960s 1966, Edvard Munch 1973, Vasily Kandinsky 1997; museum catalogues on: Vasily Kandinsky, Paul Klee, Edvard Munch, Egon Schiele, etc.; articles and contributions to numerous art journals. *Leisure interests:* music and literature, cultural pursuits. *Address:* 205 E 77th Street, New York, NY 10021; 303 E 57th Street, New York, NY 10022 (Office); 35 Sutton Place, New York, NY 10022, USA (Home). *Telephone:* (212) 486-1393 (Office); (212) 355-8611 (Home); (212) 249-2727. *Fax:* (212) 249-2727 (Office). *E-mail:* tmmesser@aol.com (Office).

MESSIER, Jean-Marie Raymond Pierre; French government official and business executive; b. 13 Dec. 1956, Grenoble; s. of Pierre Messier and Janine Delapierre; m. Antoinette Fleisch 1983; three s. two d.; ed Lycée Champollion, Grenoble, Ecole polytechnique, Ecole Nat. d'Admin.; Inspecteur des Finances 1982; Dir Office of Minister in charge of privatization at Ministry of Econ., Finance and Privatization, then Tech. Adviser to Minister 1986–88; Man. Partner Lazard Frères et Cie 1989–94; Chair. Fonds Partenaires 1989–94; Dir, Gen. Man. and Chair. Exec. Cttee Générale des Eaux group (now Vivendi) 1994, Chair. and Man. Dir 1996–2002; Chair. and Man. Dir Cégétel 1996–2000, Cie Immobilière Phénix 1994–95, Cie Générale d'Immobilier et de Services (CGIS) 1995–96, SGE 1996–97; Dir Canal Plus 1995 (merged with Universal and Vivendi 2000) to form Vivendi Universal, Chair. and CEO 2000–02; Dir LVMH, Strafor-Facom, Saint-Gobain, UGC, Daimler-Benz, New York Stock Exchange 2001–02. *Publication:* j6m.com: faut-il avoir peur de la nouvelle économie 2000. *Leisure interests:* flying, skiing, tennis. *Address:* c/o Vivendi, 42 avenue de Friedland, 75380 Paris cedex 08, France (Office).

MESSMER, Pierre Auguste Joseph, LLD; French politician and overseas administrator; b. 20 March 1916, Vincennes; s. of Joseph Messmer and Marthe (née Farcy) Messmer; Christiane Marie Alice Terrail; ed Faculté de droit de Paris; mil. service 1937–45, with "Free French" forces 1940–45; Sec.-Gen. Interministerial Cttee for Indochina 1946; Dir of Cabinet High Comm. in Indochina 1947–48; Gov. Mauritania 1952, Ivory Coast 1954–56; High Commr Cameroon 1956–58; High Commr-Gen. French Equatorial Africa 1958, French West Africa 1958–59; Minister for the Armed Forces 1960–69; elected Deputy for Moselle, Nat. Ass. 1968, 1969, 1973, 1978, 1981, 1986; Minister of State for Overseas Depts and Territories 1971–72; Prime Minister

1972–74; mem. European Parl. 1979–84; Pres. RPR Group in Nat. Ass. 1986–88, Charles de Gaulle Inst. 1992–95, Fondation Charles de Gaulle 1992–97; Sec. in Perpetuity, Acad. des Sciences Morales et Politiques 1995–98; mem. Institut de France (Acad. des Sciences Morales et Politiques) 1988– (Chancellor 1999–), Acad. Française 1999–; Grand-Croix, Légion d'honneur, Compagnon de la Libération, Croix de guerre, Médaille de la Résistance. *Publications include:* Après tant de batailles 1992, Les Blancs s'en vont 1998, Le Rôle et la place de l'Etat au début du XXI siècle 2001. *Leisure interests:* tennis, sailing. *Address:* Institut de France, 23 quai Conti, 75006, Paris; 3 rue de Chaillot, 75116 Paris, France. *Telephone:* 1-44-41-44-95 (Office). *Fax:* 1-44-41-44-34 (Office). *E-mail:* institut-de-france@fr (Office).

MESSNER, Hon. Anthony, FCA; Australian government official; b. 24 Sept. 1939, East Melbourne, Vic.; s. of Colin Thomas Messner and Thelma Luxford Messner; ed South Australia Inst. of Tech., Adelaide; practised as chartered accountant 1965–75, 1990–97; mem. Fed. Senate for S. Australia 1975–90; Minister for Veterans' Affairs, Asst Treas. 1980–83; Shadow Minister for Social Security 1983–85, for Finance and Taxation 1985–87, for Communications 1987–88, for Public Admin. 1988–89; Admin. Norfolk Island 1997–. *Leisure interests:* rugby, reading biographies and history, music, cricket. *Address:* Office of the Administrator, New Military Barracks, Norfolk Island, 2899 (Office); Government House, Norfolk Island, Australia (Home). *E-mail:* tony.messner@dotrs.gov.au (Office); govhouse@ni.net.nf (Home).

MESSNER, Reinhold; Italian mountaineer, lecturer, author and politician; b. 17 Sept. 1944, Brixen; one s. three d.; ed Univ. of Padua; began climbing aged four with his father; joined expedition to Nanga Parbat (8,000 m), N Pakistan 1970; with partner Peter Habeler became first person to climb Mount Everest without supplementary oxygen; later climbed Everest alone by North Col route without oxygen; the first person to climb all the world's 8,000m peaks in Himalayas and adjoining ranges; made first crossing of Antarctica on foot (2,800 km.) since Shackleton 1989/90; collaborated with Dir Werner Herzog in filming his story Schrei aus Stein 1991; f. int. org. Mountain Wilderness; f. Sulden Museum, Juval Museum (collections of Asiatica); Inauguration of the Museum 'Dolomites'/Monte Rite 2002 MEP 1999–; ITAS 1975, Primi Monti 1968, Dav 1976, 1979, Sachbuchpreis for Donauland 1995, Coni 1998, Bambi Lifetime Award 2000, Royal Geographical Soc.'s Gold Medal 2001. *Publications:* Free Spirit: A Climber's Life, Antarctica, Moving Mountains 2001. *Address:* Europaallee 2, 39012 Meran (Office); Castle Juval, 39020 Kastelbell, Italy (Home). *Telephone:* (0473) 221852 (Office). *Fax:* (0473) 221852 (Office). *E-mail:* mail@reinhold-messner.de (Office). *Website:* www .reinhold-messner.de (Office).

MESTEL, Leon, BA, PhD, FRS; British professor emeritus of astronomy; b. 5 Aug. 1927, Melbourne, Australia; s. of Rabbi Solomon Mestel and Rachel née Brodetsky; m. Sylvia L. Cole 1951; two s. two d.; ed West Ham Secondary School, London and Trinity Coll., Cambridge; ICI Research Fellow, Univ. of Leeds, 1951–54; Commonwealth Fund Fellow, Princeton Univ. Observatory 1954–55; Univ. Asst Lecturer in Math., Cambridge 1955–58, Univ. Lecturer 1958–66; Fellow, St John's Coll., Cambridge 1957–66; Visiting mem. Inst. for Advanced Study, Princeton 1961–62; J. F. Kennedy Fellow, Weizmann Inst. for Science, Israel 1966–67; Prof. of Applied Math., Univ. of Manchester 1967–73; Prof. of Astronomy, Univ. of Sussex 1973–93, Prof. Emer. 1993–; Eddington Medal 1993, Gold Medal 2002 Royal Astronomical Soc. *Publications:* Stellar Magnetism 1999; papers, reviews, conf. reports on different branches of theoretical astrophysics. *Leisure interests:* reading, music. *Address:* Astronomy Centre, CPES, University of Sussex, Falmer, Brighton, BN1 9QJ; 13 Prince Edward's Road, Lewes, E Sussex, BN7 1BJ, England. *Telephone:* (1273) 606755 ext. 2430 or 8604 (Office); (1273) 472731 (Home). *Fax:* (1273) 677196 (Office). *E-mail:* lmestel@star.pact.cpes.susx.ac.uk (Office); mestel@mestel.fsnet.co.uk (Home).

MESTIRI, Mohamed Said; Tunisian professor of medicine; b. 22 June 1919, Tunis; s. of Tahar Mestiri and Khedija Kassar; m. Zohra Chenik (d. of fmr Prime Minister Mohamed Chenik) 1950; four s. one d.; ed Lycée Carnot, Tunis, Faculty of Medicine, Algiers; Intern and Resident Algiers Hosp. and Sadiki Hosp. Tunis 1947–51; Asst Surgeon, Sadiki Hosp. 1951–57; Chief Surgeon, H. Thameur Hosp. Tunis 1957–64; Chief, Dept of Gen. Surgery, La Rabta Hosp. 1965–85; Prof. of Surgery, Faculty of Medicine Tunis 1970–85, Hon. Prof. 1985–; Founder and Pres. Tunisian Soc. of Surgery 1973–85; Foreign mem. French Acad. of Surgery; Foreign Corresp. mem. Nat. Acad. of Medicine (France), Royal Belgian Acad. of Medicine; mem. Int. Soc. of Surgery; Hon. mem. Soc. Belge de Chirurgie; Commdr of Beylical Order Nichan Iftikhar 1957, Medal of Bizerta 1962, Chevalier of Tunisian Ind., Commdr Order of Tunisian Repub. *Publications include:* Moncef Bey: Le Règne 1988, Moncef Bey: L'Exil 1990, Le Ministère Chenik 1991, Le Métier et la Passion (memoirs) 1995, Abulcasis, grand Maître de la Chirurgie arabe 1997, La Chirurgie arabe ancienne et son Impact en Occident 1998. *Leisure interests:* swimming, bridge. *Address:* 5 avenue Ferhat Hached-Gammarth, 2070 La Marsa, Tunisia. *Telephone:* (1) 746-965. *Fax:* (1) 775-663 (Office); (1) 746-905 (Home). *E-mail:* said.mestiri@med.mail.com (Home).

MESTRE, Phillipe, LL.B; French politician and civil servant; b. 23 Aug. 1927, Talmont, Vendee; s. of Raoul Mestre and Anne Lapie; m. Janine Joseph 1951; one s. two d.; ed Paris Univ.; Admin. Overseas France 1951; Pvt. Sec. to High Commr, Congo 1957–60, to Indre-et-Loir Prefect 1967, to Prime Minister Raymond Barre 1978–81; Tech. Adviser to Pierre Messmer (Minister of Defence) 1964–69, to Prime Minister Jacques Chaban-Delmas 1969–70,

1971–72; Pres. Inter-ministerial Mission of Repatriation from Overseas Territories 1969–70; Prefect of Gers 1970–71, of Calvados 1973–76, of Loire-Atlantique 1976–78, of Mayotte 2001–; Pres. Serpo 1981–; Deputy of Vendée 1981–86, 1986–93; Vice-Pres. Nat. Ass. 1986–88; Minister of War Veterans 1993–95; Vice-Pres. Union pour la Démocratie Française (UDF) 1998–; Officier, Légion d'honneur, Ordre nat. du Mérite, du Mérite agricole, Croix de la Valeur militaire. *Address:* Representation du Gouvernement, B.P. 20, 97610 Dzaoudzi, Mayotte (Office); 95 rue de Rennes, 75006 Paris, France (Home).

MESYATS, Gennady Andreyevich, DSc; Russian physicist; b. 28 Feb. 1936, Kemerovo; s. of Andrei Mesyats and Anna Mesyats; m. Nina Alexandrovna (née Mashukova) Mesyats 1959; one s.; ed Tomsk Polytechnical Inst.; Sr Research Physicist, Research Inst. for Nuclear Physics, Tomsk Polytechnical Inst. 1961–64, Head of Lab. 1966–71; Deputy Dir Inst. of Atmospheric Optics, Tomsk 1971–76; Dir Prof. Inst. of High Current Electronics, Tomsk 1976–86; Dir, Prof. Inst. of Electrophysics 1987–; Corresp. mem. USSR (now Russian) Acad. of Sciences 1979, mem. 1984–, Pres. Ural Div. 1986–99, Vice-Pres. of Acad. 1987–; Int. Chair. Supreme Attestation Comm. 1999–; Pres. Demidov Foundation; Vice-Pres. Int. Unit of Science and Eng Fellowships; mem. Russian Electrical Eng Acad.; Hon. Prof. Tomsk Polytechnic Univ. 1996, Russian Technological Univ. 2000; Dr. hc (Urals State Technical Univ.) 1996; Int. Dyke's Award in Electronics 1990, E Marx Award in Pulsed Power 1991; State Prize of USSR 1978, USSR Council of Ministers Prize 1990; A. G. Stoletov Prize 1996; State Prize of Russia 1999; Order of Red Banner of Labour 1971, Badge of Honour 1981, Order of Lenin 1986, Order for Services to the Motherland 1996, 1999. *Publications:* Techniques for the Production of High-Voltage Nanosecond Pulses 1963, Generation of High-Power Nanosecond Pulses 1974, Field Emission and Explosive Processes in Gas Discharges 1982, High-Power Nanosecond X-Ray Pulses 1983, Pulsed Electrical Discharge in Vacuum 1989, Ectons 1994, About Our Science 1995, Pulsed Gas Lasers 1995, Explosive Electron Emission 1998, Physics of Pulsed Breakdown in Gases 1998, Ectons in a Vacuum Discharge: Breakdown, the Spark and the Arc 2000. *Leisure interests:* reading fiction, studying Russian history, writing articles. *Address:* Russian Academy of Sciences, 14 Leninsky Prospekt, Moscow GSP-1 117901 (Office); Apt. 29, 3 Akademika Petrovskogo, Moscow 117900, Russia (Home). *Telephone:* (095) 237-53-12 (Office); (095) 952-50-81. *E-mail:* mesyats@pran.ru (Office).

MÉSZÁROS, Márta; Hungarian film director; b. 19 Sept. 1931, Budapest; d. of László Mészáros; m. 2nd Jan Nowicki; ed Moscow Film School; emigrated with family to USSR 1936; now lives in Hungary; Golden Bear Award OCIC 1975, Béla Balázs Prize 1977; Artist of Merit 1989. *Films include:* End of September 1973, Free Breath 1973, Adopted Child 1975, Nine Months 1976, The Two of Them 1977, En Route 1979, Heritage 1980, Diary for my Children 1982, Fata Morgana Land 1983, Diary for my Loves 1986, Diary III 1989. *Address:* c/o MAFILM Studio, Lumumba utca 174, 1149 Budapest, Hungary. *Telephone:* (1) 183-1750.

META, Ilir; Albanian politician and economist; b. b. 1969, Skrapar; m.; two c.; ed Tirana Univ.; elected Deputy 1992–; Chair. Parl. Comm. for Foreign Relations 1996–97; fmr Deputy Prime Minister, Sec. of State for Integration (Ministry of Foreign Affairs) and Minister of Government Co-ordination; Prime Minister of Albania 1999–2002; Minister of Foreign Affairs 2002–; mem. Socialist Party of Albania (Steering Council 1992–); mem. Youth Eurosocialist Forum of Albania 1995–2001, Socialist Youth Int. *Leisure interest:* sports. *Address:* Ministria e Punëve të Jashtme, Bulevardi Zhan D'Ark, Tirana, Albania (Office). *Telephone:* (43) 62170. *Fax:* (42) 35899. *Website:* www.mfa.gov.al.

METCALF, John, BA; Canadian author; b. 12 Nov. 1938, Carlisle, UK; s. of Thomas Metcalf and Gladys Moore; m. Myrna Teitelbaum 1975; three s. three d.; ed Beckenham and Penge Grammar School and Univ. of Bristol; emigrated to Canada 1962; Writer-in-Residence, Univs. of NB 1972–73, Loyola of Montreal 1976, Ottawa 1977, Concordia Univ. Montreal 1980–81, Univ. of Bologna 1985; Sr Ed. Porcupine's Quill Press 1989–; Ed. Canadian Notes and Queries (literary magazine) 1997–. *Publications:* The Lady Who Sold Furniture 1970, The Teeth of My Father 1975, Girl in Gingham 1978, Selected Stories 1982, Kicking Against the Pricks 1982, Adult Entertainment 1986, What is a Canadian Literature? 1988, Volleys 1990, How Stories Mean 1992, Shooting the Stars 1992, Freedom from Culture: Selected Essays 1982–1992 1994, Acts of Kindness and of Love (jtly.) 1995, Forde Abroad 2003, An Aesthetic Underground 2003. *Leisure interest:* collecting modern first editions. *Address:* 128 Lewis Street, Ottawa, Ont., K2P 0S7, Canada. *Telephone:* (613) 233-3200.

METHENY, Pat; American jazz guitarist; b. 12 Aug. 1954, Kansas City, Mo.; ed Univ. of Miami; taught guitar at Univ. of Miami and Berklee Coll. of Music; has performed and recorded with musicians and composers including Ornette Coleman, Herbie Hancock and Steve Reich; formed Pat Metheny Group 1978; numerous awards including Grammy Award for Best Instrumental Composition 1990, 1993, Best Contemporary Jazz Performance 1995, Best Rock Instrumental Performance 1996, Orville H. Gibson Award for Best Jazz Guitarist 1996, Best Guitarist (Jazz Times Magazine) 2000. *Albums include:* American Garage 1980, Offramp 1982, Travels 1983, Still Life (Talking) 1987, Letter from Home 1989, We Live Here 1995, A Map of the World 1999. *Address:* Geffen Records, 10900 Wilshire Boulevard, Suite 1000, Los Angeles, CA 90024, USA (Office).

METZ, Johann Baptist, DPhil, DTheol; German professor of theology; b. 5 Aug. 1928, Auerbach; s. of Karl M. Metz and Sibylle Müller; ed Univs. of Bamberg, Innsbrück and Munich; Prof. of Fundamental Theology, Univ. of Münster 1963–; Prof. of Philosophy of Religion, Univ. of Vienna, Austria 1993–; mem. Founding Comm. of Univ. of Bielefeld 1966; consultant to Papal Secr. Pro Non Credendibus 1968–73; Adviser to German Diocesan Synod 1971–75; mem. Advisory Council, Inst. für die Wissenschaften vom Menschen (Vienna) 1982–; mem. Advisory Council Wissenschaftszentrum Nordrhein-Westfalen/Kulturwissenschaftliches Inst. 1989–2000; numerous guest professorships; Dr. hc (Univ. of Vienna); awards from Univ. of Innsbrück and Boston Coll., Mass. *Publications:* books on theological and political themes in several languages. *Address:* Katholisch-Theologische Fakultät, Seminar für Fundamentaltheologie, Johannisstrasse 8–10, 4400 Münster (Office); Kapitelstrasse 14, 48145 Münster, Germany. *Telephone:* (251) 83-2631 (Office); (251) 36662 (Home). *Fax:* (251) 36662 (Home). *E-mail:* j.metz@uni-muenster.de.

METZENBAUM, Howard Morton, LLB; American politician, lawyer and company executive; b. 4 June 1917, Cleveland; s. of Charles I. and Anna (Klafter) Morton; m. Shirley Turoff 1946; four d.; ed Ohio State Univ.; mem. War Labour Bd 1942–45, Ohio Bureau for Code Revision 1949–50; mem. Ohio House of Reps. 1943–46, Ohio Senate 1947–50; alt. del. to Democratic Nat. Convention 1964, del. 1968; mem. Ohio Democratic Exec. Cttee 1966, Finance Cttee 1969; U.S. Senator from Ohio 1977–95; Chair. Bd Airport Parking Co. of America 1958–66, ITT Consumer Services Corpn 1966–68; Chair. Exec. Cttee ComCorp 1969–74; Trustee, Mount Sinai Hosp., Cleveland 1961–73, Treas. 1966–73; mem. Bd of Dirs., Council of Human Relations; mem. United Cerebral Palsy Asscn, Nat. Council on Hunger and Malnutrition, American, Ohio, Cuyahoga and Cleveland Bar Asscns., American Asscn of Trial Lawyers. *Address:* 5610 Wisconsin Avenue, Bethesda, MD 20815 (Home); Consumer Federation of America, 1424 16th Street, NW, Suite 504, Washington, DC 20036, USA.

METZGER, Henry, AB, MD, FAAS; American (b. German) scientific researcher; b. 23 March 1932, Mainz, Germany; s. of Paul Alfred Metzger and Anne (Daniel) Metzger; m. Deborah Stashower 1957; two s. one d.; ed Univ. of Rochester, Columbia Univ.; emigrated to USA 1938; Intern, then Asst Resident, Col-Presbyterian Medical Center 1957–59; Research Assoc., NIAMD, Nat. Insts. of Health 1959–61, Medical Officer, Arthritis and Rheumatism Branch, Bethesda, Md 1963–73, Chief, Section on Chemical Immunology 1973–, Chief, Arthritis and Rheumatism Branch, Nat. Inst. of Arthritis and Musculoskeletal and Skin Diseases 1983–94, Dir Intramural Research Program 1987–98; Fellow Helen Hay Whitney Foundation, Dept of Biology, Univ. of Calif., San Diego 1961–63; Pres. American Asscn of Immunologists 1991–92; Pres. Int. Union of Immunological Socs. 1992–95; mem. Health Research Council BMFT, German Govt 1994–97; mem. NAS; Hon. mem. Chilean and French Socs. of Immunology; several awards. *Publications:* over 200 scientific papers and contribs. to scientific journals. *Address:* 3410 Taylor Street, Chevy Chase, MD 20815, USA (Home).

METZLER-ARNOLD, Ruth; Swiss politician and lawyer; b. 23 May 1964; m.; ed Univ. of Freiburg; chartered accountant UBS Berne 1989–90, PricewaterhouseCoopers AG, St Gallen 1990–99; Dist Judge Appenzell 1992–95; Canton Judge, Appenzell Inner Rhodes 1995–96; Governmental Adviser for Finance, Appenzell Inner Rhodes 1996–99, Financial Dir 1999; elected to Upper House of Parl. (rep. Appenzell Inner Rhodes) 1999; Fed. Dept of Justice and Police 1999–2001; Vice-Pres. of Switzerland Jan. 2003–; mem. Democratic People's Party. *Address:* Office of the Vice-President, Federal Chancellery, Bundeshaus-West, 3003 Bern, Switzerland (Office).

MEYER, Sir Christopher John Rome, KCMG, MA; British diplomatist; b. 22 Feb. 1944, Beaconsfield; s. of the late Flight Lt R. H. R. Meyer and of E. P. L. Meyer (now Landells); m. 1st Françoise Hedges 1976; two s. one step-s.; m. 2nd Catherine Laylle 1997; two step-s.; ed Lancing Coll., Lycée Henri IV, Paris, Peterhouse, Cambridge and Johns Hopkins School of Advanced Int. Studies, Bologna; Foreign Office 1966–67; Army School of Educ. 1967–68; Third Sec., later Second Sec. Moscow 1968–70; Second Sec. Madrid 1970–73; FCO 1973–78; First Sec. Perm. Representation of UK at EC 1978–82; Counsellor and Head of Chancery, Moscow 1982–84; Head of News Dept FCO 1984–88; Fellow, Center for Int. Affairs, Harvard 1988–89; Minister (Commercial), Washington, DC 1989–92, Minister and Deputy Head of Mission 1992–93; Press Sec. to Prime Minister 1994–96; Amb. to Germany 1997, to USA 1997–2003; Chair. Press Complaints Comm. 2003–; Hon. Fellow Peterhouse, Univ. of Cambridge 2001. *Leisure interests:* jazz, history, football, tennis. *Address:* c/o Foreign and Commonwealth Office, King Charles Street, London, SW1A 2AH, England (Office).

MEYER, (Donatus) Laurenz (Karl); German politician; b. 2 Feb. 1948, Salzkotten; m.; four d.; ed Univ. of Münster; fmr mem. staff VEW AG, Dortmund; mem. Hamm City Council 1975–95; Parl. Group Chair. Christian Democratic Union (CDU), Hamm 1989–95; mem. Land Parl. of N Rhine-Westphalia (NRW) 1990–92, Econ. Policy Spokesman of Land Parl. of NRW 1990–99, Vice-Chair. CDU Parl. Group of Land Parl. of NRW 1997–99, Chair. 1999–2000, Vice-Pres. Land Parl. of NRW 2000, Treas. CDU of NRW 1997–2001; mem. Fed. Party Exec., Sec.-Gen. CDU Germany 2000–; mem. Bundestag 2002–; Order of Merit (FRG). *Leisure interests:* tennis, golf. *Address:* Christlich-Demokratische Union, Konrad-Adenauer-Haus, Klingelhöferstrasse 8, 10785 Berlin, Germany (Office). *Telephone:* (30) 220700 (Office). *Fax:* (30) 22070111 (Office). *E-mail:* laurenz.meyer@cdu.de (Office). *Website:* www.cdu.de (Office).

MEYER, Edgar, BMus; American composer and bass player; b. 24 Nov. 1960, Tulsa, OK; s. of Edgar A. Meyer and Anna Mary Metzel; m. Cornelia (Connie) Heard 1988; one s.; ed Georgia Inst. of Tech., Atlanta, Indiana School of Music, Bloomington; began playing bass under tutelage of father age 5; began composing pop songs and classical pieces as a child; studied with Stuart Stanley at univ.; formed 'bluegrass' band Strength in Numbers, Nashville, Tenn. 1984; signed to MCA label; regular bass player Santa Fe Chamber Music Festival 1985–93; appeared with concert artists Emanuel Ax (piano) and Yo-yo Ma (cello); collaborated with Katty Mattea on album Where Have You Been (Grammy Award, Country Music Award, Acad. of Country Music Assn Award) 1990; premiere of Concerto for Bass 1993; joined Chamber Music Soc., Lincoln Centre, NY 1994; formed band Quintet for Bass and String Quartet, soloist debut performance 1995; premiere of Double Concerto for Bass and Cello 1995; premiere of Violin Concerto 2000; recitals with Amy Dorfman, Bela Flack and Mike Marshall; performed at Aspen, Caramoor and Marlboro Festivals; debuted with Boston Symphony Orchestra, Tanglewood, Mass. 2000; Visiting Prof. Royal Acad. of Music, London, UK; Winner, Zimmerman-Mingus Competition, Int. Soc. of Bassists 1981, Avery Fisher Prize 2000, Grammy Award for the Best Crossover Album 2001. *Music includes:* (albums) Unfolding 1986, The Telluride Sessions (Strength in Numbers) 1989, Dreams of Flight 1987, Love of a Lifetime 1988, Appalachia Waltz 1996, Uncommon Ritual 1997, Short Trip Record 1999, Bach Unaccompanied Cello Suites Performed on a Double Bass 1999, Appalachian Journey (Grammy Award 2001) 2000, Perpetual Motion 2000. *Address:* c/o Sony Classical, 550 Madison Avenue, New York, NY 10022-3211, USA (Office); c/o IMG Artists, Lovell House, 616 Chiswick High Road, London, W4 5RX, England (Office).

MEYER, Robert; Norwegian photohistorian; b. 2 Oct. 1945, Oslo; m. Ingebjørg Ydstie 1985; one s. one. d.; ed Fotoskolan, Univ. of Stockholm; photographer, Norwegian State Police 1963–64; advertising photographer 1964–; freelance photographer 1964–71; debut Exhbn LYS, Oslo 1970; photojournalist, Norwegian Broadcasting, Oslo 1971–77; Ed. and Publr Ikaros 1976–80; full-time photohistorian engaged in research work 1977–; Prof. Inst. of Photography (SHDK) Bergen 1990–; Munch stipend 1981; art stipend 1988–90; two book prizes. *Publications:* Norsk fotohistorisk Journal 1976–78, Jim Bengston in Photographs 1981, Slow Motion 1985, Simulo 1987, Norsk Landskapsfotografi 1988, Den glemte tradisjonen 1989, Splint 1991. *Address:* Institute of Photography Strømgt. 1, 5015 Bergen (Office); Professor Hansteens gate 68, 5006 Bergen, Norway (Home). *Telephone:* 55-31-22-14 (Office); 55-31-07-93 (Home). *Fax:* 55-32-67-56.

MEYER, Roelof Petrus (Roelf), BComm, LLB; South African fmr politician and business executive; b. 16 July 1947, Port Elizabeth; m. 1st Carené Lubbe 1971; two s. two d.; m. 2nd Michèle de la Rey 2002; ed Fickburg High School, Univ. of the Free State; practised as attorney, Pretoria and Johannesburg –1980; MP for Johannesburg West 1979–97; Deputy Minister of Law and Order 1986–88, of Constitutional Devt 1988–91 and of Information Services 1990–91; Minister of Defence and of Communication 1991–92, of Constitutional Devt and of Communication 1992–94, of Provincial Affairs and Constitutional Devt 1994–96; Sec.-Gen. Nat. Party 1996–97; Co-Founder United Democratic Movt 1997, Deputy Pres. 1998–2000; MP 1998–2000; Tip O'Neill Chair. in Peace Studies, Univ. of Ulster 2000–01; Chair. Civil Soc. Initiative 2000–; Chief Govt Negotiator at Multi-Party Negotiating Forum for new SA Constitution; Nat. Party, fmr Chair. Standing Cttee on Nat. Educ.; fmr Chair. Standing Cttee on Constitutional Devt, fmr Parl. Whip; Tip O'Neill Chair in Peace Studies (Univ. of Ulster) 2000–01. *Leisure interests:* reading, outdoor life, jogging. *Address:* PO Box 2271, Brooklyn Square, Pretoria 0075 (Office); 732 Skukuza Street, Faerie Glen, 0043 Pretoria, South Africa (Home). *Telephone:* (12) 3341826 (Office); (82) 9900004. *Fax:* (12) 3341867 (Office). *E-mail:* roelf.meyer@tilca.com (Office); rmeyer@lantic.net (Home). *Website:* www.tilca.com (Office).

MEYER, Ron; American theatrical agent and business executive; b. 1944; m. Kelly Chapman; one s. three d.; fmrly served with US Marine Corps; with Paul Kohner Agency 1965–70; agent William Morris Agency 1970–75; co-f., Pres. Creative Artists Agency 1975–95; Pres., COO, Vivendi Universal Entertainment. *Address:* Universal Studios Inc., 100 Universal City Plaza, Universal City, CA 91608, USA. *E-mail:* susan.fleishman@unistudios.com (Office).

MEYER, Wilhelm Olaf, MArch, ARIBA, MIA, MBA; South African architect; b. 14 May 1935, Pretoria; s. of Dr F. Meyer; m. Angela Winsome 1961; one s. one d.; ed Univs. of Witwatersrand and Pennsylvania; Partner, Moerdyk & Watson, Pretoria 1961; f. own practice, Wilhelm O Meyer & Partners, Johannesburg 1966, Consultant 1993–; Founder mem. Urban Action Group, Johannesburg 1971; mem. Council SA Council of Architects 1973–, Pres. 1983, 1985; Co-Founder, COPLAN Jt architectural practice with P.S.I. Hong Hong 1983; Pres.-in-Chief, Interbou 84 1984; opened architectural practice jtly. in London 1986; mem. Bd Faculty, School of Architecture, Univ. of Witwatersrand 1988–93; Gen. Consultant for Standard Bank Bldgs. nationwide 1993; Dir Pancom Devt Co. 1993–; many other appointments; work includes urban design, apt. bldgs, univ. bldgs, churches, Marine Parade Hotel, Durban, Johannesburg Civic Centre and Johannesburg Art Gallery; Medal of Honour for Architecture, SA Akad. vir Wetenskap en Kuns 1980; numerous

other awards and competition prizes. *Publications:* contribs to architectural journals. *Leisure interests:* music, windsurfing. *Address:* 64 Galway Road, Parkview 2193, Johannesburg, South Africa.

MEYER-LANDRUT, Andreas, PhD; German diplomatist; b. 31 May 1929, Tallinn, Estonia; s. of Bruno and Käthe (née Winter) Meyer-Landrut; m. Hanna Karatsony von Hodos 1960; one s. one d.; m. 2nd Natali Somers (née Seferov); ed Univs. of Göttingen and Zagreb; entered foreign service 1955, in Moscow, Brussels and Tokyo 1956–68, Amb. to Congo (Brazzaville) 1969; in Foreign Office, Bonn 1971–80, Head of Sub-Dept for Policy towards E Europe and GDR 1974–78, Dir Dept of Relations to Asia, Near and Middle East, Africa and Latin America 1978–80, Amb. to USSR 1980–83, 1987–89; State Sec. to Foreign Office 1983–87; Head of Fed. Pres.'s Office and State Sec. 1989–94; Man. Daimler Chrysler AG in Moscow 1994–2002; Adviser to German cos in Russia and CIS countries; Hon. Pres. German-Russian Forum Berlin, Hon. mem. German Equestrian Fed.; Grand Commdr Order of Merit. *Address:* Malaja Bronnaja ul.20a, 103104 Moscow, Russia; Auswärtiges Amt für BO, 11013 Berlin PF 117 (Office); Thielallee 93, 14192 Berlin, Germany (Home). *Telephone:* (095) 258-1454 (Russia) (Office); (095) 200-6231 (Russia); (30) 8329071 (Germany) (Home). *Fax:* (095) 258-1449 (Russia) (Office); (095) 209-1672 (Russia) (Home). *E-mail:* Andreas.Meyer-Landrut@cnc.ag.com (Office).

MEYEROWITZ, Joel; American photographer; b. 1938, Bronx, New York; fmr art dir in an advertising firm; began photography career in 1962; one-man exhbn My European Trip: Photographs from a Moving Car, Museum of Modern Art, New York 1968; selection of photographs from unpublished work Going Places shown at Expo 70, Japan; gave lessons in colour photography at Cooper Union, New York 1971; commissioned by St Louis Art Museum, Missouri to photograph Eero Saarinen's Gateway Arch 1977; photographed Empire State Bldg 1978; participant in Mirrors and Windows: American Photography since 1960, Museum of Modern Art, New York 1978; images from Cape Light exhibited at Museum of Fine Art, Boston 1979. *Publication:* Cape Light 1979.

MEYERSON, Martin, ScD, FAAS; American urban planner and former university president; b. 14 Nov. 1922, New York; s. of S. Z. Martin and Etta (née Berger) Martin; m. Margy Ellin Lazarus 1945; two s. one d. (deceased); ed Columbia Univ., Harvard Univ.; Asst Prof. of Social Sciences, Univ. of Chicago 1948; successively Research Dir, Exec. Dir, Vice-Pres., Vice-Chair., American Council to Improve Our Neighborhoods; Assoc. Prof., Prof., Univ. of Pa Inst. for Urban Studies and Dept of City and Regional Planning 1952–57; Adviser on urban problems for UN in Indonesia, Japan and Yugoslavia 1958–66; Frank Backus Williams Prof. of City Planning and Urban Research, Harvard Univ. 1957–63; Dir Jt Center for Urban Studies of MIT and Harvard Univ. 1957–63; Dean Coll. of Environmental Design, Univ. of Calif. (Berkeley), Acting Chancellor 1963–66; Pres. State Univ. of New York at Buffalo, Prof. of Policy Sciences 1966–70; Prof. of Public Policy, Univ. of Pa Foundation 1970–77, Chair. 1981–, Univ. Prof. 1977–81, Pres. Univ. of Pa 1970–81, Pres. Emer. 1981–; Chair. Monell Chem. Senses Center 1993–, Bd Marconi Int. Fellowship Foundation 1996–2001; mem. Int. Council for Educ. Devt 1971–94; Pres. Int. Asscn Univs. 1975–85, Hon. Pres. 1985–; fmr Gov. Centre for Environmental Studies, London, Gov. American Inst. of Planners; Fellow American Acad. of Arts and Sciences; mem. American Philosophical Soc., Council on Foreign Relations, Nat. Acad. of Educ.; Hon. Prof. Nat. Univ. of Paraguay, Beijing Univ. 1996–; Hon. LLD (Queens Univ., Canada, D'Youville Coll., Alfred Univ., Rutgers Univ., Univ. of Pa, Stonehill Coll.); Hon. DSc (Chattanooga); numerous hon. degrees and other decorations. *Publications:* Politics, Planning and the Public Interest (co-author) 1955, Housing, People and Cities 1962, Face of the Metropolis 1963, Boston 1966, Conscience of the City (ed.) 1970, Gladly Learn and Gladly Teach 1978. *Address:* Room 225, Van Pelt Library, University of Pennsylvania, 3420 Walnut Street, Philadelphia, PA 19104 (Office); 2016 Spruce Street, Philadelphia, PA 19103, USA (Home). *Telephone:* (215) 898-5577 (Office). *Fax:* (215) 898-2379.

MEZHIROV, Aleksandr Petrovich; Russian poet; b. 26 Sept. 1923, Moscow; s. of Pyotr Izraelevich Mezhirov and Yelizaveta Semyonovna Mezhirova; m. Yelena Yaschenko; one d.; ed Moscow Univ.; served in Soviet Army 1941–45; Prof. in Literary Inst., Moscow 1966–91; State Prize for Poetry 1986, Georgian State Prize 1989. *Publications:* more than 50 books of poetry, including Long is the Road 1947, Returns 1955, Poems and Translations 1962, Ladoga Ice 1965, Selected Works (2 Vols) 1981, The Blind Turning 1983, The Outline of Things 1984, Prose in Poetry 1985, Bormotucha 1990, The What That Has No Name 1995, Ground Wind 1997, Apologia of a Circus 1997; trans. Georgian and Lithuanian poetry, articles, critical reviews, essays on history of Russian Econs. *Leisure interest:* billiards. *Address:* 146–148 West 68 Street, Apt. 3B, New York, NY 10023, USA. *Telephone:* (212) 873-0390.

MHLABA, Mpakamisi Raymond; South African politician and civil servant; b. 12 Feb. 1920, Fort Beaufort; s. of Mxokozeli Mhlaba and Dinah (née Mnyazi) Mhlaba; m. 1st Joyce Meke 1943 (died 1960); m. 2nd Dideka Heliso 1986; three s. five d.; ed Healdtown Missionary Sch.; mem. ANC Nat. Exec. Cttee 1960–63, 1990–, Regional Exec. Cttee E Cape Br.; ANC Regional Head E Cape Region; Deputy Chair. Cen. Cttee and Politburo SA Communist Party 1990–; Vice-Chair. Mzingisi Devt Trust, Port Elizabeth 1991–; Chair. E Cape Regional Econ. Devt Forum 1992–; Premier E Cape Prov. Legislature 1994–97; High Commr in Uganda 1997–2001; Dr. hc (Unitra Transkei); Eastern Cape Award 2001. *Leisure interests:* reading, political activities and social gatherings. *Address:* 5 Millard Crescent, Summerstrand, Port Elizabeth, 6001 South Africa (Home). *Telephone:* (41) 5833558 (Home). *Fax:* (41) 5831356 (Home).

MICHAEL, Rt. Hon. Alun Edward, BA; British politician; b. 22 Aug. 1943; m.; two s. three d.; ed Keele Univ.; journalist South Wales Echo 1966–71; Youth and Community Worker, Cardiff 1972–84; Area Community Education Officer, Grangetown and Butetown 1984–87; mem. Cardiff City Council 1973–89 (fmr Chair. Finance, Planning, Performance Review and Econ. Devt, Chief Whip, Labour Group); mem. House of Commons (Labour and Co-op) for Cardiff S. and Penarth 1987–; Opposition Whip 1987–88; Opposition Front-bench Spokesman on Welsh Affairs 1988–92, on Home Affairs and the Voluntary Sector 1992–97; Minister of State, Home Office 1997–98; Sec. of State for Wales 1998–99; First Sec. of Nat. Ass. for Wales 1999–2000; Minister of State for Rural Affairs and Urban Quality of Life, Dept for the Environment, Food and Rural Affairs 2001–; mem. Nat. Ass. for Wales for Mid and W Wales May 1999–; mem. numerous parl. groups and cttees.; Vice-Pres. YHA. *Leisure interests:* opera, reading, long-distance running, classical music. *Address:* House of Commons, London, SW1A 0AA, England (Office). *Telephone:* (20) 7219-5980 (Office). *Fax:* (20) 7219-5930 (Office). *E-mail:* alunmichaelmp@parliament.uk (Office).

MICHAEL, George; British singer, composer and producer; b. 25 June 1963, Finchley; s. of Jack Kyriacus Panayiotou and the late Lesley Panayiotou; ed Bushey Meads School; has sold millions of records; creating promotional video for Coca-Cola 1989; debut in group The Executive 1979; formed (with Andrew Ridgeley) Wham! 1981, numerous consecutive hits; toured UK, France, USA, China, etc.; launched solo career 1986; Ivor Novello Award for Best Songwriter 1985, 1989, British Rock Industry Award for Best Male Artist 1988; Grammy Award for Best Album (Faith) 1989. *Singles include:* with Wham!: Wham Rap!, Young Guns Go For It, Bad Boys, Club Tropicana, Wake Me Up Before You Go Go; duet: I Knew You Were Waiting (For Me) (with Aretha Franklin, ; solo: Careless Whisper, A Different Corner, I Want Your Sex, Faith, Father Figure, Jesus to a Child 1995, Fastlove 1996. *Albums include:* Fantastic, Make It Big, Music From The Edge of Heaven, Final, Faith (solo), Listen without Prejudice 1990; contrib. to albums: Two Rooms; Celebrating the Songs of Elton John and Bernie Taupin 1991, Red, Hot and Dance 1992, A Very Special Christmas II 1992, Older 1996, Ladies and Gentlemen: The Best of George Michael 1998. *Publication:* George Michael: Bare (with Tony Parsons) 1990. *Address:* c/o Connie Filippello, 49 Portland Road, London, W11 4LJ, England. *Telephone:* (20) 7229-5400.

MICHAEL, HM King; fmr King of Romania; b. 25 Oct. 1921, Foishor Castle, Sinaïa; s. of the late King Carol II and Princess Helen of Greece; m. Princess Anne of Bourbon-Parma 1948; five d.; declared heir apparent, ratified by Parl. 4 Jan. 1926; proclaimed King 1927, deposed by his father 1930; succeeded to the throne of Romania following his father's abdication 1940; led coup d'etat against pro-Nazi dictator Ion Antonescu 1944; forced to abdicate following communist takeover of Romania 30 Dec. 1947; subsequently ran chicken farm in Herts., UK; went to Switzerland as test pilot 1956; has also worked for Lear Inc.; started electronics co. and worked as stockbroker; deported from Romania on first visit since exile Dec. 1990; returned to Romania 1992; Romanian citizenship and passport restored 1997; undertook official mission for Romania's integration into NATO and EU 1997; Collar and Grand Master, Order of Carol I of Romania, Order of Faithful Service, Order of Crown of Romania and Star of Romania, Grand Cross, Royal Victorian Order, Grand Cross, Légion d'honneur, Grand Cross, Order of Leopold (Belgium), Collar, Order of Annunciata, Grand Cross, Order of St Saviour (Greece), Marshal, Romanian Armed Forces. *Leisure interest:* restoring Second World War jeeps. *Address:* Villa Serena, C.P. 627, 1290 Versoix, Switzerland (Office). *Telephone:* (22) 755-29-68 (Office). *Fax:* (22) 755-29-69 (Office). *E-mail:* msregele@ swissonline.ch (Office).

MICHAELS-MOORE, Anthony, BA; British opera singer; b. 8 April 1957, Grays, Essex; s. of John Frederick Moore and Isabel Shephard; m. Ewa Bozena Migocki 1980; one d.; ed Gravesend School for Boys, Univ. of Newcastle, Fenham Teacher Training Coll.; prin. baritone, Royal Opera House, Covent Garden 1987–97; roles in all British opera cos.; debut La Scala, Milan (Licinius in La Vestale) 1993, New York Metropolitan Opera (Marcello in La Bohème) 1996, Vienna Staatsoper (Lescaut in Manon) 1997, San Francisco Opera (Eugene Onegin) 1997, Paris Bastille (Sharpless in Madama Butterfly) 1998; specializes in 19th-century baritone repertoire; winner Luciano Pavarotti/Opera Co. of Phila Prize 1985, Royal Philharmonic Soc. Award Winner 1997. *Television appearances include:* BBC Proms (Beethoven's Missa Solemnis, Mahler's Symphony No. 8), Carmina Burana recorded at La Scala, Milan 1996. *Music:* major recordings include: Carmina Burana, Lucia di Lammermoor, La Vestale, La Favorite, Falstaff and Il Tabarro, Aroldo, La Favorite. *Radio:* regular BBC Radio 3 broadcasts, Verdi operas from Royal Opera House, Met Opera relays from New York. *Leisure interests:* clay pigeon shooting, computer games, oriental food. *Address:* c/o IMG Artists, Media House, 3 Burlington Lane, Chiswick, London, W4 2TH, England (Office). *Telephone:* (20) 8233-5868 (Office).

MICHALCZEWSKI, Dariusz; Polish/German boxer; b. 5 May 1968, Gdańsk; m.; two s.; amateur boxer 1982–91; 133 wins in 150 amateur fights; professional boxer 1991–; 47 wins in 47 professional fights; European champion, Göteborg 1991; became World Boxing Org. (WBO) light-heavyweight champion 1994 and has defended the title 22 times; won WBO cruiserweight title in 1994 (abandoned 1995); won World Boxing Asscn (WBA), Int. Boxing Fed. (IBF) light–heavyweight titles in 1997. *Address:* Waldeweg 134B, 22393 Hamburg, Germany (Office). *Telephone:* (40) 68912656 (Office). *Website:* www .dariusz-tiger.de.

MICHALIK, Archbishop Józef, DTheol; Polish ecclesiastic; b. 20 April 1941, Zambrów; ed Acad. of Catholic Theology, Warsaw, Angelicum, St Thomas Pontifical Univ., Rome; ordained priest Łomża 1964; Vice-Chancellor Bishops' Curia, Łomża 1973–78; fmr lecturer Higher Theological Seminary, Łomża, Rector Pontifical Polish Coll., Rome 1978–86; staff mem. Pontifical Laity Council 1978–86; Bishop Gorzów Diocese 1986–92; Chair. Episcopate Cttee for Academic Ministry 1986–95; Bishop Zielona Góra and Gorzów Diocese 1992–93; Archbishop Metropolitan of Przemyśl 1993–; Chair. Episcopate's Council for Poles Abroad, Councils of Episcopates of Europe Cttee for Laity; mem. Main Council of Conf. of Episcopates of Poland, Vatican Congregation for Bishops. *Publications:* My Talks with God 1976, La Chiesa e il suo rinnovamento secondo Andrea Frycz Modrzewski 1973, Brothers Look at Your Vocation 1991, Bóg i Ojczyzna, Wiara i Naróol 1998, Mocą Twoją Panie 1998, Pan was potrzebuje 2000. *Address:* pl. Katedralny 4, 37-700 Przemyśl, Poland (Office). *Telephone:* (16) 6786694 (Office). *Fax:* (16) 6782674 (Office). *E-mail:* michalik@episkopat.pl (Office). *Website:* www.przemysl.opoka.org.pl (Office).

MICHAUD, Jean-Claude Georges; French broadcasting executive; b. 28 Oct. 1933; s. of Maurice Michaud and Suzanne Michaud; one s. one d. (from fmr marriage); ed Lycée Louis-le-Grand, Paris and Ecole Normale Supérieure, Paris; Counsellor, Ministry of Educ. 1961–62, Ministry of Information 1962–64; Asst Dir Television ORTF 1964–68, Counsellor to Dir-Gen. 1968–70; man. position, Librairie Hachette 1970–73; Deputy Dir for External Affairs and Co-operation, ORTF 1973–74; Dir of Int. Affairs and Co-operation, Télédiffusion France 1975–80, Dir of Commercial Affairs 1982–83, Overseas Dir 1983–85; Pres.-Dir-Gen. Soc. Française Radio-Télévision d'Outre-Mer (RFO) 1986–89; Pres. Dir-Gen. Sofratev 1989–98. *Publication:* Teoria e Storia nel Capitale di Marx 1960, Alain Peyrefitte 2002. *Leisure interests:* walking, skiing, reading. *Address:* 55 boulevard du Montparnasse, 75006 Paris, France. *Telephone:* 1-45-49-06-90 (Home). *Fax:* 1-42-22-58-43 (Home). *E-mail:* jeanclaudemichau@aol.com (Home).

MICHAUX-CHEVRY, Lucette; French politician and lawyer; b. 5 March 1929, Sainte-Claude, Guadeloupe; d. of Edouard Chevry and Florentine Labry; m. Émile Michaux (deceased); two c.; lawyer Basse-Terre 1955–; Municipal Councillor, Sainte-Claude 1959–65; mem. Departmental Council of Guadeloupe 1976, Chair. 1982–85; f. Political Party for Guadeloupe (L.P.G.) 1984; mem. Regional Council 1984; Deputy to Nat. Ass. 4th Constituency of Guadeloupe 1986; Mayor of Gourbeyre 1987; State Sec. for French-speaking World, Govt of France 1986–88; Chair. Regional Council of Guadeloupe 1992; Deputy to Nat. Ass. 1993; Nat. Minister with special responsibility for Humanitarian Measures and Human Rights 1993–95; Senator from Guadeloupe (RPR) 1995–; Mayor of Basse-Terre 1995–; mem. Comm. of Foreign Affairs and Nat. Defence. *Address:* Conseil Régional de la Guadeloupe, avenue Paul Lacavé, Petit Paris, 97109 Basse-Terre, Guadeloupe; Sénat, Palais du Luxembourg, 75291 Paris Cédex 06, France.

MICHEL, James Alix; Seychelles politician; b. 16 Aug. 1944; ed Teacher Training Coll., Seychelles; teacher 1960–61; with Cable & Wireless Telecommunications 1962–71; treas. and sec. staff union 1970–71; Accountant, Asst Man., then Man. Hotel des Seychelles 1971–74; mem. Exec. Cttee Seychelles People's United Party and Co-ordinator of Party Brs, also Ed. of The People 1974–77; Minister of State, Admin and Information 1977–79; mem. Cen. Exec. Cttee Seychelles People's Progressive Front 1978–, also Sec.; Chief of Staff Seychelles People's Defence Forces 1979–93; Minister of Educ., Information, Culture and Telecommunications 1979–86, of Educ., Information, Culture and Sports 1986–89, of Finance 1989–91, of Finance and Information 1991–93, of Finance, Information, Communications and Defence, also First Desig. Minister to discharge the functions of Pres. 1993–96; Vice-Pres. (retaining portfolios for Finance, Information and Communications) 1996; Vice-Pres. (with portfolios of Econ. Planning and Environment and Transport) 1998–2000; Vice-Pres. and Minister of Finance, Econ. Planning, Information Tech. and Communications 2001–; Patron Seychelles Football Fed.; Foreign mem. Russian Acad. of Natural Sciences; Gran Croce dell'Ordine al Merito Melitense, Kt of Malta. *Address:* Ministry of Finance, Economic Planning, Information Technology and Communications, Central Bank Building, PO Box 313, Victoria, Mahé, Seychelles (Office). *Telephone:* 382000 (Office). *Fax:* 225265 (Office). *E-mail:* jamichel@seychelles.net (Office).

MICHEL, Louis; Belgian politician; b. 2 Sept. 1947, Tirlemont; fmr lecturer at Inst. Supérieur de Commerce Saint-Louis; Prof. of Dutch, English and German Literature, Ecole Normale provinciale de Jodoigne 1968–78; Alderman of Jodoigne 1977–83, Mayor 1983–; Sec.-Gen. Parti Réformateur Libéral (PRL) 1980–82, Pres. 1982–90; Pres. Fed. of Local and Provincial PRL Office Holders 1990–92; Pres., parl. group in Council of Walloon Region 1991–92, in House of Reps. 1992–95; MP 1978–99; Pres. PRL 1995–2001; Deputy Pres. of Liberal Int.; Deputy Prime Minister and Minister of Foreign Affairs July 1999–; Rep. of Belgium to EU Special Convention on a European Constitution 2001–; mem. Parl. Comms. on Finance, Budget, Institutional Reforms and Comm. charged with supervising electoral expenditures; mem. Benelux Interparl. Consultative Council; Commdr Order of Leopold. *Address:* Ministry of Foreign Affairs, Foreign Trade and International Co-operation, 15 rue des Petits Carmes, 1000 Brussels, Belgium (Office). *Telephone:* (2) 501-82-11 (Office). *Fax:* (2) 511-63-85 (Office). *E-mail:* cab.ae@diplobel.org (Office). *Website:* diplobel.fgov.be (Office).

MICHEL, Smarck; Haitian politician and businessman; petrol retailer; owns rice-importing business; fmr Commerce Sec. in first Aristide Govt 1991; Prime Minister of Haiti 1994–96. *Address:* c/o Office of the Prime Minister, Port-au-Prince, Haiti.

MICHELBERGER, Pál; Hungarian engineer; b. 4 Feb. 1930, Vecsés; s. of Pál Michelberger and Mária Komáromy; m. Ilona Torma; one s. one d.; ed Technical Univ., Budapest; Assoc. Prof. Tech. Univ., Budapest 1963–68, Prof. 1968–, Rector 1990–94; mem. Bd of Mans. IKARUS Motor Coach Factory 1991–95, HUNGAROCAMION Transport Co. 1992–94; Corresp. mem. Hungarian Acad. of Sciences 1982, mem. 1990 (Vice-Pres. 1993); Chair. Cttee for Machine Design, Scientific Soc. for Mechanical Eng, Co-Pres. 1976–90, Vice-Pres. 1990–93; Councillor Fed. Int. des Techniques de l'Automobile 1974, Vice-Pres. 1978, Pres. 1992–94; Pres. (elect) Hungarian Rectors' Conf. 1994–95; mem. Perm. Cttee European Rectors' Conf. 1991–94; Corresp. mem. Verein Deutscher Ingenieure 1983–; mem. Russian Acad. of Transportation 1992, Acad. Europaea 1993–, European Acad. of Science and Arts 1998–; A. G. Pattantyus Prize 1973, L. Eötvös Prize 1994, Széchenyi Prize 1995, O. Benedikt Prize 1998, Pázmány Prize 1999. *Publications:* seven books and numerous articles on vehicle dynamics. *Leisure interest:* music. *Address:* H 2040, Budaörs, Szabadság út 141 (Office); c/o Technical University, 1521 Budapest, Műegyetem rakpart 3-9, Hungary. *Telephone:* (1) 463-1728; (23) 422-668 (Office). *Fax:* (1) 463-1783.

MICHELIN, François; French industrialist; b. 15 June 1926, Clermont-Ferrand; s. of Etienne Michelin and Madeleine (née Calliès) Michelin; m. Bernadette Montagne 1951; Man. Dir Compagnie Générale des Etablissements Michelin, "Michelin & Cie." 1959–66, Jt Man. Dir 1966–99; Man. Dir Cie Financière Michelin, Manufacture française des pneumatiques Michelin; Dir Peugeot SA; Conseiller d'Etat en service extraordinaire 1989. *Publications:* Et pourquoi pas? (jtly.) (Prix de l'excellence, Maxim's Business Club 1999) 1998. *Leisure interest:* tennis. *Address:* Michelin, 12 cours Sablon, 63000 Clermont-Ferrand, France (Office).

MICHELL, Keith; actor; b. 1 Dec. 1926, Adelaide, Australia; s. of Joseph Michell and Maud (née Aslat) Michell; m. Jeanette Sterk 1957; one s. one d.; ed Port Pirie High School, Adelaide Univ. Teacher's Coll. and School of Arts, Old Vic. Theatre School; started career as art teacher; first stage appearance Playbox, Adelaide 1947; with Young Vic. Theatre Co. 1950–51, first London appearance in And So To Bed 1951; Artistic Dir, Chichester Festival Theatre 1974–77; Top Actor Emmy Award 1971, British Film Award 1973, Logie Award 1974 and numerous others. *Stage appearances include:* Troilus and Cressida 1954, Romeo and Juliet 1954, Macbeth 1955, Don Juan 1956, Irma La Douce 1958, The Art of Seduction 1962, The Rehearsal 1963, Robert and Elizabeth 1964, The King's Mare 1966, Man of La Mancha 1968–69, Abelard and Heloise 1970, Hamlet 1972, Dear Love 1973, The Crucifer of Blood 1979, Captain Beaky Christmas Show 1981–82, The Tempest 1982, On the Rocks 1982, Amadeus 1983, La Cage aux Folles 1984–85, Jane Eyre 1986, Portraits 1987, The Royal Baccarat Scandal 1988, Henry VIII 1991, Aspects of Love 1992, Scrooge 1993–94, Monsieur Amilcar 1995, Brazilian Blue 1995, Family Matters 1998, All the World 2001, 2003. *Television includes:* The Six Wives of Henry VIII 1970, Keith Michell in Concert at Chichester 1974, Captain Beaky and His Band, Captain Beaky, Vol. 2, The Story of the Marlboroughs, Jacob and Joseph, The Story of David, The Tenth Month, The Day Christ Died, My Brother Tom 1987, Capt. James Cook 1988, Murder She Wrote (series) 1988, The Prince and the Pauper 1996. *Television / video:* The Gondoliers, The Pirates of Penzance, Ruddigore, The Six Wives of Henry VIII. *Films include:* Dangerous Exile, The Hell Fire Club, Seven Seas to Calais, The Executioner, House of Cards, Prudence and the Pill, Henry VIII and His Six Wives, Moments, The Deceivers. *One-man art shows:* Jamaica Paintings 1960, New York 1962, Portugal 1963, Outback in Australia 1965, Don Quixote series, New York 1969, Abelard and Héloise 1972, Hamlet 1972, 12 Shakespeare Sonnets lithographs 1974, Capt. Beaky & Alice in Wonderland 1982, Capt. Cook 1990, Majorcan Paintings, Retrospective 1991. *Publications:* Shakespeare Sonnet series of lithographs 1974, Captain Beaky (illustrations for poems) 1975, Captain Beaky Vol. 2 1982, Alice in Wonderland 1982, Keith Michell's Practically Macrobiotic Cookbook 1987. *Leisure interests:* cooking, painting, swimming. *Address:* c/o Chatto and Linnit, 123A King's Road, London, SW3 4PL, England. *Telephone:* (20) 7352-7722.

MICHELL, Robert H., PhD, FRS, FMedSci; British university professor; b. 16 April 1941, Yeovil; s. of Rowland C. Michell and Elsie L. (Hall) Michell; m. 1st June Evans 1967 (divorced 1971); m. 2nd Esther Margaret Oppenheim 1992; two s. one d.; ed Crewkerne School and Univ. of Birmingham; Research Fellow, Birmingham Univ. 1965–66, 1969–70, Harvard Medical School 1966–68; Lecturer, Birmingham Univ. 1970–81, Sr Lecturer 1981–84, Reader 1984–86, Prof. of Biochemi. 1986–87, Royal Soc. Research Prof. 1987–; other professional appts.; mem. Council, Royal Soc. 1996–97; Royal Soc. UK-Canada Rutherford Lecturer 1994; Biochemical Soc. Morton Lecturer 2002; CIBA Medal, Biochemical Soc. 1988. *Publications:* Membranes and their Cellular Functions (with J. B. Finean and R. Coleman) 1974, 1978, 1984, Membrane Structure (ed. with J. B. Finean) 1981, Inositol Lipids and Transmembrane Signalling (ed. with M. J. Berridge) 1988, Inositol Lipids in Cell Signalling (ed. with A. H. Drummond and C. P. Downes) 1989. *Leisure*

interests: birdwatching, photography, modern literature, wildernesses. *Address:* School of Biosciences, University of Birmingham, Birmingham, B15 2TT (Office); 59 Weoley Park Road, Selly Oak, Birmingham, B29 6QZ, England (Home). *Telephone:* (121) 414-5413 (Office); (121) 472-1356 (Home). *Fax:* 870-137-7947. *E-mail:* r.h.michell@bham.ac.uk (Office); bob_michell@yahoo.co.uk (Home).

MICHELSEN, Axel, DPhil; Danish professor of biology; b. 1 March 1940, Haderslev; s. of Erik Michelsen and Vibeke Michelsen; m. Ulla West-Nielsen 1980; two s. one d.; ed Univ. of Copenhagen; Asst Prof. of Zoophysiology and Zoology, Univ. of Copenhagen 1963–72; Prof. of Biology Odense Univ. 1973–; Chair. Danish Science Research Council 1975–78, Danish Nat. Cttee for Biophysics 1980–90, Danish Nat. Cttee for ICSU 1986–2000, Max-Planck Gesellschaft Fachbeirat 1978–82, Carlsberg Lab. 2003–; Dir Carlsberg Foundation 1986–, Centre for Sound Communication 1994–; mem. Royal Danish Acad. of Sciences and Letters, Akad. der Naturforscher Leopoldina, Academia Europaea; Corresp. mem. Akad. der Wissenschaften und der Literatur (Mainz), Bayerische Akad. der Wissenschaften; Alexander von Humboldt Prize 1990, Kt Order of Dannebrog (First Class). *Publications:* The Physiology of the Locust Ear 1971, Sound and Life 1975, Time Resolution in Auditory Systems 1985, The Dance Language of Honeybees 1992. *Leisure interests:* wines, beekeeping, gardening. *Address:* Institute of Biology, University of Southern Denmark, 5230 Odense M (Office); The Carlsberg Foundation, 35 H.C. Andersens Boulevard, 1553 Copenhagen V (Office); Rosenvænget 74, 5250 Odense SV, Denmark (Home). *Telephone:* 65-50-24-66 (Univ.) (Office); 33-43-53-63 (Foundation) (Office); 66-11-75-68 (Home). *Fax:* 65-93-04-57 (Univ.) (Office); 66-11-97-16 (Home). *E-mail:* a.michelsen@biology.sdu.dk (Office).

MICHENER, Charles Duncan, BS, PhD, FAAS; American biologist (entomology); b. 22 Sept. 1918, Pasadena, Calif.; s. of Harold and Josephine Rigden Michener; m. Mary Hastings 1940; three s. one d.; ed Univ. of California, Berkeley; Tech. Asst in Entomology, Univ. of Calif. 1939–42; Asst Curator, Lepidoptera and Hymenoptera, American Museum of Natural History, New York 1942–46, Assoc. Curator 1946–48, Research Assoc. 1949–; Curator, Snow Entomological Museum, Univ. of Kansas 1949–89, Dir 1974–83; Assoc. Prof. Entomology, Univ. of Kansas 1948–49, Prof. 1949–89, Prof. Emer. 1989–; Chair. Dept of Entomology 1949–61, 1972–75, Watkins Dist Prof. of Entomology 1959–89, of Systematics and Ecology 1969–89; State Entomologist, S. Div. of Kansas 1949–61; Ed. Evolution 1962–64; American Ed. Insectes Sociaux (Paris), 1954–55, 1962–90; Assoc. Ed. Annual Review of Ecology and Systematics 1970–90; Pres. Soc. for the Study of Evolution 1967, Soc. of Systematic Zoology 1969, American Soc. of Naturalists 1978, Int. Union for the Study of Social Insects 1977–82 (Vice-Pres. Western Hemisphere Section 1979–80); mem. NAS, American Acad. of Arts and Sciences, Corresp. mem. Acad. Brasileira de Ciências; Foreign Hon. mem. Russian Entomological Soc.; Hon. mem. Soc. of Systematic Biology; Guggenheim Fellow to Brazil 1955–56, Africa 1966–67; Fellow Royal Entomological Soc. of London; Fulbright Scholar, Australia 1957–58; Morrison Prize, NY Acad. of sciences 1943; Founder's Award, American Entomological Soc. 1981, Thomas Say Award, Entomological Soc. of America 1997, C. V. Riley Award, Entomological Soc. of America 1999, Distinguished Research Medal, Int. Soc. of Hymenopterists 2002. *Publications:* Comparative External Morphology, Phylogeny and a Classification of the Bees (Hymenoptera) 1944, American Social Insects (with M. H. Michener) 1951, The Nest Architecture of the Sweat Bees (with S. F. Sakagami) 1962, A Classification of the Bees of the Australian and S. Pacific Regions 1965, The Social Behaviour of the Bees 1974, Kin Recognition in Animals (with D. Fletcher) 1987, The Bee Genera of North and Central America (with R. J. McGinley and B. N. Danforth) 1994, The Bees of the World 2000. *Leisure interests:* travel, field work. *Address:* Snow Entomological Division, Natural History Museum, Snow Hall, University of Kansas, Lawrence, KS 66045; 1706 West 2nd Street, Lawrence, KS 66044, USA (Home). *Telephone:* (785) 864-4610 (Office); (785) 843-4598 (Home). *Fax:* (785) 864-5260 (Office). *E-mail:* michener@ku.edu (Office).

MICHIE, David Alan Redpath, OBE, FRSA; British painter and professor of art; b. 30 Nov. 1928, St Raphael, France; s. of James Beattie Michie and Anne Redpath; m. Eileen Michie 1951; two d.; ed Hawick High School, Edinburgh Coll. of Art; Lecturer in Drawing and Painting, Gray's School of Art, Aberdeen 1957–61; Vice-Prin. Edinburgh Coll. of Art 1974–77, Head of School of Drawing and Painting 1982–90, Prof. of Painting 1988–90; Prof. Emer., Heriot Watt Univ. 1991–; Visiting Artist to Acad. of Fine Art, Belgrade 1979, to Art Studio Dept, Univ. of Calif. at Santa Barbara 1992; mem. Edinburgh Festival Soc. 1976–, Royal Scottish Acad. 1972, Royal Glasgow Inst. of Fine Art 1983, Royal West of England Acad. 1991–2000, Museums and Galleries Comm. 1991–96; Guthrie Award, RSA 1964, David Cargill Award, R.G.I. 1977, Lothian Region Award 1977, Sir William Gillies Award, RSA 1980, Glasgow City of Culture Award, R.G.I. 1990, Cornelissen Prize, R.W.A. 1992. *Solo exhibitions include:* Mercury Gallery, London 1966, 1969, 1971, 1974, 1980, 1983, 1992, 1996, 1999, Mercury Gallery, Edinburgh 1986, The Scottish Gallery, Edinburgh 1980, 1994, 1998, 2003 The Lothian and Region Chambers 1977, The Loomshop Gallery, Lower Largo 1981, 1987, De Kasteel de Hooge Vursche and Mia Joosten Gallery, Amsterdam 1991. *Leisure interest:* music. *Address:* 17 Gilmour Road, Edinburgh, EH16 5NS, Scotland (Home). *Telephone:* (131) 667-2684 (Home).

MICHIE, Donald, DPhil, DSc, FRSE; British scientist; b. 11 Nov. 1923, Rangoon, Burma (now Myanmar); s. of the late James Kilgour Michie and

Marjorie Crain Michie; m. 1st Zena Margaret Davies 1949 (divorced); one s.; m. 2nd Anne McLaren 1952 (divorced); one s. two d.; m. 3rd Jean Elizabeth Hayes (née Crouch) 1971; ed Rugby School, Balliol Coll., Oxford; war service in Foreign Office Bletchley 1942–45; Research Assoc. Univ. of London 1952–58; Sr Lecturer in Surgical Science, Edin. Univ. 1958, Reader 1962, Dir of Experimental Programming Unit 1965, Chair. Dept of Machine Intelligence and Perception 1966, Prof. of Machine Intelligence 1967–84, Prof. Emer. 1984–; Dir Machine Intelligence Research Unit 1974–84; Royal Soc. Lecturer in USSR 1965; numerous visiting lectureships and professorships; Ed.-in-Chief Machine Intelligence series 1967–; Founder, Dir Turing Inst., Glasgow 1975–86, Chief Scientist 1986–92, Sr Fellow 1992–94; Tech. Dir Intelligent Terminals Ltd (Knowledgelink) 1984–92; Fellow British Computer Soc. 1971; Hon. DSc (CNAA) 1991, (Salford) 1992, (Aberdeen) 1999; Hon. DUniv (Stirling) 1996, (York) 2000; Pioneer Award (jtly.) Int. Embryo Transfer Soc. 1988, IEE Achievement Award 1995, Feigenbaum Medal, World Congress on Expert Systems 1996, Research Excellence Award, Int. Jt Conf. on Artificial Intelligence 2001. *Publications:* An Introduction to Molecular Biology (jtly.) 1964, On Machine Intelligence 1974, Machine Intelligence and Related Topics 1982, The Creative Computer (jtly.) 1984; papers in scientific journals. *Leisure interests:* writing. *Address:* Artificial Intelligence Laboratory, School of Computer Science and Engineering, University of New South Wales, Sydney, NSW 2052 (Office); Medina Apartments, 63–65 St Marks Road, Randwick, Sydney, NSW 2031, Australia. *Telephone:* (2) 9314-9800. *Fax:* (2) 9398-4509 (Home). *E-mail:* d.michie@ed.ac.uk (Office); d.michie@ed .ac.uk (Home).

MICHNIK, Adam; Polish journalist; b. 17 Oct. 1946, Warsaw; m.; one s.; ed Adam Mickiewicz Univ., Poznań; active in anti-communist movt 1965–80, spent six years in prison; Co-Founder and mem. Cttee for the Defence of Workers (KOR) 1976–80; Biuletyn Informacyjny, Krytyka, Zapis (ind. periodicals); activist Solidarity Self-governing Ind. Trade Union in the 1980s; imprisoned 1985–86; participant Round Table plenary debates 1989; Deputy to Sejm (Parl.) 1989–91; Ed.-in-Chief Gazeta Wyborcza (daily) 1989–; Dr hc (New School for Social Research, New York), (Univ. of Minnesota), (Univ. of Michigan), (Connecticut Coll.); French Pen Club Freedom Award 1982, Robert F. Kennedy Human Rights Award 1986, Alfred Jurzykowski Foundation Award, La Vie Man of the Year 1989, Shofar Award 1991, Brucke-Preis (Germany) 1995, Award of the European Journalists Asscn 1995, Medal of Imre Nagy 1995, OSCE Prize in Journalism and Democracy 1996, Officer's Cross of Merit (Hungary) 1998, The Golden Pen (Bauer Verlag) 1998, The Francisco Cerecedo Journalist Prize 1999, Bernardo O'Higgins Commdr's Order (Chile) 1999, Int. Press Inst. Freedom Hero 2000, Order for Contrib. to Polish-German Reconciliation, European Univ. Viadriana, Frankfurt 2000, Grand Prince Gedymin Order (Lithuania) 2001, Carl Bertelsmann Prize 2001, Grand Cross of Merit (Germany) 2001. *Publications:* Cienie zapomnianych przodków (The Shadows of the Forgotten Ancestors) 1975, Kościół, Lewica, Dialog (Church, The Left, Dialogue) 1977, Penser la Pologne 1983, Szanse polskiej Demokracji (Chances for Polish Democracy) 1984, Z dziejów honoru w Polsce. Wypisy więzienne (From the History of Honour in Poland. Prison Notes) 1985, Takie czasy: Rzecz o kompromisie (Such Other Times: Concerning Compromise) 1985, Listy z Białołęki (Letters from Białołęka), Polskie pytania (Polish Questions) 1987, Druga faza rewolucji 1990, Między Panem a Plebanem 1995, Diabeł naszego czasu 1995; many articles in Gazeta Wyborcza, Der Spiegel, Le Monde, Libération, El Pais, Lettre International, New York Review of Books, The Washington Post and others. *Address:* Gazeta Wyborcza, ul. Czerska 8/10, 00-732 Warsaw, Poland (Office). *Telephone:* (22) 5504000, (22) 5554002 (Office). *Fax:* (22) 8416920 (Office). *E-mail:* contact@ agora.pl (Office).

MICHON, John Albertus, PhD; Netherlands research director and university professor; b. 29 Oct. 1935, Utrecht; s. of the late J. J. Michon and of S. Ch. A. de Ruyter; m. Hetty Sommer 1960; one s. one d. (deceased); ed Utrecht Mun. Gymnasium and Univs. of Utrecht and Leiden; Research Assoc. Inst. for Perception, Soesterberg 1960–73, Head, Dept of Road User Studies 1969–73; Co-Founder, Netherlands Psychonomics Foundation 1968, Sec. 1968–72, Pres. 1975–80; Prof. of Experimental Psychology and Traffic Science, Univ. of Groningen 1971–92, Dir Inst. for Experimental Psychology 1971–92, Chair. Traffic Research Center 1977–92, Chair. Dept of Psychology 1978, 1983–92, Assoc. Dean, Faculty of Social Sciences 1983–86; mem. Bd Center for Behavioral, Cognitive and Neurosciences 1990–92, co-f. Dept of Cognitive Science 1990; Dir Netherlands Inst. for the Study of Criminality and Law Enforcement 1992–98; Prof. of Criminal Research, Leiden Univ. 1992–98, Sr Research Prof. of Psychonomics 1998–, Emer. Prof.; Pres. Int. Soc. for the Study of Time 1983–86; Co-Founder, mem. Bd European Soc. for Cognitive Psychology 1984–90; Vice-Chair. Nat. Council for Road Safety 1977–86; Ed.-in-Chief, Acta Psychologica 1971–74; Visiting Prof. Carnegie Mellon Univ., Pittsburgh, Pa 1986–87; Co-ordinator EEC DRIVE Project Generic Intelligent Driver Support 1988–92; Chair. Steering Cttee for the Cognitive Sciences, Netherlands Org. for Scientific Research NWO 2002–; mem. Royal Netherlands Acad. of Arts and Sciences (Chair. Behavioral and Social Sciences Section 1988–98, Chair. Accreditation Cttee Research Schools 2000–); mem. Acad. Europaea (London), European Acad. of Sciences and Arts (Vienna), Social Sciences Council (S.W.R.) 1994–; NATO Science Fellowship, NIAS Fellowship; Dr. hc (Liège) 1995. *Publications:* Timing in Temporal Tracking 1967, Sociale Verkeerskunde 1976, Handboek der Psychonomie 1976, 1979, Beïnvloeding van Mobiliteit 1981, Time, Mind and Behaviour 1985, Guyau and the Idea of Time 1988, Handboek der Sociale Verkeerskunde

1989, Soar: A Cognitive Architecture in Perspective 1992, Generic Intelligent Driver Behaviour 1993, Nederlanders over Criminaliteit en Rechtshandhaving 1997; approx. 250 articles and chapters in scientific journals and books. *Leisure interests:* visual arts (painting, graphics), music (bassoon playing). *Address:* Department of Psychology, Leiden University, Wassenaarseweg 52, PO Box 9555, 2300 RB Leiden, Netherlands. *Telephone:* (71) 5273801. *Fax:* (71) 5221927. *E-mail:* michon@fsw.leidenuniv.nl (Office); michonja@xs4all.nl (Home).

MICHOT, Yves Raoul; French aviation executive; b. 4 Nov. 1941, Nantes; s. of Raoul Michot and Lucienne Ruffel; m. Michèle Gouth 1964; one s. one d.; Brétigny Flight Test Centre 1965–73; Govt Concorde Project Man. 1973–75; Tech. Adviser to Nat. Armament Dir 1975–78, to Minister of Defence 1978–80; Mirage 2000 Program Man. Ministry of Defence 1980–84; Mil. Programs Gen. Man. Aérospatiale 1984, Programs Gen. Man. 1985; Exec. Vice-Pres. Aérospatiale 1987, Exec. Vice-Pres. and COO 1989, Sr Exec. Vice-Pres. and COO and Pres. Aérospatiale 1995–99, Pres., Dir-Gen. 1996–99, Pres. Bd of Dirs. 1999; Pres. European Asscn of Aerospace Industries (AECMA) 1997–, Club d'affaires franco-singapourien 1998–; Officier, Légion d'Honneur, Officier, Ordre Nat. du Mérite, Médaille de l'Aéronautique. *Address:* Aérospatiale, 37 boulevard de Montmorency, 75781 Paris, Cedex 16 (Office); 3 rue Chabrier, 78370 Plaisir, France (Home). *Telephone:* 42-24-24-24 (Office).

MICIC, Natasa; Serbia and Montenegro (Serbian) politician and lawyer; b. 11 Aug. 1965, Uzice; m.; one c.; ed Faculty of Law, Univ. of Belgrade; sec. Dist Court, Uzice; admitted to Bar 1998– Deputy Speaker, Parl. –2001; Pres. Serbian Ass. 2001, Chair. Cttee for Constitutional Issues; apptd Acting Pres. of Serbia Jan. 2003; mem. Civil Alliance of Serbia 1997–. *Address:* Office of the President, 11000 Belgrade, Andrićev venac 1, (Office); c/o Government HQ, 11000 Belgrade, 11 Nemanjina Street, Serbia and Montenegro (Office). *Website:* www.serbia.sr.gov.yu (Office).

MICOSSI, Stefano; Italian economist and international official; b. 27 Oct. 1946, Bologna; m. Daniela Zanotto; one s. one d.; ed Università Statale di Milano, Yale Univ.; economist Bank of Italy Research Dept 1974–78, Head 1980–84, Asst Dir 1984–86, Dir Int. Div. 1986–88; seconded to IMF as Asst to Italy's Exec. Dir 1978–80; Dir of Econ. Research Confindustria (Confed. of Italian Industries) 1988–94; Prof. of Macroeconomic Policy Int. Free Univ. of Social Sciences 1989–94, Prof. of Monetary Theory and Policy 1993–94; Prof. of Int. Monetary Econs, Coll. of Europe, Bruges 1990–94, Prof. of European Integration 1999–; Dir-Gen. for Industry, EC 1994–99; Dir-Gen. Asscn of Italian Ltd Cos. 1999–. *Publications:* Jt Ed. Adjustment and Integration in the World Economy 1992, The Italian Economy 1993, Inflation in Europe 1997 and books on the European Monetary System 1988, numerous articles in professional journals. *Address:* Assonmie, Piazza Venezia 11, 00187 Rome, Italy.

MIDDELHOEK, André, PhD; Netherlands civil servant; b. 13 Dec. 1931, Voorburg; s. of J. Middelhoek; m. Trudy van den Broek 1982; two d.; ed Univ. of Amsterdam; Cen. Planning Office, Govt of Netherlands 1958–69, Deputy Dir 1966–69; lecturer, Int. Inst. for Social Studies, The Hague 1960–69; Dir-Gen. of the Budget, Ministry of Finance 1969–77; mem. Court of Auditors of European Communities 1977–93; Pres. European Court of Auditors 1993–96; Pres. Cttee of Wise Men 1999–; Commdr, Order of Netherlands Lion, Grand Croix, Couronne de Chêne (Luxembourg). *Publications:* publs on econs, econ. planning, public finance, policy analysis, EU finance and audit. *Leisure interests:* swimming, tennis, genealogy, hiking. *Address:* Marnixlaan 108, 3090 Overijse, Belgium. *Telephone:* (2) 687-55-53. *Fax:* (2) 688-39-41.

MIDDELHOFF, Thomas, MBA; German business executive; b. 11 May 1953, Düsseldorf; m.; five c.; fmr Lecturer in Marketing, Münster Univ.; mem. Bd responsible for multimedia, Bertelsmann publishing, Chair. and CEO Bertelsmann AG 1998–2002; Vernon A. Walters Award 1998. *Address:* c/o Bertelsmann AG, Carl-Bertelsmann-Str. 270, 33311 Gütersloh, Germany (Office).

MIDDENDORF, J. William, II, BS, MBA; American fmr government official, diplomatist and business executive; b. 22 Sept. 1924, Baltimore, Md; s. of the late Henry Stump and Sarah Boone Middendorf; m. Isabelle J. Paine 1953; two s. two d.; ed Holy Cross Coll., Harvard Univ. and New York Graduate School of Business Admin.; U.S. Navy service during Second World War; in Credit Dept of Bank of Manhattan Co. (now Chase Manhattan Bank) 1947–52; Analyst, brokerage firm of Wood Struthers and Co. Inc., New York 1952–58, Partner 1958–62; Sr Partner investment firm of Middendorf, Colgate and Co., New York 1962–69; U.S. Amb. to the Netherlands 1969–73; Under-Sec. of the Navy 1973–74, Sec. 1974–76; Pres. and CEO of First American Bankshares, Washington, DC 1977–81; Pres. and CEO Middendorf & Co., Inc. 1989–; Chair. Middendorf SA 1989–; U.S. Amb. to O.A.S. 1981–85, to EC 1985–87; Chair. Presidential Task Force on Project Econ. Justice 1985–86; numerous hon. degrees; State Dept Superior Honor Award 1974, Dept of Defense Distinguished Public Service Award 1975, 1976, U.S. Navy Public Service Award 1976, numerous other awards, Grand Master of Order of Naval Merit (Brazil) 1974, Distinguished Service Medal (Brazil) 1976, Order of Arab Repub. of Egypt (Class A) 1979, Grand Officer of the Order of Orange Nassau Netherlands 1985, Ludwig Von Mises Inst. Free Market Award 1985, Arleigh Burke Award 1998; U.S. Nat. Sculling Champion in Masters Div. 1979, won a world masters championship in rowing at the 1985 Toronto Masters Games. *Compositions:* has composed seven symphonies, an opera and numerous marches and concertos. *Publications:* Investment Policies of Fire and Casualty Insurance Companies. *Address:* Middendorf and Associates Inc., P.O. Box 159, Great Falls, VA 22066, USA (Office).

MIDDLEMAS, Robert Keith, DPhil, DLitt, FRSA; British historian; b. 26 May 1935, Alnwick; s. of Robert James Middlemas and Eleanor Mary Middlemas (née Crane); m. Susan Mary Tremlett 1958; one s. three d.; ed Stowe School, Pembroke Coll., Cambridge; nat. service 2nd Lt Northumberland Fusiliers 1953–55; Clerk House of Commons 1958–67; Lecturer in History, Sussex Univ. 1967–76, Reader 1976–86, Prof. 1986–95, Prof. Emer. 1995–; Visiting Prof. Stanford Univ. and Hoover Inst. 1984, Univ. of Beijing 1989; Dir ESL and Network SA 1998–; mem. UK Nat. Cttee UNESCO 1980–86, Co-Founder and Ed. Catalyst, A Journal of Public Debate 1985–87; Council mem., Research Cttee mem. Foundation for Mfg and Industry 1993–99; Consultant and mem. Advisory Bd ESL and Network, SA 2000–. *Publications:* The Master Builders 1963, The Clydesiders 1965, Baldwin (jtly.) 1969, Diplomacy of Illusion 1972, Thomas Jones: Whitehall Diary (Ed.) 1969–72, Cabora Bassa: Engineering and Politics 1975, Politics in Industrial Society 1979, Power and the Party: Communism in Western Europe 1980, Industry, Unions and Government 1984, Power, Competition and the State (three Vols) 1986–91, Orchestrating Europe: Informal Politics of the Community Since 1973 1995. *Leisure interests:* rifle shooting (UK nat. team, Canada 1958), sailing, fishing, landscape gardening, building follies. *Address:* West Burton House, West Burton, Pulborough, West Sussex, RH20 1HD, England. *Telephone:* (1798) 831516.

MIDDLETON, Christopher, MA, DPhil; British professor of Germanic languages and literature; b. 10 June 1926, Truro; s. of Hubert S. Middleton and Dorothy M. Miller; m. 1953 (divorced); one s. two d.; ed Felsted School and Merton Coll. Oxford; Lektor in English, Univ. of Zürich 1952–55; Asst Lecturer in German, King's Coll. Univ. of London 1955–57, Lecturer 1957–66; Prof. of Germanic Languages and Literature Univ. of Texas at Austin 1966–98, Emer.Prof.; Sir Geoffrey Faber Memorial Prize 1964, Guggenheim Poetry Fellowship 1974–75; Nat. Endowment for Humanities Poetry Fellowship 1980; Tieck-Schlegel Translation Prize 1985, Max Geilinger Stiftung Prize 1987, etc. *Publications:* Torse 3, poems 1948–61 1962, Nonsequences/ Selfpoems 1965, Our Flowers and Nice Bones 1969, The Lonely Suppers of W.V. Balloon 1975, Carminalenia 1980, III Poems 1983, Two-Horse Wagon Going By 1986, Selected Writings 1989, The Balcony Tree 1992, Andalusian Poems 1993, Intimate Chronicles 1996, Faint Harps and Silver Voices: Selected Translations 2000, The Word Pavilion and Selected Poems 2001; Vols of prose, essays etc. *Address:* Department of Germanic Languages, University of Texas at Austin, Austin, TX 78712, USA. *Telephone:* (512) 471-4123.

MIDDLETON, Peter, BA; British business executive and diplomatist; b. 10 Feb. 1940; s. of Roy Middleton and Freda Middleton; m. 1st Yvonne Summerson 1968 (divorced 1996); two s. one d.; m. 2nd Anita Mehra 1996; ed Sorbonne, Hull Univ.; joined a monastery, Paignton, Devon; joined the foreign service, two-year posts in both Indonesia and Tanzania 1969–77; Sr Embassy Counsellor Paris 1977–82; joined Midland Bank 1985, Midland Int. 1985–87; with Thomas Cook 1987–92; CEO Lloyd's of London (Insurance) 1992–95; Chief Exec. Salomon Bros. Int. 1995–98; Chair. London Luton Airport 1999–2000; Transaction Dir Nomura Int. PLC 2000–; Chair. Football League 1998–2000; Chief. Exec. World Professional Billards and Snooker Asscn 1999–2000; Chair. Dome Europe 2000–; Hon. LLD (Teesside) 1997. *Leisure interests:* music, horse-racing, soccer. *Address:* Nomura International PLC, Nomura House, 1 St Martin's-le-Grand, London, EC1A 4NP, England (Office).

MIDDLETON, Sir Peter Edward, KCB, MA; British fmr civil servant and business executive; b. 2 April 1934; m. 1st Valerie Ann Lindup 1964 (died 1987); one s. (deceased) one d.; m. 2nd Connie Owen 1990; ed Sheffield City Grammar School, Sheffield Univ., Bristol Univ.; Sr Information Officer, HM Treasury 1962, Prin. 1964, Asst Dir, Centre for Admin. Studies 1967–69, Pvt. Sec. to Chancellor of Exchequer 1969–72, Treasury Press Sec. 1972–75, Head, Monetary Policy Div. 1975, Under-Sec. 1976, Deputy Sec. 1980–83, Perm. Sec. 1983–91; a Deputy Chair. Barclays Group 1991–98, Chair. 1999–, mem. Exec. Bd 1991–, Chair. BZW Div. 1991–98; Chair. Sheffield Urban Regeneration Co. Ltd 2001–; mem. Council Univ. of Sheffield 1991–, Pro-Chancellor 1997–99, Chancellor 1999–; mem. Bd United Utilities Group PLC 1994–, Vice-Chair. 1998–99, Chair. 1999–2000, Deputy Chair. 2000–; non-exec. mem. Bd Bass PLC 1992–, Dir 1992–2001, General Accident Fire and Life Assurance Corpn PLC (now CGU PLC) 1992–98; mem. Council Manchester Business School 1985–92; Gov. London Business School 1984–90, Ditchley Foundation 1985–; mem. Nat. Econ. Research Asscn 1991–; Chair. Inst. of Contemporary History 1993–2001, Dir 2001–; mem. Financial Reporting Council 1997–; Dir Int. Monetary Conf. 2001–; Visiting Fellow, Nuffield Coll., Oxford 1981–89; Hon. DLitt (Sheffield) 1984. *Leisure interests:* music, walking, outdoor sports. *Address:* Barclays Bank PLC, 54 Lombard Street, London, EC3P 3AH, England.

MIDDLETON, Stanley, BA, M.ED., FRSL; British author and schoolteacher (retd); b. 1 Aug. 1919, Bulwell, Nottingham; s. of Thomas Middleton and Elizabeth Ann Middleton (née Burdett); m. Margaret Shirley Charnley (née Welch) 1951; two d.; ed Bulwell St Mary's School, Bulwell Highbury School, High Pavement School, Nottingham, Nottingham Univ. Coll., Univ. of Nottingham; fmr English teacher; fmr Head of English High Pavement Coll.,

Nottingham, retd 1981; Judith Wilson Fellow Emmanuel Coll., Cambridge 1982–83; Hon. MA (Nottingham); Hon. M.Univ. (Open); Hon. DLitt (De Montfort) 1998, (Nottingham Trent) 2000; Booker Prize (for Holiday) 1974. *Publications:* 40 novels including Harris's Requiem, Wages of Virtue, Holiday, In a Strange Land, Entry into Jerusalem, Valley of Decision, A Place to Stand, Catalysts, Toward the Sea, Brief Hours, Against the Dark, Necessary Ends 1999, Small Change 2000, Love in the Provinces 2002. *Leisure interests:* music, painting. *Address:* 42 Caledon Road, Sherwood, Nottingham, NG5 2NG, England. *Telephone:* (115) 962-3085.

MIDLER, Bette; American singer, entertainer and actress; b. 1 Dec. 1945, Honolulu; m. Martin von Haselberg 1984; one d.; ed Univ. of Hawaii; début as actress in film Hawaii 1965; mem. of cast in Fiddler on the Roof, New York 1966–69, Salvation, New York 1970, Tommy, Seattle Opera Co. 1971; nightclub concert performer 1972–; After Dark Ruby Award 1973, Grammy Award 1973, Special Tony Award 1973, Emmy Award 1978. *Film appearances include:* The Rose (two Golden Globe Awards) 1979, Jinxed 1982, Down and Out in Beverly Hills 1986, Ruthless People 1986, Outrageous Fortune 1987, Big Business 1988, Beaches 1989, Stella 1990, For The Boys (Golden Globe Award) 1991, Hocus Pocus 1993, Gypsy (TV), The First Wives Club 1996, That Old Feeling 1997, Get Bruce 1999, Isn't She Great? 1999. *Recordings include:* The Divine Miss M. 1973, Bette Midler 1973, Broken Blossom 1977, Live at Last 1977, Thighs and Whispers 1979, New Depression 1979, Divine Madness 1980, No Frills 1984, Some People's Lives 1990. *Television includes:* The Tonight Show (Emmy Award) 1992, Gypsy 1993, Seinfeld 1996, Diva Las Vegas 1997, Murphy Brown 1998. *Publications:* A View From A Broad 1980, The Saga of Baby Divine 1983. *Address:* c/o All Girl Productions, 100 Universal City Plaza, Universal City, CA 91608 (Office); c/o Warner Bros. Records, 3300 Warner Boulevard, Burbank, CA 91505, USA. *Fax:* (818) 866-5871.

MIDORI; Japanese violinist; b. 25 Oct. 1971, Osaka; d. of Setsu Goto; ed The Professional Children's School and Juilliard School of Music; began violin studies with mother aged four; moved to USA 1982; début with New York Philharmonic 1982; recording début 1986 aged 14; now makes worldwide concert appearances; Founder and Pres. Midori and Friends 1992; Dorothy B. Chandler Performing Arts Award; New York State Asian-American Heritage Month Award; Crystal Award (Japan), Suntory Award 1994. *Leisure interests:* cooking, reading, listening to music, art. *Address:* Midori and Friends, 850 Seventh Avenue, Suite 1103, New York, NY 10019 (Office); c/o ICM Artists Ltd, Oxford House, 76 Oxford Street, London, W1N 0AX, England; Sony Classical, Sony Music Entertainment Inc., 550 Madison Avenue, New York, NY 10022, USA.

MIDWINTER, John Edwin, OBE, PhD, FRS, F.R.ENG., FIEE, FIEEE, FInstP; British professor of optoelectronics; b. 8 March 1938, Newbury, Berks.; s. of the late H. C. Midwinter and of V. J. (née Rawlinson) Midwinter; m. Maureen A. Holt 1961; two s. two d.; ed King's Coll., London; Sr Scientific Officer, Royal Radar Establishment 1967–68; Sr Research Physicist, Perkin-Elmer Corpn, USA 1968–70; Head, Fibre Optic Devt British Telecom Research Labs. 1971–77, Head Optical Communications Technology 1977–84; British Telecom Prof. of Optoelectronics, Univ. Coll., London 1984–91, Head, Dept of Electronic and Electrical Eng 1988–98, Pender Prof. of Electronic Eng 1991–, Vice-Provost 1994–; Vice-Pres. IEE 1994, Deputy Pres. 1998–2000, Pres. 2000–01; Hon. DSc (Nottingham) 2000, (Loughborough) 2001; IEE-J.J. Thompson Medal 1987, Faraday Medal 1997. *Publications:* Applied Non-Linear Optics 1972, Optical Fibers for Transmission 1977; over 70 papers on lasers, non-linear optics and optical communications. *Leisure interests:* walking, skiing, writing. *Address:* Department of Electronic and Electrical Engineering, University College, Torrington Place, London, WC1E 7JE, England. *Telephone:* (20) 7388-0427; (20) 7387-7050.

MIELI, Paolo; Italian journalist; b. 25 Feb. 1949, Milan; m. Barbara Parodi Delfino; two s.; ed classical lycée and univ.; Asst to Chair of History of Political Parties, Univ. of Rome; Corresp., Political Commentator at Home, Head of Cultural Desk and then Cen. Man. Ed., Espresso (weekly) 1967–85; worked for La Repubblica 1985–86; Lead Writer, La Stampa 1986–90, Ed.-in-Chief 1990–92; Ed. Corriere della Sera 1992–97; apptd Pres. RAI (Radiotelevisione Italiana) March 2003 (resgnd after five days); mem. Bd Govs. Storia Illustrata, Pagina and has collaborated with Tempi Moderni, Questi Istituzioni, Mondo operaio; Premio Spoleto 1990; Premio Mediterraneo 1991; Premio Alfio Russo 1995. *Publications:* Litigo a Sinistra, Il Socialismo Diviso, Storia del Partito Socialista Negli Anni della Repubblica, Le Storie—La Storia 1999, Storia e Politica: Risorgimento, fascismo e comunismo 2001. *Leisure interests:* ancient history, skiing. *Address:* Via Medaglie d'Oro 391, Rome 00136, Italy (Home).

MIERS, Sir David, KBE, CMG, MA; British diplomatist (retd); b. 10 Jan. 1937, Liverpool; s. of the late Col R. Miers, DSO and Honor Bucknill; m. Imelda Wouters 1966; two s. one d.; ed Winchester Coll. and Univ. Coll. Oxford; joined diplomatic service 1961; served Tokyo 1963, Vientiane 1966, Paris 1972, Tehran 1977, Beirut 1983; Asst Under-Sec. FCO 1986; Amb. to Greece 1989–93; to Netherlands 1993–96; Chair. Soc. of Pension Consultants 1998–, British-Lebanese Asscn 1998–, Anglo-Hellenic League 1999–. *Leisure interest:* open air.

MIERZEJEWSKI, Jerzy; Polish painter and academic; b. 13 July 1917, Cracow; s. of Jacek Mierzejewski and Stanisława Brzezińska; m. Krystyna Szner (died 1994), one s. one d.; ed Acad. of Fine Arts, Warsaw; Lecturer and

Prof. State Film School, Łódź; fmr Dean Film Photography Dept and Film Directory Dept, fmr Rector; fmr Pres. Union of Polish Artists and Designers, State Film School, Łódź; Minister of Culture and Art Prize (II Class) 1963, Kt.'s Cross of Polonia Restituta Order 1975, Grant-Pollok-Krasner Foundation Award 1992, 1996, Jan Cybis Award 1997, Golden Frog, Int. Film Festival of the Art of Cinematography Camerimage 1997. *Films include:* Jan Matejko 1954, Jacek Mierzejewski 1968. *Paintings include:* My Brother 1985, Garden 1986, Lake 1992, Hospital 1992, Double Landscape 1995, Brunch 1998, Studio X 1998, Sielanka 1999, Pilgrim 2000, The Moment 2001, Friend 2002. *Exhibitions include:* 30 one-man exhbns.; group exhbns. include Selective Eye, Crown Town Gallery, Los Angeles 1970; works in perm. collections Nat. Museum, Warsaw, Museum of Art Łódź, Stedelijk Museum, Amsterdam and in numerous pvt. collections. *Publications include:* Composition of Film Picture 1955, Some Aspects of Continuity of Film 1963. *Address:* ul. Śmiała 63, 01-526 Warsaw, Poland (Home). *Telephone:* (22) 8392243 (Home).

MIFFLIN, Fred J.; Canadian politician and former naval officer; b. 1938, Bonavista, Newfoundland; m. Cwenneth Mifflin; three c.; ed Nat. Defence Coll., Kingston, Ont., U.S. Naval War Coll., Newport, RI; joined Navy 1954, assumed first command at sea 1969, commanded destroyers, served in Sr positions relating to UN Confs. on Law of the Sea, fisheries protection, procurement of mil. systems and int. relations; Head Nat. Defence Secr.; MP for Bonavista-Trinity-Conception 1988–; Parl. Sec. to Minister of Nat. Defence and Veterans' Affairs 1993–95; Minister of Fisheries and Oceans 1996–97, of Veterans Affairs and Sec. of State (Atlantic Opportunities Agency) 1997–99. *Leisure interests:* cooking, country music. *Address:* House of Commons, Confederation Building, Room 207, Ottawa, Ont. K1A 0A6, Canada (Office).

MIFSUD BONNICI, Carmelo, LLD; Maltese politician and lawyer; b. 17 July 1933, Cospicua; s. of Lorenzo Mifsud Bonnici and Catherine Buttigieg; ed Lyceum, Univ. of Malta, Univ. Coll. London; legal consultant, Gen. Workers' Union 1969; Deputy Leader, Maltese Labour Movt 1980–82, Leader desig. 1982, Leader Labour Party 1984; mem. Parl. 1982–96; Minister of Labour and Social Services 1982–83; Sr Deputy Prime Minister and Minister of Educ. 1983–84; Prime Minister of Malta and Minister of the Interior and of Educ. 1985–87; Leader of Opposition 1987–92; Lecturer in Industrial and Fiscal Law, Univ. of Malta 1969. *Leisure interest:* reading.

MIFSUD BONNICI, Ugo, BA, LLD; Maltese fmr Head of State and lawyer; b. 8 Nov. 1932, Cospicua; s. of Carmelo Mifsud Bonnici and Maria Mifsud Bonnici (née Ross); m. Gemma Bianco; three c.; ed Royal Univ. of Malta; practising lawyer 1955–87; mem. Parl. 1966–94; Opposition Spokesman for Educ. 1972–87; Pres. Gen. Council and Admin. Council of Nationalist Party 1977–87; Minister of Educ. 1987, of Educ. and Interior 1990–92, of Educ. and Human Resources 1992–94, Pres. of Malta 1994–99; Hon. DLitt (Univ. of Malta), (Paris IV). *Publications:* newspaper articles. *Address:* 18 Erin Serracino Inglott Road, Cospicua, Malta (Home). *Telephone:* 826975 (Home).

MIGAŠ, Jozef, DPhil, CSc; Slovak politician; b. 7 Jan. 1954, Pušovce; m. Alena Migašová; one s. one d.; ed Univ. of Kiev; fmrly with Acad. of Sciences, Košice, Political Univ., Bratislava; f. Party of the Democratic Left, Chair. 1996–2001; diplomatist 1993–96; Chair. Nat. Council of the Slovak Repub. 1998–. *Address:* National Council of the Slovak Republic, na'meste A. Dubčeka 1, 812 80 Bratislava; Office of the Government of the Slovak Republic, Nám. Slobody 1, 813 70 Bratislava 1, Slovakia (Office). *Telephone:* (7) 593-41-201 (Office); (7) 593-41-111. *Fax:* (7) 544-15-460 (Office). *E-mail:* migajoze@nrsr.sk (Office). *Website:* www.nrsr.sk (Office).

MIGRANYAN, Andranik Movsesovich, CAND.HIS.SC.; Russian/Armenian civil servant; b. 10 Feb. 1949, Yerevan; m.; one d.; ed Moscow State Inst. of Int. Relations, Inst. of Int. Workers' Movt USSR Acad. of Sciences; teacher, Prof. Moscow Inst. of Automobile Construction 1976–85; leading researcher Inst. of Econ. and Political Studies Acad. of Sciences 1985–88; Head Cen. for Studies of Social-Political Problems and Interstate Relations of CIS 1992–93; mem. Pres.'s Council 1993–; Chief Expert Cttee on CIS countries of State Duma 1993–96; Chair. Bd Scientific Council on CIS Countries; Prof. Moscow State Inst. of Int. Relations (MGIMO) 1994–; co-f. Politika Fund; Vice-Pres. Reforma Fund. *Address:* Reforma Fund, Staromonetny per.10, 109180 Moscow (Office); MGIMO, Vernadskogo prosp. 76, 117454, Moscow, Russia (Office). *Telephone:* (095) 433-34-95.

MÍGUEZ BONINO, Rev. José, PhD; Argentine professor of theology, clergyman and international church official; b. 5 March 1924, Santa Fé; s. of José Míguez Gándara and Augustina Bonino; m. Noemi Nieuwenhuize 1947; three s.; ed Facultad Evangélica de Teología, Emory Univ., Union Theological Seminary, New York; Methodist minister in Bolivia, later in Argentina 1945–; Prof. of Theology, Facultad Evangélica de Teología, Buenos Aires 1954–70, Rector 1960–70; Prof. of Systematic Theology and Ethics, Protestant Inst. for Higher Theological Studies, Buenos Aires 1970–86, Prof. Emer. 1986–, Dean of Post-Graduate Studies 1973–86; mem. Cen. Cttee of World Council of Churches (WCC) 1968–75, a Pres. Presidium of WCC 1976–82; Visiting Prof., Facoltà Valdese di Teologia, Rome 1963, Union Theological Seminary, New York 1967–68, Selly Oak Coll., Birmingham, UK 1974, Faculté de Théologie Protestante, Strasbourg Univ. 1981, Harvard Univ. 2001–02; Observer at II Vatican Council 1962–64; Pres. Perm. Ass. for Human Rights (APDH), Argentina; mem. Nat. Constitutional Ass. 1994–, Nuremberg Human Rights Award Jury 1995–99; Hon. PhD (Candler School of Theol., Free Univ. of Amsterdam 1980); Hon. DD (Aberdeen) 1987. *Publications:* Concilio abierto 1968, Integración humana y unidad cristiana 1968, Ama y haz lo que quieras 1972, Theology in a Revolutionary Situation (trans. in Dutch, German, Italian) 1975, Espacio para ser hombres 1975, Christians and Marxists 1976, Toward a Christian Political Ethic 1983, Rostros del Protestantismo en América Latina 1996; articles in Concilium, Expository Times, Evangelische Kommentare, Evangelio y Poder: poder del evangelio y poder político, Teología y Economía 2003. *Leisure interests:* swimming, playing tennis. *Address:* Camacuá 252, 1406 Buenos Aires (Office); F. Madero 591, 1706 V. Sarmiento (Haedo) Rov., Buenos Aires, Argentina (Home). *Telephone:* (1) 4654-2184 (Home). *Fax:* (11) 4656-4239 (Office). *E-mail:* jmiguez@arnet.com.ar (Home).

MIHAJLOV, Mihajlo; Serbia and Montenegro (Serbian) author, scholar and human rights administrator; b. 26 Sept. 1934, Pančevo; s. of Nicholas Mihajlov and Vera Daniloff; ed High School, Sarajevo and Zagreb Univ.; served armed forces 1961–62; freelance writer and trans., magazines, newspapers and radio 1962–63; Asst Prof. of Modern Russian Literature, Zagreb Univ. 1963–65; freelance writer, western press 1965–66, 1970–74; imprisoned 1966–70, 1974–77; lectures, USA, Europe and Asia 1978–79; Visiting Lecturer, Yale Univ. 1981; Visiting Prof. of Russian Literature and Philosophy, Univ. of Va 1982–83; Visiting Prof. Ohio State Univ. 1983–84, Univ. of Siegen 1984, Univ. of Glasgow 1985; Commentator on Ideological Matters, Radio Free Europe/Radio Liberty Inc. 1986; Sr Fellow, Program on Transitions to Democracy, Elliott School of Int. Affairs, George Washington Univ. 1994–99, Adjunct Fellow Hudson Inst. 1999; Vice-Pres. Democracy Int.; Chair. Democracy Int. Comm. to Aid Democratic Dissidents in Yugoslavia 1990; mem. Editorial Bd int. magazine Kontinent 1975–84, Tribuna Magazine, Paris and Forum Magazine, Munich, Contributing Ed. Religion in Communist Dominated Areas, New York; mem. Int. PEN (French br. 1977, American 1982); Fellow, Nat. Humanities Cen.; mem. Int. Helsinki Group, Cttee for the Free World; mem. Bd Int. Gesellschaft für Menschenrechte 1982–, Bd of Consultants, Centre for Appeals for Freedom 1980, Nat. Cttee of Social Democrats USA 1989, Advisory Bd CAUSA Int. 1986; Trustee, World Constitution and Parl. Assn 1982–; Special Analyst for Intellectual and Ideological Events in the Soviet Union and Eastern Europe, Research Div. of Radio Free Europe 1985–86; Int. League for Human Rights Award 1978; Council against Communist Aggression Award 1975, 1978; Ford Foundation Award for the Humanities 1980. *Publications:* Moscow Summer 1965, Russian Themes 1968, Underground Notes 1976, 1982, Unscientific Thoughts 1979, Planetary Consciousness 1982, Djilas versus Marx 1990, Homeland is Freedom 1994 and hundreds of articles in newspapers, magazines and scholarly books (weekly column in Belgrade daily "Borba" (renamed "Nasa Borba" 1995) 1990–). *Leisure interests:* classical music, motoring. *Address:* Obilićev Venac 6, Stan 5, 11000 Belgrade, Serbia and Montenegro (Home). *Telephone:* (11) 629-939 (Home). *E-mail:* mishamih@yahoo.com (Home).

MIHAJLOVIĆ, Svetozar; Bosnia and Herzegovina (Serb) politician; fmr Vice-Pres. of Serb Repub. of Bosnia and Herzegovina; co-Prime Minister of Bosnia and Herzegovina 1999–2000; Minister for Civil Affairs and Communications 2001–. *Address:* Ministry for Civil Affairs and Communications, 71000 Sarajevo, Vojvode Putnika 3, Bosnia and Herzegovina (Office). *Telephone:* (33) 786822. *Fax:* (33) 786944.

MIHÓK, Peter, PhD; Slovak business administrator and fmr diplomatist; b. 18 Jan. 1948, Topolčianky; s. of Augustin Mihók and Johanna Mihoková; m. Elena Škulová 1971; two d.; with Czechoslovak Chamber of Commerce 1971–78; Commercial Counsellor, Embassy, Morocco 1978–82; Dir Foreign Relations Dept; INCHEBA (Foreign Trade Co.) 1982–90; Dir Foreign Dept, Office of Govt of Slovak Repub. 1990–91; Vice-Pres. Czechoslovak Chamber of Commerce and Industry (CCI) 1991–92; Dir Int. Politics Dept, Ministry of Foreign Affairs of Slovak Repub. 1991; Plenipotentiary of Govt of Slovak Repub. in EU, Head Negotiator in Brussels 1991–94; Pres. Slovak CCI 1992–; Vice-Chair. Supervisory Bd of Heineken Slovakia 1998–, Globtel Orange Bratislava 2001–; Vice-Chair. World Chamber Fed. Paris 2001–; Pres. Ecosoc Slovakia 2000–; Deputy Pres. Eurochambers 2001–; mem. Supervisory Bd Incheba a.s. Bratislava 1999–; Gold Medal of Hungarian CCI 1999, Officer, Order of Léopold II, Belgium 1995, Officier Ordre du Mérite, France 1996, Prominent of Economy, Slovakia 1997, Great Silver Order, Austria 1998. *Publication:* Advertising in the Market Economy. *Leisure interests:* literature, philately, swimming. *Address:* Slovak Chamber of Commerce and Industry, Gorkého 9, 816 03 Bratislava, Slovakia (Office). *Telephone:* (2) 5443-3291 (Office). *Fax:* (2) 5413-1159 (Office). *E-mail:* sopkurad@scci.sk (Office). *Website:* www.scci.sk (Office).

MIHOV, Gen. Miho, MA; Bulgarian air force officer; b. 1 Feb. 1949, Sennik; s. of Dimitar Mihov and Stanka Mihov; m. 1973; one s. one d.; ed Benkovski Air Force Acad., Dolna Mitropolia, Rakovski Nat. War Coll., Sofia, Gen. Staff Coll., Moscow, USAF Special Operations School; Training Flight Air Unit Deputy Commdr/Instructor; Air Squadron Deputy Commdr, Commdr, Air Regt, Deputy Commdr, Commdr; Air Corps Deputy Commdr; Air Defence Div. Commdr, Air Force Commdr; Chief of Gen. Staff of the Bulgarian Armed Forces 1997–2002; Adviser to Pres. of Bulgaria 2002–; Order of Merit and Valor, Medal for Service to the Bulgarian Armed Forces, Medal for the 40th Anniversary of the Victory over Hitler and Fascism, Medals and Orders of Distinguished Service, Order of Merit of Aviation (presented by King of Spain), Order presented by King of Sweden, Order presented by Pres. of Repub. of Bulgaria. *Leisure interests:* hunting, skiing. *Address:* 2 Dondoukov blvd, 1123 Sofia, Bulgaria. *Telephone:* (2) 923-91-08 (Office). *Fax:* (2) 981-75-79 (Office). *E-mail:* mihov@president.bg (Office).

MIKEREVIĆ, Dragan, DSc; Bosnia and Herzegovina (Serb) politician; b. 12 Feb. 1955, Doboj; m.; two c.; ed Univ. of Novi Sad; fmr Chief of Finance Dept., Municipality of Doboj, later Pres. Municipality Ass.; fmr Financial Dir Health Assurance Bureau, Republika Srpska; fmr Prof. of Econs, Univ. of Banja Luka, later Man. and mem. of research teams, Inst. for Economy, Univ. of Banja Luka; mem. Party of Democratic Progress 1999–; Chair. Council of Ministers (Prime Minister) of Bosnia and Herzegovina 2002, Minister for European Integration 2001–02; Prime Minister of Serb Repub. (Republika Srpska) of Bosnia and Herzegovina Jan. 2003–. *Address:* Office of the Prime Minister, 78000 Banja Luka, Republika Srpska, Bosnia and Herzegovina (Office). *Telephone:* (51) 331333 (Office); (51) 331332 (Office). *E-mail:* kabinet@vladars.net (Office). *Website:* www.vladars.net (Office).

MIKHAILOV, Felix Trofimovich; Russian philosopher; b. 12 April 1930, Chimkent, Kazakhstan; ed Moscow State Univ.; researcher, Head of Chair 2nd Pirogov Moscow Inst. of Med. (now Russian State Med. Univ.) 1957–72; Head of Lab. Research Inst. of Methods of Teaching, USSR (now Russian) Acad. of Pedagogical Sciences 1972–74, Head of Lab. Research Inst. of Gen. and Pedagogical Psychology 1974–84; Chief Researcher, Head of Sector Inst. of Philosophy, USSR (now Russian) Acad. of Sciences 1994–; visiting reader univs. in USA, UK, Canada; mem. Russian Acad. of Educ. *Publications:* numerous books, papers and articles on problems of human self-consciousness, including The Mystery of Humans. *Address:* Institute of Philosophy, Russian Academy of Sciences (IF RAN), Volkhonka str. 14m building 5, 119842 Moscow, Russia (Office). *Telephone:* (095) 203-91-09 (Office).

MIKHAILOV, Nikolai Vasilyevich, DPhil; Russian politician; b. 14 May 1937, Sevsk, Bryansk Region; m.; one s.; ed Moscow Bauman Higher School of Tech.; with defence industry enterprises 1961–96; Dir-Gen., Vympel Co. 1986–96; Deputy Sec. Security Council of Russian Fed. 1996–97; State Sec., First Deputy Minister of Defence of Russian Fed. 1997–2000; Co-Chair. Russian-American Comm. on Econ. and Tech. Co-operation 1998–, mem. Bd of Dirs. AFC Systema Co. 2001–; USSR State Prize, State Prize of Russian Fed. 1997. *Address:* Systema Financial Corporation, Leont'yevsky per. 10, 103009 Moscow, Russia. *Telephone:* (095) 229-35-15 (Office).

MIKHAILOV, Viktor Nikitovich, DTech SC.; Russian physicist and politician; b. 12 Feb. 1934, Sopronovo, Moscow Region; m.; two c.; ed Moscow Inst. of Physics and Eng; on staff All-Union Research Inst., Arsamas; worked with group of nuclear bomb constructors; f. Scientific School of Explosive Nuclear Fission; Prof., Deputy, First Deputy Minister of Machine Construction of USSR (later USSR Ministry of Atomic Energy) 1988–1992; Minister of Atomic Energy Russian Fed. 1992–98; Chair. Scientific Council 1998–; fmr mem. Security Council of Russia; mem. Russian Acad. of Sciences 1997–; Lenin Prize, USSR State Prize. *Publication:* over 200 works on nuclear energy problems. *Address:* Ministry of Atomic Energy, B. Ordynka str. 24/26, 101000 Moscow, Russia (Office). *Telephone:* (095) 233-49-08, 233-37-51 (Office).

MIKHAILOV, Vyacheslav Aleksandrovich, DR. HIST.; Russian politician; b. 13 April. 1938, Dubovka, Volgograd Region; m.; two d.; ed Lvov State Univ.; teacher, secondary school, lecturer, Lvov State Univ.; Head of Sector, Inst. of Marxism–Leninism at CPSU Cen. Cttee 1987–90; Head, Div. of Nat. Policy, CPSU Cen. Cttee 1990–91; scientific consultant, I and World (magazine), Head, Centre on Int. Problems and Protection of Human Rights 1991–93; Prof. Moscow Inst. of Int. Relations (MGIMO) 1992–93, 1999–; Deputy Chair. State Cttee on Problems of Fed. and Nationality 1993–95; First Deputy Minister on Problems of Nationality and Regional Policy Jan.–July 1995, Minister 1995–98, 1999–2000; First Deputy Sec. Security Council 1998–99. *Publications:* 3 monographs on nat. problems, numerous articles. *Address:* MGIMO, Vernadskogo Prosp. 76, 117454 Moscow, Russia. *Telephone:* (095) 206-43-26 (Office).

MIKHALCHENKO, Alla Anatolyevna, MA; Russian ballerina; b. 3 July 1957, Moscow; d. of Anatoly Alexandrovich Dmitryev and Irina Antonovna Mikhalchenko; ed Moscow Choreographic School, Russian Acad. of Theatrical Arts; dancer with Bolshoi 1976–99; lecturer Russian Acad. of Theatrical Arts 1999–; Co-ordinator Bolshoi Ballet School in Brazil 1999–2001; Chief Choreographic Chair Moscow State Inst. of Culture and Arts; First Prize, All-Soviet Competition 1976, First Prize and Distinction, Varna Ballet Competition 1976; First Prize, Moscow Int. Ballet Competition 1977; People's Artist of Russia, State Prize of Uzbekistan, Prize of Lenin's Komsomol. *Roles include:* Odette-Odile (Swan Lake), Kitri (Don Quixote), Nina (The Seagull), Giselle, Anastasia (Ivan the Terrible), Rita (Golden Age), Shirin (Legend of Love), Serene (Prodigal Son), Aegina (Spartacus), Leda (Zeus), Raymonda, Roxanne (Cyrano de Bergerac), Nikia, Gamzaty (La Bayadère), Sylphida (Les Sylphides), Dying Swan (Le Spectre de la Rose). *Films:* Spartacus, Legend of Love, Swan Lake, An Evening with the Bolshoi, I Want to Dance, Fragments of One's Biography. *Leisure interests:* learning yoga and Eastern philosophy. *Address:* Malaya Gruzinskaya Street, 12/18, 123242 Moscow, Russia. *Telephone:* 252-26-09 (Home).

MIKHALKOV, Nikita Sergeyevich; Russian film director; b. 21 Oct. 1945, Moscow; s. of Mikhalkov Sergey Vladimirovich and Konchalovskaya Natalia Petrovna; m. 1st Anastasya Vertinskaya 1966; m. 2nd Tatyana Mikhalkova 1973; two s. two d.; ed Shchukin Theatre School, State Film Inst. under Mikhail Romm; mem. State Duma 1995 (resgnd); First Sec. Russian Union of Cinematographers 1997–98, Chair. 1998–; first worked as actor in films: Strolling Around Moscow, A Nest of Gentlefolk, The Red Tent; RSFSR People's Artist 1984; Felix Prize for Best European Film

1993, State Prize of Russian Fed., Honoured Artist of Russia, Chevalier, Légion d'honneur and several other awards. *Films directed:* A Quiet Day at the End of the War, At Home Among Strangers, A Stranger at Home 1975, The Slave of Love 1976, An Unfinished Piece for Mechanical Piano 1977, Five Evenings 1978, Several Days in the Life of I. I. Oblomov 1979, Kinsfolk 1982, Without Witnesses 1983, Dark Eyes 1987, Urga 1990 (Prize at Venice Biennale 1991), Anna from 6 to 18 1994, Burned by the Sun (Acad. Award for Best Foreign Film) 1994. *Play:* An Unfinished Piece for Mechanical Piano, Rome 1987. *Leisure interests:* sport, hunting. *Address:* Maly Kozikhinsky per. 4, Apt. 16–17, 103001 Moscow, Russia.

MIKHALKOV, Sergey Vladimirovich; Russian playwright, poet and children's writer; b. 12 March 1913, Moscow; m. 1st Natalia Konchalovskaya (deceased); two s.; m. 2nd; ed Literary Inst. Moscow; began writing 1928, verses for children 1935; Jt author (with El-Registan) Soviet Anthem 1943; mem. CPSU 1950–91; Chief Ed. Fitil 1962–; First Sec. Moscow Br., RSFSR Union of Writers 1965–70, Chair. of Union 1970–91; Deputy to Supreme Soviet of RSFSR 1967–70, to USSR Supreme Soviet 1970–89; author Anthem of Russian Fed. (new version) 2000; mem. Comm. for Youth Affairs, Soviet of Nationalities; fmr Corresp. mem. Acad. of Pedagogical Sciences 1970; numerous awards. *Film script:* Frontovye podrugi (Frontline Friends) 1941. *Plays:* Tom Kenti (after Mark Twain) 1938, Krasnyi galstuk (Red Neckerchief), Selected Works 1947, Ilya Golovin, Ya khochu domoi (I Want to Go Home) 1949, Raki (Lobsters) 1952, Zaika-Zaznaika 1955, Sombrero 1958, Pamyatnik Sebe (A Monument to Oneself) 1958, Dikari (Campers) 1959, Collected Works (4 Vols) 1964, Green Grasshopper 1964, We Are Together, My Friend and I 1967, In the Museum of Lenin 1968, Fables 1970, Disobedience Day 1971, The Funny Bone (articles) 1971, Collected Works (3 Vols) 1970–71, Selected Works 1973, Slap in the Face 1974, Bibliographical Index 1975, The Scum 1975, The Lodger 1977, Echo 1980, Almighty Kings 1983, Fables 1987, A Choice for Children (English trans.) 1988. *Publications:* Dyadya Styopa (Uncle Steve) 1936 and Collected Works (poems, stories, plays) in two Vols. *Address:* Tchaikovskogo str. 28/35, Apt. 67, 121069 Moscow, Russia. *Telephone:* 291-78-15.

MIKHALKOV-KONCHALOVSKY, Andrey Sergeyevich; Russian film director and script-writer; b. 20 Aug. 1937, Moscow; s. of Sergey Mikhalkov and Natalia Konchalovskaya; m. 1st Natalia Arinbasarova 1946; m. 2nd Irina Ivanova 1960; one s. two d.; ed USSR State Inst. of Cinema, Moscow 1961–65; worked in Hollywood 1979–93; RSFSR People's Artist 1980. *Films include:* Roller and Violin (with A. Tarkovsky) 1959, The First Teacher 1965, The Story of Asya Klyachina, Who Loved but Did Not Marry 1966, A Nest of Gentlefolk 1969, Uncle Vanya 1971, Romance of Lovers 1974, Siberiada 1979, Maria's Lovers 1984, Runaway Train 1985, Duet for One 1986, Shy People 1987, Homer and Eddie 1988, Tango and Cash 1989, The Inner Circle 1991, Ryaba—My Chicken 1994, Odissea 1997, House of Fools 2002; scriptwriter (with Tarkovsky) Andrei Rublev 1969; also opera dir and theatre dir (productions at La Scala, Bastille, Mariinski Theatre). *Address:* Mosfilmovskaya str. 1, Russkaya Ruletka, 119858 Moscow (Studio); Malaya Gruzinskaya 28, Apt. 130, 123557 Moscow, Russia (Home). *Telephone:* (095) 143-93-09 (Studio); 253-50-21 (Home). *Fax:* (095) 143-91-89.

MIKHEEV, Vladimir Andreyevich, DR.PHYS.SC.; Ukrainian physicist; b. 5 Aug. 1942; m. Tatiana Mikheeva 1969; one s. one d.; ed Kharkov Polytechnic; researcher 1964–86; discovery of quantum diffusion 1972–77; Head. of Lab. of Ultralow Temperatures, Inst. for Low Temperature Physics and Eng, Ukrainian Acad. of Science 1986–; Visiting Prof. Royal Holloway and Bedford New Coll. 1992; Lenin Prize for Science and Tech. *Address:* 88 Barrington Close, Witney, Oxon., OX8 5FL, England.

MIKKELSEN, Richard, MSc(ECON.); Danish central banker (retd); b. 27 April 1920, Copenhagen; m. Ester Overgaard 1944 (died 1993); at Banken for Slagelse og Omegn 1937–45; apptd. Asst Danmarks Nationalbank 1945, Head of Section 1954, Asst Head Dept 1961, Head Dept 1961, Dir 1966, Asst Gov. 1971, Gov. 1982–90; Attaché, Danish-OEEC Del., Paris 1955–57; mem. Bd European Monetary Agreement 1970–72; Industrial Mortgage Fund 1971–81; mem. Bd Mortgage Credit Council, Supervisor 1972–81; mem. Bd Export Finance Corpn 1975–90; mem. Steering Cttee and Bd Employees Capital Pension Fund 1980–91, Industrial Mortgage Credit Fund 1981–91, Monetary Cttee of EEC 1982–90; Nordic Financial Cttee 1982–90, Econ. Policy Cttee of OECD 1982–90; Chair. Financing Fund of 1992 1992–96; Commdr. Order of Dannebrog. *Publication:* Monetary History of Denmark, 1960–90. *Address:* c/o Danmarks Nationalbank, Havnegade 5, 1093 Copenhagen K, Denmark. *Telephone:* 33-63-63-63.

MIKLOŠ, Ivan, Dip.Eng.Econ.; Slovak politician and economist; b. 2 June 1960, Svídník; m.; two c.; ed Univ. of Econs, Bratislava, LSE, UK; Asst, Univ. of Econs, Bratislava 1983–87, Chief Asst 1987–90; Adviser to Deputy Prime Minister responsible for Econ. Reform 1990; Dir Govt Dept of Econ. and Social Policy 1990–91; Minister of Privatization 1991–92; Exec. Dir and Pres. MESA 10 Org. 1992–98; Deputy Prime Minister 1998–; Minister of Finance 2002–; First Deputy Chair. Civil Democratic Union 1992–93; Chair.Democratic Party 1993–2000; First Vice-Pres. East-West Inst., New York 1998. *Publications include:* numerous articles in specialized and popular press. *Leisure interests:* tennis, windsurfing, skiing. *Address:* Ministry of Finance, Štefanovicova 5, 817 82 Bratislava, Slovakia (Office). *Telephone:* (2) 59581111 (Office). *Fax:* (2) 52498042 (Office). *E-mail:* miklos@vlada.gov.sk (Office). *Website:* www.finance.gov.sk (Office).

MIKLOŠKO, Jozef, DrSc, DR.RER.NAT.; Slovak politician, mathematician and educationist; b. 31 March 1939, Nitra; s. of Ondrej Mikloško and Marta (née Kutliková) Mikloško; m. Mária Bitterová 1964; two s. two d.; ed Pedagogical Univ., Bratislava, Komenský Univ., Bratislava; teacher, Nové Zámky 1961–62; scientific worker, Inst. of Tech. Cybernetics, Slovak Acad. of Sciences, Bratislava 1963–90; Lecturer, Faculty of Mathematics and Physics, Komenský Univ., Bratislava 1969–89; Head. Int. Base Lab. for Artificial Intelligence 1985–90; Vice-Chair. Christian-Democratic Movt 1990; Deputy to Slovak Nat. Council 1990–91; Fed. Deputy Premier for Human Rights in Czechoslovak Fed. Repub. 1990–92; Deputy to House of the People, Fed. Ass. June–Dec. 1992; Adviser to Pres. of Slovakia 1993–95; Head DACO publishing house 1995–; Sec. Justice and Peace Comm. 1995–; Lecturer and Vice-Rector Trnava Univ. 1996–; Chair. Solidarity Foundation 1993–97, Schiller Foundation for Protection of Life and Human Rights 1995–; mem. World Ecological Acad., Moscow 1994–, Int. Informatization Acad., Moscow 1995–, Slovak Asscn of Writers 1995–, Slovak Asscn of Journalists 1997–; Deputy to Town Council, Bratislava V 1994–. *Publications:* 7 books including Strong Secret 1995 and Farewell 1996; 100 scientific articles. *Leisure interests:* literature, music, sport. *Address:* Žabotova 2, 81104 Bratislava (Office); Trnava University, Hornopotočná 23, 91843 Trnava, Slovakia (Home); Romanova 22, 85102 Bratislava, Slovakia (Home). *Telephone:* (7) 496-308 (Office); (7) 6382-7763 (Home). *Fax:* (7) 496-313 (Office); 5249-7995 (Home). *E-mail:* jmiklosk@truni .sk (Office); solidari@internet.sk (Home).

MIKULSKI, Barbara Ann, BA; American politician; b. 20 July 1936, Baltimore; d. of William Mikulski and Christina Eleanor Kutz; ed Mount St Agnes Coll. and Maryland Univ.; Baltimore Dept Social Services 1961–63, 1966–70; York Family Agency 1964; VISTA Teaching Center 1965–70; Teacher, Mount St Agnes Coll. 1969; Teacher, Community Coll., Baltimore 1970–71; Democratic Nominee to U.S. Senate 1974, to House of Reps. 1976; mem. 96th–99th Congresses from 3rd Md Dist; Senator from Maryland 1987–, first woman Democrat elected to U.S. Senate in her own right; mem. Democratic Nat. Strategy Council; mem. Nat. Bd of Dirs. Urban Coalition; mem. Nat. Asscn of Social Workers; Democrat; Hon. LLD (Goucher Coll.) 1973, (Hood Coll.) 1978. *Address:* U.S. Senate, 709 Hart Office Building, Washington, DC 20510, USA.

MÍL, Jaroslav; Czech business executive; b. 10 Aug. 1958, Prague; ed Electrotech. Faculty, Czech Tech. Univ., Sheffield Business School, UK; various tech. positions, then Dir responsible for Procurement and Fuel Cycles, Czech Power Co. (ČEZ) 1985–2000, Chair. Bd and CEO 2000–, Chair. Bd and CEO Elektrárny Opatovice (EOP) 2000; mem. Bd of Govs. World Nuclear Fuel Market, Atlanta, USA 1993–99, Bd of Dirs. Škoda-ÚJP Praha 1994–2000, Supervisory Bd Severočeské doly 1998–99, Bd Czech Asscn of Employers in Energy Sector 2000–; Chair. Bd Radioactive Waste Repository Authority 1997–2000; fmr mem. ICC, Bd of Dirs. EURELECTRIC, European Nuclear Council, Int. Advisory Cttee of Soc. for Strategic Man. *Leisure interests:* family, skiing, golf, squash, cycling, hiking. *Address:* ČEZ a.s., Duhová, 14000 Prague 4, Czech Republic (Office). *Telephone:* (2) 24082201 (Office). *Fax:* (2) 24083028 (Office). *E-mail:* miljar.hsp@mail.cez.cz (Office). *Website:* www.cez .cz (Office).

MILAKNIS, Valentinas Pranas; Lithuanian politician; b. 4 Oct. 1947, Rokiskis; m. Sofija Milakniene; one s. one d.; ed Kaunas Polytech. Inst.; fmr engineer, then Head of Group, Head of Sector, Deputy Chief Engineer Control System Planning and Design Construction Bureau, Mun. Econ. Planning Inst. 1970–89; Man. Dir, then Dir.-Gen. Alna AB Co. 1989–; Minister of Nat. Economy 1999–2000. *Leisure interest:* shooting. *Address:* Alna AB, A. Domaševicius 9,Vilnius 2001, Lithuania (Office). *Telephone:* (2) 31-22-44.

MILANI, Cesare (Chez), BA, LLB; South African trade union official and lawyer; b. 27 Nov. 1966, Cape Town; m.; one d.; ed Stellenbosch Univ., Univ. of South Africa School of Business Leadership; Nat. Legal Adviser (HOS PERSA) 1994–97; Gen. Sec. Fed. of Unions of SA (FEDUSA) 1997–; mem. Pres. Mbeki's Working Group, NEDLAC Exec. Cttee and Man. Cttee, CCMA Governing Body. *Leisure interests:* antiques, sailing. *Address:* FEDUSA, PO Box 2096, Northcliff 2115, Pretoria (Office); PO Box 412, Featherbrook Estate, 1746, South Africa (Office). *Telephone:* (11) 4765188 (Office); (11) 4765189 (Office). *Fax:* (11) 4765131 (Office). *E-mail:* chez@fedusa.org.za (Office). *Website:* www.fedusa.org.za (Office).

MILBERG, Joachim, DR.-ING.; German business executive and engineer; b. 10 April 1943, Westphalia; ed Technische Univ. Berlin; Scientific Asst, Inst. of Machine Tools and Production Tech., Technische Univ., Berlin 1970–72; Exec. Man. Werkzeugmaschinenfabrik Gildemeister AG (machine tools factory) 1972, Head of Automatic Lathe Division 1978; Prof. in Ordinary, Technische Univ., Munich 1981; joined BMW AG as mem. of Bd of Man. Production 1993, mem. Bd of Man. Eng and Production 1998, Chair. Bd of Man. BMW AG 1999–2002. *Address:* c/o BMW AG, 80788, Munich, Germany (Office).

MILBRADT, Georg, Dr rer pol; German politician and academic; b. 23 Feb. 1945, Eslohe, Sauerland; m. Angelika Meeth; two s.; ed Univ. of Münster; Asst, Inst. of Finance, Univ. of Münster 1970–80, Guest Prof. 1985–; Deputy Prof. of Finance and Econs, Univ. of Mainz 1980–83; Head Dept of Finance, Münster 1983–90, later responsible for econ. devt and property man.; mem. CDU 1973–, Fed. Admin 2000–; Minister of Finance, Saxony State 1990–2001; mem. Upper House of Parl. (Bundesrates), Cttee on Mediation; mem. Saxony State Parl. 1994–; Minister-Pres. of Saxony April 2002–;

Regional Deputy Chair. Sächsischen Union 1999; Chair. Bd Sächsischen Aufbaubank, Dresden Airport, Sächsischen Landesbank; Deputy Chair. Bd Leipzig-Halle Airport; Chair. Tariff Community of German Länder (TdL). *Leisure interests:* literature, computers. *Address:* Sächsische Staatskanzlei, Archivstr. 1, 01097 Dresden, Germany (Office). *Telephone:* (351) 564-0 (Office). *Fax:* (351) 564-1199 (Office). *E-mail:* ministerpraesident:dd.sk .sachsen.de (Office). *Website:* www.sachsen.de (Office).

MILBURN, Rt. Hon. Alan, PC, BA; British politician; b. 27 Jan. 1958; m. Mo O'Tooze 1982; partner Ruth Briel; one s.; ed Stokesley Comprehensive School, Lancaster Univ.; co-ordinator Trade Union Studies Information Unit, Newcastle 1984–90; Sr Business Devt Officer N Tyneside Municipal Borough Council 1990–92; MP for Darlington 1992–; Opposition Front Bench Spokesman on Health 1995–96, on Treasury and Econ. Affairs 1996–97; Minister of State, Dept of Health 1997–98; Chief Sec. to Treasury 1998–99, Sec. of State for Health 1999–; Chair. Parl. Labour Party Treasury Cttee 1992–95; mem. Public Accounts Cttee 1994–95. *Address:* House of Commons, London, SW1A 0AA, England.

MILCHAN, Arnon; American film producer; b. 6 Dec. 1944; has worked in TV and theatre as well as film. *Plays produced:* Tomb, It's So Nice To Be Civilized, Amadeus (Paris production). *Television:* Masada 1981, The Client 1995. *Films:* The Medusa Touch 1978, The King of Comedy 1983, Once Upon a Time in America 1984, Brazil 1985, Stripper 1986, Legend 1986, Man on Fire 1987, The Adventures of Baron Munchausen 1989, Who's Harry Crumb 1989, The War of the Roses 1989, Big Man on Campus 1990, Pretty Woman 1990, Q&A 1990, Guilty by Suspicion 1991, JFK 1991, The Mambo Kings 1992, Memoirs of an Invisible Man 1992, The Power of One 1992, Under Siege 1992, Sommersby 1993, Falling Down 1993, Made in America 1993, Free Willy 1993, The Nutcracker 1993, That Night 1993, Heaven and Earth 1993, The New Age 1993, Striking Distance 1993, Six Degrees of Separation 1993, Second Best 1994, Boys on the Side 1994, The Client 1994, Bogus 1995, A Time to Kill 1996, The Mirror Has Two Faces 1996, Tin Cup 1996, L.A. Confidential 1997, The Devil's Advocate 1997, City of Angels 1998, The Negotiator 1998, A Midsummer Night's Dream 1999, Entrapment 1999, The Hunt for the Unicorn Killer 1999; Exec. Producer: Squash 2000, Noriega: God's Favorite 2000, Up at the Villa 2000, Big Momma's House 2000. *Address:* New Regency Enterprises, 10201 West Pico Boulevard, Building 12, Los Angeles, CA 90035, USA.

MILEDI, Ricardo, MD, FRS, FAAS, MRI; Mexican/American professor of neurobiology; b. 15 Sept. 1927, Mexico DF; m. Ana Mela Garces 1955; one s.; ed Universidad Nacional Autónoma de Mexico; Research Fellow, Instituto Nacional de Cardiología, Mexico 1954–56; Visiting Fellow, John Curtin School of Medical Research, Canberra, Australia 1956–58; Hon. Research Assoc., Dept of Biophysics, Univ. Coll. London 1958–59, Lecturer 1959–62, Reader 1962–65, Prof. of Biophysics 1965–75, Foulerton Research Prof. of the Royal Soc. 1975–85, Foulerton Research Prof. and Head of Dept of Biophysics 1978–85; Distinguished Prof., Dept of Psychobiology, School of Biological Sciences, Univ. of Calif., Irvine 1984–; Fellow, Third World Acad. of Sciences, American Acad. of Arts and Sciences; Hon. mem. Hungarian Acad. of Sciences; mem. NAS 1989, European Acad. of Arts, Sciences and Humanities 1995, Mexican Acad. of Medicine 1995, Mexican Acad. of Sciences 1995; Dr. hc (Univ. del País Vasco, Leioa, Spain) 1992, (Trieste Univ., Italy) 2000, (Univ. of Chihuahua, Mexico) 2000; King Faisal Foundation Int. Prize for Science, Principe de Asturias Prize (Spain) 1999, Royal Medal, Royal Soc. 1999. *Publications:* over 500 published papers. *Leisure interest:* hiking. *Address:* Department of Neurobiology and Behavior, University of California, 2205 Bio Sci II, Irvine, CA 92697-4550; 9 Gibbs Court, Irvine, CA 92616, USA (Home). *Telephone:* (949) 824-4721 (Office); (949) 856-2677 (Home). *Fax:* (949) 824-6090. *E-mail:* rmiledi@uci.edu (Office).

MILES, (Henry) Michael (Pearson), OBE; British business executive; b. 19 April 1936; s. of the late Brig. H. G. P. Miles and Margaret Miles; m. Carol Jane Berg 1967; two s. one d.; ed Wellington Coll., Nat. Service, Duke of Wellington's Regt; joined John Swire & Sons 1958, Dir John Swire & Sons (HK) Ltd 1970–99, Chair. 1984–88; Man. Dir John Swire & Sons (Japan) Ltd 1973–76; Man. Dir Cathay Pacific Airways Ltd 1978–84, Chair. 1984–88; Chair. Swire Pacific 1984–88; Exec. Dir John Swire & Sons Ltd 1988–99, Adviser to Bd 1999–; Dir Johnson Matthey PLC 1990–2003, Chair. 1998–2002; Chair. Schroders Jan. 2003–; Dir Baring PLC 1989–95 (Jt Deputy Chair. 1994–95), Portals Holdings 1990–95, BICC 1996–2002; Dir (non-exec.) HSBC Holdings 1984–88, ING Baring Holdings Ltd 1989–2002, BP PLC 1994–, Pacific Assets Trust PLC; Chair. Hong Kong Tourist Asscn 1984–88, Korea-Europe Fund Ltd; Vice-Pres. China Britain Business Group 1995–2000; Gov. Wellington Coll. 1988–. *Leisure interests:* golf, tennis. *Address:* Schroders, 31 Gresham Street, London, EC2V 7QA (Office); Shalbourne House, Shalbourne, nr. Marlborough, Wilts, SN8 3QH, England (Home). *Telephone:* (20) 7658-6000 (Office). *Website:* www.schroders.com (Office).

MILES, John Arthur Reginald, CBE, MA, MD, FRACP, FRSNZ; New Zealand microbiologist and epidemiologist; b. 13 May 1913, Sidcup, Kent, England; s. of Albert E. Miles and Mary Watson; m. 1st Ruth H. French 1951 (died 1980); m. 2nd Violet C. Miller 1985; two d.; ed Monkton Combe School, Bath, Gonville & Caius Coll. Cambridge and St Thomas's Hosp., London; Capt. Royal Army Medical Corps 1942–46; Huddersfield Lecturer in Special Pathology, Cambridge 1946–50; Medical Research Fellow, Inst. of Medical and Veterinary

Science, Adelaide 1951–55; Prof. of Microbiology Univ. of Otago 1955–79, Prof. Emer. 1979–; Pres. Royal Soc. of NZ 1966–70; Hon. Dir NZ MRC Virus Research Unit 1960–79; mem. M.R.C. of NZ 1966–72; mem. NZ Health Dept Epidemiology Advisory Cttee 1961–79; mem. NZ Nat. Comm. for UNESCO 1972–76; Pres. Pacific Science Asscn 1979–83; many other professional appts; Hon. Life Fellow, Pacific Science Asscn; NZ Asscn of Scientists Service to Science Award 1972, K. F. Meyer Award, American Soc. of Veterinary Epidemiologists 1983. *Publication:* Infectious Diseases Colonising the Pacific 1996. *Leisure interests:* ornithology, fishing, gardening. *Address:* P.O. Box 17, 132 Capell Avenue, Lake Hawea, Otago 9192, New Zealand. *Telephone:* (3) 443-1695.

MILES, Roy Edward; British art dealer; b. 9 Feb. 1935, Liverpool; s. of Edward Marsh and Elsa McKinley; m. Christine Rhodes 1970 (died 1997); ed Sorbonne, Paris; Dir and sole owner, Roy Miles Gallery (largest pvt. gallery in London) 1975–89; dealer in British art and fine paintings; organizer of major exhbns of Victorian and Russian art. *Television:* contributions to numerous art programmes. *Publications:* The Conceit of That Plum: Priceless: Memoirs and Mysteries of Britain's No. 1 Art Dealer (autobiog.) 2003; articles in magazines, newspapers and journals. *Leisure interests:* classical music, history. *Address:* 10 Ennismore Gardens, London, SW7 1NP, England. *Telephone:* (20) 7581-7969.

MILES, Sarah; British actress; b. 31 Dec. 1941; m. Robert Bolt 1967 (divorced 1976), remarried 1988 (died 1995); ed Royal Acad. of Dramatic Art, London; first film appearance in Term of Trial 1962; with Nat. Theatre Co. 1964–65; Shakespeare stage season 1982–83. *Films include:* Those Magnificent Men in Their Flying Machines 1964, I Was Happy Here 1966, The Blow-Up 1966, Ryan's Daughter 1970, Lady Caroline Lamb 1972, The Hireling 1973, The Man Who Loved Cat Dancing 1973, Great Expectations 1975, Pepita Jiminez 1975, The Sailor Who Fell From Grace With the Sea 1976, The Big Sleep 1978, Venom 1981, Hope and Glory 1987, White Mischief 1988, The Silent Touch 1993. *Theatre appearances include:* Vivat! Vivat Regina!, Asylum 1988. *Television appearances:* James Michener's Dynasty, Great Expectations, Harem, Queenie, A Ghost in Monte Carlo, Dandelion Dead, Ring Around the Moon, The Rehearsal. *Publications:* Charlemagne (play) 1992, A Right Royal Bastard (memoirs) 1993, Serves Me Right (memoirs) 1994, Bolt from the Blue (memoirs) 1996.

MILIBAND, David Wright, BA, MSc; British politician; b. 15 July 1965; s. of the late Ralph Miliband and Marion Miliband (née Kozak); m. Louise Shackelton 1998; ed Corpus Christi Coll., Oxford, Massachusetts Inst. of Tech., USA; Research Fellow Inst. of Public Policy Research 1989–94; Sec. Comm. on Social Justice 1992–94; Head of Policy, Office of Leader of Opposition 1994–97; Head, Prime Minister's Policy Unit 1997–2001; MP (South Shields) 2001–, Labour Party. *Publications:* Reinventing the Left (Ed.) 1994, Paying for Inequality: The Economic Cost of Social Injustice (jt ed.) 1994. *Leisure interests:* supporting Arsenal Football Club, Hoping for South Shields Football Club. *Address:* House of Commons, Westminster London, SW1A 0AA, England (Office).

MILINGO, Most Rev. Archbishop Emmanuel, DipEd; Zambian ecclesiastic; b. 13 June 1930; s. of Yakobe Milingo and Tomaida Lumbiwe; m. Maria Sung 2001 (divorced); ed St Mary's Presbyteral School, Fort Jameson and Kasina Junior Seminary and Kachebere Major Seminary, Nyasaland (now Malawi); Curate, Minga Mission 1958–61; studied Pastoral Sociology (Diploma), Rome 1961–62; Univ. Coll. Dublin, Ireland (Dip. Ed.) 1962–63; Parish Priest, St Ann's Mission, Chipata 1963–66; Sec. for Mass Media, Zambia Episcopal Conf. 1966–69; Archbishop of Lusaka 1969–83, Archbishop Emer. 1983–; Special Del. to Pontifical Comm. for Pastoral Care of Migrants, Refugees and Pilgrims 1983–. *Publications:* Amake Joni, Demarcations, The World in Between, The Flower Garden of Jesus the Redeemer, My Prayers are Not Heard, Precautions in the Ministry of Deliverance, Against Satan. *Leisure interests:* writing and preaching to make Jesus Christ known and loved. *Address:* Pontificio Consiglio della Pastorale per i Migranti e gli Itineranti, Piazza S. Calisto 16, 00153 Rome, Italy.

MILIUS, John Frederick; American film writer and director; b. 11 April 1944, St Louis; s. of William Styx Milius and Elizabeth (née Roe) Milius; m. 1st Renée Fabri 1967; two s.; m. 2nd Celia K. Burkholder 1978; ed Univ. of Southern Calif.; wrote screenplays: The Devil's 8 1969, Evel Knievel 1971, Jeremiah Johnson 1972, The Life and Times of Judge Roy Bean 1973, Magnum Force 1973, Purvis FBI (for TV) 1974, Apocalypse Now 1979 (Acad. Award for Best Screenplay 1980), 1941 (with Francis Ford Coppola) 1979, Geronimo: An American Legend (co-writer), Clear and Present Danger (co-writer); wrote and directed: Dillinger 1973, The Wind and the Lion 1975, Big Wednesday 1978, Conan the Barbarian 1981, Red Dawn 1984, Farewell to the King 1989, Navy Seals 1990, Flight of the Intruder 1991, The Texas Rangers 1994, The Northmen 1999. *Address:* c/o Jeff Berg International Creative Management, 8942 Wilshire Boulevard, Beverly Hills, CA 90211, USA (Office).

MILLAN, Rt Hon Bruce, PC, CA; British politician (retd); b. 5 Oct. 1927, Dundee, Scotland; s. of David Millan; m. Gwendoline Fairey 1953; one s. one d.; ed Harris Acad., Dundee; worked as Chartered Accountant (Inst. of Chartered Accountants of Scotland) 1950–59; MP for Craigton Div. of Glasgow 1959–83, for Govan Div. of Glasgow 1983–88; EEC (now EU) Commr for Regional Policy 1989–95; Parl. Under-Sec. of State for Defence (RAF) 1964–66, for Scotland 1966–70; Minister of State, Scottish Office 1974–76,

Sec. of State for Scotland 1976–79; Opposition Spokesman for Scotland 1979–83; Labour; Hon. FRSE 1995; Hon. Fellow (Paisley) 1991; Hon. LLD (Dundee) 1989, (Abertay Dundee) 1994, (Glasgow) 1995; Hon. DLitt (Heriot-Watt) 1991; Dr. hc (Panteios, Athens) 1995, (Sheffield Hallam) 1996. *Address:* 1 Torridon Avenue, Glasgow, G41 5LA, Scotland (Home). *Telephone:* (141) 427-6483 (Home).

MILLAR, Fergus Graham Burtholme, MA, DPhil, DLitt, FBA, FSA; British academic; b. 5 July 1935, Edinburgh; s. of J. S. L. Millar and J. B. Taylor; m. Susanna Friedmann 1959; two s. one d.; ed Edinburgh Acad., Loretto School, Trinity Coll., Oxford; Fellow, All Souls Coll., Oxford 1958–64; Fellow and Tutor in Ancient History, The Queen's Coll., Oxford 1964–76; Prof. of Ancient History, Univ. Coll., London 1976–84; Camden Prof. of Ancient History, Univ. of Oxford 1984–2002; Fellow, Brasenose Coll., Oxford 1984–2002; Pres. Soc. for the Promotion of Roman Studies 1989–92 (Vice-Pres. 1977–89, 1992–2001, Hon. Vice-Pres. 2001–); Pres. Classical Asscn 1992–93; Publications Sec. British Acad. 1997–2002; Corresp. mem. German Archaeological Inst. 1977, Bavarian Acad. 1987, Finnish Acad. 1989, Russian Acad. 1999; Hon. DPhil (Helsinki) 1994. *Publications:* several historical studies, The Roman Near East 1993, The Crowd in Rome in the Late Republic 1998, The Roman Republic in Political Dispute 2002. *Address:* Oriental Institute, Pusey Lane, Oxford, OX1 2LE (Office); 80 Harpes Road, Oxford, OX2 7QL, England (Home). *Telephone:* (1865) 288093 (Office); (1865) 515782 (Home). *Fax:* (1865) 278190 (Office). *E-mail:* fergus.millar@brasenose.oxford.ac.uk (Office).

MILLAR, Sir Oliver Nicholas, GCVO, FBA; British art historian and administrator; b. 26 April 1923, Standon, Herts.; s. of Gerald Millar and Ruth Millar; m. Delia Mary Dawnay, CVO 1954; one s. three d.; ed Rugby School and Courtauld Inst. of Art, Univ. of London; Asst Surveyor of the King's Pictures 1947–49, Deputy Surveyor of the King's (Queen's from 1952) Pictures 1949–72, Surveyor 1972–88, Surveyor Emer. 1988–; Dir of the Royal Collection 1987–88; Trustee Nat. Portrait Gallery 1972–95; mem. Reviewing Cttee on Export of Works of Art 1975–87, Exec. Cttee Nat. Art Collections Fund 1986–98; Trustee Nat. Heritage Memorial Fund 1988–92. *Publications:* English Art 1625–1714 (with M. D. Whinney) 1957, Abraham van der Doort's Catalogue 1960, Tudor, Stuart and Georgian Pictures in the Collection of HM The Queen 1963, 1969, Inventories and Valuations of The King's Goods 1972, The Queen's Pictures 1977, Victorian Pictures in the Collection of HM The Queen 1992; numerous catalogues including William Dobson 1951, Age of Charles I 1972, Sir Peter Lely 1976, Van Dyck in England 1982 and for The Queen's Gallery 1992. *Leisure interests:* grandchildren, drawing, gardening, cricket, listening to music, reading. *Address:* The Cottage, Rays Lane, Penn, Bucks., England. *Telephone:* (1494) 812124.

MILLER, Aleksei Borisovich, CAND.ECONS; Russian business executive; b. 1962, Leningrad; m.; one s.; ed Leningrad Inst. of Finance and Econs; mem. Cttee on Foreign Econ. Relations, Office of the Mayor of St Petersburg 1991–96; Dir Sea Port, St Petersburg 1996–99; Dir-Gen. Baltic Pipeline Systems 1999–2000; Deputy Minister of Energy 2000–01; Chair. Bd Dirs. GAZPROM May 2001–. *Address:* GAZPROM, Nametkina str. 18, 117420 Moscow, Russia (Office). *Telephone:* (095) 719-21-09 (Office). *Fax:* (095) 719-47-86 (Office).

MILLER, Andrew, CBE, MA, PhD, FRSE; British academic; b. 15 Feb. 1936, Kelty, Fife; s. of William Hamilton Miller and Susan Anderson (née Auld) Miller; m. Rosemary Singleton Hannah Fyvie 1962; one s. one d.; ed Beath High School, Univ. of Edinburgh; Asst Lecturer in Chem., Univ. of Edin. 1960–62; Post-Doctoral Fellow, CSIRO Div. of Protein Chem., Melbourne 1962–65; Staff Scientist MRC Lab. of Molecular Biology, Cambridge 1965–66; Lecturer in Molecular Biophysics, Oxford Univ. 1966–83; First Head European Molecular Biology Lab., Grenoble Antenne, France 1975–80; Prof. of Biochem., Edinburgh Univ. 1984–94, Vice-Dean of Medicine 1991–93, Vice-Provost, Medicine and Veterinary Medicine 1992–93, Vice-Prin. 1993–94; Prin. and Vice-Chancellor, Univ. of Stirling 1994–2001, Prof. Emer. 2001–; Interim Chief Exec. Cancer Research, UK 2001–; mem. Science and Eng Research Council Biological Sciences Cttee 1982–85; Council mem., Inst. Laue-Langevin, France 1981–85; mem. Univ. Grants Cttee Biological Sciences Cttee 1985–88; Dir of Research, European Synchrotron Radiation Facility, Grenoble 1986–91; Fellow Wolfson Coll., Oxford 1967–83, Hon. Fellow 1995–; mem. Univ. Funding Council-Biological Science Advisory Panel, Medical Advisory Panel 1989; mem. Council, Grenoble Univ. 1990–91, Royal Soc. of Edin. 1986 (Gen. Sec. 2001–), Council Open Univ. 2001–; mem. Minister of Educ.'s Action Group on Standards in Scottish Schools 1997–99 Scottish Exec. Science Strategy Group 1999–2000, UNESCO UK Science Cttee 2000–; Adviser to Wellcome Trust on UK-French Synchrotron 1999–2000; Chair. Int. Centre for Mathematical Sciences, Edin. 2001–; Visiting Prof. Univ. of Edin. 2001–; Leverhulme Emer. Prof. 2001–03; Hon. DUniv (Stirling) 2002. *Publications:* Minerals in Biology (co-ed.) 1984; 170 research papers. *Leisure interests:* reading, walking, music. *Address:* General Secretary's Office, Royal Society of Edinburgh, 22–26 George Street, Edinburgh, EH2 2PQ, Scotland (Office). *Telephone:* (131) 240-5000 (Office).

MILLER, Arthur, AB; American playwright; b. 17 Oct. 1915, New York; s. of Isidore Miller and Augusta (Barnett) Miller; m. 1st Mary Grace Slattery 1940 (divorced 1956); one s. one d.; m. 2nd Marilyn Monroe 1956 (divorced 1961); m. 3rd Ingeborg Morath 1962; one s. one d.; ed Univ. of Michigan; Prof. of Contemporary Theatre, Univ. of Oxford 1995–; Pres. Int. PEN Clubs Org. 1965–69; Fellow St Catherine's Coll., Oxford; Hon. DLitt (Univ. of E Anglia)

1984, (Oxford) 1995, (Harvard) 1997; received Hopwood Award for Playwriting, Univ. of Mich. 1936 and 1937, Theatre Guild Nat. Award 1938, New York Drama Critics Circle Award 1947 and 1949, Pulitzer Prize for Drama 1949, Antoinette Perry Award 1953, American Acad. of Arts and Letters Gold Medal for Drama 1959, Anglo-American Award 1966, Creative Arts Award, Brandeis Univ. 1970, Kennedy Center Award 1984, Nat. Medal of Arts 1993, Olivier Award 1995, Dorothy and Lilian Gish Prize 1999, Antoinette Perry Lifetime Achievement Award 1999, Prix Molière 1999, Praemium Imperiale Award, Japan Art Asscn 2001, Prince of Asturias Prize for Literature 2002, Jerusalem Prize, Israel 2003. *Publications:* The Man Who Had All the Luck 1943, Situation Normal 1944, Focus 1945, All My Sons 1947, Death of a Salesman 1949, The Crucible 1953, A View From The Bridge 1955, A Memory of Two Mondays 1955, Collected Plays 1958, The Misfits (screenplay) 1959, After the Fall 1964, Incident at Vichy 1964, I Don't Need You Any More (short stories) 1967, The Price (play) 1968, In Russia (with Inge Morath) 1969, The Creation of the World and Other Business (play) 1972, Up From Paradise 1974, Chinese Encounters 1979, The American Clock 1980, Playing for Time (play) 1981, Elegy for a Lady (play) 1983, Some Kind of Love Story (play) 1983, Salesman in Beijing (journal) 1984, Two Way Mirror 1985, Danger: Memory! (plays) 1986, The Archbishop's Ceiling 1986, Timebends: A Life (autobiog.) 1987, Everybody Wins (screenplay) 1989, The Ride Down Mt. Morgan 1990, The Last Yankee 1990 (play), Broken Glass (play) 1994, Homely Girl (novella—made into play Eden in which he made acting debut 2001) 1995, The Crucible (screenplay) 1995, Mr. Peters' Connections (play) 2000, Echoes Down the Corridor (essays) 2000. *Address:* c/o ICM, 40 W 57th Street, New York, NY 10019 (Office); Tophet Road, Roxbury, CT 06783, USA (Home).

MILLER, Billie A.; Barbadian politician and lawyer; b. 8 Jan. 1944; ed Queen's Coll., Barbados, King's Coll., Durham Univ., UK; Chair. NGO Planning Cttee for Int. Conf. on Population and Devt, Cairo, Egypt 1994, Exec. Cttee Commonwealth Parl. Asscn 1996–99, Caribbean Tourism Org. 1997–98, Asscn of Caribbean States Ministerial Council 2001–02, IDB's Advisory Council on Women in Devt; Pres. Int. Planned Parenthood Fed., Western Hemisphere Region 1991–97, African, Caribbean and Pacific States Council of Ministers 1998; currently Deputy Prime Minister and Minister of Foreign Affairs and Foreign Trade; Pres. Bd of Dirs. Inter-American Parl. Group on Population and Devt for Caribbean and Latin America; Vice-Chair. Commonwealth Ministerial Action Group; mem. Barbados Family Planning Asscn, Barbados Nat. Trust; Queen's Silver Jubilee Medal 1977, Barbados Centennial Award 2000, Grantley Adams Award, Barbados Labour Party 2001; Grand Officer, Nat. Order of Benin 2000, Nat. Order of Juan Mora Fernandez, Costa Rica 2001. *Publications:* numerous papers and articles on population and women's issues. *Leisure interests:* reading, interior design, Ikebana. *Address:* Ministry of Foreign Affairs and Foreign Trade, 1 Culloden Road, St Michael, Barbados (Office). *Telephone:* 429-7108 (Office). *Fax:* 429-6652 (Office). *E-mail:* barbados@foreign.gov.bb (Office). *Website:* www.foreign.barbadosgov.org (Office).

MILLER, George "Kennedy", AO, MB, BS; Australian film director, producer, writer and doctor; b. 3 March 1945, Brisbane; s. of James Miller and Angela (Balson) Miller; m. Sandy Gore 1985; one d.; ed Sydney Boys' High School, Univ. of New South Wales Medical School; Resident Medical Officer, St Vincent's Hosp., Sydney 1971–72; f. Kennedy Miller film co. with the late Byron Kennedy 1977, Chair. 1977–; Writer and Dir Violence in the Cinema, Part 1 1975, Co-Writer and Dir Mad Max 1979, Mad Max II (The Road Warrior) 1981, Exec. Producer and Dir The Dismissal (mini-series) 1982, Dir The Twilight Zone Movie 1983, Producer Bodyline (mini-series) 1983, The Cowra Breakout (mini-series) 1984, Co-Writer, Producer, Co-Dir Mad Max Beyond Thunderdome 1985, Producer Vietnam (mini-series) 1986, Dir Witches of Eastwick 1986, Producer The Riddle of the Stinson, The Clean Machine, Fragments of War 1987, Co-Producer Dead Calm, The Year My Voice Broke 1988, The Bangkok Hilton (mini-series), Flirting 1989, Over the Hill, Dir, Co-Writer, Co-Producer Lorenzos Oil 1990, Co-Producer, Co-Writer Babe (Golden Globe Award for Best Picture 1996) 1994; Dir Contact 1996; Pres. Jury Avoriaz Film Festival 1984; mem. Jury Cannes Film Festival 1988; Chair. Byron Kennedy Memorial Trust 1984–; mem. Bd of Dirs. Museum of Contemporary Art, Sydney 1987–; Best Dir, Australian Film Inst. 1982; Best Dir TV Drama, Penguin Awards 1983, Grand Prix Avoriaz 1983, Best Foreign Film, LA Film Critics 1983 and numerous other prizes and awards. *Leisure interests:* art, music, sport. *Address:* 30 Orwell Street, King's Cross, NSW 2011, Australia. *Telephone:* (2) 357-2322.

MILLER, G. (George) William, BS, JD; American business executive; b. 9 March 1925, Sapulpa, Okla; s. of James Dick Miller and Hazel Deane (née Orrick) Miller; m. Ariadna Rogojarsky 1946; ed US Coast Guard Acad., New London, Univ. of Calif. School of Law, Berkeley; served as line officer in Pacific area, stationed in China for a year; lawyer with Cravath, Swaine and Moore, New York, NY 1952–56; joined Textron Inc. as Asst Sec. 1956, Vice-Pres. 1957–60, Pres. 1960–74, CEO Officer 1968–78, Chair. 1974–78; Chair. Fed. Reserve Bd 1978–79, Sec. of the Treasury 1979–81; Chair. G. William Miller & Co. Inc. 1981–; Chair. Federated Stores Inc. 1990–92; Dir Repligen Corpn, GS Industries Inc., H. John Heinz Center, Simon Property Group Inc., Bd of Trustees Marine Biological Lab. *Address:* 1215 19th Street, NW, Washington, DC 20036, USA. *Telephone:* (202) 429-1780. *Fax:* (202) 429-0025. *E-mail:* miller@gwmco.com (Office).

MILLER, Heidi G., PhD; American business executive; ed Princeton Univ., Yale Univ.; Chief Financial Officer Citigroup; Sr Exec. Vice-Pres., Strategic Planning and Admin. Priceline.com 2000; Vice-Chair. Marsh & McLennan Co., Inc. 2001–. *Address:* Marsh & McLennan Co. Inc., 1166 Avenue of the Americas, New York, NY 10036, USA (Office).

MILLER, Jacques Francis, AO, BA, MD, PhD, DSc, FAA, FRS; Australian medical research scientist; b. 2 April 1931, Nice, France; s. of the late Maurice Miller and Fernande Debarnot; m. Margaret D. Houen 1956; ed Univs. of Sydney and London; Jr Resident Medical Officer, Royal Prince Alfred Hosp., Sydney 1956; pathological research, Univ. of Sydney 1957, fmr Prof. of Experimental Immunology, now Prof. Emer.; cancer research, Chester Beatty Research Inst., London 1958–65; Head, Experimental Pathology and Thymus Biology Unit, Walter and Eliza Hall Inst., Melbourne 1966–96; various other professional appts; Foreign Assoc., NAS; numerous awards and honours including Esther Langer-Bertha Teplitz Memorial Prize 1965, Paul Ehrlich-Ludwig Darmstaedter Prize 1974, Inaugural Sandoz Prize for Immunology 1990, Florey-Faulding Medal and Prize 2000, Copley Medal, Royal Soc. 2001. *Publications:* over 400 papers in scientific journals, mostly on immunology and cancer research. *Leisure interests:* art, photography, music, literature. *Address:* Walter and Eliza Hall Institute of Medical Research, Royal Melbourne Hospital, Grattan Street, Parkville, Vic. 30502 (Office); 5 Charteris Drive, East Ivanhoe, Vic. 3079, Australia (Home). *Telephone:* 9345-2555 (Office); 9499-3481 (Home).

MILLER, James Clifford, III, PhD; American government official, academic and business executive; b. 25 June 1942, Atlanta, Ga; s. of James Clifford Miller, Jr and Annie Moseley; m. Demaris Humphries 1961; one s. two d.; ed Univs. of Georgia and Virginia; Asst Prof. Ga State Univ. Atlanta 1968–69; Economist, U.S. Dept of Transport 1969–72; Assoc. Prof. of Econs Texas A & M Univ. 1972–74; Economist, U.S. Council of Econ. Advisers, Washington, DC 1974–75; Asst Dir U.S. Council of Wage and Price Stability 1975–77; Resident Scholar, American Enterprise Inst. 1977–81; Admin., Office of Information and Regulatory Affairs, Office of Man. and Budget and Exec. Dir Presidential Task Force on Regulatory Relief 1981; Chair Fed. Trade Comm., Washington, DC 1981–85; Dir Office of Man. and Budget 1985–89; Distinguished Fellow, Center for Study of Public Choice, George Mason Univ. and Chair. Citizens for a Sound Econ. 1988–; serves on several business bds. and non-profit bds.; Thomas Jefferson Fellow 1965–66; DuPont Fellow 1966–67, Ford Foundation Fellow 1967–68. *Publications:* Why the Draft? The Case for a Volunteer Army 1968, Economic Regulation of Domestic Air Transport; Theory and Policy 1974, Perspectives on Federal Transportation Policy 1975, Benefit—Cost Analyses of Social Regulation 1979, Reforming Regulation 1980, The Economist as Reformer 1989, Fix the U.S. Budget! 1994, Monopoly Politics 1999. *Leisure interests:* politics, economics. *Address:* Citizens for a Sound Economy, 1250 H Street, NW, Washington, DC 20005, USA.

MILLER, Jonathan; American media executive; b. 1957; fmrly with cable operations section, Nat. Basketball Asscn; helped launch Nickelodeon (children's cable TV channel) in UK; Chief of Information Services Unit (in charge of Ticketmaster, Expedia, CitySearch and Match.com), USA Interactive –2002; CEO America Online (AOL) Aug. 2002–. *Address:* America Online, 200 AOL Way, Dulles, VA, 20166-9323, USA (Office). *Telephone:* (703) 265-1000 (Office). *Website:* www.aol.com (Office).

MILLER, Sir Jonathan Wolfe, Kt, CBE, MB, BCh; British stage and film director and physician; b. 21 July 1934, London; s. of the late Emanuel Miller; m. Helen Rachel Collet 1956; two s. one d.; ed St Paul's School, St John's Coll., Cambridge and Univ. Coll. Hosp. Medical School, London; co-author of and appeared in Beyond the Fringe 1961–64; Dir John Osborne's Under Plain Cover, Royal Court Theatre 1962, Robert Lowell's The Old Glory, New York 1964 and Prometheus Bound, Yale Drama School 1967; Dir at Nottingham Playhouse 1968–69; Dir Oxford and Cambridge Shakespeare Co. production of Twelfth Night on tour in USA 1969; Research Fellow in the History of Medicine, Univ. Coll., London 1970–73; Assoc. Dir Nat. Theatre 1973–75; mem. Arts Council 1975–76; Visiting Prof. in Drama, Westfield Coll., Univ. of London 1977–; Exec. Producer Shakespeare TV series 1979–81; Artistic Dir Old Vic 1988–90; Research Fellow in Neuropsychology, Univ. of Sussex; Fellow, Univ. Coll. London 1981–; Dir of the Year, Soc. of West End Theatre Awards 1976; Hon. Fellow, St John's Coll. Cambridge, Royal Coll. of Physicians 1997, Royal Coll. of Physicians (Edin.) 1998; Dr hc (Open Univ.) 1983; Hon. DLitt (Leicester) 1981, (Kent) 1985, (Leeds) 1996, (Cambridge) 1996; Silver Medal (Royal Television Soc.) 1981, Albert Medal (Royal Soc. of Arts) 1992. *Productions:* for Nat. Theatre, London: The Merchant of Venice 1970, Danton's Death 1971, The School for Scandal 1972, The Marriage of Figaro 1974, The Wind in the Willows 1990; other productions The Tempest, London 1970, Prometheus Bound, London 1971, The Taming of the Shrew, Chichester 1972, The Seagull, Chichester 1973, The Malcontent, Nottingham 1973, Arden Must Die (opera) 1973, The Family in Love, Greenwich Season 1974, The Importance of Being Earnest 1975, The Cunning Little Vixen (opera) 1975, All's Well That Ends Well, Measure For Measure, Greenwich Season 1975, Three Sisters 1977, The Marriage of Figaro (ENO) 1978, Arabella (opera) 1980, Falstaff (opera) 1980, 1981, Otello (opera) 1982, Rigoletto (opera) 1982, 1984, Fidelio (opera) 1982, 1983, Don Giovanni (opera) 1985, The Mikado (opera) 1986, Tosca (opera) 1986, Long Day's Journey into Night 1986, Taming of the Shrew 1987, The Tempest 1988, Turn of the Screw 1989, King Lear 1989, The Liar 1989, La Fanciulla del West (opera) 1991, Marriage of Figaro (opera), Manon Lescaut (opera), Die Gezeichneten (opera) 1992, Maria Stuarda (opera), Capriccio (opera), Fedora (opera), Bach's St Matthew Passion 1993, Der Rosenkavalier (opera), Anna Bolena (opera), Falstaff (opera), L'Incoronazione di Poppea (opera), La Bohème (opera) 1994, Così fan Tutte (opera) 1995, Carmen (opera) 1995, Pelléas et Mélisande (opera) 1995, She Stoops to Conquer, London 1995, A Midsummer Night's Dream, London 1996, The Rake's Progress, New York 1997, The Beggar's Opera 1999; films: Take a Girl Like You 1969 and several films for television including Whistle and I'll Come to You 1967, Alice in Wonderland 1967, The Body in Question (series) 1978, Henry the Sixth, part one 1983, States of Mind (series) 1983, Subsequent Performances 1986, The Emperor 1987, Jonathan Miller's Opera Works (series) 1997. *Publications:* McLuhan 1971, Freud: The Man, his World, his Influence 1972, The Body in Question 1978, Subsequent Performances 1986, The Don Giovanni Book: Myths of Seduction and Betrayal (Ed.) 1990, On Reflection 1998. *Leisure interest:* deep sleep. *Address:* c/o IMG Artists, 616 Chiswick High Road, London, W4 5RX, England.

MILLER, Karl Fergus Connor; British professor of English literature; b. 2 Aug. 1931; s. of William Miller and Marion Miller; m. Jane E. Collet 1956; two s. one d.; ed Royal High School, Edinburgh and Downing Coll., Cambridge; Asst Prin., HM Treasury 1956–57; BBC TV producer 1957–58; Literary Ed. The Spectator 1958–61, New Statesman 1961–67; Ed. The Listener 1967–73; Lord Northcliffe Prof. of Modern English Literature, Univ. Coll., London 1974–92; Ed. London Review of Books 1979–92, Co-Ed. 1989–92; James Tait Black Prize 1975, Scottish Arts Council Book Award 1993. *Publications:* Cockburn's Millennium 1975, Doubles: Studies in Literary History 1985, Authors 1989, Rebecca's Vest (autobiog.) 1993, Boswell and Hyde 1995, Dark Horses (autobiog.) 1998; ed. of several anthologies. *Leisure interest:* football. *Address:* 26 Limerston Street, London, SW10 0HH, England. *Telephone:* (20) 7351-1994.

MILLER, Lajos; Hungarian baritone; b. 23 Jan. 1940, Szombathely; s. of Lajos Miller and Teréz Sebestyén; m. Zsuzsa Dobránszky; one s.; studied at Music Acad. of Budapest under Jenö Sipos;. mem. Hungarian State Opera 1968–; has sung with maj. cos. in France, Germany, Italy, Monaco, Switzerland, Austria, UK, USA, Belgium, Venezuela, Canada, Chile, Japan, Argentina, Russia; Grand Prix, Fauré singing contest, Paris 1974, first prize, "Toti dal Monte" singing contest, Treviso, Italy 1975; Liszt Prize 1975, Kossuth Prize 1980. *Operatic roles include:* (Verdi) Renato, Rodrigo, Simon Boccanegra, Don Carlos, Rolando (Battaglia di Legnano), Iago, Nabucco, Conte di Luna, Miller, Germont, (Gluck) Orpheus, Orestes, (Mozart) Don Giovanni, Guglielmo, (Giordano) Carlo Gérard, (Leoncavallo) Silvio, (Rossini) Figaro, Guglielmo Tell, (Tchaikovsky) Eugene Onegin, Yeletsky, (Puccini) Scarpia, (Bizet) Escamillo, (Verdi) Commandante Ivo, (Donizetti) Enrico, (Rimsky-Korsakov) Grasnoi, (Puccini) Sharpless. *Recorded roles:* Don Carlos (Ernani), Simon Boccanegra, Lycidas, Sharpless (Madame Butterfly), Fanuel, Valentin (Faust), Andrei (War and Peace), Manfredo (Il Giuramento), Chelkalov (Boris Godunov), Belfagor, Zosimo (Maria Egiziaga), Falásar (Semirama), Arias by Verdi. *TV films:* Enrico (Lucia di Lammermoor), Marcello (Tabarro), Silvio (Pagliacci), Loth (Madarasz 'Loth), two portrait films 1995, Angelica (Iber), Elisir Damor (Donizetti), Rigoletto (Verdi). *Leisure interests:* tennis, surfing, skiing, photography, making films. *Address:* 3232 Mátrafüred, Hegyalja u. 32; State Opera, Andrássy ut 22, 1061 Budapest, Hungary. *Telephone:* (61) 331-2550.

MILLER, Leszek, MPolSci; Polish politician; b. 3 July 1946, Żyrardów; m. Aleksandra Borowiec; one s.; ed Higher School of Social Sciences; electrician Enterprise of Linen Industry, Żyrardów 1963–70; mem. Polish United Workers' Party (PZPR) 1966–90, Staff mem. Cen. Cttee 1977–86; First Sec. Voivodeship's Cttee of Skierniewice 1986–89, mem. Cen. Cttee 1989–90; mem. Politburo Cen. Cttee 1989–90; Participant Round Table Talks 1989; Deputy to Sejm (Parl.) 1991– (Chair. Left Alliance Caucus 1997–2001); Minister of Labour and Social Policy 1993–96, of Interior and Admin. 1997; Minister, Head Council of Ministers Office 1996; Chair. Democratic Left Alliance (SLD) 1999–; mem. and Co-founder Social Democracy of Repub. of Poland 1990–2001 (Gen. Sec. 1990–93, Vice-Chair. 1993–97, Chair. 1997–2001); Prime Minister of Poland 2001–; Golden Cross of Merit 1979, Kt.'s Cross of Polonia Restituta Order 1984, Goodwill Amb., Polish Cttee of UNICEF 2000, Chevalier of the Order of the Smile. *Leisure interests:* angling, literature. *Address:* Chancellery of the Prime Minister, AP. Ujazdowskie 1/3, 00-583 Warsaw, Poland (Office). *Telephone:* (22) 621-76-77 (Office). *Fax:* (22) 628-68-46 (Office). *E-mail:* leszek.miller@miller.pl (Office); cirinfo@kprm.gov .pl (Office). *Website:* www.miller.pl (Office); www.kprm.gov.pl.

MILLER, Sir Peter North, Kt, MA, DSc; British insurance broker; b. 28 Sept. 1930, London; s. of Cyril T. Miller and Dorothy N. Miller; m. Jane Miller 1991; one s.; two s. one d. by previous marriage; ed Rugby School and Lincoln Coll. Oxford; joined Thos. R. Miller & Son (Insurance) 1953, Partner 1959, Sr Partner 1971–, Chair. of Miller Insurance Group 1971–83, 1988–96; mem. Cttee Lloyds Insurance Brokers' Asscn 1973–77, Deputy Chair. 1974-75, Chair. 1976–77; mem. Cttee of Lloyds 1977–80, 1982–89; Chair. of Lloyds 1984–87; mem. Cttee on Invisible Exports 1975–77; mem. Insurance Brokers' Registration Council 1977–81; Chair. British Cttee of Bureau Veritas 1980–; one of Her Majesty's Lts for City of London 1987–; Hon. Fellow Lincoln Coll., Oxford 1992–; Commendatore, Ordine al Merito della Repubblica Italiana 1989. *Leisure interests:* all forms of sport (except cricket), particularly running, riding, tennis and sailing, wine, music. *Address:* c/o Miller Insurance Group, Dawson House, 5 Jewry Street, London, EC3N 2PY (Office); Quinneys, Camilla Drive, Westhumble, Dorking, Surrey, RH5 6BU, England. *Telephone:* (20) 7488-2345.

MILLER, Robert Joseph, BA, J.D; American lawyer and politician; b. 30 March 1945, Evanston, Ill.; s. of Ross Wendell Miller and Coletta Jane Doyle; m. Sandra Ann Searles; one s. two d.; ed Santa Clara and Loyola Univs.; First Legal Advisor Las Vegas Metropolitan Police Dept 1973–75; JP 1975–78; Deputy Dist Attorney, Clark Co., Las Vegas 1971–73, Dist Attorney 1979–86; Lt Gov. of Nevada 1987–89, 1989–90, Gov. 1991–98; Chair. Nev. Comm. on Econ. Devt, Nev. Comm. on Tourism 1987–91; mem. Nat. Govs. Asscn (Vice-Chair. Exec. Cttee 1995–96, Chair. 1996–97, fmr Chair. Cttee on Justice and Public Safety, Chair. Legal Affairs Cttee 1992–94, Lead Gov. on Transport 1992–); Sr. Partner Jones Vargas, Las Vegas 1999–; Democrat. *Address:* Jones Vargas, 3rd Floor, South 3773 Howard Hughes Parkway, Las Vegas, NV 89109, U.S.A. (Office).

MILLER, Robert Stevens, Jr., AB, MBA, JD; American business executive; b. 4 Nov. 1941, Portland, Ore.; s. of Robert Stevens Miller and Barbara Weston Miller; m. Margaret Rose Kyger 1966; three s.; ed Stanford Univ. and Harvard Law School; mem. financial staff, Ford Motor Co., Dearborn, Mich. 1968–71; Investment Man., Ford Motor de Mexico, Mexico City 1971–73; Dir of Finance, Ford Asia Pacific, Melbourne, Australia 1974–77; Vice-Pres. (Finance) Ford Motor de Venezuela, Caracas 1977–79; Vice-Pres.-Treas., Chrysler Corpn, Detroit, Mich. 1980–81, Exec. Vice-Pres. (Finance) 1981–85, 1985–88, Exec. Vice-Pres. 1988–92; Sr Partner James D. Wolfensohn Inc. 1992–93; Chair. Morrison Knudson Corpn 1995–96, Waste Man. Inc. 1997–; Chair., CEO Bethlehem Steel 2001–; Dir Fed.-Mogul, Pope and Talbot, Coleman, Symantec, Morrison Knudson; mem. Int. Advisory Bd, Creditanstalt Bankverein, Vienna, Austria. *Leisure interest:* model railroading. *Address:* Waste Management Inc., 3003 Butterfield Road, Oak Brook, IL 60523, U.S.A. (Office); Federal-Mogul Corporation, 26555 Northwestern Highway, Southfield, MI 48034 (Office).

MILLER, Stanley Lloyd, PhD; American chemist and educator; b. 7 March 1930, Oakland, Calif.; s. of Nathan Harry Miller and Edith (Levy) Miller; ed Univs. of California (Berkeley) and Chicago; F. B. Jewett Fellow, Calif. Inst. of Tech. 1954–55; Instructor and Asst Prof., Dept of Biochem. and Chem., Coll. of Physicians and Surgeons, Columbia Univ. 1955–60; Asst, Assoc. then Full Prof., Dept of Chem., Univ. of Calif., San Diego 1960–; mem. NAS; Hon. Councillor, Higher Council of Scientific Research of Spain; Oparin Medal, Int. Soc. for the Study of the Origin of Life. *Publication:* The Origins of Life on the Earth (with L. E. Orgel) 1974. *Address:* University of California, San Diego, Department of Chemistry, 9500 Gilman Drive, La Jolla, CA 92093-0506, USA. *Telephone:* (619) 534-3365. *Fax:* (619) 534-4864 (Office). *E-mail:* smiller@ucsd .edu (Office).

MILLER, Thomas J., MA, PhD; American diplomatist; b. 1948, Chicago; ed Univ. of Michigan; mem. Sr Foreign Service at rank of Minister-Counselor; joined State Dept 1976; analyst for Vietnam, Laos and Cambodia 1976–77; Special Asst to Under-Sec. for Political Affairs 1977–79; Deputy Prin. Officer, US Consulate, Chiang Mai, Thailand 1979–81; served twice on Israeli Desk (once as Dir); Head Office of Maghreb Affairs; Acting Dir of an office on counter-terrorism; political section, Athens Embassy 1985–87; Deputy Chief of Mission, Athens 1994–97; Special Coordinator for Cyprus (with rank of Amb.) 1997–99; Amb. to Bosnia and Herzegovina 1999–2001, to Greece 2001–; Equal Opportunity Award (Dept. of State), Superior Honor Award (five times) (Dept of State), Meritorious Award (Dept of State) and many others. *Address:* American Embassy, Alipašina 43, 71000 Sarajevo, Bosnia and Herzegovina (Office). *Telephone:* (71) 659969 (Office). *E-mail:* MillerTJ@State.gov.

MILLER, Walter Geoffrey Thomas, AO; Australian diplomatist; b. 25 Oct. 1934, Tasmania; s. of Walter T. Miller and Gertrude S. Galloway; m. Rachel C. Webb 1960; three s. one d.; ed Launceston High School and Univs. of Tasmania and Oxford; served in Australian missions in Kuala Lumpur, Djakarta and at UN, New York; Deputy High Commr, India 1973–75; Amb. to Repub. of Korea 1978–80; Head, Int. Div. Dept of the Prime Minister and Cabinet, Canberra 1982; Deputy Sec. Dept of Foreign Affairs 1985–86; Amb. to Japan 1986–89; Dir-Gen. Office of Nat. Assessments Canberra 1989–95; High Commr in NZ 1996–2000; Pres. Australian Inst. of Int. Affairs 2000–; Rhodes Scholar 1956. *Leisure interests:* international relations, literature, ballet, tennis, reading, golf. *Address:* 85 Union Street, McMahons Point, NSW 2060, Australia.

MILLER, William (see Miller, G. (George) William).

MILLER, Zell Bryan, MA; American politician; b. 24 Feb. 1932, Young Harris, Ga; s. of Stephen G. Miller and Birdie Bryan; m. Shirley Carver 1954; two s.; ed Young Harris Coll., Univ. of Georgia; Prof. of Political Science and History, Univ. of Ga, Young Harris Coll. 1959–64, 1999–; mem. Ga Senate 1960–64; Dir Ga Bd of Probation 1965–67; Deputy Dir Ga Dept of Corrections 1967–68; Exec. Sec. to Gov. of Ga 1968–71; Exec. Dir Democratic Cttee of Ga 1971–72; mem. State Bd of Pardons and Paroles, Atlanta 1973–75; Lt-Gov. of Ga 1975–91; Gov. of Georgia 1990–98, Senator of Georgia 2000–; Pres. Council State Govts. 1991–; Vice-Chair. Southern Gov.'s Asscn 1991–; Democrat. *Publications:* The Mountains Within Me, Great Georgians, They Heard Georgia Singing. *Address:* 1175 Peachtree Street, NE #100–300, Atlanta, GA 30361, USA (Office); US Senate, 257 Dirksen Senate Office Building, Washington, DC 220510.

MILLER SMITH, Charles, MA; British business executive; b. 7 Nov. 1939, Glasgow; s. of William Smith and Margaret Wardrope; m. Dorothy Adams 1964 (died 1999); one s. two d.; ed Glasgow Acad. and St Andrew's Univ.;

Financial Dir Vinyl Products, Unilever 1970–73, Head of Planning 1974; Finance Dir Walls Meat Co. 1976; Vice-Chair. Industan Lever 1979–81; Speciality Chemicals Group 1981; Chief Exec. PPF Int. 1983; Chief Exec. Quest Int. 1986; Financial Dir Unilever Bd 1989; Exec. Unilever Foods 1993–94; Exec. Dir ICI PLC 1994–95, Chief Exec. 1995–99, Chair. 1999–2001; Chair. Scottish Power PLC 2000–; Dir (non-exec.) HSBC Holdings PLC 1996–; Int. Adviser Goldman Sachs 2002–; Hon. LLD (St Andrew's) 1995. *Leisure interests:* reading, walking. *Address:* Scottish Power PLC, Corporate Office, 1 Atlantic Quay, Glasgow, G2 8SP, Scotland (Office). *Telephone:* (141) 248-8200 (Office). *Fax:* (141) 248-8300 (Office). *Website:* www.scottishpower.plc.uk (Office).

MILLERON, Jean-Claude; French economist; b. 8 Jan. 1937, Paris; s. of Pierre A. Milleron and Geneviève Hedouin; m. Marie-France Dannaud 1966; two s. one d.; ed Ecole Polytechnique, Paris, Ecole Supérieure des Sciences Econ., Paris; with Nat. Inst. of Statistics and Econ. Studies (INSEE), Paris 1963–70, Dir-Gen. 1987–92; Visiting Research Dept of Econs, Univ. of Calif. at Berkeley 1970–71; Deputy Dir Nat. School of Statistics and Econ. Admin. (ENSAE), Paris 1971–78; Head of Dept of Econs, Planning Commissariat-Gen., Paris 1978–81; Dir of Forecasting French Ministry of Econ. and Finance 1982–87; Under-Sec.-Gen. Dept of Econ. and Social Information and Policy Analysis, UN, New York 1992–97; Special Adviser to French Minister of Econ., Finance and Industry 1997–98; apptd. Exec. Dir of IMF and IBRD 1998; apptd. Financial Minister Embassy, Washington 1998; Fellow Econometric Soc. *Publications:* various books and articles on econ. theory and public Econs. *Leisure interests:* jogging, hiking, opera. *Address:* c/o Ministry of the Economy, Finance and Industry, 139 rue de Bercy, 75572 Paris, France.

MILLETT, Baron (Life Peer), cr. 1998, of St Marylebone in the City of Westminster; **Peter Julian Millett,** PC; British judge; b. 23 June 1932; s. of the late Dennis Millett and Adele Millett; m. Ann Harris 1958; three s. (one deceased); ed Harrow School and Univ. of Cambridge; called to Bar, Middle Temple 1955, Lincoln's Inn 1959, Singapore 1976, Hong Kong 1979; at Chancery Bar 1958–86; Lecturer in Practical Conveyancing and Examiner Council of Legal Educ. 1962–76; mem. Gen. Council of the Bar 1971–75; Judge, High Court of Justice, Chancery Div. 1986–94, Lord Justice of Appeal 1994–98, Lord of Appeal in Ordinary 1998–; mem. House of Lords 1998–; Non-Perm. Judge of the Court of Final Appeal, Hong Kong 2000–; Hon. LLD (Queen Mary and Westfield Coll., London). *Address:* House of Lords, London, SW1A 0PQ, England (Office). *Telephone:* (20) 7219-3107 (Office). *Fax:* (20) 7219-5979 (Office).

MILLIKEN, Peter, LLB, MA; Canadian politician and lawyer; b. 12 Nov. 1946, Kingston, Ont.; ed Queen's Univ., Kingston, Wadham Coll., Oxford Univ., UK, Dalhousie Univ., Halifax; called to Bar of Ont., Solicitor of Supreme Court of Ont. 1973; solicitor, Cunningham, Little, Kingston (law firm) 1973–78, partner, Cunningham, Little, Bonham and Milliken 1978–89; MP for Kingston and the Islands 1988–; served as Asst House Leader, Vice-Chair. Standing Cttee on Privileges and Elections; Parl. Sec. to Leader of Govt in House of Commons 1993–96; Deputy Chair. Cttees. of Whole House 1996, Deputy Speaker and Chair. Cttees. of Whole House 1997, Speaker House of Commons 2001–; Chair. Bd of Internal Economy; Lecturer in Business Law, School of Business, Kingston 1973–81; Hon. LLD (State Univ. of New York) 2001. *Publication:* Question Period: Developments from 1960 to 1967 1968. *Address:* House of Commons, Ottawa, Ont., K1A 0A6 (Office); Quaker Valley, R.R. No. 1, Elginburg, Ont., K0H 1M0, Canada (Home). *Telephone:* (613) 992-5042 (Office); (613) 548-7889 (Home). *Fax:* (613) 947-2816 (Office). *E-mail:* millip9@parl.gc.ca (Office). *Website:* www.petermilliken.com (Office).

MILLON, Charles, L. ÈS SC.ECON.; French politician; b. 12 Nov. 1945, Belley, Ain; s. of Gabriel Millon and Suzanne Gunet; m. Chantal Delsol 1970; three s. two d.; ed Ecole Sainte-Marie, Lyon, Faculté de Droit et de Sciences Economiques de Lyon; univ. tutor 1969; legal and taxation adviser 1970–; Mayor of Belley 1977–2001; Deputy 1981–86, 1988–93, First Vice-Pres. Ass. Nat. 1986–88, Leader Union pour la Démocratie Française in Nat. Ass. 1989; Minister of Defence 1995–97; Local Councillor, Ain 1985–88; Vice-Pres. Regional Council, Rhône-Alpes 1981–88, Pres. 1988–, Pres. 1988–98; Founder and Pres. la Droite Movt 1998–99; Leader Droite Libérale Chrétienne 1999–; Municipal Councillor and Urban Community Councillor, Lyon 2001–. *Publications:* L'Extravagante histoire des nationalisations 1984, L'Alternance-vérité 1986, La Tentation du Conservatisme 1995, La Paix civile 1998. *Leisure interests:* reading, walking, mountaineering. *Address:* Droite Libérale Chrétienne (DLC), 21 rue de Bourgogne, 75007 Paris (Office); 11 bis rue des Barons, 01300 Belley, France (Home). *E-mail:* contact@d-l-c.org (Office). *Website:* www.d-l-c.org (Office).

MILLS, Dame Barbara Jean Lyon, DBE, QC, MA; British lawyer; b. 10 Aug. 1940; m.; four c.; ed St Helen's School, Northwood and Lady Margaret Hall, Oxford; called to bar, Middle Temple, London 1963, Bencher 1990; Jr Prosecuting Counsel to Inland Revenue 1977, Sr Prosecuting Counsel 1979; Jr Treasury Counsel, Cen. Criminal Court 1981; Recorder, Crown Court 1982–92; QC 1986; Dept of Trade and Industry Insp. under Section 177 of Financial Services Act 1986 (re Jenkins-British Commonwealth) 1986; mem. Criminal Injuries Compensation Bd 1988–90; Legal Assessor to Gen. Medical Council and Gen. Dental Council 1988–90; mem. Parole Bd 1990; Dir Serious Fraud Office 1990–92; mem. Gen. Advisory Council of BBC 1991–92; QC (NI) 1991; Dir of Public Prosecutions and Head, Crown Prosecution Service 1992–98; The Adjudicator 1999–; Chair. Forum UK 1999–2001, Council of Man., Women's Library 2000–; Dir (non-exec.) Royal Free Hampstead Nat. Health Service Trust 2000–; Gov. London Guildhall Univ. 1999–; Trustee Victim Support 1999–; mem. The Competition Comm. 2001–; Hon. Vice-Pres., Inst. for Study and Treatment of Delinquency 1996; Hon. Fellow, Lady Margaret Hall, Oxford 1991, Soc. for Advanced Legal Studies 1997; Companion of Honour, Inst. of Man. 1993; Hon. LLD (Hull, Nottingham Trent) 1993, (London Guildhall) 1994. *Address:* 72 Albert Street, London, NW1 7NR, England. *Telephone:* (20) 7388-9206. *Fax:* (20) 7388-3454.

MILLS, Hayley Cathrine Rose Vivien; British actress; b. 18 April 1946, London; d. of Sir John Mills (q.v.) and Lady Mills (Mary Hayley Bell); m. Roy Boulting 1971 (divorced 1977); two s.; Elmhurst Ballet School, Inst. Alpine Vidamanette; first film appearance in Tiger Bay 1959; on contract to Walt Disney; first stage appearance as Peter Pan 1969; Silver Bear Award, Berlin Film Festival 1958, British Acad. Award; Special Oscar (USA), TV Best Actress Award 1982. *Films include:* Pollyanna 1960, The Parent Trap 1961, Whistle Down the Wind 1961, Summer Magic 1962, In Search of the Castaways 1963, The Chalk Garden 1964, The Moonspinners 1965, The Truth about Spring 1965, Sky West and Crooked 1966, The Trouble with Angels 1966, The Family Way 1966, Pretty Polly 1967, Twisted Nerve 1968, Take a Girl Like You 1970, Forbush and the Penguins 1971, Endless Night 1972, Deadly Strangers 1975, The Diamond Hunters 1975, What Changed Charley Farthing? 1975, The Kingfisher Caper 1975, Appointment with Death 1987, After Midnight 1992. *Stage appearances include:* The Wild Duck 1970, Trelawny 1972, The Three Sisters 1973, A Touch of Spring 1975, Rebecca 1977, My Fat Friend 1978, Hush and Hide 1979, The Importance of Being Earnest (Royal Festival Theatre, Chichester), The Summer Party 1980, Tally's Folly 1982, The Secretary Bird 1983, Dial M for Murder 1984, Toys in the Attic 1986, The Kidnap Game 1991, The King and I (Australian and New Zealand tour) 1991–92, The Card 1994, Fallen Angels 1994, Dead Guilty 1995–96, Brief Encounter 1997–98, The King and I (U.S. tour) 1997–98, Suite in Two Keys (New York) 2001, A Little Night Music (USA) 2001, The Vagina Monologues (New York) 2001. *Television appearances include:* The Flame Trees of Thika 1981, Parent Trap II 1986, Good Morning Miss Bliss, Murder She Wrote, Back Home, Tales of the Unexpected, Walk of Life 1990, Parent Trap III, IV, Amazing Stories. *Publication:* My God (with Marcus Maclaine) 1988. *Leisure interests:* riding, reading, children, cooking, scuba-diving. *Address:* c/o Chatto and Linnit, Prince of Wales Theatre, Coventry Street, London, W1V 7FE, England.

MILLS, Ian Mark, BSc, DPhil, FRS; British academic; b. 9 June 1930; s. of John Mills and Marghuerita Alice Gertrude Mills (née Gooding); m. Margaret Maynard 1957; one s. one d.; ed Leighton Park School, Univ. of Reading, St John's Coll. Oxford; Research Fellow, Univ. of Minn. 1954–56; Research Fellow in Theoretical Chem., Corpus Christi Coll., Cambridge 1956–57; Lecturer in Chem. Univ. of Reading 1957–64, Reader 1964–66, Prof. of Chemical Spectroscopy 1966–95; Prof. Emer. 1995–, Leverhulme Emer. Research Fellow 1996–98; Ed. Molecular Physics 1972–77, 1995–; mem. and Chair. of various cttees. of IUPAC; Vice-Pres. Faraday Div. of the RSC 1984–86; mem. British Nat. Cttee for IUPAC of RSC 1992–, Chair. 1998–; Pres. of the Consultative Cttee on Units of the Bureau Int. des Poids et Mesures 1995–; Chair. British Standards Inst. Cttee on Symbols and Units 1996–; mem. Council Royal Inst. 2000–; Lomb Medal 1960, Fellow 1974, Lippincott Medal of Optical Soc. of America 1982; Spectroscopy Award of RSC 1990. *Publications:* Quantities, Units and Symbols in Physical Chemistry 1988 (Jt author); various papers in learned journals on quantum mechanics and molecular spectroscopy. *Leisure interests:* sailing, walking. *Address:* Department of Chemistry, University of Reading, Reading, RG6 6AD (Office); 57 Christchurch Road, Reading, RG2 7BD, England (Home). *Telephone:* (118) 931-8456 (Office); (118) 987-2335 (Home). *Fax:* (118) 931-6331 (Office). *E-mail:* i.m.mills@reading.ac.uk (Office).

MILLS, Sir John, Kt, CBE; British actor; b. 22 Feb. 1908, North Elmham, Suffolk; s. of Lewis Mills; m. Mary Hayley Bell 1941; one s. two d. (Hayley Mills, q.v.); ed Norwich High School; debut in chorus of The Five O'Clock Girl 1929; appeared in repertory 1929–30; appeared as The Aunt in Charley's Aunt, London, 1930; has since appeared in numerous West End productions including the following plays by his wife Mary Hayley Bell: Men in Shadow 1942, Duet for Two Hands 1945, Angel 1947, The Uninvited Guest 1952; mem. Council Royal Acad. of Dramatic Art 1965–; mem. Bd Govs of British Film Inst., Soc. of Film and TV Arts (Vice-Pres.); Chair. Stars Org. for Spastics 1975; Patron, Life mem. Variety Club; other stage appearances include: Noel Coward's Cavalcade 1931 and Words and Music 1932, Give Me a Ring 1933, Jill Darling 1934, Red Night 1936, A Midsummer Night's Dream, She Stoops to Conquer, The Damascus Blade 1950, Figure of Fun 1951, The Uninvited Guest 1952, Ross (Broadway production) 1961, Powers of Persuasion 1963, Veterans 1972, At the End of the Day 1973, The Good Companions (musical) 1974, Great Expectations (musical) 1975, Separate Tables 1977, Goodbye, Mr. Chips (musical) 1982, The Housekeeper 1983, Little Lies 1983 and 1984, The Petition 1986, Pygmalion 1987, When the Wind Blows (TV play) 1987; Pres. Mountview Theatre School 1983–; Vice-Pres. Greater London Fund for the Blind 1998–; numerous theatre and film awards include Best Actor of the Year (for Of Mice and Men) 1939, Best Actor (for Great Expectations) 1947, Venice Film Festival Best Actor Award (for Tunes of Glory) 1960, San Sebastian Film Festival Best Actor Award (for The Family Way) 1968; Acad. Award (Oscar) for role in Ryan's Daughter 1971; BAFTA Award for Outstanding Contrib. to World Cinema 2002. *Film appearances include:* The Midshipmaid, Those

Were the Days, Doctor's Orders, Royal Cavalcade, Tudor Rose, O.H.M.S., Goodbye Mr. Chips (1937), Four Dark Hours, Black Sheep of Whitehall, The Young Mr Pitt, In Which We Serve, Waterloo Road, This Happy Breed, The Way to the Stars, Scott of the Antarctic, The History of Mr Polly, The Rocking Horse Winner, Morning Departure, Hobson's Choice, The Colditz Story, Above Us The Waves, Escapade, War and Peace, The Baby and the Battleship, Round the World in 80 Days, Dunkirk, Ice Cold in Alex, Monty's Double, Summer of the Seventeenth Doll, Tiger Bay, Swiss Family Robinson, Tunes of Glory, The Singer Not the Song, Flame in the Streets, Tiara Tahiti, King Rat, The Chalk Garden, Operation Crossbow, The Wrong Box, The Family Way, Chuka, Cowboy in Africa, Adam's Woman, Lady Hamilton, Oh! What a Lovely War, Run Wild, Run Free, A Black Veil for Lisa, Ryan's Daughter, Dulcima, Young Winston, Oklahoma Crude, The Human Factor, Trial by Combat, The Big Sleep, Thirty-Nine Steps, Zulu Dawn, Dr Strange, Love Boat, Quatermass (TV), Young at Heart (TV) 1980/82, A Woman of Substance (TV), The Masks of Death (TV), Murder with Mirrors (TV), Gandhi 1980, Sahara 1983, A Woman of Substance, Tribute to Her Majesty (film documentary) 1986, A Tale of Two Cities (TV) 1989, Ending Up (TV) 1989, Harnessing Peacocks 1993, The Big Freeze, Martin Chuzzlewit (TV) 1994. *Publications:* Up in the Clouds Gentlemen Please 1980, Book of Famous Firsts 1984, Still Memories (autobiog.) 2000. *Leisure interests:* skiing, golf, painting. *Address:* c/o I.C.M. Ltd, 76 Oxford Street, London, W1R 1RB, England.

MILLS, John Evans Atta, PhD; Ghanaian politician and academic; b. 21 July 1944, Cape Coast, Cen. Region; m. Ernestina Naadu; ed Univ. of Ghana, London School of Econs, School of Oriental and African Studies, London Univ., Stanford Law School, Calif.; lecturer, Faculty of Law, Univ. of Ghana 1971–80, Assoc. Prof. of Law 1992; Visiting Prof., Temple Law School, Phila, USA 1978–79, 1986–87, Leiden Univ., Netherlands 1985–86; Acting Commr Internal Revenue Service 1986–93, Commr 1993–96; Nat. Democratic Congress (NDC) cand. Presidential Election 2000; Vice-Pres. of Ghana 2000. *Address:* c/o National Democratic Congress, 641/4 Ringway Close, Kokomlemle, P.O. Box 5825, Accra-North, Ghana (Office).

MILNE, Alasdair David Gordon, BA; British broadcasting official; b. 8 Oct. 1930; s. of Charles Gordon Shaw Milne and Edith Reid Clark; m. Sheila Kirsten Graucob 1954 (died 1992); two s. one d.; ed Winchester Coll., New Coll., Oxford; served with 1st Bn, Gordon Highlanders 1949; joined BBC 1954, Deputy Ed. 1957–61, Ed. of Tonight Programme 1961–62, Head of Tonight Productions 1963–65; Partner Jay, Baverstock, Milne & Co. 1965–67; rejoined BBC 1967, Controller BBC Scotland 1968–72, Dir of Programmes, BBC TV 1973–77, Man. Dir TV 1977–82, Deputy Dir-Gen. BBC 1980–82, Dir-Gen. 1982–87; Chair., Darrell Waters Ltd 1988–90; Dir ABU TV Ltd 1988–93; Pres. Commonwealth Broadcasting Asscn 1984–87; BBC Visiting Prof., Univ. of Miami 1989; Hon. Fellow New College, Oxford; Dr. hc (Stirling) 1983; Cyril Bennett Award 1987. *Publication:* DG: The Memoirs of a British Broadcaster 1988. *Leisure interests:* piping, salmon fishing, golf. *Address:* 30 Holland Park Avenue, London, W11 3QU, England.

MILNES, Sherill, M.MUS.ED.; American opera singer; b. 10 Jan. 1935, Hinsdale, Ill.; s. of James Knowlton and Thelma Roe Milnes; m. 2nd Nancy Stokes 1969; one s.; one s. one d. by first marriage; m. 3rd Maria Zouves 1996; ed Drake Univ., Northwestern Univ.; studied with Boris Goldovsky, Rosa Ponselle, Andrew White, Hermanes Baer; with Goldovsky Opera Co. 1960–65, New York City Opera Co. 1964–67, debut with Metropolitan Opera Co., New York 1965, leading baritone 1965–; has performed with all American city opera cos. and maj. American orchestras 1962–73; performed in Don Giovanni, Vespri Siciliani and all standard Italian repertory baritone roles, Metropolitan Opera and at San Francisco Opera, Hamburg Opera, Frankfurt Opera, La Scala, Milan, Covent Garden, London, Teatro Colón, Buenos Aires, Vienna State Opera, Paris Opera and Chicago Lyric Opera; recordings for RCA Victor, London Decca, EMI Angel, Phillips, Deutsche Grammophon, 60 albums 1967–; most recorded American opera singer 1978; Chair. of Bd Affiliate Artists Inc.; three hon. degrees, Order of Merit (Italy) 1984, three Grammy Awards. *Leisure interests:* table tennis, swimming, horse riding. *Address:* c/o Herbert Barrett, 1776 Broadway, Suite 1610, New York, NY 10019, USA.

MILO, Paskal, PhD; Albanian politician; b. 22 Feb. 1949, Vlorë; s. of Koço Petromilo and Parashqevi Petromilo; m. Liliana Balla-Milo 1976; one s. two d.; ed Univ. of Tirana; journalist 1971–74; high school teacher 1975–80; Lecturer in History Univ. of Tirana 1981–91, Dean Faculty of History and Philology 1991–92, Prof. 1996; Sec. of State for Educ. 1991; MP 1992–96, 1997–, Chair. Parl. Comm. for Educ. and Science 1992–96, Minister of Foreign Affairs 1997–2002; Chair. S.-E. European Co-operation Process (SEECP). *Publications:* The End of an Injustice 1984, Albania and Yugoslavia 1918–27 1992, A Good Understanding and Cooperation in the Balkans, From Utopia to Necessity 1997, Albania and the Balkan Entente 1997, Constitutional Rights and Minorities in the Balkans: A Comparative Analysis 1997, The Soviet Union and Albania's Foreign Policy 1944–46 1997, Albania in East-West Relations 1944–45 1998. *Leisure interests:* football, music. *Address:* c/o Ministria e Punëve të Jashtme, Bul. Zhan D'Ark, Tirana, Albania.

MILONGO, André; Republic of Congo politician; Prime Minister of the Congo 1991–93; Leader Parti congolais du travail (PCT) 1991; Leader Union pour la démocratie et la République 1992–; Presidential Cand. 1992; Leader Alliance pour la démocratie et le progrès (opposition coalition) 2001–. *Address:* Alliance pour la démocratie et le progrès (ADP), Brazzaville, Republic of the Congo (Office).

MILOŠEVIĆ, Slobodan; Serbia and Montenegro (Serbian) politician; b. 20 Aug. 1941, Požarevac; m. Mirjana Milošević; one s. one d.; ed Belgrade Univ.; mem. League of Communists of Yugoslavia (LCY) 1959–; active in student politics; Adviser on Econ. Affairs to Mayor of Belgrade; Deputy Dir Tehnogas Co. 1960–73, Dir-Gen. 1973–78; Head, Belgrade Information Service 1966–69; Pres. Beogradska Udružena Banka (Jt Bank of Belgrade) 1978–83; mem. Presidium, LCY Cen. Cttee 1983–84; Chair. Belgrade City Cttee of LCY 1984–86; mem. Presidency of League of Communists of Serbia, Pres. 1986–88; mem. Presidency, Belgrade City Cttee of League of Communists; mem. Fed. Council's Comm. for Long-Term Stabilization Program; Pres. collective Presidency of Serbia 1989–90; Pres. of Serbia 1990–97; Pres. Socialist Party of Serbia 1990–91; Pres. of Yugoslavia 1997–2000 (now Serbia and Montenegro); Serb actions in Kosovo lead to NATO mil. air strikes against Serb forces in Kosovo and Yugoslavia March–June 1999, culminating in the withdrawal of all Serb forces from Kosovo; ousted following riot in Belgrade Oct. 2000; indicted by Int. Criminal Tribunal, The Hague, for crimes against humanity; arrested on corruption charges in Yugoslavia April 2001; handed over to custody of UN war crimes tribunal in The Hague 28 June 2001, trial ongoing as at May 2003; Order of Labour with Gold Wreath; Order of Labour with Red Flag. *Publication:* Years of Outcome 1989.

MIŁOSZ, Czesław; Polish/American writer; b. 30 June 1911, Szetejnie, now Lithuania; s. of Aleksander Miłosz and Weronika (Kunat) Miłosz; m. 1st Janina Dlusta 1943 (died 1986); two s.; m. 2nd Carol Thigpen 1992 (died 2002); ed Univ. of Wilno (now Vilnius, Lithuania); helped form literary group Żagary; first collection of poems published 1933; studied in Paris 1934–35; programmer with Polish Nat. Radio 1935–39; active in Polish resistance, World War II; brought out "underground" an anti-Nazi anthology of poems Pieśń niepodległa (Invincible Song) and other publications; diplomatic service, Washington Embassy, later Paris 1946–50; went into exile, Paris 1951; with Polish emigrant publishing house Instytut Literacki, Paris 1951–60, still writes for house magazine Kultura; went to USA 1960, became naturalized American 1970; Prix Littéraire Européen (jtly) for novel Zdobycie władzy (first published in French as La prise du pouvoir) 1953; Visiting Lecturer, Univ. of Calif. at Berkeley 1960, Prof. of Slavic Languages and Literatures 1960–78, Prof. Emer. 1978–; Dr hc (Univ. of Michigan, Ann Arbor) 1977, (Catholic Univ. of Lublin 1981), (Brandeis Univ.) 1985, (Harvard Univ.) 1989, (Jageiollonian Univ.) 1989, (Univ. of Bologne) 1992, (Rome Univ.) 1992; mem. American Acad. of Arts and Letters; Polish PEN Club award for poetry translation 1974; Guggenheim Prize 1976; Books Abroad/Neustadt Prize 1978; Nobel Prize for Literature 1980; Order of the White Eagle (Poland) 1994, Order of Gedyminas (Lithuania) 1997. *Publications include:* prose: Zniewolony umysł (The Captive Mind) 1953, Zdobycie władzy (The Usurpers) 1955, Dolina Issy (The Issa Valley) 1955, Native Realm: A Search for Self-Definition 1968, The History of Polish Literature 1969, Emperor of the Earth: Modes of Eccentric Vision (essays) 1977, Striving Towards Being 1997; translations into Polish: The Gospel According to St Mark, The Book of Psalms, The Book of Job, Five Megloth, Book of Wisdom; into English: Post-war Polish Poetry 1965; Ziemia Ulro (The Land of Ulro) 1977, The Separate Notebooks (poems) 1984, The Unattainable Earth (poems) 1986, Collected Poems 1988, Provinces (poems) 1991, Beginning with My Streets: Baltic Reflections (memoirs) 1992, A Year of the Hunter 1994, A Book of Luminous Things 1996, Striving Towards Being 1996, Roadside Dog 1998, Expedition in the Twenties 1999, Szukanie ojczyzny (In Search of a Homeland) 2001; numerous essays, translations; poetry: Światło dzienne (Daylight) 1953, Traktat poetycki (Poetic Treatise) 1957, Król Popiel i inne wiersze (King Popiel and Other Poems) 1962, Gucio zaczarowany (Bobo's Metamorphosis) 1964, Miasto bez imienia (City Without a Name) 1969, Gdzie słońce wschodzi i kędy zapada (From Where the Sun Rises to Where It Sets) 1974, Bells in Winter (poems) 1978, Kroniki (Chronicles) 1988, Facing the River 1994, A Book of Luminous Things 1996, Striving Towards Being 1996, Dzieta zebrane (Collected Works) 1999, To (It) 2000, Traktat poetycki z komentarzem autora (Poetic Treatise with Author's Commentary) 2001, Druga przestrzeń (The Second Space) 2002, Orfeusz i Eurydyka (Orpheus and Euridice) 2002. *Address:* ul. Bogusławskiego 6/5a, 31-048 Kraków; Polish Writers' Association, ul. Kanonicza 7, 31-002 Kraków, Poland (Office). *Telephone:* (12) 4231210 (Office). *Fax:* (12) 4311546 (Office). *E-mail:* ora@labora.pl (Office).

MILOW, Keith; British artist; b. 29 Dec. 1945, London; s. of Geoffrey Keith Milow and the late Joan Ada; ed Camberwell School of Art and Royal Coll. of Art; experimental work at Royal Court Theatre, London 1968; teacher, Ealing School of Art 1968–70; Artist in Residence, Leeds Univ. (Gregory Fellowship) 1970; worked in New York (Harkness Fellowship) 1972–74; teacher, Chelsea School of Art 1975; teacher, School of Visual Arts, New York City 1981–85; lives and works in New York; many one-man exhbns. in England, USA, Belgium, France, Netherlands and Switzerland; over 50 group exhbns. in several countries; works in public collections in 6 countries including Tate Gallery and Victoria and Albert Museum, London, Guggenheim Museum and Museum of Modern Art, New York; Calouste Gulbenkian Foundation Visual Arts Award 1976; equal First Prize Tolly Cobbold/Eastern Arts 2nd Nation Exhbn 1979; Arts Council of GB Major Award. *Address:* 32 West 20th Street, New York, NY 10011, USA. *Telephone:* (212) 929-0124.

MILSOM, Stroud Francis Charles, QC, FBA; British academic; b. 2 May 1923, Merton, Surrey; s. of Harry Lincoln Milsom and Isobel Vida Collins; m. Irène Szereszewski 1955 (died 1998); ed Charterhouse School, Trinity Coll. Cambridge and Univ. of Pennsylvania Law School (as Commonwealth Fund Fellow); Fellow, Trinity Coll. 1948–55; Fellow, Tutor and Dean, New Coll. Oxford 1956–64; Prof. of Legal History, LSE 1964–76; Prof. of Law, Cambridge Univ. 1976–90, Fellow of St John's Coll. 1976–; called to Bar 1947, Hon. Bencher, Lincoln's Inn 1970, QC 1985; Literary Dir Selden Soc. 1964–80, Pres. 1985–88; mem. Royal Comm. on Historical Manuscripts 1975–98; Foreign mem. American Philosophical Soc.; Hon. LLD (Glasgow) 1981, (Chicago) 1985; Ames Prize, Harvard 1972; Swiney Prize, RSA 1974. *Publications:* Novae Narrationes 1963, Introduction to reissue of History of English Law (Pollock and Maitland) 1968, Historical Foundations of the Common Law 1969, 1981, Legal Framework of English Feudalism 1976, Studies in the History of the Common Law 1985. *Address:* St John's College, Cambridge, CB2 1TP; 113 Grantchester Meadows, Cambridge, CB3 9JN, England (Home). *Telephone:* (1223) 354100 (Home).

MILTON-THOMPSON, Sir Godfrey James, KBE, MA, MB, FRCP; British naval surgeon; b. 25 April 1930, Birkenhead, Cheshire; s. of the late Rev. James Milton-Thompson and May L. Hoare; m. Noreen H. F. Fitzmaurice 1952; three d.; ed Eastbourne Coll., Queens' Coll. Cambridge and St Thomas's Hospital, London; joined RN 1955, Sr Specialist in Medicine, RN Hospital, Malta 1962–66; Consultant Physician, RN Hospital, Plymouth 1966–69, 1971–75; Hon. Research Fellow, St Mark's Hospital 1969–70; Prof. of Naval Medicine 1975–80; promoted Surgeon Capt. 1976; Royal Coll. of Defence Studies 1981, Deputy Medical Dir-Gen. (Naval) 1982–84, Medical Dir-Gen. (Naval) 1985–90, Deputy Surgeon-Gen. (Research and Training) 1985–87; promoted Surgeon Rear Adm. 1984, Surgeon Rear-Adm. (Operational Medical Services) 1984; Surgeon Gen., Defence Medical Services in the rank of Surgeon Vice-Adm. 1988–90; Hon. Physician to HM the Queen 1982–90; Chair. Cornwall Community Healthcare Trust 1991–93; Chair. Bd of Govs, St Mary's School, Wantage 1996–; Vice-Pres. British Digestive Foundation 1997–; Warden, St Katharine's House, Wantage 1993–98; Hospitaller, Order of St John 1991–95; Hon. Col 211 (Wessex) Field Hosp., RAMC (V) 1990–95; Chair. St John Council for Cornwall 2000–; KStJ; Errol-Eldridge Prize 1974; Gilbert Blane Medal 1976. *Publications:* contributions to medical and scientific literature on gastroenterology. *Leisure interests:* fishing, literature, collecting East Anglian paintings. *Address:* Pool Hall, Menheniot, Cornwall, PL14 3QT, England.

MILUTINOVIĆ, Milan, LLM; Serbia and Montenegro (Serbian) politician, diplomatist and lawyer; b. 19 Dec. 1942, Belgrade; s. of Aleksandar Milan Milutinović and Ljubica Vladimir Jokić; m. Olga Branko Spasojević; one s.; ed Belgrade Univ.; mem. Presidency of Socialist Youth Union of Yugoslavia 1969–71; MP 1969–74; Sec. Communal Cttee of League of Communists 1972–74; Sec. for Ideology, City Cttee of League of Communists 1974–77; Minister of Science and Educ. of Serbian Repub. 1977–82; Dir Serbian Nat. Library 1983–87; Head of Sector for Press, Information and Culture, Sec. for Foreign Affairs 1987–89; Amb. to Greece 1989–95; Minister of Foreign Affairs Fed. Repub. of Yugoslavia 1995–97; Pres. of Serbia 1997–2003; accused of crimes against humanity and violations of the customs of war by UN War Crimes Tribunal 2001, charged with crimes against humanity and war crimes by Int.Court of Justice, on trial in The Hague Jan. 2003; Order of Merit with Silver Star 1974, Medal for work with Gold Coronet 1980. *Publications include:* University – Eppur si muove! 1985. *Leisure interest:* philately. *Address:* c/o Office of the President, Andrićev venac 1, 11000 Belgrade; Koste Glavinica 9, 11000 Belgrade, Serbia and Montenegro (Home).

MILYUKOV, Yuri Aleksandrovich, CAND. PHYS. AND MATH. SC.; Russian banker; b. 29 April 1957; m.; two s.; ed Moscow Inst. of Physics Eng; researcher, Lebedev Inst. of Physics USSR (now Russian) Acad. of Sciences 1984–87; Chair. Council of Altair 1989–91; f. Moscow Commodity Exchange (MTB) 1990–, Pres. 1993–; mem. Council on Business, Govt of Russian Fed. 1992–; mem. Bd Dirs, Russian Industrialists and Entrepreneurs Union 1992–; mem. Presidium, All-Russian Movt Businessmen for New Russia 1993–94; mem. Co-ordination Council, Round Table of Russian Business 1994–; mem. Beer Lovers Party; mem. Cen. Cttee 1995–; mem. Political Consultative Council of Russian Presidency 1996; Chair. Rosmed; Chair. Russian Union of Stock Exchanges 1991–; Chair. Stock Cttee, Moscow Stock Exchange 1996–; First Deputy Chair. Bd MDM Bank 1997–. *Leisure interest:* theatre. *Address:* Stock Exchange, Mira Prospekt 69, 129223 Moscow (Office); MDM Bank, Zhitnaya Str. 14, 117049 Moscow, Russia (Office). *Telephone:* (095) 187-98-26; (095) 797-95-00 (Office).

MIN HUIFEN; Chinese musician and university professor; b. Nov. 1945, Yixing Co., Jiangsu Prov.; ed Shanghai Music Inst.; Prof. Shanghai Music Inst. 1993–; mem. 5th Nat. Cttee CPPCC 1978–82, 6th 1983–87, 7th 1988–92, 8th 1993–; Prize for Performance, Spring of Shanghai. *Address:* Room 1101 Bldg 151, Weihai Road, Shanghai 200003, People's Republic of China.

MINAH, Francis Misheck, LLM; Sierra Leonean politician and lawyer; b. 19 Aug. 1929, Pujehun; m. Gladys Emuchay; four c.; ed Methodist Boys' High School, Freetown, King's Coll. (London Univ.), Grays Inn, London; Pres. Sierra Leone Students' Union of GB and Ireland 1960–62; mem. House of Reps. 1967–87; Minister of Trade and Industry 1973–75, of Foreign Affairs 1975–77, of Justice 1977–78; Attorney-Gen. 1978; Minister of Finance 1978–80, of Health 1980–82; Attorney-Gen. and Minister of Justice 1982–84; First Vice-Pres. 1985–87; UNESCO Fellowship to study community Devt in India and Liberia; barrister-at-law.

MINCATO, Vittorio; Italian energy company executive; b. 14 May 1936, Torrebelvicino, Vicenza; joined Ente Nazionale Idrocarburi (Eni) Group SpA (oil and gas co.) 1957, various positions including Admin. and Finance Man. Lanerossi (textile co.) 1957–77, Admin. Man. Eni SpA 1977–84, Asst to Chair. 1984–88, Man. Human Resources and Org. 1988–92, Chair. Savio (textile machinery) and Head of Fertilizers Section EniChem 1990–92, Deputy Chair. and Man. Dir EniChem 1993–95, Chair. EniChem 1996–98, Man. Dir Eni SpA 1998–, CEO 2002–, dir numerous other Eni cos including Agip, Lanerossi, Immobiliare Metanopoli, Sofid and Polimeri Europa; mem. Bd Il Sole 24 Ore SpA 2000–, Fondazione Eni Enrico Mattei, Exec. Bd Assonime (Asscn of Italian Ltd Liability Cos) 2001–, Bd Dirs Fondazione Teatro alla Scala, Man. Bd Assolombarda (industrialists' asscn); Cavaliere del Lavoro 2002. *Leisure interests:* classical music (especially Wagner), reading. *Address:* Eni SpA, Piazzale Mattei 1, 00144 Rome, Italy (Office). *Telephone:* (06) 59821 (Office). *Fax:* (06) 59822141 (Office). *E-mail:* segreteriasocietaria.azionisti@eni.it (Office). *Website:* www.eni.it (Office).

MINCKWITZ, Bernhard von; German business executive; b. 11 Aug. 1944, Göttingen; m. Cornelia Böhning; mem. Man. Bd Bertelsmann AG; mem. Bd Süddeutscher Verlag, Man. Dir Süddeutscher Verlag Hüthig Fachinformationen –2002. *Address:* c/o Süddeutscher Verlag GmbH, Emmy-Noether-Str. 2, 80992 Munich, Germany (Office).

MINDADZE, Aleksander Anatol'yevich; Russian scriptwriter; b. 28 April 1949, Moscow; m. Galina Petrovna Orlova; two d.; ed All-Union State Inst. of Cinematography; screenplays since 1972; Merited Worker of Art of Russia, State Prize of Russia 1984, Silver Pegas Prize of Cultural Asscn Ennio Flaiano 1985, USSR State Prize 1991. *Film scripts include:* Say of the Defence 1977 (Prize of All-Union Film Festival, Prize of Lenin's Komsomol), Spring Mobilization 1977 (A. Dovzhenko Silver Medal), Turn 1979, Fox Hunt 1980, The Train has Stopped 1982, Parade of Planets 1985, Plumbum or Dangerous Game 1986, Servant 1991, Armavir 1991, Play for a Passenger 1994, Time for a Dancer 1997. *Address:* Usiyevicha str. 8, Apt. 89, 125319 Moscow, Russia. *Telephone:* (095) 155-75-34 (Home).

MINETA, Norman Yoshio, BS; American politician, insurance broker and transportation executive; b. 12 Nov. 1931, San Jose, Calif.; s. of Kay Kunisaku Mineta and Kane Mineta (née Watanabe); m. Danealia Mineta; two s. two step-s.; ed Univ. of California at Berkeley; agent/broker Mineta Insurance Agency 1956–89; mem. Advisory Bd, Bank of Tokyo in Calif. 1961–75; mem. San Jose City Council 1967–71; Vice-Mayor, City of San Jose 1969–71, Mayor 1971–75; mem. House of Reps. from 13th (now 15th) Calif. Dist 1975–95, Subcttee. on Surface Transportation 1989–92; Sr Vice-Pres. and Man. Dir Transportation Systems and Services, Lockheed Martin 1995–2001; Sec. of Transportation Jan. 2001–; Chair. Nat. Civil Aviation Revenue Comm. 1997; Commr San Jose Human Relations Comm. 1962–64, San Jose Housing Authority 1966–; mem. Bd of Regents, Santa Clara Univ., Smithsonian Nat. Bd 1996–; Hon. DH (Rust Coll.) 1993. *Address:* Department of Transportation, 400 Seventh Street SW, Washington, DC 20590, USA (Office). *Telephone:* (202) 366-5580 (Office). *Fax:* (202) 366-7202 (Office). *Website:* www.dot.gov (Office).

MINFORD, (Anthony) Patrick (Leslie), CBE, PhD; British economist; b. 17 May 1943; s. of Leslie Mackay Minford and Patricia Mary Sale; m. Rosemary Irene Allcorn 1970; two s. one d.; ed Horris Hill, Winchester Coll., Oxford Univ., LSE; Econ. Asst, Ministry of Overseas Devt 1966; Economist, Ministry of Finance, Malawi 1967–69; Econ. Adviser Courtaulds Ltd 1970–71; HM Treasury 1971–73; HM Treasury Del. Washington, DC 1973–74; Visiting Hallsworth Fellow Manchester Univ. 1974–75; Edward Gonner Prof. of Applied Econs, Univ. of Liverpool 1976–97; Visiting Prof. Cardiff Business School 1993–97, Prof. of Econs 1997–; Dir Merseyside Devt Corpn 1988–89; mem. Monopolies and Mergers Comm. 1990–96, Treasury Panel of Independent Econ. Forecasters 1993–96; Ed. Nat. Inst. for Econ. and Social Research Review 1975–76, Liverpool Quarterly Econ. Bulletin 1980–. *Publications:* Substitution Effects, Speculation and Exchange Rate Stability 1978, Unemployment – Cause and Cure 1983, Rational Expectations and the New Macroeconomics 1983, The Housing Morass 1987, The Supply-Side Revolution in Britain 1991, The Cost of Europe (ed.) 1992, Rational Expectations Macroeconomics 1992, Markets not Stakes 1998, Britain and Europe: Choices for Change (with Bill Jamieson) 1999, Advanced Macroeconomics – A Primer (with David Peel) 2002; articles in journals. *Address:* Cardiff Business School, University of Wales Cardiff, Cardiff, CF1 3EU, Wales.

MINGHELLA, Anthony, CBE; British director and playwright; b. 6 Jan. 1954, Isle of Wight; s. of Eddie Minghella and Gloria Minghella; m. Carolyn Choa; one s.and one d. from previous marriage; ed St John's Coll., Sandown High School, Univ. of Hull; fmr drama lecturer, Univ. of Hull; TV includes first series of Inspector Morse (screenplay); Chair. Bd of Govs BFI; Hon. DLitt (Hull) 1997; First Hon. Freeman, Isle of Wight 1997. *Films directed include:* Truly, Madly, Deeply 1991, Mr Wonderful, The English Patient 1997 (Acad. Award for Best Dir, BAFTA for Best Adapted Screenplay), The Talented Mr Ripley 2000. *Plays:* One 1992, Driven to Distraction: A Case for Inspector Morse 1994, Two 1997, The English Patient (screenplay) 1997. *Publications:* Whale Music 1983, Made in Bangkok 1986, Jim Henson's Storyteller 1988, Interior—Room, Exterior—City 1989. *Address:* MacCartendale & Holton,

1640 Fifth Street, Suite 05, Santa Monica, CA 90401, USA (Office); c/o British Film Institute, National Film Theatre, Belvedere Road, South Bank, Waterloo, London, SE1 8XT, England. *E-mail:* anthony.minghella@bfi.org.uk. *Website:* www.bfi.org.uk.

MING-LIANG, Tsai; Taiwanese film director; Venice Golden Lion Award (for Vive l'Amour) 1994, Berlin Silver Bear Award (for The River) 1996. *Films include:* Rebels of the Neon God 1992, Vive l'Amour 1994, The River 1996, The Hole, Last Dance, Dong.

MINGOS, David Michael Patrick, DPhil, FRS; British university professor; b. 6 Aug. 1944, Basrah, Iraq; s. of Vasso Mingos and Rose Enid Billie Griffiths; m. Stacey Mary Hosken 1967; one s. one d.; ed Harvey Grammar School, Folkestone, King Edward VII School, Lytham, Univ. of Manchester, Univ. of Sussex; Fulbright Fellow Northwestern Univ. Ill., USA 1968–70; ICI Fellow Univ. of Sussex 1970–71; lecturer Queen Mary Coll., London Univ. 1971–76; Lecturer in Inorganic Chem. Univ. of Oxford 1976–90, Reader 1990–92; Fellow Keble Coll., Oxford 1976–92; Univ. Assessor 1991–92; Sir Edward Frankland BP Prof. of Inorganic Chem., Imperial Coll., Univ. of London 1992–99; Dean, Royal Coll. of Science 1996–99; Prin. St Edmund Hall, Oxford 1999–; Visiting Prof. Imperial Coll. 1999–2002; visiting professorships in USA, Canada, France, Germany, Switzerland and consultant for various UK and U.S. chem. cos.; Gov. Harrow School; mem. numerous editorial bds.; Hon. DSc (UMIST) 2000, (Sussex) 2001, Corday Morgan Medal, Noble Metal Prize, Tilden Medal of RSC, Manchott Prize 1995, Michael Collins Award for Innovation in Microwave Chemistry 1996, Alexander von Humboldt Forschungs Prize 1999. *Publications:* An Introduction to Cluster Chemistry, Essentials of Inorganic Chemistry 1 1996, Essential Trends in Inorganic Chemistry 1998, Essentials of Inorganic Chemistry 2 1998. *Leisure interests:* cricket, tennis, walking, gardening, travel. *Address:* St. Edmund Hall, Oxford OX1 4AR, England (Office). *Telephone:* (1865) 279003 (Office). *Fax:* (1865) 279030 (Office); (8165) 279033 (Home). *E-mail:* michael.mingos@seh.ox.ac.uk (Office).

MINKIN, Vladimir Isaakovich; Russian chemist; b. 4 March 1935; m.; one d.; ed Rostov State Univ.; Asst, Docent, Prof. Rostov State Univ.; Corresp. mem. USSR (now Russian) Acad. of Sciences 1990, mem. 1994; works on physical and organic chem., quantum chem. of organic compounds, organic photochemistry; mem. Comm. of IUPAC; USSR State Prize. *Publications include:* Dipole Moments in Organic Chemistry 1968, Quantum Chemistry of Organic Compounds 1986. *Leisure interests:* chess, literature. *Address:* Institute of Physical and Organic Chemistry, Stachki pr. 194/3, 344104 Rostov on Don, Russia. *Telephone:* (8632) 28-54-88 (Office).

MINKS, Wilfried; German stage director and designer; b. 21 Feb. 1930, Binai, Czechoslovakia; twin s.; ed Akad. der Künste, Berlin; theatre engagements in Ulm through Intendant Kurt Hübner (worked with Peter Zadek, Peter Palitzsch); Hübner (Intendant), Zadek, Minks, Bremen 1962–73; worked as stage designer with Fassbinder, Gruber, Stein, Zadek, Palitzsch; Prof. of Stage Design, Hochschule für Bildende Kunst, Hamburg 1970–; cr. German Pavilion, Expo 1970, Osaka, Japan; began working as theatre dir 1971; screenplay and direction for film Die Geburt der Hexe 1979. *Exhibition:* Scénographe, Centre Pompidou, Paris 1994. *Address:* Wellingsbüttler Landstr. 166, 22337 Hamburg, Germany. *Telephone:* (40) 503600.

MINNELLI, Liza; American actress and singer; b. 12 March 1946, Los Angeles; d. of the late Vincente Minnelli and Judy Garland; m. 1st Peter Allen 1967 (divorced 1972); m. 2nd Jack Haley, Jr 1974 (divorced 1979); m. 3rd Mark Gero 1979 (divorced 1992); m. 4th David Gest 2002. *Films:* Charlie Bubbles 1968, The Sterile Cuckoo 1969, Tell Me That You Love Me, Junie Moon 1971, Cabaret (played Sally Bowles) 1972 (Acad. Award for Best Actress, The Hollywood Foreign Press Golden Globe Award, the British Acad. Award and David di Donatello Award, Italy), Lucky Lady 1976, A Matter of Time 1976, New York, New York 1977, Arthur 1981, Rent-a-Cop 1988, Arthur 2: On the Rocks 1988, Sam Found Out 1988, Stepping Out 1991, Parallel Lives 1994. *Television includes:* Liza, Liza with a Z (Emmy Award) 1972, Goldie and Liza Together 1980, Baryshnikov on Broadway 1980 (Golden Globe Award), A Time to Live 1985 (Golden Globe Award), My Favourite Broadway: The Leading Ladies 1999. *Theatre:* Best Foot Forward 1963, Flora, the Red Menace 1965 (Tony Award), Chicago 1975, The Act 1977–78 (Tony Award), Liza at the Winter Garden 1973 (Special Tony Award), The Rink 1984, Victor-Victoria 1997. *Recordings:* Liza with a Z, Liza Minnelli: The Singer, Liza Minnelli: Live at the Winter Garden, Tropical Nights, The Act, Liza Minnelli: Live at Carnegie Hall, The Rink, Liza Minnelli at Carnegie Hall, Results 1989, Maybe This Time 1996, Minelli on Minelli 2000. *Address:* Angel EMI Guardian Records, 304 Park Avenue South, New York, NY 10010; Capitol Records Incorporated, 1750 Vine Street, Hollywood, CA 90028, USA.

MINNER, Ruth Ann; American state official; b. 17 Jan. 1935, Milford; m. 1st Frank Ingram (deceased); three s.; m. 2nd Roger Minner (died 1991); ed Del. Tech. and Community Coll.; receptionist to Gov. of Del. 1972–74; mem. Del. House of Reps 1974–82, House Majority Whip; mem. Del. Senate, del. to Gen. Ass. 1982–92; Lt Gov. 1993–2001, Gov. of Del. 2001–. *Leisure interest:* family. *Address:* Office of the Governor, Legislative Hall, Wilmington, DE19801, USA (Office). *Website:* www.state.de.us (Office).

MINOGUE, Kylie Ann; Australian singer and actress; b. 28 May 1968, Melbourne; started acting aged 11 years in Skyways, The Sullivans, then Neighbours 1986 (all TV series); first female vocalist to have her first

(released) five singles obtain silver discs in UK, 9 Logies (Australian TV Industry awards); Woman of the Decade award 1989; Best Int. Solo Female Artist and Best Int. Album 2002. *Records include:* singles include: I Should Be So Lucky 1988, Got To Be Certain 1988, The Loco-Motion 1988, Je Ne Sais Pas Pourquoi 1988, Especially For You (with Jason Donovan, 1988, Hand On Your Heart 1989, Wouldn't Change a Thing 1989, Never Too Late 1989, Tears On My Pillow 1990, Better the Devil You Know 1990, Step Back in Time 1990, What Do I Have To Do 1991, Shocked 1991, If You Were With Me Now (with Keith Washington) 1991, Give Me Just A Little More Time 1992, Confide In Me 1994, Where the Wild Roses Grow (with Nick Cave and The Bad Seeds) 1995, Some Kind of Bliss 1997, Breathe 1998, Spinning Around 2000, On a Night Like This 2000, Kids (with Robbie Williams) 2000, Please Stay 2000, Can't Get You Out of My Head 2001, In Your Eyes 2002, Love at First Sight 2002; albums: Kylie 1988, Enjoy Yourself 1989, Rhythm of Love 1990, Let's Get To It 1991, Kylie – Greatest Hits 1992, Kylie Minogue 1994, Kylie Minogue (Impossible Princess) 1998, Light Years 2000, Fever 2001. *Films:* The Delinquents 1989, Streetfighter 1994, Biodome 1996, Sample People 1999, Cut 1999, Moulin Rouge 2001. *Play:* The Tempest 1999. *Publications:* Kylie 1999. *Address:* c/o Terry Blamey Management Pty Ltd, 329 Montague Street, Albert Park, Vic. 3206, Australia; c/o Terry Blamey Management, PO Box 13196, London, SW6 4WF England. *Telephone:* (20) 7371-7627. *Fax:* (20) 7731-7578. *E-mail:* info@terryblamey.com (Office). *Website:* www.kylie.com (Office).

MINOR, Halsey; American computer executive; ed Univ. of Virginia; investment banker Merrill Lynch Capital Markets, San Francisco 1991; f. Global Publishing Corpn, San Francisco; f. CNET: The Computer Network, San Francisco 1992, Chair., CEO 1992–2000; Chair. CNET Networks Inc. 2000–. *Address:* CNET Networks Inc., 150 Chestnut Street, San Francisco, CA 94111, USA (Office).

MINOVES TRIQUELL, Juli F., MA, M.PHIL.; Andorran diplomatist; b. 15 Aug. 1969, Andorra la Vella; ed Yale Univ.; Counsellor first Perm. Mission of Andorra to the UN 1993–94, Deputy Perm. Rep. and Chargé d'affaires 1994–95, Perm. Rep. 1995–; Alt. Head Andorran del. to World Summit on Social Devt, Copenhagen, Special Plenipotentiary Rep. of Andorran Govt in negotiations to est. diplomatic relations with various govts. 1994–95; Minister of Foreign Affairs 2001–; contrib. to Andorra 7 magazine; literary and journalism awards. *Publications:* a novel and a collection of short stories. *Address:* Ministry of Foreign Affairs, Carrer Prat de la Creu 62–64, Andorra la Vella, Andorra (Office); Permanent Mission of Andorra to the United Nations, 2 United Nations Plaza, 25th Floor, New York, NY 10017, USA (Office). *Telephone:* 875700 (Andorra) (Office); (212) 750-8064 (Office). *Fax:* 869559 (Andorra) (Office); (212) 750-6630 (Office). *E-mail:* andorra@un.int.

MINOW, Newton N., JD; American lawyer; b. 17 Jan. 1926, Milwaukee, Wis.; s. of Jay A. Minow and Doris (Stein) Minow; m. Josephine Baskin 1949; three d.; ed Northwestern Univ.; Law Clerk to Supreme Court Chief Justice Vinson 1951; Admin. Asst to Gov. of Illinois 1952–53; served Stevenson's law firm 1955–57, Partner 1957–61; Chair. Fed. Communications Comm. 1961–63; Exec. Vice-Pres. Gen. Counsel Encyclopaedia Britannica, Chicago 1963–65; mem. Bd of Trustees, Rand Corpn 1965–75, 1976–86, 1987, Chair. 1970–72; Partner, Sidley Austin Brown & Wood (fmrly Leibman, Williams, Bennett, Baird & Minow (and fmrly Sidley & Austin) 1965–91, of counsel 1991–; mem. Bd of Trustees, Carnegie Corpn of New York 1987–97, Chair. 1993–97; Annenberg Univ. Prof., Northwestern Univ. 1987–; Dir The Annenberg Washington Program 1987–96, Big Flower Press 1997–99; Trustee Northwestern Univ. 1975–87 (Life Trustee 1987); Life Trustee, Univ. of Notre Dame; Chair. Arthur Andersen & Co. Public Review Bd 1974–83, Public Broadcasting Service 1978–80; Democrat; Hon. Chair. and Dir Chicago Educational TV Asscn; Hon. LLD (Wisconsin) 1963, (Brandeis) 1963, (Northwestern Univ.) 1965, (Columbia Coll.) 1972, (Notre Dame) 1994, (Santa Clara) 1998. *Publications:* Equal Time: The Private Broadcaster and the Public Interest 1964, Presidential Television (co-author) 1973, Electronics and the Future (co-author) 1977, For Great Debates (co-author) 1987, Abandoned in the Wasteland: Children, Television and the First Amendment 1995. *Leisure interest:* reading. *Address:* Sidley Austin Brown & Wood, 10 S. Dearborn Street, Suite 4800, Chicago, IL 60603 (Office); 179 E Lake Shore Drive, Chicago, IL 60611, USA (Home). *Telephone:* (312) 853-7555 (Office). *Fax:* (312) 853-7036 (Office). *E-mail:* nminow@sidley.com (Office).

MINTER, Alan; British boxer (retd); b. 17 Aug. 1951, Penge, London; s. of Sidney Minter and Anne Minter; m. Lorraine Bidwell 1974; one s. one d.; ed Sarah Robinson School, Ifield; amateur boxer 1965–72; Amateur Boxing Assn (ABA) champion 1971; Olympic bronze medallist 1972; 145 amateur fights, 125 wins; professional boxer 1972–82; won British middleweight championship 1975; won Lonsdale Belt outright 1976; won European championship from Germano Valsecchi Feb. 1977, lost it to Gratien Tonna Sept. 1977; forfeited British title Feb. 1977, regained it Nov. 1977; won vacant European title v. Angelo Jacopucci July 1978, retained it v. Tonna Nov. 1978; relinquished British title Nov. 1978; won world middleweight title from Vito Antuofermo, Las Vegas March 1980 (first British boxer to win a world championship in USA for 63 years); retained title v. Antuofermo June 1980, lost it to Marvin Hagler Sept. 1980; lost European title to Tony Sibson Sept. 1981; retd from boxing Feb. 1982. *Publication:* Minter: An Autobiography 1980. *Leisure interest:* golf.

MINTOFF, Dominic, BSc, B.E.&A., MA, A.&C. E.; Maltese politician; b. 6 Aug. 1916, Cospicua; s. of Lawrence Mintoff and Concetta née Farrugia (deceased); m. Moyra de Vere Bentinck 1947; two d.; ed Univs. of Malta and Oxford; civil engineer in Great Britain 1941–43; practised in Malta as architect 1943–; rejoined and helped reorganize Maltese Labour Party 1944; elected to Council of Govt and Exec. Council 1945; mem. Legis. Ass. 1947; Deputy Leader of Labour Party, Deputy Prime Minister and Minister for Works and Reconstruction 1947–49; resigned Ministry, Leader of Labour Party 1949–85; Prime Minister and Minister of Finance 1955–58; Leader of the Opposition 1962–71; Prime Minister 1971–84, also Minister of Foreign and Commonwealth Affairs 1971–81 (redesig. Ministry of Foreign Affairs 1978), of the Interior 1976–81, 1983–84; Special Adviser to Prime Minister 1985–87; mem. House of Reps. 1987–98; Chair. Malta Counter Trade Co. Ltd. *Publications:* several scientific, literary and artistic works. *Leisure interests:* swimming, water skiing, bocci, horse riding. *Address:* "The Olives", Tarxien, Malta.

MINTON, Yvonne Fay, CBE; Australian mezzo-soprano; b. 4 Dec. 1938, Sydney; d. of R. T. Minton; m. William Barclay 1965; one s. one d.; ed Sydney Conservatorium of Music and studied in London with H. Cummings and Joan Cross; sang with several opera groups in London; début Covent Garden 1965, Prin. Mezzo-soprano 1965–71; U.S. début, Lyric Opera, Chicago (Octavian in Der Rosenkavalier) 1972; Guest Artist, Cologne Opera 1969–, Australian Opera 1972–73, also with Hamburg State Opera and at Bayreuth, Paris, Salzburg, Metropolitan Opera, New York, Munich and San Francisco; recordings include Der Rosenkavalier, Figaro, La Clemenza di Tito, Mozart's Requiem, Elgar's The Kingdom; many concert appearances; created role of Thea in Tippett's The Knot Garden 1970; Hon. ARAM. *Leisure interests:* reading, gardening. *Address:* c/o Ingpen and Williams, 26 Wadham Road, London, SW15 2LR, England. *Telephone:* (20) 8874-3222. *Fax:* (20) 8877-3113.

MINTZ, Shlomo; Israeli violinist; b. 30 Oct. 1957, Moscow; s. of Abraham Mintz and Eve (Labko) Mintz; m. Corina Ciacci; two s.; ed Juilliard School of Music, New York; went to Israel when very young; many concert tours; Premio Accad. Musicale Chigiana, Siena, Italy 1984; Music Dir, conductor, soloist Israel Chamber Orchestra 1989–93; Artistic Adviser Limburg Symphony Orchestra, Netherlands 1994; guest conductor and soloist for numerous orchestras world-wide. *Recordings include:* Violin Concertos by Mendelssohn and Bruch (Grand Prix du Disque, Diapason d'Or) 1981, J. S. Bach Complete Sonatas and Partitas for Solo Violin, The Miraculous Mandarin by Bartok (with Chicago Symphony Orchestra, conducted by Abbado), Compositions and Arrangements by Kreisler (with Clifford Benson, piano), Twenty-four Caprices by Paganini, Two Violin Concertos by Prokofiev (with London Symphony Orchestra, conducted by Abbado), The Four Seasons by Vivaldi (with Stern, Perlman, Mehta). *Address:* ICM Artists Ltd, 40 West 57th Street, Floor 16, New York, NY 10019, USA.

MIOT, Jean Louis Yves Marie; French journalist; b. 30 July 1939, Châteauroux (Indre); s. of René Miot and Madeleine Moreau; two s. three d.; ed Lycée Jean Giraudoux de Châteauroux and Univ. de Poitiers; Ed. Centre Presse, Poitiers 1964–68; journalist, French Antilles 1968–70; Ed.-in-Chief, later Political Dir Havre-Presse 1970–74; Man. Dir France Antilles Martinique Guadeloupe, launched France-Guyane (weekly) 1974–76; Head, Legis. Elections Service, Le Figaro 1977–78; Man. Dir Berry Républicain, Bourges 1978; Dir Groupe de Presse Robert Hersant 1978–79; Political corresp. L'Aurore 1979–80; mem. Man. Bd Société de Gestion and Assoc. Dir Le Figaro 1980–93; Pres. Advisory Bd Le Figaro 1993–96; Pres. Syndicat de la Presse Parisienne 1986–96; Pres. Féd. Nat. de la Presse Française 1993–96; Pres. Agence-France-Presse (AFP) 1996–99, Syndicat des agences de presse de nouvelles (SANOV) 1996–99; Pres.-Dir Gen. Codalie, Financière-CDP and CD-Presse 1999–; mem. Conseil Econ. et Social 1993–96, Comm. de réflexion sur la justice 1997; Dir Société Financière de Radio-Diffusion (SOFIRAD) 1995; many other professional appts.; Chevalier, Légion d'honneur, Officier de l'Etoile Civique, Officer, Order of Lion (Senegal). *Address:* SARL Codalie, 59 avenue Victor Hugo, 75116 Paris (Office); 10 rue Matre Albert, 75005 Paris, France (Home); CD-Presse, 3 chemin du Clos, 95650 Puiseux-Pontoise. *E-mail:* janmio@wanadoo.fr (Home).

MIOU-MIOU; French film actress; b. 22 Feb. 1950, Paris; one d. by the late Patrick Dewaere; one d. by Julien Clerc; worked as child in Les Halles wholesale market; apprenticed in upholstery workshop; with comedian Coluche helped create Montparnasse café-theatre 1968; stage appearance in Marguerite Duras' La Musica 1985. *Films:* La cavale 1971, Themroc 1972, Quelques missions trop tranquilles 1972, Elle court la banlieue 1972, Les granges brûlées 1972, Les aventures de Rabbi Jacob 1972, Les valseuses 1973, La grande Vadrouille 1974, Lily aime-moi 1974, Pas de Problème 1974, Un génie, deux associés, une cloche 1975, La marche triomphale 1975, F. comme Fairbanks 1976, On aura tout vu 1976, Jonas qui aura vingt ans en l'an 2000 1976, Portrait de province en rouge 1977, Dites-lui que je l'aime 1977, Les routes du Sud 1978, Au revoir à lundi 1978, Le grand embouteillage 1978, La Dérobade 1978, La femme flic 1980, Est-ce bien raisonnable? 1980, La gueule du loup 1981, Josépha 1981, Guy de Maupassant 1982, Coup de foudre 1983, Attention, une femme peut en cacher une autre! 1983, Canicule 1983, Blanche et Marie 1984, Tenue de soirée 1986, Ménage, Les portes tournantes 1988, La lectrice, Milou en mai, Netchaiev is Back, The Jackpot, Le Bal des Casse-Pieds, Germinal.

MIQUEL, Pierre Gabriel Roger; French social historian, broadcaster and administrator; b. 30 June 1930, Montluçon, Allier; s. of Jean Miguel and

Suzanne Montagne; m. Maryvonne Jaume 1956; three s.; ed Lycée de Montluçon, Lycée Henri-IV, Paris, Univ. de Paris; teacher, Lycée d'Avignon 1955–56, de Melun 1956–57, Carnot, Paris 1958–59; Asst Faculté des lettres, Univ. de Paris 1961-64, Asst Lecturer, Nanterre 1964–70; Lecturer, Faculté des Lettres, Univ. de Lyon 1970–71, Head Dept Humanities 1971–72, Head Dept TV Documentaries 1972–74; Lecturer, Inst. d'études politiques, Paris 1970–70; Prof. of Mass Communications, Sorbonne 1975–, fmr Admin. Bibliothèque Nat.; at Ministry of Works 1957–58, Ministry of Co-operation 1959–61; Head of Documentaries Antenne 2 1975; Pres. Inst. pratique de journalisme 1978–; Commentary for Les oubliés de l'histoire, France-Inter 1987; Chevalier Palmes académiques, Légion d'honneur, Officer, Arts et Lettres, Diplome d'études supérieures de philosophie, Agrégé d'histoire, Docteur d'Etat. *Publications:* numerous books on social and media history, including L'affaire Dreyfus 1959, Poincaré 1961, La paix de Versailles et l'opinion politique française 1971, Histoire de la radio et de la télévision 1973, Histoire de la France 1976, La véritable histoire des Français 1977, Les oubliés de l'histoire 1978, Les guerres de religion 1980, La quatrième république 1982, La grande guerre 1983, Histoire de la radio et de la télévision, au temps de la grande guerre 1984, La seconde guerre mondiale 1986, La lionne de Belfort 1987, Les hommes de la Grande Guerre 1987, Vive la France 1988, La Grande Révolution 1988, La Troisième République 1989, Les Gendarmes 1990, La Campagne de France de Napoléon ou les Eclairs du Génie 1991, Histoire du monde contemporain 1945–91 1991, Le magasin de chapeaux (novel) 1992, Le Second Empire 1993, La guerre d'Algérie 1993, Les Polytechniciens 1994, Le Monde Bascule 1995, Mourir à Verdun 1995, Vincent de Paul 1996, Petite histoire des fleurs de l'histoire 1997, La main courante, les archives indiscrètes de la police parisienne 1997, Les Poilus d'Orient 1998, Ce siècle avait mille ans 1999, Vive la République, quand même! 1999, Le film du millénaire 2000, Les Poilus 2000, La France et ses paysans 2001, Une histoire du monde rural au XXᵉ siècle 2001, Les rois de l'Elysée 2001. *Leisure interest:* collecting replicas (in tin) of soldiers of the First Empire. *Address:* 24 rue de la Gare, 77135 Pontcarré, France (Home).

MIRAKHOR, Abbas, PhD; Iranian international banking executive and economist; b. 1 July 1941, Tehran; m. Loretta Thomas 1965; two s.; ed Kansas State Univ., USA; Asst and Assoc. Prof. and Chair. Dept of Econs, Univ. of Alabama 1968–77, Prof. and Chair. Dept 1977–79, Vice-Chancellor 1979–80; Az-Zahra Univ., Tehran; Prof. and Chair. Grad. Study Dept, Alabama A&M Univ. 1980–83; Prof. of Econs Fla Inst. of Tech. 1983–84; Economist, IMF 1984–87, Sr Economist 1987–90, Exec. Dir 1990–. *Publications:* numerous articles on Econs. *Address:* International Monetary Fund, 700 19th Street, N.W., Washington, DC 20431, USA (Office). *Telephone:* (202) 623-7370 (Office). *Fax:* (202) 623-4966 (Office). *E-mail:* amirakhor@imf.org (Office).

MIRANI, Aftab Shahban; Pakistani politician; b. Shikarpur; s. of Ghulam Kadir Shahban Mirani and Begum Sharfunisa Shahban Mirani; m.; one s. three d.; ed studies in farm man. and agric. in USA; fmr Pres. Shikarpur Municipality; mem. Sindh Provincial Ass. (Pakistan People's Party) 1977–90; Chief Minister of Sindh –1990; mem. Nat. Ass. 1990–; Minister of Defence 1993–96. *Leisure interests:* walking, swimming. *Address:* Shikarpur, Pakistan.

MIRICIOIU, Nelly; Romanian opera singer; b. 31 March 1952, Adjud; d. of Voicu Miricioiu and Maria Miricioiu; ed Conservatoire G. Enesco, Iassy; professional début as Queen of the Night in The Magic Flute in Romania 1970; western European début as Violetta in Scottish Opera production of La Traviata 1981; début at Convent Garden as Nedda in Pagliacci 1982, at La Scala as Lucia in Lucia di Lammermoor 1983; has since appeared at many of the other opera houses of the world including Verona, San Francisco, Vienna, Berlin, Hamburg, Madrid, Florence and in recitals and concerts; repertoire includes Mimi (La Bohème), Julietta (I Capuleti e I Montecchi), Gilda (Rigoletto), Marguerite and Elena (Mefistofele), Michaela (Carmen), Marguerite (Faust), Violetta (La Traviata), Manon Lescaut; repertoire also includes Anna Bolena and Lucrezia Borgia (by Donizetti), Norma (Bellini), Tancredi (Rossini), Elisabeth (Don Carlos) 1996; made first recording, recital Wigmore Hall, London 1986; winner of 10 int. competitions. *Leisure interests:* literature, television, cooking, socializing. *Address:* c/o Royal Opera House (Contracts), Covent Garden, London, WC2E 9DD (Office); 53 Midhurst Avenue, Muswell Hill, London, N.10, England. *Telephone:* (20) 8883-8596.

MIRONOV, Oleg Orestovich, LLD; Russian lawyer; b. 5 June 1939, Pyatigorsk; m.; one s.; ed Saratov Inst. of Law; local investigator Pyatigorsk 1964; teacher, Prof. Constitutional Law Dept Saratov Inst. of Law; State Duma Deputy with CP of Russian Fed. 1993–95; mem., State Duma for Saratov Region 1995–98; mem. Cttee on Law and Legal Reform; mem. Central Cttee of CP of Russian Fed. –1998; Commr on Human Rights (Ombudsman) in Russian Fed. 1998–; mem. Interparl. Ass. of CIS, Acad. of Social Sciences, Russian Acad. of Lawyers; Honoured Jurist of Russian Fed. *Publications:* about 200 articles including monographs on problems of constitutional law, theory of state and law, politology. *Leisure interests:* mountain tourism, sports. *Address:* Office of the Commissioner on Human Rights in the Russian Federation, Myasnitskaya str. 47, Moscow, Russia. *Telephone:* (095) 207-76-30 (Office).

MIRONOV, Sergey Mikhailovich, CAND.JUR; Russian politician and jurist; b. 14 Feb. 1953, Pushkin, Leningrad region; m.; one s. one d.; ed Plekhanov Ore Inst., St Petersburg State Tech. Univ., North-Western Acad. of Civil Service, St Petersburg State Univ.; army service 1971–73; engineer Rusgeophysica (production co.), Sr Geophysicist in Mongolia until 1991; Exec. Dir Russian Trade Chamber 1991–93, Construction Corpn – Restoration of St Petersburg 1993–94; mem., First Deputy Chair., then Chair. Legis. Ass. of St Petersburg 1994–2000; Head Political Council Volya Peterburga (regional, political, public Movt), St Petersburg 2000–01; Rep. of St Petersburg Ass. to Council of Feds., June 2001, Chair. Council of Fed. Nov. 2001–. *Address:* Council of Federation, B. Dmitrovka str. 26, 103426 Moscow, Russia (Office). *Telephone:* (095) 292-06-89 (Office). *Fax:* (095) 292-65-45 (Office).

MIRONOV, Yevgeniy Vitalyevich; Russian actor; b. 29 Nov. 1966, Saratov; s. of Vitaly Sergeyevich Mironov and Tamara Petrovna Mironova; ed Saratov School of Theatre Art, Studio School of Moscow Art Theatre; actor Oleg Tabakov Theatre-Studio 1990–; Merited Artist of Russia 1996. *Films include:* roles in films by A. Kaidanovsky, A. Mitta, V. Todorovsky, Khotinenko, D. Yevstigneyev, N Mikhalkov, S. Gazarov including Flutist (Wife of a Keroseneman 1989), Volodya (Lost in Siberia 1989), Sasha (Love 1990-Prize for best Kinotaurus Festival 1992), Constellation 1992, Young Stars of Europe, Geneva 1992, Cinema Critics Prize-Best Actor of the Year 1992, Volodya Poletayev (Encore, Another Encore 1991-Prize of Cinema Critics-Best Actor of the Year 1993), Kolya (Moslem 1995-Cinema Critics Prize-Best Actor of the Year 1995), Misha Vuloch (Limita 1994-Nika Prize 95), Kolya (Burnt of the Sun 1993-Prize for Supporting Actor, Constellation-95), Khlestakov (Inspector-Prize for Best Actor Role, Ural Festival 1996). *Theatre roles include:* David Schwartz (Matrosskaya Tishina, A. Galich), Aleksander Aduyev (Common Story, Goncharov), Bumbarash (Passions over Bumbarash, Kim), Orestes (Oresteia, Aeschylus), Ivan Karamazov (The Brothers Karamazov and Hell, Dostoyevsky), Maratov (The Last Night of the Last Tsar, Radzinsky). *Address:* Oleg Tabakov Theatre-Studio, Chaplygina str. 12A, Moscow, Russia. *Telephone:* (095) 916-21-21 (Office); 264-15-58 (Home).

MIRREN, Helen; British actress; b. 26 July 1945, London; m. Taylor Hackford 1997; first experience with Nat. Youth Theatre culminating in appearance as Cleopatra in Antony and Cleopatra, Old Vic 1965; joined RSC 1967 to play Castiza in The Revenger's Tragedy and Diana in All's Well that Ends Well; Dr. hc (St. Andrews) 1999. *Other roles include:* Cressida in Troilus and Cressida, Hero in Much Ado About Nothing, RSC, Stratford 1968; Win-the-Fight Littlewit in Bartholomew Fair, Aldwych 1969, Lady Anne in Richard III, Stratford, Ophelia in Hamlet, Julia in The Two Gentlemen of Verona, Stratford 1970 (the last part also at Aldwych), Tatyana in Enemies, Aldwych 1971; title role in Miss Julie, Elyane in The Balcony, The Place 1971; with Peter Brook's Centre International de Recherches Théâtrales, Africa and USA 1972–73; Lady Macbeth, RSC, Stratford 1974 and Aldwych 1975; Maggie in Teeth 'n' Smiles, Royal Court 1975; Nina in The Seagull and Ella in The Bed Before Yesterday, Lyric for Lyric Theatre Co. 1975; Margaret in Henry VI (Parts 1, 2 and 3), RSC 1977–78; Isabella in Measure for Measure, Riverside 1979; The Duchess of Malfi, Manchester Royal Exchange 1980 and Roundhouse 1981; The Faith Healer, Royal Court 1981; Antony and Cleopatra 1983, 1998, The Roaring Girl, RSC, Barbican 1983, Extremities (Evening Standard Award) 1984, Madame Bovary 1987, Two Way Mirror 1989; Sex Please, We're Italian, Young Vic 1991; The Writing Game, New Haven, Conn. 1993, The Gift of the Gorgon (New York) 1994; A Month in the Country 1994, Orpheus Descending 2001, Dance of Death (New York) 2001. *Films include:* Age of Consent 1969, Savage Messiah, O Lucky Man! 1973, Caligula 1977, The Long Good Friday, Excalibur 1981, Cal (Best Actress, Cannes) 1984, 2010 1985, White Nights 1986, Heavenly Pursuits 1986, The Mosquito Coast 1987, Pascali's Island 1988, When the Whales Came 1988, Bethune: The Making of a Hero 1989, The Cook, the Thief, His Wife and Her Lover 1989, The Comfort of Strangers 1989, Where Angels Fear to Tread 1990, The Hawk, The Prince of Jutland 1991, The Madness of King George 1995, Some Mother's Son 1996, Killing Mrs Tingle 1998, The Pledge 2000, No Such Thing 2001, Greenfingery 2001, Gosford Park (Screen Actors' Guild Award for Best Supporting Actress) 2001. *Television includes:* Miss Julie, The Apple Cart, The Little Minister, As You Like It, Mrs. Reinhardt, Soft Targets 1982, Blue Remembered Hills, Coming Through, Cause Celebre, Red King White Knight, Prime Suspect (BAFTA Award) 1991, Prime Suspect II 1992, Prime Suspect III 1993, Prime Suspect: Scent of Darkness 1996 (Emmy Award 1996), Painted Lady 1997, The Passion of Ayn Rand 1998. *Address:* c/o Ken McReddie Ltd, 91 Regent Street, London, W1R 7TB, England.

MIRRLEES, Sir James Alexander, Kt, MA, PhD, FBA; British professor of economics; b. 5 July 1936, Scotland; s. of the late George B. M. Mirrlees; m. 1st Gillian M. Hughes 1961 (died 1993); two d.; m. 2nd Patricia Wilson 2001; ed Edinburgh Univ. and Trinity Coll., Cambridge; Adviser, MIT Center for Int. Studies, New Delhi 1962–63; Asst Lecturer in Econs and Fellow, Trinity Coll., Univ. of Cambridge 1963, Univ. Lecturer 1965; Research Assoc. Pakistan Inst. of Devt Econs 1966–67; Fellow, Nuffield Coll. and Edgeworth Prof. of Econs Univ. of Oxford 1968–95; Prof. of Political Economy, Univ. of Cambridge, Fellow Trinity Coll. 1995–; Adviser to Govt of Swaziland 1963; Visiting Prof. MIT 1968, 1970, 1976, 1987; Ford Visiting Prof., Univ. of Calif. at Berkeley 1986; Visiting Prof., Yale Univ. 1989; mem. Treasury Cttee on Policy Optimization 1976–78; Pres. Econometric Soc. 1982, Royal Econ. Soc. 1989–92, European Econ. Asscn 2000; Foreign Assoc. NAS; Hon. DLitt (Warwick) 1982, (Portsmouth) 1997, (Oxford) 1998; Hon. DScS (Brunel) 1997; Hon. DSc (Social Sciences) (Edin.) 1997; Nobel Prize for Econ. 1996; Foreign Hon. mem. American Acad. of Arts and Sciences; Hon. mem. American Econ. Asscn; Hon. Fellow Royal Soc. of Edin. *Publications:* Jt author of three books and articles in academic journals. *Leisure interests:* music, travel, computing. *Address:* Trinity College, Cambridge, CB2 1TQ, England. *Telephone:* (1223) 339516. *Fax:* (1223) 335475. *E-mail:* jam28@cam.ac.uk (Office).

MIRSAIDOV, Shukurulla Rakhmatovich, DEcon; Uzbekistan politician; b. 14 Feb. 1938, Leninabad; m.; four c.; ed Tashkent Finance and Econ. Inst.; mem. CPSU 1962–91; on staff State Planning Org. 1964–84; Head Cen. Statistical Dept, Uzbek SSR 1984–85; Chair. Tashkent City Council 1985–86; Head of Dept, CP of Uzbekistan 1988–89; Deputy Premier of Uzbekistan SSR 1989–90; Chair. Council of Ministers 1990–92; Vice-Pres. of Uzbekistan 1991–92; State Sec. for Pres. Karimov 1992; rep. Int. Fund for Privatization and Investments in Uzbekistan 1992–95; now in pvt. business. *Address:* International Fund for Privatization, Tashkent, Uzbekistan.

MIRVISH, David, CM; Canadian theatrical producer; b. 29 Aug. 1944; s. of Edwin Mirvish (q.v.), CBE and Anne Macklin; producer and owner of the Old Vic Theatre, London and The Royal Alexandra and The Princess of Wales Theatres, Toronto; productions and co-productions include: Candide and Too Clever by Half (London), Into the Woods (London), Les Misérables (Canada), The Good Times Are Killing Me (New York), Miss Saigon, Crazy for You, Tommy (Toronto); Dir Williamstown Theatre Festival, USA –1992, Nat. Gallery of Canada, Nat. Theatre School of Canada 1989–91, Toronto French School; mem. Canadian Cultural Property Export Review Bd 1983–86; Rayne Award (Royal Nat. Theatre); Toronto Theatre Alliance (Dora) Humanitarian Award, Toronto Arts Award 1994. *Address:* The Old Vic, Waterloo Road, London, SE1 8NB, England; Mirvish Productions, 266 King Street W, Toronto, Ont., Canada. *Telephone:* (20) 7928-2651 (London); (416) 593-0351 (Toronto).

MIRVISH, Edwin (Ed), OC, CBE; Canadian impresario; b. 24 July 1914, Colonial Beach, Va, USA; m. Anne Maklin 1941; one s. (David Mirvish, q.v.); opened Honest Ed's (Bloor Street Retail Bargain Emporium), Markham St, Toronto in 1940s; bought Royal Alexandra Theatre, Toronto 1962, bought Old Vic Theatre, London, UK 1982; Pres. and CEO Honest Ed's Ltd, Royal Alexandra Theatre; Dir Mirvish Enterprises; opened Ed's Unusual Theatre Museum 1991; bought (with son) Canadian rights to musical Les Misérables 1988; built Princess of Wales Theatre, Toronto 1993; Markham St, Toronto officially renamed Mirvish Village 1984; Mirvish Productions have won Dora Awards in Canada and 5 Olivier Awards in UK, nominated for Tony Awards in USA; Hon. LLD (Trent, Waterloo, McMaster, York); numerous honours and awards including Order of Ont., Order of Merit, City of Toronto, Distinguished Retailer of the Year Award, Retail Council of Canada, Drama Bench (Toronto) Award for distinguished contrib. to Canadian theatre, Freeman City of London. *Publications:* How to Build an Empire on an Orange Crate (autobiog.) 1993, There's No Business Like Showbusiness 1997. *Leisure interest:* ballroom dancing. *Address:* Honest Ed's Ltd, 581 Bloor Street W, Toronto, Ont., M6G 1K3, Canada (Office). *Telephone:* (416) 537-2111.

MIRZA, Jamil Ahmed; Pakistani artist and industrialist; b. 21 Feb. 1921, Delhi, India; c. of Mirza Noor Ahmed and of Sughra Begum; m.; three s. two d.; ed St. Joseph High School, Bombay (now Mumbai), India, Sir J. J. School of Art, Bombay; Film Art Dir, Calcutta (now Kolkata), India 1945–49; f. Elite Publishers Ltd, Karachi 1951, developed photo-offset printing, electronic colour scanning and invented computerised Urdu calligraphy 1981; Fellow Sir J. J. School of Arts 1944; mem. Rotary Club 1965, Dist Gov. 1974; DLitt hc (Karachi) 1999; numerous art, civil and professional awards, including First Prize, Dolly Gursetji Mural Decoration 1942, three Best Entry Awards, All India Art in Industry 1943, Tamgha-I-Imtiaz (Medal of Distinction), Govt of Pakistan 1982, Rotary Int. Meritorious Services Award 1993, Lifetime Achievement Award, Pakistan Asscn of Printing and Graphics Art Industry 2001. *Exhibitions include:* Bombay Art Soc. 1928–43, The Children's Royal Acad., London, UK 1936, Royal Drawing Soc., London, UK 1936–37, All India Art Industry 1943–45. *Publications include:* Urdu Lexicon of Ligatures 1995. *Leisure interests:* painting, travelling, sports. *Address:* Elite Publishers Ltd., D-118, SITE, Karachi 75700 (Office); Al-Noor, 23-B/6, PECHS, Karachi 75400, Pakistan (Home). *Telephone:* (21) 2562351 (Office); (21) 4547880 (Home). *Fax:* (21) 2564720 (Office); (21) 4559011 (Home). *E-mail:* elite@elite.com.pk (Office); ami@elite.com.pk (Home).

MIRZABEKOV, Andrei Daryevich, D.CHEM.; Russian molecular biologist; b. 19 Oct. 1937, Baku; m. Nataly Romanov 1964; one d.; ed Inst. of Fine Chemical Technology, Moscow; Lab. Asst W Engelhardt Inst. of Molecular Biology of USSR Acad. of Sciences 1961, later Jr Researcher, Chief of Dept, Deputy Dir 1984, Dir 1985–; fmr Academician-Sec. Biophysics, Biochem. and Chem. of Physiologically Active Compounds Div. USSR Acad. of Sciences; Visiting Scientist, MRC Lab. of Molecular Biology, Cambridge, UK 1971, Calif. Inst. of Tech. Pasadena and Harvard Univ. 1975; Vice-Pres. Int. Human Genome Org. (HUGO) 1989–; mem. USSR (now Russian) Acad. of Sciences 1987, Academia Europaea 1990; USSR State Prize 1969; FEBS Anniversary Prize 1978; Gregor Mendel Medal, Deutsche Akad. der Naturforscher Leopoldina. *Publications:* contribs. to professional journals. *Leisure interests:* philosophy, hiking, skiing. *Address:* W. A. Engelhardt Institute of Molecular Biology, Vavilov Street 32, Moscow 117984, Russia. *Telephone:* (095) 135-23-11 (Office); (095) 331-32-79 (Home).

MIRZOEFF, Edward, CVO, CBE, MA; British television producer, director and executive producer; b. 11 April 1936, London; s. of the late Eliachar Mirzoeff and of Penina Asherov; m. Judith Topper 1961; three s.; ed Hasmonean Grammar School, Queen's Coll. Oxford; market researcher, Social

Surveys (Gallup Poll) Ltd 1958–59, Public Relations Exec., Duncan McLeish & Assocs. 1960–61; Asst Ed. Shoppers' Guide 1961–63; with BBC TV 1963–2000, Exec. Producer, Documentaries 1983–2000; Dir and producer of many film documentaries including: (with Sir John Betjeman) Metro-land 1973, A Passion for Churches 1973, The Queen's Realm 1977; Police – Harrow Road 1975, The Regiment 1977, The Front Garden 1979, The Ritz 1981, The Englishwoman and The Horse 1981, Elizabeth R (marking the Queen's 40th anniversary) 1992, Torvill and Dean – Facing the Music 1994, Treasures in Trust 1995, John Betjeman – The Last Laugh 2001; Ed. 40 Minutes (BBC) 1985–89; Ed. many documentary series including Real Lives 1985, Pandora's Box 1992, The Ark 1993, True Brits 1994, Situation Vacant 1995, The House 1995, Full Circle with Michael Palin 1997, The Fifty Years War: Israel and the Arabs 1998, Children's Hosp. 1998–2000; Producer, Richard Dimbleby Lectures 1972–82, A. J. P. Taylor Lectures (three series); Exec. Producer, The Lord's Tale 2002; Chair. BAFTA 1995–97 (Vice-Chair., TV 1991–95); Trustee BAFTA 1999–; Trustee Grierson Memorial Trust 1999–, Vice-Chair 2000–02, Chair. 2002–; mem. Bd Directors' and Producers' Rights Soc. 1999–; Salisbury Cathedral Council 2002–; BAFTA Awards: Best Documentary 1981, Best Factual Series 1985, 1989, Alan Clarke Award for outstanding creative contribution to TV 1995; Samuelson Award, Birmingham Festival 1988, BFI TV Award 1988, British Video Award 1992, Broadcasting Press Guild Award 1996, Royal Philharmonic Soc. Music Award 1996, Int. Emmy 1996. *Leisure interests:* exploring the London Library, walking in Wiltshire, visiting Venice, mowing lawns. *Address:* 9 Westmoreland Road, London, SW13 9RZ, England. *Telephone:* (20) 8748-9247.

MIRZOYAN, Edvard Mikhailovich; Armenian composer; b. 12 May 1921, Gori, Georgian SSR; s. of Mikhail Mirzoyan and Luciné Mirzoyan; m. Elena M. Stepanyan 1951; two c.; ed Yerevan Conservatory, Moscow Conservatory; teacher Komitas Conservatory, Yerevan, Armenia 1948–, Prof. 1965–; mem. CPSU 1952–90; Pres. Union of Composers of Armenian SSR 1957–91; Sec. USSR Union of Composers 1962–90; mem. Cen. Cttee of Armenian CP 1964–90; Deputy of Supreme Soviet of Armenian S.S.R.C.P. 1959–90; People's Deputy of USSR 1989–91; mem. USSR Supreme Soviet 1990–91; Pres. Armenian Peace Fund 1978–; Armenian Meritorious Artist 1958; Armenian People's Artist 1963; USSR People's Artist 1981; Order of Cyril and Methodius, Bulgaria 1981. *Compositions include:* Symphonic Dances 1946, Soviet Armenia (cantata), To the Heroes of the War (Symphonic poem), Symphony of Light (ballet), Symphony for strings and timpani 1962, Sonata for cello and piano 1967, Poem for Piano, Lyrical Picture "Shushanik" 1973, In Memory of Aram Khachaturyan 1988, Album for my Granddaughter 1988, Poem for Cello and Piano 1995, Circle "Seasons" based on the words of Chinese poets 1997; string quartet, romances, instrumental pieces, songs, film-music. *Address:* c/o Armenian Composers' Union, Demirchyan Street 25, Apt. 9, 375002 Yerevan, Armenia. *Telephone:* (2) 52-92-59. *Fax:* (2) 72-36-39.

MIRZOYEV, Gasan Borisovich; Russian lawyer; b. 11 Dec. 1947, Baku, Azerbaijan; ed Azerbaijan State Univ., Moscow Inst. of Man.; State Arbiter of Moscow 1987–; Founder and Chair. Moscow State Center on Legal Assistance, later Moscow Legal Centre 1993–, leading to creation of Russian Lawyers Guild; Rector and mem. Russian Bar Acad.; Vice-pres. Russian Acad. of Natural Sciences; Pres. Human Rights Bd Int. Informatization Acad.; mem. Political Council, Union of Right Forces; Pres. Russian Lawyers Guild 1994–; Deputy State Duma of Russian Fed. 1999–; Chair. Ed. Bd Rossiyskiy Advokat; Merited Lawyer of Russia. *Publications:* over 100 including monographs on problems of legal protection of business in Russia and protection of human rights; essays and articles. *Leisure interest:* chess. *Address:* Russian Lawyers Guild, Maly Poluyaroslavsky per. 3/5, 107120 Moscow, Russia. *Telephone:* (095) 916-12-48 (Office). *Fax:* (095) 975-24-16 (Office). *E-mail:* grusadvocat@mtu-net.ru (Office).

MIRZOYEV, Ramason Zarifovich; Tajikistan diplomatist; b. 15 Feb. 1945, Kulyab Region; m.; six c.; ed Tadjik Inst. of Agric.; worked with construction teams Kulyab Region; in Afghanistan 1975–78; since 1983 worked in CP bodies and orgs.; USSR People's Deputy 1989–92; Deputy Chair. USSR Supreme Soviet 1989–91; Man. Council of Ministers Repub. of Tajikistan 1992–95; Amb. of Tajikistan to Russian Fed. 1995–2001; Amb. to Iran 2001–. *Address:* Ministry of Foreign Affairs, Rudaki Prosp. 42, 73405 Dushanbe, Tajikistan. *Telephone:* (2) 211808.

MISCHNICK, Wolfgang; German politician; b. 29 Sept. 1921; s. of Walter Mischnick and Marie Rölig; m. Christine Dietzsch 1949; two s. one d.; ed High School, Dresden; Co-Founder, Liberal Democratic Party, Dresden 1945; town official, Dresden 1946–48; mem. Cen. Cttee of Liberal Democratic Party, Soviet Zone 1946–48; fled to FRG 1948; mem. Prov. Ass., Hesse, 1954–57, Parl. Leader of FDP; Fed. Chair. FDP Youth Movement and Ed. Stimmen der jungen Generation 1954–57; mem. Bundestag 1957–94; Deputy Chair. FDP, Hesse 1957–67, Chair. 1967–77; Fed. Minister for Refugees 1961–63; Deputy Chair. FDP 1964–88, FDP Chair. in Bundestag 1968–77; Chair. Supervisory Bd Gröditzer Stahlwerke GmbH 1991; Hon. Chair. FDP Hessen. *Leisure interests:* sport (especially football), music, history.

MISHCON, Baron (Life Peer), cr. 1978, of Lambeth in Greater London; **Victor Mishcon;** British solicitor and politician; b. 14 Aug. 1915; s. of Rabbi Arnold Mishcon and Queenie Mishcon; m. Joan Estelle Conrad 1976; two s. one d. by previous marriage; ed City of London School; mem. Lambeth Borough Council 1945–49, Chair. Finance Cttee 1947–49; mem. for Brixton London Co. Council 1946–65, Chair. Public Control Cttee 1947–52, Gen.

Purposes Cttee 1952–54, Council 1954–55, Supplies Cttee 1956–57, Fire Brigade Cttee 1958–65; mem. for Lambeth, GLC 1964–67, Chair. Gen. Purposes Cttee 1964–67; mem. Inner London Educ. Authority 1964–67; contested parl. seat (Labour) Leeds NW 1950, Bath 1951, Gravesend 1955, 1959; mem. Jt Cttee on Consolidation of Bills 1983–85, Law Sub-Cttee, House of Lords European Communities Cttee 1978–86, House of Lords Select Cttee on Procedure 1981–83, House of Lords Select Cttee on Medical Ethics 1993; Opposition Spokesman on Home Affairs, House of Lords 1983–90, on Legal Affairs 1983–92; Vice-Chair. Lords and Commons Solicitors Group 1983–; solicitor, later Sr Partner Mishcon de Reya (fmrly Victor Mishcon and Co.) 1988–92, now Consultant; Gov. and Chair. Bd of Govs. various schools in UK 1947–85; mem. Standing Jt Cttee, Co. of London Sessions 1950–65, Vice-Chair. 1959–61, Nat. Theatre Bd 1965–67, 1968–90, South Bank Theatre Bd 1977–82, London Orchestra Bd 1966–67, Exec. Cttee London Tourist Bd 1965–67; mem. Govt Cttee of Enquiry into London Transport 1953–54, Departmental Cttee on Homosexual Offences and Prostitution 1954–57; Vice-Chair. Council of Christians and Jews 1976–77; Vice-Pres. Bd of Deputies of British Jews 1967–73; Hon. Pres. British Technion Soc.; Vice-Pres. (Past Pres.) Asscn of Jewish Youth; Pres. British Council of the Shaare Zedek Hosp., Jerusalem; Hon. QC 1992; Hon. Fellow Univ. Coll. London 1993; Hon. LLD (Birmingham) 1991; Commdr Royal Swedish Order of North Star 1954, Star of Ethiopia 1954, Star of Jordan 1995; DL Greater London 1954. *Leisure interests:* theatre, music, reading. *Address:* House of Lords, London, SW1A 0PW; 21 Southampton Row, London, W.C.1, England.

MISTRY, Dhruva, RA, MA; Indian sculptor; b. 1 Jan. 1957, Kanjari; s. of Pramodray Mistry and Kantaben Mistry; ed Univ. of Baroda and RCA, London; British Council Scholar 1981–83; Artist in Residence Churchill Coll., Cambridge 1984–85; Freelance Sculptor-Agent Nigel Greenwood Gallery, London; Sculptor in Residence, Victoria and Albert Museum, London 1988; Rep. GB for the Grand Rodin Prize Exhbn, Japan 1990; public collections Tate Gallery, British Council, Arts Council, Victoria and Albert Museum, Walker Art Gallery, Nat. Museum of Wales, Hakone Open Air Museum, Japan; Hon. CBE. *Solo exhibitions include:* Kettle's Yard Gallery, Cambridge 1985, tour to Arnolfini, Bristol 1986, Mostyn Art Gallery, Llandudno 1986, Walker Art Gallery, Liverpool 1986, Nigel Greenwood Gallery, London 1987, 1990, Collins Gallery, Strathclyde 1988. *Publications:* (Exhbn catalogues) Sculptures and Drawings 1985, Cross-sections 1988, Dhruva Mistry, Bronzes 1985–1990. *Leisure interests:* photography, reading, walking. *Address:* c/o Anthony Wilkinson Gallery, 242 Cambridge Heath Road, London, E2 9DA, England.

MISTRY, Rohinton, BA; Canadian author; b. 3 July 1952, Bombay (now Mumbai), India; m. Freny Elavia 1975; ed St Xavier's High School, Bombay, Univ. of Bombay, Univ. of Toronto, Canada; took lessons in music theory and composition; mem. folk-singing band; moved to Canada 1975; clerk and accountant Canadian Imperial Bank of Commerce, Toronto 1975–85; began writing short stories 1982; novels have been translated into German, Swedish, Norwegian, Danish and Japanese; Hon. PhD (Ottawa) 1996; Hart House Literary Prize (two) 1985, Contributor's Prize, Canadian Fiction Magazine 1985, Gov.-Gen.'s Award 1991, Commonwealth Writer's Prize for Best Book 1991, First Novel Award, W.H. Smith/Books in Canada 1991, Giller Prize 1995, Winfried Holtby Prize, RSL 1995, Los Angeles Times Award for Fiction 1996. *Publications include:* Coming Attraction (short stories) 1986, Tales from Firozsha Baag 1987, Swimming Lessons and Other Stories from Firozsha Baag (short stories) 1989, Such a Long Journey (novel) 1991, A Fine Balance (novel) 1995, Family Matters (novel) 2002. *Address:* c/o Bruce Westwood, Westwood Creative Artists Ltd., 94 Harbord Street, Toronto, Ont. M5S 1G6, Canada (Office).

MITA, Katsushige, BEE; Japanese business executive; b. 6 April 1924, Tokyo; s. of Yoshitaro and Fuji Mita; m. Toriko Miyata 1957 (died 1989); two d.; ed Univ. of Tokyo; joined Hitachi Ltd 1949; Gen. Man. Omika Works Aug.–Nov. 1971, Kanagawa Works 1971–75, Dir 1975; Man. Computer Group 1976–78, Exec. Man. Dir 1977–79, Sr Exec. Man. Dir 1979–80, Exec. Vice-Pres. 1980–81; Pres. and Rep. Dir Hitachi Ltd 1981–91, Chair. and Rep. Dir 1991–2000; Vice-Chair. Keidanren (Japan Fed. of Econ. Orgs.) 1992–; Dr. hc (Tufts Univ., USA) 1991; Blue Ribbon Medal (Japan) 1985; Officier, Légion d'honneur 1993; DSPN Dato (Malaysia) 1993; Will Rogers Award (USA) 1994. *Leisure interests:* golf, gardening. *Address:* 2423-277, Nara-machi, Aoba-ku, Yokohama-shi, Kanagawa-ken, 227, Japan (Home).

MITCHELL, Adrian; British poet and playwright; b. 24 Oct. 1932, London; s. of James Mitchell and Kathleen Mitchell; ed Christ Church Coll., Oxford; Fellowships at Univs of Lancaster 1967–69, Wesleyan Coll. 1972, Cambridge 1980–81, Royal Soc. of Literature 1987; Dr hc (N London Univ.); Gold Medal of the Theatre of Poetry, Varna, Bulgaria; Shadow Poet Laureate (apptd by Red Pepper magazine). *Films:* Man Friday 1975, The Tragedy of King Real 1982. *Music:* The Ledge (opera libretto) 1961, Houdini (opera libretto) 1977, Start Again (oratorio) 1998, The Princess Robot (opera libretto) 2003. *Plays:* Tyger and Tyger Two, Man Friday, Mind Your Head, A Seventh Man, White Suit Blues, Uppendown Money, Hoagy, In the Unlikely Event, Satie Day/ Night, The Pied Piper, The Snow Queen, Jemima Puddleduck, The Siege, The Heroes, The Lion, the Witch and the Wardrobe, The Mammoth Sails Tonight, Alice in Wonderland and Through the Looking Glass, Peter Rabbit, Tom Kitten, Robin Hood and Marian, King of Shadows. *Radio plays:* Animals Can't Laugh, White Suit Blues, Anna on Anna. *Poetry:* Paradise Lost and Paradise Regained; five programmes on Brecht's poetry 1998. *Television:* Man Friday

1972, Daft as a Brush 1975, Glad Day 1978, Pieces of Peace 1992. *Publications:* novels: If You See Me Coming, The Bodyguard, Wartime; plays: Plays with Songs; poetry: Out Loud, Heart on the Left, Blue Coffee, All Shook Up; for children: Robin Hood and Maid Marian, Nobody Rides the Unicorn, Maudie and the Green Children, Zoo of Dreams; also adaptations of numerous foreign plays. *Leisure interest:* dog (Golden Retriever) and cat. *Address:* c/o PFD, Drury House, 34–43 Russell Street, London, WC2B 5HA, England (Office).

MITCHELL, Arthur; American dancer, choreographer and artistic director; b. 27 March 1934, New York; s. of Arthur Mitchell and Willie Mae Mitchell; ed School of American Ballet; with Ballet Theater Workshop 1954; with John Butler Co., 1955; Prin. Dancer, NY City Ballet 1955–72; dancer, choreographer and actor, Spoleto Festival of Two Worlds 1960; Founder and Artistic Dir American Negro Dance Co. 1966–; Founder, Choreographer and Artistic Dir Nat. Ballet Co., Brazil 1967; Founder, Dir and Choreographer Dance Theater of Harlem, NY City 1969–; Teacher of Dance, Karel Shook Studio, Melissa Hayden School, Cedarhurst, Long Island, Jones-Haywood School of Ballet, Washington; Choreographer (with Rod Alexander) Shinbone Alley; has appeared in numerous productions; hon. degrees include: Hon. D.Arts (Columbia Coll., Chicago) 1975; Hon. DFA (NC School of the Arts) 1981, (Fordham Univ.) 1983, (Princeton Univ., Williams Coll.) 1986, (Juilliard School) 1990; Hon. D.A. (Harvard) 1987; awards include: Ebony Magazine American Black Achievement Award 1983; Paul Robeson Award, Actors Equity Asscn, N.A.A.C.P. Image Awards Hall of Fame 1986; Arnold Gringrich Memorial Award 1987; Banquet of the Golden Plate 1989; Kennedy Center Honor for Lifetime Achievement 1993; Handel Medallion, City of NY, American Acad. of Arts and Letters Award for Distinguished Service to the Arts, Barnard Coll. Medal of Distinction, Zenith Award for Fine Arts 1994, Nat. Medal of Arts 1995. *Address:* Dance Theater of Harlem, 466 West 152nd Street, New York, NY 10031, USA (Office).

MITCHELL, Basil George, MA, DD, FBA; British academic; b. 9 April 1917, Bath; s. of George William Mitchell and Mary Mitchell; m. Margaret Collin 1950; one s. three d.; ed King Edward VI School, Southampton and The Queen's Coll., Oxford; served RN 1940–46; Lecturer Christ Church, Oxford 1946–47; Fellow and Tutor Keble Coll., Oxford 1947–67; Nolloth Prof. of the Philosophy of the Christian Religion, Oxford Univ. and Fellow of Oriel Coll. 1968–84, Prof. Emer. 1984–; Stanton Lecturer, Cambridge Univ. 1959–62; Edward Cadbury Lecturer, Birmingham Univ. 1966–67; Gifford Lecturer, Glasgow Univ. 1974–76; Norton Lecturer, Southern Baptist Theological Seminary, Louisville 1989; Sarum Lecturer, Oxford Univ. 1992; Visiting Prof. Princeton Univ., USA 1963, Colgate Univ., USA 1976; Nathaniel Taylor Lecturer, Yale Univ., USA 1986; mem. Church of England Doctrine Comm. 1978–85; Chair. Ian Ramsey Centre, Oxford 1985–89; Hon. DD (Glasgow); Hon. D.Lit.Hum. (Union Coll., Schenectady). *Publications:* Faith and Logic (Ed.) 1957, Law, Morality and Religion in a Secular Society 1967, The Philosophy of Religion (Ed.) 1971, The Justification of Religious Belief 1973, Morality: Religious and Secular 1980, How to Play Theological Ping Pong and Other Essays on Faith and Reason 1990, Faith and Criticism 1994. *Leisure interests:* gardening, flower arranging. *Address:* Bartholomew House, 9 Market Street, Woodstock, Oxon., OX20 1SU, England.

MITCHELL, Sir Derek, KCB, CVO; British fmr civil servant and company director; b. 5 March 1922, Wimbledon; s. of the late Sidney Mitchell and Gladys Mitchell; m. Miriam Jackson 1944 (died 1993); one s. two d.; ed St Paul's School, London and Christ Church, Oxford; served Royal Armoured Corps and HQ London District 1942–45; served in HM Treasury 1947–63, Principal Private Sec. to Chancellor of the Exchequer 1962–63; Principal Private Sec. to Prime Minister 1964–66; Deputy Under-Sec. of State, Dept of Econ. Affairs 1966–67; Ministry of Agric., Fisheries and Food 1967–69; Econ. Minister, British Embassy, Washington and Exec. Dir IBRD, IMF, etc. 1969–72; Second Perm. Sec. (Overseas Finance) HM Treasury 1973–77; Dir Guinness Mahon 1977–78; Sr Adviser, Shearson Lehman Brothers International 1979–88; Dir Bowater Corpn 1979–84, Bowater Industries PLC 1984–89, Bowater Inc. 1984–93, Standard Chartered PLC 1979–89; mem. Nat. Theatre (now Royal Nat. Theatre) Bd 1977–96; mem. Bd French Theatre Season 1997 1996–98; Trustee Nat. Theatre (now Royal Nat. Theatre) Foundation 1982–2002, Chair. 1989–2002; mem. Council of Univ. Coll., London 1978–82; Port of London Authority 1979–82; Independent Dir The Observer Ltd 1981–93; Dir The Peter Hall Production Co. Ltd 1989–90; Trustee Nuffield Trust (fmrly Nuffield Prov. Hosps. Trust) 1978–99. *Address:* 9 Holmbush Road, Putney, London, SW15 3LE, England. *Telephone:* (20) 8788-6581. *Fax:* (20) 8788-6948.

MITCHELL, Duncan, MSc, PhD, F.R.S.S.AF.; South African professor of physiology; b. 10 May 1941, Germiston; s. of Thomas Mitchell and Maud K. (née Abercrombie) Mitchell; m. Lily May Austin 1966; one s. one d.; ed St John's Coll., Johannesburg, Univ. of Witwatersrand; mem. scientific staff, Research Org. of Chamber of Mines of SA 1964–72, Nat. Inst. for Medical Research, London 1973–75; Prof. of Physiology, Medical School, Univ. of Witwatersrand 1976–; Gold Medal, Zoological Soc. of SA 2000. *Publications:* over 160 papers in thermal, pain and sleep physiology. *Leisure interests:* nature conservation, ballet. *Address:* School of Physiology, Medical School, University of Witwatersrand, Parktown 2193, South Africa; 73A Fourth Street, Linden, Johannesburg 2195 (Home). *Telephone:* (11) 717-2359 (Office);

(11) 888-2671 (Home); (83) 260-7205. *Fax:* (11) 643-2765 (Office). *E-mail:* 057dunc@chiron.wits.ac.za (Office); duncanmitchell@hotmail.com (Home). *Website:* www.wits.ac.za./fac/med/physiol/physiol.html (Office).

MITCHELL, George John, BA, LLB; American politician and lawyer; b. 20 Aug. 1933, Waterville, Me; s. of George J. Mitchell and Mary (née Saad) Mitchell; one d.; called to Bar 1960; Trial Attorney US Dept of Justice, Washington 1960–62; Exec. Asst to Senator Edmund Muskie 1962–65; partner Jensen & Baird, Portland 1965–77; US Attorney for Maine 1977–79; US Dist Judge 1979–80; US Senator from Maine 1980–95; Majority Leader, US Senate 1988–95; Chair. Maine Democratic Cttee 1966–68; mem. Nat. Cttee Maine 1968–77; Special Adviser to Pres. Clinton for Econ. Initiatives in Ireland 1995; Chair. Cttee on NI 1995; Democrat; Chancellor (desig.) Queen's Univ. Belfast 1999–; Adviser Thames Water 1999–; Hon. LLD (Queen's, Belfast) 1997; Hon. KBE 1999; shared Houphouët-Boigny Peace Prize 1999, Presidential Medal of Freedom 1999, Tipperary Int. Peace Award 2000. *Address:* c/o Piper Rudnick LLP, 901 15th Street, NW, #700, Washington, DC 20005, USA (Office).

MITCHELL, Rt. Hon. Sir James Fitzallen, KCMG, PC; Saint Vincent and the Grenadines politician, agronomist and hotelier; b. 15 May 1931, Bequia, Grenadines; s. of Reginald Mitchell and Lois (née Baynes) Mitchell; m. Patricia Parker 1965 (divorced); four d.; ed St Vincent Grammar School, Imperial Coll. of Tropical Agric., Trinidad and Univ. of British Columbia; Agricultural Officer, Saint Vincent 1958–61; Ed. Pest Control Articles and News Summaries, Ministry of Overseas Devt, London 1964–65; MP for the Grenadines 1966–; Minister of Trade, Agric., Labour and Tourism 1967–72; MP (as an ind.) for the Grenadines 1972–79, re-elected in by-election 1979–2001; Premier of St Vincent 1972–74; Prime Minister of Saint Vincent and the Grenadines 1984–2000, also Minister of Finance and Planning and fmr Minister of Foreign Affairs; Founder New Democratic Party 1975, then Pres.; Chair. Caribbean Democrat Union 1991; Vice-Chair. Int. Democrat Union 1992–; mem. Inst. of Biologists, London 1965–; Order of the Liberator (Venezuela) 1972, Grand Cross Knights of Malta 1998 and other awards. *Publications include:* World Fungicide Usage 1965, Caribbean Crusade 1989, Guiding Change in the Islands 1996, A Season of Light 2001. *Leisure interests:* sailing, farming. *Address:* c/o New Democratic Party (NDP), Murray Road, P.O. Box 1300, Kingstown, Saint Vincent (Office); c/o Prime Minister's Office, Kingstown. *Telephone:* 457602 (Home).

MITCHELL, John; New Zealand rugby football player and coach; b. 23 March 1964, Hawera; made 134 appearances for Waikato Chiefs rugby team (86 as Capt.) and set record for most tries scored in a NZ season (21); made six mid-week appearances for NZ; Asst Coach England rugby team 1997–2000; returned to coach Waikato Chiefs 2001 season; All Blacks Coach 2001–. *Address:* c/o James Funnell, Media Centre, All Blacks Rugby Union Club, Wellington, New Zealand (Office). *E-mail:* mediacentre@nzrugby.com (Office).

MITCHELL, Joni (Roberta Joan Anderson); Canadian singer and songwriter; b. 7 Nov. 1943, Fort Macleod, Alberta; d. of William A. Anderson and Myrtle (née McKee) Anderson; m. 1st Chuck Mitchell 1965 (divorced); m. 2nd Larry Klein 1982; one d. by Brad McGrath; ed Alberta Coll.; Jazz Album of Year and Rock-Blues Album of Year for Mingus, Downbeat Magazine 1979, Juno Award 1981, Century Award, Billboard Magazine 1996, Polar Music Prize (Sweden) 1996, Gov. Gen.'s Performing Arts Award 1996, Nat. Acad. of Songwriters Lifetime Achievement Award 1996; inducted into Rock & Roll Hall of Fame 1997, into Nat. Acad. of Popular Music–Songwriters Hall of Fame 1997. *Albums include:* Song to a Seagull, Clouds, Ladies of the Canyon 1970, Blue 1971, For the Roses, Court and Spark 1974, Miles of Aisles, The Hissing of Summer Lawns 1975, Hejira 1976, Don Juan's Reckless Daughter, Mingus 1979, Shadows and Light 1980, Wild Things Run Fast 1982, Dog Eat Dog 1985, Chalk Mark in a Rain Storm 1988, Night Ride Home 1991, Turbulent Indigo 1994 (Grammy Awards for Best Pop Album, Best Art Direction 1996), Hits 1996, Misses 1996, Taming the Tiger 1998, Both Sides Now 2000, Travelog 2002. *Songs include:* Both Sides Now, Michael from Mountains, Urge for Going, Circle Game. *Television includes:* Joni Mitchell: Intimate and Interactive (Gemini Award 1996). *Publication:* Joni Mitchell: The Complete Poems and Lyrics. *Address:* c/o Reprise Records, 3300 Warner Boulevard, Burbank, CA 91505 (Office); c/o S. L. Feldman & Associates, 1505 W 2nd Avenue, Suite 200, Vancouver, BC, V6H 3Y4, Canada.

MITCHELL, Julian; British author; b. 1 May 1935; s. of the late William Moncur Mitchell and Christine Mitchell (née Browne); ed Winchester and Wadham Coll., Oxford; mem. Literature Panel, Arts Council 1966–69, Welsh Arts Council 1988–92; John Llewellyn Rhys Prize 1965; Somerset Maugham Award 1966. *Publications:* novels: Imaginary Toys 1961, A Disturbing Influence 1962, As Far As You Can Go 1963, The White Father 1964, A Circle of Friends 1966, The Undiscovered Country 1968; Biography: Jennie: Lady Randolph Churchill (with Peregrine Churchill); Plays: Half Life 1977, The Enemy Within 1980, Another Country 1981 (SWET Award 1982, filmed 1984), Francis 1983, After Aida (or Verdi's Messiah) 1986, Falling over England 1994, August 1994 (adapted from Uncle Vanya, filmed 1995). *Films:* Arabesque 1965, Vincent and Theo 1990, Wilde 1997; television plays and adaptations; translation of Pirandello's Henry IV. *Leisure interests:* fishing, local history. *Address:* 47 Draycott Place, London, SW3 3DB, England. *Telephone:* (20) 7589-1933.

MITCHELL, Katie; British theatre director; b. 23 Sept. 1964; d. of Michael Mitchell and Sally Mitchell; Pres. Oxford Univ. Dramatic Soc. 1984; awarded a Winston Churchill Memorial Trust Award to research Eastern European theatre in Russia, Lithuania, Georgia, Poland and Germany 1989; f. Classics on a Shoestring Theatre Co. 1990; Assoc. Dir RSC 1997–98; Assoc. Dir Royal Court Theatre, London 2001–; Assoc. Dir Abbey Theatre, Dublin 2000; Evening Standard Award for Best. Dir 1996. *Plays directed:* Titus Andronicus, The Master Builder, The Man Who Came to Dinner, King Lear, The Plain Dealer, The Man of Mode, Much Ado About Nothing (all as Asst Dir, RSC) 1990–91; Arden of Faversham, Vassa Zheleznova and Women of Troy (with Classics on a Shoestring) 1990; A Woman Killed with Kindness 1991, The Dybbuk 1992, Ghosts 1993, Henry VI 1994, The Phoenician Women 1995, The Mysteries 1997, The Beckett Shorts 1997, Uncle Vanya 1998 (RSC); Rutherford and Son 1994, The Machine Wreckers 1995, The Oresteia 1999, Ivanov 2002, Three Sisters 2003, (Royal Nat. Theatre); The Widowing of Mrs Holroyd 1995 (BBC); Endgame 1996 (Donmar Warehouse); Don Giovanni 1996, Jenůfa 1998, Katya Kabanova 2001, Jephtha 2003 (Welsh Nat. Opera); Attempts on Her Life 1999 (Piccolo Theatre, Milan); The Maids 1999 (Young Vic, London); The Country 2000, Mountain Language Ashes to Ashes 2001, Nightsongs 2002 (Royal Court); Thelastones 1996, Iphigenia in Aulis 2001 (Abbey Theatre, Dublin). *TV work includes:* The Widowing of Mrs Holroyd 1995, The Stepdaughter 2000 (BBC). *Leisure interests:* accordion, travel. *Address:* c/o Sebastian Born, The Agency, 24 Pottery Lane, London, W11 4LZ, England.

MITCHELL, Keith Claudius, MS, PhD; Grenadian politician; b. 12 Nov. 1946, St George's; m. Marietta Mitchell; one s.; ed Presentation Coll., Grenada, Univ. of West Indies, Barbados, Howard Univ. and American Univ., Washington, DC; cand. for Grenada Nat. Party in 1972 elections; Gen. Sec. New Nat. Party (NNP) 1984–89, Leader 1989–; Minister of Communication, Works, Public Utilities, Transportation, of Civil Aviation and Energy 1984–87, of Communications, Works, Public Utilities, Co-operatives, Community Devt, Women's Affairs and Civil Aviation 1988–89; Prime Minister of Grenada and Minister of Finance, External Affairs, Mobilization, Trade and Industry, Information and Nat. Security 1995–99; Prime Minister and Minister of Nat. Security and Information 1999–; Capt. Grenada Nat. Cricket Team 1971–74; Order of the Brilliant Star (Taiwan) 1995. *Leisure interest:* playing cricket. *Address:* Office of the Prime Minister, 6th Floor, Ministerial Complex, Botanical Gardens, The Carenage, St. George's, Grenada. *Telephone:* 440-2383 (Office); 440-4116. *E-mail:* gndpm@caribsurf.com (Office). *Website:* www.spiceisle.com/economicaffairs.

MITCHELL, Thomas Noel, PhD, LittD; Irish academic; b. 7 Dec. 1939; s. of Patrick Mitchell and Margaret Mitchell; m. Lynn S. Hunter 1965; three s. one d.; ed Nat. Univ. of Ireland and Cornell Univ. NY; Instructor Cornell Univ. 1965–66; Asst Prof. Swarthmore Coll. 1966–73, Assoc. Prof. 1973–78, Prof. of Classics 1978–79; Prof. of Latin, Trinity Coll. Dublin 1979–91, Fellow 1980–, Sr Dean 1985–87, Sr Lecturer 1987–90, Provost 1991–2001; Cornell Visiting Prof. Swarthmore Coll. 1986; mem. Royal Irish Acad. (Vice-Pres. 1989); mem. American Philosophical Soc. 1996–; Distinguished Visiting Prof. Victoria Univ. Melbourne 2001–; Visiting Fellow, The Hoover Inst. Stanford Univ. Calif. 2002; Hon. Fellow RCPI 1992, R.C.S.I. 1993; Hon. LLD (Queen's Univ. Belfast) 1992, (Nat. Univ. of Ireland) 1992; Hon. D.Hum.Litt. (Swarthmore) 1992, (Lynn Univ., USA) 1998, (State Univ. of New York) 1998; Hon. PhD, (Charles Univ., Prague) 1998, (Dublin Inst. of Tech.) 1999; Hon. DLitt (Victoria Univ. of Tech.) 2000. *Publications:* Cicero, The Ascending Years 1979, Cicero, Verrines II.1. 1986, Cicero the Senior Statesman 1990; numerous articles and reviews on Cicero and Roman History. *Leisure interest:* gardening. *Address:* The Rubrics, Trinity College, Dublin 2 (Office); Dodona, Blackwood Lane, Malahide, Co. Dublin, Ireland (Home). *Telephone:* (1) 6081843 (Office).

MITCHISON, John Murdoch, FRS, FRSE, FIBiol; British cell biologist; b. 11 June 1922, Oxford; s. of the late Lord Mitchison and of Naomi M. Mitchison (née Haldane); m. Rosalind Mary Wrong 1947 (died 2002); one s. three d.; ed Winchester Coll., Trinity Coll., Univ. of Cambridge; Army Operational Research 1941–46; Sr and Research Scholar, Trinity Coll., Univ. of Cambridge 1946–50, Fellow 1950–54; Lecturer in Zoology, Univ. of Edinburgh 1953–59, Reader in Zoology 1959–62, Prof. of Zoology 1963–88, Dean of Faculty of Science 1984–85, Univ. Fellow 1988–92, Prof. Emer. 1988– and Hon. Fellow; J. W. Jenkinson Memorial Lecturer, Univ. of Oxford 1971–72; mem. Edinburgh Univ. Court 1971–74, 1985–88; mem. Council Scottish Marine Biological Asscn 1961–67; mem. Exec. Cttee Int. Soc. for Cell Biology 1964–72; mem. Biology Cttee SRC 1976–79, Science Bd 1976–79; mem. Royal Comm. on Environmental Pollution 1974–79, Academia Europaea 1989; mem. Working Group of Biological Manpower, Dept of Educ. and Science 1968–71; Pres. British Soc. for Cell Biology 1974–77; mem. Advisory Cttee on Safety of Nuclear Installations, Health and Safety Exec. 1981–84. *Publications:* The Biology of the Cell Cycle 1971, numerous papers in scientific journals. *Address:* Institute of Cell, Animal and Population Biology, West Mains Road, Edinburgh, EH9 3JT (Office); Great Yew, Ormiston, East Lothian, EH35 5NJ, Scotland (Home). *Telephone:* (1875) 340530. *Fax:* (131) 667-3210 (Office). *E-mail:* jmmitchison@ed.ac.uk.

MITCHISON, (Nicholas) Avrion, DPhil, FRS; British professor of zoology and comparative anatomy; b. 5 May 1928, London; s. of the late Baron Mitchison and Naomi Mitchison; m. Lorna Margaret Martin 1957; two s. three d.; ed Leighton Park School and Univ. of Oxford; Lecturer, later Reader in

Zoology, Univ. of Edin. 1956–62; Head, Div. of Experimental Biology, Nat. Inst. for Medical Research, Mill Hill 1962–71; Jodrell Prof. of Zoology and Comparative Anatomy, Univ. Coll. London 1970–89; Scientific Dir Deutsches Rheuma-Forschungszentrum, Berlin 1990–96; Sr Fellow, Dept of Immunology, Univ. Coll. London 1996–; Hon. Dir Imperial Cancer Research Fund, Tumour Immunology Unit, Univ. Coll. London; Hon. MD (Edin.); Paul Ehrlich Prize. *Address:* Department of Immunology, University College London, Windeyer Building, 46 Cleveland Street, London, W1P 6DB (Office); 14 Belitha Villas, London, N1 1PD, England (Home). *Telephone:* (20) 7380-9349. *Fax:* (20) 7380-9357. *E-mail:* n.mitchison@ucl.ac.uk (Office).

MITREVA, Ilinka, MA, PhD; Macedonian politician, academic and international official; b. 11 Feb. 1950, Skopje; ed Univ. of Skopje, Univ. of Belgrade; Head Group of Romance Languages and Literature, Philological Faculty, Univ. of Skopje 1974–94; mem. Ass. of the Repub. 1994–, Head Ass. Group for Co-operation with European Parl.; Minister of Foreign Affairs 2001, 2002–; Head Macedonian Parl. Del. in Cen. European Initiative (CEI); mem. Initiative Bd for NATO Club Est.; Chevalier, Ordre nat. du Mérite. *Address:* Ministry of Foreign Affairs, Dame Gruev 6, 1000 Skopje, Republic of Macedonia (Office). *E-mail:* mailmnr@mnr.gov.mk. *Website:* www.mnr.gov.mk.

MITROFANOV, Aleksey Valentinovich; Russian politician; b. 16 March 1962, Moscow; s. of Zoya Mitrofanova; m. Marina Lillevyali; ed Moscow Inst. of Int. Relations; with Ministry of Foreign Affairs 1985–88; researcher, Inst. of USA and Canada 1988–91; producer TV programmes, Leisure Centre Sokol; mem. Higher Council, Liberal Democratic Party of Russia 1991–93; Minister of Foreign Affairs, Shadow Cabinet of Liberal Democratic Party 1992–; mem. State Duma 1993–; Deputy Chair. Cttee on Int. Relations 1993–96, Chair. Cttee on Geopolitics 1996–99; mem. State Duma 1999–. *Films:* scriptwriter: Pchiojka (A Little Bee); numerous documentaries including Yury Andropov 1993; Andrey Gromyko 1993. *Publications include:* Steps of New Geopolitics, Secret Visit of Professor Voland. *Leisure interest:* chess. *Address:* State Duma, Okhotny ryad 1, 103265 Moscow, Russia. *Telephone:* (095) 292-56-23 (Office). *Fax:* (095) 292-34-21 (Office).

MITROFANOV, Alexandr, BPhil; Czech political journalist; b. b. 27 June 1957, Rostov, Russia; divorced; one d.; ed Rostov State Univ., Russia; Ed. Skodovák, Škoda Plzeň 1980–88, Právo Lidu 1992–95; contrib. Právo 1995–, Deputy Political Ed., Political Commentator; undertook sabbatical study in UK 1994, 1997; Křepelky Prize, Czech Literary Fund 1994, Ferdinand Peroutka Prize for Journalism 2001. *Publications:* Behind the Façade of Lidový dům, Czech Social Democracy, People and Events 1992–1998 1998, Politics Under Lid (with Markéta Maláčova) 2002. *Leisure interest:* reading and writing books. *Address:* Právo, Slezská 13, 120 00 Prague 2, Czech Republic (Office). *Telephone:* (2) 21001315 (Office). *Fax:* (2) 21001361 (Office). *E-mail:* alm@pravo.cz (Office). *Website:* www.pravo.cz (Office).

MITROPOLSKY, Yuriy Alekseyevich, D.MATH.SC; Ukrainian mathematician; b. 3 Jan. 1917, Shishaki, Poltava Region; s. of Alexy Savvich Mitropolsky and Vera Vasilevna (née Charnish) Mitropolskaya; m. Olexandra (née Lihacheva) Mitropolskaya 1941; one s. one d.; ed Kiev State Univ., Kazakh State Univ.; army service 1943–45; scientific researcher, Inst. of Bldg Mechanics 1946–51; Inst. of Math. Ukrainian Acad. of Sciences 1951–58, Dir 1958–88, Hon. Dir 1988–; mem. Ukranian Acad. of Sciences 1961, Acad.-Sec. Dept of Math. and Cybernetics 1963–93, Scientific Consultant 1993–; lecturer, Prof. Ukranian State Univ. 1949–89; mem. USSR (now Russian) Acad. of Sciences 1984; Foreign Corresp. mem. Accademia di Bologna 1971–; Lenin Prize 1965; Hero of Socialist Labour 1986. *Publication:* over 500 scientific articles and papers and 25 monographs including Group-theoretical Approach in Asymptotic Methods of Nonlinear Mechanics 1988, Nonlinear Mechanics, Groups and Symmetry 1995, Nonlinear Mechanics, One-Frequency Oscillations 1997. *Leisure interest:* travel. *Address:* Ukrainian Academy of Sciences, Vladimirskaya 54, 01034, Kiev 34 (Office); B. Khemelnitskogo Street 42, Apt. 10, 01030 Kiev 30, Ukraine (Home). *Telephone:* (44) 235-23-84, (44) 235-31-93 (Office); (44) 235-20-10 (Home). *Fax:* (44) 235-20-10 (Office).

MITSOTAKIS, Constantine; Greek politician; b. 18 Oct. 1918, Chania, Crete; m. Marika Yianoukou; one s. three d.; ed Univ. of Athens; served in army 1940–41; active in Cretan resistance against Nazi occupation, twice arrested and sentenced to death; after War, republished newspaper KIRYX; MP for Chania 1946–74, 1977–; Under-Sec. of State for Finance, then Acting Minister for Communications and Public Works 1951; Minister for Finance 1963–64, for Econ. Co-ordination 1965; arrested by mil. junta 1967, released, under house arrest, escaped and lived in exile; returned to Greece 1974; f. Neoliberal Party; joined New Democracy Party 1978, Leader 1984–93; Minister for Econ. Co-ordination 1978-80, for Foreign Affairs 1980–81; Prime Minister of Greece, also with responsibility for the Aegean 1990–93. *Address:* 1 Aravantinou Street, 106 74 Athens, Greece.

MITTA, Aleksander Naumovich; Russian film director; b. 29 March 1933, Moscow; ed Moscow Inst. of Construction Eng, All-Union Inst. of Cinematography; with Mosfilm studio 1961; Prof. Hamburg Univ. 1995–; Merited Worker of Arts of Russia 1974. *Films:* My Friend Kolka 1961, Without Fear and Reproach 1963, One is Ringing, Open the Door 1966 (Grand Prix Int. Festival in Venice), Period, Period, Comma 1973, Twinkle, Twinkle, My Star 1970, The Crew 1980 (Prize of All-Union Film Festival), The Tale of Wandering 1983, Safety Margin 1988, A Step 1988, Lost in Siberia 1991, Alfred Schnittke and His Friends (TV) 1994, Border of the State (TV Series)

1999–2000. *Publication:* Cinema Between Hell and Paradise. *Address:* Malaya Gruzinskaya str. 28, Apt. 105, 123557 Moscow, Russia (Home). *Telephone:* (095) 253-73-20 (Home, Moscow); (40) 4123-41-69 (Home, Hamburg). *Fax:* (095) 253-80-67.

MITTAL, Lakshmi N.; Indian steel industry executive; b. 15 June 1950, Sadulpur, Rajasthan; m. Usha Mittal; one s. one d.; ed St Xavier's Coll., Calcutta; began career in family's steelmaking business; Founder, Chair., CEO The LNM Group; f. Caribbean Ispat 1989; acquired Ispat Mexicana 1992, Ispat Sidbec, Canada 1994, Ispat Hamburger Stahlwerke, Germany 1995, Karmet, Kazakhstan 1995, Irish Ispat 1996, Thyssen's Long Product Div., Germany 1997, Ispat Unimetal Group 1999, Chair., CEO of all mem. cos. of LNM Group Inc., Ispat Int. N.V., Ispat Karmet, Ispat Indo, Ispat Coal; Dir ICICI Ltd; mem. Advisory Bds. of Wharton and Kellogg Schools of Man., USA; Steelmaker of the Year Award 1996, Willy Korf Steel Vision Award 1998. *Leisure interests:* swimming, yoga, golf. *Address:* Ispat International (UK) Ltd., 7th Floor, Berkeley Square House, Berkeley Square, London, W1J 6DA, England (Office). *Telephone:* (20) 7629-7988 (Office).

MITTERRAND, Gen. Jacques; French aerospace executive; b. 21 May 1918, Angoulême, Charentes; s. of Joseph Mitterrand and Yvonne (née Lorrain) Mitterrand; brother of the late François Mitterrand; m. Gisèle Baume 1948; two d.; ed St Paul Coll., Angoulême, St Louis Lycée, Paris, St Cyr Mil. Acad.; served in Air Force 1937–75; participated in Devt and institution of French Nuclear Force; mem. Del. to NATO Perm. Group, Washington, DC 1961–64; Gen., Asst Commdr French Strategic Air Forces 1965–67, Commdr 1970–72; Deputy Chief of Staff of Air Force 1968, of Armed Forces 1968–70; Insp. Gen. of Air Force 1972–75; mem. Supreme Air Council 1970–75; Chair. Bd and Chief Exec., Soc. Nat. Industrielle Aérospatiale (SNIAS) 1975–81; Counsellor to Chair. French Atomic Energy Agency 1975; First Vice-Chair. French Aerospace Industries Asscn (GIFAS), Chair. 1981–84; Chair. Asscn Européenne des Constructeurs de Matériel Aérospatial (AECMA) 1978–83; Pres. Office Gén. de l'Air (Oga) 1984–93, Hon. Pres. 1993–; Vice-Chair. Supervisory Bd of Airbus Industry; Vice-Pres. Turbomeca 1983; mem. Bd Inst. of Air Transport; Dir Intertechnique, Turbomeca, Hurel Dubois; Grand Croix, Légion d'honneur, Croix de guerre, Croix de la Valeur militaire, Croix du Combattant; Médaille de l'Aéronautique. *Address:* Oga, 33 Avenue des Champs-Elysées, Paris 75008 (Office); 87 boulevard Murat, 75016 Paris, France (Home).

MITYUKOV, Mikhail Alekseyevich, CAND.JUR.SC.; Russian politician, lawyer and professor; b. 7 Jan. 1942, Ust-Uda, Irkutsk Region; m. Ludmila Aleksandrovna Mityukova; two s. one d.; ed Irkutsk State Univ.; worked in Khakassia Autonomous Region (now Repub.), Deputy Chair. regional court 1968–87; Sr Teacher, Head of Chair of History and Law Abakan State Pedagogical Inst. 1987–90; Russian Fed. People's Deputy and mem. Supreme Soviet, Deputy Chair. then Chair. Cttee on Law 1990–93; First Deputy Minister of Justice 1993–94; mem. State Duma (Parl.) 1993–95, First Deputy Chair. 1994–95; participated in drafting new Russian Constitution; First Deputy Sec., Security Council of Russia 1996–98; Plenipotentiary Rep. of Russian Pres. in Constitutional Court 1998–; Prof. Inst. of Econs, Man. and Law Russian State Humanitarian Univ. (RGGU) 2001–; Merited Jurist of the Russian Fed. award, several medals. *Publications:* over 200 scientific works and monographs including Constitutional Courts on Post-Soviet Territory 1999, A History of Constitutional Justice in Russia 2002. *Address:* Ipat'yevski per. 4-10, 103132 Moscow, Russia (Office). *Telephone:* (095) 206-44-18 (Office). *E-mail:* Shubert_T@maindir.gov.ru (Office).

MITZNA, Amram, MA; Israeli politician and army general (retd); b. 1945; ed Haifa Univ.; joined Israeli Armed Forces 1960s; served as Brig. in Six-Day war 1967, Yom Kippur War 1973; resgnd in protest at Israeli treatment of Palestinians in Sabra and Shatila, Lebanon 1982; re-apptd Defence Force Commdr in West Bank during Palestinian uprising 1987–93, later Gen. of the Cen. Region Command; Mayor of Haifa 1993–; Chair. Israel Labour Party 2002–, advocates removal of West Bank and Gaza settlements and direct negotiations with Yasser Arafat. *Address:* Israel Labour Party, POB 62033, Tel-Aviv 61620, Israel (Office). *Telephone:* 3-6899444 (Office). *Fax:* 3-6899420 (Office). *E-mail:* avoda@inter.net.il (Office).

MIYAKE, Issey; Japanese fashion designer; b. Kazunaru Miyake, 22 April 1939, Tokyo; ed Tama Art Univ. Tokyo and La Chambre Syndicale de la Couture Parisienne, Paris; Asst Designer to Guy Laroche, Paris 1966–68, to Hubert de Givenchy, Paris 1968–69; Designer, Geoffrey Beene (ready-to-wear firm), New York 1969–70; est. Miyake Design Studio, Tokyo 1970; Dir Issey Miyake Int., Issey Miyake & Assocs., Issey Miyake Europe, Issey Miyake USA and Issey Miyake On Limits (Tokyo); Exec. Adviser and Planner, First Japan Culture Conf., Yokohama 1980; work has been exhibited in Paris, Tokyo and at MIT and appears in collections of Metropolitan Museum of Art, New York and Victoria & Albert Museum, London; Dr. hc (RCA) 1993; Japan Fashion Editors' Club Awards, 1974, 1976, Mainichi Design Prize 1977, Pratt Inst. Award (New York) 1979.

MIYAMOTO, Kenji; Japanese politician and writer; b. 17 Oct. 1908, Yamaguchi; s. of Sutekichi Miyamoto and Miyo Miyamoto; m. Sueko Omori 1956; two c.; ed Tokyo Imperial Univ.; mem. Japanese CP 1931–, (imprisoned 1933–45), mem. Cen. Cttee 1933–97, Gen. Sec. of Cen. Cttee 1958–70, Chair. Presidium Cen. Cttee 1970–82, Chair. Cen. Cttee 1982–97, Chair. Emer. 1997–2000, Officer Emer. 2000–; mem. House of Councillors 1977–89. *Publications:* Problems of Democratic Revolution 1947, Advance Towards

Freedom and Independence 1949, Twelve Years' Letters 1952, World of Yuriko Miyamoto 1954, Perspective of Japanese Revolution 1961, The Path of Our Party's Struggle 1961, Selections from Literary Critiques of Kenji Miyamoto 1966–80, The Road towards a New Japan 1970, Actual Tasks and the Japanese Communist Party 1970, Standpoint of the Japanese Communist Party 1972, Dialogues with Kenji Miyamoto 1972, Kenji Miyamoto with Pressmen 1973, Interviews with Kenji Miyamoto 1975, Kenji Miyamoto on Our Time 1975, Kenji Miyamoto Before the Court under Militarism 1976, Dialogues with Kenji Miyamoto (sequel) 1977, Kenji Miyamoto on Contemporary Politics 1978, Kenji Miyamoto on the 1980s 1981–83, Now Is Turn for JCP 1983, Dialogues on Developments in the World and Japan 1984, Road to Elimination of Nuclear Weapons 1985, People in Retrospect 1985, Selected Works 1985, Kenji Miyamoto on the 1980s (sequel) 1983–86, Fundamental Problems of the Communist Movement 1988, Works in the Early Postwar Period 1987–88, No Future for the Current Against History 1991, Immortal Party Based on Scientific Socialism 1991, Twentieth Century and Vitality of Socialism 1992, Japan: Its Present and Future Course 1994, Basic Course of Party Building 1995, Features of Some Party Members 1995, Toward the Progressive Future 1997. *Address:* Central Committee of the Japanese Communist Party, Sendagaya 4-26-7, Shibuya-ku, Tokyo, Japan. *Telephone:* (3) 5474-8421. *Fax:* (3) 3746–0767. *E-mail:* intl@jcp.or.jp (Office). *Website:* www.jcp.or.jp.

MIYASHITA, Sohei; Japanese politician; mem. LDP; fmr civil servant in Finance Ministry; mem. for Nagano House of Reps.; Dir-Gen. Defence Agency 1991–92, Environment Agency 1994–95; Minister of Health and Welfare 1998–99; Chair. Social Security Reform Study Group 2001–. *Address:* c/o Liberal Democratic Party, 1-11-23 Nagata-cho, Chiyoda-ku, Tokyo 100-8910, Japan (Office).

MIYAZAWA, Kiichi; Japanese politician; b. 8 Oct. 1919, Tokyo; m. Yoko Miyazawa 1943; two c.; ed Tokyo Imperial Univ.; Finance Ministry 1942–52, Pvt. Sec. to Minister of Finance 1949; mem. House of Councillors 1953–65; Parl. Vice-Minister of Educ. 1959–60; Minister of State, Dir-Gen. of Econ. Planning Agency 1962–64, 1966–68, 1977–78; mem. House of Reps. 1967–; Minister of Int. Trade and Industry 1970–71, of Foreign Affairs 1974–76, of Finance 1986–88; Deputy Prime Minister and Minister of Finance 1987–88; Minister of State, Chief Cabinet Sec. 1980–82; Chair. Exec. Council LDP 1984–86; Pres. 1991–93; Prime Minister of Japan 1991–93; Minister of Finance 1999–2001. *Publications:* Tokyo-Washington no Mitsudan (Tokyo-Washington Secret Talks) 1956, Shakaito tono taiwa (Dialogue with the Socialist Party), Utsukushii Nippon heno Chosen (Challenge for Beautiful Japan) 1984. *Leisure interests:* Noh theatre, reading. *Address:* c/o Liberal Democratic Party, 1-11-23 Nagata-cho, Chiyoda-ku, Tokyo 100-8910, Japan.

MIYET, Bernard; French diplomatist; b. 16 Dec. 1946, Bourg de Léage; m. Dominique Bourguignon 1974; one d.; ed Inst. of Political Studies, Grenoble, Nat. School of Admin.; Chief of Staff, Ministry of Communications 1981–82; Chair. and CEO Soc. Française de radiodiffusion 1983–84; Special Adviser to Chair. Schlumberger Ltd 1985; Consul Gen. of France, LA 1986–89; Deputy Dir-Gen. Office of Cultural, Scientific and Tech. Relations, Ministry of Foreign Affairs, Paris 1989–91; Amb. and Perm. Rep. of France to UN, Geneva 1991–93; Amb. responsible for audio-visual services to GATT Uruguay Round, Ministry of Foreign Affairs, Paris 1993–94; Amb. and Perm. Rep. of France to Org. for Security and Co-operation in Europe, Vienna 1994–97; Under Sec.-Gen. for Peacekeeping Operations, UN, New York 1997–2000; Chair. Bd of Dirs. Société des auteurs, compositeurs et éditeurs de musique (Sacem) 2001–; Chevalier Ordre nat du Mérite, Officier des Arts et Lettres. *Leisure interests:* opera, cinema, theatre. *Address:* Sacem, 225 avenue Charles de Gaulle, 92528 Neuilly-sur-Seine Cédex (Office); 7 rue Coëtlogon, 75006 Paris (Home); Le Vivier, 26300 Beauregard-Baret, France.

MIYOSHI, Shunkichi; Japanese business executive; b. 16 March 1929; ed Univ. of Tokyo; joined NKK Corpn 1951, mem. Bd Dirs. 1982–, Man. Dir 1985–88, Sr Man. Dir 1988–90, Exec. Vice-Hon. Adviser 2002–; Pres. 1990–92, Pres. 1992–97, Chair. of Bd 1997–2002; Pres. Iron and Steel Inst. of Japan 1992–94; Chair. Japan Inst. of Construction Eng 1997–, Japan Vocational Ability Devt Asscn 1998–, Weights and Measures Admin. Council 1998–; Vice-Chair. Japan Fed. of Employers' Asscns. 1997–; Dir Japan Iron and Steel Fed. 1992–97, Vice-Chair 1993–94, 1996–97; Exec. mem. Bd of Dirs. Japan Fed. of Econ. Orgs. 1992–97; mem. Coal Mining Council 1992–97, Electric Power Devt Co-ordination Council 1996–2001 (disbanded), Trade Council 1997–, Cen. Environment Council 1997–99, Electric Power Devt Cttee 2001–; Trustee Japan Asscn of Corp. Executives 1995–. *Address:* NKK Corporation, 1-1-2 Marunouchi, Chiyoda-ku, Tokyo 100-8202, Japan (Office). *Telephone:* (3) 3212-7111. *Fax:* (3) 3214-8401.

MIYOSHI, Toru, LLB; Japanese judge (retd); b. 31 Oct. 1927; ed Univ. of Tokyo; Asst Judge, Tokyo Dist Court and Tokyo Family Court 1955; Judge, Hakodate Dist Court and Hakodate Family Court 1965; Judge, Tokyo Dist Court (Presiding Judge of Div.) 1975; Pres. Research and Training Inst. for Court Clerks 1982; Pres. Oita Dist Court and Oita Family Court 1985; Pres. Nagano Dist Court and Nagano Family Court 1986; Chief Judicial Research Official of Supreme Court 1987; Pres. Sapporo High Court 1990, Tokyo High Court 1991; Justice of Supreme Court 1992; Chief Justice of Supreme Court 1995–97.

MIZRAHI, Isaac; American fashion designer; b. 14 Oct. 1961, Brooklyn, New York; s. of Zeke Mizrahi and Sarah Mizrahi; ed Yeshiva, Flatbush, High

School of Performing Arts, Manhattan, Parsons School of Design; apprenticed to Perry Ellis 1982, full-time post 1982–84; worked with Jeffrey Banks 1984–85, with Calvin Klein 1985–87; started own design firm in partnership with Sarah Hadad Cheney 1987, first formal show 1988, first spring collection Nov. 1988, first menswear line launched April 1990, announced closure of firm Oct. 1998.

MKAPA, Benjamin William, BA; Tanzanian politician, journalist and diplomatist; b. 12 Nov. 1938, Masasi; s. of William Matwani and Stephania Nambanga; m. Anna Joseph Maro 1966; two s.; ed Makerere Univ. Coll.; Admin. Officer, Dist Officer 1962; Foreign Service Officer 1962; Man. Ed. Tanzania Nationalist and Uhuru 1966, The Daily News and The Sunday News 1972; Press Sec. to Pres. 1974; Founding Dir Tanzania News Agency 1976; High Commr in Nigeria 1976; Minister for Foreign Affairs 1977–80, for Information and Culture 1980–82; High Commr in Canada 1982–83; Amb. to USA 1983–84; Minister for Foreign Affairs 1984–90; MP for Nanyumbu 1985–95; Minister for Information and Broadcasting 1990–92, for Science, Tech. and Higher Educ. 1992–95; Pres. of Tanzania and C-in-C of Armed Forces Nov. 1995–; Chair. Chama Cha Mapinduzi (CCM) party 1996–; Dr. hc (Soka Univ., Tokyo) 1998; Hon. DHumLitt (Morehouse Coll., Atlanta, USA) 1999. *Leisure interest:* reading. *Address:* Office of the President, P.O. Box 9120, Dar es Salaam, Tanzania. *Telephone:* (22) 2116898 (Office). *Fax:* (22) 2113425 (Office).

MKHATSHWA, Smangaliso, ThM, PhD; South African ecclesiastic; b. 26 June 1939, Barberton; s. of Elias Mkhatshwa and Maria Mkhatshwa (née Nkosi); ordained Catholic priest 1965; Gen. Sec. Southern African Catholic Bishops' Conf. 1980–88; Patron of the United Democratic Front 1983; Gen. Sec. Inst. for Contextual Theology 1988–94; mem. Parl. (ANC) 1994–, mem. Reconstruction and Devt Standing Cttee and Educ. Standing Cttee; Deputy Minister of Educ. 1996–; Trustee Kagiso Trust, Matla Trust; Pres. Cen. Transvaal Civics Asscn (later renamed SANCO Pretoria); Dr. hc (Tübingen, Germany, Georgetown, USA); Steve Biko Award, Indicator Newspaper Award. *Publications:* articles on theology and politics. *Leisure interests:* tennis, music, reading, theatre. *Address:* Private Bag X895 Pretoria 0001; Private Bag X9023, Cape Town, 8000, South Africa.

MKRTUMYAN, Yuri Israelovich, CandHisSc; Armenian ethnographist; b. 1 Jan. 1939, Tbilisi; ed Moscow State Univ.; lab. asst, jr researcher Inst. of Archaeology and Ethnography, Armenian Acad. of Sciences 1962–71, Prof. 1996–; Sr Lecturer Yerevan State Univ. 1971–89; Head Chair of Ethnography, Yerevan State Univ. 1989–94; Sec. CP Cttee Yerevan State Univ.; mem. Cen. CPSU Cttee, mem. Bureau Cen. Cttee Armenian CP 1990–91; counsellor to Minister of Foreign Affairs, Repub. of Armenia April–June 1994; Amb. to Russia 1994–96; Dir Inst. of Ethnography and Archaeology 1997–. *Publications:* over 40 scientific works on theoretical and regional ethnography in Russian, Armenian and English. *Address:* Institute of Ethnography and Archaeology, Armenian Academy of Sciences, Charentsa Street 15, 375025 Yerevan, Armenia. *Telephone:* (2) 55-68-96 (Office).

MLECZKO, Andrzej; Polish graphic designer and illustrator; b. 5 Jan. 1949, Tarnobrzeg; one d.; ed Kraków Technical Univ.; illustrator of books, paintings, drawings; contrib. to magazines in Poland and abroad 1971–; Andrzej Mleczko Author's Gallery, Kraków 1983–, Warsaw 2002–; has designed over 10,000 graphics, drawings and posters. *Art exhibitions:* 136 one-man exhbns in Poland and 28 exhbns abroad. *Publications:* numerous albums and books. *Address:* Andrzej Mleczko Author's Gallery, ul. św. Jana 14, 31-018 Kraków (Office); ul. Marszatkowska 140, 00-061 Warsaw, Poland (Office). *Telephone:* (12) 4217104 (Office); (22) 8295760 (Office). *Fax:* (12) 4217104 (Office). *E-mail:* galeria@pro.onet.pl (Office). *Website:* www.mleczko.onet.pl (Office).

MLYNÁRIK, Ján, CSc, PH. D.; Slovak historian; b. 11 Feb. 1933, Filakova; m.; five c.; ed Charles Univ., Prague; Prof., Acad. of Music and Dramatic Arts, Bratislava 1957–59, Acad. of Performing Arts (AMU), Prague 1959–60; manual worker (for political reasons) 1970–81; political prisoner in Ruzyne 1981–82; expelled from Czechoslovakia 1982; Prof., Univ. of Munich 1982–89; worked on Radio Free Europe 1982–89; mem. Parl. 1990–92; Prof., Charles Univ., Prague 1990–. *Publications include:* Way to Stars 1989, M. R. Štefánik 1999. *Leisure interests:* literature, music. *Address:* Charles University, Nám. J. Palacha 2, Prague 1, 11000 Czech Republic (Office). *Telephone:* (2) 22319762 (Office). *Fax:* (2) 222328405 (Office).

MMARI, Geoffrey Raphael Vehaeli, DipEd, PhD; Tanzanian university teacher and administrator; b. 24 June 1934, Moshi; s. of the late Vehaeli Mmari and of Luisia Mmari; m. Salome Mmari 1959; one s. three d.; ed Univ. of E Africa, Univ. of N Iowa, USA, Univ. of Dar es Salaam; teacher and admin. 1966–69; univ. teacher 1969–; Vice-Chancellor Sokoine Univ. of Agric. 1984–88, Univ. of Dar es Salaam 1988–91; Co-ordinator Open Univ. Planning Office 1991–, Vice-Chancellor Open Univ. 1993–. *Publications:* Mwalimu: The Influence of Julius Nyerere (ed. with Colin Legum) 1995; ed. secondary math. books series; articles in journals and chapters in books 1960–. *Leisure interests:* reading, travelling, walking. *Address:* The Open University, P.O. Box 23409, Dar es Salaam, Tanzania. *Telephone:* (22) 266-8445. *Fax:* (22) 266-8759. *E-mail:* avu.out@vudsm.ac.tz (Office).

MNANGAGWA, Emmerson; Zimbabwean politician; b. 15 Sept. 1946; fmr Admin. Sec. Zanu-PF; Head Cen. Intelligence Org. (CIO) 1980s; fmr Minister of State Security; fmr Minister of Justice, Legal and Parl. Affairs; currently Speaker of Parl.; reported to have organised secret talks for Pres. Robert

Mugabe's succession 2003. *Address:* Parliament of Zimbabwe, Nelson Mandela/3rd Street, Box CY298, Causeway, Zimbabwe (Office). *Telephone:* 7001810, 25293655 (Office). *Fax:* 252935 (Office). *E-mail:* clerk@parlzim.gov .zw (Office). *Website:* www.parlzim.gov.zw (Office).

MNOUCHKINE, Ariane; French theatre director; has staged productions with the Paris-based Théâtre du Soleil since the 1960s. *Stage productions include:* Les Atrides.

MO, Timothy; British author; b. 30 Dec. 1950, Hong Kong; s. of Peter Mo Wan Lung and Barbara Helena Falkingham; ed Mill Hill School and St John's Coll., Univ. of Oxford; fmrly worked for Times Educational Supplement and New Statesman; fmr reporter for Boxing News and P.A.Y.E. clerk; Hawthornden Prize. *Publications include:* The Monkey King 1979 (Geoffrey Faber Memorial Prize 1979), Sour Sweet 1982, An Insular Possession 1986, The Redundancy of Courage 1991 (EM Forster Award 1992), Brownout on Breadfruit Boulevard 1995, Renegade or Halo² 1999 (James Tait Black Memorial Prize 1999). *Leisure interests:* weight training, scuba diving. *Address:* c/o Paddleless Press, BCM Paddleless, London, WC1N 3XX, England. *Telephone:* timothymo@eudoramail.com.

MO YAN; Chinese novelist; b. Guan Moyan, 1955, Gaomi, Shandong Prov.; ed PLA Acad. of Arts, Beijing Normal Univ.; joined PLA 1976. *Publications:* Red Sorghum Family, The Song of Heaven's Garlic Shoots, Thirteen Steps, The Herbivora Family, Jiuguo.

MOBBS, Sir (Gerald) Nigel, Kt; British business executive; b. 22 Sept. 1937, Birmingham; s. of Gerald Aubrey Mobbs and Elizabeth Lanchester; m. Hon. Pamela Jane Berry 1961; one s. two d.; ed Marlborough Coll. and Christ Church, Oxford; Chair. and CEO Slough Estates PLC 1976–; Chair. Kingfisher PLC 1995–96 (Dir 1982–96); Chair. Bovis Homes Group PLC 1996–; numerous directorships including Barclays Bank PLC 1979–, The Charterhouse Group PLC 1974–84, Cookson Group PLC 1985–93; Chair. Univ. of Buckingham; mem. Commonwealth War Graves Comm. 1988–97, Cttee on Corp. Governance 1995–98; Lord Lt of Buckinghamshire 1997–; Chair. Wembley Task Force 1999–2002, Historic Royal Palaces 2003–; Commr Royal Hosp. Chelsea 2000–; Hon. DUniv (Buckingham Univ.) 1993; Hon. DSc (City Univ.); Hon. LLD (Reading Univ.). *Leisure interests:* hunting, skiing, golf, riding, travel. *Address:* Widmer Lodge, Pink Road, Parslows Hillock, Princes Risborough, Bucks. HP27 0RJ; 234 Bath Road, Slough, Berks., SL1 4EE, England. *Telephone:* (1753) 537171.

MOBY; American musician; b. Richard Melville Hall, 11 Sept. 1965, Harlem, New York; s. of James Hall and Elizabeth Hall; ed Royle Grammer School, Darien, CT, Univ. of CT; cr. first band 1979, new wave/punk rock band Vatican Commandos 1980, new wave band AWOL 1982; DJ The Beat, Port Chester, New York 1984, Mars, Palladium, Palace de Beaute, MK, New York 1989; signed with Instinct Records 1989, Elektra Records and Mute Records 1992, V2 Records 1999; performed at the Palladium, New York 1990; toured with the Shamen 1992, the Prodigy and Richard Hawtin 1993, Orbital and Aphex Twin 1994, Lollapalooza and the Red Hot Chili Peppers 1995; composed music for films including the James Bond Theme 1997; MTV Europe Award, MTV USA Award, VH-1 Award. *Music includes:* singles: Hit Squad with God (Vatican Commandos) 1983, AWOL (AWOL) 1984, Move 1993, Time's Up 1989, Mobility 1990, Go (One of Best Records of All Time, Rolling Stone magazine) 1991; albums: The Story so Far, Voodoo Child 1991, Ambient, Early Underground, Everything is Wrong (Album of the Year, Spin) 1995, Animal Rights 1996, I Like To Score 1997, Mobysongs, Play (platinum in 25 countries) 1999, 18 2000. *Address:* DEF Management, POB 2477, London, NW6 6NQ, England (Office). *E-mail:* info@d-e-f.com (Office). *Website:* www .moby.com (Office).

MOCK, Alois, LLD; Austrian politician; b. 10 June 1934, Euratsfeld; s. of August and Mathilde Mock; m. Dr. Edith Mock (née Partik) 1963; ed Univ. of Vienna, Johns Hopkins Univ., Bologna and Free Univ., Brussels; mem. Austrian mission to OECD 1962–66; Private Sec. to Fed. Chancellor 1966, Head of Private Office 1968; Minister of Educ. 1969–70; mem. Parl. 1970–; Leader, Austrian People's Party (ÖVP) 1979–89; Leader of Opposition 1979–87; Vice-Chancellor 1987–89; Minister of Foreign Affairs 1987–95; Pres. European Democratic Union, Vienna 1979–88; Pres. Int. Democratic Union, London 1983–87; Hon. Chair. ÖVP 1995–. *Publication:* Standpunkte 1983. *Address:* c/o Österreichische Volkspartei, Lichtenfelsgasse 7, 1010 Vienna, Austria.

MOCUMBI, Pascoal Manuel; Mozambican politician; b. 10 April 1941, Maputo; s. of Manuel Mocumbi Malume and Leta Alson Cuhle; m. Adelina Isabel Bernardino Paindane 1970; two s. two d.; fmr Minister of Health, fmr Minister of Foreign Affairs; Prime Minister of Mozambique 1994–; mem. Frente de Libertação de Moçambique (FRELIMO). *Leisure interests:* jogging, squash, reading. *Address:* Praça da Marinha, Maputo, Mozambique. *Telephone:* (1) 426861. *Fax:* (1) 426881. *E-mail:* dgpm.gov@teledata.mz (Office).

MOCZULSKI, Leszek Robert, LLM; Polish political leader, lawyer, journalist and historian; b. 7 June 1930, Warsaw; s. of Stanisław Moczulski and Janina (née Reimer) Moczulska; m. 1st Małgorzata (née Smogorzewska) Moczulska 1951 (deceased); m. 2nd Maria-Ludwika (née Różycka) Moczulska 1968; one d.; ed Acad. of Political Science, Warsaw, Warsaw Univ.; reporter on Życie Warszawy (daily) 1950–53, on dailies and weeklies, including Dookoła Świata, Warsaw 1955–57; imprisoned on charges of slandering Poland in foreign press 1957–58, acquitted; assoc. (pseud. Leszek Karpatowicz) Więź (monthly) 1959–62; Head History Section Stolica (weekly) 1961–77; ed. of underground journals Opinia 1977–78, Droga 1978–80, Gazeta Polska 1979–80; arrested Aug. 1980 and sentenced to 7 years on charge of attempting to overthrow regime, amnestied Aug. 1984; sentenced to 4 years on charge of heading illegal org. March 1985, amnestied Sept. 1986; victim of reprisals 1946–89, including repeated 48 hr. custody (250 times 1976–80), forbidden to publish, refused passport, prevented from finishing PhD; mem. Polish Journalists' Asscn 1951–, Theatre Authors and Composers' Union 1960– (mem. Bd 1972–77), Polish Historical Soc.; active in Movt for Rights of Man and Citizen (ROPCiO) 1977–80; Deputy to Sejm (Parl.) 1991–97; Hon. Chair. Parl. Club of Confed. of Independence of Poland (KPN) 1993–97; Chair. Parl. Cttee for Polish Connection Abroad 1993–97; mem. Confed. for an Independent Poland (KPN) 1979– (one of founders, temporary chair. 1979–80, Chair. 1980–); mem. Polish del. to Parl. Ass., Council of Europe 1992–93, 1994–96; Gold Badge of Honour; Officer's Cross of Polonia Restituta Order (London) 1987. *Publications:* numerous contribs. on history, politics and int. affairs, over 20 books including Wojna polska (War) 1939 1972, Rewolucja bez rewolucji (Revolution Without Revolution) 1979, Trzecia Rzeczpospolita – zarys ustroju politycznego (A Constitutional System for Independent Poland) 1984, U progu niepodległości (Gateway to Independence) 1990, Bez wahania (Without Hesitation) 1992, Trzy drogi (Three Ways)1993, Demokracja bez demokracji (Democracy Without Democracy) 1995, Geopolityka (Geopolitics) 1999, Investigation 2001. *Leisure interests:* horse riding, old automobiles, sailing, old maps. *Address:* ul. Jaracza 3 m. 4, 00-378 Warsaw, Poland. *Telephone:* (22) 625 26 39 (Home). *E-mail:* lmski@poczta.onet.pl (Home). *Website:* www.moczulski.pl.

MODI, Narendra Damodardas, MA; Indian politician; b. Sept. 1950, Vadnagar, Mehsana Dist; ed Gujarat Univ.; mem. Nava Nirman Andolan movt 1972–77; joined Bharatiya Janata Party (BJP) 1986, Gen. Sec. for Gujarat 1988, elected to Ass. 1995, Nat. Sec., Delhi 1995, re-elected in Gujarat 1998, Gen. Sec. for Himachai, Punjab and Haryana 1998–2001, Nat. Gen. Sec. 1999–; Chief Minister of Gujarat 2001–03, 2003–. *Publications include:* Sangharsha ma Gujarat (Gujarat under Struggle), Setu Bandh, Patra Roop Guruji. *Address:* Office of the Chief Minister, Block No. 1, 5th Floor, Ganghinagar 382 010, India (Office). *Telephone:* 3232611/9 (Office); 3243721 (Home). *Fax:* 3222101 (Office); 3222020 (Home). *E-mail:* webmaster@gujaratindia.com (Office). *Website:* www.gujaratindia.com (Office).

MODI, Vinay Kumar, B.TECH.CHEM.ENG.; Indian industrialist; b. 31 May 1943, Modinagar; s. of the late Rai Bahadur Gujar Mal Modi and Dayawati Modi; m. Chander Bala 1965; one s. one d.; ed Scindia School, Gwalior, Indian Inst. of Tech., Kanpur; Dir Modi Industries Ltd 1965–; Vice-Chair., Man. Dir Modi Rubber Ltd 1976–; Chair. Gujarat Guardian Ltd, Modi Mirrlees Blackstone Ltd, Shree Acids and Chemicals Ltd; various awards from Govt for export performance; prizes from several asscns. *Publications:* various articles on steel, tyres and cement production. *Leisure interests:* golf, tennis, billiards. *Address:* DDA Shopping Centre, New Friends Colony, New Delhi 110065; Modi Bhavan, Civil Lines, Modinagar 201204, India; 55A, Friends Colony (East), New Delhi 110065 (Home). *Telephone:* (11) 6835766, (11) 6830703 (Office); (11) 6833633, (11) 6833088 (Home). *Fax:* (11) 6830868 (Office); (11) 6846175 (Home). *E-mail:* modivinay@hotmail.com (Office).

MODIANO, Patrick Jean; French novelist; b. 30 July 1945, Boulogne-Billancourt; s. of Albert Modiano and Luisa Colpyn; m. Dominique Zehrfuss 1970; two d.; ed schools in Biarritz, Chamonix, Deauville, Thônes, Barbizon, coll. in Paris; Prix Roger Nimier 1968, Prix Felix Fénéon 1969, Grand Prix de l'tAcadémie Française 1972, Prix Goncourt 1978; Chevalier des Arts et des Lettres; prix Pierre de Monaco 1984; Grand prix du Roman de la Ville de Paris 1994, Grand prix de littérature Paul Morand de l'Académie française 2000. *Publications:* La place de l'étoile 1968, La ronde de nuit 1969, Les boulevards de ceinture 1972, Lacombe Lucien (screenplay) 1973, La polka (play) 1974, Villa triste (novel) 1975, Interrogatoire d'Emmanuel Berl 1976, Livret de famille (novel) 1977, Rue des boutiques obscures 1978, Une jeunesse 1981, Memory Lane 1981, De si braves garçons (novel) 1982, Poupée blonde 1983, Quartier perdu 1985, Dimanches d'août 1986, Une aventure de Choura 1986, La fiancée de Choura 1987, Remise de peine (novel) 1988, Catherine Certitude 1988, Vestiaire de l'enfance (novel) 1989, Voyage de noces 1990, Fleurs de ruine (novel) 1991, Un cirque passe (novel) 1992, Chien de Printemps 1993, Du plus loin de l'oubli 1995, Dora Bruder 1997, Des inconnues 1999, La Petite bijou 2001. *Address:* c/o Editions Gallimard, 5 rue Sébastien Bottin, 75007 Paris, France.

MODIGLIANI, Franco, DJur, DSc; American professor of economics; b. 18 June 1918, Rome, Italy; s. of Enrico Modigliani and Olga Flaschel; m. Serena Calabi 1939; two s.; ed Liceo Visconti, Univ. of Rome, New School for Soc. Research, New York; Lecturer, New School for Soc. Research, New York, 1943–44, Asst Prof. of Math. Econ. and Econometrics 1946–48; Assoc. Prof. of Econs, Univ. of Ill. 1949–50, Prof. 1950–52; Prof. of Econs and Industrial Admin., Carnegie Inst. of Tech. 1952–60; Prof. of Econs, Northwestern Univ. 1960–62; Prof. of Econs and Finance, MIT 1962–88, Inst. Prof. 1970–88, Prof. Emer. 1988–; Academic Consultant, Bd of Govs., Fed. Reserve System 1966, mem. Cttee on Monetary Statistics, 1974–76; Sr Adviser, Brookings Panel on Econ. Activity 1971; Vice-Pres. Int. Econ. Asscn 1976–83, Hon. Pres. 1983–; Pres. American Finance Asscn 1981; fmr Pres. Econometric Soc., American Econ. Asscn; mem. NAS, American Acad. of Arts and Sciences; Hon. LLD (Univ. of Chicago) 1967; Hon. Dr.Econs. (Univ. Catholique de Louvain, Belgium) 1974; Hon. Dr. of Econs and Commerce (Istituto Universitario di Bergamo) 1979; Hon. D.Hum. Litt. (Bard Coll., New York) 1985, (Brandeis Univ.) 1986; Dr. hc (Ill.) 1990; Journal of Business Award 1961, Graham and Dodd Award 1975, 1980, Nobel Prize for Economic Science 1985, Premio Scanno 1997. *Publications:* National Incomes and International Trade 1953, Planning Production, Inventories and Work Force 1960, Role of Anticipations and Plans in Economic Behavior and Their Use in Economic Analysis and Forecasting 1961, New Mortgage Designs for Stable Housing in an Inflationary Environment 1975, The Collected Papers of Franco Modigliani (3 Vols) 1980, (4th and 5th Vols) 1989, Adventures of an Economist 2001; co-author of several Publs. *Leisure interests:* sailing, swimming, skiing, tennis. *Address:* Massachusetts Institute of Technology, Sloan School of Management, Room E53-417, 50 Memorial Drive, Cambridge, MA 02142 (Office); 1010 Memorial Drive, #20-B, Cambridge, MA 02138, USA (Home). *Telephone:* (617) 253-7153 (Office); (617) 354-0025 (Home).

MODROW, Hans, DR.; German politician; b. 27 Jan. 1928, Jasenitz, Ueckermuende Dist; s. of Franz Modrow and Agnes (née Krause) Modrow; m. Annemarie Straubing 1950; two d.; apprentice locksmith 1942–45; served in German army in Second World War; prisoner of war –1949; mem. SED 1949; First Sec. of East Berlin City Cttee 1953–61; mem. East Berlin City Council 1953–71; SED Party School 1954–58; cand. mem. SED Cen. Cttee 1958–67, mem. Cen. Cttee 1967–90; Deputy to People's Chamber (Volkskammer) 1958–90; First Sec. SED Dist Cttee, Berlin-Köpernick 1961–67; Head Dept for Agitation and Propaganda, SED Cen. Cttee 1967–71; First Sec., SED Dresden Dist Cttee 1973–89; Prime Minister of GDR 1989–90; mem. Bundestag 1990–94, Hon. Chair. Party of Democratic Socialism 1990–; MEP 1999–; on trial for alleged vote-rigging April 1993; found guilty and fined May 1993; to stand trial again for the same offence after appeal court decision that fine was too small; retrial ordered Nov. 1994; given nine-month suspended sentence for electoral fraud 1995; Ddecorations include Order of Merit of Fatherland 1959, Silver 1969, Gold 1975, Karl Marx Order 1978. *Publications:* Aufbruch und Ende 1991, Ich wollte ein neues Deutschland, Die Perestroika–wie ich sie sehe. *Leisure interests:* politics, culture, sport (active skier). *Address:* Karl-Marx-Allee 62, 10243 Berlin, Germany. *Telephone:* (30) 2912789.

MODRZEJEWSKI, Andrei Mikołaj, MSc; Polish business executive; b. 16 Dec. 1950, Szczecin; s. of Stanisław Modrzejewski and Sabina Modrzejewska; ed Nicolaus Copernicus Univ. Toruń; liquidator, Nowosądecki Kombinat Budowlany, Nowy Sącz 1992–94; Dir of Investment E. Kwiatkowski Nat. Investment Fund SA 1995–98, Pres. 1998–99; Pres. and CEO Polski Koncern Naftowy Orlen SA 1998–. *Leisure interests:* literature, mountain tourism, skiing, music. *Address:* PKN Orlen SA, ul. Chemików 7, 09-411 Płock (Office); Poreba Wielka 278, 34-535 Niedźwiedź, Poland (Home). *Telephone:* (24) 3653150 (Office). *Fax:* (24) 3654040 (Office). *E-mail:* prezes@orlen.pl (Office). *Website:* www.orlen.pl (Office).

MOE, George Cecil Rawle, C.H.B., QC, MA, LLM; Barbadian fmr politician and barrister-at-law; b. 12 March 1932, Barbados; s. of Cecil S. Moe and Odessa M. (née Marshall) Moe; m. Olga Louise Atkinson 1957; two s. one d.; ed Harrison Coll., Oxford Univ. and Columbia Univ., New York; called to the Bar, Middle Temple, London; Magistrate 1960–62; Acting Asst Legal Draftsman 1962–63; Acting Crown Counsel 1963–66; Sr Crown Counsel 1967–71; Acting Perm. Rep. to UN 1970–71; Attorney-Gen. and Minister of Legal Affairs 1971–76, also Minister of External Affairs 1972–76; Leader of Senate 1972–76; pvt. practice 1976–79; Puisne Judge (Belize) 1979–81, Chief Justice (Belize) 1982–85; Justice of Appeal, Eastern Caribbean Supreme Court 1985–91, Justice of Appeal, Supreme Court of Barbados 1991–. *Leisure interests:* music, cricket, gardening, swimming. *Address:* Supreme Court, Judiciary Office, Coleridge Street, Bridgetown (Office); P.O. Box 1004, Bridgetown, Barbados. *Telephone:* 426-3461 (Office); 432-2357. *Fax:* 246-2405 (Office).

MOE, Thorvald, PhD; Norwegian economist; b. 4 Oct. 1939, Oslo; s. of Thorvald Moe and Marie Cappelen Moe; m. Nina Kjeldsberg 1968; one s. one d.; ed Stanford Univ.; held various Sr posts in Ministry of Finance; Dir-Gen. Econ. Policy Dept Ministry of Finance 1978–86, Chief Econ. Adviser and Deputy Perm. Sec. 1989–; Amb. to OECD 1986–89; Deputy Sec.-Gen. OECD 1997–. *Leisure interests:* history, tennis. *Address:* OECD, 2 rue André-Pascal, 75775 Paris Cédex 16, France. *Telephone:* 1-45-24-82-00. *Fax:* 1-45-24-85-00. *E-mail:* webmaster@oecd.org (Office). *Website:* www.oecd.org (Office).

MOELLER, Bernd, DTheol; German professor of Church history; b. 19 May 1931, Berlin; s. of the late Max Moeller and Carola Bielitz; m. Irene Müller 1957; three d.; ed Univs. of Erlangen, Mainz, Basle, Munich and Heidelberg; Research Asst Univ. of Heidelberg 1956–58, Privatdozent 1958–64; Prof. of Church History, Univ. of Göttingen 1964–, Rector 1971–72; Chair. Verein für Reformationsgeschichte, Heidelberg 1976–2001; mem. Akad. der Wissenschaften zu Göttingen, Academia Europaea; Dr hc (Zürich) 1998. *Publications:* Reichsstadt und Reformation 1962, Geschichte des Christentums in Grundzügen 1965, Spätmittelalter 1966, Oekumenische Kirchengeschichte (with R. Kottje) I-III 1970–74, Deutschland im Zeitalter der Reformation 1977, Die Reformation und das Mittelalter 1991, Kirchengeschichte. Deutsche Texte (1699–1927) 1994, Städtische Predigt in der Frühzeit der Reformation (with K. Stackmann) 1996, Luther—Rezeption 2001. *Address:* Herzberger Landstrasse 26, 37085 Göttingen, Germany. *Telephone:* (551) 42850.

MOERDANI, Leonardus Benjamin; Indonesian army officer; b. 2 Oct. 1932, Cepu; m. Theresia Hartini Moerdani 1964; one d.; served under Gen. Soeharto in mil. operation to take back Irian Jaya from Netherlands 1962;

played key role in restoring diplomatic relations with Malaysia following Pres. Soekarno's armed conflict over Sabah and Sarawak 1963–66; Consul Gen., Kuala Lumpur 1967–71, Seoul 1971–74; Asst for Intelligence, Dept of Defence & Security 1974–83; Head Strategic Intelligence Center 1977, Vice-Chief State Intelligence Co-ordinating Agency 1978–83; C-in-C of the Armed Forces, Commdr Security & Order Restoration Command, Chief of Strategic Intelligence Agency 1983–88; Minister of Defence and Security 1988–93. *Leisure interest:* golf. *Address:* c/o Ministry of Defence and Security, Jalan Merdeka Barat 13, Jakarta 10110, Indonesia.

MOERSCH, Karl; German politician and journalist; b. 11 March 1926, Calw/Württ.; s. of Karl F. Moersch; m. Waltraut Schweikle 1947; one s.; ed Univ. of Tübingen; journalist in Ludwigshafen, Bad Godesberg (Deutscher Forschungsdienst) and Frankfurt (Ed. of Die Gegenwart) 1956–58; Head of Press Dept, Freie Demokratische Partei (FDP) 1961–64; freelance journalist 1964–; fmr mem. Bundestag; Parl. Sec. of State, Minister of State, Ministry of Foreign Affairs 1970–76; mem. Exec. Bd of UNESCO 1980–85; Ludwig-Uhland Prize 1997. *Publications:* Kursrevision–Deutsche Politik nach Adenauer 1978, Europa für Anfänger 1979, Sind wir denn eine Nation? 1982, Bei uns im Staate Beutelsbach 1984, Geschichte der Pfalz 1987, Sueben, Württemberger und Franzosen 1991, Sperrige Landsleute 1996, Es geht seltsam zu – in Württemberg 1998, Immer wieder war's ein Abenteuer–Erinnerungen 2001, Kontrapunkt Baden-Württemberg 2002; and numerous newspaper articles, etc. *Address:* Gebhard-Müller-Allee 14, 71638 Ludwigsburg, Germany. *Telephone:* (7141) 905745. *Fax:* (7141) 905643.

MOFAZ, Lieut.-Gen. Shaul, BA; Israeli politician and army officer; b. 1948, Iran; m. Orit Mofaz; four c.; ed Bar-Ilan Univ., US Marine Corps Command and Staff Coll., Va, USA; immigrated to Israel 1957; paratrooper Israel Defense Forces (IDF) 1966, served in Six-Day War 1967; command positions in Paratroop Brigade; Commdr Paratroop Reconnaissance Unit 1973; Deputy Commdr Paratroop Brigade; infantry brigade commdr 1982; Commdr IDF Officers School 1984; Commdr Paratroop Brigade 1986–88; promoted Brig.-Gen. 1988; Sr Officer Ground Corps Command 1988–90; Commdr Galilee Div. 1990–92; Commdr IDF forces in Judea and Samaria 1993–94; promoted Maj.-Gen. 1994; GOC Southern Command 1994–96; Chief of Planning Directorate Gen. Staff 1996–97; Deputy Chief Gen. Staff 1997; 16th Chief of Gen. Staff 1998–2002; Minister of Defence Nov. 2002–. *Address:* Ministry of Defence, Kaplan Street, Hakirya, Tel-Aviv 67659, Israel (Office). *Telephone:* 3-5692010 (Office). *Fax:* 3-6916940 (Office). *E-mail:* public@mod.gov.il (Office). *Website:* www.mod.gov.il (Office).

MOFFAT, Sir Brian Scott, Kt, OBE, FCA; British business executive; b. 6 Jan. 1939; s. of Festus Moffat and Agnes Moffat; m. Jacqueline Cunliffe 1964; one s. (and one s. deceased) one d.; ed Hulme Grammar School; with Peat Marwick Mitchell & Co. 1961–68; joined British Steel Corpn (later British Steel PLC, now Corus Group PLC) 1968, Man. Dir Finance 1986–91, Chief Exec. 1991–99, Chair. 1993–2003; Dir (non-exec.) Enterprise Oil PLC 1995–, HSBC Holdings 1998–; Deputy Chair. and Sr Ind. Dir (non-exec.) 2001–; Dir (non-exec.) Bank of England 2000–; Hon. DSc (Warwick) 1998, (Sheffield) 2001. *Leisure interests:* farming, fishing, shooting. *Address:* Springfield Farm, Earlswood, Chepstow, Monmouthshire, NP6 6AT, England (Home). *Telephone:* (1291) 650959. *Fax:* (1291) 650747.

MOFFAT, Leslie Ernest Fraser, BSc, MB, CH.B., MBA, FRCSE, FRCS(GLASG.), FRCPE; British urologist; b. 3 Nov. 1949; m.; three d.; ed Univs of Edinburgh and Stirling; Professorial House Officer posts City Hosp., Royal Infirmary, Edin. 1974–75; Sr House Officer Dept of Surgery, Royal Infirmary, Edin. 1976, Surgical Registrar 1977–79; Munro Prosector, Royal Coll. of Surgeons Edin. 1977–78; Research Registrar, Clinical Shock Study Group, Western Infirmary, Glasgow 1980–81; Urological Sr Registrar, Glasgow Teaching Hosps. 1982–86; Clinical Sr Lecturer, Univ. of Aberdeen 1986–; Pres. Grampian Div. BMA 1994; Trustee Prostate Cancer charity, Hammersmith Hosp., London; Chair. Urological Cancer Working Party in Scotland; Founding Ed. UroOncology 1999–; Chair. Urological Cancer Working Party in Scotland 1999–; Medical and Specialist Adviser to CancerBACUP; Urological Consultant to British Antarctic Survey; Hon. Consultant Royal Marsden Hosp. London; Burgess of Aberdeen 1999. *Publications:* Prostate Cancer – The Facts (co-author), Urological Cancer: A Practical Guide to Management; over 98 publs including 6 book chapters. *Leisure interests:* country life, opera. *Address:* UroOncology, Polwarth Building, Medical School, Foresterhill, Aberdeen, AB25 2ZD (Office); Tillery House, Udny, Ellon, Aberdeenshire, Scotland (Home). *Telephone:* (1224) 849136 (Office); (1651) 842898 (Home). *Fax:* (1224) 403618 (Office). *E-mail:* uro-oncology@abdn.ac.uk (Office).

MOFFATT, Henry Keith, ScD, FRS; British professor of mathematical physics; b. 12 April 1935, Edinburgh; s. of the late Frederick Henry Moffatt and Emmeline Marchant Fleming; m. Katharine (Linty) Stiven 1960; two s. (one deceased) two d.; ed Edinburgh and Cambridge Univs; Asst Lecturer, then Lecturer, Cambridge Univ. 1961–76, Prof. of Mathematical Physics 1980–; Fellow of Trinity Coll., Cambridge 1961–76, 1980–, Tutor 1971–74, Sr Tutor 1975; Prof. Applied Mathematics, Bristol Univ. 1977–80; Dir Isaac Newton Inst. for Mathematical Sciences 1996–2001; Pres. Int. Union of Theoretical and Applied Mechanics 2000–; part-time Prof. Ecole Polytechnique, Paris 1992–99; Chair. Int. de Recherche Blaise Pascal 2002–03; Ed. Journal of Fluid Mechanics 1966–83; mem. Academia Europaea 1994; Foreign mem. Royal Netherlands Acad. of Arts and Sciences 1991, Acad. des Sciences, Paris 1998, Acad. Scienzia Lincei 2001; Dr. hc (INPG Grenoble)

1987, (State Univ. of New York) 1990, (Edin.) 2001; Smiths Prize 1960; Officier des Palmes Académiques 1998; Panetti-Ferrari Prize and Gold Medal 2001. *Publications:* Magnetic Field Generation in Electrically Conducting Fluids 1978, Topological Fluid Mechanics (Ed. with A. Tsinober) 1990, Topological Aspects of the Dynamics of Fluids and Plasmas (Ed. jtly.) 1992. *Leisure interests:* French country cooking, hill walking. *Address:* Trinity College, Cambridge, CB2 1TQ (Office); 6 Banhams Close, Cambridge, CB4 1HX, England (Home). *Telephone:* (1223) 363338. *E-mail:* hkm2@damtp.cam.ac.uk (Office).

MOFFO, Anna; American opera singer; b. 27 June 1932, Wayne, Pa, USA; d. of Nicholas Moffo and Regina (Cinti) Moffo; m. Robert Sarnoff 1974; ed Curtis Inst.; appeared in TV opera Madame Butterfly, Italy 1956; singer opera houses in Paris, London, Salzburg, Vienna, Milan, numerous others abroad; American debut at Lyric Opera Co., Chicago 1957, Metropolitan Opera Co., New York 1959; appeared Voice of Firestone telecast 1957; recital tours, US; numerous recordings; Order of Merit (Italy); Young Artists award, Philadelphia Orchestra; Fulbright Award for study in Europe; Liebe Augustin Award. *Roles include:* soprano Norma, La Bohème, Mignon, Rigoletto, Falstaff, Madame Butterfly, The Barber of Seville, La Traviata, Thaïs, The Daughter of the Regiment, Stiffelio, Tosca, Hansel and Gretel, Faust, Don Pasquale, Romeo and Juliet, The Magic Flute, Turandot, La Juive, The Marriage of Figaro, Otello, Il Trovatore, Luisa Miller, La Belle Hélène, The Gypsy Princess. *Address:* c/o Metropolitan Opera, Lincoln Center, New York, NY 10023, USA (Office).

MOGAE, Festus Gontebanye, MA; Botswana politician; b. 21 Aug. 1939, Serowe; s. of Ditlhabano and Dithunya Mogae; m. Barbara Gemma Modise 1968; three d.; ed Moeng Secondary School, North West London Polytechnic, Univs. of Oxford and Sussex; Planning Officer, Ministry of Devt Planning 1968–69, Ministry of Finance and Devt Planning 1970, Sr Planning Officer 1971, Dir Econ Affairs 1972–74, Perm. Sec. 1975–76; Alt. Exec. Dir of IMF 1976–78, Exec. Dir 1978–80; Alt. Gov. for Botswana, IMF 1971–72, African Devt Bank 1971–76, IBRD 1973–76; Dir Botswana Devt Corpn 1971–74 (Chair. 1975–76), De Beers Botswana Mining Co. Ltd 1975–76, Bangwato Concessions Ltd 1975–76, BCL Sales Ltd 1975–76, Bank of Botswana 1975–76 (Gov. 1980–81); Gov. IMF 1981–82; Perm. Sec. to Pres. of Botswana 1982–89, Minister of Finance and Devt Planning 1989–98, Vice-Pres. 1992–98; Pres. of Botswana April 1998–; Pres. Botswana Soc., Botswana Soc. of the Deaf; mem. Jt Devt Cttee of World Bank and IMF on the transfer of real resources to developing countries 1992–, Kalahari Conservation Soc., Commonwealth Parl. Assoc., Parliamentarians for Global Action, Global Coalition for Africa; Rep., Commonwealth Fund for Tech. Co-operation 1971–; Hon. Fellowship Botswana Inst. of Bankers 1999; Officier, Ordre Nat. Côte d'Ivoire 1979, Mali 1997, Presidential Order of Honour of Botswana 1989; Hon. LLD (Botswana) 1998; Achievement Awards for AIDS Leadership (USA 2000, Gaborone 2001). *Leisure interests:* reading, tennis, music. *Address:* Office of the President, Private Bag 001, Gaborone, Botswana (Office). *Telephone:* 350850 (Office); 353391 (Home). *Fax:* 357800 (Office); 356866 (Home). *E-mail:* kmadisa@gov.bw (Office).

MOGG, John Frederick; British European Community official; b. 5 Oct. 1943, Brighton; s. of Thomas W. Mogg and Cora M. Mogg; m. Anne Smith 1967; one d. one s.; ed Univ. of Birmingham; fmrly with Rediffusion group; First Sec. UK Perm. Representation at EC, Brussels 1979–82; various appts. in UK civil service 1982–89; Deputy Head, European Secr. Cabinet Office 1989–90; Deputy Dir-Gen. Internal Market and Industrial Affairs, European Comm. 1990–93, Dir-Gen. Internal Market (fmrly DG XV) Directorate-Gen. 1993–. *Address:* European Commission, DG Internal Market, B-1049 Brussels, Belgium. *Telephone:* (2) 295-03-07 (Office). *Fax:* (2) 295-65-00 (Office). *E-mail:* john.mogg@cec.eu.int (Office). *Website:* europa.eu.int/comm/internal_market/.

MOGGACH, Deborah, BA, FRSL; British writer; b. 28 June 1948, London; d. of Richard Hough and Helen Charlotte Hough; m. Anthony Moggach 1971 (divorced); one s. one d.; ed Camden School for Girls, Bristol Univ.; Chair. Soc. of Authors 1999–2001; TV dramas: To Have and To Hold 1986, Stolen 1990, Goggle-Eyes (adaptation) 1989 (Writers' Guild Award for Best Adapted TV Serial), Seesaw 1998, Close Relations 1998, Love in a Cold Climate (adaptation) 2001; play for theatre Double Take. *Publications:* (novels) You Must Be Sisters 1978, Close to Home 1979, A Quiet Drink 1980, Hot Water Man 1982, Porky 1983, To Have and To Hold 1986, Driving in the Dark 1988, Stolen 1990, The Stand-in 1991, The Ex-Wives 1993, Seesaw 1996, Close Relations 1997, Tulip Fever 1999, Final Demand 2001; (short stories) Smile 1987, Changing Babies 1995. *Leisure interests:* swimming in rivers, walking round cities. *Address:* c/o Curtis Brown, 28/29 Haymarket, London, SW1Y 4SP, England. *Telephone:* (20) 7396-6600. *Fax:* (20) 7396-0110.

MOGGIE, Datuk Leo, MA, MBA; Malaysian politician; b. 1 Oct. 1941, Kanowit, Sarawak; ed Univs. of Otago and Pennsylvania State Univ.; Dist Officer, Kapit, Sarawak 1966–68; Dir Borneo Literature Bureau, Kuching, Sarawak 1968–69; attached to Office of Chief Minister, Kuching 1969–72; Deputy Gen. Man. Borneo Devt Corpn Kuching 1973–74; elected to Sarawak State Legis. Ass. and Parl.; Sec.-Gen. Sarawak Nat. Party (SNAP) 1976; Minister of Welfare Services, State Govt of Sarawak 1976–77, of Local Govt 1977–78; Minister of Energy, Telecommunications and Posts 1978–89, of

Works and Public Utilities 1989–90, of Public Works 1990–95. *Address:* c/o Ministry of Public Works, Jalan Sultan Salahuddin, 50580 Kuala Lumpur, Malaysia.

MOGWE, Archibald Mooketsa, MBE, BA, P.M.S., P.H.; Botswana politician and teacher; b. 29 Aug. 1921, Kanye; s. of Rev. Morutwana T. Mogwe and Mary (née Leepo) Mogwe; m. Lena Mosele Senakhomo 1953; one s. two d.; ed schools in Bechuanaland Protectorate, teacher training in S. Africa, Univs. of Reading and Oxford; teacher 1944–57; Educ. Officer 1957–64; transferred to Secr. 1964, Perm. Sec. 1966; worked in Foreign Office 1966–, Sr Perm. Sec., Sec. to Cabinet and Head of Public Service 1968–74; Minister of Foreign Affairs 1974–84, of Mineral Resources and Water Affairs 1984–89, 1990–94. *Leisure interests:* soccer, classical music, shooting. *Address:* c/o Ministry of Mineral Resources and Water Affairs, Private Bag 0018, Gaborone, Botswana. *Telephone:* 353180 (Home).

MOHAMED, Caabi el Yachroutou; Comoran politician; Minister of Finance 1993–94; Prime Minister of Comoros April–Oct. 1995; Interim Pres. 1995–96; mem. Rally for Democracy and Renewal.

MOHAMMAD RABBANI, Haji Mola; Afghanistan politician; Chair. Taliban Interim Council of Ministers 2001. *Address:* c/o Office of the Council of Ministers, Shar Rahi, Sedarat, Kabul, Afghanistan (Office).

ISHMAEL, Mohammed Ali Odeen; Guyanese diplomatist; m.; two c.; fmr teacher; served in Ministry of Foreign Affairs 1970s; Amb. to USA 1993–; Perm. Rep. to OAS 1993–, Vice-Chair. Perm. Council 1993, Chair. 1994; mem. Del. of Guyana to UN Gen. Ass. 1993–; Chief Negotiator Summit of the Americas 1994, 1998; Head Del. of Guyana to CARICOM 1997–, to Org. of Islamic Conf., Tehran 1999; mem. Cen. Cttee Progressive Youth Org. (PYO), People's Progressive Party (PPP); Cacique Crown of Honor (CCH) 1997; Gandhi Centenary Medal, Univ. of Guyana 1974. *Publications include:* Problems of Transition of Education in the Third World, Towards Education Reform in Guyana, Amerindian Legends of Guyana, The Trail of Diplomacy; numerous articles on educ., Guyanese history and int. political issues. *Address:* Embassy of Guyana, 2490 Tracy Place, NW, Washington, DC 20008, USA (Office). *Telephone:* (202) 265-6900 (Office). *Fax:* (202) 232-1297 (Office). *E-mail:* guyanaembassy@hotmail.com (Office). *Website:* www.guyana.org/govt/embassy.html (Office).

MOHAMMED VI, King of Morocco; b. 21 Aug. 1963, Rabat; s. of the late King Hassan II; succeeded to the throne on death of his father 30 July 1999; m. Salma Bennani 2002; one s. Prince Moulay Hassan, b. 2003; ed Collège Royal, Université Mohammed V, Faculté des Sciences Juridiques, Economiques et Sociales de Rabat; Head Moroccan del., 7th Summit of Non-Aligned Nations, New Delhi 1983, 10th Franco–African Conf., Vittel 1983; apptd Co-ordinator Admin. and Services, Armed Forces 1985; rank of Gén. de Div. 1994; Hon. Pres. Asscn Socio–Culturelle du Bassin Méditerranéen 1979–; Chair. Org. Cttee 9th Mediterranean Games, Casablanca 1982. *Address:* Royal Palace, Rabat, Morocco.

MOHAMMED ZAHIR SHAH, fmr King of Afghanistan; b. 15 Oct. 1915; m. Lady Homira, 4 Nov. 1931 (died 2002); c. Princess Bilqis, Prince Ahmad Shah, Princess Maryam, Prince Mohammed Nadir, Prince Shah Mahmoud, Prince Mohammed Daoud, Prince Mirvis; ed Habibia High School, Istiqlal Coll. (both in Kabul), Lycée Janson-de-Sailly and Lycée of Montpellier, France; graduated with honours; attended Infantry Officers' School, Kabul 1932; Asst Minister in Ministry of Nat. Defence 1932–33; acting Minister of Educ. 1933, crowned King 8 Nov. 1933; deposed 17 July 1973, abdicated 24 Aug. 1973, forced into exile 1973, stripped of citizenship 1978 after Communist takeover, citizenship restored 1991, returned to Royal Palace, Kabul after 29 years of exile Aug. 2002; adviser to Future of Afghanistan Govt Talks 2001.

MOHAN, Ramesh, PhD; Indian university vice-chancellor and fmr professor of English; b. 20 March 1920, Meerut (UP); s. of Madan Mohan and Kamal Kumari; m. Vimala Mangalik 1943; three s.; ed Lucknow Univ., Leeds Univ., UK; Lecturer in English, Lucknow Univ. 1942–55, Reader 1955–61, Prof. and Head Dept of English and Modern European Languages 1961–67; Dir Cen. Inst. of English and Foreign Languages, Hyderabad 1967–85; Vice-Chancellor, Meerut Univ. 1985–88; Visiting Prof. Univ. of Ill., Urbana, USA 1971, 1975; Consultant, Indira Gandhi Nat. Open Univ., New Delhi 1988–90; Pres. Indian Asscn of English Studies 1975–80, Asscn of Indian Univs. 1982–83; mem. Bd of Dirs., American Studies Research Centre 1969–89, Exec. Council, Univ. of Hyderabad 1974–77, Exec. Bd Sahitya Akademi, New Delhi 1978–88, Bd of Dirs., U.S. Educational Foundation of India 1980–81, Governing Council, Indian Inst. of Science, Bangalore 1980–81, Univ. Grants Comm. 1982–85, Council, Asscn of Commonwealth Univs. 1982–83, Governing Body, Indian Inst. of Advanced Studies, Simla 1984–87; Wilhelm and Jacob Grimm Prize (GDR) 1986. *Publications:* The Political Novels of Anthony Trollope 1961, George Meredith and the Political Novel 1968, Teaching of English at the University Level in India 1968, Syllabus Reform in English 1977, Some Aspects of Style and Language in Indian English Fiction 1978, Indian Writing in English (Ed.) 1978, English by Air 1979, Stylistics and Literary Interpretation 1980, Symphony (collection of poems) 1984, Nehru as a Man of Letters 1989, Radhakrishnan and Higher Education in India 1989, Religion and National Secularism 1993, English in India: Status and Creativity 1993, Crisis in Higher Education 1994, Let Me Say (essays and addresses) 1996, Benjamin Disraeli: Political Novelist 1999; numerous papers on teaching of

English and higher educ. in India. *Leisure interests:* music, theatre, reading, writing, jigsaw puzzles. *Address:* Shanti Sadan 36, Nehru Road, Meerut, Uttar Pradesh, India. *Telephone:* 642339.

MOHIEDDIN, Zakaria; Egyptian politician and army officer; b. 7 May 1918; s. of the late Abdul Magid Mohieddin and Zeinab Abdul Magid; m. Naila Moustafa 1950; one s. two d.; ed Mil. Coll. and Staff Officers' Coll., Cairo; fmr lecturer Mil. Coll. and Staff Officers' Coll. and Dir-Gen. Intelligence; mem. Revolutionary Council 1952; Minister of the Interior 1953–58; Minister of the Interior UAR 1958–62, Vice-Pres. UAR and Chair. Aswan Dam Cttee 1961–62; mem. Nat. Defence Cttee 1962–69, Presidency Council 1962–64; mem. Exec. Cttee Arab Socialist Union 1964–69; Deputy Prime Minister 1964–65, 1967–68; Prime Minister and Minister of the Interior 1965–66. *Leisure interests:* fishing, shooting, rowing, poultry farming. *Address:* 52 El-Thawra Street, Dokki, Cairo, Egypt. *Telephone:* 3499421.

MOHL, Andrew, BSc; Australian financial services executive; b. 1956; with Fed. Reserve Bank of New York 1983–84; fmr Deputy Head of Research, Reserve Bank of Australia; Man. Dir ANZ Funds Man. –1996; Gen. Man. of Retail Distribution, AMP Financial Services 1996, Man. Dir AMP Asset Man., Man. Dir AMP Australian Financial Services 1999–2002, CEO AMP Group Sept. 2002–. *Address:* AMP Ltd., AMP Sydney Cove Building, 33 Alfred Street, Sydney, NSW 2000, Australia (Office). *Telephone:* (2) 9257-2700 (Office). *E-mail:* matthew_coleman@amp.com.au (Office). *Website:* www.amp .com.au (Office).

MOHN, Christoph; German electronics and telecommunications executive; b. 1965; s. of Reinhard Mohn; great-great-grands. of Carl Bertelsmann (f. co. 1835); ed Univ. of Münster; fmr intern Bantam Doubleday Dell; with Bertelsmann Music Group (BMG), Hong Kong and New York, USA 1991–94; specialist in electronics and telecommunications, McKinsey & Co. (Germany) 1994–96; Vice-Pres. Telemedia (subsidiary of Bertelsmann) 1996–97; CEO Lycos Europe 1997–, responsible for expansion of co. into 13 European countries; mem. Bertelsmann Trust. *Address:* Lycos Europe GmbH, Carl-Bertelsmann-Strasse 180, 33311 Gütersloh, Germany (Office). *Telephone:* (52) 418041339 (Office). *Fax:* (52) 418041810 (Office). *Website:* www.lycos.de (Office).

MOHORITA, Vasil; Czech politician and businessman; b. 19 Sept. 1952, Prague; s. of Vasil Mohorita and Ludmila Mohoritová; m. Vlasta Mohoritová 1976; one s. one d.; ed Komsomol Coll., Moscow and CP of Czechoslovakia (CPCZ) Political Coll., Prague; joined CPCZ 1970, mem. Cen. Cttee 1988–90, First Sec. Cen. Cttee 1989–90; Chair. Youth Union's Czechoslovak Cen. Cttee 1987–89; mem. Czechoslovak Nat. Front Presidium 1987; Deputy, Czechoslovak Nat. Council 1985–90; mem. Presidium Fed. Ass. Jan.–Oct. 1990, Deputy to Fed. Ass. House of People 1990; Chair. Communist Deputies Club Jan.–Nov. 1990; agent for Valemo, Parfia, Jamiko, CIS Group; Chair. Bd of Supervisors E.R. Tradings; Head of Sales, Frut Ovo (pvt. co.); mem. Party of Democratic Left 1993–97; Chair. Party of Democratic Socialism 1997–98; Head of External Relations, Zbrojovka, Brno 2000–. *Publications:* numerous articles. *Leisure interests:* reading historical and political literature, playing the guitar, basketball, tennis.

MOHRT, Michel, LenD; French writer and editor; b. 28 April 1914, Morlaix; s. of Fernand and Amélie (née Gélébart) Mohrt; m. Françoise Jarrier 1955; one s.; ed Law School, Rennes; lawyer, Marseilles Bar –1942; Prof. Yale Univ., Smith Coll., Univ. Coll. LA 1947–52; Ed. and Head English Translations Section Les Editions Gallimard 1952–; mem. Acad. Française 1985; Officier, Légion d'honneur, Croix de guerre; Grand Prix du roman de l'Académie française for La Prison Maritime 1962; Grand Prix de la Critique Littéraire 1970; Grand Prix de Littérature de l'Académie française 1983. *Art Exhibition:* Aquarelles Expositions (Galeries des Orfèvres Paris). *Publications:* novels: Le répit, Mon royaume pour un cheval 1949, Les nomades, le serviteur fidèle, La prison maritime 1961, La campagne d'Italie 1965, L'ours des Adirondacks 1969, Deux Indiennes à Paris 1974, Les moyens du bord 1975, La guerre civile 1986, Le Télésiège 1989, Un soir à Londres 1991, On liquide et on s'en va 1992, L'Ile des fous 1999; essays: Les intellectuels devant la défaite de 1870, Montherlant, homme libre 1943, Le nouveau roman américain 1956, L'air du large 1969, L'air du large II 1988, plays: Un jeu d'enfer 1970, La maison du père 1979, Vers l'Ouest 1988, L'Air du temps 1991. *Leisure interests:* sailing, painting. *Address:* c/o Editions Gallimard, 5 rue Sébastien-Bottin, 75007 Paris; 4 bis rue du Cherche-Midi, 75006 Paris, France (Home). *Telephone:* 1-42-22-42-12 (Home).

MOHTASHAMI, Ali Akbar, DTheol; Iranian politician; b. 30 Aug. 1946, Tehran; s. of Seyed Hossein and Fatemeh Mohtashami; m. Fatemeh Mohtashami 1968; two s. five d.; studied theology in Iran and Iraq; mil. training in Palestinian camps, Lebanon; went to Paris with Ayatollah Khomeini 1978; returned to Iran and took part in overthrow of monarchy 1979; mem. political advisory office of Ayatollah Khomeini; Dir of Ayatollah's representative delegation in Foundation of the Oppressed 1980; mem. IRIB Supervisory Council 1980–81; Amb. to Syria 1981–85; a founder of Hezbollah in Lebanon; Minister of the Interior 1985; mem. Parl. 1989–91; Chair. Parl. Cttee on Defence; Sec.-Gen. IPU Group of Iran (Chair. 1989–91); mem. Cttee to Protect the Islamic Revolution of Palestine, Cen. Council of Combatant Clergy; Sec.-Gen. of Int. Conf. on Intifada; Deputy Chair. Bd of Trustees Qods Inst.; Social Adviser to Pres. of Iran; Man. Bayan newspaper (banned June 2000). *Publications include:* Plurality, From Iran to Iran (Memoirs) 1965–79. *Leisure interests:* study, sport (especially mountaineering and swimming). *Address:*

General Secretariat of International Conference on Palestinian Intifada, 11 Khorshid Street, Pastor Avenue, Tehran (Office); Islamic Consultative Assembly, Tehran (Office); 11, Adib-ol-Mamalek Street, Ray Street, Tehran, Iran (Home). *Telephone:* (21) 6135672 (Office); (21) 361892 (Home). *Fax:* (21) 6460046 (Office). *E-mail:* info@gods-path.org (Office). *Website:* www .gods-path.org (Office).

MOI, Daniel arap; Kenyan politician; b. 1924, Sacho, Baringo district; ed African Mission School, Kabartonjo A.I.M. School and Govt African School, Kapsabet; teacher 1945–57; Head Teacher, Govt African School, Kabarnet 1946–48, 1955–57, teacher Tambach Teacher Training School, Kabarnet 1948–54; African Rep. mem., Legis. Council 1957–63; Chair. Kenya African Democratic Union (KADU) 1960–61; mem. House of Reps. 1961–; Parl. Sec., Ministry of Educ. April–Dec. 1961; Minister of Educ. 1961–62, Local Govt 1962–64, Home Affairs 1964–67; Pres. Kenya African Nat. Union (KANU) for Rift Valley Province 1966–67; Vice-Pres. of Kenya 1967–78, concurrently Minister of Home Affairs; Pres. of Kenya and C-in-C of the Armed Forces 1978–2002; Minister of Defence 1979–2002; Chair. OAU 1981–82; mem. Rift Valley Educ. Bd, Kalenjin Language Cttee; Chair. Rift Valley Provincial Court; Kt of Grace, Order of St John 1980. *Address:* c/o Office of the President, Harambee House, Harambee Avenue, PO Box 30510, Nairobi, Kenya.

MOINOT, Pierre, LèsL; French civil servant; b. 29 March 1920, Fressines, Deux-Sèvres; m. Madeleine Sarrailh 1947; one s. four d.; ed Univs. de Paris, Caen and Grenoble; Sr Civil Servant 1946–; Tech. Adviser, Pvt. Office of André Malraux 1959–61; Dir Theatres and Cultural Action 1960–62; Admin. Union générale cinématographique 1960–; Pres. Comm. on advances in long films 1964–72, Comm. on Audiovisual Problems 1981–; French Del. to UNESCO 1966; Dir-Gen. of Arts and Letters 1966–69; Chief Adviser, Audit Office 1967, Pres. 1978, Attorney-Gen. 1983–86; mem. Acad. française 1982–; Prix du Roman de l'Académie française, Prix Sainte-Beuve, Prix des libraires de France, Prix Fémina 1979; Grand Officier Légion d'honneur, Croix de guerre, Médaille des blessés, Commdr des Arts et des Lettres, Bronze Star Medal, Chevalier des Palmes académiques, Officier du Mérite agricole and other decorations. *Publications:* Armes et bagages 1951, La chasse royale 1954, La blessure 1956, Le sable vif 1963, Héliogabale 1971, Mazarin 1978, Le guetteur d'ombre 1979, Jeanne d'Arc 1988, La descente du fleuve 1991, Tous comptes faits 1993, T. E. Lawrence en guerre 1994, Attention à la peinture 1997, Le matin vient et aussi la nuit 1999, La mort en lui 2002. *Leisure interests:* hunting, carpentry. *Address:* 44 rue du Cherche-Midi, 75006 Paris, France (Home). *Telephone:* 1-45-44-19-47. *Fax:* 1-45-44-59-85 (Home).

MOISEIWITSCH, Benjamin Lawrence, PhD, MRIA; British professor of applied mathematics; b. 6 Dec. 1927, London; s. of Jacob Moiseiwitsch and Chana Kotlerman; m. Sheelagh Mary Penrose McKeon 1953; two s. two d.; ed Royal Liberty School, Romford and Univ. Coll., London; Lecturer in Applied Math., Univ. of Belfast 1952–62, Reader in Applied Math. 1962–68, Prof. 1968–93, Prof. Emer. 1993–, Head Dept of Applied Math. and Theoretical Physics 1977–89, Dean Faculty of Science 1972–75. *Publications include:* Variational Principles 1966, Integral Equations 1977. *Leisure interest:* music. *Address:* Department of Applied Mathematics and Theoretical Physics, The Queen's University of Belfast, Belfast, BT7 1NN (Office); 21 Knocktern Gardens, Belfast, BT4 3LZ, Northern Ireland (Home). *Telephone:* (28) 9027-3158 (Office); (28) 9065-8332 (Home). *Fax:* (28) 9023-9182 (Office). *E-mail:* b .moiseiwitsch@qub.ac.uk (Office); b.moiseiwitsch@btinternet.com (Home). *Website:* www.qub.ac.uk/mp/amtpt (Office); www.b.moiseiwitsch.btinternet .co.uk (Home).

MOISEYEV, Igor Aleksandrovich; Russian choreographer; b. 21 Jan. 1906, Kiev, Ukraine; m. 1st Tamara Alekseevna Seifert; one d.; m. 2nd Irina Alekseevna Chagadaeva; ed Bolshoi Theatre School of Choreography; Artist and Ballet Master at the Bolshoi Theatre 1924–39; Dir of the Choreographic Dept of the Theatre of People's Art 1936; Founder and Art Dir of the Folk Dance Ensemble of the USSR (now Moiseyev Dance Co.) 1937–; Hon. mem. Paris Acad. of Dance; People's Artist of the USSR 1953; State Prizewinner 1942, 1947, 1952; Lenin Prize 1967; Hero of Socialist Labour 1976 and other decorations. *Publications:* articles on choreography of nat. dance. *Address:* Iverskaya str. 31, Moscow; Moiseyev Dance Company, 20 Triumfalnaya Pl., Moscow, Russia. *Telephone:* (095) 299-63-28. *Fax:* (095) 202-20-36.

MOÏSI, Dominique; French professor of international relations; b. 21 Oct. 1946, Neuilly-sur-Seine; s. of Jules Moïsi and Charlotte Tabakman; m. Diana Pinto-Moïsi 1977; two s.; ed Lycée Buffon, Paris, Institut d'études politiques, Paris, Faculté de droit de Paris, Harvard Univ., USA; Visiting Lecturer, Hebrew Univ. of Jerusalem 1973–75; Asst Lecturer, Univ. of Paris X 1975–89; Deputy Dir Institut français des relations internationales 1979–; lecturer, Ecole Nationale d'Administration 1980–85, Ecole des hautes études en sciences sociales 1988–; Sec.-Gen. Groupe d'étude et de recherche des problèmes internationaux 1975–78; Assoc. Prof., Johns Hopkins Univ. European Centre, Bologna 1983–84; Ed. Politique étrangère 1983–; Prof. Inst. d'études politiques, Paris; Bd Dirs. Salzburg Seminar, Aspen Inst., Berlin; editorial writer for Financial Times and Die Zeit. *Publications:* Crises et guerres au XXe siècle: analogies et différences 1981, Le nouveau continent: plaidoyer pour une Europe renaissante (with Jacques Rupnik) 1991 etc. *Leisure interests:* music, cinema, tennis, skiing. *Address:* Institut français des relations internationales (IFRI), 27 rue de la Procession, 75015 Paris (Office); 4 rue Saint-Florentin, 75001 Paris, France (Home). *Telephone:* 1-40-61-60-00 (Office). *Fax:* 1-40-61-60-60 (Office). *E-mail:* moisi@ifri.org (Office). *Website:* www.ifri.org (Home).

MOISIU, Alfred; Albanian politician and head of state; b. 1 Dec. 1929, Scutari; s. of Spiro Moisiu; ed in USSR; fmr mil. engineer and army gen. under Enver Hoxha; Dir 'The Genius', Ministry of Defence 1971–81; Deputy Minister of Defence 1981–82, Minister 1991–92; Leader Democratic Party of Sali Berisha 1982–94, Adviser on Defence 1992–97; Pres. of Albania 2002–; Pres. Albanian Atlantic Asscn (pro-NATO NGO) 1994–. *Address:* Office of the President, Bulevardi Deshmoret E Kombit, Tirana, Albania (Office). *Fax:* (4) 233761. *Website:* president.al.

MOITINHO DE ALMEIDA, José Carlos de Carvalho, L. EN D.; Portuguese judge; b. 17 March 1936, Lisbon; m. Maria de Lourdes Saraiva De Menezes 1959; one s. one d.; Asst to Public Prosecutor 1963–68; Public Prosecutor, Court of Appeal, Lisbon 1962–72; Chef du Cabinet to Minister of Justice 1972–73; Deputy Attorney-Gen. 1974–79; Dir Office of European Law 1980–86; fmr Judge, Court of Justice of European Union and Pres. Third and Sixth Chambers; Judge, Supreme Court of Portugal; Croix de Guerre, Ordre du Mérite (Luxembourg). *Publications:* Le contrat d'assurance dans le droit portugais et comparé, La publicité mensongère, Droit communautaire, ordre juridique communautaire, Les libertés fondamentales dans la CEE. *Leisure interests:* swimming, gardening. *Address:* Vivenda Panorama, Av. do Monaco, 2675 Estoril, Portugal (Home). *Fax:* (12) 14647999 (Home). *E-mail:* mjmoitinho@mail.telepac.pt (Home).

MOJADDEDI, Sibghatullah; Afghanistan religious leader and politician; b. 1929; ed Al-Azhar Univ., Cairo; imprisoned for involvement in plot to assassinate Soviet Prime Minister Nikita Krushchev 1959–64; f. Jami'at Ulamai Mohammadi (Org. of Muslim Clergy) 1972; f. Jebha-i-Nejat-i-Melli Afghanistan (Nat. Liberation Front of Afghanistan) 1979, Leader 1979–; acting Pres. Unity Govt 1992; Head Govt of Mujaheddin Council, Kabul 1992–94.

MOJSOV, Lazar, DIur; Macedonian journalist, politician and diplomatist (retd); b. 19 Dec. 1920, Negotino, Macedonia; s. of Dono Mojsov and Efka Mojsov; m. Liljana Jankov 1945; two d.; ed Belgrade Univ.; fmr mem. Anti-Fascist Ass. for the Nat. Liberation of Macedonia; fmr Public Prosecutor, Macedonia; Minister of Justice, Macedonia 1948–51; Dir New Macedonia 1953–58; Pres. Supreme Court of Macedonia 1953; fmr Head of Press Dept, Fed. Govt of Macedonia; mem. Yugoslav Fed. Parl. and Parl. of Macedonia; mem. Exec. Bd, Socialist League of Working People of Yugoslavia; mem. Exec. Cttee of Cen. Cttee, Macedonian League of Communists; mem. Cen. Cttee League of Communists of Yugoslavia –1989 (Pres. of Presidium 1980–81); Amb. to USSR 1958–61; Dir Inst. for Study of Workers' Movements 1961–62; Dir and Chief Ed. Borba 1962–64; Pres. Int. Cttee of Fed. Conf. of Socialist Alliance of Working People of Yugoslavia 1965; Amb. to Austria 1967–69; Perm. Rep. to UN 1969–74; Chair. Security Council 1973; Deputy Fed. Sec. for Foreign Affairs 1974–78, Fed. Sec. 1982–84; mem. Collective State Presidency of Yugoslavia 1984–89, Vice-Pres. 1986–87, Pres. 1987–88; Pres. 32nd UN Gen. Ass. 1977; Partisan Memorial Medal 1941; Order of Merit for Exceptional Achievements First Class, Order of Merit for Services to the Nation, First and Third Class, Order of Brotherhood and Unity. *Publications:* The Bulgarian Working Party (Communist) and the Macedonian National Question 1948, Vasil Glavinov: First Propagator of Socialism in Macedonia 1949, Concerning the Question of the Macedonian National Minority in Greece 1954, The World Around Us 1977, Historical Themes 1978, Dimensions of Non-alignment 1980, Past and Present 1981, Nonalignment Yesterday, Today and Tomorrow 1990. *Leisure interest:* philately.

MOLCHANOV, Vladimir Kyrillovich; Russian journalist; b. 7 Oct 1950, Moscow; s. of Kyrill Molchanov; m. Consuella Segura; one d.; ed Moscow State Univ.; with Press Agency Novosti 1973–86; observer USSR State Cttee for TV and Radio 1987–91; artistic Dir studio of independent co. REN-TV 1991–, Observer Reuter-TV 1994–; regular appearances in his own TV programmes Before and After Midnight 1987–93, Before and After 1994–, Panorama 2000–, Longer than Age 2000–; mem. Acad. of Russian TV, Acad. of Natural Sciences; Prize of Journalists' Union as the Best TV Journalist 1990 and other awards. *Publications:* TV films: Remembrance, I, You, He and She, People and Years, Zone, I Still Have More Addresses, Tied with One Chain, August of 1991 (screenplays), Retribution Must Come (M. Gorky Prize 1982). *Leisure interest:* life in the country. *Address:* REN-TV, Zubovsky blvd 17, Moscow, Russia. *Telephone:* (095) 255-90-77 (Office).

MOLEFE, Popo Simon; South African politician; b. 26 April 1952, Sophiatown; m. 1st Olympia Molefe (divorced); three c.; m. 2nd Boitumelo Plaatje 1991; ed Naledi High School; microfilm machine operator, photographic printing machine operator 1976–78; mem. SASM 1973–76; mem. Black Peoples's Convention 1974, 1977; First Chair. Azanian People's Org. (AZAPO), Soweto Branch 1979–81; mem. Gen. and Allied Workers Union 1980–83; Sec. Transvaal Region, United Democratic Front (UDF) 1983, Nat. Gen. Sec. 1983–91; mem. Nat. Exec. Cttee ANC 1991–; charged with treason and murder after detention in 1985, convicted at Delmas Treason Trial, sentenced to 10 years imprisonment after being held in custody for 4 years 1988, released 1989; Chair. ANC Nat. Elections Comm. 1992–94, ANC Alexandra Br. 1990; Vice-Chair. ANC PWV Region 1990–94; Premier NW

Prov. Govt 1994–; Sec. Nat. Organizing Comm. of ANC. *Address:* Private Bag X2018, Mmabatho 8681; African National Congress, P.O. Box 61884, Marshalltown 2107, South Africa.

MOLIN, Yuri Nikolaevich; Russian chemist and physicist; b. 3 Feb. 1934; s. of N. N. Molin and A. F. Kuramova; m. N. G. Molina 1965; two d.; ed Moscow Inst. of Physics and Tech.; worked in USSR Acad. of Sciences Inst. of Chemical Physics 1957–59; various posts in USSR Acad. of Sciences Inst. of Chem. Kinetics and Combustion 1959–, Dir 1971–93, Head of Lab. 1993–; teacher in Univ. of Novosibirsk 1966–, Prof. 1974–; mem. USSR (now Russian) Acad. of Sciences 1981; Fellow Int. Electron Paramagnetic Resonance Soc. 1998; Mendeleev Lecture 1992; Lenin Prize 1986. *Publications:* Spin Exchange 1980, Spin Polarization and Magnetic Effects in Radical Reactions 1984, Infrared Photochemistry 1985. *Leisure interest:* mountain walking. *Address:* Institute of Chemical Kinetics and Combustion, Novosibirsk 630090, Russia. *Telephone:* (3832) 33-16-07 (Office); (3832) 30-25-21 (Home). *Fax:* (3832) 34-23-50 (Office). *E-mail:* molin@ns.kinetics.nsc.ru (Office).

MOLINA, Alfred; British actor; b. 24 May 1953, London; m. Jill Gascoigne; ed Guildhall School of Music and Drama; on stage has appeared with RSC and at Nat. Theatre, Royal Court Theatre and Donmar Warehouse. *Films include:* Indiana Jones and the Raiders of the Lost Ark 1981, Anyone for Denis 1982, Number One 1984, Eleni 1985, Ladyhawke 1985, A Letter to Brezhnev 1985, Prick Up Your Ears 1987, Manifesto 1988, Not Without My Daughter 1991, American Friends 1991, Enchanted April 1991, When Pigs Fly 1993, The Trial 1993, American Friends 1993, White Fang 2: Myth of the White Wolf 1994, Maverick 1994, Hideaway 1995, The Perez Family 1995, A Night of Love 1995, The Steal, Species 1995, Before and After 1996, Dead Man 1996, Scorpion Spring 1996, Mojave Moon 1996, Anna Karenina 1997, The Odd Couple II 1997, Boogie Nights 1997, The Man Who Knew Too Little 1997, The Imposters 1998, Magnolia 1999, Dudley Do-Right 1999, The Trial 2000, Chocolat 2000, Texas Rangers 2001, Agatha Christie's Murder on the Orient Express 2001, Pete's Meteor 2002, Road to Perdition 2002, Frida 2003. *Television includes:* role of Blake in series El CID, Year in Provence, Nervous Energy, Ladies Man (series). *Website:* www.alfred-molina.com (Office).

MOLINA, Mario Jose, PhD; American Mexican professor of atmospheric chemistry; b. 19 March 1943, Mexico City; s. of Roberto Molina-Pasquel and Leonor Henriquez; m. Luisa Y. Tan 1973; one s.; ed Acad. Hispano Mexicana, Univ. Nacional Autónoma de Mexico (UNAM), Univ. of Freiburg and Univ. of Calif. at Berkeley; Asst Prof. UNAM 1967–68; Research Assoc. Univ. of Calif. Berkeley 1972–73; Research Assoc. Univ. of Calif. at Irvine 1973–75, Asst Prof. 1975–79, Assoc. Prof. 1979–82; Sr Research Scientist, Jet Propulsion Lab., Calif. 1983–89; Prof. Dept of Earth, Atmospheric and Planetary Sciences and Dept of Chem. MIT 1989–97, Inst. Prof. 1997–; mem. NAS; Max Planck Research Award 1994–96; UNEP Ozone Award 1995; Nobel Prize for Chem. 1995; many other awards and distinctions. *Publications:* articles in scientific journals. *Leisure interests:* music, reading, tennis. *Address:* Department of Earth, Atmospheric and Planetary Sciences, Massachusetts Institute of Technology, Room 54-1814, Cambridge, MA 02139 (Office); 8 Clematis Road, Lexington, MA 02421, USA. *Telephone:* (617) 253-5081 (Office). *Fax:* (617) 258-6525 (Office). *E-mail:* mmolina@mit.edu (Office).

MOLINA BARRAZA, Col Arturo Armando; Salvadorean fmr Head of State and army officer; b. 6 Aug. 1927, San Salvador; s. of Mariano Molina and Matilde Barraza de Molina; m. María Elena Contreras de Molina; four s. one d.; ed Escuela Militar, El Salvador, Escuela Superior de Guerra, Mexico, Escuela de Infanteria, Spain; Section and Co. Commdr, Escuela Militar; Artillery Garrison, Asst Dir Escuela de Armas, Section and Dept Chief, Staff HQ; Del. 6th Conf. of American Armed Forces, Peru 1965, 7th Conf. Buenos Aires; Gen. Co-ordinator, 2nd and 3rd Confs. of Defence Council of Cen. American States; Dir Exec. Comm. for Shipping; Dir Nat. Cttee of Caritas, El Salvador; Pres. of El Salvador 1972–77.

MOLISA, Sela; ni-Vanuatu politician; b. 15 Dec. 1950, Santo; s. of Mandei Rongtuhun and Ruth Rongtuhun; one d. two s.; ed Onesua High School, Malaba Coll., Efate, Univ. of the S. Pacific, Fiji, Fifi School of Medicine; banker 1974–77; Gen. Man. Co-operative Fed. 1977–81; MP 1982–; Minister of Internal Affairs 1983, of Foreign Affairs 1983–87, of Finance 1987–91, 2002–, of Trade, Commerce and Industry 1996, of Finance and Econ. Man. 1998–99, of Lands and Natural Resources 2001–02; apptd Govt Special Rep. to negotiate with rebels during attempted secession of Santo from Vanuatu 1980; involved in design and implementation of Vanuatu Comprehensive Reform Programme 1997–. *Leisure interests:* reading, swimming, listening to music, watching sports. *Address:* Ministry of Finance, PMB 058, Port Vila (Office); POB 252, Port Vila, Vanuatu (Home). *Telephone:* 23032 (Office); 23081 (Home). *Fax:* 27937 (Office); 23081 (Home).

MÖLK, Ulrich, DPhil; German professor of Romance Literature; b. 29 March 1937, Hamburg; s. of Heinrich Mölk and Berta Mölk; m. Renate Mölk 1962; ed Univs. of Hamburg and Heidelberg; Prof. of Romance Literature, Univ. of Giessen 1967; Prof. of Romance Literature Univ. of Göttingen and Dir Inst. für Lateinische und Romanische Philologie des Mittelalters 1974–; mem. Acad. of Göttingen, Vice-Pres. 1990–92, Pres. 1992–94. *Publications:* Guiraut Riquier, Las cansos 1962, Trobar clus 1968, Répertoire métrique de la poésie lyrique française 1972, Trotzki, Literaturkritik 1973, Trobadorlyrik 1982, Flaubert, Une Nuit de Don Juan, Edition 1984, Vita und Kult des hl. Metro von Verona 1987, Lohier et Malart 1988, Romanische Frauenlieder 1989, Die europäische Bedeutungsgeschichte von 'Motiv' 1992, Julien Sorel vor dem

Schwurgericht 1994, Impressionistischer Stil 1995, Literatur und Recht 1996, Europäische Jahrhundertwende 1999, Albéric: le poème d'Alexandre 2000. *Address:* Institut f. Latein u. Roman. Philologie des Mittelalters, Humboldtallee 19, 37073 Göttingen; Höltystr. 7, 37085 Göttingen, Germany. *Telephone:* (551) 399255 (Office); (551) 47978. *Fax:* (551) 398151 (Office). *E-mail:* sekretariat.latromma@phil.uni-goettingen.de.

MOLL, Kurt; German bass; b. 11 April 1938, Buir; m. Ursula Pade 1968; one s. two d.; ed Staatliche Hochschule für Musik, Cologne; operatic début Cologne; subsequently sang operatic roles at Aachen, Mainz, Wuppertal, Hamburg; appeared Bayreuth 1968, Salzburg 1970, La Scala, Milan 1972, Covent Garden, London 1975, Metropolitan Opera, New York 1978; Prof. Staatliche Hochschule für Musik, Cologne 1991–; mem. Hamburg, Bavarian and Vienna State Operas. *Address:* Grosse Theaterstrasse 34, 20354 Hamburg (Office); Voigtelstr. 22, 50933 Cologne, Germany.

MÖLLEMANN, Jürgen W.; German politician; b. 15 July 1945, Augsburg; s. of the late Wilhelm Mölleman and Franziska Reisner; m. Carola M. Appelhoff 1975; three d.; ed Münster Teachers' Coll.; joined Christian Democratic Union (CDU) 1962, resgnd 1969; joined Free Democratic Party (FDP) 1970; mem. Deutscher Bundestag 1972–2000; Educ. Policy Spokesman for FDP Parl. Party in Bundestag 1972–75; mem. FDP Fed. Exec. 1981–; FDP Deputy State Chair. N. Rhine Westphalia 1982–83, Chair. 1983–94, 1998–2002, FDP Rep. in Landtag 2000–; Minister of State, Foreign Office 1982–87; Fed. Minister of Educ. and Science 1987–91, of Econs 1991–93; Health Policy Spokesman for FDP Parl. Party 1994–; Pres. German-Arab Soc. 1993–; Pres. German-Arab Chamber of Trade and Ind. 1996–; Chair. Ausschuss für Bildung, Forschung und Technikfolgenabschätzung 1998–. *Leisure interest:* modern literature, parachuting. *Address:* Platz der Republik, 11011 Berlin (Office); Coesfeldweg 59, 48161 Münster, Germany (Home). *Telephone:* (30) 22773240 (Office); (251) 868282 (Home). *Fax:* (30) 22776326 (Office); (251) 867119 (Home). *E-mail:* juergen.moellemann@bundestag.de (Office).

MÖLLER, Erwin; German business executive; b. 23 Jan. 1939; m.; ed Tech. Univ. of Darmstadt; Chair. Supervisory Bd Metaleurop SA, Foutenay-sous-Bois, VTG Vereinigte Tanklager und Transportmittel GmbH, Hamburg; Chair. Exec. Bd Preussag A.G.; mem. Supervisory Bd Hannoversche Lebensversicherung AG, Hannover, Kabelmetal Electro GmbH, Hannover, Salzgitter Stahl GmbH, Düsseldorf; mem. Governing Council DSL Bank, Bonn; Chair. Bd, Dir Amalgamated Metal Corp. PLC, London; Hon. Consul Grand-Duchy of Luxembourg.

MOLLER, Gordon Desmond, DIP. ARCH., FNZIA, FRSA; New Zealand architect; b. 26 July 1940, Hastings; s. of Oscar Carl Moller and Winifred Daisy Moller; m. Sylvia Anne Liebezeit 1962; one s. two d.; ed Wellington Coll., Hutt Valley High School, Univ. of Auckland; Dir Craig, Craig, Moller architectural practice 1969–; Chair. Arts Marketing Bd, Aotearoa 1994, 1995, Site Safe NZ; Pres. Wellington Architectural Centre 1972, 1973; Professorial Teaching Fellow Victoria Univ. School of Architecture 1990, 1991; Pres. NZ Inst. of Architects 2003–(05); mem. Design Consortium Wellington Civic Centre 1992, 1998; Ed. New Zealand Architect 1976–83; Trustee Wellington City Gallery Foundation; NZ Inst. of Architects Gold Medal for Architecture 1983, 1988; 40 design awards 1970–2000. *Designs include:* School of Architecture, Wellington 1994, Sky Tower, Auckland 1994–97, numerous houses, Macau Tower and Entertainment Centre, Macau 1997–2001, Point Apartments, Auckland 2000, New Galleries, Te Papa Wellington 2001, Viaduct Point Apartments, Auckland 2002, Sky City Conf. Centre 2002, Sky City Grand Hotel 2003. *Leisure interests:* photography, music, motoring, landscape gardening, design, travel, visual and performing arts. *Address:* PO Box 105293, Auckland, New Zealand; 121 Customs Street West, Auckland (Home); West Plaza, 3 Albert Street, Auckland (Office). *Telephone:* (9) 357-1140 (Office); (9) 357-0686. *Fax:* (9) 357-0689 (Office). *E-mail:* gordon@ccm.co.nz (Office). *Website:* www.ccm.co.nz (Office).

MØLLER, Maersk Mc-Kinney; Danish shipowner; b. 13 July 1913, Copenhagen; s. of Arnold Peter and Chastine Estelle Mc-Kinney Møller; m. Emma (née Neergaard Rasmussen) Mc-Kinney Møller 1940; three d.; Partner A. P. Møller 1940–, Sr Partner 1965–; mem. Int. Council Morgan Guaranty Trust Co., New York 1967–84; mem. Bd IBM Corpn, USA 1970–84, Advisory Bd 1984–93; Chair. Steamship Co. of 1912 Ltd, Steamship Co. Svendborg Ltd, Odense Steel Shipyard Ltd; mem. Bd of Dirs. Maersk Olie og Gas A/S; Chair. The A. P. Møller and Chastine Mc-Kinney Møller Foundation; Hon. mem. Baltic Exchange, London 1991; Peace and Commerce Medal, US Dept of Commerce 1991; Hon. KBE 1990; Knight of the Order of the Elephant 2000. *Address:* Esplanaden 50, 1098 Copenhagen K, Denmark.

MØLLER, Per Stig, MA, Ph.D; Danish politician; b. 1942; s. of Poul Møller and Lis Møller; ed Univ. of Copenhagen; Lecturer, Sorbonne Univ., Paris 1974–76; Cultural Ed. Radio Denmark 1973–74, Deputy Head, Culture and Society Dept 1976–79, Chief of Programmes 1979–84; Vice-Chair. Radio Council 1985–86, Chair. 1986–87; Commentator, Berlingske Tidende 1984–2001; Chair. Popular Educ. Assocn (FOF) 1983–89; MP (Danish Conservative Party) 1984–, mem. Exec. Cttee 1985–89, 1993–98, Chair. 1997–98, Parl. Leader 1997–98, Foreign Policy Spokesman 1998–2001; mem. Council of Europe 1987–90, 1994–97, 1998–2001; Minister for the Environment 1990–93; Chair. Security Policy Cttee 1994–96, mem. Foreign Policy Cttee 1994–2001; Minister for Foreign Affairs 2001–; Nat. Chair. Union of Conservative Gymnasium Students 1960–61, Vice-Chair. Conservative Students' Asscn 1961–62,

Pres. Students' Union; Commdr, Order of the Dannebrog, Chevalier, Ordre nat. du Lion 1975, Chevalier des Arts et des Lettres 1986, Grosskreuz des Verdienstordens der Bundesrepublik Deutschland 2002, Commdr, Ordre nat. du Benin 2003; Sound and Environment Award 1993, Georg Brandes Award 1996, Einer Hansen Research Fund Award 1997, G-1930s Politician of the Year 1997, Cultural Award of the Popular Educ. Asscn 1998, Raoul Wallenberg Medal 1998, Kaj Munk Award 2001, Rosenkjaer Award 2001. *Publications include*: La Critique dramatique et littéraire de Malte-Brun 1971, Erotismen 1973, København-Paris (trans.) 1973, På Sporet af det forsvundne Menneske 1976, Livet I Gøgereden 1978, Fra Tid til Andren 1979, Tro, Håb og Faellesskab 1980, Midt I Redeligheden 1981, Orwells Håb og Frygt 1983, Hat uden Daggry 1985, Mulighedernes Samfund 1985, Stemmer fra Øst 1987, Historien om Estland, Letland og Litauen 1990, Kurs mod Kastrofer? 1993, Miljøproblemer 1995, Den naturlige Orden: Tolv år der flyttede Verden 1996, Spor: Udvalgte Skrifter om det åbne Samfund og dets Vaerdier 1997, Magt og Afmagt 1999, Munk 2000, Mere Munk 2003. *Address*: Ministry of Foreign Affairs, Asiatisk Plads 2, 1448 Copenhagen K, Denmark (Office). *Telephone*: 33-92-00-00 (Office). *Fax*: 32-54-05-33 (Office). *E-mail*: um@um.dk (Office). *Website*: www.um.dk (Office).

MOLLISON, Patrick Loudon, CBE, MD, FRS; British professor of haematology and medical author; b. 17 March 1914, London; s. of William M. Mollison and Beatrice M. Walker; m. 1st Margaret D. Peirce 1940 (divorced 1964); three s.; m. 2nd Jennifer A. Jones 1973; ed Univ. of Cambridge and St Thomas's Hosp. Medical School, London; worked in London Blood Transfusion Service for MRC 1939–43, then in RAMC; Dir MRC Blood Transfusion Research Unit (later Experimental Haematology Unit) at Postgrad. Medical School; in charge of Haematology Dept St Mary's Hosp., London 1960–79; Prof. of Haematology, Univ. of London 1962–79, Prof. Emer.; Hon. Consultant Immunohaematologist N London Blood Transfusion Centre 1983–; several awards and honours. *Publications*: Blood Transfusion in Clinical Medicine 1951; some 200 papers in scientific journals. *Leisure interests*: opera, gardening. *Address*: North London Blood Transfusion Centre, Colindale Avenue, London, NW9 5BG (Office); 60 King Henry's Road, London, NW3 3RR, England (Home). *Telephone*: (20) 7722-1947 (Home).

MOLLOY, Patrick; Irish banker; b. 4 Jan. 1938; m. Ann Lynch; three s. two d.; ed Trinity Coll. Dublin, Harvard Business School; Asst Gen. Man. Bank of Ireland 1975–78, Gen. Man. Area East 1978–83, Man. Dir 1983–91, Group CEO 1991–; Dir Eircom PLC 2001–. *Leisure interests*: fishing, shooting. *Address*: Bank of Ireland, Lower Baggot Street, Dublin 2, Ireland. *Telephone*: (1) 6615933. *Fax*: (1) 6615193. *Website*: www.bankofireland.ie (Office).

MOLLOY, Robert M., BComm; Irish politician; b. 6 July 1936, Salthill, Galway; s. of Michael Edward Molloy and Rita (Stanley) Molloy; m. Phyllis Barry 1972; two s. two d.; ed St Ignatius Coll., Univ. Coll. Galway; became mem. Dáil Éireann (House of Reps) 1965, House Cttee of Public Accounts 1965–69, House Cttee on Constitution 1967; Parl. Sec. to Minister for Educ. 1969–70; Minister for Local Govt 1970–73, for Defence 1977–79, of Energy 1989–92, of State to the Govt 1997–, and fmrly at the Dept of the Environment and Local Govt with special responsibility for Housing and Urban Renewal; mem. Galway Co. Council 1967–70, 1974–77, 1985–91, Galway Borough Council 1967–70, 1985–91; Mayor of Galway 1968–69; Chair. Galway Harbour Bd 1974–77, 1985–91, Lough Corril Navigation Trustees 1985–91; Chair. House Cttee on Bldg Land; mem. House Cttee on State-Sponsored Bodies 1982–87, 1994–, on the Irish Language 1992–, on Enterprise and Econ. Strategy 1994–; mem. Council of Europe 1996–; mem. Governing Body, Univ. Coll. Galway 1977; mem. Exec., Inter-Parl. Asscn; Dir Salthill Failte Ltd 1985–91; Progressive Democrat. *Leisure interests*: swimming, sailing, golf. *Address*: St Mary's, Rockbarton, Salthill, Galway, Ireland (Home). *Telephone*: (91) 521765 (Home). *Fax*: (91) 520304 (Home). *E-mail*: molloyr@eircom.net (Home).

MOLNÁR, Lúdovít, RNDr., DSc; Slovak computer scientist and university administrator; b. 11 Oct. 1940, Komjatice Dist; m.; three c.; ed Slovak Univ. of Tech., Bratislava; various teaching positions, Slovak Univ. of Tech., Bratislava 1962–, currently Rector; research periods in UK 1969–70, 1991, USSR 1974, Italy 1978, Cyprus 1983. *Publications include*: numerous computer tech. manuals and textbooks. *Leisure interest*: literature. *Address*: Office of the Rector, Slovak University of Technology, Vazovova 5, 812 43 Bratislava 16, Slovakia (Office). *Telephone*: (2) 52497196 (Office). *Fax*: (2) 57294333 (Office). *E-mail*: zahran@vm.stuba.sk (Office). *Website*: www.stuba.sk (Office).

MOLONEY, Thomas Walter, MA, MBA, M.P.H.; American foundation executive; b. 8 Feb. 1946, New York; s. of Thomas Walter Moloney and Anne Heney; ed Colgate Univ., Columbia Univ.; Program Dir Nat. Center for the Deaf-Blind, New York 1971–72; Special Asst to Dir and Dean, Cornell Univ. Medical Center 1973–74; Asst Vice-Pres. Robert Wood John Foundation 1975–80; Visiting Lecturer, Princeton Univ. 1975–80; Sr Vice-Pres., The Commonwealth Fund, New York 1980–92; Dir of Public Policy and Health Programmes, Inst. for the Future 1992–99; Partner, Owner Future Inc. 1997–; mem. Bd Dirs. New England Medical Center, Boston 1982–89; mem. Bd Grantmakers in Health, New York 1984–, Chair. 1984–88; Policy Scholar Eisenhower Center, Columbia Univ., New York 1992–, Inst. of Health Policy Studies, Univ. of Calif. at San Francisco 1992–; mem. Nat. Bd of Medical Examiners 1986–90, Health Advisory Cttee, Gen. Accounting Office, Washington, DC 1987–; Bd, Foundation Health Services Research, Washington,

DC 1989 and other bds.; Fellow of the American Acad. of Arts and Sciences; mem. Inst. of Medicine, NAS. *Publications*: Ed. New Approaches to the Medicaid Crisis 1983; numerous articles. *Address*: S/B Futures Inc., Floor 8, 1170 North Ocean Boulevard, Palm Beach, FL 33480 (Office); 72 Norwood Avenue, Upper Montclair, NJ 07043, USA.

MOLSON, Eric H., AB; Canadian business executive; b. 16 Sept. 1937, Montreal, PQ; s. of Thomas H. P. Molson and Celia F. Cantlie; m. Jane Mitchell 1966; three c.; ed Selwyn House School, Montreal, Bishop's Coll. School, Lennoxville, Le Rosey, Switzerland, Princeton and McGill Univs. and US Brewers Acad. New York; served as apprentice brewer with Molson Breweries of Canada Ltd, rising through various appts. to Pres.; Chair. Bd Molson Inc. 1988–. *Address*: Molson Inc., 1555 Notre Dame Street East, Montreal, Que., H2L 2R5, Canada. *Telephone*: (514) 597-1786.

MOLTKE, Gebhardt von; German diplomatist; b. 28 June 1938, Wernersdorf, Silesia; m. Dorothea von Moltke 1965; one s. one d.; ed Univs. of Heidelberg, Grenoble, Berlin, Freiburg im Breisgau; practical legal training 1963–67; with Fed. Foreign Office, Bonn 1968–71, Personnel Admin. 1977–82, Head of US Dept 1986–91; Embassy, Moscow 1971–75; Embassy, Yaoundé 1975–77; Embassy, Washington, DC 1982–86; Asst Sec.-Gen. for Political Affairs NATO 1991–97; Amb. to UK 1997–99; Perm. Rep. to NATO 1999–; Hon. Dr Jur. (Birmingham) 2000; Hon. GCVO, Great Cross (Hungary), Grand Cross (Germany). *Leisure interests*: tennis, music, drawings (old masters). *Address*: Permanent Mission of Germany to NATO, 39 boulevard Leopold III, 1110 Brussels, Belgium. *Telephone*: (2) 727-76-29. *Fax*: (2) 727-77-30.

MOLTMANN, Jürgen, DTheol; German theologian; b. 8 April 1926, Hamburg; m.; four d.; POW during Second World War; with Dept of Theology, Univ. of Göttingen 1948–52, Prof. of Theology 1957–; fmr Minister, Bremen; Prof. and Rector Wuppertal Church Univ. 1958–; Visiting Prof. in USA 1967–68; Comenius Medal 1992, Ernst Bloch Prize 1994. *Publications*: Christliche Petzel und das Calvinismus in Bremen 1958, Prädestination und Perseveranz 1961, Anfänge Dialektische Theologie 1963, Theologie der Hoffnung (Isla of Elba Literary Prize) 1964, Mensch 1971, Der gekreuzigte Gott 1972, Der Sprache der Befreiung 1972, Das Experiment Hoffnung 1974, Kirche in der Kraft des Geistes 1975, Zukunft der Schöpfung 1977, Trinität und Reich Gottes 1980, Gott in der Schöpfung 1985, Das Weg Jesu Christi 1989, Der Geist des Lebens 1991, Das Kommen Gottes (Grawemeyer Religion Award) 1995. *Address*: Liebermeister Strasse 12, 72076 Tübingen, Germany.

MOLYNEAUX OF KILLEAD, Baron (Life Peer), cr. 1997, of Killead in the County of Antrim; **James Henry Molyneaux,** KBE; British politician; b. 28 Aug. 1920, Crumlin; s. of William Molyneaux and Sarah Gilmore; ed Aldergrove School, Co. Antrim; served RAF 1941–46; mem. Antrim Co. Council 1964–73; Vice-Chair. Eastern Special Care Hosp. Man. Cttee 1966–73; Chair. Antrim Branch NI Asscn for Mental Health 1967–70; Hon. Sec. S. Antrim Unionist Asscn 1964–70; MP for Antrim South 1970–83, for Lagan Valley 1983–97; Vice-Pres. Ulster Unionist Council 1974; Leader Ulster Unionist Party, House of Commons 1974–97; Leader Ulster Unionist Party 1979–95; mem. NI Ass. 1982–86; fmr JP (resgnd 1987); Deputy Grand Master of Orange Order and Hon. Past Grand Master of Canada; Sovereign Grand Master, Commonwealth Royal Black Inst. 1971–98. *Leisure interests*: music, gardening. *Address*: House of Lords, London, SW1A 0PW; Aldergrove, Crumlin, County Antrim, Northern Ireland BT29 4AR. *Telephone*: (28) 9442-2545 (Crumlin).

MOMOH, Maj.-Gen. Joseph Saidu, OBE; Sierra Leonean fmr Head of State and army officer; b. 26 Jan. 1937, Binkolo, Northern Prov.; m. Hannah V. Wilson (died 1996); two d.; ed West Africa Methodist Collegiate Secondary School, Officers' Training School, Ghana, School of Infantry, Hythe, UK, Nigeria Defence Acad., Kaduna, Mons Officers' Cadet School, Aldershot, UK and Mil. Training Dept, Zaria, Nigeria; commissioned, Royal Sierra Leone Mil. Forces 1963, Deputy Asst Adjutant and Quartermaster-Gen. 1968, Commdr First Bn 1969, Acting Force Commdr 1971, Brig. 1973, Maj.-Gen. 1983; mem. Parl. 1973–85; Minister of State 1973–85; Pres. of Sierra Leone 1985–92; Minister of Defence and Public Services 1986–92; charged with treason April 1998; sentenced to ten years' imprisonment for conspiracy 1998; found not guilty of treason; Order of the Rokel; Order of Nat. Security Merit (Repub. of Korea); Hon. DCL. *Leisure interests*: reading, sport.

MOMPER, Walter; German politician; b. 21 Feb. 1945, Sulingen; mem. Berlin Chamber of Deputies 1975–95, 1999–; Party Whip SPD, Berlin 1985–89, Chair. –1992; Gov. Mayor of Berlin 1989–91; Vice-Pres., then Pres. Lower House, Berlin 1999–. *Address*: Abgeordnetenhauses, Seydelstrasse 28, 10117 Berlin, Germany. *Telephone*: 20623698.

MONBERG, Torben Axel, DPhil; Danish anthropologist; b. 25 July 1929, Copenhagen; s. of Axel S. S. Monberg and Elna Elsa Johansson; m. 1st Bodil B. Melbye (died 1976); m. 2nd Hanne (née Schou) Birthe 1985; one s. two d.; ed Univ. of Copenhagen; Asst Prof. of Cultural Sociology, Univ. of Copenhagen 1965–69, Prof. 1969–75; Chief. Curator Nat. Museum of Denmark 1975–80; Prof., Univ. of Hawaii 1972; Hon. Chief Bellona Island, Solomon Islands 1984; field work on Rennell and Bellona Islands 1958–84, on Tikopia (with Raymond Firth) 1966; mem. Danish Acad. of Sciences. *Publications*: From the Two Canoes, Oral Traditions of Rennell and Bellona Islands (with Samuel H. Elbert) 1965, The Religion of Bellona Island 1966, Mobile in the Trade Wind 1976, Mungiki, Kulturen og dens religion på øen Bellona i Stillehavet 1979,

Bellona Island: Beliefs and Ritual Practices 1991; scientific and popular papers. *Address:* Veksebovej 10, 3480 Fredensborg, Denmark. *Telephone:* 42-28-10-31. *Fax:* 42-28-45-31.

MONCADA, Salvador Enrique, MD, PhD, FRCP, FRS; British academic, doctor and scientist; b. 3 Dec. 1944, Tegucigalpa, Honduras; s. of Salvador Moncada and Jenny Seidner; m. 1st 1966; one s. (deceased) one d.; m. 2nd HRH Princess Esmeralda of Belgium 1998; one s. one d.; ed Univ. of El Salvador; Assoc. Prof. of Pharmacology and Physiology, Univ. of Honduras 1974–75; Section Leader, Wellcome Research Laboratories, Beckenham, Kent 1975–77, Head of Prostaglandin Research 1977–84, Dir of Therapeutic Research 1984–86, Dir of Research 1986–95; Dir of the Wolfson Inst. for Biomedical Research 1996–; Fellow of the Third World Acad. of Sciences 1988, mem. Academia Europaea 1992, Foreign mem. NAS 1994, Hon. mem. Asscn of Physicians of GB and Ireland 1997, American Soc. of Hematology 1999; Prince of Asturias Prize for Science and Tech. 1990, Amsterdam Prize for Medicine 1992, First Roussel Uclaf Prize, Royal Medal 1994, Louis and Artur Lucian Award 1997, Galen Medal in Therapeutics, Dale Medal, Gold Medal of the Spanish Soc. of Cardiology 1999, Gold Medal of the Royal Soc. of Medicine 2000; Hon. DMed (Universidad Complutense de Madrid) 1986, (Antwerp) 1997, Academico de Honor a la Real Academia Nacional de Medicina 1993; Hon. DSc (Sussex) 1994, Mount Sinai School of Medicine New York, (Nottingham) 1995, (Univ. Pierre and Marie Curie, Paris) 1997, (Edin.) 2000. *Publications:* co-ed. Nitric oxide from L-arginine: a bioregulatory system 1990, The Biology of Nitric Oxide, (Vols 1–7) 1992–2000. *Leisure interests:* theatre, literature, music, walking, diving. *Address:* The Wolfson Institute for Biomedical Research, University College London, Gower Street, London, WC1E 6BT, England (Office). *Telephone:* (20) 7679-6666 (Office). *Fax:* (20) 7209-0470 (Office). *E-mail:* s.moncada@ucl.ac.uk (Office). *Website:* www.ucl.ac.uk/wibr (Office).

MONCAYO, Gen. Paco, MSc; Ecuadorean army officer and politician; b. 1941; m.; four c.; fmr Prof. of Cen. Univ. of Ecuador; fmr Pres. of Rumiñahui Bank; fmr C-in-C of Armed Forces; fmr Head of the Ministry of Agric.; Nat. Deputy; Mayor of Quito 2000–. *Address:* Alcaldía de Quito, Quito, Ecuador (Office).

MONDALE, Walter Frederick, LLB; American politician and lawyer; b. 5 Jan. 1928, Ceylon, Minn.; s. of Rev. and Mrs. Theodore Sigvaard Mondale; m. Joan Adams 1955; two s. one d.; ed Minnesota public schools, Macalester Coll., Univ. of Minnesota and Univ. of Minnesota Law School; admitted to Minn. Bar 1956, pvt. practice 1956–60; Attorney-Gen., Minn. 1960–64; US Senator from Minnesota 1964–77; Vice-Pres. of the US 1977–81; mem. Nat. Security Council 1977–81; fmr Regent Smithsonian Inst.; Counsel with firm Winston and Strawn 1981–87; Partner, Dorsey and Whitney 1987–93; Amb. to Japan 1993–96; fmr mem. Bd Control Data, Columbia Pictures; Democrat-Farm Labor Party; Democratic Cand. for Presidency 1984. *Publication:* The Accountability of Power: Towards a Responsible Presidency 1975. *Leisure interest:* fishing. *Address:* c/o Department of State, 2201 C Street, NW, Washington, DC 20520, USA.

MONDUZZI, HE Cardinal Dino; Italian ecclesiastic; b. 2 April 1922, Brisighella; ordained priest 1945; titular Bishop of Capri 1987; Prefect of the Pontifical Household; cr. Cardinal 1998. *Address:* Via Monfe della Farina 64, 00186 Rome, Italy. *Telephone:* (06) 69883273. *Fax:* (06) 69885863.

MONEO, José Rafael, DArch; Spanish architect and professor of architecture; b. May 1937, Tudela, Navarra; s. of Rafael Moneo and Teresa Vallés; m. Belén Feduchi 1963; three d.; ed Madrid Univ. School of Architecture; Fellow, Acad. in Rome 1963–65; Asst Prof. Madrid School of Architecture 1966–70; Prof. Barcelona School of Architecture 1970–80; Visiting Fellow, Inst. for Architecture and Urban Studies, Cooper Union School of Architecture New York 1976–77; Chair. Dept of Architecture Harvard Univ. Grad. School of Design 1985–90, Josep Lluís Prof. 1992–; mem. American Acad. of Arts and Sciences, Academia di San Luca di Roma; Hon. Fellow, American Inst. of Architects; Premio di Roma 1962; Gold Medal for Achievement in Fine Arts, Govt of Spain 1992; Brunner Memorial Prize, American Acad. of Arts and Letters; Schock Prize in the Visual Arts 1993, Antonio Fettinelli Prize 1998; RIBA Gold Medal 2003; Dr hc (Leuven) 1993, and other distinctions. *Work includes:* Bankinter Bank, Madrid; Nat. Museum of Roman Art, Mérida; Thyssen Bornemisza Museum; San Pablo Airport, Seville; Manzana Diagonal, Barcelona; Davis Museum, Wellesley Coll. USA; City Hall Extension, Orcia 1998; Barcelona Concert Hall 1999; Kursaal Concert Hall, San Sebastian 1999; Audrey Jone Beck Building, Houston Museum of Fine Arts 2000. *Address:* Harvard University, Graduate School of Design, Cambridge, MA 02138, USA; Calle Miño 5, Madrid 28002, Spain. *Telephone:* (1) 5642257. *Fax:* (1) 5635217.

MONETTE, Richard Jean, OC, CM, BA; Canadian actor and artistic director; b. 19 June 1944, Montreal, PQ; ed Concordia Univ. Montreal (fmrly Loyola Coll.); debut as the Prince in Cinderella, St Michael's Playhouse, Winooski, Vt 1962; has appeared in numerous productions at Stratford Festival, especially in works of Shakespeare 1965–; Dir of numerous productions, Stratford Festival 1978–, Assoc. Dir 1988–90, Artistic Dir 1994–; other appearances at Theatre Toronto, Welsh Nat. Theatre, Open Air Theatre, London, Open Space Theatre, London, St Lawrence Centre etc.; Artistic Dir Citadel Theatre Young Co. 1989; regular TV and film appearances 1963–; Dr. hc (Univ. of Windsor) 1995; Tyrone Guthrie Award 1967, Queen's Silver Jubilee Medal 1977, Derek F. Mitchell Artistic Dir.'s Award, Stratford 1984;

Dora Mavor Moore Award for Outstanding Direction, St Joan, Theatre Plus 1991. *Leisure interests:* gardening, cooking. *Address:* Stratford Festival, Box 520, Stratford, Ont., N5A 6V2, Canada. *Telephone:* (519) 271-4040. *Fax:* (519) 271-4904. *Website:* www.stratford-festival.on.ca (Office).

MONGE, Luis Alberto; Costa Rican politician; b. 29 Dec. 1925, Palmares, Alajuela; s. of Gerardo Monge Quesada and Elisa Alvarez Vargas; ed Univs. of Costa Rica and Geneva; mem. Cen. de Trabajadores Rerum Novarum 1947, subsequently Pres.; fmr Vice-Pres. Inter-American Labor Confed. (CIT); militant mem. Nat. Liberation Army 1948; mem. Nat. Constituent Ass. (Social Democrat) 1949; Co-Founder Nat. Liberation Party 1951, Sec.-Gen. for 12 years; worked for ILO, Geneva for 3 years; Sec.-Gen. Interamerican Labor Org. (ORIT) for 6 years; served at Ministry of the Presidency, Govt of José Figueres 1955; mem. Legis. Ass. 1958, 1970, Pres. of Congress 1970–74; Prof. Inter-American School of Democratic Educ. and Dir Center of Democratic Studies for Latin America (CEDAL); Pres. of Costa Rica 1982–86.

MONGO BETI (pseudonym of Alexandre Biyidi-Awala); Cameroonian writer and teacher; b. 1932, Mbalmayo; s. of Oscar Awala and Régine Alomo; m. Odile Marie Jeanne Lebossé 1963; two s. one d.; ed Lycée de Yaoundé, Univ. d'Aix-en-Provence and Sorbonne, Paris; exiled from Cameroon, became teacher and writer in Paris; undertook research in sociology, Paris Univ. 1957–59; currently Prof. Lycée Corneille, Rouen; Founder of bi-monthly journal, Peuples Noirs-Peuples Africains 1978; Prix Sainte-Beuve for Mission Terminée 1958. *Publications:* Le pauvre Christ de Bomba 1956 (trans. in English), Mission terminée 1957 (trans. in English), Le roi miraculé 1958 (trans in English), Main basse sur le Cameroun, autopsie d'une décolonisation (political essay) 1972 (banned in France), Remember Ruben 1974, Perpétuité et l'habitude du malheur 1974, La ruine presque cocasse d'un polichinelle (novel) 1979.

MONGUNO, Shettima Ali; Nigerian politician and educationist; b. 1926, Borno; s. of Rahma and Fanna Monguno; m. 1st Ashe Meta 1948 (died 1994); two s. five d.; m. 2nd Fatima Monguno 2001; ed Borno Middle School, Bauchi Teacher Training Coll., Katsina Higher Coll., Univ. of Edin., Coll. of Arts, Science and Tech., Zaria, Moray House Coll. of Educ., Edin.; teacher, Borno Middle School 1952–56; MP 1956–66; Councillor for Educ., Borno Native Authority 1961–65; Fed. Minister of Air Force 1965, of Int. Affairs 1965–66; Fed. Commr for Trade and Industry 1967–71, for Mines and Power, Petroleum and Energy 1971–75; Pres. of OPEC 1972–73; Chair. Maiduguri Metropolitan Council 1976–79; Pro-Chancellor Calabar Univ. 1976–80, Univ. of Nigeria 1980–84; mem. Constituent Ass. 1978–79; Deputy Nat. Chair. Nat. Party of Nigeria 1980–84; political detainee 1984–85 (cleared by mil. tribunal); del. to UN Gen. Ass., UNCTAD 1968 and other int. confs.; mem. Bd of Trustees West African Examinations Council 1976–99; Chair. Bd of Dirs. FRUCO Co. Nigeria Ltd 1987–2000; Chair. Bd of Trustees Borno Educ. Endowment Fund 1986–87; Co-Pres. Provisional World Constitution and Parl. Asscn 1992–; mem. Bd of Trustees, World Environmental Movt for Africa 1986; mem. Commonwealth Countries League Educ. Fund 1996–, Transparency Int. Nigeria 1997–; Life mem. Britain-Nigeria Asscn; Patron and Life mem. Nigeria-USA Council 1998; Hon. DLitt (Sokoto) 1984, (Maiduguri) 1996, (Univ. of Nigeria Nsuka) 2001; UNESCO Medal; Hon. Citizen cities of Oklahoma, Lima, Quito; Hon. Mayor Oklahoma City; Key to City of New York 1964, Commdr, Order of Fed. Repub. (Nigeria) 1983, Distinguished Friend of Council, W African Exams Council 2002; and awards from Egypt, Cameroon, Sudan and Ethiopia. *Publications:* Corruption – Why it Thrives in Nigeria 1983. *Leisure interests:* gardening, reading, cycling, farming. *Address:* 5 Muhammed Monguno Road, Old Gra, Maiduguri, Borno State (Office); PO Box 541, Maiduguri, Borno State, Nigeria (Home). *Telephone:* (76) 231170, 342140 (Maiduguri); (1) 5837572, 2619534 (Lagos). *Fax:* (76) 231170, 342140 (Maiduguri).

MONICELLI, Mario; Italian film director; b. 16 May 1915; ed Università degli Studi, Pisa; fmr Asst to Pietro Germi; writer of film Riso Amaro; film Dir 1949–; Golden Lion, Venice Film Festival; Silver Medal, Berlin Film Festival; Silver Laurel Medal, San Francisco Film Festival. *Films include:* Guardie e Ladri 1948, The Big Deal of Madonna Street 1955, The Great War 1958, The Organiser 1960, Casanova '70 1963, L'Armata Brancaleone 1965, Vogliamo i Colonnelli, Romanzo popolare, Caro Michele, Amici miei, Un borghese piccolo piccolo, Viaggio con Anita, Temporale Rosy, Camera d'Albergo 1979, Il Marchese del Grillo 1980, 2nd part of Amici Miei 1982, Viva Italia!, Lovers and Liars, Bertoldo, Bertoldino, E Cacasenna, The Two Lives of Mattia Pascal, I Picari, Let's Hope It's a Girl (also wrote screenplay), The Rogues (also co-wrote screenplay), The Obscure Illness (co-wrote screenplay), Looking for Paradise. *Address:* Via del Babuino 135, 06 6780448 Rome, Italy.

MONK, Meredith Jane; American composer, director and choreographer; b. 20 Nov. 1942; d. of Theodore G. Monk and Audrey Lois (Zellman); ed Sarah Lawrence Coll; Founder and Artistic Dir House Foundation for the Arts 1968–; formed Meredith Monk & Vocal Ensemble 1978–; Dr. hc (Bard Coll.) 1988, (Univ. of the Arts) 1989, (Juilliard School of Music) 1998, San Francisco Art Inst. 1999; Golden Eagle Award 1981, Nat. Music Theatre Award 1986, German Critics' Award for Best Recording of the Year 1981, 1986, Samuel Scripps Award 1996 and many other awards. *Works include:* Break 1964, 16 Millimeter Earrings 1966, Juice: A Theatre Cantata 1969, Key 1971, Vessel: An Opera Epic 1971, Paris 1972, Education of the Girlchild 1973, Quarry 1976, Songs from the Hill 1976, Dolmen Music 1979, Specimen Days: A Civil War Opera 1981, Ellis Island 1981, Turtle Dreams Cabaret 1983, The Games

1983, Acts from Under and Above 1986, Book of Days 1988, Facing North 1990, Three Heavens and Hells 1992, Atlas: An Opera in Three Parts 1991, New York Requiem 1993, Volcano Songs 1994, American Archaeology 1994, The Politics of Quiet 1996, Magic Frequencies 1998. *Leisure interests:* gardening, horseback riding. *Address:* 228 West Broadway, New York, NY 10013, USA (Office).

MONKS, John Stephen, BA; British trades union official; b. 5 Oct. 1945, Manchester; s. of Charles Edward Monks and Bessie Evelyn Monks; m. Francine Jacqueline Schenk 1970; two s. one d.; ed Nottingham Univ.; joined TUC Org. Dept 1969, Asst Sec. Employment and Manpower Section 1974, Head Org., Employment Law and Industrial Relations Dept 1977–87, Deputy Gen.-Sec. 1987–93, Gen.-Sec. 1993–2003; Sec.-Gen. European Trade Union Confed. (ETUC) May 2003–; mem. Council Advisory, Conciliation and Arbitration Service (ACAS), 1979–95; mem. British Govt and EU Competitiveness Councils 1997–; mem. Exec. Council, European TUC and Int. Confed. of Free Trade Unions; Trustee Nat. Museum of Labour History 1988–; Visiting Prof., School of Man., UMIST 1996–; Dr hc (Nottingham, UMIST, Salford, Cranfield, Cardiff, Kingston and Southampton Univs.). *Leisure interests:* hiking, music, squash. *Address:* European Trade Union Confederation, 5 Boulevard Roi Albert II, 1210, Brussels, Belgium. *Telephone:* (2) 224-04-11. *Fax:* (2) 224-04-54. *E-mail:* etuc@etuc.org (Office). *Website:* www.etuc.org (Office).

MONNIER, Claude Michel, PhD; Swiss journalist; b. 23 March 1938, Rwankéri, Rwanda; s. of Henri Monnier and Olga Pavlov; m. Estela Troncoso Balandrán 1958; two s.; ed Univs of Geneva and Mexico, Graduate Inst. of Int. Studies, Geneva; educational tour in Asia and America 1956–58; Research Fellow, Swiss Nat. Fund for Scientific Research, Tokyo 1963–66; Tokyo Corresp. Journal de Genève 1963–66, Foreign Ed. 1966–70, Ed.-in-Chief 1970–80; Ed. Le Temps Stratégique, Genève 1982–2001; mem. Bd French-speaking Swiss TV and radio 1989–2000; mem. Academic Council, Univ. of Lausanne 1998–, Bd Médias et Société Foundation, Geneva; adviser Edipresse Publishing 2001–. *Publications:* Les Américains et sa Majesté l'Empereur: Etude du conflit culturel d'où naquit la constitution japonaise de 1946 1967, Alerte, citoyens! 1989, L'année du Big-Bang 1990, La terre en a marre 1991, La déprime, ça suffit! 1992, Dieu, que la crise est jolie! 1993, Les Rouges nous manquent 1994, La bonté qui tue 1995, Envie de bouffer du lion 1996, Programme d'un agitateur 1997, Le temps des règlements de compte 1998, Le Culte douteux de l'action 1999, La trahison de l'an 2000 2000, Morts de trouille 2001, If faut nous faire soigner! 2002. *Leisure interests:* walking, light aircraft flying. *Address:* Chemin de Saussac 2, 1256 Troinex, Geneva, Switzerland (Home). *Telephone:* (22) 343-95-55 (Home). *Fax:* (22) 343-95-55 (Home).

MONOD, Jérôme; French businessman; b. 7 Sept. 1930, Paris; s. of Olivier Monod and Yvonne (née Bruce) Monod; m. Françoise Gallot 1963; three s.; ed Wesleyan Univ., USA, Institut d'Etudes Politiques, Ecole Nat. d'Admin; Auditeur, Cour des Comptes 1957; Rapporteur, Study mission of Sec.-Gen. for Algerian Affairs 1958; Chargé de mission, Prime Minister's Office 1959–62; Conseiller Référendaire à la Cour des Comptes 1963; Chief Exec. Dél. à l'Aménagement du Territoire 1967–75; Special Asst to Prime Minister Jacques Chirac 1975–1976; Sec.-Gen. Rassemblement pour la République (RPR) 1976–78; Chair. Bd, Centre Français du Commerce Extérieur 1980–83; Pres. French Canadian Chamber of Commerce in Paris 1984–86; Vice-Pres. Société Lyonnaise des Eaux 1979–80, Chair. and CEO 1980–97; Vice-Chair. General Waterworks Corpn (USA) 1983–93; Vice-Chair., Compagnie de Suez 1995–97, Chair. Supervisory Bd, Suez Lyonnaise des Eaux 1997–2000, Chair. Lyonnaise des Eaux de Casablanca 1997–2000; Chair. Sino French Holding (China) 1996–; Adviser to Pres. of France 2000–02; mem. Bd of Dirs Total (Cie Française des Pétroles), Aguas de Barcelona (Spain), Dic-Degrémont (Japan), Lyonnaise American Holding (USA), Groupe GTM, GTM-Entrepose, Métropole Télévision; mem. Consultative Council Banque de France, Business Advisory Council, IFC (USA); mem. Int. Advisory Bd, NatWest Bank; mem. Steering Cttee, European Round Table 1995–2000; Commdr, Légion d'honneur, Officier des Arts et des Lettres, Chevalier des Palmes académiques. *Publications:* L'aménagement du territoire 1971, Transformation d'un pays: pour une géographie de la liberté 1975, Propositions pour la France 1977, Manifeste pour une Europe souveraine 1999. *Leisure interests:* swimming, climbing. *Address:* c/o Présidence de la République, 55-57 rue du Faubourg-Saint-Honoré, 75800 Paris, France (Office); 94 rue du Bac, 75007 Paris, France (Home).

MONORY, Jacques; French artist; b. 25 June 1934, Paris; s. of Luis José Monory and Angel Foucher; m. 1st Sabine Monirys 1959 (divorced 1968); one s.; m. 2nd Paule Moninot 1993; ed Ecole de Beaux Arts, Paris; numerous one-man exhbns. in France and throughout Europe since 1955 including Galerie Kléber, Paris 1955, Galerie H. Legendre 1965, Musée de l'Art Moderne, Paris 1971, 1984, Palais des Beaux Arts, Brussels 1971, Stedelijk Museum, Amsterdam 1972, Centre nat. d'art contemporain, Paris 1974, Louisiana Museum 1975, Galerie Maeght, Zürich 1975, Galerie Maeght, Paris 1976, 1978, 1981, Galerie Maeght, Barcelona 1980, Fuji TV Gallery, Tokyo 1984, Galerie Lelong, Paris 1987, 1989, 1991, 1994, Mayer-Schwartz Gallery, Los Angeles 1990, Galerie Andata Ritorno, Geneva 1992, Champclose 1995, Théâtre, Centre Culturel, Cherbourg 1996, Galerie Grand Café, St-Nazaire 1996, Villa Tamaris, La Seyne sur Mer 1996, Galerie Nova Sim, Prague 1997, Municipal Art Museum, Reykjavik 1997, Musée des Beaux Arts, Sables d'Olonne 1998, Musée des Beaux Arts, Chartres 1998, Musée des Beaux Arts, Dole 1999, Galerie Zannettacci, Geneva 1999, Palais des Congrès, Paris 1999, FIAC, Paris 2000, Galerie Antonio Prates, Lisbon 2001, Galerie Ernst Hilger,

Vienna 2002; work represented in numerous public collections in Europe, USA and Japan. *Films:* Ex 1968, Brighton Belle 1973, La Voleuse (video) 1986, Le Moindre Geste peut faire signe 1986. *Art exhibitions include:* Mythologies quotidiennes, Musée d'Art Moderne, Paris 1964, Les Immatériaux, Musée National d'Art Moderne, Paris 1985, Espace Venice Biennale 1986, Planetarium, Cité des Sciences de la Villette, Paris 1986, Accrochage, Musée National d'Art Moderne, Paris 2000, Figuration Narrative, La Seyne sur Mer, Kunst Museum, Bergen, Art Museum, Reykjavik 2000. *Leisure interests:* shooting, swimming. *Address:* 9 Villa Carnot, Cachan 94230, France. *Telephone:* 46-65-08-67. *Fax:* 46-65-08-67.

MONORY, René Claude Aristide; French politician and administrator; b. 6 June 1923, Loudun; s. of Aristide Monory and Marguerite (Devergne) Monory; m. Suzanne Cottet 1945; one d.; ed Ecole primaire supérieure de Thouars; dealer in vehicles and agricultural machinery 1952; Chair. agricultural machinery and oil cos.; Mayor of Loudun 1959–99; Pres. Mayors' Asscn of Vienne; Councillor, Canton of Loudun 1961; municipal judge; Senator for Vienne 1968–77, 1981–86, Rapporteur, Senate Finance Comm. 1976–77; Minister of Industry and Trade 1977–78, of the Economy 1978–81, of Educ. 1986–88; Pres. Conseil général de la Vienne 1979–; Chair. Interim Cttee of Bd of Govs, IMF 1981; Pres. Asscn de l'union républicaine des présidents de conseils généraux 1983–86; mem. Centre des démocrates sociaux (fmr nat. sec.), First Vice-Pres. 1984; mem. Union pour la démocratie française; Pres. Conseil régional Poitou-Charentes 1985–86; Senator for Vienne 1988–; Pres. of Senate 1992–98; f. Futuroscope 1987, Pres. 1987–2000. *Publications:* Combat pour le bon sens 1983, Des clés pour le futur 1995. *Leisure interests:* big-game fishing, hunting. *Address:* Conseil général de la Vienne, Place Aristide Briand, 86000 Poitiers (Office); Palais de Luxembourg, 15 rue de Vaugirard, 75291 Paris Cedex 06, France. *Telephone:* 1-56-54-31-44, 1-56-54-31-40. *Fax:* 1-56-54-31-45.

MONREAL LUQUE, Alberto, D.ECON.SC.; Spanish politician and economist; b. 18 Nov. 1928, Madrid; s. of Federico Monreal and Irene Luque; m. Maria Elena Alfageme 1961; two s. one d.; ed Univ. de Madrid; mem. Cuerpo de Economistas del Estado 1957–; Prof. Faculty of Econ. Sciences, Univ. de Madrid 1957–68; Tech. Sec. Ministry of Public Works 1965–68; Sec. of State, Ministry of Educ. and Science 1968–69; Minister of Finance 1969–73; Pres. Tabacalera (Tobacco Monopoly Co.) 1974–82; Pres. Eurotabac 1994–; Econ. Consultant, Superior Council of Commerce, Ministry of the Economy; Deputy Chair. Grupo Anaya (publishers). *Address:* Eurotabac, Monte Esquinza 28, Madrid 28010, Spain. *Fax:* 3104286.

MONTAGNA, Gilberto Luis Humberto; Argentine civil engineer; b. 1936; m.; four c.; Sec. Chamber of Food Industrialists (CIPA) 1964–84, Vice-Pres. 1984; Sec. Fed. of Food and Derivatives Industries (FIPAA) 1975–84, Pres. 1984–87; Sec. to Coordinator of Food and Derivates Industry (COPAL) 1975–79, now Pres.; Sec. Industrial Transitory Comm. (COTEI) of Union Industrial Argentina (UIA) 1978–79, mem. Advising Exec. Comm. of UIA Comptrolling 1979–81, First Vice-Pres. UIA 1981–89, Pres. 1989; Tech. Adviser, ILO, Geneva 1978; Alt. Del. to ILO 1979, 1980, 1981; Founder, currently Vice-Pres. Action for Pvt. Initiative; Vice-Pres. Establecimientos Modelo Terrabusi SAIC; Dir Terra Garba Sacai y F, Atilena SCA. *Address:* c/o Union Industrial Argentina, Avda Leandro N Arem 1067, 11°, 1001 Buenos Aires, Argentina.

MONTAGNE SÁNCHEZ, Gen. Ernesto; Peruvian politician and army officer; b. 18 Aug. 1916, Barranco, Lima; s. of Gen. Ernesto Montagne Markholtz and Raquel de Montagne; m. Isabel Landázuri de Montagne; one s. one d.; ed Military School of Chorrillos; Capt. 1944, Lt-Col 1953, Col 1958, Brig.-Gen. 1963, Gen. of Div. 1968; taught at various mil. schools; several posts as Div. Chief of Staff; Dir Chorrillos Mil. School; Dir Escuela Superior de Guerra; Prefect of Lima; Gen. Commdr 3rd Mil. Zone; Minister of State for Educ.; Dir of Personnel; Deputy Chief of Staff of Army; Gen. Commdr 1st Mil. Zone and Insp. Gen. of Army; Gen. Commdr of Army, Pres. of Council of Ministers and Minister of War 1968–72; Orden Militar de Ayacucho, Cruz Peruana al Mérito Militar, Orden del Sol, Orden de San Gregorio Magno and numerous other foreign awards. *Leisure interest:* sailing.

MONTAGNIER, Luc, LèsL, DMed; French research scientist; b. 18 Aug. 1932, Chabris; s. of Antoine Montagnier and Marianne Rousselet; m. Dorothea Ackermann 1961; one s. two d.; ed Univs. of Poitiers and Paris; Asst in Faculty of Science, Paris 1955–60, Attaché 1960, Head 1963, Head of Research 1967; Dir of Research CNRS 1974–; Head of Lab. Inst. of Radium 1965–71; Head of Viral Oncology Unit, Pasteur Inst. 1972–; Prof. Pasteur Inst. 1985–; Pres. World Foundation for AIDS Research and Prevention (WFARP) 1993; Vice-Pres. Scientific Council AIDS Research Agency 1989–; Prof. Queens Coll., New York 1997; mem. Acad. Nat. de Médecine 1989, Acad. des Sciences 1990; Commdr, Légion d'honneur, Commdr Ordre nat. du Mérite; Lauréat du CNRS 1964, 1973, Prix Rosen de Cancérologie 1971, Prix Galien 1985, Prix de la Fondation Louis-Jeantet 1986, Prix Lasker 1986, Prix Gairdner 1987, Japan Prize 1988, King Faisal Prize 1993, Warren Alpert Foundation Prize 1998, Prince of Asturias Prize for Literature 2000, and many other prizes. *Publications:* Vaincre le SIDA 1986, SIDA: les faits, l'espoir 1987, SIDA et infection par VIH (jtly.) 1989, Des virus et des hommes 1994, Oxidative Stress in Cancer, AIDS and Neurodegenerative Diseases (Jt) 1997, New Concepts in Aids Pathogenesis (Jt), Virus () 2000, numerous scientific papers. *Leisure* *interests:* piano playing, swimming. *Address:* World Foundation for AIDS Research and Prevention, UNESCO, 1 rue Niollis, 75015 Paris (Office); Institut de France, 23 quai Conti, 75006 Paris, France.

MONTAGUE, Diana, ARCM; British mezzo-soprano opera and concert singer; b. 8 April 1953, Winchester; d. of Mr. and Mrs. N. H. Montague; m. Philip Doghan 1978; one s.; ed Testwood School, Totton, Hants., Winchester School of Art and Royal Northern Coll. of Music; professional début at Glyndebourne 1977; principal mezzo-soprano, Royal Opera House, Covent Garden 1978; freelance artist 1984–; has toured throughout Europe and USA appearing at Metropolitan Opera and Bayreuth, Aix-en-Provence, Salzburg and Glyndebourne festivals; sang at Promenade Concerts, London 1991; composed Ariadne auf Naxos for Opera North 1998. *Leisure interests:* horse-riding, country life in general. *Address:* c/o IMG Artists, Lovell House, 616 Chiswick High Road, London, W4 5RX, England (Office).

MONTANA, Claude; French fashion designer; began career designing jewellery in London, then worked for leather and knitwear firms; first ready-to-wear show 1976; f. Claude Montana Co. 1979; Designer in Charge of Haute Couture, House of Lanvin 1989–.

MONTANA, Joseph C., Jr (Joe), B.B.A.; American football player (retd); b. 11 June 1956, New Eagle, Pa; s. of Joseph C. Montana, Sr and Theresa Montana; m. 1st Kim Monses 1975 (divorced); m. 2nd Cass Castillo (divorced 1983); m. 3rd Jennifer Wallace 1984; two d.; ed Univ. of Notre Dame; quarterback, San Francisco 49ers 1979–93, Kansas City Chiefs 1993–95, commentator NBC TV 1995–; partner Target-Chip Ganassi Racing Team 1995–; mem. Super Bowl Championship Team 1982, 1985, 1989; played in Pro Bowl 1982–85; fmrly with New Business Devt Dept, Viking Components Inc. 1999; voted Most Valuable Player in the Super Bowl 1982, 1985, 1990 (record), NFL Player of the Year 1989, 1990. *Publication:* Cool Under Fire (with Alan Steinberg) 1989. *Address:* Viking Components Inc., 30200 Avenue de las Banderas, Rancho Santa Margarita, CA 92688 (Office); Super Joe Official J. Montana Fan Club, P.O. Box 2409, Menlo Park, CA 94026 (Office); c/o IMG, 1 Erieview Plaza, Suite 1300, Cleveland, OH 44114, USA.

MONTAÑO, Jorge, PhD; Mexican diplomatist; b. 16 Aug. 1945, Mexico City; s. of Jorge Montaño and Lucia Montaño; m. Luz Maria Valdes; one s. one d.; ed Nat. Autonomous Univ. of Mexico, London School of Econs, UK; posts with Nat. Inst. of Fine Arts, Ministry of Public Educ., Nat. Autonomous Univ. of Mexico; Dir-Gen., Office for UN Specialized Agencies, then Dir-in-Chief for Multilateral Affairs, Ministry of Foreign Affairs 1979–82; fmr Int. Affairs Adviser to Pres. Salinas de Gortari; fmr univ. lecturer, Mexico and UK; Perm. Rep. to UN 1989–93; Amb. to USA 1993–95. *Publication:* The United Nations and the World Order 1945–1992 1992. *Address:* Chimalistac No. 6, Colonia San Angel, 01070 México, DF, Mexico. *Telephone:* (5) 661-9765.

MONTAZERI, Ayatollah Hussein Ali; Iranian religious leader; b. 1922, Najafabad, Isfahan; s. of Montazeri Ali and Sobhani Shah Baigom; m. Rabbani, Khadijeh 1942; three s. four d.; ed Isfahan Theological School; teacher of science and philosophy, Theological School, Qom; arrested after riots over Shah's land reform 1963; visited Ayatollah Khomeini in Iraq 1964; arrested several times and exiled to rural parts of Iran 1964–74; imprisoned 1974–78; Leading Ayatollah of Tehran 1979–80; returned to Qom Feb. 1980; named Grand Ayatollah 1984; resgnd as successor to Ayatollah Khomeini March 1989; placed under house arrest 1997, released 2003. *Address:* Madresseh Faizieh, Qom, Iran.

MONTEFIORE, Rt Rev Hugh William, MA, BD; British ecclesiastic (retd); b. 12 May 1920, London; s. of Charles Edward Sebag-Montefiore OBE and Muriel Alice Ruth de Pass; m. Elisabeth Mary Macdonald Paton 1945 (deceased); three d.; ed Rugby School, St John's Coll., Oxford and Westcott House, Cambridge; Chaplain and Tutor, Westcott House 1951–53, Vice-Prin. 1953–54; Fellow and Dean, Gonville and Caius Coll., Cambridge 1954–63; Vicar of Great St Mary's, Cambridge 1963–70; Bishop of Kingston-upon-Thames 1970–78; Bishop of Birmingham 1978–87; Hon. Asst Bishop, Diocese of Southwark 1987–; Chair. Transport 2000 1987–92, Friends of the Earth Trust 1992–98, Nat. Trust for the Homeless 1992–97, Natural Justice 2000–; Hon. Fellow St John's Coll. Oxford, Gonville and Caius Coll. Cambridge; Hon. DD (Aberdeen) 1976, Birmingham 1985. *Publications include:* Commentary on the Epistle to the Hebrews 1964, The Question Mark 1969, The Probability of God 1985, So Near and Yet So Far 1986, Communicating the Gospel in a Scientific Age 1988, God, Sex and Love 1989, Christianity and Politics 1990, Reclaiming the High Ground (Ed.) 1990, The Gospel and Contemporary Culture 1992, The Womb and the Tomb 1992, Preaching for Our Planet 1992, Credible Christianity 1994, Oh God, What Next? 1995, Reaffirming the Church of England 1995, Time to Change 1997, On Being a Jewish Christian 1998, Looking Afresh 2002, The Paranormal – A Bishop Investigates 2002. *Address:* White Lodge, 23 Bellevue Road, Wandsworth Common, London, SW17 7EB, England. *Telephone:* (20) 8672-6697. *Fax:* (20) 8672-6697. *E-mail:* hugh5000@onetel.net.uk.

MONTEGRIFFO, Peter Cecil Patrick, LLB; British barrister; b. 28 Feb. 1960, Gibraltar; s. of Dr. Cecil Montegriffo and Lily Zammitt; m. Josephine Perera 1985; two s.; ed Bayside Comprehensive School, Univ. of Leeds and Lincoln's Inn/Council of Legal Educ.; called to the Bar 1982; practitioner in law firm J. A. Hassan & Partners (now Hassans), Partner 1988–; mem. Exec. Gibraltar Labour Party/Assen. for Advancement of Civil Rights (GLP/AACR) 1982–88, Deputy Leader 1988–89; Leader Gibraltar Social Democrats (GSD)

1989–91; Deputy Chief Minister and Minister for Trade and Industry 1996–2000. *Leisure interests:* literature, economics, music, travel. *Address:* Hassans, 57 Line Wall Road, Gibraltar (Office); 10 Gardiner's Road, Gibraltar (Home). *Telephone:* 79000 (Office); 79912 (Home). *Fax:* 71966 (Office); 42772 (Home). *E-mail:* peter.montegriffo@hassans.gi (Office); pcm@gibnet.gi (Home). *Website:* www.gibraltarlaw.com (Office).

MONTGOMERIE, Colin Stuart, MBE; British golfer; b. 23 June 1963, Glasgow, Scotland; s. of James Montgomerie; m. Eimear Wilson 1990; one s. two d.; ed Baptist Univ., Texas, USA; won Scottish Stroke Play Championship 1985, Scottish Amateur Championship 1987; turned professional 1987; won Portuguese Open 1989, Scandinavian Masters 1991, 1999, 2001, Heineken Dutch Open, Volvo Masters 1993, Peugeot Open de España, Murphy's English Open, Volvo German Open 1994, Volvo German Open, Trophée Lancôme, Alfred Dunhill Cup 1995, Dubai Desert Classic, Murphy's Irish Open 1996, 1997, 2001, Canon European Masters, Million Dollar Challenge 1996, World Cup (Individual), Andersen Consulting World Champion 1997, PGA Championship 1998, 1999, 2000, German Masters 1998, Compaq European Grand Prix 1997, King Hassan II Trophy 1997, British Masters 1998, Benson and Hedges Int. Open 1999, BMW Int. Open 1999, Cisco World Matchplay 1999, Loch Lomond Invitational 1999, Skins Game (US) 2000, Novotel Perrier Open de France 2000, Ericsson Australian Masters 2001, Volvo Masters Andalucia, TCL Classic 2002; mem. European Ryder Cup team from 1991–2001 (undefeated in Ryder Cup singles); 28 tournament wins as at end Dec. 2002; signed contract to play Ben Hogan irons and golf balls from 2003; Hon. LLD (St Andrews); seven times winner of Volvo Order of Merit Trophy 1993–99. *Publications:* Real Monty: The Autobiography of Colin Montgomerie, The Thinking Man's Guide to Golf. *Leisure interests:* music, cars, DIY, films. *Address:* c/o IMG, Pier House, Strand-on-the-Green, London, W4 3NN, England.

MONTGOMERY, David; American photographer; b. 8 Feb. 1937, Brooklyn, New York; m. 1st (divorced); two d.; m. 2nd Martine King 1983; one s. one d.; ed Midwood High School; toured USA as musician; freelance photographer/dir. 1960–; regular contrib. to Sunday Times Colour Magazine, Vogue, Tatler, Rolling Stone, Esquire, Fortune, New York Sunday Times, House and Garden magazines; has photographed HM Queen Elizabeth II, HM Queen Elizabeth the Queen Mother, T.R.H. Duke and Duchess of York, Rt Hon Margaret Thatcher, Rt Hon Pierre Trudeau, Mick Jagger, Clint Eastwood, Lord Mountbatten, Lord Hume, HM King Hussein, HRH Queen Noor, Rt Hon Edward Heath, Rt Hon James Callaghan, Baron Thyssen-Bornemisza, Prince and Princess Thurn und Taxis, HE Cardinal Basil Hume; numerous awards for photography. *Leisure interests:* flowers and fish keeping, photography, day-dreaming. *Address:* Studio B, 11 Edith Grove, London, S.W.10, England. *Telephone:* (20) 7352-6667/8.

MONTGOMERY, David John, BA; British newspaper executive; b. 6 Nov. 1948, Bangor, Northern Ireland; s. of William John Montgomery and Margaret Jean Montgomery; m. 1st Susan Frances Buchanan Russell 1971 (divorced 1987); m. 2nd Heidi Kingstone 1989 (divorced 1997); m. 3rd Sophie, Countess of Woolton 1997; ed Queen's Univ., Belfast; Sub-Ed., Daily Mirror London, Manchester 1973–76, Asst Chief Sub-Ed. 1976–80; Chief Sub-Ed. The Sun 1980; Asst Ed. Sunday People 1982; Asst Ed. News of the World 1984, Ed. 1985–87; Ed. Today 1987–91 (Newspaper of the Year 1988); Man. Dir News UK 1987–91; Chief Exec. London Live TV 1991–92, Dir 1991–; Chief Exec. Mirror Group 1992–99; Dir Satellite Television PLC 1986–91, News Group Newspapers 1986–91, Donohue Inc. 1992–95, Newspaper Publishing 1994–98, Scottish Media Group 1995–99, Press Assen 1996–99; Chair. Tri-Mex Group PLC 1999–, Mecom 2000–, Yava 2000–, Africa Lakes PLC 2000–, Integrated Educ. Fund Devt Bd, NI 2000–, Espresso 2001–. *Leisure interests:* music, family. *Address:* ALC, 7–10 Chandos Street, London, W1G 9DQ; 15 Collingham Gardens, London, SW5 0HS, England. *Telephone:* (20) 7323-5440 (Office); (20) 7373-1982 (Home). *E-mail:* dmontgomery@tri-mex.com (Office).

MONTGOMERY, Tim; American athlete; b. 28 Jan. 1975, Gaffney, SC; pnr. Marion Jones (q.v.); one d.; ed Gaffney High School, Blinn Coll. JC, Norfolk State Coll.; fmrly American football and baseball player; ran 100m in 9.96 seconds age 19; World Record Holder (9.78 seconds 100m), Grand Prix Final, 2002; ran fastest 60m (6.48 seconds), Dortmund 2002; coached by Trevor Graham; (ranked 2nd): JUCO Indoor 1994, USA Championships 100m 1997, USA Indoors 60m 1997, USATF Outdoor Championship 100m 2002, Golden Gala 100m 2002, Norwich Union Grand Prix 100m 2002; (ranked 1st): Bislett Golden Gala 100m 2001, Zurich 100m 2001, Sparkassen 100m 2002, Engen GP 100m 2002, Prefontaine 100m 2002, DN Galan 100m 2002, Weltklasse 100m 2002, Memorial Van Damme 100m 2002, Grand Prix Final 100m 2002; (Bronze Medal): World Championships 100m 1997; (Silver Medal): Olympics 4x100m relay 1996, 1999, Goodwill Games 100m 2001, World Indoors 60m 2001, World Championships 100m 2001; (Gold Medal): World Championships 4x100m relay 1999, Olympics 4x100m relay 2000. *Address:* c/o Vector Sports Management, 417 Keller Parkway, Keller, TX 76248, USA (Office). *E-mail:* info@vectorsportsmgmt.com (Office). *Website:* www.vectorsportsmgmt.com (Office).

MONTGOMERY, William D., BA, MBA; American diplomatist; b. 8 Nov. 1945, Carthage, Mo.; m. Lynne Germain; one s. two d.; ed Buckness and George Washington Univs., Nat. War Coll.; served US Army 1967–70; joined Foreign Service 1974, Econ.-Commercial Officer, Belgrade, Commercial Officer, Moscow, Political Officer, Moscow, Deputy Chief of Mission, Dar es

Salaam; several posts in Dept of State; Deputy Chief of Mission, Sofia 1989–91; Amb. to Bulgaria 1993–96; Special Adviser to Pres. and Sec. of State for Bosnian Peace Implementation 1996–97; Amb. to Croatia 1998–2000, to Yugoslavia 2000–; several Army decorations including Bronze Star; Distinguished Honor Award and other awards from Dept. of State; Order of Prince Trpimir, Croatia, Order of Star Planina, First Class, Bulgaria, Order of Madara Horseman, First Class, Bulgaria. *Leisure interests:* skiing, tennis. *Address:* Embassy of USA, Kneza Miloša 50, 11000 Belgrade, Yugoslavia (Office). *Telephone:* (11) 3613816 (Office). *Fax:* (11) 3613825 (Office). *E-mail:* billmont@aol.com (Office).

MONTI, Mario; Italian international organization official and economist; b. 19 March 1943, Varese; m.; two c.; ed Bocconi Univ., Milan and Yale Univ., USA; Assoc. Prof. Univ. of Trento 1969–70; Prof. Univ. of Turin 1970–79; Prof. of Monetary Theory and Policy, Bocconi Univ. 1971–85, Prof. of Econs, Dir Inst. of Econs 1985–94, f. Paolo Baffi Centre for Monetary and Financial Econs 1985, f. Innocenzo Gasparini Inst. of Econ. Research 1989, Rector Bocconi Univ. 1989–94, Pres. 1994; Econ. Commentator, Corriere della Sera 1978–94; Rapporteur Treasury Cttee on savings protection 1981, Chair. Treasury Cttee on banking and financial system 1981–82, mem. Competition Act drafting Cttee 1987–88, mem. Treasury Cttee on debt man. 1988–89, on banking law reform 1989–91; mem. working party preparing Italy for single market 1988–90; mem. Macroecon. Policy Group, European Comm. and Center for Econ. Policy Studies (CEPS) 1985–86; mem. European Comm., responsible for internal market, financial services and financial integration, Customs, Taxation 1995–99, for Competition 1999–(2004). *Address:* European Commission, 200 rue de la Loi, 1049 Brussels, Belgium (Office). *Website:* www.europa.eu.int/comm/commissioners/monti (Office).

MONTKIEWICZ, Zdzislaw; Polish business executive; b. 28 June 1944, Sokolów Podlaski; ed Mil. Tech. Acad.; mem. staff Polish Acad. of Sciences 1972–74, Ministry of Foreign Affairs 1974–78, UN Security Council 1978–82; Dir-Gen. Dernan & Sental Mfrg. and Financial Group 1983–88; Dir-Gen. Poland office, IBM World Trade/Europe/Middle East/Africa Corpn 1988–91; Pres. Ciech S.A. 1994–97; Pres. Prudential/Prumerica Financial Poland 1997–2001; currently Chair. Powszechny Zaklad Ubezpieczen (PZU) S.A.; Founder mem. Polish Trade and Finance Union; mem. Zacheta Art Society. *Leisure interests:* reading historical books. *Address:* Powszechny Zaklad Ubezpieczen S.A., al. Jana Pawla II 24, 00-133 Warsaw, Poland (Office). *Telephone:* (22) 5822810 (Office). *Fax:* (22) 5822811 (Office). *Website:* www.pzu.pl (Office).

MONTWILL, Alexander, PhD, DSc, MRIA, F.INST. P.; Irish professor of physics; b. 28 Oct. 1935, Riga, Latvia; s. of Stanislaw Montwill and Jadwiga Huszcza; m. Ann O'Doherty 1966; one s. four d.; ed Belvedere Coll., Westland Row Christian Brothers' School, Dublin and Univ. Coll. Dublin; lecturer, Univ. Coll. Dublin 1959–81, Assoc. Prof. 1981–85, Prof. of Experimental Physics 1985, Head Dept of Physics 1986–95; Visiting Assoc. Prof. City Coll. of New York 1966–68; Visiting Scientist, CERN, Geneva 1965–, Prof. Emer. 2002–. *Television includes:* Understanding the Universe (six-part series) R.T.E. Television. *Radio includes:* 150 segments on physics, RTE Radio. *Publications:* 43 Ppubls on high-energy physics. *Leisure interest:* bridge. *Address:* Department of Physics, University College, Belfield, Dublin 4, Republic of Ireland. *Telephone:* (1) 7062210. *Fax:* (1) 2837275.

MONTY, Jean C., MA, MBA; Canadian business executive; b. 26 June 1947, Montreal; m. Jocelyne Monty; two s.; ed Coll. Sainte-Marie, Montreal and Univs of W. Ontario and Chicago; Merrill Lynch, New York, Toronto and Montreal 1970–74; Bell Canada, Montreal 1974; Pres. Télébec Ltée. 1976; Nat. Defence Coll. Kingston, Ont. 1979–80; Bell Canada 1980–92, Pres. 1989, Pres. and CEO 1991–92; Pres. and COO Northern Telecom Ltd 1992, Pres. and CEO 1993–98; CEO BCE Inc. 1998–, now Pres.; Pres. and CEO Bell Canada 1998–; Dir Bank of Montreal, Bell-Northern Research Ltd; mem. Supervisory Bd Lagardère Group, Paris. *Leisure interest:* golf. *Address:* BCE Incorporated, Suite 3700, 1000 Rue de la Gauchetière, Québec, H3B 4Y7, Canada. *Telephone:* (514) 397-7244. *E-mail:* bcecomms@bce.ca (Office). *Website:* www.bce.ca (Office).

MONYAKE, Lengolo Bureng, MSc, UED; Lesotho public servant; b. 1 April 1930, Lesotho; s. of Bureng L. Monyake and Leomile Monyake; m. Molulela Mapetla 1957; two s. one d.; ed Fort Hare Univ. Coll., Univ. of Toronto, Carleton Univ., London School of Economics; Headmaster, Jordan High School 1958–61; Dir of Statistics, Govt of Lesotho 1968–74, Perm. Sec. 1974–76, Deputy Sr Perm. Sec. 1976–78; Amb. 1979–83; Man. Dir Lesotho Nat. Devt Corpn 1984–86; Minister for Foreign Affairs 1986–88, for Works 1988; Alt. Exec. Dir IMF 1988–90, Exec. Dir 1990–92; Deputy Exec. Sec. Southern African Devt Community 1993–. *Leisure interests:* tennis, table tennis, music, photography. *Address:* Southern African Development Community, Private Bag 0095, Gaborone, Botswana. *Telephone:* 314016. *Fax:* 372848.

MOODY-STUART, Sir Mark, KCMG, MA, PhD, FGS; British oil company executive and geologist; b. 15 Sept. 1940, Antigua, West Indies; s. of Sir Alexander Moody-Stuart and Judith Moody-Stuart (née Henzell); m. Judith McLeavy 1964; three s. one d.; ed Shrewsbury School and St John's Coll. Cambridge; with Shell Internationale Petroleum Mij. 1966–67, Koninklijke Shell E & P Lab. 1967–68, worked with Shell cos. in Spain, Oman, Brunei 1968–72, Chief Geologist, Australia 1972–76, Shell UK 1977–78, Brunei Shell Services Man. 1978–79, Gen. Man. Shell 1978–79, Man. Western Div. Shell

Nigeria 1979–82, Gen. Man. Shell Turkey 1982–86, Chair. and CEO Shell Malaysia 1986–89, Exploration and Production Co-ordinator, Royal Dutch/Shell 1990, Dir Shell Transport & Trading Co. PLC 1990–, Chair. 1997–2001, Man. Dir Royal Dutch/Shell Group 1991–2001, Chair. Cttee of Man. Dirs. 1998–2001; Chair. Anglo American PLC 2002–; Jt Chair. Task Force on Devt of Renewable Sources of Energy 2000; Dir Accenture 2001–, HSBC Holdings PLC 2001–; Chair. Business Action for Sustainable Devt 2001–02; Pres. Liverpool School of Tropical Medicine 2001–, Geological Soc. of London 2002–; mem. UN Sec. Gen.'s Advisory Council for the Global Compact 2001–; mem. Bd Global Reporting Initiative 2001–; Gov. Nuffield Hosps. 2001–; Hon. Fellow Inst. of Chemical Engineers 1997, St John's Coll. Cambridge Univ. 2001–; Hon. DBA (Robert Gordon) 2000; Cadman Medal Inst. of Petroleum 2002. *Publications:* papers in scientific journals. *Leisure interests:* sailing, travel, reading. *Address:* Anglo American PLC, 20 Carlton House Terrace, London, SW1Y 5AN (Office); 9 Gun House, 122 Wapping High Street, London, E1W 2NL, England (Home). *Telephone:* (20) 7698-8709 (Office); (20) 7702-4456 (Home). *Fax:* (20) 7698-8888 (Office). *E-mail:* markmoodystuart@aol.com (Home). *Website:* www.angloamerican.co.uk.

MOOG, Robert Arthur, PhD; American electrical engineer; b. 23 May 1934, New York; s. of George Conrad Moog and Shirley Jacobs Moog; m. Ileana Grams; one s. three d.; one step-d.; ed Queen's Coll., New York, Columbia Univ., Cornell Univ.; Pres. Moog Music Inc. 1954–77; Ind. Consultant 1978–84; Vice-Pres. for new product research, Kurzweil Music Systems, Waltham, Mass. 1985–89; Research Prof. Univ. of NC at Asheville 1989–92; Pres. Big Briar Inc. 1978–2002; Chief Tech. Officer Moog Music Inc. 2002–; Dr hc (Polytech. Univ., New York) 1984, (Berkeley Coll. of Music Boston) 2002, (Univ. of the Arts Phila) 2003; Billboard Magazine Trendsetters Award 1970, NARAS Trustees' Award 1970, Silver Medal, Audio Eng Soc. 1980, Seamus Award 1991, Polar Music Prize 2001, Naras Technical Grammy 2002. *Leisure interests:* gardening, reading, family. *Address:* Moog Music Inc., 554-C Riverside Drive, Asheville, NC 28801 (Office); 332 Barnard Avenue, Asheville, NC 28804, USA (Home). *Telephone:* (828) 251-0090 (Office); (828) 254-2750 (Home). *Fax:* (828) 254-6233 (Office). *E-mail:* bobm@moogmusic.com (Office). *Website:* www.moogmusic.com (Office).

MOONEY, Harold Alfred, MA, PhD; American professor of biology; b. 1 June 1932, Santa Rosa, Calif.; s. of Harold Walter Stefany and Sylvia A. Hart; m. Sherry L. Gulmon 1974; three d.; ed Univ. of Calif., Santa Barbara and Duke Univ.; Instructor to Assoc. Prof. Univ. of Calif., LA 1960–68; Assoc. Prof. Stanford Univ. 1968–73, Prof. 1975–, Paul S. Achilles Prof. of Environmental Biology 1976–; Guggenheim Fellow 1974; mem. NAS, American Acad. of Arts and Sciences, American Philosophical Soc.; Mercer Award (Ecology Soc. of America) 1961, Humboldt Award 1988, Inst. of Ecology Prize 1990. *Publications:* 12 books. *Address:* Department of Biological Sciences, 477 Herrin Lab., Stanford University, Stanford, CA 94305 (Office); 2625 Ramona Street, Palo Alto, CA 94306, USA (Home).

MOONS, Charles M. J. A., DIur; Netherlands jurist; b. 30 May 1917, Gemert; s. of A. J. W. M. Moons and A. M. van der Heyden; m. H. S. de Vriese 1949; three s. two d.; ed Univ. of Nijmegen; Substitute Public Prosecutor 1940–56, Public Prosecutor 1956–58; Advocate-Gen. Court of Appeal 1958–61; Advocate-Gen. Hoge Raad der Nederlanden (Supreme Court) 1961–64, Judge 1966–76, Vice-Pres. 1976–81, Pres. 1981–87; Judge, Benelux Court 1976–79, Vice-Pres. 1979–83, Pres. 1983; mem. Council of Govs., Leiden Univ. 1968–72; mem. Council of Govs., Royal Mil. Acad. 1970–; Appointing Authority Iran-U.S. Claims Tribunal 1983; Commdr Orde van de Nederlandsche Leeuw, Orde van Oranje-Nassau; Groot Officier Kroonorde van Belgie; Grand Officier, Ordre Grand-Ducal de la Couronne de Chène. *Publications:* Conclusions Advocate-General Nederlandse Jurispendentie, 1961–67, De Hoge Raad der Nederlanden, een Portret de Strafkamer 1988. *Leisure interest:* computer science. *Address:* Wassenaarseweg 81, 2596 CM, 's-Gravenhage, Netherlands. *Telephone:* (70) 3243571.

MOORBATH, Stephen Erwin, DPhil, DSc, FRS; British earth scientist; b. 9 May 1929, Magdeburg, Germany; s. of Heinz Moorbath and Else Moorbath; m. Pauline Tessier-Varlêt 1962; one s. one d.; ed Lincoln Coll., Oxford; Asst Experimental Officer, Atomic Energy Research Est., Harwell 1948–51; Scientific Officer, AERE 1954–56; Research Fellow, Univ. of Oxford 1956–61, Sr Research Officer, 1962–78, Reader in Geology 1978–92, Prof. of Isotope Geology 1992–96, Prof. Emer. 1996–, Professorial Fellow Linacre Coll. 1990–96, Fellow Emer. 1996; Research Fellow, MIT 1961–62; several awards. *Publications:* numerous contribs. to books and scientific journals. *Leisure interests:* music, philately, travel, linguistics. *Address:* Department of Earth Sciences, Oxford University, Parks Road, Oxford, OX1 3PR (Office); 53 Bagley Wood Road, Kennington, Oxford, OX1 5LY, England (Home). *Telephone:* (1865) 274584 (Office); (1865) 739507 (Home). *E-mail:* stephen.moorbath@earth.ox.ac.uk.

MOORCOCK, Michael John; British novelist; b. 18 Dec. 1939, London; s. of Arthur Moorcock and June Moorcock; m. 1st Hilary Bailey 1963 (divorced 1978); one s. two d.; m. 2nd Jill Richies 1978 (divorced 1983); m. 3rd Linda M. Steele 1982; one s. two d.; ed Michael Hall School, Sussex; worked as musician and journalist; Ed. Outlaws Own 1951–53, Tarzan Adventures 1957–59, Sexton Blake Library 1959–61, Current Topics 1961–62; Consulting Ed. New Worlds 1963–; Nebola Award (for Behold the Man) 1967, August Derleith Prize, Guardian Fiction Prize (for Condition of Muzak) 1977, World Fantasy Award (for Gloriana) 1979. *Publications include:* The Eternal Champion sequence 1963–98, Behold the Man 1968, Condition of Muzak 1976, Gloriana 1977, Byzantium Enclaves 1981, The Laughter of Carthage 1984, Mother London 1988, Jerusalem Commands 1992, Blood 1994, The War Amongst Angels 1996, Tales from the Texsas Woods 1997, King of the City 2000, Silverheart (co-author) 2000, London Borne 2001, The Dreamthief's Daughter 2001. *Leisure interests:* climbing, travelling, walking, cats, birds. *Address:* c/o Nomads Association, 21 Honor Oak Road, London, SE23 3SH, England (Office); P.O. Box 1230, Bastrop, TX 78602, USA; c/o Hoffman, 77 Boulevard St. Michel, 75005 Paris, France. *Telephone:* (512) 321-5000 (USA). *Fax:* (512) 321-5000 (USA).

MOORE, Ann S., BSc, MBA; American publisher and media executive; b. 1950, McLean, Va; m. Donovan Moore; one s.; ed Vanderbilt Univ., Nashville, Harvard Univ. Business School; financial analyst Time Inc. 1978, served in various exec. positions including Publr and Pres. People magazine (est. spin-offs Teen People, Instyle, Real Simple, People en Español 2001), cr. Sports Illustrated for Kids 1989, Exec. Vice-Pres. Time Inc. 2001–02, Chair. and CEO 2002–, responsible for Time magazine, People, Fortune, Money, Entertainment Weekly and 135 other titles (first woman in position). *Leisure interests:* Washington Redskins, cooking, reading. *Address:* Time Inc., Rockefeller Plaza, New York, NY 10019, USA (Office). *Telephone:* (212) 484-8000 (Office). *Website:* www.aoltimewarner.com (Office).

MOORE, Carole Irene, MS; Canadian librarian; b. 15 Aug. 1944, Berkeley, Calif., USA; ed Stanford and Columbia Univs.; Reference Librarian Columbia Univ. Libraries 1967–68, Univ. of Toronto Library 1968–73; Asst Head Reference Dept, Univ. of Toronto Library 1973–74, Head 1974–80; Head Bibliographic Processing Dept, Univ. of Toronto Library 1980–86, Assoc. Librarian, Tech. Services 1986–87, Chief Librarian 1986–; Research Libraries Group Dir 1994–96; mem. Bd Dirs. Univ. of Toronto Press 1994–; Columbia Univ. School of Library Service Centenary Distinguished Alumni Award 1987. *Publications:* Labour Relations and the Librarian (ed.) 1974, Canadian Essays and Collections Index 1972–73 1976. *Leisure interest:* gardening. *Address:* Robarts Library, 130 St George Street, Toronto, Ont., M5S 1A5, Canada (Office).

MOORE, Charles Hilary, BA; British journalist; b. 31 Oct. 1956, Hastings; s. of Richard Moore and Ann Moore; m. Caroline Baxter 1981; twin s. and d.; ed Eton Coll. and Trinity Coll. Cambridge; editorial staff, Daily Telegraph 1979–81, leader writer 1981–83; Asst Ed. and Political Columnist, The Spectator 1983–84, Ed. 1984–90, fortnightly columnist ('Another Voice') 1990–; weekly columnist, Daily Express 1987–90; Deputy Ed. Daily Telegraph 1990–92; Ed. Sunday Telegraph 1992–95, Daily Telegraph 1995–; Trustee T. E. Utley Memorial Fund, Benenden Council, ShareGift. *Publications:* 1936 (ed. with C. Hawtree) 1986, The Church in Crisis (with A. N. Wilson and G. Stamp) 1986, A Tory Seer: The Selected Journalism of T. E. Utley (ed. with S. Heffer) 1986. *Address:* Daily Telegraph, 1 Canada Square, Canary Wharf, London, E14 5DT, England. *Telephone:* (20) 7538-6300. *Fax:* (20) 7538-7654 (Office). *E-mail:* charles.moore@telegraph.co.uk (Office).

MOORE, Demi; American actress; b. Demi Guynes, 11 Nov. 1962, Roswell, New Mexico; d. of Danny Guynes and Virginia Guynes; m. Bruce Willis (q.v.) (divorced 2000); three d.; began acting with small part in TV series; worked as a model, Los Angeles. *Films:* Blame It on Rio, No Small Affair, St Elmo's Fire, One Crazy Summer, About Last Night..., Wisdom, The Seventh Sign, Ghost, Mortal Thoughts (also co-producer), The Butcher's Wife, A Few Good Men, Indecent Proposal, Disclosure, The Scarlet Letter, Striptease 1995, The Juror 1996, G.I. Jane 1996, The Hunchback of Notre Dame, Now and Then (also co-producer), Deconstructing Harry 1997, Austin Powers: International Man of Mystery (producer) 1997, Passion of Mind 2000, Airframe. *Television:* General Hospital (series), Bedroom. *Theatre:* The Early Girl (Theater World award). *Address:* Creative Artists Agency Inc., 9830 Wilshire Boulevard, Beverly Hills, CA 90212, USA.

MOORE, (Georgina) Mary, MA; British administrator and writer; b. 8 April 1930, Oxford; d. of the late Prof. V. H. Galbraith and Dr. Georgina R. Cole-Baker; m. Antony R. Moore 1963 (died 2000); one s. two step-d.; ed The Mount School, York and Lady Margaret Hall, Oxford; joined HM Foreign (later Diplomatic) Service 1951; served Budapest 1954, UK Perm. Del. at UN, New York 1956; First Sec. 1961; resgnd on marriage 1963; Prin. St Hilda's Coll., Oxford 1980–90, Hon. Fellow 1990; Trustee, British Museum 1982–92, Rhodes Trust 1984–96, Pilgrim Trust 1991– (Chair. 1993–); mem. Council for Industry and Higher Educ. 1986–90; Hon. D.L.L. (Mount Holyoake). *Television includes:* The Trial of Madame Fatimy (under pseudonym Helena Osborne), Granada TV 1981. *Publications:* (all under pseudonym Helena Osborne) novels: The Arcadian Affair 1969, Pay Day 1972, White Poppy 1977, The Joker 1979; plays for radio. *Leisure interests:* theatre, travel. *Address:* Touchbridge, Brill, Aylesbury, Bucks., HP18 9UJ, England. *Telephone:* (1844) 238247.

MOORE, Gillian, MBE, BMus, MA, FRCM; British music administrator; b. 20 Feb. 1959, Glasgow; d. of Charles Moore and Sara Queen; partner Bruce Nockles; one s.; ed Univ. of Glasgow, Royal Scottish Acad. of Music and Drama, Univ. of York, Harvard Univ.; Educ. Dir London Sinfonietta 1983–93, Artistic Dir 1998–; Head of Educ. Royal Festival Hall 1993–96, Music Audience Devt Man. 1996–; Artistic Dir ISCM World Music Days, Manchester 1997–98; Visiting Prof. R.C.M. 1996–; Gov. Nat. Youth Orchestra of GB; mem. British Govt Nat. Curriculum Working Group on Music; freelance work as broadcaster, lecturer and writer in music, consultant on music and educ.;

Hon. Mem. Guildhall School of Music 1993; Sir Charles Grove Award for Outstanding Contrib. to British Music 1992, Asscn of British Orchestras Award for Contrib. of Most Benefit to Orchestral Life in the UK 1999. *Address:* London Sinfonietta, 4 Maguire Street, London S.E.1 (Office); 108 Waller Road, London, SE14 5LU, England (Home). *Telephone:* (20) 7928-0828 (Office); (20) 7639-6680 (Home). *Fax:* (20) 7928-8557 (Office); (20) 7639-6675 (Home).

MOORE, John A(lexander), PhD; American biologist; b. 27 June 1915, Charles Town, W Va; s. of George Douglas and Louise Hammond Blume Moore; m. Anna Betty Clark 1938; one d.; ed Columbia Coll. and Columbia Univ.; Asst Zoology Dept, Columbia Univ. 1936–39, Chair. 1949–52, Prof. 1954–68; Prof. Biology Dept Univ. of Calif. (Riverside) 1969–82, Prof. Emer. 1982–; Tutor of Biology, Brooklyn Coll. 1939–41; Instructor at Queens Coll. 1941–48; Asst Prof. Zoology Barnard Coll. 1943–47, Assoc. Prof. 1947–50, Prof. 1950–68, Chair. Zoology Dept 1948–52, 1953–54, 1960–66; Walker Ames Prof. Univ. of Washington 1966; Fulbright Research Scholar, Australia 1952–53; mem. Nat. Research Council Comm. on Human Resources 1979–82; Biological Sciences Curriculum Study 1959–76, Comm. on Science Educ. 1967–73 (Chair. 1971–73), AAAS Project 2061 1985–89, Nat. Research Council: Co-ordinating Council for Educ. 1991–95, Cttee on Under-graduate Science Educ. 1992–, Nat. Science Resource Center 1994–, Cttee K-12 Science Educ. 1996–, Marine Biology Lab., AAAS; mem. Genetics Soc. of America, American Soc. of Zoologists (Pres. 1974), American Soc. of Naturalists (Pres. 1972), Soc. for Study of Evolution (Pres. 1963), American Acad. Arts and Sciences, NAS; Guggenheim Fellowship Award 1959. *Publications:* Principles of Zoology 1957, Heredity and Development 1963, 1972, A Guide Book to Washington 1963, Biological Science: An Inquiry into Life 1963, 1968, 1973 (Supervisor), Physiology of the Amphibia (Ed.) 1964, Ideas in Modern Biology (Ed.) 1965, Interaction of Man and the Biosphere (co-author) 1970, 1975, 1979, Ideas in Evolution and Behavior (Ed.) 1970, Science for Society: A Bibliography 1970, 1971, Readings in Heredity and Development 1972, Dobzhansky's Genetics of Natural Populations (Ed.) 1981, Science as a Way of Knowing – Evolutionary Biology 1984, Science as a Way of Knowing—Human Ecology 1985, Science as a Way of Knowing – Genetics 1986, Science as a Way of Knowing – Developmental Biology 1987, Science as a Way of Knowing – Form and Function 1988, Genes, Cells and Organisms (12 Vols, Ed.) 1988, Science: A Way of Knowing – A Conceptual Framework for Biology (Part I) 1989, (Part II) 1990, (Part III) 1991, Science as a Way of Knowing: The Foundations of Modern Biology 1993. *Leisure interests:* photography, history of American science, history of illumination. *Address:* Department of Biology, University of California, Riverside, CA 92521; 11522 Tulane Avenue, Riverside, CA 92507-6649, USA (Home). *Telephone:* (909) 787-3142 (Office); (909) 684-0412 (Home). *Fax:* (909) 787-4286 (Office); (909) 789-4286. *E-mail:* jamore@ucr.aci.ucr.edu (Office).

MOORE, Hon. John Colinton, BCom, AASA; Australian fmr politician and company director; b. 16 Nov. 1936, Rockhampton; s. of T. R. Moore and D. S. Moore; m. 2nd Jacquelyn Moore; two s. one d. from previous m.; ed Armidale School, Queensland Univ.; stockbroker 1960; mem. Brisbane Stock Exchange 1962–74; Vice-Pres. and Treas. Queensland Liberal Party 1967–73, Pres. 1973–76, 1984–90; MP for Ryan 1975–2001; Minister for Business and Consumer Affairs 1980–82; Opposition Spokesman for Finance 1983–84, for Communications 1984–85, for Northern Devt and Local Govt 1985–87, for Transport and Aviation 1987, for Business and Consumer Affairs 1987–89, for Business Privatization and Consumer Affairs 1989–90; Shadow Minister for Privatization and Public Admin. 1994, for Privatization 1994–95, for Industry, Commerce and Public Admin. 1995–96; Minister for Industry, Science and Tourism 1996–97, of Industry, Science and Tech. 1997–98, for Defence 1998–2001; Vice-Pres. Exec. Council 1996–98; Dir William Brandt & Sons (Australia), Phillips, First City, Brandt Ltd, Merrill Lynch, Pierce, Fennell and Smith (Australia) Ltd, Citinat, Agricultural Investments Australia Ltd; mem. various bd. dels, Council Order of Australia. *Leisure interests:* tennis, cricket, reading, golf. *Address:* PO Box 2191, Toowong, Brisbane 4066; 47 Dennis Street, Indooroopilly, Brisbane, Australia (Home). *Telephone:* 419 704764 (Office); (7) 3217-7427 (Home). *Fax:* (7) 3876-8088 (Office). *E-mail:* john_moore1@bigpond.com.au (Home).

MOORE, Capt. John Evelyn, RN, FRGS; British editor, author and retd naval officer; b. 1 Nov. 1921, Sant' Ilario, Italy; s. of William John Moore and Evelyn Elizabeth (née Hooper); m. 1st Joan Pardoe 1945; one s. two d.; m. 2nd Barbara Kerry; ed Sherborne School, Dorset; entered RN 1939, specialized in hydrographic surveying, then submarines, commanded HM Submarines Totem, Alaric, Tradewind, Tactician, Telemachus; RN staff course 1950–51; Commdr 1957; attached to Turkish Naval Staff 1958–60; subsequently Plans Div., Admiralty, 1st Submarine Squadron, then 7th Submarine Squadron in command; Capt. 1967; served as Chief of Staff, C-in-C Naval Home Command; Defence Intelligence Staff; retd list at own request 1972; Ed. Jane's Fighting Ships 1972–87; Ed. Jane's Naval Review 1982–87; Hon. Prof. of Int. Relations, Aberdeen Univ. 1987–90, St Andrews Univ. 1990–92. *Publications:* Jane's Major Warships 1973, The Soviet Navy Today 1975, Submarine Development 1976, Soviet War Machine (jtly.) 1976, Encyclopaedia of World's Warships 1978, World War 3 1978, Seapower and Politics 1979, Warships of the Royal Navy 1979, Warships of the Soviet Navy 1981, Submarine Warfare: Today and Tomorrow (jtly.) 1986; ed. The Impact of Polaris 1999. *Leisure interests:* gardening, archaeology. *Address:* 1 Ridgelands Close, Eastbourne, East Sussex, BN20 8EP, England. *Telephone:* (1323) 638836.

MOORE, Maj.-Gen. Sir (John) Jeremy, KCB, OBE, MC; British Royal Marines officer; b. 5 July 1928, Lichfield, Staffs.; s. of Lt-Col C. P. Moore, MC and Alice Hylda Mary Bibby; m. Veryan Acworth 1966; one s. two d.; ed Cheltenham Coll.; with Royal Marines 1947–83; Staff Coll., Australia 1963–64; Chiefs of Staff Secr., London 1966–68; CO 42 Commando, Royal Marines 1972–73; Purveyor in Mil. Music to RN 1973–75; Royal Coll. of Defence Studies 1976; Commdr 3rd Commando Brigade, Royal Marines 1977–79; Maj.-Gen. commanding commando forces, Royal Marines 1979–82; Commdr of British Land Forces in Falklands conflict 1982, accepted Argentine surrender 14 June 1982, Col Commdt 1990–93; Specialist Adviser Commons Select Cttee on Defence 1984–91; defence consultant; Dir-Gen. Food Mfrs Fed. 1984–85, Food and Drink Fed. 1984–85; Chair. Ranleigh Enterprises Ltd, Task (International) Ltd; Pres. Royal Marines Assen 1990–93; Hon. Col Wiltshire Army Cadet Force 1991–93; Hon. Pres. British Biathlon team 1984–88; mem. Parish Council, Bratton, Wilts. 1987–91. *Leisure interests:* governor of two schools, music, sailing, hill-walking.

MOORE, Julianne, BA; American actress; b. 3 Dec. 1961, Fayetteville, NC; ed Boston Univ. School for Arts; with the Guthrie Theater 1988–89. *Stage appearances include:* Serious Money 1987, Ice Cream with Hot Fudge 1990, Uncle Vanya, The Road to Nirvana, Hamlet, The Father. *Film appearances include:* Tales from the Darkside 1990, The Hand That Rocks the Cradle 1992, The Gun in Betty Lou's Handbag 1992, Body of Evidence 1993, Benny and Joon 1993, The Fugitive 1993, Short Cuts 1993, Vanya on 42nd Street 1994, Roommates 1995, Safe 1995, Nine Months 1995, Assassins 1995, Surviving Picasso 1996, Jurassic Park: The Lost World 1997, The Myth of Fingerprints 1997, Hellcab 1997, Boogie Nights 1997, The Big Lebowski 1998, Eyes Wide Shut, The End of the Affair 1999, Map of the World 1999, Magnolia 1999, Cookie's Fortune 1999, An Ideal Husband 1999, Hannibal 2000, The Shipping News 2002, Far From Heaven (Best Actress, Venice Film Festival) 2002, The Hours 2002. *Television appearances include:* As the World Turns (series), The Edge of Night (series), Money, Power Murder 1989, Lovecraft 1991, I'll Take Manhattan, The Last to Go, Cast a Deadly Spell. *Address:* c/o Kevin Huvane, Creative Artists Agency, 9830 Wilshire Boulevard, Beverly Hills, CA 90212, USA.

MOORE, Michael; American author, filmmaker and political commentator; b. 1954, Davison, Michigan; elected to high school bd age 18; active in student politics; began career as journalist The Flint Voice, later Ed., expanded into The Michigan Voice; Ed. Mother Jones magazine, San Francisco 1986–88; writer, producer and dir award-winning documentary Roger and Me (based on Gen. Motors Co. activities in Flint) 1989, Roger and Me, Pets or Meat: The Return to Flint. *Television includes:* TV Nation (NBC) 1994, (FOX-TV) 1995, The Awful Truth (Channel 4) 1999. *Film appearances include:* Pony Express 1953, Lucky Number 1999, EdTV 1999, Bowling for Columbine (also producer and screenwriter—Acad. Award for Best Documentary 2003) 2002. *Films directed include:* Talion 1966, Paradise Hawaiian Style 1966, An Eye for an Eye 1966, The Fastest Guitar Alive 1968, Buckskin 1968, Canadian Bacon 1994, The Big One 1997, Bowling for Columbine (Jury Award, Cannes Film Festival 2002) 2002. *Publications include:* Downsize This!: Random Threats From An Unarmed America 1996, Stupid White Men (after Random House decided to cancel launch following Sept. 11 2001 attacks, email campaign spearheaded by librarians forced release of book; Book of the Year, British Book Awards 2003) 2002. *Address:* c/o Random House Inc., 299 Park Avenue, New York, NY 10170, USA (Office).

MOORE, Michael, CBE, MBA, MA; British business executive; b. 15 March 1936; s. of Sir Rodney Moore and Olive Marion Robinson; m. Jan Moore; one s.; ed Eton Coll., Magdalen Coll. Oxford and Harvard Business School; called to the Bar 1961; Chair. Tomkins PLC 1984–95, Quicks Group PLC 1993–, Linx Printing Technologies PLC 1993–, London Int. Group PLC 1994–, Status Holdings PLC 2000–; Jt Deputy Chair., Clerical Medical & Gen. Life Assurance Soc. 1996–; Chair. Nat. Soc. for Prevention of Cruelty to Children (NSPCC) 1988–95; Chair. Which? 1997–; Trustee Public Concern at Work 1996–. *Leisure interests:* reading, music (especially opera), visiting ruins, tennis. *Address:* 35 New Bridge Street, London, EC4V 6BJ, England.

MOORE, Rt Hon Michael Kenneth, PC, MP; New Zealand politician and international organization official; b. 28 Jan. 1949, Whakatane; s. of the late Alan Moore and Audrey Moore; m. Yvonne Dereaney 1975; fmr social worker, printer etc.; MP for Eden 1972–75, Papanui, Christchurch 1978–84, Christchurch N 1984–96, Waimakariri 1996–99; Minister of Overseas Trade and Marketing, also Minister of Tourism and Publicity and of Recreation and Sport 1984–87; Minister of Overseas Trade and Marketing and of Publicity 1987–88, 1989–90, of External Relations and Int. Trade 1988–90; Minister of Foreign Affairs Jan.–Oct. 1990; Prime Minister Sept.–Oct. 1990; Leader of the Opposition 1990–93; fmr Assoc. Minister of Finance; Dir-Gen. WTO 1999–2002. *Publications:* six books including A Pacific Parliament, Hard Labour, Fighting for New Zealand 1993, Children of the Poor 1996, A Brief History of the Future 1998. *Address:* c/o Privy Council, Government of New Zealand, Parliament Buildings, Wellington, New Zealand.

MOORE, Nicholas G., JD, BS; American finance company executive; m. Jo Anne Moore; four c.; ed St Mary's Coll., Calif., Hastings Coll. of Law, Univ. of Calif. at Berkeley; joined Coopers & Lybrand 1968, Partner 1974, Head of Tax Practice, San José office 1974–81, Man. Partner San José Office 1981, mem. firm council 1984, Exec. Cttee 1988, Vice-Chair. W Region 1991–92, Client Service Vice-Chair. 1992, Chair., CEO Coopers & Lybrand USA 1994,

Chair. Coopers & Lybrand Int. 1997, Chair. PricewaterhouseCoopers (formed from merger of Coopers & Lybrand Int. and Price Waterhouse) 1999–; mem. Calif. Bar Asscn; Trustee Financial Accounting Foundation 1997–; Chair. Co-operation Ireland; mem. Bd of Trustees Cttee for Econ. Devt; Vice-Chair. Business Cttee, Metropolitan Museum of Art. *Address:* Pricewaterhouse-Coopers LLP, 1301 Avenue of the Americas, New York, NY 10019, USA (Office).

MOORE, Sir Patrick Alfred Caldwell-, Kt, CBE, FRS; British astronomer and author; b. 4 March 1923, Pinner, Middx; s. of the late Capt. Caldwell-Moore, MC and Gertrude Lilian Moore (née White); ed privately; Officer, Bomber Command, RAF 1940–45; BBC TV series, The Sky at Night 1957–, radio broadcasts; Ed. Year Book of Astronomy 1962–; Dir Armagh Planetarium 1965–68; freelance 1968–; composed Perseus and Andromeda (opera) 1975, Theseus 1982; Pres. British Astronomical Asscn 1982–84, now Life Hon. Vice-Pres.; Hon. DSc (Lancaster) 1974, (Hatfield Polytechnic) 1989, (Birmingham) 1990, (Portsmouth) 1997, (Leicester) 1996; Dr hc (Keele) 1994; Goodacre Medal (British Astronomical Asscn) 1968; Jackson Gwilt Gold Medal (Royal Astronomical Soc.) 1977; Klumpke Medal (Astronomical Soc. of the Pacific) 1979; Minor Planet No. 2602 is named in his honour; BAFTA Special Award 2002. *Plays:* Quintet (Chichester) 2002. *Television includes* Sky at Night, BBC 1957–. *Radio:* frequent broadcaster on radio. *Publications:* numerous, including Guide to the Moon 1976, Atlas of the Universe 1980, History of Astronomy 1983, The Story of the Earth (with Peter Cattermole) 1985, Halley's Comet (with Heather Couper) 1985, Patrick Moore's Armchair Astronomy 1985, Stargazing 1985, Exploring the Night Sky with Binoculars 1986, The A–Z of Astronomy 1986, Astronomy for the Under Tens 1987, Astronomers' Stars 1987, The Planet Uranus (jtly.) 1988, Space Travel for the Under Tens 1988, The Planet Neptune 1989, Mission to the Planets 1990, The Universe for the Under Tens 1990, A Passion for Astronomy 1991, Fireside Astronomy 1992, Guinness Book of Astronomy (revised edn) 1995, Passion for Astronomy 1995, Stars of the Southern Skies 1995, Teach Yourself Astronomy 1996, Eyes on the Universe 1997, Brilliant Stars 1998, Patrick Moore on Mars 1999, Yearbook of Astronomy AD 1000 (with Allan Chapman) 1999, Data Book of Astronomy 2001. *Leisure interests:* music, cricket, chess, tennis. *Address:* Farthings, 39 West Street, Selsey, Sussex, PO20 9AD, England. *Telephone:* (1243) 603668.

MOORE, Robin James, MA, PhD, DLit, FAHA; Australian professor of history; b. 29 April 1934, Melbourne; s. of the late F. E. Moore; m. 2nd Rosemary Sweetapple 1976; ed Univs. of Melbourne and London; Exec. Containers Ltd 1955–60, Western Mining Corpn 1960–62; Sir Arthur Sims Travelling Scholar 1962–64; Lecturer in Modern Indian History SOAS, London Univ. 1964–71; Prof. of History, Flinders Univ. of South Australia 1971–2003, mem. of Council 1986–89, Dean Faculty of Social Sciences 1988–97, Emer. Prof. of History 2003–; Smuts Visiting Fellow in Commonwealth Studies, Cambridge Univ. 1974–75; Australian Vice-Chancellor's Cttee Visiting Fellow, India 1979; Chapman Visiting Fellow Inst. of Commonwealth Studies, Univ. of London 1980–81; Gov. Adelaide Festival of Arts Inc. 1980–94; Pres. Australian Historical Asscn 1985–86; mem. Bd Wakefield Press 1985–86; Visiting Prof. Univ. of Tulsa, Okla 1987. *Publications:* Sir Charles Wood's Indian Policy 1853–1866 1966, Liberalism and Indian Politics 1872–1922 1966, The Crisis of Indian Unity 1917–40 1974, Churchill, Cripps and India 1939–45 1979, Escape from Empire 1983, Making the New Commonwealth 1987, Endgames of Empire 1988, Paul Scott's Raj 1990. *Leisure interests:* music, theatre, reading, walking. *Address:* 2 Palm Street, Medindie, SA 5081, Australia.

MOORE, Roger, CBE; British actor; b. 14 Oct. 1927, London; m. 1st Doorn van Steyn (divorced 1953); m. 2nd Dorothy Squires 1953 (divorced 1969, died 1998); m. 3rd Luisa Mattioli; two s. one d.; ed Royal Acad. of Dramatic Art; Special Amb. for UNICEF 1991–. *Films include:* Crossplot 1969, The Man With the Golden Gun 1974, That Lucky Touch 1975, Save Us From Our Friends 1975, Shout At The Devil 1975, Sherlock Holmes in New York 1976, The Spy Who Loved Me 1976, The Wild Geese 1977, Escape To Athena 1978, Moonraker 1978, Esther, Ruth and Jennifer 1979, The Sea Wolves, 1980, Sunday Lovers 1980, For Your Eyes Only 1980, Octopussy 1983, The Naked Face 1983, A View to a Kill 1985, Key to Freedom 1989, Bed and Breakfast 1989, Bullseye! 1989, Fire, Ice and Dynamite 1990, The Quest 1997. *Television appearances include:* The Alaskans, The Saint 1962–69, The Persuaders 1972–73, The Man Who Wouldn't Die 1992, The Quest 1995. *Publication:* James Bond Diary 1973.

MOORE OF LOWER MARSH, Baron (Life Peer), cr. 1992, of Lower Marsh in the London Borough of Lambeth; **John Edward Michael Moore;** British politician; b. 26 Nov. 1937; s. of Edward O. Moore; m. Sheila S. Tillotson 1962; two s. one d.; ed London School of Econs; with Royal Sussex Regt Korea 1955–57; Pres. Students' Union LSE 1959–60; banking and stockbroking, Chicago 1962–65; Dir Dean Witter Int. Ltd 1968–79, Chair. 1975–79; underwriting mem. Lloyds 1978–92; Exec. Chair. Crédit Suisse Asset Man. 1991–, Energy Saving Trust Ltd 1992–95 (Pres. 1995–); mem. Parl. for Croydon Cen. 1974–92; Parl. Under-Sec. of State, Dept of Energy 1979–83; Econ. Sec. to HM Treasury June–Oct. 1983, Financial Sec. to HM Treasury Oct. 1983–86; Sec. of State for Transport 1986–87, for Dept of Health and Social Security 1987–88, for Social Security 1988–89; Dir Monitor Inc. 1990– (Chair. Monitor Europe 1990–), Blue Circle Industries 1993–, Camelot PLC 1994–96, Rolls-Royce PLC (Deputy Chair. 1996–), Crédit Suisse Investment Man. Australia 1995–, Cen. European Growth Fund PLC 1995–, BEA Assocs USA 1996–98,

TIG Inc. 1997–, Pvt. Client Partners, Zurich 1999–; mem. Court of Govs LSE 1977–. *Address:* Credit Suisse Asset Management Ltd, Beaufort House, 15 St. Botolph Street, London, EC3A 7JJ (Office); House of Lords, Westminster, London, SW1A 0PW, England. *Telephone:* (20) 7426-2626 (Office). *Fax:* (20) 7426-2618 (Office).

MOORER, Adm. Thomas Hinman, DSM, DFC; American naval officer (retd); b. 9 Feb. 1912, Mount Willing, Ala; s. of the late Dr. Richard Randolph Moorer and Hulda Hinson; m. Carrie Ellen Foy 1935; three s. one d.; ed U.S. Naval Acad.; service in U.S. warships 1933–35, aviation squadrons 1936–43; Commdr of bombing squadron 1943; Gunnery and Tactical Officer, Staff of Commdr, Naval Air Force, Atlantic 1944–45; Strategic Bombing Survey, Japan 1945–56; Naval Aviation Ordnance Test Station 1946–48; Exec. Officer aircraft carrier Midway 1948–49; Operations Officer on Staff of Commdr Carrier Div. Four, Atlantic Fleet 1949–50; Naval Ordnance Test Station, Inyokern 1950–52; Capt. 1952; Staff of Commdr, Naval Air Force, Atlantic Fleet 1953–55; Aide to Asst Sec. of Navy for Air 1955–56; Commdr USS Salisbury Sound 1956–57; Special Asst, Strategic Plans Div., Office of Chief of Naval Operations, Navy Dept 1957–58; Rear-Adm. 1958; Asst Chief of Naval Operations (War Gaming Matters) 1958–59; Commdr Carrier Div. Six 1959–60; Dir Long Range Plans 1960–62; Vice-Adm. 1962; Commdr U.S. Seventh Fleet, W Pacific 1962–64; Adm. 1964; C-in-C U.S. Pacific Fleet 1964–65; C-in-C U.S. Atlantic Fleet, C-in-C Atlantic and Supreme Allied Commdr Atlantic (NATO Forces) 1965–67; Chief of Naval Operations, U.S. 1967–70; Chair. U.S. Jt Chiefs of Staff 1970–74; Dir Blount Inc., Montgomery, Ala 1974–; mem. Asscn of Naval Aviation (Chair. 1974–); Silver Star Medal 1942, Legion of Merit 1945, Gray Eagle of U.S. Navy Award 1972, Defense Distinguished Service Medal 1973, included in Nat. Aviation Hall of Fame 1987, Nat. Football Foundation and Hall of Fame Gold Medal 1990 and many U.S. and foreign decorations. *Leisure interests:* football, golf, hunting, fishing. *Address:* 9707 Old Georgetown Road, Bethesda, MD 20814, USA (Home).

MOORES, Sir Peter, Kt, CBE, DL; British business executive; b. 9 April 1932; s. of Sir John Moores; m. Luciana Pinto 1960 (divorced 1984); one s. one d.; ed Eton Coll., Christ Church, Oxford, Wiener Akademie der Musik und darstellender Kunste; worked opera, Glyndebourne and Vienna State Opera; Dir The Littlewoods Org. 1965–93 (Chair. 1977–80); f. Peter Moores Foundation 1964; pioneered opera recordings in English trans. by ENO and Opera Rara; annual Peter Moores Foundation Scholarships awarded to promising young opera singers, Royal Northern Coll. of Music; endowed Faculty Directorship and Chair of Man. Studies, Oxford Univ. 1992; est. Scotland Beef Project, Barbados (land conservation and self-supporting farming practice) 1993, Transatlantic Slave Trade Gallery, Merseyside Maritime Museum 1994; Benefactor, Chair of Tropical Horticulture, Univ. of W. Indies, Barbados 1995; f. Compton Verney House Trust 1993, Peter Moores Charitable Trust 1998; Dir Singer & Friedlander 1978–92, Scottish Opera 1988–92; Trustee Tate Gallery 1978–85; Gov. BBC 1981–83; Hon. RNCM 1985; Hon. MA (Christ Church, Oxford) 1975; Gold Medal of Italian Repub. 1974; DL (Lancs.). *Leisure interests:* opera, shooting. *Address:* Parbold Hall, Parbold, nr Wigan, Lancs., WN8 7TG, England (Home).

MOOREY, (Peter) Roger (Stuart), FBA, FSA, DPhil; British fmr museum curator and college officer; b. 30 May 1937, Bush Hill Park, Middx; s. of the late Stuart Moorey and of Freda (née Harris) Moorey; ed Mill Hill School, Corpus Christi Coll., Oxford; Asst Keeper, Ashmolean Museum, Oxford 1961–73; Sr Asst Keeper 1973–83, Keeper, Dept of Antiquities 1983–2002 (Acting Dir 1997–98); Pres. British School of Archaeology, Jerusalem 1990–99; Fellow of Wolfson Coll., Oxford 1976–2002, Senior Research Fellow 2002–; Vice-Gerent 2002–. *Publications:* Catalogue of the Ancient Persian Bronzes in the Ashmolean Museum 1971, Biblical Lands 1975, Kish Excavations 1923–33 1978, Cemeteries at Deve Hüyük 1980, Excavation in Palestine 1981, Materials and Manufacture in Ancient Mesopotamia 1985, The Bible and Recent Archaeology (with Kenyon) 1987, Ancient Near Eastern Seals in the Ashmolean Museum, Vols 2 and 3 (with Buchanan) 1984, 1988, A Century of Biblical Archaeology 1991, Ancient Mesopotamian Materials and Industries 1994. *Leisure interests:* travelling, walking. *Address:* Wolfson Coll., Oxford, OX2 6UD (Office); 343 Iffley Road, Oxford, OX14 4DP England (Home). *Telephone:* (1865) 274109 (Office); (1865) 248655 (Home).

MOORMAN van KAPPEN, Olav, LLD; Netherlands legal historian; b. 11 March 1937, The Hague; s. of Karel S. O. van Kappen and Johanna J. Moorman; m. Froukje A. Bosma 1963; one s. one d.; ed Huygens Lyceum and Utrecht Univ.; Research Asst Faculty of Law, Utrecht Univ. 1961–64, Jr Lecturer 1965–68; Sr Lecturer Faculty of Law, Amsterdam Univ. 1968–71; Asst Prof. Faculty of Law, Leyden Univ. 1971–72; Prof. of Legal History, Nijmegen Univ. 1971–2000, Co. Dir Gerard Noodt Inst. for Legal History 1972–2000, Emer. Prof. 2000–; Visiting Prof. Munster Univ. 1982–83, Poitiers Univ. 1986, 1991 Düsseldorf Univ. 1989–90, Univ. René Descartes (Paris V) 1992, 1995, 1999; mem. Bd of Govs Netherlands School for Archivists 1979–81, Chair. 1981–95; mem. Netherlands Council of Archives 1979–89, Vice-Pres. 1986–89, Pres. 1990–95; mem. Nat. Council of Cultural Heritage 1990–95; mem. editorial Bd, Legal History Review 1983–; mem. Dutch Soc. of Sciences at Haarlem 1982, Royal Netherlands Acad. of Sciences 1986; Corresp. mem. Acad. of Sciences, Göttingen 1996; Dr hc (Univ. René Descartes (Paris V)); Cross of Merit 1st Class (FRG), Officier, Ordre des Palmes Académiques (France), Officier, Ordre van Oranje-Nassau (Netherlands). *Publications:* over 360 books and numerous articles on various aspects of legal history. *Address:* Institute of Legal Science of Nijmegen University, PO Box 9049, 6500 KK Nijmegen, Netherlands. *Telephone:* (24) 3612186. *Fax:* (24) 3616145.

MOOSA, Mohammed Valli, BSc; South African politician; b. 9 Feb. 1957, Johannesburg; m. Elsabé Wessels; ed Lenasia State Indian High School, Univ. of Durban-Westville; active in SA Students' Org., Nat. Indian Congress and other political and trade-union activities; teacher 1979–82; involved in est. of Anti-SA Indian Council Cttee 1982, revival of Transvaal Indian Congress 1983; Founder mem. and fmr mem. Nat. Exec. Cttee United Democratic Front; fmr Leader Mass Democratic Movt; detained 1987, escaped 1988; planned Defiance Campaign; detained 1989; involved in Conf. for a Democratic Future 1989; mem. Nat. Reception Cttee for released ANC leaders 1989–90; with ANC 1990–, mem. Nat. Exec. Cttee 1991, fmr mem. Nat. Working Cttee, rep. of negotiating team Convention for a Democratic South Africa 1991–94; Deputy Minister of Provincial Affairs and Constitutional Devt 1994, Minister 1996–99, Minister of Environmental Affairs and Tourism 1999–. *Address:* Ministry of Environmental Affairs and Tourism, Fedsure Forum Building, North Tower, corner Van der Walt and Pretorius Streets, Private Bag X447, Pretoria 0001, South Africa (Office). *Telephone:* (12) 3103611 (Office). *Fax:* (12) 3220082 (Office). *E-mail:* vmoosa@ozone.pwv.gov.za (Office). *Website:* www.environment.gov.za (Office).

MORA GRAMUNT, Gabriel; Spanish architect; b. 13 April 1941, Barcelona; s. of Evaristo Mora Gramunt and Josefa Mora Gramunt; m. Carmina Sanvisens Montón 1985; one s.; ed Tech. Univ. of Architecture, Barcelona (ETSAB); Assoc. Piñón-Viaplana 1967; tutor, ETSAB 1973; in partnership with Jaume Bach Nuñez, Bach/Mora Architects 1976–; Prof. of History of Modern Architecture, EINA School of Design 1978; Design Tutor, ETSAB 1978–; Visiting Prof. Univ. of Dublin 1993; Various professional awards. *Work includes:* Grass Hockey Olympic Stadium, Terrassa 1992, cen. telephone exchange, Olympic Village, Barcelona 1992, apt. bldgs., agric. complex, health clinic etc. *Publications include:* Junge Architekten in Europa (jtly.) 1983, Young Spanish Architects (jtly.) 1985. *Address:* Passatge Sant Felip, 12 bis, 08006 Barcelona, Spain.

MORAES, Dominic; Indian writer and poet; b. 19 July 1938; s. of the late Frank Moraes; m. Leela Naidu 1970; ed St Mary's High School, Bombay and Jesus Coll., Oxford; Consultant UN Fund for Population Activities 1973– (on loan to India); Man. Ed. The Asia Magazine Hong Kong 1972–; fmr Ed. Indian Express; Hawthornden Prize for A Beginning 1957. *Publications include:* A Beginning 1957, Gone Away 1960, My Son's Father (autobiog.) 1968, The Tempest Within 1972–73, The People Time Forgot 1972, A Matter of People 1974, Voices for Life (essays) 1975, Mrs. Gandhi 1980, Bombay 1980, Collected Poems 1957–87 1988, Serendip 1990 (poems), Never At Home 1994 (autobiog.), In Cinnamon Shade (poems) 2001. *Address:* 12 Sargent House, Allana Marg, Mumbai 400039, India.

MORAES DE ABREU, José Carlos; Brazilian business executive; b. 15 July 1922; ed Univ. de São Paulo (USP); Man. Dir Itaúsa (Investimentos Itaú SA) 1966, Exec. Vice-Pres. 1966–76, 1979–83, Pres. 1976–79, CEO 1983–, mem. Admin. Council 2001–; mem. Nat. Monetary Council 1975–84; Hon. LLB (São Paulo) 1944. *Address:* Office of the Chief Executive, Praça Alfredo Egydio de Souza Aranha 100, Torres Itaúsa, São Paulo 04344-902, Brazil (Office). *Telephone:* (11) 5019-1677 (Office). *Fax:* (11) 5019-1114 (Office). *Website:* www.itausa.com.br (Office).

MORAHAN, Christopher Thomas; British theatre, television and film director; b. 9 July 1929; s. of the late Thomas Morahan and Nancy Barker; m. 1st Joan Murray 1954 (died 1973); m. 2nd Anna Carteret 1974; two s. three d. (one deceased); ed Highgate School and Old Vic Theatre School; Dir Greenpoint Films and Head, plays, BBC TV 1972–76; Assoc. Dir Royal Nat. Theatre 1977–88; BAFTA Best TV Series 1984, Int. Emmy 1984, 1993, 1994, Evening Standard Best Dir 1984, Prix Italia 1987 and many other awards. *Films include:* Clockwise 1986, Papermask 1990. *Stage productions include:* Little Murders, This Story of Yours, The Caretaker, Flint, Melon, Major Barbara, The Handyman, Letter of Resignation, Racing Demon, Equally Divided, The Importance of Being Earnest, Semi Detached, Quartet, The Retreat from Moscow, Beyond a Joke, Heartbreak House, Naked Justice, the Winslow Boy, Hock and Soda Water; for Nat. Theatre: State of Revolution, The Philanderer, Brand, Richard III, Strife, The Wild Duck, Man and Superman, Wild Honey, The Devil's Disciple. *Radio includes:* Art, BBC Radio 3. *Television productions include:* The Jewel in the Crown 1984, In the Secret State 1985, After Pilkington 1987, Troubles 1988, The Heat of the Day 1989, Old Flames 1990, Can You Hear Me Thinking? 1990, Ashenden 1991, The Common Pursuit 1992, Unnatural Pursuits 1992, The Bullion Boys 1993, Summer Days Dream 1994, It Might be You 1995, The Peacock Spring 1996, Element of Doubt, A Dance to the Music of Time (two episodes) 1997. *Leisure interests:* photography, birdwatching. *Address:* c/o Whitehall Artists, 10 Lower Common South, London, SW15 1BP; Highcombe Farmhouse, The Devil's Punchbowl, Thursley, Godalming, Surrey, GU8 6NS, England. *Telephone:* (20) 8785-3737; (1428) 607031. *Fax:* (20) 8788-2340 (Office); (1428) 607989. *E-mail:* chrismorahan@solutions-inc.co.uk (Home).

MORAIS, José Pedro de; Angolan politician and economist; b. 20 Dec. 1955; ed in France; fmr Sec. of State for Construction Materials; Minister of Planning and Econ. Co-ordination 1992; Angola's nominee to Bd of IMF 1990s; Minister of Finance Dec. 2002–. *Address:* Ministry of Finance, Avda 4 de

Fevereiro 127, CP 592, Luanda, Angola (Office). *Telephone:* (2) 338548 (Office). *Fax:* (2) 332069 (Office). *E-mail:* gm@minfin.gv.ao (Office). *Website:* www.minfin.gv.ao (Office).

MORALES, Armando; Nicaraguan artist; b. 15 Jan. 1927, Granada; ed Inst. Pedagógico de Varones, Managua, Escuela de Bellas Artes, Managua and Pratt Graphic Art Center, New York; first one-man Exhbn Lima 1959, subsequently at Toronto, New York, Washington, DC, Panama, Bogotá, Detroit, Caracas, Mexico City; Group exhbns. all over N and S. America and in Europe; numerous awards for painting in the Americas including Carnegie Int. 1964 and award at Arte de América y España Exhbn, Madrid.

MORALES ANAYA, Juan Antonio, PhD; Bolivian economist and social scientist; ed Catholic Univ. of Leuven, Belgium; Dir of Socio-Econs Research Inst. 1974–95; Catholic Univ. of Bolivia 1974–95; Dir Cen. Bank of Bolivia 1993–95, now Pres. *Address:* Banco Central de Bolivia, Avda Ayacucho esq. Mercado, Casilla Postal 3118, La Paz, Bolivia (Office). *Telephone:* 37-4151 (Office). *Fax:* 39-2398 (Office). *E-mail:* jam@mail.bcb.gov.bo, vmarquez@mail .bcb.gov.bo (Office). *Website:* www.bcb.gov.bo (Office).

MORALES BERMÚDEZ, Gen. Francisco; Peruvian politician and army officer; b. 4 Oct. 1921, Lima; grandson of the late Col Remiro Morales (President of Peru, 1890–94); m. Rosa Pedraglio de Morales Bermúdez; four s. one d.; ed Chorillos Mil. School; Founder mem. Dept of Research and Devt, Army Gen. Staff; taught at School of Eng and at Army Acad. of War; Chief of Staff of First Light Div., Tumbes; Asst Dir of Logistics, Dir of Econ., War Ministry; advanced courses at Superior Acad. of War, Argentina and Centre for Higher Mil. Studies, Peru; apptd. to reorganize electoral registration system 1962; Minister of Econ. and Finance 1968–74; Chief of Army Gen. Staff 1974–75: Prime Minister, Minister of War and Commdr-Gen. of Army Feb.–Aug. 1975; Pres. of Peru 1975–80.

MORAN, 2nd Baron, (cr. 1943), of Manton; **(Richard) John McMoran Wilson,** KCMG; British diplomatist (retd); b. 22 Sept. 1924, London; s. of the late Sir Charles McMoran Wilson, 1st Baron Moran and Dorothy Dufton; m. Shirley Rowntree Harris 1948; two s. one d.; ed Eton, King's Coll., Cambridge; served in World War II; HMS Belfast 1943, Sub-Lt RDVR in motor torpedo boats and HM Destroyer Oribi 1944–45; Foreign Office 1945; Third Sec., Ankara 1948, Tel Aviv 1950; Second Sec., Rio de Janeiro 1953; First Sec., Foreign Office 1956; Washington, DC 1959; Foreign Office 1961; Counsellor, S Africa 1965; Head of W African Dept of FCO 1968–73, concurrently Amb. to Chad 1970–73; Amb. to Hungary 1973–76, to Portugal 1976–81; High Commr in Canada 1981–84; sits as ind. peer, House of Lords; Chair. All Party Conservation Group of both Houses of Parl. 1992–2000, Wildlife and Country-side Link 1992–95, Regional Fisheries Advisory Cttee, Welsh Region, NRA 1989–94, Jt Fisheries Policy and Legislation Working Group (The Moran Cttee) 1997, Salmon and Trout Asscn 1997–2000 (Exec. Vice-Pres. 2000–); Pres. Welsh Salmon and Trout Angling Asscn 1988–95, 2001–, Radnorshire Wildlife Trust 1994–; Vice-Chair. Atlantic Salmon Trust 1983–95, Vice-Pres. 1995–; mem. Council RSPB 1989–94 (Vice-Pres. 1997–98), Agricultural Sub-Cttee 1991–95, 1997–2000; Grand Cross of the Order of the Infante (Portugal) 1978. *Publications:* C.B., a Life of Sir Henry Campbell-Bannerman 1973 (Whitbread Award for biography), Fairfax 1985. *Leisure interests:* fishing, fly-tying, bird watching. *Address:* c/o House of Lords, Westminster, London, SW1A 0PW, England.

MORÁN LÓPEZ, Fernando; Spanish politician; b. 1926, Avilés; m. Maria Luz Calvo-Sotelo; one s. two d.; ed Institut des Hautes Etudes Internationales, Paris, London School of Econs; began diplomatic career 1954; Asst Consul, Spanish Consulate-Gen., Buenos Aires 1956; Sec. Spanish Embassy, Pretoria; transferred to Ministry of Foreign Affairs 1963, specialized in African affairs, Asst Dir-Gen. for Africa, Near and Middle East, Political Dir Dept of Foreign Policy, later in charge of Africa, Near and Middle East 1971, Dir-Gen. of African Affairs 1975–77; First Sec. Spanish Embassy, Lisbon; Consul-Gen. Spanish Embassy, London 1974; Partido Socialista Popular cand. for elections to Congress of Deputies 1977; elected Partido Socialista Obrero Español Senator for Asturias, Socialist Spokesman for Foreign Affairs in Senate; Minister of Foreign Affairs 1982–85; Perm. Rep. to the UN 1985–87; MEP 1989–99; Légion d'honneur, Grand Cross of Carlos III, Grand Cross Order of Isabel la Católica 1985, Grand Cross of Christ (Portugal). *Publications:* También se muere el Mar 1958, Una política exterior para España, El dia en que 1997. *Address:* Alvarez de Baena 5, 28006 Madrid, Spain (Home). *Telephone:* (1) 5643719 (Home).

MORATTI, Letizia; Italian media executive and politician; fmr Chair. RAI; Dir (non-exec.) BSkyB May–Sept. 1999; Chair. News Corpn Europe 1998–99; Minister of Educ., Univs and Scientific Research 2001–. *Address:* Ministry of Education, Universities and Scientific Research, Viale Trastevere 76A, 00153 Rome, Italy (Office). *Telephone:* (06) 58491 (Office). *Fax:* (06) 5803381 (Office). *Website:* www.istruzione.it (Office).

MORAUTA, Sir Mekere, Kt, BEcons; Papua New Guinea politician and banker; b. 12 June 1946; s. of Morauta Hasu and Morikoai Elavo; m. Roslyn Morauta; two s.; ed Univ. of Papua New Guinea, Flinders Univ. of S. Australia; research officer, Dept of Labour 1971; economist, Office of the Econ. Adviser 1972; fmr dir of numerous cos; Sec. for Finance, Govt of Papua New Guinea 1973–82; Man. Dir Papua New Guinea Banking Corpn 1983–92; Chair. Nat. Airline Comm. 1992–94; Gov. Bank of Papua New Guinea 1993–94; Exec. Chair. Morauta Investments Ltd 1994–97; MP for Moresby

NW 1997–; Minister for Planning and Implementation 1997, for Fisheries 1998–99; Prime Minister and Treas. of Papua New Guinea 1999–; mem. Bd Dirs Angco; Hon. DTech (Univ. of Tech., Lae) 1987. *Publications:* numerous econs-related papers. *Address:* Prime Minister's Office, P.O. Box 639, Naigani, NCD, Papua New Guinea (Office). *Telephone:* 3276544 (Office). *Fax:* 3277380 (Office). *E-mail:* primeminister@pm.gov.pg (Office). *Website:* www .pm.gov.pg/pmsoffice/PMsoffice.nsf (Office).

MORAVČÍK, Jozef, LLD, CSc; Slovak politician; b. 19 March 1945, Očová Zvolen Dist; m.; two d.; ed Charles Univ., Komenský Univ.; clerk with Chemapol (trade co.) Bratislava; lecturer Law Faculty, Komenský Univ., Bratislava 1972–85, Head of Dept of Business Law 1985–90; Dean, Law Faculty 1990–91; Deputy to Slovak Nat. Council 1991–92; mem. Movt for Democratic Slovakia (MDS) 1991–94; Minister of Foreign Affairs of Č.S.F.R. July–Dec. 1992; Chair. Council of Ministers of C.S.C.E. July–Dec. 1992; Minister of Foreign Affairs, Slovak Repub. 1993–94; Premier, Govt of Slovakia March–Dec. 1994; Chair. Democratic Union of Slovakia 1994–97; Chair. Policy Planning Council 1997–; Mayor of Bratislava 1998–2002. *Address:* Magistrát hlavného mesta SR Bratislavy, Primaciálne hám. 1, PO Box 192, 81422 Bratislava, Slovakia. *Telephone:* (7) 5443-5324 (Office). *Fax:* (7) 5443-5405 (Office). *E-mail:* primator@bratislava.sk (Office). *Website:* www .bratislava.sk (Office).

MORAVEC, Ivan; Czech pianist and academic; b. 9 Nov. 1930, Prague; m. 1st (deceased); m. 2nd; one s., one d.; ed Conservatoire, Prague 1946–51; teacher Acad. of Musical Arts, Prague 1969–, Prof. 2000–; soloist with Czech Philharmonic Orchestra; concert tours Europe, USA, Japan; festivals Salzburg, Edin., Aldeburgh, Prague Spring, Schleswig-Holstein, Tanglewood, etc.; Charles IV Prize 2000; Cannes Classical Award 1999, Gold CD Award, Supraphon 2000, Medal for Merit 2000, Int. Prize Charles Univ. 2000, Harmonie Prize 2001, Classical Award for Lifetime Achievement, Cannes. *Music:* Recordings for Nonesuch, Supraphon, Dorian, Vox, Connoisseur Soc., Hänssler (numerous record of the year listings). *Leisure interest:* culture. *Address:* Pod Vyhlídkou 520, 160 00 Prague 6, Czech Republic (Home). *Telephone:* (2) 2312-36-96 (Home). *Fax:* (2) 3334-3696 (Home).

MORCELI, Noureddine; Algerian athlete; b. 28 Feb. 1970, Tenes; coached by his brother Abderrahmane Morceli; world champion, 1,500m Tokyo 1991, Stuttgart 1993, Gothenburg 1995; fmr world record-holder at 1,500m, one mile, 2,000m, 3,000m; gold medal Atlanta 1996; announced intention to compete in 2003 over 5,000m and 10,000m; IAF Athlete of the Year 1994. *Address:* c/o Ministry of Youth and Sports, 3 rue Mohamed Belouizdad, Algiers, Algeria.

MORDACQ, Patrick; French government official; b. 20 May 1934, Bordeaux; m. Marie Thérèse de Yturbe 1967; one s. one d.; ed Ecole Nat. d'Admin; Commissariat Gen. du Plan d'Equipement et de la Productivité 1963–67; Office of Minister of Equipment and Housing 1968; Head, Office of Foreign Investment, Treasury 1969; Deputy Chair. Comm. of Industry for VIth Plan 1970; Head, Office of Loans, Aid and Guarantees to Business, Treasury 1971–74; Finance Dir Groupe Jacques Borel Int. 1974–77; Head, Finance Service, Commissariat Gen. du Plan d'Equipement et de la Productivité 1977; Financial Counsellor, French Embassy, Bonn 1979; Head, Regulation of Finance, Treasury 1984–86; Govt Commr Centre Nat. des Caisses d'Epargne et de Prévoyance 1984–86; CEO Comm. des Opérations de Bourse 1986–91; Dir for France EBRD (London) and Financial Counsellor, French Embassies, Poland, Romania and Bulgaria 1991–96; Conseiller-Maître, Cour des Comptes 1996–2002; Chair. Bd of Auditors OECD 2002–; Chevalier Legion d'honneur, Commdr Ordre du Mérite de l'Allemagne. *Address:* OECD, 2 rue André Pascal, 75775 Paris Cédex 16, France (Office). *Telephone:* 1-45-24-82-48 (Office). *E-mail:* patrick.mordacq@oecd.org (Office).

MORDECHAI, Yitzhak, MA; Israeli politician and fmr army officer; b. 1944, Iraq; m. (divorced); two c.; ed Staff and Command Colls., Tel Aviv and Haifa Univs; emigrated to Israel aged five; served in Israeli Defence Forces (IDF) 1962–95, Commdr of a paratroop unit in the Sinai, 1967 Six Day War, paratroop Bn on Suez Canal front, 1973 Yom Kippur War, Chief Infantry and Paratroopers Officer 1983–86, apptd. Head of IDF HQ Training Dept, rank of Maj.-Gen. 1986, Officer in Command of IDF Southern Command 1986, of Cen. Command 1989, of Northern Command 1991; joined Likud party 1995; mem. Knesset (Parl.) 1996–2001, Minister of Defence 1996–99, of Transport and Energy 1999–2001, also fmr Deputy Prime Minister; convicted on three counts of indecent acts towards subordinates, received suspended sentence 2001; mem. Likud-Tzomet-Gesher group. *Address:* c/o Likud, 38 Rehov King George, Tel-Aviv 61231, Israel (Office).

MORDKOVITCH, Lydia, PhD, FRNCM; Israeli (b.Russian) violinist; b. 30 April 1944, Saratov, USSR (now Russia); d. of Mendel Shtimerman and Golda Shtimerman; m. 1st Leonid Mordkovitch 1962 (divorced); one d.; m. 2nd Malkia Chayoth 1977 (divorced 1983); ed School for Talented Children, Kishinev, Stoliarski School, Odessa, Nejdanova Conservatoire, Odessa, Tchaikovsky Conservatoire, Moscow and studied with David Oistrakh; went to Israel 1974; has lived in UK since 1980; Sr Lecturer, Kishinev Inst. of Art 1970–73; Sr Lecturer, Rubin Acad. of Music, Jerusalem 1974–80; Prof. of Violin, Royal Northern Coll. of Music, Manchester, England 1980–, RAM, London 1995–; soloist in recitals, concerts, on radio and TV, USSR, then Europe, USA, S and Cen. America 1974–; Hon. ARAM; Prizewinner Young Musicians Competition, Kiev 1967, Long-Thibaud Competition, Paris 1969, Gramophone Award (for Shostakovich concertos) 1990, three Diapason d'Or

Awards, Woman of the Year Award, American Biog. Inst. 1996, 1997, 1998, 1999, 2000, Outstanding Woman of the 20th Century, Outstanding Woman of the 21st Century, American Biog. Inst. *Leisure interests:* theatre, literature, art. *Address:* Royal Academy of Music, Marylebone Road, London, NW1 (Office); 11 Deansway, London, N2 0NJ, England. *Telephone:* (20) 7873-7373 (Office); (20) 8815-1292 (Home). *Fax:* (20) 8815-1292 (Home).

MORDYUKOVA, Nonna (Noyabrina) Viktorovna; Russian actress; b. 27 Nov. 1925, Otradnaya, Kuban Territory; ed All-Union Inst. of Cinematography; debut in 1948 film Young Guard; over 60 films; USSR People's Actress 1974; USSR State Prize 1949; prize winner int. and all-union festivals. *Film appearances (leading parts) include:* Somebody Else's Kinsfolk, Ekaterina Voronina, Paternal House, Simple Story, Chairman, Commissar, Small Crane, Russian Field, Quagmire, Relatives, Diamond Hand, Railway Station for Two. *Publications:* That's Our Life (novel), short stories. *Address:* Rublevskoye Shosse 34, korp. 2, Apt. 549, 121609 Moscow, Russia.

MOREAU, Jeanne, FBA; French actress; b. 23 Jan. 1928, Paris; d. of Anatole-Désiré Moreau and Katherine Buckley; m. 1st Jean-Louis Richard 1949 (divorced); one s.; m. 2nd William Friedkin 1977 (divorced); ed Collège Edgar-Quinet, Conservatoire national d'art dramatique; stage actress with Comédie Française 1948–52; Théâtre Nat. Populaire 1953; Pres. Cannes Film Festival July 1995; Paris Int. Film Festival 1975; Pres. Acad. des Arts et Techniques du Cinéma 1986–88; Pres. Comm. des avances sur recettes 1993–94; mem. Académie des Beaux-Arts, Inst. de France (Acad. of Modern Art) 2000–, jury of December Prize 2001–; Fellow BAFTA; Officier, Légion d'honneur, Officier Ordre nat. du Mérite, Commdr des Arts et Lettres, Molière Award 1988; European Cinema Prize, Berlin 1997; Hon. Acad. 1998, Golden Bear, Int. Film Festival, Berlin 2000. *Films include:* Touchez pas au grisbi, Le salaire du péché, Ascenseur pour l'échafaud, Les amants, Moderato Cantabile, Les liaisons dangereuses, Dialogue des Carmélites, Jules et Jim, Eve, The Victors, La baie des anges, Peau de banane, Le train, Le journal d'une femme de chambre, Mata Hari—H21, The Yellow Rolls-Royce 1964, Viva Maria 1965, Mademoiselle 1965, Chimes at Midnight 1966, L'amour à travers les âges 1967, The Sailor from Gibraltar 1967, The Bride Wore Black 1967, The Great Catherine 1968, Le corps de Diane 1970, Une histoire immortelle, Monte Walsh, L'humeur vagabonde, Comptes rebours 1971, Chère Louise 1972, Jeanne, la Française 1972, Nathalie Granger 1972, Je t'aime 1973, Les valseuses 1973, La race des seigneurs 1973, Pleurs 1974, Le jardin qui bascule 1974, Souvenirs d'en France 1974, Lumière (also dir) 1976, The Last Tycoon 1976, Mr. Klein 1976, Le Petit Théâtre de Jean Renoir 1976, L'adolescente 1978, Madame Rosa 1978, L'intoxe 1980, Plein Sud 1981, Mille milliards de dollars 1982, Au-delà de cette limite votre billet n'est plus valable 1982, Querelles 1982, La truite 1982, Le paltoquet 1986, Sauve-toi Lola 1986, Alberto Express 1989, Nikita 1990, Anna Karamazoff 1989–90, La femme fardée 1990, The Suspended Step of the Stork 1991, Till the End of the World 1991, La Vieille qui marchait dans la Mer 1991, La Nuit de l'océan 1992, A Demain 1992, The Summer House 1994, Les Cent et Une Nuits 1995, The Proprietor 1996, Un amour de sorcière 1997, A tout jamais (une histoire de Cendrillon) 1999, Lisa 2001, Cet amour là 2001. *Plays include:* L'heure éblouissante, La machine infernale, Pygmalion, La chatte sur un toit brûlant, La bonne soupe, La chevauchée sur le lac de Constance, Lulu, L'intoxe, Night of the Iguana, Le Récit de la Servante Zerline 1986, La Célestine 1989, Un trait de l'espirit 2000. *Leisure interest:* reading. *Address:* Spica Productions, 4 Square du Roule, 75008 Paris, France.

MOREL, Claude Syvestre; Seychelles diplomatist; b. 25 Sept. 1956, Victoria, Mahé; m.; one s. one d.; ed Seychelles Coll., Univ. of Lille, France, Cairo Inst. of Diplomatic Studies, Inst. Int. d'Admin. Publique, Paris; Chief of Protocol, Ministry of Foreign Affairs 1983–87, Dir Bilateral/Multilateral Affairs 1987–88; Chargé d'affaires, Embassy, Paris 1988–90; Dir.-Gen. Ministry of Foreign Affairs 1990–96; Amb. to EU (also Accred to Benelux and Germany) 1997–98; Perm. Rep. to UN, Amb. to USA and Canada 1998–. *Leisure interests:* sports in general, travelling. *Address:* Permanent Mission of Seychelles to the United Nations, 800 Second Avenue, Room 400c, New York, NY 10017, USA (Office). *Telephone:* (212) 972-1785 (Office). *Fax:* (212) 972-1786 (Office). *E-mail:* seychelles@un.int (Office).

MOREL, Pierre Jean Louis Achille; French diplomatist; b. 27 June 1944, Romans (Drôme); s. of André Morel and Janine Vallernaud; m. Olga Bazanoff 1978; three c.; ed Lycée du Parc, Lyon, Paris, Ecole nat. d'admin; Europe Dept, Ministry of Foreign Affairs 1971–73, Analysis and Forecasting Centre 1973–76, First Sec. then Second Counsellor, Embassy, Moscow 1976–79, Ministerial Rep., Gen. Secr. Interministerial Cttee on European Econ. Co-operation 1979–81, Office of Pres. of Repub., Technical Adviser to Gen. Secr. 1981–85, Dir Political Affairs, Ministry of Foreign Affairs 1985–86, Amb. and France's Rep. Disarmament Conf. Geneva 1989, Head French Del. Preparatory Cttee Conf. on Security and Co-operation in Europe 1990, Diplomatic Adviser, Office of Pres. of Repub. 1991–92, Amb. to Georgia 1992–93, to Russia (also Accred to Moldova, Turkmenistan, Mongolia, Tadjikistan and Kyrgyzstan) 1992–96, to China 1996–2002; Amb. to Vatican City 2002–; Chevalier, Légion d'honneur, Officier Ordre nat. du Mérite. *Publications:* trans. Mantrana 1984, Sauts de Temps 1989, Serpentara 1998 by Ernst Jünger. *Address:* French Embassy to the Vatican City, Villa Bonaparte, Via Piave 23, 00186 Rome, Italy (Office). *Telephone:* (6) 42030900 (Office). *Fax:* (6) 42030968 (Office). *E-mail:* ambfrssg@tin.it (Office).

MORELLET, François Charles Alexis Albert; French painter and sculptor; b. 30 April 1926, Cholet, Maine-et-Loire; s. of Charles Morellet and Madeleine Guérineau; m. Danielle Marchand 1946; three s.; ed Lycée Charlemagne, Institut Nat. des Langues et Civilisations Orientales, Paris; Commercial Dir then Man. Dir Morellet-Guérineau 1948–76; artist 1942–; monumental works include mural at 22 Reade St, Lower Manhattan, New York 1988, neon piece, Grande halle de la Villette, Paris 1988, steel sculpture, La Défense, Paris 1991, neon piece, Debis Potsdamerplatz, Berlin 1998, transparent films on glass, Obayashi Corpn., Tokyo 1998, neon pieces, Bundestag, Berlin 2000, marble piece, Jardin des Tuileries, Paris 2000, Gold Leaves, French Embassy, Berlin 2003; Grand prix nat. de sculpture 1987. *Exhibitions:* Van Abbemuseum, Eindhoven 1971, Centre Nat. d'art contemporain, Paris 1971, Nat. Gallery, West Berlin 1977, Brooklyn Museum, New York 1985, Musée nat. d'art moderne, Paris 1986, Stedelijk Museum, Amsterdam 1986, Musée Rodin, Paris 1990, Städtische Galerie in Lenbachhaus, Munich 1995, Kunstmuseum, Bonn 1997, Jeu de Paume, Paris 2000, Haus Konstruktiv Konkrete Kunst, Zürich 2002, Musée des Beaux Arts, Nancy 2003, Musée Matisse, Cateau Cambrésis 2003. *Publication:* Mais comment taire mes commentaires 1999. *Leisure interests:* travel, underwater fishing. *Address:* 83 rue Porte Baron, 49300 Cholet; 8 rue Fallempin, 75015 Paris, France.

MORENA, Alma-Rosa, MA; Mexican diplomatist and financial officer; ed Instituto Tecnológico Autónomo de México, El Colegio de México, Univ. of New York, USA; held various positions Ministry of Finance and Public Credit, served as Pres. Nat. Service for Tax Admin (SAT), Gen. Co-ordinator for Income and Tax Policies, Head of Liaison Unit with Mexican Congress, Special Adviser to Sec. of Finance on Income Policies and Federalism, Dir-Gen. for Income Policies; fmr Deputy Dir for Planning, Promotion and Tech. Assistance Nat Bank of Public Works and Services (Banobras); fmr Exec. Dir Reconstruction and Syndicated Loans Multibanco Comermex; researcher Centre for Econ. Investigation and Educ. in Mexico 2000; Amb. to UK 2001–;. *Address:* Embassy of Mexico, 42 Hertford Street, London, W1J 7JR, England (Office). *Telephone:* (20) 7499-8586 (Office). *Fax:* (20) 7495-4035 (Office). *E-mail:* mexuk@easynet.co.uk (Office). *Website:* www.mexicanembassy.co.uk (Office).

MORENILLA, José María, DR.IUR; Spanish judge; b. 29 Aug. 1926, Granada; s. of Carlos Morenilla and Clotilde Morenilla; m. Joanne Allard 1962; one s. one d.; ed School of Law, Granada, Columbia Univ., Univ. of Granada; Judge of First Instance 1952; Legal Adviser (in int. law) Ministry of Justice 1978–87; Supreme Court Judge Criminal Section 1987–90, Admin. Section 1990–; Agent/Rep. of Spanish Govt before European Comm. of Human Rights 1988–90; apptd Judge European Court of Human Rights 1990; Cross of Honour of San Raimundo de Peñafort. *Publications:* Organization of the Courts and Judicial Reform in the United States 1968, Poder Judicial en los Estados Unidos 1979, La Igualdad (Jurídica) de la Mujer en España 1980, Medidas Alternativas de la Prisión 1983, Protección Internacional de los Derechos Humanos 1984, Convenio Europeo de Derechos Humanos—Ambito, Organos, Procedimientos 1985. *Leisure interests:* music (opera), reading. *Address:* Juan Ramón Jiménez 2, 9°C, 28036 Madrid, Spain. *Telephone:* (91) 4574591.

MORENO BARBERÁ, Adm.-Gen. Antonio; Spanish naval officer; b. 17 April 1940, Madrid; m. Pepa Deckler Andreu; four c.; ed Naval War Coll.; joined Spanish navy 1956, Lt Jr Grade 1961, then Lt, served on board destroyer Alava, submarines Almirante García de los Reyes (S-31), Delfín (S-61) and Marsopa (S-63) and on Submarine Flotilla Staff; Lt Commdr 1975, commanding submarine Tonina (S-62) and later Galerna (S-71); Commdr 1983, commanding frigate Asturias (F-74); promoted to rank of Capt. 1988, Commdr Submarine Flotilla 1989; Leading Lecturer on Logistics, Naval Warfare Coll., also Lecturer on Tactics, Submarine School; Chief Tactical Studies Dept at Naval Staff; Exec. Asst to Chief of Naval Staff; promoted to Rear-Adm. and apptd Commdr Fleet Amphibious Force (DELTA Group) 1992; promoted to Vice-Adm. and apptd Chief of Rota Naval Base 1994; apptd Chief of Jt Defence Staff 1995; promoted to Adm. and apptd Chief of Naval Staff 1997; Chief of Defence Staff 2000–; Commdr of US Legion of Merit; four Naval Merit Crosses, Sahara Medal (Combat Zone), Brazilian Naval Merit Medal, Grand Cross of St Hermenegildo, Naval Merit Grand Cross, Military Merit Grand Cross, Chilean Great Star Military Merit Cross, Brazilian Naval Merit Grand Cross. *Address:* Ministry of Defence, Paseo de la Castellana 109, 28071 Madrid, Spain (Office). *Telephone:* (91) 5555000 (Office). *Fax:* (91) 5563958 (Office). *E-mail:* infodefensa@mde.es (Office). *Website:* www.mde.es (Office).

MORENO-MEJÍA, Luis Alberto, BA, MBA; Colombian diplomatist; b. 3 May 1953, Philadelphia, USA; m. Gabriela Febres-Cordero 1970; one s. one d.; ed Florida Int. Univ., Thunderbird Univ., Phoenix, AZ and Harvard Univ.; Div. Man. Praco 1977–82; exec. producer of nationwide nightly news programme and other entertainment and children's programmes 1982–90; Neiman Fellow, Harvard Univ. 1990–91; Pres. Inst. de Foment Industrial 1991–92; telecommunications adviser and pvt. consultant, Luis Carlos Sarmiento Org., Bogotá 1994–97; Partner Westsphere Andean Advisers 1997–98; Minister of Econ. Devt 1992–94; Campaign Man. of Andrés Pastrana 1994; Amb. to USA 1998–. *Address:* Embassy of Colombia, 2118 Leroy Place, NW, Washington, DC 20008, USA (Office). *Telephone:* (202) 387-8338 (Office). *Fax:* (202) 797-3917 (Office). *E-mail:* emwas@colombiaemb.org (Office).

MORENO OCAMPO, Luis; Argentine lawyer; b. 1953, Buenos Aires; ed Univ. of Buenos Aires; Deputy Public Prosecutor in trials against mil. junta

1985–87; Dist Attorney Fed. Circuit, City of Buenos Aires 1987–92; in pvt. practice (specializing in corruption control programmes and ethical advice for large cos) 1992–; Prosecutor (first in position), Int. Criminal Court (ICC) 2003–; Sub-Dir Research Centre, Univ. of Buenos Aires Law School 1984, currently Adjunct Prof. of Penal Law; Visiting Prof. of Law, Harvard Univ., USA; co-f. Poder Ciudadano; mem. Advisory Cttee Transparency Int., Pres. for Latin-America and the Caribbean. *Publications include:* In Self Defense: How to Avoid Corruption 1993, When Power Lost the Trial: How to Explain the Dictatorship to our Children 1996. *Address:* International Criminal Court (ICC), Maanweg 174, 2516 AB, The Hague, The Netherlands (Office). *Telephone:* (70) 5158515 (Office). *Fax:* (70) 5158555 (Office). *Website:* www.icc-cpi .int.

MORGAN, Howard James, MA; British artist; b. 21 April 1949, N Wales; s. of Thomas James Morgan and Olive Victoria Morgan (née Oldnall); m. Susan Ann Sandilands 1977 (divorced 1998); two s. one d.; one s. one d. (with Sarah Milligan); ed Fairfax High School, Sutton Coldfield, Univ. of Newcastle-upon-Tyne; career artist; numerous Royal and pvt. comms.; perm. display of work at Nat. Portrait Gallery, London; mem. Royal Soc. of Portrait Painters 1986–. *Exhibitions include:* Anthony Mould 1983, Claridges 1984, Richmond Gallery 1986–91, Thomas Agnew 1989, 1996, 1998 and 2000, Cadogan Contemporary Watercolours 1988–92 and 1995, Leighton House 1993, Sara Stewart Watercolours 1998, Opera Pictures 2001. *Leisure interests:* riding, 1938 Citröen, books. *Address:* Studio 401½ Wandsworth Road, Battersea, London, SW8 2JP; 12 Rectory Grove, Clapham Old Town, London, SW4 0EA, England (Home). *Telephone:* (20) 7720-1181 (Studio). *E-mail:* howard@j-morgan.demon.co.uk (Office). *Website:* www.howard-morgan.co.uk (Office).

MORGAN, Rt. Hon. (Hywel) Rhodri, PC, MA; British politician; b. 29 Sept. 1939; s. of the late Thomas John Morgan and of Huana Morgan; m. Julie Edwards 1967; one s. two d.; ed St John's Coll. Oxford, Harvard Univ., USA; Research Officer, Cardiff City Council, Welsh Office and Dept of Environment 1965–71; Econ. Adviser, Dept of Trade and Industry 1972–74; Industrial Devt Officer, S Glamorgan Co. Council 1974–80; Head of Bureau for Press and Information, European Comm. Office for Wales 1980–87; Labour MP for Cardiff W, House of Commons 1987–2001; Opposition Spokesman on Energy 1988–92, Welsh Affairs 1992–97; Sec. for Econ. Devt, Nat. Ass. for Wales 1999–2000; First Minister, Nat. Ass. for Wales Feb. 2000–. *Publication:* Cardiff: Half and Half a Capital 1994. *Leisure interests:* long-distance running, wood carving, marine wildlife. *Address:* Welsh Ass. Govt, Cardiff Bay, Cardiff, CF99 1NA (Office); Lower House, Michaelston-le-Pit, Dinas Powys, South Glamorgan, CF64 4HE, Wales (Home). *Telephone:* (29) 2089-8765 (Office); (29) 2051-4262 (Home). *Fax:* (29) 2089-8198 (Office). *E-mail:* rhodri .morgan@wales.gsi.gov.uk (Office).

MORGAN, James N., PhD; American economist; b. 1 March 1918, Corydon, Ind.; s. of John Jacob Brooke and Rose Ann Davis Morgan; m. Gladys Lucille Hassler 1945; three s. one d.; ed Northwestern Univ. and Harvard; Asst Prof. of Econs Brown Univ. 1947–49; Carnegie Research Fellow Inst. for Social Research, Univ. of Mich. 1949–51, Fellow Center for Advanced Study in the Behavioral Sciences 1955–56, Program Dir Survey Research Center, Inst. for Social Research 1956–88, Prof. of Econs 1957–88, Prof. Emer. 1988–; Fellow Wissenschaftskolleg zu Berlin 1983–84; mem. NAS; Fellow American Statistical Asscn, mem. American Acad. of Arts and Sciences, Fellow American Gerontological Asscn; Distinguished Faculty Award 1997, Woytinsky Lecture 1999. *Publications:* Income and Welfare in the United States 1962, Economic Behavior of the Affluent 1965, Economic Survey Methods 1971, Five Thousand American Families (Ed.) 10 Vols 1972–84, Economics of Personal Choice 1980, Household Survey of Grenada 1985. *Leisure interests:* travel, photography. *Address:* Institute for Social Research, Thompson Street, Ann Arbor, MI 48104 (Office); 1217 Bydding Road, Ann Arbor, MI 48103, USA (Home). *Telephone:* (734) 764-8388 (Office); (734) 668-8304 (Home). *Fax:* (734) 647-4575 (Office). *E-mail:* jnmorgan@umich.edu (Office).

MORGAN, Keith John, BSc, MA, DPhil, FRSC, F.R.A.C.I., FAIM; British/Australian university vice-chancellor; b. 14 Dec. 1929; s. of C. F. J. Morgan and W Morgan; m. Hilary A. Chapman 1957 (divorced 1999); one d.; ed Manchester Grammar School and Brasenose Coll. Oxford; Sr Research Fellow, Ministry of Supply 1955–57; ICI Research Fellow 1957–58; lecturer, Univ. of Birmingham 1958–64; AEC Research Fellow, Purdue Univ. 1960–61; lecturer, Univ. of Lancaster 1964–65, Sr Lecturer 1965–68, Prof. 1968–86, Pro-Vice-Chancellor 1973–78, Sr Pro-Vice-Chancellor 1978–86; Vice-Chancellor, Univ. of Newcastle, NSW 1987–93; Visiting Prof. Kobe Univ., Japan 1993; Chair. Hunter Foundation for Cancer Research –1993; Deputy Chair. Hunter Tech. Devt Centre 1987–93, Hunter Econ. Devt Council 1989–93, Hunter Fed. Task Force 1991–93; Prof. Univ. of Electro-Communications, Tokyo 1993–95; Visiting Prof., Hiroshima Univ. 1995–99, Nagoya Univ. 2002; Hon. DSc (Newcastle) 1993. *Publications:* various scientific, managerial, economic and educational papers. *Leisure interests:* Mozart, mountains, cricket. *Address:* 9B Castle Hill, Lancaster, LA1 1YS, England. *E-mail:* keith .j.morgan@lineone.net.

MORGAN, Baron (Life Peer), cr. 2000, of Aberdyfi in the County of Gwynedd; **Kenneth Owen Morgan,** DPhil, DLitt, FBA, FRHistS; British historian; b. 16 May 1934, Wood Green; s. of David James Morgan and Margaret Morgan (née Owen); m. Jane Keeler 1973 (died 1992); one s. one d.; ed University Coll. School, London, Oriel Coll., Univ. of Oxford; Lecturer History Dept Univ. Coll., Swansea 1958–66, Sr Lecturer 1965–66; Fellow and Praelector Modern History and Politics The Queen's Coll., Univ. of Oxford 1966–89; Prin., Univ. Coll. of Wales, Aberystwyth 1989–95; Pro-Vice-Chancellor, Univ. of Wales 1989–93, Vice-Chancellor 1993–95, Prof. 1989–99, Emer. Prof. 1999–; Ed. Welsh History Review 1961–; Jt Ed. 20th Century British History 1994–99; mem. House of Lords Constitutional Cttee 2001–; Election Commentator BBC Wales 1964–79; Fellow American Council of Learned Socs. Columbia Univ. 1962–63, Visiting Prof. 1965; Visiting Prof. Univ. of Witwatersrand 1997–2000, Univ. of Bristol 2000; Hon. Fellow Univ. Coll., Swansea 1985, Hon. Prof. 1995–; Hon. Fellow The Queen's Coll., Oxford 1992, Univ. of Wales, Cardiff 1997, Trinity Coll., Carmarthen 1998; Supernumerary Fellow, Jesus Coll., Oxford 1991–92; Hon. DLitt (Wales), (Glamorgan) 1997. *Publications:* Wales in British Politics 1963, David Lloyd George 1963, Freedom or Sacrilege? 1966, Keir Hardie 1967, The Age of Lloyd George 1971, Lloyd George: Family Letters (ed.) 1973, Lloyd George 1974, Keir Hardie: Radical and Socialist 1975, Consensus and Disunity 1979, Portrait of a Progressive (with Jane Morgan) 1980, Rebirth of a Nation: Wales 1880–1980 1981, David Lloyd George 1981, Labour in Power 1945–51 1984, The Oxford Illustrated History of Britain (ed.) 1984, Labour People 1987, The Oxford History of Britain (ed.) 1988, The Red Dragon and The Red Flag 1989, Academic Leadership 1991, The People's Peace: British History 1945–90 1992, Modern Wales: Politics, Places and People 1995, Young Oxford History of Britain and Ireland (Gen. Ed.), 1996, Callaghan: A Life 1997, Crime, Protest and Police in Modern British Society (ed.) 1999, The Twentieth Century 2000, The Great Reform Act 2001. *Leisure interests:* music, sport, travel, architecture. *Address:* House of Lords, London, SW1A 0PW (Office); The Croft, 63 Millwood End, Long Hanborough, Witney, Oxon., OX29 8BP, England. *Telephone:* (20) 7219-8616 (Office); (1993) 881341 (Home). *Fax:* (1993) 881341 (Home). *E-mail:* k .morgan@online.rednet.co.uk (Home).

MORGAN, Michèle (pseudonym of Simone Roussel); French actress; b. 29 Feb. 1920; d. of Louis Roussel; m. 1st Bill Marshall; one s.; m. 2nd Henri Vidal (deceased); studied with R. Simon (Paris); actress 1936–; Cannes Festival Prize for Best Actress (in Symphonie pastorale) 1946; French "Victoire" for Best Actress 1946, 1948, 1950, 1952, 1955; Médaille de vermeil, Paris 1967; Grand Officier, Légion d'honneur, Officier, Ordre nat. du Mérite, Commdr des Arts et des Lettres. *Films include:* Quai des brumes, Symphonie pastorale, Fabiola, Les sept péchés capitaux, Les orgueilleux, Obsession, Les grandes manoeuvres, Marguerite de la nuit, Marie Antoinette, Si Paris nous était conté, Le miroir à deux faces, Femmes d'un été, Pourquoi viens-tu si tard? Les scélérats, Fortunat, Le puits aux trois vérités, Les lions sont lâches, Rencontres, Le crime ne paie pas, Landru, Constance aux Enfers, Les yeux cernés, Dis-moi qui tuer, Les centurions, Benjamin, Le chat et la souris 1975, Ils vont tous bien 1989; has also appeared on TV and in theatre. *Publications:* Mes yeux ont vu 1965, Avec ces yeux-là 1977, Le fil bleu 1993. *Address:* Agents Associés, 201 rue du Faubourg Saint-Honoré, 75008 Paris, France.

MORGAN, Peter William Lloyd, MA; British business executive; b. 9 May 1936, Neath; s. of the late Matthew Morgan and of Margaret Gwynneth (née Lloyd) Morgan; m. Elisabeth Susanne Davis 1964; three d.; ed Llandovery Coll., Trinity Hall, Cambridge; served Royal Signals 1954–56; joined IBM UK Ltd 1959, Data Processing Sales Dir 1971–74, Group Dir of Data Processing Marketing, IBM Europe, Paris 1975–90, Dir IBM UK Ltd 1980–87, IBM UK Holdings Ltd 1987–89; Dir Gen. Inst. of Dirs. 1989–94; Dir South Wales Electricity PLC 1989–95, Chair. 1996; Dir Nat. Provident Inst. 1990–95, Chair. 1996–99; Dir Firth Holdings PLC (now Hyder Consulting PLC) 1994–, Zergo Holdings PLC (now Baltimore Technologies PLC) 1994–, (Chair. 2000–), Oxford Instruments PLC 1999–; Chair. Pace Micro Tech. PLC 1996–99, KSCL Ltd 1999–2000, Technetix PLC 2002–; Dir IDP SA (Paris) 2000–02; Dir Asscn of Lloyd's Mems. 1997–, Council mem. Lloyd's of London 2000–, Dir Lloyds.com 2001–; mem. Econ. and Social Cttee, EU 1994–2002, Advisory Cttee Business and the Environment 2001–; Master, Co. of Information Technologists; Radical of the Year, Radical Soc. 1990. *Leisure interests:* music, history, gardening, skiing, wine, dog walking. *Address:* Baltimore Technologies PLC, Innovation House, Mark Road, Hemel Hempstead, Hertfordshire HP2 7DN, England. *Telephone:* (118) 903-8905 (Office); (1428) 642757 (Home). *Fax:* (1653) 600066 (Office); (1428) 643684 (Home). *E-mail:* petermorgan@baltimore.com (Home). *Website:* www.baltimore.com (Office).

MORGAN, Piers Stefan; British journalist; b. 30 March 1965, Guildford; s. of Anthony Pughe-Morgan and Gabrielle Oliver; m. Marion E. Shalloe 1991; three s.; ed Cumnor House Preparatory School, Chailey School, Sussex, Lewes Priory Sixth Form Coll. and Harlow Journalism Coll.; reporter, Surrey and S London newspapers 1987–89; Showbusiness Ed. The Sun 1989–94; Ed. The News of the World 1994–95, Daily Mirror (now The Mirror) 1995–; Atex Award for Nat. Newspaper Ed. of Year 1994, Newspaper of the Year Award, What the Papers Say 2001, GQ Ed. of the Year 2002, Newspaper of the Year, British Press Awards 2002. *Publications:* Private Lives of the Stars 1990, Secret Lives of the Stars 1991, Phillip Schofield, To Dream a Dream 1992, Take That, Our Story 1993, Take That: On the Road 1994. *Leisure interests:* cricket, Arsenal Football Club. *Address:* The Mirror, 1 Canada Square, Canary Wharf, London, E14 5AP, England. *Telephone:* (20) 7293-3000. *Fax:* (20) 7293-3098. *E-mail:* c/o k.buckley@mirror.co.uk (Office).

MORGAN, William Newton, MArch, FAIA; American architect; b. 14 Dec. 1930, Jacksonville, Fla; s. of Thomas Morgan and Kathleen Fisk Morgan; m. Bernice Leimback 1954; two s.; ed Duncan U. Fletcher High School, Harvard Coll., Harvard Grad. School of Design and Università degli Studi per Stranieri, Perugia; US Navy 1952–55; Lehman Fellow, Harvard Univ. 1956–57; Fulbright Grantee, Italy 1958–59; Pres. William Morgan Architects, P.A. 1961–; maj. architectural designs: Fla State Museum Gainsville 1969–70, Jacksonville Police Admin. Bldg 1971–75, Pyramid Condominium, Ocean City, Md 1972–74, First Dist Court of Appeal, Tallahassee 1983–85, Westinghouse H.Q., Orlando 1984–86, US Embassy, Khartoum 1987–91, US Courthouses, Fort Lauderdale 1976–78, Tallahassee 1992–98, Neiman-Marcus, Fort Lauderdale 1980–82; Wheelwright Fellow, Harvard Grad. School of Design 1964–65, Visiting Critic 1981–82; Nat. Endowment of the Arts Fellow 1980; Adjunct Prof. of Art History, Jacksonville Univ. 1995–, Univ. of N. Fla 1997, Univ. of Fla 1998; Beineke-Reeves Distinguished Prof. of Architecture, Univ. of Fla 1998–2000; numerous awards and distinctions, including AIA Honor for Design Excellence 1974, AIA Honor for Research and Recording Ancient American Architecture 1998, Gibbons Eminent Scholar of Architecture and Urban Design, Univ. of S. Fla 1990. *Publications:* Prehistoric Architecture in the Eastern United States 1980, Prehistoric Architecture in Micronesia 1988, Ancient Architecture of the Southwest 1994, Pre-Columbian Architecture in Eastern North America 1999; The Architecture of William Morgan (by Paul Spreiregen) 1987, The Master Architect Series: Selected Works of William Morgan (by Robert McCarter) 2002; numerous articles. *Address:* William Morgan Architects, P.A., 220 East Forsyth Street, Jacksonville, FL 32202 (Office); 1945 Beach Avenue, Atlantic Beach, FL 32233, USA (Home). *Telephone:* (904) 356-4195 (Office). *Fax:* (904) 356-2808 (Office). *E-mail:* wnmorgan@aol.com (Office). *Website:* www .williammorganarchitects.com (Office).

MORGAN OF HUYTON, Baroness (Life Peer), cr. 2001, of Huyton in the County of Lancashire; **Sally Morgan,** MA; British politician; b. 28 June 1959, Liverpool; d. of Albert Edward Morgan and Margaret Morgan; m. John Lyons 1984; two s.; ed Belvedere Girls' School, Liverpool, Durham and London Univs.; secondary school teacher 1981–85; Labour Party Student Organizer 1985–87, Sr Targeting Officer 1987–93, Dir of Campaigns and Elections 1993–95, Head of Party Liaison for Leader of Opposition 1995–97; Political Sec. to Prime Minister 1997–2001; Minister of State for Women June–Nov. 2001; Dir of Govt Relations 2001–; mem. House of Lords 2001–. *Leisure interests:* relaxing with friends, cooking, gardening, walking. *Address:* House of Lords, London, SW1A 0PW, England (Office). *Telephone:* (20) 7930-4433 (Office). *Fax:* (20) 7930-9572 (Office).

MORGENTHAU, Robert Morris, LLB; American lawyer; b. 31 July 1919, New York; s. of Henry Morgenthau, Jr and Elinor (née Fatman) Morgenthau; m. 1st Martha Pattridge (deceased); one s. four d.; m. 2nd Lucinda Franks 1977; one s. one d.; ed Deerfield Acad., Amherst Coll., Yale Univ.; barrister, New York 1949; Assoc. of Patterson, Belknap & Webb, New York 1948–53, Partner 1954–61; U.S. Attorney S. Dist New York 1961–62, 1962–70; Dist Attorney New York County 1975–; mem. New York Exec. Cttee State of Israel Bonds; Democratic Candidate for Gov., New York 1962; mem. Bd of Dirs. P.R. Legal Defense and Educ. Fund; Trustee Baron de Hirsch Fund, Fed. of Jewish Philanthropies; Co. Chair. New York Holocaust Memorial Comm.; Pres. Police Athletic League 1962; mem. Bar Asscn City of New York; Dr. hc (New York Law School) 1968, (Syracuse Law School) 1976, (Union Univ., Albany Law School) 1982, (Colgate Univ.) 1988, Frank Hogan Award, NY State Dist Attorney's Asscn 2000, Lone Sailor Award, USN Memorial Foundation 2000, Award for Excellence in Public Service, NY State Bar Asscn 2001. *Address:* Office of District Attorney, 1 Hogan Place, New York, NY 10013, USA.

MORI, Hanae; Japanese fashion designer; b. 1926, Shimane; m.; two s.; graduate in Japanese literature; began career as costume designer for films in 1950s and has designed for over 500 films; opened first shop in Shinjuku, Tokyo 1951; now has 67 Hanae Mori shops in Japan, a store in New York, three shops in Paris and one in Monaco; first overseas show New York 1965; couture business and ready-to-wear; mem. Chambre Syndicale de la Haute Couture, Paris (first Asian mem.) 1977–; retrospective exhbn at The Space, Hanae Mori Bldg Tokyo 1989; Co-Founder Asscn for 100 Japanese books; launched Hanae Mori perfume brand 1995; Order of Cultural Merit (Japan); Chevalier Légion d'honneur, Ordre des Arts et des Lettres; numerous awards and prizes. *Address:* Hanae Mori Haute Couture, 17–19 avenue Montaigne, 75008 Paris, France.

MORI, Hideo, BA; Japanese business executive; b. 1 April 1925, Osaka City; s. of Shigekazu Mori and Ikue Mori; m. Masako (née Okano) Mori; two s.; ed Kyoto Univ. 1947; joined Sumitomo Chemical Co. Ltd 1947, Dir 1977, Man. Dir 1980, Sr Man. Dir 1982, Pres. 1985–93, Chair. 1993–; Chair. Sumitomo Pharmaceuticals Co. Ltd, ICI-Pharma Ltd, Japan Upjohn Ltd, Nippon Wellcome KK; Dir and Counsellor Japan Petrochemical Ind. Asscn; Exec. Dir Japan Fed. of Employers' Asscns.; Dir Japan Tariff Asscn, Nihon Singapore Polyolefin Co. Ltd; Pres. Japan Chemical Industry Asscn 1990; mem. Bd of Exec. Dirs., Fed. of Econ. Orgs. (Keidanren); Blue Ribbon Medal 1987. *Leisure interest:* golf. *Address:* Sumitomo Chemical Co. Ltd, 2-27-1, Shinkawa 2-chome, Chuo-ku, Tokyo 104-8260, Japan. *Telephone:* (3) 5543-5102. *Fax:* (3) 5543-5901. *Website:* www.sumitomo-chem.co.jp (Office).

MORI, Kazuhisa, BSc; Japanese nuclear non-profit organization representative; b. 17 Jan. 1926, Hiroshima; s. of Tsunezo Mori and Kayo Mori; m. Reiko Iizuka 1953; two s.; ed Kyoto Univ.; mem. editorial staff, Chuokoron-sha Inc. 1948–55; Chief of Nuclear Energy Devt Electric Power Devt Co., Ltd 1956–65; Man. Programming Div. Tokyo Channel 12 TV, Ltd 1963–65; Japan Atomic Industrial Forum Inc. (JAIF) 1956–, Exec. Man. Dir 1978–, Vice-Chair. 1996–,

Exec. Vice-Chair. 1998–; Dir Nuclear Safety Research Asscn 1965–; Vice-Pres. Japan Atomic Energy Relations Org. 1976–; Councillor Univ. Alumni Asscn 1994–; Chevalier, Ordre Nat. du Mérite (France), Order of Civil Merit Seogryu Medal (Korea). *Publications:* Economics of Atomic Power 1956, Atomic Power 1960. *Leisure interests:* fishing, Go (traditional Japanese game). *Address:* Japan Atomic Industrial Forum Inc., 2–13 Shiba-Daimon 1-chome, Minato-ku, Tokyo 105-8605 (Office); 5-20, Sakuragaoka 1-chome, Kugenuma, Fujisawa City, Kanagawa, Japan. *Telephone:* (3) 5777-0761 (Office); (466) 26-6228 (Home).

MORI, Yoshiro; Japanese politician; b. 14 July 1937; m. Chieko Mori; one s. one d.; ed Waseda Univ.; with Sankei Newspapers, Tokyo 1960–62; mem. House of Reps, for Ishikawa Pref. Dist 1 1969–96, Dist 2 1996–; Deputy Dir-Gen. Prime Minister's Office 1975–76; Deputy Chief Cabinet Sec. 1977–78; Dir Educ. Div., Policy Research Council, Liberal Democratic Party (LDP) 1978–81, Deputy Sec.-Gen. LDP 1978–79, 1984–85, Chair. Special Cttee on Educational Reform, Policy Research Council 1984–87, Acting Chair. Policy Research Council 1986, Acting Chair. Gen. Council 1986–87, Chair. Nat. Org. Cttee 1987–88, Chair. Research Comm. on Educational System, Policy Research Council 1989–91, Chair. Policy Research Council 1991–92, Sec.-Gen. LDP 1993–95, Chair. Gen. Council 1996–98, Sec.-Gen. LDP 1998–2001; Chair. Standing Cttee on Finance, House of Reps. 1981–82, on Rules and Admin. 1991; Minister of Educ. 1983–84, of Int. Trade and Ind. 1992–93, of Construction 1995–96; Prime Minister of Japan 2000–01. *Address:* c/o Liberal Democratic Party, 1-11-23 Nagata-cho, Chiyoda-ku, Tokyo, 100-8910, Japan.

MORIKAWA, Kosuke, PhD; Japanese scientist; b. 28 Sept. 1942, Tokyo; m. Keiko Tanaka 1966; ed Koyamadai High School, Tokyo Univ.; instructor Tokyo Univ. 1971–75, research assoc. Aarhus Univ., Denmark 1975–77, MRC Lab. of Molecular Biology, Cambridge, UK 1978–80; instructor Kyoto Univ. 1980–86, Dir First Dept Protein Eng Research Inst. 1986–, Research Dir Biomolecular Eng Research Inst. (BERI) 1996–. *Leisure interest:* listening to classical music, particularly by Bach and Mozart. *Address:* Department of Structural Biology, Biomolecular Engineering Research Institute, 6-2-3 Furuedai, Suita, Osaka 565-0874 (Office); 1-22-16 Hiyoshidai, Takatsuki, Osaka 569-1022, Japan. *Telephone:* (726) 89- 0519 (Home); (6) 6872-8211 (Office). *Fax:* (6) 6872-8219. *E-mail:* morikawa@beri.or.jp (Office). *Website:* www.beri .jp (Office).

MORIKAWA, Toshio, LLB; Japanese banker; b. 3 March 1933, Tokyo; m. Sawako Morikawa; two d.; ed Univ. of Tokyo; joined Sumitomo Bank Ltd, 1955, Dir 1980, Man. Dir 1984, Sr Man. Dir 1985, Deputy Pres. 1990, Pres. 1993–97, Chair. 1997–; Chair. Fed. of Bankers' Asscns. 1994–95. *Leisure interests:* golf, driving. *Address:* Sumitomo Bank Ltd, 4-6-5 Kitahama, Chuo-ku, Osaka 541-0041, Japan. *Telephone:* (6) 6227-2111. *Website:* www .sumitomobank.co.jp (Office).

MORILLON, Gen. Philippe; French army officer; b. 24 Oct. 1935, Casablanca; m. Anne Appert 1958 (deceased); three d.; ed Saint Cyr Mil. Acad.; platoon leader, French Foreign Legion during Algerian war of independence; fmr Div. Commdr of French units stationed in Germany; Deputy Under-Sec. for Int. Relations, Ministry of Defence in late 1980s; Commdr UN Forces in Bosnia-Herzegovina 1992–93; Adviser on Defence to Govt of France 1993; Commdr Force d'Action Rapide 1994–96; M.E.P. 1999–; numerous decorations. *Publications:* Croire et Oser 1993, Paroles de Soldat 1996, Mon Credo 1999. *Leisure interest:* reading. *Address:* European Parliament, 97–113 rue Wiertz, 1047 Brussels, Belgium (Office); Ministère de la Défense, 14 rue Saint-Dominique, 75700 Paris, France.

MORIN, Edgar, LenD; French scientific researcher; b. 8 July 1921, Paris; s. of Vidal Nahoum and Luna Beressi; m. Edwige Lannegrace; two d.; resistance fighter 1942–44; Head Propaganda Dept, French military government, Germany 1945; Ed.-in-Chief Paris newspaper 1947–50; researcher, CNRS 1950–, Dir of Research 1970–93, Dir Emer. 1993; Dir Review Arguments 1957–62, Communications 1972–; Dir Centre d'études transdisciplinaires (sociologie, anthropologie, politique) (Cetsap), of Ecole des hautes études en sciences sociales 1977–93; Prix européen de l'Essai Charles Veillon 1987, Prix média de l'Asscn des Journalistes Européens 1992, Prix Internacional Catalunya 1994; Commdr Légion d'honneur, Commdr des Arts et des Lettres; Dr hc (Brussels, Perugia, Palermo, Geneva, Natal, João Pessoa, Odense, Porto-Alegre, Milan, Guadalajara). *Publications include:* L'Homme et la mort 1951, Le Cinéma ou l'homme imaginaire 1956, Autocritique 1959, Le Vif du sujet 1969, Le Paradigme perdu: la nature humaine 1973, La méthode (5 Vols) 1977–2001, De la nature de l'URSS 1983, Penser l'Europe 1987, Vidal et les siens 1989, Terre-Patrie 1993, Mes démons 1994, Amour, poésie, sagesse 1998; numerous other publs. *Leisure interests:* music, theatre, movies, literature. *Address:* 7 rue Saint-Claude, 75003 Paris, France. *Telephone:* 1-42-78-90-99. *Fax:* 1-48-04-86-35.

MORIN, Jean, LenD; French civil servant; b. 23 June 1916, Melun; s. of Alexis Morin and Berthe France; m. Janine Lamouroux 1942; one s. two d.; ed Ecole Libre des Sciences Politiques, Institut de Statistique, Paris; Sec.-Gen. Inst. Scientifique des Recherches Economiques et Sociales 1939; Auditeur, Cour des Comptes 1941; Dir of Personnel, Ministry of the Interior 1944; Prefect, Manche 1946; Deputy Dir du Cabinet to Pres. of Provisional Govt 1946, to Minister of Foreign Affairs 1947–48; Tech. Adviser, Minister of the Interior 1948–49; Prefect, Maine-et-Loire 1949; Conseiller Référendaire, Cour des Comptes 1949; Prefect, Haute-Garonne and Extraordinary Insp.-Gen. of Admin. (5th Region) 1958–60; Del.-Gen. in Algeria 1960–62; Sec.-Gen. of

Merchant Navy 1962–68; Pres. Ass., Inter-Governmental Maritime Consultative Org. 1962–68; Pres. Société auxiliaire minière du Pacifique (Saumipac) 1968–72, Cie française industrielle et minière du Pacifique 1969–72; Dir Publicis SA 1970, Vice-Pres. 1972, Dir Publicis Conseil, Pres. 1972–73, mem. Conseil de Surveillance de Publicis SA 1987–90; Pres. Communication et Publicité 1972, Intermarco 1974–84, Comité de surveillance Intermarco (Amsterdam); Chair. and Man. Dir Régie-Presse 1974–83; Vice-Pres. Comité de surveillance Holding Farner (Zürich); Pres. Inst. de la Mer 1974–97, now Hon. Pres., Acad. de Marine 1990–92; Hon.Préfet, Conseiller Maître Cour des Comptes; Grand Officier, Légion d'honneur, Croix de guerre, Médaille de la Résistance avec rosette and other French and Foreign decorations. *Publication:* De Gaulle et l'Algérie 1999. *Leisure interests:* history, bridge. *Address:* 19 avenue du Maréchal-Franchet-d'Esperey, 75016 Paris, France. *Telephone:* 1-46-47-59-10.

MORIN, Roland Louis, LenD; French public servant; b. 6 Sept. 1932, Taza, Morocco; s. Fernand Morin and Emilienne (Carisio) Morin; m. Catherine Roussy 1961; one s. one d.; ed Lycée Gouraud, Rabat, Faculty of Law and Humanities, Bordeaux and Ecole Nat. d'Administration; Auditor, Audit Office 1960; Asst to Prime Minister and Chargé de Mission, Algeria 1960–61; Pvt. Recorder Comm. for Verification of Public Accounts, Asst to Recorder-Gen. 1964; Tech. Counsellor Louis Joxe Cabinet (Minister of State for Admin. Reform) 1966–67, Edmond Michelet Cabinet (Minister of State for Public Office) 1967-68; Referendary Counsellor Audit Office 1967; Asst to Prime Minister, Departmental Head for Econ. and Financial Programmes and Affairs 1968; Dir of Financial Affairs, Gen. Del. for Scientific and Tech. Research 1969, Asst to Del.-Gen. 1974, Asst Del.-Gen. 1974, Dir 1978; rejoined Audit Office 1980; Prof. Inst. d'Etudes Politiques de Paris 1965–90; Chargé de Mission with Jean-Pierre Chevènement (Minister of State, Minister for Research and Tech.) 1981–82, Dir Gen. Research and Tech., Ministry of Research and Industry 1982–86; Conseiller maître, Cour des comptes 1986, Pres. 1993–2000; mem. Comité nat. d'évaluation de la recherche (CNER) 1989–94, Commission nationale des comptes de campagne et des financements politiques (CCFP) 1997–2000 (Vice-Pres. 2000–); Officier, Légion d'honneur, Ordre Nat. de Mérite, Chevalier, Palmes Académiques, Mérite Agricole. *Publications:* Les sociétés locales d'économie mixte et leur contrôle 1964, Théorie des grands problèmes économiques contemporains. *Leisure interest:* tennis. *Address:* 24 Résidence des Gros-Chênes, 91370 Verrières-le-Buisson, France (Home); Villa Ej-Jemaïa, 903 rocade des Playes, 83140 Six-Fours-les-Plages.

MORISHIMA, Michio, MA, FBA; Japanese professor of economics; b. 18 July 1923, Osaka; s. of Kameji Morishima and Tatsuo Morishima; m. Yoko Tsuda 1954; two s. one d.; ed Univ. of Kyoto; Asst Prof. Univ. of Kyoto 1950–51; Asst Prof. and Prof. Univ of Osaka 1951–69; Rockefeller Foundation Fellow, Oxford and Yale Univs. 1956–58; Visiting Sr Fellow, All Souls Coll., Oxford 1963–64; Prof. Univ. of Essex 1968–70; Sir John Hicks Prof. of Econs LSE 1984–88 (Prof. of Econs 1970–84), Prof. Emer. 1988–; mem. Econometric Soc., Pres. 1965; Hon. mem. American Econ. Asscn 1976; Foreign Hon. mem. American Soc. of Arts and Sciences; Bunka Kunsho 1976. *Publications:* Equilibrium, Stability and Growth 1964, Theory of Economic Growth 1969, The Working of Econometric Models 1972, The Theory of Demand: Real and Monetary 1973, Marx's Economics 1973, The Economic Theory of Modern Society 1975, Walras's Economics 1977, Value, Exploitation and Growth 1978, Why Has Japan "Succeeded"? 1982, The Economics of Industrial Society 1984, Ricardo's Economics 1989, Capital and Credit 1992, Dynamic Economic Theory 1996, Japan at Deadlock 2000, Collaborative Development in Northwest Asia 2000. *Address:* STICERD, London School of Economics and Political Science, Houghton Street, London, WC2A 2AE (Office); Ker, 31 Greenway, Hutton Mount, Brentwood, Essex, CM13 2NP, England (Home). *Telephone:* (20) 7955-7032 (Office). *Fax:* (20) 7055-6951 (Office).

MORISSETTE, Alanis; Canadian rock singer and songwriter; b. 1 June 1974, Ottawa; acted in TV serial You Can't Do That on Television aged 10; signed contract as songwriter with MCA Publishing aged 14, recorded two albums for MCA's recording div.; moved to Toronto, later to LA, USA; numerous awards including Brit Award for Best Int. Newcomer, four Grammy Awards including Album of the Year and Best Rock Album, Best Female Award, MTV European Music Awards 1996. *Albums include:* Jagged Little Pill 1995 (co-written with Glen Ballard; 16 million (copies sold worldwide), Supposed Former Infatuation Junkie 1998, Under Rug Swept 2002. *Film:* Dogma 1999. *Address:* Maverick Recording Company, 9348 Civic Center Drive, Suite 100, Beverly Hills, CA 90210, USA (Office).

MORITS, Yunna Petrovna; Russian poet; b. 2 June 1937, Kiev; m. Yuri Grigor'yevich Vasil'yev; one s.; ed Gorky Literary Inst.; began publishing poetry 1954; has participated in int. poetry festivals London, Cambridge, Toronto etc.; has made recordings of recitations of her poetry; mem. Russian PEN, Int. Fed. of Journalists, Russian Acad. of Natural Sciences; Golden Rose (Italy) 1996, Triumph Prize (Russia) 2000. *Publications:* eleven collections of poetry (trans. in many languages), including The Vine 1970, With Unbleached Thread 1974, By Light of Life 1977, The Third Eye 1980, Selected Poems 1982, The Blue Flame 1985, On This High Shore 1987, In the Den of Vice 1990, A Bunch of Cats 1997, The Face 2000, In This Way 2000 and 6 books for children, including The Great Secret for a Small Company 1987; poems appeared in journal Oktyabr 1993–97; also short stories, essays, scripts for animated cartoons. *Leisure interests:* painting and drawing. *Address:* Astrakhansky per. 5, Apt 76, 129010 Moscow, Russia. *Telephone:* (095) 280-08-16. *E-mail:* yunna_morits@mtu-net.ru.

MORIYAMA, Raymond, OC, M.ARCH, FRAIC, M.C.I.P., RCA, FRSA; Canadian architect and planner; b. 11 Oct. 1929, Vancouver; s. of John Michi and Nobuko Moriyama; m. Sachiko Miyauchi 1954; three s. two d.; ed Univ. of Toronto, McGill Univ.; Raymond Moriyama Architects and Planners 1958–70; partner, Moriyama and Teshima Architects 1970–, Prin. 1980–; winner int. competition for Nat. Saudi Arabian Museum, Riyadh 1996; Design Tutor, Univ. of Toronto 1961–63; Chair. Ecological Research Ltd 1970; Chair. Mid-Canada Conf., Task Force on Environmental and Ecological Factors 1969–70; mem. Bd and Life mem. Royal Canadian Inst.; Dir Canadian Guild of Crafts 1973–75; mem. of Council, Ont. Coll. of Arts 1972–73; mem. Advisory Cttee, MBA Programme in Arts Admin., York Univ. 1982; Founding mem. Asia Pacific Foundation of Canada 1982; mem. Bd, Multilingual TV; mem. Bd of Trustees, Royal Ont. Museum; mem. Council's Advisory Cttee, N York Gen. Hosp.; Fellow Toronto Soc. of Architects 1998; eight hon. doctorates including Univ. of Toronto, McGill Univ., York Univ.; Civic Awards of Merit (Toronto and Scarborough), Gov.-Gen.'s Medal for Architecture (four times), P.A. Award 1989, Toronto Arts Award 1990, Order of Ont. 1992, Gold Medal, Royal Architectural Inst. of Canada 1997, Best Architect in Toronto Award 1997, 1998 and many other awards. *Publications:* Great American Goose Egg Co. (Canada) Ltd, The Global Living System and Mid-Canada Task Force Committee on Ecological and Environmental Factors 1970, Can Your Life Become a Work of Art 1975, The Satisfactory City: The Survival of Urbanity 1975, Into God's Temple of Eternity, Drive a Nail of Gold, TANT—Time, Appropriateness, Nature and Transition 1982, Architect as Nature's Collaborator (lecture at McGill Univ.) 1996. *Leisure interests:* fishing, sailing. *Address:* 32 Davenport Road, Toronto, Ont. M5R 1H3, Canada. *Telephone:* (416) 925-4484. *Fax:* (416) 925-4736. *E-mail:* raymond@mtarch.com (Office). *Website:* www.mtrach.com (Office).

MORJANE, Kamel; Tunisian international organization official and diplomat; b. 1948, Hammam-Sousse; two c.; ed Univ. of Tunis, Ecole Nat. d'Admin Tunis, Univ. of Geneva; worked as journalist; Asst Prof. Univ. of Geneva; joined staff UNHCR 1977, Asst High Commr 2001–; apptd Perm. Rep. to UN, Geneva 1996, later UN Sec.-Gen.'s Special Rep. for Democratic Repub. of Congo 1999. *Address:* UNHCR, CP 2500, 1211 Geneva 2 dépôt, Switzerland (Office). *Telephone:* (22) 7398668. *Fax:* (22) 7397382. *E-mail:* morjane@unhcr.ch. *Website:* www.unhcr.ch.

MØRK, Truls; Norwegian cellist; b. 25 April 1961, Bergen; s. of John Mørk and Turid Otterbech; two s. one d.; studied under his father, with Frans Helmerson at Swedish Radio Music School, in Austria with Heinrich Schiff and in Moscow with Natalia Shakovskaya; debut, BBC Promenade Concerts 1989; has since appeared with leading European, American and Australian orchestras, including the Berlin Philharmonic, Rotterdam Philharmonic, London Philharmonic, Pittsburgh Symphony Orchestra, City of Birmingham Symphony Orchestra, Orchestre de Paris, NHK Symphony Orchestra, Royal Concertgebouw Orchestra and Cleveland, Los Angeles and Gewandhaus Symphony Orchestras; regular appearances at int. chamber music festivals; Artistic Dir of own chamber music festival in Stavanger; prizewinner, Moscow Tchaikovsky Competititon 1982; First Prize, Cassado Cello Competition, Florence 1983, W Naumburg Competition, New York 1986; UNESCO Prize, European Radio-Union Competition, Bratislava 1983. *Recordings include:* Dvorak and Shostakovich cello concertos, Haydn concertos with Norwegian Chamber Orchestra, the Britten Cello Symphony and Elgar Cello Concerto with Sir Simon Rattle and the City of Birmingham Symphony Orchestra; Britten cello suites and recital discs of works by Grieg, Sibelius, Brahms, Rachmaninov and Myaskovksy. *Address:* c/o Harrison/Parrott, 12 Penzance Place, London, W11 4PA, England. *Telephone:* (20) 7229-9166. *Fax:* (20) 7221-5042.

MORLEY, Malcolm, ARCA; British artist; b. 1931, London; ed Royal Coll. of Art and Camberwell School of Arts and Crafts, London; one-man exhbns. in New York, Paris, Amsterdam, Cologne, Toronto, Zurich, London, etc.; numerous group exhbns. throughout USA and Europe; "Malcolm Morley", maj. retrospective Exhbn organized by Whitechapel Art Gallery, London, travelled to Kunsthalle, Basle, Museum Boymans-van Beuningen, Rotterdam, Whitechapel Art Gallery, London, Corcoran Gallery of Art, Washington DC, Museum of Contemporary Art, Chicago and Brooklyn Museum, New York 1983–84, Centre Pompidou, Paris 1993; many solo exhbns. in Europe, Canada, USA; 1st Annual Turner Prize, The Tate Gallery, London 1984, 1991, Skowhegan School of Painting and Sculpture Award 1992. *Address:* c/o Mary Boone Gallery, 745 Fifth Avenue, New York, NY 10151, USA.

MOROCCO, King of (see Mohammed VI).

MOROSS, Manfred David, BSc, MBA; business executive; b. 30 Aug. 1931; s. of Dr H. Moross and A. Moross; m. Edna Fay Jacobson 1956; three s. one d.; ed Witwatersrand and Harvard Univs; Dir Whitehall Financial Group, New York, Whitehall Investment Corpn, New York, Siem Industries Inc., Bermuda; Hon. PhD Weizmann Inst. of Science. *Leisure interests:* tennis, reading. *Address:* 7 Princes Gate, London, SW7, England (Home). *Telephone:* (20) 7589-9020 (Home). *Fax:* (20) 7938-1393.

MOROZ, Oleksandr Oleksandrovich; Ukrainian politician; b. 29 Feb. 1944, Buda, Kiev Region; m. Valentina Andriivna Moroz; two d.; ed Ukrainian Agric. Acad., Higher C.P. School; trained as engineer in Kiev; engineer and mechanic in state farm professional school, Dist and regional enterprises of Selkhoztechnika 1965–76; sec. regional trade union, First Sec. Dist CP Cttee; Head of Agric. Div. Regional CP Cttee; People's Deputy of Ukrainian SSR (later of Ukraine); one of founders and head Socialist Party of Ukraine 1994–; Chair. Verkhovna Rada (Parl.) 1994–98, mem. 1998–; Pres. Cand. 1994, 1998; leader of opposition to Pres. Kuchma. *Publications:* author and co-author of a number of legal projects including Code on Land: Where Are We Going?, Choice, Subjects for Meditation and articles. *Address:* Verkhovna Rada, M. Hrushevskoho 5, 252019 Kiev, Ukraine. *Telephone:* (44) 226-28-25, 293-23-15.

MOROZOV, Oleg Viktorovich, C.PHIL.SC.; Russian politician; b. 5 Nov. 1953, Kazan; m.; one d.; ed Kazan State Univ.; docent, Kazan State Univ.; Head of Div. Tatar Regional CP Cttee 1987–89; instructor, Asst to Sec., CPSU Cen. Cttee 1989–91; consultant, Office of USSR Pres. 1991–92; Deputy Dir-Gen., Biotekhnologiya; mem. State Duma 1993– (re-elected as mem. Otechestvo—Vsya Russia Movt 1999); mem. Deputies' group New Regional Politics 1994–96; Chair. Deputies' Group Russian Regions 1997–; joined Yedinstvo Party 2001. *Leisure interests:* collecting toy hippopotamuses, serious classical music. *Address:* State Duma, Okhotny ryad 1, 103265 Moscow, Russia. *Telephone:* (095) 292-83-52 (Office). *Fax:* (095) 292-91-69 (Office).

MOROZOV, Vladimir Mikhailovich; Russian opera singer (bass); b. 12 Feb. 1933, Leningrad; m.; one s.; ed Leningrad State Conservatory; soloist with Kirov (now Mariinsky) Opera 1959–; mem. CPSU 1965–91; Prof. Head of Faculty, A. Gersten Russian State Pedagogic Univ.; Glinka Prize 1974, USSR State Prize 1976; RSFSR People's Artist 1976; USSR People's Artist 1981. *Roles include:* Varlaam (Boris Godunov), Ivan the Terrible (The Women from Pskov), Grigory (Quiet Flows the Don), Peter the Great (Peter I), Dosifey (Khovanshchina). *Address:* c/o Mariinsky Theatre, Teatralnaya pl. 1, St Petersburg, Russia.

MORRICE, Norman Alexander; British choreographer; b. 10 Sept. 1931, Agua Dulce, Mexico; s. of Norman Morrice and Helen Vickers; ed Rambert School of Ballet; joined Ballet Rambert as dancer 1952, Prin. Dancer 1958, Asst Dir 1966–70, Dir 1970–74; freelance choreographer 1974–77; Dir Royal Ballet Co. 1977–86, Dir Royal Ballet Choreographic Group 1987–96, Head Choreographic Studies, Royal Ballet School 1987–; first success as choreographer with Two Brothers 1958; second ballet Hazaña (première, Sadler's Wells Theatre, London) 1958; ballet Hazard, Bath Festival 1967; 10 new ballets for Ballet Rambert by 1968; Elizabeth II Coronation Award for services to British ballet. *Ballets include:* 1-2-3, Them and Us, Pastorale Variée, Ladies, Ladies!, Spindrift. *Leisure interests:* literature, music, films. *Address:* c/o Royal Opera House, Covent Garden, London, W.C.2, England. *Telephone:* (20) 7240-1200.

MORRICONE, Ennio; Italian film score composer; b. 10 Nov. 1928, Rome; s. of Mario Morricone and Libera Morricone; m. Maria Travia; two s. two d.; ed Acad. of Santa Cecilia, Rome. *Film scores include:* The Federal, The Basilisks, A Fistful of Dollars (Silver Ribbon Award), For a Few Dollars More, The Good, Bad and the Ugly, Once Upon a Time in the West, Battle of Algiers, Partner, China is Near, Teorema, Decameron, Investigation of a Senior Citizen Above Suspicion, Orca, 1900, The Five Man Army, Fräulein Doktor, The Guns of San Sebastian, A Fine Pair, Pardon, Let's Make Love, Once Upon a Time in the Country, Escalation, Grazie Zia, The Harem, La Cage aux Folles I, II & III, The Mission, The Untouchables, Cinema Paradiso, Casualties of War, Frantic, Hamlet, Bugsy, City of Joy, The Bachelor, In the Line of Fire, A Pure Formality, Frantic, Wolf, Disclosure, Love Affair, Lolita, Phantom of the Opera, Bulworth, The Legend of 1900, Canone Inverso.

MORRILL, Rev. John Stephen, DPhil, FBA; British historian and academic; b. 12 June 1946, Manchester; s. of William Henry Morrill and Marjorie Morrill (née Ashton); m. Frances Mead 1968; four d.; ed Altrincham Grammar School, Trinity Coll. Oxford; Research Fellow, Trinity Coll. Oxford 1970–74; Lecturer in History, Univ. of Stirling 1974–75; Fellow Selwyn Coll. Cambridge 1975–, Sr Tutor 1989–92, Vice-Master 1994–; Lecturer in History, Cambridge Univ. 1975–92, Reader in Early Modern History 1992–98, Prof. of British and Irish History 1998–; mem. Council, Royal Historical Soc. 1988–92, Vice-Pres. 1992–96. *Publications:* Cheshire 1630–1660 1974, The Revolt of the Provinces 1976, Reactions to the English Civil War 1981, Oliver Cromwell and the English Revolution 1989, The Impact of the English Civil War 1991, Revolution and Restoration 1992, The Nature of the English Revolution 1992, The British Problem 1534–1707 1996, The Oxford Illustrated History of Tudor and Stuart Britain 1996, Revolt in the Provinces 1998, Soldiers and Statesmen of the English Revolution (jtly.) 1998; 40 articles in learned journals. *Leisure interests:* music, theology, beer, cricket. *Address:* Selwyn College, Cambridge, CB3 9DQ (Office); 1 Bradford's Close, Bottisham, Cambridge, CB5 9DW, England (Home). *Telephone:* (1223) 335895 (Office); (1223) 811822 (Home). *Fax:* (1223) 335837.

MORRIS, Christopher, FCA, F.S.P.I.; British chartered accountant (retd); b. 28 April 1942; s. of Richard Archibald Sutton Morris, M.C. and Josephine Fanny Mary (née Galliano) Morris; m. Isabel Ramsden (divorced); two s.; qualified 1967; partner Touche Ross & Co. (later Deloitte & Touche) 1972–2000; Sr Partner Corp. Recovery; cases have included liquidation of

Laker Airways 1982, British Island Airways, British Air Ferries, Rush & Tompkins, London & County Securities, Polly Peck Int., Banco Ambrosiano, Bank of Credit and Commerce International (BCCI). *Leisure interests:* racing, wine, the countryside. *Address:* Hill House, Little New Street, London, EC4A 3TR, England.

MORRIS, Sir Derek James, Kt, MA, DPhil; British economist; b. 23 Dec. 1945, Harrow; s. of Denis William Morris and Olive Margaret Morris; m. Susan Mary Whittles 1975; two s.; ed Harrow Co. Grammar School, St Edmund Hall and Nuffield Coll., Oxford; Research Fellow Univ. of Warwick 1969–70; Fellow and Tutor of Econs Oriel Coll., Oxford 1970–98; Econ. Dir Nat. Econ. Devt Office 1981–84; Chair. Oxford Econ. Forecasting Ltd 1984–98; mem. Monopolies and Mergers Comm. 1991–95, Deputy Chair. 1995–98, Chair. 1998–99, Chair. Competition (fmrly Monopolies and Mergers) Comm. 1999–. *Publications include:* The Economic System in the UK (Ed.) 1971, Industrial Economics and Organisation (with D. Hay) 1985, Chinese State-Owned Enterprises and Economic Reform 1994; numerous journal articles on Econs. *Leisure interests:* skiing, rugby. *Address:* Competition Commission, New Court, 48 Carey Street, London, WC2A 2JT, England. *Telephone:* (20) 7271-0114 (Office). *Fax:* (20) 7271-0203 (Office). *E-mail:* derek.morris@competition-commission.gsi.gov.uk (Office). *Website:* www.competition-commission.org.uk (Office).

MORRIS, Desmond John, DPhil; British zoologist; b. 24 Jan. 1928, Purton, Wilts.; s. of Capt. Harry Howe Morris and Marjorie (née Hunt) Morris; m. Ramona Joy Baulch 1952; one s.; ed Dauntsey's School, Wilts., Birmingham Univ. and Oxford Univ.; Head of Granada TV and Film Unit at Zoological Soc. of London 1956–59; Curator of Mammals at Zoological Soc. of London 1959–67; Dir Inst. of Contemporary Arts, London 1967–68; Research Fellow at Wolfson Coll., Oxford 1973–81; now privately engaged in writing books on animal and human behaviour; artist; Hon. DSc (Reading) 1998. *Television:* Zootime (Granada) 1956–67, Life in the Animal World (BBC) 1965–67, The Human Race (Thames TV) 1982, The Animals Roadshow (BBC) 1987–89, The Animal Contract 1989, Animal Country 1991–95, The Human Animal 1994, The Human Sexes 1997. *Solo exhibitions include:* Swindon Museum and Art Gallery 1976, Galerie D'Eendt Amsterdam 1978, Mayor Gallery London 1987, 1989, 1991, 1994, 1997, 1999, Keitelman Gallery Brussels, 1998, Jessy Van der Velde Gallery Antwerp 1998 and many others. *Publications:* The Ten-spined Stickleback 1958, The Biology of Art 1962, The Mammals: A Guide to the Living Species 1965, Men and Snakes (with Ramona Morris) 1965, Men and Apes (with Ramona Morris) 1966, Men and Pandas (with Ramona Morris) 1966, Primate Ethology (Editor) 1967, The Naked Ape 1967, The Human Zoo 1969, Patterns of Reproductive Behaviour 1970, Intimate Behaviour 1971, Manwatching: A Field-Guide to Human Behaviour 1977, Gestures, Their Origins and Distribution 1979, Animal Days (autobiog.) 1979, The Giant Panda 1981, The Soccer Tribe 1981, Inrock (fiction) 1983, The Book of Ages 1983, The Art of Ancient Cyprus 1985, Bodywatching 1985, The Illustrated Naked Ape 1986, Dogwatching 1986, Catwatching 1986, The Secret Surrealist 1987, Catlore 1987, The Animals Roadshow 1988, Horsewatching 1988, The Animal Contract 1990, Animal-Watching 1990, Babywatching 1991, Christmas Watching 1992, The World of Animals 1993, The Naked Ape Trilogy 1994, The Human Animal 1994, Body Talk: A World Guide to Gestures 1994, The Illustrated Catwatching 1994, Illustrated Babywatching 1995, Catworld: A Feline Encyclopedia 1996, Illustrated Dogwatching 1996, The Human Sexes 1997, Illustrated Horse-Watching 1998, Cool Cats 1999, Body Guards 1999, Cosmetic Behaviour and the Naked Ape 1999, The Naked Eye 2000, Dogs, a Dictionary of Dog Breeds 2001, People-Watching 2002. *Leisure interest:* archaeology. *Address:* c/o Jonathan Cape, 20 Vauxhall Bridge Road, London, SW1V 2SA, England. *Fax:* (1865) 512103. *E-mail:* dmorris@patrol.i-way.co.uk (Home). *Website:* www.desmond-morris.com/ (Home).

MORRIS, Dick, BA; American political strategist, consultant and journalist; b. 1952, New York; s. of Eugene Morris; m. Eileen McGann; ed Stuyvesant High School, New York, Columbia Univ.; freelance adviser to politicians, including Eugene McCarthy in presidential campaign 1968; organized a poll for Bill Clinton in governorship election, Arkansas 1978; worked for Clinton's election campaigns 1980–96; adviser to many Democratic cands.; currently political analyst, FOX News. *Publications:* Behind the Oval Office 1997, The New Prince: Machiavelli Updated for the Twenty-First Century 1999.

MORRIS, Doug; American record company executive, producer and songwriter; f. Big Tree label (sold to Atlantic Records); Head ATCO, Atlantic Records, Warner Music USA; Co-Chair. and CEO Warner Music Group –1995; co-cr. Interscope Records; Chair. and CEO Universal Music Group 1995–, f. Universal Records; Co-founder (with Jimmy Iovine, q.v. Jimmy and Doug's Farm Club (project comprising a record label, website and cable TV show) 1999–; jt owner Pressplay (subscription-based music download website); has worked with Tori Amos, Phil Collins, INXS, Led Zepplin, Bette Midler, Stevie Nicks, The Rolling Stones, Pete Townsend. *Compositions include:* Sweet Talkin' Guy, The Chiffons 1996. *Address:* Universal Music Group, Universal Studios, 100 Universal City Plaza, Universal City, CA 91608, USA (Office). *Website:* www.umusic.com (Office); www.farmclub.com (Office).

MORRIS, Estelle, BEd; British politician; b. 17 June 1952; d. of Charles Richard Morris and Pauline Morris; ed Whalley Range High School, Manchester, Coventry Coll. of Educ., Warwick Univ.; teacher 1974–92; Councillor, Warwick Dist Council 1979–91, Labour Group Leader 1981–89; MP for

Birmingham, Yardley 1992–; Opposition Whip 1994–95, Opposition Front-bench Spokeswoman on Educ. 1995–97; Parl. Under-Sec. of State, Dept for Educ. and Employment (DFEE) 1997–98, Minister of State 1998–2001, Sec. of State for Educ. and Skills 2001–02. *Address:* House of Commons, Westminster, London, SW1A 0AA, England (Office). *Telephone:* (20) 7219-3000 (Office).

MORRIS, James (Humphry) (see Morris, Jan).

MORRIS, James Peppler; American opera singer; b. 10 Jan. 1947; s. of James Morris and Geraldine Peppler; m. 1st Joanne F. Vitali 1971; one d.; m. 2nd Susan Quittmeyer 1987; one s. one d. (twins); ed Univ. of Maryland, Peabody Conservatory and Acad. of Vocal Arts; debut at Metropolitan Opera, New York 1970; opera and concert appearances throughout USA, Canada, S. America, Europe, Japan and Australia. *Recordings include:* Wotan in the New Ring Cycles, The Flying Dutchman, operas by Wagner, Offenbach, Mozart, Verdi, Donizetti, Bellini. *Title roles include:* The Flying Dutchman, Don Giovanni, Le Nozze di Figaro, Macbeth, Boris Godunov, Faust, Billy Budd, Otello. *Address:* c/o Colbert Artists Management Inc., 111 West 57th Street, New York, NY 10019, USA.

MORRIS, James T., BS, MBA; American international organization official and business executive; b. 18 April 1943, Terre Haute, Ind.; m. Jacqueline Harrell Morris; three c.; ed Indiana Univ., Butler Univ.; Chief of Staff to Mayor of Indianapolis 1967–73; Dir of Community Devt, Lilly Endowment 1973, Vice-Pres., Pres. 1984–89; Chair. and CEO IWC Resources Corpn, Indiana Water Co. 1989–; Exec. Dir World Food Programme (WFP) April 2002–; Chair. Bd of Trustees Indiana Univ.; Treas. US Olympic Cttee; mem. Bd of Govs American Red Cross. *Address:* World Food Programme, Via Cesare Giulio Viola 68, Parco dei Medici, 00148 Rome, Italy (Office). *Telephone:* (06) 65131 (Office). *Fax:* (06) 6590632 (Office). *E-mail:* wfpinfo@wfp.org (Office). *Website:* www.wfp.org (Office).

MORRIS, Jan, MA, FRSL, CBE; Welsh writer; b. 2 Oct. 1926; editorial staff The Times 1951–56, editorial staff The Guardian 1957–62; Commonwealth Fellowship, USA 1954; George Polk Memorial Award for Journalism (USA) 1961; mem. Yr Academi Gymreig; mem. Gorsedd of Bards, Welsh Nat. Eisteddfod; Hon. Fellow, Univ. Coll. Wales; Hon. FRIBA; Dr. hc (Univ. of Wales) 1993, (Univ. of Glamorgan) 1996; Heinemann Award for Literature 1961. *Publications:* (as James Morris) Coast to Coast 1956, Sultan in Oman 1957, The Market of Seleukia 1957, Coronation Everest 1958, South African Winter 1958, The Hashemite Kings 1959, Venice 1960, The Upstairs Donkey (for children) 1962, The Road to Huddersfield 1963, Cities 1963, The Presence of Spain 1964, Oxford 1965, Pax Britannica 1968, The Great Port 1970, Places 1972, Heaven's Command 1973, Farewell the Trumpets 1978; (as Jan Morris) Conundrum 1974, Travels 1976, The Oxford Book of Oxford 1978, Destinations, The Venetian Empire, My Favourite Stories of Wales, 1980, The Small Oxford Book of Wales, Wales The First Place, A Venetian Bestiary, Spectacle of Empire 1982, Stones of Empire 1983, Journeys 1984, The Matter of Wales 1984, Among the Cities 1985, Last Letters from Hav 1985, Stones of Empire: The Buildings of the Raj 1986, Scotland, The Place of Visions 1986, Manhattan, '45 1987, Hong Kong: Xianggang 1988, Pleasures of a Tangled Life 1989, Ireland Your Only Place 1990, O Canada 1992, Sydney 1992, Locations 1992, Travels with Virginia Woolf (ed.) 1993, A Machynlleth Triad 1994, Fisher's Face 1995, 50 Years of Europe 1997, Lincoln: A Foreigner's Quest 1999, Our First Leader 2000, A Writer's House in Wales 2001, Trieste and the Meaning of Nowhere 2001. *Address:* Trefan Morys, Llanystumdwy, Gwynedd, LL52 0LP, Wales. *Telephone:* (1766) 522222. *Fax:* (1766) 522426. *E-mail:* janmorris1@msn.com. (Home).

MORRIS, Mark William; American choreographer and dancer; b. 29 Aug. 1956, Seattle, Wash.; s. of William Morris and Maxine Crittenden Morris; Artistic Dir Mark Morris Dance Group 1980–; Dir of Dance, Théâtre Royal de la Monnaie, Brussels 1988–91; Co-Founder White Oak Dance Project (with Mikhail Baryshnikov) 1990; performed with various dance cos including Lar Lubovitch Dance Co., Hannah Kahn Dance Co., Laura Dean Dancers and Musicians, Eliot Feld Ballet, Dance Umbrella and Koleda Balkan Dance Ensemble; cr. over 70 works for Mark Morris Dance Group including Mythologies 1986, L'Allegro, il Penseroso ed il Moderato 1988, Dido and Aeneas 1989, Nutcracker 1991, Lucky Charms 1994, Rondo 1994, The Office 1994, Peccadillos 2001, Grand Duo 2001, I Don't Want to Love 2001, V 2001; has cr. dances for many other ballet cos including San Francisco Ballet, Paris Opera Ballet and American Theatre Ballet; Guggenheim Fellowship 1986; Fellow MacArthur Foundation 1991; New York Dance and Performance Award 1984, 1990. *Address:* Mark Morris Dance Group, 3 Lafayette Avenue, Brooklyn, NY 11217, USA. *Telephone:* (718) 624-8400 (Office). *Fax:* (718) 624-8900 (Office). *Website:* www.mmdg.org (Office).

MORRIS, Michael Jeremy, MA; British performing arts producer; b. 30 March 1958, London; s. of Lawrence Morris and Monica Morris; m. Sarah Culshaw 1991; one s. one d.; ed Oundle School, Keble Coll. Oxford and City Univ. London; Assoc. Dir of Theatre, ICA 1981–84, Dir of Performing Arts 1984–87; mem. Drama and Dance Panel, British Council 1984–90; Founding Dir Cultural Industry Ltd (presenting and producing contemporary theatre, music and dance) 1987–; Co.-Dir The Artangel Trust (commissioning outstanding artists to create new work) 1991–; Dir first production and co-author of libretto of Michael Nyman's opera The Man Who Mistook His Wife for a Hat 1986; Dir first production and author of libretto of Mike Westbrook's opera

Coming Through Slaughter 1994. *Leisure interests:* world music, fine wine, foreign food, popular art. *Address:* 36 St John's Lane, London, EC1M 4BJ, England. *Telephone:* (20) 7336-6781. *Fax:* (20) 7336-6782.

MORRIS, Sir Peter John, Kt, MB, BS, PhD, FRCS, FMedSci, FRS; Australian professor of surgery; b. 17 April 1934, Horsham, Vic.; s. of Stanley Henry Morris and Mary Lois (née Hennessy) Morris; m. Jocelyn Mary Gorman 1960; three s. two d.; ed Univ. of Melbourne; Resident Surgical Officer, St Vincent's Hosp. 1958–61; Surgical Registrar, Southampton Gen. Hosp., UK 1963–64; Clinical Assoc. and Fellow, Mass. Gen. Hosp., Boston, USA 1964–66; Asst Prof. of Surgery, Medical Coll., Richmond, Va, USA 1967; Dir Tissue Transplantation Labs., Univ. of Melbourne, Australia 1968–74; Reader in Surgery 1971–74; Consultant Surgeon, Lymphona Clinic, Cancer Inst., Melbourne 1969–74; Nuffield Prof. of Surgery, Univ. of Oxford, UK 1974– (now Prof. Emer.), Dir Oxford Transplant Centre; Pres. The Transplantation Soc. 1984–86, European Surgical Asscn 1996–98, Int. Surgical Soc. 2001–; Vice-Chair. Clinical Medicine Bd, Univ. of Oxford 1982–84; Vice-Pres. Royal Coll. of Surgeons of England 2000–01, Pres. 2001–; Chair. Council, Inst. of Health Sciences, Univ. of Oxford 2000–; Scientific mem. MRC, London 1983–87; Ed. Transplantation 1979–; Fellow, Balliol Coll., Univ. of Oxford 1974–; mem. UFC 1989–92; Hon. FRCSE, FACS 1986, FRACS 1996; Gov. Foundation 1998–; Hon. Fellow American Coll. of Surgeons, American Sugical Asscn, Royal Australasian Coll. of Surgeons; Hon. DSc (Hong Kong) 2000; Selwyn Smith Prize (Australia); Lister Medal (UK) 1998. *Publications:* Kidney Transplantation 1978, Tissue Transplantation 1982, Transient Ischaemic Attacks 1982, Progress in Transplantation 1984, Oxford Textbook of Surgery (with R. Malt) 1993. *Leisure interests:* golf, tennis. *Address:* Royal College of Surgeons, 35–43 Lincoln's Inn Fields, London, WC2A 3PE (Office); 19 Lucerne Road, Oxford, OX2 7QB, England (Home). *Telephone:* ((20) 7869-6000 (Office). *Fax:* (20) 7869-6005 (Office). *E-mail:* allison.elliott@reseng.ac .uk (Office); peterj.morris@virgin.net (Home).

MORRIS, Richard Graham Michael, MA, DPhil, FMedSci, FRSE, FRS; British neuroscientist; b. 27 June 1948, Worthing; s. of Robert Morris and Edith Morris; m. Hilary Ann Lewis 1985; two d.; ed Cambridge and Sussex Univs; Lecturer in Psychology Univ. of St Andrews 1977–86, MRC Research Fellow 1983–86; Reader, then Prof. of Neuroscience Univ. of Edin. 1986–, Dir Centre for Neuroscience 1993–97; Chair. Dept of Neuroscience 1998–; Chair. Brain Research Asscn 1991–95; Sec. Experimental Psychology Soc. 1983–87; mem. MRC Neuroscience Research Grants Cttee 1983–87, Neuroscience and Mental Health Bd 1993–97, Innovation Bd 1998–2000, MRC Strategy Group 2000–02; Fellow Acad. of Medical Sciences 1998–; Decade of the Brain Lecturer 1998, Zotterman Lecturer 1999, Forum Fellow at World Econ. Forum 2000, Life Sciences Co-ordinate OST Foresight Project on Cognitive Systems 2002–03; Yngve Zotterman Prize, Karolinska Inst. 1999, Henry Dryerre Prize, Royal Soc. of Edin. 2000. *Publications:* scientific papers on neural mechanisms of memory. *Leisure interest:* sailing. *Address:* Department of Neuroscience, University of Edinburgh, 1 George Square, Edinburgh, EH8 9JZ, Scotland. *Telephone:* (131) 650-3520. *Fax:* (131) 650-6530.

MORRIS, Richard Keith, OBE, BPhil, MA, FSA; British writer, archaeologist and composer; b. 8 Oct. 1947; s. of John Richard Morris and Elsie Myra Wearne; m. Jane Whiteley 1972; two s. one d.; ed Denstone Coll., Staffs., Pembroke Coll., Oxford and Univ. of York; musician 1971–72; Research Asst York Minster Archaeological Office 1972–75; Churches Officer Council for British Archaeology 1975–77, Research Officer, 1978–88, Dir 1991–99; Hon. Lecturer School of History, Leeds Univ. 1986–88; Lecturer Dept of Archaeology, York Univ. 1988–91; Hon. Visiting Prof. York Univ. 1995; Hon. Vice-Pres. Council for British Archaeology; Commr English Heritage 1996–; Chair. Ancient Monuments Advisory Cttee for England 1996–2001, Historic Settlements and Landscapes Cttee 2001–, Bede's World 2004–; writer 1999–; Frend Medal, Soc. of Antiquaries 1992. *Opera:* Lord Flame (jtly). *Publications:* Cathedrals and Abbeys of England and Wales 1979, The Church in British Archaeology 1983, Churches in the Landscape 1989, Guy Gibson (jtly) 1994, Cheshire: The Biography of Leonard Cheshire, VC, OM 2000, The Triumph of Time 2003. *Leisure interests:* aviation history, natural history, 20th-century music and opera. *Address:* 13 Hollins Road, Harrogate, N. Yorks., HG1 2JF, England (Home). *Telephone:* (1423) 817283 (Home). *E-mail:* rkmorris@dial .pipex.com (Home).

MORRIS, William (Bill), FRSA; British trade union official; b. 19 Oct. 1938, Jamaica; s. of William Morris and Una Morris; m. Minetta Morris 1957 (died 1990); two s.; ed Mizpah School, Manchester, Jamaica; Dist Officer, Transport & Gen. Workers' Union (TGWU), Nottingham 1973, Dist Sec. Northampton 1977, Nat. Sec. Passenger Services 1979–85, Deputy Gen. Sec. TGWU 1986–92, Gen. Sec. 1992–2003; mem. TUC Gen. Council 1988–2003; mem. Comm. for Racial Equality 1977–87, IBA Gen. Advisory Council 1981–86, ITF Exec. Bd 1986–, Prince of Wales Youth Business Trust 1987–90, BBC Gen. Advisory Council 1987–88, Employment Appeals Tribunal 1988–, Econ. and Social Cttee EC 1990–, NEDC 1992, Royal Comm. on Lords Reform 1999, Bd of Govs. South Bank Univ. 1997, Comm. for Integrated Transport 1999–; Dir (non-exec.) Court of the Bank of England 1998–; Bd mem. Project Fullemploy 1985–88; Dir Unity Trust Bank 1994–; Chancellor Univ. of Tech., Jamaica 2000–; Hon. Fellow City & Guilds 1992, Royal Soc. of Arts; Dr hc (S Bank Univ.) 1994, (Open Univ.) 1995; Hon. DLitt (Westminster) 1998 and several other hon. degrees; Order of Jamaica 2002; Public Figure of the Year, Ethnic

Multicultural Media Awards (EMMA) 2002. *Leisure interests:* walking, gardening, watching sports, jazz concerts. *Address:* 156 St Agnells Lane, Grove Hill, Hemel Hempstead, Herts., HP2 6EG, England.

MORRIS OF ABERAVON, Baron (life Peer), cr. 2001, of Aberavon in the County of West Glamorgan and of Ceredigion in the County of Dyfed; **John Morris**, Kt, PC, QC, LLD; British politician and barrister; b. 5 Nov. 1931, Aberystwyth; s. of the late D. W. Morris and of Mary Olwen Ann Morris; m. Margaret M. Lewis JP 1959; three d.; ed Ardwyn, Aberystwyth, Univ. Coll. of Wales, Aberystwyth, Gonville and Caius Coll., Cambridge and Acad. of Int. Law, The Hague; commissioned Royal Welch Fusiliers and Welch Regt; called to Bar, Gray's Inn 1954, Bencher 1985; Labour MP for Aberavon 1959–2001; Parl. Sec. Ministry of Power 1964–66; Jt Parl. Sec. Ministry of Transport 1966–68; Minister of Defence for Equipment 1968–70; Sec. of State for Wales 1974–79; a Recorder, Crown Court 1982–97; Legal Affairs and Shadow Attorney-Gen. 1983–97; Attorney-Gen. 1997–99; Chancellor Univ. of Glamorgan; fmr Deputy Gen. Sec. and Legal Adviser, Farmers' Union of Wales; mem. UK Del., Consultative Ass., Council of Europe and WEU 1963–64; mem. Cttee of Privileges 1994–97, Select Cttee on Implementation of the Nolan Report 1995–97; Chair. Nat. Pneumoconiosis Jt Cttee 1964–66, Nat. Road Safety Advisory Council 1967–68, Jt Review of Finances and Man. British Railways 1966–67; mem. N Atlantic Ass. 1970–74; HM Lord Lt for Dyfed; Pres. London Welsh Asscn; Hon. Fellow Univ. Coll. of Wales, Aberystwyth and Swansea, Trinity Coll., Carmarthen, Gonville and Caius Coll. Cambridge; Hon. LLD (Wales). *Address:* c/o House of Lords, London, SW1A 0PW, England.

MORRISON, Graham, MA, DIP.ARCH., RIBA; British architect; b. 2 Feb. 1951, Kilmarnock, Scotland; s. of Robert Morrison and Robina G. Morrison; m. Michelle Lovric; one s. one d.; ed Brighton Coll., Jesus Coll. Cambridge; partner, Allies and Morrison 1983–; architect, Royal Festival Hall, London 1993–; mem. RIBA council 1991–94, Dir RIBA Journal 1993–97; external examiner, Univ. of Cambridge 1994–97; Royal Fine Arts Commr 1998–99; mem. Arts Council Architecture Advisory Cttee 1996–97, CABE Design Review Panel 2000–, London Advisory Cttee, English Heritage 2001–; RIBA Awards to Allies and Morrison for The Clove Bldg 1990, Pierhead, Liverpool 1995, Sarum Hall School 1996, Nunney Square, Sheffield 1996, Newnham Coll. Cambridge 1996, British Embassy, Dublin 1997, Abbey Mills, Stratford 1997, Goldsmiths Coll., London 1997, Blackburn House, London 2000. *Exhibitions:* New British Architecture, Japan 1994, Allies and Morrison retrospective, USA 1996–98; also exhbns. in Helsinki, Delft, Strasbourg 1999. *Leisure interest:* Venice. *Address:* Allies and Morrison, 62 Newman Street, London, W1T 3EE (Office); 5 Winchester Wharf, 4 Clink Street, Southwark, London, SE1 9DL, England (Home). *Telephone:* (20) 7612-7100 (Office); (20) 8852-6209 (Home). *Fax:* (20) 7612-7101 (Office); (20) 8852-6209 (Home). *E-mail:* info@alliesandmorrison.co.uk, gmorrison@alliesandmorrison.co.uk (Office).

MORRISON, James Douglas, AO, DSc, PhD, FAA, FRSE, F.R.A.C.I.; Australian mass spectrometrist; b. 9 Nov. 1924, Glasgow, Scotland; s. of James K. Morrison and Rose Ann Wheeler; m. Christine B. Mayer 1947; three s.; ed Lenzie Acad., Scotland and Univ. of Glasgow; Instructor Dept of Chem. Univ. of Glasgow 1946–48; Research Officer, CSIRO 1949, Chief Research Officer 1965–67; Foundation Prof. of Chem. La Trobe Univ. 1967–90, Prof. Emer 1990–; Resident Head, Chisholm Coll. 1972–77; Adjunct Prof. Univ. of Utah 1975–, Univ. of Delaware 1987–; Commonwealth Fund Fellow, Chicago Univ. 1956–57; Visiting Prof. Princeton Univ. 1964, Univ. of Utah 1971; mem. Council, Royal Soc. of Victoria, Pres. 1975–76; mem. Council, Australian Acad. of Science, Vice-Pres. 1986–87; Rennie and Smith Medals, Royal Australian Chemical Inst. *Publications:* articles in scientific journals. *Leisure interests:* fossil hunting, Byzantine studies, travel. *Address:* 40 Central Avenue, Mooroolbark, Vic. 3138, Australia.

MORRISON, (Philip) Blake, PhD, FRSL; British author; b. 8 Oct. 1950, Lancashire; s. of the late Arthur Morrison and Agnes O'Shea; m. Katherine Ann Drake 1976; two s. one d.; ed Ermysted's Grammar School, Skipton, Nottingham Univ., McMaster Univ., Univ. Coll. London; Poetry and Fiction Ed., Times Literary Supplement 1978–81; Deputy Literary Ed. The Observer 1981–86, Literary Ed. 1987–89; Literary Ed. The Independent on Sunday 1990–94; freelance writer 1995–; Eric Gregory Prize 1980, Somerset Maugham Prize 1984, Dylan Thomas Prize 1985, E. M. Forster Prize 1987, Waterstones/Esquire Prize 1994, J. R. Ackerley Prize 1994. *Film:* Bicycle Thieves 1979. *Television documentaries:* Little Angels, Little Devils 1994, The Great Divide 1997. *Publications:* The Movement 1980, Seamus Heaney 1982, Penguin Book of Contemporary British Poetry (Ed.) 1982, Dark Glasses (poetry) 1984, The Yellow House (children's book) 1987, The Ballad of the Yorkshire Ripper (poetry) 1987, And When Did You Last See Your Father? (memoir) 1993, The Cracked Pot (play) 1996, As If 1997, Too True (essays and stories) 1998, Dr. Ox's Experiment (libretto) 1998, Selected Poems 1999, The Justification of Johann Gutenberg (novel) 2000, Oedipus (play) 2001, Things My Mother Never Told Me (memoir) 2002. *Leisure interests:* soccer, tennis. *Address:* 54 Blackheath Park, London, SE3 9SJ, England. *Telephone:* (20) 8318-9599. *Fax:* (20) 8318-9599. *E-mail:* blakemorr@aol.com (Office).

MORRISON, Toni (Chloe Anthony Morrison), MA; American novelist; b. 18 Feb. 1931, Lorain, Ohio; d. of George Wofford and Ella Ramah (Willis) Wofford; m. Harold Morrison 1958 (divorced 1964); two c.; ed Howard Univ., Cornell Univ.; taught English and Humanities, Tex. Southern Univ. 1955–57,

Howard Univ. 1957–64; Ed., Random House, New York 1965–; Assoc. Prof. of English, State Univ. of New York 1971–72, Schweitzer Prof. of the Humanities 1984–89; Robert F. Goheen Prof. of the Humanities, Princeton Univ. 1989–; mem. Council, Authors Guild; Nobel Prize for Literature 1993; Commdr Ordre des Arts et des Lettres; Nat. Medal of Arts 2000. *Publications:* The Bluest Eye 1970, Sula 1974, Song of Solomon 1977, Tar Baby 1983, Beloved 1987 (Pulitzer Prize and Robert F. Kennedy Book Award 1988), Jazz 1992, Playing in the Dark: Whiteness and the Literary Imagination 1992, Nobel Prize Speech 1994, Birth of a Nationhood: Gaze, Script and Spectacle in the O. J. Simpson Trial 1997. *Address:* Princeton University, Writing Program, 185 Nassau Street, Princeton, NJ 08544; c/o Suzanne Gluck, International Creative Management, 40 57th Street West, New York, NY 10019, USA.

MORRISON, Van, OBE; British singer, songwriter and instrumentalist; b. George Ivan Morrison, 31 Aug. 1945, Belfast; one d.; left school aged 15; joined The Monarchs, playing in Germany; formed Them, Belfast, disbanded 1966; moved to New York; Grammy Award for Best Pop Collab. with Vocals 1995. *Albums include:* Blowin' Your Mind 1967, Astral Weeks, Moondance 1970, Van Morrison: His Band and Street Choir 1970, Tupelo Honey 1971, Saint Dominic's Preview 1972, Hardnose the Highway 1973, It's Too Late To Stop Now 1970, Veedon Fleece 1974, A Period of Transition 1977, Wavelength 1978, Into the Music 1979, Beautiful Vision 1982, Inarticulate Speech of the Heart 1983, Live At The Royal Opera House, Belfast 1984, A Sense of Wonder 1985, No Guru, No Method, No Teacher 1986, Poetics Champion Compose 1987, Irish Heartbeat 1988, Avalon Sunset 1989, Enlightenment 1990, Hymns to the Silence 1991, Bang Masters 1991, The Best of Van Morrison 1993, Too Long in Exile 1993, A Night in San Francisco 1994, Days Like This 1995, The Healing Game 1997, Tell Me Something 1997, Brown Eyed Girl 1998, The Masters 1999, Super Hits 1999, Back On Top 1999, The Skiffle Sessions: Live in Belfast 1998, 2000.

MORRITT, Hon. Sir (Robert) Andrew, Hon. Mr. Justice Morritt, Kt, PC, CVO, QC; British judge; b. 5 Feb. 1938; s. of Robert Augustus Morritt and Margaret Mary Tyldesley Jones; m. Sara Simonetta Merton 1962; two s.; ed Eton Coll., Magdalene Coll. Cambridge; 2nd Lt Scots Guards 1956–58; called to Bar, Lincoln's Inn 1962, Bencher 1984, QC 1977; Jr Counsel to Sec. of State for Trade in Chancery Matters 1970–77, to Attorney-Gen. in Charity Matters 1972–77; Attorney-Gen. to HRH The Prince of Wales 1978–88; a Judge of High Court of Justice, Chancery Div. 1988–94; a Lord of Appeal in Ordinary 1994–2000; Vice-Chancellor, Head of Chancery Div. 2000–; Pres. Council of the Inns of Court 1997–2000; mem. Gen. Council of Bar 1969–73, Advisory Cttee on Legal Educ. 1972–76, Top Salaries Review Body 1982–87. *Leisure interests:* fishing, shooting. *Address:* c/o Royal Courts of Justice, Strand, London, WC2A 2LL, England.

MORROW, Sir Ian Thomas, J.DIP., MA, CA, FCMA; British chartered accountant; b. 8 June 1912, Manchester; s. of the late Thomas George Morrow and Jamesina Hunter; m. 1st Elizabeth Mary Thackray 1940 (divorced 1967); one s. one d.; m. 2nd Sylvia Jane Taylor 1967; one d.; ed Dollar Acad., Scotland; Chartered Accountant 1936; Asst Accountant Brocklehurst-Whiston Amalgamated Ltd 1937–40; Partner, Robson, Morrow & Co. 1942–51; Financial Dir The Brush Electrical Eng Co. Ltd (now The Brush Group Ltd) 1951–52, Deputy Man. Dir 1952–56, Jt Man. Dir 1956–57, Man. Dir 1957–58; Jt Man. Dir H. Clarkson & Co. Ltd 1961–72; Chair. Rowe Bros. & Co. (Holdings) Ltd 1960–70, Associated Fire Alarms Ltd 1965–70, Crane Fruehauf Trailers Ltd 1969–71, Rolls-Royce (1971) Ltd (Deputy Chair. and Man. Dir 1971–73), MAI (fmrly Mills and Allen Int. PLC) 1974–94, Scotia Holdings PLC (fmrly Efamol Holdings) 1986–95, Beale Dobie & Co. Ltd 1989–97, Scotia Pharmaceuticals Ltd 1986–95, Walbrook Insurance Co. Ltd 1990–92, Fintauro SIM SpA (Milan) 1992–93, Thurne Group Ltd 1993–99; mem. Bd Scotia Pharmaceuticals Ltd 1986–95, Insport Consultants 1988–93, etc.; fmr Dir The Laird Group PLC (fmr Chair.) 1973–92, Dir Hambros Industrial Man. Ltd, Zeus Management Ltd –1993, Psion PLC 1987–98, CE Heath PLC 1988–97, Harlow Ueda Savage (Holdings) Ltd 1985–88 and numerous other cos.; Council mem. Chartered Inst. of Man. Accountants 1952–70 (Pres. 1956–57; Gold Medallist 1961); Pres. Inst. of Chartered Accountants of Scotland 1981–82; mem. Press Council until 1981; Liveryman, Worshipful Co. of Spectaclemakers; Hon. DLitt (Heriot-Watt) 1982; Hon. DUniv (Stirling) 1979; Freeman, City of London. *Leisure interests:* reading, music, golf, skiing. *Address:* Broadacres, Seven Devils Lane, Saffron Walden, CB11 4BB, England (Home).

MORSCHAKOVA, Tamara Georgyevna, D.JUR.SC.; Russian judge; b. 28 March 1938, Moscow; m.; one d.; ed Moscow State Univ.; Jr researcher Inst. of State and Law, USSR Acad. of Sciences 1958–71; Sr researcher, chief, then leading researcher All-Union Research Inst. of Soviet Construction and Law 1971–91; mem. Scientific-Consultative Council, Supreme Court of Russian Fed. 1985–; Prof. Moscow State Juridical Acad. 1987–; Justice, Constitutional Court of Russian Fed. 1991–95, Deputy Chair. 1995–2002; Honoured Jurist of Russian Fed., Honoured Scientist of Russian Fed. *Publications:* books include Efficiency of Justice 1975, Reform of Justice 1990, Commentary to Legislation on Judiciary 2003, Criminal Procedure Law 2003. *Address:* Constitutional Court of Russian Federation, Ilyinka str. 21, 103132 Moscow, Russia (Office). *Telephone:* (095) 206-16-29 (Office).

MORSE, Sir (Christopher) Jeremy, KCMG; British banker; b. 10 Dec. 1928, London; s. of the late Francis J. Morse and Kinbarra (née Armfield-Marrow)

Morse; m. Belinda M. Mills 1955; three s. one d.; ed Winchester and New Coll., Oxford; fmrly with Glyn, Mills & Co., Dir 1964; Dir Legal and Gen. Assurance Society Ltd 1963–64, 1975–87; Exec. Dir Bank of England 1965–72, Dir (non-exec.) 1993–97; Alt. Gov. IMF 1966–72; Chair. of Deputies of "Cttee. of Twenty", IMF 1972–74; Deputy Chair. Lloyds Bank Ltd 1975–77, Chair. 1977–93; Chair. Lloyds Merchant Bank Holdings 1985–88; Dir (non-exec.) ICI 1981–93, Zeneca 1993–99; Chair. Cttee of London Clearing Bankers 1980–82, City Communications Centre 1985–87; mem. Council, Lloyd's 1987–98; mem. NEDC 1977–81; Pres. Inst. Int. d'Études Bancaires 1982–83, Int. Monetary Conf. 1985–86, Banking Fed. of EC 1988–90, Chartered Inst. of Bankers 1992–93; Vice-Pres. Business in the Community 1986–98; Chair. City Arts Trust 1977–79, Per Jacobsson Foundation 1987–99, Governing Bodies Asscn 1994–99; Chancellor Bristol Univ. 1988–; Pres. Classical Asscn 1989–90; Fellow, All Souls Coll., Oxford 1953–68, 1983–; Chair. Trustees, Beit Memorial Fellowships for Medical Research 1976–; Fellow, Winchester Coll. 1966–83, Warden 1987–97; Hon. life mem. British Chess Fed. 1988–; Hon. D.Litt (City) 1977; Hon. DSc (Aston) 1984; Hon. LLD (Bristol) 1989. Publication: Chess Problems: Tasks and Records 1995. Leisure interests: poetry, golf, problems and puzzles, coarse gardening. Address: 102A Drayton Gardens, London, SW10 9RJ, England (Home). Telephone: (20) 7370-2265.

MORTELL, Michael Philip, MSc, MS, PhD; Irish university administrator; b. 9 Feb. 1941, Cork; m. Patricia Yule 1967; two d.; ed Charleville Christian Bros. School, Univ. Coll. Cork and Calif. Inst. of Tech.; Asst Prof. and Assoc. Prof. Center for Application of Math. Lehigh Univ. 1967–72; Lecturer in Math. Univ. Coll. Cork 1972–89, Registrar 1979–89, Pres. 1989–99, Prof. Applied Scholar Math. 2000–; Visiting Prof. Univ. of British Col 1976–77, Univ. of Queensland 1979; Visiting Assoc. Caltech and New York Univ. 1999–2000; Vice-Chancellor Nat. Univ. of Ireland; Chair. Conf. of Heads of Irish Univs.; Hon. LLD (Dublin, Queen's Univ. Belfast, Limerick). Publications: some 30 papers on nonlinear acoustics. Leisure interests: reading, art, gardening, sport. Address: Department of Applied Mathematics, University College, Cork, Ireland. Telephone: (21) 4903402 (Office). Fax: (21) 4270813 (Office). E-mail: m.mortell@ucc.ie (Office).

MORTIER, Gerard; Belgian music director; b. 25 Nov. 1943, Ghent; ed Univ. of Ghent; engaged in journalism and communications 1966–67; Admin. Asst Flanders Festival 1968–72; Artistic Planner, Deutsche Oper am Rhein, Düsseldorf 1972–73; Asst Admin. Frankfurt Opera 1973–77; Dir of Artistic Production, Hamburg Staatsoper 1977–79; Tech. Programme Consultant, Théâtre Nat. de l'Opéra, Paris 1979–81; Dir-Gen. Belgian Nat. Opera, Brussels 1981–91; Dir Salzburg Music Festival 1992–2001. Address: c/o Viktor Schoner, KULTUR RUHR GmbH, Leifhestr. 35, 45886 Gelsenkirchen, Germany. Telephone: (209) 167-1719 (Office). Fax: (209) 167-1710/1738 (Office). E-mail: v.schoner@kulturruhr.com (Office).

MORTIER, Roland F. J., DPhil; Belgian university professor; b. 21 Dec. 1920, Ghent; s. of the late Arthur Mortier and Berthe Baudson; m. Loyse Triffaux 1948; one s.; ed Antwerp Atheneum, Univ. Libre de Bruxelles and Univ. of Ghent; Prof., Univ. Libre de Bruxelles 1955–85, Prof. Emer. 1990; Visiting Prof. Toronto, Stanford, Yale, Paris, Cologne, Jerusalem, London, Cleveland, Maryland, Duisburg, Pisa; Vice-Pres. Inst. des Hautes Etudes de Belgique; past Pres. Société Diderot, FCLA, ISECS; mem. Acad. Royale de Langue et Littérature Française, Belgium; Foreign mem. Hungarian Acad. of Sciences; corresp. Fellow, British Acad., Academia Europaea; mem. Inst. de France 1993; other professional appts and affiliations; Dr hc (Montpellier, Göttingen, Jerusalem), Prix Francqui 1965, Prix Montaigne 1983, Prix Counson 1985, Prix de l'Union rationaliste de France 1993, Giltsilver Medal of the French Acad. 2001; Chevalier, Légion d'honneur 2001. Publications: Diderot en Allemagne 1954, Clartés et Ombres du Siècle des Lumières 1969, Le Tableau littéraire de la France au XVIIIe Siècle 1972, La Poétique des Ruines en France 1974, L'Originalité, une nouvelle catégorie esthétique 1982, Le coeur et la raison 1990, Anacharsis Cloots, ou l'Utopie Foudroyée 1995, Les combats des lumières 2000, Le prince d'Albanie 2000; critical edns of Voltaire and Diderot, of Prince de Ligne 2001, Le 18e siècle français au quotidien 2002. Leisure interests: reading, walking, swimming, travel. Address: 10 avenue Général de Longueville, B.P. 12, 1150 Brussels, Belgium. Telephone: (2) 772-01-94. Fax: (2) 772-01-94.

MORTIMER, H. Roger, LVO, BSc, MA; British diplomatist; b. 19 Sept. 1949, Salisbury; ed Cheltenham Coll., Univ. of Surrey, King's Coll. London; joined FCO 1973, served Rome, Singapore, UN, New York; on secondment to German Ministry of Foreign Affairs 1990; Deputy Head of Mission, Berlin 1991–94, FCO 1994–95, Ankara 1997–2000; Amb. to Slovenia 2001–. Leisure interests: jogging, guitar playing, cinema. Address: Embassy of UK, 4th Floor Trg Republike 3, 1000 Ljubljana, Slovenia (Office). Telephone: (1) 2003910 (Office). Fax: (1) 4250174 (Office). E-mail: hugh.mortimer@fco.gov.uk (Office).

MORTIMER, Sir John (Clifford), Kt, CBE, QC; British author, barrister and playwright; b. 21 April 1923, Hampstead, London; s. of Clifford and Katherine (née Smith) Mortimer; m. 1st Penelope Fletcher (Penelope Mortimer, 1949 (divorced 1972); one s. one d.; m. 2nd Penelope Gollop; two d.; ed Harrow, Brasenose Coll., Oxford; called to the Bar 1948, Master of the Bench, Inner Temple 1975; mem. Bd of Nat. Theatre 1968–; Chair. Council Royal Soc. of Literature 1989; Chair. Council Royal Court Theatre 1990–2002; Pres. Howard League for Penal Reform 1991–; British Acad. Writers' Award 1979, 1980; Dr. hc (Exeter) 1986; Hon. LLD (Susquehanna Univ.) 1985; Hon.

DLitt (St Andrews) 1987, (Nottingham) 1989; Hon. DUniv (Brunel) 1990. Plays include: The Wrong Side of the Park 1960, Two Stars for Comfort 1962, The Judge 1967, A Voyage Round My Father 1970 (adapted for TV 1982, Int. Emmy Award), I, Claudius (adaptation from Robert Graves) 1972, Collaborators 1973, Mr. Luby's Fear of Heaven (radio) 1976, Heaven and Hell 1976, The Bells of Hell 1977, The Lady from Maxim's (trans. from Feydeau) 1977, Flea in Her Ear, A Little Hotel on the Side (trans. from Feydeau), TV adaptations of Rumpole of the Bailey (six series), Brideshead Revisited 1981, Unity Mitford 1981, The Ebony Tower 1984, adaptation of Die Fledermaus 1989, (TV) A Christmas Carol 1994, Naked Justice 2001, Hock and Soda Water 2001; Under the Hammer (TV series) 1993. Publications: novels: Charade 1947, Rumming Park 1948, Answer Yes or No 1950, Like Men Betrayed 1953, Three Winters 1956, Will Shakespeare 1977, Rumpole of the Bailey 1978, The Trials of Rumpole 1979, Rumpole's Return 1981, Rumpole and the Golden Thread 1983, Paradise Postponed 1985, Rumpole's Last Case 1987, Rumpole and the Age of Miracles 1988, Rumpole à la Carte 1990, Clinging to the Wreckage (autobiog.) 1982, In Character 1983, Character Parts (interviews) 1986, Summer's Lease 1988, The Narrowing Stream, Titmuss Regained 1990, Dunster 1992, Rumpole on Trial 1992, The Best of Rumpole 1993, Murderers and Other Friends (autobiog.) 1993, Rumpole and the Angel of Death 1995, Rumpole and the Younger Generation 1996, Felix in the Underworld 1997, Rumpole's Return 1997, The Third Rumpole Omnibus 1997, The Sound of Trumpets 1998, The Summer of a Dormouse (autobiog.) 2000, Rumpole Rests His Case 2001, Rumpole and the Primrose Path 2002; trans. Die Fledermaus 1988; Great Law and Order Stories 1991, The Oxford Book of Villains 1992; numerous articles in magazines. Leisure interests: working, gardening, going to the opera. Address: Turville Heath Cottage, Henley on Thames, Oxon., England. Telephone: (1491) 638237 (Home). Fax: (1491) 638861 (Home).

MORTON, Sir Alastair (see Morton, Sir Robert Alastair).

MORTON, Donald Charles, PhD, FAA; Canadian astronomer; b. 12 June 1933, Canada; s. of Charles O. Morton and Irene M. Wightman; m. Winifred Austin 1970; one s. one d.; ed Univ. of Toronto and Princeton Univ.; astronomer, US Naval Research Lab. 1959–61; from Research Assoc. to Sr Research Astronomer (with rank of Prof.), Princeton Univ. 1961–76; Dir Anglo-Australian Observatory (Epping and Coonabarabran, NSW) 1976–86; Dir-Gen. Herzberg Inst. of Astrophysics, Nat. Research Council of Canada 1986–2000, Researcher Emer. 2001–; mem. Int. Astronomical Union, Royal Astronomical Soc. (Assoc. 1980), Astronomical Soc. of Australia (Pres. 1981–83, Hon. mem. 1986), Canadian Astronomical Soc.; Fellow Australian Acad. of Sciences. Publications: research papers in professional journals. Leisure interests: mountaineering, marathon running. Address: Herzberg Institute of Astrophysics, National Research Council of Canada, 5071 W Saanich Road, Victoria, BC, V9E 2E7, Canada. Telephone: (250) 363-8313. Fax: (250) 363-0045.

MORTON, Sir (Robert) Alastair, Kt, MA; British business executive; b. 11 Jan. 1938, Johannesburg, South Africa; s. of the late Harry Newton Morton and Elizabeth Markino; m. Sara Stephens 1964; one s. one d.; ed St John's Coll., Johannesburg, Univ. of Witwatersrand, Johannesburg, Univ. of Oxford and MIT; with Anglo-American Corpn of S Africa, London and Cen. Africa 1959–63; with World Bank Group, Washington, DC 1964–67, Industrial Reorganisation Corpn, London 1967–70; Exec. Dir Investment Trust Group 1970–72; Chair. and CEO, Draymont Securities Ltd 1972–76; (first) Man. Dir British Nat. Oil Corpn (BNOC) 1976–80; Co-int. energy consultancy 1980–81; CEO Guinness Peat Group PLC 1982–87, Chair. 1987; Chair. Guinness Mahon & Co. 1986–87; Dir British Steel Corpn (BSC) 1979–82; Chair. Eurotunnel PLC 1987–96, CEO, Eurotunnel Group 1990–94, Co-Chair. 1987–90, 1994–96; (first) Chair. Kent Training and Enterprise Council 1989–95; Chair. Strategic Rail Authority 1999–2001; Dir National Power PLC 1989–, Lucas Industries PLC 1993–96, Lonrho 1998–; Chair. Pvt. Finance Panel advising Chancellor of the Exchequer 1993–95, Strategic Adviser 1997–; Hon. LLD (Bath) 1990; Hon. DCL (Kent) 1992; Hon. DUniv (Brunel) 1992; Hon. DSc (Warwick) 1994, (Cranfield) 1994; Gold Medal, Inst. of Civil Engineers 1994; Commdr Légion d'honneur. Leisure interests: yachting, walking. Address: 26 Old Queen Street, London, SW1H 9HP, England.

MOSBACHER, Robert Adam, BSc; American politician and oil and gas executive; b. 11 March 1927, New York; s. of Emil Mosbacher and Gertrude (née Schwartz) Mosbacher; m. Georgette Paulsin 1986; one s. three d.; ed Washington and Lee Univs; Ind. oil and gas producer 1948–89; Pres. Mosbacher Energy Corp., Houston 1995–; Sec. of Commerce, Washington 1989–92; Chair., CEO Mosbacher Energy Co., Houston; Dir Texas Bankshares, Houston, New York Life Insurance Co.; Chair. Bd Dirs., Choate School, Wallingford, Conn.; Dir Aspen Inst. Center for Strategic and Int. Studies; Chair. Nat. Finance, George Bush for Pres.; Pres. Ford Finance Cttee; Gen. Campaign Chair., then Chief Fundraiser 1992 Republican Presidential Campaign; Gen. Chair. Finance, Republican Nat. Cttee, Washington, DC 1992–; Dir Texas Heart Inst.; mem. Mid-Continent Oil and Gas Asscn (fmr Chair.), American Petroleum Inst. (Dir, Exec. Cttee), Nat. Petroleum Council (fmr Chair.), All American Wildcatters Asscn (fmr Chair.), American Asscn Petroleum Landmen; Hon. LLD (Lee Univ.) 1984. Address: Mosbacher Energy Corp., 712 Main Street, Suite 2200, Houston, TX 77002, USA.

MOSBAKK, Kurt; Norwegian politician; b. 21 Nov. 1934, Orkdal; s. of Henrik Mosbakk and Jenny Mosbakk; m. Grete Tidemandsen 1975; two s. one d.; ed Norwegian Coll. Econs and Business Admin.; Pvt. Sec. to Minister of Defence 1964–65; Minister of Trade and Shipping 1986–88; County Exec. of Østfold 1988–; Deputy Chair. Norwegian Defence Comm. 1990–92; fmr Deputy Mayor Lørenskog; Chair. Akershus Co. Labour Party 1969–74; Chief Co. Exec. Finnmark Co. 1976; Chair. Bd Norwegian State Housing Bank 1988–; Chair. Norwegian Tourist Bd 1990–. *Leisure interest:* literature. *Address:* NORTRA, Drammensvn 40, P.O. Box 2893 Solli, 0230 Oslo, Norway.

MOSCOSO DE GRUBER, Mireya Elisa; Panamanian politician; b. 1 July 1946, Panama; d. of Plinio Antonio Moscoso and Elisa Rodríguez de Moscoso; m. Arnulfo Arias (died 1988); one s.; ed Colegio Comercial María Inmaculada, Miami Dade Community Coll.; fmr Exec. Sec. Social Security Agency; fmr Sales Man., Deputy Man. and Gen. Man. Arkapal SA (coffee co.); Govt rep. on numerous int. missions; spent ten years in exile in USA; Pres. Partido Arnulfista; Pres. of Panama Sept. 1999–; fmr Pres. Arias Foundation, Madrid; mem. Asscn of Boquete Coffee Growers, Asscn of Milk Producers, Nat. Asscn of Ranchers. *Address:* Office of the President, Palacio Presidencial, Valija 50, Panamá 1, Panama (Office). *Telephone:* 227-4062 (Office). *Fax:* 227-0076 (Office). *E-mail:* ofasin@presidencia.gob.pa (Office).

MOSCOVICI, Pierre; French politician; b. 16 Sept. 1957; s. of Serge Moscovici and Marie Bromberg; ed Univ. of Paris X, I, IV, Ecole nat. d'administration; official, Cour des Comptes 1984–88; Adviser, pvt. office of Minister of Nat. Educ., Youth and Sport 1988–89, Special Adviser to Minister 1989–90; Head. Gen. Planning Comm.'s Public Sector Modernization and Finance Dept 1990; mem. Parti Socialiste (PS) Nat. Council and Nat. Bureau 1990, Nat. Sec. responsible for policy research and devt 1990–92, 1995–97, Nat. Treas. 1992–94; mem. Doubs Gen. Council, Sochaux-Grand-Charmont canton 1994; Montbéliard municipal councillor 1995; mem. European Parl. 1994–97; Nat. Ass. Deputy for 4th Doubs constituency 1997–; Minister Del. attached to Minister for Foreign Affairs, with responsibility for European Affairs 1997–2002; Rep. Convention on the Future of Europe 2002; Regional Councillor Franche-Comté. *Publications include:* A la recherche de la gauche perdue 1994, L'urgence, plaidoyer pour une autre politique 1997, Au coeur de l'Europe 1999, L'Europe, une puissance dans la mondialisation 2001. *Leisure interests:* tennis, skiing. *Address:* c/o Assemblée Nationale, Paris, France.

MOSELEY BRAUN, Carol, BA; American politician and lawyer; b. 16 Aug. 1947; d. of Joseph J. Moseley and Edna A. Moseley (née Davie); m. Michael Braun 1973 (divorced 1986); one s.; ed Univ. of Illinois; fmr Asst Attorney, Davis, Miner & Barnhill; fmr Attorney, Jones, Ware & Grenard; fmr Asst U.S. Attorney for Northern Dist of Ill.; mem. Ill. House of Reps. 1978–88; Cook Co. Recorder of Deeds 1988; Senator from Illinois (first African-American woman to be elected to Senate) 1993–99; Amb. to N.Z. 1999–2001; Democrat. *Address:* c/o Department of State, 2201 C Street, NW, Washington, DC 20520, USA.

MOSER, Lord Claus Adolf Moser, Baron (Life Peer), cr. 2001, of Regents Park in the London Borough of Camden, KCB, CBE, FBA; British statistician; b. 24 Nov. 1922, Berlin; s. of the late Dr. Ernest Moser and Lotte Moser; m. Mary Oxlin 1949; one s. two d.; ed Frensham Heights School, London School of Econs; RAF 1943–46; Asst Lecturer in Statistics, LSE 1946–49, Lecturer 1949–55, Reader in Social Statistics 1955–61, Prof. of Social Statistics 1961–70; Statistical Adviser Cttee on Higher Educ. 1961–64; Dir LSE Higher Educ. Research Unit 1964–; Dir Royal Opera House Covent Garden 1965–87, Chair. 1974–87; Dir Cen. Statistical Office, Head of Govt Statistical Service 1967–78; Visiting Fellow, Nuffield Coll. 1972–80; Vice-Chair. N. M. Rothschild and Sons 1978–84, Dir 1978–90; Dir The Economist 1979–93, Chair. Economist Intelligence Unit 1978–84; Warden of Wadham Coll., Oxford 1984–93, Pres. 1989–90; Chair. AS Konas Holt Ltd 1990–2002, British Museum Devt Trust 1993–, Basic Skills Agency 1997–2002; Dir Equity & Law Life Assurance Soc. 1980–87, Int. Medical Statistics Inc. 1982–88, Octopus Publishing Group 1982–87, Property and Reversionary Investments 1986–87; Chancellor, Univ. of Keele 1986–2002, Open Univ. of Israel 1994–; Pres. British Asscn 1989–95; Pro-Vice-Chancellor Oxford Univ. 1991–93; Trustee Soros Foundation 1993–; Gov. Royal Shakespeare Theatre 1982–93, British American Arts Asscn 1982–, Pilgrim Trust 1982–99, Nat. Comm. on Educ. 1991–95; mem. Gov. Body, Royal Ballet School 1974–87; Hon. Fellow, RAM 1970, LSE 1976, Inst. of Educ., Univ. of London 1997; Hon. DScS (Southampton) 1975, (Leeds, Surrey, Keele, York, Sussex, City Univs) 1977; Hon. DTech (Brunel) 1981; Hon. DSc (Wales) 1990, (Liverpool) 1991; Hon. DScEcon (London) 1991; Dr hc (Brighton) 1994; Commdr Ordre nat. du Mérite 1976; Commdr's Cross, Order of Merit (FRG) 1986. *Publications:* Measurement of Levels of Living 1957, Survey Methods in Social Investigation 1958, Social Conditions in England and Wales (co-author) 1958, British Towns (co-author) 1961 and papers in statistical journals. *Leisure interest:* music. *Address:* 3 Regents Park Terrace, London, NW1 7EE, England (Home). *Telephone:* (20) 7485-1619 (Home).

MOSEROVÁ, Jaroslava, MD, PhD, DSc; Czech international organization official, plastic surgeon (burns specialist), politician, writer and artist; b. 17 Jan. 1930, Prague; d. of the late Jaroslav Moser and of Anna Moserová; m. Milan David; one s.; ed Warren Coll., Swannanoe, NC, Arts Students League, NY, Charles Univ., Prague; house surgeon Surgical Dept, Duchcov 1955–60; specialist Burns Centre, Charles Univ. 1960–65, Head of Research 1965–90; mem. Czech Nat. Council 1990–91; Amb. to Australia and New Zealand 1991–93; Sec.-Gen. Czech Comm. for UNESCO 1993–95, mem. UNESCO Exec. 1995–99, Pres. Gen. Conf. 1999–2001; elected mem. Parl. Senate of Czech Repub. 1996–, Vice-Pres. 1997; first woman candidate for Pres. 2003; has also written films and plays, illustrated children's books and translated English literature texts; mem. PEN Int., Rotary Int., Czech Writers' Asscn, Czech Translators' Asscn, Czech Fine Arts Asscn, Olga Havel's Good Will Foundation, Prague School of Fine Arts; Europe Integration Prize, Hungary, Med. Acad. Medal, Poland, Charles Univ. Med. School Gold Medal, UNESCO Gold Medal. *Films:* (screenplays) Killing with Kindness, Double Role. *Radio Plays:* Such a Nice Boy, A Letter to Wollongong. *Publications:* The Atlas of Plastic Surgery, The Healing and Treatment of Skin Defects; Historky (short stories) 2003; translations of over 50 works, including novels by Dick Francis, Jacob Bronowski and John Mortimer. *Leisure interests:* education, science and culture, ethics and perception of human dignity in different parts of the world, music. *Address:* Parliamentary Senate of the Czech Republic, Valdštejnské nám. Č. 4, 118 01 Prague 1 (Office); Pošta Làzně Bohdaneč, 53341 Prague 43, Czech Republic (Home). *Telephone:* (2) 57072375 (Office). *Fax:* (2) 57534500 (Office). *E-mail:* moserovaj@senat.cz (Office). *Website:* www .moserova.cz (Office).

MOSES, Edwin, BSc, MBA; American athlete, sports administrator, diplomatist and businessman; b. 31 Aug. 1955, Dayton, Ohio; m. Myrella Bordt Moses 1982; ed Fairview High School and Morehouse Coll., Atlanta, Ga; won gold medal for 400m hurdles, Olympic Games, Montreal 1976 (in world record time), LA 1984; one of only three men to break 48 secs. for 400m hurdles; holds record for greatest number of wins consecutively in any event; winner 122 straight races 1977–87, lost to Danny Harris June 1987; at one time held 13 fastest times ever recorded; retd 1988, comeback 1991; competed int. for USA in bobsleigh and 2- and 4-man sleds; mem. Jt Olympic Cttee Athletes Comm., Exec. Bd of U.S.O.C., Bd of Dirs. Jesse Owens Foundation; US Rep. to Int. Amateur Athletic Fed. 1984–; Pres. Int. Amateur Athletics Asscn; dynamics engineer, Pomona, Calif.; fmr Chair. U.S.O.C. Substance Abuse Cttee; Founding Partner Platinum Group (representing athletes' business interests); Financial Consultant with Solomon Smith Barney; Vice-Chair US Olympic Foundation; Jesse Owens Int. Award 1981, US Track and Field Hall of Fame 1994, Speaker of the Athletes' Oath at 1984 Olympic Games. *Leisure interests:* aviation, scientific breakthroughs in athletics, scuba diving. *Address:* Robinson-Humphrey Co., 3333 Peachtree Road NE, Atlanta, GA 30326, U.S.A.

MOSES, Lincoln Ellsworth, PhD; American professor of statistics; b. 21 Dec. 1921, Kansas City; s. of Edward Walter Moses and Virginia (née Holmes) Moses; m. 1st Jean Runnels 1942; m. 2nd Mary Louise Coale 1968; two s. three d.; ed Stanford Univ.; Asst Prof. of Educ., Columbia Univ. 1950–52; Asst Prof. of Statistics, Stanford Univ. and Stanford Medical School 1952–55, Assoc. Prof. 1955–59, Prof. 1959–, Assoc. Dean of Humanities and Sciences 1965–68, 1985–86, Dean of Graduate Studies 1969–75; (First) Admin. Energy Information Admin., U.S. Dept of Energy 1978–80; Guggenheim Fellow, Fellow at Center for Advanced Study in Behavioral Sciences. *Publications:* (with Herman Chernoff) Elementary Decision Theory 1959, Biostatistics Casebook (Jt Ed.) 1980, Think and Explain with Statistics 1986. *Leisure interests:* birds, chess. *Address:* Division of Biostatistics, Stanford University Medical Centre, Stanford, CA 94305, USA. *Telephone:* (650) 851-8182 (Home); (650) 723-6910. *Fax:* (650) 725-6951 (Office).

MOSHER, Gregory Dean, BFA; American theatre producer and director; b. 15 Jan. 1949, New York; s. of Thomas Edward Mosher and Florence Christine Mosher; ed Oberlin Coll., Ithaca Coll., Juilliard School; Dir Stage 2 Goodman Theatre, Chicago 1974–77, Artistic Dir 1978–85; Dir Lincoln Center Theater 1985–92, Resident Dir 1992–; producer of new works by Tennessee Williams, Studs Terkel, David Mamet, John Guare, Michael Weller, Wole Soyinka, Elaine May, David Rabe, Mbongeni Ngema, Edward Albee, Spalding Gray, Arthur Miller, Leonard Bernstein, Stephen Sondheim, Richard Nelson, Jerome Robbins; producer: Samuel Beckett's first directing work in US, Krapp's Last Tape 1979, Endgame 1980; Dir Glengarry Glen Ross (David Mamet), Broadway 1984–85, American Buffalo 1975, A Life in the Theater 1977, Edmond 1982, Speed-the-Plow (David Mamet), Danger: Memory (Miller premiere) 1987, Broadway 1988, London 1989, Our Town (50th anniversary production, Thornton Wilder), Broadway 1988, Oh Hell, Lincoln Center Theater 1989, Uncle Vanya 1990, Mr Gogol and Mr Preen 1991, A Streetcar Named Desire 1992; two Tony Awards (as producer of revivals: Anything Goes, Our Town). *Address:* Lincoln Center Theater, 150 W 65th Street, New York, NY 10023, USA. *Telephone:* (212) 362-7600.

MOSHINSKY, Elijah, BA; British opera director; b. 8 Jan. 1946; s. of Abraham Moshinsky and Eva Moshinsky; m. Ruth Dyttman 1970; two s.; ed Melbourne Univ. and St Antony's Coll. Oxford; apptd. to Royal Opera House 1973, Assoc. Producer 1979–; work for Royal Opera includes original productions of Peter Grimes 1975, Lohengrin 1978, The Rake's Progress 1979, Un Ballo in Maschera 1980; Macbeth 1981, Samson et Dalila 1981, Tannhäuser 1984, Otello 1987, Die Entführung aus dem Serail 1987, Attila 1990, Simon Boccanegra 1991, Stiffelio 1993, Aida 1994, Otello 1994, The Makropoulos Case 1996, The Queen of Spades 1998; has also produced work for ENO, Australian Opera, Metropolitan Opera, New York, Holland Festival, Maggio Musicale, Florence etc. *Theatre productions include:* Troilus and Cressida (Nat. Theatre) 1976, The Force of Habit (Nat. Theatre) 1976, Three Sisters (Albery) 1987, Light Up the Sky (Globe) 1987, Ivanov (Strand) 1989, Much Ado About Nothing (Strand) 1989, Another Time (Wyndham's) 1989, Shadowlands (Queen's) 1989, Cyrano de Bergerac 1992, Genghis Cohn 1993, Danton 1994; Dir Matador (Queen's) 1991, Becket (Haymarket) 1991, Reflected Glory (Vaudeville) 1992, Richard III 1998, The Female Odd Couple (Apollo) 2001;

productions for BBC TV of works by Shakespeare, Ibsen and Sheridan. *Leisure interests:* painting, telephone conversation. *Address:* 28 Kidbrooke Grove, London, SE3 0LG, England. *Telephone:* (20) 8858-4179.

MOSIER, Frank Eugene; American oil executive; b. 15 July 1930, Kersey, Pa; s. of Clarence Mosier and Helen Mosier; m. Julia M. Fife 1961; one s. one d.; ed Univ. of Pittsburgh; joined Standard Oil Co. Cleveland 1953, Vice-Pres. (supply and distribution) 1972–76, (supply and transport) 1976–77, Sr Vice-Pres. (marketing and refining) 1977–78, (supply and transport) 1978–82, (downstream petroleum Dept) 1982–85, Exec. Vice-Pres. 1985–86, Pres. and COO 1986–88; with BP America Inc. (following 1987 merger of BP and Standard Oil), Cleveland 1987–, Pres. 1987–88, Vice-Chair. 1988–.

MOSIMANN, Anton; Swiss chef and restaurateur; b. 23 Feb. 1947; s. of Otto Mosimann and Olga Mosimann; m. Kathrin Roth 1973; two s.; ed pvt. school in Switzerland; apprentice, Hotel Baeren, Twann; worked in Canada, France, Italy, Sweden, Japan, Belgium, Switzerland 1962–; cuisinier at Villa Lorraine, Brussels, Les Prés d'Eugénie, Eugénie-les-Bains, Les Frères Troisgros, Roanne, Paul Bocuse, Collonges au Mont d'Or, Moulin de Mougins; joined Dorchester Hotel, London 1975, Maître Chef des Cuisines 1975–88; owner, Mosimann's (fmr Belfry Club) 1988–, Mosimann's Party Service 1990–, The Mosimann Acad. 1995–, Creative Chefs 1996–; owner Château Mosimann, Switzerland 2001–; TV programmes include series Cooking with Mosimann 1990, Anton Mosimann Naturally 1991–92, Natürlich, Leichtes Kochen (Swiss TV) 1997, Mosimann's Culinary Switzerland (Swiss TV) 1998; World Pres. Les Toques Blanches Internationales 1989–93; Hon. mem. Chefs' Asscns of Canada, Japan, Switzerland, SA; Dr of Culinary Arts hc (Johnson and Wales Univ., USA); Hon. DSc (Bournemouth Univ.) 1998; Chevalier du Mérite Agricole; Personalité de l'Année Award 1986, Glenfiddich Award (for TV programme Anton Goes to Sheffield) 1986; Freedom of City of London 1999, Royal Warrant from HRH the Prince of Wales for Caterers 2000, Restaurateur of the Year, Int. Food and Beverage Forum, Rhode Island 2000; numerous awards in int. cookery competitions etc. *Publications:* Cuisine à la Carte 1981, A New Style of Cooking: The Art of Anton Mosimann 1983, Cuisine Naturelle 1985, Anton Mosimann's Fish Cuisine 1988, The Art of Mosimann 1989, Cooking with Mosimann 1989, Anton Mosimann—Naturally 1991, The Essential Mosimann 1993, Mosimann's World 1996. *Leisure interests:* jogging, travel, collecting art. *Address:* c/o Mosimann's, 11B West Halkin Street, London, SW1X 8JL, England.

MOSISILI, Bethuel Pakalitha; Lesotho politician; fmrly Deputy Prime Minister, Minister of Home Affairs, Local Govt and Rural and Urban Development; fmrly Deputy Leader Lesotho Congress for Democracy, Leader June 1997–; Prime Minister of Lesotho and Minister of Defence and Public Service May 1998–. *Address:* Office of the Prime Minister, P.O. Box 527, Maseru 100, Lesotho. *Telephone:* 311030. *Fax:* 310102.

MOSKOVSKY, Col-Gen. Aleksey Mikhailovich; Russian army officer; b. 1947, Smolensk; ed Kiev Higher Military Engineering Radio Technical School, Novosibirsk State Univ.; worked in devt and testing of armaments and mil. tech.; Deputy State Mil. Insp. of Russia, Sec. Council of Defence 1997–98; Deputy Sec. Russian Council of Security 1998–2001, supervised security in defence, tech. and scientific areas; Deputy Minister of Defence, Head of Armaments 2001–; State Prize of Russian Fed., Prize of Council of Ministers for devt of new weapons. *Address:* Ministry of Defence, Znamenka str. 19, 103160 Moscow, Russia (Office). *Telephone:* (095) 296-18-00 (Office).

MOSLEY, Max Rufus; British fmr motor racing driver and lawyer; b. 13 April 1940; s. of the late Sir Oswald Mosley and of the Hon. Lady Diana Mosley (née Freeman-Mitford); m. Jean Marjorie Taylor 1960; two s.; ed Christ Church Oxford; called to Bar (Gray's Inn) 1964; fmr Dir March Cars Ltd, Legal Adviser to Formula One Constructors Asscn, fmr Formula Two racing driver, Co-Founder March Grand Prix Team; Pres. Fed. Internationale du Sport Automobile (FISA) 1991–93, Fed. Int. de l'Automobile 1993–; Chair. Mfrs Comm. 1986–91; Hon. Pres. European Parl. Automobile Users Group 1994–99; Chair. European New Car Assessment Prog. 1997–; Vice-Chair. Supervisory Bd ERTICO Intelligence Transport System Europe 1999–2001, Chair. 2001–; Order of Merit (Italy) 1994, Order of Madarksi Kannik, First Degree (Bulgaria) 2000, Castrol/Inst. of the Motor Industry Gold Medal 2000, Quattroruote Premio Speciale per la Sicurezza Stradale (Italy) Gold Medal 2001, Der Goldene VdM-Dieselring (Germany) 2001. *Leisure interests:* walking, snowboarding. *Address:* Fédération Internationale de l'Automobile, 8 place de la Concorde, 75008 Paris, France. *E-mail:* mmosley@ait.fia.ch (Office). *Website:* www.fia.com (Office).

MOSLEY, Nicholas (see Ravensdale, 3rd Baron).

MOSLEY, Walter; American writer; b. 1952, Los Angeles; m. Joy Kellman; ed Johnson State Coll. *Publications include:* Devil in a Blue Dress 1990 (Shamus Award 1990, adapted into film 1995), A Red Death 1991, White Butterfly 1992, RL's Dream 1995, A Little Yellow Dog 1996, Gone Fishin' 1997, Always Outnumbered, Always Outgunned 1997, Bad Boy Brawly Brown 2002. *Address:* c/o W. W. Norton, 500 5th Avenue, Floor 6, New York, NY 10110, USA.

MOSS, Kate; British model; b. 16 Jan. 1974, Addiscombe; d. of Peter Edward Moss and Linda Rosina; partner Jefferson Hack; one d.; ed Croydon High School; has modelled for Face, Harpers and Queen, Vogue, Dolce & Gabana, Katherine Hamnett, Versace (q.v.), Yves Saint Laurent; exclusive contract world-wide with Calvin Klein (q.v.) 1992–; named Female Model of the Year

VH-1 Awards 1996. *Film:* Unzipped 1996. *Publication:* Kate 1994. *Address:* Storm Model Management, 1st Floor, 5 Jubilee Place, London, SW3 3TD, England. *Telephone:* (20) 7376-7764.

MOSS, Sir Stirling, Kt, OBE; British racing driver; b. 17 Sept. 1929, London; s. of Alfred Moss and Nora Aileen Moss; m. 1st Katherine Stuart Moson 1957 (divorced 1960); m. 2nd Elaine Barbarino 1964 (divorced 1968); one d.; m. 3rd Susie Paine 1980; one s.; ed Haileybury and Imperial Service Coll.; bought his first racing car, a Cooper 500, with prize money from show-jumping 1947; British Champion 1951; built his own car, the Cooper-Alta 1953; drove in H.W.M. Formula II Grand Prix team 1950, 1951, Jaguar team 1950, 1951; Leader of Maserati Grand Prix team 1954; mem. Mercedes team 1955; leader of Maserati Sports and Grand Prix teams 1956, Aston Martin team 1956; mem. Vanwall, Aston Martin, Maserati teams 1958; winner of Tourist Trophy (TT) race, UK 1950, 1951, 1953, 1955, 1958, 1959, 1960, 1961, Gold Coupe des Alpes (3 rallies without loss of marks) 1954, Italian Mille Miglia 1955, Sicilian Targa Florio 1955, 8 int. events including New Zealand, Monaco Grand Prix, Nurburgring 1,000 km. (FRG) 1956, Argentine 1,000 km. UK, Pescara (Italy), Moroccan Grand Prix 1957, 11 events incl. Argentine, Netherlands, Italian Grand Prix and Nurburgring 1,000 km. 1958, 19 events including New Zealand, Portuguese, U.S. Grand Prix 1959, 19 events including Cuban, Monaco, Austrian, S. African Grand Prix 1960, 27 events including Monaco, German, Pacific Grand Prix, Nassau Tourist Trophy 1961; competed in 529 events, finishing in 387, winning 211, during motor racing career 1947–62; retd from racing after accident at Goodwood, UK April 1962, attempted comeback 1980; subsequently took part in many business ventures, consultancy work on vehicle evaluation, property conversion, design; Man. Dir Stirling Moss Ltd; Dir 28 cos.; also journalism and lecturing; Pres. or Patron of 28 car clubs; Hon. FIE 1959; Gold Star, British Racing Drivers' Club 10 times 1950–61, Driver of the Year (Guild of Motoring Writers) (twice); Sir Malcolm Campbell Memorial Award 1957. *Publications include:* Stirling Moss 1953, In the Track of Speed 1957, Le Mans '59 1959, Design and Behaviour of the Racing Car 1963, All But My Life 1963, How to Watch Motor Racing 1975, Motor Racing and All That 1980, My Cars, My Career 1987, Stirling Moss: Great Drives in the Lakes and Dales 1993, Motor Racing Masterpieces 1995, Stirling Moss (autobiog.) 2001. *Leisure interests:* water and snow skiing, theatre and cinema, designing houses, model making, motor trials, historic racing, swimming, interior decorating, woodwork, horse jumping and riding. *Address:* c/o Stirling Moss Ltd, 46 Shepherd Street, Mayfair, London, W1Y 8JN (Office); 44 Shepherd Street, London, W1Y 8JN, England (Home). *Telephone:* (20) 7499-3272/7967. *Fax:* (20) 7499-4104. *E-mail:* stirlingmossltd@aol.com (Office).

MÖSSBAUER, Rudolf L., PhD; German physicist; b. 31 Jan. 1929, Munich; s. of Ludwig Mössbauer and Erna Mössbauer; m.; one s. two d.; ed Tech. Hochschule, Munich; Research Asst Max-Planck Inst., Heidelberg 1955–57; Research Fellow, Tech. Hochschule, Munich 1958–60; Research Fellow, Calif. Inst. of Tech. 1960, Sr Research Fellow 1961, Prof. of Physics Dec. 1961; Prof. of Experimental Physics, Tech. Univ. of Munich 1964–72, 1977–97, Prof. Emer. 1997–; Dir Inst. Max von Laue and of German-French-British High Flux Reactor, Grenoble, France 1972–77; Foreign mem. American Acad. of Arts and Sciences, Accad. Nazionale di Roma; mem. Deutsche Physische Gesellschaft, Deutsche Gesellschaft der Naturforscher, Leopoldina, American Physical Soc., European Physical Soc., Indian Acad. of Sciences, American Acad. of Sciences, NAS, Acad. of Sciences of the USSR, Pontifical Acad. of Sciences, Hungarian Acad. of Sciences; Hon. DSc (Oxford) 1973, (Lille) 1973, (Leicester) 1975, (Birmingham) 1999; Dr hc (Grenoble) 1974; Research Corpn Award 1960, Röntgen Prize, Univ. of Giessen 1961, Elliot Cresson Medal of Franklin Inst., Philadelphia 1961, Nobel Prize for Physics 1961; Grosses Bundesverdienstkreuz. *Publications:* papers on recoilless nuclear resonance absorption and on neutrino physics. *Leisure interests:* piano, hiking, photography, languages. *Address:* Fachbereich Physik, Physik Department E 15, Technische Universität Munich, D-85747 Garching, Germany (Office). *Telephone:* (89) 28912522 (Office). *Fax:* (89) 28912680 (Office). *E-mail:* beatrice.vbellen@ph.tum.de (Office). *Website:* www.e15.physik .tu-muenchen.de (Office).

MOSTELLER, Frederick, MA, PhD; American professor of mathematical statistics; b. 24 Dec. 1916, Clarksburg, Va; s. of William R. Mosteller and Helen (Kelley) Mosteller; m. Virginia Gilroy 1941; one s. one d.; ed Carnegie Inst. of Tech. and Princeton Univ.; Instructor in Math. Princeton Univ. 1942–43, Research Mathematician 1944–45; Lecturer, Dept of Social Relations Harvard Univ. 1946–48, Assoc. Prof. 1948–51, Prof. of Mathematical Statistics 1951–87, Prof. Emer. 1987–, Chair. Dept of Statistics 1957–69, 1975–77, Chair. Dept of Biostatistics, School of Public Health 1977–81, Chair. Dept of Health Policy & Man. Harvard School of Public Health 1981–87, Roger I. Lee Prof. 1978–87, Dir. Tech. Assessment Group 1987–, Dir Center for Evaluation American Acad. of Arts and Sciences 1994–; mem. Faculty, Harvard Medical School 1977–; Miller Research Prof. Univ. of Calif. at Berkeley 1974–75; Charles M. and Martha Hitchcock Prof. Univ. of Calif. at Berkeley 1984–85; mem. American Acad. of Arts and Sciences, American Philosophical Soc., NAS, Royal Statistical Soc.; five hon. degrees; Myrdal Prize 1978, Lazarsfeld Prize 1979; S. S. Wilks Award 1986, R. A. Fisher Award 1987. *Publications:* articles in related field and co-author of numerous books. *Address:* Department of Statistics, Harvard University, 1 Oxford Street, Cambridge, MA 02138, USA. *Telephone:* (617) 495-2583.

MOTEJL, Otakar, DIur; Czech judge and politician; b. 10 Sept. 1932, Prague; s. of Jirí Motejl and Eliška Motejl; m. Anna Motejl (died 1995); one d.; ed Charles Univ., Prague; solicitor in Banska Bystrica, Slovakia 1955–1966, later in Kladno and Prague; researcher Law Inst., Ministry of Justice 1966–1968; Judge, Supreme Court of Prague 1968–1970; resumed law practice 1970–89; mem. Cttee for Investigation of Events of 17 Nov. 1989 (Velvet Revolution); Pres. Supreme Court of Czech and Slovak Fed. Repub. 1990–92, Supreme Court of Czech Repub. 1993–98; Minister of Justice 1998–2000; Ombudsman 2000–; Commdr., Légion d'Honneur 2000. *Publications include:* articles in law journals. *Leisure interests:* literature, music. *Address:* Office of the Ombudsman, Údolní 39, 60200 Brno (Office); Mělnická 1, 15500 Prague 5, Czech Republic (Home). *Telephone:* (5) 42542111 (Office). *Fax:* (5) 42542112 (Office). *E-mail:* kancelar@ochrance.cz (Office). *Website:* www.ochrance.cz (Office).

MOTION, Andrew, M.LITT., FRSA; British biographer and poet; b. 26 Oct. 1952; s. of Andrew R. Motion and Catherine G. Motion; m. 1st Joanna J. Powell 1973 (dissolved 1983); m. 2nd Janet Elisabeth Dalley 1985; two s. one d.; ed Radley Coll. and Univ. Coll., Oxford; Lecturer in English, Univ. of Hull 1977–81; Ed. Poetry Review 1981–83; Poetry Ed. Chatto & Windus 1983–89, Editorial Dir 1985–87; Prof. of Creative Writing Univ. of E Anglia, Norwich 1995–2003; Chair. Literature Advisory Panel Arts Council of England 1996–98; Hon. DLitt (Hull) 1996, (Exeter) 1999, (Brunel) 2000, (A.P.U.) 2001, (Open Univ.) 2002; Rhys Memorial Prize for Dangerous Play 1984, Somerset Maugham Award for The Lamberts 1987, Whitbread Biography Award 1993; Poet Laureate 1999. *Publications:* poetry: The Pleasure Steamers 1978, Independence 1981, The Penguin Book of Contemporary British Poetry (anthology) 1982, Secret Narratives 1983, Dangerous Play 1984, Natural Causes 1987, Love in a Life 1991, The Price of Everything 1994, Selected Poems 1996–97 1998, Horn to Eternity (autobiog.) 2000, Public Property 2001; criticism: The Poetry of Edward Thomas 1981, Philip Larkin 1982, William Barnes Selected Poems (ed.) 1994, Salt Water 1997; biography: The Lamberts 1986, Philip Larkin: A Writer's Life 1993, Keats 1997, Wainewright the Poisoner 2000; novel: The Invention of Dr Cake 2003. *Leisure interest:* filming. *Address:* c/o Dept of English and American Studies, University of East Anglia, Norwich, NR4 7TJ; c/o Faber & Faber, 3 Queen Square, London, WC1N 3AU, England.

MOTLANA, Nthato Harrison, BSc, MB, B.CH.; South African community worker and medical practitioner; b. 1925, Marapyane, Pretoria Dist; m. Sally Maunye 1953; three s. one d.; ed Kilnerla High School and Univs. of Fort Hare and Witwatersrand; Sec. ANC Youth League 1949; participated in ANC Defiance Campaign 1952; arrested, received suspended sentence, banned for five years 1952–57; Resident Houseman, Baragwanath Hosp. 1955–56, subsequently Medical Officer; own medical practice 1957–; Founder mem. Black Community Programmes 1972; Vice-Chair. Black Parents Asscn 1976; detained for six months 1976; Chair. Cttee of Ten est. to organize civic affairs in Soweto 1977; imprisoned 1977–78; Pres. Soweto Civic Assocn; active in campaign to ban Black Local Authority Election 1983; frequent guest of overseas govts.; Chair. Population Devt Council of S. Africa 1993–, Metropolitan Life 1993–, Corporate Africa, Metlife Holdings 1993–, etc.; numerous other professional and public appts.; Dr. hc (Dartmouth, USA); Citation for Outstanding Community Services (Univ. of Witwatersrand). *Address:* c/o Metropolitan Life Ltd, 7 Coen Steytler Avenue, Foreshore, Cape Town, South Africa.

MOTSPAN, Dumitru; Moldovan politician; b. 3 May 1940, Selishte vill.; engineer, worked as head agric. enterprises, head local admin.; Chair. Agrarian-Democratic Party; Deputy Chair. of Parl. 1994–97, Chair. 1997–2000. *Address:* Parliament House, Stefan Celmari prosp. 105, 277033 Chișinău, Moldova (Office). *Telephone:* (2) 23-25-28 (Office).

MOTSUENYANE, Samuel Mokgethi, B.SC.(AGRIC.); South African business executive; b. 11 Feb. 1927, Potchefstroom; s. of the late Solomon P. Motsuenyane and Christina D. Motsuenyane; m. Jocelyn Mashinini 1954; six s.; ed N Carolina State Univ., USA, Jan Hofmeyr School of Social Work; Nat. Organizing Sec. African Nat. Soil Conservation Assocn 1952–59; NC State Univ., USA 1960–62; Pres. NAFCOC 1968–92; Chair. African Business Publications, African Business Holdings, NAFCOC Permanent, Venda Nat. Devt Corpn, New-Real African Investments; Dir African Devt and Construction Holdings, NAFCOC Nat. Trust, Barlow Rand, Blackchain Ltd, numerous other cos.; Chancellor, Univ. of the North (SA) 1985–90; Pres. Motsuenyane Comm. to investigate torture and disappearances in ANC detention camps 1992–93; Pres. Boy Scouts of SA 1976–81; Leader of Senate 1994–96; serves on bds. of numerous cos. and orgs.; Dr. hc (Univ. of Witwatersrand) 1983; Hon. D.Econ.Sc. (Cape Town) 1986; Harvard Business Award 1977. *Publications:* numerous articles. *Leisure interests:* gardening, reading. *Address:* P.O. Box 911407, Rosslyn 0200, South Africa.

MOTTISTONE, Lord, 4th Baron, cr. 1933, of Mottistone; **David Peter Seely,** CBE, FIEE, FCIPD; British naval officer (retd); b. 16 Dec. 1920, London; s. of Maj.-Gen. J. E. B. Seely, 1st Lord Mottistone and Lady Mottistone (née Murray) of Elibank; m. Anthea Christine McMullan 1944; two s. three d. (one deceased); ed Royal Naval Colls., Dartmouth and Greenwich; promoted to Commdr, RN 1955, Special Asst NATO Chief of Allied Staff, Malta 1956–58, in command HMS Cossack 1958–59, rank of Capt. RN 1960, Deputy Dir Signals Div., Admiralty 1961–63, in command HMS Ajax and 24th Escort Squadron 1964–65, Naval Adviser to UK High Commr, Ottawa 1965–66, retd

from RN in protest at govt.'s defence policy 1967; Peer of Parl. 1966–99; Dir of Personnel and Training, Radio Rentals Group of Cos. 1967–69; Dir Distributive Industries Training Bd 1969–75, Cake & Biscuit Alliance 1975–82; Lord Lt of Isle of Wight 1986–95, Gov., Capt. and Steward of Isle of Wight 1992–95; KStJ; Hon. DLitt (Bournemouth) 1994. *Leisure interest:* yachting. *Address:* The Old Parsonage, Mottistone, Isle of Wight, PO30 4EE, England.

MOTTRAM, Sir Richard Clive, KCB, BA; British civil servant; b. 23 April 1946; s. of John Mottram and Florence Yates; m. Fiona Margaret Erskine 1971; three s. one d.; ed King Edward VI Camp Hill School, Birmingham, Univ. of Keele; joined Civil Service 1968, assigned to Ministry of Defence, Asst Pvt. Sec. to Sec. of State for Defence 1971–72, Prin. Naval Programme and Budget 1973, Cabinet Office 1975–77, Pvt. Sec. to Perm. Under-Sec., Ministry of Defence 1979–81, Pvt. Sec. to Sec. of State for Defence 1982–86, Asst Under-Sec. of State (programmes) 1986–89, Deputy Under-Sec. of State (Policy) 1989–92, Perm. Sec. Office of Public Service and Science, Cabinet Office 1992–95, Ministry of Defence 1995–98, Dept of the Environment, Transport and the Regions 1998–2001, Dept for Transport, Local Govt and the Regions 2001–; Hon. DLitt (Keele) 1996. *Leisure interests:* cinema, theatre, tennis. *Address:* Department for Transport, Local Government and the Regions, 6th Floor, Eland House, Bressenden Place, London, SW1E 5DU, England.

MOTULSKY, Arno Gunther, BS, MD; American medical geneticist; b. 5 July 1923, Germany; s. of Herman Motulsky and Rena (née Sass) Motulsky; m. Gretel Stern 1945; one s. two d.; ed YMCA Coll., Chicago, Yale Univ., Univ. of Illinois Medical School; Intern, Fellow, Asst and Sr Resident (Internal Medicine) Michael Reese Hosp., Chicago 1947–51; Staff mem. in charge of Clinical Investigation, Dept of Hematology, Army Medical Service Graduate School, Walter Reed Army Medical Center; Research Assoc. in Internal Medicine, George Washington Univ. School of Medicine, Washington 1952–53, Instructor 1953–55, Asst Prof. 1955–58, Assoc. Prof. 1958–61, Prof. Dept of Medicine 1961–, Prof. Dept of Genetics 1961–, Dir Medical Genetics Training Program 1961–89, Dir Center for Inherited Diseases 1972–89; Prof. Emer. of Medicine and Genetics 1994–; Pres. Int. Congress of Human Genetics 1986; Ed. American Journal of Human Genetics 1969–75, Human Genetics 1969–98; mem. American Soc. of Human Genetics, NAS 1976, American Acad. of Arts and Sciences 1978; Hon. DSc (Illinois) 1982; Hon. MD (Würzburg) 1991; William Allan Memorial Award 1970, Alexander von Humboldt Award 1984, San Remo Int. Prize for Genetic Research 1988; Excellence in Educ. Award 1999. *Publications:* Human Genetics—Problems and Approaches (with F. Vogel) 1996; more than 300 medical and scientific articles. *Leisure interests:* reading, collecting African art, antique maps. *Address:* University of Washington, Medicine and Genome Sciences, Health Sciences Bldg K336-B, PO Box 357730, Seattle, WA 98195-7730 (Office); 4347 53rd NE, Seattle, WA 98105, USA (Home). *Telephone:* (206) 543-3593 (Office). *Fax:* (206) 616-4196 (Office). *E-mail:* agmot@u.washington.edu (Office).

MOTYL, Vladimir Yakovlevich; Russian film director; b. 26 June 1927, Lepel, Belarus; s. of Yakov Motyl and Vera Levina; m. Ludmila Podaruyeva; one d.; ed Sverdlovsk Inst. of Theatre, Ural State Univ.; Chief Stage Dir Sverdlovsk Theatre of Young Spectators 1955–57; work in cinema 1957–; mem. Exec. Bd Union of Cinematographers; Sec. Union of Cinematographers of Moscow; Founder film studio Serial; Artistic Dir Higher Courses for Scriptwriters and Film Dirs. 1995–; State Prize of Russian Fed. 1997, Prize of the Union of Cinematographers 1963, Prize of All-Union Film Festival 1964, Hon. Diploma Best Films of the World, Int. Film Festival, Belgrade 1977, Prize of Golden Ostap Film Festival, St Petersburg 1995; Merited Worker of Arts 1992. *Films:* Children of Tamir 1963, Zhenya, Zhenechka and Katyusha (jtly.), White Sun of the Desert 1969, The Star of Wonderful Happiness 1975, Forest 1980, Let Us Part As Long As We Are Good 1991, The Horses Are Carrying Me 1996. *Television:* Once There Lived Shishlov... 1987. *Leisure interests:* travelling, history, sciences. *Address:* Higher Courses for Scriptwriters and Film Directors, Bolshoi Tishinsky per. 12, 123557 Moscow (Office); Dovzhenko str. 12, korp. 1, Apt. 45, 119590 Moscow, Russia (Home). *Telephone:* (095) 253-64-88 (Office); (095) 143-68-00 (Home).

MOTZFELDT, Jonathan; Greenlandic politician; b. 25 Sept. 1938, Qassimut, Greenland; m. Kristjana Gudrum Gudmundsdóttir 1992; ed Greenland Teacher's College, Univ. of Copenhagen; teacher; Lutheran pastor; mem. and Vice-Chair. Greenland Ass. 1971–79; mem. Greenland Parl. (Landsting) 1979–, Chair. 1979–88, 1997, 2002–; Prime Minister of Greenland 1979–91, 1997–2002; Co-Founder Siumut Party, Chair. 1977–79, 1980–87, 1998–2001; Hon. Dr rer. pol (Fairbanks USA); Nersornaat in gold, K; Ordre de la Couronne (Belgium) and other foreign decorations and medals. *Address:* Greenland Home Rule Government, PO Box 1015, 3900 Nuuk, Greenland. *Telephone:* 395000. *Fax:* 325002. *Website:* www.homerule.gl (Office).

MOTZFELDT, Joseph; Greenlandic politician; b. 1941; trained as teacher; Minister of Trade and Traffic 1984–88; mem. Parl. 1987–; Chair. Inuit Ataqatigiit Party 1994–; Minister of Finance 1999–2001; Minister of Economy (Greenland Home Rule Govt.) Dec. 2002–Jan. 2003. *Address:* Greenland Home Rule Government, POB 1015, 3900 Nuuk, Greenland (Office). *Telephone:* 395000 (Office). *Fax:* 325002 (Office). *Website:* www.homerule.gl (Office).

MOUBARAK, Samir, PhD; Lebanese diplomatist; b. 23 March 1943, Beirut; s. of Moussa Moubarak and Nada Aboussouan; ed Ecole des Hautes Etudes Commerciales, Paris, Sorbonne, Paris; Political Section, Ministry of Foreign

Affairs, Beirut 1967–69; mem. Lebanese Del., Perm. Mission of Lebanon to UN, New York 1969–73; First Sec., Embassy, Paris 1973–77, Chargé d'affaires a.i., Embassy, Madrid; Special Adviser to Minister of Foreign Affairs, Beirut 1977–82; Amb. to Sweden 1982–88, to Spain 1999–; Amb., Ministry of Foreign Affairs 1988–94; Perm. Rep. of Lebanon to UN, New York 1994–99, Vice-Pres. 50th Session UN Gen. Ass. 1995, Vice-Pres. ECOSOC, New York 1996. *Address:* Lebanese Embassy, Paseo de la Castellana 178, 3° Izqda, 28046 Madrid, Spain. *Telephone:* (91) 3451368. *Fax:* (91) 3455631. *E-mail:* leem_e@teleline.es (Office).

MOUGEOTTE, Etienne Pierre Albert; French journalist; b. 1 March 1940, La Rochefoucauld; s. of Jean Mougeotte and Marcelle Thonon; m. Françoise Duprilot 1972; one s. two d.; ed Lycée Buffon, Lycée Henri-IV, Paris, Inst. d'études politiques de Paris, Inst. Français de presse; reporter France-Inter 1965-66, Beirut Corresp. 1966–67; Ed. Europe Numéro 1 1968–69; Chief Reporter, Asst Ed.-in-Chief Information Première (TV) 1969–72; Producer l'Actualité en question 1972; journalist Radio-Télé Luxembourg 1972–73; Ed.-in-Chief Europe 1 1973, News Dir 1974–81; monthly contrib. Paradoxes 1974–; Editorial Dir Journal du Dimanche 1981–83, Télé 7 Jours 1983–87; Dir Gen. Broadcasting TF1 1987–89, Dir Gen. 1987–89, Vice-Pres. Broadcasting 1989–; Vice-Pres. French Fed. of Press Agencies 1975–81; mem. Interprofessional communication group (Gic) 1985–87; Pres. Nat. Videocommunication Syndicate 1982–87, TF1 Films, Tricom; Dir TF1 1991–; Pres. TF1 Films Productions; Dir TFI Films 1991–, Pres. TFI Films and TFI Digital 2000–; Officier Légion d'honneur, Ordre nat. du Mérite. *Leisure interests:* tennis, golf. *Address:* TF1, 1 quai du Point-du-Jour, 92656 Boulogne-Billancourt cedex, France.

MOULAERT, Jacques, LLD, MPA; Belgian banker; b. 23 Oct. 1930, Ostend; s. of the late Albert Moulaert and of Marie de Neckere; m. Christiane Laloux 1957; four d.; ed St Barbara Coll. Ghent, Univ. of Ghent and Harvard Univ.; Gen. Sec. Aleurope SA 1961; Asst Man. Compagnie Lambert 1967; Man. Compagnie Bruxelles Lambert (CBL) 1972; Man. Dir Groupe Bruxelles Lambert 1979; Chair. Bd Bank Brussels Lambert (BBL) 1993–; Officier, Ordre de la Couronne; Commdr, Ordre de St-Sylvestre; Commdr, Ordre de Léopold. *Address:* Bank Brussels Lambert, 24 avenue Marnix, 1000 Brussels, Belgium (Office). *Telephone:* (2) 547-21-11 (Office). *Fax:* (2) 547-38-44 (Office). *E-mail:* info@bbl.be (Office). *Website:* www.bbl.be (Office).

MOULAYE, Mohamed, DSc; Mauritanian politician and public official; b. 1 Oct. 1936, Ouagadougou, Burkina Faso; s. of El Hassan Moulaye and Maimouna Dem; m. Ginette Marcin 1962; three s. five d.; Founder-mem. Asscn de la Jeunesse de Mauritanie (AJM) 1956; Sec.-Gen. Section P.R.M. Boutilimit 1960; mem. Nat. Ass. 1965–75; Directeur des finances 1966; Contrôleur financier 1967–75; Minister of Finance 1975–77, 1979; Parl. rapporteur to Comm. des Finances; fmr mem. IPU; Dir Office of Pres. of Mauritania 1979–80; Conseiller Econ. et Financier du Chef de l'Etat, Prés. de la Comm. Centrale des Marchés Publics; Pres. Parti du Centre démocratique mauritanien 1992, now Democratic Centre Party (DCP); First Vice-Pres. Action pour le Changement; mem. Conseil général, Banque Centrale de Mauritanie 1980–; Dir Personnel Air Afrique, Financial Dir 1985–; Chair. and Man. Dir Arrachad, Nouackchott 1990; Chevalier, Ordre nat. du mérite (France). *Leisure interests:* reading, cinema. *Address:* B.P. 289, Nouackchott, Mauritania.

MOULE, Rev. Charles Francis Digby, CBE, FBA; British university professor (retd) and ecclesiastic; b. 3 Dec. 1908, Hangchow, China; s. of Henry W. Moule and Laura C. Pope; ed Weymouth Coll., Dorset, Emmanuel Coll., Cambridge and Ridley Hall; ordained deacon 1933, priest 1934; Tutor, Ridley Hall 1933–34; Curate, St Andrew's, Rugby 1934–36; Vice-Prin., Ridley Hall 1936–44; Fellow, Clare Coll., Cambridge 1944–, Dean 1944–51; Asst Lecturer in Divinity, Univ. of Cambridge 1944–47, Lecturer 1947–51, Lady Margaret's Prof. 1951–76; Hon. Fellow, Emmanuel Coll., Cambridge; Hon. DD (St Andrews), (Cambridge); Collins Biennial Book Prize; Burkitt Medal (British Acad.). *Publications:* Idiom Book of New Testament Greek 1953, Commentary on Colossians and Philemon 1957, The Birth of the New Testament 1962, The Origin of Christology 1977, Essays in New Testament Interpretation 1982, Forgiveness and Reconciliation 1998. *Address:* 1 King's Houses, Pevensey, East Sussex, BN24 5JR, England. *Telephone:* (1323) 762436.

MOULINE, Larbi; Moroccan business executive, diplomatist and consultant; b. 10 Nov. 1934, Rabat; s. of Mohamed Mouline and Habiba Balafrej; m. Naima Mouline 1959; three s. one d.; ed Ecole Nat. Supérieure des Mines, St Etienne, France; Man. Dir O.C.P. (phosphate co.) 1959–74, Pres. Amicale des Hors-Cadres; Gen. Man. Sonasid (steel co.) 1975–83; Amb. to India 1984–86, to Greece 1987–88; Adviser to Minister of Privatization and Econ. Affairs, Minister of Agric. 1989–94; now pvt. consultant; Sec.-Gen. Asscn des Intervenants Scientifiques (ASSIST), Rabat; Kt of the Throne (Morocco); Order of Phoenix (Greece). *Publications:* A Study on Economic Development Linked to a Steel Complex in Morocco 1977, A Study on Mechanization in Phosphate Mines. *Leisure interests:* reading, music, golf, travel. *Address:* 27 rue Cadi Sanhaji, Souissi, Rabat, Morocco. *Telephone:* (37) 750282. *Fax:* (37) 639501. *E-mail:* imouline@iam.net.ma (Home).

MOULTON, Alexander Eric, CBE, R.D.I., MA, F.R.ENG., FIMechE, F.P.R.I., FRSA; British engineer; b. 9 April 1920, Stratford-on-Avon; s. of John Coney Moulton and Beryl Latimer Moulton; ed Marlborough Coll., King's Coll., Cambridge; worked in Engine Research Dept, Bristol Aeroplane Co. 1939–44, Personal

Asst to Sir Roy Fedden 1940–42; est. Research Dept of George Spencer, Moulton & Co. Ltd, originating work on rubber suspensions for vehicles and designing Flexitor, Works Man. then Tech. Dir 1945–56; f. Moulton Devts. Ltd, Man. Dir 1956–, Devt work on own designs of rubber suspensions including Hydrolastic and Hydragas 1956, Chair. 1956–67, Man. Dir 1956–; designed Moulton Coach; f. Moulton Bicycles Ltd to produce own design Moulton Bicycle 1962, Chair. and Man. Dir 1962–67, Dir 1967–; Dir Alex Moulton Ltd; Dir SW Regional Bd, Nat. Westminster Bank 1982–87; Hon. Dr. RCA; Hon. DSc (Bath); Design Centre Award 1964, Amb. Award 1964, Bidlake Memorial Plaque 1964, Gold Medal Milan Triennale 1964, Queens Award to Industry for Tech. Innovation (Moulton Devts. Ltd) 1967, Soc. of Industrial Artists and Designers Design Medal 1976, Council of the Inst. of Mechanical Engineers James Clayton Prize, Crompton Lanchester Medal (from Automobile Div.), Thomas Hawksley Gold Medal, 1979. *Publications:* various papers on vehicle suspension. *Leisure interests:* steamboating, canoeing, cycling, shooting. *Address:* The Hall, Bradford-on-Avon, Wiltshire, BA15 1AJ, England. *Telephone:* (1225) 862991.

MOUNGAR, Fidèle; Chadian politician and medical practitioner; b. Logone Region; fmr head of surgery, Peronne Hosp., Somme, France; Prime Minister of Chad 1993; currently leader Action tchadienne pour l'unité et le socialisme (ACTUS), Collectif des partis pour le changement (COPAC). *Address:* Action tchadienne pour l'unité et le socialisme, N'Djamena, Chad.

MOUNT, (William Robert) Ferdinand, FRSL; British author and journalist; b. 2 July 1939, London; s. of the late Robert Mount and Julia Mount; m. Julia Lucas 1968; two s. one d.; ed Eton Coll., Christ Church, Oxford; Political Ed. The Spectator 1977–82, 1985, Literary Ed. 1984–85; Head Prime Minister's Policy Unit 1982–84; Political Columnist, The Times 1984–85, Daily Telegraph 1985–90; Ed. Times Literary Supplement 1991–2002; Sr Columnist The Sunday Times 2002–; Fellow RSL 1991, Council 2002–; Hon. Fellow (Univ. of Wales Lampeter) 2002; Hawthornden Prize (for Of Love and Asthma) 1992. *Publications:* Very Like a Whale 1967, The Theatre of Politics 1972, The Man Who Rode Ampersand 1975, The Clique 1978, The Subversive Family 1982, The Selkirk Strip 1987, Of Love and Asthma 1991, The British Constitution Now 1992, Communism 1992, Umbrella 1994, The Liquidator 1995, Jem (and Sam) 1998, Fairness 2001. *Address:* 17 Ripplevale Grove, London, N1 1HS, England. *Telephone:* (20) 7607-5398.

MOUNTCASTLE, Vernon Benjamin, MD; American neurophysiologist (retd) and educator; b. 15 July 1918, Shelbyville, Ky; s. of Vernon B. Mountcastle and Anna-Francis Marguerite Waugh; m. Nancy Clayton Pierpont 1945; two s. one d.; ed Roanoke Coll., Salem, Va and Johns Hopkins Univ. School of Medicine; House Officer, Surgery, The Johns Hopkins Hosp. Baltimore, Md 1943; with USN Amphibious Forces 1943–46; through jr ranks, The Johns Hopkins Univ. School of Medicine 1948–59, Prof. of Physiology 1959, Dir of Dept of Physiology 1964–80, Univ. Prof. of Neuroscience 1980–92, Prof. Emer. 1992; Dir Bard Labs of Neurophysiology, Johns Hopkins Univ. 1981–91; Pres. Neurosciences Research Foundation 1981–85; Dir Neuroscience Research Program 1981–84; Penfield Lecturer, American Univ., Beirut 1971; Sherrington Lecturer, Liverpool Univ. 1974; Sherrington Lecturer, Royal Soc. of Medicine, London, Mellon Lecturer, Univ. of Pittsburgh 1976, Visiting Prof. Collège de France, Paris 1980 and numerous other hon. lectureships; Nat. Pres. Soc. for Neuroscience 1971–72; mem. NAS, American Acad. of Arts and Sciences, American Phil. Soc.; Foreign Fellow, Royal Soc. (UK); Hon. DSc (Pa) 1976, (Roanoke) 1968, (Northwestern) 1985; Hon. MD (Zurich) 1983, (Siena) 1984; Lashley Prize, American Phil. Soc. 1974, F. O. Schmitt Prize and Medal, MIT 1975, Gold Medal, Royal Soc. of Medicine 1976, Horwitz Prize, Columbia 1978, Gerard Prize, Soc. for Neuroscience 1980, Int. Prize, Fyssen Foundation Paris 1983, Lasker Award 1983, Nat. Medal of Sciences 1986, McGovern Prize and Medal, AAAS 1990, Neuroscience Award Fidia Fed. 1990, Australia Prize 1993, Neuroscience Prize, NAS 1998. *Publications:* The Mindful Brain (with G. M. Edelman) 1978, Medical Physiology (two vols) (ed. and major contrib.) 14th edn 1980, Perceptual Neuroscience: The Cerebral Cortex 1998 and more than 50 articles in scientific journals on the physiology of the central nervous system especially on the neuronal mechanisms in sensation and perception. *Leisure interests:* sailing, horsemanship. *Address:* The Krieger Mind-Brain Institute, Johns Hopkins University, 3400 N Charles Street, Baltimore, MD 21218 (Office); 15601 Carroll Road, Monkton, MD 21111, USA (Home). *Telephone:* (410) 516-4271 (Office); (410) 472-2514 (Home). *Fax:* (410) 516-8648 (Office). *E-mail:* vernon@fastfire.mb.jhu.edu (Office).

MOUNTER, Julian D'Arcy; British journalist, television director, producer and broadcasting executive; b. 2 Nov. 1944, Cornwall; s. of Francis Mounter and Elizabeth Moore; m. Patricia A. Kelsall-Spurr 1983; two s.; ed Skinners Grammar School, Tunbridge Wells and Grenville Coll.; reporter various local newspapers 1961–65; journalist The Times 1966–71; Weekend World, London Weekend TV 1971–73; Head of Current Affairs and Documentaries, Westward TV 1973–74; Reporter/Dir. Panorama and Midweek, BBC TV 1974–78; Ed., Inside Business, Thames TV 1978–79, Exec. Producer, Current Affairs 1979–81, Controller, Children's and Young Adults' Dept 1981–84; Dir Programmes and Production, Thorn–EMI Satellite and Cable 1984–86; Dir Cosgrove Hall Ltd 1981–84, JRA Ltd 1980–85, Cameralink Ltd 1980–85, Blackwell Videotec Ltd 1980–85; Dir-Gen. and CEO Television New Zealand 1986–91; Chair. South Pacific Pictures Ltd, Broadcast Communications Ltd 1988–91; Dir The Listener, Visnews (UK) Ltd 1987–89, Reuters TV Ltd 1989–91; Chief Exec. and Pres. Star TV Ltd Hutchvision Ltd, Media Assets

Ltd, Asia News Ltd 1992–93; Chair. New Media Investments 1994–98, Majestic Films and TV Ltd 1993–95, Swoffers Ltd 1995–96, Renown Leisure Group Ltd 1995–; CEO and Man. Dir Seven Network Ltd 1998–2000; Dir CTV Ltd; 1994–99; Trustee Int. Inst. of Communications 1988–95; Dir Int. Council of Nat. Acad. of Television Arts and Sciences, USA 1993–; Queen's Medal 1990, for Services to NZ; Jt Winner, IPC Investigative Journalism Award; various TV awards. *Leisure interests:* ocean sailing, naval history, music. *Address:* c/o Seven Network Ltd, Television Centre, Mobbs Lane, Epping, NSW 2121, Australia.

MOUREAUX, Philippe; Belgian politician; b. 12 April 1939, Etterbeek; m.; four c.; secondary school teacher 1961–62; Asst, subsequently Prof., Université Libre de Bruxelles 1967–; Adviser, Deputy Prime Minister's Office 1972–73, on staff Prime Minister's Office 1973–74, Chef de cabinet to Deputy Prime Minister 1977–80, Minister of the Interior and Institutional Reforms 1980, of Justice and Institutional Reforms 1980–81, Minister and Chair. Exec. of French Community, responsible for cultural affairs, budget and foreign affairs 1981–85, Feb.–May 1988, Deputy Prime Minister and Minister for the Brussels Region and Institutional Reforms 1988–89, 1990–92, of Social Affairs 1992–93.

MOUSAWI, Faisal Radhi al-, MB, B.CH., FRCSE; Bahraini government minister and orthopaedic surgeon; b. 6 April 1944, Bahrain; one s. three d.; ed Univ. of Cairo, Egypt; fmr Rotary Intern., Cairo Univ. Hosp., House Officer, Sr House Officer, Dept of Surgery, Govt Hosp., Bahrain, Sr House Officer, Accident and Orthopaedic Surgery, Cen. Middx Hosp., London, Orthopaedic Surgery, St Helier Hosp., Carshalton, Surrey, Gen. Surgery, Nelson Hosp., London, St Bartholomew's Hosp., London, registrar, Orthopaedic Surgery, Whittington Hosp., London, Gen. and Traumatic Surgery, Wexford Co. Hosp., Ireland; locum consultant, Whittington Hosp. 1983–84; consultant Orthopaedic Surgeon, Salmaniya Medical Centre, Bahrain 1976–, Chair. Dept of Surgery 1982–84, Chief of Medical Staff June–Aug. 1982, Chair. Dept of Orthopaedic Surgery; Asst Prof. Coll. of Medicine and Medical Sciences, Arabian Gulf Univ.; Asst Under-Sec., Ministry of Health 1982–85, Minister of Health 1995–; mem. Scientific Council, Arab Bd for Surgery 1979–; Chair. Arab Bd Cttee for Sub-specialities in Surgery, Arab Bd for Orthopaedic Surgery 1990–, Chair. Training Cttee 1988–; Chair. Nat. Arab Bd Cttee and Co-ordinator, Arab Bd Programme in Surgery, Bahrain; Examiner, Ministry of Health Qualification Examination 1982–, Royal Coll. of Surgeons, Ireland, Part B Fellowship Examination; mem. Editorial Bd Bahrain Medical Bulletin; Pres. Gulf Orthopaedic Asscn; mem. European Soc. for Sport Medicine, Knee Surgery and Arthroscopy; Fellow British Orthopaedic Asscn, Royal Coll. of Surgeons, Ireland. *Publications:* numerous papers and articles. *Leisure interest:* tennis. *Address:* Ministry of Health, P.O. Box 12, Sheikh Sulman Road, Manama, Bahrain. *Telephone:* 289810. *Fax:* 289864. *E-mail:* hid1@ batelco.com.bh (Office). *Website:* www.batelco.com.bh/mhealth (Office).

MOUSKOURI, Nana (Joanna); Greek singer; b. 13 Oct. 1936, Canea; m. 1st George Petsilas (divorced); one s. one d.; m. 2nd Andre Chapelle 2003; ed Athens Nat. Conservatory; several gold albums since 1959, also over 300 gold and platinum records world-wide; living in Paris 1962–; UNICEF Amb. 1993–94; MEP 1994–99; Greek Broadcasting Festival Award 1959, Barcelona Festival Award and numerous awards and prizes. *Address:* c/o Polygram, 20 rue des Fossés Saint-Jacques, 75005 Paris, France; Aharnon 289, GR112 53, Athens, Greece. *Telephone:* (1) 8561902 (Greece). *Fax:* (1) 9600555.

MOUSSA, Amr Muhammad, LLB; Egyptian politician and diplomatist; b. 3 Oct. 1936, Cairo; ed Cairo Univ.; joined Ministry of Foreign Affairs 1957; served in several diplomatic posts abroad, including Amb. to India 1987–90; Perm. Rep. to the U.N. 1990–91; Minister of Foreign Affairs 1991–2001; Sec.-Gen. Arab League March 2001–. *Address:* Arab League, P.O. Box 11642, Tahrir Square, Cairo, Egypt (Office). *Telephone:* (2) 5750511 (Office). *Fax:* (2) 5775626 (Office).

MOUSSA, Pierre L.; French banker; b. 5 March 1922, Lyon; m. Anne-Marie Trousseau 1957; ed Ecole Normale Supérieure; Insp. of Finances 1946–50; Tech. Adviser to Sec. of State for Finance 1949–51, Dept of External Econ. Relations 1951–54, Dir Econ. Affairs and Planning, Ministry for Overseas Territories 1954–59; Dir of Civil Aviation, Ministry of Public Works and Transport 1959–62; Dir Dept of Operations for Africa, World Bank 1962–64; Pres. French Fed. of Assurance Cos. 1965–69; Pres. Banque de Paris et des Pays-Bas 1969–81, Chair. 1978–81; Chair. Finance and Devt Inc. 1982–86, Pallas Holdings 1983–92, Dillon, Read Ltd 1984–87, France Développement (Frandev) 1986–90, Cresvale Partners 1987–94, Pallas Invest 1988–90, Pallas Monaco 1988–96, The Managed Convertible Fund 1990–95, Pallas Ltd 1992–93, Strand Assocs. Ltd 1993–, Strand Partners Ltd 1993–94, The Prometheus Fund 1993–95, Forum pour l'Afrique 1995–, West Africa Growth Fund 1997–, Fondation pour l'Entreprise Africaine 1999–; Dir numerous cos.; Officier, Légion d'honneur 1976, Officier, Ordre national du Mérite. *Publications:* L'économie de la zone franc, Les chances économiques de la communauté Franco-Africaine, Les nations prolétaires, Les Etats-Unis et les nations prolétaires, La roue de la fortune: souvenirs d'un financier, Caliban naufragé: les relations Nord/Sud à la fin du XXe siècle. *Address:* 49 Devonshire Close, London, W1G 7BG (Office); 14 Pelham Place, South Kensington, London, SW7 2NH, England (Home). *Telephone:* (20) 7436-4500. *Fax:* (20) 7323-0885. *E-mail:* pierremoussa@btinternet.com (Office).

MOUSSAVI, Farshid; Iranian architect; b. 1965, Tehran; m. Alejandro Zaera-Polo; ed London School of Architecture, UK, Yale Univ., USA; moved to London with family 1978; with Office for Metropolitan Architecture, Rotterdam 1991–93; Co-Founder and Owner (with husband Alejandro Zaera-Polo) Foreign Office Architects Ltd (FOA), London 1993–; teacher Architectural Assocn (AA) 1993–2000; Visiting Critic Princeton Univ., Univ. of Calif. at LA, Columbia Univ., Berlage Inst. Amsterdam, Sint-Lucas Inst., Ghent; Prof., Acad. of Fine Arts, Vienna 2002–; represented UK at Architecture Biennale, Venice, Italy 2002. *Architectural Works include:* Yokohama Int. Ferry Terminal (Japan) 1996–2002; Bermondsey Square, London 1997; Belgo Restaurant Notting Hill Br., London 1998 (Bristol 1999, New York 1999); Hotel, Groningen, Germany; Municipal Police HQ, Joiosa, Spain 2000–; Public Square and Theatre, nr Alicante 2001–; Coastal Park, nr Barcelona 2002–; T'Raboes Harbour Facilities, Amersfoort, The Netherlands 2002–; Selfridges Shopping Centre, Bristol 2002–. *Major exhibitions include:* AA, London 1996, Ministerio de Fomento, Madrid 1998, Museum of Modern Art, New York 2000, British Pavilion, 8th Venice Biennale 2002, TN Probe Gallery, Tokyo 2003. *Publications include:* The Yokohama Project 2002, FOA's ARC 2002; numerous monographs. *Address:* Foreign Office Architects, 58 Belgrave Road, London, SW1V 2BP, England (Office). *Website:* www.f-o-a .net (Office).

MOUSSAVI, Mir Hussein; Iranian politician; b. 1942, Iran; ed Nat. Univ., Tehran; joined Islamic Soc. at univ. in Tehran and active in Islamic Socs. since; imprisoned briefly for opposition to the Shah 1973; a founder mem. Islamic Republican Party (IRP) 1979; appointed Chief Ed. IRP newspaper Islamic Republic 1979; Foreign Minister Aug.–Oct. 1981; elected Prime Minister by Majlis (consultative ass.) 1981–89, Adviser to the Pres. 1989. *Address:* c/o Office of the President, Palestine Avenue, Azerbaijan Intersection, Tehran, Iran.

MOUSTIERS, Pierre Jean (Rossi), LenD; French author and producer; b. 13 Aug. 1924, La Seyne (Var); ed Univs of Aix-Marseilles and Neuchâtel; Attaché at the Office des Changes, French zone in Germany 1947–49; Chief, Information Services, Nat. Information and Protection Centre for Construction (C.N.I.P.) 1950–60; medical del., pharmaceutical lab. MERCK, Darmstadt 1961, later regional insp.; literary critic Nice-Matin 1970, Radio-Marseille; Hommes et Lectures Prize 1962, Grand Prix de littérature sportive, Grand Prix du Roman, Acad. Française for La Paroi 1969, Prix des Maisons de la Presse for L'Hiver d'un Gentilhomme 1972, Grand Prix littéraire de Provence for Une place forte 1975, Prix Louis Philippe Kammans for Une place forte, Prix des libraires for Un crime de notre temps 1977, Grand Prix du Scénario for La ronde de nuit, Prix Acad. Balzac for TV adaptation of Curé de Tours 1980, Sceptre d'Or for L'Affaire Caillaux, Prix Jean Giono, Italy 1986; Officier des Arts et Lettres; Médaille des Combattants de la Résistance. *Television:* L'hiver d'un gentilhomme 1973, La mort du Pantin 1975, Une place forte 1976, Un crime de notre temps 1977, La ronde de nuit 1978, Le Coq de Bruyère 1980, Le Curé de Tours 1980, Antoine et Julie 1981, Bel Ami 1983, L'Affaire Caillaux 1985, Le Coeur du Voyage 1986, L'Eté de la Revolution 1989, Les Grandes Familles 1989, L'Interdiction 1992, Pris au piège 1993, Eugénie Grandet 1993, Un si bel orage 1995. *Play:* Les Trois Chaînes (Théâtre de Boulogne-Billancourt) 1976. *Publications:* Le journal d'un geôlier 1957, La mort du Pantin 1961, Le pharisien 1962, La paroi 1969, L'hiver d'un gentilhomme 1971, Une place forte 1974, Un Crime de notre temps 1976, Prima Donna 1978, Le Coeur du voyage 1981, La grenade 1984, Un Aristocrate à la lanterne 1986, L'Eclat 1990, Un si bel orage 1991, lLa Flambée 1993, L'Or du torrent 1995, A l'Abri du Monde (Prix Chateaubriant) 1997, Saskia 1999, Ce fils unique 2000; Hervé Bazin ou le romancier en mouvement (essay) 1973, Ce Fils Unique 2000, De Rêve et de Glace 2001, Le Dernier Mot d'un Roi 2003. *Leisure interests:* mountaineering, reading, painting and drawing, taxidermy. *Address:* Campagne Sainte Anne, boulevard des Acacias, 83100 Toulon, France.

MOUT, Marianne Elisabeth Henriette Nicolette, DLitt; Netherlands historian; b. 31 May 1945, Wassenaar; d. of Arie Mout and Maria Helena van Tooren; m. 1st Robbert Salomon van Santen (divorced 1979); m. 2nd Peter Felix Ganz 1987; ed Rijnlands Lyceum, Wassenaar, Univ. of Amsterdam; research student Czechoslovakia 1966, 1967; Asst Keeper, Jewish Historical Museum, Amsterdam 1969; Ed., Martinus Nijhoff publrs 1970; Lecturer in Modern History, Utrecht Univ. 1975–76; Sr Lecturer in Dutch History, Leiden Univ. 1976–94; Prof. of Cen. European Studies 1990–, Prof. of Modern History 1994–; Man. Ed. Tijdschrift voor Geschiedenis 1981–86; Fellow Netherlands Inst. for Advanced Studies, Wassenaar 1987–88, 1993–94; mem. Bd, Inst. of Netherlands History (Instituut voor Nederlandse Geschiedenis) 1989–; mem. Royal Netherlands Acad. of Arts and Sciences; Corresp. mem. Austrian Acad. of Sciences; Pres. Conseil International pour l'édition des oeuvres d'Erasme. *Publications:* Komenský v Amsterodamu (with J. Polišenský) 1970, Bohemen en de Nederlanden in de zestiende eeuw 1975, Plakkaat van Verlatinge 1581 1979, Die Kultur des Humanismus 1998; numerous articles, mainly on 16th–17th century Dutch and Cen. European history of ideas and cultural history; Ed. and Co-Ed. of several books, including Gerhard Oestreich, Antiker Geist und moderner Staat bei Justus Lipsius 1989, Erasmianism Idea and Reality 1997. *Address:* Department of History, P.B. 9515, 2300 RA Leiden (Office); Oranje Nassaulaan 27, 2361 LB Warmond, Netherlands (Home). *Telephone:* (71) 5272759, 5272651 (Office). *Fax:* (71) 5272652 (Office). *E-mail:* m.e.h.n.mout@let.leidenuniv.nl (Office). *Website:* www.let.leidenuniv.nl/history/sub/ag/mout.htm (Office).

MOUTAKWEL, Nawal el-; Moroccan athlete (retd) and sports administrator; b. 15 April 1962, Casablanca; m.; two c.; ed Iowa State Univ., USA;

gold medallist, 400m. hurdles, Olympic Games, Los Angeles 1988 (first Moroccan, African and Muslim woman to win Olympic Gold); Asst Coach, Iowa State Univ.; Dir Nat. School of Track and Field, Casablanca br. 1991; Vice-Pres. Moroccan Track and Field Fed. 1992; mem. Moroccan Nat. Olympic Cttee; Sec. of State for Sport and Youth 1997; Sr Exec., Fondation Banque Marocaine du Commerce Exterieur; mem. Athletes' Comm., Int. Asscn Athletics Feds 1989–, mem. Council 1995–, mem. Devt Sub-Comm. for Women; mem. Int. Olympic Cttee (first Muslim woman) 1998–, (mem. Working Group on Women and Sport 1996–), mem. Electoral Coll.; mem. Comité Int. des Jeux Mediterranéens, Comité Int. des Jeux de la Francophonie, Laureus World Sports Acad.; Chevalier, Ordre nat. du Mérite Exceptionnel (Morocco) 1983; Chevalier, Ordre nat. du Lion (Senegal) 1988. *Address:* c/o International Olympic Committee, Château de Vidy, Lausanne, 1007, Switzerland (Office).

MOUTINOT, Laurent; Swiss politician and lawyer; b. 2 March 1953, Geneva; m.; three c.; advocate, Geneva Bar 1978–97; Pres. Asloca romande 1990–93, Vice-Pres. Asloca suisse 1990–97; Deputy Grand Council of Geneva 1993–97; Leader of Parl. Group 1994–96; elected (Parti socialiste) to Council of State of Geneva (Département de l'aménagement, de l'équipement et du logement) 1997–, Vice-Pres. 2001–02, Pres. 2002–03. *Address:* Conseil d'Etat, Rue David-Dufour 5, case postale, 1211 Geneva 8, Switzerland (Office). *Telephone:* (22) 3274940 (Office). *Website:* www.geneve.ch/chancellerie/conseil/ (Office).

MOWAT, Farley McGill, OC, BA; Canadian author; b. 12 May 1921, Belleville, Ont.; s. of Angus Mowat and Helen (née Thomson) Mowat; m. 1st Frances Mowat 1947; two s.; m. 2nd Claire Mowat 1963; ed Toronto Univ.; served in the Canadian Army 1939–45; Arctic exploration 1947–49; full-time writer 1950–; Hon. DLitt (Laurentian Univ.) 1970, (Univ. of Victoria) 1982, (Lakehead Univ.) 1986, (Univ. Coll. of Cape Breton) 1996; Hon. D.Laws (Lethbridge, Toronto, Prince Edward Island, Queen's Univ.); Hon. DH (McMaster Univ., Hamilton) 1994; Hon. LLD (Queen's Univ.) 1995; Fourth Nat. Prize for Foreign Literature Books, Beiyue Literature and Art Publishing House, People's Repub. of China 1999; Gov.-Gen.'s Award, Canadian Centennial Medal, Leacock Medal for Humour, Hans Christian Andersen Award, Anisfield Wolf Award, Mark Twain Award, Gemini Award (Best Documentary Script), Award of Excellence (Atlantic Film Festival) 1990, Canadian Achievers Award, Take Back the Nation Award, Council of Canadians 1991, Author's Award, Author of the Year, Foundation for Advancement of Canadian Letters 1993. *Publications:* People of The Deer 1952, The Regiment 1955, Lost in The Barrens 1956, The Dog Who Wouldn't Be 1957, Coppermine Journey 1958, The Grey Seas Under 1958, The Desperate People 1959, Ordeal by Ice 1960, Owls in the Family 1961, The Serpent's Coil 1961, The Black Joke 1962, Never Cry Wolf 1963, Westviking 1965, The Curse of the Viking Grave 1966, Canada North 1967, The Polar Passion 1967, This Rock Within the Sea 1968, The Boat Who Wouldn't Float 1969, Sibir 1970, A Whale for the Killing 1972, Tundra 1973, Wake of the Great Sealers (with David Blackwood) 1973, The Snow Walker 1975, Canada North Now 1976, And No Birds Sang 1979, The World of Farley Mowat 1980, Sea of Slaughter 1984, My Discovery of America 1985, Virunga (Woman in the Mist, USA) 1987, The New Founde Land 1989, Rescue the Earth 1990, My Father's Son 1992, Born Naked 1993, Aftermath 1995, A Farley Mowat Reader 1997; TV documentary: Sea of Slaughter 1990, The Farfarers 1998, Walking on the Land 2000. *Leisure interests:* travel, all facets of nature. *Address:* c/o Writers Union of Canada, 24 Ryerson Avenue, Toronto, Ont., M4T 2P3 (Office); 18 King Street, Port Hope, Ont., L1A 2R4, Canada.

MOWLAM, Rt Hon Marjorie (Mo), PC, PhD; British politician; b. 18 Sept. 1949, Watford; d. of Frank and Tina Mowlam; m. Peter Jonathan Norton 1995; two step-c.; ed Coundon Court Comprehensive School, Coventry, Durham Univ., Iowa Univ., USA; fmr lecturer and coll. admin.; elected Labour MP for Redcar 1987–2001; fmr mem. Opposition NI team; mem. Treasury team, with special responsibility for City and Corp. Affairs 1990–92; mem. Shadow Cabinet, Shadow Minister for Citizens' Charter and Women's Affairs 1992–93, for Nat. Heritage 1993–94, Shadow Sec. of State for NI 1994–97; Sec. of State for NI 1997–99; Minister for the Cabinet Office and Chancellor of Duchy of Lancaster 1999–2001; mem. Int. Crisis Group 2001–; Hon. LLD (Queen's) 1999, (Teesside), (Newcastle), (Durham). *Television:* numerous appearances on news programmes and chat shows. *Publications:* Debate on Disarmament (Jt) 1982, Momentum Momentum. *Leisure interests:* jigsaws, swimming, photography, fly fishing. *Address:* 38A Albion Terrace, London, E8 4LX, England (Home). *Telephone:* (20) 7684-1822 (Office); (20) 7684-1822 (Home). *Fax:* (20) 7684-2199 (Office). *E-mail:* MoMwlm@cs.com (Office).

MOXLEY, John Howard, III, MD, FACP; American physician and business executive; b. 10 Jan. 1935, Elizabeth, NJ; s. of John Howard Moxley, Jr and Cleopatra Mundy Moxley; m. Doris Banchik; three s.; ed Williams Coll. and Univ. of Colorado School of Medicine; hosp. posts 1961–63; Clinical Assoc. Nat. Cancer Inst., Solid Tumor Branch 1963–65; Sr Resident Physician, Peter Bent Brigham Hosp. 1965–66; mem. Lymphoma Task Force Nat. Cancer Inst. 1965–77; Instructor in Medicine and Asst to the Dean, Harvard Medical School 1966–69; Dean, Univ. of Md School of Medicine and Assoc. Prof. of Medicine 1969–73; Vice-Chancellor for Health Sciences and Dean of School of Medicine, Univ. of Calif., San Diego and Assoc. Prof. of Medicine 1973–80; Asst Sec. of Defense for Health Affairs, Dept of Defense, Washington, DC 1979–81; Sr Vice-Pres., Corp. Planning and Alternative Services, American Medical Int. Inc. 1981–87; Pres. and CEO, MetaMedical Inc., Beverly Hills,

Calif. 1987–89; Man. Dir Korn Ferry Int. 1989–; Dir Nat. Fund for Medical Educ. 1986–, Chair. 1993–; Fellow American Fed. for Clinical Research; mem. Inst. of Medicine (NAS), American Soc. of Clinical Oncology, American Medical Asscn; Dir Henry M. Jackson Foundation for the Advancement of Mil. Medicine 1983; Sec. of Defense Medal for Distinguished Public Service and other awards. *Publications:* numerous papers in scientific journals. *Address:* Korn/Ferry International, 1800 Century Park East, Suite 900, Los Angeles, CA 90067 (Office); 8180 Manitoba Street 210, Playa del Rey, CA 90293, USA (Home). *Telephone:* (310) 843-4123 (Office). *E-mail:* moxleyj@kornferry.com (Office).

MOXON, (Edward) Richard, MB, BChir, FRCP; British medical doctor; b. 16 July 1941, Leeds; s. of the late Gerald Richard Moxon and Margaret Forster Mohun; m. Marianne Graham 1973; two s. one d.; ed Shrewsbury School, St John's Coll., Cambridge and St Thomas' Hosp. Medical School, London; with Hosp. for Sick Children, Great Ormond St, London 1969; Research Fellow in Infectious Diseases, Children's Hosp. Medical Center, Boston, Mass., USA 1971–74; Asst Prof. of Pediatrics, Johns Hopkins Hosp., Baltimore, Md, USA 1974–80; Dir Eudowood Pediatric Infectious Diseases Unit 1982–84; Action Research Prof. of Paediatrics, Oxford Univ. 1984–; Head, Molecular Infectious Diseases Group, Inst. of Molecular Medicine, John Radcliffe Hosp. 1988–; Visiting Scientist, Dept of Molecular Biology, Washington Univ., St Louis, Mo. 1990–91; Fellow, Jesus Coll. Oxford 1984–; Founder and Chair. Oxford Vaccine Group 1994–; mem. Steering Group, Encapsulated Bacteria, WHO 1987–93; Chair. MRC Sub-Cttee Polysaccharide Vaccines 1986–90; convenor, BPA Immunology and Infectious Diseases Group 1984–89; Founder Fellow Acad. of Medical Sciences 1998; mem. American Soc. Clinical Investigation; Fellow Infectious Diseases Soc. of America, American Soc. Pediatric Research; Mitchell Lecture, Royal Coll. of Physicians 1992, Bob Deich Memorial Lecture, Univ. of Rochester, NY 1995, Teale Lecturer, Royal Coll. of Physicians 1998, Burroughs-Wellcome Lecturer, Univ. of Pennsylvania 1998, Dolman Lecture, Univ. of British Columbia 1999, J.H.P. Jonxis Lecturer, Beatrix Children's Hosp., Groningen, Netherlands 2001. *Publications:* Neonatal Infections (with D. Isaacs) 1991, A Practical Approach to Paediatric Infectious Diseases (with D. Isaacs) 1996, Longman Handbook of Neonatal Infections (with D. Isaacs) 1999; Modern Vaccines (ed. adviser) 1990, Progress in Vaccinology (ed.) 2000; more than 300 scientific articles on infections, molecular basis of bacterial virulence and vaccines published in major journals. *Leisure interests:* music, literature, sports. *Address:* Department of Paediatrics, John Radcliffe Hospital, Headington, Oxford, OX3 9DU (Office); 17 Moreton Road, Oxford, OX2 7AX, England (Home). *Telephone:* (1865) 221074 (Office). *Fax:* (1865) 220479.

MOYA PALENCIA, Mario; Mexican politician and lawyer; b. 14 June 1933, México, DF; s. of Mario Moya Iturriaga and Concepción Palencia de Moya; m. Marcela Ibáñez de Moya Palencia 1959; one s. one d.; ed Univ. Nacional Autónoma de México; Public Relations Dept, Ferrocarriles Nacionales de México 1955–58; in Dept of Nat. Property 1959–64; Dir Gen. of Cinematography, Dept of Interior 1964–68; Pres. of Bd of Dirs. of Productora e Importadora de Papel, SA (PIPSA) 1968–69; Under-Sec., Dept of Interior 1969; Sec. of Interior 1970–76; fmr Perm. Rep. to UN; Prof. of Constitutional Law, Univ. Nacional Autónoma de México 1977; Dir-Gen. Organización Editorial Mexicana (OEM) 1977–79, Fondo Nacional de Fomento al Turismo (FONATUR) 1979–82, Banco Nacional de Turismo 1982; Exec. Pres. Ocean Garden Products Inc. 1983–; Gen. Man. Exportadores Asscn SA de CV 1983–; numerous foreign awards and decorations. *Publications:* La reforma electoral 1964, Temas Constitucionales 1978, Democracia y Participación 1982. *Leisure interests:* reading, riding. *Address:* Insurgentes Sur Torre B, 4o. piso, C.P. 1000, México 20, DF, Mexico. *Telephone:* 548-91-84.

MOYANA, Kombo James, MA, M.PHIL., PhD; Zimbabwean banker; b. 4 July 1942, Chipinge; m.; one s. three d.; ed Columbia Univ. New York; Research Fellow, Inst. de Développement Economique et de Planification, Dakar 1972; Fellow, UNITAR, New York 1973; int. finance economist, Div. of Money, Finance and Devt UNCTAD, New York and Geneva 1974–80; seconded to Ministry of Econ. Planning and Devt of Govt of Zimbabwe 1980; Deputy Gov. Reserve Bank of Zimbabwe 1980, Gov. 1983; Alt. Gov. IMF 1983; Pres. Inst. of Bankers (Zimbabwe) 1985–86; Exec. Sec. Preferential Trading Area (PTA) of Eastern, Cen. and Southern African States until 1991; Chair. Asscn of African Cen. Banks (AACB) 1991–93. *Leisure interest:* farming. *Address:* P.O. Box 1283, Harare, Zimbabwe. *Telephone:* 790731; 7910721.

MOYERS, Bill D., FAAS; American journalist; b. 5 June 1934, Hugo, Okla; s. of Henry Moyers and Ruby Johnson; m. Judith Davidson 1954; two s. one d.; ed Univ. of Texas, Edinburgh Univ. and Southwestern Baptist Theological Seminary; Exec. Asst to Senator Lyndon Johnson 1959–60; Assoc. Dir U.S. Peace Corps 1961–63, Deputy Dir 1963; Special Asst to Pres. Johnson 1963–66, Press Sec. to Pres. 1965–66; Publr of Newsday, Long Island, NY 1966–70; host of This Week, weekly current affairs TV programme 1970; Ed.-in-Chief Bill Moyers Journal, Public Broadcasting Service 1971–76, 1978–81; Contrib. Newsweek 1974–76; Chief Corresp. CBS Reports 1976–78, Sr News Analyst, CBS News 1981–86; Exec. Ed. Public Affairs TV Inc. 1987–; news analyst NBC News 1995–; Pres. Florence and John Schumann Foundation 1991–; mem. American Philosophical Soc.; Emmy Awards 1983–90, Gold Baton Award 1991, 1999, American Jewish Cttee Religious Liberty Award 1995, Walter Cronkite Award 1995, Fred Friendly First Amendment Award 1995, Charles Frankel Prize 1997, George Peabody Award 2000. *Publications:* Listening to America 1971, The Secret Government 1988, Joseph Campbell and the Power of Myth 1988, A World of Ideas 1989, Healing and the Mind 1993, Genesis: A Living Conversion 1996, Fooling with Words 1999. *Address:* Public Affairs TV Inc., 450 West 33rd Street, New York, NY 10001, USA.

MOYO, Jonathan, BSc, MPA, PhD; Zimbabwean politician; b. 12 Jan. 1957; m.; mem. ZANU-PF; currently Minister of State for Information and Publicity; mem. Pres. Robert Mugabe's 'Gang of Four' politicians; architect of Zimbabwe's highly-controlled press regime. *Leisure interests:* philosophy, classics, music, composition, tennis, scriptwriting. *Address:* Ministry of Information and Publicity, Linquenda House, Baker Avenue, POB CY825, Causeway, Harare, Zimbabwe (Office). *Telephone:* (4) 702731 (Office). *Fax:* (4) 729311 (Office).

MPALANYI-NKOYOYO, Most Rev. Livingstone, DD; Ugandan ecclesiastic; b. 4 Oct. 1939, Namukozi Village, Ssingo Co., Mityana Dist; s. of the late Erisa Wamala Nkoyoyo; m. Ruth Nkoyoyo; three s. two d.; ed Bishop Lutaaya Theological Coll., Buwalasi Theological Coll., Legoni Trinity Coll. Ghana, Cranmer Theological House; worked as a mechanic 1959–62; lay reader Church of Uganda 1962; curate Kasubi Parish 1970, priest 1971–74; parish priest, Nsangi Parish 1975–76; Archdeacon, Namirembe Archdeaconry 1977; Asst Bishop, Namirembe Diocese 1980; Suffragan Bishop, Mukono Area 1982; Bishop, Mukono Diocese 1984; Archbishop of Uganda and Bishop of Kampala 1995–. *Address:* Church of Uganda, P.O. Box 14123, Mengo, Kampala, Uganda (Office). *Telephone:* (41) 270218 (Office); (41) 271138 (Home). *Fax:* (41) 251925 (Office). *E-mail:* couab@uol.co.ug (Office).

MPHAHLELE, Es'kia (Ezekiel), MA, PhD, DLitt; South African author; b. 17 Dec. 1919, Marabastad; s. of Moses Mphahlele and Eva Mphahlele; m. Rebecca Nnana Mphahlele 1945; four s. one d.; ed teacher training and private study; teacher of English and Afrikaans, Orlando, Johannesburg until 1957; Fiction Ed. Drum magazine 1955; Lecturer in English Literature, Dept of Extra-Mural Studies, Univ. Coll., Ibadan, Nigeria 1957; fmr Dir African Programme for the Congress for Cultural Freedom, Paris; circuit schools inspector Lebowa 1978; Educ. Adviser and Chair. of Bd Funda Centre, Soweto 1986–; Researcher African Studies Inst., Univ. of Witwatersrand 1979, Prof. of African Literature 1979–88, Head of African Literature 1983–88, Prof. Emer. 1988–; fmr lecturer Univ. of Nairobi, Univ. of Denver, Univ. of Penn., Dir Council for Black Educ.; numerous hon. degrees. *Publications include:* Man Must Live, The Living and the Dead (short stories), Down Second Avenue (autobiog.), The Wanderers (novel) 1972, In Corner B (short stories), The African Image (essays), Voices in the Whirlwind (essays), Chirundu (novel) 1981, Afrika My Music (autobiog.) 1984, Father Come Home (novel) 1984, Creative Writing Guides: Let's Talk Writing, Prose and Let's Talk Writing, Poetry; The Story of African Literature 1986, Renewal Time 1989; numerous other essays and poems. *Leisure interests:* music, theatre. *Address:* 5444, Zone 5, Pimville, Johannesburg, South Africa. *Telephone:* (11) 9332273.

MPINGA KASENDA, PhD; Democratic Republic of the Congo politician and university professor; b. 30 Aug. 1937, Tshilomba; ed Elisabethville (now Lubumbashi) High School of Social Sciences, Catholic Univ. of Lovanium and Univ. of Bordeaux, France; Teacher, Tshilomba Secondary School 1957–59; studied at Lubumbashi and Lovanium Univ. 1959–65; Asst Lecturer, Lovanium Univ. 1965–66; Prof. 1966–70; Adviser to the Chancellor, Nat. Univ. of Zaire and to the Minister of Public Admin. 1971–72; mem. Political Bureau Mouvement Populaire de la Révolution (MPR) 1972, mem. Perm. Cttee 1974–80; Deputy People's Commr 1975, First State Commr 1977–80; Dir Makanda Kabobi Inst. (MPR school) 1974–; Commdr, Nat. Order of Zaire and Dem. People's Repub. of Korea, Grand Officier Ordre du Mérite national (Mauritania). *Publications:* Ville de Kinshasa, Organisation politique et administrative 1968, L'administration publique du Zaire 1973, Les reformes administratives au Zaire 1975. *Address:* Institut Makanda Kabobi, avenue de la Gombe, Kinshasa (Office); 384 Quartier Gombele, Kinshasa/Lemba, P.O.B. 850, Democratic Republic of the Congo (Home).

MROUDJAE, Ali; Comoran politician; b. 2 Aug. 1939, Moroni; s. of Chohezi Mroudjae and Charif Zahara; m. Nourdine Batouli 1967; three s. five d.; Minister of Foreign Affairs and Co-operation 1979–82; Prime Minister of the Comoros 1982–85; Minister of State for Internal and Social Affairs Jan.–Sept. 1985; and numerous other portfolios; currently Leader Parti Comorien pour la Démocratie et le Progrès (PCDP). *Leisure interests:* reading, swimming, travelling. *Address:* PCDP, Route Djivani, B.P. 179, Moroni; B.P. 58, Rond Point Gobadjou, Moroni, Comoros. *Telephone:* (73) 1733 (PCDP); (73) 1266. *Fax:* (73) 0650 (PCDP).

MROŻEK, Sławomir; Polish writer; b. 26 June 1930, Borzęcin nr Brzesk; m.; fmr cartoonist, satirist and journalist; mem. Polish Writers' Asscn 1951–71, 1978–; numerous prizes include Silver Cross of Merit 1953, Julian Brano Prize 1954, Kościelscy Foundation Award (Switzerland) 1962, Prix de l'Humour Noir 1964, Alfed Jurzykowski Award 1964, 1985, State Prize (Austria) 1972, Prix Crédit Industriel et Commercial Paris Théâtre (France) 1993. *Publications include:* prose includes: Maleńkie lato (novel) 1956, The Elephant (short stories) 1957, Wesele w Atomicach (Wedding in Atomice) 1959, The Rain (short stories) 1962, Moniza Clavier (short story) 1967, The Ugupu Bird (short stories) 1968, Dwa listy 1974, Małe listy 1981, Dziennik powrotu 2000; plays include: The Police 1958, What a Lovely Dream, Indyk (Turkey) 1961, Karol 1961, Striptease 1964, Tango 1964, On the High Seas, Vatzlav 1970, Druga zmiana (Second Service) 1970, Testarium 1970, Blessed Event 1973, Rzeźnia (Butchery) 1973, Emigrants 1974, Garbus (Humpback) 1975, Utwory sceniczne nowe 1976, Krawiec (Tailor) 1977, Drugie danie (Second

Dish), Pieszo 1983, Miłość na Krymie (Love in Crimea) 1993, Wielebni 2001; series of satirical drawings: Polska w obrazach (Poland in Pictures) 1957, Postępowiec (Progressive man) 1960, Rysunki 1982, Polska w obrazach i polskie cykle (Poland in Pictures and the Other Polish Series) 1998. *Address:* Związek Literatów Polskich, ul. Królewska 84 m. 18, 30-079 Cracow, Poland (Office). *Telephone:* (12) 636-29-66 (Office).

MROZIEWICZ, Robert; Polish politician; b. 20 Sept. 1942, Warsaw; m. Elżbieta Nowik; two s.; ed Univ. of Warsaw; Asst Prof. Inst. of History, Polish Acad. of Sciences 1965–68, Asst Warsaw Univ. 1966–68, Polish Inst. of Int. Affairs 1968–70; Inst. of History, Polish Acad. of Sciences 1971–89; Minister-Adviser Ministry of Foreign Affairs; Deputy Perm. Rep. to UN, New York, then Perm. Rep. of UN, New York 1990–92; Under-Sec. of State in Ministry of Foreign Affairs; Pres. of UN Social and Economic Council 1992–97, Pres. of Gen. Ass. 1992; Under-Sec. of State for Co-operation with Abroad and Integration with NATO in Ministry of National Defence 1997; mem. Solidarity Trade Union 1980–99; Commdr.'s Cross of Order Polonia Restituta 1995. *Publications:* author and co-author of 6 monographs and various scientific articles. *Address:* c/o Ministry of National Defence, ul. Królewska 1, 00-909 Warsaw 60, Poland.

MSIKA, Joseph; Zimbabwean politician; m. Maria Msika; Co-Vice-Pres. Zimbabwe African Nat. Union (ZANU) Dec. 2000–; Co-Vice-Pres. of Zimbabwe Jan. 2001–. *Address:* Office of the Vice-Presidents, Munhumutapa Building, Samora Machel Avenue, Private Bag 7700, Harare, Zimbabwe (Office). *Telephone:* (4) 707091 (Office).

MSIMANG, Mendi, BA; South African diplomatist and civil servant; b. 1928, Johannesburg; m. Mantombazana Tshabalala; four c. from previous marriage; ed Univ. Coll. of Rome, Lesotho; with Rand Steam Laundries, organizer Laundry Workers' Union; asbestos assayer Costa Rican consulate; joined ANC, Personal Sec. to then Sec.-Gen. Walter Sisulu; with Nelson Mandela (q.v.) and Oliver Tambo's law practice –1960; left for UK; Rep. ANC Mission to UK and Ireland; Co-Founder South Africa in Fact (ANC newsletter); Ed. Spotlight on South Africa (ANC journal); Admin. Sec. ANC Nat. Exec. Cttee in Exile, E Africa br.; collaborated with Oliver Tambo to est. Solomon Mahlangu Freedom Coll., Tanzania; ANC Educ. Officer; Admin. Sec. Treas.-Gen. of ANC's office, Zambia; ANC Chief Rep. to India 1969, to UK 1988; returned to SA 1990; elected mem. ANC Nat. Exec. Cttee 1991, Nat. Ass. 1994 (fmr Chair.); fmr Chair. ANC Parl. Caucus; High Commr in UK 1995–98; Treasurer ANC 1998–; Chair. Nelson Mandela Children's Fund; Vice-Pres. Royal Over-Seas League, London; Fellow Rotarian, Rotary Club of London. *Leisure interests:* watching football, golf, jazz/blues, reading, theatre. *Address:* P.O. Box 25929, Monument Park, Pretoria 0105, South Africa.

MSUYA, Cleopa David, BA; Tanzanian politician and civil servant; b. 4 Jan. 1931, Chomvu Usangi, Mwanga Dist; s. of David Kilenga and Maria Ngido; m. Rhoda Christopher 1959; four s. two d.; ed Makerere Univ. Coll., Uganda; Civil Service, Community Devt Officer 1956–61, Commr for Community Devt 1961–64, Prin. Sec. to Ministry of Community Devt and Nat. Culture 1964, to Ministries of Land Settlement and Water Devt 1965–67, to Ministry of Econ. Affairs and Devt Planning 1967–70 and to Treas. 1970–72; Minister of Finance 1972–75, 1983–85, for Finance, Econ. Affairs and Planning 1985–89, for Industries 1975–80, for Industries and Trade 1990–95; Prime Minister 1980–83, 1994–95; First Vice-Pres. 1994–95; mem. Nat. Ass.; Gov. ADB, IMF; mem. Bd of Dirs. of several public corpns. *Address:* c/o Office of the Prime Minister and First Vice-President, P.O. Box 980, Dodoma, Tanzania.

MSWATI III, HM Makhosetive; King of Swaziland; b. 19 April 1968; s. of the late King Sobhuza II and Queen Ntombi Laftwala; m. to seven wives (Emakhosikati); ed Sherborne School, England; crowned King of Swaziland 25 April 1986. *Leisure interests:* swimming, rugby. *Address:* Lozitha Palace, Mbabane, Swaziland.

MTHEMBI-MAHANYELE, Sankie (Rebecca Matlou), BA; South African politician and diplomatist; b. 23 March 1951, Sophiatown; d. of the late Mkhomazi Mthembi and Emma Gabaza Mthembi; m. Mohale Mahanyele; three d.; ed Sekano-Ntoane High School, Univ. of the North; fmr punch card operator Standard Bank; became involved in ANC underground, left SA 1977 to work for ANC, with Radio Freedom 1977–81, Ed. women's journal Voice of Women 1979–87, fmr sub-Ed. Dawn, mem. Nat. Exec. Cttee of Women 1980–87, 1987–89, Admin. Sec. mission in West Africa 1986–89, Admin. Sec. mission in Sweden 1983–84, Chief Rep. mission for Germany and Austria 1989–93, mem. Nat. Exec. 1993–; Deputy Head Dept of Int. Affairs 1993–94; Deputy Minister of Welfare 1994–95; Minister of Housing 1995–99, 1999–. *Publications:* as Sankie Mthembi: Flames of Fury (poetry anthology), One Never Knows (short story); as Rebecca Matlou: also published in other poetry anthologies including Poets to the People, Mahbongwe: Poetry is Their Weapon, Return of the Amasi, Whispering Land. *Leisure Interests:* music, reading. *Address:* Ministry of Housing, 240 Walker Street, Sunnyside, Pretoria 0001 (Office); Private Bag X645, Pretoria 0001, South Africa (Office). *Telephone:* (12) 4211310 (Office). *Fax:* (12) 3418513 (Office). *Website:* www .housing.gov.za (Office).

MU GUOGUANG; Chinese university professor; b. 22 Jan. 1931, Liaoning; m. Chi Yuanxiang; one s. one d.; ed Nankai Univ.; Pres. Nankai Univ. 1986–95, Chair. Academic Cttee, Dir Inst. of Modern Optics; Pres.Chinese Optical Soc.; mem. Chinese Acad. of Sciences 1991; mem. 4th Presidum of Depts, Chinese Acad. of Sciences 2000–; Fellow Optical Soc. of America, Third World Acad. of Science, Int. Soc. of Optical Eng; Hon. PhD (Kyoto Limengkom); several scientific awards. *Publications:* Optics (univ. textbook). *Leisure interest:* swimming. *Address:* Nankai University, Institute of Modern Optics, 94 Weijin Road, Tianjin 300071, People's Republic of China. *Telephone:* (22) 2350-2275 (Office); (22) 2350-1688 (Home). *Fax:* (22) 23240-3118 (Office); (22) 2350-2896 (Home). *E-mail:* mugg@nankai.edu.cn (Home).

MU'ALLA, HH Sheikh Rashid bin Ahmad al-, Ruler of Umm al-Qaiwain; b. 1930; apptd. Deputy Ruler of Umm al-Qaiwain, succeeded as Ruler on the death of his father Feb. 1981; Chair. Umm al-Qaiwain Municipality 1967; constituted the Emirate's first municipal council 1975. *Address:* Rulers' Palace, Umm al-Qaiwain, United Arab Emirates.

MUBARAK, Lt-Gen. (Muhammad) Hosni, B.MIL.SCI., BA; Egyptian politician and air force officer; b. 4 May 1928, Kafr El-Moseilha, Minuffya Governorate; m. Suzanne Sabet; two s.; ed Mil. Acad., Air Acad.; joined Air Force 1950, Lecturer Air Force Acad. 1952–59; Commdr Cairo West Air Base 1964; Dir-Gen. Air Acad. 1967–69; Air Force Chief of Staff 1969–72; C-in-C 1972–75; promoted to Lt-Gen. 1974; Vice-Pres. of Egypt 1975–81; Pres. Oct. 1981– (Cand. of NDP); Vice-Pres. Nat. Democratic Party (NDP) 1979, Pres. 1982; mem. Higher Council for Nuclear Energy 1975–; Sec.-Gen. NDP and Political Bureau 1981–82, Chair. 1982–; Chair. OAU 1989–90, 1993–94, Arab Summit 1996–, GI5 1998, 2000; Pres. Emergency Arab Summit 2000, D-8 Summit 2001, COMESA Summit 2001; Dr hc (Bulgaria) 1998, (Beijing) 1999, (St. Johns) 1999, (George Washington) 1999; Order of Star of Honour 1964, 1974, Medal of the Star of Sinai of the First Order 1983, Louise Michel Prize 1990, Prize of Democratic Human Rights, Social and Political Studies Centre, Paris 1990, UN Prize of Population 1994 and numerous other awards and foreign decorations, honours. *Leisure interest:* squash. *Address:* Presidential Palace, Abdeen, Cairo, Egypt.

MUDD, Roger Harrison, MA; American news broadcaster; b. 9 Feb. 1928, Washington; s. of Kostka Mudd and Irma Iris (née Harrison) Mudd; m. Emma Jeanne Spears 1957; three s. one d.; ed Washington and Lee Univ. and Univ of North Carolina; served with U.S. Army 1945–47; teacher Darlington School, Rome, Ga 1951–52; Reporter Richmond (Va) News Leader 1953; News Dir Station WRNL, Richmond 1953–56; Reporter, radio and TV Station WTOP, Washington 1956–61; Corresp. CBS 1961–80; Chief Washington Corresp. NBC 1980–87, Congressional Corresp. MacNeil/Lehrer News Hour 1987–92; Host The History Channel 1995–; Prof. of Journalism, Princeton Univ. 1992–94, Washington & Lee Univ. 1995–96; Dir Berlin Comm. 1996–99, Va Foundation for Ind. Colls. 1997–, Nat. Portrait Gallery Comm. 1997–; Bd Dirs. Media Gen. 1998–2001, Civil War Trust 1999–2001. *Publication:* Great Minds of History 1999. *Address:* 7167 Old Dominion Drive, McLean, VA 22101, USA (Home). *Fax:* (703) 356-1341 (Office). *E-mail:* rhmudd@aol.com (Office).

MUDENDA, Elijah Haatukali Kaiba; Zambian politician and agriculturist; b. 6 June 1927; ed Makerere Univ. Coll., Uganda, Fort Hare Univ. Coll., S. Africa and Univ. of Cambridge; agricultural expert until 1962; mem. Legis. Ass. 1962–64; Parl. Sec. for Agric. 1962–64; mem. Zambian Parl. 1964–; Minister of Agric. 1964–67, of Finance 1967–68, of Foreign Affairs 1968–69, 1970–73, of Devt and Finance 1969–70; Prime Minister 1975–77, also Minister of Nat. Guidance and Culture 1975–76; mem. Cen. Cttee United Nat. Independence Party (UNIP), Chair. Political Sub-Cttee 1973–75, Rural Devt Sub-Cttee 1977–78, Social and Economic Sub-Cttee 1978–81, Econs and Finance Sub-Cttee 1981; Chair. Nat. Comm. for Devt Planning April–July 1977. *Address:* United National Independence Party, Freedom House, P.O. Box 302, Lusaka, Zambia.

MUDENGE, Isack Stanislaus Gorerazvo, BA, PhD; Zimbabwean politician; b. 17 Dec. 1941, Bawa, Zimuto, Masvingo; ed Univ. of Rhodesia and Nyasaland, Gonakudzingwa, Univ. of York, UK and Univ. of London, UK; Lecturer, then Sr Lecturer Fourah Bay Coll., Sierra Leone and Nat. Univ. of Lesotho 1971–80; joined Zimbabwe African Nat. Union (ZANU) party 1963, mem. Cen. Cttee 1993–; Sec. for External Affairs, ZANU Br., Lesotho 1977–80; Permanent Sec. of Foreign Affairs 1980–85; Permanent Rep. to the UN 1985–90, Chair. Co-ordinating Cttee of the Non-aligned Nations at the UN 1986–89, Vice-Pres. UN Gen. Ass. 1989; Sec. for Educ. ZANU, Munyambe S. Dist 1990–91; Sr Permanent Sec. of Political Affairs 1990–92; Deputy Sec. for Commissariat and Culture, Masvingo Prov. 1991–93; Minister of Higher Educ. 1992–95; Deputy Sec. for Educ., Politburo ZANU; Minister of Foreign Affairs 1995–; mem. Int. Cttee for the Release of the ZANU Leadership Arrested in Zambia 1975–76; Int. Treas. World Univ. Service, Geneva 1974–76, Pres. 1976–78; Treas. Int. Congress of African Studies 1976–78, 1986–92, Pres. 1992–; Exec. mem. Bd of the Donors on African Educ., World Bank 1993. *Publications:* A Political History of Munhumutapa: 1400–1902; contribs. to Journal of Southern African Studies 1979–80; several other books and articles in learned journals. *Address:* Ministry of Foreign Affairs, Munhumutapa Building, Samora Machel Avenue, P.O. Box 4240, Causeway, Harare, Zimbabwe (Office). *Telephone:* (4) 727005 (Office). *Fax:* (4) 705161 (Office).

MUDGE, Dirk; Namibian politician; b. 16 Jan. 1928, Otjiwarongo; m. Stienie Jacobs; two s. three d.; Chair. of Turnhalle Constitutional Conf. 1977; Vice-Chair. of Nat. Party and mem. SW Africa Exec. Council Sept. 1977; formed Republican Party of SW Africa 1977; Chair. Democratic Turnhalle Alliance (now DTA of Namibia) 1977; mem. Constituent Ass. 1978–79, Nat. Ass. 1979–83; Pres. Ministers' Council 1980–83, Minister for Finance and Governmental Affairs 1985–89; mem. Nat. Ass. 1991–93. *Address:* DTA of Namibia, P.O. Box 173, Windhoek 9000, Namibia.

MUDIMBE, Valentin Y., DÈsL; Congolese professor of literature and writer; ed Univ. of Louvain, Univ. of Paris–VII, France; fmr Lecturer Univs of Louvain, Paris-Nanterre, Zaire and Haverford Coll.; specialist in phenomenology and structuralism; Prof. Literature Program, Stanford Univ. 1994–2000; currently Newman Ivey White Prof. of Literature Duke Univ., NC, USA; Gen.-Sec. Soc. for African Philosophy in N. America (SAPINA); Chair. Bd African Philosophy, Univ. of London, Int. Africa Inst., SOAS; discussant The Crossing Conf., Inst. St. Eugène de Mazenod, Kinshasa 2002. *Publications include:* L'odeur du père 1982, The Invention of Africa 1988, Parables and Fables 1991, The Idea of Africa 1994, Tales of Faith 1997; (Ed.): The Surreptitious Speech 1992, The American Society of French Philosophy, Nations, Identities, Cultures 1997, Diaspora and Immigration 1999; (Co-Ed.): Africa and the Disciplines 1993, Le corps glorieux des mots et des êtres 1994; seventy articles; three collections of poetry. *Address:* Duke University, Literature Program, 111 Art Museum, Box 90670, N. Carolina, USA (Office). *Telephone:* (919) 684-4240 (Office). *E-mail:* vmudimbe@duke.edu (Office). *Website:* www.duke.edu (Office).

MUELLER, Robert Swan, III, MA, JD; American intelligence officer, lawyer and federal official; b. 7 Aug. 1944, New York City; s. of Robert Swan Mueller Jr. and Alice Mueller (née Truesdale); m. Ann Standish 1966; two d.; ed Princeton Univ., New York Univ. and Univ. of Virginia; Capt. U.S. Marine Corps 1967–70; Assoc. Pillsbury, Madison & Sutro, San Francisco 1973–76; Asst U.S. Attorney, U.S. Attorney's Office, Northern Dist Calif., San Francisco 1976–80, Chief, Special Prosecutions Unit 1980–81, Criminal Div. 1981–82; Chief, Criminal Div. Mass. Dist, U.S. Attorney's Office, Boston 1982–85, First Asst U.S. Attorney in Boston 1985, U.S. Attorney for Mass. Dist 1986–87, Deputy U.S. Attorney for Mass. Dist 1987–88; Partner Hill and Barlow, Boston 1988–89; Asst to Attorney Gen. for criminal matters, U.S. Dept of Justice, Washington 1989–90, Asst Attorney Gen. for criminal div. 1990–93, Interim U.S. Attorney, Northern Dist Calif. 1998–2001; lawyer Hale & Dorr, Washington 1993–; Dir FBI Aug. 2001–; Bronze Star, Purple Heart, Vietnamese Cross of Gallantry. *Address:* U.S. Department of Justice, Federal Bureau of Investigation, J. Edgar Hoover Building, 950 Pennsylvania Avenue, NW, Washington, DC 20530, USA (Office).

MUELLER-STAHL, Armin; German actor; b. 17 Dec. 1930, Tilsit, East Prussia (now Russia); ed Berlin Conservatory; began career with music studies (violin), subsequently became actor; moved to FRG 1980; Hon. DHumLitt (Chicago); Bundesfilmpreis 1981, Silver Bar Award 1992, Australian Film Prize (for Shine) 1996. *Films:* Naked Among the Wolves, The Third, Jacob the Liar, The Flight, Lite Trap, Lola, Wings of Night, Veronika Voss, A Cop's Sunday, A Love in Germany, Thousand Eyes, Trauma, Colonel Redl, L'Homme Blessé, God Doesn't Believe in Us Anymore, Angry Harvest, The Blind Director, Following the Führer, Momo, The Jungle Mission, Lethal Obsession, Midnight Cop, Music Box, Das Spinnenetz, Just for Kicks, Avalon, Bronstein's Children, Kafka, The Power of One, Night on Earth, Utz, The House of the Spirits, Holy Matrimony, The Last Good Time, A Pyromaniac's Love Story, Taxandria, Shine, Theodore Rex, Peacemaker, The Game, Commissioner. *Television:* (mini-series) Amerika. *Publications:* Verordneter Sonntag (Lost Sunday), Drehtage, Unterwegs Nach Hause (On the Way Home).

MUFAMADI, Fholisani Sydney; South African politician; b. 28 Feb. 1959, Alexandra; m. Nomsa Mboweni; two d.; pvt. teacher Lamula Secondary School 1980; Gen. Sec. Gen. and Allied Workers' Union 1982; Publicity Sec. United Democratic Front (UDF); Asst Gen. Sec. Congress of SA Trade Unions 1985; mem. Nat. Peace Cttee, helped draft Nat. Peace Accord 1991; mem. ANC Nat. Exec. Cttee, ANC Working Cttee, Cen. Cttee of SA Communist Party, Political Bureau; ANC Rep. at Transitional Exec. Council on Law and Order, Safety and Stability 1993–94; Minister of Safety and Security, Govt of Nat. Unity 1994–99, of Provincial Affairs and Local Govt 1999–. *Address:* Ministry of Provincial Affairs and Local Government, 87 Hamilton Street, Arcadia, Pretoria 0083, South Africa (Office). *Telephone:* (12) 3340600 (Office). *Fax:* (12) 3340604 (Office). *E-mail:* editor@dso.pwv.gov.za (Office). *Website:* www .local.gov.za (Office).

MUGABE, Robert Gabriel, BA, BAdmin, BEd, MSc(Econ), LLM; Zimbabwean politician and fmr teacher; b. 21 Feb. 1924, Kutama; m. 1st Sarah Mugabe (died 1992); one s. (deceased); m. 2nd Grace Marufu 1996; ed Kutama and Empandeni Mission School, Fort Hare Univ. Coll., S. Africa, Univs. of S. Africa and London; teacher, at Drifontein Roman Catholic School, Umvuma 1952, Salisbury S. Primary School 1953, in Gwelo 1954, Chalimbana Teacher Training Coll. 1955, in Accra, Ghana 1958–60; entered politics 1960; Publicity Sec. of Nat. Dem. Party 1960–61; Publicity Sec. Zimbabwe African People's Union 1961; detained Sept.–Dec. 1962, March–April 1963; escaped to Tanzania April 1963; Co-founder of Zimbabwe African Nat. Union (ZANU) Aug. 1963; Sec.-Gen. Aug. 1963; in detention in Rhodesia 1964–74; Pres. ZANU; mem. Politburo ZANU 1984–; Jt Leader of Patriotic Front (with Joshua Nkomo) 1976–79; contested Feb. 1980 elections as Leader of ZANU (PF) (name changed to ZANU 1984) Party, Pres. 1988–; Prime Minister of Zimbabwe 1980–87; Pres. of Zimbabwe 1988–; Minister of Defence 1980–87, also fmrly of Public Works, Industry and Tech.; Chancellor Univ. of Zimbabwe; attended Geneva Constitutional Conf. on Rhodesia 1976, Malta Conf., 1978, Lancaster House Conf. Sept.–Dec. 1979; Newsmaker of the Year Award (S. African Soc. of Journalists) 1980, Africa Prize 1988; Dr hc (Ahmadu Bello Univ., Nigeria) 1980, (Edin. Univ.) 1984; Int. Human Rights Award (Howard

Univ., Washington) 1981, Jawarhal Nehru Award 1992. *Address:* Office of the President, Munhumutapa Building, Samora Machel Avenue, Private Bag 7700, Causeway, Harare, Zimbabwe. *Telephone:* (4) 707091 (Office).

MUGLER, Thierry; French fashion designer; b. 1946, Strasbourg; ed in Strasbourg; fmr ballet dancer, Opéra du Rhin, Strasbourg; later window-dresser and clothing designer, Gudule boutique, Paris; designer of fashion collection for André Peters, London; subsequently began career as freelance clothing designer in Amsterdam, later in Paris where he launched Café de Paris collection; designer of menswear and fashion accessories; launched own Thierry Mugler fashion label, Paris 1973; launched Thierry Mugler Diffusion fashion co,; opened own boutique, Place des Victoires, Paris; clothing also sold in dept stores in USA and Japan.

MUHAMMAD, Ali Nasser; Yemeni politician; b. 1939, Dathina Rural District; active mem. of Nat. Liberation Front (NLF) 1963–67; Gov. of the Islands 1967, of Second Province 1968; mem. Nat. Front Gen. Command March 1968; Minister of Local Govt 1969, of Defence 1969–77, of Educ. 1974–75; mem. Front Exec. Cttee 1970; mem. Presidential Council of People's Democratic Repub. of Yemen 1971–78, Chair. June–Dec. 1978; Chair. Council of Ministers (Prime Minister) 1971–85; mem. Supreme People's Council (SPC) 1971, Chair. Presidium of SPC (Head of State) 1980–86 (overthrown in coup Jan. 1986); mem. Political Bureau of Nat. Front 1972–75, of United Political Org. Nat. Front 1975–78, of Yemen Socialist Party (YSP) 1978–86, Sec.-Gen. of YSP 1980–86.

MUHEIM, Franz Emmanuel, LèsL; Swiss diplomatist (retd) and academic; b. 27 Sept. 1931, Berne; s. of Hans Muheim and Hélène Ody; m. Radmila Jovanovic 1962; ed Univs. of Fribourg, Geneva and Paris; joined Fed. Dept of Foreign Affairs 1960, served successively in Belgrade, Rabat and London 1961–70, Council of Europe, UN and Int. Orgs. Section, Dept of Foreign Affairs, Berne 1971–77, Deputy Head of Mission, Minister Plenipotentiary, Washington, DC 1978–81, Deputy Dir Political Affairs and Head, Political Div. Europe and N America, with rank of Amb., Berne 1982–83, Dir Int. Orgs., Dept of Foreign Affairs 1984–89, Amb. to UK 1989–94; Pres. Swiss Red Cross 1996–2001; Vice-Pres. Int. Fed. of Red Cross and Red Crescent Socs. 1996–2001; Head of Swiss dels. to int. confs. including UNESCO, Int. Red Cross, Non-Aligned Movement; Fellow Center for Int. Affairs, Harvard Univ., USA 1981–82; Prof. Bologna Center of Johns Hopkins Univ. 1995–96; Pres. Fribourg Festival of Sacred Music. *Exhibitions:* Photographs from China (Boston, USA and Bezu, Switzerland) 1980. *Publications:* (Jt Ed.) Einblick in die Schweizerische Aussenpolitik: Festschrift für Staatssekretär Raymond Probst 1984; (contrib.) Les organisations internationales entre l'innovation et la stagnation 1984, Multilateralism Today, Geburtstag von a. Ständerat Franz Muheim 1993. *Leisure interests:* walking, mountaineering, skiing, photography, classical music. *Address:* Es Chesaux, 1646 Echarlens, Switzerland. *Telephone:* (26) 9152474. *Fax:* (26) 9152450. *E-mail:* franz.e.muheim@ mcnet.ch (Home).

MÜHLEMANN, Lukas, MBA; Swiss business executive; b. 1950; ed Univ. of St Gallen and Harvard Univ.; fmr systems engineer IBM; man. consultant McKinsey & Co. 1977–94, Prin. 1982, Dir 1986, Man. Dir McKinsey's Swiss offices 1989, mem. Bd Dirs McKinsey & Co., Inc., New York 1990; CEO Swiss Re 1994, Man. Dir 1994, Deputy Chair. 1996; CEO Credit Suisse Group 1997–2002, Chair. Bd Dirs 2000–02, mem. Bd Dirs Credit Suisse, Credit Suisse First Boston; mem. Bd Tonhalle Foundation, Zurich, Zurich Opera House, Banco Gen. de Negocios; Pres. Harvard Club of Switzerland. *Address:* c/o Credit Suisse Group, Paradeplatz 8, P.O. Box 1, CH-8070 Zurich, Switzerland.

MUIR, (Isabella) Helen (Mary), CBE, MA, DPhil, DSc, FRS; British biochemist; b. 20 Aug. 1920, Naini Tal, Uttar Pradesh, India; d. of the late Basil Fairlie Muir and Gwladys Helen Muir; ed Somerville Coll., Univ. of Oxford; Research Fellow Univ. of Oxford 1947–48; Research Scientist Nat. Inst. for Medical Research 1948–54; at St Mary's Hosp. 1954–66, Empire Rheumatism Council Fellow 1954–58, Pearl Research Fellow 1959–66; Head of Div. Kennedy Inst. of Rheumatology 1966–86, Dir 1977–90; Bunim Lecturer U.S. Arthritis Assen 1978; Visiting Prof. of Biochem., Queen Elizabeth Coll. 1981–85, Newcastle Univ. 1995, Manchester Univ. 1997–; Hon. Prof. of Biochem. Charing Cross Hosp. Medical School 1979–90; Gov. Strangeways Research Lab. 1980–90; mem. Arthritis and Rheumatism Council Research Sub-Cttee 1962–75; mem. Editorial Bd Biochemical Journal 1964–70, Annals of Rheumatic Diseases 1971–77, Connective Tissue Research 1971–85, Journal of Orthopaedic Research 1983–; Scientific mem. MRC 1973–77; Hon. Fellow Somerville Coll., Oxford 1978; Hon. mem. American Soc. Biological Chemists; Foreign mem. Royal Swedish Acad. of Sciences 1989; mem. Council Royal Soc. 1982–83, Council Chelsea Coll. 1982–85; Wellcome Trustee 1982–90; Hon. DSc (Edin.) 1982, (Strathclyde) 1983, (Brunel) 1990; numerous awards including Heberden Orator and Medallist 1976, Feldberg Prize 1977, Bunim Medal of American Arthritis Assen 1978, Co-Winner Basic Science Section Volvo Prize 1980, Neil Hamilton Fairley Medal 1981, CIBA Medal Biochemical Soc. 1981, Steindler Award Orthopaedic Research Soc., USA 1982, CIBA Int. Award 1993. *Publications:* over 200 articles, mainly on biochem. of connective tissues in relation to arthritis and inherited diseases; contrib. several specialist books. *Leisure interests:* gardening, music, horses, natural history, ballet. *Address:* School of Biological Sciences, University of Manchester, Stopford

Building, Oxford Road, Manchester, ML3 9PT (Office); Langlands House, Hornby, Bedale, North Yorkshire, DL8 1NG, England. *Telephone:* (161) 275-5074 (Office); (1677) 450307.

MUIR, Richard John Sutherland, CMG, BA; British diplomatist; b. 25 Aug. 1942, London; s. of John Muir and Edna Hodges; m. Caroline Simpson 1965; one s. one d; ed Stationers' Co. School and Univs. of Reading and Strasbourg; entered HM Diplomatic Service 1966; Second Sec. Jeddah 1967–70, Tunis 1970–72; FCO 1972–75; First Sec. Washington, DC 1975–79; Prin. Dept of Energy 1979–81; Counsellor, Jeddah 1981–85; FCO 1985–91; Under-Sec. and Chief Insp. Diplomatic Service 1991–94; Amb. to Oman 1994–98, to Kuwait 1999–. *Leisure interests:* walking, sailing, fishing, opera. *Address:* United Kingdom Embassy, P.O. Box 2, 13001 Safat, Arabian Gulf Street, Kuwait City, Kuwait (Office); c/o Foreign and Commonwealth Office, London, SW1A 2AH, England. *Telephone:* 2403336 (Office). *Fax:* 2426799 (Office). *E-mail:* bmtemb@kems.net (Office).

MUIR WOOD, Sir Alan (Marshall), Kt, MA, F.R.ENG., FRS, FICE; British consulting civil engineer; b. 8 Aug. 1921, London; s. of Edward Stephen Wood and Dorothy Wood (née Webb); m. Winifred Leyton Lanagan (Dr W. L. Wood) 1943; three s.; ed Abbotsholme School, Derbyshire and Peterhouse, Cambridge; Engineer Officer, RN 1942–46; Asst Engineer, British Rail 1946–50; Research Asst, Docks Exec. 1950–52; Engineer, Sir William Halcrow & Partners 1952–64, Partner, then Sr Partner 1964–84, Consultant 1984–; Pres. Inst. of Civil Engineers 1977–78; Fellow, Imperial Coll. London; Foreign mem. Royal Swedish Acad. of Eng Sciences; Hon. Fellow, Peterhouse, Portsmouth Polytechnic; Hon. DSc (City Univ.) 1978, (Southampton) 1986; Hon. LLD (Dundee) 1985; Hon. DEng (Bristol) 1991; Telford Medal (ICE) 1976, Ewing Medal (ICE and Royal Soc.) 1984, ICE Gold Medal 1998. *Publication:* Coastal Hydraulics 1969, 2nd edn with C. A. Fleming 1981, Tunnelling: Management by Design 2000. *Leisure interests:* music, arts and the countryside. *Address:* Franklands, Bere Court Road, Pangbourne, Berkshire, RG8 8JY, England.

MUJURU, Joyce Teurai-Ropa; Zimbabwean politician; b. 15 April 1955, Mt. Darwin; m. Tapfumanei Ruzambu Solomon Mujuru (Nhongo) 1977; four d.; Minister of Youth, Sport and Recreation 1980–81, of Community Devt and Women's Affairs 1981–88, of Community and Co-operative Devt 1989–92, of Rural Resources and Water Devt 1996–; Gov. and Resident Minister of Mashonaland Cen. Prov. 1993–96. *Leisure interests:* church and women's meetings, knitting, sewing, cooking, outdoor life. *Address:* Ministry of Rural Resources and Water Development, Makombe Complex, Private Bag 7701, Causeway, Harare, Zimbabwe. *Telephone:* (4) 706081 (Office).

MUKHAMEDOV, Irek Javdatovich, OBE; Russian/Tatar ballet dancer; b. 8 Feb. 1960; m. Maria Zubkova; one d.; ed Moscow Choreographic Inst.; joined Moscow Classical Co.; debut with Bolshoi Ballet in title role of Grigorovich's Spartacus 1981; other roles include Ivan IV in Ivan the Terrible, Jean de Brienne in Raymonda, Basil in Don Quixote, Romeo in Grigorovich's Romeo and Juliet, Boris in Grigorovich's The Golden Age; toured extensively with Bolshoi Ballet and made worldwide guest appearances; joined The Royal Ballet 1990; Covent Garden debut in MacMillan's pas de deux Farewell (with Darcey Bussell) 1990; f. Irek Mukhamedov & Co. 1991–; appeared in musical The King and I, London 1995. *Address:* c/o Royal Ballet, Royal Opera House, Covent Garden, London, WC2E 9DD, England. *Telephone:* (20) 7240-1200.

MUKHAMETSHIN, Farid Khairullovich, DScS; Russian/Tatar politician; b. 22 May 1947, Almetyevsk, Tatarstan; m.; two c.; ed Almetyevak Higher Professional Tech. School, Ufa Inst. of Oil; metal turner in factories; CP functionary: Sec. Almetyevsk City CP Cttee; Chair. Exec. Cttee, Almetyevsk City Soviet; Deputy Chair. Council of Ministers, Minister of Trade of Tatar ASSR 1970–91; Chair. Supreme Soviet of Tatarstan Repub., 1991–94; mem. Council of Fed. 1991–94, 1998–; Prime Minister of Tatarstan Repub.1995–98; Chair. State Council of Tatarstan 1998–; leader Tatarstan New Age political Movt 1999–. *Address:* Parliament Building, Svobody pl. 1, 420060 Kazan, Tatarstan, Russia. *Telephone:* (8432) 67-63-00 (Office). *Fax:* (8432) 92-73-59 (Office). *E-mail:* first@gossov.tatarstan.ru (Office). *Website:* www.gossov .tatarstan.ru (Office).

MUKHERJEE, Bharati; American (b. Indian) lecturer and author; b. 27 July 1940, Calcutta; s. of Sudhir Lal Mukherjee and Bina Banerjee; m. Clark Blaise 1963; two s.; ed Univs of Calcutta, Baroda and Iowa; Prof. of English, McGill Univ.; lecturer Skidmore Coll.; Lecturer in Literature and Creative Writing, Queen's Coll., New York; Prof. Univ. of Calif. at Berkeley 1990–. *Publications include:* The Tiger's Daughter 1971, The Tiger's Daughter and Wife 1975, Days and Night in Calcutta 1977, Darkness 1985, The Sorrow and the Terror (with Clark Blaise) 1987, The Middleman and Other Stories (Nat. Book Critics Circle Award for Fiction 1988) 1988, Jasmine 1989, The Holder of the World 1993, Leave it to Me 1996. *Address:* c/o Janklow and Nesbit, 598 Madison Avenue, New York, NY 10022; 130 Rivoli Street, San Francisco, CA 94117, U.S.A. *Telephone:* (415) 681-0345. *Fax:* (415) 759-9810.

MUKHERJEE, Pranab Kumar, MA, LLB; Indian politician; b. 11 Dec. 1935, Kirnahar, Birbhum District, W Bengal; s. of Kamada Kinkar Mukherjee and Rajlakshmki Mukherjee; m.; two s. one d; ed Univ. of Calcutta; started career as lecturer; Ed. Palli-O-Panchayat Sambad (Bengali monthly); Founder-Ed. Desher Dak (Bengali weekly) 1967–71; mem. Rajya Sabha 1969–, Leader 1980–88; Deputy Minister of Industrial Devt, Govt of India 1973; Deputy Minister for Shipping and Transport Jan.–Oct. 1974; Minister of State,

Ministry of Finance 1974–75; Minister for Revenue and Banking 1975–77; Minister of Commerce 1980–82, of Finance Jan.–Sept. 1982, of Finance 1982–85, of Commerce 1993–95, of External Affairs 1995–96; Deputy Chair. Planning Comm. with Cabinet rank; f. Rashtriya Samajwadi Congress 1987–; mem. Exec. Cttee Congress (I) Party 1972–73, All India Congress Cttee 1986; Treas. Congress (I) Party, mem. Working Cttee, Deputy Leader in Rajya Sabha; Pres. W Bengal Pradesh Congress Cttee; Hon. DLitt. *Publications:* Bangla Congress: An Aspect of Constitutional Problems in Bengal 1967, Mid-term Election 1969, Off the Track 1987, Challenges before the Nation 1992. *Leisure interests:* reading, gardening, music. *Address:* 2-A, 1st Floor, 602/7 Kabi Bharti Sarni (Lake Road), Calcutta 700 029, India; 13 Talkatora Road, New Delhi 110 001 (Home); S-22, Greater Kailash-II, New Delhi 110 048 (Office). *Telephone:* (11) 3737623 (Office); (11) 6435656 (Home); (11) 6474025. *E-mail:* pkm@sansad.nic.in (Office).

MUKUMBAYEV, Usup Mukambayevich; Kyrgyzstan politician; b. 28 Jan. 1941, Dzholgolot, Kyrgyzia; m. Galina Mukumbayeva; two d.; ed Kyrgyz State Univ., Higher Courses USSR Cttee of State Security; army service; shepherd Kolkhoz Ak-Suy Region; Sec. CP Cttee of State Security Cttee Kyrgyz Repub. 1970–78; Deputy Dir Dept of State Security Cttee Osh Region 1978–80; Dir Dept of State Security Cttee Talass and Osh Regions 1980–86; First Deputy Dir State Security Cttee Kyrgyz Repub. 1986–91; Minister of Justice 1991–95; mem. Parl. (Zhogorku Kenesh) of Kyrgyzstan 1990–2000, Chair 1996–2000; Pres.'s Rep. in Parl. 2001–; Chair. Legislation Asscn Kyrgyz Parl. *Address:* Zhogorku Kenesh, 720003 Bishkek, Kyrgyzstan (Office). *Telephone:* (3312) 22-55-23 (Office).

MULAMBA NYUNYI WA KADIMA, Gen. (Léonard); Democratic Republic of the Congo politician, army officer and diplomatist; b. 1928, Luluabourg (now Kananga); s. of Kadima Mulamba and Ngalula Mulamba; m. Adolphine N'galula 1956; six s. two d.; ed Mil. School, Luluabourg; commissioned 1954; Maj. and Deputy Dir of Cabinet, Ministry of Defence 1961–64; Lt-Col 1962; Col, Chief of Staff and Commr of Eastern Province (now Haut Zaïre) after re-occupation of Kivu Province 1964–65; Prime Minister 1965–66; Pres. Soc. nationale d'Assurances (SONAS) 1966; Amb. to India 1967–69; Amb. to Japan 1969–76, also Accred to Repub. of Korea 1971–76; Amb. to Brazil 1976–79; Gén. de Division, Gén. de Corps d'Armée 1979; Mil. Medal, Cross of Bravery, Commdr Ordre de la Couronne (Belgium), Grand Officier Ordre nat. du Léopard (Zaire), Ordre du Mérite (Cen. African Republic), Compagnon de la Révolution. *Leisure interests:* hunting, reading. *Address:* c/o Chancellerie des Ordres Nationaux, B.P. 2014, Kinshasa, Democratic Republic of Congo.

MULCAHY, Sir Geoffrey John, Kt, BSc, MBA; British business executive; b. 7 Feb. 1942, Sunderland; s. of Maurice Mulcahy and Kathleen (née Blankinsop) Mulcahy; m. Valerie Elizabeth Mulcahy 1965; one s. one d.; ed King's School, Worcester, Univ. of Manchester, Harvard Univ.; started career in labour relations, marketing and planning with Esso Corpn; Finance Dir Norton Abrasives' European Div., then for British Sugar; joined Woolworth Holdings (now Kingfisher PLC) 1983, firstly as Group Financial Dir, then Group Man. Dir 1984–86, CEO 1986–93, Chair. 1990–95, Group Chief Exec. Kingfisher Group 1995–2002. *Leisure interest:* sailing. *Address:* PO Box 35466, London, NW8 9WG, England.

MULDOON, Paul Benedict, BA; Irish poet and university professor; b. 20 June 1951, Portadown; s. of Patrick Muldoon and Brigid Regan; m. Jean Hanff Korelitz 1987; one s. one d.; ed St Patrick's Coll., Armagh, Queen's Univ., Belfast; Radio and TV Producer, BBC NI 1973–86; has taught at Cambridge Univ., Univ. of E. Anglia, Columbia Univ., Univ. of Calif. at Berkeley, Univ. of Mass. 1986–; Lecturer, Princeton Univ. 1990–95, Prof. 1995–; Hon. Prof. of Poetry Oxford Univ. 1999–; Guggenheim Fellowship 1990; T. S. Eliot Prize for The Annals of Chile 1995, American Acad. of Arts and Letters Award for Literature 1996. *Publications:* New Weather 1973, Mules 1977, Why Brownlee Left 1980, Quoof 1983, Meeting the British 1987, Madoc: A Mystery 1990, The Annals of Chile 1995; Selected Poems 1968–83 1986, New Selected Poems 1968–1994 1996, Hay (poems) 1999, Poems 1968–1998 2001; Ed. The Faber Book of Beasts 1997, Moy Sand and Gravel (Pulitzer Prize for Poetry) 2002. *Address:* Creative Writing Programme, Princeton University, Princeton, NJ 08544, USA. *Website:* www.paulmuldoon.net (Home).

MULDOWNEY, Dominic John, BPhil; British composer; b. 19 July 1952, Southampton; s. of William Muldowney and Barbara Muldowney (née Lavender); m. Diane Ellen Trevis 1986; one d.; ed Taunton's Grammar School, Southampton and York Univ.; Composer-in-Residence to Southern Arts Asscn 1974–76; Music Dir, Royal Nat. Theatre 1976–; Prof. of Composition, RAM 1999–; has composed music for British and int. festivals, for many films and TV and over 50 scores for the theatre; Prix Italia 1993, 1997. *Publications:* Piano Concerto 1983, Saxophone Concerto 1984, Sinfonietta 1986, Ars Subtilior 1987, Lonely Hearts 1988, Violin Concerto 1989, Three Pieces for Orchestra 1990, Percussion Concerto 1991, Oboe Concerto 1992, Trumpet Concerto 1993, Concerto for 4 Violins 1994 The Brontës (ballet) 1995, Trombone Concerto 1996, Clarinet Concerto 1997, The Fall of Jerusalem (oratorio) 1998, God's Plenty (ballet) 1999. *Leisure interest:* driving through France and across America. *Address:* c/o Carlin Music, 3 Bridge Approach, Chalk Farm, London, NW1 8BD, England. *Telephone:* (20) 7734-3251 (Office).

MULLAN, Peter, BSc; British actor and film director; b. b.1954, Glasgow; ed Univ. of Glasgow; debut with Wildcat Theatre Co. 1988; Hon. MA (Caledonian Univ., Glasgow) 2000. *Film appearances include:* Riff-Raff 1990, The Big Man

1991, Shallow Grave 1994, Braveheart 1995, Ruffian Hearts 1995, Good Day for the Bad Guys 1995, Trainspotting 1996, Fairytale: A True Story, My Name is Joe (Best Actor Award, Cannes Film Festival 1998) 1998, Duck 1998, Miss Julie 1999, Mauvaise passe 1999, Ordinary Decent Criminal 2000, The Claim 2000, Session 9 2001, The Magdalene Sisters 2000, Entering Blue Zone 2002, Young Adam 2002. *Films written and directed include:* Good Day for the Bay Guys 1995, Fridge 1996, Orphans (Golden Lion Award, Venice Film Festival 1998) 1997, The Magdalene Sisters (Golden Lion Award, Venice Film Festival 2002) 2002. *Films produced include:* Caesar 2000. *Television includes:* Rab C. Nesbitt (series) 1990, Jute City (film) 1991, Nightlife (film) 1996, Cardiac Arrest (series) 1996–97, Bogwoman (film) 1997.

MÜLLER, Claus, Dr rer. nat; German university professor and consultant; b. 20 Feb. 1920, Solingen; s. of Michael Müller and Grete (née Porten) Müller; m. Irmgard Döring 1947; two s. one d.; ed Univs. of Bonn and Munich; service in German army and navy 1941–45; Asst Prof. Göttingen Univ. 1945–46; lecturer Bonn Univ. 1947–55; lecturer, Univ. Coll. Hull 1949; Prof. and Dir Inst. of Math. Sciences, Tech. Univ. of Aachen 1955–85, Prof. Emer. 1985–; Fellow Peterhouse, Cambridge 1948; Visiting Prof. Princeton Inst. 1952, Courant Inst., New York, Math. Research Center Madison, Boeing Scientific Research Lab. 1955–65; Saragossa Acad. 1968, North-Rhine Acad. 1970. *Publications:* Foundations of the Mathematical Theory of Electromagnetic Waves, Spherical Harmonics, Analysis of Spherical Symmetries 1997; specialist articles in math. *Leisure interest:* music. *Address:* Horbacher Strasse 33, 52072 Aachen, Germany. *Telephone:* (241) 12661.

MÜLLER, Gerhard, DTheol; German ecclesiastic; b. 10 May 1929, Marburg/ Lahn; s. of Karl Müller and Elisabeth Landau; m. Ursula Herboth 1957; two s.; ed Marburg, Göttingen and Tübingen; priest in Hanau/Main 1956–57; Deutsche Forschungsgemeinschaft scholarship, Italy 1957–59; Asst, Ecumenical Seminar, Univ. of Marburg 1959–61, Docent, Faculty of Theology 1961–66; guest lecturer, German Historical Inst., Rome 1966–67; Prof. of Historical Theology (Modern Church History), Univ. of Erlangen 1967–82; Evangelical-Lutheran Bishop of Brunswick 1982–94; Hon. Prof. Univ. of Göttingen 1983–; mem. Mainz, Netherlands Acads. and Braunschweiger Wissenschaftliche Gesellschaft; Hon. DTheol (St Andrews). *Publications:* Franz Lambert von Avignon und die Reformation in Hessen 1958, Nuntiaturberichte aus Deutschland 1530–1532 (2 Vols) 1963, 1969, Die römische Kurie und die Reformation 1523–1534 1969, Die Rechtfertigungslehre 1977, Reformation und Stadt 1981, Zwischen Reformation und Gegenwart 1983, Zwischen Reformation und Gegenwart II 1988, Causa Reformationis 1989, Die Mystik oder das Wort? 2000; ed. works of Andreas Osiander and a 34-vol. theological encyclopaedia. *Address:* Sperlingstr. 59, 91056 Erlangen, Germany. *Telephone:* (9131) 490939. *Fax:* (9131) 490939.

MÜLLER, K. Alex, PhD; Swiss physicist; b. 20 April 1927, Chur; ed Swiss Fed. Inst. of Tech.; Lecturer, Univ. of Zurich 1962, Titular Prof. 1970, Prof. 1987–; joined IBM Zurich Research Lab. Rüschlikon in 1963, Man. Dept of Physics, Fellow 1973–92, Researcher 1985–, Fellow Emer. 1992–98; Fellow American Physics Soc.; mem. European Physics Soc., Swiss Physics Soc.; Hon. DSc from 17 univs.; Nobel Prize for Physics (with G. Bednorz) for discovery of new superconducting materials 1987, Hewlett-Packard Europhysics Prize 1988, APS Int. Prize for New Materials Research 1988, Minnie Rosen Award, Ross Univ., New York 1989, Special Tsukuba Award 1989, Int. 'Aldo Villa' Prize, Italian Ceramic Soc. 1991. *Publications;* over 400 Publs. *Address:* University of Zürich, Physik-Institut Winterthurerstr. 190, 8057 Zürich (Office); Haldenstr. 54, 8909 Hedingen, Switzerland (Home). *Telephone:* (1) 6355721 (Office). *Fax:* (1) 6355704 (Office).

MÜLLER, Klaus-Peter; German banker; b. 16 Sept. 1944, Duppach; m.; one c.; apprenticeship in banking, Bankhaus Friedrich Simon KGaA, Düsseldorf 1962–64; with Düsseldorf Br., Commerzbank AG 1966–68, New York Rep. Office and Br. 1968–73; Jt Man. Düsseldorf and Duisburg Br. 1973–82, Jt Man. New York Br. 1982–86, Exec. Vice-Pres. 1986–90, Head of Corp. Banking Dept 1990–2001, mem. Bd of Man. Dirs. 1990–, Chair. 2001–. *Address:* Commerzbank AG, 60261 Frankfurt/Main, Germany (Office). *Telephone:* (69) 13620 (Office). *Fax:* (69) 285389 (Office). *E-mail:* info@commerzbank.com (Office). *Website:* www.commerzbank.com, www.commerzbank.de (Office).

MÜLLER, Lothar; German financier; b. 27 Jan. 1927, Munich; m. Irmgard Mueller; one s. three d.; with tax authority of Bavaria 1954; Head Bavarian Finance Ministry 1977–79; Pres. Landeszentralbank, Bavaria 1979–94; mem. Cen. Bank Council of the Deutsche Bundesbank; Bayerischer Verdienstorden, Grosses Bundesverdienstkreuz. *Publications:* publs on public finance, company and tax law, monetary and economic policy. *Address:* Waldparkstrasse 35c, 85521 Riemerling, Germany. *Telephone:* (89) 28893200. *Fax:* (89) 28893890.

MÜLLER, Peter; German lawyer and politician; b. 25 Sept. 1955, Illingen; m. Astrid Gercke-Müller; three s.; ed Lebach Grammar School, Univs. of Bonn and Saarbrücken; trainee lawyer 1983–86; Asst Lecturer Univ. of Saarland 1983–86, later Chair. Constitutional and Admin. Law; Judge Saarbrücken Regional Court –1990; mem. CDU Parl. Party, Saarland Parl. 1990–; Minister Pres. of Saarland Sept. 1999–; Dr h c (Univ. of Tokyo) 2001. *Publication:* Nach dem Pisa-Shock. Plädoyers für eine Bildungsreform (co-ed.) 2002. *Leisure interests:* active footballer, plays chess and skat, clarinet and saxophone. *Address:* Landtag des Saarlandes, Postfach 101833, 66081 Saarbrücken (Office); Saarländische Staatskanzlei, Am Ludwigsplatz 14, Postfach

102431, 66024 Saarbrücken, Germany (Office). *Telephone:* (681) 5011122 (Office). *Fax:* (681) 5011159 (Office). *E-mail:* p.mueller@staatskanzlei .saarland.de (Office). *Website:* www.saarland.de, www.staatskanzlei .saarland.de (Office).

MULLER, Steven, PhD; American university and hospital administrator; b. 22 Nov. 1927, Hamburg, Germany; s. of Werner A. and Marianne (Hartstein) Muller; m. 1st Margie Hellman 1951; two d.; m. 2nd Jill E. McGovern 2000; ed Hollywood High School, Los Angeles, Univ. of Calif., Los Angeles, Oxford Univ., Cornell Univ.; Instructor in Political Science, Wells Coll. 1953; U.S. Army 1954–55; Research Fellow in Social Science, Cornell Univ. 1955–56; Asst Prof. of Political Science, Haverford Coll. 1956–58; Asst Prof. of Govt, Cornell Univ. 1958–61, Assoc. Prof. and Dir Center for Int. Studies 1961–66, Vice-Pres. for Public Affairs 1966–71; Provost, Johns Hopkins Univ. 1971–72, Pres. 1972–90, Pres. Emer. 1990–; Prof. School of Advanced Int. Studies 1993; Pres. Johns Hopkins Hosp. 1972–83; Chair. 21st Century Foundation 1990–96; Chair. of Bd St Mary's Coll. of Md; Co-Chair. American Inst. for Contemporary German Studies; Dir Law/Gibb Corpn, Org. Resources Counselors, Inc., Atlantic Council of the U.S., German Marshall Fund of the U.S.; fmr mem. Bd of Dirs., CSX Corpn, Millipore Corpn, Beneficial Corpn, Alex. Brown & Sons Inc., Van Kampen Closed End Funds; Commdr.'s Cross of the Order of Merit (FRG). *Publications:* Documents on European Government 1963, From Occupation to Cooperation 1992 (co-ed.), In Search of Germany 1996 (co-ed.), Universities in the Twenty-First Century 1996; articles in learned journals. *Leisure interest:* philately. *Address:* Johns Hopkins University, School of Advanced International Studies, 1619 Massachusetts Avenue, NW, Suite 406, Washington, DC 20036 (Office); 2315 Bancroft Place, NW, Washington, DC 20008-4005, USA (Home). *Telephone:* (202) 663-5821 (Office); (202) 387-2777 (Home). *Fax:* (202) 663-5822 (Office); (202) 387-6777 (Home). *E-mail:* kareese@mail.jhuwash.jhu.edu (Office); catalina53@juno .com (Home).

MÜLLER, Werner; German politician and business executive; b. 1 June 1946, Essen; m.; two c.; ed Univs. of Mannheim, Duisberg and Bremen; teacher Ludwigshafen Polytechnic 1970–72; Dept Chief Rheinisch-Westfälische electricity co. (RWE) 1973–80; gen. rep. and Chief Exec. VEBA power co. 1980–87; Adviser to Minister-Pres. of Lower Saxony 1991–; ind. industrial consultant 1997–98; Fed. Minister of Econ. and Tech. 1998–; Independent. *Address:* Ministry of Economics and Technology, Scharnhorststrasse 34–37, 10115 Berlin, Germany. *Telephone:* (1888) 6150. *Fax:* (1888) 6157010. *E-mail:* info@bmwi.bund.de (Office). *Website:* www.bmwi.de (Office).

MÜLLER-SEIDEL, Walter, DPhil; German professor of modern literature; b. 1 July 1918, Schöna; s. of Martin Müller-Seidel and Rosa (née Seidel) Müller; m. Ilse Peters 1950; one s.; ed Univs. of Leipzig and Heidelberg; lecturer Univ. of Cologne 1958, Privat-dozent 1958–59; Prof. Univ. of Munich 1960–65; Ordinary Prof. 1965, now Emer.; mem. Bayerischen Akad. der Wissenschaften 1974. *Publications:* Versehen und Erkennen: Eine Studie über Heinrich von Kleist 1961, Probleme der literarischen Wertung 1965, Theodor Fontane: Soziale Romankunst in Deutschland 1975, Die Geschichtlichkeit der deutscher Klassik 1983, Die Deportation des Menschen, Kafkas Erzählung 'In der Strafkolonie' im europäischen Kontext 1986, Arztbilder im Wandel. Zum literarischen Werk Arthur Schnitzlers 1997, Alfred Erich Hoche: Lebensgeschichte im spannungsfeld von Psychiatrie 1999, Strafrecht und Literatur 1999. *Address:* Pienzenauerstrasse 164, 81925 Munich, Germany. *Telephone:* (89) 988250.

MULLIS, Kary Banks, PhD; American biochemist; b. 28 Dec. 1944, Lenoir, NC; s. of Cecil Banks Mullis and Bernice Alberta Barker Fredericks Mullis; two s. one d.; ed Georgia Inst. of Tech., Univ. of California, Berkeley; Lecturer in Biochem. Univ. of Calif., Berkeley 1972; Postdoctoral Fellow, Univ. of Kan. Medical School 1973–76, Univ. of Calif., San Francisco 1977–79; researcher Cetus Corp. 1979–86; Dir Molecular Biology Xytronyx, Inc., San Diego 1986–88; consultant 1988–96; Chair. StarGene, Inc.; Vice-Pres. Histotec, Inc., Vyrex lnc.; Visiting Prof. Univ of SC; Partner in Questar Int. 1998; devised polymerase chain reaction; Preis Biochemische Analytik Award 1990, Allan Award 1990, Gairdner Foundation Award 1991, Nat. Biotech. Award 1991, R&D Magazine Scientist of the Year 1991, Koch Award 1992, Chiron Corpn Award 1992, Japan Prize 1992, Calif. Scientist of the Year 1992, shared Nobel Prize for Chem. 1993, Japanese Science and Tech. Foundation Award 1993. *Publications:* numerous articles.

MULLOVA, Viktoria; Russian violinist; b. 27 Nov. 1959, Moscow; d. of Raissa Mullova and Yuri Mullov; one s. two d.; studied in Moscow at Cen. Music School and Moscow Conservatory under Leonid Kogan; left USSR 1983; has appeared with most maj. orchestras and conductors and at int. festivals; first prize at Sibelius Competition, Helsinki 1980, Gold Medal, Tchaikovsky Competition, Moscow 1982. *Recordings include:* Tchaikovsky and Sibelius Violin Concertos with Boston Symphony under Seiji Ozawa (Grand Prix du disque); Bartok, Bach and Paganini solo works; Shostakovich Concerto No. 1, Prokofiev Concerto No. 2; Brahms Violin Sonatas; J. S. Bach Partitas for violin and piano; Mendelssohn Concertos; J. S. Bach Partitas for Solo Violin; Brahms Violin Concerto; Janáček, Prokofiev and Debussy Sonatas; J. S. Bach Violin Concertos, Concerto for Violin and Oboe; Stravinsky Concerto; Bartok Concerto no. 2, Through the Looking Glass (incl. works by Miles Davis and Yousso N'Dour), Mozart Concertos Nos. 1, 3 and 4. *Leisure interests:* reading,

cinema, skiing, tennis, mountain climbing. *Address:* c/o Askonas Holt, Lonsdale Chambers, 27 Chancery Lane, London, WC2A 1PF, England. *Telephone:* (20) 7400-1700. *Fax:* (20) 7400-1799.

MULRONEY, Rt Hon (Martin) Brian, PC, CC, LLD; Canadian politician, business executive and lawyer; b. 20 March 1939, Baie Comeau, Québec.; s. of Benedict Mulroney and Irene (O'Shea) Mulroney; m. Mila Pivnicki 1973; three s. one d.; ed St Francis Xavier Univ. and Univ. Laval; called to Bar of Québec 1965; Partner, Ogilvy, Cope, Porteous, Montgomery, Renault, Clarke & Kirkpatrick, Montreal 1965–76, Sr Partner, Ogilvy Renault 1993–; Exec. Vice-Pres. (Corp. Affairs), Iron Ore Co. of Canada 1976–77, Pres. and Dir 1977–83; Leader, Progressive Party of Canada 1983–93; mem. Parl. 1983–93; Leader of Opposition 1983–84; Prime Minister of Canada 1984–93; Chair. Forbes Global (New York), Int. Advisory Bd Barrick Gold Corpn, Bd Quebecor World Inc.; Dir Barrick Gold Corpn, Archer Daniels Midland Co., Cendant Corpn,Trizec Properties Inc., AOL Latin America; mem. Int. Advisory Council, JP Morgan Chase & Co., China Int. Trust and Investment (CITIC), Independent News and Media PLC; Senior Counsellor to Hicks, Muse, Tate and Furst; Trustee Montreal Heart Inst., Freedom Forum, Int. Advisory Council Les Hautes Etudes Commerciales Univ. of Montreal, First Amendment Center Vanderbilt Univ. Nashville; Grand Officier Ordre Nat. du Québec; numerous hon. degrees and awards. *Publication:* Where I Stand 1983. *Leisure interests:* tennis, swimming. *Address:* Ogilvy Renault, 1981 McGill College Avenue, Suite 1100, Montreal, Québec H3A 3C1 (Office); 47 Forden Crescent, Westmount, Québec H3Y 2Y5, Canada (Home). *Telephone:* (514) 847-4779 (Office). *Fax:* (514) 286-1238 (Office). *E-mail:* bmulroney@ ogilvyrenault.com (Office).

MULUZI, Bakili; Malawi politician and business executive; b. 17 March 1943, Machinga; m. Patricia Shanil; seven c.; ed Huddersfield Tech. Coll., Thirsted Tech. Coll. and coll. in Denmark; clerk, colonial civil service of Nyasaland; fmr Sec.-Gen. Malawi Congress Party (resgnd 1982); mem. Parl. 1975; held various Cabinet portfolios including Educ. and Minister without Portfolio; business interests in transport, merchandise distribution and real estate; Leader, United Democratic Front 1992–; Pres. of Malawi 1994–(2004); Hon. DJur (Lincoln, MO), (Glasgow); Hon. Dr rer. pol (Nat. Chengchi, Taipei). *Publication:* Democracy with a Price 2000. *Leisure interests:* reading, watching football, assisting the needy. *Address:* Office of the President, State House, P.O. Box 40, Zomba, Malawi. *Telephone:* 634566. *Fax:* 523222.

MUMBENGEGWI, Simbarashe Simbanenduku, BA, DipEd; Zimbabwean diplomatist, politician and public servant; b. 20 July 1945, Chivi Dist; s. of the late Chivandire Davis Mumbengegwi and Dzivaidzo Shuvai Chimbambo; m. Emily Charasika 1983; one s. four d.; ed Monash Univ., Melbourne, Australia, Univ. of Zimbabwe; active in Zimbabwe African Nat. Union (ZANU) Party 1963–, in exile, Australia 1966–72, Deputy Chief Rep. in Australia and Far East 1973–76, Chief Rep. 1976–78, Chief Rep. in Zambia 1978–80, mem. Cen. Cttee 1984–94; elected MP 1980, 1985; Deputy Minister of Foreign Affairs 1981–82, Minister of Water Resources and Devt 1982, of Housing 1982–84, of Public Construction and Nat. Housing 1984–88, of Transport 1988–90; Perm. Rep. to UN 1990–95; Amb. to Belgium, the Netherlands and Luxembourg, Perm. Rep. to EU 1995–99; Perm. Rep. to Org. for the Prohibition of Chemical Weapons (OPCW) 1997–99, Chair. Conf. of the State Parties 1997–98, mem. Exec. Council 1997–99; High Commr in UK and Amb. to Ireland 1999–. *Leisure interests:* reading, photography, jogging, tennis, golf. *Address:* Embassy of Zimbabwe, Zimbabwe House, 429 Strand, London, WC2R 0QE, England (Office). *Telephone:* (20) 7836-7755 (Office). *Fax:* (20) 7379-1167 (Office).

MUMFORD, David Bryant, PhD; American professor of mathematics; b. 11 June 1937, Sussex, England; s. of William Bryant Mumford and Grace Schiott; m. 1st Erika Jentsch 1959 (died 1988); three s. one d.; m. 2nd Jenifer Moore 1989; ed Harvard Univ.; Prof. of Maths. Harvard Univ. 1967–77, Higgins Prof. 1977–97, Chair. Maths Dept 1981–84, MacArthur Fellow 1987–92; Prof. of Maths. Brown Univ. 1996–; Pres. Int. Math. Union 1995–98; mem. NAS, American Acad. of Arts and Sciences, American Philosophical Soc.; Hon. DSc (Warwick) 1983, (Norwegian Univ. Science and Tech.) 2000, (Rockefeller); Fields Medal 1974. *Publications:* Geometric Invariant Theory 1965, Abelian Varieties 1970, Algebraic Geometry I 1976, Two and Three Dimensional Patterns of the Face 1999, Indra's Pearls 2002. *Leisure interest:* sailing. *Address:* Brown University, 182 George Street, Providence, RI 02912 (Office); 65 Milton Street, Milton, MA 02186, USA (Home). *Telephone:* (401) 863-3441 (Office); (617) 364-3954 (Home). *Fax:* (401) 863-1355 (Office). *E-mail:* david_mumford@brown.edu (Office). *Website:* www.dam.brown.edu/ people/mumford (Office).

MUNA, Solomon Tandeng; Cameroonian politician (retd); b. 1912, Ngyn-Mbo, Momo Division; s. of Muna Tayim and Ama Keng Muna; m. Elizabeth Fri Muna 1937; seven s. one d.; ed Teacher Training Coll., Kumba and Univ. of London Inst. of Educ.; MP for Bamenda Dist 1951; Eastern Nigeria Minister for Public Works 1951; Minister of Works, subsequently Minister of Commerce and Industries, Minister of Finance, Southern Cameroon Region; Fed. Minister of Transport, Mines, Posts and Telecommunications of Cameroon 1961–68; Prime Minister of W Cameroon 1968–72, also Vice-Pres. Fed. Repub. of Cameroon 1970–72; Minister of State 1972–73; Pres. Nat. Ass. 1973–88; Co-Pres. ACP-EEC States Consultative Ass. 1978–82; fmrly Chair. Bd of Dirs. Cameroon Railways, Chair. Higher Cttee on Cameroon Ports; has represented Cameroon at various int. confs.; mem. Bureau of the Cameroon

People's Democratic Movt (CPDM) 1973–88; Chief Scout of Cameroon 1970–77; Chair. African Scout Cttee 1973–77, mem. World Bureau of Scouts 1975, Vice-Chair. World Scout Cttee 1977–81; Commdr, Ordre de la Valeur du Cameroun, Officier, Légion d'honneur and numerous other foreign decorations. *Leisure interests:* horseback riding, stamp collecting, scouting, gardening, inland fish-farming. *Address:* P.O. Box 15, Mbengwi, Momo Division, North West Province, Cameroon. *Telephone:* 36-12-62.

MUNDELL, Robert Alexander, PhD; Canadian professor of economics; b. 24 Oct. 1932, Kingston, Ont.; s. of William Campbell Mundell and Lila Teresa Mundell; m. Barbara Sheff 1957 (divorced 1972); two s. one d.; ed Univ. of British Columbia, Univ. of Washington, Massachusetts Inst. of Tech., London School of Econs, Univ. of Chicago; Instructor, Univ. of BC 1957–58; economist, Royal Comm. on Price Spreads of Food Products, Ottawa 1958; Asst Prof. of Econs, Stanford Univ., USA 1958–59; Prof. of Econs, Johns Hopkins Univ., School of Advanced Int. Studies, Bologna, Italy 1959–61; Sr Economist, IMF 1961–63; Visiting Prof. of Econs, McGill Univ. 1963–64, 1989–90; Prof. of Int. Econs, Grad. Inst. of Int. Studies, Geneva, Switzerland 1965–75; Prof. of Econs Univ. of Chicago 1966–71; Prof. of Econs and Chair. Dept of Econs, Univ. of Waterloo, Ont. 1972–74; Prof. of Econs Columbia Univ., USA 1974–; Ed. Journal of Political Economy 1966–71; Annenburg Distinguished Scholar in Residence, Univ. of Southern Calif. 1980; Richard Fox Visiting Prof. of Econs, Univ. of Pa 1990–91; First Rockefeller Visiting Research Prof. of Int. Econs, Brookings Inst. 1964–65; Guggenheim Fellow 1971; Marshall Lectures, Cambridge Univ. 1974; Distinguished Lecturer, Ching-Hua Inst., Taipei, Taiwan 1985; Pres. N American Econ. and Financial Asscn 1974–78; Dr. hc (Univ. of Paris) 1992, (People's Univ. of China) 1995; Jacques Rueff Prize and Medal 1983, Nobel Prize for Econs 1999. *Publications:* The International Monetary System: Conflict and Reform 1965, Man and Economics 1968, International Economics 1968, Monetary Theory: Interest, Inflation and Growth in the World Economy 1971, Global Disequilibrium in the Lloyd Economy (co-author) 1989, Building the New Europe (co-author) 1991, Inflation and Growth in China (co-author) 1996; numerous papers and articles in journals. *Leisure interests:* painting, tennis, hockey, skiing, art history. *Address:* Department of Economics, Columbia University, 420 West 118th Street, New York, NY 10027; 35 Clarement Avenue, New York, NY 10027, USA (Home); Palazzo Mundell, Santa Colomba, Siena, Italy (June–Aug.). *Telephone:* (212) 854-3669 (Office); (212) 749-0630 (Home, USA); (0577) 57068 (Italy). *Fax:* (212) 854-8059.

MUNGOSHI, Charles Muzuva; Zimbabwean writer, poet and playwright; b. 2 Dec. 1947, Chivhu; m. Jesesi Jaboon 1976; four s. one d.; ed secondary school; clerk in bookshop, Harare 1969–74; Ed. with the Literature Bureau 1974–81; Dir and Ed. publisher in Zimbabwe 1981–88; Writer-in-Residence, Univ. of Zimbabwe 1985–87; Visiting Arts Fellow, Univ. of Durham 1990; Noma Award for Publishing in Africa, Book Centre/PEN Award, Commonwealth Writers Award (Africa Region). *Film:* The Axe (writer and Dir) 1999. *Publications:* (novels) Makunun'unu Maodzamwoyo (in Shona) 1970, Waiting for the Rain 1975, Ndiko Kupindana Kwamazuva (in Shona) 1975, Kunyarara Hakusi Kutaura? (in Shona) 1983; (short stories) Coming of the Dry Season 1972, Some Kinds of Wounds 1980, Setting Sun and Rolling World 1987, One Day Long Ago: Tales from a Shona Childhood (folk tales) 1991, Walking Still 1997; (poetry) The Milkman Doesn't Only Deliver Milk 1981. *Leisure interests:* travelling reading, acting. *Address:* P.O. Box 1688, Harare (Business); 47/6156 Uta Crescent, Zengeza 1, Chitungwiza, Zimbabwe.

MUNITZ, Barry, PhD; American foundation administrator and professor of English literature; b. 26 July 1941, Brooklyn, New York; s. of Raymond J. Munitz and Vivian LeVoff Munitz; m. Anne Tomfohrde 1987; ed Brooklyn Coll., Princeton Univ., Univ. of Leiden; Asst Prof. of Literature and Drama, Univ. of Calif. at Berkeley 1966–68; Staff Assoc. Carnegie Comm. on Higher Educ. 1968–70; mem. Presidential staff, then Assoc. Provost Univ. of Ill. 1970–72, Academic Vice-Pres. 1972–76; Vice-Pres., Dean of Faculties Cen. Campus Univ. of Houston 1976–77, Chancellor 1977–82; Pres., COO Federated Devt Co. 1982–91; Vice-Chair. Maxxam Inc., LA 1982–91; Chancellor Calif. State Univ., Long Beach 1991–98, Prof. of English Literature, LA 1991–; Pres., COO J. Paul Getty Trust, LA 1998–; Woodrow Wilson Fellow 1963. *Publications:* The Assessment of Institutional Leadership 1977; articles and monographs. *Address:* J. Paul Getty Trust, Suite 400, 1200 Getty Center Drive, Los Angeles, CA 90049, U.S.A. (Office).

MUNK OLSEN, Birger, DLitt; Danish professor of medieval culture and philology; b. 26 June 1935, Copenhagen; m. 1st Annalise Bliddal 1964 (divorced 1988); m. 2nd Gudrun Haastrup 1994; two d.; ed Ecole Normale Supérieure, Sorbonne, Paris and Pontificia Univ. Gregoriana, Rome; Assoc. Prof. of Romance Philology, Univ. of Copenhagen 1961–68; Lecturer Univ. Paris-Sorbonne 1968–74; Prof. of Romance Philology, Univ. of Copenhagen 1974–83, Prof. of Medieval Culture and Philology 1983–; Chair. Danish Nat. Research Council for the Humanities 1987–90; Danish Rep. Standing Cttee for the Humanities, European Science Foundation 1988–92; mem. Royal Danish Acad. 1985– (Vice-Pres., Chair. Humanities Section 1989–95, Pres. 1996–), Danish Council for Research Planning and Policy 1987–89, Acad. Europaea 1988– (Exec. Council 1989–92); Corresp. mem. Acad. des Inscriptions et Belles Lettres (Inst. de France) 1996, mem. 1998–; Vice-Pres. Soc. Int. de Bibliographie Classique 1994–99, Pres. 1999–; Hon. mem. Academia Română 2000; mem. European Science and Tech. Ass. (ESTA) 1997–2000, Corresp. Fellow Royal Soc. of Edin.; Prix Brunet 1984; Kt Order of Dannebrog, Officier Légion d'Honneur, Ordre Nat. du Mérite, Commandor Ordinul

Național Pentru Merit (Romania). *Publications:* Les "Dits" de Jehan de Saint-Quentin 1978, L'étude des auteurs classiques latins aux XIe et XIIe siècles, Vols I–IV 1982–89, I classici nel canone scolastico altomedievale 1991, L'atteggiamento medievale di fronte alla cultura classica 1994, La réception de la littérature classique au Moyen Age 1995. *Address:* Ny Kongensgade 20, 1557 Copenhagen V, Denmark; 51 rue de Tolbiac, 75013 Paris, France; Torshoj 1, Veddinge, 4540 Faarevejle, Denmark. *Telephone:* 33-91-91-81 (Copenhagen); 1-45-84-27-18 (Paris); 20-21-72-17 (Faarevejle). *Fax:* 35-32-81-55 (Office).

MUNRO, Alice; Canadian writer; b. 10 July 1931, Wingham, Ont.; d. of Robert E. Laidlaw and Anne Chamney; m. 1st James A. Munro 1951 (divorced 1976); three d.; m. 2nd Gerald Fremlin 1976; recipient of Gov.-Gen.'s Award for Literature 1968, Canadian Booksellers' Award 1971, Canada-Australia Literary Prize 1994, Fiction Prize, Nat. Book Critics Circle 1999. *Publications:* Dance of the Happy Shades 1968, Lives of Girls and Women 1971, Something I've Been Meaning to Tell You 1974, Who Do You Think You Are? (appeared as The Beggar Maid in USA and UK) 1978, The Moons of Jupiter 1982, The Progress of Love 1986, Friend of My Youth 1990, Open Secret 1994, Selected Stories 1996, The Love of A Good Woman 1998, Hateship, Friendship, Courtship, Loveship, Marriage 2001. *Address:* The Writers Shop, 1325 Avenue of the Americas, Floor 16, New York, NY 10019, USA (Office); P.O. Box 1133, Clinton, Ont., N0M 1L0, Canada (Home).

MUNRO, J. Richard, BA; American publishing executive; b. 1931; m.; ed Colgate, Columbia and New York Univs.; joined Time Inc. 1957; Pres. Pioneer Press Inc. (Time subsidiary) 1969; Publr Sports Illustrated 1969–71; Vice-Pres. Time Inc. 1971–75, Group Vice-Pres. for Video 1975–79, Exec. Vice-Pres. 1979–80, Pres. 1980–86, CEO 1980–90, Chair. 1986–90, Chair. Exec. Comm. 1990, also Dir; Chair. Genentech Inc. 1997–; Dir IBM Corpn; Hon. LittD (Richmond Univ.) 1983; Purple Heart with two Clusters. *Address:* Time Inc., Time & Life Building, 75 Rockefeller Plaza, New York, NY 10019, USA.

MUNS ALBUIXECH, Joaquín, PhD; Spanish university professor and international civil servant; b. 25 June 1935, Barcelona; m. M. Tardà; one s.; ed Univ. of Barcelona and London School of Econs; Economist, Nat. Studies Div. of OECD 1962–63; Asst Prof. of Econs Univ. of Barcelona 1963–65, Prof. of Econs Univ. of Barcelona 1968–73, Sr Prof. of Int. Econ. Org. 1973–, Jean Monnet Prof. of European Integration 1991–; Economist, Western Hemisphere Dept of IMF 1965–68, Exec. Dir IMF 1978–80; Exec. Dir IBRD 1980–82; Econ. Adviser to Barcelona City Council 1968–73; Econ. Adviser to Govt of Spain and to various public and pvt. insts. 1973–78; Adjunct Prof. SIS American Univ. 1982; mem. European Parl. (Liberal Group) 1987–89; mem. Vatican Council of Econ. Advisers 1988–94; mem. Governing Council Bank of Spain 1994–; economic journalist; Cross of St George (Catalonia) 1984, Best Researcher Catalan Research Foundation 1995. *Publications:* (in English): Adjustment, Conditionality and International Financing (ed.) 1984; (in Spanish): Industrialization and Growth in the Developing Countries 1972, The European Option for the Spanish Economy 1973, The International Economic Crisis: Thoughts and Proposals 1975, Crisis and Reform of the International Monetary System 1978, History of the Relations between Spain and the IMF 1958–82, Twenty-five Years of the Spanish Economy 1986, The EMU and its Future 1992, Radiography of the Crisis 1993, Spain and the World Bank 1994, Spain and the Euro: Risks and Opportunities (Ed.) 1997, The Culture of Stability and the Consensus of Washington (with M. Guitián) 1999, Readings on Economic Integration: The European Union (ed.) 2001; over 30 essays and articles, with special reference to problems of the int. econ. orgs. *Leisure interests:* travel, music. *Address:* Diagonal 690, 08034 Barcelona (Office); C. Muntaner, 268, 08021 Barcelona, Spain (Home). *Telephone:* (93) 4021939; (93) 2094534 (Home). *Fax:* (93) 4021934 (Office); (93) 4140697 (Home). *E-mail:* muns@eco.ub.es (Office). *Website:* www.ub.es/muns/personal.html (Office).

MUNTEANU, Mihai; Moldovan opera and concert singer (tenor); b. 15 Aug. 1943, Kriva, Briceni; s. of Ion Muntean and Elizaveta Muntean; m. Rosentul Galina Andrian 1969; one s. one d.; ed Kishinev Inst. of Arts, La Scala, Milan; Prin. Tenor with Moldovan State Acad. Theatre of Opera and Ballet 1971–, Gen. Dir 1996–97; Prof. Chair of Vocal Arts, Music Acad. of Moldova 1993–; Provost Art Inst., Mil. Acad. Stefan Cel Mare 1996–; Pres. Centre for Devt and Support of Culture Mihai Munteanu 1998–; Hon. Prof. Modern Humanitarian Inst. Moscow 1997–; Verdi Award 1978, USSR People's Artist, 1986, Moldovan State Award 1984, Award of the Republic 1993. *Opera roles include:* Lensky (Eugene Onegin), Riccardo (Un Ballo in Maschera), Don Carlo (Don Carlo), Cavaradossi (Tosca), Calaf (Turandot), Hermann (The Queen of Spades), Radames (Aida), Turriddu (Cavalleria Rusticana), Otello (Otello), Canio (Pagliacci), Manrico (Il Trovatore), Samson (Samson et Dalila), Ismael (Nabucco), Don José (Carmen), Don Alvaro (La Forza del Destino), Pinkerton (Madame Butterfly); performances and concerts throughout the world. *Leisure interests:* collecting books, family, children, music. *Address:* 16 N Iorga Str., Apt. 13, 2012 Chișinău, Moldova. *Telephone:* 911-7577 (Office); (2) 23-75-19. *Fax:* (2) 23-75-19. *E-mail:* mihai.muntean@excite.com (Home).

MÜNTEFERING, Franz; German politician; b. 16 Jan. 1940, Neheim; s. of Franz Müntefering and Anna Schlinkmann; m. Ankepetra Rettich 1995; two d.; apprenticeship in industrial admin. 1954–57; industrial admin. in Eng firm 1957–61; mil. training 1961; mem. Social Democratic Party of Germany (SPD) 1966–, sub-Dist Chair. Hochsauerland 1984–88, mem. Dist Exec. W Westphalia 1984–, Dist Chair. 1992–98, Fed. Business Man. 1995–99, Chair.

state org. North Rhine Westphalia 1998, Gen. Sec. 1999–; mem. Sudern City Council 1969–79; mem. Bundestag 1975–92, Parl. Business Man. SPD Bundestag Parl. Group 1991–92; mem. North Rhine Westphalia Landtag 1996–98; Fed. Minister of Transport, Construction and Housing 1998–99; mem. IG Metall (Eng TU) 1967–. *Address:* SPD, 10963 Berlin, Wilhelmstr. 141, Germany (Office). *Telephone:* (30) 259910. *Fax:* (30) 25991410. *Website:* www.spd.de (Office).

MURAD, Ferid, BA, MD, PhD; American professor of pharmacology; b. 14 Sept. 1936, Whiting, Indiana; s. of John Murad and Henrietta Josephine Bowman; m. Carol A. Leopold 1958; one s. four d.; ed DePauw Univ., Ind. and Western Reserve Univ., Cleveland, Ohio; Dir Clinical Research Center, School of Medicine, Univ. of Va 1971–81, Div. of Clinical Pharmacology 1973–81, Prof. Depts. of Internal Medicine and Pharmacology 1975–81; Prof. Depts. of Internal Medicine and Pharmacology, Stanford Univ. 1981–89, Acting Chair. Dept of Medicine 1986–88; Chief of Medicine Palo Alto Veterans Admin. Medical Center, Calif. 1981–86; Adjunct Prof. Dept of Pharmacology, Northwestern Univ., Chicago 1988–96; Chair. Dept of Integrative Biology and Pharmacology, Univ. of Texas Medical School, Houston 1997– (Prof. and Dir Depts. of Pharmacology and Physiology), Dir Inst. of Molecular Medicine 1999–; Vice-Pres. Pharmaceutical Research and Devt, Abbott Labs. 1988–92; CEO and Pres. Molecular Geriatrics Corpn, Lake Bluff, Ill. 1993–95; Albert and Mary Lasker Award for Basic Research 1996; Nobel Prize in Medicine or Physiology 1998. *Publications:* Discovery of Some of the Biological Effects of Nitric Oxide and its Role in Cellular Signaling (Nobel Lecture 1998) 1999. *Leisure interests:* golf, carpentry. *Address:* Department of Integrative Biology and Pharmacology, University of Texas, P.O. Box 20708, Houston, TX 77225, USA (Office). *Telephone:* (713) 500-7509 (Office). *Fax:* (713) 500-0790 (Office). *E-mail:* Ferid.Murad@uth.tmc.edu (Office).

MURADOV, Sakhat, D.TECH.SC.; Turkmenistan politician (retd); b. 7 May 1932, Ivanovo, Russia; s. of Nepes Muradov and Nursoltan Muradova; m. Sona Muradova 1954; two s. one d.; ed Turkmenistan Agric. Inst.; fmr mem. CP; Head Dept of Science and Educ. Central Cttee Turkmenistan CP 1965–70; Rector, Turkmenistan State Univ. 1970–79; Minister for Higher Educ. 1979–85; Rector, Turkmenistan Polytechnic Inst. 1985–90; Deputy to Supreme Soviet of Turkmenistan, 8th and 12th convocations, fmr First Deputy Chair. Supreme Soviet of Turkmenistan, Chair. 1990–92; Chair. Turkmenistan Majlis (legislature) 1992–2001; Order of Red Banner of Labour (twice), Star of Pres. of Turkmenistan; Certificate of Honour (Presidium of Turkmenistan Supreme Soviet). *Publications:* three books, more than 50 articles. *Leisure interests:* sport, tourism, literature. *Address:* c/o Turkmenistan Majlis, 17 Bitarap Kuchesinde, 744000 Ashkhabad, Turkmenistan. *Telephone:* (3632) 35-31-25. *Fax:* 35-31-47.

MURAKAMI, Haruki; Japanese writer; b. 12 Jan. 1949, Kyoto; ed Kobe High School, Waseda Univ.; opened a jazz bar in Tokyo. *Publications:* fiction: Hear the Wind Sing 1979 (Gunzo New Writer Award), Wild Sheep Chase 1982 (Noma Shinjin Literary Award for New Writers), Hard Boiled Wonderland and The End of the World 1985 (Junichi Tanizaki Award), Norwegian Wood 1987, The Elephant Vanishes, Dance Dance Dance, The Wind-Up Bird Chronicle (Yomiuri Literary Award), South of the Border, West of the Sun, Sputnik Sweetheart 2001; non-fiction: Underground 1987, Underground II (Kuwahara Takeo Award) 1998; has translated works by F. Scott Fitzgerald, Raymond Carver, Truman Capote, Paul Theroux, etc. *Leisure interests:* running marathons, music, jazz, classical etc. *Address:* c/o International Creative Management (Att. Amanda Urban), 40 West 57th Street, New York, NY 10019, USA (Office).

MURALITHARAN, Muttiah; Sri Lankan cricketer; b. 17 April 1972, Kandy; s. of Muttiah Sinnasamy; ed St. Anthony's Coll.; right-arm off-break bowler, lower-order right-hand batsman; teams: Tamil Union Cricket and Athletic Club, Lancashire, Sri Lanka; quickest and youngest player to reach 400 Test wickets (in 72 matches); world's highest wicket-taker 2000, 2001; took 437 wickets (average 23.53) in 78 Tests (to Nov. 2002); 297 wickets (average 23.29) in 200 One Day Ints. (to Nov. 2002); 777 first-class wickets (average 19.83) in 141 matches (to Jan. 2002); Wisden Cricketer of the Year 1999, CEAT Int. Cricketer of the Year 2000, rated best-ever Test bowler by Wisden Dec. 2002. *Address:* c/o Board of Control for Cricket in Sri Lanka, A. P. B. Tennekoon, 35 Maitland Place, Colombo 7,Sri Lanka. *Telephone:* (1) 691439. *E-mail:* cricket@sri.lanka.net.

MURALIYEV, Amangeldy Mursadykovich; Kyrgyzstan politician; b. 7 Aug. 1947, Kum-Aryk; ed Bishkek Polytechnical Inst., Acad. of Nat. Econ. USSR Govt; Eng Frunze (Bishkek) factories 1970–80; Dir heavy machine construction factory 1980–82, Kirgizavtomash factory 1982–88; Chair, Frunze City Council 1988–91; Chair State Cttee on Economy, State Sec. 1991–92; Min. Chair Fund of State Property 1994–96; Deputy Prime Minister 1996; Gov. Osh region 1996–99; Prime Minister of Kyrgyzstan 1999–2000; Co-ordinator Political Bd Union Party of Kyrgyzstan 2001–; Pres. Kyrgyzstan Stock Exch. 2001–; Pres. Kyrgyzstan Football Union; mem. Kyrgyzstan Eng Acad. *Address:* Kyrgyz Stock Exchange, Moskovskaya 172, 720010 Bishkek, Kyrgyzstan (Office).

MURAOKA, Takamitsu, PhD, FAHA; Japanese academic; b. 9 Feb. 1938, Hiroshima; m. Keiko Kageyama 1965; two s. one d.; ed Tokyo Kyoiku, The Hebrew Univ., Jerusalem; Lecturer in Semitic Languages, Dept of Near Eastern Studies, Univ. of Manchester, UK 1970–80; Prof. of Middle Eastern Studies, Chair. Dept, Melbourne Univ. 1980–91; Prof. of Hebrew, Univ. of Leiden 1991–; Ed. Abr-Nahrain (Leiden) 1980–92; Academic Assoc., The Oxford Centre for Hebrew and Jewish Studies; Visiting Prof. Univ. of Göttingen, Germany 2001–02; Alexander von Humboldt Research Award 2001–02. *Publications:* A Greek-Hebrew/Aramaic Index to I Esdras 1982, Emphatic Words and Structures in Biblical Hebrew 1985, Classical Syriac for Hebraists 1987, A Grammar of Biblical Hebrew (with P. Joüon) 1991, Studies in Qumran Aramaic (ed.) 1992, A Greek-English Lexicon of the Septuagint (Twelve Prophets) 1993, Studies on the Hebrew of the Dead Sea Scrolls and Ben Sira (ed. with J. F. Elwolde) 1997, A Grammar of Egyptian Aramaic (with B. Porten) 1998, Classical Syriac—A Basic Grammar with a Chrestomathy 1997, Hebrew/Aramaic Index to the Septuagint Keyed to the Hatch-Redpath Concordance 1998. *Leisure interest:* angling. *Address:* Postbus 9515, Hebreeuws, Rijksuniversiteit, 2300 RA Leiden, Netherlands.

MURATA, Makoto, BEng; Japanese business executive; b. 26 Dec. 1926, Nagano Pref.; s. of Ichiro Murata and Misue Murata; m. Yukio Kurashina 1953; one s.; ed Univ. of Tokyo; joined Showa Denko KK (SDK) 1948, Dir 1973, Man. Dir 1978–83, Senior Man. Dir 1983–87, Rep. Dir and Exec. Vice-Pres. 1983–87, Rep. Dir, Pres. and CEO 1987–97, Rep. Dir, Chair. 1997–2001, Adviser 2001–; Chair. Japan Ammonium Sulphate & Urea Industry Asscn 1988–90, Japan Carbon Asscn 1991–93, Acetic Acid Mfrs Asscn 1991–93, Japan Hygienic Olefine and Styrene Plastics Asscn 1993–94, Japan Petrochemical Industry Asscn 1993–94, Japan Chemical Industry Asscn 1996–98, Asscn for the Progress of New Chem. 1998–2000, Japan Chemical Innovation Inst. 1999–2000, Chemical Products Council of MITI 1999–2000; Exec. mem. Bd of Dirs., Japan Fed. of Econ. Orgs. (Keidanren) 1994–2001. *Leisure interest:* golf. *Address:* Showa Denko KK, 1-313-9, Shiba Daimon, Minato-ku, Tokyo 105-8518 (Office); 2–12, Miyazaki 6-chome, Miyamae-ku, Kawasaki, Japan (Home). *Telephone:* (3) 5470-3111 (Office); 44-854-2551 (Home). *Fax:* (3) 3436-2625 (Office). *E-mail:* pr-office@hq.sdk.co.jp (Office). *Website:* www.sdk.co.jp (Office).

MURATA, Ryohei, LLB; Japanese diplomatist; b. 2 Nov. 1929, Kyoto; s. of Tahei Murata and Yoshiko Murata; m. Reiko Akama 1958; one d.; ed Kyoto Univ.; joined Ministry of Foreign Affairs 1953; Deputy Dir-Gen. Middle Eastern and African Affairs Bureau 1974–76, Treaties Bureau 1976–78; Amb. to UAE 1978–80; Dir-Gen. Middle Eastern and African Affairs Bureau 1980–82, Econ. Affairs Bureau 1982–84; Amb. to Austria 1985–87; Deputy Minister for Foreign Affairs 1987, Vice-Minister 1987–89; Amb. to USA 1989–91, to Germany 1992–94; Adviser to the Foreign Minister 1994–, to the Sanwa Bank and to Hotel Okura 1995–, to Nippon Foundation 2000–. *Publications:* Between Friends 1985, OECD 2000, Ocean, World and Japan 2001, Why Has the Quality of the Foreign Ministry Deteriorated? 2002. *Leisure interest:* contract bridge. *Address:* c/o Nipipon-Foundation, 1-2-2, Akasaka, Minato-ku, Tokyo (Office); 2-37-15, Eifuku, Suginami-ku, Tokyo 168-0064, Japan (Home). *Telephone:* (3) 6229-5209 (Office); (3) 3327-7633 (Home). *Fax:* (3) 6229-5120 (Office); (3) 3327-7610 (Home). *E-mail:* r_murata@ps.nippon-foundation.or.jp (Office).

MURATOVA, Kira Georgievna; Russian/Ukrainian film director; b. 5 Nov. 1934, Soroki, Moldavia; m. 1st Alexandre Muratov (divorced); m. 2nd Yevgeni Golubenko; ed All-Union Inst. of Cinematography with Sergey Gerasimov; debut feature film with A. Muratov On Steep Bank; acted in several films; USSR State Prize 1989; Int. Andrzey Wajda Prize 2000. *Films include:* Our Harvest Bread 1965, Short Meetings 1968, Long Partings 1972 (Fipressi Prize, Locarno 1987), Cognizing the White World 1980, Among Grey Stones 1983, Change of Fate 1988, Asthenic Syndrome 1990 (Nika Prize 1990), The Sentimental Militiaman 1991, Animations 1994, Three Stories 1996. *Address:* Proletarsky blvd 14B, apt. 15, 270015 Odessa, Ukraine. *Telephone:* 28-65-51 (Home).

MURAYAMA, Tomiichi; Japanese politician; b. 3 March 1924; m. Yoshie Murayama; two d.; ed School of Political Science and Econs, Meiji Univ.; fmr sec. of a trade union of Oita Pref. Govt employees; entered local Govt 1955; mem. Japanese Socialist Party (JSP), now Social Democratic Party of Japan (SDPJ), renamed Democratic League 1995, renamed Shakai Minshuto (Social Democratic Party); Chair. Oita Pref. of JSP, Chair. Diet Affairs Cttee 1991–93, Chair. SDPJ 1993–96; mem. House of Reps. 1972–; Prime Minister 1994–96; mem. Lower House's Cttee on Social and Labour Affairs. *Publications:* several books on social and labour affairs. *Leisure interest:* drama appreciation. *Address:* Social Democratic Party, 1-8-1, Nagata-cho, Chiyoda-ku, Tokyo 100-0014 (Office); 3-2-2 Chiyomachi, Oita, Oita 870, Japan (Home). *Telephone:* (3) 3580-1171 (Office); (975) 32-0033 (Home). *Fax:* (3) 3580-0691. *E-mail:* sdpjmail@omnics.co.jp (Office). *Website:* www.omnics.co.jp (Office).

MURCH, Walter; American film maker; b. 1943, New York City; m. Muriel Murch; two c.; ed Johns Hopkins Univ., Univ. of Southern California; worked with George Lucas, Francis Ford Coppola and Anthony Minghella as film ed. and sound designer; Acad. Award for Best Sound (Apocalypse Now), BAFTA Award and two Acad. Awards (The English Patient). *Films include:* The Godfather (sound-effects ed.) 1972, American Graffiti (sound designer) 1973, The Godfather, Part II (sound designer) 1974, The Conversation (ed. and sound designer) 1974, Julia (ed.) 1977, Apocalypse Now (and sound designer) 1979, Return to Oz (Dir) 1985, The Unbearable Lightness of Being (ed.) 1988, The English Patient (ed. and sound mixer) 1996, The Talented Mr Ripley (ed.) 1999. *Publication:* In the Blink of an Eye: A Perspective on Film Editing (with Francis Ford Coppola) 1995. *Address:* c/o Mirisch Agency, 1801 Century Park E, Suite 1801, Los Angeles, CA 90067, USA (Office).

MURDOCH, Anna Maria, MA; Australian media executive; b. 30 June 1944, Scotland; d. of J. Torv; m. Rupert Murdoch (q.v.) 1967 (divorced 1999); two s. one d.; ed Univ. of New York; journalist Daily Telegraph, Daily Mirror, Sunday Mirror, Australia; Dir, Vice-Pres. News America Publishing Inc., News America Holdings; Dir News Corpn Ltd 1990–98; Chair. Bd Regents, Children's Hosp., LA; Pres. Bd Children's Inst. Int. (fmr Sec.). *Publications:* In Her Own Image 1985, Family Business 1988, Coming to Terms 1991. *Address:* News Corporation Ltd., P.O. Box 4245, Sydney, N.S.W. 2001, Australia (Office).

MURDOCH, Elisabeth, BA; British media executive; d. of Rupert Murdoch (q.v.) and Anna Maria Murdoch (née Torv); m. 1st Elkin Kwesi Pianim (divorced); two d.; m. 2nd Matthew Freud 2001; one d.; ed Vassar Coll., Poughkeepsie, New York; presentation and promotions Asst Nine Network Australia 1990–91, researcher and producer 1991–93, Man. of Programming and Promotion Fox TV LA 1993, Programme Dir KSTU Fox 13 Salt Lake City 1993–94, Dir of Programme Acquisitions FX Cable Network LA 1994–95, Pres., CEO, EP Communications 1995–96 (Peabody Award for Broadcast Excellence 1995); Gen. Man. Broadcasting Dept, BSkyB Ltd 1996, Dir of Programming 1996–98, Man. Dir Sky Networks 1998–2000; Dir Future Publishing 2000–; Co-Founder Shine Entertainment 2001, Chair. and CEO 2001–. *Address:* c/o British Sky Broadcasting Ltd, Grant Way, Isleworth, Middx., TW7 5QD, England (Office).

MURDOCH, James; American media executive; s. of Rupert Murdoch (q.v.); m.; ed Harvard Univ.; f. record label Rawkus Entertainment 1995; Exec. Vice-Pres. News Corpn 1999–; f. and Pres. News Digital Media 1997–99, mem. Exec. Cttee. News Digital systems; CEO and Chair. Star TV 2000–; Dir (non-exec.) BSkyB 2003–; mem. Bd YankeeNets, Inner City Scholarship Fund, Jump Start, Harvard Lampoon Trustees. *Leisure interests:* reading, painting. *Address:* Star TV Headquarters, 8th Floor, One Harbourfront, 18 Tak Fung Street, Hunghom, Kowloon, Hong Kong Special Administrative Region, People's Republic of China (Office); The News Corporation Ltd, 2 Holt Street, Surrey Hills, NSW 2010, Australia. *Telephone:* (852) 2621-8888 (Office). *Fax:* (852) 2621-8000 (Office). *E-mail:* webmaster@startv.com (Office). *Website:* www.startv.com (Office).

MURDOCH, (Keith) Rupert, AC; American (b. Australian) publisher, broadcaster and media business developer; b. 11 March 1931, Melbourne, Victoria; s. of the late Sir Keith Murdoch and of Dame Elisabeth Murdoch; m. 1st Patricia Booker (divorced); one d.; m. 2nd Anna Maria Torv 1967 (divorced); two s. one d.; m. 3rd Wendy Deng 1999; one d.; ed Geelong Grammar School, Victoria and Worcester Coll., Oxford; inherited Adelaide News 1954; has since built up Cruden Investments, a Murdoch family co. which owns 30 per cent of News Corpn (Group CEO 1979–, Chair. 1991–); has acquired newspapers, magazines and other interests in Australia, UK, USA, Latin America, Europe and Asia, including: Australia—newspapers: The Australian (national), Daily Telegraph, Sunday Telegraph, Daily Mirror (Sydney), Sunday Sun (Brisbane), The News and Sunday Mail (Adelaide), The Sunday Times (Perth); USA—New York Post; UK—newspapers: Sun, News of the World (national, acquired 1969); acquired Times Newspapers Ltd 1981, group includes The Times, The Sunday Times, The Times Literary Supplement, The Times Educational Supplement, The Times Higher Education Supplement; Dir Times Newspapers Holdings 1981–, Chair. 1982–90, 1994–; magazines: Weekly Standard; television: British Sky Broadcasting (UK), STAR (Asia); other interests include: acquired 20th Century Fox 1985–; Chair., CEO Fox Entertainment Group USA 1992–; Commdr of the White Rose (First Class) 1985; Kt Order of St Gregory the Great 1998. *Leisure interests:* sailing, skiing. *Address:* 1 Virginia Street, London, E98 1EX, England; News Ltd, 2 Holt Street, Surrey Hills, NSW 2010, Australia; News Corporation, 1211 Avenue of the Americas, New York, NY 10036, USA.

MURDOCH, Lachlan Keith, BA; American (b. Australian) business executive; b. 8 Sept. 1971; s. of Keith Rupert Murdoch (q.v.) and Anna Maria Murdoch (q.v.); m. Sarah O'Hare 1999; ed Trinity School, Manhattan, Aspen Country Day School, Andover, Princeton Univ.; fmr Reporter San Antonio Express News, The Times (UK); fmr Sub-Ed., The Sun UK; Gen. Man. Queensland Newspapers Pty Ltd 1994–95; Exec. Dir News Ltd 1995; Dir Beijing P.D.N. Xinren Information Tech. Co. Ltd 1995–; Exec. Chair. and CEO News Ltd 1997–; Deputy Chair. Star Television 1995–; Deputy Chief Exec., News Ltd 1995–96; Sr Exec. Vice-Pres. U.S. Print Operations News Corpn 1999–; Dir The Herald & Weekly Times Ltd 1996–, News Corpn 1996– (Deputy COO 2000–), Ind. Newspapers Ltd (NZ) 1997–. *Leisure interests:* Greek philosophy, ancient history, rock climbing, sailing, reading. *Address:* News Ltd, 2 Holt Street, Surry Hills, NSW 2010, Australia.

MURERWA, Herbert; Zimbabwean politician; m.; mem. ZANU-PF; Minister of Finance Aug. 2002– (second time in position). *Address:* Ministry of Finance and Economic Development, Munhumutapa Building, Samova Machel Avenue, Private Bag 7705, Causeway, Harare, Zimbabwe (Office). *Telephone:* (4) 794571 (Office). *Fax:* (4) 792750 (Office).

MURKOWSKI, Frank Hughes, BA; American politician and banker; b. 28 March 1933, Seattle, Wash.; s. of Frank Michael and Helen (Hughes) Murkowski; m. Nancy R. Gore 1954; two s. four d.; ed Santa Clara Univ., Seattle Univ.; with Pacific Nat. Bank of Seattle 1957–59, Nat. Bank of Alaska, Anchorage 1959–67, Vice-Pres. in Charge of Business Devt, Anchorage 1965–67; Commr, Dept of Econ. Devt, Alaska State, Juneau 1967–70; Pres. Alaska Nat. Bank of the North 1971–80, Alaska State Chamber of Commerce

1977; Senator from Alaska 1981–2003, Chair. Cttee on Energy and Natural Resources –2001; Gov. of Alaska 2003–; Vice-Pres. Bd of Trade, BC (Canada) and Alaska; mem. American and Alaskan Bankers' Asscns.; Republican. *Leisure interests:* hunting, fishing, skiing, tennis, golf. *Address:* Office of the Governor, PO Box 110001, Juneau, Alaska 99811-0001, USA. *Telephone:* (907) 465-3500 (Office). *E-mail:* webmaster@gov.state.ak.us (Office). *Website:* www.gov.state.ak.us (Office).

MUROFUSHI, Minoru, BA; Japanese business executive; ed Tokyo Univ.; joined C Itoh 1956, Gen. Man. Coal Dept, New York 1963–71, Vice-Pres. C Itoh (America) (now ITOCHU) 1971, mem. Bd 1985, Chief Exec. 1990–98, also Chair. Bd 1999–, Pres.; mem. Bd HSBC Holdings 1992–2002. *Address:* ITOCHU Corporation, 5-1 Kita-Aoyama 2-chome, Minato-ku, Tokyo 107-8077, Japan. *Telephone:* (3) 3497-2022 (Office). *Fax:* (3) 3497-2002 (Office).

MURPHY, Dervla Mary; Irish author and critic; b. 28 Nov. 1931, Cappoquin; d. of Fergus Murphy and Kathleen Rochfort-Dowling; one d.; ed Ursuline Convent, Waterford; American Irish Foundation Literary Award 1975; Ewart-Biggs Memorial Prize 1978; Irish American Cultural Inst. Literary Award 1985. *Publications:* Full Tilt 1965, Tibetan Foothold 1966, The Waiting Land 1967, In Ethiopia with a Mule 1968, On a Shoestring to Coorg 1976, Where the Indus is Young 1977, A Place Apart 1978, Wheels Within Wheels 1979, Race to the Finish? 1981, Eight Feet in the Andes 1983, Muddling Through in Madagascar 1985, Ireland 1985, Tales from Two Cities 1987, Cameroon with Egbert 1989, Transylvania and Beyond 1992, The Ukimwi Road 1993, South from the Limpopo 1997, Visiting Rwanda 1998, One Foot in Laos 1999, Through the Embers of Chaos: Balkan Journeys 2002. *Leisure interests:* music, reading, swimming, cycling, walking. *Address:* Lismore, Co. Waterford, Ireland.

MURPHY, Eddie (Edward Regan); American film actor; b. 3 April 1951, Brooklyn, New York; s. of Vernon Lynch (stepfather) and Lillian Lynch; m. 2nd Nicole Mitchell; five c.; feature player in Saturday Night Live TV show 1980–84; film debut in 48 Hours 1982; tours with own comedy show; comedy albums: Eddie Murphy 1982, Eddie Murphy: Comedian 1983, How Could I Be 1984, So Happy 1989; has also released seven record albums of comedy and songs; recipient of numerous awards and nominations. *Films include:* 48 Hours 1982, Trading Places 1983, Delirious 1983, Best Defence 1984, Beverly Hills Cop 1984, The Golden Child 1986, Beverly Hills Cop II 1987, Eddie Murphy Raw 1987, Coming to America 1988, Harlem Nights 1989, 48 Hours 2 1990, Boomerang 1992, Distinguished Gentleman 1992, Beverly Hills Cop III 1994, The Nutty Professor 1996, Dr. Dolittle 1998, Holy Man 1998, Life 1998, Bowfinger 1999, Toddlers 1999, Pluto Nash 1999, Nutty Professor II: The Klumps 2000, Shrek 2001, Dr. Doolittle 2 2001, Showtime 2002, I Spy 2003.

MURPHY, Gerry, MBS, PhD; Irish business executive; b. 1955; m.; two s.; ed Univ. Coll. Cork, Univ. Coll. Dublin; fmrly with Grand Metropolitan PLC (now Diageo), Ireland, UK and USA; CEO Greencore Group PLC, Dublin 1991–95, Exel PLC (fmrly NFC) 1995–2000, Carlton Communications PLC 2000–02, Kingfisher 2002–. *Address:* Kingfisher PLC, 3 Sheldon Square, London, W2 6PX, England (Office). *Telephone:* (20) 7372-8008 (Office). *Fax:* (20) 7644-1001 (Office). *Website:* www.kingfisher.co.uk.

MURPHY, John A., BSc, JD; American business executive; b. 15 Dec. 1929, New York; s. of John A. Murphy and Mary J. Touhey; m. Carole Ann Paul 1952; four s. two d.; ed Villanova Univ. and Columbia Univ. Law School; mem. of New York law firm Conboy, Hewitt, O'Brien and Boardman, then joined Philip Morris Inc. as Asst Gen. Counsel 1962, held various posts in the group, then apptd. Dir 1971, Pres. 1985–91, Vice-Chair. 1991–92; Pres. and CEO Miller Brewing Co. 1971–78, Chair. and CEO 1978–84, Pres. 1984–91; mem. Bd of Dirs. Nat. Westminster Bank, USA; mem. American and New York Bar Asscns. and Business Cttee, Metropolitan Museum of Art; Roberto Clemente Award, Nat. Asscn for Puerto Rican Civil Rights, Distinguished Public Service Award, Anti-Defamation League Appeal, Blackbook Humanitarian Award 1982, New York Boys' Club Harriman Award 1982. *Address:* Philip Morris Companies Inc., 100 Park Avenue, New York, NY 10017, USA. *Telephone:* (212) 880-5000.

MURPHY, John Michael; British artist; b. 7 Sept. 1945, St Albans; s. of James Murphy and Maureen (née Tarrant) Murphy; ed St Michael's Coll., Hitchin, Luton and Chelsea Schools of Art; has participated in several group exhbns. in Britain, Europe and USA; Arts Council of GB Award 1980. *Solo exhibitions include:* Jack Wendler Gallery, London 1973, Museum of Modern Art, Oxford 1975, The New Gallery, ICA, London 1976, Barry Barker Gallery, London 1976, Galerie Arno Kohnen, Düsseldorf 1978, Piwna Warsawa 1980, Arts Council of Northern Ireland Gallery, Belfast 1981, Orchard Gallery, Derry 1982, Vereniging voor het Museum van Hedendaagse Kunt, Ghent 1983, Serpentine and Lisson Galleries, London 1984, Whitechapel Art Gallery, London 1987, Arnolfini, Bristol 1988, Galerie Marca Paz, Madrid 1988, Asher/Faure Gallery, LA 1989, Lisson Gallery, London 1990, 1992, John Weber Gallery, New York 1991, Christine Burgin Gallery, New York 1991, Galerie Yvon Lambert, Paris 1992, Project Room, John Weber Gallery, New York 1992, Galerie Bruges La Morte, Bruges 1992, Douglas Hyde Gallery, Dublin 1996, Galerie de Luxembourg 1996, Villa Arson, Nice 1997, Galerie Yvon Lambert, Paris 1998, Southampton City Art Gallery 1999, Galerie Erna Hécey, Luxembourg 2003. *Address:* c/o Lisson Gallery, 67 Lisson Street, London, NW1 5DA, England.

MURPHY, Paul Peter, PC, MA; British politician; b. 25 Nov. 1948; s. of the late Ronald Murphy and Marjorie Murphy; ed Oriel Coll., Oxford; man. trainee Co-operative Wholesale Soc. 1970–71; Lecturer in History and Govt, Ebbw Vale Coll. of Further Educ. 1971–87; mem. Torfaen Borough Council 1973–87 (Chair. Finance Cttee 1976–86); Sec. Torfaen Constituency Labour Party 1974–87; MP for Torfaen 1987–; Opposition Front Bench Spokesman for Wales 1988–94, on NI 1994, on Foreign Affairs 1994–95, on Defence 1995–97; Minister of State, NI Office 1997–99; Sec. of State for Wales 1999–02, for NI 2002–; Kt of St Gregory 1997; Hon. Fellow Oriel Coll. Oxford. *Leisure interest:* music. *Address:* Northern Ireland Office, 11 Millbank, London, SW1P 4PN, England (Office). *Telephone:* (20) 7210-3000 (Office). *Fax:* (20) 7210-0249. *E-mail:* press.nio@nics.gov.uk. *Website:* www.nio.gov .uk.

MURPHY, Tom (Thomas); Irish playwright; b. 23 Feb. 1935, Tuam, Co. Galway; s. of John (Jack) Murphy and Winifred Shaughnessy; m. Mary Lindisfarne Hamilton-Hippisley 1966; two s. one d.; ed Tuam Vocational School, Vocational Teachers' Training Coll., Dublin; metalwork teacher 1957–62; playwright and theatre Dir 1962–; Writer-in-Asscn Druid Theatre Co., Galway 1983–; Hon. DLitt (Dublin) 1998, (Galway NUI) 2000; Irish Acad. of Letters Award 1972, Harveys Award 1983, 1985, Sunday Tribune Arts Award 1985, Independent Newspapers Award 1983, 1989, Drama-Logue Critics' Award 1995, Irish Times ESB Theatre Awards Special Tribute 1997, 2000. *Stage plays:* On the Outside 1959, A Whistle in the Dark 1961, A Crucial Week in the Life of a Grocer's Assistant 1966, The Orphans 1968, Famine 1968, The Morning After Optimism 1971, The White House 1972, The Vicar of Wakefield (adaptation) 1974, On the Inside 1974, The Sanctuary Lamp 1975, The J. Arthur Maginnis Story 1976, The Blue Macushla 1980, The Informer (adaptation) 1981, The Gigli Concert 1983, Conversations on a Homecoming 1985, Bailegangaire 1985, A Thief of a Christmas 1986, Too Late for Logic 1989, The Patriot Game 1991, The Seduction of Morality (novel) 1994, Cup of Coffee (In the Apiary) and She Stoops to Folly 1995, The Wake 1998, Plays (four Vols) 1998, Too Late for Logic 1998, The House 2000, The Cherry Orchard 2003, The Drunkard 2003; and Tom Murphy at the Abbey (Irish Nat. Theatre) 2001. *Leisure interests:* music, gardening. *Address:* c/o Alexandra Cann Representation, 12 Abingdon Road, London, W8 6AF, England (Office); 4 Garville Road, Dublin 6, Ireland. *Telephone:* (20) 7938-4002 (Office). *Fax:* (20) 7938-4228 (Office).

MURPHY-O'CONNOR, HE Cardinal Cormac, STL, PhL; British ecclesiastic; b. 24 Aug. 1932, Reading, Berks.; s. of the late Dr Patrick George Murphy-O'Connor and Ellen Theresa Cuddigan; ed Prior Park Coll., Bath, The Venerable English Coll., Rome and Gregorian Univ., Rome; ordained Priest 1956; Asst Priest, Corpus Christi Parish, Portsmouth 1956–63, Sacred Heart Parish, Fareham 1963–66; Pvt. Sec. Chaplain to Bishop of Portsmouth 1966–70; Parish Priest, Portswood, Southampton 1970–71; Rector Venerable English Coll., Rome 1971–77; Bishop of Arundel and Brighton 1977–2000; Archbishop of Westminster 2000–; cr Cardinal 2001; First Chair. Bishops' Cttee for Europe 1980–83; Jt Chair. Anglo-RC Int. Comm. 1983–2000; Chair. TVS Religious Advisers Panel 1985–90; Pres. Catholic Bishops' Conf. of England and Wales 2000– (Dept for Mission and Unity 1993–); Vice-Pres. Council of the Episcopal Confs of Europe 2001–; mem. Presidential Cttee of Pontifical Council for the Family 2001–, Congregation for Divine Worship and the Discipline of the Sacraments 2001–, Admin of Patrimony of the Holy See 2001–, Council for the Study of Org. and Econ. Problems of the Holy See 2001–, Pontifical Council for Culture 2002–, Pontifical Comm. for Cultural Heritage of the Church 2002–, Pontifical Council for Promoting Christian Unity 2002–; Hon. Bencher of the Inner Temple 2001, Freeman of the City of London 2001, Prior of British and Irish Del. of Constantinian Order 2002, Bailiff Grand Cross of Sovereign Mil. Order of Malta 2002; Hon. DD (Lambeth) 1999. *Publication:* The Family of the Church 1984. *Leisure interests:* music, walking, reading, sport. *Address:* Archbishop's House, Westminster, London, SW1P 1QJ, England. *Telephone:* (20) 7798-9033. *Fax:* (20) 7798-9077 (Office). *E-mail:* archbishop@rcdow.org.uk (Office). *Website:* www.rcdow.org .uk/archbishop/ (Home).

MURRAY, Dame A. Rosemary, DBE, DPhil, JP; British university vice-chancellor and chemist; b. 28 July 1913, Havant; d. of the late Admiral A. J. L. Murray and Ellen Maxwell Spooner; ed Downe House School, Newbury and Lady Margaret Hall, Oxford; Lecturer in Chem., Royal Holloway Coll. 1938–41, Univ. of Sheffield 1941–42; WRNS 1942–46; Fellow and Tutor, Girton Coll., Cambridge 1946–54; Pres. New Hall, Cambridge 1954–81; Univ. Demonstrator in Chem. 1947–52, Vice-Chancellor Cambridge Univ. 1975–77; JP, Cambridge 1953–83; Pres. Nat. Inst. of Adult Educ. 1977–80; Dir Midland Bank 1978–84, Ind. Dir The Observer 1981–93; DL (Cambridgeshire) 1982; Chair., mem. cttees. and councils in univs., colls. of educ., schools, Wages Councils, Armed Forces Pay Review Body and others; Hon. DSc (Ulster) 1972, (Leeds) 1975, (Pa) 1975, (Wellesley Coll., Mass.), (S. Calif.) 1976; Hon. DCL (Oxford) 1976; Hon. LLD (Sheffield) 1977, (Cambridge) 1988; Liveryman Goldsmiths Co. 1976. *Leisure interests:* foreign travel, gardening, book binding. *Address:* 3 Oxford Road, Old Marston, Oxford, OX3 0PQ, England.

MURRAY, Ann; Irish opera singer; b. 27 Aug. 1949, Dublin, Ireland; m. Philip Langridge 1981; one s.; ed Royal Northern Coll. of Music; fmrly performed with ENO, Royal Opera; European recital tours 1990, 1993, 1994; has performed in festivals at Aldeburgh, Edin., Munich, Salzburg. *Address:* c/o Askonas Holt Ltd., Lonsdale Chambers, 27 Chancery Lane, London, WC2A 1PF, England.

MURRAY, Bill; American actor and writer; b. 21 Sept. 1950, Evanston, Ill.; m. 1st Margaret Kelly 1980 (divorced 1996); four s.; m. 2nd Jennifer Murray; ed Loyola Acad., Regis Coll., Denver, Second City Workshop, Chicago; performer off-Broadway Nat. Lampoon Radio Hour; regular appearances TV series Saturday Night Live; appeared in radio series Marvel Comics' Fantastic Four; Emmy Award for best writing for comedy series 1977. *Films include:* Meatballs 1977, Mr Mike's Mondo Video 1979, Where the Buffalo Roam 1980, Caddyshack 1980, Stripes 1981, Tootsie 1982, Ghostbusters 1984, The Razor's Edge 1984, Nothing Lasts Forever 1984, Little Shop of Horrors 1986, Scrooged 1988, Ghostbusters II 1989, What About Bob? 1991, Mad Dog and Glory 1993, Groundhog Day 1993, Ed Wood 1994, Kingpin 1996, Larger Than Life 1996, Space Jam 1996, The Man Who Knew Too Little 1997, With Friends Like These 1998, Veeck as in Wreck 1998, Rushmore 1998, Wild Things 1998, The Cradle Will Rock 1999, Hamlet 1999, Company Man 1999, Charlie's Angels 2000, The Royal Tenenbaums 2001, Osmosis Jones 2001; co-producer, dir, actor film Quick Change 1990; Writer, NBC-TV series Saturday Night Live 1977–80. *Address:* c/o Jessica Tuchinsky, Creative Artists Agency, 9830 Wilshire Boulevard, Beverly Hills, CA 90212, USA.

MURRAY, Denis James, OBE; British journalist; b. 7 May 1951; s. of the late James Murray and Helen Murray; m. Joyce Linehan 1978; two s. two d.; ed St Malachy's Coll. Belfast, Trinity Coll. Dublin, Queen's Univ. Belfast; grad. trainee Belfast Telegraph 1975–77, also reporter; Belfast Reporter Radio Telefís Éireann 1977–82; Dublin Corresp. BBC 1982–84, NI Political Corresp. 1984–88, Ireland Corresp. 1988–. *Leisure interests:* music, reading, sports, family. *Address:* c/o BBC, Ormeau Avenue, Belfast, BT2 8HQ, Northern Ireland. *Telephone:* (28) 9033-8000.

MURRAY, John Loyola, BL, SC; Irish judge; b. 27 June 1943, Limerick; s. of John C. Murray and Catherine Casey; m. Gabrielle Walsh 1969; one s. one d.; ed Crescent Coll., Rockwell Coll., Univ. Coll. Dublin and King's Inns, Dublin; Pres. Union of Students of Ireland 1964–66; Barrister-at-law 1967; Bencher, Kings Inns 1986; Sr Counsel, Bar of Ireland 1981; Attorney-Gen. Aug.–Dec. 1982, 1987–91; mem. Council of State 1987–91; Judge, Court of Justice of European Communities 1991–99; Hon. LLD (Limerick). *Leisure interests:* yachting, travel, art.

MURRAY, Joseph Edward, MD, DSc; American plastic surgeon (retd); b. 1 April 1919, Milford, Mass.; s. of William A. Murray and Mary DePasquale; m. Virginia Link 1945; three s. three d.; ed Holy Cross Coll. and Harvard Univ.; Chief Plastic Surgeon, Peter Bent Brigham Hosp. Boston 1964–86, Emer. 1986–; Chief Plastic Surgeon, Children's Hosp. Medical Center, Boston 1972–85, now Emer.; Prof. of Surgery, Harvard Medical School 1970–86; mem. American Surgical Asscn, American Soc. of Plastic and Reconstructive Surgery, American Asscn of Plastic Surgeons etc.; Hon. Fellow, Royal Australasian Coll. of Surgeons, Royal Coll. of Surgeons of England; Hon. DSc (Holy Cross Coll.) 1965, (Rockford (Ill.) Coll.) 1966, (Roger Williams Coll.) 1986; hon. award, American Acad. of Arts and Sciences 1962; Gold Medal, Int. Soc. of Surgeons 1963; Nobel Prize for Medicine 1990; Bigelow Medal, Boston Surgical Soc. 1992, Pontifical Medal 1997, Mass. Medical lifetime Achievement Award 1998. *Achievements:* performed first human kidney transplant 1954. *Leisure interests:* tennis, biking, swimming. *Address:* 108 Abbott Road, Wellesley, MA 02481, USA. *Telephone:* (781) 235-4356 (Home). *Fax:* (781)-235-2612 (Office). *E-mail:* josmurray@aol.com (Office).

MURRAY, Leslie Allan (Les), BA, AO; Australian poet; b. 17 Oct. 1938; s. of the late Cecil Allan Murray and Miriam Pauline Murray (née Arnall); m. Valerie Gina Morelli 1962; three s. two d.; ed Univ. of Sydney; acting ed., Poetry Australia 1973–80; ed. New Oxford Book of Australian Verse 1985–97; literary ed., Quadrant 1987–; Petrarca Prize, Germany 1995, T. S. Eliot Prize 1997, Queen's Gold Medal for Poetry 1999. *Publications:* Collected Poems 1976, The Boys Who Stole the Funeral (verse novel) 1980, The Paperbark Tree (selected prose) 1991, Fivefathers (Ed.) 1995, Subhuman Redneck Poems 1996, A Working Forest (prose) 1997, Fredy Neptune (verse novel) 1998, Learning Human – New Selected Poems 2001, Poems the Size of Photographs 2002. *Leisure interests:* cinema, gossip, ruminative driving. *Address:* c/o Margaret Connolly & Associates, 16 Winton Street, Warrawee, N.S.W. 2074, Australia.

MURRAY, Hon. Lowell, PC, MA; Canadian politician; b. 26 Sept. 1936, New Waterford, Nova Scotia; s. of the late Daniel Murray and Evelyn Young; m. Colleen Elaine MacDonald 1962; two s.; ed St Francis Xavier Univ., Queen's Univ., Ont.; fmr Chief of Staff to Minister of Justice and Minister of Public Works; Progressive Conservative Nat. Campaign Chair. in Gen. Election 1977–79, 1981–83; Senator 1979–, Co-Chair. Jt Senate-House of Commons Cttee on Official Languages 1980–84; Chair. Standing Cttee on Banking, Trade and Commerce 1984–86; Chair. Standing Senate Cttee on Nat. Finance 1995–96, 1999– Chair. Standing Senate Cttee on Social Affairs, Science and Tech. 1997–99; Leader of Govt in the Senate 1986–93 and Minister of State for Fed.-Provincial Relations 1986–91; Minister responsible for Atlantic Canada Opportunities Agency 1987–88; Acting Minister for Communications 1988–89; mem. Bd of Trustees, Inst. for Research on Public Policy 1984–86, Trilateral Cttee 1985–86, Bd of Dirs. Sony of Canada 1995–; Progressive Conservative. *Address:* The Senate, Room 502, Victoria Building, Ottawa, Ont., K1A 0A4, Canada. *Telephone:* (613) 995-2407 (Office). *Fax:* (613) 947-4730 (Office). *E-mail:* murral@sen.parl.gc.ca (Office).

MURRAY, Noreen Elizabeth, CBE, PhD, FRS, FRSE; British professor emeritus of genetics; b. 26 Feb. 1935, Burnley, Lancs.; d. of John Parker and Lilian

G. Parker; m. Kenneth Murray 1958; ed Lancaster Girls' Grammar School, King's Coll., Univ. of London, Univ. of Birmingham; Research Assoc. Dept of Biological Sciences, Stanford Univ., Calif. 1960–64; Research Fellow Botany School, Univ. of Cambridge 1964–67; at Dept of Molecular Biology, Univ. of Edinburgh, Lecturer, then Sr Lecturer 1974–80, Reader 1982–88, Prof. of Molecular Genetics 1988–; mem. MRC Molecular Genetics Unit 1968–74; Group Leader, European Molecular Biology Lab., Heidelberg 1980–82; mem. European Molecular Biology Org. 1981–, Biotech. and Biosciences Research Council 1994–; Pres. Genetical Soc. of GB 1987–90; Dr hc (Birmingham) 1995, (UMIST) 1995, (Warwick) 2001; Gabor Medal, Royal Soc. 1989. *Publications:* numerous articles in specialist Publs and journals. *Leisure interest:* gardening. *Address:* Institute of Cell and Molecular Biology, University of Edinburgh, King's Buildings, Mayfield Road, Edinburgh EH9 3JR, Scotland. *Telephone:* (131) 650-5374.

MURRAY, Patty, BA; American politician; b. 11 Oct. 1950, Bothell, Wash.; d. of David L. Johns and Beverly A. Murray (née McLaughlin); m. Robert R. Murray 1972; one s. one d.; ed Washington State Univ.; teacher, Shoreline Community Coll. 1984–87; campaigned against proposed closure of Wash. State Parent Educ. Programme 1980; fmr mem. Wash. State Senate; instructor Shoreline Community Coll. Seattle 1984–88; US Senator from Wash. 1993–; Vice-Chair. Senate Democratic Policy Cttee; mem. Budget Cttee, Appropriations Cttee etc.; Democrat. *Address:* U.S. Senate, 173 Russell Senate Office Bldg, Washington, DC 20510; 528 NW 203rd Place, Seattle, WA 98177, USA.

MURRAY, Robin MacGregor, MD, DSc, FRCP; British psychiatrist; b. 31 Jan. 1944, Glasgow, Scotland; s. of James. A. C. Murray and Helen MacGregor; m. Shelagh Harris 1970; one s. one d.; ed Glasgow and London Univs.; Jr posts with Glasgow Univ., Dept of Medicine 1970–72, with Maudsley Hosp. 1972–75; Sr Lecturer Inst. of Psychiatry, London 1978–82, Dean 1982–89, Prof. of Psychological Medicine 1989–99; Lilly Int. Fellow Nat. Inst. for Mental Health, Bethesda, Md 1976–77; Prof. of Psychiatry King's Coll. London 1999–; Pres. Asscn of European Psychiatrists 1995–96; Gaskell Gold Medal and Research Prize (Royal Coll. of Psychiatrists) 1976, Sr Leverhulme Research Fellow (Royal Soc.) 1993; Kurt Schneider Award 1994, Adolf Meyer Award 1997, Paul Hoch Award 1998, Stanley Dean Award 1999. *Publications:* Schizophrenia 1996, Psychosis in the Inner City 1998, First Episode Psychosis (co-author) 1999; Publs on schizophrenia, depression, psychiatric genetics and epidemiology, alcoholism and analgesic abuse. *Leisure interests:* Scottish and Jamaican music, swimming. *Address:* Department of Psychiatry, Institute of Psychiatry, de Crespigny Park, London, SE5 8AF, England. *Telephone:* (20) 7703-6091. *Fax:* (20) 7710-9044.

MURRAY, Dame Rosemary (see Murray, Dame A. Rosemary).

MURRAY, Simon; British banker; b. 25 March 1940, Leicester; s. of Patrick G. Murray and Maxine M. K. Murray; m. Jennifer A. Leila 1966; one s. two d.; ed Bedford School (Sr exec. programme) and Stanford Business School; Jardine Matheson & Co., Ltd 1966–73; Dir Matheson & Co., London 1973–75; Man. Dir Jardine Eng Corpn 1975–80; Man. Dir Davenham Investments Ltd 1980–84; Group Man. Dir Hutchison Whampoa Ltd 1984–93; Exec. Chair. (Asia/Pacific) Deutsche Bank 1994–. *Publication:* The Legionnaire 1979. *Leisure interests:* squash, jogging, reading.

MURRAY, Stuart, FRAIA, RIBA; Australian architect and planner; b. 27 Oct. 1926, Sydney; s. of Cyril Hargreaves Murray and Daphne Williams; m. 1st Elizabeth Grime 1952 (divorced 1965); two s. two d.; m. 2nd Adrienne Solti 1982; ed Fort Street High School, Sydney, Sydney Tech. Coll. School of Architecture and Univ. of Sydney; Office of Burley Griffin 1944–46; Office of Sydney Ancher 1947–49; Office of Denis Clarke Hall, London 1950–52; partner, Ancher Mortlock & Murray 1953–64; Dir Ancher Mortlock Murray & Woolley, Architects 1965–75; Stuart Murray & Assocs., Architects & Planners 1976–; Dir N Sydney Planning Consultants 1968–72; work includes Great Hall, Univ. of Newcastle (winner, Limited Competition 1968) 1971, Aeronautics School, Univ. of Sydney 1974, North Sydney Devt Control Plan 1974, Polo Club, Forbes, NSW 1987, school and univ. bldgs., homes and apts. etc. *Publications:* papers on civic design and urban environment. *Leisure interests:* architecture, art, music, literature, philosophy, cooking, travel, walking. *Address:* Stuart Murray & Associates, Suite 1, 144 High Street, North Sydney, NSW 2060, Australia. *Telephone:* (2) 9955-4779.

MURRAY OF EPPING FOREST, Baron (Life Peer), cr. 1985, of Telford in the County of Shropshire; **Rt Hon Lionel (Len) Murray,** PC, OBE; British trade unionist; b. 2 Aug. 1922; m. Heather Woolf 1945; two s. two d.; ed Wellington Grammar School, Univ. of London, New Coll., Oxford; with Econ. Dept, TUC 1947, Head of Dept 1954–69; Asst Gen. Sec. TUC 1969–73, Gen. Sec. 1973–84; mem. Social Science Research Council 1965–70, NEDC 1973–84; Vice-Pres. European Trade Union Confed. 1974–84, Int. Confed. Free Trade Unions 1973–84; mem. Cttee to Review Functioning of Financial Insts. 1977–80; Bd of Trustees, Anglo-German Foundation for the Study of Industrial Soc. 1977–86; Vice-Pres. Nat. Children's Home, Hearing and Speech Trust, Ironbridge Museum Trust, Wesley's Chapel, Nat. Youth Theatre; Hon. Fellow, New Coll., Oxford 1975, Sheffield City Polytechnic 1979, Queen Mary Coll., London; Hon. DSc (Aston) 1977, (Salford) 1978; Hon LL.D (St Andrews) 1979, (Leeds) 1985. *Address:* 29 The Crescent, Loughton, Essex 1G10 4PY, England. *Telephone:* (20) 8508-4425.

MURTAGH, Peter, MA; Irish journalist; b. 9 April 1953, Dublin; s. of Thomas Murtagh and Olive de Lacy; m. Moira Gutteridge 1988; one s. one d.; ed The High School, Dublin and Trinity Coll. Dublin; reporter, The Irish Times 1981–84; ed. Insight, The Sunday Times, London 1985; reporter, Deputy Foreign Ed. and News Ed. The Guardian, London 1986–94; Ed. The Sunday Tribune, Dublin 1994–97; Journalist of the Year, Ireland 1983; Reporter of the Year, UK 1986. *Publications:* The Boss: Charles J. Haughey in Government (with J. Joyce) 1983, Blind Justice: The Sallins Mail Train Robbery (with J. Joyce) 1984, The Rape of Greece 1994. *Leisure interests:* family, newspapers, Ireland. *Address:* Penhanboon, Somerby Road, Greystones, Co. Wicklow, Ireland (Home). *Fax:* (1) 6615302 (Office).

MUSA, Said, LLB; Belizean politician and attorney-at-law; b. 19 March 1944, San Ignacio; s. of Hamid Musa and Aurora Musa (née Gibbs); ed St John's Coll., Belize City, Manchester Univ., England; called to the Bar London 1966; worked as barrister, Gray's Inn, London 1966–67; circuit magistrate Belize 1967–68, Crown Counsel 1968–70; lawyer pvt. practice 1970–79, 1984–89, 1993–98 (Sr Counsel 1983–); Pres. Public Service Union 1969; f. People's Action Cttee, Soc. for Promotion of Educ. and Research (SPEAR) 1969; obliged to leave public service because of political activities; joined People's United Party (PUP); Chair. Fort George Div. PUP 1974–; Chair. PUP 1986–94, Deputy Leader 1994–96, Leader 1996–; Co-Founder Journal of Belizean Affairs 1972; apptd. Senator to Nat. Ass. by George Price 1974; negotiator in talks to safeguard territorial integrity of Belize on independence 1975–81; mem. House of Reps. for Fort George constituency 1979–84, 1993–98; Attorney-Gen. and Minister for Educ., Sports and Culture 1979–84; Minister of Foreign Affairs, Econ. Devt and Educ. 1989–93 (negotiated recognition of Belizean sovereignty by Guatemala 1991); Leader of the Opposition 1996–98; Prime Minister of Belize, Minister of Finance and Foreign Affairs, then of Finance and Econ. Devt 1998–. *Publications:* People's Assemblies, People's Government and articles in nat. press. *Leisure interests:* reading, int. affairs, human rights, music, tennis. *Address:* Office of the Prime Minister, New Administrative Building, Belmopan, Belize. *Telephone:* (8) 22346. *Fax:* (8) 20071.

MUSALIA MUDAVADI, Wycliffe; Kenyan economist and politician; b. 21 Sept. 1960, Vihiga Dist; m.; three c.; fmr employee Tysons Ltd (property consultants firm) –1989; elected to govt 1989; Minister of Supplies and Marketing 1989–93, of Finance 1993–97, of Agric. 1997, of Transport and Communications –2002; Vice-Pres. of Kenya 2002–. *Address:* Office of the Vice President, Jogoo House 'A', Taifa Road, POB 30520, Nairobi, Kenya (Office). *Telephone:* (20) 228411 (Office).

MUSAMBACHIME, Mwelwa C., PhD; Zambian diplomatist and fmr university professor; b. 13 May 1945, Mansa; m.; four c.; ed Univs. of Zambia, Wisconsin, USA Uppsala, Sweden; primary, secondary school teacher, then lecturer primary school teachers' coll. 1964–74; Lecturer Univ. of Zambia 1997, Prof. 1997–2000; Perm. Rep. to UN, New York 2000–. *Publications:* four books, over 70 papers in journals. *Address:* Permanent Mission of Zambia to the UN, 800 Second Avenue, 9th Floor, New York, NY 10022 (Office); 201 Wyndcliff Road, Scarsdale, New York, NY 10853, USA (Home). *Telephone:* (212) 888-5770 (Office); (914) 722-4885 (Home). *Fax:* (212) 888-5213 (Office); (914) 722-4887 (Home). *E-mail:* zambianmission@msn.com (Office); mwelwamusambachime@msn.com.

MUSEVENI, Yoweri Kaguta; Ugandan head of state; b. 1944, Ntungamo, Mbarara; s. of Amos Kaguta and Esteri Kokundeka; m. Janet Kataaha; four c.; ed Mbarara High School, Ntare School, Univ. Coll. of Dar es Salaam; Research Asst Office of fmr Pres. Milton Obote (q.v.) 1971; in Tanzania planning overthrow of regime of Idi Amin 1971–79; f. Front for Nat. Salvation (FRONASA) 1972; taught at Moshi Co-operative Coll., Tanzania 1972; participated in Tanzanian invasion of Uganda 1979; Defence Minister in interim Govt of Uganda Nat. Liberation Front (UNLF) following overthrow of Amin 1979–80; following election of Dr. Obote, amid allegations of ballot-rigging, in 1980, spent five years as leader of Nat. Resistance Army (NRA) waging a guerrilla war 1981–86; Pres. of Uganda (following overthrow of Govt by NRA forces) and Minister of Defence, then Pres. and C-in-C of Armed Forces 1986–; Chair. Preferential Trade Area (PTA) 1987–88, 1992–93, OAU 1990–91. *Publications:* Selected Essays 1985, Selection of Speeches and Writings, Vol. I: What is Africa's Problem? 1992, Vol. II 1997, Sowing the Mustard Seed—The Struggle for Freedom and Democracy 1997. *Leisure interest:* football. *Address:* Office of the President, Parliament Building, P.O. Box 7168, Kampala, Uganda. *Telephone:* (41) 258441. *Fax:* (41) 256143. *E-mail:* info@gouexecutive.net (Office). *Website:* www.gouexecutive.net (Office).

MUSGRAVE, Thea, CBE, MusDoc; British composer; b. 27 May 1928, Edinburgh; d. of James Musgrave and Joan (née Hacking) Musgrave; m. Peter Mark 1971; ed Edinburgh Univ. and Paris Conservatoire (under Nadia Boulanger); Lecturer, Extra-Mural Dept, London Univ. 1958–65; Visiting Prof. Univ. of Calif., Santa Barbara 1970; Guggenheim Fellow 1974–75, 1982–83; Distinguished Prof., Queen's Coll., City Univ. of New York 1987; Hon. DMus (Council for Nat. Academic Awards, Smith Coll. and Old Dominion Univ.); Koussevitzky Award 1972. *Works include:* Chamber Concertos 1, 2 & 3 1966, Concerto for Orchestra 1967, Clarinet Concerto 1968, Beauty and the Beast (ballet) 1969, Night Music 1969, Horn Concerto 1971, The Voice of Ariadne (chamber opera) 1972–73, Viola Concerto 1973, Space Play 1974, Mary, Queen of Scots (opera) 1976–77, A Christmas Carol (opera)

1978–79, An Occurrence at Owl Creek Bridge (radio opera) 1981, Harriet, A Woman Called Moses 1980–84, Black Tambourine for women's chorus and piano 1985, Pierrot 1985, For the Time Being for chorus 1986, The Golden Echo 1984, Narcissus 1988, The Seasons (orchestral) 1988, Rainbow (orchestral) 1990, Simón Bolívar (opera) 1993, Autumn Sonata 1993, Journey through a Japanese Landscape (marimba concerto) 1993, On the Underground (vocal) 1994, Helios (oboe concerto) 1995, Phoenix Rising (orchestral) 1997; chamber music, songs, choral music, orchestral music. *Leisure interests:* cooking, cinema, reading. *Address:* c/o Novello & Co., 8/9 Frith Street, London, W1V 5TZ, England.

MUSGROVE, Ronnie, JD; American state official and lawyer; b. 29 July 1956; m. Melanie Ballard; three c.; ed Northwest Miss. Jr Coll., Univ. of Miss.; partner Smith, Musgrove & McCord, Miss.; Lt Gov. State of Miss. 1996–99, Gov. of Miss. 2000–; Fellow Miss. Bar Foundation; mem. Miss. State Bar, Miss. Bar Assn, Miss. Young Lawyers' Assn, Panola Co. Bar Assn, Tri Co. Bar Assn. *Address:* Office of the Governor, P.O.B. 139, Jackson, MS 39205, USA (Office).

MUSHARRAF, Gen. Pervez; Pakistani head of state and army officer; b. 11 Aug. 1943, Delhi, India; m. one s. one d.; ed Saint Patrick's High School, Karachi, Forman Christian Coll., Lahore, Command and Staff Coll., Nat. Defense Coll., Royal Coll. of Defense Studies, UK; spent early childhood in Turkey 1949–56; joined Pakistan Mil. Acad. 1961; Commdr in Artillery Regiment 1964; fought in 1965 war with India (Imtiazi Sanad Gallantry Award); spent much of mil. career in Special Services Group; Company Commdr Commando Battalion Indo-Pakistan War 1971; Dir-Gen. Mil. Operations, Gen. HQ 1993–95; apptd. C-in-C of Pakistani Army Oct. 1998; Chair. Jt Chiefs of Staff Cttee 1999; led mil. coup 1999; Chief Exec. Nat. Security Council of Pakistan 1999–; Pres. of Pakistan June 2001–. *Address:* Office of the President, Islamabad, Pakistan (Office). *Telephone:* (51) 9206060 (Office). *Fax:* (51) 9211018 (Office). *E-mail:* ce@pak.gov.pk (Office).

MUSHKETIK, Yuri Mikhailovich; Ukrainian author; b. 21 March 1929, Verkiivka, Chernigiv Region; s. of Mikhail Petrovich Mushketik and Uliana Onufriivna Mushketik; m. Lina Sergiivna Mushketik (née Lushnikova); two d.; ed Kiev State Univ.; mem. CPSU 1951–91; Chair. Bd Union of Writers of Ukraine 1987–; Ed. in Chief Dnipro journal; Chair. Nat. Cttee. of UNESCO; first works published 1952; T. Shevchenko Ukrainian State Prize 1980. *Publications include:* Fires in the Middle of the Night 1959, Black Bread 1960, The Heart and the Stone 1961, Drop of Blood 1964, A Bridge Across the Night 1975, White Shadow 1975, Position 1979, Pain 1981, The Boundary 1987, Selected Works (2 Vols) 1989, Hetman's Treasure (novel) 1993, Brother Against Brother (novel) 1995. *Leisure interests:* reading American literature, history of Ukrainian Cossacks. *Address:* Suvorova Str. 3, Apt. 10, 252010 Kiev, Ukraine. *Telephone:* (44) 290-80-04.

MUSOKE, Kintu; Ugandan politician; fmr Minister of State for Security; Prime Minister of Uganda 1994–2000. *Address:* c/o Office of the Prime Minister, P.O. Box 341, Kampala, Uganda.

MUSOKOTWANE, Kebby Sililo Kambulu; Zambian politician and educationist; b. 5 May 1946, Musokotwane; s. of the late Chief Musokotwane and Rhoda Chambwa; m. Regina Muzya Sibulowa 1966; four s. three d.; ed Monze Secondary School, David Livingstone Teachers' Training Coll., Univ. of Zambia; primary school teacher 1965, Demonstration Teacher 1965–71, Deputy Head Teacher 1968–69, Head Teacher 1970, Lecturer 1972–73; MP 1973–89; Minister of Water and Natural Resources 1977–78, of Youth and Sport 1979, of Finance and Tech. Co-operation 1979–83, of Gen. Educ. and Culture 1983–85, of Educ., Sport and Culture 1989; Prime Minister 1985–89; High Commr in Canada 1990; Pres. United Nat. Independence Party (UNIP) 1992. *Leisure interest:* playing tennis. *Address:* Freedom House, P.O. Box 30302, Lusaka, Zambia.

MUSONDA, Moses, PhD; Zambian diplomatist; ed Bryn Mawr Univ.; fmr Amb. to People's Repub. of China and to Malta; Amb. to UK –2002, to India 2002–. *Address:* Embassy of Zambia, C-79 Anand Niketan, New Delhi 110 021, India (Office). *Telephone:* (11) 4101289 (Office). *Fax:* (11) 4101520 (Office). *E-mail:* zambiand@nde.vsnl.net.in (Office).

MUSONGE, Peter Mafany; Cameroonian politician; fmr Gen. Man. Cameroon Devt Corp. (CDC); mem. Rassemblement démocratique du peuple camerounais (RDPC); Prime Minister of Cameroon Sept. 1996–. *Address:* Office of the Prime Minister, Yaoundé, Cameroon. *Telephone:* 23-80-05. *Fax:* 23-57-35. *E-mail:* spm@spm.gov.cm. *Website:* www.spm.gov.cm.

MUSSA, Michael; American economist; b. 1944; ed Univs. of Calif. and Chicago; Asst Prof. of Econs Univ. of Rochester; Research Fellow, LSE and Grad. Inst. of Int. Studies; William H. Abbott Prof. of Int. Business, Univ. of Chicago Grad. School of Business 1980–; Research Assoc. Nat. Bureau of Econ. Research 1981–; fmr mem. U.S. Council of Econ. Advisers; fmr Visiting Prof. Asian and Research Depts. of IMF; Econ. Counsellor and Dir Research Dept IMF 1991–2001, Special Adviser to Man. Dir 2001–; Sr Fellow Inst. for Int. Econs. *Address:* Institute for International Economics, 1750 Massachusetts Avenue, N.W., Washington, DC 20036, USA.

MUSTILL, Baron (Life Peer), cr. 1992, of Pateley Bridge in the County of North Yorkshire; **Michael John Mustill,** Kt, PC, FBA; British judge; b. 10 May 1931; s. of Clement Mustill and the late Marion Mustill; m. 1st Beryl R. Davies (divorced); m. 2nd Caroline Phillips; two s. one step d.; ed Oundle

School and St John's Coll. Cambridge; called to Bar, Gray's Inn 1955, Bencher 1976, QC 1968; Deputy Chair. Hants. Quarter Sessions 1971; Recorder, Crown Court 1972–78; Judge, High Court, Queen's Bench Div. 1978–85; Presiding Judge, NE Circuit 1981–84; a Lord Justice of Appeal 1985–92; Lord of Appeal in Ordinary 1992–97; Hon. Prof. of Law Univ. of Birmingham 1995–; Pres. British Maritime Law Assn 1995–, Chartered Inst. of Arbitrators 1995–98, Assn of Average Adjusters 1996–97, Seldon Soc. 1997–2000; Yorke Distinguished Visiting Fellow Univ. of Cambridge 1996–; mem. Comité Maritime Arbitration 1996–. *Publications:* The Law and Practice of Commercial Arbitration in England (with S. C. Boyd) 1982, Anticipatory Breach of Contract 1990; articles in legal journals. *Address:* House of Lords, London, SW1A 0PW; 42 Laurier Road, London, NW5 1SJ, England. *Telephone:* (20) 7813-8000 (Office). *Fax:* (20) 7813-8080 (Office).

MUSTONEN, Olli; Finnish pianist, composer and conductor; b. 7 June 1967, Helsinki; s. of Seppo Mustonen and Marja-Liisa Mustonen; m. Raija Kerppo 1989; began studies with harpsichord, studied piano with Ralf Gothóni and Eero Heinonen, composition with Einojuhani Rautavaara; has played with many of the world's leading orchestras; has appeared at festivals including Berlin, Hollywood Bowl, BBC Proms and Salzburg; Artistic Dir Turku Music Festival 1990–92, Ludus Mustonalis concert series, Helsinki Festival Orchestra; Edison Award 1992, Gramophone Award for Best Instrumental Recording 1992. *Major compositions:* Fantasia (for piano and strings) 1985, Toccata (for piano, string quartet and double bass) 1989, two Nonets (for two string quartets and double bass) 1995, 2000, Triple Concerto (for three violins and orchestra) 1998. *Leisure interests:* mathematics, nature, politics, sports. *Address:* c/o van Walsum Management Ltd, 4 Addison Bridge Place, London, W14 8XP, England. *Telephone:* (20) 7371-4343. *Fax:* (20) 7371-4344. *Website:* www.vanwalsum.co.uk (Office).

MUSYOKA, (Stephen) Kalonzo, LLB; Kenyan politician and lawyer; b. 24 Dec. 1953; ed Univ. of Nairobi and Mediterranean Inst. of Man., Nicosia, Cyprus; lawyer with Kaplan & Stratton Advocates; Sr Partner Musyoka & Wambua Advocates; entered politics 1985; fmr Minister of Educ. and Minister of Tourism and Information; Minister of Foreign Affairs 1993–98; fmr Vice-Chair. KANU party; defected from KANU to Democratic Party just before Dec. 2002 presidential elections; Minister of Foreign Affairs and Int. Co-operation Jan. 2003–. *Address:* Ministry of Foreign Affairs and International Co-operation, Treasury Building, Harambee Avenue, POB 30551, Nairobi, Kenya (Office). *Telephone:* (20) 334433 (Office).

MUTALIBOV, Ayaz Niyazi Ogly; Azerbaijani politician; b. 12 May 1938, Baku; m. Adilia Khanum; two s.; ed M. Azizbekov Azerbaijani Inst. of Oil and Chem.; mem. CPSU 1963–91; engineer, later Dir Baku Refrigerator Manufacturing Plant; Dir Baku Assn for Production of Refrigerators and Household Equipment 1974–77; Second Sec. of Narimanov Dist Party Cttee 1977–79; Minister of Local Industry for Azerbaijan SSR 1979–82; Vice-Chair. Council of Ministers Azerbaijan SSR 1982–89, Chair. 1989–91; Pres. Gosplan for Repub. 1982–89; First Sec., Cen. Cttee Azerbaijan CP 1990–91; USSR People's Deputy 1989–91; mem. CPSU Politburo 1990–91; Pres. of Azerbaijan 1990–92; charged with organizing a coup and impeached 1992; lives in Moscow.

MUTALOV, Abdulkhashim Mutalovich; Uzbekistan politician and business executive; b. 1947, Telyau, Tashkent Region; ed All-Union Inst. of Food Industry; worker Tashkent Factory of Bread Products; army service 1965–79; Dir Akhangaran Enterprise of Bread Products 1979–86; Deputy Minister of Bread Products Uzbek SSR 1986–87, Minister 1987–91; Deputy Chair. Cabinet of Ministers 1991–92; Prime Minister of Uzbekistan 1992–96; Chair. State grain co. Uzdon Makhsulot 1996–. *Address:* Uzdon Makhsulot (State Grain Company), Tashkent, Uzbekistan (Office). *Telephone:* (712) 39-82-95 (Home). *Fax:* 39-86-01.

MUTEBI II, HM Kabaka of Buganda; (Ronald Muwenda Mutebi); b. 13 April 1955, Kampala; s. of the late Kabaka Sir Edward Mutesa II (King Freddy) and Lady Sarah Nalule Kisosonkole; m. Lady Sylvia 1999; ed Univ. of Cambridge; lived in exile in England, following overthrow of his father by fmr Pres. of Uganda Milton Obote 1966–87; worked as journalist; returned to Uganda 1987; crowned 37th Kabaka (King) of Buganda, marking restoration of ancient kingdom of Buganda, 31 July 1993. *Leisure interest:* squash. *Address:* Mengo Palace, P.O. Box 58, Kampala, Uganda.

MUTI, Riccardo; Italian conductor; b. 28 July 1941, Naples; s. of Domenico Muti and Gilda Sellitto; m. Cristina Mazzavillani 1969; two s. one d.; ed San Pietro Conservatory, Majella, Naples and Milan Conservatory of Music; Prin. Conductor, Maggio Musicale, Florence 1969–, Philharmonia Orchestra, London 1973–82, Music Dir 1979–82, Conductor Laureate 1982–; Prin. Guest Conductor Philadelphia Orchestra 1977–80, Prin. Conductor and Music Dir 1980–92, Conductor Laureate 1992–; Music Dir La Scala (Milan) 1986–; Prin. Conductor Filarmonica della Scala 1988–; concert tours in USA with Boston, Chicago and Philadilphia Orchestras; concerts at Salzburg, Edinburgh, Lucerne, Flanders and Vienna festivals; also conducted Berlin Philharmonic, Bayerische Rundfunk Sinfonie Orchester, Vienna Philharmonic, New York Philharmonic and Concertgebouw Amsterdam; opera: Florence, Munich, Covent Garden, La Scala, Ravenna, Vienna; Accad. di Santa Cecilia, Rome; Accademico Dell'Accademia Cherubini, Florence; Hon. PhD (Weizmann Inst. of Science); Dr hc (Pennsylvania, Philadelphia, Bologna, Urbino, Milan, Cremona, Lecce); Grand Golden Medal of the City of Monaco; Grand Silver Ehrenkreuz Medal (Austria); Officer Order of Merit (Germany); 'Guido

Cantelli' Award 1967, Diapason d'Oro; Premio Critica Discografia Italiana; Prix Académie nat. du disque 1977; Verdienstkreuz (First Class, Germany) 1976, Cavaliere Gran Croce (Italy) 1991, Légion d'honneur (France), Deutscher Schallplatten Preis, 'Bellini d'Oro', Abbiati Prize, Grand Prix du disque for La Traviata (Verdi), Requiem in C minor (Cherubini) 1982; Disco d' Oro for Music for Films; Wolf Prize 2000, Hon. KBE 2000, Russian Order of Friendship 2001, Silver Medal of the Salzburg Mozarteum 2001. *Address:* Teatro alla Scala, Via Filodrammatici 2, Milan 20121, Italy. *Telephone:* (02) 88791 (Office).

MUTO, Kabun; Japanese politician; b. 18 Nov 1926; s. of Kaichi Muto; m. Hisako Koketsu 1951; two s.; ed Kyoto Univ.; worked in family brewing business; mem. House of Reps. 1967–; Parl. Vice-Minister of Home Affairs 1972–73, Minister of Agric., Forestry and Fisheries 1979–80, of Int. Trade and Industry Feb.–Dec. 1990, of Foreign Affairs April–Aug. 1993, Dir-Gen. Man. and Coordination Agency (State Minister) 1996–97; Chair. Liberal-Democratic Party (LDP) Commerce and Industry Div. 1974–76; Deputy Sec.-Gen. LDP 1978–79; mem. Standing Cttee on Budget, House of Reps., LDP Finance Cttee; Vice-Pres. LDP Cttee on Small and Medium Enterprises, LDP Tax Policy Cttee etc. *Publications:* Kusa-no-Ne Minshushugi (Grassroots Democracy), Jiminto Saisei no Teigen, Nihon no Sentaku (Japan's Choice) etc. *Address:* c/o Ministry of Foreign Affairs, 2-2 Kasumigaseki, Chiyoda-ku, Tokyo, Japan.

MUTOLA, Maria; Mozambican athlete; b. 27 Oct. 1972, Maputo; d. of João Mutola and Catarina Mutola; ed Eugene High School; gold medallist, World Indoor Championships 1993, 1995, 1997, 2001; gold medallist World Championships 1995, 2001; bronze medallist, 800m., Olympic Games 1996, gold medallist 2000; world record-holder at 1,000m. indoor; African record-holder at 800m. and 1,000m. (outdoor); between 1992 and 1995 she won all the 42 races she competed in. *Address:* c/o Confédération Africaine d'Athlétisme, Stade de l'Amitié, BP 88, Dakar, Senegal.

MUTTER, Anne-Sophie; German violinist; b. 29 June 1963, Rheinfelden/ Baden; m. Dithelf Wunderlich 1989 (deceased); studied with Prof. Aida Stucki, Winterthur, Switzerland; began musical career playing piano and violin 1969; played in the Int. Music Festival, Lucerne 1976; début with Herbert von Karajan at Pfingstfestspiele, Salzburg 1977; soloist with major orchestras of the world; also plays with string trio and quartet; Guest Teacher RAM, London 1985; est. foundation promoting gifted young string players throughout the world; Hon. Pres. Mozart Soc., Univ. of Oxford 1983; Youth Music Prize (FRG) for violin 1970, for piano 1970, for violin 1974; Artist of the Year, 'Deutscher Schallplattenpreis', Grand Prix Int. du Disque, Record Acad. Prize, Tokyo 1982, Internationaler Schallplattenpreis 1993; Order of Merit (of Germany, of Bavaria). *Leisure interests:* graphic arts, sport. *Address:* c/o Kaye Artists Management, Barratt House, 7 Chertsey Road, Woking, GU21 5AB (Office); Effnerstrasse 48, 81925 Munich, Germany; c/o London Symphony Orchestra, Barbican Hall, London, EC1, England. *Telephone:* (89) 984418 (Germany). *Fax:* (89) 9827186 (Germany).

MUZENDA, Simon Vengay; Zimbabwean politician; b. 28 Oct. 1922; m. Mandy Muzenda 1950; three s. five d. (one deceased); returned to S. Rhodesia (now Zimbabwe) 1950; Sec.-Gen. Voice Asscn 1953; Chair. Umvuma Branch, Nat. Democratic Party, later Organizing Sec. Victoria Prov. 1960–61; Founder mem. Zimbabwe African People's Union (ZAPU) and Admin. Sec. Victoria Prov. 1961–62; imprisoned 1962–64; Founder mem. Zimbabwe African Nat. Union (ZANU) 1963, mem. Cen. Cttee 1964; activity restricted 1964–71; mem. Exec., African Nat. Council and Sec. of Law and Order 1971; Deputy Admin. Sec. ZANU 1975–76; co-ordinated activities of ZANU from Zambia and formed Zimbabwe People's Army (ZIPA) in conjunction with ZAPU leadership; Deputy Leader of ZANU 1976, Vice-Pres. 1977–, mem. Politburo; Deputy Prime Minister 1980–88, Vice-Pres. of Zimbabwe 1988–; Minister of Foreign Affairs 1980–81, of Energy and Water Resources 1984–85. *Leisure interests:* wrestling, music, traditional music. *Address:* Office of the Vice-Presidents, Munhumutapa Building, Samora Machel Avenue, Private Bag 7700, Causeway, Harare (Office); ZANU-PF, 88 Manica Road, Harare, Zimbabwe. *Telephone:* (4) 707091 (Office).

MUZI-FALCONI, Livio; Italian diplomatist; b. 1 Sept. 1936, Oslo, Norway; s. of Baron Filippo Muzi Falconi and Marion Barton; m. Marina Chantre 1961; two s. two d.; ed Tamalpais School for Boys, San Rafael, CA, Lowell High School, Univ. of San Francisco, Univ. of Genoa; joined Italian diplomatic corps 1960; Lieut, Italian Air Force 1962; Vice Consul Buenos Aires 1963–67; First Sec. Madrid Embassy 1967–70; Dept of Migratory Affairs Ministry of Foreign Affairs 1970–72; Counsellor London Embassy 1972–77; Consul Gen. Addis Ababa 1977–79; Coordinator European Affairs Ministry of Foreign Affairs 1979–83; Amb. to Nigeria (also Accred to Benin) 1983–87; Minister Embassy, London 1987–92; Deputy Head Italian State Protocol 1992–95; Chief of Protocol Exec. Office of Sec.-Gen. of UN 1995–98; elected rep. Italian diplomatic and others Trade Union 1969–73, 1977–79, 1992–95; currently Head of Task Force, Ministry of Foreign Affairs; Grand Official Order of Repub. 1990; Hon. KCMG 1991. *Address:* Ministry of Foreign Affairs, Piazzale della Farnesina, 00194 Rome, Italy.

MUZOREWA, Abel Tendekayi, MA, DD, DHL; Zimbabwean ecclesiastic; b. 14 April 1925, Old Umtali; s. of Philemon Haadi Muzorewa and Hilda Takaruda Muzorewa (née Munangatire); m. Margaret Muzorewa (née Chigodora); four s. one d.; ed Old Umtali Secondary School, Nyadiri United Methodist Mission, Cen. Methodist Coll., Fayette, Mo., Scarritt Coll., Nash-

ville, Tenn., USA; Pastor, Chiduku N Circuit 1955–57; studied in USA 1958–63; Pastor, Old Umtali Mission 1963; Dir of Youth Work, Rhodesia Annual Conf. 1965; Jt Dir of Youth Work, Rhodesia Christian Council 1965; Travelling Sec. Student Christian Movt 1965; Resident Bishop, United Methodist Church 1968–92; Pres. African Nat. Council (ANC) 1971–85, All-Africa Conf. of Churches; Rep. of UANC at Geneva Conf. on Rhodesia 1976; mem. Transitional Exec. Council to prepare transfer to majority rule in Rhodesia 1978–79, Prime Minister of Zimbabwe Rhodesia, Minister of Defence and Combined Operations June–Dec. 1979; attended Lancaster House Conf. 1979; contested March 1980 election as Leader of UANC; detained Nov. 1983–Sept. 1984; fled to USA 1985, returned to Zimbabwe Nov. 1986; Pres. of United Parties 1994–98; Pres. Coll. of Bishops United Methodist Church of Cen. Africa 1988–92; Bishop of Zimbabwe and Head of United Methodist Church; Hon. DD (Cen. Methodist Coll., Mo.) 1960; UN Prize for Outstanding Achievement in Human Rights 1973. *Publications:* Manifesto for African National Council 1972, Rise Up and Walk (autobiog.) 1978. *Leisure interests:* vegetable and flower growing, poultry raising. *Address:* P.O. Box 3408, Harare; P.O. Box 353, Borrowdale, Harare, Zimbabwe. *Telephone:* (4) 704127. *Fax:* (4) 745303.

MWAANGA, Vernon Johnson; Zambian diplomatist, politician and businessman; b. 1939; ed Hodgson Tech. Coll., Lusaka, Stanford Univ., USA and Oxford Univ., UK; joined Zambian independence movement 1960; mem. United Nat. Independence Party (UNIP) 1961, later Regional Party Sec., Monze and Choma Areas; Deputy High Commr for Zambia in UK 1964–65; Amb. to USSR 1965–68; Perm. Rep. to UN 1968–72; Ed.-in-Chief Times of Zambia 1972–73; Minister of Foreign Affairs 1973–75, 1991–92; Minister of Information and Broadcasting Services Jan. 2002–; mem. UNIP Cen. Cttee 1975; Sr Business Exec. 1975–; Chair. Curray Ltd, Bank of Credit and Commerce (Zambia) Ltd, Zambia Safaris Ltd; mem. Int. Public Relations Asscn; Fellow, London Inst. of Dirs; convicted of drug-trafficking in early 1990s. *Address:* Ministry of Information and Broadcasting Services, Independence Avenue, P.O. Box 32186, Lusaka, Zambia. *Telephone:* (1) 228202. *Fax:* (1) 253457. *Website:* www.information.gov.zm.

MWAKAWAGO, Daudi Ngelautwa; Tanzanian politician; b. Sept. 1939; ed Makerere Univ., Uganda, Victoria Univ. of Manchester, England; Tutor at Kivukoni Coll., Dar es Salaam 1965–72, Vice-Principal 1970, Principal 1971, 1977; Nat. MP 1970–75; Minister for Information and Broadcasting 1972–77; Constituent MP 1975; mem. Party of Constitution Comm. 1976; mem. Constituent Ass. 1977, Cen. Cttee Chama cha Mapinduzi 1977–; Minister of Information and Culture 1982–84, of Labour and Manpower Devt 1984–86, of Industries and Trade 1986–88; now Perm. Rep. to UN, New York; fmr mem. Historical Asscn of Tanzania, Nat. Adult Educ. Asscn of Tanzania, African Adult Educ. Asscn, Income Tax Local Cttee, Bd of Inst. of Adult Educ., Nat. Advisory Council on Educ.; fmr Dir Nat. Devt Corpn, Nat. Museum; Chair. Wildlife Corpn 1979–; Vice-Chair. Co-operative Coll., Moshi; mem. TIRDO. *Address:* Permanent Mission of United Republic of Tanzania to the United Nations, 205 East 42nd Street, 13th Floor, New York, NY 10017, USA (Office). *Telephone:* (212) 972-9160 (Office). *Fax:* (212) 682-5232 (Office). *E-mail:* tanzania@un.int (Office).

MWANAWASA, Levy Patrick, LL.B.; Zambian lawyer and politician; b. 3 Sept. 1948, Mufulira; m. Maureen Kakubo Mwanawasa 1988; two s. two d.; ed Univ. of Zambia and Law Practice Inst. Lusaka; admitted to Zambian Bar 1975; worked in pvt. law firms 1975–78; est. Mwanawasa & Co. legal practice 1978, Sr Partner –1992; Vice-Chair. Law Asscn of Zambia 1981–83; Solicitor-Gen. for Zambia 1986–87; Legal Chair. Interim Cttee of Movt for Multi-Party Democracy (MMD) 1990, Vice-Pres. 1991, Leader 2002–; Vice-Pres. of Zambia 1991–94, Pres. of Zambia and Minister of Defence Jan. 2002–. *Address:* Office of the President, P.O. Box 30208, Lusaka (Office); Movement for Multi-Party Democracy (MMD), P.O. Box 30708, Lusaka, Zambia. *Telephone:* (1) 218282 (Office). *Website:* www.statehouse.gov.zm (Office).

MWANSA, Kalombo T., LLM, MPhil, PhD; Zambian politician and professor of law; b. 9 Sept. 1955, Nchelenge; two s. two d.; ed Univ. of Zambia, Harvard Univ., USA, Univs of Cambridge and London, UK; Tutor in Law, Univ. of Zambia 1979–80, Lecturer in Law and Criminology 1983–88, Acting Dean of Law School 1992–93; Perm. Sec. Ministry of Home Affairs 1993–98; Acting Chair. Police and Prisons Service Comm. 1994–96; Perm. Sec. of Admin Cabinet Office 1998–99; Deputy Sec. to Cabinet 1999–2002, Acting Sec. 2001, 2002; Minister of Foreign Affairs 2002–; elected Mem. Parl. 2002–; Livingstone Scholar, Jesus Coll. Cambridge 1982–83; Commonwealth Scholar, SOAS 1988–92. *Leisure interests:* reading, vegetable gardening, soccer. *Address:* Ministry of Foreign Affairs, POB RW50069, Lusaka (Office); Plot No. 283/401 (A), Makeni, Zambia (Home). *Telephone:* 253427 (Office); 272937 (Home). *Fax:* 254256 (Office).

MWENCHA, J. E. O. (Erastus), MA; Kenyan economist and international finance official; m.; three c.; ed Univ. of Nairobi, York Univ., Canada; entered civil service 1974, becoming Prin. Industrial Devt Officer; Dir Kenya Medical Research Inst.; Dir Kenya Industrial Research and Devt Inst.; Sec. Industrial Sciences Advisory Council; Sr Industrial Expert, Econ. Comm. for Africa 1983; Dir of Industry, Energy and Environment, Preferential Trade Area for Eastern and Southern Africa 1987–97; Acting Sec.-Gen. Common Market for Eastern and Southern Africa (COMESA) 1997–98, Sec.-Gen. 1998–; Order of the Moran of the Burning Spear 1998. *Address:* COMESA Centre, Ben Bella

Road, P.O. Box 30051, 10101 Lusaka, Zambia (Office). *Telephone:* (1) 229726 (Office). *Fax:* (1) 227318 (Office). *E-mail:* comesa@comesa.int (Office). *Website:* www.comesa.int (Office).

MWINYI, Ali Hassan; Tanzanian politician, teacher and diplomatist; b. 8 May 1925, Kivure, Tanganyika; m. Siti A. Mwinyi 1960; five s. four d.; moved to Zanzibar as a child; schoolteacher, later Prin. Zanzibar teacher-training Coll.; Prin. Perm. Sec. of Educ. Zanzibar 1963–64; Asst Gen. Man. Zanzibar State Trading Corpn 1964–70; Minister of State, Office of Pres., Tanzania 1970; later Minister of Health and Home Affairs; Minister of Natural Resources and Tourism 1982–83, of State in Vice-Pres.'s Office 1983–84; interim Pres. of Zanzibar Feb.–April 1984, Pres. April 1984; Vice-Pres. of Tanzania 1984–85, Pres. 1985–95, also fmr Minister of Defence and Nat. Service; fmr C.-in.-C. of Armed Forces; mem. Chama Cha Mapinduzi (CCM or Revolutionary Party, Chair. 1990–96). *Address:* c/o State House, Dar es Salaam, Tanzania.

MWIRARIA, David; Kenyan politician; retd from Civil Service to enter politics 1992; elected MP (Democratic Party—DP) for N. Imenti 1992–; fmr Perm. Sec. in various ministries; Minister of Finance Jan. 2003–; Founder mem. and Leader Cen. Kenya Parl. Group; Deputy Chair. DP;. *Address:* Ministry of Finance, Treasury Building, Harambee Avenue, POB 30007, Nairobi, Kenya (Office). *Telephone:* (20) 338111 (Office). *Fax:* (20) 330426 (Office). *E-mail:* mof@form-net.com (Office).

MYAGKOV, Andrei Vasilyevich; Russian actor; b. 8 July 1938, Leningrad; ed Leningrad Inst. of Chemical Tech., Studio-School, Moscow Art Theatre; began acting in Sovremennik Theatre 1965–77, with Moscow Art Theatre 1977–; USSR State Prize, RSFSR State Prize, RSFSR People's Artist. *Theatre includes:* Aduyev in Ordinary Story, Trubetskoy in Decembrists, Repetilov in Trouble from Intelligence, Misail in Boris Godunov. *Films include:* Adventures of a Dentist, Brothers Karamazov, Hope, Silver Pipes, Morning Round, Garage, Business Romance, Merciless Romance, Lethargy Afterword. *Address:* General Yermolov str. 6, Apt. 42, 121293 Moscow, Russia. *Telephone:* (095) 148-93-64.

MYAING, U Linn, BSc; Myanmar diplomatist; m.; two d.; ed Defence Studies Acad.; commissioned as officer in Myanmar Navy 1967–93; joined Ministry of Foreign Affairs 1993; Amb. to France (also accred. (non-resident) to Belgium, The Netherlands, UNESCO and EU) 1999–2001; Amb. to USA 2001–02. *Address:* c/o Ministry of Foreign Affairs, Pyay Rd, Dagon Township, Yangon, Myanmar (Office).

MYASNIKOV, Vladimir Stepanovich, DR.HIST.; Russian historian and sinologist; b. 15 May 1931, Moscow; ed Moscow State Inst. of Int. Relations; researcher Inst. of Sinology 1956–60, Inst. of Peoples' of Asia 1963–64, Inst. of Econs of World Socialist System 1964–66; researcher, Scientific Sec., Head of Div. Inst. of Far E Russian Acad. of Sciences 1966–85, Deputy Dir 1985–; Head Centre for Chinese and Russian Relations 1992–; Corresp. mem. Russian Acad. of Sciences 1990, mem. 1997. *Publications:* over 150 published works, books, monographs. *Address:* Institute of Far East, Russian Academy of Sciences, Nakhimovsky prosp. 32, 117218 Moscow (Office); Novocheremoushkinskaya str. 49, 160 Moscow, Russia (Home). *Telephone:* (095) 124-07-22 (Office). *Fax:* (095) 718-96-56 (Office). *E-mail:* ifes@cemi.rssi.ru (Office).

MYASOYEDOV, Boris Fedorovich; Russian chemist; b. 2 Oct. 1930; m.; one s.; ed Moscow I. Mendeleyev Inst. of Chem. and Tech.; Jr, Sr Researcher, Head of Lab, Deputy Dir V. Vernadsky Inst. of Geochem. and Analytical Chem.; Corresp. mem. USSR (now Russian) Acad. of Sciences 1990, mem. 1994; research in chem. of radioactive elements, radionucleides, creation and application of chem. sensors and analysers; USSR State Prize, V. Khlopin Prize Acad. of Sciences. *Publications:* Chemical Sensors: Possibilities and Perspectives 1990. *Leisure interests:* music, stamp collecting. *Address:* Institute of Geochemistry and Analytical Chemistry, Kosygin str. 19, 117975 Moscow, Russia. *Telephone:* (095) 137-41-47 (Office); 420-90-81 (Home). *Fax:* (095) 938-20-54.

MYERS, Barton, MArch, FAIA; American/Canadian architect, planner and professor; b. 6 Nov. 1934, Norfolk, Va; s. of Barton Myers and Meeta (Burrage) Myers; m. Victoria George 1959; one d.; ed Norfolk Acad., U.S. Naval Acad. and Univ. of Pennsylvania; Partner, A. J. Diamond & Barton Myers, Toronto 1968–75; Founder and Prin. Barton Myers Assocs., Toronto 1975–86, Barton Myers Assocs Inc. LA 1981–; Asst Prof. of Architecture Univ. of Toronto 1968–70; mem. Advisory Cttee Nat. Capital Comm., Ottawa 1968–74; Founder and Pres. Bd of Dirs., Trace Magazine 1980–82; Visiting Prof. Harvard Grad. School of Design 1981; Sr Prof. School of Architecture and Urban Design, UCLA 1981–; mem. Royal Canadian Acad. of Arts, American Inst. of Architects, Soc. of Architectural Historians, GSA Nat. Register of Peer Professionals; numerous design awards, including Royal Architectural Inst. of Canada Gold Medal 1994, several AIA awards. *Major works by Diamond & Myers Assocs. include:* York Square, Toronto; Ont. Medical Asscn, Toronto; Myers & Wolf Residences, Toronto; Housing Union Bldg, Univ. of Alberta Citadel Theatre, Edmonton; Dundas-Sherborne Housing, Toronto. *Major works by Barton Myers Assocs. include:* Seagram Museum, Waterloo, Ont.; Howard Hughes Center, LA; Wang Tower, LA; Performing Arts Center, Portland, Ore.; Pasadena City Center; Music Center Expansion, LA; CBC Network HQ, Toronto; Cerritos Center for the Performing Arts, Calif.; Woodsworth Coll., Univ. of Toronto; NW Campus Housing, UCLA; Art Gallery of Ont. expansion (competition winner); York Univ. Fine Arts Bldg expansion,

Toronto; USC Education Bldg, USC Plaza, LA; New Jersey Performing Arts Center, Newark (New Jersey Golden Trowel Award, Int.Masonry Inst., Chicago Athenaeum Award 1998); The Ice House Renovation, Beverly Hills, Calif.; UCSD/Scripps Ocean Atmosphere Research Facility, La Jolla, Calif.; Univ. of New Mexico, Albuquerque (Master Devt Plan); Federal Courthouse, San Diego, Calif. 1998; Sotheby's Renovation, Beverly Hills, Calif. 1998; Hall of Justice, Sacramento, Calif. (Historial Preservation Award Calif. Preservation Foundation 2002); Montecito Film Co./Post Production Facility, Carpinteria, Calif.; House and studio at Toro Canyon, Montecito, Calif.(CCAIA Honor Award in Design 2000, AIA PIA Housing Award for Innovation in Housing Design 2002); 421 South Beverly Drive, Beverly Hills, Calif. (Beverly Hills Architectural Design Award 2002); 8820 Wilshire blvd, LA. *Publications:* Barton Myers Selected and Current Works (in The Master Architect series) 1994, New Stage for a City (monograph) 1998, 3 Steel Houses (House Design series) 2003. *Leisure interests:* travel, reading. *Address:* 1025 Westwood Boulevard, Los Angeles, CA 90024 (Office); 949 Toro Canyon Road, Santa Barbara, CA 93108, USA (Home). *Telephone:* (310) 208-2227. *Fax:* (310) 208-2207. *E-mail:* mail@bartonmyers.com (Office).

MYERS, Dale Dehaven, B.S.A.E.; American engineer, business executive and consultant; b. 8 Jan. 1922, Kansas City, Mo.; s. of Wilson A. Myers and Ruth Myers; m. Marjorie Williams 1943; two d.; ed Univ. of Washington, Seattle; Aerophysics Dept, N American 1946, Chief Engineer Missile Div. 1954, Vice-Pres. and Program Man. Hound Dog Air Launched Missile Program 1957; Vice-Pres. and Program Man., Apollo Command and Service Modules, N American 1964; Assoc. Admin. for Manned Space Flight, NASA Headquarters 1970–74, Deputy Admin., NASA 1986–89; U.S. Govt Rep. to AGARD 1988–89; Pres. N American Aircraft Operations, Rockwell Int. Corpn 1974–77, Corporate Vice-Pres. 1974–77; Under-Sec., Dept of Energy, Washington 1977–79; Pres. and COO Jacobs Eng Group Inc., Pasadena 1979–84; Pres. Dale Myers and Assocs., Leucadia, 1984–86, 1989–; mem. Bd of Dirs. Ducommun Inc., 1982–86, Jacob's Eng Group 1979–86, MacNeal Schwendler Corpn 1990–98, SYS 1984–86, SAIC's GSC 1993–97, San Diego Aerospace Museum 1992–; mem. NASA Advisory Comm. 1984–86, NASA Aero Comm. 1994–97; Fellow, American Astronautical Soc.; Hon. Fellow, American Inst. of Aeronautics and Astronautics; mem. Nat. Acad. of Engineers 1974, Int. Acad. of Astronautics 1991; Hon. PhD (Whitworth Coll.); NASA Public Service Award 1969, NASA Distinguished Service Medal 1971, 1974, DSM (Dept of Energy) 1979. *Leisure interests:* golf, old cars. *Address:* P.O. Box 232518, Encinitas, CA 92023, USA. *Telephone:* (760) 753-4043.

MYERS, Margaret Jane (Dee Dee), BS; American government official, broadcaster and magazine editor; b. 1 Sept. 1961, Quonset Point, RI; d. of Stephen George Myers and Judith Ann Burleigh; one d.; ed Univ. of Santa Clara; Press Asst Mondale for Pres. Campaign, LA 1984, to deputy Senator Art Torres, LA 1985; Deputy Press Sec. to Maj. Tom Bradley, LA 1985–87, Tom Bradley for Gov. Campaign 1986; Calif. Press Sec. Dukakis for Pres. Campaign, LA 1988; Press Sec. Feinstein for Gov. Campaign, LA and San Francisco 1989–90; Campaign Dir Jordan for Mayor Campaign, San Francisco 1991; Press Sec. Clinton for Pres. Campaign, Little Rock 1991–92, White House, Washington 1993–94; Co-host Equal Time, CNBC, Washington 1995–97; Ed. Vanity Fair magazine, Washington 1995–; mem. Bd Trustees, Calif. State Univ. 1999–; Robert F. Kennedy Award, Emerson Coll., Boston 1993. *Leisure interests:* running, cycling, music, major league baseball. *Address:* c/o White House, 1600 Pennsylvania Avenue, NW, Washington, DC 20500, USA.

MYERS, Mike; Canadian actor and writer; b. 25 May 1963, Toronto, Ont.; s. of Eric Myers and Bunny (née Hind) Myers; m. Robin Ruzan 1993; Canadian Comedy Award 2000. *Stage appearances:* The Second City, Toronto 1986–88, Chicago 1988–89; actor and writer: Mullarkey & Myers 1984–86. *Television includes:* John and Yoko (TV film) 1985, Saturday Night Live 1989–94 (Emmy Award for Outstanding Writing in a Comedy or Variety Series 1989), Russell Gilbert Show 1998, Dir The Bacchae (TV Film) 1999. *Films:* Wayne's World 1992, So I Married an Axe Murderer 1992, Wayne's World II 1993, Austin Powers: International Man of Mystery 1997, Meteor 1998, McClintock's Peach 1998, Just Like Me 1998, It's A Dog's Life 1998, 54 1998, Austin Powers: The Spy Who Shagged Me 1998, Pete's Meteor 1999, Shrek 2001, Austin Powers 3 2002. *Address:* c/o Creative Artists Agency, 9830 Wilshire Boulevard, Beverly Hills, CA 90212, USA.

MYERS, Norman, CMG, PhD; British scientist; b. 24 Aug. 1934, Whitewell, Yorks.; s. of John Myers and Gladys Myers (née Haworth); m. Dorothy Mary Halliman 1965 (separated 1992); two d.; ed Clitheroe Royal Grammar School, Lancs., Oxford Univ., Univ. of Calif. at Berkeley; ind. scientist and consultant in Environment and Devt with focus on Third World regions of the tropics 1970–; has worked for many int. orgs and govt agencies; Man. Dir Norman Myers Scientific Consultancy Ltd 1982–; lectures at American univs; Amb. to World Wide Fund for Nature UK; Foreign Assoc. NAS; Hon. Visiting Fellow Green Coll. Oxford; Hon. degree (Kent); WWF Int. Gold Medal 1983, Order of the Golden Ark (Netherlands) 1983, Kt of the Golden Ark (Netherlands) 1992, Volvo Environment Prize 1992, UNEP/Sasakawa Environment Prize 1995, Blue Planet Prize 2001. *Publications:* The Long African Day 1973, The Sinking Ark 1979 (five scientific/literary awards), A Wealth of Wild Species 1983, The Primary Source 1984, Economics of Ecosystem Management 1985, The Gaia Atlas of Planet Management 1985, Future Worlds: Challenge and Opportunity in an Age of Change 1991, Population, Resources and the Environment: The Critical Challenges (for UN Population Fund) 1991,

Tropical Forests and Climate (Ed.) 1992, Ultimate Security: The Environmental Basis of Political Stability 1993, Scarcity or Abundance: A Debate on the Environment 1994, Environmental Exodus: An Emergent Crisis in the Global Arena 1995, Biodiversity Hotspots 1999, Towards a New Green Print for Business and Society (in Japanese) 1999, Perverse Subsidies 2001. *Leisure interests:* marathon running, mountaineering, professional photography. *Address:* Upper Meadow, Headington, Oxford, OX3 8NT, England. *Telephone:* (1865) 750387. *Fax:* (1865) 741538. *E-mail:* myers1n@aol.com (Office).

MYERS, Richard B., BS, MBA; American air force officer; b. 1942, Kansas City, Mo.; m.; two d. one s.; ed Kansas State Univ., Auburn Univ., Air Command/Staff Coll., Ala, US Army War Coll., Pa and Harvard Univ.; commissioned 2nd Lieut. USAF 1965; fighter pilot, Vietnam 1969; various assignments to Commdr US Forces, Japan and 5th Air Force, Yakota Air Base, Japan 1993–96; Asst to Chair. Jt Chiefs of Staff, The Pentagon, 1996–97; rank of Gen. 1997; Commdr Pacific Air Forces, Hickam Air Force Base, Hawaii 1997–98; C-in-C N American Aerospace Defense Command/US Space Command, Peterson Air Force Base, Colo 1998–2000; Vice-Chair. Jt Chiefs of Staff 2000–01, Chair. 2001–; Defense Distinguished Service Medal with Oak Leaf Cluster, Distinguished Service Medal, Legion of Merit, Distinguished Flying Cross with Oak Leaf Cluster, Meritorious Service Medal with Three Oak Leaf Clusters, Air Medal with 18 Oak Leaf Clusters, Air Force Commendation Medal. *Address:* c/o Department of Defense, The Pentagon, Washington, DC 20301, USA (Office). *Telephone:* (703) 697-5737 (Office). *Fax:* (703) 695-1149 (Office). *Website:* www.defenselink.mil (Office).

MYERSON, Jacob M., MA; American economist and diplomatist; b. 11 June 1926, Rock Hill, SC; s. of Solomon Myerson and Lena (née Clein) Myerson; m. 1st Nicole Neuray 1965 (died 1968); one d.; m. 2nd Helen Hayashi 1974 (died 1995); ed Washington, DC, Pennsylvania State Coll., George Washington Univ.; entered US Foreign Service 1950; Economic Analyst for the Office of the US High Commr, Berlin 1950–52, mem. US Regional Mission for the OEEC and Marshall Plan, Paris 1953–56; State Dept Desk Officer for EC and European Free Trade Area Affairs 1956–60; Chief of Political Section of US Mission to the European Communities, Brussels 1960; Special Asst to the Under-Sec. of State, Officer in Charge of NATO Political Affairs, State Dept, then Deputy Political Adviser and Counsellor to the US Mission to NATO, Brussels 1965–68, Adviser to the US del. at several ministerial sessions of the N Atlantic Council 1966–70; Econ. Counsellor US Mission to the European Communities, Brussels, then Deputy Chief and Minister Counsellor 1970–75; Amb. to UN Econ. and Social Council, New York 1975–77; Minister Counsellor for Econ. and Commercial Affairs, US Embassy, Paris 1977–80; Deputy Sec.-Gen. of the OECD 1980–88; Rivkin Award American Foreign Service Assoc. 1969, Order of the Sacred Treasure of Japan 1990. *Leisure interest:* twentieth century art. *Address:* 2 rue Lucien-Gaulard, 75018 Paris, France.

MYINT MAUNG, U; Myanmar diplomatist and administrator; b. 10 March 1921, Magwe; m.; three c.; ed Univ. of Rangoon; joined Army 1942; has held the following positions: Head of Co-operative Dept; Chief of Admin. Div. of Burma Socialist Programme Party, also mem. Party Inspection Cttee; mem. Pyithu Hluttaw (People's Congress) for Magwe Constituency; mem. Bd of Dirs of People's Bank of the Union of Burma, Exec. Cttee of Burma Sports and Physical Fitness Cttee, Cen. Cttee of Burma Red Cross Soc.; Chair. Resettlement Cttee of Cen. Security and Admin. Cttee, Independence Award Cttee; Perm. Rep. to UN 1975–77; Minister of Foreign Affairs 1977–79; Amb. to China –1989; mem. State Council and Attorney-Gen. 1988. *Address:* c/o Ministry of Foreign Affairs, Yangon, Myanmar.

MYNBAEV, Sauat M., CAND.ECON.; Kazakhstan politician; b. 19 Nov. 1962, Taldy-Kurgan; s. of Mukhametbai Mynbaev and Oralbaeva Rakhima; m. Kalieva Zhanar Mynbaev; one s. one d.; ed Moscow State Univ.; teacher Almaty Inst. of Nat. Economy, later Assoc. Prof. 1989–; Pres. Kazakhstan Exchange 1991–92; First Deputy Chair., Dir Kazkommerts Bank 1992–95; Deputy Minister of Finance and Dir of Treasury 1995–98, Minister of Finance 1998–99; Deputy Head of Pres.'s Admin. 1999; Minister of Agric. 1999–2001; Pres. Devt Bank of Kazakhstan 2001–; Dir European Bank of Devt from Kazakhstan 2001–. *Address:* Development Bank of Kazakhstan, Pobeda Avenue, Astana Tower, Office 12/1, 473000 Astana, Kazakhstan (Office). *Telephone:* (2) 580-02-60 (Office). *Fax:* (2) 580-02-69 (Office). *E-mail:* info@kdb .kz (Office).

MYNERS, Paul, FRSA; British business executive; b. 1 April 1948; m.; five c.; ed Univ. of London; finance writer, Daily Telegraph –1974; N. M. Rothschild 1974–85; CEO Gartmore Investment Man. 1985–87, Chair. 1987–2001; Deputy Chair. Powergen 1999–2001; Exec. Dir Nat. Westminster Bank 1999–2000; Dir City Disputes Panel, Financial Reporting Council, Lloyds of London Investment Cttee; Chair. Guardian Media Group 2001–; Dir (nonexec.) mmO$_2$ 2001–, Bank of NY, Marks & Spencer 2002; Chair. Tate St Ives; mem. Royal Acad. Trust, United Response. *Leisure interest:* London Symphony Orchestra. *Address:* Guardian Media Group, 75 Farringdon Road, London, EC1M 3JX (Office); Gartmore House, 8 Fenchurch Place, London, EC3M 4PH, England. *Telephone:* (20) 7278-2332 (Guardian) (Office); (20) 7782-2000. *Fax:* (20) 7242-0679 (Guardian) (Office).

MYRDAL, Jan; Swedish writer; b. 19 July 1927, Stockholm; s. of the late Gunnar Myrdal and Alva Reimer; m. 1st Nadja Wiking 1948; m. 2nd Maj Liedberg 1953; m. 3rd Gun Kessle 1956; one s. one d.; Sunday columnist (politics, culture) Stockholms-Tidningen 1963–66, Aftonbladet 1966–72; Chair. and Publr Folket i Bild/Kulturfront 1971–72, columnist 1972–; Hon.

DLit (Upsala Coll., NJ) 1980; Hon. PhD (Nankai Univ., China) 1993; Chevalier, Ordre des Arts et des Lettres 1990. *Works include:* films: Myglaren 1966, Hjalparen 1968, Balzac or The Triumphs of Realism 1975, Mexico: Art and Revolution 1991; TV documentaries: Democratic Kampuchea 1978–79, Guerilla Base Area of Democratic Kampuchea 1979, China 1979, 20 films on history of political caricature and posters 1975–87. *Publications:* (in Swedish) novels: Hemkomst 1954, Jubelvår 1955, Att bli och vara 1956, Badrumskranen 1957, Karriär 1975, Barndom 1982, En annan värld 1984; drama: Folkets Hus 1953, Moraliteter 1967, Garderingar 1969, B. Olsen 1972; travel: Resa i Afghanistan 1960, Bortom berg och öknar 1962, Turkmenistan 1966, En världsbild (co-author) 1977, Sidenvägen 1977, Indien väntar 1980; politics: Kina: Revolutionen går vidare 1970, Albansk utmaning 1970, Ett 50-tal 1972, lag utan ordning, Kinesiska frågor, Tyska frågor 1976, Kina efter Mao Tse-tung 1977, Kampuchea och kriget 1978, Kampuchea hösten 1979, Den albanska utmaningen 1968–86, 1987, Mexico, Dröm och längtan 1996; art: Bartom Bergen 1983; essays: Söndagsmorgon 1965, Skriftställning 1968, Skriftställning II 1969, Skriftställning III 1970, Skriftställning IV 1973, V 1975, Klartexter 1978, Skriftställning X 1978, Balzac und der Realismus (in German) 1978, Strindberg och Balzac 1981, Ord och Avsikt 1986, Det nya Stor, Tyskland 1993; autobiography: Rescontra 1962, Samtida bekännelser 1964, Inför nedräkningen 1993, När morgondagarna sjöng 1994, En kärlek 1998, Maj: En kärlek 1998; art: Ansikte av sten, Angkor 1968, Ondskan tar form 1976; Dussinet fullt 1981, Den trettonde 1983, Franska revolutionens bilder 1989, 5 ar av frihet 1830–35 1991, När Västerlandet tradde fram 1992, André Gill 1995, Drömmen om det goda samhallet; Kinesiska affischer 1966–1976 1996; wine: Jan Myrdal on vin 1999; biography: Johan August Strindberg 2000; (in English) Report from a Chinese Village 1965, Chinese Journey 1965, Confessions of a Disloyal European 1968, Angkor: an essay on art and imperialism 1970, China: The Revolution Continued 1971, Gates to Asia 1971, Albania Defiant 1976, The Silk Road 1979, China Notebook 1975–78 1979, Return to a Chinese Village 1984, India Waits 1984, Childhood 1991, Another World 1993, 12 Going on 13 1995. *Leisure interests:* collecting Meccano, computing for fun. *Address:* Kalvängen 70 D, 739 91 Skinnskatteberg, Sweden. *Telephone:* (223) 51-012. *Fax:* (223) 51-007. *E-mail:* myrdal@ myrdal.pp.se (Office).

MYSEN, Bjorn O., MA, PhD; American research scientist; b. 20 Dec. 1947, Oslo, Norway; s. of Martin Mysen and Randi Mysen; m. Susanna Laya 1975; two c.; ed Univ. of Oslo and Pennsylvania State Univ.; Carnegie Foundation Fellow 1974–77; Sr Scientist, Experimental Geochemist, Carnegie Inst. Washington 1977–; mem. Royal Norwegian Acad. of Sciences; Fellow, Mineralogy Soc. of America; F. W. Clarke Medal; Reusch Medal. *Publications:* Structure and Properties of Silicate Melts 1988; more than 210 other scientific publications. *Address:* Geophysical Laboratory, Carnegie Institution of Washington, 5251 Broad Branch Road, NW, Washington, DC 20015, USA (Office). *Telephone:* (202) 478-8975. *Fax:* (202) 478-8901 (Office). *E-mail:* mysen@gl.ciw.edu (Office). *Website:* www.gl.civw.edu/~mysen (Office).

MYŚLIWSKI, Wiesław; Polish writer; b. 25 March 1932, Dwikozy nr Sandomierz; m. Wacława Stec; one s.; ed Catholic Univ. of Lublin; worked at People's Publishing Cooperative until 1976, Ed. quarterly magazine Regiony 1975–99; Ed. fortnightly Sycyna 1994–99; numerous awards include Stanisław Piętak Prize 1968, 1973, Prize of Ministry of Culture and Art 1971, State Prize 1986, Nike Literary Prize 1997, Reymont Prize 1997; Alfred Jurzykowski Foundation Award, New York 1998. *Novels:* Nagi sad (Naked Orchard) 1967, Pałac (Palace) 1970, Kamień na kamieniu (Stone on Stone) 1984, Widnokrąg (Horizon) 1996. *Screenplays include:* Przez dziewięć mostów (Across Nine Bridges) 1972, Droga (Way), Popielec (Ash Wednesday) 1983, Kamień na kamieniu (Stone on Stone) 1995. *Plays:* Złodziej (Thief) 1973, Klucznik (Steward) 1978, Drzewo (Tree) 1989, Requiem dla gospodyni (Requiem for a Landlady) 2000. *Address:* ul. Nowoursynowska 119C, 02-797 Warsaw, Poland (Home).

MYTARAS, Dimitris; Greek artist; b. 1934, Chalkis; s. of Basilis Mytaras and Efrosini Mytaras; m. Chariklia Mytaras 1961; one s.; ed Athens School of Fine Arts and Ecole des Arts Décoratifs, Paris; Prof. Athens School of Fine Arts; has exhibited in many of the world's capitals and has participated in most important Biennales; assoc. with Kreonidis Gallery, Athens, Metropolis Art Galleries, New York, the Inter Art Group, Tokyo and Galerie Flak, Paris; main periods of his painting are: Mirrors 1960–64, Dictatorship 1966–70, Epitaphs 1971–76, Portraits 1977–87, Theatre Scenes 1988–91. *Publications:* D. Mytaras: Peinture 1982, D. Mytaras: Peinture 1990, D. Mytaras: Drawings 1994, D. Mytaras: Parepiptonda. *Address:* Kamariotou 15, 115-24 N Filothei, Athens, Greece. *Telephone:* 6913658. *Fax:* 6928327.

MYTTON, Graham Lambert, PhD, FRSA; British marketing consultant; b. 21 Oct. 1942, Sanderstead; s. of Peter Mytton and Joan Jackson; m. Janet Codd 1966; two d.; ed Trinity School, Croydon, Purley Grammar School and Univs. of Liverpool, Manchester and Dar es Salaam; Man. BBC Radio studio 1964–66; Research Fellow, Zambia Broadcasting 1970–73; radio producer, BBC African Service 1973–75; current affairs producer, BBC Radio Four 1976; Head, Hausa Language Section, BBC African Service 1976–82; Head, Int. Broadcasting Audience Research, BBC World Service 1982–91, Head, Audience Research and Correspondence 1991–96, Controller, Marketing 1996–98; ind. consultant and trainer in audience, opinion and market research 1999–; Dir Intermedia, Washington, DC 2001–; AT&T Guest lecturer, George Washington Univ. 1995; Silver Medal, Market Research Soc. 1997. *Publications:* Mass Communications in Africa 1983, Global Audiences (ed.) 1993, Handbook on Radio and TV Audience Research 1993. *Leisure interests:* stamp collecting, singing. *Address:* Roffeys, The Green, Coldharbour, Dorking, Surrey, RH5 6HE, England. *Telephone:* (1306) 712122. *Fax:* (1306) 712958. *E-mail:* gmytton@gn.apc.org (Office).

MZALI, Mohamed, LIC.EN.PHIL.; Tunisian politician; b. 23 Dec. 1925, Monastir; m.; six c.; ed Sadiky School, Tunis, Univ. of Paris; Teacher at Sadiky School, Lycée Alaoui and Univ. of Zitouna 1950–56; Chef de Cabinet, Ministry of Educ. 1956–58; mem. Nat. Ass. 1959–; Dir of Youth and Sports, President's Secr. 1959–64; Dir-Gen. Radiodiffusion Télévision Tunisienne (RTT) 1964–67; Sec. of State for Nat. Defence 1968–69; Minister of Youth and Sports 1969–70, of Educ. 1969–70, 1971–73, 1976–80, of Health 1973–76; Coordinator of Govt Activities, Dept of the Pres. March–April 1980; Prime Minister 1980–84, Prime Minister and Minister of the Interior 1984–86; mem. Neo-Destour Party (now Parti Socialiste Destourien) 1947–, mem. Cen. Cttee 1971–, Sec.-Gen. 1980–86; mem. IOC (First Vice-Pres. 1976–80) 1976–; Municipal Councillor, Tunis 1960, 1963; First Vice-Pres. Tunis Town Council 1960–63, Pres. Culture, Youth and Sports Comm. 1960–66; Pres. Ariana Town Council 1959–72; Founder El Fikr (monthly cultural review) 1955; Pres., Tunisian Olympic Cttee 1962–, Union des Ecrivains Tunisiens 1970–; Pres. Int. Cttee Jeux Méditerranéens 1979–; mem. Arab Language Acad.,

Cairo 1976–, Baghdad 1978–, Damascus 1980–, Jordan 1980–; mem. French Sports Acad. 1978–; Living in France in self-imposed exile; fined and sentenced to 15 years forced labour after *in absentia* conviction for corruption 1987; Grand Cordon, Ordre de l'Indépendance, Ordre de la République, Grand Officier Légion d'honneur and numerous foreign decorations. *Publications:* La Démocratie 1955, Recueil d'Editoriaux d'El Fikr 1969, Prises de positions 1973, Etudes 1975, Points de vue 1975, Les Chemins de la pensée 1979, The Word of the Action 1984, The Olympism Today 1984.

MZIMELA, Rev. Sipo E., PhD; South African ecclesiastic and civil servant; b. 1937, Durban; m.; three d.; in exile 1961, W Germany 1964–74, USA 1974; Rector Epiphany Church New Jersey; ordained Episopal Priest New York 1976; worked with SA refugees; teacher St Paul's United Theological Coll., Kenya 1984; Founder SA Educ. Fund 1987; Assoc. Priest St Bartholomew's Episcopal Church, Atlanta 1987; Inkatha Freedom Party Rep. to USA 1990; fmr Minister of Works, KwaZulu Govt 1994; Minister of Correctional Services, Govt of Nat. Unity 1994–99. *Publications include:* Apartheid. South African Nazism, Whither South Africa Now?, Marching to Slavery—South Africa's Descent to Communism 1983. *Address:* c/o Private Bag X853, Pretoria 0001, South Africa.

N

NÄÄTÄNEN, Risto Kalervo, PhD; Finnish professor of psychology; b. 14 June 1939, Helsinki; s. of Prof. Esko K. Näätänen and Rauni (née Raudanjoki) Näätänen; m. Marjatta Kerola 1960; three s.; ed Univ. of Helsinki; Asst Dept of Psychology, Univ. of Helsinki 1965–69, Prof. of Psychology 1975–, Dir Cognitive Brain Research Unit 1991–; Researcher Acad. of Finland 1969–75, Research Prof. 1983–, Acad. Prof. 1995–; Scientific Organizer (with Prof. G. Rizzolatti) of European Science Foundation Winter School 1990; Fellowships, Dept of Psychology, UCLA 1965–66, Univ. Dundee, Scotland 1979–80, Univ. Marburg, Germany 1980–81, The Neurosciences Inst., New York 1985–86, Inst. for Advanced Study, Berlin 1988–89; Vice-Pres. Fed. of European Psychophysiology 1994–96, Pres. 1996–; mem. Brain Research Soc. of Finland (Pres. 1983–91), Int. Brain Research Org. (Governing Council 1985–91), Nordic Psychophysiology Soc. (Pres. 1992–95), Advisory Council, Int. Asscn for the Study of Attention and Performance, Governing Council, Fed. of European Psychophysiology Socs.; mem. Finnish Acad. of Science and Letters 1980–, Academia Europaea 1991– (Council 2000–); Foreign mem. Russian Acad. of Sciences 1994–; Hon. Dr (Jyväskylä), (Tartu) 2000; Purkinje Medal (Prague) 1988, Finnish Cultural Foundation Prize 1990, First Science Prize (Finland) 1997, State Traffic Safety Medal 1992; Kt, First Class, Order of the White Rose of Finland. *Publications:* Selective Attention and Evoked Potentials 1967, Road-User Behaviour and Traffic Accidents (with H. Summala) 1976, Attention and Brain Function 1992, The Orienting Response in Information Processing (with E.N. Sokolov, J.A. Spinks & H. Lyytinen; numerous articles. *Leisure interests:* sports, the Green Movement, traffic safety. *Address:* Cognitive Brain Research Unit, The Department of Psychology, University of Helsinki, Siltavuorenpenger 20 C, 00170 Helsinki; Mäkipellontie 12 D, 00320 Helsinki, Finland (Home).

NABARRO, Frank Reginald Nunes, MBE, DSc, FRS; British physicist; b. 7 March 1916, London; s. of Stanley Nunes Nabarro and Leah (née Cohen) Nabarro; m. Margaret Constance Dalziel 1948 (died 1997); three s. two d.; ed Nottingham High School, New Coll. Oxford, Univ. of Bristol; Sr Experimental Officer Ministry of Supply 1941–45; Royal Soc. Warren Research Fellow, Univ. of Bristol 1944–49; Lecturer in Metallurgy, Univ. of Birmingham 1949–53; Prof. of Physics, Univ. of the Witwatersrand, Johannesburg 1953–84, Prof. Emer. 1985–; Consultant, South African Council for Scientific and Industrial Research 1985–, Fellow 1994–; Pres. Royal Soc. of SA 1989–92; Founder mem. South African Acad. of Science 1995; Hon. mem. South African Inst. of Physics, Microscopy Soc. of South Africa; Foreign Assoc. US Nat. Acad. of Eng 1996–; Hon. FRSSA; Hon. Pres. Johannesburg Musical Soc.; Beilby Memorial Award, South African Medal (South African Asscn for the Advancement of Science) 1972, De Beers Gold Medal 1980, Claude Harris Leon Foundation Award of Merit 1983, J.F.W. Herschel Medal 1983, R.F. Mehl Award 1995, Platinum Medal, Inst. of Materials 1997; Hon. DSc (Witwatersrand) 1987, (Natal) 1988, (Cape Town) 1988, (Pretoria) 2003. *Publications:* Theory of Crystal Dislocations 1967, Ed. Dislocations in Solids (9 vols) 1979–92, Vol. 10 (with M. S. Duesbery) 1996, Vol. 11 2003, Physics of Creep (with H. Filmer) 1995. *Leisure interests:* gardening, music. *Address:* 32 Cookham Road, Auckland Park, Johannesburg 2092, South Africa; School of Physics, University of the Witwatersrand, Private Bag 3, WITS 2050, Johannesburg, South Africa (Office). *Telephone:* (11) 7176875 (Office); (11) 7267745 (Home). *Fax:* (11) 7176879. *E-mail:* nabarro@physnet.phys.wits.ac.sa (Office).

NACHTIGALL, Dieter, Dr rer. nat; German physicist; b. 4 Feb. 1927, Berge; s. of Walter Nachtigall and Emma (née Eisermann) Nachtigall; two s. one d.; ed Humboldt Univ., Berlin; schoolteacher, GDR 1946–49, lecturer, Teacher's Coll. 1949–50; Scientific Asst and Lecturer, Tech. Univ. of Dresden 1956–59; Research Group Leader Nuclear Research Establishment, Juelich, FRG 1959–65; Research Assoc. CERN, Geneva 1965–66; Group Leader EURATOM BCNM, Geel 1966–71; Prof. of Physics Educ., Paed. Hochschule, Dortmund 1971–81, Univ. of Dortmund 1981–92, Prof. Emer. 1992–, Dean Dept of Physics 1990–92; Advisory Prof., East China Normal Univ., Shanghai 1989–, Guangxi Normal Univ. 1995; mem. Int. Comm. on Physics Educ. 1987–93; Hon. Prof. Xian Highway Inst. 1988; Hon. Prof. Normal Univ. of Chengdu/Sichuan 1993, South West China Normal Univ. at Chongqing 1994; Medal of Int. Comm. on Physics Educ. 1998. *Publications:* Table of Specific Gamma Ray Contents 1969, Physikalische Grundlagen für Dosimetrie und Strahlenschutz Thiemig 1971, Skizzen zur Physik-Didaktik Lang 1986, Neues Physiklerinnen-Das Teilchen-Konzept Lang 1989, Das Feldkonzept 1990, Das Wellenkonzept 1990, Internalizing Physics–Making Physics Part of One's Life (UNESCO) 1995. *Address:* Otto Hahn Strasse 4, 4422A Dortmund (Office); Auf'm Hilmkamp 15, 58739 Wickede Wiehagen, Germany (Home). *Telephone:* (231) 7552989 (Office); (2377) 3548 (Home). *Fax:* (231) 7555175 (Office); (2377) 6134 (Home). *E-mail:* nachtigall@didaktik.physik.uni-dortmund.de (Office); dieternachtigall@t-online.de (Home).

NADAR, Shiv; Indian business executive and electrical engineer; b. 1946; m.; systems analyst Cooper Eng; Sr Man. Trainee DCM Ltd 1968; f. HCL Overseas (later HCL Consulting, now HCL Technologies) 1991, HCL Group. *Address:* HCL Infosystems Ltd, E-4, 5, 6 Sector 11, Noida 201 301, Uttar Pradesh, India (Office). *Telephone:* (91) 4526518 (Office). *Fax:* (91) 4550923 (Office). *E-mail:* webhost@hclinfosystems.com (Office). *Website:* www.hclinfosystems.com (Office).

NADER, Ralph; American lawyer, author and consumer advocate; b. 27 Feb. 1934, Winsted, Conn.; s. of Nadra Nader and Rose Bouziane; ed Princeton and Harvard Univs; admitted to Conn. Bar 1958, Mass. Bar 1959, also US Supreme Court; US Army 1959; law practice in Hartford, Conn. 1959–; Lecturer in History and Govt, Univ. of Hartford 1961–63; fmr Head of Public Citizen Inc. 1980; Lecturer, Princeton Univ. 1967–68; Co-founder Princeton Project 55 1989; launched new political Movt Democracy Rising 2001; presidential cand. 2001; mem. ABA; has advanced cause of consumer protection, particularly with regard to car safety in USA; f. Clean Water Action Project, Disability Rights Center, int. network of Public Interest Research Groups (PIRGs) across univ. campuses and other orgs; Woodrow Wilson Award (Princeton Univ.) 1972. *Publications:* Unsafe at Any Speed 1965, Who Runs Congress? 1972, Ed. The Consumer and Corporate Accountability 1974, Taming the Giant Corporation (co-author) 1976, The Menace of Atomic Energy (with John Abbotts) 1979, The Lemon Book 1980, Who's Poisoning America? 1981, The Big Boys 1986, Winning the Insurance Game (co-author) 1990, Good Works 1993, No Contest: Corporate Lawyers and the Perversion of Justice in America 1996, The Ralph Nader Reader 2000; Contributing Ed. Ladies Home Journal 1973–81, syndicated columnist 1972–. *Address:* Democracy Rising, 320 SW Stark Street, Suite 2002, Portland, OR 97204, USA.

NADIR, Asil; Turkish-Cypriot business executive; b. 1 May 1941, Paphos; s. of Irfan Nadir; m. Ayesha Nadir twice (divorced twice); two s.; ed Univ. of Istanbul; settled in East End of London, England 1963; formed Wearwell cash-and-carry clothing co., Tower Hamlets 1967; est. cardboard-box factory for fruit-packing in Northern Cyprus following partition of island in 1974; Chair. Polly Peck Int. PLC 1980–90; business expanded to include citrus fruit, colour television factory in Turkey, hotels, leisure complexes, Pizza Hut franchise in Turkey, etc.; acquired control of Sansui electronics co.; bought tropical fruit arm of Del Monte Co., making Polly Peck world's third largest fruit trader; cos. became largest employers in Northern Cyprus; owner of several leading Turkish newspapers; set up charitable trust Nadir Health and Educ. Foundation 1989; Polly Peck empire valued at nearly £2 billion when it collapsed and was placed in hands of administrators Oct. 1990; arrested 15 Dec. 1990 following inquiries into his business affairs by Inland Revenue and Serious Fraud Office; indicted on counts of theft and false accounting faced further charges rearrested Sept. 1991; declared bankrupt Nov. 1991; jumped bail and fled to "Turkish Federated State of Northern Cyprus" May 1993. *Address:* c/o Dome Hotel, Kyrenia, "Turkish Federated State of Northern Cyprus".

NAFEH, Ibrahim; Egyptian journalist; b. 1934, Suez; m.; two c.; diplomatic corresp., Cairo Radio 1956–60; Econ. Ed., Al-Gumhuriya newspaper 1960–62; Econ. Ed. of Al-Ahram (newspaper) 1962–67; Middle East specialist in IBRD, Information Dept 1971–73; Head of Al-Ahram Econ. Dept 1974–75; Chief Ed. Al-Ahram 1975, then Chair. and Ed. in Chief; currently Pres. Arab Journalists' Union. *Publication:* Translation into Arabic of Lester Pearson's Report: Partners in Devt 1971. *Address:* c/o Al-Ahram, Sharia al Galaa, Cairo 11511, Egypt.

NAFFAH, Fouad Georges, LIC. EN DROIT; Lebanese politician and lawyer; b. 1 March 1925, Zouk Mikhaël; s. of Georges Naffah and Malvina Takla; m. Zbeide Sfeir; three s. one d.; ed Coll. des Frères Maristes, Coll. d'Antoura, Univ. St Joseph, Beirut; elected Deputy for Kesrouan 1960, 1972; Lecturer in Constitutional Law and Lebanese Constitution, Coll. de la Sagesse and Univ. Libanaise; Minister of Agric. March–May 1972, of Finance 1972–73, of Foreign Affairs 1973–74; mem. Centre Bloc.

NAGAI, Kiyoshi, PhD, FRS; Japanese biologist; s. of Otoyï Nagai and Naoko Nagai (née Matsumoto); m. Yoshito Mayïma 1974; one s. one d.; ed Osaka Univ. Morimoto Lab.; Prof. MRC Lab. of Molecular Biology 1981–; Leader, Nagai Group (research projects); Fellow Darwin Coll. Cambridge 1993–; organizer RNA Club (Darwin Coll.), Novartis Medal and Prize, Biochem. Soc. 2000. *Leisure interests:* reading, playing cello in chamber groups. *Address:* Structural Studies Division, Medical Research Council Laboratory of Molecular Biology, Hills Road, Cambridge, CB2 2QH, (Office); 100 Mowbray Road, Cambridge, CB1 7TG, England. *Telephone:* (1223) 402292 (Office). *Fax:* (1223) 213556 (Office). *E-mail:* kn@mrc-lmb.cam.ac.uk (Office). *Website:* www2.mrc-lmb.cam.ac.uk (Office).

NAGAKURA, Saburo, DrSc; Japanese scientist; b. 3 Oct. 1920, Shizuoka Pref.; m. Midori Murayama 1953; one s.; ed Shizuoka High School and Tokyo Imperial Univ.; Assoc. Prof., Univ. of Tokyo 1949–59, Prof. 1959–81; Head of Physical Organic Chem. Lab., Inst. of Physical and Chemical Research 1961–81; mem. Science Council of Japan 1972–75; mem. Science Council, Ministry of Educ., Science and Culture 1974–86, 1988–96, Univ. Council 1987–93; Dir-Gen. Inst. for Molecular Science 1981–87; Pres. Int. Union of Pure and Applied Chem. 1981–83, Chem. Soc. of Japan 1984–85, Okazaki Nat. Research Insts 1985–88, Grad. Univ. for Advanced Studies 1988–95, Japanese Centre for Int. Studies in Ecology 1993–, Kanagawa Acad. of Science and Tech. 1995–; mem. Japan Acad., Int. Acad. of Quantum Molecular Science, Deutsche Akad. der Naturforscher Leopoldina; Foreign mem. Royal Swedish Acad. of Sciences; Foreign Fellow Indian Nat. Science Acad.; Hon. mem. Royal Institution, London, Chem. Soc. of Japan, Korean Acad. of

Science and Tech.; Hon. Fellow Chinese Chem. Soc., Indian Acad. of Sciences; Hon. DSc (Nebraska); Chem. Soc. of Japan Prize 1966, Asahi Prize 1971, Japan Acad. Prize 1978, Jawaharlal Nehru Birth Centenary Medal 1996; Person of Cultural Merit 1985, Order of Cultural Merit 1990. *Publications:* Electronic Theory for Organic Chemistry 1966 and many publs on electronic structure and dynamic behaviour of excited molecules. *Leisure interest:* appreciation of Japanese paintings. *Address:* 2-7-13 Higashi-cho, Kichijoji, Musashino, Tokyo 1800002, Japan. *Telephone:* (422) 22-5777.

NAGANO, Kent; American conductor; b. 22 Nov. 1951, Berkeley, Calif.; studied under Ozawa, Boulez and Bernstein; first achieved int. recognition when he conducted Boston Symphony Orchestra in performance of Mahler's Symphony No. 9 1984; conducted US premiere of Messiaen's The Transfiguration; debut at Paris Opera conducting world premiere of Messiaen's St François d'Assise; debut, Metropolitan Opera, New York conducting Poulenc's Dialogues de Carmelites 1994; Music Dir Berkeley Symphony Orchestra, Calif. 1978–; Music Dir Opera de Lyon 1989; Assoc. Prin. Guest Conductor, London Symphony Orchestra 1990, Music Dir 1994–99; Music Dir Hallé Orchestra 1992–2000; Artistic Dir Deutsches Sinfonie-Orchester Berlin 2000–; Prin. Conductor Los Angeles Opera 2001–; several awards for operatic recording. *Address:* c/o Van Walsum Management Ltd, 4 Addison Bridge Place, London, W14 8XP, England. *Telephone:* (20) 7371-4343 (Office). *Fax:* (20) 7371-4344 (Office).

NAGARE, Masayuki; Japanese sculptor; b. Nagasaki; m. (divorced); one d.; enrolled in Zen Temple; apprentice to a sword maker; fighter pilot volunteer World War II; several one-man exhbns. *Works include:* Cloud Fortress, New York, Nagare Park, Okushiri, as well as over 2,000 other pieces.

NAGASHIMA, Shigeo, BA; Japanese baseball player; b. 20 Feb. 1936, Chiba Pref.; s. of Toshi Nagashima and Chiyo Nagashima; m. Akiko Nishimura 1965; two s. two d.; ed St Paul's Univ., Tokyo; professional baseball player, Tokyo Yomiuri Giants 1958–74, Man. 1975–81, 1993–2001; Rookie of the Year 1958, Most Valuable Player of the Year (five times), Best Average Hitter of the Year (six times), Most Home-run Hitter of the Year (twice), Most Runs batted in Hitter of the Year (five times), Man. of Champion Team of the Year three times. *Leisure interest:* golf. *Address:* 3-29-19, Denenchofu, Ohta-ku, Tokyo 145, Japan. *Fax:* (3) 3722-3766.

NAGEL, Andrés; Spanish artist; b. 15 Aug. 1947, San Sebastián; qualified as an architect. *Exhibitions include:* Tasende Gallery, LA and La Jolla, Calif., Galerie Maeght, Barcelona, Galerie Didier Imbert, Paris, Ulysses Gallery, New York, Koldo Mitxelena, Donostia, Galería Antonia Puyó, Zaragoza, Museo Tamayo, México, DF, Meadows Museum, Dallas, Tex., Museo de Bellas Artes, Bilbao, San Carlo Gallery, Milan, Galeria Marlborough, Madrid. *Address:* Caserío Paradar 36, 20015 San Sebastián, Guipúzcoa, Spain (Office). *Fax:* (943) 293589 (Office).

NAGEL, Günter; German landscape architect; b. 2 Feb. 1936, Dresden; s. of Heinrich Nagel and Erna (née Hempel) Nagel; m. Helga Jähnig 1962; one c.; ed Dresden, Humboldt Univ., Berlin and Berlin Tech. Univ.; Scientific Asst Garden and Landscape Design, Berlin Tech. Univ. 1962–70, lectureship in Design, Garden and Landscape; freelance landscape architect; lectureships at Fine Arts Univ., Berlin (Prof. 1974) and Tech. Univ. Brunswick 1970–74; Prof. and Dir Inst. for Park Planning and Garden Architecture, Univ. of Hannover 1977–2000; mem. German Soc. for Garden Design and Preservation of Natural Resources; mem. Deutscher Werkbund; mem. Bd of Trustees, Fritz Schumacher Foundation and Karl Foerster Foundation; mem. Acad. of Arts, Berlin, German Acad. of Town and Country Planning; Exhbn "Wohnen in den Stadten?" (with H. Luz and F. Spengeli) 1984. *Publications:* Gärten in Cornwall 1975, Freiräume in der Stadtentwicklung 1978, Erholungsraum Stadtlandschaft 1980, Stadtumbau Grunfunktionen im Hamburger Hafen 1983, Gestaltung und Nutzung des Freiraums Strasse 1985, Verbesserung des Wohnumfeldes 1985, Qualität öffentlicher Freiräume 1986. *Address:* c/o Institut für Grünplanung und Gartenarchitektur, Universität Hannover, Herrenhäuser Strasse 2, 30419 Hannover, Germany.

NAGEL, Ivan; German professor of aesthetics and history of performing arts; b. 28 June 1931, Budapest, Hungary; ed Univs. of Heidelberg, Paris, Frankfurt and Durham; Theatre and Music Critic, Deutsche Zeitung 1959–61, Süddeutsche Zeitung 1969–71; Artistic Adviser, Münchner Kammerspiele 1962–69; Gen. Man. Deutsches Schauspielhaus, Hamburg 1972–79; Pres. Int. Theatre Inst. 1972–79; Cultural Corresp. Frankfurter Allgemeine, New York 1980–83; Fellow, Wissenschaftkolleg, Berlin 1983–84, 1988–89; Dir Stadt Theatre, Stuttgart 1985–88; Prof. for Aesthetics and History of the Performing Arts, Hochschule der Künste, Berlin 1988–96; Dir Drama Section Salzburg Festival 1997–98; Founder and Pres. Theater der Welt (int. theatre festival), Hamburg 1979, 1989, Cologne 1981, Stuttgart 1987; mem. Akad. der Künste, Berlin, Akad. für Sprache und Dichtung, Darmstadt und Akad. der Darstellenden Künste, Frankfurt; mem. PEN Club; Merck Award 1998, Kortner Award 1998, Moses Mendelssohn Award 2000, Berlin Merit Order 2002. *Publications:* Autonomie und Gnade: Über Mozarts Opern 1985, Gedankengänge als Lebensläufe: Versuche über das 18. Jahrhundert 1987, Kortner Zadek Stein 1989, Johann Heinrich Dannecker: Ariadne auf dem Panther 1993, Vier Regisseure: Bondy, Castorf, Sellars, Wilson 1996, Der Künstler als Kuppler: Goyas Nackte und Bekleidete Maja 1997, Streitschriften 2001. *Leisure interest:* music. *Address:* Keithstr. 10, 10787 Berlin, Germany. *Telephone:* (30) 2114710. *Fax:* (30) 2114710.

NAGEL, Thomas, PhD; American professor of philosophy and law; b. 4 July 1937, Belgrade, Serbia; s. of Walter Nagel and Carolyn Baer Nagel; m. 1st Doris Blum 1968 (divorced 1972); m. 2nd Anne Hollander 1979; ed Cornell, Oxford and Harvard Univs.; Asst Prof. of Philosophy, Univ. of Calif. at Berkeley 1963–66; Asst Prof. of Philosophy, Princeton Univ. 1966–69, Assoc. Prof. 1969–72, Prof. 1972–80; Prof. New York Univ. 1980–, Prof. of Philosophy and Law 1986–; Fellow, American Acad. of Arts and Sciences, British Acad. *Publications:* The Possibility of Altruism 1970, Mortal Questions 1979, The View from Nowhere 1986, What Does It All Mean? 1987, Equality and Partiality 1991, Other Minds 1995, The Last Word 1997. *Address:* New York University Law School, 40 Washington Square South, New York, NY 10012, USA. *Telephone:* (212) 998-6225. *Fax:* (212) 995-4526.

NAGGAR, Zaghloul Raghib el-, PH.D.; professor of geology; ed Univ. of Wales, UK; taught at Ain Shams Univ., Cairo, King Saud Univ., Riyadh, Univ. Coll. of Wales, Aberystwyth, Kuwait Univ., Univ. of Qatar, Doha; fmr Prof. of Geology, King Fahd Univ. of Petroleum and Minerals, Dhahran; now at Arab Devt Inst.; mem. Geological Soc., London, Geological Soc. of Egypt, American Soc. of Petroleum Geologists, Tulsa; Fellow, Inst. of Petroleum, London, Islamic Acad. of Sciences, mem. Council 1994; Secondary Educ. Award (Egypt), Best Papers Award (Arab Petroleum Congress) 1970. *Address:* Islamic Academy of Sciences, P.O. Box 830036, Amman, Jordan (Office). *Telephone:* 5522104 (Office). *Fax:* 5511803 (Office).

NAHNAH, Sheikh Mahfoud; Algerian politician; b. 1939; took part in war of independence against France; f. Harakat el-Mouwahidine (The Unifiers) underground movt 1970; sentenced to 15 years' imprisonment for terrorist activities, released 1981; mem. Islamic Algerian Hamas party (renamed Movt for a Peaceful Soc. 1997), now Leader; cand. in presidential election Dec. 1995. *Address:* Mouvement de la société pour la paix, 163 Hassiba Ben Bouali, Algiers, Algeria (Office). *E-mail:* bureau@hms-algeria.net (Office). *Website:* www.hms-algeria.net (Office).

NAHORNY, Włodzimierz; Polish pianist and composer; b. 5 Nov. 1941, Radzyń Podlaski; m. Anna Woźniakowska; has performed in numerous concerts in Europe 1964–, including Int. Jazz Workshop, Hamburg 1965–69, Jazz Festival, Edin. 2000, Shanghai Music Festival 2001; winner 1st Prize Jazz nad Odrą, Int. Jazz Festival, Vienna 1967, Polish Song Festival, Opole 1972, 1973; Musician of the Year, Jazz Forum magazine 1967, Meritorious Activist of Culture 1974, 1986, Grand Prix Jazz Melomani, Łódź 1997, Fryderyk Polish Music Award 2000. *Compositions:* soundtracks: Rondo, Pełnia; for theatre: Medea, Księżniczka Turandot; songs: Her Portrait, Chianti; *Recordings include:* Nahorny–Chopin Polish Fantasy, Nahorny–Szymanowski Myths, Nahorny–Karłowicz Concerto Dolce Far Niente. *Leisure interests:* books, garden, theatre. *Address:* ul. Nałęczowska 62/14, 02-922 Warsaw, Poland (Office). *Telephone:* (22) 642-76-81 (Office). *Fax:* (22) 642-76-81 (Office).

NAHYAN, Sheikh Sultan bin Zayed an-; Abu Dhabi government official and soldier; b. 1955; ed in Abu Dhabi, Lebanon, UK, Sandhurst Univ. Coll.; Commdr Western Mil. Dist 1976; Gen. Commdr UAE Armed Forces 1978; now Deputy Commdr Abu Dhabi Defence Forces; Deputy Prime Minister 1991. *Address:* P.O. Box 831, Abu Dhabi, United Arab Emirates. *Telephone:* (2) 651881.

NAHYAN, Sheikh Zayed bin Sultan an-, Ruler of Emirate of Abu Dhabi; b. 1926; m.; appointed by his brother Sheikh Shakhbut bin Sultan (Ruler of Abu Dhabi 1928–66) as his personal rep. at inland oasis of Al Ain 1946; paid first official visit to Europe and UK with his brother 1953; Ruler of Abu Dhabi 1966–; Pres. Fed. of UAE 1971–; played leading role in establishment of Gulf Cooperation Council. *Leisure interests:* hunting, falconry. *Address:* Presidential Palace, Abu Dhabi, United Arab Emirates.

NAIDOO, Beverley, PhD; South African/British writer and educationalist; b. 21 May 1943, Johannesburg, South Africa; d. of Ralph Henry Trewhela and Evelyn Levison; m. Nandhagopaul Naidoo 1969; one s. one d.; ed Univs of Witwatersrand, York and Southampton; NGO worker, SA 1964; detained without trial, SA 1964; teacher, London then Dorset, UK 1969–89; educ. adviser on English and cultural diversity, Dorset 1990–97; writer 1985–; held int. writers' workshops 1991–; Hon. Visiting Fellow School of Educ., Univ. of Southampton 1992–; Hon. DLitt (Southampton) 2002; Hon. DUniv (Open Univ.) 2003; The Other Award, UK 1985, Child Study Children's Book Award, USA 1986, 1998, Vlag en Wimpel Award, Netherlands 1991, African Studies Asscn Children's Book Award, USA 1998, Arts Council Writer's Award, UK 1999, Smarties Silver Medal for Children's Books, UK 2000, Carnegie Medal for Children's Literature, UK 2000, Jane Addams Book Award, USA 2002. *Radio:* The Other Side of Truth (BBC) 2003. *Publications:* Censoring Reality: An Examination of Non-fiction Books on South Africa 1985, Journey to Jo'burg 1985, Chain of Fire 1989, Through Whose Eyes? Exploring Racism: Reader, Text and Context 1992, Letang and Julie (series – illustrator Petra Rohr-Rouendall) 1994, No Turning Back 1995, The Other Side of Truth 2000, Out of Bounds 2001, Baba's Gift (with Maya Naidoo, illustrator Karin Littlewood) 2003. *Leisure interests:* reading, theatre, walking. *Address:* c/o Hilary Delamere, The Agency, 24 Pottery Lane, London, W11 4LZ, England (Office). *Telephone:* (20) 7727-1346 (Office). *Fax:* (20) 7727-9037 (Office). *E-mail:* info@theagency.co.uk (Office). *Website:* www .beverleynaidoo.com (Office).

NAIDOO, Jay; South African trade union official; b. 20 Dec. 1954, Durban; m. L. Page 1992; two s. one d.; ed Sastri Coll., Durban and Univ. of Durban-Westville; mem. SASO 1977; involved in community orgs., Natal 1976–79; Organizer Fed. of South African Trade Unions (FOSATU) 1980; Gen. Sec. Sweet Food & Allied Workers Union 1982, Congress of South African Trade Unions (COSATU) 1985–93; Minister, Office of the Pres., Govt of Nat. Unity 1994–96; Minister of Posts and Telecommunications and Broadcasting 1996–99. *Leisure interests:* jazz, skiing cross-country, kids, cycling. *Address:* c/o Private Bag X860, Pretoria 0001, South Africa.

NAIDU, K. Muppavarapu Venkaiah, BA, BL; Indian politician; b. 1 July 1949, Chavatapalem, Nellore Dist, Andhra Pradesh; s. of the late Rangaiah Naidu and Ramanamma Naidu; m. M. Usha; one s. one d.; fmr agriculturalist; political activist, imprisoned during Nat. Emergency 1975–77; Pres. Youth Wing of Janata Party, Andhra Pradesh (AP) 1977–80, State Univ. of Bharatiya Janata Party (BJP—Indian People's Party) 1988–93, Student Union, Andhra Univ. 1973–74; Vice-Pres. Youth Wing of All-India BJP 1980–83, Leader of BJP Legis. Party, AP 1980–85, Gen. Sec. All-India BJP 1993–2002, Pres. BJP 2002–; mem. Legis. Ass., AP 1978–83, 1983–85; elected to Rakya Sabha 1998; Minister of Rural Devt 2000–02. *Address:* Bharatiya Janata Party (BJP), 11 Ashok Road, New Delhi 110 001, India (Office). *Telephone:* (11) 3382234 (Office). *Fax:* (11) 3782163 (Office). *E-mail:* bjpco@del3.vsnl.net.in (Office). *Website:* www.bjp.org (Office).

NAIDU, M. VENKAIAH; Indian politician; b. 1949, Andra Pradesh; Sec.-Gen. Bharatiya Janata Party (BJP) 1993–2001, Party Spokesperson 1999–2001, Pres. 2002–; Minister of Rural Devt 2001–02. *Address:* Bharatiya Janata Party, 11 Ashok Road, New Delhi 110 001, India (Office). *Telephone:* (11) 3382234 (Office). *Fax:* (11) 3382234 (Office). *E-mail:* bjpco@del3.vsnl.net.in (Office). *Website:* www.bjp.org (Office).

NAIPAUL, Sir Vidiadhar Surajprasad, Kt, CLit, BA; Trinidadian-born writer; b. 17 Aug. 1932; m. 1st Patricia Ann Hale 1955 (died 1996); m. 2nd Nadira Khannum Alvi 1996; ed Queen's Royal Coll., Port-of-Spain and Univ. Coll. Oxford; for two years freelance broadcaster with the BBC, producing programmes for the Caribbean area; fiction reviewer on New Statesman 1958–61; grant from Trinidad Govt to travel in Caribbean and S America 1961; in India 1962–63, 1975, 1988–89, in Uganda 1965–66, in USA 1969, 1978–79, 1987–88, in Argentina 1972, 1973–74, 1977, 1991, in Venezuela 1977, 1985, in Iran, Pakistan, Malaysia and Indonesia 1979–80, 1995; Hon. DLitt (Univ. of the W Indies, St Augustine) 1975, (St Andrews) 1979 (Columbia) 1981, (Cambridge) 1983, (London) 1988, (Oxford) 1992; John Llewelyn Rhys Memorial Prize 1958, Somerset Maugham Award 1961, Phoenix Trust Award 1962, Hawthornden Prize 1964, W. H. Smith Award 1968, Booker Prize 1971, Jerusalem Prize 1983, Ingersoll Prize 1986, David Cohen British Literature Prize 1993, Nobel Prize for Literature 2001. *Publications:* The Mystic Masseur 1957, The Suffrage of Elvira 1958, Miguel Street 1959, A House for Mr. Biswas 1961, The Middle Passage 1962, Mr. Stone and the Knights Companion 1963, An Area of Darkness 1964, The Mimic Men 1967, A Flag on the Island 1967 (collection of short stories), The Loss of El Dorado 1969, In a Free State 1971, The Overcrowded Barracoon (essays) 1972, Guerrillas 1975, India: A Wounded Civilization 1977, A Bend in the River 1979, The Return of Eva Perón 1980, Among the Believers 1981, Finding the Center 1984, The Enigma of Arrival 1987, A Turn In The South 1989, India: A Million Mutinies Now 1990, A Way in the World 1994, Beyond Belief 1998, Letters Between a Father and Son 1999, Reading and Writing: a Personal Account 2000, Half a Life 2001. *Address:* c/o Gillon Aitken Associates Ltd, 29 Fernshaw Road, London, SW10 0TG, England.

NAIR, C. V. Devan (see Devan Nair, C. V.).

NAIR, Dileep, B.MECH.ENG., MPA; Singaporean international organization official; ed McGill Univ., Montreal, Canada, Kennedy School of Govt, Harvard Univ., USA; with Housing and Devt Bd 1974–79; joined Admin. Service 1979, various posts including Dir in charge of expenditure control, Deputy Sec. Ministry of Trade and Industry 1986–89, Ministry of Defence 1989–97; CEO Post Office Savings Bank of Singapore 1997–98, Man. Dir Devt Bank of Singapore (DBS) 1998–2000; Under-Sec.-Gen. for Internal Oversight Services, UN 2000–(05); fmr Vice-Pres. Singapore Indian Devt Asscn, mem. Hindu Advisory Bd, mem. Bd of Govs. Raffles Inst.; Colombo Plan Scholar 1969–73. *Address:* UN Office of Internal Oversight Services, United Nations Plaza, New York, NY 10017, USA (Office). *Website:* www.un.org/depts/oios (Office).

NAIR, Mira; Indian film director and producer; b. 1957, Bhubaneswar, Orissa; m. 1st Mitch Epstein; m. 2nd Mahmood Mamdan; one s.; ed Irish Catholic boarding school, Simla, Univ. of Delhi and Harvard Univ., USA; performed with experimental theatre co., Calcutta (now Kolkata); began career as documentary and feature film-maker at Harvard Univ.; Asst Prof. Dept of Arts, Columbia Univ., N.Y. *Films:* India Cabaret (American Film Festival Award for Best Documentary of 1985) 1985, Children of Desired Sex (documentary), Salaam Bombay! (Cannes Film Festival Camera d'Or Award for Best First Feature by a New Dir, Prix du Publique) 1988, Mississippi Masala (three awards at Venice Film Festival) 1991, Buddha, The Perez Family 1996, Kama Sutra 1996, My Own Country 1998, The Laughing Club of India 1999, Monsoon Wedding (Golden Lion Award, Venice Film Festival) 2002, Hysterical Blindness 2002. *Address:* c/o Department of Arts, Columbia University, Morningside Heights, New York, NY 10027, USA (Office). *Website:* www.columbia.edu (Office).

NAIRNE, Rt Hon. Sir Patrick Dalmahoy, PC, GCB, MC, MA; British civil servant and university administrator; b. 15 Aug. 1921, London; s. of the late C. S. Nairne and E. D. Nairne; m. Penelope Chauncy Bridges 1948; three s. three d.; ed Radley Coll., Univ. Coll., Oxford; entered civil service 1947; Pvt. Sec. First Lord of Admiralty 1958–60; Defence Sec. 1965–67; Deputy Sec. Ministry of Defence 1970–73; Second Perm. Sec. Cabinet Office 1973–75; Perm. Sec. Dept of Health and Social Security 1975–81; Master, St Catherine's Coll. Oxford 1981–88; Chancellor of Essex Univ. 1983–97; Dir Gen. ITV 1982–92; Chair., W Midlands Bd 1990–92, Nuffield Council on Bioethics 1991–96; mem. Civil Service Security Appeals Panel 1982, Cttee of Inquiry into the events leading to the Argentine invasion of the Falklands 1982; UK Monitor, Anglo-Chinese Agreement on Hong Kong 1984; Gov. and mem. Council of Man. Ditchley Foundation 1988–; Chair. Comm. on the Conduct of Referendums 1996; Church Commr 1993–98; Trustee Nat. Maritime Museum 1981–91, Joseph Rowntree Foundation 1982–96, Nat. AIDS Trust 1987–96; Pres. Seamen's Hosp. Soc. 1982–2002, Oxfordshire Craft Guild 1993–97; Chair. Advisory Bd, Museum of Modern Art, Oxford 1988–98, Pres. 1998; Chair. Irene Wellington Educational Trust 1986–2002; Hon. LLD (Leicester) 1980, (St Andrews) 1984; Hon. DUniv (Essex) 1983. *Painting exhibitions:* Clarges Gallery, London 1971, 1977, 1983, 1997, 1999; Oliver Swan Gallery, London 1989, 1992. *Leisure interests:* water-colour painting, calligraphy. *Address:* Yew Tree, Chilson, Chipping Norton, Oxon., OX7 3HU, England. *Telephone:* (1608) 676456.

NAISH, Bronwen, ARCM; British solo double bass player; b. 19 Nov. 1939, Burley, Hants.; d. of E. F. E. Naish and G. J. Grant; m. Roger Best 1959 (divorced 1981); two s. three d.; ed Holyhead Grammar School and Royal NorthernColl. of Music; began playing double bass 1966; performance and teaching in northern England and sub-prin. bass, Northern Sinfonia 1967–73; début recital, King's Hall, Newcastle-upon-Tyne 1971; London début, Purcell Room 1974; returned to N Wales to concentrate on solo career 1976; Channel Island tours 1980, 1988; Australian tour 1988; est. Slap & Tickle with pianist Maurice Horhut 1988; Edin. Fringe Festival 1989, 1990; commissioning new works for musical saw (recent acquisition) 1990; examiner, Assoc. Bd of Royal Schools of Music. *Publication:* Another String to my Bow 1982. *Leisure interests:* beekeeping, do-it-yourself. *Address:* Moelfre, Cwm Pennant, Garndolbenmaen, Gwynedd, LL5 9AX, North Wales. *Telephone:* (176) 675356.

NAJDER, Zdzisław Marian; Polish civic leader and author; b. 31 Oct. 1930, Warsaw; s. of Franciszek Najder and Józefa Najder (née Kowalska); m. Halina Paschalska 1965; one s.; ed Warsaw Univ., Oxford Univ.; Asst Inst. for Literary Research of Polish Acad. of Sciences 1952–57; Sr Asst Aesthetics, Warsaw Univ. 1958–59; staff Twórczość (monthly) 1957–81; taught Polish literature at Columbia and Yale Univs. 1966 and Univ. of Calif., Berkeley 1966–67; Prof. of Philosophy 1967–68, Regents' Prof. Univ. of Calif. at Davis 1968–69; Prof. of English Literature Northern Ill. Univ. 1971–72; Visiting Scholar Stanford Univ. 1974–75; adviser to Solidarity Trade Union 1980–90; Visiting Fellow St Antony's Coll., Oxford 1981, 1988; Head Polish section of Radio Free Europe, Munich 1982–87; charged with spying, sentenced to death in absentia by Warsaw Mil. Tribunal in 1983, stripped of Polish citizenship 1985, sentence revoked 1989, case dismissed 1990; mem. editorial staff Kontakt, Paris 1988–91; Chair. Nat. Civic Cttee 1990–92; Chief Adviser to the Prime Minister 1992; Pres. Civic Inst. 1991–97, Atlantic Club 1991–93; Chair. Joseph Conrad Soc. (Poland) 1994–; Prof. of English Literature, Univ. of Opole 1997–; Adviser to Chair. Cttee for European Integration 1998–2001; mem. Polish Writers' Union 1956–83, PEN Club 1957–; f. Polish Agreement for Independence 1976; Juliusz Mieroszewski Award 1982, Prize of Modern Language Asscn 1984, Polish PEN Club Prize 1988; Commdr's Cross, Order of Polonia Restituta 1983; Commdr Ordre Nat. du Mérite (France) 1991. *Publications:* studies and essays including Conrad's Polish Background 1964, Nad Conradem 1965, Values and Evaluations 1975, Życie Conrada-Korzeniowskiego 1981, Ile jest dróg? 1982, Wymiary polskich spraw 1990, Jaka Polska 1993, Z Polski do Polski poprzez PRL 1995, Conrad in Perspective: Essays on Art and Fidelity 1997, W sercu Europy 1998. *Leisure interests:* travel, walks in forest, 12th-century Romanesque art. *Address:* ul. Tyniecka 31 m. 7, 02-621 Warsaw, Poland. *Telephone:* (22) 8448536. *Fax:* (22) 8448536. *E-mail:* zdzislaw.najder@uni.opole.pl (Home).

NAJJAR, Mgr Raouf, PhD; Jordanian ecclesiastic; b. 1932, Haifa, Israel; ed Latin Seminary, Beit-Jala, nr Jerusalem, Lateran Univ., Rome; ordained Priest, Nazareth 1955; Pres. Church Court (Officialis) 1963–88; Canon of the Holy Sepulchre 1971; Mgr 1971; acting for Apostolic Del. in Jordan 1988–, for the Apostolic Nunciature 1994–; Pres. Bethlehem Univ. 1988–; Chair. and Gen. Dir Jordanian Acad. of Music; owner and Ed.-in-Chief Voice of the Holy Land 1968–; Chair. and Gen. Dir Al Wasifiyyah Vocational Centre 1968–; mem. Bd Int. Fed. of Catholic Univs., Paris; Distinguished Leadership Award in Church Law, American Biographical Inst.; Prelate ad honorem 1991; Commdr Italian Repub., Order of Jordan Independence (2nd Degree), Commdr Ordre Int. de la Paix, Grand Chevalier, Order of St John of Jerusalem. *Address:* Bethlehem University, P.O. Box 9, Bethlehem, West Bank, via Israel (Office); Apostolic Nunciature, P.O. Box 5634, Amman 11183, Jordan. *Telephone:* (2) 741241 (Office); (6) 694095. *Fax:* (6) 692502.

NAKAE, Toshitada; Japanese journalist; b. 4 Oct. 1929, Chiba City; m. Yohko Nakae 1959; three s.; ed Tokyo Univ.; local reporter Asahi Shimbun 1953–58, econ. reporter 1972–76, Econ. Ed. 1972–76, Asst Man. Ed. 1976–78, Man. Ed. 1978–83, Dir 1982–97, Pres. 1989–96, Special Adviser 1996–; Pres. Japan Newspaper Publrs' and Eds' Asscn 1991–95; Commdr des Arts et des

Lettres 1994. *Publications:* (in English trans.) Cities 1966, The Pulitzer Prize Story 1970, The News Media 1971, The Economy of Cities 1971. *Leisure interests:* driving, listening to music, karaoke. *Address:* 1-11-1-401 Hamadayama, Suginami-ku, Tokyo, Japan. *Telephone:* (3) 3302-7087. *Fax:* (3) 3302-7087 (Home).

NAKAE, Yosuke; Japanese diplomatist; b. 30 Dec. 1922, Osaka; s. of Yasuzo Nakae and Itsu Kawase; m. Yasuko Takakura 1959; one s. one d.; ed Kyoto Univ.; Dir-Gen. of Asian Affairs Bureau, Ministry of Foreign Affairs 1975; Amb. to Yugoslavia 1978, to Egypt 1982, to People's Repub. of China 1984–87; Commr Japan Atomic Energy Comm. 1987–91; Pres.'s Adviser, Mitsubishi Heavy Industries Co. Ltd 1991–99; Grand Cordon of the Order of the Sacred Treasure 1995. *Ballet scenarios performed include:* Creature 1975, Mobile et Immobile 1984, Friendship across the Strait 1987, Magpies' Bridge 1998. *Publications:* ballet scenarios: Creature 1975, Mobile et Immobile–Mirage à l'Abu-Simbel 1983, Magpies' Bridge 1998; books: Future of China 1991, An Unsuitable Ambassador talks 1993. *Leisure interest:* writing scenarios for ballet. *Address:* 3-21-5, Eifuku, Suginami, Tokyo 168-0064, Japan. *Telephone:* (3) 3325-7359. *Fax:* (3) 3325-7359.

NAKAGAWA, Shoichi; Japanese politician; b. Hokkaido; s. of Ichiro Nakagawa; fmr banker; mem. for Hokkaido, House of Reps.; Minister of Agric., Forestry and Fisheries 1998–99; Head Policy Research Council of LDP on Agric. and Forestry. *Address:* c/o Ministry of Agriculture, Forestry and Fisheries, 1-2-1, Kasumigaseki, Chiyoda-ku, Tokyo 100, Japan.

NAKAJIMA, Fumio, DLitt; Japanese professor; b. 11 Nov. 1904, Tokyo; m. Chizu Takaba 1935; ed First Prefectural School, First Nat. Coll. and Univ. of Tokyo; Asst Prof., Univ. of Keijo, Seoul 1928, Assoc. Prof. 1933, Prof. of English Philology 1939; Prof. of English Philology, Univ. of Tokyo 1947–65, Prof. Emer. 1965–; Prof. Tsuda-juku Coll. 1965–73, Pres. 1973–80; Pres. English Literary Soc. of Japan 1952–64, Shakespeare Soc. of Japan 1964–75; mem. Japan Acad. 1974–; Order of the Sacred Treasure (2nd Class) 1975. *Publications:* Imiron 1939, Eigo-no-Joshiki 1944, Bunpo-no-Genri 1949, Eibunpo-no-taikei 1961, Eigo-no-Kozo 1980, Nihongo-no-Kozo 1985. *Address:* 2-24-10, Nishi-koigakubo, Kokubunji, Tokyo 185, Japan. *Telephone:* (423) 24-5580.

NAKAMURA, Hajime, DLitt; Japanese professor of philosophy; b. 28 Nov. 1912, Matsue City; s. of Kiyoji Nakamura and Tomo Nakamura; m. Rakuko Nakamura 1944; two d.; ed Univ. of Tokyo; Prof. of Indian and Buddhist Philosophy, Univ. of Tokyo 1943–73; Founder and Dir Eastern Inst. Inc. 1973–; mem. Japan Acad. of Sciences 1984–; corresp. mem. Acad. of Sciences, Göttingen, Austrian Acad. of Sciences; Hon. Fellow Royal Asiatic Soc. of Great Britain; Imperial Prize (Japan Acad. of Sciences); Order of Merit. *Publications:* A Comparative History of Ideas 1986, Ways of Thinking of Eastern Peoples, A History of Early Vedànta Philosophy. *Address:* Kugayama 4-37-15, Suginami-ku, Tokyo, Japan.

NAKAMURA, Hisao; Japanese business executive; b. 11 Nov. 1923, Kyoto Pref.; s. of Kinjiro Nakamura and Masao Nakamura; m. Fusako Nagai 1955; one s. one d.; ed Kyoto Univ.; joined Kuraray Co. Ltd 1950, Dir 1972, Man. Dir 1976, Exec. Vice-Pres. 1981, Pres. 1985–93, Chair. 1993–; Chair. Kurray Trading Co. Ltd 1984–; Pres. Kyowa Gas Chemical Industries Co. Ltd 1985–. *Leisure interests:* golf, car-driving, reading. *Address:* 1-12-39 Umeda, Kita-ku, Osaka 530; 52 Nigawa-dai, Takarazuka, Hyogo 665, Japan.

NAKAMURA, Kuniwo; Palauan politician; Vice-Pres. of Palau 1989–92; Pres. of Palau 1993–2001; Leader Ta Belau party. *Address:* Ta Belau, c/o Olbiil era Kelulau, Koror, PW 96940, Palau (Office).

NAKAMURA, Shozaburo; Japanese politician; fmr businessman; mem. LDP; mem. for Minami Kanto bloc. House of Reps.; fmr Dir-Gen. Environment Agency, Parl. Vice-Minister of Finance (three times); Minister of Justice 1998–99. *Leisure interests:* skiing, scuba diving. *Address:* c/o Ministry of Justice, 1-1-1, Kasumigaseki, Chiyoda-ku, Tokyo 100, Japan.

NAKASONE, Hirofumi; Japanese politician; mem. House of Councillors; fmr Deputy Dir (LDP) Commerce and Industry Div.; fmr Chair. LDP Policy Bd, House of Councillors; Minister of Educ. and Dir-Gen. Science and Tech. Agency 1999–2000. *Address:* c/o Ministry of Education, Science, Sport and Culture, 3-2-2, Kasumigaseki, Chiyoda-ku, Tokyo 100-0013, Japan (Office).

NAKASONE, Yasuhiro; Japanese politician; b. 27 May 1917, Takasaki, Gumma Prov.; s. of Matsugoroh and Yuku Nakasone; m. Tsutako Kobayashi 1945; one s. two d.; ed Tokyo Imperial Univ.; mem. House of Reps.; fmr Minister of State, Dir-Gen. of Science & Tech. Agency; Chair. Nat. Org. Liberal-Democratic Party (LDP), Jt Cttee on Atomic Energy, Special Cttee on Scientific Tech., Chair. LDP Exec. Council 1971–72, Sec.-Gen. LDP 1974–76, Chair. 1977–80; Minister of Transport 1967–68; Minister of State and Dir-Gen. Defence Agency 1970–71; Minister of Int. Trade and Industry 1972–74; Minister of State and Dir-Gen. of Admin. Man. Agency 1980–82; Prime Minister of Japan 1982–87; Chair. and Pres. Inst. for Global Peace 1988–89, Inst. for Int. Policy Studies 1988–; after involvement in Recruit affair resigned from LDP, rejoined April 1991. *Publications:* Ideal of Youth, Frontier in Japan, The New Conservatism, Human Cities–a proposal for the 21st Century 1980, Tenchiyujou (autobiog.) 1996. *Leisure interests:* golf, swimming, painting. *Address:* 3-22-7, Kamikitazawa, Setagaya-ku, Tokyo, Japan (Home). *Telephone:* (3) 3304-7000 (Home).

NAKAYAMA, Masaaki; Japanese politician; mem. House of Reps.; fmr Dir.-Gen. Man. and Co-ordination Agency; fmr Posts and Telecommunications Minister; Chair. House of Reps. Cttee on Budget; Minister for Construction and Dir.-Gen. Nat. Land Agency 1999–2000. *Address:* c/o Ministry of Construction, 2-1-3, Kasumigaseki, Chiyoda-ku, Tokyo 100-0013, Japan (Office).

NAKAYAMA, Taro, MD, PhD; Japanese politician; b. 27 Aug. 1924, Osaka; ed Osaka Medical Coll.; mem. Osaka Pref. Ass. 1955–68; mem. House of Councillors 1968-86, Parl. Vice-Pres. Labor Party 1971; Chair. Cttee on Cabinet 1976, Chair. Cttee on Rules and Admin. 1979; Dir-Gen. Prime Minister's Office 1980; Chief Okinawa Devt Agency 1980; Chair. Parl. Affairs Cttee of Liberal-Democratic Party (LDP) 1982, LDP Financial Cttee 1988, LDP Political Reform HQ 1998, LDP Research Comm. on Foreign Affairs 1999; mem. Gen. Council of LDP 1998–; mem. House of Reps. 1986–; Minister of Foreign Affairs 1989–91; Chair. Research Comm. on Constitution of House of Reps. 2000–; Chair. Asian Population and Devt Asscn and numerous int. parliamentarians' friendship leagues; Grand Cordon, First Order of Rising Sun, 1997. *Publications:* five books including Scientific Strategy for the Post-Oil Age 1979. *Address:* 1-7-1 Nagata-Cho, Chiyoda-ku, Tokyo, Japan.

NAŁĘCZ, Maciej, Prof.Tech.; Polish scientist; b. 27 April 1922, Warsaw; s. of Aleksander Nałęcz and Stefania Nałęcz; m. Zofia Bozowska 1952; one s.; ed Warsaw Tech. Univ.; scholarship to Case Inst. of Tech., Cleveland, USA 1961–62; Assoc. Prof. 1962–72, Prof. 1972–; Corresp. mem. Polish Acad. of Sciences (PAN) 1967–73, Ordinary mem. 1974–, Presidium mem. and Sec. Tech. Sciences Section 1972–80, Deputy Gen. Sec. PAN 1981–83, Deputy to Sejm (Parl.) 1985–89, mem. Presidium 1972–89; Dir Inst. of Automatic Control 1962–72; Chair. Biomedical Eng Cttee of Section IV 1972–; Dir Inst. of Biocybernetics and Biomedical Eng 1975–93; Dir Int. Centre of Biocybernetics 1988–; Chair. Nat. Cttee for Pugwash Confs. 1972–, elected Chair. Pugwash Council 1974, 1977, 1982, 1987, 1992–97; Visiting Prof. Polytechnic Inst. of Brooklyn 1967–68, Univ. of Hanover, W Germany 1990; Distinguished Visiting Prof. Ohio State Univ. 1979–80, Campinas Univ., Brazil 1985, Cleveland Clinic Foundation 1985, Waseda Univ., Japan 1988; Scholar in Residence, Int. Fogarty Foundation, NIH, USA 1991–92; mem. Int. Measurement Confed. (IMEKO), Cttee on Data for Science and Tech. (CODATA) of ICSU, Exec. Cttee Int. Fed. of Automatic Control 1972–, Int. Soc. of Artificial Organs, Admin. Bd Int. Fed. for Medical and Biological Eng 1988–94, Gen. Bd European Soc. of Engineers and Physicians (Co-founder) 1991–, Int. Acad. for Medical and Biological Eng 1997–; Co-founder and Vice-Pres. European Soc. for Eng and Medicine (ESEM) 1995–98; Foreign mem. USSR (now Russian) Acad. of Sciences 1976–, Georgian Acad. of Sciences 1996–; Hon. mem. World Org. of Gen. Systems and Cybernetics 1979, Soc. for Theoretical and Applied Electrotechnics 1980, Polish Soc. for Medical Eng 1995; State Prize, 2nd Class 1972, Nobel Peace Prize (for Pugwash) 1995; Award med tack för värdefull insats (Sweden) 1957, Kt's, Officer's, Commdr's with Star Cross (and Great Cross 2002), Order Polonia Restituta, Order Banner of Labour, 2nd Class 1972, 1st Class 1978, Copernicus Medal, Polish Acad. of Science, Krizik Medal, Czechoslovakian Acad. of Science 1988, Int. Fogarty Center Medal, USA 1991. *Publications:* The Technology of Hall Generators and Their Use in Measurement and Conversion 1972, Trends in Control Components 1974, Control Aspects of Biomedical Engineering (ed. and contrib.) 1987, Computers in Medicine (ed. and contrib.) 1987, Problems of Biocybernetics and Biomedical Engineering (ed. and contrib.) Vols I–VI 1990–91, State of Art and Development of BME in Poland (monograph, ed. and co-author) 1994, Biocybernetics and Biomedical Engineering 2000 (9 vols, monograph, ed. and co-author) 2003. *Leisure interest:* summer house. *Address:* International Centre of Biocybernetics, Polish Academy of Sciences, ul. Trojdena 4, 02-109 Warsaw, Poland. *Telephone:* (22) 658-28-77 (Office). *Fax:* (22) 658-28-72 (Office). *E-mail:* maciej.nalecz@ibib.waw.pl (Office).

NALLET, Henri Pierre; French politician; b. 6 Jan. 1939, Bergerac (Dordogne); s. of Jean Nallet and France Lafon; m. Thérèse Leconte 1963; one s.; ed Inst. d'Etudes Politiques, Bordeaux; Sec.-Gen. Jeunesse Étudiante Catholique 1963–64; Inst. de Formation des Cadres Paysans 1965–66; Féd. Nat. des Syndicats d'Exploitants Agricoles (FNSEA) 1966–70; Dir of Research, Dept of Econ. and Rural Sociology, Inst. Nat. de Recherche Agronomique (INRA) 1970–81; agricultural adviser, Sec. Gen. of Presidency of Republic 1981–85; Minister of Agric. 1985–86; Socialist Deputy to Nat. Ass. 1986–88; Minister of Agric. and Forestry 1988–90, Garde des Sceaux, Minister of Justice 1990–92; Conseiller-Gen. of Yonne 1988–2001; Mayor of Tonnerre 1989–2000; Conseiller d'état 1992–; Deputy for Yonne 1997–99; Pres. Del. of Nat. Ass. to EU; mem. Parl. Ass. of Council of Europe and of WEU; Consultant IBRD 1992–, EU 1992–; Vice-Chair. European Socialist Party 1997; Nat. Sec. for Int. Affairs of Socialist Party 1999–; Pres. World Council of Nutrition 1985–87; Officier Légion d'honneur 2001. *Publications:* Tempête sur la justice 1992, Les Réseaux multidisciplinaires. La Documentation française 1999. *Address:* 12 rue Rougemont, 89700 Tonnerre; Parti Socialiste, 10 rue de Solférino, 75333 Paris Cedex 07, France.

NAM DUCK-WOO, PhD; South Korean politician, economist and government official; b. 10 Oct. 1924; s. of Nam Sang-Bom and Cha Soon Noy; m. Hye Sook Choi 1953; two s. one d.; ed Kook Min. Coll., Seoul, Seoul Nat. Univ. Oklahoma State and Stanford Univs.; with Bank of Korea 1952–54; Asst Prof., Assoc. Prof., Prof., Dean of Econ. Dept, Kook Min Coll. 1954–64; Prof. Sogang Univ. and Dir Research Inst. for Econ. and Business 1964–69; Minister of Finance 1969; Gov. for Korea, IMF, IBRD, ADB 1969–72, Chair. Bd of Govs. Asian Devt Bank 1970; Deputy Prime Minister and Minister of Econ. Planning Bd

1974–78; Special Asst for Econ. Affairs to the Pres. Jan.–Dec. 1979; Prime Minister of Repub. of Korea 1980–82; mem. Advisory Cttee on Evaluation of Econ. Devt Plan, Nat. Mobilization Bd 1964–69; Adviser to Korea Devt Bank 1964–69; Assoc. mem. Econ. and Scientific Council 1967–69. *Publications:* History of Economic Theory 1958, Price Theory 1965, History of Economic Theory (co-author) 1962, The Determinants of Money Supply and Monetary Policy: in the case of Korea 1954–64 1966, Social Science Research and Population Policy (jt author) 1980, Changes in the Pattern of Trade and Trade Policy in a Pacific Basin Community 1980. *Leisure interests:* reading, music appreciation.

NAMALIU, Rt Hon Sir Rabbie Langanai, KCMG, PC, MA; Papua New Guinea politician; b. 3 April 1947, Raluana, E New Britain Prov.; s. of Darius Namaliu and Utul Ioan Namaliu; m. 1st Margaret Nakikus 1978 (died 1993); two s. one step-d.; m. 2nd Kelina Tavul 1999; one s.; ed Keravat High School, Univ. of Papua New Guinea, Univ. of Victoria, BC; fmrly scholar and Fellow Univ. of Papua New Guinea; tutor and Lecturer in History, Univ. of Papua New Guinea; Prin. Pvt. Sec. to Chief Minister 1974; fmr Prov. Commr, E New Britain and Chair. Public Services Comm.; held sr positions in the Office of the Prime Minister and Leader of the Opposition under Mr Somare; MP for Kokopo Open 1982–; Minister for Foreign Affairs and Trade 1982–84, for Primary Industry 1984–85; Deputy Leader Pangu Pati 1985–88, Leader 1988–92; Prime Minister 1988–92; Speaker Nat. Parl. 1994–97; Sr Minister for State 1997–98, for Petroleum and Energy 1998–99; Pres. African Caribbean Pacific Council of Ministers 1984; Co-Pres. ACP/EEC Jt Council of Ministers 1984; Vacation Scholar ANU 1968; Visiting Fellow Univ. of Calif., Center for Pacific Studies, Santa Cruz, Calif., USA 1976; Hon. LLD, MA (Victoria, BC) 1983; Independence Medal 1975, Queen's Silver Jubilee Medal 1977; Pacific Man of the Year 1988. *Leisure interests:* reading, fishing, walking, golf. *Address:* National Parliament, PO National Parliament, Waigani, National Capital District; PO Box 6655, Boroko, National Capital District, Papua New Guinea. *Telephone:* 3277752/54/55. *Fax:* 3277753.

NAMANGONIY, Juma; Uzbekistan guerrilla leader; b. 1969, Ferghana Valley; conscripted into Soviet army 1987, active service in Afghanistan; f. radical Islamic anti-Govt Movt 1991; in exile, fought with United Tajik Opposition in Tajik civil war 1992–97; Leader and Field Commdr Islamic Movt of Uzbekistan (also known as Islamic Party of Turkestan from 2001), in armed opposition to Uzbek and Kyrgyz forces 1999–. *Address:* c/o Islamic Movement of Uzbekistan, Muslim Board of Central Asia, Tashkent, Zarrkainar 103, Uzbekistan (Office).

NAMIR, Ora; Israeli politician; b. 1930; ed Levinsky and Givat Hashlosha teacher seminaries, Hunter Coll., NY; officer Israel Defence Forces, War of Independence; Sec. Mapai Knesset faction; Sec. Coalition Exec.; Sec.-Gen. Na'amat (Working Women and Volunteers Org.) 1967; Chair. Prime Minister's Cttee on the Status of Women 1975, Educ. and Culture Cttee 1977–84, Labour and Social Welfare Cttee 1984–92; Minister of the Environment 1992–94; fmr Minister of Labour; mem. Knesset (Parl.) 1973–. *Address:* c/o Knesset, Jerusalem, Israel.

NAMPHY, Lt.-Gen. Henri; Haitian politician and soldier; fmr Chief of Haitian Gen. Staff; Head of State and Pres. Nat. Governing Council (formed after overthrow of Jean-Claude Duvalier, q.v., in coup) 1986–88; Vice-Chair. Legis. 1987–88; now living in exile in Dominica.

NAMYSŁOWSKI, Zbigniew; Polish jazz musician and composer; b. 9 Sept. 1939, Warsaw; m. Maria Małgorzata Ostaszewska; two d. one s.; ed in Warsaw; trombone player, leader of Modern Dixielanders 1957–60, sideman with Zygmunt Wichary Group 1960, New Orleans Stompers 1960–61, alto sax player and leader of Jazz Rockers 1961–62, Air Condition 1980–82, Zbigniew Namysłowski Quartet and Quintet 1973–; Air Condition 1980–83; Kalatówki Big Band 2001–03, sideman in the Wreckers 1962–63, Krzysztof Komeda Quintet 1965; mem. Polish Composer Asscn 1972–; participant in festivals include Students' Group Festival, Wrocław (Award for the Best Soloist – trombone) 1957, Int. Jazz Festival, Prague (Award for the Best Soloist) 1964, Lugano 1961, Tauranga (New Zealand) 1969, 1978, Bombay (now Mumbai) 1969, 1978, Paris 1974, Ivrea (Italy) 1979, Montréal 1984, Copenhagen 1989, Århus 1989, several times Jazz Jamboree, Warsaw and Molde, Kongsberg, Bergen (Norway), Zürich, Christianstadt, Stockholm, North Sea-Haag, Pori Jazz Festival (Finland), Red Sea (Israel) 1991, Int. Festival Wien, Kuwait 2002 and others; has toured in countries including Denmark, USA, Italy, New Zealand, Australia, India, Netherlands, Greece, Canada, Mexico, Sweden, Norway, Switzerland; State Prize (First Class) 1984, Fryderyk (Polish music award for Best Polish Jazz Record of the Year–Zbigniew Namysłowski Quartet and Zakopane Highlanders Band) 1995, Jazz Forum Award 1997, 1998, Gold Cross of Merit 1974, Meritorious Activist of Culture Award 1982. *Compositions include:* Der Schmalz Tango 1976, Convenient Circumstances 1980, Speed Limit 1981, Kuyawiak Goes Funky 1984, After Perturbation 1985, Quiet Afternoon 1985, Double-Trouble Blues 1985, Cuban Tango Mojito 1986, Seven-Eleven 1987, Western Ballade 1992, Oriental Food 1994, Mazurka Uborka 1996; *Recordings include:* Polish Jazz–Zbigniew Namysłowski Quartet, Kuyawiak Goes Funky, Zbigniew Namysłowski with Symphony Orchestra, Song of the Pterodactil, Jasmine Lady, Song of Innocence, Double Trouble, Open, Without Talk; adaptations of compositions by Mozart, Gershwin and Chopin for string quartet, clarinet and jazz band. *Leisure interests:* travelling, tennis, skiing, bicycling. *E-mail:* quartet@poczta .onet.pl (Office).

NAN ZHENZHONG; Chinese journalist and politician; b. May 1942, Lingbao, He'nan Prov.; ed Zhengzhou Univ.; joined CCP 1978; fmrly Vice-Chief, then Chief Shandong Br., Xinhua News Agency; Assoc. Ed. then Ed., Vice-Dir 1993–2000, Chief Ed. 2000–. *Publications:* The Eyes of a Correspondent, The Reflections of a Correspondent. *Address:* Xinhua (New China) News Agency, 57 Xuanwumen Xidajie, Beijing 100803, People's Republic of China. *Telephone:* (10) 63071114. *Fax:* (10) 63071210. *Website:* www .xinhuanet.com (Office).

NANDAN, Satya Nand, CBE; Fijian diplomatist and lawyer; b. 10 July 1936, Suva; s. of Shiu Nandan and Rajkuar Nandan; m. 1st Sreekumari Nandan 1966 (died 1971); m. 2nd Zarine Merchant 1976; one s.; ed John McGlashan Coll. Dunedin, NZ, DAV Coll. Suva and Univs of Wellington and London; called to Bar, Lincoln's Inn, London 1965; barrister and solicitor, Supreme Court of Fiji 1966–; pvt. law practice, Suva 1965–70; Counsellor then Amb. Perm. Mission of Fiji to UN 1970–76; Leader, Fiji Del. to Third UN Conf. on Law of Sea 1973–82; Amb. to EEC (also accred to Belgium, France, Italy, Luxembourg, Netherlands) 1976–80; Perm. Sec. for Foreign Affairs, Fiji 1981–83; UN Under-Sec.-Gen. for Ocean Affairs and the Law of the Sea and Special Rep. of UN Sec.-Gen. for Law of the Sea 1983–92; mem. Perm. Mission of Fiji to UN 1993–2001; Chair. UN Conf. on Straddling Fish Stocks and Highly Migratory Fish Stocks 1993–95; Rep. of Fiji to Int. Seabed Authority 1994–95, Pres. 1996–; Int. Law Adviser to Govt of Fiji 1994–95; del. to numerous int. confs etc.; Visiting Lecturer, Columbia Univ. New York and Univ. of Va, Charlottesville; Sr Visiting Fellow, US Inst. of Peace 1992; many other professional appts; Hon. LLD (Newfoundland) 1995; Dr hc (Univ. of the South Pacific) 1996; Grand Cross Order of Merit (FRG) 1996, Companion Order of Fiji 1999. *Publications include:* Commentary on 1982 UN Convention on Law of Sea (7 vols) (ed.); numerous articles on UN and aspects of Law of the Sea. *Leisure interests:* history, int. law, reading, swimming. *Address:* International Seabed Authority, 14–20 Port Royal Street, Kingston, Jamaica (Office); 301 East, 48th Street, New York NY 10017, USA (Home). *Telephone:* (876) 922-9105. *Fax:* (876) 922-0195. *E-mail:* webmaster@isa.org.jm. *Website:* www.isa.org.jm.

NANO, Fatos Thanas; Albanian politician; b. 1952, Tirana; fmr Sec.-Gen. of Council of Ministers, Deputy Chair. Jan.–Feb. 1991, Chair. 1991–92; Chair. Socialist Party of Albania 1991–; stripped of immunity from prosecution to face charges of embezzlement July 1993; convicted of misappropriation of state funds, of dereliction of duty and of falsifying state documents April 1994; sentenced to 12 years' imprisonment; released and pardoned March 1997; Prime Minister of Albania 1997–98, 2002–. *Address:* Socialist Party of Albania (Partia Socialiste e Shqipërisë), Tirana; Office of the Prime Minister, Council of Ministers, Këshilli i Ministrave, Tirana, Albania. *Telephone:* (42) 28210 (Office). *Fax:* (42) 27888 (Office).

NAPIER, John; British stage designer; b. 1 March 1944; s. of James Edward Thomas Napier and Lorrie Napier (née Godbold); m. 1st Andreanne Neofitou; one s. one d.; m. 2nd Donna King; one s. one d.; ed Hornsey Coll. of Art, Cen. School of Arts and Crafts; Production designs include: A Penny for a Song, Fortune and Men's Eyes, The Ruling Class, The Fun War, Muzeeka, George Frederick (ballet), La Turista, Cancer, Isabel's a Jezebel, Mister, The Foursome, The Lovers of Viorne, Lear, Jump, Sam Sam, Big Wolf, The Devils (ENO), Equus, The Party, Knuckle, Kings and Clowns, Lohengrin (Covent Garden), Macbeth, Richard III, Hedda Gabler, Twelfth Night, The Greeks, Nicholas Nickleby, Cats, Starlight Express, Time, Les Misérables, Miss Saigon, Sunset Boulevard, Burning Blue, Jesus Christ Superstar, Idomeneo (Glyndebourne), Who's Afraid of Virginia Woolf?, An Enemy of the People, Peter Pan, Martin Guerre, Candide, Jane Eyre, Nabucco (Metropolitan Opera), South Pacific; Designer, co-Dir Siegfried & Roy Show, Las Vegas 1990; film designs include Hook 1991; numerous stage and TV set designs worldwide; Hon. Fellow London Inst. 2001; Royal Designer for Industry, Royal Soc. of Arts 1996; five Tony Awards. *Leisure interest:* photography. *Address:* c/o M.L.R., Douglas House, 16–18 Douglas Street, London, SW1P 4PB, England. *Telephone:* (20) 7834-4646. *Fax:* (20) 7834-4949.

NAPIER, John Alan, MA(Econs); British business executive; b. 22 Aug. 1942; s. of the late William Napier and Barbara Napier (née Chatten); m. 1st Gillian Reed 1961; two s. one d.; m. 2nd Caroline Denning 1992; one d. two step-s. one step-d.; ed Colchester Royal Grammar School and Emmanuel Coll., Cambridge; jr and middle man. positions, Int. Publishing Corp. and Reed Int. 1960–69; Man. Dir Index Printers 1969–72; Man. Dir QB Newspapers 1972–76; Exec. Dir (Australia) James Hardie Industries 1976–86; Group Man. Dir AGB PLC 1986–90; Group Man. Dir Hays PLC 1991–98; Chair. Booker PLC 1998–2000; Exec. Chair. Kelda Group PLC 2000–02, Chair. (nonexec.) Sept. 2002–; Chair. Yorkshire and Humber Rural Affairs Forum; Chair. Royal & Sun Alliance Insurance Group Jan. 2003–. *Leisure interests:* rural matters, outdoor activities, people, philosophy. *Address:* Royal & Sun Alliance, Worldwide Group Office, 30 Berkeley Square, London, W1J 6EW, England (Office). *Telephone:* (20) 7636-3450 (Office). *Fax:* (20) 7636-3451 (Office). *Website:* www.royalsunalliance.com (Office).

NAPIER, HE Cardinal Wilfrid Fox, B.PH., B.TH., MA; South African ecclesiastic; b. 8 March 1941, Matatiele; s. of Thomas D. Napier and Mary Davey; ed Little Flower School, Ixopo, Natal, Univ. of Ireland, Galway and Catholic Univ., Louvain, Belgium; ordained priest 1970; Asst Pastor, St Anthony's Parish, Lusikisiki 1971; Parish Priest, St Francis Parish, Tabankulu 1973; Apostolic Administrator, Diocese of Kokstad 1978; Bishop of Kokstad 1981;

Archbishop of Durban 1992–; Vice-Pres. S African Catholic Bishops' Conf. 1984, Pres. 1987–92, First Vice-Pres. 1994–; cr. Cardinal 2001. *Leisure interests:* gardening, tennis, golf, DIY mechanics, fishing. *Address:* Archbishop's House, 154 Gordon Road, Durban 4001; PO Box 47489, Greyville 4023, South Africa. *Telephone:* (31) 3031417. *Fax:* (31) 231848. *E-mail:* chancery@durban-archdiocese.co.za (Office).

NAPOLI, Jacopo; Italian composer; b. 26 Aug. 1911; ed S. Pietro a Majella Conservatoire of Music, Naples; obtained diplomas in Composition, Organ and Piano; Chair. of Counterpoint and Fugue at Cagliari Conservatoire and at Naples Conservatoire; Dir S. Pietro a Majella Conservatoire of Music, Naples 1955, 1962; Dir Giuseppe Verdi Conservatoire of Music, Milan –1972, then Dir St Cecilia Conservatory, Rome; Dir Scarlatti Arts Soc. 1955–; works performed in Germany, Spain and on Italian radio. *Works:* (operas) Il Malato Immaginario 1939, Miseria e Nobiltà 1946, Un curioso accidente 1950, Masaniello 1953, I Pescatori 1954, Il Tesoro 1958, (oratorio) The Passion of Christ, Il Rosario 1962, Il Povero Diavolo 1963, Piccola Cantata del Venerdì Santo 1964, (orchestral works) Overture to Love's Labours Lost 1935, Preludio di Caccia 1935, La Festa di Anacapri 1940. *Address:* 55 Via Andrea da Isernia, 80122 Naples, Italy.

NAPOLITANO, Janet Ann, BS, JD; American state official and lawyer; b. 29 Nov. 1957, New York City; d. of Leonard Michael Napolitano and Jane Marie Napolitano (née Winer); ed Univ. of Santa Clara, Univ. of Va; assoc. Lewis & Roca, Phoenix 1984–89, partner 1989–93, attorney 1997–98; U.S. Attorney, Phoenix, Ariz. 1993–97; Attorney-Gen. of Ariz. 1999–2002; Gov. of Ariz. 2003–; mem. Ariz. Bar Asscn, Maricopa Co. Bar Asscn, American Judicature Soc., Ariz. Women Lawyers' Asscn, Ariz. Women's Forum, Charter 100; Fellow Ariz. Bar Foundation; Leader of Distinction, Anti Defamation League, Woman of Distinction, Crohns and Colitis Disease Foundation, Women Making History Award, Nat. Museum of Women's History. *Publications:* numerous contribs. to legal journals. *Leisure interests:* hiking, trekking, travel, reading, film, sports. *Address:* Office of the Governor, State Capitol, West Wing, 1700 West Washington Street, Phoenix, AZ 85007, USA (Office).

NARANTSATSRALT, Janlav, PhD; Mongolian politician; b. 10 June 1957, Ulan Bator; s. of T. Janlav and D. Orgo; m. M. Altantsetseg 1978; two s.; ed Moscow Land Tenure Systems Univ., Nat. Univ. of Mongolia; Sr Engineer and Gen. Specialist Land Tenure Inst., Ministry of Agriculture 1981–89; Scientific Researcher and Head of Dept, Land Policy Inst. 1989–91; Head Urban Devt and Planning Bd, Ulan Bator Municipality 1991–95; Sr Specialist Office of the Mayor, Ulan Bator 1995–96; Head Land Dept, Ulan Bator 1996; Acting Mayor Ulan Bator 1996–97, Mayor 1997–98; Prime Minister of Mongolia 1998–99; Prof., Ulan Bator State Univ. 1999–2000; mem. State Great Hural (Parl.) 2000–; Medal of Labour, Anniversary Medals. *Publications:* Land Management Issues in the New Market, Economic Conditions in Mongolia. *Leisure interest:* travelling. *Address:* c/o State House, Ulan Bator 12, Mongolia. *E-mail:* narantsatsralt@mail.parl.gov.mn.

NARASIMHA RAO, P. V., BSc, LLB; Indian politician; b. 28 June 1921, Karimnagar, Andhra Pradesh; widower; three s. five d.; ed Osmania, Bombay and Nagpur Univs.; mem. Andhra Pradesh Legis. Ass. 1957–77, Minister, Govt of Andhra Pradesh 1962–71, Chief Minister 1971–73; Gen. Sec. All India Congress Cttee 1975–76; mem. Lok Sabha (Congress (I) Party) 1977–96, Minister of External Affairs, Govt of India 1980–85, of Defence and Acting Minister of Planning 1985, of Human Resources Devt and Health and Family Welfare 1985–88, of Human Resources Devt Feb.–June 1988, of External Affairs 1988–90; Acting Leader, then Pres. Congress (I) 1991–96; Prime Minister of India 1991–96, numerous other portfolios; Chair. Telugu Acad., Andhra Pradesh 1968–74; Vice.-Pres. Dakshin Bharat Hindi Prachar Sabha 1972. *Publications:* The Insider; trans. into Telugu and Hindi of several famous works; many articles in journals on political matters and allied subjects. *Leisure interests:* Indian Philosophy and culture, writing poems in Telugu and Hindi, music, theatre and cinema. *Address:* Vangara Post, Karimnagar District, Andhra Pradesh, India (Home); 9 Moti Lal Nehru Marg, New Dehli 110011 (Office). *Telephone:* (11) 3015550 (Office).

NARASIMHAM, Maidavolu; Indian government official; b. 3 June 1927, Bangalore; s. of M. Seshachelapati; m. Shanthy Sundaresan; one s.; ed Presidency Coll., Madras and St John's Coll. Cambridge; joined Reserve Bank of India, Bombay 1950, Sec. 1967, Gov. 1977; Chief of S. Asia Div., IMF 1960–63, Exec. Dir of IMF for India, Bangladesh and Sri Lanka 1980–82; Exec. Dir IBRD 1978–80; Additional Sec. Ministry of Finance 1972, Sec. Banking Dept 1976–78, Sec. Dept of Econ. Affairs 1982; Finance Sec., Govt of India 1983; Prin. Admin. Staff Coll. of India, Hyderabad 1983–85, Chair. 1991–; Vice-Pres. Asian Devt Bank, Manila 1985–88; Norton Prize (Madras Univ.); Padma Vibhushan 2000, Telugu Talli Award 2001, Lifetime Achievement Award 2001. *Publications include:* World Economic Environment and Prospects for India 1988, Economic Reforms: Development and Finance 2002, From Reserve Bank to Finance Ministry and Beyond: Some Reminiscences 2002. *Leisure interests:* reading, music. *Address:* "Sukruti", 8-2-681/7, Road No. 12, Banjara Hills, Hyderabad 500 034, India (Home). *Telephone:* (40) 23310994 (Office); 23396511 (Home). *Fax:* (40) 23310994/23312954.

NARAYANAN, Kocheril Raman, MA, BSc; Indian head of state and diplomatist; b. 27 Oct. 1920, Uzhavoor, Kerala; s. of the late Raman Vaidyan; m. Usha Ma Tint Tint 1951; two d.; ed Travancore Univ. and London School of Econs, Univ. of London; Lecturer in English Literature, Travancore Univ. 1943; worked in Editorial Dept of The Hindu newspaper, Madras 1944–45; Reporter, Times of India 1945; London Corresp. of Social Welfare (weekly), Bombay 1945–48; entered Foreign Service 1949; Jt Dir of Orientation Centre for Foreign Technicians, Delhi School of Econs 1954–55; served Rangoon, Tokyo, London and in Ministry of External Affairs 1949–60; Acting High Commr in Australia 1961–62; Consul-Gen., Hanoi 1962–63; Dir of China Div., Ministry of External Affairs 1963–67; Amb. to Thailand 1967–69; Joint Sec. for Policy Planning in Ministry 1969–70; Jawaharlal Nehru Fellow 1970–72; Hon. Prof., Jawaharlal Nehru Univ. 1970–72; Amb. to Turkey 1973–75; Additional Sec. for Policy Planning Div. of Ministry 1975–76; Sec. for the East, Ministry of External Affairs April–May 1976; Amb. to People's Repub. of China 1976–78; mem. Indian Del. to UN Gen. Ass. 1979; Amb. to USA 1980–84; mem. Lok Sabha for Ottapalath, Kerala 1984–; Minister of State for Planning, Govt of India 1985, for External Affairs 1985–86, for Atomic Energy, Space, Electronics and Ocean Devt 1986–87, for Science and Tech. 1986–89; Vice-Pres. of India 1992–97, concurrently Chair. Rajya Sabha (Council of States); Pres. of India 1997–2002; Vice-Pres. Council of Scientific and Industrial Research 1986–; Vice-Chancellor Jawaharlal Nehru University 1979–80; Co-Chair. Indo-US Sub-Comm. on Educ. and Culture 1980; mem. Indian Council for Social Science Research, New Delhi, Exec. Council, Children's Book Trust, Inst. of Defence Studies and Analysis, Indian Asscn of Social Science Inst., Universal Acad. of Cultures, Paris; Hon. Fellow, LSE 1972–, Jawaharlal Nehru Centre for Advanced Scienctific Research, Bangalore, Centre for Devt Studies, Kerala; Hon. DSc (Toledo) 1987; Hon. LLD (ANU) and several other hon. degrees. *Publications:* India and America—Essays in Understanding, Images and Insights, Non-Alignment in Contemporary International Relations (with Prof. KP Mishra), Nehru and his Vision; and other works on int. relations, Indian politics, literary subjects. *Leisure interests:* int. affairs, literature, philosophy, fine arts, folk and classical music. *Address:* c/o Office of the President, Rashtrapati Bhavan, New Delhi 110 004, India.

NARITA, Yoriaki, DJur; Japanese professor of law; b. Tokyo; s. of Masaji Narita and Masako Narita; m. Akiko Narita 1956; two d.; lecturer, Faculty of Econs, Yokohama Nat. Univ. 1929, Asst Prof. 1933, Prof. 1943, Dean of Econs 1982–86, Dir and Prof., Grad. School of Int. and Business Law 1990–93; Man. Dir Japan Energy Law Inst. 1993–. *Publications:* Introduction to Modern Administrative Law, Legal Theories and Reform of Local Self-government, Land Policy and Law. *Leisure interest:* collecting stamps. *Address:* 2-20-2, Tomigaya, Shibuya-ku, Tokyo 151-0063, Japan.

NARJES, Karl-Heinz; German politician and public servant; b. 30 Jan. 1924, Soltau; m.; two c.; ed Hamburg Univ.; submarine Commdr during World War II; with Minstry of Foreign Affairs; Chef de Cabinet to Pres. of European Comm. 1963; Dir-Gen. Press and Information Directorate of Comm. 1968–69; Minister of the Econ. and of Transport, Schleswig-Holstein Prov. 1969–73; mem. Bundestag 1972–88, Bundestag Foreign Affairs Comm. 1972–76, 1980–88, Bundestag Econ. Affairs Comm. (Pres. 1972–76, 1980–); Commr for Internal Market and Industrial Innovation, Customs Union, Environment and Consumer Protection and Nuclear Safety, Comm. of the European Communities 1981–84, for Economic Affairs and Employment 1985–86, for Industrial Affairs, Information Tech., Science and Research, Jt Research Centre 1986–88, Vice-Pres. Comm. of the European Communities 1985–88.

NARLIKAR, Jayant Vishnu, PhD, ScD; Indian scientist; b. 19 July 1938, Kolhapur; s. of Prof. and Mrs V. V. Narlikar; m. Mangala S. Rajwade 1966; three d.; ed Banaras Hindu Univ. and Fitzwilliam Coll. Cambridge; Berry Ramsey Fellow, King's Coll. Cambridge 1963–69; Grad. Staff Mem., Inst. of Theoretical Astronomy, Cambridge 1966–72; Sr Research Fellow, King's Coll. 1969–72; Jawaharlal Nehru Fellow 1973–75; mem. Science Advisory Council to the Prime Minister 1986–90; Dir Inter-Univ. Centre for Astronomy and Astrophysics, Pune 1988–; Hon. Prof. Jawaharlal Nehru Centre for Advanced Scientific Research; Homi Bhabha Prof. 1998–; Pres. Cosmology Comm. of Int. Astronomical Union 1994–97; Fellow, Indian Nat. Science Acad. (INSA), Assoc. Royal Astronomical Soc., London; Hon. DSc (Calcutta) 2000; awarded Padma Bhushan by the Indian Govt 1965, S. S. Bhatnagar Award 1978, Rashtrabhushan Award of FIE Foundation 1981, Rathindra Award 1985, INSA Vainu Bappu Award 1988, INSA Indira Gandhi Award for Science Popularization 1990, UNESCO Kalniga Award 1996. *Publications:* articles on cosmology, general relativity and gravitation, quantum theory, astrophysics etc. in the Proceedings of the Royal Soc., London, The Monthly Notices of the Royal Astronomical Soc., London, The Astrophysical Journal, Nature, Observatory and scientific articles in various magazines; Action at a Distance in Physics and Cosmology (with Sir F. Hoyle) 1974, The Structure of the Universe 1977, General Relativity and Cosmology 1978, The Physics Astronomy Frontier (with Sir F. Hoyle) 1980, Violent Phenomena in the Universe 1982, The Lighter Side of Gravity 1982, Introduction to Cosmology 1983, From Black Clouds to Black Holes 1985, Gravity Gauge Theories and Quantum Cosmology (with T. Padmanabhan) 1986, The Primeval Universe 1988. *Address:* IUCAA, Post Bag 4, Ganeshkhind, Pune 411007, India. *Telephone:* (20) 351414; (20) 5651414. *Fax:* (20) 5656417.

NARS, Kari, DrSc; Finnish banker; m.; two c.; ed Univ. of Helsinki, Helsinki Swedish School of Econs; economist, Bank of Finland 1964–66, Sec. of Bank 1967, Head Foreign Exchange Policy Dept 1972–75, Dir (Int.) 1977–83; Exec. Man. Dir Bank of Helsinki 1984–85; Economist, IMF, Washington, DC 1967–71; Dir Council of Econ. Orgs. 1975–76; Dir of Finance, Ministry of Finance 1986–91, 1994–; Exec. Dir EBRD, London 1991–94; Chair Admin. Cttee, Social Devt Fund of Council of Europe 1993–, currently Pres. Governing Bd, Council of Europe Devt Bank; Alt. Gov. for Finland, IMF 1981–82; mem. Bd Nordic Investment Bank 1989–91; Co-Chair. Govt Borrowers' Forum 1988–91. *Publications include:* Corporate Foreign Exchange Strategies 1980, Foreign Financing and Foreign Exchange Strategy (co-author) 1981, Financial Sector Study on Mozambique – a World Bank study (co-author) 1992, Cross Currency Swaps (contrib.) 1992; numerous articles and speeches. *Address:* Council of Europe Development Bank, 67075 Strasbourg Cédex, France; Ministry of Finance, Snellmaninkatu 1A, 00170 Helsinki, Finland.

NARUHITO, Crown Prince, MA; Japanese Crown Prince; b. 23 Feb. 1960, Tokyo; s. of Emperor Akihito and Empress Michiko; m. Masako Owada (now Crown Princess Masako); ed Gakushuin Univ., Merton Coll., Univ. of Oxford. *Leisure interests:* music, playing viola and violin, mountaineering, tennis.

NARVEKAR, Prabhakar R.; American (born Indian) international civil servant; b. 5 Jan. 1932, Mumbai; s. of Ramkrishna Manjunath Narvekar and Indira Narvekar; m. (wife deceased); one s. one d.; ed Bombay, Columbia and Oxford Univs; Research Asst IMF 1953; subsequently held various positions in Asian and European Depts of IMF; Dir Asian Dept IMF 1986–94; Deputy Man. Dir IMF 1994–97; Special Adviser to Pres. of Indonesia 1998; Sr Adviser to the Pres. Nikko Securities, Japan 1997–2000; Vice-Chair. Centennial Group of Consultants. *Leisure interest:* reading. *Address:* Centennial Group, 3105 38th Street NW, Washington, DC 20016 (Office); 4701 Willard Avenue, Chevy Chase, MD 20815, USA (Home). *Telephone:* (301) 654-7065 (Home); (202) 393-6663 (Office). *Fax:* (202) 393-6556 (Office); (301) 654-5133 (Home). *E-mail:* pnarvekar@narvekar.com (Office).

NASCIMENTO, Lopo Fortunato Ferreira do; Angolan politician; b. 10 July 1940, Luanda; s. of Vaz I. do Nascimento and Arminda F. do Nascimento; m. Maria do Carmo Assis 1969; two s. one d.; mem. Presidential Collegiate in transitional Govt before independence from Portugal Jan.–Nov. 1975; Prime Minister of Angola 1975–78; Minister of Internal Trade 1977–78, of Foreign Trade 1979–82, of Planning 1980–86; Deputy Exec. Sec. UN ECA, Addis Ababa 1979; Head Fifth Mil. Region 1986–90; Gov. Huila Prov. 1986–90; Presidential Adviser for Special Political Affairs 1990–; Head Govt Del. at negotiations on a peace agreement for Angola 1991; Minister of Territorial Admin. 1991; Sec.-Gen. Movimento Popular de Libertação de Angola (MPLA) –1993; Deputy Speaker of Parl. *Leisure interests:* music, writing, walking. *Address:* 93, Amilcar Cabral Street, 1st Floor, Luanda; 47 Ambuíla Street, P.O. Box 136, Luanda, Angola. *Telephone:* (2) 399640 (Office); (2) 444220 (Home); (24461) 205732. *Fax:* (2) 399639 (Office); (2) 448532 (Home); (2) 443088. *E-mail:* mcir@netangola.com (Office).

NASH, Charles; Irish boxer; b. 10 May 1951, Londonderry, Northern Ireland; s. of Alexander Nash and of the late Bridget Nash; m. Elizabeth Nash; one s. one d.; ed St Joseph's Secondary School, Londonderry; five times Irish amateur lightweight champion; boxed for Ireland in Olympic Games and European championships; won Irish title in first professional contest Oct. 1975; won vacant British lightweight title v. Johnny Claydon Feb. 1978; won vacant European title v. Andre Holyk June 1979, retained title v. Ken Buchanan Dec. 1979; relinquished British and European titles Jan. 1980 to challenge, unsuccessfully, for world title v. Jim Watt, Glasgow March 1980; regained European title from Francisco Leon Dec. 1980; 25 fights, 23 wins. *Leisure interests:* football, snooker, table tennis, coaching amateur boxers.

NASH, David, RA; British sculptor; b. 14 Nov. 1945, Surrey; s. of Lt-Col W. C. E. Nash and Dora Nash (née Vickery); m. Claire Langdown 1972; two s.; ed Brighton Coll., Kingston Art School and Chelsea School of Art; has exhibited widely in Britain, Europe, USA and Japan; first exhbn Briefly Cooked Apples, York Festival 1973; works in over 80 public collections including Tate Gallery and Guggenheim Museum; Research Fellow Dept of Visual and Performing Arts, Univ. of Northumbria 1999–2002; Dr hc (Kingston) 1999; Hon. DH (Glamorgan) 2002. *One-man shows include:* Loosely Held Grain, Arnolfini Gallery, Bristol 1976, 30 days 2 beech, Kröller-Müller Museum, Netherlands 1982, Ki No Inoichi: Ni No Katachi, Japan 1984, Spirit of Three Seasons, Otoineppu, Japan (touring exhbn) 1993–94, Voyages and Vessels, Joslyn Art Museum, USA (touring exhbn) 1994–95, Line of Cut, Henry Moore Inst., Leeds 1996, Wood Quarry, Market Hall, Blaenau Ffestiniog 2001; major group exhbns: British Art Now, Guggenheim Museum, New York 1980, Aspects of British Art Today, Japan 1982. *Publications:* Forms into Time, The Sculpture of David Nash, Black and Light, Twmps. *Address:* Capel Rhiw, Blaenau Ffestiniog, Gwynedd, LL41 3NT, Wales; c/o Annely Juda Fine Art, 23 Dering Street, London, W1R 9AA, England. *Telephone:* (20) 7629-7578 (London). *Fax:* (1766) 831179 (Blaenau Ffestiniog); (20) 7491-2139 (London).

NASH, John Forbes, Jr, PhD; American mathematician and economist; b. 13 June 1928, Bluefield, W Va; s. of John F. Nash and Margaret Virginia Martin Nash; m. Alicia Larde 1957; one s.; ed Carnegie Mellon Univ., Princeton Univ.; Research Asst, Instructor, Princeton Univ. 1950–51; Moore Instructor, MIT 1951–53, Asst Prof. 1953–57, Assoc. Prof. 1957–59; Research Assoc. in Mathematics 1966–67; Visiting Research Collaborator, Princeton Univ. 1995–, visiting mem. Inst. of Advanced Study 1956–57, 1961–62, 1963–64; mem. NAS 1996; Fellow of Econometric Soc., Sloan Fellow, NSF Fellow, Westinghouse Scholar; Hon. ScD (Carnegie-Mellon) 1999, Hon. PhD (Athens) 2000; awarded Von Neumann Medal of Operations Research Soc. of America; shared Nobel Prize for Econs 1994 for pioneering work on game theory; Business Week Award, Erasmus Univ., Rotterdam 1998; Leroy P. Steele Prize, American Mathematical Soc. 1999. *Publications:* Essays on

Game Theory; articles on econometric and mathematical theory. *Address:* Department of Mathematics, Princeton University, Fine Hall, Princeton, NJ 08544, USA.

NASHASHIBI, Nassiriddin; Palestinian journalist; b. 1924; ed American Univ. of Beirut; Arab Office, Jerusalem 1945–47; Chief Chamberlain, Amman, Jordan 1951; Dir Gen. Hashemite Broadcasting 1952; Ed. Akhbar al Youm, Cairo; Chief Ed. Al-Gumhuriyah, 1959–65; Rep. of the Arab League 1965–67; Diplomatic Ed. Al-Ahram; freelance journalist in Europe and the Middle East; Diplomatic Commentator, Jordanian, Israeli and other Middle Eastern TV stations; Order of Independance, Order of the Jordanian Star. *Publications:* What Happened in the Middle East 1958, Political Short Stories 1959, Return Ticket to Palestine 1960, Some Sand 1962, An Arab in China 1964, Roving Ambassador 1970, The Ink is Very Black 1976 and 40 other books. *Address:* 55 Avenue de Champel, Geneva, Switzerland; P.O. Box 1897 Jerusalem 91017, Israel; 26 Lowndes Street, London, SW1, England. *Telephone:* (22) 3463763 (Geneva) (Office); (20) 7235-1427 (London) (Office).

NASIM, Anwar, PhD; Pakistani professor of genetics; b. 7 Dec. 1935, Pasrur; ed Univ. of the Punjab, Univ. of Edinburgh; lecturer, Govt Coll., Multan and Lahore 1957–62; Research Officer, Atomic Energy of Canada Ltd, Chalk River, Canada 1966–73; Sr Research Officer, Nat. Research Council of Canada 1973–89; Adjunct Prof. Carleton Univ., Ottawa 1984–89, Univ. of Ottawa 1983–89; Prin. Scientist and Head, Molecular Genetics Group, Biology and Medical Research Dept, King Faisal Specialist Hosp. and Research Centre, Riyadh 1989–93; Exec. Sec. Pakistan Acad. of Sciences 1994–96; Adviser (Science) COMSTECH 1996–; Fellow, Third World Acad. of Sciences 1987, Islamic Acad. of Sciences 1998, Pakistan Acad. of Medical Sciences 2000; Foreign Fellow, Pakistan Acad. of Sciences 1988; Civil Award Prime of Performance in Molecular Genetics 1995, Award for Outstanding Service (Overseas Pakistanis Inst.) 1995, Sitara-e-Imtiaz Civil Award in Molecular Genetics 1999Gold Medal, MSc (Punjab). *Publications:* Repairable Lesions in Microorganisms (with A. Hurst) 1984, Recombinant DNA Methodology (with J. R. Dillon and E. R. Nestmann) 1985, Molecular Biology of the Fission Yeast (with P. Young and B. F. Johnson) 1989, Genetic Engineering and Biotechnology (with V. L. Chopra) 1990, Genetic Engineering – State of the Art (monograph) 1992, Biotechnology for Sustainable Development (with A. Malik Kauser and M. Khalid Ahmed) 1995; more than 100 scientific papers published in int. journals since 1965. *Leisure Interests:* reading literature, music. *Address:* COMSTECH Secretariat, 3 Constitution Avenue, G-5, Islamabad 44000, Pakistan (Office); 237, Street 23, F-11/2, Islamabad (Home). *Telephone:* (51) 9226813 (Office); (51) 2299838 (Home). *Fax:* (51) 9221115/ 92220265. *E-mail:* comstech@isb.comsats.net.pk (Office); comstech@isb .apollo.net.pk (Office); anwar_nasim@yahoo.com (Home).

NASIR, Agha, MA; Pakistani television executive and playwright; b. 9 Feb. 1937, Meerut, UP, India; s. of Ali Ahmad Khan and Ghafari Begum; m. Safia Sultana 1957; one s. two d.; Programmes Man. Pakistani TV 1967–68, Additional Gen. Man. 1967, Gen. Man. 1969–72, Dir Programmes Admin. 1972–86, Deputy Man. Dir 1986–87, Man. Dir 1987–88; Man. Dir Nat. Film Devt Corpn 1979; Dir-Gen. Pakistan Broadcasting Corpn 1989–92; Chief Exec. Shalimar Recording and Broadcasting Co. 1992–97; media consultant 1997–; recipient of numerous awards for radio and TV plays; Pride of Performance Award from Pres. of Pakistan for services in field of broadcasting 1993. *Radio:* has written a large number of features and plays for radio and produced more than 500 programmes. *Television:* has written more than 20 plays for TV and has produced about 100. *Publications:* Saat Dramey (plays), Television Dramey (TV plays); Gumshuda Log – a collection of pen pictures of eminent personalities. *Leisure interests:* reading, walking. *Address:* Geo TV Network, 40 Blue Area, Fazal-ul-huq Rd, Islamabad (Office); House No. 23, Street No. 3, F-8/3, Islamabad, Pakistan (Home). *Telephone:* (51) 2263685; (51) 2852619 (Home). *Fax:* (51) 2827396 (Office); (51) 2263685 (Home). *E-mail:* geotvpk@yahoo.com (Office); isloo@isb.compol.com (Home).

NASIR, Amir Ibrahim; Maldivian politician; b. 2 Sept. 1926, Malé; s. of Ahmed Didi and Aishath Didi; m. 1st Aishath Zubair 1950; m. 2nd Mariyam Saeed 1953; m. 3rd Naseema Mohamed Kalegefaan 1969; four s. one d.; ed Ceylon (now Sri Lanka); Under-Sec. of State to Minister of Finance and to Minister of Public Safety, Repub. of Maldives 1954; Minister of Public Safety 1956, of Home Affairs Aug. 1957; Prime Minister (1st term) Dec. 1957, Prime Minister (2nd term) and Minister of Home Affairs, Finance, Educ., Trade, External Affairs and Public Safety Aug. 1959, Prime Minister (3rd term) and Minister of Finance, Educ., External Affairs and Public Safety 1964; Pres. of the Repub. of Maldives 1968–78; in exile in Singapore, tried in absentia 1980 on charges of embezzling public funds and illegally collecting taxes, banished for 25 years, granted pardon by Pres. Gayoom (q.v.) July 1990; Award of Nishan Ghazee ge Izzatheri Veriya, Ranna Bandeiri Kilegefaan; Hon. KCMG. *Leisure interests:* fishing, yachting, gardening.

NASR, Farouk Mahmoud Sayf an-; Egyptian politician; b. Dec. 1922; fmr Pres. Supreme Constitutional Court; Dir Tech. Office, Ministry of Justice; worked on the preparation of laws, on Nationalist Councils; Minister of Justice 1987–. *Address:* Ministry of Justice, Justice and Finance Building, Sharia Majlis ash-Sha'ab, Lazoughli Square, Cairo, Egypt. *Telephone:* (2) 7951176. *Fax:* (2) 7955700. *E-mail:* mojeb@idsc1.gov.eg (Office).

NASR, Seyyed Hossein, MS, PhD; Iranian/American professor of Islamic studies; b. 7 April 1933, Tehran; s. of Valiallah Nasr and Ashraf Kia; m. Soussan Daneshvari 1958; one s. one d.; ed Mass. Inst. of Tech. and Harvard

Univ.; Teaching Asst Harvard Univ. 1955–58, Visiting Prof. 1962, 1965; Assoc. Prof. of History of Science and Philosophy, Tehran Univ. 1958–63, Prof. 1963–79, Dean, Faculty of Letters 1968–72, Vice-Chancellor 1970–71; Chancellor (Pres.) Aryamehr Univ. 1972–75; First Prof. of Islamic Studies, American Univ. of Beirut 1964–65; Prof. of Islamic Studies, Temple Univ. 1979–84; Univ. Prof. of Islamic Studies, George Washington Univ. 1984–; Visiting Prof. Harvard Univ. 1962, 1965, Princeton Univ. 1975, Univ. of Utah 1979; A. D. White Prof.-at-Large, Cornell Univ. 1991–98; Founder and first Pres. Iranian Acad. of Philosophy 1974–79; mem. Inst. Int. de Philosophie, Greek Acad. of Philosophy, Royal Acad. of Jordan; Dr hc (Uppsala) 1977, (Lehigh) 1996. *Publications:* over 30 books and some 300 articles in Persian, Arabic, English and French in leading int. journals. *Leisure interests:* classical music (both Western and Eastern), tennis, hiking. *Address:* 709R Gelman Library, The George Washington University, Washington, DC 20052, USA. *Telephone:* (202) 994-5704. *Fax:* (202) 994-4571.

NASREEN, Taslima; Bangladeshi feminist, author and doctor; b. 1962, Mymensingh, E Pakistan; d. of Royab Ali; m. 3rd (divorced); ed Mymensingh Medical Coll., Dhaka Univ.; practised as a gynaecologist; columnist Ajker Kagoj 1989; books banned in Bangladesh, fatwa (death threat) pronounced against her 1993; left Bangladesh to live in self-imposed exile in Sweden and France 1994; has published 16 books; winner Sakharov Prize (European Parl.) 1994. *Publications include:* Fera (Return), Nirbachito Column (selected columns), Laija (Shame) (novel) 1993, Utal Hawa 2002.

NASSER, Jacques A. (Jac), AO; Australian business executive; b. 12 Dec. 1947, Lebanon; m.; ed Royal Melbourne Inst. of Tech.; with Ford of Australia 1968–73, mem. financial staff N American Truck operations, Ford Motor Co. 1973, Mman. profit analysis, product programming Ford Motor Co., Australia 1973–75, various positions, Int. Automotive Operations, Ford Motor Co. 1975–87, Dir, Vice-Pres. Finance and Admin., Autolatina jt venture, Brazil and Argentina 1987–90, Pres., CEO Ford of Australia 1990–93, Chair. Ford of Europe 1993–96, Vice-Pres. Ford Motor Co. 1993–96, CEO 1999–2001, Chair. Ford of Europe, Pres. Ford Automotive Operations, Exec. Vice-Pres. 1996–2002; Sr Partner, One Equity Partners LLC (Bank One Corpn) 2002–; Chair. (non-exec.), Polaroid Corpn 2002–; mem. Int. Advisory Bd Allianz AG; mem. Bd Dirs BSkyB; Order of the Cedar (Lebanon). *Leisure interest:* opera. *Address:* One Equity Partners LLC, 320 Park Avenue, 18th Floor, New York, NY 10022; 100 Bloomfield Hills Parkway, Suite 175, Bloomfield Hills, MI 48304 (Home). *Website:* www.bankone.com.

NĂSTASE, Adrian, LLM, PhD; Romanian academic and politician; b. 22 June 1950, Bucharest; s. of Marin Năstase and Elena Năstase; m. Daniela Miculescu 1985; two s.; ed Bucharest Univ.; Research Fellow, Inst. of Legal Research, Bucharest 1973–90; Prof. of Public Int. Law, Bucharest Univ. 1990–, Titu Maiorescu, Dimitrie Cantemir and Nicolae Titulescu pvt. univs. 1992–; Assoc. Prof. of Public Int. Law, Paris-Panthéon Sorborne I 1994–; Minister of Foreign Affairs 1990–92; Speaker Chamber of Deputies 1992–96, Deputy Speaker 1996–; Exec. Pres. Social Democracy Party of Romania 1992–97, First Vice-Pres. 1997, Pres. 2000; Prime Minister of Romania 2000–; mem. Romanian Parl. Del. to Parl. Asscn Council of Europe 1996–; Vice-Pres. Asscn of Int. Law and Int. Relations, Bucharest 1977–; Dir of Studies, Int. Inst. of Human Rights, Strasbourg 1984; Pres. Titulescu European Foundation 1990–92 (Hon. Pres. 1992–); Exec. Pres. Euro-Atlantic Centre, Bucharest 1991–92; mem. Bd of Dirs. Inst. for East-West Studies, New York 1991–97; mem. Human Rights Information and Documentation System; mem. French Soc. of Int. Law 1984–, American Soc. of Int. Law 1995–; lecturer at numerous univs. and insts. of int. relations and human rights and speaker at many int. confs.; Nicolae Titulescu Prize, Romanian Acad. 1994, The Political Man of 1995, Turkish Businessmen's Asscn; Order of Diplomatic Service Merit 1991, Gwanghwa Medal, Repub. of Korea 1991, Grande Croix de Mérite, Sovereign Order of Malta 1992, Global Leader for Tomorrow Prize 1993. *Publications include:* Human Rights: an End-of-the-Century Religion 1992, International Law: Achievements and Prospects (co-author) 1992, Human Rights, Civil Society, Parliamentary Diplomacy 1994, Public International Law (co-author) 1995, Nicolae Titulescu – Our Contemporary 1995, Parliamentary Humour 1996, International Economic Law II 1996, Romania and the New World Architecture 1996, Documenta universales: I (with law documents) 1997, 1998, The Treaties of Romania (1990–1997) 1998, Documenta universales: II The Rights of Persons Belonging to National Minorities 1998, Battle for the Future 2000, Contemporary International Law-Essential Texts 2001; more than 240 articles and papers. *Leisure interests:* hunting, music, modern art, collecting antiques, gardening, tennis. *Address:* Office of the Prime Minister, Piata Victoriei, nr 1, sect. 1, 71201 Bucharest, Romania (Office). *Telephone:* (1) 3131450 (Office). *Fax:* (1) 3132436 (Office). *E-mail:* prim .ministru@guv.ro (Office). *Website:* www.guv.ro (Office).

NĂSTASE, Ilie; Romanian tennis player; b. 19 July 1946, Bucharest; m. 1st; one d.; m. 2nd Alexandra King 1984; nat. champion (13–14 age group) 1959, (15–16 age group) 1961, (17–18 age group) 1963, 1964; won the Masters Singles Event, Paris 1971, Barcelona 1972, Boston 1973, Stockholm 1975; winner of singles at Cannes 1967, Travemünde 1967, 1969, Gauhati 1968, Madras 1968, 1969, New Delhi 1968, 1969, Viareggio 1968, Barranquilla 1969, Coruna 1969, Budapest 1969, Denver 1969, Salisbury 1970, Rome 1970, 1973, Omaha 1971, 1972, Richmond 1971, Hampton 1971, Nice 1971, 1972, Monte Carlo 1971, 1972, Baastad 1971, Wembley 1971, Stockholm 1971, Istanbul 1971, Forest Hills 1972, Baltimore 1972, Madrid 1972, Toronto 1972, South Orange 1972, Seattle 1972, Roland Garros 1973, US Open 1973; winner of doubles at Roland Garros (with Ion Ţiriac) 1970, Wimbledon (with Rosemary Casals) 1970, 1972, (with Jimmy Connors, 1975; winner of ILTF Grand Prix 1972, 1973; won 108 pro titles in his career; played 130 matches for the Romanian team in the Davis Cup; elected to the Nat. Council of Romania's Social Democracy Party 1995; Pres. Romanian Tennis Fed.; Best Romanian Sportsman of the Year 1969, 1970, 1971, 1973; Int. Tennis Hall of Fame 1991; mem. Laureus World Sports Acad. *Publication:* Breakpoint 1986. *Address:* Clubul sportiv Steaua, Calea Plevnei 114, Bucharest, Romania.

NATADZE, Nodar; Georgian politician and academic; b. 27 May 1929, Tbilisi; s. of Revas Natadze and Tina Natadze (née Tatiana); m. Nana Gadyatska 1968; two s.; Philologist and Head Dept, Inst. of Philosophy, Georgian Acad. of Sciences; Leader Popular Front of Georgia 1989–, Nat. Cttee of United Republican Party of Georgia; mem. Supreme Council (Parl.) of Georgia 1989–90, 1990–91, 1992–95. *Leisure interests:* mountaineering, skiing, literary criticism. *Address:* Panaskerteli str. 16, Apt. 57, Tbilisi, Georgia. *Telephone:* (32) 381632.

NATAPEI, Edward; Ni-Vanuatu politician; b. 1955; Pres. (acting) of Vanuatu March 1999; Prime Minister of Vanuatu April 2001–; Pres. Vanuaaku Pati (Our Land Party). *Address:* Prime Minister's Office, PMB 053, Port Vila, Vanuatu (Office). *Telephone:* 22413 (Office). *Fax:* 22863 (Office).

NATHAN, S. R. (Sellapan Ramanathan); Singaporean head of state and civil servant; b. Ramanathan Sellapan, 3 July 1924; s. of V. Sellapan and Mdm Abirami; m. Urmila (Umi) Nandey; one s. one d.; ed Victoria School and Univ. of Malaya, Singapore; almoner Medical Dept, Gen. Hosp. 1955–56; Seaman's Welfare Officer, Ministry of Labour 1956–62; Asst Dir Labour Research Unit 1962–63, Dir 1964–66; Asst Sec. Ministry of Foreign Affairs Feb.–June 1966, Prin. Asst Sec. 1966–67, Deputy Sec. 1967–71; Dir Security and Intelligence Div. Ministry of Defence 1971–79; First Perm. Sec. Ministry of Foreign Affairs 1979–82; Exec. Chair. The Straits Times Press 1982–88; High Commr in Malaysia 1988–90; Amb. to USA 1990–96; Amb.-at-Large, Ministry of Foreign Affairs 1996–99; Dir Inst. of Defence and Strategic Studies, Nanyang Technological Univ. 1996–99; Pres. of Singapore 1999–; Pro-Chancellor Nat. Univ. of Singapore; Chair. Hindu Endowments Bd, Mitsubishi Singapore Heavy Industries (Pte) Ltd; mem. Bd of Trustees NTUC Research Unit, Singapore Indian Devt Asscn; Dir Singapore Nat. Oil Co. (Pte) Ltd, New Nation Publishing Berhad, Times Publishing Berhad, Singapore Press Holdings Ltd, Marshall Cavendish Ltd, Singapore Mint (Pte.) Ltd, Singapore Int. Media (Pte.) Ltd; mem. Bd of Govs Civil Service Coll.; Friend of Labour Award 1962, Public Service Star 1964, Public Admin. Medal (Silver) 1967, Meritorious Service Medal 1974, NTUC May Day Meritorious Service Award 1984. *Leisure interests:* walking, reading. *Address:* President's Office, Istana, Orchard Road, Singapore 238823 (Office). *Telephone:* 7375522 (Office). *Website:* www.istana.gov.sg (Office).

NATOCHIN, Yury Viktorovich, DSc; Russian physiologist; b. 6 Dec. 1932, Kharkov, USSR (now Ukraine); s. of Victor Natochin and Frida Kohan; m. 1957; one s. one d.; ed Novosibirsk High Medical School; Jr, then Sr Researcher Inst. of Evolutionary Physiology and Biochemistry 1959–64, Head of Lab. 1964–; Dean Medical Faculty 1995–2002; Head Physiology Dept, St Petersburg State Univ. 1996–; Corresp. mem. USSR (now Russian) Acad. of Sciences 1987, mem. 1992, Acad.-Sec. Dept of Physiology 1996–2002; Ed.-in-Chief Russian Journal of Physiology 1995–; main research in physiology of kidney, functional nephrology, molecular physiology; mem. Int. Acad. of Astronautics, Academia Europaea; Hon. mem. Hungarian Physiology Soc. 1984; L. A. Orbeli Prize 1980, S. Rach Medal 1968, Jan Parkinje Gold Medal 1982, S. Korolev Medal 1992; Science Prize of Govt of Russia 1997, I. Pavlov Gold Medal 2001. *Publications include:* Ion-Regulating Function of Kidney 1976, Physiology of Kidney 1982, Problems of Evolutional Physiology of Water-Salt Balance 1984, Kidney 1997, Fluid and Electrolyte Regulation in Spaceflight 1998. *Leisure interests:* photography, poetry, travelling. *Address:* Sechenov Institute of Evolutionary Physiology and Biochemistry, 44 M. Thorez prospekt, 194223 St Petersburg; Presidium of Russian Academy of Sciences, Leninsky prospekt 32A, 117334 Moscow, Russia. *Telephone:* (812) 552-30-86 (St Petersburg), (095) 938-51-10 (Moscow). *Fax:* (812) 552-30-86 (St Petersburg). *E-mail:* natochin@iephb.ru (Office).

NATSUKI, Shizuko; Japanese novelist; b. (Shizuko Idemitsu), 21 Dec. 1938, Tokyo; m. Yoshihide Idemitsu 1963; one s. one d.; ed Keio Univ.; screenplay for Only I Know (Japanese TV); followed by numerous novels, short stories and screenplays; Mystery Writers of Japan Prize 1973, Prix du Roman d'Aventures (France) 1989, Nishinippon Shinsbeen Cultural Award 1999, Fukuoka Prefecture Cultural Award 2001. *Films:* Tragedy of W 1984. *Plays:* novels adapted for the stage: Tragedy of W 1993, Actress X 1994. *Works adapted for television include:* The Angel Vanishes 1972 and more than 200 others. *Publications:* 39 novels including The Angel Vanishes 1970, Disappearance 1973, Murder at Mt. Fuji 1984, Dome 1986 The Third Lady 1987, Portal of the Wind 1990, Mariko 1999, The Punishment 2001 and nearly 240 novelettes and short stories. *Leisure interests:* Golf & Go (started own Go Tournament using go stone she developed herself). *Address:* 2-6-1 Ooike, Minami-ku, Fukuoka-shi 815-0073, Japan. *Telephone:* (92) 553-1893. *Fax:* (92) 552-0181.

NATTRASS, E. M. B. (Sue), AO, FAIM, FAIAM; Australian arts administrator and director; b. 15 Sept. 1941, Horsham, Vic.; d. of John Elliott Nattrass and Elizabeth Claven Saul; ed Univ. of Melbourne and Melbourne Business School; Stage Man., Lighting Designer and Production Dir 1963–79; Gen.

Man. J. C. Williamson Productions Ltd 1980–83; Dir Playbox Theatre Co. 1981–84; Theatre Operations Man., Victorian Arts Centre 1983–88, Deputy Gen. Man. 1988–89, Gen. Man. 1989–96; Artistic Dir Melbourne Int. Festival of the Arts 1998–; Exec. Dir Producer Services Millmaine Entertainment 2000–; CEO Artistic Dir Adelaide Festival 2002; numerous public appts. including mem. Drama Advisory Panel, Vic. Ministry for the Arts 1983–85, 1987–88, mem. Bicentennial Arts and Entertainment Cttee 1987–88; mem. Ministerial Advisory Cttee, Queen Victoria Women's Centre 1993–94, Patron 1996–2001; Pres. Australian Entertainment Industry Asscn 1994–; Deputy Pres. Victorian Coll. of Arts 1992–2002, Pres. 2002–; Dir Leadership Vic. 1996–, Theatre Royal Hobart 2000–, Fed. Square Pty Ltd 2000–, Harold Mitchell Foundation 2000–; mem. Melbourne and Olympics Parks Trust 2000–; Patron Victorian Theatres Trust and the Song Room Inc.; Premier Award, The AGE Performing Arts Awards, St Michael's Medal 1996, Vic. Day Award for Community and Public Service 1999. *Leisure interests:* cooking, walking, staring at trees, the bush. *Address:* 7 Martin Street, South Melbourne, Vic. 3205 (Office); 5 Havelock Street, St Kilda, Vic. 3182 Australia (Home). *Telephone:* 9534-6269; (3) 9690-9766 (Office). *Fax:* 9525-4392. *E-mail:* suen@millmaine.com.au (Office); nattrass@smart.net.au (Home). *Website:* www.millmaine.com.au (Office).

NAUDÉ, Rev. (Christiaan) Beyers; South African clergyman; b. 1915; s. of Jozua François Naudé and Adriana Johanna Naudé; m. Ilse Weder 1940; three s. one d.; co-f. multi-racial Christian Inst of S Africa; given seven-year Govt banning order 1977; Gen. Sec. SA Council of Churches 1985–87; mem. A.N.C. Del. for talks with South African Govt 1990; Hon. DTheol (Amsterdam) 1972; Hon. LLD (Witwatersrand) 1974, (Notre Dame, USA) 1985, (Limburg) 1989, (Durban–Westville) 1993; Hon. DLitt (Cape Town) 1983, (Univ. of the North) 1995; many int. humanitarian awards, including Bruno Kreisky Award, Austria 1979, Robert F. Kennedy Human Rights Award 1985, Herbert Haag Prize, FRG, Hoof-Offisier van die Orde van Oranje-Nassau, Netherlands 1995, Order of Meritorious Service (Gold) 1997. *Address:* 26 Hoylake Road, Greenside 2193, South Africa.

NAUGHTIE, (Alexander) James, MA; British journalist; b. 9 Aug. 1951, Aberdeen; s. of Alexander Naughtie and Isabella Naughtie; m. Eleanor Updale 1986; one s. two d.; ed Univs of Aberdeen and Syracuse; journalist The Scotsman (newspaper) 1977–84, The Guardian 1984–88, also Chief Political Corresp.; presenter The World at One, BBC Radio 1988–94, The Proms, BBC Radio and TV 1991–, Today, BBC Radio 4 1994–, Book Club BBC Radio 4 1998–; mem. Council Gresham Coll. 1997–; Hon. LLD (Aberdeen), (St Andrews); Hon. DUniv (Stirling). *Publication:* The Rivals 2001. *Leisure interests:* books, opera. *Address:* BBC News Centre, London, W12 8QT, England. *Telephone:* (20) 8624-9644.

NAUMAN, Bruce, MFA; American artist; b. 6 Dec. 1941, Fort Wayne, Ind.; ed Univ. of Wisconsin (Madison) and Univ. of Calif. (Davis); studied with Italo Scango, William Wiley, Robert Arneson, Frank Owen, Stephen Kaltenbach; Instructor San Francisco Art Inst. 1966–68, Univ. of Calif. (Irvine) 1970; has participated in numerous group exhbns. in USA and Europe; work in many perm. collections including Whitney Museum, LA County Museum of Art; retrospective Kunsthaus Zurich 1995; Dr. hc (San Francisco Art Inst.) 1989; Artist Fellowship Award, Nat. Endowment for the Arts 1968, Max Beckmann Prize (Frankfurt) 1990, Wolf Prize 1993, Aldrich Prize 1995. *Solo exhibitions include:* LA 1972, 1988, 1993, 1994, Düsseldorf 1974, 1989, 1994, Paris 1974, New York 1975, 1976, 1982, 1990, 1991, 1993, 1994, Amsterdam 1978, Basel 1990, Barcelona 1991, Frankfurt am Main 1991, Vienna 1991, London 1991, 1992, 1994, Tel Aviv 1992, Munich 1993, Madrid 1993, Washington, DC 1995, Copenhagen 1993, Chicago 1995, Athens 1995. *Publications:* Pictures of Sculptures in a Room 1966, Clear Sky 1968, Burning Small Fires 1968, Bruce Naumann 1988, Bruce Naumann Prints 1989.

NAUMANN, Gen. Klaus, OBE; German army officer (retd); b. 25 May 1939, Munich; m. Barbara Linke; one s. one d.; joined Bundeswehr 1958, Col staff of German Mil. Rep.–NATO Mil. Cttee, Brussels 1981–84; Brigade Commdr Armoured Infantry Brigade, Ellwangen 1984–86; Brig. Dept Head of Force Planning, Gen. Staff, Ministry of Defence 1986–88; Maj.-Gen., Head of Defence Policy and Operations staff 1988–90; Adviser in two-plus-four negotiations on German Unification 1990; Lt-Gen., Commdr first German corps April–Oct. 1991; Insp.-Gen. of the Bundeswehr 1991; Chair. NATO Mil. Cttee 1996–99; Great Distinguished Service Cross 1993, Commdr Legion of Merit 1993, Grand Officer, Légion d'honneur 1994, Grosses Bundesverdienstkreuz mit Stern 1998 and numerous other awards and honours. *Leisure interests:* politics, history, art, photography, Latin American culture. *Address:* c/o NATO HQ, Boulevard Leopold III, 1110 Brussels, Belgium.

NAUMANN, Michael, DPhil; German publisher; b. 8 Dec. 1941, Köthen; s. of Eduard Naumann and Ursula Naumann (née Schönfeld); m. Christa Wessel 1969 (divorced); one s. one d.; ed Univ. of Munich and Queen's Coll. Oxford; Asst Prof. Univ. of Bochum 1971–76; Florey Scholar Queen's Coll. Oxford 1976–78; Ed., Foreign Corresp. Die Zeit, Hamburg 1978–82; Sr Foreign Ed. Der Spiegel, Hamburg 1982–84; Publr Rowohlt Verlag, Reinbek 1984–95; Pres. and CEO Henry Holt and Co., New York 1996–; Minister of State for Culture 1998–2000; Ed.-in-Chief Die Zeit 2001–; Commdr Légion d'honneur. *Publications:* Der Abbau einer Verkehrten Welt 1969, Amerika liegt in Kaliforniuen 1983, Strukturwandel des Heroismus 1984, Die Geschichte ist offen 1990, Die schönste Form der Freiheit 2001. *Leisure interests:* books,

motor-cycling, sailing. *Address:* Die Zeit, Pressehaus, Speersort 1, 20095 Hamburg, Germany (Office). *Telephone:* (40) 32800 (Office); (40) 327111. *Website:* www.zeit.de (Office).

NAUMI, Najeeb al-, PhD; Qatari lawyer and politician; b. 21 March 1954, Doha; m.; four s. one d.; ed Alexandria Univ., Egypt, Dundee Univ., UK; Legal Adviser Qatar Gas and Petrochemical Co. 1981–88, Diwan Amiri 1988–92; Minister and Legal Adviser, Office of HH The Heir Apparent and Minister of Defence 1992–95; Minister of Justice 1995–97; advocate and legal consultant 1997–. *Publication:* International Legal Issues Arising under the United Nations Decade of International Law 1995. *Leisure interests:* boating, Internet, reading, writing. *Address:* P.O. Box 9952, Doha, Qatar (Office). *Telephone:* (974) 675374 (Office). *Fax:* (974) 675378.

NAUMOV, Vladimir Naumovich; Russian film director and script writer; b. 6 Dec. 1927, Leningrad (now St. Petersburg); m. Natalia Belokhvostikova; one s. one d.; ed Dept of Directing, State Inst. of Cinematography (under I. A. Savchenko); Artistic Dir workshop unit at Mosfilm 1961–89 (with A. Alov until 1983); Chair. Bd Mosfilm Studios Co. 1989–; Prof. VGIK 1980–; currently CEO Navona film production company, Pres. Nat. Acad. of Film Arts and Sciences; Meritorious Art worker 1965, People's Artist of the RSFSR 1974, People's Artist of USSR 1983, USSR State Prize 1984; Order of Honour 1971, Order of the Red banner of Labour 1972, Order of the Friendship of Peoples 1987, Order of Merit for the Country 1997. *Films include:* (in collaboration with Alov to 1983) Uneasy Youth 1955, Pavel Korchagin (based on Ostrovsky's novel How the Steel Was Tempered) 1957, Wind 1959, Peace to Him Who Enters (two prizes at 22nd Venice Film Festival) 1961, A Nasty Story (based on Dostoevsky) 1966 (banned, shown 1989), Flight (based on M. Bulgakov's play) 1971, How the Steel Was Tempered (TV series) 1974, Legend about Til (three prizes at All-Union Festival, First Prize Int. Festival Haugesunde, Norway, Int. Festival Brussels) 1976, Tehran-43 (Golden Prize at 12th Int. Film Festival, Moscow, Golden Prize All-Union Festival) 1981, The Shore (First Prize at 17th Int. Film Festival, Kiev) 1984, The Choice 1987, The Law 1989, Ten Years of Confinement 1990, The White Holiday (two prizes Int. Festival Rimini 1995) 1994, Nardo's Mystery (aka White Dog's Dream) (Moscow Film Festival Prize 1998) 1998, Clock Without Hands (Russian "Window to Europe" Film Festival Prize 2000, Grand Gold Pegasus Prize from the Moscow Film Festival 2001, Moscow Mayor's Prize 2001) 2000. *Address:* Bolshaya Gruzinskaya 39, Apt. 214, 123056 Moscow, Russia. *Telephone:* (095) 147-23-10 (Office); (095) 253-87-32. *Fax:* (095) 938-20-88.

NAVA-CARRILLO, Germán, DR.; Venezuelan diplomatist and politician; b. 21 Aug. 1930, Maracaibo; m.; two c.; ed Universidad Central de Venezuela; joined Ministry of Foreign Affairs 1955; Minister Plenipotentiary, Chargé d'affaires, London; Asst Dir-Gen. of Int. Politics and Chief Div. of Inter-American Affairs, Ministry of Foreign Affairs; Minister-Counsellor, Perm. Mission at UN 1967–69; Amb. and Deputy Perm. Rep. to UN 1969–70; Amb. to Egypt, also accred to Ethiopia 1970–72; Dir of Protocol, Ministry of Foreign Affairs 1972–74; Amb. to Costa Rica 1974–75; Dir of Int. Politics, Ministry of Foreign Affairs 1975–78, Gen. Dir of Int. Politics and Vice-Minister 1978–79; Perm. Rep. to UN 1979–81; Vice-Minister, Ministry of Foreign Affairs 1984–88, Minister of Foreign Affairs 1988–89; Rep. of Venezuela to several UN and other int. confs; Prof., Int. Studies School, Cen. Univ. of Venezuela 1981. *Address:* c/o Ministry of Foreign Affairs, Casa Amarilla, Biblioteca Central, esq. Principal, Caracas 1010, Venezuela.

NAVARETTE LÓPEZ, Jorge Eduardo; Mexican economist and diplomatist; b. 29 April 1940, Mexico City; m. Martha L. López; one s.; ed Autonomous Univ. of Mexico (UNAM); Prof., Nat. School of Econs and Nat. School of Political and Social Sciences, UNAM 1964–71; various positions with Foreign Trade Nat. Bank 1966–72; Ed. Comercio Exterior; with Secr. of Finance and Public Credit –1972; Amb. to Venezuela 1972–75, to Austria 1975–77, to Yugoslavia 1977–78, to UK 1986–89, to People's Repub. of China 1989–93, to Chile 1993–95, to Brazil 1997–2001, to Germany 2002–; Rep. of Mexico at Int. Conf. for Co-operation and Devt, Paris 1976–77; Deputy Perm. Rep to UN and Vice-Pres. Econ. and Social Council 1978–79, Perm. Rep to UN 2001–02; Under-Sec. for Econ. Affairs, Secr. of Foreign Relations 1979–86; Under-Sec. for Policy and Devt, Secr. of Energy 1995–97; fmr consultant for Inter-American Bank and UNDP; fmr Perm. Rep. to UNIDO; fmr mem Bd Govs. IAEA; fmr mem. South Comm. *Publications include:* The International Transference of Technology: The Mexican Case (with Gerardo Bueno and Miguel Wionczek) 1969, Mexico: The Economic Policy of the New Government 1971, The Latin American External Debt 1986. *Address:* Embassy of Mexico, Klingelhöferstr. 3, Berlin 10785, Germany (Office). *Telephone:* (30) 2693230 (Office). *Fax:* (30) 269323700 (Office). *E-mail:* mail@embamexale.de (Office). *Website:* www.embamex.de (Office).

NAVARRO BERMÚDEZ, Leopoldo, PhD; Nicaraguan politician; Vice-Pres. of Nicaragua 2000–01; Pres. Partido Liberal Constitucionalista (PLC); mem. Asamblea Nacional. *Address:* Colonial Los Robles 211, Managua, Nicaragua (Office). *Telephone:* (2) 78-8705 (Office). *Fax:* (2) 78-1800 (Office).

NAVARRO NAVARRO, Miguel; Spanish sculptor; b. 29 Sept. 1945, Mislata; s. of Vicente Navarro Lopez and Valentina-Francisca Navarro Hernandez; ed Escuela Superior de Bellas Artes de San Carlos, Valencia; began career as a painter; from 1972 devoted himself mainly to sculpture; works in public spaces include: public fountains Valencia 1984, Turis (Valencia) 1986, Minerva Paranoica (sculpture), Castellón 1989, Torre del Sonido (sculpture), Universidad Carlos III, Getafe 1990, Fraternitat (sculpture), Barcelona 1992,

Boca de Luna (fountain), Brussels 1994, Casco Industrial (sculpture) Bilbao 1999, Vigía (sculpture) Las Palmas 2000; works in public collections including: Guggenheim Museum, New York, Fundació Caixa de Pensions, Barcelona, Instituto Valenciano de Arte Moderno, Valencia, Museo Nacional Centro de Arte Reina Sofía, Madrid, Fondation Lambert, Brussels, Diputación Prov. de Valencia, Centre Georges Pompidou, Paris, Museu d'Art Contemporani, Barcelona, Colección Argentaria, Madrid, Colección Banco de España, Madrid, Fundación Coca Cola España, Madrid, Fundazion I.C.O., Madrid, Universidad Politécnica de Valencia, Museo de Arte Contemporáneo Sofía Imbert, Caracas, Mie Prefectural Art Museum, Japan; Premio Nacional Artes Plast. 1986, Premio Alfons Roig, Valencia 1987, Premio Valencianos para el Siglo XXI 2001. *Exhibitions include:* New York 1980, Madrid 1985, 1988, 1989, 1991, 2000, 2001, Venice 1986, 2000, London 1986, Valencia 1988, 1990, 1996, 2001, Barcelona 1988, Paris 1994, 2001, Derry, NI 1996, Mexico 1997, Chicago 1998, Buenos Aires 1999, Duisburg 1999, São Paulo 1999, The Hague 2000, Naples 2001. *Leisure interests:* cooking, countryside. *Address:* c/o San Martín 13, 46920 Mislata (Valencia), Spain. *Telephone:* (6) 3792624.

NAVASKY, Victor Saul, AB, LLB; American writer and editor; b. 5 July 1932, New York; s. of Macy Navasky and Esther Goldberg; m. Anne Landey Strongin 1966; one s. two d.; ed Swarthmore Coll., Yale Univ. Law School; Special Asst to Gov. G. Mennen Williams, Mich. 1959–60; Ed. and Publisher, Monocle Magazine 1961–65; Ed. New York Times magazine 1970–72; Ed.-in-Chief The Nation magazine 1978–94, Editorial Dir and Publr 1995–; Delacorte Prof. of Journalism, Columbia Univ. 1999–; mem. Bd PEN, Authors' Guild, Cttee to Protect Journalists, Man. Bd Swarthmore Coll. 1991–94; American Book Award (for Naming Names) 1981. *Play:* Starr's Last Tape (with Richard R. Lingeman). *Publications:* Kennedy Justice 1971, Naming Names 1980, The Experts Speak (Co-Ed. with C. Cerf) 1984, The Best of the Nation (with Katrina van den Heuvel). *Address:* The Nation, 33 Irving Place, 8th Floor, New York, NY 10003 (Office); 33 W 67th Street, New York, NY 10023, USA (Home). *Telephone:* (212) 209-5411 (Office). *Fax:* (212) 982-9000 (Office). *E-mail:* vic@thenation.com (Office).

NAVITSKY, Genadz; Belarus politician and engineer; b. 2 Jan. 1940, Mogilev; ed Belarus State Polytech. Inst.; foreman, job superintendent, chief engineer, Mogilev Construction Trust 1971–77, instructor Mogilev Regional CP Cttee 1977–81, Head of Construction Div. 1985; Head Mogilev Regional Agric. Construction Dept until 1994; Minister of Architecture and Construction 1994–97; Deputy Prime Minister responsible for Construction 1997–2001; Deputy Chair., then Chair. (Prime Minister) Cabinet of Ministers of Belarus Jan. 2000–01, Prime Minister Oct. 2001–. *Address:* House of Government, 220010 Minsk, Belarus (Office). *Telephone:* (17) 222-60-47 (Office). *Fax:* (17) 222-61-05 (Office).

NAVON, Itzhak; Israeli politician and teacher; b. 9 April 1921, Jerusalem; s. of Yosef Navon and Miriam Ben-Atar; m. Ofira Reznikov-Erez; one s. one d.; ed Hebrew Univ. of Jerusalem; Dir, Hagana Arabic Dept, Jerusalem 1946–49; Second Sec., Israel Legation in Uruguay and Argentina 1949–51; Political Sec. to Foreign Minister 1951–52; Head of Bureau of Prime Minister 1952–63; Head, Dept of Culture, Ministry of Educ. and Culture 1963–65; mem. Knesset (Parl.) 1965–78; fmr Deputy Speaker; fmr Chair. Knesset Defence and Foreign Affairs Cttee; Chair. World Zionist Council 1973–78; Pres. of Israel 1978–83; Vice-Premier and Minister of Educ. and Culture 1984–90; mem. Mapai Party 1951–65, Rafi 1965–68, Israel Labour Party 1968–; Chair. Acad. of Music and Dance, Nat. Authority of Ladino, Neot Kedumim (Biblical Gardens). *Television:* Out of Spain – series of five programmes on the history of the Jews in Spain. *Play:* The Sephardic Orchard. *Publications:* Romancero Sephardi, Six Days and Seven Gates; collection of articles on Ben Gurion. *Leisure interests:* theatre, folklore, cantorial music. *Address:* 31 Hanevi'im Street, Jerusalem (Office); 39 Jabotinsky Street, Jerusalem, Israel (Home).

NAVRATILOVA, Martina; American (b. Czechoslovakian) tennis player; b. 18 Oct. 1956, Prague; d. of Miroslav Navratil and Jana Navratilova; professional since 1975, the year she defected to USA; ranked No. 1 1982–85; Wimbledon singles champion 1978, 1979, 1982, 1983, 1984, 1985, 1986, 1987, 1990, finalist 1988, 1989, 1994; (doubles 1976, 1979, 1982, 1983, 1984, 1985); French champion 1982, 1984; Australian champion 1981, 1983, 1985; Avon champion 1978, 1979, 1981; US Open champion 1983, 1984, 1986, 1987; 54 Grand Slam titles (18 singles, 37 women's doubles); holder of 167 singles and 165 doubles titles (more than any other player, male or female); world No. 1 for 332 weeks at retirement (Nov. 1994); 19 Wimbledon titles (1995); set professional women's record for consecutive victories 1984; won 100th tournament of career 1985; only player to win 100 matches at Wimbledon 1991; record of 158 wins (Feb. 1992) in singles beating the record of Chris Evert Lloyd; Pres. Women's Tennis Assn 1979–80, 1983–84, 1994–95; world champion 1980; played Federation Cup for Czechoslovakia 1973, 1974, 1975; 1,400 victories (Oct. 1993); designer own fashion wear; made comeback (in doubles only) 2000; winner Mixed Doubles, Australian Open 2003 (at age 46.3 months, oldest winner of a grandslam title); Dr hc (George Washington) 1996; Female Athlete of the Decade for the 1980s, Nat. Sports Review, Sportswomen of the Year 1982–84, Women's Sports Foundation, Int. Tennis Hall of Fame 2000. *Publications:* Being Myself (autobiog.) 1985, The Total Zone (novel with Liz Nickles) 1994, The Breaking Point (with Liz Nickles) 1996, Killer Instinct (with Liz Nickles) 1998. *Leisure interests:* golf, snowboarding, skiing, basketball. *Address:* IMG, 1360 E 9th Street, Cleveland, OH 44114, USA.

NAWAR, Ahmed, PhD; Egyptian arts administrator; b. 3 June 1945, El sheen Gharbia; s. of Mohamed Ismail Nawar and Fakiha Karam Mostafa Ghali; m. Wafaa Mossallem 1969; three d.; ed Cairo Univ. and St Fernando Acad., Madrid; Prof. of Graphics, Faculty of Fine Art, Helwan Univ. 1967–; Dean and f. Faculty of Fine Art, Menia Univ. 1983–88; Head Nat. Centre for Fine Arts, Ministry of Culture 1988–; Head Museums Service, Higher Council for Antiquities 1994–; Gen. Supervisor Nubia Savings Fund 1996–98; State Order of Arts and Sciences, First Class 1979, Nobel Gold Medal 1986, Order of Merit (Spain) 1992, Officier, Ordre des Arts et des Sciences and other awards and honours. *Address:* 54 Dimashk, Madenat Al Mohandeseen, Flat 16, Giza, Cairo, Egypt. *Telephone:* (2) 3488279. *Fax:* (2) 3488279.

NAWAWI AYOB, Ahmad, PhD; Malaysian professor of botany and university vice-chancellor; b. 11 Jan. 1937, Perak; m.; two c.; ed Queen's Univ., Belfast; Demonstrator in Botany, Mycology and Plant Pathology, Queen's Univ., Belfast 1963–65; botanist and plant pathologist Ministry of Agric., Malaysia 1966–67; Post-doctoral Research Fellow Wageningen Agricultural Univ., Netherlands 1970, Queen's Univ. Belfast 1971–72; Lecturer in Botany, Univ. of Malaya 1967–74, Assoc. Prof. 1974–78, Head Dept of Botany 1974–75, Prof. of Botany 1978, Dean Faculty of Sciences 1976–78, Acting Deputy Vice-Chancellor 1977, Deputy Vice-Chancellor for Finance and Devt 1983–86, Acting Vice-Chancellor 1986, Deputy Vice-Chancellor 1991; Pres. Malaysian Soc. for Microbiology 1986–87; Pres. Malaysian Soc. for Microbiology 1986–87; fmr Pres. Malaysian Soc. Applied Biology; mem. Council Malaysian Agricultural Research and Devt Inst., Malaysian Nat. Science Council 1981–, Man. Cttee Nat. Scientific Research and Devt Trust Fund 1981–; mem. Council Nat. Inst. of Public Admin.; Fellow Islamic Acad. of Sciences, Malaysian Acad. of Sciences; Hon. DSc (Portsmouth), (Belfast) 1995; Johan Mangku Negara 1982, Datuk Paduka Cura Si Manja Kini 1986. *Publications:* over 60 specialized publs. *Address:* Islamic Academy of Sciences, PO Box 830036, Amman, Jordan (Office). *Telephone:* 5522104 (Office). *Fax:* 5511803 (Office).

NAWAZ SHARIF, Mohammed; Pakistani politician and industrialist; b. 25 Dec. 1949, Lahore; s. of Mian Mohammad Sharif; m. 1971; two s. two d.; ed Govt Coll. and Punjab Univ. Law Coll., Lahore; started work in Ittefaq faction industrial group 1969; Finance Minister, Govt of the Punjab 1981–85, Chief Minister of Punjab 1985–90; Prime Minister of Pakistan 1990–93 (dismissal ruled unconstitutional), resgnd July 1993, Prime Minister 1997–99 (removed in coup), concurrently Minister of Defence and Finance; sentenced to life imprisonment for terrorism and hijacking April 2000; released from imprisonment, in exile in Jeddah, Saudi Arabia Dec. 2000–(03); Pres. Pakistan Muslim League, Punjab 1985, Islami Jamhoori Ittehad 1988. *Leisure interests:* social work, photography, hunting, playing cricket. *Address:* 180-181-H, Ittefaq Colony, Model Town, Lahore, Pakistan. *Telephone:* 856069 (Home).

NAZARBAYEV, Nursultan Abishevich; Kazakhstan politician; b. 6 July 1940, Chemolgan; s. of Abish Nazarbayev and Aizhan Nazarbayev; m. Sarah Alplisovna Kounakaeva 1962; three d.; ed Higher Tech. Course at Karaganda Metallurgical Combine and Higher Party School of Cen. Cttee CPSU; mem. CPSU 1962–91; worked for Karaganda Metallurgical Plant 1960–64, 1965–69; Sec. Temirtau City Cttee of Kazakh CP 1969–84; Sec. party Cttee of Karaganda Metallurgical Combine 1973–77; Second, then First Sec. Karaganda Dist Cttee of Kazakh CP 1977–79; Sec. Cen. Cttee of Kazakh CP 1979–84; Chair. Council of Ministers of Kazakh SSR 1984–89; USSR People's Deputy 1989–91; First Sec. Cen. Cttee of Kazakh CP 1989–91, Socialist Party 1991–; Chair. Kazakh Supreme Soviet 1989–90; Pres. Kazakh SSR 1990–91, Kazakh Repub. 1991–; Chair. World Kazakh Union 1992–. *Publications:* 9 books; numerous articles on economics. *Leisure interests:* tennis, water-skiing, horses, reading history books. *Address:* Respubliki sq. 4, 480091 Almaty, Kazakhstan. *Telephone:* (3272) 62-30-16, 15-11-53.

NAZARENKO, Tatyana Georgievna; Russian painter; b. 24 June 1944, Moscow; m.; ed Moscow Surikov State Fine Arts Inst.; worked Studio of USSR Acad. of Fine Arts 1969–72; mem. USSR (now Russian) Union of Painters 1969; solo exhbns France, USA, Spain, Russia, Germany 1987–; Acad. of Arts Silver Medal 1987, Russian State Prize 1993. *Address:* Moscow Artists' Union, Starosadsky Per. 5, 101000 Moscow, Russia. *Telephone:* (095) 921-51-88.

NAZAROV, Talbak Nazarovich, DEconSc; Tajikistan politician and academic; b. 15 March 1938, Kulyab; m. Tatyana Grigorievna Teodorovich 1959; one s. one d.; ed Leningrad Inst. of Finance and Econs; Asst, then Deputy Dean Econs Faculty, Tajik State Univ. 1960–62, Head of Dept, Dean 1965–80, Rector 1982–88; Chair Supreme Soviet Tajik SSR 1986–88; Minister of Public Educ. 1988–90; USSR People's Deputy 1989–92; First Deputy Chair. Tajikistan Council of Ministers, Chair. State Planning Cttee 1990–91; Minister of Foreign Affairs 1994–; mem. Tajikistan Acad. of Sciences 1980–; Vice-Pres. 1991–94; Merited Worker of Science and many other awards and medals. *Publications:* books and articles on Tajikistan's economy and external policies. *Address:* Ministry of Foreign Affairs, Rudaki 42, 734051 Dushanbe, Tajikistan (Office). *Telephone:* (2) 21-02-59 (Office); (2) 21-18-08.

NAZDRATENKO, Yevgeny Ivanovich; Russian politician; b. 16 Feb. 1949, Severo-Kurilsk, Sakhalin Region; m.; two s.; ed Far East Inst. of Tech.; served with Pacific Fleet; Head of sector Bor Co.; mechanic, Vice-Pres., Pres. Primorsk Mining Co., Vostok 1980–93; Peoples' Deputy of Russian Fed. 1990–93; Head of Admin. Primorsk Territory 1993–95, Gov. 1995–2001; mem. Council of Fed. of Russia 1996–2001; Chair. State Cttee for Fisheries 2001–; Dr hc (St Petersburg Mining Univ.), (Seoul Univ.); Order for Personal Courage

1994, Hon. Citizen of Russia 1995. *Address:* State Committee for Fisheries, Rozhdestvensky blvd 12, 103031 Moscow, Russia. *Telephone:* (095) 923-76-34 (Office). *Website:* www.gkr.ru (Office).

NAZER, Sheikh Hisham Mohi ed-Din; Saudi Arabian politician; b. 1932; ed Univ. of California; legal adviser 1958; assisted in foundation of OPEC 1960; Deputy Minister of Petroleum 1962–68; with Ministry of Planning 1975–, Acting Minister of Planning 1986–91; Minister of Petroleum and Mineral Resources 1986–95; Pres. Cen. Org. for Planning 1968–; mem. Supreme Council for Petroleum and Minerals 1968–; Chair. SAMAREC, Saudia Arabian Oil Co. *Address:* c/o Ministry of Petroleum and Mineral Resources, P.O. Box 247, Riyadh 11191, Saudi Arabia.

NAZIR-ALI, Rt Rev Michael James, BA, MLitt, ThD; British/Pakistani ecclesiastic; b. 19 Aug. 1949, Karachi; s. of James Nazir-Ali and Patience Nazir-Ali; m. Valerie Cree 1972; two s.; ed St Paul's High School, Karachi, St Patrick's Coll., Karachi, Univ. of Karachi, Fitzwilliam Coll. Cambridge, Ridley Hall, Cambridge, St Edmund Hall, Oxford and Australian Coll. of Theology in Asscn with Centre for World Religions, Harvard; Tutorial Supervisor in Theology, Univ. of Cambridge 1974–76; Tutor then Sr Tutor, Karachi Theological Coll. 1976–81; Assoc. Priest Holy Trinity Cathedral, Karachi 1976–79; Priest-in-Charge St Andrew's Akhtar Colony, Karachi 1979–81; Provost Lahore Cathedral 1981–84; Bishop of Raiwind 1984–86; fmr Visiting Lecturer, Centre for Study of Islam and Muslim-Christian Relations, Birmingham; Asst to Archbishop of Canterbury; Co-ordinator of Studies for 1988 Lambeth Conf. 1986–89; Gen. Sec. Church Mission Soc. 1989–94; Asst Bishop, Diocese of Southwark 1990–94; Canon Theologian Leicester Cathedral 1992–94; Bishop of Rochester 1994–; mem. House of Lords 1999–; Chair. Mission Theological Advisory Group 1992–2001, Chair. Governing Council, Trinity Coll. Bristol 1996–; Dir Oxford Centre for Mission Studies, Christian Aid; mem. Design Group for 1998 Lambeth Conf., Anglican Roman Catholic Int. Comm. 1991–, Bd of Mission Gen. Synod, Church of England 1992–94, 1996–, Human Fertilization and Embryology Authority 1998– (Chair. of Ethics Cttee); Fellow St Edmund Hall, Oxford 1998–; Visiting Prof. of Theological and Religious Studies, Univ. of Greenwich 1996–; mem. Archbishop's Council 2001–, House of Bishop's Standing Cttee. 2001–, Anglican-Roman Catholic Jt Working Group 2001–, Chair. Working Party on Women in the Episcopate; Hon. DLitt (Bath), (Greenwich); Radio Pakistan Prize for English Language and Literature 1964; Burney Award (Cambridge) 1973, 1975; Oxford Soc. Award for Grads 1973; Langham Scholarship 1974. *Publications:* Islam, a Christian Perspective 1982, Frontiers in Christian–Muslim Encounter 1985, Martyrs and Magistrates: Toleration and Trial in Islam 1989, The Roots of Islamic Tolerance: Origin and Development 1990, From Everywhere to Everywhere 1991, Mission and Dialogue 1995, The Mystery of Faith 1995, Citizens and Exiles 1998, Shapes of the Church to Come 2001, Understanding My Muslim Neighbour 2002; numerous articles on Islam, Christianity, mission, inter-faith dialogue, Anglican and ecumenical affairs. *Leisure interests:* cricket, hockey, table tennis and reading, poetry. *Address:* House of Lords, London, SW1A 0PW (Office); Bishopscourt, Rochester, Kent, ME1 1TS, England. *Telephone:* (1634) 842721. *Fax:* (1634) 831136. *E-mail:* bishops.secretary@rochester.anglican.org.

NAZRUL-ISLAM, Jamal, PhD; Bangladeshi professor of mathematics; b. 24 Feb. 1939, Jhenidah, Jessore; ed Trinity Coll. Cambridge, Calcutta Univ.; Postdoctoral Fellow, Dept of Physics and Astronomy, Univ. of Md 1963–65; staff mem. Inst. of Theoretical Astronomy, Univ. of Cambridge 1967–71; Visiting Assoc. in Physics, Calif. Inst. of Tech. 1971–72; Sr Research Assoc., Dept of Astronomy, Univ. of Wash. 1972–73; Lecturer in Applied Math., King's Coll., London 1973–74; Science Research Council Fellow, Univ. Coll. Cardiff 1975–78; Lecturer and Reader, Dept of Math., City Univ., London 1978–84; Prof. Math., Founder and Dir Centre for Math. and Physical Sciences, Univ. of Chittagong; Fellow, Third World Acad. of Sciences, Cambridge Philosophical Soc., Royal Astronomical Soc., Bangladesh Acad. of Sciences, Islamic Acad. of Sciences; Gold Medal, Bangladesh Acad. of Sciences for Physical Sciences, Sr. Group 1985. *Address:* Department of Mathematics, University of Chittagong, Chittagong, Bangladesh (Office). *Telephone:* (31) 210133 (Office). *Fax:* (31) 210141 (Office).

NCUBE, Most Rev. Pius Alick, LTh; Zimbabwean ecclesiastic; b. 1 Jan. 1947, Mtshabezi, Gwanda; s. of Amos Ncube; ed Chishawasha Major Seminary, Harare, Lateran Univ., Rome, Italy; ordained Priest, Bulawayo 1973, Parish Priest, St Patrick's 1986–90, St Mary's Cathedral 1990–1995; Vicar Gen., Bulawayo Archdiocese 1995–98, Archbishop of Bulawayo 1998–. *Publications include:* Imfundiso. Yebandla. Elikhatholike (Catholic catechism). *Leisure interests:* reading, writing articles. *Address:* Archbishop's House, cnr Lobenguela Street and Ninth Avenue, POB 837, Bulawayo, Zimbabwe (Office). *Telephone:* (9) 63590 (Office). *Fax:* (9) 60359 (Office). *E-mail:* archdbyo@mweb.co.zw (Office).

NDAYIZEYE, Domitien; Burundian politician; Sec.-Gen. opposition pro-Hutu party Front pour la démocratie au Burundi (FRODEBU); Vice-Pres. of Burundi responsible for Political and Admin. Affairs 2001–03; Pres. of Burundi May 2003–. *Address:* Office of the President, Bujumbura, Burundi (Office). *Telephone:* 226063 (Office).

NDEBELE, Njabulo Simakahle, PhD; South African academic and writer; b. 4 July 1948, Johannesburg; m. Kathleen Mpho; one s. two d.; ed Univs of Botswana, Lesotho and Swaziland, Cambridge Univ., UK; Head of Dept, Nat. Univ. of Lesotho, Dean of Humanities Faculty 1987, Pro-Vice-Chancellor 1988; Chair. and Head of Dept of African Literature, Wits Univ.; Vice-Rector, Univ. of the Western Cape; Vice-Chancellor and Prin., Univ. of the North, Scholar in Residence, Ford Foundation; Vice-Chancellor, Univ. of Cape Town July 2000–; Chair. S African Broadcasting Policy Project, Ministry of Post, Telecommunications and Broadcasting, S African Univs Vice-Chancellors' Asscn –2000; mem. Exec. Bd AA4, AC4; Dr hc (Natal Univ., Chicago State Univ., Vrije Univ. Amsterdam, Soka Univ. Japan); President's Award, Lincoln Univ.; Fiftieth Anniversary Distinguished Service Award, Nat. Univ. of Lesotho; NOMA Award for Publishing in Africa; Sanlam Award for Outstanding Fiction; Pringle Prize for Outstanding Criticism. *Publications:* Fools and Other Stories 1983, Bonolo and the Peach Tree 1991, Rediscovery of the Ordinary 1991, The Prophetess 1992, Sarah, Rings and I 1993, Death of a Son 1996. *Leisure interests:* bird watching, computer simulation games. *Address:* University of Cape Town, Private Bag, Rondebosch 7701, Cape Town (Office); Glenara, Burg Road, Rondebosch 7700, Cape Town, South Africa (Home). *Telephone:* (21) 6502105, (21) 6502106 (Office). *Fax:* (21) 6892440 (Office). *E-mail:* vc@bremner.uct.ac.za (Office). *Website:* www.uct.ac.za (Office).

N'DIAYE, Babacar; Senegalese banker; b. 11 June 1936, Conakry, Guinea; joined African Devt Bank 1965, subsequently Group Dir of Finance, then Vice-Pres. for Finance, Pres. 1985–95; Chair. African Business Round Table; LLD (Clark Atlanta Univ., Ga) 1992, (Lincoln Univ., Pa) 1993. *Address:* c/o African Development Bank, 01 BP 1387, Abidjan 01, Côte d'Ivoire.

NDIMIRA, Pascal-Firmin; Burundian politician; fmrly univ. rector, IBRD official; fmrly Minister of Agric.; Prime Minister of Burundi 1996–98.

N'DONG, Léon; Gabonese diplomatist; b. 15 Feb. 1935, Libreville; s. of the late Jean-Martin Bikègne and of Marthe Kemeboune; m. Chantal Annette Bekale 1971; four s. one d.; ed School of Law and Econ. Sciences, Rennes, France; Under-Sec.-Gen. of Ministry of Foreign Affairs, later Sec.-Gen.; Teacher, Nat. School of Admin. 1969–72; Amb. to Cen. African Repub. and Sudan 1972–73, to Morocco 1973–74, to UN Office at Geneva 1974–76, to UN 1976–80, to UK 1980–86, to FRG 1986–90 (also accred to Norway, Denmark, Finland and Sweden); Amb. du Gabon, Diplomatic Adviser to Prime Minister 1990–; High Commr, Office of Prime Minister 1997–; Commdr de l'Etoile Equatoriale, Grand Cordon of Order of the Brilliant Star (China), Commdr, Order of Devotion (Malta), Commdr Nat. Order of Dahomey, Order of Nile (Sudan), Ordre Nat. du Mérite (Gabon), Diplomatic Order of Repub. of Korea, Ordre de la Pléïade (France), Grand Officier Etoile Equatoriale, Grand Officier Ordre du Mérite, Officier Courtoisie française. *Leisure interests:* swimming, walking, music, reading, fishing, gardening. *Address:* B.P. 848, Libreville, Gábon (Home); Office of the Prime Minister, B.P. 91, Libreville, Gábon (Office). *Telephone:* (241) 747321/721976 (Office); (241) 263175/071952 (Home). *Fax:* (241) 772004 (Office).

N'DOUR, Youssou; Senegalese pop singer; b. 1959, Dakar; began career with Star Band; formed band Etoile de Dakar (later Super Etoile) 1979; has performed with Peter Gabriel, Paul Simon, Bob Dylan, Branford Marsalis; sings in English, French, Fulani, Serer and native Wolof; Goodwill Amb. to UN, UNICEF, Int. Bureau of Work; Best African Artist 1996, African Artist of the Century 1999. *Singles include:* Nelson Mandela, Sinebar, Toxic Wastes, Jaam, Birima, Seven Seconds (with Neneh Cherry). *Albums include:* Immigres 1988, St Louis 1997, Best of the 80s 1998, The Lion (Gainde) 1989, Set 1990, Eyes Open 1992, The Guide (Wommat) 1994, Lii 1996, Inedits (1984–1985) 1988, Rewmi 1999, Joko: From Village to Town 2000, Batay 2001, Le Grand Bal, Bercy 2000, Le Grand Bal 1 & 2 2001, Birth of a Star 2001, Et Ses Amis 2002, Nothing's in Vain 2002; numerous guest appearances on albums. *Leisure interest:* football. *Address:* Youssou N'Dour Head Office, 8 Route des Almadies Parcelle, BP 1310, Dakar, Senegal (Office). *Telephone:* 865-1039 (Office). *Fax:* 865-1068 (Office). *E-mail:* yncontact@yahoo.fr (Office). *Website:* www.youssou.com (Office).

NDUNGANE, Most Rev. Winston Njongonkulu, MTh, BD, DD, AFTS; South African ecclesiastic; b. 2 April 1941, Kokstad; s. of Foster Ndungane and Tingaza Ndungane; m. 1st Nosipo Ngcelwane 1972 (died 1986), 2nd Nomahlubi Vokwana 1987; one step-s. one step-d.; ed Lovedale High School, Univ. of Cape Town, Fed. Theological Seminary and King's Coll. London; Rector, St Nicholas Church, Matroosfontein, Cape Town 1980–81; Provincial Liaison Officer, Johannesburg 1982–84; Prin., St Bede's Theological Coll. Umtata 1985–86; Exec. Officer, Church of the Prov. of Southern Africa (Anglican) 1987–91; Bishop of Kimberley and Kuruman 1991–96; Archbishop of Cape Town 1996–; mem. Bd SABC, Johannesburg 1992–96; Chair. Hearings into Poverty in S. Africa; Patron Jubilee 2000 1998–; Hon. DD (Rhodes) 1997, (Protestant Episcopal Theological Seminary, Va.) 2000; Hon. D. Hum.Litt (Worcester State Coll, Mass.) 2000; Hon. DScS (Natal) 2001. *Publications:* The Commuter Population for Claremont, Cape 1973, Human Rights and the Christian Doctrine of Man 1979, A World with a Human Face: A Voice from Africa 2003. *Leisure interests:* music, walking. *Address:* Bishopscourt, 20 Bishopscourt Drive, Claremont 7708, South Africa. *Telephone:* (21) 761-2531. *Fax:* (21) 797-4193. *E-mail:* archbish@bishopscourt-cpsa.org.za (Home).

NDUWAYO, Antoine; Burundian politician; mem. Union pour le progrès national (UPRONA); Prime Minister of Burundi 1995–96.

NEAGU, Paul; British sculptor, painter and fine art lecturer; b. 22 Feb. 1938, Bucharest, Romania; s. of the late Tudor Neagu and of Rozalia Neagu; m. 1st Sibyla Oarcea 1966 (divorced 1972); m. 2nd M. Omescu 1998 (separated); ed Inst. Fine Art, Bucharest 1959–65; freelance artist 1965–; emigrated to

England 1969; Lecturer in Fine Art, Hornsey School of Art 1972–79; Visiting Lecturer and External Assessor throughout UK 1975–; Asst Prof. Concordia Univ. of Montréal 1982–83; part-time lecturer, Slade School of Art 1985–90; Founder and Co-Dir Generative Art Trust 1995–; Sargant Fellow, British School at Rome 1991–92; Tolly Cobbold Prize 1977; Westminster City Sculpture Prize (Charing Cross Station) 1987; Krasner-Pollock Foundation Award 1995, Blue Ribbon Medal, Japanese Govt 1996, Leverhulme Trust Research Award 1997. *Exhibitions include:* Bauzentrum, Hamburg 1969, Modern Art Museum, Oxford 1975, Leeds Polytechnic Gallery 1976, Serpentine Gallery, London 1976, 1987, I.C.A. London 1979, Epagoge Flowers East, London 1992, Endlessedge Hyphen, Flowers East, London 1998. *Publications and exhbns.:* Palpable Art Manifesto! 1969, Generative Art 1972, Gradually Going Tornado 1974, Generative Arts Group 1975, Hyphen 1975, Nine Catalytic Stations 1987, Triple Starhead (monument, British High Comm., Ottawa) 1987–98, Deep Space and Solid Time 1988, Unnamed 1988, Epagoge 1988–93, Tossing Fish Over Gate 1992, New Hyphen 1993, Ten right angles, ten right angles 1994, Last 1995, Reorganization of nothing 1996, Unnamed–Eschaton 1997, Century's Cross (monument, Bucharest) 1997, Endless edge–Hyphen 1998, Isotope 1998, Tao-hyphen (monument Guanxi-Guilin, China) 1999, A-cross (monument, Timisoara) 1999, A Whirlblast for Brancusi, New York 2000, A Derridean Tornado (book), London 2000. *Leisure interests:* philosophy, psychology, cycling, swimming, walking, cinema, travelling. *Address:* G.A.T. Atelier, 16–32 Conistone Way, London, N7 9DD (Office); c/o 31C Jackson Road, London N7 6ES, England. *Telephone:* (20) 7607-7858; (20) 7700-7268 (Office). *Fax:* (20) 7700-7268 (Office). *E-mail:* atelier16@btinternet.com; generativeart@lineone.net (Office).

NEAL, Sir Eric James, Kt, AC, CVO, CEng, F.I.GAS.E., F.I.E.AUST., FAIM, F.A.I.C.D., KStJ; Australian state governor, business executive and chartered engineer; b. 3 June 1924, London, UK; s. of James Neal and May Neal (née Johnson); m. Thelma Joan Bowden 1950; two s.; ed South Australian School of Mines; Dir Boral Ltd 1972–92, Chief Exec. 1973–82, Man. Dir 1982–87; Dir Oil Co. of Australia NL 1982–87, Chair. 1984–87; Dir Westpac Banking Corpn 1985–92, Chair. 1989–92; Dir Atlas Copco Australia Ltd 1987–96, Chair. 1990–96; Dir Metal Manufactures Ltd 1987–96, Chair. 1990–96; Dir Wormald Int. Ltd 1978–85, John Fairfax Ltd 1987–88, Cola-Cola Amatil Ltd 1987–96, BHP 1988–94; Gov. S. Australia 1996–2001; Chancellor The Flinders Univ. of S. Australia 2001–; mem. Gen. Motors Australia Advisory Council 1987–94; Chief Commr Council of City of Sydney 1987–88; Int. Trustee, The Duke of Edinburgh's Award Int. Foundation 1987–97; Chair. of Trustees, Sir David Martin Foundation 1991–94; Nat. Pres. Australian Inst. of Co. Dirs 1990–93; Hon. DEng (Sydney) 1989; Hon. DUniv (S. Australia), (Flinders) 2001; numerous awards and medals. *Leisure interests:* reading, walking, motor boating, sailing, naval and eng history, opera. *Address:* Office of the Chancellor, The Flinders University of South Australia,G.P.O. Box 2100, Adelaide 5001 (Office); 82/52 Brougham Place, North Adelaide 5006, South Australia (Home). *Telephone:* (8) 8201-2721 (Office); (8) 8361-7014 (Home). *Fax:* (8) 8276-2271 (Office); (8) 8267-1715 (Home).

NEAL, Patricia; American actress; b. 20 Jan. 1926, Packard, Ky; d. of William Burdette Neal and Eura Mildred Petrey; m. Roald Dahl 1953 (divorced 1983, died 1990); one s. three d. (and one d. deceased); ed Northwestern Univ., Ill.; numerous TV appearances; public lectures in America and abroad; Academy Award for film Hud 1963; Antoinette Perry Award (Tony) 1946. *Stage appearances include:* Another Part of the Forest 1946, The Children's Hour 1953, A Roomful of Roses 1954, Suddenly Last Summer 1958, The Miracle Worker 1959. Films: John loves Mary 1949, The Hasty Heart 1949, The Fountainhead 1949, The Breaking Point 1950, Three Secrets 1950, Raton Pass 1951, The Day the Earth Stood Still 1951, Diplomatic Courier 1952, Something for the Birds 1953, A Face in the Crowd 1957, Breakfast at Tiffany's 1961, Hud 1963, The Third Secret 1964, In Harms Way 1965, The Subject was Roses 1968, The Road Builder 1970, The Night Digger 1970, The Boy 1972, Happy Mother's Day Love George 1973, Baxter 1973, Widow's Nest 1976, The Passage 1978, All Quiet on the Western Front 1979, Ghost Story 1981, An Unremarkable Life 1989. *Publication:* As I Am (autobiog.) 1988. *Leisure interests:* needlepoint, gardening, cooking. *Address:* 45 East End Avenue, New York, NY 10028, USA. *Telephone:* (212) 772-1268.

NEAME, Ronald, CBE; British film director; b. 23 April 1911, London; s. of Elwin Neame and Ivy Close; m. 1st Beryl Heanly 1933; one s.; m. 2nd Dona Friedberg 1994; messenger and tea boy, British Int. Film Studios 1925, became Dir of Photography 1932; with Sir David Lean and Anthony Havelock-Allen, formed Cineguild and produced Great Expectations 1946, Oliver Twist 1947 and The Passionate Friends 1948; film dir 1950–; teacher of film direction, Univ. of Calif., LA 1992–. *Films photographed include:* Drake of England 1934, The Gaunt Stranger 1937, Four Just Men, Major Barbara 1940, One of Our Aircraft is Missing 1942, In Which We Serve 1942, This Happy Breed 1943, Blithe Spirit 1945. *Films directed include:* Take My Life 1947, The Golden Salamander 1950, The Card 1950, The Million Pound Note 1953, The Man Who Never Was 1956, Windom's Way 1958, The Horse's Mouth 1959, Tunes of Glory 1960, I Could Go On Singing 1962, The Chalk Garden 1964, Mr. Moses 1965, A Man Could Get Killed 1966, Gambit 1966, The Prime of Miss Jean Brodie 1968, Scrooge 1970, The Poseidon Adventure 1972, The Odessa File 1974, Meteor 1978, Hopscotch 1979, First Monday in October 1980, Foreign Body 1985, The Magic Balloon 1989. *Leisure interests:*

painting, photography, stereo and hi-fi equipment. *Address:* 2317 Kimridge Road, Beverly Hills, CA 90210, USA. *Fax:* (310) 271-3044. *E-mail:* rnfilm@aol.com (Home).

NÉAOUTIYNE, Paul; New Caledonian politician; b. 1952, St Michel Village; ed Univ. of Lyon; teacher of econs at secondary coll. in Nouméa until 1980; jailed for participation in pro-independence demonstration 1980; reinstated as teacher 1983; Aide to Jean-Marie Tjibaou (Pres. Northern Regional Council) 1985; Leader, Party of Kanak Liberation (Palika); Mayor of Poindimie; mem. Northern Provincial Govt; currently Leader Parti de Libération Kanak (PALIKA) (merged with Kanak Socialist Nat. Liberation Front 1984). *Address:* Kanak Socialist National Liberation Front, Nouméa, New Caledonia. *Telephone:* 272599.

NEARY, J. Peter, DPhil; Irish economist; b. 11 Feb. 1950, Drogheda; s. of Peter Neary and Anne Loughran; m. 1st Frances Ruane 1972 (divorced); two s.; m. 2nd Mairéad Hanrahan 1997; two d.; ed Clongowes Wood Coll., Co. Kildare, Univ. Coll. Dublin, Oxford Univ.; Jr Lecturer, Trinity Coll. Dublin 1972–74, lecturer 1978–80; Prof. of Political Economy, Univ. Coll. Dublin 1980–; Heyworth Research Fellow, Nuffield Coll. Oxford 1976–78; Visiting Prof., Princeton Univ. 1980, Univ. of Calif. at Berkeley 1982, Queen's Univ., Ont. 1986–88, Univ. of Ulster at Jordanstown 1992–93; Research Assoc. Centre for Econ. Performance, LSE 1993–; Dir de Recherche, Ecole Polytechnique, Paris 1999–2000; Fellow Centre for Econ. Policy Research, London 1983–; mem. Council Royal Econ. Soc. 1984–89, European Econ. Asscn 1985–92, Econometric Soc. 1994–99; Co-Ed. Journal of Int. Econs 1980–83; Assoc. Ed. Econ. Journal 1981–85, Econometrica 1984–87, Review of Econ. Studies 1984–93, Economica 1996–2000; Ed. European Econ. Review 1986–90; Fellow Econometric Soc. 1987–; mem. Academia Europaea 1989–, Royal Irish Acad. 1997–; Pres. Irish Econ. Asscn 1990–92, Int. Trade and Finance Soc. 1999–2000, European Econ. Asscn 2002. *Publications:* three edited books and over 80 publs, mostly on int. econs. *Leisure interests:* family, travel, reading, music. *Address:* Department of Economics, University College Dublin, Belfield, Dublin 4 (Office); 56 St. Alban's Park, Sandymount, Dublin 4, Ireland (Home). *Telephone:* (1) 7168334 (Office); (1) 2837198 (Home). *Fax:* (1) 2830068 (Office). *E-mail:* peter.neary@ucd.ie (Office). *Website:* www.ucd.ie/~economic/staff/pneary/neary.htm (Office).

NEARY, Martin Gerard James, LVO, MA, FRCO; British conductor and organist; b. 28 March 1940; s. of the late Leonard W. Neary and of Jeanne M. Thébault; m. Penelope J. Warren 1967; one s. two d.; ed City of London School and Gonville & Caius Coll. Cambridge; Asst Organist, St Margaret's Westminster 1963–65, Organist and Master of Music 1965–71; Prof. of Organ, Trinity Coll. London 1963–72; Organist and Master of Music, Winchester Cathedral 1972–87; Organist and Master of Choristers, Westminster Abbey 1988–98; has led Westminster Abbey Choir on tours to France, Germany, Switzerland, Hungary, USA, Russia, Ukraine; Founder and Conductor Martin Neary Singers 1972–; Chair. Church Services Cttee, Musicians Benevolent Fund 1993–, Herbert Howells Soc. 1993–; Conductor Waynflete Singers 1972–87; Pres. Cathedral Organists Asscn 1985–88; Pres. Royal Coll. of Organists 1988–90, 1996–98; Guest Conductor Australian Youth Choir 1999–; Visiting Artistic Dir Paulist Boy Choristers of Calif. 1999–2000; many organ recitals and broadcasts in UK, Europe, USA, Canada, the Far East and Australia; many choral premières; guest conductor English Chamber Orchestra, London Symphony Orchestra; numerous recordings; Hon. RAM; Hon. F.T.C.L.; Hon. Fellow Royal School of Church Music. *Publications:* editions of early organ music, contribs to organ journals. *Leisure interest:* watching cricket. *Address:* 71 Clancarty Road, Fulham, London, SW6 3BB, England. *Telephone:* (20) 7736-5268. *Fax:* (20) 7610-6995.

NEČAS, Petr, DrScNat; Czech politician; b. 11 Nov. 1964, Uherské Hradiště; m. Radka Nečas; two s. two d.; ed Univ. Brno; research engineer Tesla Rožnov 1988–92; mem. Civic Democratic Party 1991–, Jt Vice-Chair. 1999–; MP 1992–; mem. Parl. Cttee for Foreign Affairs 1992–96; Deputy Minister of Defence 1995–96; Chair. Parl. Cttee for Defence and Security 1996–. *Leisure interest:* history. *Address:* Parliament Buildings, Sněmovní 4, Prague 1, 118 26, Czech Republic (Office). *Telephone:* (2) 57171111 (Office). *Fax:* (2) 57534421 (Office). *E-mail:* petr.necas@synergy-vs.cz (Office). *Website:* www.petr-necas.cz (Office); www.psp.cz.

NECHAEV, Andrey Alekseevich, DEcon; Russian politician and economist; b. 2 Feb. 1953, Moscow; s. of Aleksey Nechaev and Marseliesa Nechaev; m. 1st Elena Belyanova 1975; one d.; m. 2nd Margarita Kitova 1986; m. 3rd Svetlana Sergeenko; ed Moscow State Univ.; Sr Researcher Cen. USSR Acad. of Sciences 1979–90, Deputy Dir Inst. of Econ. Policy Acad. of Nat. Sciences 1990–91; First Deputy Minister of Econ. and Finance of Russia 1991–92; Minister of Econ. 1992–93; Pres. Russian Financial Corpn 1993–, Moscow Finance Club 1994–; mem. Political Consultative Council under Pres. of Russia 1996–2000, Scientific Council under Security Council of Russia 1997–; Prof. Russian Acad. of Econs; Chair. Bd of Dirs United Nat. Insurance Co., First Russian Banking Holding Co. Posinbank; Co-Chair. Business Roundtable of Russia; Vice-Pres. Moscow Actors Charity Fund; mem. Acad. of Nat. Econ., Int. Acad. of Informatization Bd of Dirs East–West Inst., Nat. Econ. Council, Advisory Bd Charity Fund Sanctuaries of Russia; State Medal 1997, Public Recognition Prize 2001. *Radio:* econ. analyst on Russian radio. *Television:* author and presenter of TV programme Money Question. *Publications:* 200 publs on econs and econ. policy. *Leisure interests:* theatre, publicity, history, tennis, gardening. *Address:* Russian Financial Corporation, Georgievsky per. 1, 103009 Moscow, Russia. *Telephone:* (095) 292-74-82 (Office). *Fax:* (095) 292-35-62 (Office). *E-mail:* rfc@rfk.girmet.ru (Office); nechaev@rfk .girmet.ru (Home). *Website:* rfc.girmet.ru (Office); russianpartner.com (Office).

NEDERKOORN, Erik Jan; Netherlands business executive; b. 22 Aug. 1943, Haarlem; m.; two s. one d.; Vice-Pres. Fokker (aircraft mfrs) 1988–91, Chair. Bd of Man. and CEO 1991–94; mem. Bd Deutsche Telekom 1996–. *Address:* c/o Deutsche Telekom, PO Box 2000, 53105 Bonn, Germany.

NEDERLANDER, James Morton; American impresario; b. 31 March 1922, Detroit, Mich.; s. of David T. Nederlander and Sarah L. Applebaum; m. Charlene Saunders 1969; one s. two d.; ed Pontiac Sr High School and Detroit Inst. of Tech.; former usher, box-office asst and press agent for father's Schubert-Lafayette Theatre; served in USAF during World War II; Man. Lyceum Theatre, Minneapolis for eight years; returned to Detroit to assist in devt of Nederlander theatre chain in Detroit and Chicago in 1950s; chain expanded to Broadway with purchase of Palace Theatre 1965; now Chair. Bd Nederlander Org. 1966–, owners and operators of largest chain of theatres in world including 11 Broadway theatres and Adelphi and Aldwych theatres, London and producers and backers of maj. Broadway musicals such as Annie, La Cage aux Folles and Will Roger Follies; est. Nederlander TV and Film Production (creating films, mini-series, etc. for TV) in 1980s. *Address:* Nederlander Organization Inc., 1450 Broadway, Floor 6, New York, NY 10018, USA.

NEEDHAM, James J.; American business consultant (retd); b. 18 Aug. 1926, Woodhaven, NY; s. of the late James Joseph Needham and Amelia Pasta Needham; m. 1st Dolores A. Habick 1950 (died 1993); three s. two d.; m. 2nd Patricia H. Campo 1995; ed Cornell and St John's (Brooklyn) Univs.; with Price Waterhouse & Co., then Partner, Raymond T. Hyer & Co.; joined A. M. Pullen & Co. 1957, subsequently partner, in charge of New York office and mem. Exec. Cttee; Commr Securities and Exchange Comm. 1969–72; Chair. New York Stock Exchange 1972–76; Vice-Pres. Int. Fed. of Stock Exchanges, Pres. 1976–; fmrly Distinguished Prof., Grad. Dir, Coll. of Business Admin., St John's Univ.; Amb. and Commr-Gen. of U.S. Int. Exposition, Japan 1985; Hon. LLD (St John's Univ.) 1972. *Leisure interests:* golf, fishing. *Address:* 92 Coopers Farm Road, Unit 1, Southampton, NY 11968, USA. *Telephone:* (516) 204-0859 (Home).

NEEDLEMAN, Jacob, PhD; American professor of philosophy; b. 6 Oct. 1934, Philadelphia; s. of Benjamin Needleman and Ida Needleman; m. 1st Carla Satzman 1959 (divorced 1989); one s. one d.; m. 2nd Gail Anderson 1990; ed Research Assoc., Rockefeller Inst., New York 1960–61, Harvard Coll., Yale Univ.; Assoc. Prof. of Philosophy, San Francisco State Univ. 1962–66, Prof. 1967–; Dir, Center for the Study of New Religions, Graduate Theological Union, Berkeley, Calif. 1977–83; Vice-Pres. Audio Literature Co. 1987–; Rockefeller Humanities Fellow, Fulbright Scholar. *Publications:* The New Religions 1970, A Sense of the Cosmos 1975, Lost Christianity 1980, The Heart of Philosophy 1982, The Way of the Physician 1985, Sorcerers 1986, Money and the Meaning of Life 1991, A Little Book on Love 1996, Time and the Soul 1998, The American Soul 2002. *Address:* San Francisco State University, Department of Philosophy, 1600 Holloway Avenue, San Francisco, CA 94132, USA. *Telephone:* (415) 338-1596 (Office). *Website:* www .jacobneedleman.com (Office).

NEEMAN, Yaakov, JSD; Israeli politician and lawyer; b. 1939, Tel Aviv; m.; six s.; ed Hebrew Univ. of Jerusalem, New York Univ. Law School; mem. Israeli Bar Asscn 1966–; Sr Partner Herzog Fox & Neeman 1972– (with two-year interruption); Visiting Prof. of Law Univ. of Calif. at LA, USA 1976, Tel Aviv Univ. 1977–79, New York Univ. 1989–90, Hebrew Univ. of Jerusalem 1990, 1994; Dir-Gen. Ministry of Finance 1979–81; Chair. Cttee of Inquiry into Inter-Relation between Tax Laws and Foreign Currency Restrictions 1977–78, Public Cttee on Allocation of Distributions by Ministry of Interior 1991–92; mem. Investigation Cttee on Temple Mount Affair 1991; fmr mem. several other public cttees.; mem. Bd of Govs. Bank of Israel 1977–79, 1992–; mem. Cen. Cttee of World Bank; Minister of Justice 1996, of Finance 1997. *Publications:* seven books and over 30 articles on taxation, Corpn and securities law. *Address:* c/o Ministry of Finance, P.O. Box 13191, 1 Rehov Kaplan, Kiryat Ben-Gurion, Jerusalem 91008, Israel. *Telephone:* 5317111. *Fax:* 5637891.

NE'EMAN, Yuval, DipIng, DEM, DIC, PhD; Israeli professor of physics; b. 14 May 1925, Tel-Aviv; s. of Gedalia Ne'eman and Zipora Ne'eman; m. Dvora Rubinstein 1951; one d. one s.; ed Herzliya High School, Tel-Aviv, Israel Inst. of Tech., Haifa and London Univ.; Hagana volunteer, taking part in activities against British rule in Palestine 1946–47; Hydrodynamical Design Engineer 1946–47; Capt., Israeli Defence Forces (Infantry) 1948, Maj. 1949, Lt-Col 1950; Head of Defence Planning 1952–55; Deputy Dir Defence Intelligence Div. 1955–57; Defence Attaché, London 1958–60; resigned from Israeli Defence Forces active service May 1960; took part in six day war June 1967; Scientific Dir Israel Atomic Energy Establishment 1961–63; Research Assoc., Calif. Inst. of Tech., Pasadena 1963–64, Visiting Prof. of Theoretical Physics 1964–65; Prof. of Physics and Head of Dept, Tel-Aviv Univ. 1965–73; Prof. of Physics and Dir Centre for Particle Theory, Univ. of Texas (Austin) 1968–; Pollak Prof. of Theoretical Physics, Tel-Aviv Univ. 1968–76, Wolfson Prof. Extraordinary in Theoretical Physics 1977–97; Vice-Pres. Tel-Aviv Univ. 1965–66, Pres. 1971–75; Dir Sackler Inst. of Advanced Studies, Tel-Aviv Univ. 1979–97; Adviser to Head of Mil. Intelligence 1973–74; Special Adviser

to Israel Defence Ministry 1975–76; mem. Knesset (Parl.) 1981–90; Minister of Science and Devt 1982–84, of Science, Devt and Energy 1990–92; Chair. Steering Cttee Mediterranean–Dead Sea Conduit 1977–83; Chair. Israel Space Agency 1983–; mem. Israel Atomic Energy Cttee 1966–84, Israel Nat. Acad. of Sciences 1966–; co-discoverer of Unitary Symmetry Theory; conceived basic field explaining compositeness of nuclear particles (quarks in their final format); Foreign Hon. mem. American Acad. Arts and Sciences; Hon. Life mem. New York Acad. of Sciences 1973–; Foreign Assoc. Nat. Acad. of Sciences; Hon. Pres. Int. Soc. for Interdisciplinary Study of Symmetry, Budapest 1989; Hon. DSc (Israel Inst. of Tech.) 1966, (Yeshiva Univ., New York) 1972; Weizmann Prize for Sciences 1966, Rothschild Prize 1968, Israel Prize for Sciences 1969, Albert Einstein Medal and Prize for Physics 1970, Wigner Medal 1982, Birla Award 1997. *Publications:* The Eightfold Way (with M. Gell-Mann) 1964, Algebraic Theory of Particle Physics 1967, One Way to Unitary Symmetry, The Past Decade in Particle Theory (with E. C. G. Sudarshan) 1973, Symétries, Jauges et Variétés de Groupes 1979, Group Theoretical Methods in Physics (with L. P. Horwitz) 1980, To Fulfil a Vision 1981, Twentieth Century Physics (Hebrew) 1981, The Particle Hunters (in Hebrew, with Y. Kirsch) 1983, Policy from a Sober Viewpoint 1984, Dynamical Groups (with A. Barut and A. Bohm) 1989; about 350 articles on physics, astrophysics and philosophy of science and about 50 on defence matters. *Leisure interests:* music, history, linguistics. *Address:* School of Physics and Astronomy, Tel Aviv University, Ramat Aviv, Tel Aviv 69978, Israel. *Telephone:* 3-6408560. *Fax:* 3-6424264. *E-mail:* matildae@tauex.tau.ac.il (Office).

NEESON, Liam, OBE; British actor; b. 7 June 1952, Ballymena, Northern Ireland; m. Natasha Richardson 1994; two s.; ed St Mary's Teachers' Coll., London, Queen's Univ., Belfast; worked as forklift operator, then as architect's asst; acting debut with Lyric Players' Theatre, Belfast, in The Risen 1976. *Theatre includes:* Of Mice and Men (Abbey Theatre Co., Dublin), The Informer (Dublin Theatre Festival), Translations (Nat. Theatre, London), The Plough and the Stars (Royal Exchange, Manchester), The Judas Kiss. *Films include:* Excalibur, Krull, The Bounty, The Innocent, Lamb, The Mission, Duet for One, A Prayer for the Dying, Suspect, Satisfaction, High Spirits, The Dead Pool, The Good Mother, Darkman, The Big Man, Under Suspicion, Husbands and Wives, Leap of Faith, Ethan Frome, Ruby Cairo, Schindler's List, Rob Roy, Nell, Before and After, Michael Collins (Best Actor Evening Standard Award 1997), Les Misérables (1998), The Haunting, Star Wars: Episode 1 – The Phantom Menace, Gun Shy 1999, Gangs of New York 2000, K19: The Widowmaker 2002, Love Actually 2003. *Television includes:* Arthur the King, Ellis Island, If Tomorrow Comes, A Woman of Substance, Hold the Dream, Kiss Me Goodnight, Next of Kin, Sweet As You Are, The Great War. *Address:* c/o Ed Limato, ICM, 8942 Wilshire Boulevard, Beverly Hills, CA 90211, USA.

NEEWOOR, Anund Priyay, BA; Mauritian diplomatist; b. 26 June 1940; m. Chandranee Neewoor 1971; two s. one d.; ed Delhi Univ., Makerere Univ., Uganda; Teacher, Prin. Northern Coll. (secondary school), Mauritius 1964–67; joined Ministry of External Affairs, Tourism and Emigration (in charge of UN affairs and West Asia affairs) 1970; Admin. Asst, Civil Service 1972; Second Sec., High Comm., London 1973–75; First Sec., High Comm., New Delhi 1975–81; Minister-Counsellor, Embassy, Washington, DC 1982; Amb. to Pakistan 1983, to USA 1993–96; High. Commr in India 1983–93; Amb. in Ministry of External Affairs in charge of Multilateral Econ. Affairs 1996; Sec. for Foreign Affairs 1996–99; apptd. Amb. and Perm. Rep. to UN 1999; rep. to numerous UN and int. confs. 1972–. *Leisure interests:* reading, sports. *Address:* c/o Ministry of Foreign Affairs and Regional Co-operation, New Government Centre, Level 5, Port Louis, Mauritius.

NEFEDOV, Oleg Matveyevich, DSc; Russian chemist; b. 25 Nov. 1931, Dmitrov, Moscow region; s. of Matvey Kondrat'evich Nefedov and Mariya Adolfovna Teodorovich; m. Galina Gimelfarb 1954; one s. one d.; ed D.I. Mendeleyev Inst. of Chem. and Tech.; worked as Jr then Sr researcher, Head Lab. Zelinsky Inst. of Organic Chem., USSR (now Russian) Acad. of Sciences 1957–; corresp. mem. USSR (now Russian) Acad. of Sciences 1979–87, mem. 1987–, Academic Sec. Div. of Gen. and Applied Chem. 1988–91, Vice-Pres. 1988–97; USSR People's Deputy 1989–91; USSR State Prize 1983, 1990, ND Zelinsky Prize 1987, Prize of USSR and Hungarian Acads. 1988, N Semyonov Prize 1991, A. Karpinsky Prize 1993. *Publications:* The Structure of Cyclopropane Derivatives 1986, Chemistry of Carbenes and Small-sized Cyclic Compounds (ed.) 1989, Carbenes Chemistry 1990; 627 articles and 201 patents. *Leisure interests:* sport, gathering mushrooms. *Address:* Zelinsky Institute of Organic Chemistry, GSP-1, Leninsky prospekt 47, Moscow, Russia. *Telephone:* (095) 237-45-32. *Fax:* (095) 938 1837.

NEGAHBAN, Ezatollah, PhD; Iranian archaeologist; b. 1 March 1926; s. of Abdol Amir Negahban and Roghieh Dideban; m. Miriam Lois Miller 1955; five s.; ed Tehran and Chicago Univs.; Assoc. Prof. Univ. of Tehran 1956–62, Prof. 1962, Founder and Dir Univ. Inst. of Archaeology 1957, Head, Dept Archaeology 1968–75, Dean Faculty of Letters and Humanities 1975–78; Prof. Univ. Chicago 1964; Tech. Dir Iranian Archaeological Service 1960–65; Tech. Adviser to Ministry of Culture 1965–79; Visiting Curator Univ. Museum, Visiting Prof., Univ. of Pa 1980–; Dir Museum Iran Bastan 1966–68, Iranian Archaeological Asscn 1957–65; Sec.-Gen. Int. Congress, Iranian Art and Archaeology, Dir 5th Congress; excavated at Mehranabad 1961, Marlik 1961–62, Haft Tepe 1966; Dir Gazvin Plain Expedition (Zaghe, Qabrestan and Sagzabad) 1970; archaeological survey of NE Iran 1965, Mazandaran Highlands 1975; mem. German Archaeological Inst., Exec. Cttee and Perm.

Council, Congress of Pre- and Proto-History; Highest Decoration of Cultural Heritage, Org. for Cultural Heritage, Iran 1999. *Publications:* The Buff Ware Sequence in Khuzistan 1954, Preliminary Report on the Marlik Excavation 1961–1962 1964, Archaeology of Iran 1973, Metal Vessels from Marlik 1983, Excavations at Haft Tepe 1991 (Book of the Year, Ministry of Culture of Iran 1996), Final Report of Marlik Excavation 1994, Weapons from Marlik 1995, Final Report of Marlik Excavation 1996, Susa: The Earliest Urban Centre (in Farsi) 1996, A Look at 50 Years of Iranian Archaeology (in Farasi) 1997 and numerous excavation reports and articles in journals. *Leisure interest:* Persian calligraphy. *Address:* 5226 Rexford Road, Philadelphia, PA 19131, USA. *Telephone:* (215) 898-4057 (Office); (215) 877-1821 (Home).

NEGISHI, Takashi, PhD; Japanese economist and professor; b. 2 April 1933, Tokyo; s. of Setsuko Negishi and Suteta Negishi; m. Aiko Mori 1964; one d.; ed Univ. of Tokyo; Research Asst, then Research Assoc., Stanford Univ., Calif. 1958–60; Research Asst, Univ. of Tokyo 1963–65, Assoc. Prof. 1965–76, Prof. 1976–94, Dean Faculty of Econs 1990–92; Prof., Aoyama Gakuin Univ. 1994–2001; Fellow Econometric Soc. 1966–, Vice-Pres. 1992–93, Pres. 1994; Pres. Japan Asscn of Econs and Econometrics 1985; Pres. The Soc. for the History of Econ. Thought, Japan 1997–99; mem. Exec. Cttee Int. Econ. Asscn 1989–92, Science Council of Japan 1985–88, Japan Acad. 1998–; Foreign Hon. mem. American Econ. Asscn 1989; Japan Acad. Prize 1993. *Television:* Introduction to History of Economic Thought, Univ. of the Air, Japan 2001. *Publications:* General Equilibrium Theory and International Trade 1972, Microeconomic Foundations of Keynesian Macro Economics 1979, Economic Theories of a Non-Walrasian Tradition 1985, History of Economic Theory 1989, The Collected Essays of Takashi Negishi 1994, 2000. *Address:* 2-10-5-301, Motoazabu, Minato-ku, Tokyo 106-0046, Japan. *Telephone:* 3440-0630. *E-mail:* tnegishi@bk9,so-net.ne.jp.

NEGMATULLAEV, Sabit, D.TECH.SC.; Tajikistan physicist; b. 16 Sept. 1937, Ura-Tube; ed Tajik Polytech. Inst.; mem. CPSU 1966–91; Jr researcher Inst. of Seismology, Tajik Acad. of Sciences, Scientific Sec. 1964–65, Vice-Dir 1965–69, Dir 1969–; mem. Tajik Acad. of Sciences 1987, Pres. 1988–95; Chair. Scientific-Publishing Council of Acad. of Sciences; mem. Cen. Cttee CPSU 1990–91. *Address:* Academy of Sciences of Tajikistan, Rudaki Prospect 33, 734029 Dushanbe, Tajikistan. *Telephone:* (3772) 22-50-83.

NEGRI, Barjas; Brazilian politician; ed Methodist Univ. of Piracicaba; Prof. of Econs Univ. of Piracicaba 1974–95; researcher and lecturer UNIVCAMP Univ. 1986–; Sec. of Educ., São Paulo State Parl. 1979–82, Sec. of Planning 1993–94; Sec. Dept of Educ., Fed. Govt 1995–96; Sec. Dept of Health 1997–2001, Minister for Health 2002–. *Address:* Ministry of Health, Esplanada dos Ministérios, Bloco G, 5° Andar, 70048 Brasília DF, Brazil (Office). *Telephone:* (61) 223-3169 (Office). *Fax:* (61) 322-6817 (Office). *Website:* www.saude.gov.br (Office).

NEGRI SEMBILAN, Yang di-Pertuan Besar, Tuanku Ja'afar ibni Al-Marhum Tuanku Adbul Rahman; Malaysian Ruler; b. 19 July 1922; m. Tuanku Najihar binti Tuanku Besar Burhanuddin 1943; three s. three d.; ed Malay School Sri Menanti, Malay Coll. and Nottingham Univ.; entered Malay Admin. Service 1944; Asst Dist Officer, Rembau 1946–47, Parti 1953–55; Chargé d'affaires, Washington, DC 1947; First Perm. Sec., Malayan Perm. Mission to the UN 1957–58; First Sec., Trade Counsellor, rising to Deputy High Commr, London 1962–63; Amb. to United Arab Repub. 1962; High Commr concurrently in Nigeria and Ghana 1965–66; Timbalan Yang di-Pertuan Agong (Deputy Supreme Head of State) 1979–84, 1989–94, Yang di-Pertuan Agong (Supreme Head of State) 1994–99. *Leisure interests:* well-planned housing schemes, sports.

NEGRITOIU, Misu, MS, PhD; Romanian politician, economist and banker; b. 26 May 1950, Dăbuleni, Dolj Co.; s. of Marin Negritoiu and Floarea Negritoiu; m. Paulina Urzica 1977; one s. one d.; ed Bucharest Acad. of Econ. Studies, Law School, Bucharest Univ., HDS Hertfordshire Univ.; foreign trade economist and then foreign trade co. dir 1973–90; Minister-Counsellor, Embassy, Washington; Pres. Romanian Devt Agency 1990–92; Deputy Prime Minister, Chair. Council for Strategy and Econ. Reform Co-ordination 1993; Chief Econ. Adviser to Pres. of Romania 1994–96; mem. Parl. 1996–; Deputy Gen. Man., Dir of Corp. Finance, ING Barings Romania 1997–; Prof. Acad. of Econ. Studies, School of Political Studies and Public Admin., Bucharest; Chair. Bd of Dirs Grad. School of Man., MBA Canadian Programme; mem. Romanian Econ. Soc. (SOREC), Romanian Soc. for Club of Rome, Romanian Asscn for Energy Policy (APER), American Asscn for Arbitration, Centre for European Policy Studies, Econ. Policy Forum, Faculty for International Economics and Business, Business Advisory Council – South-East European Co-operation Initiative/Stability Pact. *Publications:* Jumping Ahead–Economic Development and FDI 1996, International Finance (textbook) 1994, Management in International Trade 1997; numerous studies and articles on int. and domestic economic issues, presentations to int. and domestic conferences and seminars. *Address:* ING Building, 11–13 Kiseleff Boulevard, Bucharest 1 (Office); Str. Mexic 2, ap. 16, sector 1, Bucharest, Romania (Home). *Telephone:* (21) 2222097 (Office); (21) 2229385. *Website:* www.ingbank.com (Office).

NEGROPONTE, John Dimitri, BA; American diplomatist; b. 21 July 1939, UK; s. of Dimitri J. Negroponte and Catherine C. Negroponte; m. Diana Mary Villiers 1976; two s. three d.; ed Yale Univ.; entered Foreign Service 1960, Amb. to Honduras 1981–85; Asst Sec. of State 1985–87; Deputy Asst to Pres. for Nat. Security Affairs 1987–89; Amb. to Mexico 1989–93, to the Philippines 1993–95; Special Co-ordinator for post-1999 U.S. Presence in Panama 1996–97; Exec. Vice-Pres. Global Markets McGrawHill 1997–; Perm. Rep. to UN 2001–; Chair. The French-American Foundation 1998–. *Leisure interests:* swimming, skiing, reading, history. *Address:* Permanent Mission of the U.S.A. to the United Nations, 799 United Nations Plaza, New York, NY 10017; McGraw-Hill Companies, 49th Floor, 1221 Avenue of the Americas, New York, NY 10020 (Office); 4936 Lowell Street, NW, Washington, DC 20016, USA (Home). *Telephone:* (212) 415-4000. *Fax:* (212) 415-4443. *E-mail:* john_negroponte@mcgraw-hill.com (Office); usa@un.int (Office); jdneg@erols.com (Home). *Website:* www.un.int/usa (Office).

NEHER, Erwin; German research scientist; b. 20 March 1944, Landsberg; s. of Franz Xaver Neher and Elisabeth Neher; m. Dr. Eva-Maria Neher 1978; three s. two d.; ed Tech. Univ. Munich, Univ. of Wisconsin, Madison, USA; Research Assoc., Max-Planck-Institut für Psychiatrie, Munich 1970–72, Max-Planck-Institut für biophysikalische Chemie, Göttingen 1972–75, 1976–83, Research Dir 1983–; Research Assoc., Yale Univ., New Haven, Conn., USA 1975–76; Fairchild Scholar, Calif. Inst. of Tech. 1988–89; shared Nobel Prize for Medicine 1991; several nat. and int. scientific awards; Bundesverdienstkreuz mit Stern und Schulterband 1998. *Publications:* Elektronische Messtechnik in der Physiologie 1974, Single Channel Recording (Ed.) 1983. *Address:* Max-Planck-Institut für biophysikelische Chemie, Am Fassberg 11, 37077 Göttingen (Office); Domäne 11, 37120 Bovenden, Germany. *Telephone:* (551) 2011630 (Office); (5594) 93135. *Fax:* (551) 2011688 (Office). *E-mail:* eneher@gwdg.de (Office). *Website:* www.mpibpc.gwdg.de (Office).

NEIL, Andrew Ferguson, MA, FRSA; British editor, writer, broadcaster and publisher; b. 21 May 1949, Scotland; s. of James Neil and Mary Ferguson; ed Paisley Grammar School, Univ. of Glasgow; with Conservative Party Research Dept 1971–73; with The Economist 1973–83, Ulster Political then Industrial Corresp. 1973–79, American Corresp. 1979–82, UK Ed. 1982–83; Ed. The Sunday Times 1983–94; Exec. Ed. Fox TV News, USA 1994; Exec. Chair. Sky TV 1988–90; Publr The Business, The Scotsman, Scotland on Sunday, Edinburgh Evening News 1996–; Chair. Business Europe.com. 1999–; regular anchorman and TV commentator UK and USA; anchorman The Daily Politics (BBC2) and This Week (BBC1), Contrib. Ed. Vanity Fair, New York 1994–; writer, speaker and broadcaster 1994–; Lord Rector Univ. of St Andrews 1999–2002; Hon. DLit (Napier Univ.) 1998; Hon. DUniv (Paisley) 2001; Hon. Dr of Laws. *Publications:* The Cable Revolution 1982, Britain's Free Press: Does It Have One? 1989, Full Disclosure 1996, British Excellence 1999, 2000, 2001. *Leisure interests:* dining out in New York, London, Aspen and Côte d'Azur, skiing. *Address:* Glenburn Enterprises, P.O. Box 584, London, SW7 3QY, England. *Telephone:* (20) 7240-9968. *E-mail:* afneil@aol.com (Office).

NEILAND, Brendan Robert, MA, RA; British artist and professor of painting; b. 23 Oct. 1941, Lichfield; s. of Arthur Neiland and Joan Whiley; m. Hilary Salter 1970; two d.; ed St Philip's Grammar School, Birmingham, St Augustine's Seminary, Ireland, Birmingham School of Art and Royal Coll. of Art; painter and printmaker; gallery artist, Angela Flowers Gallery 1970–78, Fischer Fine Art 1978–92, Redfern Gallery 1992–; one-man shows and group shows throughout Europe, Middle East, America and Australia; Lecturer in Fine Art, Brighton Univ. 1983–, Prof. of Painting 1996–98; Keeper of the Royal Acad. 1998–; Visiting Prof. of Fine Art, Loughborough Univ. 1999; Daler Rowney Award, Royal Acad. Summer Exhbn 1989. *Publication:* Upon Reflection 1997. *Leisure interests:* cricket, golf, fine wines. *Address:* 2 Granard Road, London, SW12 8UL, England (Home); Crepe, La Grévé sur Mignon, 17170 Courcon, France. *Telephone:* (20) 8673-4597 (Home); (5) 46-01-62-97 (France).

NEILD, Robert Ralph; British economist; b. 10 Sept. 1924, Peterborough; s. of Ralph Neild and Josephine Neild; m. 1st Nora Clemens Sayre (dissolved 1961); 2nd Elizabeth W. Griffiths 1962 (divorced 1986); one s. four d.; ed Charterhouse and Trinity Coll. Cambridge; RAF 1943–44, Operational Research, RAF, 1944–45; Secr., UN Econ. Comm. for Europe, Geneva 1947–51; Econ. Section, Cabinet Office (later Treasury) 1951–56; Lecturer in Econs, Fellow and Steward of Trinity Coll. Cambridge 1956–58; Nat. Inst. of Econ. and Social Research 1958–64; Econ. Adviser to Treasury 1964–67; mem. Fulton Cttee on the Civil Service 1966–68; Dir Stockholm Int. Peace Research Inst. 1967–71, mem. Governing Bd 1972–82; Prof. of Econs, Cambridge Univ. 1971–84, Emer. 1984–; mem. Governing Body Queen Elizabeth Coll. Oxford 1978–87; Fellow, Trinity Coll. 1971–, Acorn Investment Trust 1988. *Publications:* Pricing and Employment in the Trade Cycle 1964, The Measurement and Reform of Budgetary Policy (with T. S. Ward) 1978, How to Make up your Mind about the Bomb 1981, An Essay on Strategy 1990, The Foundations of Defensive Defence (ed. with A. Boserup) 1990, The English, the French and the Oyster 1995, Public Corruption: The Dark Side of Social Evolution 2002. *Leisure interests:* painting, oysters. *Address:* Trinity College, Cambridge, CB2 1TQ, England. *Telephone:* (1223) 338400.

NEILL, Rt. Hon. Sir Brian (Thomas) Neill, Kt, PC, MA; British judge; b. 2 Aug. 1923; s. of Sir Thomas Neill and Lady (Annie Strachan) Neill (née Bishop); m. Sally Margaret Backus 1956; three s.; ed Highgate School, Corpus Christi Coll. Oxford; served Rifle Brigade 1942–46; called to Bar, Inner Temple 1949, Bencher 1976; QC 1968; a Recorder of the Crown Court 1972–78; a Judge of the High Court, Queen's Bench Div. 1978–84; a Lord Justice of Appeal 1985–96; Justice of Court of Appeal, Gibraltar 1997–, Pres. 1998–; mem. Departmental Cttee to examine operation of Section 2 of Official Secrets Act 1971; Chair. Advisory Cttee on Rhodesia Travel Restrictions

1973–78; mem. Court of Assistants 1972–, Master 1980–81; mem. Worshipful Co. of Turners. *Publication:* Defamation (with Colin Duncan) 1978. *Address:* 20 Essex Street, London, W.C.2, England.

NEILL, Sam, OBE; New Zealand actor; b. 14 Sept. 1947, Northern Ireland; m. Noriko Watanabe; one d.; one s. by Lisa Harrow; ed Univ. of Canterbury; toured for one year with Players Drama Quintet; appeared with Amamus Theatre in roles including Macbeth and Pentheus in The Bacchae; joined NZ Nat. Film Unit playing leading part in three films 1974–78; moved to Australia 1978, to England 1980. *Films:* Sleeping Dogs 1977, The Journalist, My Brilliant Career, Just Out of Reach, Attack Force Z, The Final Conflict (Omen III), Possession, Enigma, Le Sang des Autres, Robbery Under Arms, Plenty, For Love Alone, The Good Wife, A Cry in the Dark, Dead Calm, The French Revolution, The Hunt for Red October, Until the End of the World, Hostage, Memoirs of an Invisible Man, Death in Brunswick, Jurassic Park, The Piano, Sirens, Country Life, Restoration, Victory, In the Month of Madness, Event Horizon, The Horse Whisperer, My Mother Frank, Molokai: The Story of Father Damien, Bicentennial Man, The Dish 2000, Monticello, The Zookeeper 2001, Jurassic Pack III 2001, Dirty Deeds 2002, Perfect Strangers 2002. *Television appearances include:* From a Far Country, Ivanhoe, The Country Girls, Reilly: Ace of Spies, Kane and Abel (mini-series), Submerged (film) 2001, Framed (film) 2002, Dr Zhivago (mini-series) 2002. *Address:* c/o ICM, 8942 Wilshire Boulevard, Beverly Hills, CA 90211, USA. *Website:* www.samneill.com (Office).

NEILL OF BLADEN, Baron (Life Peer), cr. 1997, of Briantspuddle in the County of Dorset; **Francis Patrick Neill,** Kt, QC; British lawyer; b. 8 Aug. 1926; s. of the late Sir Thomas Neill and of Annie Strachan Neill (née Bishop); m. Caroline Susan Debenham 1954; three s. two d. (and one s. deceased); ed Highgate School and Magdalen Coll. Oxford; served with Rifle Brigade 1944–47; GSO III (Training), British Troops Egypt 1947; called to the Bar, Gray's Inn 1951; Recorder of the Crown Court 1975–78; Judge of the Court of Appeal of Jersey and Guernsey 1977–94; Fellow of All Souls Coll., Oxford 1950–77, Sub-Warden 1972–74, Warden 1977–95; Vice-Chancellor Oxford Univ. 1985–89; Chair., Justice–All Souls Cttee for Review of Admin. Law 1978–87, Press Council 1978–83, Council for Securities Industry 1978–85; mem. DTI Cttee of Inquiry into Regulatory Arrangements at Lloyds 1986–87; Bencher, Gray's Inn 1971, Vice-Treasurer 1989, Treasurer 1990; mem. Bar Council 1967–71, Vice-Chair. 1973–74, Chair. 1974–75; Chair. Senate of the Inns of Court and the Bar 1974–75; Chair. Cttee on Standards in Public Life 1997–2001; Dir Times Newspapers Holdings Ltd 1988–97; Hon. Fellow Magdalen Coll. Oxford 1988; Hon. Prof. of Legal Ethics, Birmingham Univ. 1983–84; Hon. DCL (Oxford) 1987; Hon. LLD (Hull) 1978, (Buckingham) 1994. *Publication:* Administrative Justice: Some Necessary Reforms 1988. *Leisure interests:* music, forestry. *Address:* House of Lords, London, SW1A 0PW (Office); 1 Hare Court, Temple, London, EC4Y 7BE, England.

NEIMAN, LeRoy; American artist; b. 8 June 1921, St Paul, Minn.; s. of Charles Runquist and Lydia Runquist (née Serline); m. Janet Byrne 1957; ed Art Inst., Chicago, Univ. of Illinois and DePaul Univ.; Instructor Art Inst., Chicago 1950–60, Saugatuck (Mich.) Summer School of Painting 1957–58, 1963, School of Arts and Crafts, Winston-Salem, NC 1963; Instructor in painting Atlanta Youth Council for Poverty Program 1968–69; contrib. to features Playboy magazine 1956–; graphics printmaker 1971–; artist Olympic Games, Munich, ABC TV 1971, official artist Olympic Games, Montréal, ABC TV 1976, US Olympics 1980, 1984; computer artist Superbowl, New Orleans CBS TV 1978; official artist Goodwill Games, Moscow, CNN TV 1986; first official artist Ky Derby, Louisville 1997; one-man shows in Chicago, London, Paris, New York, Atlanta, Dublin, Caracas, Leningrad, Tokyo, Helsinki, Stockholm, Cadaqués (Spain), Elkhart (Ind.), Oklahoma, Moscow, Youngstown (Ill.) etc.; retrospective exhbns in Minn., Houston, Tokyo, Ohio, Ky, Paris; two-man show Neiman–Warhol, LA Inst. of Contemporary Art 1981; group shows in USA, Paris, Milan, London, Munich, Tokyo, St Petersburg; rep. in perm. collections Minneapolis Inst. of Arts, State Museum, Springfield, Joslyn Museum, Omaha, Wadham Coll. Oxford, Nat. Art Museum Sport, New York, Museo de Bellas Artes, Caracas, Hermitage Museum, St Petersburg, The Armand Hammer Collection, Los Angeles, The Art Inst. of Chicago, Whitney Museum, NY; work commissioned for Baseball Hall of Fame, Coca Cola, Gen. Mills, Gen. Motors, Ky Derby, Los Angeles Dodgers 100th Anniversary, Nat. Football League, Newport Jazz Festival, Rocky II, III, IV and V films; executed murals at Merchant Nat. Bank, Hammond, Ind., Continental Hotel, Chicago, Swedish Lloyd ship S.S. Patricia, Stockholm, Sportsmans Park, Chicago; donor and mem. advisory cttee, LeRoy Neiman Center for Print Studies, School of the Arts, Columbia Univ. 1995, LeRoy Neiman Center for Study of American Soc. and Culture, Univ. of Calif. at LA; mem. advisory Cttee New York Comm. for Cultural Affairs 1995; numerous hon. doctorates including Franklin Pierce Coll. 1976, St Francis Coll. 1998, St Bonaventure Univ. 1999; numerous prizes including Gold Medal, Salon d'Art Moderne, Paris 1961, Award of Merit, Outstanding Sports Artist, AAU 1976, Gold Plate Award, American Acad. of Achievement 1977, Olympic Artist of Century Award 1979, Gold Medal Award, St John's Univ. 1985, Hofstra Univ. 1998. *Publications include:* Art and Lifestyle 1974, Illustrations for new edn of Moby Dick 1975, Horses 1979, Posters 1980, Carnaval 1981, Winners 1983, Monte Carlo Chase 1988, Big Time Golf 1992, An American in Paris 1994, LeRoy Neiman on Safari 1997, The Prints of LeRoy Neiman 1991–2000, Casey at the Bat 2001. *Address:* Hammer Galleries, 33 West 57th Street, New York, NY 10019; Knoedler Publishing, 19 East 70th Street, New York, NY 10021; LeRoy Neiman Inc., 1 West 67th Street, New York, NY 10023, USA. *Telephone:* (212) 644-4400 (Hammer Galleries); (212) 794-0571 (Knoedler Publishing).

NEISS, Hubert; Austrian international finance official; b. 1935; ed Hochschule für Welthandel and Univ. of Kansas, USA; Economist, European Dept IMF 1967; Chief, S. Pacific Div. 1973; Resident Rep. of IMF in Indonesia; Deputy Dir Asian Dept 1980–91; Dir Asian Regional Dept IMF 1991–2000; Chair. Deutsche Bank Asia 2001.

NEIZVESTNY, Ernst Iosifovich; Russian artist and sculptor; b. 9 April 1925, Sverdlovsk; ed V. I. Surikov State Inst. of Arts (M. G. Maniser's studio); Soviet Army 1942–45; sculptor at studios of USSR Agricultural Exhbn (later Econ. Achievements of USSR Exhbn) 1953–54; mem. Artists' Union of USSR 1955–57; granted permission to emigrate to Geneva 1976; Soviet citizenship restored 1990; mem. Royal Acad. of Fine Arts, Sweden, New York Acad. of Sciences 1986, European Acad. of Arts, Sciences and Humanities, Paris, Swedish Acad. of Sciences; Prof. Columbia Univ., NY; Order of Red Star 1945, Russian State Award for Merit 1995, Russian Govt Award for Achievement in the Arts 1996, Order of Honour 2000. *Television:* Monumental Statues 1998, Cold War Postscript, CNN 1999. *Exhibitions include:* Le Monde de l'Art, Paris and Jewish Museum, Washington, DC 1992, Jewish Museum, New York 1995, Pushkin Museum, Moscow 1996, UN Palace of Nations, Geneva 1997, Tretiakov Gallery, Moscow 1999. *Main works:* Kremlin Builder, First Wings, The Youth, Mother, series: War–is ...; Robots and Semi-robots, Great Mistakes, Nikita Krushchev Memorial, Lotus Blossom, Aswan Dam, Egypt 1968, Monument to the Golden Child, Odessa, Ukraine 1995, Monument to Victims of Stalinism, Magadan, Russia 1990–96, Bust of Boris Yeltsin 1996, Monument to the Kalmykia Deportation 1996, The Great Centaur, Palace of Nations, Geneva 1997; illustrations to works of Dante, Beckett and Dostoyevsky. *Publications:* Space, Time and Synthesis in Art 1990, Artist's Fate 1992. *Leisure interests:* building sculpture garden on Shelter Island, New York. *Address:* 81 Grand Street, New York, NY 10013, USA. *Telephone:* (212) 226-2677 (Office). *Fax:* (212) 226-2603. *E-mail:* enstudio@yahoo.com (Office). *Website:* www.enstudio.com (Office).

NEJAD-HOSSEINIAN, Seyed Mohammad Hadi, MS; Iranian diplomatist and politician; b. 2 Feb. 1947, Karbala; s. of Hossein Nejad Hosseinian and Razie Haj Tarkhani; m. Fatemeh Tadbir; two s. two d.; ed Tehran Univ., George Washington Univ., Washington, DC; Deputy, Plan and Budget Org. 1980–81; Minister for Road and Transportation 1981–85; Deputy Minister of Oil 1985–89, 1994–97; Minister for Heavy Industry 1989–94; Amb. and Perm. Rep. to UN 1998–. *Address:* Permanent Mission of Iran to the United Nations, 622 Third Avenue, 34th Floor, New York, NY 10017, USA (Office). *Telephone:* (212) 687-2020 (Office). *Fax:* (212) 867-7086 (Office). *E-mail:* iran@un.int (Office). *Website:* www.un.int/iran (Office).

NEKIPELOV, Alexander Dmitriyevich, DrEcon; Russian economist; b. 16 Nov. 1951, Moscow; m.; one d.; ed Moscow State Univ.; Jr researcher, Sr researcher, head of sector, Deputy Dir Inst. of. Int. Econ. and Political Studies Russian Acad. of Sciences 1973–98, Dir 1998–; mem. Russian Acad. of Sciences 1997; Medal of Order for Service to Motherland. *Publications:* numerous scientifc publs including monograph Essays on Economics of Postcommunism 1996. *Leisure interest:* chess. *Address:* Institute of International Economic and Political Studies, Novocheremushkinskaya str. 46, 117418 Moscow, Russia (Office). *Telephone:* (095) 128-91-35 (Office).

NEKROŠIUS, Eimuntas; Lithuanian theatre director and actor; b. 21 Nov. 1952, Pažobris; s. of Petras Nekrošius and Elena Nekrošienė; m. Nadezhda Gultyaeva 1976; two s.; ed State Inst. of Theatre Art in Moscow; Theatre Dir Kaunas Drama Theatre 1978–79; Theatre Dir Youth Theatre Lithuanian SSR (now Lithuania), Vilnius 1979–91, Dir LIFE Int. Theatre Festival 1993–97; f. Meno Fortas Theatre Studio; USSR State Prize 1987, Award of European Theatre Union 1991, Baltic Ass. Award 1994, Nat. Culture and Art Award, Order of Grand Duke Gediminas. *Productions include:* A Taste of Honey 1976, Duokishkis Ballad 1978, Ivanov 1978, Square 1980, Pirosmani 1981, Love and Death in Verona 1982, The Day Lasts More Than Ages 1983, Uncle Vanya 1986, Mozart and Salieri, Don Juan, Plague 1994, Three Sisters 1995, Hamlet 1997, Macbeth 1999, Othello 2001, Ivanov 2002, Veridi's Macbeth 2002, The Seasons 2003. *Film roles include:* Girenas in Flight Through Atlantics 1983, Father in Lessons of Hatred 1984, Minister in Team 1985. *Address:* Bernardinų 8/8, 2000 Vilnius, Lithuania. *Telephone:* (52) 685816. *Fax:* (52) 685817 (Office). *E-mail:* info@menofortas.lt (Office). *Website:* www.menofortas.lt.

NEKVASIL, Lt-Gen. Jiří; Czech army officer and diplomatist; b. 24 April 1948, Benešov; m. 1st Jaroslava Papežová; m. 2nd Danuše Kadlečková; two s. two d.; ed Tech. Inst. Liptovský Mikuláš, Mil. Acad., Kalinin, Acad. of Gen. Staff of Mil. Forces, Moscow, NATO Defence Coll., Rome; 2nd in Command Czech AF and Anti-Air Defence System 1990–92; Commdr of Gen. Staff 1993–98; Adviser to Ministry of Defence 1998–99; Amb. to Georgia 2000–; Order of Red Star (Czecholsavakia) 1985, Commdr Legion of Merit 1996, Legion d'honneur 1996, Bundeswehr Gold Cross (Germany) 1998, Gold Cross (Austria) 1998. *Leisure interests:* mushrooming, tennis, gardening, photography. *Address:* c/o Ministry for Foreign Affairs, Loretánské nam. 5, Prague 1, 118000 Czech Republic. *Telephone:* (2) 24182555. *E-mail:* czechembassy@ti.net.ge (Office). *Website:* www.mzv.cz.

NELDER, John Ashworth, MA, DSc, FRS; British statistician; b. 8 Oct. 1924, Dulverton, Somerset; s. of Reginald Charles Nelder and Edith May Ashworth (née Briggs); m. Mary Hawkes 1955; one s. one d.; ed Blundell's School, Tiverton, Sidney Sussex Coll., Cambridge Univ.; Head of Statistics Section, Nat. Vegetable Research Station, Wellesbourne 1950–68; Head of Statistics Dept, Rothamsted Experimental Station, Harpenden 1968–84; Sr Research Fellow London Business School 1984–87; Originator statistical computer programs Genstat and GLIM; Visiting Prof. Imperial Coll., London 1971–; fmr Pres. Int. Biometric Soc.; Pres. Royal Statistical Soc. 1985–86; Guy Medal (Silver) of Royal Statistical Soc. *Publications:* Generalized Linear Models (with P. McCullagh), Computers in Biology; more than 150 papers in scientific journals. *Leisure interests:* ornithology, music (especially playing piano). *Address:* Cumberland Cottage, 33 Crown Street, Redbourn, St Albans, Herts., AL3 7JX, England. *Telephone:* (1582) 792907. *E-mail:* jnelder@imperial.ac.uk (Office); jnelder@ntlworld.com (Home).

NELISSEN, Roelof J., MA; Netherlands politician and banker; b. 4 April 1931, Hoofdplaat, Zeeland Prov.; m. A. M. van der Kelen; three s. one d.; ed grammar school at Dongen and Faculty of Law, Catholic Univ. of Nijmegen; various posts in employers' asscns., Amsterdam and The Hague 1956–69; mem. Second Chamber, States-Gen. (Parl.) 1963–70; Minister of Econ. Affairs 1970–71; First Deputy Prime Minister, Minister of Finance 1971–73; mem. Bd Man. Dirs Amsterdam-Rotterdam Bank N.V. 1974–, Vice-Chair. 1979–82, Chair. 1983–92; Chair. Bd Man. Dirs ABN-AMRO Holding N.V. 1990–92. *Address:* P.O. Box 552, 1250 AN Laren, Netherlands.

NELLIGAN, Kate; Canadian actress; b. 16 March 1951, London, Ont.; d. of Patrick Joseph Nelligan and Alice (née Dier) Nelligan; ed St Martin's Catholic School, London, Ont., York Univ., Toronto and Cen. School of Speech and Drama, London, England; professional stage début as Corrie in Barefoot in the Park, Little Theatre, Bristol 1972; other parts there and at Theatre Royal for Bristol Old Vic 1972–73 include: Hypatia in Misalliance, Stella Kowalski in A Streetcar Named Desire, Pegeen Mike in The Playboy of the Western World, Grace Harkaway in London Assurance, title role in Lulu, Sybil Chase in Private Lives; London début as Jenny in Knuckle, Comedy Theatre 1974; joined Nat. Theatre Co. at Old Vic 1975 to play Ellie Dunn in Heartbreak House, also in Plenty and Moon for the Misbegotten 1984; As You Like It for RSC, Stratford; Serious Money, Broadway 1988, Spoils of War 1988, Eleni; Evening Standard Best Actress Award 1978. *Films include:* The Count of Monte Cristo, The Romantic Englishwoman, Dracula 1979, Patman, Eye of the Needle 1980, Agent 1980, Without a Trace 1983, Eleni 1986, White Room, The Prince of Tides, Frankie and Johnny, Shadows and Fog, Fatal Instinct, Wolf, How to Make An American Quilt, Up Close and Personal, U.S. Marshals, Stolen Moments (voice), Boy Meets Girl, The Cider House Rules 1999, Love is Strange 1999, Blessed Stranger 2000, Walter and Henry 2001. *Television includes:* The Onedin Line, The Lady of the Camellias, Licking Hitler, Measure for Measure, Thérèse Raquin 1980, Forgive our Foolish Ways 1980, Count of Monte Cristo, Victims, Kojak, Love and Hate, Old Times, Love is Strange, Swing Vote. *Leisure interests:* reading, cooking. *Address:* Innovative Artists, Suite 2850, 1999 Avenue of the Stars, Los Angeles, CA 90067, USA (Office).

NELSON, Bill, JD; American government official; b. 29 Sept. 1942, Miami, Fla; s. of C. W. Nelson and Nannie Nelson; m. Grace H. Cavert 1972; one s. one d.; ed Yale Univ., Univ. of Va; with U.S. Army Reserves 1965–75, Army 1968–70, rank of Capt.; admitted to Bar, Fla; pvt. law practice Melbourne, Fla 1970–79; mem. House of Reps, Fla 1972–78, U.S. Congress 1979–91, Chair. Space Sub-Cttee of the Science, Space and Tech. Cttee. (flew with crew on 24th flight of NASA Space Shuttle); State Treas., Insurance Commr and Fire Marshall, Fla 1995–2000, Senator from Fla 2000–, mem. Senate Foreign Relations, Armed Services, Budget and Commerce Cttees. *Address:* United States Senate, Washington, DC 20510, USA (Office). *Telephone:* (202) 224-5274 (Office). *Fax:* (202) 228-2183 (Office). *Website:* www.billnelson.senate .gov (Office).

NELSON, E. Benjamin, MA, JD; American politician and lawyer; b. 17 May 1941, McCook, Neb.; s. of Benjamin E. Nelson and Birdella Nelson; m. Diane Nelson (née Gleason); two s. two d. from previous marriage; one step-s. one step-d.; ed Univ. of Nebraska; Instructor Dept of Philosophy, Univ. of Neb. 1963–65; Dir of Compliance Neb. Dept of Insurance 1965–72, Dir 1975–76; admitted to Neb. Bar 1970; Gen. Counsel, Cen. Nat. Insurance Group of Omaha 1972–74, Exec. Vice-Pres. 1977, Pres. 1978–79, Pres. and CEO 1980–81; Attorney of Counsel Kennedy, Holland DeLacy and Svoboda, Omaha 1985–90; Gov. of Nebraska 1990–98, Senator from Nebraska Jan. 2001–; mem. of counsel Lumson, Dugan and Murray 1999–; Exec. Vice-Pres. Nat. Asscn of Insurance Commrs 1982–85; Chair. Nat. Educ. Goals Panel 1992–94, Govs' Ethanol Coalition (also f.) 1991, 1994, Midwestern Govs' Conf. 1994; fmr Chair. Interstate Oil and Gas Compact Comm., Western Govs' Asscn and Co-Lead Gov. on Int. Trade; Pres. Council of State Govts 1994; Chair. Nat. Resources Cttee and Co-Lead Gov. on Federalism, Nat. Govs' Asscn; Co-Chair. Nat. Summit on Federalism 1995; fmr Vice-Chair. Democratic Govs' Asscn; Hon. LLD (Creighton Univ.) 1992, (Peru State Coll.) 1993; Hon. DHumLitt (Coll. of St Mary) 1995; numerous awards. *Leisure interests:* spending time with my family, hunting and fishing, reading and collecting clocks. *Address:* Lamson, Dugan and Murray, 10306 Regency Parkway Drive, Omaha, NE 68114 (Office); U.S. Senate, 720 Hart Senate Office Building, Washington, DC 20510, USA (Office).

NELSON, Gaylord Anton, LLB; American politician and lawyer; b. 4 June 1916, Clear Lake, Wis.; s. of Anton Nelson and Mary Bradt; m. Carrie Lee Dotson 1947; two s. one d.; ed Clear Lake High School (Polk County, Wis.), San José State Coll., Calif. and Wisconsin Univ. Law School; army service 1942–46; admitted to Wis. Bar 1942; Practising Attorney, Madison, Wis. 1946–58; Wisconsin State Senator 1949–58; Gov. of Wisconsin 1958–62; U.S. Senator from Wisconsin 1963–80; Counsellor Wilderness Soc., Washington, DC 1981–; Founder of Earth Day 1970; Democrat; UN Environmental Programme "Environmental Leadership" Award 1982, UN Environment Programme "Only One Earth" Award 1992, Presidential Medal of Freedom 1995. *Address:* Wilderness Society, 900 17th Street, NW, Washington, DC 20006 (Office); 3611 Calvend Lane, Kensington, MD 20895, USA (Home).

NELSON, Judith, BA; American singer; b. 10 Sept. 1939; d. of Virgil D. Nelson and Genevieve W. Manes; m. Alan H. Nelson 1961; one s. one d.; ed St Olaf Coll., Northfield, Minn.; Alfred Hertz Memorial Fellowship, Univ. of Calif. at Berkeley 1972–73; European début 1972; specializes in baroque repertoire; has appeared with most of the maj. baroque orchestras in USA and Europe including Acad. of Ancient Music, Tafelmusik, Toronto, Philharmonia, San Francisco; has performed with San Francisco, St Louis, Baltimore and Washington Nat. Symphony Orchestras and LA Philharmonic; has appeared in opera in Boston, LA, Brussels, Innsbruck, Venice, Turin and Rome and at Md Handel Festival; master classes at UCLA, Univ. of Chicago, Bath Summer School, Bruges Festival, Jerusalem Music Center; Hon. DFA (St.Olaf Coll.) 1979. *Leisure interests:* languages, support of local arts orgs, local politics. *Address:* 2600 Buena Vista Way, Berkeley, CA 94708, USA. *Telephone:* (415) 848-1992.

NELSON, Ralph Alfred, MD, PhD, FACP; American professor of medicine; b. 19 June 1927, Minneapolis; s. of Alfred Walter Nelson and Lydia Nelson (née Johnson); m. Rosemarie Pokela 1954; three s. two d.; ed Univ. of Minnesota; Pathology Residency, Univ. of Minnesota 1954–55; Fellowship in Physiology, Mayo Graduate School, Mayo Clinic, Rochester 1957–60, Resident Internal Medicine 1976–78; Asst Prof. of Nutrition, Cornell Univ. 1961–62; Assoc. Prof. of Physiology, Assoc. Prof. of Nutrition, Mayo Medical School, Rochester 1967–78; Prof. of Nutrition, Dept of Medicine, Univ. of Ill. 1979–, Prof. of Medicine, Food Science, Prof. of Physiology, Univ. of Ill. 1979–84, Exec. Head, Dept of Internal Medicine, Univ. of Ill. Coll. of Medicine at Urbana-Champaign 1979–, Head Dept of Medicine 1989–; Consultant for Nutritional Support Service, Danville Veterans Admin. Hosp.; Dir of Research, Carle Foundation Hosp., Urbana 1979–; mem. American Physiological Soc., American Inst. of Nutrition, American Soc. of Clinical Nutrition, American Soc. of Gastroenterology; Fulbright Scholar 1988; Mayo Clinic Alumni Award for Outstanding Research 1959. *Publications:* Mayo Clinic Renal Diet Cook Book 1974, numerous learned papers, including over 140 on the metabolism of bears and clinical nutrition. *Leisure interests:* walking, bicycling, canoeing, mountain hiking. *Address:* Carle Foundation Hospital, Department of Medical Research, 611 West Park Street, Urbana, IL 61801 (Office); 2 Illinois Circle, Urbana, IL 61801, USA (Home). *Telephone:* (217) 383-3036 (Office); (217) 344-4676 (Home). *Fax:* (217) 383-3993 (Office). *E-mail:* r-nelson@uiuc .edu (Office).

NĚMEC, Jaroslav, DrTech, DrSc; Czech engineer and metallurgist (retd); b. 15 March 1921, Horažďovice, Klatovy Dist; s. of Karel Němec and Bohuslava Němcová; m. Zdenka Němcová 1944 (died 1996); ed Eng Faculty, Tech. Univ. of Prague (ČVUT); design engineer 1942–45; Dir of Research and Devt, ČKD Sokolovo 1945–53; Prof., Coll. of Transport (VŠD), Dean 1953–55, Deputy Rector 1955–59; Prof., Head of Materials Dept and Dept of Specialization, Faculty of Nuclear and Physical Eng, ČVUT 1969–86, Deputy Dean 1967–74, Deputy Rector 1973–79; Corresp. mem. Czechoslovak (now Czech) Acad. of Sciences (ČSAV) 1972–75, mem. ČSAV 1975–, mem. Presidium 1979–87, Dir Acad. Inst. of Theoretical and Applied Mech., Prague 1979–87, Consultant 1991–; mem. Czechoslovak Atomic Comm.; Expert Adviser, Skoda Works, ČKD and others; Hon. mem. Int. Conf. on Fracture, Nat. Tech. Museum; mem. various foreign scientific and eng socs; Dr hc (Pardubice) 1999; All States Prize of Sciences 1965, 1974, Kaplan Medal 1968, Felber Medal 1971, Křižík Medal 1976, Order of Labour 1981, Nat. Prize 1985, Komensky Medal 1986, Medal of Sciences and Humanities, Acad. of Sciences 1986 and many others. *Exhibitions include:* 20 solo exhbns of painting. *Publications:* over 400 original papers on mechanics, elasticity and strength; 24 books including: Strength of Pressure Vessels under Different Operational Conditions, Toughness and Strength of Steel Parts, Failure of Strength of Plastics (with Acad. Serensen, Moscow), Shape and Strength of Metal Bodies (with Prof. Puchner), New Methods of Calculations of Rigidity and Strength of Machines (with Prof. Valenta), Fracture Dynamics, Dynamics and Reliability of Locomotive Parts, The Problem of Nuclear Equipment, with Special Reference to Reliability and Safety, Endurance of Mechanical Structures (with Dr Drexler), Strength and Lifetime of Gas Pipes (jtly). *Leisure interest:* painting. *Address:* UTAM, Czech Academy of Sciences, Prosecka 74, Prague 9 (Office); Letohradská 60, 7 Prague 17000, Czech Republic (Home). *Telephone:* (2) 86885382, (2) 86882121 (Office); (2) 33376423. *Fax:* (2) 86884634 (Office). *E-mail:* gajdos@itam.cas.cz (Office). *Website:* www.itam.cas.cz (Office).

NEMEIRY, Field Marshal Gaafar Mohammed al- (see Nemery, Field Marshal Gaafar Mohammed al-).

NEMERY, Field Marshal Gaafar Mohammed al-; Sudanese political leader and army officer; b. 1 Jan. 1930, Omdurman; ed Sudan Military Coll.; fmr Commdr Khartoum garrison; campaigns against rebels in Southern Sudan; placed under arrest on suspicion of plotting to overthrow the Govt; led successful mil. coup May 1969; promoted from Col to Maj.-Gen. May 1969, to Field Marshal May 1979; Chair. Revolutionary Command Council (RCC) 1969–71, C-in-C of Armed Forces 1969–73, 1976–85; Minister of Defence May–June 1969, 1972–73, 1974–76, 1978–79; Prime Minister 1969–76, 1977–85; Minister of Foreign Affairs 1970–71, of Planning 1971–72, of Finance 1977–78, of Agric. and Irrigation 1982, of Defence 1983–85; Pres. of Sudan 1971–85 (overthrown in coup); Supreme Commdr of Armed Forces 1985; stripped of rank of Field Marshal in absentia June 1985; in exile in Egypt for 14 years, returned May 1999; Pres. Political Bureau Sudanese Socialist Union 1971–85, Sec.-Gen. 1971–76, 1979–82; Pres. of OAU 1978–79.

NÉMETH, János, PH.D; Hungarian judge and academic; b. 31 July, 1933, Újpest; s. of János Németh and Erzsébet Németh (née Nemes); m. Izabella Vass 1959, two d.; ed Eötvös Loránd Univ. of Budapest; Jr legal official in law firm 1957, Teacher at Dept of Civil Procedural Law at Eötvös Loránd Univ. 1982–97, Head of Dept, Prof. 1983–91, Vice-Chancellor 1993–97; Ed. of the Hungarian Law (journal) 1991–, Chief Ed. Pres. of the Comm. for Hungarian Lawyers Asscn; mem. of Nat. Legal Comm. of Hungarian Acad. of Sciences, Nat. Legal Cttee of Experts for Doctorates at Hungarian Acad. of Sciences; Head of Békés-Németh-Vékás and Co. Law firm; Chair. of Nat. Electoral Cttee. 1990–97; judge of Constitutional Court of Hungary 1997–98, Pres. 1998–. *Publications:* over 100 legal publs. *Leisure interest:* hunting. *Address:* ELTE Polgári Eljárásjogi Tanszék, 1053 Budapest, Egyetem tér 1-3 (Office); Alkotmánybíróság, 1015 Budapest, Donáti u. 35-45, Hungary (Office). *Telephone:* (1) 266-4930, (1) 488-3110 (Office). *E-mail:* nemeth@mkab.hu (Office).

NÉMETH, Miklós; Hungarian politician; b. 24 Jan. 1948, Monok; s. of András Németh and Margit Németh (née Stajz); m. Erzsébet Szilágyi 1971; two s.; ed Karl Marx Univ. of Budapest; Lecturer in Political Economy Karl Marx Univ. 1971–77; deputy section head Nat. Planning Office 1977–81; worked on staff, later as deputy leader, of HSWP Cen. Cttee Dept of Political Economy, Dept Leader 1987–88; mem. of Cen. Cttee, Secr. 1987–88; mem. Political Cttee 1987–88; MP 1988–90; Prime Minister of Hungary 1988–90; apptd to four-mem. Presidium of HSWP 1989; mem. Presidium, Hungarian Socialist Party (HSP) Oct.–Dec. 1989 (resgnd); Vice-Pres. (Personnel and Admin.) EBRD 1991–2000. *Leisure interests:* sailing, tennis, classical music. *Address:* c/o 1029 Budapest II, Keszi u.7, Hungary.

NEMITSAS, Takis; Greek-Cypriot fmr politician and industrialist; b. 2 June 1930, Limassol; s. of Xanthos Nemitsas and Vassiliki Nemitsa; m. 1st Daisy Petrou 1958 (died 1983); three d.; m. 2nd Louki Loucaides 1986; mem. House of Reps. 1976–81; fmr Pres. Parl. Cttee on Commerce and Industry; Minister of Commerce and Industry 1988–93; Chair. and Man. Dir Nemitsas Group 1993–95, Chair. Bd of Dirs. 1995–; fmr mem. Bd Bank of Cyprus, Cyprus Employers' and Industrialists' Fed., Chamber of Commerce and Industry, Cyprus Tourism Org.; fmr Deputy Chair. Woolworth Cyprus; Grand Cross of Leopold II (Belgium), Grand Officer Kt of the Order of Merit (Italy). *Publications:* Environmental policy and the EU, Recycling of Scrap Metal in Cyprus. *Leisure interest:* swimming. *Address:* 153 Franklin Roosevelt Avenue, Limassol (Office); Nemitsas Ltd, P.O. Box 50124, 3601 Limassol, Cyprus. *Telephone:* (25) 569222 (Office); (25) 636844 (Home). *Fax:* (25) 569275 (Office); (25) 636050 (Home). *E-mail:* central@nemitsas.com (Office). *Website:* www.nemitsas.com (Office).

NEMTSOV, Boris Yefimovich, CTechSc; Russian politician; b. 9 Oct. 1959, Sochi; m.; one d.; ed Gorky (now Nizhny Novgorod) State Univ.; researcher then Sr researcher Research Inst. of Radiophysics 1981–91; rep. of Pres. of Russia in Nizhny Novgorod Region 1991; Gov. of Nizhny Novgorod Region 1991–97; People's Deputy of Russia 1990–93; mem. Council of Fed. (Upper House of Parl.) 1993–97; First Deputy Chair. Russian Govt 1997–98 (resgnd); Minister of Fuel and Power Eng March–Nov. 1997; f. Young Russia Movt; joined pre-election coalition Pravoye delo 1999; mem. State Duma (Parl.) 1999–, Deputy Chair. Feb.–June 2000; Leader Union of Right Forces faction 2000–01; Chair. Political Council Eight Forces Party 2001–. *Publication:* The Provincial 1997. *Leisure interests:* tennis, windsurfing, fishing. *Address:* State Duma, Okhotny Ryad 1, 103265 Moscow, Russia (Office). *Telephone:* (095) 292-57-77 (Office). *Fax:* (095) 291-18-18 (Office).

NEOH, Anthony Francis, LL.B, QC, JP; Chinese lawyer; b. 9 Nov. 1946, Hong Kong; ed Univ. of London; teacher 1964–66; Hong Kong Civil Service 1966–79; pvt. practice, Hong Kong Bar 1979–95, Calif. Bar 1984–95; Hong Kong public service in educ., health etc. 1985–; People's Repub. of China public service in teaching, Govt advisory work etc. 1985–; Visiting Scholar, Harvard Univ., USA 1990–91; now Chair. Securities and Futures Comm. Hong Kong; Chair. IOSCO Tech. Cttee 1996. *Leisure interests:* reading, music. *Address:* 12th Floor, The Landmark, 15 Queen's Road Central, Hong Kong Special Administrative Region, People's Republic of China. *Telephone:* 28409201. *Fax:* 28101872.

NEPTUNE, Yvon; Haitian politician and architect; b. 8 Nov. 1946, Cavaillon; m.; two c.; ed Brothers of the Christian Instruction, Coll. Philippe Guerrier of Cayes, Port-au-Prince Lycée Alexandre Petion, Univ. of State of Haiti Faculty of Science, New York Inst. of Tech., USA; architect with Emery Roth and Sons, New York, USA; political activist, opponent of coup d'etat in Haiti 1991, produced radio broadcasts and helped org. of exiles, adviser to Bertrand Aristide, returned to Haiti 1994; mem. Lavalas Party, also Spokesman and Rep.; elected to Senate 2002, currently Pres.; Prime Minister of Haiti March 2002–. *Address:* Office of the Prime Minister, Villa d'Accueil, Delmas 60, Musseau, Port-au-Prince, Haiti (Office). *Telephone:* 245-0007 (Office). *Fax:* 245-1624 (Office).

NERETTE, Justice Joseph; Haitian politician and judge; fmr mem. Supreme Court of Haiti; named Pres. of Haiti after mil. coup overthrew Govt of Father Jean Aristide 1991–92.

NERLOVE, Marc L., PhD; American professor of agricultural economics; b. 12 Oct. 1933, Chicago; s. of Samuel Henry Nerlove and Evelyn Nerlove (née Andelman); two d.; ed Univ. of Chicago and Johns Hopkins Univ.; Analytical Statistician, U.S. Dept of Agric., Washington, DC 1956–57; Assoc. Prof., Univ. of Minn., Minneapolis 1959–60; Prof., Stanford Univ. 1960–65, Yale Univ. 1965–69; Prof. of Econs, Univ. of Chicago 1969–74; F. W. Taussig Research Prof., Harvard Univ. 1967–68; Visiting Prof., Northwestern Univ., 1973–74, Cook Prof. 1974–82; Prof. of Econs, Univ. of Pa 1982–86, Univ. Prof. 1986–93; Prof. of Agric. and Resource Econs Univ. of Md, Coll. Park 1993–; mem. NAS; John Bates Clark Medal 1969, P. C. Mahalinobis Medal 1975. *Publications:* Dynamics of Supply 1958, Distributed Lags and Demand Analysis 1958, Estimation and Identification of Cobb-Douglas Production Functions 1965, Analysis of Economic Time Series: A Synthesis 1979, Household and Economy: Welfare Economics of Endogenous Fertility 1987; numerous articles. *Address:* Department of Agriculture and Research Economics, Maryland University, College Park, MD 20742, USA.

NERO, Franco; Italian actor; b. Francesco Sparanero, 23 Nov. 1941, Parma; m. Vanessa Redgrave (q.v.). *Films:* The Bible 1966, Ojango, Camelot, The Hired Killer, The Wild, Wild Planet, The Brute and the Beast, The Day of the Owl, Sardinia, Mafia, Vendetta, Companeros, Detective Belli, The Mercenary, A Quiet Place in the Country, Tristana, The Virgin and the Gypsy, Battle of the Neretva, Confessions of a Police Captain, The Vacation, Pope Joan, Deaf Smith and Johnny Ears, The Last Days of Mussolini, Force Ten from Navarone, The Roses of the Danzig, Mimi, The Man With Bogart's Face, Enter the Ninja, Mexico in Flames, Querelle, Kamikaze '89, The Salamander, Wagner, Victory March, The Day of the Cobra, Ten Days That Shook the World, Der Falke, The Repenter, The Forester's Sons, Garibaldi: The General, The Girl, Sweet Country, Die Hard 2, Brothers and Sisters, A Breath of Life, Jonathan of the Bears, Conflict of Interest, The Dragon's Ring, Talk of Angels, The Innocent Sleep, The King and Me. *Television includes:* The Last Days of Pompeii, Moyles: The Legend of Valentino, 21 Hours at Munich, The Pirate, Young Catherine, The Versace Murder, Das Babylon Komplott.

NESHAT, Shirin, MFA, MA; Iranian photographer and video artist; b. 1957, Qazvin; ed Univ. of California at Berkeley, USA; immigrated to USA to attend univ.; returned to Iran in early 1990s to explore status as a self-imposed artist in exile; Artist in Residence, Henry Street Settlement, New York 1991–92; Louis Comfort Fiffany Foundation Grant 1996; several grants and fellowships including Sponsored Project Grant, New York State Council on the Arts 1989, Tiffany Foundation Grant 1996, New York Foundation for Arts Photography Fellowship 1996, Gold Lion, Venice Biennale 1999. *Works include:* series of photographs Women of Allah 1993–97; split-screen video installations: Turbulent 1998, Rapture 1999, Fervor 2000, Pulse 2001, Passage 2001. Solo *exhibitions include:* Franklin Furnace, New York 1993, Annina Nosei Gallery, New York 1995, 1997, Lucio Amelio Gallery, Naples 1996, Marco Noire Contemporary Arts, Turin 1996, Centre d'Art Contemporain, Fribourg 1996, Lumen Travo, Amsterdam 1997, Galleria d'Arte Moderna, Bologna 1997, Moderna Galerija, Ljubljana, Slovenia 1997, Kunsthalle Wien, Whitney Museum of American Art, Tate Gallery, London, Serpentine Gallery, London 2000, Hamburger Kunsthalle 2001. *Group exhibitions include:* Venice Biennale 1999, Malmö Konsthall 2000. *Address:* c/o Union Chapel Administration, The Vestry, Compton Avenue, London, N1 2XD, England (Office).

NESTERENKO, Yevgeniy Yevgeniyevich; Russian singer (bass); b. 8 Jan. 1938, Moscow; s. of Yevgeniy Nikiforovich Nesterenko and Velta Woldearovna Baumann; m. Yekaterina Dmitrievna Alexeyeva 1963; one s.; ed Leningrad Eng Inst. and Leningrad Conservatoire (V. Lukanin's class); soloist with Leningrad Maly Opera and Ballet Theatre 1963–67; soloist with Kirov Opera 1967–71; teacher of solo singing at Leningrad Conservatoire 1967–71; soloist with Bolshoi 1971–; mem. CPSU 1974–91; mem. staff, Moscow Musical Pedagogical Inst. 1972–74; Chair. of Singing at Moscow Conservatoire 1975–93, Prof. 1981–93; Prof. Vienna Acad. of Music 1993–; USSR People's Deputy 1989–91; USSR People's Artist, Hero of Socialist Labour, Lenin Prize 1982, Giovanni Zenatello Prize, Verona 1986, Viotti d'Oro Medal, Chaliapin Prize 1992, Wilhelm Furtwängler Prize 1992, Austrian Kammersänger 1992, Golden Disc, Japan. *Roles include:* Boris Godunov, Dosifey (Khovanshchina), Prince Igor, Mephistopheles (Gounod's Faust), Grigori (Dzerzhinsky's Quiet Flows the Don), Kutuzov (War and Peace), Filippo II (Don Carlo), Attila, Zaccaria (Nabucco), Don Pasquale, Sarastro (Magic Flute). *Publication:* Thoughts on My Profession 1985. *Leisure interest:* tea testing. *Address:* Bolshoi Theatre, Teatralnaya pl. 1, 103009 Moscow (Office); Frunzenskaya nab. 24, korp. 1, Apt. 178, 119146 Moscow, Russia (Home). *Telephone:* (095) 242-47-89 (Home).

NESTERIKHIN, Yuri Yefremovich; Russian physicist; b. 10 Oct. 1930, Ivanovo; s. of Yefrem Nesterikhin and Maria Morozova; m. 1954; one s. one d.; ed Moscow Univ.; mem. CPSU 1960–91; with Inst. of Atomic Energy 1954–61, 1987–, Inst. of Nuclear Physics 1961–67; Prof. 1970; Corresp. mem. of USSR (now Russian) Acad. of Sciences 1970, mem. 1981–; Dir of Inst. of Automation and Electrometrics, Siberian Branch of Acad. of Sciences

1967–87; Head of Synchrotron and Applied Electronics Divs. Kurchatov Inst., Moscow 1987–; Dir Multimedia Centre, Acad. of Nat. Economy 1992–; mem. Bd Ranet (jt stock co.) 1992–95; most important works on plasma physics and thermonuclear synthesis. *Leisure interest:* sauna. *Address:* Kurchatov Institute, Kurchatova ploshchad 46, D-182 Moscow (Office); Leninski Prosp. 13, Apt. 93, 117071 Moscow, Russia. *Telephone:* (095) 196-97-79 (Office); (095) 237-43-47 (Home). *Fax:* (095) 420-22-66.

NESTEROVA, Natalia Igorevna; Russian painter; b. 23 April 1944, Moscow; one s.; ed Moscow Surikov State Fine Arts Inst.; mem. USSR (now Russian) Union of Painters; Stage Designer Bolshoi Theatre 1958; participated in over 170 exhbns including solo exhbns Russia, Europe, N America 1988– (Moscow 1997); Prof. Russian Acad. of Theatre Art 1992–; works in collections of Tretyakov Gallery, Moscow, Ludwig Collection, Germany, Guggenheim Museum, New York; State Prize of Russia 1998. *Address:* Moscow Artists Union, Starosadsky per. 5, 101000 Moscow, Russia. *Telephone:* (095) 921-51-88.

NESTEROVA, Natalya Vasilyevna; Russian academic; b. 1952; ed Moscow State Univ., Moscow Pedagogical Inst.; worked in different higher educ. insts. of Moscow; Founder and Pres., Moscow Centre of Educ. 1990–; Founder Humanitarian Gymnasium of N. Nesterova 1991–; Founder and Rector, New Humanitarian Univ. and Acad. of Dance N. Nesterova 1992–; Founder Acad. of Painting 1994–. *Address:* New Humanitarian Centre of Education, Varshavskoye shosse 38, 115230 Moscow, Russia. *Telephone:* (095) 113-55-44 (Office).

NETANYAHU, Benjamin, MSc; Israeli politician and diplomatist; b. 21 Oct. 1949, Tel-Aviv; m.; three c.; ed MIT; Man. Consultant, Boston Consulting Group 1976–78; Exec. Dir Jonathan Inst. Jerusalem 1978–80; Sr Man. Rim Industries, Jerusalem 1980–82; Deputy Chief of Mission, Israeli Embassy, Washington, DC 1982–84; Perm. Rep. to UN 1984–88; Deputy Minister of Foreign Affairs 1988–91; Deputy Minister, Prime Minister's Office 1991–92; Prime Minister of Israel, Minister of Housing and Construction 1996–99; Leader Likud 1993–99; Minister of Foreign Affairs 2002–03, of Finance 2003–; mem. Knesset 1988–. *Publications:* Yoni's Letters (Ed.) 1978, Terror: Challenge and Reaction (Ed.) 1980, Terrorism: How the West Can Win (Ed.) 1986, International Terrorism: Challenge and Response (Ed.) 1991, A Place Among the Nations: Israel and the World 1993, Fighting Terrorism: How Democracies Can Defeat Domestic and International Terrorism 1995, A Durable Peace 2000. *Address:* Ministry of Finance, POB 13191, 1 Rehov Kaplan, Kiryat Ben-Gurion, Jerusalem 91008, Israel (Office). *Telephone:* 2-5317111 (Office). *Fax:* 2-5637891 (Office). *E-mail:* sar@mof.gov.il (Office). *Website:* www.mof.gov.il (Office).

NETHERLANDS, HRH Prince of the, (Bernhard Leopold Frederik Everhard Julius Coert Karel Godfried Pieter), Prince zur Lippe-Biesterfeld; b. 29 June 1911, Germany; s. of HSH the late Prince Bernhard zur Lippe and Princess Armgard, Baroness von Sierstorpff-Cramm; m. Juliana Louise Emma Marie Wilhelmina, Queen of the Netherlands (1948–80) 1937; four d.; ed Gymnasiums at Zuellichau and Berlin and Univs of Lausanne, Munich and Berlin; assumed Netherlands nationality 1936; studied at Netherlands Staff Coll.; apptd. mem. State Council; after German invasion of Holland, May 1940, evacuated family to England and returned to Continent with army until fall of France; returned to England and qualified as pilot 1941; appointed Hon. Air Cdre RAFVR 1941; subsequently Chief Netherlands Liaison Officer with British Forces, Col later Maj.-Gen. and Chief of Netherlands Mission to War Office; visited war fronts in N Africa and Normandy; maintained liaison throughout the war between Netherlands Underground and the Allied Govts.; appointed Supreme Commdr (Lt.-Gen.) Netherlands Armed Forces 1944 and played important part in liberation of Netherlands; decorated for his services in this operation by HM Queen Wilhelmina (MWO) and HM King George VI (GBE); subsequently resigned from office of Supreme Commdr 1945; mem. Council for Mil. Affairs of the Realm and mem. Jt Defence, Army, Admiralty and Air Force Councils; Insp.-Gen. of Armed Forces; Adm., Gen. Royal Netherlands Air Force, Gen. (Army) 1954–76; Hon. Air Marshal RAF 1964; Hon. Cdre RNZAF 1973; mem. Bd of the Netherlands Trade and Industries Fair; has greatly contributed to post-war expansion of Netherlands trade; Founder and Regent Prince Bernhard Fund for the Advancement of Arts and Sciences in the Netherlands; Regent Praemium Erasmianum Foundation; Founder-Pres. World Wildlife Fund Int., Pres. WWF (Worldwide Fund for Nature) Netherlands, Pres. Rhino Rescue Trust; Chair. Achievement Bd ICBP; Hon. mem. Royal Aeronautical Soc., Royal Inst. Naval Architects, Aeromedical Soc., Royal Spanish Acad.; Hon. degrees (Utrecht) 1946, (Delft) 1951, (Montréal) 1958, (British Columbia) 1958, (Amsterdam) 1965, (Michigan) 1965, (Basel) 1971; many decorations. *Leisure interests:* golf, skiing, filming, photography, hunting. *Address:* Soestdijk Palace, Baarn, Netherlands.

NEUBER, Friedel; German banker; b. 10 July 1935, Rheinhessen; Chair. Man. Bd, Westdeutsche Landesbank Girozentrale (WestLB), Düsseldorf/Münster 1981–2001; Chair. Supervisory Bd, Preussag AG, Hanover/Berlin, Deutsche Babcock AG, Oberhausen, LTU Lufttransport Unternehmen GmbH & Co. KG, Düsseldorf, LTU Touristik GmbH, Düsseldorf, WestLB (Europa) AG, Düsseldorf; mem. Supervisory Bd Deutsche Bahn AG, Frankfurt, Douglas Holding AG, Hagen, Friedr. Krupp AG Hoesch-Krupp, Essen, KD Cologne-Düsseldorfer Deutsche Rheinschiffahrt AG, Düsseldorf, RWE AG, Essen, STEAG, Essen, VIAG Aktiengesellschaft, Munich, Bank Austria,

Vienna, UAP SA, Paris; Chair. Bd, Verband öffentlicher Banken e.V., Bonn/Bad Godesberg; Pres. Handelshochschule Leipzig 1997–; mem. Bd of Dirs. Deutsche Girozentrale-Deutsche Kommunalbank, Frankfurt and of numerous other bds.; Hon. DUniv (Duisburg). *Address:* c/o Westdeutsche Landesbank Girozentrale, Herzogstr. 15, 40217 Düsseldorf, Germany. *Telephone:* (211) 82601. *Fax:* (211) 8266119. *E-mail:* presse@westlb.de (Office). *Website:* www.westlb.de (Office).

NEUBERGER, Rabbi Julia Babette Sarah, MA; British rabbi; b. 27 Feb. 1950, London; d. of the late Walter Schwab and Alice Schwab; m. Anthony John Neuberger 1973; one s. one d.; ed South Hampstead High School, Newnham Coll. Cambridge and Leo Baeck Coll. London; Rabbi, S. London Liberal Synagogue 1977–89; Lecturer and Assoc. Fellow, Leo Baeck Coll. 1979–97; Assoc. Newnham Coll. Cambridge 1983–96; Sec. and Chief Exec. The King's Fund 1997–; Chancellor, Univ. of Ulster 1994–2000; Chair. Rabbinic Conf. Union of Liberal and Progressive Synagogues 1983–85; Camden and Islington Community Health Services NHS Trust 1993–97; mem. Policy Planning Group, Inst. of Jewish Affairs 1986–90, NHS Complaints Review 1993–94, Gen. Medical Council 1993–2001, Council, Univ. Coll. London 1993–97, MRC 1995–2000, Council, Save the Children Fund 1995–96; Visiting Fellow, King's Fund Inst. 1989–91; Trustee, Runnymede Trust 1990–97; Chair. Patients Asscn 1988–91, Royal Coll. of Nursing Comm. on Health Service; mem. Nat. Cttee Social Democratic Party 1982–88, Funding Review of BBC 1999, Cttee on Standards in Public Life 2001–; Civil Service Commr 2001–; mem. Bd of Visitors, Memorial Church, Harvard Univ. 1994–; Trustee Imperial War Museum 1999–; other public and charitable appts.; presenter, Choices, BBC TV 1986, 1987; Harkness Fellow, Commonwealth Fund of New York; Visiting Fellow, Harvard Medical School 1991–92; Hon. Fellow, City and Guilds Inst., Mansfield Coll. Oxford; Dr. hc (Open Univ., City Univ. London, Humberside, Ulster, Stirling, Oxford Brookes, Teesside, Nottingham, Queen's Belfast). *Publications:* The Story of Judaism 1986, Days of Decision (ed.) 1987, Caring for Dying Patients of Different Faiths 1987, Whatever's Happening to Women? 1991, A Necessary End (ed. with J. White) 1991, Ethics and Healthcare: the role of Research Ethics Committees in the UK 1992, The Things that Matter 1993, On Being Jewish 1995, Dying Well–A Health Professional's Guide to Enabling a Good Death 1999; contribs. to various books on cultural, religious and ethical factors in nursing; contribs. to Nursing Times; reviews in journals and newspapers. *Leisure interests:* riding, sailing, Irish life, opera, setting up the old girls' network, children. *Address:* The King's Fund, 11–13 Cavendish Square, London, W1G 0AN, England. *Telephone:* (20) 7307-2400. *Fax:* (20) 7307-2803.

NEUBERGER, Michael, PhD, FRS; research scientist; b. 2 Nov. 1953, London; s. of the late Albert Neuberger and of Lilian Neuberger (née Dreyfus); m. Gillian A. Pyman 1991; two s. two d.; ed Westminster School, Trinity Coll. Cambridge, Imperial Coll. London; Sr mem. scientific staff MRC Lab. of Molecular Biology, Cambridge 1980–, Jt Head of Div. of Protein and Nucleic Acid Chemistry 2002–; mem. European Molecular Biology Org.; Int. Research Scholar Howard Hughes Medical Inst.; Novartis Medal, Biochemical Soc. 2002, William Hardy Bate Prize (Cambridge Philiosophical Soc.) 2002, Prix J-P Lecocq (Institut de France) 2002; Hon. Prof. (Cambridge) 2002. *Publications:* papers on molecular immunology in learned journals. *Address:* Medical Research Council Laboratory of Molecular Biology, Hills Road, Cambridge, CB2 2QH, England (Office). *Telephone:* (1223) 248011 (Office). *Fax:* (1223) 412178 (Office).

NEUHARTH, Allen H.; American business executive; b. 22 March 1924, Eureka, S. Dakota; s. of Daniel J. Neuharth and Christina Neuharth; m. 1st Loretta F. Helgeland 1946 (divorced 1972); one s. one d.; m. 2nd Lori Wilson 1973 (divorced 1982); m. 3rd Rachel Fornes 1993; two adopted s. four adopted d.; ed Univ. of S. Dakota; reporter, The Associated Press, Sioux Falls, S. Dakota 1950–52; launched weekly tabloid SoDak Sports 1952; reporter, rising to Asst Man. Ed., Miami Herald 1954–60; Asst Exec. Ed. Knight's Detroit (Mich.) Free Press 1960–63; joined Gannett (newspaper and communications group) 1963, Exec. Vice-Pres. 1966, Pres. and COO 1970, Pres. and CEO 1973, Chair., Pres. and CEO 1979, Chair. and CEO 1984–86, Chair. 1986–89, Founder and Chair. The Freedom Forum 1991–97, Trustee 1991–98, Sr Advisory Trustee 1998–; Founder Florida Today 1966, USA Today 1982; Chair. and Pres. American Newspaper Publishers' Asscn 1979, 1980; numerous awards and 14 hon. degrees. *Publication:* Confessions of an S.O.B. 1989. *Address:* Freedom Forum, 1101 Wilson Boulevard, Suite 2300, Arlington, VA 22209, USA (Home).

NEUHAUSER, Duncan von Briesen, PhD, MBA, M.H.A.; American professor of epidemiology and biostatistics; b. 20 June 1939, Philadelphia, Pa; s. of Edward B. D. Neuhauser and Gernda von Briesen Neuhauser; m. Elinor Toaz Neuhauser 1965; one s. one d.; ed Harvard Univ. and Univs. of Michigan and Chicago; Research Assoc. (Instructor), Center for Health Admin. Studies, Univ. of Chicago 1965–70; Asst Prof., then Assoc. Prof., Harvard School of Public Health 1970–79; Assoc. Chair., Program for Health Systems Man., Harvard Business School 1972–79; Consultant in Medicine, Mass. Gen. Hosp. 1975–80; Prof. of Epidemiology and Biostatistics, Case Western Reserve Univ. 1979–, Prof. of Organizational Behaviour 1979–, Prof. of Medicine 1981–, Keck Foundation Sr Research Scholar 1982–, Prof. of Family Medicine 1990–, Charles Elton Blanchard Prof. of Health Man. 1995–; Adjunct Prof. of Nursing, Vanderbilt Univ. 1998–; mem. bioscientific medical staff, Cleveland Metropolitan Gen. Hosp. 1981–; Adjunct mem., Medical Staff, Cleveland Clinic Foundation 1984–99; Co-Dir Health Systems Man. Centre, Case

Western Reserve Univ. 1985–; Ed. Medical Care 1983–97, Health Matrix 1982–90; mem. Inst. of Medicine (NAS) 1983–; Visiting Prof. of Health Man. Karolinska Inst., Stockholm, Sweden; Festschrift Issue of Medical Care, Aug. 1998; The Duncan Neuhauser PhD Endowed Chair in Community Health Improvement created at Case Western Reserve Univ. in Jan. 2003. *Publications:* (Co-author) Health Services in the US 1976, The Efficient Organization 1977, The Physician and Cost Control 1979, Clinical Decision Analysis 1980, Competition, Co-operation or Regulation 1981, The New Epidemiology 1982, Coming of Age 1984, 1995, Clinical CQI 1995, Health Services Management 1997, Health Services Management Case Studies 1997 and scientific papers. *Leisure interests:* sailing, curling. *Address:* Department of Epidemiology and Biostatistics, Medical School, Case Western Reserve University, 10900 Euclid Avenue, Cleveland, OH 44106-4945 (Office); 2655 North Park Boulevard, Cleveland Heights, OH 44106-3622 (Home, winter); Parker Point Road, P.O. Box 932, Blue Hill, ME 04614, USA (Home, summer). *Telephone:* (216) 368-3726 (Office); (216) 321-1327 (Cleveland Heights); (207) 374-5325 (Blue Hill). *Fax:* (216) 368-3970 (Office). *E-mail:* dvn@po.cwru.edu (Office).

NEUKIRCHEN, Karl Josef, Dr rer. pol; German business executive; b. 17 March 1942, Bonn; Chair. Man. Bd Klöckner-Humboldt-Deutz AG, Cologne until 1988, Hösch AG, Dortmund 1991–92; Chair. Supervisory Bd Klöckner-Werke AG Duisburg 1992–95, Dynamit Nobel AG 1994–; CEO Metallgesellschaft AG Dec. 1993–. *Address:* c/o Metallgesellschaft AG, 60271 Frankfurt am Main, Bockenheimer Landstrasse 73–77, Germany. *Telephone:* (69) 711990 (Office). *Website:* www.mg-ag.de.

NEUMEIER, John, BA; American choreographer and ballet director; b. 1942, Milwaukee, Wis.; s. of Albert Neumeier and Lucille Neumeier; ed Marquette Univ., Milwaukee; dance training in Milwaukee, Chicago, Royal Ballet School, London and in Copenhagen with Vera Volkova; soloist, The Stuttgart Ballet 1963; Ballet Dir Frankfurt 1969; Ballet Dir and Chief Choreographer, The Hamburg Ballet 1973–; Prof. of Hamburg 1987; Dir Hamburg Ballet 1996, Balletintendant 1997–; f. John Neumeier ballet centre, Hamburg 1989; noted for his creation of new works and original interpretations of well-known ballets; f. a ballet training school in Hamburg 1978; appears as soloist, notably in The Chairs with Marcia Haydée, a ballet cr. for them by M. Béjart; Golden Camera Award for TV series of his Ballet Workshops 1978; Dance Magazine Award 1983; Deutscher Tanzpreis 1988; Bundesverdienstkreuz; Hon. DFA (Marquette); Diaghilev Prize 1988, Ordre des Arts et des Lettres, Benois de la Danse 1992, Medal of Honour (City of Tokyo) 1994, Carina-Ari Gold Medal (Sweden) 1994, Nijinsky Medal (Polish Ministry of Culture) 1996. *Works choreographed include:* A Midsummer Night's Dream (Mendelssohn/Ligeti), ballets to the Mahler symphonies, Le Sacre (Stravinsky), The Lady of the Camellias (Chopin), Bach's St Matthew Passion, A Streetcar Named Desire (Prokofiev/Schnittke), Messiah (Handel/Pärt), Nijinsky (Chopin/Rimsky-Korsakov/Shostakovich). *Address:* Hamburg Ballet, Ballettzentrum Hamburg, Caspar-Voght-Str. 54, 20535 Hamburg, Germany. *E-mail:* www.hamburgballett.de.

NEURRISSE, André, DenD, DèsScEcon; French historian and economist; b. 21 April 1916, Pomarez; m. Louise Marie Verdier 1942; two d.; ed Univs. of Bordeaux and Paris; civil servant, Ministry of Finance 1941–58; Treas.-Paymaster Gen. 1958–82; Consultant to IMF, World Bank and UN 1982–; Man. Dir Société d'Etudes et des Participations (SEP) 1984–89; Man. Dir Banque Internationale de Financement et de Négociation (BIFEN) 1985–91; Pres., Dir-Gen. Union Commerciale de crédit multiservices 1989–91; Médaille d'Or de l'Educ. Physique et des Sports 1958, Lauréat de l'Inst. (Prix Joseph Dutens) 1964; Officier des Palmes académiques 1964, Officier Légion d'Honneur 1970, Commdr Mérite National 1980. *Publications:* Précis de droit budgétaire 1961, La comptabilité économique française 1963, Les règlements internationaux 1972, Histoire du Franc 1974, Les jeux de casino 1977, Histoire de l'impôt 1978, L'économie sociale 1983, Le Trésorier-Payeur Général 1986, Le Franc C.F.A. 1987, Les jeux d'argent et de hasard 1990, Deux mille ans d'impôts 1994, Histoire de la Fiscalité en France 1996; contribs. to collective works and numerous articles in La Revue du trésor. *Address:* 9 rue Docteur Blanche, 75016 Paris, France. *Telephone:* 1-45-25-89-32. *Fax:* 1-45-25-89-32.

NEUSTADT, Richard Elliott, PhD; American political scientist; b. 26 June 1919, Philadelphia; s. of Richard Neustadt and Elizabeth Neufeld; m. 1st Bertha Cummings 1945 (died 1984); one s. one d.; m. 2nd Shirley Williams (now Baroness Williams of Crosby, q.v., 1987; ed Univ. of Calif. at Berkeley and Harvard Univ.; Economist, Office of Price Admin. 1942; US Naval Reserve 1942–46; Staff mem., Bureau of Budget 1946–50, White House 1950–53; Prof. of Public Admin. Cornell Univ. 1953–54, of Govt, Columbia Univ. 1954–65, Harvard Univ. 1965–78; Lucius N. Littauer Prof. of Public Admin. John F. Kennedy School of Govt 1978–86, Assoc. Dean 1965–75, Dir Inst. of Politics 1966–71; Douglas Dillon Prof. of Govt, Harvard 1986–89, Prof. Emer. 1989–; Visitor, Nuffield Coll. Oxford 1961–62, Assoc. mem. 1965–67, 1990–93; Visiting Prof. of Govt, Univ. of Essex 1994–95; Special Consultant, Sub-Cttee on Nat. Policy Machinery, US Senate 1959–61; mem. Advisory Bd on Comm. on Money and Credit 1960–61; Special Consultant to Pres.-Elect Kennedy 1960–61, to Pres. Kennedy 1961–63; to Bureau of Budget 1961–70, to Dept of State 1962–69; Consultant to Pres. Johnson 1964–66, to Rand Corpn 1964–78; mem. Council on Foreign Relations, Inst. for Strategic Studies, American Political Science Assn, Nat. Acad. of Public Admin., American Philosophical Soc.; Fellow American Acad. of Arts and Sciences, Center for Advanced Study in the Behavioral Sciences 1978–79; Chair.

Advisory Cttee to Comm. on Presidential Debate 1988–96; Trustee, Radcliffe Coll. 1977–80; Democrat; Woodrow Wilson Award, American Political Science Assn 1962, Grawemeyer Award, Univ. of Louisville 1989, Hubert H. Humphrey Award, American Political Science Assn 1994, Paul Peck Prize, Smithsonian Inst. 2002. *Publications:* Presidential Power 1960 (revised 1990), Alliance Politics 1970, The Epidemic That Never Was (with Harvey Fineberg) 1983, Thinking in Time (with Ernest May) 1986, Report to JFK 1999, Preparing To Be President 2000. *Address:* Kennedy School of Government, Harvard University, Cambridge, MA 02138, USA. *Telephone:* (617) 495-1196. *Fax:* (617) 496-6886.

NEUVO, Yrjö A., PhD, FIEEE; Finnish research professor; b. 21 July 1943, Turku; s. of Olavi Neuvo and Aune (née Vaisala) Neuvo; m. Tuula Halsas 1968; two s. one d.; ed Cornell Univ. and Helsinki Univ. of Tech.; Acting Prof. Helsinki Univ. of Tech. 1975–76; Prof. of Electronics, Tampere Univ. of Tech. 1976–92; Sr Vice-Pres., Tech. Nokia Corpn 1993–; Sr Research Fellow Acad. of Finland 1979–80, Research Prof. 1984–; Visiting Prof. Univ. of Calif. 1981–82; Hon. MD (Tampere Univ. of Tech.) 1992; Commdr Order of Lion of Finland 1992; IEEE Bicentennial Award 1986, Assn in Finland Hon. Prize 1988; Nokia Prize 1989. *Publications:* over 300 scientific publs on computer eng and new technologies. *Address:* Nokia Corporation, P.O. Box 226, 00101 Helsinki, Finland. *Telephone:* (0) 18071. *Fax:* (0) 176015.

NEVANLINNA, (Eero) Olavi, DipEng, DTech; Finnish professor of mathematics; b. 17 April 1948, Helsinki; m. Marja Lähdesmäki 1968; three s. one d.; ed Helsinki Univ. of Technology; Asst Math. Helsinki Univ. of Tech. 1971–74; Sr Researcher Acad. of Finland 1975–77; Assoc. Prof. Applied Math. Oulu Univ. 1978–79; Prof. Math. Helsinki Univ. of Tech. 1980–; Research Prof. Acad. of Finland 1986–92; Visiting Prof. at several U.S. univs. and at ETH, Zürich; Chair. Rolf Nevanlinna Inst. 1989–90; Chair. Supervisory Bd Suomi Mutual Life Assurance Co. 1996–98; Pres. Int. Council for Industrial and Applied Math. 1999–2003; mem. Bd Pohjola Insurance Co. Ltd 1997–99; mem. Finnish Acad. of Tech. Sciences 1984, Finnish Acad. of Sciences and Letters 1986, Ed. Bd BIT, Nat. Cttee in Math. 1984–. *Publications:* Convergence of Iterations for Linear Equations 1993, Birkhäuser, Meromorphic Functions and Linear Algebra 2003. *Address:* Institute of Mathematics, Helsinki University of Technology, P.O. Box 1100, 02015 HUT, Finland. *Telephone:* (9) 4513034. *Fax:* (9) 4513016. *E-mail:* olavi.nevanlinna@hut.fi (Office).

NEVES, José Maria Pereira; Cape Verde politician; Chair. Partido Africano da Independência de Cabo Verde (PAICV); Prime Minister of Cape Verde Feb. 2001–. *Address:* Office of the Prime Minister, Palácio do Governo, Várzea, C.P. 16, Praia, Santiago, Cape Verde (Office). *Telephone:* 61-05-13 (Office). *Fax:* 61-30-99 (Office).

NEVILLE, John, OBE; British actor and theatre director; b. 2 May 1925, Willesden, London; s. of Reginald D. Neville and Mabel L. Fry; m. Caroline Hooper 1949; three s. three d.; ed Chiswick County Grammar School and Royal Acad. of Dramatic Art, London; with Bristol Old Vic Co., London 1953, played Othello, Iago, Hamlet, Aguecheek and Richard II; mem. Chichester Theatre Co. 1962; created part of Alfie (Alfie by Bill Naughton), London 1963; Dir Nottingham Playhouse 1963–68, Newcastle Playhouse 1967; Hon. Prof. of Drama, Nottingham Univ. 1967–; Drama Adviser to Howard and Wyndham Ltd; in musical Mr. & Mrs. 1968; series of TV plays 1968; presented four plays at Fortune Theatre, London with the Park Theatre Co.; appeared in the Apple Cart, Mermaid Theatre, London 1970, The Beggar's Opera, Chichester 1972, Happy Days, Nat. Theatre, London 1977, The School for Scandal, Nat. Theatre 1990, The Dance of Death, Almeida 1995, Beethoven's Tenth, Chichester 1996, Krapp's Last Tape, Nottingham Playhouse 1999; went to Canada 1973; staged The Rivals, Nat. Arts Theatre, Ottawa; Dir opera Don Giovanni, Festival Canada, Ottawa; played Prospero (The Tempest), Judge Brack (Hedda Gabler), Sir George Croft (Mrs. Warren's Profession), in Sherlock Holmes, New York 1975; Artistic Dir of Citadel Theatre, Edmonton, Alberta 1973–78; Artistic Dir Neptune Theatre, Halifax, Nova Scotia 1978–83; with Stratford Festival Theatre, Ont. 1983–89, Artistic Dir 1985–89; Dir Hamlet 1986, Mother Courage, Othello 1987, Three Sisters 1989; film (in title role) Adventures of Baron Munchhausen 1987–88; acted in School for Scandal, Nat. Theatre 1990; Hon. Dr. Dramatic Arts (Lethbridge Univ., Alberta) 1979; Hon. DFA (Nova Scotia Coll. of Art and Design) 1981, Dr. hc (Ryerson Univ.) 1999. *Films acted in include:* Mr. Topaz, Oscar Wilde, Billy Budd, A Study in Terror, Adventures of Baron Munchausen. *Leisure interests:* watching football, listening to music (all kinds), thinking about gardening. *Address:* 139 Winnett Avenue, Toronto, Ont., M6C 3L7, Canada.

NEVO, Ruth, PhD; Israeli painter and fmr professor of humanities; b. 1924, Johannesburg, SA; d. of Benjamin Weinbren and Henrietta Weinbren (née Goldsmith); m. Natan Nevo 1952; three s.; ed Univ. of the Witwatersrand, Johannesburg and Hebrew Univ., Jerusalem; tutor Dept of English, Hebrew Univ. 1952, Prof. 1973; Renee Lang Prof. of Humanities 1982–87; full-time painter 1987–; solo exhbns. 1987, 1991, 1992, 1995, 1997, 1998, 2000; mem. Israel Acad. 1985–, Israel Assocn of Painters and Sculptors 1989–. *Publications:* The Dial of Virtue 1963, Tragic Form in Shakespeare 1972, Comic Transformations in Shakespeare 1980, Shakespeare's Other Language 1987; trans. Selected Poems by Bialik 1981, Travels by Amichai 1986. *Address:* Hehalutz 22, Jerusalem; Department of English, Hebrew University, Mount Scopus, Jerusalem, Israel. *Telephone:* 2-6523752.

NEWALL, James Edward Malcolm, OC, BComm; Canadian business executive; b. 20 Aug. 1935, Holden, Alberta; m. Margaret Elizabeth Lick; ed Prince Albert Coll. Inst., Univ. of Saskatchewan; joined Du Pont Canada Inc. 1957, various posts in marketing and gen. man. in fibres business, leading to Dir Fibres Group 1972, Vice-Pres., Corp. Devt 1974, Marketing 1975, Exec. Vice-Pres. 1975, Dir 1976, Pres. and CEO 1978–89, Chair. 1979, Chair. and CEO du Pont Canada –1994 and responsible for E.I. du Pont's int. businesses outside Canada and USA 1989–91, Sr Vice-Pres. E.I. du Pont de Nemours Agricultural Products 1989–91; Vice-Chair., CEO and Dir Nova Corpn of Alberta 1991–98, Chair. 1998–; Chair. Maritime Transport Services 1994–, Newall & Assocs. 1998–, Nova Chems. 1998–; Chair. Business Council on Nat. Issues; Dir Alcan Aluminium Ltd, BCE Inc., The Molson Cos. Ltd, Pratt & Whitney Canada Inc., The Royal Bank of Canada; Chair. Business Council on Nat. Issues; fmr Chair. and Dir Conf. Bd of Canada; mem. Advisory Group to Prime Minister on exec. compensation in the public service. *Address:* Newall & Associates, 2015 Bankers Hall, 855 2nd Street, SW, Calgary, Alberta T2P 4J7, Canada (Office).

NEWBERY, David Michael Garrood, PhD, FBA; British academic economist; b. 1 June 1943, Bucks.; m. Dr. Terri E Apter 1975; two d.; ed Portsmouth Grammar School, Trinity Coll. Cambridge; Economist, Treasury of Tanzanian Govt 1965–66; Asst Lecturer, Faculty of Econs and Politics, Cambridge Univ. 1966–71, Lecturer 1971–86, Reader in Econs 1986–88, Prof. of Applied Econs and Dir Dept of Applied Econs 1988–, Fellow Churchill Coll. 1966–; Div. Chief, World Bank 1981–83; Fellow Econometric Soc. 1989; Vice-Pres. European Econ. Asscn 1994–95, Pres. 1996; Frisch Medal, Econometric Soc. 1990, Harry Johnson Prize (jtly), Canadian Econ. Asscn 1993. *Publications:* Project Appraisal in Practice (co-author) 1976, The Theory of Commodity Price Stabilization: A Study in the Economics of Risk (with J. E. Stiglitz) 1981, The Theory of Taxation for Developing Countries (with N. H. Stern) 1987, Hungary: An Economy in Transition (with I. Székely) 1993, Tax and Benefit Reform in Central and Eastern Europe 1995, A European Market for Electricity? (co-author) 1999, Privatization, Restructuring and Regulation of Network Utilities 2000; numerous articles. *Address:* Department of Applied Economics, Sidgwick Avenue, Cambridge, CB3 9DE (Office); 9 Huntingdon Road, Cambridge, CB3 0HH, England (Home). *Telephone:* (1223) 335247 (Office); (1223) 360216 (Home). *Fax:* (1223) 335299.

NEWBIGGING, David Kennedy, OBE; British business executive; b. 19 Jan. 1934, Tientsin, China; s. of the late D. L. and of L. M. Newbigging; m. Carolyn S. Band 1968; one s. two d.; ed Oundle School; joined Jardine, Matheson & Co., Ltd 1954, Dir 1967, Man. Dir 1970, Chair. and Sr Man. Dir 1975–83; Chair. Hongkong & Kowloon Wharf & Godown Co., Ltd 1970–80; Chair. and Man. Dir Hongkong Land Co., Ltd 1975–83; Dir Hongkong & Shanghai Banking Corpn 1975–83; Dir Hongkong Electric Holdings Ltd 1975–83, Chair. 1982–83; Dir Hongkong Telephone Co., Ltd 1975–83; Chair. Jardine, Fleming & Co., Ltd 1975–83; Dir Rennies Consolidated Holdings Ltd 1975–83; Dir Safmarine and Rennies Holdings Ltd 1984–85; Dir Provincial Insurance PLC 1984–86, Deputy Chair. Provincial Group PLC 1985–91; Deputy Chair. Ivory & Sime PLC 1990–95, Chair. 1992–95 (Dir 1987–95); Dir NM UK (Chair. 1990–93), Rentokil Group PLC 1986–94 (Chair. 1987–94), PACCAR (UK) Ltd 1986–97, Mason Best Int. Ltd 1986–90 (Chair. 1987–90), Int. Financial Markets Trading Ltd 1986–93, United Meridian Corpn 1987–97, Thai Holdings Ltd 1989–91, Merrill Lynch Inc., USA 1997–, Ocean Energy Inc., USA 1998–, PACCAR Inc., USA 1999–; Deputy Chair. Benchmark Group PLC 1996–; Chair. Redfearn PLC March–Dec. 1988; Chair. Faupel Trading Group PLC 1994– (Dir 1989–), London Capital Holdings PLC March–Dec. 1994; Dir Wah Kwong Shipping Holdings Ltd 1992–99, Lloyd's Market Bd 1993–95, Friends' Provident PLC 1993– (Chair. 1998–); Chair. Equitas Holdings Ltd 1995–98, Maritime Transport Services Ltd 1993–95; Trustee, King Mahendra UK Trust for Nature Conservation 1988–; Chair. of Trustees, Wilts Community Foundation 1991–97; Chair. of Council, Mission to Seafarers (fmrly Mission to Seaman) 1993–; Deputy Chair., Council of Trustees, Cancer Research UK 2002–; mem. Legis. Council of Hongkong 1978–82, mem. Exec. Council 1980–84; mem. Int. Council, Morgan Guaranty Trust Co. of New York 1977–85, Supervisory Bd DAF Trucks NV 1997–99; mem. British Coal Corpn (fmrly Nat. Coal Bd) 1984–87, CIN Man. 1985–87; Deputy Lt of Wiltshire 1994–, High Sheriff of Wiltshire 2003–04. *Leisure interests:* most outdoor sports, Chinese art. *Address:* 15 Old Bailey, London, EC4M 7EF, England. *Telephone:* (20) 7506-1000. *Fax:* (20) 7248-6332.

NEWBY, (George) Eric, CBE, MC, FRSL, FRGS; British author; b. 6 Dec. 1919, London; s. of George A. Newby and Hilda Pomroy; m. Wanda Skof 1946; one s. one d.; ed St Paul's School; with Dorland Advertising, London 1936–38; apprentice and ordinary seaman, four-masted Finnish barque 1938–39; mil. service 1939–45, Black Watch (commissioned 1940) and Special Boat Section, prisoner-of-war 1942–45; women's fashion business 1946–56; exploration in Nuristan 1956; with Secker and Warburg (publisher) 1956–59; fashion buyer, John Lewis Partnership 1959–63; Travel Ed., The Observer and Gen. Ed. Time Off Books 1964–73; Hon. DLitt (Bournemouth) 1994; Dr. hc (Open Univ.) 1996. *Publications:* The Last Grain Race 1956, A Short Walk in the Hindu Kush 1958, Something Wholesale 1962, Slowly Down the Ganges 1966, Time Off in Southern Italy 1966, Grain Race: Pictures of Life Before the Mast in a Windjammer 1968, The Wonders of Britain (jtly) 1968, The Wonders of Ireland (jtly.) 1969, Love and War in the Apennines 1971, The World of Evelyn Waugh (jtly.) 1973, Ganga 1973, World Atlas of Exploration 1975, Great Ascents 1977, The Big Red Train Ride 1978, A Traveller's Life 1982, On the Shores of the Mediterranean 1984, A Book of Traveller's Tales 1985, Round Ireland in Low Gear 1987, What the Traveller Saw 1989, A Small Place in Italy 1994, A Merry Dance Around the World 1995, Learning the Ropes 1999, Departures and Arrivals 2000, Around the World in Eighty Years 2000. *Leisure interests:* walking, cycling. *Address:* Pine View House, 4 Pine View Close, Chilworth, Surrey, GU4 8RS, England. *Telephone:* (1483) 571430; (1483) 571430 (Office).

NEWBY, Sir Howard Joseph, KCMG, CBE, PhD, FRSA; British university vice-chancellor; b. 10 Dec. 1947, Derby; s. of Alfred J. Newby and Constance A. Potts; m. Janet Elizabeth Craddock 1970; two s.; Lecturer in Sociology, Univ. of Essex 1972–75, Sr Lecturer 1975–79; Prof. of Sociology, Univ. of Wis. 1979–83, Univ. of Essex 1983–88; Chair. Econ. & Social Research Council 1988–94, Chief Exec. 1994; mem. Rural Devt Comm. 1991–99, S. & W. Regional Health Authority 1994–96, European Sciences and Technology Asscn 1997–; Vice-Chancellor, Univ. of Southampton 1994–2001; Chair. Cttee of Vice-Chancellors and Prins 1999–2001; Chair Centre for Exploitation of Science and Tech. 1995–; Chief Exec. Higher Educ. Funding Council for England 2001–; visiting appts Univs of New South Wales 1976, Sydney 1976, Wis. 1977–78, Newcastle-upon-Tyne 1983–84; seven hon. degrees. *Publications include:* Community Studies (jtly) 1971, The Deferential Worker 1977, Property, Paternalism and Power (jtly) 1978, Green and Pleasant Land? 1979, The Problem of Sociology (jtly) 1983, Country Life 1987, The Countryside in Question 1988, Social Class in Modern Britain 1988 (jtly), The National Trust: The Next 100 Years 1995. *Leisure interests:* family life, gardening, Derby County, railway enthusiasms. *Address:* HEFCE, Northavon House, Coldharbour Lane, Bristol, BS16 1QD (Office); The Old Mill, Mill Lane, Corston, Malmesbury, Wilts., SN16 0HH, England. *Telephone:* (117) 931-7300. *E-mail:* chief.executive@hefce.ac.uk (Office).

NEWCOMBE, John David, AO, OBE; Australian professional tennis player; b. 23 May 1944, Sydney; s. of George Ernest Newcombe and Lillian Newcombe; m. Angelika Pfannenberg (fmr German pro tennis player) 1966; one s. two d.; ed Sydney Church of England Grammar School; winner of Wimbledon Singles Championship 1967 (last amateur), 1970, 1971, USA Singles Championship 1967, 1973, Australia Singles Championship 1973, 1975, World Championship Tennis Crown 1974, Wimbledon Doubles Championship 1965–66, 1968–70, 1974; won 73 pro titles; played with Australian Davis Cup Team 1963–67, 1973–76, Capt. (non-playing) 1994–2000; set up a tennis camp, the John Newcombe Tennis Ranch, in Texas in 1968; Pres. Asscn of Tennis Professionals (Int.) 1976–78, Nat. Australia Day Council 1981–91; Chair. Player Devt Bd Tennis Australia 1985–94; Hon. Life mem. Australian Wheelchair Tennis Asscn; mem. Bd McDonald's System of Australia; Dr hc (Bond, Queensland) 1999; inducted Int. Tennis Hall of Fame 1986. *Television:* has appeared as a commentator for various networks on numerous tennis tournaments in Australia, America and the UK. *Publications:* The Family Tennis Book 1975, The Young Tennis Player 1981, Bedside Tennis 1983, Newk 2002. *Leisure interests:* skiing, waterskiing, golf, fishing. *Address:* c/o Tennis Australia, Batman Avenue, Melbourne, Vic. 3000, Australia.

NEWELL, Frances Mary, FRSA, FCSD; British design consultant; b. 19 Jan. 1947, Surrey; d. of the late Alexander C. Newell and of Julie S. Newell; m. John William Sorrell 1974; two s. one d.; Founder and Chair. Newell & Sorrell (identity & design consultants, merged with Interbrand 1997) 1976–97; apptd. Group Creative Dir Interbrand Newell and Sorrell 1997; Chair. City & Guilds Nat. Advisory Cttee on Art, Craft and Design 1994–96, mem. Colour Group 1996–, City & Guilds Sr Awards Cttee 1996–; Bd Dir Royal Acad. Enterprises 1996–99; mem. Exec. Cttee Mencap Blue Sky Appeal 1996–98, Advisory Bd of Nat. Museum of Photography, Film and TV; 11 DBA Design Effectiveness Awards, 5 Silver D&ADs, 5 Clios, 1 Grand Award for British Airways Corp. Identity and 5 Gold Awards in New York Festivals, 2 Art Directors' Club of Europe Awards. *Leisure interests:* art, travel, gardening. *Address:* c/o Interbrand Newell and Sorrell, 4 Utopia Village, Chalcot Road, London, NW1 8LH, England.

NEWELL, Mike; British film director; b. 1942, St Albans, Herts.; s. of Terence William Newell and Mollie Louise Newell; m. Bernice Stegers 1979; one s. one d.; ed Univ. of Cambridge; trainee Dir Granada TV 1963; Dir European premiere of Tennessee Williams' The Kingdom of the Earth, Bristol Old Vic. *Films:* The Man in the Iron Mask 1976, The Awakening 1979, Bad Blood 1980, Dance with a Stranger (Prix de la Jeunesse, Cannes) 1984, The Good Father 1985, Amazing Grace and Chuck 1986, Soursweet 1987, Common Ground 1990, Enchanted April 1991, Into the West 1992, Four Weddings and a Funeral (BAFTA Award for Best Film and Best Achievement in Direction 1995, Cesar Award for Foreign Film) 1994, An Awfully Big Adventure 1994, Donnie Brasco 1997, Pushing Tin 1998, Mona Lisa Smile 2003; exec. producer on Photographing Fairies 1997, 200 Cigarettes 1999, Best Laid Plans 1999, High Fidelity 2000, Traffic 2000. *TV Films:* Ready when you are, Mr McGill, Tales out of School, Birth of a Nation (Prix Futura, Berlin), The Melancholy Hussar, Lost Your Tongue, Baa Baa Black Sheep, Common Ground (for CBS), Blood Feud (for Fox) 1983. *TV work includes:* Mr and Mrs Bureaucrat, Destiny, The Gift of Friendship, Brassneck (play), Just your Luck (play). *Leisure interests:* reading (anything but fiction), walking. *Address:* c/o ICM, Oxford House, 76 Oxford Street, London, W1N 0AX, England.

NEWELL, Norman Dennis, PhD; American palaeontologist and geologist; b. 27 Jan. 1909, Chicago, Ill.; s. of Virgil Bingham Newell and Nellie Clark; m. 1st Valerie Zirkle 1928 (died 1972); m. 2nd Gillian Wendy Wormall 1973;

ed Univ. of Kansas and Yale Univ.; Geologist, Kansas Geological Survey 1929–37; Faculty mem., Univ. of Kansas 1934–37; Assoc. Prof. of Geology Univ. of Wis. 1937–45; Prof. of Geology Columbia Univ. 1945–77, Prof. Emer. 1977–; Curator American Museum of Natural History, New York 1945–77, Curator Emer. 1977–; Consultant on Petroleum Geology, Govt of Peru 1942–45; mem. NAS, American Acad. of Arts and Sciences, American Philosophical Soc., Geological Soc. of America, London Geological Soc., Paleontology Soc. (Pres. 1960–61), Soc. for the Study of Evolution (Pres. 1949), Soc. of Systematic Zoology (Pres. 1972–73); Hon. mem. Canadian Soc. of Petroleum Geologists 1993; awards include NAS Mary Clarke Thompson Medal 1960, Yale Univ. Verrill Medal 1966, American Museum of Natural History Gold Medal for Achievement in Science 1978, Palaeontological Soc. Medal 1979 and AAAS Scientific Freedom and Responsibility Award 1987, Geological Soc. of America Penrose Medal 1990, American Asscn of Petroleum Geologists Special Award 1996, Geological Soc. of Peru Medal 1997, Int. Symposium on the Paleobiology and Evolution of the Bivalvia Festschrift 1998. *Publications:* Late Paleozoic Pelecypods 1937–42, Geology of the Lake Titicaca Region 1943, Upper Paleozoic of Peru 1953, Permian Reef Complex of the Guadalupe Mountains Region 1953, Geological Reconnaissance of Raroia Atoll 1956, Classification of the Bivalvia 1965, Revolutions in the History of Life 1967, Creation and Evolution: Myth or Reality? 1982, Pectinoid Bivalves of the Permian-Triassic Crisis 1995 and scientific and popular articles on evolution, extinction. *Address:* Division of Paleontolgy, Department of Invertebrates, American Museum of Natural History, Central Park West and 79th Street, New York, NY 10024 (Office); 135 Knapp Terrace, Leonia, NJ 07605, USA (Home). *Telephone:* (212) 769-5736 (Office); (201) 944-5596 (Home). *Fax:* (212) 769-5222 (Office); (201) 944-1553 (Home). *E-mail:* newell@amnh.org (Office); gwnewel@attglobal.net (Home).

NEWHOUSE, Samuel I., Jr; American publishing executive; b. 1928; m. Victoria Newhouse; Chair. Condé Nast Publs Inc., New York; Chair., CEO Advance Publs Inc., New York; fmr mem. Bd NY Museum of Modern Art; Henry Johnson Fisher Award, Magazine Publishers' Asscn 1985. *Address:* Advance Publishers Inc., 950 Fingerboard Road, Staten Island, NY 10305, USA.

NEWMAN, Arnold; American photographer; b. 1918, New York; ed Univ. of Miami; began career at a photographic studio in Philadelphia 1941; first show Sept. 1941; moved to New York 1945; worked as freelance photographer for numerous magazines including Newsweek, Fortune, Life, Esquire; Infinity Award for Master of Photography 1999.

NEWMAN, Edwin Harold; American journalist; b. 25 Jan. 1919, New York; s. of Myron Newman and Rose Parker Newman; m. Rigel Grell 1944; one d.; ed Univ. of Wisconsin, Louisiana State Univ.; Washington Bureau, Int. News Service 1941, United Press 1941–42, 1945–46; U.S. Navy 1942–45; CBS News, Washington, DC 1947–49; freelance, London 1949–52; NBC News, London Bureau 1952–, Rome Bureau 1957–58, Paris Bureau 1958–61; Corresp. and Commentator, NBC News, New York 1961–83; Moderator of Presidential Cand. debates Ford-Carter 1976, Reagan-Mondale 1984; Columnist, King Features Syndicate 1984–89; freelance journalist and lecturer; appeared as self in numerous TV comedy series and films including The Pelican Brief and Spies like Us; Peabody Award, Overseas Press Club Award, Emmy Award, Univ. of Mo. School of Journalism Award, Chevalier, Légion d'honneur and others. *Publications:* Strictly Speaking 1974, A Civil Tongue 1976, Sunday Punch 1979, I Must Say 1988; articles for Punch, Esquire, Atlantic, Harper's, New York Times, Saturday Review, Chicago Tribune, TV Guide, Sports Illustrated. *Leisure interests:* music, reading. *Address:* c/o Richard Fulton Inc., 66 Richfield Street, Plainview, NY 11803, USA.

NEWMAN, Frank, BA; American banker; b. 20 April 1942, Quincy, Mass.; m. Lizabeth Newman; one s.; ed Harvard Univ.; Man. Peat Marwick Livingston & Co. 1966–69; Vice-Pres. Citicorp 1969–73; Exec. Vice-Pres., Chief Financial Officer Wells Fargo Bank 1973–86; Vice-Chair., Chief Financial Officer Bank America Corp. 1986–93; Under-Sec., Deputy Sec. Treasury Dept 1993–95; Sr Vice-Chair. Bankers Trust Co. 1995–, Chair., CEO, Pres. 1996–99, resgnd as Chair.; mem. Bd Deutsche Bank 1999; Alexander Hamilton Award (Treasury Dept). *Address:* Bankers Trust, 130 Liberty Street, New York, NY 10006, USA. *Telephone:* (212) 250-2500.

NEWMAN, Jocelyn Margaret, LLB; Australian politician; b. 8 July 1937; ed Melbourne Univ.; Senator (Liberal Party) for Tasmania 1986–2001; Shadow Minister for Defence, Science and Personnel 1988–92, Veterans' Affairs 1990–92; Shadow Minister Assisting Leader on Status of Women 1989–93; Shadow Minister for the Aged and Veterans' Affairs 1992–93; Shadow Minister for Family Health, Shadow Minister Assisting Leader on Family Matters, Chair. Health, Welfare and Veterans' Affairs Group 1993–94; Shadow Minister for Defence 1994–96; Minister for Social Security and Minister Assisting Prime Minister on Status of Women 1996–98, for Family and Community Services and Minister Assisting Prime Minister on Status of Women 1998–2001. *Address:* c/o Parliament House, Canberra, ACT 2600, Australia.

NEWMAN, Sir Kenneth (Leslie), Kt, GBE; British police officer; b. 15 Aug. 1926; s. of John William and Florence Newman; m. Eileen Lilian Newman 1949; one s. one d.; ed Univ. of London; with RAF 1942–46; mem. Palestine Police 1946–48; with Metropolitan Police, London 1948–73, Commdr New Scotland Yard 1972; with Royal Ulster Constabulary 1973–79, Sr Deputy Chief Constable 1973, Chief Constable 1976–79; Commandant, Police Staff

Coll. 1980–82; Insp. of Constabulary 1980–82; Commr Metropolitan Police 1982–87; Prof. of Law, Bristol Univ. 1987–88; Registrar Imperial Soc. of Kts. Bachelor 1991–98; Dir Control Risks 1987–92; Chair. Disciplinary Cttee, Security Systems Inspectorate, British Security Industry Asscn 1987–95, Asscn for Prevention of Theft in Shops 1987–91; Pres. Asscn of Police and Public Security Suppliers 1993–2000; Vice-Pres. Defence Mfrs Asscn 1987–2000; Trustee Community Action Trust 1987–99, World Humanity Action Trust 1993–98; CIMgt 1977; KStJ 1984; Queen's Police Medal 1982, numerous foreign decorations. *Leisure interests:* bridge, walking. *Address:* c/o New Scotland Yard, Broadway, London, S.W.1, England.

NEWMAN, Maurice Lionel, AM; Australian banker; b. 20 April 1938, Ilford, England; s. of J. Newman; m. 1st 1963 (divorced); two s.; m. 2nd Jeanette Newman 1994; ed Univ. of Sydney; partner Bain and Co. 1966–73, Man. Dir Bain and Co. Group 1983–85; Exec. Chair. Deutsche Bank Australia Group (fmrly Deutsche Morgan Grenfell Group) 1985–; Chair. Australian Stock Exchange Ltd 1994–, Australian-Taiwan Business Council 1995–, E Asian and Oceanic Stock Exchanges Fed. 1995–96, Axiom Funds Man. Ltd 1997–, Benchmark Securities Man. Ltd 1997–, Commercial Investment Trust 1998–, Financial Sector, Advisory Council 1998–; Dir Financial Futures Market 1990–, Securities Industry Research Centre Australia; mem. Australian Inst. of Co. Dirs; Trustee Stock Exchange Superannuation and Accumulation Fund 1990–. *Leisure interests:* cycling, horse riding, tennis. *Address:* Australian Stock Exchange Ltd, P.O. Box H224, Australia Square, Sydney, NSW 2000 (Office); 35 Burran Avenue, Mosman, NSW 2088, Australia (Home). *Telephone:* (2) 9321-4000 (Office). *Fax:* (2) 9235-0056 (Office). *Website:* www.asx.com.au.

NEWMAN, Nanette; British actress and writer; b. Northampton; d. of Sidney Newman and Ruby Newman; m. Bryan Forbes (q.v.) 1955; two d.; ed Sternhold Coll., London, Italia Conti Stage School, Royal Acad. of Dramatic Art. *Film appearances include:* The L-Shaped Room 1962, The Wrong Arm of the Law 1962, Seance on a Wet Afternoon 1963, The Wrong Box 1965, The Whisperers 1966, The Madwoman of Chaillot 1968, The Raging Moon (Variety Club Best Actress Award) 1971, The Stepford Wives 1974, International Velvet 1978. *Television appearances include:* The Fun Food Factory, London Scene, Stay with me till Morning, Jessie, Let There Be Love, Late Expectations, The Endless Game 1988, Ideal Home Cooks, Newman Meets (series), Celebrations (series). *Publications:* God Bless Love 1972, Lots of Love 1973, All Our Love 1978, Fun Food Factory 1976, The Root Children 1978, Amy Rainbow 1980, That Dog 1980, Reflections 1981, Dog Lovers Coffee Table Book 1982, Cat Lovers Coffee Table Book 1983, My Granny was a Frightful Bore 1983, Christmas Cookbook 1984, Cat and Mouse Love Story 1984, The Best of Love 1985, Pigalev 1985, Archie 1986, The Summer Cookbook 1986, Small Beginnings 1987, Bad Baby 1988, Entertaining with Nanette Newman 1988, Charlie the Noisy Caterpillar 1989, Sharing 1989, ABC 1990, 123 1991, Cooking for Friends 1991, Spider, The Horrible Cat 1992, There's a Bear in the Bath 1993, There's a Bear in the Classroom 1996, Take 3 Cooks 1996, Up to the Skies and Down Again 1999, To You with Love 1999, Bad Baby Good Baby 2002. *Leisure interests:* needlepoint, china painting. *Address:* Chatto & Linnit Ltd, 123A King's Road, London, SW3 4PL, England.

NEWMAN, Paul, BA, LHD; American actor; b. 26 Jan. 1925, Cleveland, Ohio; s. of Arthur Newman and Theresa Fetzer; m. 1st Jacqueline Witte 1949; one s. (died 1978) two d.; m. 2nd Joanne Woodward (q.v.) 1958; three d.; ed Kenyon Coll. and Yale Univ. School of Drama; mil. service 1943–46; Pres. Newman's Own Foundation Inc. (organic food co.); Best Actor, Acad. of Motion Pictures, Arts and Sciences 1959, 1962, 1964, Hon. Acad. Award 1986; Head cos Newman's Own, Newman's Own Spaghetti Sauce, Newman's Own Popcorn etc.; Hon. DHumLitt (Yale) 1988; Franklin D. Roosevelt Four Freedoms Medal 1991, Kennedy Center Honor 1992, Jean Hersholt Humanitarian Award 1994. *Stage appearances include:* Picnic 1953–54, Desperate Hours 1955, Sweet Bird of Youth 1959, Baby Want a Kiss 1964. *Films include:* (actor) The Rack 1955, Somebody Up There Likes Me 1956, Cat on a Hot Tin Roof 1958, Rally Round the Flag, Boys 1958, The Young Philadelphians 1958, From the Terrace 1960, Exodus 1960, The Hustler 1962, Hud 1963, The Prize 1963, The Outrage 1964, What a Way to Go 1964, Lady L 1965, Torn Curtain 1966, Hombre 1967, Cool Hand Luke 1967, The Secret War of Harry Frigg 1968, Butch Cassidy and the Sundance Kid 1969, WUSA 1970, Pocket Money 1972, The Life and Times of Judge Roy Bean 1973, The Mackintosh Man 1973, The Sting 1973, The Towering Inferno 1974, The Drowning Pool 1975, Buffalo Bill and the Indians 1976, Silent Movie 1976, Slap Shot 1977, Absence of Malice 1981, The Verdict 1982, Harry and Son (dir) 1984, The Color of Money 1986, Fat Man and Little Boy, Blaze 1989, Mr. and Mrs. Bridge 1990, The Hudsucker Proxy 1994, Nobody's Fool 1994, Message in a Bottle 1999, (dir) Rachel, Rachel 1968, The Effect of Gamma Rays on Man in the Moon Marigolds 1973, The Shadow Box 1980, When Time Ran Out 1980, Fort Apache: the Bronx 1981, The Glass Menagerie 1987, Super Speedway 1997, Twilight 1998, Where the Money Is 2000, Road to Perdition 2002. *Address:* Newman's Own, 246 Post Road East, Westport, CT 06880, USA. *Website:* www.newmansown.com (Office).

NEWMAN, Peter C., CC, CD; Canadian author and journalist; b. 10 May 1929, Vienna, Austria; s. of Oscar Newman and Wanda Newman; m. 1st Christina McCall (divorced); m. 2nd Camilla J. Turner 1978; two d.; m. 3rd Alvy Björklund 1992; ed Upper Canada Coll., Toronto, Univ. of Toronto and McGill Univ.; Asst Ed. The Financial Post 1951–55; Ottawa Ed. Maclean's 1955–64; Ottawa Ed. Toronto Daily Star 1964–69, Ed.-in-Chief 1969–71; Ed.-

in-Chief, Maclean's 1971–82, Sr Contributing Ed. 1982–; Dir Maclean Hunter Ltd 1972–83, Key Radio Ltd 1983–; Prof. Creative Writing, Univ. of Victoria 1985–90; Prof. Creative Writing, Univ. of British Columbia; several honours and awards including Kt Commdr Order of St Lazarus; Hon. LLD (Brock) 1974, (Wilfrid Laurier) 1983, (Royal Mil. Coll.) 1986, (Queens) 1986; Hon. DLitt (York) 1975, (British Columbia) 1998. *Publications:* Flame of Power 1959, Renegade in Power 1963, The Distemper of our Times 1968, Home Country 1973, The Canadian Establishment: Vol. I 1975, Bronfman Dynasty 1978, The Acquisitors – The Canadian Establishment: Vol. II 1981, The Establishment Man 1982, True North – Not Strong and Free 1983, Debrett's Illustrated Guide to the Canadian Establishment 1983, Company of Adventurers 1985, Caesars of the Wilderness 1987, Sometimes A Great Nation 1988, Merchant Princes 1991, The Canadian Revolution 1995, Defining Moments 1996, Titans: How the New Canadian Establishment Seized Power 1998. *Leisure interest:* sailing. *Address:* 1444 Sasamat, Vancouver, BC VGR 4G4, Canada. *Telephone:* (604) 222-8274 (Office); (604) 222-8274 (Home). *Fax:* (604) 222-8275 (Office). *E-mail:* petercnewman@home.com (Home).

NEWMAN, Ronald Charles, PhD, FRS, FInstP; British scientist; b. 10 Dec. 1931; s. of Charles Henry Newman and Margaret Victoria May Newman (née Cooper); m. Jill Laura Weeks 1956; two d.; ed Imperial Coll. of Science and Tech.; research scientist, Assoc. Electrical Industries Cen. Research Lab., Aldermaston Court 1955–63, Sr Research Scientist, Rugby 1963–64; Lecturer Dept of Physics, Univ. of Reading 1964–69, Reader 1969–75, Prof. 1975–89, Visiting Prof. 1989–; Prof. of Physics, Univ. of London 1989–99, Prof. Emer. 1999–; Sr Research Fellow, Dept of Physics, Imperial Coll., London 1999–; Assoc. Dir Industrial Reorganization Corpn for Semiconductor Materials, Imperial Coll. 1989–99; Visiting Prof., Dept of Electrical Eng and Electronics, UMIST 2000–. *Publications:* Infra-Red Studies of Crystal Defects 1973; (contrib.) Semiconductors and Semimetals 1993, Handbook on Semiconductors 1994 and numerous contribs to learned journals. *Leisure interests:* music, foreign travel. *Address:* 23 Betchworth Avenue, Earley, Reading, Berks., RG6 7RH, England (Home). *Telephone:* (118) 966-3816 (Home).

NEWMARCH, Michael George, BSc (ECON.); British insurance executive; b. 19 May 1938, London; s. of George Langdon Newmarch and Phillis Georgina Newmarch; m. Audrey Ann Clarke 1959; one s. two d.; ed Tottenham County Grammar School, London Univ.; joined Econ. Intelligence Dept Prudential Assurance Co. Ltd 1955; Exec. Dir Prudential Corpn 1985, CEO Prudential Financial Services 1987, Chair. Prudential Holborn 1986–89, CEO and Deputy Chair. Prudential Portfolio Mans. Ltd 1980–90, CEO Prudential Corpn 1990–95; Dir (non-exec.) Celltech PLC 1996–; Chair. Weston Medical Ltd 1999–; Consultant Price Waterhouse 1997–99; Chair. Bourne End Properties PLC 1997–2001, Transacsys PLC 2000–; Vice-Chair. Princess Royal Trust for Carers 1994–; Trustee Berkshire Community Trust 1996–; mem. Advisory Council, Orchestra of the Age of Enlightenment 1994–; mem. Council Univ. of Reading 1997–. *Leisure interests:* salmon fishing, fly-tying, bridge, music, theatre, cinema, travel. *Address:* 7 The Bromptons, Rose Square, London, SW3 6RS (Home); Craven View, Craven Hill, Hamstead Marshall, nr Newbury, Berks., RG20 0JG, England (Home).

NEWSOM, David Dunlop, AB, MS; American diplomatist, professor and academic administrator (retd); b. 6 Jan. 1918, Richmond, Calif.; s. of Fred Stoddard and Ivy Elizabeth (née Dunlop) Newsom; m. Jean Frances Craig 1942; three s. two d.; ed Richmond Union High School and California and Columbia Univs.; Reporter, San Francisco Chronicle 1940–41; U.S. Navy 1941–45; Newspaper Publr 1945–47; Information Officer, U.S. Embassy, Karachi 1947–50; Consul, Oslo 1950–51; Public Affairs Officer, U.S. Embassy, Baghdad 1951–55; Dept of State 1955–59; U.S. Nat. War Coll. 1959–60; First Sec. U.S. Embassy, London 1960–62; Dir Office of Northern African Affairs, State Dept 1962–65; Amb. to Libya 1965–69; Asst Sec. of State for African Affairs 1969–73; Amb. to Indonesia 1974–77, to Philippines 1977–78; Under-Sec. of State for Political Affairs 1978–81; Sec. of State ad interim 1981; Marshall B. Coyne Research Prof. of Diplomacy, Georgetown Univ.; Cumming Memorial Prof. of Int. Relations, Univ. of Va 1991–98; interim dean School of Foreign Service Georgetown Univ., Washington 1995–96; mem. Nat. Acad. of Sciences Cttee on Science, Tech. and Foreign Policy 1999; Dept of State Meritorious Service Award 1958, Nat. Civil Service League Career Service Award 1971, Rockefeller Public Service Award 1973, Dept of State Distinguished Honor Award 1981, John Adams Memorial Fellow in Int. Relations 1986, Lifetime Award, American Foreign Service Asscn 2000. *Publications:* The Soviet Brigade in Cuba, Diplomacy and the American Democracy, The Public Dimension of Foreign Policy, The Imperial Mantle 2001. *Address:* 2409 Angus Road, Charlottesville, VA 22901, USA.

NEWTON, Sir (Charles) Wilfrid, Kt, CBE, FRSA, FCIT; British business executive; b. 11 Dec. 1928, Johannesburg, South Africa; s. of the late Gore M. Newton and of Catherine K. Newton; m. Felicity Mary Lynn 1954; two s. two d.; ed Highlands North High School, Johannesburg, Univ. of Witwatersrand; Territory Accounting and Finance Man., Mobil Oil Corpn of South Africa 1955–62; Controller, Mobil Sekiyu KK, Tokyo 1962–63, Finance Dir 1965–68; Financial Man. and Deputy Gen. Man., Mobil Oil East Africa Ltd 1963–65; Chief Financial Officer, Mobil Interests Japan 1965–68; Finance Dir, Turner and Newall Ltd 1968–74; Man. Dir Finance and Planning 1974–76, Man. Dir Plastics, Chemicals and Mining Divs 1976–79, Group Man. Dir 1979–82, CEO 1982–; Chair. Mass Transit Railway Corpn, Hong Kong 1983–89, Hong Kong Futures Exchange Ltd 1987–89, Chair. Jacobs Holdings PLC 1994–2002, Raglan Properties PLC 1994–99; Chair. and CEO London Regional Transport

1989–94, London Underground Ltd 1989–93; Chair. G. Maunsell Int. Ltd 1996–98; Dir (non-exec.) Hong Kong and Shanghai Banking Corpn 1986–92, Sketchley PLC 1990–99, HSBC Holdings PLC 1990–99, Midland Bank PLC 1992–99, Mountcity Investments Ltd 1994–, Maunsell Holdings Ltd; mem. Inst. of Chartered Accountants of South Africa; Fellow Hong Kong Man. Asscn; Hon. FREng; Hon. Fellow Hong Kong Inst. of Engineers. *Leisure interests:* sailing, reading, current affairs, economics. *Address:* Newtons Gate, Ramley Road, Pennington, Lymington, Hants., SO4 8GQ, England. *Telephone:* (20) 7629-1339 (Office); (1590) 679750 (Home). *Fax:* (20) 7629-0728 (Office); (1590) 677440 (Home). *E-mail:* wilfridn@sutanet.com (Home).

NEWTON, Christopher, CM, MA, FRCM; Canadian actor, director and author; b. 11 June 1936, Deal, Kent; s. of Albert E Newton and Gwladys M. Emes; ed Sir Roger Manwood's School, Sandwich, Kent, Univs. of Leeds and Illinois and Purdue Univ.; actor, Stratford Festival, New York; founding Artistic Dir Theatre Calgary, Calgary, Alberta 1968–71; Artistic Dir Vancouver Playhouse and Founder (with the late Powys Thomas), The Playhouse Acting School 1973–79; Artistic Dir The Shaw Festival, Niagara-on-the-Lake 1979–; Hon. Fellow Ryerson Univ.; Hon. LLD (Brock Univ., Guelph, Toronto); Hon. DLitt (Wilfrid Laurier Univ.); Hon. DHL (State Univ. of NY at Buffalo), Gov.-Gen.'s Award. *Plays directed include:* (for the Shaw Festival) Easy Virtue, The Doctor's Dilemma, Lady Windmere's Fan, Caesar and Cleopatra, The Return of the Prodigal, (for Melbourne Theatre Co.) Misalliance, (for Vancouver Playhouse) She Stoops to Conquer, Hamlet, Julius Caesar, Taming of the Shrew, (for Theatre Calgary) An Inspector Calls, (for YPT) Great Expectations. *Operas directed include:* (for Canadian Opera Co.) Madama Butterfly, Patria I, (for Nat. Arts Centre and Vancouver Opera) The Barber of Seville, (for Opera Hamilton) I due Fascari. *Publications:* plays: You Two Stay Here the Rest Come with Me, Slow Train to St Ives, Trip, The Sound of Distant Thunder, The Lost Letter. *Leisure interest:* landscape architecture. *Address:* c/o Shaw Festival, Box 774, Niagara-on-the-Lake, Ont., L0S 1J0 (Office); 22 Prideaux Street, Niagara-on-the-Lake, Ont., L0S 1J0, Canada (Home). *Telephone:* (905) 468-2153 (Office); (905) 468-4169 (Home).

NEWTON, David A., MA, FBIM, F.INST.D.; British company director; b. 6 Oct. 1942; s. of Alexander Newton and Hazel Newton (née Little); m. Kathleen Mary Moore 1965; one s. one d.; ed Morecombe Grammar School, Wyvern Business Studies Coll.; Man. Trainee J. Bibby & Sons Ltd 1964–67; Gen. Man. Anglian Hatcheries Ltd 1967–73; Agric. Dir Sovereign Poultry 1973–81; Man. Dir Ross Poultry Ltd 1981–83, Buxted Poultry Ltd 1983–86; Dir Hillsdown Holdings Ltd UK 1985–96, CEO 1993–96, COO 1992–93; Chair., Pres., CEO Maple Leaf Mills, Toronto 1987–92, Pres., Deputy Chair. 1992–95; Pres., CEO Canada Packers Inc., Toronto (subsequently Maple Leaf Foods Inc.) 1990–92; Dir Carr's Milling Industries 1996– (Chair. 1997–), Bodfari Ltd 1996–, Bernard Matthews PLC 1996–, Prism Rail PLC 1997–, MRCT Ltd 1997–; Partner K&D Partnership 1997–; rep. Lancashire County Rugby, Soccer. *Leisure interests:* golf, music, watching sports. *Address:* Carr's Milling Industries, Old Croft, Stanwix, Carlisle, CA3 9BA, England. *Telephone:* (1228) 528291.

NEWTON, Helmut; Australian photographer; b. 31 Oct. 1920, Berlin; m. June F. Browne (pseudonym Alice Springs, q.v.) 1948; ed Heinrich von Treitschke Realgymnasium, Berlin and American School, Berlin; apprentice to fashion and theatre photographer Yva (Else Simon) 1936–38; emigrated to Australia; served Australian Army 1940–45; freelance photographer Melbourne in 1940s; moved to Paris; freelance photographer working for Jardin des Modes, Elle, Queen, Playboy, Nova, Marie-Claire, Stern and French and US edns of Vogue, etc., 1958–; participant in numerous group shows; work in numerous public collections; Best Photography Award, Art Dirs Club, Tokyo 1976; American Inst. of Graphic Arts Award 1977, 1980; Gold Medal, Art Dirs. Club, Germany 1978, 1979, Photographers Award for Outstanding Achievements and Contribs. to Photography in 1960s and 1970s, Photographic Soc. of Japan 1989, Grand Prix de la Ville de Paris 1989, Grand Prix Nat. for Photography, France 1990, World Image for Best Portrait Photography, New York 1991; Grosses Verdienstkreuz, Chevalier des Arts, Lettres et Sciences (Monaco), Commdr des Arts et des Lettres. *Solo exhibitions include:* Paris 1975, 1979, 1981, 1984, 1992, 1993, LA 1976, New York 1978, Munich 1982, Shiga, Japan 1990, London 1991, 1995, Milan 1993, Monte Carlo 1995. *Publications include:* White Women 1976, Sleepless Nights 1978, Special Collection: 24 Photo Lithos 1979, 47 Nudes 1982, World Without Men 1984, Private Property 1984, Pola-Woman 1992, Naked and Dressed in Hollywood 1992, Immorale 1993, Helmut Newton's Illustrated No. 4–Dr. Phantasme 1995.

NEWTON, John Oswald, MA, PhD, DSc, FAA; Australian/British professor of nuclear physics; b. 12 Feb. 1924, Birmingham; s. of O. J. Newton and R. K. Newton; m. 2nd Silva Dusan Sablich 1964; two s. one d.; ed Bishop Vesey's Grammar School, Sutton Coldfield, St Catharine's Coll. Cambridge, Cavendish Lab., Cambridge; Jr Scientific Officer, Telecommunications Research Establishment, Great Malvern 1943–46; Harwell Fellow 1951–54; Prin. Scientific Officer, AERE Harwell 1954–59; Sr Lecturer, Univ. of Manchester 1959–67, Reader 1967–70; Prof. of Nuclear Physics, ANU 1970–89, Head of Dept of Nuclear Physics, Inst. of Advanced Studies 1970–88, Emer. Prof. and Visiting Fellow in Dept of Nuclear Physics 1990–; Visiting Physicist, Lawrence Berkeley Lab. (several times since 1956); Visiting Prof. Univ. of Manchester 1985–86. *Publications:* more than 100 Ppubls in Nuclear Physics and several book chapters. *Leisure interests:* painting, chess, music, walking, tennis. *Address:* Department of Nuclear Physics, IAS, Australian National

University, Canberra, ACT 0200 (Office); 8 Mackenzie Street, Hackett, ACT 2602, Australia (Home). *Telephone:* (2) 6215-2074 (Office). *Fax:* (2) 6215-0748 (Office).

NEWTON, Thandie; British actress; b. 6 Nov. 1972, Zimbabwe; d. of Nick Newton and Nyasha Newton; m. Oliver Parker 1998; ed Downing Coll. Cambridge. *Films include:* Flirting 1990, Jefferson In Paris 1995, Interview with a Vampire, Beloved 1998, It Was an Accident, The Leading Man 1998, Besieged 1999, Mission Impossible 2 2000, The Truth About Charlie 2003.

NEWTON, Sir Wilfrid (see Newton, Sir (Charles) Wilfrid).

NEWTON-JOHN, Olivia, OBE; British singer and actress; b. 26 Sept. 1948, Cambridge; d. of Brin Newton-John and Irene Born; m. Matt Lattanzi 1984; one d.; co-owner Koala Blue 1982–; UNEP Goodwill Amb. 1989–; Humanitarian Award U.S. Red Cross 1999 and numerous other awards. *Recordings include:* Let Me Be There, If You Love Me, Let Me Know, Clearly Love, Come On Over, Don't Stop Believin', Making a Good Thing Better, Totally Hot, Physical, The Rumour, Gaia, Heathcliff, Back with a Heart, The Main Event. *Film appearances include:* Grease 1978, Xanadu 1980, Two of a Kind 1983, It's My Party 1995, Sordid Wives 1999. *Television appearances:* numerous, including It's Cliff Richard (BBC series). *Leisure interests:* horse riding, song writing, cycling, astrology, conservation, animals. *Address:* MCA, 70 Universal City Plaza, North Hollywood, CA 91608 (Office); P.O. Box 2710, Malibu, CA 90265, USA (Home). *Website:* www.onlyolivia.com (Office).

NEWTON OF BRAINTREE, Baron (Life Peer), cr. 1997, of Coggeshall in the County of Essex; **Antony Harold (Tony) Newton,** OBE, PC; British politician; b. Aug. 1937; m. 1st Janet Huxley 1962 (divorced 1986); two d.; m. 2nd Patricia Gilthorpe 1986; one step-s. two step-d.; ed Friends' School, Saffron Walden, Trinity Coll. Oxford; Pres. Oxford Union 1959; fmr Sec. and Research Sec. Bow Group; Head Econ. Section, Conservative Research Dept 1965–70, Asst Dir 1970–74; Parl. Cand. for Sheffield, Brightside 1970; MP for Braintree 1974–97; Asst Govt Whip 1979–81; Lord Commr, Treasury 1981–82; Parl. Under-Sec. for Social Security 1982–84 and Minister for the Disabled 1983–84, Minister of State 1984–86; Minister of State (Health) and Chair. Nat. Health Service Man. Bd 1986–88; Chancellor Duchy of Lancaster 1988–89; Sec. of State for Social Security 1989–92; Lord Pres. of the Council and Leader of the House of Commons 1992–97; Chair. NE Essex Mental Health Nat. Health Service Trust 1997–, E Anglia's Children's Hospices 1998–; Professional Standards Dir, Inst. of Dirs. 1998–; mem. Further Educ. Funding Council 1998–. *Address:* c/o House of Lords, London, SW1A 0PW, England.

NEY, Edward Noonan, BA; American business executive; b. 26 May 1925, St Paul, Minn.; s. of John Ney and Marie Noonan Ney; m. 1st Suzanne Hayes 1950 (divorced 1974); one s. two d.; m. 2nd Judith I. Lasky 1974; ed Amherst Coll.; Account Exec., Young & Rubicam Inc. 1951, Vice-Pres. 1959–63, Sr Vice-Pres. 1963–67, Exec. Vice-Pres. 1967–68, Pres. Int. Div. 1968–70, Pres. and CEO 1970–72, Pres., CEO and Chair. 1972–83, Chair. and CEO 1983–85, Chair. 1985–86, Chair. PaineWebber/Young Rubicam Ventures 1987–89, Young and Rubicam Ventures 1989–, Vice-Chair. PaineWebber 1987–89; Chair. Bd of Advisers Burton-Marsteller 1992–98; Amb. to Canada 1989–92; Vice-Chair. The Advertising Council 1984–87, Chair. 1987–88; mem. Bd Int. Broadcasting 1984–, Bd of Govs. Foreign Policy Asscn 1980– (Vice-Chair. 1984–87); Dir Center for Communications 1986–; Chair. Manteller Advertising 1996–98; Trustee, Nat. Urban League 1974–, Amherst Coll. 1979–, New York Univ. Medical Center 1979–, Museum of Broadcasting 1982–; mem. Council on Foreign Relations 1974; mem. Bd Advisory Council, Center for Strategic and Int. Studies 1986–. *Leisure interests:* tennis, paddle tennis, reading. *Address:* Young Rubicam Advertising, 285 Madison Avenue, New York, NY 10017, USA (Office). *Telephone:* (212) 210-3199 (Office). *Fax:* (212) 880-7540 (Office).

NEYELOVA, Marina Mstislavovna; Russian actress; b. 8 Jan. 1948; m. Kyrill Gevorgyan; one d.; ed Leningrad Inst. of Theatre, Music and Cinema; actress Moscow Theatre Studio of Film Actors 1968–71, Mossoviet Theatre 1971–74, Sovremennik 1974–; prin. roles in classical and contemporary repertoire including Chekhov's plays; debut in cinema 1968; numerous roles in films including Old, Old Tale 1970, Monologue 1973, Autumn Marathon 1979 (State Prize of Russia), Prison Romance; People's Artist Russian Fed. 1980; USSR State Prize 1990, Prize Nika (film I Have Only You) 1994; Order Friendship of Peoples 1996, State Prize of Russia 2000. *Address:* Potapovsky per. 12, Apt. 24, 117333 Moscow, Russia (Home).

NEZVAL, Jiří; Czech automobile executive; b. 5 April 1941, Brno; s. of František Nezval and Květa Nezvalová 1963; two d.; ed Railway Coll. Žilina and Polytechnic Inst. Brno; designer and design office man. in automation of rail transport, Prague; involved in Czechoslovak Scientific and Tech. Soc., Peace Movt; Fed. Minister of Transport 1990–92; mem. Civic Movt Party 1991–93, Free Democrats Party 1993– (merged with Liberal Nat. Social Party 1995); Dir Denzel Praha Co. 1992–; Chair. Union of Motor Car Importers 1995–; Exclusive Mitsubishi dealership in Czech Repub. 1997–. *Leisure interests:* computer art, management systems, reading books, sports (skiing, cycling, volleyball). *Address:* Denzel Praha s.r.o., Revoluční 2, Prague 1, Czech Republic. *Telephone:* (2) 24810836 (Office). *Fax:* (2) 22315926 (Office).

NG, Daniel; Chinese business executive, entrepreneur and arts administrator; fmr Chair. McDonald's Restaurants (Hong Kong Special Admin.

Region); Chair. Bd Dirs. Arts4All Ltd, New York 2000–. *Address:* Arts 4All Ltd, 2 West 45 Street, Suite 500, New York, NY 10036, USA (Office). *E-mail:* info@arts4all.com (Office). *Website:* www.arts4all.com (Office).

NGAPO NGAWANG-JIGME (see Ngapoi Ngawang Jigme).

NGAPOI NGAWANG JIGME, Lt-Gen.; Chinese politician; b. 1911, nr Lhasa, Tibet; captured by Communist troops, Qamdo (Tibetan Mil. Region under his control) 1950; Vice-Chair. Qamdo Liberation Cttee 1950; First Deputy Commdr Tibet Mil. Region 1952; Vice-Chair. and Sec. Gen. 1959; Deputy for Xizang, 1st NPC 1954; mem. Nat. Defence Council 1954–Cultural Revolution; Sec.-Gen. Preparatory Cttee for Establishment of Tibet Autonomous Region (AR) 1956, Vice-Chair. 1959, Acting Chair. 1965; Vice-Chair. Standing Cttee, 3rd CPPCC 1959–64; Head, Cadre School, Lhasa 1961; Vice-Chair. Standing Cttee, 3rd NPC 1965–75, 4th NPC 1975–78, 5th NPC 1978–86, 6th NPC 1983–87, 7th NPC 1988–93; Chair. Tibet AR 1965; Vice-Chair. Tibet AR Revolutionary Cttee 1968–79; Chair. People's Congress, Tibet AR 1979; Exec. Chair. Presidium 6th NPC 1986; Chair. Tibet Autonomous Regional 5th People's Congress 1988–93; Chair. Nationalities Cttee, NPC, 1979–; Chair. China-Tibet Devt Foundation April 1992–, Vice-Chair. CPPCC 8th Nat. Cttee 1993–98, 9th Nat. Cttee 1998–; Hon. Pres. Asscn for Well-Known Chinese Figures 1993–. *Publication:* Tibet (jtly.). *Address:* National Committee of Chinese People's Political Consultative Conference, 23 Taipingqiao Street, Beijing, People's Republic of China.

NGEI, Paul, B.SC.(ECON.); Kenyan politician; b. 1923, Machakos; grandson of Akamba Paramount Chief Masaku; ed Makerere Coll., Kampala; Army Service, Second World War; f. Wasya wa Mukamba newspaper and Swahili magazine Uhuru wa Mwafrika 1950; Deputy Gen. Sec. Kenya African Union 1951–52; imprisoned and under restriction for connection with Mau-Mau 1953–61; Pres. Kenya African Farmers' and Traders' Union 1961; f. African Peoples' Party 1962; Chair. Maize Marketing Bd 1963–64; Minister for Co-operatives and Marketing 1964–65, for Housing and Social Services 1965–66, for Housing 1966–74, of Local Govt 1974–75, unseated by High Court ruling; MP for Kagunda 1976–; Minister of Co-operative Devt 1976–79, of Works 1979–82, of Livestock Devt 1982–83, of Lands and Settlement 1983–84, of Environment and Nat. Resources 1984–85, of Water Devt 1985–87, of Livestock Devt 1987–88, Minister of Culture and Social Services 1988–89, of Manpower Devt and Employment 1989–90; Man. Dir Akamba Carving and Industrial Co. *Address:* c/o Ministry of Manpower Development and Employment, Nairobi, Kenya.

NGEMA, Mbongeni; South African playwright, producer and composer; b. Hlabisa; mem. Gibson Kente's acting co., f. Cttee Artists; est. S. African struggle theatre on London and New York stages 1981; song Amandiya (Indians) banned by Broadcasting Complaints Comm. 2002. *Plays include:* Woza Albert! (with Barney Simon and Percy Mtwa) 1981, Asinimali (writer and producer), Sarafina!, Sarafina! 2. *Address:* c/o Universal Music South Africa, Johannesburg, South Africa (Office). *Telephone:* (11) 7843490 (Office). *Fax:* (11) 8832184 (Office).

NGO, Quang Xuan; Vietnamese diplomatist; b. 1 Jan. 1951, Nghe An; s. of Ngo Tri Tai and Dau Thi Nghiem; m. Le Thi Hoa 1975; two d.; ed Inst. of Int. Relations, Hanoi, Inst. des Hautes Etudes Internationales, Geneva, Diplomatic Acad. of Moscow; Deputy Gen. Dir Dept for Multilateral Econ. and Cultural Co-operation, Foreign Ministry 1988–91, Deputy Dir Int. Orgs. Dept 1992–93, Dir of Ministry 1995–; Nat. Rep. to Francophone Community 1990–93; Acting Perm. Rep. to UN 1993–95, Perm. Rep. 1995–2000; Medal for Diplomatic Service. *Leisure interests:* classical music, tennis. *Address:* c/o Ministry of Foreign Affairs, 1 Ton That Dam, Hanoi, Viet Nam (Office).

NGO DINH NHU, Madame; Vietnamese politician; sister-in-law of the late Pres. Ngo Dinh Diem; m. Ngo Dinh Nhu (deceased); arrested by Viet Minh, escaped 1946; organized first popular demonstration in support of Govt of Prime Minister Ngo Dinh Diem 1954; Official Hostess for Pres. Ngo Dinh Diem 1955–63; fmr Deputy, Nat. Assembly, author of "Family Bill"; f. programme of paramility service for women 1961; Founder-Pres. Vietnamese Women's Solidarity Movt.

NGOUPANDE, Jean-Paul; Central African Republic politician and fmr diplomatist; b. 6 Dec. 1948, Dekoa; m.; three s. three d.; Dean Faculty of Letters Univ. de Bangui 1982–85; Minister of Educ. 1985–87; fmr Amb. to France and to Côte d'Ivoire; Prime Minister of Cen. African Repub. 1996–97; MP 1998–; Leader Parti pour l'union national; Commdr Meritorious Order of Cen. African Rep., Commdr Ordre de Palmes Académiques, Grand Officier Ordre Nat. de Côte d'Ivoire. *Publications include:* Racines historiques et culturelles de la crise africaine 1994, Chronique de la crise centrafricaine 1997. *Leisure interests:* reading, music. *Address:* National Assembly of Central African Republic, Bangui (Office); P.O. Box 179, Bangui, Central African Republic (Home). *Telephone:* 61-82-96. *Fax:* 61-78-66 (Home).

NGUBANE, Ben, MB, CH.B.; South African politician and doctor; b. 22 Oct. 1941, Camperdown; m. Sheila Buthelezi; four c.; ed St Francis Coll., Marrianhill, Durban Medical School, Univ. of Witwatesrand, Natal Medical School; fmr Latin teacher; mem. Inkatha Freedom Party Cen. Cttee Exec. 1977–; mem. KwaZulu Legis. Ass. 1978–; led KwaZulu Govt del. to Constitutional negotiations; Minister of Health, KwaZulu Govt 1991–94, Premier 1997–99; Minister of Arts, Culture, Science and Tech. 1994–96, 1999–; mem. SA Red Cross Soc. 1977–, Regional Counsellor 1978–; mem. Council Univ. of Zululand; mem. Nat. Boxing Bd of Control 1991–. *Leisure interests:* tennis, reading, photography. *Address:* Ministry of Arts, Culture, Science and Technology, Oranje Nassau Building, 188 Schoeman Street, Pretoria 0002 (Office); Empangeni, KwaZulu-Natal, South Africa (Home). *Telephone:* (12) 3378378 (Office); (12) 3242687. *E-mail:* frans@dacst.pwv.gov.za (Office). *Website:* www.dacst.gov.za (Office); www.gov.za (Home).

N'GUESSAN, Pascal Affi; Côte d'Ivoirian politician; b. 1953, Bouadikro; ed Lycée Moderne de Dimbokro, Lycée Technique d'Abidjan; Dir of Studies and Work Placements, École Nat. Supérieure des Postes et Télécommunications 1989–1993; Vice-Pres. Union des villes et commune de Côte d'Ivoire (UVI-COCI) 1990–95; mem. nat. directorate, Front populaire ivoirien—FPI (Ivorian Popular Front) 1990–, Pres. 2001–; Special Adviser to the Regional Dir, Ci-Télécom, Bouaké 1993–97; Head Dept of Resources and Standards, Côte d'Ivoire Télécom 1997–2000; Campaign Man. for Laurent Gbagbo in presidential elections 2000; Minister of Industry and Tourism 2000; Prime Minister of Côte d'Ivoire 2000–03; Minister for Planning and Devt 2000–03; Officier du mérite sportif 1995. *Address:* Front populaire ivoirien (FPI), 22 BP 302, Abidjan 22, Côte d'Ivoire (Office). *Telephone:* 21-24-36-76 (Office). *Fax:* 21-35-35-50 (Office). *E-mail:* president@fpi-ci.org. *Website:* www.fpi-ci.org.

NGUGI, Wa Thiong'o (James); Kenyan novelist; b. 1938, Limuru; ed Makerere Univ. Coll., Uganda and Leeds Univ., England; Lecturer in Literature, Univ. Nairobi 1967–69; Fellow in Creative Writing, Makerere Univ. 1969–70; Visiting Assoc. Prof. Northwestern Univ., USA 1970–71; Sr Lecturer, then Assoc. Prof. and Chair. Literature Dept, Univ. Nairobi; arrested and detained Dec. 1977, released Dec. 1978; in exile in London 1982–; Lecturer in Politics and Literature, Yale Univ. *Publications:* The Black Hermit (play) 1962, Weep Not Child 1964, The River Between 1965, A Grain of Wheat 1967, Homecoming (essays) 1972, Secret Lives (short stories) 1973, Petals of Blood (novel) 1977, The Trial of Dedan Kimathi (with Micere Mugo) 1977, Detained: A Writer's Prison Diary 1981, I'll Marry When I Want (with Ngugi wa Mirii) 1982, Devil on the Cross 1982, Writers in Politics (essays) 1982, Barrel of a Pen (essays) 1983, Decolonising the Mind (essays) 1986, Writing Against Neo-Colonialism 1986, Matigari ma Ngirũũngi (novel in Gĩkũyũ language) 1986, Moving the Centre 1992.

NGUYEN CAO KY, Air Vice-Marshal; Vietnamese politician and air force officer; b. 8 Sept. 1930; ed High School, Hanoi and Officers' Training School, Hanoi; Flight Training, Marrakesh until 1954; commanded Transport Squadron 1954, later Commdr Tan Son Nhât Air Force Base, Repub. of Viet Nam; spent six months at U.S. Air Command and Staff Coll., Maxwell Field, Ala, USA; later Commdr Air Force, Repub. of Viet Nam; Prime Minister 1965–67; Vice-Pres. Repub. of Viet Nam 1967–71; went to USA April 1975; owns liquor store. *Publication:* Twenty Years and Twenty Days 1977.

NGUYEN KHANH, Lt-Gen.; Vietnamese politician and army officer; b. 1927; ed Viet Nam Mil. Acad., Dalat, Army Staff Schools, Hanoi and France and U.S. Command and Gen. Staff Coll., Fort Leavenworth; French Colonial Army 1954, Vietnamese Army 1954; Chief of Staff to Gen. Duong Van Minh 1955; took part in coup against Pres. Diem Nov. 1963; Prime Minister Jan.-Oct. 1964; Chair. Armed Forces Council 1964–65; led coup Jan. 1965; Roving Amb. 1965; mem. Secr. CP of Viet Nam; Vice-Prime Minister and Gen. Sec. Council of Ministers 1987. *Address:* 1 Hoang Van Thu, Hanoi, Viet Nam.

NGUYEN PHU DUC, LLD, DJur; Vietnamese diplomatist; b. 13 Nov. 1924, Son-Tay; m.; two s.; ed Univ. of Hanoi, Harvard Law School, USA; Perm. Observer to UN 1964–65; Special Asst for Foreign Affairs to Pres. Thieu 1968; Envoy to Thailand, Khmer Repub., Laos, Indonesia, USA 1972; Minister of Foreign Affairs 1973; Amb. to Belgium 1974–75; attended confs. on Viet Nam 1966, 1967, 1968, 1969, 1973, active in negotiations leading to Paris Conf. 1968 and to Paris Agreement 1973.

NGUYEN THANH CHAU, MA; Vietnamese diplomatist; b. 17 Sept. 1945, Phu Tho; m.; two c.; ed Australian Nat. Univ.; Lecturer Inst. of Int. Relations, Ministry of Foreign Affairs, Hanoi; Second Sec., Perm. Mission to UN 1983–86; various positions with Viet Nam Comm. for UNESCO including Sec.-Gen. 1987–92; Amb. to Australia, (also accred to NZ, Papua New Guinea, Vanuatu and Fiji) 1992–96; Dir Int. Orgs Div., Ministry of Foreign Affairs 1996–2000; Perm. Rep. to UN 2000–. *Address:* Permanent Mission of Viet Nam to the United Nations, 866 United Nations Plaza, Suite 435, New York, NY 10017, USA (Office). *Telephone:* (212) 644-0594 (Office). *Fax:* (212) 644-5732 (Office). *E-mail:* vietnam@un.int (Office). *Website:* www.un.int/vietnam (Office).

NGUYEN THI BINH, Madame; Vietnamese politician; b. 1927; ed Saigon; student political leader in Saigon; organized (with Nguyen Huu Tho) first anti-American demonstration 1950; imprisoned by French authorities 1951–54; Vice-Pres. S. Vietnamese Cttee for Solidarity with the American People; Vice-Pres. Union of Women for the Liberation of S. Viet Nam; mem. Cen. Cttee Nat. Liberation Front (NLF); apptd. NLF spokesman to four-party peace talks, Paris Nov. 1968; Minister for Foreign Affairs, Provisional Revolutionary Govt of S. Viet Nam 1969–76 (in Saigon 1975–76); Minister of Educ., Socialist Repub. of Viet Nam 1976–87; Vice-Pres. Vietnamese Women's Union, Hanoi 1976–; Vice-Pres. of Viet Nam 1992–93; Vice-Pres. OSPAA. *Address:* c/o Ministry of Education, 21 Le Thanh Tong, Hanoi, Viet Nam.

NGUYEN VAN LOC, LLM; Vietnamese politician, lawyer and writer; b. 24 Aug. 1922, Vinh-Long; s. of Nguyen Van Hanh and Tran Thi Ngo; m. Nguyen Thi Mong Hoa; two s.; ed Univs. of Montpellier and Paris, France; Lawyer, Saigon Court of Appeal 1955; Lecturer, Nat. Inst. of Admin. 1965; Chair.

People's and Armed Forces Council 1966, People's and Armed Forces Council Political Cttee 1966; Vice-Chair. Constituent Ass. Electoral Law Preparation Cttee; mem. Barristers Fraternity 1961–67; Del. in charge of campaigning, Cttee for Aid to War Victims (Viet Nam Red Cross); Counsellor, Viet Nam Asscn for Protection of Human and People's Rights; Sec.-Gen., Inter-Schools Asscn 1965–67; Prime Minister of Repub. of Viet Nam 1967–68; Prof. Univ. of Hóa-Hao 1970; Founder and Rector, Cao-Dai Univ. 1971–75; escaped to Singapore 1983. *Publications:* Uprising (novel) 1946, Rank 1948, New Recruits (novel) 1948, Poems on Liberation (collection) 1949, Recollections of the Green Years 1960, Free Tribune (collection) 1966, Poisonous Water (novel) 1971.

NGUYEN VAN VY, Lt-Gen.; Vietnamese politician; b. 16 Jan. 1916, Hanoi; ed Univ., Tong Officers' School and School of Command and Staff, Paris; Chief Mil. Cabinet of Chief of State 1952; Commdr Coastal Interzone 1954; Acting Chief, Gen. Staff, Vietnamese Army Oct. 1954; Insp.-Gen. Dec. 1954; Asst Chief of Staff for Training, Republic of Viet Nam Air Force (RVNAF) Jan. 1964; Asst to C-in-C Nov. 1964; Commdt Quang Trung Training Centre Feb. 1965; Commdr Training Command, RVNAF June 1966; Chief-of-Staff Jt Gen. Staff RVNAF 1966–67; Minister of Defence 1968–72; Grand Officer Nat. Order of Viet Nam; Army and Air Force Distinguished Service Orders; Officier, Légion d'Honneur.

NGUZA KARL-I-BOND; Democratic Republic of the Congo politician and diplomatist; b. 1938, Musumba; m. N'Landu Kavidi; ed Catholic schools, Elisabethville (now Lubumbashi) and Univ. of Louvain, Belgium; Announcer, Radio Lubumbashi 1957–60, Radio Kinshasa 1964; mem. of Prime Minister Tshombe's pvt. cabinet 1964; Counsellor, Congolese Embassy, Brussels 1964–66; Govt Commr Union Minière 1965–66; Counsellor, Congolese Del. to UN, New York 1966–68; Deputy Perm. Rep. to UN 1968; Minister, later Amb. and Perm. Rep. at UN Office, Geneva 1970–72; State Commr for Foreign Affairs 1972–74, 1976–77, 1979–80, for Foreign Affairs and Int. Co-operation 1988–90, Minister of State in Office of the Pres. 1992–93; First Deputy Prime Minister in charge of Defence by Pres. Mobutu 1993–94; First State Commr (Prime Minister) 1980–81, 1991–92; Amb. to USA 1986–88; mem. Political Bureau of the Mouvement populaire de la révolution 1972–77, 1979–81, Nat. Security Council 1979–81, Dir 1974–77; Vice-Pres. Exec. Council, presiding over Political, Econ. and Finance Comm. Feb.-Aug. 1977; arrested Aug. 1977; accused of treason and sentenced to death, sentence commuted to life imprisonment Sept. 1977, reinstated March 1979; resgnd posts while in Brussels April 1981; in exile 1982; returned to Zaire 1985. *Publications:* Mobutu ou l'Incarnation du Mal Zaïrois, Le Zaire de Demain 1984, Un Avenir pour le Zaire 1985. *Address:* c/o Office of the President, Kinshasa Gombe, Democratic Republic of the Congo.

NHASSÉ, Alamara; Guinea-Bissau politician; b. 1957; Pres. Partido para a Renovação Social (PRS); Minister of Internal Admin. 2001; Prime Minister of Guinea-Bissau 2001–02. *Address:* c/o Office of the Prime Minister, Avda Unidade Africana, C.P. 137 Bissau, Guinea-Bissau.

NHU, Madame (see Ngo Dinh Nhu, Madame).

NI CHIH-FU (see Ni Zhifu).

NÍ DHOMHNAILL, Nuala, BA; Irish poet; b. 16 Feb. 1952, St Helens, Lancs., England; d. of Séamus Ó Dhomhnaill and Eibhlín Ní Fhiannachta; m. Dogan Leflef 1973; one s. three d.; ed Laurel Hill Convent, Limerick and Univ. Coll., Cork; travel overseas 1973–80; Writer-in-Residence Univ. Coll., Cork 1992–93; various Oireachtas awards 1982, 1984, 1990, Irish American O'Shaughnessy Award 1988, Ireland Fund Literary Prize 1991. *Publications:* An Dealg Droighinn 1981, Feár Suaithinseach 1984, Feís 1991. *Leisure interests:* swimming, mountain walks, reading. *Address:* 2 Little Meadow, Pottery Road, Cabinteely, Co. Dublin, Ireland. *Telephone:* (1) 2857465. *Fax:* (1) 2834327.

NI RUNFENG; Chinese business executive; b. 1944, Rongcheng, Shandong Prov.; ed Dalian Polytechnic; Chair. and Gen. Man. Changhong Electronics Group Inc. 1988–; winner of Nat. Wuyi Labour Medal. *Address:* Changhong Electronics Group, Chengdu, Sichuan Province, People's Republic of China (Office).

NI ZHENGYU, DJur; Chinese international jurist; b. 28 July 1906, Wujiang, Jiangsu Prov.; m. Zhang Fengzhen 1930; one d.; ed Dongwu Univ., Shanghai, Stanford Univ., Johns Hopkins Univ., USA; mem. Shanghai Bar Asscn 1931–; Prosecutor, Int. Mil. Tribunal for the Far East 1946–48; attended many int. confs. as legal consultant to Govt del. of People's Repub. of China; legal adviser to Chinese Foreign Ministry; fmr mem. UN Int. Law Comm.; Judge, Int. Court of Justice 1985–94; Assoc. mem. l'Institut de Droit 1987–; Pres. Maritime Law Soc. 1995; Hon. LLD; Ni Prize in Int. and Chinese Law (est. in his hon.), Stanford Law School 2001. *Publications:* The Question of Judicial Jurisdiction in International Law, The Judicial Systems in the United States and the United Kingdom, The Theory and Practice Concerning Jurisdictional Immunities of States. *Address:* c/o The Ministry of Justice, 11 Xiaguangli, Chayang Gu, Beijing, People's Republic of China.

NI ZHIFU; Chinese party official; b. 1933, Chuansha Co., Shanghai; ed elementary school 1945–48; errand boy for a Japanese oil company 1944; apprentice, a Shanghai printing machine factory 1948; joined trades union 1950; mechanic, Yongding Machine Tool Factory 1953; joined CCP 1958; promoted engineer 1962; active participation in the criticism movt during the

Cultural Revolution; mem. 9th Cen. Cttee CCP 1969; Chair. Municipal Trade Union Council, Beijing 1973; Second Sec. CCP Cttee, Beijing 1973–76; alt. mem. Politburo, 10th Cen. Cttee CCP 1973; Vice-Chair. Municipal Revolutionary Cttee, Beijing 1974–78; Second Sec. CCP Cttee, Shanghai 1976–78; First Vice-Chair. Municipal Revolutionary Cttee, Shanghai 1976–78; mem. Politburo, 11th Cen. Cttee CCP 1977; Pres. All-China Fed. of Trade Unions 1978–93; mem. Politburo 12th CCP Cen. Cttee 1982–87; mem. 13th CCP Cen. Cttee 1987–92, 14th CCP Cen. Cttee 1992–97, 15th CCP Cen. Cttee 1997–2002; Sec. Tianjin Municipal Cttee of CCP 1984–87; Vice-Chair. 7th NPC Standing Cttee 1988–92; Vice-Chair. Standing Cttee 8th NPC 1993–98; Hon. Chair. Bd Dirs Beijing Science and Eng Univ. 1995–; Adviser Chinese Asscn for Promotion of Population Culture 1993–. *Address:* 10 Fuxingmenwai Street, Beijing, People's Republic of China.

NIANG, Souleymane, PhD; Senegalese university administrator; b. Dec. 1929, Matam; ed Univ. of Toulouse; teacher, Lycée Fermat, Toulouse, William Ponty Teachers' School, Daker 1956–60; lecturer Faculty of Sciences, Univ. of Dakar 1960, Sr Lecturer 1964, Prof. 1969–; Dir Research Inst. on the Teaching of Math., Physics and Tech. 1970; Rector and Pres. Univ. of Dakar 1986–; fmr Pres. Scientific Section, UNESCO Nat. Comm., Nat. Cttee of Int. Comm. for Teaching Math.; Pres. Math. and Physics Section, Africa and Mauritius Advisory Cttee on Higher Educ.; mem. Office of African Comm. for Teaching Math., Scientific Council, OAU; Officer, Ordre Nat. du Lion, Ordre Nat. du Mérite, Chevalier, Ordre des Palmes Académiques Sénégalaises, Commdr. Ordre des Palmes Académiques. *Address:* University of Dakar, B.P. 5005 Dakar-Fann, Senegal (Office). *Telephone:* 825-05-30 (Office). *Fax:* 825-52-19 (Office).

NIASSE, Cheikh Moustapha; Senegalese politician and United Nations official; b. 4 Nov. 1939; ed Lycée Faidherbe, St Louis, Univs. of Dakar and Paris, Nat. School of Admin., Dakar; Dir for Information and Press Affairs, Ministry of Information 1968–69; Dir de Cabinet at Presidency 1970–78; Minister of Town Planning, Housing and Environment March–Sept. 1978, of Foreign Affairs 1978–84; Minister of Foreign Affairs of the Confed. of Sengambia 1982–84; fmr Minister of State, Minister of Foreign Affairs and Senegalese Abroad; Presidential cand. 2000; Prime Minister of Senegal April 2000–01; UN Special Envoy to Peace Process of the Democratic Repub. of the Congo June 2002–; Political Sec. Union Progressiste Sénégalaise until 1984; Founder and Leader Alliance des forces de progrès (AFP) 1999–. *Address:* Alliance des forces de progrès (AFP), B.P. 5825, Dakar, Senegal (Office). *Telephone:* 825-40-21 (Office). *Fax:* 825-77-70 (Office). *E-mail:* admin@afp-senegal.org (Office). *Website:* www.afp-senegal.org (Office). *Address:* Special Envoy to the Democratic Republic of the Congo, United Nations, New York, NY 10017, USA.

NIBBERING, Nicolaas Martinus Maria, PhD; Netherlands professor of chemical mass spectrometry; b. 29 May 1938, Zaandam; s. of Dirk Nibbering and Hendrika Clijnk; m. Christina A. de Waart 1964; three s. one d.; ed Gymnasium B Zaanlands Lyceum Zaandam and Univ. of Amsterdam; mem. Faculty, Univ. of Amsterdam 1967–75, Assoc. Prof. 1975–80, Prof. of Organic Mass Spectrometry 1980–88, Prof. of Chemical Mass Spectrometry 1988–, Scientific Dir Inst. of Mass Spectrometry 1988–2000; Visiting faculty mem. Cornell Univ. 1974; Guest Prof. Univ. of Colorado 1980; Chair. 12th Int. Mass Spectrometry Conf., Amsterdam 1991; Chair. European Soc. for Mass Spectrometry 1993–97, Pres. 1997–2000; Treas. Int. Mass Spectrometry Soc. 1997–2000, Pres. 2000–; Co-Ed. Scientific Journal of Mass Spectrometry Reviews 1991–2000; Ed. Scientific Journal of Mass Spectrometry 1995–2000; mem. Royal Netherlands Acad., New York Acad. of Sciences; Hon. mem. Netherlands Soc. for Mass Spectrometry 1999, Life mem. Indian Soc. for Mass Spectrometry 2000, Unilever Chemistry Prize 1964, Shell Research Chemistry Prize 1968, J. J. Thomson Award 1991, Joannes Marcus Marci Award 1992, Hon. Life mem. British Mass Spectrometry Soc. 1999. *Publications:* articles in books and journals. *Leisure interests:* motorbike races, classical music, opera, musicals, travelling, history. *Address:* Laser Centre and Chemistry Department, Vrÿe Universiteit, De Boelelaan 1083, 1081 HV Amsterdam (Office); Janshof 39, 1391 XK Abcoude, Netherlands (Home). *Telephone:* (20) 4447646 (Office); (294) 283211 (Home). *Fax:* (20) 4447643 (Office); (294) 283211 (Home). *E-mail:* nibberin@chem.vu.nl (Office).

NICHOLAS, Sir David, Kt, CBE; British television executive and editor; b. 25 Jan. 1930, Tregaron; m. Juliet Davies 1952; one s. one d.; ed Neath Grammar School, Univ. Coll. of Wales; Nat. Service 1951–53; journalist with Yorkshire Post, Daily Telegraph, Observer; joined Ind. TV News 1960, Deputy Ed., Ed. 1963–77, Ed. and CEO 1977–89, Chair. 1989–91; Dir (non-exec.) Channel 4 TV 1992–97; Chair. Sports News TV 1996–; Visiting Ed. 10 US Schools of Journalism 1992–99; Hon. LLD (Univ. Coll. of Wales, Aberystwyth), Hon. D. Hum.Litt. (Univ. of S. Illinois). *Leisure interests:* walking, sailing, golf. *Address:* Lodge Stables, 2F Kidbrooke Park Road, London, SE3 0LW, England. *Telephone:* (20) 8319-2823. *Fax:* (20) 8319-2417. *E-mail:* newscons@dircon.co.uk (Home).

NICHOLAS, Nicholas John, Jr., MBA; American communications executive; b. 3 Sept. 1939, Portsmouth, NH; s. of Nicholas John Nicholas; m. Llewellyn Jones 1972; two s. three d.; ed Princeton and Harvard Univs.; Dir of Financial Analysis, Time Inc., New York 1964–69, Asst to Pres. 1970, Asst Treas. 1971–73, Vice-Pres. 1975–86, Pres. and COO 1986–; Pres. Manhattan Cable TV 1973–76; Pres. Home Box Office, New York 1976–80, Chair. 1979–81, Chief Financial Officer 1982–. *Address:* Time Inc., Time & Life Building, Rockefeller Center, New York, NY 10020, USA.

NICHOLLS OF BIRKENHEAD, Baron (Life Peer), cr. 1994, of Stoke D'Abernon in the County of Surrey; **Donald James Nicholls,** PC, MA, LLB; British judge; b. 25 Jan. 1933, Bebington, Cheshire; s. of the late William Greenhow and of Eleanor J. Nicholls; m. Jennifer Mary Thomas 1960; two s. one d.; ed Birkenhead School, Univ. of Liverpool and Trinity Hall, Cambridge; called to Bar, Middle Temple 1958; in practice at Chancery Bar, London 1958–83; QC 1974; Judge, High Court of Justice, Chancery Div. 1983–86; Lord Justice of Appeal 1986–91; Vice-Chancellor, Supreme Court 1991–94; a Lord of Appeal in Ordinary 1994–; Chair. Lord Chancellor's Advisory Cttee on Legal Educ. and Conduct 1996–97, Jt Cttee on Parl. Privilege 1997–99; a non-perm. Judge, Hong Kong Court of Final Appeal 1998–; Hon. Fellow, Trinity Hall, Cambridge 1986; Treas. Middle Temple 1997; Hon. LLD (Liverpool) 1987. *Leisure interests:* history, music, walking. *Address:* House of Lords, London, SW1A 0PW, England.

NICHOLS, Mike; American entertainer and stage and film director; b. Michael Igor Peschowsky, 6 Nov. 1931, Berlin, Germany; s. of Paul Nikolaievich Peschowsky and Brigitte Landauer; m. 1st Patricia Scot 1957 (divorced); m. 2nd Margot Callas 1974 (divorced); one d.; m. 3rd Annabel Nichols (divorced); m. 4th Diane Sawyer 1988; ed pvt. schools and Univ. of Chicago; started Playwrights Theatre Club, Chicago which became the Compass Players and later Second City; formed improvised nightclub double-act with Elaine May, touring for two years and recording TV programmes and record albums; appeared in An Evening with Mike Nichols and Elaine May, New York 1961–62; acted in Shaw's St Joan and directed The Importance of Being Earnest, Vancouver; Antoinette Perry (Tony) awards for direction Barefoot in the Park, Luv, The Odd Couple, Plaza Suite, The Real Thing; Acad. Award for The Graduate; Emmy award for TV programme Julie and Carol at Carnegie Hall; Nat Asscn Theatre Owners' Achievement Award for direction for Who's Afraid of Virginia Woolf? *Directed shows:* Barefoot in the Park, New York 1963, The Knack 1964, Luv 1964, The Odd Couple 1965, The Apple Tree 1966, The Little Foxes 1967, Plaza Suite 1968. *Directed films:* Who's Afraid of Virginia Woolf? 1966, The Graduate 1967, Catch-22 1969, Carnal Knowledge 1971, Day of the Dolphin 1973, The Fortune 1975, Gilda Live 1980, Silkwood 1983, Heartburn 1985, Biloxi Blues 1987, Working Girl 1988, Postcards From the Edge 1990, Regarding Henry, Wolf 1994 (co-producer), Mike Nicholas 1995, The Birdcage (co-producer), Primary Colors 1998, What Planet Are You From? (also producer) 2000, All the Pretty Horses (producer) 2000. *Directed plays:* Streamers 1976, Comedians 1976, The Gin Game 1978, Lunch Hour 1980, The Real Thing 1984, Hurlyburly 1984, Waiting for Godot 1988, Death and the Maiden 1992, Blue Murder 1995, The Seagull 2001; producer Annie (New York) 1977. *Leisure interest:* Arabian horse breeding.

NICHOLS, Peter Richard, FRSL; British playwright; b. 31 July 1927; s. of the late Richard G. Nichols and of Violet A. Poole; m. Thelma Reed 1960; one s. two d. (and one d. deceased) ed Bristol Grammar School, Bristol Old Vic School and Trent Park Training Coll.; actor, mostly in repertory 1950–55; schoolteacher 1958–60; mem. Arts Council Drama Panel 1973–75; playwright-in-residence, Guthrie Theatre, Minneapolis; Visiting Writer, Nanyang Coll., Singapore 1994; directed revivals of Joe Egg and Forget-me-not Lane (Greenwich), National Health (Guthrie, Minneapolis) and first productions of Born in the Gardens (Bristol), A Piece of My Mind (Southampton), Blue Murder (Bristol), Nicholodeon (Bristol); Tony Award, New York 1985; recipient of several SWET and four Evening Standard Drama Awards; Ivor Novello Award for Best Musical. *Plays:* A Day in the Death of Joe Egg 1967, The National Health 1969, Forget-me-Not Lane 1971, Chez Nous 1973, The Freeway 1974, Privates on Parade 1977, Born in the Gardens 1979, Passion Play 1980, Poppy (musical) 1982, A Piece of My Mind 1986, Blue Murder 1995, So Long Life 2000, Nicholodeon 2000. *Films:* Catch Us If You Can 1965, Georgy Girl 1967, Joe Egg 1971, The National Health 1973, Privates on Parade 1983. *Television:* plays include Promenade, Ben Spray, The Gorge, The Common and Greeks Bearing Gifts (in the Inspector Morse series). *Publications:* Feeling You're Behind (memoirs) 1984, Nichols: Plays One and Two 1991, Diary 1969–71. *Leisure interests:* listening to jazz, looking at cities. *Address:* c/o Alan Brodie Representation, 211 Piccadilly, London, W1V 9LD, England.

NICHOLS, Most Rev. Vincent Gerard, STL, PhL, MA, M.ED.; British ecclesiastic; b. 8 Nov. 1945, Crosby; s. of Henry Joseph Nichols and Mary Russell; ed St Mary's Coll., Crosby, Gregorian Univ., Rome, Manchester Univ. and Loyola Univ., Chicago; Chaplain St John Rigby VI Form Coll., Wigan 1972–77; Priest in inner city of Liverpool 1978–81; Dir Upholland Northern Inst., Lancs. 1981–84; Gen. Sec. Catholic Bishops' Conf. of England and Wales 1984–91; Auxiliary Bishop of Westminster 1992–2000; Archbishop of Birmingham 2000–; Adviser to HE Cardinal Hume and Archbishop Worlock at the Int. Synods of Bishops 1980, 1983, 1985, 1987, 1990, 1991; Del. of Bishops' Conf. to Synod of Bishops 1994, 1999. *Publication:* Promise of Future Glory–Reflections on the Mass 1997. *Address:* Archbishop's House, 8 Shadwell Street, Birmingham, B4 6EY, England. *Telephone:* (121) 236-9090. *Fax:* (121) 212-0171 (Office). *E-mail:* archbishop@rc-birmingham.org (Office).

NICHOLSON, Sir Bryan Hubert, Kt, MA, FRSA, CBIM, FCIM; British business executive; b. 6 June 1932, Rainham, Essex; s. of the late Reginald H. Nicholson and of Clara Nicholson; m. Mary E. Harrison 1956; one s. one d.

(and one s. deceased); ed Palmers School, Grays and Oriel Coll. Oxford; Man. trainee, Unilever 1955–58; Dist Man. Van den Berghs 1958–59; Sales Man. Three Hands/Jeyes Group 1960–64; joined Sperry Rand 1964, Sales Dir UK Remington Div. 1964–66, Gen. Man. Australia, Remington Div. 1966–69, Man. Dir UK and France, Remington Div. 1969–72; Dir Operations, Rank Xerox (UK) 1972–76, Dir Overseas Subsidiaries 1976, Exec. Dir 1976–84, Chair. Rank Xerox (UK) and Rank Xerox GmbH 1979–84; Chair. Manpower Services Comm. 1984–87, The Post Office 1987–92; Chair. BUPA 1992–2001, Varity Holdings Ltd (now Varity Europe Ltd) 1993–96, Cookson Group PLC 1998–; Dir (non-exec.) Newsquest PLC 1997–99, Action Centre for Europe Ltd 1997–, Accountancy Foundation 2000–; Pres. Involvement and Participation Asscn 1990–94; Chair. CBI Vocational Educ. and Training Task Force 1988–89, CNAA 1988–91, Nat. Council for Vocational Qualifications 1990–93, CBI Educ. and Training Affairs Cttee 1990–93, Industrial Soc. 1990–93, Deputy Pres. CBI 1993–94, Pres. 1994–96; Non-exec. Dir GKN 1990–2000, Varity Corpn, USA 1993–96, LucasVarity 1996–99, Equitas Holdings Ltd 1996–; mem. Nat. Econ. Devt Council 1985–92; Pres. Oriel Soc. 1988–92; Vice-Pres. Nat. Children's Home 1990–2002, Industrial Trust 1999–; Deputy Chair. Education Development Int. 2003–; Chancellor Sheffield Hallam Univ. 1992–2001; Pro-Chancellor and Chair. of Council The Open Univ. 1996–; Chair. United Oxford and Cambridge Univ. Club 1995–97, Financial Reporting Council 2001–, Goal PLC 2001–02; mem. Int. Advisory Bd Active Int. 2001–; Hon. FCGI 1988; Hon. Fellow Oriel Coll. Oxford 1989, Manchester Metropolitan Univ. 1990, Scottish Vocational Ed. Council 1994, Scottish Qualifications Authority 1997; Hon. Companion Inst. of Personnel and Devt 1994; Hon. DEd (CNAA) 1994; Dr hc (Open Univ.) 1994, (Sheffield Hallam) 2001; Hon. DLitt (Glasgow Caledonian) 2000. *Leisure interests:* tennis, bridge, opera, political history. *Address:* Point Piper, Lilley Drive, Kingswood, Surrey, KT20 6JA, England. *Telephone:* (1737) 832208 (Home).

NICHOLSON, Ernest Wilson, PhD, DD, FBA; British university professor; b. 26 Sept. 1938, Northern Ireland; s. of Ernest Tedford Nicholson and Veronica Muriel Nicholson; m. Hazel Jackson 1962; one s. three d.; ed Trinity Coll. Dublin, Univ. of Glasgow; Lecturer in Semitic Languages, Trinity Coll. Dublin 1962–67; Lecturer in Divinity, Cambridge Univ. 1967–79, Fellow Univ. Coll. (now Wolfson Coll.) Cambridge 1967–69, Fellow and Chaplain Pembroke Coll. Cambridge 1969–79, Dean 1973–79; Oriel Prof. of The Interpretation of Holy Scripture, Oxford Univ. 1979–90, Provost of Oriel Coll. 1990–; Pro-Vice-Chancellor, Oxford Univ. 1993–; Chair. Jardine Foundation 1993–2000; Hon. Fellow Trinity Coll. Dublin, Wolfson Coll. Cambridge, St Peter's Coll. Oxford; Commdr Order of Merit Italian Repub. *Publications:* Deuteronomy and Tradition 1967, Preaching to the Exiles 1970, Exodus and Sinai in History and Tradition 1973, The Book of Jeremiah 1–25 1973, Kimchi's Commentary on Psalms 120–150 1973, The Book of Jeremiah 26–52 1974, God and His People 1986, The Pentateuch in the Twentieth Century 1998. *Leisure interests:* country walking, music. *Address:* Oriel College, Oxford, OX1 4EW, England. *Telephone:* (1865) 276533.

NICHOLSON, Jack; American actor and film maker; b. 22 April 1937, Neptune, NJ; s. of John Nicholson and Ethel May Nicholson; m. Sandra Knight 1961 (divorced 1966); two d.; Cecil B. De Mille Award 1999, Kennedy Center Honor 2001; Commdr des Arts et des Lettres. *Films include:* Cry-Baby Killer 1958, Studs Lonigan 1960, The Shooting (produced and acted), Ride the Whirlwind (wrote, produced and acted), Hell's Angels on Wheels 1967, The Trip (wrote screenplay) 1967, Head (co-scripted, co-produced) 1968, Psych-Out 1968, Easy Rider 1969 (Acad. Award for Best Supporting Actor), On a Clear Day You Can See Forever 1970, Five Easy Pieces 1971, Drive, He Said (dir) 1971, Carnal Knowledge 1971, The King of Marvin Gardens 1972, The Last Detail 1973, Chinatown 1974, The Passenger 1974, Tommy 1974, The Fortune 1975, The Missouri Breaks 1975, One Flew over the Cuckoo's Nest 1975 (Acad. Award for Best Actor 1976), The Last Tycoon 1976, Goin' South (actor, dir) 1978, The Shining 1980, The Postman Always Rings Twice 1981, Reds 1981, The Border 1982, Terms of Endearment 1984 (Acad. Award for Best Supporting Actor), Prizzi's Honor 1984, Heartburn 1985, The Witches of Eastwick 1986, Ironweed 1987, Batman 1989, The Two Jakes (actor, dir) 1989, Man Trouble, A Few Good Men 1992, Hoffa 1993, Wolf 1994, The Crossing Guard 1995, Mars Attacks!, The Evening Star, Blood and Wine 1996, As Good As It Gets 1997, The Pledge 2001, About Schmidt (Golden Globe for Best Dramatic Actor 2003) 2002, Anger Management 2003. *Address:* Bresler Kelly and Associates, 11500 West Olympic Boulevard, Suite 510, Los Angeles, CA 90064, USA (Office).

NICHOLSON, Jim; American diplomatist and business executive; b. 1938, Struble, Iowa; ed West Point, Columbia Univ., Univ. of Denver; army ranger, paratrooper, army reserve, retd with rank of Col; partner in pvt. law practice; f. Nicholson Enterprises, Inc. 1978–; Pres. Renaissance Homes, Denver 1987–; elected mem. for Col., Republican Nat. Cttee (RNC) 1986–2000, Vice-Chair. 1993–97, Chair. 1997–2000; Amb. to the Holy See 2001–; Kt, Sovereign Military Order of Malta; Dr hc (Regis, Denver) 2001; Bronze Star Medal, Combat Infantry Badge, Meritorious Service Medal, Vietnamese Cross for Gallantry, two Air Medals, Horatio Alger Award. *Address:* Embassy of the USA, Villa Domiziana, Via delle Terme Deciane 26, 00153 Rome, Italy (Office). *Telephone:* (06) 46741 (Office). *Fax:* (06) 5758346 (Office). *E-mail:* embassyvatican@libero.it (Office). *Website:* ww.usembassy.it/usembvat .Ambassador (Office).

NICHOLSON, Robin, CBE, MA, MSc; British architect; b. 27 July 1944, Hertford; m. Fiona Mary Bird; three s.; ed Eton Coll., Magdalene Coll.

Cambridge, Bartlett School, Univ. Coll. London; worked for James Stirling Chartered Architects, London 1969–76; Boza Lührs Muzano, Santiago, Chile 1973; Polytechnic of North London 1976–79; Edward Cullinan Architects 1979– (now Dir.); mem. RIBA; Hon. Fellow Inst. of Structural Eng; RIBA Student Design Prize 1969. *Publication:* Innovations in Healthcare Design 1995. *Leisure interest:* gardening. *Address:* Edward Cullinan Architects, 1 Baldwin Terrace, London, N1 7RU, England (Office). *Telephone:* (20) 7704-1975 (Office). *Fax:* (20) 7354-2739 (Office).

NICHOLSON, Sir Robin Buchanan, Kt, PhD, FEng, FRS; British metallurgist; b. 12 Aug. 1934, Sutton Coldfield; s. of the late Carroll and of Nancy Nicholson; m. 1st Elizabeth Mary Caffyn 1958 (died 1988); one s. two d.; m. 2nd Yvonne Appleby 1991; ed Oundle School and St Catharine's Coll. Cambridge; Demonstrator in Metallurgy, Univ of Cambridge 1960–64, lecturer 1964–66, Fellow of Christ's Coll. 1962–66; Prof. of Metallurgy, Univ. of Manchester 1966–72; Dir of Research Lab., Inco Europe Ltd 1972–76, Dir 1975–81, Man. Dir 1976–81; Co.-Chair. Biogen N.V. 1979–81; Chief Scientist, Cen. Policy Review Staff 1981–83; Chief Scientific Adviser, Cabinet Office 1983–86; Chief. Exec., Chair. Electro-Optical Div., Pilkington PLC 1986–, Dir Pilkington PLC (fmrly Pilkington Bros. PLC) 1986–96; Dir Rolls-Royce 1986–, BP PLC 1987–; Chair. Centre for Exploitation of Science and Tech. 1987–90, Advisory Council on Science and Tech. 1990–93, Pilkington Optronics Ltd 1991–; Pres. Inst. of Materials 1997–98; mem. Council, Royal Soc. 1983–85, Council for Science and Tech. 1993–, Scottish Advisory Cttee Imperial Cancer Research Fund 1994–; Hon. DSc (Cranfield, Aston) 1983, (Manchester) 1985, Hon. D.Met. (Sheffield) 1984, Hon. DEng (Birmingham) 1986; Rosenhain Medal, Inst. of Metals 1971; Platinum Medal, Metals Soc. 1981. *Publications:* Precipitation Hardening (with A. Kelly) 1962, Electron Microscopy of Thin Crystals (with Sir P. Hirsch and others) 1965, Strengthening Methods in Crystals (ed. and contrib. with A. Kelly) 1971. *Leisure interests:* family life, gardening, music. *Address:* c/o Pilkington Optronics Ltd, Glascoed Road, St Asaph, Denbighshire, LL17 0LL (Office); Penson Farm, Diptford, Totnes, Devon, TQ9 7NN, England. *Telephone:* (1745) 588003 (Office).

NICKELL, Stephen, BA, MSc; British economist; b. 25 April 1944; s. of John Edward Hilary Nickell and Phyllis Nickell; m. Susan Elizabeth Pegden; one s. one d.; ed Merchant Taylors' School, Pembroke Coll., Cambridge, London School of Econs; maths teacher, Hendon Co. School 1965–68; lecturer, LSE 1970–77, Reader 1977–79, Prof. of Econs 1979–84, 1998–; Dir Inst. of Econs and Statistics, Prof. of Econs and Fellow, Nuffield Coll. Oxford Univ. 1984–98; mem. Academic Panel, HM Treasury 1981–89; mem. of Council of Royal Econ. Soc. 1984–94, Econ. and Social Research Council 1990–94; mem. Monetary Policy Cttee Bank of England June 2000–; Pres. Royal Econ. Soc. 2001–(04); Fellow, Econometric Soc. 1980, British Acad. 1993; Hon. mem. American Econ. Asscn 1997; Hon. Fellow, Nuffield Coll. Oxford 2003. *Publications:* The Investment Decisions of Firms (jtly) 1978, The Performance of the British Economy (jtly) 1988, Unemployment (jtly) 1991, The Unemployment Crisis 1994, The Performance of Companies 1995; numerous articles in learned journals. *Leisure interests:* reading, riding, cooking. *Address:* Bank of England, Threadneedle Street, London, EC2R 8AH (Office); The Old Bakehouse, Horn Hill, Barford St Michael, Banbury, Oxon., OX15 0RG, England (Home). *Telephone:* (20) 7601-3768 (Office). *Fax:* (20) 7601-4610 (Office). *E-mail:* stephen.nickell@bankofengland.co.uk (Office).

NICKLAUS, Jack William; American golfer; b. 21 Jan. 1940, Columbus, Ohio; s. of L. Charles Nicklaus and Nicklaus Helen (née Schoener); m. Barbara Bash 1960; four s. one d.; ed Ohio State Univ.; professional golfer 1961–; won US Amateur Championship 1959, 1961; US Open Championship 1962, 1967, 1972, 1980, US Masters 1963, 1965, 1966, 1972, 1975, 1986, US PGA Championship 1963, 1971, 1973, 1975, 1980, British Open Championship 1966, 1970, 1978; by 1973 had won more maj. championship titles (totals now: 18 as professional, 2 as amateur) than any other player; Australian Open Champion six times, World Series winner five times, record three times individual winner World Cup, six times on winning team; rep. USA six Ryder Cup matches; 97 tournament victories, 76 official tour victories, 58 times second, 36 times third; joined Seniors Tour 1990; won US Sr Open, USA; 136 tournament appearances 1996; played in 154 consecutive majors 1999; has also designed over 100 golf courses in 26 countries; Co-Chair. The First Tee's Capital Campaign, More Than A Game 2000; Hon. LLD (St Andrews) 1984; five times US PGA Player of the Year; Golfer of the Century 1988; Athlete of the Decade Award 1970s; Golf World's Golf Course Architect of the Year 1993. *Publications:* My Story 1997 and numerous books about golf. *Leisure interests:* fishing, hunting, tennis. *Address:* Golden Bear International Inc., 11780 U.S. Highway 1, North Palm Beach, FL 33408, USA (Office).

NICKLES, Don; American politician and business executive; b. 6 Dec. 1948, Ponca City, Okla; s. of Robert Nickles and Coeweene Nickles; m. Linda Morrison 1968; one s. three d.; mem. Nat. Guard 1971–76; mem. Okla State Senate 1978–80, U.S. Senator from Oklahoma, 1981–; Asst Majority Leader, U.S. Senate; Vice-Pres., Gen. Man. Nickles Machine Co. 1972–80; Republican. *Address:* 133 Hart Senate Office Building, Washington, DC 20510, USA (Office). *Telephone:* (202) 224-5754 (Office). *Fax:* (202) 224-6008 (Office). *E-mail:* senator@nickles.senate.gov (Office). *Website:* www.senate.gov/ ~nickles (Office).

NICKS, Stevie (Stephanie); American singer and songwriter; b. 26 May 1948, Calif.; songwriter with Lindsey Buckingham; recorded album Buckingham Nicks 1973; joined group Fleetwood Mac 1973; albums with Fleetwood Mac include: Fleetwood Mac 1975, Rumours 1977, Tusk 1979, Fleetwood Mac Live 1980, Mirage 1982, Tango in the Night 1987, Behind the Mask 1990, 25 Years–The Chain 1992; solo albums include: Bella Donna 1981, The Wild Heart 1983, Rock a Little 1985, Time Space 1991, Street Angel 1994; composer of songs Rhiannon, Landslide, Leather and Lace, Dreams, Sara, Edge of Seventeen, If Anyone Falls (with Sandy Stewart), Stand Back (with Prince Rogers Nelson), I Can't Wait (with others), The Other Side of the Mirror, Time Space, Street Angel, Seven Wonders (with Sandy Stewart). *Address:* WEA Corporation, 79 Madison Avenue, Floor 7, New York, NY 10016, USA.

NICKSON, Baron (Life Peer), cr. 1994, of Renagour in the District of Stirling; **David Wigley Nickson,** KBE, FRSE ; British business executive (retd); b. 27 Nov. 1929, Eton; s. of Geoffrey W. Nickson and Janet M. Nickson; m. Helen L. Cockcraft 1952; three d.; ed Eton and Royal Mil. Acad. Sandhurst; man. trainee, Wm. Collins, Publrs Glasgow 1954, Dir 1961, Jt Man. Dir 1967, Vice-Chair. 1976, Vice-Chair. and Group Man. Dir 1979–82, Non-exec. Dir 1982–85; Non-exec. Dir Scottish & Newcastle Breweries PLC 1981–95, Deputy Chair. 1982, Chair. 1983–89; Chair. Atlantic Salmon Trust 1989–96 (Vice-Chair. 1985–88), Sec. of State for Scotland's Atlantic Salmon Task Force 1996, Scottish Devt Agency 1989–90, Scottish Enterprise 1990–92; Deputy Chair. Clydesdale Bank PLC 1989–91, (Chair. 1991–98), Gen. Accident 1993–98; Dir (non-exec.) Gen. Accident Fire & Life Assurance Corpn PLC, Edin. Investment Trust PLC 1983–94; Pres. Confed. of British Industry (CBI) 1986–88; Chair. Top Salaries Review Body 1989–95; Chancellor Glasgow Caledonian Univ. 1993–; Vice-Lord-Lt of Stirling and Falkirk 1997–; Hon. DL, Hon. DUniv (Stirling) 1986; Hon. DBA (Napier Univ.) 1990, (Paisley Univ.) 1991; Hon. DUniv (Glasgow) 1993. *Leisure interests:* fishing, birdwatching, shooting, the countryside. *Address:* The River House, Doune, Perthshire, FK16 6DA, Scotland (Home). *Telephone:* (1876) 841614 (Home). *Fax:* (1876) 841062 (Home).

NICODIM, Ion; Romanian painter, engraver and sculptor; b. 26 March 1932, Constanța; ed Coll. of Fine Arts, Bucharest; mem. of the Romanian Artists' Union; exhbns. Bucharest, Cluj, Venice, Turin, Rome, São Paulo, Cagnes-sur-Mer, Yugoslavia, Vienna, Warsaw, Prague, Paris, Baden-Baden, Copenhagen; Prize of the Romanian Artists' Union 1964, 1977; Prize of the Romanian Acad. 1975, Gottfried von Herder Prize, Vienna 1992. *Exhibitions include:* Venice Biennale 1982, Museum of Fine Arts, Bucharest 1987, Grand Palais Fiac Edition Saga, Paris 1989–90, L'Amore dall' Olimpo all' Alcova, Turin 1992. *Works:* frescoes, mosaics, tapestries including Praise to Man, at the UN headquarters in New York, painting, graphics, glass, furniture, design, engravings, monumental decorative designs. *Publication:* La Surface et le Cri 1986. *Address:* Str. E. Broeșeanu nr. 17, Bucharest, Romania; 60 rue de Domrémy, 75013 Paris, France. *Telephone:* 45-70-87-04 (Paris); (1) 2111398 (Bucharest).

NICOL, Donald MacGillivray, PhD, FBA, FRHistS; British professor of Byzantine history; b. 4 Feb. 1923, Portsmouth; s. of George Manson Nicol and Mary Patterson (née MacGillivray); m. Joan Mary Campbell 1950; three s.; ed King Edward VII School, Sheffield, St Paul's School, London; Pembroke Coll. Cambridge and British School of Archaeology at Athens; Lecturer in Classics and Ancient History, Univ. Coll. Dublin 1952–64; Visiting Fellow, Dumbarton Oaks, Washington, DC 1964–65; Visiting Prof. of Byzantine History, Indiana Univ., USA 1965–66; Reader in Byzantine History, Univ. of Edin. 1966–70; Koraës Prof. of Modern Greek and Byzantine History, Language and Literature, King's Coll. London 1970–88, now Emer.; Dir Gennadius Library, Athens 1989–92; Fellow and fmr Vice-Prin. King's Coll.; Birkbeck Lecturer, Cambridge Univ. 1976–77; Pres. Ecclesiastical History Soc. 1975–76; mem. Royal Irish Acad. *Publications:* The Despotate of Epirus 1957, Meteora: The Rock Monasteries of Thessaly 1963, The Byzantine Family of Kantakouzenos (Cantacuzenus) c. 1100–1460 1968, The Last Centuries of Byzantium 1972, Church and Society in the Last Centuries of Byzantium 1979, The Despotate of Epiros: A Contribution to the History of Greece in the Middle Ages 1267–1479 1984, Studies in Late Byzantine History and Prosopography 1986, Byzantium and Venice. A Study in Diplomatic and Cultural Relations 1988, A Biographical Dictionary of the Byzantine Empire 1991, The Immortal Emperor, The Life and Legend of Constantine Palaiologos, Last Emperor of the Romans 1992, Ten Byzantine Ladies 1250–1500 1994, The Reluctant Emperor: A Biography of John Cantacuzene, Byzantine Emperor and Monk c. 1295–1383 1996, Theodore Spandounes, On the Origin of the Ottoman Emperors (ed. and trans.) 1997. *Leisure interest:* bookbinding. *Address:* 4 Westberry Court, Pinehurst, Grange Road, Cambridge, CB3 9BG, England. *Telephone:* (1223) 360955.

NICOLAIDES, Maj.-Gen. Cristino; Argentine army officer; b. 2 Jan. 1925, Mercedes; ed Mil. Acad.; Second Lt, Corps of Engineers, Mil. Acad. 1947; Capt. 1954; Staff Officer army high command; Col 1970; Dir School for Combat Services 1974; Brig.-Gen. 1975; led mil. campaign against leftist guerrillas, Córdoba; Commdr 1st Army Corps 1981–82; C.-in-C of the Army and mem. mil. junta 1982–83; indicted for human rights abuses (by Spain) Oct. 1999.

NICOLAS, Gwenael, BA; French interior designer and graphic designer; b. 6 June 1969, Rosporden; ed Ecole supérieure d'art graphique et d'architecture d'intérieure, Royal Coll. of Art; Pres. Curiosity Inc.; Nintendo Game Boy Advance Design Consultant 2000; American Inst. of Architecture Citation 1998, I.D. Magazine Distinction 1999, 2000. *Achievements:* Issey Miyake 'Pleats Please' shop design: New York 1998, Paris 1999, Tokyo 2000; bottle and package design for perfumes 'Le Feu d'Issey' 1998, 'Le Feu d'Issey Light' 2000; Olympus Digital Camera design 1999. *Address:* Curiosity Inc., 2-45-7 Honmachi, Shibuya-ku, Tokyo 151-007 1, Japan (Office). *Telephone:* (3) 5333-8525 (Office). *Fax:* (3) 5371-1219 (Office). *E-mail:* nicolas@curiosity.co.jp (Office). *Website:* www.curiosity.co.jp (Office).

NICOLET, Claude; French professor of Roman history; b. 15 Sept. 1930, Marseilles; s. of Edmond Nicolet and Suzanne Nicolet; m. 1st Michelle Brousset 1956 (divorced, deceased); one s.; m. 2nd Hélène Pierre 1963; three s.; ed Ecole Normale Supérieure and Ecole Française de Rome; served on Staff of Minister of State Pierre Mendès-France 1956; Editorial Sec. Cahiers de la République 1956–57; mem. Ecole Française de Rome 1957–59; Lecturer Univ. of Tunis 1959–61; Lecturer and Prof. Univ. of Caen 1961–69; Prof. of Roman History, Univ. of Paris/Sorbonne 1969–; Dir of Studies, Ecole Pratique des Hautes Etudes (Section IV) 1969–; mem. Inst. for Advanced Studies, Princeton 1966–67, 1972; Prof. Univ. Paris I 1971–; Dir Era 757, CNRS 1978–91; Dir Centre Gustav Glotz 1981–92, Ecole Française de Rome 1992–95; Pres. Soc. for Latin Studies 1983, Conseil scientifique du Centre d'études et des prévisions du ministère de l'Interieur 1998; mem. Acad. des Inscriptions et Belles Lettres (Inst. de France); Assoc. mem. Academia dei Lincei; Corresp. Fellow British Acad. 1987; Prix Galileo Galilei des Rotary italiens 1994, Grand Prix Nat. (histoire) 1996, Prix des Culbori di Roma 1997; Chevalier, Légion d'honneur; Officier des Palmes académiques. *Publications:* numerous books including Nation, Histoire, République 2000, Censeurs et Publicains 2000. *Address:* Institut de France, 23 quai Conti, 75006 Paris; 2 rue de Paradis, 75010 Paris, France. *Telephone:* 1-47-70-02-91.

NICOLI, Eric Luciano, BSc; British business executive; b. 5 Aug. 1950, Pulham Market, Norfolk; s. of Virgilio Nicoli and Ida Nicoli; m. Rosalind West 1977; one s. one d.; ed Diss Grammar School, Norfolk, King's Coll. London; worked briefly in market research, then various positions with Rowntree Marketing Dept 1972–80; Sr Marketing Controller, Biscuit Div., United Biscuits 1980–81, Marketing Dir, Biscuits 1981–84 and Confectionery 1982–84; UK Business Planning Dir 1984, Man. Dir UB Frozen Foods 1985, UB Brands 1986–89, apptd. to Bd of UB (Holdings) PLC 1989, CEO, European Operations 1989–90, Group CEO United Biscuits (Holdings) PLC 1991–99, Acting Chair. 2001–; Chair. EMI Group PLC 1999–, HMV Media Group PLC 2001–; Deputy Chair. BITC 1991–, Per Cent Club 1993–; Dir (non-exec.) Thorn EMI PLC 1993–, Tussauds Group Ltd 1999– (Chair. 2001–); Trustee Comic Relief 1999–. *Leisure interests:* all sports (especially golf), music, food. *Address:* EMI Group PLC, 4 Tenterden Street, Hanover Square, London, W1A 2AY, England. *Telephone:* (20) 7355-4848 (Office).

NICOLIN, Curt René; Swedish company executive; b. 10 March 1921, Stockholm; s. of Felix Nicolin and Anna-Lisa Nicolin; m. Ulla Sandén 1946 (died 1999); three s. two d.; ed Royal Inst. of Tech., Stockholm; with STAL Finspong 1945–61; Interim Pres. Scandinavian Airlines System (SAS) 1961–62; Swedish Chair. SAS 1973–91; Pres. ASEA AB, Västerås 1961–76, Chair. of Bd 1976–91, Incentive AB 1991–92; Co-Chair. ABB Asea Brown Boveri 1988–91; Hon. Chair. ASEA AB 1991; Hon. DTech 1974; Hon. Dr. Laws 1991; Hon. DEcon 1994; Lucia Trade Award 1996; Commdr, Order of Vasa, First Class 1974, Medal, Order of Seraphim 1991. *Publications:* Private Industry in a Public World 1973, New Strategy for Sweden 1996, Ethics in Society, Business and Management 1989–99. *Leisure interests:* tennis, sailing.

NICORA, Most Rev. Attilio; Italian ecclesiastic; b. 16 March 1937, Varese; ordained Priest 1964; Auxiliary Bishop of Milan 1977–92; Bishop of Verona 1992–97; Bishop of Roman Curia 1997–2002, Pres. Patrimony of the Apostolic See, Roman Curia 2002–; oversaw revision of Concordat between Italy and the Vatican 1984. *Address:* Administration of the Patrimony of the Holy See, Palazzo Apostolico, 00120 Città de Vaticano, Italy (Office). *Telephone:* (06) 69893403 (Office). *Fax:* (06) 69883141 (Office). *E-mail:* apsa-ss@apsa.va (Office).

NICULESCU, Alexandru A.; Romanian diplomatist and international organization official; b. 1 Jan. 1941, Bucharest; s. of Alexandru Niculescu and Elisabeth Niculescu; m.; three c.; ed Polytech. Inst. and Univ. of Law, Bucharest; Chargé d'affaires, Perm. Mission to UN, Geneva 1990–91, Deputy Perm. Rep. 1991–95; Dir Div. for UN and Specialized Agencies, Ministry of Foreign Affairs, Bucharest 1995–98; Deputy Perm. Rep. to UN, New York 1999–2000, Amb. and Perm. Rep. 2000–. *Publications:* essays and articles on world econ. relations, globalization and UN system's activities. *Leisure interests:* music, economic literature (on globalization), art. *Address:* Permanent Mission of Romania to the United Nations, 573–577 Third Avenue, New York, NY 10016, USA (Office); 13A, Dumbrava Rosie Street, Ap. 6, Sector 2, Bucharest, Romania (Home). *Telephone:* (212) 6823273 (Office); (1) 2117877 (Home). *Fax:* (212) 6829746 (Office). *E-mail:* romania@un.int (Office); alniculescu@hotmail.com (Home).

NICULESCU, Ştefan; Romanian composer; b. 31 July 1927, Moreni, Dîmbovița Co.; s. of Lazar Niculescu and Maria Niculescu; m. Colette Demetrescu 1952; ed Acad. of Music and Theatrical Art, Bucharest Coll. of Engineering, Bucharest, C. Porumbescu Conservatory of Music, Bucharest; studies in electronic music Munich 1966; researcher Inst. for Art History of the Romanian Acad., Bucharest 1960–63; Prof. Acad. of Music, Bucharest 1963–87, 1992–; Sec. for Symphonic, Chamber and Opera Music Romanian Composers' Union 1990–93; Guest, Deutscher Akademischer Austauschdienst, West Berlin 1971–72, Internationaler Frienkurse für Neu Musik, Darmstadt 1992;

Corresp. mem. Romanian Acad. 1993–, mem. 1996–; Romanian Acad. Prize 1962, French Acad. Prize 1972, Prizes of the Romanian Composers' Union 1972, 1975, 1977, 1979, 1981, 1982, 1984, 1985, 1986, 1988, 1994, Festival Montreux Prize, Int. Record Critics Award 1985, Herder Prize, Vienna 1994, George Apostu Grand Award 1994. *Works include:* symphonies, cantatas, chamber music; Aphorismes d'Héraclite, for mixed choir of 20 soloists 1969, Ison I–II for orchestra 1971–76, Sincronie I–IV for instruments 1979–87, Opus Dacicum for orchestra 1981, Ricercare in uno, for synthesizer, clarinet and violin 1983, Cantos for saxophone and orchestra 1985, Octuplum 1987, Invocatio (choral symphony) 1988, Axion for choir and saxophone 1992, Psalmus for 6 voices 1993, Deisis for orchestra 1995, Litanies for orchestra 1997, Undecimum for 11 instruments 1998; stage and film music. *Publications:* Reflectii despre Musică (Reflections about Music) 1980, Un Nouvel "Esprit de Temps" en Musique 1987, Global Language in Music 2000. *Address:* Intr. Sublocotenent Stăniloiu 4, 73228 Bucharest 39, Romania (Home); Calea Victoriei 141, 70149 Bucharest (Office). *Telephone:* 6424370 (Home). *Fax:* 2527945 (Home).

NIE LI (LILI), Maj.-Gen.; Chinese administrator; b. 1930; d. of the late Marshal Nie Rongzhen; m. Ding Henggao; Vice-Chair. of Scientific and Tech. Cttee under Comm. of Science, Tech. and Industry for Nat. Defence 1983; promoted Maj.-Gen. PLA 1988; Vice-Chair. of Nat. Examination Cttee for Science Award; mem. 8th NPC 1994–98; Vice-Pres. All-China Women's Fed. 1992–; mem. Internal and Judicial Affairs Cttee. *Address:* National Examination Committee for Science Award, Sanlihe, Beijing, People's Republic of China.

NIELSON, Poul, MSc; Danish politician and civil servant; b. 1943, Copenhagen; m.; three c.; ed Univ. of Århus; Chair. Nat. Social Democratic Students Org. 1966–67; mem. Social Democratic Foreign Affairs Cttee 1965–79 (Chair. 1974–79); MP 1971–73, 1977–84, 1986–99; Head of Section, Ministry of Foreign Affairs 1974–79, 1984–85; Chair. Danish European Movt 1977–79; Chair. Parl. Commerce Cttee 1979; Minister of Energy 1979–82; Asst Prof., Danish School of Public Admin. 1985–86; CEO LD-Energy Inc. 1988–94; Minister for Devt Co-operation 1994–99; EU Commr for Devt and Humanitarian Aid 1999–. *Publictions:* The Wage Earners and the Company Act, Power Play and Security, Politicians and Civil Servants. *Address:* Commission of the European Communities, 200 rue de la Loi, 1049 Brussels (Office); Avenue du Fort Jaco 75, 1180 Brussels, Belgium (Home). *Telephone:* (2) 298-10-00 (Office). *Fax:* (2) 298-10-98.

NIEMCZYCKI, Zbigniew; Polish business executive; b. 23 Jan. 1947, Nisko; m. Katarzyna Frank; one d. three s.; ed Warsaw Univ. of Tech.; owner and Chair. Curtis Group; Founder, Chair. Polish Eagles Aviation Foundation; Pres. Bd Polish Business Roundtable; Vice-Pres. Main Council Business Centre Club; Businessman of the Year 1992, Leader of Polish Business 1992; Kt's Cross, Order of Polonia Restituta, St Gregory Cross. *Leisure interests:* piloting helicopters and planes, tennis. *Address:* Curtis Development, ul. Wołoska 18, 02-675 Warsaw, Poland (Office). *Telephone:* (22) 848-65-53 (Office). *Website:* www.curtisgroup.pl (Office).

NIEMEYER, Oscar; Brazilian architect; b. 15 Dec. 1907, Rio de Janeiro; s. of Oscar Niemeyer Soares; m. Anita Niemeyer; one d.; ed Escola Nacional de Belas Artes, Rio de Janeiro; in office of Lúcio Costa 1935; designed Ministry of Educ. and Health Bldg, Rio de Janeiro 1937–43, Brazilian Pavilion, New York World Fair 1939, with others designed UN Bldg, New York 1947; Dir of Architecture for new capital of Brasília and given a free hand in design of public and other bldgs. 1957–; Designer of Bienal Exhbn Hall, São Paulo, urban area of Grasse (near Nice) 1966, French CP Bldg, Paris 1966, Palace of Arches (for Foreign Ministry) Brasília; Lenin Peace Prize 1963, Prix Int. de l'Architecture d'aujourd'hui 1966, shared Pritzker Prize 1988, Prince of the Asturias Prize for the Arts 1989, Royal Gold Medal for Architecture 1998. *Address:* 3940 avenida Atlàntica, Rio de Janeiro, RJ, Brazil.

NIEMI, Irmeli, DPhil; Finnish fmr civil servant and university professor; b. 3 Feb. 1931, Helsinki; d. of Taneli Kuusisto and Kyllikki Valtonen; m. Mikko Niemi 1953; one s. two d.; ed Univ. of Helsinki; freelance translator, literature and theatre critic; Ed. 1950–68; Jr Research Fellow, Acad. of Finland 1968–69; Assoc. Prof. of Comparative Literature and Drama, Univ. of Turku 1970–78, Prof. 1978–81, 1984–90; Dir-Gen. Dept of Culture, Ministry of Educ. 1990–96; Sr Teacher, Theatre Acad. Helsinki 1964–96; Research Prof. Acad. of Finland 1981–84; Chair. Finnish Research Council for the Humanities 1986–88, Arts Council of Finland 1989–90, Bd of Finnish Nat. Opera 1996–2001, Finland Festivals 1998–; Council of the Finnish Inst. in London 1996–; mem. Science Policy Council of Finland 1986–90. *Publications:* Maria Jotunin näytelmät 1964, Nykydraaman ihmiskuva 1969, Nykyteatterin juuret 1975, The Role of the Spectator 1984, Suomalainen alueteatteri 1978–82 1984, Arki ja tunteet Maria Jotunin elämä ja kirjailijantyö 2001. *Leisure interests:* modern music, forest walks, travel. *Address:* Osmalahdentie 437, 21570 Sauvo, Finland. *Telephone:* (2) 4701833. *Fax:* (2) 4701893. *E-mail:* irniemi@saunalahti.fi (Home).

NIETO GALLO, Gratiniano; Spanish art official; b. 6 March 1917, La Aguilera, Burgos; s. of Francisco and Genoveva Nieto Gallo; m. María de Mergelina Cano-Manuel; one s. one d.; ed Institución Teresiana, Instituto Ramiro de Maeztu and Univ. de Madrid; Prof., Univ. de Valladolid 1940–52; Dir Colegio Mayor Santa Cruz de Valladolid 1943–52; Sec. School of Art and Archaeology, Univ. de Valladolid 1940–52; Dir Colegio Mayor Nebrija, Univ. de Madrid 1952–56; Tech. Sec.-Gen. Directorate of Archives and Libraries

1956–61; attached to Univ. de Murcia 1959–61; Dir-Gen. of Fine Arts 1961–68; Dir Cen. Inst. for Conservation and Restoration of Works of Art 1968–; Prof. Univ. Madrid 1968–; Pres. Univ. Autónoma de Madrid 1973; decorations from Spain, Portugal, Malta, Fed. Repub. of Germany, Italy, France and Peru. *Publications:* La Necrópolis Ibérica del Cabecito del Tesoro 1940, 1944, 1947, Las tablas flamencas de la Igl. del Salvador de Valladolid 1941, Criterio de Reconstrucción de Objetos Arqueológicos 1941, El Oppidum de Iruña 1949, Guía Artística de Valladolid 1954, Historia de los Monumentos de Lerma 1959, La cueva artificial del Bronco I de Alguazas 1959, Tendencias Actuales de la Arqueología 1959, Guía de la Exposición Conmemorativa de la Paz de los Pirineos 1963, Las Bellas Artes en España 1963, Conservación del Patrimonio Artístico 1968, Museos de Artes y Costumbres Populares 1968, Conservación de Objetos Arqueológicos 1969, Panorama de los Museos Españoles y cuestiones museológicas 1971, Reflexiones sobre la Universidad 1973. *Leisure interests:* swimming, rowing, mountaineering. *Address:* Universidad Autónoma de Madrid, Km. 15 Carretera de Colmenar Viejo, Canto Blanco, 28049 Madrid, Spain. *Telephone:* (91) 3975000. *Fax:* (91) 3974123. *Website:* www.uam.es (Office).

NIGHTINGALE, (William) Benedict (Herbert), BA; British author and theatre critic; b. 14 May 1939, London; s. of R. E. Nightingale and Hon. Mrs. Nightingale (née Gardner); m. Anne B. Redmon 1964; two s. one d.; ed Charterhouse School, Magdalene Coll. Cambridge and Univ. of Pennsylvania; gen. writer, The Guardian 1963–66; Literary Ed. New Society 1966–67; Theatre Critic, New Statesman 1968–86; Prof. of English, Theatre and Drama Univ. of Mich. 1986–89; Chief Drama Critic The Times 1990–; Sunday theatre critic, New York Times 1983–84. *Publications:* Charities 1972, Fifty British Plays 1982, Fifth Row Center 1986, The Future of the Theatre 1998; numerous articles on cultural and theatrical matters in British and American journals. *Leisure interests:* music, literature, watching soccer. *Address:* 40 Broomhouse Road, London, SW6 3QX, England.

NIGHY, Bill; British actor; b. Caterham, Surrey; s. of Alfred Nighy and Catherine Whittaker; partner Diana Quick; one d.; ed John Fisher Grammar, Purley; Peter Sellers Comedy Award, Barclays Best Actor Award. *Stage appearances include:* Arcadia, A Map of the World, The Seagull, Skylight, Blue Orange, Mean Tears, Pravda, Betrayal, A Kind of Alaska. *Film appearances include:* Still Crazy, Lawless Heart, Lucky Break, Blow-dry, I Capture the Castle, Underworld, Love Actually, Fairytale. *Radio:* Lord of the Rings, No Commitments, Bleak House, and numerous others. *Television appearances include:* The Men's Room, Absolute Hell, Dreams of Leaving, The Lost Prince, Ready When You Are Mr McGill, and numerous others. *Leisure Interests:* reading, rhythm and blues. *Address:* c/o Markham & Froggatt Ltd, 4 Windmill Street, London W1P 1HF, England (Office).

NIILUS, Leopoldo Juan (Leopoldo Johannes); Argentine lawyer; b. 19 Jan. 1930, Tallinn, Estonia; s. of the late Jaan Eduard Niilus and Meta Kiris; m. Malle Reet Veerus 1961; one d.; ed Faculty of Law, Univ. Buenos Aires, Argentina, Southern Methodist Univ., Dallas, Tex., USA; left Estonia 1944; fmrly practising lawyer, Buenos Aires; fmr Chair. Argentine Student Christian Movt; fmr mem. World Student Christian Fed. (WSCF); Dir Argentine Dept River Plate Centre of Christian Studies 1966–67; Gen. Sec. ISAL (Comm. for Church and Soc. in Latin America) 1968–69; Dir Comm. of the Churches on Int. Affairs of WCC, Geneva 1969–81; Dir Int. Ecumenical Relations, Middle East Council of Churches (MECC) 1982–95; Consultant on int. affairs and human rights, Lutheran World Fed. 1988–95; ind. political consultant 1996–; participated in mediation for Sudan peace negotiations 1972, Guatemala peace negotiations, signed as witness, Oslo accords on Guatemala 1990; Order of Two Niles, 1st Grade (Sudan). *Publications:* On Penal Law (essays); numerous articles and essays in ecumenical publs on peace, disarmament, North–South relations, Middle East, Central America. *Address:* 7 chemin du Champ d'Anier, 1209 Geneva, Switzerland (Home). *Telephone:* (22) 7983259 (Home). *Fax:* (22) 7884448 (Home). *E-mail:* leopoldo_niilus@compuserve.com (Home).

NIINISTÖ SAULI, Väinämö; Finnish politician and lawyer; b. 24 Aug. 1948, Salo; m. (wife deceased); two s.; own law office in Salo 1978–88; Sr Sec. Turku Court of Appeal 1976; mem. Salo City Council 1977–; Chair. 1989–92, mem. City Bd 1977–88; mem. Nat. Coalition Party (KOK) Council 1979–81, Party Chair. 1994; mem. Parl. 1987–; Chair. Constitutional Cttee of Parl. 1993–95; Deputy Prime Minister 1995–2001; Minister of Justice 1995–96; Minister of Finance 1996–2003; Chair. European Democratic Union (EDU) 1998–. *Address:* c/o Ministry of Finance, PO Box 28, 00023 Government, Finland (Office).

NIJENHUIS, Emmie te, PhD; Netherlands ethnomusicologist; b. 11 Nov. 1931, Bussum; d. of Dirk te Nijenhuis and W. Margarete Küchenthal; m. 1965–70; one s.; ed Utrecht Conservatory and Utrecht Univ.; Teacher of Theory and History of Western Music, Zwolle Conservatory 1958–61; Reader Indian Musicology, Utrecht Univ. 1964–88; Visiting Lecturer Oxford and Basel Univs 1978, 1984; mem. Royal Netherlands Acad. of Sciences 1978. *Publications:* Dattilam: Compendium of Ancient Indian Music 1970, Indian Music, History and Structure 1974, The Ragas of Somanatha, 2 vols 1976, Musicological Literature 1977, Sacred Songs of India: Muttusvami Diksitar's Cycle of Hymns to the Goddess Kamala, 2 vols 1987, Saṅgītaśiromani, A Medieval Handbook of Indian Music 1992, Varnam: Selected Concert Studies for the South Indian Lute 2001. *Address:* Verlengde Fortlaan 39, 1412 CW Naarden, Netherlands. *Telephone:* (35) 6949322.

NIKOLAYEV, Army Gen. Andrei Ivanovich; Russian army officer (retd) and politician; b. 21 April 1949, Moscow; m. Tatyana Yuryevna Nikolayeva; two s.; ed Moscow Gen. Troops Commdg School of RSFSR Supreme Soviet, M. Frunze Mil. Acad., Gen. Staff Acad.; Commdr of platoon, co., Regt; First Deputy Head Main Admin. of Gen. Headquarters of USSR Armed Forces; First Deputy Head of Gen. HQ of Russian Army 1992–94; C-in-C of Border troops of Russian Fed. 1994–; Head of Fed. Border Troops Service 1995–97; mem. State Duma (Parl.) 1998–; Chair. Cttee of Defence 2000–; f. Union of People's Power and Labour 1998–. *Leisure interests:* theatre, organ music. *Address:* State Duma, Okhotny Ryad 1, 103265 Moscow, Russia. *Telephone:* (095) 292-80-24. *Fax:* (095) 292-95-77.

NIKOLAYEV, Mikhail Yefimovich; Russian/Yakut politician; b. 13 Nov. 1937, Ordzhonikidze Region, Yakutia; m.; three c.; ed Omsk Veterinary Inst., Higher CP School; worked as veterinarian, then Sec. Zhigan Regional Comsomol Cttee, First Sec. Yakut Comsomol Cttee, Sec., then First Sec. Verkhneviluysk Regional CP Cttee 1971–75; Deputy Chair. Council of Ministers Yakut ASSR 1975–79; Minister of Agric. 1979–85; Sec. Yakut Regional CP Cttee 1985–89; Chair. Presidium of Supreme Soviet Yakut ASSR 1989–91; Pres. Repub. of Sakha (Yakutia) 1991–2001; mem. Council of Fed. of Russia 1993–, Rep. Sakha-Yakutia Rep. In Council of Fed. 2001–, Deputy Chair. 2002–; Order of Red Banner of Labour, Order of Friendship, Order for Prominent Services to the Fatherland and other honours. *Publications include:* My People are My Republic 1992, The Arctic: The Pain and Hope of Russia 1994, The Arctic. XXI Century 1999. *Address:* Council of Federation, Bolshaya Dmitrovka 26, 103426 Moscow, Russia; House of Government, Kirova str. 11, 677022 Yakutsk, Russia. *Telephone:* (4112) 43-50-50 (Office). *Fax:* (4112) 24-06-24 (Office).

NIKOLSKY, Boris Vassilyevich; Russian politician; b. 1 May 1937, Moscow; m.; two c.; ed Moscow Inst. of Agric. Eng, Higher School Cen. Cttee CPSU; master, chief engineer in a factory; Deputy Chair. Moscow Municipal Exec. Cttee on problems of energy and eng 1976–82; Sec. Moscow City CP Cttee 1982–84; Sec., then Second Sec. Cen. Cttee of Georgian CP 1984–; First Deputy Chair. Moscow City Planning Cttee 1989–; First Deputy Chair. Moscow City Construction Cttee 1990–91; Deputy Prime Minister Moscow Govt 1991–92, First Deputy Chair. 1992–2002; Moscow Rep. to Council of Fed. 2002–. *Address:* Moscow Government, Tverskaya str. 13, 103032 Moscow, Russia (Office). *Telephone:* (095) 229-24-24 (Office). *Fax:* (095) 230-20-69. *E-mail:* mayor@mos.ru (Office).

NIKOLSKY, Sergey Ivanovich; Russian physicist; b. 5 June 1923; m.; one s.; ed Moscow State Univ.; served in Soviet Army 1941–43; mem. of staff of Inst. of Physics, USSR (now Russian) Acad. of Sciences 1948–, Head of Section 1970–73, Deputy Dir 1973–93, Dir Dept of Nuclear Physics 1993–, Corresp. mem. 1984–; numerous publs on space research, nuclear physics, solid state physics 1947–90; Lenin Prize 1982. *Leisure interest:* history of civilization. *Address:* P. N. Lebedev Institute of Physics, Leninsky Prospekt 53, 117924 Moscow, Russia. *Telephone:* 135-50-11 (Office); 135-00-93 (Home).

NIKONENKO, Sergey Petrovich; Russian actor, film director and scriptwriter; b. 16 April 1941, Moscow; s. of Peter Nikonenko and Nima Nikonenko; m. Yekaterina Voronina-Nikonenko; one s.; ed All-Union Inst. of Cinematography; mem. Union of Cinematographers 1968–; f. Yesenin Cultural Foundation 1994–; Comsomol Prize 1976, Order of Honour 1971, A. Dovzhenko Medal 1988, Grand Prix Int. Film Festival in Oberhausen (Germany), People's Artist of Russia 1991. *Film appearances include:* War and Peace 1965–67, Wings 1966, They are Ringing, Open the Door 1966, Strange People 1969, Journalist, I Have Come This Way, Crime and Punishment, White Explosion 1969, Sing a Song, Poet 1971, Inspector of Road Police 1982, Unfinished Piece for a Mechanical Piano 1976, Winter Evening in Gagry 1986, Tomorrow was War 1987, The Red Wine of Victory 1990, Family Man 1991, Unwilling to Marry 1992, Time of the Dancer 1996, Kids of Monday 1997, Sinful Love 1997, Chinese Service 1999, Classic 1998, Kamenskaya 2000. *Films directed include:* Gypsy's Happiness, Birds Above the Town, Love. Wait. Lyonya, I Want Your Husband. *Leisure interests:* classical literature and music, opera music, painting. *Address:* Sivtsev Vrazhek str. 44, Apt. 20, 121000 Moscow, Russia (Home). *Telephone:* (095) 241-78-72 (Home).

NIKONOV, Vyacheslav Alekseyevich, DrHis; Russian politician and academic; b. 5 June 1956, Moscow; s. of Aleksey Dmitrievich Nikonov and Svetlana Vyacheslavovna Molotova; grandson of Vyacheslav Molotov; m. 1st Viktoria Makarovna Kostyuk 1976; m. 2nd Olga Mikhailovna Rozhkova 1987; three s.; ed Moscow State Univ.; researcher Moscow State Univ.; on staff Admin. Cen. Cttee CPSU 1989–90; on staff of Pres. Gorbachev 1990–91; Asst to Chair. USSR State Security Cttee (KGB) 1991–92; counsellor Dept of Political Problems Int. Foundation of Econ. and Social Reforms (Foundation Reforma) 1992–93; Pres. Politika Foundation 1993–; mem. State Duma (Parl.); Chair. Subcttee on Int. Security and Arms Control 1994–95; Deputy Chair. Cttee to Re-elect the Pres. 1996; Dean of History and Political Science Moscow Int. Univ. 2001; Deputy Chair. Editorial Bd Russia in Global Affairs 2002. *Publications:* Republicans: From Eisenhower to Nixon 1984, Iran-Contra Affair 1988, Republicans: From Nixon to Reagan 1989, The Age of Change: Russia in the 90s as Viewed by a Conservative 1999, Contemporary Russian Politics (Ed.) 2003. *Leisure interests:* reading, gardening. *Address:* Politika Foundation, Zlatoustinsky per. 8/7, 101000 Moscow, Russia (Office). *Telephone:* (095) 206-81-49 (Office). *Fax:* (095) 206-86-61 (Office). *E-mail:* polity@online.ru (Office). *Website:* www.polity.ru (Office).

NILEKANI, Nandan M., BEng; Indian business executive; ed Indian Inst. of Tech.; Co-Founder, Dir Infosys 1981–, later Man. Dir, Pres. and COO, CEO, Pres. and Man. Dir 2002–; Co-Founder India's Nat. Asscn of Software and Service Cos. (NASSCOM), Bangalore Chapter of the IndUS Entrepreneurs (TiE); mem. Asia Pacific Regional Advisory Bd, London Business School, Global Advisory Council, The Conf. Bd; Co-Chair. Business Leaders Dialogue, Initiative for Social Innovation Through Business (ISIB), Aspen Inst.; Co-Chair. Advisory Bd, IIT Bombay Heritage Fund; Chair. Govt of India's IT for the Power Sector task force, Bangalore Agenda task force; Alumnus Award, Indian Inst. of Tech. 1999. *Address:* Infosys, Plot No. 44&97A, Electronics City, Hosur Road, Bangalore 561 229, India (Office). *Telephone:* (80) 8520261 (Office). *Fax:* (80) 8522390 (Office). *E-mail:* indiasales@infosys.com (Office). *Website:* www.infosys.com.

NILES, Thomas Michael Tolliver, MA; American diplomatist; b. 22 Sept. 1939, Lexington, Ky; s. of John Jacob Niles and Rena Niles (née Lipetz); m. Carroll C. Ehringhaus 1967; one s. one d.; ed Harvard Univ. and Univ. of Kentucky; Foreign Service Officer, Dept of State 1962; posts in Moscow, Belgrade and Brussels; Amb. to Canada 1985–89, to Greece 1993–97; Perm. Rep. to the EEC, Brussels 1989; Vice-Pres. Nat. Defense Univ. 1997–; Pres. U.S. Council of Int. Business 1998–99; Superior Honor Award, Dept of State 1982, 1985. *Address:* c/o National Defense University, Fort McNair, Washington, DC 20319, USA.

NILSSON, Birgit (Fru Bertil Niklasson); Swedish opera singer (soprano); b. 17 May 1918, Karup; m. Bertil Niklasson 1948; ed Stockholm Royal Acad. of Music; with Stockholm Opera 1947–51; sang at Glyndebourne Festival (England) 1951, Bayreuth Festival 1954, 1957–70, Munich 1954–58, Hollywood Bowl, Buenos Aires and Florence 1956, London (Covent Garden) 1957, 1962, 1963, 1973, Milan (La Scala), Naples, Vienna, Chicago and San Francisco 1958, New York (Metropolitan) 1959, Moscow 1964; sang in Turandot, Paris 1968, Elektra, London 1969; particularly well known for her Wagnerian roles (Brünnhilde, Isolde, etc.); Royal Court singer 1954; retd 1985; Austrian and Bavarian Kammersängerin; Hon. mem. of the Vienna State Opera 1968, Royal Acad. of Music (London) 1970; Dr. hc Andover Music Univ., Mass., USA, Manhattan School of Music, New York, Mich. State Univ. of Fine Arts, Sibelius Acad. Helsinki 1997; Medal Litteris et Artibus 1960, Medal for Promotion of Art of Music, Royal Acad. of Music, Stockholm 1968, First Commdr, Order of Vasa 1974, Commdr Order of St Olav 1st Class (Norway) 1975, Swedish Gold Medal 1978; Commdr. des Arts et des Lettres 1991; Prof. h.c., Swedish Govt. 1999, Royal Music School Stockholm 2000. *Publications:* My Memories in Pictures 1977, La Nilsson 1995. *Address:* c/o Kungliga Teatern, P.O. Box 16094, 10322 Stockholm (Office); P.O. Box 527, 10130, Stockholm C, Sweden.

NIMATALLAH, Yusuf A., PH.D.(Econs); Saudi Arabian economist; b. 1936; ed American Univ., Beirut and Univ. of Mass., USA; with Banque de l'Indochine 1952–57; Teaching Asst in Econs, Univ. of Mass. 1963–65; Prof. Monetary and Int. Econs, Univ. of Riyadh (King Saud Univ. 1982–) 1965 (on leave 1973); Adviser to Minister of Finance on Money and Banking, Oil Finance and Planning 1967–73; Adviser to Sultan of Oman on Oil, Finance, Money and Banking; Deputy Chair. and Pres. Cen. Bank of Oman 1975–78; Deputy Chair. UBAF Arab American Bank, New York 1976–78; Exec. Dir Fund for Saudi Arabia 1979–89. *Address:* c/o Ministry of Finance and National Economy, Airport Road, Riyadh 11177, Saudi Arabia.

NIMERI, Field Marshal Gaafar Mohammed al- (see Nemery, Field Marshal Gaafar Mohammed al-).

NIMOY, Leonard; American actor and director; b. 26 March 1931, Boston; s. of Max Nimoy and Dora (née Spinner) Nimoy; m. 1st Sandi Zober 1954 (divorced); one s. one d.; m. 2nd Susan Bay 1988; ed Boston Coll. and Antioch Univ.; served in U.S. Army 1954–56; trained at the Pasadena Playhouse, Calif. 1960-63; numerous stage appearances. *Television appearances include:* Star Trek 1966–69, Eleventh Hour, The Virginian, Rawhide, Dr. Kildare. *Film appearances include:* Queen for a Day, Rhubarb 1951, Kid Monk Baron, Francis Goes to West Point 1952, Old Overland Trail 1953, Satan's Satellites 1958, The Balcony 1963, Deathwatch 1966, Valley of Mystery (co-producer) 1967, Catlow (co-producer) 1971, Invasion of the Bodysnatchers (co-producer) 1978, Star Trek–the Motion Picture (co-producer) 1979, Star Trek–the Wrath of Khan (co-producer) 1982, Star Trek III–the Search for Spock (also Dir) 1984, Star Trek IV–the Voyage Home (also Dir) 1986, Star Trek V–The Final Frontier 1989, Star Trek VI–The Undiscovered Country 1991, Bonanza: Under Attack 1995, Carpati: 50 Miles, 50 Years 1996, A Life Apart: Hasidism in America (voice) 1997, David 1997, Brave New World 1998, Sinbad 2000, Atlantis: The Lost Empire 2001; also directed Three Men and a Baby 1987, The Good Mother 1988, Funny About Love 1990, Holy Matrimony 1994, The Pagemaster (voice) 1994. *Publications:* I Am Not Spock (autobiog.) 1975, We Are All Children 1977, Come Be With Me 1979. *Address:* c/o Gersh Agency Inc., 232 North Cannon Drive, Beverly Hills, CA 90210, USA.

NIMR, Nabih An-; Jordanian diplomatist; b. 26 Oct. 1931, Tubas; m. Rabab Al-Nimr 1961; one s. one d.; ed Alexandria Univ.; Amb. to Syria 1974–78, to FRG (also accred to Sweden, Denmark, Norway and Luxembourg) 1978–81, to Tunisia and Perm. Rep. to the Arab League 1981–85, to UK 1985–87, (also accred to Ireland 1986–87), to Egypt 1988–; Sec. Gen. Ministry of Foreign Affairs 1987–88. *Address:* Embassy of Jordan, 6 Sharia Juhaini, Cairo, Egypt. *Telephone:* (2) 3485566 (Office). *Fax:* (2) 3601027 (Office).

NIN-CULMELL, Joaquín María; Spanish composer, pianist and conductor; b. 5 Sept. 1908, Berlin, Germany; s. of Joaquín Nin and Rosa Culmell; ed Schola Cantorum and Nat. Conservatoire, Paris; studied privately with Manuel de Falla; Instructor, Middlebury Coll., Vt 1938, 1939, 1940, Williams Coll. 1940–50; Prof. of Music, Univ. of Calif. 1949–74, Emer. Prof. 1974–, Inst. of Creative Arts 1965–66; has appeared as pianist and conductor with the San Francisco Symphony and other orchestras in the USA and Europe; Corresp. mem. Royal Acad. of Fine Arts of San Fernando (Madrid 1962). *Compositions:* Piano Concerto, El burlador de Sevilla (ballet), Piano Quintet, Sonata Breve, Tonadas (piano), Twelve Cuban Dances (piano), Three Old Spanish Pieces (orchestra), Diferencias (orchestra), Concerto for cello and orchestra (after Padre Anselmo Viola), Mass in English (for mixed chorus and organ), La Celestina (opera), Cantata for voice and harpsichord or piano and strings (after Padre José Pradas), Le rêve de Cyrano (ballet), incidental music for Shakespeare's Cymbeline, Federico García Lorca's Yerma, Six Sephardic Folksongs (for voice and piano), Te Deum (for chorus, organ and symbols) 1999, songs, choral pieces, organ symphony, pieces for guitar, etc. *Publications:* Ed. Spanish Choral Tradition, Prefaces in English and French for the early diaries of Anaïs Nin (Vols I–IV). *Address:* 5830 Clover Drive, Oakland, CA 94618, USA. *Fax:* (510) 658 0477.

NINAGAWA, Yukio; Japanese theatre director; known for his direction of Western classic plays, especially Shakespeare, in a Japanese style; his co. appeared at Edin. Festival with samurai-style Macbeth 1985, Suicide of Love, Nat. Theatre, London 1989, Medea, Suicide for Love and a Noh-inspired version of The Tempest, Barbican Theatre, London 1992; also Dir Tango at the End of Winter, King Lear 1999; Hon. Dr. hc (Univ. of Edin.) 1992.

NINEHAM, Rev. Canon Dennis Eric, MA, DD; British professor of theology and ecclesiastic (retd); b. 27 Sept. 1921, Southampton; s. of Stanley Martin Nineham and Bessie Edith Gain; m. Ruth Corfield Miller 1946; two s. two d.; ed King Edward VI School, Southampton, Queen's Coll. Oxford and Lincoln Theological Coll.; Chaplain Queen's Coll. Oxford 1944–54, Fellow 1946–54; Prof. of Biblical and Historical Theology London Univ. 1954–58, Prof. of Divinity 1958–64; Regius Prof. of Divinity Cambridge Univ. 1964–69; Fellow of Emmanuel Coll. 1964–69; Warden Keble Coll. Oxford 1969–79; Prof. of Theology Bristol Univ. 1980–86; Visiting Prof. Rikkyo Univ., Tokyo 1994; Fellow King's Coll. London; Hon. Canon Emer. Bristol Cathedral; Hon. Fellow Keble Coll. Oxford, Queen's Coll. Oxford; Hon. DD (Yale) 1965, (Birmingham) 1972. *Publications:* The Gospel of St Mark 1963, The Use and Abuse of the Bible 1976, Explorations in Theology 1977, Christianity Medieval and Modern: A Study in Religious Change 1993. *Leisure interests:* walking and reading. *Address:* 9 Fitzherbert Close, Iffley, Oxford, OX4 4EN, England (Home). *Telephone:* (1865) 715941.

NINN-HANSEN, Erik, LLD; Danish politician; b. 12 April 1922, Skørpinge, Western Zealand; s. of Christian Hansen; in pvt. law practice 1955–; mem. Folketing (Parl.) 1953–94; Minister of Defence 1968–71, of Finance 1971, of Justice 1982–89; Pres. of the Folketing Jan.–Oct. 1989; Nat. Chair. Conservative Youth 1948–50. *Publication:* Syv år for VKR 1974, Fra Christmas til Baunsgaard 1985, Ret Fœrd mellem jura og politik 1990, Christmas Møller, En stridsmand i dansk politik 1991, Vaerelse 28 Dansk politik 1974–94 (1997). *Address:* Bregnegårdsvej 11, 2920 Charlottenlund, Denmark.

NIRENBERG, Louis, PhD; American professor of mathematics; b. 28 Feb. 1925, Hamilton, Ont., Canada; s. of Zuzie Nirenberg and Bina Katz; m. Susan Blank 1948 (deceased); one s. one d.; ed McGill and New York Univs.; Instructor, New York Univ. 1949–51, Asst Prof. 1951–54, Assoc. Prof. 1954–57, Prof. 1957–; Dir Courant Inst. of Mathematical Sciences 1970–72; mem. NAS, American Acad. of Arts and Sciences, American Philosophical Soc., Accad. dei Lincei, Acad. des Sciences, France, Istituto Lombardo Accad. di Scienze e Lettere, Italy; Hon. Prof. Nankai Univ., Zhejiang Univ.; Hon. DSc (McGill Univ., Univ. of Pisa, Univ. of Paris, Dauphine, McMaster Univ.); Bôcher Prize and Steele Prize of American Mathematical Soc, Crafoord Prize (Royal Swedish Acad. of Sciences) 1982. *Publications:* various papers in mathematical journals. *Leisure interests:* classical music, reading, cinema, walking. *Address:* 221 West 82nd Street, New York, NY 10024, USA (Home). *Telephone:* (212) 998-3192 (Office); (212) 724-1069 (Home). *Fax:* (212) 995-4121 (Office); (212) 724-1069 (Home). *E-mail:* nirenl@cims.nyu.edu (Office).

NIRENBERG, Marshall Warren, PhD; American biochemist; b. 10 April 1927; s. of Harry Edward and Minerva (née Bykowsky) Nirenberg; m. Perola Zaltzman 1961; ed Univ. of Florida and Univ. of Michigan; Postdoctoral Fellow, American Cancer Soc., NIH 1957–59, U.S. Public Health Service, NIH 1959–60; mem. staff, NIH 1960–, research biochemist 1961–62; research biochemist, Head of Section for Biochemical Genetics, Nat. Heart Inst. 1962–66; Chief, Lab. of Biochemical Genetics, Nat. Heart, Lung and Blood Inst. 1962–; has researched on mechanism of protein synthesis, genetic code, nucleic acids, regulatory mechanism in synthetic macromolecules; mem. New York Acad. of Sciences, AAAS, NAS, Pontifical Acad. of Sciences 1974, Deutsche Leopoldina Akad. der Naturforscher; Foreign Assoc. Acad. des Sciences (France) 1989; Hon. mem. Harvey Soc.; Molecular Biology Award, Nat. Acad. of Sciences 1962; Medal from Dept of Health, Educ. and Welfare 1963, Modern Medicine Award 1964, Nat. Medal for Science, Pres. Johnson 1965, Nobel Prize for Medicine (with Holley and Khorana) for interpreting the genetic code and its function in protein synthesis 1968, Louisa Gross Horwitz

Prize for Biochem. 1968. *Address:* Laboratory of Biochemical Genetics, National Heart, Lung and Blood Institute, Building 36, Room IC06, Bethesda, MD 20892, USA.

NISBET, Robin George Murdoch, MA, FBA; British classical scholar; b. 21 May 1925, Glasgow; s. of Robert George Nisbet and Agnes Thomson Husband; m. Anne Wood 1969; ed Glasgow Acad., Glasgow Univ. and Balliol Coll. Oxford; Fellow and Tutor in Classics, Corpus Christi Coll. Oxford 1952–70, Prof. of Latin 1970–92; Hon. Fellow Balliol Coll. 1989, Corpus Christi Coll. 1992; Kenyon Medal, British Acad. 1997. *Publications:* Commentary on Cicero, In Pisonem 1961, Horace, Odes I, II (with M. Hubbard) 1970, 1978, Collected Papers on Latin Literature 1995. *Address:* 80 Abingdon Road, Cumnor, Oxon., OX2 9QW, England. *Telephone:* (1865) 862482.

NISHIDA, Mamoru; Japanese politician; b. Ehime Pref.; mem. LDP; mem. for Shikoku, House of Reps.; fmr Dir-Gen. Nat. Land Agency; Minister of Home Affairs 1998–99. *Address:* c/o Ministry of Home Affairs, 2-1-2, Kasumigaseki, Chiyoda-ku, Tokyo 100, Japan.

NISHIHARA, Haruo, LLD; Japanese professor of law; b. 13 March 1928, Tokyo; s. of Keiichi Nishihara and Makoto Tateyama Nishihara; m.; one s.; ed Waseda Univ.; Asst, School of Law, Waseda Univ. 1953–59, Asst Prof. 1959–63, Assoc. Prof. 1963–67, Prof. 1967–, Dean School of Law and mem. Bd of Trustees 1972–76, Exec. Dir 1978–80, Vice-Pres. 1980–82, Pres. and mem. Bd of Trustees 1982–95; Hon. LLD (Korea Univ.) 1985, (Earlham Coll.) 1988; D.Univ. (Sydney) 1989; Educational Man. Prize (De La Salle Univ.) 1988. *Publications:* On the Theory of "mittelbare Täterschaft" 1962, Traffic Accidents and the Principle of Trust 1962, Particular Aspects of Criminal Law 1974, 1983, General Aspects of Criminal Law 1977, What Governs the Criminal Law? 1979. *Leisure interests:* swimming, skiing. *Address:* 619-18 Nohgaya-cho, Machida-shi, Tokyo, Japan.

NISHIMATSU, Chikara, BSME; Japanese business executive; b. 3 Nov. 1931, Osaka; m. Michiko Yamada 1959; two s. one d.; ed Pratt Inst.; joined Itochu Co., Ltd 1959, mem. Bd Dirs 1984–91, Gen. Man. Itochu Asian Operations 1985, Man. Dir 1986, Gen. Man. Itochu Europe and Africa Operation 1989–91; Pres. and CEO Matsubo Co. Ltd (fmrly. known as Matsuzaka Co. Ltd) 1992–98, Chair. and CEO 1998–2000, Adviser 2000–02; CEO The Mirai Creative Co. Inc. *Address:* 3-21-6, Katsuta-Dai, Yachiyo City, Chiba-ken 276-0023, Japan (Home). *Telephone:* (47) 480-1436 (Home). *Fax:* (47) 480-1436 (Home). *E-mail:* chik-ni@ma.kcom.ne.jp (Home).

NISHIMURA, Kiyohiko G., PhD; Japanese professor of economics; b. 30 March 1953, Tokyo; s. of Giichi Nishimura and Sumiko Otsuka; m. Yukiko Kurihata 1979; two d.; ed Univ. of Tokyo, Yale Univ., USA; Arthur Okun Research Fellow, Brookings Inst., USA 1981–82; Assoc. Prof. of Econs, Univ. of Tokyo 1983–94, Prof. 1994–; Assoc. Ed. Economic Studies Quarterly 1989–93; Research Assoc. US–Japan Center, New York Univ. 1989–; Dir Tokyo Centre for Econ. Research 1990–91; Visiting Scholar, MIT, USA 1991–92; Visiting Research Fellow Inst. for Int. Econ. Studies, Sweden 1993; Visiting Prof., Louis Pasteur Univ. 1994, Aarhus Univ. 1996; Special mem. Econ. Council, Japanese Govt 1994–98; mem. Regulatory Reform Cttee, Japanese Govt 1999–2001; mem. Council Japanese Econ. Asscn 1999–; mem. Statistic Council, Japanese Govt 2003–, Financial System Council, Japanese Govt 2003–; Nikkei Prize 1993, Japan Economist's Prize 1997, Nakahara Prize, Japanese Econ. Asscn 1998. *Publications:* Stock and Land Prices in Japan (in Japanese) 1990, The Distribution System in Japan (ed., in Japanese) 1991, Imperfect Competition, Differential Information and Microfoundations of Macroeconomics 1992, Macroeconomics of Price Revolution 1996, The Grief of a Prairie Dog (fiction) 1998, The Distribution in Japan 2002. *Leisure interest:* painting. *Address:* Faculty of Economics, 7-3-1, Hongo, Bunkyo-ku, Tokyo 113-0033 (Office); 1-2-26-403, Higashi-Gotanda, Shinagawa-ku, Tokyo 141-0022, Japan (Home). *Telephone:* (3) 5841-5524. *Fax:* (3) 5841-5521. *Website:* www.e.u-tokyo.ac.jp/~nisimura/e-index.html (Office).

NISHIZAKI, Takako; Japanese violinist; d. of Shinjii Nishizaki; ed Toho School of Music, Juilliard School, New York; studied with father, then became first student of Shinichi Suzuki, creator of Suzuki Method of violin teaching. *Recordings include:* complete Fritz Kreisler Edn. (ten vols.), many contemporary Chinese violin concertos, concertos by Spohr, Briot, Crui, Respighi, Rubinstein and Joachim; for Naxos: Vivaldi's Four Seasons, Mozart's Violin Concertos, sonatas by Mozart and Beethoven, also Bach, Mendelssohn, Tchaikovsky, Beethoven, Bruch and Brahms Concertos.

NISHIZAWA, Jun-ichi, DEng, FIEE; Japanese electrical engineer and academic; b. 12 Sept. 1926, Sendai; s. of Kyosuke Nishizawa and Akiko (née Ishii) Nishizawa; m. Takeko Hayakawa 1956; one s. two d.; ed Tohoku Univ.; Research Asst, Electrical Communication Research Inst., Tohoku Univ. 1953–54, Asst Prof. 1954–62, Prof. 1962–90, Dir 1983–86, 1989–90, Pres. of Univ. 1990–96; Dir Semiconductor Research Inst., Sendai 1968–; Pres. Iwate Prefectural Univ.; approx. 615 patents in Japan, 345 patents abroad; mem. Japan Acad.; Foreign mem. Polish Acad. of Sciences, Russian Acad. of Sciences, Korea Acad. of Science and Tech., Yugoslav Acad. of Engineering; Laudise Prize IOCG, Kenneth J. Button Prize, Edison Medal, Inst. of Electrical and Electronics Engineers 2000. *Publications:* Semiconductor Devices 1961, Semiconductor Materials 1968, Optoelectronics 1977. *Leisure interests:* classical music, reading, pottery, pictures (especially Impressionist school). *Address:* Semiconductor Research Institute, Kawauchi, Aoba-ku, Sendai 980-0862, Japan. *Telephone:* (22) 223-7287. *Fax:* (22) 223-7289.

NISSEL, Siegmund Walter, OBE; British musician; b. 3 Jan. 1922, Munich, Germany; s. of Isidor Nissel and Malvine Nissel; m. Muriel Nissel 1957; one s. one d.; ed Mittelschule Vienna, London Univ. and violin tuition pvtly. with Prof. Max Weissgärber, Vienna and Prof. Max Rostal, London; Leader, London Int. Orchestra 1947; Founder mem. Second Violin, Amadeus Quartet 1948–87; Prof. of Chamber Music, Musikhochschule, Cologne, Fed. Repub. of Germany 1978–, RAM, London 1986– (Dir for Chamber Music); Hon. mem. RAM; Hon. DMus (York, London); Grosses Verdienstkreuz, Germany; Ehrenkreuz für Wissenschaft und Kunst, Austria, 1. Klasse. *Leisure interests:* opera and theatre. *Address:* 11 Highgrove Point, Mount Vernon, Frognal Rise, London, NW3 6PZ, England. *Telephone:* (20) 7681-7078 (Office). *Fax:* (20) 7681-7269 (Home).

NISSIM, Moshe, LLD, MJ; Israeli politician and lawyer; b. 1935, Jerusalem; s. of Isaac Nissim (Chief Rabbi of Israel) and Victoria Nissim; m.; five c.; ed Hebrew Univ. of Jerusalem; elected to Knesset (Parl.) (youngest-ever member) 1959–96 (as rep. of Union of Gen. Zionists 1959, subsequently as rep. of Gahal faction of the Liberal Party, then of the Likud Bloc); has served on Defence, Foreign Affairs and Security, Constitution Law and Legislation, Labour and Housing Cttees. in the Knesset; Co-Chair. Likud Group 1975–79; Chair. Exec. Cttee, Likud Feb. 1978–; Minister without Portfolio 1978–80, 1988–89; Minister of Justice 1980–86, of Finance 1986–88, of Trade and Industry 1989–92; Deputy Prime Minister 1990–92; Head of Law Office Moshe Nissim, Rinkov, Senderovitch; Dr hc (Ben-Gurion Univ.). *Address:* 3A Jabotinsky Street, Haya'lom Tower, Ramat-Gan 52520 (Office); 6 Shlom Aleichem Street, Jerusalem 92148, Israel (Home). *Telephone:* 3-6133333 (Office); 2-5619414 (Home). *Fax:* 3-6133334 (Office); 2-5617155 (Home). *E-mail:* nrs@nrs-law.com (Office).

NISSINEN, Mikko; Finnish artistic director, teacher and ballet dancer; b. 1962, Helsinki; ed Stanford Univ., USA; began dance training Finnish Nat. Ballet School 1973; began performing soloist age 1977; joined Kirov Ballet School 1979; performer with Dutch Nat. Ballet and Basel Ballet; Prin. Dancer San Francisco Ballet, USA 1986–96; guest artist at numerous int. galas; Artistic Dir Marin Ballet, San Rafael, Calif., USA 1996–98, Alberta Ballet, Calgary, Canada 1998–2001; Artistic Dir Boston Ballet and Boston Ballet Center for Dance Educ. Sept. 2001–; mem. Artistic Cttee, NY Choreographic Inst.; First Prize, Nat. Ballet Competition, Kuopio 1978. *Address:* Boston Ballet, 19 Clarendon Street, Boston, MA 02116-6100, USA (Office). *Telephone:* (617) 695-6950 (Office). *Fax:* (617) 695-6995 (Office). *E-mail:* eolds@bostonballet.com (Office). *Website:* www.bostonballet.com (Office).

NITTVE, Lars; Swedish museum director and writer; b. 1953, Stockholm; fmr Stockholm newspaper critic; fmr journalist for Artforum; Sr Curator Moderna Museet (nat. contemporary art museum) 1986–89, Dir Nov. 2001–; Dir Rooseum, Malmö 1990–95, Louisiana Museum of Modern Art, Humlebæk, Denmark 1995–98, Tate Modern, London 1998–2001. *Address:* Moderna Museet, Box 163 82, 103 27 Stockholm, Sweden (Office). *Telephone:* (8) 5195-52-00 (Office). *E-mail:* info@modernamuseet.se (Office). *Website:* www.modernamuseet.se (Office).

NITZE, Paul Henry, AB; American political adviser; b. 16 Jan. 1907, Amherst, Mass.; s. of William A. Nitze and Anina Nitze (née Hilken); m. 1st Phyllis Pratt 1932 (deceased); two s. two d.; m. 2nd Elisabeth Scott Porter 1993; ed Harvard Univ.; New York Investment Banker 1929–41; Financial Dir Office of Co-ordinator of Inter-American Affairs 1941–42; Chief, Metals and Minerals Br., Bd of Econ. Welfare, Dir Foreign Procurement and Devt 1942–43; Vice-Chair. Strategic Bombing Survey 1944–46; Deputy Dir Office of Int. Trade Policy 1946–48; Deputy to Asst Sec. of State for Econ. Affairs 1948–49; Dir Policy Planning Staff, Dept of State 1950–53; Pres. Foreign Service Educ. Foundation 1953–61; Asst Sec. of Defense for Int. Security Affairs 1961–63; Sec. of the Navy 1963–67; Deputy Sec. of Defense 1967–69; mem. U.S. Del. to Strategic Arms Limitation Talks (SALT) 1969–74; Consultant, System Planning Corpn 1974–81; Head of U.S. Del. to the Intermediate Range Nuclear Forces Negotiations with USSR 1981–83; Adviser on Arms Control Matters to the Pres. and the Sec. of State 1984–89; Founder, Diplomat-in-Residence and Distinguished Research Prof. in Strategic Studies and American Foreign Policy, Paul H. Nitze School of Advanced Int. Studies, Johns Hopkins Univ.; mem. and fmr Pres. Advisory Council, Paul H. Nitze School of Advanced Int. Studies; mem. Bd of Dirs. Marshall Foundation, Atlantic Council of the U.S., Center for Naval Analyses, Washington Opera, St Mary's Coll. of Maryland; mem. Council on Foreign Relations; Chair. Washington Inst. of Foreign Affairs; Hon. Vice-Pres. Int. Inst. for Strategic Studies; Hon. LLD (Brown Univ., Johns Hopkins Univ., William Coll.); George C. Marshall Medal, Sec. of State's Distinguished Service Award, Sylvanus Thayer Award, Theodore Roosevelt Distinguished Service Medal, Jefferson Award for Public Service, Eric M. Warburg Prize, Sec.-Gen. of NATO Atlantic Award, James Doolittle Award; Medal of Merit, Medal of Freedom, Kt Commdr.'s Cross (Badge and Star) of Order of Merit, Fed. Repub. of Germany, Grand Officier, Ordre de la Couronne, Belgium, Grosses Goldene Ehrenzeichen des Landes Steiermark, Austria and awards from the Netherlands and Italy. *Publications:* From Hiroshima to Glasnost: At the Center of Decision–A Memoir 1989, Tension Between Opposites 1993 and numerous articles on U.S. foreign policy, nat. security policy and int. affairs. *Leisure interests:* horseback riding, skiing, tennis. *Address:* Paul H. Nitze School of Advanced International Studies, Johns Hopkins University, 1730 Massachu-

setts Avenue, NW, Washington, DC 20036 (Office); 3122 P. Street, NW, Washington, DC 20007, USA (Home). *Telephone:* (202) 965-1774 (Home). *Fax:* (202) 965-2626 (Office).

NIU HAN; Chinese poet; b. Shi Chenghan, 1923, Dingxiang, Shanxi Prov.; m. Wu Ping; one s. one d.; ed Northwest Univ.; fmrly Sec. Research Dept Renmin Univ.; Dir Cultural and Educational Office, Political Dept of Northeast Air Force; Exec. Assoc. Chief Ed. Chinese Literature; Chief Ed. Historical Records of New Literature Movt; Dir Editorial Office of May 4th Literature; Sr Ed. People's Publishing House; Creative Literary Works Award 1981–82, Nation's Best New Poem. *Publications:* Motherland, In Front of the Motherland, Coloured Life, Hot Spring, Love and Songs, Earthworm and Feather, Selected Lyric Poems of Niu Han, Notes Taken While Learning to Write Poems. *Leisure interest:* fine arts. *Address:* People's Literature Publishing House, 166 Chaoyangmen Nei Dajie, Beijing 100705, People's Republic of China (Office). *Telephone:* (10) 65138394 (Office); (10) 85836410 (Home). *Fax:* (10) 65138394 (Home). *E-mail:* fangjia2001@yahoo.com.cn (Home).

NIU MAOSHENG; Chinese government official; b. 1939, Beijing; ed Beijing Agric. Inst.; joined CCP 1961; Vice-Minister of Water Resources 1988–93, Minister 1993–98; Deputy Gov. Hebei Prov. 1998–99, Gov. 1999–; Deputy Head, Nat. Gen. Headquarters for Flood Prevention and Drought Control; mem. 15th CCP Cen. Cttee 1997–. *Address:* Governor's Office, Shijiazhuang City, Hebei Province, People's Republic of China.

NIU QUN; Chinese actor; b. Dec. 1949, Tianjin; joined PLA 1971; actor Zhanyou Art Troupe of PLA Beijing Mil. Command 1974–93; actor China Broadcasting Art Troupe 1993–; performs comic dialogues with Feng Gong; numerous prizes. *Publications:* In Various Ingenious Names (5 cassettes of comic dialogues). *Address:* China Broadcasting Art Troupe, Beijing, People's Republic of China.

NIWA, Yuya; Japanese politician; mem. House of Reps.; fmr Parl. Vice-Minister for Health and Welfare; fmr Health and Welfare Minister; fmr Chair. LDP Policy Research Council; Minister for Health and Welfare 1999–2000. *Address:* Ministry of Health and Welfare, 1-2-2, Kasumigaseki, Chiyoda-ku, Tokyo 100-0013, Japan (Office). *Telephone:* (3) 3503-1711 (Office). *Fax:* (3) 3501-2532 (Office). *E-mail:* www-admin@mhw.ho.jp (Office).

NIXON, Sir Edwin Ronald, Kt, CBE, DL, MA; British business executive (retd); b. 21 June 1925, Leicester; s. of William Archdale Nixon and Ethel Nixon (née Corrigan); m. 1st Joan Lilian Hill 1952 (died 1995); one s. one d.; m. 2nd Bridget Diana Rogers 1997; ed Alderman Newton's Grammar School, Leicester and Selwyn Coll. Cambridge; served RAF 1943–47; Man. Accountant, Dexion Ltd 1950–55; joined IBM as a data processing salesman 1955, various man. posts 1955–65, Man. Dir 1965–79; Chair. and CEO IBM United Kingdom Holdings Ltd 1979–86, Chair. 1986–90; Dir Nat. Westminster Bank PLC 1975–96, Deputy Chair. 1987–96; Dir Amersham Int. PLC 1987–96, Chair. 1988–96; Dir UK-Japan 2000 Group Ltd –1996, Partnership Sourcing Ltd –1996, Lloyd Instruments PLC 1987–91, NatWest Bancorp Inc. 1991–96, Nat. Westminster Bank USA 1992–96; Chair. London Classical Radio PLC 1989-92, NatWest Pension Trustees Ltd 1991–96, Leicester BioSciences Ltd 1996–99; mem. Council CBI 1971–96; Council mem. The Open Univ. 1986–92, Univ. of Leicester; Gov. United World Coll. of the Atlantic; Vice-Pres. Opportunities for the Disabled, London Int. String Quartet Competition; Hon. Trustee Inst. of Econ. Affairs; mem. Royal Nat. Theatre Devt Council 1984–96, Advisory Council The Prince's Youth Business Trust 1987–, The Macmillan Appeal Devt Bd 1994–96; Trustee Inst. for Man. Devt –1996, Jean Sainsbury Royal Opera House Trust, Monteverdi Choir and Orchestra (Chair. 1988–2001); Friend of Lambeth Palace Library; Patron Asscn Internationale des Etudiants en Sciences Economiques et Commerciales, GB –1996; Fellow Queen Mary and Westfield Coll. London; Hon. Fellow Selwyn Coll. Cambridge, Chartered Inst. of Marketing; Dr. hc (Stirling, Manchester, Aston, Brunel, Leeds Metropolitan, Leicester). *Leisure interests:* music, golf, reading. *Address:* Starkes Heath, Rogate, Petersfield, Hants., GU31 5EJ, England. *Telephone:* (1730) 821504. *Fax:* (1730) 821504 (Home).

NIXON, John Forster, PhD, DSc, FRS, FRSA; British professor of chemistry; b. 27 Jan. 1937, Whitehaven, Cumberland (now Cumbria); s. of Edward Forster Nixon, MBE and Mary Nixon (née Lytton); m. "Kim" Smith 1960; one s. one d.; ed Univs. of Manchester and Cambridge; Research Assoc. in Chem., Univ. of Southern Calif., LA 1960–62; ICI Fellow, Cambridge Univ., Inorganic Chem. Dept 1962–64; Lecturer in Inorganic Chem. Univ. of St Andrews 1964–66; Lecturer in Chem., Univ. of Sussex 1966, Reader 1976, Subject Chair. in Chem. 1981–84, Prof. of Chem. 1986–, Dean School of Chem. and Molecular Sciences 1989–92; Visiting Assoc. Prof. of Chem., Victoria, BC 1970–71; Visiting Prof. Simon Fraser Univ., Vancouver BC 1975; Chair. Downland Section, Chemical Soc. 1973–74; mem. Int. Cttee on Phosphorus Chem. 1983–2001; elected titular mem. IUPAC Comm., Inorganic Nomenclature 1985; mem. Inorganic Chem. Panel SERC Cttee 1986–89; Royal Soc.-Leverhulme Sr Research Fellow 1993; Visiting Prof. Indian Inst. of Science, Bangalore 2002; Corday-Morgan Medal and Prize 1973, Main Group Element Prize 1985, Tilden Lectureship 1991–92, Ludwig Mond Lectureship and Prize 2002–03 (all Royal Soc. of Chem.), Alexander von Humbold Prize Winner 2001–02. *Publications:* Phosphorus: The Carbon Copy (co-author) 1998 and over 350 publs in chemical journals and invited lectures to int. chemical socs. *Leisure interests:* walking, theatre, music, watching cricket, playing tennis, badminton and squash. *Address:* School of Chemistry, Physics and Environmental Science, University of Sussex, Brighton, Sussex, BN1 9QJ (Office); Juggs Barn, The Street, Kingston, Lewes, Sussex, BN7 3PB, England (Home). *Telephone:* (1273) 678536 (Office); (1273) 483993 (Home). *Fax:* (1273) 677196 (Office). *E-mail:* j.nixon@sussex.ac.uk (Office).

NIXON, Patrick Michael, CMG, OBE; British diplomatist; b. 1 Aug. 1944, Reading, Berks.; s. of John Moylett Gerard Nixon and of the late Hilary Mary Paterson; four s.; ed Downside School, Magdalene Coll. Cambridge; joined Diplomatic Service 1965, served Middle East Centre for Arab Studies, Lebanon, Cairo, Lima, Tripoli, British Information Services, New York 1980–83; Asst, later Head Near East and N Africa Dept, FCO 1983–87; Amb. to Qatar 1987–90; Counsellor, FCO 1990–93; High Commr in Zambia 1994–97; Dir FCO 1997–98; Amb. to UAE 1998–2003.

NIYAZOV, Saparmurad; Turkmenistan politician; b. 19 Feb. 1940, Ashkhabad; m. Muza Alexeevna Niyazova; one s. one d.; ed Leningrad Polytechnic Inst.; mem. CPSU 1962–91; instructor with Trade Union Org. of mineral prospecting works in Turkmenistan 1959–67; instructor, then deputy head of section of Cen. Cttee of Turkmenistan CP 1970–79; head of section and first sec. of Ashkhabad City Cttee of Turkmenistan CP 1979–84; party work with Cen. Cttee of CPSU 1984–85; mem. Cen. Cttee of CPSU 1986–91; mem. CPSU Politburo 1990–91; Pres. of Council of Ministers of Turkmenistan SSR 1985; First Sec. of Cen. Cttee of CP of Turkmenistan SSR 1985–91; Chair. Turkmenistan Supreme Soviet Jan.–Nov. 1990; Pres. of Turkmenistan 1991–, concurrently Prime Minister 1991–; Chair. Democratic Party of Turkmenistan 1991; Pres. Humanitarian Asscn of Turkmenistan People of the World; Mukhtumikuli Prize 1992; title of Turkmenbashi (Father of Turkmenistan People) conferred by Parl. 1993, title of Pres. for Life conferred by Parl. 1999. *Address:* Office of the President, Karl Marx str. 24, 744017 Ashgabat; Democratic Party of Turkmenistan, Gogolya str. 28, 744014 Ashgabat, Turkmenistan. *Telephone:* (3632) 35-45-34.

NJIE-SAIDY, Isatou; Gambian politician and teacher; m.; four c.; started work as schoolteacher 1970; active in Nat. Women's Council; currently Sec. of State for Women's Affairs, Vice-Pres. of The Gambia 1997–. *Address:* Office of the Vice-President, State House, Banjul, The Gambia (Office). *Telephone:* 227605 (Office). *Fax:* 224012 (Office).

NJOJO, Rt Rev. Patrice Byankya; Congolese ecclesiastic; b. 1935, Boga; m. Kamanyoho Njojo; seven c.; teacher, schools inspector, priest, currently Bishop of Boga; Archbishop of the Prov. of the Congo 1992–2002. *Address:* P.O. Box 25586, Kampala, Uganda (Office); Bishop's Residence, CAC-Boga, P.O. Box 25586, Kampala, Uganda (Home). *Telephone:* 77665099. *E-mail:* eac-mags@infocom.co.ug (Office).

NKOMO, John Landa; Zimbabwean politician; b. 22 Aug. 1934; s. of Lufele Nkomo; m. Georgina Nkomo 1963; five s. one d.; school teacher 1957–64; mem. Cen. Cttee Zimbabwe African People's Union (ZAPU) 1975–89, mem. Political Bureau Zimbabwe African Nat. Union-Patriotic Front (ZANU-PF) and Cen. Cttee 1989–; MP for Bulawayo Constituency 1980–; Deputy Minister of Industry 1981–82; Minister of State, Prime Minister's Office 1982–84; Minister of Labour, Manpower Planning and Social Welfare 1988; Pres. Int. Labour Conf. 1989–; Minister of Local Govt and Nat. Housing–2001; Minister of Home Affairs 2001–02; Minister for Special Affairs in the Pres.'s Office 2002–; mem. Public Accounts Cttee 1980–81; Chair. Cttee of Estimates of Expenditure 1985–87, African Regional Labour Centre; Exec. mem. S. Rhodesia Teachers' Asscn; Trustee Devt Trust of Zimbabwe, The Pres. Fund; Hon. Life Pres. Matebeleland Turf Club; mem. Highlanders Football Club, Bulawayo Club; Zimbabwe Gold Liberation Medal. *Leisure interest:* reading. *Address:* c/o Ministry of Home Affairs, Mukwati Building, Samora Machel Avenue, Causeway, Private Bag 7703, Harare, Zimbabwe (Office).

NOAH, Harold Julius, MA, PhD; American academic; b. 21 Jan. 1925, London; s. of Abraham Noah and Sophia Cohen; m. 1st Norma Mestel 1945 (divorced 1966); m. 2nd Helen Claire Chisnall 1966; two s. two d.; ed Stratford Grammar School, LSE, King's Coll. London, Teachers Coll. Columbia Univ., New York; Asst Master then Head of Econs, Henry Thornton School, London 1949–60; Asst, Assoc. and Gardner Cowles Prof. Emer. of Econs and Educ. Teachers Coll., Columbia Univ., New York 1964–81; Dean 1976–81; Prof. of Educ., State Univ. of New York, Buffalo 1987–91; has received numerous academic honours and awards. *Publications include:* Educational Financing and Policy Goals for Primary Schools: General Report (with Joel Sherman) 1979, The National Case Study: An Empirical Comparative Study of Twenty-one Educational Systems (with Harry Passow and others) 1976, Canada: Review of National Policies for Education 1976, International Study of Business/Industry Involvement in Education 1987, Secondary School Examinations: International Perspectives on Policies and Practice 1993, Doing Comparative Education: Three Decades of Collaboration (with Max Eckstein) 1998; Fraud in Education: The Worm in the Apple 2001. *Address:* Teachers College, Columbia University, Box 211, New York, NY 10027, USA. *E-mail:* hjn9@columbia.edu (Office).

NOAKES, Michael; British portrait and landscape painter; b. 28 Oct. 1933, Brighton, Sussex; s. of the late Basil Noakes and Mary Noakes; m. Vivien Langley 1960; two s. one d.; ed Downside, Reigate School of Art, The Royal Acad. Schools; mil. service 1954–56; has painted numerous portraits of mems. of royal family including Queen Elizabeth II, Queen Elizabeth The Queen Mother, Prince of Wales, Prince Philip, the Duke and Duchess of York, the Princess Royal, Princess Margaret, The Duchess of Kent, Princess Alice

Countess of Athlone and of other leading figures, including Earl Mountbatten, Earl of Snowdon, Lady Thatcher as Prime Minister, Pres. Clinton, Archbishop Hope when Bishop of London, Duke of Norfolk, HE Cardinal Hume, Lord Aberconway, Princess Ashraf of Iran, Lord Charteris, Lord Denning, Sir Alec Guinness, Haham Dr. Solomon Gaon, Gen. Sir John Hackett, Robert Hardy, Cliff Michelmore, Robert Morley, Malcolm Muggeridge, Airey Neave, Valerie Hobson Profumo, Sir Ralph Richardson, Lord Runcie when Archbishop of Canterbury, Dame Margaret Rutherford, Dennis Wheatley, Sir Mortimer Wheeler; etc.; exhbns. internationally, including Royal Acad., Royal Inst. of Oil Painters, Royal Soc. of British Artists, of Marine Artists, of Portrait Painters, Nat. Soc. etc.; represented in perm. collections, The Queen, The Prince of Wales, The British Museum, Nat. Portrait Gallery, House of Commons, Frank Sinatra, etc.; mem. Royal Inst. of Oil Painters 1964, Vice-Pres. 1968–72, Pres. 1972–78, Hon. mem. Council 1978–; mem. Royal Soc. of Portrait Painters 1967–, served Council, 1969–71, 1972–74, 1978–80, 1993–95; Gov. Fed. of British Artists 1972–83, a Dir 1981–83; Liveryman Co. of Woolmen; fmr Chair. Contemporary Portrait Soc.; designed Crown Piece (£5 coin) as a mark of 50th Birthday of Prince of Wales and the work of the Prince's Trust 1998; throughout 1999 illustrated The Daily Life of The Queen: An Artist's Diary; has broadcast frequently in UK and also in USA on art subjects; Freeman City of London; Hon. mem. numerous socs. including Nat. Soc., United Soc.; Platinum Disc Award for record sleeve, Portrait of Sinatra 1977. *Publications:* A Professional Approach to Oil Painting 1968, The Daily Hope of the Queen 2000, numerous contribs. to art journals and books on art. *Leisure interest:* idling. *Address:* 146 Hamilton Terrace, St John's Wood, London, NW8 9UX, England. *Telephone:* (20) 7328-6754. *Fax:* (20) 7625-1220. *E-mail:* noakes@noakesnet.freeserve.co.uk (Office). *Website:* www.michael-noakes.co.uk (Office).

NOAKES, Baroness (Life Peer), cr. 2000, of Goudhurst in the County of Kent; **Sheila (Valerie) Masters,** DBE, LLB, FCA; British business executive; d. of Albert Frederick Masters and Iris Sheila Ratcliffe; m. Colin Barry Noakes 1985; ed Univ. of Bristol; joined Peat Marwick Mitchell & Co. 1970; seconded to HM Treasury 1979–81; partner KPMG (fmrly Peat Marwick Mitchell & Co., then KPMG Peat Marwick) 1983–2000; seconded to Dept of Health as Dir of Finance, Nat. Health Service Man. Exec. 1988–91; Dir Bank of England 1994–2001, Chair. Cttee of Non-Exec. Dirs 1998–2001; mem. Council, Inst. of Chartered Accountants in England and Wales 1987– (Deputy Pres. 1999–2000), Inland Revenue Man. Bd 1992–99, Chancellor of Exchequer's Pvt. Finance Panel 1993–97; Dir (non-exec.) Carpetright PLC 2001–, Solutions in Staffing and Software PLC 2001–; Assoc. Inst. of Taxation; Trustee Reuters Founders Share Co. 1998–; mem. Bd ENO 2000–; Gov. London Business School 1998–, Eastbourne Coll. 2000–, Marlborough Coll. 2000–; Hon. LLD (Warwick) 2000, (Bristol) 2000; Hon. DSc (Buckingham) 2001. *Leisure interests:* early classical music, horse racing, skiing. *Address:* House of Lords, London, SW1A 0PW, England (Office).

NOBILO, Mario, MA, PhD; Croatian diplomatist; b. 15 June 1952, Lumbarda, Korcula Island; s. of Donko I. Nobilo and Frana Mušić; m. Marijana Kujundzić; two s. one d.; ed Univ. of Zagreb; Research Assoc. Dept of Political and Strategic Studies, Inst. for Int. Relations, Zagreb 1979–89; Guest Prof. in USA, Germany and Spain 1985–90; co-founder and Vice-Pres. Croatian Council of European Movt 1990–92; Spokesman and Foreign Policy Adviser to Pres. of Croatia 1991–92; Perm. Rep. of Croatia to UN 1992–96, to OSCE 1996–; Decoration of Homeland War 1993. *Publications:* Western Sahara 1984, Namibia 1985, South Africa 1986, Atlas 1989, War Against Croatia 1992, Croatian Phoenix 2000. *Leisure interests:* diving, fishing, sailing, do-it-yourself skills. *Address:* Croatian Mission to OSCE, Habsburgergasse 6/18, 1010 Vienna (Office); Goldeggasse 2-22, 1040 Vienna, Austria (Home). *Telephone:* (1) 5350137 (Office). *Fax:* (1) 5350134 (Office). *E-mail:* misija.oess.@aon.at (Office); gombek2@aol.com (Home). *Website:* www.osce.org (Office).

NOBLE, Adrian Keith, BA; British theatre director; b. 19 July 1950; s. of the late William John Noble and of Violet Ena Noble (née Wells); m. Joanne Pearce 1991; one d. one s.; ed Chichester High School for Boys, Bristol Univ., London Drama Centre, Trinity Arts Centre, Birmingham; Resident Dir then Assoc. Dir Bristol Old Vic 1976–79; Resident Dir Royal Shakespeare Co. (RSC) 1980–82, Assoc. Dir 1982–90, Artistic Dir 1991–2003; Guest Dir Royal Exchange Theatre, Man. 1980–81; Visiting Prof. London Inst. 2001; Hon. Bencher Middle Temple; Hon. DLitt (Birmingham) 1994, (Bristol) 1996, (Exeter) 1999, (Warwick) 2001. *Film directed:* A Midsummer Night's Dream 1995. *Stage productions include:* Ubu Rex 1977, A Man's a Man 1977, A View from a Bridge 1978, Titus Adronicus 1978, The Changeling 1978, Love for Love 1979, Timon of Athens 1979, Recruiting Officer 1979, Duchess of Malfi 1980, Dr Faustus 1981, The Forest (Best Revival, Drama Awards) 1981, A Doll's House 1981, King Lear 1982, Antony and Cleopatra 1982, A New Way to Pay Old Debts 1983, Comedy of Errors 1983, Measure for Measure 1983, Henry V 1984, The Winter's Tale 1984, As You Like It 1985, Mephisto 1986, The Art of Success 1986, Macbeth 1986, Kiss Me Kate 1987, The Plantagenets 1989, The Master Builder 1989, The Fairy Queen (Aix-en-Provence), The Three Sisters 1990, Henry IV (parts 1 and 2) 1991, The Thebans 1991, Hamlet, Winter's Tale 1992, Travesties, King Lear, Macbeth 1993, A Midsummer Night's Dream 1994, Romeo and Juliet 1995, The Cherry Orchard 1995, Little Eyolf 1996, Cymbeline 1997, Twelfth Night 1997, The Tempest 1998, The Lion, the Witch and the Wardrobe 1998, The Seagull, The Family Reunion 2000, The Secret Garden 2000–01, Chitty Chitty Bang Bang 2002;

The Return of Ulysses (Aix-en Provence) 2000, Don Giovanni (Kent Opera) 1983. *Address:* c/o Royal Shakespeare Company, Royal Shakespeare Theatre, Waterside, Stratford-upon-Avon, Warwicks. CV37 6BB, England.

NOBLE, Denis, CBE, PhD, FRS, FRCP; British professor of physiology; b. 16 Nov. 1936, London; s. of George Noble and Ethel Rutherford; m. Susan Jennifer Barfield 1965; one s. (adopted) one d.; ed Emanuel School and Univ. Coll. London; Asst Lecturer Univ. Coll. London 1961–63; Fellow, Lecturer and Tutor in Physiology Balliol Coll. Oxford 1963–84, Praefectus Balliol Graduate Centre 1971–89, Burdon Sanderson Prof. of Cardiovascular Physiology, Oxford Univ. 1984–, Professorial Fellow 1984–; Visiting Prof., Alberta 1969–70; Ed. Progress in Biophysics 1967–; Founder Dir Oxsoft Ltd 1984–, Physiome Sciences Inc. 1994–, Chair. Jt Dental Cttee 1984–90; Pres. Medical Section British Asscn 1992; Gen.-Sec. Int. Union of Physiological Sciences 1993–; Hon. Sec. Physiological Soc. 1974–80, Foreign Sec. 1986–92; Darwin Lecturer British Asscn 1966; Nahum Lecturer Yale Univ. 1977; Fellow University Coll. London 1986; Founder Fellow Acad. of Medical Sciences 1998; Lloyd Roberts Lecturer 1987; Bowden Lecturer, Alderdale Wyld Lecturer 1988; Hon. mem. Acad. de Medécine de Belgique; Hon. mem. American Physiological Soc., Academia Europaea 1989, Japanese Physiological Soc. 1998, The Physiological Soc. 1999; Hon. FRCP; Scientific Medal, Zoological Soc. 1970, British Heart Foundation Gold Medal and Prize 1985, Pierre Rijlant Prize (Belgian Royal Acad.) 1991, Baly Medal, Royal Coll. of Physicians (London) 1993. *Publications:* Initiation of the Heartbeat 1975, Electric Current Flow in Excitable Cells 1975, Electrophysiology of Single Cardiac Cells 1987, Goals, No Goals and Own Goals 1989, Sodium-Calcium Exchange 1989, Logic of Life 1993, Ionic Channels and the Effect of Taurine on the Heart 1993, Ethics of Life 1997; scientific papers mostly in Journal of Physiology. *Leisure interests:* Occitan language and music, Indian and French cooking, classical guitar. *Address:* University Laboratory of Physiology, Parks Road, Oxford, OX1 3PT (Office); 49 Old Road, Oxford, OX3 7JZ, England. *Telephone:* (1865) 272533 (Office); (1865) 762237 (Home). *Fax:* (1865) 272554 (Office). *E-mail:* denis.noble@physiol.ox.ac.uk (Office).

NOBLE, Ronald Kenneth, BA, JD; American law enforcement executive; ed Univ. of New Hampshire, Stanford Univ. Law School; fmr Asst to US Attorney, then Deputy Asst to Attorney-Gen., Dept of Justice; Pres. Financial Action Task Force (26 mem. multi-nat. org. est. to fight money-laundering by G7) 1989; Chief Law Enforcement Officer, US Treasury Dept 1989–96, responsible for The Secret Service, Customs Service, Bureau of Alcohol, Tobacco and Firearms, Fed. Law Enforcement Training Center, Financial Crimes Enforcement Network, Office of Foreign Assets Control and Criminal Investigation Div. of Internal Revenue Service; Prof. of Law, New York Univ. School of Law; fmr mem. Exec. Cttee INTERPOL, Sec.-Gen. Nov. 2000–. *Address:* International Criminal Police Organization (INTERPOL), 200 quai Charles de Gaulle, 69006 Lyon, France (Office). *Telephone:* 4-72-44-70-00 (Office). *Fax:* 4-72-44-71-63 (Office). *E-mail:* cp@interpol.int. *Website:* www .interpol.int (Office).

NOBOA, Alvaro; Ecuadorean industrialist and politician; b. 21 Nov. 1950, Guayaquil; s. of Luis Noboa Naranjo; m. Anabella Azín; three s.; ed Universidad de Guayaquil, in Europe and USA; inherited Noboa Corpn following death of father 1995, Pres. Noboa Corpn (controls 105 cos in Ecuador, Europe, USA and New Zealand with interests in coffee, bananas, real estate and flour) 1995–, cos include Bonita Bananas (largest banana co. in Ecuador), four shipping cos, one bank, two insurance cos, La nica (edible oils), Valdez (sugar refinery), Los Álamos and 14 other banana plantations, mines, media cos and other Ecuadorean businesses; Presidential Cand. for Partido Roldosista Ecuatoriano—PRE 1998, for Partido Renovador Institucional Acción Nacional—PRION 2002. *Address:* Corporacion Noboa, El Oro y La Ria, Guayaquil, Ecuador (Office). *Website:* www.alvaronoboa.com (Office).

NOBOA BEJARANO, Gustavo, PhD; Ecuadorean politician and academic; b. 21 Aug. 1939, Guayaquil; m. Marta Baquerizo; six c.; teacher of social sciences and politics 1962–; fmr Rector of Catholic Univ. of Guayaquil; fmr Rector of Public Univ. of Guayaquil; Gov. of Guayas Province 1983; mem. of peace comm. on border dispute with Peru 1996; Vice-Pres. of Ecuador 1998–2000, Pres. 2000–02; Order of St Sylvester, Commdr. State of the Vatican. *Address:* c/o Office of the President, Palacio Nacional, Garcia Moreno 1043, Quito, Ecuador (Office).

NOBU, (Nobuyuki Matsuhisa); Japanese chef; b. Tokyo; m.; two d.; served apprenticeship in sushi bars in Tokyo; opened sushi bar in Peru, later moving to Argentina, Japan and Alaska; opened Matsuhisa restaurant in Beverly Hills, Calif. Jan. 1987, Aspen, Colo 1999; opened Nobu restaurant in New York Aug. 1994, London 1997, Tokyo 1999; now owns chain of 14 restaurants. *Address:* c/o Nobu, 105 Hudson Street, New York, NY 10013, USA (Office). *Telephone:* (212) 219-0500 (Office).

NODA, Seiko; Japanese politician; b. 1961; ed Sophia Univ.; fmr mem. staff Imperial Hotel; elected mem. Gifu Prefectural Ass. 1987; mem. Liberal Democratic Party (LDP); mem. for Gifu, House of Reps.; fmr Parl. Vice-Minister of Posts and Telecommunications, Minister 1998–99. *Address:* c/o Ministry of Posts and Telecommunications, 1-3-2, Kasumigaseki, Chiyoda-ku, Tokyo 100, Japan.

NODA, Takeshi; Japanese politician; mem. House of Reps., constituency Kumamoto-1; Chair. Liberal Democratic Party (LDP) Nat. Campaign HQ., Cttee on Commerce and Industry House of Reps.; fmr Construction Minister,

LDP Deputy Sec. Gen.; Dir Gen. Econ. Planning Agency (State Minister) 1991–92; Minister for Home Affairs Jan–Oct. 1999, 2000. *Address:* c/o Ministry of Home Affairs, 2-1-2 Kasumigaseki, Chiyoda-ku, Tokyo 100, Japan.

NODA, Tetsuya, MA; Japanese print-making artist and university professor; b. 5 March 1940, Kumamoto Pref.; s. of Tesshin Noda and Sakae Noda; m. Dorit Bartur 1971; one s. one d.; ed Tokyo Nat. Univ. of Fine Art and Music; Visiting Artist at Alberta Univ., Canada 1984, Betzalel Art Acad., Israel 1985, Canberra Art School, Australia 1990, Columbia Univ., USA 1998; Prof. Tokyo Nat. Univ. of Fine Arts and Music 1990–; mem. Int. Jury for the British Int. Print Biennale 1976, Korean Int. Print Biennale 1996; prizes include Int. Grand Prize (Tokyo Int. Print Biennale) 1968, Grand Prize (Ljubljana Int. Print Biennale) 1977 and Grand Prize of Honour 1987, Grand Prize (Norwegian Int. Print Biennale) 1978, Friends of Bradford Art Galleries and Museum Prize (British Int. Print Biennale) 1986, Gen Yamaguchi Memorial Grand Prize, City of Numazu 1993. *Solo exhibitions include:* Fuji TV Gallery 1978, 1983, 1987, 1992. *Group exhibitions include:* São Paulo Biennale 1971, Venice Biennale (Graphic Int.) 1972, The Mechanized Image (touring), UK, Printed Art, A View of Two Decades, Museum of Modern Art, New York 1980, Japanese Prints since 1900, British Museum, London 1983, PhotoImage: Printmaking 60s to 90s, Museum of Fine Arts, Boston 1988, The Unfinished Century: Legacies of 20th-Century Art, Nat. Museum of Modern Art, Tokyo 2002. *Publications:* several woodcut and silkscreen prints. *Leisure interest:* gardening. *Address:* 2-12-4 Kikkodai, Kashiwa-shi, Chiba-ken, 299-0031, Japan. *Telephone:* (471) 63-5332. *Fax:* (471) 63-5332. *E-mail:* tetsuyanoda@ hotmail.com (Home).

NOE PINO, Hugo, PhD; Honduran economist; b. 11 Jan. 1955, Tegucigalpa; s. of Roberto Noe and Elidia Pino; m. Vivian Bustamante; two s. one d.; ed Universidad Nacional Autonoma de Honduras (UNAH), Univ. of Texas at Austin, USA; fmr teaching Asst, Dept of Econs, Univ. of Tex.; Pres. Cen. Bank of Honduras 1994–97; Dir Master's Programme in Econs for Cen. American and Caribbean Region, UNAH; Pres. Asscn of Economists of Honduras; mem. Editorial Council of various magazines published in Honduras; Spokesman of Shadow Cabinet 1993; Amb. to USA to 1999–. *Publications:* An Assessment of the Campesino Associative Enterprise of Isletas 1987, Honduras: Structural Adjustment and Agrarian Reform 1992. *Leisure interests:* reading, music. *Address:* Honduras Embassy, 3007 Tilden Street N.W., Suite 4-M, Washington, DC 20008, USA. *Telephone:* (202) 966-7702 (Office). *Fax:* (202) 966-9751 (Office). *E-mail:* embassy@hondurasemb.org (Office). *Website:* www .hondurasemb.org (Office).

NOELLE, Elisabeth, DPhil; German professor of communications research; b. 19 Dec. 1916, Berlin; d. of Dr. Ernst Noelle and Eva Schaper; m. 1st Erich P. Neumann 1946 (died 1973); m. 2nd Heinz Maier-Leibnitz 1979 (died 2000); ed Univs of Königsberg and Munich, School of Journalism, Univ. of Missouri, Univ. of Berlin; Founder and Dir Inst. für Demoskopie Allensbach (first German survey research inst.) 1947–; Lecturer in Communications Research, Free Univ. of Berlin 1961–64; Prof. of Communications Research, Univ. of Mainz 1964–, also Dir Inst. für Publizistik (until 1983); f. Allensbach Foundation for Public Opinion Research 1996; Public Opinion Analyst, Frankfurter Allgemeine Zeitung (newspaper) 1978–; Visiting Prof., Dept of Political Science, Univ. of Chicago 1978–91, Univ. of Munich 1993–94; Hon. Prof. Moscow External Univ. of the Humanities; Co-Ed. Int. Journal of Public Opinion Research; Hon. Citizen of Allensbach 1977; Dr.oec. hc (St Gallen); Grosses Bundesverdienstkreuz 1976, Alexander Rüstow Medal 1978, Nürnberger Trichter Award 1985, Viktor Matajy Medal 1987, Order of Merit, Baden-Württemberg 1990, Helen Dinerman Award 1990, Boveri Award 1997, Schleyer Foundation Award 1999; Hon. mem. German Univ. Asscn 2000. *Publications include:* Jahrbücher der Demoskopie (11 Vols) (Ed.) 1947–2002, The Germans, (Vol. I) 1967, (Vol. II) 1980, Fischer Lexikon Publizistik–Massenkommunikation (Co-Ed.) 1971, 1989, 1994, 1998, 2002, Umfragen in der Massengesellschaft: Einführung in die Methoden der Demoskopie 1963, revised Edn, Alle, nicht jeder: Einführung in die Methoden der Demoskopie (with T. Petersen) 1996, 1998, 2000, Öffentlichkeit als Bedrohung 1977, 1979, Die Schweigespirale: Öffentliche Meinung—unsere soziale Haut 1980, 2001, Eine demoskopische Deutschstunde 1983, Macht Arbeit krank? 1984 (with B. Strümpel), Die verletzte Nation (with R. Köcher) 1987, Öffentliche Meinung: Die Entdeckung der Schweigespirale 1989, 1991, 1996, Demoskopische Geschichtsstunde 1991, Kampa: Meinungsklima und Medienwirkung im Bundestagwahlkampf 1998, 1999, Die soziale Natur des Menschen 2002. *Leisure interests:* painting, strolling by Lake Constance. *Address:* Institut für Demoskopie Allensbach, Radolfzeller Str. 8, 78476 Allensbach am Bodensee, Germany. *Telephone:* 07533/8050. *Fax:* 07533 805-108 (Office); 07533/3048. *E-mail:* enoelle-neumann@ifd-allensbach.de (Office). *Website:* www.ifd-allensbach.de (Office).

NOGHAIDELI, Zurab; Georgian politician; b. 22. Oct. 1964, Kobuleti; s. of Mai Katamadre; m. Nino Tsintsabadze; one s.; ed Moscow Lomonosov State Univ., USSR (now Russian Fed.); MP, Chair. Environment Protection and Natural Resources Cttee, Exec. Sec. Georgian Greens 1992–; Co-ordinator Secr. of Parl. 1995–; Int. Relations Sec., Citizens' Union of Georgia 1995–98; Del. of Supreme Council, Ajara Autonomous Rep. 1996–; Chair. Tax and Income Cttee 1999–; Minister of Finance 2000–. *Address:* c/o Ministry of

Finance, Abashidze 70, 380062 Tbilisi, Georgia (Office); Governmental Residence of Tskneti, Georgia (Home). *Telephone:* (32) 226805 (Office). *Fax:* (32) 931922 (Office). *E-mail:* minfin@access.sanet.ge (Office).

NOGUCHI, Teruhisa, PhD; Japanese business executive; b. 22 Oct. 1924, Chiba Pref.; m.; one s. three d.; ed Schools of Medicine, Kanazawa and Tokyo Univs.; with Nihon Soda Co. 1949–72; with Teijin Ltd 1972–79, Dir 1973, Dir Teijin Inst. for Biomedical Research 1976; with Suntory Ltd 1979–92, Dir 1979, Exec. Man. Pharmaceutical Div. 1981, Sr Man. Dir 1987–, Chief Exec. 1991; Exec. Vice-Pres. Yamanouchi Pharmaceutical Co. Ltd 1992–; Adjunct Prof., The Rockefeller Univ. 1984–; Fellow American Acad. of Microbiology; several prizes and awards. *Publications include:* Biochemistry of Interferons 1982, New Trends in Neuro-Science 1984. *Leisure interests:* fine arts, golf. *Address:* 2-18-11, Kugenuma Kaigan, Fujisawa City, Kanagawa Prefecture 251, Japan.

NOIRET, Philippe; French actor; b. 1 Oct. 1930, Lille; s. of Pierre Noiret and Lucy Heirman; m. Monique Chaumette 1962; one s.; ed Lycée Janson-de-Sailly, Paris and Coll. des oratoriens, Juilly; Prix Orange 1972, César for Le vieux fusil 1976, Best Actor at Rio de Janiero Film Festival for Les Ripoux 1984, David Award, Best Foreign Actor for Life and Nothing But 1990. *Stage appearances include:* La Nuit des rois, Le Cid, Richard II, Drôle de couple, Les Côtelettes. *Films include:* La Pointe courte 1954, Zazie dans le métro, Les Amours célèbres, Tout l'or du monde, Thérèse Desqueyroux, Ballade pour un voyou, Clementine chérie 1963, Cyrano et d'Artagnan, Monsieur 1964, L'une et l'autre 1967, Le vieux fusil 1975, Le taxi mauve, Une semaine de vacances 1980, Les Ripoux 1984, Masques 1987, La femme de mes amours 1989, La vie et rien d'autre (Life and Nothing But) 1989, Cinema Paradiso 1989, Ripoux contre ripoux 1990, Oublier Palerme 1990, Faux et usage de faux 1990, Le Cop 2 1991, J'embarrasse pas 1991, Nous deux 1992, Le Chien leu 1992, Max et Jérémie 1992, Tango 1993, Il Postino 1995, D'Artagnan's Daughter 1995, Le Roi de Paris 1995, Les Grands ducs 1996, Fantôme avec chauffeur 1996, Les Palmes de M. Schultz 1997, Le Roi de Paris 1999, Le Pique-rique de Lulu Kreutz 2000. *Address:* c/o Artmédia, 20 avenue Rapp, 75007 Paris, France.

NØJGAARD, Morten, DPhil; Danish professor of romance philology; b. 28 July 1934, Holbaek; s. of Niels Nøjgaard and Annie Nøjgaard (née Bay); m. Stina Lund 1962; two s. two d.; secondary school teacher Roedovre Statskole 1960–63; research scholar Univ. of Copenhagen 1963–65; Prof. of Romance Philology, Univ. of Odense 1966–; Chief Ed. Orbis Litterarum 1968–; Pres. Asscn of French Prof. 1962–63, Alliance Française, Odense 1970–; mem. Soc. of Letters (Lund, Sweden) 1978, Royal Danish Acad. of Science 1982, Royal Norwegian Acad. of Science 1991, Royal Swedish Acad. of Antiquities 1997; Fnske Bladfond Research Award 1975, Ordre du Mérite 1980. *Publications:* La Fable Antique, (Vols I–II) 1964–67, Elévation et Expansion. Les deux dimensions de Baudelaire 1973, An Introduction to Literary Analysis 1975, Romain-Gary-Emile Ajar, Homo Duplex 1986, Les Adverbes français, Vol. I 1992, Vol. II 1993, Vol. III 1995, Plaisir et vérité, Le paradoxe de l'évaluation littéraire 1993, Le Temps de la littérature. Sur Paul Ricoeur et les paradoxes du temps raconté 1999 and numerous scientific articles. *Address:* Odense University, Campusvej 55, 5230 Odense M (Office); Aløkken 48, 5250 Odense SV, Denmark. *Telephone:* 65-50-10-00 (Office); 65-96-18-06. *Fax:* 65-93-51-41 (Office); 65-93-51-49. *E-mail:* mno@litcul.ou.dk (Office).

NOLAN, Baron (Life Peer), cr. 1994, of Brasted in the County of Kent; **Michael Patrick Nolan,** Kt, PC; British judge; b. 10 Sept. 1928; s. of James T. Nolan and Jane Walsh; m. Margaret Noyes 1953; one s. four d.; ed Ampleforth and Wadham Coll. Oxford; called to Bar, Middle Temple 1953, Bencher 1975; QC 1968; called to Bar, Northern Ireland 1974; QC (Northern Ireland) 1974; a Recorder of Crown Court 1975–82; Judge, High Court of Justice, Queen's Bench Div. 1982–91; Presiding Judge, Western Circuit 1985–88; Lord Justice of Appeal 1991–93; a Lord of Appeal in Ordinary 1994–98; Chair. Comm. of Inquiry into Standards in Public Life 1994–97; Chair. Bd Inst. of Advanced Legal Studies 1994–2000, Review on Child Protection in the Catholic Church of England and Wales 2000–; Chancellor Essex Univ. 1997–; Dr. hc (Essex) 1996, (Surrey) 1996, Hon. LL.D (Warwick) 1998, (Exeter) 1998, (Bournemouth) 2000. *Leisure interest:* fishing. *Address:* House of Lords, London, SW1A 0PW, England.

NOLAN, Philip, MBA, PhD; British telecommunications executive; b. Enniskillen, NI; ed Queens Univ., Belfast, London Business School; fmr Lecturer of Geology Univ. of Ulster; with British Petroleum (BP) Exploration –1996, numerous roles including Man. of Acquisitions and Disposals; Dir Transco East Area, BG Group 1996–97, Man. Dir Transco 1997–, CEO 1999–2000, mem. Bd BG Group 1998–2000; C.E.O. Lattice Group (fmrly. part of the BG Group) 2000–02; C.E.O. Eircom 2002–. *Address:* Eircom plc., 114 St. Stephen's Green, Dublin 2, Ireland (Office). *Website:* www.eircom.ie.

NOLAND, Kenneth Clifton; American artist; b. 10 April 1927, Asheville, NC; s. of Harry C. Noland and Bessie (née Elkins) Noland; m. 1st Cornelia Langel (divorced); one s. two d.; m. 2nd Stephanie Gordon 1967; m. 3rd Peggy Schiffer (divorced); one s.; m. 4th Paige Rense 1994; ed Black Mountain Coll., North Carolina and Paris; Teacher Inst. of Contemporary Arts 1950–52, Catholic Univ. 1951–60, Bennington Coll. 1968; work in perm. collections in Museum of Modern Art, Guggenheim Museum, Whitney Museum, Tate Gallery, Stedelijk Museum (Amsterdam), Zürich Kunsthaus and others; North Carolina Medal of Arts 1995. *One-man shows include:* Galerie Creuze, Paris 1949, Tibor de Nagy, New York 1957, 1958, French and Co., New York 1959, André Emmerich Gallery, New York 1967, 1973, 1975, 1977–78

1980–83, 1988, 1998, André Emmerich Gallery, Zürich 1973, 1976, 1979, 1982, Nicholas Wilder Gallery, LA 1967, Salander New York 1989, 1991, O'Reilly Galleries, Gana Art Gallery, Seoul, Korea 1995, CHAC-Mool Gallery, Calif. 1999, also Toronto, Florida, Atlanta, Houston, Beverly Hills, Berlin, Edmonton, Madrid, Milan, Paris, London. *Address:* North Bennington, VT 05257, USA.

NOLL, João Gilberto, BA; Brazilian writer; b. 15 April 1946, Porto Alegre; s. of João Noll and Ecila Noll; columnist Folha de São Paulo newspaper; writer-in-residence Univ. of Calif. at Berkeley, also teaching Brazilian Literature 1996, 1997, 1998; Guggenheim Fellowship 1999–2000; Prêmio Jabuti on three occasions. *Play:* Quero Sim 1992. *Publications:* (short stories) O cego e a dançarina; (novels) A fúria do corpo, Bandoleiros, Hotel Atlântico, Harmada, A céu aberto, Canoas e marolas, Rastros do verão, O quieto animal da esquina. *Leisure interests:* music, travelling. *Address:* Rua José do Patrocínio 557/306, 90050-003 Porto Alegre, R.S., Brazil. *Telephone:* (50) 224-8766. *Fax:* (50) 224-8766.

NOLTE, Nick; American film actor; b. 8 Feb. 1941, Omaha; m. Rebecca Linger 1984 (divorced 1995); one s.; ed Pasadena City Coll., Phoenix City Coll.; stage appearance in The Last Pad 1973; TV films 1974–75 and drama series Rich Man, Poor Man 1976; also appeared in repertory groups. *Films:* Return to Macon County 1975, The Deep 1977, Who'll Stop the Rain 1978, North Dallas Forty 1979, Heartbeat 1980, Cannery Row 1982, 48 Hours 1982, Under Fire 1983, The Ultimate Solution of Grace Quigley 1984, Teachers 1984, Down and Out in Beverly Hills 1986, Weeds 1987, Extreme Prejudice 1987, Farewell to the King 1989, New York Stories 1989, Three Fugitives, Everybody Wins, Q & A 1990, Prince of Tides 1990, Cape Fear 1991, Lorenzo's Oil 1992, Blue Chips 1994, I'll Do Anything 1994, Love Trouble 1994, Jefferson in Paris 1994, Mulholland Falls 1996, Mother Night 1996, Afterglow 1997, Affliction 1998, U-Turn, Breakfast of Champions 1998, The Thin Red Line 1998, Trixie 2000, The Golden Bowl 2000, Investigating Sex 2001, Double Down 2001, The Good Thief 2003. *Address:* 6153 Bonsall Drive, Malibu, CA 90265, USA.

NOMIYAMA, Akihiko, LLB; Japanese business executive; b. 15 June 1934, Fukuoka Pref.; one s. one d.; ed Tokyo Univ.; joined Nippon Mining Co. 1957, assignments in budget control, corp. financing, Gen. Man. Admin. Dept, Petroleum Operation 1981–92, Man. Dir Japan Energy Corpn (formed from merger with Kyodo Oil Co.) 1992–96, Pres., CEO and Dir 1996–; Vice-Chair. Petroleum Asscn of Japan. *Leisure interests:* golf, classical music. *Address:* Japan Energy Corporation, 10-1 Toranomon, 2-chome, Minato-ku, Tokyo 105, Japan.

NOMURA, Masayasu, PhD; American molecular biologist and academic; b. 27 April 1927, Hyogo-Ken, Japan; s. of Hiromichi Nomura and Yaeko Nomura; m. Junko Hamashima 1957; one s. one d.; ed Univ. of Tokyo; Research Assoc., Prof. S. Spiegelman's Lab., Univ. of Ill. and Prof. J. D. Watson's Lab., Harvard Univ. 1957–59; Prof. S. Benzer's Lab., Purdue Univ. 1959–60; Asst Prof., Inst. for Protein Research, Osaka Univ. 1960–63; Assoc. Prof., Dept of Genetics, Univ. of Wis. 1963–66, Prof. 1966–70; Elvehjem Prof. of Life Sciences, Inst. for Enzyme Research, with Jt appointments in Depts. of Genetics and Biochem. 1970–84; Grace Bell Prof. of Biological Chem., Univ. of Calif. at Irvine 1984–; Fellow AAAS; mem. American Acad. of Arts and Sciences, NAS; Foreign mem. Royal Danish Acad. of Sciences and Letters, Royal Netherlands Acad. of Arts and Sciences; U.S. Steel Award in Molecular Biology (NAS); Japan Acad. Award 1972; Y. D. Mattia Award (Roche Inst.). *Leisure interests:* hiking, reading. *Address:* University of California, Department of Biological Chemistry, Med. Sci. I, D240, Irvine, CA 92697-1700 (Office); 74 Whitman Court, Irvine, CA 92612, USA (Home). *Telephone:* (949) 824-4564 (Office); (949) 854-3482 (Home). *Fax:* (949) 824-3201 (Office). *E-mail:* mnomura@uci.edu (Office). *Website:* www.ucihs.uci.edu/biochem/faculty/nrmura.html (Office).

NOMURA, Yoshihiro; Japanese professor of law; b. 3 Jan. 1941, Nagoya City; s. of Akio Nomura and Michiko Nomura; m. 1966; three s. one d.; ed Univ. of Tokyo; Asst Researcher in Law, Univ. of Tokyo 1963; Lecturer Tokyo Metropolitan Univ. 1966, Assoc. Prof. 1967, Prof. of Civil and Environmental Law 1977–. *Publication:* Automobile Accident Damages 1970, Environmental Law 1981. *Leisure interest:* nature watching. *Address:* Faculty of Law, Tokyo Metropolitan University, Minami-Ohsawa 1-1, Hachiohji-City, Tokyo 192-0397, Japan. *Telephone:* (45) 973-2612. *Fax:* (45) 972-0592.

NOOR, Dato Mohamad Yusof, MA, PhD; Malaysian politician and teacher; b. 5 Feb. 1941, Raja, Terangganu; m.; two c.; ed Islamic Coll., Klang, Selangor, Al Azhar Univ., Ein Shams Univ. and Univ. of Cairo; secondary school teacher 1969–70; Insp. of Secondary Schools, Terengganu State 1970; Prin., Sultan Zainal Abidin Secondary Religious School 1970; Lecturer and Head of Coll., Nat. Univ. of Malaysia 1974, Dean, Faculty of Islamic Studies 1975–79, Deputy Vice-Chancellor for Student Affairs 1980–84; mem. Senate 1984; Deputy Minister responsible for Islamic Affairs, Prime Minister's Dept 1984; mem. House of Reps. 1987–; mem. Supreme Council, United Malays Nat. Org. (UMNO) 1987–; Minister, Prime Minister's Dept 1987; Chair. Religious Council for Fed. Territory; many other appointments in Islamic and religious field. *Publications:* numerous articles in fields of educ. and Islamic affairs. *Address:* c/o House of Representatives, Parliament Building, Kuala Lumpur, Malaysia.

NOOR AL-HUSSEIN, HM Queen of Jordan, BA; b. Lisa Najeeb Halaby,, 23 Aug. 1951; m. King Hussein I of Jordan (died 1999) 1978; four c.; ed Princeton Univ., USA; architectural and urban planning projects in Australia, Iran and Jordan 1974–78; f. in Jordan: Royal Endowment for Culture and Educ. 1979, annual Arab Children's Congress 1980, annual int. Jerash Festival for Culture and Arts 1981, Jubilee School 1984, Noor Al-Hussein Foundation 1985, Nat. Music Conservatory 1986; Chair. Nat. Task Force for Children, Advisory Cttee for UN Univ. Int. Leadership Acad., Amman; Patron, Gen. Fed. of Jordanian Women, Nat. Fed. of Business and Professional Women's Clubs, Royal Soc. for Conservation of Nature and various cultural, sports and nat. devt orgs; Hon. Pres. Jordan Red Crescent; Patron, Int. Union for Conservation of Nature and Natural Resources 1988, Landmine Survivors Network 1998; Founding mem. Int. Comm. on Peace and Food 1992; Pres. United World Colls. 1995; Dir Hunger Project; Hon. Pres. Birdlife Int. 1996–; mem. Int. Eye Foundation, Hon. Bd mem. Gen. Ass. SOS-Kinderdorf Int.; mem. Int. Council Near East Foundation; Trustee Mentor Foundation; many other affiliations; numerous hon. doctorates, int. awards and decorations for promotion of environmental conservation and awareness, econ. and social devt of women, children and communities, cross cultural exchange, int. understanding and world peace. *Publication:* Leap of Faith: Memoirs of an Unexpected Life 2002. *Leisure interests:* skiing, riding, tennis, sailing, reading, photography. *Address:* Royal Palace, Amman, Jordan.

NORDAL, Jóhannes, PhD; Icelandic economist and banker; b. 11 May 1924, Reykjavik; s. of Prof. Sigurdur Nordal and Olöf Jónsdóttir; m. Dóra Gudjónsdóttir; one s. five d.; ed Reykjavik Grammar School and LSE, London; Chief Economist, Nat. Bank of Iceland 1954–59, Gen. Man. 1959–61; Gov., Cen. Bank of Iceland (Sedlabanki Islands) 1961–93, (Chair. Bd of Govs. 1964–93); Chair. of Bd Nat. Power Co. (Landsvirkjun) 1965–96; Gov. IMF for Iceland 1965–93; Ed. Fjármálatíáindi (Financial Review) 1954–94; Co.-Ed. Nýtt Helgafell (literary periodical) 1955–59; Chair. Humanities Div. of Science Fund for Iceland 1958–87, Icelandic Council of Science 1987–94, Nat. Library Bd 1994–; mem. Soc. Scientiarum Islandica 1959–; Grand Kt Order of Falcon 1966. *Publications:* Iceland 1966, 1974, 1986, Iceland–The Republic 1996. *Leisure Interests:* fly-fishing, books. *Address:* Sedlabanki Islands, Kalkofnsvegur 1, 150 Reykjavik (Office); Laugarásvegur 11, Reykjavik, Iceland (Home). *Telephone:* 5699600 (Office); 5533350 (Home). *Fax:* 5699609 (Office).

NORDH, Sture, BPA; Swedish trade union official; b. 3 June 1952, Skellefteå; m. Gudrun Nordh (née Nygren); one d. one s.; ed Univ. of Umeå; Union Sec. Swedish Union of Local Govt Employees (SKTF) 1975–79, Gen.-Sec. 1979–83, Pres. 1983–96; State Sec. Ministry of Labour 1996–98; Deputy Dir-Gen. Nat. Inst. of Working Life 1999; Pres. Swedish Confed. of Professional Employees (TCO) 1999–. *Publication:* Future of the Welfare State (co-author with Bengt Westerberg). *Leisure interests:* skiing, literature. *Address:* Tjänstemännens Centralorganisation (TCO), Linnégt. 14, 114 94 Stockholm (Office); Gyllenstiernsg. 10, 115 26 Stockholm, Sweden (Home). *Telephone:* 87-82-91-00 (Office); 86-61-34-23 (Home). *Fax:* 87-82-91-15 (Office); 86-62-16-75 (Home). *E-mail:* ordforande@tco.se (Office); sture.nordh@telia.com (Home). *Website:* www.tco.se (Office).

NORDHAGEN, Per Jonas, DPhil; Norwegian professor of history of art; b. 30 Oct. 1929, Bergen; s. of Rolf Nordhagen and Elisabeth M. Myhre; m. Inger K. Noss 1978; one s. four d.; ed Univ. of Oslo; Lecturer, Univ. of Oslo 1962; Assoc. Prof. Univ. of Bergen 1969; Dir Norwegian Inst. Rome 1973; Sr Lecturer, Univ. of Oslo 1977; Prof. of History of Art, Univ. of Bergen 1986–2000; mem. Norwegian Acad. of Sciences. *Publications:* The Frescoes of John VII (705–707 AD) in S. Maria Antiqua, Rome 1968, Frescoes of the Seventh Century 1978, The Capri Papers (novel) 1986, Collected Papers in the History of Byzantine and Early Medieval Art 1990, Bergen–Guide and Handbook 1992, The Wooden Architecture of Bergen 1994, The Technique of Early Christian and Byzantine Mosaics 1997, Art and Architecture of Norway: an Outline 1997. *Leisure interests:* skiing, hiking, books, botany. *Address:* c/o Institute of Art History, University of Bergen, Parkv. 22B, 5014 Bergen, Norway.

NORDHEIM, Arne; Norwegian composer; b. 20 June 1931, Larvik; m. 1st 1956; m. 2nd 1981; two c.; ed Oslo Conservatory of Music and electronic music studies in Paris, Utrecht, Warsaw and Stockholm; began to compose 1950; first maj. work Stringquartett 1956; since composed several works for orchestra and solo instruments and symphonic music, voice or electronic sound and one ballet score; worked as music critic for several daily newspapers 1959–67; critic Dagbladet, Oslo 1960–68; fmr Prof. of Electronic Music; mem. Royal Swedish Acad. of Music; Hon. mem. Int. Soc. for Contemporary Music 1996–; Nordic Council Music Prize 1972, Prix Italia 1980, awarded Norwegian State Residence of Honour 1982, Steffens Prize 1993, Commdr Order of St Olav 1997, Commdr Order al Merito (Italy) 1998, Commdr Orderu Zasługi Rzeczy pos Politej Polskie (Poland) 1999. *Music:* approx. 180 works including Epitaffio, Canzona, Floating, Wirklicher Wald, The Tempest (ballet) and solo concertos for cello, oboe and accordion. *Address:* Wergelandsveien 2, 0167 Oslo, Norway. *Telephone:* 22-11-28-27. *Fax:* 22-11-38-47.

NORDLI, Odvar; Norwegian politician; b. 3 Nov. 1927, Stange, Hedmark; ed in business admin.; Asst Baerum Municipal Auditor's Office 1948–49; Chief Clerk, Hedmark County Auditor's Office 1949–57; Dist Auditor, Vang and Löten 1957–61; mem. Storting (Parl.) 1961; mem. and Deputy Chair. Stange Municipal Council 1952; Chair. Municipal Cttee of Hedmark Labour Party 1960–; Deputy mem. Cen. Cttee of Labour Party 1965, Chair. Hedmark Labour Party 1968; Chair. Trade Union and Labour Party Tax Cttee 1967–68; Vice-Chair. Parl. Municipal Cttee 1965–69; Chair. Parl. Social Welfare Cttee 1969–71; Minister of Labour and Municipal Affairs 1971–72; Chair. Comm. of Defence 1974–75; Prime Minister 1976–81; Vice-Pres. Parl. 1981; Leader Parl. Labour Party 1973–76.

NORDLING, Carl, PhD; Swedish professor emeritus of physics; b. 6 Feb. 1931, Edmonton, Canada; s. of Jarl Nordling and Karin Thorén; m. Gunhild Söderström 1954; two s. one d.; ed Univ. of Uppsala; Asst Prof. Univ. of Uppsala 1959–61, Lecturer 1962–64, Assoc. Prof. 1965–69, Prof. of Atomic and Molecular Physics 1970–95, Prof. Emer. 1995–; Sec.-Gen. Swedish Nat. Science Research Council 1987–93; Chair. Nobel Cttee for Physics 1992–96. *Publications:* ESCA-Atomic, Molecular and Solid State Structure Studied by Means of Electron Spectroscopy (co-author) 1967, ESCA Applied to Free Molecules (co-author) 1969, Physics Handbook (co-author) 1982; 150 scientific papers on electron, X-ray and laser spectroscopy. *Address:* Department of Physics, University of Uppsala, Box 530, 751 21 Uppsala (Office); Malma Ringv. 45B, 75645 Uppsala, Sweden (Home). *Telephone:* (18) 471-35-45 (Office); (18) 30-22-21 (Home). *Fax:* (18) 51-22-27. *E-mail:* carl.nordling@fysik.uu.se (Office).

NORÉN, Lars; Swedish playwright and director; b. 9 May 1944, Stockholm; s. of Matti Norén and Britt Norén; m. 1st Titti Mörk 1979; m. 2nd Charlott Neuhauser 1993; two d.; started career as a poet; wrote first play 1968; has written 55 plays, performed worldwide; De Nio's Pris 1985, Expressens Reviewers' Prize 1993, Pilot Prize 1994 and many other prizes and awards. *Plays include:* Courage to Kill 1978, Munich-Athens 1981, Night is Day's Mother 1982, Comedians 1985, Hebriana 1987, Autumn and Winter 1987, And Give Us the Shadows 1988, Trick or Treat 1989, Lost and Found 1991, Leaves in Vallombrosa 1992, Blood 1994, Some Kind of Hades 1994, The Clinic 1995, Personkrets 3:1 1997, 7:3 1998, The Shadow Boys 1991. *Leisure interests:* fishing, hunting. *Address:* c/o Ulla Orre, Draken Teaterförlag, Södermannagatan 27 NB, SE-11640 Stockholm (Agent); Östermalmsgatan 33, S-11426 Stockholm, Sweden, (Home). *Telephone:* (8) 642-71-06 (Agent). *Fax:* (8) 643-81-08. *E-mail:* draken@mbox307.swipnet.se (Office). *Website:* home.swipnet.se/draken (Office).

NØRGAARD, Carl Aage, DJur; Danish professor of law; b. 15 Sept. 1924; s. of Edvard Nørgaard and Jensine Kristine Kristensen; m. Hedvig Hauberg 1951; one d.; ed Univs. of Aarhus, Cambridge and Geneva; Asst Faculty of Law, Univ. of Aarhus 1955–58, Lecturer 1958–64, Prof. 1964–89, Head of Inst. of Public Law 1964–86; Rockefeller Fellowship, Univ. of Geneva 1959–60; mem. European Comm. of Human Rights 1973–95, Second Vice-Pres. 1976–81, Pres. 1981–95, Ind. Legal Adviser for UN concerning the release of political prisoners in Namibia 1989–90; Legal Adviser to S. African Truth and Reconciliation Comm. 1994–98; Hon. DJur (Lund) 1994; Danish Grand Cross, German Grand Order of Merit with star and sash; Prix de la Tolérance and Prix Marcel Rudloff, Strasbourg 1998. *Publications:* The Position of the Individual in International Law 1962, Forvaltningsret-Sagsbehandling 1972, Administration og Borger (with Claus Haagen Jensen) 1972, 1984, 1988 and articles in legal periodicals. *Leisure interests:* rowing, gardening. *Address:* Skjoldsbjergvej 2A, Skórring, 8464 Galten, Denmark. *Telephone:* 89-42-11-33 (Office); 86-94-40-47 (Home).

NORIEGA, Gen. Antonio; Panamanian army officer; b. 11 Feb. 1940, Panama City; m. Felicidad Sieiro; three d.; ed Univ. of Panama, Mil. Acad., Peru; First Lt Panama Nat. Guard 1962; Head Panama Intelligence Services 1970; mem. Jt Chiefs of Staff, Guardia Nacional 1970–81, Chief 1982–83; C-in-C Panama Defence Forces 1983–89; overthrown, sought refuge in Vatican Embassy, Panama; extradited on drug charges to Miami, USA Jan. 1990; residing in high security prison, facing 12 charges of drug trafficking 1990–92; found guilty of 8 of 10 charges (money laundering, cocaine manufacturing and distribution, racketeering and the bldg of a drug lab. in Panama) April 1992; sentenced to 40 years' imprisonment; further sentence in absentia of 20 years' imprisonment for murder Oct. 1993; currently in a fed. prison in Miami; numerous medals. *Publication:* Immortal Ayacucho.

NORMAN, Rt. Hon Archie John, MA, MBA; British business executive and politician; b. 1 May 1954, London; s. of Archibald Percy Norman and Aleida Elizabeth Norman; m. Vanessa Peet 1982; one d.; ed Univ. of Minnesota, Emmanuel Coll. Cambridge, Harvard Business School; with Citibank N.A. 1975–77; Partner, McKinsey & Co. Inc. 1979–86; Group Finance Dir Kingfisher PLC 1986–91; Chief Exec. Asda Group PLC 1991–96, Chair. 1996–97; Chair. (non-exec.) French PLC 1999–2001; MP for Tunbridge Wells 1997–; Vice-Chair. Conservative Party 1997–98; Chief Exec. and Deputy Chair. Conservative Party 1998–99; Shadow Foreign Affairs Post 1999–2000; Shadow Spokesman on Environment, Transport and the Regions 2000–01; Dir (non-exec.) Geest 1988–91, British Rail 1992–94, Railtrack 1994–2000; Chair. Energis 2002–. *Leisure interests:* farming, music, opera, tennis, football. *Address:* House of Commons, Westminster, London, SW1A 0AA, England. *Telephone:* (20) 7219-3000.

NORMAN, Barry Leslie, CBE; British writer and broadcaster; b. 21 Aug. 1933, London; s. of Leslie Norman and Elizabeth Norman; m. Diana Narracott 1957; two d.; ed Highgate School, London; Entertainments Ed. Daily Mail, London 1969–71; weekly columnist The Guardian 1971–80; Writer and Presenter of BBC 1 Film 1973–81, 1983–98, The Hollywood Greats 1977–79, 1984, The British Greats 1980, Omnibus 1982, Film Greats 1985, Talking

Pictures 1988, Barry Norman's Film Night, BSkyB 1998–2001; Radio 4 Today 1974–76, Going Places 1977–81, Breakaway 1979–80; Hon. DLitt (E Anglia) 1991, (Herts.) 1996; Richard Dimbleby Award, BAFTA Award 1981, Columnist of the Year award 1990. *Publications:* Novels: The Matter of Mandrake 1967, The Hounds of Sparta 1968, End Product 1975, A Series of Defeats 1977, To Nick a Good Body 1978, Have a Nice Day 1981, Sticky Wicket 1984, The Birddog Tape 1992, The Mickey Mouse Affair 1995, Death on Sunset 1998; non-fiction: Tales of the Redundance Kid 1975, The Hollywood Greats 1979, The Movie Greats 1981, The Film Greats 1985, Talking Pictures 1987, The Good Night In Guide 1992, 100 Best Films of the Century 1992, And Why Not? 2002. *Leisure interest:* cricket. *Address:* c/o Curtis Brown Ltd, Haymarket House, 28–29 Haymarket, London, SW1Y 4SP, England. *Telephone:* (20) 7396-6600.

NORMAN, Denis; Zimbabwean politician and farmer; b. 1931, Oxfordshire, UK; m.; four c.; emigrated to Rhodesia (now Zimbabwe) 1953; employed as a farm man.; started farming in own right 1959; served on various agricultural cttees. 1961–; Chair. Commercial Grain Producers 1974–76; Minister of Agric. 1980–85, 1995–96, of Transport and Energy 1990–95; Vice-Pres. Commercial Farmers' Union 1976–78, Pres. 1978–80; Pres. Zimbabwe Agricultural Soc. 1993–. *Address:* c/o Ministry of Agriculture, Ngungunyana Building, Private Bag 7701, Causeway, Harare, Zimbabwe.

NORMAN, Gregory John (Greg), AO; Australian golfer; b. 10 Feb. 1955, Queensland; s. of M. Norman; m. Laura Andrassy 1981; one s. one d.; ed Townsville Grammar School, High School, Apsley, Queensland; turned professional 1976; won Westlakes Classic, Australia 1976, Martini Int., New S. Wales Open, South Seas Classic, Fiji 1978, Martini Int., Hong Kong Open 1979, Australian Open, French Open, Scandinavian Open 1980, Australian Masters, Martini Int., Dunlop Masters 1981, Dunlop Masters, State Express Classic, Benson & Hedges Int. 1982, Australian Masters, Nat. Panasonic New S. Wales Open, Hong Kong Open, Cannes Invitational, Suntory World Match Play Championship 1983, Canadian Open, Victorian Open, Australian Masters, Toshiba Australian PGA Championship 1984, Toshiba Australian PGA Championship, Nat. Panasonic Australian Open 1985, European Open, British Open, Suntory World Matchplay Championship, Panasonic-Las Vegas Invitational, Kemper Open 1986, Australian Masters, Nat. Panasonic Australian Open 1987, Palm Meadows Cup, Australia, PGA Nat. Tournament Players Championship, Australia, Panasonic NSW Open, Lancia Italian Open 1988, Australian Masters, PGA Nat. Tournament Players Championship 1989, Australian Masters, The Memorial Tournament 1990, Canadian Open 1992, British Open, Taiheyo Masters, Japan 1993, Johnnie Walker Asian Classic, The Players Championship 1994, Australian Open, Memorial Tournament, Canon Greater Hartford Open 1995, Doral-Ryder Open, SA Open 1996, World Championship, FedEx St Jude Classic 1997; apptd. Australian Amb. for Sport by Prime Minister 1998; inducted into World Golf Hall of Fame 2001. *Publications:* My Story 1983, Shark Attack 1988, Greg Norman's Better Golf 1994. *Leisure interests:* fishing, hunting, scuba diving. *Address:* Great White Shark Enterprise Inc., 501 North A1A, Jupiter, FL 33477, USA. *Website:* www.shark.com.

NORMAN, Jessye, M.MUS.; American concert and opera singer; b. 15 Sept. 1945, Augusta, Ga; d. of Silas Norman and Janie Norman (née King); ed Howard Univ., Washington, DC, Peabody Conservatory, Univ. of Michigan; Vocal Winner, Int. Musikwettbewerb, Bayerischer Rundfunk, Munich, Fed. Repub. of Germany 1968; operatic début Deutsche Oper Berlin 1969; début La Scala, Milan 1972, Royal Opera House, Covent Garden 1972; American operatic début, Hollywood Bowl 1972; performer Lincoln Centre 1973–; tours in N. and S. America, Europe, Middle East, Australia; int. festivals including Aix-en-Provence, Aldeburgh, Berliner Festwochen, Edin., Flanders, Helsinki, Lucerne, Salzburg, Tanglewood, Spoleto, Hollywood Bowl, Ravinia; with leading orchestras from USA, UK, Israel, Australia; Hon. Mus.Doc. (Howard) 1982, (Univ. of the South, Sewance) 1984, (Univ. of Mich.) 1987, (Edin.) 1989; Hon. DMus (Cambridge) 1989; Grand Prix du Disque (Acad. du Disque Français) 1973, 1976, 1977, 1982; Deutsche Schallplatten Preis für Euryanthe 1975; Cigale d'Or (Aix-en-Provence Festival) 1977; Grammy Award 1980, 1982, 1985, Musician of the Year (Musical America) 1982, IRCAM Record Award 1982, Alumna Award (Univ. of Michigan) 1982; Commdr, Ordre des Arts et des Lettres 1984. *Leisure interests:* reading, cooking, houseplant growing, fashion designing. *Address:* L'Orchidee, PO Box South, Crugers, NY 10521; Philips Records Polygram, 825 8th Avenue, New York, NY 10019, USA.

NORMAN, Marsha; American playwright; b. 21 Sept. 1947, Louisville; d. of Billie Williams and Bertha Conley; m. 1st Michael Norman (divorced 1974); m. 2nd Dann C. Byck Jr 1978 (divorced); m. 3rd. Timothy Dykman; one s. one d.; ed Agnes Scott Coll. and Univ. of Louisville; Rockefeller playwright-in-residence grantee 1979–80; American Acad. and Inst. for Arts and Letters grantee; Pulitzer Prize for Drama 1983; Tony Award 1991; many other awards and prizes. *Publications:* plays: Getting Out 1977, Third and Oak 1978, Circus Valentine 1979, The Holdup 1980, 'Night, Mother 1982, Traveler in the Dark 1984, Sarah and Abraham 1987, Four Plays by Marsha Norman (collection) 1988, D. Boone 1992, Loving Daniel Boone 1992, Trudy Blue 1995; The Secret Garden (book of musical lyrics) 1991; TV plays: It's the Willingness 1978, In Trouble at Fifteen 1980, The Laundromat 1985, Third and Oak: The Pool Hall 1989, Face of a Stranger 1991; The Fortune Teller (novel) 1987;

books of musicals and lyrics; The Secret Garden 1991, The Red Shoes 1992. *Address:* c/o Jack Tantleff, 375 Greenwich Street, Suite 700, New York, NY 10013, USA.

NORODOM RANARIDDH, Prince; Cambodian politician; b. 2 Jan. 1944; s. of King Norodom Sihanouk; m. 1968; two s. one d.; Pres. United Nat. Front for an Ind., Neutral, Peaceful and Co-operative Cambodia (FUNCINPEC); Co-Chair. Provisional Nat. Govt of Cambodia, also Minister of Nat. Defence, Interior and Nat. Security June–Sept. 1993; mem. Nat. Ass. May 1993–; Co-Prime Minister and mem. Throne Council Sept.–Oct. 1993; First Prime Minister of Royal Govt of Cambodia 1993–97; Chair. Nat. Devt Council 1993–97; found guilty of conspiracy with Khmer Rouges to overthrow the Govt, sentenced to 30 years imprisonment; in exile; returned from exile May 1998; Prof. of Public Law. *Leisure interest:* aviation.

NORODOM SIHANOUK, Samdech Preah, King of Cambodia; b. 31 Oct. 1922, Phnom Penh; s. of the late King Norodom Suramarit and Queen Kossamak Nearireath; m. Princess Monique; fourteen c. (six deceased); ed Chasseloup-Labaut High School, Saigon (now Ho Chi Minh City), Viet Nam, School of Instruction, Army Cavalry and Armoured Div., Saumur, France; mil. training in Saumur, France; elected King by Council of the Crown April 1941, claimed and obtained independence of Cambodia from France 1952–53, abdicated in favour of his father HM Norodom Suramarit March 1955, granted rank of Samdech and title of Upayuvareach of Cambodia; f. Sangkum Reastr Niyum (People's Socialist Community) 1955, (Leader 1955–70), won 82% of vote at legislative elections 1955; Prime Minister and Minister of Foreign Affairs Oct. 1955, March 1956, Sept. 1956, April 1957; Co-Founder Movt of Non-aligned Countries 1956; Perm. Rep. to UN Feb.-Sept. 1956; elected Head of State after death of his father 1960, took oath of fidelity to vacant throne 1960, deposed while on official visit to Soviet Union by forces of Lon Nol and Siri Matak March 1970; became Pres. Cambodian Resistance (FUNC – Nat. United Front of Cambodia) March 1970; resided in Peking (now Beijing), People's Repub. of China; est. Royal Govt of Nat. Union of Cambodia (GRUNC) May 1970; restored as Head of State (Pres.) of Democratic Kampuchea when FUNC forces overthrew Khmer Repub. April 1975, resgnd April 1976; Special Envoy of Khmer Rouge to UN 1979; f. Nat. United Front for an Ind., Neutral, Peaceful Co-operative Kampuchea 1981–89; Head of State in exile of Govt of Democratic Kampuchea and Head Cambodian Nat. Resistance 1982–88, 1989–90; in exile 13 years, returned to Cambodia Oct. 1991; Chair. Supreme Nat. Council 1991–93; Pres. of Cambodia 1991–93; crowned King of Cambodia Sept. 1993–; C-in-C of Armed Forces June 1993–; musician and composer; producer of films including Le Petit Prince. *Publications:* L'Indochine vue de Pékin (with Jean Lacouture) 1972, My War With the C.I.A. (with Wilfred Burchett) 1973, War and Hope: The Case for Cambodia 1980, Souvenirs doux et amers 1981, Prisonnier des Khmers Rouges 1986, Charisme et Leadership 1989. *Leisure interests:* badminton, film making in DPR Korea, French style cooking in Beijing. *Address:* Khemarindra Palace, Phnom Penh, Cambodia.

NORRBACK, Johan Ole; Finnish politician; b. 18 March 1941, Overmark; m. Vivi-Ann Lindqvist 1959; teacher 1966–67; Dist Sec. Swedish People's Party in Ostrobothnia 1967–71; Exec. Man. Provincial Union of Swedish Ostrobothnia 1971–91; Political Sec. to Minister of Communications 1976–77; mem. Parl. 1979–87, 1991–99; mem. Exec. Cttee Swedish People's Party 1983–, Chair. 1990–99; Minister of Defence 1987–90, of Educ. and Science 1990–91, of Transport and Communications 1991–95, for Europe and Foreign Trade 1995–99; Amb. to Norway 1999–. *Address:* Embassy of Finland, Thomas Heftyesgt. 1, 0244 Oslo, Norway. *Telephone:* 22-12-49-00. *Fax:* 22-12-49-49. *E-mail:* finland@online.no. *Website:* www.finland.no.

NORRINGTON, Sir Roger Arthur Carver, Kt, OBE; British conductor; b. 16 March 1934; s. of Sir Arthur Norrington and Edith Joyce Carver; m. 1st Susan Elizabeth McLean May 1964 (divorced 1982); one s. one d.; m. 2nd Karalyn Mary Lawrence 1986; one s.; ed Dragon School, Oxford, Westminster School, Clare Coll. Cambridge, Royal Coll. of Music; freelance singer 1962–72; Prin. Conductor, Kent Opera 1966–84; Guest Conductor many British and European orchestras, appearances BBC Promenade Concerts and City of London, Bath, Aldeburgh, Edin. and Harrogate festivals; regular broadcasts UK, Europe, USA; Prin. Conductor Bournemouth Sinfonietta 1985–89; Assoc. Chief Guest Conductor London Philharmonic Orchestra 1993–; Chief Conductor South German Radio Orchestra 1997–, Camerata Academica Salzburg 1997–; conductor Radio Sinfonie Orchester, Stuttgart 1998–; Musical Dir London Classical Players 1978–97, London Baroque Players 1975–, Schütz Choir of London 1962, Orchestra of St Lukes, NY 1990–94; Co.-Dir Early Opera Project 1984–, Historic Arts 1986–; many gramophone recordings; Hon. DMus (Kent) 1994; Cavaliere, Ordine al Merito della Repubblica Italiana, Ehrenkreuz Erster Klasse (Austia) 1999. *Leisure interests:* reading, walking, sailing.

NORRIS, David Owen, MA, FRCO, FRAM; British pianist and broadcaster; b. 16 June 1953, Northampton; s. of Albert Norris and Margaret Norris; two s.; ed Keble Coll. Oxford and Royal Acad. of Music; Prof. Royal Acad. of Music 1977–89; Dir Petworth Festival 1986–92; Artistic Dir Cardiff Festival 1992–95; Gresham Prof. of Music 1993–97; Prof. Royal Coll. of Music 2000–; Chair. Steans Inst. for Singers, Chicago 1992–98; Research Fellow Southampton Univ. 2000–; First Gilmore Artist Award 1991. *Recordings:* CDs of Elgar's complete piano music and the world's first piano concertos. *Achievements:* gave world premières of Schubert's First Song Cycle and Elgar's Piano

Concerto. *Leisure interests:* naval and detective fiction. *Address:* 17 Manor Road, Andover, Hants., SP10 3JS, England. *Telephone:* (1264) 355409. *Website:* davidowennorris.co.uk.

NORRIS, Steve; British film producer; fmrly with Rank Org.; fmr exec. Columbia Pictures, Warner Brothers, Enigma, USA; fmr Vice-Pres. Producers' Alliance for Cinema and TV, Chair. Film Cttee; British Film Commr 1998–2000; several awards, including Golden Globe for The Burning Season. *Films include:* Memphis Belle, Being Human, War of the Buttons, The Burning Season, Le Confessionnal, My Life So Far.

NORRIS, Steven, MA; British politician; b. 24 May 1945, Liverpool; s. of John Francis Birkett and Eileen Winifred Walsh; m. 1st Peta Veronica Cecil-Gibson 1969 (divorced); two s.; m. 2nd Emma Courtney 2000; one s.; ed Liverpool Inst. High School, Worcester Coll., Oxford; Berks. Co. Councillor 1977–85; various man. positions in industry –1983; Chair. Abingdon Conservative Asscn 1979; MP for Oxford E 1983–87, for Epping Forest 1988–97; Parl. Pvt. Sec. to William Waldegrave, Minister of State, Dept of Environment 1985–87, to Nicholas Ridley, Sec. of State for Trade and Industry 1990, to Kenneth Baker, Home Sec. 1991–92; Minister for Transport in London 1992–96; Dir.-Gen. Road Haulage Asscn 1997–99; Conservative Cand. for Mayoralty of London 2000; Vice-Chair. Conservative Party 2000–01; Fellow Chartered Inst. of Transport, Inst. of Highways and Transportation; Freeman of the City of London, Liveryman of the Worshipful Co. of Coachmen and Coach Harness Makers, Trustee London Action Trust; mem. Bd Transport for London –2001. *Publication:* Changing Train 1996. *Leisure interests:* football, opera, reading. *Address:* Citigate Public Affairs, 26 Grosvenor Gardens, London, SW1W 0GT, England (Office).

NORSHTEIN, Yuri Borisovich; Russian film director, animator and scriptwriter; b. 15 Sept. 1941, Andreyevka, Penza Region; s. of Berko Leibovich Norshtein and Basya Girshevna Krichevskaya; m. Francesca Alfredovna Yarbusova; one s. one d.; ed Soyuzmultfilmstudio courses; debut as film dir The 25th is the First Day 1968 (co-dir with Arkady Tyurin); cutout film Battle at Kerzhenets 1971 (co-dir with I. Ivanov-Vano); later with his wife (art dir Yarbusova): Fox and Hare 1973, Heron and Crane 1974, Hedgehog in Mist 1975, The Tale of Tales 1979, Great Coat 2002; Tale of Tales voted best animated film of all time 1984 in int. survey, LA Animation Olympiad; Tarkovsky Prize 1989; Grand Prix Zagreb Animation Festival 1980; USSR State Prize 1979, Triumph Prize 1995. *Address:* Butlerov str. 4, korp. 2, Apt. 88, 117485 Moscow, Russia (Home). *Telephone:* (095) 335-08-21 (Home).

NORTH, Alastair Macarthur, OBE, PhD, DSc; British professor of chemistry (retd); b. 2 April 1932, Aberdeen; s. of Norman R. North and Anne North; m. Charlotte Muriel Begg 1957; two s. two d.; ed Univs. of Aberdeen and Birmingham; Lecturer, Dept of Inorganic, Physical and Industrial Chem., Univ. of Liverpool; apptd. to Burmah Chair of Physical Chem., Univ. of Strathclyde 1967, subsequently Dean of School of Chemical and Materials Science, then Vice-Prin. of the Univ.; Pres. Asian Inst. of Tech. 1983–96; mem. several nat. cttees on formation of science policy; ScD hc (Politechnika Lodzka); Hon. PhD (Ramkhamhaeng Univ.); DUniv hc (Strathclyde); Dr hc (Inst. Nat. Polytechnique de Toulouse), DTech. hc (AIT), LLD hc (Aberdeen); Commdr des Palmes académiques; Commdr Order of King Leopold II (Belgium); Prasidda Prabala Gorkha Dakshin Bahu (Nepal). *Leisure interests:* golf, scuba diving. *Address:* 79/78 Soi 7/1 Mooban Tararom, Ramkhamhaeng Soi 150, Sapansoong, Bangkok 10240, Thailand. *Telephone:* (2) 373-2818. *Fax:* (2) 373-3052.

NORTH, Douglass Cecil, PhD; American professor of economics; b. 5 Nov. 1920, Cambridge, Mass.; s. of Henry North and Edith Saitta; m. Elisabeth Willard Case 1972; three s. by previous m.; ed Univ. of Calif. at Berkeley; Asst Prof. Univ. of Washington 1950–56, Assoc. Prof. 1957–60, Prof. of Econs 1960–63, Prof. Emer. 1983–, Chair. Dept of Econs 1967–79; Dir Inst. of Econ. Research 1960–66, Nat. Bureau of Econ. Research 1967–87; Luce Prof. of Law and Liberty, Prof. of Econs Washington Univ. St Louis 1983–, Olin Prof. in Arts and Sciences 1996–; Pitt Prof. of American History and Inst. Cambridge Univ. 1981–82; mem. Bradley Foundation 1986–; Fellow, Center for Advanced Study on Behavioral Sciences 1987–88; Guggenheim Fellow 1972–73; Fellow, American Acad. of Arts and Sciences; mem. American Econ. Asscn, Econ. History Asscn; Dr. rer. pol. hc (Cologne) 1988, (Zürich) 1993, (Stockholm School of Econs) 1994, (Prague School of Econs) 1995; shared Nobel Prize for Econs 1993. *Publications:* The Economic Growth of the U.S. 1790–1860 1961, Growth and Welfare in the American Past 1971, Institutional Change and American Economic Growth (with L. Davis) 1971, The Economics of Public Issues (with R. Miller) 1971, The Rise of the Western World (with R. Thomas) 1973, Structure and Change in Economic History 1981, Institutions, Institutional Change and Economic Performance 1990. *Address:* Washington University, Campus Box 1208, St Louis, MO 63130, USA.

NORTH, John David, MA, BSc, DPhil, DLitt, FBA; British professor of the history of philosophy and the exact sciences; b. 19 May 1934, Cheltenham; s. of J. E North and G. A. North; m. Marion J. Pizzey; one s. two d.; ed Merton Coll. Oxford and Univ. of London; Nuffield Foundation Research Fellow Univ. of Oxford 1963–68, Museum of History of Science, Univ. of Oxford 1968–77; Visiting Prof. of History of Science, Aarhus Univ. 1974, Prof. of the History of Philosophy and the Exact Sciences, Univ. of Groningen, 1977–99, Prof. Emer. 1999–; Visiting Prof. Univs. in Germany, Denmark and USA; Dean of the Cen. Interfaculty 1981–84, 1991–93; Sec. Perpétuel, Acad. int. d'histoire

des sciences, Paris 1983–89, Hon. Sec. Perpétuel 1990–; mem. Royal Netherlands Acad. (mem. Council 1990–93), Deutsche Akad. der Naturforscher Leopoldina; Foreign mem. Royal Danish Acad.; Corresp. Fellow, British Acad. 1992–2001, Ordinary Fellow 2001–; Koyré Medal, Acad. Int. d'Histoire des Sciences 1989; Kt Order of the Netherlands Lion 1999. *Publications:* The Measure of the Universe 1965, Richard of Wallingford (3 Vols) 1976, The Light of Nature (Ed.) 1985, Horoscopes and History 1986, Chaucer's Universe 1988, Stars, Minds and Fate 1989, The Universal Frame 1989, The Fontana History of Astronomy 1994, Stonehenge: Neolithic Man and the Cosmos 1996, The Ambassadors' Secret: Holbein and the World of the Renaissance 2002. *Leisure interest:* archaeology. *Address:* 28 Chalfont Road, Oxford, OX2 6TH, England. *Telephone:* (1865) 558458.

NORTH, Oliver L.; American marine officer; b. 7 Oct. 1943, San Antonio, Texas; s. of Oliver Clay North and Ann North; m.; c.; ed U.S. Naval Coll., Annapolis; joined marines, platoon Commdr Viet Nam; marine instructor 1969; leader marine mission, Turkey 1980; mem. Nat. Security Council as Deputy Dir for Political Mil. Affairs 1981–86; dismissed Nov. 1986 because of involvement with secret operation to sell arms to Iran and the diversion of proceeds from the sales to aid anti-Govt "Contra" guerrillas in Nicaragua; rank of Lt-Col 1983, retd from Marines 1988; on trial Feb. 1989, found guilty on three counts May 1989, appeal court reversed one count 1990, three convictions set aside 1990; cleared of all charges 1991; Head V-PAC (political action group); own radio show 1995–; Dr. hc (Liberty Univ.) 1988. *Publication:* Under Fire: An American Story 1991.

NORTH, Sir Peter Machin, Kt, CBE, QC, MA, DCL, FBA; British academic; b. 30 Aug. 1936, Nottingham; s. of Geoffrey Machin North and Freda Brunt North (née Smith); m. Stephanie Mary Chadwick 1960; two s. one d.; ed Oakham School, Rutland, Keble Coll. Oxford; Teaching Assoc., Northwestern Univ. Law School, Chicago 1960–61; Lecturer, Univ. Coll. of Wales, Aberystwyth 1961–63, Univ. of Nottingham 1964–65; Fellow and Tutor in Law, Keble Coll. Oxford 1965–76; Chair., Faculty of Law, Univ. of Oxford 1971–75; Prin. Jesus Coll. Oxford 1984–; Pro-Vice-Chancellor, Oxford 1988–93, 1997–, Vice-Chancellor 1993–97; Ed. Oxford Journal of Legal Studies 1987–92; Law Commr for England and Wales 1976–84; mem. Lord Chancellor's Advisory Cttee on Legal Educ. 1973–75, Council of Man., British Inst. of Int. and Comparative Law 1976–, Econ. and Social Research Council Cttees. 1982–87, Council, Univ. of Reading 1986–89; Chair. Conciliation Advisory Cttee 1985–88, Road Traffic Law Review 1985–88, Ind. Review of Parades and Marches in Northern Ireland 1996–97, Ind. Cttee for Supervision of Standards of Telephone Information Services; Hon. Bencher, Inner Temple; mem. Inst. de droit int.; Hon. Fellow, Keble Coll. Oxford, Univ. Coll. of N. Wales, Bangor, Trinity Coll., Carmarthen, Univ. of Wales, Aberystwyth; Hon. LLD (Reading) 1992, (Nottingham) 1996, (Aberdeen) 1997, (New Brunswick) 2002. *Publications:* Occupier's Liability 1971, Modern Law of Animals 1972, Chitty on Contracts (ed.) 1968–89, Private International Law of Matrimonial Causes 1977, Contract Conflicts (ed.) 1982, Cases and Materials on Private International Law (with J.H.C. Morris) 1984, Cheshire and North's Private International Law (ed.) 1970–99, Private International Law Problems in Common Law Jurisdictions 1993, Essays in Private International Law 1993. *Address:* Jesus College, Oxford, OX1 3DW, England. *Telephone:* (1865) 279701. *Fax:* (1865) 279696. *E-mail:* principal@jesus.ox.ac.uk (Office).

NORTHCOTE, Donald Henry, DS, FRS; British plant biochemist; b. 27 Dec. 1921, Plymouth; s. of F. Northcote and F. Corbin; m. Eva Marjorie Mayo 1948; two d.; ed Univs. of London and Cambridge; Demonstrator in Biochem., Univ. of Cambridge 1948, Prof. of Plant Biochem. 1972–, Master of Sidney Sussex Coll. 1976–92; Fellow St John's Coll. Cambridge 1960, now Fellow Emer.; Hon. Fellow, Downing Coll. Cambridge 1979; Ciba Medal, Biochemical Soc. *Publications:* 300 papers on plant cell growth and differentiation 1948–. *Leisure interests:* sailing, reading and computing. *Address:* 100 North Street, Burwell, Cambridge, CB5 0BB, England. *Telephone:* (1638) 743924. *E-mail:* dhn21@cam.ac.uk (Home).

NORTON, Edward, BA; American actor; b. 18 Aug. 1969, Boston, Mass.; s.of Edward Norton and the late Robin Norton (née Rouse); ed Wilde Lake High School, MD, Yale Univ., CT, Columbia School for Theatrical Arts, MD; fmr consultant Enterprise Foundation, Osaka, Japan, currently mem. Nat. Bd; mem. Signature Theatre Repertory Co. 1994–, performed in the premiere of Edward Albee's Fragments, mem. Bd 1996–. *Films include:* Primal Fear (Golden Globe, Best Supporting Actor) 1996, Everyone Says I LoveYou 1996, The People Vs. Larry Flint 1996, American History X 1998, Rounders 1998, Fight Club 1999, Keeping the Faith (also dir and producer), The Score, Death to Smoochy, Red Dragon 2002, The 25th Hour 2001, Frida 2002 (also co-wrote screenplay). *Address:* c/o Endeavor Talent Agency, 9701 Wiltshire Boulevard, 10th Floor, Beverly Hills, CA 90210, USA (Office).

NORTON, Gale Ann, BA, JD; American politician and lawyer; b. 11 March 1954, Wichita, Kan.; d. of Dale Bentsen Norton and Anna Jacqueline Norton (née Lansdowne); m. John Goethe Hughes 1990; ed Univ. of Denver; lawyer Colo. 1978, U.S. Supreme Court 1981; judicial clerk Colo. Court of Appeals 1978–79 Sr. Attorney, Mountain States Legal Foundation 1979–83; Nat. Fellow, Hoover Inst., Stanford Univ. 1983–84; Asst. to Deputy Sec., USDA 1984–85; Assoc. Solicitor, Dept. of Interior 1985–87; pvt. law practice 1987–90; Attorney-Gen., Colo. 1991–99; attorney, Brownstein, Hyatt & Farber, P.C., Sr. Counsel 1999–2001; Sec. of the Interior Jan. 2001–; Transportation Law Program Dir., Univ. of Denver 1978–79; lecturer, Univ. of

Denver Law School 1989; Past Chair. Nat. Asscn. of Attorneys Environmental Cttee.; Co.-Chair Nat. Policy Forum Environmental Council; Chair. Environmental Comm. of Republican Nat. Lawyers Asscn.; Policy Analyst, Presidential Council on Environmental Quality 1985–88; Young Lawyer of the Year 1991, Mary Traiblazer Award, Col Women's Bar Asscn 1999. *Leisure interest:* skiing. *Address:* Department of the Interior, 1849 C Street, NW, Washington, DC 20240, U.S.A. (Office). *Telephone:* (202) 208-3171 (Office). *Fax:* (202) 208-5048 (Office). *Website:* www.usgs.-doi.gov.

NORTON, Hugh Edward, BA; British business executive; b. 23 June 1936, London; s. of Lt-Gen. Edward F. Norton and I. Joyce Norton; m. 1st Janet M. Johnson 1965 (died 1993); one s.; m. 2nd F. Joy Harcup 1998; ed Winchester Coll., Trinity Coll. Oxford; joined British Petroleum Co. 1959, Exploration Dept 1960, in Abu Dhabi, Lebanon and Libya 1962–70, subsequently held appointments. in Supply, Cen. Planning, Policy Planning, Regional Directorate Middle East and Int. and Govt Affairs depts.; Man. Dir BP's assoc. cos., Singapore, Malaysia, Hong Kong 1978–81, Dir of Planning 1981–83, Regional Dir for Near East, Middle East and Indian sub-continent 1981–86, Dir of Admin. 1983–86, Man. Dir and CEO BP Exploration Co. 1986–89, Chair. 1989–95, Man. Dir The British Petroleum Co. PLC 1989–95; Chair. BP Asia Pacific Pvt. Co. Ltd 1991–95; Dir Inchcape PLC 1995–, Standard Chartered PLC 1995–, Lasmo PLC 1997–; mem. Council Royal Inst. of Econ. Affairs 1991–. *Leisure interests:* painting, ornithology, tennis, travel. *Address:* c/o BP Asia Pacific Pte Ltd, BP Tower, 25th Storey, 396 Alexandra Road, Singapore 0511.

NORVIK, Harald; Norwegian administrator and executive; b. 21 June 1946, Vadsø; ed Norwegian School of Econs and Business Admin., Bergen; Adviser, Nat. Inst. of Tech. 1971–73; Group Sec. for Industrial and Financial Affairs 1973–75; Trainee course Ministry of Foreign Affairs 1975–76; Personal Sec. to Prime Minister 1976–79; Minister of Petroleum and Energy 1979–81; Dir of Finance Aker mek. Verksted A/S 1981–85, Sr Exec. Vice-Pres. 1985–86; Pres. Astrup Hoyer A/S 1986–87; now Pres. and Chair. Exec. Bd Statoil Group; alternating Chair. Bd Dirs. SAS Norge A.S.A., Scandinavian Airlines System (S.A.S.); Chair. Supervisory Bd Den Norske Bank; mem. Bd Orkla Borregaard A.S., Supervisory Council Nycomed A.S.A.; Commdr Order of the Lion of Finland (1st Class), Grosses Bundesverdienstkreuz.

NORWICH, 2nd Viscount, cr. 1952, of Aldwick; **John Julius Cooper,** CVO, FRSL, FRGS; British author and broadcaster; b. 15 Sept. 1929; s. of 1st Viscount Norwich, PC, GCMG, DSO and of the late Lady Diana Cooper; m. 1st Anne Clifford 1952 (divorced 1985); one s. one d.; m. 2nd Mollie Philipps 1989; ed Upper Canada Coll. Toronto, Eton Coll., Univ. of Strasbourg and New Coll. Oxford; entered Foreign Office 1952; Third Sec. Belgrade 1955–57; Second Sec. Beirut 1957–60; Foreign Office and British del. to Disarmament Conf. Geneva 1960–64; Chair. British Theatre Museum 1966–71, Venice in Peril Fund 1970–99, World Monuments Fund in Britain 1994–; mem. Exec. Cttee Nat. Trust 1969–95; mem. Franco-British Council 1972–79; mem. Bd English Nat. Opera 1977–81; Ed. New Shell Guides to Britain 1987–91; Dir Robclif Productions Ltd 1991–94; has made some 30 documentary films for TV, mainly on history and architecture; Commendatore, Ordine al Merito della Repubblica Italiana. *Publications:* (as John Julius Norwich): Mount Athos (with R. Sitwell) 1966, The Normans in the South 1967, Sahara 1968, The Kingdom in the Sun 1970, A History of Venice (Vol. I) 1977, (Vol. II) 1981, Christmas Crackers 1970–79 1980, Britain's Heritage (ed.) 1982, The Italian World (ed.) 1983, Fifty Years of Glyndebourne 1985, A Taste for Travel (anthology) 1985, Great Architecture of the World (general ed.) 1975, The Architecture of Southern England 1985, Byzantium, the Early Centuries 1988, More Christmas Crackers 1980–89 1990, Venice: a Traveller's Companion 1990, Byzantium: The Apogee 1991, Byzantium: Decline and Fall 1995, Shakespeare's Kings 1999, Still More Christmas Crackers 1990–99 2000. *Leisure interests:* sight-seeing, walking at night through Venice, nightclub piano. *Address:* 24 Blomfield Road, London, W9 1AD, England. *Telephone:* (20) 7286-5050. *Fax:* (20) 7266-2561. *E-mail:* jjnorwich@dial.pipex.com (Home).

NORWOOD, Mandi; British magazine editor; b. 9 Oct. 1963, Oldham, Lancs.; m. Martin Kelly 1995; two d.; ed Lord Lawson Comprehensive School, Park View Grammar School, Darlington Coll. of Tech. and London Coll. of Fashion; Sub-Ed. then Deputy Chief Sub Look Now magazine 1984–86; freelance journalist 1986–87; Features Ed. Clothes Show magazine Aug.–Oct. 1987; Deputy Ed. More! magazine 1987–89; Ed. Looks magazine 1989–90, Company magazine 1990–95, Cosmopolitan 1995–2000; Ed.-in-Chief Mademoiselle, New York 2000–01; mem. British Soc. of Magazine Eds. 1990; mem. Periodical Publrs. Asscn Editorial Cttee; Women's Magazine Ed. of the Year Award, British Soc. of Magazine Eds. 1993, 1999. *Address:* Condé Nast Publications Inc., 4 Times Square, New York, NY 10036 (Office); 312 East 69th Street, New York, NY 10021, USA (Home).

NOSIGLIA, Enrique; Argentine politician; b. 28 May 1949, Posadas; m. Nina Ciarlotti; four c.; ed Universidad Nacional de Buenos Aires; joined Unión Cívica Radical 1972; mem. Nat. Exec. Movimiento de Renovación y Cambio 1975–80; Sec. Comité de la Capital (Wealth) 1983–87, Pres. 1987; Under-Sec. for Health and Social Affairs, Ministry of Health and Social Affairs 1983–85; Sec. Exec. Comm. Programa Alimentario Nacional (PAN) 1983–85; mem. Consejo para la Consolidación de la Democracia 1986; Minister of the Interior 1987–89; Sec. for Institutional Relations, Unión Cívica Radical.

NOSSAL, Sir Gustav Joseph Victor, AC, CBE, MB, BS, PhD, FRCP, FRACP, FRCPA, FRCPath, FRSE, FTSE, FAA, FRS; Australian medical research scientist; b. 4 June 1931, Bad Ischl, Austria; s. of R. I. Nossal and I. M. C. Lowenthal; m. Lyn B. Dunnicliff 1955; two s. two d.; ed St Aloysius Coll., Sydney, Univs. of Sydney and Melbourne; jr and sr resident officer, Royal Prince Alfred Hosp., Sydney 1955–56; Research Fellow, The Walter and Eliza Hall Inst. of Medical Research, Melbourne 1957–59; Asst Prof., Dept of Genetics, Stanford Univ. School of Medicine, Calif. 1959–61; Deputy Dir (Immunology), The Walter and Eliza Hall Inst. of Medical Research 1961–65, Dir 1965–96; Prof. of Medical Biology, Univ. of Melbourne 1965–96, Prof. Emer., Dept of Pathology 1996–; Chair. WHO Global Programme for Vaccines and Immunization 1992–; Partner Foursight Assocs. Pty Ltd 1996–; Dir, CRA Ltd 1977–97; Pres. Australian Acad. of Science 1994–98; Foreign Assoc. NAS (USA); mem. or hon. mem. many other nat. and foreign acads. and learned socs.; Hon. FRACOG; Hon. LLD (Monash, Melbourne); Hon. MD (Mainz, Newcastle, Leeds, Univ. W.A.); Hon. DSc (Sydney, Queensland, ANU, Univ. NSW, La Trobe, McMaster); Robert Koch Gold Medal, Albert Einstein World Award of Science, Emil von Behring Prize, Rabbi Shai Shacknai Prize and many other awards and prizes. *Publications:* Antibodies and Immunity 1968, Antigens, Lymphoid Cells and Immune Response 1971, Medical Science and Human Goals 1975, Nature's Defences (1978 Boyer Lectures), Reshaping Life: Key issues in Genetic Engineering 1984; 500 publications on immunity. *Leisure interests:* golf, literature. *Address:* Department of Pathology, University of Melbourne, Parkville, Vic. 3010 (Office); 46 Fellows Street, Kew, Vic. 3101, Australia (Home). *Telephone:* (3) 8344-6946 (Office). *Fax:* (3) 9347-5242 (Office).

NOSSOL, Archbishop Alfons, PhD; Polish ecclesiastic and professor of theology; b. 8 Aug. 1932, Brożec, Opole Prov.; ed Higher Ecclesiastical Seminary in Opole Silesia, Catholic Univ. of Lublin (KUL); Asst Prof. 1976, Prof. 1981; ordained Priest, Opole 1957; Lecturer Higher Ecclesiastical Seminary in Opole Silesia 1962–; lecturer Catholic Univ. of Lublin 1968, Head Second Dept of Dogmatic Theology 1977, Prof. 1981, Head Ecumenical Inst. 1983; Prof. Theological Dept Jan Gutenberg Univ., Mainz 1977; Prof. Pontifical Theology Dept, Wrocław 1978; Prof. Diocesan Theology and Pastoral Inst., Opole 1981; Ordinary Bishop Opole Diocese 1977–; Archbishop ad personam 1999; High Chancellor and Prof. Opole Univ. Theological Dept 1994–; mem. Main Council of the Polish Episcopate; mem. Scientific Council of the Episcopate of Poland; Chair. Episcopate Cttee for Ecumenism; Vice-Leader Episcopate Cttee for Catholic Learning; mem. Christian Unity Pontifical Council, int. cttees for theological dialogue with the Orthodox Church and the Lutheran Church; mem. European Acad. of Science and Art, Salzburg; Dr. hc (Munster Univ.) 1991, (Mainz Univ.) 1992, (Opole Univ.) 1995, (Christian Acad. of Theology, Warsaw) 1997, (Bamberg Univ.)1998, (Olomuniec Univ.) 2000; Augsburger Friedenspreis 1997, Kulturpreis Schlesien des Landes Niedersachsen 2001. *Publications:* Theology for the Service of Faith 1968, Cognito Dei experimentalis 1974, Karol Barth Christology 1979, Truth and Love 1982, Towards a Civilization of Love 1984, Theology Closer to Life 1984, Der Mensch braucht Theologie 1986, Love the Victor of Truth 1987, Gelebte Theologie Heute 1991, By Truth to Love 1994, Love Rejoices Together with Truth 1996, Ecumenism as Imperative of Christian Conscience 2001, Brücken bauen Wege zu einem christlichen Europa von Morgen 2002. *Leisure interests:* classical literature, philosophy, the history of art. *Address:* Kuria Diecezjalna, ul. Książat Opolskich 19, 45-005 Opole, Poland. *Telephone:* (77) 454-24-18. *Fax:* (77) 453-79-61. *E-mail:* kuria@diecezja.opole.pl.

NOTAT, Amélie; Belgian author; b. 1967, Kobe, Japan; d. of Patrick Nothomb; ed Université Libre de Bruxelles; novel Fear and Trembling released as film 2002. *Publications include:* Hygiène de l'assassin 1992, Le Sabotage amoureux 1993, Les combustibles 1994, Les Catalinaires 1995, Péplum 1996, Attentat 1997, Mercure 1998, Stupeur et tremblements (Grand Prix du Roman, Académie française) 1999, Métaphysique des tubes 2000, The Character of Rain, Robert des Noms Propres. *Address:* c/o Editions Albin Michel, 22 rue Huyhens, 75014 Paris, France (Office).

NOTE, Kessai H.; Marshall Islands politician; b. 7 Aug. 1950, Ailinglablab Atoll; m. Mary Note; five c.; fmr Speaker of Nitijela (Parl.); mem. United Democratic Party (UDP); Pres. of the Marshall Islands Jan. 2000–. *Address:* Office of the President, P.O. Box 2, Majuro, MH 96960, Marshall Islands. *Telephone:* (625) 3445. *Fax:* (625) 4021. *E-mail:* presoff@ntamar.com (Office).

NÖTH, Heinrich; German university professor; b. 20 June 1928, Munich; s. of Hans Nöth and Eugenie Nöth; m. 1951; two d.; ed Univ. of Munich; Scientific Asst Univ. of Munich 1952–55, 1957–62, Research Officer 1956, Lecturer 1962–64, Assoc. Prof. 1964–65, Prof. 1965–, Head Inst. of Inorganic Chem. 1969–97, Prof. Emer. 1997–; Pres. German Chemical Soc. 1988–89, 1991–92, Hon. mem.; Pres. Bavarian Acad. of Sciences 1998–2000; Foreign mem. Russian Acad. of Sciences, Mexican Acad. of Sciences; Corresp. mem. Acad. of Sciences, Göttingen; Hon. mem. Austrian Chemical Soc., Royal Soc. of Chem.; Dr hc (Marburg); DSc hc (Leeds); Alfred Stock Medal, IMEBORON Award; Bavarian Order of Maximilian for Science and Art. *Publications:* Nuclear Magnetic Resonance of Boron Compounds and more than 780 original research papers. *Leisure interests:* hiking, gardening, music. *Address:* Department of Chemistry, University of Munich, Butenandt str. 5-13, 81377 Munich (Office); Eichleite 25A, 82031 Grünwald, Germany. *Telephone:* (89) 21807454 (Office). *Fax:* (89) 21807455 (Office). *E-mail:* H.Noeth@lrz .uni-muenchen.de (Office).

NOTT, Rt Hon. Sir John William Frederic, KCB, PC, BA; British fmr politician and business executive; b. 1 Feb. 1932; s. of Richard Nott and Phyllis Nott (née Francis); m. Miloska Sekol 1959; two s. one d.; ed Bradfield Coll. and Trinity Coll. Cambridge; Lt with 2nd Gurkha Rifles, (regular officer) 1952–56; called to the Bar, Inner Temple 1959; MP for St Ives, Cornwall 1966–83; Minister of State at Treasury 1972–74; Sec. of State for Trade 1979–81, for Defence 1981–83; Man. Dir Lazard Brothers 1983–90, Chair. and CEO 1985–90; Chair. Hillsdown Holdings PLC (now Hillsdown Holdings Ltd.) 1993–99 (Dir 1991–), Maple Leaf Foods Inc., Toronto 1993–95; Deputy Chair. Royal Insurance PLC 1986–89; Chair. (non-exec.) Etam 1991–95; Dir Apax Partners & Co. Capital 1996–, Apax Partners & Co. Asset Man. Ltd 1997–; Pres. Cambridge Union 1959. *Publication:* Here Today, Gone Tomorrow. *Leisure interests:* farming, fishing, golf. *Address:* 31 Walpole Street, London, SW3 4QS, England. *Telephone:* (20) 7730-2351. *Fax:* (20) 7730-9859.

NOTT, Rt Rev Peter John, MA; British ecclesiastic; b. 30 Dec. 1933, Belfast; s. of Cecil Frederick Wilder Nott and Rosina Mabel Nott; m. Elizabeth May Maingot 1961; one s. three d.; ed Bristol Grammar School, Dulwich Coll., London, RMA Sandhurst and Fitzwilliam House and Westcott House, Cambridge; served in regular army, commissioned RA 1951–55; Curate of Harpenden 1961–64; Chaplain and Fellow of Fitzwilliam Coll. Cambridge 1966–69, Hon. Fellow 1993; Chaplain of New Hall, Cambridge 1966–69; Rector of Beaconsfield 1969–77; Bishop of Taunton 1977–85; Bishop of Norwich 1985–99; Asst Bishop, Diocese of Oxford 1999–; Archbishop's Adviser to HMC 1980–85; Vice-Chair. Archbishops' Comm. on Rural Areas 1988–90; Pres. SW Region of Mencap 1978–84, Somerset Rural Music School 1981–85, Royal Norfolk Agricultural Asscn 1996; Dean of the Priory of England, Order of St John 1999–2003; KStJ; Council of Nat. Army Museum 2001. *Publication:* Bishop Peter's Pilgrimage: His Diary and Sketchbook 1996. *Leisure Interests:* gardening, sketching, fishing. *Address:* 16 St. Joseph's Mews, Candlemas Lane, Beaconsfield, Bucks., HP9 1GA, England. *Telephone:* (1494) 678007.

NOUMAZALAY, Ambroise; Republic of the Congo politician; b. 23 Sept. 1933, Brazzaville; ed Mathematics Faculty Univ. of Toulouse, France; First Sec. Nat. Revolutionary Movt (MNR); Dir of Econ. Affairs 1964–66; mem. Nat. Revolutionary Council (CNR) and Sec. Org. Cttee of the CNR Aug.–Oct. 1968; Prime Minister and Minister of Planning 1966–68; Minister of State in charge of Planning Aug.-Dec. 1968, for Agric., Water Resources and Forests 1968–69; Second Sec. responsible for the Execution of the Plan 1970–71; sentenced to life imprisonment March 1972; gained amnesty Oct. 1973; Minister of Industry and Manufacturing 1984–85, of Industry and Fisheries 1985–88, of Crafts 1986–88, of Forestry 1988–89; fmr Sec. Gen. Parti congolais du travail (PCT). *Address:* Parti congolais du travail, Brazzaville, Republic of the Congo.

NOURBAKHSH, Mohsen, PhD; Iranian banker; b. 1948, Isfahan; s. of the late Hossein Nourbakhsh and of Heshmat Pasra Nourbakhsh; m. Moazzam Karbasizadeh 1976; two s. two d.; ed Univ. of Tehran, Univ. of Calif., USA; fmr Faculty mem. Shahid Beheshti Univ., Tehran; Deputy Minister of Econ. Affairs and Finance 1979–81, Minister 1989–93; Gov. Cen. Bank (Bank Markazi Johhouri Islami Iran) 1981–86, 1994–; MP 1988–89; Deputy to the Pres., Econ. Affairs 1993–94. *Leisure interest:* swimming. *Address:* Bank Markazi Johhouri Islami Iran, 23 Ferdowsi Avenue, P.O. Box 11365-8551, Tehran, Iran. *Telephone:* (21) 3110231. *Fax:* (21) 3115674. *E-mail:* g.secdept@cbi.gov.ir (Office). *Website:* www.cbi.iranet.net (Office).

NOURISSIER, François; French writer and journalist; b. 18 May 1927, Paris; s. of Paul E. E. Nourissier and Renée Heens; m. 1st Marie-Thérèse Sobesky 1949; two s.; m. 2nd Cécile Muhlstein 1962; one d.; ed Lycée St Louis, Lycée Louis-le-Grand, Paris, Ecole libre des Sciences Politiques, Paris and Faculté de Droit, Paris; mem. staff Secours Catholique Int. and worked with Int. Refugee Org. 1949–51; Dir Chalet Int. des Etudiants, Combloux (World Univ. Service) 1951–52; Sec.-Gen. Editions Denoël 1952–56; Ed.-in-Chief La Parisienne (review) 1956–58; Literary Adviser to Editions Grasset 1958–95; Literary Dir Vogue (French) 1964–66, Contributing Ed. Vogue (American) 1964–; Literary Critic Les Nouvelles littéraires 1963–72; Cinema Critic L'Express 1970–72; Literary Critic Le Point 1972–, Le Figaro 1975–, Figaro-Magazine 1978–; mem. l'Acad. Goncourt 1977, Sec.-Gen. 1983–96, Pres. 1996–2002; Prix Félix Fénéon 1952, Grand Prix de la Guilde du Livre 1965 (Swiss), Grand Prix du Roman de l'Acad. française 1966, Prix Fémina 1970, Prix Prince Pierre de Monaco 1975; Grand Prix de la Ville de Paris 1987, Prix Mondial Cino Del Duca 2002; Commdr, Légion d'honneur, Commdr, Ordre nat. du Mérite, Commdr des Arts et des Lettres. *Publications:* L'eau grise (novel) 1951, Lorca (essay) 1955, Les orphelins d'Auteuil (novel) 1956, Le corps de Diane (novel) 1957, Portrait d'un indifférent 1957, Bleu comme la nuit 1958, Un petit bourgeois 1964, Une histoire française 1966, Les Français (essay) 1967, Le maître de maison 1968, The French (trans. of Les Français) 1970, Cartier-Bresson's France 1971, La crève (novel) 1970, Allemande (novel) 1973, Lettre à mon chien (essay) 1975, Lettre ouverte à Jacques Chirac (essay) 1977, Le musée de l'homme (essay) 1979, L'empire des nuages (novel) 1981, La fête des pères (novel) 1986, En avant, calme et droit (novel) 1987, Bratislava (essay) 1990, Autos Graphie (essay) 1990, Le Gardien des ruines (novel) 1992, Mauvais genre (essay) 1994, Le Bar de l'escadrille (novel) 1997, Les Plus belles histoires d'amour (anthology) 1997, A défaut de génie (autobiog.) 2000. *Leisure interests:* walking, dogs. *Address:* Editions Grasset, 61 rue des Saints-Pères, 75006 Paris, France (Office); Gallimard, 5 rue Sébastien Bottin, 75007 Paris.

NOUVEL, Jean; French architect; b. 12 Aug 1945, Fumel, Lot-et-Garonne; s. of Roger Nouvel and Renée Barlangue; m. Catherine Richard 1992; one d. two s. by Odil Fillion; ed Ecole des Beaux Arts, Paris; first major bldg, medical centre, Bezons; began Nemausus housing projects, Nîmes 1985; Hon. Prof. Univ. of Buenos Aires; in 1992 completed designs for La Tour Sans Fins, a 1,400 ft (425m) glass tower to be built in Paris, completed Opéra Lyon, opened 1993, Fondation Cartier, opened 1994, Galeries Lafayette Berlin, opened 1996, Centre de Culture et de Congrès de Lucerne, Switzerland, opened 1998, Musée de la Publicité au Louvre, opened 1999; mem. Acad. d'Architecture 2002; Chevalier ordre nat. du Mérite, des Arts et des Lettres; Grand Prix de l'Architecture for Arab cultural centre, Paris 1987, Praemium Imperiale Award, Japan Art Asscn 2001, Francesco Borromini Int. Architecture Prize 2001. *Address:* Architectures Jean Nouvel, 10 Cité d'Angoulême, 75011 Paris, France.

NOVÁK, Jiří, LLD; Czech politician and lawyer; b. 11 April 1950, Hranice, Přerov Dist; m.; one s. one d.; ed J.E. Purkyně (now Masaryk) Univ., Brno; lawyer 1976–89; mem. Standing Comm. of the Presidium of Czech Nat. Council for Prison System Issues 1989–92; Deputy to Czech Nat. Council Feb.–June 1990; mem. Presidium, Czech Nat. Council 1990–92; Chair. Cttee on Law and Constitution of Czech Nat. Council 1990–92; Minister of Justice, Czech Repub. 1992–96; Chair. Legis. Council of Govt of Czech Repub. Feb.–July 1992; mem. Parl. 1996–98; Chair. Parl. Cttee for Petitions 1996–98; Vice-Chair. Interdepartmental Antidrug Comm. 1996; mem. Civic Democratic Party 1991–98; advocate 1998–. *Address:* Sokolská 60, 120 00 Prague 2 (Office); nám. T. G. Masaryka 15, Lipník/Bečvou, Czech Republic (Home). *Telephone:* (2) 22494146. *E-mail:* advokati@broz-sokol.cz.

NOVAK, Michael, B.T., MA; American theologian and writer; b. 9 Sept. 1933, Johnstown, Pa; s. of Michael J. Novak and Irene Sakmar; m. Karen R. Laub 1963; one s. two d.; ed Stonehill Coll., North Easton, Mass. and Gregorian Univ., Rome; Teaching Fellow, Harvard Univ. 1961–63; Asst Prof. of Humanities, Stanford Univ. 1965–68; Assoc. Prof. of Philosophy and Religious Studies, State Univ. of NY, Old Westbury 1969–71; Assoc. Dir Humanities, Rockefeller Foundation 1973–74; Ledden-Watson Distinguished Prof. of Religion, Syracuse Univ. 1976–78; Resident Scholar American Enterprise Inst. 1978–, George Frederick Jewett Prof. of Public Policy Research 1983–, Dir Social and Political Studies 1987–; Visiting Prof. Univ. of Notre Dame 1987–88; columnist, The Nat. Review 1979–86, Forbes Magazine 1989–; f., Publr Crisis 1982–95, Ed.-in-Chief 1993–95; mem. Bd for Int. Broadcasting 1983; Judge, Nat. Book Awards, DuPont Awards in Broadcast Journalism; Head, U.S. Del. to UN Human Rights Comm., Geneva 1981, 1982, to CSCE, Berne 1996; other public appointments; numerous hon. degrees and awards, including Templeton Prize 1994, Boyer Award 1999, Masaryk Medal 2000; Kt of Malta. *Publications include:* Belief and Unbelief 1965, The Rise of the Unmeltable Ethnics 1972, Choosing Our King 1974, The Spirit of Democratic Capitalism 1982, Freedom with Justice: Catholic Social Thought and Liberal Institutions 1984, Taking Glasnost Seriously 1988, Free Persons and the Common Good 1989, This Hemisphere of Liberty 1990, The Catholic Ethic and the Spirit of Capitalism 1993, Business as a Calling 1996, The Experience of Nothingness 1998, Tell Me Why 1998, On Cultivating Liberty 1999, A Free Society Reader (ed.) 2000, Three in One 2001 and over 500 articles in journals. *Address:* American Enterprise Institute, 1150 17th Street, NW, Washington, DC 20036, USA. *Telephone:* (202) 862-5839. *Fax:* (202) 862-5821 (Office). *E-mail:* mnovak@aei.org (Office). *Website:* www.aei.org (Office).

NOVELLO, Antonia Coello, MD, M.P.H.; American public health official; b. 23 Aug. 1944, Fajardo, Puerto Rico; m. Joseph Novello 1970; ed Univ. of Puerto Rico and Johns Hopkins Univ.; intern, Mott Children's Hosp., Univ. of Mich., Ann Arbor 1970–71; Univ. of Mich. Medical Center 1971–73; postgrad. training in nephrology, Dept of Internal Medicine, Univ. of Mich. Medical Center 1973–74, Dept of Pediatrics, Georgetown Univ. 1974–75; pvt. practice in pediatrics, Springfield, Va 1976–78; entered U.S. Public Health Service 1978; various posts at Nat. Insts. of Health, Bethesda, Md 1978–90, Deputy Dir Nat. Inst. of Child Health and Human Devt 1986–90; Clinical Prof. of Pediatrics, Georgetown Univ. Hospital, Washington, DC 1986, 1989, Uniformed Services Univ. of the Health Services, Bethesda, Md 1989; Adjunct Prof. of Pediatrics and Communicable Diseases, Univ. of Mich.; Surgeon-Gen. U.S. Public Health Service 1990–93, UNICEF Special Rep. for Health and Nutrition 1993–; numerous professional appointments, memberships and affiliations; recipient of numerous awards, honours and hon. degrees. *Address:* c/o UNICEF, 3 United Nations Plaza, Room 634, New York, NY 10017, USA.

NOVIKOV, Sergey Petrovich; Russian mathematician; b. 20 March 1938, Gorky (now Nizhniy Novgorod); s. Petr Novikov and Ludmila Keldysh; m. Eleonora Tsoi 1962; one s. two d.; ed Moscow Univ., Steklov Math. Inst.; Corresp. mem. of USSR (now Russian) Acad. of Sciences 1966–, mem. 1981–; Prof. Moscow Univ. 1966–; Head Dept, Landau Inst. for Theoretical Physics 1975–, Chair. Dept of Geometry and Topology, Moscow Univ. 1984–; Head Dept, Steklov Math. Inst. 1983–; Distinguished Univ. Prof., Univ. of Maryland 1997–; Foreign mem. NAS, Acad. dei Lincei; Hon. mem. London Math. Soc., Serbian Acad. of Art and Science 1988, Academia Europaea 1990, Pontifical Acad. of Sciences 1996; Dr hc (Athens) 1989, (Tel-Aviv) 1999; Moscow Math. Soc. Prize 1964, Lenin Prize 1967, Field's Medal, Int. Math. Union 1970, Lobachevsky Int. Prize, USSR Acad. of Sciences 1981. *Publications:* Algebraic and Differential Topology 1960, General Relativity 1971–75, Theory of Solitons 1974, Topological Phenomena in Physics 1981,

Riemannian Geometry and Poisson Structures 1983. *Leisure interest:* history. *Address:* University of Maryland at College Park, College Park, IPST, MD 20742, USA; Landau Institute for Theoretical Physics, Kosygina 2, 117334 Moscow, Russia. *Telephone:* (301) 405-4836 (USA) (Office); (095) 137-32-44 (Russia) (Office); (301) 779-7472 (USA) (Home); (095) 135-12-24 (Russia) (Home). *Fax:* (301) 314-9363 (USA). *E-mail:* novikov@ipst.umd.edu (Office).

NOVODVORSKAYA, Valeria Ilyinichna; Russian politician; b. 17 May 1950; ed Krupskaya Moscow Region Pedagogical Inst.; in dissident movt since late 1960s, arrested as student on charge of organizing underground anti-Soviet group 1969; trans. Second Moscow Medicine Inst. 1975–90; organized political action against invasion of Czechoslovakia Dec. 1969; arrested, discharged 1972; initiator and participant of anti-Soviet meetings; was arrested 17 times 1985–91; imprisoned for anti-Soviet activities 1978, 1985, 1986, 1991; mem. Co-ordination Council of Democratic Union, participated in political seminar Democracy and Humanism 1988; Leader Party of Democratic Union 1992; political reviewer Khozyain 1993–95, Stolitsa 1995–96. *Publications:* articles in newspapers and magazines. *Leisure interests:* reading, mountain climbing, swimming. *Address:* Democratic Union, Onezhskaya str. 4, Apt. 113, Moscow, Russia. *Telephone:* (095) 453-37-76.

NOVOTNÁ, Jana; Czech tennis player; b. 2 Oct. 1968, Brno (in fmr Czechoslovakia); d. of František Novotný and Libuše Novotná; won US Open Jr Doubles 1986; turned professional 1987; won her first title Adelaide 1988; Olympic silver medal in doubles with Helena Suková 1988; won Australian and US Open Mixed Doubles with Pugh 1988; won six women's doubles titles 1989; with Suková won Australian Open, French Open and Wimbledon Doubles 1990; reached quarter-finals French Open 1991; won 7 doubles titles with Savchenko Neiland 1992; won singles titles Osaka and Brighton 1993; singles titles Leipzig, Brighton and Essen 1994; Olympic bronze medal in singles, silver medal in doubles with Suková, Atlanta 1996; won Wimbledon Singles 1998, Wimbledon Women's Doubles 1998; Czech Fed. Cup Team 1978–93, 1995–98; announced retirement 1999, having won 17 Grand Slam titles (1 singles, 12 doubles, 4 mixed doubles); now lives in USA; 5–time winner of the WTA Tour Doubles Team of the Year award (4 different partners), Int. Tennis Fed. Doubles Team of the Year 1997 (with Lindsay Davenport. *Leisure interests:* soccer, ice hockey, golf, rollerskating, skiing, motorcycles, music.

NOVOTNÝ, Petr; Czech actor, writer and producer; b. 6 Aug. 1947, Olomouc; m. Miroslava Novotný; four c.; ed Charles Univ., Prague; mem. Laterna Magika Theatre, Prague; owner of Firma 6P and Amfora Football Club. *Awards:* Best Comedian and Best Programme (Novotný), TYTY Awards 1999, Most Popular Male Actor, TYTY Awards 2000. *Theatre productions directed:* Sugar (Some Like It Hot), Gypsies Go to Heaven, Libuse (opera) 1995, Hello Dolly! 1996, My Fair Lady, Evita 1999, Pokuseni sv. Antonina 2001. *Television includes:* Big Ear; writer and presenter of numerous programmes. *Leisure interests:* football, cooking. *Address:* Firma 6P—Petr Novotný, s.r.o, Koterovská 833, 15500 Prague 5, Czech Republic (Office). *Telephone:* (2) 57960560 (Office). *Fax:* (2) 57960562 (Office). *E-mail:* firma6p@decent3000.cz (Office). *Website:* www.firma6p.cz; www.petr-novotny.cz (Office).

NOVOZHILOV, Genrikh Vasilievich; Russian mechanical engineer; b. 27 Oct. 1925, Moscow; m.; one s.; ed Moscow Aviation Inst.; mem. CPSU 1951–91; constructor, constructing engineer, leading engineer, Sec. CP Cttee aviation plant 1948–57; Deputy Constructor-in-Chief, Chief Constructor, Constructor-Gen. USSR Ministry of Aviation Industry 1958–86; simultaneously First Deputy Constructor-Gen. Moscow Ilyushin Machine Constructing Plant 1964–, Constructor-Gen. 1976–2000, Adviser 2000–; Deputy to USSR Supreme Soviet 1974–89, USSR People's Deputy, 1989–91; mem. Cen. CPSU Cttee 1986–91; Head of Production of IL76T, IL86 and IL96-300 aircraft; Hero of Socialist Labour (twice), Lenin Prize and other decorations. *Publications:* works in the field of new samples of aviation tech., including Theory and Practice of Designing Passenger Aircraft 1976, Design, Testing and Production of Wide-Fuselage Passenger Aircraft 1980, essays on History of Constructions and Systems of Aircraft 1983. *Leisure interests:* tennis, photography. *Address:* S. Ilyushin Machine Construction Plant, Leningradsky prospekt 45G, 125319 Moscow, Russia. *Telephone:* (095) 251-52-93, 155-31-16.

NOWAK, Arkadiusz; Polish Roman Catholic ecclesiastic and charity worker; b. 28 Nov. 1966, Rybnik; ed Pontifical Faculty of Theology, Warsaw, Szczecin Univ.; mem. Camillian Order (Ordo Clericorum Regularium Ministrantium Infirmis–OSCam.) 1985–; Dir Centre of Re-adaptation Ministry of Health, Konstancin (brs in Piastów and Anielin) 1990–; ordained priest 1993; Co-Founder Polish Humanitarian Aid Foundation Res Humanae 1993–; Adviser on issues of AIDS and Drugs to Minister of Health 1995–2001, Plenipotentiary 2001; numerous prizes include Medal of St Georges (Tygodnik Powszechny award) 1993, Order of Smile 1995, Award for Acting Against Intolerance, Xenophobia and Racialism (Finland), Global Leader for Tomorrow, World Econ. Forum 2000, UN Award for Breaking the Silence on HIV/AIDS 2000. *Address:* National Aids Centre, ul. Samsonowska 1, 02–829 Warsaw, Poland (Office). *Telephone:* (22) 6418301 (Office). *Fax:* (22) 6412190 (Office). *E-mail:* arknowak@poczta.onet.pl (Office).

NOWAK-JEZIORAŃSKI, Jan; Polish publicist and writer; b. 15 May 1913, Warsaw; ed Poznań Univ.; Sr Asst Poznań Univ. 1937–39; Lt Officer Cadet 2nd Horse Artillery Div. Sept. 1939; served in Home Army 1941–43, courier and emissary 1943–45; ed. Polish BBC Section, London 1948–51; Dir Polish Service Radio Free Europe, Munich 1951–76; Nat. Dir and Vice-Chair. Polish-

American Congress, Washington 1978–98; consultant Nat. Security Council, USA 1979–92; Cross of Valour 1943, Virtuti Militari 1944, King's Medal for Courage, Great Ribbon, Order of Polonia Restituta (London) 1990, Commdr.'s Cross of Merit with Star, White Eagle Order 1994, Presidential Medal of Freedom 1996, Order of Grand Duke Gedyminas (Lithuania) 1998; Hon. citizenships include Baltimore, Gdynia, Poznań, Wrocław, Cracow; Dr hc (Adam Mickiewicz Univ., Poznań), (Wrocław Univ.), (Warsaw Univ.), (Jagiellonian Univ., Cracow); Awards include: Wiktor (Polish TV Award), Golden Microphone (Polish Radio Award). *Publications:* 63 Days: Warsaw Uprising 1945, Polska droga ku Wolności (Polish Road to Freedom) 1974, Polska pozostała sobą (Poland Did Not Change) 1980, Kurier z Warszawy (Courier from Warsaw) 1982, Wojna w eterze (War on Ether) 1986, Polska z oddali (Poland from Afar) 1988, Rozmowy o Polsce (Talks about Poland) 1995, Polska wczoraj, dziś i jutro (Poland Yesterday, Today, Tomorrow) 1999, Fakty, wydarzenia, opinie (Facts, Events, Opinion) 2001. *Leisure interests:* collecting polonica, tourism. *Address:* Stowarzyszenie Piscwzy Polskich, ul. Krakowskie Pnedmiescie 87/89, Warsaw, Poland (Office). *Telephone:* (22) 8260589 (Office).

NOWINA-KONOPKA, Piotr Maria, MSc(Econs), PhD; Polish politician, economist, publicist and scholar; b. 27 May 1949, Chorzów; s. of Mikołaj Nowina-Konopka and Anna Nowina-Konopka; m. Wanda Nowina-Konopka 1975; two d.; ed Higher School of Econs, Sopot and Gdańsk Univ. 1972; Asst Gdańsk Tech. Univ. 1972–74; Deputy Head, Centre of Revocatory Maritime Chamber, Gdynia 1977–79; Lecturer, Foreign Trade Econs Inst. of Gdańsk Univ. 1979–; Co-Founder and Sec. Catholic Intelligentsia Club in Gdańsk 1980–81; mem. Solidarity Independent Self-governing Trade Union 1980–1990, Press Spokesman 1988–89, Chief of Press 1989; mem. Civic Cttee attached to Lech Wałęsa (q.v.) 1988–91; Lecturer, Gdańsk Theology Inst. 1988–; Minister of State in Chancellery of Pres. of Poland 1989–90; Sec.-Gen. Democratic Union 1990–94; Union for Freedom Sec. for Foreign Affairs 1994–98; Deputy to Sejm (Parl.) 1991–2001, Vice-Chair. Cttee for the European Treaty 1992–97; Sec. of State Office of the Cttee for European Integration 1998; Sec. of State in Chancellery of Prime Minister 1998–99; Deputy Chair. Jt Parl. Cttee Poland-European Parl. 1993–97; mem. Foreign Affairs Comm. 1991–2001; Pres. Polish Robert Schuman Foundation 1996–; Vice-Rector Coll. of Europe, Bruges/Warsaw 1999–; Deputy Chief Negotiator for negotiations with EU 1998–99; Chevalier Ordre du Mérite, Verdienstkreuz Erste Klasse des Verdienstordens. *Publicatons:* weekly columnist in Wprost, political articles in different books/periodicals. *Leisure interests:* family life, reading, social sciences, yachting, riding, skiing. *Address:* College of Europe, Rezydencja Natolin, ul. Nowoursynowska 84, Box 120, 02-797 Warsaw, Poland (Office). *Telephone:* (22) 545-94-02/545-94-00 (Office). *Fax:* (22) 648-98-23/649-13-52 (Office). *E-mail:* pnk@natolin.edu.pl (Office). *Website:* www.coleurop.be (Office).

NOWRA, Louis; Australian writer and scriptwriter; b. 12 Dec. 1950; Prix Italia 1990, Australia/Canada Award 1993. *Publications:* The Misery of Beauty 1977, Inner Voices 1978, Inside the Islands 1980, The Golden Age 1985, Palu 1988, Byzantine Flowers 1990, Map of the Human Heart 1991, Summer of the Aliens 1991, The Watchtower 1992, Cosi (play) 1992, Radiance (play) 1993, Crow 1994, The Temple 1994, The Incorruptible 1995, Heaven's Burning 1997, Red Nights 1997, Twisted (play) 1997, The Matchmaker (play) 1997, The Twelfth of Never (memoir) 1997, Abaza: A Modern Encyclopaedia 2002. *Leisure interests:* cricket, mycology. *Address:* Level 18, Plaza 11, 500 Oxford Street, Bondi Junction, NSW 2011, Australia. *Telephone:* (2) 389-6400.

NOYCE, Phillip; Australian film director; b. 1950; ed Univ. of Sydney, Australian Film and Television School. *Films directed include:* documentaries: Castor and Pollux (Rouben Mamoulien Award, Sydney Film Festival) 1974, God Knows Why But It Works 1975, Backroads (writer, dir and producer) 1977, Newsfront 1978; feature films: Dead Calm 1989, Patriot Games 1992, Sliver 1993, Clear and Present Danger 1994, The Saint 1997, The Bone Collector 1999, Rabbit Proof Fence (dir and producer) 2002, The Quiet American 2002. *Address:* c/o Endeavor Talent Agency, 9701 Wiltshire Boulevard, #1000, Beverly Hills, CA 90212, USA (Office); c/o The Cameron Creswell Agency Pty Ltd., 5/2 New McLean Street, Edgcliff, NSW 2027, Australia.

NOYER, Christian; French central banker and civil servant; b. 6 Oct. 1950, Soisy; ed Univs. of Rennes and Paris, Inst. of Political Science, Ecole Nat. d'Admin.; mil. service as naval officer 1972; joined French Treasury 1976, Chief of Banking Office, then of Export Credit Office 1982–85, Deputy Dir in charge of Int. Multilateral Issues 1988–90, then of Debt Man., Monetary and Banking Issues 1990–92, Dir of Dept responsible for public holdings and public financing 1992–93, Dir of Treasury 1993–95; financial attaché French Del. to EC, Brussels 1980–82; Econ. Adviser to Minister for Econ. Affairs and Finance, Edouard Balladur 1986–88, Chief of Staff to E. Alphandéry 1993, to Jean Arthuis 1995–97; Dir Ministry for Econ. Affairs, Finance and Industry 1997–98; Vice-Pres. European Cen. Bank 1998–2002; Alt. Gov. IMF and World Bank 1993–95; alt. mem. European Monetary Cttee 1988–90, mem. 1993–95, 1998; alt. mem. G7 and G10 1993–95; mem. Working Party No. 3 OECD 1993–95; Chair. Paris Club of Creditor Countries 1993–97; mem. European Econ. and Financial Cttee 1999–2002; Chevalier Légion d'honneur, Ordre nat. du Mérite, Commdr Nat. Order of Lion, Senegal, Grand Cross, Orden del Mérito, Spain. *Publications:* Banks: The Rules of the Game 1990; various articles. *Leisure interest:* sailing. *Address:* c/o European Central Bank, Kaiserstrasse 29, 60311 Frankfurt am Main, Germany (Office).

NOYORI, Ryoji, M.SC, PhD; Japanese scientist; b. 3 Sept. 1938, Kobe; m. Hiroko Oshima; two s.; ed Univ. of Kyoto, Harvard Univ., USA; Research Assoc. Dept of Industrial Chemistry, Kyoto Univ. 1963–68; Assoc. Prof. Dept of Chemistry, Nagoya Univ. 1968–72, Prof. 1972–; Dir Chemical Instrument Center 1979–91, Dean Grad. School of Science 1997–99, Dir Research Center for Materials Science 2000–; Dir ERATO Molecular Catalysis Project, Research Devt Corpn of Japan 1991–96; Science Adviser Ministry of Educ., Science and Culture 1992–96, mem. Scientific Council 1996–; Prof. Inst. for Fundamental Research on Organic Chemistry, Kyushu Univ. 1993–96; Cttee Chair. Research for the Future Program on Advanced Processes, Japan Soc. for the Promotion of Science 1996–; Pres. Soc. of Synthetic Organic Chemistry 1997–99; mem. numerous professional bodies including The Chemical Soc. of Japan, The Pharmaceutical Soc. of Japan, The American Chemical Soc., The Royal Soc. of Chemistry (UK); Visiting Prof. at numerous int. univs.; mem. editorial Bd of 30 learned journals; numerous hon. degrees.; Nobel Prize in Chemistry Nov. 2001 (Jt recipient); numerous other awards and prizes including Chemical Soc. of Japan Award 1985, Japan Acad. Prize 1995, several awards from the American Chemical Soc. *Address:* Department of Chemistry, Graduate School of Science, Nagoya University, Chikusa, Nagoya 464-8602, Japan (Office); 135-417 Shinden, Umemori-cho, Nisshin, Aichi 470-0132, Japan (Home). *Telephone:* (52) 789-2956 (Office). *Fax:* (52) 783-4177 (Office). *E-mail:* noyori@chem3.chem.nagoya-u.ac.jp (Office).

NOZIÈRES, Philippe Pierre Gaston François; French physicist; b. 12 April 1932, Paris; s. of Henri Noziéres and Alice Noël; m. Catherine Michel 1982; one d. and one s. (one d. by previous m.); ed Ecole Normale Supérieure and Princeton Univ., USA; Prof. of Physics, Univ. of Paris 1961–72; Physicist, Laue-Langevin Inst. 1972–76; Prof. of Physics, Grenoble Univ. 1976–83; Prof. of Statistical Physics, Coll. de France 1983–2001; mem. Acad. des Sciences (Inst. de France); Foreign Assoc. NAS (USA); Holweck Prize 1976, Prix du CEA (Acad. des Sciences) 1979, Wolf Prize 1985, Gold Medal CNRS 1988, Feenberg Medal 2000. *Publications:* papers on theoretical and statistical physics. *Address:* ILL, BP 156, 38042 Grenoble Cedex (Office); 15 route de Saint Nizier, 38180 Seyssins, France (Home). *Telephone:* (4) 76-20-72-74 (Office); (4) 76-21-60-28 (Home). *Fax:* (4) 76-88-24-16. *E-mail:* nozieres@ill.fr (Office).

NSEKELA, Amon James, MA, DipEd, FIBA; Tanzanian fmr diplomatist, civil servant and banker; b. 4 Jan. 1930, Lupepo, Rungwe; s. of the late Ngonile Reuben Nsekela and of Anyambilile Nsekela (née Kalinga); m. Christina Matilda Kyusa 1957; two s.; ed Rungwe Dist School, Malangali Secondary School, Tabora Govt Sr Secondary School, Makerere Univ. Coll. and Univ. of the Pacific, Calif., USA; teacher 1955–59; Admin. Officer 1960–62; Perm./Prin. Sec. Ministries of External Affairs and Defence, Industries, Mineral Resources and Power and Treasury 1963–67; Chair. and Man. Dir Nat. Bank of Commerce 1967–74, 1981–91; Chair. Nat. Insurance Corpn of Tanzania 1967–69, Tanzania Investment Bank 1981–91, Inst. of Devt Man., Mzumbe, Morogoro 1982–91; High Commr in UK 1974–81 (also Accred to Ireland) 1980–81; Dir Tanzania-Zambia Railway Authority 1982–, Computers & Telecoms Systems 1993–; Chair., Council, Univ. of Dar es Salaam 1970–74, Pensioners' Union of Tanzania 1992–; Vice-Pres. Britain–Tanzania Soc.; Hon. DLit (Dar es Salaam) 1990; African Insurance Org. Award 1982; Order of the United Republic of Tanzania. *Publications:* Minara ya Historia ya Tanganyika: Tanganyika hadi Tanzania, Demokrasi Tanzania, Socialism and Social Accountability in a Developing Nation, The Development of Health Services in Mainland Tanzania: Tumetoka Mbali (with Dr. A. L. Nhonoli), Towards National Alternatives 1984, A Time to Act 1984. *Leisure interests:* swimming, darts, reading and writing. *Address:* 9 Lupa Way, P.O. Box 722, Mbeya, Tanzania. *Telephone:* (65) 3487. *Fax:* (65) 2541.

NSIMBAMBI, Apolo; Ugandan politician; fmr Minister of Educ. and Sports; Prime Minister of Uganda April 1999–; mem. Nat. Resistance Movt (NRM). *Address:* Office of the Prime Minister, P.O. Box 341, Kampala, Uganda (Office). *Telephone:* (41) 259518 (Office). *Fax:* (41) 242341 (Office).

N'SINGA UDJUU ONGWABEKI UNTUBE, Joseph; Democratic Republic of the Congo politician; b. Joseph N'Singa Udjuu, 29 Sept. 1934, Nsontin, Bandundu Prov.; s. of Nshue O. N'singa and Monkaju Medji; m. Mbu Modiri Marie; four s. four d.; ed Kokoro and Kabue Seminaries, Bandundu Prov., Univ. of Lovanium (now Kinshasa); Juridical adviser of the provisional Govt, Inongo, Bandundu Prov. 1963; Provincial Minister of the Interior (Home Affairs) and Information 1963–64; elected Nat. Deputy 1964; Vice-Minister of the Interior (Home Affairs) 1965, of Justice 1965; Minister of Justice 1966–69; Minister of State for Home Affairs 1968; Minister of State at the Presidency Sept. 1970; Chair. Nat. Inst. of Social Security 1975–80; Co-founder and mem. Cen. Cttee, Mouvement Populaire de la Révolution (MPR) 1980–83 (Exec. Sec. 1981–83), First Vice-Pres. 1980–83; Chair. 1990–91; Prime Minister (first State Commissary) 1981; Pres. Judiciary Council 1987–90; mem. Sovereign Nat. Conf. and elected Counsellor of the Repub. during Nat. Conf.; mem. transition Parl.; Minister of Transportation 1994–95, of Justice 1995–96, of Reconstruction and Planning 1997; participant at nat. consultation assizes conf., Kinshasa 2000; mem. Jt Comm. Cttee in charge of Law Review 2001; Founder and Pres. own political party Union chrétienen pour le renouveau et la justice (UCRJ); Grand Cordon of the Leopard Nat. Order, Commdr of the Belgian King Leopold II Cross, Commdr of the Cen. African Repub. Order of Merit. *Leisure interests:* walking, jogging. *Address:* 68 Avenue Uvira, #5 Commune de Gombe, Kinshasa, Democratic Republic of the Congo (Home). *E-mail:* nsinga5@hotmail.com.

N'TCHAMA, Caetano; Guinea-Bissau politician; Prime Minister of Guinea-Bissau. 2000–01. *Address:* c/o Office of the Prime Minister, Avda Unidade Africana, C.P. 137, Bissau, Guinea-Bissau (Office).

NTETURUYE, Marc; Burundian diplomatist; b. 22 Nov. 1954, Murambi; m.; six c.; ed Univ. of Burundi, Inst. Int. d'Admin. Publique, Paris; taught history in a Jesuit secondary school 1978–81; Dir of secondary school 1981–82; Adviser to Pres. of Repub. on press and information matters 1982–85; First Counsellor, Embassy in Tanzania 1981–87; Amb. to Kenya 1987–91 (also Accred to Somalia and Namibia and to Rwanda 1991–93); Perm. Rep. to UNEP and UN Habitat 1990–91; Diplomatic and Political Adviser to Prime Minister 1994–95; Dir Office of Prime Minister 1995–96; Dir External Intelligence 1997–98; Perm. Rep. to UN (also Accred to Cuba) 1999–. *Publications:* A Study of the Problem of Energy in the Rural Villages of Burundi 1978, A Study on the Role of Sorghum in the Socio-Culture of Burundi. *Address:* Permanent Mission of Burundi to the United Nations, 336 East 45th Street, 12th Floor, New York, NY 10017 (Office); 16 Murray Hill Road, Scarsdale, NY 10583, USA (Home). *Telephone:* (212) 499-0001 (Office); (914) 722-0915 (Home). *Fax:* (212) 499-0006 (Office). *E-mail:* burundi@un.int (Office).

NTIBANTUNGANYA, Sylvestre; Burundian politician; b. 8 May 1956, Nyamutobo; m. Eusebie Ntibantunganya (deceased); ed Nat. Audiovisual Inst. Paris; worked for Burundi State TV and Radio for two years; joined Nat. Secr. Unity for Nat. Progress (UPRONA); in exile in Rwanda 1979–83; founding mem. Sahwanya-Frodebu Party, mem. Exec. Cttee 1991, Leader 1993–; Chief Ed. Aube de la Démocratie (Frodebu Party newspaper) until 1993; Deputy for Gitega 1993; Minister for External Relations 1993; fmr Speaker of Parl.; Pres. of Burundi 1994–96; Chair. Nat. Security Council 1996. *Address:* National Security Council, Bujumbura, Burundi.

NTOUTOUME EMANE, Jean-François; Gabonese politician; Minister of State, Minister of Land Registry, Town Planning and Housing and Minister for State Control, Decentralization, Territorial Admin. and Regional Integration 1997–99; Prime Minister of Gabon and Head of Govt Jan. 1999–, also fmrly Minister of Housing and Urbanization. *Address:* Office of the Prime Minister, B.P. 546, Libreville, Gabon (Office). *Telephone:* 77-89-81 (Office).

NUAIMI, Ali ibn Ibrahim an-, MS; Saudi Arabian politician and fmr oil industry executive; b. 1935, Eastern Prov.; m. 1962; four c.; ed Int. Coll. Beirut, American Univ. Beirut and Lehigh Univ., Pennsylvania and Stanford Univs., USA; Asst Geologist, Exploration Dept, Aramco 1953, Hydrologist and Geologist 1963–67, worked in Econs and Public Relations Dept 1967–69, Vice-Pres. Aramco 1975, Sr Vice-Pres. 1978, Dir 1980, Exec. Vice-Pres., Operations 1982, Pres. 1984, CEO 1988; Minister of Petroleum and Mineral Resources 1995–. *Leisure interests:* hunting, hiking. *Address:* Ministry of Petroleum and Mineral Resources, P.O. Box 247, King Abd al-Aziz Road, Riyadh 11191, Saudi Arabia. *Telephone:* (1) 478-1661. *Fax:* (1) 478-1980.

NUAIMI, HH Sheikh Humaid bin Rashid an-, Ruler of Ajman; Ruler of Ajman 1981–; mem. Supreme Council of UAE 1981–; Patron, Sheikh Humaid bin Rashid Prizes for Culture and Science 1983–. *Address:* Ruler's Palace, P.O. Box 1, Ajman, United Arab Emirates.

NUGIS, Ulo; Estonian politician and business executive; b. 28 April 1944, Tallinn; ed Minsk Polytech. Inst.; Chief Engineer Tegur Factory 1970–73; Dir Ehitusdetail (experimental factory) 1974–80; Dir Dunamo (ski mfg factory) 1980–86; Dir-Gen. Production Asscn Estoplast 1986–1990; mem. Congress of Estonia and Speaker Supreme Soviet of Estonian Repub. 1990–92; mem. Republican Coalition Party (now People's Party of Republicans and Conservatives) 1990–; Chair. Riigikogu (State Ass.) 1992–95, mem. 1995–. *Address:* Riigikogu, Lossi-plats 1A, 15165 Tallinn, Estonia (Office). *Telephone:* (6) 31-63-50.

NUJOMA, Sam; Namibian politician; b. 12 May 1929, Etunda Village, Ongandjera Dist; s. of the late Daniel Uutoni Nujoma and of Helvi Mpingana Kondombolo; m. Kovambo Theopoldine Katjimune 1956; three s. one d.; ed Okahoal Finnish Mission School, St Barnabas School, Windhoek; with State Railways until 1957; Municipal Clerk, Windhoek 1957; clerk in wholesale store 1957–59; elected Leader of Ovamboland People's Org. (OPO) 1959; arrested Dec. 1959; went into exile 1960; Founder, with Herman Toivo ja Toivo (q.v.) and Pres. SWAPO (SW Africa People's Org.) April 1960–; appeared before UN Cttee on SW Africa June 1960; set up SWAPO provisional HQ in Dar es Salaam, Tanzania March 1961; arrested on return to Windhoek and formally ordered out of the country March 1966; turned to armed struggle after rejection by Int. Court of Justice of SWAPO complaint against S. Africa Aug. 1966; gave evidence at UN Security Council Oct. 1971; led SWAPO negotiations at numerous int. negotiations culminating in implementation in March 1989 of UN Resolution 435 providing for independence of Namibia; returned to Namibia Sept. 1989; mem. Constituent Ass. 1989–90; Pres. of Namibia March 1990–, also Minister of Home Affairs 1995–96; Hon. LLD (Ahmadu Bello Univ., Nigeria) 1982, (Lincoln Univ., USA) 1990, (Ohio Cen. State Univ., USA) 1993, (State Univ. of NJ, USA) 1997; Hon. DTech (Fed. Univ. of Tech., Minna) 1992; Hon. DEd (Univ. of Namibia) 1993; Dr hc (Academic Council 1998, Russian Econ. Acad.) 1998, (People's Friendship Univ. of Russia); Grand Master, Order of Merit Grand Cruz (Brazil); Lenin Peace Prize 1973, Frederic Joliot Curie Gold Medal 1980, Ho Chi Minh Peace Award 1988, Indira Gandhi Peace Prize 1990, Africa Prize for Leadership for Sustainable End to Hunger, New York 1995, order of Friendship Award (Viet

Nam) 2000; numerous honours and awards. *Publication:* To Free Namibia 1994. *Address:* Office of the President, State House, Robert Mugabe Avenue, Private Bag 13339, Windhoek, Namibia. *Telephone:* (61) 2707111. *Fax:* (61) 221780.

NUKAGA, Fukushiro; Japanese politician and fmr journalist; b. 1944; ed Waseda Univ.; fmr political and econ. reporter for Sankei Shimbun; fmr mem. Ibaraki Prefectural Ass.; mem. LDP; mem. for Ibaraki, House of Reps.; fmr Deputy Chief Cabinet Sec.; Dir-Gen. Defence Agency 1998–2000, of Econ. Planning Agency 2000–01. *Address:* Jiyu-Minshuto, 1-11-23, Nagata-cho, Chiyoda-ku, Tokyo 100-0014, Japan (Office).

NUMAIRI, Field Marshal Gaafar al- (see Nemery).

NUMAN, Yasin Said; Yemeni politician; fmr Deputy Prime Minister and Minister of Fisheries; Prime Minister of Democratic Republic of Yemen 1986–90, Minister of Labour and Civil Service 1986.

NUNES, Manuel Jacinto, PhD; Portuguese banker and politician; b. 27 Jan. 1926, Lisbon; s. of José and Lourença da Conceição Nunes; m. Lutgarda da Silva Rodrigues Nunes 1950; one d.; Prof., Inst. for Advanced Mil. Studies 1953–74; Sec. of State for Finance 1955–59; Vice-Gov. Banco de Portugal 1960–74, Gov. 1974–75, 1980–85; Pres. Caixa Geral de Depósitos 1976–80; Deputy Prime Minister and Minister of Finance and the Plan 1978–79; Econ. Adviser 1985–89; Pres. Lisbon Acad. of Sciences 1980–90; Vice-Pres. Nat. Geographic Soc. 1974–79; Chair. Consultative Comm. for European Econ. Integration; Chair. Portuguese-American Foundation for Devt; Grand Officer, Order of Christ, Grand Officer, Order of the Southern Cross, Grand Cross of the Viscount of Rio, Distinguished Service Silver Medal, Grand Cross of Prince d. Henrique, Grand Cross of Public Educ., Officier, Légion d'honneur (France), Hon. CBE (UK). *Publications:* Structure of the Portuguese Economy 1954, National Income and Budgetary Balance 1957, Economic Growth and Budget Policy 1961, Economic Development and Planning, The Monetary Controversy, From Rome to Maastricht, The Keynes Thinking 1998, Epistemology and Methodology of Economics; numerous articles. *Leisure interests:* history, politics, philosophy, economics. *Address:* Fundação Luso-Americana, Rua do Sacramento à Lapa 21, 1249-090 Lisbon (Office); R. S. Francisco De Sales, 17-A, 1° Esq., 1250-230 Lisbon, Portugal (Home). *Telephone:* (21) 3935831 (Office); (21) 3886408 (Home). *Fax:* (21) 3963358 (Office). *E-mail:* jacinto.nunes@flad.pt (Office); jacinto.nunes@mail.kgnet.pt (Home).

NUNGESSER, Roland, LenD; French politician; b. 9 Oct. 1925, Nogent-sur-Marne; s. of Léon Nungesser and Aline Sanguinolenti; m. 1st Michèle Jeanne Elizabeth Selignac 1957 (divorced 1981); three d.; m. 2nd Marie-Christine Ventrillon 1981; ed Ecole Libre des Sciences Politiques, Paris Law Faculty; Commissaire-général du Salon Nautique Int. 1957–62; Vice-Pres. Chambre Syndicale des Industries Nautiques; Pres. Conseil Nat. de la Navigation de Plaisance 1961–67; Regional Chair. 1962; Deputy for Seine 1958–67, Val-de-Marne 1967–95; Sec. Nat. Ass. 1958–60; Sec. of State for Housing 1966–67; Sec. of State at Ministry of Economy and Finance 1967–68; Minister of Youth and Sports May–July 1968; Mayor of Nogent-sur-Marne 1959–95; Pres. Franco-Soviet (then Franco-Russian 1992) Chamber of Commerce 1969–98, Liaison Cttee for Local Councillors 1971, Union of Parisian Region Mayors 1983, Soc. for Protection of Animals (SPA) 1984–88 (Hon. Pres. 1988–); Vice-Pres. Nat. Ass. 1969–74; Pres. Conseil Général du Val de Marne 1970–76; Vice-Pres. Movt Nat. des élus locaux 1976–95; Pres. Carrefour du Gaullisme 1979–, Asscn des Maires de l'Ile-de France 1983–95, now Hon. Pres.; mem. Rassemblement pour la République; mem. various socs. and asscns; Chevalier Légion d'honneur, Mérite commercial. *Publications:* Le Chevalier du ciel, La Revolution qu'il faut faire. *Leisure interests:* motor yachting, athletics. *Address:* 18 avenue Duvelleroy, 94130 Nogent-sur-Marne, France. *Telephone:* 1-48-77-76-76. *Fax:* 1-48-77-99-16 (Home).

NUNN, Sam, LLB; American politician and lawyer; b. 8 Sept. 1938, Macon, Ga; s. of Samuel Augustus Nunn and Elizabeth Cannon Nunn; m. Colleen O'Brien 1965; one s. one d.; ed Georgia Inst. of Tech., Emory Univ. and Emory Univ. Law School, Atlanta; pvt. law practice 1964–72; mem. Ga House of Reps. 1968–72; US Senator from Georgia 1972–96, mem. Armed Services Cttee, Govt Affairs Cttee, Small Business Cttee; Sr Partner King & Spalding, Atlanta 1997–; Democrat. *Leisure interest:* golf, reading. *Address:* King & Spalding, Suite 4900, 191 Peachtree Street, Atlanta, GA 30303, USA. *Telephone:* (404) 572-4949.

NUNN, Trevor Robert, CBE; British theatre director; b. 14 Jan. 1940, Ipswich; s. of Robert Alexander Nunn and Dorothy May Nunn (née Piper); m. 1st Janet Suzman (q.v.) 1969 (divorced 1986); one s.; m. 2nd Sharon Lee Hill 1986 (divorced 1991); two d.; m. 3rd Imogen Stubbs 1994; one s. one d.; ed Northgate Grammar School, Ipswich and Downing Coll. Cambridge; Trainee Dir Belgrade Theatre, Coventry; Assoc. Dir Royal Shakespeare Co. 1964–86, Artistic Dir 1968–78, CEO 1968–86, Jt Artistic Dir 1978–86, Dir Emer. 1986–; f. Homevale Ltd and Awayvale Ltd; Artistic Dir Royal Nat. Theatre 1996–2001; toured USA, Australia with own version of Hedda Gabler 1975; mem. Arts Council of England 1994–; Hon. LittD (Warwick) 1982; Hon. MA (Newcastle-upon-Tyne) 1982; Hon. DLitt (Suffolk) 1997; London Theatre Critics' Best Dir Award for The Revenger's Tragedy and The Winter's Tale 1969, Soc. of Film and TV Arts Award for Antony and Cleopatra 1975, Ivor Novello Award for Best British Musical of 1976 for The Comedy of Errors (Lyrics), Soc. of West End Theatre Awards, Best Musical of the Year, for The Comedy of Errors 1977, Plays and Players Award 1978, 1979 for Best

Production (Dir) and Sydney Edwards Award for Best Director in Evening Standard Drama Awards 1978, 1979, both for Once in a Lifetime, Soc. of West End Theatres Awards, including Best Dir, Best New Play, Evening Standard Award, Best Dir, Drama Award for Best Dir, Mr. Abbott Award (Broadway) (all for The Life and Adventures of Nicholas Nickleby). *Productions:* Tango 1965, The Revenger's Tragedy 1965, 1969, The Taming of the Shrew, The Relapse, The Winter's Tale 1969, Hamlet 1970, Henry VIII 1970, Roman Season: Antony and Cleopatra, Coriolanus, Julius Caesar, Titus Andronicus 1970, Macbeth 1974, 1976, Hedda Gabler (own version) 1975, Romeo and Juliet 1976, Comedy of Errors 1976, Winter's Tale (co-dir) 1976, King Lear (co-dir) 1976, Macbeth 1976, The Alchemist 1977, As You Like It 1977, Every Good Boy Deserves Favour 1977, Three Sisters 1978, The Merry Wives of Windsor 1979, Once in a Lifetime 1979, Juno and the Paycock 1980, The Life and Adventures of Nicholas Nickleby 1980 (with John Caird) (New York 1981), Cats 1981, All's Well That Ends Well 1981, Henry IV (Parts I & II) 1981, 1982, Peter Pan (with John Caird) 1982, Starlight Express 1984, Les Misérables (with John Caird) 1985, Chess 1986, The Fair Maid of the West 1986, Aspects of Love 1989, Othello 1989, The Baker's Wife 1989, Timon of Athens 1991, The Blue Angel 1991, Measure for Measure 1991, Heartbreak House 1992, Arcadia 1993, Sunset Boulevard 1993, Enemy of The People 1997, Mutabilitie 1997, Not About Nightingales 1998, Oklahoma! 1998, Betrayal 1998, Troilus and Cressida 1999, The Merchant of Venice 1999, Summerfolk 1999, Love's Labour's Lost 2002. *Television:* Antony and Cleopatra 1975, Comedy of Errors 1976, Every Good Boy Deserves Favour 1978, Macbeth 1978, Shakespeare Workshops Word of Mouth (written and directed by T. Nunn) 1979, The Three Sisters, Othello 1989, Porgy and Bess 1992, Oklahoma! 1999. *Films:* Hedda (own scripted version), Lady Jane 1985, Twelfth Night 1996. *Operas:* Idomeneo 1982, Porgy and Bess 1986, Così fan tutte 1991, Peter Grimes 1992, Katya Kabanova 1994, Sophie's Choice 2002. *Publication:* British Theatre Design 1989. *Address:* c/o Royal National Theatre, Upper Ground, South Bank, London, SE1 9PX, England.

NURSE, Sir Paul Maxime, Kt, MA, PhD, FRS; British scientist; b. 25 Jan. 1949, Norfolk; s. of Maxime Nurse and Cissie Nurse (née White); m. Anne Teresa Talbott 1971; two d.; ed Harrow County Grammar School, Univ. of Birmingham, Univ. of East Anglia; Research Fellow, Dept of Zoology, Univ. of Edin. 1974–78; Sr Research Fellow, School of Biology, Univ. of Sussex 1980–84; Head Cell Cycle Control Lab., Imperial Cancer Research Fund (ICRF), London 1984–87; Iveagh Prof. of Microbiology, Univ. of Oxford 1987–91, Napier Research Prof. of Royal Soc. 1991–93; Dir of Research (Labs) and Head Cell Cycle Lab., ICRF 1993–96, Dir-Gen. ICRF 1996–2002, Dir-Gen. (Science) and CEO Cancer Research UK 2002–; Fleming Lecturer, Soc. of Gen. Microbiology 1984; Florey Lecturer, Royal Soc. 1990; Marjory Stephenson Lecturer, Soc. of Gen. Microbiology 1990; mem. EMBO 1987–; Pres. Genetical Soc. 1990–93; mem. Academia Europaea 1991; Foreign Assoc. NAS 1995–; Hon. FRCP; Hon. FRCPath 2000; Feldberg Prize for Medical Research (UK/Germany) 1991, CIBA Medal (Biochem. Soc.) 1991, Louis Jeantet Prize for Medicine in Europe, Switzerland 1992, Gairdner Foundation Int. Award, Canada 1992, Royal Soc. Wellcome Medal 1993, Jiménez Díaz Memorial Award and Medal, Spain 1993, Purkyne Medal (Czech Acad.) 1994, Pezcoller Award for Oncology Research (Italy) 1995, Royal Soc. Medal 1995, Dr Josef Steiner Prize, Switzerland 1996, Dr H. P. Heineken Prize for Biochem. and Biophysics, The Netherlands 1996, Alfred P. Sloan Jr Prize and Medal, General Motors Cancer Research Foundation 1997, Berkan Judd Award (USA) 1998, Albert Lasker Award (USA) 1998, Nobel Prize for Physiology or Medicine 2001. *Publications:* numerous articles in scientific journals concerned with cell and molecular biology. *Leisure interests:* gliding, astronomy, talking. *Address:* Cancer Research UK, P.O. Box 123, Lincoln's Inn Fields, London, WC2A 3PX, England. *Telephone:* (20) 7269-3436 (Office). *Fax:* (20) 7269-3610 (Office). *E-mail:* paul.nurse@cancer.org.uk (Office). *Website:* www.cancerresearchuk.org (Office).

NUSSBAUM, Martha Craven, MA, PhD; American professor of philosophy and classics; b. 6 May 1947, New York; d. of George Craven and Betty Craven; m. Alan J. Nussbaum 1969 (divorced 1987); one d.; ed New York and Harvard Univs.; Jr Fellow, Soc. of Fellows, Harvard Univ. 1972–75, Asst Prof. of Philosophy and Classics 1975–80; Assoc. Prof. 1980–83; Assoc. Prof. of Philosophy and Classics, Brown Univ. 1984–85, Prof. of Philosophy, Classics and Comparative Literature 1985–87, David Benedict Prof. 1987–89, Prof. 1989–95; Visiting Prof. of Law, Univ. of Chicago 1994, Prof. of Law and Ethics 1995–96, Prof. of Philosophy 1995–, Prof. of Divinity 1995–, Ernst Freund Prof. 1996–99, Assoc. mem. Classics Dept 1996–; Fellow, American Acad. of Arts and Science; mem. American Philosophical Asscn (Chair. Cttee on Status of Women 1994–97); Brandeis Creative Arts Award 1990; PEN Spielvogel-Diamondstein Award 1991. *Publications:* Aristotle's De Motu Animalium 1978, The Fragility of Goodness 1986, Love's Knowledge 1990, The Therapy of Desire 1994, The Quality of Life (ed. with A. Sen) 1993, Passions and Perceptions (with J. Brunschwig) 1993, Women, Culture and Development (with J. Glover) 1995, Poetic Justice 1996, For Love of Country 1996, Cultivating Humanity 1997, Sex and Social Justice 1998. *Leisure interests:* music, running, hiking. *Address:* The Law School, University of Chicago, 1111 East 60th Street, Chicago, IL 60637, USA (Office).

NÜSSLEIN-VOLHARD, Christiane, PhD, FRS; German scientist; b. 20 Oct. 1942, Magdeburg; d. of Rolf Volhard and Brigitte Volhard (née Haas); ed Univ. of Tübingen; Research Assoc., Lab. of Dr Schaller, Max-Planck-Inst. für Virusforschung, Tübingen 1972–74; Postdoctoral Fellow (EMBO Fellowship),

Lab. of Prof. Dr W. Gehring, Biozentrum Basel, Switzerland 1975–76, Lab. of Prof. Dr K. Sander, Univ. of Freiburg 1977; Head Group, European Molecular Biology Lab. (EMBL), Heidelberg 1978–80; Group Leader, Friedrich-Miescher-Laboratorium, Max-Planck-Gesellschaft, Tübingen 1981–85, Scientific mem. Max-Planck-Gesellschaft and Dir Max-Planck-Institut für Entwicklungsbiologie, Tübingen 1985–90, Dir Dept of Genetics 1990–; mem. NAS; Hon. ScD (Yale) 1990; Dr. hc (Utrecht) 1991, (Princeton) 1991, (Harvard) 1993; Albert Lasker Medical Research Award, New York 1991, Prix Louis Jeantet de Médicine, Geneva 1992, Ernst Schering Prize, Berlin 1993, Novel Prize in Medicine 1995, Grosses Verdienstkreuz mit Stern 1996, Ordre pour le Mérite 1997. *Publications:* 135 Zebra Fish: A Practical Approach 2002; scientific articles. *Address:* Max-Planck-Institut für Entwicklungsbiologie, Spemannstrasse 35/III, 72076 Tübingen, Germany. *Telephone:* (7071) 601487. *Fax:* (7071) 601 384 (Office). *Website:* www.eb.tuebingen.mpg.de/dept3 (Office).

NUTT, Jim, BFA; American artist; b. 28 Nov. 1938, Pittsfield, Mass.; s. of Frank E. Nutt and Ruth Tureman Nutt; m. Gladys Nilsson 1961; ed School of Art Inst. of Chicago, Washington Univ. and Univ. of Pennsylvania; Prof. of Art, Calif. State Univ. Sacramento 1968–75, School of Art Inst. of Chicago 1990; Cassandra Foundation Award 1969; Nat. Endowment for the Arts Award 1975, 1990. *Solo exhibitions include:* Museum of Contemporary Art, Walker Art Center, Minneapolis, Whitney Museum of American Art, New York 1974, San Francisco Art Inst. 1975, Rotterdamse Kunstichting, Rotterdam 1980, Kunsthalle Basel 1992–93, Centro de Arte Reina Sofía, Madrid 1992–93, Setagaya Art Museum 1992–93. *Address:* c/o Phyllis Kind Gallery, 136 Greene Street, New York, NY 10012, USA.

NYAKYI, Anthony Balthazar, BA; Tanzanian diplomatist; b. 8 June 1936, Moshi; m. Margaret Mariki 1969; two s. two d.; ed Umbwe Secondary School, Moshi, Holy Ghost Secondary School, Pugu, Makerere Univ. Coll., Kampala, Uganda; Dir Political Div., Ministry of Foreign Affairs 1966–68; Amb. to Netherlands 1968–70, to FRG (also Accred to the Holy See 1970 and Romania 1972) 1970–72; Prin. Sec. Ministry of Foreign Affairs 1972–78, Ministry of Defence and Nat. Service 1978–80; High Commr in Zimbabwe 1980–81, in UK 1981–89; Perm. Rep. to UN 1989–94; UN Special Rep. for Liberia 1994–98; Amb. to Burundi 1998–. *Address:* Tanzanian Embassy, B.P. 1653, Bujumbura, Burundi.

NYAMDOO, Gendengiyin, PhD; Mongolian diplomatist; b. 1 April 1934; m.; three c.; ed Inst. of Int. Relations, Moscow; served in Mongolian Dept of Legal Affairs and Dept of Int. Orgs., Ministry of Foreign Affairs 1962–68, Chief of Section of Legal Affairs 1969–72, Dir of Dept of Treaties and Legal Affairs 1972–76, 1980–84; Counsellor of Mongolian Mission to the UN 1976–78, Perm. Rep. to UN 1984–88; Amb. to USA 1989–91, to the UK 1995; Foreign Policy Adviser to Prime Minister 1991–92; mem. Constitutional Court 1992–. *Address:* c/o Ministry of External Relations, Government Building 6, Ulan Bator, Mongolia.

NYAMOYA, Albin; Burundian politician; b. 27 July 1924, Ibuye, Ngozi Prov.; s. of Pierre Nkikanyi and Marie Inamabubwe; m. Mélanie Sinduhije 1946; six s. (one deceased) four d. (one deceased); ed Ecole Supérieure, Astrida (now Butare, Rwanda); qualified as veterinary surgeon; held various posts at the Ministry of Agric. and Stockbreeding, Ruanda-Urundi 1945–61, Minister of Agric. and Stockbreeding 1961–62; Minister of Interior and Information, Burundi 1962–63; Prime Minister and Minister of State 1964–65; Minister of State 1965–66; Deputy to Nat. Ass. 1963–66; various posts in Ministry of Agric. and Stockbreeding 1966–72, Dir-Gen. 1970–71, Minister 1971–72; Prime Minister and Minister of the Interior 1972–73; Nat. Exec. Sec., mem. Cen. Cttee, Political Bureau, Unity and Nat. Progress Party until 1973; engaged in pvt. livestock farming and research 1973–76, 1980–; mem. Party Bureau, Chair. Political Comm., mem. Rural Villagization Comm. 1976–78; Adviser to Minister of Agric., Livestock and Rural Devt 1978–80, to Dept of Livestock 1980; elected mem. Nat. Ass. 1982, mem. various Govt comms. 1982–; Councillor, Mwumba Commune, Ngozi Prov. 1985–91; mem. Party Prov. Cttee, Bujumbura 1991–; mem. Nat. Comm. studying Nat. Unity 1988–91, Centre de Développement et de Solidarité 1990–91, Comm. de Commercialisation du Café, Office du Café 1991–92; mem. Bd Société Régionale de Développement du Buyenzi 1983–87, Bureau Pharmaceutique Vétérinaire 1988–91; Commdr Ordre du Mérite Civique 1985.

NYANDA, Lt-Gen. Siphiwe (Gebhuza), BA; South African army officer; b. b. 22 May 1950, Soweto; s. of Henry Nyanda and Betsy Nyanda; two s. four d.; ed Orlando High School, Soweto and Univ. of S. Africa; fmrly sports journalist; trained in fmr GDR and USSR as platoon Commdr, artilleryman and in intelligence; mem. African Nat. Congress, fmrly guerrilla fighter for A.N.C., Commissar of Transvaal Region 1979–86, mem. Nat. Exec. Cttee 1991–96; Deputy Chief South African Nat. Defence Force 1997–98, Chief 1998–; Mil. Merit Medal 1995, Gold Star of South Africa 1998, American Legion of Honor and other decorations. *Leisure interests:* reading, watching soccer, playing golf, aerobics. *Address:* c/o Ministry of Defence, Armscor Building, Block 5, Nossob Street, Erasmusrand 0181; Private Bag X603, Pretoria 0001; 301 Edward Street, Waterkloof Ridge, Pretoria, South Africa (Home). *Telephone:* (12) 3556000 (Office); (12) 3465604 (Home). *Fax:* (12) 3556016 (Office).

NYANJA, Rt Rev Peter Nathaniel; Malawi ecclesiastic; b. 10 June 1940; m. Irene Matrida Kayamba 1964; seven s. one d.; ed secondary school; primary school teacher 1963–67; parish priest 1972–77; Diocesan Bishop, Diocese of Lake Malawi 1978–. *Leisure interest:* gardening. *Address:* Diocese of Lake Malawi, P.O. Box 30349, Capital City, Lilongwe 3, Malawi. *Telephone:* 731966 (Office); 722670 (Home).

NYE, John Frederick, MA, PhD, FRS; British professor emeritus of physics; b. 26 Feb. 1923, Hove; s. of Haydn Percival Nye and Jessie Mary Nye (née Hague); brother of Peter Nye (q.v.); m. Georgiana Wiebenson 1953; one s. two d.; ed Stowe School, King's Coll. Cambridge; Demonstrator, Dept of Mineralogy and Petrology, Univ. of Cambridge 1949–51; mem. of Tech. Staff, Bell Telephone Labs., NJ 1952–53; Lecturer in Physics, Bristol Univ. 1953–65, Reader 1965–69, Prof. 1969–88, Prof. Emer. 1988–; Pres. Int. Glaciological Soc. 1966–69, Int. Comm. of Snow and Ice 1971–75; Foreign mem. Royal Swedish Acad. of Sciences 1977; glacier in Palmer Peninsula, Antarctica officially named Nye Glacier 1963; Seligman Crystal Int. Glaciological Soc. 1969, Antarctic Service Medal (ed.) 1974, Charles Chree Medal and Prize, Inst. of Physics 1989. *Publications:* Physical Properties of Crystals 1957, Natural Focusing and Fine Structure of Light 1999; numerous papers in scientific journals on glaciers, physics of ice, waves and mathematical catastrophes. *Leisure interest:* gardening. *Address:* H. H. Wills Physics Laboratory, Tyndall Avenue, Bristol, BS8 ITL (Office); 45 Canynge Road, Bristol, BS8 3LH, England (Home). *Telephone:* (117) 928 8727 (Office); (117) 973 3769 (Home).

NYE, Joseph S(amuel), Jr, PhD; American university dean and professor of political science; b. 19 Jan. 1937; s. of Joseph Nye and Else Ashwell; m. Molly Harding 1961; three s.; ed Princeton, Oxford and Harvard Univs; Prof. of Govt Harvard Univ. 1969–, also Dir Centre for Int. Affairs 1989–93; Deputy Under-Sec. Dept of State, Washington, DC 1977–79, Chair. Nat. Intelligence Council 1992–; Asst Sec. of Defense for Int. Security Affairs 1994–95, Dean and Don K. Price Prof. of Public Policy, John F. Kennedy School of Govt 1995–; mem. Trilateral Comm.; Fellow, American Acad. of Arts and Sciences, Aspen Inst.; mem. Council, Int. Inst. of Strategic Studies; mem. Council on Foreign Relations; Dept of State Distinguished Honor Award 1979, Intelligence Distinguished Service Award 1994, Dept of Defense Distinguished Service Medal 1995. *Publications:* Power and Independence (co-author) 1977, The Making of America's Soviet Policy (ed. and co-author) 1984, Hawks, Doves and Owls (co-author and ed.) 1985, Nuclear Ethics 1986, Fateful Visions (co-ed.) 1988, Bound to Lead: The Changing Nature of American Power (co-ed.) 1990, Understanding International Conflicts: An Introduction to Theory and History 1993, Governance in a Globalizing World 2000, The Paradox of American Power 2002. *Leisure interests:* fly-fishing, skiing, hiking, squash, gardening. *Address:* Harvard University, JFK School of Government, Office of the Dean, 79 John F. Kennedy Street, Cambridge, MA 02138, USA (Office).

NYE, Peter Hague, BSc, MA, FRS; British soil scientist; b. 16 Sept. 1921, Hove, Sussex; s. of Haydn P. Nye and Jessie M. Hague; brother of John Nye (q.v.); m. Phyllis M. Quenault 1953; one s. one d. (and one d. deceased); ed Charterhouse, Balliol Coll. Oxford and Christ's Coll. Cambridge; agricultural chemist, Gold Coast 1947–50; Lecturer in Soil Science, Univ. Coll. of Ibadan, Nigeria 1950–52; Sr Lecturer in Soil Science, Univ. of Ghana 1952–60; Research Officer, Vienna 1960–61; Reader in Soil Science, Univ. of Oxford 1961–88, Emer. Reader 1988–; Professorial Fellow, St Cross Coll. Oxford 1966–88 (Sr Fellow 1982–83), Emer. Fellow 1988–; Pres. British Soc. of Soil Science 1968–69; mem. Council, Int. Soc. of Soil Science 1968–74; Gov. Nat. Vegetable Research Station 1972–88; Visiting Prof. Cornell Univ. 1974, 1981, Univ. of W. Australia 1979, Royal Veterinary and Agricultural Univs Copenhagen 1990; Hon. Research Prof. Scottish Crop Research Inst. 1995–2000; Fellow Inst. of Professional Soil Scientists; Messenger Lectures, Cornell Univ. 1989; IMPHOS Award 1982. *Publications:* The Soil Under Shifting Cultivation 1961, Solute Movement in the Soil-Root System (co-author) 1977, Solute Movement in the Rhizosphere (co-author) 2000; numerous papers, mainly in Journal of Soil Science and Plant and Soil. *Leisure interests:* watching cricket, computing. *Address:* Hewel Barn, Common Road, Beckley, Oxon., OX3 9UR, England. *Telephone:* (1865) 351607 (Home). *Fax:* (1865) 351607 (Home).

NYE, Robert, FRSL; British poet, novelist and critic; b. 15 March 1939, London; s. of Oswald William Nye and Frances Dorothy Weller; m. 1st Judith Pratt 1959 (divorced 1967); three s.; m. 2nd Aileen Campbell 1968; one d. one step-s. one step-d.; ed Southend High School; freelance writer 1961–; contributes critical articles and reviews to British periodicals, including The Times and The Scotsman; Poetry Critic, The Times 1971–96; Eric Gregory Award 1963, Guardian Fiction Prize 1976, Hawthornden Prize 1977, Soc. of Authors Travelling Scholarship 1991. *Publications include:* (poetry) Juvenilia 1 1961, Juvenilia 2 1963, Darker Ends 1969, Divisions on a Ground 1976, A Collection of Poems 1955–1988 1989, Collected Poems 1995, 1998, New and Selected Poems 2003; (novels) Doubtfire 1967, Falstaff 1976, Merlin 1978, Faust 1980, The Voyage of the Destiny 1982, The Memoirs of Lord Byron 1989, The Life and Death of My Lord Gilles de Rais 1990, Mrs. Shakespeare: The Complete Works 1993, The Late Mr. Shakespeare 1998, and several children's books, plays. *Address:* Thornfield, Kingsland, Ballinhassig, Co. Cork, Ireland.

NYEMBO SHABANI, D.SC.(ECON.); Democratic Republic of the Congo politician and professor of economics; b. 5 Aug. 1937, Kayanza; ed Inst. Saint Boniface, Elisabethville (now Lubumbashi) and Univ. Catholique de Louvain, Belgium; Dir, Bureau of Econ. Co-operation attached to the Prime Minister's Office 1964–65; Research in Econs Univ. Catholique de Louvain 1967–76; Prof. Faculty of Econ. Science, Nat. Univ. of Zaire Oct. 1976; State Commr for

Nat. Econ. and Industry Feb.–Aug. 1977, for Nat. Econ. 1977–78, for the State Portfolio (Investments) 1978–80, for Agric. and Rural Devt 1980–81, 1983–84, for Econ., Industry and Foreign Trade 1982–83, for Finance and Budget 1986–88, for Agric. 1988–89; Pres. Gécamines Holdings 1985. *Publications:* L'industrie du cuivre dans le monde, Le progrès économique du Copperbelt Africain, Bruxelles, La Renaissance du Livre 1975. *Address:* B.P. 3. 824, Kinshasa 1, Democratic Republic of the Congo (Home).

NYKVIST, Sven; Swedish cinematographer; b. 3 Dec. 1922, Moheda; ed Stockholm Municipal School for Photographers; asst photographer, Sandew movie studios 1941–59; photographer, Cinecitta, Rome; filmed nearly 40 feature-length films and several documentaries in Africa including Vördnad för Livet (Albert Schweitzer); Dir of Photography for Ingmar Bergman from 1960; has worked with many other famous dirs including John Huston, Caspar Wrede, Richard Fleischer, Roman Polanski, Louis Malle, Alan J. Pakula and Andrei Tarkovsky; numerous Swedish and int. honours and awards inc. Acad. Award for Photography in Bergman's Cries and Whispers 1973. *Films include:* with Bergman: The Virgin Spring 1960, Through a Glass Darkly 1960, Winter Light 1963, The Silence 1963, All These Women 1964, Persona 1966, Hour of the Wolf 1968, A Passion 1969, The Touch 1971, Cries and Whispers 1973, Scenes from a Marriage 1973, The Magic Flute 1975, Face to Face 1976, The Serpent's Egg 1977, The Autumn Sonata 1978, The Postman Always Rings Twice 1980, Star 80 1982, The Tragedy of Carmen 1983, Swann in Love 1985, The Sacrifice, Agnes of God 1987, Dream Lover, The Unbearable Lightness of Being 1987, Katinka, Another Woman 1989, The Ox (Dir only) 1991, New York Stories, Crimes and Misdemeanors, Chaplin, Sleepless in Seattle, With Honors, Kirsten Lavrandatter, Only You, Mixed Nuts, Something to Talk About 1995, Confession. *Publications:* three books. *Address:* c/o Svenska Filminstitutet, Filmhuset Borgvagen 1–5, Box 27126, 10252 Stockholm 27, Sweden. *Telephone:* (8) 665-11-00.

NYRUP RASMUSSEN, Poul; Danish politician; b. 15 June 1943, Esbjerg, Western Jutland; s. of Olof Nyrup Rasmussen and Vera Nyrup Rasmussen; m. 1st (divorced); m. 2nd (divorced); m. 3rd Lone Dybkjar; one c. (deceased); ed Esbjerg Statsskole and Univ. of Copenhagen; worked for Danish Trade Union Council 1981; Man. Dir Employees' Capital Pension Fund 1986–88; Deputy Chair. Social Democratic Party 1987–92, Chair. 1992–; mem. Parl. 1988–; Prime Minister of Denmark 1993–2001. *Address:* Office of the Prime Minister, Christiansborg, Prins Jørgens Gaard 11, 1218 Copenhagen K, Denmark. *Telephone:* 33-92-33-00. *Fax:* 33-11-16-65. *E-mail:* stm@stm.dk. *Website:* www.stm.dk.

NZAMBIMANA, Lt-Col Edouard; Burundian politician and army officer; Minister of Public Works, Transport and Equipment 1974–76; participated in coup which overthrew Pres. Micombero Nov. 1976; Prime Minister 1976–78 and Minister of Planning 1976–78, of Agric., Livestock and Rural Devt 1978, of Foreign Affairs and Co-operation 1978–82; currently Chair. Union Commerciale d'Assurances et de Réassurance (UCAR). *Address:* Union Commerciale d'Assurances et de Réassurance, B.P. 3012, Bujumbura, Burundi. *Telephone:* 223638. *Fax:* 223695.

O

Ó MÓRÁIN, Dónall; Irish public official; b. 6 Sept. 1923, Co. Kerry; s. of Mícheál Ó Móráin and Eibhlín Ní Loingsigh; m. Maire Beaumont 1949; three s. two d.; ed Coláiste Muire, Dublin, Univ. Coll., Dublin and King's Inns, Dublin; called to the Bar 1946; Man. Ed. of Retail Food Trade Journal 1946–50; Gen. Man., printing and publishing firm 1951–63; Founder, Gael-Linn (voluntary nat. cultural and social asscn) 1953, Chair. 1953–63, Dir-Gen. 1963–88, Chair. and Life mem. of Bd 1988–; Chair. Convocation of Nat. Univ. of Ireland 1955–84; Chair. Inisfree Handknits Group 1965–; mem. Radio Telefís Éireann Authority 1965–70, Chair. 1970–72, 1973–76; mem. Language Consultative Council, Dept of Finance 1965–75; Dir Glens of Antrim Tweed Co. Ltd 1967–79; mem. Irish Comm. for UNESCO 1966–, Irish Film Industry Comm. 1967–69; Chair. Consultative Council to Radio na Gaeltachta (first local radio service in Ireland) 1971–76; Founder and Man. Dir Anois, Sunday newspaper 1984–96; Man. Dir Gael-Linn Educational Publications 1996–; Hon. LLD (Nat. Univ. of Ireland) 1979. *Leisure interests:* fowling, salmon fishing. *Address:* 32 Sydney Avenue, Blackrock, Dublin, Ireland. *Telephone:* (1) 2880541. *Fax:* (1) 6767030.

OAKLEY, Ann, PhD; British sociologist and writer; b. 17 Jan. 1944; d. of Richard Titmus; m. Robin Oakley (divorced); three c.; ed Chiswick Polytechnic and Somerville Coll., Oxford; Prof. of Sociology and Social Policy, Dir Social Science Research Unit, Inst. of Educ., Univ. of London 1991–; Hon. Prof. Univ. Coll. London 1996–; Hon. Fellow Somerville Coll. Oxford 2001–; Hon. DLitt (Salford) 1995. *Publications include:* (novels) The Men's Room (adapted for TV 1991) 1988, Only Angels Forget 1990, Matilda's Mistake 1991, The Secret Lives of Eleanor Jenkinson 1992, Scenes Orginating in the Garden of Eden 1993, A Proper Holiday 1996, Overheads 2000; (non-fiction) Sex Gender and Society 1972, Women Confined: Towards a Sociology of Child-birth 1980, Subject Women 1981, Essays on Women, Medicine and Health 1993, Man and Wife: Richard and Kay Titmus, My Parents, Early Years 1996, Experiments in Knowing: Gender and Method in the Social Sciences 2000, Gender on Planet Earth 2002. *Leisure interests:* cycling, grandchildren. *Address:* Social Science Research Unit, Institute of Education, 18 Woburn Square, London, WC1H 0NR, England (Office). *Telephone:* (20) 7612-6391 (Office). *Fax:* (20) 7612-6400 (Office). *E-mail:* a.oakley@ioe.ac.uk (Office). *Website:* www.ioe.ac.uk/SSRU/ (Office).

OATES, Joyce Carol, MA; American author; b. 16 June 1938, Lockport, NY; d. of Frederic J. Oates and Caroline Bush; m. Raymond J. Smith 1961; ed Syracuse Univ. and Univ. of Wisconsin; Prof. of English, Univ. of Detroit 1961–67, Univ. of Windsor, Ont. 1967–87; Writer-in-Residence, Princeton Univ. 1978–81, Prof. 1987–; mem. American Acad., Inst. of Arts and Letters; Guggenheim Fellow 1967–68; O. Henry Prize Story Award 1967, 1968, Rea Award for Short Story 1990, Elmer Holmes Bukst Award 1990. *Publications include:* novels: With Shuddering Fall 1965, A Garden of Earthly Delights 1967, Wonderland 1971, Do With Me What You Will 1973, The Assassins 1975, Childwold 1976, The Triumph of the Spider Monkey 1977, Son of the Morning 1978, Unholy Loves 1979, Cybele 1979, Bellefleur 1980, A Sentimental Education 1981, Angel of Light 1981, A Bloodsmoor Romance 1982, Mysteries of Winterthurn 1984, Solstice 1985, Wild Nights 1985, The Lives of the Twins 1987, You Must Remember This 1988, American Appetites 1989, Because It Is Bitter and Because It Is My Heart 1990, Black Water 1992, Foxfire 1993, What I Lived For 1994, Man Crazy 1997, My Heart Laid Bare 1998, The Collector of Hearts 1999, Broke Heart Blues 1999, Blonde: A Novel 2000, several volumes of poems including Them 1969 (Nat. Book Award 1970); Nemesis (under pseudonym of Rosamond Smith) 1990, I Lock the Door Upon Myself 1990; George Bellows: American Artist 1995 (biog.); plays, stories, essays; fiction in nat. magazines; Ed. The Oxford Book of American Short Stories 1993. *Address:* Department of Creative Writing, Princeton University, 117/185 Nassau Street, Princeton, NJ 08544 (Office); c/o John Hawkins, 71 W 23rd Street, Suite 1600, New York, NY 10010, USA.

OBAID, Thoraya Ahmed, PhD; Saudi Arabian international organization official; b. 2 March 1945, Baghdad, Iraq; m.; two d.; ed Mills Coll., Oakland, USA, Wayne State Univ., Detroit, USA; mem. League of Arab States working group for formulating the Arab Strategy for Social Devt 1984–85; mem. Editorial Bd Journal of Arab Women 1984–90; mem. Int. Women's Advisory Panel, Int. Planned Parenthood Fed. 1993; Chair. UN Inter-agency Task Force on Gender, Amman 1996; mem. UN Inter-agency Gender Mission to Afghanistan Nov. 1997; mem. UN Strategic Framework Mission to Afghanistan 1997; Assoc. Social Affairs Officer (Women and Devt), Econ. and Social Comm. for W Africa (ESCWA) Social Devt and Population Div. (SDPD) 1975–81, Women and Devt Programme Man. ESCWA SDPD 1981–92, Chief ESCWA SDPD 1992–93, Deputy Exec. Sec. ESCWA 1993–98; Dir Div. for Arab States and Europe, UN Fund for Population Activities (UNFPA) 1998–2000, Exec. Dir UNFPA 2001–. *Address:* UN Fund for Population Activities, 220 East 42nd Street, 19th Floor, New York, NY 10017, USA (Office). *Telephone:* (212) 297-5020 (Office). *Fax:* (212) 297-4911 (Office). *Website:* www.unfpa.org (Office).

OBAME-NGUEMA, Paulin; Gabonese politician; mem. Union nationale pour la démocratie et le développement (UNDD); Prime Minister of Gabon 1994–99. *Address:* c/o Office of the Prime Minister, BP 546, Libreville, Gabon.

OBANDO Y BRAVO, HE Cardinal Miguel; Nicaraguan ecclesiastic; b. 2 Feb. 1926, La Libertad (Chontales), Juigalpa; ordained 1958; consecrated Bishop (Titular Church of Puzia di Bizacena) 1968–, Archbishop of Managua 1970–; cr. Cardinal 1985; Chair. Nat. Reconciliation Comm. for Nicaragua 1987; currently Pres. Nicaragua Bishops' Conf. *Address:* Conferencia Episcopal de Nicaragua, Ferretería Long 1c al. Norte, 1c al. Este, Zona 3, Las Piedrecitas, Apdo 2407, Managua (Office); Arzobispado, Apartado 3058, Managua, Nicaragua. *Telephone:* (2) 66-6292 (Office); (2) 277-1754. *Fax:* (2) 66-8089 (Office); (2) 276-0130. *E-mail:* cen@tmx.com.ni (Office).

O'BANNON, Frank Lewis, BA, JD; American lawyer and politician; b. June 1930, Louisville, Ky; s. of Robert Pressley O'Bannon and Rosella Faith Dropsey; m. Judith Asmus 1957; one s. two d.; ed Indiana Univ.; pvt. practice, Corydon, Ind.; partner Hays, O'Bannon, Funk, Corydon 1966–80, O'Bannon, Funk and Simpson 1990–94, Funk, Simpson, Thompson and Byrd 1995–97; mem. Ind. Senate 1970–89, Asst Minority Floor Leader 1972–76, Minority Floor Leader 1979–89; Lt-Gov. of Ind. 1989–97, Gov. 1997–2000; Chair. and Dir O'Bannon Co. Inc.; mem. American Judicature Soc., American Bar Asscn; Democrat. *Address:* c/o Office of the Governor, State House, 200 West Washington Street, Indiana, IN 46204, USA.

OBASANJO, Gen. Olusegun; Nigerian politician and fmr army officer; b. 5 March 1937, Abeokuta, Ogun State; m. 1st Oluremi Akinbwon; two s. four d.; m. 2nd Stella Abebe; ed Abeokuta Baptist High School and Mons Officers' Cadet School, UK; joined Nigerian Army 1958, commissioned 1959; served in Congo (now Democratic Repub. of the Congo) 1960; promoted Capt. 1963, Maj. 1965, Lt-Col 1967, Col 1969, Brig. 1972, Lt-Gen. 1976, Gen. 1979; Commdr Eng Corps 1963, later Commdr 2nd Div. (Rear), Ibadan; G.O.C. 3rd Infantry Div. 1969; Commdr 3rd Marine Commando Div. during Nigerian Civil War, accepted surrender of Biafran forces Jan. 1970; Commdr Eng Corps 1970–75; Fed. Commr for Works and Housing Jan.–July 1975; Chief of Staff, Supreme HQ 1975–76; mem. Supreme Mil. Council 1975–79; Head of Fed. Mil. Govt and C-in-C of Armed Forces 1976–79; mem. Advisory Council of State 1979; farmer 1979–; arrested March 1995, interned 1995; Pres. of Nigeria and C-in-C of Armed Forces May 1999–; Fellow, Univ. of Ibadan 1979–81; mem. Ind. Comm. on Disarmament and Security 1980, mem. Exec. Cttee Inter Action Council of fmr Heads of Govt; Chair. Africa Leadership Forum and Foundation; Co-Chair. Eminent Persons Group on S. Africa (EPG) 1985; Hon. D.Hum.Litt (Howard); Hon. LLD (Maiduguri) 1980, (Ahmadu Bello Univ., Zaria) 1985, (Ibada) 1988; Grand Commdr Fed. Repub. of Nigeria 1980. *Publications:* My Command 1980, Africa in Perspective 'Myths and Realities' 1987, Nzeogwu 1987, Africa Embattled 1988, Constitution for National Integration and Development 1989, Not My Will 1990, Elements of Development 1992, Elements of Democracy 1993, Africa: Rise to Challenge 1993, Hope for Africa 1993. *Leisure interests:* table tennis, squash, reading, writing. *Address:* Office of the Head of State, New Federal Secretariat Complex, Shehu Shagari Way, Central Area District, Abuja, Nigeria (Office). *Telephone:* (9) 5233536 (Office).

OBASI, Godwin Olu Patrick, DSc; Nigerian meteorologist, statistician and manager; b. 24 Dec. 1933, Ogori; s. of A. B. P. Obasi and R. A. Akande; m.; one s. five d.; ed McGill Univ., Montreal, Canada and Massachusetts Inst. of Tech., USA; joined Nigerian Meteorological Dept as Asst Meteorological Officer 1956, later apptd. Sr Meteorologist in charge of Research and Training and of Nat. Meteorological Centre for Forecasting Services; Visiting Research Scientist, Fla State Univ. and Nat. Center for Atmospheric Research, Boulder, Colo, USA 1973; Sr Lecturer in Meteorology for WMO/UNDP, Univ. of Nairobi, Kenya 1967–74; Prof., Chair. Dept of Meteorology and Dean Faculty of Science 1974–76; Adviser in Meteorological Research and Training, Fed. Govt of Nigeria, Head Nigerian Inst. for Meteorological Research and Training 1976–78; Vice-Pres. and mem. Advisory Working Group, Comm. for Atmospheric Sciences 1978; Dir Educ. and Training Dept, WMO Secr., Geneva 1978–84, Sec.-Gen. WMO 1984–; mem. British Inst. of Statisticians, Int. Acad. of Sciences of Nature and Society (Armenia br.) 1998; Fellow African Acad. of Sciences 1993, Third World Acad. of Sciences 1996 (Vice-Pres. 1999–), Int. Energy Foundation 1998, meteorological socs. of Dominican Repub., Ecuador, Colombia, Nigeria, Africa, America; Hon. mem. Acad. of Agricultural and Forestry Sciences, Romania, Kenya Meteorological Soc., Hellenic Meteorological Soc.; Hon. Fellow Meteorological Socs. of Cuba, Burkina Faso, India; Hon. Dr. Physics (Bucharest) 1991; Hon. LLD (Univ. of Philippines) 1992; Hon. DSc (Fed. Univ. of Tech., Nigeria) 1992, (Alpine Geophysical Research Inst., Russian Fed.) 1993, (Univ. of Nairobi) 1998; Gold Plaque Merit Award for Science and Art, Czechoslovakian Acad. of Sciences 1986, Gold Medal for Meteorology and Hydrology, Paraguay 1988, Cross Medal of Air Force, Venezuela 1989, Ogori Merit Award, Kogi State, Nigeria 1991, Washington Climate Award, USA 1990, Gold Medal Award, African Meteorological Soc. 1993, Recognition of Merit, Nat. Univ. of Asunción, Paraguay 1993, Medal of Merit for Devt of Hydrology and Meteorology, Slovak Hydrometeorological Inst. 1994, Balkan Physical Union Golden Medal Award, Greece 1997, Medal of Honour and Certificate of Merit, Front for Ebira Solidarity, Okene, Nigeria 1995, Award for Promotion of Hydrometeorology, Viet Nam 1998, Nat. Roll of Honour for Environmental Achievement, Nigeria 1999 and other awards; Officer Order of Fed. Repub. of Nigeria; Commdr Nat. Order Côte d'Ivoire, Benin, Burkina Faso; Commdr Nat. Order of Lion,

Senegal, Medal of Freedom of Ho Chi Minh City, Viet Nam, Order of Grand Duke of Gediminas and Medal Order of Gediminas, Lithuania, Presidential Award Medal of Friendship, Viet Nam and other distinctions. *Publications:* many scientific and tech. papers on meteorology and hydrometeorology. *Leisure interests:* tennis, gardening, reading. *Address:* World Meteorological Organization, 7 bis avenue de la Paix, CP 2300, 1211 Geneva 2, Switzerland (Office). *Telephone:* (22) 7308111 (Office). *Fax:* (22) 7308181 (Office). *E-mail:* ipa@gateway.wmo.ch (Office). *Website:* www.wmo.ch (Office).

OBEID, Atif Muhammad, MA, PhD; Egyptian politician; m.; two c.; ed Faculty of Commerce, Cairo Univ. and Univ. of Illinois; mem. Arab League Media Policy Co-ordinating Cttee 1970; fmr Prof. of Business Admin. Faculty of Commerce, Cairo Univ. and Pres. Int. Man. Centre; Minister of Cabinet Affairs and Minister of State for Admin. Devt 1985–93, Minister of the Public Enterprise Sector 1993–99; Prime Minister of Egypt Oct. 1999–. *Address:* Sharia Majlis ash-Sha'ab, Lazoughli Square, Cairo, Egypt. *Telephone:* (2) 3553192 (Office). *Fax:* (2) 3558016 (Office). *E-mail:* primemin@idsc.gov.eg (Office).

OBEIDAT, Ahmad Abdul-Majeed; Jordanian politician; b. 1938, Hartha, Irbid; m.; five c.; ed Salahiyah School and Univ. of Baghdad; Teacher, Min. of Educ. 1957; Customs Officer 1961; First Lt-Gen. Security Service 1962–64; Asst Dir Gen. Intelligence Service 1964–74, Dir 1974–82; Minister of the Interior 1982–84; Prime Minister of Jordan and Minister of Defence 1984–85; partner Law and Arbitration Centre 1985–. *Address:* Law and Arbitration Centre, P.O. Box 926544, Amman, Jordan. *Telephone:* 672222.

OBENG, Letitia Eva, PhD, FRSA; Ghanaian scientist and research director; b. Takyibea Asihene, 10 Jan. 1925, Anum; d. of Rev. E. V. Asihene and Dora Asihene; m. George A. Obeng 1953; two s. one d.; ed Achimota Coll., Ghana, Univs. of Birmingham and Liverpool, UK; Lecturer, Coll. of Science and Tech. Kumasi 1952–59; Research Scientist, Nat. Research Council, Ghana 1960–62; research staff, Ghana Acad. of Sciences 1963–65; built and first Dir Inst. of Aquatic Biological Council for Scientific and Industrial Research (CSIR), Ghana 1965–74; Sr Programme Officer and Chair. Soil and Water Task Force, UNEP, Nairobi 1974–80; Dir and Regional Rep. of UNEP to Africa 1980–85; Dir. Environmental Man. Services 1986; Distinguished Int. Visitor, Radcliffe Coll., Cambridge, Mass., USA 1992; mem. Exec. Council, Africa Leadership Forum 1991; Trustee, Bd of Int. Rice Research Inst., Int. Irrigation Man. Inst., Human Ecology Foundation; Dir Bd of Stockholm Environment Inst., PANOS etc. 1986–95; Fellow, Ghana Acad. of Arts and Sciences, New York Acad. of Sciences 1995; Silver Medal, Royal Soc. of Arts, Ghanoa Council for Scientific and Industrial Research (CSIR) Award 1997, Ghana Govt Award 1998, CSIR Bldg named The Letitia Obeng Block 1998; featured on nat. commemorative postage stamp. *Publications:* Man-made Lakes (ed.) 1969, Environment and the Responsibility of the Privileged, Environment and Population, The Right to Health in Tropical Agriculture; Parasites: The Sly and Sneaky Enemies Inside You 1997, Ephraim Amu – A Portrait of Cultured Patriotism; scientific articles; book chapters. *Leisure interests:* poetry, painting flowers, Akan culture and traditions. *Address:* P.O. Box C223, Accra, Ghana.

OBERMEIER, Georg, DPhil; German business executive; b. 21 July 1941, Munich; m.; Knorr-Bremse GmbH 1964–72; Bayernwerk AG, Munich, latterly Dir of Finance and Org. 1973–89; mem. Man. Bd VIAG AG 1989–, Chair. 1995–98; Chair. Supervisory Bd Isar-Amperwerke AG, Munich, Rheinhold & Mahla AG, Munich, SKW Trostberg AG, Trostberg; mem. Supervisory Bd Bayernwerk AG, Munich, Didier-Werke AG, Wiesbaden, Gerresheimer Glas AG, Düsseldorf, Klöckner & Co. AG, Duisburg, Kühne & Nagel Int. AG, Schindellegi, Mobil Oil AG, Hamburg, Schmalbach-Lubeca AG, Brunswick, Thomassen & Drijver Verblifa NV, Deventer, Thyssengas GmbH, Duisburg, VAW Aluminium AG, Berlin/Bonn. *Address:* c/o VIAG AG, Nymphenburger Strasse 37, 80335 Munich, Germany.

OBETSEBI-LAMPTEY, Jake; Ghanaian politician and advertising executive; b. 4 Feb. 1946, Accra; scriptwriter, commentator and TV and radio presenter, Ghana Broadcasting Corpn 1966–69; Account Exec. and radio and TV producer Lintas West African advertising agency 1969, Client Service Man., Ghana 1971, wrote, co-ordinated and executed Ghana Nat. Family Planning Programme motivation campaign, Gen. Man. Lintas Ghana Ltd 1974–84; devised operation manuals and presentations for WHO and SOMARC Futures Group 1984–99; Nat. Campaign Man. for New Patriotic Party (NPP), presidential elections 2000; Minister of Information and Presidential Affairs and Chief of Staff 2001–; fmr Pres. Advertising Asscn of Ghana. *Publications:* Using Commercial Resources in Family Planning Programmes: the International Experience, The Handbook for AIDS Prevention in Africa. *Address:* Ministry of Information and Presidential Affairs, P.O.B. 1627, Osu, Accra, Ghana (Office).

OBI, Onyeabo C., LLB, FCIA; Nigerian international business lawyer; b. 20 Nov. 1938, Ogidi; s. of Chief Z.C. Obi; m. Evelyn Nnenna Obioha 1967; two s. three d.; ed London School of Econs, London Univ.; admitted to Bar (Gray's Inn) 1962; in pvt. practice as barrister and solicitor of Supreme Court of Nigeria 1963–; Dir Nigerian Rubber Bd 1977–79; Senator of Fed. Repub. of Nigeria 1979–83; mem. of Council (and Vice-Chair. Cttee on Procedures for Settling Disputes), Section on Business Law, Int. Bar Asscn 1986–92; mem. Advisory Cttee on Rules of the Supreme Court of Nigeria (by appt. of Hon. Chief Justice) 1986–92. *Leisure interest:* lawn tennis. *Address:* Western House

(13th Floor), 8-10 Broad Street, P.O. Box 4040, Lagos, Nigeria (Office). *Telephone:* (1) 263-0843 (Office); (1) 263-4604 (Office). *Fax:* (1) 263-7609 (Office). *E-mail:* abobi@hyperia.com (Office).

OBIALA, Edmund, MESc; Polish/Australian civil and construction engineer; b. 9 Feb. 1946, Poland; m. Grażyna Guth; ed Poznań Univ. of Technology, Bydgoszcz Univ. Technology; geodesist Pomeranian Mil. Dist 1966–72; construction designer, head designer team Eltor, Bydgoszcz 1972–78; research worker Ibmer Warsaw, constructed works in Bydgoszcz 1977–80; mem. staff Civil and Civic Pty Ltd, Sydney 1982–88, Multiplex Constructions Pty Ltd 1988–2000, Bovis Lend Lease Ltd 2000–; Award for Excellence, Concrete Inst. of Australia 1999, Grand Award for Excellence in Arboriculture, Nat. Arborist Asscn 1999, British Construction Award for Olympic Stadium in Sydney 2000, Structural Special Award 2000. *Works:* constructions designed include Nat. Bank of Australia, Sydney 1982–85, sports stadium Parramatta and football stadium, Sydney 1985–88, Chiefley Tower, Coles Myer Centre and rebuilding of Chelsea football team stadium, London 1988–2000. *Achievements:* project director on major constructions including Olympic Stadium, Sydney 1994–99, Wembley Stadium 1999–2001, Chelsea Stadium 1999–2001, Munich City Tower 2001–02. *Leisure interests:* cinema, literature, tennis, volley-ball. *Address:* Bovis Lend Lease Ltd, Bovis House, Northolt Road, Harrow, Middlesex, HA2 OEE, England (Office); 4/26–32 Princess Street, Manchester, M1 4LB (Home). *Telephone:* (20) 8271-8000 (Office); (161) 839-9000 (Office); (161) 228-7284 (Home). *E-mail:* Edmund.Obiola@eu .Bovislendlease.com (Office); guta@bigpond.com (Home); eobiola@onetel.net .uk (Home).

OBOTE, (Apollo) Milton; Ugandan politician; b. 1924; s. of the late Stanley Opeto; labourer, clerk, salesman, Kenya 1950–55; founder-mem. Kenya African Union; mem. Uganda Nat. Congress 1952–60; mem. Uganda Legis. Council 1957–71; formed and mem. of Uganda People's Congress 1960–71, then Leader; Leader of the Opposition 1961–62; Prime Minister 1962–66; Minister of Defence and Foreign Affairs 1963–65; assumed full powers of Govt Feb. 1966; Pres. of Uganda 1966–71 (deposed by mil. coup); in exile in Tanzania 1971–80; returned to Uganda May 1980, re-elected Pres. 1980–85, Minister of Foreign Affairs and Finance 1980–85; deposed by mil. coup 1985; resident in Zambia 1985–.

OBRAZTSOV, Ivan Filippovich; Russian mechanical engineer; b. 28 July 1920, Tver, Tverskaya Prov.; s. of Philipp I. Obraztsov and Pelageia I. Obraztsova; m. Rosa I. Mavrina 1945; two d.; ed Moscow Aviation Inst.; active service with Soviet Army; mem. CPSU 1944–91; teaching 1944–58; Rector of Moscow Aviation Inst. 1958–72; RSFSR Minister of Higher and Intermediate Special Educ. 1972–89; Dir Inst. of Applied Mechanics, USSR (now Russian) Acad. of Sciences 1989–96, Scientific Man. 1996–; Pres. Nat. Cttee for Theoretical and Applied Mechanics 1981–; mem. of USSR (now Russian) Acad. of Sciences, 1974; cand. mem. of CPSU Cen. Cttee 1981–90, USSR People's Deputy 1989–91; State Prize 1976, Lenin Prize 1988. *Publications:* works on building, mechanics and theory of cohesion of flying machines. *Leisure interest:* classical music. *Address:* Institute of Applied Mechanics, Leninsky Prosp. 32a, 117334 Moscow, Russia. *Telephone:* (095) 938-18-36 (Office); (095) 202-82-24 (Home).

OBRAZTSOVA, Elena Vasilyevna; Russian mezzo-soprano; b. 7 July 1939, Leningrad (now St Petersburg); d. of Vasily Alekseevich Obraztsov and Nataliya Ivanovna Obraztsova (née Bychkova); m. 1st Vyacheslav Makarov (divorced 1983); one d.; m. 2nd Algis Žiuraitis 1983 (died 1998); ed Leningrad Conservatoire (under tuition of Prof. Grigoriyeva); Prof., Moscow Conservatoire 1973–94; mem. and Prin. Soloist Bolshoi Theatre, Moscow 1964–; Dir St Petersburg Elena Obraztsova Cultural Center 1999–; has appeared at most leading opera houses of Europe and America, including Vienna State Opera 1975, Metropolitan Opera New York 1976, La Scala Milan 1976, Salzburg 1978, Covent Garden, London 1981 and has toured extensively in Russia and throughout world; gives masterclasses in Europe and Japan; judge of int. vocal competitions; est. Int. Elena Obraztsova Competition for young opera singers, St Petersburg 1999 and for chamber music singers, Moscow 2000; Academician Acad. of Russian Art 1999–; Hon. mem., Russian Acad. of Art Critics and Musical Performance 1999–; Hon. mem. Pushkin Acad. 1995, Russian Acad. of Art Critics and Music Performing 1999; gold medals at competitions Helsinki 1962, Moscow 1962, 1970, Barcelona 1970, Medal of Granados 1971, Gold Pen of Critics, Wiesbaden 1972, Award of Merit, San Francisco 1977, Gold Verdi, Italy 1978, Bartók Memorial Medal, Hungary 1982; State Prize of Russia 1974, Lenin Prize 1976; People's Artist of USSR 1976, Gold Star-Hero of Labour 1990, Order for Services to the Fatherland 1999 and other decorations. *Roles include:* Marina Mniszek in Boris Godunov (debut, Bolshoi 1963), Countess in Queen of Spades, Konchakovna in Prince Igor, Marfa in Khovanshina, Lyubasha in The Tsar's Bride, Helene Bezukhova in War and Peace, Frosia in Semionkotko, Princess de Bouillon in Adriana Lecouvreur, Jocasta in Oedipus Rex, Oberon in A Midsummer Night's Dream, Silvana in La Fiamma, Giovanna Seymour in Anna Bolena, Herodiade, Amneris in Aida, Azucena in Il Trovatore, Eboli in Don Carlos, Santuzza in Cavelleria Rusticana, Ulrica in Un Ballo in Maschera, Adalgiza in Norma, Orfeo in Orfeo ed Euridice, Neris in Medea, Leonora in La Favorita, Aunt Princess in Suor Angelica, Frederica in Louise Miller, Carmen, Charlotte in Werther, Delilah in Samson and Delilah, Judith in Duke Bluebeard's Castle, Granny in The Gambler and others; recital repertoire includes works by more than 100 composers; staged Werther at Bolshoi Theatre 1986. *Film:* Cavalleria Rusticana 1981. *Recordings:* over 50 recordings for Melodia,

Polydor, DG, EMI, CBS, Philips etc. including operas, oratorios, cantatas, solo discs of arias and chamber music. *Play:* Amalia in Antonia von Elba 1999. *Television includes:* My Carmen 1977, And My Image will Rise Before You 1979, The Merry Widow 1984, Higher Than The Love 1991, Elena The Great 1995. *Publication:* Bolshoi (poetry) 2001. *Leisure interests:* dogs, horses, fishing, mushrooms. *Address:* c/o Bolshoi Theatre, Teatralnaya pl. 1, 125009 Moscow (Office); Ermolaevsky per. 9-6, 125001 Moscow, Russia. *Telephone:* (095) 292-31-08 (Office); (095) 292-06-58 (Office); (095) 292-66-90 (Office); (095) 209-17-67 (Home). *Fax:* (095) 292-66-90 (Office); (095) 292-66-32 (Office); (095) 292-16-74 (Home). *E-mail:* pr@bolshoi.ru (Office).

O'BRIEN, Conor Cruise, PhD; Irish writer and diplomatist; b. 3 Nov. 1917, Dublin; s. of Francis Cruise O'Brien and Katherine Sheehy; m. 1st Christine H. Foster 1939 (divorced 1962); one s. one d. (and one d. deceased); m. 2nd Maire MacEntee 1962; one s. one d. (both adopted); ed Sandford Park School, Dublin, Trinity Coll., Dublin; entered Dept of External Affairs of Ireland 1944, Counsellor, Paris 1955–56, Head UN Section and mem. Irish Del. to UN 1956–60, Asst Sec.-Gen., Dept of External Affairs of Ireland 1960; Rep. of Sec.-Gen. of UN in Katanga, Congo (later Shaba, Zaïre) May-Dec. 1961; Vice-Chancellor, Univ. of Ghana 1962–65; Regent's Prof. and Holder of Albert Schweitzer Chair in Humanities, New York Univ. 1965–69; mem. Dáil Eireann (House of Reps) for Dublin (Labour) 1969–77; Minister for Posts and Telegraphs 1973–77; resgnd from Labour Party; Senator for Dublin Univ. 1977–79; Ed.-in-Chief The Observer, London 1978–81, Consultant Ed. 1981; Contributing Ed. The Atlantic, Boston; Pro-Chancellor Univ. of Dublin 1973–; Visiting Fellow, Nuffield Coll., Oxford 1973–75; Fellow, St Catherine's Coll., Oxford 1978; Visiting Prof. Dartmouth Coll., USA 1984–85; mem. Royal Irish Acad.; Hon. DLitt (Bradford) 1971, (Ghana) 1974, (Edin.) 1976, (Nice) 1978, (Liverpool) 1987; Hon. LLD (Glasgow) 1990; Valiant for Truth Media Award 1979. *Publications:* Maria Cross (under pseudonym Donat O'Donnell) 1952, Parnell and his Party 1957, The Shaping of Modern Ireland (ed.) 1959, To Katanga and Back 1962, Conflicting Concepts of the United Nations 1964, Writers and Politics 1965, The United Nations: Sacred Drama 1967, Murderous Angels (play) 1968, Power and Consciousness (ed.) 1969, Conor Cruise O'Brien Introduces Ireland 1969, Edmund Burke's Reflections on the Revolution in France (ed.) 1969, Camus 1969, A Concise History of Ireland (with Máire Cruise O'Brien) 1972, The Suspecting Glance 1972, States of Ireland 1972, Herod's Reflections on Political Violence 1978, Neighbours: Ewart-Biggs memorial lectures 1978–79 1980, The Siege: the Saga of Israel and Zionism 1986, Passion and Cunning 1988, God Land: Reflections on Religion and Nationalism 1988, The Great Melody: A Thematic Biography of Edmund Burke 1992, Ancestral Voices 1994, On the Eve of the Millennium 1996, The Long Affair: Thomas Jefferson and the French Revolution 1996, Memoir: My Life and Themes 1998. *Leisure interest:* travelling. *Address:* Whitewater, Howth Summit, Dublin, Ireland. *Telephone:* (1) 8322474.

O'BRIEN, Edna; Irish author; b. Tuamgraney, Co. Clare; d. of Michael O'Brien and Lena Cleary; m. Ernest Gébler 1954 (divorced 1964); two s.; ed convents, Pharmaceutical Coll. of Ireland; engaged in writing from an early age; Hon. DLitt (Queen's) 1999; Yorkshire Post Novel Award 1971, Kingsley Amis Award, Writers' Guild of GB Award 1993, European Prize for Literature 1995, American Nat. Arts Gold Medal. *Publications include:* The Country Girls 1960 (film 1983), The Lonely Girl 1962, Girls in Their Married Bliss 1963, August is a Wicked Month 1964, Casualties of Peace 1966, The Love Object 1968, A Pagan Place 1970 (play 1971), Night 1972, A Scandalous Woman (short stories) 1974, Mother Ireland 1976, Johnny I Hardly Knew You (novel) 1977, Arabian Days 1977, Mrs. Reinhardt and other stories 1978, Virginia (play) 1979, Mrs. Reinhardt (adapted for TV) 1981, The Dazzle (children's book), Returning: A Collection of New Tales 1982, A Christmas Treat 1982, A Fanatic Heart (Selected Stories) 1985, Madame Bovary (play) 1987, Vanishing Ireland 1987, Tales for the Telling (children's book) 1987, The High Road (novel) 1988, On the Bone (poetry) 1989, Scandalous Woman and Other Stories 1990, Lantern Slides (stories) 1990, Time and Tide (novel) 1992, House of Splendid Isolation (novel) 1994, Down By the River (novel) 1997, Maud Gonne (screenplay) 1996, James Joyce 1999, Wild Decembers 1999, In the Forest (novel) 2002, Iphigenia (play) 2003. *Leisure interests:* reading, walking, meditating. *Address:* c/o David Godwin Associates, 55 Monmouth Street, London, WC2H 9DG, England. *Telephone:* (20) 7240-9992.

O'BRIEN, Gregory Michael St. Lawrence, PhD; American university chancellor; b. 7 Oct. 1944, New York; s. of Henry J. O'Brien and Mary A. McGoldrick; m. Mary K. McLaughlin 1968; two d.; ed Lehigh Univ., Pa and Boston Univ.; Dean and Prof. School of Social Welfare, Univ. of Wisconsin-Milwaukee 1974–78; Provost and Prof. of Psychology, Univ. of Mich.-Flint 1978–80; Prof. of Psychology, Univ. of S. Fla 1980–87, also Prof. of Social Work 1980–87, Prof. of Man. 1986–87, Vice-Pres. for Academic Affairs 1980–87, Univ. Provost 1983–87; Chancellor, Univ. of New Orleans 1987–; Chair. Metro Council Govts. Metrovision 1992–; Vice-Chair. State of LA Film and Video Comm. 1993-94 (mem. 1994–); Supt New Orleans Public Schools 1999–2000; mem. Kellogg Comm. on Future of Land Grant Colls. and State Univs. 1996–; Gambit Weekly's New Orleanian of the Year 1999. *Address:* Office of the Chancellor, University of New Orleans, Lakefront, New Orleans, LA 70148 (Office); 2468 Lark Street, New Orleans, LA 70122, USA (Home). *Telephone:* (504) 280-6201 (Office); (504) 288-4878 (Home).

O'BRIEN, Most Rev. Keith Michael Patrick, BSc, DipEd; British ecclesiastic; b. 17 March 1938, Ballycastle; s. of Mark Joseph O'Brien and Alice Mary Moriarty; ed St Patrick's High School, Dumbarton, Holy Cross Acad., Edin.,

Univ. of Edin., St Andrew's Coll., Drygrange and Moray House Coll. of Educ.; ordained to priesthood 1965; Chaplain and teacher St Columba's High School, Dunfermline 1966–71; Asst Priest St Patrick's, Kilsyth 1972–75, at St Mary's, Bathgate 1975–78; Spiritual Dir St Andrew's Coll. 1978–80; Rector St Mary's Coll., Blairs 1980–85; RC Archbishop of St Andrews and Edin. 1985–; Sovereign Mil. Order of Malta, Grand Cross Conventual Chaplain 1985; Equestrian Order of Holy Sepulchre of Jerusalem, Kt Commdr with Star 1991, Grand Prior of Scottish Lieutenancy of Equestrian Order of Holy Sepulchre of Jerusalem 2001. *Address:* 42 Greenhill Gardens, Edinburgh, EH10 4BJ, Scotland. *Telephone:* (131) 447 3337. *Fax:* (131) 447 0816.

O'BRIEN, (Michael) Vincent; Irish racehorse trainer (retd); b. 9 April 1917, Cork; s. of Daniel P. O'Brien and Kathleen O'Brien (née Toomey); m. Jacqueline Wittenoom 1951; two s. three d.; ed Mungret Coll., Limerick; started training in Co. Cork 1944, moved to Co. Tipperary 1951; won all principal English and Irish steeplechases, including 3 consecutive Champion Hurdles, 3 consecutive Grand Nationals and 4 Gold Cups; concentrated on flat racing from 1959; trained winners of 16 English classics, including 6 Derbys; trained Nijinsky, first Triple Crown winner since 1935, also trained winners of 27 Irish Classics (including 6 Irish Derbys); other major training triumphs include the French Derby, Prix de l'Arc de Triomphe (3), King George VI and Queen Elizabeth Diamond Stakes (2), Washington Int., Breeders' Cup Mile; Hon. LLD (Nat. Univ. Ireland) 1983; Dr hc (Ulster) 1995. *Publications:* Vincent O'Brien: The Man and the Legend. *Leisure interests:* golf, fishing. *Address:* Ballydoyle House, Cashel, Co. Tipperary, Ireland. *Telephone:* (62) 61222. *Fax:* (62) 61677.

O'BRIEN, Patrick Karl, BSc(Econ.), MA, DPhil, FRSA, FRHistS, FBA; British professor of economic history; b. 12 Aug. 1932, London; s. of William O'Brien and Elizabeth O'Brien Stockhausen; m. Cassy Cobham 1959; one s. two d.; ed London School of Economics, Nuffield Coll. Oxford; lecturer, SOAS, London Univ. 1963–70; Reader in Econs and Econ. History, London Univ. 1967–70; Univ. Lecturer in Econ. History and Faculty Fellow, St Antony's Coll. Oxford 1970–84, Univ. Reader in Econ. History and Professorial Fellow 1984–90; Prof. of Econ. History, London Univ. 1990–98; Sr Research Fellow and Convener of Programme in Global History, Inst. of Historical Research, London Univ. 1998– (now Dir); Centennial Prof. of Econ. History, LSE 1999–; Fellow Academia Europaea; Dr hc (Carlos III Univ., Madrid) 1999, (Uppsala) 2000. *Publications:* The Revolution in Egypt's Economic System 1966, The New Economic History of Railways 1977, Two Paths to the 20th Century: Economic Growth in Britain and France 1978, The Economic Effects of the Civil War 1988. *Leisure interests:* theatre, Western art, foreign travel. *Address:* Department of Economic History, London School of Economics, Houghton Street, Aldwych, London, WC2A 2AE (Office); 66 St Bernard's Road, Oxford, OX2 6EJ, England (Home). *Telephone:* (1865) 512004 (Home).

O'BRIEN, Vincent (see O'Brien, Michael Vincent).

O'BRIEN QUINN, James Aiden, BA, LLB, QC; Irish lawyer; b. 3 Jan. 1932, Tipperary; s. of the late William Patrick Quinn and Helen Mary Quinn (née Walshe); m. Christel Mary Tyner 1960; two s. one d.; ed Presentation Coll., Bray, Univ. Coll. Dublin and King's Inns, Dublin; studied banking, Nat. City Bank, Dublin 1949–53; Crown Counsel and Acting Sr Crown Counsel, Nyasaland (Malawi) 1960–64; Asst Attorney-Gen. and Acting Attorney-Gen., West Cameroon 1964–66, Attorney-Gen. 1966–68; Avocat-Général près la Cour Fédérale de Justice, Cameroon 1966–68; Conseiller à la Cour Fédérale de Justice, Yaoundé, Cameroon 1968–72; Président du Tribunal Administratif du Cameroon Occidental 1968–72; Conseiller Technique (Harmonisation des Lois), Yaoundé, Cameroon 1968–72; Attorney-Gen. of Seychelles and British Indian Ocean Territory 1972–76; Chief Justice of Seychelles 1976–77; Acted as Deputy Gov. of Seychelles for a period during 1974; mem. Seychelles dels on self-govt and independence constitutions 1975, 1976; Chief Justice of Gilbert Islands (later Kiribati), Pacific Ocean 1977–81; Judge of High Court of Solomon Islands 1977–81; Special Prosecutor, Falkland Is. 1980; Chief Justice of Botswana 1981–87; Chair. of Judicial Service Comm., Botswana 1981; Adjudicator Immigrations Appeals 1990–96; Vice-Pres. Immigration Appeal Tribunal 1996–; BESO Adviser, Dominica 1992; Third Place, Inst. of Bankers in Ireland 1950; QC, Seychelles 1973; Chevalier de l'Ordre National de la Valeur, Cameroon 1967; Kiribati Independence Medal 1979. *Publications:* Ed. W Cameroon Law Reports 1961–68 and Gilbert Islands Law Reports, Kiribati Law Reports 1977–79; Magistrates' Courts' Handbook, W Cameroon 1968, Magistrates' Courts' Handbook, Kiribati 1979. *Leisure interests:* swimming, reading, languages, travel. *Address:* Field House, 15–25 Bream's Buildings, London, EC4A 1DZ (Office); 9 Lorane Court, Langley Road, Watford, Herts., WD1 3LZ, England. *Telephone:* (1923) 232861.

OBUKHOV, Alexei Aleksandrovich, PhD; Russian diplomatist; b. 12 Nov. 1937, Moscow; s. of Alexander Oboukhov and Klaudia Oboukhov; m. Olga Oboukhov; two s.; ed Moscow Inst. of Int. Relations and Univ. of Chicago; joined Ministry of Foreign Affairs 1965; served in Embassy in Thailand; took part in Soviet-American Strategic Arms Limitation Talks and in the talks on Threshold Test Ban Treaty (TTBT), Moscow 1974; Deputy Dir U.S. Dept, Ministry of Foreign Affairs 1980–86; mem. Soviet negotiating team in arms control talks, responsible for negotiations on long-range strategic weapons, subsequently for negotiations on medium-range nuclear weapons, Geneva 1985; Deputy Head Soviet Del., Nuclear and Space Talks, Geneva 1987; Head 1988; Head, Dept of USA and Canada, Ministry of Foreign Affairs 1989–90;

Deputy Minister of Foreign Affairs 1990–91; Amb. to Denmark 1992–96; Amb.-at-Large 1996–, Head of Del. to Russian-Lithuanian talks on border issues 1996–; Chair. Cttee of Sr Officers (CSO) of the Barents Euro/Arctic Council 2000–01, CSO of the Council of Baltic Sea States 2001–02. *Publications:* numerous texts on diplomatic affairs. *Address:* 40/7/71 Bolshaya Yakimanka str., 117049 Moscow, Russia. *Telephone:* (095) 244-25-96; (095) 238-00-48.

OCAMPO, José Antonio, PhD; Colombian United Nations official; b. 20 Dec. 1952; m.; three c.; ed Univ. of Notre Dame, Yale Univ., USA; researcher, Centre for Devt Studies, Univ. de los Andes 1976–80, Dir 1980–82; at Foundation for Higher Educ. and Devt 1983–93, Deputy Dir 1983–84, Exec. Dir 1984–88, Sr Researcher and mem. Bd of Dirs.; Minister of Agric. 1993–94, of Planning 1994–96, of Finance and Public Credit 1996–97; Exec. Sec. UN Econ. Comm. for Latin America and the Caribbean 1998–; Nat. Dir Employment Mission 1985–86; Adviser, Colombian Foreign Trade Bd 1990–91; Adviser, Colombian Nat. Council of Entrepreneurial Asscn; mem. Tech. Comm. on Coffee Affairs, Public Expenditure Comm., Advisory Comm. for Fiscal Reform, Mission on Intergovernmental Finance; consultant to IBRD, IDB and UN; mem. Colombian Acad. of Econ. Science 1987; Visiting Fellow Univ. of Oxford, England, Yale Univ.; Nat. Science Prize 1988. *Address:* Economic Commission for Latin America and the Caribbean, Edif. Naciones Unidas, Avda Dag Hammarskjöld, Casilla 179D, Santiago, Chile (Office). *Telephone:* (2) 2102000 (Office). *Fax:* (2) 2080252 (Office). *E-mail:* dpisantiago@eclac.cl (Office).

O'CATHAIN, Baroness, cr. 1991 (Life Peer), of The Barbican in the City of London; **Detta O'Cathain,** OBE, BA, FCIM; British business executive; b. 3 Feb. 1938, Cork, Ireland; d. of Caoimhghin O'Cathain and Margaret Prior; m. William Ernest John Bishop 1968 (died 2001); ed Loreto School, Rathfarnham, Co. Dublin, Laurel Hill, Limerick, Univ. Coll. Dublin; Asst Economist, Aer Lingus 1961–66; Group Economist, Tarmac Ltd 1966–69; Econ. Adviser, Rootes Motors Ltd 1969–72; Sr Economist, Carrington Viyella 1972; Market Planning Dir, British Leyland 1973–76; Corp. Planning Exec., Unigate PLC 1976–81; Head of Strategic Planning, Milk Marketing Bd 1981–83, Dir and Gen. Man. 1983, Man. Dir Milk Marketing 1984–88; Man. Dir Barbican Centre, London 1990–95; Dir (non-exec.) Midland Bank PLC 1984–93, Tesco PLC 1985–2000, Sears PLC 1987–94, British Airways 1993–, BET PLC 1994–96, BNP Paribas (UK) PLC 1995–, Thistle Hotels 1996–; Pres. Chartered Inst. of Marketing 1998–2001, Southeast Water PLC 1998, Allders PLC 2000–, William Baird PLC 2000–02. *Leisure interests:* music, reading, swimming, gardening. *Address:* House of Lords, London, SW1A 0PW (Office); Eglantine, Tower House Gardens, Arundel, West Sussex, BN18 9RU, England (Home). *Telephone:* (20) 7219-0662 (Office); (1903) 883775 (Home). *Fax:* (20) 7219-5979. *E-mail:* ocathaind@parliament.uk (Office).

OCCHETTO, Achille; Italian politician; b. 1936, Turin; joined Italian Communist Party (PCI) and Young Communists' Fed. 1953, apptd. Nat. Sec. Young Communists 1962; Sec. PCI Palermo 1969, subsequently Regional Sec. for Sicily; moved to Rome, held succession of party posts 1976; Deputy Leader PCI (name changed to Partito Democratico della Sinistra 1991) 1987–88, Gen.-Sec. 1988–94. *Address:* c/o Partito Democratico della Sinistra, Via delle Botteghe Oscure 4, 00186 Rome, Italy.

OCCHIUTO, Antonino, BEcons AND DIPL.; Italian central banker; b. 21 Dec. 1912, Naples; s. of late Stefano Occhiuto and Margherita Ruggiero; m. Valeria Marcucci 1952; one s. two d.; ed Univ. of Naples; Head of Gen. Secr., Banca d'Italia 1961–64, Head of Personnel Dept 1965–67, Gen. Insp. 1967–69, Deputy Dir-Gen. 1969–76, Hon. Dir-Gen. Banca d'Italia 1976–; mem. Bd of Dirs., BIS 1975–; Chair. Luigi Einaudi Inst. for Monetary, Banking and Financial Studies 1976–; Pres. Istituto Italiano di Credito Fondiario, Istituto di Credito per le Imprese di Pubblica Utilità (ICIPU) 1979–; Grande Ufficiale dell'Ordine al Merito della Repubblica Italiana. *Address:* Via Nomentana 293, Rome, Italy.

OCHI, Michio; Japanese politician; mem. House of Reps.; fmr Deputy Chief Cabinet Sec.; fmr Dir.-Gen. Defence Agency; fmr Construction Minister; Chair. Financial Reconstruction Comm. 1999–2000. *Address:* House of Representatives, Tokyo, Japan (Office).

OCHIRBAT, Punsalmaagin, DSc; Mongolian politician; b. 23 Jan. 1942, Tudevtei Dist, Zavkhan Prov.; s. of Gonsiin Gendenjav and Tsogtiin Punsalmaa; m. Sharaviin Tsevelmaa 1965; two d.; ed Mining Inst. of USSR; apptd. official at Ministry of Industry 1966, Chief Engineer Sharyn Gol coal mine 1967, Deputy Minister, Ministry of Fuel and Power Industry and Geology 1972–76, Minister 1976; Chair. State Cttee External Econ. Relations 1985–87, Minister 1987; elected mem. Mongolian People's Revolutionary Party (MPRP) Cen. Cttee 17th, 18th and 19th Party Congresses at 1990 Extraordinary Congress; resgnd from MPRP 1991; elected Deputy to Great People's Hural 9th, 10th and 11th elections, Chair. 1990; Pres. of Mongolia 1990–97, C-in-C of the Armed Forces 1993–97; Pres. Ochirbat Fund 1997–; Altan Gadas 1972, Mu Gung Hwa (Repub. of Korea) 1991, Liberty Award (USA) 1995. *Publications:* Black Gold, Art of Management, Organisation and Management of Fuel and Energy Complex, Heavenly Hour, Without the Right to Mistakes, Ecolog-Steady Development. *Address:* Tengeriin Tsag Co. Head Office, Olympic Street 14, Ulan Bator, Mongolia. *Telephone:* (1) 327215. *Fax:* (1) 327233. *E-mail:* crmongolia@magicnet.mn (Office).

OCHMAN, Wiesław; Polish tenor, producer and painter; b. 6 Feb. 1937, Warsaw; s. of Jan Ochman and Bronisława Ochman; m. Krystyna Ochman 1963; one s. one d.; ed Acad. of Mining and Metallurgy, Cracow 1960, studied with Prof. Gustaw Serafin, Cracow and with Prof. Maria Szłapak, Jerzy Gaczek and Sergiusz Nadgryzowski; début Silesian Opera, Bytom 1960; soloist: Silesian Opera, Bytom 1960–63, Opera in Cracow 1963–64, Great Theatre, Warsaw 1964–75, Deutsche Staatsoper 1967, Hamburgische Staatsoper 1967–, Metropolitan Opera, New York 1975–, La Scala, Milan 1981; Festivals at Glyndebourne, Salzburg, Orange; guest performances in operas in Paris, Munich, Frankfurt am Main, San Francisco, Miami, Chicago, Geneva, Budapest, Washington, Staatsoper in Vienna, Grand Theatre in Moscow, Staatsoper and Deutsche Oper in W Berlin, Teatro Colón in Buenos Aires, Gran Teatre del Liceu in Barcelona, Accademia Santa Cecila in Rome, Carnegie Hall in New York, Teatro de la Maestranza in Seville; participation in TV films including Eugene Onegin, Tcharevitch, Salome, Don Giovanni; numerous recordings; mem. Pres. Council for Culture 1992–95; Goodwill Amb. for UNICEF 1996; Minister of Culture and Art Prize 1973, The City of Warsaw Prize 1976, Pres. of Radio and TV Cttee Prize (1st Class) 1976, Prime Minister Prize (1st Class) 1979, Minister of Foreign Affairs Diploma 1977, 1986, Medal Maecenas of Art 1976, The City of Cracow Gold Award, Medal of Merit for Nat. Culture 1986; Commdr's Cross with Star, Order of Polonia Restituta 2001. *Exhibitions:* 75 one-man exhbns of paintings. *Operatic roles include:* Faust, Don Carlos, Tosca (Cavaradossi), Carmen (Don José), Boris Godunov (Dimitri), Lucia di Lammermoor (Edgardo), I vespri siciliani (Arrigo), La Traviata (Alfredo), Don Carlos (Don Carlos), The Hunted Manor (Stefan), Cavalleria Rusticana (Turiddu), Eugene Onegin (Lensky), Pique Dame (Herman), Der Zauberflöte (Tamino), Idomeneo (Idomeneo), La clemenza di Tito (Titus), Der Fliegende Holländer (Eric), Fidelio (Florestan), King Roger (Shepherd), Les pêcheurs de perles (Bizet), Salome (Herod), Khovanshchina (Prince Golitsyn), Halka (Jontek), Jenůfa (Laca), Rigoletto (Prince), Don Giovanni (Don Ottavio). *Operas directed:* Don Giovanni (Mozart), Traviata (Verdi) 2000, Tcharevitch (Lehar) 2001, Eugene Onegin (Tchaikovsky) 2002. *Leisure interests:* painting, collecting objects of art. *Address:* ul. Miączyńska 46B, 02-637 Warsaw, Poland. *Telephone:* 603-640-845 (Office).

OCHOJSKA-OKOŃSKA, Janina; Polish charity administrator; b. 12 March 1955, Gdańsk; m. Michał Okoński; ed Nicolaus Copernicus Univ., Toruń; Asst Astrophysics Lab. of Astronomy Centre of Polish Acad. of Sciences (PAN), Toruń 1980–92; co-f. EquiLibre Foundation 1989, Dir (and co-founder) Warsaw br. 1992–94; Co-Founder and Pres. Polish Humanitarian Org. 1992–. *Leisure interests:* music, books, cooking. *Address:* Polish Humanitarian Organisation, ul. Szpitalna 5 lok. 3, 00-031 Warsaw, Poland (Office). *Telephone:* (22) 8288882 (Office). *Fax:* (22) 8319938 (Office). *E-mail:* pah@pah.org.pl (Office). *Website:* www.pah.org.pl (Office).

OCKRENT, Christine; Belgian journalist; b. 24 April 1944, Brussels, Belgium; d. of Roger Ockrent and Greta Bastenie; m. Bernard Kouchner (q.v.); one s.; ed Collège Sévigné, Paris, Cambridge Univ., England and Institut d'études politiques de Paris; journalist, Information Office, EEC 1965–66; Researcher, NBC News, USA 1967–68; producer and journalist, CBS News, USA 1968–77; Journalist and Producer, FR3, France 1976–80; Ed. and Anchor, news programme on Antenne 2 1980–85; Chief Ed. RTL 1985–86; Deputy Dir-Gen. TF1 1986–87; Ed., anchor and producer, news programmes on Antenne 2 1988–92, on France 3 1992–95; Chief Ed. L'Express 1995–96; Deputy Dir BFM 1996–2000; Ed.-in-Chief Dimanche Soir programme France 3 1996–98; Ed.-in-Chief and Presenter France Europe Express 1997–; Pres. BFMbiz.com; columnist La Provence, Dimanche CH; Chevalier Légion d'honneur 2000. *Publications:* Dans le Secret des Princes 1986, Duel 1988, Les Uns et Les Autres 1993, Portraits d'ici et d'ailleurs 1994, La Mémoire du cœur 1997, Les Grands patrons (jtly) 1998, L'Europe racontée à mon fils, de Jules César à l'euro 1999, La double vie d'Hillary Clinton 2000. *Leisure interests:* riding, skiing, tennis. *Address:* France 3, esplanade Henri de France, 75907 Paris cedex 15, France. *Website:* www.bfmbiz.com

O'CONNOR, Charmian Jocelyn, CBE, JP, PhD, DSc, FRSNZ, CChem, FRSC, FNZIC; New Zealand professor of chemistry and university administrator; b. 4 Aug. 1937, Woodville; d. of Cecil J. Bishop and Kathrene M. Bishop; m. Peter S. O'Connor 1963 (divorced 1970); one s. one d.; ed Univ. of Auckland; Postdoctoral Fellow, Univ. Coll. London 1967, Univ. of Calif. Santa Barbara 1967–68; lecturer, Univ. of Auckland 1958–66, Sr Lecturer 1967–71, Assoc. Prof. 1972–85, Prof. of Chem. 1986–, Deputy Vice-Chancellor 1994, Asst Vice-Chancellor 1988–97; Visiting Prof. Texas A & M Univ. 1972, Nagasaki Univ. 1982, 1986, 1987, Tokushima Univ. 1987, Nagoya Inst. of Tech. 1994, 1996, 1998; numerous awards and prizes. *Publications:* three books, over 300 articles in journals and several book chapters. *Leisure interests:* swimming, knitting, tapestry, watching television, looking after grandchildren. *Address:* Department of Chemistry, The University of Auckland, Private Bag 92019, Auckland, New Zealand. *Telephone:* (9) 373-7599. *Fax:* (9) 373-7422. *E-mail:* cj.oconnor@auckland.ac.nz (Office).

O'CONNOR, Sandra Day; American judge; b. 26 March 1930, El Paso, Tex.; d. of Harry A. and Ada Mae (née Wilkey) Day; m. John Jay O'Connor III 1952; three s.; ed Stanford Univ.; pvt. practice Phoenix, Ariz. 1959–65; served in Arizona Senate 1969–74, Majority Leader 1973–74; elected Superior Court Judge, Ariz. 1975, Judge of Appeals 1979–81; Judge (Assoc. Justice), U.S. Supreme Court Sept. 1981–; mem. Nat. Bd Smithsonian Assocs. 1981–, Exec. Bd Cen. E European Law Initiative 1990–; 25 hon. degrees; Fordham-Stein Prize, Fordham Univ. 1992; numerous awards including Service to Democracy Award, American Ass. 1982, Award of Merit, Stanford Law School 1990, Nat. Women's Hall of Fame, Seneca Falls, NY 1995, ABA Medal 1997. *Address:* U.S. Supreme Court, 1 First Street, NE, Washington, DC 20543, USA. *Telephone:* (202) 479-3151 (Office).

O'CONNOR, Sinead; Irish singer; b. 8 Dec. 1967, Dublin; d. of John O'Connor and the late Marie O'Connor; m. John Reynolds (divorced); one s. one d.; ed Dublin Coll. of Music; band mem. Ton Ton Macoute 1985–87; refused to accept Grammy Award for Best Alternative Album 1991; now Catholic priest Sister Bernadette. *Singles include:* Heroin 1986, Mandinka 1987, Jump in the River 1988, Nothing Compares 2 U 1990 (MTV Best Video, Best Single Awards 1990, also Best Female Singer), Three Babies 1990, You Do Something To Me (for the Red Hot and Blue compilation) 1990, Silent Night 1991, My Special Child 1991, Visions of You (with Jah Wobble's Invaders of the Heart) 1992, Emperor's New Clothes 1992, Secret Love 1992, Success Has Made a Failure of Our Home 1992. *Albums include:* The Lion and the Cobra 1987, I Do Not Want What I Have Not Got 1990 (Grammy Award for Best Alternative Album 1991, also Rolling Stone Artist of the Year Award 1991, BRIT Award for Best Int. Solo Artist 1991), Am I Not Your Girl? 1992, Universal Mother 1994, Gospeloak 1997, Sean-Nós Nua 2002. *Video films:* Value of Ignorance 1989, The Year of the Horse 1991. *Television:* Hush-a-Bye-Baby. *Address:* c/o Principle Management, 30–32 Sir John Rogersons Quay, Dublin 2, Ireland (Office). *Telephone:* (20) 7336-8802.

ODA, Shigeru, LLM, JSD, LLD; Japanese lawyer; b. 22 Oct. 1924; s. of Toshio and Mioko Oda; m. Noriko Sugimura 1950; one s. one d.; ed Univ. of Tokyo, Yale Univ.; Research Fellow, Univ. of Tokyo 1947–49; Lecturer Univ. of Tôhoku 1950–53, Assoc. Prof. 1953–59, Prof. 1959–76, Prof. Emer. 1985–; Tech. Adviser, Atomic Energy Comm. 1961–64; Special Asst to Minister for Foreign Affairs 1973–76; mem. Science Council of Ministry of Educ. 1969–76, of Council for Ocean Devt in Prime Minister's Office 1971–76, Advisory Cttee for Co-operation with UN Univ. 1971–76; Judge, Int. Court of Justice 1976–85, 1985–94, 1994–, (Vice-Pres. 1991–94); del. to UN Confs. on Law of the Sea 1958, 1960, 1973–75; Rep. at 6th Gen. Conf. of Inter-Governmental Oceanographic Comm. 1969; consultative positions with bodies concerned with marine questions; Counsel for Fed. Repub. of Germany before Int. Court of Justice 1968; Ed.-in-Chief, Japanese Annual of International Law 1973–77; Assoc. Inst. de Droit Int. 1969 (mem. 1979); mem. Curatorium, Hague Acad. of Int. Law 1989–, Bd of Dirs., Int. Devt Law Inst., Rome 1994–, Int. Council of Arbitration for Sport 1994–; mem. Japan Acad. 1994; Hon. mem. American Soc. of Int. Law 1975; Hon. DJur (Bhopal Univ.) 1980, (New York Law School) 1981. *Publications:* in Japanese: International Law of the Sea 1956–85 (8 Vols), International Law and Maritime Resources 1971–75, Judicial Decisions relating to International Law before Japanese Courts 1978; in English: International Control of Sea Resources 1962, The International Law of Ocean Development (4 Vols) 1972–79, The Law of the Sea in Our Times (2 Vols) 1977, The Practice of Japan in International Law 1961–70 1982, The International Court of Justice 1987; various articles. *Address:* International Court of Justice, Peace Palace, Carnegieplein 2, 2517 KJ The Hague, Netherlands (Office). *Telephone:* (70) 302-23-23 (Office). *Fax:* (70) 364-99-28 (Office). *E-mail:* information@icj-cij.org (Office). *Website:* www.icj-cij.org (Office).

ODDSSON, David; Icelandic politician; b. 17 Jan. 1948, Reykjavik; s. of Oddur Ólafsson and Ingibjörg Kristín Lúðvíksdóttir; m. Ástríður Thorarensen 1970; one s.; ed Reykjavik Coll., Univ. of Iceland; mem. Reykjavik City Council 1974–99; Mayor of Reykjavik 1982–91; Vice-Chair. Independence Party 1989–91, Chair. 1991–; MP 1991–; Prime Minister of Iceland 1991–; Minister of the Statistical Bureau of Iceland; Hon. LLD (Univ. of Manitoba) 2000. *Publications:* Plays: For My Country's Benefit (Nat. Theatre 1974–75), Icelandic Confabulations (Reykjavik Theatre 1975–76). TV Dramas: Robert Eliasson Returns From Abroad 1977, Stains on the White Collar 1981; Anders Küng-Estonia, a Small Nation under the Yoke of a Foreign Power 1973; Novel: A Couple of Days Without Gudny 1997. *Leisure interests:* bridge, salmon fishing, forestry. *Address:* Stjórnarráðshusið v/Laekjartorg, 150 Reykjavik, Iceland. *Telephone:* 5609400. *Fax:* 5624014. *E-mail:* postur@for.stjr.is (Office). *Website:* www.raduneyti.is (Office).

ODENT, Michel; French obstetrician and writer; developed maternity unit, Pithiviers; f. Primal Health Research Centre, London, for study of long-term consequences of early experiences; Contributing Ed. Midwifery Today, USA. *Publications:* 10 books, including Birthing Normally: A Personal Growth Approach to Childbirth, Birth Reborn, The Scientification of Love; numerous medical articles. *Address:* c/o Midwifery Today, Inc., P.O. Box 2672-350, Eugene, OR 97402, USA (Office). *Telephone:* (541) 344-7438 (Office). *Fax:* (541) 344-1422 (Office).

ODGERS, Sir Graeme David William, Kt, MA, MBA; British business executive; b. 10 March 1934, Johannesburg, SA; s. of the late William Arthur Odgers and of Elizabeth Minty (née Rennie); m. Diana Patricia Berge 1957; one s. three d. (one deceased); ed St John's Coll., Johannesburg, Gonville and Caius Coll., Cambridge, Harvard Business School, USA; Investment Officer, IFC, Washington DC 1959–62; Man. Consultant, Urwick Orr & Partners Ltd 1962–64; Investment Exec., Hambros Bank Ltd 1964–65; Dir Keith Shipton Ltd 1965–72, C. T. Bowring (Insurance) Holdings Ltd 1972–74; Chair. Odgers & Co. Ltd (Man. Consultants) 1970–74; Dir Industrial Devt Unit, Dept of Industry 1974–77; Assoc. Dir (Finance) Gen. Electric Co. 1977–78; Group Finance Dir, Tarmac PLC, 1979–86, Group Man. Dir 1983–86, Non-exec. Dir 1986–87; Non-exec. Dir Dalgety PLC 1987–93; Part-time Bd mem. British

Telecommunications PLC 1983–86, Govt Dir 1984–86, Deputy Chair. and Chief Finance Officer 1986–87, Group Man. Dir 1987–89; Chief. Exec. Alfred McAlpine 1990–93; Chair. Monopolies and Mergers Comm. 1993–97; Dir (non-exec.) Southern Electric PLC 1998–; Dir Scottish and Southern Energy PLC 1999–; Chair. Locate in Kent Ltd 1998–, Kent and Medway Econ. Bd 2001–; DL Co. of Kent 2002–. *Leisure interest:* golf. *Address:* 5 The Coach House, Springwood Park, Tonbridge, TN11 9LZ, England.

ODIO BENITO, Elizabeth; Costa Rican politician and lawyer; ed Univ. of Costa Rica, Univ. of Buenos Aires; Minister of Justice and Attorney-Gen. 1978–82, Minister of Justice 1990–94, Second Vice-Pres. of Costa Rica and Minister of Environment and Energy 1998–2002; Perm. Rep. to UN, Geneva 1993; mem. Sub-Comm. for the Prevention of Discrimination and Minoritites Protection, Human Rights Comm., UN 1980–83, Special Rapporteur, Sub-Comm. on Discrimination and Intolerance Based on Religion or Creed 1983–86, Vice-Pres. of the Criminal Tribunal for the fmr Yugoslavia Tribunal 1993–95, mem. Admin. Tribunal of the Inter-American Devt Bank 1997–98, mem. and Vice-Pres. Bd Dirs Univ. para la Paz, UNESCO 1999–, Pres. Working Group on Optional Protocol for the Int. Convention against Torture 1998, Judge, Int. Tribunal for the fmr Yugoslavia 1993–98, mem. Costa Rican Nat. Group to the Perm. Court of Arbitration 2000–03, Judge, Int. Criminal Court 2003–; Visiting Prof. Univs of Strasbourg, France 1986, Utrecht, Netherlands 1995, Zaragoza, Spain 1996, Leiden, Germany 1998, Barcelona, Spain 1998; Prof. Univ. of Costa Rica 1986–94, Vice-Pres. of Academic Affairs 1988–90, Prof. Emer. 1994–; Prof. Inter-American Inst. of Human Rights, Costa Rica 1992–; mem. Costa Rican Law Asscn, Steering Cttee Asser Inst., The Hague, Bd Dirs Inter-American Inst. of Human Rights, Int. Comm. of Jurists. *Address:* International Criminal Court (ICC), Maanweg 174, 2516 AB, The Hague, The Netherlands (Office); PO Box 2292/1000, San José, Costa Rica. *Telephone:* (70) 5158515 (Office); (506) 2809654 (Home). *Fax:* (70) 5158555 (Office); (506) 253-6984 (Home). *E-mail:* pio@icc-cpi.int (Office); eodio@racsa.co.cr (Home). *Website:* www.icc-cpi.int (Office).

ODJIG, Daphne, CM; Canadian artist and muralist; b. 11 Sept. 1919, Wikwemikong (Manitoulin Island), Ont.; d. of Dominic Odjig and Joyce Emily (Peachey) Odjig; m. Chester Beavon 1963; two s. two step-s. one step-d.; mem. Odawa Tribe; numerous solo exhbns. Canada 1967–; numerous group exhbns. in Canada, also London, UK 1976, São Paulo, Brazil 1977, Okla, USA 1978; commissions include: Earthmother, for Canadian Pavilion, Expo 1970, Osaka, Japan; mural depicting Indian legend, Creation of the World, Museum of Man 1972, From Mother Earth Flows the River of Life, Cultural Devt Div., Ministry of Indian and Northern Affairs 1974; The Indian in Transition, for Nat. Museum of Man. 1978; works in collections of Winnipeg Art Gallery, Ministry of Indian and Northern Affairs, Winnipeg, Nat. Museum of Man, Man. Indian Brotherhood, Canadian Council Art Bank, McMichael Canadian Coll., Kleinberg, Ont., Tom Thompson Gallery, Sir Wilfrid Laurier Univ., Govt of Israel, Jerusalem and other; Founding mem. Professional Native Indian Artists' Asscn Inc. 1973–; mem. Royal Canadian Acad. of Art 1989; LLD hc (Laurentian Univ.) 1982, (Toronto) 1985, Hon.D.Ed. (Nipissing Univ., Ont.) 1996; Swedish Brucebo Foundation Scholarship 1973, Man. Arts Council Bursary 1973, Canadian Silver Jubilee Medal 1977, Eagle Feather presented by Chief Wakageshig, Wikwemikong Reserve in recognition of artistic accomplishments 1978, Commemorative Medal, 125th Anniversary of Confed. of Canada 1992, Aboriginal Award, Toronto 1998. *Publications:* Nanabush Indian Legends for Children (Author and Illustrator; 10 books) 1971, A Paintbrush in my Hand 1992, The Art of Daphne Odjig 2001. *Address:* 101–102 Forest Brook Place, Penticton, British Columbia, V2A 7N4, Canada. *Telephone:* (250) 493-7475 (Home).

ODLING-SMEE, John Charles, MA; British official; b. 13 April 1943; s. of late Rev. Charles William Odling-Smee and Katherine Hamilton Odling-Smee (née Aitchison); m. Carmela Veneroso 1996; ed Durham School, St John's Coll. Cambridge; Jr Research Officer Dept of Applied Econs, Cambridge 1964–65; Asst Research Officer Inst. of Econs and Statistics, Oxford 1968–71, 1972–73; Econ. Research Officer Govt of Ghana 1971–72; Sr Research Officer Centre for Urban Econs LSE 1973–75; Econ. Adviser Cen. Policy Review Staff, Cabinet Office 1975–77; Sr Econ. Adviser HM Treasury 1977–80; Sr Economist IMF 1981–82; Under-Sec. HM Treasury 1982–89; Deputy Chief Econ. Adviser HM Treasury 1989–90; Sr Adviser IMF 1990–91, Dir IMF European II Dept 1992–. *Publications:* Housing Rent Costs and Subsidies 1978, British Economic Growth 1856–1973 1982; various articles in books and learned journals. *Address:* c/o IMF, 700 19th St, NW, Washington, DC 20431, USA.

ODONE, Cristina, MA; Italian journalist and writer; b. 11 Nov. 1960, Nairobi, Kenya; d. of Augusto Odone and Ulla Sjöström; ed Oxford Univ.; Vice-Pres. Odone Assocs. consultancy, Washington; Ed. The Catholic Herald, UK 1992–96; Diary journalist The Times 1991–; TV reviewer Daily Telegraph 1996–98; Deputy Ed. The New Statesman 1998–. *Publications:* The Shrine 1996, Renewal 1997, A Perfect Wife 1997. *Leisure interests:* travel, walking, entertaining, swimming. *Address:* New Statesman, Victoria Station House, 7th Floor, 191 Victoria Street, London, SW1E 5NE (Office); Capel & Land, 29 Wardour Street, London, W10 6PS, England. *Telephone:* (20) 7828-1232 (Office); (20) 7734-2414 (Capel & Land). *Fax:* (20) 7828-1881 (Office). *E-mail:* info@newstatesman.co.uk (Office).

O'DONNELL, Augustine Thomas 'Gus', CB, BA, MPhil; British economist; b. 1 Oct. 1952, London; s. of James O'Donnell and Helen O'Donnell (née

McLean); m. Melanie Timmis 1979; one d.; ed Salesian Coll., Battersea, Univ. of Warwick and Nuffield Coll., Oxford; lecturer Dept of Political Economy, Univ. of Glasgow 1975–79; economist 1979–85; First Sec. (Econ.) Embassy, Washington 1985–88; Sr Econ. Adviser, HM Treasury 1988–89, Press Sec. to Chancellor of the Exchequer 1989–90; Press Sec. to Prime Minister 1990–94; Under-Sec. (monetary group) HM Treasury 1994–95, Deputy Dir Macroeconomic Policy and Prospects Directorate 1995–96, Minister (Econs) British Embassy, Washington, UK Exec. Dir IMF, World Bank 1997–98, Macroeconomic Policy and Prospects Directorate 1998–2000 (Man. Dir 2000–); Head of Govt Econ. Service, HM Treasury 1998–2002, Perm. Sec. (with responsiblity for Euro entry tests) 2002–. *Publications:* various articles in econ. journals. *Leisure interests:* football, cricket, tennis. *Address:* HM Treasury, 1 Horse Guards Road, London, SW1A 2HQ, England.

O'DONNELL, Chris; American actor; b. 26 June 1970, Winnetka, Ill; m. Caroline Fentress 1997. *Films include:* Men Don't Leave 1990, Fried Green Tomatoes 1991, Scent of a Woman 1992, School Ties 1992, The Three Musketeers 1993, Blue Sky 1994, Circle of Friends 1995, Mad Love 1995, Batman Forever 1995, The Chamber, In Love and War, Batman and Robin, Cookie's Fortune 1998, The Bachelor (producer and actor) 1999, Vertical Limit 2000. *Address:* c/o Josh Lieberman, C.A.A., 9830 Wilshire Boulevard, Beverly Hills, CA 90212, USA.

O'DONOGHUE, John, BCL, LLB; Irish politician; b. 28 May 1956, Cahirciveen, Co. Kerry; m. Kate Ann Murphy; two s. one d.; ed Christian Brothers' Secondary School, Cahirciveen, Univ. Coll., Cork, Inc. Law Soc. of Ireland; fmrly solicitor; mem. Dáil Éireann Feb. 1987–; Minister of State Dept of Finance 1991–92; fmr Fianna Fáil Spokesperson on Justice; Minister of Justice, Equality and Law Reform June 1997–2002, for Arts, Sport and Tourism 2002–; mem. Kerry Co. Council (Chair. 1990–91), mem. various council cttees., Southern Health Bd Psychiatric Services Cttee, British-Irish Parl. Body. *Leisure interests:* English literature, history, Gaelic games, horse racing. *Address:* Department of Arts, Sport and Tourism, Kildare Street, Dublin 2 (Office); Garranearagh, Cahirciveen, Co. Kerry, Ireland (Home). *Telephone:* (1) 6789181 (Office); (66) 72413 (Home). *Fax:* (1) 6785906 (Office); (66) 72667 (Home). *E-mail:* ministersoffice@dast.gov.ie (Office). *Website:* www.gov.ie/arts-sport-tourism (Office).

ODROWĄŻ-PIENIĄŻEK, Janusz; Polish writer, literary historian and museum director; b. 2 July 1931, Opatowice; m. Izabella Romanowska; one s.; ed Warsaw Univ.; scientific worker, Inst. of Literary Research, Polish Acad. of Science, Warsaw 1956–72; Dir Adam Mickiewicz Museum of Literature, Warsaw 1972–; Ed.-in-Chief Muzealnictwo (journal) 1981–; mem. Asscn of Friends of Books 1958–, Adam Mickiewicz Literature Asscn 1952–, Soc. of Authors ZAIKS 1962–, Pen Club 1969–, Accademia di Storia e Letteratura Polacca e Slava 'Adamo Mickiewicz', Bologna 1976–, Deutsche Schillergesellschaft (Marbach am Neckar) 1995–, mem. Polish Nat. Cttee, ICOM 1972–, Vice-Chair. 2002–; Pres. Int. Cttee Museum of Literature ICOM 1995–2001; mem. Man. Bd SEC 1975–; Vice-Chair. Polish Writers' Asscn 1996–99, Chair. 1999–2002; Golden Cross of Merit 1974, Kt's Cross, Order of Polonia Restituta 1988, Commdr's Cross 1999. *Publications:* short stories: Opowiadania paryskie 1963, Ucieczka z ciepłych krajów 1968, Wielki romans w Bucharze 1984; poetical prose: Teoria fal 1964, głosz suiflady 2002; novels: Małżeństwo z Lyndą Winters 1971, Mit Marii Chapdelaine 1985; essays: Polonika zbierane po świecie 1992, Mickiewicziana zbierane po świecie 1998; Paul Cazin, diariste, epistolier, traducteur (co-author) 1997. *Leisure interest:* travelling. *Address:* Adam Mickiewicz Museum of Literature, Rynek Starego Miasta 20, 00-272 Warsaw, Poland (Office). *Telephone:* (22) 8314061 (Office). *E-mail:* muzeum.literatury@poczta.wp.pl (Office).

ODUBER, Nelson O.; Aruban politician; b. 1947; Leader Movimentu Electoral di Pueblo (People's Electoral Movt); Prime Minister of Aruba 1989–94, 2001–; Minister of Gen. Affairs 1989–94. *Address:* MEP, Cumana 84, Oranjestad, Aruba.

ODUBER QUIRÓS, Daniel; Costa Rican politician and diplomatist; b. 25 Aug. 1921, San José; s. of Porfirio Oduber and Ana María Quirós; m. Marjorie Elliott Sypher 1950; one s.; ed Univ. de Costa Rica, McGill Univ., Canada and Univ. de Paris; Amb. to UN 1949; Head of Public Relations, Partido de Liberación Nacional (PLN) 1951–53, Sec.-Gen. 1956–58, Pres. 1970–77; Minister of Foreign Affairs 1962–64; Head various dels. to UN Gen. Ass.; coordinator at the meeting of Presidents of Cen. America USA and Panama 1963; PLN Presidential Cand. 1965; Pres. of Congress 1970–74; Pres. of Costa Rica 1974–78; Dr. hc (Yale) 1986; Grand Cross Order of Malta, Gran Cruz, Orden de Isabel la Católica (Spain) and numerous other foreign decorations. *Leisure interests:* sports, reading, travel. *Address:* c/o Casa Presidencial, San José, Costa Rica.

ODUMEGWU-OJUKWU, Gen. Chukwuemeka; Nigerian politician and army officer; b. 4 Nov. 1933, Zungeru; s. of Sir Odumegwu Ojukwu, KBE. and Grace Ojukwu; m. Bianca Olivia Odinaka Onoh 1994; ed C.M.S. Grammar School and King's Coll., Lagos, Epsom Coll., UK, Lincoln Coll., Oxford, Eaton Hall Officer Cadet School, UK and Joint Services Staff Coll., UK; Admin. Officer, Nigerian Public Service 1956–57; joined Nigerian Army 1957; at Nigerian Army Depot, Zaria 1957; army training in UK 1957–58; joined 5th Bn. Nigerian Army 1958; Instructor, Royal West African Frontier Force Training School, Teshie 1958–61; returned to 5th Bn. Nigerian Army 1961; Maj. Army HQ 1961; Deputy Asst Adjutant and Quartermaster-Gen. Kaduna Brigade HQ 1961; Congo Emergency Force 1962; Lt-Col and Quartermaster-

Gen. 1963–64; Commdr 5th Bn., Kano 1964–66; Mil. Gov. of E Nigeria 1966–67; Head of State of Repub. of Biafra (E Region of Nigeria) 1967–70; sought political asylum in Ivory Coast 1970–82; returned to Nigeria 1982; joined Nat. Party of Nigeria 1983–84; imprisoned Jan.–Oct. 1984; then released; disqualified from Presidential candidacy Feb. 1993; left SDP May 1993. *Publications:* Biafra: Random Thoughts 1969, Because I am Involved 1982. *Leisure interests:* sports, music, art, photography, poetry. *Address:* Villaska, 29 Queen's Drive, Ikoyi, Lagos, Nigeria.

O'DWYER, Thomas, MS, PhD; Irish European Union official; b. 13 April 1937, Tipperary; m. Margaret M. Tuohy 1963; three s.; ed Christian Brothers School, Tipperary, Univ. Coll. Dublin and Cornell Univ.; Marketing Dept Agricultural Inst. Dublin 1968–73; Head, Dairy Div. European Comm. 1973; Chef de Cabinet to Commr for Personnel and Admin. 1981; Dir Org. of Markets in Livestock Products Dec. 1981; Chef de Cabinet to Commr for Agric. and Rural Devt 1989; Dir-Gen. for Co-ordination of Structural Policies and mem. Bd Dirs. EIB 1990; Dir-Gen. for Educ., Training and Youth (DG XXII) 1993–98; First Pres. European Foundation for Vocational Training 1994–. *Publications:* contribs. to agricultural and econ. journals 1968–73. *Leisure interests:* reading, golf. *Address:* Avenue Xavier Henrard 30, 1150 Brussels, Belgium (Home). *Telephone:* (2) 295-32-51.

OË, Kenzaburo, BA; Japanese author; b. 31 Jan. 1935; m. Yukari Itami 1960; two s. one d.; ed Tokyo Univ.; first stories published 1957; first full-length novel Pluck The Flowers, Gun The Kids 1958; represented young Japanese writers at Peking (now Beijing) 1960; travelled to Russia and Western Europe writing a series of essays on Youth in the West 1961; Commdr Légion d'Honneur 2002; Akutagawa prize for novella The Catch 1958, Shinchosha Literary Prize 1964; Tanizaka Prize 1967; Nobel Prize for Literature 1994. *Publications:* The Catch 1958, Pluck The Flowers, Gun The Kids 1958, Our Age 1959, Screams 1962, The Perverts 1963, Hiroshima Notes 1963, Adventures in Daily Life 1964, A Personal Matter 1964 (English 1969), Football in The First Year of Mannen 1967, The Silent Cry 1989, Nip the Buds Shoot the Kids 1995, Japan, The Ambiguous and Myself (Nobel Prize speech and other lectures) 1995, A Healing Family 1996, A Quiet Life 1998, Rouse Up, O Young Men of The New Age 2002. *Address:* Marion Boyars Publishers Ltd, 24 Lacy Road, London SW15 1NL, England (Office); 585 Seijo-machi, Setagaya-ku, Tokyo, Japan. *Telephone:* 482-7192.

OELZE, Christiane; German opera and concert singer (soprano); b. 9 Oct. 1963, Cologne; m. Bodo Primus; one d.; studied with Klesie Kelly-Moog and Erna Westenberger; won several Lieder competitions including Hugo-Wolf-Wettbewerb 1987, Hochschule Wettbewerb für Lied-Duo 1988; recital tours USA, S. America, Japan; has worked with many maj. int. conductors and has appeared on all important European concert stages and at int. festivals, including Salzburg Festival; began singing in opera 1990. *Roles include:* Despina (Ottawa), Pamina (Leipzig, Lyon, Hamburg, Munich), Konstanze (Salzburg, Zürich), Anne Trulove (Glyndebourne), Regina (in Mathis der Maler, Covent Garden), Zdenka (Covent Garden), Zerlina (Covent Garden), Ännchen (in Der Freischütz, Covent Garden), Mélisande (Glyndebourne), Servilia (in La Clemenza di Tito, Covent Garden), Susanna (Salzburg), Ilia (in Idomeneo, Glyndebourne), Igluno (Palestina, Covent Garden), Sophie (in Rosenkavalier, Hamburg). *Recordings include:* several solo recitals, concert arias, Mass in C minor (Mozart), Christmas Oratorio, St John and St Matthew Passions, Webern songs and cantatas, Le Nozze di Figaro and many others. *Television:* Pelléas et Mélisande, Glyndebourne 1999. *Address:* c/o Artists Management HRA, Sebastienplatz 3, 80331 Munich, Germany. *Telephone:* (89) 2602 4333 (Office); (172) 6423344 (Mobile). *Fax:* (89) 2602 4344 (Office). *E-mail:* AgenturHRA@aol.com (Office).

OERTER, Alfred A.; American athlete; b. 19 Sept. 1936, Astoria, NY; s. of Alfred and Mary Oerter (née Strup); m. 1st Corinne Benedetto 1958 (divorced 1975); two d.; m. 2nd Cathy Carroll 1983; ed Univ. of Kansas; competed Olympic Games, winning gold medals at discus, Melbourne 1956, Rome 1960, Tokyo 1964, Mexico 1968; first athlete to win gold medals at four successive Olympic Games; held world records (four times) at discus, is the only athlete ever to set four Olympic records and was first man to throw over 200 feet; retd 1969, made comeback 1976 and in 1980 recorded a personal best; motivational speaker athletic and corporate promotions; currently an exhibiting artist; mem. track and field Hall of Fame; Olympic Hall of Fame, Olympic Order 1982; honorary torch bearer at the 1996 Atlanta Olympic Games. *Address:* 4753 Estero Boulevard # 1401, Ft. Myers Beach, FL 33931, USA. *Website:* www.aloerter.com.

OESTERHELT, Jürgen, LLD, MCL; German diplomatist (retd); b. 19 Aug. 1935, Munich; s. of Dr Egon Oesterhelt and Trude Pfohl; m. Katharina Galeiski 1964; one s. one d.; ed Univ. of Munich and Columbia Univ.; int. lawyer, Paris 1963–64; entered diplomatic service, Bonn 1964; served Moscow 1964–65, New York (UN) 1966–71, Sofia 1971–74, Athens 1977–80; Ministry of Foreign Affairs 1980–92; Amb. to Turkey 1992–95, to UK 1995–97, to the Holy See 1997–2000; Grosses Bundesverdienstkreuz; decorations from Greece, Finland, Austria. *Leisure interests:* reading, music, sports. *Address:* Auf der Königsbitze, 4, 53639 Königswinter, Germany. *Telephone:* (2223) 27109 (Home). *Fax:* (2223) 904075 (Home). *E-mail:* juergen@oesterhelt.de (Home).

OESTREICHER, Rev. Canon Paul, MA; British/New Zealand clergyman and journalist; b. 29 Sept. 1931, Meiningen, Germany; s. of Paul Oestreicher, MD and Emma Oestreicher (née Schnaus); m. 1st Lore Feind 1958 (died 2000);

two s. (one deceased) two d.; m. 2nd Dr Barbara Einhorn 2002; ed Otago and Victoria Univs., NZ, Bonn Univ., Fed. Repub. of Germany, Lincoln Theological Coll., UK; emigrated to New Zealand with parents 1939; Ed. Critic student newspaper, Otago Univ. 1952–53; Humboldt Research Fellow, Bonn Univ. 1955, Berlin 1992; studied industrial mission (Opel, Gen. Motors), Rüsselsheim 1958–59; ordained in Church of England 1959; freelance journalist and broadcaster in Fed. Repub. of Germany and UK 1959–; Curate in Dalston, London 1959–61; Programme Producer, Religious Dept, BBC Radio 1961–64; Assoc. Sec., Dept of Int. Affairs, British Council of Churches, with special responsibility for East-West relations 1964–69, Hon. Sec. East-West Relations Cttee 1969–81, Asst Gen. Sec. and Div. Sec. for Int. Affairs 1981–86; Vicar, Church of the Ascension, Blackheath, London 1968–81; Dir of Lay Training, Diocese of Southwark 1969–72; mem. Gen. Synod of Church of England 1970–86, 1996–97, Int. Affairs Cttee. 1965–2001; mem. Exec. Council Amnesty Int. (UK Section) 1969–80, Chair. 1974–79; Founder and Trustee, Christian Inst. (of Southern Africa) Fund 1974–94, Chair. Trustees 1983–94; Hon. Chaplain to Bishop of Southwark 1975–80; Hon. Canon of Southwark Cathedral 1978–83, Canon Emer. 1983–86; Public Preacher, diocese of Southwark 1981–86; Dir Int. Ministry of Coventry Cathedral 1986–97, Canon Residentiary 1986–97, Canon Emer. 1998–; int. consultant 1997–2000; Chair. Christians Aware 1999–2000; mem. Council Keston Coll. 1975–83; mem. Nat. Council Campaign for Nuclear Disarmament 1980–82, Vice-Chair. 1983–85, Vice-Pres. 1985–; mem. Religious Soc. of Friends (Quakers) 1982; Hon. D. Litt.; Hon. Citizen Meiningen 1995; Bundesverdienstkreuz (First Class), Germany 1995, Wartburg Prize for Promotion of European Unity 1997, City of Coventry Order of Merit 2002. *Publications:* Ed.: Gollwitzer: The Demands of Freedom (English Edn) 1965, The Christian Marxist Dialogue 1969, (with J. Klugmann) What Kind of Revolution 1969, The Church and the Bomb (jtly.) 1983, The Double Cross 1986; trans. Schulz: Conversion to the World 1967; contrib. to British Council of Churches working party reports on Eastern Europe and Southern Africa. *Address:* 97 Furze Croft, Furze Hill, Brighton, BN3 1PE, England (Home). *Telephone:* (1273) 728033 (Home).

OETKER, Rudolf-August; German shipowner and industrialist; b. 20 Sept. 1916, Bielefeld; s. of Rudolf Oetker; m. 3rd Maja von Malaisé 1963; eight c.; Owner Dr. August Oetker, Bielefeld 1944–, Hamburg-Südamerika Dampfschiffahrts-Gesellschaft Eggert und Amsinck, Hamburg 1951–; holder of controlling interest of Bankhaus Hermann Lampe KG, Bielefeld; numerous other business interests. *Leisure interests:* art, tennis. *Address:* Lutterstrasse 14, 33617 Bielefeld, Germany. *Telephone:* (521) 1550.

O'FARRELL, Anthony Gilbert, PhD, MRIA; Irish professor of mathematics; b. 28 May 1947, Dublin; s. of Patrick O'Farrell and Sheila O'Farrell, née Curtis; m. Lise Pothin 1972; three s. one d.; ed Univ. Coll. Dublin, Brown Univ., USA; Meteorological Officer, Irish Meteorological Service 1967–68; Fellow and Teaching Asst, Brown Univ. 1970–73; Asst Prof., Univ. of Calif., LA 1973–75; Prof. of Math., Maynooth Coll. 1975–, Head of Computer Science 1992–95; Research Assoc., Dublin Inst. for Advanced Studies 1979–; mem. Irish Math. Soc. (Pres. 1982–84, Sec. 1984–85, 1987–89), London Math. Soc., Société Mathématique de France, American Math. Soc., Math. Asscn of America, Irish Meteorological Soc.; Nat. Univ. Travelling Studentship 1969. *Publications:* numerous research papers. *Leisure interests:* literature, walking, music. *Address:* Mathematics Department, NUI Maynooth, Co. Kildare, Ireland. *Telephone:* (1) 7083914. *Fax:* (1) 7083913. *E-mail:* aof@maths.may.ie (Office).

O'FARRELL, Patrick James, PhD; New Zealand professor of history; b. 17 Sept. 1933, Greymouth; s. of P. V. O'Farrell; m. Deidre G. MacShane 1956; three s. two d.; ed Marist Bros. High School, Greymouth, Univ. of Canterbury, Christchurch and Australian Nat. Univ. (ANU), Canberra; Research Scholar ANU 1956–59; Lecturer, Sr Lecturer, Assoc. Prof. Univ. of NSW 1959–72, Prof. of History 1972–; Visiting Prof. Univ. Coll. and Trinity Coll., Dublin 1965–66, 1972–73, Scientia Prof. 1998, Prof. Emer. 1999–; NSW Premier's Literary Award 1987. *Publications:* Harry Holland: Militant Socialist 1964, The Catholic Church in Australia 1968, Documents in Australian Catholic History 1969, Ireland's English Question 1971, England and Ireland since 1800 1975, The Catholic Church and Community in Australia 1977, Letters from Irish Australia 1825–1929 1984, The Irish in Australia 1986, Vanished Kingdoms: Irish in Australia and New Zealand 1990, Through Irish Eyes: Australian and New Zealand Images of the Irish, 1788–1948 1994, UNSW: A Portrait 1998. *Leisure interest:* reading thrillers. *Address:* School of History, University of New South Wales, NSW 2052, Australia. *Telephone:* (2) 9427-4656 (Home). *Fax:* (2) 9428-2770 (Home).

OFFICER, David Adrian, MA, FRSA; British artist, art lecturer, television presenter and producer; b. 24 Aug. 1938, Belfast, Northern Ireland; s. of Adrian Charles Officer and Eileen Officer (née Sterritt); ed Hutcheson's Grammar School, Glasgow, Univ. of Durham and Moray House Coll. of Educ. Edinburgh; Head of Art Dept Rhyl Grammar School, lecturer in Fine Art, Harrow School 1970–71; lecturer in Art Educ. W Australian Inst. of Tech. (now Curtin Univ.) Perth 1972–78; ABC TV lecturer, Melbourne and Sydney 1973–78; Festival Artist, Perth 1974; Art Consultant, Whittaker (USA), Tabuk Mil. Hosp. Saudi Arabia 1979–83; lecturer in Art and Design, United Coll. of Educ. Zimbabwe 1983–85; weekly art and design programmes, ZTV Television, Zimbabwe 1985–87; lecturer in Fine Art, Hillside Teacher's Coll. Bulawayo 1985–87; lecturer in Fine Art and World Art History, Univ. of Anatolia, Turkey 1987–89; Visiting Examiner in Art, Cambridge Univ. 1991–;

freelance artist, display artist, art educator, Exhbn organizer; exhbns. in most maj. European cities and in Sydney, Adelaide, Melbourne and Perth. *Publications:* articles in Liverpool Gazette, festival magazines etc. *Leisure interests:* fine arts, drawing, painting, calligraphy, typography, stained glass, rugby, cricket. *Address:* 86 London Road, Plaistow, London, E.13, England.

OFFORD, Robin Ewart, MA, PhD; British professor of medical biochemistry; b. 28 June 1940, Stondon; s. of Frank Offord and Eileen Offord; m. Valerie Wheatley 1963; one s. two d.; ed Dame Alice Owen's School, London, Peterhouse Coll., Cambridge; scientific staff (part-time) UKAEA 1959–62; grad. student MRC Lab. for Molecular Biology 1962–65, on scientific staff 1965–66; scientific staff Lab. of Molecular Biophysics, Oxford 1966–72; Fellow Univ. Coll., Oxford Univ. 1968–73, Univ. lecturer in Molecular Biophysics, Oxford 1972–80, tutor in Biochem. and Official Fellow Christ Church Coll., Oxford Univ. 1973–80; Prof., Dir Dept of Medical Biochem., Univ. of Geneva 1980–, Pres. Pre-Clinical Medicine 1994–; Dir Geneva Bioinformatics SA 1999–2000; Pres. and Exec. Vice-Chair. GeneProt Inc. 2000–01; Agefi Man. of the Year Award (Switzerland) 2002. *Publications:* author, co-author and ed. six scientific books; author and co-author over 170 articles in scientific journals. *Leisure interests:* scuba diving, windsurfing, cross-country skiing, comparative linguistics. *Address:* Department of Medical Biochemistry, University Medical Center, 1 rue Michel Servet, 1211 Geneva 4, Switzerland. *Telephone:* (22) 7025470. *Fax:* (22) 3468758.

OFILI, Chris, MA; British artist; b. 1968, Manchester; ed Chelsea School of Art, Royal Coll. of Art, Hochschule der Kunst, Berlin; has exhibited as solo artist in Southampton and at Serpentine Gallery, London and at Manchester City Art Gallery; fmr winner Whitworth Young Contemporaries Exhbn; Turner Prize 1998. *Address:* c/o Victoria Miro Gallery, 21 Cork Street, London, W1X 1HB, England. *Telephone:* (20) 7734-5082. *Fax:* (20) 7494-1787.

OGATA, Sadako, PhD; Japanese international organization official; b. 1927; one s. one d.; ed Univ. of Sacred Heart, Tokyo, Georgetown Univ., Univ. of Calif., Berkeley; Minister, Japan's Mission to UN 1978–79; UN special emissary investigating problems of Cambodian refugees on Thai-Cambodian border; rep. of Japan on UN Comm. for Human Rights 1982–85; fmr Chair. Exec. Bd UNICEF; fmr Dir Inst. of Int. Relations, Sophia Univ. Tokyo; Dean, Faculty of Foreign Studies, Sophia Univ. until 1990; UN High Commr for Refugees 1991–2000; Prime Minister's Special Rep. for Afghanistan 2002–; Dr. hc (Harvard) 1994, Hon. DCL (Oxford) 1999; UNESCO Houphouët-Boigny Peace Prize 1996; Ramon Magsaysay Award for Int. Understanding 1997, Seoul Peace Prize 2000, Delta Prize for Global Understanding 2002. *Address:* c/o Ministry of Foreign Affairs, 2-11-1, Shiba-Koen, Minato-ku, Tokyo 105-8519, Japan (Office).

OGATA, Shijuro, MA; Japanese fmr banker; b. 16 Nov. 1927, Tokyo; s. of Taketora Ogata and Koto Ogata; m. Sadako Nakamura 1961; one s. one d.; ed Seikei Higher School, Tokyo, Univ. of Tokyo and Fletcher School of Law and Diplomacy; joined Bank of Japan 1950, Asst Rep. in London 1962–64, Rep. in New York 1975–78, Adviser to Gov. 1978–79, Dir Foreign Dept 1979–81, Exec. Dir 1981–84, Deputy Gov. for Int. Relations 1984–86; Deputy Gov. The Japan Devt Bank 1984–91; Dir Barclays Bank 1991–95, Fuji Xerox 1991–2001, Horiba Ltd 1995–; Auditor Fuji Xerox 2001–02; Adviser Swire Group 1991–98, Yamaichi Securities 1991–97; Chair. Barclays Trust & Banking Co. (Japan) Ltd 1993–97; Co-Chair. Study Group on UN Financing 1992–93; Japan Soc. Award 1992. *Publications:* International Financial Integration: The Policy Challenges (co-author) 1989, The Yen and the Bank of Japan 1996; several articles on int. monetary issues. *Leisure interests:* reading, writing. *Address:* 3-29-18 Denenchofu, Ota-ku, Tokyo 145-0071, Japan. *Telephone:* (3) 3722-4801.

OGI, Adolf; Swiss politician and international consultant; b. 18 July 1942, Kandersteg; s. of Adolf Ogi and Anna Ogi; m.; two c.; ed Ecole Supérieure de Commerce, La Neuveville, Swiss Mercantile School, London; Man. Soc. for the Devt and Improvement of Meiringen and the Hasli Valley 1963–64; joined Swiss Ski Asscn 1964, Tech. Dir 1969–74, Dir 1975–81; Maj. in Army 1981–83, Staff Liaison Officer 1984–87; mem. Swiss People's Party 1978–, Chair. 1984–87; mem. Parl. 1979–; mem. Fed. Council 1987, Vice-Pres. 1999; Head Fed. Dept of Transport, Communications and Energy 1988–95; Pres. of Switzerland Jan.–Dec. 1993, Jan.–Dec. 2000; Special Adviser to UN Sec.-Gen. on Sport for Devt and Peace 2001–; Head Fed. Mil. Dept 1995–97, Fed. Dept of Defence, Civil Protection and Sports 1998–2002; Chair. Candidature Cttee for winter Olympic Games Sion 2006 1998–99; Vice-Chair. Int. and European Cttee. Int. Ski Fed. 1971–83; Dir-Gen. and mem. of Bd Intersport Schweiz Holding AG 1981–; Hon. Pres. Swiss Olympic Asscn; Citizen of Honour, Kandersteg 1992, Fraubrunnen 1999, Sion 2000. *Address:* United Nations, New York, NY 10017, U.S.A. (Office).

OGI, Chikage; Japanese politician; b. Hiroko Hayashi, 10 May 1933, Hyogo; m. Nakamura Ganjiro; ed Kobe High School; fmr actress, singer and broadcaster; mem. House of Councillors 1977–89, 1993–; Minister of State, Dir-Gen. Nat. Land Agency 2000–; Minister of Land, Infrastructure and Transport 2001–; Head Hoshuto (New Conservative Party) 2000–01. *Address:* Ministry of Land, Infrastructure and Transport, 2-1-3, Kasumigaseki, Chiyoda-ku, Tokyo 100-8989, Japan (Office). *Telephone:* (3) 5253-8111 (Office). *Fax:* (3) 5253-1562 (Office). *Website:* www.mlit.go.jp (Office).

OGILVIE, Dame Bridget Margaret, DBE, ScD, FIBiol, FRCPath, FMedSci; Australian scientist; b. 24 March 1938, Glen Innes; d. of late John Mylne

Ogilvie and Margaret Beryl McRae; ed New England Girls School, Armidale, NSW, Univ. of New England, NSW, Univ. of Cambridge; Fellow Wellcome Animal Health Trust 1963–66; mem. scientific staff MRC 1966–81; mem. staff of The Wellcome Trust (various capacities) 1979–, Dir 1991–98; Visiting Prof. Univ. Coll. London 1998–; Dir (non-exec.) Lloyds Bank 1995–96, Lloyds TSB Group PLC 1996–2000, Zeneca Group PLC 1997, AstraZeneca 1999–; mem. UK Council for Science and Tech. 1993–2000, Advisory Council for Chem., Univ. of Oxford 1997–2001, Australian Health and Medical Research Strategic Review 1998; Trustee Nat. Museum of Science and Industry 1992–2002, Royal Coll. of Veterinary Surgeons Trust Fund 1998–2001, Nat. Endowment for Science and Tech. and the Arts 1998–2002, Cancer Research Campaign 2000–02, Research UK 2002–; Chair. Governing Body Inst. for Animal Health 1997–, Cttee on the Public Understanding of Sciences 1998–2002, British Library Advisory Cttee for Science and Business 1999–2002; High Steward Univ. of Cambridge 2002–; Chair. Asscn of Medical Research Charities 2002–; Chair. Lister Inst. Governing Body 2002–; Ian McMaster Fellow 1971–72; Hon. mem. British and American Socs. of Parasitology, British Veterinary Asscn, Hon. MRCP, Hon. FRCP; Hon. Assoc. Royal Coll. of Veterinary Surgeons; Hon. Fellow Univ. Coll. London, Girton Coll. Cambridge, St Edmunds Coll. Cambridge, Royal Australian Coll. of Physicians, Inst. of Biology, Royal Soc. of Medicine; Foundation Hon. Fellow Royal Veterinary Coll.; Hon. MD (Newcastle); Hon.D.Sc. (Univs. of Nottingham, Salford, Westminster, Bristol, Glasgow, ANU, Buckingham, Dublin, Nottingham Trent, Oxford Brookes, Greenwich, Auckland, Durham, Kent, Exeter, London, Leicester, Manchester, St Andrews); Hon. LLD Trinity Coll., Dundee; Dr. h.c. (Edin.); Univ. Medal (Univ. of New England), Inaugural Distinguished Alumni Award (Univ. of New England), Lloyd of Kilgerran Prize 1994, Wooldridge Memorial Medal 1998, Australian Soc. of Medical Research Medal 2000. *Publications:* various scientific papers, reviews, book chapters on the immune response to parasitic infections of man and animals 1964–84. *Leisure interests:* the company of friends, looking at landscape, swimming, walking, music, gardening. *Address:* c/o Medical Administration, University College London, Gower Street, London, WC1E 6BT, England. *Telephone:* (20) 7679-6939. *Fax:* (20) 7383-2462. *E-mail:* rachel.chapman@ucl.ac.uk (Office).

OGILVIE THOMPSON, Julian, MA; South African business executive; b. 27 Jan. 1934, Cape Town; s. of the late the Hon. Newton and Eve Ogilvie Thompson; m. the Hon. Tessa M. Brand 1956; two s. two d.; ed Diocesan Coll., Rondebosch and Worcester Coll., Oxford; Chair. De Beers Consolidated Mines Ltd 1985–97, Deputy Chair. 1998–2001, Dir 2002–; Chair, Mineral and Resources Corpn 1982–99; Deputy Chair. Anglo-American Corpn of SA Ltd 1983–90, Chair. 1990–2002, Chair. Anglo-American PLC 1999–2002; Dir Anglogold Ltd 1998–, Nat. Business Initiative; Rhodes Scholar 1953; Hon. LLD (Rhodes Univ.); Commdr, Order of Leopold (Belgium), Grand Official, Order of Bernardo O'Higgins (Chile), Presidential Order of Honour (Botswana). *Leisure interests:* golf, fishing, shooting. *Address:* P.O. Box 61631, Marshalltown 2107 (Office); Froome, Froome Street, Athol Ext. 3, Sandton, Gauteng, South Africa (Home). *Telephone:* (11) 274-2040 (Office); 884-3925 (Home). *Fax:* (11) 643-2720 (Office).

OGILVY, HRH Princess Alexandra, the Hon. Lady, GCVO; b. 25 Dec. 1936; d. of the late Duke of Kent (fourth s. of King George V) and Princess Marina (d. of late Prince Nicholas of Greece); m. Hon. Angus James Bruce Ogilvy (second s. of late 12th Earl of Airlie, KT, GCVO, MC) 1963; one s. one d.; ed Heathfield School, Ascot; Chancellor, Univ. of Lancaster; Col-in-Chief, The King's Own Royal Border Regt, The Queen's Own Rifles of Canada and the Canadian Scottish Regt (Princess Mary's); Deputy Col-in-Chief, The Light Infantry; Deputy Hon. Col, The Royal Yeomanry (Territorial Army Voluntary Reserves); Deputy Col-in-Chief Queen's Royal Lancers 1993–; Patron and Air Chief Commdt, Princess Mary's Royal Air Force Nursing Service; Patron, Queen Alexandra's Royal Naval Nursing Service; Pres. or Patron of many charitable and social welfare orgs.; Hon. Liverywoman, Worshipful Co. of Clothworkers; rep. HM Queen Elizabeth II at independence celebrations of Nigeria 1960 and St Lucia 1979, 150th anniversary celebrations, Singapore 1969; Hon. Freeman, City of Lancaster, City of London; Hon. Fellow, Royal Coll. of Physicians & Surgeons of Glasgow, Royal Coll. of Anaesthetists, Royal Coll. of Obstetricians & Gynaecologists, Royal Coll. of Physicians; Hon. degrees (Queensland, Hong Kong, Mauritius, Liverpool); decorations from Mexico, Peru, Chile, Brazil, Japan, Finland, Luxembourg, the Netherlands, Canada. *Leisure interests:* music, reading, tapestry, outdoor recreations including swimming, skiing, riding. *Address:* Buckingham Palace, London, SW1A 1AA, England. *Telephone:* (20) 7024-4270.

OGRIS, Werner, DrIur; Austrian professor of law; b. 9 July 1935, Vienna; s. of Alfred Ogris and Maria Erber; m. Eva Scolik 1963; two s.; ed Univ. of Vienna; Asst Inst. für Deutsches Recht, Vienna 1958–61; Prof. Freie Univ. Berlin 1962, Univ. of Vienna 1966–; mem. Austrian Acad. of Sciences; corresp. mem. Saxon Acad.; Foreign mem. Royal Netherlands Acad.; Hon. DrIur (Prague, Bratislava); Prize of Theodor-Körner-Stiftung 1961, Brothers Grimm Prize, Univ. of Marburg 1997. *Publications:* Der mittelalterliche Leibrentenvertrag 1961, Der Entwicklungsgang der österreichischen Privatrechtswissenschaft im 19. Jahrhundert 1968, Die Rechtsentwicklung in Österreich 1848–1918 1975, Personenstandsrecht 1977, Recht und Macht bei Maria Theresia 1980, Goethe—amtlich und politisch 1982, Jacob Grimm. Ein politisches Gelehrtenleben 1986, Friedrich der Grosse und das Recht 1987, Joseph von Sonnenfels als Rechtsreformer 1988, Zur Entwicklung des Ver-

sicherungsaufsichtsrechts und des Versicherungsvertragsrechts in Österreich von 1850 bis 1918 1988, Mozart und das Eherecht seiner Zeit 1991, Deutsche und österreichische Rechtsgeschichte in Japan 1991, Tatort Rechtsgeschichte 1994, Vom Galgenberg zum Ringtheaterbrand 1997, Tatort Rechtsgeschichte 2 1998, Mozart im Familien und Erbrecht seiner Zeit 1999, Die Universitätsreform des Ministers Leo Graf Thun-Hohenstein 1999. *Leisure interest:* tennis. *Address:* Vienna University, Juridicum, Institut für Österreichische und Europäische Rechtsgeschichte, Schottenbastei 10–16, 1010 Vienna (Office); Mariahilferstrasse 71/21, 1060 Vienna, Austria (Home). *Telephone:* (1) 4277-34567 (Office); (1) 586-41-57 (Home). *Fax:* (1) 4277-34599. *E-mail:* werner.ogris@univie.ac.at (Office). *Website:* www.univie.ac.at/rechtsgeschichte (Office).

O'HALI, Abdulaziz A., PhD; Saudi Arabian business executive; b. 1935, Onayza; one s. three d.; ed Univ. of Puget Sound, Tacoma, Wash. and Claremont Graduate School, Calif.; entered Govt service 1957, held various posts, including Mil. Advisory Dir, Prime Minister's Office, Acting Dir of Planning and Budgeting, Dir Cultural and Educ. Directorate, Ministry of Defense and Aviation; retd with rank of Col 1979; founding shareholder United Saudi Commercial Bank, Nat. Industrialization Co. 1983; Chair. Saudi Investment Bank; Man. Dir Gulf Center Man. Consultants; mem. Jt Econ. and Tech. Comm. of Saudi Arabia and USA, of Saudi Arabia and Germany. *Address:* Saudi Investment Bank, P.O. Box 3533, Riyadh 11481; Gulf Center Management Consultants, P.O. Box 397, Riyadh 11411, Saudi Arabia. *Telephone:* 476-0287. *Fax:* 478-1557.

O'HANLON, Rory; Irish politician and doctor; b. 7 Feb. 1934, Dublin; s. of Michael O'Hanlon and Anna Mary O'Hanlon; m. Teresa Ward 1962; four s. two d.; ed Blackrock Coll. Dublin and Univ. Coll. Dublin; mem. Dáil 1977–; mem. Monaghan County Council 1979–; Minister of State, Dept of Health and Social Welfare Oct.–Dec. 1982; Minister of Health 1987–91, for the Environment 1991–92; Chair. Fianna Fáil Parl. Party 1997–; Deputy Speaker of Dáil 1997–; Fellow Royal Acad. of Medicine; mem. British-Irish Parl. Group 1992–, Jt Cttee on Foreign Affairs 1993–. *Leisure interests:* swimming, reading, walking, computers. *Address:* Dáil Éireann, Dublin 2 (Office); Mullinary, Carrickmacross, Co. Monaghan, Ireland (Home). *Telephone:* (1) 6183457 (Office); (42) 9661530 (Home). *Fax:* (1) 6184111 (Office); (42) 9663220 (Home). *E-mail:* rory.ohanlon@oireachtas.irlgov.ie (Office). *Website:* www.roryohanlon.com (Office).

O'HARA, Michael John, MA, PhD, FRS, FRSE; British scientist; b. 22 Feb. 1933, Sydney, Australia; s. of late Michael Patrick O'Hara and Dorothy Winifred Avis; m. 1st Janet Prudence Tibbits 1962 (divorced 1977); one s. two d.; m. 2nd Susan Howells 1977; two s. one d.; ed Dulwich Coll. Prep., London, Cranleigh School, Surrey and Peterhouse, Cambridge; Univ. of Edin., Grant Inst. of Geology 1958–78, Reader 1967, Prof. 1971–; Research Fellow, Carnegie Inst. of Washington Geophysical Lab. 1962–63; Prof., Univ. Coll. Aberystwyth, Dept of Geology 1978–88, Head of Dept 1978–87, Prof., Inst. of Earth Sciences 1988–93; Distinguished Research Prof. Earth Sciences Dept, Cardiff Univ. 1994–, Sherman-Fairchild Distinguished Visiting Scholar, Calif. Inst. of Tech. 1984–85; Visiting Prof. Dept of Earth Sciences, Harvard Univ. 1986; Prof. and Head of Dept, Sultan Qaboos Univ., Oman 1988–90; mem. Natural Environment Research Council 1986–88; mem. Univ. Grants Cttee 1987–89; Chair. Univ. Grants Cttee Earth Sciences Review; Geochem. Fellow, Jt geochemical socs. of America and Europe 1997; Hon. mem. Geological Soc. France; Geological Soc. of London Murchison Medal 1983; American Geophysical Union Bowen Award 1984. *Publications:* over 100 articles in scientific journals. *Leisure interests:* mountaineering, hill walking. *Address:* University of Wales, College of Cardiff, P.O. Box 914, Cardiff, CF1 3YE, Wales. *Telephone:* (29) 2087-4830. *Fax:* (29) 2087-4326.

O'HARE, Joseph Aloysius, MA, PhL, STL, PhD; American university president and Jesuit priest; b. 12 Feb. 1931, New York; ed Berchmans Coll., Cebu City, Philippines, Woodstock Coll., Md and Fordham Univ. New York; Instructor in Humanities, Ateneo de Manila Univ. 1955–58, Assoc. Prof. in Philosophy 1967–72; Assoc. Ed. America Magazine, New York 1972–75, Ed.-in-Chief 1975–84; Pres. Fordham Univ. 1984–; Chair. NY City Campaign Financial Bd; numerous hon. degrees. *Leisure interests:* contemporary fiction, Irish folk music. *Address:* Office of the President, Fordham University, New York, NY 10458, USA. *Telephone:* (718) 817-3000. *Fax:* (718) 817-3005 (Office). *E-mail:* johare@fordham.edu (Office).

OHGA, Norio, BMus; Japanese business executive; b. 29 Jan. 1930, Numazu, Shizuoka Pref.; s. of Shoichi Ohga and Toshi Mizuno; m. Midori Matsubara 1957; ed Tokyo Nat. Univ. of Art, Kunst Universität, Berlin; joined Tokyo Tsushin Kogyo KK (Tokyo Telecommunications Eng Corpn) as Consultant and Adviser 1953, co. name changed to Sony Corpn 1958; Gen. Man. Tape Recorder Div. and Product Planning (also in charge of Industrial Design) 1959, Dir 1964; Sr Man. Dir CBS/Sony Inc. 1968, Pres. 1970; Man. Dir Sony Corpn 1972, Sr Man. Dir 1974, Deputy Pres. 1976, Pres. 1982–95, Chair. 1995–2003, Rep. Dir 1999–2000, Chair. Bd of Dirs. 2000–03, Hon. Chair. 2003–; Chair. CBS/Sony Group Inc. 1980–90; Chair. Sony USA Inc. 1988–2003, CEO Sony Corpn 1989–2003, Pres. 1989–95, Chair. Sony Software Corpn 1991–2003; Vice-Chair. Tokyo Chamber of Commerce and Industry 1989–; Chair. Cttee on New Business, Keidanren 1994–; fmr Chair. Electronic Industries Asscn of Japan 1995; Vice-Chair. Keidanren 1998–; Int. CEO of the Year (George Washington Univ.) 1994; Commdr.'s Cross First Class of the Order of Merit (Austria) 1987; Medal of Honour with Blue Ribbon

(Japan) 1988; Commdr's Cross Order of Merit (Germany) 1994, Grande Ufficiale dell' Ordine Al Merito (Italy) 1998. *Leisure interests:* yachting and flying. *Address:* c/o Sony Corporation, 6-7-35 Kita Shinagawa 6-chome, Shinagawa-ku, Tokyo 141-0001, Japan.

OHKUCHI, Shunichi; Japanese business executive; b. 15 Jan. 1918, Tokyo; s. of Tatsuzo and Takae Ohkuchi; m. Kazuko Ohkuchi 1948; two s.; ed Tokyo Imperial Univ.; Ministry of Agric. and Forestry 1941; mil. service 1942–48; Chief, Import Planning Div., Food Agency, Ministry of Agric. and Forestry; First Sec. Embassy, London 1956–59; Dir Overseas Fishery Dept, Fishery Agency, Ministry of Agric. and Forestry 1961–64; Deputy Vice-Minister of Agric. and Forestry 1965, Vice-Minister 1968–69; Dir-Gen. Food Agency, Ministry of Agric. and Forestry 1966–68; retd from Govt service 1969; Adviser, Nippon Suisan Kaisha Ltd 1970, Man. Dir, Sr Man. Dir, then Vice-Pres. 1971–75, Exec. Vice-Pres. 1975–80, Pres. 1980–86, apptd Chair. 1986. *Leisure interests:* golf, audio (classical music), billiards. *Address:* c/o Nippon Suisan Kaisha Ltd, 2-6-2, Otemachi, Chiyoda-ku, Tokyo 100-8686, Japan.

OHLSSON, Garrick; American pianist; b. 1948, White Plains, New York; winner Chopin Int. Piano Competition, Warsaw 1970; appears regularly with maj. orchestras including New York Philharmonic, Chicago Symphony, Boston Symphony, Philadelphia Orchestra, Los Angeles Philharmonic and with orchestras in recital series throughout the world. *Recordings include:* Complete Solo Works of Chopin and numerous other recordings. *Address:* c/o Jenny Vogel, ICM Artists Ltd, 8942 Wilshire blvd, Beverly Hills, CA 90211, USA. *Telephone:* (310) 550-4477 (Office). *Fax:* (310) 550-4460 (Office).

OHLSSON, Per Evald Torbjörn; Swedish journalist; b. 3 March 1958, Malmö; s. of Ulla Ohlsson and Torsten Ohlsson; m. Maria Rydqvist-Ohlsson 1989; one s.; ed Univ. of Lund; Ed. Lundagård 1980–81; editorial writer Expressen, Stockholm 1981–85; New York Corresp. Sydvenska Dagbladet 1985–88, Ed.-in-Chief 1990–; Soderberg Foundation Prize for Journalism 1998. *Publications:* Over There – Banden Över Atlanten 1992, Gudarnas Ö 1993, 100 År Av Tillväxt 1994. *Leisure interests:* music, literature, sports. *Address:* Sydvenska Dagbladet, 205 05 Malmö, Sweden (Office). *Telephone:* 40-28-12-00 (Office). *Fax:* 40-28-13-86 (Office). *E-mail:* per.t.ohlsson@sydsvenskan.se (Office).

OHNISHI, Minoru; Japanese business executive; b. 28 Oct. 1925, Hyogo Pref.; s. of Sokichi and Mitsu Ohnishi; m. Yaeko Yui 1951; two s.; ed School of Econs, Tokyo Univ.; joined Fuji Photo Film Co. Ltd 1948, Man. Tokyo Sales Dept of Consumer Products Div. 1957–61, Sales Dept of Industrial Products Div. 1961–62, Fukuoka Br. Office 1962–64, Exec. Vice-Pres. Fuji Photo Film USA Inc. 1964–68, Man. Export Sales Div. Fuji Photo Film Co. Ltd 1968–76, Dir 1972–, Man. Dir 1976–79, Sr Man. Dir 1979–80, Pres. 1980–96, Chair. 1996–; Pres. Photo-Sensitized Materials Mfrs Asscn of Japan 1980–96; mem. Photography Soc. of Japan (Chair. 1997–). *Leisure interests:* golf, reading. *Address:* Fuji Photo Film Company Ltd, 2-26-30 Nishiazabu, Minato-ku, Tokyo 106-8620, Japan. *Telephone:* (3) 3406-2111. *Fax:* (3) 3406-2193. *Website:* www.home.fujifilm.com (Office).

OHTA, Tomoko, PhD; Japanese geneticist; b. 7 Sept. 1933, Aichi-Ken; d. of Mamoru Harada and Hatsu Harada; m. Yasuo Ohta 1960 (divorced 1972); one d.; ed Tokyo Univ., North Carolina State Univ.; researcher Kihara Inst. for Biological Research 1958–62; Post Doctoral Fellow Nat. Inst. of Genetics 1967–69, Researcher 1969–76, Assoc. Prof. 1976–84, Prof. 1984–97, Prof. Emer. 1997–, Head Dept of Population Genetics 1988–97; Vice-Pres. Soc. for the Study of Evolution 1994; Foreign hon. mem. American Acad. of Arts and Sciences 1984, Fellow AAAS 2000; Saruhashi Prize 1981, Japan Acad. Prize 1985, Weldon Memorial Prize (Oxford Univ.) 1986, Foreign Assoc. NAS 2002, Japanese Cultural Achievement Award 2002. *Publications:* Evolution and Variation of Multigene Families, Lecture Notes in Biomathematics Vol. 37 1980. *Leisure interest:* reading. *Address:* 20-20 Hatsunedai, Mishima-shi, Shizuoka-ken 411-0018, Japan. *Telephone:* (559) 724-638. *E-mail:* tohta@lab.nig.ac.jp (Office).

OHTANI, Ichiji; Japanese textile executive; b. 31 Aug. 1912, Kobe; s. of Kyosuke Ohtani and Tama Ohtani; m. Atsuko Suzuki 1943; two s. one d.; ed Kobe Univ.; Dir Toyobo Co. Ltd 1964–68, Man. Dir 1968–72, Sr Man. Dir 1972–74, Deputy Pres. 1974, Pres. 1974–78, Chair. 1978–83, Counsellor 1983–92, Hon. Sr Adviser 1992–; Dir Toyobo Petcord Co. Ltd 1969–83, Chair. Toyobo Co. Ltd 1978–83, Counsellor 1983–; Vice-Pres. Industrias Unidas, SA 1973–79; Exec. Dir Fed. of Econ. Orgs. 1976–83; Chair. Japan Spinners' Asscn 1976–79, Diafibres Co. Ltd 1977–88; Vice-Pres. Japan Textile Fed. 1976–79; Jr Vice-Pres. Int. Textile Mfrs Fed. 1976–78, Sr Vice-Pres. 1978–80, Pres. 1980–82, Hon. Life mem. 1982–; Blue Ribbon Medal 1979; Order of the Rising Sun (Second Class) 1984. *Leisure interest:* sports. *Address:* Toyobo Co. Ltd, 2-8 Dojima Hama 2-chome, Kita-ku, Osaka 530 (Office); 7-18 Yamate-cho, Ashiya-shi 659, Japan (Home).

OHTANI, Monshu Koshin, MA; Japanese ecclesiastic; b. 12 Aug. 1945, Kyoto; s. of Kosho Ohtani and Yoshiko Ohtani; m. Noriko Tanaka 1974; two s. two d.; ed Tokyo Univ. and Ryukoku Univ.; ordained Priest of Jodo Shinshu Hongwanji-ha Aug. 1960, Monshu (Ecclesiastic Patriarch) Apparent 1970–1977, Monshu April 1977–; Pres. All-Japanese Buddhist Fed. 1978–80, 1988–90, 2002–. *Leisure interests:* classical music, skiing. *Address:* Horikawa-dori, Hanayacho-sagaru, Shimogyo-ku, Kyoto 600-8501, Japan. *Telephone:* (75) 371-5181 (Office). *Fax:* (75) 351-1211 (Office). *Website:* www.hongwanji.or.jp (Office).

O'HUIGINN, Sean; Irish diplomatist and civil servant; b. Co. Mayo; m.; two c.; ed St Jarlath's Coll., Tuam, Univ. Coll. Galaway, Univ. of Bordeaux, France; joined Foreign Service 1969, served in Berne, Switzerland and Copenhagen, Denmark; Consul-Gen. in New York, USA; Amb. to Saudi Arabia, to USA (also accred(non-resident) to Mexico 1997–2002, to Germany 2002–; Head Irish Del. to Anglo–Irish Secr., Belfast, NI 1987–91; Head of Anglo–Irish Div., Dublin 1991–97; involved in Devt of NI Peace Process including negotiation of Downing Street Declaration 1993, Framework Document 1995, paramilitary cease-fires and all-party talks. *Address:* Embassy of Ireland, Berlin Friedrichstr. 200, Berlin 10117, Germany (Office). *Telephone:* (30) 220720 (Office). *Fax:* (30) 22072299 (Office). *E-mail:* berlin@iveagh.irlgov.ie (Office). *Website:* www.botschaft-irland.de.

OIZERMAN, Teodor Ilyich; Russian philosopher; b. 14 May 1914, Petroverovka; s. of Ilya Davidovich Oizerman and Yelizaveta Abramovna Nemirovskaya; m. Genrietta Kasavina; two s. one d.; ed Moscow Inst. of History, Philosophy and Literature; Industrial worker 1930–33; Postgraduate 1938–41; Army service 1941–46; Asst Prof., Moscow Inst. of Econs 1946–47; Asst Prof., Prof. Moscow Univ. 1952–54, Head of Chair 1954–68; corresp. mem. USSR (now Russian) Acad. of Sciences 1966–81, mem. 1981–; Foreign mem. Acad. of Sciences, GDR 1981–90; mem. Int. Inst. of Philosophy 1982–; Head Dept of History of Philosophy, Inst. of Philosophy of Acad. of Sciences 1971–87, Adviser to Acad. of Sciences 1987–; Vice-Pres. USSR (now Russian) Philosophical Soc. 1982–95; Dr hc (Jena); Order of the Red Star 1944, Order of the Patriotic War 1945, 1985, Order of the Badge of Honour 1961; Lomonosov Prize 1965, Plekhanov Prize 1981, State Prize 1983. *Publications:* (works have been translated into German, French, English and more than 10 other foreign languages), Development of Marxist Theory in Experience of the Revolution of 1848 1955, Philosophie Hegels 1959, The Making of Marxist Philosophy 1962, 1974, 1986, On the History of pre-Marxist Philosophy 1961, Alienation as an Historical Category 1965, Problems of Historical-Philosophical Science 1969, Principal Philosophical Trends 1971, Crisis of Contemporary Idealism 1973, Problems of the History of Philosophy 1973, Philosophy of Kant 1974, Dialectic Materialism and the History of Philosophy 1982, Principles of the Theory of the Historical Process in Philosophy 1986, The Main Trends in Philosophy 1988, Philosophical and Scientific World Outlook of Marxism 1989, Kant's Theory of Knowledge 1991, Philosophy as a History of Philosophy 1999; and over 550 articles on philosophical problems, including more than 220 articles in foreign languages. *Leisure interest:* walking. *Address:* Institute of Philosophy, Russian Academy of Sciences, Volchonka str. 14, Moscow (Office); Mendeleyev str. 1, Apt. 168, 117234 Moscow, Russia (Home). *Telephone:* 203-91-98 (Office); 939-01-37 (Home).

OJEDA PAULLADA, Pedro; Mexican lawyer; b. 19 Jan. 1934, México, DF; s. of Manuel Ojeda Lacroix and Adela Paullada de Ojeda; m. Olga Cárdenas de Ojeda 1959; two s. three d.; ed Univ. Nacional Autónoma de México; Head of Personnel and lawyer, Técnica y Fundación, SA de CV 1955, Sub-Man. 1955–57; Gen. Man. Industria Química de Plásticos SA 1957–58; Deputy Dir-Gen. Juntas Federales de Mejoras Materiales 1959–65; Dir-Gen. of Legal Affairs, SCT 1966–70; Sec.-Gen. Presidential Secr. 1970–71; Attorney-Gen. 1971–76; Sec. of Labour and Social Welfare 1976–81; Minister of Fisheries 1982–88; Gen. Coordinator Nat. Food Comm. 1988–91; Pres. Fed. Court of Conciliation and Arbitrage 1995–; Prof. of Law and Economics UNAM (Nat. Autonomous Univ. of Mexico), Prof. of Social Security; represented Mexico on many int. and regional comms. etc., including Pres. Perm. Conf. of Political Parties of Latin America (COPPAL) 1981–82, Chair. World Conf. of Int. Women's Year 1975, 64th Int. Conf. of ILO 1978, World Conf. on Fishing Devt (FAO) 1984; Fed. Congressman 1991–94; Pres. Energy Comm. of the Mexican Congress 1991–94, Nat. Fed. of Lawyers in the Service of Mexico (FENASEM) 1992–, Tech. Comm. of Foreign Relations of Fundación Mexicana Luis Donaldo Colosio, AC 1992–94, Mexican Coll. of Lawyers 1994–, Mexican Acad. of Law and Econs 1995–; Mexican Soc. of Geography and Statistics, 1994–97; mem. Institutional Revolutionary Party (PRI) 1951–, Pres. Nat. Exec. Cttee 1981–82; mem. Nat. Acad. of History and Geography, American Law and Econs Assocn 1991–; Order of Merit (Italy), Gran Cruz al Mérito (Italy), Orden de Isabel la Católica (Spain) and other orders. *Leisure interests:* art, dominoes, reading, tennis. *Address:* Avenida del IMAN 660, 3° piso, Col Pedregal del Maurel, C.P. 04720, Del. Coyoacan, Mexico, DF, Mexico. *Telephone:* (5) 568-1878; (5) 606-8881. *Fax:* (5) 606-9070.

OJEDA Y EISELEY, Jaime de, LLB; Spanish diplomatist; b. 5 Aug. 1933; ed Univ. of Madrid, Int. Acad. of The Hague, Naval War Coll. of Madrid and Sr Center for Nat. Defence Studies (CESEDEN), Madrid; Prof. of Political Law, Complutense Univ. of Madrid 1958; joined diplomatic service 1958; served Washington, DC 1962–69; Minister-Counsellor, Beijing 1973–76; Consul-Gen. of Spain in Hong Kong and Macao 1976–79; Fellow Center for Int. Relations, Harvard Univ. 1979–80; Deputy Perm. Rep. to North Atlantic Council 1982–83, Perm. Rep. to NATO 1983–90; Amb. to USA 1990–97; Pres. Sr Council on Foreign Affairs 1997–98; Amb.-in-Residence Shenandoah Univ. 1998–; Great Cross, Mil. Merit, Great Cross Civil Merit, Kt Order of Carlos III. *Publications:* El 98 en el Congreso y en la Prensa de los Estados Unidos 1999; trans. Alice in Wonderland 1971, Through the Looking Glass 1974, Spain and America: The Past and the Future 1994. *Leisure interests:* music, botany, sailing. *Address:* 3770 Leed's Manor Road, Markham, VA 22643, USA. *Telephone:* (540) 364-2275. *Fax:* (540) 364-9281.

OJUKWU, Gen. Chukwuemeka Odumegwu- (see Odumegwu-Ojukwu, Gen. Chukwuemeka).

OJULAND, Kristiina; Estonian politican; b. 17 Dec. 1966, Kohtla-Jarve; m.; ed Tartu Univ., Estonian School of Diplomacy; specialist Dept of Draft Legislation, Ministry of Justice 1990–92; First Sec. Political Dept, Ministry of Foreign Affairs 1992–94, Rep. to Council of Europe; Man. Dir Estonian Broadcasting Asscn 1994–96; Mem. Riigikogu (Parl.) 1994–2001; Euro-Integration Dir Concordia Int. Univ. 1997–2001; Mem. Tallinn City Council 1996–2001; Vice-Pres. of Parl. Ass., Council of Europe 1996–2002, Pres. LDR Group, Parl. Ass., Council of Europe 1999–2002; Minister of Foreign Affairs 2002–. *Leisure interests:* tennis, reading. *Address:* Ministry of Foreign Affairs, Ryavala pst 9, EE0001 Tallinn, Estonia (Office). *Telephone:* (2) 631-70-00 (Office).

OKA, Takeshi, PhD, FRSC, FRS; Canadian (born Japanese) university professor; b. 10 June 1932, Tokyo, Japan; s. of Shumpei Oka and Chiyoko Oka; m. Keiko Nukui 1960; two s. two d.; ed Univ. of Tokyo; Fellow Japan Soc. for the Promotion of Science 1960–63; Postdoctoral Fellow Nat. Research Council of Canada 1963–65; Research Physicist, Herzberg Inst. of Astrophysics 1965–81; Prof. of Chem. and Astronomy and Astrophysics, Enrico Fermi Inst., Univ. of Chicago, USA 1981–, Robert A. Millikan Distinguished Service Prof. 1989–; Fellow American Acad. of Arts and Sciences; Hon. DSc (Waterloo) 2001; Steacie Prize 1972, Plyler Prize 1982; Meggers Award 1997, Lippincott Award 1998, Wilson Award 2002. *Leisure interest:* history of science. *Address:* Department of Chemistry, Astronomy and Astrophysics, University of Chicago, Chicago, IL 60637 (Office); 1463 East Park Place, Chicago, IL 60637, USA. *Telephone:* (773) 702-7070 (Office). *Fax:* (773) 702-0805 (Office). *E-mail:* t-oka@uchicago.edu (Office). *Website:* www.fermi.uchicago.edu/oka.

OKALIK, Paul, LLB; Canadian politician; b. Baffin Island; s. of Auyaluk; first Inuit law grad.; called to the Bar 1999; mem. Nunavut Ass. 1999–; first Premier of Nunavut, Minister of Exec. and Intergovernmental Affairs and Minister of Justice April 1999–. *Address:* Office of the Premier, Government of Nunavut, P.O. Box 2410, 2nd Floor Legislative Building, Iqaluit, Nunavut X0A 0H0, Canada (Office).

O'KANE, Dene Philip; New Zealand professional snooker player; b. 24 Feb. 1963, Christchurch; s. of Robert John O'Kane and Lesley Joan Marshall; youngest-ever NZ Champion 1980; turned professional 1984; twice World Championship quarter-finalist 1987, 1992; finalist Hong Kong Open 1989; quarter-finalist many other world-ranking events including British Open, European Open, Asian Open; Chair. NZ Confed. of Billiard Sports; Overseas (non-British) Player of the Year 1987. *Leisure interests:* golf, skin-diving, Formula One motor-racing, wine, clothes.

O'KANE, Maggie, BA; Irish journalist; b. 8 June 1962, Ardglas, Co. Down, Northern Ireland; d. of Peter O'Kane and Maura McNeil; m. John Mullin 1995; one s.; ed Loreto Convent (Balbriggan, Co. Dublin), Univ. Coll. Dublin, Coll. de Journalistes en Europe, Paris and Coll. of Commerce, Dublin; reporter on Irish TV 1982–84, for Sunday Tribune newspaper 1984–87; reporter, TV Producer and Presenter 1987–89; Foreign Corresp. and Feature Writer, The Guardian 1989–; has reported from world trouble spots: Eastern Europe 1989–91, Baghdad 1991, Kurdistan 1991–92, Yugoslavia 1992–94, Bosnia, Haiti, Cuba 1994–96, Afghanistan, Cambodia, Kosovo, Yugoslavia 2000, etc.; writer and presenter various TV documentaries; Journalist of the Year 1992, Foreign Corresp. of the Year 1992, Reporter of the Year (commended) (jt award) 1994, Amnesty Int. Foreign Corresp. of the Year 1993, James Cameron Award for Journalism 1996, European Journalist of the Year 2002, 2003. *Films:* (documentaries) Milosevic: Puppet Master of the Balkans (Channel 4) (Royal TV Soc. Documentary of the Year 1993), Bloody Bosnia (Royal TV Soc. Documentary of the Year 1994), Looking for Karadzic (Guardian Films) (European Journalist of the Year 2002). *Publications:* A Woman's World: Beyond the Headlines 1996, Mozambique. *Leisure interests:* swimming, cooking, triathlon training in Co. Mayo. *Address:* The Guardian, 119 Farringdon Road, London, EC1R 3ER, England. *Telephone:* (20) 7278-2332. *Fax:* (20) 7239-9787. *E-mail:* maggie.okane@guardian.co.uk.

OKASHA, Sarwat Mahmoud Fahmy, DèsSc; Egyptian author, fmr diplomatist and politician; b. 18 Feb. 1921, Cairo; s. of Mahmoud Okasha and Saneya Okasha; m. Islah Abdel Fattah Lotfi 1943; two s. one d.; ed Military Coll., Cairo Univ. and Univ. of Paris; Cavalry Officer 1939; took part in Palestine war 1948–49, Egyptian Revolt 1952: Mil. Attaché, Berne 1953–54, Paris 1954–56; Counsellor in Presidency of Repub. 1956–57; Egyptian Amb. to Italy 1957–58; UAR Minister of Culture and Nat. Guidance 1958–62; Chair. and Man. Dir Nat. Bank 1962–66; Deputy Prime Minister and Minister of Culture 1966–67; Minister of Culture 1967–71; Asst to the Pres. 1971–72; Visiting Prof. Coll. de France 1973; Pres. of Supreme Council for Literature, Art and Social Sciences; Pres. Egypt–France Asscn 1965–; mem. Exec. Bd UNESCO 1962–70 (masterminded int. campaign to save temples of Abu Simbel, etc. from the rising waters of the Aswan Dam); Pres. Consultative Cttee, Inst. du Monde Arabe (Paris) 1990–93; Corresp. Fellow British Acad.; Hon. DHumLitt (American Univ., Cairo) 1995; Commdr des Arts et des Lettres 1964, Légion d'honneur 1968; numerous other awards including UNESCO Gold Medal 1970 and State Award for the Arts 1988. *Publications:* 55 works (including trans): Ovid's Metamorphoses and Ars Amatoria, Khalil Gibran's works, Etienne Drioton's Le Théâtre Egyptien, studies of the works of Wagner, The Development of European Music (in Arabic), History of Art (25 vols), The Muslim Painter and the Divine 1979, Ramsès Recouronné, The Renaissance 1996, The Baroque 1997, The Rococo 1998, Indian Art 2000,

Chinese Art 2001, Japanese Art 2001, Egypt in the Eyes of Foreigners 2001. *Leisure interests:* horse-riding, golf, music. *Address:* 34 Street 14, Villa 34, Maadi, Cairo, Egypt. *Telephone:* 3585075.

OKE, Timothy R., MA, PhD, FRSC; Canadian/British professor of geography; b. 22 Nov. 1941, Kingsbridge, Devon; s. of late Leslie and Kathleen Oke; m. Margaret 1967; one s. one d.; ed Lord Wandsworth Coll., Univ. of Bristol and McMaster Univ.; Asst Prof. McGill Univ. 1967–70; Asst Prof. Univ. of British Col 1970–71, Assoc. Prof. 1971–78, Prof. of Geography 1978–, Head, Dept of Geography 1991–96; Ed.-in-Chief, Atmosphere-Ocean 1977–80; Hooker Distinguished Visiting Prof. McMaster Univ. 1987; Visiting Fellow, Keble Coll. Oxford 1990–91; Research Scholar (Rockefeller Foundation) Bellagio, Italy 1991; consultant to WMO and other orgs.; Pres. Int. Asscn for Urban Climate 2000–; Fellow, Royal Canadian Geographical Soc.; Guggenheim Fellow 1990; Pres.'s Prize, Canadian Meteorological Soc. 1972, Killam Prize 1988; Award for Scholarly Distinction, Canadian Asscn of Geographers 1986, Outstanding Service Award, World Meteorological Org. 1997, American Meteorological Soc. Outstanding Achievement in Biometeorology Award 2002. *Publications:* Boundary Layer Climates 1978, Vancouver and its Region 1992, The Surface Climates of Canada 1997; more than 100 articles on climate of cities. *Leisure interests:* golf, music, walking, painting. *Address:* Department of Geography, University of British Columbia, 1984 West Mall, Vancouver, BC, V6T 1Z2 (Office); 3776 West 39th Avenue, Vancouver, BC, V6N 3A7, Canada (Home). *Telephone:* (604) 822-2900 (Office); (604) 263-7394 (Home). *Fax:* (604) 822-6150. *Website:* www.geog.ubc.ca (Office).

O'KEEFE, Sean; American space research administration official; b. 1956; fmr staff dir and professional staff mem. Defense Subcttee. of Senate Appropriations Cttee; Comptroller, Dept of Defense 1989, Sec. of the Navy 1992–93; Prof. of Business Admin., Sr Vice-Pres. for Research, Dean of Grad. School Pennsylvania State Univ. 1993–96; Louis A. Bantle Prof. of Business and Govt Policy, Maxwell Grad. School of Citizenship and Public Affairs, Syracuse Univ., New York 1996–2001, Dir Nat. Security Studies, Syracuse Univ. and Johns Hopkins Univ. 1996–2001; Deputy Dir Office of Man. and Budget March–Dec. 2001; Admin. NASA Dec. 2001–. *Address:* Office of the Administrator, National Aeronautics and Space Administration HQ, 300 East Street, SW, Washington, DC 20546, USA (Office). *Telephone:* (202) 453-8400 (Office).

O'KENNEDY, Michael, MA; Irish politician; b. 21 Feb. 1936, Nenagh, Co. Tipperary; s. of Éamonn O'Kennedy and Helena (Slattery) O'Kennedy; m. Breda Heavey 1965; one s. two d.; ed St Flannan's Coll., Ennis, Univ. Coll. Dublin, King's Inns, Dublin; practised as barrister 1961–70, as Senior Counsel 1973–77, 1982–; mem. Senate 1965–69, 1993–, Front Bench Spokesman on Educ. and Justice, Senate Statutory Instruments Cttee on the Constitution until 1967; mem. Dáil for North Tipperary 1969–80, 1982–93, 1997–2002; Parl. Sec. to Minister of Educ. 1970–72, Minister without Portfolio 1972–73, Minister for Transport and Power 1973; Opposition Spokesman on Foreign Affairs 1973–77; Minister for Foreign Affairs 1977–79, of Finance 1979–80; mem. Comm. of European Communities 1980–82; Commr for Personnel, Consumer Affairs, Environment 1981–82; Opposition Spokesman for Finance 1982–87, Minister of Agric. 1987–92; mem. All-Parties Cttee on Irish Relations, Chair. 1973–80; mem. Informal Cttee on Reform of Dáil Procedure until 1972, Dáil and Senate Joint Cttee on Secondary Legislation of EEC 1973–80, Anglo-Irish Parl. Body 1993– (Co-Chair. 1997–); mem. Inter-Parl. Union, mem. Exec. of Irish Council of European Movement; Pres. EEC Council of Ministers July–Dec. 1979; Pres. EC Council of Agric. Ministers Jan.–June 1990; Pres. Re-negotiation EEC/ACP at 2nd Lomé Convention 1979; Nat. Trustee Fianna Fáil. *Leisure interests:* reading, philosophy, history, politics, drama, music, sports. *Address:* Gortlandroe, Nenagh, Co. Tipperary, Ireland. *Telephone:* (67) 31366 (Home).

OKEZIE, Chief Josiah Onyebuchi Johnson, L.S.M., F.M.C.G.P.; Nigerian politician and physician; b. 26 Nov. 1924, Umuahia-Ibeku; s. of Chief Johnson Okezie and Esther Okezie; m. Rose Chioma Onwucheka 1966; three s. one d.; ed Higher Coll., Yaba, Achimota Coll., Ghana, Yaba Coll. of Medicine, Univ. Coll., Ibadan and Royal Coll. of Surgeons, UK; Asst Medical Officer, Nigerian Civil Service 1950–54; Founder and Medical Supt Ibeku Central Hosp., Umuahia-Ibeku 1958–69; Sr Medical Officer in charge of Queen Elizabeth Hosp., Umuahia-Ibeku 1970; Assoc. Ed., The Nigerian Scientist 1961–62; Sec. E Nigerian Science Asscn 1961–63; mem. Nigerian Medical Council 1965–66; mem. E Nigeria House of Ass. 1961–66; Leader, Republican Party 1964–66; Rep. of E Central State, Fed. Exec. Council 1970; Fed. Commr for Health 1970–71, for Agric. and Natural Resources 1971–74; mem. Constituent Ass. to draw up 1979 Constitution of Nigeria 1977–78; Chair. Imo State Br., Nigerian Medical Asscn 1976, Alvan Ikoku Coll. of Educ., Owerri 1980–82; Chair. Bd of Dirs. African Continental Bank Ltd 1982–84; Sec. Nigerian Medical Asscn (E Region Branch) 1960–70; Life mem. Nigerian Bible Soc. 1972; Pres. Imo State Scout Council 1976–; Pres.-Gen. Ibeku Egwu ASA Devt Asscn 1981–84; Patron Grad. Nurses Asscn of Nigeria 1987–, Imo State Red Cross Soc., Soc. for Promoting Igbo Language and Culture, Govt Coll. Umuahia Old Boys' Asscn 1990–; mem. Gov. Council Imo State Univ., Okigwe 1991–; Kt of St Christopher, Anglican Church 1988, Pres. Council of Kts., Umuahia Diocese 1994–97, patron Council of Kts. 1998; installed Chief Ezeomereoha of Bende 1974; invested Ochiagha of Ibeku 1982, traditional title of Eze Udo of Abiriba 1983, title of Onunekwuru Igbo of Umuopara Abia State 1997. *Publications:* The Evolution of Science 1959, Atomic Radiation

1961. *Leisure interests:* English literature, reading poetry, gardening, keeping animals (peacocks, antelopes and rabbits). *Address:* P.O. Box 306, Umuahia-Ibeku, Abia State, Nigeria. *Telephone:* (88) 220673.

OKHOTNIKOV, Nikolai Petrovich; Russian bass; b. 5 July 1937, Glubokoye, Kazakh Repub.; s. of P. Y. Okhotnikov and K. A. Okhotnikov; m. Larkina Tamara 1973; two s.; ed Leningrad Conservatoire (pupil of I. I. Pleshakov); mem. CPSU 1974–90; soloist with Leningrad Concert Union; with Maly Theatre, Leningrad 1967–71, with Kirov (now Mariinsky) Opera 1971–; teacher of singing at Leningrad (now St Petersburg) Conservatoire 1976–; Grand Prix, Barcelona 1972, People's Artist of USSR 1983, USSR State Prize 1985. *Major roles include:* Kochubey in Mazeppa, René in Iolanta, the Miller in Rusalka, Susanin in Glinka's Ivan Susanin, Dosifey in Mussorgsky's Khovanshchina, Kutuzov in Prokofiev's War and Peace, Philip II in Don Carlos, Heinrich in Lohengrin, Gremin in Eugene Onegin, Boris Godunov and Pimen in Boris Godunov, Don Basilio in The Barber of Seville. *Leisure interests:* fishing, photography. *Address:* The Mariinsky Theatre, Teatralnaya pl.1, St Petersburg; Canal Griboedova 109, Apt. 13, 190068 St Petersburg, Russia (Home). *Telephone:* 310-57-38.

OKINAGA, Shoichi, MD, PhD; Japanese university president; b. 29 June 1933, Tokyo; s. of Shobei Okinaga and Kin Ino-Okinaga; m. Yoko Ishida 1968; two s.; ed Univ. of Tokyo; Prin. Teikyo Commercial and Eng Sr High School 1961–71; founder and Pres. Teikyo Women's Jr Coll. 1965–; founder and Pres. Teikyo Univ. 1966–, Prof. of Medicine 1971–; pvt. practice in obstetrics and gynaecology 1971–; Pres. Teikyo Special School of Medical Tech. 1969–; f. Teikyo Univ. of Tech. 1987; Chair. Bd of Trustees, Teikyo Univ. Foundation 1987–; Chair. Judo Fed. of Tokyo 1987–; f. Teikyo School UK 1989, Nishi-Tokyo Univ. 1990; Chair. Salem-Teikyo Univ., USA 1990–, Teikyo-Loretto Heights Univ., USA 1990–, Teikyo Westmar Univ., USA 1990, Teikyo Marycrest Univ., USA 1991–, Teikyo Post Univ., USA 1991–; Fellow, Wadham Coll. Oxford 1991, St Edmund's Coll. Cambridge 1991. *Publication:* Hitasura No Michi (autobiog.) 1984. *Leisure interest:* judo. *Address:* Teikyo University, 2-11-1, Kaga, Itabashi-ku, Tokyo 173, Japan.

OKODI, Benjamin, LLB; Ugandan lawyer; b. 23 Feb. 1943, Busia; m. Veronica Odoki; three s. one d.; ed Kings Coll. Budo, Kampala, Univ. of Dar-es-Salaam; state attorney 1969–74; advocate High Court of Uganda 1970; Dir and Sr Lecturer, Law Devt Centre 1974–78; Judge High Court of Uganda 1978–86, Dir Public Prosecution 1981–84; Judge Supreme Court 1986–89; Chair. Uganda Constitutional Comm. 1989–93; Chair. Judicial Service Comm. 1997–2000; Chief Justice of Uganda Jan. 2001–; Independence Medal 1974, Order of Merit, Uganda Law Soc. 1998, Distinguished Jurist, Law Soc. 2002. *Publications include:* A Guide to Criminal Procedure, An Introduction to Juridical Conduct and Practice, Criminal Investigation and Prosecutions. *Leisure interests:* music, fine art, drama. *Address:* Office of the Chief Justice, Courts of Judicature, POB 7085, Kampala (Office); Plot 4 Philip Road, Kololo, Kampala, Uganda (Home). *Telephone:* (41) 343576 (Home). *E-mail:* bodoki@yahoo.com (Home).

OKOGIE, Mgr Anthony Olubunmi, STL, DD; Nigerian ecclesiastic; b. 16 June 1936, Lagos; s. of Prince Michael Okogie and Lucy Okogie; ed St Gregory's Coll., Lagos, St Theresa Minor Seminary, Ibadan, St Peter and St Paul's Seminary, Ibadan, Urban Univ., Rome; ordained priest 1966; Act. Parish Priest, St Patrick's Church, Idumagbo, Lagos; Asst Priest, Holy Cross Cathedral, Lagos; Religious Instructor, King's Coll., Lagos; Dir of Vocations, Archdiocese of Lagos; Man. Holy Cross Group of Schools, Lagos; Master of Ceremonies, Holy Cross Cathedral; Broadcaster of religious programmes, NBC/TV; Auxiliary Bishop of Oyo Diocese 1971–72; Auxiliary Bishop to the Apostolic Admin., Archdiocese of Lagos 1972–73; Archbishop of Lagos April 1973–; Vice-Pres. Catholic Bishops' Conf. of Nigeria 1985–88, Pres. 1988–94; Nat. Pres. Christian Assocn of Nigeria 1988–96; mem. Prerogative of Mercy, Religious Advisory Council; Commdr Order of the Niger 1999. *Leisure interests:* reading, watching films, table tennis. *Address:* Archdiocese of Lagos, 19 Catholic Mission Street, P.O. Box 8, Lagos, Nigeria. *Telephone:* (1) 2633841; (1) 2635729 (Home). *Fax:* (1) 2633841. *E-mail:* arclagos@infoweb.abs.net (Office).

OKPAKO, David Tinakpoevwan, PhD, CBiol, FIBiol, FNIBiol, FAAS, FAS, FRPharms; Nigerian pharmacologist; b. 22 Nov. 1936, Owahwa, Delta; s. of the late Okun Okoro-Okpako Tsere and Obien Rebayi-Tsere; m. Kathleen Gweneth Jones-Williams 1967; one s. one d.; ed Urhobo Coll. Effurun, Nigerian Coll. of Arts, Science & Tech. Ibadan, Univ. of Bradford and Univ. Coll. London; Visiting Fellow, Corpus Christi Coll. Cambridge 1973–74, 1983–84; Prof. and Head, Dept of Pharmacology and Therapeutics, Univ. of Ibadan 1978–81, 1986–87, Dean, Faculty of Pharmacy 1987–91; Pres. W African Soc. for Pharmacology 1987–90; Foundation Pres. Nigeria Inst. of Biology 1990–92; Chair. Council, Nigerian Field Soc. 1991–2000; Visiting Prof. Univ. of the Western Cape, SA 1995–96; Visiting Fellow, Humanities Research Centre, ANU, Canberra 1996, Fitzwilliam Coll. Cambridge 1997; Visiting Scientist, Research Inst. Hosp. for Sick Children, Univ. of Toronto; now working as consultant pharmacist and pharmacologist. *Publications:* Principles of Pharmacology—A Tropical Approach 1991, Pharmacological Methods in Phytotherapy Research, Vol. 1. Selection, Preparation and Pharmacological Evaluation of Plant Material (with E. M. Williamson and F. J. Evans) 1996; articles in professional journals; book chapters. *Leisure interests:* golf, tennis, reading, fishing. *Address:* P.O. Box 20334, University of Ibadan Post

Office, Oyo Road, Ibadan; 22 Sankore Avenue, University of Ibadan, Ibadan, Nigeria. *Telephone:* (234) 28107602 (Home). *E-mail:* dpc@skannet.com.ng (Office).

OKRI, Ben, OBE, FRSL; Nigerian/British author; b. 15 March 1959, Minna; s. of Silver Okri and Grace Okri; ed John Donne's School, Peckham, London, Children's Home School, Sapele, Nigeria, Christ High School, Ibadan, Urhobo Coll. Warri and Univ. of Essex, UK; staff writer and librarian, Afriscope magazine 1978; poetry ed. West Africa magazine 1983–86; broadcaster with BBC 1983–85; Fellow Commoner in Creative Arts, Trinity Coll. Cambridge 1991–93; mem. Int. PEN, a Vice-Pres. English Centre of Int. PEN 1997–; mem. Bd Royal Nat. Theatre of GB 1999–; mem. Soc. of Authors; Hon. DLitt (Westminster) 1997, (Essex) 2002; Commonwealth Prize for Africa 1987, Paris Review Aga Khan Prize for Fiction 1987, Premio Letterario Internazionale, Chianti Ruffino-Antico Fattore 1992, Premio Grinzane Cavour 1994, The Crystal Award (World Econ. Forum, Switzerland) 1995, Premio Palmi 2000. *Play:* In Exilus (The Studio, Royal Nat. Theatre of GB) 2001. *Television:* Great Railway Journey: London to Arcadia 1996. *Publications:* Flowers and Shadows 1980, The Landscapes Within 1982, Incidents at the Shrine 1986, Stars of the New Curfew 1988, The Famished Road (Booker Prize) 1991, An African Elegy (vol. of poems) 1992, Songs of Enchantment 1993, Astonishing the Gods 1995, Birds of Heaven (essays) 1996, Dangerous Love (novel) 1996, A Way of Being Free (non-fiction) 1997, Infinite Riches (novel) 1998, Mental Fight (epic poem) 1999, poems, essays, short stories. *Leisure interests:* chess, music, travel, theatre, dancing, cinema, art, games, riddles, silence. *Address:* c/o Orion Books, Orion House, 5 Upper St Martin's Lane, London, WC2H 9EA, England.

OKUDA, Hiroshi; Japanese business executive; b. 29 Dec. 1932; ed Hitotsubashi Univ.; fmr Exec. Dir Toyota Motor Corpn, Pres. 1995–, now Chair.; Deputy Chair. Keidanren. *Leisure interests:* music appreciation, reading. *Address:* Toyota Motor Corporation, 1 Toyota-cho, Toyota, Aichi 448-8671, Japan (Office). *Telephone:* (565) 28-2121 (Office). *Fax:* (565) 23-5800 (Office). *Website:* www.global.toyota.com (Office).

OKULOV, Valery Mikhailovich; Russian business executive and pilot; b. 22 April 1952, Kirov; m. Yelena Yeltsin (d. of fmr Pres. Boris Yeltsin, q.v.); one s. two d.; ed Acad. of Civil Aviation; navigator, instructor, Sverdlovsk aviation team 1976–85; leading navigator, First Deputy Dir-Gen. Aviation Co. Aeroflot 1996–97, Dir-Gen. 1997–. *Leisure interest:* boating. *Address:* Aeroflot, Leningradsky prosp. 37, korp. 9, 125836 Moscow, Russia. *Telephone:* (095) 156-80-19 (Office).

OKUN, Daniel A., ScD; American professor emeritus of environmental engineering and consulting engineer; b. 19 June 1917, New York; m. Beth Griffin 1946; one s. one d.; ed Cooper Union, New York, California Inst. of Tech., Pasadena and Harvard Univ.; Sanitary Engineer, US Public Health Service 1940–42; served U.S. Army 1942–46; Assoc., Malcolm Pirnie Inc., Consulting Engineers 1948–52; Assoc. Prof., then Kenan Prof., Univ. of NC 1952–87, Kenan Prof. Emer. 1987–; Head, Dept of Environmental Sciences and Eng 1955–73, Dir Inst. of Environmental Health Studies 1965–73, Dir Int. Programmes, Dept of Environmental Sciences and Eng 1954–84, Chair. of Faculty, Univ. of NC 1970–73; Consultant to local, State and Nat. Govts., int. agencies and industry 1952–; mem. Environmental Advisory Council Rohm and Haas Inc. 1985–92; Chair. Water Science and Tech. Bd, Nat. Research Council 1991–94; Pres. Chapel Hill Chapter NC Civil Liberties Union 1991–93; Kappe Lecturer, American Acad. of Environmental Engineers; mem. Nat. Acad. of Eng, Inst. of Medicine (NAS), Comm. on Human Rights NAS 1991–94; Hon. ScD (NC) 2000; Hon. mem. American Soc. of Civil Engineers; Eddy and Fair Medals, Water Environment Fed.; Fair Award, American Acad. of Environmental Engineers; Billard Award, New York Acad. of Sciences; Freese Award, American Soc. of Civil Engineers; Friendship Medal, British Inst. of Water and Environmental Man.; Best Paper Award, Educ. Div. and Abel Wolman Award of Excellence, American Waterworks Assocn, Boyd Award, Assocn of Metropolitan Water Agencies, Founders' Award, Assocn of Environmental Eng Professionals, Thomas Jefferson Award, Univ. of NC, Daniel A. Okun Distinguished Professorship in Environmental Eng, Univ. of NC est. 2002, Gano Dunn Medal, The Cooper Union for the Advancement of Science and Art, New York. *Publications:* Water and Wastewater Engineering (with Fair and Geyer), Elements of Water Supply and Wastewater Disposal (with Fair and Geyer), Regionalization of Water Management in England and Wales, Community Wastewater Collection and Disposal (with George Ponghis), for WHO, Surface Water Treatment for Communities in Developing Countries (with Schulz). *Leisure interests:* squash, tennis, reading. *Address:* Department of Environmental Sciences and Engineering, CB 7431, University of North Carolina, Chapel Hill, NC 27599 (Office); 204 Carol Woods, 750 Weaver Dairy Road, Chapel Hill, NC 27514-7431, USA (Home). *Telephone:* (919) 918-3500 (Home). *Fax:* (919) 966-7115 (Office); (919) 918-3349 (Home). *E-mail:* dokun@unc.edu (Office); dokun@unc.edu (Home).

OKUN, Lev Borisovich; Russian theoretical physicist; b. 7 July 1929, Sukhinichi, Kaluga Dist; s. of B. G. Okun and B. R. Ginzburg; m. Erica Gulyaeva 1954; one s. two d.; ed Moscow Physics and Eng Inst.; mem. of staff of Inst. of Experimental and Theoretical Physics, now Head of Lab. 1954–; Prof. Moscow Inst. of Physics and Tech. 1967–; main work has been on the theory of elementary particles; Corresp. mem. of USSR (now Russian) Acad. of Sciences 1966–90, mem. 1990–, mem. Bureau Nuclear Physics Div., mem.

Bureau Div. of Physical Sciences 2002–; mem. Science Policy Cttee CERN 1981–86, Super Conducting Super Collider Lab., Dallas 1989–93; mem. Extended Scientific Council of DESY 1992–98, Bd Int. Science Foundation 1993–97, Council of Scientists of Int. Asscn for the Promotion of Co-operation with Scientists from the Ind. States of the fmr Soviet Union (INTAS), Brussels 1993–97; mem. Acad. Europaea 1991; Loeb Lecturer, Harvard Univ. 1989; Regents Prof. Univ. Calif. Berkeley 1990; Buhl Lecturer, Carnegie Mellon Univ. 1991, Visiting Prof., CERN 1992; Fermi Lecturer, Scuola Normale Superiore, Pisa 1993, Schrödinger Professorship (Univ. of Vienna) 1994, AUI Distinguished Lecturer, Brookhaven Nat. Lab. (USA) 1995, Henry Primakoff Lecturer, Penn. Univ. 2001; invited lecturer numerous maj. int. confs on high energy physics; Hon. Life mem. New York Acad. of Sciences 1993; Matteucci Prize (Italy) 1988, Lee Page Prize (Yale Univ.) 1989, Karpinsky Prize (F.V.S. Foundation, FRG) 1990, Humboldt Research Award 1993, Bruno Pontecorvo Prize (Jt Inst. for Nuclear Research, Dubna) 1996, Open Soc. Inst. Prize 1997, L.D. Landau Gold Medal, Russian Acad. of Sciences 2003. *Publications include:* The Weak Interaction of Elementary Particles 1963, Leptons and Quarks 1981, Particle Physics: The Quest for the Substance of Substance 1984, A Primer in Particle Physics 1987, The Relations of Particles 1991; more than 200 research and review articles in leading physics journals. *Address:* Institute of Theoretical and Experimental Physics, B. Cheremushkinskaya 25, 117218 Moscow, Russia. *Telephone:* (095) 123-31-92 (Office); (095) 124-19-41 (Home). *Fax:* (095) 127-08-33.

OLAFSSON, Thröstur; Icelandic government official and business consultant; b. 4 Oct. 1939, Husavík; m. 1st Monika Büttner 1966 (divorced); m. 2nd Thorunn Klemenzdóttir 1975; three s. one d. (and one s. deceased); ed Akureyri Gymnasium, Free Univ. of Berlin, Ruhr Univ., Bochum, Germany; economist, Nat. Bank of Iceland 1968–69, Civil Servants' Org. 1969–71; specialist adviser to Minister of Industry 1971–73; Man. Dir Mál og Menning (publishing co.) 1973–80; Asst to Minister of Finance 1980–83; Man. Dir Gen. Workers and Transport Union 1983–88; Exec. Dir Mikligardur Ltd 1989–90; Political Asst to Minister of Foreign Affairs 1991–95; Chair. Bd of Dirs Cen. Bank of Iceland 1994–98; Sec.-Gen. Social Democratic Party's Parl. Group 1995–97; consultant 1997–98; Chair. Bd Icemarkt Ltd 1989–, Icelandic Int. Devt Agency 1991–95, Social Housing Co. Felagsbustadir Ltd; Gen. Man. Iceland Symphony Orchestra 1998–; mem. Bd Edda Ltd publishing co.; mem. Admin. Council of Europe Devt Bank. *Publications:* numerous articles on Icelandic econs and politics. *Leisure interests:* music, literature, skiing, forestry. *Address:* Brædraborgarstígur 21B, 101 Reykjavik, Iceland. *Telephone:* 5622255 (Office). *Fax:* 5624475 (Office); 5519698 (Home). *E-mail:* throl@sinfonia.is (Office).

OLAH, George Andrew, PhD; American professor of chemistry; b. 22 May 1927, Budapest, Hungary; s. of Julius Olah and Magda Krasznai; m. Judith Lengyel 1949; two s.; ed Tech. Univ. Budapest; mem. Faculty, Tech. Univ. Budapest 1949–54; Assoc. Dir Centre for Chemical Research, Hungarian Acad. of Sciences 1954–56; research scientist, Dow Chemical Canada Ltd 1957–64, Dow Chemical Co. Framingham, Mass. 1964–65; Prof. of Chem. Case Western Reserve Univ. 1965–69, C. F. Mabery Research Prof. 1969–77; Donald P. and Katherine B. Loker Distinguished Prof. of Chem. and Dir Hydrocarbon Research Inst. Univ. of S. Calif. LA 1977–; consultant to industry; numerous visiting professorships; Fellow, AAAS, Chemical Inst. of Canada; Foreign Fellow Royal Soc. (UK), Canadian Royal Soc.; mem. NAS, Italian Acad. of Sciences, Hungarian Acad. of Sciences, European Acad. of Arts, Sciences and Humanities, German, British and Swiss Chem. Socs etc.; Hon. mem. Royal Chem. Soc.; Dr hc (Durham) 1988, (Budapest) 1989, (Munich) 1990, (Crete) 1994, (Southern Calif., Case Western, Szeged, Veszprem) 1995, (Montpellier) 1998, (NY State Univ.) 1998; Alexander von Humboldt Sr US Scientist Award 1979; Pioneer of Chem. Award, American Inst. of Chemists 1993; Nobel Prize for Chem. 1994; other awards and distinctions. *Publications:* Friedel-Crafts Reactions (Vols I–IV) 1963–64, Carbonium Ions (Vols I–V) 1969–76 (with P. Schleyer), Friedel-Crafts Chemistry 1973, Carbocations and Electrophilic Reactions 1973, Halonium Ions 1975, Superacids (with G. K. S. Prakash and J. Somer) 1984, Hypercarbon Chemistry (with others) 1987, Nitration (with R. Malhotra and S. C. Narang) 1989, Cage Hydrocarbons 1990, Electron Deficient Boron and Carbon Clusters (with K. Wade and R. E. Williams) 1991, Synthetic Fluorine Chemistry (with Chambers and Prakash) 1992, Hydrocarbon Chemistry 1995, Onium Ions (jtly) 1998, A Life of Magic Chemistry 2001; book chapters; numerous scientific papers. *Leisure interests:* reading, swimming. *Address:* Loker Hydrocarbon Research Inst., University of Southern California, Los Angeles, CA 90007 (Office); 2252 Gloaming Way, Beverly Hills, CA 90210, USA (Home). *Telephone:* (213) 740-5976. *Fax:* (213) 740-5087. *E-mail:* olah@usc.edu (Office).

OLARREAGA, Manuel; Uruguayan international civil servant and academic; b. 1 June 1937, Salto; s. of Manuel Olarreaga and Hilda Leguisamo; m. Marina Rico 1966; three s.; ed Univ. of Paris; Minister-Counsellor, Uruguay's Perm. Del. to GATT 1982–87; First Exec. Sec. Latin American and Caribbean Program of Commercial Information to Support Foreign Trade 1988–91; Co-ordinator, Admin. Secr. of MERCOSUR 1991–96, Head Regulations Div. 1997–, Ed. Official Bulletin of MERCOSUR 1997–; Prof. of Int. Marketing, Catholic Univ. of Uruguay 1993–; Chair. Cttee of Countries Participating in Protocol Relating to Trade between Developing Countries, GATT; Deputy Chair. 18th, 19th and 20th Consultative Groups, UNCTAD–GATT Int. Trade Centre. *Publications:* several publs on int. trade.

Leisure interests: reading, collecting antique keys. *Address:* Luis Piera 1992, Piso 1°, CP 11200, Montevideo (Office); Tomás Diago 769, Ap. 601, CP 11300, Montevideo, Uruguay. *Telephone:* (2) 412-90-24 (Office); (2) 710-24-33 (Home). *Fax:* (2) 418-05-57 (Office).

ÓLASON, Vésteinn, PhD; Icelandic academic and university administrator; b. 14 Feb. 1939, Höfn; s. of Óli K. Gudbrandsson and Adalbjörg Gudmundsdóttir; m. Unnur Alexandra Jónsdóttir 1960; one s. one d.; ed Menntaskólinn Laugarvatni, Univ. of Iceland; Lecturer in Icelandic Language and Literature Univ. of Copenhagen 1968–72, in Comparative Literature Univ. of Iceland 1972–80, docent Icelandic Literature 1980–85; Prof. of Icelandic Univ. of Oslo 1985–91; Prof. of Icelandic Literature Univ. of Iceland 1991–99, Dean Faculty of Arts 1993–95, Prorektor 1993–94; mem. Icelandic Soc. for Sciences 1983–, Norwegian Acad. of Sciences 1994–, Icelandic Research Council 1994–, Royal Gustaf Adolfs Acad. of Letters 1999–; Dir Árni Magnússon Inst. 1999–; Iceland Literary Prize for Non-Fiction 1993. *Publications:* Sagnadansar: Edition and Study 1979, The Traditional Ballads of Iceland 1982, Islensk Bókmenntasaga I–II (History of Icelandic Literature 870–1720) 1992–93, Dialogues with the Viking Age: Narration and Representation in the Sagas of the Icelanders 1998; over 100 articles in professional publs. *Address:* Arni Magnússon Institute, Reykjavik (Office); Nylendugata 43, IS-101 Reykjavik, Iceland (Home). *Telephone:* 5254011 (Office); 5521792 (Home). *Fax:* 5254035.

OLAYAN, Khaled S.; Saudi Arabian business executive; s. of Suleyman Saleh Olayan; Chair. Olayan Group 2002–. *Address:* c/o Olayan Financing Co., P.O.B. 8772, Riyadh, Saudi Arabia (Office). *Telephone:* (1) 477-8740 (Office). *Fax:* (1) 478-0988 (Office). *Website:* www.olayangroup.com (Office).

OLAZABAL, José María; Spanish golfer; b. 5 Feb. 1966, Fuenterrabía, Spain; s. of Gaspar and Julia Olazabal; won Italian Open, Spanish Open and British Boys' Amateur Championships 1983, Belgian Int. Youth Championship 1984, Spanish Open Amateur Championship 1984, British Youths' Amateur Championship 1985; turned professional 1985; winner World Series of Golf 1990, 1994, The Int. (USA) 1991, US Masters 1994, 1999, Dubai Desert Classic 1998, Benson and Hedges Int. Open 2000, French Open 2001, Buick Invitational 2002; mem. European Ryder Cup Team 1987, 1989, 1991, 1993, 1997; golf-course designer (11 designed at end of 2002). *Leisure interests:* cinema, music, hunting, wildlife, ecology. *Address:* c/o PGA, 100 Avenue of Champions, Palm Beach Gardens, FL 33418, USA. *Website:* www.aboutgolf.com/jmo.

OLBRYCHSKI, Daniel; Polish actor; b. 27 Feb. 1945, Łowicz; m.; one s. one d.; ed State Higher School of Drama, Warsaw; Actor Nat. Theatre 1969–77; mem. Polish Film Union; State Prize (2nd Class) 1974; numerous awards at Polish and foreign film festivals; Officier ordre des arts et des lettres. *Roles include:* Koral in Wounded in the Forest 1964, Rafał Olbromski in Ashes 1965, boxer in Boxer 1966, Marek in Jowita 1967, Daniel in All for Sale 1968, Azja in Michael Wołodyjowski 1969, Angel of Death in Agnus Dei 1970, Tadeusz in Landscape After Battle 1970, Bolesław in The Birch Wood 1971, Wit in Family Life 1971, Pan Młody in The Wedding 1972, Mateusz in Pilatus und Andere 1972, Kmicic in The Deluge 1974, Karol Borowiecki in The Promised Land 1975, Przybyszewski in Dagny 1976, Wiktor in The Maids of Wilko 1978, Jan in Little Tin Drum 1978, Saint-Genis in The Trout 1982, Pisarz in Flash-Back 1983, Love in Germany 1983, I'm Against 1985, Leon in Rosa Luxemburg 1986, Scope in Ga-ga 1986, Michał Kątny in Siekierezada 1986, Pitt in Tiger's Fight 1987, Borys in Pestka 1995, Old Tuchajbej in With Fire and Sword 1998, Gerwazy in Last Foray in Lithuania 1999, Dyndalski in Revange 2002. *Stage appearances:* Hamlet 1970, Rhett in Gone With the Wind, Rodric in Cyd 1985, Cześnik in Revenge 1998. *Television:* Raskolnikow in Crime and Punishment 1980, Chello 1985, Kean 1993. *Leisure interests:* tennis, horses, family life.

OLDENBURG, Claes; American artist; b. 28 Jan. 1929, Stockholm, Sweden; s. of Gösta Oldenburg and Sigrid E. Lindfors; brother of Richard Oldenburg (q.v.); m. 1st Pat Muschinski 1960 (divorced 1970); m. 2nd Coosje van Bruggen 1977; ed Yale Coll. and Art Inst. of Chicago; Apprentice reporter, City News Bureau, Chicago 1950–52; various odd jobs 1952–53; moved to New York 1956; part-time job at Cooper Union Museum Library 1956–61; works included in XXXII Biennale, Venice 1964; IX Bienal do Museu de Arte Moderno, São Paulo 1967; installed Giant Soft Fan in Buckminster Fuller's dome for US Pavilion, Expo 67, Montreal 1967; mem. American Acad., Inst. of Arts and Letters; Dr hc (RCA) 1996; Wilhelm Lehmbruck Sculpture Award 1981, Wolf Prize for the Arts 1989, Lifetime Achievement Award, International Sculpture Center, NY 1994, National Medal of Arts, Washington DC 2000, mem. American Acad. Inst. of arts and Letters, American Acad. of Arts and Sciences and numerous other awards. *Exhibitions:* first group exhbn, Club St Elmo, Chicago 1953; participated in other local shows, Chicago and Evanston 1953–56; exhibited in group show, Red Grooms's City Gallery 1958–59; first public one-man show, Judson Gallery, New York 1959; two-man show with Jim Dine, Judson Gallery Nov.–Dec. 1959; has since participated in numerous exhbns of contemporary art throughout USA and Europe; several one-man shows at Sidney Janis Gallery, New York; travelling one-man exhbn sponsored by Museum of Modern Art, New York shown at Tate Gallery, London and other European galleries 1970; recent one-man shows include Nat. Gallery of Art, Washington DC 1995, Museum of Contemporary Art, Los Angeles 1995, Kunst-und-Ausstellunghalle der Bundesrepublik Deutschland, Bonn 1996, Hayward Gallery, London 1996, Whitney Museum of American Art, New York 2002. *Publications:* Store Days: Documents from

"The Store" (1961) and Ray Gun Theater (1962) 1967, Claes Oldenburg, Proposals for Monuments and Buildings 1965–69 1969, Claes Oldenburg, Drawings and Prints 1969, Notes in Hand 1971, Raw Notes 1973, Claes Oldenburg: Multiples in Retrospect 1991; (co-author with Coosje van Bruggen) Claes Oldenburg: Sketches and Blottings Toward the European Desk Top Large Scale Projects 1994, Claes Oldenburg Coosje van Bruggen 1999, Down Liquidambar Lane: Sculpture in the Park 2001. *Address:* 556 Broome Street, New York, NY 10013, USA. *Fax:* 212-226-4315 (Office). *Website:* www.oldenburgvanbruggen.com (Office).

OLDENBURG, Richard Erik, AB; American museum director; b. 21 Sept. 1933, Stockholm, Sweden; s. of Gösta Oldenburg and Sigrid E Lindfors; brother of Claes Oldenburg (q.v.) ; m. Harriet L. Turnure 1960 (died 1998); ed Harvard Coll.; Man. Ed., The Macmillan Co. 1964–69; Dir of Publications, Museum of Modern Art, New York 1969–71; Acting Dir Museum of Modern Art Jan.–June 1972, Dir 1972–94, Dir Emer., Hon. Trustee 1995–; Chair. Sotheby's N. and S. America 1995–2000, Hon. Chair. 2000–. *Leisure interest:* reading. *Address:* Sotheby's Inc., 1134 York Avenue, New York, NY 10021 (Office); 447 East 57th Street, New York, NY 10022, USA (Home).

OLDFIELD, Bruce, OBE; British fashion designer; b. 14 July 1950; brought up in Dr. Barnardo's charity home, Ripon; ed Ripon Grammar School, Sheffield City Polytechnic, Ravensbourne Coll. of Art and St Martin's Coll. of Art; est. own fashion house, producing designer collections 1975; began making couture clothes for individual clients 1981; opened retail shop selling couture and ready-to-wear 1984; designed for films Jackpot 1974, The Sentinel 1976; Vice-Pres. Barnardo's 1998; Trustee Royal Acad. 2000–; Gov. London Inst. 1999–; Hon. Fellow Sheffield Polytechnic 1987, RCA 1990, Durham Univ. 1991; Hon. DCL (Northumbria) 2001. *Exhibition:* retrospective Exhbn Laing Galleries, Newcastle upon Tyne 2000. *Publication:* Seasons 1987. *Leisure interests:* music, reading, gardening, working, cooking. *Address:* 27 Beauchamp Place, London, SW3 1NJ, England. *Telephone:* (20) 7584-1363. *Fax:* (20) 7584-6972.

OLDMAN, Gary; British actor; b. 21 March 1958, New Cross, S. London; m. 1st Lesley Manville; one s.; m. 2nd Uma Thurman (q.v.) 1991 (divorced 1992); m. 3rd Donya Fiorentino (separated 2001); two c.; ed Rose Bruford Drama Coll.; studied with Greenwich Young People's Theatre; acted with Theatre Royal, York and then with touring co.; appeared at Glasgow Citizens Theatre in Massacre at Paris, Chinchilla, Desperado Corner, A Waste of Time; London stage appearances: Minnesota Moon, Summit Conference, Real Dreams, The Desert Air (RSC), War Play I, II, III (RSC), Serious Money (Royal Court), Women Beware Women (Royal Court), The Pope's Wedding; appeared in The Country Wife, Royal Exchange Theatre, Manchester. *Films:* Sid and Nancy, Prick Up Your Ears, Track 29, Criminal Law, We Think The World of You, Chattahoochee, State of Grace, Exile, Before and After Death, Rosencrantz and Guildenstern are Dead, JFK, Dracula, True Romance, Romeo is Bleeding, Immortal Beloved, Murder in the First, Dead Presidents, The Scarlet Letter, Basquiat, Nil by Mouth (BAFTA Award) 1997, The Fifth Element 1997, Air Force One 1997, Lost in Space 1998, Anasazie Moon 1999, Hannibal 2000, The Contender 2000. *Television appearances include:* Remembrance, Meantime (Channel 4); Honest, Decent and True (BBC); Rat in the Skull (Central), The Firm, Heading Home, Fallen Angels. *Address:* c/o Douglas Urbanski, Douglas Management Inc., 515 N. Robertson Boulevard, Los Angeles, CA 90048, USA.

O'LEARY, Hazel, BA; American politician and lawyer; b. 17 May 1937, Newport News, Va; d. of Russell Reid and Hazel Palleman; m. John F. O'Leary 1980 (deceased); one s.; fmr prosecutor, then an Asst Attorney-Gen., NJ; Vice-Pres. and Gen. Counsel, O'Leary Assocs. (consultants on energy econs and planning) 1981–89, Pres. O'Leary and Assocs 1997–2000; COO Blaylock & Partners, NY 2000–; fmr mem. staff Dept of Energy and Fed. Energy Admin., joined Northern States Power Co., Minn. 1989, subsequently Exec. Vice-Pres.; Sec. of Energy 1993–97; Democrat. *Address:* Blaylock & Partners L P, 609 5th Avenue, New York, NY 10017, USA (Office).

O'LEARY, John, BA, LLB; American diplomatist and lawyer; b. 16 Jan. 1947, Portland, Maine; ed Yale Coll. and Law School; Mellon Fellow, Clare Coll., Cambridge 1969–71; lawyer 1974–; partner Pierce Atwood law firm; Amb. to Chile 1998–2001; Deputy Chief of Mission in Mali 2001–; Chair. Standing Cttee on Environmental Law, American Bar Asscn 1996, Nat. Resources and Environmental Protection Cttee, Inter-American Bar Asscn; Chair. Devt, the Environment and Dispute Resolution in the Americas Conf., American Bar Asscn, Argentina 1997. *Address:* American Embassy, Rue Rochester NY and rue Mohamed V, B.P. 34, Bamako, Mali (Office). *E-mail:* ipc@usa.org.ml.

O'LEARY, Michael; Irish politician and barrister; b. 8 May 1936, Cork; s. of John O'Leary and Margaret McCarthy; ed Univ. Coll., Cork, Kings Inns Dublin; Deputy Pres. Nat. Students' Union 1960–61; Educ. Officer, Irish TUC 1962–65; TD for Dublin North Cen. 1965–82, for Dublin SW 1982–87; spokesman on Industry and Commerce, Labour, Foreign Affairs and Educ. 1965–73; Minister for Labour 1973–77; Deputy Prime Minister and Minister of Energy 1981–82; fmr Leader, Labour Party (resgnd); Pres. 2nd European Regional Conf., ILO 1974, Annual Conf. 1976, EEC Council of Ministers for Social Affairs Jan.–June 1975; mem. European Parl. 1979–81; resgnd from Labour Party 1982 and joined Fine Gael party; mem. Hon. Soc. of the Middle Temple. *Address:* Áras Uí Dhálaigh, Inns Quay, Dublin 7, Ireland (Office).

O'LEARY, Terence Daniel, CMG, MA; British diplomatist (retd); b. 18 Aug. 1928, London; s. of the late Daniel O'Leary and Mary O'Leary (née Duggan);

m. Janet Douglas Berney 1960 (died 1997); twin s. one d.; ed Dulwich Coll., St John's Coll., Cambridge; commissioned, served in Queen's Royal Regt 1946–48, Capt. TA 1951–55; worked in industry 1951–53; Asst Prin. Commonwealth Relations Office (later FCO) 1953, subsequently served New Zealand, India, Tanganyika, Australia, South Africa and in Cabinet Office and as Sr Directing Staff, Nat. Defence Coll. 1978–81; High Commr in Sierra Leone 1981–84, in New Zealand and concurrently W Samoa and Gov. of Pitcairn 1984–87; mem. S.B.O. EC Monitoring Mission, Zagreb, Croatia 1991–92; Chair. Petworth Preservation 1989–97; Councillor, Petworth 1993–97. *Leisure interests:* gardening, croquet, walking.

OLEKSY, Józef, DEcon; Polish politician and economist; b. 22 June 1946, Nowy Sącz; s. of Józef Oleksy and Michalina Oleksy; m. Maria Oleksy 1983; one s. one d.; ed Warsaw School of Econs, European Faculty of Comparative Law, Strasbourg; researcher Faculty of Foreign Trade, Vice-Dir Int. Law Dept Warsaw School of Econs (SGH) 1969–; Founder, Pres. Movt of Young Scientists in Poland 1969–72; Minister, mem. of Council of Ministers 1989; mem. Polish Group of IPU; Deputy to Sejm (Parl.) 1989–; Marshal (Speaker) of Sejm 1993–95; Prime Minister of Poland 1995–96; mem. Polish United Workers' Party (PZPR) 1968–90, First Sec. Voivod. Cttee 1987–89; mem. Parliamentary Asscn of the OSCE 1989–93; mem.Governing Bd of the Council for Social Democracy of the Repub. of Poland (SDRP) 1990–, Vice-Chair. 1992–96, Chair. 1996–97; Pres. Polish Council of Young Scientists 1969–76; participant Historical Compromise in Poland Round Table 1989; mem. Cttee on Foreign Affairs and Cttee on European Integration; Rep. EU–Poland Jt Parliamentary Cttee 1997, Co-Chair. 2001–; Chair. European Cttee of Sejm 2001–. *Publications:* numerous articles on econ. and int. affairs. *Leisure interests:* walking, hunting, history, futurology, parapsychology, cosmology. *Address:* Sejm RP, ul. Wiejska 4/6/8, 00-902 Warsaw, Poland (Office). *Telephone:* (22) 6942226 (Office); (22) 6942651 (Office). *Fax:* (22) 6254529 (Office).

OLESEN, Poul; Danish physicist; b. 28 April 1939, Aalborg; s. of Viktor Olesen and Herdis Olesen; m. Birgitte Sode-Mogensen 1984; ed Univ. of Copenhagen; Research Assoc. Univ. of Rochester, New York 1967–69; Research Assoc. CERN, Geneva 1969–71; Visiting Fellow 1985; Assoc. Prof. of Theoretical Physics, The Niels Bohr Inst. Copenhagen 1971–97, Prof. 1997–, Chair. Research Cttee 1993–95, mem. Governing Body 1996–99; mem. Faculty of Science Council, Univ. of Copenhagen 1989–, Exec. Cttee 1990–93, Research Cttee 1998–; mem. Royal Danish Acad.; Hermer Prize. *Publications:* articles in int. journals on particle physics. *Address:* The Niels Bohr Institute, Blegdamsvej 17, 2100 Copenhagen Ø (Office); Malmmosevej 1, 2840 Holte, Denmark (Home). *Telephone:* 31-42-16-16 (Office).

OLHAYE, Roble, M.B.I.M.; Djibouti diplomatist; b. 24 April 1944; m.; five c.; ed Commercial School of Addis Ababa; worked in area of financial and admin. man. in various orgs in Ethiopia engaged in communication, printing, export trade, insurance and mfg 1964–73; regional accountant, TAW Int. Leasing Corpn Nairobi 1973, Financial Dir 1975; ind. consultant 1980–82; Hon. Consul of Djibouti to Kenya 1980–85; f. (as jt venture with Middle East Bank of Dubai) Banque de Djibouti et du Moyen Orient, SA 1982; Perm. Rep. to UNEP and UN Centre for Human Settlements (Habitat), Nairobi 1986–88; Amb. to USA 1988–, to Canada (non-resident) 1989–; Perm. Rep. to UN 1988–; Pres. of Council 1994, Chair. of Sanctions Cttee 1994, mem. Security Council Mission to Mozambique 1994, Dean of African Diplomatic Corps 1999, Chair. Second Cttee (Econ. and Social) 1999–; Fellow Asscn of Int. Accountants, UK; mem. British Inst. of Man. *Address:* Permanent Mission of Djibouti to the United Nations, 866 United Nations Plaza, Suite 4011, New York, NY 10017, USA. *Telephone:* (212) 753-3163 (Office). *Fax:* (212) 223-1276 (Office). *E-mail:* djibouti@nyct.net (Office).

OLINS, Wally (Wallace), CBE, MA, FCSD; British business executive; b. 19 Dec. 1930; s. of Alfred Olins and Rachel Olins (née Muscovitch); m. 1st Renate Steinart 1957 (divorced 1989); two s. one d.; m. 2nd Dornie Watts 1990; one d.; ed Highgate School, St Peter's Coll., Oxford; nat. service with army in Germany 1950–51; with S.H. Benson Ltd, London 1954–57; with Benson, India 1957–62; with Caps Design Group, London 1962–65; co-f. Wolff Olins 1965, Chair. –2001; Vice-Pres. SIAD 1982–85; visiting lecturer Design Man. London Business School 1984–89; Visiting Prof. Man. School Imperial Coll., London 1987–89, Lancaster Univ. 1992–, Copenhagen Business School 1993–, Duxx, Centro de Excelencia Empresarial, Mexico 1992–2001, Said Business School, Oxford 2001–; Chair. Design Dimension Educ. Trust 1987–93, Saffron Brand Consultants 2001–; Trustee Design Museum 1988–93; mem. Council RSA 1989–95; mem. Devt Trust Royal Philharmonic Orchestra 1994–; Dir Glasgow 1999 1996–; Dir Health Educ. Authority 1996–99; mem. Master's Council St Peter's Coll., Oxford 1995–; RSA Bicentenary Medal 2000. *Publications:* The Corporate Personality 1978, The Wolff Olins Guide to Corporate Identity 1983, The Wolff Olins Guide to Design Management 1985, Corporate Identity 1989, International Identity 1995, New Guide to Identity 1996, Trading Identitites 1999, numerous articles in design and man. publs. *Leisure interests:* looking at buildings, shopping for books, theatre, old cars. *Address:* Grahamsfield, Goring-on-Thames, Reading, RG8 9AD (Home); 126 Montagu Mansions, London W1U 6LG, England. *Telephone:* (20) 7224-2121 (Office). *Fax:* (20) 7224-1922 (Office). *E-mail:* wally@wallyolins.com. *Website:* www.wallyolins.com.

OLIPHANT, Patrick, DHumLitt; American political cartoonist, artist and sculptor; b. 24 July 1935, Adelaide, Australia; copyboy, press artist, Adelaide Advertiser 1953–55, cartoonist 1955–64; cartoonist, Denver Post 1964–75,

Washington Star 1975–81; ind. cartoonist syndicated through Universal Press Syndicate 1980–; Hon. LHD (Dartmouth Coll.) 1981; awards include Pulitzer Prize 1967, Nat. Cartoonist of Year Award 1968, 1972, Washington Journalism Review 'Best in the Business' Award 1985. *Exhibitions:* retrospective Exhbn Nat. Portrait Gallery, Washington DC 1990, Seven Presidents, San Diego Museum of Art 1995, Oliphants Anthem, Library of Congress, Washington, DC 1998, travelling exhbns. in Eastern Europe and USA. *Publications:* The Oliphant Book 1969, Four More Years 1973, An Informal Gathering 1978, Oliphant, A Cartoon Collection 1980, The Jellybean Society 1981, Ban This Book 1982, But Seriously Folks 1983, The Year of Living Perilously 1984, Make My Day! 1985, Between Rock and a Hard Place 1986, Up to Here in Alligators 1987, Nothing Basically Wrong 1988, What Those People Need is a Puppy 1989, Fashions for the New World Order 1991, Just Say No 1992, Waiting for the Other Shoe to Drop 1994, Off to the Revolution 1995, Maintain the Status Quo 1996, So That's Where They Came From 1997, Are We There Yet? 1999, Now We'll Have to Spray for Politicians! 2000. *Address:* Universal Press Syndicate, 4520 Main Street, Suite 700, Kansas City, MO 64112; c/o Susan Conway Gallery, 1214 Thirtieth Street Northwest, Washington DC 20007, USA.

OLITSKI, Jules, MA; American painter and sculptor; b. 27 March 1922, Snovsk, Russia; s. of late Jevel Demikovsky and of Anna Zarnitsky; m. 1st Gladys Katz 1944 (divorced 1951), one d.; m. 2nd Andrea Hill Pearce 1956 (divorced 1974); one d.; m. 3rd Kristina Gorby 1980; ed Beaux Arts Inst., NY, New York Univ.; Assoc. Prof. of Art, State Univ. Coll., New Paltz 1954–55; Curator New York Univ. Art Gallery 1955–56; Art Instructor, Co-ordinator Fine Arts Dept, C. W. Post Coll., Long Island Univ. 1956–63; Art Teacher Bennington Coll., Vt 1963–67; one-man exhbns of paintings, drawings and sculpture in USA at Corcoran Gallery, Washington, DC 1967, 1974, 1975, Metropolitan Museum of Art, New York 1969, retrospective exhbn at Museum of Fine Arts, Boston 1973, Galleria dell'Ariete, Milan 1974, Knoedler Contemporary Arts, New York 1974–77, Waddington Gallery, London 1975, Boston Museum of Fine Art 1977, Galeria Wentzel, Fed. Repub. of Germany 1975, 1977, Hirshhorn Museum, Washington 1977, Edmonton Art Gallery, Canada 1978; solo exhbns at Galerie Huit, Paris 1950, Kasmin Gallery, London 1964–75, 1989, David Mirvish Gallery, Toronto 1964–78, André Emmerich Gallery, New York 1966–89, 1995, Zürich 1973–74, Gallery One, Toronto 1981–89, Yares Gallery, Ariz. 1983–89, Gallery Camino Real, Fla 1988–97, Salander-O'Reilly Galleries, New York 1989–94, Long Fine Art, New York 1994–97, Annandale Galleries, Sydney, Australia 2000, Bunnington Gallery, Nottingham 2001 and many others in USA and abroad; numerous group exhbns in USA, Canada, France, Fed. Repub. of Germany, Switzerland, Spain; represented in many perm. collections in USA; Fellow American Acad. of Arts and Sciences 1993; Assoc. Nat. Academician, Nat. Acad. of Design 1993; chosen for Carnegie Int. 1961, 1967, for Venice Biennale 1966; Second Prize Carnegie Int. 1961, First Prize Corcoran Biennal 1967, Award for Distinction in the Arts Univ. Union (S. Carolina) 1975. *Publications:* The Courage of Conviction (essay) 1985, How I Got My First New York Show (essay) 1989, A Letter to Kristina: The Courage to Grow Old (essay) 1989, Small Mountains (co-author, illustrator) 2000. *Address:* c/o Salanders O'Reilly Galleries Inc., 20 E 79th Street, New York, NY 10021, USA. *E-mail:* jolitski@sover.net (Office).

OLIVA, L. Jay, PhD; American university president; b. 23 Sept. 1933, Walden, NY; s. of Lawrence Oliva and Catherine Mooney; m. Mary E. Nolan 1961; two s.; ed Manhattan Coll. and Univs. of Freiburg and Paris; Univ. Fellow, Syracuse Univ. 1955–57, Research Assoc. 1957–58, Univ. Research Inst. 1959–60; Instr., Assoc. Prof. of History, New York Univ. 1960–69, Prof. of History 1969–, Deputy Vice-Chancellor 1970–75, Vice-Pres. for Academic Planning and Service 1975–77, Vice-Pres. for Academic Affairs 1977–80, Provost and Exec. Vice-Pres. for Academic Affairs 1980–83, Chancellor and Exec. Vice-Pres. for Academic Affairs 1983–91, Pres. 1991–2002; mem. Council on Foreign Relations 1992–2002; other academic and professional appointments; Hon. DHumLit (Manhattan Coll.) 1987, (Hebrew Union Coll.) 1992; Hon. LLD (St Thomas Aquinas Coll.); Hon. DLit (Univ. Coll. Dublin) 1993; Medal of the Sorbonne 1992. *Publications include:* Misalliance: A Study of French Policy in Russia During the Seven Years War 1964, Russia and the West from Peter to Kruschev (ed.) 1965, Russia in the Era of Peter the Great 1969, Peter the Great (ed.) 1970, Catherine the Great (ed.) 1971. *Leisure interests:* athletics, music, reading. *Address:* 33 Washington Square West, New York, NY 10011, USA (Home); c/o New York University, 70 Washington Square South, New York, NY 10012. *Telephone:* (212) 998-2345. *Fax:* (212) 995-3679.

OLIVE, David Ian, CBE, MA, PhD, FRS; British professor of theoretical physics; b. 16 April 1937, Staines; m. Jenifer Tutton 1963; two d.; ed Royal High School, Edinburgh and Univs. of Edinburgh and Cambridge; Fellow, Churchill Coll., Cambridge 1963–70; Asst Lecturer, Lecturer, Univ. of Cambridge 1965–71; staff mem. CERN Theory Div. 1971–77; Lecturer, Reader, Blackett Lab. Imperial Coll., London 1977–84; Prof. of Theoretical Physics 1984–92; Research Prof. in Physics, Univ. of Wales, Swansea 1992–2002; Dirac Medal and Prize (Italy) 1997. *Publications:* The Analytic S-Matrix (jtly) 1965; many scientific papers and articles on the theory of elementary particles and their symmetries. *Leisure interests:* golf, listening to music. *Address:* Department of Physics, University of Wales Swansea, Singleton Park, Swansea, SA2 8PP (Office); 4 Havergal Close, Caswell, Swansea, SA3 4RL, Wales (Home). *Telephone:* (1792) 295842 (Office).

OLIVEIRA, Manoel de; Portuguese film director; b. 1908, Oporto. *Films include:* Douro, Faina Fluvial 1931, Aniki-Bóbó 1942, O Pinto e a Cidade 1956, O Pão 1959, O Acto da Primavera 1963, A Caça 1964, O Passado e Presente 1972, Benilde ou A Virgem Mãe 1975, Amor de Perdição 1979, Francisca 1981.

OLIVER, Jamie; British chef; b. May 1975; m. Jools Oliver 2000; two d.; ed Westminster Catering Coll.; began cooking at parents' pub/restaurant The Cricketers, Cambridge; fmr Head Pastry Chef, The Neal Street Restaurant; fmr Chef The River Café; Presenter The Naked Chef (Optomen TV), Jamie's Kitchen; advertising contract with Sainsbury's Co.; cookery show tour The Happy Days Tour, UK, NZ and Australia 2001; designed range of cooking and tableware for Royal Worcester; Consultant Chef Monte's Restaurant, London; est. restaurant Fifteen, London 2003; Food Ed. GQ magazine (UK), Marie Claire magazine (UK); contrib. to Saturday Times Magazine. *Publications include:* The Naked Chef (3 cookery books), Jamie's Kitchen 2002. *Leisure interests:* pasta and bread-making, plays drums in band Scarlet Division. *Address:* Fifteen, Westland Place, London, N1 7LP, England (Office). *Telephone:* (20) 7251-1515 (Office). *Fax:* (20) 7251-2749 (Office). *Website:* www .jamieoliver.net (Office).

OLIVER, Roland, PhD, FBA; British Africanist; b. 30 March 1923, Srinagar, Kashmir; s. of Douglas Gifford Oliver and Lorimer Janet Donaldson; m. 1st Caroline Linehan 1947 (died 1983); one d.; m. 2nd Suzanne Miers 1990; ed Cambridge Univ.; Lecturer, SOAS, Univ. of London 1948–49, 1950–57, Reader 1958–63, Prof. of African History 1963–86, Hon. Fellow 1992; organized first confs. on history and archaeology of Africa, London Univ. 1953, 1957, 1961; f. and edited Journal of African History 1960–73; Pres. British Inst. in E Africa 1981–93; Chair. Minority Rights Group; Distinguished Africanist Award, American African Studies Asscn 1989. *Publications:* The Missionary Factor in East Africa 1952, Sir Harry Johnston and the Scramble for Africa 1957, The Dawn of African History 1961, Short History of Africa (with J. D. Fage) 1962, History of East Africa (with G. Mathew) 1963, Africa since 1800 (with A. Atmore) 1967, Africa in the Iron Age (with B. M. Fagan) 1975, The African Middle Ages 1400–1800 (with A. Atmore) 1980, The African Experience 1991, The Realms of Gold 1997, Medieval Africa (with A. Atmore) 2001; Gen. Ed. Cambridge History of Africa 8 Vols 1975–86. *Address:* Frilsham Woodhouse, near Thatcham, Berkshire, RG18 9XB, England. *Telephone:* (1635) 201407. *Fax:* (1635) 202716.

OLIVER OF AYLMERTON, Baron (Life Peer), cr. 1986, of Aylmerton in the County of Norfolk; **Peter Raymond Oliver,** Kt, PC; British lawyer; b. 7 March 1921; s. of David Thomas Oliver and Alice Maud Oliver; m. 1st Mary Chichester Rideal 1945 (died 1985); one s. one d.; m. 2nd Wendy Anne Oliver 1987; ed The Leys, Cambridge, Trinity Hall, Cambridge; mil. service 1941–45; called to Bar, Lincoln's Inn 1948, Bencher 1973; QC 1965; Judge of the High Court of Justice, Chancery Div. 1974–80; mem. Restrictive Practices Court 1976–80; Chair. Review Body on Chancery Div. of High Court 1979–81; Lord Justice of Appeal 1980–85; Lord of Appeal in Ordinary 1986–92; Hon. Fellow, Trinity Hall, Cambridge 1980. *Leisure interests:* gardening, music. *Address:* House of Lords, London, SW1A 0PW (Office); The Canadas, Sandy Lane, West Runton, Norfolk, NR27 9ND, England (Home).

OLLILA, Esko Juhani, LLM; Finnish bank executive; b. 14 July 1940, Rovaniemi; s. of Heikki Armas Ollila and Lempi Maria Ollila (née Häggman); m. Riitta Leena, née Huhtala 1963; two s.; Man. Dir Rovaniemi Savings Bank 1971–75; Man. Dir and Chair. Bd Regional Devt Fund of Finland 1975–79; mem. Bd Skopbank 1979–83; Minister of Trade and Industry 1982–83; Minister of Finance 1986–87; mem. Bd Bank of Finland 1983–2000; Chair. Finnish Nat. Fund for Research and Devt (SITRA) 1991–95, mem. 1995–; mem. Supervisory Bd Finnish Guarantee Bd 1995–; Chair. Advisory Bd Baltic Investment Fund 1995–.

OLLILA, Jorma, MSc; Finnish business executive; b. 15 Aug. 1950, Seinäjoki; m. Liisa Annikki Metsola; two s. one d.; ed Univ. of Helsinki, London School of Econs and Helsinki Univ. of Tech.; mem. Man. Bd Citibank Oy 1983–85; Vice-Pres. Int. Operations, Nokia 1985–86, mem. Group Exec. Bd 1986–, Sr Vice-Pres. Finance 1986–89, Deputy mem. Bd of Dirs 1989–90, Pres. Nokia Mobile Phones 1990–92, Pres. Nokia 1992–99, CEO 1992–99, Chair. Bd Dirs, CEO, Chair. Group Exec. Bd 1999–; Chair. Bd MTV Oy; mem. Bd Oy Dipoli Ab, ICI PLC; mem. Supervisory Bd NKF Holding NV, Tietotehdas Oy, Industrial Mutual Insurance Co., Pohjola Insurance Co. Ltd, Sampo Insurance Co. Ltd, Pension-Varma Mutual Insurance Co., Oy Rastor AB; mem. Bd and Exec. Cttee Confed. of Finnish Industries and Employers; Chair. Council, Finnish Foreign Trade Asscn; Vice-Chair. Bd, Finnish Section, Int. Chamber of Commerce, and many other positions; Hon. PhD (Helsinki) 1995, Hon. DSc (Helsinki Univ. of Tech.) 1998; Kt, Order of White Rose of Finland 1996, Commdr's. Cross Order of Merit, Germany 1997, Commdr's Cross, Order of Merit, Poland 1999. *Address:* Office of the President, Nokia Group, Keilalahdentie 4, P.O. Box 226, 00045 Helsinki, Finland. *Telephone:* (71) 8008000 (Office).

OLLOQUI, Javier Viar; Spanish arts administrator; b. 1946, Bilbao; poet, novelist, art critic and historian; mem. Bd Bilbao Fine Arts Museum late 1980s–, Dir 2002–; fmr mem. Acquisitions Advisory Bd, Guggenheim Bilbao; fmr mem. Dept of Culture, Basque Govt; organizer of numerous int. and nat. exhbns; Euskadi Literature Award, City of Irun Short Story Prize 1992. *Address:* Museo de Bellas Artes, Plaza del Museo 2, 48011 Bilbao, Spain (Office).

OLMERT, Ehud, BA, LLB; Israeli politician and lawyer; b. 1945, Binyamina; m.; four c.; ed Hebrew Univ. of Jerusalem; served in Israeli Defence Force (IDF) as combat infantry unit officer; mil. corresp. for IDF journal Bamachane; mem. Likud Party; mem. Knesset 1973–98, 2003–; Minister without Portfolio responsible for Minority Affairs 1988–90; Minister of Health 1990–92; Mayor of Jerusalem 1993–2003; Vice-Premier of Israel and Minister of Industry and Trade 2003–. *Address:* Ministry of Industry and Trade, POB 299, 30 Rehov Agron, Jerusalem 94190, Israel (Office). *Telephone:* 2-6220661 (Office). *Fax:* 2-6222412 (Office). *E-mail:* dover@moit.gov.il (Office). *Website:* www.tamas.gov.il (Office).

OLMI, Ermanno; Italian film director; b. 24 July 1931, Bergamo; fmr clerk, Edison-Volta electric plant; later Dir and producer sponsored documentary films; made first feature film 1959, f. production co. 22 December SpA 1961 and helped found Hypothesis Cinema. *Films include:* Il Tempo si è Fermato 1959, Il Posto 1961, I Fidanzati 1963, E Venne un Uomo 1965, Un Certo Giorno 1969, I Recuperanti 1970, Durante l'Estate 1971, La Circostanza 1974, L'Albero degli Zoccoli (Palme d'Or, Cannes) 1978, Legend of a Holy Drinker 1988, Il Segreto Del Bosco Vecchio, The Profession of Arms 2001.

OLOVSSON, Ivar (Olov Göte), DrSc; Swedish professor emeritus of inorganic chemistry; b. 15 Oct. 1928, Rödön; s. of Erik Olovsson and Anna Andersson; m. Kristina Jonsson 1950; three s. one d.; ed Univ. of Uppsala; Teaching Asst Univ. of Uppsala 1953–57, Asst Prof. 1961–64, Assoc. Prof. 1965–69, Prof. of Inorganic Chem. 1969–93, Prof. Emer. 1993–; Research Assoc. Univ. of Calif. Berkeley 1957–59, 1964–65; Guest Prof. Lab. de Cristallographie, Grenoble 1977–78, Univ. of Konstanz 1982–83, 1999; Visiting Miller Prof. Berkeley 2002; mem. Royal Soc. of Sciences 1970 (Pres. 1996–97), Royal Acad. of Sciences of Sweden 1974; Gold Medal, Royal Acad. of Sciences of Sweden 1961; Gold Medal, Swedish Chem. Soc. 1965; Kt of Northern Star 1975; Chevalier des Palmes Académiques 1981. *Publications:* about 90 scientific papers, mainly in field of structural chem. *Leisure interests:* outdoor life, mountaineering, skiing, music. *Address:* Ångström Laboratory, Materials Chemistry, P.O. Box 538, SE–751 21 Uppsala, Sweden (Office); Murklevägen 27, SE–756 46 Uppsala, Sweden (Home). *Telephone:* (18) 471-37-21 (Office); (18) 30-22-76 (Home). *Fax:* (18) 51-35-48 (Office). *E-mail:* ivar .olovsson@mkem.uu.se (Office); ivar.olovsson@mkem.uu.se (Home).

OLSEN, Olaf, PhD; Danish archaeologist, historian and fmr museum director; b. 7 June 1928, Copenhagen; s. of the late Prof. Albert Olsen and of Agnete Bing; m. 1st Jean Catherine Dennistoun Sword; one s; m. 2nd Rikke Agnete Clausen 1971; ed Copenhagen Univ.; Asst, Medieval Dept, Nat. Museum 1950–58, Asst Keeper 1958–71, State Antiquary and Dir Nat. Museum 1981–95; Prof. of Medieval Archaeology, Aarhus Univ. 1971–81; Dir Hielmstierne-Rosencrone Foundation 1979–; Vice-Pres. Det kgl. nordiske Oldskriftselskab 1981–95, Royal Danish Acad. of Sciences and Letters 1983–89; founding mem. Academia Europaea 1988; Dir numerous archaeological excavations, mainly of Viking ships and fortresses and medieval churches and monasteries; Hon. Fellow, Soc. of Antiquaries; Dr. hc (St Petersburg Univ.) 1994; GEC Gad Foundation Prize 1966, 1992, Hartmann Prize 1995, Westerby Prize 2002. *Publications:* numerous books and papers on history and medieval archaeology. *Address:* Strevelshovedvej 2, Alrø, 8300 Odder, Denmark. *Telephone:* 86-55-21-28. *Fax:* 86-55-21-28. *E-mail:* olaf .olsen@rikkeslyst.dk (Home).

OLSON, Lyndon L., Jr; American insurance executive, politician and diplomatist; b. 7 March 1947, Waco, Texas; m. Kay Woodward Olson 1982; ed Baylor Univ., Baylor Law School, Tex.; mem. Texas State House of Reps. 1973–78; Chair. Cttee on Higher Educ., House Standing Cttee on Local Govt; Chair. Texas State Bd of Insurance 1979–81, 1983–87; CEO Nat. Group of Insurance Cos. 1987–; helped negotiate U.S.–Israeli Free Trade Agreement; led Trade Del. on Financial Services to Russia and China 1985; Amb. to Sweden 1997–2001; Pres. Nat. Asscn of Insurance Commrs. 1982; Pres. and CEO Travellers Insurance Holdings Inc. 1990–98, Assoc. Madison Cos. Inc.; Elder Cen. Pres. Church, Texas; Gates of Jerusalem Award (Israel), Baylor Young Outstanding Alumni Award, Distinguished Public Official (Texas Med. Asscn). *Address:* c/o Department of State, 2201 C Street, N.W., Washington, DC 20520, U.S.A.

OLSSON, Curt G., BScEcon; Swedish banker; b. 20 Aug. 1927, Mjällby; s. of N. E. Olsson and Anna Olsson (née Nilsson); m. Asta Olsson 1954; two d.; Man. Dir Swedish Bank Giro Centre 1959; Deputy Man. and Head of Marketing, Skandinaviska Banken, Stockholm 1964; Man. and Head of Cen. Group 1966, Man. Dir (Stockholm Group) 1970; Man. Dir Skandinaviska Enskilda Banken, Stockholm Group 1972; Man. Dir and Chief Exec. Head Office, Stockholm 1976–82, 1st Deputy Chair. of Bd 1982–84, Chair. 1984–96; Dir Fastighets AB Hufvudstaden; mem. Royal Swedish Acad. of Eng Sciences; Consul Gen. hc for Finland 1990–99; Hon. DEcon; Kt, Order of Vasa, HM King Carl XVI Gustaf's Gold Medal, Commdr Royal Norwegian Order of Merit, Commdr Order of the Lion of Finland. *Address:* c/o Skandinaviska Enskilda Banken, Kungsträdgårdsgt. 8, 106 40 Stockholm, Sweden.

OLSSON, Karl Erik; Swedish politician; b. 1938, Häglinge, Kristianstad; m. Sonja Olsson; three c.; ed Colleges of Agric.; farmer Nygård Farm 1963–; Chair. Nat. Centre Party Youth League 1971–74; mem. Centre Party Nat. Bd 1981–92, Asst Vice-Chair. 1986–87, Vice-Chair. 1987–92; MP 1976–79, 1985–; mem. Bd Nuclear Power Inspectorate 1977–91, Foundation for the Promotion of Literature 1980–91, Swedish Univ. of Agric. Sciences 1986–91;

Chair. Standing Cttee on Agric. 1985–91; Minister of Agric. 1991–94. *Publications:* Bonde i lokalsamhället, Tankar. *Address:* c/o Ministry of Agriculture, Drottninggt. 21, 103 33 Stockholm, Sweden.

OLSZEWSKI, Jan Ferdynand; Polish politician and lawyer; b. 20 Aug. 1930, Warsaw; m.; ed Warsaw Univ.; mem. underground Boy Scouts WWII; Research Asst Legal Sciences Dept Polish Acad. of Sciences 1954–56; journalist Po prostu 1956–57; banned from working as a journalist 1957; mem. Crooked Circle Club 1956–62; Trial Lawyer 1962–68; suspended from the Bar by Justice Minister for defending students involved in anti-Communist demonstrations 1968; returned to work as Attorney 1970; Defence Counsel for anti-Communist Ruch Organization 1972; founder leader Polish Independence Alliance 1975–81; co-founder Workers' Defence Cttee (KOR) 1976–77; drafted (jtly.) Statute of the Free Trade Union of Coast Workers 1980; Adviser Solidarity Nat. Comm. 1980–; Legal Adviser Secretariat of Polish Episcopate; Plenipotentiary to family of Father Jerzy Popiełuszko during trial of his murderers; Rep. Solidarity opposition in sub-comm. on legal and judicial reform 1989; mem. Pres. Lech Wałęsa's Advisory Cttee Jan.–Nov. 1991; Deputy to Sejm (Parl.) 1991–93, 1997–; Prime Minister of Poland 1991–92; Co-founder and Pres. Movt for the Repub. 1992–94; co-founder and Leader Movt for the Reconstruction of Poland (ROP) 1995–; Leader Homeland Patriotic Movt 1997; Founder-mem. Civic Inst. and Atlantic Club. *Address:* Biuro Poselskie, Al. Ujazdowskie 13, 00-567 Warsaw, Poland. *Telephone:* (22) 6941051 (Office). *Fax:* (22) 6941051 (Office).

O'MALLEY, Desmond Joseph, BCL; Irish politician and solicitor; b. 2 Feb. 1939, Limerick; s. of Desmond J. O'Malley and Una O'Malley; m. Patricia McAleer 1965; two s. four d.; ed Crescent Coll., Limerick, Nat. Univ. of Ireland; practised as solicitor 1962; mem. Dáil (House of Reps.) for Limerick East 1968–; mem. Limerick Corpn 1974–77; Parl. Sec. to Taoiseach (Prime Minister) and to Minister for Defence 1969–70; Minister for Justice 1970–73; Opposition Spokesman on Health 1973–75, on Industry and Commerce 1975–77; Minister for Industry and Commerce 1977–81, 1989–92, for Energy 1977–79; Opposition Spokesman on Industry and Commerce 1981–82; Minister for Trade, Commerce and Tourism 1982; Opposition Spokesman on Energy 1983–84; fmrly Fianna Fáil (expelled 1984); co-f. and Leader of Progressive Democrats Party 1985–93; Party Whip; Chair. Foreign Affairs Cttee 1997–. *Leisure interest:* golf. *Address:* Leinster House, Kildare Street, Dublin 2, Ireland. *Telephone:* (1) 6183750. *Fax:* (1) 6184166.

OMAN, Julia Trevelyan, CBE, RDI, DESRCA, FCSD; British designer; b. 11 July 1930, London; d. of Charles Chichele Oman and Joan Trevelyan; m. Dr. (now Sir) Roy Strong (q.v.) 1971; ed Royal Coll. of Art, London; Designer BBC TV 1955–67 (including TV film Alice in Wonderland 1966); designer for theatre: Brief Lives (London and New York) 1967, 1974, Country Dance 1967, Forty Years On 1968, The Merchant of Venice 1970, Othello 1971, Getting On 1971, The Importance of Being Earnest (Burgtheater, Wien) 1976; ballet: Enigma Variations (Royal Ballet, London) 1968; opera: Eugene Onegin (Covent Garden) 1971, Un Ballo in Maschera (Hamburg) 1973, La Bohème (Covent Garden) 1974, A Month in the Country (Royal Ballet, London) 1976, Die Fledermaus (Covent Garden) 1977, Le Papillon (Ashton, Pas-de-Deux) 1977; films: The Charge of the Light Brigade (art Dir) 1967, Laughter in the Dark (art Dir) 1968, Julius Caesar (production designer) 1969, Straw Dogs (design consultant) 1971; exhbns: Samuel Pepys (Nat. Portrait Gallery) 1970, Hay Fever (Danish TV) 1979; Designer Mme Tussaud's Hall of Historical Tableaux 1979, Hay Fever (Lyric, Hammersmith) 1980, The Wild Duck (Lyric, Hammersmith) 1980, Sospiri (Ashton, Pas-de-Deux) 1980, The Bear's Quest for the Ragged Staff—A Spectacle, Warwick Castle 1981, Swan Lake, Boston Ballet 1981, The Shoemaker's Holiday, Nat. Theatre 1981, Die Csárdasfürstin, Kassel, Fed. Repub. of Germany 1982, Separate Tables 1982, Otello, Stockholm 1983, Arabella, Glyndebourne Opera 1984, Nutcracker, Royal Ballet Covent Garden 1984, The Consul, Edin. and USA 1985, Mr. & Mrs. Nobody 1986, A Man for All Seasons (Chichester Festival and Savoy, London) 1987, The Best of Friends 1988, Enigma Variations (Birmingham Royal Ballet) 1994, Beatrix (Chichester) 1996; Dept Educ. and Science Visiting Cttee, Royal Coll. of Art 1980; Dir Oman Productions Ltd; Royal Scholar, Royal Coll. of Art; elected Royal Designer for Industry (RDI); Designer, Royal Coll. of Art; Hon. DLitt (Bristol) 1987; Silver Medal, RCA; Designer of the Year Award 1967, ACE Award for Best Art Dir, NCTA, USA 1983. *Publications:* Street Children (with B. S. Johnson) 1964, Elizabeth R. (with Roy Strong) 1971, Mary Queen of Scots (with Roy Strong) 1972, The English Year (with Roy Strong) 1982, A Celebration of Gardens (with Roy Strong) 1991, A Country Life (with Roy Strong) 1994, On Happiness (with Roy Strong) 1997, Garden Party (with Roy Strong) 2000. *Address:* c/o Oman Productions, The Laskett, Much Birch, Herefordshire, HR2 8HZ, England.

OMAND, David Bruce, KCB, BA; British civil servant; b. 15 April 1947, Glasgow, Scotland; s. of the late J. Bruce Omand and Esther Omand; m. Elizabeth Wales 1971; one s. one d.; ed Glasgow Acad., Corpus Christi Coll., Cambridge; Asst Prin. Ministry of Defence 1970, Pvt. Sec. to Chief Exec. (Procurement Exec.) 1973, Asst Pvt. Sec. to Sec. of State 1973–75, 1979–80, Prin. 1975, Asst Sec. 1981, Pvt. Sec. to Sec. of State 1981–82; Asst Under Sec. of State (Man. Strategy) 1988–91, Deputy Under Sec. of State (Policy) Ministry of Defence 1993–96, Dir Govt Communications HQ 1996–97; Perm. Under Sec. of State Home Office 1998–2001; Defence Counsellor FCO UK Del. to NATO, Brussels 1985–88; Chair. Centre for Man. and Policy Studies, Cabinet Office 2001–02, Perm. Sec. Cabinet Office, also Security and Intelligence Co-ordinator 2002–. *Leisure interests:* opera, walking. *Address:* Cabinet Office, 70 Whitehall, London, SW1A 2AS, England (Office). *Telephone:* (20) 7270-3000 (Office). *E-mail:* david.omand@cabinet-office.x.gsi.gov.uk (Office).

OMAR, Dato Abu Hassan Bin Haj; Malaysian politician; b. 15 Sept. 1940, Bukit Belimbing, Kuala Selangor; m. Datin Wan Noor bint Haj Daud; five c.; ed Univ. of Hull; fmr Deputy State Sec. State of Selangor and Deputy Sec.-Gen. Ministry of Land and Fed. Devt; mem. Parl. 1978–; Parl. Sec. Ministry of Commerce and Industry 1978–80; Deputy Minister of Defence 1980–81, of Transport 1981–84; Minister of Welfare Services 1984–86, of Fed. Territory 1986–87, of Foreign Affairs 1987–91, of Domestic Trade and Consumer Affairs 1991; mem. UMNO Supreme Council 1978–; recipient of several awards. *Leisure interests:* gardening, photography. *Address:* c/o Ministry of Domestic Trade and Consumer Affairs, Tingat 19, 22–24 and 40, Menara Maybank, 100 Jalan Tun Perak, 50050 Kuala Lumpur, Malaysia.

OMAR, Chamassi Said; Comoran politician; fmr naval officer; Prime Minister of Comoros 1998–99.

OMAR, Dullah, BA, LLB; South African politician and legal representative; b. 26 May 1934, Cape Town; m. Farida Ally; three c.; ed Trafalgar High School, Cape Town, Univ. of Cape Town; defence lawyer for political prisoners serving sentences on Robben Island; legal rep. to trade unions, civic and religious orgs.; Nat. Vice-Pres. Nat. Asscn of Democratic Lawyers, Pres. Cape Town br.; Attorney and Advocate Supreme Court 1982; Chair. United Democratic Front W Cape Region 1987–88, Vice-Pres. 1988–91; Dir Community Law Centre, Univ. of W Cape –1994; Minister of Justice (also with responsibility for intelligence services 1995) Govt of Nat. Unity 1994–99, of Transport 1999–; Commr Human Rights Comm. of SA; mem. ANC Nat. Exec. Comm., ANC Constitutional Comm.; Trustee SA Legal Defence Fund. *Address:* Ministry of Transport, Forum Building, Cnr. Struben and Bosman Streets, Pretoria 0002, South Africa (Office). *Telephone:* (12) 3093131 (Office). *Fax:* (12) 3283194 (Office). *E-mail:* mabasam@ndot.pwv.gov.za (Office). *Website:* www.transport .gov.za (Office).

OMAR, Ibrahim Amin, BA; Egyptian civil servant; b. 1 Dec. 1936, Kfr El-Moseillha; s. of Amin Ebraim Omar; m. Afaf Ghazy 1971; three d.; ed Cairo Univ.; mem. Nat. Guards 1953; Bd mem. Menufia Governorate 1967; Head, Safag Port 1982, Areesh City 1990; Sec.-Gen. Al Aswan Governorate 1995–; Sec., Head Cttee of Interior Front 1969; mem. Nat. Democratic Party 1981; mem. Red Sea Ports Corpn Council 1983–84; Head of Salam District, Nasser suburb 1992; State Prize, Science Day 1957, Gen. Syndicate of Engineers Medal for efforts in reconstructing Sinai and other awards. *Publication:* Planning and Developing Education Policy in Egypt. *Leisure interests:* reading, swimming, shooting. *Address:* 28 Abdel Aziz Fahmay Street, Kafr El Mosselha, Menufia, Egypt; Shebin El-Kom, Menofiya Governorate, Egypt (Home). *Telephone:* 329944.

OMAR, Mola Mohammad; Afghanistan guerrilla leader and political leader; b. 1959, Uruzgan Prov.; m. Guljana Omar 1995; two other wives; five c. (one s. died 2001); studied in several Islamic schools; joined jihad (Islamic holy war) against Soviet occupation in 1980s, became a deputy chief commdr Mujaheddin guerrilla movt fighting USSR occupation forces; helped form, recruit for and consolidate the Taliban regime (with Osama bin Laden) 1994; declared Afghanistan a 'complete' Islamic State (Islamic Emirate of Afghanistan); Leader Taliban-apptd Interim Council of Ministers 1996–2001, given title Emir al-Mo'menein (Commdr of the Faithful); went into hiding during US-led mil. action against Taliban and al-Qaida targets in Afghanistan, following suspected al-Quaida terrorist attacks in USA Sept. 2001.

OMAR, Dato Napsiah binti, MSc; Malaysian politician; b. 21 April 1943; m. (husband deceased); ed Australian Nat. Univ. Canberra and Cornell Univ. New York; Admin. Officer, Fed. Land Devt Authority, Kuala Lumpur 1967–69; started Women's and Family Devt Programme 1967; lecturer, Agricultural Coll. Malaya Serdang 1972; Co-ordinator, Food Tech., Home and Food Tech. Div. Agricultural Univ. 1972–73, Deputy Head, Dept of Home Tech. 1973–76, Head, Dept of Human Devt Studies 1978–80, Warden, Fourth Residential Coll. 1974–82; Assoc. Prof. Dept of Human Devt Studies 1981; Deputy Minister of Housing and Local Govt 1981–87; Minister of Public Enterprises 1988–90; mem. Exec. Cttee UMNO Women Malaysia and Chair. of Unity Bureau, UMNO Malaysia 1987–90; Chair. Econ. Bureau, UMNO 1986–88. *Address:* c/o Ministry of Public Enterprises, WISMA PKNS, 3rd Floor, Jalan Raja Lant, 50652 Kuala Lumpur, Malaysia.

O'MEARA, Mark Francis; American golfer; b. 13 Jan. 1957, Goldsboro, NC; m. Alicia O'Meara; one s. one d.; ed Long Beach State Univ.; professional golfer 1980–; mem. Ryder Cup team 1985, 1989, 1991, 1997, 1999; won US Amateur Championship 1979, Greater Milwaukee Open 1984, Bing Crosby Pro-Am 1985, Hawaiian Open 1985, Fuji Sankei Classic 1985, Australian Masters 1986, Lawrence Batley Int. 1987, AT&T Pebble Beach Nat. Pro-Am 1989, 1990, 1992, 1997, H-E-B Tex. Open 1990, Walt Disney World/Oldsmobile Classic 1991, Tokia Classic 1992, Argentine Open 1994, Honda Classic 1995, Bell Canada Open 1995, Mercedes Championships 1996, Greater Greensboro Open 1996, Buick Invitational 1997, US Masters 1998, British Open 1998, World Matchplay 1998; best finish 2002, 2nd in Buick Invitational and 2nd in Buick Open; All-American Rookie of Year, Long Beach State Univ. 1981; PGA Tour Player of the Year 1998. *Leisure interests:* golf course consulting, hunting, fishing. *Address:* c/o PGA, Box 109601, Avenue of Champions, Palm Beach Gardens, FL 33410, USA.

OMOROGBE, Oluyinka Osayame, LLM; Nigerian university lecturer, legal practitioner and energy consultant; b. 21 Sept. 1957, Ibadan; d. of Samuel O Ighodaro and Irene E. B. Ighodaro; m. Allan Omorogbe 1984; one s. two d.; ed Univ. of Ife and LSE; Nat. Youth Service 1979–80; Pvt. Legal Practitioner 1980–81; Lecturer Dept of Jurisprudence and Int. Law, Univ. of Benin 1983–90, Head of Dept 1988–89; Sr Lecturer Univ. of Lagos 1990–; Dir Centre for Petroleum, Environment and Devt Studies, Lagos 1996–; E-Publisher and Consultant 2001–; mem. Exec. Cttee Petroleum Energy and Mining Law Asscn of Nigeria 1986–; mem. Acad. Advisory Group, Section on Energy and Natural Resources Law, Int. Bar Asscn, African Soc. of Int. and Comparative Law; Treas. Nigerian Soc. of Int. Law 1994–97, Sec. 1997–. *Publications:* The International Oil and Gas Industry: Exploration and Production Contracts, Oil and Gas Law in Nigeria; numerous articles on petroleum and energy law and int. econ. law in int. journals. *Leisure interests:* cooking, baking, handicrafts. *Address:* P.O. Box 9261, Ikeja, Lagos; Inter Linear Ltd, Pees Galleria, 2A Osborne Road, I Koyi, Lagos, Nigeria. *Telephone:* (1) 2695790 (Office). *E-mail:* linear@petrojournal.com (Office). yomorogbe@petrojournal.com (Office). *Website:* petrojournal.com (Office).

OMRANA, Abderrahim, PhD; Moroccan economist; b. 1947, Quezane; m.; three c.; with Govt Gen. Inspection Dept 1970; Head of Mission, Treasury Dept, Ministry of Finance 1973; Asst Lecturer, Univ. of Rabat 1974, Sr Lecturer 1975–78; Exec. Attaché, Banque Nationale pour le Développement Economique 1975–78; Lecturer, Univ. of Dakar, Senegal 1978–79; Gen. Man. ICOMA and NASCOTEX 1989–95; Sec. and Dir Islamic Devt Bank 1996–2001. *Address:* c/o Islamic Development Bank, P.O. Box 5925, Jeddah 21432, Saudi Arabia (Office).

ONDAATJE, Michael; Canadian author; b. 12 Sept. 1943, Colombo, Sri Lanka; s. of Philip Mervyn Ondaatje and Enid Doris Gratiaen; two s.; ed Dulwich Coll. London, Queen's Univ. and Univ. of Toronto, Canada. *Publications include:* poetry: The Dainty Monsters 1967, The Man with Seven Toes 1968, There's a Trick with a Knife I'm Learning to Do 1979, Secular Love 1984, The Cinnamon Peeler 1991, Handwriting 1998; fiction: The Collected Works of Billy the Kid, Coming Through Slaughter, Running in the Family, In the Skin of a Lion, The English Patient (shared the Booker Prize for Fiction 1992), Anil's Ghost (Prix Medicis) 2000. *Address:* 2275 Bayview Avenue, Toronto, Ont., N4N 3M6, Canada.

ONDAATJE, (Philip) Christopher, CBE, OC, FRGS; Canadian financier; b. 22 Feb. 1933; s. of Philip Mervyn Ondaatje and Enid Doris Gratiaen; m. Valda Bulins 1959; one s. two d.; ed Blundell's School, UK; Nat. and Grindlays Bank, London 1951–55; Burns Bros & Denton, Toronto 1955–56; Montrealer Magazine and Canada Month Magazine 1956–57; Maclean-Hunter Publishing Co. Ltd, Montreal 1957–62; Financial Post, Toronto 1963–65; Pitfield Mackay, Ross & Co. Ltd, Toronto 1965–69; founder Pagurian Corpn Ltd 1967–89, Loewen, Ondaatje, McCutcheon & Co. Ltd 1970–88; Pres. Ondaatje Foundation 1975–; maj. donor to Ondaatje Wing, Nat. Portrait Gallery, London 2000 and to the Ondaatje Theatre, Royal Geographical Soc.; mem. Advisory Bd Royal Soc. of Portrait Painters, Council Royal Geographical Soc.; Patron Somerset Co. Cricket Club; Trustee Nat. Portrait Gallery; mem. Canadian Bob-Sled Team 1964; Chair. Royal Soc. of Portrait Painters; Hon. LLD (Dalhousie) 1994. *Publications:* Olympic Victory 1964, The Prime Ministers of Canada (1867–1985) 1985, Leopard in the Afternoon 1989, The Man-Eater of Punanai 1992, Sindh Revisited 1996, Journey to the Source of the Nile 1998. *Leisure interests:* golf, tennis, adventure, photography. *Address:* Glenthorne, Countisbury, nr Lynton, N Devon, EX35 6NQ, England (Home).

O'NEAL, E. Stanley, BS, MBA; American business executive; ed Kettering Univ., Harvard Univ.; joined treasury Dept, Gen. Motors 1978; Dir of Investment Banking, Merrill Lynch 1986–91, Man. Dir of High Yield Finance and Restructuring 1991–95, Head of Capital Markets Group 1995–98, Exec. Vice-Pres. and Co-Head of Corp. and Institutional Client Group 1997–99, Pres. US Pvt. Client Group 1999–2001, COO, mem. Bd Dirs and Exec. Man. Cttee Merrill Lynch 2001–, CEO 2002–, Chair. 2003–; Co-Head CICG 1997–, CFO 1998–2000, Pres. 2000–; Vice-Chair. Securities Industry Asscn; mem. Advisory Cttee New York Stock Exchange; Dir Nasdaq Stock Market; mem. Bd Nat. Urban League, McDonald House of New York, Catalyst, Buckley School; mem. Advisory Council, Bronx Preparatory Charter School. *Address:* Merrill Lynch International, 2 King Edward Street, London EC1A 1HQ, England (Office). *Telephone:* (20) 7772-1000 (Office). *Fax:* (20) 7772-2919 (Office). *Website:* www.ml.com (Office).

O'NEAL, Ralph T.; British Virgin Islands politician; b. 1933; Leader Virgin Islands Party (VIP); Chief Minister and Minister for Finance 1995–. *Address:* Office of the Chief Minister, Road Town, Tortola, The British Virgin Islands (Office). *Telephone:* 494-3701 (Office). *Fax:* 494-4435 (Office). *E-mail:* pcsm@ bvigovernment.org (Office).

O'NEAL, Ryan; American actor; b. 20 April 1941, Los Angeles; s. of Charles O'Neal and Patricia O'Neal (née Callaghan) ; m. 1st Joanna Moore 1963 (divorced 1967), one s. one d. (Tatum O'Neal, q.v.); m. 2nd Leigh Taylor-Young 1967, one s.; one s. by Farrah Fawcett.; ed US Army High School, Munich, Germany. *Television appearances include:* Dobie Gillis, Two Faces West, Perry Mason, The Virginian, This is the Life, The Untouchables, My Three Sons, Bachelor Father, Empire, Peyton Place. *Films include:* The Big Bounce 1969, Love Story 1970, The Wild Rovers 1971, What's Up, Doc? 1972, The Thief Who Came to Dinner 1973, Paper Moon 1973, Oliver's Story 1978, The Main Event 1979, So Fine 1981, Partners 1982, Irreconcilable Differences

1983, Fever Pitch 1985, Tough Guys Don't Dance 1986, Chances Are 1989, Faithful 1996, Hacks 1997, Burn Hollywood Burn 1997, Zero Effect 1998, Coming Soon 1999, Epoch 2000.

O'NEAL, Shaquille Rashaun; American professional basketball player; b. 6 March 1972, Newark; s. of Philip A. Harrison and Lucille O'Neal; m. Shaunie Nelson 2002; two c.; two c. from previous relationships; ed Louisiana State Univ.; Centre Orlando Magic 1992–96; LA Lakers 1996–; mem. Nat. Basketball Asscn (NBA) All-Star team 1993, Dream Team 11 1994; mem. gold-medal winning World Championship team 1994 and US Olympic team, Atlanta 1996. *Films:* Blue Chips 1994, Kazaam 1996. *Music:* has released five rap albums; owns record label Twism. *Address:* c/o Los Angeles Lakers, 3900 West Manchester Boulevard, Inglewood, CA 90305, USA.

O'NEAL, Tatum; American actress; b. 5 Nov. 1963, Los Angeles; d. of Ryan O'Neal (q.v.) and Joanna Moore; m. John McEnroe (q.v.) 1986 (divorced 1994); two s. one d. *Film appearances include:* Paper Moon 1973, The Bad News Bears 1976, Nickelodeon 1976, International Velvet 1978, Little Darlings 1980, Circle of Two 1980, Certain Fury 1985, Little Noises 1992, Basquiat 1996. *Address:* c/o Innovative Artists, 1999 Avenue of the Stars, Suite 2850, Century City, CA 90067, USA.

O'NEIL, William Andrew, OC, BSc, FRSA, FREng, FILT, PEng; Canadian international public servant and engineer; b. 6 June 1927, Ottawa; s. of Thomas Wilson O'Neil and Margaret (Swan) O'Neil; m. Dorothy Muir 1950; one s. two d.; ed Univ. of Toronto; engineer, Fed. Dept of Transport, Ottawa 1949–53, Resident Engineer, Special Projects Br. 1954; Div. Engineer, St Lawrence Seaway Authority 1955–59, Regional Dir 1960–63, Dir of Construction 1964–70; Deputy Admin., Marine Services, Canadian Marine Transportation Admin. 1975–79; Commr, Canadian Coast Guard and Deputy Admin., Marine Admin. 1979–89; Pres. St Lawrence Seaway Authority 1980–89; Chair. Council Int. Maritime Org. 1980–89, Sec.-Gen. 1990–; mem. Bd of Govs. World Maritime Univ. 1983–89, subsequently mem. Exec. Council of Bd of Govs. and Bd of Trustees of Capital Fund; Chair. Governing Bd, Int. Maritime Law Inst., Malta 1991–; Canadian del. to Perm. Int. Asscn of Navigation Congresses 1984–90; Chair. Canadian Cttee Lloyd's Register of Shipping 1987–88; mem. Int. Maritime Bureau 1991–; Chancellor World Maritime Univ. 1991–; Dir Canarctic Shipping Co.; Pres. Seaway Int. Bridge Corpn; mem. Bd of the Thousand Islands Bridge Authority 1980–90; mem. Asscn of Professional Engineers of Ont., American Soc. of Civil Engineers; Foreign mem. Royal Acad. of Eng (UK); Fellow Inst. of Logistics and Transport; Hon. Commodore, Canadian Coast Guard; Hon. mem. Canadian Maritime Law Asscn, Honourable Co. of Master Mariners, UK, Int. Maritime Pilots Asscn, Int. Fed. of Shipmasters' Asscns, NUMAST (Nat. Union of Marine Aviation and Shipping Transport Officers) (UK), Soc. of Naval Architects and Marine Engineers (USA), Singapore, Int. Asscn of Lighthouse Authorities, Co. of Master Mariners, India 1998; Hon. Fellow The Nautical Inst., UK 1996, Royal Inst. of Naval Architects 1998, Royal Inst. of Navigation; Hon. Titular mem. Comité Maritime Int.; Hon. Dip. Canadian Coast Guard Coll.; Hon. LLD (Malta) 1993, (Memorial Univ. of Newfoundland) 1996; Hon. DSc (Nottingham Trent) 1994; Eng Medal, Asscn of Professional Engineers of Ont. 1972, Distinguished Public Service Award, US Govt, Admirals' Medal 1994, Seatrade Personality of the Year Award 1995, NUMAST Award (UK) 1995, Professional Engineers Ont. Gold Medal 1995, mem. Eng Alumni Hall of Distinction, Univ. of Toronto 1996, Silver Bell Award, Seamen's Church Inst. New York 1997, Vice Adm. 'Jerry' Land Medal, Soc. of Naval Architects and Marine Engineers, USA 1999; Commdr, Ordre Nat. des Cèdres (Lebanon) 1995, Grand Cross, Orden Vasco Núñez de Balboa (Panama) 1998, Cdre Award, Conn. Maritime Asscn 1998, Dioscun Prize, Lega Navale Italiana (Italy) 1998, Halert C. Shepheard Award (USA) 2000, Medal for Distinguished Services to the Directorate Gen. for Maritime Affairs, Colombia 2001, CITIS Lifetime Achievement Award UK 2002, Freeman of the Worshipful Company of Shipwrights (hc) UK 2002, Golden Jubilee Medal, Canada 2002, "15 November 1817 Medal", Uruguay 2002. *Leisure interests:* reading, swimming, golf. *Address:* International Maritime Organization, 4 Albert Embankment, London, SE1 7SR (Office); 15 Ropers Orchard, London, SW3 5AX, England (Home). *Telephone:* (20) 7587-3100. *Fax:* (20) 7587-3210. *E-mail:* info@imo.org. *Website:* www.imo.org.

O'NEILL, Brendan, PhD, FCMA; British business executive; b. 6 Dec. 1948; s. of John Christopher O'Neill and Doris Monk; m. Margaret Maude O'Neill 1979; one s. two d.; ed Churchill Coll., Cambridge, Univ. of E Anglia; with Ford Motor Co. 1973–75, British Leyland 1975–81, BICC PLC 1981–83; Group Financial Controller Midland Bank 1983–87; Dir of Financial Control Guinness PLC 1987, Finance Dir 1988–90, Man. Dir Int. Regulation, United Distillers 1990–92, Guinness Brewing Worldwide 1993–97, CEO Guinness Diageo PLC 1997–98; COO ICI PLC 1998–99, CEO 1999– (Dir 1998–); Dir EMAP PLC 1995–, Diageo 1997–98; Life Gov. Imperial Cancer Research Fund 1994–2002; Trustee Cancer Reserch UK 2002–. *Leisure interests:* music, reading. *Address:* ICI PLC, 9 Millbank, London, SW1P 3JF, England (Office). *Telephone:* (20) 7834-4444 (Office).

O'NEILL, Paul H., MPA; American business executive and fmr government official; b. 4 Dec. 1935, St Louis, Mo.; s. of John Paul O'Neill and Gayland Elsie Irvin; m. Nancy Jo Wolfe 1955; one s. three d.; ed Fresno State Coll., Indiana Univ., Claremont Grad. School and George Washington Univ.; computer systems analyst, US Veterans Admin.; later engineer, Morris-Knudsen, Anchorage, Alaska; mem. staff, Office of Man. and Budget 1967–77, Deputy Dir 1974–77; Vice-Pres. Planning, Int. Paper Co. 1977, Sr Vice-Pres. Planning and Finance 1981, Sr Vice-Pres. paperboard and packaging Div. 1983, Pres. 1985–87; Chair., CEO Aluminum Co. of America (Alcoa) 1987–99, Chair. 1999–2000; Sec. of Treasury 2001–02; Dir Manpower Demonstration Research Group, Aluminum Co. of America, Lucent Technologies, Eastman Kodak Co.; Chair. Rand; many other business and community affiliations; Dr hc (Clarkson Univ.) 1993. *Address:* c/o Department of the Treasury, 1500 Pennsylvania Avenue, N.W., Washington, DC 20220, USA.

O'NEILL, Robert John, AO, MA, BE, DPhil, F.A.S.S.A.; Australian historian and army officer; b. 5 Nov. 1936, Melbourne; s. of Joseph Henry O'Neill and Janet Gibbon O'Neill; m. Sally Margaret Burnard 1965; two d.; ed Scotch Coll. Melbourne, Royal Mil. Coll. of Australia, Melbourne Univ., Brasenose Coll. Oxford; served in Australian army 1955–68, Fifth Bn Royal Australian Regt, Vietnam (despatches) 1966–67, Maj. 1967–68 (resgnd); Rhodes scholar, Vic. 1961; Official Australian Historian for the Korean War 1969–82; Head Strategic and Defence Studies Centre, Australian Nat. Univ. 1971–82; Dir Int. Inst. for Strategic Studies, London 1982–87; Chichele Prof. of the History of War Oxford Univ. 1987–2001; Dir Grad. Studies Modern History Faculty, Oxford 1990–92; Fellow All Souls Coll. Oxford 1987, Hon. Fellow Brasenose Coll. Oxford, Sr Fellow in Int. Relations Australian Nat. Univ. 1969–77, Professorial Fellow 1977–82; Trustee Imperial War Museum 1990–, Deputy Chair. 1996–98, Chair. 1998–2001; Gov. Ditchley Foundation 1989–, Int. Peace Acad. 1990–; Chair. Bd Centre for Defence Studies and Bd Centre for Australian Studies, Univ. of London 1990–95; Chair. Council, Int. Inst. of Strategic Studies 1996–2001; Dir The Shell Transport and Trading Co. 1992– and two mutual funds of Capital Group, LA 1992–; mem. Advisory Bd Investment Co. of America 1988–; mem. Commonwealth War Graves Comm. 1990, The Rhodes Trust 1995–; Hon. Col 5th (V) Bn, The Royal Greenjackets 1993–99; Hon. DL (ANU) 2001. *Publications:* The German Army and the Nazi Party 1933–39 1966, Vietnam Task 1966, General Giap: politician and strategist 1969, (ed.) The Strategic Nuclear Balance 1975, (ed.) The Defence of Australia: fundamental new aspects 1977, (ed.) Insecurity: the spread of weapons in the Indian and Pacific Oceans 1978, (co-ed.) Australian Dictionary of Biography Vols 7–12, 1891–1939, 1979–91, (co-ed.) New Directions in Strategic Thinking 1981, Australia in the Korean War 1950–53: Vol. I Strategy and Diplomacy 1981, Vol. II Combat Operations 1985, (co-ed.) Australian Defence Policy for the 1980s 1982, (ed.) Security in East Asia 1984, (ed.) The Conduct of East–West Relations in the 1980s 1985, (ed.) New Technology and Western Security Policy 1985, (ed.) Doctrine, the Alliance and Arms Control 1986, (ed.) East Asia, the West and International Security 1987, (ed.) Security in the Mediterranean 1989, (co-ed.) The West and the Third World 1990, (co-ed.) Securing Peace in Europe 1945–62 1992, (co-ed.) War, Strategy and International Politics 1992, Alternative Nuclear Futures 1999; articles in numerous journals. *Leisure interests:* local history, walking.

O'NEILL, Terence Patrick; British photographer; b. 30 July 1938, London; s. of Leonard Victor O'Neill and Josephine Mary O'Neill; m. 1st Vera Day; one s. one d.; m. 2nd Faye Dunaway (q.v.) 1981; one s.; ed Gunnersbury Grammar School; fmr modern jazz drummer in leading London jazz clubs; army service as physical training instructor; subsequently took up photography, took first photographs of Beatles and Rolling Stones early 1960s; went to Hollywood 1962; has photographed leading actors and actresses, rock and classical musicians, political and sports personalities, mems. of British and other royal families; work published in The Sunday Times, Time, Life, Newsweek, Tatler, Elle, Paris Match, Stern etc. and other newspapers and magazines, in 52 countries and used on about 500 front covers worldwide a year. *Publication:* Legend S. *Leisure interests:* music, food, wine, art in all forms, literature.

O'NEILL OF BENGARVE, Baroness (Life Peer), cr. 1999, of The Braid in the County of Antrim; **Onora Sylvia O'Neill,** CBE, PhD, FBA, FMedSci; British philosopher and college principal; b. 23 Aug. 1941, Aughafatten, N Ireland; d. of late Sir Con O'Neill and of Lady Garvey (née Rosemary Pritchard); m. Edward Nell 1963 (divorced 1976); two s.; ed St Paul's Girls' School, London, Somerville Coll. Oxford and Harvard Univ., USA; Asst Prof. Barnard Coll. Columbia Univ. 1970–76, Assoc. Prof. 1976–77; Lecturer, Univ. of Essex 1977–78, Sr Lecturer 1978–82, Reader 1982–87, Prof. 1987–92; Prin. Newnham Coll. Cambridge 1992–; Chair. Nuffield Foundation 1998–, Human Genetics Advisory Cttee 1997–99; Dr hc (E Anglia) 1995, (Essex) 1996, (Nottingham) 1999, (Aberdeen) 2001, (Dublin) 2002; Hon. Bencher of Gray's Inn 2002. *Radio:* The Reith Lectures 2002. *Publications:* Faces of Hunger: An Essay on Poverty, Development and Justice 1986, Constructions of Reason: Explorations of Kant's Practical Philosophy 1989, Towards Justice and Virtue: A Constructive Account of Practical Reasoning 1996, Bounds of Justice 2000, Autonomy and Trust in Bioethics 2002, A Question of Trust 2002. *Leisure interests:* walking, talking. *Address:* Newnham College, Cambridge, CB3 9DF, England. *Telephone:* (1223) 330469. *Fax:* (1223) 359155.

ONER, Gulsen, MD, PhD; Turkish professor of physiology; b. 3 Jan. 1944, Kemah, Erzincan; ed Istanbul Univ., Hacettepe Univ.; Asst Prof., Surgical Research Centre, Hacettepe Medical School 1972–76; Medical Research Centre, Univ. Coll. Hosp. London 1976; Assoc. Prof. and Sr Researcher, Surgical Research Centre, Hacettepe Medical School 1976–85; Dept of Pharmacology, Faculty of Medicine, Univ. of Calgary 1980, Dept of Endocrinology, Coll. of Medicine, Univ. of Saskatchewan 1981–82; Prof. of Physiology, Head Dept of Physiology and Biophysics and Dir Medical Research Centre, Antalya Medical School. *Publications:* over 50 scientific medical Publs on endocrinology, serology and allergy diseases. *Address:* Antalya Medical School,

Akdeniz University, Antalya, Turkey (Office). *Telephone:* (242) 227-52-66 (Office). *Fax:* (242) 227-55-40 (Office). *E-mail:* webmaster@akdeniz.edu.tr (Office). *Website:* www.akdeniz.edu.tr (Office).

ONG, John Doyle, MA, L.L.B.; American business executive; b. 29 Sept. 1933, Uhrichsville, Ohio; s. of Louis Brosee and Mary Ellen Ong (née Liggett); m. Mary Lee Schupp 1957; two s. one d.; ed Ohio State Univ., Harvard Univ.; admitted to Ohio Bar 1958; Asst Counsel B. F. Goodrich Co., Akron 1961–66, Group Vice-Pres. 1972–73, Exec. Vice-Pres. 1973–74, Vice-Chair. 1974–75, Pres. 1975–84, Dir 1975–77, COO 1978–79, Chair. Pres. and CEO 1979–84, Chair. 1984–97, CEO 1984–96, Chair. Emer. 1997–; Asst to Pres. Int. B. F. Goodrich Co., Akron 1966–69, Vice-Pres. 1969–70, Pres. 1970–72; Dir Cooper Industries, The Kroger Co., Ameritech Corpn; Chair. Ohio Business Roundtable 1994–95; mem. Bd Dirs. Nat. Alliance for Business; Pres. Bd of Trustees, Western Reserve Acad., Hudson 1977–95; Trustee John S. and James L. Knight Foundation 1995–, Univ. of Chicago 1991–, Ohio Historical Soc. 1998–. *Leisure interests:* fishing, hunting. *Address:* 230 Aurora Street, Hudson, OH 44236, USA (Home).

ONG, Tan Sri Haji Omar Yoke-Lin; Malaysian politician and diplomatist; b. 23 July 1917, Kuala Lumpur; m. Toh Puan Datin (Dr.) Hajjah Aishah 1974; three s. one d.; mem. Kuala Lumpur Municipal Council 1952–55; co-founder Alliance Party; mem. Fed. Legis. Council 1954; Malayan Minister of Posts and Telecommunications 1955–56, of Transport 1956–57, of Labour and Social Welfare 1957–59, of Health and Social Welfare 1959–72; MP 1959–72; Vice-Pres. Commonwealth Parl. Asscn 1961; Amb. to UN 1962–64, to USA 1962–72, also Accred to Canada 1966–72 and Brazil 1967–72; Minister without Portfolio 1964–73; Pres. of the Senate 1973–80; Chair. Asian Int. Merchant Bankers Bhd., Malaysian Oxygen Bhd., Omariff Holdings Sdn. Bhd., Syarikat Ong Yoke Lin Sdn. Bhd., OYL Industries Sdn. Bhd., Raza Sdn. Bhd.; Dir Esso Malaysia Berhad, Hume Industries (Malaysia) Berhad, Malayan Flour Mills Bhd., United Chemical Industries Bhd.; Pro-Chancellor Nat. Univ. of Malaysia 1987; Council mem. Inst. of Strategic Studies, Malaysia; Vice-Pres. UN Malaysia Asscn; Hon. LLD (Hanyang Univ. Seoul) 1978, Hon. PhD (Malaysia); SSM 1972; Panglima Mangku Neyara (Malaysia) 1959; Order of First Homayon (Iran) 1969, Grand Cross (1st Class) Fed. Rep. of Germany; Order of Civil Merit (1st Class) Rep. of Korea, Commdr Ordre nat. du Mérite. *Leisure interests:* golf, photography, swimming. *Address:* Asian International Merchant Bankers Ltd, UMBC Annexe 9-11 Floors, Jalem Salaiman, Kuala Lumpur (Office); Malaysian Oxygen Bhd., 13 Jalan 222, 46100 Petaling Jaya, Selangor Darul Ehsan; 44 Pesiaran Duta, Kuala Lumpur, Malaysia (Home). *Telephone:* (3) 2749011 (Office); (3) 2546637 (Home).

ONG, Romualdo Añover, BSc; Philippine diplomatist; b. 25 April 1939, Manila; s. of late Juan Salido Ong and of Adelaida Añover; m. 1st Cecilia Hidalgo 1964 (deceased); m. 2nd Farita Aguilucho 1994; two s. two d.; ed Ateneo de Manila and Univ. of the Philippines; joined Ministry of Foreign Affairs 1968; served Bonn 1971–75, Geneva 1975–79, Minister Counsellor, Beijing 1979–82; Special Asst to Deputy Minister for Foreign Affairs 1983; Asst Minister for ASEAN Affairs 1984–85; Sr Econ. Consultant, Tech. Secr. for Int. Econ. Relations/Bd. of Overseas Econ. Promotion 1985; Amb. to Australia (also Accred to Vanuatu) 1986–89; Asst Sec. for Asian and Pacific Affairs, Dept of Foreign Affairs, Manila 1990–93; Amb. to Russia 1993–94, to People's Repub. of China 1994–2000; Dir Foreign Service Inst. 2000–. *Leisure interests:* reading, car driving, basketball, hiking, movies, listening to music. *Address:* Foreign Service Institute, 5th Floor, DFA Building, 2330 Roxas Blvd, 1300 Pasay City, Metro Manila, The Philippines. *Website:* www.fsi.gov .ph.

ONG KENG SEN; Singaporean director; fmr Artistic Dir TheatreWorks, Singapore; Artistic Dir 'In Transit' Arts Festival, Berlin 2001–. *Theatre includes:* Continuum: Beyond the Killing Fields, Yale Univ., USA and Singapore 2001. *Address:* c/o Berliner Festspiele GmbH, Schaperstrasse 24, D-10719 Berlin, Germany (Office). *Telephone:* (30) 254890 (Office). *Fax:* (30) 25489111 (Office). *Website:* www.berlinerfestspiele.de (Office).

ONG KENG YONG, LLB; Singaporean international organization official and diplomatist; b. 6 Jan. 1954; m. Irene Tan Lee Chen; ed Univ. of Singapore, Georgetown Univ., Washington DC, USA; Charge d'affaires Embassy in Riyadh 1984–88; Counsellor High Comm. in Kuala Lumpur 1989–91; Minister Counsellor and Deputy Chief of Mission Embassy in Washington DC 1991–94; Press Sec. to Minister of Foreign Affairs and Ministry Spokesperson 1994–95; High Commr to India and Amb. to Nepal 1996–98; Press Sec. to Prime Minister 1998–2002; Deputy Sec. Ministry of Information, Communication and the Arts 1998; Chief Exec. Dir The People's Asscn (PA) 2002; Sec.-Gen. ASEAN 2003–; Public Admin Medal. *Address:* Association of South East Asian Nations (ASEAN), 70A Jalan Sisingamangaraja, POB 2072, Jakarta 12110, Indonesia (Office). *Telephone:* (21) 7262991 (Office). *Fax:* (21) 7398234 (Office). *E-mail:* public@asean.or.id (Office). *Website:* www.aseansec.org (Office).

O'NIONS, Sir Robert Keith, Kt, MA, PhD, FRS; British geochemist; b. 26 Sept. 1944, Birmingham; s. of William Henry O'Nions and Eva Stagg; m. Rita Bill 1967; three d.; ed Univ. of Nottingham, Univ. of Alberta; Postdoctoral Fellow, Univ. of Alberta 1969–70; Unger Vetlesen Postdoctoral Fellow, Univ. of Oslo 1970–71; Demonstrator in Petrology, Univ. of Oxford 1971–72, Lecturer in Geochem. 1972–75; Assoc. Prof. and Prof. of Geology, Columbia Univ. 1975–79; Royal Soc. Research Prof., Univ. of Cambridge 1979–95;

Fellow Clare Hall Cambridge 1980–95; Prof. of Physics and Chem. of Minerals, Univ. of Oxford 1995– (on leave of absence); Chief Scientific Adviser, Ministry of Defence 2000–; Fellow St Hugh's Coll. Oxford 1995–; Fellow American Geophysical Union; Foreign Fellow Indian Nat. Science Acad.; mem. Norwegian Acad. of Sciences; Foreign mem. India Acad. of Sciences; Hon. Fellow Univ. of Cardiff; J. B. Macelwane Award 1979; Bigsby Medal 1983, Holmes Medal 1995, Lyell Medal 1995, Urey Medal 2001. *Publications:* numerous Publs in scientific journals on the subject of geochem. *Address:* Ministry of Defence, Whitehall, London, SW1A 2HB, England (Office).

ONKELINX, Laurette, BL; Belgian politician; b. 2 Oct. 1958, Ougrée; lecturer in Admin. Sciences 1982–85; barrister, Liège 1981–; Parti Socialiste (PS) Deputy for Liège 1988; Chair. Interfed. Comm. of Socialist Women; Vice-Chair. Socialist Group, House of Reps.; mem. PS Party Office 1988; Chair. Justice Cttee, House of Reps.; Vice-Pres. House of Reps.; Minister for Social Integration, Health and Environment 1992–93; Minister-Pres. in Govt of Communauté française in charge of Civil Service, Childhood and Promotion of Health 1993–95, Minister-Pres. in charge of Educ., Audio-visual, Youth Help and Promotion of Health 1995–99; Deputy Prime Minister and Minister for Employment (later Employment and Equal Opportunities) July 1999–. *Publications:* Continuons le débat, Théâtre du jeune public. *Address:* Cabinet of the Deputy Prime Minister and Minister for Employment, Handelstraat 76–80, rue du commerce, 1040 Brussels, Belgium (Office). *Telephone:* (2) 233-51-11 (Office). *Fax:* (2) 230-10-67 (Office). *E-mail:* lauretteonkelinx@win.be (Office).

ÖNNERFORS, Alf, PhD; Swedish university professor; b. 30 Nov. 1925, Hovmantorp; s. of Carl-Oscar Önnerfors and Karin Widerström; m. 1st Ingrid Åhlén 1949; m. 2nd Ute Michaelis 1964; three s.; ed Univ. of Uppsala; Lecturer, then Assoc. Prof., Univ. of Uppsala 1957–62, Univ. of Lund 1962–63; Prof., Freie Universität Berlin, West Berlin 1963–70, Univ. of Cologne, Fed. Repub. of Germany 1970–91; research into Latin language and literature; mem. Rheinisch-Westfälische Akademie der Wissenschaften, Ed. Lateinische Sprache u. Literatur des Mittelalters 1974–93. *Publications:* Pliniana (dissertation) 1956, In Medicinam Plinii studia philologica 1963, Die Hauptfassungen des Sigfrid-Offiziums 1968, Vaterporträts in der römischen Poesie 1974, Willem Jordaens, Conflictus virtutum et viciorum 1986, Antike Zaubersprüche 1991, Das medizinische Latein von Celsus bis Cassius Felix 1993, Magische Formeln im Dienste römischer Medizin 1993, Zu Person und Werk des Publius Flavius Vegetius Renatus 1993, Classica et Mediaevalia. Abhandlungen und Aufsätze 1997; critical edns of Cicero, Ad Atticum 13-16 1960, Medicina Plinii (Corpus Med. Lat.) 1964, C. de Bridia, Hystoria Tartarorum 1967, Physica Plinii Bambergensis (ed. princeps) 1975, Tacitus, Germania (Teubner) 1983, Vegetius, Epitoma rei militaris 1995 Pliny the Elder, Natural History Book VII (Swedish trans.) 2000; Plautus, Miles gloriosus, Miles gloriosus (Swedish trans.) 2001 about 100 papers and essays in int. reviews and journals of Classical and Medieval Philology; historical short stories 2000, 2003. *Leisure interests:* riding (military), chemistry, pharmacology. *Address:* Rudeboksvägen 199, 22655 Lud; 36051 Hovmantorp, Sweden. *Telephone:* (46) 15-88-87; (478) 19-039.

ONWUMECHILI, Ozo Ochendo Cyril Agodi, PhD, DSc; Nigerian professor of physics and administrator; b. 20 Jan. 1932, Inyi; s. of Nwaime Onwumechili and Akuviro Onwumechili (née Orji); m. Cecilia Bedeaka (née Anyadibe) 1958; two s. one d.; ed King's Coll., Lagos, Univ. Coll., Ibadan and Univ. of London; Prof. 1962–; Dir of chain of observatories 1960–66; Dean, Faculty of Science, Univ. of Ibadan 1965–66; Prof. and Head of Dept Univ. of Nigeria 1966–73, 1976–78, Dean, Faculty of Science 1970–71, Dean, Faculty of Physical Sciences 1973–76, 1978; Visiting Prof. of Geophysics, Univ. of Alaska 1971–72; Consultant, Inst. for Space Research, Nat. Research Council of Brazil 1972; Vice-Chancellor, Univ. of Ife, Ile-Ife 1979–82; Deputy Pres. Anambra State Univ. of Tech., Enugu 1983–84, Pres. 1984–85, Vice-Chancellor 1985–86; Consultant U.N. Econ. Comm. for Africa 1987; Commonwealth Science Council 1988; Vice-Chair. Div.II Int. Asscn of Geomagnetism and Aeronomy 1987–91, Chair. Interdivisional Comm. 1991–95; mem. Int. Scientific Programmes Cttee, Int. Symposia on Equatorial Aeronomy 1972–, UN Advisory Cttee on Science and Tech. for Devt 1981–83; Chair. Man. Cttee UNESCO African Network of Scientific and Technological Insts. (ANSTI) 1985–90; Vice-Pres. Asscn of African Univs 1984–89, Consultant 1990–2002, Chair. Scientific Cttee 1993–; mem. American Geophysical Union, Soc. for Terrestrial Magnetism and Electricity of Japan; Fellow UK and Nigerian Inst. of Physics 1969; Foundation Ed.-in-Chief Nigerian Journal of Science 1964–67; Visiting Prof. of Physics, Univ. of Wales at Cardiff 1987–88; Foundation Fellow and Former Pres. Nigerian Acad. of Science; UK Chartered Physicist 1986; Fellow African Acad. of Sciences 1987, Third World Acad. of Sciences 1989; Foundation Fellow, Science Asscn of Nigeria 1974; Hon. DSc (Ife) 1977, (Enugu State Univ.) 1992, (Univ. of Nigeria) 2001. *Publications:* Geomagnetic Variations in the Equatorial Zone 1967, University Administration in Nigeria: the Anambra State University of Technology Approach I 1991, Cost Effectiveness and Efficiency in African Universities 1993, The Equatorial Electrojet 1997, Igho Enwe Eze?: The 2000 Ahiajoku Lecture; numerous scientific articles. *Leisure interests:* swimming, table tennis, lawn tennis. *Address:* 4813 Lackawanna Street, College Park, MD 20740, USA (Home); 69 Lansdowne Drive, Hackney, London, E8 3EP,

England; P.O. Box 9059, Uwani, Enugu, Nigeria. *Telephone:* (301) 446-0312 (Home); (20) 7249-3260 (London); (42) 254987 (Enugu). *Fax:* (212) 829-0146 (Home). *E-mail:* cagodionwumechili@yahoo.com (Home).

ONYEAMA, Charles Dadi, LLB; Nigerian judge; b. 5 Aug. 1917, Eke, Enugu; s. of Chief Onyeama; m. 1st Susannah Ogwudu 1950; m. 2nd Florence Wilcox 1966; five s. two d.; ed King's Coll., Lagos, Achimota Coll., Gold Coast, Univ. Coll., London and Brasenose Coll., Oxford; Cadet Admin. Officer, Nigeria 1944; mem. Legis. Council of Nigeria and Eastern House of Ass. 1946–51; mem. Nigerianization Comm. and mem. Gen. Conf. and Constitutional Drafting Cttee 1948–50; Chief Magistrate, Nigeria 1952–56; Acting High Court Judge, W Nigeria 1956–57; High Court Judge, Lagos 1957–64; Acting Chief Justice, Lagos High Court 1961 and 1963; Justice of Supreme Court of Nigeria 1964–66; Judge Int. Court of Justice, The Hague 1967–76; Chair. Cttee on the Prerogative of Mercy, Nigeria 1976–79, Ife Univ. Teaching Hospitals Complex Bd 1976–79, Orthopaedic Hospitals Man. Bd 1979–; Judge, World Bank Admin. Tribunal 1982–; Hon. LLD; Commdr of the Fed. Repub. of Nigeria. *Leisure interest:* reading. *Address:* 1 Church Road, P.O. Box 602, Enugu, Nigeria.

ONYSZKIEWICZ, Janusz, DMath; Polish government official and mathematician; b. 18 Dec. 1937, Lvov; s. of Stanislaw and Franciszka Onyszkiewicz; m. 1st Witoslawa Boretti (died 1967); m. 2nd Alison Chadwick (died 1978); m. 3rd Joanna Jaraczewska 1983; two s. three d.; ed Warsaw Univ.; Asst, Math. Engines Inst., Polish Acad. of Sciences, Warsaw 1958–61; Asst, later Sr Asst Faculty of Math., Informatics and Mechanics, Math. Inst., Warsaw Univ. 1963–67, lecturer 1967–75, now Sr lecturer; lecturer, Univ. of Leeds 1976–79; lectured at many univs. abroad; mem. Polish Teachers' Union (ZNP) 1969-80, Ind. Self-governing Trade Union of Science, Tech. and Educ. Workers 1980, Deputy Chair. Br. at Warsaw Univ. Sept.–Oct. 1980; adviser to Interfactory Founding Cttee of Solidarity Ind. Self-governing Trade Union–Mazovia Region, subsequently mem. Presidium of Nat. Comm. of Solidarity Trade Union, Bd and Press Spokesman of Mazovia Region of Solidarity Trade Union; Press Spokesman Nat. Understanding Comm. and First Nat. Congress of Solidarity Trade Union 1980–81; interned 1981–82; arrested April 1983, released under amnesty July 1983; sentenced to six weeks' confinement May 1988; Press Spokesman Nat. Exec. Comm., Solidarity Trade Union; mem. Civic Cttee attached to Lech Wałęsa (q.v.) 1988–91; participant Round Table debates, mem. team for mass media and opposition press spokesman Feb.–April 1989; Deputy to Sejm (Parl.) 1989–2001; Vice-Minister of Nat. Defence 1990–92, Minister 1992–93, 1997–2000; Chair. Defence Cttee, Council of Ministers 1997–99; mem. Democratic Union Parl. 1991–94, Freedom Union Parl. 1994–; Vice-Pres. Polish Asia-Pacific Council 1996–; mem. Nat. Council Freedom Union 1996; mem. Euro-Atlantic Asscn 1994– (Pres. 1994–98); Pres. Polish Mountaineering Fed. 2001–; mountaineer and speleologist, participant mountaineering expeditions in Himalayas, Hindu Kush, Karakoram, Pamir; Hon. DSc (Leeds) 1991; Gold Medal (For Outstanding Sporting Achievements), Manfred Wörner Medal, Great Cross of Gedymin (Lithuania), Great Cross of King Leopold II (Belgium). *Publications:* 15 works on foundations of math., including Complete Abstract Logics 1979; co-author Zdobycie Gasherbrumów 1977. *Leisure interests:* climbing, caving, tourism, classical music. *Address:* Center for International Relations, ul. Emilii Plater, 00-688, Warsaw, Poland (Office). *Telephone:* (22) 6465267 (Office). *Fax:* (22) 6465258 (Office). *E-mail:* onyszkiewicz@csm.org.pl (Office); janusz.onyszkiewicz@n17.waw.pl (Home). *Website:* www.csm.org.pl (Office).

OOKA, Makoto; Japanese writer and professor; b. 16 Feb. 1931, Mishima City; s. of Hiroshi Ooka and Ayako Ooka; m. Kaneko Aizawa 1957; one s. one d.; ed Tokyo Nat. Univ.; journalist with Yomiuri (newspaper), foreign news section 1953–63; Asst Prof. Meiji Univ., Tokyo 1965–70, Prof. 1970–87; Pres. Japan Poets' Asscn 1979–81; Prof. Nat. Univ. for Fine Arts and Music 1988–93; Pres. Japan PEN Club 1989–93; mem. Int. Advisory Bd of Poetry Int., Rotterdam; mem. Japan Art Acad. 1995–; Yomiuri Prize for Literature, Kikuchi Kan Prize, Hanatsubaki Prize for Poetry, Golden Wreath Prize, Struga Poetry Evenings Macedonia 1996, Asahi Prize 1996, Person of Cultural Merit 1997, Japan Foundation Prize 2002; Officier des Arts et des Lettres. *Publications:* Poetry: Memories and the Present 1956, For a Girl in Springtime 1978, City of Water 1981, Odes to the Waters of my Hometown 1989, The Afternoon in the Earthly Paradise 1992, The Last Will of Fire 1995; Criticism: The Banquet and the Solitary Mind, Aesthetics of Japanese Poetry 1978; English translations: Japanese Poetry; Past and Present, A Poet's Anthology 1979–, an anthological series for the newspaper Asahi, A String Around Autumn 1982, Elegy and Benediction 1991, The Colours of Poetry—Essays on Classic Japanese Verse 1991, What the Kite Thinks, a linked poem with three American poets 1994, The Range of Japanese Poetry 1994, Beneath the Sleepless Tossing of the Planets 1995, The Poetry and Poetics of Ancient Japan 1997; French translations: Poèmes de tous les jours 1993, Propos sur le vent et autres poèmes 1995, Poésie et Poétique du Japon Ancien 1995, Dans l'Océan du Silence 1998, Citadelle de Lumière 2002. *Address:* 2-18-1-2606, Iidabashi, Chiyoda-ku, Tokyo 102-0072, Japan.

OPERTTI BADDAN, Didier, PhD; Uruguayan lawyer and politician; b. 1937, Montevideo; m.; four c.; ed Univ. of Uruguay; fmr Asst Prof. of Int. Pvt. Law, Univ. of Uruguay, Prof. of Int. Relations 1986; Dir Office of Codification and Devt of Int. Law, Gen. Secr., OAS 1979–81, Perm. Rep. to OAS 1988–93, Pres. OAS Perm. Council's Comm. of Juridical and Political Matters 1989, Pres. OAS Perm. Council 1990; Dir Diplomatic Law Advisory Council, Ministry of Foreign Affairs 1985–88; Prof. of Int. Pvt. Law, Int. Law Acad., The Hague; Prof. of Int. Pvt. Law, Catholic Univ. of Uruguay 1994; Minister of the Interior 1995–98, of Foreign Affairs Feb. 1998–; Pres. 53rd Session of UN Gen. Ass. 1998–2000; Special Counsellor for MERCOSUR issues to IDB and Inst. for Integration of Latin America and the Caribbean 1993–94; mem. UN Law Comm.; fmr mem. Uruguayan Nat. Group of Perm. Court of Arbitration; founder and Bd mem. Int. Law Asscn of Uruguay; mem. and Dir Uruguayan Comparative Law Inst.; mem. Lawyers Asscn of Uruguay, Portuguese-Spanish American Int. Law Inst., Int. Law Asscn of Argentina, Int. and Comparative Law Acad. of Brazil. *Address:* Ministry of Foreign Affairs, Avda 18 de Julio 1205, Montevideo, Uruguay (Office). *Telephone:* (2) 9021007 (Office). *Fax:* (2) 9021327 (Home). *E-mail:* webmaster@mrree.gub.uy (Office). *Website:* www.mree.gub.uy (Office).

OPIE, Julian Gilbert, BA; British artist; b. 12 Dec. 1958, London; s. of Roger G. Opie and Norma Opie; m. Lisa K. Milroy 1984; ed Magdalen Coll. School, Oxford, Chelsea School of Art, London and Goldsmiths' School of Art, London; exhibited Young Blood, Riverside Studios, London 1983, Sculpture 1983, Rotterdam 1983, The Sculpture Show, Hayward Gallery, London 1983, Making Sculpture, Tate Gallery, London 1983, Perspective, Basle Art Fair, Basle 1984, Home and Abroad, Serpentine Gallery, London 1984, Myth and Symbol, Tokyo Museum of Modern Art 1984, The British Show touring Australia 1984, Paris Biennale, Paris 1985, Anniotanta, Ravenna 1985, British Sculpture Louisiana Museum, Denmark 1986, De Sculptura, Vienna 1986, Correspondence Europe, Stedelijk Museum, Amsterdam 1986, Prospect 86, Frankfurt 1986; one-person exhbns. at Lisson Gallery, London 1983, Kunstverein Cologne, Cologne 1984 and Groningen Museum, Netherlands 1985, ICA, London 1985, Lisson Gallery 1985, 1986, Franco Toselli Gallery, Milan 1985; works in the collections of The British Council, The Contemporary Arts Soc., Tate Gallery, Cincinnati Museum of Modern Art, Documenta 8, Kassel 1987, Stedelijk Museum, Amsterdam. *Publications:* Julian Opie, Kunstverein Cologne: Catalogue of Works 1984, Julian Opie Drawings, ICA, London, Julian Opie New Works, Lisson Gallery. *Leisure interests:* art, music, films, books, architecture, travel, a 1981 Chevrolet Caprice Classic, supermarkets, fast food restaurants, hotel lobbies, petrol stations. *Address:* Lisson Gallery, 66–68 Bell Street, London, NW1 6SP, England. *Telephone:* (20) 7262-1539.

OPIE, Lionel Henry, MD, PhD, MRCP, FACC, FRSSA; South African professor of medicine; b. 6 May 1933, Hanover, SA; s. of Prof. William Henry Opie and Marie Opie (née Le Roux); m. Carol June Sancroft Baker 1969; two d.; ed Diocesan Coll., Rondebosch, Cape Town, Univ. of Cape Town, Oxford Univ., England; Intern, Groote Schuur Hosp. 1956; Sr House Officer, Dept of Neurology, Radcliffe Infirmary, Oxford, England 1957–59; House Physician (Endocrinology), Hammersmith Hosp., London 1959; Asst in Medicine, Peter Bent Brigham Hosp., Boston, Mass., USA, Samuel A. Levine Fellow in Cardiology, Harvard Medical School 1960–61; Asst Resident in Medicine, Toronto Gen. Hosp., Canada 1961–62; Consultant Physician, Karl Bremer Hosp. and Univ. of Stellenbosch, SA; Out-Patient Asst Physician, Radcliffe Infirmary, Wellcome Research Fellow, Dept of Biochem., Oxford Univ. 1964–66; Part-Time Registrar, Hammersmith Hosp., London 1966–67; Research Fellow, Dept of Biochem., Imperial Coll., London 1966–68; Sr Registrar in Medicine (Cardiology), Hammersmith Hosp. 1967–69, Consultant in Medicine 1969; Sr Specialist Physician, Groote Schuur Hosp. 1971; Assoc. Prof. of Medicine, Univ. of Cape Town 1975, Dir MRC Research Unit for Ischaemic Heart Disease 1976, Personal Chair in Medicine, Prof. of Medicine 1980; Dir Hypertension Clinic 1979–; Visiting Prof. Div. of Cardiovascular Medicine, Stanford Univ. School of Medicine, Calif., USA 1991–94; British Heart Foundation Sr Fellow and Visiting Prof. St Thomas' Hosp., London 1992; Pres. Southern Africa Cardiac Soc. 1980–82; Chair. Council on Cardiac Metabolism, Int. Soc. and Fed. of Cardiology 1980; Pres. Southern Africa Hypertension Soc. 1986; Chair. Cttee Cardiovascular Drugs, Int. Soc. and Fed. Cardiology 1990; mem. British Cardiac Soc., Physiological Soc. (UK), SA Socs. of Cardiology, Pharmacology, Biochem. and Hypertension, Int. Hypertension Soc. *Publications:* over 300. *Address:* Heart Research Unit, Department of Medicine, University of Cape Town Medical School Observatory 7925; 66A Dean Street, Newlands 7700, South Africa (Home). *Telephone:* 471250; 6853855 (Home).

OPLE, Blas F.; Philippine politician; b. 3 Feb. 1927, Hagonoy, Bulacan; s. of Felix Ople and Segundina Fajardo; m. Susana Vasquez 1949; five s. two d.; ed Philippine public and pvt. schools, Far Eastern Univ. and Manuel L. Quezon Univ., Manila; copy Ed. and columnist The Daily Mirror, Manila 1950–53; Asst to Pres. Ramon Magsaysay on labour and agrarian affairs 1954–57; writer and labour leader 1958–64; Head, Propaganda Div., Ferdinand E. Marcos' presidential campaign 1965; Special Asst to Pres. Marcos and Commr Social Security System 1966; Sec. of Labour 1967–78, Minister of Labour and Employment 1978–86; Founder and Leader Partido Nacionalista ng Pilipinas (PNP) 1986–; Sec. of Foreign Affairs July 2002–; Chair. Nat. Manpower and Youth Council 1967–71; mem. Bd of Trustees, Land Bank 1968; Chair. Govt Group, Int. Labour Conf. 1969, Pres. Int. Labour Conf. 1975–76; Chair. Asian Labour Ministers' Conf. 1967; various govt and civic awards. *Address:* Partido Nacionalista ng Pilipinas, Metro Manila (Office); Department of Foreign Affairs, DFA Building, 2330 Roxas Boulevard, Passay City, Metro Manila, Philippines. *Telephone:* (2) 8344000. *Fax:* (2) 8321597.

OPPENHEIM, Dennis A., MFA; American artist; b. 6 Sept. 1938, Electric City, Wash.; s. of David Oppenheim and Katherine Belknap; m. Karen Cackett (divorced); one s. two d.; ed School of Arts and Crafts, Oakland, Calif.,

Stanford Univ.; Prof. of Art, Yale Univ. 1969, State Univ. of New York at Stony Brook 1969; Guggenheim Foundation Sculpture Grant 1972; Nat. Endowment for the Arts Sculpture Grant 1974; numerous individual and group exhbns. at galleries in USA and Europe since 1968; works in many public collections including Museum of Modern Art, New York, Tate Gallery, London, Stedelijk Museum, Amsterdam and Musée d'Art Moderne, Paris. *Publications:* Indentations 1974, Proposals 1967–1974 1975; articles in journals. *Leisure interest:* films. *Address:* 54 Franklin Street, New York, NY 10013, USA (Office). *Telephone:* (212) 962-0178 (Office). *Fax:* (212) 587-3314 (Office). *E-mail:* dennisoppenheim@earthline.net (Office). *Website:* dennisoppenheim.com (Office); dennisoppenheim.net (Home).

OPPENHEIMER, Nicholas Frank, MA; South African business executive; b. 8 June 1945, Johannesburg; s. of Harry F. Oppenheimer; m. Orcillia M. L. Lasch 1968; one s.; ed Harrow School and Christ Church, Oxford; Chair. De Beers Consolidated Mines Ltd, Non-exec. Dir Anglo-American Corpn of SA Ltd; Dir Anglogold Ltd, De Beers Industrial Corpn Ltd, E. Oppenheimer & Son. (Pty) Ltd. *Leisure interests:* squash, golf. *Address:* P.O. Box 61631, Marshalltown 2107, South Africa.

OPPENLÄNDER, Karl Heinrich, DEcon; German economist; b. 17 Jan. 1932, Dörzbach; m. Cäcilie Oppenländer 1958; one s. one d.; ed Univ. of Munich; entered IFO Inst. for Econ. Research 1958, Head of Dept 1966, mem. Exec. Cttee 1972, Pres. (Prof.) 1976–99; Lecturer, Univ. of Tübingen 1975, Univ. of Munich 1976–, Univ. of Augsburg 1980–83. *Publications:* Die moderne Wachstumstheorie 1963, Der investitionsinduzierte technische Fortschritt 1976.

ORAYEVSKY, Victor Nikolayevich, DPhysMathSc; Russian physicist; b. 9 March 1935, Poltava, Ukraine; ed Kharkov State Univ.; Jr researcher Inst. of Nuclear Physics, USSR Acad. of Sciences (Siberian br.) 1958–65, Head of Div. Inst. of Earth Magnetism, Ionosphere and Radiowaves Propagation (IZMIRAN) 1979–89, Dir 1989–, Head of int. Sputnik projects; Sr researcher Inst. of Physics, Ukrainian Acad. of Sciences 1965–70, Head of Div. Inst. of Nuclear Studies 1970–74; Head of Scientific Production Div., Energia Co. 1974–79, Head of Lab., Head of Dept 1979–89; mem. Int. Acad. of Astronautics, NY Acad. of Sciences, Russian Acad. of Sciences, Int. Acad. of Informatics; State Prize of Ukrainian SSR, USSR State Prize 1987, Merited Worker of Science, Russian Fed. 1996. *Address:* IZMIRAN, 142092 Troitsk, Moscow, Russia (Office). *Telephone:* (095) 334-01-20 (Office).

ORAZMUKHAMEDOV, Nury Orazovich; Turkmenistan politician and diplomatist; b. 1949, Mary; ed Turkmenistan Polytech. Inst.; master, engineer, chief engineer Turkmencentrstroi 1971–; head Ashkhabad construction units; Deputy Chair. State Construction Cttee 1990–91; Minister of Construction of Turkmenistan 1991–94; Minister of Construction and Architecture 1994–95; Head of Admin. Khikim Ashkhabad Feb. 1995; Amb. to Russian Fed. 1996–2001. *Address:* c/o Ministry of Foreign Affairs, Ashgabat, Turkmenistan (Office).

ORBÁN, Viktor, LLD, PhD; Hungarian politician and lawyer; b. 31 May 1963, Székesfehérvár; s. of Győző Orbán; m.; one s. three d.; ed Loránd Eötvös Univ. of Budapest and Pembroke Coll., Oxford; researcher Middle Europe Research Group 1989–91; co-f. Hungarian opposition group Fed. of Young Democrats (FIDESZ) 1988, Spokesman 1989; represented FIDESZ political sub-Cttee of Opposition Round Table Discussion 1989; MP, leader of FIDESZ Parl. Group 1990–94, Prime Minister (FIDESZ) 1998–2002; Chair. Parl. Cttee on European Integration Affairs 1994–98; Pres. FIDESZ 1993–2000, New Atlantic Initiative Hungarian Cttee 1996–98; Vice-Pres. Liberal Int. 1992–2000, mem. Bureau 1993–2002; Vice-Pres. Christian Democrat and People's Parties Int. 2001–; Hon. Senator European Acad. of Sciences and Arts 2000; Freedom Prize American Inst. 2001, Vesek and Maria Polák Prize 2001, Franz Josef Strauss Prize 2001, Capo Circeo Prize 2001, Grande Croix de l'ordre Nat. du Mérite (France) 2001. *Publications:* National Policy 1988–1998. *Leisure interest:* playing soccer. *Address:* Christian Democrat and People's Parties International, CDI Headquarters, rue d'Arlon 67, 1040 Brussels, Belgium. *Telephone:* (2) 285-41-60. *Fax:* (2) 285-42-66. *E-mail:* idc@idc-cdi.org. *Website:* www.idc-cdi.org.

ORDE, Hugh Stephen Roden, OBE, BA; British police officer; b. 27 Aug. 1958; s. of Thomas Ordre and Stella Ordre; m. Kathleen Helen Ordre; one s.; ed Univ. of Kent; joined London Metropolitan Police 1977, apptd Sergeant, Brixton 1982, Police Staff Coll. 1983, Insp., Greenwich 1984–90, Chief Insp., Deputy Asst Commdr SW London 1990, Chief Insp., Hounslow 1991–93, Superintendent Territorial Support 1993–95, Commdr (Community Safety and Partnership) 1997–98, Commdr (Crime), S. London 1998–99, Deputy Asst Commr attached to Commr's Pvt. Office, New Scotland Yard 1999–2002; Chief Constable Police Service Northern Ireland—PSNI 2002–. *Leisure interests:* marathon running, wine, gardening. *Address:* Office of the Chief Constable, PSNI Headquarters, "Brooklyn", 65 Knock Road, Belfast BT5 6LE, Northern Ireland (Office). *Telephone:* (28) 9056-1613 (Office). *Fax:* (28) 9056-1645 (Office). *E-mail:* comsec@psni.police.uk (Office). *Website:* www.psni.police.uk (Office).

ORDJHONIKIDZE, Yosif Nikolayevich; Georgian/Russian politician; b. 9 Feb. 1948, Borzhomi, Georgia; m.; two c.; ed Tbilisi Polytech. Inst.; different posts Tbilisi Aviation factory; more than 20 years' Komsomol service; First Sec. Regional Komsomol Cttee, First Sec. Cen. Komsomol Cttee of Ga Sec. USSR Cen. Komsomol Cttee; Pres. Union of Innovation Enterprises 1989; Deputy

Chair., First Deputy Chair. Exec. Cttee Moscow City Council 1990–; Deputy Prime Minister Moscow Govt, Head Dept of Int. Econ. Relations 1992–. *Address:* Moscow Government, Tverskaya str. 13, 103032 Moscow, Russia (Office). *Telephone:* (095) 229-63-60 (Office); (095) 229-08-12 (Office).

ORDZHONIKIDZE, Sergei Alexandrovitch; Russian politician and diplomatist; b. 14 Mar. 1946, Moscow; m.; two s.; ed Moscow State Inst. of Int. Relations; mem. staff USSR Ministry of Foreign Affairs –1991; Deputy Perm. Rep. to UN, New York 1991–96; Head Dept of Int. Orgs Ministry of Foreign Affairs 1996–99, Deputy Minister of Foreign Affairs 1999–2002; Under-Sec.-Gen. UN and Dir-Gen. UN Office at Geneva 2002–. *Publications:* numerous publications on international and legal affairs, in particular on UN problems. *Leisure interests:* tennis, skiing, cycling. *Address:* United Nations, Palais des Nations, 1211 Geneva 10, Switzerland (Office). *Telephone:* (22) 9172100 (Office). *Fax:* (22) 917 0002 (Office).

OREFFICE, Paul F(austo), BS; American company executive; b. 29 Nov. 1927, Venice, Italy; s. of Max and Elena (Friedenberg) Oreffice; m. Franca Giuseppina Ruffini 1956; one s. one d.; ed Purdue Univ.; joined Dow Chemical Int., Midland, Mich. 1953, Mediterranean Area Sales Man., Milan, Italy 1955–56, Man. Dow Quimica do Brazil, São Paulo 1956–63, Gen. Man. Dow. Int., Spain 1963–65, Gen. Man. Dow Chemical Latin America 1965–67, Pres. Dow Chemical Inter-American Ltd 1967–69, Financial Vice-Pres. The Dow Chemical Co. 1969–75, Dir Dow Chemical Co. 1971–, Pres. Dow Chemical USA 1975–78, Chair. Exec. Cttee Dow Chemical Co. 1978–87, Pres. and CEO 1978–86, Chair., Pres. and CEO 1986–87, Chair. Bd 1987–92; Dir Cigna Corpn, Northern Telecom Ltd 1983, The Coca-Cola Company 1985, Morgan Stanley Group Inc. 1987; Chair. American Enterprise Inst., Bd of Overseers Inst. for Civil Justice; Bd of Govs. Nat. Parkinson Foundation; mem. The Business Council; Hon. DEng (Purdue) 1976, Hon. Dr. Industrial Management (Lawrence Inst. of Tech.), Science (Saginaw Valley State Coll.), Business Admin. (Tri-State Univ.); Encomienda del Mérito Civil (Spain) 1966. *Leisure interests:* tennis, bridge, golf, various other sports. *Address:* c/o 2030 Willard H. Dow Center, Midland, MI 48674, USA (Office).

O'REGAN, (Andrew) Brendan, CBE; Irish business executive; b. 15 May 1917, Co. Clare; s. of James and Norah O'Regan; m. (Rita) Margaret Barrow 1950; two s. three d.; ed Blackrock Coll., Dublin; Comptroller, Sales and Catering, Shannon Airport 1943–73; Chair. Bord Fáilte Eireann 1957–73, Shannon Free Airport Devt Co. 1959–78; Jt Pres., State Agencies Devt Co-operation Org. (DEVCO) 1974–79, 1988–89; Chair. Co-operation N 1979–82, Pres. 1982–; Pres. Co-operation Ireland Inc. (NY) 1982–90; Chair. Irish Peace Inst. 1984–90, Pres. 1990–; Chair. Shannon Centre for Int. Co-operation 1987–90, Pres. 1990–; Founder mem. OBAIR Enterprise, Newmarket-on-Fergus 1993; Fellow, Inst. of Engineers of Ireland 1977, Irish Hotel and Catering Inst. 1977; Hon. LLD (Nat. Univ. of Ireland) 1978, (Queen's Univ., Belfast) 1999, (Univ. of Limerick) 2001; United Dominions Trust Endeavour Award for Tourism 1973, American Soc. of Travel Agents—Hall of Fame 1977, British Airways Tourism Endeavour Award 1980, Clareman of the Year 1983, Rotary's Paul Harris Award, Freeman of City of Limerick 1995, Duty Free News Int. and Möet & Chandon Lifetime Achievement Award 1999, Co-Operation Ireland 'Peace Dove' Award 2000. *Publications:* numerous speeches and articles on peace through managed co-operation. *Leisure interests:* reading, walking. *Address:* 12 The Sycamores, Gorve Road, Malahide, Co. Dublin, Ireland. *Telephone:* (61) 368408 (Office); (1) 8454523 (Home). *Fax:* (61) 368717 (Office). *E-mail:* obairnewmarket@eirom.net (Office).

O'REILLY, Sir Anthony (John Francis), Kt, BCL; Irish company executive; b. 7 May 1936, Dublin, Ireland; s. of John Patrick O'Reilly and Aileen (O'Connor) O'Reilly; m. 1st Susan Cameron 1962 (divorced); three s. three d.; m. 2nd Chryss Goulandris 1991; ed Belvedere Coll., Dublin, Univ. Coll., Dublin; qualified as solicitor 1958; Demonstrator and Lecturer, Univ. Coll., Cork 1960–62; Personal Asst to Chair., Suttons Ltd, Cork 1960–62; Dir Robert McCowen & Sons Ltd, Tralee 1961–62; Gen. Man. Bord Bainne (Irish Dairy Bd) 1962–66; Man. Dir and CEO, Comhlucht Siuicre Eireann Teo. (Irish Sugar Co.) 1966–69; Jt Man. Dir Heinz-Erin Ltd 1967–70, Man. Dir H. J. Heinz Co. Ltd, UK 1969–71, Sr Vice-Pres. N America and Pacific H. J. Heinz Co. 1971–72, Exec. Vice-Pres. and COO 1972–73, Pres. and COO 1973–79, Chair. 1978–2000, Pres. 1979–90, CEO 1979–98; Chair. Ind. Newspapers PLC 1980–, Waterford Wedgwood PLC 1993–; Chair. European Advisory Bd Bankers Trust 1992–; Chair. Ind. News and Media 2000–, Fitzwilton PLC, Atlantic Resources, Dublin, Eircom PLC 2001–; numerous other commercial appointments; Fellow BIM, RSA; Dr hc (Bradford) 1991, Hon. LLD (Leicester) 1992. *Publications:* Prospect 1966, Developing Creative Management 1970, The Conservative Consumer 1971, Food for Thought 1972. *Leisure interests:* tennis, rugby. *Address:* Independent News and Media, 2023 Bianconi Avenue, City West, Dublin 24 (Office); Castlemartin, Kilcullen, Co. Kildare, Ireland (Home).

O'REILLY, Francis Joseph, BA, BAI, LLD, MRIA; Irish university chancellor and fmr banker; b. 15 Nov. 1922, Dublin; s. of Lt-Col C. J. O'Reilly and Dorothy Mary Martin; m. Teresa Williams 1950; three s. seven d.; ed Ampleforth Coll. and Trinity Coll. Dublin; Chair. Irish Distillers Group 1966–83; Dir Ulster Bank 1961–90, Chair. 1982–89; Dir Nat. Westminster Bank 1982–89; Chair. Coll. des Irlandais, Paris 1988–2000; Chancellor, Univ. of Dublin 1985–98; Hon. LLD (Dublin) 1978, (Nat. Univ. of Ireland) 1986, Hon. Fellow (Trinity Coll. Dublin) 1999; Grand Cross, Order of St Lazarus of Jerusalem 1982,

Knight Commdr, Order of St Gregory the Great 2002. *Leisure interests:* racing, gardening, reading. *Address:* Rathmore, Naas, Co. Kildare, Ireland (Home). *Telephone:* (45) 862136 (Home). *Fax:* (45) 862012 (Home).

OREJA AGUIRRE, Marcelino, LLD; Spanish diplomatist and government official; b. 13 Feb. 1935; m. Silvia Arburua 1967; two s.; ed Univ. of Madrid; entered diplomatic service 1958; Dir Tech. Office of Minister of Foreign Affairs 1962; fmr Asst Dir, Prof. of Foreign Affairs at Escuela Diplomática; mem. Dels. to UN, IMF, IDB, OECD; mem. interministerial Cttee drafting bill for religious freedom; Dir of Int. Relations, Banco de España 1971–74; Under-Sec. for Information and Tourism 1974, for Foreign Affairs Dec. 1975; Minister of Foreign Affairs 1976–80; elected Deputy for Guipúzcoa and Alava in 1979 and 1982; Govt Rep. in Basque Country 1980–82; Sec. Gen. Council of Europe 1984–89; EC Commr for Energy, Euratom Supply Agency and Transport 1994–95, for Relations with European Parl., with mem. States, Culture and Public Affairs 1995–99; Senator by royal appointment June 1977. *Address:* The Senate, Madrid, Spain (Office); 81 Núñez de Balboa, 28006 Madrid, Spain. *Telephone:* (91) 5759101.

OREKHOV, Ruslan Gennadyevich; Russian politician; b. 14 Oct. 1963, Kalinin (now Tver); m.; two c.; ed Kazakh State Univ.; engineer-researcher Kazakh State Univ. 1985–87; Head of div. Alma-Ata Dist Exec. Cttee 1987–88; instructor Moscow Dist Exec. Cttee 1989–90; expert USSR Union of Lawyers 1990; leading expert Cttee on Law Supreme Soviet of Russian Fed. 1990–91; Head Div. of Service of State Counsellors Russian Fed. 1991–93; Head State Dept of Law; Russian Presidency 1993–94; Co-Chair. Expert Council on Law, Russian Presidency 1994–96; Deputy Head of Admin. Russian Presidency, Head Dept of State Law 1996–2000, Pres. World Bank Group for Russia 2001. *Address:* The World Bank, Sadovo-Kudrinskaya str. 3, 123242 Moscow, Russia (Office). *Telephone:* (095) 745-70-00 (Office). *Fax:* (095) 253-06-12.

ORELLANA, José Roberto, MS; Salvadorean banker; b. 20 Jan. 1944, San Salvador; s. of Roberto Orellana and Aida Milla; m. Julia Raquel Aguilar 1977; four c.; ed Trinity Coll., Conn., USA, Stanford Univ.; Vice-Pres., Gen. Man. Banco Cuscatlán 1971–81; Dir Fundación Salvadoreña para el Desarrollo Económico y Social (FUSADES) 1984–89; fmr Pres. Banco Cen. de Reserva de El Salvador; Alt. Gov. Interamerican Devt Bank 1989–95, IMF, World Bank, Banco Centroamericano de Integración Económica. *Address:* c/o Banco Central de Reserva de El Salvador, Alameda Juan Pablo II y 17 Avenida Norte, San Salvador, El Salvador.

ORGAD, Ben Zion; Israeli composer; b. 21 Aug. 1926, Germany; two s.; ed Acad. of Music in Jerusalem and Brandeis Univ., USA; studied violin with Kinory and Bergman and composition with Paul Ben-Haim and Josef Tal; studied in USA under Aaron Copland and Irving Fine; Supervisor of Musical Educ., Israel Ministry of Educ. and Culture 1950–88; Chair. Israel Composers' League; recipient of several awards for compositions. *Compositions include:* cantatas: The Story of the Spies (UNESCO Koussevitzky Prize 1952), Isaiah's Vision; orchestral: Building a King's Stage, Choreographic Sketches, Movements on 'A', Kaleidoscope, Music for Horn and Orchestra, Ballad for Orchestra, Dialogues on the First Scroll; Hatsvi Israel (baritone and orchestra), Suffering for Redemption (mezzo-soprano, choir and orchestra), Out of the Dust (for solo and instruments); Ballada (for violin), Taksim (for harp), Monologue (for viola); works for soloists and orchestra, songs, piano pieces, etc. *Address:* 14 Bloch Street, Tel Aviv 64161, Israel (Home). *Telephone:* 5242833.

ORGAN, (Harold) Bryan; British artist; b. 31 Aug. 1935, Leicester; s. of the late Harold Victor and Helen Dorothy Organ; m. 2nd Sandra Mary Mills 1982; ed Loughborough Coll. of Art; Royal Acad. Schools, London; Lecturer in Drawing and Painting, Loughborough 1959–65; Represented: Kunsthalle, Darmstadt 1968, Mostra Mercatao d'Arte Contemporanea, Florence 1969, 3rd Int. Exhbns. of Drawing Germany 1970, São Paulo Museum of Art, Brazil; Works in pvt. and public collections in England, France, Germany, Italy, Switzerland, USA, Canada, Brazil; Hon. MA (Loughborough) 1974, Hon. DLitt (Leicester) 1985. *Solo exhibitions include:* Leicester Museum and Art Gallery 1959, Redfern Gallery, London 1967, 1969, 1971, 1973, 1975, 1978, 1980, Leicester 1973, 1976, New York 1976, Baukunst, Cologne 1977, Turin 1981. *Portraits include:* Sir Michael Tippett 1966, David Hicks 1968, Mary Quant 1969, Princess Margaret 1970, Elton John 1973, Viscount Stockton 1980, The Prince of Wales 1980, The Princess of Wales 1981, Lord Denning 1982, Sir James Callaghan 1982, HRH The Duke of Edinburgh 1983. *Leisure interest:* cricket. *Address:* c/o Redfern Gallery, 20 Cork Street, London, W1X 2HL; The Stables, Marston Trussell, Nr. Market Harborough, Leics., LE16 9TX, England. *Telephone:* (20) 7734-1732 (London).

O'RIORDAN, Timothy, MA, PhD, FRSA, FBA; British professor of environmental sciences; b. 21 Feb. 1942, Edinburgh; s. of Kevin O'Riordan and of late Norah O'Riordan; m. Ann Philip 1968 (died 1992); two d.; ed Univs. of Edinburgh and Cambridge and Cornell Univ.; Asst Prof. Dept of Geography, Simon Fraser Univ. Vancouver, BC 1967–74; Visiting lecturer, Univ. of Canterbury, New Zealand 1970; Visiting Assoc. Prof. Clark Univ., Worcester, Mass. 1972; Reader Univ. of East Anglia 1974, Prof. of Environmental Sciences 1980–; Chair. Environment Cttee Broads Authority 1989–, Environment Science & Soc. Programme, European Science Foundation 1989–; Adviser Environmental Research Directorate 1996–97; mem. Environmental Advisory Council, Dow Chemicals 1992–, Eastern Group PLC 1995–; DL (Norfolk) 1998; Fellow British Acad. 1999; mem. UK Sustainable Devt Cmm.

2000–03; Gill Memorial Prize, Royal Geographical Soc. *Publications:* Environmentalism 1976, Countryside Conflicts 1986, Sizewell B: An Anatomy of the Inquiry 1987, The Greening of the Machinery of Government 1990; ed. Interpreting the Precautionary Principle 1994, The Politics of Climate Change in Europe 1996, Ecotaxation 1996, The Transition to Sustainability in Europe 1998, Environmental Science for Environmental Management 2000, Globalism, Localism and Identity 2001, Reinterpreting the Precautionary Principle 2001. *Leisure interests:* classical double bass playing, jogging, cycling, swimming, intuition. *Address:* School of Environmental Sciences, University of East Anglia, Norwich, NR4 7TJ; Wheatlands, Hethersett Lane, Colney, Norwich, NR4 7TT, England. *Telephone:* (1603) 810534. *Fax:* (1603) 250588. *E-mail:* t.oriordan@uea.ac.uk (Office).

ORITA, Masaki; Japanese diplomatist; diplomatic postings to GB 1967, USSR during 1970s, OECD, Paris 1977–79; mem. staff Gaimusho (Ministry of Foreign Affairs) 1979–89, 1994–2002; Personal Asst to Prime Minister 1989–1994; Amb. to UK 2002–. *Address:* Embassy of Japan, 101–104 Piccadilly, London W1J 7JT, England (Office). *Telephone:* (20) 7465-6500 (Office). *Fax:* (20) 7491-9348 (Office). *E-mail:* info@embjapan.org.uk (Office). *Website:* www.embjapan.org.uk (Office).

ORLOV, Viktor Petrovich, CandGeolSc, DEconSc; Russian politician and geologist; b. 23 March 1940, Chernogorsk, Krasnoyarsk Region; s. of Petr Orlov and Eva Orlova; m.; three d.; ed Tomsk State Univ., Acad. of Nat. Econ. at USSR Council of Ministers; geologist, chief geologist, team leader W Siberian Geological Survey 1968–75; Chief Engineer Geological Exploration, Iran 1975–78; chief geologist, Deputy Head Geological Div. Amalgamation Tsentrgeologiya 1979–81, Dir Gen. 1986–90; Deputy Head Geology and Production Depts, Ministry of Geology Russian Fed. 1981–84, 1986–; Deputy Minister of Geology USSR 1990–91; First Deputy Chair. State Cttee on Geology Russian Fed. 1991–92; Chair. Cttee on Geology and Use of Mineral Resources Russian Fed. 1992–96; Minister of Natural Resources Russian Fed. 1996–98, 1998–99; Pres. Russian Geological Soc. 2000–01; mem. Council of Fed., Fed. Ass. of the Russian Fed., Rep., Admin, Koryak Autonomous Area 2001–; Laureate, RF State Prize in Science and Engineering 2001Honoured Geologist of Russia 1990, Order for Services to the Native Land, IVth degree, 2001. *Publications:* Geological Forecasting 1991, Iron-Ore Base of Russia 1998, Mineral Resources and Geological Service of Russia during the Economic Reforms 1999, Reforms in Geology 2000; more than 200 scientific articles. *Leisure interests:* fishing, hunting. *Address:* Russian Geological Society, Zvenigorodskoye Shosse 9, 123022 Moscow, Russia (Office); Council of Federation, Bolshaya Dmitrovka str.26, Moscow (Office); Palana, Portova str.22, 684620 Kamchatka region, Karyak autonomous district, Russia (Office). *Telephone:* (095) 292-75-43 (Geological Soc.) (Office); (095) 926-69-53 (Council of Fed.) (Office); (095) 259-79-53; (8415-43) 3-13-80 (Palana) (Office). *Fax:* (095) 292-75-43. *E-mail:* VPOrlov@council.gov.ru (Office).

ORME, Baron (Life Peer), cr. 1997, of Salford in the County of Greater Manchester; **Stanley Orme,** PC; British politician; b. 5 April 1923, Sale, Cheshire; s. of Sherwood Orme; m. Irene Mary Harris 1951; ed elementary and tech. schools, Nat. Council of Labour Colls. and Workers' Educ. Assn classes; Shop Steward, Amalgamated Union of Eng Workers (AUEW) 1949–64; Councillor, Sale Borough Council 1957–65; MP for Salford W 1964–83, for Salford E 1983–97; Minister of State, Northern Ireland Office 1974–76, Dept of Health and Social Security April-Sept. 1976; Minister for Social Security 1976–79; Chair. AUEW Parl. Group of Labour M.P.s 1977; Opposition Spokesman for Health and Social Security 1979–80, for Industry 1980–83, for Energy 1983–87; Chair. Parl. Labour Party 1987–92; Hon. Dr.SC. (Salford) 1985. *Address:* 8 Northwood Grove, Sale, Cheshire, M33 3DZ, England (Home).

ORMESSON, Comte Jean d'; French author, journalist and international official; b. 16 June 1925; s. of Marquis d'Ormesson; nephew of late Comte Wladimir d'Ormesson; m. Françoise Béghin 1962; one d.; ed Ecole Normale Supérieure; Deputy Sec.-Gen. Int. Council for Philosophy and Humanistic studies (UNESCO) 1950–71, Sec.-Gen. 1971; staff of various Govt ministers 1958–66; Deputy Ed. Diogène (int. journal) 1952–72, mem. Man. Cttee 1971–; mem. Council ORTF 1960–62, Programme Cttee 1973; mem. Control Comm. of Cinema 1962–69; mem. Editorial Cttee Editions Gallimard 1972–74; Ed.-in-Chief, Columnist, Le Figaro 1974–77, Dir-Gen. 1976, leader writer, columnist 1977–; mem. Acad. Française 1973; Pres., Soc. des amis de Jules Romains 1974–; Grand Prix du Roman (Acad. Française) for novel La gloire de l'empire 1971; Officier, Légion d'honneur, Commdr des Arts et des Lettres, Officier, Ordre nat. du Mérite, Chevalier des Palmes académiques. *Publications:* L'amour est un plaisir 1956, Du côté de chez Jean 1959, Un amour pour rien 1960, Au revoir et merci 1966, Les illusions de la mer 1968, La gloire de l'empire 1971, Au plaisir de Dieu 1974, Le vagabond qui passe sous une ombrelle trouée 1978, Dieu, sa vie, son oeuvre 1981, Mon dernier rêve sera pour vous 1982, Jean qui grogne et Jean qui rit 1984, Le vent du soir 1985, Tous les hommes en sont fous 1985, Bonheur à San Miniato 1987, Garçon de quoi écrire (jtly.) 1989 (prix de Mémorial 1990), Histoire du juif errant 1991, Tant que vous penserez à moi, entretien avec Emmanuel Berl 1992, La Douane de mer 1994, Presque rien sur presque tout 1996, Casimir mène la grande vie 1997, Une autre histoire de la littérature française 1997, Le rapport Gabriel (Prix Jean Giono) 1999, Voyez comme on danse 2001, C'était bien 2003; numerous articles in Le Figaro, Le Monde, France-Soir, Paris

Match, etc. *Leisure interests:* skiing, sailing. *Address:* c/o Le Figaro, 37 rue du Louvre, Paris 75001 (Office); 1 rue Miollis, 75015 Paris (Office); 10 avenue du Parc-Saint-James, 92200 Neuilly-sur-Seine, France (Home).

ORMOND, Julia; British actress; b. 4 Jan. 1965; m. Rory Edwards (divorced); ed Guildford High School, Cranleigh School, Farnham Art School and Webber Douglas Acad.; worked in repertory, Crucible Theatre, Sheffield, Everyman Theatre, Cheltenham and on tour with Royal Exchange Theatre, Manchester; appeared in Faith, Hope and Charity (Lyric, Hammersmith), Treats (Hampstead Theatre); West End debut in Anouilh's The Rehearsal (Almeida), My Zinc Bed (Royal Court) 2000. *Films:* The Baby of Macon 1993, Legends of the Fall 1994, First Knight 1995, Sabrina 1995, Smilla's Sense of Snow 1997, The Barber of Siberia 1998. *Television appearances:* Traffik (Channel 4 series), Ruth Rendell Mysteries, Young Catherine 1990.

ORMOND, Richard Louis, CBE, MA; British museum director and art historian; b. 16 Jan. 1939, Bath; s. of Conrad E. Ormond and Dorothea Gibbons; m. Leonée Ormond 1963; two s.; ed Marlborough Coll., Brown Univ. USA and Christ Church, Oxford; Asst Keeper, Nat. Portrait Gallery 1965–75, Deputy Dir 1975–83; Head of Picture Dept Nat. Maritime Museum 1983–86; Dir Nat. Maritime Museum 1986–2000; Dir J. S. Sargent Catalogue Raisonné project. *Publications:* J. S. Sargent 1970, Catalogue of Early Victorian Portraits in the National Portrait Gallery 1973, Lord Leighton 1975, Sir Edwin Landseer 1982, The Great Age of Sail 1986, F.X. Winterhalter and the Courts of Europe 1987, Frederic, Lord Leighton (co-author) 1996, Sargent Abroad (co-author) 1997, John Singer Sargent: The Early Portraits (co-author) 1998, John Singer Sargent (co-author) 1998, Sargent (co-author) 1998, Sargent e l'Italia (co-author) 2001, John Singer Sargent: Portraits of the 1890s (co-author) 2002. *Leisure interests:* opera, theatre, cycling. *Address:* 8 Holly Terrace, London, N6 6LX, England. *Telephone:* (20) 7839-3125.

ORMOS, Mária, DSc; Hungarian historian; b. 1 Oct. 1930, Debrecen; d. of János Ormos and Elza Förster; one s. one d.; ed Kossuth Lajos Univ., Debrecen; Asst lecturer, Historic Science Inst. 1963; mem. Hungarian Acad. of Sciences 1993, mem. of Presidium; Univ. Prof. 1982; Rector Janus Pannonius Univ. of Pécs 1984–92; mem. Nat. Cttee of Historians; Pres. Italian-Hungarian Mixed Cttee of Historians; Vice-Pres. Asscn d'histoire des relations internationales; mem. European Acad. of Arts, Sciences and Humanities; Széczhenyi Prize 1995, Szentgyörgyi Prize 1995, Leo Sziliard Prize 2000, Deák Ferenc Prize 2000, Pulitzer Prize 2000. *Publications:* Franciaország és a keleti biztonság 1931–36 (France and the Eastern Security) 1969, Merénylet Marseilleben (Assassination in Marseille) 1984, Mussolini: a political portrait 1987, Nazism and Fascism, 1987, Never as long as I shall live 1989, Civitas fidelissima 1921 1990, From Padova to Trianon 1991, Hitler 1993, Magyarország a világháborúk korában 1914–45 (Hungary in the Age of the World Wars 1914–45) 1997, Európa a nemzetközi Küzdőtéren. Felemelkedés és hanyatlás 1814–1945 (Europe in the International Arena. Rise and Decline) (co-author) 1998, Hitler–Sztálin (Hitler-Stalin) (co-author 1999), Kozma Miklós, Egy magyar Médiavezér (Nikolaus Kozma, Life of Hungarian Media Leader) 2000, Governments and Politics 1848–2000 (jtly.) 2001. *Leisure interests:* music, books, theatre. *Address:* c/o Janus Pannonius University, 7621 Pécs, Rókus u. 2, Hungary. *Telephone:* (72) 315-942.

ORNSTEIN, Donald Samuel, PhD; American professor of mathematics; b. 30 July 1934; s. of Harry Ornstein and Rose (Wisner) Ornstein; m. Shari Richman 1964; two s. one d.; ed Swarthmore Coll. and Univ. of Chicago; mem. Inst. for Advanced Study, Princeton 1956–58; Instructor, Univ. of Wisconsin 1958–60; Asst Prof. Stanford Univ. 1960–63, Sloan Fellow and Assoc. Prof. 1963–65, Assoc. Prof. 1965–66, Prof. of Math. 1966–; Visiting Prof. Cornell Univ. and New York Univ. (Courant Inst.) 1967–68, Hebrew Univ. Jerusalem 1975–76, Mathematical Sciences Research Inst. Berkeley 1983–84; mem. NAS 1981, American Acad. of Arts and Sciences 1991; Bocher Prize 1974. *Publications:* Ergodic Theory Randomness and Dynamical Systems 1974; mathematical papers in many journals since 1959. *Address:* Department of Mathematics, Stanford University, Stanford, CA 94305-2125 (Office); 857 Tolman Drive, Stanford, CA 94305, USA (Home). *Fax:* (415) 725-4066 (Office).

O'ROURKE, Mary, BA; Irish politician; b. 31 May 1937, Athlone; d. of P. J. Lenihan; m. Enda O'Rourke (died 2001); two s.; ed St Peter's Convent, Univ. Coll. Dublin and St Patrick's Coll. Maynooth, Co. Kildare; fmr secondary school teacher; mem. Westmeath County Council 1979–87; mem. Dáil 1982; Minister for Educ. 1987–91, of Health 1991–92, for Trade and Marketing 1992–93, for Labour Affairs 1993–94, for Public Enterprise 1997–2002; Deputy Leader Fianna Fáil 1995–2002; Leader of Seanad Eireann. *Address:* Seanad Eireann, Leinster House, Kildare Street, Dublin 2 (Office); Aisling, Arcadia, Athlone, Co. Westmeath, Ireland. *Telephone:* (1) 6183860 (Office); (902) 75065. *Fax:* (1) 6184790 (Office); (902) 78218. *E-mail:* mary.orourke@ oireachtas.ie (Office).

ORR, Christopher John, RA; British artist; b. 8 April 1943, London; s. of Ronald Orr and Violet Townley; m. Catherine Terris 1985; one s. one d.; ed Royal Coll. of Art; worked as artist and teacher, latterly as a tutor and visiting lecturer, Royal Coll. of Art 1976–, Prof. and Course Dir of Printmaking 1998–; one man touring exhbns The Complete Chris Orr 1976, Many Mansions 1990; numerous exhbns. worldwide; Fellow Royal Soc. of Painters and Printmakers, elected Royal Academician 1995. *Publications:* Many Mansions 1990, The Small Titanic 1994, Happy Days 1999, Semi-antics 2001. *Address:* Royal

College of Art, Kensington Gore, London, SW7 (Office); 7 Bristle Hill, Buckingham, MK18 1EZ, England. *Telephone:* (1280) 815255. *Fax:* (1280) 815255. *E-mail:* chrisorr@aol.com (Home).

ORR, Sir David Alexander, Kt, MC, LLD, FRSA; British business executive; b. 10 May 1922, Dublin, Ireland; s. of the late Canon A. W. F. Orr and Grace Robinson; m. Phoebe R. Davis 1949; three d.; ed High School and Trinity Coll., Dublin; with Unilever 1948–82; Marketing Dir, Hindustan Lever, Bombay 1955; mem. Overseas Cttee, Unilever 1960; Vice-Pres. Lever Brothers Co., New York 1963, Pres. 1965; Dir Unilever PLC 1967–82, Vice-Chair. 1970–74, Chair. 1974–82; Chair. British Council 1985–92; Dir Rio Tinto-Zinc Corpn 1981–92, Shell Transport and Trading Co. 1982–92, Inchcape PLC 1982–92 (Chair. 1983–86, 1991–92, Deputy Chair. 1986–91), Bank of Ireland 1982–90; Chair. Sea Perfect PLC 1994–96; Pres. Liverpool School of Tropical Medicine 1981–89, Vice-Pres. 1989–; Pres. Coll. of Speech and Language Therapists 1992–96, Children's Medical Charity 1990–96; Trustee Leverhulme Trust 1979–81, Chair. 1982–91; Chair. Charles Wallace (India) Trust 1991–98; Chancellor The Queen's Univ. Belfast 1992–99; Council mem. LSE; Hon. LLD (Trinity Coll. Dublin) 1978, (Liverpool Univ.) 1989, (Queen's Univ., Belfast) 1992, (Nat. Univ. of Ireland) 1993; Hon. DUniv (Surrey) 1982; Commdr of Order of Oranje Nassau (Netherlands) 1979. *Leisure interests:* books, travel, golf, rugby. *Address:* 81 Lyall Mews West, London, SW1X 8DJ; Home Farm House, Shackleford, Godalming, Surrey, GU8 6AH, England. *Telephone:* (1483) 810350 (Home).

ORREGO VICUÑA, Francisco, PhD; Chilean lawyer and diplomatist; b. 12 April 1942, Santiago; m. Soledad Bauza; three c.; ed schools in Chile, Argentina, Spain and Egypt, Univ. of Chile and LSE; fmr Dir Inst. of Int. Studies Univ. of Chile; fmr Visiting Prof. Stanford Univ., Univ. of Paris II Law School, Univ. of Miami Law School; participated in projects for Acad. of Int. Law, The Hague, UNITAR and various studies and projects undertaken by univs. in Europe, USA, Asia and Latin America; fmr legal adviser to OAS; fmr del. Law of Sea Conf.; fmr int., El Mercurio (daily newspaper); Amb. to UK 1983–85; Prof. of Int. Law, Inst. of Int. Studies, Law School, Univ. of Chile 1985–; Pres. Chilean Council on Foreign Relations 1989–2000, Chilean Acad. of Social Sciences 1995–2000; mem. Chilean-U.S. Comm. for Settlement of Disputes; mem. Advisory Cttee on Foreign Policy, Ministry of Foreign Affairs; Conciliator and Arbitrator of ICSID 1995–; Judge and Vice-Pres. Admin. Tribunal of IBRD, Pres. 2001–; Commr UN Compensation Comm. 1998–2000; new Arbitrator Int. Chamber of Commerce, London Court of Int. Arbitration; mem. Inst. of Int. Law; Nat. Award for the Humanities and Social Sciences 2001. *Publications:* Antarctic Resources Policy 1983, Antarctic Mineral Exploitation 1988, The Exclusive Economic Zone 1989, The Changing International Law of High Seas Fisheries 1999 and other books and articles. *Address:* Institute of International Studies, University of Chile, P.O. Box 14187 Suc. 21, Santiago 9, Chile (Office). *Telephone:* 2745377. *Fax:* 2740155. *E-mail:* forrego@uchile.cl (Office).

ORRELL-JONES, Keith, MA, CInstM, FRSA; British business executive; b. 15 July 1937; s. of Francis George Orrell-Jones and Elsie Orrell-Jones; m. Hilary Kathleen Orrell-Jones (née Pegram) 1961; four s.; ed The High School, Newcastle-under-Lyme, St John's Coll., Cambridge; Chief Exec. ARC Ltd 1986–89; Dir Consolidated Gold Fields PLC 1989; Dir Blue Circle Industries PLC 1990, Chief Exec. 1992–99; Chair. FKI PLC 1999–; Dir (non-exec.) Smiths Group PLC 1990, Chair. 1998–. *Leisure interests:* music (particularly opera), field sports, art, walking. *Address:* Smiths Group PLC, 765 Finchley Road, London, NW11 8DS, England. *Telephone:* (20) 8457-8245 (Office).

ORSENNA, Erik, D.ÈS SC.ECON.; French author and academic; b. Erik Arnoult, 22 March 1947, Paris; s. of Claude Arnoult and Janine Arnoult (née Bodé); m. 2nd Catherine Clavier; one s. one d.; ed Ecole Saint-Jean de Béthune, Versailles, Univ. de Sciences Économiques, Inst. des Sciences Politiques, Paris; lecturer Inst. d'Etudes Politiques, Paris 1975–80, Ecole Normale Supérieure 1977–81, Sr Lecturer Univ. de Paris I 1978–81; Tech. Adviser to Ministry of Co-operation and Devt 1981–83, Cultural Adviser to Presidency 1983–85, Personal Adviser to Minister of Foreign Affairs 1990–92; Literary Ed. Editions Ramsay 1977–81; Counsel Conseil d'Etat 1985–, Sr mem. 2000–; Pres. Centre Int. de la Mer 1991–; Ecole Nat. Supérieure du Paysage 1995–; Vice-Pres. Cytale Soc. 2000–; mem. Acad. Française 1998. *Publications:* Espace national et déséquilibre monétaire 1977, La Vie comme à Lausanne 1997, Une comédie française 1980, L'Exposition coloniale (Prix Goncourt) 1988, Grand Amour 1993, Histoire du monde en neuf guitares 1996, Longtemps 1998, Portrait d'un homme heureux, André Le Nôtre 1613–1700 2000, La Grammaire est une chanson donce 2001. *Address:* Conseil d'Etat, Place du Palais Royal, 75001 Paris, France (Office); Institut de France, 23 quai Conti, 75006 Paris.

ORSETTI, Christian Ernest, LenD; French diplomatist; b. 1 April 1923, Montpellier; s. of Antoine Orsetti and Marie-Louise Couffinhal; m. Marie-Antoinette Vincent 1946; three d.; ed Univ. of Montpellier, Ecole Libre des Sciences Politiques; holder of numerous Govt posts since 1945, including: Sec.-Gen. for Haute-Marne 1952, Tarn-et-Garonne 1955, Fougères 1960; Cabinet Dir for Minister of Agric. 1962–64, then Minister for Material Resources 1966–67; Auditor to Inst. des Hautes Etudes de Défense Nat. 1972–73; Prefect for Martinique 1973–75; with Ministry of Foreign Affairs 1977; Hon. Prefect 1989; Amb. of Monaco to France 1977–; Vice-Pres. and Pres. Jury du Prix des Ambassadeurs; mem. and Chair. Bd Dirs. Institut de paléontologie humaine, Fondation Prince Albert de Monaco; Officier Légion d'honneur, Commdr Ordre nat. du Mérite, Ordre du Mérite Agricole, Officier des Palmes Académiques, etc. *Address:* Ambassade de la Principauté de Monaco, 22 boulevard Suchet, 75116 Paris (Office); 12 avenue Georges-Mandel, 75116 Paris (Office); 6 rue Foucault, 75116 Paris, France (Home). *Telephone:* 1-45-04-74-54 (Office). *Fax:* 1-45-04-45-16 (Office).

ORSZULIK, Alojzy; Polish Roman Catholic ecclesiastic; b. 21 June 1928, Baranowice Śląskie; ed Catholic Univ. of Lublin; ordained Priest 1957; lecturer Higher Ecclesiastic Seminar, Ołtarzew 1962–89; mem. staff Secr. of Episcopate of Poland 1962–68, Head Press Bureau 1968–93, Deputy Sec. 1989–94, Chair. Comm. for Social Communications 1984–94; Adviser Pontifical Council for Social Communications 1974–2000; Sec. Joint Comm. of Gov. and Episcopate of Poland 1980–; mem. Working Group for Legis. Affairs 1981-83, 1987–89; Legis. Council of Episcopate of Poland 1993–; rep. of Catholic Church during Round Table Talks 1989; Suffragan of Siedlce and Curate-Gen. 1989–92; del. of the Holy See for negotiations with Polish Govt about the concordat 1990–93; Ordinary of Łowicz Diocese 1992–. *Publications:* numerous articles on canon law. *Address:* Bishops Curie, Stary Rynek 20, 99-400 Łowicz, Poland (Office). *Telephone:* (46) 837-43-49 (Office).

ORTEGA GAONA, Amancio; Spanish retail executive; b. March 1936, León; fmr shop assistant; f. Confecciones Goa (mfrs of bathrobes) 1963, f. Zara (chain of fashion stores, 700 outlets world-wide) 1975, is now majority shareholder of Inditex group (Industrias de Diseño Textil SA), including Zara, Massimo Dutti and Pull & Bear brands. *Address:* Inditex SA, Avenida de la Diputación, 15142 Arteixo, A Coruña, Spain (Office). *Telephone:* (98) 1185400 (Office). *Website:* www.inditex.com (Office).

ORTEGA SAAVEDRA, Daniel; Nicaraguan politician and fmr resistance leader; b. 11 Nov. 1945, La Libertad, Chontales; s. of Daniel Ortega and Lidia Saavedra; m. Rosario Murillo; seven c.; ed Univ. Centroamericano, Managua; joined Frente Sandinista 1963; active in various underground resistance movts against regime of Anastasio Somoza from 1959 and was several times imprisoned and tortured for revolutionary activities; ed. El Estudiante, official publ of Frente Estudiantil Revolucionaria and directed org. of Comités Cívicos Populares in Managua 1965; mem. Nat. Directorate of FSLN (Sandinista Liberation Front) 1966–67; imprisoned 1967–74; resumed position with FSLN and with José Benito Escobar became involved in further revolutionary activities; fought on front in two-year mil. offensive which overthrew Somoza regime 1979; mem. Junta of Nat. Reconstruction Govt 1979, Co-ordinator of Junta 1981–85, Pres. of Nicaragua 1985–90; presidential cand. 2001; currently Gen. Sec. FSLN. *Address:* Frente Sandinista de Liberación Nacional, Costado Oeste Parque El Carmen, Managua, Nicaragua. *Telephone:* (2) 66-0845. *Fax:* (2) 66-1560. *Website:* www.fsln.org.ni (Office).

ORTIZ, Cristina; Brazilian concert pianist; b. 17 April 1950, Bahia; d. of Silverio M. Ortiz and Moema F. Ortiz; m. Jasper W Parrott 1974; two d.; ed Conservatório Brasileiro de Música, Rio de Janeiro, Acad. Int. de Piano (with Magda Tagliaferro), Paris and Curtis Inst. of Music, Philadelphia (with Rudolph Serkin); New York recital debut 1971; has appeared in concerts with the Vienna Philharmonic, Berlin Philharmonic, the Concertgebouw, Chicago Symphony, NY Philharmonic, Israeli Philharmonic, LA Philharmonic, leading British orchestras and has undertaken many tours of North and South America, the Far East, NZ and Japan; appeared with NHK Symphony, the Bergen Philharmonic and Philharmonia under Janowski 1997; has recorded extensively for EMI, Decca, Pantheon, Collins Classics and Pickwick Records; First Prize Van Cliburn Int. Competition, Texas 1969. *Leisure interests:* tennis, swimming, gardening, reading, hiking, holidaying. *Address:* c/o SPNM 4th Floor, St Margaret's House, 18–20 Southwark Street, London, SE1 ITJ (Office); c/o Harrison-Parrott Ltd, 12 Penzance Road, London, W11 4PA, England. *Telephone:* (20) 7229-9166.

ORTIZ, Francis Vincent, MS, LLD; American diplomatist (retd); b. 14 March 1926, Santa Fe; s. of Frank V. Ortiz and Margaret Delgado Ortiz; m. Mary Dolores Duke 1953; three s. one d.; ed Georgetown, George Washington, New Mexico, Madrid Univs. and American Univ. of Beirut, Lebanon; diplomatic posts in Ethiopia and Mexico 1957–60; Special Asst to Under-Sec. of State 1957–60, to Amb. to Mexico 1961–63; Country Dir for Spain and Portugal 1963–67, for Argentina, Uruguay and Paraguay 1973–75; Head, Political Section and Chargé d'Affaires, Peru and Uruguay 1967–73; Deputy Exec. Sec. of State 1975–77; Amb. to Barbados, Grenada, St Lucia and Dominica 1977–79, to Guatemala 1979–80, to Peru 1981–83, to Argentina 1983–86; Diplomat in Residence, Latin American Inst., New Mexico Univ. 1986–88; Special Asst to Under-Sec. of State for Man. 1988–90; Political Adviser, C-in-C, Southern Command 1980–81; Regent, Museum of N.M. 1999–; mem. American Foreign Service Asscn; Hon. DrIur (New Mexico); Superior Service Award, Kt. Grand Cross of Civil Merit of Spain, Order of the Kts. of Malta; Meritorious Honor Award, Presidential Chamizal Medal (Mexico), Grand Cross Order of Mayo (Argentina) and others. *Leisure interests:* history, tennis. *Address:* 663 Garcia Street, Santa Fe, NM 87501, USA. *Telephone:* (505) 984-2586. *Fax:* (505) 984-2741. *E-mail:* fvo14@aol.com (Home).

ORTIZ BOSCH, Milagros María; Dominican Republic politician; b. 23 Aug. 1936, Santo Domingo; one s.; niece of fmr Pres. Juan Bosch Gaviño; ed Univ. of Santo Domingo; Adviser, Chamber of Deputies 1982–90; mem. Senate 1990–2000; Vice-Pres. of the Dominican Republic May 2000–; Sec. of State for Educ. 2000–; Vice-Pres. Revolutionary Democratic Party (PRD) 1991–. *Address:* Administrative Secretariat of the Presidency, Palacio Nacional,

Avda México, esq. Dr. Delgado, Santo Domingo, DN, Dominican Republic (Office). *Telephone:* 686-4771 (Office). *Fax:* 688-2100 (Office). *Website:* www.presidencia.gov.do (Office).

ORTIZ DE ROZAS, Carlos; Argentine diplomatist and lawyer; b. 26 April 1926, Buenos Aires; s. of late Alfredo Ortiz de Rozas and Susana del Valle; m. Carmen Sarobe 1952; ed Univ. de Buenos Aires School of Diplomacy; entered foreign service 1948; Chargé d'Affaires, Bulgaria 1952–54; Sec. Greece 1954–56; mem. Cabinet, Argentine Ministry of Foreign Affairs 1958–59; Counsellor, Argentine Mission at UN 1959–61; subsequently Dir-Gen. Policy Dept, Ministry of Foreign Affairs and later Minister at embassies in UAR and UK; Amb. to Austria 1967–70; Chief Rep. to Conf. of Cttee on Disarmament, Geneva 1969 (Chair. of Cttee 1979); Perm. Rep. to UN 1970–77; Amb. to UK 1980–82, to France 1984–89, to USA 1991–93; Under-Sec. of State for Foreign Relations 1990; Head of Argentine Special Mission to Holy See 1982–83; Pres. UN Security Council 1971, 1972; mem Advisory Bd to Sec.-Gen. on Disarmament 1978–92; Prof. of Int. Relations, Univ. of Belgrano, Buenos Aires 1995–; Dir and Pres. Del. of Conf. on Law of the Sea 1973, First (Political and Security) Cttee of the 29th General Ass. 1974; has held several teaching posts including Prof. of Public Law and Int. Relations, Univ. del Salvador, Buenos Aires (now mem. Bd of Dirs); Pres. Bunge and Born Foundation 1994–99, Alliance Française de Buenos Aires 1999–2001; mem. Exec. Bd Argentine Council for Int. Relations 1994–; decorations from Italy, Chile, Brazil, Greece, Japan, Peru, Thailand, Egypt, Austria, Nicaragua, the Republic of Korea, Spain, Holy See and France. *Publications:* Paths to Peace – The UN Security Council and its Presidency 1981, La reunion de Palm Beach – J.F. Kennedy – A. Frondizi 1994, Contribuciones Argentinas a las Naciones Unidas 1995. *Address:* Avenida Gelly y Obes 2263, 1425 Buenos Aires, Argentina. *Telephone:* (11) 4803-3630 (Home). *Fax:* (11) 4804-6791 (Home). *E-mail:* crozas1@attglobal.net (Home).

ORTLEB, Rainer, Dr rer. nat, DR.SC.TECH.; German politician and computer scientist; b. 5 June 1944, Gera; m.; one s. one d.; ed Dresden Tech. Univ. and Rostock Univ.; Asst lecturer, Dresden Tech. Univ. 1971–82; Sr Asst lecturer, Computer Centre, Rostock Univ. 1982–84, lecturer, Computer Science Dept 1984, lecturer, Ship Eng Dept 1986, Assoc. Prof. 1989; Chair. Rostock Liberal Party Org. 1987–90; fmr Chair. Liberal LDPD Party and mem. fmr GDR Parl. 1990; mem. Bundestag 1990–; Deputy Fed. Chair. Free Democratic Party (FDP) 1990–; Fed. Minister for Special Tasks 1990–91; Fed. Minister for Educ. and Science 1991–94. *Leisure interests:* art, music. *Address:* 10117 Berlin, Reinhardtstr. 14, Germany.

ORTOLI, François-Xavier; French economist; b. 16 Feb. 1925, Ajaccio, Corsica; s. of Antoine Ortoli and Angèle Tessarech; m. Yvonne Calbairac 1946; one s. three d.; ed Hanoi Faculty of Law and Ecole Nat. d'Administration, Paris; Insp. of Finances 1948–51; Tech. Adviser to the Office of the Minister of Econ. Affairs and Information 1951–53; Technical Adviser, Office of the Minister of Finances 1954; Asst Dir to the Sec. of State for Econ. Affairs and Sec.-Gen. Franco-Italian Cttee of EEC 1955; Head, Commercial Politics Service of Sec. of State for Econ. Affairs 1957; Dir-Gen. of the Internal Market Div. of EEC 1958; Sec.-Gen. Inter-Ministerial Cttee for Questions of European Econ. Co-operation, Paris 1961; Chef de Cabinet to Prime Minister 1962–66; Commr-Gen. of the Plan 1966–67; Minister of Works 1967–68, of Educ. 1968, of Finance 1968–69, of Industrial and Scientific Devt 1969–72; Pres. Comm. of European Communities 1973–76; Vice-Pres. for Econ. and Monetary Affairs 1977–84; Pres., Dir Gen. TOTAL 1984–90, Hon. Chair. 1990–; Pres. Conseil nat. du patronat français int. (now Mouvement des entreprises de France int. 1989–), Asscn Ouest-Atlantique 1996–; Dr. hc (Oxford and Athens Univs.); Commdr Légion d'honneur, Médaille militaire, Croix de guerre 1945, Médaille de la Résistance, etc. *Address:* Tour Total, 24 cours Michelet, 92069 Paris la Défense (Office); 18 rue de Bourgogne, 75007 Paris, France (Home). *Telephone:* 1-41-35-31-84 (Office). *Fax:* 1-41-35-33-46.

OSBALDESTON, Hon. Gordon Francis, PC, CC, BComm, MBA, LLD; Canadian company director; b. 29 April 1930, Hamilton, Ont.; s. of John E. Osbaldeston and Margaret (Hanley) Osbaldeston; m. Geraldine M. Keller 1953; three s. one d.; ed St Jerome's Coll., Kitchener, Ont. and Univs of Toronto and Western Ontario; Sec. Treasury Bd 1973–76; Deputy Minister, Dept of Industry, Trade and Commerce 1976–78; Sec. Ministry of State for Econ. Devt 1978–82; Under-Sec. of State for External Affairs 1982; Clerk of Privy Council and Sec. to Cabinet 1982–86; Sr Fellow, School of Business Admin., Univ. of Western Ontario 1986–95, Prof. Emer., Ivey School of Business, Univ. of W Ont. 1995–; Dir Du Pont Canada, Great West Lifeco Inc., London Life Insurance Co.; Vanier Medal, Inst. of Public Admin. of Canada 1990; Hon. DrIur (Western Ontario), (Carleton), (Dalhousie)Companion, Order of Canada. *Publications:* Keeping Deputy Ministers Accountable 1989, Organizing to Govern 1992. *Leisure interests:* golf, stamp collecting. *Address:* 1353 Corley Drive, London, Ont., N6G 4L4, Canada. *Telephone:* (519) 438-9772 (Home). *Fax:* (519) 433-7605 (Home). *E-mail:* gordon5304@aol.com (Home).

OSBORN, Eric Francis, PhD, DD, FAHA; Australian professor of New Testament and early church history; b. 9 Dec. 1922, Melbourne; s. of William F. Osborn and Hilda P. Osborn; m. Lorna G. Grierson 1946; two s.; ed Wesley Coll. Melbourne, Queen's Coll., Univ. of Melbourne and Queens' Coll., Cambridge; army service 1942–44; Methodist Minister in country parishes 1948–51, 1954–57; research student, Cambridge 1952–54; Prof. of New Testament and Early Church History, Queen's Coll. Univ. of Melbourne

1958–87, Pres. United Faculty of Theology 1987; Guest Prof. Univ. of Strasbourg 1981–82; Visiting Prof. La Trobe Univ. 1990–; Guest Prof. Augustinianum Lateran Univ., Rome 1997; Professorial Fellow Univ. of Melbourne 1998–; Centenary Medal for Services to Australian Society and the Humanities 2003. *Publications:* The Philosophy of Clement of Alexandria 1957, Justin Martyr 1973, Ethical Problems in Early Christian Thought 1976, The Beginning of Christian Philosophy 1981, La Morale dans la Pensée Chrétienne Primitive 1984, Anfänge Christlichen Denkens 1986, The Emergence of Christian Theology 1993, Tertullian, First Theologian of the West 1997, Irenaeus of Lyons 2001. *Leisure interests:* swimming, running. *Address:* 2 Ocean Road, Point Lonsdale, Vic. 3225, Australia. *Telephone:* (3) 5258-2827 (Home); (3) 9347-2249.

OSBORN, Frederic (Derek) Adrian, C.B., BA, BPhil; British government official; b. 14 Jan. 1941, Dorset; s. of late Rev. George Osborn and Betty Osborn; m. Caroline Niebuhr Tod 1971; one s. one d.; ed Leys School, Cambridge and Balliol Coll. Oxford; Ministry of Housing and Local Govt 1965–70; with Dept of Transport 1975–77, Dept of Environment 1977–95, Dir-Gen. (Deputy Sec.) 1990–95; Chair. European Environment Agency 1995–99; Chair. UNED, UK (name changed to Stakeholder Forum for Our Common Future 2002) 1996–, Earth Centre 1996– (mem. Bd 1996–), Joseph Rowntree Foundation Steering Group on Reconciling Environmental and Social Objectives 1998–, UK Round Table on Sustainable Devt 1999–; mem. Bd England and Wales Environment Agency 1996–98, Severn Trent PLC 1998–; Special Adviser House of Commons Environmental Audit Cttee 1998–99; Chair. Jupiter Global Green Investment Trust 2001–; mem. Royal Soc. for Protection of Birds 1996–; Visiting Fellow Green Coll., Oxford 1996–97; Visiting Prof., School of Public Policy, Univ. Coll., London 1998–. *Publications:* Earth Summit II 1998, contribs. to Journal of Environmental Law etc. *Leisure interests:* music, reading. *Address:* Stakeholder Forum for Our Common Future, c/o United Nations Association, 3 Whitehall Court, London SW1A 2EL, England. *Telephone:* (20) 7839-1784. *Fax:* (20) 7930-5893.

OSBORNE, John A.; Montserratian politician; Leader People's Liberation Movement 1978–96, People's Progressive Alliance 1996–2001, New People's Liberation Movement 2001–; Chief Minister of Montserrat 1978–91, 2001– (also Minister of Finance, Economic Devt, Trade, Tourism and Media). *Address:* Office of the Chief Minister, Government Headquarters, P.O. Box 292, Plymouth, Montserrat (Office). *Telephone:* 491-3463 (Office). *Fax:* 491-6780 (Office).

OSBOURNE, Ozzy (John); British musician; b. 3 Dec. 1948, Aston, Warwicks.; m. Sharon Arden; one s. two d.; vocalist with Black Sabbath (fmrly. Earth) 1967–79; solo artist with backing group Blizzard of Ozz, 1979–; cr. annual touring festival Ozz Fest 1996–; recorded with numerous artists, including Alice Cooper, Mötorhead, Ringo Starr (q.v.), Rick Wakeman; Grammy Award 1994. *Concerts include:* Madison Square Garden, New York 1975, Live Aid, Phila 1985, US Festival 1983, Rock In Rio festival 1984, Monsters of Rock Festival, Castle Donington 1986, Moscow Music Peace Festival 1989, No More Tears world tour 1992. *Singles include:* with Black Sabbath: Paranoid, Iron Man, War Pigs, Never Say Die; solo/with Blizzard of Ozz: Crazy Train 1980, Bark at the Moon 1983, The Ultimate Sin 1986, Close My Eyes Forever (with Lita Ford) 1989, No More Tears 1991, Perry Mason 1995. *Albums include:* with Black Sabbath: Black Sabbath 1969, Paranoid 1970, Sabbath Bloody Sabbath 1973, Sabotage 1975, Technical Ecstasy 1976, Never Say Die 1978; solo/with Blizzard of Ozz: Blizzard of Ozz 1980, Bark at the Moon 1983, The Ultimate Sin 1986, No Rest for the Wicked 1988, Just Say Ozzy 1990, No More Tears 1991, Ozzmosis 1995, The Ozzman Cometh 1997, OzzFest Vol. 1: Live 1997, Diary of a Madman/Bark at the Moon/Ultimate 1998. *Television series:* The Osbournes 2001–. *Address:* Sharon Osbourne Management, POB 15397, Beverly Hills, CA 90209, USA (Office).

OSCARSSON, Per Oscar Heinrich; Swedish actor; b. 28 Jan. 1927, Stockholm; s. of Ing. Einar Oscarsson and Theresia Küppers; m. Bärbel Krämer 1960; one s. two d.; ed Royal Dramatic School; Royal Dramatic Theatre 1947–52, Gothenburg Town Theatre 1953–59, TV-Theatre 1966–67; now works mainly as freelance film-actor; Best Actor Award, Cannes 1966; New York Critics Award for Best Actor 1968; Silver Hugo Best Actor Award, Chicago Int. Film Festival 1969. *Films include:* The Doll 1962, My Sister My Love 1965, Hunger 1965, Ole Dole Doff 1967, It's Up to You 1968, Close to the Wind 1970, A Last Valley, Salem Comes to Supper 1971. *Stage appearances include:* Hamlet 1953, Candida 1961, Waiting for Godot 1963. *Leisure interests:* reading, riding.

O'SHEA, Timothy Michael Martin, PhD; British university principal and professor of computer science; b. 28 March 1949, Hamburg; s. of John Patrick O'Shea and Elisabeth Hedwig Oberhof; m. Eileen Scanlon 1982; two s. two d.; ed Royal Liberty School Havering, Univ. of Sussex, Univ. of Leeds; Research Fellow, Dept of Artificial Intelligence, Univs of Texas at Austin and Edin. 1974–78; joined Open Univ. 1978–, f. Computer Assisted Learning Research Group 1978, Lecturer, Inst. of Educational Tech. 1980–82, Sr Lecturer 1983–87, Prof. of Information Tech. and Educ. 1987–97, Pro-Vice Chancellor of Quality Assurance and Research 1994–97, Visiting Research Prof. in Computer Supported Collaborative Learning 1997–; Master Birkbeck Coll. and Chair in Information and Communication Tech., Univ. of London 1998–2002, Gov. City Literary Inst. 1998–2000, Gov. SOAS 1998–2002, Curator School of Advanced Study 1999–2002, Gov. St George's Medical School 2000–02, Provost Gresham Coll. 2000–02, Pro-Vice-Chancellor Univ.

of London 2001–02; Prin., Univ. of Edin. 2002–; Visiting Scientist, Xerox PARC, and Visiting Scholar, Univ. of Calif. at Berkeley, USA 1986–87; Chair. Advanced Educational Tech. Programme, NATO 1988–90; Chair. Artificial Intelligence Soc. of Britain 1979–82, London Metropolitan Network Ltd 1999–2002, Information Systems Sectory Group, CVCP 1999–, Higher Educ. and Research Opportunities Ltd (HERO) 2000–; Dir Edexcel Foundation 1998–2001 (mem. Exec. Cttee 1998–2001), Univs and Colls Staff Devt Agency 1999–2000; mem. HEFCE Cttee on Equal Opportunities, Access and Lifelong Learning 1998–, Jt Information Systems Cttee 2000–; mem. Bd UUK 2001–; Pres. Pyschology Section, BAAS 1991–92; Trustee Eduserv 1999–2000; mem. Council, RCM 2001–; . *Television:* The Learning Machine (series-presenter and author) 1985. *Publications include:* Self-Improving Teaching Systems 1979, Learning and Teaching with Computers (co-author) 1983, Artificial Intelligence: Tools, Techniques and Applications (co-author) 1984; ed. Advances in Artificial Intelligence 1985, Intelligent Knowledge-based Systems: An Introduction (co-ed.) 1987, Educational Computing (co-ed.) 1987, New Directions in Educational Tech. (co-ed.) 1992. *Address:* Office of the Principal, University of Edinburgh, Old College, South Bridge, Edinburgh, EH8 9YL, Scotland (Office). *Telephone:* (131) 650-2150 (Office). *Fax:* (131) 650-6519 (Office). *E-mail:* principal@ed.ac.uk. *Website:* www.ed.ac.uk (Office).

OSHEROFF, Douglas Dean, PhD; American physicist and researcher; b. 1 Aug. 1945, Aberdeen, Wash.; s. of William Osheroff and Bessie Anne (Ondov) Osheroff; m. Phyllis S. K. Liu 1970; ed California Inst. of Tech., Cornell Univ.; mem. tech. staff Bell Labs., Murray Hill, NY 1972–82, Head Solid State and Low Temperature Physics Research Dept 1982–87; Prof. Stanford Univ., Calif. 1987–, J. G. Jackson and C. J. Wood Prof. of Physics 1992–, Chair. Physics 1993–96; co-discoverer superfluidity in liquid 3He 1971, nuclear antiferromagnetic resonance in solid 3He 1980; Fellow American Physical Soc., American Acad. of Arts and Sciences, N.A.A.; co-recipient Simon Memorial Prize, British Inst. of Physics 1976, Oliver E. Buckley Solid State Physics Prize 1981, John D. and Catherine T. MacArthur Prize Fellow 1981, shared Nobel Prize for Physics 1996. *Address:* Department of Physics, Stanford University, Stanford, CA 94305-4060, USA.

OSHIMA, Kenzo; Japanese diplomatist and United Nations official; b. 1943; ed Tokyo Univ.; served in diplomatic posts in Australia, France, India, USA and at Perm. Mission to UN; Dir-Gen. Econ. Co-operation Bureau, Ministry of Foreign Affairs; Sec.-Gen. Secr. for Int. Peace Co-operation HQ, Office of the Prime Minister –2000; UN Under-Sec.-Gen. for Humanitarian Affairs and Emergency Relief Co-ordinator 2001–. *Address:* Office for the Co-ordination of Humanitarian Affairs, United Nations Plaza, New York, NY 10017, USA (Office). *Telephone:* (212) 963-1234 (Office). *Fax:* (212) 963-1312 (Office). *E-mail:* ochany@un.org (Office).

OSHIMA, Nagisa; Japanese film director; b. 31 March 1932, Kyoto; m. Akiko Koyama 1960; two s.; ed Kyoto Univ.; with Shochiku Co. 1954–59; formed own film co. 1959; Pres. Dirs'. Guild of Japan 1980–; has also directed TV films. *Films:* Ai To Kibo No Machi (A Town of Love and Hope) 1959, Seishun Zankoku Monogatari (Cruel Story of Youth) 1960, Taiyo No Hakaba (The Sun's Burial) 1960, Nihon No Yoru To Kiri (Night and Fog in Japan) 1960, Shiiku (The Catch) 1961, Amakusa Shiro Tokisada (The Rebel) 1962, Etsuraku (The Pleasures of the Flesh) 1965, Yunbogi No Nikki (Yunbogi's Diary) 1965, Hakuchu No Torima (Violence at Noon) 1966, Ninja Bugeicho (Band of Ninja) 1967, Nihon Shunka-ko (A Treatise on Japanese Bawdy Song) 1967, Muri Shinju Nihon No Natsu (Japanese Summer: Double Suicide) 1967, Koshikei (Death By Hanging) 1968, Kaettekita Yopparai (Three Resurrected Drunkards) 1968, Shinjuku Dorobo Nikki (Diary of a Shinjuku Thief) 1968, Shonen (Boy) 1969, Tokyo Senso Sengo Hiwa (He Died After the War, or The Man Who Left His Will on Film) 1970, Gishiki (The Ceremony) 1971, Natsu No Imoto (Dear Summer Sister) 1972, Ai no Corrida (In the Realm of the Senses) 1976, Ai no Borei (Empire of Passion) 1978, Merry Christmas, Mr. Lawrence 1982, Max, mon amour 1985, Kyoto, My Mother's Place 1991, Gohatto 2001.

OSIPOV, Victor Ivanovich; Russian geologist; b. 15 April 1937; ed Moscow State Univ.; Dir seismic station 1959–61; lecturer. Prof. Moscow State Univ. 1964–90; Deputy Dir Inst. of Lithosphere 1990; Dir Centre of Eng Geology and Geoecology (now Inst. of Geoecology) Russian Acad. of Sciences; corresp. mem., USSR (now Russian) Acad, of Sciences 1987, mem. 1991; main research in Eng geology, environmental protection; State Prize 1988. *Leisure interests:* travelling, sports, gardening. *Address:* Institute of Geoecology, Ulansky per. 13, 101000 Moscow, Russia. *Telephone:* (095) 135-83-25 (Office).

OSIPOV, Yuri Sergeyevich, DPhys-MathSc; Russian mathematician and technician; b. 7 July 1936, Tobolsk; m.; one d.; ed Urals State Univ.; corresp. mem. USSR (now Russian) Acad. of Sciences 1984, mem. 1987, Pres. 1991–; staff mem., Inst. of Mechanics and Math., Urals Scientific Cen. Acad. of Sciences 1959, Dir 1990–93; Prof., Urals Univ. 1961–70; fmr Head of Chair of Moscow State Univ.; Dir Steklov Math. Inst. 1993–; mem. American Math. Soc., American Acad. of Sciences, Mongolian Acad. of Sciences, Armenian Acad. of Sciences, Santiago Univ., Chile; Dr hc (Bar-Ilan Univ., Israel), (Santiago Univ., Chile); Lenin Prize 1976, USSR State Prize. *Publications:* more than 150 works on the theory of man., differential equations and their application. *Address:* Russian Academy of Sciences, Leninsky prospekt 14,

117901 GSP-1, Moscow; Steklov Mathematical Institute, 42 Vavilov Street, 117966 Moscow, Russia. *Telephone:* (095) 954-35-06 (Acad.); (095) 135-22-91 (Inst.).

OSIPYAN, Yuri Andreyevich, DPhys-MathSc; Russian physicist; b. 15 Feb. 1931, Moscow; m.; three c.; ed Moscow Steel Inst.; mem. CPSU 1959–91; on staff of Cen. Inst. of Metallo-Physics (Sr Researcher) 1955–62; Deputy Dir of USSR (now Russian) Acad. of Sciences Inst. of Crystallography 1962–63; on staff of USSR (now Russian) Acad. of Sciences Inst. of Solid State Physics 1963–, Prof. 1970–, Deputy Dir then Dir 1973–; Corresp. mem. of USSR (now Russian) Acad. of Sciences 1972, mem. 1981–, Vice-Pres. 1988–97, mem. Presidium 1997–2002; Dean, Prof. and Head of Faculty of Moscow Inst. of Physics and Tech. 1963–73; mem. Pres. Council 1990–91; Pres. Int. Union for Theoretical and Applied Physics 1990–; Hero of Socialist Labour 1986; USSR People's Deputy 1989–91; P.N. Lebedev Gold Medal 1984, A. P. Karpinsky Prize, City of Hamburg 1991. *Publications:* works on solid state physics. *Address:* Institute of Solid State Physics, Chernogolovka, Moscow region, 142432, Russia. *Telephone:* (095) 993-27-55 (Office); (095) 913-23-24. *Fax:* (095) 52-49-701 (Office). *E-mail:* ossipyan@issp.ac.ru (Office).

OSKANYAN, Vartan; Armenian politician; b. 7 Feb. 1955, Syria; m.; two s.; ed Yerevan Polytechnic Inst., Tufts Univ. Massachusetts, Harvard Univ., Fletcher School of Law and Diplomacy; f. and Ed. Armenian Int. Magazine; on staff Armenian Ministry of Foreign Affairs 1992–; Deputy Head, Middle E Dept, Head, Dept of N America 1992–94; Prin. negotiator in Misk process on Nagorno-Karabakh conflict 1994–97; Deputy Foreign Minister 1994–97, First Deputy Foreign Minister 1997–98, Minister of Foreign Affairs April 1998–. *Address:* Ministry of Foreign Affairs, 2 Republic Square, 375010 Yerevan, Armenia (Office). *Telephone:* (2) 52-35-31 (Office). *Fax:* (2) 15-10-42 (Office). *E-mail:* comgroup@ns.r.am (Office).

OSKARSON, Peter; Swedish theatre director; b. 13 June 1951, Stockholm; s. of Per-Otto Oskarson and Margareta Du Rietz; m. Gunilla Kindstrand 1983; one s. four d.; ed Actors' School, Stockholm; Artistic Dir Skånska Teatern Landskrona 1973–82, Folkteatern Gävleborg 1982–90; Head, Helsingegården, inst. for theatre and popular arts, N Scandinavia 1990–; Artistic Dir Orion Theatre 1993–2000; Gen. Man. Folkteatern Gävleborg 1997–; Artistic Adviser Peking Opera, Anhui, Hefei, China 1996–; Artistic Dir World Theatre Project 1999–; plays produced also at Royal Opera House and at Royal Dramatic Theatre, Stockholm, Drottningholm Theatre, Staatsoper, Stuttgart, Intiman, Seattle, USA, Oper der Stadt, Bonn, Festwochen, Vienna, Schwetzingen Festspiele, Swedish TV etc.; mem. Swedish Theatre Acad. 1993–, Swedish World Culture Forum 1998–2001, Framtidens Kultur 2003–; Alf Sjöberg Prize, Swedish Acad. Theatre Prize, Svenska Dagbladet Thalia Prize, Expressen Theatre Prize, Gävle and Gävleborg Culture Prize, Malmö Thalia Prize. *Address:* Helsingegården, S-820 40 Järvsö, Sweden. *Telephone:* (651) 40999. *Fax:* (651) 41595. *E-mail:* peter@oskarson.se (Office). *Website:* www.gavlefolkteater.se (Office).

OSMAN, Osman Ahmed, BSc; Egyptian civil engineer (retd); b. 1917, Ismailia; s. of Ahmed Mohamed Osman; m. Samia Ismail Wahbi 1947; four s. one d.; ed Cairo Univ.; Chair. The Arab Contractors (Osman Ahmed Osman & Co) 1949–73 and of its assoc. cos., Saudi Enterprises, Kuwaiti Eng Co., The Arab Contractors (Libya), The Libyan Co. for Contracting and Devt, The Osman Ahmed Osman & Co. (Abu Dhabi, Arabian Gulf); Minister of Reconstruction 1973–76 and of Housing 1975–76; Deputy Premier, responsible for Popular Devt Jan.–May 1981; mem. People's Ass. 1976–, Pres. Chamber of Reps. (Speaker) 1984–92; mem. Consultative Council 1957; Chair. Syndicate of Engineers March 1979; mem. Inter Action Council (union of fmr heads of states and govts.) 1983; Hon. LLD (Ricker Coll. of North East) 1976; Repub. Medal (1st Class), Soviet Hero of Labour Medal, Nile Medal (1st Class) 1980. *Major projects include:* (in Egypt) Aswan High Dam, Suez Canal deepening and widening, Port Said Shipyard, Cairo Int. Airport, Salhia reclamation project, High Dam Electric Power Transmission Lines, Giza Bridge and Ramsis Bridge over the Nile; (in Saudi Arabia) Dhahran Airport, Riyadh Mil. Coll., Dammam Mil. Barracks; (in Kuwait) Municipality Centre, Kuwait sewer system, secondary schools, Sabahia roads and drainage system; (in Libya) Benghazi drainage system, Stadium and Highway; (in Iraq) Kirkuk Feeder Canal No. 2 and 3; (in Jordan) Khaled Ibn El-Walid Dam and Tunnels; (in Abu Dhabi) Zayed City, Ruler's Palace Kharj Mil. Base and City, Taif Mil. Base, numerous airports, hospitals and land reclamation. *Publications:* The High Dam (lecture) 1966, My Experience 1981. *Leisure interests:* fishing, football. *Address:* c/o Osman Ahmed Osman & Co., 34 Adly Street, Cairo, Egypt. *Telephone:* 3935011. *Fax:* 3937674.

OSMOND, Charles Barry, FRS, FAA, PhD; Australian professor of biology; b. 20 Sept. 1939, Australia; s. of Edward Charles Osmond and Joyce Daphne Osmond (née Krauss); m. 1st Suzanne Ward 1962 (divorced 1983); one s. one d.; m. 2nd Cornelia Gauhl 1983; ed Wyong High School and Univs of New England and Adelaide; Postdoctoral fellow, Univ. of Calif. at LA 1965–66, Univ. of Cambridge 1966–67; Research Fellow, Dept of Environmental Biology, Research School of Biological Sciences, ANU 1967, subsequently Fellow, Sr Research Fellow, Prof. of Biology 1978–87, Dir 1991–98, Prof. Photo Bioenergetics Group 1998–; Exec. Dir Biological Science Center, Desert Research Inst., Univ. of Nevada 1982–86; Arts and Sciences Prof., Dept of Botany, Duke Univ. 1987–91; Dir Research School of Biol. Sciences, ANU 1991–98, also Visiting Fellow; Pres. and CEO Biosphere 2 Center, Columbia Univ. 2000; Sr Fulbright Fellowship, Univ. of Calif. (Santa Cruz) 1973–74;

Guest Prof., Technical Univ., Munich 1974; Overseas Fellow, Churchill Coll., Cambridge 1980; mem. Australian Nat. Comm. for UNESCO 1980–82; mem. Council, Australian Acad. of Sciences 1982–85; Forschungspreis, Alexander von Humboldt Foundation, Univs. of Darmstadt and Göttingen 1997–2000; Mitgleider Deutsche Akad. der Naturforscher, Leopoldina 2001. *Publications:* numerous Publs on plant physiology. *Address:* 7 Needham Place, Stirling, ACT 2611, Australia; Biosphere 2 Centre, Columbia University, Box 689 Oracle, AZ 85623, USA (Office). *Telephone:* (520) 838-5096 (USA) (Office); (2) 6287-1487 (Australia) (Office). *Fax:* (520) 838-6429 (USA) (Office). *E-mail:* osmond@bio2.edu (Office).

OSPEL, Marcel; Swiss banker; b. 8 Feb. 1950; ed Higher School of Econs and Man., Basel; joined Dept of Planning and Marketing Swiss Bank Corpn (SBC) 1977, with SBC Capital Markets, London, New York 1980, Dir 1987, mem. Enlargement Group 1990, CEO Capital Markets and Treasury 1992, SBC Warburg 1995, Group Pres. 1996–; CEO Union Bank of Switzerland 1998–2000, Pres. and CEO 2000–. *Address:* Union Bank of Switzerland, Bahnhofstr. 45, 8021 Zürich; Swiss Bank Corporation, Aeschenplatz 6, 4002 Basel, Switzerland. *Telephone:* (61) 2311111. *Fax:* (61) 2365111. *E-mail:* info@ubs.com (Office). *Website:* www.ubs.com (Office).

OST, Friedhelm; German politician; b. 15 June 1942, Castrop-Rauxel; s. of Franz Ost and Barbara Ost; m. Erika Herrmann 1968; three s. two d.; ed Univs. of Freiburg and Cologne; bank employee 1966–69; Adviser, Bundesverband Deutscher Banken 1969–72; Econ. Ed., moderator and commentator, Zweites Deutsches Fernsehen (ZDF) 1973–85; State Sec. and Head, Govt Press and Information Dept 1985–89; Econ. and Political Adviser to German Fed. Chancellor and freelance journalist and public relations consultant 1989–90; Gen. Man. Wirtschaftsvereinigung Bergbau –1990; mem. CDU 1980–; mem. Bundestag 1990–, Chair. Econ. Cttee; Adviser Frankfurter Rothschild GmbH 1997–; now Gen. Rep. Deutsche Vermögensberatungs AG; mem. Russian Acad. of Sciences. *Leisure interests:* football, tennis. *Address:* Deutsche Vermögensberatungs AG, Querstr. 1, 60322 Frankfurt-am-Main, Germany (Office).

OSTAPCIUC, Eugenia; Moldovan politician and engineer; b. 19 Oct. 1947, Fyntynitsa, Soroka region; m.; two s.; ed Chişinău Trade Higher School, Moscow Inst. of Nat. Econs; engineer, Deputy Dir, then Dir Dietary Dept 1966–88; Dir-Gen. Dept of Trade Soroka 1988–95; Deputy Dir Asscn Logos, Chişinău 1995–98; Sec. Parl. faction, Party of Communists of Repub. of Moldova; mem. Perm. Comm. on Social Protection, Public Health and Family 1998–2001; Chair. Parl. of Moldova March 2001–. *Address:* House of Parliament, Stefan Celmari prosp. 105, 277073 Chişinău, Moldova (Office). *Telephone:* (2) 23-75-86 (Office). *Fax:* (2) 54-65-79 (Office).

OSTEN, Suzanne (Carlota); Swedish playwright and theatre and film director; b. 20 June 1944, Stockholm; d. of Carl Otto Osten and Gud Osten; m.; one d.; ed Lund Univ.; started directing while a student 1963; ran fringe theatre group performing in schools, prisons, public areas, etc.; joined City Theatre, Stockholm 1971; f. Unga Klara Stadsteatern ind. repertory co. 1975; has written and directed over 30 plays, numerous radio and TV productions; began directing films 1980; Prof. Dramatic Inst. 1995–; Nat. Theatre Critics Prize 1982; Guldbagge Award for Direction (for The Mozart Brothers) 1986; Paris-Creteil Prize 1993; several other awards and prizes. *Films include:* Mamma—Our Life is Now 1982, The Mozart Brothers 1986, Lethal Film 1988, Guardian Angel 1990, Speak Up It's So Dark 1992, Only You and Me 1994, Carmen's Revenge 1996. *Address:* Upplandsgt. 19, 113 60 Stockholm, Sweden. *Telephone:* (8) 32-54-23.

OSTERBROCK, Donald E., PhD; American astronomer; b. 13 July 1924, Cincinnati, Ohio; s. of William C. Osterbrock and Elsie W. Osterbrock; m. Irene Hansen 1952; one s. two d.; ed Univ of Chicago; Instructor Princeton Univ. 1952–53; Instructor, then Asst Prof. Calif. Inst. of Tech. 1953–58; Asst Prof., then Assoc. Prof., Univ. of Wis. 1958–61, Prof. of Astronomy 1961–73, Chair. Dept of Astronomy 1967–68, 1969–72; Visiting Prof., Univ. of Chicago 1963–64; Letters Ed., Astrophysical Journal 1971–73; Prof. of Astronomy, Univ. of Calif., Santa Cruz 1972–92, Prof. Emer. 1993–; Dir Lick Observatory 1972–81; Hill Family Prof., Univ. of Minn. 1977–78; Visiting Prof., Ohio State Univ. 1980, 1986; Guggenheim Fellow 1960–61, 1982–83, Nat. Science Sr Foundation Fellow 1968–69; Assoc., Royal Astronomical Soc. 1976; mem. Nat. Acad. of Sciences, American Acad. of Arts and Sciences, American Philosophical Soc., Wisconsin Acad. of Sciences, Arts and Letters, American Astronomical Soc. (Vice-Pres. 1975–77, Pres. 1988–90); Corresp. mem. Mexican Acad. of Sciences 1998; Henry Norris Russell Lectureship, American Astronomical Soc. 1991; Hon. DSc (Ohio State Univ.) 1986, (Univ. of Chicago) 1992, (Univ. of Wis.-Madison) 1997; Univ. of Chicago Alumni Asscn Professional Achievement Award 1982, Catherine W. Bruce Medal, Astronomical Soc. of the Pacific 1991, Antoinette de Vancouleurs Memorial Lectureship and Medal (Univ. of Texas) 1994, Gold Medal, Royal Astronomical Soc. 1997, Alumni Medal, Univ. of Chicago 2000. *Publications:* Astrophysics of Gaseous Nebulae 1974, James E. Keeler, Pioneer American Astrophysicist and the Early Development of American Astrophysics 1984, Astrophysics of Gaseous Nebulae and Active Galactic Nuclei 1989, (with J. R. Gustafson and W. J. S. Unruh) Eye on the Sky: Lick Observatory's First Century 1988, Pauper and Prince: Ritchey, Hale and Big American Telescopes 1993; numerous scientific papers in Astrophysical Journal and Publications of the Astronomical Society of the Pacific, etc. *Leisure interests:* drama, hiking, conservation. *Address:* Lick Observatory,

University of California, Santa Cruz, CA 95064; 120 Woodside Avenue, Santa Cruz, CA 95060, USA (Home). *Telephone:* (831) 459-2605 (Office). *Fax:* (831) 426-3115. *E-mail:* don@ucolick.org (Office).

ÖSTMAN, Arnold; Swedish conductor; b. 1939, Malmo, Sweden; m. Kristina Modig; ed Univs. of Paris and Stockholm; fmr Lecturer State Acad. of Music and Drama, Stockholm; Artistic Dir Vadstena Acad. 1969, f. Norrlands Operan 1974, Gen. Admin. and Artistic Dir Drottningholm Court Theatre 1979–92; has conducted at opera houses including: Covent Garden, Parma, Paris Bastille, Trieste, Cologne, Bonn, Toulouse, Nice, Vienna, Wexford, Washington, Lausanne; symphonic conductor with orchestras including: the German radio orchestras of Hamburg, Cologne, Stuttgart and Baden-Baden, the Stuttgart Philharmonic, Orchestre nat. de France, de Lille, orchestra of La Fenice, Venice, Adelaide Symphony Orchestra, Orchestra Sinfonia Siciliana, Scottish Chamber Orchestra, Acad. of Ancient Music, London, Royal Concertgebouw Orchestra, Amsterdam, Oslo Philharmonic Orchestra, Minneapolis Symphony Orchestra, Sydney Symphony Orchestra, Melbourne Symphony Orchestra; works regularly with Netherlands Radio Chamber Orchestra (symphonic and operatic); mem. Royal Swedish Acad. of Music; Hon. PhD; Chevalier, Légion d'honneur. *Recordings include:* Così fan tutte, Le Nozze di Figaro, Don Giovanni, Die Zauberflöte (Diapason d'Or and Deutsche Schallplattenpreis), Gluck's Alceste for Naxos; co-producer two TV films: Christina the Winter Queen, Gustav III (both winners of Prix d'Italia). *Address:* Haydn Rawstron (UK) Ltd, 36 Station Road, London, SE20 7BQ, England. *Telephone:* (20) 8659-2659. *Fax:* (20) 8676-9119.

OSTRIKER, Jeremiah (Paul), PhD; American professor of theoretical astrophysics; b. 13 April 1937, New York; s. of Martin Ostriker and Jeanne Sumpf; m. Alicia S. Suskin 1958; one s. two d.; ed Harvard Univ. and Univ. of Chicago; Postdoctoral Fellow, Cambridge Univ., England 1964–65; Research Assoc. and Lecturer, Princeton Univ. 1965–66, Asst Prof. 1966–68, Assoc. Prof. 1968–71, Prof. 1971–, Chair. Dept of Astrophysical Sciences and Dir Observatory 1979–95, Charles A. Young Prof. of Astronomy 1982–; Provost, Princeton Univ. 1995–2001; Plumian Prof. of Astronomy and Experimental Physics, IOA, Univ. of Cambridge UK 2001–; mem. Editorial Bd and Trustee, Princeton Univ. Press 1982–84, 1986; Visiting Prof. Harvard Univ. and Regents Fellow Smithsonian Inst. 1984–85, 1987; mem. NAS 1974–, mem. Council 1992–95, mem. Bd of Govs. 1993–95; mem. American Acad. of Arts and Sciences 1975–, American Astronomical Soc., Int. Astronomical Union, American Philosophical Soc. 1994–; Assoc. mem. Royal Astronomical Soc. 1994–; Fellow AAAS 1992; Foreign mem. Royal Netherlands Acad. of Arts and Sciences; Nat. Science Foundation Fellowship 1960–65; Alfred P. Sloan Fellowship 1970–72; Sherman Fairchild Fellowship of CalTech 1977; Trustee American Museum of Nat. History 1997–; Hon. FRAS 1994; Hon. DSc (Univ. of Chicago) 1992; Helen B. Warner Prize (American Astronomical Soc.) 1972, Henry Norris Russell Prize 1980; Vainu Bappu Memorial Award (Indian Nat. Science Acad.) 1993, Karl Schwarzschild Medal, Astronomische Gesellschaft (Germany) 1999, U.S. Nat. Medal of Science 2000, American Acad. of Achievement Golden Plate Award 2001. *Leisure interest:* squash. *Address:* Department of Astrophysical Sciences, Princeton University, Princeton, NJ 08544 (Office); 33 Philip Drive, Princeton, NJ 08540, USA (Home). *Telephone:* (609) 258-4267 (Office); (609) 924-5737 (Home). *Fax:* (609) 258-1020 (Office). *E-mail:* jpo@astro.princeton.edu (Office).

OSTROUMOVA, Olga Mikhailovna; Russian actress; b. 21 Sept. 1947, Buguruslan; ed Moscow Inst. of Theatre Arts; actress Moscow Theatre of Young Spectators until 1973, Moscow Theatre on Malaya Bronnaya 1973–83, Moscow Mossoviet Theatre 1983–; USSR Official State Prize 1979, RSFSR Merited Actress 1982, Peoples' Actress of Russian Fed. 1993; Silver Nymph Prize, Sorrento and Naples 1973, Golden Dovzhenko Medal 1982. *Films include:* And Dawns Here are Quiet, Earthly Love, Vassily and Vassilisa, Garage, Stop Kidding, Fate, Snake's Spring, Let's Live up to Monday. *Music:* (CDs) Tribute to Vladimir Visotsky 2000, A Song about Earth, A Novel about Girls 2002. *Theatre includes:* White Guard, Madame Bovary, At the Threshold of the Tsardom, Cherry Orchard 2001, A Husband, a Wife and a Lover, The Eternal Husband (Dostoevsky) 2003. *Leisure interest:* travelling. *Address:* Moscow Mossoviet Theatre, B. Sadovaya str. 16, 103050 Moscow (Office); Arboit str. 17, 4, apt 9, 121002 Moscow, Russia (Home). *Telephone:* (095) 299-33-77 (Office); (095) 202-01-88 (Home).

OSTROVSKY, Mikhail Arkadievich, DBiolSc; Russian physiologist and biophysicist; b. 22 Feb. 1935, Leningrad; m. Raisa Brook; two s.; ed Moscow State Univ.; Jr, then Sr researcher Inst. of Higher Nervous Activity and Neurophysiology 1959–70, Head of Sensory Reception Lab., Inst. of Chemical Physics USSR (now Russian) Acad. of Sciences 1970–; Prof. Moscow State Univ. 1977–; Visiting Prof., Univ. of Md at Coll. Park 1994–; Corresp. mem. USSR (now Russian) Acad. of Sciences 1990, mem. 1994; Ed. Russian Sensory Systems 1987–; Chair. Expert Comm. on Physiology and Medicine of Russian Foundation for Basic Research 1992–; mem. Int. Brain Research Organization 1980, Russian Pavlov Physiological Soc. 1976, Int. Eye Research Asscn 1989; mem. Bd and Chair. Cttee for Relations with E European Neuroscience Asscns. *Publications:* more than 100 articles and papers on photoreception, visual pigments, phototransduction, eye screening pigments, light damage to eye structures; patents for devices and methods in biochem., medicine and optics; invented UV blue light-absorbing intraocular lenses. *Address:* ul. Kosygina 4, 119991 Moscow, Russia. *Telephone:* (095) 135-70-73 (Office); (095) 939-73-57 (lab.); (095) 434-15-35 (Home). *Fax:* (095) 137-41-01. *E-mail:* ostrovsky@sky.chph.ras.ru (Office); ostrovsky@eye.phys.msu.su (Home).

OSTRY, Sylvia, CC, PhD, FRSC; Canadian economist; b. Winnipeg; d. of Morris J. Knelman and B. (Stoller) Knelman; m. Bernard Ostry; two s.; ed McGill and Cambridge Univs.; Chief Statistician, Statistics Canada 1972–75; Deputy Minister of Consumer and Corp. Affairs and Deputy Registrar Gen. 1975–78; Chair. Econ. Council of Canada 1978–79; Head, Econ. and Statistics Dept, OECD 1979–83; Deputy Minister (Int. Trade) and Co-ordinator for Int. Econ. Relations, Dept of External Affairs 1984–85; Amb., Multilateral Trade Negotiations and Personal Rep. of the Prime Minister, Econ. Summit, Dept of External Affairs 1985–88; Per Jacobsson Foundation Lecture, Washington 1987; Sr Research Fellow, Univ. of Toronto 1989–90; Volvo Distinguished Visiting Fellow, Council on Foreign Relations, New York 1989; Chair. Centre for Int. Studies, Univ. of Toronto 1990–97, Distinguished Research Fellow 1997–; Chancellor, Univ. of Waterloo 1991–97; Western Co-Chair. Blue Ribbon Comm. for Hungary's Econ. Devt 1990–94; Chair. Council Canadian Inst. for Int. Affairs 1990–94; Dir Power Financial Corpn; Chair. Int. Advisory Council, Bank of Montreal; mem. several learned socs and professional orgs; Fellow American Statistical Asscn; Sylvia Ostry Foundation annual lecture series launched 1992; 18 hon. degrees; Outstanding Achievement Award, Govt of Canada 1987, Career Achievement Award, Canadian Policy Research 2000. *Publications include:* International Economic Policy Co-ordination (with Michael Artis) 1986, Governments and Corporations in a Shrinking World: The Search for Stability 1990, The Threat of Managed Trade to Transforming Economies 1993, Technonationalism and Technoglobalism: Conflict and Cooperation (with Richard Nelson) 1995, Rethinking Federalism: Citizens, Markets and Governments in a Changing World (jtly) 1995, The Halifax G7 Summit: Issues on the Table (ed. with Gilbert Winham) 1995, Who's On First? The Post Coldwar Trading System 1997, The Future of the World Trading System 1999, Convergence and Sovereignty: Policy Scope for Compromise 2000, Business, Trade and the Environment 2000, The Changing Scenario in International Governance 2000; articles on labour econs, demography, productivity, competition policy. *Leisure interests:* films, theatre, contemporary reading. *Address:* Munk Center for International Studies, University of Toronto, 1 Devonshire Place, Room 361S, Toronto, Ont. M5S 3K7, Canada (Office). *Telephone:* (416) 946-8958 (Office). *Fax:* (416) 946-8915 (Office). *E-mail:* sylvia.ostry@utoronto.ca (Office). *Website:* www .utoronto.ca/cis/ostry.html (Office).

O'SULLEVAN, Sir Peter John, Kt, CBE; racing correspondent and commentator; b. 3 March 1918; s. of the late Col John Joseph O'Sullevan and Vera O'Sullevan; m. Patricia Duckworth 1951; ed Hawtreys, Charterhouse and Collège Alpin, Switzerland; attached to Chelsea Rescue Services 1939–45; then editorial work and MSS. reading with Bodley Head Publr; Racing Corresp., Press Asscn 1945–50, Daily Express 1950–86, Today 1986–87; race-broadcaster 1946–98 (from Australia, S. Africa, Italy, France, USA etc.); first regular TV (BBC) horse-racing commentator to work without a race-reader; commentator on first televised Grand National 1960, world's first televised electronic horse race from Atlas computer at London Univ. (transmitted by BBC) 1967, first horse race transmitted live via satellite from New York 1980; Dir Int. Racing Bureau 1979–93, Racing Post Ltd 1985–95; mem. Jockey Club 1986–; Chair. Osborne Studio Gallery 1999–; numerous awards for services to horse-racing include Derby Award for Racing Journalist of the Year (with the late Clive Graham) 1971, Racehorse Owner of the Year Award, Horserace Writers' Asscn 1974, Sport on TV Award, Daily Telegraph 1994, Services to Racing Award, Daily Star 1995, Lester's Award, Jockeys' Asscn 1996, Special Award, TV and Radio Industries Club 1998. *Publication:* Calling the Horses: A Racing Autobiography 1989. *Leisure interests:* travel, reading, art, food and wine. *Address:* 37 Cranmer Court, London, SW3 3HW, England. *Telephone:* (20) 7584-2781.

O'SULLIVAN, David, BA; Irish international civil servant; b. 1 March 1953, Dublin; m. Agnes O'Hare; one s. one d.; ed Trinity Coll. Dublin, Collège d'Europe, Bruges; Dept of Foreign Affairs, Dublin 1976–79; mem. staff External Relations, EC 1979–81, First Sec. (Econ. and Commercial), Del. of EC in Japan 1981–85; mem. Cabinet of Commr P. Sutherland 1985–89; Head of Unit (Educ. and Youth, Training) 1989–92; mem. Cabinet of Commr P. Flynn 1993–96, Deputy Head 1994–96; Dir Social Affairs, European Social Fund 1996–98, Social Affairs, Man. of Resources 1998–99; Dir-Gen. DGXXII 1999; Head of Cabinet of Pres. of Comm. 1999–2000; Sec.-Gen. European Comm. 2000–; European of the Year (Irish Council of the European Movt) 1999. *Leisure interests:* tennis, fitness, cinema, music. *Address:* European Commission, 1049 Brussels (Office); 87 rue Langeveld, 1180 Brussels, Belgium (Home). *Telephone:* (2) 295-09-48 (Office); (2) 374-98-12 (Home). *Fax:* (2) 299-32-29 (Office). *E-mail:* david.osullivan@cec.eu.int (Office). *Website:* www .cc.cec (Office).

O'SULLIVAN, John, OBE, BA; British editor and journalist; b. 25 April 1942, Liverpool; s. of Alfred M. O'Sullivan and Margaret (née Corner) O'Sullivan; ed London Univ.; Jr Tutor Swinton Conservative Coll. 1965–67, Sr Tutor 1967–69; Ed. Swinton Journal 1967–69; London Corresp. Irish Radio and TV 1970–72; Editorial Writer and parl. sketchwriter Daily Telegraph 1972–79; Ed. Policy Review 1979–83; Asst Ed. Daily Telegraph 1983–84; Columnist The Times 1984–86, Assoc. Ed. 1986–87; Editorial Page Ed. New York Post 1984–86; Ed. Nat. Review 1988–97, Ed.-at-Large 1998–; Columnist Sunday Telegraph 1988–; Dir of Studies Heritage Foundation 1979–83; Special Adviser to the Prime Minister 1987–88; Founder, Co-Chair. The New Atlantic Initiative 1996–; Conservative cand. for Parl. 1970; mem. Exec. Advisory Bd Margaret Thatcher Foundation, Advisory Council Social Affairs Unit, Hon.

Bd Civic Inst., Prague; Fellow Inst. of Politics, Harvard Univ. 1983. *Leisure interests:* reading, cinema, theatre, dining out. *Address:* National Review, 215 Lexington Avenue, New York, NY 10016, USA. *Telephone:* (212) 679-7330.

O'SULLIVAN, Sonia; Irish athlete; b. 28 Nov. 1969, Cóbh, Co. Cork; d. of John O'Sullivan and Mary O'Sullivan; partner Nick Bedeau; two d.; ed Villanova Univ., USA; gold medal 1500m, silver sedal 3000m, World Student Games 1991; holds seven nat. (Irish) records; set new world record (her first) in 2,000m TSB Challenge, Edinburgh 1994, new European record in 3,000m TSB Games London 1994, gold medal in 3,000m European Athletic Championships, Helsinki 1994; winner Grand Prix 3,000m, second overall 1993; silver medal, 1,500m, World Championships, Stuttgart 1993; gold medal, 5,000m, World Championships, Gothenburg 1995; gold medal World Cross Country Championships 4km, 8km 1998; gold medal European Championships 5,000m, 10,000m 1998; silver medal 5,000m 2000 Olympic Games; silver medal 5,000m, 10,000m European Championships 2002; Female Athlete of the Year 1995, Texaco Sports Star of the Year (Athletics) 2002. *Publication:* Running to Stand Still. *Leisure interests:* mountain biking, reading, films, cooking, playing with children. *Address:* c/o Kim McDonald, 201 High Street, Hampton Hill, Middx, TW12 1NL, England. *Telephone:* (20) 8941-9732. *Fax:* (20) 8979-8325. *E-mail:* sonia@osullivan.net (Home). *Website:* www.soniaosullivan.com.

OSWALD, Sir (John) Julian (Robertson), GCB, FRSA; British naval officer and company director; b. 11 Aug. 1933, Selkirk, Scotland; s. of George Oswald and Margaret Oswald (née Robertson); m. Veronica Thompson 1958; two s. three d.; ed Beaudesert Park, Minchinhampton, Britannia Royal Naval Coll., Royal Coll. of Defence Studies; joined RN 1947; served in HM ships Devonshire, Vanguard, Verulam, Newfoundland, Jewel, Victorious, Naiad; specialised in Gunnery 1960; commanded HMS Yarnton 1962–63, HMS Bacchante 1971–72, HMS Newcastle 1977–79; Ministry of Defence 1972–75; RN Presentation Team 1979–80; Capt. Britannia, RN Coll. 1980–82; Asst Chief of Defence Staff (Programmes) 1982–84, (Policy and Nuclear) 1985; Flag Officer, Third Flotilla, Commdr Anti-Submarine Warfare, Striking Fleet 1985–87; C-in-C, Fleet, Allied C-in-C, Channel and C-in-C, E Atlantic Area 1987–89; First Sea Lord and Chief of Naval Staff 1989–93; First and Prin. Aide-de-Camp to HM the Queen 1989–93; Chair. Aerosystems Int. 1995–; Dir Sema Group PLC 1993–2001 (Chair. 1999–2001), BAe Sema 1995–98, James Fisher & Sons 1993–2001, Marine and Gen. Mutual Life Assurance 1994–; Chair. Maritime Trust 1994–; Nat. Historic Ships Cttee 1995–, Ends of the Earth 1996–, Naval Review 1999–; Pres. Sea Cadet Asscn 1994–; Gov. Portsmouth Univ. 1994–99; Hon. DBA (CNAA) 1992, Hon. LLD (Portsmouth) 2000. *Publications:* The Royal Navy Today and Tomorrow 1993; defence and strategy articles in specialized journals, book reviews. *Leisure interests:* gliding, travel, stamp collecting, music, tennis. *Address:* Aerosystems International, Alvington, Yeovil, Somerset, BA22 8UZ; c/o Naval Secretary, Victory Building, HM Naval Base, Portsmouth, PO1 3LS, England. *Telephone:* (1935) 443116 (Office). *Fax:* (1935) 443169 (Home).

OSYKA, Sergey Grigorovich, CandJur; Ukrainian politician; b. 27 March 1955; m.; one s.; ed Kiev State Univ.; worked as researcher and teacher Kiev State Univ., then chief consultant Comm. of Foreign Affairs Verkhovna Rada (Parl.) of Ukraine 1991–92; adviser to Prime Minister Kuchma 1992–93; Deputy, First Deputy Minister of External Econ. Relations 1993–94, Minister of Foreign Econ. Relations and Trade 1994–99, Deputy Prime Minister Jan.–July 1995. *Address:* c/o Ministry of External Economic Relations, Lvivska pl. 8, 252053 Kiev, Ukraine. *Telephone:* (44) 226-27-33.

OTA, Seiichi; Japanese politician; b. 1946, Fukuoka Pref.; ed Keio Univ.; fmr Asst Prof. of Econs, Fukuoka Univ.; mem. LDP; mem. Shinshinto 1994–95; mem. for Fukuoka, House of Reps.; fmr Parl. Vice-Minister of Finance, Chair. House of Reps. Finance Cttee; Dir-Gen. Man. and Co-ordination Agency 1998–99. *Address:* c/o Management and Co-ordination Agency, 3-1-1, Kasumigaseki, Chiyoda-ku, Tokyo 100, Japan.

OTAKA, Tadaaki; Japanese conductor; b. 8 Nov. 1947, Kamakura; s. of Hisatada Otaka and Misaoko Otaka; m. Yukiko Otaka 1978; ed Toho Music School, Toho Music Acad., Vienna Acad.; began studying violin 1951; apptd. Chief Conductor Tokyo Philharmonic Orchestra 1971–, Conductor Laureate 1991–; Chief Conductor Sapporo Symphony 1981–86, Prin. Conductor 1998–; Prin. Conductor BBC Welsh Symphony Orchestra (now BBC Nat. Orchestra of Wales) 1987–95, Conductor Laureate 1996–; Chief Conductor Yomiuri Nippon Symphony Orchestra 1992–98; Music Adviser and Prin. Conductor Kioi Sinfonietta (Tokyo) 1995–; Dir Britten Pears Orchestra 1998–2001; has conducted BBC Proms, and orchestras including City of Birmingham Symphony, Royal Liverpool Philharmonic, Royal Scottish National, Bournemouth Symphony, BBC Symphony, London Philharmonic, London Philharmonic, Rotterdam Philharmonic, Bamberg Symphony and Strasbourg Philharmonic; Hon. CBE 1997; Hon. Fellowship (Welsh Coll. of Music and Drama) 1993; Dr hc (Univ. of Wales) 1993; 2nd Prize Min-On Conductors' Competition 1969, Suntory Music Award 1992, Elgar Medal 2000. *Music:* many recordings with BBC Now including works by Takemitsu and Franck, and Britten's Peter Grimes with Yomiuri Nippon. *Leisure interests:* fishing, tennis, cooking. *Address:* c/o Askonas Holt, Lonsdale Chambers, 27 Chancery Lane, London, WC2A 1PF, England. *Telephone:* (20) 7400-1700 (Office). *Fax:* (20) 7400-1799 (Office). *E-mail:* info@askonasholt.co.uk (Office).

OTČENÁŠEK, Karel, DTheol; Czech ecclesiastic; b. 13 April 1920, České Meziříčí nr Opočno; s. of František Otčenášek and Žofie Otčenášková; ed

Papal Lateran Univ., Rome; ordained priest 1945; secretly made bishop of Hradec Králové Diocese without approval from communist authorities 1950; sentenced to 13 years' imprisonment by communist regime 1954; pardoned 1962; labourer 1962–65; ecclesiastical admin. 1965–89; Bishop of Hradec Králové Diocese 1990–98, Archbishop ad pars. 1998–; Dr hc (Pedagogical Univ. Hradec Králové) 1996; Golden Medal of Honour, Charles Univ. Prague 1995; Scout Orders of Lily of Honour and of Silver Wolf; Order of T. G. Masaryk 1996; František Ulrich Prize, Hradec Králové 1998. *Leisure interests:* scouting, travelling, social service. *Address:* Biskupství Královéhradecké, Velké náměstí 35, 500 01 Hradec Králové, Czech Republic. *Telephone:* (49) 551-23-11. *Fax:* (49) 551-28 50.

OTCHAKOVSKY-LAURENS, Paul, LenD; French publisher; b. 10 Oct. 1944, Valreas, Vaucluse; s. of Zelman Otchakovsky and Odette Labaume; adopted s. of Berthe Laurens; m. Monique Pierret 1970; one s. one d.; ed Coll. and Lycée de Sablé sur Sarthe, Coll. Montalembert de Courbevoie, Coll. St Croix de Neuilly and Faculté de Droit, Paris; Reader, Editions Christian Bourgois 1969–70; Dir of Collection, Editions Flammarion 1970–77; Dir of Collections, then Dir of Dept Editions Hachette 1977–82; Pres. Dir-Gen. Editions P.O.L. 1983–; Commdr Ordre des Arts et des Lettres, Chevalier Légion d'honneur. *Address:* Editions P.O.L., 33 rue Saint-André-des-Arts, 75006 Paris, France. *Telephone:* 1-43-54-21-20. *E-mail:* otchakov@pol-editeur.fr (Office).

OTHMAN BIN WOK; Singaporean company director, fmr journalist and politician; b. 8 Oct. 1924, Singapore; m. Asnah Bte Suhaimi (now called Lina Binte Abdullah) 1975; one s. two d.; ed Telok Saga Malay School, Raffles Inst. and London School of Journalism; worked on Utusan Melayu as reporter, News Ed. then Deputy Ed. 1946–63; mem. People's Action Party 1954–; MP for Pasir Panjang Constituency 1963–81; Minister for Social Affairs 1963–77; Amb. to Indonesia (also accred to Papua New Guinea) 1977–80; Dir Overseas Investment Pte Ltd 1981–, Overseas Trustees Ltd 1982–, Overseas Investment Nominees Pte Ltd 1982–, Biohealth Int. (S) Pte Ltd 1983–99, Autologous Blood Bank (S) Pte Ltd 1987–99, Sembawang Eng Pte Ltd 1989–97, Utusan Melayu (S) Pte Ltd 1988–2001, Gainall Pte Ltd 1992–, Property Services Int. 1993–99, Hale Medical Clinic (Concourse) Pte Ltd 1995–, Bright Steel Pte Ltd 1996–, Genesis School for Special Educ. 1998–; The Hale Medical Group 2001–, Dimas (S) Pte Ltd 2001–, Ms Twilight Pte Ltd 2001–, Chair. Lion Asiapac Ltd 1996–, Mainstream Techs Pte Ltd 2000–, Mindsets Tech. Pte Ltd 2000–, d'Oz International Pte Ltd; Perm. mem. Presidential Council for Minority Rights 1981–; mem. Singapore Tourist Promotion Bd 1981–94, Sentosa Devt Corpn 1981–97 Singapore Professional Execs Co-operative Ltd 2000–, Ang Mo Kio Community Hosp. 2002; Hon. Consul Principality of Monaco 1996–99; Jasa Utama Star for Outstanding Services (Indonesia) 1980, Order of Nila Utama for Distinguished Service 1983. *Leisure interests:* reading, music, keep-fit exercise, golf. *Address:* Overseas Investment Private Ltd, 300 Beach Road, # 02-01, The Concourse, Singapore 199555 (Office); "Wisma Bahagia", 35 Carmen Street, Singapore 459756, Singapore (Home). *Telephone:* (65) 63929881. *Fax:* (65) 63929901 (Office).

OTMAN ASSED, Mohamed; Libyan politician; b. Oct. 1922, Fezzan; s. of Ahmed al-Badawi Assed and Fatima Nuweir; m. Lola Seif 1959; nine s.; ed Libyan religious and Arabic schools; Teacher 1942–43; in Liberation Movt; Head of Fezzan Del. in Legis. Ass. 1950–51; Rep. for Fezzan, UN Council for Libya 1951; Deputy 1952–64; Minister of Health, Fed. Govt 1951–58, of Econ. Affairs Feb.–Oct. 1960; Prime Minister 1960–63; pvt. business 1964–; emigrated to Morocco 1969; Order of Independence 1954, Order of Independence (Tunisia) 1957, Order of the Throne (Morocco) 1962, Mohamed Ali al-Sanoussi Medal 1964. *Address:* Villa Rissani, Route Oued Akrach, Souissi, Rabat, Morocco. *Telephone:* 75-16-25; 75-11-83.

O'TOOLE, Peter Seamus; Irish actor; b. 2 Aug. 1932, Connemara, Co. Galway; s. of Patrick Joseph O'Toole; m. 1st Siân Phillips (q.v.) 1960 (divorced 1979); two d.; m. 2nd Karen Brown 1983 (divorced); one s.; ed Royal Acad. of Dramatic Art; office boy, later reporter for Yorkshire Evening News; Nat. Service as signalman, Royal Navy; joined Bristol Old Vic Theatre Co., playing 73 parts 1955–58; West End debut in musical play Oh, my Papa 1957; toured England in play The Holiday; appeared in The Long, the Short and the Tall 1959; Stratford season 1960, playing Shylock, Petruchio and Thersites; stage appearances in Pictures in the Hallway 1962, Baal 1963, Ride a Cock Horse, Waiting for Godot 1971, Dead Eyed Dicks 1976, Present Laughter 1978; Bristol Old Vic Theatre Season 1973; inaugurated Britain's Nat. Theatre Co.; appeared with Abbey Theatre Co. in Waiting for Godot, Man and Superman 1976; fmr Assoc. Dir Old Vic Theatre Co.; Artistic Dir, North American Tour of Royal Alexandra Theatre Co. playing Present Laughter and Uncle Vanya 1978; Macbeth, Old Vic 1980; Man and Superman 1982–83, Pygmalion 1984, 1987, The Apple Cart 1986, Jeffrey Bernard is Unwell 1989, 1991, 1999, Our Song 1992; Commdr des Arts et des Lettres 1988; Outstanding Achievement Award 1999; Hon. Acad. Award for Lifetime Achievement 2003. *Films include:* Kidnapped 1959, The Day they Robbed the Bank of England 1959, Lawrence of Arabia 1960, Becket 1963, Lord Jim 1964, The Bible 1966, What's New Pussycat? 1965, How to Steal a Million 1966, Night of the Generals 1967, Great Catherine 1967, The Lion in Winter 1968, Goodbye Mr. Chips 1969, Brotherly Love 1970, Country Dance 1970, Murphy's War 1971, Under Milk Wood 1972, The Ruling Class 1972, Man of La Mancha 1972, Rosebud 1974, Man Friday 1975, Foxtrot 1975, Rogue Male (TV) 1976, Caligula 1977, Power Play 1978, Stuntman 1978, Zulu Dawn 1978, Masada (TV) 1981, The Antagonists 1981, My Favourite Year 1981, Svengali (TV) 1982, Supergirl

1984, Banshee (TV) 1986, Club Paradise 1986, The Last Emperor 1986, High Spirits 1988, On a Moonlit Night 1989, The Dark Angel (TV) 1989, Creator 1990, King Ralph 1990, Wings of Fame 1991, Rebecca's Daughters 1992, Our Song 1992, Civies (TV) 1992, Fairytale: the True Story 1997, Coming Home (TV) 1998. *Publications:* Loitering with Intent 1992, Loitering with Intent 2: The Apprentice 1996. *Address:* c/o William Morris Agency, Stratton House, Stratton Street, London, W1X 5FE; Guyon House, Hampstead High Street, London, NW3, England.

O'TOOLE, Shane, BArch, FRIAI, RIBA; Irish architect and critic; b. 5 July 1955, Dublin; s. of James Patrick O'Toole and Caroline Louise O'Toole (née Hannan); m. Maeve O'Neill 1984; one s. one d.; ed Franciscan Coll., Gormanston, Co. Meath, Univ. Coll. Dublin; Lynch O'Toole Walsh Architects, Dublin 1979–86; Project Man. Energy Research Group, Univ. Coll. Dublin (UCD) 1986–92; Co-Founder and Dir urban design consortium Group 91 Architects 1990–99; Shane O'Toole Architects 1991–97; Co. Architect Tegral Bldg Products Ltd 1994–; architecture critic, The Sunday Times, London and Dublin 1999–; Visiting Lecturer UCD 1992–96; Visiting Tutor Univ. of Edin. 1993–95, 2001; External Examiner Dublin Inst. of Tech. 2001; Pres. Architectural Assen of Ireland 1982–83; Vice-Pres. Royal Inst. of the Architects of Ireland 1988, 1997; founder and convenor Docomomo Ireland 1990–; Adviser to Mies van der Rohe Award for European Architecture 1992–; Adviser to Veronica Rudge Green Prize in Urban Design, (Harvard Prize in Urbanism) Harvard Univ. Grad. School of Design 2000–; Adviser to Nation Bldg (TV series on architecture in Ireland 1922–2000) 2000; mem. Editorial Bd A+D Architecture and Design, Stuttgart 1995–, and other journals; Hon. mem. Architectural Assen of Ireland 1995–; Grand Prix Cracow Biennale 1989, Irish Bldg of the Year Award 1996, Architectural Assen of Ireland Downes Medal 1996, European Architectural Award (RIBA) 1997, Int. Union of Architects Sir Patrick Abercrombie Prize for Town Planning and Territorial Devt 2002, and other prizes and awards. *Achievements:* Co-Dir Architectural Framework Plan for Regeneration of Temple Bar, Dublin 1992–2000; Co-Designer The Ark, Europe's first cultural centre for children 1992–95; represented in architecture exhbns including 40 Under 40: Emerging British Architects, UK and USA 1988–89, The New Breed, Sydney 1988, Making a Modern Street, Zurich 1991, 20 Young Architects of the World, London 1993; cr. exhbn, The Pillar Project, Dublin 1988, Tales from Two Cities: Emerging Architects in Dublin and Edinburgh (Edin. Dublin, Berlin, London) 1994. *Publications:* Collaboration: The Pillar Project 1988, Tales from Two Cities 1994; (Co-Ed.) Kevin Roche Architect 1983, Aldo Rossi 1983, Making a Modern Street 1991. *Leisure interests:* family, football, films, food, good buildings, a glass of wine. *Address:* 68 Irishtown Road, Dublin 4, Ireland (Home). *Telephone:* (1) 6609843 (Home). *E-mail:* shane_otoole@hotmail.com (Home).

OTSASON, Rein, DEconSc; Estonian economist; b. 24 May 1931, Tartu; s. of August Otsason and Marta Otsason; m. Valentina Otsason 1979; one s.; Dir Inst. of Econ., Acad. of Sciences of Estonia; Deputy Chair. Council of Ministers of Estonian SSR (now Estonia) 1988–89, State Planning Cttee 1988–89; Pres. Bank of Estonia 1989–91, Credit Bank of Estonia 1992–. *Publications:* works on monetary policy and currency reforms. *Address:* Eesti Krediidipank, Narva Mnt. 4, 15014 Tallinn, Estonia. *Telephone:* 669-0900 (Office). *Fax:* 661-6037 (Office). *E-mail:* reino@ekp.ee (Office).

OTTEWILL, Ronald Harry, OBE, MA, PhD, FRS; British professor emeritus of physical chemistry; b. 8 Feb. 1927, Southall, Middx; s. of Harry A. Ottewill and Violet D. Ottewill (née Bucklee); m. Ingrid G. Roe 1952; one s. one d.; ed Southall County School, Queen Mary Coll., London and Fitzwilliam Coll., Cambridge; Asst Lecturer, Queen Elizabeth Coll., London 1951–52; Nuffield Fellowship, Dept of Colloid Science, Univ. of Cambridge 1952–55, Sr Asst in Research 1955–58, Asst Dir of Research 1958–63; Lecturer in Physical Chem., Univ. of Bristol 1964–66, Reader in Colloid Science 1966–71, Prof. of Colloid Science 1971–82, Leverhulme Prof. of Physical Chem. 1982–92, Emer. Prof. of Physical Chem. 1992–, Dean, Faculty of Science 1988–90, Head of School of Chem. 1990–92; Sr Research Fellow Univ. of Bristol 1996–; mem. NATO Research Grants Cttee 1980–84, Chair. 1984; mem. Science Bd SERC 1982–85, Chair. Neutron Beam Cttee 1982–85; mem. Scientific Council Inst. Laue Langevin 1981–86; mem. Council Faraday Soc. (now Faraday Div. of Royal Soc. of Chem.) 1981–99, Hon. Treas. 1985–89, Vice-Pres. 1986–89, 1991–99, Pres. 1989–91; Monsanto Lecturer 1979, Alexander Lecturer, Royal Australian Chem. Inst. 1982; Liversidge Lecturer, Royal Soc. of Chem. 1985–86; Founders Lecturer SCI 1985; Xerox Lecturer, Canada 1987; Rideal Lecture, Royal Soc. of Chem. 1990, Dunning Lecture, Univ. of Bristol 1992; Langmuir Lecturer, ACS 1988; Orica Lecture, Melbourne Univ. 1998; Chem. Soc. Medal 1974, Wolfgang Ostwald Prize, Kolloid Gesellschaft 1979, Bude Medal, Collège de France 1981, Liversidge Medal, Royal Soc. of Chem. 1985, Presidential Medal, Faraday Div. 1991, Faraday Soc. C.I.S.G. Medal 1993. *Publications:* over 300 papers in scientific journals; ed. 10 books. *Leisure interests:* gardening, walking, music. *Address:* School of Chemistry, Cantock's Close, University of Bristol, Bristol, BS8 1TS (Office); The Glen House, Holt Close, Wickham, Hants., PO17 5EY, England (Home). *Telephone:* (117) 928-7647 (Office); (1329) 834745 (Home). *Fax:* (1329) 834745 (Office); (117) 925-1295 (Home). *E-mail:* ron.ottewill@bris.ac.uk (Office).

OTTEY, Merlene, BA; Jamaican athlete; b. 10 May 1960, Pondside, Cold Springs; d. of Hubert and Joan Ottey; m. Nathaniel Page 1984; ed Nebraska Univ., USA; set 200m. indoor record (21.87) 1993; winner 100m. finals 57 consecutive times from Sept. 1987 to Aug. 1991; winner 200m. finals 36 consecutive times from May 1989 to Aug. 1991; winner 7 Olympic medals; tested positive for nandrolone 1999, one-year ban lifted after Int. Assen of Athletics Feds. (IAAF) ruled that Swiss lab. had mishandled sample; co-owner TMG Co., Slovenia; Roving Amb. for Jamaica; granted citizenship of Slovenia 2002; IAAF Patron for the Year of Women in Athletics 1998. *Publication:* Merlene Ottey: Unyielding Spirit (autobiog.). *E-mail:* otteyfanclub@hotmail .com.

OTTO, Michael; German business executive; b. 12 April 1943; Chair. Bd Dirs. Otto Versand, Hamburg 1981– (Dir 1971–); Chair. Bd Dirs. Spiegel Inc., Chicago 1982–; Binding Prize for Protection of Nature and Environment 1996, Alexander-Rüstow-Plakette 1998. *Address:* Wandsbeker Str. 3–7, 22179 Hamburg, Germany.

OTUNBAYEVA, Rosa Isakovna, CPhilSc; Kyrgyzstan politician and diplomatist; b. 23 Aug. 1950; m.; one s. one d.; ed Moscow Univ.; Sr teacher, Head of Chair Kyrgyz Univ. 1975–81; Second Sec. Regional CP Cttee in Frunze, Sec. City CP Cttee 1979–86; Vice-Chair. Council of Ministers, Minister of Foreign Affairs of Kyrgyz SSR 1986–89; Exec. Sec. USSR Comm. on UNESCO Problems 1989–90, Chair. 1990–91; Amb. of USSR to Malaysia 1991–92; Vice-Prime Minister and Minister of Foreign Affairs of Repub. of Kyrgyzstan Feb.–May 1992; Amb. of Kyrgyzstan to USA 1992–94 (also Accred to Canada); Minister of Foreign Affairs 1994–97; Amb. to UK 1997–. *Address:* Embassy of Kyrgyzstan, 119 Crawford Street, London, W1H 1AF, England. *Telephone:* (20) 7935-1462. *Fax:* (20) 7935-7449.

OTUNGA, HE Cardinal Maurice Michael; Kenyan ecclesiastic; b. Jan. 1923, Chebukwa; ordained priest 1950; consecrated titular Bishop of Tacape 1957; Bishop of Kisii 1961; titular Archbishop of Bomarzo 1969; Archbishop of Nairobi 1971; cr. Cardinal by Pope Paul VI 1973; Primate of Kenya 1983–; Dir Castrense for Kenya. *Address:* Archbishop's House, P.O. Box 14231, Nairobi, Kenya. *Telephone:* (2) 441919. *Fax:* (2) 471320.

OTUNNU, Olara; Ugandan diplomatist and United Nations official; b. Sept. 1950, Mucwini, northern Uganda; guardian of six c.; ed Makerere Univ. (Uganda), Univ. of Oxford (England), Harvard Law School (USA); practised law in USA; Asst Prof. of Law, Albany Law School, USA; participated in resistance activities against regime of Idi Amin; Perm. Rep. to UN 1980–85, Pres. Security Council 1981, Vice-Pres. Gen. Ass. 1982–83; Minister of Foreign Affairs 1985–86; Pres. Int. Peace Acad. 1990–97; Special Rep. of UN Sec.-Gen. for Children and Armed Conflict Aug. 1997; UN Under-Sec.-Gen. for Children and Armed Conflict 1998–. *Address:* United Nations, United Nations Plaza, New York, NY 10017, USA (Office). *Telephone:* (212) 963-1234 (Office). *Fax:* (212) 963-4879 (Office).

OUAIDOU GUELENGDOUKSIA, Nassour; Chadian politician; fmrly Sec.-Gen. in Office of the Pres.; Prime Minister of Chad 1997–99. *Address:* c/o Office of the Prime Minister, N'Djamena, Chad.

OUANE, Moctar, MA; Malian diplomatist; b. 11 Oct. 1955, Bidi; m.; two c.; ed Univ. of Dakar, Senegal; with Gen. Secr. of Govt 1982–86, Chief Div. of Int. Agreements and Conventions, Foreign Ministry March–June 1986, Diplomatic Counsellor, Office of the Prime Minister 1986–88, Prin. Pvt. Sec. to Minister Sec.-Gen., Office of the Pres. and Diplomatic Counsellor to the Pres. 1988–91; mem. del. to UN Gen. Ass. 1988–91, 1993, mediation del., Senegal–Mauritania and Liberian conflicts; Diplomatic Counsellor, Office of the Head of State 1991–92, Office of the Prime Minister June–Oct. 1992, Tech. Counsellor, Political and Diplomatic Affairs, Foreign Ministry 1994–95; Perm. Rep. to the UN 1995–; f. and Pres. Democracy and Repub. Club, Mali. *Address:* Permanent Mission of Mali to the United Nations, 111 East 69th Street, New York, NY 10021, USA (Office). *Telephone:* (212) 737-4150 (Office). *Fax:* (212) 472-3778 (Office). *E-mail:* mali@un.int (Office).

OUATTARA, Alassane Dramane, DSc; Côte d'Ivoirian politician and financial official; b. 1 Jan. 1942, Dimbokro; s. of Dramane Ouattara and Nabintou Cissé; m.; four c.; ed Drexel Inst. of Tech., Phila and Univ. of Pennsylvania, USA; Economist, IMF 1968–73; Sr Staff mem. in charge of missions Banque Centrale des Etats de l'Afrique de l'Ouest (BCEAO) 1973–75, Special Adviser to the Gov. and Dir of Research 1975–82, Vice-Gov. 1983–84, Gov. 1988–90; Dir African Dept, IMF 1984–88, Counsellor to Man. Dir 1987–88; Prime Minister of Côte d'Ivoire and Minister of Economy and Finance 1990–93; Deputy Man. Dir IMF 1994–99; Pres. UNCTAD 1979–80; mem. Bd Dirs, Global Econ. Action Inst.; Expert Adviser Comm. on Transnat.Corpns; Hon. Gov. BCEAO; Pres. Rassemblement des républicains (RDR) 1999–; in exile in Gabon; being also a citizen of Burkina Faso he was barred from standing in 2000 presidential elections of Côte d'Ivoire; granted Côte d'Ivorian citizenship 2002; Commdr Ordre du Lion du Sénégal, Ordre du Mono du Togo, Ordre Nat. du Niger, Grand Officier Ordre Nat. de Côte d'Ivoire. *Address:* Rassemblement des républicains (RDR), 8 rue Lepic, Cocody, 06 BP 1440, Abidjan, Côte d'Ivoire (Office). *Telephone:* 22-44-33-51 (Office). *E-mail:* rdrci@rdrci.org (Office). *Website:* www.rdrci.org (Office); www.ado.ci (Home).

OUCHI, Tsutomu, DEcon; Japanese professor of economics; b. 19 June 1918, Tokyo; s. of Hyoe Ouchi; m. Setsuko Otsuka 1944; one s. one d.; ed The Daiichi Kotogakko and Tokyo Imperial Univ.; researcher Japan Inst. of Agric. 1942–46; Assoc. Prof. Univ. of Tokyo 1947–60, Prof. 1960–79, Prof. Emer. 1979–; Prof. Shinshu Univ. 1979–84, Prof. Emer. 1984–; Prof. Daito Bunka Univ. 1987–91; Dean Faculty of Econs, Univ. of Tokyo 1968–69; Vice-Pres. Univ. of Tokyo 1972–73; Dir Nat. Fed. of Univ. Co-operative Assens 1988–99; Dir Nat. Fed. of Co-operatives of Aged People of Japan 2001–; Chair. Central

Cttee for Security of Employment 1976–88, Employment Cttee, Ministry of Labour 1988–96; mem. Japan Acad. 1981–; Mainichi Press Prize, Nasu Prize, Nihon Keizai Press Prize. *Publications:* Agricultural Crisis 1954, American Agriculture 1965, State Monopolistic Capitalism 1970, American Agriculture in the 1960's 1975, Japanese Agriculture 1978, Methodology of Economics 1980, Principles of Economics (2 vols) 1981–82, Imperialism (2 vols) 1984–85, World Economy 1991, Japanese Economy 2000. *Leisure interests:* skiing, trekking. *Address:* 26-19 Hyakunin-cho II, Shinjuku-ku, Tokyo 169 0073, Japan. *Telephone:* (3) 3371-3760.

OUEDDEI, Goukouni; Chadian politician; b. 1944, Zouar; formed the Second Army of the Front de Libération Nationale du Tchad (FROLINAT) 1972; head of Northern Armed Forces Command Council 1977–; Chair. Revolutionary Cttee, Popular Armed Forces of FROLINAT 1978–84; Chair. Provisional State Council of Chad after Kano peace agreement March–April 1979, in charge of Information; Minister of State for the Interior in Shawa Govt April–Sept. 1979; Pres. of Chad and Head of State (Gouvernement d'union nationale de transition-GUNT) 1979–82 (deposed); Pres. GUNT forces in N Chad 1982–86, Pres. Conseil suprême de la Révolution 1985–86; leader FROLINAT.

OUEDRAOGO, Ablassé; Burkinabè international organization official; b. 30 June 1953, Burkina Faso; Deputy Resident Rep. of UNDP, Kinshasa 1991–93; Head of Regional Office for E Africa of UN Sudano-Sahélienne Office (also Accred to OAU, ECA, UNEP) 1993–94; Minister of Foreign Affairs 1994–99; Special Adviser to Pres. of Burkina Faso Feb. 1999–; Jt Deputy Dir-Gen. World Trade Org. 1999–2000; Officer of Nat. Order of Burkina Faso 1997, Officer of Equatorial Order of Gabon 2000. *Publications:* Réflexions sur la crise industrielle en France 1979, Les firmes multinationales et l'indus-trialisation des pays en voie de développement 1981. *Address:* 10 ch. Colladon, 1209 Geneva, Switzerland.

OUÉDRAOGO, Gérard Kango; Burkinabè politician; b. 19 Sept. 1925, Ouahigouya; s. of Jean Ouédraogo and Christine Ouédraogo; m. 1947; Rep. to French West African Fed. 1952; Deputy to French Nat. Ass. 1956–59; co-founder Mouvement Démocratique Voltaïque; mem. Parl. 1957–65; Minister of Finance 1958–59; Amb. to UK 1961–66; Adviser, Ministry of Foreign Affairs; Pres. Union Démocratique Voltaïque 1970–74, now Commr; Prime Minister 1971–74; Pres. Nat. Ass. 1978–80; Jr Pres. ACP/EEC Lomé Convention 1970–80; fmr Leader Rassemblement Démocratique Africain (RDA); Deputy and Pres. Parl. Group RDA, Assemblée des Députés du Peuple; Grand Officier Ordre Nat. Burkina Faso; Grand Officier du Mérite Français; Grand Officier Légion d'honneur; several other decorations. *Address:* ADF-RDA, 01 BP 2061, Ouagadougou, Burkina Faso. *Telephone:* 31-15-15.

OUEDRAOGO, Idrissa; Burkinabè film director; ed film school in Burkina Faso; Grand Jury Prize, Cannes Film Festival 1990; Etalon de Yenenga (Grand Prix) for Tilaï, Pan-African Film Festival (Fespaco), Ouagadougou 1991. *Films include:* Yaaba, Tilaï, Samba Traore 1993, Lumiè et Compagnie 1995, Kini and Adams 1997. *Address:* FEPACI, 01 B.P. 2524, Ouagadougou, Burkina Faso.

OUEDRAOGO, Kadré Désiré; Burkinabè politician; fmr Gov. of Cen. Bank of West African States; Prime Minister of Burkina Faso 1996–2000; currently Amb. to the EU (also Belgium, Luxembourg, Netherlands and UK). *Address:* 16 Place Guy d'Arezzo – 1180 Brussels (Office); Mission of Burkina Faso to the European Union, 16 place Guy d'Arezzo, 1180 Brussels, Belgium. *Telephone:* (322) 3459912 (Office). *Fax:* (322) 3450612 (Office). *E-mail:* ambassade .burkina@skynet.be.

OUEDRAOGO, Pathe; Burkinabè designer; cr. clothing line Pathe'O; boutiques in Ivory Coast, Mali, Burkina Faso, Cameroon; clients include Nelson Mandela, Miriam Makeba, Laurent Gbagbo.

OUÉDRAOGO, Youssouf; Burkinabè politician; b. 1942; State Minister and Minister of Foreign Affairs 2000–. *Address:* Ministry of Foreign Affairs, 03 B.P. 7038, Ouagadougou 03, Burkina Faso (Office). *Telephone:* 32-47-34 (Office). *Fax:* 30-87-92 (Office). *E-mail:* mamadou.kone@mae.gov.bf (Office). *Website:* www.mae.gov.bf/newdefault.htm (Office).

OUELLET, Hon. André, PC, BA, LLL; Canadian fmr politician and lawyer; b. 6 April 1939, St-Pascal, Québec; s. of Dr. Albert Ouellet and Rita Turgeon; m. Edith Pagé 1965; two s. two d.; ed Pensionnat St-Louis de Gonzague, Québec Seminary, Ottawa and Sherbrooke Univs; MP for Papineau 1967–93; Parl. Sec. to Minister for External Affairs 1970, to Minister for Nat. Health and Welfare 1971; Postmaster Gen. 1972–74; Minister for Consumer and Corp. Affairs 1974–76, 1980–84, for Urban Affairs 1976–79, for Public Works 1978–79, for Canada Post Corpn 1980–83, for Labour 1983, for Regional Econ. Devt 1983–84; Pres. Privy Council 1984; Govt Leader of Commons 1984; Opposition Transport Critic 1984; Opposition External Affairs Critic 1987; Opposition Critic for Fed. Provincial Relations 1990; Minister for Foreign Affairs 1993–96; Chair. Canada Post Corpn 1996–99, Pres. and CEO 1999–. *Leisure interests:* tennis, swimming, squash, skiing, reading and collecting works of art. *Address:* Canada Post Corporation, 2701 Riverside Drive, Suite N1250, Ottawa, Ont., K1A 0B1, Canada.

OUMAROU, Mamane; Niger politician; m.; Prime Minister of Niger 1988–90; mem. Mouvement Nat. de la société de développement (MNSD). *Address:* c/o Office of the Prime Minister, Niamey, Niger.

OURISSON, Guy, DrSc, PhD; French chemist; b. 26 March 1926, Boulogne-sur-Seine; s. of Jacques Ourisson and Colette Ourisson (née de Bosredon); m. 1st Paula Baylis 1950 (deceased 1958); m. 2nd Nicole Heiligenstein 1959 (divorced); one s. two d. from previous m.; ed Ecole Normale Supérieure, Paris, Harvard Univ.; Maître de Conférences, Univ. Louis Pasteur, Strasbourg 1955–58, Prof. of Chem. 1958–, Pres. of Univ. Louis Pasteur 1971–75; Dir of Univ. Studies, Ministry of Educ. Nat. 1981–82; Dir Inst. of Chem. of Natural Products, CNRS, Gif/Yvette 1984–89; Chair. Scientific Council, Rhône-Poulenc 1988–92, Compagnie Générale des Eaux 1998–2000; Pres. of many scientific cttees. in France; Chair. Publications Cttee, IUPAC 1973–77, Sec.-Gen. 1975–83; Regional Ed. Tetrahedron Letters 1965–; Vice-Pres. Acad. of Sciences 1997–99, Pres. 1999–2001; Pres. Fondation Alfred Kastler; mem. Acad. Leopoldina (Halle), European Acad. of Arts and Sciences, American Acad. of Arts and Sciences, Danish, Swedish, Indian, Rheinland-Westphalia, Serbian and French Acads. of Sciences; Hon. mem. Chemical Socs. of Belgium, UK, Switzerland; awards from Chemical Socs of France, Fed. Repub. of Germany, Belgium, UK, USA; Commdr, Légion d'honneur; Commdr, Ordre nat. du Mérite; Commdr des Palmes académiques; Order of Sacred Treasure (Japan). *Publications:* over 400 on chem. and on ethics of science. *Address:* Centre de Neurochimie, 5 rue Blaise Pascal, 67084 Strasbourg (Office); 10 rue Geiler, 67000 Strasbourg, France (Home). *Telephone:* (3) 88-60-05-13; (3) 88-11-04-21 (Home). *Fax:* (3) 88-60-76-20; (3) 88-60-76-20 (Office). *E-mail:* ourisson@chimie.u-strasbg.fr (Office).

OUSELEY, Baron Herman (George), (cr. Life Peer 2001), Kt; British civil servant and race relations adviser; various public service posts 1963–86; Race Relations Adviser Lambeth Borough Council 1979–81, GLC 1981–84; Dir of Educ. ILEA 1986–88, Chief Exec. 1988–90; Chief Exec. London Borough of Lambeth 1990–93; Chair. Comm. for Racial Equality 1993–2000; Man. Dir Different Realities Partnership Ltd 2000–; Dir Focus Consultancy Ltd 2000–; mem. Council Policy Studies Inst. 1988–, Inst. of Race Relations 1990–, Inst. of Educ., Univ. of London 1995–; mem. Advisory Council Prince's Youth Business Trust 1993–; Chair. Uniting Britain Charitable Trust 1997–, Presentation Educ. and Employment Charitable Trust 1997–; Patron Presentation Housing Asscn 1990–; Dr. hc (Edin.) 1999. *Publications:* The System 1981, pamphlets and articles on local Govt, public services, employment, training and race equality issues. *Address:* Different Realities Partnership, 254 High Street, Croydon, Surrey, CR0 1NF, England (Office).

OUSMAN, Ahmad, LLB, LLM; Moroccan politician and diplomatist; b. 3 Jan. 1930, Oujda; m. HRH Princess Lalla Nezha (sister of King Hassan II) 1965; one s.; ed Royal High School, Rabat, Univ. of Rabat and Univ. of Bordeaux, France; Head of the Legal Section, Royal Cabinet 1956; joined Ministry of Foreign Affairs 1957; Sec.-Gen. Ministry of Nat. Defence 1959–61; Amb. to Fed. Repub. of Germany 1961–62; Under Sec.-of-State for Industry and Mines 1963–64; Pres. and Gen. Man. Moroccan Navigation Co. 1964–67; Amb. to USA, Canada and Mexico 1967–70; Minister of Admin. Affairs 1970–71; Dir of Royal Cabinet 1971–72; Prime Minister 1972–79; Parl. Rep. for Oujda 1977–; Leader Rassemblement nat. des indépendants 1978–; mem. Nat. Defence Council 1979–; Minister of State 1983; Pres. Chamber of Reps. 1984; participated in UN sessions 1957, 1958, 1960, 1961, 1968, Conf. on Maritime law 1958, Conf. of the League of Arab States 1961. *Leisure interests:* bridge, sports, reading, swimming. *Address:* Rassemblement national des indépendants, 6 rue Laos, avenue Hassan II, Rabat, Morocco. *Telephone:* (3) 7721420. *Fax:* (3) 7733824.

OUSMANE, Sembene; Senegalese writer and film-maker; b. 1 Jan. 1923, Ziguinchor, Casamance region; plumber, bricklayer, apprentice mechanic; served in Europe in World War II; docker in Marseille; studied film production in USSR under Marc Donski; Founder Ed. first Wolof language monthly, Kaddu; first prize for novelists at World Festival of Negro Arts, Dakar 1966; numerous int. awards. *Films:* Borom Sarret 1963, niaye 1964, La noire de ... 1966, Mandabi 1968, Taaw 1971, Emitai 1971, Xala 1974, Ceddo 1977, Camp de Thiaroye 1988 (Jury Prize, Venice), Guelwaar 1992. *Publications:* novels: Le docker noir 1956, O pays mon beau peuple 1957, Les bouts de bois de Dieu 1960, Voltaïque 1962, L'harmattan 1964, Vehi-Ciosane suivi du mandat 1966, Xala 1974, Fat Ndiay Diop 1976, Dernier de l'empire 1979, Niiwam 1987, God's Bits of Wood 1995, Guelwaar 1996. *Address:* P.O. Box 8087, Yoff, Dakar, Senegal. *Telephone:* 823-51-66. *Fax:* 823-51-66.

OUSSET, Cécile; French pianist; b. 23 Jan. 1936, Tarbes; ed Paris Conservatoire; French début with Orchestre de Paris; British début, Edin. Festival 1980; U.S. début with LA Philharmonic 1984; first recital at Théâtre des Champs-Elysées 1987–88; played Debussy's Preludes on BBC TV 1988; prizewinner, Van Cliburn, Queen Elisabeth of Belgium, Busoni and Marguerite Long-Jacques Thibaud competitions; Grand Prix du Disque for recording of Brahms 2nd Piano Concerto. *Recordings include:* concertos by Rachmaninov, Liszt, Saint-Saëns, Ravel, Grieg and Mendelssohn and recitals of Chopin, Debussy and Liszt. *Address:* c/o Intermusica Artists' Management, 16 Duncan Terrace, London, N1 8B7, England (Office).

OUTRAM, Dorinda, MA, PhD; British historian; b. 11 Dec. 1949, Leicester; d. of Albert Ernest Outram and Rosemary Elenor Collins; m. 1976 (divorced 1980); one s.; ed Univ. of Cambridge; Research Fellowship British Acad. 1974, Univ. of Reading 1975; Lectureship and Research Fellowships, Univ. of London 1977–81; Asst Prof. Univ. of Montreal 1981–82; Research Fellowship, Girton Coll., Cambridge 1982–84; Lecturer in Modern History, Univ. Coll., Cork 1984–98; Clark Prof. of History, Univ. of Rochester, NY 1998–; Visiting

Prof. Griffith Univ., Australia 1990; Landon Clay Visiting Assoc. Prof. Harvard Univ. 1991–92; Editorial Dir, Comité int. pour l'édition de la correspondance de Georges Cuvier 1983–; mem. Editorial panel, Dictionary of Irish Biography 1984–; Ed. Bulletin of the Irish Asscn for Research in Women's History 1987–88; Trustee, British Soc. for History of Science; Hon. Sec. Irish Nat. Cttee for Research in Women's History 1988–; Vellacott Historical Essay Prize, Cambridge 1971; Royal Soc. of London Research Award 1982; CNRS Research Award, Paris 1982. *Publications:* Science, Vocation and Authority in Post-Revolutionary France; Georges Cuvier 1984, Uneasy Careers and Intimate Lives: Women in Science 1987, The Body and the French Revolution 1989, The Enlightenment 1994; numerous articles. *Leisure interests:* walking, talking, learning languages, visiting France, Italy and Germany. *Address:* Department of History, University of Rochester, Rochester, NY 14627, USA.

OUVRIEU, Jean-Bernard; French diplomatist; b. 13 March 1939; m. Arabella Cruse 1968; one s. two d.; ed Ecole Nat. d'Admin.; Head of Mission, Office of Prime Minister 1968–69; served Perm. Mission to European Communities, Brussels 1971–74, Baghdad 1975–77, Washington 1977–79; Deputy Dir, Office of Minister of Foreign Affairs 1979–80; Rep. to Governing Council of IAEA 1981–85; Amb. to Repub. of Korea 1985–87; Dir of Econ. and Financial Affairs, Ministry of Foreign Affairs 1987–89; Amb. to Brazil 1989–93, to Japan 1993–98; Personal Rep. of Minister of Defence 1998–2002; Officier, Légion d'honneur, Officier, Ordre nat. du Mérite. *Address:* c/o Ministry of Defence, 14 rue St.-Dominique, 00450 Armées; 23 Square des Peupliers, 75013 Paris, France.

OUYAHIA, Ahmed; Algerian politician and diplomatist; b. 1953, Kabylie; fmr Sec. of State for Co-operation and Maghreb Affairs; Prime Minister of Algeria 1996–98, 2003–; Minister of Justice –2002; Minister of State, Personal Rep. of the Pres. of the Repub. 2002–03; Sec.-Gen. Rassemblement nat. démocratique. *Address:* Office of the Prime Minister, rue Docteur Saâdane, Algiers, Algeria (Office). *Telephone:* (21) 73-23-40 (Office). *Fax:* (21) 71-79-27 (Office).

OUYANG ZIYUAN, MSc; Chinese scientist; b. Oct. 1935, Jian City, Jiangxi Prov.; ed Beijing Coll. of Geology, Inst. of Geology, Beijing, Univ. of Science and Tech., Beijing, Inst. of Atomic Energy; Asst Prof. Inst. of Geology Chinese Acad. of Sciences 1960–66, Assoc. Prof. Inst. of Geochem. 1966–78, Prof., Vice-Dir then Dir 1978–94, Prof. 1994–, Dir Bureau of Resources and Environmental Sciences 1991–93; Vice-Pres. People's Congress of Guizhou Prov. 1993–; Chair. Asscn for Science and Tech. Guizhou Prov. 1993–; Pres. Chinese Soc. of Mineralogy, Petrology and Geochem. 1994–; Guest Prof. Beijing, Nanjing and other univs. 1993–; Standing Vice-Pres. Chinese Soc. of Mineralogy, Petrology and Geochem. 1976–94; Vice-Pres. Chinese Soc. of Space Sciences; Chair. Cttee of Space Chem. and Space Geology, Assoc. Ed.-in-Chief Journal of Space Science, Chinese Journal of Geochemistry 1980–; Ed.-in-Chief Journal of Environmental Science, Journal of Geology-Geochemistry, Bulletin of Mineralogy, Petrology and Geochemistry 1985–; Vice-Pres. Chinese Soc. of Geology 1992–96; Academician Chinese Acad. of Sciences 1991–; First-Class Award of Natural Science Prize, Chinese Acad. of Sciences Nat. Science Conf. Prize. *Publications:* Progress of Selenology Research, Space Chemistry, Progress of Geology and Geochemistry during the 1980s, Progress of Mineralogy, Petrology and Geochemistry Research in China, Riddle of Dinosaur Depopulation, Formation and Evolution of the Planets and the Earth. *Leisure interests:* music, literature, tourism, photography. *Address:* Chinese Society for Mineralogy, Petrology and Geochemistry, 73 Guanshui Road, Guiyang 550002, Guizhou Province (Office); Institute of Geochemistry, China Academy of Sciences, Guiyang City, Guizhou Province, People's Republic of China. *Telephone:* (851) 5895328 (Office); (851) 5891338 (Office). *Fax:* (851) 5891923 (Office); (851) 5891379 (Home). *E-mail:* ouyangziyuan@ ms.gyig.ac.cn (Home); kydhtb@263.net (Home). *Website:* www.gyig.ac.cn (Office).

OVCHINIKOV, Vladimir Pavlovich; Russian pianist; b. 1 Jan. 1958, Beleby, Urals; ed pvtly. under Anna Artobolevskaya and Moscow Conservatoire (under Alexey Nasedkin); London debut, Barbican Hall 1987; has since given recitals in UK, Europe, USA, Canada and Japan and appeared with BBC Symphony, Royal Liverpool Philharmonic, Netherlands Philharmonic, Moscow Philharmonic and other maj. orchestras; lecturer, Keyboard Studies, Royal Northern Coll. of Music 1994–; Silver Medal (jtly. with Peter Donohoe), Moscow Tchaikovsky Competition 1982; First Prize, Leeds Int. Piano Competition 1987. *Address:* c/o Manygate Management, 13 Cotswold Mews, 30 Battersea Square, London, SW11 3RA, England. *Telephone:* (20) 7223-7265. *Fax:* (20) 7585-2830.

OVCHINNIKOV, Col-Gen. Vyacheslav Victorovich; Russian army officer; b. 25 Oct. 1946, Tambov Region; m.; two s.; ed Leningrad Artillery Higher School, Kalinin Mil. Artillery Acad.; various posts in internal troops; service in Dept of Internal Affairs; fmr Deputy Head of Gen. Staff, Ministry of Internal Affairs, Head Dept of Punishments 1989–99, Deputy Minister of Internal Affairs 1999; Commdt of Stepanakert during Karabakh Conflict 1992, of N Osetia during Osetia-Ingush Conflict, of Grozny during mil. operations in Chechnya; First Deputy C-in-C Internal Troops, Ministry of Internal Affairs 1999, C-in-C 1999–2000, Adviser to Dir-Gen. Rosoboronexport Co. 2001; Order for Personal Courage, Order for Service to Motherland and numerous other medals. *Address:* Rosoboronexport, Gogolevski blvd 21, 119865 Moscow, Russia (Office). *Telephone:* (095) 239-52-66 (Office).

OVENDEN, Graham Stuart, MA, ARCA, ARCM; British art historian, artist and poet; b. 11 Feb. 1943, Alresford, Hants.; s. of the late Henry Ovenden and Gwendoline D. Hill; m. Ann. D. Gilmore 1969; one s. one d.; ed Alresford Dames School, Itchen Grammar School, Southampton, Southampton Coll. of Art, Royal Coll. of Art; corresp. mem. and critic, Architecture Design Magazine; Founder mem. South West Acad. of Fine and Applied Art. *Publications:* Illustrators of Alice 1971, Victorian Children 1972, Clementina, Lady Harwarden 1973, Pre-Raphaelite Photography 1972, Victorian Erotic Photography 1973, Aspects of Lolita 1975, A Victorian Album (with Lord David Cecil) 1976, Satirical Poems and Others 1983, The Marble Mirror (poems) 1984, Lewis Carroll Photographer 1984; Graham Ovenden...A Monograph with Essays by Laurie Lee, etc. 1987, Sold With All Faults (poems) 1991; photographs: Alphonse Mucha 1973, Hill & Adamson 1973, Graham Ovenden—Childhood Streets (Photographs 1956–64) 1998; contribs on art to numerous journals. *Leisure interests:* music (very seriously indeed), architecture, social science. *Address:* Barley Splatt, Panters Bridge, Mount, nr Bodmin, Cornwall, England.

OVERBEEK, Jan Theodoor Gerard, DRS.CHEM., PhD; Dutch professor of physical chemistry; b. 5 Jan. 1911, Groningen; s. of Dr. A. A. Overbeek and J. C. (van Ryssel) Overbeek; m. Johanna Clasina Edie 1936; four d.; ed Univ. of Utrecht; Asst at Univ. of Ghent, Belgium 1935–36, Univ. of Utrecht 1936–41; Scientific Officer, N V. Philips, Eindhoven 1941–46; Prof. of Physical Chem., Univ. of Utrecht 1946–81, Vice-Pres. of Univ. 1971–76; Visiting Prof., MIT, Cambridge, Mass., USA 1952–53, 1966–67, 1969–81, 1984–88, Columbia Univ., New York 1956, Univ. of Southern Calif., LA 1959–60; Ed. Advances in Colloid Interface Science –1967, Ed. Emer. 1990–; mem. Bd Verenigde Bedrijven Bredero, Utrecht 1963–83; mem. Royal Netherlands Acad. of Arts and Sciences 1953–; Emer. mem. American Chemical Soc.; Foreign mem. Royal Flemish Acad. of Sciences (Belgium) 1957–; Hon. mem. Royal Netherlands Chem. Soc. 1993–; Kolloid-Gesellschaft 1993–; Foreign Hon. mem. American Acad. of Arts and Sciences 1969–; Hon. Fellow Royal Soc. of Chem. (London) 1983; Hon. DSc (Clarkson Coll. of Tech., Potsdam, NY) 1967, (Univ. of Bristol) 1984; Wolfgang-Ostwald-Preis (Kolloid-Gesellschaft) 1989; Kt, Order of Netherlands Lion 1971. *Publications:* Theory of Stability of Lyophobic Colloids (with E. J. W. Verwey) 1948, Colloid Science (with H. R. Kruyt) Vol. I 1952, Vol. II 1949, The Electrical Double Layer (with A. L. Loeb, P. H. Wiersema) 1960; An Introduction to Physical Chemistry (with H. R. Kruyt) 1954, Colloid and Surface Chemistry Vols I–IV 1971–74, Electrochemistry Vols I, II & III 1981; numerous articles and study guides on colloid and surface science. *Leisure interests:* outdoor activities, hiking, photography. *Address:* Zweerslaan 35, 3723HN Bilthoven, Netherlands (Home). *Telephone:* (30) 2532391 (Office); (30) 2282882 (Home).

OVERHAUSER, Albert Warner, PhD; American physicist; b. 17 Aug. 1925, San Diego; s. of Clarence Albert Overhauser and Gertrude Irene (Pehrson) Overhauser; m. Margaret Mary Casey 1951; four s. four d.; ed Univ. of California at Berkeley; service with USNR 1944–46; Research Assoc., Univ. of Ill. 1951–53; Asst Prof. of Physics, Cornell Univ. 1953–56, Assoc. Prof. 1956–58; Supervisor, Solid State Physics, Ford Motor Co., Dearborn, Mich. 1958–62, Man. Theoretical Sciences 1962–69, Asst Dir of Physical Sciences 1969–72, Dir 1972–73; Prof. of Physics Purdue Univ., W. Lafayette, Ind. 1973–74, Stuart Distinguished Prof. of Physics 1974–; Fellow American Physics Soc., American Acad. of Arts and Sciences; mem. NAS; Hon. DSc (Chicago) 1979; Hon. LLD (Simon Fraser Univ., Canada) 1998; Oliver E. Buckley Solid State Physics Prize (American Physical Soc.) 1975, Alexander von Humboldt Sr US Scientist Award 1979, Nat. Medal of Science 1994. *Address:* Department of Physics, Purdue University, West Lafayette, IN 47907 (Office); 236 Pawnee Drive West, Lafayette, IN 47906, USA (Home). *Telephone:* (765) 494-3037 (Office). *Fax:* (765) 494-0706 (Office). *E-mail:* awo@ physics.purdue.edu (Office).

OVERY, Richard James, PhD, FRHistS, FBA; British professor of history; b. 23 Dec. 1947, London; s. of James Herbert Overy and Margaret Grace Overy (née Sutherland); m. 1st Tessa Coles 1969 (divorced 1976); m. 2nd Jane Giddens 1979 (divorced 1992); m. 3rd Kim Turner 1992; one s. four d.; ed Sexey's Blackford Grammar School, Somerset, Gonville and Caius Coll., Cambridge; Research Fellow Churchill Coll., Cambridge 1972–73; Fellow and Coll. lecturer Queen's Coll., Cambridge 1973–79; Univ. Asst Lecturer Cambridge Univ. 1976–79; lecturer in History King's College, Univ. of London 1980–88, Reader in History 1988–92, Prof. of Modern History 1992–; T. S. Ashton Prize 1983, Cass Prize for Business History 1987, Samuel Eliot Morison Prize 2001. *Publications:* The Air War 1939–45 1980, Goering: The 'Iron Man' 1984, The Road to War 1989, War and Economy in the Third Reich 1994, Why the Allies Won 1995, Times Atlas of the Twentieth Century 1996, Russia's War 1997, The Battle 2000, Interrogations: The Nazi Elite in Allied Lands 1945 2001. *Leisure interests:* opera, art, football. *Address:* Department of History, King's College, Strand, London, WC2R 2LS, England. *Telephone:* (20) 7848-1080. *Fax:* (20) 7873-2052.

OVETT, Stephen Michael (Steve), OBE; British athlete; b. 9 Oct. 1955, Brighton, Sussex; m. Rachel Waller 1981; ed Brighton College of Art; European Jr Champion at 800 m 1973; European Champion at 1500m 1978 and silver medallist at 800m 1974 and 1978; competed Olympic Games, Montreal 1976, finished 5th in 800m, reached semi-final of 1,500m; Moscow 1980, won gold medal at 800m and bronze medal at 1,500m; set four world records; holder of record for greatest number of mile/1,500m victories (45 to 1980); also winner of maj. titles at 5,000m. *Publication:* Ovett: An Autobiography. *Leisure interest:* art.

OVITZ, Michael; American film industry executive; b. Dec. 1946, Chicago; m. Judy Reich 1969; three c.; ed Birmingham High School and Univ. of Calif., LA; tour guide at Universal Studios while at coll.; joined William Morris Agency, Beverly Hills 1968; with three others formed Creative Artists Agency (CAA) 1975, Pres. 1975–95; Pres. Walt Disney Co. 1995–97; Head Livent Inc. Toronto 1998–; f., CEO Artists Man. Group 1998–; agency represents many of top Hollywood actors, writers, dirs., producers. *Address:* Artists Management Group, 9465 Wilshire Boulevard, Suite 212, Beverly Hills, CA 90212, USA (Office).

OWADA, Hisashi, LLB; Japanese diplomatist and international lawyer; b. 18 Sept. 1932, Niigata; s. of Takeo Owada and Shizuka Tamura; m. Yumiko Egashira 1962; three d.; (one d. Masako; m. Crown Prince Michiko); ed Univs. of Tokyo and Cambridge; Pvt. Sec. to Prime Minister 1976–78; Minister-Plenipotentiary, USSR 1981–84; Dir-Gen. Treaties Bureau and Office for Law of the Sea 1984–87; Deputy Vice-Minister, Ministry of Foreign Affairs 1987–88; Amb. to OECD 1988–89; Deputy Minister, Ministry of Foreign Affairs 1989–91, Vice-Minister for Foreign Affairs 1991–93; Adviser to Minister for Foreign Affairs 1993–94, 1999–; Adjunct Prof. Tokyo Univ. 1963–88, Col Law School 1994–2000; Visiting Prof. Harvard Univ. 1979–81, 1987, 1989, NY Univ. Law School; Amb. and Perm. Rep. to UN 1994–98; Pres. Japan Inst. of Int. Affairs 1999–; Associé de l'Institut de Droit Int. *Publications:* U.S.–Japan Economic Interaction in an Independent World 1981, Japanese Perspectives on Asian Security 1982, Practice of Japan in International Law 1984, From Involvement to Engagement: A New Course for Japanese Foreign Policy 1994, Diplomacy 1997. *Leisure interests:* music, skiing, mountain walking. *Address:* Japan Institute of International Affairs, Kasumigaseki Bldg 11/F, 3-2-5 Kasumigaseki, Chiyoda-ku, Tokyo 100-6011, Japan. *Telephone:* (3) 3503-6625. *Fax:* (3) 3503-7292; (3) 3503-7411. *E-mail:* owada@jiia.or.jp (Office). *Website:* www.jiia.or.jp (Office).

OWEN, Clive; British actor; b. 1965; m. Sarah-Jane Fenton.; ed Royal Acad. of Dramatic Arts. *Television appearances include:* Precious Bane, Vroom, Chancer (series), Sharman (series). *Film appearances include:* Close My Eyes 1991, Century, Bent 1998, Croupier 1998, Greenfingers 2000, Ambush 2001, Powder Keg 2001, The Follow 2001, Gosford Park 2001, A Day in the Death of Joe Egg 2001, Beyond Borders 2002, The Bourne Identity 2002. *Stage appearances include:* Design for Living 1994, Closer 1997.

OWEN, Baron (Life Peer), cr. 1992, of the City of Plymouth; **David Anthony Llewellyn Owen,** CH, PC, MA, MB, BChir; British politician and business executive; b. 2 July 1938, Plymouth; s. of Dr. John William Morris Owen and Mary Llewellyn; m. Deborah Schabert 1968; two s. one d.; ed Bradfield Coll., Sidney Sussex Coll., Cambridge, St Thomas' Hosp.; house appointments, St Thomas' Hosp. 1962–64, Neurological and Psychiatric Registrar 1964–66, Research Fellow, Medical Unit 1966–68; MP for Sutton Div. of Plymouth 1966–74, for Devonport Div. of Plymouth 1974–92; Parl. Pvt. Sec. to Minister of Defence, Admin. 1967; Parl. Under-Sec. of State for Defence, Royal Navy 1968–70; Opposition Defence Spokesman 1970–72, resgnd over party policy on EEC 1972; Parl. Under-Sec. of State, Dept of Health and Social Security (DHSS) March-July 1974; Minister of State, DHSS 1974–76, FCO 1976–77; Sec. of State for Foreign and Commonwealth Affairs 1977–79; Opposition Spokesman for Energy 1979–80; co-f. Social Democratic Party (SDP) 1981; Chair. Parl. Cttee 1981–82; Deputy Leader SDP 1982–83, Leader 1983–87, 1988–92; now Ind. Social Democrat; Chair. Decision Tech. Int. 1970–72, Palme Comm. on Disarmament and Security Issues 1980–89, Ind. Comm. on Int. Humanitarian Issues 1983–88; EC Co-Chair. Int. Conference on fmr Yugoslavia 1992–95, Carnegie Comm. on Preventing Deadly Conflict 1994–2000; Exec. Chair. Global Natural Energy 1995–; Dir (non-exec.) Coats Viyella 1994–2001; Dir Abbott Laboratories 1996–; Chair. New Europe 1999; Chair. Yukos Int. 2002; Chancellor Liverpool Univ. 1996–; Dir Center for Int. Health and Co-operation; Freeman, City of Plymouth 2000. *Publications:* Ed.: A Unified Health Service 1968; Contrib.: Social Services for All 1968; Author: The Politics of Defence 1972, In Sickness and in Health—The Politics of Medicine 1976, Human Rights 1978, Face the Future 1981, A Future that Will Work 1984, A United Kingdom 1986, Personally Speaking to Kenneth Harris 1987, Our NHS 1988, Time to Declare (autobiog.) 1991, Seven Ages (Poetry) 1992, Balkan Odyssey 1995; articles in Lancet, Neurology and Clinical Science. *Leisure interest:* sailing. *Address:* House of Lords, London, SW1A 0PW; 78 Narrow Street, Limehouse, London, E14 8BP, England (Home). *Telephone:* (20) 7787-2751 (Office); (20) 7987-5441 (Home). *Fax:* (1442) 876108. *E-mail:* lordowen@nildram.co.uk.

OWEN, Sir Geoffrey (David), Kt, MA; British newspaper editor; b. 16 April 1934; s. of L. G. Owen; m. 1st Dorothy J. Owen 1961 (died 1991); two s. one d.; m. 2nd Miriam Marianna Gross 1993; ed Rugby School and Balliol Coll. Oxford; joined Financial Times as feature writer and industrial corresp. 1958, U.S. corresp. 1961, industrial 1967; Exec. Industrial Reorganization Corpn 1967–69; Dir of Admin. Overseas Div. British Leyland Int. 1969, Dir of Personnel and Admin. 1972; Deputy Ed. Financial Times 1974–80, Ed. 1981–90; Dir Business Policy Programme, Centre for Economic Performance, LSE 1991–98, Sr Fellow Inter-disciplinary Inst. of Man. 1998–; mem. Council Foundation for Mfg and Industries 1993–; Chair. Wincott Foundation 1999–; Dir Laird Group 2000–. *Publications:* Industry in the USA 1966, From Empire

to Europe 1999. *Address:* London School of Economics and Political Science, Houghton Street, London, WC2A 2AE, England. *Telephone:* (20) 7405-7686. *Fax:* (20) 7242-0392. *Website:* www.lse.ac.uk (Office).

OWEN, Michael; British football player; b. 14 Dec. 1979, Chester; s. of Terence Owen and Jeanette Owen; partner Louise Bonsall; one d.; ed Idsall High School; player Liverpool FC since High School, scored during debut against Wimbledon May 1997 (youngest ever Liverpool player to score); player England nat. team 1998–, scored hat-trick in 5-1 victory over Germany in World Cup qualifier 2001; 19 goals for Liverpool in European competition (one less than Ian Rush's club record) and 19 goals in 40 int. matches for England (to 13 Dec. 2002); Professional Footballers' Asscn Young Player of the Year 1997, BBC Sports Personality of the Year 1998, European Footballer of the Year 2001. *Leisure interests:* golf, table-tennis, snooker. *Address:* c/o Liverpool Football Club, Anfield Road, Liverpool, L4 0TH, England (Office).

OWEN, Ray David, PhD, ScD; American biologist; b. 30 Oct. 1915, Genesee, Wis.; s. of Dave Owen and Ida Hoeft Owen; m. June Johanna Weissenberg 1939; one s.; ed Carroll Coll., Wis., Univ. of Wisconsin; Research Fellow, Wisconsin 1941–43, Asst Prof. of Genetics and Zoology 1943–47; Gosney Fellow, Calif. Inst. of Tech. 1946–47, Assoc. Prof. 1953–83, Chair. Div. of Biology 1961–68, Vice-Pres. for Student Affairs and Dean of Students 1975–80, Prof. Emer. 1983–; Research Participant, Oak Ridge Nat. Lab. 1957–58; mem. Genetics Soc. of America (Treas. 1957–60, Vice-Pres. 1961, Pres. 1962), Nat. Acad. of Sciences, American Acad. of Arts and Sciences, American Philosophical Soc., Soc. for the Study of Evolution, American Asscn of Immunologists (Excellence in Mentoring Award 1999); served on numerous scientific cttees; Mendel Award, Czechoslovak Acad. of Sciences 1965, Morgan Award, Genetics Soc. of America 1995, Medawar Award, Transplantation Soc. 2000. *Publications:* General Genetics (with Srb and Edgar) 1952, 1965; numerous research papers. *Address:* Division of Biology, 156-29, California Institute of Technology, Pasadena, CA 91125, USA (Office). *Telephone:* (626) 395-4960 (Office). *Fax:* (626) 449-0756.

OWEN, Robert John Richard, MA; British financial official; b. 11 Feb. 1940, London; s. of Thomas R. Owen and Margaret Fletcher; m. Beatrice M. Voelker 1962 (divorced); two s. one d.; ed Repton School and Oriel Coll. Oxford; Foreign Office 1961–68, served British Embassy, Washington 1964–68; HM Treasury 1968–70; Morgan Grenfell & Co., Ltd 1970–79, Dir 1973; Dir Merchant Banking Div. Lloyds Bank Int., Ltd 1979–82, Dir Far East Div. 1982–84; Dir of Investment Banking, Lloyds Bank PLC and Chair. Lloyds Merchant Bank, Ltd 1984–88; Adviser to Hong Kong Govt on implementation of Securities Review Cttee Report 1988–89; Chair. Securities and Futures Comm. of Hong Kong 1989–92; Dir European Capital Co. Ltd 1992–, Regulatory Bd and Council of Lloyd's of London 1993–95; Deputy Chair. Nomura Int. Ltd, Hong Kong 1993–; Dir Yaohan Int. Holdings 1993–, Int. Securities Consultancy Ltd 1995–, Regent Pacific Group Ltd 1998–, ECK and Partners Ltd 1999–, TechPacific Ltd 1999–. *Leisure interests:* mountain walking, collecting oriental paintings and carvings. *Address:* c/o European Capital Co. Ltd, 3 Lombard Street, London, EC3V 9AA, England.

OWEN-JONES, Lindsay, CBE, BA; British business executive; b. 17 March 1946, Wallasey; s. of Hugh A. Owen-Jones and Esmee (Lindsay) Owen-Jones; m. 1st; one d.; m. 2nd Cristina Furno 1994; ed Univ. of Oxford and European Inst. of Business Admin. (INSEAD); Product Man. L'Oréal 1969, Head, Public Products Div., Belgium 1971–74, Man. SCAD (L'Oréal subsidiary), Paris 1974–76, Marketing Man. Public Products Div., Paris 1976–78, Gen. Man. SAIPO (L'Oréal subsidiary, Italy) 1978–81, Chair. 1991–, Pres. COSMAIR Inc. (exclusive L'Oréal agent) USA 1981–83, Vice-Pres. L'Oréal Man. Cttee 1984, mem. Bd of Dirs. 1984, Pres. and COO 1984–88, Chair. and CEO Sept. 1988–; Dir Banque Nat. de Paris 1989–, Lafarge 1993–2001, Air Liquide 1994–; Hon. DSc (Cranfield School of Man.); Officier, Légion d'honneur. *Leisure interest:* sailing. *Address:* L'Oréal, 41 rue Martre, 92117 Clichy Cedex, France (Home). *Telephone:* 1-47-56-70-00 (Office).

OWENS, Bill, BA, MPA; American politician; b. 22 Oct. 1950, Fort Worth; m. Frances Owens; one s. one d.; ed Austin State Univ., Univ. of Texas; fmrly with Touche Ross & Co., Gates Corpn; State Treas., Colorado 1994–99; Gov. of Colorado 1999–; fmrly guest host Mike Rosen, Ken Hamblin and Chuck Baker talk shows; Republican. *Publications:* contrib. to professional journals. *Address:* Office of the Governor, State Capitol Building, Room 136, Denver, CO 80203, USA.

OWUSU, Victor; Ghanaian politician; b. 26 Dec. 1923, Agona-Ashanti; ed Univs. of Nottingham and London; called to the Bar, Lincoln's Inn 1952; practising barrister 1952–67; MP for Agona-Kwabre 1956–61; Attorney-Gen. 1966–69; concurrently Minister of Justice 1967–69; Minister of External Affairs April 1969, 1969–71; Attorney-Gen. and Minister of Justice 1971–72; Leader fmr Popular Front Party 1979 (political activity suspended by Flt.-Lt Jerry Rawlings Jan. 1982); Presidential Cand. 1979; has served on several Govt comms. and corpns.; fmr mem. Council of Univ. of Ghana, Legon, Council of Univ. of Science and Technology, Kumasi and Cen. Legal Council of Ghana. *Address:* Popular Front Party, Accra, Ghana.

OXBURGH, Baron (Life Peer), cr. 1999, of Liverpool in the County of Merseyside; **Ernest Ronald Oxburgh,** Kt, KBE, PhD, FRS; British geologist; b. 2 Nov. 1934, Liverpool; s. of Ernest Oxburgh and Violet Bugden; m. Ursula Mary Brown 1934; one s. two d.; ed Liverpool Inst., Univ. of Oxford and Univ. of Princeton, USA; Departmental Demonstrator, Univ. of Oxford 1960–61,

Lecturer in Geology 1962–78, Fellow, St Edmund Hall 1964–78, Emer. Fellow 1978, Hon. Fellow 1986; Prof. of Mineralogy and Petrology, Univ. of Cambridge 1978–91, Head of Dept of Earth Sciences 1980–88; Chief Scientific Adviser, Ministry of Defence 1988–93; Rector Imperial Coll. of Science, Tech. and Medicine 1993–2001; Fellow, Trinity Hall Cambridge 1978–82, Hon. Fellow 1983; Pres. Queens' Coll. Cambridge 1982–89, Hon. Fellow 1989; Dir Shell Transport and Trading 1996–, Nirex 1996–97; Sherman Fairchild Distinguished Scholar, Calif. Inst. of Tech. 1985–86; Pres. European Union of Geosciences 1985–87; mem. Nat. Cttee of Inquiry into Higher Educ. (Dearing Cttee) 1996–97; Trustee Natural History Museum 1993–2002, Chair. of Trustees 1999–2002; Chair. House of Lords Select Cttee on Science and Tech. 2001–; Chair. SETNET 2001–; Foreign mem. Venezuelan Acad. of Sciences 1992, Deutsche Acad. der Naturforscher Leopoldina 1994; Hon. mem. Geologists' Asscn; Hon. Fellow Univ. Coll., Oxford 1983; Hon.DSc (Paris) 1986, (Leicester) 1990, (Loughborough) 1991, (Edin.) 1994, (Birmingham, Liverpool) 1996, Hon. FREng 2002; Bigsby Medal, Geological Soc. of London 1979. *Publications:* The Geology of the Eastern Alps (Ed. and Contrib.) 1968, Structural, Metamorphic and Geochronological Studies in the Eastern Alps 1971 and contribs. to Nature, Journal of Geophysical Research, Tectonophysics, Journal of the Geological Soc. of London and other learned journals. *Leisure interests:* reading, walking and various sports. *Address:* House of Lords, London, SW1A 0PW, England.

ØYE, Harald Arnljot, DTech; Norwegian professor of inorganic chemistry; b. 1 Feb. 1935, Oslo; s. of Leiv C. Øye and Ingrid H. Øye; m. Tove Stiegler 1963; two s. one d.; ed Norwegian Inst. of Tech.; Postdoctoral Fellow, Argonne Nat. Lab. Ill. USA 1963–64; Assoc. Prof. Inst. of Inorganic Chem. Norwegian Inst. of Tech. 1965–72, Prof. and Head of Inst. Norwegian Univ. of Science and Tech. (fmrly Norwegian Inst. of Tech.) 1973–90, 1992–98, Prof. Chemistry Dept 1999–; Pres. Norwegian Acad. of Tech. Sciences 1985–92, Hon. Fellow 1993–; guest scientist at various insts. in Germany, Italy, USA, France, New Zealand, Switzerland, UK; Brotherton Distinguished Prof. Univ. of Leeds 1985; Hon. Prof. North-Eastern Univ., Shenyang, People's Repub. of China; Prize for Outstanding Research, Research Council of Norway 1997; Guldberg-Waage Medal, Norwegian Chemical Soc. 1998, Max Bredig Award, Electrochemical Soc., USA 1998; Kt First Class, Royal Norwegian Order of St. Olav. *Publications:* Cathodes in Aluminium Electrolysis (with M. Sørlie) 1991; more than 300 publs on electrowinning of aluminium and magnesium, characterization of silicon, carbon technology, transport properties, molten salt chem., spectroscopy and thermodynamics of high temperature systems. *Leisure interests:* reading, outdoor activities. *Address:* Department of Chemistry, Norwegian University of Science and Technology, 7491 Trondheim (Office); Steinhaugen 5, 7049 Trondheim, Norway (Home). *Telephone:* 73-59-40-16 (Office); 73-93-75-58 (Home). *Fax:* 73-59-39-92 (Office). *E-mail:* oye@chembio .ntnu.no (Office). *Website:* www.chembio.ntnu.no/users/haoye (Office).

OYÉ-MBA, Casimir, DenD; Gabonese banker; b. 20 April 1942, Nzamaligue Village, Libreville; s. of Ange Mba and Marie-Jeanne Nse; m. Marie-Françoise Razafimbelo 1963; one s. two d.; ed Univs. of Rennes and Paris; trainee Banque Centrale, Libreville 1967–69, Asst Dir 1969–70, Dir 1970–73; Nat. Dir Banque pour le Gabon 1973–76; Asst Dir-Gen. Banque Centrale 1977–78; Gov. Banque des Etats de l'Afrique Centrale 1978–90; Prime Minister of Gabon 1990–94; Minister of Foreign Affairs and Co-operation 1994–99; currently Minister of State for Planning and Devt; Acting Gov. IMF for Gabon 1969–76; apptd. Pres. Asscn des Banques Centrales Africaines 1987; Rep. of Komo-Mondah Dist 1990–; mem. political bureau, Gabonese Democratic Party 1991; Campaign Man. for Pres. Omar Bongo 1993; Légion d'honneur; Gabon, Cameroon, Congo and Equatorial Guinea decorations. *Leisure interests:* football, tennis, cinema, reading. *Address:* Ministry of Planning and Development, Libreville, Gabon.

OYELOWO, David Oyetokunbo; British actor; b. 1 April 1976, Oxford; m. Jessica Oyelowo; one s.; ed Model Coll., Lagos, Nigeria, Highbury Grove Boys, Islington Sixth Form Centre, London Acad. of Music and Dramatic Art; left drama school early to do work on BBC TV series Maisie Raine 1998; joined the RSC Jan. 1999; went to play Henry VI 2000, first black actor to play an English King at the RSC; London Acad. of Music and Dramatic Arts (LAMDA) Scholarship of Excellence, Ian Charleson Award for Best Newcomer 2001. *Films:* Dog Eat Dog 2000. *Television:* Maisie Raine 1998, Brothers and Sisters 1998, Spooks 2002, Tomorrow La Scala (film) 2002. *Radio:* The Faerie Queen (BBC), Man Talk, Woman Talk (BBC), Oroonoko (BBC). *Plays:* The Suppliants (Gate Theatre, London) 1998; Oroonoko, Volpone, Antony and Cleopatra (RSC) 1999; Henry VI Parts 1, 2, 3 (RSC) 2001, Richard III. *Publications:* Actors on Shakespeare: Henry VI 2003. *Leisure interests:* drawing, film, tennis, football, travel. *Address:* Hamilton Asper Management, 24 Hanway Street, London, W1P 9DD, England (Office). *Telephone:* (20) 7636-1221 (Office). *Fax:* (20) 7636-1226 (Office).

ÖYMEN, Onur Basaran, PhD; Turkish diplomatist; b. 1940, Istanbul; s. of Münir Raşit Öymen and Nebahat Öymen; m. Nedret Gürsel 1971; one s. one d.; ed Galatasay Lisesi, Istanbul, Univ. of Ankara; joined Ministry of Foreign Affairs 1964; mil. service 1964–66; Second Sec. NATO Dept, Ministry of Foreign Affairs 1966–68, First Sec. Perm. Del. to Council of Europe, Strasbourg 1968–72, Chief of Section, Policy Planning Dept, Ministry of Foreign Affairs 1972–74, Counsellor Turkish Embassy, Nicosia 1974–78; Special Adviser to Minister of Foreign Affairs 1978–80; Counsellor Turkish Embassy, Prague 1980–82, Turkish Embassy, Madrid 1982–84, Head Policy Planning Dept, Ministry of Foreign Affairs 1984–88, Amb. to Denmark 1988–90, to Germany 1990–95; Under-Sec. Ministry of Foreign Affairs 1995–97; Perm. Rep. to NATO 1997–; Bureaucrat of the Year, Nokta Review 1995, Diplomat of the Year, Asscn of Turkish Industrialists and Business 1995, 1996, 1997; Abdi Ipekçi Special Peace Award, Milliyet newspaper 1997. *Publications:* Türkiye'nin Gücü (Turkish Strength) 1998, trans. into Turkish of Science and Common Sense by Oppenheimer. *Address:* Turkish Delegation to NATO, Boulevard Léopold III, 1110 Brussels, Belgium. *Telephone:* (2) 707-41-11. *Fax:* (2) 707-45-79. *E-mail:* natodoc@hq.nato.int (Office). *Website:* www.nato.int (Office).

OYUN, Sanjaasurengin, DPhil; Mongolian politician; b. 1964; ed Univ. of Cambridge; worked as exploration geologist on surveys in Mongolia and for Rio Tinto-Zinc; Founder and Chair. Civil Courage Party ('Irgenii Zorig Nam') 1999–, mem. Opposition in Parl. *Address:* Civil Courage Party ('Irgenii Zorig Nam'), P.O. Box 49, Ulan Bator, Mongolia (Office). *Telephone:* 323045 (Office). *Fax:* 322866 (Office). *E-mail:* oyun@mail.parl.gov.mn (Office).

OZ, Amos, BA; Israeli author; b. 4 May 1939, Jerusalem; m. Nily Zuckermann 1960; three c.; ed Hebrew Univ. Jerusalem; Kibbutz Hulda 1957–86; teacher of literature and philosophy, Hulda High School and Givat Brenner Regional High School 1963–86; Visiting Fellow, St Cross Coll. Oxford; Writer-in-residence Hebrew Univ. Jerusalem 1975; Visiting Prof. Univ. of Calif. at LA (Berkeley); Writer-in-Residence and Prof. of Literature Colorado Coll., Colorado Springs 1984–85; Prof. of Hebrew Literature, Ben Gurion Univ. 1987–, Agnon Chair in Modern Hebrew 1990–; Visiting Prof. of Literature, Writer in Residence, Boston Univ. 1987; Writer-in-Residence, Hebrew Univ. 1990– and Prof of Literature, Princeton Univ. 1997; Officier des Arts et des Lettres; Holon Prize 1965, Brenner Prize 1976; Zeev Award for Children's Books 1978; Bernstein Prize 1983, Bialik Prize 1986, Prix Femina, Paris 1989 (for novel Black Box), German Publrs' Int. Peace Prize 1992, Luchs Prize for Children's Books (Germany) 1993, Hamore Prize 1993, Israeli Prize for Literature 1998, Freedom of Speech Prize, Wirters' Union of Norway 2002. *Publications:* novels: Elsewhere, Perhaps 1966, My Michael 1968, Touch the Water, Touch the Wind 1973, A Perfect Peace 1982, Black Box 1987, To Know a Woman 1989, Fima 1991, Don't Pronounce It Night 1994; novellas and short stories: Where the Jackals Howl 1965, Unto Death 1971, The Hill of Evil Counsel 1976; essays: Under this Blazing Light 1979, In the Land of Israel 1983, The Slopes of Lebanon 1987, Israel, Palestine and Peace 1994; Different People (selected anthology) 1974; Soumchi (children's story) 1978, Panther in the Basement (novel) 1995, A Story Begins 1996, All Our Hopes 1998. *Address:* Ben Gurion University of the Negev, P.O. Box 653, Beersheva 84105, Israel. *Telephone:* (8) 6461111. *Fax:* (8) 6237682. *E-mail:* acsec@bgumail.bgu.ac.il (Office). *Website:* www.bgu.ac.il (Office).

OZAL, Kurkut; Turkish engineer, administrator and politician; b. 29 May 1929, Malatya; m.; five c.; ed Istanbul Tech. Univ.; chief engineer Water Works Dept, Malatya Region 1951–55; Regional Dir Water Works Dept, Euphrates and Tigris River Basins 1957–60; instructor, then Asst Prof., then Assoc. Prof. Middle East Tech. Univ., Ankara 1960–67; Chair., CEO Turkish State Petroleum Corpn, Prof. Middle East Tech. Univ. 1967–71; Prof. Bosphorus Univ., Consultant Shell Group 1972–73; mem. Nat. Ass.; Minister of Agric., of the Interior 1973–80; CEO of cos. dealing in Islamic banking, construction and int. oil trade 1981–85; fmr Dir Islamic Research and Training Inst., Islamic Devt Bank; Founding Fellow Islamic Acad. of Sciences 1986. *Address:* Islamic Academy of Sciences, P.O. Box 830036, Amman, Jordan (Office). *Telephone:* 5523385 (Office). *Fax:* 5511803 (Office). *E-mail:* secretariat@ias-worldwide.org (Office). *Website:* www.ias-worldwide.org (Office).

OZAWA, Ichiro, BA; Japanese politician; b. 24 May 1942, Mizusawa, Iwate Pref.; s. of Saeki Ozawa and Michi Ozawa; m. Kazuko Fukuda 1973; three s.; ed Keio Univ.; mem. House of Reps.; Minister of Home Affairs 1985–87; fmr Deputy Chief Cabinet Sec.; fmr Dir-Gen. Liberal-Democratic Party (LDP) Election Bureau; Sec.-Gen. LDP 1989–91; Chair. Cttee on Rules and Admin.; left LDP 1993; co-founder Shinseito (Japan Renewal Party) 1993; Sec.-Gen. Shinshinto (New Frontier Party) 1994–95, Pres. 1995–97; Founder and Pres. Jiyuto (Liberal Party) 1998–. *Publication:* Blueprint for a New Japan 1993. *Leisure interests:* fishing, go. *Address:* Liberal Party, Kokusai Kogyo Building, 2-2-12 Akasaka, Minato-ku, Tokyo 107-0052 (Office); 2-38 Fukuro-machi, Mizusawa-shi, Iwate-ken 023-0814, Japan (Home). *Telephone:* (3) 5562-7111 (Office). *E-mail:* liberal@mx5.mesh.ne.jp (Office). *Website:* www.jiyuto.or.jp (Office).

OZAWA, Seiji; Japanese conductor; b. 1 Sept. 1935, Shenyang, China; m. 1st Kyoko Edo; m. 2nd Vera Ilyan; one s. one d.; ed Toho School of Music, Tokyo (under Prof. Hideo Saito), Tanglewood, USA and in West Berlin under Herbert von Karajan; Asst Conductor (under Leonard Bernstein), New York Philharmonic 1961–62 (including tour of Japan 1961); guest conductor, San Francisco Symphony, Detroit Symphony, Montreal, Minneapolis, Toronto and London Symphony Orchestras 1961–65; Music Dir Ravinia Festival, Chicago 1964–68; Music Dir Toronto Symphony Orchestra 1965–69, San Francisco Symphony Orchestra 1970–76, Boston Symphony Orchestra 1973–2002, Vienna State Opera 2002–; toured Europe conducting many of the maj. orchestras 1966–67; Salzburg Festival 1969; toured USA, France, Fed. Repub. of Germany, China 1979, Austria, UK 1981, Japan 1981, 1986, toured England, Netherlands, France, Germany, Austria and Belgium 1988; now makes frequent guest appearances with most of the leading orchestras of America, Europe and Japan; has conducted opera at Salzburg, Covent

Garden, La Scala, Vienna Staatsoper and Paris Opera; conducted world premiere, Messiaen's St Francis of Assisi, Paris 1983; many recordings; Hon. DMus (Univ. of Mass., New England Conservatory, Wheaton Coll., Norton, Mass.); First Prize, Int. Competition of Orchestra Conductors, France 1959, Koussevitsky Prize for outstanding student conductor 1960, Laureate, Fondation du Japon 1988. *Leisure interests:* golf, tennis, skiing. *Address:* c/o Ronald A. Wilford Columbia Artists Management Inc., Conductors Division, 165 West 57th Street, New York, NY, USA; c/o Harold Holt Ltd, 31 Sinclair Road, London, W14 0NS, England.

OZBEK, (Ibrahim Mehmet) Rifat, BA; Turkish/British couturier; b. 8 Nov. 1953, Istanbul; s. of Melike Osbek and Abdulazim Mehmet Ismet; ed St Martin's School of Art, London; worked with Walter Albini for Trell; designer Monsoon Co.; launched O for Ozbek (now Future Ozbek) 1987; presented first collection 1984; British Fashion Council Designer of the Year 1988, 1992. *Address:* 18 Haunch of Venison Yard, London, W1Y 1AF, England. *Telephone:* (20) 7408-0625. *Fax:* (20) 7629-1586.

OZDAS, Mehmet Nimet, DipEng, PhD; Turkish professor of engineering and administrator; b. 6 March 1921, Istanbul; m.; two c.; ed Istanbul Tech. Univ., Univ. of London; Visiting Prof. Case Western Reserve Univ., Ohio 1953–59; Research Fellow MIT 1955–56; Prof. Istanbul Tech. Univ. 1961; Founding Dir Computer Centre 1961; Founding Sec.-Gen. Turkish Scientific Council (TUBITAK) 1964–66, mem. Science Bd 1968–72; Founding Dir Marmara Scientific and Industrial Research; Pres. NATO Science Cttee 1973–79; mem. Bd Von Karman Inst. and Steering Cttee AGARD 1973; Minister of State for Science and Tech. 1980–83; Prof. Dept of Mechanical and Control Eng, Istanbul Tech. Univ. 1983–; Fellow Islamic Acad. of Sciences; Pres. Turkish Org. for Automatic Control. *Address:* Department of Mechanical and Control Engineering, Istanbul Technical University, Ayazaga, Istanbul, 80626, Turkey (Office). *Telephone:* (212) 2853000 (Office). *Fax:* (212) 2852916 (Office). *Website:* www.mkn.itu.edu.tr (Office).

OZICK, Cynthia, MA; American author; b. 17 April 1928, New York; d. of William Ozick and Celia Regelson; m. Bernard Hallote 1952; one d.; ed New York Univ. and Ohio State Univ.; mem. PEN, Authors League, American Acad. of Arts and Sciences, American Acad. of Arts and Letters; Founder mem. Acad. Universelle des Cultures; Guggenheim Fellow 1982; Hon. LHD (Yeshiva) 1984, (Hebrew Union Coll.) 1984, (Williams Coll.) 1986, (Hunter Coll.) 1987, (Jewish Theological Seminary) 1988, (Adelphi) 1988, (State Univ. of NY) 1989, (Brandeis) 1990, (Bard Coll.) 1991, (Spertus Coll.) 1991, (Seton Hall Univ.) 1999, (Rutgers Univ.) 1999, (Asheville) 2000; Mildred and Harold Strauss Living Award, American Acad. of Arts and Letters 1983; Rea Award for short story 1986, PEN/Spiegel-Diamonstein Award for the Art of the Essay 1997, Harold Washington Literary Award, City of Chicago 1997, John Cheever Award 1999, Lotos Club Medal of Merit 2000, Lannan Foundation Award 2000, Nat. Critics' Circle Award for Criticism 2001, Koret Foundation Award for Literary Studies 2001. *Publications:* Trust 1966, The Pagan Rabbi and Other Stories 1971, Bloodshed and Three Novellas 1976, Levitation: Five Fictions 1982, Art & Ardor: Essays 1983, The Cannibal Galaxy 1983, The Messiah of Stockholm 1987, Metaphor & Memory: Essays 1989, The Shawl 1989, What Henry James Knew: And Other Essays on Writers 1993, Blue Light (play) 1994, Portrait of the Artist as a Bad Character and Other Essays on Writing 1995, The Shawl (play) 1996, Fame & Folly: Essays 1996, The Puttermesser Papers (novel) 1997, The Best American Essays 1998 (guest ed.), Quarrel & Quandary (essays) 2000 and fiction in numerous periodicals and anthologies. *Address:* c/o Alfred A. Knopf Co., 201 E 50th Street, New York, NY 10022; 34 Soundview Street, New Rochelle, NY 10805, USA (Home). *Telephone:* (914) 636-1970. *Fax:* (914) 654-6583.

OZIM, Igor; Slovenian violinist; b. 9 May 1931, Ljubljana; s. of Rudolf Ozim and Marija Kodric; m. Dr. Breda Volovsek 1963; one s. one d.; ed Akad. za glasbo Ljubljana, Royal Coll. of Music; studied with Prof. Max Rostal; Prof. of Violin, Akad. za glasbo Ljubljana 1960–63, Staatliche Hochschule für Musik, Cologne 1963–96, Berne Conservatoire 1985–, Hochschule für Musik, Vienna 1996–; concerts throughout Europe; First Prize, Int. Carl-Flesch Competition, London 1951, Munich 1953. *Leisure interests:* photography, table tennis. *Address:* Breibergstrasse 6, 50939 Cologne 41, Germany.

ÖZKÖK, Gen. Hilmi; Turkish army officer; b. 1940, Turgutlu, Manisa; m. Özenç Özkök; two c.; ed Isiklar Mil. High School, Turkish Mil. Acad., Field Artillery School, Army War Coll., NATO Defence Coll.; Artillery 3rd Lt 1959; Platoon Leader and Anti-Aircraft Battery Commdr 1972; Chief of Operations and Training Br, 15th Training Brigade; Staff Officer, Plan and Policy Dept of Shape, HQ; Chief of Defence Research Section, Plan and Policy Dept of Shape, HQ; Dir Exec. Office of Sec.-Gen. of Nat. Security Council; Commdr Cadet Regiment, Turkish Mil. Acad.; rank of Brig.-Gen. 1984; Chief of Planning and Operations Dept, Turkish Gen. Staff (TGS) 1984–86; Commdr 70th Infantry Brigade 1986–88; rank of Maj.-Gen. 1988; Commdr 28th Infantry Div. 1988–90; Chief of Personnel, Dept of TGS 1990–92; rank of Lt-Gen. 1992; Chief of Turkish Mil. Del. to NATO, Brussels 1992–95; Commdr 7th Corps 1995–96; rank of Gen. 1996; Command of Allied Land Forces South-Eastern Europe 1996–98; Deputy Chief of TGS 1998–99; 1st Army Commdr 1999–2000; Commdr of Turkish Army 2000–; Chief of the Gen. Staff 2002–; Turkish Armed Forces Medal of Honour, Turkish Armed Forces Medal of Distinguished Service, Medal of Distinguished Service and Self-Sacrifice, Legion of Merit (USA), Medal of Nishan-I Imtiaz (Pakistan), Great Cross for Military Merit (Spain), Tong-II Medal (Repub. of Korea). *Address:* c/o Ministry of National Defence, Milli Savunma Bakanlığı, 06100 Ankara, Turkey (Office).

OZSOYLU, Sinasi, MD; Turkish physician; b. 29 Aug. 1927, Erzurum; s. of Ahmet Ozsoylu and Azime Fazil Ozsoylu; m. Selma Ozsoylu; two s. one d.; ed Istanbul Univ., Ankara Univ.; pediatrician, Washington Univ. Medical School, St Louis, USA 1960; Haematologist, Harvard Univ. Medical School, Boston, Mass. 1963; Assoc. Prof. of Pediatrics, Hacettepe Univ., Ankara 1964–69, Prof. 1969–94, Head of Haematology 1970–94, of Pediatrics 1976–77; Prof. of Pediatrics and Haematology, Fatih Univ., Ankara 1996–; Visiting Prof. Md Univ. Medical School, Baltimore 1972; mem. Turkish Medical Soc. 1953–, Turkish Pediatrics Soc. 1958–, Turkish Haematology Soc. 1974–, Int. Pediatrics Soc. 1974–; Pres. European Soc. of Haematology and Immunology 1991–93; Hon. Mem. American Pediatric Soc. 1992–; Fellow Islamic Acad. of Sciences 1989–; Hon. Fellow American Acad. of Pediatrics 1995–; Ed. Turkish Journal of Medical Sciences 1989–94, Hon. Ed. 1994–; Ed. Yeni Tip Dergisi 1994–; invited to speak at numerous specialist congresses; numerous awards and prizes including Exceptional Scientific Achievement Award, Hacettepe Univ. 1991. *Publications:* several hundred papers on pediatrics, haematology, liver disorders, etc. *Leisure interests:* gardening, music. *Address:* Kenedi Cad. No. 148/14, GOP 06700, Ankara, Turkey (Home); Fatih University, Medical School Hospital, Alpaslan Turkes Cad. No. 57, Emek. 06510, Ankara (Office). *Telephone:* (312) 2126262 (Office); (312) 4280975 (Home). *Fax:* (312) 2213276 (Office). *E-mail:* sinasi.ozsoylu@ fatihmed.edu.tr (Office).

P

PAAR, Vladimir, DSc; Croatian physicist; b. 11 May 1942, Zagreb; s. of Vladimir Paar and Elvira Paar; m. Nada Paar-Pandur 1968; three s. one d.; ed Zagreb Univ.; Research Assoc. Zagreb Univ. 1973–76, Prof. 1981; Visiting Prof. in Copenhagen, Julich, Paris, Moscow, Munich, Amsterdam, Livermore (Calif.) and Rio de Janeiro; participation in numerous int. confs; mem. Croatian Acad. of Arts and Sciences, Croatian Physical Soc., European Physical Soc. *Several TV series including:* Deterministic Chaos, Energy Crisis, Physics in Educ. *Publications:* author and ed. of several books and over 300 papers on atomic nucleus structure, symmetry, supersymmetry and deterministic chaos, energetics and scientific econ. devt. *Leisure interests:* soccer, tennis, presenting science in the media. *Address:* Gajeva 26, Samobor, Croatia (Office). *Telephone:* (1) 4680321 (Office). *Fax:* (1) 4680336.

PAASIO, Pertti Kullervo, MSc; Finnish politician; b. 2 April 1939, Helsinki; s. of Rafael Paasio and Mary Wahlman; m. Kirsti Johansson 1967; two s. two d.; ed Turku Univ.; regional organizer, Nuoret Kotkat (Young Falcons) 1963–66; mem. Turku City Council 1965–91; Sec. for Tourism, City of Turku 1967–73; Political Sec. Ministry of Finance 1972; Head of Turku Labour Exchange 1973–87; Vice-Pres. Int. Falcon Movt 1975–81; Chair. Young Falcons Fed. 1978–81; Political Sec. to Prime Minister 1975; mem. Parl. 1975–79, 1982–96; mem. Exec. Cttee Social Democratic Party of Finland 1978–91; mem. Presidential Electoral Coll. 1978, 1982, 1988; Leader, Social Democratic Parl. Group 1984–87; Chair. Social Democratic Party 1987–91; Deputy Prime Minister, Minister for Foreign Affairs 1989–91; Chair. Parl. Cttee for Foreign Affairs 1991–96; mem. European Parl. 1996, Quaestor 1997–. *Leisure interests:* photography, caravanning. *Address:* Eerikinkatu 30, 20100 Turku, Finland. *Telephone:* (2) 4145002 (Finland). *Fax:* (2) 4145003 (Finland).

PAČES, Václav, DSc; Czech biochemist; b. 2 Feb. 1942, Prague; m. Magdalena Tomková Pačes 1966; two s.; ed Charles Univ., Prague, Univ. of Chicago, McMaster Univ., Canada; scientific worker, Inst. of Organic Chemistry, Czech Acad. of Sciences, Prague 1970–77; Group Leader Inst. of Molecular Genetics Czech Acad. of Sciences 1977–86; Yale Univ., New Haven, Conn., 1990–91; Vice-Pres. Czech Acad. of Sciences 1993–97; Dir Inst. of Molecular Genetics Czech Acad. of Sciences 1998–; mem. EMBO; State Prize for Science 1989; Prize for Popularization of Science 1992. *Publications:* Molecular Biology of the Gene, Prague 1982; Molecular Genetics 1983; Antibiotics, Mechanism of Action and Resistance (jtly.) 1987; Highlights of Modern Biochemistry 1989. *Leisure interests:* skiing, golf, music, hiking. *Address:* Institute of Molecular Genetics, Czech Acad. of Sciences, Flemingovo nám. 2, Prague 6 – 160 00, Czech Republic. *Telephone:* (2) 4310234 (Office). *Fax:* (2) 4310955 (Office). *E-mail:* office@img.cas.cz. *Website:* www.img.cas.cz.

PACHAURI, Rajendra K., MS, DEcon, DEng; Indian research director; b. 20 Aug. 1940, Nainital; s. of A. R. Pachauri; m. Saroj Pachauri; three d.; ed North Carolina State Univ., USA; Asst Prof. NC State Univ. 1974–75; mem. Sr Faculty, Admin. Staff Coll. of India 1975–79, Dir Consulting and Applied Research Div. 1979–81; Dir Tata Energy Research Inst. New Delhi 1981–; Visiting Prof. W Va Univ. 1981–82; Visiting Fellow, Energy Dept IBRD 1990; Pres. Int. Asscn for Energy Econs 1988, Chair. 1988–90; Pres. Asian Energy Inst. 1992–; mem. World Energy Council 1990–93; Adviser on Energy and Sustainable Man. of Natural Resources to the Admin., UNDP 1994–99; Vice-Chair. Intergovernmental Panel on Climate Change (IPCC) 1997, Chair. 2002–; mem. Bd of Dirs. Inst. for Global Environmental Strategies 1999; McCluskey Fellow, Yale Univ. Sept.–Dec. 2000; Millennium Pioneer Award 2000, Padma Bhushan 2001. *Publications:* The Dynamics of Electrical Energy Supply and Demand 1975, Energy and Economic Development in India 1977, International Energy Studies 1980, Energy Policy for India: An Interdisciplinary Analysis 1980, The Political Economy of Global Energy 1985, Global Energy Interactions 1986, Contemporary India 1992, Climate Change in Asia and Brazil: The Role of Technology Transfer (ed. with Preety Bhandari) 1994, Population, Environment and Development (ed. with Lubina F. Qureshy) 1997; Energy in the Indian Sub-Continent (ed. with Gurneeta Vasudeva) 2000; scientific papers; newspaper articles. *Leisure interests:* cricket, flying, golf. *Address:* Intergovernmental Panel on Climate Change, World Meteorological Organization, 7 bis, ave de la Paix, CP 2300, 1211 Geneva 2, Switzerland; 160 Golf Links, New Delhi 110003, India (Home). *Telephone:* (11) 4634663 (Home). *Website:* www.ipcc.ch (Office).

PACHE, Bernard; French business executive and engineer; b. 13 Oct. 1934, Sallanches; s. of Joseph Pache and Sabine Pache (née Minjoz); m. Yvette Vitaly 1959; three s. (one deceased); ed Ecole Polytechnique de Paris and Ecole des Mines de Paris; mining engineer 1957–; Asst to Dir of Mines 1963–65; Tech. Adviser to Minister of Industry 1965–67; Chief Mining Engineer 1967; joined Compagnie Pechiney 1967, Asst to Dir, Uranium and Nuclear Activity Dept, then Dir of Mines Div., Nuclear Branch of Pechiney Ugine Kuhlmann 1969–73; Gen.-Man. Société des Electrodes et Refractaires Savoie (SERS) 1972–73; Chair. Compagnie Générale d'Electrolyse du Palais 1972–76; Gen.-Man. Société Cefilac 1973–74; Dir and Gen. Man. Société Française d'Electrométallurgie 1974–79; Dir of Industrial Policy, Pechiney Ugine Kuhlmann Group 1979–83, Deputy Dir of Pechiney 1983–84, Chair. and CEO 1985–86, Hon. Pres. 1986–; Dir-Gen. Charbonnages de France 1986, Chair. and CEO 1987–92, Hon. Pres. 1992–; Pres., Dir-Gen. Cie des Machines Bull 1992–93, Hon. Pres. 1993–; Pres. Directoire de l'Entreprise minière et chimique 1994–99, Hon. Pres. 1999–, la Fondation Georges 1994–99; Chair. IDTEC 1999–; Officier Légion d'honneur; Officier Ordre nat. du Mérite. *Address:* 7 Résidence de l'Observatoire, 8 rue Bel Air, 92190 Meudon, France (Home). *Telephone:* 1-46-26-32-90 (Home).

PACHECO, Abel; Costa Rican head of state, psychiatrist and writer; b. 1934; fmr TV commentator and producer of documentaries; Pres. Partido Unidad Social Cristiana (PUSC); Pres. of Costa Rica April 2002–. *Publications:* six books on Costa Rica. *Address:* Ministry of the Presidency, 2010 Zapote, Apdo 520, San José, Costa Rica (Office). *Telephone:* 224-4092 (Office). *Fax:* 253-6984 (Office).

PACHECO, Máximo, MBA; Chilean economist; b. 12 Feb. 1953, Santiago; s. of Máximo Pachecho and Adriana Matte; m. Soledad Flanagan 1976; four d.; ed Univ. of Chile; Man. Banco Osorno; Man. Planning, Banco Talca; Gen. Man. Leasing Andino 1983–90; Exec. Dir Cabildo SA 1982–90, Jucosa 1987–90; Pres. Chilean Leasing Asscn 1984–90; Faculty mem. Univ. de Chile; COO Codelco-Chile; Exec. Vice-Pres. for Chile and Latin America, Carter Holt Harvey 1994–; Pres. Latin America–Int. Paper 2000. *Address:* Miraflores 222, 13th Floor, Santiago, Chile. *Telephone:* (2) 638-3585. *Fax:* (2) 632-9311. *E-mail:* maximo.pacheco@ipaper.com (Office).

PACINO, Al (Alfredo James); American actor; b. 25 April 1940, New York; s. of Salvatore Pacino and Rosa Pacino; ed High School for the Performing Arts, New York, The Actors Studio; worked as messenger and cinema usher; Co-artistic Dir The Actors Studio, Inc., New York 1982–83; mem. Artistic Directorate Globe Theatre 1997–; Broadway début in Does a Tiger Wear a Necktie? 1969; appeared with Lincoln Center Repertory Co. as Kilroy in Camino Real 1970; other New York appearances include The Connection, Hello Out There, Tiger at the Gates and The Basic Training of Pavlo Hummel 1977, American Buffalo 1981 (UK 1984), Julius Caesar 1988, Salome 1992; appearances at Charles Playhouse, Boston, include: Richard III 1973 (repeated on Broadway 1979), Arturo Ui 1975, Rats (director) 1970. *Films include:* Me, Natalie 1969, Panic in Needle Park 1971, The Godfather 1972, Scarecrow 1973, Serpico 1974, The Godfather Part II 1974, Dog Day Afternoon 1975, Bobby Deerfield 1977, And Justice For All 1979, Cruising 1980, Author! Author! 1982, Scarface 1983, Revolution 1985, Sea of Love 1990, Dick Tracy 1991, The Godfather Part III 1990, Frankie and Johnny 1991, Glengarry Glen Ross 1992, Scent of a Woman (Acad. Award for Best Actor 1993) 1992, Carlito's Way 1994, City Hall 1995, Heat 1995, Donny Brasco 1996, Looking for Richard 1996 (also producer, Dir), Devil's Advocate 1997, The Insider 1999, Chinese Coffee 1999, Man of the People 1999, Any Given Sunday 1999, Insomnia 2002, Simone 2002; Nat. Soc. of Film Critics Award, The Godfather; British Film Award, The Godfather Part II, Tony Award 1996. *Address:* c/o Rick Nicita, CAA, 9830 Wilshire Boulevard, Beverly Hills, CA 90212, USA.

PACKER, James Douglas; Australian media company executive; b. 8 Sept. 1967; s. of Kerry Francis Packer (q.v.) and Roslyn Packer; m. Jodie Meaves 1999; ed Cranbrook School, Sydney; worked as a 'jackeroo' on a family-owned cattle station, Newcastle Walters; joined family business as magazine sales rep.; Dir Publishing & Broadcasting Ltd (PBL) 1991–, Man. Dir 1996–99, Exec. Chair. 1998–; Dir Australian Consolidated Press Group Ltd 1991–, Gen. Man. 1993–; Dir Nine Network Australia Ltd 1992–, Huntsman Corpn (Utah) 1994–, Optus Vision Pty Ltd 1995–, Valassas Inserts, USA, Ecorp Ltd. 1999–, Challenger Int. 1999–, Crown Ltd. 1999–, Hoytes Cinemas Ltd. 1999–. *Address:* Consolidated Press Ltd, Level 3, 54–58 Park Street, Sydney, NSW 2000, Australia.

PACKER, Kerry Francis Bullmore, AC; Australian business executive; b. 17 Dec. 1937, Sydney; s. of late Sir Frank and Lady Packer; m. Roslyn Weedon 1963; one s. one d.; ed Cranbrook School, Geelong Church of England Grammar School; Chair. Consolidated Press Holdings Ltd 1974–; Dir Publishing and Broadcasting Ltd 1994–; business interests include pastoral property, ski resort, investment portfolio, magazine publishing and TV broadcasting. *Leisure interests:* polo, golf, cricket, tennis. *Address:* Consolidated Press Holdings Ltd, 54 Park Street, Sydney, NSW 2000, Australia. *Telephone:* (2) 9282-8000. *Fax:* (2) 9264-6969.

PACKER, Sir Richard John, KCB, MSc; British government official; b. 18 Aug. 1944; s. of the late George Packer and Dorothy Packer; m. 1st Alison Sellwood; two s. one d.; m. 2nd Lucy Neville-Rolfe; four s.; ed City of London School and Univ. of Manchester; joined Ministry of Agric., Fisheries and Food (MAFF) 1967; on secondment, First Sec., Office of Perm. Representation to EEC 1973–76; Prin. Pvt. Sec. to Minister, Ministry of Agric., Fisheries and Food 1977–78; Asst Sec. 1979–85, Under-Sec. 1985–89, Deputy Sec. 1989–93, Perm. Sec. 1993–2000. *Leisure interests:* philosophy, history, arts, sport. *Address:* 113 St. George's Road, London, SE1 6HY, England.

PACKER, William John; British artist, art critic and teacher; b. 19 Aug. 1940, Birmingham; s. of Rex Packer and Molly Wornham; m. Clare Winn 1965; three d.; ed Windsor Grammar School, Wimbledon School of Art; teacher 1964–77; art critic, Financial Times 1974–; first exhibited Royal Acad. 1963; most recent one-man exhbn Piers Feetham Gallery, London 1996, 2001; mem. Fine Art Bd of Council for Nat. Academic Awards and Specialist Adviser

1976–83, Specialist Adviser 1983–87; mem. Advisory Cttee to Govt Art Collection 1977–84, Crafts Council 1980–87; sole selector first British Art Show (Arts Council) 1979–80, external examiner at various art schools 1980–2000; Inaugural Henry Moore Memorial Lecture, Florence 1986; Hon. Fellow Royal Coll. of Art; Hon. RBA; Hon. RBS; Nat. Diploma in Design. *Publications:* Fashion Drawing in Vogue 1983, Henry Moore 1985. *Leisure interests:* hockey, riding, Venice. *Address:* 39 Elms Road, Clapham, London, SW4 9EP, England. *Telephone:* (20) 7622-1108. *Fax:* (20) 7622-1108.

PADGAONKAR, Dileep, PhD; Indian journalist; b. 1 May 1944, Poona; s. of Vasant Padgaonkar and Shakuntala Padgaonkar (née Kattakar); m. Latika Tawadey 1968; two s.; ed Fergusson Coll., Poona, Institut des Hautes Etudes Cinématographiques, Paris, Sorbonne, Paris; Paris Corresp. of The Times of India 1968–73, Asst Ed., Bombay and Delhi 1973–78, Assoc. Ed. 1986–88, Ed. 1988–; Information Chief for Asia and Pacific, UNESCO 1978–81; Deputy Dir Office of Public Information, Paris 1981–85, Acting Dir 1985–86, Acting Dir Communication Sector 1986. *Publication:* When Bombay Burned (Ed.) 1993. *Leisure interests:* reading, classical music, contemporary art, cooking. *Address:* The Times of India, Times House, 7 Bahadur Shah Zafar Marg, New Delhi 110002 (Office); C-313, Defence Colony, New Delhi 110024, India (Home). *Telephone:* (11) 3312277 (Office); (11) 4697949 (Home). *Fax:* (11) 3323346. *Website:* www.timesofindia.com (Office).

PADILLA ARANCIBIA, Gen. David; Bolivian politician and army officer; Career officer with regional commands; Pres. of Bolivia and C-in-C of the Armed Forces 1978–79.

PADMANABAN, A., MA; Indian civil servant and writer; b. 14 Dec. 1928, Pinji, Ranipet, Tamil Nadu; m. Seetha Padmanaban 1961; two s. one d.; fmrly with Indian Admin. Service; Chief Sec. Govt of Tamil Nadu 1986–87, adviser to Gov. 1988–89; mem. Union Public Service Comm. 1989–93; Gov. of Mizoram 1998–2000; Indian Ed. Poet Int.; Pres. Authors' Guild of India; Vice-Pres. World Acad. of Arts and Culture, USA; Gov. Indian Council for Cultural Affairs; Eminent Poet Award, Int. Acad., India, Nat. Integration Award 1994, Michael Madhusudan Award. *Publications:* (biographical sketches) Dalits at the Cross-Roads: Their Struggle Past and Present 1996, (poetry) Rain Drops 1986, Light a Candle 1987, Buddha 1987, Untouchable's Journey 1991, My Dream 1992, Cosmic Accident 1995. *Leisure interests:* freelance writing, social work. *Address:* c/o Ananda Illam 14, 9th Cross Street, Shastri Nagar, Chennai 600020, India.

PADOA-SCHIOPPA, Tommaso, M.SC.ECON.; Italian banker and economist; b. 23 July 1940, Belluno; s. of Fabio Padoa and Stella Schwarz; m. Fiorella Kostoris 1966; one s. two d.; ed Università Commerciale Luigi Bocconi, Milan, Massachusetts Inst. of Tech., USA; with insurance co., Bremen, Fed. Repub. of Germany 1959–60, C. & A. Brenninkmeyer 1966–68; Economist, Research Dept, Banca d'Italia, Rome 1970–79, Head, Money Market Dept 1975–79, Direttore Centrale for Econ. Research 1983–84, Deputy Dir-Gen. 1984–97; Economic Adviser, the Treasury 1978–79; Dir-Gen. Econ. and Financial Affairs, Comm. of EC 1979–83; mem. Group of Thirty; Chair. Banking Advisory Cttee, Comm. of EC 1988–91, Cen. Bank's Working Group on EC Payment Systems 1991–, Group of Ten Basle Cttee on Banking Supervision at BIS 1993–; mem. Exec. Bd European Cen. Bank 1998–; Hon. Prof. Univ. of Frankfurt am Main 1999; Hon. Dr. (Trieste) 1999. *Publications include:* The Management of an Open Economy with One Hundred Per Cent Plus Wage Indexation (with F. Modigliani, in Essays in International Finance) 1978, Money, Economic Policy and Europe 1985, The Road to Monetary Union in Europe 1994, Il governo dell'economia 1997, Che cosa ci ha insegnato l'avventura europea 1998. *Address:* Banca d'Italia, Via Nazionale 91, 00187 Rome, Italy; European Central Bank, Kaiserstrasse 29, 60311 Frankfurt am Main, Germany (Office). *Telephone:* (69) 13447170 (Frankfurt) (Office). *Fax:* (69) 13447163(Frankfurt) (Office). *Website:* www.ecb.int.

PADVA, Genrikh Pavlovich; Russian barrister; b. 20 Feb. 1931, Moscow; s. of Pavel Padva and Eva Rappoport; one d.; ed Moscow Inst. of Law; Kalinin Pedagogical Inst.; mem. Kalinin Bar 1953, Presidium 1965–71, of Moscow Bar 1971–, of the Presidium 1986, Dir Research Inst. of Bar; one of founders of the USSR (now Russian) Union of Barristers, Deputy-Chair. of the Exec. Board 1990; Vice-Pres. of the Int. Asscn of Lawyers 1990, acted as a barrister on maj. political and economic trials in 1970s, was a lawyer for many dissidents, rendered legal advice to the families of Andrei Sakharov, singer Vladimir Vysotsky, Anatoliy Lukyanov (q.v.), Pavel Borodin; investigated some maj. econ. and criminal cases in late 1980s–1990s, a founder and Dir-Gen. of Russian-American Int. Lawyers Co.; Chief Partner Padva, Rosenberg and Partners Co. 1990–; Honoured Barrister of Russian Fed., FN Plevako Gold Medal. *Publications:* articles in specialized journals and newspapers on legal problems. *Address:* Padva and Partners, Bolshoi Golovin 6, Moscow (Office); B. Sukharevskiy per. 15 Apt. 15, 103051 Moscow, Russia (Home). *Telephone:* (095) 737-43-03 (Office); (095) 234-46-00 (Home). *Fax:* (095) 737-43-08 (Office); (095) 974-24-25. *E-mail:* padva@col.ru (Office). *Website:* www.advpadva.harod.ru (Office).

PAEK NAM SUN; North Korean government official and diplomatist; b. 1929, Kilchu, North Hamgyong Prov.; ed Kim Il-Song Univ.; Deputy Dir, Workers' Party Int. Dept 1968–74; Vice-Chair. Cttee for Cultural Relations with Foreign Countries 1972; Amb. to Poland 1974–79; apptd Deputy Dir, Workers' Party Propoganda Dept 1979; Del. to Inter-Korean talks; Sec.-Gen. Cttee for Peaceful Reunification of the Fatherland; Chair. Reunification

Policy Cttee., Supreme People's Ass. 1990; Deputy Head Gen. Fed. of Trade Unions 1973, Journalists Union 1985; Minister of Foreign Affairs 1998–. *Address:* Ministry of Foreign Affairs, Pyongyang, Democratic People's Republic of Korea (Office).

PAENIU, Bikenibeu, MSc; Tuvaluan politician and economist; b. 10 May 1956, Bikenibeu, Tarawa; two s. two d.; ed King George V School, Tarawa, Univ. of S. Pacific, Suva and Univ. of Hawaii; worked in Agric. Div. Tuvalu; later Asst Economist, South Pacific Comm. Nouméa; returned to Tuvalu 1988; Prime Minister of Tuvalu 1989–93, 1996–99. *Address:* c/o Office of the Prime Minister, Fongafale, Tuvalu.

PAFFRATH, Hans-Georg; German art dealer; b. 12 April 1922, Düsseldorf; s. of Hans Paffrath and Eleonore Paffrath (née Theegarten); m. Helena née Baroness Åkerhielm 1958; two s. three d.; ed Gymnasium; war service 1941–45; art dealer 1945–2000; fmr Royal Swedish Consul-Gen. for North Rhine Westphalia; Commdr Nordstjerne Orden, Verdienstorden des Landes Nordrhein-Westfalen, Medalj för förtjänster om utrikes förvaltningen. *Leisure interest:* riding. *Address:* Königsallee 46, Düsseldorf 40212, Germany. *Telephone:* (211) 323128 (Home). *Fax:* (211) 320216.

PAGANO, Gino; Italian industrialist; b. 2 Sept. 1921, Naples; ed Naples Univ.; joined ANIC (Associazione Nazionale dell'Industria Chimica) 1951, Man. Dir 1967–, Vice-Pres. 1970–72, Pres. 1972–76, 1980; co-ordinator, chemical and nuclear sector, ENI –1975; Pres. SIR Finanziaria SpA 1980–; Consultant Bastogi SpA 1978–80; Pres. SAPIR Porto Intermodale Ravenna SpA 1974–76, 1980–; Vice-Pres. Associazione Italiana di Ingegneria Chimica 1973–; mem. Bd Dirs. Hydrocarbons Int., Consultative Bd Liquifar Agropecuaria do Brasil 1981–. *Address:* c/o ANIC, San Donato Milanese, Milan, Italy. *Telephone:* (02) 53531.

PAGBALHA GELEG NAMGYAI; Chinese administrator; b. 1940, Litang Co., Sichuan Prov.; was confirmed by the Qangdin Lamasery as 11th incarnation of a living Buddha 1942; Vice-Chair. CPPCC 1959; mem. Presidium 4th NPC 1975–78; mem. Presidium 5th NPC 1978–82; Vice-Chair. People's Govt of Tibet Autonomous Region 1979–83; Vice-Pres. Buddhist Asscn of China 1980–; Exec. Chair. 6th CPPCC 1983–88; Acting Chair., Tibet Autonomous Region People's Congress 1983–86; Vice-Chair. Tibetan Autonomous Region Cttee of CPPCC and Vice Chair. Standing Cttee of Tibetan Autonomous Regional People's Congress 1983–88; Vice-Chair, CPPCC 7th Nat. Cttee 1988–92; Vice-Chair. Standing Cttee 8th NPC 1993–98, 9th NPC 1998–; Chair. People's Political Consultative Conference of Tibetan Autonomous Region 1993–; Pres. China Tibet Devt Foundation. *Address:* Standing Committee of National People's Congress, Beijing, People's Republic of China.

PAGE, Ashley; British classical dancer, choreographer and artistic director; b. 9 Aug. 1956, Rochester, Kent; s. of John H. Laverty and Sheila R. Medhurst; m. Nicola J. Roberts; one s. one d.; ed St Andrew's, Rochester, Royal Ballet, Lower and Upper Schools; joined Royal Ballet Co. 1975, soloist 1980, Prin. 1984, House Choreographer; leading roles in classical and modern repertoire; cr. numerous roles for MacMillan, Ashton and other leading choreographers; Choreographer Royal Opera House 1984; with numerous cos in London, Europe; Artistic Dir Scottish Ballet 2002–; Frederick Ashton Choreographer Award 1982, Frederick Ashton Memorial Comm. Award 1990, Time Out Dance Award 1994, Olivier Award for Best New Dance Production 1995. *Productions include:* 19 works for the Royal Ballet, 2 for the Dutch Nat. Ballet, 3 for the Rambert Dance Co. and several for Dance Umbrella, West Australian Ballet and other cos. *Films:* (all dance) Savage Water (Channel 4) 1989, Soldat (BBC) 1990; (art films) Pull-Dance for the Camera 1998. *Leisure interests:* fine arts, driving, film, music, reading, theatre, travel, photography, family, friends. *Address:* Scottish Ballet, 261 West Princes Street, Glasgow, G4 9EE, England. *Telephone:* (141) 331-6263 (Office). *Fax:* (141) 331-2629 (Office). *E-mail:* ashley.page@scottishballet.co.uk (Home).

PAGE, Bruce; British journalist and publisher; b. 1 Dec. 1936, London; s. of Roger and Amy B. Page; m. 1st Anne Gillison 1964 (divorced 1969); m. 2nd Anne L. Darnborough 1969; one s. one d.; ed Melbourne High School and Melbourne Univ.; trained as journalist, Melbourne Herald 1956–60; Evening Standard, London 1960–62; Daily Herald, London 1962–64; various exec. posts, Sunday Times, London 1964–76; Assoc. Ed. Daily Express 1977; Ed. New Statesman 1978–82; Dir Direct Image Systems and Communications 1992–95; various awards for journalism. *Publications:* co-author: Philby, the Spy who Betrayed a Generation, An American Melodrama, Do You Sincerely Want to be Rich?, Destination Disaster, Ulster (contrib.), The Yom Kippur War, The British Press. *Leisure interests:* reading, sailing, computers. *Address:* 32 Lauderdale Tower, Barbican, London, EC2Y 8BY; Beach House, Shingle Streeet, Shottisham, Suffolk, IP12 3BE, England. *Telephone:* (20) 7628-3847; (1394) 411427. *E-mail:* bruce@pages.dircon.co.uk (Home).

PAGE, Geneviève (pseudonym of Geneviève Bonjean); French actress; b. 13 Dec. 1927, Paris; d. of Jacques Bonjean and Germaine Lipmann; m. Jean-Claude Bujard 1959; one s. one d.; ed Lycée Racine, Paris, Sorbonne, Paris, Conservatoire nat. d'art dramatique; prin. actress in the Comédie Française, the Jean-Louis Barrault company and TNP Jean Vilar; has appeared in many famous classical and tragic stage roles, including Les larmes amères de Petra von Kant (Critics' Prize for Best Actress 1980), La nuit des rois, L'aigle à deux têtes, Angelo, tyran de Padoue 1984, Perséphone 1988, Mère Courage 1988, Le balcon 1991, Paroles de poètes 1992, La peste 1992, La femme sur le lit 1994 (Colombe Prix, Plaisir du Théâtre Best Actress), Les orandes forêts 1997,

Delicate Balance 1998; Chevalier Légion d'honneur, Chevalier du Mérite sportif. *Films include:* Ce siècle a cinquante ans, Pas de pitié pour les femmes, Fanfan la tulipe, Lettre ouverte, Plaisirs de Paris, Nuits andalouses, L'étrange désir de M. Bard, Cherchez la femme, L'homme sans passé, Foreign Intrigue, The Silken Affair, Michael Strogoff, Un amour de poche, Song Without End, Le bal des adieux, El Cid, Les égarements, Le jour et l'heure, L'honorable correspondance, Youngblood Hawke, Le majordome, Les corsaires, Trois chambres à Manhattan, Grand Prix, Belle de jour, Mayerling, A Talent for Loving, The Private Life of Sherlock Holmes, Les Gémeaux, Décembre, Buffet froid, Beyond Therapy 1987, Les bois noirs 1991, Lovers 1999. *TV:* La Nuit des rois 1962 (Best Actress TV 1962), La chambre 1964, La chasse aux hommes 1976, Athalie 1980, Les gens ne sont pas forcément ignobles 1990. *Leisure interests:* ancient artefacts, skiing. *Address:* 52 rue de Vaugirard, 75006 Paris, France.

PAGE, Jennifer Anne, CBE, BA; British civil servant and business executive; b. 12 Nov. 1944; d. of Edward Page and Olive Page; m. Jeremy David Orme 2001; ed Barr's Hill Grammar School, Coventry and Univ. of London; entered civil service 1968, Prin. Dept of Environment 1974, Asst Sec. Dept of Transport 1980; seconded BNOC 1981, London Dockland's Devt Corpn 1983; Sr Vice-Pres. Pallas Invest SA 1984–89; Chief Exec. English Heritage (Historic Bldgs. and Monuments Comm.) 1989–95, Millennium Comm. 1995–97, New Millennium Experience Co. Ltd 1997–2000; mem. Bd Railtrack Group 1994–2001, Equitable Life Assurance Soc. 1994–2001; Dir London Acad. of Music and Dramatic Art 2001–. *Address:* c/o Railtrack Group PLC, Railtrack House, Euston Square, London, NW1 2EE, England.

PAGLIA, Camille, BA, M.PHIL., PhD; American professor of humanities; b. 2 April 1947, Endicott, NY; d. of Pasquale Paglia and Lydia Paglia; ed State Univ of New York at Binghamton, Yale Univ.; Faculty mem. Bennington Coll. 1972–80; Visiting Lecturer, Wesleyan Univ. 1980, Yale Univ. 1980–84; Asst Prof., Phil. Coll. of Performing Arts (now Univ. of the Arts) 1984–87, Assoc. Prof. 1987–91, Prof. of Humanities 1991–2000; Univ. Prof. and Prof. of Humanities and Media Studies 2000–; columnist Salon.com 1995–2001; Contributing Ed. Interview magazine 2001–. *Publications:* Sexual Personae: Art and Decadence from Nefertiti to Emily Dickinson 1990, Sex, Art and American Culture: Essays 1992, Vamps and Tramps: New Essays 1994, Alfred Hitchcock's The Birds 1998. *Address:* University of the Arts, 320 South Broad Street, Philadelphia, PA 19102, USA. *Telephone:* (212) 421-1700 (agent) (Office); (215) 717-6265. *Fax:* (212) 980-3671 (agent).

PĄGOWSKI, Andrzej; Polish graphic designer; b. 19 April 1953, Warsaw; ed High School of Fine Arts, Poznań; illustrator of books, covers of compact discs; designer of posters, TV and film billboards, TV programme credits, satirical drawings; has designed over 1,000 posters including Husband and Wife and series highlighting dangers of alcohol, tobacco and drug abuse; numerous awards include: Silver Medal, Biennale Polish Poster 1983, 1993, First Prize Int. Competition for the Best Film and TV Poster, Los Angeles 1980–1993, Silver Hugon, Golden and Silver Badge (twice) Int. Competition Film Poster, Chicago 1982–1987, Clio Poland Award 1993. *Art exhibitions:* numerous solo and group exhbns in Poland and abroad; works in numerous pvt. and public collections including Metropolitan Museum, NY. *Address:* Andrzej Pągowski Studio P, ul. Balaton 8, 01-981 Warsaw, Poland (Office). *Telephone:* (22) 8649293 (Office). *Fax:* (22) 8649290 (Office). *E-mail:* pagowski .a@studio-p.pl (Office).

PAHAD, Aziz Goolam Hoosein, MA; South African politician; b. 25 Dec. 1940, Schweizer-Reneke, Western Transvaal; s. of Goolam Hoosein Ismail Pahad and Amina Pahad; m. Sandra Pahad 1994; two s. one d.; ed Cen. Indian High School, Johannesburg, Univ. of Witwatersrand, Univ. Coll., London, Univ. of Sussex; in exile 1964–90; worked in London office of African Nat. Congress (ANC) from 1968, later mem. ANC Revolutionary Council until its dissolution in 1983; rep. of ANC Revolutionary Council in Angola and Zambia; mem. ANC Nat. Exec. Cttee 1985–; Deputy Head, ANC Dept of Int. Affairs 1991; mem. Nat. Peace Exec. Cttee 1991–92; mem. Sub-Council on Foreign Affairs of Transitional Exec. Council 1993–94; MP 1994–; Deputy Minister of Foreign Affairs 1994–, re-elected 1999–. *Address:* Room 1725, 120 Plein Street, Cape Town (Office); Room 283, East Wing, Union Buildings, Pretoria, South Africa (Office). *Telephone:* (21) 4643711 (Cape Town) (Office); (12) 3510105 (Pretoria) (Office). *Fax:* (21) 4618090 (Cape Town) (Office); (12) 3510259 (Pretoria) (Office). *E-mail:* depmin@foreign.gov.za (Office). *Website:* www.dfa.gov.za.

PAHANG, HRH Sultan of, Sultan Haji Ahmad Shah Al-Mustain Billah ibni Al-Marhum Sultan Abu Bakar Ri'Ayatuddin Al-Muadzam Shah, D.K.P.; Malaysian Ruler; b. 24 Oct. 1930, Istana Mangga Tunggal, Pekan; m. Tengku Hajjah Afzan binti Tengku Muhammad 1954; ed Malay Coll. Kuala Kangsar, Worcester Coll., Oxford, Univ. Coll., Exeter; Tengku Mahkota (Crown Prince) 1944; Capt. 4th Battalion, Royal Malay Regt 1954; Commdr of 12th Infantry Battalion of Territorial Army 1963–65, Lt-Col; mem. State Council 1955; Regent 1956, 1959, 1965; succeeded as Sultan 1974; Timbalan Yang di Pertuan Agong (Deputy Supreme Head of State of Malaysia) 1975–79, Yang di Pertuan Agong (Supreme Head of State) 1979–84, 1985; Constitutional Head of Int. Islamic Univ. 1988; Hon. DLitt (Malaya) 1988; Hon. LLD (Northrop, USA) 1993. *Address:* Istana Abu Bakar, Pekan, Pahang, Malaysia.

PAHLAVI, Farah Diba, fmr Empress of Iran; b. 14 Oct. 1938; d. of Sohrab and Farida Diba; m. H.I.M. Shah Mohammed Reza Pahlavi 1959 (died 1980); two s. two d.; ed Jeanne d'Arc School and Razi School, Tehran and Ecole Spéciale d'Architecture, Paris; Foreign Assoc. mem. Fine Arts Acad., France 1974; fmr Patron Farah Pahlavi Asscn (admin. of Social Educ. Asscn), Iran Cultural Foundation and 34 other educational, health and cultural orgs.; left Iran Jan. 1979; living in Egypt June 1980.

PAHR, Willibald P., DrIur; Austrian administrator and politician; b. 5 June 1930, Vienna; m. Ingeborg Varga 1960; one s. one d.; ed Univ. of Vienna and Coll. of Europe, Bruges, Belgium; Asst in Inst. of Int. Law and Int. Relations, Univ. of Vienna 1952–55; served Fed. Chancellery 1955–76, Head of Section 1968, Head of Dept 1973, Dir-Gen. 1975–76; Fed. Minister for Foreign Affairs 1976–83; Amb. to Fed. Repub. of Germany 1983–85; Sec.-Gen. World Tourism Org. 1986–88; Special Commr for Refugees and Migration 1990–95. *Publications:* Der österreichische Status der dauernden Neutralität 1967, several articles in Revue des Droits de l'Homme, numerous articles on current int. problems in various periodicals; co-ed. Grundrechte, die Rechtsprechung in Europa (journal). *Address:* ICMPD, Möllwaldplatz 4, 1040 Vienna, Austria.

PAIGE, Elaine, OBE; British singer and actress; b. 5 March 1948, Barnet; d. of Eric Bickerstaff and Irene Bickerstaff; ed Aida Foster Stage school; West End theatre appearances in Hair 1968, Jesus Christ Superstar 1973, Grease (played Sandy) 1973, Billy (played Rita) 1974, created roles of Eva Perón in Evita 1978 and Grizabella in Cats 1981, Abbacadabra (played Carabosse) (London) 1983, Chess (played Florence) 1986, Anything Goes (played Reno Sweeney) 1989, Piaf 1993–94, Sunset Boulevard (played Norma Desmond) 1995–96, The Misanthrope (played Célimène) 1998, The King and I 2000; 14 solo albums; 4 multi-platinum albums, 8 consecutive gold albums; Soc. of West End Theatre Award (Best Actress in a Musical for the role of Eva Perón in Evita) 1978, Variety Club Award for Showbusiness Personality of the Year and Recording Artist of the Year 1986, British Asscn of Songwriters, Composers and Authors (BASCA) Award 1993, Lifetime Achievement Award, Nat. Operatic and Dramatic Asscn 1999. *Leisure interests:* antiques, gardening, skiing, tennis. *Address:* c/o E.P. Records, Sanctuary House, 45–53 Sinclair Road, London W14 0NS, England. *Telephone:* (20) 7300-1865. *Fax:* (20) 7300-1864.

PAIGE, Rod, PhD; American politician and educational administrator; b. Monticello, Miss.; ed Jackson State Univ., Indiana Univ.; mem. Bd of Educ., Houston Ind. School Dist 1989, Pres. 1992; Supt of Schools 1994; Dean Coll. of Educ. Texas Southern Univ.; Sec. of Educ. 2001–; mem. Houston Job Training Partnership Council; Community Advisory Bd of Texas Commerce Bank, NAACP; consultant, Greater New Orleans Educ. Foundation; Sec.-Treas. Council of the Great City Schools; Richard R. Green Award 1998, Outstanding Urban Educator Award 1999, McGraw Prize in Educ. 2000, Supt of the Year Award 2000, 2001. *Address:* Department of Education, 400 Maryland Avenue, SW, Washington, DC 20202, USA. *Telephone:* (202) 401-3000 (Office). *Fax:* (202) 401-0596 (Office). *Website:* www.ed.gov (Office).

PAIK, Nam June; South Korean/American kinetic artist; b. 1932, South Korea; ed Univ. of Tokyo, Japan; left S. Korea 1949, moved permanently to NY 1964; mem. Fluxus (anarchic, neo-dadaist Movt) 1961. *Major works include:* Urmusik 1961, Opera Sextronique, performed NY 1967, The K-456 Robot. *Exhibitions include:* Galerie Parnassus, Wuppertal, Germany 1963, Video Works 1963–68, Hayward Gallery, London 1988.

PAIK KUN-WOO; South Korean pianist; b. 10 March 1946; ed Juilliard School, New York and in London and Italy; interpreter of piano works of Ravel, Liszt, Scriabin and Prokofiev; has played with orchestras throughout N America and Europe, notably Indianapolis Symphony, Rotterdam Philharmonic, Royal Philharmonic, London Symphony, BBC Symphony (soloist, Last Night of the Proms 1987), Orchestre Nat. de France, Polish Radio Nat. Symphony; lives in Paris; recitals at all maj. European music festivals; three Diapason d'Or awards.

PAIN, Emil Abramovich, PhD; Russian sociologist; b. 6 Dec. 1948, Kiev; m.; one s.; ed Voronezh State Univ., Moscow State Univ.; researcher on problems of regional sociology and ethnology, problems of nat. conflicts, Voronezh State Univ. and Inst. of Ethnography USSR Acad. of Sciences 1974–91; during perestroika was expert of Deputies' Comm. on Deported Peoples and Problems of Crimea Tartars 1989–91; Chief Adviser Int. Asscn of Foreign Policy 1991–92; Dir-Gen. Cen. Ethnopolitical and Regional Studies (CEPRI) 1993–; mem. Pres.'s Council 1993–97; mem. Expert-Analytical Dept of Pres. of Russia 1994–98; Adviser to Pres. 1996–99; Prof. Inst. of Int. Relations 1992–99, Moscow Univ. 1999–. *Publications:* numerous articles on relations between nations, prevention of social conflicts, sociology and ethnology. *Address:* CEPRI, Krzhizhanovskogo str. 24/35 Korp. 5, Suite 522, 117259 Moscow, Russia. *Telephone:* (095) 128-56-51 (Office); (095) 431-56-07 (Home). *Fax:* (095) 128-56-51 (Office); (095) 431-56-07 (Home).

PAINTAL, Autar Singh, MD, PhD, FRCP, FRS, FRSE; Indian professor of physiology; b. 24 Sept. 1925; s. of Dr. Man Singh and Rajwans Kaur; one s. two d.; ed Forman Christian Coll., Lahore, Lucknow and Edinburgh Univs.; lecturer, King George's Medical Coll. Lucknow Univ. 1949; Rockefeller Fellow 1950; lecturer, Univ. of Edin. 1951; Control Officer, Tech. Devt Establishment Labs., Ministry of Defence, Kanpur 1952–54; Prof. of Physiology, All India Inst. of Med. Sciences, Delhi 1958–64; Prof. of Physiology and Dir Vallabhbhai Patel Chest Inst., Delhi Univ. 1964–; now Dir-Gen. Indian Council of Medical Research; Dean Faculty of Med. Sciences, Delhi Univ. 1966–77; Fellow, Indian Acad. of Medical Sciences, Indian Nat. Science Acad. and other learned socs.; Pres. Nat. Coll. of Chest Physicians 1981–86, Indian Science Congress

1984–85; numerous awards and distinctions including R.D. Birla Award 1982, Nehru Science Award 1983, Acharya J. C. Bose Medal 1985; Hon. DSc (Benares Hindu Univ.) 1982, (Delhi) 1984, (Aligarh Muslim Univ.) 1986, other hon. degrees. *Publications:* articles in professional journals. *Leisure interests:* swimming, rowing, bird watching. *Address:* Indian Council of Medical Research, Ansari Nagar, New Delhi 110029 (Office); DST Centre for Visceral Mechanisms, Vallabhbhai Patel Chest Institute, Delhi University, P.O. Box 2101, Delhi 110007, India. *Telephone:* (11) 7257749.

PAISLEY, Rev. Ian Richard Kyle, DD, MP, FRGS; British politician and minister of religion; b. 6 April 1926; s. of Rev. J. Kyle Paisley and Isabella Paisley; m. Eileen E Cassells 1956; two s. (twins) three d.; ed Ballymena Model School, Ballymena Tech. High School and S. Wales Bible Coll. and Reformed Presbyterian Theological Coll., Belfast; ordained 1946; Minister, Martyrs Memorial Free Presbyterian Church 1946–; Moderator, Free Presbyterian Church of Ulster 1951; f. The Protestant Telegraph 1966; MP (Democratic Unionist) 1974– (Protestant Unionist 1970–74) resgnd seat Dec. 1985 in protest against Anglo-Irish Agreement; re-elected Jan. 1986; MP (Protestant Unionist) for Bannside, Co. Antrim, Parl. of N Ireland (Stormont) 1970–72, Leader of the Opposition 1972, Chair. Public Accounts Cttee 1972; mem. N Ireland Ass. 1973–74, elected to Second N Ireland Ass. 1982; MEP 1979–; MP for Antrim N, N.I. Ass. 1998–2000; mem. Constitutional Convention 1975–76; Leader (co-founder) of Democratic Unionist Party 1972; Chair. Agric. Cttee and Cttee of Privileges 1983; Pres. Whitefield Coll. of the Bible, Laurencetown, Co. Down 1979–; Co-Chair. World Congress of Fundamentalists 1978; mem. Political Cttee European Parl., N.I. Ass. 1998–; mem. Int. Cultural Soc. of Korea 1977. *Publications:* History of the 1859 Revival 1959, Christian Foundations 1960, Ravenhill Pulpit Vol. I 1966, Vol. II 1967, Exposition of the Epistle to the Romans 1968, Billy Graham and the Church of Rome 1970, The Massacre of Saint Bartholomew 1972, Paisley, the Man and his Message 1976, America's Debt to Ulster 1976, Ulster—the Facts 1981 (jtly.), No Pope Here 1982, Dr. Kidd 1982, Those Flaming Tennents 1983, Crown Rights of Jesus Christ 1985, Be Sure: 7 Rules for Public Speaking 1986, Paisley's Pocket Preacher 1986, Jonathan Edwards, The Theologian of Revival 1987, Union with Rome 1989, The Soul of the Question 1990, The Revised English Bible: An Exposure 1990, What a Friend We Have in Jesus 1994, Understanding Events in Northern Ireland: An Introduction for Americans 1995, My Plea for the Old Sword 1997, The Rent Veils at Calvary 1997, A Text a Day Keeps the Devil Away 1997. *Address:* House of Commons, London, SW1A 0AA, England (Office); The Parsonage, 17 Cyprus Avenue, Belfast, BT5 5NT, N Ireland.

PAK GIL YON; North Korean diplomatist; m.; three c.; ed Univ. of Int. Relations; joined Ministry of Foreign Affairs 1964, served as Officer, Consul in Singapore and Myanmar, Section Chief, Deputy Dir, Dir of Ministry 1978–1983, Vice-Minister 1983–84, 1996–; Perm. Rep. to UN, New York 1984–96, 2001–; Kim Il Sung Order. *Address:* Permanent Mission of Democratic People's Republic of Korea to the UN, 820 Second Avenue, 13th Floor, New York, NY 10017, USA (Office). *Telephone:* (212) 972-3105 (Office). *Fax:* (212) 972-3154 (Office). *E-mail:* dprk@un.int (Office).

PAK SONG CHOL; North Korean politician; b. 1913; Amb. to Bulgaria 1954; commanded unit in Korean War, retd as Lt-Gen.; Minister of Foreign Affairs 1959; mem. Cen. Cttee Workers' Party of Korea (WPK) 1961, mem. Political Bureau 1980–; Vice-Premier and Minister of Foreign Affairs 1966; Second Vice-Premier 1970; Political Commissar of WPK 1970; Premier 1976–77; mem. Cen. People's Cttee 1977; Vice-Pres. Democratic People's Repub. of Korea 1977–98; mem. Presidium, Democratic Front for Reunification of Fatherland 1991; Hon. Vice-Pres. Presidium Supreme People's Ass. 1998–. *Address:* c/o Supreme People's Assembly, Pyongyang, Democratic People's Republic of Korea.

PAKENHAM, Hon. Michael, CMG, MA; British diplomatist; b. 3 Nov. 1943, Oxford; s. of the late Earl of Longford and of Elizabeth Pakenham, Countess of Longford; brother of Antonia Fraser (q.v.); m. Mimi Doak; two d.; ed Ampleforth Coll., N Yorks., Trinity Coll. Cambridge, Rice Univ., Tex., USA; joined FCO 1965, served in Warsaw, New Delhi, Paris, Washington, DC; mem. staff British Representation to EU 1987–91; Amb. to Luxembourg 1991–94; seconded to Cabinet Office 1971–74, Deputy Sec. to Cabinet, Chair. Jt Intelligence Cttee and Cen. Intelligence Co-ordinator 1997–2000; Amb. to Poland 2001–03. *Leisure interests:* golf, tennis, museums, military history. *Address:* c/o Foreign and Commonwealth Office, London, England (Office).

PAKSAS, Rolandas; Lithuanian politician and engineer; b. 10 June 1956, Telsiai; m. Laima Paksienė; one s. one d.; ed Vilnius Inst. of Civil Eng, Leningrad Inst. of Civil Aviation; flight instructor –1984; Chair. Vilnius Darius ir Girenas Aero Club, Aviation Dept, Voluntary Nat. Defence Service 1985–92; Pres. Construction Co. Restako 1992–97; elected to Vilnius City Council, Mayor of Vilnius 1997–99; Prime Minister of Lithuania 1999–2000; adviser for special tasks to Lithuanian Pres. 1999–2000; Pres. of Lithuania 2003–; fmr Chair. Lithuanian Liberal Union. *Address:* Office of the President, S. Daukanto 3/8, Vilnius 2008, Lithuania (Office). *Telephone:* (526) 28986 (Office). *Fax:* (521) 26210 (Office). *E-mail:* info@president.lt (Office). *Website:* www.president.lt (Office).

PÁL, László; Hungarian politician and electrical engineer; b. 5 Sept. 1942, Budapest; m.; two c.; ed Inst. of Energetics, Moscow, Political Acad., Budapest; Research Inst. for Electrical Eng 1966–69; mem. Nat. Cttee for Technological Devt 1969–89; State Sec. Ministry of Industry 1989–90; mem. of Parl. 1990–97; Minister of Industry 1994–95; Chair. Bd Hungarian Oil and

Gas Co.; Lóránd Eötvös Award 1986, János Neumann Award 1988. *Address:* 1117 Budapest, Okt. 23. str. 18, Hungary. *Telephone:* (1) 209-0101. *Fax:* (1) 209-0051.

PÁL, Lénárd; Hungarian physicist; b. 7 Nov. 1925, Gyoma; s. of Imre Pál and Erzsébet Varga; m. Angela Danóci 1963; one d.; ed Budapest and Moscow Univs.; Dept Head, Cen. Research Inst. for Physics, Budapest 1953–56, Deputy Dir 1956–69, Dir 1970–74, Dir-Gen 1974–78; Prof. of Nuclear Physics, Eötvös Lóránd Univ. Budapest 1961–77, 1989–98; Pres. State Office for Tech. Devt 1978–80, 1984–85, Nat. Atomic Energy Comm. 1978–80, 1984–85; mem. Science Policy Cttee, Council of Ministers 1978–85; Sec. Cen. Cttee Hungarian Socialist Workers' Party 1985–88; Corresp. mem. Hungarian Acad. of Sciences 1961–73, mem. 1973, Gen. Sec. 1980–84, Pres. Intercosmos Council 1980–84; Foreign mem. Acad. of Sciences of the USSR 1976, of GDR 1982, of Czechoslovakia 1983, Russian Acad. of Sciences 1996; mem. Leibniz Soc. e.V. 1994; Gold Medal, Order of Labour 1956, 1968; Kossuth Prize 1962; Memorial Medal 25th Anniversary of the Liberation 1970; Kurtchatov Memory Medal (USSR) 1970; Gold Medal of the Hungarian Acad. of Sciences 1975, Eötvös Lóránd Physical Soc. Medal 1976, Red Banner Order of Labour (USSR) 1975, Red Banner of Work 1985, Wigner's Award 2001. *Publications:* Science and Technical Development 1987, Science and Technology Policies in Finland and Hungary 1985, Foundation of Probability Calculus and Statistics 1995; approx. 275 articles in Hungarian and foreign scientific journals. *Leisure interests:* hunting, angling. *Address:* Széher út 21/A, 1021 Budapest II, Hungary. *Telephone:* 275-0725. *Fax:* 275-0725.

PAL SINGH, Krishna; Indian politician; b. 2 Aug. 1922, V. Birhuli, Shahdol Dist, Madhya Pradesh; politically active at school and in higher educ.; Pres. Students' Union, Rewa, organized students' congress and congress volunteer corps; worked with Sindhi refugees during communal riots of 1947–48; became follower of Bhai Paramanandji 1942, joined Quit India Movt, arrested and served prison sentence; after independence became trades union leader, continuing to campaign for causes of students, kisans, colliery workers and other labourers; Vice-Pres. MP Unit of All India Trades Union Congress; joined Socialist Party 1946 and became Pres. of party in fmr Vindya Pradesh and Pres. Samyukta Socialist Party, MP; joined Congress Party 1965; mem. A.I.C.C. and M.P.C.C., later Gen. Sec. and Vice-Pres. M.P.C.C. and special invitee A.I.C. Working Cttee; MP Vidhan Sabha 1962–90; served five times as Minister with many different portfolios, finance, law, etc., becoming Deputy Leader; fmr Gov. of Gujarat; party and political observer gen. and party elections in Indian states; Pres. Friends of Soviet Union, India-China Soc., MP Unit of Nepal Friendship Soc., India-Africa Friendship Asscn and Gen. Sec. All India Indo-Arab Friendship Soc.

PALACIO, Alfredo, MD; Ecuadorean politician and cardiologist; b. 22 Jan. 1939, Guayaquil; ed Colegio San José La Salle, Universidad de Guayaquil; worked at various hosps in USA 1969–74, including Mount Sinai Hosp., Cleveland, OH 1969–71, Veterans Admin. Hosp., Missouri 1971–72, Barnes Hosp., Washington Univ. 1972–74; Dir Nat. Inst. of Cardiology 1980–; Prin. Prof. of Cardiology, Faculty of Medicine, Univ. of Guayaquil 1989–, Prof. of Public Health 2001–; Minister of Public Health 1994–96; Vice-Pres. of Ecuador Jan. 2003–; fmr Regional Dir Equador Inst. of Social Security (IESS); Fellow American Coll. of Cardiology, American Coll. of Chest Physicians, American Coll. of Physicians; mem. American Acad. of Sciences, Ecuador Acad. of Medicine, and numerous other medical socs; Commdr Al Mérito Atahualpha, Ministry of Nat. Defence 1995, Recognition of Merit, Ecuador Nat. Civil Defence 1996, Recognition of Merit, Gran Cruz, Pres. of Ecuador 1996; American Medical Asscn Award 1976, Eugenio Espejo Award, Quito Municipality 1982, Scientific Merit Award, Guayaquil Municipality 1982, 1987. *Publications include:* Atlas de Ecocardiografía Bidimensional 1981, Atlas of 2D Echocardiography 1983, Cardiopatía Isquémica (Ed.) 1985, Estudio Guayaquil 1991, Hacia un Humanisco Científico 1997. *Address:* Office of the Vice-President, Manuel Larrea y Arenas, Edif. Consejo Provincial de Pichincha, 21, Quito, Ecuador (Office). *Telephone:* (2) 250-4953 (Office). *Fax:* (2) 250-3379 (Office). *E-mail:* info@alfredopalacio.com (Office). *Website:* www.alfredopalacio.com (Office).

PALACIO VALLELERSUNDI, Ana; Spanish politician and lawyer; b. 22 Aug. 1948, Madrid; MEP (PPE, PP) 1994–, mem. Cttee on Transport and Tourism, on the Rules of Procedure, on the Verification of Credentials and Immunities, Del. for Relations with SE Europe; Pres. Cttee on Legal Affairs and the Internal Market, European Parl. 1999–2002; Minister of Foreign Affairs July 2002–; Pres. Exec. Council Europäische Rechtsakad.; Vice-Pres. Consejo de los Colegios de Abogados Europeos; Hon. mem. Bar of England and Wales (including the Inner Temple). *Address:* Ministry of Foreign Affairs, Plaza Marqués de Salamanca 8, 28071 Madrid, Spain (Office). *Telephone:* (91) 3798300 (Office). *Fax:* (91) 3667098 (Office). *Website:* www.mae.es (Office).

PALADE, George Emil; American scientist; b. 19 Nov. 1912, Iaşi, Romania; s. of Emil Palade and Constanţa Cantemir; m. 1st Irina Malaxa 1941 (died 1969), one s. one d.; m. 2nd Marilyn Farquhar 1970; ed Hasdeu Lyceum, Buzău, Univ. of Bucharest; went to the USA 1946; naturalized U.S. citizen 1952; Instructor, Asst Prof. of Anatomy, School of Medicine, Univ. of Bucharest 1935–45; Visiting Investigator, Asst, Assoc., Prof. of Cell Biology, Rockefeller Univ. 1946–73; Prof. of Cell Biology, Yale Univ. 1973–83; Sr Research Scientist 1983–90; Dean Scientific Affairs, Univ. of Calif. San Diego, School of Medicine 1990–; Fellow American Acad. of Arts and Sciences; mem. NAS, Pontifical Acad. of Sciences; Foreign mem. Royal Soc.; Albert Lasker

Basic Research Award 1966, Gairdner Special Award (Canada) 1968, Hurwitz Prize 1970, Nobel Prize for Medicine 1974, Nat. Medal of Science 1986. *Leisure interest:* history. *Address:* University of California at San Diego, Division of Cellular and Molecular Medicine, M-002, La Jolla, CA 92093, USA.

PALAU, Luis; American evangelist and writer; b. 27 Nov. 1934, Buenos Aires, Argentina; s. of Luis Palau Sr; m. Patricia Marilyn Scofield 1961; four s.; ed St Alban's Coll., Buenos Aires, Multnomah School of the Bible, Portland, Ore., USA; mem. staff Bank of London, Buenos Aires and Cordoba 1952–59; moved to USA 1960; worked as interpreter for Billy Graham 1962; began Spanish radio broadcasts as missionary in Colombia 1967; began evangelistic ministry as part of Overseas Crusades 1968; made crusade broadcasts to all Latin America 1975; named Pres. Overseas Crusades 1976; f. Luis Palau Evangelistic Asscn 1978; first major crusade in USA, San Diego 1981; crusades on four continents 1982; Dr. hc (Talbot Theological Seminary) 1977, (Wheaton Coll.) 1985. *Publications:* Heart After God 1978, My Response 1985, Time To Stop Pretending 1985, So You Want To Grow 1986, Calling America and the Nations to Christ 1994; 26 books and booklets in Spanish; works have been transl. into 30 languages. *Leisure interest:* family. *Address:* Luis Palua Evangelistic Association, 1500 NW 167th Place, Beaverton, OR 97006, USA.

PALECKIS, Justas Vincas; Lithuanian diplomatist and politician; b. 1 Jan. 1942, Samara, Russia; s. of Justas Paleckis and Genovaite Paleckiene; m. Laima Paleckienė; two s. one d.; ed Vilnius State Univ., Higher Diplomatic School, USSR Ministry of Foreign Affairs; contrib. Komjaunimo Tiesa (daily) 1963–66; Third Sec. USSR Embassy to Switzerland; Second, First Sec., Counsellor, USSR Embassy to GDR 1969–82; Deputy Dir, Dir of sector Lithuanian CP Cen. Cttee 1983–89; Sec., Ind. Lithuanian CP Cen. Cttee 1989–90; Deputy Chair. Foreign Affairs Cttee, Lithuanian Repub. Supreme Council (Parl.) 1990–92; lecturer Inst. of Journalism, Vilnius State Univ. 1990–93; lecturer Inst. of Int. Relations and Political Science, Vilnius State Univ. 1993–95; adviser on Foreign Affairs to Lithuanian Pres. 1993–96; Amb. to UK 1996–2001 (also accred to Ireland 1997–2001); Deputy Minister of Foreign Affairs 2001–. *Publications:* Swiss Pyramids 1974, At the Foot of Swiss Pyramids 1985. *Leisure interests:* reading, theatre, gardening, tennis, swimming (fmr mem. Lithuanian water polo team). *Address:* Ministry of Foreign Affairs, J. Tumo-Vaizganto g. 2, 2600 Vilnius (Office); K. Donelaicio 20-5, 2000 Vilnius, Lithuania (Home). *Telephone:* 2362420 (Office); 2635445 (Home). *Fax:* 2362485 (Office). *E-mail:* justas.paleckis@urm.lt. *Website:* www .urm.lt (Office).

PALECZNY, Piotr; Polish pianist and academic; b. 10 May 1946, Rybnik; m.; one s.; ed State Higher School of Music, Warsaw (studied under Prof. Jan Ekier); f. master courses in music, Bordeaux, Amsterdam, Paris, Buenos Aires, Tokyo, Lugano, Warsaw; soloist with orchestras including Grand Symphonic Orchestra of Polish Radio and TV, Katowice, Chicago Symphony, Royal Philharmonic, Concertgebouw, BBC London, RAI Roma, Nat. Orchestra Madrid; Artistic Man. Chopin Int. Festival, Duszniki Zdrój; Prof. F. Chopin Acad. of Music, Warsaw; winner pianist competitions in Sofia 1968, Monachium 1969, Warsaw 1970, Pleven 1971, Bordeaux 1972; Grand Prix VIII Chopin Competition 1970; judge int. music competitions; Kt's Cross, Order of Polonia Restituta, Gold Cross of Merit. *Recordings include:* K. Szymanowski Concert Symphony No. 4, works by Chopin, Paderewski, Szymanowski, Lutosławski. *Address:* F. Chopin Academy of Music, ul. Okólnik 2, 00-368 Warsaw, Poland (Office). *Telephone:* (22) 8277241 (Office).

PALEY, Grace; American writer and teacher; b. 11 Dec. 1922, The Bronx, New York; d. of Isaac Goodside and Manya Ridnik Goodside; m. 1st Jess Paley 1942; one s. one d.; m. 2nd Robert Nichols 1972; ed Hunter Coll. and New York Univ.; teaching staff Sarah Lawrence Coll. 1966, Columbia Univ., New York 1984; mem. Inst. of American Writers, American Acad., Inst. of Arts and Letters; Guggenheim Fellow; Edith Wharton Award, New York State. *Publications:* The Little Disturbances of Man 1959, Enormous Changes at the Last Minute 1974, Later the Same Day 1984, Leaning Forward (poems) 1985, Long Walks and Intimate Talks 1991, New and Collected Poems 1992, The Collected Stories 1994, Just As I Thought 1998, Begin Again Poems 2000. *Address:* P.O. Box 620, Thetford, VT 05074, USA.

PALIN, Michael Edward, CBE, BA; British actor and writer; b. 5 May 1943; s. of the late Edward Palin and Mary Palin; m. Helen M. Gibbins 1966; two s. one d.; ed Birkdale School, Sheffield, Shrewsbury School, Brasenose Coll. Oxford; Pres. Transport 2000; actor and writer: Monty Python's Flying Circus, BBC TV 1969–74, Ripping Yarns, BBC TV 1976–80; actor: Three Men in a Boat, BBC 1975: writer: East of Ipswich, BBC TV 1987, Number 27, BBC TV, The Weekend (play for stage) 1994; actor and co-author, films: And Now for Something Completely Different 1970, Monty Python and the Holy Grail 1974, Monty Python's Life of Brian 1979, Time Bandits 1980, Monty Python's "The Meaning of Life" 1982; actor, writer and co-producer The Missionary 1982; actor, co-scriptwriter American Friends 1991; actor in: Jabberwocky 1976, A Private Function 1984, Brazil 1985, A Fish Called Wanda 1988 (Best Supporting Film Actor, BAFTA Award 1988), GBH (Channel 4 TV) 1991, Fierce Creatures 1997; TV series: contrib. to Great Railway Journeys of the World, BBC TV 1980, 1993, presenter Around the World in 80 Days 1989, Pole to Pole 1992, Palin's Column 1994, Full Circle 1997, Fierce Creatures 1997, Michael Palin's Hemingway Adventure 1999; Dr hc (Sheffield) 1992, (Queen's, Belfast) 2000. *Publications include:* Monty Python's Big Red Book 1970, Monty Python's Brand New Book 1973, Montypythonscrapbook 1979, Dr. Fegg's Encyclopaedia of All World Knowledge 1984, Limericks 1985,

Around the World in 80 Days 1989, Pole to Pole 1992, Hemingway's Chair 1995, Full Circle 1997, Michael Palin's Hemingway Adventure 1999; for children: Small Harry and the Toothache Pills 1981, The Mirrorstone 1986, The Cyril Stories 1986, Michael Palin's Hemingway Adventure 1999, Sahara 2002. *Leisure interests:* reading, running, railways. *Address:* Mayday Management, 34 Tavistock Street, London, WC2E 7PB, England. *Telephone:* 020) 7497-1100. *Fax:* 020) 7497-1133.

PALIS, Jacob, PhD; Brazilian mathematician; b. 15 March 1940, Uberaba; ed Fed. Univ. of Rio de Janeiro, Univ. of California at Berkeley; Prof., Instituto de Matemática Pura e Aplicada (IMPA), Rio de Janeiro; Visiting Prof. Univ. of Warwick, Inst. des Hautes Etudes Scientifiques, France, Univ. of Dijon, Ecole Polytechnique, Paris, City Univ. of New York, Steklov Inst., Moscow, ETH-Zurich, Univs of Nagoya, Tokyo, Kyoto, Toulouse, Rome, Paris-Orsay, Nice, Collège de France 1969–94; Guggenheim Fellow 1993; mem. Brazilian Acad. of Sciences 1973, Third World Acad. of Sciences 1991 (Math. Prize 1988); Nat. Prize for Science and Tech., Inter-American Prize for Science, OAS 1995. *Publications:* Geometric Theory of Dynamical Systems (with W. de Melo) 1982, Hyperbolicity and Sensitive-Chaotic Dynamics and Homoclinic Bifurcations, Fractal Dimensions and Infinitely Many Attractors (with F. Takens) 1994; numerous scientific papers. *Address:* Instituto Matemática Pura e Aplicada, Estrada Dona Castorina 110, Jardim Botânico, 22460-320 Rio de Janeiro, RJ, Brazil (Office). *Telephone:* (21) 2529-5270 (Office). *Fax:* (21) 512-4112 (Office). *E-mail:* jpalis@impa.br (Office).

PALITZSCH, Peter; German theatre director; b. 11 Sept. 1918, Deutmannsdorf; s. of Alwin Palitzsch and Johanna Strauss; m. Tanja von Oertzen 1974; Dramatic Adviser and Stage Dir Berliner Ensemble 1948–61; Dir Württemberg State Theatre 1967–72; Dir of Production, Schauspiel Stuttgart; mem. Bd of Dirs. Schauspiel Frankfurt am Main 1972–80; freelance Dir throughout Germany and other European countries. *Address:* Pestalozzistrasse 1A, 39539 Havelberg; Bundesratufer 5, 10555 Berlin, Germany. *Telephone:* (39) 38779427 (Havelberg); (30) 3912757 (Berlin).

PALLANT, John, BA; British advertising executive; b. 10 Aug. 1955; s. of Dennis Pallant and Doreen Pallant (née Hirst); ed St John's Coll., Southsea, Univ. of Reading; copywriter Griffin & George Ltd 1977, Acroyd Westwood Assocs. 1977, Collett Dickenson Pearce 1980, Gold Greenless Trott 1982, Boase Massimi Politt 1978, copywriter and creative group head 1983; copywriter Saatchi & Saatchi 1988, Group Head 1991, Deputy Creative Dir and Exec. Bd Dir 1995, Creative Dir 1996–97, Jt Exec. Creative Dir 1997–98, Deputy Exec. Creative Dir 1999–; numerous awards. *Address:* Saatchi & Saatchi, 80 Charlotte Street, London, W1A 1AQ, England. *Telephone:* (20) 7636-5060. *Fax:* (20) 7637-8489.

PALLASMAA, Juhani Uolevi; Finnish architect and university professor; b. 14 Sept. 1936, Hämeenlinna; s. of Harry Alexander Pallasmaa and Aili Pallasmaa (née Kannisto); m. 1st 1957; two d.; m. 2nd Hannele Jäämeri 1980; one s. one d.; ed Helsinki Univ. of Tech.; Dir Exhbn Dept, Museum of Finnish Architecture, Helsinki 1968–72, 1974–83, Dir of Museum 1978–83; Rector Coll. of Crafts and Design, Helsinki 1970–72; Assoc. Prof. Haile Selassie Univ., Addis Ababa, Ethiopia 1972–74; own architectural practice, Juhani Pallasmaa Architects, Helsinki 1983–; State Artist Prof., Helsinki 1983–88; Prof. Faculty of Architecture, Univ. of Tech., Helsinki 1991–97; Raymond E. Maritz Visiting Prof. Washington Univ., St Louis, Mo. 1999–; participant in numerous exhbns of architecture and visual arts, designer numerous nat. and int. exhbns of architecture and visual arts, designer numerous nat. and int. exhbns on town planning, architecture, design and visual arts; Dr hc (Helsinki Univ. of Industrial Arts) 1993, (Helsinki Univ. of Tech.) 1998; Finnish State Award for Architecture 1992, Helsinki City Culture Award 1993, Russian Fed. Architecture Award 1996, Fritz Schumacher Prize for Architecture, Germany 1997, Int. Union of Architects Jean Tschumi Prize for Architectural Criticism 1999, Finland Award 2000. *Publications:* Language of Wood 1987, Animal Architecture 1995, The Melnikov House 1996, The Eyes of the Skin: Architecture and the Senses 1996, Alvar Aalto, Villa Mairea 1938–39 1998, Architecture of Image: Existential Space in Cinema 2001, Sensuous Minimalism 2002. *Leisure interests:* philosophy and psychology of artistic phenomena. *Address:* Tehtaankatu 13 B 28, 00140 Helsinki (Office); Huvilakatu 14 A 8, 00150 Helsinki, Finland (Home). *Telephone:* (9) 669740 (Office); (9) 666625 (Home). *Fax:* (9) 669741 (Office). *E-mail:* pallasm@clinet.fi (Office).

PALLISER, Rt. Hon. Sir (Arthur) Michael, GCMG, PC, MA, FRSA; British diplomatist; b. 9 April 1922, Reigate, Surrey; s. of late Admiral Sir Arthur Palliser, KCB, DSC and of Lady Palliser (née Margaret E King-Salter); m. Marie M. Spaak (d. of late Paul-Henri Spaak) 1948 (died 2000); three s.; ed Wellington Coll. and Merton Coll., Oxford; war service in Coldstream Guards (mentioned in despatches) 1942–46; entered diplomatic service 1947; Foreign Office 1947–49, 1951–56; posted to Athens 1949–51, Paris 1956–60; Head of Chancery, Dakar 1960–62; Counsellor and seconded to Imperial Defence Coll. 1963; Head of Planning Staff, Foreign Office 1964; a Pvt. Sec. to Prime Minister 1966–69; Minister, Paris 1969–71; Amb. and Head, UK Del. to EEC 1971–72; Amb. and UK Perm. Rep. to EC 1973–75; Perm. Under-Sec., Head of Diplomatic Service 1975–82; Chair. Council, Int. Inst. for Strategic Studies 1983–90; Deputy Chair. Midland Bank PLC 1987–91; Deputy Chair. Midland Montagu (Holdings) 1987–93; Vice-Chair. Samuel Montagu and Co. Ltd 1983–84, 1993–96 (Chair. 1984–85, 1986–93); Dir, Arbor Acres Farm Inc., Booker PLC, BAT Industries PLC, Eagle Star (Holdings), Shell Transport and Trading Co. PLC 1983–92, United Biscuits PLC 1983–89; Pres. China-Britain

Trade Group 1992–96; Deputy Chair. British Invisible Exports Council 1987–95; Dir XCL Ltd 1994–2000; Chair. Major Projects Asscn 1994–98; Vice-Chair. Salzburg Seminar 1996–; Pres. Int. Social Service (UK) 1982–96; Chair. City and E London Confed. of Medicine and Dentistry 1989–95; Gov. Wellington Coll. 1982–92; mem. Security Comm. 1983–92; mem. Bd Royal Nat. Theatre 1988–96; Assoc. Fellow Centre for Int. Affairs, Harvard Univ. 1982; Hon. Fellow Merton Coll., Oxford 1986, Queen Mary Coll., London Univ. 1990; Chevalier, Order of Orange-Nassau, Commdr, Légion d'honneur. *Address:* 12B Wedderburn Road, London, NW3 5QG, England. *Telephone:* (20) 7794-0440 (Home). *Fax:* (20) 7916-2163 (Home).

PALMAR, Sir Derek, Kt, FCA; British business executive; b. 25 July 1919, Romford; s. of the late Lt-Col F. J. Palmar and Hylda (née Smith) Palmar; m. 1st Edith Brewster 1946 (died 1990), one s. one d.; m. 2nd Shuna Pyman 1992; ed Dover Coll.; RA 1941–46; Staff Coll.; Lt-Col 1945; with Peat, Marwick Mitchell & Co. 1937–57; Dir Hill Samuel Group 1957–70, Industrial Adviser Dept of Econ. Affairs 1965–67; Pres. Bass PLC 1987–89 (Dir 1970–76, CEO 1976–84, Chair. 1976–87); Chair. Yorkshire TV 1982–93, Boythorpe 1986–93; Dir Grindlays Bank Ltd 1973–85, Grindlays Holdings PLC 1979–85, United Newspapers 1986–93, Centre for Policy Studies Ltd 1983–88, CM Group Holdings Ltd 1986–93, Consolidated Venture Trust PLC 1984–93, Drayton Consolidated Trust PLC 1982–93; mem. Dover Harbour Bd 1964–75, British Railways Bd 1969–72, Prince's Trust 1984–; Chair British Rail Southern Regional Advisory Bd 1972–79; Chair. Leeds University Foundation Trust 1986–89, Zoological Soc. of London Devt Trust 1986–88; Accounting Standards Comm. 1982–84; World Wildlife Fund (UK) 1982–85; Trustee, Civic Trust 1979–89, Police Dependants' Trust 1979–, Queen Elizabeth's Foundation for Disabled People Devt Trust 1993–96; Vice-Pres. Brewers' Soc. 1982– (Chair. 1982–84); mem. Alcohol Educ. and Research Council 1982–87, Ct. Brewers' Co. 1982–88; Freeman, City of London. *Leisure interests:* shooting, gardening. *Address:* Church Farm, Naunton, Cheltenham, Glos., England.

PALMER, Andrew Clennel, PhD, FRS, FREng, FICE; British civil engineer and professor of engineering; b. 26 May 1938, Colchester; s. of Gerald Basil Coote Palmer and Muriel Gertrude Palmer (née Howes); m. Jane Rhiannon Evans 1963; one d.; ed Cambridge Univ., Brown Univ., USA; lecturer, Univ. of Liverpool 1965–67, Univ. of Cambridge 1968–75; Chief Pipeline Engineer, R. J. Brown & Assocs. 1975–79, Vice-Pres. Eng 1982–85; Prof. of Civil Eng, UMIST 1979–82; Man. Dir and Tech. Dir Andrew Palmer & Assocs. 1985–96; Research Prof. of Petroleum Eng, Cambridge Univ. 1996–; Fellow Churchill Coll., Cambridge 1996–. *Publications:* Structural Mechanics 1976; papers in learned journals. *Leisure interests:* travel, languages, glassblowing. *Address:* University Engineering Department, Trumpington Street, Cambridge, CB2 1PZ (Office); 49 Ashley Gardens, Ambrosden Avenue, London, SW1P 1QF, England (Home). *Telephone:* (1223) 332718 (Office); (20) 7828-8843 (Home). *Fax:* (1223) 339713 (Office). *E-mail:* acp24@eng.cam.ac.uk (Office).

PALMER, Arnold Daniel; American professional golfer and business executive; b. 10 Sept. 1929, Latrobe, Pa; s. of Milfred J. Palmer and Doris Palmer; m. Winifred Walzer 1954 (died 1999); two d.; ed Wake Forest Univ., NC; US Coast Guard 1950–53; US Amateur Golf Champion 1954; professional golfer 1954–; winner of 92 professional titles, including British Open 1961, 1962, US Open 1960, US Masters 1958, 1960, 1962, 1964, Canadian PGA 1980, US Srs Championship 1981; mem. US Ryder Cup team 1961, 1963, 1965, 1967, 1971, 1973, Captain 1963, 1975; joined Seniors (Champions) Tour 1980, finished first 10 times; Pres. Arnold Palmer Enterprises, one automobile agency, Latrobe Country Club, Bay Hill Club; mem. Bd of Dirs Latrobe Area Hospital; Hon. Nat. Chair. Nat. Foundation March of Dimes 1971–90; Chair. Bd Golf Channel; mem. of numerous golf clubs and Hon. Life mem. Carnoustie Golf 1992–; designer numerous golf courses; Hon. LLD (Wake Forest, Nat. Coll. of Educ.), Hon. DH (Thiel Coll.), Hon. DHL (Fla Southern Coll., St Vincent Coll.); Athlete of Decade, Associated Press 1970; Sportsman of the Year, Sports Illustrated 1960; Hickok Belt, Professional Athlete of Year 1960. *Publications:* My Game and Yours 1965, Situation Golf 1970, Go for Broke 1973, Arnold Palmer's Best 54 Golf Holes 1977, Arnold Palmer's Complete Book of Putting 1986, Play Great Golf 1987, Arnold Palmer: A Personal Journey (with Thomas Hauser) 1994, A Golfer's Life (with James Dodson) 1999, Playing by the Rules 2002. *Leisure interests:* bridge, occasional hunting, fishing, aviation, business, clubmaking. *Address:* PO Box 52, Youngstown, PA 15696, USA (Home and Office). *Telephone:* (724) 537-7751 (Office); (724) 537-7751 (Home). *Fax:* (724) 537-9355 (Office).

PALMER, Frank Robert, MA, DLitt, FBA; British professor of linguistics; b. 9 April 1922, Westerleigh, Glos.; s. of George Samuel Palmer and Gertrude Lilian Palmer (née Newman); m. Jean Elisabeth Moore 1948; three s. two d.; ed Bristol Grammar School, New Coll., Oxford, Merton Coll., Oxford; Lecturer in Linguistics, School of Oriental and African Studies (SOAS), Univ. of London 1950–60; Prof. of Linguistics, Univ. Coll. of North Wales, Bangor 1960–65; Prof. of Linguistic Science, Univ. of Reading 1965–87, Dean, Faculty of Letters and Social Sciences 1969–72; Vice-Pres., Philological Soc.; Chair. Linguistics Asscn (GB) 1965–68, Ed. Journal of Linguistics 1969–79, Linguistic Soc. of America Prof., Buffalo, USA 1971; Distinguished Visiting Prof. Univ. of Del., Newark, USA 1982. *Publications:* The Morphology of the Tigre Noun 1962, A Linguistic Study of the English Verb 1965, Ed. Selected Papers of J. R. Firth (1951–58) 1968, Ed. Prosodic Analysis 1970, Grammar 1971, 1984, The English Verb 1974, 1987, Semantics 1976, 1981, Modality and the English Modals 1979, 1990, Mood and Modality 1986, 2001, Jt Ed. Studies in the History of Western Linguistics in Honour of R. H. Robins 1986, Grammatical Roles and Relations 1994, Ed. Grammar and Meaning: Essays in Honour of Sir John Lyons 1995. *Leisure interests:* gardening, crosswords. *Address:* 'Whitethorns', Roundabout Lane, Winnersh, Wokingham, Berks., RG41 5AD, England. *Telephone:* (118) 978-6214. *E-mail:* f.r.palmer@reading.ac.uk (Home).

PALMER, Rt. Hon. Sir Geoffrey Winston Russell, KCMG, PC, AC, BA, LLB, JD; New Zealand fmr politician and professor; b. 21 April 1942, Nelson; s. of Leonard R. and Jessie P. Palmer; m. Margaret E Hinchcliff 1963; one s. one d.; ed Nelson Coll., Victoria Univ. of Wellington and Univ. of Chicago; solicitor, Wellington 1964–66; Lecturer in Political Science, Vic. Univ. 1968–69; Prof. of Law, Univ. of Iowa and Univ. of Va, USA 1969–73; Principal Asst to Australian Nat. Comm. of Inquiry on Rehabilitation and Compensation 1973; Prof. of English and New Zealand Law, Victoria Univ. 1974–79, Prof. of Law 1991–95; Visiting Fellow, Wolfson Coll., Oxford 1978; mem. Parl. for Christchurch Cen. 1979–90; Deputy Leader NZ Labour Party 1983–89; Deputy Prime Minister, Minister of Justice and Attorney-Gen. 1984–89, for the Environment 1987–90; Prime Minister of New Zealand 1989–90; Minister in Charge of NZ Security Intelligence; Prof. of Law Victoria Univ. 1991–95, Univ. of Iowa 1991–95; Partner Chen, Palmer & Partners, Wellington 1995–; Ida Beam Distinguished Visiting Prof. of Law, Univ. of Iowa 1991; UN Environment Programme Global 500 Laureate 1991. *Publications:* Unbridled Power?—An Interpretation of New Zealand's Constitution and Government 1979, Compensation for Incapacity—A Study of Law and Social Change in Australia and New Zealand 1979, Environmental Politics—A Greenprint for New Zealand 1990, New Zealand's Constitution in Crisis 1992, Public Law in New Zealand (with Mai Chen) 1993, Environment—the international challenge 1995, Bridled Power 1997. *Leisure interests:* cricket, golf, playing the trumpet, fishing. *Address:* 63 Roxburgh Street, Mount Victoria, Wellington, New Zealand. *Telephone:* (4) 801-5185.

PALMER, Thomas Joseph, CBE, MA; British business executive; b. 11 Sept. 1931, Cheddar; m. Hilary Westrup 1955; two s. two d.; ed King's School, Bruton and Trinity Coll. Cambridge; Gen. Man. (Admin.), Legal & General Group PLC 1972–78, Gen. Man. (Int.) 1978–84, Group Chief Exec. 1984–91, Dir 1972–91; Chair. Asscn of British Insurers 1989–91, Laser Richmount Ltd 1991–93, Personal Investment Authority 1993–2000, Springman Tipper Campbell Partnership 1993–; Dir Nat. Power PLC 1991–96, S.I.B., Halifax Bldg Soc. 1991–93, Sedgwick Group PLC, Investors Compensation Scheme 1992–93; Hon. Fellow, London Business School. *Leisure interests:* mountain walking, langlauf, gardening, reading. *Address:* 1 Canada Square, Canary Wharf, London, E14 5AZ, England. *Telephone:* (20) 7538-8860.

PALMISANO, Samuel J.; American business executive; ed Johns Hopkins Univ.; joined IBM, Baltimore, Md 1973, subsequently Sr Man. Dir of Operations, IBM Japan, Pres., CEO ISSC (IBM subsidiary) 1993, mem. Worldwide Man. Council IBM 1994, in charge of IBM's strategic outsourcing business 1995, Sr Vice-Pres. and Group Exec. Enterprise Systems Group, IBM Global Services, Personal Systems Group, mem. Corp. Exec. Cttee 1998, Pres. and COO 2000–02, CEO 2002–; mem. Bd of Dirs. IBM, Gannett Co. Inc. *Address:* IBM Corporation, New Orchard Road, Armonk, NY 10504, U.S.A. (Office). *Telephone:* (914) 499-1900 (Office). *Website:* www.ibm.com (Office).

PALMSTIERNA, Jacob, CBE; Swedish banker; b. 28 April 1934, Lund; s. of Carl Palmstierna and Anne-Marie Palmstierna; m. Hanne Wedell-Wedellsborg 1994; two s. one d.; ed Wharton School of Finance, Stockholm School of Econ.; with Stockholms Enskilda Bank 1960–69; Exec. Vice-Pres. Skandinaviska Enskilda Banken 1969–76, Pres. 1976–89, Man. Exec., CEO, Chair. 1989–91; Vice-Chair. Nord Banken 1991–92, Chair. 1992–98; Chair. Siemans-Elema AB 1996–, Bilia AB 1997–; Vice-Chair. Merita Nord Banken 1998–99, apptd. Chair. 1999; Hon. D.Econ.; King Carl X Gustaf's Medal (Sweden); Grosses Verdienstkreuz (Germany). *Leisure interests:* golf, hunting.

PALOCCI FILHO, António; Brazilian politician and physician; b. 4 Oct. 1960; s. of António Palocci and Antonia de Castro Palocci; m. Margareth Rose Silva Palocci; one s. two d.; ed Univ. de São Paulo-USP; physician specializing in preventive medicine; mem. Partido dos Trabalhadores—PT 1980–, Municipal Party Exec. 1988–89, Regional Party Directorate 1990–91 (Pres. 1997–99), Nat. Party Directorate 1996–97, Deputy Leader 2000; Pres. Rocha Lima Centre USP 1981; Regional Dir DCE Alexandre Vanucci Leme USP 1982; Pres. Ass. Resident Physicians of Ribeirão Pret 1984–85; Regional Dir SIMESP 1985; Pres. Regional CUT Ribeirão Preto 1985; Regional Dir Sanitary Monitoring Service São Paulo 1986–88; Mayor of Ribeirão Preto 1993–96, 2001–02; Fed. Deputy 1999–2000; Co-ordinator government transition team Oct.–Dec. 2002; Minister of Finance Jan. 2003–; UNICEF "Child and Peace" Prize 1995, Juscelino Kubitschek Prize, Serviço Brasileiro de Apoio às Micro e Pequenas Empresas–SEBRAE 1996. *Publications include:* Saúde do trabalhador (Health of the Worker) 1994, A reforma do Estado e os municípios: a experiência de Ribeirão Preto (State and City Reform: The Experience of Ribeirão Preto) 1996. *Address:* Ministry of Finance, Esplanada dos Ministérios, Bloco P, 5 Andar, 70048-900, Brasília, DF, Brazil (Office). *Telephone:* (61) 412-2518 (Office). *Fax:* (61) 412-1721 (Office). *E-mail:* acs@fazenda.gov.br (Office). *Website:* www.fazenda.gov.br (Office).

PALOUŠ, Radim, PhD; Czech university rector (retd); b. 6 Nov. 1924, Prague; m. Anna Štausová 1949; two s.; ed Charles Univ. of Prague, Pedagogical Univ.; mem. student anti-Nazi resistance movt; lecturer in Analytical Chem., Faculty of Natural Sciences 1957–59, Inst. of Univ. Studies, Tech. Univ. of

Prague; after 1959 suffered intermittent persecution from Communist regime; Chair. Educ. Techniques Dept, Faculty of Pedagogics, Prague 1968–69; Charter 77 spokesman; Rector Charles Univ. 1990–94; Vice-Chair. Czechoslovak Asscn of the Roman Club 1991–; mem. numerous acads and orgs; Dr. hc (Pittsburgh) 1990, (Omaha) 1990, (Int. Acad. for Philosophy) 1991, (Cracow) 1991, (Moravian Coll., USA) 1991, (York) 1992, Seoul 1993, (Edin.) 1993; Czechoslovak Acad. of Sciences Prize 1990, Comenius Scheidegger Prize, Netherlands 1992, T.G. Masaryk Order 1997. *Publications include:* Die Schule den Alten 1979, The Time of Education 1983, The Czech Experience 1994, Das Weltzeitalter 1993, Totalism and Holism 1995, Letters to Godchildren of the Present Age 2001. *Address:* Charles University, Ovocný trh 3-5, 116 36 Prague 1 (Office). *E-mail:* rpalous@ruk.cuni.cz.

PALSSON, Gunnar, PhD; Icelandic diplomatist; b. 25 Jan. 1955; m.; three c.; ed Univ. Coll. Dublin, Karl Eberhardt Univ., Tübingen, Germany, State Univ. of New York, Buffalo; First Sec., Ministry of Foreign Affairs, Reykjavík 1984-86, officer, Div. of Political Affairs, NATO Int. Staff, Brussels 1986–88, Counsellor, Ministry of Foreign Affairs 1988–90, Amb. to CSCE, Negotiations on Confidence and Security-Bldg Measures (CSBM) and Negotiations on Conventional Forces in Europe (CFE), Vienna 1991–92, Deputy Perm. Under-Sec. for Political Affairs, Reykjavík 1992–94; Amb. and Perm. Rep. to UN, New York 1994–98, to NATO and WEU, Brussels and the Org. for the Prohibition of Chemical Weapons (OPCW), The Hague 1998–. *Address:* Boulevard Leopold III 39, 1110 Brussels, Belgium (Office). *Telephone:* (2) 707-50-58 (Office). *Fax:* (2) 726-45-31 (Office). *E-mail:* gunnar.palsson@utn.stjr.is (Office). *Website:* www.iceland.org (Office).

PÁLSSON, Thorsteinn; Icelandic politician; b. 29 Oct. 1947; m. Ingibjörg Rafnar; three c.; ed Commercial Coll., Reykjavik and Univ. of Iceland; Chair. Vaka (student's union) 1969–70; Ed. Vísir 1975; Dir Confed. of Icelandic Employers 1979–83; MP 1983–99; Chair. Independence Party 1983–91; Minister of Finance 1985–87, Prime Minister of Iceland 1987–88, Minister of Fisheries 1991–99, of Justice 1991–99, also of Ecclesiastical Affairs –1999; Amb. to UK 1999–. *Address:* Embassy of Iceland, 2A Hans Street, London, SW1X 0JE, England (Office); Háteigsvegur 46, 105 Reykjavik, Iceland. *Telephone:* 020) 7259-3999 (Office). *Fax:* 020) 7245-9649 (Office). *E-mail:* icemb.london@utn.stjr.is (Office). *Website:* www.iceland.org.uk (Office).

PALTRIDGE, Garth William, PhD, FAA; Australian research scientist; b. 24 April 1940, Brisbane; s. of T.B. Paltridge and A.T. Savage; m. Kay L. Petty 1965; one s. one d.; ed Brisbane Boys' Coll. and Queensland and Melbourne Univs.; Postdoctoral Fellow, New Mexico Tech. 1965; Sr Scientific Officer RSRS, UK 1966; research scientist, CSIRO Div. of Meteorological Physics 1967; Exec. Dir PIECE of Australian Inst. of Petroleum 1980; Chief Research Scientist, CSIRO Div. of Atmospheric Research 1981–89; Dir Co-operative Research Centre for Antarctic and Southern Ocean Environment, Univ. of Tasmania 1991–2002; WMO Research Prize. *Publications:* Radiative Processes in Meteorology and Climatology; 100 research papers on environmental topics. *Leisure interests:* golf, history, furniture and cabinet making. *Address:* Antarctic Co-operative Research Centre, University of Tasmania, GPO 252-80, Hobart, Tasmania 7001 (Office); 9 Waymouth Avenue, Sandy Bay, Tasmania 7005, Australia (Home).

PALTROW, Gwyneth; American actress; b. 29 Sept. 1973, Los Angeles; d. of the late Bruce Paltrow and of Blythe Danner; ed Spence School, New York and Univ. of California at Santa Barbara. *Films include:* Flesh and Bone 1993, Hook, Moonlight and Valentino, The Pallbearer, Seven, Emma 1996, Sydney, Kilronan, Great Expectations 1998, Sliding Doors 1998, A Perfect Murder 1998, Shakespeare in Love (Acad. Award for Best Actress) 1998, The Talented Mr Ripley 1999, Duets 1999, Bounce 2000, The Intern 2000, The Anniversary Party 2001, Shallow Hal 2001, The Royal Tenenbaums 2002, Possession 2002, View from the Top 2003. *Play:* Proof (Donmar Warehouse, London) 2002. *Address:* c/o Rick Kurtzman, CAA, 9830 Wilshire Boulevard, Beverly Hills, CA 90212; Screen Actors Guild, 5757 Wilshire Boulevard, Los Angeles, CA 90036, USA.

PALTSEV, Mikhail Alexandrovich, DrMed; Russian pathologist; b. 9 Nov. 1949, Russia; m.; one d.; ed 1st Moscow Sechenov Inst. of Med.; Prof. Moscow Sechenov Acad. of Medicine; active as pathology anatomist and organizer of medical sciences; mem. Presidium of Russian Acad. of Sciences; Pres. Asscn of Medical and Pharmaceutical Educ.; Ed.-in-Chief Journal Vrach, Molecular Medicine, Pathology Archives; mem. Int. Acad. of Pathology, Exec. Cttee European Soc. of Pathology; Rector and Head of Pathology Dept Moscow Sechenov Acad. of Medicine 1997–; Order of Friendship Between Peoples, USSR State Prize 1991, Russian Govt's Prize 2000. *Publications:* Pathological Anatomy (with N. Anichkov) 2001, Pathology (textbook, jt writer) 2002. *Address:* Moscow Sechenov Academy of Medicine, Bolshaya Pirogovskaya str. 2/6, 119881 Moscow, Russia (Office). *Telephone:* (095) 248-05-53 (Office). *Fax:* (095) 248-02-14 (Office). *E-mail:* mma-sechenov@mtu-net.ru.

PALUMBO, Baron (Life Peer), cr. 1991, of Walbrook in the City of London; **Peter Garth Palumbo,** MA; British property developer; b. 20 July 1935, London; s. of Rudolph Palumbo and Elsie Palumbo; m. 1st Denia Wigram 1959 (died 1986), one s. two d.; m. 2nd Hayat Morowa 1986, one s. two d.; ed Eton Coll. and Worcester Coll., Oxford; Gov. LSE 1976–94; Hon. mem. Emmanuel Coll., Cambridge 1994–; Trustee, Mies van der Rohe Archive 1977–, The Tate Gallery 1978–85, Whitechapel Art Gallery Foundation 1981–87; Trustee and Hon. Treas. Writers and Scholars Educational Trust 1984–99; Chair. The Tate Gallery Foundation 1986–87, Painshill Park Trust Appeal 1986–96;

Chair. The Arts Council of GB 1989–94; Chancellor Univ. of Portsmouth 1992–; mem. bd and Dir Andy Warhol Foundation for the Arts 1994–97; Trustee Natural History Museum 1994–, Design Museum 1995–; mem. Council, Royal Albert Hall 1995–99; Gov. RSC 1995–2000, Whitgift School 2002–; Hon. FRIBA 1986; Hon. Fellow Inst. of Structural Eng 1994; mem. Livery, Salters' Co. 1965; Dr hc (Portsmouth) 1993; Nat. Order of Southern Cross, Brazil; Cranbrook Patronage of the Arts Award, Detroit, USA 2002. *Leisure interests:* music, travel, gardening, reading. *Address:* 2 Astell Street, London, SW3 3RU, England. *Telephone:* (20) 7351-7371. *Fax:* (20) 7352-5660.

PAMFILOVA, Ella Aleksandrovna; Russian politician; b. 12 Sept. 1953, Tashkent Region, Uzbekistan; d. of Aleksandr Lekomtsev and Polina Lekomtseva; m. 1st Nikita Leonidovich Pamfilov 1976 (divorced 1993); one d.; m. 2nd; ed Moscow Inst. of Power Eng; foreman Cen. factory Mosenergo, Part. trade union at factory 1981–89; USSR People's Deputy 1989–91; Sec. Comm. of Supreme Soviet on Privileges Jan.–Nov. 1991; Russian Fed. Minister for Social Security 1991–94; mem. State Duma (Parl.) 1993–99, mem. Cttee on Security 1995–98; Chair. Council on Social Policy under Presidential Admin. 1994; Founder and Head Movt for Healthy Russia (later Movt for Civic Dignity) 1996; Chair. Pres.'s Cttee on Human Rights 2002–; Pres. Acad. Revival. *Leisure interest:* gardening. *Address:* Movement For Healthy Russia, Palikha str. 4, Bldg 2, 103055 Moscow, Russia (Office). *Telephone:* (095) 978-82-98 (Office).

PAN, Marta; French sculptor; b. 12 June 1923, Budapest, Hungary; m. André Wogenscky; ed School of Fine Art, Budapest, Paris; numerous public sculptures, fountains and monuments in Japan, USA, Saudi Arabia, Lebanon, Italy, Netherlands, France, Luxembourg, Germany, UK, etc.; Commdr des Arts et Lettres, Chevalier Légion d'honneur; Médaille des Arts Plastiques, Acad. d'Architecture 1986, Prix Int. de l'Eau, de la Création et des Arts UNESCO 2001, Praemium Imperiale (Japan) 2001. *Exhibitions include:* Sculpture flottante, Musée Kröller-Müller 1961, Patio and Fountain, 26 Champs Elysées, Paris 1982, Les Lacs, Brest 1988, Floating Sculpture, Santomato di Pistoia, Italy 1990, Signe infini, nr Lyon 1994, Jardin de la ligne blanche, Osaka 1994, Fragment de paysage, Tokyo 1994, Floating Sculpture 3 Islands, Luxembourg 1999, Monument, Atami, Japan 2000, Fragment of a Landscape, nr London 2001. *Leisure interests:* music, gardening. *Address:* 80 avenue du Général Leclerc, 78470 Saint-Rémy-les-Chevreuse, France (Home). *Fax:* 1-30-52-73-20 (Home).

PAN HONG; Chinese film actress; b. 4 Nov. 1954, Shanghai; m. Mi Jingshan (divorced 1990); ed Shanghai Drama Acad. 1973–76; actress, Shanghai Film Studio, Shanghai 1977–80, Omei Film Studio, Chengdu 1980–; mem. 5th Nat. Cttee, Fed. of Literary and Art Circles 1988–; 3rd Golden Rooster Best Actress Award for A Middle-aged Women 1983; 8th Golden Rooster Best Actress for Well 1988. *Films include:* The Last Aristocrat, A Slave's Daughter, Camel Bell in the Desert, A Bitter Smile. *Address:* Omei Film Studio, Tonghui Menwai, Chengdu City, Sichuan Province, People's Republic of China. *Telephone:* (28) 22991.

PAN RONGWEN, MD; Chinese physician; b. 1 July 1931, Jiangsu Prov.; d. of Pan Yu Qi and Pan Cao Shi; m. Lu Shi Cai 1960; one s. one d.; alt. mem. 12th CCP Cen. Cttee 1982; Physician-in-Charge, Changzheng Hosp. 1982, Vice-Pres. 1983–; Prof. 1986–. *Address:* Changzheng Hospital, 428 Feng Yang Road, Shanghai 200003, People's Republic of China. *Telephone:* (21) 3275997.

PAN XIA; Chinese director; b. Aug. 1937, Yidu, Shandong Prov.; ed Tongji Univ. Shanghai; Ed. and Dir Literature and Arts Dept, Chinese People's Cen. Radio Station 1959–75; Dir TV Drama Troupe, Cen. Broadcasting Art Co. 1975–83; Dir China TV Drama Centre 1983–; Best TV Drama Award 1980, Flying Apsaras Award 1982, several Gold Eagle Awards; awarded the titles of Nat. Jinguo Pacesetter for Meritorious Service 1991 and Nat. Sanba Standard-Bearer 1992. *Television:* The Sacred Mission, Multi-Prism, Walking into the Storm, Xiang Jingyu, The Pioneers' Footsteps, Madame Sun Yatsen and Her Sisters. *Publications:* over 20 research papers. *Address:* China Television Drama Centre, Beijing, People's Republic of China (Office).

PANAYIDES CHRISTOU, Tasos, MA, MPA; Cypriot diplomatist; b. 9 April 1934, Ktima-Paphos; s. of Christos Panayi and Efrosini Savva; m. Pandora Constantinides 1969; two s. one d.; ed Paphos Gymnasium, Cyprus Teacher's Training Coll., Univ. of London and Univ. of Indiana; Teacher, Cyprus 1954–59; First Sec. to Pres. (Archbishop Makarios), then Dir President's Office 1960–69; Amb. to Fed. Repub. of Germany (also to Austria and Switzerland) 1969–79; Sec. and Dean, Commonwealth Group, Bonn 1976–79; High Commr in UK (also Amb. to Denmark, Iceland, Norway and Sweden) 1979–90; Perm. Sec. of Ministry of Foreign Affairs and Amb. to Iceland 1990–94; Amb. to Sweden 1994–96 (also to Denmark, Finland, Iceland, Norway, Latvia, Lithuania and Estonia); Chair. AVRA Shipmanagement SA 1997–; Chair. Commonwealth Foundation Grants Cttee 1985–88, Commonwealth Fund for Tech. Co-operation (CFTC) 1986–89, Finance Cttee of Commonwealth Secr. 1988–90, SCOSO (Commonwealth Steering Cttee of Senior Officials) 1994–95; Rep. to IAEA 1976–79; Fellow, Ealing Coll.; Hon. LLD (Birmingham) 1991; Grand Cross (with Star and Sash) of Fed. Repub. of Germany, Grand Cross (with Star and Sash) of Austria, Thyateira Archbishopric Grand Cross (in Gold), Grand Cross (in Gold) of the Patriarchate of Antioch 1984, Freeman of City of London 1984; Hon. GCVO 1990. *Leisure interests:* history, swimming, reading. *Address:* 116 Kolokotroni Street, 185-35 Piraeus, Greece. *Telephone:* (1) 4181601. *Fax:* (1) 4181608.

PANCIROLI, Most Rev. Romeo; Vatican ecclesiastic; b. 21 Nov. 1923, Italy; s. of Anthony Panciroli and Celestine Cavazzoni; ordained Priest 1949; teacher of natural ethics and sociology 1951–59; Vatican Secr. of State 1960; Attaché to Apostolic Nunciature, Nigeria 1961–64; Sec. to Pontifical Comm. for Social Communications 1965–76; Consultant to Pontifical Cttee for revision of Canon Law 1975–83; Dir Vatican Press Office and Spokesman of Holy See 1976–84; Information Officer and mem. Papal Suite with Pope John Paul II in his journeys to 54 countries 1978–84; Titular Archbishop of Noba 1984–; Apostolic Pro-Nuncio to Liberia, Guinea, The Gambia 1984–92; Apostolic Del. to Sierra Leone 1984–92; Apostolic Nuncio to Iran 1992–99. *Publications:* Words on the Faith, Papal Messages in Asia and Australia, Audience Pontifical Suite, Paul VI Apostolic Pilgrim. *Leisure interests:* reading, fine arts, classical music, travelling. *Address:* Borgo S. Spirito, 10 00193 Rome, Italy. *Telephone:* (06) 69885505. *Fax:* (06) 69885378.

PANDAY, Basdeo, BLL, B.SC.ECONS.; Trinidad and Tobago politician; b. 25 May 1933, Prince's Town; m. 1st Norma Mohammed (died 1981); one d.; m. 2nd Oma Ramkisson; three d.; ed Lincoln's Inn, Univ. of London; entered politics as mem. of Workers' and Farmers' Party 1966; trade union legal adviser; Pres.-Gen. All Trinidad Sugar and Gen. Workers' Trade Union 1973, Sugar Industry Staff Asscn 1975; founder mem. United Labour Front (ULF); Leader of the Opposition 1976–86; Minister of Foreign Affairs 1986–91; mem. Nat. Alliance for Reconciliation (NAR), expelled 1988; f. and Leader United Nat. Congress (UNC); Prime Minister of Trinidad and Tobago 1995–2001. *Address:* United National Congress, Rienzi Complex, 78–81 Southern Main Road, Couva; La Fantasie Gardens, St Ann's, Port of Spain, Trinidad and Tobago (Home).

PANDE, Arvind, MA; Indian business executive; b. 7 Sept. 1942; ed Allahabad Univ., Cambridge Univ.; Adviser to Exec. Dir for India, Bangladesh and Sri Lanka, IBRD 1971–74; Dept of Econ. Affairs, Ministry of Finance 1974–78; Special Sec., Govt of Madhya Pradesh 1978–81; Jt Sec. to Prime Minister of India 1981–86; Dir (Corp. Planning) Steel Authority of India Ltd (SAIL) 1986–90, (Personnel and Corp. Planning) 1990–93, Vice-Chair. 1993–97, Chair. (CEO) 1997–2002; Chair. Indian Iron and Steel Co. Ltd; Pres. Nat. HRD Network; Council mem. Indian Inst. of Metals, Confed. of Indian Industry; mem. Bd of Govs. Int. Man. Inst.; Dir Int. Iron and Steel Inst., Belgium; mem. Bureau of Indian Standards. *Address:* B-249, Asian Games Village, New Delhi 110 049, India (Home). *Telephone:* 6493167 (Home).

PANDIT, Jasraj, DMus; Indian musician; b. 28 Jan. 1930, Hissar, Hariyana; s. of Motiram Pandit and Krishnabai Pandit; m. Madhura Pandit 1962; one s. one d.; studied under elder brother Maniram Pandit; belongs to Mewati Gharana (school of music); has conducted extensive research in Haveli Sangeet and presented the original Pure Haveli Sangeet with its devotional content intact; has est. an Ashram Motiram Sangeet Natale Acad. with main object of propagating Indian classical music by teaching students free of charge; mem. advisory Bd of radio and TV; numerous awards and honours, including Rajiv Gandhi Award for professional excellence, Padma Bhushan and Sangeet Martand. *Works include:* compositions for opera, ballet and short films etc., including Kan Khani Sunyo Kare, Geet Govindam, Sur, Laya Aur Chhanda. *Publication:* Sangeet Saurabh. *Leisure interests:* teaching, travel, sport. *Address:* Rajkamal Building, 138 Shivaji Park, Mumbai 400016, India. *Telephone:* 4456281. *Fax:* 4147654.

PANDOLFI, Filippo Maria, PhD; Italian politician; b. 1 Nov. 1927, Bergamo; fmr company Dir; mem. Chamber of Deputies for Brescia-Bergamo 1968; mem. Comm. on Finance and the Treasury; fmr Under-Sec. of State in Ministry of the Budget; Minister of Finance 1976–78, of the Treasury 1978–80, of Industry 1980–81, 1982–83, of Agric. 1983–88; EEC Commr for Science, Research, Telecommunications and Information Tech. 1989–92; Christian Democrat.

PANETTA, Leon, LLB; American politician and lawyer; b. 28 June 1938, Monterey, Calif.; s. of Carmelo Panetta and Carmelina Panetta; m. Sylvia Varni 1962; three s.; ed Univ. of Santa Clara; served U.S. Army 1964–66; Legis. Asst to Senator Thomas Kuchel, Washington 1966–69; Dir U.S. Office of Civil Rights 1969–70; Exec. Asst to Mayor of New York 1970–71; partner Panetta, Thompson and Panetta, Monterey 1971–76; mem. U.S. House of Reps. 1977–93, mem. House Budget Cttee 1979–85, Chair. 1989–92; Head of Office of Man. and Budget 1993–94; Chief of Staff to Pres. Clinton 1994–97; Founder Panetta Inst., Calif. State Univ., Monterey 1998–; Democrat. *Address:* Panetta Institute, California State University at Monterey, 100 Campus Centre, Building 86E, Seaside, CA 93955, USA.

PANFILOV, Gleb Anatolyevich; Russian film director; b. 21 May 1934, Magnitogorsk; m. Inna Mikhailovna Churikova; one s.; grad. Sverdlovsk Polytechnic Inst. as chemical engineer and Mosfilm Studios (course in directing); work as Dir in Sverdlovsk, Leningrad (now St Petersburg), Moscow 1976–; RSFSR People's Artist 1984, RSFSR State Prize 1985. *films include:* No Ford in the Fire (scenario: Yevgeniy Gabrilovich) 1968 (Grand Prix Locarno 1969), Début 1970, both starring Inna Churikova, I Wish to Speak 1975, Valentina 1981, Vassa Zheleznova 1983, The Theme 1986, The Mother 1991; stage productions at Lenkom Theatre incl. Hamlet 1986, Sorry (A. Galin) 1992, Romanovs: The Crowned Family 2000. *Address:* Universitetski Prosp. 6, Korp. 4, Apt. 68, 117333 Moscow, Russia. *Telephone:* (095) 137-89-67.

PANGALOS, Theodoros, PhD; Greek politician and lawyer; b. Aug. 1938, Elefsis; m.; three s. one d.; ed Athens and Sorbonne Univs.; a founder of the Grigoris Lambrakis Youth Movt; stood as EDA cand. in 1964 election; active in dissident Movt during mil. dictatorship; deprived of Greek citizenship by junta 1968; Lecturer and Researcher specializing in Econ. Devt, Programming and Town and Country Planning, Sorbonne, Paris and Head of Econ. Devt Inst. 1969–78; practises as lawyer in Athens; Legal Adviser to trade unions in Megarida; active in Movt to protect environment, a founder mem. of Citizens Against Pollution, Socialist MP for Attica; Deputy Minister of Commerce 1982–84, of Foreign Affairs 1984–89, 1993–94; Minister of Transport and Communications 1989–90; Minister of Foreign Affairs 1996–99, of Culture 2000; currently Head of Greek Del. WEU Ass. and Council of Europe; an Ed. of newspapers The Thriasio and the Megara and periodical ANTI; 17 awards or honours from various countries. *Publications:* several works on econs, sociology and philosophy. *Leisure interests:* wine production, fishing, mountain walking, opera and symphonic music. *Address:* 16–18 Pireos Street, 104 31 Athens, Greece. *Telephone:* (1) 5231142. *Fax:* (1) 5231178. *E-mail:* pangalos@otenet.gr (Office). *Website:* www.pangalos.gr (Office).

PANGELINAN, Lourdes; Guam international organization official; held various positions in judicial, legislative and exec. brs. of Guam Govt, including Chief of Staff in Office of the Gov.; Deputy Dir-Gen. Pacific Community 1996–99, Dir-Gen. 2000–. *Address:* Pacific Community, BP D5, 98848 Nouméa Cedex, New Caledonia (Office). *Telephone:* 26-20-00 (Office). *Fax:* 26-38-18 (Office). *E-mail:* spc@spc.org.nc (Office). *Website:* www.spc.org.nc (Office).

PANGGABEAN, Gen. Maraden Saur Halomoan; Indonesian politician and army officer; b. 29 June 1922, Tarutung, N Sumatra; s. of M. Patuan Natoras and Katharina Panjaitan; m. Meida Seimima Matiur Tambunan; one s. three d.; studied mil. affairs in various mil. acads. including the Advanced Infantry Officer Course, USA; mil. posts include C-in-C of the Army 1968, Vice-Commdr Armed Forces 1969–73, C-in-C 1973–78; Deputy Commdr for Restoration of Security and Order 1968, Commdr 1969–73, Exec. Officer Command 1973–78; Minister of State for Defense and Security 1969–73, Minister 1973–78; Acting Minister of Home Affairs 1973; Minister Co-ordinator for Political and Security Affairs 1978–83; Acting Foreign Minister 1978–83; Chair. Bd of Guidance, GOLKAR 1973–78, Vice-Chair. 1978–83; Chair. Exec. Presidium, Bd of Guidance, GOLKAR 1978–83; mem. People's Consultative Ass. 1973–78, 1978–83, 1983–; War of Independence Medal, Service Award Medal, Best Son of the Nation Medal, Rep. of Indonesia Medal and numerous other medals and awards. *Leisure interests:* golf, jogging, gymnastics, hunting, reading. *Address:* Jalan Teuku Umar 21, Jakarta, Indonesia. *Telephone:* 378012.

PANHOFER, Walter; Austrian concert pianist; b. 3 Jan. 1910, Vienna; s. of Josef and Maria Panhofer; m. Gertraut Schmied 1956; two s.; ed Akademie für Musik und darstellende Kunst, Hochschule für Musik und darstellende Kunst, Vienna; concerts in Austria, Germany, England, Switzerland, Italy and Yugoslavia; performed with Vienna Philharmonic and Vienna Symphony Orchestras and Royal Philharmonic and London Chamber Orchestras, England; has toured with and made records with Vienna Octet; master classes in Brussels, Vienna and in Italy; has adjudicated many times at Int. Beethoven piano competition, Vienna; Ehrenkreuz für Wissenschaft und Kunst. *Leisure interests:* mountains, books. *Address:* Erdbergstrasse 35/9, 1030 Vienna, Austria. *Telephone:* 7147902 (Home). *Fax:* 7147902 (Home).

PANIAGUA CORAZAO, Valentín; Peruvian politician, professor of constitutional law and lawyer; Deputy 1963–68, 1980–85; Minister of Justice and Religion 1965–66; Pres. Chamber of Deputies 1982–83; Minister of Educ. 1984; Sec.-Gen. Acción Popular 1998–2000; Speaker and Head of Congress Dec. 2000; interim Pres. of Peru Jan.–July 2001; lecturer, Catholic Univ., Lima; Prof. of Constitutional Law, Univ. of Lima 1980–96, Extraordinary Prof. 1996; Vice-Pres. Comm. for Constitutional Reform of the Coll. of Lawyers, Lima; Hon. Prof. (Nat. Univ. San Antonio Abad), Hon. Mem. Academia Nacional de la Salud. *Address:* c/o Acción Popular, Paseo Colén 218, Lima 1, Peru (Office).

PANIČ, Milan; Serbia and Montenegro (Serbian) politician and business executive; b. 20 Dec. 1929, Belgrade; one s. two d.; ed Belgrade, South Carolina and Heidelberg Univs; emigrated to USA 1956; Founder and Chair. ICN Pharmaceuticals Inc. 1960–2002; returned to Yugoslavia 1991; Prime Minister of Yugoslavia July–Dec. 1992; cand. for Presidency of Serbia 1992; Founder and owner of MP Global Enterprises 2003–; Dir Galenica Co., Belgrade and Moscow; mem. Bd Fund for Interdisciplinary Scientific Research (ISRF); Corresp. mem. Californian Inst. of Tech.; mem. American Nuclear Soc., Swiss Chemical Soc., Int. Soc. of Haemotherapy; mem. Bd Freedoms Foundation of Valley Forge; Wall Street Journal European of the Year. *Leisure interests:* tennis, cycling (fmr Yugoslav Champion). *Address:* MP Global Enterprises, 650 Town Center Drive, No. 660, Costa Mesa, CA 92626 (Office); 1050 Arden Road, Pasadena, CA 91106, USA (Home). *Telephone:* (714) 384-4000 (Office). *Fax:* (714) 384-4010 (Office).

PANICHAS, George Andrew, FRSA, MA, PhD, LittD; American writer and university professor; b. 21 May 1930, Springfield, Mass.; s. of Andrew Panichas and Fannie Dracouli Panichas; ed Springfield Classical High School, American Int. Coll., Trinity Coll. and Nottingham Univ., England; Instructor in English, Univ. of Maryland 1962, Asst Prof. 1963, Assoc. Prof. 1966, Prof. 1968–92; Co-Dir of Conf. "Irving Babbitt: Fifty Years Later" 1983;

mem. Richard M. Weaver Fellowship Awards Cttee 1983–88; Academic Bd Nat. Humanities Inst. 1985–, Advisory Bd Humanitas 1993–; Editorial Adviser, Modern Age: A Quarterly Review 1972–77, Assoc. Ed. 1978–83, Ed. 1984–; mem. Advisory Bd Continuity: A Journal of History 1984; Ingersoll Prizes Jury Panel 1986; Earhart Foundation Award 1982. *Publications:* Adventure in Consciousness: The Meaning of D. H. Lawrence's Religious Quest 1964, Renaissance and Modern Essays: Presented to Vivian de Sola Pinto in Celebration of his Seventieth Birthday (Ed. with G. R. Hibbard and A. Rodway) 1966, Epicurus 1967, Mansions of the Spirit: Essays in Literature and Religion (Ed.) 1967, Promise of Greatness: The War of 1914–1918 (Ed.) 1968, The Politics of Twentieth-Century Novelists (Ed.) 1971, The Reverent Discipline: Essays in Literary Criticism and Culture 1974, The Burden of Vision: Dostoevsky's Spiritual Art 1977, The Simone Weil Reader (Ed.) 1977, Irving Babbitt: Representative Writings (Ed.) 1981, The Courage of Judgment: Essays in Criticism, Culture and Society 1982, Irving Babbitt in Our Time (Ed. with C. G. Ryn) 1986, Modern Age: The First Twenty-Five Years. A Selection (Ed.) 1988, The Critic as Conservator: Essays in Literature, Society and Culture 1992, In Continuity: The Last Essays of Austin Warren (Ed.) 1996, The Critical Legacy of Irving Babbitt: An Appreciation 1999, Growing Wings to Overcome Gravity: Criticism as the Pursuit of Virtue 1999; also numerous articles, trans. and reviews for books and journals published in USA and Europe. *Leisure interests:* hiking, playing racquetball, keeping physically fit, listening to music. *Address:* P.O. Box AB, College Park, MD 20741 (Office); 4313 Knox Road, Apartment 402, College Park, MD 20740, USA (Home). *Telephone:* (301) 779-1436 (Home).

PANIGRAHI, Sanjukta; Indian dancer and choreographer; b. 24 Aug. 1934, Berhampur; d. of late Abhiram Mishra and of Shakuntala Mishra; m. Raghunath Panigrahi 1960; two s.; first performance aged four; has toured extensively in Europe giving lecture demonstrations and performances in Odyssi style; has appeared at int. festivals of music. dance and drama in India, Russia, Australia, Japan, Indonesia, UK etc.; conducts regular workshops at cultural and educ. insts. abroad; Life Pres. Kalinga Kala Kshetra and the Natyotkala; mem. Gen. Council Orissa Sangeet Natak Acad.; mem. Gov. Bd Utkal Sangeet Mahavidyalaya, Bhubaneswar; mem. various social and cultural orgs.; several awards including Cen. Sangeet Natak Akad. Award. 1976, State Akad. Award 1977, Padmashree (Govt of India) 1978, Tirupati Nat. Award 1987, All-India Critics Asscn Award 1989. *Publications:* articles in journals in India and abroad. *Address:* Plot No. 4114/A, Ashok Nagar East, Unit II, Bhubaneswar 751009, Orissa, India. *Telephone:* 50638.

PANINA, Yelena Vladimirovna, CandEconSci; Russian civil servant; b. 29 April 1948, Smolensk Region; m. Aleksandr Andreyevich Panin; one d.; ed Moscow Inst. of Finance, Higher School of Econs; on staff Control-Audit Dept Ministry of Finance, Russian Fed. 1970–75; Head of Dept, Deputy Dir-Gen. Production Union 1975–86; Sec. Dist CP Cttee Moscow Region 1986–88; Head of Dept Moscow CP City Cttee 1988–91; Dir-Gen. USSR Trade Chamber 1991–92; mem. Exec. Bd Russian Union of Businessmen 1992–; Chair. Russian Zemsvto Movt 1993–; Deputy Head World Russian People's Sobor 1995–; Co-Chair., Co-ordinator Moscow Confed. of Businessmen 1992–; Chair. Moscow Confed. of Industrialists and Entrepreneurs 2000–; Dir-Gen. Centre of Business Projects (Interbusinessproekt) 1992–97; mem. State Duma 1997–99. *Address:* Moscow Confederation of Industrialists and Entrepreneurs, Novy Arbat 21, Moscow, Russia (Office). *Telephone:* (095) 291-98-74 (Office).

PANITCHPAKDI, Supachai; Thai politician and international organization official; b. 1946; ed in the Netherlands and UK; with Bank of Thailand for 12 years; fmr Deputy Prime Minister and Minister of Commerce; Dir.-Gen. World Trade Org. Oct. 2002–. *Address:* World Trade Organization, Centre William Rappard, rue de Lausanne 154, 1211 Geneva, Switzerland (Office). *Telephone:* (22) 7395111 (Office). *Fax:* (22) 7314206 (Office). *E-mail:* enquiries@wto.org (Office). *Website:* www.wto.org (Office).

PANKE, Helmut, PhD; German business executive; b. 1946; Head of Corp. Strategy and Co-ordination, BMW AG 1990–93, Chair. and CEOBMW (US) Holding Corpn 1993–96, mem. Bd Man. (Personnel and Information Tech.) 1996–99, mem. Bd Man. (Finance) 1999–2002, Chair. Bd Man. BMW AG May 2002–. *Address:* BMW AG, Recruiting, PM-1, 80788 Munich, Germany (Office). *Website:* www.bmw.de (Office); www.bmwgroup.com (Office).

PANKIN, Boris Dmitriyevich; Russian diplomatist (retd) and essayist; b. 20 Feb. 1931, Frunze (now Bishkek); m.; two s. one d.; ed Moscow State Univ.; journalist and literary critic 1957–; Ed. Komsomolskaya Pravda 1965–73; Chair. Bd USSR Copyright Agency 1973–82; USSR Amb. to Sweden 1982–90, to Czechoslovakia 1990–91; Foreign Minister Aug.–Dec. 1991; Russian Amb. to UK 1991–94; now living in Sweden; USSR State Prize 1982. *Publications:* Severe Literature, Time and Word, Boundaries and Books, The Last 100 Days of the Soviet Union, Four I of Konstantin Simonov. *Telephone:* (46) 880-7871.

PANNENBERG, Wolfhart Ulrich, DTheol; German professor of systematic theology; b. 2 Oct. 1928, Stettin; s. of Kurt B. S. Pannenberg and Irmgard Pannenberg; m. Hilke S. Schütte 1954; ed Heidelberg Univ.; ordained as Lutheran Minister 1955; Privatdozent, Heidelberg 1955; Prof. of Systematic Theology, Wuppertal 1958, Univ. of Mainz 1961, Univ. of Munich 1967–94; Head, Inst. of Ecumenical Theology, Munich; mem. Bavarian Acad. of Sciences, British Acad. of Sciences; Hon. DD (Glasgow, Manchester, Trinity Coll. Dublin, St Andrews, Madrid-Comillas, Cambridge). *Publications:* What is Man? 1962, Jesus: God and Man 1968, Revelation as History 1969, Theology

and the Kingdom of God 1969, Basic Questions in Theology (Vol. I) 1970, (Vol. II) 1971, The Apostle's Creed 1972, Theology and the Philosophy of Science 1976, Human Nature, Election and History 1977, Anthropology in Theological Perspective 1985, Christianity in a Secularized World 1989, Metaphysics and the Idea of God 1990, Systematic Theology (Vols 1–III) 1991–98, Grundlagen der Ethik 1996, Theologie und Philosophie 1996, Problemgeschichte der neueren evangelischen Theologie in Deutschland 1997. *Leisure interests:* history, music, philosophy. *Address:* Sudetenstrasse 8, 82166 Gräfelfing, Germany. *Telephone:* (89) 855915.

PANNI, Marcello; Italian conductor and composer; b. 24 Jan. 1940, Rome; s. of Arnaldo Panni and Adriana Cortini; m. Jeanne Colombier 1970; one d.; ed Accademia di Santa Cecilia, Rome under Goffredo Petrassi and Conservatoire Nat. Supérieur, Paris; conducting début, Festival of Contemporary Music, Venice 1969; has since achieved renown in field of avant-garde music conducting first performances of works by Berio, Bussotti, Cage, Feldman, Donatoni, Clementi, Sciarrino, and others at all major European festivals and for Italian Radio; regular guest conductor for Accademia di Santa Cecilia, the Italian radio orchestras and other European orchestras performing full range of baroque, classical and modern works; Musical Dir Bonn Opera House 1994–97, Nice Opera House 1997–2001; Artistic Dir San Carlo Opera House, Naples 2001–02; opera début with The Barber of Seville, Hamburg 1977 and has since conducted opera in all the principal opera houses in Europe; American debut with Elisir d'amore, Metropolitan Opera, New York 1988; conducted world premiere of Bussotti's Cristallo di Rocca (opera) at La Scala 1983; Milhaud Prof. of Composition and Conducting, Mills Coll., Oakland, Calif. 1980–84. *Works include* symphonic and chamber music and music for experimental theatrical works; operas: Hanjo (one act) 1994, Il giudizio di Paride (one act) 1996, The Banquet 1998. *Leisure interests:* arts, sport. *Address:* 3 Piazza Borghese, 00186 Rome, Italy. *Telephone:* (06) 6873617.

PANNICK, David Philip, QC, BCL, MA; British barrister; b. 7 March 1956, London; s. of Maurice A. Pannick and Rita L. Pannick; m. Denise Sloam 1978 (died 1999); two s. one d.; ed Bancroft's School, Essex and Hertford Coll. Oxford; called to the Bar 1979, QC 1992; Fellow, All Souls Coll. Oxford 1978–; Jr Counsel to the Crown (Common Law) 1988–92; columnist on law, The Times 1991–; Hon. LLD (Hertfordshire) 1998. *Publications:* Sex Discrimination Law 1985, Judges 1987, Advocates 1992, Human Rights Law and Practice (jtly with Lord Lester of Herne Hill) 1999. *Leisure interests:* theatre, cinema, jogging. *Address:* Blackstone Chambers, Temple, London, EC4Y 7BH, England. *Telephone:* 020) 7583-1770. *Fax:* 020) 7822-7222.

PANNONE, Rodger John, DL, FRSA; British solicitor; b. 20 April 1943, Minehead, Somerset; s. of Cyril Pannone and Violet Weeks; m. Patricia Todd 1966; two s. one d.; ed St Brendan's Coll. Bristol and Coll. of Law, London and Manchester Polytechnic; articled clerk, Casson & Co. Salford; joined W.H. Thompson 1969, later partner; joined Conn Goldberg (now Pannone & Partners) 1973, Sr Partner 1991–; lecturer and broadcaster on legal affairs; mem. Lord Chancellor's Advisory Cttee on Civil Justice; fmr mem. Supreme Court Rule Cttee; Gov. Coll. of Law; Chair. Gov. Coll. of Law, Council Manchester Univ.; Fellow, Manchester Metropolitan Univ.; mem. Council, Law Society of England and Wales, Pres. 1993–94; Hon. mem. Canadian Bar Asscn; Hon. Fellow Soc. of Chiropodists, Birmingham Univ. 1998; Deputy Lieutenant Lt Greater Manchester; DLitt hc (Salford), Hon. LLD (Nottingham Trent). *Publications:* legal articles. *Leisure interests:* walking slowly, food and drink. *Address:* Pannone & Partners, 123 Deansgate, Manchester, M3 2BU, England. *Telephone:* (161) 909-3000. *Fax:* (161) 909-4444. *E-mail:* law@pannone.co.uk (Office). *Website:* www.pannone.com (Office).

PANOFSKY, Wolfgang Kurt Hermann, AB, PhD; American scientist; b. 24 April 1919, Berlin, Germany; s. of Erwin Panofsky and Dorothea Mosse Panofsky; m. Adele Dumond 1942; three s. two d.; ed Princeton Univ. and California Inst. of Tech.; in USA 1934–; mem. of staff Radiation Laboratory, Calif. Univ. 1945–51; Asst Prof. 1946–48, Assoc. Prof. 1948–51; Prof. Stanford Univ. 1951–89, Prof. Emer. 1989–, Dir High Energy Physics Laboratory 1953–61, Dir Linear Accelerator Center 1962–84, Dir Emer. 1984–; Consultant Office of Science and Tech., Exec. Office of Pres. 1965–73; Consultant, Arms Control and Disarmament Agency 1968–81; mem. President's Science Advisory Cttee 1960–64; mem. Panel Office of Science and Tech. Policy 1977–; mem. Cttee on Int. Security and Arms Control (CISAC), Nat. Acad. of Science 1981–; mem. NAS, American Physical Soc. (Vice-Pres. 1974, Pres. 1975), American Acad. of Arts and Sciences, Accad. Naz. dei Lincei 1994; Foreign mem. Chinese Acad. of Sciences 2002; Officier, Légion d'honneur 1977; many honorary doctorates including Hon. DSc (Case Inst. of Tech., Saskatchewan, Columbia, Hamburg, Yale, Rome); Dr hc (Princeton, Beijing, Uppsala); Guggenheim Fellowship 1959, 1973, Lawrence Prize, US Atomic Energy Comm. 1961; Calif. Scientist of Year Award 1967, Nat. Medal of Science 1969, Franklin Medal 1970, Enrico Fermi Award, Dept of Energy 1979, Shoong Foundation Award for Science 1983, Hilliard Roderick Prize, AAAS 1991, Matleuci Medal, Rome 1997. *Publications:* Classical Electricity and Magnetism (with M. Phillips) 1995; about 100 scientific papers in professional journals. *Leisure interest:* music. *Address:* Stanford Linear Accelerator Center, Stanford University, P.O. Box 20450, Stanford, CA 94309 (Office); SLAC, 2575 Sand Hill Road, Menlo Park, CA 94025; 25671 Chapin Road, Los Altos, CA 94022, USA (Home). *Telephone:* (650) 926-3988 (Office); (650) 948-6286 (Home). *Fax:* (650) 926-2395 (Office). *E-mail:* pief@slac.stanford.edu (Office).

PANOV, Alexander Nikolayevich, CandHist Sc; Russian diplomatist; b. 6 July 1944, Moscow; m. 1967; one d.; ed Moscow Inst. of Int. Relations; diplomatic service 1968–; translator attaché Embassy, Japan 1968–71; teacher, Asst. Prof. Moscow Inst. of Int. Relations 1971–77; Third, Second Sec. Perm. USSR Mission to UN, New York 1977–82; First Sec. Second Far East Dept USSR Ministry of Foreign Affairs 1982–83; First Sec., Counsellor Embassy, Japan 1983–88; Deputy Chief, Chief of Div., Deputy Chief Dept of Countries of Pacific Ocean and South-East Asia, USSR Ministry of Foreign Affairs 1988–90, Chief 1990–92; Russian Amb. to Korean Repub. 1992–94; Deputy Minister of Foreign Affairs 1994–96; Amb. to Japan 1996–; Order of Merit. *Publications:* Postwar Reforms in Japan 1945–52, Japanese Diplomatic Service, Beyond Distrust to Trust; articles in periodicals. *Leisure interest:* photography. *Address:* Russian Embassy, Minato-ku, Azabu-dai 2-1-1, Tokyo, Japan. *Telephone:* (3) 83583-4224.

PANSA CEDRONIO, Paolo, LLD, LIC.POL.SC.; Italian diplomatist; b. 15 Nov. 1915, Naples; s. of Ciro Pansa Cedronio and Elina Stammelluti; ed Univs. of Naples and Florence; entered Italian diplomatic service 1940; Sec., Italian Embassy, Washington 1945–49; Sec., Italian Del. to NATO, London and Paris 1951–55; Head of Service, Ministry of Foreign Affairs, Rome 1955–61; Minister, Italian Embassy, London 1961–66; Amb. to Chile 1966–70, to Canada 1970–71; Deputy Sec.-Gen. NATO 1971–78; Amb. to USA 1978–81; mem. Cttee of Patrons, Atlantic Treaty Asscn, Paris; alt. Pres. NATO Appeals Bd, Brussels; fmr mem. Consiglio del Contenzioso Diplomatico, Ministry of Foreign Affairs, Rome; mem. Bd Comitato Atlantico; mem. Istituto Studi Ricerca Difesa, Centro Conciliazione Internazionale, Circolo Studi Diplomatici, Rome; Croce di Guerra, Cavaliere di Gran Croce al Merito della Repubblica Italiana, Gran-Cruz Orden al Mérito de Chile, Officier, Légion d'honneur, etc. *Leisure interests:* golf, horse riding, sailing. *Address:* Palazzo Borghese, Largo Fontanella Borghese 19, 00186 Rome, Italy. *Telephone:* (06) 6876128.

PANT, Krishna Chandra, MSc; Indian politician; b. 10 Aug. 1931, Bhowali, Nainital Dist; s. of late Pandit Govind Ballabh Pant; m. Ila Pant 1957; two s.; ed St Joseph's Coll., Nainital, Univ. of Lucknow; Mem. Lok Sabha for Nainital 1962–77, 1978–; Minister of Finance 1967–69, of Steel and Heavy Eng 1969–70, of Home Affairs and Head, Depts. of Science, Electronics and Atomic Energy 1970–73; Minister of Irrigation and Power 1973–74, of Energy 1974–77, 1979–80, of Educ. Jan.–Sept. 1985, of Steel and Mines 1985–87, of Defence 1987–89; Chair. Advisory Bd on Energy 1983–84; First Vice-Pres. Human Rights Comm. 1966; Leader del. to Int. Conf. on Human Rights, Tehran 1968; Deputy Chair. Planning Comm.; del. to various other int. confs.; mem. Nat. Integration Council; Hon. Fellow Inst. of Engineers; Hon. DSc (Udaipur). *Leisure interests:* welfare work, reading, travelling, sports. *Address:* Yojana Bhavan, Sansad Marg, New Delhi 110001, India (Office); 22 Dakshineswar, 10 Hailey Road, New Delhi 110001. *Telephone:* (11) 3716354 (Office); (11) 3012618. *Fax:* (11) 3717681 (Office).

PANTO, György; Hungarian geochemist and academic; b. 1936, Budapest; s. of Endre Pantó and Ilona Botár; m. Márta Juhász; one s. one d.; ed Loránd Eötvös Univ.; mine geologist Hungarian Mineral and Ore Mines 1959–62; postgrad. scholarship Hungarian Acad. of Sciences 1962–65, Sr researcher Hungarian Acad. of Sciences Lab. for Geochemical Research 1965–76, Dir 1976–2000; Dir-Gen. Hungarian Acad. of Sciences Research Centre for Earth Sciences 1998–; mem. Hungarian Acad. of Sciences, Pres. Earth Sciences Section; Foreign mem. Serbian Acad. of Arts and Sciences; mem. editorial bd Acta Geologica Hungarica; Szèchenyi Prize 2000. *Publications:* numerous articles, books and contribs. on geochem. *Leisure interests:* gardening, tourism. *Address:* Hungarian Academy of Sciences Research Centre for Earth Sciences, 1112 Budapest, Budaörsi út 45, Hungary (Office). *Telephone:* (1) 319-3145 (Office). *Fax:* (1) 319-3145 (Office). *E-mail:* panto@sparc.core.hu (Office).

PANULA, Jorma; Finnish conductor, composer and academic; b. 10 Aug. 1930, Kauhajoki; ed Sibelius Acad., Helsinki; Artistic Dir Turku Philharmonic Orchestra, Finland Aarhus Symphony, Denmark 1963–97; Prin. Conductor Helsinki Philharmonic 1965–72; Prof. of Orchestral Conducting, Sibelius Acad., Helsinki 1973–93; trains conductors in USA, Russia, Sweden, Italy and Australia; fmr Visiting Prof. Music Acads of Stockholm and Copenhagen, Yale Univ., Bartók Seminar, Hungary; Music Prize, Royal Swedish Acad. of Science 1997. *Music:* (operas) Jaakko Ilkka, The River Opera; musicals, church music, a violin concerto, a jazz capriccio and vocal music. *Address:* c/o Sibelius Academy, P. Rautatiekatu 9, 00100 Helsinki 10, Finland (Office).

PANYARACHUN, Anand; Thai diplomatist and politician; b. 9 Aug. 1932; s. of Phya and Khunying Prichanusat; m. M. R. Sodsee Panyarachun Chakrabandh 1956; two d.; ed Bangkok Christian Coll., Dulwich Coll., London and Univ. of Cambridge; joined Ministry of Foreign Affairs 1955; Sec. to Foreign Minister 1959; First Sec. Perm. Mission to UN 1964, Counsellor 1966, Acting Perm. Rep. 1967–72, concurrently Amb. to Canada; Amb. to USA concurrently Perm. Rep. to UN 1972–75, Amb. to Fed. Repub. of Germany 1977; Perm. Under-Sec. of State for Foreign Affairs 1975–76; del. to several sessions of UN Gen. Ass. and SEATO Council; Chair. Group of 77 on Law of Sea 1973; Rep. to UN Econ. and Social Council 1974–75; Chair. Thai Del. to 7th Special Session of UN Gen. Ass., Vice-Chair. Ad Hoc Cttee 7th Special Session, Sept. 1975; Chair. Textport Int. Corpn Ltd; Pres. ASEAN-CCI Council 1980; Vice-Chair. Saha-Union Corpn Ltd 1979; Vice-Pres. Asscn Thai Industries; Vice-Chair. ASEAN-U.S. Business Council 1980; Dir Sime Darby 1982; Acting Prime Minister 1991–92; Prime Minister of Thailand 1992; UNICEF Amb. for Thailand 1996; Ramon Magsaysay Award 1997. *Leisure interests:* tennis, squash, reading. *Address:* Government House, Thanon Nakhon Pathom, Bangkok 10300, Thailand.

PANZA di BIUMO, Giuseppe, DJur; Italian art collector; b. 23 March 1923, Milan; s. of Ernesto Panza di Biumo and Maria Mantegazza; m. Rosa G. Magnifico 1955; four s. one d.; ed self-taught in art history; 80 works of art acquired by Museum of Contemporary Art, LA 1984; 220 works of art acquired by Guggenheim Museum 1990; 150 works of art in gift to Guggenheim Museum, 200 works of art in gift to Museo Cantonale d'Arte, Lugano, 70 to Museum of Contemporary Art, LA, 133 works of art and the 18th-century villa in Biumo. *Publications:* Art of the Sixties and Seventies 1988, Panza di Biumo: The Eighties and Nineties from the Collection 1992. *Address:* P.O. Box 3183, 6901 Lugano; Sentiero Vinorum 2, 6900 Massagno, Switzerland. *Telephone:* (91) 9676021; (91) 9682353. *Fax:* (91) 9676125.

PAO, Eugene; Chinese jazz guitarist; ed Univ. of Washington; played in local groups while at univ.; joined father's trading co. upon return to Hong Kong; began playing at Rick's Café; subsequently joined Hong Kong's Jazz Club where he leads a four-man band 1988–; CDs include By the Company You Keep.

PAOLILLO, Felipe; Uruguayan diplomatist and lawyer; b. 8 Oct. 1931; Prof. of Int. Public Law, Univ. of Uruguay 1967–74, 1985–87; Assoc. Prof. New York Univ. School of Law 1977–84; Perm. Rep. to UN 1987–90, 2000–01, to Holy See and FAO 1996–2000; Chair. UN Gen. Ass. Credentials Cttee May 2002–; mem. Inst. of Int. Law; mem. Interamerican Judicial Council. *Address:* United Nations General Assembly, New York, NY 10017, U.S.A. (Office). *Telephone:* (212) 963-1234. *Fax:* (212) 963-4879. *Website:* www.un.org.

PAOLOZZI, Sir Eduardo Luigi, Kt, CBE, RA; British sculptor; b. 7 March 1924, Leith, Scotland; s. of Alfonso Rudolfo Paolozzi and Carmella (Rossi) Paolozzi; m. (divorced); three d.; ed Edinburgh Coll. of Art and Slade School of Fine Art, Oxford and London; first exhibitions, Mayor Gallery, London 1947, 1948, 1949; teacher of textile design, Cen. School of Art and Design 1949–55; Lecturer in sculpture, St Martin's School of Art 1955–58; Visiting Prof. Hochschule für Bildende Künste, Hamburg 1960–62; Visiting Lecturer, Univ. of Calif., Berkeley 1968; tutor in Ceramics, Royal Coll. of Art 1968–89; Prof. in Ceramics, Fachhochschule, Cologne 1976–81, Prof. of Sculpture at Akad. der Bildenen Künste, Munich 1981–90; Visiting Prof. RCA 1989–; Prof. Master Class, Int. Summer Acad., Salzburg 1982; one-man exhbns have included Hanover Gallery, London 1958, 1967, Betty Parsons Gallery, NY 1960, 1962, Robert Fraser Gallery, London 1964, 1966, Museum of Modern Art, NY 1964, Pace Gallery, NY 1966, 1967, Stedelijk Museum, Amsterdam 1968, Tate Gallery, London 1971, Victoria and Albert Museum 1977, Nationalgalerie, Berlin retrospective 1975, Cologneischer Kunstverein, Cologne 1979, Museum für Kunst und Gewerbe, Hamburg 1982, Royal Scottish Acad. 1984, Lenbachhaus, Munich 1984, Museum Ludwig, Cologne 1985, Museum of Mankind, London 1986, Royal Acad., London 1986, Serpentine Gallery, London 1987, Nat. Portrait Gallery, London 1988, Talbot Rice Art Gallery, Edinburgh 1989, Stadtmuseum, Munich 1990, Goethe Inst., London 1991, Yorkshire Sculpture Park, West Bretton 1994, Fitzwilliam Museum, Cambridge 1995, Jason and Rhodes, London 1997, Dean Gallery, Edin. 1999–, Univ. of Northambria 2000, Flowers East, London 2001 and other galleries in UK, USA, Canada, Netherlands, Germany; has participated in numerous group exhbns including Venice Biennale 1952, 1960, São Paulo Biennale 1957, 1963, New Images of Man, Museum of Modern Art, NY 1959, 2nd 3rd and 4th Int. Biennial Exhbns of Prints, Museum of Modern Art, Tokyo 1960, 1962, 1964, British Art Today (travelling exhbn, tour of USA) 1962, 7th Int. Art Exhbn, Tokyo 1963, Neue Realisten und Pop Art, Akad. der Künste, Berlin 1964, Premier Bienniale Exhbn, Cracow 1966, Sculpture from Twenty Nations, Guggenheim Museum, NY 1967, Pop Art Redefined, Hayward Gallery, London 1969, Expo 70, Osaka 1970, Hayward Annual Arts Council Exhbn 1977, Nat. Gallery of Scotland 1980, 20th Century British Sculpture, London 1981, West-Kunst, Cologne 1981, English Painters 1900–82, Museo Municipal of Madrid 1983, British Museum, London 1990, Pompidou Centre, Paris 1990, Royal Acad., London 1991 Spellbound, Hayward Gallery, London 1996, Un siècle de sculpture anglaise, Gal. Nat. de Jeu de Paume, Paris; designed mosaics for Tottenham Court Road underground station, London; Fellow, Univ. Coll. London 1986; apptd Her Majesty's Sculptor-in-Ordinary for Scotland 1986; Trustee Nat. Portrait Gallery 1988–, Dean Gallery, Paolozzi Collection, Edinburgh; corresp. mem. Bayerische Akad. der Schönen Künste 1990; Hon. Fellow Royal Glasgow Inst. of Fine Arts 1993; Hon. Fellow Jesus Coll. Cambridge 1994; Dr hc (RCA, London); Hon. DLitt (Univ. of Glasgow) 1980, (Heriot-Watt Univ., Edinburgh) 1987, (London) 1987, (St Andrews) 1994, (Birmingham) 1996; British Critics' Prize 1953, Copley Foundation Award 1956, Bright Foundation Award 1960, Blair Prize, 64th Annual American Exhbn, Chicago 1961, 1st Prize for Sculpture, Carnegie Int. Exhbn, Pittsburgh 1967, Saltire Soc. Award 1981, Grand Prix d'honneur, 15th Int. Print Biennale, Ljubljana 1983; Invited Artist, Cleveland Sixth Int. Drawing Biennale 1983, Goethe Medal 1991; Cavaliere Ufficiale, Ordine al Merito (Italy) 1991. *Address:* 107 Dovehouse Street, London, SW3 6JZ, England.

PAPACOSTEA, Serban, DHist; Romanian historian; b. 25 June 1928, Bucharest; s. of Petre G. Papacostea and Josefina Papacostea; ed Univ. of

Bucharest; scientific researcher and Dir, "Nicolae Iorga" Inst. of History, Bucharest; mem. editorial Bd Revue Roumaine d'Histoire, Studii si materiale de istorie medie (Studies and Materials of Medieval History), Il Mar Nero (Rome); Corresp. mem. Romanian Acad., Accademia Ligure di Scienze e Lettere; Prize of the Roman Acad. 1971. *Publications:* Istoria României (The History of Romania) (in collaboration) 1964, 1998, 2002, Istoria poporului român (History of the Romanian People) (in collaboration) 1970, Nochmals Wittenberg und Byzanz: die Moldau im Zeitalter der Reformation 1970, Oltenia sub stăpînirea austriacă, 1718–1739 (Oltenia under Austrian Rule, 1718–1739) 1971, Venise et les Pays Roumains au Moyen Age, in Venezia e il Levante fino al secolo XV, 1973, Stephan der Grosse, Fürst der Moldau 1975, Kilia et la politique orientale de Sigismond de Luxembourg 1976, Die politischen Voraussetzungen für die wirtschaftliche Vorherrschaft des Osmanischen Reiches im Schwarzmeergebiet 1453–1484 1978, La fondation de la Valachie et de la Moldavie et les Roumains de Transylvanie 1978, "Quod non iretur ad Tanam": Un aspect fondamental de la politique génoise dans la Mer Noire au XIVe siècle 1979, Inceputurile politicii comerciale a Tării Româneşti şi Moldovei (The Beginnings of Trade Policy in Wallachia and Moldavia) 1983, La fin de la domination génoise à Licostomo 1985, La Valachie et la crise de structure de l'Empire Ottoman (1402–1413) 1986, La Mer Noire: du monopole byzantin à la domination des Latins aux Détroits 1988, La première crise des rapports byzantino-génois après Nymphaion: le complot de Guglielmo Guercio (1264) 1988, Geneza statului in Evul mediu Românesc (The Formation of the Medieval Romanian State) 1988, Gênes, Venise et la Mer Noire à la fin du XIIIe siècle 1990, Byzance et la Croisade au Bas-Danube à la fin du XIVe siècle 1991, Jews in the Romanian Principalities during the Middle Ages 1993, Romanii in Secolul XIII intre Cruciata şi Imperial Mongol 1993, Une révolte antigénoise en Mer Noire et la riposte de Gênes (1432–1434) 1994, Captive Clio: Romanian Historiography under Communist Rule 1996, Un tournant de la politique génoise en Mer Noire au XIVe siècle 1997, Gênes, Venise et la Croisade de Varna 1997, Between the Crusades and the Mongol Empire 1998, Evul Mediu românesc (The Romanian Middle Ages) 2001, Welthandel und Weltpolitik im Spätmittealter 2001. *Leisure interest:* pre-classical music. *Address:* Institutul de Istorie "Nicolae Iorga", Bd Aviatorilor 1, Bucharest (Office); Caragea Vodă 19, 71149 Bucharest, Romania (Home). *Telephone:* 6509045 (Office); 2114455 (Home).

PAPADEMOS, Lucas D., PhD; Greek economist; b. 11 Oct. 1947, Athens; ed Athens Coll.,MIT, USA; Prof. of Econs Columbia Univ., NY 1975–84, Univ. of Athens 1988–; Sr Economist Fed. Reserve Bank of Boston; Econ. Adviser Bank of Greece 1985–93, Head of Econ. Research Dept 1988–92, Deputy Gov. 1993–94, Gov. 1994–2002; Vice-Pres. ECB 2002–; mem. Cttee of Alts of Govs. of EC Cen. Banks 1985–93, Council of Econ. Advisers 1985–88, 1991–94, EMI and various bds; Grand Commdr, Order of Honour 1999. *Address:* European Central Bank, Kaiserstrasse 29, Postfach 160319, 60066 Frankfurt am Main, Germany (Office). *Telephone:* (69) 13440 (Office). *Fax:* (69) 13446000 (Office). *E-mail:* info@ecb.int. *Website:* www.ecb.int (Office).

PAPADIMITRIOU, George, DJur; Greek professor of law; b. 1944, Thessaloniki; s. of Alexandros Papadimitriou and Argiri Papadimitriou; m. Anna Papadimitriou Tsatsou 1976; one s.; ed Univs of Thessaloniki, Heidelberg and Paris I; Research Fellow, Inst. für Int. Recht, Kiel 1971–72, Max Planck Inst. of Foreign, Public and Int. Law, Heidelberg 1972–74; lecturer, Thessaloniki Univ. Law School 1975–79; Prof. of Constitutional Law, Thrace Univ. 1979–84, Univ. of Athens 1984–; Dean, Dept of Political Science and Public Admin. Univ. of Athens 1993; Legal Adviser to Prime Minister 1996–; mem. several nat. and foreign learned socs. *Publications include:* Die Stellung der allgemeinen Regeln des Voelkerrechts im innerstaatlichen Recht 1972, The Dispute of the Aegean Shelf and the Cyprus Problem 1975, Constitutional Law. The Electorate 1981, The European Parliament: Problems, Realities and Perspectives 1984, Constitutional Problems 1989–91, Democracy and European Integration 1993, Constitutional Problems 1992–93 1995. *Address:* 30 Sina Street, Athens 10672 (Office); 8 Ivodotou Street, Athens 10675, Greece (Home). *Telephone:* (1) 3635137 (Office); (1) 3617443 (Office); (1) 6437414 (Home). *Fax:* (1) 3629353. *E-mail:* gpapdim@ath.forthnet.gr (Office).

PAPADONGONAS, Alexandros; Greek politician and naval officer; b. 11 July 1931, Tripolis; s. of Dionisios and Vasiliki Papadongonas; m. Niki Maidonis 1976; one s. one d.; ed Greek Naval Acad., Naval War Coll., U.S. Naval Schools, NATO Defence Coll.; has served on Greek fleet vessels and submarines and has held staff positions; organized with other Navy officers Movt of Navy against the dictatorship; arrested May 1973 and removed from service; returned to Navy July–Nov. 1974; MP 1974–93; Minister of Merchant Shipping 1974–77, of Communications 1977–80; Deputy Minister of Defence 1990–91, Minister of Merchant Shipping 1992–93; mem. Council of Europe 1982–89, 1991; Pres. Greek Del. to Parl. Ass. of OSCE 1993–; mem. North Atlantic Ass.; New Democracy Party; Medal of Mil. Valour, Commdr Order of the Phoenix, Officer Order of George I. *Leisure interests:* sailing, scuba diving, underwater archaeology. *Address:* 11 Nikis Street, Athens 105 57, Greece. *Telephone:* (1) 3255150.

PAPADOPOULOS, Tassos; Cypriot politician and lawyer; b. 1934, Nicosia; m. Photini Michaelides; two s. two d.; actively participated in EOKA struggle for independence 1955–59; Rep. of Greek Cypriot side in Constitutional Cttee (which drafted constitution); mem. House of Reps 1970–, Pres. of House 1976; elected Deputy Democratic Party (Diko) 1991, 1996, Leader 2000–; fmr Minister of the Interior, of Finance, of Labour and Social Insurance, of Health, of Agric. and Natural Resources; Interlocutor 1976; fmr mem. Nat. Council; fmr Chair. Standing Parl. Cttee on European Affairs, Cttee on Selection, Cttee on Financial and Budgetary Affairs; fmr co-Chair. Jt EU–Cyprus Parl Cttee; Pres. of Cyprus March 2003–. *Address:* Presidential Palace, Dem. Severis Avenue, 1400 Lefkosia (Nicosia), Cyprus (Office). *Telephone:* 665016 (Office). *Fax:* 661333 (Office). *Website:* www.pio.gov.cy (Office).

PAPAIOANNOU, Miltiades; Greek politician and lawyer; b. 1946, Kalavryta, Achaia; ed Panteio Univ., Law Faculty of Athens; Panhellenic Socialist Movt (PASOK) MP; Deputy Minister, Ministry of Internal Affairs 1982–85, Minister of Justice 1985, Deputy Minister, Prime Minister's Dept and Govt Spokesman 1985–86, Gen. Sec. Ministry of Nat. Economy 1993–96; Minister of Labour and Social Security 1998–2000; Minister of State 2000–02; mem. Exec. Bureau and Cen. Cttee PASOK. *Publications:* numerous articles on politics, econs, public admin, local govt and regional devt. *Address:* c/o Ministry of Labour and Social Security, Odos Pireos 40, 104 37 Athens, Greece.

PAPANDREOU, George A., MSc; Greek politician; b. 16 June 1952, St Paul, Minn., USA; m. Ada Papandreou; one s. one d.; ed Amherst Coll., Md, USA, Stockholm Univ., Sweden, LSE; Panhellenic Socialist Movt (PASOK) MP for Achaia (Patras) 1981–96, for First District of Athens 1996–; Under-Sec. for Cultural Affairs 1985–87, Minister of Educ. and Religious Affairs 1988–89, Deputy Minister of Foreign Affairs 1993–94, Minister of Educ. and Religious Affairs 1994–96, Alt. Foreign Minister 1996–99, Foreign Minister 1999–; mem. Cen. Cttee PASOK 1984–, Exec. Cttee 1987–88, mem. Exec. Office and Political Bureau 1996–; Govt Co-ordinator 2004 Athens Olympic bid 1997; mem. Bd Foundation of Mediterranean Studies, for Research and Self-Educ.; Fellow Center for Int. Affairs, Harvard Univ. 1992–93; Botsis Foundation for Promotion of Journalism Award 1988, SOS against Racism Award 1996, Abdi Ipekci Special Award for Peace and Friendship 1997, Statesman of the Year Award, Eastwest Inst. 2000. *Address:* Ministry of Foreign Affairs, Odos Zalokosta 2, 106 71 Athens, Greece. *Telephone:* (1) 3610581. *Fax:* (1) 3624195. *Website:* www.papandreou.gr (Office).

PAPANDREOU, Vasiliki (Vasso), PhD; Greek politician; b. 1953, Valimitika Aeghiou; ed Athens, London and Reading Univs; lecturer, Athens Univ.; Research Asst Exeter and Oxford Univs; Dir Hellenic Org. of Small and Medium-sized Businesses, Athens 1981–85; founder mem. Panhellenic Socialist Party (PASOK) 1974, mem. Cen. Cttee Exec. Bureau 1984–88, 1996–; MP 1985–89, 1993–, Deputy Minister for Industry, Energy and Tech. 1985–89, Alt. Minister 1986–87, Alt. Minister for Trade 1988–89; Commr for Social Affairs, Employment, Educ., Comm. of European Communities 1989–92; Head Greek Del. Council of Europe Parl. Ass. 1993–96, Vice-Pres. 1995–96; Minister for Devt 1996–99, of the Interior, Public Admin and Decentralization 1999–2001, of the Environment, Physical Planning and Public Works 2001–; Hon. LittD (Sheffield) 1992; Dr hc (CNAA, London) 1992, (P. Sabatier, Toulouse) 1993; Chevalier Légion d'honneur, France 1993, Grand-Croix, Belgium 1993, Great Cross of the Order of the North Star 1999. *Publications:* Multinational Companies and Less Developed Countries: The Case of Greece 1981; numerous papers on politics and econs. *Address:* Ministry of the Environment, Physical Planning and Public Works, Odos Amaliados 17, 115 23 Athens; 15 Omirou Street, 10672 Athens, Greece. *Telephone:* (1) 06431461 (Office). *Fax:* (1) 06432589 (Office). *E-mail:* minister@minenv.gr (Office). *Website:* www.minenv.gr (Office).

PAPANTONIOU, Ioannis, PhD; Greek politician; b. 1949; three c.; ed Univs. of Athens, Wisconsin, USA, Paris, Cambridge; lecturer Dept of Econs, Univ. of Athens, Researcher Centre of Planning and Econ. Research 1977–78; staff mem. Econs Dept OECD, Paris 1978–81; Panhellenic Socialist Movt (PASOK) MEP 1981–84; Special Adviser to Prime Minister on EC Affairs; Deputy Minister for Nat. Economy 1985–89, Minister of Trade 1989; MP for first Dist of Athens 1989–; Alt. Minister for Nat. Economy 1993–94, Minister of Nat. Economy and Finance 1994–2001, of Nat. Defence 2001–. *Address:* Ministry of National Defence, Stratopedo Papagou, Holargos, Athens, Greece. *Telephone:* (1) 06552001. *Fax:* (1) 06443832. *E-mail:* epyetha@mod.gr (Office). *Website:* www.mod.gr (Office).

PAPATHANASSIOU, Aspassia; Greek actress; b. 1918, Amphissa; m. Kostas Mayrommatis 1944; ed Dramatic Art School of National Theatre of Greece; played a variety of leading roles with various Greek theatrical groups; founder-mem. Piraikon Theatre 1957, Intellectual and Artistic Asscn 1974, Inst. for Study of Greek Tragedies 1990; has toured extensively in Europe and N and S America; appeared at int. festivals in Berlin, Paris, Florence and Vienna; has given over 450 performances of ancient tragedy; appeared on TV in England, Russia, USA and several other countries; mem. Patriotic Front (PAM); Officier des Arts et des Lettres 1991; Paris Théâtre des Nations 1st Prize; Gold Medal of City of Athens 1962; Silver Palladium Medal for best European actress 1963. *Address:* 38 Xenokratous Street, 106 76 Athens, Greece. *Telephone:* (1) 7242243. *Fax:* (1) 7214050.

PAPAZYAN, Vahan, CHisSc; Armenian politician, diplomatist and historian; b. 26 Jan. 1957, Yerevan; m.; one s.; ed Yerevan Univ.; researcher Inst. of History, Armenian Acad. of Sciences 1980–91; Counsellor to Pres. of Armenia 1991–92; Chargé d'Affaires of Armenia to France 1992–93; Minister of Foreign Affairs 1993–96; on staff Acad. of Sciences 1996–. *Publications:* works on history of Armenian-Iranian relations and trade routes in Middle Ages. *Address:* Academy of Sciences, Marshal Bagramian Avenue 24, 375019 Yerevan, Armenia. *Telephone:* (3742) 523531. *Fax:* (3742) 527022.

PAPIERNIK-BERKHAUER, Emile, DenM, FRCOG; French obstetrician and gynaecologist; b. 14 Feb. 1936, Paris; s. of Motel Papiernik and Pesa Bonk; m. Martine Czermichow 1961; two s. one d.; ed Univ. of Paris; Asst Prof. Faculté de Médecine René Descartes, Paris and Maternité de Port-Royal, Paris 1966–; Prof. of Obstetrics and Gynaecology, Univ. of Paris-Orsay and Chair. Dept of Obstetrics and Gynaecology, Hôpital Béclère, Clamart 1972–90; Dir Research Unit 187, Inst. de la santé et de la recherche médicale (INSERM) (Physiology and Psychology of Human Reproduction) 1979–; Bd Dirs. Collège nat. des gynécologues-accouchers; Fellow, American Acad. of Pediatrics, Royal Coll. of Obstetricians and Gynaecologists; Chevalier, Légion d'honneur. *Publication:* Le prix de la vie 1988, Le Guide Papiernik de la grossesse (jtly.) 1991, Le passeur de vie, entretien avec Emile Papiernik (jtly.) 1998. *Leisure interest:* collector of contemporary painting. *Address:* Maternité de Port Royal Baudeloque, 123 blvd de Port Royal, 75674 Paris cedex 14 (Office); 35 rue Imbergeres, 92330 Sceaux, France (Home).

PAPON, Maurice Arthur Jean, LenD; French politician; b. 3 Sept. 1910, Gretz-Armainvilliers (Seine-et-Marne); s. of Arthur Papon and Marie Dussiau; m. Paulette Asso 1932; one s. two d.; ed Lycée Louis-le-Grand and Facultés de Droit et de Lettres, Paris; Ed., Ministry of Interior 1935–36; Attachée, Cabinet of the Under-Sec. of State 1936, Foreign Affairs 1937–39; Sec.-Gen. Gironde 1942–44; Prefect and Dir of Cabinet of the Comm. of the Repub. of France 1944–45; Deputy Dir for Algeria at Ministry of Interior 1946–47; Prefect of Corsica 1947–49, Constantine, Algeria 1949–51; Sec.-Gen., Prefecture of Police 1951–54, Protectorate of Morocco 1954–55; Tech. Adviser, Cabinet of Sec. of State for Interior 1956; Insp.-Gen. for Admin., E Algeria 1956–58; Prefect of Police, Paris 1958–66; Pres., Dir-Gen. Sud-Aviation 1967–68; elected Deputy for Cher, Nat. Ass. 1968, 1973, 1978; Pres. Ass. Finance Comm. 1972–73, Rapporteur 1973–78; Minister of the Budget 1978–81; Mayor of Saint-Amand-Montrond 1971–82; Chair. and Man. Dir Verreries champenoises, Rheims; Hon. Prefect of Police 1972; sentenced to ten years' imprisonment for crimes against humanity April 1998, conviction on appeal 2001, released Sept. 2002; Commdr, Légion d'honneur, Commdr, Ordre du Mérite Civil and mil. awards. *Publications:* L'ère des responsables 1954, Vers un nouveau discours de la méthode 1965, Le Gaullisme ou la loi de l'effort 1973, Les chevaux du pouvoir 1988.

PAPOULIAS, George Dimitrios; Greek diplomatist; b. 19 May 1927; s. of Dimitrios G. Papoulias and Caterina Kontopoulou; m. Emily Pilavachi 1974; one d.; ed Univ. of Athens; entered diplomatic service 1955; served Athens, New Delhi, Bonn; Deputy Perm. Del. to UN and int. orgs. Geneva 1964–69; Dir Political Affairs, Ministry of Northern Greece 1969–70; Minister, Paris and Perm. Rep. to UNESCO 1971–74; mem. Bd of Dirs Resettlement Fund, Council of Europe 1971–74; Perm. Rep. to UN, New York 1975–79; Amb. to Turkey 1979–83, to USA 1983–89; Alt. Minister and Minister for Foreign Affairs 1989, 1990; Amb. to UK (also Accred to Iceland) 1990–93; Commdr Order of the Phoenix, Order of George I; other foreign orders and decorations. *Leisure interests:* archaeology, history. *Address:* Rigillis 16, Athens 10674, Greece. *Telephone:* (1) 7229888.

PAPOULIAS, Karolos, PhD; Greek politician and lawyer; b. 1929; s. of late Maj.-Gen. Gregorios Papoulias; ed Univs. of Athens, Madrid, Bonn and Cologne; fmr practising lawyer in Athens; lived in Germany 1962–74; worked for Greek radio programme of Deutsche Welle; mem. Greek democratic del. at Gen. Ass. of Council of Europe during period of mil. dictatorship in Greece; mem. Parl. 1977–; mem. Cen. Cttee Panhellenic Socialist Movt (PASOK); Sec.-Gen. Centre for Mediterranean Studies, Athens; Deputy Minister for Foreign Affairs 1981–84, Alt. Minister 1984–85, Minister of Foreign Affairs 1985, 1993–96; Alt. Minister for Defence 1989–90. *Address:* c/o Parliament Buildings, Syntagma Square, Athens, Greece.

PAPOUTSIS, Christos; Greek politician and economist; b. 11 April 1953, Larissa; m.; one d.; Pres. Greek Nat. Union of Students 1978–80; Special Adviser on Public Admin. Ministry of Presidency of Govt 1981–84; mem. Exec. Bureau Pan-Hellenic Socialist Movt (PASOK); MEP 1984–, Vice-Pres. Socialist Group 1987–; leader, PASOK del. to European Parl.; mem. Presidium, Party of European Socialists 1988–; Commr for Energy and Euratom Supply Agency, Small and Medium Enterprises (SME) and Tourism, European Comm. 1995–99. *Publication:* European Journeys 1994. *Address:* Filikis Etairids 21, 10673 Athens, Greece.

PAPP, László; Hungarian boxer; b. 25 March 1926; s. of Imre Papp and Erzsébet Burgus; m. Erzsébet Kovács 1950; one s.; original profession mechanic; 288 wins from 300 amateur contests; unbeaten as professional (28 wins, 2 draws); first boxer to win three Olympic gold medals (middleweight 1948, light-middleweight 1952, 1956) and twice European champion; professional boxer 1956–64, European champion 1962–64; professional licence withdrawn by Hungarian authorities 1965; official coach with the Hungarian Amateur Boxing Fed. 1971–92; Labour Order of Merit, Sport Order of Merit, Olympic Silver Order of Merit, World Boxing Council Order 1989, Int. Fair Play Prize 1993; mem. Athletes of the Century 1999, Boxing Hall of Fame and Museum 2001. *Leisure interest:* angling. *Address:* Ora-utca 6, 1125 Budapest, Hungary.

PAPPALARDO, HE Cardinal Salvatore, DST; Italian ecclesiastic; b. 23 Sept. 1918, Villafranca; s. of the late Alfio Pappalardo and Gaetana Coco; ed Pontifical Univ. Lateranensis; ordained Priest 1941; Counsellor, Vatican Secr. of State 1947–65; Apostolic Pronuncio, Indonesia 1965–69; Pres. Pontif-ical Ecclesiastical Acad., Rome 1969–70; Archbishop of Palermo 1970–96; Archbishop Emer. 1996–; cr. Cardinal by Pope Paul VI 1973. *Address:* Piazza Baida 1, 90136 Palermo, Italy. *Telephone:* (091) 223893 (Home).

PAPPANO, Antonio; conductor and pianist; b. London; studied piano, composition and conducting in USA with Norma Verrilli, Arnold Franchetti and Gustav Meier; worked as pianist and Asst conductor with New York City Opera, Gran Teatro del Liceo, Barcelona, Frankfurt Opera, Lyric Opera of Chicago and the Bayreuth Festival (Asst to Daniel Barenboim for Tristan und Isolde, Parsifal and the Ring cycle); opera conducting debut with Norwegian opera, later Music Dir; has also conducted opera at Vienna Staatsoper (debut conducting new production of Wagner's Siegfried 1993), San Francisco Opera, Théâtre du Châtelet, Berlin Staatsoper, ENO, Covent Garden (debut conducting La Bohème 1990) and the Teatro Comunale, Florence; has conducted many world-class orchestras including Chicago Symphony Orchestra, Cleveland Orchestra, LA Philharmonic, LSO, Berlin Philharmonic, Orchestre de Paris, Oslo Philharmonic, Munich Philharmonic; Prin. Guest Conductor Israel Philharmonic Orchestra 1997–2000; Music Dir Royal Opera House, Covent Garden March 1999–2002; Music Dir Théâtre Royal de la Monnaie, Brussels 1992–2002; opera repertory includes Britten, Wagner, Strauss, Verdi, Shostakovich, Debussy, Puccini, Berg, Janacek and Bellini; piano accompanist for La Monnaie int. recital series. *Recordings include:* Puccini's La Rondine (Gramophone Award for Best Opera Recording and Record of the Year 1997), Il Trittico 1999, Britten's The Turn of the Screw (Théâtre Royal de la Monnaie production) (Choc du Monde de la Musique, Prix de l'Acad. du Disque Lyrique Grand Prix Int., Orphée d'Or) 1999, Werther 1999, Manon Gramophone Award for Best Opera Recording 2001. *Address:* c/o IMG Artists, Hovell House, 616 Chiswick High Road, London, WC2E 9DD, England (Office).

PAPPAS, Spyros; Greek civil servant and European Union official; b. 1 Jan. 1953, Athens; m. Frady Karkanis; one s. one d.; ed Univ. of Athens, Panteios School of Econ. and Political Studies, Univ. of Paris, Directorate for European Affairs, INSEAD; fmr naval Petty Officer; barrister, Athens 1976; Auditor Council of State 1978, Counsel 1983; Special Adviser in Prime Minister's Legal Office 1981; mem. Comm. for Drafting of Laws 1982; est. Nat. Centre of Public Admin., Sec.-Gen. 1985; est. Inst. of Permanent Training 1985; Assoc. Prof. European Inst. of Public Admin., Maastricht 1988, Dir of Faculty 1989, Dir-Gen. 1990, Prof. of European Law 1992; Dir-Gen. for Consumer Policy EC 1995, for Information, Communication, Culture and Audiovisual Media 1997–99; Chair. Bd of Govs. Int. East–West Acad.; mem. Supreme Council Church of Greece 1984, Comm. of Information on National Affairs, Inst. for Admin. Studies, Asscn of the Judges of the Council of State, Inst. of Public Admin., Cttee for Drafting of the Encyclopedia of Admin., Centre for European Policy Studies Int. Advisory Council, Scientific Council of Academia Istropolitana Bratislava Inst. of Advanced Studies, Foundation for Hellenic Culture; assoc. mem. Asscn of European Magistrates for Democracy and Liberty (MEDEL); substitute Bd mem. Open Univ., Athens; cr. European Centre of Judges and Lawyers 1992; hon. State Scholar 1970–73; Scholar of Council of Europe 1977; First Prize Michel Stassinopoulos Foundation for Admin. Law 1976; Officer Order of Merit, Luxembourg 1994. *Publications:* La constitution de la Grèce de 1975 1976, Le régime de planification en Grèce 1977, Le Tribunal de Première Instance 1990, Tendances actuelles et évolution de la jurisprudence de la cour de justice des Communautés européennes: suivi annuel Vol. I 1993, Vol. II 1995 (Ed.), Procédures administratives nationales: préparation et mise en oeuvre des décisions communautaires: études comparatives (Ed.) 1994, EC Competition Law: Financial Aspects (Co-Ed.) 1994, The Changing Role of Parliaments in the European Union (Co-Ed.) 1995, The European Union's Common Foreign and Security Policy: The Challenges of the Future 1996, Politiques publiques dans l'Union européenne 1996.

PAQUET-SEVIGNY, Thérèse, PhD; Canadian United Nations official; b. 3 Feb. 1934, Sherbrooke, Québec; d. of René Paquet and Marie-Reine Cloutier; m. Robert Sévigny 1956; one s. one d.; ed Sorbonne-Paris Univ. and Univ. of Montreal; journalism and communications research for La Tribune and L'Actualité, Montreal and for Montreal and Laval Univs. 1952–61; Man. Dir for Consumer Research, Steinberg Limitée 1961–66; various appts. at Communications Depts. Montreal Univ., McGill Univ. and Ecole des Hautes Etudes Commerciales, Montreal 1969–76; Vice-Pres. for Research and Planning, BCP Publicité Limitée 1969–71, Vice-Pres. and Man. Dir 1974–81, Pres. and Chief of Operations 1981–83; Vice-Pres. RSGL Publicité Limitée 1971–74; Vice-Pres. for Communications, Canadian Broadcasting Corpn (CBC) 1983–87; Under-Sec.-Gen. for Public Information, United Nations 1987; Prof. of Communications, Québec Univ., Montreal (UQAM) 1993–; Dir, UNESCO Chair in Communication and Int. Devt 1993–; Int. Consultant 1993–; Sec.-Gen. Orbicom (Int. Network of UNESCO Chairs in Communications) 1993–98, Sr Adviser 1999–; Dr. hc (Sherbrooke) 1991, (Bishop's Univ.) 1991. *Publications:* articles in books and journals. *Leisure interests:* reading, films, walking, friends. *Address:* P.O. Box 8888, Downtown Station, Montreal, Que. H3C 3P8 (Office); 1509 Sherbrooke Street, West, Apartment 29, Montreal, Que., H3G 1M1, Canada.

PARAMONOVA, Tatyana Vladimirovna; Russian banker; b. 24 Oct. 1950; one s.; ed Moscow Plekhanov Inst. of Nat. Economy; economist, later Head of Dept, USSR State Bank 1972–92; Vice-Pres. Petrocommerz Bank 1992; Deputy Chair. Cen. Bank of Russian Fed. 1992–94, 1995–97, Acting Chair. 1994–95, First Deputy Chair. 1998–, mem. Bd of Dirs 2002–; Deputy Chair.

Bd of Dirs Elbimbank 1997–, Chair. 1998; Pres. Russian Nat. Commercial Bank 1998. *Address:* Central Bank of Russian Federation, Neglinnaya str. 12, 103016 Moscow, Russia (Office). *Telephone:* (095) 923-16-41 (Office). *Fax:* (095) 924-65-24 (Office). *E-mail:* webmaster@www.cbr.ru (Office). *Website:* www.cbr.ru (Office).

PARASKEVA, Janet, BA, JP; British administrator; b. 28 May 1946; d. of Antonis Paraskeva and Doris Paraskeva (née Fowler); m. Alan Hunt 1967 (divorced 1983); two d., two step s.; ed Open Univ., UK; HM Insp. of Schools Dept of Educ. and Science (now Dept for Educ. and Employment) 1983–88; Dir Nat. Youth Bureau 1988–91; CEO Nat. Youth Agency 1991–95; Dir Nat. Lotteries Charities Bd, England 1995–2000; CEO Law Soc. of England and Wales 2000–; mem. Fosse Community Nat. Health Service Trust 1992–2000, Council of Leicester Univ. 1998–2000. *Leisure interests:* golf, riding, gardening. *Address:* c/o The Law Society's Hall, 113 Chancery Lane, London, WC2A 1PL, England (Office). *Telephone:* (20) 7242-1222 (Office). *Fax:* (20) 7320-5759 (Office). *E-mail:* janet.paraskeva@lawsociety.org.uk (Office). *Website:* www.lawsoc.org.uk (Office).

PARAYRE, Jean-Paul-Christophe; French building and civil engineering executive; b. 5 July 1937, Lorient; s. of Louis Parayre and Jeanne (Malarde) Parayre; m. Marie-Françoise Chaufour 1962; two s. two d.; ed Lycées in Casablanca (Morocco) and Versailles, Ecole Polytechnique, Paris, Ecole Nat. des Ponts et Chaussées; Engineer, Dept of Highways 1963–67; Tech. Adviser, Ministry of Social Affairs 1967, Ministry of Econ. and Finance 1968; Dir of Mech. Industries at Ministry of Industry and Research 1970–74; Chief Adviser to Pres. and Gen. Man. Banque Vernes et Commerciale 1974; Man. of Planning, Automobile Div. of Peugeot 1975; Man. Automobile Div. of Peugeot-Citroën 1976, Chair. Bd of Dirs. Peugeot SA 1977–84, mem. advisory Bd 1984; mem. Supervisory Bd Soc. Dumez 1977–84 (Dir-Gen. 1984, Chair. 1988–90, Pres. 1991–92); Pres., Dir-Gen. Fided Financière (affil. to Dumez) 1985; Vice-Pres., Dir-Gen. Lyonnaise des Eaux-Dumez 1990–92, Vice-Pres. 1990–93; Pres. Supervisory Bd Razel 1991; Pres. Bolloré Technologies Jan–Sept. 1994, Scac-Delmas-Vieljeux 1994, Pres. Saga 1996–99; Vice-Pres. Bolloré Group 1994–99; Dir Bolloré Investissement 1994, Carillion PLC 1999, Stena UK 1999; Chair. Advisory Bd Vallourec 2000; Officier, Légion d'honneur, Commdr Ordre nat. du Mérite. *Leisure interests:* golf, tennis. *Address:* Stena UK 4/5 Arlington Street, London, SW1 1RA (Office); 31/32 Ennismore Gardens, London, SW7 1AE, England (Home). *Telephone:* 020) 7409-0124 (Office). *Fax:* 020) 7409-2873 (Office); 020) 7581-1707 (Home).

PARDEE, Arthur Beck, MA, PhD; American biochemist; b. 13 July 1921, Chicago, Ill.; s. of Charles A. Pardee and Elizabeth Beck; m. Ruth Sager (died 1997); three s. from previous m.; m. Ann Goodman; ed Univ. of California (Berkeley), California Inst. of Tech.; Postdoctoral Fellow, Univ. of Wisconsin 1947–49; Instructor, Asst and Assoc. Prof. Univ. of Calif. (Berkeley) 1949–61; Sr Postdoctoral Fellow, Pasteur Inst. 1957–58; Prof. Biochemical Sciences and Donner Prof. of Science, Princeton Univ. 1961–75; Prof. Biological Chem. and Molecular Pharmacology, Harvard Medical School Boston 1975–97, Prof. Emer. 1997–; Prof. Emer. Harvard Univ. 1998–; Chief, Div. Cell Growth and Regulation, Dana Farber Cancer Inst. 1975–98; mem. NAS, American Chemical Soc., American Soc. of Biological Chemists (Treasurer 1964–70, Pres. 1980); American Asscn for Cancer Research (Pres. 1985), American Acad. of Arts and Sciences, American Soc. of Microbiologists, Japanese Biochemical Soc.; mem. Council American Cancer Soc. 1967–71; Hon. Faculty mem. Nanjing Univ. 1999; Fellow Int. Inst. for Advanced Studies Nara, Japan 1999, American Philosophical Soc. 2001; Dr hc (Paris) 1993; Paul Lewis Award (American Chemical Soc.) 1960, Krebs Medal (Fed. of European Biochemical Socs.) 1973, Rosensteil Award (Brandeis Univ.) 1975, Princess Takamatsee Award Japan 1990, Boehringer Bioanalytica Award 1998 and numerous other honours and awards. *Publications:* more than 500 articles on subjects including bacterial physiology and enzymology in synchronous cultures, cell division cycle events, growth regulation in cancer and normal cells, enzymology of DNA synthesis, repair of damaged DNA; Experiments in Biochemical Research Techniques (co-author) 1957. *Leisure interests:* music, tennis, travel, art. *Address:* Dana Farber Cancer Institute, 44 Binney Street, Boston, MA 02115 (Office); 987 Memorial Drive, Unit 271, Cambridge, MA 02138 (Home). *Telephone:* (617) 732-3372 (Office). *Fax:* (617) 632-4680 (Office). *E-mail:* pardee@mbcrr.harvard.edu (Office).

PARDO, Luis María de Pablo; Argentine professor of law and politician; b. 15 Aug. 1914, Buenos Aires; s. of Augusto de Pablo Pardo and Luisa Gosset; m. Aida Quinteros Sánchez de Bustamente; one s. two d.; ed Law Faculty, Univ. de Buenos Aires, postgraduate Univ. of Georgetown (Washington, DC); Dir of Courses, Law and Social Sciences Faculty, Univ. de Buenos Aires, Prof. adjunct of Int. Public Law, Faculty of Econ. Sciences 1947–51; Prof. titular of Int. Public Law, Univ. Católica, Argentina, then Prof. titular of Int. Relations 1961–; also Prof. of Int. Public Law and Int. Policy, Naval War School and lecturer at Aeronautical Staff's Officers School 1966–; imprisoned 1951, 1952 and 1953 for anti-Peronist activities, exiled to Brazil until 1955; Minister of the Interior designate 1955; Legal Adviser to Ministry for Foreign Relations and Worship 1958–61; Rep. UN 2nd Sea Law Conf. 1960; Tech. Adviser at 5th, 6th and 7th "Reunión de Consulta" of American Foreign Ministers; Amb. to Chile 1961; Legal Adviser of Chancellery at the "Rio Encuentro" Affair; Legal Adviser of the "Tech. Argentine-Uruguayan Mixed Comm. for the Salto Grande"; Minister for Foreign Relations and Worship 1970–72; Judge adjunct of Supreme Court; Grand Cross of Orders Cruzeiro del Sur, Rio Branco (Brazil), Bernardo O'Higgins (Chile), Del Sol (Peru), Al Mérito (Ecuador) and many other decorations, incl. from German and Japanese Govts. *Publications:* manual of International Public Law for use of Navy Officers, The Geographic Position of Argentina as a Factor of its Foreign Policy 1947, The Tendency towards Federation within Interamerican Relations 1947, Dominant Economics within the International Order, Foreign Policy 1952, The Contemporary International System and Argentine International Policy 1973. *Address:* Paraná 976, Buenos Aires (Office); Avenida Quintane 325, 1014 Buenos Aires, Argentina (Home). *Telephone:* 44-43-50 (Office); 44-27-34 (Home).

PARET, Peter, PhD, DLit, LittD, DH; American historian; b. 13 April 1924, Berlin, Germany; s. of Dr. Hans Paret and Suzanne Aimée Cassirer; m. Isabel Harris 1961; one s. one d.; ed Univ. of California and Univ. of London; Research Assoc. Center of Int. Studies, Princeton Univ. 1960–62; Visiting Asst Prof. Univ. of California, Davis 1962–63, Assoc. Prof. 1963–66, Prof. of History 1966–69; Prof. of History, Stanford Univ. 1969–77, Raymond A. Spruance Prof. in Int. History 1977–86; Andrew W Mellon Prof. in the Humanities, Inst. for Advanced Study, Princeton 1986–97, Andrew W Mellon Prof. Emer. 1997–; mem. American Philosophical Soc., Historische Kommission zu Berlin; Fellow, American Acad. of Arts and Sciences, Royal Historical Soc., Leo Baeck Inst.; Hon. Fellow LSE, Clausewitz Gesellschaft; Thomas Jefferson Medal, Samuel Eliot Morison Medal; several hon. degrees; Officer's Cross, German Order of Merit. *Publications:* Guerrillas in the 1960s (with John Shy) 1961, French Revolutionary Warfare 1964, Yorck and the Era of Prussian Reform 1966, The Berlin Secession 1980, Makers of Modern Strategy (ed.) 1986, Art as History 1988, Carl von Clausewitz: On War (ed. and trans. with Michael Howard) 1976, 1984, Clausewitz and the State 1985, Carl von Clausewitz, Historical and Political Writings (ed. and trans.) 1991, Understanding War 1992, Persuasive Images (with Beth Lewis and Paul Paret) 1992, Sammler, Stifter und Museen (ed. with Ekkehard Mai) 1993, Imagined Battles 1997, German Encounters with Modernism 2001. *Address:* School of Historical Studies, Institute for Advanced Study, Princeton, NJ 08540, USA. *Telephone:* (609) 734-8344. *Fax:* (609) 924-8399.

PARFIT, Derek, MA, FBA; British academic; b. 11 Dec. 1942, Chengtu, China; s. of Norman Parfit and Jessie Browne; ed Oxford Univ.; Fellow All Souls Coll., Oxford 1967–, Sr Research Fellow 1984–; Visiting Prof. Dept of Philosophy, Harvard, Princeton and New York Univs; Fellow American Acad. of Arts and Sciences. *Publication:* Reasons and Persons 1984. *Leisure interest:* architectural photography. *Address:* All Souls College, Oxford, OX1 4AL, England. *Telephone:* (1865) 279282. *Fax:* (1865) 279299.

PARFITT, David; British film producer; b. 8 July 1958; s. of the late William Parfitt and of Maureen Collinson; m. 1st Susan Coates (divorced 1993); one s.; m. 2nd Elizabeth Barron 1996; two s.; ed Barbara Speake Stage School, London; actor 1970–88; producer 1985–; Man. Dir Renaissance Theatre Co. 1987–, Trademark Films 1999–; mem. Bd London Film Comm. 1999–; mem. Council BAFTA 2000–; Dr. hc (Sunderland) 2000; Hon. Dr. Drama (Royal Scottish Acad. of Music and Drama) 2001. *Films include:* Henry V, Peter's Friends, Swan Song, Much Ado About Nothing, Mary Shelley's Frankenstein, The Madness of King George, Twelfth Night, The Wings of a Dove, Shakespeare in Love (Acad. Award), Gangs of New York (consultant), I Capture the Castle. *Address:* Trademark Films, Phoenix Theatre, 110 Charing Cross Road, London, WC2H 0JP, England (Office). *Telephone:* (20) 7240-5585 (Office). *Fax:* (20) 7240-5586 (Office). *E-mail:* mail@trademarkfilms.co.uk (Office).

PARIZEAU, Jacques, PhD; Canadian politician; b. 9 Aug. 1930, Montreal; s. of Gérard Parizeau and Germaine Parizeau (née Biron); m. 1st Alicja Poznanska 1956, one s. one d.; m. 2nd Lisette Lapointe 1992; ed Ecole des Hautes Etudes Commerciales, Montreal, Institut d'Etudes Politiques, Paris, London School of Econs; Adviser to Govt of Québec 1961–65; elected Deputy for Assomption, Montreal 1976–84, 1989–; fmr Minister of Finance, Prov. of Québec (resgnd 1985); mem. Exec. Cttee Parti Québecois 1969, Pres. 1988–96; Premier of Québec 1994–95 (resgnd). *Publications:* The Terms of Trade of Canada 1966, Initiation à l'économie du Québec 1975, Pour un Québec souverain 1997, numerous articles. *Leisure interests:* reading, music.

PARÍZEK, Pavol, Dip.Ing.Econ.; Slovak finance executive; b. 19 Feb. 1951, Bratislava; m.; two s.; ed Univ. of Econs, Bratislava; with State Bank of Czechoslovakia 1974–82, 1985, Živnostenská banka London br. 1982–84; Chief of Export. Econ. Section, Fed. Ministry of Finance 1986–90, secondment to USA 1990–91; Dir-Gen. Export Guarantee and Insurance Corpn (EGAP) 1992–2001, Vice-Pres. EGAP 2001–. *Leisure interests:* classical music, nature. *Address:* Export Guarantee and Insurance Corporation (EGAP), Vodickova 34, 11121 Prague 1 (Office); Matejkova 1089/3, 19000 Prague 9, Czech Republic (Home). *Telephone:* (2) 22841111 (Office); (2) 66317490 (Home). *Fax:* (2) 22844001 (Office). *Website:* www.egap.cz (Office).

PARK, Charles Rawlinson, AB, MD; American professor of physiology; b. 2 March 1916, Baltimore, Md; s. of Edwards A. Park and Agnes Bevan Park; m. Jane Harting 1953; one s.; ed Harvard Coll. and Johns Hopkins School of Medicine; Intern in Medicine, Johns Hopkins 1942; Asst Resident then Chief Resident, Harvard 1943–44; US Army 1944–47; Welch Fellow in Biochemistry, Wash. Univ. 1947–52; Prof. of Physiology and Chair. of Dept, Vanderbilt School of Medicine 1952–84, Prof. of Molecular Physiology and Biophysics, Emer. 1984–; Adjunct Prof. Biochemistry, Meharry Medical Coll. 1993–; mem. Bd, Life Insurance Fund, Howard Hughes Medical Inst. 1964–84, Juvenile Diabetes Foundation, Int. Inst of Cellular and Molecular Pathology,

Nat. Inst. of Heart, Lung and Blood (Nat. Insts of Health); mem. Editorial Bd, Journal of Biological Chem.; mem. American Physiological Soc., American Soc. of Biological Chemists, American Soc. of Clinical Investigation (Vice-Pres. 1961), Asscn of American Physicians, NAS; Banting Medal for Research, American Diabetes Asscn, Nat. Acad. of Sciences. *Publications:* approx. 120 scientific papers in journals of biochemistry and physiology 1942–; major topics concern action of hormones, diabetes, metabolic regulation, sugar and fat transport into mammalian cells. *Leisure interests:* music, reading, outdoor sports. *Address:* Oxford House 212, Vanderbilt School of Medicine, Nashville, TN 37232 (Office); 5325 Stanford Drive, Nashville, TN 37215, USA (Home). *Telephone:* (615) 936-0721 (Office); (615) 665-1228 (Home). *Fax:* (615) 936-3027 (Office); (615) 322-7236. *E-mail:* charles.park@vanderbilt.edu (Office).

PARK, Dame Merle Florence, DBE; British ballerina; b. 8 Oct. 1937, Salisbury, Rhodesia (now Harare, Zimbabwe); m. 1st James Monahan, CBE 1965 (divorced 1970, died 1985), one s.; m. 2nd Sidney Bloch 1971 (died 2000); ed Elmhurst Ballet School and Royal Ballet School; joined Royal Ballet 1954; first solo role 1955; opened own ballet school 1977; Dir Royal Ballet School 1983–99; Prin. Royal Ballet; Adeline Genée Medal, Queen Elizabeth Award, Royal Acad. of Dancing 1982 and many other certificates and medals. *Repertoire includes:* Façade, Coppelia, Sleeping Beauty, La Fille Mal Gardée, Giselle, Les Sylphides, The Dream, Romeo and Juliet, Triad, The Nutcracker, La Bayadère, Cinderella, Shadow Play, Anastasia, Pineapple Poll, Swan Lake, The Firebird, Walk to the Paradise Garden, Dances at a Gathering, Shadow, Don Quixote, Deux Pigeons, Serenade, Scène de Ballet, Wedding Bouquet, Les Rendezvous, Mirror Walkers, Symphonic Variations, Daphnis and Chloë, In the Night, Laurentia, Mamzelle Angot, Manon, Apollo, Flower Festival, Le Corsaire, The Moor's Pavane, Aureole, Elite Syncopations, Lulu, The Taming of the Shrew, Mayerling, Birthday Offering, La Fin du Jour, Adieu, Isadora, Raymonda, etc. *Leisure interests:* coaching young dancers, laying in the sun, listening to music and being with my family. *Address:* c/o Royal Ballet School, 144 Talgarth Road, London, W14 9DE, England (Office).

PARK, Nicholas W., CBE, BA; British film animator; b. 6 Dec. 1958, Preston, Lancs.; ed Sheffield Art School and Nat. Film and TV School, Beaconsfield; joined Aardman Animations 1985, partner 1995–; BAFTA Award for Best Short Animated Film for A Grand Day Out 1990, Acad. Awards for Creature Comforts 1991, A Grand Day Out 1994, A Close Shave 1996. *Films include:* A Grand Day Out 1989, Creature Comforts 1990, The Wrong Trousers 1993, A Close Shave 1995, Chicken Run (co-dir) 2000. *Address:* Aardman Animations Ltd, Gas Ferry Road, Bristol, BS1 6UN, England. *Telephone:* (117) 984-8485. *Fax:* (117) 984-8486.

PARK OF MONMOUTH, Baroness (Life Peer), cr. 1990, of Broadway in the County of Hereford and Worcester; **Daphne Margaret Sybil Désirée Park,** CMG, OBE; British fmr diplomatist and college principal; b. 1 Sept. 1921; ed Rosa Bassett School and Somerville Coll. Oxford; W.T.S. (Field Aid Nursing Yeomanry) 1943–47; entered Foreign Office 1948; served UK Del. to NATO 1952, Moscow 1954, Léopoldville 1959, Lusaka 1964, Consul-Gen. Hanoi 1969–70, Chargé d'Affaires a.i. Ulan Bator 1972, F.C.O. 1973–79, retd; Hon. Research Fellow, Univ. of Kent 1971–72; Prin. Somerville Coll. Oxford 1980–89, Pro-Vice-Chancellor, Univ. of Oxford 1985–89; Chair. Royal Comm. on Historical Monuments of England 1989–94; Vice Patron Atlantic Council Appeal 2001–; mem. Thatcher Foundation 1992–; other public appts.; Hon. LLD (Bristol) 1988. *Leisure interests:* good talk, politics, difficult places. *Address:* House of Lords, London, SW1A 0PW, England.

PARK SEUNG, PH.D.; South Korean central banker and professor of economics; b. 16 Feb. 1936; ed Seoul Nat. Univ. and State Univ. of New York, USA; economist at Bank of Korea 1961–76, Gov. March 2002–, fmr mem. Monetary Bd; Assoc. Prof., Chung-Ang Univ. 1976, Prof. 1982–88, 1990–, Dean Coll. of Politics and Econs 1984–87, Dean Grad. School 1988; Sr Sec. for Econs, Presidential Secr. 1988; Minister of Construction 1988–89; Chief Dir Korea Nat. Housing Corpn 1993–96; Chief Dir Korea Transport Inst. 1997; Chair. Korea Econ. Asscn 1999; Head Public Funds Man. Cttee –2002; Pres. Korea Int. Econ. Asscn 1986. *Address:* Bank of Korea, 110, 3-ga, Namdaemun-no, Jung-gu, Seoul 100-794, Republic of Korea (Office). *Telephone:* (2) 759-4114 (Office). *Fax:* (2) 759- 4139 (Office). *E-mail:* bokdiri@bok.or.kr (Office). *Website:* www.bok.or.kr (Office).

PARKER, Sir Alan William, Kt, CBE; British film director and writer; b. 14 Feb. 1944, London; s. of William Parker and Elsie Parker; m. Annie Inglis 1966 (divorced 1992); three s. one d.; ed Owen's School, Islington, London; Advertising Copywriter 1965–67; TV Commercials Dir 1968–78; wrote screenplay Melody 1969; Chair. Dirs Guild of GB 1982–86, British Film Inst. 1998–99; Chair. Film Council 1999–; mem. British Screen Advisory Council 1985–; British Acad. of Film and TV Arts Michael Balcon Award for Outstanding Contrib. to British Film, Nat. Review Bd Best Dir Award for Mississippi Burning 1988, Lifetime Achievement Award Dirs Guild of Great Britain. *Wrote and directed:* No Hard Feelings 1972, Our Cissy 1973, Footsteps 1973, Bugsy Malone 1975, Angel Heart 1987, A Turnip Head's Guide to the British Cinema, Come See the Paradise 1989, The Road to Wellville 1994, Angela's Ashes 1999. *Directed:* The Evacuees 1974, Midnight Express 1977, Fame 1979, Shoot the Moon 1981, The Wall 1982, Birdy 1984, Mississippi Burning 1988, The Commitments (BAFTA Award for Best Dir) 1991, Evita 1996, The Life of David Gale 2003. *Publications:* (novels) Bugsy

Malone 1976, Puddles in the Lane 1977; (cartoon) Hares in the Gate 1983; Making Movies 1998. *Leisure interest:* cartooning. *Address:* c/o Creative Artists' Agency, 9830 Wilshire Boulevard, Beverly Hills, CA 90212, USA.

PARKER, Sir Eric Wilson, Kt, FCA; British business executive; b. 8 June 1933, Shrewsbury; s. of Wilson Parker and Gladys Edith Wellings; m. Marlene Teresa Neale 1955; two s. two d.; ed The Priory Grammar School for Boys, Shrewsbury; articled clerk with Wheeler, Whittingham & Kent, Shrewsbury 1950–55; nat. service, Pay Corps 1956–58; Taylor Woodrow Group 1958–64; joined Trafalgar House Group 1965, Finance/Admin. Dir 1969, Deputy Man. Dir 1973, Group Man. Dir 1977, Group Chief Exec. 1983–92, Deputy Chair. 1988–93; Chair. Caradon PLC 1998–99; Pres. Racehorse Owners Asscn 1998–2001; Dir (non-exec.) Criterion Properties 1997–, Ministry of Defence Quartermaster Gen. Bd 1997–2000, British Borneo PLC 1998–2000, European Real Estates, Sweden 1998–2000, British Horseracing Bd 1999–, Horserace Betting Levy Bd 2000, Job Partners 2000–02; Cttee mem. Teenage Cancer Trust; owns Crimbourne Stud. *Leisure interests:* golf, horse racing, wines. *Address:* Crimbourne Stud, Crimbourne Lane, Wisborough Green, nr Billingshurst, West Sussex, RH14 0HR, England (Home). *Telephone:* (1403) 700400. *Fax:* (1403) 700776. *E-mail:* crimbournestud@ecosse.com (Office).

PARKER, Eugene N., PhD; American physicist (retd); b. 10 June 1927, Houghton, Mich.; s. of Glenn H. Parker and Helen M. Parker; m. Niesje Meuter 1954; one s. one d.; ed Mich. State Univ. and California Inst. of Tech.; Instructor, Dept of Mathematics and Astronomy, Univ. of Utah 1951–53, Asst Prof., Dept of Physics 1953–55; at Univ. of Chicago 1955–, Prof. Dept of Physics 1962–95, Prof. Dept of Astronomy 1967–95; mem. NAS 1967–, Norwegian Acad. of Sciences 1988–; Hon. DSc (Michigan State Univ.) 1975; Dr hc (Utrecht) 1986; Space Science Award, AIAA 1964, John Adam Fleming Award, American Geophysical Union 1968, Henryk Arctowski Medal, NAS 1969, Henry Norris Russell Lecture, American Astronomical Soc. 1969, George Ellery Hale Award, Solar Physics Div. American Astronomical Soc. 1978, Sydney Chapman Medal, Royal Astronomical Soc. 1979, Distinguished Alumnus Award, Calif. Inst. of Tech. 1980, James Arthur Prize Lecture, Harvard Smithsonian Center for Astrophysics 1986, US Nat. Medal of Science 1989, William Bowie Medal, American Geophysical Union 1990, Karl Schwarzschild Medal (FRG) 1990, Gold Medal (Royal Astronomical Soc.) 1992, Bruce Medal (Astronomical Soc. of the Pacific) 1997, ADION Medal (Observatoire de Nice) 1997. *Publications:* Interplanetary Dynamical Processes 1963, Cosmical Magnetic Fields 1979, Spontaneous Current Sheets in Magnetic Fields 1994. *Leisure interests:* hiking, history, wood-carving. *Address:* 1323 Evergreen Road, Homewood, IL 60430, USA (Home). *Telephone:* (708) 798-3497 (Home).

PARKER, Franklin, BA, MS, EdD; American writer and educationalist; b. 2 June 1921, New York; m. Betty June Parker 1950; ed Berea Coll., Ky, Univ. of Illinois, Peabody Coll. Vanderbilt Univ., Nashville, Tenn.; Librarian and Speech Teacher, Ferrum Coll., Va 1950–52, Belmont Coll., Nashville, Tenn. 1952–54, Peabody Coll. Vanderbilt Univ. 1955–56; Assoc. Prof. of Educ., State Univ. Coll., New Paltz, NY 1956–57, Univ. of Tex. 1957–64; Prof., Univ. of Okla 1964–68; Claude Worthington Benedum Prof. of Educ., West Va Univ., Morgantown 1968–86; Distinguished Prof. Emer., Center for Excellence in Educ. 1986–89; Visiting Distinguished Prof. Western Carolina Univ. 1989–94; Consultant Macmillan Merrill (Publrs), Teachers Coll. Press, William C. Brown 1988–; several visiting professorships; Sr Fulbright Research Scholar, Zambia 1961–62; Distinguished Alumnus Award, Peabody Coll., Vanderbilt Univ. 1970, Berea Coll., Kentucky 1989. *Publications include:* African Development and Education in Southern Rhodesia 1960, Government Policy and International Education 1965, Church and State in Education 1966, Strategies for Curriculum Change: Cases from 13 Nations 1968, International Education: Understandings and Misunderstandings 1969, George Peabody, A Biography 1971, American Dissertations on Foreign Education: Abstracts of Doctoral Dissertations (20 Vols) 1971–91, What We Can Learn From China's Schools 1977, Education in Puerto Rico and of Puerto Ricans in the USA Vol. 1 1978, Vol. 2 1984, British Schools and Ours 1979, Women's Education (2 Vols) 1979–81, US Higher Education: Guide to Information Sources 1980, Education in the People's Republic of China, Past and Present: Annotated Bibliography 1986, Education in England and Wales: Annotated Bibliography 1991, Academic Profiles in Higher Education 1993, Tennessee Encyclopaedia of History and Culture (mem. editorial bd) 1998, many articles, contribs. to encyclopaedias.

PARKER, Michael D., BChemEng, MBA; American/British business executive; m. Noreen Parker; one s. one d.; ed Univ. of Manchester and Manchester Business School, UK; joined Dow Chemical Co. 1968, later served with Dow Int. Research and Devt, Freeport, TX, field sales post, Birmingham, UK 1972, Dist Sales Man. 1975, Product Marketing Man. for Epoxy Resins, Dow Europe, later Dir Marketing for Inorganic Chemicals, then Dir Marketing for Organic Chemicals, Commercial Dir Functional Products Dept, Dow Europe 1983, Gen. Man. Specialty Chemicals Dept, Dow USA, Midland, MI 1984, Commercial Vice-Pres. Dow Pacific, Hong Kong 1987, Pres. 1988–93, Group Vice-Pres. (Chemicals and Hydrocarbons) 1993–95, Pres. Dow N America 1995–96, mem. Bd Dirs. 1995–, mem. Exec. Cttee Bd, Chair. Corp. Operating Bd, Exec. Vice-Pres. 1996–2000, Pres. and CEO 2000–, also mem. Bd Dirs. and Exec. Cttee Dow Corning Corpn 2000–, mem. Mems. Cttee of Dow Agrosciences; Dir Univation Technologies, LLC 2001–;Dir Nat. Legal Center for the Public Interest; mem. Exec. Cttee American Chem. Council; mem.

Exec. Cttee, Soc. of Chemical Industry-American Section 2001–. *Address:* The Dow Chemical Company, 2030 Dow Center, Midland, MI 48642, USA (Office). *Telephone:* (989) 636-1000 (Office). *Fax:* (989) 636-3518 (Office). *Website:* www .dow.com (Office).

PARKER, Robert Brown, PhD; American writer; b. 17 Sept. 1932, Springfield, Mass.; s. of Carroll Snow Parker and Mary Pauline (née Murphy) Parker; m. Joan Hall 1956; two s.; ed Colby Coll., Boston Univ.; served with US Army 1954–56; Co-Chair. Parker-Farman Co. 1960-62; lecturer Boston Univ. 1962–64; mem. faculty Lowell State Coll., Mass. 1964–66; lecturer Suffolk Univ. 1965–66; mem. faculty Bridgewater State Coll. 1966–68; Asst Prof. of English Northeastern Univ., Boston 1968–73, Assoc. Prof. 1973–76, Prof. 1976–79; screenwriter with Joan Parker 1985–; mem. Writers Guild of America; Hon. DLitt (Northeastern Univ.) 1987. *Screenwriting includes:* Spenser: For Hire 1985–88 (series), Blues for Buder 1988, High Rise 1988, A Man Called Hawk (series) 1989–90, Spenser: Ceremony 1993, Spenser: Pale Kings and Princes 1993, Spencer: Small Vices 1999. *Publications include:* Promised Land 1976 (Edgar Allen Poe Award for Best Novel, Mystery Writers of America 1976), Three Weeks in Spring (with Joan Parker) 1978, A Savage Place 1981, Surrogate: A Spenser Short Story 1982, Love and Glory 1983, Parker on Writing 1985, Pale Kings and Princes 1987, Poodle Springs (with Raymond Chandler) 1989, Stardust 1990, A Year at the Races 1990, Paper Doll 1993, All Our Yesterdays 1994, Spenser's Boston 1994, Thin Air 1995, Chance 1996, Small Vices 1997, Night Passage 1997, Sudden Mischief 1998, Trouble in Paradise 1998, Family Honor 1999, Hush Money 1999, Hugger Mugger 2001.

PARKER, Robert M., Jr., BA, LLB; American writer and wine critic; b. 23 July 1947, Baltimore; m. Patricia Parker 1969; one d.; ed Univ. of Maryland; attorney, Sr attorney and later Asst Gen. Counsel for Farm Credits, Bank of Baltimore 1973–84; Founder, Writer and Publr The Wine Advocate 1978–; Contributing Ed. Food and Wine Magazine; wine critic for L'Express magazine (first non-French holder of post); Hon. Citizen of Châteauneuf du Pape 1995, Chevalier, Ordre nat. du Mérite 1993, Chevalier, Légion d'honneur 1999; Loyola Coll. Marylander of the Year Award 1992, James Beard Foundation Wine and Spirits Professional of 1997. *Publications include:* Bordeaux (Glenfiddich Award 1986, Int. Asscn of Cooking Professionals Award for 2nd Edn 1992, Goldene Feder Award (Germany) for 3rd Edn 1993, Moët-Hennessy Wine and Vine Communication Award for French Edn 1993) 1985, Parker's Wine Buyer's Guide 1987, The Wines of the Rhône Valley and Provence (Tastemaker's Award, USA 1989, Wine Guild's Wine Book of the Year Award, UK 1989) 1987, Burgundy (Moët-Hennessy Wine and Vine Communication Award for French Edn 1993) 1990; contribs. to The Field. *Address:* The Wine Advocate, Inc., P.O. Box 311, Monkton, MD 21111, USA (Office). *Telephone:* (410) 329-6477 (Office). *Fax:* (410) 357-4504 (Office). *E-mail:* wineadvocate@erobertparker.com (Office). *Website:* www .erobertparker.com (Office).

PARKER, Sarah Jessica; American actress; b. 25 March 1965, Nelsonville, Ohio; m. Matthew Broderick 1997; one s. *Stage appearances include:* The Innocents 1976, The Sound of Music 1977, Annie 1978, The War Brides 1981, The Death of a Miner 1982, To Gillian on Her 37th Birthday 1983–84, Terry Neal's Future 1986, The Heidi Chronicles 1989, How To Succeed in Business Without Really Trying 1996, Once Upon A Mattress 1996, Wonder of the World 2001. *Television appearances include:* Equal Justice 1990–91, Sex and the City (Golden Globe for Best Actress in a TV series 2001) 1998–. *Film appearances include:* Rich Kids 1979, Somewhere Tomorrow 1983, Firstborn 1984, Footloose 1984, Girls Just Want to Have Fun 1985, Flight of the Navigator 1986, LA Story 1991, Honeymoon in Vegas 1992, Hocus Pocus 1993, Striking Distance 1993, Ed Wood 1994, Miami Rhapsody 1995, If Lucy Fell 1996, Mars Attacks! 1996, The First Wives Club 1996, Extreme Measures 1996, A Life Apart: Hasidism in America 1997, 'Til There Was You 1997, Isn't She Great 1999, Dudley Do-Right 1999, State and Main 2000. *Address:* c/o Jane Berliner, Creative Artists Agency, 9830 Wilshire Boulevard, Beverly Hills, CA 90212, USA.

PARKER, Sir (Thomas) John, Kt, DSc(Eng), ScD, FREng; British business executive; b. 8 April 1942, Downpatrick, Northern Ireland; s. of Robert Parker and Margaret Elizabeth Parker (née Bell); m. Emma Elizabeth Blair 1967; one s. one d.; ed Belfast Coll. of Tech.; Ship Design Staff, Harland and Wolff PLC 1963–69, Ship Production Man. 1969–71, Production Drawing Office Man. 1971–72, Sales and Projects Dept Gen. Man. 1972–74; Man. Dir Austin & Pickersgill 1974–78; Bd mem. for Shipbuilding (Marketing and Operations), British Shipbuilders 1978–80, Corpn Deputy Chief Exec. 1980–83; Chair. and CEO Harland and Wolff Holdings PLC 1983–93, Dir (non-exec.) 1993–; Chair. Harland-MAN Engines 1983–93; Bd mem. Industrial Devt Bd for Northern Ireland 1983–87; mem. Gen. Cttee Lloyds Register of Shipping 1983– (Chair. Tech. Cttee 1996–); Bd mem. QUBIS 1984–93; British Coal Bd mem. 1986–93; Deputy Chair. 1993–94, Chief Exec. Babcock Int. Group PLC 1993–2000, Chair. 1994–2001; Dir (non-exec.) GKN PLC 1993–, BG PLC 1997–2000, P&O Princess Cruises PLC; Chair. (non-exec.) Lattice Group PLC 2000–, Firth Rixson PLC 2001–; Deputy Chair. RMC 2001–; Vice-Pres. Royal Inst. of Naval Architects 1985–93, Pres. 1996–99; Chair. Council of European Shipbuilders Asscn 1993; Fellow Royal Acad. of Eng, Royal Inst. of Naval Architects, Inst. of Marine Engineers; Hon. DSc (Trinity Coll. Dublin, Ulster, Abertay); Man. of the Year Award, Ireland 1986 and other awards. *Publications:* A Profile of British Shipbuilders 1979, British Shipbuilders—A Period of Constructive Change (Marintec Conf., Shanghai) 1981, The Chal-

lenge of Change in Shipbuilding Today (ICCAS '85 Conf., Trieste) 1985. *Leisure interests:* reading, music, ships, sailing. *Address:* Lattice Group PLC, 130 Jermyn Street, London, SW7 4UR, England (Office). *Telephone:* (20) 7389-3206. *Fax:* (20) 7389-3204 (Office).

PARKHOMENKO, Sergey Borisovich; Russian journalist; b. 13 March 1964, Moscow; m.; two s.; ed Moscow State Univ.; , then Sr, then head of div. Teatre (magazine) 1985–90; political observer Nezavisimaya Gazeta 1990–92; mem. Bd Segodnya (newspaper) 1993–95; co-founder Moscow Charter for Journalists 1994; Ed.-in-Chief Itogi (magazine) 1996–2001, Weekly (journal) 2002–. *Leisure interest:* computer games. *Address:* c/o Itogi, Leningradskoye shosse 5a, 125871 Moscow, Russia (Office).

PARKINSON, Baron (Life Peer), cr. 1992, of Carnforth in the County of Lancashire; **Cecil Edward Parkinson,** PC, MA; British politician and chartered accountant; b. 1 Sept. 1931; s. of Sidney Parkinson; m. Ann Mary Jarvis 1957; three d.; one d. by Sarah Keays; ed Royal Lancaster Grammar School and Emmanuel Coll., Cambridge; joined Metal Box Co. as man. trainee; joined West, Wake, Price & Co. (chartered accountants) as articled clerk 1956, Partner 1961–71; f. Parkinson Hart Securities Ltd 1967, Chair. 1967–79, Dir 1967–79, 1984–; Dir several other cos 1967–79; Branch Treas. Hemel Hempstead Conservative Asscn 1961–64, Constituency Chair. 1965–66, Chair. and ex-officio mem. all cttees 1966–69; Chair. Herts. 100 Club 1968–69; Pres. Hemel Hempstead Young Conservatives 1968–71, Northampton Young Conservatives 1969–71; contested Northampton, Gen. Election 1970; MP for Enfield West 1970–74, for Hertfordshire South 1974–83, for Hertsmere 1983–92; Sec. Conservative Backbench Finance Cttee 1971–72; Parl. Pvt. Sec. to Minister for Aerospace and Shipping 1972–74; Asst Govt Whip 1974, Opposition Whip 1974–76; Opposition Spokesman on Trade 1976–79; Minister of State for Trade 1979–81; Paymaster-Gen. 1981–83; Chair. Conservative Party 1981–83, 1997–98; Sec. of State for Trade and Industry June–Oct. 1983, for Energy 1987–89, for Transport 1989–90; Chair. Conservative Way Forward Group 1991–; Chancellor of the Duchy of Lancaster 1982–83; Leader, Inst. of Dirs. Parl. Panel 1972–79; Sec. Anglo-Swiss Parl. Group 1972–79, Chair. 1979–82; Chair. Anglo-Polish Conservative Soc. 1986–98, Chemical Dependency Centre Ltd 1986–, Jarvis (Harpenden) Holdings, Usborne 1991–, Midland Expressway Ltd 1993–, Dartford River Crossing Ltd 1993–; Dir Babcock Int. 1984–87, Sports Aid Foundation, Save and Prosper 1984–87, Tarmac 1984–87, Sears PLC 1984–87. *Publication:* An Autobiography: Right at the Centre 1992. *Leisure interests:* skiing, reading, golf. *Address:* c/o House of Lords, London, SW1A 0PW, England.

PARKINSON, Michael, CBE; British television and radio presenter and writer; b. 28 March 1935, Barnsley; m. Mary Heneghan 1959; three s.; ed Barnsley Grammar School; began career as journalist with local paper, then worked on The Guardian, Daily Express, Sunday Times, Punch, The Listener etc.; joined Granada TV as interviewer/reporter 1965; joined 24 Hours (BBC) as reporter; Exec. Producer and Presenter, London Weekend TV 1968; Presenter Cinema 1969–70, Tea Break, Where in the World 1971, host own chat show "Parkinson" 1971–82, 1998–, The Boys of '66 1981, Presenter TV-AM 1983–84, Give Us a Clue 1984–92, All Star Secrets 1984–86, The Skag Kids 1985, Desert Island Discs (BBC Radio 4) 1986–88, The Help Squad 1991–92, Ghost Watch 1992, Parkinson on Sport (BBC Radio 5) 1994–97, Going for a Song 1995–99, A League Apart, 100 Years of Rugby League (BBC 2) 1995, Parkinson: The Interviews 1995–97, Parkinson's Sunday Supplement (BBC Radio 2) 1996–, Auntie's All Time Greats 1997, Parkinson's Choice (BBC Radio 2) 1999–; columnist for Daily Mirror 1986–90, for Daily Telegraph 1991–; Parkinson One-to-One 1987–88; Ed., Catalyst 1988–; has worked extensively on Australian TV; Founder and Dir Pavilion Books 1980–97; Sports Feature Writer of the Year (British Sports Journalism Awards) 1995, 1998, Fellow BFI for contrib. to TV 1997, Yorks. Man of the Year 1998, Sony Radio Award 1998, Sports Writer of the Year, British Press Award 1998, BAFTA Award for Best Light Entertainment (for "Parkinson") 1999, Media Soc. Award for Distinguished Contrib. to Media 2000; Hon. Dr (Lincs. and Humberside) 1999. *Publications:* Football Daft 1968, Cricket Mad 1969, Sporting Fever 1974, George Best: An Intimate Biography 1975, A-Z of Soccer (Jt author) 1975, Bats in the Pavilion 1977, The Woofits 1980, Parkinson's Lore 1981, The Best of Parkinson 1982, Sporting Lives 1992, Sporting Profiles 1995, Michael Parkinson on Golf 1999, Michael Parkinson on Football 2001. *Leisure interests:* cricket, golf. *Address:* c/o Kate Stephenson, CSS-Stellar Management Ltd, 1st Floor, Drury House, 34–43 Russell Street, London, WC2B 5HA, England (Office). *Telephone:* (20) 7344-1073 (Office). *Fax:* (20) 7836-9544 (Office). *E-mail:* cbaxendale@pfd.co.uk (Office).

PARLY, Jeanne-Marie; French civil servant; b. 1 April 1935, Toulouse; Sr lecturer Univ. de Clermont-Ferrand 1967–68; fmrly Sr lecturer, Prof. Univ. of Paris IX, Prof. 1985–89; with Ministry of Nat. Educ. 1984, 1993–, adviser 1997–98, Dir 1998–; Rector Acad. of Caen 2001–. *Address:* c/o Ministry of National Education, 110 rue de Grenelle, 75007 Paris, France.

PARMINTER, Kate; British charity administrator; b. 24 June 1964; d. of James Parminter and June Parminter; m. Neil Sherlock; one d.; fmrly grad. trainee Nestlé; fmrly mem. Horsham Dist Council; fmrly Head Press and Public Affairs RSPCA; Dir Council for the Protection of Rural England 1998–. *Address:* Campaign to Protect Rural England, 128 Southwark Street, London, SE1 0SW, England. *Telephone:* (20) 7981-2800 (Office). *Fax:* (20) 7981-2899 (Office). *E-mail:* katep@cpre.org.uk (Office).

PARODI, Anton Gaetano; Italian journalist and playwright; b. 19 May 1923, Castanzaro Lido (Calabria); s. of Luigi Parodi and Grazia Scicchitano; m. Piera Somino 1952; two c.; ed Università degli Studi, Turin and Genoa; journalist 1945–; professional journalist 1947–; Corresp. of Unità, Budapest 1964–; Premio nazionale di teatro Riccione 1959, 1965, Premio nazionale di teatro dei giovani 1947 and numerous other prizes. *Plays include:* Il gatto, Il nostro scandalo quotidiano, L'ex-maggiore Hermann Grotz, Adolfo o della nagia, Filippo l'Impostore, Una corda per il figlio di Abele, Quel pomeriggio di domenica, Dialoghi intorno ad un'uovo, Una storia della notte, Pioggia d'estate, Cielo di pietra, I giorni dell'Arca, Quello che dicono.

PARR, Robert Ghormley, PhD, AB; American physical chemist and educator; b. 22 Sept. 1921, Chicago, Ill.; s. of Leland Wilbur Parr and Grace Ghormley; m. Jane Bolstad 1944; one s. two d.; ed Western High School, Washington, DC, Brown Univ., Univ. of Minnesota; Asst Prof. of Chem., Univ. of Minn. 1947–48; Asst Prof. to Prof. of Chem., Carnegie Inst. of Tech. 1948–62, Chair. of Gen. Faculty 1960–61; Prof. of Chem. Johns Hopkins Univ. 1962–74, Chair. of Dept of Chem. 1969–72; William R. Kenan, Jr Prof. of Theoretical Chem. Univ. of NC 1974–90, Wassily Hoeffding Prof. of Chemical Physics 1990–; Guggenheim Fellow and Fulbright Scholar Univ. of Cambridge 1953–54; Sloan Fellow 1956–60; Visiting Prof. at Univ. of Ill. 1962, State Univ. of New York at Buffalo and Pa State Univ. 1967, Japan Soc. for Promotion of Sciences 1968, 1979; Firth Prof. Univ. of Sheffield 1976; Visiting Prof. Univ. of Berlin 1977, Duke Univ. 1996–97; Fellow Univ. of Chicago 1949, Research Assoc. 1957; Nat. Science Foundation Sr Postdoctoral Fellow, Univ. of Oxford and CSIRO, Melbourne 1967–68; mem. of numerous academic and scientific socs, including AAAS, American Physical Soc., American Chemical Soc., NAS, American Acad. of Arts and Sciences; mem. Int. Acad. of Quantum Molecular Science, Vice-Pres. 1973–79, Pres. 1991–97; Trustee Inst. for Fundamental Chemistry Kyoto 1988–2000; Dr hc (Louvain) 1986, (Jagiellonian) 1996; NC Inst. of Chemists Distinguished Chemists Award 1982, Langmuir Award in Chemical Physics, American Chemical Soc. 1994, North Carolina Award in Science 1999. *Publications:* The Quantum Theory of Molecular Electronic Structure 1963; Density—Functional Theory of Atoms and Molecules 1989; more than 200 scientific articles in specialist publs, fmr mem. editorial bd numerous specialist magazines and reviews. *Address:* Department of Chemistry, University of North Carolina, Chapel Hill, NC 27599 (Office); 701 Kenmore Road, Chapel Hill, NC 27154, USA (Home). *Telephone:* (919) 929-2609 (Home).

PARRA, Nicanor; Chilean poet; b. 5 Sept. 1914, San Fabián; s. of Nicanor P. Parra and Clara S. Navarrete; m. 1st Ana Troncoso 1948; m. 2nd Inga Palmen; seven c.; ed Univ. de Chile, Brown Univ., USA and Oxford; Prof. of Theoretical Mechanics, Univ. de Chile 1964–; has given poetry readings in LA, Moscow, Leningrad, Havana, Lima, Ayacucho, Cuzco; Premio Municipal de Poesía, Santiago 1937, 1954; Premio Nacional de Literatura 1969. *Publications:* Poetry: Cancionero sin nombre 1937, Poemas y antipoemas 1954, La cueca larga 1958, Antipoems 1958, Versos de salón 1962, Discursos (with Pablo Neruda) 1962, Deux Poèmes (bilingual) 1964, Antología (also in Russian) 1965, Antología de la Poesía Soviética Rusa (bilingual) 1965, Canciones Rusas 1967, Defensa de Violeta Parra 1967; Scientific Works: La Evolución del Concepto de Masa 1958, Fundamentos de la Física (trans. of Foundation of Physics by Profs Lindsay and Margenau) 1967, Obra Gruesa 1969. *Address:* Julia Bernstein, Parcela 272, Lareina, Santiago, Chile.

PARRA-ARANGUREN, Gonzalo; Venezuelan judge and university professor; b. 5 Dec. 1928, Caracas; ed Cen. Univ. of Venezuela, Inter-American Law Inst., Univ. of New York, Ludwig-Maximilians Univ., Munich; Prof., Cen. Univ. of Venezuela, Caracas 1956–, Andrés Bello Catholic Univ., Caracas 1957–; Judge, Second Court of First Instance (commercial matters), Fed. Dist and State of Miranda, Caracas 1958–71; First Assoc. Judge, Chamber of Cassation (civil, commercial and labour matters) of Supreme Court of Justice 1988–92, elected Alt. Judge 1992; mem. nat. group for Venezuela, Perm. Court of Arbitration, The Hague 1985; Judge Int. Court of Justice 1991–; has acted as arbitrator in Venezuela and abroad on pvt. commercial matters; mem. Legal Advisory Cttee of Ministry of Foreign Affairs 1984–, of Nat. Congress 1990–; mem. Acad. of Political and Social Sciences of Caracas 1966– (Pres. 1993–95), Inst. of Int. Law 1979–; rep. Venezuela at several sessions of The Hague Conf. on Pvt. Int. Law. *Publications:* several books and numerous articles in Venezuelan and foreign journals on law of nationality, pvt. int. law and int. civil procedural law. *Address:* International Court of Justice, Peace Palace, Carnegieplein 2, 2517 KJ The Hague, Netherlands. *Telephone:* (70) 3022323. *Fax:* (70) 3649928. *E-mail:* information@icj-cij.org (Office). *Website:* www.icj-cij.org.

PARRATT, James Roy, DSc, DSc(Med), PhD, FESC, FRCPath, FRSE; British professor of cardiovascular pharmacology; b. 19 Aug. 1933, London; s. of James J. Parratt and Eunice E. King; m. Pamela J. Lyndon 1957; two s. one d.; ed St Clement Danes Holborn Estate Grammar School, London and Univ. of London; Nigerian School of Pharmacy 1958–61; Dept of Physiology, Univ. Coll. Ibadan, Nigeria 1961–67; Univ. of Strathclyde, Glasgow 1967–, Reader 1970, Personal Prof. 1975, Prof. of Cardiovascular Pharmacology 1983–, now Prof. Emer., Head, Dept of Physiology and Pharmacology 1986–90, Chair. School of Pharmacy and Pharmacology 1988; Visiting Prof. Albert-Szent-Györgyi Medical Univ., Szeged 1995–; Vice-Pres. European Shock Soc.; Fellow Royal Pharm. Soc., Inst. of Biology; mem. Council, Int. Soc. for Heart Research (European Section); Hon. mem. Hungarian Pharmacological Soc., Slovak Medical and Cardiological Socs, Czech Cardiological Soc.; Hon. MD (Albert-Szent-Gyorgyi Univ. Medical School); Gold Medal, Univ. of Szeged, Hungary, Gold J.E. Purkyne Medal, Acad. of Sciences of the Czech Repub. *Leisure interests:* active within Baptist denomination in Scotland and in Christian mission. *Address:* Department of Physiology and Pharmacology, University of Strathclyde, Strathclyde Institute for Biomedical Sciences, 27 Taylor Street, Glasgow, G4 0NR; 16 Russell Drive, Bearsden, Glasgow, G61 3BD, Scotland. *Telephone:* (141) 548-2858 (Office); (141) 942-7164 (Home). *Fax:* (141) 552-2562. *E-mail:* j.r.parratt@strath.ac.uk (Office).

PARRIS, Matthew; British writer and broadcaster; b. 7 Aug. 1949, Johannesburg, S Africa; s. of Leslie F. Parris and Theresa E. Parris (née Littler); ed Waterford School, Swaziland, Clare Coll., Cambridge and Yale Univ.; FCO 1974–76; with Conservative Research Dept 1976–79; mem. Parl. (Conservative) for W Derbyshire 1979–86; presenter Weekend World 1986–88; Parl. Sketch Writer for The Times 1988–2001; columnist for The Times 1988–, for The Spectator 1992–; mem. Broadcasting Standards Council 1992–97; various journalistic awards. *Publications:* Chance Witness (memoir) 2001; various books about travel, politics, insult, abuse and scandal. *Address:* c/o The Times, Pennington Street, London, E1 9XN; The Spout, Gratton, Bakewell, Derbyshire, DE45 1LN, England.

PARROTT, Andrew Haden, BA; British conductor and scholar; b. 10 March 1947, Walsall; s. of R. C. Parrott and E. D. Parrott; m. 1st Emma Kirkby 1971; m. 2nd Emily Van Evera 1986; one d.; ed Queen Mary's Grammar School, Walsall, Merton Coll., Oxford; Dir of Music Merton Coll., Oxford 1969–71; Founder, Conductor and Dir, Taverner Choir, Taverner Consort and Taverner Players 1973–; Music Dir and Prin. Conductor London Mozart Players 2000–; Music Dir New York Collegium 2002–; BBC Promenade Concerts début 1977; fmr musical asst to Sir Michael Tippett; freelance orchestral and operatic conductor; occasional writer, lecturer and continuo player; Open Postmastership, Merton Coll. 1966–69; Leverhulme Fellowship 1984–85; Hon. Research Fellow, Royal Holloway, Univ. of London 1995–; Hon. Sr Research Fellow, Univ. of Birmingham 2000–. *Recordings include:* medieval, renaissance and 20th-century music, Monteverdi, Purcell, Vivaldi, Bach, Handel, Mozart. *Publications include:* New Oxford Book of Carols 1992, The Essential Bach Choir 2000. *Address:* Allied Artists, 42 Montpelier Square, London, SW7 1JZ, England. *Telephone:* (20) 7589-6243. *E-mail:* name@alliedartists.co.uk.

PARROTT, Jasper William, BA; British impresario and agent; b. 8 Sept. 1944, Stockholm, Sweden; s. of the late Prof. Sir Cecil Parrott and of Lady Parrott; m. Cristina Ortiz; two d.; ed Tonbridge School, Peterhouse Coll. Cambridge; joined Ibbs and Tillett Ltd 1965–69; f. Harrison Parrott Ltd 1969, Chair. and Man. Dir 1987–; Dir Japan Festival 1991, Swiss Festival in UK 1991; Dir Rambert Dance Co. 1993–98; Hon. Trustee Kew Foundation, Royal Botanical Gardens 1991–. *Publication:* Beyond Frontiers: Vladimir Ashkenazy. *Leisure interests:* reading, theatre, history, tennis, landscape and water gardening, languages. *Address:* Harrison Parrott, 12 Penzance Place, London, W11 4PA, England (Office). *Telephone:* (20) 7229-9166 (Office). *Fax:* (20) 7221-5042 (Office). *E-mail:* info@harrisonparrott.co.uk (Office). *Website:* www.harrisonparrott.co.uk (Office).

PARRY, Eric Owen, MA, RIBA; British architect; b. 24 March 1952, Kuwait; s. of the late Eric Parry and of Marion Parry; m. Jane Anne Parry (née Saunders); one d.; ed Univ. of Newcastle upon Tyne, Royal Coll. of Art, London, Architectural Asscn, London; Founder and Prin. Eric Parry Architects 1983–, est. Eric Parry Assocs 1983, including Eric Parry Architects Ltd 1990; Lecturer, Univ. of Cambridge 1983–97, Harvard Univ. Grad. School of Design 1988, Univ. of Houston 1988, 1990, Tokyo Inst. of Tech. 1996; mem. RIBA Awards Group 2000–02, Chair. 2002–; mem. Arts Council of England (ACE) Architecture Unit 1991–, ACE Lottery Architecture Advisory Cttee 1991–99, ACE Visual Arts Panel 1996–; mem. Council Architectural Asscn 1995–99; External Examiner Univ. of Canterbury, John Moore's Univ., Univ. of Cardiff and Univ. Coll. London; Hon. Librarian Architectural Asscn. *Architectural works include:* Artists' Studio, London 1986–88, Stockley Park Office Bldg W3, London 1989–91, Foundress Court, Pembroke Coll. Cambridge (RIBA Award 1998) 1993–98, Damai Suria Luxury Apts, Kuala Lumpur 1996–97, Southwark Information Centre, London Bridge (RIBA Award 1999) 1997–99, Mandarin Oriental, Hyde Park, London (FX Int. Interior Award for the Spa 2001) 1997–2000, 30 Finsbury Square, London 1999–2002, King Edward Court, Paternoster Square (HQ for London Stock Exchange) 2000–03, St Martin-in-the-Fields, London 2002–. *Publications include:* On Certain Possibilities of the Irrational Embellishment of a Town (co-author with Peter Carl) 1999, Eric Parry Architects Vol. 1 2002. *Leisure interests:* walking, drawing, general cultural pursuits. *Address:* Eric Parry Architects Ltd, 87–89 Saffron Hill, London, EC1N 8QU, England (Office). *Telephone:* (20) 7831-4464 (Office). *Fax:* (20) 7831-4074 (Office). *E-mail:* eric.p@ericparryarchitects.co.uk (Office). *Website:* www.ericparryarchitects.co.uk (Office).

PARRY, Martin, OBE, PhD; British environmentalist; b. 12 Dec. 1945; s. of John Fyson Parry and Frances Joan Stewart; m. Cynthia Jane Mueller 1968; two d.; ed Durham and West Indies Univs.; Prof. of Environmental Man. and Dir Oxford Univ. Environmental Change Unit 1991–94; Prof. of Environmental Man., Dept of Geography, Univ. Coll. London 1996–99; Prof. of Environmental Sciences and Dir Jackson Environment Inst., Univ. of East Anglia 1996–; fmrly with Birmingham Univ.; Chair. UK Climate Change Review Group; Royal Geographical Soc. Peek Award 1991, WMO Gerbier-Mumm Int. Award 1993. *Publications:* Climatic Change, Agric. and Settlement 1976, Climate Change and World Agriculture 1990, Economic Implications of Climate Change in Britain 1995. *Leisure interests:* riding, sailing. *Address:* School of Environmental Sciences, Jackson Environment Institute, University of East Anglia, Norwich, NR4 7TJ, England (Office). *Telephone:* (1603) 592318 (Office). *Fax:* (1603) 507719 (Office). *E-mail:* Martin.Parry@ uea.ac.uk (Office). *Website:* www.jei.uea.ac.uk/parry_m.html (Office).

PARSONS, Charles Dacre, PhD; American professor of philosophy; b. 13 April 1933, Cambridge, Mass.; s. of Talcott Parsons and Helen Walker Parsons; m. Marjorie Louise Wood 1968; one s. one d.; ed Harvard Coll., King's Coll., Cambridge, Harvard Univ.; Jr Fellow, Soc. of Fellows, Harvard Univ. 1958–61; Asst Prof. of Philosophy, Cornell Univ. 1961–62, Harvard Univ. 1962–65; Assoc. Prof. of Philosophy, Columbia Univ. 1965–69, Prof. 1969–89, Chair. Dept of Philosophy 1976–79, 1985–89; Prof. of Philosophy, Harvard Univ. 1989–, Edgar Pierce Prof. of Philosophy 1991–; Ed. The Journal of Philosophy 1966–90, consulting ed. 1990–; Sec. Asscn for Symbolic Logic 1971–76, Vice-Pres. 1986–89, Pres. 1989–92; Santayana Fellow, Harvard 1964–65, NEH Fellow 1979–80, Guggenheim Fellow 1986–87; Fellow Center for Advanced Study in The Behavioral Sciences 1994–95; Fellow American Acad. of Arts and Sciences 1982–; Foreign mem. Norwegian Acad. of Science and Letters 2002–. *Publications:* Mathematics in Philosophy 1983, Kurt Gödel, Collected Works, Vols III–V (Ed. with Solomon Feferman et al.) 1995, 2003; articles on logic and philosophy. *Address:* Department of Philosophy, Emerson Hall, Harvard University, Cambridge, MA 02138 (Office); 16 Ellery Square, Cambridge, MA 02138, USA (Home). *Telephone:* (617) 495-2191 (Office). *E-mail:* parsons2@fas.harvard.edu (Office). *Website:* www.fas .harvard.edu/~phildept/ (Office).

PARSONS, Peter John, MA, FBA; British academic; b. 24 Sept. 1936, Surbiton, Surrey; s. of Robert John Parsons and Ethel Ada Parsons (née Frary); ed Raynes Park County Grammar School and Christ Church, Oxford; Lecturer in Documentary Papyrology, Oxford Univ. 1960–65, Lecturer in Papyrology 1965–89, Regius Prof. of Greek 1989–2003; Student (Fellow) Christ Church Oxford 1964–; J. H. Gray Lecturer, Cambridge Univ. 1982; Hon. PhD (Berne) 1985, Hon. DLitt (Milan) 1994, Hon. PhD (Athens) 1995. *Publications:* The Oxyrhynchus Papyri (jtly) Vols XXXI 1966, XXXIII and XXXIV 1968, LIV 1987, LIX 1992, LX 1994, LXVI 1999, (solely) vol. XLII 1973, Supplementum Hellenisticum (with H. Lloyd-Jones) 1983; articles in learned journals. *Leisure interests:* music, cinema, cooking, eating. *Address:* Christ Church, Oxford, OX1 1DP, England. *Telephone:* (1865) 276223.

PARSONS, Richard D.; American entertainment executive; ed Univ. of Hawaii, Albany Law School, Union Univ.; began career with various positions in state and fed. service, including counsel for Nelson Rockefeller and Sr White House aide under Pres. Gerald Ford; fmr. Man. Partner Patterson, Belknap, Webb & Tyler; fmr Chair. and CEO Dime Bancorp Inc.; joined Time Warner Inc. (later AOL Time Warner), mem. Bd of Dirs 1991–, Pres. 1995–, Co-COO –2002, CEO May 2002–, Chair. 2003–; Co-Chair. Pres.'s Comm. to Strengthen Social Security 2001–; mem. bd Citigroup, Estée Lauder, Colonial Williamsburg Foundation, Lincoln Center, Museum of Modern Art, Howard Univ.; Chair. Apollo Theatre Foundation. *Address:* AOL Time Warner Inc., 75 Rockefeller Plaza, New York, NY 10019, USA (Office). *Website:* www .aoltimewarner.com (Office).

PARSONS, Roger, DSc, PhD, FRS; British professor of chemistry; b. 31 Oct. 1926, London; s. of Robert H. A. Parsons and Ethel Fenton; m. Ruby M. Turner 1953; three s. one d.; ed King Alfred School, London, Strathcona High School, Edmonton, Alberta and Imperial Coll., London; Asst Lecturer, Imperial Coll. 1948–51; Deedes Fellow, Univ. Coll., Dundee 1951–54; Lecturer, Univ. of Bristol 1954–63, Reader 1963–79; Dir Lab. d'Electrochimie Interfaciale du CNRS, Meudon, France 1977–84; Prof. of Chem. Univ. of Southampton 1985–92, Prof. Emer.; Pres. Faraday Div., Royal Soc. of Chemistry 1991–93; D. Univ. (Buenos Aires) 1997; Prix Pascal, Palladium Medal, Breyer Medal, Galvani Medal, Frumkin Memorial Medal. *Publications:* Electrochemical Data 1956, Electrical Properties of Interfaces (with J. Lyklema); Co-Ed. Standard Potentials in Aqueous Solution 1985, Electrochemistry in Research and Development 1985; over 200 scientific papers. *Leisure interests:* listening to music, going to the opera. *Address:* 16 Thornhill Road, Bassett, Southampton, SO16 7AT, England. *Telephone:* (23) 8079-0143. *E-mail:* roger .parsons@care4free.net (Home).

PARSURAMAN, Armoogum (Dassen), BA; Mauritian politician; b. 30 June 1951; m.; ed Univ. of Mauritius; mem. Legis. Ass. June 1982–; Minister of Educ., Arts and Culture 1983–92, of Educ. and Science 1992–95; Chair. Parti Socialiste Mauricien (PSM); Vice-Pres. MSM 1986–; mem. MSM/PMSD/ Labour Party Govt –1990, MSM/MMM Govt 1990–; Chair. Public Accounts Cttee 1982–83, Mauritius Ex-Servicemen Welfare Fund; mem. Local Govt Comm., Select Cttee on Industrial Relations Act. *Address:* c/o Ministry of Education, Science and Technology, Government Centre, Port Louis, Mauritius.

PÄRT, Arvo; Estonian composer; b. 11 Sept. 1935, Paide; ed Tallinn Conservatory (student of Heino Eller); worked as sound producer for Estonian radio 1957–67; teacher at Tallinn Conservatory 1967–78; emigrated to Berlin 1980; Hon. DMus. (Sydney) 1996; Hon Dr (Tartu) 1998, (Durham) 2002; Triumph Award (Russia) 1997, Culture Prize 1998, Herder Award (Germany) 2000. *Works include:* Orchestral music: 3 symphonies 1963, 1966, 1971, Collage über B-A-C-H 1964, Cantus in Memory of Benjamin Britten 1977, Tabula Rasa 1977, Psalom, 1985/91/95, Festina lente, 1988, Trisagion 1992,

1994, Orient and Occident 1999, Lamentate 2002; Vocal music: Credo 1968, An den Wassern zu Babel sassen wir und weinten . . . 1976, 1984 and other versions, Summa 1977, several other versions, Missa Syllabica 1977, 1995, 1996, Passio 1982, Te Deum 1984/85, 1992, Stabat Mater 1985, Magnificat 1989, Miserere 1989, Berliner Messe 1990/97, Litany 1994, Kanon Pokajanen 1997, Triodion 1998, Como anhela la cierva 1999, Cecilia 2000, Littlemore Tractus 2001; Chamber music: Für Alina 1976, Pari intervallo 1976, Fratres 1977 (several other versions). *Address:* c/o Universal Edition Ltd., 48 Great Marlborough Street, London, W1F 7BB, England. *Telephone:* (20) 7437-6880 (Office). *Fax:* (20) 7437-6115 (Office). *E-mail:* uclondon@universaledition.com (Office). *Website:* www.universaledition.com (Office).

PARTON, Dolly Rebecca; American singer and composer; b. 19 Jan. 1946, Sevier County, Tenn.; d. of Robert Lee and Avie Lee (née Owens) Parton; m. Carl Dean 1966; owner of the Dollywood Entertainment Complex, including Dollywood Theme Park; Vocal Group of the Year award (with Porter Wagoner) 1968, Vocal Duo of the Year, All Country Music Asscn 1970, 1971; Nashville Metronome Award 1979; Female Vocalist of the Year 1975, 1976; Country Star of the Year 1978; People's Choice 1980; Female Vocalist of the Year, Academy of Country Music 1980; Hall of Fame 1988. *Films include:* Nine to Five 1980, The Best Little Whorehouse in Texas 1982, Rhinestone 1984, Steel Magnolias 1989, Straight Talk 1991, The Beverly Hillbillies. *Albums include:* Here You Come Again (Grammy award 1978), Real Love 1985, Just the Way I Am 1986, Heartbreaker, Great Balls of Fire, Rainbow 1988, White Limozeen 1989, Home for Christmas 1990, Eagle When She Flies 1991, Slow Dancing with the Moon 1993, Honky Tonk Angels 1994, The Essential Dolly Parton 1995, Just the Way I Am 1996, Super Hits 1996, I Will Always Love You and Other Greatest Hits 1996 (with others), Hungary Again 1998 Grass is Blue 1999, Best of the Best-Porter 2 Doll 1999, Halos and Horns 2002. *Composed numerous songs including:* Nine to Five (Grammy Award 1981). *Radio includes:* Grand Ole Opry, WSM Radio, Cass Walker Program. *Publication:* Dolly: My Life and Other Unfinished Business 1994. *Address:* RCA, 6 W 57th Street, New York, NY 10019, USA.

PARTRIDGE, Frank David Peregrine; British art dealer; b. 14 Sept. 1955, London; s. of John A. Partridge and Caroline M. Cust; m. Susan A. Hince 1982; three d.; ed Elstree and Harrow Schools; Dir Partridge Fine Arts PLC 1981–. *Leisure interests:* shooting, tennis, skiing, golf, sailing, bridge. *Address:* Partridge Fine Arts PLC, 144–146 New Bond Street, London W1S 2PF (Office); 7 Thurloe Square, London, SW7 2TA, England. *Telephone:* (20) 7629-0834 (Office). *Fax:* (20) 7495-6266 (Office).

PARTRIDGE, John Albert, CBE, RA, FRIBA; British architect; b. 26 Aug. 1924, London; s. of George Partridge and Gladys Partridge; m. Doris Foreman 1953 (died 2000); one s. one d.; ed Shooter's Hill Grammar School, Woolwich and Polytechnic School of Architecture, London; London County Council Housing Architects' Dept 1951–59; Sr and Founding Partner, Howell, Killick, Partridge & Amis (HKPA) 1959–95; John Partridge Consultancy 1995–; Vice-Pres. RIBA 1977–79, Concrete Soc. 1979–81; RIBA Hon. Librarian 1977–81; Chair. RIBA Architectural Research Steering Cttee 1978–84, Clients Advisory Steering Cttee 1990–94; Gov. Building Centre, London 1981–96; Chair. Trustees Eric Lyons Memorial Fund 1982–; Chair. Asscn of Consultant Architects 1983–85; mem. NEDO Construction Research Strategy Cttee 1983–86; Architect mem. FCO Advisory Bd on the Diplomatic Estate 1985–94; External Examiner in Architecture, Univ. of Bath 1975–78, 1992, Thames Polytechnic 1978–86, Univ. of Cambridge 1979–81, Univ. of Manchester 1982–, South Bank Polytechnic (London) 1981–86, Brighton Polytechnic 1987–91, Royal Coll. of Art 1991–94. *Exhibition:* Royal Museum and Art Gallery, Canterbury 2001. *Major works include:* Wolfson Rayne and Gatehouse Bldg, St Anne's Coll., Oxford, New Hall and Common Room, St Antony's Coll., Oxford, Weston Rise Housing, Islington, Wells Hall, Univ. of Reading, Middlesex Polytechnic Coll. of Art, Cat Hill, Medway Magistrates Court, The Albany, Deptford, Hall of Justice, Trinidad & Tobago, in Asscn with ACLP, Trinidad; Warrington Crown Courthouse, Basildon Courthouse, Haywards Heath Magistrates Courthouse, Chaucer Coll., Univ. of Kent; exhbns. of HKPA work at Heinz Gallery, London 1983, Puck Bldg, New York 1983; 35 Nat. Design Awards for HKPA 1965–. *Publications:* articles in the tech. press and architectural papers to conferences. *Leisure interests:* looking at buildings and gardens, travel, sketching, taking photographs, listening to music. *Address:* Cudham Court, Cudham, Nr. Sevenoaks, Kent, TN14 7QF, England. *Telephone:* (1959) 571294. *Fax:* (1959) 570478. *E-mail:* john .partridge1@btinternet.com.

PARTRIDGE, Linda, BA, DPhil, FRS, FRSE; British biometrist; b. 18 March 1950, Bath; d. of George Albert Partridge and Ida Partridge (née Tucker); m. 1st Vernon French (divorced 1989); m. 2nd Michael John Morgan 1996; ed Convent of Sacred Heart, Tunbridge Wells, Univ. of Oxford; demonstrator, then lecturer, Reader, Prof. of Evolutionary Biology Univ. of Edinburgh 1976–1993; Weldon Prof. of Biometry Univ. Coll. London 1994–; NERC Research Prof. 1997–2002, British Biological Sciences Research Council Research Prof. 2002–; London Zoological Soc. Frink Medal 2000, American Soc. of Naturalists Sewall Wright Award 2002. *Leisure interests:* sailing, gardening. *Address:* Department of Biology, University College London, Darwin Building, Gower Street, London, WC1E 6BT, England (Office). *Telephone:* (20) 7679-2983 (Office). *Fax:* (20) 7679-7096 (Office). *Website:* www .gene.ucl.ac.uk/flies/partridge.html (Office).

PARTRIDGE, Sir Michael John Anthony, KCB, MA; British civil servant; b. 29 Sept. 1935, Stourbridge, Worcs.; s. of Dr. John Henry Partridge and Ethel Green; m. Joan Elizabeth Hughes 1968; two s. one d.; ed Merchant Taylors' School, St John's Coll., Oxford Univ.; joined Home Civil Service (Ministry of Pensions and National Insurance—MPNI) 1960, Pvt. Sec. to Perm. Sec. 1962–64, Prin. MPNI 1964–71, Asst Sec. 1971–76, Under Sec. 1976–81, Deputy Sec. 1981–83; Deputy Under-Sec. of State, Home Office 1983–87; Second Perm. Sec. Dept of Health and Social Security 1987–88; Perm. Sec. Dept of Social Security 1988–95; Sr Treas. Methodist Church Finance Div. 1980–96; Hon. Fellow St John's Coll. Oxford 1991–; Dir (non-exec.) Methodist Ministers' Pensions Trust 1992–, Epworth Investment Man. 1995, Commercial Gen. and Norwich Union 1996–, Stationery Office 1997–99; Gov. Middx Univ. 1992,Chair. Bd of Govs 1996–2002, Pro-Chancellor 2001–; Vice-Chair. Harefield Research Foundation 2001–; mem. Council Sheffield Univ. 2001–; Gov. Merchant Taylors' School 1992–99; Trustee Harefield Hosp. Heart Transplant Trust 1992–; Liveryman Merchant Taylors' Co. 1987. *Leisure interests:* do-it-yourself, Greece, reading, skiing. *Address:* 27 High View, Pinner, Middx, HA5 3NZ, England. *Telephone:* 020) 8868-0657. *Fax:* 020) 8429-4532.

PARTS, Juhan; Estonian politician; Chair. Union for the Repub. Res Publica 2002–; Prime Minister of Estonia 2003–. *Address:* Prime Minister's Office, State Chancellery, The Stenbock House, 3 Rahukohtu str., Tallinn 15161, Estonia. *Telephone:* (2) 6935701 (Office). *Fax:* (2) 6935704 (Office). *E-mail:* peaminister@riik.ee. *Website:* www.peaminister.ee.

PASANELLA, Giovanni, FAIA; American architect; b. 13 Jan. 1931, New York; two s.; ed Cooper Union, New York, Yale Univ.; designer, Edward L. Barnes, New York 1959–64; Prin. Giovanni Pasanella, New York 1964–76; co-owner Pasanella & Klein, New York 1976–; Architecture Critic, Univ. of Ky, Lexington 1963, Yale Univ. 1964; Adjunct Prof. of Architecture, Columbia Univ. 1965–87, Project Dir Inst. of Urban Environment 1965–68; Visiting Fellow Urban Studies, Inst. of Architecture 1975; Consultant Architect to Chair. New York City Planning Comm. 1967; mem. Bd of Trustees Il Piccolo Teatro dell'Opera, Brooklyn, New York 1986; Yale Univ. Travelling Fellow 1958–59; Fellow AIA; mem. Soc. of Architectural Historians; Architecture Award, Architectural Record 1974, 1975. *Address:* Pasanella & Klein, 330 W 42nd Street, New York, NY 10036, USA; Villa Cannizzaro, via Fondi Camaiore, Lucca, Italy. *Telephone:* (0584) 989297.

PASCAL, Jean-Baptiste Lucien, LenD, DIPL.; French banker; b. 26 Nov. 1930, Bordeaux; s. of Ernest Pascal and Paule de Battisti; m. Christiane Gardelle 1962; three s. (one deceased); ed Univ. of Paris; attached to Banque Nat. pour le Commerce et l'Industrie 1954; Head of Supplies Mission for the Devt of Algeria and Jt Govt Commr for Crédit Populaire de France in Algeria 1959; Head of Bureau for Financial Co-operation to Sec. of State for Algerian Affairs 1963; mem. Crédit Commercial de France (CCF) 1965, Deputy Dir Cen. Admin. CCF 1967, Dir-Gen. d'Interbail 1971, Dir Cen. Admin. 1973–, Admin. Dir-Gen. 1974, Vice-Pres. Dir-Gen. d'Interbail 1978–96; Dir Crédit Commercial de France 1977; Pres. Dir-Gen. Banque Hervet 1986–89; Pres. Admin. Council SOFEC 1991; Pres. GOBTP 1993–97, Pres. Conseil de Surveillance du GOBTP 1997–99, Interbail 1996– (Chair. Bd Dirs. 1996–97); Dir French Asscn of Financial Cos., Vice-Pres. 1995–97; Chevalier, Légion d'honneur. *Publication:* La Décolonisation de l'Europe—Querelle des Continents 1964. *Leisure interests:* alpinism, hunting. *Address:* BAC, 21 avenue George V, 75008 Paris (Office); 14 rue Jules Claretie, 75116 Paris, France (Home).

PASCAL-TROUILLOT, Ertha; Haitian politician and attorney; b. 13 Aug. 1943, Pétionville; d. of Thimocles Pascal and Louise Clara Dumornay; m. Ernst Trouillot 1971 (died 1987); one d.; ed State Univ. of Haiti; attorney-at-law; Judge, Civil Court 1979–85, Supreme Court 1986–90; Acting Pres. of Haiti 1990–91; mem. French Writers' Asscn 1973–; Lauréate du Concours de l'Alliance Française, Prix Littéraire 1965. *Publications:* Code de Lois Usuelles (Vols 1 and 2) 1978–98. *Leisure interests:* travelling, music, theatre (classical and modern), cinema, sports (wrestling). *Address:* P.O. Box 150, Port-au-Prince (Office); Christ-Roi 21, Port-au-Prince, Haiti (Home). *Telephone:* 245-6760 (Office). *Fax:* 245-6760 (Office).

PASCHKE, Fritz, DTechSc; Austrian electrical engineer; b. 2 March 1929, Graz/Goesting; s. of late Eduard Paschke and Stefanie Mittellehner; m. Gertrud P. Kutschera 1955; two d.; ed Tech. Univs of Graz and Vienna; Asst Tech. Univ. Vienna 1953–55; consultant, New York 1955–56; mem. tech. staff, RCA David Sarnoff Research Center 1956–61; Components Div. Siemens AG, Munich 1961–66; Prof. of Gen. Electronics, Tech. Univ. Vienna 1965–97, Prof. Emer. 1997–, Dean, School of Electrical Eng 1970–71, Rector/Pro-Rector 1971–76, Head, Inst. für Allgemeine Elektrotechnik und Elektronik 1980–97; Vice-Pres. Austrian Nat. Science Foundation 1974–82; Dr hc (Budapest) 1974; Ludwig Boltzmann Award 1977, HE Cardinal Innitzer Award 1984, Erwin Schrödinger Award (Austrian Acad.) 1988, Award of City of Vienna for Science and Tech. 1988 etc., Leonardo da Vinci Medal of SEFI 1996. *Leisure interests:* art, hiking, swimming. *Address:* Technical University of Vienna, Karlsplatz 13, 1040 Vienna, Austria. *Telephone:* (1) 58801-36653. *Fax:* (1) 58801-36699. *E-mail:* fritz.paschke@tuwien.ac.at (Office); fritz.paschke@chello.at (Home). *Website:* www.iemw.tuwien.ac.at (Office).

PASCHKE, Karl Theodor; German diplomatist; b. 12 Nov. 1935, Berlin; s. of Adolf Paschke and Adele Cornill; m. Pia-Irene Schwerber 1963; one s. one d.; ed Univs of Munich and Bonn; Consul, New Orleans, La., USA 1964–68;

Deputy Chief of Mission, Kinshasa 1968–71; Dean, Foreign Office Training School, Bonn 1972–77; Press Counsellor, Washington, DC 1977–80; Spokesman, German Foreign Office, Bonn 1980–84; Amb. to UN Orgs. Vienna 1984–86; Minister, Washington, DC 1987–90; Dir-Gen. for Personnel & Man. German Foreign Office, Bonn 1990–94; Under-Sec.-Gen. for Internal Oversight Services, UN, New York 1994–99; Special Insp. Foreign Office 2000–. *Publication:* Reform der Attache-Ausbildung 1975. *Leisure interest:* music, especially jazz. *Address:* Ministry of Foreign Affairs, Werderscher Markt 1, 10117 Berlin, Germany (Office). *Telephone:* (1888) 170 (Office). *Fax:* (1888) 1703402 (Office). *E-mail:* poststell@auswaertiges-amt.de (Office). *Website:* www.auswaertiges-amt.de (Office).

PASCO, Richard Edward, CBE; British actor; b. 18 July 1926, Barnes; s. of Cecil George Pasco and Phyllis (née Widdison) Pasco; m. 1st Greta Watson 1956 (divorced 1964); one s.; m. 2nd Barbara Leigh-Hunt 1967; ed Colet Court and King's Coll. School, Wimbledon, Cen. School of Speech and Drama; first appearance on stage, Q Theatre 1943; served in HM forces 1944–48; Old Vic Co. 1950–52; Birmingham Repertory Co. 1952–55; played Fortinbras in Hamlet (Moscow and London) 1955; English Stage Co. 1957, played in The Member of the Wedding, Look Back in Anger, The Entertainer, Man from Bellac and The Chairs; toured USA and Europe 1967 (with RSC), Japan, Australia 1970, Japan 1972; joined RSC 1969, Nat. Theatre 1987; now Hon. Assoc. Artist RSC; has made broadcasts and recordings of plays and verse, including complete sonnets of Shakespeare. *Roles include:* The Entertainer (New York) 1958, Moscow Youth Festival in Look Back in Anger 1959, Teresa of Avila (Dublin Theatre Festival and Vaudeville) 1961, Henry V, Love's Labour's Lost (Bristol Old Vic, Old Vic and tour to Europe) 1964; Hamlet, Bristol Old Vic, 1965, Measure for Measure, Peer Gynt, Man and Superman, Hamlet 1966, Polixenes in The Winter's Tale, Proteus in The Two Gentlemen of Verona, Buckingham in Henry VIII 1969, Major Barbara, Richard II, Duchess of Malfi 1971, Becket in Murder in the Cathedral, Medraut in the Island of the Mighty 1972, Richard and Bolingbroke in Richard II 1973–74; The Marrying of Ann Leete 1975, Jack Tanner in Man and Superman 1977, Trigorin in The Seagull 1978, Timon in Timon of Athens 1980, Clarence in Richard III 1980, Arkady Schatslivtses in The Forest 1981, La Ronde 1982, Father in Six Characters in Search of an Author 1987, Pavel in Fathers and Sons 1987, Charlie Southwark in Racing Demon, Sir Peter Edgcombe in Murmuring Judges, Mr Birling in An Inspector Calls, Malcolm Pryce in Absence of War, Boss Findley in Sweet Bird of Youth 1994, Sorin in The Seagull, Stratford, Barbican 2000. *Television appearances include:* Henry Irving, The Three Musketeers, Savages, As You Like It, Julius Caesar, British in Love, Trouble with Gregory, Philby, The House Boy, Number 10—Disraeli, The Plot to Murder Lloyd George, Let's Run Away to Africa, Sorrell and Son, Drummonds, etc. *Films include:* Room at the Top, Yesterday's Enemy, The Gorgon, Rasputin, Watcher in the Woods, Wagner, Arch of Triumph, Inspector Morse, etc. *Publications:* Time and Concord: Aldeburgh Festival Recollections (contrib.) 1997, Acting in Stratford (contrib.) 1997. *Leisure interests:* music, gardening, preservation of rural England. *Address:* c/o Michael Whitehall Ltd, 10 Lower Common South, London, SW15 1BP, England.

PASCOE, B. Lynn, MA; American diplomatist; b. 1943, Mo.; m. Diana Pascoe; two d.; ed Univ. of Kansas, Columbia Univ.; served on Soviet and China Desks; postings to Moscow, Hong Kong, Bangkok, Beijing (twice) and Taiwan; Prin. Deputy Asst Sec., East Asian and Pacific Bureau, State Dept; Deputy Chief of Mission, American Embassy, Beijing; Deputy Exec. Sec., Dept of State; Special Asst to Deputy Sec. of State; Dir American Inst., Taiwan 1993–96; Sr Adviser, Bureau of East African and Pacific Affairs and at U.S. Mission to the UN; Special Negotiator for Nagorno-Karabakh and Regional Conflicts; Co-Chair. O.S.C.E. Minsk Group; Amb. to Malaysia 1999–. *Address:* American Embassy, 376 Jalan Tun Razak, P.O. Box 10035, 50700 Kuala Lumpur, Malaysia (Office). *Telephone:* (3) 21685000 (Office). *Fax:* (3) 21684961 (Office).

PASCUAL, Ramon, DSc; Spanish professor of physics; b. 4 Feb. 1942, Barcelona; s. of Josep Montserrat; m. Maria Lluisa Roca 1966; two s. one d.; Junta de Energía Nuclear, Madrid 1963–64; Teaching Asst Univ. of Valencia 1964–67; Asst Prof. of Quantum Mechanics, Univ. Complutense de Madrid 1967–70; Prof. of Mathematical Physics, Univ. of Zaragoza Jan.–Sept. 1970; Prof. Univ. Autónoma de Madrid 1970–71; Prof. of Theoretical Physics, Univ. Autónoma de Barcelona 1971–, Dean, Faculty of Science 1976–79, Vice-Rector for Academic Affairs 1979–80, Rector 1986–90; Visiting Scientist, CERN, Geneva, 1969, 1970, 1977, 1978, 1981, 1983, 1986, Faculty of Science, Paris (Orsay) 1972, 1975, Rutherford Appleton Lab. Oxford 1975; mem. Real Sociedad Española de Física y Química, European Physical Soc., Real Acad. Ciencias y Artes de Barcelona. *Publications:* over 40 articles in scientific journals etc. *Address:* Universitat Autónoma de Barcelona, Edificio C, 08193 Bellaterra, Barcelona, Spain. *Telephone:* (3) 5811307. *Fax:* (3) 5813213. *E-mail:* pascual@ifae.es (Office). *Website:* www.ifae.es (Office).

PASHIN, Valentin Mikhailovich, DSc, CEng; Russian naval engineer; b. 25 July 1937, Saratov Region; m.; two c.; ed St Petersburg State Marine Tech. Univ.; on staff A.N. Krylov Research Inst. 1960; Jr, Sr Researcher, Head of Dept, Tech. Dir; Science Prin. and Dir Krylov Shipbuilding Research Inst. 1990–; Corresp. mem. Russian Acad. of Sciences 1991, mem. 1997; USSR State Prize 1985, Gold Star Medal of Hero of the Russian Fed. and several other awards. *Publications:* monographs, scientific articles and reports. *Address:* Krylov Shipbuilding Research Institute, Moskovskoye shosse 44,

196158 St Petersburg (Office); Sofiyskaya ulitsa 30, Bldg 2, Flat 69, 192236 St. Petersburg, Russia (Home). *Telephone:* (812) 443-54-82 (Office); (812) 123-66-23 (Office). *Fax:* (812) 127-95-95 (Office). *E-mail:* krylov@krylov.spb.ru (Office); krsi@pop3.rcom.ru (Office); pashin@krylov.spb.ru (Office). *Website:* www.krylov.com.ru (Office).

PASINETTI, Luigi Lodovico, MA, PhD; Italian professor of economics; b. 12 Sept. 1930, Bergamo; s. of Giovanni Pasinetti and Romilda Arzuffi; m. Carmela Colombo 1966; one s.; ed Univ. Cattolica del Sacro Cuore, Milan, Univ. of Cambridge, Harvard Univ.; Research Fellow, Nuffield Coll., Oxford 1960–61; Fellow and Lecturer in Econs, King's Coll., Cambridge 1961–73; Lecturer, then Reader in Econs, Univ. of Cambridge 1961–76; Prof. Faculty of Econs, Univ. Cattolica del Sacro Cuore 1976–, Chair. 1980–83; Wesley Clair Mitchell Visiting Research Prof. of Econs, Columbia Univ., New York 1971, 1975; Visiting Research Prof., Indian Statistical Inst., Calcutta and New Delhi 1979; Visiting Prof. of Econs, Univ. of Ottawa, Carleton Univ. 1981, Kyoto Univ. 1984, Univ. of Southern Calif. 1985; Visiting Fellow, Gonville and Caius Coll., Cambridge 1989; McDonnell Distinguished Scholars Fellow, WIDER, the UN Univ., Helsinki 1992; Visiting Prof. Univ. of Sydney 1993; Visiting Fellow Trinity Coll. Cambridge 1997, 1999; mem. Council and Exec. Cttee Int. Econ. Asscn 1980–99; Pres. Italian Econ. Asscn 1986–89; Pres. Confed. European Econ. Asscns. 1992–93; Pres. European Soc. for the History of Econ. Thought 1995–97; Fellow Econometric Soc. 1978–; mem. Accademia Lincei, Rome 1986–, Inst. Lombardo Accademia di Scienze e Lettere, Milan 1995–; Hon. Fellow, Gonville and Caius Coll., Cambridge 1999–; Dr hc (Fribourg) 1986; St Vincent Prize for Econs 1979, 2002, Invernizzi Prize for Econs 1997; Gold Medal (First Class) for Educ., Culture and Arts 1982. *Publications:* Growth and Income Distribution 1974, Lectures on the Theory of Production 1977, Structural Change and Economic Growth 1981, Structural Change and Adjustment in the World Economy (with P. Lloyd) 1987, Structural Economic Dynamics 1993, Economic Growth and the Structure of Long-Term Development (with R. M. Solow) 1994, The Impact of Keynes in the 20th Century (with B. Schefold) 1999; numerous articles on income distribution, capital theory and economic growth. *Leisure interests:* tennis, climbing, music. *Address:* c/o Faculty of Economics, Università Cattolica del Sacro Cuore, Largo A. Gemelli 1, 20123 Milan, Italy. *Telephone:* (02) 72342470. *Fax:* (02) 72342406.

PASKAI, HE Cardinal László; Hungarian ecclesiastic; b. 8 May 1927, Szeged; joined Franciscan Order, professed his vows 1949; assumed diocesan service 1950; ordained priest 1951; Episcopal liturgist 1952–55, Szeged; Prof. of Philosophy, Theological Acad., Szeged 1955–65, simultaneously Prefect 1955–62, Spiritual 1962–65; Spiritual Prefect, Central Seminary of Budapest 1965–69; commissioned lecturer 1965–67, leading Prof. of Philosophy, Theological Academy, Budapest 1967–78; Rector of Seminary 1973–78; appointed titular Bishop of Bavagaliana and Apostolic Gov. of Veszprém 1978; Diocesan Bishop of Veszprém 1979, coadjutor with right of succession to Archbishop of Kalocsa 1982; Archbishop of Esztergom (now Esztergom-Budapest) and Primate of Hungary 1987–2003; created Cardinal 1988; Chair. Hungarian Catholic Bench of Bishops 1986–90. *Address:* Úri u. 62, 1014 Budapest, Hungary. *Telephone:* (1) 202-5611. *Fax:* (1) 202-5458.

PASQUA, Charles Victor; French politician; b. 18 April 1927, Grasse; s. of André Pasqua and Françoise Rinaldi; m. Jeanne Joly 1947; one s.; ed College de Grasse, Inst. d'Etudes Juridiques, Nice and Faculté de Droit, Aix-en-Provence; Rep. Société Ricard 1952, Insp. 1955, Regional Dir 1960, Dir French Sales 1962, Dir-Gen. French Sales and Export 1963; Pres.-Dir-Gen. Société Euralim 1967–71; Commercial Consultant 1972–; Deputy to Nat. Ass. (UDR) 1968–73; Sec.-Gen. UDR 1974–76; Senator, Hauts de Seine 1977–86, 1988–93, 1995–99; Pres. RPR Group in Senate 1981–86, 1988–93; Minister of the Interior and Administration 1986–88, 1993–95; Political adviser Exec. Comm. of RPR 1998–99; co.-f. Rassemblement pour la France 1999–; MEP 1999–; Chevalier, Légion d'honneur; Médaille de la France libre. *Publications:* La libre entreprise – un état d'esprit 1964, L'ardeur nouvelle 1985, Que demande le peuple 1992, Demain, la France (Vol. I): la priorité sociale (jtly.) 1992, Tous pour la France 1999. *Address:* European Parliament, 97–113 rue Wiertz, 1047 Brussels, Belgium; Conseil Général, Hôtel du Département, 2–16 Blvd Soufflot, 92015 Nanterre Cedex, France.

PASQUAL, Lluís; Spanish theatre and opera director; b. 5 June 1951; founder and Dir Lliure Theatre, Barcelona 1976; worked in Poland; became Asst to Giorgio Strehler, Italy 1978; apptd. Dir Centro Dramático Nacional, Teatro María Guerrero, Madrid 1983; Dir Odéon, Théâtre de l'Europe, Paris 1990–; Teacher Inst. Teatral de Barcelona; numerous prizes; Officier des Arts et des Lettres, France. *Plays directed include:* Luces de Bohemia (Valle Inclán) 1984, Sans Titre (Lorca) 1990, Le Balcon (Genet) 1991, Tirano Banderas (Valle Inclán) 1992, Le Chevalier d'Olmédo (Lope de Vega) 1992, El Público (Lorca) 1986. *Operas directed include:* (Teatro de la Zarzuela, Madrid); Samson et Dalila (Saint-Saëns) 1982, Falstaff (Verdi) 1983, Don Carlo (Verdi) 1985, Il Trittico (Puccini) 1987, Il Turco in Italia (Rossini) 1990; La Vera Storia (Berio), Paris 1985, Maggio Musicale, Florence 1986, Falstaff, Bologna 1987. *Address:* c/o Théâtre National de l'Odéon, 1 place Paul Claudel, 75006 Paris, France. *Telephone:* 1-43-25-80-92. *Fax:* 1-40-46-95-31.

PASQUINI, Pierre Emile Joseph, LenD, LèsL; French politician and lawyer; b. 16 Feb. 1921, Sétif, Algeria; s. of Aimé Pasquini and Clotilde Tabet; one s. one d.; ed Lycée Louis-le-Grand, Paris, Facultés de Droit et des Lettres, Algiers; Admin. Overseas Territories 1945; lawyer, Bar of Nice 1946–; Deputy

Mayor of Nice 1947–65; Deputy (UNR) to Nat. Ass. 1958–67; RPR Deputy to Nat. Ass. 1978–81, 1986, 1988–95; Vice-Pres. Nat. Ass. 1962–65, 1978–79; Minister of War Veterans and Victims of War May–Nov. 1995; Deputy Minister (with responsibility for Veterans and War Victims) 1995–97; Commdr Légion d'honneur, Commdr Ordre Nat. du Mérite, Croix de Guerre. *Publications:* Virginie, Le Guérisseur (comedies); Elle a parlé (book); Vol nuptial (ballet); L'Ane de Zigliara (screenplay); L'éclatement de la société française 2002, Je n'ai pas voulu le tuer 2002. *Address:* 40 rue Pastorelli, 06000 Nice, France. *Telephone:* 4-93-85-98-60. *Fax:* 4-93-80-04-17.

PASSACANTANDO, Franco, DEcon; Italian economist; b. 7 Aug. 1947, Rome; m. Miriam Veronesi 1987; three s. one d.; ed Rome and Stanford Univs.; Head Money Market Div., Research Dept, Bank of Italy 1981–85, Task Force on the Reform of the Italian Payment System 1986–89, Dir Monetary and Financial Sector, Research Dept 1990–95; mem. Group of Experts in Banking, Financial Markets Cttee OECD 1979–86, Group of Monetary Experts 1991; mem. Group of Experts on Payment Systems BIS 1980–90, Working Party on Multilateral Netting Obligations, Cttee on Interbank Netting Schemes 1990, Eurocurrency Standing Cttee 1991–92; Exec. Dir IBRD 1995–, Chair. Budget Cttee; Fulbright, Einaudi and Stringher fellowships. *Publications:* White Paper on the Payment System in Italy 1988, Le Banche e il Finanziamento delle Imprese 1997 and articles on monetary policy in professional journals. *Leisure interests:* making movies, art. *Address:* International Bank for Reconstructional and Development, 1818 H Street, NW, Washington, DC 20433 (Office); 3434 - 30th Street, N.W., Washington, D.C. 20008, U.S.A. (Home). *Telephone:* (202) 458-1169 (Office); (202) 362-2930 (Home). *Fax:* (202) 477-3735 (Office). *E-mail:* fpassacantando@worldbank.org (Office). *Website:* www .worldbank.org (Office).

PASTRANA-ARANGO, Andrés, LLD; Colombian politician; b. 17 Aug. 1954, Bogotá; s. of Misael Pastrana-Borrero (fmr Pres. of Colombia) and María Cristina Arango de Pastrana; m. Nohra Puyana Bickenbach; one s. two d.; ed Colegio San Carlos de Bogotá, Colegio Mayor de Nuestra Señora del Rosario Law School, Harvard Univ.; Man. Dir Revista Guión (publ.) 1978–79; Man. Dir Datos y Mensajes SA News Broadcasting Co. 1979–80; Dir TV Hoy News 1980–87; Councillor Bogotá City Council 1982–86, Chair. Jan.–April 1983, 1984–85; Mayor of Bogotá 1988–90; Senator 1991–93; founder and Presidential Cand. of Nueva Fuerza Democrática 1994; Pres. of Colombia 1998–2002; mem. Int. Union of Local Authorities (IULA), Exec. Cttee 1989, Pres. Latin American Chapter 1988–89; Vice-Pres. Latin American Union of Capital Cities; Co-Dir World Mayors' Conf. on Drug Addiction, New York 1989, Madrid 1990; Sec. Gen. Union of Latin American Parties 1992–; Adviser to UN Univ., Tokyo 1994; Dir and f. UN Leadership Acad., Jordan; fmr Chair. Bogotá Telephone Co., Bogotá Aqueduct and Sewerage Co., Electricity and Public Utilities Co. of Bogotá, Inst. for Urban Devt, Dist Planning; Colombian Jr Chamber Exec. of the Year 1981, King of Spain Int. Journalism Award 1985, Simón Bolívar Nat. Journalism Award 1987, King of Spain Nat. Journalism Award 1987, Bogotá Circle of Journalists Nat. Award 1987, Nat. Police Distinguished Service Order, UNESCO Order, Grand Cross, Civilian Order of Merit 1988, Order of Merit, Colombian Publishing Industry 1988, Civilian Defence Order 1989, Order of Santa Bárbara, Colombian Navy 1990, José María Córdova Order of Mil. Merit 1990. *Publication:* Hacia la formulación de un derecho ecológico (Towards the formulation of an ecological law). *Address:* c/o Oficina del Presidente, Carrera 8A, No 7-26, Santafé de Bogotá, Colombia (Office).

PASTUKHOV, Boris Nikolayevich; Russian politician; b. 10 Oct. 1933, Moscow; m. Janna Pastukhova; two d.; ed Bauman Higher Tech. Coll., Moscow; mem. CPSU 1959–91; First Sec. Bauman Regional Komsomol Cttee, Moscow 1959–61; Second Sec. Moscow City Komsomol Cttee 1961–62, First Sec. 1962–64; Second Sec. All-Union Komsomol Cttee 1964–77, First Sec. 1977–82; Chair. USSR State Cttee for Publishing, Printing and Bookselling, USSR Goskomizdat 1982–86; mem. Presidium, Supreme Soviet of the USSR 1978–83; USSR Amb. to Denmark 1986–89, to Afghanistan 1989–92; Deputy Foreign Minister of Russia 1989–96; First Deputy Foreign Minister 1996–98; mediator in negotiations between Georgia and Abkhazia; Minister for CIS Affairs 1998–99; Chair. Govt Cttee on CIS; mem. State Duma Otechestvo faction 1999–, Cttee on Connections with Compatriots 2000–. *Address:* State Duma, Okhotny Ryad 1, 103265, Moscow, Russia. *Telephone:* (095) 292-59-95. *Fax:* (095) 292-41-90.

PASTUSIAK, Longin, PhD; Polish politician and professor of international affairs; b. 22 Aug. 1935, Łódź; m. Anna Ochab; one s. one d.; ed Warsaw Univ., American Univ.; Prof. and Head Dept Polish Inst. of Int. Affairs 1963–93; Deputy to Sejm (Parl.) 1991–2001, Vice-Chair. Foreign Affairs Cttee 1993–2001; Head Polish Del. to WEU Ass. 1993–; Head Polish Del. to NATO Parl. Ass. 1993–, Vice-Pres. 2002–; Senator 2001–, Speaker of the Senate 2001–; Prof. of Int. Relations Gdansk Univ.; Silver Cross of Merit 1972, Knight's Cross 1985, Parliamentarian of the Year 1997. *Publications:* 600 scholarly publs and over 3,000 articles in daily and weekly journals on American history and foreign policy, German studies, East–West relations, Polish foreign policy, Polish–American relations and theoretical aspects of int. relations; over 60 books including Poland–Canada 1945–1961 1994, United States Diplomacy, 18th and 19th Century 1997, Chicago: Portrait of the City 1997, Will the World Come to an End? 1999, From the Secrets of the Diplomatic Archives: Polish–American Relations 1948–1954 1999, Ladies of the White House 2000, Presidents of the USA 2002. *Leisure interest:* tennis. *Address:* Senate, ul. Wiejska 6/8, 00-902 Warsaw (Office); al. Niepodleglosci

151, Apt 21, 02-555 Warsaw, Poland (Home). *Telephone:* (22) 6941439 (Office). *Fax:* (22) 6942701 (Office). *E-mail:* pastusiak@nw.senat.gov.pl. *Website:* www .senat.gov.pl (Office).

PASUGSWAD, Suwan, MA; Thai international civil servant; b. 19 March 1937, Songkhla; s. of Dam Pasugswad and Kate Pasugswad; m. 1973; two d.; ed Thammasat Univ. of Bangkok and Queen's Univ. Ont., Canada; Asst to Exec. Dir IBRD and affiliates 1975–78; Alt. Exec. Dir Asian Devt Bank, Manila 1985–87, Exec. Dir 1987–89; Deputy Dir-Gen. Fiscal Policy Office, Ministry of Finance 1992–94; Exec. Dir IBRD and affiliates 1994–97. *Leisure interests:* swimming, gardening. *Address:* 123/4 Soi Bangkrabue, Samsen Road, Dusit, Bangkok, Thailand. *Telephone:* (2) 669-0340. *Fax:* (2) 669-0340.

PATAIL, Abdul Gani; Malaysian lawyer; b. 1955; involved in numerous high profile cases; led the prosecution of fmr Deputy Prime Minister Anwar Ibrahim in trials involving corruption and sodomy 1998; Sr Public Prosecutor in Chambers of Attorney-Gen. –2001, Attorney-Gen. Jan. 2002–. *Address:* Attorney-General's Chambers, c/o Federal Court of Malaysia, Bangunan Sultan Abdul Samad, Salan Raja, 50506 Kuala Lumpur, Malaysia (Office).

PATAKI, George, BA; American politician and lawyer; b. 24 June 1945, Peekskill, NY; m. Elizabeth Rowland; two s. two d.; ed Yale Univ.; Assoc. Dewey Ballantine PC (law firm), New York 1970–74; partner, Plunkett & Jaffee PC (law firm), White Plains and New York; co-owner, Pataki's Farm, Peekskill, NY; Mayor of Peekskill 1982–84; fmr mem. New York State Ass.; mem. New York State Senate 1993–95; Gov. of New York 1996–; Republican. *Address:* State Capitol, Office of the Governor, Albany, NY 12224, USA.

PATASSÉ, Ange-Félix; Central African Republic politician; b. 25 Jan. 1937; ed French Equatorial Coll.; Agricultural inspector 1959–65; Dir of Agric. 1965; Minister of Devt 1965; Minister of State for Transport and Power 1969–70, concurrently Minister of State for Devt and Tourism 1969–70; Minister of State for Agric., Stock-breeding, Waters and Forests, Hunting, Tourism, Transport and Power Feb.–June 1970; Minister of State for Devt June–Aug. 1970; Minister of State for Transport and Commerce 1970–72, for Rural Devt 1972–73, of Health and Social Affairs 1973–74; Minister of State for Tourism, Waters, Fishing and Hunting 1974–76, Prime Minister 1976–78, also Keeper of the Seals Sept.–Dec. 1976; Vice-Pres. Council of the Cen. African Revolution Sept.–Dec. 1976; Leader Mouvement pour la libération du peuple centrafricain; under house arrest Oct. 1979, escaped, recaptured and detained Nov. 1979; Cand. in Pres. Election March 1981; took refuge in French Embassy March 1982, fled to Togo April 1982; lived in France, returned to Cen. African Repub.; Pres. of Cen. African Repub. 1993–2003 (overthrown in coup); in exile in Togo March 2003–.

PATCHETT, Ann, BA, MFA; American writer; b. 2 Dec. 1963, Los Angeles; ed Sarah Lawrence Coll. and Univ. of Iowa Writers Workshop; Writer-in-Residence Allegheny Coll. 1989–90; Yaddo Fellow 1990; Millay Fellow 1990; Resident Fellow, Fine Arts Work Center, Provincetown 1990–91; Visiting Asst Prof. Murray State Univ. 1992; Bunting Fellow, Mary Ingraham Bunting Inst., Radcliffe Coll. 1993; Guggenheim Fellowship 1994; American Library Asscn Notable Book 1992, Nashville Banner Tenn. Writer of the Year Award 1994. *Publications include:* The Patron Saint of Liars (James A. Michener/ Copernicus Award, Univ. of Iowa for a book in progress 1989, TV film 1997) 1992, Taft (Janet Heidinger Kafka Prize 1994, novel optioned by Morgan Freeman, q.v., for film) 1994, The Magician's Assistant 1997, Bel Canto (PEN/ Faulkner Award 2002, Orange Prize 2002) 2001; contribs. to The New York Times Magazine, Chicago Tribune, Boston Globe, Vogue, GQ, Elle and Gourmet. *Address:* c/o Carol Fass Ivy Publishing, 201 East 50th Street, New York, NY 10022, USA. *Website:* www.annpatchett.com (Office).

PATE, John Stewart, PhD, FAA, FRS; British professor of botany; b. 15 Jan. 1932; s. of H. S. Pate and M. M. Pate; m. Elizabeth L. Sloan 1959; three s.; ed Campbell Coll. Belfast and Queen's Univ. Belfast; lecturer in Botany, Univ. of Sydney 1957–60; lecturer in Botany, Queen's Univ. Belfast 1960–65, then Reader, Personal Chair. in Plant Physiology 1970–83; Prof. of Botany, Univ. of W Australia 1974–2001, Emer. Prof. 2001–; Australian Minerals and Energy Research Foundation Award 1999, Commonwealth Centenary Medal 2003. *Publications:* Restionaceae and Allied Families of Australia 1999 (co.-ed.); over 350 books, research articles, reviews, chapters for textbooks and conf. proceedings. *Leisure interests:* music, reading, nature study, committed Christian. *Address:* Department of Botany, University of Western Australia, Nedlands, WA 6009 (Office); RMB 1452, Denmark, WA 6333, Australia. *Telephone:* (9) 848-1096.

PATEL, A. K., MB; Indian politician and medical practitioner; b. 1 July 1931, Vadu, Mehsana Dist, Gujarat; s. of Kalidas Patel; m.; two s. one d.; ed B.J. Medical Coll., Ahmedabad; mem. Gujarat Legis. Ass. –1984; mem. for Mehsana, Lok Sabha 1984–, Minister of State for Chemicals and Fertilizers 1998–99; Pres. Bharatiya Janata Party, Gujarat 1982–85; mem. Rajya Sabha; Man. Trustee S.R.S.T. Gen. Hosp., Vijapur, Asha Educ. Trust, Girls' Coll., Vijapur; Trustee St Joseph Public School, Vijapur. *Leisure interests:* reading, swimming, riding, sports. *Address:* 30 Canning Lane, New Delhi, 110001 (Office); nr T.B. Hospital, Bhavsor, Vijapur, Dist. Mahesaona, Gujarat, India. *Telephone:* (11) 3722922.

PATEL, Indraprasad Gordhanbhai, PhD; Indian economist; b. 11 Nov. 1924, Sunav; s. of Gordhanbhai Patel and Kashiben Patel; m. Alaknanda Dasgupta 1958; one d.; ed Baroda Coll., Bombay Univ., King's Coll., Cambridge and Harvard Univ.; Prof. of Econs and Principal Baroda Coll., Maha-

raja Sayajirao Univ., Baroda 1949–50; Economist and Asst Chief, Financial Problems and Policies Div., IMF 1950–54; Deputy Econ. Adviser, Indian Ministry of Finance 1954–58; Alt. Exec. Dir for India, IMF 1958–61; Chief Econ. Adviser, Ministry of Finance, India 1961–63, 1965–67, Econ. Adviser Planning Comm. 1961–63; Special Sec. Ministry of Finance 1968–69, Sec. 1970–72; Deputy Admin., UN Devt Programme 1972–77; Gov. Reserve Bank of India 1977–82; Dir Indian Inst. of Man., Ahmedabad, India 1982–84; Dir LSE 1984–90; Chair. Indian Council for Research on Int. Econ. Relations, Delhi 1997–, Hindustan Gil Exploration Ltd 1999–; mem. Bd of Dirs State Bank of India 1996–; Visiting Prof., Delhi School of Econs, Delhi Univ. 1964; Hon. Fellow King's Coll., Cambridge 1986, LSE 1990; Hon. DLitt (Sardar Patel Univ.) 1980, (MS Univ. of Baroda) 1993, (Univ. of Roorkee) 1997; Hon. Dr Civil Laws (Univ. of Mauritius) 1990; Hon. KBE 1990; Padmavibhushan 1990. *Publications:* On the Economics of Development 1986, Essays in Economic Policy and Economic Growth 1986, Economic Reform and Global Change 1998, Glimpses of Indian Economic Policy 2002, and articles on inflation and econ. devt, monetary and credit policy, etc. *Leisure interests:* reading, music. *Address:* 12 Amee Co-operative Housing Society, Diwali Pura, Old Padra Road, Vadodara 390015, India. *Telephone:* (265) 339026. *Fax:* (265) 333658.

PATEL, Sir Praful Raojibhai Chaturbhai, Kt; British company director; b. 7 March 1939, Jinja, Uganda; s. of Raojibhai Chaturbhai Patel and Maniben Jivabhai Lalaji Patel; ed Govt Secondary School and London Inst. of World Affairs (Extra-Mural Dept, Univ. Coll., London); Sec. Uganda Students' Union 1956–58; del. to Int. Youth Assembly, New Delhi 1958; studied and lectured on politics and Econs in Africa and Middle East before arrival in Britain as student 1958, where developed commercial activities 1962; spokesman for Asians in UK following Commonwealth Immigrants Act 1968; Hon. Sec. All Party Parl. Cttee on UK Citizenship 1968–82; Founder and mem. Council, UK Immigrants Advisory Service 1970–82; mem. Uganda Resettlement Bd 1972–74, Hon. Sec. Uganda Evacuees Resettlement Advisory Trust 1974–2000; Pres. Nava Kala India Socio-Cultural Centre, London 1962–75; Chair. Bd of Trustees, Swaminarayan Hindu Mission, UK 1970–76; Jt Convenor, Asian Action Cttee 1976; Convener Manava Trust 1979–; Chair. Asia Fund Ltd 1984–; Hon. Sec. Indo-British Cultural Exchange 1980–82, Dir 2002–; Trustee Charutar Arogya Mandal Trust 1980–, India Overseas Trust 2002–, Kailas Manasarovar Trust 2002–; mem. Indian Govt Consultative Cttee on Non-resident Investments 1986–91; frequent appearances on radio and TV programmes concerned with immigration and race relations; Queen's Scout 1956, Asian Times Award for achievement 1986, Neasden Swaminarayan Mandir Award. *Publications:* many articles in newspapers and journals on race relations and immigration. *Leisure interests:* cricket, campaigning and lobbying, current affairs, promoting traditional Ayurveda medicines, interfaith co-operation. *Address:* 60 Bedford Court Mansions, Bedford Avenue, London, WC1B 3AD, England; Puja Corporation Ltd, Readymoney Mansion, 3rd Floor, 43 Veer Nariman Road, Mumbai, 400023 India. *Telephone:* (20) 7580-0897 (London); (22) 2049248 (India). *Fax:* (20) 7436-2418 (London); (22) 2048938 (India). *E-mail:* prcpatel@vsnl.com.

PATERSON, Sir Dennis Craig, Kt, BS, MD, FRCS, FRACS; Australian orthopaedic surgeon; b. 14 Oct. 1930, Adelaide; s. of Gilbert Charles Paterson and Thelma Drysdale Paterson; m. Mary Mansell Hardy 1955; one s. three d.; ed Collegiate School of St Peter, Adelaide, Univ. of Adelaide; Resident Medical Officer, Royal Adelaide Hosp. 1954, Adelaide Children's Hosp. 1956; Registrar, Robert Jones and Agnes Hunt Orthopaedic Hosp., Oswestry, Shropshire, England 1958–60; Sr Registrar, Royal Adelaide Hosp. 1960–62; Consultant Orthopaedic Surgeon, Repatriation Gen. Hosp., Adelaide 1962–70; Asst Hon. Orthopaedic Surgeon, Adelaide Children's Hosp. 1964–66, Sr Hon. Orthopaedic Surgeon 1966–70; Dir and Chief Orthopaedic Surgeon 1970–95, mem. Bd of Man., Chair. Medical Advisory Cttee, Medical Staff Cttee 1976–84; Sr Hon. Orthopaedic Surgeon, Queen Victoria and Modbury Hosps, Adelaide 1970–95; Sr Visiting Consultant Orthopaedic Surgeon, Royal Adelaide Hosp. 1962–85; Clinical Assoc. Prof. Orthopaedic Surgery Univ. of Adelaide 1990–; mem. Bd of Orthopaedic Surgery, RACS 1974–82, 1984–87, Chair. 1977–82, mem. Court of Examiners 1974–84; Censor-in-Chief, Australian Orthopaedic Asscn 1976–80, Dir Continuing Educ. 1982–86; Pres. Crippled Children's Asscn of S. Australia 1970–84; Pres. Int. Soc. of Orthopaedic Surgery and Traumatology (SICOT) 1987–90; Chair. S Australia Road Safety Consultative Council 1994–99, Trauma Systems Cttee of S Australia 1994–2000; mem. Bd Man. McLaren Vale and Fleurian Visitor Centre 1995–2001, Chair. 1998–2001; Chair. Southern Partnership 1997–2000; mem. Archbishops' Appeal Cttee 1993–; Queen's Jubilee Medal 1977; L.O. Betts Medal in Orthopaedic Surgery 1980. *Publications:* Electrical Stimulation and Osteogenesis (Thesis) 1982; over 80 articles in refereed scientific journals. *Leisure interests:* golf, tennis, gardening. *Address:* 26 Queen Street, Glenunga, South Australia 5064, Australia (Home). *Telephone:* (8) 8379-2669 (Home). *Fax:* (8) 8379-6449 (Home). *E-mail:* paterson@senet.com.au (Home).

PATERSON, Rt Rev John Campbell, BA, LTh; New Zealand ecclesiastic; b. 4 Jan. 1945, Auckland; s. of Thomas Paterson and Mary Paterson; m. Marion Reid Anderson 1968; two d.; ed King's Coll., Univ. of Auckland, St John's Coll.; Asst curate Whangarei 1969–71; vicar Waimate N Maori pastorate 1971–76; priest-in-charge Hokianga 1973–74, Bay of Islands 1974–75; chaplain Queen Victoria School 1976–82; Asst priest Maori Mission 1976–82; Sec. Bishopric of Aotearoa 1978–87; provincial sec. 1986–92; mem. Anglican Consultative Council 1990–96, Chair. 2002; Gen. Sec. of Anglican Church, Aotearoa,

Polynesia and NZ 1992–95, Presiding Bishop and Primate 1998–; Bishop of Auckland 1995–. *Leisure interests:* literature, music. *Address:* Bishopscourt, P.O. Box 37242, Parnell 1033, New Zealand. *Telephone:* (9) 302-7202. *Fax:* (9) 377-6962.

PATERSON, Mervyn Silas, FAA, ScD; Australian geophysicist; b. 7 March 1925, South Australia; s. of Charles Paterson and Edith M. Michael; m. Katalin Sarosy 1952; one s. one d.; ed Adelaide Technical High School, Univs. of Adelaide and Cambridge; research, Aeronautical Research Labs. Melbourne 1945–53; ANU, Canberra 1953–, Prof. Research School of Earth Sciences 1987–90, Visiting Fellow and Emer. Prof. 1990–; Consultant Australian Scientific Instruments Pty Ltd; Fellow, American Mineralogical Soc., American Geophysical Union; Hon. Fellow, Geological Soc. of America. *Publications:* Experimental Rock Deformation: The Brittle Field 1978; about 110 research papers in rock deformation and materials science. *Leisure interests:* walking, reading. *Address:* Research School of Earth Sciences, Australian National University, Canberra 0200, Australia. *Telephone:* (2) 6125-2497 (Office). *Fax:* (2) 6125-0738.

PATERSON, William Edgar, OBE, MSc, PhD, FRSE, FRSA; British academic; b. 26 Sept. 1941, Blair Atholl, Scotland; s. of William Edgar Paterson and Winnie Paterson (née McIntyre); m. 1st Jacqueline Cramb 1964 (died 1974); two s.; m. 2nd Phyllis MacDowell 1979; one d. one step-s. one step-d.; ed Morrison's Acad., Univ. of St Andrews, London School of Econs; lecturer in Int. Relations Aberdeen Univ. 1967–70; Volkswagen Lecturer in German Politics, Warwick Univ. 1970–75, Sr Lecturer 1975–82, Reader 1982–89, Prof. and Chair. of Dept 1989–90; Salvesen Prof. and Dir of Europa Inst. Edin. Univ. 1990–94; Dir Inst. for German Studies, Birmingham Univ. 1994–; Chair. Asscn for the Study of German Politics 1974–76, Univ. Asscn for Contemporary European Studies 1989–94; Vice-Chair. German–British Forum 1996; mem. Econ. and Social Research Council Research Priorities Bd 1994–99, British Königswinter Cttee 1995–, Kuratorium Allianz Kulturstiftung 2001–; Co-ed. German Politics 1991–2001, Journal of Common Market Studies 2003–; Officer's Cross of Order of Merit (Germany) 1999, Academician of Acad. of Learned Socs in Social Sciences 2000. *Publications include:* The Federal Republic of Germany and the European Community (with Simon Bulmer) 1987, Government and the Chemical Industry (with Wyn Grant) 1988, Developments in German Politics II 1996, The Kohl Chancellorship (with Clay Clemens) 1998, The Future of the German Economy (with Rebecca Harding) 2000; 20 other books and over 100 articles in learned journals. *Leisure interest:* walking. *Address:* Institute for German Studies, University of Birmingham, Edgbaston, Birmingham, B15 2TT (Office); 220 Myton Road, Warwick, CV34 6PS, England (Home). *Telephone:* (121) 414-7183 (Office); (1926) 492492 (Home). *Fax:* (121) 414-7329 (Office); (1926) 492492 (Home). *E-mail:* w.e.paterson@bham.ac.uk (Office); patersons@onetel.net.uk (Home).

PATHAK, Rahunandan Swarup, LLB, MA; Indian judge; b. 25 Nov. 1924, Bareilly, Uttar Pradesh; s. of Gopal Swarup Pathak (fmr Vice-Pres. of India) and Prakashwati Pathak; m. Asha Pathak; three s.; ed Allahabad Univ.; enrolled as advocate, Allahabad High Court 1948, Supreme Court of India 1957; Additional Judge, Allahabad High Court 1962–63, Judge 1963–72; Chief Justice, Himachal Pradesh High Court 1972–78; Judge, Supreme Court of India 1978–86; Chief Justice of India 1986–89; Judge, Int. Court of Justice, The Hague 1989–91; Pro-Chancellor Univ. of Delhi 1986–89; Hon. Pres. World Peace Through Law Center, Washington, DC; Pres. Indian Law Inst. 1986–89, Indian Soc. of Int. Law, Int. Law Asscn (Regional Branch) India 1986–89; Pres. Indian Council of Legal Aid and Advice, Indian Soc. of Int. Law 1989–93; Pres. Commonwealth Games, Kuala Lumpur 1998; Vice-Pres. Olympic Games, Nagano 1998; mem. Indian Council of Arbitration 1991–, Int. Council for Arbitration of Sport 1994–, Perm. Court of Arbitration, The Hague 1997–; del. to numerous int. confs., cttees. etc.; Hon. Bencher, Gray's Inn, London; Hon. LLD (Agra, Punjab and Varanasi Univs), Hon. D.Litt. (Kashi Vidhyapeeth). *Publications:* numerous lectures and research papers. *Leisure interests:* golf, photography. *Address:* Permanent Court of Arbitration, Peace Palace, Carnegieplein 2, 2517 KJ The Hague, Netherlands (Office); 7 Sardar Patel Marg, Diplomatic Enclave, New Delhi, 110021, India. *Telephone:* (11) 3017161. *Fax:* (11) 3017170.

PATNAIK, Janki Ballav, MA; Indian politician; b. 3 Jan. 1927, Khurda District, Orissa; s. of Gokulanand Devi and Rambha Devi; m. Jayanti Patnaik; one s. two d.; ed Banaras Univ.; Sub-Ed. Eastern Times 1949, Jt Ed. 1950, Ed. (also for Prajatantra) 1952–67; Ed. Paurusha; led tenants' agitation in Madhupur, Cuttack District 1953; mem. Sahitya Akademi, Orissa 1956–57, Lok Sabha 1971–77; Minister of State for Defence, Govt of India 1973–77; Minister of Tourism, Civil Aviation and Labour Jan.–Dec. 1980; Chief Minister of Orissa State 1980–89, 1995–99; Pres. Pradesh Congress Cttee, Orissa 1999–; Hon. PhD (Jagannath Sanskrit Univ.), Hon. DLitt (Tirupati Sanskrit Univ.); Orissa Sahitya Akademi Puraskar. *Publications:* Life History of the Lord Buddha; collections of poems and essays. *Leisure interests:* reading, writing creative literature. *Address:* Qrs. No. S.G.O.-5, Type—VIII, Unit-6, Bhubaneswar, Orissa (Office); 201, Forest Park, Bhubaneswar, Orissa, India (Home). *Telephone:* (674) 406078 (Office). *Fax:* (674) 418400 (Office); (674) 406177 (Home).

PATON, Boris Yevgenovich, D.TECH.SC.; Ukrainian metallurgist; b. 27 Nov. 1918, Kiev; s. of Evgen Oskarovich Paton and Natalya Viktirovna Paton; m. Olga Borisivna Milovanova 1948; one d.; ed Kiev Polytechnic Inst.; Dir E.

O. Paton Electric Welding Institute of Ukrainian SSR (now Ukrainian) Acad. of Sciences 1953–; corresp. mem. Ukrainian SSR (now Ukrainian) Acad. of Sciences 1951–58, mem. 1958–, Pres. 1962–; mem. USSR (now Russian) Acad. of Sciences 1962, mem. Presidium 1963–; Pres. Engineering Acad. 1991–; Chair. of Co-ordination Council on Welding in USSR (now Russia) 1958–; Chair. of Scientific Council of USSR (now Russian) Acad. of Sciences "New processes of production and treatment of metallic materials" 1964–; Chair. of Co-ordination Bd of CMEA on joint works in the field of welding 1972–; Chair. of USSR (now Russian) Nat. Cttee on Welding 1976–; mem. of editorial bd and ed.-in-chief of a number of scientific and tech. journals; author of numerous books, articles and inventions; Honoured Scientist of Ukrainian SSR 1968; Honoured Inventor of USSR 1983; Foreign mem. of Acad. of Sciences of Bulgaria 1969, Czechoslovakia 1973, Bosnia and Herzegovina 1975, GDR 1980, Royal Swedish Acad. of Engineering 1986; mem. CPSU 1952–91, cand. mem. Cen. Cttee of CPSU 1961–1966, mem. 1966–91; mem. Central Cttee of CP of Ukraine 1960–91; Deputy to USSR Supreme Soviet 1962–89; Vice-Chair. Soviet of the Union USSR Supreme Soviet 1966–89; Deputy to Ukrainian SSR Supreme Soviet 1959–90, mem. of Pres. 1963–80; People's Deputy of the USSR 1989–91; State Prize 1950, Lenin Prize 1957 and numerous other awards. *Leisure interest:* tennis. *Address:* E. O. Paton Electric Welding Institute, 11 Bozhenko Street, Kiev-5, Ukraine. *Telephone:* (44) 227-31-83.

PATRUSHEV, Col Gen. Nikolai Platonovich; Russian security official; b. 11 July 1951, Leningrad (now St Petersburg); m.; two s.; ed Leningrad Inst. of Vessel Construction; on staff KGB, Karelia 1974; in Leningrad Region 1974–92; Minister of Security Karelian Autonomous Rep. 1992–94; Head Dept of Self-Security, Fed. Security Service 1994–98, Deputy Dir, then Head Dept of Econs 1998–99, Dir Aug. 1999–; Head of Presidential Control Dept May–Aug. 1998; Deputy Head Admin. of Russian Presidency Aug.–Oct. 1998; Deputy Dir Fed. Security Service of Russia, Head of Econ. Security Dept 1998, First Deputy Dir April–Aug. 1999, Dir Aug. 1999–. *Address:* Federal Security Service, B. Lubyanka str. 1/3, 101000 Moscow, Russia (Office). *Telephone:* (095) 924-31-58, (095) 224-62-24 (Office).

PATSATSIA, Otar; Georgian politician; b. 15 May 1929, Zugdidi; s. of Ambako Patsatsia and Luba Patsatsia; m. Nunu Gulua 1957; one s. one d.; ed Leningrad Inst. of Tech.; engineer, Deputy Dir, Dir Zugdidi Paper Factory 1955–65; elected First Sec. Zugdidi Regional CP Cttee but removed for his refusal to follow orders of Cen. CPSU Admin.; Dir-Gen. Gruzbumprom, Zugdidi 1966–92, on initiative of E. Shevardnadze appointed Head of Zugdidi Region Admin, controlled by adversaries of fmr Pres. Gamsakhurdia 1992–93; Prime Minister of Georgia 1993–95; USSR People's Deputy 1989–90; mem. Georgian Parl. 1995–; Hero of Socialist Labour. *Leisure interest:* hunting. *Address:* Parliament Building, Tbilisi, Georgia.

PATSEV, Aleksander Konstantinovich; Russian diplomatist; b. 29 June 1936, Moscow; m.; two c.; ed Moscow State Inst. of History and Archives, Higher Diplomatic School at Ministry of Foreign Affairs; Komsomol functionary 1959–66; mem. staff Ministry of Foreign Affairs 1966–69; Head of Sector, Dept of Information 1985–87, Deputy Head Gen. Secr. 1987–89; Amb. to Oman 1990–96, to Uzbekistan 1997–99, to Finland 1999–. *Address:* Russian Embassy, Tchtaankatu 18, 00140 Helsinki, Finland (Office). *Telephone:* (9) 661876 (Office). *Fax:* (9) 661006 (Office).

PATTAKOS, Stylianos; Greek politician; b. 8 Nov. 1912, Crete; s. of George and Maria Pattakos; m. Dimitra Nickolaidou 1940; two d.; ed high school, cadet school, War Coll. and Nat. Defence Acad.; commissioned 1937, promoted Maj.-Gen. Dec. 1967, retd; Minister of the Interior 1967–73, Deputy Premier Dec. 1967; First Deputy Premier 1971–73; arrested Oct. 1974, sentenced to death for high treason and insurrection Aug. 1975 (sentence commuted to life imprisonment).

PATTEN, Brian; British poet and author; b. 7 Feb. 1946, Liverpool; s. of Ireen Stella Bevan; Regents Lecturer, Univ. of Calif. at San Diego; Freedom of City of Liverpool 2000, Hon. Fellow John Moores Univ. 2002. *Radio:* History of 20th-Century Poetry for Children, BBC Radio 2000. *Publications include:* (poetry): The Mersey Sound 1967, The Home Coming 1969, At Four O'Clock in the Morning 1971, Walking Out: The Early Poems of Brian Patten 1971, Love Poems 1981, New Volume 1983, Storm Damage 1988, Grinning Jack: Selected Poems 1990, Armada 1996; (ed) Clare's Countryside: A Book of John Clare 1981; (children's): Grizzelda Frizzle and Other Stories 1992, The Magic Bicycle 1993, Impossible Parents 1994, Frognapped! and Other Stories 1994, The Utter Nutters 1995, The Blue and Green Ark 1999, Juggling with Gerbils 2000, Little Hotchpotch 2000, Impossible Parents Go Green; (ed) The Puffin Book of 20th Century Children's Verse 1991, The Story Giant 2001. *Address:* c/o Rogers, Coleridge and White, 20 Powys Mews, London, W11 1JN, England.

PATTEN, Rt. Hon. Christopher, CH, PC; British politician; b. 12 May 1944; s. of the late Francis Joseph Patten and Joan McCarthy; m. Mary Lavender Thornton 1971; three d.; ed St Benedict's School, Ealing, Balliol Coll., Oxford; worked in Conservative Party Research Dept 1966–70, Dir 1974–79; seconded to Cabinet Office 1970; at Home Office, then personal asst to Lord Carrington, Party Chair. 1972–74; MP for Bath 1979–92; Parl. Pvt. Sec. (PPS) to Leader of the House 1979–81, to Social Services Sec. 1981–83; Parl. Under-Sec. for Northern Ireland 1983–85; Minister of State for Educ. 1985–86; Overseas Devt Minister 1986–89; Sec. of State for the Environment 1989–90; Chancellor of the Duchy of Lancaster and Chair. of the Conservative Party 1990–92; Gov. of Hong Kong 1992–97; Chair. Comm. charged with reform of

Royal Ulster Constabulary 1998–99; Chancellor Newcastle Univ. 1999–, Oxford Univ. 2003–; EU Commr for External Relations 1999–; Dir Ind. Newspapers 1998–99; Hon. FRCP (Edin.) 1994, Hon. Fellow Balliol Coll., Oxford 1999; Hon. DCL (Newcastle) 1999. *Publication:* The Tory Case 1983, East and West 1998. *Leisure interests:* reading, tennis, gardening. *Address:* European Commission, 200 rue de la Loi, 1049 Brussels, Belgium.

PATTERSON, Harry (pseudonym Jack Higgins), B.SC.(SOC.), FRSA; British/ Irish novelist; b. 27 July 1929; s. of Henry Patterson and Rita Higgins Bell; m. 1st Amy Margaret Hewitt 1958 (divorced 1984), one s. three d.; m. 2nd Denise Leslie Ann Palmer 1985; ed Roundhay School, Leeds, Beckett Park Coll. for Teachers, London School of Econs; N.C.O., The Blues 1947–50, tried numerous jobs including clerk and circus tent hand 1950–58; schoolmaster, lecturer in liberal studies, Leeds Polytechnic, Sr Lecturer in Educ., James Graham Coll. and Tutor in School Practice, Leeds Univ. 1958–72; full-time writer since age of 41; Hon. DUniv (Leeds Metropolitan Univ.) 1995. *Publications include:* (as Jack Higgins) Prayer for the Dying 1973 (filmed 1985), The Eagle has Landed 1975, Storm Warning 1976, Day of Judgement 1978, Solo 1980, Luciano's Luck 1981, Touch the Devil 1982, Exocet 1983, Confessional 1985 (filmed 1985), Night of the Fox 1986, A Season in Hell 1989, Memoirs of a Dancehall Romeo 1989, The Dark Side of the Island 1989, The Cold Harbour 1989, The Eagle Has Flown 1990, Thunder Point 1993, Angel of Death 1995, Year of the Tiger 1996, The President's Daughter 1996, Drink with the Devil 1998, Day of Reckoning 1999, Midnight Runner 2001; (as Harry Patterson) The Valhalla Exchange 1978, To Catch a King 1979 (filmed 1983), Dillinger 1983, Walking Wounded (play) 1987; others under pseudonyms Martin Fallon, Hugh Marlowe, Henry Patterson. *Leisure interests:* tennis, old movies. *Address:* c/o Ed Victor Ltd, 6 Bayley Street, London, WC1B 3HB, England.

PATTERSON, James, MA; American novelist and fmr advertising executive; b. Newburgh, New York; m.; one s.; ed Manhattan Coll., Vanderbilt Univ.; wrote first novel 1976; joined J. Walter Thompson as jr copywriter 1971, subsequently Exec. Creative Dir, CEO, Chair. 1990–96. *Publications:* The Thomas Berryman Number 1976 (Edgar Award for best first mystery novel), Along Came a Spider, Kiss the Girls (made into film 1997), Jack & Jill, Cat & Mouse, Pop Goes the Weasel, Cradle and All, When the Wind Blows, Hide & Seek, Roses are Red, Miracle on the 17th Green (with Peter de Jonge); (non-fiction): The Day America Told the Truth (with Peter Kim). *Address:* c/o Warner Books, 1271 Avenue of the Americas, New York, NY 10020, USA (Office).

PATTERSON, Rt Hon Percival James, PC, QC; Jamaican politician and lawyer; b. 10 April 1935, Cross Road, St Andrew; s. of Henry Patterson and Ina James; m. (divorced); one s. one d.; ed Univ. of West Indies, London School of Econs; called to Bar, Middle Temple 1963, Jamaican Bar 1963; mem. People's Nat. Party (PNP) 1958–, Party Organizer 1958–60, mem. Nat. Exec. Council, mem. Party Exec. 1964–69; nominated to Senate 1967, Leader of Opposition Business in Senate 1969–70; mem. for SE Westmoreland, House of Reps. 1970–80, 1989–; Minister for Industry, Foreign Trade and Tourism 1972–77; Deputy Prime Minister and Minister for Foreign Trade 1978–80; Campaign Dir for PNP, elections 1972, 1976, 1989; Deputy Prime Minister and Minister for Devt, Planning and Production 1989–90, for Finance and Planning 1990–91, of Defence 1993–; Prime Minister 1992–; Queen's Counsel, Inner Bar 1984; Adviser to Govt of Belize 1982; Pursell Trust Scholarship, Leverhulme Scholarship; Hon. DLitt (Northeastern, Boston), Hon. LLD (Brown, RI); Order of Aguila Aztec, Mexico 1990, Order of San Martí, Argentina 1992, Order of the Volta, Ghana 1999, Juan More Fernández Great Silver Cross, Costa Rica 2001, FAO Agricola Medal 2001 and other awards. *Leisure interests:* jazz, Jamaican music, spectator sports including cricket, boxing, track and field events and tennis. *Address:* Office of the Prime Minister, Jamaica House, 1 Devon Road, P.O. Box 272, Kingston 10, Jamaica. *Telephone:* (809) 927-9941 (Office). *Fax:* (809) 929-0005 (Office). *E-mail:* pmo@ opm.gov.jm.

PATTERSON, Walter Cram, MSc; Canadian/British analyst and writer; b. 4 Nov. 1936, Winnipeg; s. of Walter Thomas Patterson and Thirza Helen Cram; m. Cleone Susan Davis 1966; two d.; ed Kelvin High School, Winnipeg, Univ. of Manitoba; Ed. Your Environment 1970–73, European Ed. Bulletin of the Atomic Scientists 1979–81; First 'Energy Campaigner' Friends of the Earth 1972–78; ind. analyst, writer 1978–93; with Gorleben Int. Review 1978–79; Course tutor Open Univ. 1981–91; Series Adviser BBC TV Drama Edge of Darkness 1984–85; Specialist Adviser House of Commons Select Cttee on Environment 1985–86, on Energy 1991–92; Assoc. Fellow Energy and Environmental Programme Royal Inst. of Int. Affairs 1991–93, (Sr Research Fellow 1993–2000), 2001–; Companion, Inst. of Energy 1991; Melchett Medal, Inst. of Energy 2000. *Publications:* Nuclear Power 1976–86, The Fissile Society 1977, Coming to a Boil 1978, The Plutonium Business 1984, Going Critical 1985, Advanced Coal-Use Technology 1987, The Energy Alternative 1990, Coal-Use Technology in a Changing Environment 1990, Coal-Use Technology: New Challenges, New Responses 1993, Power from Plants 1994, Rebuilding Romania: Energy, Efficiency and the Economic Transition 1994, Electric Futures 1997, Transforming Electricity 1999. *Leisure interests:* baseball, beer, computers, languages, music, orchids, playing with the family, travel. *Address:* Royal Institute of International Affairs, Chatham House, St James's Square, London, SW1Y 4LE (Office); Little Rushmoor, High Bois

Lane, Chesham Bois, Bucks., HP6 6DQ, England (Home). *Telephone:* (7971) 840036 (Office); (1494) 726748 (Home). *E-mail:* waltpattersn@gn.apc.org (Home). *Website:* www.riia.org (Office).

PATTINSON, Rev. Sir (William) Derek, Kt, MA; British administrator; b. 31 March 1930, Barrow-in-Furness; s. of late Thomas William Pattinson and Elizabeth Pattinson; ed Whitehaven Grammar School, The Queen's Coll., Oxford; Home Civil Service 1952–70; Asst Prin., Inland Revenue Dept 1952, Pvt. Sec. to Chair. of Bd 1955–58, Prin. 1957; Prin., HM Treasury 1962–65; Asst Sec., Inland Revenue 1965–68; Asst Sec., HM Treasury 1968–70; Assoc. Sec.-Gen., Gen. Synod of Church of England 1970–72, Sec.-Gen. 1972–90; ordained deacon 1991, priest 1992; Asst Curate, St Gabriel's, Pimlico 1991–2000; Prin. Soc. of Faith 1992–2001; Chair. Liddon Trustees 1972–2001; Master, Worshipful Co. of Parish Clerks 1986, Vice-Pres. SPCK; Stanhope Historical Essay Prize, Oxford 1951. *Address:* 9 Strutton Court, Great Peter Street, London, SW1P 2HH, England. *Telephone:* (20) 7222-2397.

PATTISON, Sir John (Ridley), Kt, BSc, MA, BChir, DM, FRCP, FMedSci; British medical scientist; b. 1 Aug. 1942; s. of Tom Frederick Pattison and Elizabeth Pattison; m. Pauline Evans 1965; one s. two d.; ed Barnard Castle School, Univ. Coll. Oxford; Asst Lecturer in Pathology, later lecturer in Virology, Middx Hosp. Medical School 1970–75; Lecturer, later Sr Lecturer in Virology, St Bartholomew's and London Hosp. Med. Colls 1976–77; Prof. of Medical Microbiology, King's College Hosp. Medical School 1977–84, Hon. Consultant, Univ. Coll. London Medical School 1984–, Dean 1990–98, Vice-Provost 1994–99; Dir of Research, Analysis and Information, Dept of Health and Nat. Health Service 1999–; mem. Medical Research Council 1992–95, 1999–, Sr Medical Advisor 1996–99; mem. Spongiform Encephalopathy Advisory Cttee 1994–95, Chair. 1995–99; mem. Council, Int. Journal of Experimental Pathology 1979–2001, Soc. of Gen. Microbiology 1981–87; mem. bd, Inst. of Child Health 1992–96, Inst. of Neurology 1995–97; mem. Man. Cttee King's Fund 1993–, Deputy Chair. 1994–99; founder Fellow of Acad. of Medical Science 1998; Ed.-in-Chief, Epidemiology & Infection 1980–94; Hon. Fellow Imperial and Univ. Colls London; hon. degrees (Middlesex Univ., Univ. of South-ampton, Mount Sinai School of Medicine). *Publications:* Principles & Practice of Clinical Virology (Jt Ed.) 1987, Practical Guide to Clinical Virology (Jt Ed.) 1989, Practical Guide to Clinical Bacteriology (Jt Ed.) 1995; numerous papers on medical virology. *Leisure interests:* family, reading, music, theatre. *Address:* Department of Health, Richmond House, 79 Whitehall, London, SW1A 2NS, England (Office). *Telephone:* (20) 7210-5556 (Office). *E-mail:* john .pattison@doh.gsi.gov.uk.

PATTISON, Seamus, DIP.SOC., ECON.SC.; Irish politician and trade union official; b. 19 April 1936, Kilkenny; s. of James Pattison and Ellen Fogarty; ed St Kieran's Coll., Kilkenny, Univ. Coll., Dublin; mem. Dáil Eireann 1961–; MEP 1981–83; Minister of State Dept of Social Welfare 1983–87; mem. British–Irish Parl. Body 1991–97; Chair. Select Cttee on Social Affairs 1993–97; Speaker Dáil Eireann 1997–2002, Father of the House 1997–, Deputy Speaker 2002–; fmr Labour Party spokesman on Educ. 1963–67, on Justice 1967–72, 1991–92, on Lands 1972–73, on Defence and Marine Affairs 1987, on Energy and Forestry 1989–91; mem. Parl. Ass. of Council of Europe 1989–90, 1996–97; mem. Kilkenny Co. Council 1964–97 (Chair. 1975–76 and 1980–81); alderman Kilkenny Corpn 1964–97; Mayor of Kilkenny 1967–68, 1976–77, 1992–93; mem. Kilkenny Vocational Educ. Cttee 1964–97 (Vice-Chair. 1990–97), South Eastern Health Bd 1971–84. *Leisure interests:* reading, theatre, travel and sport. *Address:* Dáil Eireann, Leinster House, Kildare Street, Dublin 2 (Office); 6 Upper New Street, Kilkenny, Ireland (Home). *Telephone:* (1) 6183444 (Office); (56) 21295 (Home). *Fax:* (1) 6184111 (Office); (56) 52533 (Home). *E-mail:* leascc@oireachtas.ie (Office). *Website:* www.irlgov.ie/oireachtas (Office).

PATTON, Paul E., B.Eng; American state official; b. Fallsburg; ed Univ. of Ky; with coal co. –1979, Deputy Sec. for Transportation; Judge Exec., Pike Co. 1981; Lieut.-Gov., Sec. for Econ. Devt, Pres. State of Ky 1991–95; Gov. of Ky 1995–; Chair. Ky Democrats 1981–83; served numerous terms Pike Co. Democrats Exec. Comm.; Bd Overseers Bellarmine Coll., Bd Trustees Pikeville Coll. *Address:* Office of the Governor, State Capitol, 700 Capitol Avenue, Frankfort, KY 40601, USA (Office).

PATTULLO, Sir (David) Bruce, Kt, CBE, BA, F.C.I.B.S., FRSE; British banker; b. 2 Jan. 1938, Edinburgh; s. of late Colin Pattullo and Elizabeth Bruce; m. Fiona Nicholson 1962; three s. one d.; ed Rugby School and Hertford Coll. Oxford; Gen. Man. Bank of Scotland Finance Co. Ltd 1973–77; Dir British Linen Bank Ltd 1977–98, Chief Exec. 1977–78; Deputy Treas. Bank of Scotland 1978, Treas. and Gen. Man. (Chief Exec.) 1979–88, Dir 1980–98, Group Chief Exec. 1988–96, Deputy Gov. 1988–91, Gov. 1991–98; Chair. Cttee of Scottish Clearbankers 1981–83, 1987–89; three hon. degrees; Bilsland Prize, Inst. of Bankers in Scotland 1964. *Leisure interests:* tennis, hill walking. *Address:* 6 Cammo Road, Edinburgh, EH4 8EB, Scotland. *Telephone:* (131) 339-6012 (Home).

PATZAICHIN, Ivan; Romanian canoeist; b. 26 Nov. 1949, Mila, Tulcea Co.; m.; one d.; ed Coll. for Physical Educ. and Sport, Bucharest; world champion: simple canoe 1,000 m (Tampere 1973, Sofia 1977) and 10,000 m (Belgrade 1978, 1982); double canoe 500 m (Duisburg 1979) and 1,000 m (Copenhagen 1970, Nottingham 1981, Tampere 1983); Olympic champion simple canoe 500 m (Munich 1972) and double canoe 1,000 m (Mexico City 1968, Moscow 1980,

Los Angeles 1984); numerous silver and bronze medals at world and Olympic championships; 25 times nat. champion of Romania. *Address:* Clubul Sportiv Unirea Tricolor, Soseaua Stefan cel Mare nr 9, Bucharest, Romania.

PATZIG, Günther, DPhil; German professor of philosophy; b. 28 Sept. 1926, Kiel; s. of Admiral Conrad Patzig and Gertrud Patzig (née Thomsen); m. Christiane Köhn 1948; one s. one d.; ed Gymnasiums in Kiel and Berlin-Steglitz, Univs. of Göttingen and Hamburg; Asst Philosophisches Seminar, Göttingen 1953–60, Privatdozent 1958–60, Prof. of Philosophy 1963–91; Prof. of Philosophy, Univ. of Hamburg 1960–63; UNESCO Fellowship in Philosophy 1951–52; Howison Memorial Lecturer, Berkeley 1971; Keeling Lecturer, London 1992; mem. Göttingen Acad. of Sciences 1971– (Pres. 1986–90), Wissenschaftskolleg, Berlin 1984–85, J. Jungius-Gesellschaft, Hamburg 1989–, Oslo Acad. of Sciences 1997–; Lower Saxony Prize for Science 1983, Heisenberg Medal 1998, Ernst-Hellmut-Vits-Preis 2000. *Publications:* Die aristotelische Syllogistik 1959, Sprache und Logik 1970, Ethik ohne Metaphysik 1971, Tatsachen, Normen, Sätze 1980, Aristoteles Metaphysik Z: Text, Übersetzung, Kommentar (with M. Frede) 1988, Gesammelte Schriften Vols I–IV 1993–96, Die Rationalität der Moral 1996. *Address:* Philosophisches Seminar, Universität Göttingen, Humboldtallee 19, 37073 Göttingen; Ottfried-Müller-Weg 8, 37075 Göttingen, Germany. *Telephone:* (551) 394742 (Office); (551) 42929. *Fax:* (551) 399607. *E-mail:* mpelz@gwdg.de.

PAU, Louis-François, PhD, DSc, MBA; French computer and aerospace technology expert and expert in telecommunications technology; b. 29 May 1948, Copenhagen, Denmark; s. of Louis Pau and Marie-Louise Von Jessen; m. 1st Miki Miyamoto 1983 (divorced 1990); one d.; m. 2nd Maria Joukovskaia; ed Ecole Nat. Supérieure de l'Aéronautique et de l'Espace, Paris Univ., Inst. d'Etudes Politiques, Paris; dancer, Royal Ballet, Copenhagen 1957–66; served in Air Force 1970–72; Asst Prof., Tech. Univ., Denmark 1972–74; Prof. and Dept Head, Ecole Nat. Supérieure Télécommunications, Paris 1974–82; Assoc. Prof., MIT, USA 1977–78; Science and Tech. Counsellor, French Embassy, Washington, DC 1979–82; Professorial Lecturer, Univ. of Md, College Park, Md 1980–82; Sr Scientist, Battelle Memorial Inst. 1982–86; Research Prof., Tech. Univ., Denmark 1986–90; CSK Prof., Univ. of Tokyo 1988–90; Tech. Dir, Digital Equipment Corpn (Europe) 1990–95; Gen. Man. Ericsson Core Network Products, Sweden 1995–; Prof. Mobile Commerce, Rotterdam School of Man. 2001–; consultant to several int. corpns; adviser to several govts and govt agencies, USA, Asia and Europe; mem. review bds, Singapore, EEC, USA; Vice-Pres. (Tech.) Int. Fed. of Automatic Control 1982–86; FIEEE; Fellow Japan Soc. of Promotion Sciences; Fellow British Computer Soc.; many awards and prizes. *Publications:* eight books (Author), 12 books (Ed.), more than 250 papers on computers and software, aerospace tech. and financial/econ. models. *Leisure interests:* ballet, flying, travel. *Address:* Ericsson, PO Box 1505, 12525 Älvsjö, Sweden (Office). *Telephone:* (8) 727-30-00, (70) 590-13-39 (Office). *Fax:* (8) 647-82-76 (Office). *E-mail:* louis-françois.pau@uab.ericsson.se (Office).

PAUK, György; British violinist; b. 26 Oct. 1936, Budapest, Hungary; m. Susan Mautner 1959; one s. one d.; ed Franz Liszt Acad. of Music, Budapest under Zathureczky, Leo Weiner and Zoltán Kodály; concerts all over East Europe 1952–58 and the rest of the world; settled in Western Europe 1958, The Netherlands 1958–61, England 1961–; Prof. of Violin, Royal Acad. of Music 1987–; Artistic Dir Mozart Bicentenary Festival, London 1991; Hon. mem. and Prof. Guildhall School of Music and Drama, London, Royal Acad. of Music 1987; Hon. RAM 1990; Paganini Prize 1956, Sonata Competition Prize, Munich 1957, Jacques Thibaud Prize 1959, Grand Prix for Bartók Records (Ovation Magazine, USA) 1982, Best Record of 1983 (Gramophone Magazine), Grammy nomination for most recent Bartók records 1995; Highest civilian award, Hungarian Govt 1998. *Recordings include:* numerous concertos, the complete violin/piano music of Mozart and Schubert, all Handel's sonatas, all Brahms's sonatas, Mozart string quintets, all Bartók's music for solo, duo and sonatas; first performances of Penderecki's violin concerto, UK, Japan, Sir Michael Tippett's Triple Concerto, London 1980, Lutoslawski's Chain 2, UK, Netherlands, Hungary, with composer conducting, Sir Peter Maxwell Davies' violin concerto, Switzerland, Germany. *Leisure interests:* football, tennis, theatre, reading, swimming, my family. *Address:* c/o Royal Academy of Music, Marylebone Road, London, NW1 5HT, England.

PAUL, Robert (Robin) Cameron, CBE, MEng, F.R.ENG., FIChemE; British chemical engineer; b. 7 July 1935, Uxbridge; m. Diana Kathleen Bruce 1965 (died 2001); two d.; ed Rugby School and Corpus Christi Coll., Cambridge; Nat. Service (2nd Lt in Royal Engineers) 1953–55; Imperial Chemical Industries (ICI) 1957–86; Deputy Chair. ICI Mond Div. 1979–86; Deputy Chair. and Man. Dir Albright and Wilson 1986–95, Chief Exec. 1995–97; Dir (non-exec.) Courtaulds PLC 1994–98; Pres. Chemical Industries Asscn 1995–97; Hon. DEng; S.C.I. Centenary Medal 1996. *Leisure interests:* music (piano) and golf. *Address:* 2 Devonshire Place, Kensington, London, W8 5UD, England (Home).

PAUL, Baron (Life Peer), cr. 1996, of Marylebone in the City of Westminster; **Swraj Paul,** MSc, FRSA; British industry executive; b. 18 Feb. 1931, India; s. of Payare Paul and Mongwati Paul; m. Aruna Vij 1956; three s. one d. (and one d. deceased); ed Punjab Univ., Massachusetts Inst. of Tech., USA; joined family-owned Apeejay Surrendra Group as Partner 1953; moved to UK and est. Natural Gas Tubes Ltd 1966; Founder-Chair. Caparo Group Ltd 1978–, Caparo Industries PLC 1981–; Chair. Caparo Inc., USA 1988–, Armstrong Equipment Ltd 1989–, CREMSA, Spain 1989–, ENSA, Spain 1989–; Founder-Chair. Indo-British Asscn 1975–; Pres. Family Service Unit 1997–; Chancellor, Univ. of Wolverhampton 1999–; Trustee Police Foundation 1997–; Hon. PhD (American Coll. of Switzerland, Leysin) 1986; Hon. DSc (Econ.) (Hull) 1992; Hon. DLitt (Westminster) 1996; Hon. DHL (Chapman) 1996; Hon. DUniv (Bradford) 1997, (Cen. England) 1999; Hon. DSc (Buckingham) 1999; Corp. Leadership Award, MIT 1987; Padma Bhushan 1983. *Publications:* Indira Gandhi 1984, Beyond Boundaries 1998. *Address:* Caparo House, 103 Baker Street, London, WIU 6LN, England. *Telephone:* (20) 7486-1417. *Fax:* (20) 7935-3242 (Office).

PAULA, Alejandro Felippe "Jandi"; Netherlands Antilles prime minister and librarian; Govt Librarian 1973–93; Prime Minister of Netherlands Antilles 1993–94. *Address:* c/o Office of the Prime Minister, Curaçao, Netherlands Antilles.

PAULAUSKAS, Arturas; Lithuanian politician; b. 23 Aug. 1953; m. Jolanta Paulauskienė; one s. one d. (and two s. from previous m.); ed Vilnius State Univ.; Deputy Prosecutor Kaisiadoris 1979–82; Prosecutor Varena 1982–87; instructor Cen. Cttee CP 1987; Deputy Prosecutor-Gen., Prosecutor-Gen. of Lithuania 1987–95; Deputy Prosecutor-Gen. of Lithuania 1995; Cand. in Pres. Elections 1997; barrister 1997–2000, Chair. Seimas (Parl.) of Lithuania 2000–. *Leisure interests:* sport, reading. *Address:* Seimas of the Republic of Lithuania, Gedimino pr.53, LT 2600 Vilnius, Lithuania. *Telephone:* (2) 39-65-55 (Office). *Fax:* (2) 39-64-00 (Office). *E-mail:* arturas.paulauskas@lrs.lt (Office); a.paulauskas@takas.lt (Home).

PAULS, Raymond; Latvian composer and jazz pianist; b. 12 Jan. 1936, Riga; ed Latvian Conservatory; Artistic Dir and Chief Conductor of Latvian State Radio and TV 1985–88; Chair. Latvian State Cttee for Culture, later Minister of Culture 1988–93 (first non-communist minister in USSR since 1920s); Counsellor to Pres. 1993–97; mem. Parl. (Saeima) 1998–; Latvian State Prize 1979; USSR People's Artist 1985. *Compositions include:* musicals Sister Kerry, Sherlock Holmes; many popular songs, jazz pieces. *Address:* Veidenbaum Str. 41/43, Apt 26, 6001 Riga, Latvia. *Telephone:* (2) 27-55-88.

PAULSON, Henry Merritt, Jr, BA, MBA; American investment banker; b. 28 March 1946, Palm Beach, Fla; s. of Henry Merritt and Marianna (Gallaeur) Paulson; m. Wendy Judge 1969; one s. one d.; ed Dartmouth Coll., Harvard Univ.; Staff Asst to Asst Sec. of Defense (Comptroller), Pentagon, Washington, DC 1970–72; Staff Asst to Pres.'s Domestic Council, The White House, Washington, DC 1972–73; Assoc. Goldman Sachs & Co., Chicago 1974–77, Vice-Pres. 1977–82, partner Investment Banking Dept 1982–, partner in charge of investment banking Midwest Region 1984–90, Man. Cttee Co-Head Investment Banking Div., Vice-Chair., COO 1990–99, CEO, Chair. 1999–; Trustee Chicago Symphony Orchestra; Dir The Peregrine Fund Inc. *Leisure interests:* skiing, fishing, canoeing, tennis. *Address:* Goldman Sachs Group, 85 Broad Street, New York, NY 10004 (Office); 101 West 67th Street, Apt. 50A, New York, NY 10023, USA (Home).

PAVAROTTI, Luciano, DMus; Italian opera singer; b. 12 Oct. 1935, Modena; s. of Fernando Pavarotti and Adele (née Venturi) Pavarotti; m. 1st Adua Veroni 1961 (divorced); three d.; m. 2nd Nicoletta Mantovani 2003; one d.; ed Istituto Magistrale; tenor range; début as Rodolfo in La Bohème at Reggio nell'Emilia 1961, Staatsoper Vienna, Royal Opera House, London 1963, La Scala 1965, Metropolitan Opera House, New York 1968, Paris Opera and Lyric Opera of Chicago 1973; début as Edgardo in Lucia di Lammermoor in USA (Miami) 1965; La Scala tour of Europe 1963–64; recitals and concerts abroad including the USA and Europe 1973–, tour of USSR 1990; Pavarotti in the Park (London) 1991; performed Cavaradossi at the Met 1999, Radames 2001, Tosca at Covent Garden 2002; about 30 albums 1964–79; appeared in MGM film Yes, Giorgio 1981; hon. degree (Pa) 1979; Noce d'Oro Nat. Prize, Luigi Illica int. prize, first prize Gold Orfeo (Acad. du Disque Lyrique de France), Grammy Award for best classical vocal soloist 1981, Kennedy Center Honor 2001, and many other prizes; Grand Officer, Italian Repub., Légion d'honneur. *Publications:* Pavarotti: My Own Story (with William Wright), Grandissimo Pavarotti 1986, Pavarotti: My World (with William Wright) 1995. *Leisure interests:* tennis, painting, equitation. *Address:* c/o Herbert Breslin, 119 West 57th Street, New York, NY 10019, USA (Office); Via Giardini 941, 41040 Saliceta, Modena, Italy (Home).

PAVIĆ, Milorad, DPhil; Serbia and Montenegro (Serbian) poet, novelist and historian; b. 15 Oct. 1929, Belgrade; m. 1st Branka Pavić; one s. one d.; m. 2nd Jasmina Mihailović; ed Belgrade Univ.; journalist, Radio Belgrade 1958–63, Prosveta Publrs. 1963–74; Prof., Dean, Faculty of Philosophy, Novy Sad Univ. 1974–82; Prof., Belgrade Univ. 1982–94; lecturer, Univ. of Paris (Sorbonne); mem. Serbian Acad. of Sciences and Arts; numerous prizes and awards. *Publications:* 6 novels, 6 collections of short stories, 2 collections of poetry, 3 plays, more than 10 historical and literary monographs, including: (novels): Dictionary of Kharzars 1984, Landscape Painted with Tea 1988, The Inner Side of the Wind 1991, The Last Love in Constantinople 1994, The Writing Box 1999, The Star Cape 2000, Seven Deadly Sins 2002; (short stories): The Iron Curtain 1973, St Mark's Horses 1978, Borzoi 1979, The Inverted Glove 1989, Glass Snail (fiction for Internet) 1998, Horror Love Stories 2001; numerous articles and essays. *Address:* Brace Baruh 2, Belgrade, Serbia and Montenegro. *E-mail:* mpavic@eunet.yu (Home). *Website:* www.khazars.com (Home).

PAVLE, Patriarch (secular name Gojko Stojcevic); Serbia and Montenegro (Serbian) ecclesiastic; b. 11 Sept. 1914, Kućanci, Slavonia; ed High School, Belgrade, Orthodox Theological Faculty, Belgrade and Theological Faculty, Athens; worked as catechist of refugee children at Holy Trinity Monastery, Ovcar during World War II; took monastic vows, ordained deacon 1948; mem. Raca Monastery 1949–55; teacher, Theological Seminary, Prizren, Kosovo 1950–51; ordained priest 1954; Bishop, Raska-Prizren Diocese/Kosovo-Metohija 1957–90; 44th Patriarch of Serbia 1990–, Archbishop of Péc, Metropolitan of Belgrade-Karlovci; Dr. hc (Theological Faculty, Belgrade) 1992, (St Vladimir Theological Seminary, New York) 1992. *Publications:* Some Questions concerning Our Faith; ed. of liturgical books in Serbian and in Old Church Slavonic; articles in liturgics in monthly journal Glasnik. *Address:* Kralja Petra 5, P.O. Box 182, 11001 Belgrade, Serbia and Montenegro. *Telephone:* (11) 638161, 635699. *Fax:* (11) 638161.

PAVLETIĆ, Vlatko, PhD; Croatian literary researcher and politician; b. 2 Sept. 1930, Zagreb; s. of Mate Pavletić and Mira Pavletić; m. Neda Majnarić; one s.; ed Zagreb Univ.; started as drama man. at Croat Nat. Theatre (HNK); Prof. Zagreb Drama Arts Acad.; Artistic Dir Adria Filmstudio; Fellow, Vice-Pres. Croatian Acad. of Sciences and Arts 1992; Minister of Educ., Culture and Sports of Croatian Repub. 1990–92; mem. of Parl. (Sabor) 1992–95, 1999–; Pres. of Parl. 1995–99, Vice-Pres. 2000–; mem. Croatian Writers' Asscn; mem. Croatian PEN; Grand Order of Petar Kresimir IV with Sash and Star, Order of the Croatian Star, Vukovar Memorial Medal and several other honours and awards. *Achievements:* citations in numerous works dealing with Croatian literature. *Publications:* A Door-knocker in Your Hand 1952, The Destiny of an Automaton 1955, How Writers Wrote 1956, Croatian Literary Critics 1958, A Moment of the Present 1960, An Analysis One Cannot Do Without 1961, Plays by Ivo Vojnovic 1962, Goran with Himself 1963, Croatian Poets between Two Wars, The Golden Book of Croatian Poetry 1970, Against Barbarism 1971, Work in Reality 1971, Ujevic in the Paradise of His Hell 1978, The Restrained Wrath 1978, Essays and Reviews 1982, The Witness of the Apocalypse 1983, Men's Life 1987, Key to Modern Poetry 1986, A Trap for Generations 1987, A Puzzle without a Solution 1987, How to Read Poetry 1987, Common Life's Poesy 1991, Baudelaire's Flowers of Evil 1993, The Contemplative Sensation of a Place 1995, Critical Miniatures (a panorama of Croatian writers and works) 1997. *Leisure interest:* walking. *Address:* Rubetićeva str. 7, 10000 Zagreb, Croatia (Home). *Telephone:* (1) 4616000 (Home).

PAVLÍČEK, František, PhD; Czech playwright; b. 20 Nov. 1923, Lukov, Zlín Dist; s. of František Pavlíček and Růžena Šmídová; m. 1st Alena Břízová 1971, one s. one d.; m. 2nd Eva Košlerová 1991; ed Charles Univ., Prague; Script Ed.-in-Chief, Czechoslovak Film Co. 1956–65; Dir Theatre Na Vinohradech 1965–70, signed Charter 77, served long-term prison sentence; Dir-Gen. Czechoslovak Radio, Prague 1990–91; Czechoslovak State Prize 1968, Medal of Merit 2002. *Works:* 15 plays for stage and TV, including The Little Mermaid 1992, In Praise of Debauchery 1994, Muž v pozadí (Mastermind) 1995, 20 screenplays, 80 radio plays and The End of the Patriarchate (novel) 1992, Zrcadlení (The Reflection) 1997. *Leisure interests:* writing plays, history. *Address:* K. Brance 1012/19, 150 00 Prague 5, Czech Republic (Home). *Telephone:* (235) 521799.

PAVLOVSKY, Gleb Olegovich; Russian journalist and historian; b. 5 March 1951, Odessa; m.; one s. four d.; ed Odessa State Univ.; with Samizdat 1972–86; co-f., mem. Bd Poiski (magazine) 1978–80; Chair. Bd of Dirs Postfactum (information agency) 1988–93; mem. ed. bd Obshchaya Gazeta 1993–; Ed.-in-Chief Twentieth Century and World; Co.-Publr Sreda (Russian-European review) 1993–95; took part in election campaign of Pres. Vladimir Putin 2000; Founder and Pres. Fund of Efficient Policy 1995–. *Address:* Fund of Efficient Policy, Zubovsky blvd 4 entr. 8, 119021 Moscow, Russia (Office). *Telephone:* (095) 745-52-25 (Office).

PAVLYCHKO, Dmytro Vasylovych; Ukrainian poet and politician; b. 28 September 1929, Ivano-Frankivsk; s. of Vasyl Pavlychko and Paraska Bojchuk; ed Lviv Univ.; started publishing in early 1950s; mem. CPSU 1954–88; keen advocate of de-Stalinization from 1962; f. Taras Shevchenko Ukrainian Language Soc. 1988, for protection of language; Chair. inaugural Congress of the Popular Movt of the Ukraine for Perestroika (Rukh); Deputy to Ukrainian Supreme Soviet 1990; Chair. Parl. Cttee for Int. Affairs 1991; Amb. to Slovakia 1995–98, to Poland 1999–. *Publications include:* My Land 1955, The Day 1960, Bread and Banner 1968, Sonnets 1978, Turned to the Future 1986, Repentance Psalms 1994, Nostalgia 1998. *Address:* Embassy of Ukraine, 7 J. S. Such Avenue, 00-580, Warsaw, Poland (Office). *Telephone:* (22) 62-50-127 (Office). *Fax:* (22) 629-81-03 (Office).

PAWAR, Sharadchandra Govindrao, BCom; Indian politician; b. 12 Dec. 1940, Katychiwadi, Poona; s. of Govindrao Jijaba Pawar; m.; one d.; Head State Level Youth Congress; Gen. Sec. Maharashtra Pradesh Congress Cttee; elected to State Legis. 1967, held Portfolios of Home and Publicity and Rehabilitation; Minister of State and Educ. and Youth Welfare, Home, Agric. and Industries and Labour; Chief Minister of Maharashtra 1978–80, 1988–91, Minister of Defence 1991–92; Pres. Nat. Congress (opposition) 1981–86; rejoined Congress (I) 1986; fmr Pres. Congress Forum for Socialist Action; Sec. Defence Cttee; mem. Lok Sabha 1996–; Leader of Opposition 1998–99; Pres. Nationalist Congress Party 1999–; Pres. Maharashtra Kabbadi Asscn, Maharashtra Olympic Asscn, Agricultural Devt Foundation, Mumbai Cricket Asscn. *Address:* Nationalist Congress Party, 10 Dr Bish-

ambhar Das Marg, New Delhi 11001 (Office); Ramalayan, 44-A Pedder Road, Mumbai 400026, India (Home). *Telephone:* (11) 3359218 (Office); (22) 3659191 (Home). *Fax:* (11) 3352112 (Office).

PAWLAK, Waldemar, MSc; Polish politician; b. 5 Sept. 1959, Pacyna, Płock Prov.; m.; two s. one d.; ed Warsaw Univ. of Tech.; farm man. 1984–; mem. United Peasant Party (ZSL) 1984–90; Deputy to Sejm (Parl.) 1989–; mem. Polish Peasant Party (PSL) 1992– (Chair. 1992–97); Chair. Council of Ministers (Prime Minister) of Poland June–July 1992, 1993–95; Chair. Union of Volunteer Fire Brigades 1992–; Chair. Warsaw Commodity Exchange 2001–. *Leisure interests:* philosophy, information science, computers. *Address:* Zarząd Główny ZOSP RP, ul. Oboźna 1, 00-340 Warsaw, Poland (Office). *Telephone:* (22) 828-00-74 (Office).

PAWLENTY, Tim, BA; American state official; b. 1960, South St. Paul; m. Mary Pawlenty; two d.; ed South St. Paul High School, Univ. of Minn.; fmr prosecutor Minn. School Dist; mem. Egan City Council –1992; mem. Senate, Minn. 1992–2002, Majority Leader 1999–2002; Gov. of Minn. 2003–. *Address:* Office of the Governor, 130 State Capitol Building, 75 Constitution Avenue, St. Paul, MN 55155, USA (Office). *Telephone:* (651) 296-3391 (Office). *Fax:* (651) 296-0039 (Office).

PAWSON, Anthony James, OC, PhD, FRS, FRSC; British/Canadian molecular biologist; b. 18 Oct. 1952, Maidstone; s. of Henry Anthony Pawson and Hilarie Anne Pawson (née Bassett); m. Margaret Ann Luman 1975; two s. one d.; ed London Univ., Cambridge Univ.; Asst Prof. Dept of Microbiology, Univ. of British Columbia 1981–85; Sr Scientist Samuel Lunenfeld Research Inst., Mount Sinai Hosp., Toronto 1985–, Head of Programme in Molecular Biology and Cancer 1994–, Research Dir 2002–; Assoc. Prof. Dept of Medical Genetics, Univ. of Toronto 1985-88, Prof. 1989–; Gairdner Foundation Int. Award 1994; Dr. H. P. Heineken Prize for Biochemistry and Biophysics, Royal Netherlands Acad. of Arts and Sciences 1998; American Asscn for Cancer Research-Pezcoller Foundation Award for Cancer Research 1998, Flavelle Medal of the Royal Soc. of Canada 1998, Distinguished Scientist of the Medical Research Council of Canada 1998; Izaak Walton Killam Memorial Prize 2000, J. Allyn Taylor Int. Prize 2000, Ontario Platinum Research Medal 2002, Prix Galien Canada 2002, Michael Smith Prize for health research 2002. *Publications:* over 275 papers in various scientific journals. *Leisure interests:* reading, theatre, fly-fishing. *Address:* Samuel Lunenfeld Research Institute, Mount Sinai Hospital, 600 University Avenue, Room 1084, Toronto, Ont. M5G 1X5, Canada. *Telephone:* (416) 586-8262. *Fax:* (416) 586-8869. *E-mail:* pawson@ mshri.on.ca (Office). *Website:* pawson.mshri.on.ca.

PAWSON, John; British architect; b. 6 May 1949; s. of late Jim Pawson and Winifred Ward; m. Catherine Berning 1989; two s.; ed Eton; lived three years in Japan before studying architecture; pvt. architectural practice 1981–; pvt. bldgs. designed include Neundorf House, Majorca, Klein Apartment, NY; commercial bldgs. designed include Calvin Klein Store, Madison Ave., NY, Jigsaw clothes store, Bond St, London, Cathey Pacific First Class Lounge, Chep Lap Kok Airport, Hong Kong, Novy Dvur Monastery, Czech Rep. *Major exhibition:* John Pawson IVAM, Valencia 2002. *Publications:* Minimum 1996, Living and Eating (with Annie Bell) 2001, Themes and Projects 2002. *Address:* Unit B, 70–78 York Way, London, N1 9AG, England. *Telephone:* (20) 7837-2929. *Fax:* (20) 7837-4949. *E-mail:* email@johnpawson.co.uk (Office).

PAXMAN, Jeremy Dickson, MA; British journalist and author; b. 11 May 1950, Leeds; s. of Arthur Keith Paxman and Joan McKay Dickson; one s. two d.; ed Malvern Coll., St Catharine's Coll., Cambridge; journalist, Northern Ireland 1973–77; reporter, BBC TV Tonight and Panorama programmes 1977–85, presenter BBC TV Breakfast Time 1986–89, Newsnight 1989–, Univ. Challenge 1994–, Start the Week, Radio 4, 1998–2002; Fellow St Edmund Hall, Oxford, St Catharine's Coll. Cambridge 2001; Dr. h.c. (Leeds, Bradford) 1999; Royal TV Soc. Award for Int. Reporting, Richard Dimbleby Award, BAFTA 1996, 2000, Interview of the Year, Royal TV Soc. 1997, 1998, 2001, Voice of the Viewer and Listener Presenter of the Year 1994, 1997, Variety Club Media Personality of the Year 1999. *Publications:* A Higher Form of Killing (co-author) 1982, Through the Volcanoes 1985, Friends in High Places 1990, Fish, Fishing and the Meaning of Life 1994, The Compleat Angler 1996, The English 1998, The Political Animal 2002; numerous articles in newspapers and magazines. *Leisure interests:* fly-fishing, daydreaming. *Address:* c/o BBC TV, London, W12 7RJ, England.

PAYÁ SARDIÑAS, Oswaldo José; Cuban human rights activist; b. 29 Feb. 1952; m. Ofelia Acevedo Maura Payá Sardiñas 1986; three c.; ed Maristas Brothers Catholic School and Univ. of Havana; sentenced to hard labour in Isla de Pinos and Camagüey Prov. for openly criticizing communist regime 1969–72; later forced to abandon his teaching post for refusing to join Cuban Communist Party (PCC); specialist in electronic medical equipment for Public Health Dept 1980s–; del. of Havana Diocese at Church Nat. Meeting, presented document 'Faith and Justice' defending right of Catholics to practise their religion 1986; f. 'La Peña del Pensamiento Cubano'; prohibited from publishing 'Peña Cristiana' by Bishop of Havana 1988; f. Movimiento Cristiano Liberación (MCL) 1988; detained and interrogated by State Security 1990; drafted Transitory Program 1992, collected signatures for referendum on Transitory Program 1993; Co-Organizer of Cuban Council 1995; drafted Varela Project to secure referendum on guaranteeing basic human rights 1996–97, collected required number of signatures under Cuban Constitution to make Varela Project become a bill of law May 2002; move blocked when ordinary session of Nat. Ass. suspended by Fidel Castro July

2002; Homo Homini Prize 1999, European Parl. Sakharov Award for Human Rights and Freedom of Thought 2002. *Publications include:* Pueblo de Dios (God's Nation) 1987, Todos Unidos (All Together) 1999. *Address:* Buró de Información del Movimiento Cubano de Derechos Humanos, 999 South Brickell Bay Drive, 1704 Miami, FL 33131 (Office); c/o Cuba Free Press, P.O. Box 652035, Miami, FL 33265-2035, USA; Movimiento Cristiano Liberación, Havana, Cuba. *Website:* www.infoburo.org; www.cubaproyectovarela.org.

PAYE, Jean-Claude; French diplomatist; b. 26 Aug. 1934, Longué; s. of Lucien Paye and Suzanne (née Guignard) Paye; m. Laurence Jeanneney 1963; two s. two d.; ed Inst. d'Etudes Politiques and Ecole Nat. d'Admin; Head, private office of Mayor of Constantine 1961–62; Sec. of Embassy, Algiers 1962–63; Ministry of Foreign Affairs 1963–65; special adviser, Office of Sec. of State for Scientific Research 1965, Office of Minister for Social Affairs 1966; Head of private office of M. Barre (Vice-Pres. of Comm. of European Communities) 1967–73; Counsellor, Bonn 1973–74; Deputy Head, Office of Minister for Foreign Affairs 1974–76; Counsellor to Prime Minister Raymond Barre 1976–79; Sec.-Gen. Interministerial Cttee for European Econ. Co-operation questions 1977–79; Dir Econ. and Financial Affairs, Ministry for External Relations 1979–84; Sec.-Gen. OECD 1984–96; Conseiller d'Etat en Service Extraordinaire 1996–2000, au cabinet Gide Loyrette Nouel 2001–; ministre plénipotentiaire hors classe 1986; Chevalier, Légion d'honneur, Commdr, Ordre nat. du Mérite. *Address:* Cabinet d'Avocats Gide Loyrette Nouel, 26 Cours Albert Ier, 75008 Paris (Office); 1 place Alphonse Deville, 75006 Paris, France (Home). *Telephone:* 1-40-75-35-86 (Office); 1-45-49-20-30 (Home). *Fax:* 1-45-49-20-06 (Home). *E-mail:* paye@gide.fr (Office).

PAYNE, Alexander, BA, MFA; American film director and screenwriter; b. 1961, Omaha, NE; m. Sandra Oh 2003; ed Stanford Univ. and UCLA; began making films aged six; employee Universal Pictures; completed several shorts for Propaganda Films and screened on Playboy Channel; feature film debut with Citizen Ruth (co-wrote screenplay with Jim Taylor) 1996. *Films include:* The Passion of Martin (thesis film, dir) 1989, Inside Out (dir and screenwriter) 1992, Citizen Ruth (dir and screenwriter—First Prize, Munich Film Festival) 1996, Election (dir and jt screenwriter with Jim Taylor—Best Screenplay Award: WGA, New York Film Critics Circle and Ind. Spirit, Best Film and Best Dir, Ind. Spirit Awards) 1999, Jurassic Park III (screenplay) 2001, Sideways (dir), About Schmidt (dir and jt screenwriter with Jim Taylor—Best Movie of the Year, Los Angeles Film Critics Asscn 2002, Golden Globe for Best Screenplay 2003) 2002. *Address:* c/o New Line Cinema Corporation, 116 North Robertson Blvd, Los Angeles, CA 90048, USA (Office).

PAYNE, Anthony Edward, BA; British composer; b. 2 Aug. 1936, London; s. of the late Edward Alexander Payne and (Muriel) Margaret Payne; m. Jane Manning (q.v.); ed Dulwich Coll., London and Durham Univ.; freelance musical journalist, musicologist, lecturer, etc. with various publs and BBC Radio, active in promoting "new music", serving on Cttee of Macnaghten Concerts (Chair. 1967) and Soc. for the Promotion of New Music (Chair. 1969–71), composed part-time 1962–73; full-time composer 1973–; tutor in Composition, London Coll. of Music 1983–85, Sydney Conservatorium 1986, Univ. of W Australia 1996; Milhaud Prof., Mills Coll., Oakland, Calif. 1983; Artistic Dir Spitalfields Festival; Composition Tutor Univ. of Western Australia 1996; Contrib. Daily Telegraph 1964–, The Times 1964–, The Independent 1986–, Country Life 1995–; mem. Cttee Asscn Frank Bridge Trust, RVW Trust, MBF Awards and Trusts; Hon. DMus (Birmingham) 2000, (Kingston) 2002; Radcliffe Award 1975, Int. Jury Choice for Int. Soc. for Contemporary Music Festival 1976 (Concerto for Orchestra), Gramophone Critics' Choice 1977 (The Music of Anthony Payne); South Bank Show Award 1998, Evening Standard Classical Music Award 1998, New York Critics' Circle Nat. Public Radio Award 1999, Classical CD Award 1999. *Compositions:* Paraphrases and Cadenzas 1969, Phoenix Mass 1972, Concerto for Orchestra 1976, The World's Winter 1976, String Quartet 1978, The Stones and Lonely Places Sing 1979, Song of the Clouds 1980, A Day in the Life of a Mayfly 1981, Evening Land 1981, Spring's Shining Wake 1981, The Spirit's Harvest 1985, The Song Streams in the Firmament 1986, Fanfares and Processional 1986, Half Heard in the Stillness 1987, Consort Music 1988, Sea-Change 1988, Time's Arrow 1990, The Enchantress Plays 1991, Symphonies of Wind and Rain 1991, A Hidden Music 1992, The Seeds Long Hidden 1993, Empty Landscape-Heart's Ease 1995, completion of Elgar's Third Symphony 1997, Piano Trio 1998, Scenes from The Woodlanders 1999, Of Knots and Skeins 2000, Betwixt Heaven and Charing Cross 2001, Visions and Journeys 2002, Adelstrop and After 2003. *Publications:* Schoenberg 1968, The Music of Frank Bridge 1984, Elgar's Third Symphony: The Story of the Reconstruction 1998. *Leisure interests:* English countryside, cinema. *Address:* 2 Wilton Square, London, N1 3DL; c/o Boosey & Hawkes, 295 Regent Street, London W1B 2JH, England. *Telephone:* (20) 7359-1593. *Fax:* (20) 7226-4369. *E-mail:* tony@wiltonsq.demon.co.uk (Home).

PAYNE, Julien David, QC, LLD, FRSC; Canadian/British professor of law; b. 4 Feb. 1934, Nottingham; s. of Frederick Payne and Kathleen Payne (née Maltby); m. Marilyn Ann Payne; five c.; ed Univ. of London; Asst Lecturer, Queens Univ. Belfast 1956–60; Prof. of Law in various Canadian univs 1960–2001; admitted as solicitor and barrister, Prov. of Ont. 1965; served as advocate, mediator and arbitrator of family law disputes across Canada (pioneer of no-fault divorce and Unified Family Courts); adviser to fed. and prov. govts on family and law reform 1966–; Dir Family Law Project, Law Reform Comm. of Canada 1972–75; Prof., Common Law Section, Univ. of Ottawa 1974–99; Chair. Law Foundation of Saskatchewan 1999–2001;

Founding mem. Int. Soc. on Family Law 1972; visiting univ. fellowships or chairs include Manchester, Santa Clara, Calif., Vic., British Columbia, Hong Kong Univ., City Univ. of Hong Kong, Saskatchewan; Simon Sr Fellowship, Univ. of Manchester 1968, Hon. Life Fellow, Canadian Inst. for Conflict Resolution, St Paul's Univ., Ottawa, Hon. Life Mem. Bd Ontario Asscn for Family Mediation 1992; Hon. Life Mem. Bd Dirs, Ont. Asscn of Family Mediation, Ottawa; Law Soc. of Upper Canada, Medal for Contribs to Legal Profession 2002. *Publications include:* Power on Divorce 1964, Conceptual Analysis of Unified Family Courts, Law Reform Commission of Canada 1973, Payne on Divorce 1996, Canadian Family Law 2001, Child Support Guidelines in Canada 2003. *Address:* 1188 Morrison Drive, Ottawa, Ont. K2H 7L3, Canada. *Telephone:* (613) 829-1905. *E-mail:* j.d.payne@sympatico.ca (Office); j_d_payne@yahoo.com (Home).

PAYNE, Nicholas; British opera company director; b. 4 Jan. 1945, Bromley; m. Linda Jane Adamson 1986; two s.; ed Eton Coll. and Trinity Coll. Cambridge; joined finance Dept of Royal Opera House; Subsidy Officer, Arts Council of GB 1970–76; Financial Controller, Welsh Nat. Opera 1976–82; Gen. Admin. Opera North 1982–93; Dir The Royal Opera 1993–98; Gen. Dir ENO 1998–2002.

PAZ ZAMORA, Jaime, LIC.; Bolivian politician; b. 15 April 1939, Cochabamba; ed Colegio Jesuita, Sucre, Seminario Mayor de Villa Allende en Córdoba, Argentina and Catholic Univ. of Louvain, Belgium; Pres. de la Fed. de Estudiantes Latino-Americanos (Belgium); Prof. of Sociology, Univ. Mayor de San Andrés; Prof. of Int. Relations, Dir Univ. Extension; f. Movimiento de la Izquierda Revolucionaria; cand. Vice-Pres. 1978 and 1980; first Vice-Pres. of the Andean Parl.; Vice-Pres. Repub. of Bolivia and Pres. Nat. Congress 1982–84; Pres. Repub. of Bolivia 1989–93; presidential cand. 2002; mem. Exec. Cttee of the Assoc. Latino-Americana de Derechos Humanos; mem. Movimiento de la Izquierda Revolucionaria (MIR). *Address:* Movimiento de la Izquierda Revolucionaria, Avda América 119, 2°, La Paz, Bolivia (Office). *E-mail:* mir@coibo.entelnet.bo (Office). *Website:* www.cibergallo.com (Office).

PAZNIAK, Zianon Stanislavavich; Belarus politician; b. 24 Apr. 1944; fmr anti-Communist dissident; founder mem. Belorussian Popular Front (BPF) Oct. 1988, Leader 1989–99, Chair. Conservative Christian Party of the BPF (breakaway faction) 1999–; elected to Supreme Soviet as mem. Belorussian Democratic Bloc 1990–; cand. in Pres. elections 1994; lives in Warsaw. *Address:* c/o Conservative Christian Party of the BPF, PO Box 208, 220040 Minsk, Belarus.

PEACOCK, Sir Alan, Kt, DSC, MA, FBA, FRSE; British economist; b. 26 June 1922, Ryton-on-Tyne; s. of Alexander D. Peacock and Clara M. Peacock; m. Margaret Martha Astell-Burt 1944; two s. one d.; ed Grove Acad., Dundee High School, Univ. of St Andrews; RN 1942–45; lecturer in Econs, Univ. of St Andrews 1947–48; lecturer in Econs, LSE 1948–51, Reader in Public Finance 1951–56; Prof. of Econ. Science, Univ. of Edinburgh 1956–62; Prof. of Econs, Univ. of York 1962–78; Prof. of Econs and Prin. Univ. Coll. at Buckingham 1980–83, Vice-Chancellor 1983–84, Prof. Emer. 1985–; Research Prof. in Public Finance, Heriot-Watt Univ. 1987–; Chief Econ. Adviser, Dept of Trade and Industry 1973–76; Pres. Int. Inst. of Public Finance 1966–69, Hon. Pres. 1975–; mem. Royal Comm. on Constitution 1970–73, Social Science Research Council 1971–72; Trustee, Inst. of Econ. Affairs; mem. Council, London Philharmonic Orchestra 1975–79; Chair. Arts Council Enquiry into Orchestral Resources 1969–70, Cttee on Financing the BBC 1985–86, Scottish Arts Council 1986–92; mem. Bd of Dirs. English Music Theatre Ltd 1975–77; Chair. Hebrides Ensemble 1994–2000; mem. Council of Man., Nat. Inst. of Econ. and Social Research 1977–86; non-exec. Dir Economist Intelligence Unit 1977–84; Exec. Dir David Hume Inst. 1985–90, Hon. Pres. 2002–(05); non-exec. Dir Caledonian Bank PLC 1989–96; Hon. mem. Royal Soc. of Musicians 1999–; Hon. Pres. Atlantic Econ. Soc. 1981–82; Hon. Fellow LSE 1980–; Foreign mem. Accademia Naz. dei Lincei, Rome 1996–; Keynes Lecturer, British Acad. 1994; Dr. hc (Stirling) 1974, (Catania) 1991, (Brunel) 1989, (York) 1997, (Lisbon) 2000, (Turin) 2001; Hon. DEcon (Zürich) 1984; Hon. DSc (Buckingham) 1986; Hon. D.Soc.Sci. (Edinburgh) 1990; Hon. LLD (St Andrews, Dundee) 1990; Scottish Free Enterprise Award 1987, Royal Soc. of Edinburgh 2002. *Publications:* Economics of National Insurance 1952, Growth of Public Expenditure in United Kingdom (with J. Wiseman) 1961, Economic Theory of Fiscal Policy (with G. K. Shaw) 1971, The Composer in the Market Place (with R. Weir) 1975, Welfare Economics: A Liberal Reinterpretation (with Charles Rowley), The Credibility of Liberal Economics 1977, The Economic Analysis of Government 1979, The Political Economy of Taxation (ed. with Francesco Forte) 1980, The Regulation Game (Ed.) 1984, Public Expenditure and Government Growth (Ed. with F. Forte) 1985, Corporate Takeovers and the Public Interest (with G. Bannock) 1991, Public Choice Analysis in Historical Perspective 1991, Paying the Piper: Culture, Music and Money 1993, Cultural Economics and Cultural Policies (Ed. with Ilde Rizzo), The Political Economy of Economic Freedom 1997, The Political Economy of Heritage (Ed.) 1998, What Price Civil Justice (with B. Main) 2000, Calling the Tune 2001, The Enigmatic Sailor 2003; and numerous articles in professional journals on economics, public finance, social policy. *Leisure interest:* trying to write music, wine spotting. *Address:* David Hume Institute, 25 Buccleuch Place, Edinburgh, EH8 9LD; 5/24 Oswald Road, Edinburgh, EH9 2HE, Scotland. *Telephone:* (131) 667-9609 (Office); (131) 667-5677 (Home). *Fax:* (131) 667-9609 (Office). *E-mail:* hume.institute@ed.ac.uk (Office); peacock@ebs.hw.ac.uk (Home). *Website:* www.ed.ac.uk/~hume/.

PEACOCK, Hon. Andrew Sharp, AC, LLB, MP; Australian diplomatist and fmr politician; b. 13 Feb. 1939, Melbourne; s. of the late A. S. Peacock and Iris Peacock; m. 1st Susan Peacock (divorced), three d.; m. 2nd Margaret Peacock 1983 (divorced); ed Scotch Coll., Univ. of Melbourne; Pres., Victorian Liberal Party 1965–66; mem. House of Reps. for Kooyong, Vic. 1966–94; fmr partner Rigby and Fielding, solicitors; fmr Chair. Peacock & Smith Pty Ltd, engineers; Minister for the Army and Minister Assisting the Prime Minister 1969–71, Assisting the Treas. 1971–72; Minister for External Territories 1972; mem. Opposition Exec. 1973–75, Spokesman on Foreign Affairs 1973–75; Minister for Foreign Affairs 1975–80, for the Environment Nov.–Dec. 1975, for Industrial Relations 1980–81, for Industry and Commerce 1982–83; Leader Parl. Liberal Party 1983–85; Opposition Spokesman on Foreign Affairs 1985–87; Deputy Leader of the Opposition and Shadow Treas. 1987–89; Leader of the Opposition 1989–90; Shadow Attorney-Gen. and Shadow Minister for Justice 1990–92; Shadow Minister for Trade 1992–93, for Foreign Affairs 1993–94; Chair. Parl. Political Strategy Cttee 1994; Amb. to USA 1997–2000; Chair. Int. Democrat Union 1989–92, Australian Horse Council 1996. *Leisure interests:* horse racing, Australian Rules Football, surfing, reading. *Address:* 19 Queens Road, Melbourne, Vic. 3004, Australia (Home).

PEACOCK, William James, AC, PhD, FRS, FAA, FAIAS, FTSE; Australian research scientist; b. 14 Dec. 1937, Leura, NSW; s. of William Edward Peacock and Evelyn Alison Peacock; m. Margaret Constance Woodward 1961; one s. two d.; ed Univ. of Sydney; Visiting Research Scientist, Genetics, CSIRO, Canberra 1963; Fellow, Dept of Biology, Univ. of Oregon 1963–64, Visiting Assoc. Prof. 1964–65; Research Consultant, Biology Div., Oak Ridge Nat. Lab., USA 1965; Sr Research Scientist, Div. of Plant Industry, CSIRO, Canberra 1965–69, Prin. Research Scientist 1969–73, Sr Prin. Research Scientist 1973–77, Chief Research Scientist 1977–78, Chief 1978–; Pres. Australian Acad. of Science 2002–; Adjunct Prof. of Biology, Univ. of Calif., San Diego 1969–70; Visiting Prof. of Biochem., Stanford Univ. 1970–71; Visiting Distinguished Prof. of Molecular Biology, Univ. of Calif., Los Angeles 1977; Scientific Adviser, Australian Genetic Eng Ltd; Foreign Fellow, Indian Nat. Science Acad. 1990; Foreign Assoc., NAS 1990; Hon. DSc 1996; Edgeworth David Medal, Royal Soc. of NSW 1967, Lemberg Medal, Australian Biochemical Soc. 1978, N.I. Vavilov Medal 1987, BHP Bicentennial Prize 1988, Burnet Medal, Australian Acad. of Science 1989, CSIRO Medal 1989, Farrer Memorial Medal 1999, Prime Minister's Science Prize 2000. *Publications:* 310 research papers on molecular biology, cytogenetics and evolution; ed. of six books. *Leisure interests:* squash, bush-walking. *Address:* CSIRO Plant Industry, G.P.O. Box 1600, Canberra, ACT 2601 (Office); 16 Brassey Street, Deakin, ACT 2600, Australia (Home). *Telephone:* (2) 6246-5250 (Office); (2) 6281-4485 (Home). *Fax:* (2) 6246-5530. *E-mail:* jim.peacock@csiro.au (Office).

PEACOCKE, Christopher Arthur Bruce, DPhil, FBA; British professor of philosophy; b. 22 May 1950, Birmingham; s. of Arthur Peacocke and Rosemary Peacocke; m. Teresa Rosen 1980; one s. one d.; ed Magdalen Coll. School, Exeter Coll. Oxford and Harvard Univ. (Kennedy Scholar); Sr Scholar, Merton Coll. Oxford 1972–73; Jr Research Fellow, Queen's Coll. Oxford 1973–76; Visiting Lecturer, Univ. of Calif. Berkeley 1975–76; Prize Fellow, All Souls Coll. Oxford 1975–79; Visiting Prof. Univ. of Mich. 1978; Fellow, New Coll., Oxford and Common Univ. Fund Lecturer in Philosophy, Oxford Univ. 1979–85; Visiting Prof. Univ. of Calif. Los Angeles 1981; Visiting Fellow, Australian Nat. Univ. Canberra 1981, 1998; Fellow, Center for Advanced Study in Behavioural Sciences, Stanford 1983–84; Susan Stebbing Prof. of Philosophy, King's Coll. London 1985–88; Pres. Mind Asscn 1986; Waynflete Prof. of Metaphysical Philosophy, Oxford Univ. and Fellow of Magdalen Coll. Oxford 1989–2000; Leverhulme Research Professorship 1996–2000; Visiting Prof. New York Univ. 1996–2000, Prof. of Philosophy 2000–; Wilde Prize 1971, Webb-Medley Prize 1971, John Locke Prize 1972; Whitehead Lecturer, Harvard Univ. 2001. *Publications:* Holistic Explanation: Action, Space, Interpretation 1979, Sense and Content 1983, Thoughts: An Essay on Content 1986, A Study of Concepts 1992, Being Known 1999; papers in Philosophical Review, Journal of Philosophy etc. *Leisure interests:* music, visual arts. *Address:* Department of Philosophy, Room 503, New York University, 100 Washington Square East, Main Building, New York, NY 10003, USA (Office). *Telephone:* (212) 998-3559. *Fax:* (212) 995-4179.

PEARCE, Sir Austin William, Kt, CBE, F.R.ENG., PhD; British business executive; b. 1 Sept. 1921, Plymouth; s. of late William T. Pearce and of Florence Pearce; m. 1st Maglona Winifred Twinn 1947 (died 1975), 2nd Florence Patricia Grice 1979 (died 1993); three d. and two step-d.; ed Devonport High School for Boys, Birmingham Univ. and Harvard Business School; joined Esso Petroleum Co. 1945, Dir 1963–80, Man. Dir 1968–71, Chair. 1972–80, Dir Esso Europe Inc. 1972–80; Chair. Irish Refining Co. Ltd 1965–71, UK Petroleum Industry Advisory Cttee 1977–80; Pres. Inst. of Petroleum 1968–70; Pres. Pipeline Industries Guild 1973–75; Pres. Oil Industries Club 1975–76; Pres. UK Petroleum Industry Asscn 1979–80; Vice-Pres. Soc. of British Aerospace Cos. 1981–82, Pres. 1982–83; Vice-Pres. Eng Employers' Group 1983–87; Dir Williams and Glyn's Bank Ltd 1974–85, Deputy Chair. 1980–83, Chair. 1983–85; Dir Royal Bank of Scotland Group 1978–92, a Vice-Chair. 1985–92; Dir British Aerospace 1977–87, Chair. 1980–87; Chair. Oxford Instruments 1987–91; Dir Pearl Assurance PLC 1985–91, Jaguar PLC 1986–93, Smiths Industries 1987–92, Home Group Ltd 1998–2001, Pres. 2001–; Chair. CBI Industrial Policy Cttee 1982–85; Chair. Warden Housing Asscn 1994–2001, Martlets Hospice 1994–98; mem. Advi-

sory Council on Energy Conservation 1974–80, Energy Comm. 1977–79; mem. of Bd, English-Speaking Union 1974–80; mem. Comm. on Energy and the Environment 1978–81; Chair of Trustees Science Museum, London 1986–94; Pro-Chancellor Univ. of Surrey 1985–94, Pro-Chancellor Emer. 1994–; mem. Takeover Panel 1987–92; Patron Nat. Training Awards 1988; Treasurer Royal Soc. of Arts 1988–93; Hon. DSc (Exeter, Southampton) 1985, (Salford, Cranfield) 1987; Hon. D.Eng (Birmingham) 1986; Hon. D.Univ. (Surrey) 1993. *Leisure interests:* golf, general handicrafts. *Address:* Treeps House, 2 High Street, Hurstpierpoint, West Sussex, BN6 9TY, England. *Telephone:* (1273) 832927. *Fax:* (1273) 832927 (Home).

PEARCE, Sir (Daniel Norton) Idris, Kt, CBE, TD, DL, FRICS; British chartered surveyor; b. 28 Nov. 1933, Neath; s. of Lemeul George Douglas Pearce and Evelyn Mary Pearce; m. Ursula Helene Langley 1963 (divorced 1997); two d.; ed West Buckland School, Coll. of Estate Man.; joined Richard Ellis 1959, Partner 1961–92, Man. Partner 1981–87, Consultant 1992–2000; Chair. English Estates 1989–94; Chair. Higher Educ. Funding Council for Wales 1992–96; mem. Advisory Panel for Institutional Finance in New Towns 1974–80; mem. Property Services Agency Advisory Bd 1981–86; Property Adviser to Nat. Health Service Man. Bd 1985–90; mem. FCO Advisory Panel on Diplomatic Estate 1982–85, Financial Reporting Review Panel 1991–92, UFC 1991–93; Vice-Chair. Greater London TA & VRA 1991–94; mem. Gen. Council The Royal Inst. of Chartered Surveyors 1989–95, mem. Exec. Cttee 1984–91, Pres. 1990–91, Chair. Int. Assets Valuation Standards Cttee 1981–86; mem. Higher Educ. Funding Council for England 1992–96; Deputy Chair. Urban Regeneration Agency 1993–2000; Dir (non-exec.) Swan Hill 1993–2002, Nat. Mortgage Bank 1992–97, Innisfree Man. Ltd 1996–, Redburgh Ltd 1996–98, Millennium and Copthorne Hotels PLC 1996–; Gov. Peabody Trust 1992–; Pro-Chancellor Surrey Univ. 1994–; Chair. Council Surrey Univ. 1997–2000; Hon. DSc (City Univ., London, Salford Univ., Oxford Polytechnic); Hon. DSc Tech. (Univ. of E London); Hon. DEng (Bristol, Univ. of W of England); Thames Polytechnic, Centenary Fellowship 1991; Hon. Fellow, Coll. of Estate Man., Univ. of Wales, Cardiff 1997; Hon. Col, 135 Independent Topographic Squadron Royal Engineers (V). *Publications:* Profession of the Land—A Future; articles on valuation and property matters. *Leisure interests:* reading, opera, ballet, travel.

PEARCE, David William, OBE, MA, D.SC.; British professor of economics; b. 11 Oct. 1941, Harrow; s. of William Pearce and Gladys Pearce; m. Susan M. Reynolds 1966; two s.; ed Harrow Weald County Grammar School and Lincoln Coll. Oxford; Sr lecturer in Econs Southampton Univ. 1967–74; Dir Public Sector Econs Research Centre, Leicester Univ. 1974–77; Prof. of Econs Aberdeen Univ. 1977–83, Univ. Coll. London 1983–; Dir Centre for Social and Econ. Research on the Global Environment (CSERGE), Univ. Coll. London 1990–2001; Sr Assoc. Oxera Ltd 2000–; Adviser to Sec. of State for Environment 1989–92; UN Global 500 Award for Services to World Environment; Giuseppe Mazzotti Prize for Literature. *Publications:* Blueprint for a Green Economy 1989, Economics of Natural Resources and the Environment 1990, Sustainable Development 1990, Economic Valuation and the Natural World 1993, World Without End (jtly) 1993, Economics of Biodiversity 1994, The Causes of Tropical Deforestation (jtly) 1994, Blueprint 4: Sustaining the Earth: Capturing Global Value 1995, Blueprint 5: The Social Costs of Road Transport (jtly) 1996, Acid Rain: Counting the Cost (Co-Ed.) 1997, Economics and the Environment 1999, Blueprint 6: Towards a Sustainable Economy 2000. *Leisure interests:* collecting antique porcelain/china, birdwatching. *Address:* Department of Economics, University College London, Gower Street, London, WC1E 6BT (Office); Whitefriars Farm, Duddenhoe End, Saffron Walden, Essex, CB11 4UU, England (Home). *Telephone:* (20) 7679-5898 (Office); (1763) 838332 (Home). *Fax:* (20) 7916-2772 (Office); (1763) 837106 (Home). *E-mail:* d.pearce@ucl.ac.uk (Office); d.pearce@ucl.ac.uk (Home).

PEARCE, Reynold, MA; British fashion designer; ed Nottingham Trent Univ., Cen. St Martin's Coll. of Art and Design; worked for John Galliano (q.v.); design asst for Roland Klein; launched Pearce Fionda collection with Andrew Fionda (q.v.) 1994; with Andrew Fionda received British Apparel Export Award for Best New Designer 1994, New Generation Award Lloyds Bank British Fashion Award 1995, Int. Apparel Fed. World Young Designers Award 1996, Glamour Category Award (British Fashion Awards) 1997. *Address:* Pearce Fionda, The Loft, 27 Horsell Road, Highbury, London, N5 1XL, England. *Telephone:* (20) 7609-6470. *Fax:* (20) 7609-6470. *E-mail:* pearce@dircon.co.uk.

PEARL, Valerie Louise, DPhil, F.R.H.S., FSA; British professor of history and college president; b. 31 Dec. 1926, Newport, Mon.; d. of the late C. R. Bence, MP and F. Bowler; m. Morris L. Pearl 1949; one d.; ed King Edward VI High School, Birmingham and St Anne's Coll. Oxford; Sr Research Studentship, Westfield Coll. London 1962; Leverhulme Research Award 1962; Graham Research Fellow, lecturer in History, Somerville Coll. Oxford 1965–68; Reader in History of London, Univ. Coll. London 1968–76, Prof. 1976–81; Pres. New Hall, Cambridge 1981–1995; Founder and Ed.-in-Chief, The London Journal 1973–77; McBride Visiting Prof. Bryn Mawr Coll. Pennsylvania 1974; Woodward Lecturer, Yale Univ. 1974; Literary Dir Royal Historical Soc. 1975–77; Gov. Museum of London 1978–92; Stow Commemorative Lecturer 1979; Ford Special Lecturer, Oxford 1980; Syndic, Cambridge Univ. Library, Cambridge Univ. Press 1982–92; Commr Royal Comm. on Historical Manuscripts 1983–92; Hon. Fellow St Anne's Coll. Oxford. *Publications:* London and the Outbreak of the Puritan Revolution 1625–43 1961, Contrib.

to The Interregnum; Puritans and Revolutionaries, Co-Ed. and Contrib. History and Imagination (vol. in honour of Hugh Trevor-Roper) 1981, Ed. Stow's Survey of London 1985, Change and Continuity in 17th-Century London 1981 (Japanese Edn 1992); articles and contribs. to books, encyclopedias and learned journals. *Leisure interests:* walking, gardening, swimming. *Address:* c/o New Hall, Cambridge, CB3 0DF, England. *Telephone:* (1223) 351721.

PEARLSTEIN, Philip, MA; American artist; b. 24 May 1924, Pittsburgh; s. of David Pearlstein and Libbie Kalser; m. Dorothy Cantor 1950; one s. two d.; ed Carnegie Inst. of Tech. and New York Univ.; Instructor Pratt Inst. 1959–63; visiting critic, Yale 1962–63; Asst Prof. to Prof., Art Dept Brooklyn Coll. 1963–82, now Distinguished Prof. Emer.; participant in numerous group exhbns at Whitney Museum of American Art and elsewhere; work in perm. collections including Whitney Museum and Museum of Modern Art, New York; mem. American Acad. of Arts and Letters; Fulbright Fellow 1958–59; Guggenheim Fellow 1971–72. *Solo exhibitions include:* Allan Frumkin Gallery, New York 1962–83, Frumkin Gallery Chicago 1960–81, Galerie Rudolph Zwirner, Cologne, Germany 1991, Il Politico, Rome 1997, Simon Capstick Dale, London 1998, Daniel Templon Paris 1998, Galerie Chariotte Moser, Geneva 1999 and other galleries in USA, UK and Europe.

PEARLSTINE, Norman, LLB; American journalist; b. 4 Oct. 1942, Philadelphia; s. of Raymond Pearlstine and Gladys Pearlstine (née Cohen); m. Nancy Colbert Friday 1988; ed Haverford Coll., Univ. of Pennsylvania; staff reporter Wall Street Journal, Dallas, Detroit, LA 1968–73, Tokyo Bureau Chief 1973–76, Man. Ed. Asian Wall Street Journal, Hong Kong 1976–78; Exec. Ed. Forbes Magazine, LA 1978–80; Nat. News Ed. Wall Street Journal, New York 1980–82, Ed. and Publr Wall Street Journal Europe, Brussels 1982–83, Man. Ed. and Vice-Pres. Wall Street Journal, New York 1983–91, Exec. Ed. 1991–92; Pres. and CEO Friday Holdings L.P., New York 1993–94; Ed.-in-Chief Time Inc. 1994–; mem. New York Historical Soc., Council on Foreign Relations; Ed. of Year Award, Nat. Press Foundation 1989. *Address:* Time Inc., 1271 Avenue of the Americas, New York, NY 10020, USA.

PEARSE, Barbara Mary Frances, BSc, PhD, FRS; British/Swiss scientist; b. 24 March 1948, England; d. of Reginald W. B. Pearse, DSc, FRAS and Enid Alice (née Mitchell) Pearse; m. Mark Steven Bretscher 1978; one s. one d.; ed Lady Eleanor Holles School and Univ. Coll., London; Postdoctoral Fellow MRC Lab. of Molecular Biology 1972–81, staff scientist 1981–; Visiting Prof. Stanford Medical Center, USA 1984–85; mem. European Molecular Biology Org; Fellow Univ. Coll. London 1996; Jack Drummond Prize 1968, K.M. Stott Prize 1979, European Molecular Biology Org. Gold Medal 1987. *Publication:* European Molecular Biology Org. Review 1987. *Leisure interests:* garden and woodland. *Address:* Medical Research Council, Laboratory of Molecular Biology, Hills Road, Cambridge, CB2 2QH (Office); Ram Cottage, 63 Commercial End, Swaffham Bulbeck, Cambridge, CB5 0ND, England (Home). *Telephone:* (1223) 248011 (Office); (1223) 811276 (Home). *Fax:* (1223) 412142 (Office). *Website:* www2.mrc-lmb.cam.ac.uk (Office).

PEARSE, Sir Brian, Kt, FCIB; British banker; b. 23 Aug. 1933; s. of Francis and Eileen Pearse; m. Patricia M. Callaghan 1959; one s. two d.; ed St Edward's Coll., Liverpool; joined Martin's Bank Ltd 1950; joined Barclays Bank 1969, Local Dir, Birmingham 1972, Gen. Man. 1977, CEO, N America 1983, Finance Dir Barclays Bank PLC 1987–91; Chief Exec. Midland Bank 1991–94; Pres. Chartered Inst. of Bankers 1993–94; Chair. Housing Corpn 1994–97, British Invisibles 1994–97, Lucas Industries PLC 1994–96, Lucas-Varity PLC 1996–98; Dir British American Chamber of Commerce 1987–98; Dir (non-exec.) Smith & Nephew 1993–; Dir British Overseas Trade Board 1994–97; Gov. Univ. of Plymouth 1997– (Vice-Chair. 1999–); Deputy Chair. Britannic Assurance PLC 1997–; mem. Bd of Banking Supervision 1998–. *Leisure interests:* rugby football, opera. *Address:* Flat 7, 14 Glouster Street, London, SW1V 2DN, England (Home).

PEARSON, Ralph Gottfried, PhD; American professor of chemistry; b. 12 Jan. 1919, Chicago, Ill.; s. of Gottfried Pearson and Kerstin Pearson (née Larson); m. Lenore Johnson 1941 (died 1982); two s. one d.; ed Lewis Inst., Northwestern Univ.; First Lt USAF 1944–46; Asst Prof. Chem. Dept, Northwestern Univ. 1946–52, Assoc. Prof. 1952–57, Prof. 1957–76; Prof. of Chem. Univ. of Calif., Santa Barbara 1976–89, Prof. Emer. 1989–; mem. NAS; fmr Guggenheim Fellow; Inorganic Award, American Chemical Soc., Chemical Pioneer Award, American Inst. of Chemists 1995. *Publications:* Kinetics and Mechanism 1953, Mechanisms of Inorganic Reactions 1958, Hard and Soft Acids and Bases 1974, Symmetry Rules for Chemical Reactions 1976, Chemical Hardness 1997. *Leisure interests:* classical music, hiking. *Address:* c/o Chemistry Department, University of California, Santa Barbara, CA 93106 (Office); 715 Grove Lane, Santa Barbara, CA 93105, USA (Home). *Telephone:* (805) 893-3745 (Office); (805) 687-7890 (Home). *Fax:* (805) 893-4120 (Office).

PEARSON, W. Robert, BA, LLB; American diplomatist; b. 28 June 1943; ed Vanderbilt Univ., Univ. of Virginia; posted to New Zealand 1976–78, China 1981–83, NATO, Brussels 1987–90, 1993–97, Paris 1997–2000; Amb. to Turkey 2000–. *Leisure interest:* golf. *Address:* Embassy of USA, Ataturk Bul. 110, Kavaklidere, Ankara, Turkey (Office). *Telephone:* (312) 4555555 (Office).

PEART, Sir (William) Stanley, Kt, MB, BS, MD, FRCP, FRS; British professor of medicine; b. 31 March 1922, South Shields; s. of J. G. Peart and M. Peart; m. Peggy Parkes 1947 (died 2002); one s. one d.; ed King's Coll. School, Wimbledon and St Mary's Hospital Medical School, London; Lecturer in Medicine, St Mary's Hospital, London 1950–56, Prof. of Medicine 1956–87, Prof. Emer. 1987–; Master, Hunterian Inst. Royal Coll. of Surgeons 1988–92; Chair. Medical Research Soc. 1968, Beit Trust Advisory Bd 1980, Northwick Park Inst. for Medical Research 1994–; mem. Medical Research Council 1969; mem. Advisory Bd for the Research Councils 1973; Trustee, Wellcome Trust 1975–94 (Deputy Chair. 1991–94, Consultant 1994–99); Councillor, Royal Coll. of Physicians 1977; Stouffer Prize 1968; Buchanan Medal, Royal Soc. 2000. *Publications:* Clinical Atlas of Hypertension 1991; articles in The Biochemical Journal, Journal of Physiology, The Lancet; chapters in textbooks on renal disease and high blood pressure. *Leisure interests:* reading, photography, astronomy. *Address:* 17 Highgate Close, London, N6 4SD, England. *Telephone:* (20) 8341-3111. *Fax:* (20) 8341-3111.

PEASE, Rendel Sebastian, MA, ScD, FRS; British physicist; b. 2 Nov. 1922, Cambridge; s. of Michael Stewart Pease and Helen Bowen Pease (née Wedgwood); m. 1st Susan Spickernell 1952 (died 1996); two s. three d.; m. 2nd Jean Frances White 1998 (died 2000); ed Bedales School and Trinity Coll., Cambridge; Scientific Officer, Ministry of Aircraft Production at Operational Research Unit, HQ, RAF Bomber Command 1942–46; Research at AERE, Harwell 1947–61; Div. Head, Culham Lab. for Plasma Physics and Nuclear Fusion, UK Atomic Energy Authority (UKAEA) 1961–67, Dir of Culham Lab. 1968–81, Programme Dir of Fusion 1981–87; Gordon-Godfrey Visiting Prof. of Theoretical Physics, Univ. of NSW 1984, 1988, 1991; Chair. British Pugwash Group 1988–2002, Council mem. Pugwash Confs. on Science and World Affairs 1992–; Consultant Pease Partners 1988–96; Royal Soc. Assessor, Nuclear Physics Board, SERC 1987–93; Visitor, Blackett Lab., Imperial Coll. 1991–2000; Visiting Scientist, Princeton Univ. 1964–65; Asst Dir UKAEA Research Group 1967; Vice-Pres. Inst. of Physics 1973–77, Pres. 1978–80; Vice-Pres. Royal Soc. 1986–87; Chair. Int. Fusion Research Council 1976–84, Plasma Physics Comm., IUPAP. 1976–78, W Ilsley Parish Council 1996–2000; Hon. DUniv (Surrey) 1973; Hon. DSc (Aston) 1981, (City) 1987; Hon. Fellow European Nuclear Soc. 1990; Kelvin Premium (IEE) 1959, Glazebrook Medal (I.O.P.) 1988. *Publications:* Controlled Thermonuclear Reactions 1964, Does Britain Need Nuclear Weapons? (co-author) 1995, An End to British Nuclear Weapons (co-author) 2002. *Leisure interest:* music. *Address:* The Poplars, West Ilsley, Newbury, Berks. RG20 7AW, England. *Telephone:* (1635) 281237. *Fax:* (1635) 281688. *E-mail:* baspease@w-ilsley .freeserve.co.uk (Office).

PÉBEREAU, Georges Alexandre; French engineer and business executive; b. 20 July 1931, Digne, Basses-Alpes; s. of Alexandre Pébereau and Yvonne Raybaud; m. Bernadette Potier 1954; three d.; ed Lycées Buffon, Saint-Louis, Paris, Ecole Polytechnique; engineer roads and bridges in various wards 1955–64; Pres. Asscn des ingénieurs des ponts et chaussées 1964; teacher of Urban Man. École nat. des ponts et chaussées 1964; Chief-Eng, Dept Seine-St-Denis 1965, Tech. Counsellor to Ministry of Equipment 1966, Dir Office Ministry of Equipment and Housing 1967–68; Dir Land and Urban Man. 1966–68; Vice-Pres. Cttee action concertée Urbanisation 1967–68; at Cie industrielle des télécommunications (Cit) 1968–70, Jt Dir-Gen. 1968–69, Dir-Gen. 1969–70; Admin.-Dir-Gen. Cie industrielle des télécommunications (Cit-Alcatel) 1970–83, Pres., Dir-Gen. 1982–86, Hon. Pres. 1986–; at Cie Gén d'électricité 1970–86, Dir then Jt Dir-Gen. 1970–72, Admin. 1971, Dir-Gen. 1972, then Chair., Pres. and CEO Admin., Dir –1986; Hon. Pres. 1986; Co-owner Cie Privée de Banque 1987; Chair. Marceau Investissements 1997–, Indra Finance 1987–95; Pres. Délia Finance 1997–; Dir numerous Eng cos.; mem. Cttee de direction et de conseil d'admin. 1970–; mem. conseil d'admin. de la Société des sucreries de Bourbon 1995–, of Musée du Louvre 1996; Commdr Légion d'honneur, Commdr, Ordre nat. du Mérite. *Address:* Marceau investissements, 10-12 Avenue de Mesine, 75008 Paris (Office); 19 avenue Charles Floquet, 75007 Paris, France (Home).

PÉBEREAU, Michel Jean Denis; French banker; b. 23 Jan. 1942, Paris; s. of Alexandre Pébereau and Yvonne Raybaud; m. Agnès Faure 1962; two s. two d.; ed Lycées Buffon and Louis-le-Grand, Paris, Ecole Polytechnique and Ecole Nat. d'Admin.; various appts. in Ministry of Economy and Finance 1970–81; Man. Dir Crédit Commercial de France 1982–87; Chair. and CEO 1987–93; Chair. and CEO Banque Nationale de Paris (BNP) 1993–2000; Dir BNP, Cie Européenne de Publication, SA des Galeries Lafayette, Lafarge Coppée, Saint-Gobain, Lagardère Groupe, Rhône Poulenc, Elf, U.A.P., Renault, Financière BNP, Cie d'Investissements de Paris, Banque Pour l'Expansion Industrielle, BNP UK Holdings Ltd; Chair. Banking Operations Comm. of Asscn Française des Banques; Deputy Chair. Comm. for Control of Cinema Films 1981–85, Comm. for Selective Aid for Film Distribution 1987–88; Lecturer Inst. d'Etudes Politiques Paris 1967–78, Prof. 1980–, mem. Man. Cttee 1984–; Lecturer Ecole Nat. de Statistiques et d'Admin. Economique 1968–79; Inspecteur Général des Finances; mem. Supervisory Bd Axa-UAP 1997–, Dresdner Bank 1997–; mem. Int. Capital Markets Advisory Cttee Fed. Reserve Bank, New York 1998; Pres. Comm. d'exploitation bancaire de l'Association française des banques 2000; Chair. Paribas 1999–; Officier, Légion d'honneur; Officier, Ordre nat. du Mérite. *Publications:* La politique économique de la France (3 Vols); science fiction book reviews for scientific magazine La Recherche 1983–. *Leisure interest:* piano. *Address:* BNP Paribas, 16 boulevard des Italiens, 75009 Paris; 14 bis rue Mouton-Duvernet, 75014 Paris, France. *Website:* www.bnpparibas.com (Office).

PECK, Gregory, BA; American actor; b. 5 April 1916, La Jolla, Calif.; m. 1st Greta Konen Rice 1942 (divorced 1954); two s. (one s. deceased); m. 2nd Veronique Passani 1955, one s. one d.; ed California Univ.; mem. Nat. Council on Arts 1965–67, 1968–; Pres. Acad. of Motion Picture Arts and Sciences 1967–70; Medal of Freedom Award 1969; Acad. Award (Oscar) best actor 1962; Screen Actors' Guild Annual Award for Outstanding Achievement 1970; Acad. of Motion Picture Arts and Sciences Jean Hersholt Humanitarian Award 1968, Life Achievement Award 1988, Career Award, Cannes Film Festival 1989, Mama Anderson Award 1999; Commdr, Ordre des Arts et des Lettres (France), Kennedy Center Honor 1991, Officier, Légion d'honneur. *Appeared in plays including:* The Doctor's Dilemma, The Male Animal, Once in a Lifetime, The Play's the Thing, You Can't Take it With You, The Morning Star, The Willow and I, Sons and Soldiers. *Films include:* Days of Glory 1943, Keys of the Kingdom 1944, Spellbound 1945, The Valley of Decision 1945, Duel in the Sun 1946, The Macomber Affair 1947, Gentleman's Agreement 1947, The Paradine Case 1948, Yellow Sky 1949, Twelve O'Clock High 1949, The Great Sinner 1949, Captain Horatio Hornblower 1951, David and Bathsheba 1951, The Snows of Kilimanjaro 1952, Roman Holiday 1953, The Purple Plain 1954, The Man in the Grey Flannel Suit 1956, Moby Dick 1956, Designing Woman 1957, The Big Country, The Bravados 1958, Pork Chop Hill 1959, On the Beach 1959, Beloved Infidel 1959, Guns of Navarone 1961, Cape Fear 1962, To Kill a Mocking Bird 1962, How the West Was Won 1963, Captain Newman, MD 1963, Behold a Pale Horse 1964, Mirage 1964, Arabesque 1965, The Stalking Moon 1968, Mackenna's Gold 1969, The Chairman 1969, Marooned 1969, I Walk the Line 1970, Shoot Out 1971, Billy Two-Hats 1972, The Omen 1976, MacArthur 1977, The Boys from Brazil 1978, The Sea Wolves 1980, The Blue and the Gray 1981 (TV), The Scarlet and the Black 1983 (TV), Amazing Grace and Chuck 1987, The Old Gringo 1989, Other People's Money, Cape Fear 1991, Sinatra: 80 Years My Way 1995, A Salute to Martin Scorsese 1997, Moby Dick 1998; producer The Dove 1974, The Portrait 1993. *Address:* c/o Academy of Motion Picture Arts and Sciences, 8949 Wilshire Boulevard, Beverly Hills, CA 90211, USA.

PECKER, David J., CPA; American publishing executive; b. 24 Sept. 1951; m. Karen Balan 1987; ed Pace and New York Univs; fmrly Sr Auditor Price Waterhouse & Co.; fmrly Man. Financial Reporting Diamandis Communications Inc., also Dir Financial Reporting, Dir Accounting, Asst Controller; Exec. Vice-Pres. Hachette Magazines Inc. 1990–91, Pres. 1991–92, Pres., CEO 1992–99; Chair., CEO American Media Inc. 1999–; mem. Fashion Group's Int. Advisory Bd, NY City Partnership Cttee, American Man. Asscn; mem. Bd Dirs. Pace Univ., Drug Enforcement Agents Foundation 1995–. *Address:* American Media Inc., 600 East Coast Avenue, Lake Worth, FL 33464, USA (Office).

PECKER, Jean-Claude (Jean-Claude Pradel); French astronomer; b. 10 May 1923, Reims; s. of Victor-Noel Pecker and Nelly Catherine Herrmann; m. 2nd Annie A. Vormser 1974 (died 2002); one s. two d. (by previous m.); ed Lycée de Bordeaux, Univs of Grenoble and Paris (Sorbonne) and Ecole Normale Supérieure; Research Asst CNRS 1946–52; Assoc. Prof. Univ. of Clermont-Ferrand 1952–55; Assoc. Astronomer, Paris Observatory 1955–62, Astronomer 1962–65; Dir Nice Observatory 1962–69; Dir Inst. of Astrophysics, Paris 1972–79; Prof. Coll. de France 1963–89, Hon. Prof. 1989–; Asst Gen. Sec. Int. Astronomical Union 1961–63, Gen. Sec. 1964–67; Pres. Comité Nat. Français d'Astronomie 1970–73; Dir Inst. Astrophysique, Paris 1971–78; Pres. Soc. Astronomique de France 1973–76; Pres. French Asscn for Advancement of Science 1978; Chair. Orientation Cttee, Sciences-Industries Museum, La Villette 1983–85; Chair. Nat. Cttee Scientific and Tech. Culture 1985–87; Vice-Chair. French Comm. for UNESCO 1991–96; Perm. Rep. to UNESCO of Int. Humanist and Ethical Union; Vice-Chair. Scientific Cttee Musées de France 1988–; Assoc. Royal Soc. of Science, Liège 1967; Corresp. Bureau des Longitudes 1968; Assoc. Royal Astronomical Soc. 1968; Corresp. mem. Acad. des Sciences, France 1969, mem. 1977; mem. Acad. Nat. Bordeaux 1977, Acad. Royale Belgique 1979, Acad. European of Science, Arts and Letters 1982, Int. Acad. of Humanism 1983 (Sec.), Acad. Europaea 1988 (Council mem., Vice-Pres. 1989–92), Pres. Asscn française d'information scientifique 1999–2001; Prix Forthuny, Inst. de France, Prix Stroobant Acad. des Sciences de Belgique 1965, Prix Manley-Bendall de l'Acad. de Bordeaux 1966, Prix des Trois Physiciens 1969; Janssen Medal Astronomical Soc., France 1967, Prix Jean Perrin, Soc. Française de Physique 1973, Medal Univ. de Nice 1972, Adion Medal 1981, Prix Union Rationaliste 1983, Personnalité de l'année 1984, Janssen Medal (Photographic Soc. of France) 1989, Lodén Prize, Royal Astronomical Soc. of Sweden 1996; Commdr, Palmes académiques, Commdr Légion d'honneur, Grand Officier, Ordre nat. du Mérite. *Art exhibitions include:* murals at Collège de France and Int. Council of Scientific Unions; collective exhbns at Clermont-Ferrand and Paris. *Radio includes:* many programmes on popular astronomy 1957–. *Television includes:* many programmes on popular science. *Publications include:* L'astronomie au jour le jour (with P. Couderc and E. Schatzman) 1954, Astrophysique générale (with E. Schatzman) 1959, Le ciel 1959, L'astronomie expérimentale 1969, Les laboratoires spatiaux 1969, Papa, dis-moi: L'astronomie, qu'est-ce que c'est? 1971; Ed. L'astronomie nouvelle 1971, Clefs pour l'astronomie 1981, Sous l'étoile soleil 1984, Astronomie (Ed.) 1985, Pour comprendre l'univers (with Delsemme and Reeves) 1988, L'avenir du soleil 1990, Le promeneur du ciel 1992, Le soleil est une étoile 1992, Débat sur les phénomènes paranormaux 1997, Understanding the Universe 2001, L'Univers 2003. *Leisure interests:* painting, poetry, swimming, sailing. *Address:* Annexe du Collège de France, 3 rue d'Ulm, 75005 Paris (Office); Pusat-Tasek, Les Corbeaux, 85350 L'Ile d'Yeu, France (Home). *Telephone:* 1-44-27-16-95 (Collège de France). *Fax:* 1-44-27-11-85 (Collège de France); 2-51-59-43-59 (L'Ile d'Yeu). *E-mail:* j.c.pecker@wanadoo.fr (Office); j.c.pecker@wanadoo.fr (Home).

PECKHAM, Sir Michael John, Kt, MA, MD, FRCP, FRCPath, FRCR, FRCS; British medical practitioner and university professor; b. 2 Aug. 1935, Panteg, Wales; s. of Gladys Mary Peckham (née Harris) and William Stuart Peckham; m. Catherine Stevenson King 1958; three s.; ed St Catharine's Coll. Cambridge, Univ. Coll. Hosp. Medical School; Sr Lecturer, Inst. of Cancer Research 1972–74, Prof. and Hon. Consultant, Inst. of Cancer Research and Royal Marsden Hosp. 1974–86, Dean Inst. of Cancer Research 1984–86; Dir British Postgrad. Medical Fed. 1986–90; Ed.-in-Chief European Journal of Cancer 1990–95; Dir of Research and Devt, Dept of Health 1991–95; Dir School of Public Policy, Univ. Coll. London 1996–2000; Vice-Chair. Imperial Cancer Research Fund 1987–90; Chair. Office of Science and Tech. Healthcare Foresight Programme 1999–2000, Nat. Educational Research Forum 2000–, Develt Forum 2000–; Founding Pres. British Oncological Asscn 1986–88; Pres. Fed. of European Cancer Socs. 1989–91, European Soc. for Therapeutic Radiology and Oncology 1983–85; Foreign Assoc. mem. NAS Inst. of Medicine 1994–; Hon. Fellow St Catharine's Coll., Cambridge 1998; Hon. Dr. (Besançon); Dr. hc (Catholic Univ. of Louvain) 1993; Hon. DSc (Loughborough), (Exeter) 1996. *Art Exhibitions:* ten solo exhbns., Edin., London, Oxford. *Publications:* Oxford Textbook of Oncology (Jt) 1995, Clinical Futures 1999, A Model for Health: Innovation and the Future of Health Services 2000. *Address:* School of Public Policy, University College London, 29 Tavistock Square, London, WC1H 9QU; 9 Ennismore Mews, London, SW7 1AP, England (Home). *Telephone:* (20) 7679-4966 (Office). *Fax:* (20) 7679-4969. *E-mail:* m.peckham@ucl.ac.uk (Office).

PECKOVÁ, Dagmar; Czech opera singer (mezzo soprano); b. 4 April 1961, Chrudim; m. 1st J. Vejvoda; m.2nd Aleš Kaspřík 1997; one s.; m. 3rd Klaus Schiesser; one d.; ed Prague Conservatory; with Music Theatre, Prague 1982–85; soloist with numerous cos including Czech Philharmonic 1985–, with Semper Opera, Dresden 1985–88, with State Opera Berlin 1989–91; concert tours Austria, Switzerland, Germany, UK, France, USA 1997–99; charity concerts after floods in Czech Repub. 2002; lives in Germany 2002–; First Prize Antonin Dvořák Competition 1982; European Foundation for Music prize 1993; Thalia Prize (for Carmen) 2000. *Recent roles include:* Leonora (Basel), Cherubino in The Marriage of Figaro (London), Rosina in The Barber of Seville (Berlin, Dresden), Carmen (Prague), Varvara in Katya Kabanova (Salzburg, Barcelona). *Recordings include:* Martinů — Nipponari 1991, Mozart — Che Bella 1994, Janáček — Moravian Folk Poetry in Song 1994, Mahler — Adagietto, Kindertotenlieder 1996, Songs of Mahler and Berio 1997, Janáček—Kátă Kabanová 1997, Janáček—Diary of One Who Disappeared 1999, recital of music by Wagner, Schoenberg, Zemlinsky and Brahms 2000, Lieder by Strauss, Schoeck, Berg 2001, Lieder by Dvořák 2001, Arias (live) 2002. *Leisure interests:* reading, driving. *Address:* Okrouhlo 45, 254 01, Czech Republic (Office). *Telephone:* (2) 41406665 (Office). *Fax:* (2) 41407599 (Office). *E-mail:* bellamaya@iplus.cz (Office).

PÉCSI, Márton, PhD, DSc; Hungarian geographer; b. 29 Dec. 1923, Budapest; s. of Dani de Pécsi and Róza Simon; m. Dr Éva Donáth 1954; one d.; ed Pázmány Péter Univ. Budapest; Lecturer, Faculty of Natural Sciences, Eötvös Loránd Univ., Budapest 1949, Prof. 1966–; Ed.-in-Chief, Studies in Geography in Hungary; mem. ed. bd six int. geographical periodicals; Pres. Hungarian Geographical Soc. 1981–89, Hon. Pres. 1989–; Visiting Prof. at several foreign univs; mem. Hungarian Acad. of Sciences Research Inst. of Geography 1952–; corresp. mem. Hungarian Acad. of Sciences 1965, Full mem. 1976–; Assoc. Prof. Eötvös Loránd Univ., Dir Hungarian Acad. of Scientific Research, Inst. of Geography 1963–95, Scientific Adviser 1990–; mem. Österreichische Akad. der Wissenschaften 1981–, Deutsche Akad. der Naturforscher Leopoldina, Halle 1985, Acad. of Sciences of Slovenia, Acad. Scientiarium Gottingensis 1989–, Acad. of Sciences of Poland 1993–, New York Acad. of Sciences 1998–; Hon. mem. several nat. geographic socs; Hon. mem. Int. Union for Quaternary Research INQUA; Pres. INQUA Comm. on Loess 1977–91, on Paleographic Atlas of the Quaternary 1991–96; Humboldt Medal 1958; State Prize 1975, Széchenyi Prize 1990, World Lifetime Achievement Award 1993, Universal Accomplishment Award 2001 and other awards. *Publications:* A magyarországi Dunavölgy kialakulása (Development and Geomorphology of the Danube Valley in Hungary) 1960, Geomorphology 1975; co-author and ed. Landscapes of Hungary (six Vols), National Atlas of Hungary 1989, Atlas of Paleoclimates and Paleoenvironments of the Northern Hemisphere 1992, Quaternary and Loess Research 1993, Löss: Herkunft, Gliederung, Landschaften 1996, Geomorphological Regions of Hungary 1996, Landform Evolution in Hungary 1999; and more than 500 articles. *Leisure interest:* photography. *Address:* Geographical Research Institute of the Hungarian Academy of Sciences, PO Box 64, 1112 Budaörsi út 43-45, 1388 Budapest (Office); Dozsa u. 7, 2747 Törtel, Hungary (Home). *Telephone:* (1) 309-2600 (Office); (53) 376-243 (Home). *Fax:* (1) 309-2628 (Office); (53) 376-243 (Home). *E-mail:* pema@matavnet.hu (Home).

PEDDER, Anthony P. (Tony), MSc; British steel industry executive; b. 1949; m.; two. s.; ed London Univ.; joined steel industry 1972; several Sr man. positions in British Steel (now Corus Group), Man. Dir of Stainless Steel business 1986, Man. Dir of Gen. Steels business 1989, Head of Group's procurement and logistics operations 1991, mem. bd British Steel 1992, mem. bd Corus Group (after merger with British Steel) 1999, CEO 2001–03; Vice-Chair. AvestaPolarit; Dir (non-exec.) Delta PLC 1998–, Caparo Merchant Bar PLC. *Address:* c/o Corus Group PLC, 30 Millbank, London, SW1P 4WY, England (Office).

PEDERSEN, Gert K., MSc, DPhil; Danish mathematician; b. 13 April 1940, Copenhagen; m. Dorte Olesen 1971; two s. one d.; ed Univ. of Copenhagen; Lecturer, Univ. of Copenhagen 1968–75, Prof. of Math. 1975–; Co-ordinator Danish Operator Algebra Group 1988–2003, European Network in Operator Algebra 1994–2000; Chair. Danish Math. Soc. 1974–78; mem. Royal Danish Acad., Vice-Pres. 1987–93; mem. Royal Norwegian Acad.; awarded Knud Sand Domicile 1988; Kt of Dannebrog 1990, Kt of 1st Degree 2000. *Publications:* C*-algebras and Their Automorphism Groups 1979, Analysis Now 1988; numerous articles on operator algebra in scientific journals. *Leisure interests:* music, history. *Address:* Department of Mathematics, Universitetsparken 5, 2100 Copenhagen Ø (Office); Kildeskovsvej 81, 2820 Gentofte, Denmark (Home). *Telephone:* 35-32-07-23 (Office); 39-68-17-44 (Home). *Fax:* 35-32-07-04 (Office); 39-68-17-88 (Home). *E-mail:* gkped@math.ku.dk (Office). *Website:* www.math.ku.dk/~gkped.

PEDERSEN, K. George, OC, PhD; Canadian professor and university president (retd); b. 13 June 1931, Peace River, Alberta; s. of Hjalmar Pedersen and Anna Jensen; m. 1st Joan Vanderwarher 1953 (died 1988), 2nd Penny Jones 1988; one s. one d.; ed Chilliwack Sr High School and Univs. of BC, Washington and Chicago; school teacher, N Vancouver school system 1952–56; Vice-Prin., North Star Elementary School 1956–59; Prin. Carisbrooke Elementary School 1959–61; Vice-Prin., Handsworth Secondary School 1961–63; Prin., Balmoral Secondary School 1963–65; Research Assoc. Univ. of Chicago 1965–68; Asst Prof. Ont. Inst. for Studies in Educ. and Univ. of Toronto 1968–70; Assoc. Dir Midwest Admin. Center, Univ. of Chicago 1970–72; Dean, Faculty of Educ. Univ. of Vic. 1972–75, Vice-Pres. (Academic) 1975–78; Pres. and Vice-Chancellor Simon Fraser Univ. 1979–83, Univ. of BC 1983–85, Univ. of Western Ont. 1985–94, Univ. of Northern BC 1995–, Royal Roads Univ. 1995–96; Chancellor Univ. of Northern BC 1998–; Fellow, Canadian Coll. of Teachers, Royal Soc. for Encouragement of Arts; Univ. of Chicago Scholarships 1965–68, Canada Council Scholarships 1966–68; Ford Foundation Fellowship 1967–68; Hon. LLD (McMaster) 1996, (Simon Fraser Univ.) 2003, Hon. DLitt (Emily Carr Inst. of Art and Design) 2003; Commemorative Medal 1992, Order of Canada 1993, Queen's Jubilee Medal 2002. *Publications:* The Itinerant Schoolmaster 1973; book chapters and numerous articles. *Leisure interests:* fishing, golf, gardening, cooking, carving. *Address:* 2232 Spruce Street, Vancouver, BC, V6H 2P3, Canada. *Telephone:* (604) 733-2400. *Fax:* (604) 733-2430; (604) 733-2400. *E-mail:* pedersen@sfu.ca (Home).

PEDERSEN, Thor; Danish politician; b. 14 June 1945, Gentofte; s. of Laurits Pedersen; ed Copenhagen Univ.; fmr mem. staff, Assessments Div.; fmr Man. Dir of a construction co., North Zealand; fmr Mayor of Helsinge; mem. Folketing (Parl.) 1985–; Minister of Housing 1986–87, of the Interior 1987–93, of Nordic Affairs 1988, of Econ. Affairs 1992–93, of Finance 2001–. *Address:* Ministry of Finance, Christiansborg Slotsplads 1, 1218 Copenhagen K (Office); Folketing, Copenhagen, Denmark. *Telephone:* 33-92-33-33 (Office). *Fax:* 33-32-80-30 (Office). *E-mail:* fm@fm.dk (Office); www.fm.dk (Office).

PEDLEY, Timothy John, PhD, FRS; British professor of fluid mechanics; b. 23 March 1942, Leicester; s. of Richard Rodman Pedley and Jeanie Mary Mudie Pedley; m. Avril Jennifer Martin Uden 1965; two s.; ed Rugby School, Trinity Coll. Cambridge; Post-doctoral Fellow, Johns Hopkins Univ., USA 1966–68; Research Assoc. and lecturer, Imperial Coll. London 1968–73; lecturer, Dept of Applied Maths. and Theoretical Physics, Cambridge 1973–89, Reader in Biological Fluid Dynamics, Univ. of Cambridge 1989, G. I. Taylor Prof. of Fluid Mechanics 1996–, Head Dept. of Applied Math. and Theoretical Physics 2000–; Fellow Gonville & Caius Coll. Cambridge 1973–89, 1996–; Prof. of Applied Math., Univ. of Leeds 1990–96; Foreign Assoc. Nat. Acad. of Eng (USA) 1999–; Adams Prize, Cambridge Univ. 1977. *Publications:* The Mechanics of the Circulation (co-author) 1978, Scale Effects in Animal Locomotion (ed.) 1977, The Fluid Mechanics of Large Blood Vessels 1980, Biological Fluid Dynamics (co-ed.) 1995. *Leisure interests:* birdwatching, running, reading. *Address:* Department of Applied Mathematics and Theoretical Physics (DAMTP), University of Cambridge, Silver Street, Cambridge, CB3 9EW (Office); Oakhurst Farm, 375 Shadwell Lane, Leeds, LS17 8AH, England (Home). *Telephone:* (1223) 339842 (Office); (113) 266-2854 (Home). *Fax:* (1223) 337918 (Office). *E-mail:* t.j.pedley@damtp.cam.ac.uk (Office). *Website:* www.damtp.cam.ac.uk (Office).

PEDNYCYA, Kazys; Lithuanian lawyer; b. 16 Nov. 1949, Plaskunai, Kaisiadoriai Region, Lithuania; m. Viktorija Pednyciene; two s.; ed Vilnius State Univ.; interrogator Kedainai Regional Public Prosecutor's Office 1972–76; Asst Public Prosecutor Panevezys City 1976–84; Supervision Prosecutor, Lithuanian Repub. Reformatories 1984–91; Judge, Lithuanian Repub. Supreme Court 1991–92; Sr Customs Official, Lithuanian Repub. 1992–93; Asst Dir-Gen. Lithuanian Nat. Security Dept 1993–97; Gen. Public Prosecutor 1997–2001. *Address:* Justiniskiu 36-20, 2000 Vilnius, Lithuania (Home). *Telephone:* (2) 22-83-38 (Home).

PEDROSO, Ivan; Cuban athlete; b. 17 Dec. 1972, Havana; long jumper; gold medallist, World Indoor Championships 1993, 1995, 1997, 1999, 2001; gold medallist, Olympic Games 2000; voted Best Cuban Sportsman 1998. *Address:* c/o Cubadeportes SA, 710 Calle 20 no. 710 e/ 7ma y 9na, Miramar, Havana, Cuba.

PEERS, Most Rev. Michael Geoffrey, BA (HONS.), LTh; Canadian ecclesiastic; b. 31 July 1934; s. of Geoffrey H. Peers and Dorothy E. Mantle; m. Dorothy E. Bradley 1963; two s. one d.; ed Univs. of British Columbia and Heidelberg and Trinity Coll. Toronto; ordained priest 1960; Curate, Ottawa 1959–65; Univ. Chaplain, Diocese of Ottawa 1961–66; Rector, St Bede's, Winnipeg 1966–72; St Martin's, Winnipeg with St Paul's Middlechurch 1972–74; Archdeacon of Winnipeg 1969–74; Rector, St Paul's Cathedral, Regina 1974–77; Dean of Qu'Appelle 1974–77; Bishop of Qu'Appelle 1977–82; Archbishop of Qu'Appelle and Metropolitan of Rupert's Land 1982–86; Primate, Anglican Church of Canada 1986–; mem. Cen. Cttee World Council of Churches 1991–98, Jt Standing Cttee of Anglican Communion 1994–2003; Hon. DD (Trinity Coll. Toronto) 1978, (Wycliffe Coll. Toronto) 1981, (St John's Coll. Winnipeg) 1981, (Univ. of Kent) 1988, (Montreal Diocesan Coll.) 1989, (Coll. of Emmanuel and St Chad, Saskatoon) 1990, (Thornloe Univ. Sudbury) 1993, (Huron Coll., London, Ont.) 1998; Hon. DCL (Bishop's Univ., Lennoxville) 1993, (Huron Univ. Coll.) 1998, (Lutheran Theological Seminary Saskatoon) 2001. *Address:* 600 Jarvis Street, Toronto, Ont., M4Y 2J6; 195 Westminster Avenue, Toronto, Ont., M6R 1N9, Canada. *Telephone:* (416) 924-9192. *Fax:* (416) 924-0211. *E-mail:* primate@national.anglican.ca.

PEERTHUM, Satteeanund; Mauritian diplomatist; b. 15 March 1941; m.; three c.; ed People's Friendship Univ., Moscow; Sr Research Fellow Inst. of Oriental Studies, Moscow 1973–74; Head History Dept, Bhojoharry Coll., Mauritius several times between 1975 and 1987; Sr Research Fellow School of Mauritian Asian and African Studies, Mahatma Gandhi Inst. 1985–87; founding mem. Mouvement Socialiste Militant; mem. Mauritian Parl. and Minister of Labour and Industrial Relations 1982–83; Chair. Sugar Industry Devt Fund Boards of Mauritius 1984–87; Perm. Rep. to UN 1987–96; Chair. Nat. Steering Cttee for the Teaching of Mauritian History; mem. Advisory Cttee African Cultural Centre of Mauritius 1986–87; fmr mem. Court Nat. Univ. of Mauritius. *Address:* c/o Ministry of Foreign Affairs, International and Regional Co-operation, Level 5, New Government Centre, Port Louis, Mauritius.

PEI IEOH MING, MArch, FAIA, RIBA; American architect; b. 26 April 1917, Canton, China; s. of Tsu Yee Pei and Lien Kwun Chwong; m. Eileen Loo 1942; three s. one d.; ed Shanghai, Massachusetts Inst. of Tech. and Harvard Univ.; in USA 1935–; naturalized citizen 1954; architectural practice 1939–, Webb and Knapp Inc. 1948–55, Pei, Cobb, Freed & Partners (fmrly I. M. Pei & Partners) 1955–96, ind. architect 1996–; Asst Prof. Harvard Graduate School of Design 1945–48; Wheelwright Traveling Fellowship, Harvard Univ. 1951; MIT Traveling Fellowship 1940; Fellow AIA; mem. Nat. Council on the Humanities 1966–70, American Acad. of Arts and Sciences, Nat. Acad. of Design, American Acad. of Arts and Letters (Chancellor 1978–80), Nat. Council on the Arts 1981–84, RIBA, Urban Design Council (New York), Corpn of MIT 1972–77, 1978–83, American Philosophical Soc., Institut de France (Foreign Assoc.); Hon. DFA (Pennsylvania) 1970, (Rensselaer Polytechnic Inst.) 1978, (Northeastern Univ.) 1979, (Univs. of Mass., Rochester, Brown) 1982, (New York Univ.) 1983; Hon. LLD (Chinese Univ. of Hong Kong) 1970, Hon. DHL (Columbia Univ., Univs. of Colorado, Rochester, Hong Kong, American Univ. of Paris); Hon. Prof. Tonji Univ., Shanghai 1985; Brunner Award, Nat. Inst. of Arts and Letters 1961; Medal of Honor NY Chapter AIA 1963, The Thomas Jefferson Memorial Medal for Architecture 1976, Gold Medal (American Acad. of Arts and Letters) 1979, Gold Medal (American Inst. of Architects) 1979, La Grande Medaille d'Or (Académie d'Architecture) 1981, Pritzker Architecture Prize 1983, Asia Soc. Award 1984, Medal of Liberty 1986, Nat. Medal of Arts 1988, Praemium Imperiale (Japan Art Asscn) 1989, Univ. of Calif. Gold Medal 1990, Calbert Award for Excellence 1991, Presidential Medal of Freedom 1992, Edward MacDowell Medal 1998, Commdr, Ordre des Arts et des Lettres, Officier, Légion d'honneur 1988. *Projects include:* Mile High Center (Denver); MIT Earth Science Bldg (Cambridge, Mass.); U.S. Embassy Bldg (Montevideo); East-West Center, Univ. of Hawaii; redevt. projects in New York, Philadelphia, Washington, Chicago, Pittsburgh and Singapore; Nat. Center for Atmospheric Research (Boulder, Colorado); Grave of Robert F. Kennedy; Nat. Airlines Terminal (Kennedy Int. Airport); Washington Sq. East (Philadelphia); Everson Museum of Art (Syracuse NY); Nat. Gallery of Art East Bldg (Washington, DC); Wilmington Tower (Wilmington, Del.); John Fitzgerald Kennedy Library Complex (Boston, Mass.); Canadian Imperial Bd of Commerce Complex (Toronto); Des Moines Art Center Addition (Des Moines, Iowa); Cleo Rogers Memorial County Library (Columbus, Ind.); planning projects in Boston, Oklahoma City and New York; Master Plan Columbia Univ. (NY) 1970; Dallas Municipal Bldg (Dallas); Raffles City (Singapore); Overseas-Chinese Banking Corpn Centre (Singapore); Herbert F. Johnson Museum of Art (Ithaca, NY); New West Wing, Museum of Fine Arts (Boston, Mass.); Mellon Art Center, The Choate School (Wallingford, Conn.); Sunning Plaza (Hong Kong); Fragrant Hills Hotel (Beijing); Javits Convention Center, Texas Commerce Tower (Houston); Meyerson Symphony Center, IBM (Purchase, NY); Le Grand Louvre (Paris); Bank of China (Hong Kong); Luce Chapel (Taiwan); Rock-and-Roll Hall of Fame in Cleveland 1995; Museum of Modern Art, Athens; Bilbao Estuary Project; Four Seasons Hotel, New York; Musee Miko, Kyoto 1998. *Address:* c/o Pei, Cobb, Freed & Partners, 600 Madison Avenue, New York, NY 10022 (Office); 11 Sutton Place, New York, NY 10022, USA (Home). *Telephone:* (212) 751-3122 (Office).

PEI YANLING; Chinese actress; b. Aug. 1947, Shuning Co., Hebei Prov.; Vice-Chair. Hebei Fed. of Literary and Art Circles 1993–, China Fed. of Literary and Art Circles 2001–; Chair. Hebei Prof. Dramatists' Asscn; Dir Pei Yanling Co. of Hebei Prov. Peking Opera Theatre; mem. 7th CPPCC 1987–92, 8th 1993–; Excellent Performing Artist Award, Ministry of Culture 1992.

Performances include: The Man and the Ghost, Lotus Lantern and others. *Address:* Hebei Federation of Literary and Art Circles, Shijiazhuang City, People's Republic of China.

PEICHL, Gustav; Austrian architect; b. 18 March 1928, Vienna; Prof. Acad. of Fine Arts, Vienna; important bldgs include: Austrian Broadcasting Stations in Salzburg, Linz, Innsbrück, Dornbirn 1970–72, Graz 1979–80, Eisenstadt 1981–83; EFA Radio Satellite Station, Aflenz 1976–79; PEA-Phosphate Elimination Plant, Berlin-Tegel; design for Papal visit to Vienna 1984; art and exhbn centre, Bonn 1986–92; extension to Städel Museum, Frankfurt am Main; ÖMV-Center, Vienna 1991–; rehearsal stage of Burgtheater, Vienna 1991–93; Award of City of Vienna for Architecture, Austrian State Award, Reynolds Memorial Award, Styria Award for Architecture, Mies van der Rohe Award, Berlin Architectural Award; Verleihung der Grossen Verdienstkreuzes des Verdienstordens 1996. *Address:* Opernring 4, 1010 Vienna, Austria. *Telephone:* 512-32-07; 512-32-48. *Fax:* 512-32-48.

PEIMBERT, Manuel, PhD; Mexican astronomer; b. 9 June 1941, Mexico City; s. of Gonzalo Peimbert and Catalina Sierra; m. Silvia Torres-Peimbert 1962; one s. one d.; ed Universidad Nacional Autónoma de México (UNAM) and Univ. of California Berkeley; Research Asst Instituto de Astronomía, UNAM 1960–63; Research Asst Univ. of Calif. Berkeley 1963–64, Postdoctoral Fellow 1967–68; Prof. Faculty of Sciences, UNAM 1968–, Instituto de Astronomía 1970–; on sabbatical leave at Univ. Coll. London 1976, Tokyo Astronomical Observatory 1986; Vice-Pres. Int. Astronomical Union 1982–88; Foreign Assoc. NAS; Fellow, Third World Acad. of Sciences (Vice-Pres. 1998–2002); Assoc. Royal Astronomical Soc.; Science Prize, Acad. de la Investigación Científica 1971; Guillaume Budé Medal, Coll. de France 1974; Investigador ad Honorem, F. J. Duarte Center for Astronomy, Venezuela 1981; Mexican Nat. Prize in Science and Arts 1981; UNAM Science Prize 1988. *Publications:* more than 170 research papers in int. journals of astronomy and astrophysics. *Address:* Instituto de Astronomía, Universidad Nacional Autónoma de México, Apartado Postal 70-264, México DF, Mexico 04510. *Telephone:* (5) 622-3906. *Fax:* (5) 616-0653.

PEINEMANN, Edith; German concert violinist; b. 3 March 1939, Mainz; d. of Robert Peinemann and Hildegard (née Rohde) Peinemann; ed Guildhall School of Music, London; studied under her father and later with Heinz Stauske and Max Rostal; since then has performed with leading orchestras and conductors worldwide; Carnegie Hall debut 1965; performed at Salzburg, Lucerne and Mamboro Chamber Music Festivals; Prof. of Music, Frankfurt; First Prize, ARD competition, Munich 1956. *Leisure interests:* art, hiking, cooking, cross-country skiing. *Address:* c/o Pro Musicis, Ruetistrasse 38, 8032 Zurich, Switzerland.

PEIRIS, Gamini Lakshman, DPhil, PhD; Sri Lankan politician and academic; b. 13 Aug. 1946, Colombo; s. of Glanville S. Peiris and Lakshmi C. Salgado; m. Savitri N Amarasuriya 1971; one d.; ed St Thomas' Coll. Mount Lavinia, Univ. of Ceylon and New Coll. Oxford; Prof. of Law, Univ. of Colombo 1979, Dean, Faculty of Law 1982–88; Vice-Chancellor, Univ. of Colombo –1994; Dir Nat. Film Corpn of Sri Lanka 1973–88; Commr Law Comm. of Sri Lanka 1986–; mem. Inc. Soc. of Legal Educ. 1986–; Visiting Fellow, All Souls Coll. Oxford 1980–81; Butterworths Visiting Fellow, Inst. of Advanced Legal Studies, Univ. of London 1984; Distinguished Visiting Fellow, Christ's Coll. Cambridge 1985–86; Smuts Visiting Fellow in Commonwealth Studies, Univ. of Cambridge 1985–86; Chair. Cttee of Vice-Chancellors of the Univs of Sri Lanka; Minister of Justice, Constitutional Affairs, Ethnic Affairs and Nat. Integration and Deputy Minister of Finance 1994–99; Minister of Enterprise Devt, Industrial Policy and Investment Promotion and of Constitutional Affairs 1999–; Vice-Chair. Janasaviya Trust Fund; mem. Securities Council of Sri Lanka 1987–; mem. Pres. Comm. on Youth Unrest 1989; mem. Nat. Educ. Comm., Exec. Cttee of Asscn of Teachers and Researchers in Intellectual Property Law, Bd of Govs. of Inst. of Fundamental Studies; assoc. mem. Int. Acad. of Comparative Law; Presidential Award 1987. *Publications:* Law of Unjust Enrichment in South Africa and Ceylon 1971, General Principles of Criminal Liability in Ceylon 1972, Offences under the Penal Code of Sri Lanka 1973, The Law of Evidence in Sri Lanka 1974, Criminal Procedure in Sri Lanka 1975, The Law of Property in Sri Lanka 1976, Landlord and Tenant in Sri Lanka 1977; numerous articles on comparative and admin. law and law of evidence. *Leisure interest:* walking. *Address:* Ministry of Enterprise Development, Industrial Policy and Investment Promotion and of Constitutional Affairs, Colombo, Sri Lanka. *Website:* www.industry.gov.lk.

PEIROTES, Yves Jean-Marie, MSc; French business executive; b. 7 Nov. 1940, Epinal, Vosges; s. of Marcel Georges Peirotes and Germaine Eugénie Schaeffer; m. 1st Victoria Longacre 1968 (divorced 1981); two s.; m. 2nd Viviane France Bastiani 1987; ed Lycée de Belfort, Lycée Kleber, Strasbourg, Ecole Polytechnique, Paris, Ecole Nat. Supérieure du Génie Maritime, Paris, Univ. of Calif. at Berkeley; prin. engineer Maritime Eng, Del. Ministérielle pour l'Armement 1966–70; Head of Logistics, Strafor, Strasbourg 1971–72, Tech. and Industrial Devt Dir 1972–77; Gen. Man. Industrial Equipment Div., Forges de Strasbourg 1997–81; Man. Dir Air Industrie 1981–84; Chair., Man. Dir Sofiltra Poelman 1981–84; Deputy Man. Dir Cie Industrielle et Financière de Pompey 1984–85; Gen. Man. White Goods Div. Electrolux France 1985–90, White Goods & Floor Care Appliances Div. 1990–94, Man. Dir Electrolux SA 1995–97, Chair. and Man. Dir 1997–; Chair. Usines et Fonderies Arthur Martin 1985–; Pres. Bureau Départemental d'Industrialisation des Ardennes 1987–91; mem. Advisory Bd Senlis branch, Banque de France 1995–; Chevalier, Ordre nat. du Mérite. *Leisure interests:* skiing, jogging, swimming. *Address:* Electrolux, 43 ave. Félix Louat, B.P. 20139, 60300 Senlis (Office); 6 place Winston Churchill, 92200 Neuilly sur Seine, France (Home). *Telephone:* (3) 44-62-28-00 (Office). *Fax:* (3) 44-62-2189. *E-mail:* yves.peirotes@notes.electrolux.fr (Office).

PEISACH, Max, PhD, DSc, FRSSA, F.R.P.S.L.; South African nuclear analytical chemist; b. 3 Aug. 1926, Birzai, Lithuania; s. of Hyman Peisach and Sonia Kantor; m. Eunice Sheila Glick 1950; one s. three d.; ed Boys' High School, Worcester, SA, Univ. of Cape Town; demonstrator, Univ. of Cape Town 1948–49, Jr lecturer 1949–50, lecturer 1950–53; Research Officer, Nat. Chemical Research Lab., S. African Council for Scientific and Industrial Research 1953–57, Sr Research Officer 1957–60; Head, Isotope Production, Israel Atomic Energy Comm. 1960–63; Head Chem. Div., Southern Univs. Nuclear Inst. 1963–83; Head Nuclear Analytical Chem. Div., Nat. Accelerator Centre 1983–91, Chief Specialist Researcher 1986–91; mem. Int. Cttee on Modern Trends in Activation Analysis 1969–91, Hon. Life mem. 1994–; Nat. Rep., IUPAC Comm. on Radiochemistry 1985–96; Research Consultant, Witwatersrand Chem. Ion-Beam Analysis Group 1992–98; Research Fellow, Solid State and Materials, Nat. Accelerator Centre 1994; Research Adviser, Dept of Materials and Interfaces, Weizmann Inst., Rehovot, Israel 1995–; Assoc. Royal Soc. of Chem. (London) 1951–61, Fellow 1962–86; Fellow Royal Soc. of SA 1984–; Royal Philatelic Soc. London 1966–; mem. S. African Chemical Inst. 1952–96, Sr mem. 1996–98, Life mem. 1998–; AE & CI Gold Medal 1965, Roll of Distinguished Philatelists (SA) 1966, Int. Hevesy Medal 1981, SA Chemical Inst. Gold Medal 1986; Hon. Citizen, State of Tenn., USA 1965, Order of the Postal Stone (SA) 1988. *Publications:* Elemental Analysis by Particle Accelerators; many scientific papers; research papers on nuclear analytical chem.; book chapters on specialized analytical topics; research articles on philately of South Africa and Israel. *Leisure interests:* philately, numismatics, judging philatelic exhbns. *Address:* Sderot Ye'elim 30/4, Beer-sheba 84739 (Home); P.O.Box 3581, Beersheba 84135, Israel. *Telephone:* 8-6442232. *E-mail:* mpeisach@bezeqint.net (Home).

PEKHTIN, Vladimir Alekseyevich, DR.TECH.SCI.; Russian politician and engineer; b. 9 Dec. 1950, Leningrad; m.; one s.; ed Leningrad Polytech. Inst.; engineer in Kolymagestroi, then Kolymaenergo 1974–97; Chair. Magadan Regional Duma 1994; Chair. Council of Feds. of Russia 1997–; mem. State Duma (Parl.) 1999–, Head Cttee on Property; Head Yedinstvo faction in State Duma (Parl.) 2001–; mem. Co-ordination Council of Centrist Parties 2001–; Order, Friendship of Peoples, Merited Constructor of Russia. *Leisure interests:* hunting, shooting (Master of Sports). *Address:* State Duma of Russian Federation, Okhotny Ryad 1, 103265 Moscow, Russia (Office). *Telephone:* (095) 292-83-01 (Office). *Fax:* (095) 292-34-76 (Office).

PEKKANEN, Raimo Oskari, LLD; Finnish judge; b. 29 July 1927, Kivennapa; m. Eeva Niittyla 1953; two s.; ed Univ. of Helsinki; State Admin. 1950–60; researcher and teacher, Helsinki School of Econ. and Univ. of Tampere 1961–67; Acting Prof. in Labour Law, Univ. of Helsinki 1967–68; Justice, Supreme Admin. Court of Finland 1969–90; Sec.-Gen. Ministry of Justice (on leave of absence from Supreme Admin. Court) 1982–90; Judge, European Court of Human Rights 1990–98; Chair. Sub-Cttee on Medical Research Ethics, Nat. Advisory Bd on Health Care Ethics 2000–; Commdr Order of Finnish Lion, Order of Finnish White Rose. *Publications:* Mixed Type Contracts of Employment 1966, On the Commencement and Termination of Employment Relationships 1968, On Participation in Water System Regulation 1968; articles in legal publs. *Leisure interests:* fly-fishing, skiing. *Address:* Nyyrikintie 8, 02100 Espoo, Finland. *Telephone:* (9) 4554557.

PELÉ, (Edson Arantes do Nascimento); Brazilian football player and author; b. 23 Oct. 1940, Três Corações, Minas Gerais State; s. of João Ramos do Nascimento and Celeste Arantes; m. 1st Rosemeri Cholbi 1966 (divorced 1978); one s. two d.; m. 2nd Assiria Lemos 1994; ed Santos Univ.; first played football at Baurú, São Paulo; mem. Baurú Atlético Clube; joined Santos F.C. 1955, Dir 1993–; first int. game v. Argentina; played in World Cup 1958, 1962, 1966, 1970; finished career with New York Cosmos; Chair. Pelé Soccer Camps 1978–82; Special Minister for Sports, Govt of Brazil 1994–98; Dir Soccer Clinics; three World Cup winners' medals; two World Club Championship medals; 110 int. caps, 97 goals for Brazil; 1,114 appearances for Santos 1,088 goals; career total 1,282 goals in 1,364 games, 9 league championship medals, 4 Brazil cup medals; most goals in season 53 (1958); has appeared in several films, including Escape to Victory 1981, A Minor Miracle 1983, Hot Shot 1986; has composed numerous songs in Samba style; Goodwill Amb. for 1992, UN Conf. on Environment and Devt, Rio de Janeiro; Int. Peace Award 1978, Athlete of the Century 1980, WHO Medal 1989; Hon. KBE 1997; FIFA World Footballer of the Century 2000. *Publications:* Eu Sou Pelé 1962, Jogando com Pelé 1974, My Life and the Beautiful Game 1977, Pelé Soccer Training Program 1982, The World Cup Murders (novel) 1988. *Address:* 75 Rockefeller Plaza, New York, NY 10019, USA.

PELEVIN, Victor Olegovich; Russian writer; b. 1962, Moscow; ed Moscow Power Inst., Moscow Literary Inst.; army service; journal Science and Religion; author of numerous novels and stories 1995; Small Booker Prize for Blue Lantern 1994, Wanderer Prize 1995. *Publications:* Reconstructor 1991, Omon Ra 1992, Prince of Gosplan 1993, Life of Insects 1993, Yellow Arrow 1994, Ivan Kublakhanov 1994, Chapayev and Emptiness 1995. *Address:* c/o Vagrius Publishing House, Tikhvinskaya str. 7/1, 129090 Moscow, Russia. *Telephone:* (095) 785-09-63.

PELHAM, Hugh Reginald Brentnall, MA, PhD, FRS; British research scientist; b. 26 Aug. 1954, Shawford; s. of late Reginald Arthur Pelham and of Pauline Mary Pelham; ed Marlborough Coll. and Christ's Coll., Cambridge; Research Fellow, Christ's Coll., Cambridge 1978–84; Postdoctoral Fellow, Carnegie Inst. of Washington, Baltimore, Md 1979–81; mem. Scientific Staff, MRC Lab. of Molecular Biology, Cambridge 1981–, Head Cell Biology Div. 1995–, Deputy Dir 1996–; mem. European Molecular Biology Org. 1985, Acad. Europaea 1990, Acad. of Medical Sciences 1998; Colworth Medal 1988, European Molecular Biology Org. Medal 1989, Louis Jeantet Prize for Medicine 1991, King Faisal Int. Prize for Science 1996. *Publications:* articles on molecular and cell biology in scientific journals. *Address:* MRC Laboratory of Molecular Biology, Hills Road, Cambridge, CB2 2QH, England. *Telephone:* (1223) 248011. *Fax:* (1223) 412142. *Website:* www.mrc-lmb.cam.ac.uk (Office).

PELIKAN, Jaroslav, PhD; American professor of history; b. 17 Dec. 1923, Akron; s. of Rev. Jaroslav Pelikan and Anna Buzek; m. Sylvia Burica 1946; two s. one d.; ed Concordia Jr Coll. Fort Wayne, Ind., Concordia Theological Seminary, St Louis and Univ. of Chicago; mem. Faculty, Valparaiso Univ. 1946–49, Concordia Theological Seminary 1949–53, Univ. of Chicago 1953–62; Titus Street Prof. Yale Univ. 1962–72, Sterling Prof. 1972–96, Dean, Grad. School 1973–78, William C. DeVane Lecturer 1984–86; Vice-Pres. American Acad. of Arts and Sciences 1976–79, Pres. 1994–97; mem. Council, American Philosophical Soc. 1984–87, Smithsonian Inst. 1984–90; Dir Univ. Support Services Inc. 1992–94; Visiting Prof. Annenberg School of Communications, Univ. of Pa 1998–; Distingushed Visiting Scholar, Library of Congress 2002–; mem. Council of Scholars, Library of Congress; mem. Bd Nat. Humanities Center; mem. American Acad. of Politics and Social Sciences, Pres. 2000–; many other professional appts; recipient of numerous awards, medals and hon. degrees. *Publications include:* From Luther to Kierkegaard 1950, Fools for Christ 1955, The Riddle of Roman Catholicism 1959, Luther the Expositor 1959, The Shape of Death 1961, The Light of the World 1962, Obedient Rebels 1964, The Finality of Jesus Christ in an Age of Universal History 1965, Spirit versus Structure 1968, Development of Doctrine 1969, Historical Theology 1971, The Christian Tradition (5 Vols) 1971–89, Scholarship and its Survival 1983, The Vindication of Tradition 1984, Jesus through the Centuries 1985, The Mystery of Continuity 1986, Bach among the Theologians 1986, The Excellent Empire 1987, The Melody of Theology 1988, Confessor Between East and West 1990, Imago Dei 1990, Eternal Feminines 1990, The Idea of the University: A Reexamination 1992, Christianity and Classical Culture (Gifford Lectures) 1993, Faust the Theologian 1995, The Reformation of the Bible/The Bible of the Reformation 1996, Mary Through the Centuries 1996, The Illustrated Jesus Through the Centuries 1997, What Has Athens To Do With Jerusalem? 1997; Ed. of many other vols. *Address:* c/o Department of History, Yale University, 1504A, Yale Station, New Haven, CT 06520-7425 (Office); 156 Chestnut Lane, Hamden, CT 06518, USA (Home). *Telephone:* (203) 432-1375 (Office); (203) 288-3030 (Home). *Fax:* (203) 248-7402.

PELISSIER, Jacques Daniel Paul; French civil servant and railway administrator; b. 4 Feb. 1917, Versailles; s. of Jean Pelissier and Camille Bertrand; m. Jeanine Picard 1946 (died); one s.; ed Lycée Pasteur, Lycée Hoche, Lycée Chaptal, Inst. Nat. Agronomique; engineer, external service of Ministry of Agric. 1938–44; Sec.-Gen. Landes 1944, Ardennes 1945; Sous-préfet hors cadre, Chef du Cabinet to Minister of Agric. 1946; Asst Chef du Cabinet, Minister of Industry and Commerce 1948; Sec.-Gen. Indre-et-Loire 1950; Sous-préfet, Saumur 1954; Dir for Gen. Govt of Algeria, in Ministry for Algeria and in Gen. Del. of Govt in Algeria 1956–60; Préfet hors cadre 1957; Préfet, Aude 1960, Hérault and Region of Languedoc-Roussillon 1964, Ille-et-Vilaine and Region of Brittany 1967, Rhône and Region of Rhône-Alpes 1972; Préfet hors cadre, Dir-Gen. of Admin., Ministry of the Interior April 1974; Dir du Cabinet for Prime Minister May 1974; Chair. Bd of Dirs. Soc. Nat. des Chemins de Fer Français 1975–81; Pres. Office de Tourisme de Paris 1983; Adviser to Prime Minister 1986–88; Prés. délégué Supervisory Bd of Palais Omnisports Paris-Bercy 1988–; Hon. Préfet, Admin. de la Cie Int. des Wagons-Lits et du Tourisme; Grand Officier, Légion d'honneur, Grand croix, Ordre nat. du Mérite, Croix de guerre, Médaille de la Résistance. *Address:* 14 rue des Barres, 75004 Paris, France.

PELIZA, Maj. Sir Robert John, KBE, OBE, ED, M.H.A.; British soldier, businessman and politician; b. 16 Nov. 1920, Gibraltar; s. of Robert Peliza and Emily Victory; m. Irma Risso 1950; three s. four d.; ed Christian Brothers' Coll., Gibraltar; served in Royal Gibraltar Reg. 1939–61, Hon. Col 1993–98; co. Dir 1962–; City Councillor 1945–48; Leader, Integration with Britain Party 1967; elected mem. House of Ass. 1969–84; Chief Minister of Gibraltar 1969–1972; Leader of the Opposition 1972; Speaker, House of Assembly 1989–96; Founder Gibraltar branch of European Movt 1976– (Patron 1995–); Pres. Gibraltar branch, Commonwealth Parl. Asscn 1989–96; Freeman of Gibraltar 1998. *Leisure interests:* painting, writing, swimming, walking and sports in general. *Address:* 125 Beverley Drive, Edgware, Middx HA8 5NH, England (Home); 203 Water Gardens, Gibraltar. *Telephone:* (20) 8952-1712 (England), 78387 (Gibraltar). *E-mail:* rjpeliza@pelizar.freeserve.co.uk (England), rjpeliza@gibrynet.gi (Gibraltar).

PELL, Claiborne de Borda, AM; American politician; b. 22 Nov. 1918, New York City; s. of Herbert Claiborne and Matilda (née Bigelow) Pell; m. Nuala O'Donnell 1944; two s. two d.; ed Princeton and Columbia Univs; Limited Partner, Auchinloss, Parker and Redpath; U.S. Coastguard 1941–45; Capt. U.S.C.G.R. (retd); U.S. Foreign Service Officer; instructor and Lecturer, Naval and Mil. Govt Schools 1944–45; served State Dept, Czechoslovakia, Italy, Washington 1945–52; Co.-Dir and trustee 1952–60; Consultant, Dem. Nat. Cttee 1953–60; U.S. Del. to Inter-Govtl. Maritime Consultative Org. (IMCO) London 1959; Senator from Rhode Island 1961–97; Chair. Foreign Relations Cttee 1987–95; Del. to UN 1997–; Distinguished Visiting Prof. Salve Regina Univ., R.I. 1997–; Democrat; 46 hon. degrees; Légion d'honneur, Crown of Italy, six Grand Crosses, etc. *Publications:* Rochambeau and Rhode Island 1954, Megalopolis Unbound 1966, Challenge of the Seven Seas (with Harold L. Goodwin) 1966, Power and Policy 1972. *Address:* Ledge Road, Newport, RI 02840, USA.

PELLEGRINO, Edmund Daniel, MD; American professor of medicine; b. 22 June 1920, Newark, NJ; m. Clementine Coakley; two s. four d.; ed Xavier High School, New York, St John's Univ., Jamaica and New York; Prof. and Chair. Dept of Medicine, Univ. of Ky Medical Center 1959–66; Vice-Pres. for Health Sciences, Dean of School of Medicine, Dir of Health Services Center and Prof. of Medicine, State Univ. of New York 1966–73; Chancellor and Vice-Pres. for Health Affairs, Univ. of Tenn. and Prof. of Medicine and Medical Humanities, Univ. of Tenn. Center for Health Sciences 1973–75; Pres. and Chair. Bd of Dirs. Yale-New Haven Medical Center and Prof. of Medicine, Yale Univ. 1975–78; Pres. and Prof. of Philosophy and Biology, Catholic Univ. of America, Washington, DC, concurrently Prof. of Clinical Medicine and Community Medicine, Georgetown Univ. Medical School 1978–82; John Carroll Prof. of Medicine and Medical Humanities, Georgetown Univ. Medical Center 1982–, Dir Kennedy Inst. of Ethics 1983–88, Dir Centre for Advanced Study Ethics 1988–94, Dir for Clinical Bioethics 1991–99, Chief (a.i.) Div. of Gen. Internal Medicine 1993–94; Ed. Journal of Medicine and Philosophy 1983–; Fellow or mem. of 20 scientific, professional and honorary socs. including Inst. of Medicine of NAS; mem. numerous nat. cttees. and bds.; recipient of 39 hon. degrees; Kt of Malta; Kt Order St Gregory the Great, Kts. of the Holy Sepulchre; Pres. Medal Georgetown Univ. 1990, Distinction in Bioethics Award 1993, Abraham Flexner Award 1997, Lifetime Achievement Award 1998 and many other honours and awards. *Publications:* ten books and more than 500 research papers in learned journals. *Leisure interests:* music, cooking, reading. *Address:* Center for Clinical Bioethics, Georgetown University, Washington, DC 20007, USA (Office).

PELLI, César, MArch; American architect and professor of architecture; b. 12 Oct. 1926, Tucumán, Argentina; s. of Victor Vicente Pelli and Teresa S. Pelli (née Suppa); m. Diana Balmori 1950; two s.; ed Univs of Tucumán, Illinois at Urbana Champaign; Project Designer Eero Saarinen Offices, Mich., Conn. 1954–64; Dir of Design Daniel, Mann, Johnson and Medenhall (DMJM) 1964–68; Partner in Charge of Design Gruen Assocs 1968–77; Prof. of Architecture 1977–, Dean Yale School of Architecture 1977–84; Prin. César Pelli and Assocs 1977–; mem. American Acad. of Arts and Letters; Fellow AIA; numerous awards and prizes including UN City Competition First Prize, Vienna 1969, Arnold W. Brunner Prize Nat. Inst. Arts and Letters 1978, AIA Honor Award for Fed. Office Bldg, Lawndale, San Bernardino City Hall, Calif., Arnold M. Brunner Memorial Prize Nat. Acad. of Design 1991, AIA Honor Award 1994; AIA Firm Award 1989, Gold Medal 1995. *Buildings include:* Pacific Design Centre, LA, Calif. 1973, US Embassy, Tokyo, Japan 1975, Museum of Modern Art, New York 1984, Herring Hall, Rice Univ. 1984, World Financial Centre, New York 1985–87, Canary Wharf Tower, London 1990, Carnegie Hall Tower, New York 1991, Cincinnati Arts Theatre 1995, New Terminal, Wash. Nat. Airport 1998 (Design Award AIA 1998, Design for Transportation Award 2000). *Publications:* César Pelli (monograph) 1991, César Pelli, in The Master Architect series 1993; various articles in specialist journals. *Address:* c/o Janet Kagan, César Pelli and Associates, 1056 Chapel Street, New Haven, CT 06510, USA. *E-mail:* mailroom@cesar-pelli.com.

PËLLUMBI, Servet, PhD; Albanian politician; b. 14 Dec. 1936, Korçë; s. of Ismail Pëllumbi and Hazize Pëllumbi; ed State Univ. of St Petersburg; Prof. of Philosophy 1960–74; Univ. Prof. of Philosophy 1974–91; Vice-Chair. Socialist Party of Albania 1991–96; MP 1992–2003; Speaker of the Parl. of Albania (acting) 2002–; Academic Dir Inst. of Political and Social Studies; Dir Publishing Bd Policy & Society magazine. *Publications include:* Think Differently, Transition in its Light-Shade, Endeavour in Political Sociology, Sociology Tracing, Dictionary of Philosophy 1974, 1982; univ. text books and numerous articles on policy and soc. *Leisure interests:* sports, reading, books, music, community devt activities, writing memories. *Address:* Office of the Speaker of the Parliament, Parliament of Albani, Bulevardi "Dëshmorët e Kombit", nr 4, Tirana (Office); Rruga "Brigada e tetë", Pallati Havari, shk. 2, Ap. 7/1, Tirana, Albania (Home). *Telephone:* (5) 4228333 (Office); (5) 4271500 (Home). *Fax:* (5) 4227673 (Office). *E-mail:* ndokle@parlament.al (Office). *Website:* www.parlament.al (Office).

PELLY, Derek ("Derk") Roland, MA, AIB; British banker; b. 12 June 1929, Welwyn Garden City; s. of the late Arthur Roland Pelly and Phyllis Elsie Henderson; m. Susan Roberts 1953; one s. two d.; ed Marlborough Coll. and Trinity Coll., Cambridge; joined Barclays Bank Ltd (various positions) 1952, Local Dir, Chelmsford 1959, Sr. Local Dir, Luton 1969; Vice-Chair. Barclays Bank Int. Ltd 1977, full-time Vice-Chair. 1979; Group Vice-Chair. Barclays Bank PLC 1985, Group Deputy Chair. and Chair. Barclays Int. Ltd 1986–88; Gov. London House for Overseas Grads. 1985–91; Dir The Pvt. Bank and Trust Co. 1989–94. *Leisure interest:* painting. *Address:* Kenbank, St John's Town of Dalry, Kircudbrightshire, DG7 3TX, Scotland. *Telephone:* (1644) 430424.

PELOSI, Nancy; American politician; b. Baltimore; d. of Thomas D'Alesandro, Jr; m. Paul Pelosi; one s. four d.; ed Trinity Coll., Washington, DC; Democratic Nat. Committeewoman 1976–96, Chair. Democratic Nat. Convention Host Cttee 1984, Chief Fundraiser for Nat. Democratic Senatorial Campaign Cttee 1986, State and Northern Chair. Calif. Democratic Party –1987; Rep. (Democrat) 8th Congressional Dist of Calif. 1987–, mem. House Perm. Select Cttee on Intelligence, House Democratic Whip 2001–2003, Minority Leader 2003–; Sr mem. House Appropriations Cttee, mem. Appropriations SubCttee on Labor, Health and Human Services and Educ.; Chair. Congressional Working Group on China; Co-Chair. AIDS Task Force of House Democratic Caucus, Bio-Medical Research Caucus; fmr Ranking Democrat on Appropriations Sub-cttee on Foreign Operations and Export Financing; fmr mem. House Cttee on Standards of Official Conduct (Ethics). *Address:* Office of the Democratic Leader, H-204 The Capitol, Washington, DC 20515-0001, USA (Office).

PELTASON, Jack W., PhD; American university president (retd); b. 29 Aug. 1923, St Louis, Mo.; s. of Walter Peltason and Emma Hartman; m. Suzanne Toll 1945; one s. two d.; ed Univ. of Missouri and Princeton Univ.; Asst Prof. Smith Coll. 1947–51; Asst Prof. of Political Science, Univ. of Ill., Urbana-Champaign 1951–52, Assoc. Prof. 1953–59, Dean Coll. of Liberal Arts and Sciences 1960–64, Chancellor 1967–77; Vice-Chancellor Univ. of Calif. Irvine 1964–67, Chancellor 1984–92, Chancellor Emer. 1992–; Pres. Univ. of Calif. 1992–95, Pres. Emer. 1995–; Pres. American Council on Educ. 1977–84, Bren Foundation 1997–; mem. numerous bds., cttees. etc.; Fellow, American Acad. of Arts and Sciences; 22 hon. degrees and other awards. *Publications include:* Federal Courts in the Political Process 1955, Fifty-Eight Lonely Men: Southern Federal Judges and School Desegregation 1961, Understanding the Constitution 1997, Government by the People; co-author of several other books; articles in journals and encyclopedias and book chapters etc. *Leisure interests:* reading, writing, family. *Address:* Department of Political Science, University of California at Irvine, Irvine, CA 92697-5100 (Office); 18 Whistler Court, Irvine, CA 92612, USA (Home). *Telephone:* (949) 824-3938. *Fax:* (949) 824-3960. *E-mail:* jwpeltason@aol.com (Home); jwpeltason@uci.edu.

PEÑA, Federico, LLB; American politician, civil servant and lawyer; b. 15 March 1947, Laredo, Tex.; m. Ellen Hart 1988; two d.; ed Univ. of Texas; fmr partner, law firm Pena & Pena; mem. Colo Legis. 1979–83; served two terms as Mayor of Denver 1983–91; f. Pena Investment Advisors Inc. 1991; apptd. part-time legal consultant to law firm Brownstein Hyatt Farber & Strickland, Denver 1992; Sec. of Transportation 1993–97, of Energy 1997–98; Sr Adviser Vestar Capital Partners, Denver 1998–2000, Dir 2000–; Assoc. Harvard Univ. Centre for Law and Educ. *Address:* c/o Department of Energy, Forrestal Bldg, 1000 Independence Avenue, SW, Washington, DC 20585, USA.

PEÑA, Paco; Spanish flamenco guitarist; b. 1 June 1942, Córdoba; s. of Antonio Peña and Rosario Pérez; m. Karin Vaessen 1982; two d.; int. concert artist since 1968; f. Paco Peña Flamenco Co. 1970, Centro Flamenco Paco Peña, Córdoba 1981; Prof. of Flamenco, Rotterdam Conservatory, Netherlands 1985; composed Misa Flamenca 1991; produced Musa Gitana 1999; Ramón Montoya Prize 1983, Oficial de la Cruz de la Orden del Mérito Civil, Spain. *Address:* c/o Karin Vaessen, 4 Boscastle Road, London, NW5 1EG, England; c/o Wim Visser Ruysdaelkade 5, 1072 AG Amsterdam, Netherlands. *Telephone:* (20) 7681-7475 (Office). *Fax:* (20) 7681-7476 (Office); (20) 7485-2320. *E-mail:* elvee75@netscapeonline.co.uk (Office). *Website:* www.pacopena.com (Office).

PENALOSA LONDONO, Enrique; Colombian politician and accountant; ed Duke Univ., NC; Pres. of the Instituto Colombiano de Ahorro y Vivienda (ICAV); Econ. Sec. Pres. of Colombia 1986; Mayor of Bogotá 1998–. *Publications:* Democracy and Capitalism: The Challenges of the Next Century 1990; Capitalism: The Better Option 1989; numerous articles on econ. issues. *Address:* Acaldía de Bogotá, Bogotá, Colombia (Office).

PENCHAS, Shmuel, MD, DIC, MSc; Israeli professor of health administration; b. 12 Feb. 1939, Romania; s. of Nathan Penchas and Liuba Penchas; four s.; ed Hebrew Univ. Hadassah Medical School, Haifa Technion Grad. School, Imperial Coll., Univ. Coll. London, Harvard Univ.; physician, Hadassah Univ. Hosp., Jerusalem 1967–76, Dir of Computing 1977–78; Deputy Dir-Gen. Hadassah Medical Org. 1978, Dir-Gen. 1981–98; Chair. Israel Asscn of Hosp. Dirs. 1984–91, Foreign Assoc. Inst. of Medicine of NAS (USA); Consultant to Hadassah (Women's Zionist Org. of America); mem. Romanian Nat. Acad. of Science; Dr. hc. *Publications:* articles in professional journals. *Address:* Hadassah Mt. Scopus Hospital, P.O.B. 24035, Jerusalem 91240, Israel. *Telephone:* 5844300. *Fax:* 5844750. *E-mail:* penchas@netvision.net.il (Office).

PENDERECKI, Krzysztof; Polish composer and conductor; b. 23 Nov. 1933, Dębica, Cracow Prov.; s. of Tadeusz Penderecki and Zofia Penderecka; m. Elżbieta Solecka 1965; one s. one d.; ed Jagiellonian Univ., Cracow and State Higher Music School, Cracow; studied composition first with Skołyszewski, later with Malawski and Wiechowicz, Cracow; graduated from State Higher Music School, Cracow 1958; Lecturer in Composition, State Higher Music School (now Music Acad.), Cracow 1958–66, Prof. Extraordinary 1972–75, Prof. 1975–; Rector Cracow Conservatory 1972–87; Prof. of Composition, Folkwang Hochschule für Musik, Essen 1966–68; Musical Adviser, Vienna Radio 1970–71; Prof. of Composition, Yale Univ., USA 1973–78; Music Man. Sinfonia Varsovia Orchester 1997–; Guest Conductor China Philharmonic Orchestra 2000–; mem. Presidential Council of Culture 1992–; Hon. mem. RAM, London 1974; Corresp. mem. Arts Acad. of GDR, Berlin 1975; Extraordinary mem. Arts Acad. of W Berlin 1975; mem. Royal Acad. of Music, Stockholm 1976, Acad. Nat. de Sciences, Belles-Lettres et Arts, Bordeaux, American Acad. of Arts and Letters 1999, Hong Kong Acad. for the Performing Arts 2001, etc.; Hon. mem. Accad. Nazionale di Santa Cecilia, Rome 1976, Acad. Int. de Philosophie et de l'Art, Berne 1987, Musikkreis der Stadt, Duisburg 1999, Gesellschaft der Musikfreunds, Vienna 2000; Corresp. mem. Academia Nacional de Bellas Artes, Buenos Aires 1982; Fellow Royal Irish Acad. of Music; Hon. Prof. Moscow Conservatory 1997, Cen. Beijing Conservatory 1998, St Petersburg Conservatory 2003; Dr hc (Univ. of Rochester, NY) 1972, (St Olaf Coll., Northfield, Minn.) 1977, (Katholieke Univ., Leuven) 1979, (Univ. of Bordeaux) 1979, (Georgetown Univ., Washington, DC) 1984, (Univ. of Belgrade) 1985, (Univ. Autónoma, Madrid) 1987; Hon. DMus (Glasgow) 1995, (Jagiellonian Univ., Cracow) 1998, (Ukrainian Nat. Tchaikovsky Acad. of Music) 1999, (Pittsburgh) 1999, (Lucerne) 2000 and many others; Fitelberg Prize for Threnody for the Victims of Hiroshima 1960, also UNESCO award 1959, Polish Minister of Culture and Art Prize 1961, (First Class) 1981, Cracow Composition Prize for Canon 1962, North Rhine-Westphalia Grand Prize for St Luke's Passion 1966, also Pax Prize (Poland) 1966, Alfred Jurzykowski Foundation Award, Polish Inst. of Arts and Sciences in America 1966, Prix Italia 1967/68, State Prize (1st Class) 1968, Gustav Charpentier Prize 1971, Gottfried von Herder Prize 1977, Prix Arthur Honegger for Magnificat 1978, Grand Medal of Paris 1981, Sibelius Prize (Wihouri Foundation, Finland) 1983, Order of Banner of Labour (1st Class) 1983, Premio Lorenzo il Magnifico (Italy) 1985, Wolf Foundation Award 1987, Grammy Award Nat. Acad. of Recording Arts and Sciences (for Best Contemporary Composition) 1988 (for Best Instrumental Soloist Performance with Orchestra) 1999, (for Best Choral Composition) 2001, Officier, Ordre de Saint-Georges de Bourgogne (Belgium) 1990, Grawemeyer Award for Music Composition 1992, Grand Cross Order of Merit (Fed. Repub. of Germany) 1990, City of Strasbourg Medal 1995, Commdr Ordre des Arts et des Lettres 1996, Crystal Award, World Econ. Forum, Davos 1997, Business Center Club Special Award, Warsaw 1998, AFIM Indie Award 1999, Köhler-Osbahr-Siftung Music Award 1999, Ordine al Merito della Repub. Italiana 2000, Best Living Composer Award, Midem Classic Cannes 2000, Príncipe de Asturias Award 2001, North Rhine-Westphalia Award 2003. *Works include:* Psalms of David (for choir and percussion) 1958, Emanations (for 2 string orchestras) 1958, Strophes (for soprano, speaker and ten instruments) 1959, Anaklasis (for strings and percussion) 1959–60, Dimensions of Time and Silence (for 40-part mixed choir and chamber ensemble) 1959–60, String Quartet no. 1 1960, no. 2 1968, Threnody for the Victims of Hiroshima (for 52 strings) 1960, Polymorphia (for strings) 1961, Psalms (for tape) 1961, Fluorescences (for large orchestra) 1961, Sonata for Cello and Orchestra 1964, St Luke's Passion 1965–66, Capriccio per oboe e 11 archi 1965, De natura sonoris (for large orchestra) 1966, Dies irae (for soprano, tenor, bass, chorus and large orchestra) 1967, The Devils of Loudun (opera) 1968–69, Cosmogony 1970, De natura sonoris II (for wind instruments, percussion and strings) 1970, Russian Mass Utrenja 1971, Partita (for harpsichord, guitars, harp, double bass and chamber orchestra) 1972, Symphony no. 1 1972–73, Canticum Canticorum Salomonis (for 16 voices and chamber orchestra) 1970–73, Magnificat (for bass solo, voice ensemble, double choir, boys' voices and orchestra) 1973–74, When Jacob Awoke (for orchestra) 1974, Violin Concerto 1967–77, Paradise Lost (opera) 1976–78, Christmas Symphony No. 2 1979–80, Te Deum 1979–80, Lacrimosa 1980, Cello Concerto no. 2 1982, Viola Concerto 1983, Polish Requiem 1980–84, Black Mask (opera) 1984–86, Der unterbrochene Gedanke (for string quartet) 1988, Adagio (for orchestra) 1989, Symphony No. 4 (Adagio for orchestra) 1989, Sinfonietta (for orchestra) 1990–91, Symphony No. 5 (for orchestra) 1991–92, Partita (for orchestra, rev. ed.) 1991, Ubu Rex (opera) 1991, Benedicamus Domine 1992, Benedictus 1992, Flute Concerto 1992–93, Quartet for Clarinet and String Trio 1993, Violin Concerto No. 2 1992–95, Divertimento (for cello solo) 1994, Symphony No. 3 1995, Agnus Dei from Versöhnung Messe (a cappella choir) 1995, Seven Gates of Jerusalem (oratorio) 1995–96, Passacaglia (chamber music) 1995–96, Larghetto (chamber music) 1997, Sonata for Violin and Piano 2000, Sextet for Violin, Viola, Piano, Clarinet and French Horn 2000, Concerto Grosso for Three Cellos 2001, Benedictus 2002, Resurrection Piano Concerto 2002. *Leisure interest:* dendrology. *Address:* ul. Cisowa 22, 30-229 Cracow, Poland. *Fax:* (12) 4251660. *E-mail:* biuro@elzbietapenderecka.org.

PENG CHONG; Chinese politician; b. 1909, Zhangzhou, Fujian; joined CCP 1933; Political Commissar, Regt of New 4th Army 1938; Deputy Sec.-Gen. prov. People's Govt, Fujian 1950; Mayor of Nanjing 1955–59; First Sec. Municipal CCP Cttee, Nanjing 1955-60; Deputy for Jiangsu, 2nd NPC 1958; alt. Second Sec. CCP Cttee, Jiangsu 1960; Political Commissar Nanjing militia 1960; First Sec. Municipal CCP Cttee, Nanjing 1962–68; Second Sec. CCP Cttee, Jiangsu 1965–68; Vice-Chair. Prov. Revolutionary Cttee, Jiangsu 1968–74; alt. mem. 9th Cen. Cttee CCP 1969; Sec. CCP Cttee, Jiangsu 1970–74; alt. mem. 10th Cen. Cttee CCP 1973; Chair. Prov. Revolutionary Cttee, Jiangsu 1974–76; Second Political Commissar, PLA Nanjing Mil. Region 1975–80; Third Sec. CCP Cttee, Shanghai 1976–79; Second Vice-Chair. Municipal Revolutionary Cttee, Shanghai 1976–79; Chair. Municipal CPPCC Cttee, Shanghai 1977–79; mem. 11th Cen. Cttee CCP 1977; Head, Group in Charge of Snail Fever Prevention, Cen. Cttee CCP 1978–; Deputy for Shanghai, 5th NPC 1978; Vice-Chair. Nat. Cttee, 5th CPPCC 1978–80; First Sec. CCP Cttee, Shanghai 1979–80; Chair. Municipal Revolutionary Cttee, Shanghai 1979–80; Mayor of Shanghai 1980; Sec. 11th Cen. Cttee CCP 1980–82; Vice-Chair. Standing Cttee, 5th NPC 1980–83; mem. 12th Cen.

Cttee CCP 1982–87; Vice-Chair. Standing Cttee, 6th NPC 1983–88; mem. Presidium 6th NPC 1986–; Chair. Law Cttee, NPC 1983–87; Vice-Chair. 7th NPC 1988–93; mem. Presidium of 14th CCP Nat. Congress Oct. 1992; Pres. China Int. Cultural Exchange Centre 1984–; Exec. mem. China Welfare Inst. 1978–; Hon. Pres. Gymnastics Asscn 1983–, Soc. for Industry and Commerce Admin. 1991–; China Foundation for Heroism Awards. *Address:* Standing Committee, National People's Congress, Tian An Men Square, Beijing, People's Republic of China.

PENG DIXIAN; Chinese politician and economist; b. 1908, Meishan Co., Sichuan Prov.; ed in Japan; joined China Democratic League 1947, Vice-Chair. 1988–; joined CCP 1984; Perm. mem. 8th Nat. Cttee CPPCC 1993–.

PENG HUANWU, PhD; Chinese physicist; b. 1915, Changchun; ed Tsinghua Univ., Univ. of Edinburgh; Deputy Dir Inst. of Modern Physics under Acad. Sinica 1953–; Deputy, 1st NPC 1956–59, 2nd NPC 1959–64, 3rd NPC 1964–66; Deputy Dir Inst. of Atomic Energy under Acad. Sinica 1958–; Dir Inst. of Theoretical Physics under Acad. Sinica 1978–82; mem. Acad. Sinica 1955. *Address:* The Institute of Theoretical Physics, Academia Sinica, Zhong Guan Cun, Beijing 100080, People's Republic of China.

PENG LIYUAN; Chinese singer; b. Nov. 1952, Yuncheng, Shandong Prov.; ed Shandong Acad. of Arts, China Acad. of Music; solo singer Qianwei Song and Dance Troupe of Ji'nan Mil. Command 1980–84; solo singer Song and Dance Troupe, PLA Gen. Political Dept 1984–. *Address:* Song and Dance Troupe, People's Liberation Army General Political Department, Beijing, People's Republic of China (Office).

PENG MING-MIN; Taiwanese politician; b. 1923; ed in Japan and Nat. Taiwan Univ.; lost left arm during U.S. bombing raid on Nagasaki; fmr Chair. Political Science Dept, Nat. Taiwan Univ.; arrested for activities supporting self-determination for Taiwan 1964 and sentenced to eight years' imprisonment; sentence commuted to house arrest; escaped into exile in USA; returned home 1992; joined Democratic Progressive Party (DDP) 1995; DDP Cand. Presidential Elections March 1996. *Address:* Democratic Progressive Party, 14th Floor, 128 Ming Sheng East Road, Sec. 3, Taipei, Taiwan.

PENG PEIYUN; Chinese administrator; b. 1929, Liuyang Co., Hunan Prov.; ed Qinghua Univ.; joined CCP 1946; Minister of State Family Planning Comm. 1988–98; mem. 14th CCP Cen. Cttee 1992, 15th CCP Cen. Cttee 1997–; State Councillor 1993–98; Chair. Coordination Cttee for the Handicapped (State Council) 1993–; Chair. Nat. Cttee for Patriotic Public Health Campaign 1994–, Cttee for Women and Children's Work; Pres. Chinese Asscn for Promotion of the Population Culture, Soc. of Population; Vice-Chair. Standing Cttee of 9th NPC 1998–. *Address:* Standing Committee of National People's Congress, Beijing, People's Republic of China.

PENGO, HE Cardinal Polycarp, DTheol; Tanzanian ecclesiastic; b. 5 Aug. 1944, Mwazye; ed Kipapala Major Seminary, Tabora, Makerere Univ., Pontifical Lateran Univ.; ordained priest 1971; sec. to Bishop of Sumbawanga 1971–73; Rector Segerea Major Seminary 1977–90; Bishop of Nachingwea 1984–87, of Tunduru-Massai 1987–90; Archbishop Coadjutor of Dar es Salaam 1990–92, Archbishop 1992–; Cardinal 1998–; Pro-Vice-Pres. Tanzania Episcopal Conf. *Address:* Archbishop's House, P.O. Box 167, Dar es Salaam, Tanzania. *Telephone:* (22) 2113223 (Office). *Fax:* (22) 2125751 (Office). *E-mail:* nyumba@cats-net.com (Office). *Website:* www.rc.net/tanzania/tec/dsmweb/contents.htm (Office).

PENN, Arthur; American theatre and film director; b. 27 Sept. 1922, Philadelphia; m. Peggy Maurer 1955; one s. one d.; joined Army theatre company during World War II; worked in television 1951–53; produced plays for Broadway theatre including The Miracle Worker, All the Way Home, Toys in the Attic, Two for the Seesaw, Wait Until Dark, Sly Fox, Monday after the Miracle, Golden Boy, Hunting Cockroaches; Tony Award for The Miracle Worker 1960. *Films:* The Left-Handed Gun 1957, The Miracle Worker 1962, Mickey One 1964, The Chase 1965, Bonnie and Clyde 1967, Alice's Restaurant 1969, Little Big Man 1971, Night Moves 1975, The Missouri Breaks 1976, Four Friends 1981, Target 1985, Dead of Winter 1987, Penn and Teller Get Killed, The Portrait 1993, Lumière and Company 1995, Inside 1996, Law and Order 2000; Co-Dir Visions of Eight 1973. *Address:* c/o Bell and Co., 535 Fifth Avenue, 21st Floor, New York, NY 10017, USA.

PENN, Irving; American photographer; b. 16 June 1917, Plainfield, NJ; s. of Harry Penn and Sonia Penn; m. Lisa Fonssagrives 1950; one s.; painter 1941; first photographs published in Vogue 1943; retrospective exhbn Museum of Modern Art, New York 1984. *Publications:* Moments Preserved (collection of 300 photographs) 1960, Worlds in a Small Room 1974, Inventive Paris Clothes 1909–1939 1977, Flowers 1980, Passage 1991. *Address:* Irving Penn Studio, 89 Fifth Avenue, New York, NY 10003, USA.

PENN, Sean; American actor; b. 17 Aug. 1960, Burbank, Calif.; s. of Leo Penn and Eileen (née Ryan) Penn; m. 1st Madonna (q.v.) 1985 (divorced); m. 2nd Robin Wright 1996; two c. *Theatre appearances include:* Heartland (Broadway debut), Slab Boys, Hurlyburly 1988. *Films include:* Taps 1981, Fast Times at Ridgemont High 1982, Bad Boys 1983, Crackers 1984, Racing with the Moon 1984, The Falcon and the Snowman 1985, At Close Range 1986, Shanghai Surprise 1986, Colors 1988, Judgement in Berlin 1988, Casualties of War 1989, We're No Angels 1990, State of Grace 1990, Carlito's Way 1993, Dead Man Walking 1996 (Best Actor Award Berlin Film Festival 1996), U Turn 1997, She's So Lovely 1997, Hurlyburly 1998, As I Lay Dying 1998, Up

at the Villa 1998, The Thin Red Line 1998, Sweet and Lowdown, Being John Malkovich, The Weight of Water, The Pledge 2000, Up at the Villa 2000, I am Sam 2001; dir, writer The Indian Runner 1991, The Crossing Guard 1995, The Pledge 2000. *Address:* Suite 2500, 2049 Century Park East, Los Angeles, CA 90067, USA (Office).

PENNANEACH, Biova-Soumi, MSc; Togolese diplomatist; b. 5 Oct. 1941, Lomé; m. 1972; two s. four d.; ed State Univ. of Moscow and Laval Univ. Québec; active trade unionist since 1966; Head, Soils Analysis Labs. 1966–74, 1976–80; Dir Agricultural and Land Legislation Service 1980–82; Prefect of Tchaoudjo and the Lakes and Tech. Adviser, Nat. Science Inst. 1982–87; Dir Office of Minister of Rural Devt 1987–90; Under-Sec.-Gen. Nat. Confed. of Workers of Togo 1988–90; Perm. Rep. to UN 1990–96; Vice-Pres. 46th session of UN Gen. Ass. 1991. *Publications:* numerous, on conservation and environment protection. *Address:* c/o Ministry of Foreign Affairs and Cooperation, Place du Monument aux Morts, Lomé, Togo.

PENNANT-REA, Rupert Lascelles, MA; British business executive and journalist; b. 23 Jan. 1948, Harare, Zimbabwe; s. of Peter A. Pennant-Rea and Pauline E. Pennant-Rea; m. 1st Elizabeth L. Greer 1970 (divorced 1975); m. 2nd Jane Hamilton 1979 (divorced 1986), one s. one d.; m. 3rd Helen Jay 1986, one s. two step-d.; ed Peterhouse, Zimbabwe, Trinity Coll. Dublin and Univ. of Manchester; with Confed. of Irish Industry 1970–71, Gen. and Municipal Workers' Union 1972–73, Bank of England 1973–77; with The Economist 1977–93, Ed. 1986–93; Deputy Gov. of Bank of England 1993–95; Chair. The Stationery Office 1996–, Plantation and Gen. 1997–; numerous other appointments; Wincott Prize for Journalism 1984. *Publications:* Gold Foil 1979, Who Runs the Economy? (jtly) 1980, The Pocket Economist (jtly) 1983, The Economist Economics (jtly) 1986. *Leisure interests:* music, tennis, fishing, golf, family. *Address:* The Stationery Office, 51 Nine Elms Lane, London, SW8 5DR, England. *Telephone:* (20) 7873-8781. *Fax:* (20) 7873-8387. *E-mail:* rpr@tso.co.uk (Office).

PENNIE, Michael William, ARCA; British sculptor; b. 23 Oct. 1936, Wallasey, Cheshire; s. of George A. Pennie and Isabel Duff; m. 1st Norah Kimmit 1959 (divorced 1977); m. 2nd Marlene Stride 1985; two s. one d.; ed Bede Collegiate for Boys, Sunderland, Sunderland Coll. of Art and Royal Coll. of Art; Visiting Lecturer, Bath Acad. of Art, Winchester and Wimbledon Schools of Art, Norwich Coll. of Art and Brighton Polytechnic 1962–82; Sr Lecturer, Bath Spa, Univ. Coll. 1985–2001, now Prof.; Co-Organizer, Sculpture in the City, Bath 1986; Consultant, Goodwill Art Service 1992–; Chair. Bath Area Network for Artists 2001–; Consultant Horniman Museum and Gardens; Rome Scholar 1962, Gregynog Fellow, Univ. of Wales 1971. *One-man shows include:* ICA Gallery, London 1965, Welsh Arts Council Gallery, Cardiff 1971, Angela Flowers Gallery, London 1971, 1973, 1976, 1981, Ensembles, Bath 1989, Drawings of African Sculpture, SOAS, Univ. of London 1991, Michael Pennie: Carving and Drawing 1976–1995, City Art Gallery and Museum, Bristol 1995, Nat. Museum and Art Gallery, Accra, Ghana 1995; Curator touring exhbns. 'African' 1988, 'LOBI' 1994–96, 'West African Journeys' 1999–2001; numerous group shows 1961–; participant, Forma Viva, Yugoslavia 1980, Making Sculpture, Tate Gallery, London 1983; works in various public collections including Victoria and Albert Museum and Arts Council of GB, Southern Arts Coll.; twelve research trips to W Africa 1994–2000. *Publications:* Where Shall We Put This One? 1987, Smoke of the Savannah 1989, African Assortment: African Art in Museums in England and Scotland 1991, Friday's Rain Takes a Long Time to Stop 1994, Some Sculptors and African Art 1995, Marriage Poles of the Lobi 1996, Adventures with Lobi—an abc 1998, West African Journeys 2001. *Leisure interest:* African music. *Address:* 117 Bradford Road, Atworth, Melksham, Wilts., SN12 8HY, England. *Telephone:* (1225) 705409. *Fax:* (1225) 705409. *E-mail:* michael.pennie@btinternet.com (Home). *Website:* www.artworth.co.uk (Home).

PENNINGTON, Thomas Hugh, MB, PhD, F.R.C.PATH, F.R.C.P. (EDIN.), FRSE, FMedSci; British microbiologist; b. b. 19 April 1938, Edgeware; m.; two d.; ed Royal Grammar School, Lancaster, St Thomas's Medical School, Univ. of London; house appointments, St Thomas's Hosp. 1962–63, Asst Lecturer in Medical Microbiology, St Thomas's Hosp. Medical School 1963–67; Postdoctoral Fellow, Univ. of Wisconsin 1967–68; lecturer then sr lecturer in Virology, Univ. of Glasgow 1969–79; Prof. of Bacteriology, Univ. of Aberdeen 1979–, Dean of Medicine, 1987–92; Gov. Rowett Research Inst. 1980–88, 1996–; Gov. Moredun Research Inst. 2003–; Chair. Expert Group on 1996 E. Coli Outbreak in Cen. Scotland; Vice-Chair. Broadcasting Council for Scotland; Vice-Pres. Chartered Inst. of Environmental Health; mem. Scottish Food Advisory Cttee, Food Standards Agency; Hon. DSc (Lancaster) 1999, (Strathclyde) 2001; Caroline Walker Trust Consumer Advocate Award 1997, John Kershaw Memorial Prize for Notable Services to Public Health 1998, Royal Scottish Soc. of Arts Silver Medal 1999, Thomas Graham Medal, Royal Glasgow Philosophical Soc. 2001, Burgess of Guild, City of Aberdeen 2002. *Publications:* many papers, articles and book chapters on viruses and bacteria and on food safety. *Leisure interest:* collecting old books. *Address:* Department of Medical Microbiology, Medical School, University of Aberdeen, Foresterhill, Aberdeen, AB25 2ZD (Office); 13 Carlton Place, Aberdeen, AB15 4BR, Scotland (Home). *Telephone:* (1224) 553786 (Office); (1224) 645136 (Home). *Fax:* (1224) 685604 (Office). *E-mail:* mmb036@abdn.ac.uk (Office). *Website:* www.abdn.ac.uk/mmb/theme/penn.htl (Office).

PENROSE, Oliver, PhD, FRS, FRSE; British professor of mathematics; b. 6 June 1929, London; s. of Lionel S. Penrose and Margaret Leathes; m. Joan L.

Dilley 1953; three s. (one deceased) one d.; ed Central Collegiate Inst. London, Canada, Univ. Coll. London and King's Coll. Cambridge; Mathematical Physicist, English Electric Co. Luton 1952–55; Research Asst Yale Univ. 1955–56; lecturer, Reader, Imperial Coll. London 1956–69; Prof. of Math. Open Univ. 1969–86, Heriot-Watt Univ. 1986–94, Prof. Emer. 1994–. *Publications:* Foundations of Statistical Mechanics 1969; about 70 papers in scientific journals. *Leisure interests:* music, chess. *Address:* 29 Frederick Street, Edinburgh, EH2 2ND, Scotland. *Telephone:* (131) 225-5879.

PENROSE, Sir Roger, Kt, OM, PhD, FRS; British professor of mathematics; b. 8 Aug. 1931, Colchester; s. of Lionel Penrose; m. 1st Joan Wedge 1959 (divorced 1981), three s.; m. 2nd Vanessa Thomas 1988; ed Univ. Coll. School, Univ. Coll. London and St John's Coll. Cambridge; Asst Lecturer, Bedford Coll. London 1956–57; Research Fellow, St John's Coll. Cambridge 1957–60; NATO Research Fellow, Princeton and Syracuse Univs 1959–61; Research Assoc. King's Coll. London 1961–63; Visiting Assoc. Prof. Univ. of Tex. Austin 1963–64; Reader, Birkbeck Coll. London 1964–66, Prof. of Applied Math. 1966–73; Rouse Ball Prof. of Math. Univ. of Oxford 1973–98, Prof. Emer. 1998–; Gresham Prof. of Geometry, Gresham Coll. 1998; Fellow, Univ. Coll. London 1975; Hon. Fellow, St John's Coll. Cambridge 1987; Visiting Prof. Yeshiva, Princeton and Cornell Univs 1966–67, 1969; Lovett Prof. Rice Univ. Houston 1983–87; Distinguished Prof. of Physics and Math. Syracuse Univ. 1987–93, Francis and Helen Pentz Distinguished Prof. of Physics and Math., Pa State Univ. 1993–; mem. London Math. Soc., Cambridge Philosophical Soc., Inst. for Math. and its Applications, Int. Soc. for Gen. Relativity and Gravitation; Fellow Birkbeck Coll. 1998, Inst. of Physics 1999; Foreign Assoc. Nat. Acad. of Sciences, USA 1998; Dr hc, (New Brunswick) 1992, (Surrey) 1993, (Bath) 1994, (London) 1995, (Glasgow) 1996, (Essex) 1996, (St Andrew's) 1997, (Santiniketon) 1998, Hon. DUniv (Open Univ.) 1998; Adams Prize (Cambridge Univ.) 1966–67, Dannie Heinemann Prize (American Physics Soc. and American Inst. of Physics) 1971, Eddington Medal (with S. W. Hawking) (Royal Astronomical Soc.) 1975, Royal Medal (Royal Soc.) 1985, Wolf Foundation Prize for Physics (with S. W. Hawking) 1988, Dirac Medal and Prize, Inst. of Physics 1989, Einstein Medal 1990, Science Book Prize 1990, Naylor Prize, London Math. Soc. 1991. *Publications:* Techniques of Differential Topology in Relativity 1973, Spinors and Space-time (with W. Rindler), (Vol. I) 1984, (Vol. II) 1986, The Emperor's New Mind 1989, The Nature of Space and Time (with S. W. Hawking) 1996, The Large, the Small and the Human Mind 1997, White Mars (with B. Aldiss) 1999; articles in scientific journals. *Leisure interests:* three-dimensional puzzles, doodling at the piano. *Address:* Mathematical Institute, 24–29 St Giles, Oxford, OX1 3LB, England. *Telephone:* (1865) 273578. *Fax:* (1865) 273583. *E-mail:* rouse@maths.ox.ac.uk (Office).

PENZIAS, Arno Allan, PhD; American astrophysicist; b. 26 April 1933, Munich, Germany; s. of Karl Penzias and Justine Penzias; m. 1st Anne Barras Penzias 1954; one s. two d.; m. 2nd Sherry Chamovelevit 1996; ed City Coll. of New York, Columbia Univ.; mem. tech. staff Bell Laboratories, Holmdel, NJ 1961–72, Head Radiophysics Research Dept 1972–76, Dir Radio Research Lab. 1976–79, Exec. Dir Research, Communications Sciences Div. 1979–81, Exec. Dir Research, Bell Labs., Murray Hill, NJ 1979–81, Vice-Pres. Research 1981–95, Vice-Pres., Chief Scientist 1995–96; Vice-Pres., Chief Scientist Bell Labs. Innovations 1996–98; Venture Partner, New Enterprise Assocs. 1998–; Sr Tech Adviser Lucent Technologies 1998–; Lecturer, Princeton Univ. 1967–72, Visiting Prof. Astrophysical Sciences Dept 1972–85; Harvard Coll. Observatory Research Assoc. 1968–80; Adjunct Prof., S.U.N.Y. at Stony Brook 1974–84; discovered cosmic microwave background radiation 1965; Assoc. Ed., Astrophysical Journal 1978–82; mem. Editorial Bd Annual Review of Astronomy and Astrophysics 1974–78, AT & TBL Tech. Journal 1978–84 (Chair. 1981–84); mem. Bd of Trustees of Trenton State Coll. 1977–79, Visiting Cttee of Calif. Inst. of Tech. 1977–79; mem. Astronomy Advisory Panel of NSF 1978–79, Industrial Panel on Science and Tech. 1982–, Bd of Overseers, School of Eng and Applied Science Univ. of Pa 1983–86; mem. Max Planck Inst. Fachbeirat 1978–85 (Chair. 1981–83); mem. Council on Competitiveness 1989–; Vice-Chair. Cttee Concerned Scientists; mem. NAS, Nat. Acad. Eng, American Astronomical Soc., World Acad. Art and Science; Fellow AAAS, American Physical Soc.; numerous hon. degrees; Nobel Prize for Physics 1978; Henry Draper Medal, NAS 1977; Herschel Medal, Royal Astronomical Soc. 1977, Pender Award 1992, Int. Eng Consortium Fellow Award 1997 and numerous other prizes, awards, lectureships. *Publications:* Ideas and Information 1989, Digital Harmony 1995; over 100 scientific papers in various journals. *Leisure interests:* swimming, jogging, skiing. *Address:* New Enterprise Associates, 2490 Sand Hill Road, Menlo Park, CA 94025, USA (Office). *Telephone:* (650) 854-9499 (Office). *Fax:* (415) 544-0833. *E-mail:* apenzias@nea.com (Office). *Website:* www.nea.com (Office).

PEPPER, David, DPhil; British civil servant; b. 1947; m.; two s.; ed St John's Coll. Oxford; joined Govt Communications HQ (GCHQ) 1972, various positions in operational intelligence work, Dir of Personnel 1995–98, Head Corp. Devt Directorate 1998–2000, Dir of Finance 2000–03, Dir GCHQ Jan. 2003–. *Leisure interests:* music, reading, walking, cooking. *Address:* GCHQ, Priors Road, Cheltenham, Glos., GL52 5AJ, England (Office). *Telephone:* (1242) 221491 (Office). *Fax:* (1242) 574349 (Office). *E-mail:* webteam@gchq.gsi.gov.uk (Office). *Website:* www.gchq.gov.uk (Office).

PEPPER, John Ennis Jr.; American business executive; b. 2 Aug. 1938, Pottsville, Pa; s. of John Ennis Pepper, Sr and Irma O'Connor; m. Frances Graham Garber 1967; three s. one d.; ed Yale Univ.; with Procter & Gamble Co. 1963–, Gen. Man. Italian subsidiary 1974–77, Vice-Pres. and Gen. Man. packaged soap div. 1977–80, Group Vice-Pres. 1980–84, Exec. Vice-Pres. 1984–86, Pres. 1986–95, Chair., CEO 1995–99; Chair. 1999–, Exec. Cttee of the Bd 2000–; Co-Chair. Gov.'s Educ. Council of State of Ohio; Dir Xerox, Motorola; mem. adv. council Yale School of Man., other appointments. *Address:* Procter & Gamble Co., 1 Procter & Gamble Plaza, Cincinnati, OH 45202, USA.

PEPPER, Michael, ScD, FRS, FInstP; British physicist; b. 10 Aug. 1942, London; s. of Morris Pepper and Ruby Pepper; m. Dr. Jeannette D. Josse 1973; two d.; ed St Marylebone Grammer School, London, Reading Univ.; physicist, Mullard Research Lab. 1967–69; physicist engaged in solid state device research, Allen Clark Research Centre, Plessey Co. 1969–73; research at Cavendish Lab., Cambridge 1973–, Prof. of Physics, Univ. of Cambridge 1987–; Jt Man. Dir Toshiba Research Europe Ltd 1991–; Co-founder and Dir TeraView Ltd 2001; Warren Research Fellow of Royal Soc. 1978–86; Sr Research Fellow, Trinity Coll., Cambridge 1982–87, Professorial Fellow 1987–; Sr Research Fellow, GEC Hirst Research Centre 1982–87; Visiting Prof. Bar-Ilan Univ., Israel 1984; Fellow American Physical Soc.; Hon. DSc (Bar-Ilan) 1993, (Linköping) 1997; Guthrie Prize and Medal, Inst. of Physics 1985; Hewlett-Packard Prize, European Physical Soc. 1985, Hughes Medal of the Royal Soc. 1987, Mott Prize Inst. of Physics 2000. *Publications:* numerous papers on solid state physics and semiconductors in scientific journals. *Leisure interests:* travel, music, whisky tasting. *Address:* Cavendish Laboratory, Madingley Road, Cambridge, CB3 0HE; Toshiba Research Europe Ltd, 260 Cambridge Science Park, Milton Road, Cambridge, CB4 0WE, England. *Telephone:* (1223) 337330; (1223) 436900. *E-mail:* mp10000@cam.ac.uk (Office).

PEPYS, Mark Brian, PhD, MD, FRCP, FRCPath, FMedSci, FRS; British physician and academic; b. 18 Sept. 1944, Cape Town, South Africa; s. of Jack Pepys and Rhoda Pepys; m. Elizabeth Olga Winternitz 1971; one s. one d.; ed Trinity Coll., Cambridge, Univ. Coll. Hosp. Medical School, London, Harvard Medical School; house officer, Univ. Coll. Hosp., London 1968–69; Sr House Officer, Hammersmith Hosp. 1969–70, Asst Lecturer/Hon. Sr Registrar 1974–76, Prof. of Immunological Medicine 1984–99; MRC Jr Research Fellowship, Cambridge Univ., Research Scholar 1970–73, Fellow (Title A), Trinity Coll. Cambridge 1973–79, Registrar 1973–74; Sr Lecturer/Hon. Consultant and Head of Immunology Dept Royal Free Hosp. School of Medicine, London 1976–77, Head of Immunological Medicine and Hon. Consultant Physician 1977–79, Sr Lecturer 1977–81, Reader 1981–84, Prof. and Head of Medicine 1999–, Hon. Consultant Physician 1999–; Fellow Univ. Coll. London 2003; Trotter Medal for Clinical Surgery 1966; Alexander Bruce Gold Medal for Surgical Pathology, Fellowes Gold Medal for Clinical Medicine, Sir William Gowers Prize for Clinical Medicine, Liston Gold Medal for Clinical Surgery 1967; Atchison Scholarship for Clinical and Academic Attainment 1968; Royal Coll. of Physicians Goulstonian Lecturer 1982, Lumleian Lecturer 1998; Royal Coll. of Pathologists Kohn Lecturer; Royal Coll. of Surgeons of England Sir Arthur Sims Commonwealth Travelling Professorship 1991; Acad. of Medical Sciences Founder Fellow 1998; Moxon Trust Medal 1999. *Publications:* Samter's Immunologic Diseases (contrib.) 2001, Oxford Textbook of Medicine (contrib.) 2003; numerous research papers in learned journals. *Leisure interests:* tennis, surfing, skiing, wine. *Address:* Centre for Amyloidosis and Acute Phase Proteins, Department of Medicine, Royal Free and University College Medical School, Rowland Hill Street, London, NW3 2PF (Office); 22 Wildwood Road, London, NW11 6TE, England (Home). *Telephone:* (20) 7433-2802 (Office). *Fax:* (20) 7433-2803 (Office). *E-mail:* m.pepys@rfc.ucl.ac.uk (Office). *Website:* www.rfc.ucl.ac.uk (Office).

PERA, Marcello; Italian politician and professor of philosophy; b. 28 Jan. 1943, Lucca, Tuscany; ed Univ. of Pisa; Full Prof. of Theoretical Philosophy, Univ. of Catania 1989–92; Full Prof. of Philosophy of Science, Univ. of Pisa 1992; Visiting Fellow Univ. of Pittsburgh, USA 1984, Van Leer Foundation, Jerusalem 1987, MIT Dept of Linguistics and Philosophy, Cambridge, Mass. 1990; mem. Steering Cttee Forza Italia party, Deputy Leader Forza Italia Parl. Group 1996–2001; Head Judiciary Dept, Nat. Co-ordinator Convention for Liberal Reform; Senator 1996–, Pres. of Senate 2001–; mem. Cttee on Justice, Cttee on Educ. and Culture, Jt Cttee on Constitutional Reforms 1996–2001; mem. Advisory Panel Physis – Rivista internazionale di storia della scienza, Epistemologia, Perspectives on Science, Philosophical, Historical, Social; Fellow Center for the Study of Science in Soc., Univ. of Virginia; mem. Accademia Lucchese di Lettere, Scienze e Arti. *Publications include:* The Ambiguous Frog: The Galvani-Volta Controversy on Animal Electricity 1991, The Discourses of Science 1994; Ed. or Co-ed. several books including Rational Changes in Science 1987, Persuading Science. The Art of Scientific Rhetoric 1991, Scientific Controversies 2000; articles and essays. *Leisure interests:* reading essays and novels. *Address:* Office of the President, Il Senato, Rome, Italy (Office). *Telephone:* (06) 7062201 (Office). *Fax:* (06) 7062025 (Office). *E-mail:* segpres2@senato.it (Office). *Website:* www.senato.it (Office).

PERAHIA, Murray; American pianist and conductor; b. 19 April 1947, New York; s. of David Perahia and Flora Perahia; m. Naomi (Ninette) Shohet 1980; two s.; ed High School of Performing Arts, Mannes Coll. of Music; studied with Jeanette Haien, Arthur Balsam, Mieczyslaw Horszowski; début, Carnegie Hall 1968; won Leeds Int. Pianoforte Competition 1972; has appeared with many of world's leading orchestras and with Amadeus, Budapest, Guarneri and Galimir string quartets; regular recital tours N America, Europe, Japan;

Co-Artistic Dir Aldeburgh Festival 1983–89; numerous recordings including complete Mozart Piano Concertos; Avery Fisher Award 1975, Gramophone Record Award 1997, Grammy Award 1999; Kosciusko Chopin Prize 1965. *Address:* c/o Edna Landau, IMG, 825 7th Avenue, New York, NY 10019, USA.

PERAK, HH Sultan of, Sultan Azlan Muhibbuddin Shah ibni Al-Marhum Sultan Yussuf Ghafarullahu—Lahu Shah; Malaysian ruler; b. 19 April 1928, Batu Gajah; m. Tuanku Bainun Mohamed Ali 1954; two s. three d.; ed Govt English School (now Sultan Yussuf School), Malay Coll. and Univ. of Nottingham; called to Bar, Lincoln's Inn; Magistrate, Kuala Lumpur; Asst State Sec., Perak; Deputy Public Prosecutor; Pres. Sessions Court, Seremban and Taiping; State Legal Adviser, Pahang and Johore; Fed. Court Judge 1973; Chief Justice of Malaysia 1979; Lord Pres. 1982–83; Raja Kechil Bongsu (sixth-in-line) 1962, Raja Muda (second-in-line to the throne) 1983; Sultan of Perak Jan. 1984–; Yang di-Pertuan Agong (Supreme Head of State) 1989–94; Pro-Chancellor Univ. Saina Malaysia 1971, Chancellor Univ. of Malaya 1986; Hon. Col-in-Chief Malaysian Armed Forces' Engineers Corps.; Man. Malaysian Hockey Team 1972; Pres. Malaysian Hockey Fed., Asian Hockey Fed.; Vice-Pres. Int. Hockey Fed., Olympic Council of Malaysia.

PERBEN, Dominique; French politician and civil servant; b. 11 Aug. 1945, Lyon; s. of Jacques Perben and Agnès Berthier; m. 1st Annick Demoustier 1968; m. 2nd Corinne Garnier 1996; one s. two d. from previous m.; ed Paris Univ., Inst. of Political Studies, Paris; Pvt. Sec. to Maine-et-Loire Prefect 1972–75, to Norbert Ségard (Sec. of State for Postal Services and Telecommunications) 1977; Sec.-Gen. Territoire de Belfort 1975–76; Head of Mission Del. of Devt of Belfort Region 1977, Pres.'s Office Regional Council at Rhône-Alpes 1983–86; Admin. Télédiffusion de France 1980; with Ministry of the Interior 1981; Mayor of Chalon-sur-Saône 1983–; Vice-Pres. Regional Council Saône-et-Loire 1985–88, RPR Deputy 1986–93, 1997–; RPR Nat. Sec. of Local Elections 1984–86, of General Elections 1986–88, of Communication 1988–89, Asst Sec.-Gen. 1990–93; Minister of Overseas Territories 1993–95, for the Civil Service, Admin. Reform and Decentralization 1995–97; Minister of Justice May 2002–; Chevalier du Mérite agricole. *Leisure interests:* skiing, tennis. *Address:* Ministry of Justice, 13 place Vendôme, 75042 Paris cedex 01; Assemblée nationale, 126 rue de l'Université, 75355 Paris cedex 07; Mairie, BP 92, Place de l'Hôtel de Ville, 71321 Chalon-sur-Saône cedex, France. *Telephone:* 1-42-75-80-00. *Fax:* 1-44-77-70-20. *Website:* www.justice.gouv.fr.

PERCEVAL, John de Burgh, AO; Australian artist and ceramic potter; b. 1 Feb. 1923, Bruce Rock, W Australia; s. of William Perceval and Dorothy Perceval; m. 1944 (divorced); one s. three d.; ed Trinity Grammar School; began painting at age 13 (self-taught); mem. and former Sec. Contemporary Artists' Soc.; major retrospective exhbn Nat. Gallery of Vic. and Art Gallery of NSW 1992; represented in all maj. Australian art galleries, including Victoria, NSW, Queensland, S Australia, W Australia, Melbourne, Monash and Canberra, Nat. Gallery of Australia; Zwemmer Galleries, Hayward, Tate, London; Mertz Art Fund, Washington, USA; Toronto Art Gallery; pvt. collections internationally; the subject of several monographs; illustrated On My Island by Geoffery Dutton; Fellow in Creative Arts, ANU, Canberra 1965; Mona McCaughey Prize 1957, shared Wynne Prize 1961; Emer. Medal for Services to Govt, Australian Council 1995. *Address:* Unit 2/13 Terry Street, Balwyn, Vic. 3101, Australia.

PERCOVICH ROCA, Luis; Peruvian politician; b. 14 July 1931, Yungay, Ancash; s. of Alfredo Pércovich Jaramillo and Rosa Roca de Pércovich; m. Haydée Bambarén de Pércovich 1961; two s. one d.; Nat. Deputy 1963–68; Vice-Dean Chemical Pharmaceutical School of Peru 1967–68; Pres. Chamber of Deputies 1981–82; Minister of Fisheries Jan.–April 1983, Minister of the Interior 1983–84; Prime Minister of Peru and Minister of Foreign Affairs 1984–85; mem. Acción Popular (AP); Nat. Org. Sec. and Vice-Nat. Sec. Gen. Acción Popular, 1983–85; Acción Popular Del. Frente Democrático de Perú gen. election 1990. *Leisure interests:* nat. and int. econ. Devt, sport. *Address:* Los Eucaliptos 355-13A, San Isidro, Lima 27, Peru. *Telephone:* 440-1705. *Fax:* 440-4624.

PERCY, Charles Harting; American politician and business executive; b. 27 Sept. 1919, Pensacola, Fla; s. of Edward H. and Elisabeth Percy; m. Loraine Diane Guyer 1950; two s. two d.; ed Univ. of Chicago; Lt Sr Grade U.S. Naval Air Corps 1943–45; sales trainee, apprentice, Bell & Howell 1938, Man., War Co-ordinating Dept 1941–43, Asst Sec. 1943–46, Corpn Sec. 1948–49, Pres., CEO 1949–63, Chair. Bd 1961–66; Senator from Illinois 1967–85; Pres. Charles Percy and Assocs. Inc. 1985–; Chair. Foreign Relations Cttee 1981–85; Chair. Inst. of Int. Educ. 1985–89; Chair. and Pres. Hariri Foundation 1985–; Chair. U.S. Int. Cultural and Trade Center Pres. Comm. 1988–; Founding Chair. Kennedy Center for Performing Arts; Republican; Hon. LLD (Kent Coll. of Law) and various other hon. degrees. *Publications:* Growing Old In the Country of the Young 1974, I Want To Know about the United States Senate 1976. *Leisure interests:* reading, travel, swimming, tennis, skiing. *Address:* 1691 34th Street, NW, Washington, DC 20007, USA (Home). *Telephone:* (202) 337-1558 (Office); (202) 337-1691 (Home). *Fax:* (202) 337-5101 (Office); (202) 337-5101 (Home). *E-mail:* percycharles@ls.com (Office); percycharles@ls.com (Home).

PERDUE, Sonny; American state official; b. 20 Dec. 1946, Perry, Ga; s. of Ervin Perdue; m. Mary Ruff; four c.; ed Warner Robbins High School, Univ. of Ga; with USAF 1971–74; fmr veterinarian, Raleigh, NC; Propr Houston Fertilizer and Grain, Agrowstar Inc.; Democratic mem. of Senate, Ga 1991–1998, Pres. Pro Tempore, re-elected as Republican cand. 1998–2002; Gov. of Ga 2003–. *Leisure interest:* flying. *Address:* Office of the Governor, State Capitol Building, Constituent Services Room 111, Atlanta, GA 30334 (Office); P.O.B. 698, Bonaire, GA 31005, USA (Home).

PÉREC, Marie-José Juliana; French athlete; b. 9 May 1968, Basse-Terre, Guadeloupe; d. of José Pérec and Joëlle Pérec; partner Anthuan Maybank; ed Inst. Nat. du Sport et de l'Educ. Physique; 200 m European indoor champion 1989, bronze medallist European Championships 1990, gold medallist World Championships, Tokyo 1991, Olympic Games, Barcelona 1992, European Championships, Helsinki 1994, World Championships, Gothenburg 1995, Olympic Games, Atlanta 1996; gold medallist 200 m, Olympic Games, Atlanta 1996; disappeared after alleged threats when due to compete in Sydney Olympics 2000 and hasn't raced since (as at April 2003); expected to compete in World Championships, Paris 2003; also fashion model. *Leisure interest:* fashion. *Address:* c/o Ars Athletica, 20 rue de Madrid, 75008 Paris, France.

PEREIRA, Aristides Maria; Cape Verde politician; b. 17 Nov. 1923, Boa Vista; s. of Porfírio Pereira Tavares and Maria das Neves Crus Silva; m. Carlina Fortes 1959; one s. two d.; ed Lycée du Cap-Vert; began career as radio-telegraphist; Head, Telecommunications Services, Bissau, Portuguese Guinea (now Guinea-Bissau); f. Partido Africano da Independência da Guiné e Cabo Verde (PAIGC) with the late Amílcar Cabral 1956; mem. Political Bureau, Cen. Cttee, PAIGC 1956–70; fled to Repub. of Guinea 1960; Asst Sec.-Gen. PAIGC 1964–73, Sec.-Gen. 1973–81; Sec.-Gen. Partido Africano da Independência de Cabo Verde (PAICV) 1981; mem. Perm. Comm. of Exec. Cttee for Struggle in charge of Security, Control and Foreign Affairs 1970; Pres. Repub. of Cape Verde 1975–91; Dr. hc (Univs. of Rhode Island, Sacred Heart of Bridport, USA, Coimbra, Portugal, Usmane Danfodyo Univ., Sokoto, Nigeria); mem. Orders of Santiago of the Sword and Infante Dom Henrique (Portugal), Médaille, Ordre du Lyon (Senegal), Médaille Amílcar Cabral (Guinea-Bissau), Médaille de Fidélité au Peuple (Repub. of Guinea), Grand Cordon of Nat. Order of Southern Cross (Brazil), Agostinho Neto Medal, First Class (Angola), Amílcar Cabral Medal, First Class (Cape Verde). *Leisure interests:* swimming, tennis, music. *Address:* c/o Prainha, P.O. Box 172, Praia, Cape Verde. *Telephone:* 612461 (Office); 617747 (Home). *Fax:* 614302 (Office).

PEREIRA, Sir (Herbert) Charles, Kt, PhD, DSc, FRS; British agricultural scientist; b. 12 May 1913, London; m. Irene Beatrice Sloan 1941; three s. one d.; ed Prince Albert Coll., Sask., Canada, St Alban's School, Herts., England, London Univ. and Rothamsted Experimental Station, Herts.; war service with Royal Engineers in Western Desert, Italy and Germany (mentioned in dispatches); Soil Scientist Coffee Research Team Kenya 1946–52; Head of Physics Div., E African Agricultural and Forestry Research Org. 1952–55, Deputy Dir 1955–61; Dir Agricultural Research Council of Cen. Africa 1961–67; Consultant in Land Use Hydrology (IHD Programme) FAO 1968–69; Dir E Malling Research Station, Kent, England 1969–72; Chief Scientist, Deputy Sec. Ministry of Agric., Fisheries and Food 1972–77; Consultant in tropical agricultural research 1978–2000; mem. World Bank Tech. Advisory Cttee to CGIAR 1971–76; mem. Bd of Trustees, Royal Botanical Gardens, Kew 1983–86; Pres. Tropical Agric. Asscn 1990–2000; Trustee Marie Stopes Int. 1991–2000; Hon. Fellow, Royal Agricultural Soc. of England 1976; Life Fellow Inst. of Biology 1992; Hon. DSc (Cranfield) 1977; Haile Selassie Prize for Research in Africa 1966; Chevalier, Ordre du mérite agricole, Paris 1991. *Publications:* Land Use and Water Resources 1973, Policy and Practice in Watershed Management 1989, Simama 2000, scientific papers on tillage and weed competition, soil fertility and water relations, catchment area research, tropical soil structure. *Address:* Peartrees, Nestor Court, Teston, Maidstone, Kent, ME18 5AD, England (Home). *Telephone:* (1622) 813333 (Home).

PEREK, Luboš, RN.DR., DrSc; Czech astronomer (retd); b. 26 July 1919, Prague; s. of Zdeněk Perek and Vilemina (née Trapp) Perek; m. Vlasta Straková 1945; ed Masaryk Univ., Brno and Charles Univ., Prague; Asst Astronomical Inst., Masaryk Univ., Brno 1946, Head 1953; Head, Stellar Dept, Astronomical Inst. of Czechoslovak Acad. of Sciences, Prague 1956, Dir Astronomical Inst. 1968–75; Vice-Pres. Comm. of the Galactic Structure and Dynamics, Int. Astronomical Union 1961–64, Asst Gen. Sec., Int. Astronomical Union 1964–67, Gen. Sec. 1967–70; Chief, Outer Space Affairs Division, UN Secr. 1975–80; Visiting Prof., Dearborn Observatory, Evanston, Ill. 1964; mem. Czechoslovak Astronomical Soc., Exec. Cttee Int. Council of Scientific Unions 1967–70, Vice-Pres. 1968–70; Chair. Int. Astronautical Fed. 1980–82; mem. Leopoldina Acad., Int. Acad. of Astronautics, Int. Inst. of Space Law, Nat. Acad. of the Air and Space, Toulouse, Czech Learned Soc. 1999; Assoc. mem. Royal Astronomical Soc.; Dr. h.c. (Masaryk Univ., Brno) 1999; silver plaque for services to science 1969, gold plaque 1989, Janssen Medal, Paris 1992. *Publications include:* Catalogue of Galactic Planetary Nebulae (with L. Kohoutek) 1967, about 60 articles on geostationary orbits, definition of space, space debris and environment of space. *Leisure interest:* collecting seashells. *Address:* Astronomical Institute, Bočni II 1401, 141 31 Prague 4 (Office); Kouřimská 28, 130 00 Prague 3, Czech Republic (Home). *Telephone:* (2) 67103068 (Office); (2) 72744780. *Fax:* (2) 72769023. *E-mail:* perek@ig.cas.cz (Office).

PERELLA, Joseph Robert, MBA, CPA; American investment banker; b. 20 Sept. 1941, Newark; s. of Dominic Perella and Agnes Perella; m. Amy Gralnick 1974; ed Lehigh and Harvard Univs; public accountant, Haskins & Sells, New York 1964–70; consultant IBRD, Washington, DC 1971; Assoc. The First Boston Corpn New York 1972–74, Asst Vice-Pres. 1974–75, Vice-Pres. 1975-

78, Man. Dir 1978–88; Chair. Wasserstein, Perella & Co. New York 1988–93; mem. operating Cttee Morgan Stanley 1993–. *Address:* Morgan Stanley & Co. Inc., 1251 Avenue of the Americas, New York, NY 10020, USA.

PERELMAN, Ronald Owen, MBA; American business executive; b. 1943, Greensboro, NC; s. of Raymond Perelman and Claudia (née Cohen) Perelman; m. 1st Faith Golding (divorced); four c.; m. 2nd Claudia Cohen (divorced); one d.; m. 3rd Patricia Duff (divorced); one d.; m. 4th Ellen Barkin 2000; ed Univ. of Pa and Wharton School of Finance; with Belmont Industries Inc. 1966–78; Dir, Chair. and CEO MacAndrews & Forbes Group, Inc., New York City 1978–; Dir, Chair. and CEO Revlon Group, Inc., New York City 1985–; Andrews Group Inc., New York 1985–; Chair. Nat. Health Labs., La Jolla, Calif. 1985–; Chair. Technicolor Inc., Hollywood, Calif.; Pres. Solomon R. Guggenheim Museum, NY 1995–; Dir Four Star Int Inc., Compact Video Inc. *Address:* Revlon Group Inc., 625 Madison Avenue, Floor 8, New York, NY 10022 (Office); Solomark Guggenheim Museum, 1071 5th Avenue, New York, NY 10128, USA.

PERÉNYI, Miklós; Hungarian cellist and composer; b. 5 Jan. 1948, Budapest; s. of László Perényi and Erzsébet Seeger; m. Tünde Angermayer; one s.; ed Music Acad. of Budapest; started playing cello at age 6, first public recital at age 9, Budapest; Prof. of Violoncello Ferenc Liszt Acad. of Music, Budapest 1974–; numerous int. appearances; Liszt Prize 1970, Kossuth Prize 1980. *Leisure interests:* swimming, cycling. *Address:* Ferenc Liszt Academy of Music, PO Box 206, Liszt Ferenc tér 8, 1391 Budapest, Hungary.

PERES, Shimon; Israeli politician; b. 1923, Poland; s. of Isaac and Sara Persky; m. Sonia Gelman; two s. one d.; ed New York Univ., Harvard Univ.; immigrated to Palestine 1934; fmr Sec. Hano'ar Ha'oved Movt; mem. Haganah Movt 1947; Israel Naval Service, Ministry of Defence 1948; Head of Defence Mission in USA; Deputy Dir-Gen. of Ministry of Defence 1952–53, Dir-Gen. 1953–59, Deputy Minister of Defence 1959–65; mem. Knesset 1959–; mem. Mapai Party 1941–65, founder mem. and Sec.-Gen. Rafi Party 1965, mem. Labour Party after merger 1968, Chair. 1977–92, 1995–97; Minister for Econ. Devt in the Administered Areas and for Immigrant Absorption 1969–70, of Transport and Communications 1970–74, of Information March–June 1974, of Defence 1974–77, of Foreign Affairs 1992–95; Acting Prime Minister April–May 1977; Leader of the Opposition 1977–84, 1996–97; Prime Minister of Israel 1984–86; Minister of the Interior and of Religious Affairs 1984–85, of Defence 1995–96; Prime Minister 1995–96; Vice-Premier and Minister of Foreign Affairs 1986–88, Vice-Premier and Finance Minister 1988–90, Minister of Regional Co-operation –2001, of Foreign Affairs 2001–02; shared Nobel Prize for Peace 1994; Int. Council of Christians and Jews Interfaith Gold Medallion 1997. *Publications:* The Next Step 1965, David's Sling 1970, Tomorrow is Now 1978, From These Men 1979, Witness (autobiog.) 1993, The New Middle East 1993, Battling for Peace 1995 and numerous political articles in Israeli and foreign publs. *Address:* Amot Law House, 8 Shaul Hamelech Blvd, Tel Aviv, 64733; The Knesset, Jerusalem, Israel. *Telephone:* 3-6955669. *Fax:* 3-6954156. *E-mail:* s_peres@netvision.net.il.

PERESYPKIN, Oleg Gerasimovich, DHist, M.SC.ECON.; Russian diplomatist and orientalist; b. 12 Aug. 1935, Baku; s. of Gerasim Peresypkin and Anna Kochergina; m. Natalia Ushakova 1957; one d.; ed Moscow Inst. of Int. Relations; Counsellor, Embassy, Yemen Arab Repub. 1971–76; Adviser, Near Eastern Countries Dept, USSR Ministry of Foreign Affairs 1976–80; Amb. to Yemen Arab Repub. 1980–84, to Libya 1984–86; mem. Collegium of Foreign Ministry 1985–; Rector Diplomatic Acad. 1986–93; Chief Adviser on Near Eastern and N African Countries, Ministry of Foreign Affairs 1993–96; Amb. to Lebanon 1996–2000; Pres. Imperial Orthodox Palestine Soc. 1989–2000; Pres. Russian Soc. for Friendship and Cultural Co-operation with Lebanon 2001–; Order of Friendship 1995, Honoured worker of Russian diplomatic corps 2001. *Publications:* Iraqi Oil 1969, Yemen Revolution 1979, On the New East Crossroads 1979, Fifth Season 1991, Oriental Patterns 1993, Informal Notes 1997. *Leisure interests:* travelling, reading. *Address:* PO Box 44, 121069 Moscow; Vosdvijenka 14, 103885 Moscow, Russia. *Telephone:* (095) 203-03-72. *Fax:* (095) 203-03-72. *E-mail:* usfur@yandex.ru.

PERETZ, David Lindsay Corbett, CB, MA; British international finance official; b. 29 May 1943; s. of Michael Peretz and April Peretz; m. Jane Wildman 1966; one s. one d.; ed The Leys School Cambridge and Exeter Coll. Oxford; Asst Prin. Ministry of Tech. 1965–69; Head of Public Policy and Institutional Studies, Int. Bank Research Org. 1969–76; Prin. HM Treasury 1976–80, Asst Sec. External Finance 1980–84, Prin. Pvt. Sec. to Chancellor of Exchequer 1984–85, Under-Sec. (Home Finance) 1985–86, (Monetary Group, Public Finance) 1986–90; UK Exec. Dir IMF and IBRD and Econ. Minister, Washington, DC 1990–94; Deputy Dir Int. Finance, HM Treasury 1994–99; UK G7 Financial Sherpa 1994–98; Sr Adviser IBRD (World Bank) 1999–. *Leisure interests:* walking, sailing, listening to music. *Address:* World Bank, 1818 H Street, NW, Washington, DC 20433, USA (Office). *E-mail:* dperetz@worldbank.org (Office); davidperetz@compuserve.com (Office). *Website:* www.worldbank.org (Office).

PEREZ, Vincent; Swiss actor; ed Conservatoire, Paris. *Film appearances include:* Cyrano de Bergerac, La Reine Margot, Indochine, The Crow, City of Angels, Amy Foster.

PÉREZ BALLADARES, Ernesto, MBA; Panamanian politician; b. 29 June 1946, Panama City; s. of Ernesto Pérez Balladares Sr and María Enriqueta

González Revilla; m. Dora Boyd; two s. three d.; ed Univs. of Notre Dame and Pennsylvania; Dir, Corp. Credit Official for Cen. America and Panama, Citibank 1971–75; Minister of Finance and the Treasury 1976–81, of Planning and Econ. Policy 1981–82; founding mem. Partido Revolucionario Democrático (PRD) 1979, Sec.-Gen. 1982, 1992; Dir-Gen. Instituto de Recursos Hidráulicos y Electrificación (IRHE) 1983; Pres. of Panama 1994–99; Pres. Golden Fruit, SA, Inversionista el Torreón, SA; mem. Legislation Comm., PRD Political Comm.; Order of Sacred Treasure (1st class) (Japan) 1980, Orden Aguila Azteca in Grado de Bando (Mexico) 1981. *Address:* c/o Office of the President, Palacio Presidencial, Valija 50, Panamá 1, Panama.

PÉREZ DE CUÉLLAR, Javier; Peruvian diplomatist; b. 19 Jan. 1920, Lima; m. Marcela Temple; two c.; ed Catholic Univ., Lima; joined Foreign Ministry 1940, diplomatic service 1944; served as Sec. in embassies in France, UK, Bolivia, Brazil (later Counsellor); Dir Legal and Personnel Dept, Dir of Admin., of Protocol and of Political Affairs, Ministry of External Relations 1961–63; Amb. to Switzerland 1964–66; Perm. Under Sec. and Sec.-Gen. Foreign Office 1966–69, Amb. to USSR (concurrently to Poland) 1969–71, to Venezuela 1978; Perm. Rep. to UN 1971–75; mem. UN Security Council 1973–74, Pres. 1974; Special Rep. of UN Sec.-Gen. in Cyprus 1975–77; UN Under-Sec.-Gen. for Special Political Affairs 1979–81; UN Sec.-Gen. 1982–91; Prime Minister of Peru 2000–01; Amb. to France 2001–; Pres. World Comm. on Culture and Devt UN/UNESCO 1992–, Int. Disability Foundation 1992–, Fondation de l'Arche de la Fraternité 1993–; Dir Repub. Nat. Bank of New York 1992–; Pres. Cand. in 1995 Elections; fmr Prof. of Diplomatic Law, Acad. Diplomática del Perú and Prof. of Int. Relations, Acad. de Guerra Aérea del Perú; del. to First UN Gen. Ass. 1946–47 and other int. confs.; Montague Burton Visiting Prof. of Int. Relations, Univ. of Edinburgh 1985; mem. Acad. Mexicana de Derecho Int. 1988–; Hon. Dr. (Univ. of Nice) 1983, (Jagiellonian, Charles and Sofia Univs., Univ. of San Marcos and Vrije Univ., Brussels) 1984, (Carleton Univ., Ottawa, Sorbonne Univ., Paris) 1985, (Osnabruck) 1986, (Univs. of Mich., Coimbra, Mongolian State, Humbolt, Moscow State) 1987, (Univ. of Leiden) 1988, (Cambridge) 1989, (Univ. of Kuwait) 1993, (Oxford) 1993; Olaf Palme Prize for Public Service 1989; Prince of Asturias Prize for Ibero-American Co-operation; Alexander Onassis Foundation Prize 1990; Four Freedoms Award (Franklin Delano Roosevelt Inst.) 1992. *Publication:* Manual de Derecho Diplomático 1964, Anarchy or Order 1992, Pilgrimage for Peace 1997. *Address:* Embassy of Peru, 50 avenue Kléber, 75116 Paris (Office); 18 avenue de la Bourdonnais, 75007 Paris, France; Avenida A. Miro Quesada, 1071 Lima, Peru. *Telephone:* 1-53-70-42-00 (Office). *Fax:* 1-47-55-98-30 (Office). *E-mail:* amb-perou@noos.fr (Office). *Website:* www.amb-perou.fr (Office).

PÉREZ ESQUIVEL, Adolfo; Argentine human rights leader, architect and sculptor; b. 26 Nov. 1931, Buenos Aires; m. Amanda Pérez 1956; three s.; ed Nat. School of Fine Arts, Buenos Aires; trained as architect and sculptor; Prof. of Art, Manuel Belgrano Nat. School of Fine Arts, Buenos Aires 1956–71; Prof. Faculty of Architecture and Urban Studies; Univ. Nacional de la Plata; gave up teaching to concentrate on non-violent human rights movt; f. Servicio Paz y Justicia in America Latina, Buenos Aires 1973, Sec.-Gen. 1974–86, Hon. Pres. 1986–; co-founder Ecumenical Movt. for Human Rights, Argentina; Pres. Perm. Ass. for Human Rights; arrested 1977, released May 1978; visited Europe 1980; Pres. Int. League for the Rights and Liberation of Peoples 1987; fmr Rector UN Univ. for Peace; Nobel Prize for Peace 1980; Hon. Citizen of Assisi 1982. *Address:* Servicio Paz y Justicia, Piedras 730, CP 1070, Buenos Aires, Argentina.

PÉREZ GODOY, Gen. Ricardo Pío; Peruvian politician and army officer; b. 9 June 1905; ed Colegio Santo Tomás de Aquino and Escuela de Oficiales del Ejército; Dir-Gen. of Training, Peruvian Army 1956–57; Controller-Gen. of Army 1958–59; Chief of Staff of Jt Command of Armed Forces 1960–62; Prefect of Dept of Arequipa 1952–53, 1955–56; Pres. of Mil. Junta of Govt of Peru 1962–63; mem. Centro de Altos Estudios Históricos del Perú; now Gen. of a Div.; numerous decorations. *Publications:* include Teoría de la Guerra y Doctrina de Guerra, La Maniobra y la Batalla. *Address:* Blasco Núñez de Balboa 225, Miraflores, Lima, Peru.

PÉREZ-LLORCA, José Pedro; Spanish politician and lawyer; b. 30 Nov. 1940, Cadiz; s. of José and Carmen Pérez-Llorca; m. Carmen Zamora Bonilla 1965; one s. one d.; ed Madrid Central (Complutense) Univ., Univs. of Freiburg and Munich; entered diplomatic service 1964; adviser Spanish del. to 21st and 22nd Gen. Ass. of UN and 5th extraordinary emergency session; Legal Adviser to Parl. 1968; Higher Council for Foreign Affairs 1970; practised law, Madrid 1970–; mem. Cortes 1977–82; fmr parl. leader Unión de Centro Democrático (UCD); mem. Comm. for drawing up Constitution 1978; Minister of the Presidency 1979–80, Minister for Relations with Parl. Jan.–May 1980, Minister for Territorial Admin. May–Oct. 1980, Minister for Foreign Affairs 1980–82; pvt. law practice 1983–; Chair. AEG-Ibérica SA, Urquiso Leasing SA; Dir Robert Bosch Española SA; Prof. of Constitutional Law, School of Diplomacy. *Address:* Plaza de la Marina Española 8, 28071 Madrid, Spain.

PÉREZ RODRÍGUEZ, Carlos Andrés; Venezuelan politician; b. 27 Oct. 1922, Rubio; m. Blanca Rodríguez de Pérez; one s. five d.; ed Univ. Central de Venezuela; Pvt. Sec. to Pres. Rómulo Betancourt 1945; mem. Chamber of Deputies 1947–48, 1958–74; in exile 1949–58; Chief Ed. La República, San José 1953–58; Minister of the Interior 1963–64; Sec.-Gen. Acción Democrática

1968; Pres. of Venezuela 1974–79, 1989–93; suspended, to stand trial on embezzlement charges; barred from returning to office Sept. 1993; found guilty of misappropriation of public funds May 1996 and sentenced to two years and four months' imprisonment, served as house arrest owing to age.

PEREZ ROQUE, Felipe; Cuban politician; b. 28 March 1928, Havana; m.; head univ. students union 1988; fmr electronics engineer; involved with biotech. complex 1960; Pvt. Sec. to Fidel Castro; Minister of Foreign Affairs 1999–. *Address:* Ministry of Foreign Affairs, Calzada 360, Vedado, Havana, Cuba (Office). *Telephone:* (7) 324074 (Office). *Fax:* (7) 333460 (Office).

PERHAM, Richard Nelson, MA, PhD, ScD,FRS, FRSA; British professor of biochemistry; b. 27 April 1937, London; s. of Cyril Perham and Helen Thornton; m. Nancy Lane 1969; one s. one d.; ed Latymer Upper School, London and St John's Coll., Cambridge; MRC Scholar, MRC Lab. of Molecular Biology, Cambridge 1961–64; Helen Hay Whitney Fellow, Dept of Molecular Biophysics, Yale Univ. 1966–67; Univ. Lecturer in Biochemistry, Univ. of Cambridge 1969–77, Reader in Biochemistry of Macromolecular Structures 1977–89, Prof. of Structural Biochem. 1989–; Fellow, St John's Coll., Cambridge 1964–, Pres. 1983–87; Fogarty Int. Scholar, NIH, USA 1990–93; mem. European Molecular Biology Org., Academia Europaea; Max Planck Prize 1993, Novartis Medal and Prize 1998, Silver Medal, Italian Biochemical Soc. 2000. *Publications:* Instrumentation in Amino Acid Sequence Analysis; more than 250 papers and articles in learned journals. *Leisure interests:* gardening, theatre, opera, rowing, antiques (18th century). *Address:* Department of Biochemistry, University of Cambridge, 80 Tennis Court Road, Cambridge, CB2 1GA (Office); St John's College, Cambridge, CB2 1TP (Office); 107 Barton Road, Cambridge, CB3 9LL, England (Home). *Telephone:* (1223) 333663 (Office); (1223) 338764 (Coll.); (1223) 363752 (Home). *Fax:* (1223) 333667 (Office); (1223) 363752 (Home). *E-mail:* r.n.perham@bioc.cam.ac.uk (Office).

PERIGOT, François; French business executive; b. 12 May 1926, Lyons; s. of Jean-Paul Perigot and Marguerite de la Tour; m. 2nd Isabelle Paque 1986; one s. one d. from fmr marriage; ed Lycée de Bastia, Faculté de Droit, Paris and Inst. d'Etudes Politiques, Paris; joined Unilever group (France) 1955, Head of Personnel 1966; Pres.-Dir-Gen. Thibaud Gibbs et Cie 1968–70; Dir Unilever (Spain) 1971–75; Pres.-Dir-Gen. Unilever (France) 1976–86; Pres. Campagnie de Plâtre 1987–98; mem. Bd of Sodexho, Diosos, CDC lxis Pvt. Equity, Lever, Astra; mem. Exec. Council, Conseil Nat. du Patronat Français (CNPF) 1981–86, Pres. 1986–94; Vice-Pres. Union des confédérations de l'industrie et des employeurs d'Europe (UNICE) 1988–92, Pres. 1994; mem. Social and Econ. Council (CES) 1989–99; Pres. MEDEF Int. 1999, O.I.E. (Int. Org. of Employers) 2001; Commdr, Légion d'honneur; numerous foreign decorations. *Leisure interest:* golf. *Address:* 4 rue Quentin Bauchart, 75008 Paris, France. *Telephone:* 1-47-23-96-87 (Office). *Fax:* 1-47-23-61-82 (Office).

PERIN, François; Belgian politician, professor of law and writer; b. 31 Jan. 1921, Liège; ed Univ. of Liège; mem. of Socialist Party 1943–64; Asst Chef de Cabinet to Minister of Interior 1954–57; Asst to Prof. of Public Law 1954–58; Dir of Studies, Faculty of Law, Univ. of Liège 1958, Prof. of Constitutional Law 1967–86, Prof. Emer. 1986–; Deputy to Nat. Ass. 1965–; Pres. Rassemblement Wallon 1968–74; Minister of Institutional Reforms 1974–76; mem. co-founders Parti Réformateur Libéral (PRL) 1976–; author of Les invités du Dr. Klaust, staged Théâtre Arlequin, Liège 1998–99 and of Double jeu. Drame à Liège 1632–1637, staged Théâtre Arlequin 2002. *Publications:* La démocratie enrayée—essai sur le régime parlementaire belge de 1918 à 1958 1960, La Belgique au défi: Flamands Wallons à la recherche d'un état 1962, La décision politique en Belgique (co-author) 1965, Le régionalisme dans l'intégration européenne 1969, Germes et bois morts dans la société politique contemporaine 1981, Histoire d'une nation introuvable 1988, Franc parler: témoignage sur la double crise du Christianisme et du Rationalisme 1996, Tabous-chemins croisés (co-author) 2001. *Leisure interests:* music, concerts, history of religions, philosophy and science. *Address:* 10 rue Chevaufosse, 4000 Liège, Belgium. *Telephone:* (4) 223-67-82.

PERINETTI, André Louis; French administrator and theatre director; b. 7 Aug. 1933, Asnières; m. Fatiha Bel-el-Abbas 1974; two s. one d.; ed Collège Turgot, Law Faculty of Paris, Univ. of Theatre of Nations; theatre dir 1965–83; Gen. Man. Théâtre Cité Universitaire 1968–72, Nat. Theatre of Strasbourg 1972–75, Nat. Theatre of Chaillot, Paris 1974–81; Consultant, UNESCO 1974, Ministry of Culture 1982–83; Sec.-Gen. Int. Theatre Inst. (UNESCO) 1984–; Légion d'honneur, Chevalier des Arts et Lettres; hon. doctorate (Bratislava). *Leisure interests:* theatre, music, tennis. *Address:* 109 avenue Charles de Gaulle, 92200 Neuilly, France. *Fax:* 1-45-66-50-40. *E-mail:* iti@unesco.org (Office).

PERIŠIC, Zoran; Serbia and Montenegro (Serbian) film director, writer, producer and visual effects supervisor; b. 16 March 1940, Zemun; Dir Sky Bandits/Gunbus (film) 1986; Producer-Dir The Phoenix and the Magic Carpet 1994; Dir-Writer Captain Cook's Travels (TV, animated series), Magic Fountain (TV, animated series), In Search of the Real Dracula (documentary), etc.; cr. visual effects for 2001 – A Space Odyssey, Superman 1, 2 and 3, Return to Oz, Cliffhanger and other films; several patents, including ZOPTIC front-projection system and 3D cinematography; Acad. Award (Oscar) for Outstanding Achievement in Visual Effects (for Superman – the Movie), BAFTA Award for Outstanding Contrib. to the Cinema, American Acad. Tech. Achievement Award for the invention and devt of the ZOPTIC dual-zoom front-projection system. *Publications:* Special Optical Effects, The Animation Stand, Photoguide to Shooting Animation, Visual Effects Cinematography 2000. *Leisure interest:* flying (pvt. pilot's licence). *Address:* c/o Contemporary Artists, 1317 5th Street, 200 Santa Monica, CA 90401, USA. *E-mail:* zoptic@hotmail.com (Office); zoran@zoptic.force9.co.uk (Home). *Website:* zoptic.com (Office).

PERIŠIN, Ivo, DEcon; Croatian economist and university professor; b. 4 July 1925, Split; s. of Duje and Filomena Tadin Perišin; m. Magda Martinič 1949; one s. one d.; ed Zagreb Univ.; Prof. of Econ., Zagreb Univ.; Chief of post-univ. studies in banking and financial markets; fmr Under-Sec., Fed. Secr. for Finance; Gov. Nat. Bank of Yugoslavia (Narodna Banka Jugoslavije) 1969–72; Pres. Exec. Council, Socialist Repub. of Croatia 1972–74; Pres. Parl. 1974–78; Pres. Fed. Council for Devt and Econ. Policy 1978–88; mem. Croatian Acad. of Science; Partisan Memorial Award, Order of People's Merit, Order of the Repub., Medal for Valour. *Publications:* Money and Credit Policy 1964, Money and Economic Development 1961, Economics of Yugoslavia, Inflation 1965, Financial Dictionary 1967, Money, Credit and Banking 1975, Transformation of Monetary System 1975, Money, Monetary System and Associated Work 1978, Essays on the Reform of the Monetary System 1979, Interest Rates and Savings 1980, Inflation 1985, World Financial Whirlpool (a contrib. to Studies of Modern Banking and Financial Markets) 1988, Series on financial transformation 1991–98, Financial Mechanism and Our Reality 2000, Monetary Policy 2001. *Address:* Ksaverska cesta 13, Zagreb, Croatia. *Telephone:* (1) 4677212. *E-mail:* tena.perisin@zg.tel.hr (Home).

PERISSICH, Riccardo; Italian international civil servant; b. 24 Jan. 1942, Milan; m. Anne Treca 1989; one c.; writer on foreign policy for Il Punto (Rome weekly) 1962; Italconsult S.p.a. (consulting engineers) 1962–64; Head of EC Studies, Istituto Affari Internazionali, Rome 1966–70; joined Comm. of EC, Brussels 1970; Chef de Cabinet of Altiero Spinelli 1970–76, Cesidio Guazzaroni 1976; Dir Directorate A (energy savings and energy forecasts) 1977–81; Chef de Cabinet of Antonio Giolitti (regional policy) 1981–84, of Carlo Ripa di Meana (institutional affairs) 1985–86; Dir, later Deputy Dir-Gen. Directorate-Gen. for Industry 1986, Dir-Gen. 1990–94; Bd mem. and Dir Public and Econ. Affairs Pirelli SpA 1994–2001, Co-ordinator of Institutional Affairs 2001–; Dir Public and Econ. Affairs Telecom Italia Group 2001–; Chair. Seat Pagine Gialle 2002–; Vice-Chair. Assolombarda 1995–, Unione Industriali di Roma, ASSONIME (Italian Cos. Asscns.); Bd mem. European Inst. of Oncology; mem. Int. Inst. for Strategic Studies (London), Istituto Affari Internazionali, Aspen Inst. Italia. *Publications:* Gli eurocrati fra realtà e mitologia 1969, Europa America: materiali per un dibattito (with S. Silvestri) 1970. *Address:* Telecom Italia, Corso d'Italia 41, 00198 Rome, Italy.

PERISSOL, Pierre-André Daniel; French politician and engineer; b. 30 April 1947, Nice; s. of Louis Perissol and Aline Cardiec; ed Lycée Massena, Nice, Ecole Polytechnique, Ecole Nat. des Ponts et Chaussées; Dir of Planning, Saint-Quentin-en-Yvelines new town 1972–74; Adviser to Sec. of State for Housing 1974–76; Chief Eng Ecole Nat. des Ponts et Chaussées 1986; Dir-Gen. Soc. Centrale de Crédit Immobilier 1977–91, Pres., Dir-Gen. 1991–92, Pres. 1993–95; Founder and Dir.–Gen. Groupe Arcade 1980–91, Pres. 1991–95; Pres. Coopérer pour Habiter 1982, Aiguillon Construction 1987, Fed. Nat. (now Chambre Syndicale) des Sociétés de Crédit Immobilier 1988, Caisse Centrale de Crédit Immobilier 1990–93; Regional Councillor, Ile-de-France 1983–86; Councillor, Paris 1983–95; Deputy Mayor of Paris responsible for Educ. 1989–93; RPR Deputy to Nat. Ass. 1993–95; Minister of Housing May–Nov. 1995, Deputy Minister 1995–97; Mayor of Moulins 1995–; Vice-Pres. Regional Council of Auvergne 1998–; UMP Deputy to Nat. Ass. 2002–; Officier, Légion d'honneur, Ordre Nat. du Mérite. *Publications:* Le défi social 1985, En mal de toit 1995, A bonne école 2002. *Leisure interests:* travel, tennis. *Address:* Assemblée Nationale, 126 rue de l'Université, 75007 Paris, France (Office).

PERKIN, James Russell Conway, DPhil; British/Canadian university president; b. 19 Aug. 1928, Northants.; s. of William Perkin and Lily Drage; m. Dorothy Bentley 1953; two s. one d.; ed Daventry Grammar School, Northants. and Univ. of Oxford; Minister, Altrincham Baptist Church, Cheshire 1955–62; lecturer in New Testament Greek, New Coll. Edinburgh 1963–65; Assoc. Prof. of New Testament Interpretation, McMaster Divinity Coll. Hamilton, Ont. 1965–69; Prof. of Religious Studies and Head of Dept Acadia Univ. NS 1969–77, Dean of Arts 1977–80, Vice-Pres. (Academic) 1980–81, Acting Pres. 1981–82, Pres. 1982–93; mem. Soc. for New Testament Studies, Canadian Soc. for Study of Religion; Hon. DD (McMaster) 1986; Hon. DLitt (Acadia) 1995; Canada 125th Medal 1992. *Publications:* Such is Our Story (with E. A. Payne) 1955, Study Notes on Romans 1957, Resurrection in Theology and Life 1966, Handbook for Biblical Studies 1973, Scripture Then and Now 1975, In Season 1978, With Mind and Heart 1979, Crucial Questions 1980, Seedtime and Harvest 1982, Arrows in the Mind 1984, Morning in his Heart: Life and Writings of Watson Kirkconnell (with J. Snelson) 1986, Morning in his Heart: a Biographical Sketch of Watson Kirkconnell 1987, Commonplace Book 1986, Reflections and Insights 1993, Ordinary Magic 1995, Devotional Diary 1998; book chapters, essays, articles and reviews. *Leisure interests:* reading, gardening, sailing, classical music. *Address:* 46 Kent Avenue, Wolfville, NS B4P 1V1, Canada. *Telephone:* (902) 542-5501 (Home).

PERKINS, Alice Elizabeth, BA; British civil servant; b. 24 May 1949; d. of Derrick Leslie John Perkins and Elsa Rose Perkins (née Rink); m. Jack (John Whitaker) Straw (1978; one s. one d.; ed N London Collegiate School for Girls and St Anne's Coll., Oxford; joined Civil Service in Dept of Health and Social

Security (DHSS) 1971, Prin. 1976–84, Asst Sec. DHSS, then Dept of Social Security (DSS) 1984–90, Dir of Personnel 1990–93; Under-Sec. Defence Policy and Material Group, HM Treasury 1993–95, Deputy Dir of Public Spending 1995–98; Dir of Corp. Man., Dept of Health 1998–2000; Head of Civil Service Corp. Man., Cabinet Office 2000–; Trustee Whitehall and Industry Group 1993–; Dir (non-exec.) Littlewoods Org. 1997–2000. *Leisure interests:* gardening, riding, looking at paintings. *Address:* Cabinet Office, Admiralty Arch, The Mall, London, SW1A 2WH, England (Office).

PERKINS, David D(exter), PhD; American biologist and geneticist; b. 2 May 1919, Watertown, New York; s. of Dexter M. Perkins and Loretta F. (née Gardiner) Perkins; m. Dorothy L. Newmeyer 1952; one d.; ed Univ. of Rochester and Columbia Univ.; mem. Faculty, Stanford Univ. 1949, Prof. of Biology 1961–89, Prof. Emer. 1989–; Research Fellow, Univ. of Glasgow, Scotland 1954–55; Columbia Univ. 1962–63, ANU, Canberra 1968–69; mem. India-US Exchange Scientists' Program 1974; Ed. Genetics 1963–67; mem. Int. Genetics Fed. Exec. Bd 1978–83, Genetics Soc. of America (Pres. 1977), NAS; Nat. Insts. of Health Research Career Award 1964–89, Merit Award 1987–96, Guggenheim Fellow 1983–85; Genetics Soc. of America Morgan Medal 1994. *Publications:* The Cytogenetics of Neurospora (with E. G. Barry) 1977, Chromosome Rearrangements in Neurospora and Other Filamentous Fungi 1997, The Neurospora Compendium: Chromosomal Loci (co-author) 2001, Neurospora from Natural Populations: A global study (co-author) 2001. *Address:* Department of Biological Sciences, Stanford University, Stanford, CA 94305-5020 (Office); 345 Vine Street, Menlo Park, CA 94025, USA (Home). *Fax:* (650) 723-6132. *E-mail:* perklab@stanford.edu (Office).

PERKINS, Donald H., CBE, MA, PhD, FRS; British professor of physics; b. 15 Oct. 1925, Hull; s. of G. W. Perkins and G. Perkins; m. Dorothy M. Maloney 1955; two d.; ed Imperial Coll. London; Sr 1851 Scholar, Univ. of Bristol 1949–52, G. A. Wills Research Assoc. 1952–55; Visiting Scientist, Univ. of Calif. 1955–56; Lecturer, then Reader in Physics, Univ. of Bristol 1956–65; Prof. of Elementary Particle Physics, Univ. of Oxford 1965–93, Fellow St Catherine's Coll. 1965–; mem. SERC 1985–89; Hon. DSc (Sheffield) 1982, (Bristol) 1995; Guthrie Medal, Inst. of Physics 1979, Holweck Medal (Société française de physique) 1992, Royal Medal, Royal Soc. of London 1997, High-Energy Physics Prize, European Physical Soc. 2001. *Publications:* Study of Elementary Particles by the Photographic Method (with C. F. Powell and P. H. Fowler) 1959, Introduction to High Energy Physics 1972. *Leisure interests:* squash, skiing, lepidoptera. *Address:* 2A Blenheim Drive, Oxford, OX1 8DG, England (Home). *Telephone:* (1865) 311717 (Home).

PERKINS, Edward J., D.P.A.; American diplomatist and professor of political science; b. 8 June 1928, Sterlington, La.; m. Lucy Liu; two d.; ed Univ. of Maryland and Univ. of S. California; Chief of Personnel, Army and Air Force Exchange Service, Taiwan 1958–62; Deputy Chief, Okinawa, Japan 1962–64; Chief of Personnel and Admin. 1964–66; Asst Gen. Services Officer, Far East Bureau, AID 1967–69; Man. Analyst 1969–70; Deputy Dir Man. U.S. Operations, Mission to Thailand 1970–72; Staff Asst Office of Dir-Gen. of Foreign Service 1972; Personnel Officer 1972–74; Admin. Officer, Bureau of Near Eastern and South Asian Affairs 1974–75; Man. Analysis Officer, Office of Man. Operations, Dept of State 1975–78; Counsellor for Political Affairs, Accra 1978–81; Deputy Chief of Mission, Monrovia 1981–83; Dir Office of West African Affairs, Dept of State 1983–85; Amb. to Liberia 1985–86, to South Africa 1986–89; Dir-Gen. Foreign Service, Washington 1989–92; Perm. Rep. to UN 1992–93; Amb. to Australia 1993–96; William J. Crowe Chair Prof. of Geopolitics and Exec. Dir Int. Programs Center, Univ. of Okla 1996–; Bd. Dir Asscn for Diplomatic Studies and Training 1998–; Trustee Lewis and Clark Coll. 1994–, Asia Soc. 1997–2000, Inst. of Int. Educ. 1997–2000; Gov. Jt Center for Political and Econ. Studies 1996–; mem. Advisory Council Univ. Office of Int. Programs Pa State Univ. 1997–; mem. Advisory Bd Inst. of Int. Public Policy 1997–; Trustee Woodrow Wilson Fellowship Foundation 1999–; Distinguished Alumni Award, Univ. of S. Calif. 1991, Distinguished Honor Award, Dept of State 1992, Statesman of the Year Award, George Washington Univ. 1992, Dept of State Dir-Gen. Cup 2001 and numerous other awards. *Publications include:* Preparing America's Foreign Policy for the 21st Century (Ed., with David L. Boren) 1999, Democracy, Morality and the Search for Peace in America's Foreign Policy (Ed., with David L. Boren) 2002, contribs. to specialized journals and reviews. *Leisure interests:* art, jazz. *Address:* International Programs Center, University of Oklahoma, 339 W Boyd Street, Rm. 400, Norman, OK 73019 (Office); 1025 Joe Keeley Drive, Norman, OK 73072, USA (Home). *Telephone:* (405) 325-1396 (Office). *Fax:* (405) 325-7454 (Office). *E-mail:* eperkins@ou.edu (Office). *Website:* www.ou.edu/ipc/perkins (Office).

PERKINS, Frederick J., MSc; business executive; b. 2nd March 1948, Glasgow; ed Univ. of Strathclyde, Univ. of Sussex; fmr Vice-Pres. Europe, McGraw-Hill; Chief Exec. The Stationery Office (fmrly Her Majesty's Stationery Office) 1996–; Group Dir The Financial Times; Chair. Electronic Publrs. Forum 1996–, Public Policy Forum 2001–. *Address:* The Stationery Office, 51 Nine Elms Lane, London, SW8 5DR, England (Office). *Telephone:* (20) 7873-8741 (Office). *Fax:* (20) 7873-8467 (Office). *E-mail:* fjperkins@theso .co.uk (Office). *Website:* thestationeryoffice.co.uk (Office).

PERKINS, Kieren John, OA; Australian swimmer; b. 14 Aug. 1973, Brisbane; s. of Kevin Perkins and Gloria Perkins; m. Symantha Liu 1997; one s. one d.; ed Brisbane Boys' Coll., Univ. of Queensland; gold medal Olympic Games, Barcelona 1992 for 1,500 m freestyle (world record), gold medal

Olympic Games, Atlanta 1996 for 1,500 m (first swimmer to hold Olympic, World, Commonwealth and Pan Pacific titles simultaneously), two gold medals World Championships, Rome 1994 (world and Commonwealth records for 400 m freestyle), four gold medals Commonwealth Games, Canada 1994 (world and Commonwealth records for 800 m and 1,500 m freestyle); set 10 Australian, 11 Queensland and 10 Brisbane records and two Commonwealth and one Australian standard time records; silver medal 1500 m freestyle Olympic Games, Sydney 2000; then retd; World Oceania Award, LA Amateur Athletic Foundation Award 1992, Australian Sports and Tourism Amb., Australia Tourist Comm. 1993, Advance Australia Award 1993, World Male Swimmer of the Year 1994, FINA Award 1994, Australian flag-bearer Commonwealth Games 1998. *Leisure interests:* music, motorcycling, horse riding, reading, surfing, boating, fishing, jet skiing. *Address:* Kieren Perkins Management, GPO Box 232, Brisbane, Queensland 4001, Australia. *Telephone:* (7) 3211-1500. *Fax:* (7) 3211-1501.

PERKINS, Lawrence Bradford, Jr., BA, BArch, MBA; American architect; b. 13 Jan. 1943, Chicago, Ill.; s. of Lawrence B. Perkins and Margery Perkins; m. Phyllis Friedman 1966; three d.; ed Cornell and Stanford Univs. and City Coll. of New York; President, Omnidata Services 1971–73; Man. Partner, Llewellyn-Davies Assocs. 1973–77; Sr Vice-Pres., Partner, Perkins and Will 1977–81; Partner Attia & Perkins 1981–83; Pres. Perkins Eastman Architects 1983–; Dir Settlement Housing Fund 1991–, Helen Keller Int. 1993–; Dir New York City AIA, NY Foundation for Architecture; Fellow, American Inst. of Architects, Epsilon Asscn (Pres. 1993–96); various design awards. *Publications:* articles in professional journals and chapters for professional textbooks. *Address:* Perkins Eastman Architects, 115 Fifth Avenue, New York, NY 10003 (Office); 4 Rectory Lane, Scarsdale, NY 10583, USA (Home). *Telephone:* (212) 353-7200 (Office); (914) 723-8875 (Home). *Fax:* (212) 353-7676 (Office).

PERL, Martin Lewis, PhD; American research physicist, educator and enineer; b. 24 June 1927, New York; three s. one d.; ed Polytechnic Inst. of New York and Columbia Univ.; Chemical Engineer, General Electric Co. 1948–50; Asst, then Assoc. Prof. of Physics, Univ. of Mich. 1955–63; Prof. of Physics, Stanford Linear Accelerator Center, Stanford Univ. 1963–, Prof. of Physics, Stanford Univ. 1970–; research in experimental elementary particle physics 1955–; discovered the elementary particle tau lepton 1975–78; Hon. DSc (Chicago) 1990, (Polytechnic Univ.) 1997; Wolf Prize in Physics 1982, shared Nobel Prize in Physics 1995. *Publications:* High Energy Hadron Physics 1974, Reflections on Experimental Science 1996, articles on science and soc. issues and on physics educ. *Leisure interests:* mechanical antiques, gardening. *Address:* Stanford Linear Accelerator Center, Stanford University, Stanford, CA 94309; 3737 El Centro Avenue, Palo Alto, CA 94306, USA. *Telephone:* (650) 926-2652. *Fax:* (650) 926-4001.

PERLIS, HRH The Raja of; Tuanku Syed Sirajuddin ibni al-Marhum Syed Putra Jamalullail; Malaysian ruler; b. 1943; m.; one s. one d.; ed Sandhurst Mil. Acad., UK; fmr army officer; Raja of Perlis April 2000–; installed as twelfth Yang di-Pertuan Agong (Supreme Head of State) 12 Dec. 2001.

PERLMAN, Itzhak; Israeli violinist; b. 31 Aug. 1945, Tel Aviv; s. of Chaim Perlman and Shoshana Perlman; m. Toby Lynn Friedlander 1967; two s. three d.; ed Tel Aviv Acad. of Music, Juilliard School, USA; gave recitals on radio at the age of 10; went to USA 1958; studied with Ivan Galamian and Dorothy De Lay; first recital at Carnegie Hall 1963; has played with maj. American orchestras 1964–; has toured Europe regularly and played with maj. European orchestras 1966–; debut in UK with London Symphony Orchestra 1968; toured Poland, Hungary, Far East; played with Israel Philharmonic Orchestra in fmr Soviet Union; appearances at Israel Festival and most European Festivals; Prin. Guest Conductor Detroit Symphony Orchestra 2001–; numerous recordings; Hon. degrees from Univ. of S. Carolina, Yale, Harvard and Yeshivah Univs.; several Grammy awards; Medal of Liberty 1986; Nat. Medal of Arts 2001. *Leisure interest:* cooking. *Address:* c/o Askonas Holt Ltd, Lonsdale Chambers, 27 Chancery Lane, London WC2A 1PF, England (Home); c/o IMG Artists, 22 825 7th Avenue, New York, NY 10019, USA.

PERLOT, Enzo; Italian diplomatist; b. 17 Nov. 1933, Mezzolombardo; s. of the late Augusto and Ida (Paoli) Perlot; m. Ulla Segerstrale 1970; two c.; ed Univ. of Rome; entered Foreign Ministry 1959; served at Presidency of the Repub. 1965–68; Consul in Munich and Counsellor in Embassy in Vienna 1968–70; served in Office of Prime Minister 1970–72; Spokesman and Dir-Gen. of Information of EEC Comm. 1978–80; Amb. to Portugal 1983–87; Dir-Gen. for Political Affairs 1987–91; Perm. Rep. of Italy to N Atlantic Council, Brussels 1991–93, then to EU 1993–95; Amb. to Germany 1996–2002; Pres. Univ. of Trento 2002–. *Address:* Office of the President, Università degli Studi di Trento, Via Belenzani 12, 38100 Trento, Italy (Office). *Telephone:* (0461) 881111. *Fax:* (0461) 881299. *Website:* www.unitn.it.

PERNG FAI-NAN, MA; Taiwanese central banker and economist; b. 2 Jan. 1939; m.; two s.; ed Nat. Chung Hsing Univ., Univ. of Minn., USA and Int. Monetary Fund Inst.; with Bank of Taiwan 1969; Asst Specialist, Cen. Bank of China (CBC), later Deputy Div. Chief, Div. Chief, Econ. Research Dept 1971–78, Asst Dir-Gen. and Div. Chief, Econ. Research Dept 1978–80, Deputy Dir-Gen. 1980–85, Dir-Gen. 1986–89, Dir-Gen. Foreign Exchange Dept 1989–94, Deputy Gov. CBC 1994–95, Bd Dir 1995–, Gov. 1998– (also mem. Exec. Yuan (cabinet); Chair. Cen. Trust of China 1995–97, Int. Commercial

Bank of China 1997–98; Gov. for Taiwan, Asian Devt Bank 1998–, Cen. American Bank for Econ. Integration 1998–; Adjunct Prof. Nat. Chung Hsing Univ. 1986–89; Office of the Pres. Best Employee Award 1975, Cen. Bank of China Best Essay Award 1982, Excellence Magazine Outstanding Govt Official 1998, Nat. Chung Hsing Univ. Outstanding Alumnus Award 1999, Univ. of Minn. Outstanding Achievement Award 2000, Global Finance Top Central Banker Award 2000. *Publications include:* Possible Methods for the Liberalization of Foreign Exchange Control 1985, Asian Financial Crisis 1998; numerous articles. *Address:* Central Bank of China, 2 Roosevelt Road, Sec. 1, Taipei 100, Taiwan (Office). *Telephone:* (2) 2393-6161 (Office). *Fax:* (2) 2357-1974 (Office). *E-mail:* adminrol@mail.cbc.gov.tw (Office). *Website:* www .cbc.gov.tw (Office).

PERÓN, María Estela (Isabelita) (see Martínez de Perón).

PEROT, (Henry) Ross; American industrialist; b. 27 June 1930, Texarkana, Tex.; s. of Mr. and Mrs. Gabriel Ross Perot; m. Margot Birmingham 1956; five c.; ed U.S. Naval Acad.; U.S. Navy 1953–57; with IBM Corpn 1957–62; formed Electronic Data Systems Corpn 1962, Chair. of Bd and CEO 1982–86; Dir Perot Group, Dallas 1986–; f. Perot Systems Corpn, Washington 1988–, Chair. 1988–92, 1992–, mem. Bd 1988–; Chair. Bd of Visitors U.S. Naval Acad. 1970–; Cand. for Presidency of USA 1992, 1996; f. Reform Party 1995, Chair. 1995–99. *Publications:* Not For Sale at Any Price 1993, Intensive Care 1995. *Leisure interest:* horses. *Address:* The Perot Group, PO Box 269014, Plano, TX 75026, USA.

PERPIÑA-ROBERT, Fernando; Spanish diplomatist; b. 17 April 1937, San Sebastián; s. of Benito Perpiña and Cármen Peyra; m. Alba Navarro Feussier 1964; two s. two d.; ed Univ. of Barcelona; joined Diplomatic Service 1965, Consul Gen. Boston, USA 1978, Minister Counsellor, Bonn 1982, Under-Sec. of State, Ministry of Foreign Affairs, Madrid 1985, Sec. Gen. Foreign Affairs, Madrid 1988, Amb. to Germany 1991–96; numerous Spanish and foreign decorations. *Leisure interest:* bridge. *Address:* c/o Ministerio de Asuntos Exteriores, Plaza de la Provincia 1, 28071 Madrid, Spain.

PERRAULT, Dominique; French architect; b. 9 April 1953, Clermont-Ferrand; s. of Jean Perrault and Thérèse Souchon; m. Aude Lauriot-dit-Prévost 1986; three c.; ed Univ. of Paris, Ecole Nat. des Ponts et Chaussées, Ecole des Hautes Etudes en Sciences Sociales; f. architectural practice, Paris 1981; opened offices in Berlin 1992, Luxembourg 2000, Barcelona 2001; major works include Electronic Engineers Acad. Marne-la-Vallée, Bibliothèque de France (received Prix Mies Van Der Röhe 1997), Olympic swimming pool, Berlin, re-devt of town centre, Tremblay-en-France 1995, Town Hall, Innsbruck, Austria 1997, Montiagalá Stadium 1998, European Court of Justice Luxembourg (2007), tennis stadium Madrid (2012); consultant to city of Nantes 1990, Bordeaux 1992, Barcelona 2000–; Pres. Institut français d'architecture 1998–2001; mem. Salzburg Urban Cttee 1994–; Hon. mem. Royal Inst. of British Architects; Grand prix nat. d'architecture 1993; Chevalier, Légion d'honneur; numerous architectural awards and prizes. *Publication:* An Atmosphere of Falling Meteors. *Address:* Perrault Architecte, 26 rue Bruneseau, 75629 Paris Cedex 13, France (Office). *Telephone:* 1-44-06-00-00 (Office). *Fax:* 1-44-06-00-01 (Office). *E-mail:* dominique.perrault@ perraultarchitecte.com (Office). *Website:* www.perraultarchitecte.com (Office).

PERREIN, Michèle Marie-Claude; French writer; b. 30 Oct. 1929, La Réole; d. of Roger Barbe and Anne-Blanche Perrein; m. Jacques Laurent (divorced); ed Univ. of Bordeaux, Centre de Formation des Journalistes; literary contrib. to periodicals Arts-Spectacles, La Parisienne, Marie-Claire, La vie judiciaire, Votre beauté, Le point, F. magazine, Les nouvelles littéraires. *Plays:* L'Hôtel Racine 1966, a+b+c = la Clinique d'anticipation, 1971, L'alter-auto 1971; film collaborator La vérité 1959. *Publications:* La sensitive 1956, Le soleil dans l'oeil 1957, Barbastre 1960, La flemme 1961, Le cercle 1962, Le petit Jules 1965, M'oiselle S, la Chineuse 1970, La partie de plaisir 1971, Le buveur de Garonne 1973, Le mâle aimant 1975, Gemma lapidaire 1976, Entre chienne et louve 1978, Comme une fourmi cavalière 1980, Ave Caesar 1982, Les cotonniers de Bassalane 1984, La Margagne 1989. *Leisure interests:* tapestry, swimming, skating. *Address:* c/o Grasset et Fasqualle, 61 rue des Saints-pères, 75006 Paris, France (Office).

PERRY, John Richard, PhD; American professor of philosophy; b. 16 Jan. 1943, Lincoln, Neb.; s. of Ralph R. Perry and Ann Roscow Perry; m. Louise E. French 1962; two s. one d.; ed Doane Coll., Crete, Neb. and Cornell Univ.; Asst Prof. of Philosophy, Univ. of Calif. at Los Angeles 1968–72, Assoc. Prof. 1972–74; Assoc. Prof. of Philosophy, Stanford Univ. 1974–77, Prof. of Philosophy 1977–85, Henry Waldgrave Stuart Prof. of Philosophy 1985–, Chair. Dept of Philosophy 1976–82, 1990–91, Dir Center for Language and Information 1982–83, 1985–86, 1993–; Pres. American Philosophical Asscn 1993–94; Woodrow Wilson Fellow 1964; Danforth Fellow 1964–68; Guggenheim Fellow 1975–76; NEH Fellow 1980–81; Hon. DLitt (Doane Coll.) 1982; Dinkelspiel Teaching Award 1989, Humboldt Prize 1998, Nicod Prize 1999. *Publications:* A Dialogue on Personal Identity and Immortality 1978, Situations and Attitudes (with J. Barwise) 1983, The Problem of the Essential Indexical and Other Essays 1993, A Dialogue on Good, Evil and the Existence of God 1999, Knowledge, Possibility and Consciousness 2000, Reference and Reflexivity 2001, Identity, Personal Identity and the Self 2002. *Leisure interests:* reading, tennis, grandchildren. *Address:* Department of Philosophy, Stanford Uni-

versity, Building 90, Stanford, CA 94305, USA. *Telephone:* (650) 723-1619. *Fax:* (650) 723-0985. *E-mail:* john@csli.stanford.edu (Office). *Website:* www-csli.stanford.edu/~/john/ (Office).

PERRY, Matthew Langford; American actor; b. 19 Aug. 1969, Williamstown, MA; s. of John Bennett Perry and Suzanne Perry; ed Ashbury Coll., Ottawa, Canada. *Films:* A Night in the Life of Jimmy Reardon 1988, She's Out of Control 1989, Parallel Lives, Fools Rush In 1997, Almost Heroes 1998, Three To Tango, The Whole Nine Yards 2000, Serving Sara 2002. *TV appearances include:* Boys Will Be Boys, Home Free, Sydney, Who's The Boss?, The Tracy Ullman Show, Empty, The John Laroquette Show, Beverly Hills 90210, Growing Pains, 240 Roberts, Friends (NBC) 1994–. *TV films:* Deadly Relations, Call Me Anna, Dance Till Dawn 1988. *Play:* Sexual Perversity in Chicago, Comedy Theatre, London 2003. *Writing includes:* Maxwell House (sitcom sold to Universal TV), Imagining Emily (screenplay for Warner Brothers). *Leisure interests:* ice hockey, softball. *Address:* c/o William Morris Agency, 151 El Camino Drive, Beverly Hills, CA 90212, USA (Office).

PERRY, Sir Michael Sydney, Kt, GBE, MA; British business executive; b. 26 Feb. 1934, Eastbourne; s. of Sydney Albert Perry and Jessie Kate (née Brooker) Perry; m. Joan Mary Stallard 1958; one s. two d.; ed King William's Coll., Isle of Man, St John's Coll., Oxford Univ.; Chair. Lever Brothers (Thailand) Ltd 1973–77, Unilever 1997–, Nippon Lever (Japan) 1981–83, UAC Int. Ltd 1985–87, Unilever PLC 1992–96, Dunlop Slazenger Group 1996–2002; Pres. Lever y Asociados (Argentina) 1977–81; Dir Unilever NV 1985–96 (Vice-Chair. 1992–96), Bass PLC 1991–2001 (Deputy Chair. 1996–2001); Dir (non-exec.) British Gas 1994–97, Marks & Spencer 1996–2001; Chair. Shakespeare Globe Trust 1993–; Pres. Liverpool School of Tropical Medicine 1997–2002; Pres. Advertising Asscn 1993–96; Trustee Leverhulme Trust 1991–, Glyndebourne Arts Trust 1996–, Dyson Perrins Museum Trust; Commdr Order of Oranje Nassau. *Leisure interest:* music. *Address:* Bridges Stone Mill, Alfrick, Worcester, WR6 5HR, England.

PERRY, Rick (James Richard); American politician and rancher; b. 4 March 1950, Paint Creek, Tex.; s. of Ray Perry and Amelia Perry; m. Anita Perry; one s. one d.; ed Texas A&M University; served US Air Force 1972; farmer and rancher 1977–90; Commr Tex. Dept of Agric. 1991–99; Lt-Gov. of Tex. 1999–2000, Gov. 2000–; Border Texan of the Year 2001, Govt Leadership Award, Nat. Comm. Against Drunk Driving 2001, Top Cowboy of the Year Award 2001. *Address:* Office of the Governor, POB 12428, Austin, TX 78711-2428, USA (Office). *Telephone:* (512) 463-2000 (Office). *Fax:* (512) 463-1849 (Office). *Website:* www.governor.state.tx.us (Office).

PERRY, Robert Palese, PhD; American molecular biologist; b. 10 Jan. 1931, Chicago; s. of Robert P. Perry, Sr and Gertrude Hyman; m. Zoila Figueroa 1957; one s. two d.; ed Univ. of Chicago and Northwestern Univ.; Postdoctoral Fellow Oak Ridge Nat. Lab. 1956–57, Univ. of Pa 1957–59, Univ. of Brussels 1959–60; Staff mem. Inst. for Cancer Research, Fox Chase Cancer Center 1960–, Sr mem. 1969–, Stanley Reimann Chair in Research 1994–; Prof. of Biophysics, Univ. of Pa 1973–95; UNESCO Tech. Asst Expert Univ. of Belgrade 1965; Guggenheim Fellow Univ. of Paris 1974–75; Chair. Exec. Cttee Int. Cell Research Org. (UNESCO) 1982–85; mem. NAS; Dr. hc (Univ. of Paris VII). *Publications:* more than 100 articles in int. scientific journals. *Address:* Institute for Cancer Research, Fox Chase Cancer Center, 7701 Burholme Avenue, Philadelphia, Pa 19111 (Office); 1808 Bustleton Pike, Churchville, PA 18966, USA (Home). *Telephone:* (215) 728-3606 (Office); (215) 357-0272 (Home). *Fax:* (215) 728-2412 (Office). *E-mail:* rp_perry@fccc.edu (Office).

PERRY, Ruth; Liberian politician; b. Tewor Dist, Grand Cape Mount Co.; m. McDonald M. Perry (deceased); seven c.; fmrly with Chase Manhattan Bank of Liberia; Senator from Cape Mount Co. 1986–90; Chair. Council of State (of Liberian Nat. Transitional Govt) 1996–97; mem. Women's Initiatives in Liberia. *Address:* c/o Office of the President, Monrovia, Liberia.

PERRY, Simon Frank, CBE, BA; British film producer; b. 5 Aug. 1943, Farnham; s. of Frank Horace Perry and Brenda Mary Dorothea Perry; ed Eton Coll., King's Coll.; worked in theatre production (RSC, Bristol Old Vic, London West End) 1965–69, TV production (Anglia TV, Yorkshire TV) 1969–74; independent filmmaker 1974–77; entertainment trade journalist (Variety Magazine etc.) 1978–80; administrator Nat. Film Devt Fund 1980–82; feature film producer 1982–; Chief Exec. British Screen Finance 1991–2000; Chevalier des Arts et Lettres. *Films include:* Knots, Eclipse, Another Time, Another Place, Nineteen Eighty-Four, White Mischief, The Playboys. *Leisure interests:* cinema-going, cycling, European travel. *Address:* Studio C, Chelsea Studios, 416 Fulham Road, London, SW6 1EB, England. *Telephone:* (20) 7386-5119. *Fax:* (20) 7386-0017.

PERRY, Baron (Life Peer), cr. 1979, of Walton in the County of Buckinghamshire; **Walter Laing Macdonald Perry,** Kt, OBE, MD, DSc, FRCP, FRS; British university professor; b. 16 June 1921, Dundee; s. of Fletcher Smith Perry and Flora Macdonald Macdonald; m. 1st Anne Grant 1946; three s.; m. 2nd Catherine Crawley 1971; two s. one d.; ed Dundee High School and St Andrew's Univ.; Medical Officer in Colonial Service, Nigeria 1944–46, in the RAF 1946–47; Medical Research Council 1947–52; Dir Dept of Biological Standards, Nat. Inst. for Medical Research 1952–58; Prof. of Pharmacology, Edinburgh Univ. 1958–68, Vice-Prin. 1967–68; Vice-Chancellor, Open Univ. 1969–81, Fellow 1981–; Chair. Videotel Int. 1981, Pres. 1996; Consultant to

UN Univ. 1981–88; Chair. Bd of Govs. Int. Technological Univ. 1987–89; Hon. Dir Int. Centre for Distance Learning 1983; Chair. Continuing Educ. Standing Cttee 1985–88, Research Defence Soc. 1994; mem. Royal Soc. of Edinburgh 2000; British Pharmacological Soc. Gold Medal 1998; several hon. degrees. *Publications:* Open University 1976; several chapters in other books. *Leisure interests:* golf, music. *Address:* Glenholm, 2 Cramond Road South, Davidson's Mains, Edinburgh, EH4 6AD, Scotland (Home). *Telephone:* (131) 336-3666 (Home).

PERRY, William, PhD; American politician and civil servant; b. 11 Oct. 1927, Vandergift, Pa; s. of Edward Martin Perry and Mabelle Estelle Dunlop; m. Leonilla Mary Green 1947; three s. two d.; ed Stanford Univ., Pennsylvania State Univ.; Prof. School of Eng, Stanford Univ., Co-Dir Center for Int. Security and Arms Control (affil. to Stanford Univ.); Under-Sec.-of-Defense for Research and Eng 1976–81; Mil. Tech. Adviser to Pres. Clinton 1993; Deputy Sec. of Defense 1993–94, Sec. of Defense 1994–97; Prof. Stanford Univ. 1997–, Sr Fellow 1997–; Chair. Tech. Strategies and Alliances 1985–93; Dir United Technologies Corpn, FMC Corpn, Sylvania/Gen. Telephone's Electronic Defense Labs.; served on U.S. Govt.'s Foreign Intelligence Advisory Bd; mem. Nat. Acad. of Eng, NAS Cttee on Int. Security and Arms Control; Fellow American Acad. of Arts and Sciences; Trustee Carnegie Endowment for Int. Peace; several nat. and int. decorations. *Address:* School of Engineering, Stanford University, Stanford, CA 94305, USA. *Fax:* (650) 725-0920 (Office). *E-mail:* wjperry@stanford.edu (Office).

PERRY OF SOUTHWARK, Baroness (Life Peeress), cr. 1991, of Charlbury in the County of Oxfordshire; **Pauline Perry,** MA, FRSA, CIMgt; British university administrator; b. Pauline Welch, 15 Oct. 1931, Wolverhampton; d. of John Welch and Elizabeth Cowan; m. George W. Perry 1952; three s. one d.; ed Girton Coll. Cambridge; Univ. lecturer in Philosophy, Univs of Man., Mass., Exeter and Oxford 1956–59, 1961–63, 1966–70; HM Insp. 1970, Staff Insp. 1975, HM Chief Insp. of Schools 1981–86; Vice-Chancellor, South Bank Univ. (fmrly South Bank Polytechnic) 1987–93; Pres. Lucy Cavendish Coll. Univ. of Cambridge 1994–2001; Pro-Chancellor Univ. of Surrey 2001–; Chair. Dept of Trade and Industry Export Group for Educ. and Training Sector 1993–98; mem. Prime Minister's Advisory Group on the Citizen's Charter 1993–97; mem. House of Lords Select Cttee on Science and Tech. 1992–95, on Scrutiny of Delegated Powers 1995–98, on Cen. and Local Govt Relations 1995–96; mem. Jt Select Cttee on Human Rights 2001–; mem. Bd of Patrons, Royal Soc. Appeal 1995–; Vice-Pres. City & Guilds of London Inst. 1994–99; Chair. Judges Panel on Citizen's Charter 1997–; Fellow, Swedish Acad. of Sciences (Pedagogy); mem. Cambridge Univ. Foundation 1997–; Hon. Fellow Coll. of Preceptors, City and Guilds, Girton Coll. Cambridge, Lucy Cavendish Coll. Cambridge; Hon. LLD (Aberdeen, Bath); Hon. DLitt (Sussex, South Bank, City Univ.); Hon. DUniv (Surrey); Hon. DEd (Wolverhampton); Liveryman Worshipful Co. of Bakers; Freeman City of London. *Publications:* The Womb in Which I Lay 2003; four books, several chapters and numerous articles. *Leisure interests:* music, walking. *Address:* House of Lords, London, SW1A 0PW, England. *Telephone:* (20) 7219-5474 (Office). *E-mail:* pp204@ supanet.com (Home).

PERSSON, Göran; Swedish politician; b. 20 Jan. 1949, Vingaker; m. Gunnel Persson; two c.; ed Orebro Univ.; Org. Sec. Swedish Social Democratic Youth League Sörmland 1971; Studies Sec. Workers' Educ. Asscn Sörmland, 1974–76; Chair. Katrineholm Educ. Authority 1977–79; mem. Parl. 1979–84; Councillor, Chair. Municipal Exec. Bd Katrineholm 1985–89; Minister with special responsibility for schools and adult educ., Ministry of Educ. and Cultural Affairs 1989–91, of Finance 1994–96; Prime Minister of Sweden 1996–; Chair. Social Democratic Party 1996–; Vice-Chair. Bd Oppunda Savings Bank 1976–89, Nordic Museum 1983–89; Chair. Sörmland Co-operative Consumers' Asscn 1976–89; Chair. Sörmland Co. Bd of Educ. 1982–89; Nat. Auditor, Swedish Co-operative Wholesale Soc. 1988–89. *Address:* Prime Minister's Office, 103 33 Stockholm, Sweden (Office).

PERSSON, Jörgen; Swedish director of photography; b. 10 Sept. 1936, Helsingborg; s. of Erik W. Persson and Thyra Liljeroth; m. Anne von Sydow 1969; two s.; ed High School and Swedish Film School; Dir of Photography (Features) 1965–; Felix Award, Paris 1989 and Swedish awards. *Films include:* Elvira Madigan 1967, Ådalen-31 1969, My Life as a Dog 1986, Pelle the Conqueror 1988, Best Intentions 1991, Sofi 1991, Young Indy, The House of the Spirits 1993, Jerusalem 1995, Smilla's Sense of Snow 1996, Digging to China 1996, Les Misérables 1997, Faithless 2000. *Leisure interests:* off-road sport, classic cars. *Address:* Rydbolundsvagen 7, 18531 Vaxholm, Sweden.

PERT, Geoffrey James, PhD, FRS, FInstP; British physicist; b. 15 Aug. 1941, Market Harborough, Leics.; s. of Norman James Pert and Grace W. Pert; m. Janice Ann Alexander 1967; one d.; ed Norwich School, Imperial Coll., Univ. of London; Asst Lecturer, Univ. of Alberta 1967–70; lecturer, Univ. of Hull 1970–76, Sr Lecturer, Reader 1976–82, Prof. 1982–87; Prof. of Computational Physics, Univ. of York 1987–. *Publications:* numerous scientific papers. *Leisure interests:* hill-walking, gardening. *Address:* Department of Physics, University of York, Heslington, York, YO10 5DD, England. *Telephone:* (1904) 432250 (Office). *Fax:* (1904) 432214 (Office). *E-mail:* gjp@york.ac.uk (Office). *Website:* www.york.ac.uk (Office).

PERVYSHIN, Erlen Kirikovich; Russian industrial manager; b. 25 June 1932, Russia; ed Moscow Electrotechnical Inst. of Communications; mem. Int. Engineer Acad.; engineer 1955–, then Head of Ass. Section, Deputy Chief Engineer, Head of Admin., Manager of Design and Ass. Trust, Dir-Gen. All-

Union Scientific production Asscn; Deputy USSR Minister of Radio Industry 1970–74, Minister of Communications Equipment Mfg 1974–89, of Communications 1989–91; Chair. Telecom (now Mirtelecom Corpn) 1991–; Pres. ORB & TEL Co., Andrew Int. Corpn 1997–; Pres. Mirtelecom Asscn 1999–. *Address:* Mirtelecom, Gubkina str. 8, Moscow 17966, Russia. *Telephone:* (095) 748-00-01. *Fax:* (095) 748-00-02.

PESCATORE, Pierre, DIur; Luxembourg diplomatist and professor of law; b. 20 Nov. 1919, Luxembourg; s. of Ferdinand Pescatore and Cunégonde Heuertz; m. Rosalie Margue 1948; three s. one d.; Ministry of Foreign Affairs 1946–67, Sec., later mem., Del. to UN Gen. Ass. 1946–52; Legal Adviser, Min. of Foreign Affairs 1950–58; Dir for Political Affairs, Min. of Foreign Affairs 1958–64; Minister Plenipotentiary 1959; Sec.-Gen. Ministry of Foreign Affairs 1964–67; Judge, Court of Justice of the European Communities 1967–86, Perm. Court of Arbitration 1969, Pres. Luxembourg Nat. Group; Admin. Tribunal ILO 1986–; served on several GATT Panels 1989–; Prof. Law Faculty and Inst. for European Legal Studies, Univ. of Liège; Lectured Hague Acad. of Int. Law 1961; mem. Inst. de Droit Int. 1965–; Dr. hc (Nancy, Geneva, Tübingen, Leiden, Neuchâtel Univs.). *Publications:* complete bibliography to 1987 appears in Liber Amicorum Pierre Pescatore 1987; Handbook of GATT Dispute Settlement (loose-leaf) 1991–. *Address:* 16 rue de la Fontaine, 1532 Luxembourg. *Telephone:* 46-07-97 (Office); 22-40-44 (Home). *Fax:* 46-61-42.

PESCI, Joe; American film actor; b. 9 Feb. 1943, Newark, NJ. *Films include:* Death Collector 1976, Raging Bull 1980, I'm Dancing as Far as I Can 1982, Easy Money 1983, Dear Mr Wonderful 1983, Eureka 1983, Once Upon a Time in America 1984, Tutti Dentro 1984, Man On Fire 1987, Moonwalker 1988, Backtrack 1988, Lethal Weapon 2 1989, Betsy's Wedding 1990, Goodfellas (Acad. Award for Best Supporting Actor) 1991, Home Alone 1990, The Super 1991, JFK 1991, Lethal Weapon 3 1992, Home Alone II 1992, The Public Eye 1992, My Cousin Vinny 1992, A Bronx Tale 1993, With Honours 1994, Jimmy Hollywood 1994, Casino 1995, 8 Heads in a Duffel Bag 1997, Gone Fishing 1997, Lethal Weapon 4 1998.

PESCUCCI, Gabriella; Italian costume designer; b. Castiglioncello, Tuscany; ed Accademia di Belle Arti, Florence; worked as Asst to Piero Tosi on set of Luchino Visconti's films Death in Venice and Ludwig; solo debut designing costumes for Charlotte Rampling in Italian film adaptation of 'Tis Pity She's a Whore 1971; designed costumes for Maria Callas in Medea, for Sean Connery in The Name of the Rose, Montserrat Caballé in Norma at La Scala, Milan and for City of Women, Once Upon a Time in America, The Adventures of Baron Munchausen, The Scarlet Letter, The Age of Innocence (Acad. Award 1996); prizes and awards include two Donatello Davids from Italian Acad. of Cinema and two BAFTA Awards.

PEŠEK, Libor; Czech conductor; b. 22 June 1933, Prague; ed Prague Acad. of Musical Arts; studied conducting with Karel Ancerl, Vaclav Neumann and Václav Smetáček; f. Prague Chamber Harmony 1958; Chief Conductor Slovak Philharmonic 1980–81; Conductor-in-Residence Czech Philharmonic Orchestra 1982–, Germany tour 1998; Prin. Conductor and Artistic Adviser Royal Liverpool Philharmonic Orchestra 1982–97, Hon. Conductor 1997–; Visiting Conductor Prague Symphony Orchestra 1989–; Pres. Prague Spring Festival 1994–; Mem. Bd of Supervisors O.P.S. Prague European City of Culture 1999–; conducted Royal Liverpool Philharmonic Orchestra, Prague Spring Festival 2000; has conducted Philharmonia, London Symphony, Royal Philharmonic, BBC Philharmonic, Hallé, Oslo Philharmonic, Danish Radio, Los Angeles Philharmonic and Cincinnati, Dallas, Minnesota, Pittsburgh, Cleveland, Montreal, Indianapolis and Philadelphia orchestras, Orchestra of La Scala, Milan and Orchestre de Paris; charity concerts after floods in Czech Repub. 2002; Hon. KBE; Hon. mem. Preston Univ. 1997; Classic Prize for Extraordinary Merit in Musical Culture (Czech Repub.) 1997, Journal Harmonie Lifelong Contrib. to Czech Culture 2002. *Recordings include:* works by Dvořák, Suk, Janáček, Martinů and Britten. *Leisure interests:* physics, Eastern philosophy, literature. *Address:* c/o IMG Artists (Europe), Media House, 3 Burlington Lane, London, W4 2TH, England.

PESENTI, Antonio; Italian politician and economist; b. 15 Oct. 1910, Verona; s. of Romeo Pesenti and Amalia Bisoffi; m. Adriana Ghiadistri 1947; ed Univs. of Pavia, Vienna, Berne, Paris, London School of Econs; lecturer Sassari Univ. 1935; active in underground anti-Fascist movement 1930–35; took part in Italian anti-Fascist Congress in Brussels 1935; arrested and sentenced to 24 years' imprisonment by special tribunal; released Sept. 1943; Under-Sec., later Minister of Finance 1944–45; lecturer on Finance, Univ. of Rome 1945; Prof. Univ. of Parma 1948, of Pisa 1960–71, of Rome 1971; Ed. Critica Economica; fmr mem. Italian Constituent Ass.; Pres. Econ. Centre for Reconstruction; MP 1948, mem. Senate 1953–; mem. fmr CP. *Publications:* Politica finanziaria e monetaria dell'Inghilterra 1934, La politica monetaria delle Devisenverordnungen 1933, I soggetti passivi dell'obbligazione doganale 1934, Ricostruire dalle rovine 1945, Scienza delle Finanze e diritto finanziario 1961, Manuale d'Economia Politica, 2 Vols 1970. *Leisure interests:* chess, mountaineering, rowing. *Address:* Via Nomentana 372, Rome; and 41 Via Nomentana, Istituto di Economia, Rome, Italy. *Telephone:* (06) 897530.

PESIĆ, Dragiša, M.SC.ECON.; Serbia and Montenegro (Montenegrin) politician and business executive; b. Aug. 1954, Danilovgrad; s. of Lazar Pesić and Anja Pesić; m. Lela Savović; one s. one d.; ed Sarajevo Univ.; worked as financial expert; fmr Chair. Exec. Bd Municipal Ass. of Podgorica (twice); Deputy to Fed. Ass., Chair. Budget Cttee, Chamber of Citizens; Minister of Finance 1998–2001; Prime Minister of Serbia and Montenegro (fmr Fed.

Repub. of Yugoslavia) July 2001–; mem. Socialist Nat. Party of Montenegro (SNP). *Address:* Office of the Federal Government, Belgrade, Serbia and Montenegro (Office). *Telephone:* (11) 334281 (Office). *E-mail:* Dragisa.Pesic@gov.yu (Office).

PEŠIĆ, Vesna; Serbia and Montenegro (Serbian) politician, philosopher and lawyer; b. 6 May 1940, Groska; ed Belgrade Univ.; on staff Inst. of Social Sciences 1964–72, Inst. of Social Politics 1972–78; sr researcher Inst. of Philosophy and Social Theory, teacher Higher School for Social Workers 1978–91; co-f. Union for Yugoslavian Democratic Initiative (IZDI) 1991, Helsinki Cttee in Belgrade, Cen. of Antimil. Actions Daily Time; mem. Cttee for Freedom of Speech and Self-Expression; Chair. Civil Union of Serbia; active participant opposition block Union of Reform Forces of Serbia; mem. Skuptsina (Parl.) of Serbia; participant mass demonstrations of protest against S. Milošević 1996–97; author of books, articles in scientific journals and periodicals; Award for Democracy Nat. Foundation of Democracy, Washington, 1993. *Publications include:* Social Traditions and Style of Life 1977, Ethnomethodology and Sociology 1985, Social Deviations: Criticism of Social Pathology (with I. Jancović) 1981, Brief Course of Equality 1988, Theory of Changes and Parsons Concept of Contemporary Soc. 1990, Yugoslavian Military Crisis and World Movement 1992, Nationalism, War and Disintegration of Communist Federation 1993.

PESMAZOGLU, John Stevens, PhD; Greek politician, economist, university professor and central banker; b. 1 March 1918, Chios; s. of Stephanos G. Pesmazoglu and Angela Lorenzou; m. Miranda Economou 1945; two s.; ed Varvakion High School, Athens, Univ. of Athens and St John's Coll., Cambridge; served in Greek Albanian campaign 1940–41 and in liberation of Greece 1944–45; research student, Cambridge 1945–49; Lecturer in Political Economy, Univ. of Athens 1950–67, Prof. 1967–70; Dir-Gen. Greek Ministry of Co-ordination in charge of econ. devt and external financial relations 1951–55; Econ. Adviser Bank of Greece 1955–60; Alt. Gov. for Greece, IMF 1955–67; Deputy Gov. Bank of Greece 1960–67; Leader of Greek mission to negotiations for European Free Trade Area and Asscn of Greece with Common Market 1957–61; Chair. Interdepartmental Cttee for European Co-operation 1962–65; Trustee Royal Hellenic Research Foundation 1959–68; Pres. Soc. for the Study of Greek Problems 1971–72; exiled by mil. govt May–Dec. 1972; in prison April–Aug. 1973; Minister of Finance July–Oct. 1974; MP 1974–81, 1985–89; MEP 1981–84, 1989–94, Hon. mem. 1994; Co-Pres. Jt Parl. Comm. Greece-European Communities 1975–79; Pres. Party of Democratic Socialism 1979–84; Hon. Fellow St John's Coll., Cambridge; Pres. Acad. of Athens 1996; Azchon Megas Rhetor, Oecumenical Patriarchate, Grand Cross, Greek Order of Phoenix, Grand Commdr Royal Order of George I, Commdr Légion d'honneur, Grand Commdr of the Yugoslav Standard with Gold Crown, Grand Commdr German Order of Merit. *Publications:* Studies and articles on the int. trade cycle, economic devt and monetary policies and on European integration with special reference to Greece's membership of the European Community. *Leisure interest:* painting. *Address:* 6 Neophytou Vamva Street, 10674 Athens, Greece. *Telephone:* (1) 7212458. *Fax:* (1) 7236326.

PETERLE, Lojze; Slovenian politician; b. 5 July 1948, Čužnja Vas, Trebnje; ed Ljubljana Univ.; worked as consultant in town planning, environmental protection and landscape man.; Pres. Slovenian Christian Democrats (SKD) 1989–2000 (merged to form Slovenian People's Party 2000); Prime Minister of Slovenia 1990–92; Minister of Foreign Affairs 1993–94, 2000–01; Chair. Parl. Cttee on European Affairs 1997–; Vice-Pres. European Union of Christian Democrats 1993–98; Knight Grand Cross, Papal Order 1993. *Address:* c/o Slovenian People's Party, 1000 Ljubljana, Zarnikova 3, Slovenia (Office).

PETERS, Janis; Latvian diplomatist, writer and poet; b. 30 June 1939, Liepāja Region, Latvia; s. of Janis Peters and Zelma Peters; m. Baiba Kalniņa 1969; one s.; started as journalist in Latvian newspapers, later freelance; Chair. Bd of Latvian Writers' Union 1985–89; participant democratic movt for independence; Chair. Org. Cttee People's Front of Latvia 1988; USSR People's Deputy 1989–90; Perm. Rep. of Council of Ministers of Latvia to Russia 1990–91, then Amb. to Russian Fed. 1991–97; mem. govt del. to negotiations with Russia 1992–; Hon. mem. Latvian Acad. of Sciences 1990–, Latvian Univ. 1991–; Cavaliere di San Marco 1993. *Publications:* more than 30 books of poetry, prose and essays in Latvian, Russian and English. *Leisure interests:* gardening, driving. *Address:* Vesetas str. 8, Apt 12, 1013 Riga, Latvia. *Telephone:* (2) 370-774.

PETERS, Lenrie Leopold Wilfred, MA, FRCS; Gambian surgeon; b. 1 Sept. 1932, Banjul; s. of Lenrie Peters and Keria Peters; m. (divorced); ed Boys' High School, Banjul, Prince of Wales Secondary School, Freetown, Sierra Leone, Trinity Coll., Cambridge; surgeon specialist, Westfield Clinic, Banjul 1972–; farmer, Chair. and Chief Exec. Farato Farms Export Ltd 1981–99; Chair. Colloquium Cttee, Lagos 1977, Bd of Govs. Gambia Coll. 1979–87, W African Examinations Council 1988–91, Nat. Consultative Cttee The Gambia 1995–; Fellow Int. Coll. of Surgeons 1992; Distinguished Friend of W African Examinations Council; Officer of Repub. of The Gambia. *Publications:* The Second Round (novel) 1965; poems: Satellites 1967, Katchikali, Selected Poems; anthologies. *Leisure interests:* tennis, music, reading. *Address:* Westfield Clinic, Kanifing (Office); P.O. Box 142, Banjul, The Gambia (Home). *Telephone:* 392219 (Office); 495419 (Home). *Fax:* 495419.

PETERS, Wallace, MD, DSc, FRCP; British professor of parasitology; b. 1 April 1924, London; s. of Henry Peters and Fanny Peters; m. Ruth Scheidegger-Frehner 1954; ed Haberdashers Aske's Hampstead School, St Bartholomew's Hosp. Medical Coll., Univ. of London; Physician West and East Africa, including RAMC 1947–53; Scientist-Entomologist and Malariologist, WHO, in Liberia and Nepal 1953–55; Malariologist, Territory of Papua and New Guinea 1956–61; Research Assoc., CIBA Pharmaceutical Co., Basel 1961–66; Prof. of Parasitology, Liverpool School of Tropical Medicine 1966–79, Dean 1975–78; Prof. of Medical Protozoology, London School of Hygiene and Tropical Medicine 1979–89, now Prof. Emer.; Hon. Consultant in Parasitology, Camden Area Health Authority 1978–89, on malariology, to Army 1986–89; Jt Dir Public Health Lab. Service Malaria Reference Centre 1979–89; Dir Centre for Tropical Antiprotozoal Chemotherapy, Northwick Park Inst. for Medical Research 1999–; Hon. Research Fellow Int. Inst. of Parasitology (IIP) (then CABI Bioscience) 1992–99; Pres. Royal Soc. of Tropical Medicine and Hygiene 1987–88 (Vice-Pres. 1982–83, 1985–87); mem. Expert Advisory Panel on Malaria of WHO 1967–; Hon. Fellow Royal Soc. of Tropical Medicine and Hygiene; Hon. mem. American Soc. of Tropical Medicine and Parasitology; Dr hc (Univ. René Descartes, Paris) 1992; King Faisal Int. Prize, Medicine 1983, Rudolf Leuckart Medallist, German Soc. of Parasitology 1980, Le Prince Medallist, American Soc. of Tropical Medicine and Hygiene 1994. *Publications:* Checklist of Ethiopian Butterflies 1952, Chemotherapy and Drug Resistance in Malaria 1970, 1987, Rodent Malaria (co-ed.) 1978, Atlas of Tropical Medicine and Parasitology (with H. M. Gilles) 1977, 1995, Pharmacology of Antimalarials (2 Vols) (co-ed.) 1984, Leishmaniases in Biology and Medicine (co-ed.) 1987, Atlas of Arthropods in Clinical Medicine 1992, Tropical Medicine and Parasitology (with G. Pasvol) 2001. *Leisure interests:* photography, entomology, writing. *Address:* Northwick Park Institute for Medical Research, Watford Road, HA1 3UJ, England (Office). *Fax:* (20) 8422-7136 (Office); (144) 284-3044 (Home). *E-mail:* w.peters@imperial.ac.uk (Office); wallacepeters2@aol.com (Home).

PETERS, Winston R.; New Zealand politician and lawyer; MP for Tauranga; fmr Minister of Maori Affairs, Minister in charge of the Iwi Transition Agency, Chair. Cabinet Cttee on Treaty of Waitangi Issues 1990–91; independent MP 1993–, now New Zealand First Party; leader New Zealand First Party 1993–; Deputy Prime Minister and Treas. 1996–98. *Address:* c/o Parliament Buildings, Wellington; 1 Third Avenue, P.O. Box 60, Tauranga, New Zealand (Office). *Telephone:* (7) 578-1797 (Office). *Fax:* (7) 578-6207 (Office).

PETERSDORF, Robert George, MD; American physician and medical educator; b. 14 Feb. 1926, Berlin, Germany; s. of Hans H. Petersdorf and Sonja Petersdorf; m. Patricia Horton Qua 1951; two s.; ed Brown and Yale Univs; Instructor in Medicine, Yale Univ. 1957–58; Asst Prof. of Medicine, Johns Hopkins Univ. 1958–59; Assoc. Prof. of Medicine, Univ. of Washington School of Medicine 1960–62, Prof. 1962–79, Chair. Dept of Medicine 1964–79; Prof. of Medicine, Harvard Medical School 1979–81; Pres. Brigham and Women's Hosp., Boston 1979–81; Vice-Chancellor for Health Sciences and Dean, School of Medicine, Univ. of Calif., San Diego 1981–86; Pres. Asscn of American Medical Colls. 1986–94, Pres. Emer. 1994–; Prof. of Medicine Univ. of Wash. 1994–, Distinguished Prof., Sr Advisor to Dean 1998–; Distinguished Physician VA Medical Center 1994–; Distinguished Physician Veterans Health Admin., Seattle 1995–98, Sr Physician 1998–; Ed. Harrison's Principles of Internal Medicine 1968–90; mem. editorial bds. of several scientific journals; Master American Coll. of Physicians, Royal Soc. of Medicine, Royal Coll. of Physicians, London, American Acad. of Arts and Sciences, AAAS; mem. Inst. of Medicine of NAS and numerous professional orgs.; numerous hon. degrees and prizes. *Publications:* over 400 papers in professional and scientific journals. *Address:* 1219 Parkside Drive, East Seattle, WA 98112, USA.

PETERSEN, George Bouet, DSc, MA, DPhil, F.N.Z.I.C., FRSNZ; New Zealand professor of biochemistry; b. 5 Sept. 1933, Palmerston North, NZ; s. of George C. Petersen and Elizabeth S. Petersen; m. Patricia J.E. Caughey 1960; four d.; ed Univs. of Otago and Oxford; scientist, DSIR Plant Chemistry Div. Palmerston North 1959–60, 1963–67; Departmental Demonstrator in Biochemistry, Univ. of Oxford 1961–63; Head, Dept of Biochemistry, Univ. of Otago 1968–91; Prof. of Biochemistry 1968–99, Prof. Emer. 1999–; Deputy Dean, Otago Medical School 1991–95; Pres. Acad. Council Royal Soc. of NZ 1997–2000; Visiting Research Fellow, Harvard Univ. 1964; Royal Soc. Commonwealth Bursar, MRC Lab. of Molecular Biology, Cambridge 1973–74, 1981; Carnegie Corpn of New York Travel Grantee 1964; Hon. DSc (Otago) 2000; Marsden Medal, NZ Asscn of Scientists 1995; Officer, NZ Order of Merit 1997. *Publications:* numerous papers on aspects of nucleic acid chemistry and biochemistry in various scientific journals. *Leisure interests:* music, literature, book collecting. *Address:* 47 Maori Road, Dunedin, New Zealand. *Telephone:* (3) 477-0784. *E-mail:* george.petersen@stonebow.otago.ac.nz (Office).

PETERSEN, Jan; Norwegian politician; b. 11 June 1946, Oslo; m.; two c.; with Norwegian Consumers' Asscn, Norwegian Agency for Devt Co-operation (NORAD); Chair. Young Conservatives 1971–73; Mayor of Oppegård 1976–81; Chair. Standing Cttee on Foreign Affairs 1985–86, now Deputy Chair.; Leader Akershus Conservative Party 1992–94, Conservative Party (Høyre) April 1994–; mem. Storting (Parl.); mem. Storting Standing Cttee on Local Govt 1981–85; Chair. Political Cttee of N Atlantic Ass. 1996–; Minister of Foreign Affairs Oct. 2001–. *Address:* Ministry of Foreign Affairs, 7 juri pl. 1, P.O. Box 8114 Dep., 0032 Oslo; Høyre, Stortingst. 20, P.O. Box 1536 Vika, 0117 Oslo, Norway. *Telephone:* 22-24-30-00 (Office). *Fax:* 22-24-95-00 (Office).

PETERSEN, Niels Helveg, LLD; Danish politician; b. 17 Jan. 1939, Odense; ed Copenhagen Univ. and Stanford Univ., Calif., USA; mem. Folketing (Parl.)

1966–74, 1977–; Chef de Cabinet to Danish Commr for the European Communities 1974–77; mem. Parl. Foreign Affairs Cttee 1968–74, Market Cttee 1972–74, 1977–78, 1982–88, 1990–93, Parl. Politico-Econ. Cttee 1982–84; Social Liberal Party Spokesman on Political Affairs 1968–74, 1977–78, Chair. Parl. Group 1978–88; Minister for Econ. Affairs 1988–90, for Foreign Affairs 1993–2000. *Address:* Folketinget, Christiansborg, 1240 Copenhagen K, Denmark (Office). *Telephone:* 33-37-47-10 (Office).

PETERSEN, Wolfgang; German film director and producer; b. 14 March 1941, Emden; ed German Film and TV Acad.; Asst Stage Dir Ernst Deutsch Theatre, Hamburg. *Films include:* Smog (Prix Futura Award 1975), For Your Love Only, Scene of the Crime, The Consequence 1977, Black and White Like Day and Night 1978, Das Boot 1981, The Neverending Story 1984, Enemy Mine 1985, Shattered 1991, In the Line of Fire 1993, Outbreak 1995, Air Force One, The Red Corner 1997, The Perfect Storm 2000. *Address:* c/o Rand Halstan, CAA, 9830 Wilshire Boulevard, Beverly Hills, CA 90212, USA.

PETERSON, David Robert, PC, LLD, QC; Canadian politician; b. 28 Dec. 1943, Toronto; s. of Clarence Peterson; m. Shelley Matthews 1974; two s. one d.; ed Univ. of Western Ont., Univ. of Toronto; called to the Bar 1969; Chair. and Pres. C. M. Peterson Co. Ltd and Cambridge Acceptance Corpn 1969–75; MP for London Centre 1975, re-elected 1977, 1981; elected Leader Ont. Liberal Party 1982, won election for Liberal Party 1985; Premier of Ont. 1985–90; Chair. Partner Cassels Brock & Blackwell LLP; Chair. Cassels, Pouliot; numerous directorships; Founding Chair. Toronto Raptors Basketball Club, Chapters Inc.; Dir Young Pres.' Org., Council for Canadian Unity, etc; Adjunct Prof., York Univ.; Liberal; several hon. degrees; Chevalier, Légion d'honneur 1994, Commdr of the Order of St John of Jerusalem, Ordre de la Pléiade, Int. Ass. of French-speaking Parliamentarians 1995. *Leisure interests:* golf, riding, reading, gardening, skiing. *Address:* Suite 2100, 40 King Street, W, Toronto, Ont. M5H 3C2 (Office); 8 Gibson Avenue, Toronto, Ont. M5R 1T5, Canada (Home). *Telephone:* (416) 869-5451 (Office); (416) 925-0460 (Home). *Fax:* (416) 360-8877 (Office).

PETERSON, Oscar Emmanuel, O.C.C.; Canadian jazz pianist; b. 15 Aug. 1925, Montreal, Québec; s. of Daniel Peterson and Olivia John; m. 1st Lillian Alice Ann Peterson 1947; two s. three d.; m. 2nd Sandra Cynthia King 1966; m. 3rd Charlotte Peterson; one s.; m. 4th Kelly Ann Green 1990; one d.; ed Montreal High School; studied with Paul deMarky; f. Advanced School of Contemporary Music, Toronto; Chancellor York Univ. (Canada) 1991–94, Chancellor Emer. 1994–; Carnegie Hall début with Jazz at the Philharmonic 1949; leader trio with Ray Brown and Herb Ellis; more than 300 compositions, including Hymn to Freedom, Canadiana Suite; 12 hon. degrees; Genie and Gemeni film awards for music scores, 7 Grammys, American Jazz Hall of Fame 1989, Gov.-Gen.'s Award for Lifetime Achievement 1992, Glenn Gould Prize 1993, NARAS Grammy Award for Lifetime Achievement 1997, Loyola Medal 1997, Praemium Imperiale 1999; Chevalier, Order of Québec, Order of Ont. *Publications:* Oscar Peterson New Piano Solos 1965, Jazz Exercises and Pieces 1965, Jazz Playbook (Vol. 1A) 1991 (Vol. 1B) 1993. *Leisure interests:* audio, photography, astronomy, boating. *Address:* Regal Recordings Ltd, 2421 Hammond Road, Mississauga, Ont. L5K 1T3, Canada. *Telephone:* (905) 855-2370.

PETERSON, Paul E., PhD; American political scientist; b. 16 Sept. 1940, Montevideo, Minn.; s. of Alvin C. Peterson and Josephine M. Telkamp; m. Carol D. Schnell 1963; two s. one d.; ed Concordia Coll., Moorhead, Minn. and Univ. of Chicago; Asst Prof., then Assoc. Prof. and Prof., Depts of Political Science and Educ., Univ. of Chicago 1967–83, Chair. Cttee on Public Policy Studies 1981–83; Dir Governmental Studies, The Brookings Inst., Washington, DC 1983–87; Benjamin H. Griswold III Prof. of Public Policy, Dept of Political Science, Johns Hopkins Univ. 1987–88; Prof. Dept of Govt, Harvard Univ. 1988–89, Henry Lee Shattuck Prof. of Govt 1989, Dir Centre for American Political Studies 1989–2000, Dir. Program on Educ. Policy and Governance 1996–; Acad. Visitor, Dept of Govt, LSE, England 1977–78; John Simon Guggenheim Fellowship, German Marshall Fund of the US Fellowship 1977–78; mem. Nat. Acad. of Educ., American Acad. of Arts and Sciences; Gladys Kammerer Award for best book publ. 1976 on US nat. policy (for School Politics Chicago Style), Woodrow Wilson Foundation Award for best book publ. 1981 (for City Limits), Award for best book publ. 1995 on public policy (for The Price of Federalism), all from American Political Science Asscn. *Publications:* School Politics Chicago Style 1976, City Limits 1981, The Politics of School Reform, 1870–1940 1985, The New Urban Reality (Ed.) 1985, The New Direction in American Politics (Ed. with J. Chubb) 1985, When Federalism Works (with B. Rabe and K. Wong) 1987, Political Institutions and Effective Government, Can the Government Govern? 1989, Welfare Magnets (with Mark Rom) 1991, The Urban Underclass (with C. Jencks) 1991, The President, the Congress and the Making of Foreign Policy 1994, The Price of Federalism 1995 (Aaron Wildavsky Award 1996), Classifying by Race 1995, The New American Democracy (with M. Fiorina) 2001, Learning from School Choice (Ed. with B. Hassel) 1998, Earning and Learning (Ed. with S. Mayer), Charters, Vouchers and Public Education (Ed. with David E. Campbell) 2001, The Education Gap: Vouchers and Urban Schools (with William G. Howell) 2002. *Leisure interests:* tennis, piano. *Address:* Kennedy School of Government, Harvard University, 79 JFK Street, T306, Cambridge, MA 02138, USA (Office). *Fax:* (617) 496-4428. *E-mail:* ppeterson@latte.harvard.edu (Office). *Website:* www.ksg.harvard/pcpg (Office).

PETERSON, Peter G., MBA; American business executive and government official; b. 5 June 1926, Kearney, Neb.; s. of George and Venetia (née Paul) Peterson; m. 1st Sally Hornbogen 1953 (divorced 1979); four s. one d.; m. 2nd Joan Ganz Cooney 1980; ed MIT, Northwestern Univ. and Univ. of Chicago; Market Analyst, Market Facts Inc., Chicago 1947–49, Assoc. Dir 1949–51, Exec. Vice-Pres. 1951–53; Dir of Marketing Services, McCann-Erickson (advertising firm) 1953, Vice-Pres. 1954–58, Gen. Man. Chicago Office 1955–57, Dir, Asst to Pres. co-ordinating services regional offices 1957–58; Exec. Vice-Pres. and Dir Bell & Howell 1958–61, Pres. 1961–63, CEO 1963–71, Chair. of Bd 1968–71; Asst to Pres. of USA for Int. Econ. Affairs 1971–72, also Exec. Dir Council on Int. Econ. Policy; Sec. of Commerce 1972–73; Chair. Bd Lehman Bros. Kuhn Loeb Inc. (fmrly Lehman Bros. Inc.), New York 1973–83; Chair. The Blackstone Group 1985–; mem. Ind. Comm. on Int. Devt Issues, Trilateral Comm.; Pres. Clinton's Bipartisan Comm. on Entitlement Reform 1994; nominated as Amb. to Viet Nam May 1996; Dir Minnesota Mining and Mfg Co., Rockefeller Center Properties Inc.; fmr Dir Federated Dept Stores, Black and Decker Mfg Co., Gen. Foods Corpn, RCA, Continental Group, Cities Service; mem. Inst. of Int. Econs (Chair Bd); Trustee, Museum of Modern Art, New York; Per Jacobson Lecture 1984; Man of Vision Award 1994. *Publications:* Facing Up: How to Rescue the Economy from Crushing Debt and Restore the American Dream, On Borrowed Time (co-author), Readings in Market Organization and Price Policies (Ed.). *Address:* The Blackstone Group, 345 Park Avenue, Suite 3101, New York, NY 10154 (Office); 435 E 52nd Street, Apartment 11G, New York, NY 10022, USA (Home).

PETERSON, Rudolph A.; American banker; b. 6 Dec. 1904, Svenljunga, Sweden; s. of Aaron Peterson and Anna (Johannsson) Peterson; m. 1st Patricia Price 1927 (deceased); m. 2nd Barbara Welser Lindsay 1962; one s. one d. one step-s. three step-d.; ed Univ. of California (Berkeley) Coll. of Commerce; Asst Man. San Francisco, successively Vice-Pres. and Gen. Man. Mexico City, Div. Operations Man., Chicago, Commercial Credit Co. 1926–36; Dist Man. Fresno, later Vice-Pres. San Francisco, Bank of America Nat. Trust and Savings Asscn 1936–46, Vice-Chair. of Bd of Dirs. 1961–63, Pres. 1963–70, Chair. Exec. Cttee 1970–75, Hon. Dir 1975–; Pres. Allied Building Credits 1946–52; Vice-Pres. Transamerica Corpn 1952–55; Pres. Man. Exec. Officer, Bank of Hawaii, Honolulu 1956–61; Pres. and CEO BankAmerica Corpn 1963–70, Chair. Exec. Cttee 1970–76, Dir –1981, Hon. Dir 1981–98; Dir Nat. Parks Foundation 1968–70, Chair. 1980–87; Chair. The Asia Foundation 1980–90, Calif. Acad. of Sciences 1980–85, Euro-Canadian Bank 1982–94; Di Giorgio Corpn 1969–89; Dir Alza Corpn, 1969–96, etc.; Admin. UN Devt Programme (UNDP) 1972–76; Hon. DHumLitt (Univ. of Redlands) 1967, Hon. LLD (Univ. of Calif.) 1968, Commdr Royal Order of Vasa (Sweden) 1964, Grand Cross of Civil Merit of Spain 1965, Order of Merit of Italian Repub. 1967, Great Swedish Heritage Award 1996. *Leisure interests:* gardening, reading. *Address:* 86 Sea View, Piedmont, CA 94611, USA. *Telephone:* (510) 547-5461.

PETERSON, Russell Wilbur, PhD; American politician, conservationist and industrial executive; b. 3 Oct. 1916, Portage, Wis.; s. of John Anton Peterson and Emma Marie Anthony; m. 1st Eva Lillian Turner 1937; two s. two d.; m. 2nd June Bigelow-Jenkins 1995; ed Portage High School and Univ. of Wisconsin; with Du Pont Company for 26 years, various research, sales and man. assignments to Dir Research and Devt Div. of Devt Dept 1968; Vice-Pres. Nat. Municipal League 1968–78; Gov. of Delaware 1969–73; Chair. Cttee on Law Enforcement, Justice and Public Safety, Nat. Govs Conf. 1971, Mid-Atlantic Govs Conf. 1971; Vice-Chair. Council of State Govts 1971; Chair. President's Nat. Advisory Comm. on Criminal Justice Standards and Goals 1971–72; Chair. of Bd, Textile Inst.; Chair. Exec. Cttee, Comm. on Critical Choices for Americans 1973; Chair. Council on Environmental Quality 1973–76; Pres. and CEO of New Directions, citizens' action org. focused on global problems 1976–77; Special Adviser to Aspen Inst. for Humanistic Studies 1976–77; Dir AAAS 1977–82, US Asscn of Club of Rome 1975–80, Population Crisis Cttee (now called Population Action Int.) 1973–98, World Wildlife Fund 1976–82, Office of Tech. Assessment, US Congress 1978–79, Global Tomorrow Coalition 1981–91; Pres. Nat. Audubon Soc. 1979–85 (Pres. Emer. 1985–), Better World Soc. 1985–87; Chair. Advisory Bd Solar Energy Research Inst. 1979–81; mem. President's Three Mile Island Comm. 1979; Regional Councillor, Int. Union for the Conservation of Nature (IUCN) 1981–88, Vice-Pres. 1984–88; mem. World Environment Prize Cttee, UNEP 1989–; Pres. Int. Council for Bird Preservation 1982–90, Pres. Emer. 1990–; Chair. Earth Lobby 1992–97, Stand up for What's Right and Just 2000–; Visiting Prof. Dartmouth Coll. 1985, Carleton Coll. 1986, Univ. of Wisconsin-Madison 1987; mem. Linnaean Soc., American Ornithologists' Union; Democrat 1996– (fmrly Republican); Hon. DSc (Williams Coll., Butler Univ., Alma Coll., Fairleigh Dickinson) 1976, (State Univ. of NY) 1981, Hon. Dr Humanics (Springfield Coll.), Hon. DEng (Stevens Inst. of Tech.), Hon. LLD (Gettysburg Coll.), (Univ. of Wis.) 1984, (Monmouth Coll.) 1982, (Salisbury State Univ.) 1988, Hon. LHD (Ohio State Univ., Northland Coll.); Hon. DHumLitt (Meadville/Lombard Theological School) 1992, (Colby Sawyer Coll.) 2000; Vrooman Award 1964, Nat. Conf. of Christians and Jews 1966 Citizenship and Brotherhood Award, Josiah Marvel Cup for Humanitarian and Civic Work, Commercial Devt Asscn Honor Award 1971, Gold Medal Award World Wildlife Fund 1971, Golden Plate Award American Acad. of Achievement 1971, Conservationist of the Year, Nat. Wildlife Fed. 1971, Parsons Award, American Chemical Soc. 1974, Nat. Audubon Soc. Medal 1977, Swedish American of the Year 1982, Robert Marshal Award of The

Wilderness Soc. 1984, Order of the Golden Ark (Netherlands) 1985, Environmental Law Inst. Award 1990, Lifetime Achievement Award, Global Tomorrow Coalition 1994, Lifetime Achievement Award, League of Conservation Voters 1996, Liberty Bell Award, Del. Bar Asscn 1998, New Century Award, Resource Renewal Inst. 1999, Russell W. Peterson Wildlife Refuge Naming 2000, Distinguished Policy Fellow, Univ. of Delaware 2001, Paul Harris Fellow, Rotary Int. 2002, Delaware State Univ. Presidential Medal of Honor 2003. *Publications:* Rebel with a Conscience (memoirs) 1999, We Can Save the Earth (CD-Rom) 2000; various articles on autoxidation, new product developments, crime reduction, environmental quality, conservation and population. *Leisure interests:* nature study, reading. *Address:* 11 E Mozart Drive, Wilmington, DE 19807, USA. *Telephone:* (302) 995-0736. *Fax:* (302) 995-9137.

PETERSON, Thage G.; Swedish politician; b. 1933, Berg, Kronoberg; ed Inst. of Social Studies, Lund 1955–57; Municipal Treas. Community Centre Asscn 1957–59, head 1967–71; Sec. and Vice-Chair. Social Democratic Youth Union 1964–67; elected to Parl. 1970; Under-Sec. of State to Cabinet 1971–75; Chair. Stockholm County br. of Socialdemokratiska Arbetarepartiet (Social Democratic Labour Party—SDLP) 1974–89; mem. SDLP Exec. Cttee 1975–90; Minister without Portfolio 1975–76; SDLP spokesman for Industrial Policy 1976–82; mem. SDLP Parl. Group Exec. and Head of Research Div.; Minister of Industry 1982–88, of Justice 1988, of Defence 1994–97, Minister in the Prime Minister's Office 1997–; Speaker of Parl. 1988–91; Chair. Standing Cttee on the Constitution 1991–94. *Address:* Office of the Prime Minister, Rosenbad 4, 103 33 Stockholm, Sweden. *Telephone:* (8) 405-10-00. *Fax:* (8) 723-11-71.

PETERSSON, Lars-Eric Gustav, B.SC.ECON.; Swedish business executive; b. b. 21 June 1950, Mönsterås; m.; two s.; Exec. Vice-Pres. Sparbanken/Svenska Sparbanksförmingen 1984–90; Pres., later Pres. and Chair. Pronator 1990–93; with Skandia Insurance Co. Ltd as mem. Man. Group, Head Business Control/Business Devt, Exec. Man., mem. Exec. Man., Head Int. Direct Insurance and Reinsurance (IDR), Acting Head Skandia Investment Man., Deputy Chief Exec. 1993–97, Pres. and CEO Skandia Insurance Co. Ltd 1997–, Chair. Telia 2000–. *Address:* Skandia Insurance Co. Ltd, Sveavägen 44, Stockholm 103 50, Sweden (Office). *Telephone:* (8) 788-10-00 (Office). *Fax:* (8) 10-31-74 (Office). *Website:* www.skandia.se (Office).

PETHRICK, Richard Arthur, PhD, FRSC, FRSE, C. CHEM., FRSA, FIM; British professor of chemistry; b. 26 Oct. 1942, Yate; s. of Arthur T. A. Pethrick and Lavinia M. Pethrick; m. Joan Knowles Hume 1975; one s.; ed Univs. of London and Salford; Lecturer, Dept of Pure and Applied Chem. Univ. of Strathclyde 1970, Sr Lecturer 1978, Reader 1981, Prof. of Chem. 1983–, Head Dept 1992–95, 1999–; mem. Editorial Bd British Polymer Journal 1979–93, Int. Journal of Polymeric Materials 1990–, Polymer News 1991–, Trends in Polymer Science 1992–, Polymer Int. 1993–; Ed. Polymer Yearbook 1983–; Visiting Prof. Univ. of Punjab 1979; British Council Visiting Lecturer, Australia 1985, 1989; Royal Soc. Visiting Lecturer, UK-China Del., Beijing 1992; mem. Int. Swedish Tech. Review Cttee for Polymer Science 1988; mem. Polymers and Composites Cttee, SERC 1993–, Large Area Displays Cttee EPSRC 1994–; IRC Review Cttee 1995–; Chair. Science Sector Scottish Vocational Awards Council 1995–; elected to Hon. Craft of Weavers of Glasgow 1991; Elder Merrylea Church, Church of Scotland 1995. *Publications:* Molecular Motion in High Polymers 1979, Modern Methods of Polymer Characterization 1999; over 350 scientific papers and numerous book chapters and review articles. *Leisure interests:* Scottish country dancing, walking. *Address:* Department of Pure and Applied Chemistry, University of Strathclyde, Thomas Building, 295 Cathedral Street, Glasgow, G1 1XL, Scotland (Office). *Telephone:* (141) 548-2260/2795 (Office). *Fax:* (141) 548-4822 (Office). *E-mail:* r.a.pethrick@strath.ac.uk (Office).

PETIT, Roland; French dancer and choreographer; b. 13 Jan. 1924, Villemomble; s. of Edmond and Victoria (née Repetto) Petit; m. Zizi Jeanmaire (q.v.) 1954; one d.; ed Paris Opera Ballet School; Premier Danseur Paris Opera 1940–44; f. Les Vendredis de la Danse 1944, Les Ballets de Champs-Elysées 1945, Les Ballets de Paris 1948; Dir Paris Opera Ballet 1970; f. Les Ballets de Marseilles; Officier, Légion d'honneur, Officier des Arts et des Lettres, Ordre. nat. du Mérite. *Works include:* Le rossignol et la rose, Le jeune homme et la mort, Les demoiselles de la nuit, Deuil en vingt-quatre heures, Le loup, Cyrano de Bergerac, Carmen, Les forains, La belle au bois dormant, Hans Christian Andersen, Folies Bergères, L'éloge de la folie, Paradise Lost, Pelléas et Mélisande, Les intermittences du coeur 1975, La symphonie fantastique 1975, Die Fledermaus 1980, Soirée Debussy, Le mariage du ciel et de l'enfer 1985, Fantôme de l'opéra, Charlot danse avec vous, Pink Floyd Ballet, Marcel et la belle excentrique 1992, La chauve-souris 1993, Camera obscura 1994, Passcaille 1994, Clavigo 1999; numerous films and plays. *Address:* 20 boulevard Gabes, 13008 Marseille, France.

PETKOV, Petko Danev; Bulgarian politician; b. 2 March 1942, Dobrotich; ed Higher Naval School, Varna; joined Dimitrov Young Communist League 1956, Bulgarian Communist Party (BCP) 1973; worked for 1st Coast Artillery Regt, Varna, radio mechanic for Navigation Maritime Bulgare Shipping Co., designer at Resprom Plant, Varna, Deputy Man., then Man. of Radio Navigation Equipment Works, Varna, Man. Dir of Cherno More Research and Industry Combined Works; First Sec., BCP Municipal Cttee, Varna Sept. 1987–; alt. mem., BCP Cen. Cttee; alt. mem., Political Bureau Dec. 1989–. *Address:* Bulgarian Communist Party, Sofia, Bulgaria.

PETKOVSKI, Tito; Macedonian politician; b. 23 Jan. 1945, Psacha, Kriva Palanka; m. Tanja Petkovska; two d.; ed Kriva Palanka High School, Skopje Univ.; worked in Municipal court Kriva Palanka, Repub. Bureau on Urban Planning and Communal Issues; political career started as deputy in Karposh Communal Ass., deputy City Ass. Skopje; later Vice-Pres. Exec. Council City Ass. Skopje; Sec. Cen. Cttee League of Communists of Macedonia—Party for Democratic Prosperity; mem. Cttee on Constitutional Problems, Ass. Repub. of Macedonia; Vice-Pres. first multi-party Ass. of Macedonia 1994–96; co-ordinator Parl. Group Social-Democratic Union of Macedonia; mem. Council of Inter-Parl. Union; Pres. Ass. (Sobranje) Repub. of Macedonia 1996–98, Pres. Standing Inquiry Cttee for Protection of Citizens' Freedoms and Rights 1998–; cand. in presidential elections 1999. *Publications include:* legal articles on housing policy, town planning and land devt. *Address:* 11 Oktombri blvd, 91000 Skopje, Macedonia. *Telephone:* (91) 112255. *Fax:* (91) 237947 (Office).

PETO, Sir Richard, Kt, MSc, MA, FRS; British professor of medicine; b. 14 May 1943; s. of Leonard Huntley Peto and Carrie Clarinda Peto; m. 1st Sallie Messum 1970 (divorced); two s.; partner Gale Mead; two s.; ed Trinity Coll., Cambridge, Imperial Coll., London; Research Officer MRC 1967–69; with Univ. of Oxford 1969–72, lecturer Dept of Regius Prof. of Medicine 1972–75, Reader in Cancer Studies 1975–92, Imperial Cancer Research Fund Prof. of Medical Statistics and Epidemiology 1992–. *Publications include:* Natural History of Chronic Bronchitis and Emphysema 1976, Quantification of Occupational Cancer 1981, The Causes of Cancer 1983, Diet, Lifestyle and Mortality in China 1990, Mortality from Smoking in Developed Countries 1950–2000 1994, Emerging Tobacco Hazards in China 1998. *Leisure interests:* science, children. *Address:* Radcliffe Infirmary, Oxford, OX2 6HE, England. *Telephone:* (1865) 552830; (1865) 404801.

PETRAKOV, Nikolai Yakovlevich, D.ECON.SC.; Russian economist; b. 1 March 1937; m. Tat'yana Aleksandrovna; one s. one d.; ed Moscow Univ.; mem. CPSU 1964–90; mem. staff Inst. of Tech.-Econ. Research 1959–61, Econ. Inst. 1961–65, then Head of Lab.; Deputy Dir, Cen. Mathematics-Econ. Inst., USSR Acad. of Sciences 1965–91; corresp. mem. USSR (now Russian) Acad. of Sciences 1984–90, mem. 1990–; USSR People's Deputy 1989–91; Dir Inst. for Market Problems 1991–; Adviser to Pres. Yeltsin 1994; mem. Political Consultative Council 1991; mem. State Duma (Parl.) 1993–95; Chair. Bd Savings Investment Bank 1996–. *Publications:* papers and articles on the problems of pricing policies and on socialist econs. *Address:* Institute for Market Problems, Krasikova Str. 32, 117418 Moscow (Office); Acad. Zelinski Str. 38, korp. 8, Apt 40, 117334 Moscow, Russia (Home). *Telephone:* (095) 129-10-00 (Office); (095) 135-14-46 (Home).

PETRE, Zoe, PhD; Romanian historian; b. 23 Aug. 1940, Bucharest; m. (husband deceased); two s.; ed Bucharest Univ.; Prof. and fmr Dean, History Faculty, Univ. Bucharest 1990–; specialist in ancient world history; Assoc. Prof. École des Hautes Études en Sciences Sociales, Centre de Recherches Comparées sur les Sociétés anciennes, Paris 1982, 1991, 1993; Sr Adviser to Pres. of Romania 1996–; mem. Romanian socs of Classical Studies, Historical Sciences and Anthropology, Asscn pour l'encouragement des études grecques, France, East-West Inst., New York; Order of Danebrog; Commdr Légion d'honneur; Timotei Ciparius Award of the Romanian Acad., Nicolae Jorga Award, Romanian Ministry of Culture and several other honours and awards. *Publications:* Commentaire aux "Sept contre Thèbes" d'Eschyle (with Liana Lupas) 1981, Civilizaţia greacă şi originile democratiei 1993–, Virsta de Bronz 2000, Cetatea greacă, între real şi imaginar 2000; and articles in scientific journals specializing in ancient history, culture, philology. *Leisure interests:* literature, music. *Address:* Universitatea Bucureşti, B-dul M. Kogălniceanu 64, 70609 Bucharest; Str. Kiriţescu 39, 73106 Bucharest, Romania. *E-mail:* zoe@incor.ro (Home).

PETRENKO, Aleksey Vasilyevich; Russian actor; b. 26 March 1938; ed Kharkov Theatre Inst.; acted with various prov. cos in the USSR, including Lensovet Theatre 1967–81, Moscow Art Theatre 1978–83, Moscow Taganka Theatre, Russia 1985–; actor Cen. M. Gorki film studio 1983–; RSFSR People's Artist 1988, United Russia and Belarus Prize for Devt of Russia 1998, Russian Govt Prize 2001. *Films include:* King Lear 1971, Marriage 1978, Agony (role of Grigoriy Rasputin) 1981, A Cruel Romance 1984, 20 Days Out of War 1987, The Servant 1989, Balthazar's Feasts or The Night with Stalin 1990, The Small Bees 1995, The Barber of Siberia 1998, Fortune 1999, Listen! Isn't it Raining? 2000, Collectioner 2002, Belle occasion 2003, Idiot 2003 and many others. *Address:* Nikitsky Blvd 9, Apt 39, 121019 Moscow, Russia. *Telephone:* 291-48-51.

PETRESKI, Dušan; Macedonian association executive; b. 19 Jan. 1948, Mavrovo; m. Liliana Mirchevska 1973; two s.; ed Skopje Univ.; Sec. and mem. Exec. Bd Econ. Chamber of Macedonia 1984–87, Vice-Pres. 1987–90, Pres. 1990–; Vice-Pres. Asscn of Balkan Chambers 1997–98, Pres. 1998–; many state and other decorations and awards. *Publications:* professional articles in many magazines and journals. *Leisure interests:* social activities, sport, walking. *Address:* Economic Chamber of Macedonia, Dimitrie Čupovski 13, 1000 Skopje (Office); Meksička 7, 1000 Skopje, Macedonia (Home). *Telephone:* (2) 16-14-60 (Office); (2) 36-17-50 (Home). *Fax:* (2) 11-62-10 (Office). *E-mail:* president@ic.mchamber.org.mk (Office). *Website:* www.mchamber.org.mk.

PETRI, Michala; Danish musician; b. 7 July 1958, Copenhagen; d. of Kanny Sambleben and Hanne Petri; m. Lars Hannibal; two d.; ed Staatliche Hochschule für Musik und Theater, Hannover; recorder player; first concert as soloist in Tivoli 1969; since 1969 has given 2000 concerts in the USA Japan Australia and Europe; has played with Pinchas Zukerman, James Galway, Keith Jarrett and Manuel Barruelo; performs frequently with Lars; several prizes. *Recordings:* more than 30 albums. *Publications:* Ed. of several works for Wilhelm Hansen and Moeck. *Address:* Nordskraenten 3, 2980 Kokkedal, Denmark. *Telephone:* 45-86-25-77. *Fax:* 45-86-56-77. *E-mail:* mail@michalapetri.com. *Website:* www.michalapetri.com.

PETRIC, Ernest, PhD; Slovenian diplomatist and professor of international law; b. 18 Nov. 1936, Trzic; s. of Joze Petric and Angela Godnov; m. Silvestra Rogelj; three d.; ed Univ. of Ljubljana, Univ. of Vienna; Research Asst, Inst. for Ethnic Studies, Ljubljana 1961–65; Asst Prof. of Int. Law, Univ. of Ljubljana 1965–67, Prof. 1972–83; mem. Exec. Council of Slovenia, Minister of Science and Tech. 1967–72; Prof., Univ. of Addis Ababa, Ethiopia 1983–86; Dean Faculty of Social Science, Univ. of Ljubljana 1986–89; Amb. of Yugoslavia to India (also accred to Nepal) 1989–91; Amb. to USA (also accred to Mexico) 1991–97; State Sec. Ministry of Foreign Affairs 1997–2000; Perm. Rep. to UN (also Amb. to Brazil) 2000–; Kidric Award 1979, Yugoslav Silver Medal for Achievement 1986, Colorado Meritorious Service Medal, USA 1997. *Publications:* International Legal Protection of Minorities 1977, The International Legal Position of the Slovenian Minority in Italy 1981, The Right to Self-Determination 1984, From Emperor to Leader 1987. *Leisure interests:* literature, skiing, tennis. *Address:* Permanent Mission of Slovenia to the United Nations, 600 Third Avenue, 24th Floor, New York, NY 10016 (Office); 120 East End Avenue, Apt 7C, New York, NY 10028, USA (Home). *Telephone:* (212) 370-3007 (Office); (212) 734-0993 (Home). *Fax:* (212) 370-1824 (Office); (212) 535-5934 (Home). *E-mail:* slovenia@un.int (Office). *Website:* www.un.int/slovenia (Office).

PETRIDES, Paul; Greek historian and university professor; b. 19 Aug. 1947, Thessaloniki; m. Lina Voreopoulou; ed Thessaloniki and Vienna Univs; Prof. Thessaloniki Univ. 1982–; Visiting Prof. at Panteion Univ.; Chair. Hellenic Lyric Stage 1989–93; Vice-Chair. G. Papandreou Cultural Foundation, Kapodistrias Foundation; Chair. Cultural Cttee of Law Faculty, Thessaloniki Univ.; Chair. Macedonian News Agency; recipient of several awards and prizes. *Publications include:* The Diplomatic Action of John Kapodistrias for Greeks 1974, Die Jonische Frage auf den Wiener Kongress, Griechenland und Grossmaechte, Political and Social History of Greece, Contemporary Political History of Greece. *Leisure interests:* painting, music. *Address:* 5 P. Mela Street, 552 36 Panorama, Thessaloniki, Greece. *Telephone:* (31) 341-682.

PETRIE, Sir Peter (Charles), 5th Bt, cr. 1918, of Carrowcarden, CMG; British diplomatist; b. 7 March 1932, London; s. of Sir Charles Petrie, Bt, CBE and Lady Petrie; m. Countess Lydwine von Oberndorff 1958; two s. one d.; ed Westminster School and Christ Church, Oxford; Second Sec. UK del. to NATO 1958–62; First Sec. New Delhi 1961–63; Chargé d'affaires, Kathmandu 1963–64; Cabinet Office, London 1965–67; FCO 1967–69; First Sec. later Counsellor, UK Perm. Mission at UN, New York 1969–73; Counsellor, Bonn 1973–76; FCO 1976–79; Minister, Paris 1979–85; Amb. to Belgium 1985–89; Adviser to Gov. of Bank of England on European and Parl. Affairs 1989–; mem. Franco-British Council 1995, Chair. British Section 1997–2002; Acad. de Compatibilité (Paris) 1997–; mem. Council, City Univ. 1997–2002. *Leisure interests:* gardening, golf, shooting. *Address:* Bank of England, Threadneedle Street, London, EC2R 8AH (Office); 16a Cambridge Street, London, SW1V 4QH, England (Home); 40 rue Lauriston, 75116 Paris, France (Home). *Telephone:* (20) 7601-5221 (Office). *Fax:* (20) 7601-3557 (Office). *E-mail:* peter.petrie@bankofengland.co.uk (Office).

PETRITSCH, Wolfgang, PhD; Austrian diplomatist; b. 26 Aug. 1947, Klagenfurt; ed Univs. of Vienna and Southern California, USA; Adviser, Press Sec. of Austrian Fed. Chancellor 1977–83; mem. Austrian Mission to OECD, Paris 1983–84; Head Austrian Press and Information Service, NY 1984–92; Acting Head Dept for Multilateral Econ. Co-operation, Ministry of Foreign Affairs 1992–94; Head Dept for Information on European Affairs, Fed. Chancellery 1994; Head Dept for Int. Relations, City of Vienna 1995–97; Amb. to Yugoslavia 1997–99; EU Special Envoy for Kosovo 1998–99, EU Chief Negotiator at Kosovo peace talks, France Feb.–March 1999; High Rep. of the Int. Community in Bosnia and Herzegovina Aug. 1999–. *Publications include:* Kosovo-Kosova. Mythen, Daten, Fakten; Bosnien und Herzegowina fünf Jahre nach Dayton – Hat der Friede eine Chance? *Address:* 71000 Sarajevo, Emerika Bluma 1, Bosnia and Herzegovina (Office). *Telephone:* (33) 283500 (Office). *Fax:* (33) 283501 (Office). *Website:* www.ohr.int (Office).

PETROS VII, His Beatitude Pope and Patriarch; Greek-Cypriot/Egyptian ecclesiastic; b. 3 Sept. 1949, Sichari; ed Seminary of Apostle Barnabas, Nicosia, Avery High School of Alexandria, Egypt, Athens Theological School; ordained Deacon in the Holy Monastery of Macheras 1969; served as Deacon to His Beatitude Nicolaos VI, Pope and Patriarch of Alexandria 1970–74; studied theology with Ministry of Foreign Affairs scholarship, Greece 1974; ordained Priest at the Holy Monastery of Pentelis 1978; served in Holy Church of Saint Spyridon, Athens; Archimandrite in the Cathedral of Saint Nicolaos, Cairo 1978; Patriarchal Vicar, Cairo 1978; Vicar-Gen. of the Metropolis and Priest, Church of the Panagia Pantanassa, Johannesburg 1980; Bishop of Babylon and Patriarchal Vicar of Cairo 1983; consecrated Bishop 1983; Metropolitan of Accra and West Africa 1990; Patriarchal Exarch in the Archdiocese of Irinoupolis – E. Africa 1991–94; Metropolitan of Cameroon and W Africa 1994; elected Pope and Patriarch of Alexandria and All Africa 1997–. *Address:* Greek Orthodox Patriarchate, P.O.

Box 2006, Alexandria, Egypt (Office). *Telephone:* (3) 4868595 (Office). *Fax:* (3) 4875684 (Office). *E-mail:* patriarchate@greekorthodox-alexandria.org (Office). *Website:* www.greekorthodox-alexandria.org (Office).

PETROV, Aleksander Aleksandrovich; Russian scientist; b. 3 Feb. 1934, Orekhovo-Zuyevo, Moscow Region; s. of late Alexander Vasilyevich Petrov and Evgenia Nikolaevna Petrova; ed Moscow Inst. of Physics and Eng; Head of Div., Computation Centre Russian Acad. of Sciences 1975–; corresp. mem. Russian Acad. of Sciences 1991, mem. 1997–; main research in problems of evolution of econ. systems and methods of estimating potential possibilities of Econs, math. modelling of complex systems; USSR State Prize 1980. *Publication:* From Gosplan to Market Economy: Mathematics Analysis of the Evolution of the Russian Economic Structures. *Address:* Dorodnicyn Computing Centre, Russian Academy of Sciences, Vavilov St 40, 119991, Moscow, Russia. *Telephone:* (095) 135-30-23 (Office). *E-mail:* petrov@ccas.ru (Office).

PETROV, Andrei Borisovich; Russian ballet dancer and choreographer; b. 27 Dec. 1945, Moscow; s. of Boris Kholfin and Olga Petrova; m. Olga Polyanskaya; ed Moscow Higher School of Choreography, Moscow Inst. of Theatre Arts; ballet dancer Bolshoi Theatre 1965–86, head of ballet troupe 1987–89, choreographer 1989–90; Founder and Artistic Dir Theatre Kremlin Ballet; RSFSR People's Artist 1985. *Ballets include:* Don Quixote, Swan Lake, Fountain of Bakhchisarai, Raimonda, Romeo and Juliet; *Ballets directed include:* Red Snowball-Tree, Wooden Prince, Sketches, Knight of a Sorrowful Look, Ruslan and Ludmila, Nutcracker, Zeus, Napoleon Bonaparte, Nevsky Prospect. *Address:* Theatre Kremlin Ballet, Kremlin, Palace of Congresses, 03073 Moscow, Russia (Office). *Telephone:* (095) 917-23-36 (Office). *Fax:* (095) 928-52-32 (Office).

PETROV, Andrei Pavlovich; Russian composer; b. 2 Sept. 1930, Leningrad; s. of Pavel Platonovich Petrov and Olga Petrovna Vaulina; m. Natalia Fishkova 1954; one d.; ed Leningrad Conservatory; Chair. Leningrad (now St Petersburg) Composers' Union 1964–; mem. CPSU 1957–90; Dir-Gen. Spring Music Festival, St Petersburg; State Prize 1967, 1976, 1996, USSR People's Artist 1980. *Compositions include:* Radda and Loiko (Symphonic poem), Violin Concerto, Piano Concerto, Symphonies No. 1, 2, 3, 4, The Creation of the World (ballet), Peter the Great (opera), Mayakovsky Begins (opera), Pushkin (choral dance work), The Master and Margarita (ballet music), Godchildren of Katherine the Great (musical) 1995–96; also operettas, songs, music for over 80 films including The Promised Heaven 1992 (Nika Prize). *Leisure interest:* travelling. *Address:* Petrovskaya nab. 4, Apt. 75, 197046 St Petersburg, Russia. *Telephone:* (812) 232-29-63. *Fax:* (812) 311-35-48. *E-mail:* peterbass@mail.ru (Office).

PETROV, Nikolai Arnoldovich; Russian pianist; b. 14 April 1943, Moscow; m. Larisa Petrova; one d.; ed Moscow Conservatory (pupil of Yakov Zak); debut in Moscow 1962; soloist of Moscow Philharmonic 1966–; toured many countries of Europe and America as soloist and with maj. conductors and orchestras; took part in music festivals; first performer of music by contemporary Russian composers, including Rodion Shchedrin, first performances in Russia of works by Bach, Beethoven, Mozart, Debussy, Ravel, Liszt; Prof. Moscow Conservatoire 1994–; Founder and Pres. Acad. of Russian Art 1995; Vice-Pres. Int. Asscn The World of Culture 1993; State Prize of Russia 1993; People's Artist of Russia, Musician of the Year (Musikalnaya Zhizn journal) 1994. *Address:* Kutuzovsky prospekt 26, apt. 23, 121 165 Moscow, Russia. *Telephone:* (095) 561-6747.

PETROV, Rem Viktorovich, DR.MED.SC.; Russian immunologist; b. 22 March 1930, Serafimovitch; s. of Victor Ivanovich Petrov and Kutniak Evdokia Emelianovna; m. 1st Tatiana Kuk 1960 (died 1970); m. 2nd Natalia Yemetz 1978; one s. one d.; ed Voronezh Medical Inst.; mem. CPSU 1956–91; research work at various grades in USSR (now Russian) Ministry of Health Inst. of Bio-Physics 1959–83, Head of Lab. 1983–; Pres. USSR (now Russian) Immunology Soc. 1983–; Dir of USSR (now Russian) Ministry of Health Inst. of Immunology 1983–88; mem. of Acad. of Medical Sciences 1978–; concurrently Head of Dept of Immunology of Second Moscow Inst. of Medicine 1974–; mem. Int. Scientific Advisory Bd of UNESCO 1996–; mem. USSR (now Russian) Acad. of Sciences 1984–, Vice-Pres. 1988–; mem. Acad. of Agric. 1991–; Ed. Sciences in Russia 1989; mem. World Acad. of Art and Sciences 1989–, New York Acad. of Sciences 1992–, Washington Acad. of Sciences 1993–, Norwegian Acad. of Sciences 1999–; Dr. hc (Bar-Ilan Univ.) 1990, (Madrid Polytechnic Univ.) 1994; L. Mechnikov Gold Medal and Prize, Acad. of Sciences 1987; Hero of Labour 1990, Order of Lenin 1990, Achievements for the Fatherland, Third Degree 1999. *Publications:* Essays on the New Immunology 1976, Immunology and Immunogenetics 1981, Immunology 1982, Me or Not Me 1983, Suppressor B-lymphocytes 1988, Myelopeptides 1999. *Leisure interests:* fishing, hunting, woodwork. *Address:* Russian Academy of Sciences, Leninsky pr. 14, 117901 Moscow (Office); 38-8-86 Zelinskogo St, 117334 Moscow, Russia (Home). *Telephone:* (095) 954-32-76 (Office); (095) 135-10-63 (Home). *Fax:* (095) 954-32-26 (Office). *E-mail:* petrov@pran.ru (Office).

PETROVICS, Emil; Hungarian composer; b. 9 Feb. 1930, Nagybecskerek (now Zrenjanin, Yugoslavia); s. of Jovan Petrovics and Erzsébet Weninger; one d.; studied at Conservatory, graduated from Music Acad. of Budapest; Musical Dir Petöfi Theatre 1960–64; Lecturer Coll. of Dramatic and Cinematographic Arts 1964–; Prof. of Composition Music Acad., Budapest; Dir Hungarian State Opera 1986–90; mem. Hungarian Parl. 1967–85; mem. Széchenyi Acad. of Arts, Budapest 1991–, Serbian Acad. of Sciences and Arts,

Belgrade 1993–; Erkel Prize 1960, 1963, Kossuth Prize 1966, holder of titles Merited Artist 1975, Eminent Artist 1982. *Compositions for musical stage:* C'est la guerre (single act) 1961; Crime and Punishment 1969; Book of Jonah (oratorio) 1965; Lysistrate (comic opera for concert performance) 1962 (all performed in Czechoslovakia, Finland, France, Fed. Repub. of Germany, Hungary and Yugoslavia); Salome (ballet) 1984; 2nd to 5th Cantatas: There Let Me Die 1972, Fanny's Posthumous Papers 1978, We All Must Go 1980, Letters from Turkey 1981, 6th Cantata: We Take a Rest. *Instrumental music:* Concerto for Flute 1957; String Quartet 1958; Symphony for Strings 1964; Quintet for Winds 1966; Rhapsody No. 1 and No. 2 for Violin and Viola Solo 1982, 1983; Concertino for Trumpet and Orchestra 1990; 2nd String Quartet 1991; Rhapsody No 2 for Violoncello Solo 1991; Vörösmarty—Overture for Orchestra 1993; Cantata No. 7: Pygmalion, for Mixed Chorus, Narrator and Orchestra 1994–95; Lament and Consolation (three poems for tenor voice and piano) 1996; Piangendo e Meditando, for String Orchestra 1997; Cantata No. 9: By the Danube 1998; Concerto for Piano and Orchestra 1999, Symphony No. 2 for Orchestra 2001; other works for chorus, incidental film and stage music. *Publication:* Ravel 1959. *Address:* Attila utca 39, 1013 Budapest, Hungary. *Telephone:* (1) 375-6032. *Fax:* (1) 212-75-02 (Home).

PETROVSKY, Artur Vladimirovich, PhD; Russian psychologist; b. 14 May 1924, Sevastopol; s. of Vladimir Vasilievich Petrovsky and Alexandra Abramovna Petrovskaya; m. Ivetta Sinelnikova; one s., one d.; ed Moscow Pedagogical Inst.; teacher, Sr teacher Vologda Pedagogical Inst. 1947–58; Asst prof. Moscow State Pedagogical Inst., Prof. 1952–66; Chair. Psychology Dept 1966–92; Prof. RAE Univ. 1998–, Head of Theory and History of Psychology Lab.; corresp. mem. USSR Acad. of Pedagogical Sciences 1968, mem. 1971; Academician-Sec. Dept of Psychology and Age Physiology 1968–76, 1997–, Vice-Pres. 1976–79, Pres. 1992–97; mem. Russian Acad. of Educ. 1991; Consultant Russian Acad. of Educ. Univ.; Honoured Scientist, Govt Prize of Russian Fed. 1998, Order of Honour 1999. *Publications:* History of Soviet Psychology 1967, General Psychology 1970, 1976–86, Problems of History and Theory of Psychology: selected works 1984. Essays on Psychology 1985, Psychology in USSR 1990, Psychology of Each of Us 1992, History of Psychology (co-author Yaroshevsky) 1994, Foundations of Theoretical Psychology 1996–98, Psychology in Russia: 20th Century 2001, Theoretical Psychology (co-author Yaroshevsky) 2001, Memories of a Psychologist 2001. *Leisure interest:* collecting books of fiction. *Address:* RAE University, Bolshaya Polyanka Str. 58, 119180 Moscow (Office); Str. Chernyakhovskogo 4, Apt. 11, 125319 Moscow, Russia (Home). *Telephone:* (095) 237-31-51 (Office); (045) 151-98-63 (Home). *Fax:* (095) 237-45-61 (Office). *E-mail:* boris@urao.edu.

PETROVSKY, Boris Vasiliyevich; Russian surgeon; b. 27 June 1908, Essentuki; s. of Vasiliy Petrovsky and Lydia Petrovsky; m. Ekaterina Timofeeva; one d.; ed First Moscow Univ.; physician at various hospitals 1930–50; mem. CPSU 1942–91; Head of Chair of Surgery, Second Moscow Inst. of Medicine 1951–56; Head of Chair of Hospital Surgery, First Moscow Medical Inst. and Dir Inst. of Clinical and Experimental Surgery (now Scientific Centre of Surgery), Acad. of Medical Sciences 1956–; Minister of Health of USSR 1965–80; Deputy to USSR Supreme Soviet 1962–84; Cand. mem. Cen. Cttee of CPSU 1966–81; mem. USSR (now Russian) Acad. of Medical Sciences 1957–, USSR (now Russian) Acad. of Sciences 1966–, Russian Medico-technical Acad. 1994–; has studied problems of blood transfusion, oncology, surgery of vessels and organs of thoracic cavity, surgical treatment of congenital and acquired heart diseases, kidney transplant; Honoured Scientific Worker of RSFSR, Lenin Prize 1960, Hero of Socialist Labour 1968, Order of Lenin (four times) and other awards. *Publications:* Drip Transfusion of Blood and Blood-Substitute Compounds 1948, Surgical Treatment of Vascular Wounds 1949, Surgical Treatment of Carcinoma of the Oesophagus and Cardia 1950, Blood Transfusion in Surgery 1954, Surgery of Mediastinum 1960, Surgery of Patent Arterial Duct 1963, Cardiac Aneurysms 1965, Resection & Plastic Repair of Bronchi 1966, Prosthetic Replacement of Heart Valves 1966, Surgery of Diaphragm 1966, Oesophageal Diverticuli 1968, Surgery for Renovascular Hypertension 1968, Selected Lectures in Clinical Surgery 1968, Kidney Transplantation 1969, Surgery of Aortic Arch Branches 1970, Surgery of Peripheral Vessels 1970, Atlas of Thoracic Surgery 1973–74, Surgical Hepatology 1972, Microsurgery 1976, Basics of Hyperbaric Medicine 1976, Tracheo-Bronchial Surgery 1978, Surgical Treatment of Chronic Ischaemic Heart Diseases 1978, Surgical Diseases 1980, Reconstructive Surgery for Extrabiliary Duct Disorders 1980, Emergency Cardiovascular Surgery 1980, Surgeon and Life 1989, Two Persons—One Life (memoirs) 1991, Surgery for Portal Hypertension: Atlas 1994; Great Medical Encyclopaedia 30 Vols (Ed.-in-Chief). *Leisure interests:* collecting books and gardening. *Address:* National Research Centre for Surgery, Abrikosovskyi 2, Moscow 119874, Russia. *Telephone:* (095) 248-92-65 (Office); 246-43-85 (Home). *Fax:* (095) 230-24-80.

PETROVSKY, Vladimir Fyodorovich, DHist; Russian diplomatist; b. 29 April 1933, Volgograd; s. of Fyodor Petrovsky and Anna Khritinina; m. Myra Mukhina; one d.; ed Moscow Inst. of Int. Relations; with USSR (now Russian) Ministry of Foreign Affairs 1957–; staff mem. USSR Mission to UN 1957–61, mem. Office of the Foreign Minister, USSR Ministry of Foreign Affairs 1961–64; mem. UN Secr. 1964–71; with dept of planning of int. policy, USSR Ministry of Foreign Affairs 1971–78, Head of Dept 1978–79, Head Dept of Int. Orgs 1979–86, Deputy Minister 1986–91, First Deputy Minister Aug.–Dec. 1991; Exec. Sec. CSCE Conf. on Human Dimension 1991; UN Under-Sec.-

Gen. for Political Affairs 1992; Dir-Gen. UN Office, Geneva 1993–2002; Sec.-Gen. Conf. on Disarmament 1994–2002; mem. Acad. of Natural Sciences of Russian Fed. *Publications:* The Foreign Service of Great Britain 1958, The Diplomacy of 10 Downing Street 1964, US Foreign Policy Thinking: Theories and Concepts 1976, The Doctrine of National Security in US Global Strategy 1980, Disarmament: Concept, Problems, Mechanisms 1983, Security in the Era of Nuclear and Outer Space Technology 1985. *Leisure interests:* art, memoirs. *Address:* c/o Ministry of Foreign Affairs, Smolenskaya-Sennaya pl. 32/34, 121200 Moscow, Russia.

PETRUSHEVSKAYA, Liudmila Stefanovna; Russian author and playwright; b. 26 May 1938, Moscow; d. of Stefan Antonovitsh Petrushevskij and Valentina Nikolaevna Jakovleva; m. 1st Evgenij Kharatian; one s.; m. 2nd Boris Pavlov; one s. one d; ed Moscow Univ.; newspaper and radio journalist 1957–73; started writing short stories 1968, plays and folk tales 1971; stage productions and publ. of works were forbidden for many years; first underground performance 1975, first official performance, Tallinn 1979; mem. Bayerische Akad. der Schönen Kunste 1997; Int. A. Pushkin Prize (Germany) 1991, prizes for the best short story of the year from "Ogoniok" 1988, 1989 and "Oktiabr" 1993, 1996, Grand Prize for play The Time: Night, Annual All-Russian Theatre Festival of Solo Theatre, Perm 1995, Moscow-Penne Prize (Russia/Italy) 1996. *Plays include:* Two Windows 1971, Music Lessons 1973, Cinzano 1973, Love 1974, The Landing 1974, Andante 1975, The Execution, A Glass of Water, Smirnova's Birthday 1977–78, Three Girls in Blue 1980, Colombina's Flat 1981, Moscow Choir 1984, The Golden Goddess 1986, The Wedding Night 1990, The Men's Quarters 1992; co-author of screenplay Tale of Tales (prize for best animated film of all time, Los Angeles 1980). *Publications:* Immortal Love 1988, Songs of the 20th Century 1988, On the Way to the God Eros 1993, The Mystery of the House 1993; (children's books) Vasilli's Treatment 1991, Once Upon a Time There Was a Trrrr! 1994, Real Fairy Tales 1997, The Alphabet's Tale 1997; Complete Works (5 Vols) 1996, The Girl's House 1998, Find Me, My Dream 2000. *Leisure interests:* watercolour painting. *Address:* Staroslobodsky per. 2a, Apt 20, 107113 Moscow, Russia. *Telephone:* 269-74-48. *Fax:* 269-74-48.

PETRY, Heinz, DIPL. ING; German industrial executive; b. 12 Jan. 1919, Rheinhausen; s. of Heinrich Petry and Elise Petry (née Maas); m. Liselotte Petry (née Gebauer) 1945; two s. one d.; ed Berlin Tech. Coll., Stuttgart Univ.; construction engineer in dredger Mfg, Krupp Industrie- und Stahlbau, Rheinhausen 1946, Deputy Head of Dept 1959, given proxy of firm 1961, Head of Dept 1962, Deputy mem. of Man. Bd 1965, mem. 1966, Spokesman 1973; mem. Man. Bd, Friedrich Krupp GmbH, Essen 1974–, Deputy Chair. 1975–76, Chair. 1976–80; mem. Supervisory Bd AG Weser, Bremen, Krupp-Koppers GmbH, Essen. *Leisure interests:* hunting, golf, films. *Address:* Kaiserstrasse 238, 47800 Krefeld, Germany.

PETTENGILL, Gordon Hemenway, PhD; American professor of planetary physics; b. 10 Feb. 1926, Providence, RI; s. of Rodney G. Pettengill and Frances (Hemenway) Pettengill; m. Pamela Wolfenden 1967; one s. one d.; ed MIT and Univ. of California at Berkeley; staff mem., MIT Lincoln Lab. 1954–68, Assoc. Leader, Haystack Observatory 1965–68; Dir Arecibo Observatory, Puerto Rico (operated by Cornell Univ.) 1968–70; Prof. of Planetary Physics, Dept of Earth and Planetary Sciences, MIT 1970–2001, Prof. Emer. 2001–; Dir MIT Center for Space Research 1984–90; involved in the study of the solar system using radar and radio techniques; discovered 3/2 spin-orbit resonance of Mercury 1965; pioneered delay-doppler radar mapping of planets; prin. investigator of Pioneer Venus Radar Mapper 1978–81, Magellan Venus Radar Mapper 1990–93; mem. NAS, American Acad. of Arts and Sciences, AAAS, American Physical Soc., American Astronomical Soc., Int. Radio Science Union; Guggenheim Fellow 1980/81; Fellow American Geophysical Union; Magellan Premium of the American Philosophical Soc. 1994; Charles A. Whitten Medal, American Geophysical Union 1997. *Leisure interests:* ornithology, genealogy. *Address:* Room 37-582d, Massachusetts Institute of Technology, 77 Massachusetts Avenue, Cambridge, MA 02139, USA. *Telephone:* (617) 253-4281. *Fax:* (617) 253-0861 (Office). *E-mail:* ghp@space.mit.edu.

PETTIGREW, Pierre S., BA, M.PHIL.; Canadian politician; b. 18 April 1951; ed Univ. du Québec à Trois-Rivières, Univ. of Oxford; Dir Political Cttee NATO Ass., Brussels 1976–78; Exec. Asst to Leader of Québec Liberal Party 1978–81; Foreign Policy Adviser to Prime Minister, Privy Council Office 1981–84; Vice-Pres. Samson Belair Deloitte and Touche Int. (Montreal) 1985–95; elected MP 1996, re-elected 1997; Minister for Int. Co-operation and Minister with special responsibility for La Francophonie 1996–97, Minister of Human Resources Devt 1997–99, for Int. Trade 1999–; Co-Chair. First Nat. Forum on Canada's Int. Relations 1994. *Publication:* The New Politics of Confidence. *Address:* Ministry for International Trade, Lester B. Pearson Building, 125 Sussex Drive, Ottawa, Ont., K1A 0G2, Canada (Office). *Telephone:* (613) 992-7332 (Office). *Fax:* (613) 996-8924 (Office). *E-mail:* pierre.pettigrew@dfait-maeci.gc.ca (Office). *Website:* www.dfait-maeci.gc.ca (Office).

PETTIT, Philip Noel, PhD; Irish/Australian professor of social and political theory; b. 20 Dec. 1945, Ballinasloe, Ireland; s. of Michael A. Pettit and Bridget C. Molony; m. Eileen McNally 1978; two s.; ed Maynooth Coll., Nat. Univ. of Ireland, Queen's Univ. Belfast, Northern Ireland; lecturer, Univ. Coll. Dublin 1968–72, 1975–77; Research Fellow, Trinity Hall Cambridge, UK 1972–75; Prof. of Philosophy, Univ. of Bradford, UK 1977–83; Professorial

Fellow, Research School of Social Sciences, ANU, Canberra 1983–89, Prof. of Social and Political Theory 1989–2002; Visiting Prof. of Philosophy, Columbia Univ., New York 1997–2001; Prof. of Politics, Princeton Univ. 2002–; Fellow Acad. of Social Sciences, Australia, Australian Acad. of Humanities; Hon. mem. Italian Soc. for Analytical Philosophy; Hon. DLitt (Nat. Univ. of Ireland) 2000; Univ. Medal, Univ. of Helsinki 1992. *Publications:* Concept of Structuralism 1975, Judging Justice 1980, Semantics and Social Science (with G. Macdonald) 1981, Not Just Deserts: A Republican Theory of Criminal Justice (with J. Braithwaite) 1990, The Common Mind: An Essay on Psychology, Society and Politics 1992, Republicanism: A Theory of Freedom and Government 1997, A Theory of Freedom: From the Psychology to the Politics of Agency 2001, Rules, Reasons and Norms: Selected Essays 2002. *Leisure interests:* walking, tennis. *Address:* Department of Politics, Corwin Hall, Princeton University, Princeton, NJ 08544-1012, U.S.A. (Office); 605/2 Marcus Clarke St, Canberra, ACT, Australia (Home). *Telephone:* (2) 6262-7092 (Home).

PETTY, Richard; American racing driver; b. 2 July 1937, Level Cross, NC; s. of Lee Petty Lee; m. Lynda Owens Petty; one s. three d.; stock car racing driver 1958–92; Winston Cup Rookie of the Year 1959; total of 200 Career NASCAR Winston Cup Victories, NASCAR Winston Cup Champion 1964, 1967, 1971, 1972, 1974, 1975, 1979; winner Daytona 500 1964, 1966, 1971, 1973, 1974, 1979, 1981; 27 victories in one season 1967; sport's first million dollar driver; last race in 1992; f. Petty Enterprises (complete stock car racing operation); est. Richard Petty Museum 1988; Most Popular Winston Cup Driver 1962, 1964, 1968, 1970, 1974, 1975, 1976, 1977, 1978; Nat. Motorsports Press Asscn (NMPA) Myers Brothers Award 1964, 1967, 1971, 1992, NMPA Driver of the Year 1974, 1975; Nat. NC Athletic Hall of Fame 1973, Int. Motorsports Hall of Fame 1997, Automotive Hall of Fame 2002; Medal of Freedom 1992; American Auto Racing Writers & Broadcasters Asscn (AARWBA) Man of the Year 1995. *Address:* c/o The Richard Petty Museum, Level Cross, North Carolina, USA. *Website:* www.pettyracing.com (Office).

PEUGEOT, Patrick; French insurance executive; b. 3 Aug. 1937, Paris; s. of Jacques Peugeot and Edith Peugeot (née Genoyer); m. Catherine Dupont 1963; three s.; ed Lycée Hoche, Ecole Sainte-Geneviève à Versailles, Ecole polytechnique, Ecole nat. d'admin.; auditor, Cour des comptes 1965, Commissariat au plan (Public Enterprises Cttee) 1966–70; Sec.-Gen. Librairie Hachette 1972–74; Sec.-Gen. Groupe des Assurances générals de France (AGF) 1975–83, Dir-Gen. AGF-Réassurance 1979–83; tech. consultant to Ministry of Economy and Finances 1981–83; Dir-Gen. Caisse centrale de réassurance 1983–84, Pres. Advisory Bd 1984–85, Hon. Pres. 1985–; Pres. Dir-Gen. Société commerciale de réassurance (Scor) 1983–94, Hon. Pres. and Dir. 1994–; Vice-Pres. Dir-Gen. La Mondiale 1995, Chair. and CEO 1996–; Pres. Groupement des assurances des personnes (Gap) 1997–99; Pres. Réunion des organismes d'assurance mutuelle 1999–; Chevalier, Ordre nat. du Mérite. *Address:* La Mondiale, 22 boulevard Malesherbes, 75008 Paris (Office); 82 rue Notre-Dame-des-Champs, 75006 Paris, France (Home). *Website:* www.lamondiale.fr (Office).

PEUGEOT, Roland; French motor-car executive; b. 20 March 1926, Valentigney; s. of Jean-Pierre and Colette (née Boillat-Japy) Peugeot; m. Colette Mayesky 1949; two s.; ed Lycées Janson-de-Sailly and Saint-Louis, Paris and Harvard Business School, Mass., USA; Pres. Etablissements Peugeot Frères 1959–; Pres. du Conseil de Surveillance de Peugeot SA 1972–; mem. Bd Automobiles Peugeot 1982–; Pres. Peugeot Talbot Belgique 1985; Dir of subsidiaries and other cos. including L'Union et Le Phénix Espagnol 1974–, Champagne Laurent Perrier 1992–; Officier, Légion d'honneur, Officier, Ordre des Arts et des Lettres. *Address:* 75 avenue de la Grande Armée, 75116 Paris (Office); 170 avenue Victor-Hugo, 75116 Paris, France (Home).

PEVTSOV, Dmitry Anatlyevich; Russian actor; b. 8 June 1963, Moscow; m. Olga Drozdova; ed Moscow State Inst. of Theatre Arts; actor Taganka Theatre 1985–91; Moscow Theatre of Leninsky Komsomol (LENKOM) 1991–; European Prize Felix (Glasgow). *Films include:* The End of the World with a Consequent Symposium, By the Nickname of Beast, Line of Life, Queen Margo. *Plays include:* The Marriage of Figaro, The Seagull. *Address:* Teplichny per. 5, Apt. 139, 123298 Moscow, Russia (Home). *Telephone:* (095) 198-77-69 (Home).

PEYRELEVADE, Jean; French business executive; b. 24 Oct. 1939, Marseille; s. of Paul Peyrelevade and Nadia Benveniste; m. Anne Chavy 1962; three s. one d.; ed Faculté de droit de Paris, Ecole Nat. de l'aviation civile; fmr armaments and aviation engineer; Dir Dept of Foreign Business, Crédit Lyonnais 1973–82; Asst Dir Cabinet of M. Pierre Mauroy 1982; Pres. Cie Financière de Suez 1983–86; Pres. Banque Stern 1986–88; Chair. Union des Assurances de Paris 1988–93; Chair. Crédit Lyonnais Nov. 1993–; Govt Rep. on Bd of Renault 1996–2000; mem. Econ. and Social Council 1994–. *Publications:* La mort du dollar 1974, L'economie de spéculation 1978, Economie de l'entreprise 1989, Pour un capitalisme intelligent 1993, Le gouvernement d'entreprise 1999. *Leisure interests:* skiing, golf. *Address:* Crédit Lyonnais SA, 19 blvd des Italiens, 75002 Paris (Office); 61 avenue Charles de Gaulle, 92200 Neuilly-sur-Seine, France (Home).

PEYTON OF YEOVIL, Baron (Life Peer), cr. 1983, of Yeovil in the County of Somerset; **John Wynne William Peyton,** PC; British politician; b. 13 Feb. 1919, London; m. 2nd Mary Constance Wyndham 1966; two s. (one deceased) one d. from first marriage; ed Eton Coll. and Trinity Coll. Oxford; called to the Bar 1945; Conservative MP for Yeovil 1951–83; Parl. Sec., Ministry of Power

1962–64; Minister for Transport Industries 1970–74; Shadow Leader of Commons 1974–76; Opposition Spokesman for Agric. 1976–79; Chair. Texas Instruments Ltd 1974–90; Chair. British Alcan Aluminium PLC 1987–91; Chair. Zoo Operations Ltd 1988–91. *Publication:* Without Benefit of Laundry (autobiog.) 1997, Solly Zuckerman: A Scientist out of the Ordinary 2001. *Address:* The Old Malt House, Hinton St George, Somerset, TA17 8SE, England (Home).

PFAFF, Judy; American artist; b. 22 Sept. 1946, London, England; ed Wayne State Univ., Detroit, S. Illinois Univ., Univ. of Washington and Yale Univ.; Guggenheim Fellowship for Sculpture. *Solo exhibitions include:* Webb & Parsons Gallery, New York 1974, Daniel Weinberg Gallery, LA 1984. *Group exhibitions include:* Razor Gallery, New York 1973, Holly Solomon Gallery, New York 1984, Whitney Museum of American Art, Contemporary Art Museum, Houston, Tex., Wacoal Art Center, Tokyo, Japan, Brooklyn Museum, Venice Biennale, Museum of Modern Art, New York.

PFEFFER, Philip Maurice, MA; American company executive; b. 20 Jan. 1945, St Louis; s. of Philip McRae and Jeanne (Kaufman) Pfeffer; m. Pamela Jean Korte 1965; three s.; ed South Illinois Univ., Vanderbilt Univ.; joined Genesco Inc., Nashville 1968, Pres. Genesco Export co. 1970–75; Dir Financial Planning, Ingram Distribution Group Inc., Nashville 1976–77; Vice-Pres. Finance and Admin. 1977–78, Exec. Vice-Pres. 1978, Pres. and CEO 1978–81, Dir 1978–95, Chair. of Bd and CEO 1981–95, Exec. Vice-Pres. Ingram Industries Inc. 1981–95, Dir 1981–95; fmr Pres. and COO Random House; Instructor in Finance and Econs, Univ. of Tenn., Nashville 1968–77; lecturer in Corp. Finance, Vanderbilt Univ. 1972–77. *Leisure interests:* scouting, sailing, water sports, landscaping. *Address:* 836 Treemont Court, Nashville, TN 37220, USA (Home).

PFEIFFER, Didier-Bernard, LIC. EN DROIT; French business executive; b. 3 Nov. 1938, Paris; s. of Jacques Pfeiffer and Denise Pontzen; m. Maryse Bloch 1961; three c.; ed Lycée Pasteur, Neuilly, Univ. de Paris, Inst. d'études politiques de Paris, Ecole Nat. d'Admin; civil servant Treasury Dept, Ministry of Economy and Finance 1966–68, Head of Dept Office of Minister of Econ. and Finance 1968–71; Financial Attaché French Embassy, Washington 1971; a Deputy Dir World Bank 1972; Dir Financial Operations l'Union des Assurances de Paris (UAP) 1973, Dir of Investments 1976–84, Man. Dir 1984–91, Dir 1991–94, Vice-Pres. and Man. Dir 1994–96; Pres., Groupe des Assurances Nationales (GAN) 1996–98; Vice-Pres. Exec. Cttee Groupama GAN 1998–99; Pres. Supervisory Bd Fonds de Garantie des Assurances de Personnes (FGAP) 1999–; Vice-Pres. Supervisory Bd Eurazeo 2002–; Officier, Légion d'honneur, Officier, Ordre nat. du Mérite. *Address:* FGAP, 51 rue Saint-Georges, 75009 Paris, Cédex 08 (Office); 68 rue des Belles Feuilles, 75116 Paris, France (Home). *Telephone:* 1-40-22-03-09 (Office); 1-45-53-98-11 (Home). *Fax:* 1-40-22-98-73 (Office).

PFEIFFER, Michelle; American actress; b. 29 April 1957, Santa Ana, Calif.; d. of Dick Pfeiffer and Danna Ffeiffer; m. 1st Peter Horton (divorced 1987); one adopted d.; m. 2nd David E. Kelley 1993; one s.; ed Fountain Valley High School, Golden West Coll., Whitley Coll. *Films include:* Grease 2, Into the Night, The Witches of Eastwick, Sweet Liberty, Married to the Mob, Tequila Sunrise 1989, Dangerous Liaisons 1989, The Fabulous Baker Boys 1989, The Russia House 1989, Love Field, Frankie and Johnny 1991, Batman Returns 1992, The Age of Innocence 1993, Wolf 1994, My Posse Don't Do Homework 1994, Dangerous Minds, Up Close and Personal, To Gillian On Her 37th Birthday, One Fine Day 1997, A Thousand Acres 1997, Privacy 1997, The Story of Us 1999, The Deep End of the Ocean 1999, A Midsummer Night's Dream 1999, Being John Malkovich 1999, What Lies Beneath 2000, I am Sam 2001. *Address:* ICM, 8492 Wilshire Blvd., Beverly Hills, CA 90211, USA.

PHAM THE DUYET; Vietnamese fmr politician and trades union leader; economist; fmr mine man.; fmr Pres. Viet Nam Gen. Confed. of Labour; leader CP of Hanoi, Viet Nam 1987. *Address:* Communist Party of Viet Nam, 1 Hoang Van Thu, Hanoi, Viet Nam.

PHAM VAN KY; Vietnamese writer; b. 1916; ed Secondary School, Hanoi and Univ. of Paris; went to France 1939; prepared thesis on religion for the Institut des Hautes Etudes Chinoises; Grand Prix du Roman, Académie Française 1961. *Publications:* Fleurs de jade (poems) 1946, L'homme de nulle part (short stories) 1946, Frères de sang (novel) 1947, Celui qui régnera (novel) 1954, Les yeux courroucés (novel) 1958, Les contemporains (novel) 1959, Perdre la demeure (novel) 1961, Poème sur soie (poems) 1961, Des femmes assises çà et là (novel) 1964, Mémoires d'un eunuque (novel) 1966, Le rideau de pluie (play) 1974.

PHAN VAN KHAI; Vietnamese politician; b. 25 Dec. 1933, Saigon (now Ho Chi Minh City); involved in revolutionary activities from 1947, in N Viet Nam 1954–60; joined CP 1959; student, Moscow Nat. Univ. of Econs 1960–65; fmrly with Gen. Dept of State Planning Cttee, fmr econ. researcher; in communist-controlled areas of S. Viet Nam 1973; Deputy Dir Aid Planning Dept of Nat. Reunification Cttee 1974–75; Deputy Dir Planning Dept, Ho Chi Minh City 1976–78, Dir 1979–80; Deputy Mayor, Ho Chi Minh City 1979–80, Perm. Deputy Mayor 1981–84, Mayor 1985–89; Chair. People's Cttee of Ho Chi Minh City 1985–89; perm. mem. Ho Chi Minh City CP Cttee 1979–80, Deputy Sec. 1981–84; alt. mem. CP Cen. Cttee 1982–84, mem. 1984–, mem. Political Bureau 1991–; Chair. State Planning Cttee 1989–91; Deputy Chair. Council of Ministers 1991–92; Perm. Deputy Prime Minister of Viet Nam 1992–97; Prime Minister of Viet Nam Sept. 1997–. *Address:* Office of the Prime Minister, Hanoi, Viet Nam.

PHANTOG; Chinese mountaineer; b. Aug. 1939, Xigazê, Tibet; d. of Cirhen Phantog and Cijiu Phantog; m. Jia-shang Deng 1963; one s. two d.; ed Cen. Coll. of Nationalities; first Chinese woman to climb Everest 1975; Deputy Dir Wuxi Sports and Physical Culture Comm. 1981–. *Leisure interests:* table tennis, badminton. *Address:* Wuxi Sports and Physical Culture Commission, Jiangsu, People's Republic of China. *Telephone:* 225810.

PHARAON, Ghaith Rashad, PhD, MBA; Saudi Arabian business executive; b. 7 Sept. 1940, Riyadh; ed Stanford Univ., Harvard Univ.; Founder Saudi Arabia Research and Devt Corpn (Redec) 1965, now Chair. of Bd and Dir-Gen.; Chair. Bd Saudi Arabian Parsons Ltd, Saudi Automotive Industries Ltd, Redec Daelim Ltd, Interstal, Saudi Chemical Processors Ltd, Arabian Maritime Co., Saudi Inland Transport, etc.; Vice-Chair. Jezirah Bank Ltd, Saudi Light Industries Ltd, Arabian Chemical Industries Ltd; mem. Bd Okaz Publications, Tihama; Commendatore (Italy); King Abdul Aziz Award. *Address:* P.O. Box 1935, Jeddah (Office); Ghaith Pharaon Residence, Ruwais, Jeddah, Saudi Arabia (Home).

PHELAN, John Joseph, Jr, BBA; American fmr stock exchange executive and company director; b. 7 May 1931, New York; ed Adelphi Univ., New York; with Nash and Co. stockbrokers, New York 1955–62, partner 1957–62; Man. partner Phelan and Co., New York 1962–72; Sr partner Phelan, Silver, Vesce, Barry and Co., New York 1977–80; Pres. New York Stock Exchange 1980–84, Chair. and CEO 1984–1991; Chair. New York Futures Exchange 1979–85, Presidential Bd of Advisors on Pvt. Sector Initiatives 1986–; Pres. Int. Fed. of Stock Exchanges 1990–92; Chair., Bd of Trustee Adelphi Univ. 1980–84; Sr Adviser Boston Consulting Group 1991–2002; mem. Bd Dirs. Avon Products 1992–95, Eastman Kodak 1988–2001, Met Life, Merrill Lynch, Sonat Inc. 1991–2000; mem. Securities Industries Asscn (mem. Governing Bd 1978–79, Exec. Cttee 1979–80); mem. Bd of Trustees Aspen Inst. 1990–2001, Council on Foreign Relations; Hon. LLD (Adelphi) 1987, (Hamilton Coll.) 1980, (Niagara) 1985; Dr. hc (Notre Dame Univ.) 1986; Hon. Dr. (Tuslawe Univ.), (Fairfield Univ.); Kt Sovereign Mil. Order of Malta, Holy Sepulchre, Jerusalem; Chevalier, Ordre des Arts et Lettres 1987 and other awards and decorations. *Address:* 108 Forest Avenue, Locust Valley, New York, NY 11560, USA.

PHELPS, Edmund Strother, PhD; American economist; b. 26 July 1933, Evanston, Ill.; s. of Edmund S. Phelps and Florence Stone Phelps; m. Viviana Montdor 1974; ed Amherst Coll. and Yale Univ.; Research Economist, RAND Corpn 1959–60; taught Yale Univ. 1960–66; Prof., Univ. of Pa 1966–71, Columbia Univ. 1971–78, New York Univ. 1977–78, Columbia Univ. 1979–82, McVickar Prof. of Political Econs, Columbia Univ. 1982–; Sr Adviser Brookings Inst. 1976–; Econ. Adviser EBRD 1991–94; mem. NAS 1982; mem. Econ. Policy Panel, Observatoire Français des Conjonctures Economiques 1991–; Sr Adviser Consiglio Nazionale delle Ricerche 1997–2000; Distinguished Fellow, American Econ. Asscn 2000; Hon. D. H. (Amherst Coll.) 1985, (Univ. of Mannheim) 2001, (Univ. Tor Vergata, Rome) 2001; Kenan Enterprise Award 1996. *Publications:* Golden Rules of Economic Growth 1966, Microeconomic Foundations of Employment and Inflation Theory (Ed.) 1970, Studies in Macroeconomic Theory: vol. 1, 2 1979, 1980, Political Economy: an Introductory Text 1985, The Slump in Europe 1988, Seven Schools of Macroeconomic Thought 1990, Structural Slumps 1994, Rewarding Work 1997. *Leisure interest:* music. *Address:* Department of Economics, Columbia University, New York, NY 10027 (Office); 45 East 89th Street, New York, NY 10128, USA (Home). *Telephone:* (212) 854-2060 (Office); (212) 722-6688 (Home). *Fax:* (212) 854-8059 (Office). *E-mail:* esp2@columbia.edu (Office).

PHIEU, Lieut.-Gen. Le Kha; Vietnamese politician and army officer; political commissar; has held political posts throughout mil. career; Chief Political Dept, Vietnamese Army; Sec.-Gen. Vietnamese Communist Party 1997–2001. *Address:* Communist Party of Viet Nam, 1 Hoang Van Thu, Hanoi, Viet Nam. *E-mail:* www.cpv.org.vn (Office).

PHILARET, (Kyrill Varfolomeyevich Vakhromeyev), C.THEOL.; Russian/Belarus ecclesiastic; b. 21 March 1935, Moscow; s. of Varfolomey and Aleksandra V. Vakhromeyev; ed Moscow Theological Seminary and Moscow Theological Acad.; became monk 1959, ordained as a priest 1961; lecturer, Asst Prof., Moscow Theological Acad. 1961–65, Rector 1966–73; Bishop of Tikhvin 1965, of Dmitrov 1966; Vice-Chair. Dept of External Church Relations, Moscow Patriarchate 1968–71, Chair. 1981–; Archbishop 1971; Archbishop of Berlin and Middle Europe 1973–78; Metropolitan 1975, of Minsk and Byelorussia 1978, of Minsk and Grodno (later Minsk and Slutsk 1992), Patriarchal Exarch of All Byelorussia 1989; Perm. mem. Holy Synod of Russian Orthodox Church 1981–, Chair. Foreign Relations Dept 1987–89, Theological Comm. 1993–; Hon. mem. Moscow and St Petersburg Theological Acads., Medal of Frantsysk Skorina; Order of St Vladimir, Order of St Sergey of Radonezh, Order of Friendship of the Peoples, Order of Daniil of Moscow. *Publications:* Russian Orthodox Church Relations to Western Non-Orthodox Churches, St Cyril and Methodius' Works in the Territory of The Russian State in Russian Historical Literature, Patriotic Character of Patriarch Aleksiy, etc. *Address:* 220004 Minsk, 10 Osvobozdeniya Street, Belarus. *Telephone:* (172) 23-44-95; (172) 23-25-70. *Fax:* (172) 22-11-19.

PHILIPPOU, Andreas N., PhD; Cypriot politician and university professor; b. 15 July 1944, Katokopia; s. of Nicholas Philippou and Maria G. Protopapa; m. Athina Roustani 1984; three d.; ed Pancyprian Gymnasium, Athens Univ., Greece, Univ. of Wisconsin, USA; Teaching and Research Asst, Univ. of Wis., Asst Prof. of Math., Univ. of Tex., El Paso; Asst then Assoc. Prof. of Math., American Univ. of Beirut, Lebanon; Prof. of Business Admin., Beirut Univ. Coll.; Prof. of Math., subsequently Pres. of Math. Dept and Vice-Rector, Univ. of Patras, Greece; Minister of Educ. 1988–90; Pres. Preparatory Cttee for establishment of Univ. of Cyprus, then first Pres. Interim Governing Bd of Univ. 1988–90; mem. House of Reps. 1991–, mem. House Cttees. on Educ. and the Budget, Council of IPU, Rapporteur for Kosovo 1998, for the Middle East 1999–; founding mem. Cen. Cttee, Sec. of Educ. and Culture Social Democratic Movt 2000; fmr Vice-Pres. Hellenic Aerospace Industry; Hon. Pres. Math. Asscn of Cyprus 1988; Grande Ufficiale Repub. of Italy. *Publications:* 56 research papers; ed. 7 books. *Leisure interests:* swimming, sailing. *Address:* House of Representatives, Nicosia (Office); 26 Atlantis Street, 2107 Nicosia, Cyprus. *Telephone:* (2) 303451 (Office); 336360. *Fax:* (2) 666762 (Office); 336366.

PHILIPS, Sir Cyril Henry, Kt, MA, PhD, DLitt, LLD; British professor of oriental history; b. 27 Dec. 1912, Worcester; s. of William H. Philips and Mary E. Philips; m. 1st Dorcas Rose 1939 (died 1974); one s. (deceased) one d.; m. 2nd Joan Rosemary Marshall 1975; ed Rock Ferry High School and Univs of Liverpool and London; Asst Lecturer in Indian History, SOAS, London Univ. 1936, Lecturer 1939, Sr Lecturer 1945; war service 1940–46; Prof. of Oriental History and Head Dept of History, SOAS 1946–80, Dir SOAS 1957–76; Vice-Chancellor, Univ. of London 1972–76; Chair. Royal Comm. on Criminal Procedure 1978–80, India Cttee of Inter-Univ. Council and British Council 1972, Police Complaints Bd 1980–85; Adviser to Sec. of State for Home Affairs 1985–87; Pres. Royal Asiatic Soc. 1979–88; mem. Council, Chinese Univ. of Hong Kong 1965–78, Inter-University Council for Higher Educ. Overseas 1967–78; Chair. Council on Tribunals 1986–90; Hon. DLitt (Warwick) 1967, LLD (Hong Kong Univ.) 1971; Hon. DLitt (Bristol) 1983, (Sri Lanka); Bishop Chavasse Prize, Gladstone Memorial Fellow, Frewen Lord Prize (Royal Empire Soc.), Alexander Prize (Royal Historical Soc.), Sir Percy Sykes Memorial Medal, James Smart Police Medal 1979, Bengal Asiatic Soc. Gold Medal 1984. *Publications:* The East India Company 1940, 1961, Handbook of Oriental History 1951, 1960, Correspondence of David Scott 1951, Historians of India, Pakistan and Ceylon 1961, The Evolution of India and Pakistan 1962, Politics and Society in India 1963, Fort William India House Correspondence 1964, History of the School of Oriental and African Studies 1917–1967 1967, The Partition of India 1970, The Correspondence of Lord William Bentinck; Governor General of India 1828–35 1977, The Police in Politics 1982, Reform of the Police Complaints System 1984, Beyond the Ivory Tower 1995. *Address:* c/o School of Oriental and African Studies, Malet Street, London, WC1E 7HP, England. *Telephone:* (20) 7637-2388.

PHILIPSON, Lennart Carl, MD, DR.MED.SCI.; Swedish professor of microbiology; b. 16 July 1929, Stockholm; s. of late Carl Philipson and Greta Svanstrom; m. Malin Jondal 1954; three s.; ed Univ. of Uppsala; Asst Prof. Inst. of Virology, Univ. of Uppsala 1958–59; Asst Prof., Assoc. Prof. Swedish Medical Research Council, Univ. of Uppsala 1961–68; Founder and Dir Wallenberg Lab. Univ. of Uppsala 1967–76; Prof. and Chair. Dept of Microbiology, Univ. of Uppsala 1968–82; Dir-Gen. European Molecular Biology Lab., Heidelberg 1982–93; Dir Skirball Inst. of Biomolecular Medicine, New York Univ. Medical Center 1993–97; Prof. Dept of Cell Biology, New York Univ. School of Medicine 1993–; Hon. Prof. Heidelberg Univ. 1985; Dr hc (Turku) 1987, (Umeå) 1994. *Publications:* over 250 scientific publs in fields of virology, microbiology, immunology, molecular biology and biochem. *Leisure interests:* sailing, golf. *Address:* New York University Medical Center, Skirball Institute, 3rd Floor, 550 First Avenue, New York, NY 10016, USA. *Website:* www.nyu.edu (Office).

PHILLIPPE, Ryan; American film actor; b. 10 Sept. 1974, New Castle, Del.; m. Reese Witherspoon 1999; one d. *Films:* Crimson Tide 1995, White Squall 1996, I Know What You Did Last Summer 1997, Homegrown 1997, Little Boy Blue 1997, 54 1998, Playing by Heart 1999, Cruel Intentions 1999, Company Man 2000 The Way of the Gun 2000, Antitrust 2001, Igby Goes Down 2002, Gosford Park 2002. *Television includes:* One Life to Live 1992, Lake Success 1993, Natural Enemies 1993, Deadly Invasion 1995. *Website:* www .ryan-phillippe.com (Office).

PHILLIPS, Caryl, BA, FRSL; British/Saint Christopher and Nevis writer and professor of English; b. 13 March 1958, St Kitts, West Indies; ed The Queen's Coll. Oxford; Writer-in-Residence, The Factory Arts Centre, London 1980–82, Univ. of Mysore, India 1987, Univ. of Stockholm 1989; visiting writer, Amherst Coll., Mass., USA 1990–92, Writer-in-Residence and Co-Dir Creative Writing Center 1992–94, Prof. of English 1994–97, Prof. of English and Writer-in-Residence 1997–98; Prof. of English and Henry R. Luce Prof. of Migration and Social Order, Barnard Coll., Columbia Univ., New York 1998–; writing instructor, Arvon Foundation, UK 1983–; Visiting Prof. of Humanities, Univ. of W Indies, Barbados 1999–2000; Consultant Ed. Faber Inc., Boston 1992–94; Contributing Ed. Bomb Magazine, New York 1993–; Consultant Ed. Graywolf Press, Minneapolis 1994–; Dir Heartland Productions Ltd 1994–2000; Advisory Ed. Wasifiri Magazine, London 1995–; Series Ed. Faber and Faber, London 1996–2000; mem. Arts Council of GB Drama Panel 1982–85, British Film Inst. Production Bd 1985–88, Bd, The Bush Theatre, London 1985–89; Hon. Sr mem. Univ. of Kent 1988–; Fellow New York Public

Library 2002–03; Hon. AM (Amherst Coll.) 1995; Hon. DUniv (Leeds Metropolitan) 1997; British Council 50th Anniversary Fellowship 1984, Guggenheim Fellowship 1992; Lannan Literary Award 1994. *Films:* Playing Away 1986, The Mystic Masseur 2001. *Plays:* Strange Fruit 1980, Where There is Darkness 1982, The Shelter 1983. *Radio:* (plays) The Wasted Years (BBC Giles Cooper Award for Best Radio Play of the Year) 1984, Crossing the River 1985, The Prince of Africa 1987, Writing Fiction 1991; several documentaries. *Television:* The Final Passage (Channel 4) 1996. *Publications:* (fiction) The Final Passage (Malcolm X Prize for Literature) 1985, A State of Independence 1986, Higher Ground 1989, Cambridge (Sunday Times Young Writer of the Year Award) 1991, Crossing the River (James Tait Black Memorial Prize) 1993, The Nature of Blood 1997; (non-fiction) The European Tribe (Martin Luther King Memorial Prize) 1987, The Atlantic Sound 2000, A New World Order: Selected Essays 2001, A Distant Shore 2003; Ed. Extravagant Strangers 1997, The Right Set: A Tennis Anthology 1999. *Address:* c/o Georgia Garrett, A.P. Watt Ltd, 20 John Street, London, WC1N 2DR, England (Office). *Telephone:* (20) 7405-6774 (Office). *Fax:* (20) 7831-2145 (Office). *E-mail:* apw@apwatt.co.uk (Office). *Website:* www.carylphillips.com (Home).

PHILLIPS, David, OBE, PhD, FRSC; British professor of physical chemistry; b. 3 Dec 1939, Kendal, Westmorland (now Cumbria); s. of Stanley Phillips and Daphne Ivy Phillips (née Harris); m. Caroline L. Scoble 1970; one d.; ed South Shields Grammar Tech. School and Univ. of Birmingham; Postdoctoral Fellow and Fulbright Scholar, Univ. of Tex., USA 1964–66; Visiting Scientist, Acad. of Sciences of USSR 1966–67; Lecturer, Dept of Chem., Univ. of Southampton 1967–73, Sr Lecturer 1973–76, Reader 1976–80; Wolfson Prof. of Natural Philosophy, Royal Institution of GB 1980–89, Acting Dir 1986, Deputy Dir 1986–89; Prof. of Physical Chem., Imperial Coll. of Science, Tech. and Medicine 1989–, Head Dept of Chem. 1992–2002, Hofmann Prof. of Chem. 1999–, Dean of Life Sciences and Physical Sciences faculties 2002–; Spinks Lecturer, Univ. of Sask. 1979; Wilsmore Fellow, Univ. of Melbourne 1983–90; Vice-Pres. and Gen. Sec. BAAS 1987–89, Nyholm Lecturer, Royal Soc. of Chem. 1994; Faraday Award for Public Understanding of Science, Royal Soc. 1997. *Publications:* Time-Correlated Single-Photon Counting 1984, Polymer Photophysics 1985, Time-Resolved Laser Raman Spectroscopy 1987, Jet Spectroscopy and Dynamics 1994. *Leisure interests:* music, theatre, popularization of science. *Address:* Department of Chemistry, Imperial College, Exhibition Road, London, SW7 2AZ (Office); 195 Barnett Wood Lane, Ashtead, Surrey, KT21 2LP, England (Home). *Telephone:* (20) 7594-5716 (Office); (13722) 74385 (Home). *Fax:* (20) 7594-5812 (Office). *E-mail:* d.phillips@imperial.ac.uk (Office).

PHILLIPS, Sir Fred (Albert), Kt, CVO, MCL, QC; Saint Vincent and the Grenadines barrister; b. 14 May 1918; s. of Wilbert A. Phillips; ed London Univ., Toronto Univ., McGill Univ.; called to Bar, Middle Temple; legal clerk to Attorney-Gen. of St Vincent 1942–45; Prin. Officer, Secr. 1945–47; Chief Clerk, Gov.'s Office, Windward Island 1948–49, Distr. Officer/Magistrate of District III 1949–53; magistrate, Grenada and Commr of Carriacou 1953–56; Asst Admin. and mem. Exec. Council, Grenada 1957–58; Sr Asst Sec., Secr. Fed. of W Indies 1958–60, Perm. Sec. (Sec. to Cabinet) 1960–62; Acting Admin. of Montserrat 1961–62; Sr lecturer Univ. of W Indies and Sr resident tutor, Dept of Extramural Studies, Barbados 1962–63; Sr Asst Registrar Coll. of Arts and Science, Univ. of W Indies 1963–64; Sr research fellow, Faculty of Law and Centre for Developing Area Studies, McGill Univ. 1964–65; Admin. of St Christopher 1966–67, Gov. St Christopher and Nevis 1967–69; Chief Legal Adviser and Special Rep. of Cable & Wireless in the Caribbean 1969–97; Hon. LLD (W Indies) 1989. *Publications:* Freedom in the Caribbean: A Study in Constitutional Change 1977, The Evolving Legal Profession in the Commonwealth 1978, West Indian Constitutions: Post-Independence Reforms 1985, Caribbean Life and Culture: A Citizen Reflects 1991 and numerous papers in journals. *Leisure interests:* bridge, reading, legal writing. *Address:* PO Box 3298, St John's, Antigua. *Telephone:* 461-3683 (Office); 461-3683 (Home). *Fax:* 463-0350 (Office); 463-0350 (Home). *E-mail:* fredp@candw.ag (Home).

PHILLIPS, John Harber, AC, LLB; Australian judge and author; b. 18 Oct. 1933, Melbourne; s. of Anthony Phillips and I. Muriel Phillips; m. Helen Rogers 1962; two s. one d.; ed Presentation Convent, De La Salle Coll. and Univ. of Melbourne; mem. Bar of Victoria 1959–84; QC 1975; Judge, Supreme Court of Victoria 1984–90; Judge, Fed. Court of Australia 1990–91; Chief Justice of Victoria 1991–; Chair. Nat. Inst. of Forensic Science, Victoria Inst. of Forensic Medicine, Council of Australia and NZ Law Reform, Vic. Law Foundation, Vic. Council of Legal Educ., Attorney-Gen.'s Council of Law Reform; Pres. French Australian Lawyers Asscn, Lanchid Soc. (Australian and Hungarian Lawyers); Convenor in Australia, Int. Asscn of Judges; Hellenic Distinction 1992, 2000. *Publications:* Forensic Science and the Expert Witness (jtly), Advocacy with Honour, The Trial of Ned Kelly; plays: By a Simple Majority – The Trial of Socrates, Conference with Counsel, The Cab-Rank Rule, The Eureka Advocates; poetry: Wounds 2000. *Address:* Chief Justice's Chambers, 210 William Street, Melbourne 3000, Australia. *Telephone:* (3) 9603-6139. *Fax:* (3) 9603-6200.

PHILLIPS, Leon Francis, PhD, ScD; New Zealand professor of chemistry and novelist; b. 14 July 1935; m. Pamela A. Johnstone 1959; two s.; ed Westport Tech. Coll., Christchurch Boys' High School, Univs of Canterbury (NZ) and Cambridge Univ.; Upper Atmosphere Chem. Group, McGill Univ. 1961; lecturer, Univ. of Canterbury 1962, Prof. of Chem. 1966–; Pres. NZ Inst. of Chemistry 2001; Visiting Prof. Univ. of Washington 1968, Monash Univ.

1969, Univ. of Perugia 2000; Visiting Fellow, Balliol Coll. Oxford 1975, Japan Soc. for Promotion of Science 1984; Visiting Scholar, Rice Univ., Houston 1987; SERC Research Fellow Univ. Birmingham 1989; Harkness Fellow 1968; Fulbright Award 1980; Corday-Morgan Medal (Royal Soc. of Chem.), Hector Medal, (Royal Soc. of NZ), Easterfield and ICI prizes (NZ Inst. of Chem.), Univ. of Canterbury Research Medal 1999. *Publications:* Basic Quantum Chemistry, Electronics for Experimenters, Chemistry of the Atmosphere (with M. J. McEwan), First Year Chemistry (with J. M. Coxon and J. E. Fergusson); over 200 scientific papers; novels: Fire in His Hand 1978, The Phoenix Reaction 1979, Ritual Fire Dance 1980. *Leisure interests:* sailing, skiing, reading, writing. *Address:* University of Canterbury, Private Bag 4800, Christchurch 1 (Office); 12 Maidstone Road, Christchurch 4, New Zealand (Home). *Telephone:* 366-7001. *Fax:* 364-2999. *E-mail:* enquiries@regy.canterbury.ac.nz (Office). *Website:* www.canterbury.ac.nz (Office).

PHILLIPS, Leslie Samuel, OBE; British actor, producer and director; b. 20 April 1924, London; m.; early career as child actor; Vice-Pres. Royal Theatrical Fund, Disabled Living Foundation; Evening Standard Lifetime Achievement in Films Award 1997. *Films include:* A Lassie From Lancashire 1935, The Citadel, Rhythm Serenade, Train of Events, The Galloping Major, Breaking the Sound Barrier, The Fake, The Limping Man, The Price of Greed, Value for Money, The Gamma People, As Long as They're Happy, The Big Money, Brothers in Law, The Barretts of Wimpole Street, Just My Luck, Les Girls, The Smallest Show on Earth, I Was Monty's Double, The Man Who Liked Funerals, Carry on Nurse, This Other Eden, Carry on Teacher, Please Turn Over, Doctor in Love, Watch your Stern, Carry on Constable, In the Doghouse, Crooks Anonymous, The Fast Lady, Father Came Too, Doctor in Clover, The Magnificent 7 Deadly Sins, Not Now Darling, Don't Just Lie There Say Something, Out of Africa, Empire of the Sun, Scandal, King Ralph, Carry on Columbus, Caught in the Act, Day of the Jackal, Cinderella, Saving Grace, August, Lara Croft – Tomb Raider, Harry Potter and the Philosopher's Stone, Three Guesses, Thunderpants. *Radio:* numerous plays including Navy Lark, Les Miserables, Tales From the Backbench, Round the World in 80 Days, Wind in the Willows. *Television includes:* Our Man at St. Marks, Time and Motion Man, Reluctant Debutante, A Very Fine Line, Casanova 74 (series), You'll Never See Me Again, Rumpole, Summer's Lease, Chancer, Lovejoy, Boon, House of Windsor, Love on the Branch Line, Canteville Ghost, The Pale Horse, Dalziel & Pasco, The Sword of Honour, Into the Void, The Oz Trial, Take a Girl Like You, Tales of the Crypt, Who Bombed Birmingham?, Holby City, Midsomer Murder, Where the Heart Is. *Theatre includes:* Falstaff in The Merry Wives of Windsor (RSC), On the Whole Life's Been Jolly Good (Edin. Festival), Love for Love, Naked Justice, For Better or Worse, Ghosts of Albion, Charley's Aunt, Camino Real, Deadly Game, Diary of a Nobody, Man Most Likely To..., Passion Play. *Leisure interests:* restoring property, chess, poker, racing. *Address:* c/o Storm Artists, 6–10 Lexington Street, 4th Floor, London, W1F 0LB (Office); 78 Maida Vale, London, W9 1PR, England (Home). *Telephone:* (20) 7437-4313 (Office); (20) 7624-5975 (Home). *Fax:* (20) 7437-4314 (Office); (20) 7624-1250 (Office).

PHILLIPS, (Mark) Trevor, OBE, BSc, ARCS, FRSA; British journalist, broadcaster and public servant; b. 31 Dec. 1953; s. of George Milton Phillips and Marjorie Eileen Canzius; m. Asha Bhownagary 1981; two d.; ed Queens' Coll., Georgetown, Guyana, Imperial Coll., London; Pres. NUS (Nat. Union of Students) 1978–80; researcher London Weekend TV 1980–81, producer Black on Black, The Making of Britain 1981–86, Ed. London Programme 1987–92 (presenter 1987–2000), Head of Current Affairs 1992–94; reporter This Week, Thames TV 1986–87; presenter, Crosstalk 1994–2000, The Material World 1998–2000; Dir Pepper Productions 1994–; mem. and Chair. London Ass., GLA 2000–03; columnist, The Independent 1997–; Chair. Runnymede Trust 1993–98, Hampstead Theatre 1993–97, London Arts Bd 1997–2000; mem. Labour Party 2000–, Deputy Chair. 2001–02; Chair. Comm. for Racial Equality (CRE) 2003–; Journalism Award, Royal TV Soc. 1988, 1993; Hon. DLitt (Westminster). *Publication:* Windrush: The Irresistible Rise of Multi-Racial Britain 1998, Britian's Slave Trade 1999. *Leisure interests:* music, reading, running. *Address:* Commission for Racial Equality, St Dunstan's House, 201–211 Borough High Street, London, SE1 1GZ (Office); Pepper Productions, 47–49 Borough High Street, London, SE1 1NB, England (Office). *Telephone:* (20) 7939-0000 (CRE) (Office); (20) 7836-3941 (Office). *Fax:* (20) 7939-0001 (CRE) (Office). *E-mail:* info@cre.gov.uk (Office). *Website:* www.cre.gov.uk (Office).

PHILLIPS, Owen Martin, PhD, FRS; American professor of science and engineering; b. 30 Dec. 1930, Parramatta, NSW, Australia; s. of Richard Keith Phillips and Madeline Constance (Lofts); m. Merle Winifred Simons 1953; two s. two d.; ed Univ. of Sydney, Australia and Univ. of Cambridge; ICI Fellow, Univ. of Cambridge 1955–57, Fellow, St John's Coll. 1957–60; Assoc. Prof., Johns Hopkins Univ., Baltimore, Md, USA 1960–63; Asst Dir of Research, Cambridge Univ. 1961–64; Prof. of Geophysical Mechanics and Geophysics, Johns Hopkins Univ. 1963–75, Chair. Dept of Earth and Planetary Sciences 1968–78, Decker Prof. of Science and Eng 1978–98, Decker Prof. Emer. 1998–; Assoc. Ed., Journal of Fluid Mechanics 1964–95; mem. US Nat. Acad. of Eng; Hon. Fellow Trinity Coll. Cambridge, England 1997; Adams Prize, Cambridge Univ. 1965, Sverdrup Gold Medal, American Meteorological Soc. 1974. *Publications:* The Dynamics of the Upper Ocean 1966 (Russian edns 1969, 1979), The Heart of the Earth 1968, The Last Chance Energy Book 1979, Wave Dynamics and Radio Probing of the Ocean Surface (Ed.) 1985, Flow and Reactions in Permeable Rocks 1991; many research publs in the tech.

literature. *Leisure interest:* sailing. *Address:* The Johns Hopkins University, Baltimore, MD 21218; 23 Merrymount Road, Baltimore, MD 21210, USA. *Telephone:* (410) 516-7036. *Fax:* (410) 516-7933.

PHILLIPS, Siân, CBE, FRSA, BA; British actress; b. Bettws, Wales; d. of D. Phillips and Sally Phillips; m. 1st D. H. Roy 1954; m. 2nd Peter O'Toole (q.v.) 1960 (divorced 1979); two d.; m. 3rd Robin Sachs 1979 (divorced 1992); ed Pontardawe Grammar School, Univ. of Wales (Cardiff Coll.), RADA; child actress BBC Radio Wales and BBC TV Wales; newsreader and announcer and mem. BBC repertory co. 1953–55; toured for Welsh Arts Council with Nat. Theatre Co. 1953–55; Arts Council Bursary to study drama outside Wales 1955; Royal TV Soc. annual televised lecture 1992; Vice-Pres. Welsh Coll. of Music and Drama; mem. Gorsedd of Bards (for services to drama in Wales) 1960; mem. Arts Council Drama Cttee for 5 years; Gov. St. David's Trust; fmr Gov. Welsh Coll. of Music and Drama; Hon. Fellow Univ. of Cardiff 1981, Polytechnic of Wales 1988, Univ. of Wales, Swansea 1998, Trinity Coll., Carmarthen; Hon. DLitt (Wales) 1984; many awards for work in cinema, theatre and on TV including BAFTA Wales Lifetime Achievement Award 2001. *Stage appearances include:* Hedda Gabler 1959, Ondine and The Duchess of Malfi 1960–61 (first RSC season at Aldwych), The Lizard on the Rock 1961, Gentle Jack, Maxibules and the Night of the Iguana 1964, Ride a Cock Horse 1965, Man and Superman and Man of Destiny 1966, The Burglar 1967, Epitaph for George Dillon 1972, A Nightingale in Bloomsbury Square 1973, The Gay Lord Quex 1975, Spinechiller 1978, You Never Can Tell, Lyric, Hammersmith 1979, Pal Joey, Half Moon and Albery Theatres 1980 and 1981, Dear Liar 1982, Major Barbara, Nat. Theatre 1982, Peg (musical) 1984, Love Affair 1984, Gigi 1986, Thursday's Ladies 1987, Brel (musical) 1987–88, Paris Match 1989, Vanilla 1990, The Manchurian Candidate 1991, Painting Churches 1992, Ghosts (Cardiff and touring, Wales) 1993, The Lion in Winter 1994, Marlene, An Inspector Calls, Broadway 1995, A Little Night Music, Royal Nat. Theatre 1995–96, Marlene 1996–97, int. tour 1998, concert tour Middle East 1999, Marlene, Broadway 1999, Lettice and Lovage 2001, Divas at The Donmar Season 2001, My Old Lady, Doolittle Theatre, Los Angeles 2002, Promenade Theatre, New York 2003. *Films include:* Becket 1963, Goodbye Mr. Chips (Critics' Circle Award, New York Critics' Award and Famous Seven Critics' Award 1969), Laughter in the Dark 1968, Murphy's War 1970, Under Milk Wood 1971, The Clash of the Titans 1979, Dune 1983, Ewok II, The Two Mrs Grenvilles, "Siân" (Cineclaire), Valmont 1988, Dark River 1990, Age of Innocence 1992, House of America 1996, Alice Through the Looking Glass 1998, Coming and Going. *Television appearances include:* Shoulder to Shoulder 1974, How Green was my Valley (BAFTA Award) 1975, I, Claudius (Royal Television Soc. Award and BAFTA Award 1978) 1976, Boudicca, Off to Philadelphia in the Morning 1977, The Oresteia of Aeschylus 1978, Crime and Punishment 1979, Tinker, Tailor, Soldier, Spy 1979, Sean O'Casey (RTE) 1980, Churchill: The Wilderness Years 1981, How Many Miles to Babylon 1982, Smiley's People 1982, George Borrow 1983, A Painful Case (RTE), Beyond All Reason, Murder on the Exchange, The Shadow of the Noose (BBC series) 1988, Snow Spider (HTV serial) 1988, Freddie & Max, Emlyn's Moon, Perfect Scoundrels 1990, Heidi 1992, The Borrowers (series) 1992, 1993, The Chestnut Soldier 1992, Huw Weldon TV Lecture 1993, Summer Silence (HTV musical), The Vacillations of Poppy Carew (BBC), Mind to Kill (TV film series), Scolds Bridle 1997, The Aristocrats (series) 1998, Alice Through the Looking Glass (feature film) 1998, Nikita 1999, The Magician's House 1999, The Magician's House 2000. *Recordings include:* Bewitched, Bothered and Bewildered, Pal Joey, Peg, I Remember Mama, Gigi, A Little Night Music 1990, A Little Night Music (2) 1995, Marlene 1996, Both Sides Now 2002. *Radio work includes:* Phédre, Oedipus, Henry VIII, Antony and Cleopatra, Bequest to a Nation, The Maids, Henry VIII, All's Well That Ends Well, Leopard in Autumn, Bridge of San Luis Rey. *Cabaret appearances:* Falling in Love Again, New York, London and touring. *Publication:* Siân Phillips' Needlepoint 1987, Private Faces (autobiog. vol. I) 1999, Public Places (autobiog., vol. II) 2001. *Leisure interests:* travelling, gardening, painting. *Address:* c/o L. King, Peters Fraser and Dunlop, Drury House, 34–43 Russell Street, London, WC2B 5HA, England. *Telephone:* (20) 7344-1010 (Office). *E-mail:* sian@lexhamgardens.com (Home).

PHILLIPS, Tom, CBE, MA, NDD, RA, RE; British artist, writer and composer; b. 24 May 1937, London; s. of David John Phillips and Margaret Agnes Arnold; m. 1st Jill Purdy 1961 (divorced 1988), one s. one d.; m. 2nd Fiona Maddocks 1995, two step-d.; ed St Catherine's Coll., Oxford and Camberwell School of Art; one-man exhbns AIA Galleries, Angela Flowers Gallery, Marlborough Fine Art and Waddingtons, London, Galerie Ba Ma, Paris, S London Gallery, Dulwich Picture Gallery; several int. group exhbns; touring retrospective exhbn London, The Hague, Basel, Paris etc. 1975; 50 years of Tom Phillips, Angela Flowers Gallery 1987, retrospective exhbns Nat. Portrait Gallery, London 1989, NC Museum of Art, USA 1990, Royal Acad. 1992, South London Art Gallery 1998, Dulwich Picture Gallery 1998; publ. music scores 1965–; first performance opera IRMA, York Univ. 1973, revival ICA, London 1983 (CD 1986); collaborations with Jean-Yves Bosseur and John Tilbury on music works/performances 1970–84, Retrospective Concert ICA 1992; Music Works CD 1996, Six of Hearts CD 1997; worked with Peter Greenaway on TV version of Dante's Inferno, as published, translated and illustrated by the artist, broadcast 1990 (1st Prize Montreal TV Festival 1990, Italia Prize 1991); Curator exhbn "Africa: The Art of a Continent", Royal Acad. London, Gropius Bau, Berlin, Guggenheim Museum, New York 1995–96; stage design for A Winter's Tale 1997, Otello 1998, The Entertainer 2003; Vice-Chair. Copyright Council 1985–89; Chair. Royal Acad. Library, Frua Foundation 1997–2002;

Chair. Exhbns Royal Acad; mem. Royal Soc. of Painter-Etchers and Engravers; Hon. mem. Royal Soc. of Portrait Painters 1999, Royal Inst. 2000, Pastel Soc. 2001; Hon. Fellow The London Inst. 1999; Hon. Fellow St Catherine's Coll., Oxford, Leeds Univ. (Bretton Hall); Trustee Nat. Portrait Gallery 1998, British Museum 2000; John Moores Prize 1969; Frances Williams Memorial Prize, V&A 1983. *Publications:* Trailer 1971, A Humument 1973, Works and Texts to 1974 1975, Dante's Inferno 1983, Heart of a Humument 1985, Where are They Now? The Class of '47 1990, Works and Texts II 1992, Merely Connect (with Salman Rushdie) 1994, Africa: The Art of a Continent 1995, Aspects of Art 1997, Music in Art 1997, The Postcard Century 2000. *Leisure interests:* opera, ping pong. *Address:* 57 Talfourd Road, London, SE15 5NN, England. *Telephone:* (20) 7701-3978. *Fax:* (20) 7703-2800. *E-mail:* tom@tomphillips.co.uk (Home). *Website:* www.tomphillips.co.uk (Home).

PHILLIPS, Warren Henry, BA; American publisher and newspaper executive; b. 28 June 1926, New York City; s. of Abraham and Juliette Phillips; m. Barbara Anne Thomas 1951; three d.; ed Queens Coll.; Copyreader Wall Street Journal 1947–48, Foreign Corresp., Germany 1949–50, Chief, London Bureau 1950–51, Foreign Ed. 1951–53, News Ed. 1953–54, Man. Ed. Midwest Edition 1954–57, Man. Ed. Wall Street Journal 1957–65, Publr 1975–88; Exec. Ed. Dow Jones & Co. 1965–70; Vice-Pres. and Gen. Man. Dow Jones & Co. Inc. 1970–71, Editorial Dir 1971–88, Exec. Vice-Pres. 1972, Pres. 1972–79, CEO 1975–90, Chair. 1978–91, mem. Bd of Dirs. 1972–97, Dir Emer. 1997–; Pres. American Council on Educ. for Journalism 1971–73; Co-Publr Bridge Works Publishing Co. 1992–; mem. Bd of Dirs. Public Broadcasting Service 1991–97; Pres. American Soc. of Newspaper Eds. 1975–76; mem. Pulitzer Prizes Bd 1977–87; Trustee, Columbia Univ. 1980–93, Trustee Emer. 1993–; mem. Visitors' Cttee Kennedy School of Govt, Harvard Univ. 1984–90, 1992–97; mem. Corp. Advisory Bd Queens Coll. 1986–90, Foundation Bd of Trustees 1990–97; Hon. LHD (Pace) 1982, (Queens Coll.) 1987, (Long Island) 1987; Hon. JD (Portland) 1973. *Publication:* China: Behind the Mask (with Robert Keatley) 1973. *Address:* Bridge Works Publishing, P.O. Box 1798, Bridgehampton, NY 11932, USA. *Telephone:* (631) 537-3418. *Fax:* (631) 537-5092.

PHILLIPS, William D., P.H.O.; American physicist; b. 5 Nov. 1948, Wilkes-Barre, Pa; s. of William Cornelius Phillips and Mary Catherine Phillips (née Savine); m. Jane Van Wynen 1970; two d.; ed Juniata Coll., Huntington, MIT; with Nat. Inst. of Standards and Tech.; Adjunct Prof. Univ. of Md 1991–; mem. NAS; Fellow American Physical Soc., American Acad. of Arts and Sciences, Nat. Inst. of Standards and Tech., Gaithersburg, Md 1995–; shared Nobel Prize for Physics 1997 for developing methods of cooling matter to very low temperatures using lasers, Schawlow Prize in Laser Sciences 1998, Pa Soc. Gold Medal 1999. *Publications:* Laser Manipulation of Atoms and Ions 1992; numerous scientific articles. *Address:* National Institute of Standards and Technology, PHY, A157, 100 Bureau Drive, Stop 8424, Gaithersburg, MD 20899, USA.

PHILLIS, Robert Weston, BA, FRSA, FRTS; British media executive; b. 3 Dec. 1945, Croydon; s. of Francis W. Phillis and Gertrude G. Phillis; m. Jean Derham 1966; three s.; ed John Ruskin Grammar School and Univ. of Nottingham; apprentice, printing industry 1961–65; Thomson Regional Newspapers Ltd 1968–69; British Printing Corpn Ltd 1969–71; lecturer in industrial relations, Univ. of Edin. and Scottish Business School 1971–75; Visiting Fellow, Univ. of Nairobi 1974; Personnel Dir, later Man. Dir Sun Printers Ltd 1976–79; Man. Dir Independent TV Publs Ltd 1979–82; Man. Dir Cen. Independent TV PLC 1981–87, Dir Non-Exec. 1987–91; Group Man. Dir Carlton Communications PLC 1987–91; Chief Exec. Independent TV News (ITN) 1991–93; Man. Dir BBC World Service 1993–94, Deputy Dir-Gen. BBC 1993–97, Chair. BBC Worldwide 1994–97; Chief Exec. Guardian Media Group 1997–; Chair. ITV Network Programming Cttee 1984–86, ITV Film Purchase Group 1985–87, Zenith Productions 1984–91, Trader Media Group Ltd 2001–; Dir (non-exec.) ITN Ltd 1982–87; Dir and Trustee TV Trust for the Environment, Teaching Awards Trust 2001–; Vice-Chair. (Int.), Int. Council, Nat. Acad. of TV Arts and Sciences 1994–97 (Life Fellow), (Dir 1985–93); Vice-Pres. European Broadcasting Union 1996–97; Hon. Prof. Univ. of Stirling 1997; Fellow, Royal TV Soc. 1993 (Chair. 1989–92, Vice-Pres. 1994); Trustee Nat. Film and TV School Foundation; Hon. DLitt (Salford Univ.) 1999; Hon. DLit (City Univ.) 2000. *Leisure interests:* news, skiing, golf, military and political history. *Address:* Guardian Media Group, 75 Farringdon Road, London, England (Office). *Telephone:* (20) 7239-9711 (Office). *Fax:* (20) 7713-4709 (Office). *E-mail:* bob.phillis@gmgplc.co.uk (Office). *Website:* www.gmgplc.co.uk (Office).

PHOMMAHAXAY, Phantong; Laotian diplomatist; b. 2 March 1941, Vientiane; m. Amphanh (née Luangrath); three s. one d.; ed Nat. Centre for Political Studies, Vientiane; joined Ministry of Foreign Affairs 1962, Head Passport and Political Sections 1968–73, Dir NGO Section, Dept for Int. Orgs 1978–80, Deputy Dir-Gen., then Dir-Gen. Press Dept 1984–90, Dir-Gen. Asia Pacific and Africa Dept 1994–95; Attaché in Beijing, People's Repub. of China 1965–68; Second Sec., First Sec. then Chargé d'affaires in Paris, France 1974–78; First Sec., then Deputy Head of Mission to Thailand, Bangkok 1980–84; Amb. to Indonesia 1990–94, to Australia and New Zealand 1995–98, to Germany, The Netherlands, Switzerland and Austria 1998–2001, to USA 2002–. *Leisure interests:* reading, golf. *Address:* Embassy of the Lao People's

Democratic Republic, 2222 S Street, NW, Washington, DC 20008, USA (Office). *Telephone:* (202) 332-6416 (Office). *Fax:* (202) 332-4923 (Office). *Website:* www.laoembassy.com.

PHOUNSAVANH, Nouhak; Laotian politician; ed primary school; owner of bus and truck business; visited Peking (now Beijing) in a Viet-Minh del. for Conf. of Asian and Pacific Region 1952; rep. of Pathet Lao at Geneva Conf. on Indochina with Viet-Minh del. 1954; became Minister of Foreign Affairs in Free Lao Front (Neo Lao Issara) resistance Govt; Deputy for Sam Neua to Nat. Assembly 1957; arrested 1959, escaped 1960; led Lao Patriotic Front (Neo Lao Hak Sat) del. to Ban Namone peace talks 1961; mem. People's Party of Laos 1955; mem. Lao Patriotic Front, mem. Standing Cttee 1964, of Cen. Cttee; now mem. Political Bureau; Vice-Chair. Council of Ministers and Minister of Finance 1975–82, Vice-Chair. Council of Ministers 1975–90, then First Vice-Chair; Pres. of Laos 1992–98; Deputy Gen. Sec. Lao People's Revolutionary Party. *Address:* c/o Office of the President, Vientiane, Laos.

PIANO, Renzo; Italian architect; b. 14 Sept. 1937, Genoa; s. of Carlo Piano and Rosa Odone; m. 1st Magda Ardnino 1962; two s. one d.; m. 2nd Emilia Rossato 1992; ed Milan Polytechnic School of Architecture; worked with Louis I. Kahn, Phila, USA, Z.S. Makowsky, London 1965–70, with Richard Rogers (as Piano & Rogers) 1977–, with Peter Rice (as Atelier Piano & Rice) 1977–; currently has offices in Genoa, Paris, Berlin (Renzo Piano Bldg Workshop); Hon. Fellow Union Int. des Architectes 1978, AIA, 1981, RIBA, 1985, American Acad. of Arts and Letters 1994; Dr hc (Stuttgart) 1990, (Delft) 1992; Compasso d'Oro Award, Milan 1981, RIBA Gold Medal 1989, Kyoto Prize, Japan 1990, Neutra Prize, Pomona, Calif. 1991, Goodwill Amb. of UNESCO for Architecture 1994, Premio Michelangelo 1994, Art Prize of Akademie der Künste, Berlin 1995, Praemium Imperiale, Tokyo 1995, Erasmus Prize, Amsterdam 1995, The Pritzker Architecture Prize, Washington, DC 1998 and other prizes and awards; Commdr des Arts et des Lettres, Légion d'honneur, Cavaliere di Gran Croce, Officer, Ordre Nat. du Mérite. *Completed projects include:* office bldg for B&B, Como 1973, Georges Pompidou Centre, Paris 1977, IRCAM Inst. for Acoustic Research, Paris 1977, housing, Rigo Dist, Perugia 1982, office bldg for Olivetti, Naples 1984, office bldg for Lowara, Vicenza 1985, museum for Menil Collection, Houston, USA 1988, HQ for Light Metals Experimental Inst., Novara 1988, S. Nicola Football Stadium, Bari 1989, Underground stations for Ansaldo, Genoa 1990, Bercy commercial centre, Paris 1990, cruise ships for P&O 1991, housing, Paris 1991, Thomson factories, Guyancourt, France 1991, HQ for Credito Industriale Sardo, Cagliari 1992, Lingotto congress and concert hall, Turin 1994, Kansai Int. Airport, Osaka, Japan 1994, Meridien Hotel, Lingotto and Business Centre, Turin 1995, Harbour Authorities HQ, Genoa 1995, cinema, offices, contemporary art gallery, conf. centre, landscaping, Cité Int., Lyon 1996, Ushibuka Bridge, Kumamoto, Japan 1996, Museum of Science and Tech., Amsterdam 1997, Museum of Beyeler Foundation, Basel 1997, Debis Bldg HQ, Daimler Benz, Berlin 1997, Cultural Centre J.-M. Tjibao, Nouméa, New Caledonia 1998, Mercedes-Benz Design Centre, Stuttgart 1998, Daimler-Benz Potsdamer Platz project including Imax theatre, offices, housing, shops, Berlin 1998, Lodi Bank HQ, Milan 1998. *Projects in progress include:* Auditorium Rome, contemporary art gallery, Varnamö, Sweden, office block, Sydney, Australia, PTT Telecom office tower, Rotterdam, Harvard Univ. Art Gallery master plan, renovation and extension, HQ newspaper Il Sole/24 Ore, Milan Padre Pio Basilica Church, Puglia, Italy; work shown at exhbns. Europe, USA, Australia, Japan 1967–, contracted for NY Times Bldg, Manhattan 2000–; numerous lectures worldwide. *Publications:* author or co-author of 12 books on architecture. *Leisure interest:* sailing. *Address:* Renzo Piano Building Workshop, Via Rubens 29, 16158 Genoa, Italy; 34, rue des Archives, 75004 Paris, France. *Telephone:* (010) 61711 (Genoa). *Fax:* (010) 6171350 (Genoa).

PIBULSONGGRAM, Nitya, MA; Thai diplomatist; b. 30 June 1941; s. of Field Marshal Pibul Songgram and Lady La-iad Bhandhukran; m. Patricia Osmond 1965; ed Dartmouth Coll. and Brown Univ.; entered Foreign Service as Third Sec. Foreign News Div. Information Dept June 1968; served in fmr SEATO Div., Thailand's Int. Org. Dept 1969–72; Office of Sec. to Minister of Foreign Affairs 1973, Office of Under-Sec. of State, Policy Planning Div. 1974; Head Southeast Asia Div., Political Dept 1975; First Sec. Perm. Mission to UN 1976–79, Deputy Perm. Rep. 1979–80, Perm. Rep. 1988–96; Deputy Dir-Gen. Information Dept, Foreign Ministry 1980, Political Dept 1981; Amb.-at-Large 1982; Dir-Gen. Dept of Int. Org. 1983–88; Amb. to USA 1996–2001; Adviser and Special Envoy of the Minister of Foreign Affairs 2002–; Chair. Thailand–US Educational Foundation (TUSEF); Knight Grand Cross, Order of White Elephant 1984, Special Grand Cordam, Order of Crown of Thailand 1988. *Leisure interests:* tennis, golf, skiing. *Address:* Ministry of Foreign Affairs, Thanon Sri Ayudhya, Bankok, Thailand (Office); 2145 Decatur Place, NW, Washington, DC 20008, USA (Home).

PICADO, Sonia, LIC. EN D.; Costa Rican diplomatist, international civil servant and lawyer; b. 20 Dec. 1936; d. of Antonio de Picado and Odile Sotela; m. (divorced); one s. one d.; ed Univ. of Costa Rica; Dean, Law Faculty of Costa Rica 1980–84, Cathedratical Chair. 1984; Co-Chair. Int. Comm. for Central American Recovery and Devt 1987–89; mem. Cttee of Jurists, World Conf. on Refugees, UNHCR, Geneva 1988–89; Exec. Dir Inter-American Inst. of Human Rights 1988–94; Vice-Pres. Inter-American Court of Human Rights 1991–; Pres. Partido de Liberación Nacional (PLN); Amb. to USA 1994–99; Head UN Comm. of Inquiry E Timor 1999; Max Planck/Humboldt Award (Germany) 1991; Leonidas Proaño Award (Ecuador) 1991. *Publications:* Women and Human Rights 1986, Philosophical Fundamentals of Human Rights in Latin America 1987, Religion, Tolerance and Liberty: A Human Rights Perspective 1989, Peace, Development and Human Rights 1989. *Address:* c/o Ministry of Foreign Relations, Apdo 10.027, 1000 San José (Office); Partido de Liberación Nacional, Mata Redonda, 125m oeste del Ministerio de Agricultura y Ganadería, Casa Liberacionista José Figueres Ferrer, Apdo 10.051, 1000 San José, Costa Rica. *Telephone:* 232-5033. *Fax:* 231-4097. *E-mail:* palina@sol.racsa.co.cr (Office). *Website:* www.pln.org (Office).

PICARD, Dennis J.; American business executive; b. 1932; ed Northeastern Univ.; Sr Vice-Pres., Gen. Man. Missile Systems Div. Raytheon Co., Lexington, Mass., 1985–89, Pres. 1989–90, Chair. 1990–99, CEO 1990–99 (also mem. Bd Dirs.); Pres. American Inst. for Aeronautics, Va 2000–; mem. Defence Policy Advisory Cttee on Trade, President's Export Council. *Address:* AIAA, Suite 500, 1801 Alexander Bell Drive, Restan (Office); 1373 Monument Street, Concord, MA 01742, VA 20191, USA (Home).

PICASSO, Paloma; French designer; b. 19 April 1949, Paris; d. of Pablo Ruiz-Picasso and Françoise Gilot; m. Rafael Lopez-Cambil (Lopez-Sanchez) 1978 (divorced 1998); m. 2nd Eric Thevennet 1999; ed Univ. of Paris, Sorbonne; studied jewellery design and manufacture; fashion jewellery for Yves St Laurent 1969; jewellery for Zolotas 1971, costumes and sets for Parisian theatre productions, L'Interprétation 1975, Succès 1978; created Paloma Picasso brand; creations designed by her for the Paloma Picasso brand include: jewellery for Tiffany & Co. 1980, fragrance (Paloma Picasso 1984, Minotaure 1992, Tentations 1996) and cosmetics for L'Oréal, eyewear for Metzler Optik Partner AG, bone china, crystal, silverware and tiles for Villeroy & Boch, home linens for KBC, fabrics and wall coverings for Motif; pieces in perm. collections of Smithsonian Inst. (Washington, DC), Musée des Arts Décoratifs (Paris) and Die Neue Zamlang (Munich); Council of Fashion Design of America (CFDA) Accessory Award 1989. *Address:* Paloma Picasso Parfums, 1 rue Pasquier, 92698 Levallois-Perret cedex, France (Office); Quintana Roo Ltd, 291A Brompton Road, London, SW3 2DY, England; c/o Tiffany and Co., 727 Fifth Avenue, New York, NY 10022, USA. *Telephone:* (20) 7589-9030 (London). *Fax:* (20) 7589-7712 (London).

PICCARD, Jacques Ernest Jean; Swiss scientist; b. 28 July 1922, Brussels, Belgium; s. of Auguste Piccard and Marianne (née Denis) Piccard; m. Marie-Claude Maillard 1953; two s. one d.; ed Univ. of Geneva and Inst. Universitaire des Hautes Etudes Internationales, Geneva; Asst Prof. of Econs, Geneva 1946–48; consultant scientist to several American orgs for deep sea research; collaborated with father, Prof. Auguste Piccard, in construction of bathyscaph Trieste; built first mesoscaph Auguste Piccard; has made more than 100 dives in Mediterranean and Pacific, one to 35,800 feet (deepest ever dive at that time, Jan. 1960) and approx. 700 dives in European lakes with submersible F.A.-FOREL; Chief Scientist, research submarine Ben Franklin for the Grumman-Piccard Gulf Stream Drift Mission, Summer 1969; Founder and Pres. Foundation for the Study and Preservation of Seas and Lakes; built research submersible F.A.-FOREL 1978; Visiting Prof. of Oceanic Eng at Stevens Inst. of Tech., Hoboken, New Jersey; Hon. DSc (American Int. Coll. and Hofstra Univ.); Croix de guerre (France), US Distinguished Public Service award 1960, Officier, Ordre de Léopold (Belgium). *Publications:* The Sun beneath the Sea 1971, several technical papers. *Leisure interests:* reading, walking, swimming, diving.

PICCOLI, Michel; French actor; b. 27 Dec. 1925, Paris; s. of Henri Piccoli; m. 1st Juliette Gréco 1966; m. 3rd Ludivine Clerc 1978; one s. from fmr m.; ed Collège d'Annel, Collège Ste. Barbe, Paris; Man. of the Théâtre de Babylone for two years before joining the Madeleine Renaud and Jean-Louis Barrault Theatre Co.; appeared in Phèdre at the Théâtre Nationale Populaire; Best Actor, Cannes 1980 (for Salto nel Vuoto), European Prize, Taormina Theatre, Sicily 2001; Chevalier Légion d'honneur, Ordre nationale du Mérite. *Films include:* Le point du jour 1946, Parfum de la dame en noire 1949, French Cancan 1955, The Witches of Salem 1956, Le mépris 1963, Diary of a Chambermaid 1964, De l'amour 1965, Lady L 1965, La curée 1965, Les demoiselles de Rochefort 1967, Un homme de trop 1967, Belle de jour 1967, Dillinger is Dead 1968, The Milky Way 1969, Topaz 1969, The Discreet Charm of the Bourgeoisie 1972, Themroc 1972, Blow-out 1973, The Infernal Trio 1974, Le fantôme de la liberté 1974, La faille 1975, Léonar 1975, Sept morts sur ordonnance 1976, La dernière femme 1976, Savage State 1978, Le divorcement 1979, Le saut dans le vide 1979, Le mors aux dents 1979, La città delle donne 1980, Salto nel Vuoto 1980, La passante du sans-souci 1982, Adieu Bonaparte 1985, The Night is Young 1986, L'homme voilé, Maladie d'amour, La rumba 1987, Y a bon les blancs, Blanc de Chine 1988, Milou en mai 1990, Martha et moi 1991, La belle noiseuse 1991, Les equilibristes, Le voleur d'enfants 1991, Le bal des cassepieds 1992, Archipel 1993, Rupture(s) 1993, Les cent et une nuits 1995, Alors voilà (Dir) 1997, Rien sur Robert 1999, Compagne de voyage 2000, Les acteurs 2000, Je rentre à la maison 2001, La Plague noire 2001. *Publication:* Dialogues égoistes 1976. *Leisure interests:* riding, flying. *Address:* 11 rue des Lions Saint-Paul, 75004 Paris, France.

PICHLER, Joseph A., PhD; American business executive; b. 3 Oct. 1939, St Louis, Mo.; s. of late Anton Pichler and Anita Pichler; m. Susan Eyerly 1962; two s. two d.; ed Notre Dame Univ. of Chicago, Univ. of Chicago; Dean Univ. of Kan. 1974–80; Exec. Vice-Pres. Dillon Companies Inc. 1980–82, Pres. 1982–84, Pres. and CEO 1984–86, CEO 1986–88; Exec. Vice-Pres. The Kroger Co. 1985–86, Pres. and COO 1986–90, Pres. and CEO June–Sept. 1990, Chair.

of Bd and CEO Sept. 1990–; Woodrow Wilson Fellow 1961, Ford Foundation Doctoral Fellow 1962–64, Standard Oil Industrial Relations Fellow 1964; mem. Cin. Business Comm. 1991–, Chair. 1997–98; Performance Award, US Dept of Labor Manpower Admin. 1969, William Booth Award, The Salvation Army 1998, Horatio Alger Award 1999, Distinguished Service Award, Nat. Conf. Cttee of Justice 2000. *Publications:* Inequality: The Poor and the Rich in America (with Joseph W. McGuire) 1969, Ethics, Free Enterprise and Public Policy (with Richard T. De George) 1978. *Leisure interests:* fly-fishing, music, reading. *Address:* The Kroger Co., 1014 Vine Street, Cincinnati, OH 45202, USA.

PICHOIS, Claude, DèsSc; French professor of French; b. 21 July 1925, Paris; s. of Léon Pichois and Renée Bardou; m. Vincenette Rey 1961; ed Lycée Carnot, Paris, HEC, Faculté des lettres, Sorbonne, Paris; Postgrad. Trainee, then Research Asst, CNRS 1953–56; lecturer, Faculté des lettres, Aix-en-Provence 1956–61; Prof., Univ. of Basel, Switzerland 1961–70; Distinguished Professor of French, Vanderbilt Univ., Nashville, Tenn., USA 1970–98, Prof. Emer. 1998–; Visiting Prof., Inst. for Research in the Humanities, Madison, USA 1968; Prof., Facultés de Namur, Belgium 1978–79, Sorbonne Nouvelle, Paris 1979–90, Prof. Emer. 1990–; Dr hc (Neuchâtel) 1983, (Trinity Coll. Dublin) 1984, (Acad. Européenne) 1993, (Louvain) 1999; Prix Goncourt for Biography 1999. *Publications:* Le vrai visage du général Aupick, beau-père de Baudelaire 1955, L'image de la Belgique dans les lettres françaises 1957, L'image de Jean-Paul Richter dans les lettres françaises 1963, Philarète Chasles et la vie littéraire au temps du romantisme (2 vols) 1965, Baudelaire à Paris 1967, Baudelaire, études et témoignages 1967, 1976, Correspondance et oeuvres complètes de Baudelaire, (4 vols) 1973, 1975–76, Album Baudelaire 1973, Vitesse et vision du monde 1973, Album Colette 1984; (co-author) Baudelaire et Asselineau 1953, Baudelaire devant ses contemporains 1957, 1967, 1995, Iconographie de Charles Baudelaire 1960, La littérature comparée 1967, 1983, Oeuvres complètes de Gérard de Nerval, vol. I 1989, vol. II 1984, vol. III 1993, Oeuvres de Colette, vol. I 1984, vol. II 1986, vol. III 1991, vol. IV 2001, Baudelaire (biography, co-author) 1987, Le musée retrouvé de Charles Baudelaire (co-author) 1992, Baudelaire/Paris (co-author) 1993, Gérard de Nerval (biography, co-author) 1995, Poulet-Malassis, l'éditeur de Baudelaire 1996 (biography), Colette (biography, co-author) 1999, Baudelaire, nouvelles lettres 2000, Baudelaire, mon cœur mis à nu 2001, Dictionnaire Baudelaire (co-author) 2002; edns of poetry by Laforgue, five collections of letters by Colette; numerous articles. *Address:* 3 rue Pierre-Demours, 75017 Paris, France. *Telephone:* 1-45-72-05-82 (France).

PICHT, Robert, DPhil; German university rector and professor of sociology; b. 27 Sept. 1937, Berlin; s. of Georg Picht and Edith Picht-Axenfeld; m. Barbara Picht (née Heuckenkamp) 1963; six c.; ed Univs of Freiburg, Munich, Madrid, Frankfurt, Hamburg and Paris; Dir Franco-German Inst., Ludwigsburg, Germany 1972–2000; Dir Interdisciplinary Studies, Coll. of Europe, Bruges, Belgium 1994–2002, Rector 2002–; Vice-Pres. and Chair. Exec. Cttee. European Culture, Amsterdam 1978–95; Officier, Ordre nat. du Mérite 1985, Bundesverdienstkreutz 1993, Officier, Légion d'honneur 1999; Strasburg Gold Medal (FVS Hamburg) 1984, Bürgermedal of City of Ludwigsburg 1989. *Publications include:* L'identité européenne 1994, Fremde Freunde. Deutsche und Franzosen vor dem 21. Jahrhundert 1997, A Pilot Study on Innovating Education In Europe. The Role of Foundation and Corporate Funders 1998. *Leisure interests:* art, music. *Address:* College of Europe, Dijver 11, 8000 Bruges, Belgium (Office). *Telephone:* (50) 44-99-11 (Office). *Fax:* (50) 34-75-33 (Office). *E-mail:* info@coleurop.be (Office). *Website:* www.coleurop.be (Office).

PICKARD, Sir (John) Michael, Kt, FCA, CIMgt; British business executive; b. 29 July 1932, Banstead, Surrey; s. of late John Stanley and of Winifred Joan Pickard; m. Penelope Jane Catterall 1959; one d. three s.; ed Oundle School; Finance Dir British Printing Corpn 1965–68, Man. Dir Trusthouses Ltd 1968–70, Trusthouse Forte Ltd 1970–71; Chair. Happy Eater Ltd 1972–86, Grattan PLC 1978–84, Courage Ltd and Imperial Brewing & Leisure Ltd 1981–86; CEO Sears PLC 1986–92; Chair. Freemans PLC 1988–92, Bullough PLC 1996–2002 (Dir 1995–), London Docklands Devt Corpn 1992–98, Servus Holdings Ltd 1997–2001, Nat. House-Building Council 1998–, London First Centre 1998–2001; Dir (non-exec) Brown Shipley Holdings PLC 1986–93, Electra Investment Trust PLC 1989–2002, Nationwide Bldg Soc. 1991–94, Pinnacle Clubs Ltd 1992–99, Bentalls PLC 1993–2001, United Racecourses (Holdings) Ltd 1995–; mem. bd London First 1992–2002 (Deputy Chair. 1998–); mem. Cttee The Automobile Asscn 1994–99; Chair. Roedean School Council 1980–90; Gov. Oundle School 1987–2000; Chair. The Housing Forum 1999–2002, Freeport PLC 2001–; Hon. LLD (E London) 1997. *Leisure interests:* sport, education. *Address:* 16 Grosvenor Hill Court, Bourdon Street, London, W1K 3PX, England. *Telephone:* (20) 7629-6865 (Office). *Fax:* (20) 7495-4439 (Office).

PICKENS, Jo Ann; American soprano; b. 4 Aug. 1950, Robstown, Tex.; d. of Anne Belle Sanders; started singing career in Chicago Lyric Opera; has perfomed in recital and concerts around the world and appeared with conductors including Solti, Dorati, Rattle, Norrington, Pesek and Sanderling; also appears in opera, notably Berlioz's The Trojans 1987 and Armide 1988; Award, Int. Competition for Singers, Paris 1980; Metropolitan Opera Regional Auditions 1981; Benson & Hedges Gold Award 1981. *Address:* c/o Norman McCann International Artists Ltd, The Coach House, 56 Lawrie Park Gardens, London, SE26 6XJ, England.

PICKENS, Thomas Boone, Jr., BS; American oil company executive; b. 22 May 1928, Holdenville, Okla; s. of Thomas Boone Pickens and Grace Molonson Pickens; m. Beatrice L. Carr 1972; ed Oklahoma State Univ.; geologist, Phillips Petroleum Co. 1951–55; Founder, Pres., Chair. Bd Mesa Petroleum Co., Amarillo, Tex.; Gen. Partner, Mesa Inc. 1985–; mem. Nat. Petroleum Council 1970–; Founder, Chair. United Shareholders Asscn Washington. *Publication:* Boone 1987.

PICKERING, Sir Edward Davies, Kt; British journalist; b. 4 May 1912; s. of George Pickering and Louie Pickering; m. 1st Margaret Soutter 1936 (divorced 1947); one d.; m. 2nd Rosemary Whitton 1955; two s. one d.; ed Middlesbrough High School; Chief Sub-Ed. Daily Mail 1939; RA 1940–44; Staff of Supreme HQ Allied Expeditionary Force 1944–45; Man. Ed. Daily Mail 1947–49, Daily Express 1951–57, Ed. Daily Express 1957–62; Dir Beaverbrook Newspapers 1956–63; Man. Dir Beaverbrook Publications 1962–63; Editorial Dir and Dir The Daily Mirror Newspapers Ltd 1964–68; Editorial Dir Int. Publishing Corpn, Chair. I.P.C. Newspaper Div. and Chair. Daily Mirror Newspapers Ltd 1968–70; Chair. I.P.C. Magazines Ltd 1970–74; Chair. Mirror Group Newspapers Ltd 1974–77; mem. Press Council 1964–69, 1970–82, Vice-Chair. 1977–82; Chair. Commonwealth Press Union 1977–86; Exec. Vice-Chair. Times Newspapers Ltd 1982–, Chair. The Times Supplements Ltd 1989–; Dir Reed Publishing Holdings 1977–81, Times Newspapers Holdings 1981–; Treas. Int. Fed. of the Periodical Press 1971–75; Vice-Pres. Periodical Publrs. Asscn 1971–94; mem. Press Complaints Comm. 1991–94 (Consultant 1994–); Chair. William Tyndale Quincentenary Appeal 1991–94, Patron 1999–; Hon. Freeman Stationers' and Newspaper Makers' Co. 1985; Master, Guild of St Bride 1981–97; Hon. DLitt (City Univ., London) 1986; Astor Awards for distinguished service to Commonwealth Press 1986. *Address:* 23 Rutland Gate, London, SW7 1PD, England.

PICKERING, Thomas Reeve, MA; American diplomatist; b. 5 Nov. 1931, Orange, NJ; s. of Hamilton Reeve Pickering and Sarah P. Chasteney; m. Alice Jean Stover 1955; one s. one d.; ed Bowdoin Coll., Brunswick, Maine, Fletcher School of Law and Diplomacy, Medford, Mass., Univ. of Melbourne, Australia; Lt Commdr USN 1956–59; joined Dept of State 1959, Intelligence Research Specialist 1960, Foreign Affairs Officer 1961, Arms Control and Disarmament Agency 1961–62; mem. US Del. to Disarmament Conf., Geneva 1962–64; Prin. Officer, Zanzibar 1965–67; Deputy Chief of Mission, Dar es Salaam 1967–69; Deputy Dir Bureau of Politico-Mil. Affairs 1969–73; Exec. Sec. Dept of State, Special Asst to Sec. of State 1973–74; Amb. to Jordan 1974–78; Asst Sec. of State, Bureau of Oceans, Environment and Science 1978–81; Amb. to Nigeria 1981–83; Amb. to El Salvador 1983–85, to Israel 1985–88; Perm. Rep. to UN 1989–92, Amb. to India 1992–93, to Russia 1993–96; Under-Sec. of State for Political Affairs 1997–2000; named Career Amb.; Pres. Eurasia Foundation 1996–97; Sr Vice-Pres. Internal Affairs, The Boeing Co. 2001–. *Leisure interests:* archaeology, scuba, photography, carpentry. *Address:* The Boeing Company, 1200 Wilson blvd, Arlington, VA 22209, USA (Office); 2318 Kimbro Street, Alexandria, VA 22307, USA. *Telephone:* (703) 465-3471 (Office). *Fax:* (703) 465-3403 (Office).

PICKERING, William Hayward, MS, PhD; American scientist; b. 24 Dec. 1910, Wellington, NZ; s. of Albert William and Elizabeth Hayward Pickering; m. 1st Muriel Bowler 1932 (died 1992); one s. one d.; m. 2nd Inez Chapman 1994; ed California Inst. of Tech.; Calif. Inst. of Tech. 1936–, Prof. of Electrical Eng 1946–, Dir Jet Propulsion Laboratory 1954–76, Prof. Emer. 1980–; mem. Scientific Advisory Bd USAF 1945–48; Chair. Panel on Test Range Instrumentation Research and Devt Bd 1948–49; directed Devt of Army Corporal and Sergeant missiles 1950–55 and many spacecraft, including Explorer I, Ranger, the first US spacecraft to photograph the moon, Mariner II, first spacecraft to return scientific data from the vicinity of a planet (Venus), Mariner IV, first spacecraft to photograph Mars, Surveyor, first US spacecraft to soft-land on the moon and return scientific data; Dir Research Inst., Univ. of Petroleum and Minerals, Saudi Arabia 1976–78; Pres. Pickering Research Corpn, Pasadena, Calif. 1980–, Lignetics Inc. 1983– (Chair. of Bd 1995–); mem. Advisory Cttee Dept of Aeronautics and Astronautics, Univ. of Wash., US Tech. Panel on Earth Satellite Programs IGY 1956–58, Army Scientific Advisory Panel 1963–65; Pres. AIAA 1963; Fellow IEEE; Hon. Fellow AIAA; mem. NAS, American Astron Univ. Profs., American Geophysical Union, Nat. Acad. of Eng, AAAS, Royal Soc. of New Zealand, Int. Acad. of Astronautics; mem. Int. Astronautics Fed., Pres. 1965–66; Hon. mem. New Zealand Inst. of Eng and Aerospace Medical Asscn; Fellow, American Acad. of Arts and Sciences; Hon. DSc (Occidental Coll., Clark Univ., Univ. of Bologna) 1974; Meritorious Civilian Service Award US Army 1945, Distinguished Civilian Service Award US Army 1959, Columbus Gold Medal 1964, Prix Galabert Award 1965, Robert H. Goddard Memorial Trophy 1965, Crozier Gold Medal 1965, Spirit of St Louis Medal 1965, Distinguished Service Medal NASA 1965, Louis W. Hill Award 1968, Edison Medal (IEEE) 1972, Nat. Medal of Science 1975, Herman Oberth Engineering Award (Fed. Repub. of Germany) 1978, François-Xavier Bagnoud Aerospace Prize 1993, Japan Prize for Aerospace Technology 1994 and many other awards; Hon. KBE; Italian Order of Merit. *Leisure interests:* swimming, fishing, hiking, gardening. *Address:* 787 West Woodbury Road, Suite 9, Altadena, CA 91001 (Office); 294 St Katherine Drive, Flintridge, CA 91011, USA (Home). *Telephone:* (626) 797-7510 (Office). *Fax:* (626) 797-1209. *E-mail:* whpickering@aol.com (Office).

PICKETT, John Anthony, PhD, CChem, FRS, FRSC, FRES; British research chemist; b. 21 April 1945, Leicester; s. of Samuel Victor Pickett and Lilian Frances Hoar; m. Ulla Birgitta Skålén 1970; one s. one d.; ed King Edward

VII Grammar School, Coalville, Univ. of Surrey; Postdoctoral Fellowship, UMIST (organic chem.) 1970–72; Sr Scientist, Chem. Dept, Brewing Research Foundation, Surrey 1972–76; Prin. Scientific Officer, Dept of Insecticides and Fungicides, Rothamsted Experimental Station 1976–83, Individual Merit (Grade 2) and Head Dept Insecticides and Fungicides, (now Biological Chem. Div.), Inst. of Arable Crops Research (now Rothamsted Research) 1984–; Special Prof., Univ. of Nottingham 1991–; Pres. Int. Soc. of Chemical Ecology (ISCE) 1995; mem. Deutsche Akad. der Naturforscher Leopolinda 2001; Hon. mem. Academic Staff Univ. of Reading 1995; Rank Prize for Nutrition and Crop Husbandry 1995, Int. Soc. of Chemical Ecology Medal 2002. *Research:* chemical ecology and insect pheromones in particular. *Publications:* over 250 papers, including patents. *Leisure interest:* jazz trumpet playing. *Address:* Biological Chemistry Division, Rothamsted Research, Harpenden, Herts., AL5 2JQ (Office); 53 Parkfield Crescent, Kimpton, Nr. Hitchin, Herts., SG4 8EQ, England (Home). *Telephone:* (1582) 763133, Ext. 2321 (Office); (1438) 832832 (Home). *Fax:* (1582) 762595; (1582) 762595 (Office). *E-mail:* john .pickett@bbsrc.ac.uk (Office).

PICKETT-HEAPS, Jeremy David, PhD, FAA, FRS; Australian professor of botany; b. 5 June 1940, Bombay, India; m. 1st Charmian Scott 1964; one s. one d.; m. 2nd Julianne Francis 1978; two s.; ed Univ. of Cambridge; Prof., Dept of Molecular, Cellular and Developmental Biology, Univ. of Colo, Boulder, USA 1970–88; Prof. of Botany, Univ. of Melbourne 1988–. *Publication:* Green Algae. *Address:* School of Botany, University of Melbourne, Parkville, Vic. 3052 (Office); 47 St. Leonards Road, Ascot Vale, Vic. 3032, Australia (Home). *Telephone:* (3) 8344-4519 (Office); (3) 9370-1862 (Home). *Fax:* (3) 9349-3268 (Office). *E-mail:* jeremyph@unimelb.edu.au (Office).

PICULA, Tonino; Croatian politician and historian; b. 31 Aug. 1961, Mali Losinj; ed Zagreb Univ.; Assoc. Prof. and Sec. Kulturni Radnik (magazine), Cultural and Educ. Ass. 1987–89; mem. Exec. Cttee, Int. Sec. Social Democratic Party (SDP) of Croatia 1993–; counsellor Social Democratic Party Co. Ass. of Zagreb, mem. Cttee for Int. Co-operation for Local Self-Govt Devt, Pres. City Org. SDP for Velika Gorica 1997–2000; mem. Croatian Parl. 2000–; Minister of Foreign Affairs 2000–. *Address:* Ministry of Foreign Affairs, trg. Nikole Šubiča Zrinskog 7-8, 10000 Zagreb, Croatia (Office). *Telephone:* (41) 4569964 (Office). *Fax:* (41) 4569977 (Office). *E-mail:* mvp@mvp.hr. *Website:* www.mvp.hr.

PIËCH, Ferdinand; Austrian business executive; b. 17 April 1937, Vienna; ed Eidgenössische Technische Hochschule (ETH), Zürich; joined Porsche KG in engine testing 1963, Tech. Man. 1971; joined Audi NSU Auto Union AG 1972, Divisional Man. Gen. Testing 1973, mem. Bd of Man. 1975, Vice-Chair. Bd of Man. 1983, Chair. Bd of Man. of Audi AG 1988; Chair. Bd Dirs. Volkswagen AG 1993–2002, Dir, Head of Research and Devt 1995–2000, responsible for Production Optimisation and Purchasing 1996–2001, Chair. Advisory Bd 2002–; Pres. Asscn of European Automobile Mfrs 1999–2000; Chair. Scania 2000–02; Dr. tech. hc (Tech. Univ. Vienna) 1984, Dr. hc (Ben Gurion Univ.) 1997, (ETH Zurich) 1999; Distinguished Service Medal (1st Class) 1984, Automobile Business Manager of the Century 1999. *Address:* c/o Volkswagen AG, 38436 Wolfsburg, Germany.

PIEDRABUENA, Guillermo; Chilean lawyer; b. 18 Jan. 1937, Viña del Mar; m. Isabel Keymer; six c.; ed Saint George's Coll., Santiago, School of Law, Universidad de Chile, Santiago; lawyer, Consejo de Defensa del Estado 1963–76, Lawyer Counsellor 1976–96, Pres. 1990–93; Sub-Sec. Justice Dept 1970; mem. Appeal Court, Santiago 1997, Special Tribunal of Industrial Property 1993–2000; Nat. Prosecutor of Chile 2000–. *Publications include:* Breves comentarios a la reforma procesal penal 1998, El Recurso de apelación y la consulta 1999, Introducción a la reforma procesal penal 2000. *Address:* Fiscalia Nacional del Ministerio Publico, Almte. Gotuzzo 124, Piso 11, Santiago, Chile (Office). *Telephone:* (2) 870-5201 (Office). *Fax:* (2) 870-5232 (Office). *E-mail:* gpiedrabuena@minpublico.cl (Office). *Website:* www .ministeriopublico.cl (Office).

PIEL, Gerard, AB; American editor and publisher; b. 1 March 1915, New York; s. of William Piel and Loretto (née Scott) Piel; m. 1st Mary Tapp Bird 1938 (divorced 1955); two s. (one deceased); m. 2nd Eleanor Virden Jackson 1955; one d.; ed Phillips Acad., Andover, Mass. and Harvard Coll.; Editorial Assoc., Science Ed., Life 1938–45; Asst to Pres., Henry J. Kaiser Co. and associated enterprises 1945–46; Organizer, Pres. Scientific American Inc., Publr Scientific American 1947–84, Chair of Bd 1984–87, Chair. Emer. 1987; Chair. Comm. Delivery Personal Health Services, New York 1966–68, Trustees, Foundation for Child Devt; mem. Bd Overseers Harvard Univ. 1966–68, 1973–79; Trustee American Museum of Natural History, Radcliffe Coll. 1962–80, Phillips Acad., New York Botanical Garden, Henry J. Kaiser Family Foundation, Mayo Foundation, American Bd of Medical Specialities, René Dubos Center for Human Environment; mem. Council on Foreign Relations, American Philosophical Soc., Inst. of Medicine; Fellow American Acad. of Arts and Sciences, AAAS (Pres. 1985, Chair. 1986); numerous hon. doctorates; George Polk Award 1961, Kalinga Prize 1962, Bradford Washburn Award 1966, Arches of Science Award 1969, Rosenberger Medal, Univ. of Chicago 1973, A. I. Djavakhishvili Medal (Univ. of Tbilisi), Publr of the Year, Magazine Publrs. Asscn 1980. *Publications:* Science in the Cause of Man 1962, The Acceleration of History 1972, Only One World 1992, The Age of Science 2001. *Leisure interest:* fly-fishing. *Address:* 1115 Fifth Avenue, New York, NY 10128, USA (Home).

PIENAAR, Jacobus Francois, LLB; South African rugby player; b. 2 Jan. 1967, Vereeniging; s. of Johan Pienaar and Valerie Du Toit; m. Nerene Pienaar 1996; ed Patriot High School and Rand Afrikaans Univ.; capped for S. African Schools 1985, S. African Under 20 1987, S. African Barbarians 1990; Capt. Transvaal; Capt. S. African Rugby Team 1993–96, World Cup winners 1995; holds record for most tests as Capt. of SA (29); played for UK club Saracens, then Chief Exec.; motivational speaker; Int. Rugby Player of Year 1994; British Rugby Writers' Lifetime Achievement Award 1995. *Publication:* Rainbow Warrior (autobiog.). *Leisure interests:* golf, spending time at home. *Address:* c/o South African Rugby Football Union, P.O. Box 99, Newlands 7725, South Africa. *Telephone:* (21) 6853038. *Fax:* (21) 6856771.

PIENE, Otto Ludwig Wilhelm Hermann Leonhard; German artist and educator; b. 18 April 1928, Laasphe, Westphalia; s. of Otto and Anne (Niemeyer) Piene; m. Elizabeth Olson 1988; one s. three d.; ed Acad. of Fine Arts, Munich and Düsseldorf and Univ. of Cologne; organized Night Exhbns, f. Group Zero, Düsseldorf, with Heinz Mack 1957–66; Visiting Prof., Graduate School of Art, Univ. of Pa 1964; Prof. of Environmental Art, School of Architecture, MIT 1972–, Dir Center for Advanced Visual Studies, MIT 1974–94, Acting Dir 1993–94, Dir Emer. 1994–; Prof. Emer. MIT 1993–; Founder and Dir Sky Art Conf. 1981–; one-man exhbns include: Galerie Heseler, Munich 1971, 1972, 1975, 1977–79, 1981, 1983, Galerie Heimeshoff, Essen 1974, 1977, 1983, 1988, Galerie Schoeller, Düsseldorf 1976, 1977, 1980, 1984, 1987, 1991, 1995, 2000, Galerie Löhrl, Mönchengladbach 1986, 1988, 1991, 1996, Gallery 360°, Tokyo 1991, 1992; retrospective exhbn Museum am Ostwall, Dortmund 1967, Hayden Gallery, MIT 1975, Karlsruhe 1988, Städt. Kunstmuseum, Düsseldorf 1996, City Gallery, Prague 2002; group exhbns. include: Tate Gallery 1964, Düsseldorf 1973, Antwerp 1979, Paris 1983, London, Berlin 1987, New York 1988–89, Copenhagen 1992; performed works include Olympic Rainbow 1972, Sky Events, SAC 1981, 1982, 1983, 1986, Sky Dance, Guggenheim 1984, Dialogue de Têtes, Reims 1990; Les fleurs du mal, Québec 1996; works in museums in many countries; DFA hc (Univ. of Md) 1995; North Rhine-Westphalia Medal of Merit, American Acad. of Arts and Letters Sculpture Prize. *Publications:* (with Heinz Mack) Zero 1, Zero 2 1958, Zero 3 1961; More Sky 1973; author and ed. Zero 1973, Art Transition 1975–76, Centerbeam 1980, Sky Art Conference Catalog 1981, 1982, 1983, 1986, Lightsoret 1988, Feuerbilder und Texte 1988, Überblick 1991. *Address:* Center for Advanced Visual Studies, Massachusetts Institute of Technology, N51, 265 Massachusetts Avenue, Cambridge, MA 02139 (Office); 383 Old Ayer Road, Groton, MA 01450, USA (Home and Studio); Hüttenstr. 104, Atelier 40215 Düsseldorf, Germany (Studio). *Telephone:* (617) 253-4415 (Office); (978) 448-5240 (Home and Studio). *Fax:* (617) 253-1660 (Office); (978) 448-6716 (Home and Studio).

PIERANTOZZI, Sandra Sumang, BEd; Palauan politician and business executive; b. 9 Aug. 1953, Koror; d. of the late Yechadrechemai Sumang Demei and of Mitsko Wong Sumang; m. Marcello Pierantozzi; ed Palau Mission Acad., Union Coll., Lincoln, Neb., USA, Univ. of Hawaii; teacher, Micronesian Occupational Coll. 1974–79; Journal Clerk, First Palau Constitutional Convention 1979; Office Man. Koror Wholesalers 1980; owner pvt. business including MVP Construction & Realty, Belau Business Services, SPACO Finance 1980–; newscaster WALU-TV 1980–82; Clerk of the Senate 1981–91; Minister of Admin. 1991–92; Special Consultant, Nat. Congress 1992–93; Senator, Floor Leader, Chair. Cttee on Health and Social Welfare 1997–2000; Minister of Health 2001; Vice-Pres. of Palau 2001–; mem. Bd of Dirs. Palau Chamber of Commerce; Gov. and Dir Pacific Islands Devt. Bank; Senate Rep., Bd of Dirs. Asscn Pacific Island Legislatures; Sec. Center for Asia-Pacific Women in Politics; Founding Dir Palau Conservation Soc.; f. Sumang Demei Memorial Scholarship Award 1992. *Leisure interests:* philately, numismatics, environmental conservation, travel. *Address:* Office of the Vice-President, P.O. Box 100, Koror, PW 96940, Palau (Office). *Telephone:* 488-2702 (Office); 488-2335 (Home). *Fax:* 488-1310 (Office); 488-3395 (Home). *E-mail:* vprop@ palaunet.com (Office); spierantozzi@palaunet.com (Home).

PIERCE, Mary; Canadian tennis player; b. 15 Jan. 1975, Montreal, Canada; d. of Jim Pierce and Yannick Pierce; turned professional 1989; moved to France 1990; first career title, Palermo 1991; runner-up French Open 1994; winner Australian Open 1995, Tokyo Nichirei 1995; semi-finalist Italian Open, Canadian Open 1996; finalist Australian Open singles 1997, doubles (with Martina Hingis, q.v.), 2000; won singles and doubles (with Martina Hingis) French Open 2000; highest singles ranking No. 3; winner of doubles (with Martina Hingis, q.v.), Pan Pacific; French Fed. Cup team 1990–92, 1994–97; French Olympic team 1992, 1996; 24 WTA Tour singles and doubles titles (by end 2002); France's (rising star) Burgeon Award 1992, WTA Tour Comeback Player of the Year 1997. *Leisure interests:* hiking, jet skiing, boating, shopping, reading, yoga. *Address:* c/o WTA, 133 First Street NE, St Petersburg, FL 33701, USA.

PIERCY, Marge, MA; American novelist, poet and essayist; b. 31 March 1936, Detroit; d. of Robert Douglas Piercy and Bert Bernice Piercy (née Bunnin); m. Ira Wood 1982; ed Michigan and Northwestern Univs; instructor Gary Extension, Ind. Univ. 1960–62; Poet-in-Residence Kan. Univ. 1971; Distinguished Visiting Lecturer Thomas Jefferson Coll., Grand Valley State Colls 1975, 1976, 1978, 1980, Elliston Poetry Fellow Cincinnati Univ. 1986; DeRoy Distinguished Visiting Prof. Mich. Univ. 1992; mem. Writer Bd 1985–86; mem. bd dirs Transition House, Mass Foundation for the Humanities and Public Policy 1978–85; Gov.'s Appointee to Mass. Cultural Council 1990–91, Mass. Council on Arts and Humanities 1986–89; mem. Artistic

Advisory Bd ALEPH Alliance for Jewish Renewal, American Poetry Centre 1988–, Literary Advisory Panel (Poetry), NEA 1989; Ed. Leapfrog Press 1997–; Poetry Ed. Lilith 1999–; mem. PEN, NOW, American Poetry Soc. etc; Literary award, Gov. of Mass Comm. on Status of Women 1974, Nat. Endowment of Arts Award 1978, Golden Rose Poetry Prize 1990, Notable Book Award 1997, Paterson Poetry Prize 2000 and many others. *Publications:* Breaking Camp 1968, Hard Loving 1969, Going Down Fast 1969, Dance the Eagle to Sleep 1970, Small Changes 1973, To Be of Use 1973, Living in the Open 1976, Woman on the Edge of Time 1976, The High Cost of Living 1978, Vida 1980, The Moon is Always Female 1980, Braided Lives 1982, Circles on the Water 1982, Stone, Paper, Knife 1983, My Mother's Body 1985, Gone to Soldiers 1988, Available Light 1988 (May Sarton Award 1991), Summer People 1989, He, She and It 1991, Body of Glass 1991 (Arthur C. Clarke Award 1993), Mars and Her Children 1992, The Longings of Women 1994, Eight Chambers of the Heart 1995, City of Darkness, City of Light 1996, What Are Big Girls Made Of? 1997, Storm Tide 1998, Early Grrrl 1999, The Art of Blessing the Day 1999, Three Women 1999, So You Want to Write: How to Master the Craft of Writing Fiction and the Personal Narrative (with Ira Wood) 2001, Sleeping with Cats, A Memoir 2002. *Address:* PO Box 1473, Wellfleet, MA 02667, USA. *Fax:* (508) 349-1180 (Office). *Website:* margepiercy.com (Office).

PIERER, Heinrich von; German business executive; b. 26 Jan. 1941, Erlangen; ed studies in law and econs; joined Siemens' Legal Dept 1969; in charge of KWU power station unit (Siemens' power plant div.) 1977; Commercial Dir KWU 1988; mem. Admin. Bd Siemens AG 1989, Deputy Chief Exec. 1991, Chief Exec. 1992–, also Pres. *Leisure interest:* tennis. *Address:* Siemens AG, Wittelsbacherplatz 2, 80333 Munich, Germany.

PIERONEK, Bishop Tadeusz; Polish ecclesiastic and professor of theology and canon law; b. 24 Oct. 1934, Radziechowy n. Żywiec; ed Jagiellonian Univ., Kraków, Higher Ecclesiastic Seminary, Kraków, Catholic Univ. of Lublin, Lateral Univ., Rome; ordained Priest, Kraków 1957; notary Metropolitan Curia, Kraków; prefect Higher Ecclesiastic Seminary, Kraków; lecturer Catholic Theology Acad., Warsaw 1967–76, Asst prof. 1975; lecturer and head Dept of Canon Law, Pontifical Acad. of Theology, Kraków 1965–, Prof. 1985; Visiting Prof. Santa Croce Univ., Rome 1985–; Cufrut Titular Bishop 1992; Deputy Gen. Sec. Polish Episcopate 1992–93; Gen. Sec. Polish Episcopate Conf. 1993–98; Gen. Sec. Second Plenary Synod, Poland 1987; Rector Pontifical Acad. of Theology, Kraków 1998–. *Publications:* The Church Is Not Afraid of Freedom 1998 and over 100 articles. *Leisure interests:* Polish poetry, landscape tourism, cooking, classical music, painting, folklore. *Address:* Papieska Akademia Teologiczna, ul. Kanonicza 25, 31-002 Kraków, Poland. *Telephone:* (12) 421-84-16.

PIEROTH, Elmar; German politician and viticulturist; b. 9 Nov. 1934, Bad Kreuznach; s. of Philip Pieroth; m. Hannelore Ribow 1957; six c.; ed Stefan Georg Gymnasium, Bingen and Univs. of Mainz and Munich; has run Weingut Ferdinand Pieroth GmbH since 1955; creator of Pieroth-Modell; Devt work in Togo 1960; initiator Bad Kreuznach talks; mem. Bundestag 1969–81; mem. Berlin Chamber of Deputies 1981–; Senator for Economy and Labour, Berlin 1981–89, 1995–98, for Finance, Berlin 1991–95; Rep. for Eastern Europe, Fed. State of Berlin 1999–2001; mem. CDU. *Publications:* Die Union in der Opposition (with G. Golter) 1970, Chancen der Betriebe durch Umweltschutz (with L. Wicke) 1988. *Address:* 105 Martin-Luther-Strasse, 10825 Berlin, Germany.

PIERRE, Abbé (see Groués, Henri).

PIERRE, Eric; Haitian politician; fmr economist; Prime Minister of Haiti 1997–98. *Address:* c/o Office of the Prime Minister, Port-au-Prince, Haiti.

PIERRE-BROSSOLETTE, Claude, LenD; French civil servant; b. 5 March 1928, Paris; s. of Pierre Brossolette and Gilberte (née Bruel); m. Sabine Goldet 1953; two d.; ed Lycée Henri-IV, Faculty of Law of Paris Univ., Ecole nat. d'admin; Inspecteur adjoint des Finances 1952, Insp. 1955; served under two successive Ministers in Office of Minister of Econ. and Financial Affairs 1956; Asst to Financial Adviser, Embassy in USA 1957; served Direction des Finances Extérieures 1958; Tech. Adviser, Office of Minister of Finance 1960–62, Asst Dir of Office 1962, Deputy Dir 1963; Asst Dir of External Financial Affairs in Direction du Trésor 1964, later Chef de Service 1966; Sec.-Gen. Conseil nat. du Crédit 1967–71; served in office of Valéry Giscard d'Estaing, Minister of Econ. and Financial Affairs 1969–71; Dir du Trésor, Ministry of Econ. and Financial Affairs 1971; Censeur, Banque de France, Crédit nat. 1971; Vice-Chair. Caisse nat. des Télécommunications 1971–74; Dir SNCF (Nat. Railways Bd) 1971–74, Air France 1971–74; Sec.-Gen. of Presidency of the Repub. 1974–76; Chair. Crédit Lyonnais 1976–82, Omnium financier pour l'Industrie nat. (OFINA) 1976, Europartners Securities Corpn, Banque Stern 1982–86 (Vice-Chair. 1986); Assoc. Man. Worms et Cie 1986–92; Admin. Crédit Nat. 1976–81; Pres. Démachy et Assocs. 1987; mem. Conseil nat. du Crédit 1976–81, Conseil de Surveillance de la Cie Bancaire 1976, Dir Société Air-liquide, Crédit Foncier de France 1978–82, Générale Occidentale 1979–82, Péchiney Ugine Kuhlmann 1980–82, Lyonnaise des Eaux 1980, B.S.N. 1981, Norsolor 1988; Pres. Supervisory Council Câbles Pirelli 1992–; Vice-Pres. Eurofin 1992–95, Pres. 1995–96; Pres. Caisse de refinancement hypothécaire 1995; Adviser to Pres. of Merrill Lynch Int. 1993–97, Chair. Supervisory Bd Merrill Lynch France 1997–99; Dir GTM-

Enterpose 1993–; Officier, Légion d'honneur, Commdr de l'Ordre nat. du Mérite, Chevalier, Ordre des Palmes académiques, Médaille de la Résistance. *Address:* 37 avenue d'Iéna, 75116 Paris, France (Home).

PIERRET, Alain Marie, BA; French diplomatist (retd); b. 16 July 1930, Mourmelon; s. of Henri Pierret and Yvonne Delhumeau; m. Jacqueline Nanta 1958; three d. (one deceased); ed Faculties of Arts (Sorbonne) and Law, Paris and Ecole Nat. de la France d'Outre-Mer; reserve officer (navy) 1953–55; District Commr Togo 1955–59, Sahara (S. Algeria) 1959–61; Sec. of Embassy, Sierra Leone 1961–63, South Africa 1963–66; Africa Div. Ministry of Foreign Affairs 1966–69; Counsellor, Moscow 1969–72; Head, Soviet Affairs Bureau, Ministry of Foreign Affairs 1972; mem. French Del. to Conf. on Security and Co-operation in Europe Helsinki 1972–75; Counsellor, Belgrade 1975–80; Amb. to Niger 1980–82; Asst Sec. of State for UN Affairs and Int. Orgs. 1983–86; Amb. to Israel 1986–91, to Belgium 1991–93, to the Holy See 1993–95; Pres. Interministerial Cttee for Agric. and Food (CIAA) 1996–; mem. study mission into the spoliation of Jews in France during Second World War 1997–2000; Del. to Conf. on Nazi Gold, London 1997, to Conf. on Holocaust-era Assets, Washington, DC 1998; Officier, Légion d'honneur, Croix de Guerre (Vietnam), Grand Cross Order Pius IX (Holy See). *Publications include:* Ambassadeur en Israel, 1986–1991 1999. *Address:* i 117, 26 rue du Cdt. Mouchotte, 75014 Paris, France. *Telephone:* 1-43-20-53-71 (Home). *Fax:* 1-43-20-53-71 (Home). *E-mail:* alpierret@wanadoo.fr (Home).

PIERRET, Christian; French politician and economist; b. 12 March 1946, Bar-le-Duc; s. of Jean Pierret and Anne Radet; m. Marie-Odile Schibler 1978; one d. (and three d. from previous marriages); ed Faculty of Law and Econs, Paris, Inst. d'Etudes Politiques de Paris, Ecole Nat. d'Administration; civil servant, Ministry for the Economy and Finance, then Cour des Comptes 1972–78; fmr Lorraine regional councillor and mem. Vosges Gen. Council; Nat. Ass. Deputy for Vosges 1978–93, 1997–; Minister of State attached to Minister for the Economy, Finance and Industry, with responsibility for Industry 1997–2002; Mayor of St-Dié-des-Vosges 1989–97, Deputy May 1997–; Chair. Caisse Nat. d'Epargne 1986–93; Vice-Chair. Accor Hotels group 1993–96; Chair. Parl. Study Group on Textile and Clothing industry 1988–, France-Israel Parl. Friendship Group 1988–; Vice-Chair. France-Great Britain Parl. Friendship Group 1988–; Regional councillor of Lorraine 1998–; mem. Comité pour l'union monétaire de l'Europe (CUME). *Publications:* Plan et autogestion, Socialisme et multinationales; many articles in various publs. *Address:* Ministry for the Economy, Finance and Industry, 139 rue de Bercy, 75572 Paris cedex 12; Hôtel de ville, 88100 St-Dié, France. *Telephone:* 1-53-18-45-50. *Fax:* 1-53-18-95-72.

PIETRUSKI, John Michael, BS; American business executive; b. 12 March 1933, Sayreville, NJ; s. of the late John M. Pietruski, Sr and Lillian Christensen Pietruski; m. Roberta Jeanne Talbot 1954; two s. one d.; ed Sayreville High School and Rutgers Univ.; First Lt U.S. Army 1955–57; Mfg Man., Industrial Eng Man., Procter & Gamble Co. 1954–63; Pres. Medical Products and Hosp. Divs., C.R. Bard, Inc. 1963–77; Pres. Pharmaceutical Group, Sterling Drug Inc. 1977–81, Corp. Exec. Vice-Pres. 1981–83, Pres. and COO 1983–85, Chair. and CEO 1985–88, mem. Bd of Dirs. 1977–88; Pres. Dansara Co. 1988–; Chair. Bd Texas Biotech. Corp. 1990–; mem. Bd of Dirs. Irving Bank Corpn 1985–89, Associated Dry Goods Corpn 1985–88, Hershey Foods Corpn 1987–, Cytogen Corpn 1989–94, Gen. Public Utilities Corpn 1989–2001, Lincoln Nat. Corpn 1989–, McKesson Corpn 1990–99, Professional Detailing Inc. 1998–, First Energy Corpn 2001–, Xylos Corpn 2001–, Trial Card Inc.; mem. Pharmaceutical Mfrs Asscn 1985–88; Trustee Rutgers Univ. Foundation 1985–94; Regent, Concordia Coll. 1993–; Hon. LLD 1993. *Leisure interests:* boating, fishing, travelling, athletics. *Address:* Suite 3408, One Penn Plaza, New York, NY 10119; 27 Paddock Lane, Colts Neck, NJ 07722, USA (Home). *Telephone:* (212) 268-5510 (Office). *Fax:* (212) 268-5765 (Office).

PIGEAT, Henri Michel; French administrator; b. 13 Nov. 1939, Montluçon; s. of Eugène Pigeat and Odette Micard; m. Passerose Cyprienne Rueff 1976; one d.; ed Inst. des Sciences Politiques, Paris and Ecole Nat. d'Admin; Civil Servant Office of Gen. Admin. and Public Service 1965–69; Head Office of Sec. of State for Public Service 1969–71, Tech. Adviser 1971–72; Head of Information Services, Office of Sec. of State for Public Service and Information 1973; Sec.-Gen. Interministerial Cttee for Information 1973–74; Asst Gen. Dir Information, Gen. Office of Information 1974, Dir 1975–76; Dir Information and Broadcasing Service 1976–; Deputy Man. Dir Agence France-Presse 1976–79, Chair. and Man. Dir 1979–86; Chair. and Man. Dir IBIS S.A.; Prof. Univ. of Paris II; Prof. Inst. d'Etudes Politiques de Paris 1986–92; Dir Soc. nat. des entreprises de presse 1974–76; Dir Soc. financière de radiodiffusion (Sofirad) 1972–76; fmr Dir E1, R.M.C., Sud Radio, S.N.E.P., T.D.F., Europe 1, Radio Monte Carlo; Maître de confs. Inst. d'études politiques, Paris 1966–73, Ecole nat. d'admin. 1967–69, Inst. int. d'admin. 1966–73; Pres. Dir-Gen. Burson Marsteller 1987–89; Pres. Quicom SA; mem. Exec. Cttee Int. Inst. of Communications, London, Pres. of French section; Pres. and Dir Gen. L & A Editions 2000–; Pres. and CEO Ilissos Editions 2002–; mem. Int. Press Inst.; Chevalier, Ordre nat. du Mérite; Commdr Nat. Order of Fed. Repub. of Germany. *Publications:* La France contemporaine, L'Europe contemporaine (both jointly) 1966–70, Saint Ecran ou la télévision par câbles 1974, Du téléphone à la télématique, La télévision par cable commence demain 1983, Le nouveau désordre mondial de l'information 1987, Les agences de presse 1997, Médias et déontologie 1997, Tendences Economiques Internationales de la Presse 2002. *Leisure interest:* tennis. *Address:* Ilissos

Editions, 14 rue de la Sourdière, 75001 Paris (Office); 23 quai Antatole France, 75007 Paris, France (Home). *Telephone:* 1-42-60-11-03 (Office); 1-45-51-70-01 (Home). *E-mail:* edesc@wanadoo.fr.

PIGGOTT, Lester Keith; British jockey and trainer; b. 5 Nov. 1935; s. of Keith Piggott and Iris Rickaby; m. Susan Armstrong 1960; two d.; rode over 100 winners per year in UK alone in several seasons since 1955; rode 3,000th winner in UK 27 July 1974; Champion Jockey 11 times (1960, 1964–71); frequently rode in France; equalled record of 21 classic victories 1975; 4,349 winners by Oct. 1985; retd Oct. 1985; races won include: the Derby (9 times): 1954 (on Never Say Die), 1957 (on Crepello), 1960 (on St Paddy), 1968 (on Sir Ivor), 1970 (on Nijinsky), 1972 (on Roberto), 1976 (on Empery), 1977 (on The Minstrel), 1983 (on Teenoso); St Leger (8 times); Prix de l'Arc de Triomphe (3 times): 1973 (on Rheingold), 1977 and 1978 (on Alleged); Washington, DC Int. 1968 (on Sir Ivor, first time since 1922 an English Derby winner raced in USA), 1969 (on Karabas), 1980 (on Argument); trainer 1985–87; sentenced to 3 years' imprisonment for tax fraud Oct. 1987, released after 12 months, returned to racing Oct. 1990; retd as jockey 1995; achieved a record of 30 classic wins. *Leisure interests:* swimming, water skiing, golf. *Address:* Florizel, Newmarket, Suffolk, CB8 0NY, England. *Telephone:* (1683) 662584 (Office).

PIGOTT-SMITH, Tim; British actor and director; b. 13 May 1946, Rugby; s. of Harry Pigott-Smith and Margaret Pigott-Smith; m. Pamela Miles 1972; one s.; ed Bristol Univ., Bristol Old Vic Theatre School; began stage career at Bristol Old Vic; mem. RSC 1972–75; Dir Company by Samuel Beckett, Edinburgh Fringe Festival 1988; Artistic Dir Compass Theatre 1989; Dir The Royal Hunt of the Sun 1989, Playing the Wife 1992, Hamlet, Regent's Park 1994; Hon. DLitt (Leicester) 2002; BAFTA Award for Best TV actor 1984, Broadcasting Press Guild Award for Best TV Actor 1984, TV Times Award for Best Actor on TV 1984. *Stage appearances include:* As You Like it, Major Barbara, Benefactors, Sherlock Holmes 1973, Broadway 1974, Bengal Lancer 1985, Antony and Cleopatra, Coming into Land 1987, Entertaining Strangers, Cymbeline, The Winter's Tale, The Tempest 1988, Julius Caesar 1990, Amadeus 1991, Old Times, Jane Eyre 1993, The Picture of Dorian Gray 1994, Retreat, The Letter 1995, Mary Stuart 1996, The Alchemist, Heritage 1997, The Iceman Cometh 1998, Broadway 1999, Five Kinds of Silence 2000, Julius Caesar 2001. *TV appearances include:* Hamlet, Antony and Cleopatra, Glittering Prizes, North and South, Wings, Eustace and Hilda, Lost Boys, Measure for Measure, Fame is the Spur, The Hunchback of Notre Dame, The Jewel in the Crown, Dead Man's Folly, Life Story 1990, The Chief 1990, 1991, 1992, The Adventures of Christopher Columbus, Bullion Boys 1993, The Shadowy Third, Calcutta Chronicles 1995, Innocents 2000, The Vice 2001, Kavanagh QC 2001, Dr. Terrible's House of Horrible 2001, Bloody Sunday 2002, Inspector Lynley Mystries. *Film appearances include:* Aces High 1975, Joseph Andrews 1977, Sweet William, Richard's Things 1978, The Day Christ Died 1979, Clash of the Titans 1981, Escape to Victory, State of Emergency, Life Story 1986, The Remains of the Day 1993, Four Feathers 2001, Laisser Passer 2001, Bloody Sunday 2002. *Publication:* Out of India 1986. *Leisure interests:* music, reading. *Address:* c/o Actual Management, 7 Great Russell Street, London, WC1B 3NH, England. *Telephone:* (20) 7631-4422 (Office).

PIKE, Edward Roy, PhD, FRS, CPhys, C.MATH., FInstP, F.I.M.A.; British physicist; b. 4 Dec. 1929, Perth, W Australia; s. of Anthony Pike and Rosalind Irene Davies; m. Pamela Sawtell 1955; one s. two d.; ed Southfield Grammar School, Oxford, Univ. Coll., Cardiff; Royal Corps of Signals 1948–50; Instructor Physics Faculty, MIT 1958–60; Sr Scientific Officer Royal Signals and Radar Establishment Physics Group 1960, Prin. Scientific Officer 1967, Deputy Chief Scientific Officer 1973, Chief Scientific Officer 1984–91; Visiting Prof. of Math. Imperial Coll. London 1985–86; Clerk Maxwell Prof. of Theoretical Physics, Univ. of London at King's Coll. 1986–, Head School of Physical Sciences and Eng 1991–94; fmr Fulbright Scholar; Chair. Oval (114) Ltd 1984–85; Vice-Pres. for Publs Inst. of Physics 1981–85; Chair. Adam Hilger Ltd 1981–85; Dir (non-exec.) Richard Clay plc 1985–86; Chair. Stilo Tech. Ltd 1996–2002; Chair. (non-exec.) Stilo Int. PLC 2000–02, Dir (non-exec.) 2002–; Royal Soc. Charles Parsons Medal and Lecture 1975, MacRobert Award (jtly.) and lecture 1977, Worshipful Co. of Scientific Instrument Makers Annual Achievement Award (jtly.) 1978, Guthrie Medal and Prize, Inst. of Physics 1996. *Publications:* The Quantum Theory of Radiation (jtly.) 1995, Light Scattering and Photon Correlation Spectroscopy (jtly.) 1997, Scattering (jtly.) 2002; Joint Ed.: Photon Correlation and Light-Beating Spectroscopy 1974, High Power Gas Lasers 1975, Photon Correlation Spectroscopy and Velocimetry 1977, Frontiers in Quantum Optics 1986, Fractals, Noise and Chaos 1987, Quantum Measurement and Chaos 1987, Squeezed and Non-classical Light 1988, Photons and Quantum Fluctuations 1988, Inverse Problems in Scattering and Imaging 1992; numerous papers in scientific journals. *Leisure interests:* music, languages, woodwork. *Address:* Physics Department, King's College, Strand, London WC2R 2LS; 3A Golborne Mews, North Kensington, London, W10 5SB, England. *Telephone:* (20) 7848-2043 (Office). *Fax:* (20) 7848-2420 (Office). *E-mail:* erp@maxwell.ph.kcl.ac.uk (Office). *Website:* www.kcl.ac.uk/kis/schools/phys-eng/physics/staff/acad/pike.htm (Office).

PIKE, Jimmy; Australian artist; m. Pat Lowe 1987; aboriginal artist; began painting and printmaking while serving prison sentence for murder 1980–86; work is represented in nat. and state galleries of Australia and in pvt. collections in Europe and America; comms from Australian Museum, Sydney, Art Gallery of NSW, Sydney, Art Gallery of South Australia, Adelaide, Art Gallery of Western Australia, Perth, Flinders Univ. Art Museum, Adelaide, Gold Coast City Art Gallery, Surfers Paradise, Queensland, Museum and Art Gallery of the Northern Territory, Darwin, Nat. Gallery of Australia, Canberra, Nat. Gallery of Vic., Melbourne, Nat. Maritime Museum, Darwin Harbour, Sydney, Parl. House Art Collection, Canberra, Queensland Art Gallery, Brisbane, The Holmes à Court Collection, Perth. *Solo exhibitions include:* Aboriginal Artists Gallery, Melbourne 1985, Sydney 1986, Black Swan Gallery, Fremantle 1986, Ben Grade Gallery, Fremantle 1987, Tynte Gallery, Adelaide 1987, 1988, Seibu Shibuya, Tokyo 1987, Birukmarri Gallery, Sydney 1988, Capricorn Gallery, Port Douglas 1988, Blaxland Gallery, Sydney and Melbourne 1988, Rebecca Hossack Gallery, London 1991, 1998. *Group exhibitions include:* Her Majesty's Theatre, Perth, Contemporary Aboriginal Art, Praxis, Fremantle 1985, Print Council Gallery, Melbourne 1987, Recent Aboriginal Art of Western Australia, Nat. Gallery of Australia, Canberra 1987, Fourth Nat. Aboriginal Art Award Exhbn, Museum and Art Gallery of the Northern Territory, Darwin 1987, Galerie Exler, Frankfurt 1987, Art and Aboriginality, Aspec Gallery, Portsmouth, UK 1987, Addendum Gallery, Fremantle 1987, Blaxland Galleries, Sydney 1988, Australian Aboriginal Graphics from the Collection of the Flinders University Art Museum 1988, Prints by Seven Australian Aboriginal Artists (int. touring exhbn) 1989, Aboriginal Art: The Continuing Tradition, Ant. Gallery of Australia, Canberra 1989, l'Eté Australien à Montpelier, Musée Fabre Gallery, Montpellier, France 1990, Balance 1990: Views, Visions, Influences, QAG, Brisbane 1990, Contemporary Aboriginal Art from the Robert Holmes a Court Collection, Harvard Univ., Univ. of Minnesota, Lake Oswego Centre for the Arts 1990, Tagari Lia: My Family, Contemporary Aboriginal Art, Third Eye Centre, Glasgow, UK 1990, Flash Pictures, Nat. Gallery of Australia, Canberra 1991, Eighth Nat. Aboriginal Art Award Exhbn, Museum and Art Gallery of the Northern Territory, Darwin 1991, Working in the Round, Flinders Univ. Art Museum, Adelaide 1992, Crossroads – Towards a New Reality, Aboriginal Art from Australia, Nat. Museums of Modern Art, Kyoto and Tokyo 1992, Ninth Nat. Aboriginal Art Award Exhbn, Museum and Art Gallery of the Northern Territory, Darwin 1992, New Tracks Old Land: An Exhibition of Contemporary Prints from Aboriginal Australia (touring USA and Australia) 1992–93, Tenth Nat. Aboriginal Art Award Exhbn, Museum and Art Gallery of the Northern Territory, Darwin 1993, Australian Heritage Commission Nat. Aboriginal and Torres Strait Islander Art Award Exhbn, Old Parl. House, Canberra 1993, Images of Power, Aboriginal Art of the Kimberly, Nat. Gallery of Vic., Melbourne 1993. *Address:* c/o Wendy Awart, Backroom Press, POB 1870, Broome, WA 6725, Australia (Office).

PIKHOYA, Rudolf Germanovich, D.HIST.SC.; Russian historian; b. 27 Jan. 1947, Polevskoe, Sverdlovsk Region; m.; one s.; ed Ural Univ.; with Ural Univ. 1971–, Sr researcher Ural Scientific Centre, USSR Acad. of Sciences 1981–86; Pro-rector Ural Univ. 1986–90; Chair. Cttee on problems of archives, Council of Ministers of Russian Fed. 1990–, Chief, Archive Service of Russia 1992–96; participated in movt for making secret documents of the Communist period public; Vice-Pres. Int. Fund for Democracy, Dir of Research Programmes 1996–98; Prof. and Chair. Acad. of State Service 1998–. *Leisure interest:* music. *Address:* Academy of State Service, Vernadskogo prospekt 84, 117606 Moscow, Russia. *Telephone:* (095) 436-98-14.

PILARCZYK, Most Rev. Daniel Edward, MA, PhD, STD; American ecclesiastic; b. 12 Aug. 1934, Dayton, Ohio; s. of Daniel J. Pilarczyk and Frieda S. Hilgefort; ed St Gregory Seminary, Ohio, Pontifical Urban Univ. Rome, Xavier Univ. Cincinnati and Univ. of Cincinnati; ordained Roman Catholic priest 1959; Asst Chancellor, Archdiocese of Cincinnati 1961–63; Faculty, Athenaeum of Ohio (St Gregory Seminary) 1963–74, Vice-Pres. 1968–74, Trustee 1974–; Rector, St Gregory Seminary 1968–74; Synodal Judge, Archdiocesan Tribunal 1971–82; Dir of Archdiocesan Educ. Services 1974–82; Auxiliary Bishop of Cincinnati 1974–82, Archbishop 1982–; Vice-Pres. Nat. Conf. of Catholic Bishops 1986–89; Pres. Nat. Conf. of Catholic Bishops 1989–92; mem. Episcopal Bd Int. Comm. on English in Liturgy 1987–97; mem. Jt Cttee of Orthodox and Catholic Bishops 2002; numerous professional appts; Hon. LLD (Xavier Univ.) 1975, (Calumet Coll.) 1982, (Univ. of Dayton) 1990, (Marquette Univ.) 1990, (Thomas More Coll.) 1991, (Coll. of Mount St Joseph) 1994, (Hebrew Union Coll./Jewish Inst. of Religion) 1997. *Publications:* Twelve Tough Issues 1988, We Believe 1989, Living in the Lord 1990, The Parish: Where God's People Live 1991, Forgiveness 1992, What Must I Do? 1993, Our Priests: Who They Are and What They Do 1994, Lenten Lunches 1995, Bringing Forth Justice 1996, Thinking Catholic 1997, Practicing Catholic 1998, Believing Catholic 2000, Live Letters 2001, Twelve Tough Issues and More 2002; numerous articles in newspapers and journals. *Address:* 100 East Eighth Street, Cincinnati, OH 45202, USA (Home). *Telephone:* (513) 421-3131.

PILGER, John Richard; Australian journalist, film-maker and author; b. 9 Oct. 1939, Sydney; s. of Claude Pilger and Elsie Pilger (née Marheine); m. (divorced); one s. one d.; ed Sydney High School, Journalism Cadet Training, Australian Consolidated Press; journalist Sydney Daily/Sunday Telegraph 1958–62; Reuters, London 1962; feature writer, columnist and Foreign Corresp. (latterly Chief Foreign Corresp.) Daily Mirror, London 1963–86; columnist New Statesman London 1991–; freelance contrib. The Guardian, London, The Independent, London, New York Times, Melbourne Age, The Nation, New York, South China Morning Post, Hong Kong, Aftonbladet, Sweden; Documentary film-maker, Granada TV UK 1969–71, Associated Television 1972–80, Cen. Television UK 1980–; credited with alerting much of int. community to horrors of Pol Pot régime in Cambodia, also occupation of Timor-Leste; Visiting Fellow Deakin Univ. 1995; Hon. D.Litt. (Staffordshire Univ.) 1994, Hon. PhD (Dublin City Univ.) 1995, Hon. D.Arts (Oxford Brookes Univ.) 1997, Hon. Dr.Iur. (St Andrews) 1999, Hon. PhD (Kingston) 1999, Hon. DUniv (Open Univ.) 2001; Descriptive Writer of the Year, UK 1966, Journalist of the Year, UK 1967 and 1979, Int. Reporter of the Year, UK 1970, Reporter of the Year, UK 1974, Richard Dimbleby Award, British Acad. of Film and TV Arts 1991, U.S. Acad. Award (Emmy) 1991, Reporteurs sans frontières, France 1993, George Foster Peabody Award (USA) 1992. *Exhibitions:* Reporting the World: John Pilger's Great Eyewitness Photographers, The Barbican Summer Exhbn 2001. *Feature film:* The Last Day 1983. *Documentary films include:* Cambodia: Year Zero 1979 (and four other films on Cambodia), The Quiet Mutiny 1970, Japan Behind the Mask 1986, The Last Dream 1988, Death of a Nation 1994, Flying the Flag: Arming the World 1994, Inside Burma 1996, Breaking The Mirror: The Murdoch Effect 1997, Apartheid Did Not Die 1998, Welcome to Australia 1999, Paying the Price: Killing the Children of Iraq 2000, The New Rules of the World 2001. *Publications:* The Last Day 1975, Aftermath: The Struggle of Cambodia and Vietnam 1981, The Outsiders 1983, Heroes 1986, A Secret Country 1989, Distant Voices 1992, Hidden Agendas 1998, The New Rulers of the World 2002, Palestine is Still the Issue 2002. *Leisure interests:* swimming, running, reading, sunning, mulling. *Address:* 57 Hambalt Road, London, SW4 9EQ, England. *Telephone:* (20) 8673-2848. *Fax:* (20) 8772-0235. *Website:* www .johnpilger.com.

PILIKIAN, Hovhanness Israel, MA; British theatre director, author, academic and film maker; b. 15 April 1942, Nineveh-Mosul, Iraq; m. 1st Gail Rademacher (dissolved 1992, died 2000); two s. one d.; m. 2nd Clarice Stephens 1993; one s. two d.; ed Univ. of Munich, Univ. of London, Royal Acad. of Dramatic Art, Open Univ.; has directed more than 40 plays (specializing in classical Greek drama); cr. Hanano Mask Theatre Co. 1970, Cervantes Players (first all-black actors' company in Europe), London 1971; f. Spice of Life Theatre Club 1980, Bloomsbury Theatre Club 1982; Consultant, Cheltenham Int. Guitar Music Festival 2001; mem. Acad. Bd City Literature Inst. 2001–; Fellow, Royal Anthropological Inst., Deutscher Akademischer Austauschdienst; Life mem. Swedenborg Soc. of GB; mem. Turner Soc.; Visiting Prof. State Univ. of Yerevan, Dutch Drama Center, Slade School of Art, Cen. School of Art and Design, Yerevan Inst. of Literature, Armenian Acad. of Sciences; Adamian Award for Lifetime Achievement, Ministry of Culture of Armenian SSR 1985. *Films:* The New Supremes in London 1986, A King of Arabia 1987. *Plays directed include:* Euripides' Electra (Greenwich Theatre, London) 1971, Euripides' Medea (Yvonne Arnaud Theatre) 1971, William Alfred's Agamemnon (McCartur Theater, Princeton Univ.) 1973, Sophocles' Oedipus Tyrannus (Chichester Festival Theatre) 1974, Schiller's Die Räuber (Roundhouse) 1975, King Lear (Nat. Theatre of Iceland) 1977, Fat Hamlet (Shaw Theatre, London) 1993. *Achievements:* organized and produced first ever season of Armenian Cinema for the Nat. Film Theatre, London 1981; Armenian Cinema weeks in Venice 1983, Paris 1986, Montreal 2000. *Publications include:* My Hamlet 1961, An Armenian Symphony and Other Poems 1980, Armenian Cinema, A Source Book 1981, Flower of Japanese Theatre 1984, Aspects of Armenian History 1986. *Leisure interests:* book mad – pvt. library of 10,000 books and expanding... *Address:* 4 Berkeley Crescent, New Barnet, Herts., EN4 8BP, England. *Telephone:* (20) 8441-9807.

PILLAY, Navanethem, BA, LLM, SJD; South African judge and United Nations official; b. 23 Sept. 1941, Durban; m. (died); two d.; ed Natal Univ., Harvard Univ., USA; first woman to start a law practice in Natal Prov. 1967, Sr Partner 1967–95; first black woman apptd Acting Judge High Court of SA 1995; Judge, UN Int. Criminal Tribunal for Rwanda (ICTR) 1995–2003, Pres. 1999–2003; Judge, Int. Criminal Court 2003–; Chair. Equality Now 1990–95, Hon. Chair. 1995–; Pres. Advice Desk for Abused Women 1989–99, Women Lawyers' Asscn 1995–98; Vice-Chair. of Council, Univ. of Durban-Westville 1995–98; Lecturer, Dept of Public Law, Natal Univ. 1980; Trustee, Legal Resources Centre 1995–98, Lawyers for Human Rights 1998–2001; mem. Women's Nat. Coalition 1992–93, Black Lawyers' Asscn 1995–98, UN Expert Groups on Refugees and on Gender Persecution 1997, Rules Bd for Courts 1997–98, Expert Group on African Perspectives on Universal Jurisdiction, Cairo and Arusha 2001–02; currently mem. Int. Criminal Law Network, Advisory Bd Journal of Int. Criminal Justice, Bd Harvard–South Africa Scholarship Cttee, Bd of Dirs Nozala Investments (women's component of Nat. Econ. Initiative) Unifem and Noel Foundation Life Award (Los Angeles); Award for Leadership in the Fight for Human Rights, California Legislative Assembly; Dr Edgar Brookes Award, Natal Univ.; Award for Outstanding Contrib. in Raising Awareness of Women's Rights and Domestic Violence, Advice Desk for Abused Women; Award for Dedication to Human Rights, Equality Now, New York; One Hundred Heroines Award, Washington DC; Human Rights Award, Int. Assen of Women Judges; Award for High Achievement by a Woman in the Legal Profession, Center for Human Rights and Univ. of Pretoria; further awards from Assen of Law Soc. of SA, Black Lawyers' Assen, Feminist Majority Foundation. *Publications:* (contrib.): Civilians in War 2001, Essays in Memory of Judge Cassese 2003. *Address:* International Criminal Court (ICC), Maanweg 174, 2516 AB, The Hague, The Netherlands (Office); 16 Lavery Crescent, Durban 4091, South Africa (Home). *Telephone:* (70) 5158515 (Office); (31) 208-2851 (Home). *Fax:* (70) 5158555 (Office); (31) 208-8207 (Home). *E-mail:* pillayn@un.org (Office); dqnowdbn@ wn.apc.org (Home). *Website:* www.icc-cpi.int.

PILLINGER, Colin Trevor, PhD, FRS, FRAS, F.R.G.S.; British professor of planetary science; b. 9 May 1943; s. of Alfred Pillinger and Florence Honour; m. Judith Mary Hay 1975; one s. one d.; ed Kingswood Grammar School, Univ. Coll. Swansea, Univ. of Wales; Post-doctoral Fellow, Dept of Chem., Univ. of Bristol 1968–72, BSC Fellow 1972–74, Research Assoc. 1974–76; Research Assoc. and Sr Research Assoc., Dept of Earth Science, Cambridge 1976–84; Sr Research Fellow, Dept of Earth Science, Open Univ. 1984–90, Prof. of Planetary Science 1990–; Lead Scientist Beagle 2 project, Lander element of European Space Agency's Mars Express Mission 1997–; Fellow Meteoritical Soc. 1986; mem. British Mass Spectrometry Soc.; Hon. DSc (Bristol) 1985. *Publications:* numerous papers in scientific journals. *Leisure interests:* animals, farming, football. *Address:* Planetary and Space Sciences Research Institute, Open University, Milton Keynes, MK7 6AA, England (Office). *Telephone:* (1908) 652119 (Office). *Fax:* (1908) 655910 (Office).

PILLSBURY, Edmund Pennington, PhD; American museum director; b. 28 April 1943, San Francisco, Calif.; s. of Edmund P. Pillsbury and Priscilla K. (Giesen) Pillsbury; m. Mireille Marie-Christine Bernard 1969; one s. one d.; ed Yale Univ. and Univ. of London; David E. Finley Fellow, Nat. Gallery of Art, Washington, DC 1967–70; Ford Foundation Fellow, Cleveland Museum of Art 1970–71; Curator, European Art, Yale Univ. Gallery and Lecturer, History of Art, Yale Univ. 1972–76; Dir Yale Center, British Art and Adjunct Prof. of History of Art Yale Univ. 1976–80; CEO Paul Mellon Centre, Studies in British Art, London 1976–80; Dir Kimbell Art Museum and Vice-Pres. Kimbell Art Foundation 1980–; mem. Presidential Task Force on Arts and Humanities 1981, The Century Assen 1991; Adjunct Prof. Tex. Christian Univ. 1985; Chevalier, Ordre des Arts et des Lettres. *Publications:* Florence and the Arts 1971, David Hockney: Travels with Pen, Pencil and Ink 1977, The Graphic Art of Federico Barocci 1978. *Leisure interests:* skiing, running, reading. *Address:* Kimbell Art Museum, 3333 Camp Bowie Boulevard, Fort Worth, TX 76107 (Office); 1110 Broad Avenue, Fort Worth, TX 76107, USA (Home). *Telephone:* (817) 332-8451.

PILON, Jean-Guy, OC, BA, LLL; Canadian poet; b. 12 Nov. 1930, St Polycarpe; s. of Arthur Pilon and Alida Besner; m. 2nd Denise Viens 1988; two s. from 1st marriage; ed Univ. de Montreal; founded Liberté (review) 1959, Ed. 1959–79; Head of Cultural Programmes and Producer Radio-Canada 1970–88; Les Ecrits (literary review); mem. Académie des lettres du Québec 1982, Royal Soc. of Canada 1967–; Prix de Poésie du Québec 1956, Louise Labé (Paris) 1969, France-Canada 1969, van Lerberghe (Paris) 1969, du Gouverneur gén. du Canada 1970, Athanase-David 1984, Prix littéraire int. de la Paix (PEN Club Quebec) 1991; Ordre du Canada 1986, Chevalier Ordre Nat. du Québec 1987, Officier Ordre des Arts et des Lettres (France) 1992. *Publications (poems):* La fiancée du matin 1953, Les cloîtres de l'été 1954, L'homme et le jour 1957, La mouette et le large 1960, Recours au pays 1961, Pour saluer une ville 1963, Comme eau retenue 1969 (enlarged edn 1985), Saisons pour la continuelle 1969, Silences pour une souveraine 1972. *Address:* 5724 Côte St-Antoine, Montreal, PQ, H4A 1R9, Canada.

PILSWORTH, Michael John, MA; British television executive; b. 1 April 1951, Leeds; s. of Alwyne Pilsworth and Catherine Pilsworth (née Silverwood); m. Stella Frances Pilsworth (née Hore) 1972; one s. one d.; ed King Edward VI Grammar School, Retford, Univ. of Manchester; Research Asst Inst. of Advanced Studies, Manchester Polytechnic 1972–73; Research Associate Univ. of Manchester 1973–75, lecturer 1973–77; Research Fellow, Centre for TV Research 1977–79, Univ. of Leeds 1979–81; researcher, London Weekend 1982–83; Head of Programme Devt TV South 1984–86, Controller Corp. Devt 1987–88; Chief Exec. M.G.M.M. Communications Ltd 1988–89; Man. Dir Alomo Productions Ltd 1990–92, Selec TV P.L.C. 1992–93; Chief Exec. Chrysalis TV Group Ltd 1993–. *Publications:* co-author Broadcasting in the Third World 1977. *Leisure interests:* reading, cinema, gardening. *Address:* Chrysalis Group PLC, The Chrysalis Building, Bramley Road, London, W10 6SP (Office); 1 Church Lane, Eaton Bray, Beds., LU6 2DJ, England. *Telephone:* (20) 7221-2213 (Office). *Fax:* (20) 7465-6159 (Office).

PIMENTA, HE Cardinal Simon Ignatius, DCL; Indian ecclesiastic; b. 1 March 1920, Bombay (now Mumbai); s. of Joseph Pimenta and Rosie Pimenta; ordained 1949, elected to the titular Church of Bocconia 1971, consecrated bishop 1971, coadjutor bishop 1977, Archbishop of Bombay 1978–97 (retd); cr. HE Cardinal 1988. *Publications:* Priest for Ecer 1999, Memoirs and Milestones 2000, Cardinal Valerian Gracias 2002. *Address:* Archbishop's House, 21 Nathalal Parekh Marg, Mumbai 400 001, India. *Telephone:* (22) 2202-1093; (22) 2204-9696. *Fax:* (22) 2285-3872. *E-mail:* cardsp@vsnl.net.

PIMLOTT, Benjamin (Ben) John, FBA, PhD, FRHistS; British professor of politics and contemporary history; b. 4 July 1945; s. of the late John Alfred Ralph Pimlott, C.B. and Ellen Dench Howes Pimlott; m. Jean Ann Seaton 1977; three s.; ed Rokeby School, Wimbledon, Marlborough Coll. and Oxford and Newcastle Univs; Lecturer Newcastle Univ. 1970–79; Resident Assoc. LSE 1979–81; lecturer Birkbeck Coll., Univ. of London 1981–86, Reader 1986–87, Professor of Politics and Contemporary History 1987–98; Nuffield Foundation Resident Fellow 1977–78; Chair. ESRC Whitehall Programme Commissioning Panel 1993–94, Steering Cttee 1994–99; contested parl. seat at Arundel 1974, Cleveland and Whitby 1974, 1979; political columnist Today 1986–87, The Times 1987–88, New Statesman (political ed.) 1987–88, Sunday Times 1988–89; Ed. Samizdat 1988–90; Warden Goldsmiths Coll. 1998–; mem. Exec. Fabian Soc. 1987–, Chair. 1993–94; Fellow Birkbeck Coll. London 1999; Hon. Fellow St Cross Coll. Oxford 2001. *Publications:* Labour and the

Left in the 1930s 1977, Hugh Dalton 1985 (Whitbread Biography Prize), Harold Wilson 1992, Frustrate Their Knavish Tricks 1994, The Queen 1996, Elizabeth II and the Monarchy 2001, Governing London (with Nirmala Rao) 2002; Editor: Trade Unions in British Politics (with Chris Cook) 1982, Fabian Essays in Socialist Thought 1984, The Second World War Diary of Hugh Dalton 1940–45 1986, The Political Diary of Hugh Dalton 1918–40, 1945–60 1987, The Media in British Politics (with Jean Seaton) 1987, The Alternative (with A. Wright and T. Flower) 1990, Tackling the Inner Cities (with S. MacGregor) 1990; articles in learned journals and articles and reviews in nat. newspapers and other publs. *Address:* Goldsmiths College, New Cross, London, SE14 6NW (Office); 9 Milner Place, London, N1 1TN, England. *Telephone:* (20) 7919-7901 (Office); (20) 7609-1793.

PIMLOTT, Steven, MA; British theatre and opera director; b. 18 April 1953, Manchester; m. Daniela Bechly 1991; two s. one d.; ed Univ. of Cambridge; began career in regional theatre and opera; work directed includes: The Park 1984, Twelfth Night (Crucible Theatre, Sheffield) 1986, Samson et Delila (Bregenz) 1988, Carmen (Earl's Court, London) 1990, Sunday in the Park with George (Nat. Theatre) 1990, Molière's The Miser (Nat. Theatre) 1991, Joseph and the Amazing Technicolour Dreamcoat (Palladium, London) 1991, (Broadway) 1993, Julius Caesar (RSC, Stratford) 1991, Murder in the Cathedral (RSC, Stratford) 1993, La Bohème (ENO) 1993, Unfinished Business (RSC, Barbican) 1994, Butterfly Kiss (Almeida) 1994, Measure for Measure (RSC, Stratford) 1994, The Strip (Royal Court) 1995, Macbeth (Hamburg-Staatsoper) 1997, Camino Real (RSC), Never Land (Royal Court), Bad Weather (RSC), musical staging of Doctor Doolittle (Triumph Apollo) 1998, Hamlet (RSC) 2001; Dir 1996/97 RSC Season, including productions of As You Like It and The Learned Ladies, 1998/99 RSC Antony and Cleopatra, 2000 RSC Richard II, 2001 RSC Hamlet; world premiere of Ion Almeida opera L'incoronazione di Poppea, ENO; Assoc. Dir RSC 1996–2002, Assoc. Artist 2002–; Artistic Dir The Other Place RSC 1999–2001; world première of Bombay Dreams (Apollo Victoria, London) 2002; Artistic Dir Chichester Festival Theatre 2003–. *Leisure interest:* playing the oboe. *Address:* c/o Harriet Cruickshank, 97 Old South Lambeth Road, London, SW8 1XU; Old House, Old House Road, Great Horkesley, Colchester, Essex, CO6 4EQ, England.

PINA-CABRAL, João de, DPhil; Portuguese social anthropologist; b. 9 May 1954; s. of Daniel de Pina Cabral and Ana A. de Pina Cabral; ed Univ. of Witwatersrand, Johannesburg and Univ. of Oxford; Auxiliary Prof. Dept of Social Anthropology, ISCTE, Lisbon 1982–84, Assoc. Prof. 1988–; Gulbenkian Fellow in Portuguese Studies, Univ of Southampton 1984–86; Research Fellow, Inst. of Social Sciences, Univ. of Lisbon 1986–92, Sr Research Fellow 1992–, Pres. Scientific Bd; Pres. European Asscn of Social Anthropologists 2002–(04); Malinowski Memorial Lecturer 1992. *Publications:* Death in Portugal (co-ed.) 1983, Sons of Adam, Daughters of Eve 1986, Os Contextos da Antropologia 1991, Europe Observed (co-ed.) 1992, Aromas de Urze e de Lama 1993, Em Terra de Tufões 1993, Elites (co-ed.) 2000, Between China and Europe 2002. *Address:* Institute of Social Sciences, University of Lisbon, 9 Avenida A. Bettencourt, 1600-189 Lisbon, Portugal. *Telephone:* (21) 7995000. *Fax:* (21) 7964953. *E-mail:* pina.cabral@ics.ul.pt (Office).

PINARD, Hon. Yvon, BA, LLL; Canadian politician and lawyer; b. 10 Oct. 1940, Drummondville, Québec; s. of Jean-Jacques Pinard and Cécile Chassé; m. Renée Chaput 1964; two d.; ed Immaculate Conception School, Drummondville, Nicolet Seminary, Sherbrooke Univ.; Pres. Sherbrooke Univ. Law Faculty 1963; admitted to Québec Bar 1964; Pres. and founder Drummond Caisse d'Entraide Economique; Pres. Drummond Liberal Asscn 1968–70; mem. Admin. Council Centre Communautaire d'Aide Juridique Mauricie-Bois-Francs region; mem. Commonwealth Parl. Asscn and Canadian Del. Interparl. Union; mem. House of Commons 1974–84; Parl. Sec. to Pres. of Privy Council Oct. 1977; Pres. of HM the Queen's Privy Council for Canada 1980–84; Judge Federal Court of Canada, Trial Div. Judge 1984–; mem. ex-officio Fed. Court of Appeal 1984–; Liberal. *Address:* Federal Court of Canada, Ottawa, Ont., K1A 0H9, Canada.

PINAULT, François; French business executive; b. 21 Aug. 1936, Champs Géraux, Côtes-du-Nord; s. of François Pinault and Eugénie Gabillard; m. Mary Campbell 1970; two s. two d.; ed Coll. Saint-Martin, Rennes; worked in father's timber co. at age 16; f. Société Pinault, Rennes 1963, Prés.-Dir-Gén. 1970; Pres. Co. française de l'Afrique occidentale (CFAO) 1990–91; Vice-Pres. Supervisory Bd Groupe Pinault-Printemps 1992; Prés.-Dir-Gén. Artémis SA 1992; Head Christie's UK 1998–; owns vineyard Château Latour, Vail ski resort in Colo, luggage mfr. Samsonite and majority shareholding in French real estate investment co. Sefimeg; Officier, Légion d'honneur, Croix de la Valeur Militaire. *Leisure interests:* cinema, theatre, art collecting, cycling, walking. *Address:* Artémis SA, 5 blvd de Latour Maubourg, 75007 Paris, France; Christies International PLC, 8 King Street, London, SW1, England.

PINCAY, Laffit, Jr; Panamanian jockey; b. 29 Dec. 1946, Panama City; m. 1st Linda Pincay 1967 (died 1985), one s. one d.; m. 2nd Jeanine Pincay, one s.; rode first winner 1964, first U.S. winner 1966, 3,000th winner 1975; Winner Belmont Stakes 1982, 1983, 1984, Ky Derby 1984; rode 6,000th winner 1985; broke Willie Shoemaker's record of 8,834 wins 1999; first jockey to reach 9,000 wins; seven Breeders' Cup wins; Eclipse Award 1971, 1973, 1974, 1979, 1985.

PINCOTT, Leslie Rundell, CBE, FCA; British company director (retd); b. 27 March 1923, London; s. of Hubert George and Gertrude Elizabeth (Rundell) Pincott; m. 1st Mary Mae Tuffin 1944 (died 1996); two s. one d.; m. 2nd Elaine Sunderland 1997; ed Mercers School, Holborn, London, Harvard Business School, USA; Lt in RDVR 1942–46; qualified as chartered accountant; worked for Exxon 1950–1978, Man. Dir 1970–78; Chair. Oxford Univ. Business Summer School 1975–78; Vice-Chair. Remploy Ltd 1979–87 (Dir 1975–79); Dir British Railways Southern Bd 1977–86, Chair. 1986–89; Pres. Dist Heating Asscn 1977–79; Chair. Canada Perm. Trust (UK) Ltd 1978–80, Dir in Toronto; Dir George Wimpey PLC 1978–85, Brown & Root-Wimpey Highlands Fabricators Ltd 1984–91; Deputy Chair., Chair. Price Comm. 1978–80; Chair. Stone-Platt Industries Ltd 1980–82, Edman Communications Group PLC 1982–87, Printing Industries Econ. Devt Cttee 1982–88; mem. Investment Cttee, London Devt Capital Devt Fund 1984–99; Chair. The Hurlingham Club 1989–92, Trustee 1996–98; mem. bd Wandle Housing Asscn 1996, Chair. 1997–99; Chair. Hurlingham Court Ltd 1999–. *Leisure interests:* walking, travel, swimming, bowls. *Address:* 53 Hurlingham Court, Ranelagh Gardens, London, SW6 3UP, England (Home). *Telephone:* (20) 7736-1440 (Home).

PINE, Courtney, OBE; British jazz saxophonist and composer; b. 18 March 1964; m. June Guishard 1997; one s. three d.; founder mem. Jazz Warriors 1985–, The Abiba Jazz Arts 1985–; tours internationally with reggae and acoustic jazz bands; Musical Dir Windrush Gala Concert, BBC TV 1998; organizes free workshops for young people in many cos.; MOBO for Best Jazz Act 1996, Best Album of the Year for Modern Day Jazz Stories, Mercury Music Prize 1996. *Solo albums include:* Journey to the Urge Within 1986 (Silver Award), Destiny's Song and The Image of Pursuance 1988, The Vision's Tale 1989, Closer to Home 1990, Within the Realm of Our Dreams 1991, To the Eyes of Creation 1993, Modern Day Jazz Stories 1996, Underground 1997, Another Story 1998; soundtrack for History is Made at Night 1999, Back in the Day 2000; guest appearances with Mick Jagger on Wandering Spirit (album), Jazz Jamaica on Police tribute album; featured artist on The Glory of Gershwin (Larry Adler tribute album); recorded tracks for Evita soundtrack with Madonna. *Radio:* presented BBC Radio 2 series Millennium Jazz 1999. *Address:* c/o Tickety Boo Ltd, The Boathouse, Crabtree Lane, Fulham, London, SW6 6TY, England (Office); Collaboration, 23 Avenue Crescent, London, W3 8ET. *Telephone:* (20) 7610-0122 (Office).

PINEAU-VALENCIENNE, Didier; French company director; b. 21 March 1931, Paris; s. of Maurice and Madeleine (née Dubigeon) Pineau-Valencienne; m. Guillemette Rident 1964; one s. three d.; ed Lycée Janson-de-Sailly, Paris, Dartmouth Univ. (USA) and Harvard Business School; Man. Asst Banque Parisienne pour l'Industrie 1958, Prin. Man. Asst 1962, Dir 1964–67, Dir-Gen. 1969 and Admin. 1971; Pres. and Dir-Gen. Carbonisation et Charbons Actifs (CECA) 1972–74, Société Resogil 1975–76; Dir-Gen. Société Celogil 1975–76; Admin. Isorel 1976; Dir of Admin. and Strategy and Planning Rhone-Poulenc SA 1976–77, Dir-Gen. (Polymer Div.) 1978; Admin. Quartz et Silice; Admin., Vice–Pres., Dir-Gen. Schneider SA 1980–81, Pres.-Dir-Gen. 1981–98; Pres.-Dir-Gen. Jeumont-Schneider 1987–89, Pres. Schneider Industries Services Int. 1991–92, Schneider Electric SA 1993–98; Asst Admin. Société Electrorail SA 1980–; Dir Merlin-Gérin 1981–, Pres.-Dir-Gen. 1989–; Chair. Empain-Schneider Group 1981–, Société Parisienne d'Etudes et de Participations 1982–; Chair. and Man. Dir Creusot-Loire 1982–84; Vice-Chair. Crédit Suisse First Boston, London 1999–; Dir Paribas 1989–98, Whirlpool Corpn 1992–; Pres. Admin. Council, Tech. Univ. of Compiègne 1992–96; Pres. Inst. de L'Entreprise 1993–96, Hon. Pres. 1996–; Pres. Asscn française des entreprises privées 1999–; Vice-Pres. and Pres. Comm. Sociale du Conseil nat. du patronat français (CNPF) 1997; Chair. Advisory Bd Sisie 1997–98; fmr teacher Ecole des Hautes Etudes Commerciales; Officier, Légion d'honneur, Officier Ordre nat. du Mérite. *Leisure interests:* tennis, skiing, collecting books. *Address:* Afep, 63 rue de la Boétie, 75008 Paris, France (Office); Crédit Suisse First Boston, 1 Cabot Square, London, E14, England (Office).

PINHEIRO FARINHA, João de Deus; Portuguese judge; b. 8 March 1919, Redondo; s. of Simão Martins Pereira and Isabel Gapete (Pinheiro) Farinha; m. Maria das Dores Pombinho 1947; ed Liceu Nacional André da Gouveia and Univ. of Lisbon; Deputy Public Prosecutor 1943–50; Insp. of Prison Services 1944–49; Judge, Leiria Industrial Court 1950–51; Judge in lower courts 1951–66; Asst Public Prosecutor 1957–58; Pres. Corregitor (3rd Civil Chamber) 1966–70; Judge, Coimbra and Lisbon Appeal Courts 1970–74; Attorney-Gen. 1974; Minister of Justice 1975–76, of Foreign Affairs 1991–92; Commr of the European Communities (now European Comm.) for Openness, Communication and Culture 1993–95, for Relations with African, Caribbean and Pacific Countries, S. Africa, the Lomé Convention 1995–99; mem. Perm. Court of Arbitration 1977–91; Pres. Court of Accounts 1977–91; Judge, European Court of Human Rights 1977–, Supreme Court of Justice 1978–; Vice-Pres. Int. Comm. on Civil Status 1977–79, Pres. 1980; Hon. DEng (Birmingham) 1992; Gold Medal of Penitentiary Social Merit (Spain), Medal of Council of Europe. *Publications:* many legal publications. *Leisure interests:* travel, philosophy, religion. *Address:* Supremo Tribunal de Justiça, Praça do Comércio, 1149-012 Lisbon; Avenida Dr. Baraona 14, 7170 Lisbon, Portugal (Home). *Telephone:* (21) 3218900 (Office); 99197 (Home). *Fax:* (21) 3474919 (Office).

PINKAYAN, Subin, PhD; Thai politician and engineer; b. 16 June 1934, Chiang Mai; m. Boonsri Pinkayan; one s.; ed Chulalongkorn Univ., Asian Inst. of Tech. and Univ. of Colo; researcher Univ. of Colo; Eng consultant, Mekong Cttee; Irrigation Dept 1967–74; Project Dir Asian Inst. of Tech. 1974; lecturer

Chulalongkorn Univ.; Assoc. Prof. Asian Inst. of Tech.; Social Action Party MP for Chiang Mai 1983–; fmr Univ. Affairs Minister; Deputy Leader Social Action Party; Minister of Foreign Affairs Sept.–Dec. 1990. *Address:* c/o Ministry of Foreign Affairs, Saranrom Palace, Bangkok 10200, Thailand.

PINKER, Sir George Douglas, KCVO, F.R.C.S.ED., FRCOG, FRCS; British gynaecologist and obstetrician (rtd); b. 6 Dec. 1924; s. of Ronald D. Pinker and Queenie E. Dix; m. Dorothy E. Russell; three s. one d.; ed Reading School and St Mary's Hosp., London; fmrly consultant gynaecological surgeon, Bolingbroke Hosp. and resident officer, Nuffield Dept of Obstetrics, Radcliffe Infirmary, Oxford; fmrly consultant gynaecological surgeon, Queen Charlotte's Hosp., London; consulting gynaecological surgeon and obstetrician, St Mary's Hosp. Paddington and Samaritan Hosp. 1958–89; consulting gynaecological surgeon, Middx and Soho Hosps 1969–80; consultant gynaecologist, King Edward VII Hosp. for Officers, London 1974–89; Surgeon-Gynaecologist to HM Queen Elizabeth II 1973–90; mem. Royal Coll. of Obstetricians and Gynaecologists, Pres. 1987–90; Pres. Royal School of Medicine 1992–94; Hon. mem. Royal Coll. of Surgeons in Ireland, Coll. of Obstetrics and Gynaecology, USA, Coll. of Medicine, South Africa; Hon. Fellow Royal Coll. of Obstetrics and Gynocology, Australia. *Publications:* co-author of three books on obstetrics and gynaecology. *Leisure interests:* music, gardening, sailing, skiing, fell walking. *Address:* 96 Harley Street, London, W1N 1AF; Sycamore House, Willersey, Broadway, Worcs., WR12 7PJ, England.

PINKER, Robert Arthur, MSc; British professor of administration; b. 27 May 1931; s. of Dora Elizabeth Pinker and Joseph Pinker; m. Jennifer Farrington Boulton 1955 (died 1994); two d.; ed Holloway Co. School, London School of Econs; Head Sociology Dept, Goldsmiths Coll., London Univ. 1964–72, Lewisham Prof. of Social Admin., Goldsmiths Coll. and Bedford Coll. 1972–74; Prof. of Social Studies, Chelsea Coll. 1974–78; Prof. of Social Work Studies, LSE 1978–93, Prof. of Social Admin. 1993–96, Emer. Prof. of Social Admin. 1996–, Pro-Dir LSE 1985–88; Pro-Vice-Chancellor for Social Sciences, London Univ. 1989–90; Chair. Editorial Bd Journal of Social Policy 1981–86; Chair. British Library Project on Family and Social Research 1983–86; Acting Chair. Press Complaints Comm. 2002–; mem. Council, Advertising Standards Authority 1988–95, Press Complaints Comm. 1991–, Privacy Commr 1994–, Acting Chair. 2002–03, Council, Direct Mail Accreditation and Recognition Centre 1995–97, Bd of Man. London School of Hygiene and Tropical Medicine 1990–94; Chair. Govs. Centre for Policy on Ageing 1988–94; Hon. Fellow Goldsmiths Coll., Univ. of London 1999–. *Publications:* English Hospital Statistics 1861–1938 1964, Social Theory and Social Policy 1971, The Idea of Welfare 1979, Social Work in an Enterprise Society 1990. *Leisure interests:* reading, writing, travel, unskilled gardening. *Address:* Press Complaints Commission, 1 Salisbury Square, London, EC4Y 8JB (Office); 76 Coleraine Road, Blackheath, London, SE3 7PE, England (Home). *Telephone:* (20) 7955-7358 (Office); (20) 8858-5320 (Home). *Fax:* (20) 8293-4770 (Home). *E-mail:* rpinker@freenetname.co.uk (Home).

PINKER, Steven, BA, PhD; American psychologist, scientist and university professor; b. 18 Sept. 1954, Montreal, Canada; s. of Harry Pinker and Roslyn Pinker; m. Ilavenil Subbiah 1995; ed McGill Univ., Canada, Harvard Univ.; Asst Prof., Harvard Univ. 1980–81, Stanford Univ. 1981–82; Prof., MIT 1982–, Margaret MacVicar Fellow 2000–; Hon. DSc (McGill) 1999; William James Book Prize, American Psychological Asscn (for The Language Instinct) 1995, (for How the Mind Works) 1999, Golden Plate Award, American Acad. of Achievement 1999. *Publications include:* Learnability and Cognition: The Acquisition of Argument Structure 1989, The Language Instinct 1994, How the Mind Works 1997, Words and Rules: The Ingredients of Language 1999, The Blank Slate: The Modern Denial of Human Nature 2002. *Leisure interests:* bicycling, photography. *Address:* Department of Brain and Cognitive Sciences NEW20-413, Massachusetts Institute of Technology, Cambridge, MA 02139, USA (Office). *Telephone:* (617) 253-8946 (Office). *Fax:* (617) 258-8654 (Office). *E-mail:* steve@psyche.mit.edu (Office). *Website:* www.mit.edu/~pinker (Office).

PINNOCK, Trevor David, CBE, ARCM, FRAM; British harpsichordist and conductor; b. 16 Dec. 1946, Canterbury; s. of Kenneth and Joyce Pinnock; ed Canterbury Cathedral School, Royal Coll. of Music, London; Jt F. Galliard Harpsichord Trio, début, London 1966, solo début, London 1968, Dir The English Concert 1973–; Artistic Dir, Prin. Conductor Nat. Arts Centre Orchestra, Ottawa 1991–96, Artistic Adviser 1996–; has toured Western Europe, USA, South America, Canada, Australia, Japan with The English Concert, as solo harpsichordist and as orchestral/opera conductor; début Metropolitan Opera, New York 1988; Gramophone Award for Bach Partitas BWV 825-30 2001. *Recordings include:* Handel, J. S. Bach, C. P. E. Bach, Rameau, Vivaldi, Scarlatti, 16th-, 17th- and 18th-century harpsichord music and most of the standard baroque orchestral/concerto/choral repertoire. *Address:* c/o Askonas Holt Ltd, 27 Chancery Lane, London, WC2A 1PF, England.

PINOCHET UGARTE, Gen. Augusto; Chilean army officer; b. 25 Nov. 1915; m. María Lucía Hiriat Rodríguez; two s. three d.; ed Mil. Acad., School of Infantry, Acad. of War, Acad. of Nat. Defence; Army career 1933–98, Col 1966, Brig.-Gen. 1969, Div. Gen. 1970, Gen. 1973; Instructor Acad. of War 1954, Deputy Dir 1964; Asst to Under-Sec. of War 1954; mem. Chilean mil. mission to USA 1956; Instructor Acad. of War, Ecuador 1956–59; C-in-C VI Army Div., Chief of Army Staff 1969; C-in-C of Armed Forces 1973–98; Senator for Life 1998–2000; led coup to depose President Salvador Allende

Sept. 1973; Pres. Gov. Council of Chile 1973–74; Pres. of Chile 1974–90; Pres. Junta Militar; arrested in London Oct. 1998 and charged on 32 counts of torture and murder; Law Lords rule that he does not enjoy immunity from sovereign prosecution 1998; Home Sec. allows proposed extradition to Spain Dec. 1998; Lords ruling overturned 1998, ruling on immunity sustained after further hearings March 1999; Home Sec. authorizes start of further extradition proceedings April 1999; declared mentally unfit to stand trial Jan. 2000; released from Britain on "compassionate grounds" March 2000 and returned to Chile; stripped of immunity from prosecution in Chile, placed under house arrest Dec. 2000; court order annulled Dec. 2000; re-arrest ordered 2001, freed March 2001; Mil. Star, Grand Mil. Merit Cross, High Command Hon. Officer (Ecuador), Abdón Calderón Parra Medal (Ecuador), Order of Mil. Merit (Colombia), Grand Cross of Military Merit (Spain). *Publications:* Geopolítica—Diferentes Etapas para el Estudio Geopolítico de los Estados 1968, Geografía de Chile 1968, Geografía de Argentina, Perú y Bolivia 1972, Guerra del Pacífico 1879—Primeras Operaciones Terrestres 1972. *Address:* Los Barnecha District, Santiago, Chile (Home).

PINÓS, Carmen; Spanish architect; b. 23 June 1954, Barcelona; ed Escuela Superior de Arquitectura de Barcelona, Int. Lab. of Architecture with Urban Design (ILAUD), Urbino, Columbia Univ.; partnership with Enric Miralles, Barcelona 1983–91, projects included Cemetery of Igualada, Barcelona Olympics Archery Grand (Biannual Prize for European Architecture); est. own architectural practice 1991, projects include Footbridge, Petrer (Alicante), Hogar School of Morella (Nat. Prize for Architecture 1995), Mollesussa School, Torrevieja waterfront; fmr visiting Prof. Acad. Van Boukunst, Amsterdam; Ecole Speciale d'Architecture, Paris; Plym Prof. Univ. of Ill. at Urbana–Champaign 1994–95; fmr. Prof. Kunstakademie, Dusseldorf; Prof. Columbia Univ. NY 1999, Harvard Univ. School of Design, Universita Degli Studi di Sassany, Alghero; MOPU competition (1st Prize) 1982; Mies Van de Rohe Prize; Nat. Award of Architecture (Spain) 1995; numerous other awards. *Major works:* El Croquis 1986, Arte Cemento 1987, Baumeister 1989. *Address:* Av. Diagonal 490, 3º2c, 08026 Barcelona, Spain (Office). *Telephone:* (3) 416-03-72 (Office). *Fax:* (3) 415-37-19 (Office). *E-mail:* estpinos@arquired.es (Office).

PINSENT, Matthew, CBE, BA; British oarsman; b. 10 Oct. 1970, Norfolk; s. of Rev. Ewen Pinsent and Jean Pinsent; ed Eton Coll. and Univ. of Oxford; rep. UK at Jr World Championships 1987, 1988, gold medal in coxless pairs (with Tim Foster) 1988; bronze medal, coxed four, World Championships 1989, coxless pairs 1990; mem. two winning University Boat Race crews; gold medal, coxless pairs (with Steve Redgrave, q.v.) World Championships 1991, 1993, 1994, 1995, 2001, Olympic Games, Barcelona 1992, Atlanta 1996; gold medal, coxless fours 1997, 1998; gold medal, coxless fours, World Championships 1999; gold medal, coxless fours, Olympic Games, Sydney 2000; gold medal coxed pairs (with James Cracknell) World Championships 2001, 2002 (new world record); mem. Int. Olympic Cttee 2002–. *Leisure interests:* golf, flying. *Address:* c/o British International Rowing Office, 6 Lower Mall, London, W6 9DJ, England. *Telephone:* (20) 8741-7580. *Fax:* (20) 8563-2265.

PINSKY, Robert Neal, PhD; American poet; b. 20 Oct. 1940, Long Branch, NJ; s. of Milford Simon Pinsky and Sylvia Pinsky (née Eisenberg); m. Ellen Jane Bailey 1961; three d.; ed Rutgers Univ., Stanford Univ.; taught English Univ. of Chicago 1967–68, Wellesley Coll. 1968–80; Prof. of English Univ. of Calif., Berkeley 1980–89; Prof. Boston Univ. 1980–89, Prof. of Creative Writing 1989–; Poet Laureate of USA Sept. 1997–; Visiting Lecturer, Harvard Univ.; Hurst Prof. Washington Univ., St Louis; Poetry Ed. New Repub. magazine 1978, Slate Magazine 1994–2000; Guggenheim Fellow 1980; mem. AAAS; Artists Award American Acad. of Arts and Letters 1979, Saxifrage Prize 1980, William Carlos Williams Prize 1984, Shelley Memorial Award 1996, Harold Washington Literary Award 1999. *Publications:* Landor's Poetry 1968, Sadness and Happiness 1975, The Situation of Poetry 1977, An Explanation of America 1980, History of my Heart 1980, Poetry and the World 1988, The Want Bone 1990, The Inferno of Dante 1994, The Figured Wheel: New and Collected Poems 1966–96 1996, The Sounds of Poetry 1998, The Handbook of Heartbreak 1998, Americans' Favorite Poems 2000, Jersey Rain 2000. *Address:* Department of English, Boston University, 236 Bay State Road, Boston, MA 02215, USA.

PINTASILGO, Maria de Lourdes; Portuguese politician, engineer and diplomatist; b. 18 Jan. 1930, Abrantes; d. of Jaime de Matos Pintasilgo and Amélia Ruivo da Silva Pintasilgo; ed Inst. Superior Técnico, Lisbon; mem. Research and Devt Dept Companhia União Fabril (CUF) 1954–60; Pres. Pax Romana 1956–58; Int. Vice-Pres. The Grail 1965–69; mem. women's ecumenical liaison group 1966–70; mem. Corporate Chamber Comm. on Politics and Gen. Admin. 1969–74; Founder and Chair. Nat. Comm. on Status of Women 1970–74; mem. Portuguese del. to UN Gen. Ass. 1971–72; Sec. of State for Social Security, First Provisional Govt 1975; Minister of Social Affairs 1974–75; Amb. to UNESCO 1976–79, mem. Exec. Bd UNESCO 1976–80; Prime Minister 1979–80; Adviser to Pres. of Repub. 1981–85; independent cand. for Presidency of Portugal 1986; MEP 1987–89; mem. Advisory Bd World Policy Inst., New School for Social Research 1982–, UNU Council 1983–89, Club of Rome 1984–, UN Advisory Cttee on Science and Tech. for Devt 1989–91, Nat. Council of Ethics for Life Sciences 1990–; mem. InterAction Council of Fmr Heads of State and Govt 1983–94; mem. World Policy Inst. 1989–; mem., then Chair. Bd of UNU/WIDER (World Inst. for Devt Econs Research), Helsinki 1990–; Pres. Independent Comm. on Population and Quality of Life 1992–96; Chair. working group on Equality and Democracy,

Council of Europe, Strasbourg 1993–94. *Publications:* several books and articles on political issues, socio-cultural action and the women's movt. *Leisure interest:* poetry. *Address:* Alameda Santo António dos Capuchos 4–5°, 1150 Lisbon, Portugal. *Telephone:* 1-354-31-68. *Fax:* 1-314-25-14.

PINTER, Frances Mercedes Judith, PhD; American publisher; b. 13 June 1949, Venezuela; d. of George Pinter and Vera Hirschenhauser Pinter; m. David Percy 1985; Research Officer, Centre for Criminological Research, Oxford Univ., UK 1976–79; Man. Dir Pinter Publrs. 1979–94; Chair., Independent Publrs. Guild 1979–82, Publrs. Asscn E European Task Force 1990–; Man. Dir Cen. European Univ. Press 1994–96; Chair. Bd. of Trustees, Int. House 2001; Deputy Chair. Book Devt Council 1985–89; mem. Bd UK Publrs. Asscn 1987–92, IBIS Information Services 1988–90, Libra Books 1991–; Exec. Dir Centre for Publishing Devt 1994–, Open Soc. Inst. 1994–99; Visiting Fellow, London School of Econs 2000–01. *Leisure interests:* reading, travelling, hiking. *Address:* 25 Belsize Park, London, NW3 4DU, England (Home). *E-mail:* frances@pinter.org.uk (Office).

PINTER, Harold, CH, CBE, CLit; British playwright; b. 10 Oct. 1930, London; s. of J. Pinter; m. 1st Vivien Merchant 1956 (divorced 1980, died 1982); one s.; m. 2nd Lady Antonia Fraser (q.v.) 1980; ed Hackney Downs Grammar School, London; actor mainly in English and Irish prov. repertory 1949–58; playwright 1957–; Assoc. Dir Nat. Theatre 1973–83; Dir United British Artists 1983–85; Jt Ed. Publr Greville Press 1988–; Bd mem. Cricket World 1989–; Hon. Fellow (Queen Mary Coll.) 1987; Hon. DLitt (Reading) 1970, (Birmingham) 1971, (Glasgow) 1974, (East Anglia) 1974, (Stirling) 1979, (Brown) 1982, (Hull) 1986, (Sussex) 1998; Shakespeare Prize, Hamburg 1973, Austrian Prize for European Literature 1973, Pirandello Prize 1980, Commonwealth Award for Dramatic Arts, Washington, DC 1981, Donatello Prize 1982, Chilean Order of Merit 1992, David Cohen British Literature Prize 1995, Special Olivier Award 1995, Moliere d'Honneur, Paris 1997, Sunday Times Award for Literary Excellence 1997, BAFTA Fellowship 1997, RSL Companion of Literature 1998, Critics' Circle Award for Distinguished Service to the Arts 2000, Brianza Poetry Prize, Italy 2000, South Bank Show Award 2001, S. T. Dupont Golden Pen Award 2001, Premio Fiesole ai Maestri del Cinema, Italy 2001, Laurea ad honorem, Univ. of Florence 2001, World Leaders Award Toronto 2001, Hermann Kesten Medallion, German PEN, Berlin 2001. *Film:* Mansfield Park 1999. *Plays:* The Room 1957, The Dumb Waiter 1957, The Birthday Party 1957, A Slight Ache 1958, The Hothouse 1958, The Caretaker 1959, A Night Out 1959, Night School 1960, The Dwarfs 1960, The Collection 1961, The Lover 1962, Tea Party (TV play) 1965, The Homecoming 1964, The Basement (TV play) 1966, Landscape 1967, Silence 1968, Night (one act play) 1969, Old Times 1970, Monologue (one act play) 1972, No Man's Land 1974, Betrayal 1978, Family Voices 1980, Other Places 1982, A Kind of Alaska 1982, Victoria Station 1982, One for the Road 1984, Mountain Language 1988, The New World Order 1991, Party Time 1991, Moonlight 1993, Ashes to Ashes 1996, Celebration 2000, Remembrance of Things Past 2000. *Screenplays:* The Caretaker 1962, The Servant 1962, The Pumpkin Eater 1963, The Quiller Memorandum 1965, Accident 1966, The Birthday Party 1967, The Go-Between 1969, Langrishe Go Down 1970, A la Recherche du Temps Perdu 1972, The Last Tycoon 1974, The French Lieutenant's Woman 1980, Betrayal 1981, Victory 1982, Turtle Diary 1984, The Handmaid's Tale 1987, Reunion 1988, The Heat of the Day 1988, The Comfort of Strangers 1989, The Trial 1989. *Plays directed:* The Man in the Glass Booth, London 1967, NY 1968, Exiles 1970, 1971, Butley 1971, (film) 1973, Next of Kin 1974, Otherwise Engaged 1975, The Rear Column 1978, Close of Play 1979, Quartermaine's Terms 1981, Incident at Tulse Hill 1982, The Trojan War Will Not Take Place 1983, The Common Pursuit 1984, Sweet Bird of Youth 1985, Circe and Bravo 1986, Vanilla 1990, The New World Order 1991, Party Time 1991, Party Time (TV) 1992, Oleanna 1993, Ashes to Ashes 1996, Twelve Angry Men 1996, The Late Middle Classes 1999, Celebration 2000, The Room 2000, No Man's Land 2001. *Television:* A Night Out 1960, Huis Clos 1965, The Basement 1967, Rogue Male 1976, Lanerishe, Go Down 1978, The Birthday Party 1987, Breaking the Code 1997, Catastrophe 2000, Wit 2000. *Publications:* Poems and Prose 1949–77 1978, The Proust Screenplay (with Joseph Losey and Barbara Bray) 1978, Collected Poems and Prose 1986, 100 Poems by 100 Poets (co-ed.) 1986, The Dwarfs (novel) 1990, Various Voices: prose, poetry, politics 1948–1998 1999. *Leisure interests:* cricket, tennis, bridge. *Address:* c/o Judy Daish Associates, 2 St Charles Place, London, W10 6EG, England.

PINTILIE, Lucian; Romanian stage and film director; b. 9 Nov. 1933, Tarutino (Bessarabia); s. of Victor Pintilie and Amelia Pintilie; ed Bucharest Theatrical and Cinematographic Art Inst.; career at Lucia Sturdza Bulandra Theatre, directing The Cherry Orchard by Chekhov, D'ale carnavalului by I. L. Caragiale, The Inspector General by Gogol; staged several plays by Chekhov, Gorki, Ibsen, Eugène Ionesco, Pirandello and Strindberg abroad; also operas such as Rigoletto, Carmen, The Magic Flute etc; Commdr des Arts et des Lettres 2001. *Films:* Duminică la ora 6 (At Six o'Clock on Sunday), Reconstituirea (The Reconstruction) 1969, Salonul nr 6 (Ward No. 6) 1973 (Yugoslavia), De ce trag clopotele Mitică? (What Do The Bells Toll For Mitică?) 1980 and Balanţa (The Oak) 1992, O Vară de Neuitat (An Unforgettable Summer) 1994, Prea tirziu (Too Late) 1996, Terminus Paradis (Last Stop Paradise) 1998, După-amiaza unui torţionar (A Torturer's Afternoon) 2001. *Address:* 44 Mihail Kogălniceanu Blvd., Bucharest, Romania. *Telephone:* 3154715.

PINTO BALSEMÃO, Francisco José Pereira; Portuguese politician, lawyer and journalist; b. 1 Sept. 1937, Lisbon; s. of Henrique Pinto Balsemão and Maria Adelaide C. P. Pinto Balsemão; m. Mercedes Presas Pinto Balsemão 1975; three s. two d.; Ed.-in-Chief review Mais Alto 1961–63; Sec. to Man. Bd Diário Popular, later Man. –1971; f. weekly Expresso 1973; mem. Nat. Ass. during Govt of Dr. Marcello Caetano; f. Popular Democratic Party (PPD), later renamed Social Democratic Party (PSD), with late Dr. Sá Carneiro and Joaquim Magalhães Mota May 1974; Vice-Pres. Constituent Ass. 1975; Opposition Spokesman on Foreign Affairs 1977; mem. Ass. of the Repub. 1979; Minister Without Portfolio and Deputy Prime Minister 1980; Prime Minister of Portugal 1981–83; Pres. Instituto Progresso Social e Democracia, Francisco dá Carneiro 1983–; Chair. Int. Relations Cttee and mem. Political Cttee PSD, party leader 1980–83; Head Sociedad Independente de Comunicação (SIC); Pres. European Inst. for the Media 1990; Head Sociedade Independente de Comunicação; Chair. Sojornal and Controjornal (Media) Groups. *Address:* Rua Duque de Palmela, 37-2° Dt°, 1296 Lisbon Codex, Portugal. *Telephone:* 526141.

PINTO BARBOSA, António Manuel; Portuguese economist and diplomatist; b. 31 July 1917, Murtoza; s. of Manuel Maria Barbosa Junior and Mariana Vieira Pinto Barbosa; m. Maria das Dôres Soares; two s.; ed Universidade Técnica de Lisboa; teacher 1941–50; Prof. Inst. of Higher Econ. and Financial Sciences 1951–; Pres. Comm. for Reorganization of Industrial Resources 1951–54; Under-Sec. of State at Treasury 1951–54; Minister of Finance and Gov. IBRD 1955–65; mem. Council of State; Gov. Bank of Portugal and Gov. IMF 1966–74; Chair. Higher Studies Inst., Acad. of Sciences; Grand Cross, Order of Christ, Order of Prince Henry and of Isabel la Católica (Spain). *Publications:* L'industrie des conserves au Portugal 1941, L'économie, aspects positifs et aspects téléologiques 1943, L'économie du café 1945, La crise des exportations métropolitaines pour l'étranger 1950, La tâche du Ministre des Finances 1955, Banco de Fomento Nacional 1959, O sistema financeiro português 1960, L'activité du Ministre des Finances 1960, La défense de la stabilité financière 1962, Communication du Ministre des Finances sur le crédit extérieur 1962, La phase actuelle des finances portugaises 1964, La dévaluation de 1949 et le commerce extérieur portugais 1966, Portuguese Economic Development in the Presence of the Post-war Foreign Policies of the US 1969, La réforme du système monétaire international et ses vicissitudes 1973, Keynes e o accordo de Bretton-Woods 1977, O FMI e a estrutura da influência monetária internacional 1978, Problemas monetários internacionais de actualidade 1983, A reabilitação do quantitativo na economia 1984, O lado menos visível do Plano Marshall: sua actualidade, Determinantes da evasão de capitais: alguma evidência de comparações internacionais 1989, Colóquio sobre Portugal e a paz 1989, Transformações sistémicas: princípios e problemas 1992, Regulação bancária e supervisão prudencial, em contexto de globalização dos mercados financeiros, na óptica dos respectives órgãos de controle 2000. *Address:* Rua António Saldanha 3, Bairro do Restelo, 1400 Lisbon, Portugal. *Telephone:* (21) 3010463 (Home).

PINTO RUBIANES, Pedro Alfredo; Ecuadorean politician and industrialist; b. 31 Jan. 1931, Quito; ed Univ. Cen. del Ecuador, Vanderbilt Univ.; Gen. Man. Textile San Pedro SA 1967–82, 1984–97, Pres. 1997; Pres. Asscn of Textile Mfrs 1968–70; Dean Faculty of Admin., Univ. Cen. del Ecuador 1970–72; Pres. Chamber of Mfrs of Pichincha 1971–73, Fed. of Industrialists of Ecuador 1972–73; town councillor, Quito 1973–77; Dir Corporación Financiera Ecuatoriana (COFIEC) 1976–82; Minister of Finance and Public Credit 1982–84; Gov. for Ecuador, Banco Interamericano de Desarrollo (BID), IBRD 1983–84; Dir CORDES 1988, Bank of Pichincha 1993–98, Chamber of Mfrs of Pichincha 1997–98; Deputy for Pichincha 1998; Vice-Pres. of Ecuador 2001–. *Address:* Office of the Vice-President, Manuel Larrea y Arenas, Edif. Conseyo Provincial de Pichincha, 21°, Quito, Ecuador (Office). *Telephone:* (2) 504-953. *Fax:* (2) 564-531.

PIONTEK, Heinz; German writer; b. 15 Nov. 1925, Kreuzburg, Silesia; s. of Robert Piontek and Marie Piontek (née Seja); m. Gisela Dallmann 1951; ed Theologisch-Philosophische Hochschule, Dillingen; mem. Bavarian Acad. of Fine Arts 1960–, Central PEN of Fed. Repub. of Germany; Berlin Prize for Literature 1957, Andreas Gryphius Prize, Esslingen 1957, Rom-Preis, Villa Massimo 1960, Münchner Literatur Preis 1967, Eichendorff-Preis 1971, Tukan-Preis 1971, Literatur-Preis des Kulturkreises im BDI 1974, Georg-Büchner-Preis 1976, Werner-Egk-Preis 1981, Oberschlesischer Kulturpreis 1984, Bundesverdienstkreuz (1st Class) 1985, Grosser Kultur-Preis Schlesien des Landes Niedersachsen 1991, Bayerischer Verdienstorden 1992, Villa-Massimo-Preis 1995. *Publications:* Die Furt (poems) 1952, Die Rauchfahne (poems) 1953, Vor Augen (stories) 1955, Wassermarken (poems) 1957, Buchstab-Zauberstab (essays) 1959, Aus meines Herzens Grunde (anthology) 1959, John Keats: Poems (trans.) 1960, Mit einer Kranichfeder (poems) 1962, Kastanien aus dem Feuer (stories) 1963, Windrichtungen (journey reports) 1963, Neue deutsche Erzählgedichte (anthology) 1964, Klartext (poems) 1966, Die mittleren Jahre (novel) 1967, Liebeserklärungen in Prosa (essays) 1969, Männer, die Gedichte machen (essays) 1970, Die Erzählungen (stories) 1971, Tot oder lebendig (poems) 1971, Deutsche Gedichte seit 1960 (anthology) 1972, Helle Tage anderswo (travel reports) 1973, Gesammelte Gedichte (collected poems) 1974, Dichterleben (novel) 1976, Wintertage-Sommernächte (collected stories) 1977, Juttas Neffe (novel) 1979, Vorkriegszeit (poetry cycle) 1980, Was mich nicht loslässt (poems) 1981, Lieb', Leid und Zeit und Ewigkeit (anthology) 1981, Zeit meines Lebens (autobiog. vol. 1) 1984, Werke in sechs Bänden (collected works) 1985, Helldunkel (poems)

1987, Stunde der Überlebenden (autobiog. vol. 2) 1989, Werkauswahl in 2 Bänden (poems and stories) 1990, Nach Markus (story) 1991, Morgenwache (poems) 1991, Goethe unterwegs in Schlesien (almost a novel) 1993, Dichterleben (novel, new composition) 1995, Neue Umlaufbahn (poems) 1998, Schattenlinie (trans. of novel by Joseph Courad) 1999, Texte und Bilder-Catalogue of Exposition (drawing) 2001. *Address:* Dülfer Strasse 97, 80995 Munich, Germany.

PIOT, Baron Peter, MD, PhD; Belgian public health official and professor; b. 17 Feb. 1949, Leuven; m. Greet Kimzeke 1975; two c.; ed Univs of Ghent, Antwerp and Washington; Asst in Microbiology, Inst. of Tropical Medicine, Antwerp 1974–78, Prof., Head Dept of Microbiology 1981–92; Sr Fellow, Microbiology and Infectious Diseases, Washington Univ. 1978–79; Asst Prof. of Public Health, Free Univ. Brussels 1989–94; Assoc. Dir Global Program AIDS, WHO 1995, Exec. Dir Jt UN Program on HIV/AIDS, Geneva 1995–; currently Under-Sec.-Gen. UN; Dir WHO Collaborating Centre on AIDS, Antwerp; mem. Bd Dirs Project SIDA, Zaire, STD/AIDS Project, Kenya; Chair. WHO Steering Cttee on the Epidemiology of AIDS 1989–92; NATO Fellow 1978–79; mem. Royal Acad. of Medicine, Int. AIDS Soc. (Pres. 1992–), Inst. of Medicine, Washington DC, numerous socs in Europe, USA, Africa; De Kerkheer Prize for Medicine 1989, Health Research Award (Belgium) 1989, Public Health Award, Flemish Community 1990; AMICOM Award for Medicine 1991, H. Breurs Prize 1992, A. Jaunioux Prize 1992, van Thiel Award 1993, Glaxo award for infectious diseases 1995, Nelson Mandela Award 2001, Royal Acad. of Arts and Sciences Gold Medal, Belgium 2002; cr. baron by King Albert II, Officier, Ordre Nat. du Léopard (Zaire), Ordre du Lion (Senegal). *Publications:* AIDS and HIV Infection in the Tropics (with J. M. Mann) 1988, Handbook on AIDS Prevention in Africa (with P. Lamptey) 1990, AIDS in Africa 1991, Hepatitis B and STD in Heterosexuals (with F. André) 1991, AIDS in Africa: A Handbook for Physicians (co-author) 1992, Reproductive Tract Infections in Women (co-author 1992); articles on AIDS and other sexually transmitted diseases. *Leisure interests:* cooking, hiking, music, literature. *Address:* UNAIDS, 20 Avenue Appia, 1211 Geneva 27, Switzerland (Office). *Telephone:* (22) 7914510 (Office). *Fax:* (22) 7914179 (Office).

PIOTROVSKY, Mikhail Borisovich, DHist; Russian art researcher; b. 9 Dec. 1944, Yerevan, Armenia; s. of Boris Piotrovsky; m. Irina Leonidovna Piotrovskaya; one s. one d.; ed Leningrad State Univ., Cairo Univ.; researcher Leningrad Inst. of Oriental Studies USSR Acad. of Sciences 1967–91; First Deputy Dir State Hermitage, St Petersburg 1991–92, Dir. 1992–; Corresp. mem. Russian Acad. of Sciences 1997–; mem. Acad. of Humanitarian Sciences; mem. Presidium, Cttee on State Prizes of Russian Presidency, Presidium, Russian Cttee of UNESCO; mem. Int. Council of Museums; consultant to European Parl.; main research in ancient and medieval history of Near E, Muslim art in archaeology. *Publications:* over 150 scientific works. *Address:* State Hermitage, Dvortsovaya nab. 34, 191186 St Petersburg, Russia (Office). *Telephone:* (812) 110-96-01. *Fax:* (812) 311-90-09. *E-mail:* haltunen@hermitage.ru.

PIOVANELLI, HE Cardinal Silvano; Italian ecclesiastic; b. 21 Feb. 1924; ordained 1947; consecrated Bishop (Titular Church of Tubune, Mauritania) 1982; Archbishop of Florence 1983–; cr. Cardinal 1985. *Address:* Arcivescovado, Piazza S. Giovanni 3, 50129 Florence, Italy. *Telephone:* (055) 239-88-13.

PIPPARD, Sir (Alfred) Brian, Kt, MA, ScD, FRS; British professor of physics; b. 7 Sept. 1920, London; s. of Prof. A. J. S. Pippard and F. L. O. (Tucker) Pippard; m. Charlotte Frances Dyer 1955; three d.; ed Clifton Coll. and Clare Coll., Cambridge; Scientific Officer Radar Research and Devt Establishment 1941–45; Demonstrator in Physics, Cambridge Univ. 1946, Lecturer 1950, Reader 1959–60, J. H. Plummer Prof. of Physics 1960–71; Cavendish Prof. of Physics 1971–82, now Emer.; Pres. of Clare Hall, Cambridge 1966–73; Pres. Inst. of Physics 1974–76; Hughes Medal (Royal Soc.) 1959, Holweck Medal 1961, Dannie-Heineman Prize (Göttingen) 1969, Guthrie Medal (Inst. of Physics) 1970. *Publications:* Elements of Classical Thermodynamics 1957, Dynamics of Conduction Electrons 1962, Forces and Particles 1972, Physics of Vibration 1978, 1982, Response and Stability 1985, Magnetoresistance in Metals 1989; many papers in Proc. of the Royal Society, etc. *Leisure interest:* music. *Address:* 30 Porson Road, Cambridge, CB2 2EU, England. *Telephone:* (1223) 358713.

PIQUÉ I CAMPS, Josep, LLB, PhD; Spanish politician, business executive and economist; b. 21 Feb. 1955, Barcelona; ed Univ. of Barcelona; Lecturer in Econ. Theory, Univ. of Barcelona 1977–86, 1990–; economist, Studies Dept, La Caixa 1984–85; Gen. Dir of Industry, Catalan Autonomous Govt 1986–88; Gen. Man. of Corp. Strategy, Ercros SA (pvt. chemicals group) 1989–91, Man. Dir 1992, Chair. and CEO 1992–96, various posts in group including Chair. EMESA 1989–91, ERKIMIA SA 1990–96, FERTIBERIA 1993–96, FYSE 1992–93, LISAC 1992, META 1990–94, Sole Admin. FESA 1992–93, mem. Bd Prisma 1991–96, Río Tinto Minera 1991–93, Erkol 1991–96, Rhodiamul 1991–92; Minister of Industry and Energy 1996–2000; Govt Spokesman 1998–2000; Minister of Foreign Affairs 2000–02, of Science and Tech. 2002–. *Address:* c/o Ministerio de Ciencia y Tecnología, Paseo de la Castellana 160, 28071 Madrid, Spain (Office). *Telephone:* (91) 3494000 (Office). *Fax:* (91) 4578066 (Office). *E-mail:* info@mcyt.es (Office). *Website:* www.mcyt.es (Office).

PIQUET, Nelson; Brazilian racing driver; b. 17 Aug. 1952, Rio de Janeiro; m. 1st Maria Clara; m. 2nd Vivianne Leao, one s.; first Grand Prix, Germany 1978; mem. Ensign Grand Prix team 1978, BS McLaren team 1978, Brabham

team 1978–85, Williams team 1986–87, Lotus team 1988–89, Benetton team 1990; winner of 23 Grand Prix; Formula One World Champion 1981, 1983, 1987; lives in Monaco. *Leisure interest:* sports.

PIRELLI, Leopoldo; Italian business executive; b. 27 Aug. 1925, Varese; s. of Alberto Pirelli and Ludovica Zambeletti; m. Giulia Ferlito 1947; one s. one d.; ed Politecnico, Milan; Chair. Pirelli and Co., Milan 1995–99, Partner 1957–99, Hon. Pres. 1999–; Deputy Chair. Soc. Int. Pirelli, Basel 1979–99; Dir Riunione Adriatica di Sicurtà (RAS), Milan, Generale Industrie Metallurgiche, Florence; mem. confed. of Italian Industries 1957–; Cavaliere del Lavoro della Repubblica, Order of Labour Merit 1977. *Address:* Pirelli and C.A.p.A., Via Gaetano Negri 10, 20123 Milan, Italy (Office). *Telephone:* (02) 85351.

PIRES, Maria João; Portuguese pianist; b. 23 July 1944, Lisbon; m.; four c.; ed Lisbon Acad. of Music; debut recital aged four; early concert tours of Portugal, Spain and Germany; int. career from 1970, with performances in Europe, Africa and Japan; British debut 1986; debut tour of N America 1988; appearances with numerous famous orchestras and conductors world-wide; repertoire includes Mozart, Schubert, Schumann, Beethoven and Chopin; First Prize, Beethoven Int. Competition, Brussels 1970. *Recordings include:* Complete Mozart Piano Sonatas (Edison Prize, Prix de l'Acad. du Disque Français, Prix de l'Acad. Charles Cros), Debussy Etudes (Grammy Award) 1990, Concertos by Mozart (Grammy Award) 1991. *Leisure interest:* rural life. *Address:* c/o Herzberger Artists, 't Woud 1, 3862 PM Nijkerk, Netherlands (Office).

PIRES, Mario; Guinea-Bissau politician; b. 1949; m.; five c.; trained as economist; fmr Chief of Staff to Pres. Kumba Yalá; Founding mem. Social Renovation Party (SRP); Prime Minister (in caretaker govt) of Guinea-Bissau Nov. 2002–. *Address:* Gabinete do Primeiro Ministro, Avda Unidade Africana, CP 137, Bissau, Guinea-Bissau (Office). *Telephone:* 211308 (Office). *Fax:* 201671 (Office).

PIRES, Gen. Pedro Verona Rodrigues; Cape Verde politician; b. 29 April 1934, Sant' Ana, Fogo; s. of Luís Rodrigues Pires and Maria Fidalga Lopes Pires; m. Adélcia Maria da Luz Lima Barreto Pires 1975; two d.; ed Liceu Gil Eanes de São Vicente, Faculty of Science, Lisbon Univ., Portugal; left Portugal to join Partido Africano da Independência da Guiné e Cabo Verde (PAIGC) 1961; mem. PAIGC del. 1961–63; involved in preparation for liberation of Cape Verde 1963–65; mem. Cen. Cttee of PAIGC 1965, of Council of War, PAIGC 1967; re-elected mem. of Commissão Permanente do Comité Executivo da Luta (CEL) and of Council of War 1970; involved in admin. of liberated areas of southern Guinea-Bissau 1971–73; Pres. Nat. Comm. of PAIGC for Cape Verde 1973 (reaffirmed as mem. of Council of War and CEL), appointed an Asst State Commr in first Govt of Repub. of Guinea-Bissau 1973–74; negotiated independence agreements of Cape Verde and Guinea-Bissau 1974; Dir PAIGC policies during transitional govt before independence of Cape Verde 1975; elected Deputy in Nat. Popular Ass. of Cape Verde June 1975–, re-elected 1980; Prime Minister of Cape Verde 1975–91, with responsibility for Finance, Planning and Co-operation; elected Deputy Gen. Sec. Partido Africano da Independência de Cabo Verde (PAICV) 1981, Sec. Gen. 1990–93, fmr Chair. Gen. 1993; Pres. of Cape Verde Feb. 2001–; mem. Perm. Comm. of CEL 1977; Amílcar Cabral Medal 1976. *Leisure interests:* philosophy, sociology, politics. *Address:* Presidência da República, CP 100, Plateau, Praia, Santiago (Office); c/o PAICV, CP 22, Praia, Santiago, Republic of Cape Verde. *Telephone:* 61-65-66 (Office). *Fax:* 61-43-56 (Office).

PIRIE, Madsen Duncan, MA, PhD; British political philosopher; b. 24 Aug. 1940; s. of Douglas G. Pirie and Eva Madsen; ed Univs of Edinburgh and St Andrews; Republican Study Cttee 1974; Distinguished Visiting Prof. of Philosophy, Hillsdale Coll. Mich. 1975–78; Pres. Adam Smith Inst. 1978–; mem. Citizens' Charter Advisory Panel 1991–95; RC Hoiles Fellow 1975. *Publications:* Freeports 1983, Test Your IQ 1983, Book of the Fallacy 1985, Privatization 1988, Micropolitics 1988, Boost Your IQ 1990, The Sherlock Holmes I.Q. Book 1995. *Leisure interest:* calligraphy. *Address:* P.O. Box 316, London, SW1P 3DJ, England.

PIRINSKI, Georgi Georgiev; Bulgarian politician; b. 10 Sept. 1948, New York, USA; m.; two c.; ed Higher Econ. Inst., Sofia; fmr Deputy Minister of Foreign Econ. Relations and Deputy Prime Minister; mem. Parl.; Minister of Foreign Affairs 1995–97; mem. Bulgarian Socialist Party.

PIRK, Jan, MD, DSc; Czech heart surgeon; b. 20 April 1948, Prague; s. of Otto Pirk and Jitka Pirk; m. Blanka Pirk; two s.; ed Charles Univ., Prague; occupied numerous medical and surgical positions; researcher 1978–90; consultant Odensee Univ. Hosp. 1990–91, Ochsner Hosp., New Orleans 1983–84; Head IKEM Clinic for Heart Surgery 1991–. *Publications:* The Effect of Antiaggregation Drugs on the Patency of Grafts in the Arterial System 1980, Improved Patency of the Aortocoronary Bypass by Anti-Trombic Drugs (co-author) 1986, Surgery for Ischaemic Heart Disease in Patients Under Forty (co-author) 1989, An Alternative to Cardioplegia (with M. D. Kellovsky) 1995. *Leisure interests:* skiing, biking, long distance running, theatre, yachting. *Address:* IKEM Clinic for Heart Surgery, Vídeňská 1958, 140 21, 140 00 Prague 4 (Office); V. Horní Stromce 6, 130 00 Prague 3, Czech Republic (Home). *Telephone:* (2) 41723245 (Office); (2) 72741912 (Home). *Fax:* (2) 41721362 (Office). *E-mail:* japx@medicon.cz (Office).

PIRUMOV, Vladimir Semenovich, DR.MIL.SC.; Russian army officer and politician; b. 1 Feb. 1926, Kirovakan, Armenia; ed Caspian Higher Mil.

Marine School, Mil. Marine Acad.; artillery officer, Asst to Commdr of cruiser, Commdr of destroyer Baltic Navy 1948–60; Head of Dept Gen. Staff of Mil. Marine forces 1974–85; teacher, Sr teacher, Head of Chair Mil. Marine Acad. 1963–74; Prof. Mil. Acad. of Gen. Staff 1985–; mem. Russian Acad. of Nat. Sciences; Vice-Pres., Head Section of Geopolitics and Security, Russian Acad. of Sciences 1993; Pres. Cen. of Studies of Problems of Geopolitics and Security at Security Council of Russian Fed. 1993–; First Vice-Pres. Acad. of Geopolitics and Security 2000–; mem. Ed. Bd journals Geopolitica i Besopasnost, Vooruzheniye, Politika, Konversia; P. Kapitsa Silver Medal, Piotr the Great Gold Medal, State Prize of Russian Fed. 1977, Merited Worker of Science of Russian Fed. *Address:* Russian Academy of Natural Sciences, Varshawskoye shosse 8, 113105 Moscow, Russia (Office). *Telephone:* (095) 252-55-74 (Office).

PIRZADA, Syed Sharifuddin, S.PK.; Pakistani politician and lawyer; b. 12 June 1923, Burhanpur; s. of S. Vilayat Ali Pirzada and Butul Begum; m. 1st Rafia Sultana (died 1960); m. 2nd Safiya Pirzada; two s. three d.; ed Univ. of Bombay; Sec. Muslim Students Fed. 1943–45; Hon. Sec. to Quaid-i-Azam, Jinnah 1941–44; Sec. Bombay City Muslim League 1945–47; Prof., Sind Muslim Law Coll. 1947–54; Adviser to Constitution Comm. of Pakistan 1960–61; Chair. Co. Law Comm. 1962; Pres. Karachi High Court Bar Asscn. Pakistan Br. 1964–67; Attorney-Gen. of Pakistan 1965–66, 1968–72, 1977–89; Minister of Foreign Affairs 1966–68, April–Oct. 1993; Minister of Justice 1979–84; mem. or Pres. several asscns. and socs.; led Pakistan Del. to Session of UN Gen. Ass. 1966–67; Chair. UN Human Rights Sub-Cttee on Minorities 1977; mem. Panel of Perm. Court of Arbitration; mem. Int. Law Comm. 1981–86; Sec.-Gen. Org. of Islamic Conf. 1984–88; Chair. Heritage Council and Amb.-at-large with rank of Fed. Minister 1989–93; mem. Nat. Security Council of Pakistan 1999–; Hon. Sr Adviser to Chief Exec. on Foreign Affairs, Law, Justice and Human Rights 1999–; Judge (ad-hoc) Int. Court of Justice 2000; Chair. Nat. Cttee on Quaid-i-Azam Year 2001. *Publications include:* Evolution of Pakistan 1962, Fundamental Rights and Constitutional Remedies in Pakistan 1966, Some Aspects of Quaid-i-Azam's Life 1978, Collected Works of Quaid-i-Azam Mohammad Ali Jinnah (vol. I) 1985, (vol. II) 1986, Dissolution of Constituent Assembly of Pakistan 1996. *Leisure interest:* bridge. *Address:* Chief Executive Secretariat No. 11, 5th Floor, Islamabad (Office); H. No. 25/1–4, Phase-V, Zam Zam Street, Clifton, Karachi, Pakistan (Home). *Telephone:* (21) 2635151 (Office); (21) 5874414 (Home).

PISANU, Giuseppe; Italian politician; b. 2 Jan. 1937, Ittiri, Sassari; m.; three c.; Asst Man. Soc. of Finance and Industry for the Rebirth of Sardinia (SFIRS); Leader and Head Nat. Secr. Democrazia Cristiana (Christian Democrats) 1975–80; elected Deputy 1972–92; Under-Sec. of State for Treasury 1980–83; Under-Sec. of State for Defence 1986–90; elected mem. Forza Italia (Sardinia) 1994–; mem. Pres.'s cttee 1994–96, Vice-Chair. Parl. Group, then Chair.; mem. Defence Cttee; Del. of Italy to CSCE; Minister of the Interior 2002–. *Address:* Ministry of the Interior, Piazzale del Virinale, 00184 Rome, Italy (Office). *Telephone:* (06) 4651 (Office). *Fax:* (06) 4741717 (Office). *Website:* www.mininterno.it (Office).

PISCHETSRIEDER, Bernd; German business executive; b. 15 Feb. 1948, Munich; ed Technical Univ. Munich; joined BMW AG, Munich as production planning eng 1973; Production Dir BMW South Africa (Pty) Ltd 1982–85; Dir for Quality Control, BMW AG 1985–87, for Tech. Planning 1987–90; deputy mem. Admin. Bd in charge of Production 1990, mem. Admin. Bd 1991, Chair. Admin. Bd 1993–99; fmr Chair. Rover; Chair. Bd of Dirs Volkswagen AG 2002–; mem. Advisory Bd Allianz-Versicherung, Munich; Dr hc (Birmingham) 1996. *Address:* Volkswagen AG, 38436 Wolfsburg, Germany. *Telephone:* (5361) 90 (Office). *Fax:* (5361) 928282 (Office). *Website:* www.volkswagen.de (Office).

PISCHINGER, Franz Felix, DR. TECHN. E.H.; Austrian academic; b. 18 July 1930, Waidhofen; s. of Franz Pischinger and Karoline Pischinger; m. Elfriede Pischinger 1957; four s. one d.; ed Technical Univ. Graz; technical asst Technical Univ. Graz 1953–58; Head of Research Dept Inst. of Internal Combustion Engines, Prof. List (AVL) 1958–62; leading positions in research and devt Kloeckner-Humboldt-Deutz AG, Cologne, Fed. Germany 1962–70; Dir Inst. for Applied Thermodynamics, Aachen Tech. Univ. 1970–97; Pres. FEV Motorentechnik, Aachen 1978–; Vice-Pres. DFG (German Research Soc.) 1984–90; Fellow SAE 1996; Dr. hc (Tech. Univ. Graz) 1994; Herbert Akroyd Stuart Award 1962, Carl-Engler-Medaille DGMK, Deutsche Wissenschaftliche Gesellschaft für Erdöl, Erdgas und Kohle, Hamburg 1990, Medal of Honour, Verein Deutscher Ingenieure 1993, Osterreichischer Ehrenring 1954, Deutsches Bundesverdienstkreuz 1978, Cross of Honour for Science and Art, First Class (Austria) 1998, Soichiro Honda Medal, America Soc. of Mechanical Engineers 2000. *Publications:* articles in professional journals. *Address:* FEV Motorentechnik, Neuenhofstrasse 181, 52078 Aachen (Office); Im Erkfeld 4, 52072 Aachen, Germany (Home). *Telephone:* (241) 5689100 (Office); (241) 9319500 (Home). *Fax:* (241) 5689224 (Office); (241) 9319597 (Home). *E-mail:* pischinger_f@fev.de (Office). *Website:* www.fev.com (Office).

PITAKAKA, Sir Moses Puibangara, GCMG; Solomon Islands politician; b. 24 Jan. 1945, Zaru Village, Solomon Islands; m. Lois Qilariava 1967; three s. four d.; ed Univ. of Birmingham, Oxford Univ., Univ. of S. Pacific, Fiji; Dist Officer, Lands Officer and Magistrate 1972–75; Head of Foreign Affairs, Prime Minister's office 1977–79; Human Resources Devt Man. Unilever Group, Solomon Islands 1983–85; Chair. Citizenship Comm. 1978–88, Nat. Educ. Bd 1980–86, Leadership Code Comm. 1989–94; Commr Judicial and Legal Services Comm. 1982–83; Gov.-Gen. of the Solomon Islands 1994–99;

Deacon World Wide Church of God 1993–. *Leisure interests:* walking, reading, canoeing, swimming. *Address:* c/o Government House, P.O. Box 252, Honiara, Solomon Islands.

PITCHER, Sir Desmond Henry, Kt; British company executive; b. 23 March 1935, Liverpool; s. of George Charles Pitcher and Alice Marion (née Osborne) Pitcher; m. 1st Patricia Ainsworth 1961 (divorced 1973); two d.; m. 2nd Carol Ann Rose 1978 (divorced); two s.; m. 3rd Norma Barbara Niven 1991; ed Liverpool Coll. of Tech. and Commerce; Man. Dir then Vice-Pres. Int. Div. The Sperry Corpn 1961–76; Man. Dir British Leyland Truck and Bus Div. 1976–78, Plessey Telecommunications and Office Systems Ltd 1978–83; Group Chief Exec. The Littlewoods Org. PLC 1983–93, Vice-Chair. 1993–95; Chair. The Mersey Barrage Co. Ltd 1986–96, The Merseyside Devt Corpn 1991–98, The North West Water Group PLC (now United Utilities) 1993–98 (Dir 1990–98); Dir Everton Football Club Co. Ltd 1987–90, Deputy Chair. 1990–98; Dir Northern Advisory Bd of Nat. Westminster Bank PLC 1989–92, Dir (non-exec.) Nat. Westminster Bank 1994–98; Dir Liverpool School of Tropical Medicine 1996–; Chair. Royal Liverpool Philharmonic Social Devt Trust 1992–. *Leisure interests:* football, golf, 19th century history, opera, sailing. *Address:* Folly Farm, Sulhamstead, Berks., RG7 4DF, England. *Telephone:* (118) 930-2326.

PITHART, Petr; Czech politician and academic; b. 2 Jan. 1941, Kladno; s. of Vilém Pithart and Blažena Pithart (née Krystýnková); m. Drahomíra Hromádková 1964; one s. one d.; ed Charles Univ., Prague (Faculty of Law); Dept of Theory of State and Law, Charles Univ. 1964–70; scholarship Oxford Univ. 1969–70; labourer 1970–72; co. lawyer 1972–77; signed Charter 77; labourer 1977–79; clerk with Central Warehouses, Prague 1979–89; Spokesman Co-ordination Centre, Civic Forum 1989–90; Prime Minister of Czech Repub. 1990–92; Deputy to Czech Nat. Council 1990–92; mem. and Chair. Senate 1996–98, Vice-Chair. 1998–2000, Chair. 2000–; mem. Christian and Democratic Union, Czech Populist Party (KDÚ-ČSL) 1999–, Cand. presidential election 2003; Sr Research Fellow Cen. European Univ., Prague 1992–94; teacher, Faculty of Law, Charles Univ., Prague 1994–; Chief Ed. periodical The New Presence. *Publications:* numerous articles and essays; Defence of Politics 1974, "1968" 1978, History and Politics 1992, Czechs in the History of Modern Times (co-author) 1992, Who We Are 1999. *Leisure interests:* politics, history, hiking, fishing. *Address:* Senate of the Czech Republic, Valdštejnské nám. 4, 118 11 Prague 1, Czech Republic (Office). *Telephone:* (2) 57532398 (Office). *Fax:* (2) 5753-4484 (Office). *E-mail:* petr@pithart.cz (Office). *Website:* www.pithart.cz.

PITIRIM, Metropolitan of Volokolamsk and Yuriev (Konstantin Vladimirovich Netchaev), DTheol; Russian ecclesiastic; b. 8 Jan. 1926, Michurinsk; ed Moscow Theological Acad.; Deacon Moscow Patriarch Cathedral 1945–54, Archimandrite 1956; Insp. Moscow Theological Acad. 1956–, Prof. 1957–; Ed. Magazine of Moscow Patriarchy 1962–; consecrated as Bishop 1963; Bishop of Volokolamsk, Vicar of Moscow Eparchy 1963–; man. Smolensk Eparchy 1964–65; Archbishop of Volokolamsk 1971–86, Metropolitan of Volokolamsk and Yuriev 1986–94; Chair. Publishing Bd of Moscow Patriarchy 1986–; USSR People's Deputy 1989–91; Vice-Pres. Int. Foundation for Survival and Development of Humanity; co-f. Acad. of World Civilizations; Chair. of Bd Slavic Foundation of Russia. *Publications:* numerous books and articles on theological and philosophical themes. *Leisure interests:* philosophy, music. *Address:* Church of Resurrection, Bryussov per. 15/2, 103009 Moscow, Russia. *Telephone:* (095) 246-98-48.

PITMAN, Sir Brian Ivor, Kt, FIB; British banker; b. 13 Dec. 1931, Cheltenham; s. of Ronald Ivor Pitman and Doris Ivy Pitman (née Short); m. Barbara Mildred Ann Darby 1954; two s. one d.; ed Cheltenham Grammar School; Asst Gen. Man. Lloyds Bank PLC 1973–75, Jt Gen. Man. 1975–76; Exec. Dir (UK and Asia-Pacific Div.), Lloyds Bank Int. Ltd 1976–78; Deputy Chief Exec. Lloyds Bank Int. Ltd 1978–82; Deputy Group Chief Exec., Lloyds Bank PLC 1982–83, Group Chief Exec. and Dir 1983–97, Chair. 1997–99; Deputy Chief Exec. and Dir TSB Bank PLC 1995–97, Deputy Chair. 1997–2000; Group Chief Exec. and Dir Lloyds TSB Group PLC 1995–97, Chair. 1997–2001; Pres. Chartered Inst. of Bankers 1997–98; fmr Pres. British Bankers Asscn; Dir (non-exec.) Carlton Communications PLC 1998–; Chair. Next PLC 1998–; Dir (non-exec.) Tomkins PLC 2000–, Carphone Warehouse Group PLC 2001–; Adviser to Morgan Stanley 2001–; mem. Guild of Int. Bankers 2001–, Master 2002–03; Hon. DSc (City Univ.) 1996, (UMIST) 2000. *Leisure interests:* golf, cricket, music. *Address:* Morgan Stanley, 25 Cabot Square, Canary Wharf, London, E14 4QA, England (Office). *Telephone:* (20) 7425-8234 (Office). *Fax:* (20) 7425-7255 (Office). *Website:* www.morganstanley.com (Office).

PITMAN, Jennifer Susan, OBE; British consultant, fmr racehorse trainer and author; b. Jennifer Susan Harvey, 11 June 1946, Leicester; d. of George Harvey and Mary Harvey; m. 1st Richard Pitman 1965 (annulled); two s.; m. 2nd David Stait 1997; ed Sarson Secondary Girls' School; Nat. Hunt trainer 1975–99; Dir Jenny Pitman Racing Ltd 1975–99; Racing and Media Consultant, DJS Racing 1999–; winners include: Watafella (Midlands Nat. 1977), Bueche Giorod (Ferguson Gold Cup 1980), Corbiere (Welsh Nat. 1982, Grand Nat. 1983), Burrough Hill Lad (Anthony Mild Mat Peter Cazalet Gold Cup 1983, Welsh Nat. 1983, Cheltenham Gold Cup 1984, King George VI Gold Cup 1984, Hennessey Gold Cup 1984), Smith's Man (Whitbread Trophy 1985), Stears By (Anthony Mild Mat Peter Cazalet Gold Cup 1986, Welsh Nat. 1986), Gainsay (Ritz Club Chase 1987, Sporting Life Weekend Chase 1987), Willsford (Midlands Nat. 1990), Crumpet Delite (Philip Cornes Saddle of Gold Final 1988), Garrison Savannah (Sun Alliance Chase 1990, Cheltenham Gold Cup 1991), Wonder Man (Welsh Champion Hurdle 1991), Don Valentino (Welsh Champion Hurdle 1992), Superior Finish (Anthony Mild Mat Peter Cazalet Gold Cup 1993), Royal Athlete (Grand Nat. 1995), Willsford (County Hurdle 1989, Scottish Nat. 1995), Mudahim (Irish Nat. 1995), Nathen Lad (Sun Alliance Chase 1996), Indefence (Supreme Novice Hurdler 1996), Master Tribe (Ladbroke Hurdler Leopardstown 1997), Princeful (Stayers Hurdle Cheltenham 1998), Smiths Cracker (Philip Cornes Saddle of Gold Final 1998); first woman to train Grand Nat. winner 1983; numerous awards including Racing Personality of the Year, Golden Spurs 1983, Commonwealth Sports Award 1983, 1984, Piper Heidsieck Trainer of the Year 1983–84, 1989–90, Variety Club of GB Sportswoman of the Year 1984. *Publications:* Glorious Uncertainty (autobiog.) 1984, Jenny Pitman: The Autobiography 1999, On the Edge 2002, Double Deal 2002, The Dilemma 2003. *Address:* Owls Barn, Kintbury, Hungerford, Berks., RG17 9XS, England (Office). *Telephone:* (1488) 668774 (Office); (1488) 669191 (Home). *Fax:* (1488) 668999 (Office). *E-mail:* jpr@owlsbarn.fsbusiness.co.uk (Office).

PITSUWAN, Surin, PhD; Thai politician; b. 28 Oct. 1949, Nakhon Si Thammarat; s. of Ismael Pitsuwan and Sapiya Pitsuwan; m. Alisa Ariya 1983; three s.; ed Claremont McKenna Coll., Harvard Univ., USA; columnist The Nation Review and Bangkok Post newspapers 1980–92; Congressional Fellow, Office of U.S. Rep. Geraldine Ferraro (q.v.) 1983–84; Academic Asst to Dean of Faculty of Political Science and to Vice-Rector for Academic Affairs, Thammasat Univ. 1985–86; MP from Nakhon Si Thammarat Prov. 1986–; Sec. to Speaker of House of Reps. 1986; Asst Sec. to Minister of Interior 1988; Deputy Minister of Foreign Affairs 1992–95, Minister of Foreign Affairs 1997–2000; mem. Democratic Party (DP). *Leisure interest:* reading. *Address:* c/o Ministry of Foreign Affairs, 443 Sri Ayudhya Road, Bangkok 10400, Thailand.

PITT, Brad; American film actor; b. 18 Dec. 1963, Shawnee, Okla; s. of Bill Pitt and Jane Pitt; m. Jennifer Aniston 2000; ed Univ. of Missouri. *Films include:* Cutting Glass, Happy Together 1989, Across the Tracks 1990, Contact, Thelma and Louise 1991, The Favor 1992, Johnny Suede 1992, Cool World 1992, A River Runs Through It 1992, Kalifornia 1993, Legend of the Fall 1994, Interview With The Vampire 1994, 12 Monkeys 1995, Seven 1996, Sleepers, Mad Monkeys, Tomorrow Never Dies 1996, Seven Years in Tibet 1997, The Devil's Own 1997, Meet Joe Black 1998, Fight Club 1999, Snatch 2000, The Mexican 2001, Spy Game 2001, Ocean's Eleven 2001. *Television appearances include:* Dallas (series), Glory Days (series), Too Young to Die? (film), The Image (film). *Address:* c/o Kevin Huvane, Creative Artists Agency, 9830 Wilshire Boulevard, Beverly Hills, CA 90212, USA.

PITT, Harvey Lloyd, BA, JD; American lawyer; b. 28 Feb. 1945, Brooklyn, NY; s. of Morris Jacob Pitt and Sara (née Sapir) Pitt; m. Saree Ruffin 1984; one s. one d. (and one d. one s. from previous marriage); ed Columbia and St. John's Univs., NY; with SEC, Washington 1968–78, Legal Asst to Commr 1969, Ed. Institutional Investor Study 1970–71, Special Counsel, Office of Gen. Counsel 1971–72, Chief Counsel Market Regulation Div. 1972–73, Exec. Asst to Chair. 1973–75, Gen. Counsel 1975–78, Chair. 2001–02; called to Bar, NY 1969, US Supreme Court 1972, DC 1979; Man. Partner Fried, Frank, Harris, Shriver & Jacobson, Washington 1978–89, Co-Chair. 1997–; Adjunct Prof. of Law George Washington Univ. Nat. Law Centre 1974–82, Univ. of Pa Law School 1983–84; Vice-Pres. Glen Haven Civic Assen, Silver Spring, Md 1972–73, Pres. 1974; mem. ABA, Fed. Bar Assen, Admin. Conference of US, American Law Inst.; Outstanding Young Lawyer Award, Fed. Bar Assen 1975, Learned Hand Award, Inst. for Human Relations 1988. *Address:* Securities and Exchange Commission, 450 Fifth Street, NW, Washington, DC 20001 (Office); 4430 Van Ness Street, NW, Washington, DC 20016-5626, USA (Home).

PITTMAN, James A., Jr., MD; American professor of medicine; b. 12 April 1927, Orlando, Fla; s. of James A. Pittman and Jean C. Garretson; m. Constance Ming Chung Shen 1955; two s.; ed Davidson Coll. NC and Harvard Medical School; Clinical Assoc. Nat. Insts. of Health, Bethesda, Md 1954–56; Instructor in Medicine, Univ. of Alabama 1956–59, Asst Prof. 1959–62, Assoc. Prof. 1962–64, Prof. of Medicine 1964–92, Prof. of Physiology and Biophysics 1967–92, Dean, School of Medicine 1973–92, Distinguished Prof. 1992–; Consultant, Children's Hosp. Birmingham, Ala 1962–71; Prof. of Medicine, Georgetown Univ. School of Medicine, Washington, DC 1971–73; Sr Adviser Int. Council on Control of Iodine Deficiency Diseases 1994–96; Master, American Coll. of Physicians, Assen of American Physicians, American Chemical Soc. etc.; Hon. DSc (Davidson Coll.) 1980, (Alabama) 1984. *Publications:* Diagnosis and Treatment of Thyroid Disease 1963; articles in professional journals. *Leisure interests:* flying, scuba diving, hunting, sailing. *Address:* University of Alabama School of Medicine, 1924 Seventh Avenue South, Birmingham, AL 35294 (Office); 5 Ridge Drive, Birmingham, AL 35213, USA (Home). *Telephone:* (205) 934-3414 (Office). *Fax:* (205) 975-4976 (Office).

PITTMAN, Robert Warren; American media executive; b. 28 Dec. 1953, Jackson, Miss.; s. of Warren E. Pittman and Lanita (née Hurdle) Pittman; m. 1st Sandra Hill 1979 (divorced); one s.; m. 2nd Veronique Choa 1997; one c.; ed Millsaps Coll., Oakland, Pittsburg and Harvard Univs; disc jockey WJDX-FM (Miss.) 1970–72; disc jockey WRIT (Milwaukee) 1972; Research Dir WDRQ (Detroit) 1972–73; Programme Dir WPEZ (Pittsburg) 1973–74; with

WMAQ–WKQZ (NY) and NBC Radio 1974–77; with WNBC (NY) 1977–79; exec. producer Album Tracks NBC TV 1977–78; Dir, Vice-Pres., Sr Vice-Pres. Warner Amex Satellite Entertainment Co. (now MTV Networks Inc.) 1979–82, Pres., CEO 1985–86; Exec. Vice-Pres., COO MTV Networks Inc. 1983–85; Pres., CEO Quantum Media Inc. 1987–89; Exec. Adviser Warner Communications Inc. 1989–90; Pres., CEO Time Warner Enterprises 1990–95; CEO Six Flags Entertainment 1991–95; Man. Partner, CEO Century 21 Real Estate 1995–96; Pres., CEO America On-Line Networks 1996–97, Pres., COO America On-Line Inc. 1997–2001, Co-COO 2001–02; Chair. NY Shakespeare Festival 1987–94; dir numerous cos; Golden Plate Award, American Acad. of Achievement 1990, Lifetime Achievement Int. Monitor Award, Int. Teleproduction Soc. 1993 and many others. *Address:* c/o America On-Line, 2200 AOL Way, Sterling, VA 20166, USA.

PIVETTI, Irene; Italian politician; d. of Grazia Gabrielli; m. Paolo Taranta 1988 (separated 1992); ed Catholic Univ. of the Sacred Heart, Milan; journalist; mem. Parl. 1992–, Speaker 1995–96; fmr mem. Northern League; currently Pres. Unione Democratici per l'Europa (UDEUR, f. 1999). *Address:* Unione Democratici per l'Europa, Largo Arenula 34, 00186 Rome; Camera dei Deputati, Rome, Italy; (06) 684241. *Fax:* (06) 6872593. *E-mail:* udeur@udeur .org. *Website:* www.udeur.org.

PIVOT, Bernard; French journalist; b. 5 May 1935, Lyons; s. of Charles Pivot and Marie-Louise Pivot (née Dumas); m. Monique Dupuis 1959; two d.; ed Centre de formation des Journalistes; on staff of Figaro littéraire, then Literary Ed.; Figaro 1958–74; Chronique pour sourire, on Europe 1 1970–73; Columnist, Le Point 1974–77; producer and presenter of Ouvrez les guillemets 1973–74, Apostrophes, Channel 2 1975–90, Bouillon de culture 1991–2001; Ed. Lire 1975–93; Dir Sofica Créations 1986–; mem. Conseil supérieur de la langue française 1989–; Pres. Grévin Acad. 2001–; Grand Prix de la Critique l'Académie française 1983, Prix Louise Weiss, Bibliothèque Nat. 1989, Prix de la langue française décerne à la Foire 2000; Chevalier du Mérite agricole. *Publications:* L'Amour en vogue (novel) 1959, La vie oh là là! 1966, Les critiques littéraires 1968, Beaujolaises 1978, Le Football en vert 1980, Le Métier de lire. Réponses à Pierre Nora 1990, Remontrances à la ménagère de moins de cinquante ans (essay) 1998. *Leisure interests:* tennis, football, gastronomy. *Address:* France 2, 7 esplanade Henri de France, 75907, Paris cedex 15; Les Jonnerys, 69430 Quincié-en-Beaujolais, France (Home).

PIVOVAROV, Yuri Sergeyevich, Dr rer. pol; Russian political scientist; b. 25 April 1950, Moscow; m.; one s. one d.; ed Moscow Inst. of Int. Relations; Jr then Sr Researcher, Prof., Head of Div., Deputy Dir Inst. of Information on Public Sciences, USSR (now Russian) Acad. of Sciences (INION) 1976–98, Dir 1998–; mem. Exec. Bd Russian Asscn of Political Sciences; mem. Council on Politology, Presidium, Russian Acad. of Sciences; Ed.-in-Chief Gosudarstvo i Pravo (journal), Politicheskaya Nauka (periodical); Corresp. mem. Russian Acad. of Sciences 1997–. *Publications:* Political Culture of Russia after Reforms, Essays on the History of Russian Socio-political Ideas of the 19th and Early 20th Century and over 200 articles. *Address:* INION, Nakhimovsky prosp. 51/21, 117418 Moscow, Russia (Office). *Telephone:* (095) 123-88-81 (Office).

PIWOWSKI, Marek; Polish/American film director, writer, actor and journalist; b. 24 Oct. 1935, Warsaw; s. of Władysław Piwowski and Jadwiga Piwowska; ed State Acad. of Film, Łódź, Univ. of Warsaw; Visiting Prof. City Univ. of New York; actor in 11 films; Dir and writer of 17 films which have won 24 int. film festival awards; mem. American Film Inst. *Films include:* Kirk Douglas 1967, Flybeater 1967, A Cruise 1970, Psychodrama 1972, Corkscrew 1971, Blue Hair 1972, How to Recognize the Vampire 1974, Foul Play 1977, Trouble is my Business 1988, Catch 22 1990, Kidnapping Agata 1993, The Parade Step 1998, The Barracuda's Kiss 1998, The Knife in the Head of Dino Baggio 1999, Olympiad in Zakopane 1999, Executioners 2001, Martin's Law 2001, Body Language 2002. *Leisure interests:* sailing, skiing, gliders, windsurfing. *Address:* ul. Promenada 21, 00-778 Warsaw, Poland. *Telephone:* (22) 841-80-80. *Fax:* (22) 841-80-80. *E-mail:* piwek@eranet.pl (Home).

PIYASHEVA, Larisa Ivanovna, D.ECON.SC.; Russian economist; b. 10 July 1947, Moscow; m. Boris Pinsker (divorced); ed Plekhanov Inst. of Nat. Econ.; researcher Inst. of Int. Workers' Movt USSR Acad. of Sciences 1969–91; Head, Chair. of Econs, Prof., Moscow State Open Univ. 1991–93, Dean of Faculty 1996–; Head Finance-Economy Dept of Council of Fed. Staff 1994–; Dir F. von Hayek Pvt. Inst. of Econs and Law 1995–; Dir-Gen. Dept of Moscow Maj. Office Feb.–Sept. 1992. *Publications:* monographs and scientific articles on problems of Soviet economy. *Address:* Serpukhovskoy Val 17/23, Apt. 9, 113191 Moscow, Russia. *Telephone:* (095) 292-12-83.

PIZA, Arthur Luiz; Brazilian painter and printmaker; b. 1928; painter and exhibitor 1943–; moved to Paris 1952; works in many important museums and pvt. collections; Purchase Prize 1953 and Nat. Prize for Prints São Paulo Biennale 1959, Prizes at biennales at Ljubljana 1961, Santiago 1966, Venice 1966, Grenchen Triennale 1961, biennales of Norway and Mexico 1980, Puerto Rico 1991, Nat. Asscn of Critics Grand Prize, Brazil 1994. *Exhibitions:* regular exhibitor at Bienal de São Paulo 1951–63 and Biennale of Ljubljana 1957–81, at Triennali of Grenchen since 1958; one-man exhbns. in Brazil, Germany, Yugoslavia, USA, France, Switzerland, Sweden, Spain, Belgium and Italy, Triennali of Norway since since 1972. *Publication:* Larousse of Paintings (Small Larousse of Paintings, Vol. II) 1979. *Address:* 16 rue Dauphine, 75006 Paris, France.

PIZZARO, Artur; pianist; Prof. Guildhall School of Music and Drama, London; has appeared with numerous orchestras including: Philadelphia Orchestra, LA Philharmonic, Baltimore Symphony, NHK Symphony (Tokyo), Montréal Symphony, Toronto Symphony, Hong Kong Philharmonic, Leipzig Chamber Orchestra, Rotterdam Philharmonic, Vienna Symphony, Royal Philharmonic, BBC Symphony Orchestra; has recorded nine solo CDs of works by Liszt, Bach-Liszt, Kabalevsky, Rodrigo, Vorisek, Mompou, Shostakovich, Scriabin, Milhaud; won Leeds Int. Piano Competition 1990. *Address:* Guildhall School of Music and Drama, Barbican, London, E.C.2, England (Office). *Telephone:* (20) 7628-2571 (Office).

PLANCHON, Roger; French theatrical director and playwright; b. 12 Sept. 1931, Saint-Chamond; s. of Emile Planchon and Augusta (née Nogier) Planchon; m. Colette Dompietrini 1958; two s.; bank clerk 1947–49; Founder Théâtre de la Comédie, Lyon 1951; Co-Dir Théâtre de la Cité, Villeurbanne 1957–72; Dir Théâtre Nat. Populaire 1972–; Pres. Fondation Molière 1987–; aims to popularize the theatre by extending its units and recreating the classics within a modern social context; Pres. Rhône-Alpes Cinéma; Prix Ibsen (for Le cochon noir) 1974, Prix Georges Lherminier du Syndicat de la critique dramatique 1986, 1998; Chevalier des Arts et des Lettres, Croix de guerre, Chevalier Légion d'honneur. *Films include: (actor)* Le grand frère 1982, Danton 1983, Un amour interdit, La septième Cible 1984, Camile Claudel 1988, Radio Corbeau 1989, Jean Galmot, aventurier 1990, L'Année de l'éveil 1991, Louis, enfant roi 1992. *Plays:* has directed and acted in over 60 plays by Shakespeare, Molière, Racine, Marivaux, Brecht, Adamov, Vinaver, Dubillard and himself, most recently: Ionesco 1983, L'avare 1986, George Dandin 1987, Andromaque (Dir) 1989, Le Vieil Hiver 1990, Fragile Forêt 1990, Les libertins 1994, No Man's Land 1994, Occupe-Toi d'Amélie! 1995, Le Radeau de la Méduse 1995, La Tour de Nesle 1996, Le Triomphe de l'Amour 1996, Les Démons et la Dame de Chez Maxim 1998. *Films:* (wrote and directed): Dandin 1987, Louis, enfant roi 1992, Lautrec 1998. *Publications:* Plays: La remise 1961, Patte blanche 1965, Bleus, blancs, rouges ou les Libertins 1967, Dans le vent 1968, L'infâme 1969, La langue au chat 1972, Le cochon noir 1973, Gilles de Rais 1976, Fragile Forêt 1991, Le Radeau de la Méduse 1995, L'Avare 2001. *Address:* Théâtre National Populaire, 8 place Lazare Goujon, 69627 Villeurbanne Cedex, France. *Telephone:* (4) 78-03-30-30. *Fax:* (4) 78-84-03-20.

PLANT OF HIGHFIELD, Baron (Life Peer), cr. 1991, of Weelsby in the County of Humberside; **Raymond Plant,** PhD, DLitt; British academic and politician; b. 19 March 1945, Grimsby; s. of Stanley Plant and Marjorie Plant; m. Katherine Dixon 1967; three s.; ed Havelock School, Grimsby, King's Coll. London and Univ. of Hull; Lecturer, Sr Lecturer in Philosophy, Univ. of Manchester 1967–79; Prof. of Politics, Univ. of Southampton 1979–94, Pro-Chancellor 1996–2002, Prof. of European Political Thought 2000–02; Prof. of Jurisprudence, King's Coll. London 2001–; Master, St Catherine's Coll. Oxford 1994–96; Pres. Nat. Council of Voluntary Orgs., Acad. of Learned Socs. in the Social Sciences; Hon. Fellow Harris Manchester Coll. Oxford, St Catherine's Coll., Oxford, Cardiff Univ.; Stanton Lecturer, Univ. of Cambridge 1989–91; Sarum Lecturer, Univ. of Oxford 1991; Hon. Fellow Univ. of Cardiff; Hon. DLitt (Hull, London Guildhall). *Publications:* Hegel 1973, Community and Ideology 1974, Political Philosophy and Social Welfare 1981, Philosophy, Politics and Citizenship 1984, Conservative Capitalism 1989, Modern Political Thought 1991, Democracy, Representation and Elections 1992, Hegel on Religion 1997, Politics, Theology and History 2000. *Leisure interests:* music, opera, politics. *Address:* 6 Woodview Close, Bassett, Southampton, SO16 3PZ, England. *Telephone:* (23) 8059-2448 (Office); (23) 8076-9529 (Home).

PLANTEY, Alain Gilles; French government official; b. 19 July 1924, Mulhouse; m. Christiane Wioland 1955 (died 1999); four d.; ed Univs. of Bordeaux and Paris à la Sorbonne; Staff of Council of State 1949; French Del. to UN 1951–52; Master of Requests Council of State 1956–74; Legal Adviser OEEC 1956–57; Prof. Ecole Royale d'Admin., Cambodia, Faculté de Droit and Ecole Nat. d'Admin., Paris 1957–62; Gen. Sec. Agence France-Presse 1958–67; Asst Sec.-Gen. for the Community and African and Malagasy Affairs at the Presidency 1961–66; Amb. in Madagascar 1966–72; Asst Sec.-Gen. WEU 1972–82; Chair. Standing Armaments Cttee 1972–82; Conseiller d'Etat 1974–93; Chair. Int. Court of Arbitration, ICC 1989–96; Pres. Inst. de France 1996; mem. Conseil Int. de l'Arbitrage en matière de Sport (CIAS) 1994; mem. Acad. of Moral and Political Sciences (Inst. of France), American Acad. of Social and Political Science, Int. Council on Commercial Arbitration; Chair. Int. Inst. of Law; Vice-Pres. Inst. Charles de Gaulle; Grand Officier, Légion d'honneur 2000 and numerous other decorations. *Publications:* La réforme de la justice marocaine 1949, La justice répressive et le droit pénal chérifien 1950, Au coeur du problème berbère 1952, Traité pratique de la fonction publique 1956, La formation et le perfectionnement des fonctionnaires 1957, La Communauté 1962, Indépendance et coopération 1964–77, Prospective de l'État 1975, Droit et pratique de la fonction publique internationale 1977, Réformes dans la fonction publique 1978, La négociation internationale 1980, 1994, International Civil Service: Law and Management 1981, Derecho y Práctica de la Función Pública Internacional y Europea 1982, De la politique entre les Etats: Principes de diplomatie 1987, La Fonction publique, traité général 1992, Tratado de Derecho Diplomático 1992, Diplomatie 2000, La negociation internationale au XXIe siècle 2002. *Address:* 6 avenue Sully-Prudhomme, Paris 75007, France (Home). *Telephone:* 1-45-55-26-49 (Home). *Fax:* 1-44-41-43-27 (Office); 1-45-51-41-58, 45-55-26-49 (Home).

PLANTIN, Marcus; British broadcasting executive; b. 23 Oct. 1945; s. of Charles P. Plantin and Vera H. Plantin; m.1980; two s.; ed Surbiton Co. Grammar School, Guildford School of Acting; Producer BBC TV 1978–84; joined London Weekend TV, Head Light Entertainment 1985–87, Controller of Entertainment 1987–90, Dir of Programmes 1990–92, 1997; Dir London Weekend Productions and LWT Holdings 1990–92; Network Dir ITV 1992–97, Man. ITV Network Centre 1995–97; Dir of Programmes LWT Productions 1998–2000, LWT/United Productions 2000–01; Dir of Int. Entertainment Formats and Production, Granada TV 2000–01, Dir of Entertainment Content 2001–02. *Leisure interests:* gardening, swimming, travel. *Address:* LWT, London Television Centre, Upper Ground, London, SE1 9LT, England (Office). *Telephone:* (20) 7261-3444 (Office); (20) 8563-2041 (Home). *Fax:* (20) 7928-6803 (Office). *E-mail:* marcus.plantin@granadamedia.com (Office); purdenhoe@msn.com (Home).

PLANTU (pseudonym of Plantureux, Jean Henri); French artist; b. 23 March 1951, Paris; s. of Henri Plantureux and Renée Seignardie; m. Chantal Meyer 1971; three s. one d.; ed Lycée Henri IV, Paris; political cartoonist, Le Monde 1972–, L'Express 1991–; caricaturist, Droit de réponse (TV show) 1981–87; Grand Prix de l'Humour noir Granville; Prix du Reportage (film on Yasser Arafat) 1991. *Publications:* Pauvres chéris 1978, La Démocratie? Parlons-en 1979, Les Cours de caoutchouc sont trop élastiques 1982, C'est le goulag 1983, Pas nette, la planète! 1984, Politic-look 1984, Bonne année pour tous 1985, Ça manque de femmes 1986, A la Soupe 1987, Wolfgang, tu feras informatique 1988, Ouverture en bémol 1988, Des fourmis dans les jambes 1989, C'est la lutte finale 1990, Un Vagne Souvenir 1990, Reproche-Orient 1991, Le Président Hip-Hop! 1991, Le Douanier se fait la malle 1992, Ici Maastricht, les Européens parlent aux Européens 1992, Cohabitation à l'Eau de Rose 1993, Le Pire est derrière nous! 1994, Le Petit Mitterrand Illustré 1995, Le Petit Chirac et le Petit Balladur Illustrés 1995, Le Petit Raciste Illustré 1995, Le Petit Communiste Illustré 1995, Le Petit Socialiste Illustré 95, Magic Chirac 1995, Les Années vaches folles 1996, Pas de photos 1997, La France dopée 1998, Le Petit Juge Illustré 1999, L'Année PLANTU 1999, Cassettes, mensongs et vidéo 2001. *Address:* Le Monde, 21 bis rue Claude Bernard, 75005 Paris, France.

PLASTOW, Sir David Arnold Stuart, Kt, FBIM, FRSA; British business executive; b. 9 May 1932, Grimsby, Lincs.; s. of the late James Stuart Plastow and of Marie Plastow; m. Barbara Ann May 1954; one s. one d.; ed Culford School, Bury St Edmunds; apprenticed Vauxhall Motors Ltd 1950; joined Rolls-Royce Ltd, Motor Car Div. Crewe 1958, Marketing Dir Motor Car Div. 1967–71, Man. Dir 1971–72; Man. Dir Rolls-Royce Motors Ltd 1972–74, Group Man. Dir 1974–80; Regional Dir Lloyds Bank 1974–76; Dir Vickers Ltd 1975–92, Man. Dir 1980–86, Chief. Exec. 1980–92, Chair. 1987–92; Chair. Inchape PLC 1992–95; Dir GKN Ltd 1978–84; Dir Legal & General 1985–87; Guinness PLC 1986–94, Deputy Chair. 1987–89, Jt Deputy Chair. 1989–94; Deputy Chair. (non-exec.) TSB Group PLC 1991–95; Dir (non-exec.) Lloyds TSB 1996–99; Non-Exec. Dir Cable and Wireless PLC 1991–93; Trustee Royal Opera House Trust 1992–93 (Chair. 1992–93); mem. Bd Tenneco Inc. (Houston) 1985–92; Gov. (non-exec.) BUPA 1990–95 (Deputy Chair. 1992–95); Pres. Soc. of Motor Mfrs and Traders Ltd 1976–78, Deputy Pres. 1978–80; Pres. Motor Industry Research Asscn 1978–81; Vice-Pres. Inst. of Motor Industry 1974–82; Chair. Grand Council, Motor and Cycle Trades Benevolent Fund 1976–78; mem. Eng Council 1981–83, Council CBI, Council, Manchester Business School, Court of Manchester Univ., Council, Regular Forces Employment Asscn, Council, Industrial Soc., Chair. 1983–87, British Overseas Trade Bd 1980–83, British North American Cttee; Dir Tenneco Inc. 1985–92, 1996–; Chair. Medical Research Council 1990–98; Chancellor, Luton Univ. 1993–; C. I. MgT.; Patron, Coll. of Aeronautical and Automobile Eng 1972–79; Chair. of Govs Culford School, Bury St Edmunds 1979–; Liveryman, Worshipful Co. of Coachmakers and Coach Harness Makers; Hon. DSc (Cranfield Inst. of Tech.) 1978; Young Businessman of the Year Award (The Guardian) 1976. *Leisure interests:* golf, music.

PLATÉ, Nikolai Alfredovich; Russian chemist; b. 4 Nov. 1934, Moscow; m.; one s. one d.; ed Moscow State Univ.; Jr, Sr researcher, Head of Lab. Moscow State Univ. 1956, now Prof. Emer.; Dir A. Topchiev Inst. of Petrochemical Synthesis; Corresp. mem. USSR (now Russian) Acad. of Sciences 1974, mem. 1987, Vice-Pres. 1996; Deputy Acad.-Sec. Dept of Gen. and Tech. Chem, Chief Scientific Sec. 1991–96, Chief Scientific Sec. of the Acad. 2001–02, Vice-Pres. 2002–; mem. European Acad. of Sciences, Nat. Acad. of Sciences of Ukraine, American Chem. Soc.; research in polymers of medical application, chem. modifications of polymers, liquid crystal polymers, synthetic polymeric membranes; USSR State Prize 1985, V. Kargin Prize; H. Mark Medal, Austrian Inst. of Chemical Tech. 1999. *Publications:* Ed.-in-Chief Vysokomolekulyarnye Soyedinenya (Polymer Science); books and articles in scientific periodicals. *Leisure interests:* tennis, driving. *Address:* Presidium of Russian Academy of Sciences, Leninsky prospekt 14, 117901 Moscow; Institute of Petrochemical Synthesis, Leninsky prospekt 29, 117912 Moscow, Russia. *Telephone:* (095) 954-44-85 (Academy), 952-59-27 (Institute). *Fax:* (095) 954-25-49.

PLATER, Alan Frederick, FRSL, FRSA; British writer; b. 15 April 1935, Jarrow-on-Tyne; s. of Herbert Richard Plater and Isabella Scott Plater; m. 1st Shirley Johnson 1958 (divorced 1985); two s. one d.; m. 2nd Shirley Rubinstein 1986; three step-s.; ed Kingston High School and King's Coll. Newcastle-upon-Tyne; trained as architect; full-time writer 1960–; has written extensively for radio, TV, films and theatre, also for The Guardian, Listener, New Statesman, etc.; Co.-Chair. Writers' Guild of GB 1986–87, Pres. 1991–95; Visiting Prof., Univ. of Bournemouth 2001–; Hon. Fellow, Humberside Coll. of Educ. 1983; Hon. DLitt (Hull) 1985; Hon. DCL (Northumbria) 1997; Royal TV Soc. Writers' Award 1988, BAFTA Writers' Award 1988 and many other awards. *Plays include:* A Smashing Day, Close the Coalhouse Door, And a Little Love Besides, Swallows on the Water, Trinity Tales, The Fosdyke Saga, Fosdyke Two, On Your Way, Riley!, Skyhooks, A Foot on the Earth, Prez, Rent Party (musical), Sweet Sorrow, Going Home, I Thought I Heard a Rustling, Shooting the Legend, All Credit to the Lads, Peggy for You, Tales From the Backyard, Only a Matter of Time, Barriers. *Films include:* The Virgin and the Gypsy, It Shouldn't Happen to a Vet, Priest of Love, Keep the Aspidistra Flying. *Radio includes:* Only a Matter of Time, Time Added on for Injuries, The Devil's Music. *Television includes:* series: Z Cars, Softly Softly, The Beiderbecke Trilogy; adaptations: Barchester Chronicles, The Fortunes of War, A Very British Coup, Campion, A Day in Summer, A Few Selected Exits, Oliver's Travels, Dalziel and Pascoe; recent plays: Doggin' Around, The Last of the Blonde Bombshells. *Publications:* The Beiderbecke Affair 1985, The Beiderbecke Tapes 1986, Misterioso 1987, The Beiderbecke Connection 1992, Oliver's Travels 1994; plays and shorter pieces in various anthologies. *Leisure interests:* reading, theatre, snooker, jazz, grandchildren, talking and listening. *Address:* c/o Alexandra Cann Representation, 12 Abingdon Road, London, W8 6AF, England. *Telephone:* (20) 7938-4002.

PLATINI, Michel; French footballer, football coach, broadcaster and sports administrator; b. 21 June 1955, Joeuf; s. of Aldo Platini and Anna Pillenelli; m. Christele Bigoni 1977; one s. one d.; professional footballer A.S. Nancy-Lorraine 1973–79 (winners Coupe de France 1978), A.S. St-Etienne 1979–82 (French nat. champions 1981), Juventus, Turin 1982–85 where he scored 68 goals in 147 games (Italian nat. champions, winners European Cup Winners' Cup 1984, European Championship Cup 1985); player with French nat. team 1982, 1984 (winners European Cup), 1985 (winners Artemio Franqui Intercontinental Cup), 1986; French Nat. Team Coach 1987–92; co-presenter, ed. and consultant French TV 1985–88, consultant 1993–; f. and Pres. Michel Platini Foundation 1987–; Jt Pres. French 1998 World Cup Organising Cttee; Vice-Pres. French Football Fed.; Adviser to Pres. FIFA; mem. Exec. Cttee U.E.F.A. 2002–; Chevalier, Légion d'honneur, Officier, Ordre nat. du Mérite, mem. Laurens World Sports Acad.; Ballon d'or (European footballer of the year) 1983, 1984, 1985, Soulier d'or européen, Top scorer in Italian league 1983, 1984, 1985, World Footballer of the Year 1984, 1985, French Player of the Century. *Publication:* Ma vie comme un match 1987. *Address:* c/o FIFA, Hitzigweg 11, P.O. Box 85, CH 8030, Zurich 30, Switzerland (Office).

PLATONOV, Vladimir Mikhailovich, CAND.JUR.SC.; Russian politician; b. 24 Dec. 1954, Moscow; m.; one s. one d.; ed Lumumba Univ. of Peoples' Friendship; worked in machine-construction factory 1972–75; investigator Prosecutor's Office, Deputy Prosecutor Moskvoretsky Dist of Moscow 1983–91; pvt. law practice, Exec. Dir Avtum Co. 1991–94; mem. Moscow City Duma 1993, Chair. (Speaker) 1994–; mem. Party Block Choice of Russia; mem. Russian Council of Fed. 1996–; Chair. Cttee on Constitutional Law Feb. 1996–. *Address:* Moscow City Duma, Petrovka str. 22, 103051 Moscow, Russia (Office). *Telephone:* (095) 923-50-80 (Office). *Fax:* (095) 753-71-31 (Office). *E-mail:* d29@duma.munic.ru (Office).

PLATONOV, Vladimir Petrovich, DSc; Belarus mathematician; b. 1 Dec. 1939, Staiki, Byelorussian SSR; s. of Petr Platonov and Anna Platonova; m. Valentina Platonova 1974; two d.; ed Byelorussian State University; Asst Prof. Byelorussian State Univ. 1963, Prof. 1968, Head of Algebra Dept 1967–71; corresp. mem. Acad. of Sciences of Byelorussian SSR (now Belarus) 1969, mem. 1972 (Pres. 1987–92); Head Algebra Dept, Inst. of Math. 1971–93, Dir 1977–92, Lecturer; mem. Inst. for Advanced Studies, Princeton, NJ 1991–92; Prof., Univ. of Mich., USA 1993, Univ. of Bielefeld 1994, Univ. of Waterloo, Canada 1995–; mem. USSR (now Russian) Acad. of Sciences 1987, Belarus Acad. for Educ. 1995, New York Acad. of Sciences 1995; Foreign mem. Indian Nat. Science Acad.; Hon. mem. Chinese-Henan Acad. of Sciences; People's Deputy of the USSR 1989–91; Lenin Prize 1978, Humboldt Prize 1993. *Publications include:* Algebraic groups and number theory 1991, Finite-dimensional division algebras 1992. *Leisure interest:* literature. *Address:* Department of Pure Mathematics, University of Waterloo, Waterloo, Ont., N2L 3G1, Canada. *Telephone:* (519) 885-1211, ext. 3484. *Fax:* (519) 725-0160.

PLATT, Lewis Emmett, MBE; American computer executive; b. 11 April 1941, Johnson City, NY; s. of Norval Lewis and Margaret Dora Williams; m. Joan Ellen Redmund 1983; four d.; ed Cornell Univ., Univ. of Philadelphia; with Hewlett Packard, Waltham, Mass. 1966–71, Eng Man. 1971–74, Operations Man. 1976–77, Divisional Gen. Man. 1974–80, Group Gen. Man., Palo Alto, Calif. 1980–84, Vice-Pres. 1983–85, Exec. Vice-Pres. 1987–92, Pres., CEO, Chair. 1993–99; mem. Cornell Univ. Council 1992–, Computer Systems Policy Project 1993–; mem. Bd Dirs. Jt Venture, Silicon Valley 1996; Award for Business Excellence, Univ. of Calif. School of Business Admin. 1996, Tree of Life Award, Jewish Nat. Fund 1996, Leadership and Vision Award, San Francisco Chapter French-American Chamber of Commerce 1997. *Address:* c/o Hewlett-Packard Co., 3000 Hanover Street, Palo Alto, CA 94304, USA (Office).

PLATT, Nicholas, MA; American diplomatist and educational administrator; b. 10 March 1936, New York; m. Sheila Maynard; three s.; ed Harvard Coll. and Johns Hopkins Univ. School of Advanced Int. Studies; Chinese language student, Taiwan 1963; Political Officer, Hong Kong 1964–68, Beijing 1973–74, Tokyo 1974–77; staff mem. President Nixon's Del. to China 1972, later mem. U.S. Liaison Office, Beijing; Dir for Japanese Affairs, Dept of State 1977–78; Nat. Security Council staff mem. specializing in Asian Affairs 1978–79; Deputy Asst Sec. for Defense 1980–81; Acting Asst Sec. of State for UN Affairs 1981–82; Amb. to Zambia 1982–84, to the Philippines 1987–91, to Pakistan 1991–92; Pres. Asia Soc. 1992–; Special Asst to Sec. of State and Exec. Sec., Dept of State 1985–87; mem. Bd Dirs. Fiduciary Trust Int; mem. Int. Advisory Bd Financial Times 1998–. *Address:* The Asia Society, 725 Park Avenue, New York, NY 10021 (Office); 131 East 69th Street, New York, NY 10021, USA (Home).

PLATT, Stephen (Steve), B.SC.ECON.; British journalist; b. 29 Sept. 1954, Stoke-on-Trent; s. of Kenneth Platt and Joyce Pritchard; one d. by Diane Louise Paice; partner Anna Elizabeth Sutton; ed Longton High School, Stoke On Trent, Wade Deacon School, Widnes and London School of Econs; teacher, Moss Brook Special School, Widnes 1972–73; Dir Self Help Housing Resource Library, Polytechnic of N London 1977–80; co-ordinator, Islington Community Housing 1980–83; freelance writer and journalist 1983–; News Ed., subsequently Acting Ed. New Society 1986–88; Ed. Midweek 1988–89, Enjoying the Countryside 1988–; Ed. New Statesman and Society 1991–96; contributing Ed. Channel 4 TV 1996–; Website and Contributing Ed. Time Team 1999–; Dispatches Website Ed. 1999–; UKGLO Award for Outstanding Achievement 1999. *Leisure interests:* football, walking, countryside, gardening, breeding frogs, Paddington Bear, archaeology and ancient history. *Address:* 46 Tufnell Park Road, London, N7 0DT, England. *Telephone:* (20) 7263-4185. *E-mail:* plattsteve@aol.com (Home).

PLATT, Trevor, PhD, FRS, FRSC; British/Canadian oceanographer; b. 12 Aug. 1942, Salford, England; s. of John Platt and Lily Platt; m. Shubha Sathyendranath 1988; ed Nottingham, Toronto and Dalhousie Univs.; research scientist Bedford Inst. of Oceanography, Canada 1965–72, Head of Biological Oceanography 1972–; Chair. Int. Ocean-Colow Co-ordinating Group 1996–, Joint Global Ocean Flux Study 1991–93; Huntsman Medal 1992 Hutchinson Medal, Rosenstiel Medal, Plymouth Marine Medal 1999. *Publications:* numerous papers in learned journals. *Leisure interests:* cycling, fly-fishing, languages. *Address:* 33 Crichton Park Road, Dartmouth, NS, B3A 2N9, Canada (Home); Bedford Institute of Oceanography, Dartmouth, NS, B2Y 4A2. *Telephone:* (902) 426-3793. *Fax:* (902) 426-9388. *Website:* www.sap.com (Office).

PLATTNER, Hasso; German computer executive; b. 21 Jan. 1944, Berlin; ed Karlsruhe Univ.; consultant IBM 1968–72; co.-f. SAP AG 1972, Chair. SAP America, CEO SAP Markets, Co-Chair., CEO –2003, Chair. Supervisory Bd 2003–; Hon. Prof. Saarbrücken Univ. *Leisure interests:* golf, sailing. *Address:* SAP AG, P.O. Box 1461, 69185, Walldorf, Germany (Office). *Telephone:* (6227) 747474 (Office). *Website:* www.sap.com.

PLAVINSKY, Dmitri; Russian artist; b. 28 April 1937, Moscow; m. Maria Plavinskaya; three d.; ed Moscow Regional Art Coll.; painter and printmaker. *Solo exhibitions include:* Dubna 1970, Alex Edmond Gallery, New York 1993, Mimi Ferzt Gallery, New York 1995, 1998, 2000, Dom Nashchokina Gallery, Moscow 1995, Kine Gallery, Moscow 1998; numerous group exhbns. including Grosvenor Gallery, London 1964, ICA London 1977, Phillips Auctioneers, London 1989, Museum of Modern Art, New York 1967, Metropolitan Museum, New York 1977, San Francisco 1965, 1977, Florence 1969, Frankfurt 1969, Lugano 1970, Cologne 1970, Copenhagen 1971, Venice 1977, Tokyo 1978, Berne 1988, Warsaw 1994, Kassel 1995, Russian State Museum, St Petersburg 2001, Kino Gallery, Moscow 2001, Art Berlin 2002. *Publication:* Dmitri Plavinsky 2000. *Address:* 370 Fort Washington Avenue #507, New York, NY 10033, USA (Office); Arbat str. 51, korp. 2, Apt. 97, 121002 Moscow, Russia. *Telephone:* (212) 928-3260; (095) 241-32-29. *E-mail:* plavinsky@aol.com (Home).

PLAVŠIĆ, Biljana, PhD; Bosnia and Herzegovina politician and biologist; b. 1930; m. (divorced); ed Zagreb Univ., Croatia; fmr Prof. of Botany, Sarajevo Univ.; founding mem. Serbian Democratic Party; mem. 'Crisis Cttee' (military and civilian govt which ordered mass expulsion of Muslims and Croats from E and Cen. Bosnia) 1991–92; Vice-Pres., Acting Pres., then Pres. Serb Rep. of Bosnia and Herzegovina 1992–98; Chair. Serb Nat. Alliance; surrendered herself to trial at War Crimes Tribunal, The Hague Jan. 2001, charged with genocide and crimes against humanity; pleaded guilty on 2 Oct. 2002 to crimes against humanity, charge of genocide dropped by tribunal, sentenced to 11 years' imprisonment Feb. 2003.

PLAYER, Gary (Jim); South African professional golfer; b. 1 Nov. 1935, Johannesburg; s. of Francis Harry Audley Player and of the late Muriel Marie Ferguson; m. Vivienne Verwey 1957; two s. four d.; turned professional 1953; first overseas player for 45 years to win U.S. Open Championship 1965; Winner, British Open Championship 1959, 1968, 1974; Piccadilly World Match Play Champion 1965, 1966, 1968, 1971, 1973; U.S. Open Champion 1965; U.S. Masters Champion 1961, 1974, 1978; U.S. Professional Golf Assen Champion 1962, 1972; Winner, South African Open 13 times; South African P.G.A. Champion 1959, 1960, 1969, 1979, 1982; Winner, Australian Open 7 times; Quadel Sr Classic Champion 1985; third player ever to win all four major world professional titles; holds world record for lowest 18-hole score in any Open Championship (59 in the Brazilian Open 1974); Sr Tour victories include: Sr British Open 1988, 1990, 1997, Sr P.G.A. Champion 1986, 1988, 1990, Long Island Sr Classic, Sr Skins Game 2000; f. Gary Player Group, Gary Player Foundation (rural educ.); golf course designer (over 200 projects worldwide); breeds thoroughbred racehorses; Hon. LLD (St Andrews) 1995, (Ulster) 1997, (Dundee) 1999; South African Sportsman of the Century 1989, Hilton Hotel Lifetime Achievement Award 1995. *Publications:* Gary Player: The Autobiography 1991, The Golfer's Guide to the Meaning of Life 2001. *Leisure interests:* breeding thoroughbred racehorses, farming, educ., family, health, fitness. *Address:* Blair Atholl Farm, Lanseria, Johannesburg (Office); Gary Player Stud, Colesberg, South Africa (Office). *Telephone:* (11) 8833333 (Office); (11) 6592800 (Home). *Fax:* (11) 8837250 (Office). *E-mail:* garyplayer .com (Office).

PŁAŻYŃSKI, Maciej; Polish politician; b. 10 Feb. 1958, Młynary, Elbląg Prov.; m.; two s. one d.; ed Gdańsk Univ.; Co-Founder Independent Students Union (NZS) 1980, Leader NZS Univ. Board, Gdańsk 1980; participant Young Poland Movt; organizer of strikes and activist for underground Solidarity during martial law; founder and chair. Gdańsk Height Services Work Cooperative 1983 (employing many unemployed Solidarity activists); Chair. 'Lech Będkowski' Political Thought Club, Gdańsk 1988; co.-f. Liberal Congress in Gdańsk; mem. Republican Coalition 1990 (later Conservative Party); Gdańsk Voivoda 1990–96; Vice-Chair. Gdańsk Region Solidarity Election Action (AWS) 1997; co-f. and mem. Solidarity Election Action Social Movt 1997–; Deputy to Sejm (Parl.) 1997–, Sejm Marshal 1997–2001; mem. Solidarity Election Action Parl. Caucus 1997–2000; Chair. Civic Platform Caucus 2001–; Co-f. and Chair. Civic Platform 2000–; Hon. Citizen of Młynary, Puck and Pionki. *Address:* Klub Poselski Platforma Obywatelska, ul. Wiejska 4/6/8, 00-902 Warsaw, Poland. *Telephone:* (22) 6942588. *Fax:* (22) 6942590. *E-mail:* maciej.plazynski@sejm.pl (Office). *Website:* www.plazynski.pl (Office); www .platforma.org (Office).

PLEISTER, Christopher, Dr rer. pol; German banker; b. 15 May 1948, Hamburg; m.; three s.; ed Ludwig-Maximilians Univ., Munich; with LandesGenossenschaftsbank AG, Hannover 1977–81, Hallbaum, Maier & Co. Landkreditbank AG, Hannover 1981–84; Exec. Man. Norddeutsche Genossenschaftsbank AG 1984, mem. Bd of Man. 1985–90; mem. Bd of Man. DG Bank, Frankfurt-am-Main 1990–99; Chair. Bundesverbandes der Deutschen Volksbanken und Raiffeisenbanken (BVR – Fed. Asscn of German Cooperative Banks) 2000–. *Address:* BVR, Schellingstrasse 4, 10785 Berlin, Germany (Office). *Telephone:* (30) 20211000 (Office). *Fax:* (30) 20211901 (Office). *E-mail:* pleister@bvr.de (Office). *Website:* www.bvr.de (Office).

PLENDERLEITH, Ian, MA, MBA; British central banker; b. 27 Sept. 1943, York; s. of Raymond William Plenderleith and Louise Helen Plenderleith (née Martin); m. Kristina Mary Bentley; one s. two d.; ed King Edward's School, Birmingham, Christ Church, Oxford, Columbia Business School, New York; joined Bank of England 1965, seconded to IMF, Washington, DC 1972–74, Pvt. Sec. to Gov. Bank of England 1976–79; Alt. Dir EIB 1980–86, Head Gilt-Edged Div. 1982–90, Asst Dir 1986–90, Assoc. Dir 1990–94; Dir Bank of England Nominees Ltd 1994–2002, Exec. Dir Bank of England and mem. Monetary Policy Cttee 1994–2002; Alt. Dir BIS 1994–; Dir London Stock Exchange (fmrly mem. Stock Exchange Council) 1989–2001 (Deputy Chair. 1996), Chair. Stock Borrowing and Lending Cttee 1990–95; mem. G-10 Gold and Foreign Exchange Cttee 1995–2001; Co-Chair. Govt Borrowers Forum 1991–94; mem. Editorial Cttee OECD Study on Debt Man. 1990–93, Legal Risk Review Cttee 1991–92, Financial Law Panel 1992–94, Advisory Bd Inst. of Archaeology Devt Trust, Univ. Coll. London 1987–96, Bd of Overseers Columbia Business School 1991–, Fund-raising Planning Group, St Bartholomew's Hosp. 1992–94, Fund-raising Planning Cttee St Bartholomew's and The London Hosps. 1998–, Council, British Museum Friends 1993–99, 2000–; Dir City Arts Trust 1997–; Liveryman Innholders' Co. 1977–; Beta Gamma Sigma Medal 1971. *Leisure interests:* archaeology, theatre, cricket, skiing. *Address:* c/o Bank of England, Threadneedle Street, London, EC2R 8AH, England (Office).

PLENEL, Edwy; French journalist; b. 31 Aug. 1952, Nantes; s. of Alain Plenel and Michèle Bertreux; m. Nicole Lapierre; one d.; ed Institut d'études politiques, Paris; journalist Rouge 1976–78, Matin de Paris 1980; joined Le Monde 1980, Educ. Ed. 1980–82, Legal columnist 1982–90, Reporter 1991, Head Legal Dept 1992–94, Chief Ed. 1994–95, Asst Editorial Dir 1995–96, Ed. 1996–2000, Ed.-in-Chief 2000–. *Publications include:* L'Effet Le Pen 1984, La République inachevée: l'État et l'école en France 1985, Mourir à Ouvéa: le tournant calédonien 1988, Voyage avec Colomb 1991, La République menacée: dix ans d'effet Le Pen 1992, La Part d'ombre 1992, Un temps de chien 1994, Les Mots volés 1997, L'Epreuve 1999. *Address:* Le Monde, 21 bis rue Claude Bernard, 75242 Paris Cedex, France (Office). *E-mail:* plenel@lemonde .fr (Office). *Website:* www.lemonde.fr (Office).

PLESSNER, Yakir, PhD; Israeli economist; b. 18 Jan. 1935, Haifa; s. of Martin Plessner and Eva Plessner; m. Ora Ester Frenkel 1959; one s. one d.; ed Iowa State Univ., USA and Hebrew Univ. of Jerusalem; Visiting Lecturer, Pa Univ. 1971–73; Research Consultant, The World Bank 1977–78; Econ. Adviser to Israel's Minister of Finance 1981–83; Deputy Gov. Bank of Israel 1982–85; mem. Israel's Securities Authority 1982–85; Joseph and Esther Foster Visiting Prof., Brandeis Univ. 1985–86; Visiting Prof. Dartmouth Coll. 1987–88; Sr Lecturer, The Hebrew Univ. of Jerusalem 1973–; Fellow, Jerusalem Center for Public Affairs 1991; The Oded Levine Prize of the Operations Research Soc. of Israel. *Publications:* The Marketing of Israel's Citrus Fruit in Major European Markets 1976; regular columnist for Globes and Hadashot (daily newspapers); several articles in learned society journals. *Leisure interests:* music, photography, tennis.

PLEŞU, Andrei Gabriel, PH.D; Romanian philosopher; b. 23 Aug. 1948, Bucharest; s. of Radu Pleşu and Zoe Pleşu; m. Catrinel Maria Lăcrămioara, 1972; two s.; ed Acad. of Fine Arts and Univ. of Bucharest; Lecturer Acad. of Fine Arts, Bucharest 1980–82; Prof. of Philosophy of Religion 1999–97; Univ. of Bucharest 1991–97, Dir of Dilema (weekly); Rector of New Europe Coll., Bucharest 1994–2001; Minister of Culture 1989–91; Minister of Foreign Affairs 1997–99; New Europe Prize 1993, Prize of Brandenburg Acad. of Sciences, Berlin 1996; Hon. PhD (Albert-Ludwig Univ., Freiburg), Humboldt Medal (Germany) 1998, Konstantin Jireček Medal (Germany) 2000 and numerous other prizes; Gran Cruz, Orden El Sol del Perú (Peru) 1998, Grand Officier, Légion d'honneur 1999. *Publications:* Travel to the World of Forms 1974, Picturesque and Melancholy 1980, Francesco Guardi 1981, The Eye and the Things 1986, Minima Moralia 1988, The Language of Birds 1993 (books), The Diary of Tescany 1993, Faces and Masks of Transition 1996; numerous papers and articles. *Address:* Str. Paris 14, Bucharest 1, Romania (Home).

PLETNEV, Mikhail Vasilievich; Russian pianist, conductor and composer; b. 14 April 1957, Arkhangelsk; ed Moscow State Conservatory with Yakov Flier and Lev Vlasenko (piano), Albert Leman (composition); First Prize Int. Tchaikovsky competition in Moscow 1978; gave recitals and played with orchestras in maj. cities of Europe and America; gained reputation as Russian music interpreter; Founder and Chief Conductor Russian Nat. Orchestra 1990–99, Hon. Conductor 1999–; tours with orchestra in various countries; teacher in Moscow Conservatory 1981–; People's Artist of Russia 1990, State Prize of Russia 1982, 1993. *Address:* Starokonyushenny per. 33, Apt. 16, Moscow, Russia. *Telephone:* (095) 241-43-39 (Home).

PLIMPTON, George Ames, MA; American author and editor; b. 18 March 1927, New York; s. of Francis Plimpton and Pauline Ames; m. 1st Freddy M. Espy 1968 (divorced 1988); one s. one d.; m. 2nd Sarah Dudley 1991; two d.; ed Phillips Exeter Acad. and Harvard and Cambridge Univs; Ed.-in-Chief, Paris Review 1953–, Paris Review Edns (subsequently Doubleday & Co.) 1965–72, Paris Review Edns (subsequently British American Publs) 1987–; Instr. Barnard Coll. 1956–58; Assoc. Ed. Horizon 1959–61; Dir American Literature Anthology Program 1967–71; Assoc. Ed. Harper's 1972–81; Contributing Ed. Food & Wine 1978; TV Host, Dupont Plimpton Special 1967–69, Greatest Sports Legends 1979–81, The Ultimate High 1980, Survival Anglia 1980–, Writers' Workshop 1982, Masterpiece Theater 1983–, Challenge 1987; special contrib. Sports Illustrated 1968–; mem. Bd Dirs. Film Investors 1979–82, Leisure Dynamics 1983–85; curator Tennis week 1990–; Commr of Fireworks, New York 1973–; Trustee, WNET 1973–81, African Wildlife Leadership Foundation 1980–, NY Zoological Soc. 1985–, etc.; mem. Bd of Dirs Dynamite Museum, Nat. Tennis Foundation, Squaw Valley Center for Written & Dramatic Arts, Authors Trust of America, Friends of the Masai Mara, etc.; mem. Linnean Soc., PEN, American Pyrotechnics Asscn, Pyrotechnics Guild Int. etc.; numerous awards and hon. degrees. *Publications:* Rabbit's Umbrella 1956, Out of My League 1961, Paper Lion 1966, The Bogey Man 1968, Mad Ducks and Bears 1973, One for the Record 1974, Shadow-Box 1976, One More July 1976, Sports! (with N. Leifer) 1978, A Sports Bestiary (with A. Roth) 1982, Fireworks 1984, Open Net 1985, The Curious Case of Sidd Finch 1987, The X-Factor 1990, The Best of Plimpton 1990; ed. American Journey: The Times of Robert Kennedy (with J. Stein) 1970, Pierre's Book 1971, The Fancy 1973, Edie, An American Biography (with J. Stein) 1982, D.V. (with C. Hemphill) 1984 and seven vols of Writers at Work 1957–87; numerous articles. *Address:* Paris Review Inc., 541 East 72nd Street, New York, NY 10021, USA.

PLISETSKAYA, Maya Mikhailovna; Russian ballerina; b. 20 Nov. 1925, Moscow; m. Rodion Shchedrin; ed Moscow Bolshoi Theatre Ballet School; soloist Bolshoi Ballet 1943–90; Artistic Dir Ballet Roma Opera 1984–85, Nat. Ballet of Spain 1987–89; f. Maya Plisetskaya Int. Ballet Competition, St Petersburg 1994; Pres. Imperial Russian Ballet 1996–; Hon. mem. Portuguese Dance Centre; Hon. Prof. Moscow Univ. 1993; First Prize, Budapest Int. Competition 1949; People's Artist of the RSFSR 1951; People's Artist of the USSR 1959, Anna Pavlova Prize 1962, Lenin Prize 1964, Hero of Socialist Labour 1985, Légion d'honneur 1986, Triumph Prize 2000 and other decorations. *Main ballet roles:* Odette-Odile (Swan Lake, Tchaikovsky), Raimonda (Raimonda, Glazunov), Zaryema (The Fountain of Bakhchisarai, Asafiev), Kitri (Don Quixote, Minkus), Juliet (Romeo and Juliet, Prokofiev), Girl-Bird, Syunmbike (Shuralye, Yarullin), Laurencia (Laurencia, Krein), Aegina (Spartak, Khachaturian); ballets by R. Shchedrin: Carmen (Carmen Suite), Anna (Anna Karenina) 1972, Nina (The Seagull) 1980, Lady with a Lap Dog 1983, La folle de Chaillot 1992; ballets by M. Béjart: Bolero 1976, Isadora 1977, Leda 1979, Kurazuka 1995, Ave, Maya 2000. *Publication:* I, Maya Plisetskaya. *Address:* Theresien Str. 23, 80333 Munich, Germany (Home); Tverskaya 25/9, Apt. 31, 103050 Moscow, Russia (Home). *Telephone:* (89) 285834 (Munich), (095) 299-72-39 (Moscow). *Fax:* (89) 282057 (Munich), (095) 299-72-39 (Moscow) (Home).

PLOIX, Hélène Marie Joseph, MA, MBA; French business executive; b. 25 Sept. 1944, Anould; d. of René Ploix and Antoinette Jobert; m. Alexandre Lumbroso 1988; ed Calif. and Paris Univs.; Man. Consultant McKinsey and Co., Paris 1968–78; Special Asst to Cabinet of Sec. of State for Consumer Affairs 1977–78; Dir Cie Européenne de Publication 1978–82; Chair. Banque Industrielle et Mobilière Privée 1982–84; mem. of Bd Comm. des Opérations de Bourse 1983–84; Adviser to Prime Minister for Econ. and Financial Affairs 1984–86; Exec. Dir IMF and World Bank, representing France 1986–89; Deputy CEO Caisse des dépôts et consignations 1989–95; Chair. Caisse autonome de refinancement 1990–95, CDC Participations 1992–95; Chair. and CEO Pechel Industries 1997; mem. Bd of Dirs. Publicis 1998–, Lafarge 1999–, The Boots Co. PLC 2000; Chevalier Ordre Nat. du Mérite, Chevalier Légion d'honneur. *Leisure interest:* golf. *Address:* Pechel Industries, 9 avenue Percier, 75008 Paris (Office); 71 boulevard Arago, 75013 Paris, France.

PLORITIS, Marios; Greek author, journalist and director; b. 19 Jan. 1919, Piraeus; m.; ed Athens Univ.; f. mem. Art Theatre 1942; film and theatre reviewer 1945–67; Dir Niki Newspaper 1962–63; Dir Theatro Review 1965–67; Prof. at Art Theatre Dramatic School 1957–67; Dir Courrier de la Resistance Grecque, Paris 1968–69; Prof. Univ. Paris VIII 1970–72; Prof. of Philosophy Athens Univ. 1991–; fmr Chair. Union of Greek Film Reviewers, Greek Center of Theatre, Soc. of Authors; has translated into Greek more than 120 plays and has directed more than 30 plays. *Publications include:* Masks 1967, Dynasties and Tyrants 1974, Politics 1980, Brecht and Hitler 1984, Art, Language and Power 1989. *Address:* Panepistimiopolis, Zografon, 157 71 (Office); Athinisin Ethnikon Kai Kapodistriakon Panepistimion, Odos Panepistimiou 30, 106 79 Athens, Greece (Home). *Telephone:* (1) 3614301. *Fax:* (1) 3602145. *Website:* www.uoa.gr (Office).

PLOWDEN, David, BA; American writer, photographer and teacher; b. 10 Sept. 1932, Boston; s. of Roger Stanley Plowden and Mary Plowden (née Butler); m. 1st Pleasance Coggeshall (divorced 1976); m. 2nd Sandra Schoellkopf 1977; three s. one d.; ed Yale Univ.; Asst to Trainmaster, Great Northern Railway 1955–56; self-employed photographer/writer 1962–; Assoc. Prof. Ill. Inst. of Tech. Inst. of Design 1978–85; lecturer Univ. of Iowa School of Journalism 1985–88; Visiting Prof. Grand Valley State Univ. 1988–; numerous photographic exhbns.; John Simon Guggenheim Memorial Fellowship 1968; Smithsonian Inst. Award 1970–71, 1975–76; Iowa Humanities Award and Nat. Endowment for the Humanities Award 1987–88. *Publications:* Lincoln and His America 1970, The Hand of Man on America 1971, Floor of the Sky, The Great Plains 1972, Commonplace 1974, Bridges, The Spans of North America 1974, Tugboat 1976, Steel 1981, An American Chronology 1982, Industrial Landscape 1985, A Time of Trains 1987, A Sense of Place 1988, End of an Era 1992, Small Town America 1994, Imprints 1997 and co-author of numerous books. *Address:* 609 Cherry Street, Winnetka, IL 60093, USA. *Telephone:* (847) 446-2793. *Fax:* (847) 446-2795. *E-mail:* dplowden@enteract.com (Home).

PLOWRIGHT, David Ernest, CBE; British television executive; b. 11 Dec. 1930, Scunthorpe; s. of William E. Plowright and Daisy M. Plowright; m. Brenda M. Key 1953; one s. two d.; ed Scunthorpe Grammar School; reporter, Scunthorpe Star 1950; freelance correspondent and sports writer 1952; reporter, feature writer and briefly equestrian corresp., Yorkshire Post 1954; News Ed. Granada TV 1957, Producer, Current Affairs 1960, Exec. Producer, Scene at 6.30 1964, Exec. Producer, World in Action 1966, Head of Current Affairs 1968, Dir 1968, Controller of Programmes 1969, Jt Man. Dir 1975–81, Man. Dir 1981–87; Chair. Granada TV Ltd 1987–92; Dir Granada Int. 1975–92, Granada Group 1981–92, Independent TV News 1981–88, Superchannel 1986–89, British Satellite Broadcasting 1987–90; Deputy Chair. Channel 4, UK 1992–97; Visiting Prof. of Media Studies, Univ. of Salford 1992–; TV broadcast and production consultant 1992–; Dir Tate Gallery, Liverpool 1988–91; BAFTA Fellowship 1992; Hon. DLitt (Salford) 1989; Hon. Dr Arts (Liverpool) 1991. *Leisure interests:* television, theatre, yachting. *Address:* Westways, Wilmslow Road, Mottram St Andrew, Cheshire, SK10 4QT, England.

PLOWRIGHT, Joan Ann, CBE; British actress; b. 28 Oct. 1929, Brigg, Lancashire; d. of William Plowright and Daisy Plowright (née Burton); m. 1st Roger Gage 1953 (divorced); m. 2nd Sir Laurence (later Lord) Olivier 1961 (died 1989); one s. two d.; ed Scunthorpe Grammar School and Old Vic Theatre School; mem. Old Vic Company, toured South Africa 1952–53; first leading rôle in The Country Wife, London 1956; mem. English Stage Company 1956; at Nat. Theatre 1963–74; Vice-Pres. Nat. Youth Theatre; mem. Council English Stage Co.; mem. council, Royal Acad. of Dramatic Art (RADA); Best Actress (Tony) Award for A Taste of Honey, New York 1960; Best Actress (Evening Standard) Award for St Joan 1964; Variety Club Award 1976 for The Bed Before Yesterday, Best Actress Soc. of West End Theatre (Filumena) 1978, Variety Club Film Actress of the Year Award for Drowning by Numbers 1987, Golden Globe Award for Stalin 1993, Golden Globe Award for Enchanted April 1993, 18th Crystal Award for Women in Film, USA 1994. *Plays and films acted in include:* The Chairs 1957, The Entertainer 1958, Major Barbara and Roots 1959, A Taste of Honey 1960, Uncle Vanya 1962, 1963, 1964, St Joan 1963, Hobson's Choice 1964, The Master Builder 1965, Much Ado About Nothing 1967, Tartuffe 1967, Three Sisters 1967, 1969 (film 1969), The Advertisement 1968, 1969, Love's Labour's Lost 1968, 1969, The Merchant of Venice, 1970, 1971–72, Rules of the Game, Woman Killed with Kindness 1971–72, Taming of the Shrew, Doctor's Dilemma 1972, Merchant of Venice (TV film) 1973, Rosmersholm 1973, Saturday Sunday Monday 1973, Eden's End 1974, The Sea Gull 1975, The Bed Before Yesterday 1975, Equus (film) 1976, Daphne Laureola (TV film) 1977, Saturday Sunday Monday (TV film) 1977, Filumena 1977, Enjoy 1980, Who's Afraid of Virginia Woolf? 1981, Richard Wagner (film) 1982, Cavell 1982, Britannia Hospital (film) 1981, Brimstone and Treacle (film) 1982, The Cherry Orchard 1983, The Way of the World 1984, Mrs Warren's Profession 1985, Revolution 1985, The House of Bernarda Alba 1986, Drowning by Numbers (film) 1987, Uncle Vanya 1988, The Dressmaker (film) 1988, The Importance of Being Earnest (TV) 1988, Conquest of the South Pole 1989, And a Nightingale Sang 1989, I Love You

to Death 1989, Avalon (film) 1990, Time and the Conways 1991, Enchanted April (film) 1991, Stalin 1991, Denis the Menace, A Place for Annie 1992, A Pin for the Butterfly, Last Action Hero 1993, Widow's Peak (film) 1994, On Promised Land 1994, Return of the Natives 1994, Hotel Sorrento 1994, A Pyromaniac's Love Story 1994, The Scarlet Letter 1994, Jane Eyre 1994, If We Are Women (play) 1995, Surviving Picasso (film) 1995, Mr. Wrong (film) 1995, 101 Dalmatians (film) 1996, The Assistant (film) 1996, Shut Up and Dance (film) 1997, Tom's Midnight Garden (film) 1997, It May Be the Last Time (TV film) 1997, America Betrayed 1998, Tea with Mussolini (film) 1998, Return to the Secret Garden (film) 1999, Frankie and Hazel (film) 1999, Bailey's Mistake (film) 2000, Global Heresy (film) 2000. *Publications:* And That's Not All (autobiog.) 2001. *Leisure interests:* entertaining, music, reading. *Address:* c/o ICM, 76 Oxford Street, London, W1N 0AX; c/o The Malthouse, Horsham Road, Ashurst, Steyning, West Sussex, BN44 3AR, England.

PLOWRIGHT, Jonathan Daniel, ARAM; British concert pianist; b. 24 Sept. 1959, Doncaster; s. of Cyril James Plowright and Molly Plowright; m. Diane Rosemary Shaw 1990; ed Stonyhurst Coll., Royal Acad. of Music, London, Peabody Conservatory of Music, Baltimore, USA; debut Carnegie Recital Hall 1984, South Bank, London 1985; has performed with all maj. UK orchestras and numerous int. orchestras; solo recitals throughout UK and many int. tours; regular BBC broadcasts; performed world premiere Constant Lambert's piano concerto 1988; six commercial recordings; McFarren Gold Medal (RAM), Fulbright Scholarship, Countess of Munster Scholarship, Commonwealth Musician of the Year 1983, 1st Prize European Piano Competition 1989. *Leisure interests:* wine, rugby, cricket. *Address:* 25 Titian Road, Hove, East Sussex, BN3 5QR, England (Home). *Telephone:* (1273) 203559 (Home). *Fax:* (1273) 203559 (Home). *E-mail:* jdplowright@hotmail.com (Home). *Website:* jonathanplowright.com (Home).

PLOWRIGHT, Rosalind Anne, LRAM; British mezzo-soprano; b. 21 May 1949; d. of Robert Arthur Plowright and Celia Adelaide Plowright; m. James Anthony Kaye 1984; one s. one d.; ed Notre Dame High School, Wigan, Royal Northern Coll. of Music, Manchester; career began London Opera Centre 1973–75; Glyndebourne Chorus and Touring Co. 1974–77; debut with English Nat. Opera as Page in Salome 1975, Miss Jessel in Turn of the Screw 1979 (SWET award), at Covent Garden as Ortlinde in Die Walküre 1980; has sung also in Switzerland, Germany, France, Spain, Portugal, Italy, Netherlands, Denmark, Austria, Greece, USA, Argentina, Chile, Israel; has sung mezzo repertoire 1999–; Metropolitan Opera debut 2003; First Prize 7th Int. Competition for Opera Singers, Sofia 1979, Prix Fondation Fanny Heldy, Acad. Nat. du Disque Lyrique 1985. *Television:* House of Elliott 1992, The Man Who Made Husbands Jealous 1997. *Principal roles include:* Ariadne, Alceste, Médée, Norma, Tosca; title role and Elizabeth I in Mary Stuart, Maddalena in Andrea Chénier, Antonia in The Tales of Hoffman, Donna Anna in Don Giovanni, Vitellia in La Clemenza di Tito, Madame Butterfly, Manon Lescaut, Suor Angelica, Giorgetta in Il Tabarro, Aida, Abigaille in Nabucco, Desdemona in Otello, Elena in I Vespri Siciliani, Leonora in Il Trovatore, Amelia in Un Ballo in Maschera, Leonora in La Forza del Destino, Violetta in La Traviata, Kundry in Parsifal, Kostelnička in Katya Kabanova, Amneris in Aida, Cassandra in Les Troyens, Eboli in Don Carlos, Fricka in Rheingold and Walküre. *Address:* c/o Raffaella Coletti, Firenze Musicale, Via Maggio 35, Florence 50125, Italy; 83 St Mark's Avenue, Salisbury, Wilts., SP1 3DW, England (Home).

PLUMB, Baron (Life Peer), cr. 1987, of Coleshill in the County of Warwickshire; **(Charles) Henry Plumb,** Kt; British politician; b. 27 March 1925; s. of Charles Plumb and Louise Plumb; m. Marjorie Dorothy Dunn 1947; one s. two d.; ed King Edward VI School, Nuneaton; mem. Council Nat. Farmers Union 1959, Vice-Pres. 1964, 1965, Deputy-Pres. 1966–69, Pres. 1970–79; mem. Duke of Northumberland's Cttee of Inquiry on Foot and Mouth Disease 1967–68; Chair. British Agricultural Council 1975–79; Pres. Nat. Fed. of Young Farmers' Clubs 1976–86; Pres. Royal Agricultural Soc. of England 1977, Deputy Pres. 1978; Pres. Int. Fed. of Agricultural Producers 1979–82; mem. (Conservative) European Parl. 1979–99, Chair. Agricultural Cttee 1979–82, Leader, European Democratic Group (Conservative) 1982–87, 1994–97, Pres. European Parl. 1987–89, Leader British Conservatives in European Parl. 1994–97, Co-Pres. EU/ACP Jt Ass. for Africa/Caribbean/Pacific Countries 1994–99, Hon. Pres. 1999–; Vice-Pres. EPP Group in European Parl. 1994–97; Chancellor Coventry Univ. 1995–; Chair. Agricultural Mortgage Corpn 1994–95; mem. Temporary Cttee of Enquiry into BSE 1996–97; Fellow Royal Agric. Socs., Duchy; Hon. DSc (Cranfield) 1983; Hon. DL (Warwick Coll.); Order of Merit, Fed. Repub. of Germany; R.A.S.E. Gold Medal 1983 and decorations from Portugal, Luxembourg, Spain, France, Greece, Italy and others. *Leisure interests:* fishing, shooting. *Address:* House of Lords, London, SW1A 0PW; The Dairy Farm, Maxstoke, Coleshill, Warwicks., B46 2QJ, England (Home). *Telephone:* (20) 7219-1233 (Office); (1675) 463133 (Coleshill) (Home). *Fax:* (20) 7219-1649 (Office); (1675) 464156 (Coleshill). *E-mail:* plumbh@parliament.uk (Office).

PLUMBLY, Sir Derek John, BA, KCMG; British diplomatist; b. 15 May 1948, Lyndhurst, Hants.; s. of the late John Plumbly and Jean Plumbly (née Baker); m. Nadia Youssef Gohar 1979; one d. two s.; ed Brockenhurst Grammar School, Magdalene Coll. Oxford; with VSO, Pakistan 1970–71; joined FCO 1972; Arabic language training, MECAS, Lebanon 1973–74; Second Sec. in Jeddah 1975–77; First Sec. in Cairo 1977–80; FCO 1980–84; assigned to Washington DC 1984–88; Counsellor in Riyadh 1988–92; with UK

Mission to UN, New York 1992–96; Dir Drugs and Crime Dept, FCO 1996–97, Dir Middle East and North Africa Dept 1997–2000; Amb. to Saudi Arabia 2000–. *Leisure interests:* family, reading, travel. *Address:* British Embassy, POB 94351, Riyadh 11693, Saudi Arabia (Office); c/o Foreign and Commonwealth Office, King Charles Street, London, SW1A 2AH, England (Office). *Telephone:* (61) 4880077 (Office). *Fax:* (61) 4883125 (Office). *E-mail:* derek .plumbly@fco.gov.uk (Office).

PLUMBRIDGE, Robin Allan, MA; South African business executive (retd) and company director; b. 6 April 1935, Cape Town; s. of the late C. O. Plumbridge and of the late M. A. Plumbridge; m. Celia Anne Millar 1959; two s. two d.; ed St Andrew's Coll., Grahamstown, Univs of Cape Town and Oxford; joined Gold Fields of South Africa Ltd 1957, Asst Man. 1962–65, Man. 1965–69, Exec. Dir 1969–80, CEO 1980–95, Chair. 1980–97; Chair. World Gold Council 1993–95; Dir Standard Bank Investment Corpn 1980–, Newmont Mining Corpn 1983–; Hon. LLD. *Address:* PO Box 72491, Parkview 2122; 17 Woolston Road, Westcliff, Johannesburg 2193, South Africa (Home). *Telephone:* (11) 6468513 (Office). *Fax:* (11) 6468447. *E-mail:* rplum@mweb.co .za (Home).

PLUMMER, (Arthur) Christopher (Orme), CC; Canadian actor; b. 13 Dec. 1929, Toronto; m. 1st Tammy Lee Grimes 1956; one d.; m. 2nd Patricia Audrey Lewis 1962 (divorced 1966); m. 3rd Elaine Regina Taylor 1970; public and pvt. schools in Montréal, PQ; professional debut as Faulkland in The Rivals, Ottawa Repertory Theatre; Broadway debut in Starcross Story 1951–52; Maple Leaf Award 1982; numerous appearances in theatres in USA have included: Mark Antony in Julius Caesar, Ferdinand in The Tempest, Earl of Warwick in Anouilh's The Lark, The Narrator in Stravinsky's L'Histoire du Soldat, The Devil in J.B., 1951–61, The Resistible Rise of Arturo Ui and The Royal Hunt of the Sun 1965–66, The Good Doctor 1973, Iago in Othello 1981, Macbeth 1988, No Man's Land 1994, Barrymore 1996 (Tony Award for Best Leading Actor in a Play 1997); played many leading Shakespearean roles in productions by the Stratford Canadian Festival Co.; British debut in title role of Richard III, Stratford on Avon 1961 and then in London as Henry II in Anouilh's Becket; a leading actor in the Nat. Theatre Co. of Great Britain 1971–72; has appeared in Nat. Theatre productions of Amphytrion 38, Danton's Death 1971; many TV roles including Hamlet in BBC/Danish TV production, Hamlet in Elsinore, Jesus of Nazareth 1977; Theatre World Award 1955, Evening Standard Award 1961, Delia Australian Medal 1973, Antoinette Perry (Tony) Award 1974, Emmy Award 1977, Genie Award 1980, Australian Golden Badge of Honour 1982, Maple Leaf Award. *Films include:* The Fall of the Roman Empire, The Sound of Music, Inside Daisy Clover, Triple Cross, Oedipus the King, Nobody Runs Forever, Lock Up Your Daughters, The Royal Hunt of the Sun, Battle of Britain, Waterloo, The Pyx, The Spiral Staircase, Conduct Unbecoming, The Return of the Pink Panther, The Man Who Would be King, Aces High 1976, The Disappearance 1977, International Velvet 1978, The Silent Partner 1978, Hanover Street 1979, Murder by Decree 1980, The Shadow Box 1980, The Disappearance 1981, The Janitor 1981, The Amateur 1982, Dreamscape 1984, Playing for Keeps 1985, Lily in Love 1985, Dragnet 1987, Souvenir 1988, Shadow Dancing, Mindfield 1989, Where the Heart Is 1989, Star Trek VI: The Undiscovered Country 1991, Malcolm X 1992, Wolf 1994, Dolores Claiborne 1994, Twelve Monkeys 1995, Skeletons 1996, The Arrow 1997, The Insider 1999, All the Fine 1999, The Dinosaur Hunter 2000, Dracula 2000. *Leisure interests:* piano, skiing, tennis, old cars. *Address:* c/o Lou Pitt, The Pitt Group, 9465 Wilshire Boulevard, Suite 480, Beverly Hills, CA 90212, USA.

PLYUSHCH, Ivan Stepanovich; Ukrainian politician; b. 11 Sept. 1941, Borzna, Chernigov Dist; m.; one d.; ed Ukrainian Agricultural Acad., Acad. of Social Sciences of Communist Party Cen. Cttee; mem. CPSU 1962–91; worked as agronomist, Dir of collective farms, Dir Sovkhoz 1959–74, party work in Kiev Dist Cttee 1975–84; Deputy Chair. Kiev Dist Soviet 1984–90, Chair. 1990; Deputy to Ukrainian Supreme Soviet 1990–; First Deputy Chair. Supreme Council 1991–92, Chair. 1992–94, 2000–02; mem. Higher Econ. Bd 1997; mem. People's Democratic Party 1998–; mem. All-Ukrainian Union of Democratic Forces 1998–, Chair. 1999–; Yaroslav Mudzy Order 1996. *Address:* Verkhovna Rada, M. Hrushevskoho 5, 252019 Kiev, Ukraine.

POATY-SOUCHALATY, Alphonse Mouissou; Republic of Congo politician; fmr Minister of Trade and Small and Medium-sized Enterprises; Prime Minister of the Congo 1989–90; mem. Parti congolais du travail (PCT). *Address:* c/o Office of the Prime Minister, Brazzaville, Republic of the Congo.

POCHINOK, Aleksander Petrovich, CAND. ECON.; Russian politician; b. Aleksander Petrovich Pochinok, 12 Jan. 1958, Chelyabinsk; m.; one d.; ed Chelyabinsk Polytech. Inst., Inst. of Econs Urals br. USSR Acad. of Sciences; with Chelyabinsk Inst. of Econs 1985–89; People's Deputy Russian Fed.; mem. Supreme Soviet, Chair. Comm. on Budget Planning, Taxation and Prices 1990–93; mem. State Duma (Parl.), Deputy Chair., Chair. Subcttee on Budget, Taxation, Banks and Finance 1993–97; mem. Political Council Democratic Union of Russia 1994; Head State Taxation Service Russian Fed. 1997–98; Head Financial Dept of Govt Admin. 1998–; Minister of Taxation 1999–2000, of Labour and Social Devt 2000–. *Publications:* I Pay Taxes (with S. Shatalov), Principles of Tax Systems (jtly.). *Leisure interest:* sea cruises. *Address:* Ministry of Labour and Social Development, Birzhevaya Pl. 1, 103706 Moscow (Office); Sadovo-Kudrinskaya Str. 19, Apt. 23, Moscow, Russia. *Telephone:* (095) 298-06-83 (Office); (095) 201-35-05 (Home).

PODBEREZKIN, Aleksei Ivanovich, DHist; Russian historian and politician; b. 7 Feb. 1953, Moscow; m.; three d.; ed Moscow State Inst. of Int. Relations; started career as metal worker in Moscow 1968; served in the army; referent Group of Scientific Consultants, USSR Cttee of Youth Orgs 1981–85; Sr Researcher Inst. of World Econs and Int. Relations, Diplomatic Acad., Ministry of Foreign Affairs 1985–90; f. Russian-American Univ. (RAU) 1990, Pres. 1991–; Pres. Int. Non-Govt Research and Educ. Org. 1992–; adviser to Vice-Pres. of Russia 1991–93; Founder, Chair. and Sec.-Gen. All-Russian Political Movt Spiritual Heritage (Dukhovnoye Naslediye) 1994–; mem. State Duma (Parl.), mem. Communist Party faction 1995–99; Deputy Chair. Cttee on Int. Issues; Founder People's Patriotic Union of Russia 1996–; ed. Observer (analytical monthly); Ed.-in-Chief Russia: Contemporary Political History (annual) 1998–; Adviser of the Year 1998, several state decorations. *Publications:* over 1200 pubs on problems of int. relations, foreign and defence policy, state construction, ideology of state patriotism, economics and financial control. *Leisure interests:* tennis, swimming. *Address:* Dukhovnoye Nasledi diye, Bakhrushina str. 32, Building 2, 113054 Moscow (Office); B. Serpukovsky str. 70/44, Moscow, Russia. *Telephone:* (095) 959-20-45 (Office); (095) 203-88-59 (Home). *E-mail:* podberezkin_a@nasled.ru.

PODESTA, John David, BS, JD; American lawyer and government official; b. 1 Aug. 1949, Chicago, Ill.; s. of John David Podesta and Mary Kokoris; m. Mary Spieczny 1978; one s. two d.; ed Knox Coll., Illinois, Georgetown Univ. Law Center; attorney, Dept of Justice 1976–77; Special Asst to Dir, ACTION 1978–79; Counsel, Senate Judiciary Cttee 1979–81; Chief Minority Counsel, Senate Judiciary Sub-Cttee. 1981–86; Chief Counsel, Senate Agric. Cttee 1987–88; Pres., Gen. Counsel, Podesta Assocs. Inc. 1988–93; Asst to the Pres. (Staff Sec.) 1993–95; Asst to the Pres. (Deputy Chief of Staff) 1997–98; Chief of Staff to the Pres. 1998–2001; Visiting Prof. of Law, Georgetown Univ. Law Center 1995–98, Adjunct Prof. 1998–. *Publication:* Protecting Electronic Messaging 1990. *Address:* Georgetown University Law Centre, 600 New Jersey Avenue, N.W., Washington, DC 20001 (Office); The White House, 1600 Pennsylvania Avenue, NW, Washington, DC 20502; 3743 Brandywine Street, Washington, DC 20016, U.S.A. (Home). *Telephone:* (202) 456-6798 (Office). *Fax:* (202) 456-1121 (Office).

PODESTÁ SILVA, Carlos Marcial; Paraguayan politician; b. 5 June 1942, Asunción; s. of Julio Podestá Bóveda and Amalia Silva Ojeda; m.; ed Colegio "Sagrado Corazón de Jesús", Nat. Univ. of Asunción, Univ. of Guadalajara; Dir of Communications, of Planning and Public Admin., then Man. Dir Instituto de Bienestar Rural 1972–83; business consultant 1983–92; councillor Entidad Binacional Itaipú 1992–93; Pres. Nat. Emergency Cttee May 1993–; Minister of the Interior 1993–95; titular mem. Governing Bd Asociación Nacional Republicana (Partido Colorado).

PODHORETZ, John, AB; American writer and editor; b. 18 April 1961, NY; s. of Norman Podhoretz (q.v.) and Midge (née Rosenthal) Podhoretz; m. Elisabeth Hickey 1996; ed Univ. of Chicago; Exec. News Ed. Insight Magazine 1985–87; contrib. US News and World Report 1987–88; speechwriter to Pres. of USA 1988–89; Asst Man. Ed. Washington Times 1989–91; Sr Fellow Hudson Inst. 1991–94; TV critic NY Post 1994–95; Deputy Ed. The Weekly Standard 1995–97; J.C. Penney/Mo. Award for Excellence in Feature Sections 1990. *Publication:* Hell of a Ride: Backstage at the White House Follies 1989–93 1993. *Address:* 1211 Avenue of the Americas, 10th Floor, New York, NY 10036, USA.

PODHORETZ, Norman, MA, B.H.L.; American author and editor; b. 16 Jan. 1930, Brooklyn; s. of Julius Podhoretz and Helen (née Woliner) Podhoretz; m. Midge R. Decter 1956; one s. three d.; ed Columbia Univ., Jewish Theological Seminary and Univ. of Cambridge; Assoc. Ed. Commentary 1956–58, Ed.-in-Chief 1960–95, Ed.-at-Large 1995–; Ed.-in-Chief, Looking Glass Library 1959–60; Chair. New Directions Advisory Comm. U.S. Information Agency 1981–87; mem. Council on Foreign Relations, Comm. on the Present Danger, Comm. for the Free World; Sr Fellow Hudson Inst. 1995–; Fulbright Fellow 1950–51; Hon. LLD (Jewish Theological Seminary); Hon. LHD (Hamilton Coll.), (Boston) 1995, (Adelphi) 1996; Hon. D.Hum.Litt. (Yeshiva) 1991, (Boston) 1995, (Adelphi) 1996. *Publications:* Doings and Undoings, The Fifties and After in American Writing 1964, Making It 1968, Breaking Ranks 1979, The Present Danger 1980, Why We Were in Vietnam 1982, The Bloody Crossroads 1986, Ex-Friends 1999, My Love Affair with America 2000, The Prophets: Who They Were, What They Are 2002. *Address:* 165 East 56th Street, New York, New York, NY 10022, USA. *E-mail:* nhp30@hotmail.com (Office).

PÖGGELER, Otto, DPhil; German professor of philosophy; b. 12 Dec. 1928, Attendorn; m. 1959, two c.; ed Bonn Univ.; Prof. of Philosophy, Bochum Univ. 1968–94, Prof. Emer. 1994–; Dir Hegel Archives; mem. Rheinland-Westphalia Acad. of Sciences 1977–. *Publications:* Etudes hégeliennes 1985, Martin Heidegger's Path of Thinking 1987, Schritte zu einer Hermeneutischen Philosophie 1994, Heidegger in seiner Zeit 1999, Der Stein hinter Aug. Studien zu Célans Gedichten 2000, Bild und Technik-Heidegger, Klee und die Moderne Kunst 2002. *Address:* Hegel-Archiv der Ruhr-Universität, 44780 Bochum (Office); Paracelsusweg 22, 44801 Bochum, Germany (Home). *Telephone:* (234) 701160 (Home).

POGGIO, Albert Andrew, MBE; Gibraltarian diplomatist; b. 18 Aug. 1946, Ballymena, N Ireland; one d.; ed Christian Brothers Coll., Gibraltar and City of London Coll.; Rep. of Govt of Gibraltar in UK 1988–; Chair. British Overseas Territories Asscn, Vital Health Group of Cos., Westex Group of Cos., John Mowlems-CCS Ltd; Vice-Chair. Calpe House Trust; Dir Friends of

Gibraltar Heritage Soc., Medcruise (Asscn of Mediterranean Ports), Med Man. Consultants Ltd; Freeman City of London. *Leisure interests:* reading, walking, military memorabilia, sports. *Address:* Arundel Great Court, 178–179 Strand, London, WC2R 1EL (Office); The Old House, Manor Place, Chislehurst, Kent, BR7 5QJ, England (Home). *Telephone:* (20) 7836-0777 (Office). *Fax:* (20) 7240-6612 (Office). *E-mail:* A.Poggio@gibraltar.gov.uk (Office). *Website:* www.gibraltar.gov.uk (Office).

POGORELICH, Ivo; Croatian concert pianist; b. 20 Oct. 1958, Belgrade; s. of I. Pogorelich and D. Pogorelich; m. Aliza Kezeradze 1980 (died 1996); ed Tchaikovsky Conservatoire of Moscow, then studied with Aliza Kezeradze; f. Bad Wörishofen Festival (Germany) 1988; inaugurated Ivo Pogorelich Int. Solo Piano Competition, Pasadena, CA 1993; UNESCO Goodwill Amb. 1988; f. Sarajevo Charitable Foundation (to raise funds for people of Bosnia in fields of medicine and health) 1994; Fellow-Commoner, Balliol Coll. Oxford 1993; First Prize Casagrande Competition, Terni, Italy 1978; First Prize Montréal Int. Music Competition, Canada 1980; Special Prize, Int. Chopin Competition, Warsaw 1980. *Recordings:* numerous recordings for Deutsche Grammophon, starting with a Chopin recital in 1981 and including works by Beethoven, Schumann, Ravel, Prokofiev and the Tchaikovsky Piano Concerto No. 1; has appeared in major concert halls throughout the world. *Address:* c/o Kantor Concert Management, 67 Teignmouth Road, London, NW2 4EA, England. *Telephone:* (20) 8208-2480. *Fax:* (20) 8208-2490.

POGUE, Lloyd Welch, AB, LLB (JD), SJD, FRSA, FRAeS; American retd lawyer, government official and author; b. 21 Oct. 1899, nr Grant, Montgomery Co., Ia; s. of Leander Welch Pogue and Myrtle Viola Casey; m. Mary Ellen Edgerton 1926 (died 2001); three s.; ed Grinnell Coll., Ia, Univ. of Nebraska, Univ. of Michigan and Harvard Law Schools; Assoc. Ropes & Gray (law firm), Boston 1927–33, Partner in New York affiliated firm, Searle, James & Crawford 1933–38; Gen. Counsel, Fed. Civil Aeronautics Authority (later Civil Aeronautics Bd) 1939–41; mem. and Chair. Civil Aeronautics Bd 1942–46; US del. to int. aviation confs; resgnd to resume pvt. practice of law alone 1946; f. Pogue & Neal 1946; with 14 lawyers, merged with Jones, Day, Cockley & Reavis (Cleveland law firm) to form Jones, Day, Reavis & Pogue 1967; Washington Man. Partner 1967–79; author, lecturer, recorder for the blind 1981–84; Docent at Nat. Air and Space Museum 1982–95; Benjamin Franklin Fellow, Royal Soc. of Arts; mem. Nat. Aeronautic Asscn (fmr Pres.), Canadian Aeronautics and Space Inst.; mem. numerous socs.; Hon. Fellow American Helicopter Soc. 1949; Hon. mem. Wings Club 1940, AIAA 1941, Soc. of Sr Aerospace Execs. 2000, Aero Club of Washington 2000; Hon. Life mem. Helicopter Asscn Int. 1961; Achievement Awards, Golden Eagle Award (Soc. of Sr Aerospace Execs.) 1988, Elder Statesman of Aviation Award (Nat. Aeronautic Asscn) 1993, First recipient L. Welch Pogue Award for Lifetime Aviation Achievement, est. by McGraw-Hill Org. 1994, Donald D. Engen Aero Club Trophy for Aviation Excellence 2001, McGraw-Hill Laurel Legend Award and Hall of Fame 2002. *Publications:* International Civil Air Transport–Transition Following World War II 1979, Pogue/Pollock/Polk Genealogy as Mirrored in History, From Scotland to Northern Ireland/Ulster, Ohio and Westward 1990 (winner 7 awards), Airline Deregulation, Before and After: What Next? (Lindbergh Memorial Lecture) 1991, The International Civil Aviation Conference (1944) and its sequel, The Anglo-American Bermuda Air Transport Agreement (1946) 1994, The Wright Brothers Memorial Lecture 2000; numerous legal articles. *Leisure interests:* writing, genealogy, history. *Address:* 5204 Kenwood Avenue, Chevy Chase, MD 20815-6604, USA. *Telephone:* (301) 654-7233.

PÖHL, Karl Otto; German economist; b. 1 Dec. 1929, Hannover; m. Dr Ulrike Pesch; two s. two d.; ed Univ. of Göttingen; Head of Dept Ifo-Research Inst., Munich 1955–60; econ. journalist 1961–67; mem. Man. Bd of the Fed. Asscn of German Banks, Cologne 1968–69; Head of Dept Fed. Ministry of Econ. Affairs 1970–71; Head of Econ. and Fiscal Policy Dept, Fed Chancellor's Office 1971–72; State Sec. Fed. Ministry of Finance 1972–77; Vice-Chair. Deutsche Bundesbank 1977–79, Pres. 1980–91; partner Bankhaus Sal Oppenheimer Jr et Cie 1992–98; Dr hc (Georgetown, Ruhr Univ.) 1983, (Tel Aviv Univ.) 1986, (Maryland) 1987, (Buckingham, Iowa) 1992, (Johann-Wolfgang-Goethe Univ.) 2000. *Address:* Sal Oppenheim Jr & Cie, Konigsberger Strasse 29, Frankfurt am Main, Germany. *Telephone:* (69) 71345466. *Fax:* (69) 71345456.

POIROT-DELPECH, Bertrand; French writer and journalist; b. 10 Feb. 1929, Paris; s. of Jean Poirot-Delpech and Jeanne Hauvette; one s. two d.; ed Univ. of Paris; journalist 1951–; theatre critic for Le Monde 1959– and La Nouvelle Revue Française; literary critic Le Monde 1972–; Pres. Syndicat Professionel de la Critique Dramatique et Musicale 1967–71, Hon. Pres. 1986; Chair. Nat. Cttee. for the 200th anniversary of Victor Hugo 2001; mem. Acad. Française 1986; Commdr Ordre nat. du Mérite, Officier Légion d'honneur; Prix Interallié 1958, Grand Prix du roman de l'Académie Française 1970. *Publications:* Le Grand dadais 1958, La Grasse Matinée 1960, L'Envers de l'eau 1963, Finie la comédie, Au Soir le Soir 1969, La Folle de Lituanie 1970, Les Grands de ce monde 1976, Saïd et moi 1989, Marie Duplessis la Dame aux Camélias 1981, La Légende du siècle 1981, Feuilleton (1972–1982) 1983, Le Couloir du dancing 1983, L'Eté 36 1984, Bonjour Sagan 1985, Monsieur Barbie n'a rien à dire 1987, Le Golfe de Gascogne 1989, Traversées 1989, Discours de réception du commandant Cousteau sous la Coupole 1989, Discours de Réception de Michel Serres 1990, Rue des Italiens (jtly.) 1990, L'Amour de L'Humanité 1994, Diagonales 1996, Théâtre d'ombres 1998,

Monsieur le prince 1999, J'écris Paludes 2001. *Address:* Institut de France, 23 rue de Conti, 75006 Paris; Le Monde, 21 bis rue Claude Bernard, 75242 Paris (Office); 14 rue Saint-Guillaume, 75007 Paris, France (Home).

POITIER, Sidney; American actor; b. 20 Feb. 1927, Miami; s. of Reginald and Evelyn Poitier; m. 1st Juanita Hardy; four d.; m. 2nd Joanna Shimkus 1975; two d.; ed Western Senior High School, Nassau, Governors High School, Nassau; army service 1941–45; acted with American Negro Theatre 1946; appeared in Anna Lucasta 1948, A Raisin in the Sun 1959; mem. Bd of Dirs Walt Disney Co. 1994–2003, Pres. 1994–2003; Amb. to Japan from the Commonwealth of the Bahamas; Silver Bear Award, Berlin Film Festival 1958; New York Film Critics Award 1958; Acad. Award Best Actor of 1963 (for Lilies of the Field); Cecil B. De Mille Award 1982, Life Achievement Award American Film Inst. 1992, Kennedy Center Honors 1995, Hon. Acad. Award for Lifetime Achievement 2002; Hon. KBE 1974. *Films include:* Cry the Beloved Country 1952, Red Ball Express 1952, Go, Man, Go 1954, Blackboard Jungle 1955, Goodbye My Lady 1956, Edge of the City 1957, Something of Value 1957, The Mark of the Hawk 1958, The Defiant Ones 1958, Porgy and Bess 1959, A Raisin in the Sun 1960, Paris Blues 1960, Lilies of the Field 1963, The Long Ships 1964, The Bedford Incident 1965, The Slender Thread 1966, A Patch of Blue 1966, Duel at Diablo 1966, To Sir with Love 1967, In the Heat of the Night 1967, Guess Who's Coming to Dinner 1968, For Love of Ivy 1968, The Lost Man 1970, They Call Me Mister Tibbs 1970, The Organization 1971, The Wilby Conspiracy 1975, Shoot to Kill 1988, Deadly Pursuit 1988, Separate But Equal (TV) 1992, Sneakers, Children of the Dust (TV) 1995, To Sir with Love, II (TV) 1996; has appeared in and directed Buck and the Preacher 1972, Warm December 1973, Uptown Saturday Night 1974, Let's Do It Again 1975, A Piece of the Action 1977, One Man, One Vote 1996; directed Stir Crazy 1980, Hanky Panky 1982, Go for It 1984, Little Nikita 1987, Ghost Dad 1990, Sneakers 1992, The Jackal 1997, Mandela and de Klerk (TV) 1997. *Publication:* This Life 1981. *Leisure interests:* football, tennis, gardening. *Address:* c/o CAA, 9830 Wilshire Boulevard, Beverly Hills, CA 90210, USA.

POIVRE D'ARVOR, Patrick, LenD; French journalist and radio and television presenter; b. 20 Sept. 1947, Reims (Marne); s. of Jacques Poivre and Madeleine France Jeuge; m. Véronique Courcoux 1971; six c. (two deceased); ed Lycée Georges-Clemenceau, Reims, Insts. d'études politiques, Strasbourg and Paris, Faculties of Law, Strasbourg, Paris and Reims, Ecole des langues orientales vivantes; Special Corresp., France-Inter 1971, journalist 1971–74, Head Political Dept 1975–76, Deputy Chief Ed., Antenne 2 1976–83, Presenter, evening news programme 1976–83, 1987–, Deputy Dir News 1989–; Leader-writer Paris-Match, Journal du Dimanche 1983–91; Producer and Compère, A nous deux, Antenne 2 1983–86, A la folie, TF1 1986–88; Compère, Tous en Scène, Canal Plus 1984–85; Compère and Producer Ex libris 1988–; Compère Vol de nuit 1999–; Presenter and Producer magazine programme Le Droit de savoir, TF1 1990–94. *Publications:* Mai 68-Mai 78 1978, Les Enfants de l'aube 1982, Deux amants 1984, Le Roman de Virginie 1985, Les Derniers trains de rêve 1986, La Traversée du miroir 1986, Rencontres 1987, Les Femmes de ma vie 1988, L'Homme d'images 1992, Lettres à l'absente 1993, Les Loups et la bergerie 1994, Elle n'était pas d'ici 1995, Anthologie des plus beaux poèmes d'amour 1995, Un héros de passage 1996, Lettre ouverte aux violeurs de vie privée 1997, Une trahison amoureuse 1997, La fin du monde (collection) 1998, Petit homme 1999, Les rats de garde (collection) 2000, L'Irrésolu 2000 (Prix Interallié), Un enfant 2001. *Address:* TF1, 1 quai du Point du Jour, 92100 Boulogne-Billancourt, France. *Telephone:* 1-41-41-23-28 (Office). *Fax:* 1-41-41-19-63 (Office).

POKHMELKIN, Victor Valeryevich, CAND.JUR.; Russian politician and jurist; b. 3 Feb. 1960, Perm; m.; one s.; ed Perm State Univ.; docent, lecturer Higher Courses of USSR Ministry of Internal Affairs, Perm; f. and Scientific Head Research Inst. of Legal Policy; mem. State Duma (Parl.) 1993–; mem. faction Vybor Rossii; Deputy Chair. Comm. on Law and Legal Reform; mem. Political Council Demokratichesky Vybor Rossii 1994–; mem. faction Union of Rightist Forces 2000–01; now ind. *Publications:* several monographs and scientific publs. *Address:* State Duma, Okhotny Ryad 1, 103265 Moscow, Russia (Office). *Telephone:* (095) 292-77-66 (Office). *Fax:* (095) 292-32-87 (Office).

POKORNI, Zoltán, AB; Hungarian politician and academic; b. 10 Jan. 1962, Budapest; s. of János Pokorni and Klara Vincz; m. Andrea Beck 1992; three s.; ed Loránd Eötvös Univ., Budapest; Lecturer Toldy Ferenc High School, Budapest 1987–94; founding mem. 1988, spokesman 1988–93, Ed. Democratic Trades Union of Teachers' paper –1993; joined Fed. of Young Democrats—Hungarian Civic Party (Magyar Polgári Párt–FIDESZ) 1993, Vice-Pres. 1994–2002, Leader 2002– (Leader of the Opposition 2002–); MP 1994–; Deputy Head Parl. Group 1994–97, Head 1997–98, personal rep. of Budapest XIIth Dist 1998–; fmr Head FIDESZ Dept for Educational Politics; Minister of Educ. 1998–2002. *Address:* FIDESZ, Lendvay u. 28, 1062 Budapest, Hungary. *Telephone:* (1) 269-5353 (Office). *Fax:* (1) 269-5343 (Office). *E-mail:* satjo@fidesz.parlament.hu (Office). *Website:* www.fidesz.hu (Office).

POKROVSKY, Boris Aleksandrovich; Russian opera stage director; b. 23 Jan. 1912, Moscow; s. of Aleksandr Pokrovsky and Elisaveta Stulova; m. 1st Anna Nekrasova 1936; m. 2nd Irina Maslennikova 1961; one s. one d; ed Lunacharsky Inst. of Theatre; stage Dir, artistic Dir Gorky Opera Theatre 1937–43; stage Dir Moscow Bolshoi Theatre 1937–82, Dir-Gen. 1952–63, 1967–82; f. and artistic Dir Moscow Chamber Music Theatre 1972–; Prof. Lunacharsky Inst. of Theatre 1954–; Hon. Pres. Int. Inst. of Theatre 1986;

USSR People's Artist 1961, Lenin Prize 1980, State Prizes of USSR and Russia; Golden Mask Theatre Prize 1996. *Productions:* first opera productions in Bolshoi Theatre of many operas by Russian composers, including Francesca da Rimini by Rachmaninov, Semen Kotko and The Gambler by Prokofiev, Dead Souls by Shchedrin; worked with Rostropovich on new productions of Eugene Onegin 1969, Khovanshchina 1995, Bolshoi Theatre; many productions in Moscow Chamber Music Theatre, including The Rake's Progress by Stravinsky, Don Giovanni by Mozart; many productions in European countries, including Life with an Idiot by A. Schnittke, Amsterdam 1993. *Publications:* 10 books and many articles. *Leisure interests:* music, reading. *Address:* Moscow Chamber Music Theatre, Nikolskaya str. 17, 103012 Moscow, Russia. *Telephone:* (095) 929-13-24. *Fax:* (095) 921-06-72.

POKROVSKY, Valentin Ivanovich, DrMed; Russian physician; b. 1 April 1929; m. Nina Yakovlevna Pokrovskaya; one s.; ed First Moscow Medical Inst.; mem. CPSU 1959–91; mem. USSR (now Russian) Acad. of Medical Sciences 1982–, Pres. 1987–; Dir Central Scientific Research Inst. of Epidemiology 1971–; mem. of Presidium of USSR (now Russian) Fed. of Space Flight; has studied problems of AIDS treatment, meningitis and intestinal diseases; Chair. Scientific Soc. of Microbiologists, Epidemiologists and Parasitologists; mem. Physicians for the Prevention of Nuclear War; mem. WHO Expert Cttee; mem. WHO Global Cttee on AIDS and Diarrhoeal Diseases; mem. Bd Int. Fed. of Infectionists; Hon. mem. Soc. of Microbiologists of Czech Repub.; USSR People's Deputy 1989–91; V. Timakov Prize, D. Ivanovsky Prize. *Publications:* Symptoms, Treatment and Diagnostics of Salmonellosis in Adults 1981, Immuno-ferment Analysis 1985, Symptoms, Pathogenesis and Treatment of Cholera 1988, Small Medical Encylopaedia (Ed.) 1991, Encyclopaedia of Health 1992, Epidemiology of Viral Diseases 2000, Cholera in the USSR–Period of the VIIth Pandemia 2000, Social Hygiene Monitoring and Epidemiology Surveillance in Moscow 2000, Cholera–Acute Problems 2000. *Address:* Russian Academy of Medical Sciences, Solyanka str. 14, 109544 GSP Moscow, Russia. *Telephone:* (095) 298-21-52. *Fax:* (095) 298-21-64. *E-mail:* ramn@rosmail.ru.

POL, Marek; Polish politician and economist; b. 8 Dec. 1953, Słupsk; m.; one s. one d.; ed Poznań Univ. of Technology and Acad. of Economy, Poznań; mem. staff advancing to Deputy Dir for Financial and Commercial Affairs, Agric. Vehicle Factory, Antoninek, Poznań 1977–93; mem. Polish United Workers' Party (PZPR) 1976–90; Co-Founder Union of Labour (UP) 1992–, Chair. 1998–; Minister of Industry and Trade 1993–95; Govt Plenipotentiary responsible for reforming the cen. econ. admins. 1995–97; Deputy Prime Minister and Minister of Infrastructure 2001–; mem. Supervisory Bd Daewoo-FSO 2000–01. *Leisure interests:* walks with family, reading books and journals. *Address:* Ministry of Infrastructure, ul. Chałubińskiego 4/6, 00-928, Warsaw, Poland (Office). *Telephone:* (22) 6301000 (Office). *Website:* www.mtigm.gov.pl (Office).

POLAK, Julia Margaret, MD, DSc, F.R.C.PATH., FRCP, F. MED.SCI.; British professor and consultant in histopathology; b. 29 June 1939, Buenos Aires, Argentina; m. Daniel Catovsky; two s. one d.; ed Univ. of Buenos Aires; various hosp. posts, Buenos Aires 1961–67; Asst Lecturer, Dept of Histochemistry, Royal Postgrad. Medical School, London 1968–69, Lecturer 1970–73, Sr lecturer 1973–79, Reader 1982–84, Prof. 1984–, Chair. Dept 1992–; Hon. Consultant in Histopathology, Hammersmith Hosp. 1979–, Deputy Dir Dept of Histopathology 1988–; Chair. British Endocrine Pathologists Group 1988–; Chair. Cognate Research Group, Imperial Coll. School of Medicine 1997–; Pres. Tissue and Cell. Eng Soc. 1998–; Dir Tissue Eng Centre 1998–; mem. editorial bd 34 journals; mem. 34 scientific and medical socs; Hon. PhD (Univ. Complutense, Madrid), Benito Udaondo Cardiology Prize 1967, Medal of Soc. of Endocrinology 1984, Sir Eric Sharpe Prize for Oncology 1987 and others. *Publications:* 23 books, numerous articles, book chapters and case reports etc. *Address:* Tissue Engineering Centre, Imperial College School of Medicine, 3rd Floor, Chelsea & Hammersmith Hospital, 369 Fulham Road, London, SW10 9NH (Office); 11 Thames Quay, Chelsea Harbour, London, SW10 0UY, England (Home). *Telephone:* (20) 8237-2670 (Office). *Fax:* (20) 8746-5619 (Office). *E-mail:* julia.polak@ic.ac.uk (Office). *Website:* www .polak-transplant.med.ic.ac.uk (Office).

POLAŃSKI, Roman; French film director, writer and actor; b. 18 Aug. 1933, Paris; s. of Ryszard Polański and Bule Katz-Przedborska; m. 1st Barbara Kwiatkowska-Lass (divorced); m. 2nd Sharon Tate 1968 (died 1969); m. 3rd Emmanuelle Seigner; ed Polish Film School, Łódź; Dir Two Men and a Wardrobe 1958, When Angels Fall, Le Gros et Le Maigre, Knife in the Water (prize at Venice Film Festival 1962), The Mammals (prize at Tours Film Festival 1963), Repulsion (prize at Berlin Film Festival 1965), Cul de Sac (prize at Berlin Film Festival 1966), The Vampire Killers 1967, Rosemary's Baby 1968, Macbeth 1971, What? 1972, Lulu (opera), Spoleto Festival 1974, Chinatown (Best Dir Award. Soc. of Film and TV Arts 1974, Le Prix Raoul-Levy 1975) 1974, The Tenant 1976, Rigoletto (opera) 1976, Tess (Golden Globe Award) 1980, Vampires Ball 1980, Amadeus (play) 1981, Pirates 1986, Frantic 1988, Tales of Hoffmann (opera) 1992, Bitter Moon (Dir, produced, written) 1992, Death and the Maiden 1994, Dance of the Vampire (play) 1997, The Ninth Gate 1999; has acted in: A Generation, The End of the Night, See You Tomorrow, The Innocent Sorcerers, Two Men and a Wardrobe, The Vampire Killers, What?, Chinatown, The Tenant, Pirates, Metamorphosis (play) 1988, Icons, A Pure Formality, In Stuttgart 2000, The Pianist (Best Film, Cannes Film Festival 2002, Acad. Award for Best Dir 2003, BAFTA Award for Best Film and Best Dir 2003) 2002; Pris René Clair for Lifetime

Achievement, Académie Française 1999. *Publication:* Roman (autobiog.) 1984. *Address:* ICM, 8942 Wilshire Boulevard, Beverly Hills, CA 90211, USA (Office).

POLANYI, John Charles, CC, PhD, FRS, FRSC, FRSE; Canadian professor of chemistry and physics; b. 23 Jan. 1929, Berlin, Germany; s. of Michael Polanyi and Magda Polanyi (née Kemeny); m. Anne Ferrar Davidson 1958; one s. one d.; ed Manchester Grammar School and Manchester Univ., England; Postdoctoral Fellow, Nat. Research Council of Canada 1952–54; Research Assoc., Princeton Univ., USA 1954–56; Lecturer, Univ. of Toronto, Canada 1956–57, Asst Prof. 1957–60, Assoc. Prof. 1960–62, Prof. of Chem. 1962–; many visiting lectureships; mem. numerous prof. asscns.; Hon. Foreign mem. AAAS; Foreign Assoc., NAS, USA; Hon. degrees from over 30 univs.; shared Nobel Prize for Chemistry 1986; Marlow Medal, Faraday Soc. 1962; British Chemical Soc. Award 1971; Chemical Inst. of Canada Medal 1976; Henry Marshall Tory Medal, Royal Soc. of Canada 1977; Wolf Prize in Chem. (shared with G. Pimentel) 1982; Izaak Walton Killam Memorial Prize 1988; Royal Medal, Royal Soc. 1989. *Publications:* Co-Ed.: The Dangers of Nuclear War 1979; author of over 200 scientific papers. *Address:* Department of Chemistry, University of Toronto, 80 St George Street, Toronto, Ont., M5S 1A1 (Office); 142 Collier Street, Toronto, Ont., M4W 1M3, Canada (Home). *Telephone:* (416) 978-3580 (Office); (416) 961-6545 (Home).

POLE, Jack Richon, PhD, FBA, FRHistS; British historian; b. 14 March 1922, London; s. of Joseph Pole and Phoebe Rickards; m. Marilyn Mitchell 1952 (divorced 1988); one s. two d.; ed King Alfred School, London, King's Coll. London, Queen's Coll. Oxford and Princeton Univ., USA; served in army, rank of Capt. 1941–46; Instructor in History, Princeton Univ. 1952–53; Asst Lecturer, then Lecturer in American History, Univ. Coll. London 1953–63; Reader in American History and Govt, Cambridge Univ. and Fellow of Churchill Coll. 1963–79, Vice-Master of Churchill Coll. 1975–78; Rhodes Prof. of American History and Insts, Oxford Univ. and Fellow of St Catherine's Coll. 1979–89, Emer. Fellow 1989–, Emer. Prof.; Hon. Vice-Pres. Int. Comm. for the History of Rep. and Parl. Insts 1991–; Visiting Prof. Univs. at Berkeley 1960–61, Ghana 1966, Chicago 1969, Beijing 1984, William and Mary Law School 1991; Goleib Fellow New York Univ. Law School 1990; Hon. Vice-Pres. British Nineteenth Century Historians 2000–; Hon. Foreign Mem. American Historical Asscn 2002; New Jersey Prize Princeton Univ. 1953, Ramsdell Award, Southern Historical Asscn 1959. *Exhibition:* paintings and pastels, Wolfson Coll., Oxford 2001. *Publications:* Political Representation in England and the Origins of the American Republic 1966, Foundations of American Independence 1972, The Pursuit of Equality in American History 1978, (revised and enlarged edn) 1993, Paths to the American Past 1979, The Gift of Government: Political Responsibility from the English Restoration to American Independence 1983, Colonial British America 1984, The American Constitution: For and Against 1987, The Blackwell Encyclopedia of the American Revolution (Co-ed.) 1991, Freedom of Speech: Right or Privilege? 1998, Companion to the American Revolution 2000; series Co-Ed. Early America: History, Context, Culture. *Leisure interests:* cricket, painting, writing. *Address:* St Catherine's College, Oxford, OX1 3UJ (Office); 20 Divinity Road, Oxford, OX4 1LJ, England (Home). *Telephone:* (1865) 271757 (Office); (1865) 246950 (Home). *Fax:* (1865) 271768 (Office); (1865) 246950 (Home). *E-mail:* jack.pole@ntlworld.com (Home).

POLESE, Kim, BS; American computer executive; ed Univs. of California, Berkeley and Washington; Product Man. Sun Microsystems 1988–95; co-Founder Marimba Inc. 1996–, also Pres., CEO. *Address:* Marimba Incorporated, 440 Clyde Avenue, Mountain View, CA 94043, USA.

POLETTI, Alan Ronald, DPhil, FRSNZ; New Zealand professor of physics; b. 19 Oct. 1937, New Plymouth; s. of John Poletti and Pearl Poletti; m. 1st Dorothy M. Martin 1961 (died 1994); three s. one d.; m. 2nd Marcia M. Stenson 1996; ed Univ. of Oxford; Prof. of Physics, Univ. of Auckland 1969–98, Head of Dept of Physics 1986–92, now Prof. Emer. *Publications:* over 100 scientific papers. *Leisure interests:* sailing, public history. *Address:* 11 Tole Street, Ponsonby, Auckland, New Zealand (Home). *Telephone:* (9) 373-7599 .

POLETTO, HE Cardinal Severino; Italian ecclesiastic; b. 18 March 1933, Salgareda, Treviso; ordained priest 1957; Coadjutant Bishop of Fossano 1980; Bishop of Fossano 1980–89, of Asti 1989–99; Archbishop of Turin 1999–; cr. Cardinal 2001. *Address:* Via Arcivescovado 12, 10121 Turin, Italy (Office). *Telephone:* (011) 5156211 (Office). *Fax:* (011) 5156209 (Office).

POLEZHAYEV, Leonid Konstantinovich; Russian politician; b. 30 Jan. 1940, Omsk; m.; two s.; ed Omsk Inst. of Agric.; different posts in agric. orgs. Pavlodar Region, Kazakhstan; 1965–76; Head of Construction Irtysh-Karaganda Canal 1976–82; First Deputy Chair. Karaganda Regional Exec. Cttee 1982–87; Head. Omsk Regional Dept of Melioration and Water Resources 1987–89; Deputy Chair., Chair. Omsk Regional Exec. Cttee 1989–90; Head Admin. of Omsk Region 1991; Gov. Omsk Region Dec. 1995–; mem. Russian Council of Fed. 1993–2001; corresp. mem. Russian and Int. Acads. of Eng; Chair. Council of Interregional Asscn Sibirskoe Soglasheniye; Co-Chair. Consulting Council of admin. Heads of Boundary Territories of Russia and Kazakhstan; Hon. Prof. Omsk State Univ.; Peace Prize of Kazakhstan, Order of Red Banner, Order of St. Prince Vladimir and St. Prince Daniel, Medal of Valour, Medal of Virgin Lands (300th Anniversary of Russian Fleet). *Publications:* The Path Toward Oneself, Proceed with Caution, The Reform Years. *Leisure interests:* books, history, museums, sport. *Address:* Office of the

Governor, Krasny put str. 1, 644002 Omsk, Russia (Office). *Telephone:* (3812) 24-40-11, 24-14-15 (Office). *Fax:* (3812) 24-23-72 (Office). *E-mail:* vescom@ ecrel.omsk.su (Office).

POLFER, Lydie; Luxembourg politician; b. 22 Nov. 1952; m. Hubert Wurth (q.v.); one d.; ed Lycée Robert Schuman, Univ. of Grenoble, France, Univ. Centre for Int. and European Research, Grenoble; admitted to Luxembourg Bar 1977; M.P. 1979–; Mayor City of Luxembourg 1982–99; MEP 1985–89, 1990–94; Chair. Democratic Party 1994–; Deputy Prime Minister, Minister of Foreign Affairs and External Trade, Minister of Civil Service and Admin. Reform 1999–. *Address:* Ministry of Foreign Affairs and External Trade, 5 rue Notre Dame, 2240 Luxembourg, Luxembourg (Office). *Telephone:* 48-72-30-1 (Office). *Fax:* 22-32-85 (Office). *E-mail:* cecile.peysen@mae.etat.lu (Office).

POLGÁR, László; Hungarian bass opera and concert singer; b. 1 Jan. 1947, Somogyszentpál; s. of Lajos Polgár and Anna Kántor; m. Ágnes Gergely; three d.; ed Liszt Ferenc Music Acad., Budapest 1967–72; scholarship holder 1972–73; soloist State Opera House, Budapest 1973–; postgraduate study under Hans Hotter, Hochschule für Musik und Darstellende Kunst, Vienna 1979–81; Lieder recitalist; also sings Oratorio (Verdi's Requiem, etc.); Liszt Prize 1985, Merited artist 1986. *Song competition winner:* Dvořák, Karlovy Vary 1971, Schumann, Zwickau 1974, Erkel, Budapest 1975, Hungarian Radio 1977, Ostende 1977, Hugo Wolf, Vienna 1980, Pavarotti competition, Philadelphia 1981. *Performances:* début in Seneca (Monteverdi: L'Incoronazione di Poppea); appearances in Staatsoper, Vienna; Royal Opera House, Covent Garden, Salzburg Festival, Zürich, Munich, Hamburg, Hannover, Paris, Madrid, Venice, Bologna, Florence, Rome, Moscow, Prague, Dresden, Berlin, Stockholm, Buenos Aires, Metropolitan Opera, New York, Philadelphia, Los Angeles, Pittsburgh, Pa. *Operatic roles include:* Osmin, Sarastro, Leporello, Figaro, Publius (La Clemenza di Tito), Bellini: Oroveso (Norma), Rodolfo (La Sonnambula), Basilio (Il Barbiere di Sevilla), Don Geronio (Il Turco in Italia), Philippo II (Don Carlo), Il Guardiano (La Forza del Destino), Conte Walter (Luisa Miller), Fiesco (Simone Boccanegra), Ramphis (Aida), Gurnemanz (Parsifal), Marke (Tristan), Collin (La Bohème), Timur (Turandot), Bluebeard (Duke Bluebeard's Castle), Rocco (Fidelio), Gremin (Eugene Onegin), Boris Godunov. *Address:* 1113 Budapest, Ábel Jenő utca 12, Hungary. *Telephone:* (1) 668-285.

POLI, Roberto; Italian energy company executive; b. 1938; Prof. of Corp. Finance Cattolica di Milano 1966–98; fmr Chair. Rizzoli-Corriere della Sera, Publitania; Admin. Fininvest, Mondatori and Merloni; Chair. Poli Morelli & Pnrs SpA; financial adviser to Italian industrial cos; Chair. Ente Nazionale Idrocarburi (Eni) Group SpA (oil and gas co.) 2003–. *Address:* Eni SpA, Piazzale Mattei 1, 00144 Rome, Italy (Office). *Telephone:* (06) 59821 (Office). *Fax:* (06) 59822141 (Office). *E-mail:* segreteriasocietaria.azionisti@eni.it (Office). *Website:* www.eni.it (Office).

POLI BORTONE, Adriana; Italian politician; b. 25 Aug. 1943, Lecce; m.; two c.; graduated in classics; Assoc. Prof. of Latin Literature, Univ. of Lecce; Movimento Sociale Italian (MSI) Deputy 1983–94; Alleanza Nazionale Deputy 1994–; Minister of Agric. 1994–95. *Address:* c/o Ministero delle Politiche Agricole Alimentari e Forestali, Via XX Settembre, 00187 Rome, Italy.

POLIAKOFF, Stephen; British playwright and film director; b. 1952; s. of late Alexander Poliakoff and Ina Montagu; m. Sandy Welch 1983; one d. one s.; ed Westminster School and Univ. of Cambridge; Best British Film Award, Evening Standard for Close My Eyes, Critic' Circle Best Play Award for Blinded by the Sun, Prix Italia for Shooting the Past (TV). *Films:* Hidden City, Close My Eyes 1992, Century 1995, The Tribe 1998, Food of Love 1998. *Theatre:* Clever Soldiers 1974, The Carnation Gang 1974, Hitting Town 1975, City Sugar 1976, Strawberry Fields (Nat. Theatre) 1978, Shout Across the River (RSC) 1978, The Summer Party 1980, Favourite Nights 1981, Breaking the Silence (RSC) 1984, Coming in to Land (Nat. Theatre) 1987, Playing with Trains (RSC) 1989, Siena Red 1992, Sweet Panic (Hampstead) 1996, Blinded by the Sun (Nat. Theatre) 1996, Talk of the City (RSC) 1998, Remember This (Nat. Theatre) 1999. *Television:* plays: Caught on a Train (BAFTA Award), She's Been Away (Venice Film Festival Prize), Shooting the Past 1999, Perfect Strangers 2001; drama: The Lost Prince 2003. *Publications:* Plays One 1989, Plays Two 1994, Plays Three 1998, Sweet Panic and Blinded by the Sun, Talk of the City, Shooting the Past, Remember This. *Leisure interests:* watching cricket, going to the cinema. *Address:* 33 Devonia Road, London, N1 8JQ, England. *Telephone:* (20) 7354-2695.

POLING, Harold Arthur, MBA; American business executive; b. 14 Oct. 1925, Troy, Mich.; s. of Plesant Arthur Poling and Laura Elizabeth (née Thompson) Poling; m. Marian Sarita Lee 1957; one s. two d.; ed Monmouth Coll. and Ind. Univ.; with Ford Motor Co., Dearborn, Mich. 1951–59, 1960–, Asst Controller Transmissions and Chassis Div. 1964–66, Controller 1966–67, Engine and Foundry Div. 1967–69, Product Devt Group 1969–72, Vice-Pres. of Finance Ford of Europe, 1972–75, Pres. Ford of Europe, Inc., Brentwood, UK 1975–77, Chair. 1977–79, Exec. Vice-Pres. Ford Motor Co., Dearborn, Mich. 1979, Pres. and COO 1985–87, Vice-Chair. and COO 1987–90, Chair. and CEO 1990–93, Chair. 1993–94; Sec. Motor Vehicle Mfg Asscn; mem. Pres.'s Export Council, Pres.'s Comm. on Environment; mem. Bd of Dirs. Shell Oil Co.; Co-Chair. Steering Cttee Barbara Bush Foundation for Family Literacy; mem. Nat. 4-H Council and numerous other orgs.; Hon. degrees (Monmouth Coll.) 1981, (Hofstra Univ.) 1986, (Indiana) 1990, (Detroit) 1990, (Mich. State) 1992; Leadership Award, Eng Soc., Detroit 1987,

Man of the Year (Automotive Industries magazine) 1988, Horatio Alger Award 1991. *Address:* c/o Ford Motor Co., P.O. Box 1899, Room 118, Dearborn, MI 48121-1899, USA.

POLISHCHUK, Lyubov Grigoryevna; Russian actress; b. 21 May 1949, Omsk; m.; one s. one d.; ed Creative Workshop of Variety Arts at Russian Concert Agency, Moscow Lunacharsky Inst. of Theatre Art; in variety shows 1965–76; actress Theatre Hermitage 1980–87; leading actress Theatre School of Contemporary Play 1989–; in cinema 1976–; Merited Artist of Russian Fed. *Films include:* Zatsepin Family 1976, Twelve Chairs 1976, Love with Privileges, Play of Imagination, New Odeon, Golden Mine, Daphnis and Chloë. *Address:* Tsandera str. 7, Apt. 386, 129075 Moscow, Russia (Office). *Telephone:* (095) 215-66-18 (Home).

POLKINGHORNE, Rev. Canon John Charlton, Kt, KBE, MA, PhD, ScD, FRS; British ecclesiastic and physicist; b. 16 Oct. 1930, Weston-super-Mare; s. of George B. Polkinghorne and Dorothy E. Charlton; m. Ruth I. Martin 1955; two s. one d.; ed Perse School, Cambridge, Trinity Coll. Cambridge and Westcott House, Cambridge; Lecturer, Univ. of Edin. 1956–58; Lecturer, Univ. of Cambridge 1958–65, Reader 1965–68, Prof. of Math. Physics 1968–79; Fellow, Trinity Coll. Cambridge 1954–86; Curate, St Michael & All Angels, Bedminster 1982–84; Vicar of St Cosmus and St Damian in the Blean 1984–86; Fellow and Dean, Trinity Hall, Cambridge 1986–89, Hon. Fellow 1989–; Pres. Queens' Coll. Cambridge 1989–96, Fellow 1989–, Hon. Fellow 1996–; Six Preacher, Canterbury Cathedral 1996–; mem. Human Genetics Advisory Comm. 1996–99; mem. Human Genetics Comm. 2000; Hon. Prof. of Theoretical Physics, Univ. of Kent 1984–89, Hon. Fellow St Edmund's Coll., Cambridge 2002; Hon. DD (Kent) 1994, (Durham) 1999; Hon. DSc (Exeter) 1994, (Leicester) 1995; Templeton Prize 2002. *Publications:* The Analytic S-Matrix (jointly) 1966, The Particle Play 1979, Models of High Energy Processes 1980, The Way the World Is 1983, The Quantum World 1984, One World 1986, Science and Creation 1988, Science and Providence 1989, Rochester Roundabout 1989, Reason and Reality 1991, Science and Christian Belief 1994, Quarks, Chaos and Christianity 1994, Serious Talk 1995, Scientists as Theologians 1996, Beyond Science 1996, Searching for Truth 1996, Belief in God in an Age of Science 1998, Science and Theology 1998, Faith, Science and Understanding 2000, The End of the World and the Ends of God (ed with M. Welker) 2000, Faith in the Living God (with M. Welker) 2001, The Work of Love (ed.) 2001, The God of Hope and the End of the World 2002. *Leisure interest:* gardening. *Address:* Queens' College, Cambridge, CB3 9ET, England.

POLLACK, Ilana, BA; Israeli librarian; b. 13 Aug. 1946, Tel-Aviv; d. of Mala First (née Ferszt) and Leon Pinsky; m. Joseph Pollack 1977 (died 1994); two s.; ed Re'alit High School, Rishon Le Zion, Tel-Aviv Univ. and Hebrew Univ. Jerusalem; served in Israeli Army 1964–66; joined Weizmann Inst. of Science, Rehovot as Asst Librarian 1966, Librarian in charge of Physics Faculty Library 1975, Chief Librarian, Weizmann Inst. of Science 1983–. *Address:* Wix Library, Weizmann Institute of Science, Rehovot 76100 (Office); 22 Shenkin Street, Rishon Le-Zion 75282, Israel (Home). *Telephone:* 8-9343583 (Office); 3-9692186 (Home). *Fax:* 8-9344176. *E-mail:* ilana.pollack@weizmann .ac.il (Office). *Website:* www.weizmann.ac.il/WIS-library.home.htm (Office).

POLLACK, Sydney; American film director; b. 1 July 1934, Lafayette, Ind.; s. of David Pollack and Rebecca Miller; m. Claire Griswold 1958; one s. two d.; ed Neighborhood Playhouse Theatre School, New York; Asst to Sanford Meisner 1954, Acting Instructor 1954–57, 1959–60; Army service 1957–59; Exec. Dir The Actors Studio (West Coast br.); appeared on Broadway in The Dark is Light Enough 1954, A Stone for Danny Fisher 1955; TV appearances include Aloa Presents; Dir The Chrysler Theatre, Ben Casey 1962–63 (for TV); Acad. Award for Best Dir and Best Picture 1986. *Films include:* The Slender Thread 1965, This Property is Condemned 1966, The Scalphunters 1967, Castle Keep 1968, They Shoot Horses, Don't They? 1969–70, Jeremiah Johnson 1971–72, The Way We Were 1972–73, The Yakuza 1974, Three Days of the Condor 1974–75, Bobby Deerfield 1976, The Electric Horseman 1978–79, Absence of Malice 1981, Tootsie 1982 (producer), Song Writer 1984, Out of Africa 1985 (producer), Havana 1989, The Firm 1993, Sabrina 1996, Random Hearts 1999; producer The Fabulous Baker Boys 1989, The Last Ship 1990, King Ralph (co-exec. producer), Dead Again (exec. producer), Presumed Innocent 1990, Sense and Sensibility 1995 (exec. producer), The Talented Mr Ripley 1999; co-producer Bright Lights, Big City 1988; acted in The Player, Death Becomes Her, Husbands and Wives, A Civil Action, Eyes Wide Shut. *Address:* Mirage Enterprises, David Lean Building, 119, 10202 Washington Boulevard, Culver City, CA 90232 (Office); CAA, 9830 Wilshire Boulevard, Beverly Hills, CA 92012, USA.

POLLEN, Arabella Rosalind Hungerford; British couturier and business executive; b. 22 June 1961, Oxford; d. of Peregrine Pollen and Patricia Pollen; m. Giacomo Dante Algranti 1985; two s.; ed l'Ecole Française, New York, Nightingale Bamford, Hatherop Castle School, Glos., St Swithins, Winchester and Queen's Coll., London; f. Arabella Pollen Ltd in jt venture with Namara Ltd 1981; bought out Namara Ltd and entered jt partnership with Peregrine Marcus Pollen 1983–; designer for other labels 1983–. *Leisure interests:* music/ piano, literature.

POLLINI, Maurizio; Italian pianist; b. 5 Jan. 1942, Milan; s. of Gino Pollini and Renata Melotti; m. Maria Elisabetta Marzotto 1968; one s.; has played with Berlin and Vienna Philharmonic Orchestras, Bayerischer Rundfunk Orchestra, London Symphony Orchestra, Boston, New York, Philadelphia,

LA and San Francisco Orchestras; has played at Salzburg, Vienna, Berlin, Prague Festivals; recordings for Polydor Int.; First Prize Int. Chopin Competition, Warsaw 1960; Ernst von Siemens Music Prize, Munich 1996. *Address:* c/o Harrison Parrott Ltd., 12, Penzance Place, London, W11 4PA, England (Office).

POLLOCK, Griselda, PhD; British/Canadian professor of art; b. 11 March 1949, Bloemfontein, S. Africa; m. Anthony Bryant 1981; one s. one d.; ed Oxford Univ., Courtauld Inst. of Art, London Univ.; lecturer, Manchester Univ. 1974–77, Univ. of Leeds 1977–90; Prof. of Social and Critical Histories of Art 1990–; Co-Dir Centre for Cultural Studies 1987–; Dir AHRB Centre for Cultural Analysis, Theory and History 2000–. *Films:* Deadly Tales 1996, Eurydice 1997. *Television:* J'accuse . . . Van Gogh 1990. *Publications:* Millet 1977, Cassatt 1978, Old Mistresses 1981, Vision and Difference 1988, Avant-Garde Gambits 1992, Dealing with Degas 1992, Generations and Geographies 1996, Avant-Gardes and Partisans Reviewed 1996, Mary Cassatt 1998, Differencing the Canon 1999, Looking back to the Future 2000, The Case against Van Gogh 2001. *Leisure interests:* opera, skiing, music, running. *Address:* Department of Fine Art, University of Leeds, Leeds, LS2 9JT, England (Office). *Telephone:* (113) 233-1629 (Office). *Fax:* (113) 233-1629 (Office). *E-mail:* g.f.s.pollock@leeds.ac.uk (Office).

POLLOCK, Shaun; South African cricketer; b. 16 July 1973, Port Elizabeth; s. of Peter Pollock and Inez Pollock; m. Tricia Lauderdale; ed Univ. of Natal, Durban; right-hand batsman, right-arm fast-medium bowler; test debut: South Africa v. England at Centurion, 1st Test 1995–96; One Day Int. (ODI) debut: South Africa v. England at Cape Town, 1st ODI 1995–96; First-class debut: Natal B v. Western Province B at Pietermaritzburg 1991–92; major teams: SA nat. team, Natal, SA and Warwicks., UK; in Tests (up to 8 Nov. 2002) played in 65 matches for a total of 2,280 runs (average 31.66), bowling figures: 267 wickets for 5,534 runs (average 20.72); ODIs: played in 170 matches for 1,661 runs, bowling figures: 240 wickets for 5,638 runs (average 23.49); First-class: played in 135 matches for 5,282 (average 33); bowling figures: 490 wickets for 10,819 runs. *Leisure interests:* music, golf, reading. *Address:* c/o KwaZulu-Natal Cricket Union, P.O. Box 47266, Greyville, 4023, South Africa (Office).

POLOZKOVA, Lidia Pavlovna; Russian speed-skater and sports official; b. 8 March 1939, Zlatoust; d. of Pavel I. Skoblikov and Klavdia N. Skoblikova; m. Alexander G. Polozkov; one s.; six gold medals in Winter Olympic Games 1960 and 1964; all-round world champion 1963–64; won 40 gold medals, 25 at world championships and 15 in USSR; mem. CPSU 1964–91; Head Dept of Physical Educ., Moscow Higher School of the All-Union Trade Union Movt 1974–88; Sr Vice-Pres. of All-Union Trade Unions Soc. for Physical Culture and Sports 1988–92; Vice-Pres. Russian Speed-Skating Fed. 1992–95; Head, Fund for Support of Sports Veterans 1997–; Hon. mem. Russian Speed-Skating Fed. 1995–; Honoured Master of Sports 1960. *Publications:* numerous publs on sport and physical culture. *Leisure interests:* reading, theatre, forest walking, sports, knitting. *Address:* c/o Russian Speed-Skating Federation, Luzhnetskaya nab. 8, Moscow, Russia. *Telephone:* (095) 201-10-40.

POLTAVCHENKO, Lieut.-Gen. Georgy Sergeyevich; Russian politician and engineer; b. 23 Feb. 1953, Baku, Azerbaijan; m.; one s.; ed Leningrad Inst. of Aviation Machinery, Higher KGB Courses; constructor, involved in bldg Kama truck plant 1972, worked in unit Leninets, worked in local Comsomol Cttee St Petersburg; on staff in KGB orgs 1979–; with KGB, Leningrad Region 1980–92; People's Deputy of Leningrad Regional Council 1990–93; Head Dept Fed. Service of Tax Police, St Petersburg 1992–99; Rep. of Russian Pres. to Leningrad Region 1999–2000, to Cen. Fed. Dist 2000–; Pres. St Petersburg Basketball Fed. *Address:* Office of the Presidential Representative, Nikolsky per. 6, 130132 Moscow, Russia (Office). *Telephone:* (095) 206-12-76, 206-19-37 (Office).

POLTORANIN, Mikhail Nikiforovich; Russian politician and journalist; b. 22 Nov. 1939, Leninogorsk, E Kazakhstan Region; m.; two s.; ed Kazakh State Univ., Higher CP School; corresp., Ed.-in-Chief local newspapers in Altai 1966–68, Exec. Sec. Kazakhstanskaya Pravda 1970–75, Corresp. Pravda in Kazakhstan 1975–86, Ed.-in-Chief Moskovskaya Pravda 1986–88, Political corresp. Press Agency Novosti 1988–90; USSR People's Deputy 1989–91; Minister of Press and Mass Media of Russia 1990–92, Deputy-Chair. of Govt (Deputy Prime Minister) of Russia Feb.–Nov. 1992, Dir Fed. Information Agency 1992–93; mem. State Duma (Parl.) 1993–95; Chair. Cttee on Information Policy and Communications 1994–95; Chair. Bd Moment of Truth Corpn 1994–; mem. Bd of Dirs. TV-3 Russia 1998–, Exec. Dir 1999–. *Address:* TV-3, Bersenevskaya nab. 20/2, 109017 Moscow, Russia. *Telephone:* (095) 959-06-37.

POLUNIN, Vyacheslav Ivanovich; Russian mime and clown; b. 12 June 1950, Novosil, Orlov Region; s. of Pavlovich Polunin and Nikolayevna Polunina; m. Elena Ushakova; two s.; ed Leningrad Inst. of Culture; f. Theatre of Comic Pantomime Actors Litsedei 1968; f. Leningrad Mime Parade 1982; f. All-Union Festival of Street Theatres 1987, All-Union Congress of Fools 1988, Russian Acad. of Fools; took part in European Caravan of Peace 1989; tours around Europe; lives in UK; Golden Angel Prize of Edin. Festival, Golden Nose Prize, Spain, Lawrence Olivier Prize, England, Triumph Prize, Russia. *Leisure interests:* painting, sculpture, architecture, design.

POLVINEN, Tuomo Ilmari, PhD; Finnish professor of history; b. 2 Dec. 1931, Helsinki; s. of Eino Ilmari Polvinen and Ilona Vihersalo; m. Eeva-Liisa Rommi 1965; two d.; ed Univ. of Helsinki; Docent, Univ. of Helsinki 1965; Prof. of Modern History, Tampere Univ. 1968–70; Dir-Gen. Nat. Archives of Finland 1970–74; Prof. of Modern History Univ. of Helsinki 1974–93; Research Prof. Acad. of Finland 1979–95; Urho Kekkonen Prize 1981. *Publications:* Venäjän vallankumous ja Suomi 1917–1920, I-II 1967, 1971, Suomi kansainvälisessä politiikassa 1941–47, I-III 1979, 1980, 1981, Between East and West: Finland in International Politics 1944–47 1986, J. K. Paasikivi, Valtiomiehen elämäntyö Vol. 1, 1870–1918 1989, Vol. 2, 1918–1939 1992, Vol. 3, 1939–1944 1995, Vol. 4, 1944–1948 1999, Imperial Borderland: Bobrikov and the Attempted Russification of Finland, 1898–1904 1995. *Address:* Ruusulankatu 8 A 9, 00260 Helsinki, Finland. *Telephone:* 408554. *E-mail:* tuomo.polvinen@kolumbus.fi (Home).

POLWARTH, 10th Baron; Henry Alexander Hepburne Scott, TD, DL, MA, LLD, FRSE, FRSA; Scottish administrator, banker and chartered accountant; b. 17 Nov. 1916, Edinburgh; s. of Hon. Walter Thomas Hepburne Scott and Elspeth Glencairn Campbell; m. 1st Caroline Margaret Hay 1943 (divorced 1969); one s. three d.; m. 2nd Jean Jauncey (née Cunninghame Graham) 1969; two step-s. one step-d.; ed Eton Coll. and King's Coll. Cambridge; Deputy-Gov. Bank of Scotland 1960–66, Gov. 1966–72, Dir 1974–87; mem. Western Hemisphere Exports Council 1958–64; Partner Chiene and Tait, Edinburgh 1950–68; Chair. Gen. Accident, Fire and Life Assurance Co. 1968–72; Minister of State, Scottish Office 1972–74, given special responsibility for oil devt in Scotland 1973–74; Chair. Oil Devt Council for Scotland 1973–74; Dir ICI 1969–72, 1974–81, Halliburton Co. 1974–87, Canadian Pacific Ltd 1975–86, Sun Life Assurance Co. of Canada 1975–84, Brown and Root (UK) 1977; mem. Historic Bldgs. Council for Scotland 1953–66; Chancellor Univ. of Aberdeen 1966–86; Chair. Scottish Nat. Orchestra 1975–79; mem. British Section, Franco-British Council 1981–90; mem. House of Lords Select Cttee on Overseas Trade 1984–85; Vice-Lord Lt Borders Region 1975–90; Hon. LLD (Univs. of St Andrews, Aberdeen), Hon. DLitt (Heriot Watt), Dr hc (Stirling). *Leisure interests:* country pursuits, travel, the arts. *Address:* Wellfield Parva, Hawkchurch, Axminster, Devon, EX8 5UT, England. *Telephone:* (1297) 678735.

POLZE, Werner, Dr rer. pol; German banker; b. 26 March 1931, Altenburg; m. Margitta Polze 1956; one d.; ed School of Economics, Berlin, Akademie für Staats- und Rechtswissenschaften, Babelsberg (Inst. of Int. Relations); worked for Deutsche Notenbank, Berlin, GDR 1956–66; joined Deutsche Aussenhandelsbank AG 1966, Exec. Vice-Pres. 1969–78, Pres. 1978–91, Spokesman for the Bd 1991–; Deputy Chair. Supervisory Bd, DIHB Deutsche Industrie- und Handelsbank AG, Berlin 1990–. *Address:* Deutsche Aussenhandelsbank Aktiengesellschaft, Unter den Linden 26/30, 10117 Berlin, Germany.

POMERANTS, Grigory Solomonovich; Russian philosopher and writer; b. 13 March 1918, Vilnius, Lithuania; m. Mirkina Zinaida Aleksandrovna; ed Moscow Inst. of History, Philosophy and Literature; teacher Tula Pedagogical Inst. 1940–41; served in World War II, worked as corresp. of div. newspaper, expelled from CPSU for anti-party activities 1941–45; mem. staff Soyuzenerotrest, newspapers vendor 1946–49; postdoctoral thesis burnt by KGB 1950; was sent to GULAG for dissident activities 1950–53; secondary school teacher; bibliographer Library of Foreign Lit., Moscow, then Library of Public Sciences 1960s and 1970s; freelance contributor to samizdat publications 1970s. *Publications:* numerous publs banned in USSR published abroad in the 1970s including Moral Image of the Historic Personality, Unpublished 1972, Dreams of the Earth 1984, Openness to Abyss: Etudes about Dostoyevsky 1989; first three articles published in Russia 1988, Lectures on History of Philosophy 1993, Russian Richness 1994, Exit from Trance 1995, Images of the Eternal 1995.

POMMIER, Jean-Bernard; French pianist and conductor; b. 17 Aug. 1944, Beziers; two d. by Irena Podleska; ed Conservatoire de Paris; as pianist has appeared with conductors including: Herbert von Karajan, Bernard Haitink, Pierre Boulez, Riccardo Muti, Gennadi Rozhdestvensky, Leonard Slatkin, Zubin Mehta and Daniel Barenboim; has conducted numerous orchestras including Chamber Orchestra of Europe, Orchestre de Paris; debut with Royal Liverpool Philharmonic Orchestra 1991; Artistic Dir Northern Sinfonia, Newcastle-upon-Tyne 1996–; performances world-wide; masterclasses in Chicago, London, Lausanne and Melbourne; Officier, Ordre nat. du mérite; awards include Int. Competition of Young Musicians, Berlin, Prix de la Guilde des artistes solistes Français, Diapason d'Or, Tchaikovsky Prize, Moscow. *Recordings include:* Mozart Piano Concerti (with Sinfonia Varsovia), Poulenc Piano Concerti (with City of London Sinfonia), Brahms Cello Sonatas and Violin Sonatas, Complete Beethoven Piano Sonatas, complete Mozart Sonatas. *Address:* Opéra et Concert, 1 rue Volney, 75002 Paris, France (Office); Musiké Académies Productions, 12 Route Praz Gilliard, 1000 Lausanne, Switzerland. *Telephone:* (21) 7841141 (Home). *Fax:* (21) 7841148 (Office); (21) 7841148 (Home).

POMODORO, Arnaldo; Italian sculptor and theatrical designer; b. 23 June 1926, Morciano di Romagna; s. of Antonio Pomodoro and Beatrice Luzzi; has worked as jeweller and goldsmith 1950–; artist-in-residence, Stanford Univ. 1966–67, Univ. of Calif. at Berkeley 1968; lecture course, Mills Coll., Oakland, Calif. 1979–82; Hon. DLitt (Dublin) 1992, Hon. DArch (Ancona) 2001; Int. Sculpture Prize, São Paulo Biennale, Brazil 1963, Premio Nazionale di scultura, Venice Biennale 1964, Int. Sculpture Prize (Carnegie Inst., Pittsburgh) 1967, Henry Moore Grand Prize (Hakone Open-Air Museum, Japan) 1981, Praemium Imperiale for Sculpture (Japan Art Asscn) 1990; Grande Ufficiale, Ordine al Merito (Italy) 1986; Cavaliere di Gran Croce dell' Ordine al merito 1996; VII Premio Michelangelo per la Scultura 1998. *Exhibitions include:* Milan 1955, Bolles Galleries, San Francisco and NY 1960–61, Montréal World Fair 1967, Milan 1974, Marlborough Gallery, NY 1976, Musée d'art moderne de la Ville de Paris 1976, Copenhagen 1983–, Fort Belvedere, Florence 1984–, Tokyo, Osaka and San Francisco 1985, Trinity Coll. Dublin, Mills Coll., Oakland 1986, Marisa Del Re Gallery, New York 1987, 43rd Venice Biennale and Brisbane World Expo 1988, Vatican Museums 1990, Palace of Youth, Moscow 1991, Post and Telecoms HQ, Darmstadt 1992, Kanagawa, Tomaya, Kurashiki, Nishinomiya 1994, UN Plaza, New York 1996, Marlborough Gallery, New York 1996, 2000, Fortezza and Palazzo Mediceo, Varese 1998, Llonja and Cassal Balaguer, Palma de Mallorca 1999, Caserta 2000, Marlborough Monaco, Monte Carlo 2001, Jardins du Palais Rouge, Paris 2002. *Theatrical designs include:* Semiramide, Rome 1982, Orestea, Gibellina, Sicily 1983–85, Alceste, Genoa 1987, Oedipus Rex, Siena 1988, Cleopatra, Gibellina, Sicily 1989, I Paraventi at Bologna 1990, Nella solitudine dei campi di cotone by Koltès, Rome 1991, Benevento 1998, More stately mansions by O'Neill, Rome 1992, Oreste by Alfieri, Rome 1993, Stabat Mater by Tarantino, Rome 1994–95, Moonlight by Pinter, Brescia, Rome 1995, Antigone by Anouilh, Taormina 1996, Il Caso Fedra by di Martino 1997, The Tempest, Palermo 1998, Capriccio by Strauss, Naples 2002. *Publications:* L'arte lunga 1992, Arnaldo Pomodoro 1995, Scritti critici per Arnaldo Pomodoro e opere dell'artista 1955–2000 2000. *Leisure interests:* photography, theatre, literature. *Address:* Via Vigevano 5, 20144 Milan, Italy. *Telephone:* (02) 58104131. *Fax:* (02) 89401303 (Office). *E-mail:* pomod@tin .it, infopom@tin.it (Office).

PONCE ENRILE, Juan, LLM; Philippine public official and lawyer; b. 14 Feb. 1924, Gonzaga, Cagayan; s. of Alfonso Ponce Enrile and Petra Furaggan; m. Cristina Castañer 1957; one s. one d.; ed Ateneo de Manila, Univ. of the Philippines and Harvard Law School; practising Corpn lawyer and Prof. of Law 1956–64; Under-Sec. of Finance 1966–68; Acting Sec. of Finance; Acting Insurance Commr; Acting Commr of Customs; Sec. of Justice 1968–70; Sec. of Nat. Defence 1970–71 (resgnd), 1972–78, Minister 1978–86 (reappointed under Aquino Govt 1986); Chair. Cttee on Nat. Security, Defense, Peace and Order; mem. Senate and Opposition Leader (Nacionalista Party) 1987–92, 1995–2001; arrested Feb. 1990, released March 1990; mem. House of Reps 1992–95; mem. Finance, Appropriations and Steering Cttees; Chair., Bds of Dirs Philippine Nat. Bank until 1978, Nat. Investment and Devt Co., United Coconut Planters Bank, Nat. Disaster Control Center; Dir Philippine Communications Satellite Corpn; Trustee and Sec., Bd of Trustees, Cultural Centre of the Philippines; Chair. Exec. Cttee, Nat. Security Council; mem. bd, Nat. Econ. and Devt Authority, Energy Devt, Philippine Nat. Oil Co., Nat. Environmental Protection Council, Philippine Overseas Telecommunications Corpn, Philippine Crop Insurance Corpn; mem. numerous law and commercial asscns; two hon. degrees; Mahaputra Adipranada Medal, Indonesia 1975, Commander, Philippine Legion of Honor 1986. *Publications:* A Proposal on Capital Gains Tax 1960, Income Tax Treatment of Corporate Merger and Consolidation Revisited 1962, Tax Treatment of Real Estate Transactions 1964; also various articles on law, the mil. and govt. *Leisure interests:* reading, golf, tennis, swimming, water-skiing, fishing. *Address:* 3/F Vernida IV Building, Leviste Street, Salcedo Village, Makati City (Office); 2305 Morado Street, Dasmariñas Village, Makati, Metro Manila, Philippines (Home). *Telephone:* 813-7934 (Office); 844-3915 (Home). *Fax:* 818-7392 (Office). *E-mail:* jpenrile@pecabar.ph (Office).

PONCELET, Christian; French politician; b. 24 March 1928, Blaise; s. of Raoul and Raymonde (née Chamillard) Poncelet; m. Yvette Miclot 1949; two d.; ed Coll. Saint-Sulpice, Paris and Nat. Ecole Professionelle des Postes, Télégraphes et Télécommunications; Deputy to Nat. Assembly for the Vosges 1962–77; Sec. of State, Ministry of Social Affairs 1972–73, Ministry of Employment, Labour and Population 1973–74; Sec. of State for the Civil Service attached to Prime Minister March–May 1974; Sec. of State for the Budget, Ministry of Econ. Affairs and Finance 1974–77, for Relations with Parl. 1977; Conseiller Général, Remiremont 1963–73; Pres. Conseil Général des Vosges 1976–; Sénateur des Vosges 1977–, Pres. Comm. for Finance, Budgetary Control and Econ. Accounts of the Nation to the Senate 1986–98, Pres. of Senate 1998–; mem. European Parl. 1979–80; Mayor of Remiremont 1983–2001; mem. Institut de France. *Leisure interest:* hunting. *Address:* Palais du Luxembourg, 75291 Paris cedex 06; 17 rue des Etats-Unis, 88200 Remiremont, France. *Telephone:* 1-42-34-36-75 (Office). *Fax:* 1-42-34-20-94 (Office). *E-mail:* c.poncelet@senat.fr (Office).

PONOMAREV, Aleksander Sergeyevich; Russian journalist and manager; b. 13 Oct. 1956; m. Nadezhda Ponomareva; one s. one d.; ed Saratov State Univ.; Komsomol work 1979–87; Deputy Ed.-in-Chief Cen. Youth Programme Section, USSR Cen. TV 1987–88, Ed.-in-Chief 1988–91; Dir Creative Union of Experimental TV, Ostankino 1992–93, First Deputy Dir-Gen. Oskankino 1992–93; Co-founder and Vice-Pres. Moscow Ind. Broadcasting Corpn (MNVK), Dir-Gen. 1993–, First Vice-Pres. 1997–2001; Deputy Chair. All-Russian State TV Co.; Dir Cultura Camel 2001–. *Address:* Kultura TV Channel, Leningradsky prosp. 22/2, Moscow, Russia. *Telephone:* (095) 234-89-75 (Office).

PONOMAREVA, Ksenya Yuryevna; Russian journalist; b. 19 Sept. 1961, Moscow; m.; one s. one d.; ed Moscow State Univ.; schoolteacher 1984–86, teacher of Slavic languages Diplomatic Acad. 1986–88; on staff Kommersant Publrs. 1988–95, Deputy Ed. Kommersaut Daily 1992–93; Ed.-in-Chief Revisor (magazine) 1993–95; First Deputy Dir Information and Political Broadcasting Russian Public TV 1995–96; concurrently gen. producer information programmes 1996–97; mem. Bd of Dirs. Russian Public TV 1996–, Dir-Gen. 1997–98, resigned in protest against political activity of broadcaster S. Dorenko; Deputy Head of election campaign of Vladimir Putin (q.v.). *Address:* Akademika Koroleva str. 12, 127000 Moscow, Russia (Office). *Telephone:* (095) 217-98-38, 215-18-95 (Office).

PONS, Bernard Claude, DenM; French politician and doctor; b. 18 July 1926, Béziers, Hérault; s. of Claude Pons and Véronique Vogel; m. Josette Cros 1952; one s. three d.; ed Lycées, Marseilles and Toulouse and Faculté de Médecine, Montpellier; gen. practitioner, Cahors 1954; Deputy to Nat. Ass. 1967–69, 1973–86, 1988–95, 1997–, Pres. RPR Group 1988–95; Conseiller-Gen. Cajarc canton 1967–78; Sec. of State, Ministry of Agric. 1969–72; mem. Conseil-Gen. Ile-de-France 1978; Sec.-Gen. RPR 1979–84; Paris City Councillor 1983–; Pres. Admin. Council, Paris Câble 1984–; Rep. to Ass. of EC 1984–85; Minister for Overseas Departments and Territories 1986–88; Minister of Town and Country Planning, Equipment and Transport May–Nov. 1995, for Capital Works, Housing, Transport and Tourism 1995–97. *Address:* RPR, 2 boulevard Latour Maubourg, 75007 Paris (Office); Paris TV câble, 4 villa Thoréton, 75015 Paris; Assemblée nationale, 75355 Paris, France.

PONSOLLE, Patrick; French business executive; b. 20 July 1944, Toulouse; s. of Jean Ponsolle and Marie-Rose Courthaliac; m. Nathalie Elie Lefebvre 1983; two d.; ed Lycées Janson-de-Sailly and Henri IV, Paris, Ecole normale supérieure de la rue d'Ulm, Ecole Nat. d'Admin.; civil servant Ministry of Econs and Finance 1973–77; Financial Attaché Embassy, Washington 1977–79; Head of Mission for Dir of Forecasting, Ministry of Econs and Finance 1980; Sec. Gen. Nat. Accounts and Budgets Comm. 1980–81; Deputy Chief of Staff to Budget Minister 1981–83; Deputy Dir, Asst Man. Dir Compagnie de Suez 1983–87, Man. Dir 1988, Chief Exec. 1991–93; Vice-Chair., Man. Dir then Chair., Man. Dir Suez Int. 1985; Chair. Soc. financière pour la France et les pays d'outre mer (Soffo) 1990–96; Co-Chair. Eurotunnel Group, Chair. Eurotunnel SA 1994–96, Exec. Co-Chair. 1996–2001; Dir Unichem PLC 1999–; Adviser Morgan Stanley Dean Witter 1999–, Vice-Chair. Man. Dir Morgan Stanley Int. 2001–; Dir numerous cos. including France Télécom, Banque Indosuez; chair. numerous bodies. *Address:* Banque Morgan Starley Dean Witter, 25 rue Balzac, 75008 Paris (Office); 3 rue Danton, 75006 Paris, France (Home). *Website:* www.morganstanley.com.

PONTAL, Jean-François; French business executive; b. 17 April 1943, Chaton; m. Martine Lorain-Broca 1968; two c.; ed Centres d'Etudes Supérieures des Techniques Industrielles; human resources consultant Inst. Bossard; Vice-Pres. of Operations, then of Resources and Markets Carrefour, CEO Pryca (Spanish subsidiary), mem. bd with responsibility for S Europe 1993–96; Head Consumer Services Div. France Télécom 1996–2001; Exec. Vice-Pres. –2001; CEO Orange (after merger with France Télécom) 2001–; Pres. Wanadoo 2000–; Chevalier, Ordre nat. du Mérite. *Address:* France Télécom, 6 place d'Alleray, 75505 Paris, Cedex 15, France (Office). *Website:* www.francetelecom.com (Office).

PONTECORVO, Gillo; Italian film director; b. 19 Nov. 1919, Pisa; brother of the late Bruno and Guido Pontecorvo; Golden Lion Award, Venice for La Battaglia di Algeri. *Films include:* Die Windrose (or Leben der Frauen) 1957, La Grande Strada Azzurra 1958, Kapò 1960, La Battaglia di Algeri (Battle of Algiers) 1966, Queimada! 1969, Ogro 1979.

PONTI, Carlo, LLD; French film producer; b. 11 Dec. 1912, Magenta, Milan, Italy; s. of the late Leone Ponti and Maria Ponti (née Zardone); m. 1st Giulania Fiastri 1946; one s. one d.; m. 2nd Sophia Loren (q.v.) 1966; two s.; ed Università degli Studi, Milan; legal practice in office of Milan barrister 1935–38; film producer 1938–; French citizen 1965–; Officier des Arts et des Lettres. *Films include:* Roma Città Aperta 1945 (New York Critics Prize 1947), To Live in Peace 1945, Attila 1953, Ulysses 1953, La Strada 1954 (Acad. Award), War and Peace 1955, Two Women 1960, (Acad. Award for best foreign actress) Boccaccio '70 1961, Yesterday, Today, Tomorrow 1963 (Acad. Award), Marriage, Italian Style 1964, Casanova '70 1964, Lady L 1965, Dr. Zhivago 1965 (six Acad. Award), The 25th Hour 1966, Blow Up 1966 (Cannes Film Festival Award), The Girl and the General 1966, More than a Miracle 1966, Ghosts, Italian Style 1967, Smashing Time 1967, Diamonds for Breakfast 1967, Best House in London 1968, A Place for Lovers 1968, Zabriskie Point 1969, Sunflower 1969, Priest's Wife 1970, Love Stress 1971, Mortadella 1971, Red, White and … 1972, Massacre in Rome 1973, Run Run Joe 1973, Verdict 1974, The Passenger 1974, Blood Money 1975, The Cassandra Crossing 1977, The Naked Sun 1979, A Special Day, Saturday, Sunday, Monday. *Address:* Case Postale 430, 1211 Geneva 12, Switzerland.

PONTI, Michael; American concert pianist; b. 29 Oct. 1937, Freiburg, Germany; s. of Joseph Ponti and Zita Wüchner; m. 1st Carmen Wiechmann 1962 (divorced 1971); one s. two d.; m. 2nd Beatrice van Stappen 1984; one s.; studied under Prof. Gilmour McDonald and Prof. Erich Flinsch; début in Vienna 1964, in New York 1972; has toured extensively all over the world; over 80 recordings; Busoni Award, Italy 1964. *Address:* Heubergstrasse 32, 8116 Eschenlohe, Germany. *Telephone:* (8824) 594.

PONTOIS, Noëlla-Chantal; French ballet dancer; b. 24 Dec. 1943, Vendôme, Loir et Cher; d. of Jean Pontois and Josette Usal; m. Daini Kudo (divorced); one d.; entered ballet school of Opéra de Paris 1953, joined corps de ballet 1960, prima ballerina 1966, danced Sleeping Beauty with John Gilpin, London Festival Ballet 1967, named Danseuse Etoile, Opéra de Paris, danced Giselle with Rudolf Nureyev 1968, guest Danseuse Etoile 1984–93, farewell performance in The Nutcracker 1993, ballet teacher at Opéra de Paris 1988–; Prix René Blum, Prix Anna Pavlova, Gran Prix nat. de la Danse; Chevalier, Ordre du Mérite, Chevalier, Légion d'honneur, Commdr des Arts et des Lettres 2000, Officier, ordre nat. du Mérite. *Address:* c/o Théâtre national de l'Opéra, 8 rue Scribe, 75009 Paris (Office); 25 rue de Maubeuge, 75009 Paris, France (Home).

PONTZIOUS, Richard; American conductor and artistic director; has conducted orchestras, bands and choirs in Europe and Asia; Founder, Artistic and Exec. Dir Asian Youth Orchestra 1990–; Bronze Bauhina Star, Hong Kong Govt 2000. *Address:* Suite 15A, One Capital Place, 18 Luard Road, Wanchai, Hong Kong Special Administrative Region, People's Republic of China (Office). *Telephone:* (852) 28661623 (Office). *Fax:* (852) 28613340 (Office). *E-mail:* ayo@asianyouthorchestra.com (Office). *Website:* www .asianyouthorchestra.com (Office).

POOLE, David James, P.P.R.P., ARCA; British artist; b. 5 June 1931, London; s. of Thomas Herbert Poole and Catherine Lord; m. Iris Mary Toomer 1958; three s.; ed Stoneleigh Secondary Modern School, Wimbledon School of Art, Royal Coll. of Art; Sr Lecturer in Painting and Drawing, Wimbledon School of Art 1961–77; Pres. Royal Soc. of Portrait Painters 1983–91; work in HM The Queen's collection, London and in pvt. collections in Bermuda, Canada, France, Germany, Italy, S Africa, Saudi Arabia, Switzerland and USA. *Portraits include:* HM Queen Elizabeth II, HRH Prince Philip, HM Queen Elizabeth the Queen Mother, HRH Prince Charles, HRH Prince Andrew, HRH Prince Edward, HRH The Princess Royal, Lord Mountbatten, mems of govt, armed forces, industry, commmerce, medicine and acad. and legal professions. *Leisure interests:* travel and food, particularly in France. *Address:* Trinity Flint Barn, Weston Lane, Weston, Petersfield, Hants., GU32 3NN, England. *Telephone:* (1730) 265075.

POON, Dickson; Hong Kong business executive; s. of Poon Kam Kai; m. 1st Marjorie Yang (divorced); one d.; m. 2nd Michelle Yeoh (q.v.) 1988 (divorced 1991); m. 3rd Pearl Yu 1992; ed St Joseph's Coll., Hong Kong, Uppingham School, UK and Occidental Coll., Los Angeles, USA; apprenticeship in watchmaking at Chopard's, Geneva, Switzerland; returned to Hong Kong and opened first Dickson watch and jewellery shop 1980; Co-Founder (with Sammo Hung) DMV film co. 1983; Head Dickson Concepts, Hong Kong, operating more than 240 boutiques and outlets throughout SE Asia and in China; acquired French co. S.T. Dupont label 1987, sold 1997; acquired stake in Harvey Nichols, London 1991, floated co. 1996, pvt. takeover 2002, opened brs in Leeds 1997, Edin. 2002 and Manchester 2003; bought 85% stake in Hong Kong and Shenzhen brs of Japanese dept store Seibu 1996; sole benefactor of Hong Kong Univ.'s Man. Inst. *Address:* c/o Harvey Nichols, 109–125 Knightsbridge, London, SW1X 7RJ, England (Office).

POOS, Jacques F., D. ÈS SC. COMM. ET ECON.; Luxembourg politician; b. 3 June 1935; m.; three c.; ed Athénée Grand-Ducal, Univ. of Lausanne and Luxembourg Int. Univ.; Ministry of Nat. Economy 1959–62; Service d'Etudes et de Statistiques Economiques (STATEC) 1962–64; Dir Imprimerie Coopérative 1964–76; Pres. SYTRAGAZ 1970–76; Deputy 1974–76; Minister of Finance, Gov. IBRD, IMF, EIB 1976–79; Dir Banque Continentale du Luxembourg SA 1980–82, Banque Paribas (Luxembourg) SA 1982–84; Vice-Pres. Parti Socialiste 1982; Deputy Prime Minister and Minister of Foreign Affairs, Foreign Trade and Co-operation 1984–99, also of Foreign Trade and Co-operation; Pres. EC 1991; MEP 1999–, mem. Comm. for Foreign Affairs, Human Rights, Public Security and Defence Policy. *Publications:* Le Luxembourg dans le Marché Commun 1961, Le modèle Luxembourgeois 1981, La Crise Economique et Financière: est-elle encore maitrisable? 1984. *Address:* European Parliament, Centre Européene, Plateau du Kirchberg, 2929 Luxembourg. *Telephone:* 4300-1. *Fax:* 4300-7009. *Website:* www.europarl.eu.int.

POPATOV, Anatoly Victorovich; Russian politician; b. 24 July 1942, Bishkek; m. Tatyana Nikolayevna Potapova; two c.; ed Moscow Inst. of Radio Electronics and Mine Electro Mechanics; Higher Party School at Cen. CPSU Cttee; with Ministry of Foreign Affairs, numerous posts at home and abroad 1986–, Presidium and Ministry on CIS Countries; First Deputy Man. Ministry of Foreign Affairs 1986–92; Pro-Rector Moscow State Inst. of Int. Relations 1992; counsellor, Russian Fed. Embassy, China. 1992–96; Asst to Head of Russian Presidium 1996–98; Deputy Minister Ministry of CIS Affairs 1998–2001; Deputy Minister of Foreign Affairs Jan. 2002–. *Address:* Ministry of Foreign Affairs, Smolenskaya-Sennaya 32–34, 121200 Moscow, Russia (Office). *Telephone:* (095) 244-37-53 (Office). *Fax:* (095) 244-92-83 (Office). *E-mail:* popatov@mid.ru (Office).

POPESCU, Dan Mircea, DJur; Romanian politician; b. 6 Oct. 1950, Bucharest; m.; one c.; ed Faculty of Law, Bucharest Univ.; legal adviser, then researcher at Inst. of Political Sciences, Bucharest and Lecturer in Int. Relations, Acad. of Socio-Political Studies, Bucharest 1975–89; mem. Council Nat. Salvation Front, then mem. of Provisional Council of Nat. Union; Presidential Adviser for matters of domestic policy Dec. 1990; Minister of State for Living Standards and Social Security 1991; Minister of Labour and Social Protection 1991–92, Minister of State, Minister of Labour and Social

Protection 1992–96; Deputy Prime Minister 1992–96; Vice-Pres. Party of Social Democracy in Romania; Senator 1992–, Pres. Labour Comm. of Senate 1996–2000; Pres. Econ. Comm. of Senate 2000–; Dir Romanian Inst. of Social-Democratic Studies 1999–2001; mem. Exec. Bureau, Social Democrat Party 2001–; National order of faithful service. *Publications:* books and studies in the field of political science. *Address:* The Senate, Bucharest (Office); 42–46 Aurel Vlaicu Street, Bucharest, Romania (Home). *Telephone:* (1) 3120280 (Office). *E-mail:* comec@unix1.senat.ro (Office).

POPESCU, Dumitru Radu; Romanian author; b. 19 Aug. 1935, Păusa Village, Bihor County; ed Colls of Medicine and Philology, Cluj; reporter literary magazine Steaua 1956–69; Ed.-in-Chief literary magazine Tribuna 1969–82, Contemporanul 1982; alt. mem. Cen. Cttee Romanian CP 1968–79, mem. 1979–90; Chair. Romanian Writers' Union 1980–90; Corresp. mem. Romanian Acad. 1997–; in custody Jan. 1990; Prize of the Writers' Union 1964, 1969, 1974, 1977, 1980; Prize of the Romanian Acad. 1970, Grand Prize for Balkan Writers 1998, Writers' Union Prize 1994, Writers' Asscn of Bucharest Prize 1997, Grand Prize Camil Petrescu 1995. *Major works:* collections of short stories: Fuga (Flight) 1958, Fata de la miazăzi (A Girl from the South) 1964, Somnul pământului (The Earth's Sleep) 1965, Dor (Longing) 1966, Umbrela de soare (The Parasol) 1967, Prea mic pentru un război aşa de mare (Too Little for Such a Big War) 1969, Duios Anastasia trecea (Tenderly Anastasia Passed) 1967, Leul albastru (The Blue Lion) 1981, The Ice Bridge 1980, the Lame Hare 1981, God in the Kitchen 1994, Truman Capote and Nicolae 1995, Galaxy (essays) 1994, Ophelia's Complex (essays) 1998; *novels:* Zilele săptămînii (Weekdays) 1959, Vara oltenilor (The Oltenians' Summer) 1964, F 1964, Vînătoarea regală (Royal Hunt) 1973, O bere pentru calul meu (A Beer for My Horse) 1974, Ploile de dincolo de vreme (Rains beyond Time) 1976, Împăratul norilor (Emperor of the Clouds) 1976; *plays:* Vara imposibilei iubiri (The Summer of Impossible Love) 1966, Vis (Dream) 1968, Aceşti îngeri trişti (Those Sad Angels) 1969, Pisica în noaptea Anului nou (Cat on the New Year's Eve) 1970, Pasărea Shakespeare (The Shakespeare Bird) 1973, Rezervaţia de pelicani (The Pelican Reservation) 1983, Iepurele şchiop (The Lame Rabbit) 1980, Orasul îngerilor (The Angel's City) 1985, Powder Mill 1989, The Bride with False Eyelashes 1994, Love is like a Scab 1995; *poems:* Cîinele de fosfor (The Phosphorus Dog) 1981; *essays:* Virgule (Commas) 1978.

POPESCU, Ioan-Iovitz, PhD; Romanian professor of optics and plasma physics; b. 1 Oct. 1932, Burila-Mare; s. of Dumitru Popescu and Elvira Popescu; m. Georgeta-Denisa Chiru 1963; ed Univ. of Bucharest; Asst Prof. of Optics and Gaseous Electronics, Univ. of Bucharest 1955–60, Prof. Faculty of Physics 1972–, Dean 1972–77, Rector of Univ. 1981–89; Head of Plasma Physics Lab., Inst. of Physics, Bucharest 1960–67, Scientific Deputy Dir 1970–72; Dir Inst. of Physics and Radiation Tech. 1977–81, Romanian Centre for Induced Gamma Emission 1995–; Alexander von Humboldt Dozenten stipendium, Kiel Univ. 1967–69; Corresp. mem. Romanian Acad. 1974, mem. 1990 (Pres. Physics Section 1990–92); Dr. hc Univ. of Craiova) 1998; Labour Order of Romania 1964, Prize for Physics (Romanian Acad.) 1966, Scientific Merit Order 1981, Hon. Citizen Mehedintzi Co. 1997, Commdr Loyal Service Nat. Order 2000. *Publications:* Ionized Gases 1965, General Physics 1971–75, Plasma Physics and Applications 1981, Plasma Spectroscopy 1987, Optics 1988, The Nobel Prizes for Physics 1901–1998 1998; 165 scientific papers cited in about 1,500 foreign works; numerous articles on gas discharges and pioneering works in optogalvanic and multiphoton spectroscopy. *Leisure interest:* scientometrics. *Address:* IGE Foundation, PO Box 34–81, 70350 Bucharest (Office); Str. Fizicienilor 6, Bloc M4, Apt. 6, 769271 Magurele, Bucharest, Romania (Home). *Telephone:* (1) 4930334 (Office); (1) 4574180 (Home). *Fax:* (1) 4930334 (Office). *E-mail:* iovitz@pcnet.ro (Home). *Website:* alpha2.infim.ro/~ltpd/iipopescu.html (Office); www.geocities.com/iipopescu (Home).

POPLE, John Anthony, MA, PhD, FRS; British professor of theoretical chemistry; b. 31 Oct. 1925, Burnham, Somerset; s. of Keith Pople and Mary Jones; m. Joy Cynthia Bowers 1952; three s. one d.; ed Univ. of Cambridge; Research Fellow Trinity Coll. Cambridge 1951–54, Lecturer in Math. 1954–58; Research Assoc., Nat. Research Council, Ottawa during summer 1956, 1957; Supt Basic Physics Div., Nat. Physical Laboratory, Teddington (UK) 1958–64; Ford Visiting Prof. of Chem., Carnegie Inst. of Tech., Pittsburgh, Pa 1961–62; Carnegie Prof. of Chemical Physics, Carnegie-Mellon Univ., Pittsburgh 1964–74, Acting Head, Dept of Chem. 1967, John Christian Warner Univ. Prof. of Natural Sciences 1974–93; Trustees' Prof. of Chemistry, Northwestern Univ., Evanston 1993–; mem. ACS 1965–, Int. Acad. of Quantum Molecular Science 1967–; Foreign Assoc., Nat. Acad. of Sciences 1977; Fellow, American Physical Soc. 1970–, American Acad. of Arts and Sciences 1971–; Smith's Prizeman (Cambridge) 1950, Marlow Medal of Faraday Soc. 1958, ACS Awards: Irving Langmuir 1970, Harrison Howe 1971, Gilbert Newton Lewis 1973, Pittsburgh 1975, Morley Medal, American Chemical Soc. 1976, Pauling Award 1977, Oesper Award, Univ. of Cincinnati Dept of Chem. 1984, Davy Medal, Royal Soc. 1988, Wolf Prize for Chem. 1992, Nobel Prize for Chem. 1998. *Publications:* co-author: High Resolution Magnetic Resonance 1959, Approximate Molecular Orbital Theory 1970, Ab initio Molecular Orbital Theory 1986; also over 485 publs in scientific journals. *Leisure interest:* music. *Address:* Department of Chemistry, Northwestern University, 2145 Sheridan Road, Evanston, IL 60208 (Office); 1500 Sheridan Road, Apt 7K, Wilmette, IL 60091, USA (Home). *Telephone:* (847) 491-3403 (Office); (847) 251-3389 (Home). *Fax:* (847) 491-7713 (Office). *E-mail:* pople@ lithium.chem.northwestern.edu (Office).

POPOFF, Frank Peter, MBA; American business executive; b. 27 Oct. 1935, Sofia, Bulgaria; s. of Eftim Popoff and Stoyanka Kossoroff; m. Jean Urse; three s.; ed Indiana Univ.; with Dow Chemical Co. 1959–2000, Exec. Vice-Pres. 1985–87, Pres. 1987–92, CEO 1987–96, Chair. 1992–2000, Dir Emer. 2000–; Exec. Vice-Pres., then Pres. Dow Chemical European subsidiary, Switzerland 1976–85; Dir Dow Corning Corpn, Chemical Bank & Trust Co., Midland, The Salk Inst., American Express; mem. Société de Chimie Industrielle (American Section), Chemical Mfrs Asscn (Bd Dirs.); Harold A. "Red" Poling Chair. of Business and Govt, Kelley School of Business, Indiana Univ. 2001–. *Address:* Kelley School of Business, Indiana University, 1309 East Street, Bloomington, IN 47405, USA. *Telephone:* (812) 855-8100 (Office). *Website:* www.bus.indiana.edu (Office).

POPOV, Anatolii Aleksandrovich, DECONSCI; Russian/Chechen politician; b. 10 July 1960, Sovetskoye village, Volgograd Oblast ; m.; one s.; ed Volgograd Agricultural Inst.; fmr researcher agricultural scientific research inst. and irrigation farming scientific research inst.; Sec. of Gorodishchenskii Raion (dist) cttee of V.I. Lenin Young Communist League (Komsomol), Volgograd Oblast; Adviser to the Council of Ministers of the USSR; fmr Deputy to Head of Man. MENATEP bank; Financial Dir Rosoboroneksport (Russian Defence Export) State Corpn April–Sept. 1998; fmr Deputy Leader Dept of Food Resources, Govt of Moscow City; Head Centre for Econ. Strategy, Volgograd Oblast; Dir Centre of School of Investment Man. VAPK, Acad. of Nat. Economy, Govt of Russian Fed.; apptd Gen. Dir Direction for the Works of Construction–Restoration in Chechnya (state firm responsible for rebuilding Chechnya) 2001; Deputy Chair. Comm. for the Reconstruction of Chechnya 2002; Prime Minster of the Govt of Chechnya Feb. 2003–. *Address:* Office of the Prime Minister, ul. Garazhnaya 10 A, 364000 Groznyi, Chechnya, Russia (Office). *Telephone:* (095) 777-92-14 (Office).

POPOV, Dmitar; Bulgarian politician and judge; fmr judge and Chair. Sofia Municipal Court; Prime Minister of Bulgaria 1990–91.

POPOV, Gavriil Kharitonovich, DEcon; Russian politician and economist; b. 31 Oct. 1936, Moscow; s. of Khariton Popov and Theodora Popov; m. Irina Popov 1968; two s.; ed Moscow State Univ.; mem. CPSU 1959–90; teacher at Moscow Univ. 1960–89, Dean of Econ. Faculty 1977–80; introduced man. and business studies to Moscow Univ., Prof. 1971–; Ed.-in-Chief of journal Voprosy ekonomiki (Questions of Economics) 1988–90; People's Deputy of USSR 1989–91; Co-Chair. Inter-regional Group of Deputies, pressing for radical change; Chair. Moscow City Soviet 1990–91; Mayor of Moscow 1991–92 (resgnd); mem. Consultative Council 1991–2000 (Chair, Foreign Policy Cttee 1996–2000); Pres. Int. Univ. 1991–, Int. Union of Economists 1991–, Free Econ. Soc. of Russia 1991–; Chair. Russian Democratic Reform Movt (RDDR) 1992–; mem. Political Council, Social Democracy Party of Russia 2001–; M. Lomonosov Prize. *Publications include:* more than a dozen books on theory of man. and current political and econ. problems. *Leisure interest:* bees. *Address:* Nikitsky Pereulok 5, 103009 Moscow, Russia. *Telephone:* (095) 956-69-90. *Fax:* (095) 956-80-77.

POPOV, Mihai, D.HIS.SC.; Moldovan diplomatist and philologist; b. 1949, Chebruchi, Sloboza Region; ed Kishinev State Univ., Diplomatic Acad. in Moscow; worked as Komsomol and CSPU functionary in Kishinev 1973–83; diplomatic service since 1983; First Counsellor, USSR Embassy, Romania 1986–92; Minister-Counsellor, Moldovan Embassy, Russia 1992–93; Amb. to Belgium 1993–94; Minister of Foreign Affairs 1994–96; Amb. to France 1996–2002, to Belgium and Rep. to NATO and EC 2002–. *Address:* c/o Ministry of Foreign Affairs, Piaţa Marii Adunări Naţionale 1, 277033 Chişinău, Moldova. *Telephone:* (2) 23-39-40. *Fax:* (2) 23-23-02.

POPOV, Vadim Aleksandrovich; Belarus politician; b. 1940, Demidov, Smolensk region, Russia; m.; two c.; ed Minsk Higher CPSU School, Belarus State Inst. of Agriculture Mechanisation; army service 1961–64; Komsomol functionary 1964–71; Dir Sovkhoz Mogilev region 1972–76; party functionary, instructor, Head of Div. Mogilev Regional CP Cttee, First Sec. 1976–92; instructor Cen. Cttee CP of Belarus 1976–92; worked in agric. roles in complex of Mogilev region 1992–99; First Deputy Minister of Agric. and Food March–July 1999, Minister July–Nov. 2000; mem. Chamber of Reps., Nat. Ass. (Parl.) 2000–01, Chair. 2000–01, Nov. 2002–; Deputy Prime Minister March–June 2001, Prime Minister June–Nov. 2001; Speaker of the House of Reps., Belarus Nat. Ass. 2002–; Order, Labour Red Banner, three medals; Hon. Diploma Supreme Soviet Belarus SSR. *Address:* Chamber of Representatives, 220010 Minsk, Belarus (Office). *Telephone:* (17) 222-60-47 (Office). *Fax:* (17) 222-61-05 (Office).

POPOV, Viktor Ivanovich, DS; Russian diplomatist (retd); b. 19 May 1918, Moscow; m. Natalia Aleksandrovna Popova; two s.; ed Moscow Inst. of History and Philosophy, Higher Diplomatic School of USSR Ministry of Foreign Affairs; joined Ministry of Foreign Affairs 1954, Counsellor, Democratic Repub. of Viet Nam 1960–61, Embassy in Australia 1967–68, Minister-Counsellor, Embassy in UK 1968; Rector of Acad. of Diplomacy of USSR and Amb. on special assignments, including Iran and Afghanistan, UN Gen. Assembly and UNESCO 1968; Amb. to UK 1980–86; Counsellor, Foreign Ministry 1986–91; Prof. Moscow State Univ., Diplomatic Acad. 1991–; mem. Cen. Auditing Comm. of CPSU 1981–87; USSR State Prize in History, Merited Scientific Worker of the RSFSR, many other Soviet and foreign awards. *Publications:* Anglo-Soviet Relations 1927–29, Anglo-Soviet Relations 1929–37, History of Diplomacy series (co-author), The Country of Traditions Changes 1991, Margaret Thatcher 1991, Life in Buckingham Palace 1993, Queen's Counsellor–Superagent of the Kremlin 1995, Queen Elizabeth II and the Royal Family 1996 and other publications on international relations and USSR foreign policy. *Leisure interests:* tennis, angling, reading. *Address:* Leontyevski per. 14, Apt. 2, 103009 Moscow, Russia. *Telephone:* (095) 229-89-36.

POPOV, Yevgeny Anatolyevich; Russian writer; b. 5 Jan. 1946, Krasnoyarsk; m. Svetlana Anatoliyevna Vasilyeva; one s.; ed Moscow Inst. of Geological Survey; worked as geologist in various regions 1968–73; mem. USSR Union of Writers 1978, expelled 1979, readmitted 1988; Assoc. mem. Swedish PEN 1980–; a founder and mem. bd Russian PEN 1989–. *Publications:* The Merriment of Old Russia (short stories) 1981, Awaiting Untreacherous Love (short stories) 1989, Wonderfulness of Life (novel) 1990, A Plane to Cologne (short stories) 1991, On the Eve, On the Eve (novel) 1993, The Soul of a Patriot (novel) 1994, Green Musicians (novel) 1998, Thirteen (essays) 1999, Badly Tempered Piano (play), The Bold Boy (play) 2000, A Quiet Barque Named 'Hope' (short stories) 2001, Master Chaos (novel) 2002, Communists (novel) 2003. *Address:* Leningradsky prospect 26, korp. 2, Apt 52, 125040 Moscow, Russia. *Telephone:* (095) 212-33-97. *Fax:* (095) 212-33-97. *E-mail:* evg.popov@mtu-net.ru (Home).

POPOVIČ, Štĕpán, CSc; Czech engineer; b. 28 Dec. 1945, Ústí nad Labem; m. Iva Popovič; one s. one d.; ed Mechanical Eng and Textile Coll., Liberec, Econs Univ., Prague; with Sklo Union Teplice 1968–89, Dir-Gen. 1989; Dir-Gen. Glav Union 1991–; Pres. Union of Industry and Transport 1992–2000; Chair. of Bd FC Teplice 2000–01; Man. of the Year 1993, 1998. *Leisure interests:* sport, music, playing the piano. *Address:* Glaverbel Czech, Sklářská 450, Teplice, Czech Republic (Office). *Telephone:* (41) 7502100 (Office). *E-mail:* stepan.popovic@glaverbel.com.cz.

POPPER, Frank Geoffrey, DèsSc; British/French art historian; b. 17 April 1918, Prague, Czech Republic; s. of Otto Popper and Paula Goldmann; m. 1st Hella Guth 1946; m. 2nd Aline Dallier 1973; ed Univ. of Paris IV (Paris-Sorbonne); voluntary service in RAF 1941–46; Dir of shipping and travel agencies 1947–53; mem. research group Inst. of Aesthetics, Paris 1961–68; Asst Prof. of Aesthetics and the Science of Art, Univ. of Paris VIII (Vincennes à St-Denis) 1969–71, Dir of Art Dept 1970–83, Temp. Reader 1971–73, Reader 1973–75, Prof. 1975–, Full Prof. 1976–; Emer. Prof. 1985–; also organises art exhbns; Chevalier, Ordre nat. du Mérite 1998, Officier, Ordre des Arts et des Lettres 1991. *Publications include:* Kunst-Licht-Kunst (exhbn catalogue) 1966, Lumière et Mouvement (exhbn catalogue) 1967, Naissance de l'Art Cinétique 1967, Origins and Development of Kinetic Art 1968, Art, Action and Participation 1975, Agam 1976, Electra, Electricity and Electronics in the Art of the Twentieth Century (exhbn catalogue) 1983, Art of the Electronic Age 1993, Réflexions sur l'Exil, l'Art et l'Europe 1998. *Leisure interests:* chess, music, literature. *Address:* 6 rue du Marché Saint-Honoré, 75001 Paris, France. *Telephone:* 1-42-61-21-38. *Fax:* 1-42-61-21-38. *E-mail:* fpopper@club-internet.fr (Home). *Website:* www.arpla.univ-paris8.fr (Office).

POROKHOVSHCHIKOV, Aleksander Shalvovich; Russian actor, film director and scriptwriter; b. 31 Jan. 1939, Moscow; s. of Mikhail Nikolaevich Dudin and Galina Aleksandrovna Porokhovshchikova; m. Irina Valeryevna Zhukova 1995; ed Chelyabinsk Inst. of Medicine, Shchukin High School of Theatre Art; worked in Satire Theatre 1966–71, Taganka Theatre 1971–81, A. Pushkin Theatre 1981–; f. first Russian pvt. film studio Rodina 1987–; Dir Studio; Pres. Cultural Centre "House of A. A. Porokhovshchikov 1871"; Prof. Russian Acad. of Theatre Art; Main Prize Scochi Film Market (Russia) 1993, Spectators Prize, Tver Film Festival, Golden Sail Prize, St Raphaël Russian Film Festival (France) 1994 (all for Film Memory); People's Artist of Russia. *Roles in drama productions include:* Profitable Position, Inspector, Lighting but not Warming, Optimistic Tragedy. *Roles in films include:* Ring 1973, The Star of Captivating Happiness 1975, Diamonds for the Proletariat Dictatorship 1976, Seek the Wind 1979, Family Circle 1980, Living Target 1989, Heir 1992. *Films directed:* The Ninth of May 1988, dir, scriptwriter and actor: Uncensored Memory 1991. *Leisure interests:* music, piano playing, jazz band, nature, diving. *Address:* Prospekt Mira 180, Apt 169, 129366 Moscow, Russia. *Telephone:* (095) 245-26-47. *Fax:* (095) 245-26-47. *E-mail:* c/o vyatkin@npi.ru (Home).

PORPHYRIOS, Demetri; Greek architect; ed Princeton Univ., USA; teacher Architectural Asscn, London; Architect, designed an extension to Magdalen Coll., Oxford Univ.; fmr mem. Council Inst. of Architecture. *Publications include:* Classical Architecture.

PORRITT, Sir Jonathon (Espie), 2nd Bt, cr. 1963, CBE, BA; British environmentalist; b. 6 July 1950, London; s. of the late Lord Porritt; m. Sarah Staniforth 1986; two d.; ed Eton Coll. and Magdalen Coll. Oxford; school teacher, London 1975–84; Head of English, Burlington Danes School, London 1980–84; Chair. Ecology Party 1979–80, 1982–84; parl. cand. at gen. elections in 1979, 1983; Dir Friends of the Earth 1984–90; f. and Dir, Forum for the Future 1996–; Chair. UK Sustainable Devt Comm. 2000–; Chair. South W Round Table on Sustainable Devt 1999; mem. bd South W Regional Devt Agency 2000; Co-Dir Prince of Wales Business and Environment Programme. *Publications:* Seeing Green: The Politics of Ecology 1984, Friends of the Earth Handbook 1987, The Coming of the Greens 1988, Save the Earth (Ed.) 1990, Where on Earth are we going? 1991, Captain Eco (for children) 1991, Playing Safe: Science and the Environment 2000. *Leisure interests:* walking, cooking.

Address: 9 Imperial Square, Cheltenham, Glos., GL50 1QB; 9 Lypiatt Terrace, Cheltenham, Glos., GL50 2SX, England (Home). *Telephone:* (1242) 262737 (Office). *Fax:* (1242) 262757 (Office).

PORTER, Andrew, MA; British music critic; b. 26 Aug. 1928, Cape Town, SA; s. of Andrew Ferdinand and Vera Sybil (née Bloxham) Porter; ed Diocesan Coll., Rondebosch, Cape Town, University Coll. Oxford; music critic The Financial Times 1950–74; Ed. The Musical Times 1960–67; music critic The New Yorker 1972–92, The Observer 1992–97, Times Literary Supplement 1997–; Visiting Fellow All Souls Coll. Oxford 1973–74; Bloch Prof., Univ. of Calif. at Berkeley 1981; Corresp. mem. American Musicological Soc. 1993; ASCAP–Deems Taylor Award 1975, 1978, 1982, Nat. Music Theater Award 1988. *Opera:* librettos for The Tempest 1985, The Song of Majnun 1991 and numerous translations. *Publications:* A Musical Season 1974, Wagner's Ring 1976, Music of Three Seasons 1978, Music of Three More Seasons 1981, Verdi's "Macbeth": A Sourcebook (ed. with David Rosen) 1984, Musical Events: A Chronicle 1980–83 1987, 1983–86 1989, A Music Critic Remembers 2000. *Leisure interest:* architecture. *Address:* 9 Pembroke Walk, London, W8 6PQ, England.

PORTER, Sir Leslie, Kt, F.I.C.D., CBIM; British company executive; b. 10 July 1920, London; s. of the late Henry Alfred Porter and Jane (née Goldstein) Porter; m. Shirley Cohen 1949; one s. one d.; ed Holloway Coll.; served British Army 1939–46; joined Tesco PLC, superstores, supermarkets, chain stores 1959, Man. Dir and Deputy Chair. 1972–73, Chair. and Chief Exec. 1973–85, Pres. 1985–90; Chair. Sports Aid Foundation 1985–88, Hon. Vice-Pres. 1988–; fmr Pres. Inst. Grocery Distribution (IGD); mem. Pres.'s Council, Baptist Coll. of Hong Kong; Chair. Int. Bd Govs Tel-Aviv Univ. 1986–89, Hon. Chair. 1989–, Chancellor 1993–; Vice-Pres. Nat. Playing Fields Asscn; Chair. Euro-Consultants & Lampol Devts 1990–; mem. Lloyds 1994–; Hon. PhD (Tel-Aviv) 1973. *Leisure interests:* golf, yachting, tennis, bridge.

PORTER, Neil Anthony, PhD, DSc, FInstP, MRIA, FRAS; British professor of electron physics; b. 4 Sept. 1930, Manchester; s. of Francis Porter and Nora Porter; m. Sheila B. Dunn 1959; one d.; ed St Bede's Coll. Manchester, Univ. of Manchester and Dublin Inst. for Advanced Studies; Asst Univ. Coll. Dublin 1953–54; Jr and Sr Research Fellowship, AERE Harwell 1954–58; Coll. Lecturer, Univ. Coll. Dublin 1958–64, Prof. of Electron Physics 1964–88, Prof. Emer. 1989–; Visiting Prof. Univ. of Tokyo 1981, Weizmann Inst., Israel 1986–87; Hon. Consultant AERE, Harwell 1963–73; Harvard-Smithsonian Center for Astrophysics 1972–90; Dublin Symposium Award 2000. *Publications:* approximately 100 pubs on high-energy astrophysics and 10 pubs on the history of science; one book. *Leisure interests:* music, history of science, theology. *Address:* Department of Physics, University College, Belfield, Dublin 4 (Office); 5 Westerton Rise, Dublin 16, Ireland (Home). *Telephone:* (1) 7062213 (Office); (1) 2987870 (Home).

PORTER, Peter Neville Frederick, FRSL; Australian poet; b. 16 Feb. 1929, Brisbane, Australia; s. of William R. Porter and Marion Main; m. 1st Jannice Henry 1961 (died 1974); two d.; m. 2nd Christine Berg 1991; ed Church of England Grammar School and Toowoomba Grammar School; fmr journalist in Brisbane; came to UK 1951; worked as clerk, bookseller and advertising writer; full-time writer and broadcaster 1968–; Hon. DLitt (Melbourne) 1985, (Loughborough) 1987, (Sydney) 1999, (Queensland) 2001. *Publications:* Once Bitten, Twice Bitten 1961, Penguin Modern Poets, No. 2 1962, Poems, Ancient and Modern 1964, A Porter Folio 1969, The Last of England 1970, Preaching to the Converted 1972, After Martial (translation) 1972, Jonah (with A. Boyd) 1973, The Lady and the Unicorn (with A. Boyd) 1975, Living in a Calm Country 1975, New Poetry I (Jt) 1975, The Cost of Seriousness 1978, English Subtitles 1981, Collected Poems 1983 (Duff Cooper Prize), Fast Forward 1984, Narcissus (with A. Boyd) 1985, The Automatic Oracle 1987 (Whitbread Poetry Award), Mars (with A. Boyd) 1988, A Porter Selected 1989, Possible Worlds 1989, The Chair of Babel 1992, Millennial Fables 1995, New Writing (Co-Ed. with A. S. Byatt) 1997, The Oxford Book of Modern Verse (Ed.) 1997, The Shared Heritage: Australian and English Literature 1997; Ed. The Oxford Book of Modern Australian Verse 1997, Dragons in Their Pleasant Places 1997, Collected Poems 1961–1999 1999 (2 Vols 1999), Saving From the Wreck (essays) 2001, Max is Missing 2001. *Leisure interests:* buying records and listening to music, travelling in Italy. *Address:* 42 Cleveland Square, London, W2 6DA, England. *Telephone:* (20) 7262-4289.

PORTER, Robert, AC, MA, DM, DSc, FRACP, FAA; Australian professor of medical research; b. 10 Sept. 1932, Port Augusta, S Australia; s. of the late William J. and Amy Porter (née Tottman); m. Anne D. Steell 1961; two s. two d.; ed Univs of Adelaide and Oxford; House Physician and House Surgeon, Radcliffe Infirmary, Oxford 1959–60; Univ. Lecturer in Physiology, Oxford 1961–67; Medical Tutor and Fellow, St Catherine's Coll. Oxford 1963–67; Prof. of Physiology, Monash Univ. 1967–80, Dean 1989–98, Deputy Vice-Chancellor 1992–93; Dir John Curtin School of Medical Research and Howard Florey Prof. of Medical Research, ANU 1980–89; Planning Dean (Medicine) James Cook Univ. of N Queensland, Townsville 1998–99; Dir Research Devt 1999–; Rhodes Scholar 1954; Radcliffe Travelling Fellow in Medical Science 1963–64; Sr Fulbright Fellow, Washington Univ. School of Medicine, St Louis 1973; Fogarty Scholar-in-Residence, Nat. Inst. of Health, Bethesda 1986–87; Hon. DSc (Univ. of Sydney). *Publications:* Corticospinal Neurones: Their Role in Movement (with C. G. Phillips) 1977, Corticospinal Function and Voluntary Movement (with R. N. Lemon) 1993; articles on neurophysiology. *Leisure interest:* sport. *Address:* Room 119, Humanities II, James Cook University,

Townsville, Queensland 4811 (Office); 2 Denison Court, Toomulla, Qld 4816, Australia (Home). *Telephone:* (7) 4781-5330 (Office); (3) 5983-1518 (Home). *Fax:* (7) 4781-4655 (Office). *E-mail:* robert.porter@jcu.edu.au (Office).

PORTES, Richard David, CBE, DPhil; American/British professor of economics; b. 10 Dec. 1941, Chicago, Ill.; s. of Herbert Portes and Abra Halperin Portes; m. Barbara Diana Frank 1963; one s. one d.; ed Yale Univ., Balliol and Nuffield Colls Oxford; Official Fellow and Tutor in Econs, Balliol Coll. Oxford 1965–69; Asst Prof. of Econs and Int. Affairs, Princeton Univ. 1969–72; Prof. of Econs, Birkbeck Coll., London Univ. 1972–94, Head Dept 1975–77, 1980–83, 1994; Prof. of Econs, London Business School 1995–; Pres. Centre for Econ. Policy Research, London 1983–; Directeur d'Etudes, Ecole des Hautes Etudes en Sciences Sociales, Paris 1978–; fmr Rhodes Scholar, Woodrow Wilson Fellow, Danforth Fellow; Guggenheim Fellow 1977–78; British Acad. Overseas Visiting Fellow 1977–78; Research Assoc., Nat. Bureau of Econ. Research, Cambridge, Mass 1980–; Visiting Prof., Harvard Univ. 1977–78; Vice-Chair. Econs Cttee Social Science Research Council 1981–84; Sec.-Gen. Royal Econ. Soc. 1992–; mem. Bd of Dirs Soc. for Econ. Analysis 1967–69, 1972–80 (Sec. 1974–77); mem. Royal Inst. of Int. Affairs 1973– (Research Cttee 1982–94), Council on Foreign Relations 1978–, Hon. Degrees Cttee, Univ. of London 1984–89; Fellow Econometric Soc. 1983–; mem. Council, Royal Econ. Soc. 1986–92 (mem. Exec. Cttee 1987–); mem. Council, European Econ. Asscn 1992–96; Co-Chair. Bd of Govs and Sr Ed., Economic Policy 1985–; mem. and fmr mem. several editorial bds; mem. Franco-British Council 1996–2002, Comm. on the Social Sciences 2000–03; Hon. DSc (Univ. Libre de Bruxelles) 2000; Hon. PhD (London Guildhall) 2000. *Publications:* The Polish Crisis 1981, Deficits and Detente 1983; (Jt Ed.) Threats to International Financial Stability 1987; Ed.: Global Macroeconomics: Policy Conflict and Cooperation 1987, Blueprints for Exchange Rate Management 1989, Macroeconomic Policies in an Interdependent World 1989, The EMS in Transition: a CEPR Report 1989, External Constraints on Macroeconomic Policy: The European Experience 1991, The Path of Reform in Central and Eastern Europe 1991, Economic Transformation of Central Europe 1993, European Union Trade with Eastern Europe 1995, Crisis? What Crisis? Orderly Workouts for Sovereign Debtors 1995; numerous papers and contribs to learned journals. *Address:* London Business School, Regent's Park, London, NW1 4SA, England. *Telephone:* (20) 7706-6886. *Fax:* (20) 7724-1598. *E-mail:* rportes@london.edu (Office).

PORTILLO, Rt Hon Michael Denzil Xavier, PC, MA; British politician; b. 26 May 1953; s. of Luis G. Portillo and Cora W. Blyth; m. Carolyn C. Eadie 1982; ed Harrow Co. Boys' School and Peterhouse, Cambridge; Ocean Transport & Trading Co. 1975–76; Conservative Research Dept 1976–79; Special Adviser to Sec. of State for Energy 1979–81; Kerr McGee Oil (UK) Ltd 1981–83; Special Adviser to Sec. of State for Trade and Industry 1983, to Chancellor of Exchequer 1983–84; MP for Enfield, Southgate 1984–97, for Kensington and Chelsea 1999–; Asst Govt Whip 1986–87; Parl. Under-Sec. of State, Dept of Health and Social Security 1987–88; Minister of State, Dept of Transport 1988–90; Minister of State for Local Govt and Inner Cities 1990–92; Chief Sec. to the Treasury 1992–94; Sec. of State for Employment 1994–95, for Defence 1995–97; Shadow Chancellor 2000–01; freelance writer and broadcaster 1997–; adviser to Kerr McGee Corpn 1997–; Dir (non-exec.) BAE Systems 2002–; mem. Int. Comm. for Missing Persons in fmr Yugoslavia; mem. Conservative Party. *Publications:* Clear Blue Water 1994, Democratic Values and the Currency 1998. *Address:* House of Commons, London, SW1A 0AA, England (Office).

PORTILLO CABRERA, Alfonso Antonio; Guatemalan politician; ed Universidad Autónoma de Guerrero, Mexico, Universidad Autónoma de México; fmr columnist, daily newspaper Siglo Veintiuno; mem. Editorial Bd Suplemento Económico Pulso; Prof. of Law, Econs and Politics in univs in Latin America; fmr Leader of Democracia Cristiana (DC) Deputies in Congress, Chair. Comm. of Econ., Foreign Trade and Integration; Asst Gen. Sec. DC, Dir DC's Centro de Estudios Socio Políticos (IGESP); Pres. of Guatemala Jan. 2000–. *Address:* Office of the President, Guatemala City, Guatemala (Office).

PORTISCH, Lajos; Hungarian chess player and singer; b. 4 April 1937; s. of Lajos Portisch Sr and Anna Simon; mem. MTK-Sport Club; top ranking player of Hungary's selected team 1962–; nine times Hungarian champion; holder of Int. Grandmaster title 1961–; European team bronze medallist 1961, 1965, 1973, team silver medallist 1970, 1977, 1980; Olympic team bronze medallist 1956, 1966, silver 1970, 1972, 1980, gold 1978; qualified eight times as cand. for the individual chess world title; holder of Master Coach qualification; bass-baritone singer, gives regular concerts; Labour Order of Merit (golden degree). *Publication:* Six Hundred Endings (co-author with B. Sárközi) 1973. *Leisure interest:* music. *Address:* Hungarian Chess Federation, 1055 Budapest, Néphadsereg utca 10, Hungary. *Telephone:* (1) 111-6616.

PORTMAN, Natalie; American/Israeli actress; b. 9 June 1981, Jerusalem, Israel; ed Harvard Univ.; left Israel with her family aged 3 and moved to USA; discovered by modelling scout at New York pizza parlour, aged 11. *Films include:* The Professional (also known as Léon) 1994, Developing 1995, Heat 1995, Beautiful Girls 1996, Everyone Says I Love You 1996, Mars Attacks! 1996, The Diary of Anne Frank 1997, Star Wars: Episode I – The Phantom Menace (as Queen Amidala) 1999, Anywhere But Here, Where the Heart Is 2000, The Seagull 2001, Zoolander 2001, Star Wars: Episode II – Attack of the

Clones 2002, Cold Mountain 2002. *Theatre includes:* A Midsummer Night's Dream, Cabaret, Anne of Green Gables (title role), Tapestry. *Address:* c/o ICM, 8942 Wilshire Boulevard, Beverly Hills, CA 90211, USA (Office).

PORTZAMPARC, Christian de; French architect; b. 9 May 1944, Casablanca, Morocco; s. of Maurice Urvay de Portzamparc and Annick de Boutray; m. Elizabeth Jardim Neves 1982; two s.; ed Ecole Supérieure des Beaux Arts; work includes Hautes Formes housing complex, south-east Paris; City of Music, Parc de la Villette, Paris; office bldg for Crédit Lyonnais, Lille; two small housing projects in Japan and Germany, Zac Massena-Seine-Rive-gauche; retrospective exhbn, Pompidou Centre 1996; extension of Palais des Congrés de Paris 1999; French Embassy, Berlin 2000; LVMH Tower, New York (Business Week Architectural Record Prize) 2002; Pritzker Prize for Architecture 1994, Equerre d'argent Award 1995; Commdr des Arts et des Lettres. *Publications:* La Cité de la musique 1986, Scènes d'atelier, Généalogie des formes 1996, Christian de Portzamparc, Le Dantec 1995, Christian de Portzamparc 1996. *Address:* 1 rue de l'Aude, 75014 Paris, France. *E-mail:* studio@chdeportzamparc.com (Office).

POSNETT, Sir Richard Neil, KBE, CMG, MA; British colonial administrator, barrister and diplomatist (retd); b. 19 July 1919, Kotagiri, India; s. of Rev. Charles Walker Posnett and Phyllis Posnett (née Barker); m. Shirley Margaret Hudson 1959; two s. one d. (two s. one d. by previous marriage); ed Kingswood School, St John's Coll. Cambridge; RAF 1940; Colonial Admin. Service, Uganda 1941–62; barrister-at-law, Gray's Inn 1950; Chair. Uganda Olympic Cttee 1954–58; Judicial Adviser 1960; Perm. Sec. for External Affairs, Trade and Industry 1961–63; Foreign Office, UK 1964–66; UK Mission to UN 1966–70; briefly HM Commr, Anguilla 1969; Head of West Indian Dept, FCO 1970–72; Gov. and C-in-C, Belize 1972–76; mission to Ocean Island (Banaba) 1977; FCO Adviser on Dependent Territories 1977–79; High Commr in Uganda April–Nov. 1979; Gov. and C-in-C Bermuda 1981–83; UK Commr, Bd of British Phosphate Commrs 1978–81; Lord Chancellor's Panel of Ind. Inspectors 1983–89; Gov. Kingswood School 1985–93; Pres. Godalming-Joigny Friendship Asscn; mem. Royal Inst. of Int. Affairs, Royal African Soc., Royal Forestry Soc.; Fellow, Royal Commonwealth Soc.; first ascent South Portal Peak, Ruwenzori 1942; KStJ 1972. *Publications:* Looking Back at the Uganda Protectorate (contrib.) 1996, The Scent of Eucalyptus – A Journal of Colonial and Foreign Service 2001; articles in World Today and Uganda Journal. *Leisure interests:* skiing, golf, growing trees. *Address:* Bahati, Old Kiln Close, Churt, Surrey, GU10 2JH, England. *Telephone:* (1428) 714147.

POSOKHIN, Mikhail Mikhailovich; Russian architect; b. 10 July 1948, Moscow; s. of Mikhail Vasilyevich Posokhin and Galina Arkadyevna Posokhina; m. 1st (divorced); one s.; m. 2nd Vitalina Kudzyavtseva; two d.; ed Moscow Inst. of Architecture; Chief Architect Dept of Civil and Residential Construction Mosproyekt-1 1976–80; head of workshop dept for Designs of Exemplary Perspective residential area Chertanovo 1980–82; head of workshop Dept for Designs of Public Bldgs and Edifices Mosproyekt-2 1982–, Gen. Dir. 1983; fmr Vice-Chair. Cttee on Architecture and Town-planning of Moscow 1994; mem. and mem. Presidium Russian Acad. of Arts; mem. Int. Acad. of Architecture, Acad. Architectural Heritage; Merited Architect of Russia, State Prize of Russia, Public Acknowledgement Prize, The Honour Order, Sergey Radonezhsky Order (2nd and 3rd Degrees), Moscow Daneel Godly Prince Order (2nd Degree), Golden Order of Labour (Bulgary), Golden Order, Russian Acad. of Arts. *Buildings:* numerous residential complexes and public edifices including restoration of Cathedral of Christ the Saviour, the Business Centre on Kudrinskaya Square, trade complex on Manege Square, the Gosinny Dvor, reconstruction of the Kremlin and others; 101 projects. *Address:* Mosproyekt-2, 2 Brestskaya str. 5, 123056 Moscow, Russia (Office). *Telephone:* (095) 200-56-47 (Office).

POSSER DA COSTA, Guilherme; São Tomé e Príncipe politician; fmr Minister of Foreign Affairs and Co-operation; Prime Minister 1998–2001; Vice-Pres. Movimento de Libertação de São Tomé e Príncipe–Partido Social Democrata (MLSTP-PSD). *Address:* Movimento de Libertação de São Tomé e Príncipe–Partido Social Democrata, Riboque Cidade Capital, São Tomé e Príncipe (Office). *Telephone:* (12) 22253 (Office).

POST, Herschel, MA, LLB; American investment banker; b. 9 Oct. 1939; s. of the late Herschel E. Post and of Marie C. Post; m. Peggy Mayne 1963; one s. three d.; ed Yale and Harvard Univs and New Coll. Oxford; Assoc. Davis, Polk & Wordwell (attorneys) 1966–69; Exec. Dir Parks Council of New York City 1969–72; Deputy Admin., Parks, Recreation and Cultural Affairs Admin New York 1973; Vice-Pres. and Man. Euro-clear Operations, JP Morgan & Co. Brussels 1974–78; Vice-Pres. and Deputy Head, Int. Investment Dept JP Morgan, London 1978–83; Pres. Posthorn Global Asset Man. London 1984–90, Shearson Lehman Global Asset Man., London 1984–90; Deputy Chair. London Stock Exchange 1988–95, Chair. Trading Markets Managing Bd 1990–95; Trustee, Earthwatch Europe 1988– (Chair. 1997–); COO Lehman Brothers Int. Ltd 1990–94, Coutts & Co. 1994–95 (CEO, Deputy Chair. 1995–2000); Int. Man. Dir of Business Devt, Christie's Int. PLC 2000–; Chair. Woodcock Foundation 2000–; Deputy Chair. EFG Private Bank Ltd 2002–; Dir Investors Capital Trust 2000–, CRESTCO Ltd 2002–, Ahli United Bank BSC 2002–, Notting Hill Housing Group 2002–. *Address:* Christie's International PLC, 8 King Street, St James's, London, WC1Y 6QT, England (Office).

POSTE, George, CBE, BVSC, PhD, FRS, FRCVS, FRCPath, FRS; British research scientist and industry executive; b. 30 April 1944, Polegate, Sussex; s. of the late John H. Poste and of Kathleen B. Poste; m. Linda Suhler 1992; one s. two d.; ed Bristol Univ.; lecturer Royal Postgrad. Medical School, Univ. of London 1969–72; Prof. of Experimental Pathology S.U.N.Y. 1973–80; Vice-Pres. Research and Devt SmithKline Beecham 1980–88, Research and Devt Technologies 1989–92, Chair., Pres. Research and Devt 1992–97, Chief Science and Tech. Officer 1997–99; CEO Health Tech. Networks 2000–; partner Care Capital, Princeton 2000–; Research Prof. Univ. of Pa 1981–, Univ. of Tex. Medical Center 1986–; Fleming Fellow Lincoln Coll. Oxford 1995, Pitt Fellow Pembroke Coll. Cambridge 1996, Fellow, Hoover Inst., Stanford Univ. 2000–; mem. Human Genetics Advisory Cttee 1996–; mem. Bd Govs. Center for Molecular Medicine and Genetics, Stanford Univ. 1992–; mem. Alliance for Ageing 1992–97; Jt Ed. Cell Surface Reviews 1976–83, New Horizons in Therapeutics 1984–; Hon. FRCP 1993; Hon. Fellow Univ. Coll. London 1993; Hon. DSc 1987, (Sussex) 1999; Hon. LLD (Bristol) 1995, (Dundee) 1998. *Publications:* numerous reviews and papers in learned journals. *Leisure interests:* automobile racing, mil. history, photography, desert exploration. *Address:* Health Technology Networks, P.O. Box 647, Gilbertsville, PA 19525, USA (Office). *Telephone:* (610) 705-0828 (Office). *Fax:* (610) 705-0810 (Office). *E-mail:* gposte@healthtechnetwork.com (Office).

POSTGATE, John Raymond, DPhil, DSc, FRS; British professor of microbiology; b. 24 June 1922, London; s. of Raymond William Postgate and Daisy (née Lansbury) Postgate; m. Mary Stewart 1948; three d.; ed Woodstock School, Kingsbury County School, Balliol Coll. Oxford; Sr Research Investigator, Nat. Chemical Lab. 1949–50, Sr Prin. 1950–59; Prin., Sr Prin. Scientific Officer Microbiology Research Establishment 1959–63; Asst Dir AFRC Unit of Nitrogen Fixation, Royal Veterinary Coll. 1963–65; Asst Dir AFRC Unit of Nitrogen Fixation, Univ. of Sussex 1965–80, Dir 1980–87 and Prof. of Microbiology Univ. of Sussex 1965–87, Prof Emer. 1987–; Visiting Prof. Univ. of Ill. 1962–63, Ore. State Univ. 1977–78; Pres. Inst. of Biology 1982–84, Soc. for Gen. Microbiology 1984–87; Hon. DSc (Bath); Hon. LLD (Dundee). *Publications:* Microbes and Man 1969, Biological Nitrogen Fixation 1972, Nitrogen Fixation 1978, The Sulphate-Reducing Bacteria 1979, The Fundamentals of Nitrogen Fixation 1982, A Plain Man's Guide to Jazz 1973, The Outer Reaches of Life 1994, A Stomach for Dissent: The Life of Raymond Postgate (with Mary Postgate) 1994, Lethal Lozenges and Tainted Tea: A Biography of John Postgate (1820–1881) 2001. *Leisure interest:* listening to jazz and attempting to play it. *Address:* 1 Houndean Rise, Lewes, Sussex, BN7 1EG, England. *Telephone:* (1273) 472675. *E-mail:* johnp@biols.susx.ac.uk (Home).

POSTLETHWAITE, Pete; British actor; b. 16 Feb. 1945, Lancashire; partner Jacqueline Morrish; one s. one d.; ed Bristol Old Vic. Theatre School. *Theatre includes:* Macbeth, Bristol. *Films include:* The Last of the Mohicans, In the Name of the Father, Romeo and Juliet, Alien 3, Dragonheart, Distant Voices, Still Lives, Brassed Off, The Lost World: Jurassic Park, Amistad, The Serpent's Kiss, Among Giants, The Divine Ryans. *Television includes:* Between the Lines, Lost for Words, Butterfly Collectors. *Theatre includes:* Macbeth, Cyrano de Bergerac, King Lear, Midsummer Night's Dream. *Address:* c/o Markham and Froggart Ltd, 4 Windmill Street, London, W1P 1HF, England.

POTANIN, Vladimir Olegovich; Russian politician and banker; b. 3 Jan. 1961, Moscow; m.; one s., one d.; ed Moscow Inst. of Int. Relations; staff-mem. USSR Ministry of Foreign Trade 1983–90; Head Econ. Co. Interross 1991–92; Vice-Pres., Pres. Joint-Stock Commercial Bank Int. Financial Co. 1992–93; Pres. UNEXIM Bank 1993–, Interross Financial and Industrial Group 1994–; First Deputy Chair. Govt of Russian Fed. 1996–97; concurrently Head Interdept Comm. on Co-operation with Int. Financial-Econ. Orgs. and Group of Seven; mem. bds of dirs of maj. industrial cos. *Address:* Interross, Grokholski per. 12, 129010 Moscow, Russia (Office). *Telephone:* (095) 207-24-57 (Office). *Fax:* (095) 975-22-02.

POTAPOV, Alexander Serafimovich, CAND.PHIL.; Russian journalist; b. 6 Feb. 1936, Oktyabry, Kharkov Region, Ukraine; m.; one s.; ed Vilnius State Univ., Lithuania; contrib. Leninskaya Smena (newspaper) 1958–66; Head of Dept, Deputy Ed.-in-Chief Belgorodskaya Pravda (newspaper) 1966–73; Head of Dept Belgorod Regional Exec. CPSU Cttee 1973–75; Ed. Belgorodskaya Pravda 1975–76; instructor CPSU Cen. Cttee 1976–78, 1981–85; Ed.-in-Chief Trud (newspaper) 1985–; People's Deputy of Russian Fed., mem. Cttee of Supreme Soviet of Russian Fed. on Problems of Glasnost and Human Rights –1993. *Address:* Trud, Nastas'yinsky per. 4, 103792 Moscow, Russia (Office). *Telephone:* (095) 299-39-06 (Office).

POTAPOV, Leonid Vassilyevich; Russian politician; b. 4 July 1935, Llakit, Buryatia; m.; two c.; ed Khabarovsk Inst. of Railway Eng, Irkutsk Inst. of Nat. Econs; various positions from engineer to chief engineer Ulan-Ude train factory 1959–76; Head Div. of Industry, then Sec. Buryat Regional CP Cttee 1976–87; Chair. Mary Regional Exec. Cttee Turkmenia 1987–89; Chair. Supreme Soviet Turkmen SSR 1989–90; First Sec. Buryat CPSU Cttee 1990–91; Chair. Supreme Soviet Buryat Autonomous SSR (now Buryatskaya Repub.) 1991–94; Pres. of Buryatskaya Repub. 1994–; mem. Council of Fed., Russian Fed. 1993–2001. *Address:* Government House, Sukhe Bator str. 9, 670001 Ulan-Ude, Republic of Buryatia, Russia (Office). *Telephone:* (3012) 21-51-86 (Office). *Fax:* (3012) 21-25-55 (Office). *E-mail:* meconomy@icm.buryatia .ru (Office).

POTIER, Benoît; French business executive; b. 3 Sept. 1957, Mulhouse; m. Claude Menard; ed Ecole Centrale Paris; joined Research Devt Dept, Air Liquide 1981, positions in Eng and Construction Div. 1993–97, CEO 1997–, mem. Bd 2000–, Chair. Man. Bd 2001–. *Address:* Air Liquide, 75 quai d'Orsay, 75321 Paris Cedex 07, France (Office). *Telephone:* 1-40-68-55-55 (Office). *Fax:* 1-40-68-58-40 (Office). *Website:* www.airliquide.com (Office).

POTRČ, Miran; Slovenian politician and lawyer; b. 27 March 1938, Maribor, Slovenia; s. of Ivan Potrč and Olga Potrč; m. Zdenka Potrč 1992; one d.; ed Univ. of Ljubljana; with Secr. of Justice and Public Admin Maribor 1962–63; Head, Legal Dept Mariborska Livarna (Maribor Foundry) 1963–68; Sec. Communal Cttee of League of Communists of Maribor 1968–73; mem. Presidency of Cen. Cttee League of Communists of Slovenia and Pres. Comm. for Socio-Economic Matters and Social Policy 1973; mem. Exec. Cttee Presidency of Cen. Cttee of League of Communists of Slovenia 1974–78; Vice-Pres. Repub. Council of Trade Unions of Slovenia 1978–80; mem. Presidency, Trade Unions of Yugoslavia 1980–82, Pres. 1980–81; Head, Del. of Skupshtina (Parl.) of S.R. of Slovenia in Fed. Chamber of Repubs and Provs 1982–86; Pres. Skupshtina of S.R. of Slovenia 1986–90; mem. Parl. of Repub. of Slovenia, Head Parl. Group and mem. Presidium, Party of Democratic Reforms of Slovenia 1990–; Head Parl. Group United List of Social Democrats; fmr Pres. Council, Univ. of Maribor. *Address:* Assembly of the Republic of Slovenia, Tomšičeva 5, 61000 Ljubljana, Slovenia. *Telephone:* (1) 215895, (1) 4789637. *Fax:* (1) 4789866 (Office). *E-mail:* miran.potrc@dz-ns.si (Office).

POTTAKIS, Yannis A.; Greek politician; b. 1939, Corinth; m. Constantina Alexopoulou; two s. one d.; ed Univs. of Athens and Munich, Germany; founding mem. of Pasok; mem. Parl. 1977–; Alt. Minister of Nat. Economy 1982–83, Minister of Finance 1983–84, of Agric. 1985–89, of Justice 1995–96; Alt. Minister of Foreign Affairs; Chair. Council of Budget Ministers of EEC 1983. *Address:* 15 Chimaras Street, 14671 Nea Erythrea, Greece. *Telephone:* 8001-631.

POTTER, David Edwin, CBE, PhD; South African business executive; b. 4 July 1943, East London; s. of Paul James Potter and Mary Agnes Snape; m. Elaine Goldberg 1969; three s.; ed Trinity Coll. Cambridge, Imperial Coll. London; lecturer Blackett Lab., Imperial Coll. London 1970–80; Asst Prof. Univ. of Calif. at LA 1974; Founder, Chair., CEO Psion PLC 1980–; Dir Press Assoc. Ltd 1994–97 (Vice-Chair. 1995–97), London First Centre 1994–, Finsbury Tech. Trust 1995–; Chair. Symbian Ltd; mem. Nat. Cttee of Inquiry into Higher Educ. (Dearing Cttee) 1996–97, Higher Educ. Funding Council for England 1997–, Council for Science and Tech., Cabinet Office 1998–; Visiting Fellow, Nuffield Coll. Oxford 1998–; Hon. Fellow Imperial Coll. 1998, London Business School 1998; Hon. DTech (Kingston) 1998, (Brunel) 1998; Mountbatten Medal for Outstanding Services to Electronics Industry, Nat. Electronics Council 1994. *Publications:* Computational Physics 1972, contribs. to numerous physics journals. *Leisure interests:* flute, gardening, reading, tennis. *Address:* Psion PLC, 12 Park Crescent, London, W1B 1PH (Office); 8 Hamilton Terrace, St John's Wood, London, NW8 9UG, England (Home). *Telephone:* (20) 7317-4220 (Office). *Fax:* (20) 7317-4251 (Office). *E-mail:* david-potter@psion.com (Office). *Website:* www.psion.com (Office).

POUGATCHEV, Sergueï; Russian politician and banker; f. Mejprombank 1992, Dir and later Pres. –2001; co-f. Almazi Yakoutil co.; mem. (Senator) Council of the Fed. for Tver Oblast 2001–. *Address:* Representation of Tver Oblast in the Russian Federation, ul. B. Dmitrovka 26, 103426 Moscow, Russia (Office). *Telephone:* (095) 926-65-19 (Office). *Fax:* (095) 292-14-85 (Office).

POUJADE, Pierre; French newspaper executive; b. 1 Dec. 1920, St Céré; s. of Gabriel Poujade and Louise Roux; m. Yvette Seva 1944; three s. two d.; served in RAF, Second World War; after 1945 became publisher and bookseller, also active in politics; mem. St Céré Municipal Council 1951; Founder Pres. Union de Défense de Commerçants et Artisans; Founder, Union et Fraternité Française; Founder Dir Union et Défense (daily), Fraternité Française (weekly); Pres. Confédération Nat. des Travailleurs Indépendants 1970; Pres. Caisse Nat. d'Assurance Maladie Obligatoire 1971–; Pres. Nat. Asscn l'Utilisation des Resources Energetiques Français (ANUREF) 1979, Pres.-Founder l'Asscn. Occitanie-Caraïbes; mem. Comm. Nat. de Carburants de Substitution 1983; mem. Conseil Economique et Social; led econ. and social mission to Romania 1990; creator of "La Vallée Heureuse" (gastronomic and tourist centre), La Bastide-l'Evêque; Founder and Pres. Centre de Formation Avicole and Ferme Pieste, Château de Gouzou; Dir Caisse Régionale, Midi-Pyrénées 1972–; f. Union pour la Défense des Libertés 1978; Founder and Pres. Asscn Fraternité Occitanie-Roumanie 1991; Hon. Pres. Confédération européene des indépendants (Cedi) 1993; Hon. mem. Social and Econ. Council 2000; Croix du combattant volontaire, Medaille des Evadés. *Publications:* J'ai choisi le combat, A l'heure de la colère 1977, etc. *Leisure interest:* sport, particularly football and rugby. *Address:* "Vallée Heureuse", La Bastide-l'Evêque, 12200 Villefranche-de-Rouergue, France. *Telephone:* (65) 299188. *Fax:* (65) 299655.

POULIDES, Fotis George; Greek diplomatist and shipping entrepreneur; b. 21 Nov. 1914, Athens; s. of the late George F. Poulides and Theano Antonopoulou; one s.; ed Athens Coll. and Univ. of London; began career in shipping, Piraeus and London 1932; Dir of Maritime Services of Int. Red Cross (supervising ships carrying food between Canada and Greece) 1942–46; Founder and Pres. Medov SpA (shipping enterprises), Genoa 1947–; initiated regular passenger service between Italy and Australia 1949; Founder, Medov Lines 1960; Chair. of several shipping cos, shipping insts and confs; joined Cyprus diplomatic service 1961; Amb. and Perm. Rep. to UN Agencies for Food and Agric. Rome 1979–; assoc. with Baltic and Int. Maritime Council (BIMCO), Copenhagen 1946–, Vice-Pres. 1981–85, mem. Exec. Cttee 1989–92, Vice-Pres. 1993–95; nominated Counsellor 1995; honoured for 50 years' Asscn with BIMCO 1995; Cavaliere Grande Croce Ordine al Merito della Repubblica Italiana, Commdr, Order of Phoenix (Greece), Commdr, Ordre du Mérite Maritime (France). *Leisure interests:* reading, philately. *Address:* Chalet Intermezzo, 3962 Montana, Switzerland (Home). *Telephone:* (27) 4812620.

POULSEN, Ole Lønsmann, LLM; Danish diplomatist; b. 14 May 1945, Lyngby; s. of Aage Lønsmann Poulsen and Tove Alice Poulsen; m. Zareen Mehta 1973; two s.; ed Univs. of Poona, India and Copenhagen; with Danchurchaid 1969–73; Head of Section, Ministry of Foreign Affairs 1973–76, Asian Devt Bank, Manila 1976–77, First Sec., New Delhi 1977–80; Alt. Exec. Dir World Bank, Washington, DC 1980–83, Deputy Head of Dept, Ministry of Foreign Affairs 1983–85, Head of Dept 1985–88, Under-Sec. and Amb. 1988–92, Amb. in Vienna, Ljubljana and Sarajevo, Amb. to UN orgs. in Vienna 1992–93, State Sec., Amb. 1993–96, Amb. to UK 1996–2001, Amb. to People's Repub. of China 2001–; Commdr, Order of Dannebrog, Grand Cross of Austria, Hon. GCVO. *Leisure interests:* art, music, literature, sports. *Address:* 1 Dong Wu Jie, San Li Tun, Beijing 10060, People's Republic of China (Office). *Telephone:* (10) 65322431 (Office). *Fax:* (10) 65322439 (Office). *E-mail:* ambadan@public.bta.net.cn (Office). *Website:* www.dk-embassy-cn.org (Office).

POUND, Robert Vivian, MA; American physicist; b. 16 May 1919, Ridgeway, Ont., Canada; s. of V. E. Pound and Gertrude C. Prout; m. Betty Yde Andersen 1941; one s.; ed Univ. of Buffalo and Harvard Univ.; Research Physicist, Submarine Signal Co., Boston, Mass. 1941–42; Staff mem. Radiation Laboratory, MIT 1942–46; Jr Fellow, Soc. of Fellows, Harvard Univ. 1945–48, Asst Prof. 1948–50, Assoc. Prof. 1950–56, Prof. 1956–68, Mallinckrodt Prof. of Physics 1968–89, Prof. Emer. 1989–; Chair. Dept of Physics 1968–72, Dir Physics Labs 1975–83; Zernike Prof. Groningen Univ. 1982; Visiting Prof. Coll. de France 1973, Univ. of Florida 1987; Visiting Fellow, Joint Inst. for Lab. Astrophysics, Univ. of Colorado 1979–80; Visiting Scientist Brookhaven Nat. Lab. 1986–87; Research Fellow, Merton Coll. Oxford 1980; mem. NAS; Foreign Assoc. Académie des Sciences; Fellow, American Acad. of Arts and Sciences, American Physical Soc., AAAS; Fulbright Research Scholar, Oxford Univ. 1951; Fulbright Lecturer, Ecole Normale, Paris 1958; Guggenheim Fellow 1957–58, 1972–73; B. J. Thompson Memorial Award, Inst. of Radio Engineers 1948, Eddington Medal, Royal Astronomical Soc. 1965, Nat. Medal of Science (Pres. of USA) 1990. *Publications:* Microwave Mixers 1948; papers on nuclear magnetism, electric quadrupole interactions, directional correlations of gamma rays, effect of gravity on gamma rays. *Address:* Lyman Laboratory of Physics, Harvard University, Cambridge, MA 02138 (Office); 87 Pinehurst Road, Belmont, MA 02478-1502, U.S.A (Home). *Telephone:* (617) 495-2873 (Office); (617) 484-0254 (Home).

POUNDS, Kenneth Alwyne, CBE, PhD, FRS; British professor of space physics; b. 17 Nov. 1934, Leeds; s. of Harry Pounds and Dorothy Pounds (née Hunt); m. 1st Margaret Connell 1961; two s. one d.; m. 2nd Joan Mary Millit 1982; one s. one d.; ed Salt High School, Shipley, Yorks. and Univ. Coll. London; Dir X-ray Astronomy Group, Univ. of Leicester 1973–94, Prof. of Space Physics 1973–, Head of Dept of Physics and Astronomy 1986–2002 (on leave of absence 1994–98); Chief Exec. Particle Physics and Astronomy Research Council 1994–98; Pres. Royal Astronomical Soc. 1990–92; mem. Academia Europaea, Int. Acad. of Astronautics; Fellow Univ. Coll. London 1993; Gold Medal of Royal Astronomical Soc. 1990. *Publications:* over 200 scientific pubs. *Leisure interests:* sport, music. *Address:* Department of Physics and Astronomy, University of Leicester, University Road, Leicester, LE1 7RH (Office); 12 Swale Close, Oadby, Leics., LE2 4GF, England (Home). *Telephone:* (116) 252-3509 (Office); (116) 271-9370 (Home). *Fax:* (116) 252-3311 (Office). *E-mail:* kap@star.le.ac.uk (Office). *Website:* www.star.le.ac.uk (Office).

POUNGUI, Ange-Edouard; Republic of the Congo politician, economist and banker; began career in school, student unions; apptd. mem. Nat. Council for Revolution 1968, then mem. Political Bureau, Minister for Finance 1971–73, Vice-Pres. Council of State and Minister for Planning 1973–76; Prime Minister of The Congo 1984–89; fmr Pres. Union pour le Renouveau Démocratique (URD); worked for IMF and African Devt Bank, then Dir-Gen. Cen. African Bank 1976–79, then CEO Congolese Commercial Bank; Dir Cen. Bank of the Congo 1994–2001. *Address:* c/o Bank of the Central African States, P.O. Box 126, Brazzaville, Republic of the Congo.

POUNTNEY, David Willoughby, CBE, MA; British opera director; b. 10 Sept. 1947, Oxford; s. of E. W. Pountney and D. L. Byrt; m. Jane R. Henderson 1980; one s. one d.; ed St John's Coll. Choir School, Cambridge, Radley Coll. and St John's Coll. Cambridge; Dir of Productions, Scottish Opera 1976–80, ENO 1982–94; numerous productions for all maj. British cos including a Janáček cycle for Welsh Nat. Opera/Scottish Opera; has worked in USA (Chicago, Houston, San Francisco, Metropolitan Opera, New York), Paris, Berlin, Rome, Amsterdam, Vienna, Zürich and Munich; Intendant (desig.) Bregenzer Festspiele (2003)–; Janáček Medal, SWET Award, Martini Medal; Chevalier des Arts et des Lettres (France), Olivier Award. *Publications:*

Powerhouse; several trans. from German, Italian, Russian and Czech. *Leisure interests:* gardening, cooking, croquet. *Address:* Château d'Azu, 71230 St Romain sous Gourdon, France.

POUPARD, H.E. Paul; French ecclesiastic; b. 30 Aug. 1930; ordained 1954; Rector Inst. Catholique de Paris 1971–81; Titular Bishop of Usula 1979, Archbishop 1980; cr. Cardinal 1985; Priest of S. Prassede; Pres. Pontifical Council for Culture 1982–; Grand Prix Cardinal Crente, Acad. Française, Prix Robert Schuman, Prix Empedocle; Commdr. Légion d'honneur, Grand Cross Order of Merit (Germany). *Publications include:* Les Religions 1987, L'Eglise au Défi des Cultures 1989, The Church and Culture 1989, Dieu et la Liberté 1992, Nouvelle Europe 1993, Après Galilée, Science et Foi, Nouveau Dialogue 1994, What Will Give Us Happiness 1992, Dictionnaire des Religions 1993, Le Christianisme à l'aube du troisième millénaire 1999. *Address:* Piazza San Calisto, 00120 Vatican City. *Telephone:* (06) 69887393. *Fax:* (06) 69887368. *E-mail:* cultura@cultr.va (Office). *Website:* www.vatican.va (Office).

POURIER, Miguel Arcangel; Netherlands Antilles politician; b. 29 Sept. 1938, Bonaire; m.; three c.; ed Radulphus Coll., Curaçao, Univ. of Tilburg; tax inspector 1962–73, fmr Head Dept Excise and Import Duties, fmr Dir Dept of Taxes; Minister of Devt Co-operation 1973–79, also fmr Minister of Finance, of Econ. Affairs; ABN Bank 1980–91, Dir ABN Trust, Gen. Dir ABN Bank Netherlands Antilles and Aruba; Govt Adviser; fmr Pres. Asscn of Bankers; financial consultant 1991–; Prime Minister of Netherlands Antilles, Minister of Gen. Affairs and Devt Co-operation 1994–98, 1999–; Commdr Order of Oranje Nassau. *Leisure interests:* reading, chess, tennis, guitar. *Address:* Ministry of General Affairs and Development Co-operation, Plasa Horacio Hoyer 9, Willemstad, Curaçao, Netherlands Antilles (Office). *Telephone:* (9) 461-1866 (Office). *Fax:* (9) 461-1268 (Office).

POWATHIL, Most Rev. Joseph, MA, DD; Indian ecclesiastic; b. 14 Aug. 1930, Kurumpanadam; s. of Ulahannan Joseph Powathil and Mariyam Joseph Powathil; ed St Berchmans' Coll., Changanacherry, Loyola Coll., Madras, St Thomas Minor Seminary, Parel and Papal Seminary, Pune; ordained RC Priest 1962; Lecturer in Econs, St Berchmans's Coll., Changanacherry 1963–72; Auxiliary Bishop of Changanacherry 1972–77, Titular Bishop of Caesarea Philipi, 1972, consecrated Bishop 1972; 1st Bishop of Kanjirappally Diocese, Kerala 1977–85; Archbishop of Changanacherry 1985–; Chair. Kerala Catholic Bishops' Conf. (KCBC) and Chair. Educational Comm. 1993–96; Pres. Catholic Bishops' Conf. of India (CBCI) 1993–98; Perm. mem. Syro Malabar Bishops' Synod 1993; Chair. CBCI Comm. for Educ. and Clergy, KCBC Comm. for Vigilance 1998–; mem. Comm. for Devt, Justice and Peace; Chair. SMBC Comm. for Ecumenism 1993–; Chair. Inter-Church Council for Educ. 1990–; mem. Asian Synod of Bishops, Post Synodal Council (for Asia) 1998–; mem. Pontifical Comm. for Dialogue with the Orthodox Syrian Church; Chair. Religious Fellowship Foundation 1994; Hon. mem. Pro-Oriente, Vienna 1994. *Address:* Archbishop's House, P.O. Box 20, Changanacherry 686 101, Kerala, India. *Telephone:* (481) 420040, 420379, 420614, 421162. *Fax:* (481) 422540. *E-mail:* abpchry@md2.vsnl.net.in.

POWELL, Gen. Colin Luther, MBA; American army officer; b. 5 April 1937, New York; s. of Luther Powell and Maud A. McKoy; m. Alma V. Johnson 1962; one s. two d.; ed City Univ. of New York and George Washington Univ.; commissioned US Army 1958, Lt-Gen. 1986; Commdr 2nd Brigade, 101st Airborne Div. 1976–77; Exec. Asst to Sec. Dept of Energy 1979; Sr Mil. Asst to Sec. Dept of Defense 1979–81; Asst Div. Commdr 4th Infantry Div. Fort Carson, Colo 1981–83; Mil. Asst to Sec. of Defense 1983–86; assigned to US V Corps, Europe 1986–87; Nat. Security Adviser, White House, Washington 1987–88; C-in-C US Forces, Fort McPherson, Ga April–Sept. 1989; Chair. Jt Chiefs of Staff 1989–93; Sec. of State Jan. 2001–; public speaker 1993–2000; Chair. Pres.'s Summit For America's Future 1997–; Founding Chair. America's Promise–The Alliance for Youth 1997; Hon. LLD (Univ. of West Indies) 1994; Legion of Merit, Bronze Star, Air Medal, Purple Heart, Pres. Medal of Freedom, Pres. Citizen's Medal, Hon. KCB 1993, Order of Jamaica. *Publication:* A Soldier's Way (autobiog. with Joseph E. Persico) 1995. *Address:* Department of State, 2201 C. Street, NW, Washington, DC 20520, USA (Office). *Telephone:* (202) 647-5291 (Office). *Fax:* (202) 647-6738 (Office). *Website:* www.state.gov/index.html (Office).

POWELL, III, Earl Alexander, AB, AM, PhD; American art museum director; b. 24 Oct. 1943, Spartanburg, SC; s. of Earl Alexander Powell and Elizabeth Duckworth; m. Nancy Landry 1971; three d.; ed Williams Coll. and Harvard Univ.; Teaching Fellow, Harvard Univ. 1970–74; Curator, Michener Collection, Univ. of Texas, Austin 1974–76, also Asst Prof. of Art History; Museum Curator, Sr Staff Asst to Asst Dir and Chief Curator, Nat. Gallery of Art, Washington, DC 1976–78, Exec. Curator 1979–80, Dir 1992–; Dir LA Co. Museum of Art 1980–92; other professional appts.; Trustee American Fed. of Arts, Nat. Trust for Historic Preservation, White House Historical Asscn, Georgia O'Keeffe Foundation; mem. Asscn of Art Museum Dirs., Cttee for the Preservation of the White House, O'Keeffe Museum Nat. Advisory Bd, Pres.'s Cttee on the Arts and Humanities, Nat. Council on the Arts; King Olav Medal 1978, Williams Bicentennial Medal 1995, Mexican Cultural Inst. Award 1996, Grand Official, Order of the Infante D. Henrique 1995, Chevalier des Arts et des Lettres 1985, Commendatore, Ordine al Merito (Italy) 1998; Chevalier, Légion d'honneur 2000. *Publications:* American Art at Harvard 1973, Selections from the James Michener Collection 1975, Abstract Expressionists and Imagists: A Retrospective View 1976, Milton Avery 1976, The James A.

Michener Collection (catalogue) 1978, Thomas Cole monograph 1990. *Address:* Office of the Director, National Gallery of Art, 2000B South Club Drive, Landover, MD 20785, USA.

POWELL, Jonathan Leslie; British television producer; b. 25 April 1947, Faversham, Kent; s. of James Dawson Powell and Phyllis N. Sylvester (née Doubleday); m. Sally Brampton 1990; one d.; ed Sherborne School and Univ. of East Anglia; script and producer of drama, Granada TV 1970–77; producer, drama serials, BBC TV 1977–83, Head of Drama Series and Serials 1983–87; Controller BBC 1 1987–92; Dir Drama and Co-Production, Carlton TV 1993–; Royal TV Soc. Silver Award 1979–80. *Television includes:* Testament of Youth 1979 (BAFTA award), Tinker, Tailor, Soldier, Spy 1979, Pride and Prejudice 1980, The Bell 1982, Smiley's People 1982 (Peabody Medal, USA), The Old Men at the Zoo 1983, Bleak House 1985, Tender is the Night 1985, A Perfect Spy 1987. *Leisure interest:* fly-fishing. *Address:* c/o Carlton UK Television, 35–38 Portman Square, London, W1H 9FU (Office); 139 Randolph Avenue, Maida Vale, London, NW9, England (Home). *Telephone:* (20) 7486-6688 (Office).

POWELL, Jonathan Nicholas, MA; British political adviser; b. 14 Aug. 1956, Fulbeck; s. of Air Vice-Marshal John Frederick Powell and Geraldine Ysolda Powell; partner Sarah Helm; two s. two d.; ed Univ. Coll. Oxford, Univ. of Pennsylvania, USA; with BBC 1978, Granada TV 1978–79; joined FCO 1979, served in Lisbon 1980–83, FCO, London 1983–85, CSCE, Vienna 1985–89, FCO, London 1989–91, Washington 1991–95; Chief of Staff to Leader of the Opposition 1995–97, to Prime Minister May 1997–. *Leisure interests:* walking, skiing. *Address:* c/o 10 Downing Street, London, SW1A 2AA, England. *Telephone:* (20) 7270-3000.

POWELL, Michael James David, ScD, FRS; British mathematician; b. 29 July 1936; s. of William James David Powell and Beatrice Margaret Powell (née Page); m. Caroline Mary Henderson 1959; one s. (deceased) two d.; ed Eastbourne Coll. and Peterhouse, Cambridge; mathematician at AERE, Harwell 1959–76; John Humphrey Plummer Prof. of Applied Numerical Analysis, Cambridge Univ. 1976–2001, Prof. Emer. 2001–; Professorial Fellow, Pembroke Coll. 1978–; Foreigner Assoc. Nat. Acad. of Science, USA 2001–; Hon. DSc (Univ. of E Anglia) 2001; George B. Dantzig Prize in Math. Programming 1982, Naylor Prize, London Math. Soc. 1983, Gold Medal Inst. of Math. Applications 1996, Sr Whitehead Prize, London Math. Soc. 1999. *Publications:* Approximation Theory and Methods 1981; papers on numerical mathematics, especially approximation and optimization calculations. *Leisure interests:* golf, walking. *Address:* Department of Applied Mathematics and Theoretical Physics, University of Cambridge, Silver Street, Cambridge, CB3 9EW (Office); 134 Milton Road, Cambridge, CB4 1LE, England (Home).

POWELL, Michael K.; American lawyer; s. of Gen. Colin L. Powell (q.v.) and Alma V. Powell; m. Jane Knott Powell; two s.; ed Coll. of William and Mary and Georgetown Univ. Law Center; mil. service as Cavalry Platoon Leader and Troop Exec. Officer, 3/2 Armored Cavalry Reg., Amberg, Germany; fmr Policy Adviser to Sec. of Defense; fmr Judicial Clerk to Chief Judge of US Court of Appeals for DC Circuit; fmr Assoc., O'Melveny & Myers LLP, Washington; fmr Chief of Staff Antitrust Div., Dept of Justice; Chair. Fed. Communications Comm. Jan. 2001– (mem. 1997–), also Defense Chair.; mem. Bd of Visitors, Georgetown Univ. Law Center; Henry Crown Fellow, Aspen Inst. 1999. *Address:* Federal Communications Commission, 445 12th Street, SW, Washington, DC 20554, USA (Office). *Fax:* (202) 418-0232 (Office). *E-mail:* fccinfo@fcc.gov (Office).

POWELL, Mike; American athlete; b. 18 Nov. 1963, Philadelphia; ed Univ. of California; broke long jump world record (29ft. 4.5in.) at World Championships 1991 (still standing at Dec. 2002); world outdoor champion 1991, 1993; Olympic silver medallist 1988, 1992; U.S. outdoor champion (six times); retd after Olympic Games 1996; made winning comeback California Modesto Relays May 2001; volunteer Asst coach Calif. State-Fullerton; works with Olympic Aid Movt; Sullivan Award 1991. *Address:* USA Track and Field, 1 Rca Dome, Suite 140, Indianapolis, IN 46225-1023, USA (Office).

POWELL, Robert; British actor; b. 1 June 1944, Salford, Lancs.; s. of John W. Powell and Kathleen C. Powell; m. Barbara Lord 1975; one s. one d.; ed Manchester Grammar School; first job, Victoria Theatre, Stoke On Trent 1964; Hon. MA (Salford) 1990, Hon. DLitt (Salford) 2000; Best Actor, Paris Film Festival 1980, Venice Film Festival 1982. *Television roles include:* Doomwatch 1970, Jude the Obscure 1971, Jesus of Nazareth 1977, Pygmalion 1981, Frankenstein 1984, Hannay (series) 1988, The Sign of Command 1989, The First Circle 1990, The Golden Years 1992, The Detectives 1992–97. *Theatre roles include:* Hamlet 1971, Travesties (RSC) 1975, Terra Nova 1982, Private Dick 1982, Tovarich 1991, Sherlock Holmes 1992, Kind Hearts and Coronets 1998. *Films include:* Mahler 1974, Beyond Good and Evil 1976, Thirty Nine Steps 1978, Imperative 1981, Jigsaw Man 1982, Shaka Zulu 1985, D'Annunzio 1987, The Mystery of Edwin Drood 1993, The Sign of Command, Once on Chunuk Bair 1991. *Leisure interests:* golf, tennis, cricket, computers. *Address:* c/o Jonathan Altans Associates Ltd, 13 Shorts Gardens, London, WC2H 9AT, England. *Telephone:* (20) 7836-8722 (Office). *Fax:* (20) 7836-6066 (Office).

POWELL, Sandy; British costume and set designer; b. 7 April 1960; ed St Martin's Coll. of Art and Design, Cen. School of Art, London; Evening Standard Award for film of Edward II, Best Tech. Achievement Award, Evening Standard Award for Orlando 1994, Acad. Award for Shakespeare in

Love 1998, BAFTA Award for Velvet Goldmine 1998. *Designs:* costume designer for most shows by The Cholmondeleys and The Featherstonehaughs; stage sets include: Edward II (RSC), Rigoletto (Netherlands Opera) and Dr. Ox's Experiment (ENO); costumes for films include: The Last of England, Stormy Monday, The Pope Must Die, Edward II, Caravaggio, Venus Peter, The Miracle, The Crying Game, Orlando, Being Human, Interview with a Vampire, Rob Roy, Michael Collins, The Butcher Boy, The Wings of the Dove, Felicia's Journey, Shakespeare in Love, Velvet Goldmine, Hilary and Jackie, The End of the Affair, Miss Julie, Gangs of New York, Far From Heaven. *Address:* c/o PFD, Drury House, 34–43 Russell Street, London, WC2B 5HA, England. *Telephone:* (20) 7344-1000. *Fax:* (20) 7836-9543. *E-mail:* lmamy@pfd.co.uk (Office).

POWELL OF BAYSWATER, Baron (Life Peer), cr. 2000, of Bayswater; **Charles David Powell,** KCMG, BA; British fmr diplomatist, business executive and political adviser; b. 6 July 1941; s. of Air Vice-Marshal John Frederick Powell; m. Carla Bonardi 1964; two s.; ed King's School, Canterbury, New Coll. Oxford; Diplomatic Service 1963–83; Pvt. Sec. and Foreign Affairs Adviser to Prime Minister 1984–91; Sr Dir Jardine Matheson and assoc. cos. 1991–2000; Dir Nat Westminster Bank (Chair. Int. Advisory Bd 1991–2000, J. Rothschild Name Co. 1993–, LVMH Louis-Vuitton-Moët-Hennessy 1995– (Chair. LVMH (UK)), British Mediterranean Airways, Caterpillar Inc. 2001–, Textron Corpn 2001–; Chair. Singapore-British Business Council 1994–2001, Said Business School Foundation, Oxford Univ. 1997–, Sagitta Asset Man. Ltd 2001–; Pres. China-Britain Business Council 1993–; Trustee Aspen Inst. 1994–, British Museum 2002–; mem. Int. Advisory Council, Textron Corpn, European Advisory Bd Rolls-Royce, Int. Advisory Council Magna. *Address:* Fourth Floor, Berkeley Square House, Berkeley Square, London, W1J 6BL, England. *Telephone:* (20) 7543-1577 (Office). *Fax:* (20) 7543-1578 (Office).

POYNTER, John Riddoch, AO, OBE, PhD, FAHA, F.A.S.S.A.; Australian historian and university administrator; b. 13 Nov. 1929, Coleraine, Victoria; s. of Robert Poynter and Valetta Riddoch; m. 1st Rosslyn M. Rowell 1954 (divorced 1983); two d.; m. 2nd Marion Davidson 1984; ed Trinity Grammar School, Kew, Victoria, Trinity Coll. Univ. of Melbourne and Magdalen Coll. Oxford; Dean, Trinity Coll. Univ. of Melbourne 1953–64, Ernest Scott Prof. of History 1966–75, Dean, Faculty of Arts 1971–73, Pro Vice-Chancellor 1972–75, Deputy Vice-Chancellor (Research) 1975–82, Deputy Vice-Chancellor 1982–89, Deputy Vice-Chancellor (Academic) 1989–90, Dean, Faculty of Music, Visual and Performing Arts 1991–93, Asst Vice-Chancellor (Cultural Affairs) 1991–94, Prof. Emer. and Hon. Prof. Fellow 1995–; Nuffield Dominion Travelling Fellow, London and Oxford 1959; Visiting Fellow, ANU 1968, Carnegie Fellow, Fulbright Grant, USA 1968; Section Ed. Australian Dictionary of Biography 1972–90; Australian Sec. Rhodes Trust 1974–97; Chair. Melbourne Univ. Press 1976–88; mem. Bd Australian-American Educ. Foundation 1977–84; Rhodes Scholar 1951; Hon. Professorial Fellow, Australian Centre; Chevalier, Ordre des Palmes Académiques. *Publications:* Russell Grimwade 1967, Society and Pauperism 1969, A Place Apart 1996, Doubts and Certainties 1997. *Leisure interest:* music. *Address:* The University of Melbourne, Parkville, Vic. 3052 (Office); 38 Brougham Street, North Melbourne, Vic. 3051, Australia (Home). *Telephone:* (3) 8344-7202 (Office); (3) 9329-8163 (Home). *Fax:* (3) 9349-3371 (Office).

POYNTZ, Rt Rev Samuel Greenfield, MA, BD, PhD; Irish ecclesiastic; b. 4 March 1926, Manitoba, Canada; s. of Rev. James Poyntz and Catherine Greenfield; m. Noreen H. Armstrong 1952; one s. two d.; ed Portora Royal School, Enniskillen and Trinity Coll. Dublin; curate, St George, Dublin 1950–52, Bray 1952–55, St Michan and St Paul, Dublin 1955–59; Incumbent, St Stephen, Dublin 1959–67, St Ann, Dublin 1967–70, St Ann with St Stephen, Dublin 1970–78; Archdeacon of Dublin 1974–78; Examining Chaplain to the Archbishop of Dublin 1974–78; Bishop of Cork, Cloyne and Ross 1978–87; Bishop of Connor 1987–95; Chair. Irish Council of Churches 1986–88; Co-Chair. Irish Inter Church Meeting 1986–88; Vice-Pres. British Council of Churches 1987–90; DLitt hc (Univ. of Ulster) 1995. *Publications:* The Exaltation of the Blessed Virgin Mary 1953, Journey Towards Union 1975, Our Church–Praying with our Church Family 1983; contrib. A Tapestry of Beliefs 1998, Many for Earth and Heaven 2002. *Leisure interests:* stamp collecting, rugby football, travel, walking. *Address:* 10 Harmony Hill, Lisburn, Co. Antrim, BT27 4EP, Northern Ireland. *Telephone:* (28) 9267-9013.

POŽELA, Juras, D.PHYS.; Lithuanian physicist; b. 5 Dec. 1925, Moscow; s. of Karolis Požela and Eugenija Tautkaitė; m. Rima Poželienė 1953; one s. one d.; ed Vilnius State Univ. and Moscow M. Lomonosov Univ.; Researcher, Sr Researcher, Sector Man., Dir Inst. of Physics and Math., Lithuanian Acad. of Sciences 1952–67; Dir Semiconductor Physics Inst. 1967–85, Sr Researcher 1996–; mem. Seimas (Parl.) 1992–96; Academician Lithuanian Acad. of Sciences 1968, Pres. 1984–92; mem. USSR (now Russian) Acad. of Sciences 1984, European Acad. of Sciences and Arts 1991, Academia Europaea 1993; Lenin Prize 1978, Hero of Socialist Labour 1985, USSR State Prize 1988, Lithuanian State Prizes 1965, 1982, Lithuanian Merited Scientist 1965, 3rd Order of Grand Duke Gediminas (Lithuania) 1996. *Publications include:* Plasma and Current Instabilities in Semiconductors 1981, Physics of High Speed Transistors 1993; over 200 articles, 9 monographs; about 100 inventions. *Leisure interests:* hunting, chess. *Address:* Lithuanian Academy of Sciences, Gedimino Prospect 3, Vilnius 2600; Semiconductor Physics Insti-

tute, A. Goštauto 11, Vilnius 2600 (Office); M. Paco 7/2, apt. 7, 2055 Vilnius, Lithuania (Home). *Telephone:* (2) 62-71-22 (Office); (2) 72-70-22 (Home). *Fax:* (2) 62-71-23 (Office). *E-mail:* pozela@uj.pfi.lt (Office).

POZNER, Vladimir Gerald Dmitri Vladimirovich; Russian broadcaster; b. 1 April 1934, Paris; m. 1st (divorced); one d.; m. 2nd Yekaterina Orlova; ed Moscow Univ.; worked as trans. of medical biological literature, literary sec. of poet Samuel Marshak 1959–61; Sr Ed., Exec. Sec. Soviet Life 1961–67, Sputnik 1967–70; commentator USA and Britain Broadcasting Service of USSR TV and Radio Cttee 1970–86; political observer Cen. TV 1986–91; author of film scripts; Pres. Acad. of Russian TV 1996–; Communicator of the Year Prize of Soviet Journalists' Union 1986; Communicator of the Year Medal of the Better World Soc. (with Phil Donahue). *Television shows:* regular appearances in Pozner-Donahue show, Multimedia Entertainment Inc. (USA) 1991–95; Meetings with Vladimir Pozner (Moscow Channel, Russia) 1991–94, If 1995, We 1995–2000, Man in a Mask 1996–99, Time and US 1998–2000, Times 2000–. *Publications:* Parting with Illusions 1990, Remembering War (with E. Keyssar 1990), Eyewitness 1991, numerous articles in Russian and American newspapers and magazines. *Telephone:* (095) 202-71-61 (Moscow), (212) 355-3454 (New York). *Fax:* (95) 230-29-41 (Moscow), (212) 644-1193 (New York).

POZO CRESPO, Mauricio, MEconSci; Ecuadorean politician, banker and economist; ed Pontificia Univ. Católica del Ecuador, Univ. of Colorado, Univ. of Notre Dame, USA; Dir Stock Exchange, Quito; Dir Chamber of Commerce, Quito; Dir Seguros Equinoccial; Tech. Co-ordinator, Ecuadorean Sub-cttee, Pacific Econ. Co-operation Council (PECC); Pres. Investments Tech. Cttee, Inst. Ecuatoriano de Seguridad Social (IESS); Dir Tech. Div., Cen. Bank of Ecuador; Pres. Monetary Council 1981–91; Prof. of Econs, Pontificia Univ. Católica del Ecuador 1987–, Monterrey Tech. Inst. 1987–; Pres. Magna Credit Card 1991–93; Vice-Pres. Produbanco 1993–2000; Pres. Multienlace 2001–02; Minister of Economy and Finance 2003–. *Address:* Ministry of Economy and Finance, Avda 10 de Agosto 1661 y Jorge Washington, Quito, Ecuador (Office). *Telephone:* (2) 254-4500 (Office). *Fax:* (2) 253-0703 (Office). *Website:* www.minfinanzas.ec-gov.net (Office).

PRABHAKARAN, Vellupillai; Sri Lankan resistance leader; b. 26 Nov. 1954, Velvettithurai, Jaffna Penninsula; m. Mathy Parabhakaran 1984; two s. one d.; participated in Tamil protest movt. 1970s, Founder and Leader Liberation Tigers of Tamil Eelam (LTTE); accused of involvement with murder of Mayor of Jaffna 1975, Indian Prime Minister Rajiv Gandhi 1991; waged civil war against Sri Lankan Govt for 20 years with objective of securing ind. state for Tamil people.

PRABHJOT KAUR; Indian poet and politician; b. Matia, 6 July 1924, Langaryal; d. of Nidhan Singh and Rajinder Kaur; m. Brig. Narenderpal Singh 1948; two d.; ed Khalsa Coll. for Women, Lahore and Punjab Univ.; first collected poems published 1943 (aged sixteen); represented India at numerous int. literary confs; mem. Legis. Council, Punjab 1966; Ed. Vikendrit; mem. Sahitya Akademi (Nat. Acad. of Letters), later Bd 1978; mem. Cen. Comm. for UNESCO, Nat. Writers Cttee of India; Fellow Emer., Govt of India; received honours of Sahitya Shiromani 1964 and Padma Shri 1967; title of Rajya Kavi (Poet Laureate) conferred by Punjab Govt 1964, Sahitya Akademi Award 1964, Golden Laurel Leaves, United Poets Int., Philippines 1967, Grand Prix de la Rose de la France 1968, Most Distinguished Order of Poetry, World Poetry Soc. Intercontinental, USA 1974; Woman of the Year, UPLI, Philippines 1975, Sewa Sifti Award 1980, NIF Cultural Award 1982, Josh Kenya Award 1982, Delhi State Award 1983, Safdar Hashmi Award. *Television:* Ishak Shara Kee Nata (musical play). *Publications:* 50 books, including: Poems: Supne Sadhran 1949, Do Rang 1951, Pankheru 1956, Lala (in Persian) 1958, Bankapasi 1958, Pabbi 1962, Khari 1967, Plateau (French) 1968, Wad-darshi Sheesha 1972, Madhiantar 1974, Chandra Yug 1978, Dreams Die Young 1979, Shadows and Light (Bulgarian) 1980, Him Hans 1982, Samrup 1982, Ishq Shara Ki Nata 1983, Shadows (English and Danish) 1985, Charam Serma, Men Tapu Mukhatab Han–Manas Man the Gagan Mokla (collected poems in four vols); Short Stories: Kinke 1952, Aman de Na 1956, Zindgi de Kujh Pal 1982, Main Amanat Naheen (Hindi), Kuntith, Casket (English); autobiog.: Jeena vi 9k Ada Hai (two vols). *Leisure interests:* reading, travel. *Address:* D-203, Defence Colony, New Delhi 110024, India. *Telephone:* 4622756; 4626045.

PRADA, Michel André Jean Edmond; French civil servant; b. 2 April 1940, Bordeaux; s. of Robert Prada and Suzanne (née Bouffard) Prada; m. Annick Saudubray 1963; two s. three d.; ed Lycée Montesquieu Bordeaux, Faculté de Droit et Inst. d'Etudes Politiques de Bordeaux, Ecole Nat. d'Admin.; Inspecteur des Finances with Ministry of Econ. and Finance 1966–; Chargé de Mission, Inspection Générale des Finances 1969; Chargé de Mission, Direction de la Comptabilité Publique 1970, Asst Director 1974, Head of Service 1977, Dir de la Comptabilité Publique 1978–85; Dir of Budget, Ministry of the Economy, Finance and the Budget 1986–88; Chair. Bd Dirs Crédit d'équipement des petites et moyennes entreprises (CEPME) 1988–; Chair. Comm. des Opérations de Bourse 1995–2002; Chair. Orchestre de Paris 1989–2000, Inst. d'Etudes Politiques de Bordeaux 1989–, Exec. Cttee Int. Org. of Securities Comms. (IOSCO) 1996–98, Tech. Cttee of IOSCO 1998–2001; fmr mem. Econ. and Social Council, Nat. Credit Council; Commdr, Légion d'honneur, Commdr, Ordre nat. du Mérite. *Address:* Teledoc

335, 139 rue de Bercy, 75572 Paris Cedex 12 (Office); 2 rue Cart, 94160 Saint-Mandé, France (Home). *Telephone:* 1-53-18-38-60. *Fax:* 1-53-18-95-62. *E-mail:* michel.prada@igf.finances.gouv.fr.

PRADA, Miuccia, PhD; Italian fashion designer; b. 1950; d. of Luisa Prada; m. Patrizio Bertelli; c.; ed Teatro Piccolo, Milan; Head of Prada since 1979, launched collection of women's clothing 1988, Miu Miu collection 1992, men's collection 1994. *Address:* Prada, 2 via Andrea Maffei, 20135 Milan, Italy (Office). *Telephone:* (02) 76001426 (Office). *Website:* www.prada.com (Office).

PRADHAN, Om, BA; Bhutanese diplomatist and politician; b. 6 Oct. 1946; m.; three c.; ed Delhi Univ.; various posts in Ministry of Trade, Industry and Forests 1969–80; Perm. Rep. to the UN 1980–84, Amb. to India (also Accred to Nepal and Maldives) 1984–85, Head Bhutanese Del. to first and second rounds of boundary talks with China; Deputy Minister Ministry of Trade and Industry 1985–89, Head Del. to fifth round of boundary talks with China: Minister for Trade and Industry 1989–98; Perm. Rep. to the UN 1998–; mem. Nat. Ass., Council of Ministers; Chair. State Trading Corpn Chukha Hydro-electric Project Corpn and Tala Hydroelectric Project Authority; mem. Planning Comm., Nat. Environment Comm. *Address:* Permanent Mission of Bhutan to the United Nations, 2 United Nations Plaza, 27th Floor, New York, NY 10017, USA (Office). *Telephone:* (212) 826-1919 (Office). *Fax:* (212) 826-2998 (Office). *E-mail:* bhutan@un.int (Office).

PRADHAN, Trilochan, PhD; Indian scientist; b. 3 Jan. 1929, Ghanashalia, Orissa; s. of Ramachandra and Ahalya Dakshinaray; m. Sanjukta Pradhan 1959; one s. one d.; ed Utkal Univ., Benares Hindu Univ. and Univ. of Chicago; Lecturer in Physics, Ravenshaw Coll. Cuttack 1951–62; Assoc. Prof. Saha Inst. of Nuclear Physics, Calcutta 1962–67, Prof. and Head, Div. of Theoretical Nuclear Physics 1967–74; Dir Inst. of Physics, Bhubaneshwar 1974–89, Prof. Emer. 1989–; Vice-Chancellor, Utkal Univ. 1989–91; Meghnad Saha Award 1980, Padma Bhusan Award 1990. *Publications:* about 60 papers on theoretical physics in the areas of elementary particles, atomic physics, plasma physics. *Leisure interests:* gardening, indoor games. *Address:* Institute of Physics, Bhubaneswar 751005, India; 71Gajapatinagar, Bhubaneswar 751005. *Telephone:* (674) 581770. *Fax:* (674) 581142.

PRADIER, Henri Joseph Marie; French engineer; b. 5 Nov. 1931, Sainte-Colombe-lès-Vienne, Rhône; s. of Camille Pradier and Anne-Marie Côte; m. 1st Marie-France Michot (deceased); two s.; m. 2nd Brigitte Dapvril 1973; one s. one d.; ed Institution Robin, Vienne, Lycée du Parc, Lyons and Ecole Polytechnique; Consulting Engineer 1955–58; Shell Française 1958–67 and 1970–; Man. Dir Shell du Maroc 1967–79, Vice-Pres. Distribution 1975–84; Man. Dir Shell Française 1984–92, now Hon. Pres.; Dir Société pour l'Utilisation Rationnelle des Gaz (Butagaz) 1975, Shell Chimie 1984, Hosp. Works Française de L'Ordre de Malte (OHFOM) 1992–95, St Joseph and St Luke Hospital, Lyon 1994–97, Publicis 1998–; Chevalier Légion d'honneur, Officer, Order of Orange-Nassau (Netherlands). *Leisure interests:* gardening, sailing, swimming. *Address:* 52 rue du Ranelagh, 75016 Paris, France.

PRAKKE, Lucas, LLD; Netherlands professor of law; b. 20 Feb. 1938, Groningen; m. Margaretha M. O. de Bruijn Kops 1965; two s.; ed Gemeentelijk Lyceum, Doetinchem, Univ. of Amsterdam and Columbia Univ. Law School, New York; Asst Prof. of Law, Univ. of Amsterdam 1963–72, Prof. of Dutch and Comparative Constitutional Law 1972–2003, Dean, Faculty of Law 1981–83, Prof. Emer. 2003–; Judge, Civil Service Appeal Tribunal 1977–89; mem. Royal Comm. on Constitution 1982–85; mem. Royal Netherlands Acad. *Publications:* Principles of Constitutional Interpretation in the Netherlands 1970, Toetsing in het publiekrecht 1972, Pluralisme en staatsrecht 1974, Het bestuursrecht van de landen of the Europese Gemeenschappen 1986, Bedenkingen tegen het toetsingsrecht (Report of Netherlands Lawyers' Asscn) 1992, Swamping the Lords, Packing the Court, Sacking the King: Address on 'dies natalis' of University of Amsterdam 1994, Handboek van het Nederlandse staatsrecht 1995, Het staatsrecht van de landen van de Europese Unie (5th edn) 1998, Pluralisme van Staatsrecht 2003. *Leisure interests:* history, music, walking. *Address:* Faculteit der Rechtsgeleerdheid, universiteit van Amsterdam, Postbus 1030, 1000 BA Amsterdam (Office); Koedijklaan 15, 1406 KW Bussum, Netherlands (Home). *Telephone:* (20) 5253966 (Office); (35) 6989520 (Home). *Fax:* (35) 6989501 (Home).

PRAMOEDYA ANANTA TOER; Indonesian novelist; b. 20 Feb. 1925, Blora, East Java; worked with Domei Japanese news agency to 1945; studied as stenographer; wrote first book Sepulah Kepala Nika (Ten Chiefs of Nika), Jakarta 1945; manuscript lost before printing; 2nd Lt, Indonesian revolution, Bekasi, east of Jakarta; with Voice of Free Indonesia producing Indonesian language magazine; arrested by Dutch July 1947; wrote first maj. works in Bukit Duri gaol; ed Indonesian Library of Congress after release to 1951; arrested on order of Gen. A. H. Nasution in connection with book on overseas Chinese 1960; released 1961; aligned with communist-sponsored cultural groups; leading figure in Lekkra, Indonesian Communist Party cultural Asscn; arrested Nov. 1966; with first political prisoners on Buni island; released Jan. 1980; 7 novels (one published so far), one drama and 2 minor works composed in prison, Buni 1966–80; novels banned May 1981; Ramon Magsaysay Award for Journalism 1995. *Novels include:* Keluarga Guerilya, Bumi Manusia (The World of Man) 1973, Anak Seluruh Bangsa (A Child of All Nations), Jajak Langkah (Strides Forward), Bumah Kaca (The Greenhouse), The Buru Tetralogy, House of Glass.

PRANCE, Sir Ghillean Tolmie, Kt, DPhil, FRS; British botanist; b. 13 July 1937, Brandeston, Suffolk; s. of Basil Camden Prance and Margaret Hope Prance (née Tolmie); m. Anne Elizabeth Hay 1961; two d.; ed Malvern Coll., Keble Coll. Oxford; Research Asst, The New York Botanical Garden 1963–66, Assoc. Curator 1966–68, Krukoff Curator of Amazonian Botany 1968–75, Dir of Botanical Research 1975–81, Vice-Pres. 1977–81, Sr Vice-Pres. 1981–88, Dir Inst. of Economic Botany 1981–88; Dir Royal Botanic Gardens, Kew 1988–99; Dir of Research, The Eden Project 1999–; McBryde Prof. Nat. Tropical Botanical Garden 2000–; Adjunct Prof., City Univ. of New York 1968–99; Dir of Graduate Studies, Instituto Nacional de Pesquisas da Amazônia, Brazil 1973–75; Exec. Dir Org. for Flora Neotropica 1975–88; Visiting Prof. in Tropical Studies, Yale Univ. 1983–88; Visiting Prof., Reading Univ. 1988–; Chair. Bentham-Moxon Trust 1988–99, Brazilian Atlantic Rainforest Trust 1999–, Global Diversity Foundation 1999–; Pres. Linnean Soc. of London 1997–2000; Trustee Au Sable Inst. of Environmental Studies 1984–, Margaret Mee Amazon Trust 1988–96, Worldwide Fund for Nature Int. 1989–93, Horniman Museum 1990–99; Pres. Asscn of Tropical Biology 1979–80, American Asscn of Plant Taxonomists 1984–85, Systematics Asscn 1988–91, Inst. of Biology 2000–02; mem. Bd of Govs. Lovaine Trust Co. Ltd 1989–99; Council mem. Royal Horticultural Soc. 1990–2000; Corresp. mem. Botanical Soc. of America 1994; Hon. mem. British Ecological Soc. 1996–; Fil. Dr. hc (Göteborg) 1983; DSc hc (Univ. of Kent at Canterbury) 1994, (Portsmouth) 1994, (Kingston) 1994, (St Andrews) 1995, (City Univ., New York) 1998, Dr. hc (Bergen) 1996, (Sheffield) 1997, (Florida) 1997, (Liverpool) 1998, (Glasgow) 1999, (Plymouth) 1999, (Keele) 2000, (Exeter) 2000; Henry Shaw Medal, Missouri Botanical Garden 1988, Linnean Medal 1990, Int. Cosmos Prize 1993, Patron's Medal (Royal Geographical Soc.) 1994, Asa Gray Award (American Soc. of Plant Taxonomists) 1998, Int. Award of Excellence (Botanical Research Inst. of Tex.) 1998, Lifetime Discovery Award 1999, Victoria Medal of Honour, Royal Horticultural Soc. 1999, Fairchild Medal for Botanical Exploration 2000, Commendador da Ordem Nacional do Cruzeiro do Sul (Brazil) 2000, Soc. for Econ. Botany Award 2002. *Television:* Superteacher (NHK, Japan) 2002. *Publications:* Arvores de Manaus 1975, Extinction is Forever 1977, Biological Diversification in the Tropics 1981, Amazonia–Key Environments 1985, Tropical Forests and World Climate 1986, Leaves 1986, White Gold 1989, Wildflowers for All Seasons 1989, Out of the Amazon 1992, Bark 1993, Rainforests of the World 1998; Ed. 13 books; numerous scientific and gen. articles. *Leisure interests:* bird watching, stamp collecting. *Address:* The Eden Project, Bodelva, Cornwall, PL24 2SG (Office); The Old Vicarage, Silver Street, Lyme Regis, Dorset, DT7 3HS, England. *Telephone:* (1726) 811900 (Office); (1297) 444991 (Home). *Fax:* (1297) 444955 (Home). *E-mail:* gprance@edenproject.com (Office); gtolmiep@aol.com (Home).

PRAPAS CHARUSATHIRA, General (see Charusathira, General Prapas).

PRASAD, Ashoka, MD, FRHistS; Indian psychiatrist and university professor; b. 10 May 1955, Patna; s. of the late Judge Jahnavi Prasad and Usha Prasad; ed Colvin Taluqdar's Coll., Lucknow, GSVM Medical Coll. Kanpur; Resident in Paediatrics and Psychiatry, Castlebar Gen. Hosp., Eire, Resident in Psychiatry, Royal Edin. Hosp., Edin. 1980–83; Research Fellow, Depts of Biochem. and Psychiatry, Univ. of Leeds 1983–85; Kate Stillman Lecturer in Psychiatry, Univ. Coll. Hosp. and Queen Charlotte's Hosp., London 1984–86; Consultant Psychiatrist, Whipps Cross Hosp., Claybury Hosp. and Thorpe Coombe Hosp., London 1986–87; in charge of Psychopharmacology and Hon. Sr Lecturer, Mental Health Research Inst. and Monash Univ., Melbourne, Australia, Assoc. Dept of Psychiatry, Univ. of Melbourne 1987; Visiting Specialist, Kingseat Hosp., NZ 1988; Consultant Psychiatrist, Claybury Hosp., London and St Margaret's Hosp., Essex 1988–89; at Dept of Psychiatry, Dalhousie Univ., Canada, Dept of Psychology, St Mary's Univ., Canada 1989; J. Ernest Runions Fellow, Dept of Psychiatry, Univ. of BC, Vancouver 1989–90; Prof. of Psychiatry, Hahnemann Univ., Phila, USA 1990–91; Adjunct Prof. of Medical Anthropology, Columbia Univ., USA 1990–91, of Anthropology, Univ. of Pa 1991; Medical Dir Phila Consultation Center 1990–92; currently hon. consultant to several bodies, including Jain TV, India, for medical programmes, Hon. Adviser 1993–; several visiting professorships including Harvard Univ. 1986, 1991; Foreign Academician Royal Swedish Acad. of Sciences; Hon. Foreign mem. American Acad. of Arts and Sciences; Dr Med hc (Natal), (Karolinska Inst. Stockholm); Murphy Award 1987, Blueler Award 1987. *Publications:* five books including Biological Basis and Therapy of Neuroses; over 125 publns in various journals. *Leisure interests:* bird-watching, unravelling Greek myths, cricket, history of science and medicine, naturopathy. *Address:* 1 Avas Vikas, Betia Hata, Gorakhpur 273001, India. *Telephone:* (551) 334020. *Fax:* (551) 332845. *E-mail:* ashokaprasad@rediffmail.com (Home).

PRASAD, Mahabir, MA, LLB; Indian politician; b. b. 11 Nov. 1939, Ujjarpur Village, Uttar Pradesh; s. of Amar Prasad; m. Udasi Devi; two d.; Gen. Sec., Gorakhpur Uttar Pradesh Congress Cttee 1975–78 (fmr Vice-Pres. and three-times Pres.); fmr Gen. Sec. All-India Congress Cttee; mem. Uttar Pradesh Ass. 1974–77, Lok Sabha 1980, 1984, 1989, Estimates Cttee 1985–86; Deputy Minister for Railways 1986–89; Minister of State for Steel and Mines July–Nov. 1989; Gov. of Haryana 1995–2000. *Address:* Raj Bhavan, Haryana, Chandigarh, India (Office).

PRASAD, Mata; Indian politician; b. 11 Oct. 1925, Machi Shahar; s. of Rajji Devi and Jagarup Devi; m. Lekhraji Mata Prasad; three s. two d.; ed Sahitya Ratna; mem. Uttar Pradesh Ass. 1957–77, Legis. Council 1980–92; Gen. Sec. Uttar Pradesh Congress Cttee 1971–73, 1980–82; mem. Uttar Pradesh

Congress Legislature Party 1982–86, Treasurer 1986–92; Cabinet mem. 1988–89; Chair. Uttar Pradesh Congress Cttee SC/ST 1982–88; apptd. Gov. of Arunachal Pradesh 1993; fmr Vice-Pres. Al Dalit Sahitya Acad.; Sec. Uttar Pradesh Dalit Varg Sangh; mem. Housing and Devt Bd and Minority Comm., Uttar Pradesh. *Address:* Shekhpura, P.O. Box Kacheheri, P.S. Line Bazar, Jaunpur District, Uttar Pradesh, India (Home). *Telephone:* 22414 (Home).

PRASAD, Siddheshwar, DLitt; Indian politician; b. 19 June 1929, Bind; s. of Bhikari Mahton; m. Rajkumari Prasad; six c.; lecturer Nalanda Coll., Biharsharif 1953–61; mem. Lok Sabha 1962–77; Deputy Minister for Irrigation and Power 1967–71, for Industrial Devt 1971–73, for Heavy Industry Feb.–Nov. 1973, for Irrigation 1973–74, for Energy 1974–77; Minister, Govt of Bihar 1985–88; Gov. of Tripura 1995–99; Chair. Gandhi-Marx Research Inst.; Exec. Chair. Rashtra Bhasha Prachar Samiti; Sec.-Gen. Third World Hindi Conf. *Publications:* Chhayavadottar Kavya, Satyagraha Aur Vigyan, Sahitya Ka Muyankan, Upanishad Chintan Aur Adhunik Jiwan, Ekalavyon Aur Abimanyuon Se, Multi-Dimensional Transformation, Vichar Pravah, New Economic Policy, The Vedic Vision. *Address:* Sector 7, Block 1, 23 Bahadurpur HIG Cology, Kankarbagh, Patna, 800020, India (Office).

PRASAD, Sunand, MA, PhD; Indian architect; b. 22 May 1950, Dehra Dun, India; m. Susan Francis; three c.; ed Cambridge School of Architecture, Architectural Asscn, Royal Coll. of Art; partner in Edward Cullinan Architects 1976–85; Leverhulme Research Fellow RCA 1985–88; founding partner Penoyre & Prasad Architects 1988–; Vice-Pres. Architectural Asscn 1999–2001; Chair. RIBA Constructive Change Cttee 1999–2001; Commr Comm. for Architecture and the Built Environment 1999–; Eternit Award for Architecture 1989, RIBA Regional Award 1991, 1992, Lewes Dist Council Design Award, UCB Care Home Award, RIBA Award 1997, 2000, American Inst. of Architects/UK Excellence in Design Award 1998, Design Sense 1999, 7 winning design competition entries 1995–99. *Publications:* Accommodating Diversity: Housing Design in a Multi-Cultural Society 1998, Paradigms of Indian Architecture 1998. *Leisure interests:* music, sail boarding. *Address:* Penoyre & Prasad, 28–42 Banner Street, London, EC1Y 8QE (Office); 97A Shepherdess Walk, London, N1 7QD, England (Home). *Telephone:* (20) 7250-3477 (Office); (20) 7251-4218 (Home). *Fax:* (20) 7250-0844 (Office). *E-mail:* mail@penoyre-prasad.net (Office).

PRASHAR, Usha Kumari, Baroness (Life Peer), cr. 1999, of Runnymede in the County of Surrey, CBE, BA, FRSA; British civil servant; b. 29 June 1948, Nairobi, Kenya; d. of Nauhria Lal Prashar and Durga Devi Prashar; m. Vijay Kumar Sharma 1973; ed Duchess of Gloucester School, Nairobi, Wakefield Girl's High School, Univ. of Leeds, Univs of Leeds and Glasgow; Conciliation Officer, Race Relations Bd 1971–75; Asst Dir Runnymede Trust 1975–77, Dir 1977–84; Residential Fellow, Policy Studies Inst. 1984–86 (mem. Council 1992–97); Dir Nat. Council for Voluntary Orgs 1986–91; Civil Service Commr (part-time) 1990–96, First Civil Service Commr 2000–; Chair. Parole Bd of England and Wales 1997–2000; Deputy Chair. Nat. Literacy Trust 1992–2000, Chair. 2001–; Dir (non-exec.) Channel 4 1992–99, Unite PLC 2001–; Vice-Chair. British Refugee Council 1987–89; mem. Arts Council of GB 1979–81, Arts Council of England 1994–97, Study Comm. on the Family 1980–83, Social Security Advisory Cttee 1980–83, Exec. Cttee., Child Poverty Action Group 1984–85, Greater London Arts Asscn 1984–86, London Food Comm. 1984–90, BBC Educational Broadcasting Council 1987–89, Advisory Council, Open Coll. 1987–89, Solicitors' Complaints Bureau 1989–90, Royal Comm. on Criminal Justice 1991–93, Lord Chancellor's Advisory Cttee on Legal Educ. and Conduct 1991–97, Bd Energy Saving Trust 1992–98, King's Fund 2000–, Jt Cttee on Human Rights; Trustee Thames Help Trust 1984–86, Charities Aid Foundation 1986–91, Ind. Broadcasting Telethon Trust 1987–92, Acad. of Indian Dance 1987–91, Camelot Foundation 1996–, Ethnic Minority Foundation 2000–; Chair. English Advisory Cttee, Nat. AIDS Trust 1988–89; Patron Sickle Cell Soc. 1986–, Elfrida Rathbone Soc. 1988–; Chancellor De Montfort Univ. 2000– (Gov. 1996–); Hon. Vice-Pres. Council for Overseas Student Affairs 1986–; Hon. Fellow Goldsmiths' Coll., Univ. of London 1992; Hon. LLD (De Montfort) 1994, (South Bank) 1994, (Greenwich) 1999, (Leeds Metropolitan) 1999, (Ulster) 2000, (Oxford Brookes) 2000; Asian Women of Achievement Award 2002. *Publications include:* contribs to Britain's Black Population 1980, The System: A Study of Lambeth Borough Council's Race Relations Unit 1981, Scarman and After 1984, Sickle Cell Anaemia, Who Cares? A Survey of Screen, Counselling, Training and Educational Facilities in England 1985, Routes or Road Blocks, A Study of Consultation Arrangements Between Local Authorities and Local Communities 1985, Acheson and After: Primary Health Care in the Inner City 1986. *Leisure interests:* reading, music, golf, current affairs. *Address:* House of Lords, Westminster, London, SW1A 0PW, England (Office). *Website:* www .civilservicecommissioners.gov.uk.

PRATCHETT, Terry, OBE; British writer; b. 28 April 1948, Beaconsfield, Bucks.; m. Lyn Marian Purves 1968; one d.; journalist 1965–80; Press Officer Cen. Electricity Generating Bd 1980–87; Chair. Soc. of Authors 1994–95; Hon. DLitt (Warwick Univ.) 1999. *Publications:* The Carpet People 1971, The Dark Side of the Sun 1976, Strata 1981, The Colour of Magic 1983, The Light Fantastic 1986, Equal Rites 1987, Mort 1987, Sourcery 1988, Wyrd Sisters 1988, Pyramids 1989, Truckers 1989, Guards! Guards! 1989, The Unadulterated Cat 1989, Eric 1990, Good Omens (with Neil Gaiman) 1990, Moving Pictures, 1990, Diggers 1990, Wings 1990, Reaper Man 1991, Witches Abroad 1991, Small Gods 1992, Only You Can Save Mankind 1992, Lords and Ladies 1992, Johnny and the Dead 1993, Men At Arms 1993, Soul Music 1993, The Streets of Ankh-Morpork (with Stephen Briggs) 1993, The Discworld Companion (with Stephen Briggs) 1994, Interesting Times 1994, A Company Discworld 1995, Maskerade 1995, The Discworld Map (with Stephen Briggs) 1995, Johnny and the Bomb 1996, Feet of Clay 1996, Hogfather 1996, The Pratchett Portfolio (with Paul Kidby) 1996, Jingo 1997, The Last Continent 1998, A Tourist's Guide to Lancre (with Stephen Briggs) 1998, Carpe Jugulum 1998, Discworld Diary 1998, The Death Trilogy 1998, The Fifth Elephant 1999, Death Domain (with Paul Kidby) 1999, The Truth 2000, Thief of Time 2001, The Amazing Maurice and His Educated Parents (Carnegie Medal) 2002, Night Watch 2002. *Leisure interests:* astronomy, gardening, folklore. *Address:* c/o Colin Smythe, PO Box 6, Gerrards Cross, Bucks., SL9 8XA, England. *Telephone:* (1753) 886000.

PRATT, (John) Christopher, OC, CC, RCA, BFA; Canadian painter and printmaker; b. 9 Dec. 1935, St John's, Newfoundland; s. of John Kerr Pratt and Christine Emily (née Dawe) Pratt; m. Mary Frances West 1957; two s. two d.; ed Prince of Wales Coll., St John's, Newfoundland, Memorial Univ. of Newfoundland, Mount Allison Univ., Sackville, NB and the Glasgow School of Art, Scotland; taught as specialist in art, Memorial Univ. 1961–63; freelance artist 1963–; mem. Mount Carmel Town Council 1969–73, Postage Stamp Design Cttee, Ottawa 1970–73, The Canada Council 1976–82, Memorial Univ. Bd of Regents 1972–75; Hon. D. Litt. (Memorial) 1972, Hon. LLD (Mount Allison) 1973, (Dalhousie) 1986. *Exhibitions:* has exhibited widely in Europe and N America including a major retrospective organized by Vancouver Art Gallery 1985–86, 30th Anniversary Exhbn, Mira Godard Gallery, Toronto 1999. *Publications:* Christopher Pratt 1982, The Prints of Christopher Pratt (with Mira Godard) 1991, Christopher Pratt: Personal Reflections on a Life in Art 1995. *Leisure interests:* offshore sailing, walking and fly fishing. *Address:* P.O. Box 87, Mount Carmel, St Mary's Bay, Newfoundland, A0B 2M0, Canada. *Telephone:* (709) 521-2048 (Office); (709) 521-2048 (Home). *Fax:* (709) 521-2707 (Office).

PRAWER, Siegbert Salomon, MA, DLitt, PhD, LittD, FBA; British university teacher and author; b. 15 Feb. 1925, Cologne, Germany; s. of Marcus Prawer and Eleonora Prawer; brother of Ruth Prawer Jhabvala (q.v.); m. Helga Alice Schaefer 1949; one s. two d. (and one s. deceased); ed King Henry VIII School, Coventry, Jesus Coll., Christ's Coll. Cambridge; Adelaide Stoll Research Student, Christ's Coll. Cambridge 1947–48; Asst Lecturer, then Lecturer, then Sr Lecturer, Univ. of Birmingham 1948–63; Prof. of German, Westfield Coll., London Univ. 1964–69; Taylor Prof. of German Language and Literature, Oxford 1969–86, Prof. Emer. 1986–; Co-editor, Oxford Germanic Studies 1971–75, Anglica Germanica 1973–79; Visiting Prof. City Coll., New York 1956–57, Univ. of Chicago 1963–64, Harvard Univ. 1968, Hamburg Univ. 1969, Univ. of Calif. at Irvine 1975, Otago Univ., NZ 1976, Univ. of Pittsburgh 1977, Australian Nat. Univ., Canberra 1980, Brandeis Univ. 1981–82; Resident Fellow, Knox Coll., Dunedin, NZ 1976; Fellow Queen's Coll. Oxford 1969–86, Supernumerary Fellow 1986–90, Hon. Fellow 1990, Dean of Degrees 1976–93; Pres. British Comparative Literature Asscn 1984–87, Hon. Fellow 1989; Corresp. Fellow German Acad. of Literature 1989; Pres. English Goethe Soc. 1992–95, Vice-Pres. 1995–; Hon. Dir London Univ. Inst. of Germanic Studies 1967–69, Hon. Fellow 1986; Hon. mem. Modern Languages Asscn of America 1986; Hon. Fellow Jesus Coll. Cambridge 1996–; Hon. DPhil (Cologne) 1985; Hon. DLitt (Birmingham) 1988; Goethe Medal 1973, Gold Medal, German Goethe Soc. 1995; Isaac Deutscher Memorial Prize 1977, Gundolf-Prize of the German Acad. 1986. *Exhibitions:* drawings on exhbn Queen's Coll. and St Edmund Hall, Oxford and many other insts. *Publications:* German Lyric Poetry 1952, Mörike und seine Leser 1960, Heine's Buch der Lieder: A Critical Study 1960, Heine: The Tragic Satirist 1962, The Penguin Book of Lieder 1964, The Uncanny in Literature (inaugural lecture) 1965, Heine's Shakespeare, a Study in Contexts (inaugural lecture) 1970, Comparative Literary Studies: An Introduction 1973, Karl Marx and World Literature 1976, Caligari's Children: The Film as Tale of Terror 1980, Heine's Jewish Comedy: A Study of His Portraits of Jews and Judaism 1983, Coalsmoke and Englishmen 1984, A. N. Stencl–Poet of Whitechapel 1984, Frankenstein's Island–England and the English in the Writings of Heinrich Heine 1986, Israel at Vanity Fair: Jews and Judaism in the Writings of W. M. Thackeray 1992, Breeches and Metaphysics, Thackeray's German Discourse 1997, W. M. Thackeray's European Sketch Books: A Study of Literary and Graphic Portraiture 2000, The Blue Angel 2002; edited: Essays in German Language, Culture and Society (with R. H. Thomas and L. W. Forster) 1969, The Romantic Period in Germany 1970, Seventeen Modern German Poets 1971; screenplay: Das Kabinett des Dr Caligari (ed and introduction); numerous articles on German, English and comparative literature. *Leisure interest:* portrait drawing. *Address:* The Queen's College, Oxford, OX1 4AW (Office); 9 Hawkswell Gardens, Oxford, OX2 7EX, England (Home). *Telephone:* (1865) 279121 (Office); (1865) 557614 (Home).

PRAWIRO, Radius, MA; Indonesian politician, economist and banker; b. 29 June 1928, Yogjakarta; ed Senior High School, Yogjakarta, Nederlandsche Economische Hoogeschool, Rotterdam, Econ. Univ. of Indonesia; Sec. Defence Cttee, Yogjakarta during revolution 1945; with Army High Command, Yogjakarta 1946–47; Angauta Tentara Pelajar (Army) 1948–51; Officer in Govt Audit Office, Ministry of Finance 1953–65; Vice-Minister, Deputy Supreme Auditor, mem. Supreme Audit Office 1965–66; Gov. Bank Indonesia 1966–73; Chair. Indonesian Asscn of Accountants 1965–; Gov. IMF for Indonesia 1967–72, Alt. Gov. Asian Devt Bank 1967–72; Minister of Trade 1973–78, of Trade and Co-operatives 1978–83, of Finance 1983–88, Co-ordinating Minister of Econs, Finance, Industry and Devt Supervision 1988–93; Chair. Bd of Govs. IBRD, IDA, IFC 1971–72; mem. Econ. Council of the Pres. 1968, Nat. Econ. Stabilization Council 1968, Gov. Bd Christian Univ. of Indonesia, Supervisory Bd Trisakti Univ.; Order of Sacred Treasure. *Address:* Jalan Imam Bonjol 4, Jakarta, Indonesia (Home).

PRAT-GAY, Alfonso; Argentine central bank governor; ed Penn. Univ., USA; trained as economist; worked for macro-econ. consultancy, Buenos Aires –1991; country economist (Argentina), JP Morgan, NY 1994, Head of Emerging Market Proprietary Trading Desk, London –1999, Chief of Currency Strategy (cr. Liquidity and Credit Premia Index—LCPI), London 1999–2001; Prof. Univ. of Buenos Aires 2001–02; Gov. Cen. Bank of Argentina 2002–. *Address:* Banco Central de la Republica Argentina, Reconquista 266, 1003 Buenos Aires, Argentina (Office). *Telephone:* (11) 4348-3500 (Office). *Website:* www.bcra.gov.ar (Office).

PREBBLE, Mark, PhD; New Zealand civil servant; b. 12 May 1951, Auckland; s. of Archdeacon K. R. Prebble and Mary Prebble; brother of Richard William Prebble (q.v.); m. 1st Fenella Druce 1974 (died 1977); m. 2nd Lesley Bagnall 1978; two s. two d.; ed Auckland Grammar School, Auckland Univ. and Victoria Univ. of Wellington; with Treasury, Govt of NZ 1977–82, Dept of Labour 1982–85; Seconded to Prime Minister and Cabinet as Man. Change Team on Targeting Social Assistance 1991–92; Minister (Econ.) NZ High Comm., London 1992–93; Deputy Sec. of Treasury 1993–98; Chief Exec. Dept of Prime Minister and Cabinet 1998–. *Publications:* Smart Cards: Is it Smart to Use a Smart Card? 1990, Information, Privacy and the Welfare State 1990, Incentives and Labour Supply: Modelling Taxes and Benefits (ed., with P. Rebstock) 1992, New Zealand: The Turnaround Economy 1993 and articles in econ., public policy and educational journals. *Leisure interests:* walking, family and gardening. *Address:* Department of the Prime Minister and Cabinet, Parliament Buildings, Wellington, New Zealand. *Telephone:* (4) 471-9700. *Fax:* (4) 499-2109.

PREBBLE, The Hon. Richard William, CBE, BA, LLB; New Zealand politician and lawyer; b. 7 Feb. 1948, UK; s. of Archdeacon K. R. Prebble; brother of Mark Prebble (q.v.) ; m. 1st Nancy Prebble 1970; m. 2nd Doreen Prebble 1991; ed Auckland Boys' Grammar School, Auckland Technical Inst. and Auckland Univ.; admitted as barrister and solicitor, NZ Supreme Court 1971; admitted to Bar, Fiji Supreme Court 1973; MP for Auckland Cen. 1975–; Jr Opposition Whip 1978–79; Minister of Transport, of Railways, of Civil Aviation and Meteorological Services, of Pacific Island Affairs, Assoc. Minister of Finance 1984–87; Minister of State-Owned Enterprises, Postmaster-Gen., Minister of Works and Devt and Minister of Pacific Island Affairs 1987–88, of Railways, Police, State Owned Enterprises and Pacific Island Affairs Jan.–Oct. 1990; Leader ACT New Zealand 1996–. *Publications:* I've Been Thinking 1996, What Happens Next 1997, I've Been Writing. *Leisure interests:* Polynesian and Melanesian culture, opera, drama. *Address:* Parliament Buildings, Wellington, New Zealand (Office). *Telephone:* (4) 470-6638 (Office). *Fax:* (4) 473-3532 (Office). *E-mail:* richard.prebble@parliament.govt .nz (Office). *Website:* www.act.org.nz (Office).

PREBBLE, Stuart; British media executive; b. April 1951, London; s. of the late Dennis Stanley Prebble and Jean McIntosh; m.; one d.; ed Beckenham and Penge Grammar School for Boys, Newcastle Univ.; joined BBC as grad. trainee, worked as regional reporter for BBC TV in Newcastle; presenter for Granada TV; Deputy Ed. of World in Action (ITV) 1987, Ed. 1988 (fmr presenter and producer); Head of Granada's Regional Programmes 1990, Head of Factual Programmes 1992; Controller of Network Factual Programmes, ITV Network Centre 1993; CEO Granada Sky Broadcasting and Man. Dir of Channels and Interactive Media, Granada Media Group; CEO ONdigital PLC 1999–2002, ITV 2001–02; RTS Award for Best Factual Series 1995. *Publications:* A Power in the Land, The Lazarus File. *Leisure interests:* politics, cinema. *Address:* c/o ITV, 200 Gray's Inn Road, London, WC1X 8HF, England.

PREM CHAND, Lt.-Gen. D.; Indian army officer (retd) and United Nations official; b. 1916, Muzaffargarh (now West Pakistan); s. of the late Dewan Khem Chand and Mrs. Khem Chand; ed Govt Coll., Lahore and Staff Coll., Quetta; commissioned Indian Army 1937; served in Gen. Staff, Army HQ, New Delhi 1947, later apptd. Mil. Asst to Chief of Army Staff; commanded Regimental Centre of First Gurkha Rifles; Instructor, Defence Services Staff Coll., Wellington; subsequently apptd. Deputy Dir of Mil. Training, Dir of Personnel Services, Dir of Mil. Intelligence, New Delhi; Chief of Staff, HQ Western Command, Simla 1961, Commanded Brigade and Div. in Western Command; Gen.-Officer, Katanga Area, UN Operation in the Congo 1962–63; Commanded Div. in Eastern Command, Chief of Staff, HQ Eastern Command, Calcutta; Dir Gen. Nat. Cadet Corps; retd 1967 then held admin. post in industrial concern; Commdr UN Force in Cyprus (UNFICYP) 1969–76; UN Sec. Gen.'s. Rep. for Rhodesia 1977; UNTAG Force Commdr, Namibia 1989; Head of UN Transition Assistance Group, Namibia 1989; rank of Lt-Gen. 1974; Param Vishisht Seva Medal. *Leisure interests:* music and trekking. *Address:* c/o UN Information Centre, 55 Lodi Estate, New Delhi, India.

PREM TINSULANONDA, Gen.; Thai politician and army officer; b. 26 Aug. 1920; ed Suan Kularb School and Chulachomklao Royal Mil. Acad., Bangkok; started mil. career as Sub-Lt 1941; Commdr Cavalry HQ 1968; Commdr-Gen. 2nd Army Area 1974; Asst C-in-C Royal Thai Army 1977; Deputy Minister of Interior, Govt of Gen. Kriangsak Chomanan 1977; Minister of Defence 1979–87, later C-in-C; Prime Minister of Thailand 1980–88; Chair. Petroleum

Authority of Thailand (PTT) 1981; Ramathipbodi Order, King of Thailand, Seri Maharajah Mangku Negara (Malaysia) 1984. *Address:* c/o HM Privy Council, Grand Palace, Thanon Na Phra Lan, Bangkok 10200 (Office); 279 Sri Ayutthaya Road, Sisao Theves, Bangkok 10300, Thailand.

PRENDERGAST, Peter Thomas, DFA, MFA; Welsh painter and draughtsman; b. 27 Oct. 1946, Abertridwr; s. of Martin Prendergast and Mary Prendergast; m. Lesley A. Riding 1967; two s. two d.; ed Cwmaber Sec. School, Cardiff Coll. of Art, Slade School of Fine Art and Reading Univ.; part-time Lecturer, Liverpool Coll. of Art 1970–74; teacher, Ysgol Dyffryn Ogwen, Bethesda 1975–80; now part-time lecturer in Painting and Drawing at tech. coll.; comms for Rural Devt Body for Wales, Nat. Trust Gardens 1991, Nat. Museum of Wales; painting of Bethesda reproduced in book Green Bridge: Short Stories from Wales; included in book The New Wales; featured in TV film Conflicts 1991; commissioned to paint the gardens of Wales 1991–; included in exhbn 175 years of Agnews 1992; Travel Scholarship, Welsh Arts Council 1992; Govt scholarship to USA 1993; Hon. DLitt (Glamorgan) 1995; Singer Friedlander Watercolour Prize 1995. *Exhibitions:* one-man exhbns at Liverpool 1973, Bangor Univ. 1974, 1979, 1986, Welsh Arts Council Gallery 1975, Llandudno 1982, 1998, Durham 1982, Camden Arts Centre 1982, Swansea 1983, Bath 1987, Agnews, London 1993, Nat. Museum of Wales 1993, From Land and Sea, Scarborough, Swansea 1993, Boundary Gallery, London 1996, 1998, 2001, Martin Tinney Gallery, London 2000, Royal West of England Acad., Bristol 2000; group exhbns at Tate Gallery 1984, Rocks and Flesh at Norwich Art School Gallery 1985, Ways of Telling 1989, Natural Element 1989, Mixe 1990, Scarborough City Art Gallery 1991, Welsh art exhbn San Francisco 1993, Barcelona 1995, Nat. Museum of Wales 2000, Wexford Arts Centre, Ireland 2001 and elsewhere; represented in Group Wales Exhbn, Czechoslovakia 1986–87, Artists in the Parks, Victoria and Albert Museum, London, Experience of Landscape, Arts Council of GB touring exhbn. *Publications:* Road to Bethesda 1982, Hard Won Image 1984, Self Portrait 1988, Inspiration of Landscape 1989, From Land and Sea (with Len Tabner), The Gaze of Love 1998. *Leisure interests:* sport, music, reading. *Address:* c/o Agi Katz Fine Art, Boundary Gallery, 98 Boundary Road, London, NW8 0RH, England; Tan-y-Graig, Deiniolen, Caernarfon, LL55 3EE, North Wales. *Telephone:* (1248) 354683 (Caernarfon).

PRENDERGAST, Sir (Walter) Kieran, KCVO, CMG; British diplomatist; b. 2 July 1942, Campbeltown, Argyll; s. of the late Lt-Commdr J. H. Prendergast and Mai Hennessy; m. Joan Reynolds 1967; two s. two d.; ed Salesian Coll. Chertsey and St Edmund Hall, Oxford; Asst Pvt. Sec. to successive Secs of State, FCO 1976–78; has served at Istanbul, Ankara, Nicosia, The Hague, UK Mission to UN, New York and Tel-Aviv; seconded to staff of last gov. of Rhodesia (Lord Soames) during transition to independence in Zimbabwe; High Commr in Zimbabwe 1989–92, in Kenya 1992–95; Amb. to Turkey 1995–97; UN Under-Sec.-Gen. for Political Affairs 1997–. *Leisure interests:* family, reading, walking, wine. *Address:* United Nations, United Nations Plaza, New York, NY 10017, USA. *Telephone:* (212) 963-5055. *Fax:* (212) 963-5065.

PRESCOTT, John Barry, AC, BComm; Australian business executive; b. 22 Oct. 1940, Sydney; s. of John Norman Prescott and Margaret Ellen Brownie; m. Jennifer Mary Louise Cahill; one s. three d.; ed North Sydney Boys' High School, Univ. of New South Wales, Northwestern Univ. USA; Gen. Man. Transport, Broken Hill Proprietary Co. Ltd (BHP) 1982–87, Exec. Gen. Man. and CEO BHP Steel 1987–91, Dir BHP 1988–98, Man. Dir and CEO BHP 1991–98; Chair. Horizon Pvt. Equity 1998–2002; Dir Tubemakers 1988–92, Normandy Mining 1999–2001, Newmont Mining Corpn 2002–; mem. Advisory Bd Booz Allen 1991–; mem. Defence Industry Cttee 1988–93, Bd, Business Council of Australia 1995–97; Chair. Mfg Council 1990–95; Patron Australian Quality Council 1990–; mem. Int. Council of JP Morgan 1994–, Asia Pacific Advisory Cttee of New York Stock Exchange 1995–, Council of World Econ. Forum 1996–98, Bd of The Walter and Eliza Hall Inst. of Medical Research 1994–98, Bd of Trustees, The Conf. Bd 1995–2001. *Leisure interests:* tennis, golf. *Address:* Horizon Private Equity, Level 28, 140 William Street, Melbourne, Vic. 3000 (Office); 15 Accand Street, South Yarra Vic. 3141, Australia (Home). *Telephone:* (3) 9642-2518 (Office); (3) 9820-5955 (Home). *Fax:* (3) 9642-2517 (Office); (3) 9820-5944 (Home). *E-mail:* jprescott@ horizon-pe.com.

PRESCOTT, John Leslie, PC, MP, DipEconPol; British politician and trade unionist; b. 31 May 1938, Prestatyn, Denbighshire; s. of John Herbert Prescott and Phyllis Prescott; m. Pauline Tilston 1961; two s.; ed WEA correspondence courses, Ruskin Coll. Oxford, Hull Univ.; trainee chef 1953–55; steward in Merchant Navy 1955–63; Recruitment Officer, Gen. & Municipal Workers Union 1965; contested Southport for Labour 1966; Full-time official Nat. Union of Seamen 1968–70; MP Kingston upon Hull (East) 1970–83, Hull (East) 1983–97, Kingston upon Hull East 1997–; mem. Select Cttee Nationalized Industries 1973–79, Council of Europe 1972–75, European Parl. 1975–79; PPS to Sec. of State for Trade 1974–76; Opposition Spokesman on Transport 1979–81, Regional Affairs and Devolution 1981–83, on Transport 1983–84, on Employment 1984–87, on Energy 1987–89, on Transport 1988–93, on Employment 1993–94; Deputy Prime Minister and Sec. of State for the Environment, Transport and the Regions 1997–2001; Deputy Prime Minister and First Sec. of State 2001–; mem. Labour Party Nat. Exec. Cttee 1989–, Deputy Leader 1994–; mem. Shadow Cabinet 1983–97; North of England Zoological Soc. Gold Medal 1999, Priyadarshni Award 2002. *Publication:* Not Wanted on Voyage: A report of the 1966 seamen's strike

1966, Alternative Regional Strategy: A framework for discussion 1982, Planning for Full Employment 1985, Real Needs–Local Jobs 1987, Moving Britain into the 1990s 1989, Moving Britain into Europe 1991, Full Steam Ahead 1993, Financing Infrastructure Investment 1994, Jobs and Social Justice 1994. *Address:* House of Commons, London, SW1A 0AA, England. *Telephone:* (20) 7219-3000.

PRESS, Frank, PhD; American geophysicist; b. 4 Dec. 1924, Brooklyn, New York; s. of Solomon Press and Dora (née Steinholz) Press; m. Billie Kallick 1946; one s. one d.; ed Coll. of City of New York and Columbia Univ.; Research Associate, Columbia Univ. 1946–49, Instructor, Geology 1949–51, Asst Prof. of Geology 1951–52, Assoc. Prof. 1952–55; Prof. Geophysics, Calif. Inst. of Tech. 1955–65, Dir Seismological Lab. 1957–65; Co-editor Physics and Chemistry of the Earth 1957–; Chair. Dept of Earth and Planetary Sciences, MIT 1965–77, Prof. Emer. of Geophysics 2000–; Dir Office of Science and Tech. Policy, Exec. Office of Pres. and Science and Tech. Adviser to Pres. 1977–80; Consultant to U.S. Navy 1956–57, U.S. Dept of Defense 1958–62, NASA 1960–62, 1965–; mem. U.S. del. Nuclear Test Ban Conf. Geneva 1959–61, Moscow 1963; Pres. Science Advisory Comm. 1961–64; Chair. Bd of Advisors Nat. Center for Earthquake Research of the U.S. Geophysical Survey 1966–76; Planetology Subcomm. NASA 1966–70; Chair. Earthquake Prediction Panel Office of Science and Tech. 1965–66; Fellow American Acad. of Arts and Sciences 1966; Fellow Royal Astronomical Soc., mem. NAS 1958, Pres. 1981–93; Cecil & Ida Green Sr Fellow Carnegie Inst. of Washington, Washington, DC 1993–97; partner Washington Advisory Group 1996–; mem. Nat. Science Bd 1970–77; fmr Pres. American Geophysical Union; Chair. Cttee on Scholarly Communication with People's Repub. of China 1975–77; mem. U.S.-USSR Working Group in Earthquake Prediction 1973; fmr mem. Exec. Council Nat. Acad. of Sciences, Pres. Emer. 2000–; Hon. LLD (City Univ. of NY) 1972, Hon. DSc (Notre Dame Univ.) 1973, (Univ. of Rhode Island, of Arizona, Rutgers Univ., City Univ. of New York) 1979; Townsend Harris Medal Coll. of the City of New York, Royal Astronomical Soc. Gold Medal (UK) 1971, Day Medal Geological Soc. of America, Interior 1972, NASA Award 1973, Killian Faculty Achievement Award, MIT 1975, Japan Prize 1993, Nat. Medal of Science 1994, Philip Hauge Abelson Prize, AAAS 1995, Lomonosov Gold Medal, Russian Acad. of Sciences 1998. *Publications:* Earth (with R. Siever) 1986, Understanding Earth 1997. *Leisure interests:* skiing, sailing. *Address:* Suite 616 S., 2500 Virginia Avenue, Washington, DC 20037, USA. *E-mail:* fpress@theadvisorygroup.com (Office).

PRESS, Tamara Natanovna; Russian athlete and sports official; b. 10 May 1937, Kharkov; ed Leningrad Construction Engineering Inst. and Higher Party School of Cen. Cttee of CPSU; mem. CPSU 1962–91; women's champion in shot putt at Olympic Games 1960, 1964, at discus 1964, women's champion of Europe in discus throwing three times between 1958–62 and sixteen times women's champion of USSR between 1958–66; worked for All-Union Cen. Council of Trade Unions 1967–91; Deputy Chair. Russian Olympic Cttee; Vice-Pres. Sports Soc. Rossiya 1992–; writer and journalist following retirement in 1966; Order of Lenin, Order of Badge of Honour, Honoured Master of Sports of USSR 1960. *Publications:* The Price of Victory, This Tough Athletics. *Address:* Sports Society Rossiya, Tolmachevski per. 4, Moscow, Russia. *Telephone:* (095) 238-63-87.

PRESSLER, Larry, MA, JD; American politician; b. 29 March 1942, Humboldt, S.D.; s. of Antone Pressler and Loretta Claussen; m. Harriet Dent 1982; one d.; ed Univ. of South Dakota, Univ. of Oxford, England, Harvard Kennedy School of Govt and Harvard Law School; Lt in U.S. Army, Viet Nam 1966–68; mem. House of Reps. 1975–79; Senator from South Dakota 1979–97; mem. several Senate Cttees.; Congressional Del. to 47th UN Gen. Ass. 1992; mem. U.S. Comm. on Improving the Effectiveness of the UN 1993; Sec. U.S. Del. to Inter-Parl. Union 1981; Dir USAF Bd of Visitory 1987–; Chair. Commerce, Science and Transport Cttees., U.S. Senate 1995–96; Founder Pressler and Assocs., Washington 1997–; Jr Fellow Univ. of Calif. at LA 2000–; mem. Council on Foreign Relations. *Publications:* U.S. Senators from the Prairie 1982, Star Wars: The SDI Debates in Congress 1986. *Leisure interests:* running, tennis. *Address:* c/o O'Connor Hannan, 1666 K. Street, NW, # 500, Washington, DC 20006 (Office); 2440 Virginia Avenue, NW, The Diplomat 1306, Washington, DC 20037, USA (Home).

PRESTON, Paul, CBE, MA, DPhil, FRHistS; British professor of history; b. 21 July 1946, Liverpool; s. of Charles R. Preston and Alice Hoskisson; m. Gabrielle P. Ashford-Hodges 1983; two s.; ed St Edward's Coll. Liverpool, Oriel Coll. Oxford and Univ. of Reading; Research Fellow, Centre for Mediterranean Studies, Rome 1973–74; Lecturer in History, Univ. of Reading 1974–75; Lecturer in Modern History, Queen Mary Coll. London 1975–79, Reader 1979–85, Prof. of History 1985–91; Prof. of Int. History, LSE 1991–; regular contrib. to Times Literary Supplement; columnist in ABC, Diario 16 and El País, Madrid; Comendador, Orden del Mérito Civil (Spain) 1987. *Publications:* The Coming of the Spanish Civil War 1978, The Triumph of Democracy in Spain 1986, The Spanish Civil War 1986, The Politics of Revenge 1990, Franco: A Biography 1993, Las tres Españas del 36 1998, Comrades: Portraits from the Spanish Civil War 1999. *Leisure interests:* classical music, especially opera, modern fiction. *Address:* Department of International History, London School of Economics, Houghton Street, London, WC2A 2AE (Office); 10 Woodland Gardens, Muswell Hill, London, N10 3UA, England (Home). *Telephone:* (20) 7955-7107 (Office); (20) 8883-4058 (Home). *Fax:* (20) 7955-7107 (Office); (20) 8482-9865 (Home). *Website:* www.lse.ac.uk (Office).

PRESTON, Peter John, MA; British journalist; b. 23 May 1938, Barrow-upon-Soar, Leicestershire; s. of John Whittle Preston and Kathlyn Preston (née Chell); m. Jean Mary Burrell 1962; two s. two d.; ed Loughborough Grammar School and St John's Coll. Oxford; editorial trainee, Liverpool Daily Post 1960–63; Political Reporter, The Guardian 1963–64, Educ. Corresp. 1965–66, Diary Ed. 1966–68, Features Ed. 1968–72, Production Ed. 1972–75, Ed. The Guardian 1975–95; Ed.-in-Chief The Guardian 1995, Observer 1995–96; Editorial Dir Guardian Media Group 1996–98; Co-Dir Guardian Foundation 1997–; mem. Scott Trust 1976–; Chair. Int. Press Inst. 1995–97; Asscn of British Eds. 1996–99; mem. UNESCO Advisory Group on Press Freedom 2000–; Gov. British Asscn for Cen. and E Europe 2000–; Hon. DLitt (Loughborough) 1982, (E Anglia, City Univ.) 1997. *Publications:* Dunblane: Reflecting Tragedy 1996, The 51st State 1998, Bess 1999. *Leisure interests:* football, films, four children. *Address:* The Guardian, 119 Farringdon Road, London, EC1R 3ER, England. *Telephone:* (20) 7278-2332. *Website:* www.guardian.co.uk (Office).

PRESTON, Simon John, OBE, MA, MUS.B., FRAM, FRCM, FRCO, F.R.C.C.O., FRSA; British organist and conductor; b. 4 Aug. 1938, Bournemouth; ed Canford School, King's Coll. Cambridge; Sub Organist Westminster Abbey 1962–67; Acting Organist St Albans Abbey 1967–68; Organist and Lecturer in Music, Christ Church, Oxford 1970–81; Organist and Master of the Choristers Westminster Abbey 1981–87; Conductor Oxford Bach Choir 1971–74; Artistic Dir, Calgary Int. Organ Festival; Patron, Univ. of Buckingham; mem. Royal Soc. of Musicians, Council of Friends of St John's Smith Square; over 30 recordings; Edison Award 1971; Grand Prix du Disque 1979, Performer of the Year Award, American Guild of Organists 1987. *Leisure interests:* croquet, theatre, opera. *Address:* Little Hardwick, Langton Green, Tunbridge Wells, Kent, TN3 0EY, England. *Telephone:* (1892) 862042.

PRÊTRE, Georges; French conductor; b. 14 Aug. 1924, Waziers; s. of Emile Prêtre and Jeanne (née Dérin) Prêtre; m. Gina Marny 1950; one s. one d.; ed Lycée and Conservatoire de Douai, Conservatoire national supérieur de musique de Paris and Ecole des chefs d'orchestre; Dir of Music, Opera Houses of Marseilles, Lille and Toulouse 1946–55, Dir of Music Opéra-comique, Paris, 1955–59, at l'Opéra 1959; Dir-Gen. of Music at l'Opéra 1970–71; conductor of the symphonic asscns of Paris and of principal festivals throughout the world; also conducted at La Scala, Milan and major American orchestras; Conductor Metropolitan Opera House, New York 1964–65, La Scala, Milan 1965–66, Salzburg 1966; First Visiting Conductor, Vienna Symphony Orchestra 1985–, Opéra Bastille (Turandot) 1997, Opéra-Comique (Pelleas et Melisande) 1998; Officier, Légion d'honneur 1971, Haute Distinction République Italienne 1975, Commdr République Italienne 1980; Europa Prize 1982; Victoire de la musique Award for Best Conductor 1997. *Leisure interests:* riding, swimming, aviation, judo. *Address:* c/o Marcel de Valmalete, 7 rue Hoche, 92300 Levallois-Perret (Office); Château de Vaudricourt, à Naves, par Castres, 81100 France.

PRETTEJOHN, Nicholas Edward Tucker, BA; British business executive; b. 22 July 1960; s. of Edward Joseph Tucker Prettejohn and Diana Sally Prettejohn; m. 1st Elizabeth Esch 1986 (divorced 1997), 2nd Claire Helen McKenna 1997; ed Taunton School, Somerset, Balliol Coll. Oxford; Research Assoc., Bain & Co. 1982–91, Partner 1988–91; Dir Apax Partners 1991–94; Dir Corp. Strategy, Nat. Freight Corpn PLC 1994–95; Head of Strategy, Lloyd's of London 1995–97, Man. Dir Business Devt Unit 1997–99, N America Business Unit 1998–99, Chief Exec. 1999–; Dir (non-exec.) Anglo & Overseas Trust PLC 1998–; Chair. English Pocket Opera 2001–. *Leisure interests:* opera, music, theatre, horse racing, golf, cricket, rugby. *Address:* Chief Executive's Office, Lloyd's, One Lime Street, London, EC3M 7HA, England (Office). *Telephone:* (20) 7327-6930 (Office).

PRETTY, Katharine Bridget (Kate), PhD, FSA; British archaeologist and college principal; b. 18 Oct. 1945, Cheshire; d. of Maurice Walter Hughes and Bridget Elizabeth Whibley Hughes (née Marples); m. 1st Graeme Lloyd Pretty (divorced 1975); m. 2nd Tjeerd Hendrik van Andel 1988; ed King Edward VI High School for Girls, Birmingham and New Hall, Cambridge; Fellow and Lecturer New Hall, Cambridge Univ. 1972–91, Emer. Fellow 1995–, Chair, Faculty of Archaeology and Anthropology 1991–, Council of the School of Humanities and Social Sciences 1997–; Principal Homerton Coll., Cambridge Univ. 1991–; Chair. RESCUE, British Archaeological Trust 1978–83; Vice-Pres. RSA 1999; Medal, British Archaeological Awards 1998. *Publications:* The Excavations of Wroxeter Baths-Basilica 1997. *Leisure interests:* archaeology, botany and gardening. *Address:* Homerton College, Hills Road, Cambridge, CB2 2PH, England. *Telephone:* (1223) 507131. *Fax:* (1223) 507130. *E-mail:* kp10002@cam.ac.uk (Office).

PRÉVAL, René; Haitian politician; b. 17 Jan. 1943, Port-au-Prince; m.; two c.; spent ten years in exile in USA; founding mem. Group for Defence of Constitution; Chair. Cttee 'Pa Blié' investigating disappearance of persons under Duvalier regime 1987–91; Prime Minister Feb.–Sept. 1991; Pres. of Haiti 1996–2001. *Address:* c/o Office of the President, Palais National, Champ de Mars, Port-au-Prince, Haiti.

PREVIN, André George; American conductor, pianist and composer; b. (as Andreas Ludwig Priwin), 6 April 1929, Berlin, Germany; s. of Jack Previn and Charlotte (née Epstein) Previn; m. 1st Betty Bennett (divorced); two d.; m. 2nd Dory Langan 1959 (divorced 1970); m. 3rd Mia Farrow (q.v.) 1970 (divorced 1979); three s. three d.; m. 4th Heather Hales 1982 (divorced); one s.; m. 5th Anne-Sophie Mutter 2003; ed Berlin and Paris Conservatories; Music Dir

Houston Symphony, US 1967–69; Music Dir and Principal Conductor, London Symphony Orchestra 1968–79, Conductor Emer. 1979–; composed and conducted approx. 50 film scores 1950–65; Guest conductor of most major world orchestras, also Royal Opera House, Covent Garden, Salzburg, Edin., Osaka, Flanders Festivals; Music Dir London South Bank Summer Music Festival 1972–74, Pittsburgh Symphony Orchestra 1976–84, LA Philharmonic Orchestra 1984–89; Music Dir Royal Philharmonic Orchestra 1985–86, Prin. Conductor 1987–92; Conductor Laureate, London Symphony Orchestra 1992–; Television Critics Award 1972; Acad. Award for Best Film Score 1959, 1960, 1964, 1965; Hon. KBE 1996. *Television:* series of television specials for BBC and for American Public Broadcasting Service. *Major works:* Symphony for Strings 1965, Overture to a Comedy 1966, Suite for Piano 1967, Cello Concerto 1968, Four Songs (for soprano and orchestra) 1968, Two Serenades for Violin 1969, Guitar Concerto 1970, Piano Preludes 1972, Good Companions (musical) 1974, Song Cycle on Poems by Philip Larkin 1977, Every Good Boy Deserves Favour (music, drama, text by Tom Stoppard, q.v., 1977, Pages from the Calendar (for solo piano) 1977, Peaches (for flute and strings) 1978, Principals 1980, Outings (for brass quintet) 1980, Reflections 1981, Piano Concerto 1984, Triolet for Brass 1987, Variations for Solo Piano 1991, Six Songs for Soprano and Orchestra on texts by Toni Morrison 1991, Sonata for Cello and Piano 1992, The Magic Number (for soprano and orchestra) 1995, Trio for Bassoon, Oboe and Piano 1995, Sonata for Violin 1996, Sonata for Bassoon and Piano 1997, Streetcar Named Desire (opera) 1998, The Giraffes Go to Hamburg (for soprano, alto, flute and piano), Three Dickinson Songs (for soprano and piano), Diversions (for orchestra). *Publications:* Music Face to Face 1971, Orchestra (ed.) 1977, Guide to Music 1983, No Minor Chords: My Days in Hollywood 1992. *Leisure interests:* collecting contemporary art, fencing, American folk art. *Address:* c/o Columbia Artists, 165 W 57th Street, New York, NY 10019, USA; Barbican Centre, Silk Street, London, EC2Y 8DS, England.

PRICE, Antony, MA; British fashion designer; b. 5 March 1945, Yorks.; s. of Peter Price and Joan Price; ed Bradford Coll. of Art and Royal Coll. of Art; designer for Sterling Cooper 1968–72, for Plaza 1972–79; Chair. of own fashion co. 1979–; British Glamour Award 1989. *Leisure interests:* tropical plants, tropical ornithology, modern and classical music. *Address:* 17 Langton Street, London, SW10 0JL, England. *Telephone:* (20) 7376-7250. *Fax:* (20) 7376-4599.

PRICE II, Charles H.; American business executive and fmr diplomatist; b. 1 April 1931, Kansas City, Mo.; s. of Charles Harry Price and Virginia (née Ogden) Price; m. Carol Ann Swanson 1969; two s. three d.; ed Univ. of Mo.; Pres. and Dir Linwood Securities Co., Kansas City 1960–81; Chair. and CEO, Price Candy Co., Kansas City 1969–81, American Bancorpn., Kansas City 1960–81; Chair. and CEO American Bank and Trust Co., Kansas City 1973–81; Amb. to Belgium 1981–83, to UK 1983–89; Chair. Ameribanc Inc. 1989–92, Pres., COO 1990–92; Chair. Bd of Dirs. Mercantile Bank Kansas City, Mo. 1992–96, St Luke's Hosp. Kansas City 1970–81 (Hon. Dir 1989–); Hon. Fellow Regent's Coll., London 1986; several hon. degrees; William Booth Award, Salvation Army 1985, World Citizen of the Year Award, Mayor of Kansas City 1985, Trustee Citation Award Midwest Research Inst. 1987, Distinguished Service Award Int. Relations Council 1989, Mankind Award, Cystic Fibrosis Foundation 1990, Chancellor's Medal, Univ. of Mo. 1992, William F. Yates Medallion, William Jewell Coll. 1996. *Leisure interests:* shooting, golf, tennis. *Address:* One West Armour Boulevard, Suite 300, Kansas City, MO 64111-2089, USA. *Telephone:* (816) 360-6175.

PRICE, Frank; American television and cinema producer and executive; b. 17 May 1930, Decatur, Ill.; s. of William Price and Winifred (née Moran) Price; m. Katherine Huggins 1965; four s.; ed Michigan State Univ.; served with USN 1948–49; Writer and Story Ed., CBS-TV, New York 1951–53; with Columbia Pictures, Hollywood 1953–57, NBC-TV 1957–58; Producer, Writer, Universal Television, Calif. 1959–64, Vice-Pres. 1964–71, Sr Vice-Pres. 1971–73, Exec. Vice-Pres. 1973–74, Pres. 1974–78; Pres. Columbia Pictures 1978–79, Chair. and CEO 1979–83; Chair. and CEO MCA Motion Picture Group 1983–86, Price Entertainment 1991–; Chair. Columbia Pictures 1990–91; Dir Sony Pictures Entertainment, Savoy Pictures; Exec. Producer The Virginian 1961–64, Ironside 1965, Kojak, Six Million Dollar Man, Bionic Woman, Rockford Files, Quincy, Rich Man, Poor Man, The Tuskegee Airmen 1996; mem. Writers Guild America; Peabody Award 1996, NAACP Image Award 1996. *Address:* Price Entertainment Inc., 527 Spoleto Drive, Pacific Palisades, CA 90272, USA (Office).

PRICE, Rt Hon George Cadle, PC; Belizean politician; b. 15 Jan. 1919; s. of William Cadle Price and Irene Price; ed St John's Coll., Belize City and St Augustin Seminary, Mississippi; City Councillor 1947–62; founder-mem. People's United Party (PUP) 1950, Sec. PUP 1950–56, fmr Leader; Pres. Gen. Workers' Union 1947–52; mem. Legislative Council, British Honduras (now Belize) 1954–65; mem. Exec. Council 1954–57, 1961–65; Mayor, Belize City 1956–62; mem. House of Reps 1965–84, Cabinet 1965–84; fmr mem. for Nat. Resources; First Minister 1961–63, leader of del. to London for self-govt constitutional talks; Premier 1964–81, Prime Minister of Belize 1981–84, 1989–93, Minister of Finance and Econ. Planning 1965–84, of Foreign Affairs 1981–84, 1989–90; Chair. Reconstruction and Devt Corpn; Outstanding Alumnus Award (St John's Coll.) 1971. *Address:* c/o House of Representatives, Belmopan, Belize.

PRICE, James Gordon, BA, MD; American university professor; b. 20 June 1926, Brush, Colo, USA; s. of John Hoover Price and Laurette (née Dodds) Price; m. Janet Alice McSween 1949; two s. two d.; ed Univ. of Colorado; intern, Denver Gen. Hosp.; pvt. practice, family medicine, Brush, Colo 1952–78; Prof. Dept of Family Practice, Univ. of Kan. 1978–93 (Chair. 1978–90), Dean, School of Medicine 1990–93, Prof. Emer. 1993–; nationally syndicated newspaper column, Your Family Physician 1973–86; Medical Ed., Curriculum Innovations 1973–93; mem. Inst. of Medicine, NAS; Pres. American Acad. of Family Physicians 1973–, American Bd of Family Practice 1980–. *Leisure interest:* computer programming. *Address:* 12205 Mohawk Road, Shawnee Mission, Leawood, KS 66209, USA. *Telephone:* (913) 491-3072. *E-mail:* jprice@kumc.edu (Home).

PRICE, Leontyne; American soprano; b. 10 Feb. 1927, Laurel, Miss.; d. of James A. Price and Kate (née Baker) Price; m. William Warfield 1952 (divorced 1973); ed Central State Coll., Wilberforce, Ohio and Juilliard School of Music; appeared as Bess (Porgy and Bess), Vienna, Berlin, Paris, London, New York 1952–54; recitalist, soloist 1954–; soloist Hollywood Bowl 1955–59, 1966; opera singer NBC-TV 1955–58, San Francisco Opera Co. 1957–59, 1960–61, Vienna Staatsoper 1958, 1959–60, 1961; recording artist RCA-Victor 1958–; appeared Covent Garden 1958–59, 1970, Chicago 1959, 1960, 1965, Milan 1960–61, 1963, 1967, Metropolitan Opera, New York 1961–62, 1963–70, 1972, Paris Opéra as Aida 1968, Metropolitan Opera as Aida 1985 (retd); numerous recordings; Hon. Vice-Chair. US Cttee UNESCO; Fellow American Acad. of Arts and Sciences; Trustee Int. House; Hon. DMus (Howard Univ., Cen. State Coll., Ohio); Hon. DHL (Dartmouth); Hon. Dr of Humanities (Rust Coll., Miss.); Hon. DHumLitt (Fordham); Presidential Medal of Freedom, Order of Merit (Italy), Nat. Medal of Arts 1985, Essence Award 1991, 20 Grammy Awards for classical recordings. *Address:* c/o Columbia Artists Management Inc., 165 West 57th Street, New York, NY 10019; Price Enterprises, Room 920, 1133 Broadway, New York, NY 10010, USA.

PRICE, Dame Margaret Berenice, DBE; British opera singer; b. 13 April 1941, Tredegar, Wales; d. of the late Thomas Glyn Price and of Lilian Myfanwy Richards; ed Pontllanfraith Grammar School and Trinity Coll. of Music, London; operatic debut with Welsh Nat. Opera in Marriage of Figaro; renowned for Mozart operatic roles; has sung in world's leading opera houses and festivals; has made many recordings of opera, oratorio, concert works and recitals and many radio broadcasts and TV appearances; fmr performer with Bavarian State Opera, Munich; Fellow Coll. of Wales 1991; Hon. Fellow, Trinity Coll. of Music; Hon. DMus (Wales) 1983; Elisabeth Schumann Prize for Lieder, Ricordi Prize for Opera, Silver Medal of the Worshipful Co. of Musicians, Bayerische Kammersängerin. *Major roles include:* Countess in Marriage of Figaro, Pamina in The Magic Flute, Fiordiligi in Così fan tutte, Donna Anna in Don Giovanni, Konstanze in Die Entführung, Amelia in Simon Boccanegra, Agathe in Freischütz, Desdemona in Otello, Elisabetta in Don Carlo, Aida and Norma, Amelia in Ballo in Maschera. *Leisure interests:* cookery, reading, walking, swimming, driving, breeding dogs. *Address:* c/o Stefan Hahn, Artist Management HRA, Sebastianplatz 3, 80331 Munich, Germany.

PRICE, Michael F.; American financial executive; b. 1952; m. (divorced); three s.; ed Univ. of Oklahoma; with Heine Securities 1975–97, Research Asst, Man., CEO; Pres., CEO Franklin Mutual Advisers Inc. (fmrly Heine Securities) 1997–; Pres., Chair. Bd Dirs. Franklin Mutual Series Fund Inc. *Address:* Franklin Mutual Advisers Incorporated, 51 John F. Kennedy Parkway, Short Hills, NJ 07078, USA.

PRICE, Nicholas Raymond Leige (Nick); South African golfer; b. 28 Jan. 1957, Durban; m. Sue Price; one s. two d.; turned professional 1977; won Asseng Invitational 1979, Canon European Masters 1980, Italian Open, S. African Masters 1981, Vaals Reef Open 1982, World Series of Golf 1983, Trophée Lancôme, ICI Int. 1985, West End S. Australian Open 1989, GTE Byron Nelson Classic, Canadian Open 1991, Air N.Z./Shell Open, PGA Championships, H-E-B Texas Open 1992, The Players Championship, Canon Greater Hartford Open, Sprint Western Open, Federal Express St Jude Classic, ICL Int., Sun City Million Dollar Challenge 1993, British Open, ICL Int. Honda Classic, Southwestern Bell Colonial, Motorola Western Open, PGA Championship, Bell Canadian Open 1994, Alfred Dunhill Challenge, Hassan II Golf Trophy, Morocco, Zimbabwe Open 1995, MCI Classic 1997, Suntory Open 1999, CVS Charity Classic 2001, Mastercard Colonial 2002; f. golf course designers Nick Price design 2001; recipient Vardon Trophy 1993, PGA Tour Player of the Year 1986, 1993. *Publication:* The Swing 1997. *Leisure interests:* water skiing, tennis, fishing, flying. *Address:* c/o P.G.A. Tour, 100 Avenue of the Champions, Palm Beach Gardens, FL 33410, USA.

PRICE, Paul Buford, PhD; American professor of physics; b. 8 Nov. 1932, Memphis, Tenn.; s. of the late Paul Buford and Eva (née Dupuy) Price; m. Jo Ann Baum 1958; one s. three d.; ed Davidson Coll., Univ. of Virginia, Univ. of Bristol, Univ. of Cambridge; Physicist Gen. Electric Research Lab., New York 1960–69; Visiting Prof. Tata Inst. of Fundamental Research, Bombay, India 1965–66; Adjunct Prof. of Physics Rensselaer Polytechnic Inst. 1967–68; Prof. of Physics Univ. of Calif. at Berkeley 1969–, Chair. Dept of Physics 1987–91, William H. McAdams Prof. of Physics 1990–92, Dean, Physical Sciences, Coll. of Letters and Science 1992–2001, Prof. in the Grad. School 2001–; Dir Space Science Lab. 1979–85; NASA Consultant on Lunar Sample Analysis Planning Team; mem. Bd Dirs Terradex Corpn 1978–86; mem.

Visiting Cttee, Bartol Research Inst. 1991–94, Advisory Cttee, Indian Inst. of Astrophysics 1993–95; Fellow and Chair. Cosmic Physics Div. American Physical Soc.; Fellow American Geophysical Union, American Astronomical Soc.; mem. Space Science Bd, NAS, Sec. Physical and Math. Sciences Class of NAS 1985–88, Chair. 1988–91, mem. Steering Group on Future of Space Science (NAS) 1994–, Polar Research Bd (NAS) 1999–2002; Regional Dir Calif. Alliance for Minority Participation 1994–; US Ice Core Working Group 2001–; Hon. Fellow Indian Inst. of Astrophysics 2000; Hon. ScD (Davidson Coll.) 1973; Distinguished Service Award, (American Nuclear Soc.) 1964, Ernest O. Lawrence Memorial Award of Atomic Energy Comm. 1971, NASA Medal for Exceptional Scientific Achievement 1973, Scientific Symposium in Honor of P.B. Price's 65th Birthday 1997, Berkeley Citation 2002. *Publications:* (jointly) Nuclear Tracks in Solids, over 450 research papers in specialized journals. *Leisure interests:* skiing, travel. *Address:* Physics Department, University of California, Berkeley, 366 LeConte Hall, Berkeley, CA 94720 (Office); 1056 Overlook Road, Berkeley, CA 94708, USA (Home). *Telephone:* (510) 642-4982 (Office); (510) 548-5206 (Home). *Fax:* (510) 643-8497 (Office). *E-mail:* bprice@uclink4.berkeley.edu (Office). *Website:* physics .berkeley.edu/research/price/index_new.html (Office).

PRIDDLE, Robert; British international organization official; b. 9 Sept. 1938; m. Janice Elizabeth Gorham 1962; two c.; ed King's Coll. School, Wimbledon, Univ. of Cambridge; at Ministry of Aviation 1960; at Dept of Trade and Industry 1973, 1985–89; Deputy Sec., Dept of Energy 1974–, Dir-Gen., Energy Resources 1989–92; Pres. Conf. of European Posts and Telecommunications Admin. 1987–89; Chair. of Governing Bd, Int. Energy Agency 1991–92, Exec. Dir 1994–; mem. Financial Reporting Council 1992–94. *Publication:* Victoriana 1959. *Address:* International Energy Agency, 9 rue de la Fédération, 75739 Paris Cédex 15, France (Office). *Telephone:* 1-40-57-65-00 (Office). *Fax:* 1-40-57-65-09 (Office). *E-mail:* info@ iea.org (Office).

PRIDEAUX, Sir Humphrey Povah Treverbian, Kt, OBE, MA; British business executive; b. 13 Dec. 1915, London; s. of Walter Treverbian Prideaux and Marion Fenn Prideaux (née Arbuthnot); m. Cynthia V. Birch Reynardson 1939; four s.; ed St Aubyns, Eton Coll. and Trinity Coll. Oxford; Regular army officer 1936–53; Dir Navy, Army & Air Force Insts 1956–63, Chair. 1963–73; Chair. Lord Wandsworth Foundation 1966–92, Trustee 1963–92; Deputy Chair. Liebig's Extract of Meat Co. Ltd 1968–69, Dir 1966–69; Chair. Oxo Ltd 1968–72; Dir WH Smith & Son (Holdings) Ltd 1969, Vice-Chair. 1977–81; Dir Brooke Bond Oxo Ltd 1969–70; Chair. Brooke Bond Liebig 1972–81; Pres. London Life Asscn Ltd 1973–83, Dir 1964–88; Vice-Chair. Morland & Co. 1981–82, Chair. 1983–93; Dir Grindlays (Holdings) PLC 1982–85; Dir Grindlays Bank PLC 1984–85; Hon. DL (Hants.). *Leisure interests:* country pursuits. *Address:* Kings Cottage, Buryfields, Odiham, Hook, Hants., RG29 1NE, England. *Telephone:* (1256) 703658. *E-mail:* hptprideaux@aol.com (Home).

PRIDIYATHORN DEVAKULA, MBA; Thai central bank governor; b. 15 July 1947, Bangkok; s. of Prince Prididebyabongs Devakula and Mom Taengthai Devakula; m. Prapapan Devakula Na Ayudha; two s. one d.; ed Wharton School, Univ. of Penn., USA; joined Thai Farmers Bank 1971, Dir and Sr Exec. Vice-Pres. –1990; Govt Spokesperson for Prime Minister Gen. Chatichai Choonhavan 1990–91; Deputy Minister of Commerce 1991–92; Pres. Export-Import Bank of Thailand 1993–2001; Gov. of Bank of Thailand May 2001–; Hon. DBA (Chulalongkorn Univ.) 2002. *Leisure interest:* golf. *Address:* Bank of Thailand, 273 Samsen Road, Bangkhunprom, Bangkok 10200 (Office); 4/2 Moo 6, Srinakarin Road, Prawes, Bangkok 10260, Thailand (Home). *Telephone:* (2) 283-5010 (Office). *Fax:* (2) 280-0609 (Office). *E-mail:* pridiyad@bot.or.th (Office). *Website:* www.bot.or.th (Office).

PRIEDKALNS, Janis, B.V.SC., PhD, MRCVS; Latvian diplomatist and scientist; b. 28 March 1934, Barbele; s. of Karlis Priedkalns and Erna Priedkalns (née Krigers); m. 1964 (wife died 2000); three s. three d.; ed Univs. of Sydney, Australia, Minnesota, USA, Cambridge, UK; veterinary surgeon 1959–60; postgrad. studies in microanatomy, embryology, neuroendocrinology 1961–70; appts. Univ. of Minn., Harvard Medical School, Univs. of Munich and Giessen, Collège de France, Univ. of Cambridge; Elder Prof. of Anatomy and Histology, Faculty of Medicine and Dean of Science, Univ. of Adelaide 1966–96, Prof Emer. 1997–; currently Professor of Anatomy and Histology, Latvian Acad. of Medicine; mem. Parl. and Rep. to Council of Europe Parl. Ass. 1997; Perm. Rep. to UN, NY 1997–2001; Fellow Royal Soc. of S. Australia 1978–, Latvian Acad. of Sciences 1998–; mem. New York Acad. of Sciences 1989–; Pres. Asscn of Latvian Professors and Scientists 2002–; Dr. hc (Agricultural Univ., Latvia) 1997. *Address:* Latvian Academy of Medicine, Dzirciema iela 16, 1007 RigaTerbatas iela 1, Valmiera, 4200, Latvia (Office). *Telephone:* 45-97-52 (Office). *Fax:* 782-81-55 (Office). *E-mail:* priedkalns@aol .com (Home).

PRIESTMAN, Jane, OBE, FCSD; British design management consultant; b. 7 April 1930; d. of the late Reuben Stanley Herbert and Mary Elizabeth Herbert (née Ramply); m. Arthur Martin Priestman 1954 (divorced 1986); two s.; ed Northwood Coll., Liverpool Coll. of Art; design practice 1954–75; Design Man., Gen. Man. Architecture and Design British Airports Authority 1975–86; Dir Architecture and Design British Railways Bd 1986–91; Visiting Prof. De Montfort Univ. 1997–; mem. London Regional Transport Design Panel 1985–88, Jaguar Styling Panel 1988–91, Percentage for Art Steering Group, Arts Council 1989–91; Council mem., Design Council 1996–2000; Gov. Commonwealth Inst. 1987–98, Kingston Univ. 1988–96; Enabler Comm. for Architecture and the Built Environment; Hon. FRIBA, FRSA; Hon. Dr. Des. (De Montfort) 1994, (Sheffield Hallam) 1998. *Leisure interests:* textiles, city architecture, opera, travel. *Address:* 30 Duncan Terrace, London N1 8BS, England. *Telephone:* (20) 7837-4525. *Fax:* (20) 7837-4525.

PRIGOGINE, Viscount Ilya, PhD; Belgian university professor; b. 25 Jan. 1917, Moscow, USSR; s. of Roman Prigogine and Julia Wichman; m. Marina Prokopowicz 1961; two s.; ed Univ. Libre de Bruxelles; Prof. at Univ. Libre de Bruxelles 1951–87, Prof. Emer. 1987–; Dir Instituts Internationaux de Physique et de Chimie 1959–; Extraordinary Chair. Enrico Fermi Inst. for Nuclear Studies and Inst. for the Study of Metals, Univ. of Chicago, USA 1961–66; Dir Ilya Prigogine Center for Statistical Mechanics, Thermodynamics and Complex Systems, Univ. of Texas 1967–; Assoc. Dir of Studies, Ecole des Hautes Etudes en Sciences Sociales, France 1987–; mem. Exec. Council Fondation Erasme, Brussels 1983, Haut Conseil de la Francophonie, Paris 1984–88; Distinguished Visitor, Inst. for Advanced Study, Princeton Univ. 1993; Special Adviser to EC 1993; Hon. Prof. Banarashindu Univ. 1988; Hon. Pres. Univ. Philosophique Européenne, Paris 1985; mem. Académie Royale de Belgique 1958, Pres. Classe des Sciences 1968–70; Foreign Hon. mem. American Acad. of Sciences and Arts 1960; Fellow Acad. of Sciences of New York 1962; mem. Romanian Acad. of Science 1965; mem. Royal Soc. of Sciences, Uppsala, Sweden 1967; Foreign Assoc. NAS (USA) 1967; corresp. mem. de la Soc. Royale des Sciences, Liège 1967; corresp. mem. Class of Physics and Mathematics, Acad. of Sciences, Göttingen 1970, Österreichische Akad. der Wissenschaften, Vienna 1971; mem. Deutsche Akad. der Naturforscher Leopoldina 1970, Acad. Int. de Philosophie des Sciences, Acad. Européenne des Sciences, des Arts et des Lettres, Paris 1980; foreign mem. Akad. der Wissenschaften der DDR, Berlin 1980; American Chem. Soc. Centennial Foreign Fellow 1976; corresp. mem. of Rheinische Westfälische Akad. der Wissenschaften, Düsseldorf; Foreign Fellow of the Indian National Science Acad. 1979; mem. bd Lawrence Hall of Sciences, Univ. of Calif. 1982; mem. Accad. Mediterranea delle Scienze, Catania, Italy 1982; Foreign mem. USSR Acad. of Sciences 1982; Extraordinary Scientific mem. Max-Planck Foundation (Fed. Repub. of Germany) 1984; mem. Emer. Academia Europaea GB 1989; Hon. mem. Chemical Soc. of Poland 1971, Royal Chem. Soc. (Belgium) 1987, Biophysical Soc. (China); Dr hc (Univs of Newcastle-upon-Tyne 1966, Poitiers 1966, Chicago 1969, Bordeaux 1972, Uppsala 1977, Liège 1978, Aix-en-Provence 1978, Georgetown 1980, Rio de Janeiro 1981, Cracow 1981, Stevens Inst. of Tech., Hoboken 1981, Heriot-Watt, Edin. 1985, François Rabelais, Tours, 1986, Univs of Nanjing 1986, Beijing 1986, Buenos Aires 1989, Cagliari, Italy 1990, Minn., USA 1990, Siena 1990, Aristote Univ. of Thessaloniki 1998, Wesleyan Univ., Ill. 1998, Nat. Polytechnic School, Athens 2000, Odessa Medical Univ. 2000, Acad. of Slovak Repub. 2002); Hon. Prof. Int. Albert Schweitzer Univ., Geneva 2001; Prix Francqui 1955, Prix Solvay 1965; Svante Arrhenius Gold Medal, Acad. Royale des Sciences, Sweden 1969; Bourke Medal, Chemical Soc. 1972, Cothenius Gold Medal, Deutsche Akad. der Naturforscher Leopoldina (Halle) 1975, Rumford Medal 1976, Nobel Prize for Chem. 1977, Médaille Descartes 1979, Honda Prize 1983, Gold Medal, Padua Univ. 1988, Gravity Research Foundation Award for 1988, USA (with others), Artificial Intelligence Scientific Achievement Award, Tokyo 1990, Univ. Peace and Science Gold Medal, Albert Schweitzer Int. Univ. 2001, Antonio Roberti Int. Prize, Italian Inst. for Philosophic Studies, Naples 2002, and numerous other prizes and awards; Commdr des Arts et des Lettres (France), Ordre nat. du Mérite (France), Légion d'honneur (France), Order of Rising Sun, with Gold and Silver Medal, Japan. *Publications:* Traité de Thermodynamique, conformément aux méthodes de Gibbs et de De Donder (with R. Defay) 1944, 1950, Etude Thermodynamique des Phénomènes Irréversibles 1947, Introduction to Thermodynamics of Irreversible Processes 1962, The Molecular Theory of Solutions (with A. Bellemans and V. Mathot) 1957, Non-Equilibrium Statistical Mechanics 1962, Non-Equilibrium Thermodynamics, Variational Techniques and Stability (with R. J. Donnelly and R. Herman) 1966, Kinetic Theory of Vehicular Traffic (with R. Herman) 1971, Thermodynamic Theory of Structure Stability and Fluctuations (with P. Glansdorff) 1971, Self-Organization in Non-Equilibrium systems, from Dissipative Structures to order through fluctuations (with G. Nicolis) 1977, From Being to Becoming, Time and Complexity in the Physical Sciences 1980, La nouvelle alliance, les métamorphoses de la science (with I. Stengers) 1981, Order out of Chaos–Man's New Dialogue with Nature 1984, Exploring Complexity (with G. Nicolis) 1987, Entre le Temps et l'Éternité (with I. Stengers) 1988, La Fin des Certitudes 1996, La Nascita del Tiempo 1998. *Leisure interests:* music, arts. *Address:* ULB, CP 231, Boulevard du Triomphe, 1050 Brussels (Office); Avenue Fond'Roy 67, 1180 Brussels, Belgium (Home). *Telephone:* (2) 650-50-47 (Office); (2) 374-29-52 (Home). *Fax:* (2) 650-50-28 (Office). *E-mail:* njockman@ulb.ac.be (Office).

PRIGOV, Dmitri Aleksandrovich; Russian poet and artist; b. 5 Nov. 1940, Moscow; m. Nadezhda Georgiyevna Bourova; one s.; ed Moscow Higher School of Arts; worker Likhachev Automobile Factory 1957–59, 1964; architect Main Dept of Architecture of Moscow 1967–72; freelance 1972–; mem. Russian Painters' Union, Russian Writers' Union, Russian PEN Club; Pushkin Prize for Literature. *Exhibitions:* has taken part in art exhbns. in Russia, Israel, Germany, Italy, USA, South Korea, France, U.K., Spain, Denmark, Netherlands, Hungary, Czech Repub.; Metropolis, Berlin 1990, 100 Möglichkeiten, InterArt, Berlin, 1991, Russian Museum, St. Petersburg 1994, Dmitri Prigov 1975–1995, France, Germany, Hungary. *Publications include:* Black Poodle (play), Tears of Heraldic Soul 1990, Poet Ohne Personlichkeit 1991, Der Militioner und die Andere 1992, Sixty Drops of Blood 1993, The Place of God (play) 1995, The Appearance of the Verse after its Death (poetry) 1996; Collected Poems 1975–1988 1997, Soviet Texts 1997, Poems 1990–1994 1998, Texts of Our Life 1995, Katharsis (play) 1998, Collected Poems Vols I and II 1997, Live in Moscow (novel) 2000. *Leisure interests:* rambling, listening to opera, classical music. *Address:* Volgina str. 25, korp. 2, Apt. 207, 117437 Moscow, Russia (Home); 26 Abbey Drive, London, SW17 9PN, England (Home). *Telephone:* (095) 330-49-50 (Russia); (20) 8767-7386 (England). *Fax:* (095) 330-49-50 (Russia); (20) 8767-7386 (England). *E-mail:* bokrovan@aol .com (Home).

PRIKHODKO, Sergey Eduardovich; Russian government official; b. 12 Jan. 1957, Moscow; m.; two d.; ed Moscow State Inst. of Int. Relations; mem. of staff Ministry of Foreign Affairs 1980–93; Head Div. of Baltic Countries, Deputy Dir Second European Dept 1993–97; Asst to Russian Pres. on Int. Problems 1997–98, Deputy Head of Admin., Russian Presidency 1998–99, concurrently Head Dept of Admin. on Int. Policy 1998–; Public Recognition Award 1999. *Leisure interests:* theatre, literature, fishing, hunting. *Address:* Administration of the President, Staraya pl. 4, 103132 Moscow, Russia (Office). *Telephone:* (095) 206-00-27 (Office). *Fax:* (095) 206-26-77 (Office). *Website:* President.Kremlin.ru (Office).

PRIMAKOV, Yevgeniy Maksimovich, DEcon; Russian politician and economist; b. 29 Oct. 1929, Kiev; m.; one d.; ed Moscow Inst. of Oriental Studies; worked for State Comm. on Broadcasting and Television 1953–62; mem. CPSU 1959–91; Columnist and Deputy Ed. (Asia and Africa Desk), Pravda 1962–70; Deputy Dir Inst. of World Econ. and Int. Relations, USSR (now Russian) Acad. of Sciences 1970–77, Dir 1985–, Dir Inst. of Oriental Studies 1977–85; elected to Congress of People's Deputies of the USSR 1989; mem. CPSU Cen. Cttee 1989–91; cand. mem. Politburo 1989–90; Chair. Soviet of the Union June 1989–March 1990; mem. Presidential Council 1989–90; Pres. Gorbachev's Special Envoy to the Gulf 1990–91; Dir Central Intelligence Service of USSR 1991, Foreign Intelligence Service of Russian Fed. 1991–96; Minister of Foreign Affairs 1996–98; Chair of Govt (Prime Minister) 1998–99; Chair. Exec. Council of Russia and Belarus Union 1998–99; mem. Security Council 1996–98; mem. State Duma (Parl.) 1999–, Head Otechestvo faction 2000–; Pres. Russian Fed. Chamber of Commerce and Industry 2001–; corresp. mem. USSR (now Russian) Acad. of Sciences 1974, mem. 1979, Acad.-Sec., mem. of Presidium 1988–91; specialist on Egypt and other Arab countries; Chief Ed. of and contributor to a number of collective works, including: International Conflicts 1972, The Energy Crisis in the Capitalist World 1975, Years in Large-Scale Policy 1999; Nasser Prize 1975, USSR State Prize 1980, Avicenna Prize 1983. *Publications include:* Egypt under Nasser (with I. P. Belyayev) 1975, The War Which Could Be Avoided 1991, Years at the Top Level of Politics 2000, Eight Months Plus 2001. *Address:* Russian Federation Chamber of Commerce & Industry, Ilyinka str. 6, 103684 Moscow, Russia. *Telephone:* (095) 929-00-01 (Office). *Fax:* (095) 929-03-75 (Office).

PRIMAROLO, Dawn; British politician; b. 2 May 1954; m. 1st 1972 (divorced); one s.; m. 2nd Thomas Ian Ducat 1990; ed Thomas Bennett Comprehensive School, Crawley, Bristol Polytechnic, Bristol Univ.; mem. Avon Co. Council 1985–87; MP for Bristol S. 1987–; Opposition Front Bench Spokesperson on Health 1992–94, on Treasury Affairs 1994–97; Financial Sec. HM Treasury 1997–99, Paymaster Gen. 1999–; mem. Labour Party. *Address:* House of Commons, London, SW1A 0AA (Office); P.O. Box 1002, Bristol, BS99 1WH, England (Office). *Telephone:* (117) 909-0063 (Bristol). *Fax:* (117) 909-0064 (Bristol).

PRIMATESTA, HE Cardinal Raúl Francisco; Argentine ecclesiastic; b. 14 April 1919, Capilla del Señor; ordained 1942; consecrated titular Bishop of Tanais 1957; Bishop of San Rafael 1961–65; Archbishop of Córdoba 1965; cr. Cardinal by Pope Paul VI 1973; mem. Congregation for the Clergy. *Address:* c/o Arzobispado, Avenida H. Irigoyen 98, 5000 Córdoba, Argentina.

PRINCE, (Prince Rogers Nelson); American musician and actor; b. 7 June 1958, Minneapolis; s. of John L. Nelson and Mattie (née Shaw) Nelson; m. Mayte Garcia 1996; one s. (deceased); singer, songwriter and actor; recipient three Grammy awards 1985, Nat. Asscn for the Advancement of Colored People Special Achievement Award 1997. *Albums include:* For You 1978, Dirty Mind 1979, Controversy 1981, 1999 1983, Purple Rain 1984, Around the World in a Day 1985 (Best Soul/Rhythm and Blues Album of the Year, Down Beat Readers' Poll 1985), Parade 1986, Sign of the Times 1987, Lovesexy 1988, Batman (film soundtrack) 1989, Diamonds and Pearls 1991, (symbol as title) 1992, Come 1994, The Rainbow Children 2002, One Nite Alone–Live! 2002. *Films include:* Purple Rain 1984 (Acad. Award for Best Original Score), Under the Cherry Moon 1986, Graffiti Bridge 1990. *Address:* Warner Bros. Records, 75 Rockefeller Plaza, New York, NY 10019, USA.

PRINCE, Harold (Hal), LittD; American theatrical director; b. 30 Jan. 1928, New York; s. of Milton A. Prince and Blanche (née Stern) Prince; m. Judith Chaplin 1962; one s. one d.; ed Emerson Coll.; co-produced Pajama Game 1954–56 (Antoinette Perry Award), Damn Yankees 1955–57 (Antoinette Perry Award), New Girl in Town 1957–58, West Side Story 1957–59, Fiorello! 1959–61 (Antoinette Perry Award, Pulitzer Prize), Tenderloin 1960–61, A Call on Kuprin 1961, They Might Be Giants 1961, Side by Side by Sondheim 1976; produced Take Her, She's Mine 1961–62, A Funny thing Happened on the Way to the Forum 1962–64 (Antoinette Perry Award), Fiddler on the Roof 1964–72 (Antoinette Perry Award), Poor Bitos 1964, Flora the Red Menace 1965; dir, producer She Loves Me! 1963–64, London, Superman 1966, Cabaret 1966–69 (Antoinette Perry Award), London 1968, Zorba 1968–69,

Company 1970–72 (Antoinette Perry Award), London 1972, A Little Night Music 1973–74 (Antoinette Perry Award) (London 1975), Pacific Overtures 1976; co-dir, producer Follies 1971–72; co-producer, dir Candide 1974–75, Merrily We Roll Along 1981; dir A Family Affair 1962, Baker Street 1965, Great God Brown 1972–73, The Visit 1973–74, Love for Love 1974–75, On the Twentieth Century 1978, Evita, London 1978, Broadway 1979, Los Angeles 1980, Chicago 1980, Australia 1980, Vienna 1981, Mexico City 1981, Sweeney Todd, the Demon Barber of Fleet Street 1979–80, London 1980, A Doll's Life 1982, Diamonds 1984, Grind 1985, The Phantom of the Opera (Antoinette Perry Award for Best Dir 1988) 1986, Play Memory, End of the World, Rosa 1987, Grandchild of Kings (The O'Casey Project) (author and dir) 1992, Kiss of the Spider Woman (Toronto, London) 1992, (New York, Vienna) 1993, Show Boat (Toronto) 1993, (New York) 1994, (nat. tour) 1996, Candide 1997, Parade 1998; mem. Council, Nat. Endowment of the Arts, League of New York Theatres; Critics Circle awards, Best Music Award, Evening Standard; Commonwealth Award 1982; John F. Kennedy Center Awards 1994. *Films include:* (co-producer) The Pajama Game 1957, Damn Yankees 1958; (dir) Something for Everyone 1970, A Little Night Music 1978. *Operas:* Ashmedai 1976, Silverlake 1980, Don Giovanni 1989 (New York City Opera); Madame Butterfly 1982; Candide 1982; Willie Stark 1982 (Houston Opera Co.); Turandot 1983 (Vienna Staatsoper); Faust 1990, 1991 (Metropolitan Opera), La Fanciulla del West 1991 (Chicago Lyric Opera, San Francisco Opera). *Address:* Suite 1009, 10 Rockefeller Plaza, New York, NY 10020, USA.

PRINCIPI, Anthony J.; American politician, naval officer and lawyer; b. 16 April 1944, N.Y.C.; m. Elizabeth Ann Ahlering 1971; three s.; ed U.S. Naval Acad., Seton Hall Univ.; service with USN in Vietnam; Chief Defense Counsel, Judge Advocate Gen. Corps, San Diego; Staff Counsel, Commdr U.S. Pacific Fleet; Legis. Counsel, Dept of the Navy 1980; Chair. Bd, Fed. Quality Inst. 1991; Chief Counsel and Staff Dir, U.S. Senate Cttee on Armed Services 1993; Chair. Comm. on Service Mems. and Veterans Transition Assistance; COO Lockheed Martin Integrated Solutions 1995–2001; Co-founder, Pres. and Chair. of Bd, Fed. Network; Pres. QTC Medical Services; Deputy Sec. of Veterans Affairs, 1989, Acting Sec. 1992, Sec. of Veterans Affairs 2001–; Bronze Star, Vietnamese Cross of Gallantry, Navy Combat Action Medal and other decorations. *Address:* Department of Veterans Affairs, 810 Vermont Avenue, NW, Washington, DC 20420, U.S.A. (Office). *Telephone:* (202) 273-5700 (Office). *Website:* www.va.gov (Office).

PRINGLE, James Robert Henry, MA; British economist and journalist; b. 27 Aug. 1939, Surrey; s. of John Pringle and Jacqueline (née Berry) Pringle; m. Rita Schuchard 1966 (divorced 1998); ed King's School, Canterbury, King's Coll. Cambridge and London School of Econs; Asst to Ed., then Asst Ed. The Banker, London 1963–67; mem. editorial staff The Economist, London 1968; Asst Dir, later Deputy Dir Cttee on Invisible Exports 1969–72; Ed. The Banker 1972–79; Exec. Dir Group of Thirty, Consultative Group on Int. Econ. and Monetary Affairs, New York 1979–86; Sr Fellow, World Inst. for Devt Econs Research of the UN Univ. 1986–89; Sr Research Fellow, the David Hume Inst. Edinburgh 1989–91; Dir Graham Bannock and Partners 1989–97; Ed.-in-Chief, Central Banking 1990–; Head, Public Policy Centre, The World Gold Council 1997–. *Publications:* Banking in Britain 1973, The Growth Merchants 1977, The Central Banks (Co-author) 1994, International Financial Institutions 1998. *Leisure interests:* classical music, the theatre. *Address:* 9 Northwood Lodge, Oakhill Park, London, NW3 7LL, England (Home). *Telephone:* (20) 7766-2721.

PRIOR, Baron (Life Peer), cr. 1987, of Brampton in the County of Suffolk; **James Michael Leathes Prior,** PC; British politician and farmer; b. 11 Oct. 1927, Norwich; s. of the late C. B. L. Prior and A. S. M. Prior; m. Jane P. G. Lywood 1954; three s. one d.; ed Charterhouse and Pembroke Coll. Cambridge; MP for Lowestoft 1959–83, for Waveney 1983–87; Parl. Pvt. Sec. to Pres. of Bd of Trade 1963, to Minister of Power 1963–64, to Rt Hon. Edward Heath 1965–70; Vice-Chair. Conservative Party 1965, 1972–74; Minister of Agric., Fisheries and Food 1970–72, Lord Pres. of Council 1972–74; Shadow Spokesman on Home Affairs March–June 1974, on Employment June 1974–79; Sec. of State for Employment 1979–81, for Northern Ireland 1981–84; Chair. GEC 1984–98; Dir Barclays PLC 1984–89, J. Sainsbury PLC 1984–92, United Biscuits 1984–79, 1984–94; mem. Tenneco European Advisory Council 1986–97, AIG Advisory Council; Dir Arab-British Chamber of Commerce; Chair. Royal Veterinary Coll. –1998; Chancellor Anglia Polytechnic Univ. 1992–99; Deputy Chair. MSI Cellular Investments BV 1999–, Ascot Underwriting Ltd 2001–. *Publication:* A Balance of Power 1986. *Leisure interests:* cricket, tennis, golf, gardening. *Address:* House of Lords, London, SW1A 0PW, England.

PRISTAVKIN, Anatoliy Ignatevich; Russian author and government official; b. 17 Oct. 1931, Lyubertsy, Moscow; m. 1st V. Golubkova 1960 (divorced 1975); one s. one d.; m. 2nd Mary Berezhnaya 1986; one d.; ed Gorky Inst. of Literature; first works published 1956; Prof. Gorky Inst. of Literature 1981–; Leader of April Independent Asscn of Writers 1989–; Chair. Comm. for Grace, under Pres. of Russian Fed. 1992–2001; Counsellor of the Pres. of Russian Fed. 2002–; USSR State Prize 1987, Deutsche Jugendliteratur Prize 1991, Druzhba Narodov Literary Prize 1999, Aleksandr-Men Prize 2002. *Publications:* Little Stories 1959, A Lyrical Book 1969, A Golden Cloud (Nochevala tuchka zolotaya) 1987, The Small Cuckoos 1989, Ryazanka 1990, The Vine Road 1998, A Valley of Death (Dolina teni smertnoj) 2000. *Address:*

8/4 ul. Ilinka, 103132 Moscow (Office); Leningradskij prosp. 26-2, apt. 53, 125040 Moscow, Russia (Home). *Telephone:* (095) 206-43-60 (Office); (095) 212-82-36 (Home). *Fax:* (095) 206-43-38 (Office).

PRITCHARD, David E., PhD; American professor of physics; b. 15 Oct. 1941, New York; s. of Edward M. Pritchard and Blanche M. Allen Pritchard; m. Andrea Hasler; two s.; ed California Inst. of Tech. and Harvard Univ.; Postdoctoral Fellow, MIT, Cambridge, Mass. 1968, instructor 1968–70, Asst Prof. 1970–75, Assoc. Prof. 1975–80, Prof. of Physics 1980–; Div. Assoc. Ed. Physics Review Letters 1983–88; Distinguished Traveling Lecturer LSTG/ American Physical Soc. (A.P.S.) 1991–93; mem. NAS; Fellow AAAS, A.P.S., American Acad. of Arts and Sciences; Broida Prize, A.P.S. 1991. *Achievements:* mentored four Nobel Prize winners and two Thesis Award winners. *Publications:* numerous scientific papers, articles and contribs. to books. *Leisure interests:* piano playing, sailing. *Address:* Department of Physics, Massachusetts Institute of Technology, 77 Massachusetts Avenue, Room 26–241, Cambridge, MA 02139, USA. *Telephone:* (617) 253-6812. *Fax:* (617) 253-4876. *E-mail:* dpritch@mit.edu.

PRIX, Wolf D.; Austrian architect and university professor; b. 13 Dec. 1942, Vienna; ed Tech. Univ., Vienna, Architectural Asscn, London, UK, Southern Calif. Inst. of Architecture, LA, USA; co-f. and Pnr Coop Himmelb(l)au (with Helmut Swiczinsky) 1968; Prof. of Architecture 3 Masterclass, Univ. of Applied Arts, Vienna 1993–, Dean of Architecture, Industrial Design, Product Design and Stage Design 1999–; Visiting Prof. Architectural Asscn, London 1984, Harvard Univ., USA 1990; Adjunct Prof. Southern Calif. Inst. of Architecture, LA 1985–95; Faculty mem. Columbia Univ., NY 1998–; Harvey Perloff Prof. UCLA 1999, Adjunct Prof. 2001; mem. Architectural Council, Fed. Ministry of Science, Research and the Arts 1995–97; mem. Austrian Univ. Curatorial Cttee 2000–; Perm. mem. Austrian Art Senate, European Acad. of Sciences and Arts; Hon. mem. League of German Architects 1989; Officier des Arts et des Lettres 2002; Dr hc (Universidad de Palermo, Buenos Aires, Argentina) 2001; Berlin Prize for Building Art 1982, Austrian Architectural Asscn (AAA) Award 1985, PA Award 1991, European Industrial Architecture Award 1992, Erich-Schelling-Architecture Prize 1992, Tau Sigma Delta Award 1993, Grosser Österreichischer Staatspreis 1999, Gold Medal for Merits to the Fed. State of Vienna 2002. *Architectural works include:* Rooftop Remodelling Falkestrasse (City of Vienna Award for Architecture 1989) 1983–88, Funder Factory 3 (State of Carinthia Award for Superior Architecture 1989, AAA Award 1990) 1988–89, Los Angeles Art Park (PA Award 1989), Open House (PA Award 1990), Guggenheim Museum, Bilbao, Spain 1991, Centre Pompidou, Paris, France 1992–93, Groninger Museum (Dutch Nat. Steel Prize 1992) 1993–94, Seibersdorf Office and Research Centre (AAA Prize 1996) 1993–95, UFA Cinema Centre, Dresden (Neuer Sächsicher Kunstverein Prize 1996, German Architecture Prize 1999, Concrete Architectural Prize 1999, European Steel Design Award 2001) 1993–98, SEG Apt Tower (AAA Award 1999) 1994–98, SEG Remise (Austrian Cement Industry Award 2001) 1994–2000, Otis Coll. of Art and Design, LA, USA 1998, Restaurant Mosku, Guadalajara, Mexico 1999–, Expo 2002 Forum Arteplage Biel, Switzerland 1999–2002, Wassertum Hainburg (Anerkennungspreis für Architektur des Landes Niederösterreich 2002); Works in progress: Musée des Confluences, Lyon, France 2001–(06), Akron Art Museum, Ohio, USA 2001–(05). *Publications include:* The Vienna Trilogy and One Cinema 1999, Covering and Exposing: The Architecture of Coop Himmelb(l)au 2000, Blue Universe: Architectural Manifestos by Coop Himmelb(l)au 2002. *Address:* Coop Himmelb(l)au, Prix & Swiczinsky GmbH, 1010 Vienna, Austria (Office). *Telephone:* (1) 532-5535 (Office). *Fax:* (1) 532-5539 (Office). *E-mail:* office@coop-himmelblau.at (Office). *Website:* www .coop-himmelblau.at (Office).

PRLIĆ, Jadranko; Bosnia and Herzegovina (Croat) politician and university professor; b. 10 June 1959, Djakovo; m. Ankica Prlić; two d.; ed Univs. of Mostar and Sarajevo; worked as a journalist; joined teaching staff Univ. of Mostar 1987; Mayor of Mostar 1987–88; fmr Gen. Man. Apro-Mostar agricultural enterprise; Vice-Pres. Govt of Bosnia and Herzegovina 1989–91; during war 1992–95 mem. and official of highest bodies of Croatian people; following signing of Washington (1994) and Dayton (1995) Agreements: Deputy Prime Minister and Minister of Defence; mem. Parl. of Bosnia and Herzegovina and Minister of Foreign Affairs 1996–2001; mem. Council of Ministers 2001–; Deputy Minister of Foreign Trade and Econ. Relations 2001–; Founder and Pres. European Movement in Bosnia and Herzegovina; Gov. in IMF for Bosnia and Herzegovina. *Publications:* Policy of Fluctuating Foreign Exchange Rates 1990, Imperfect Peace 1998, Fuga Della Storia 2000, Return to Europe 2002; numerous articles in field of int. economy, particularly finance and political issues. *Leisure interests:* tennis, soccer, econ. and political literature, etc. *Address:* Ministry of Foreign Trade and Economic Relations, Musala Street 9, 71000 Sarajevo, Bosnia and Herzegovina. *Telephone:* (33) 208100. *Fax:* (33) 208102. *E-mail:* jprlic@bih.net.ba (Office).

PROCKTOR, Patrick, RA, RWS; British artist; b. 12 March 1936, Dublin; s. of Eric C. Procktor and Barbara W. Hopkins; m. Kirsten Andersen 1973 (died 1984); one s.; ed Highgate School and Slade School; one-man exhbns Redfern Gallery 1963–; designer of windows for AIDS recreation centre, St Stephen's Hosp. Fulham 1988; retrospective tour, England and Wales 1990; Paintings in Hosps exhbn 1999, Brighton Festival; poster for Antony and Cleopatra and exhbn at Royal Nat. Theatre. *Exhibition:* St John Baptizing the People, Chichester Cathedral 1986. *Television:* My Britain (Channel 4) 1987. *Publications:* One Window in Venice 1974, Coleridge's Rime of the Ancient

Mariner (new illustrated edn) 1976, A Chinese Journey (aquatint landscapes) 1980, Sailing through China by Paul Theroux (illustrations), Patrick Procktor Prints 1959–85 (catalogue raisonné) 1985, A Shropshire Lad by A. E Housman (new illustrated edn) 1986, Self-Portrait (memoir) 1991, P.P. by John McEwen (illustrations) 1997, Secret Classrooms by H. Shukman and G. Elliott (illustrations) 2003. *Leisure interest:* Russian ballet. *Address:* c/o Redfern Gallery, 20 Cork Street, London, W1X 2HL, England (Office).

PROCTER, Jane Hilary Elizabeth; British journalist; b. London; d. of Gordon H. Procter and Florence Bibby Procter; m. Thomas C. Goldstaub 1985; one s. one d.; ed Queen's Coll. Harley St London; Fashion Asst Vogue 1974–75; Asst Fashion Ed. Good Housekeeping 1975–77; Acting Fashion Ed. Woman's Journal 1977–78; Fashion Writer Country Life 1978–80; Freelance Fashion Ed. The Times, Daily Express 1980–87; Ed. Tatler 1990–99, Ed. Dir PeopleNews Network 1999–2001. *Publication:* Dress Your Best 1983. *Leisure interests:* skiing, sailing. *Address:* c/o PeopleNews Network, 77 Dean Street, London, W1D 3SH, England (Office). *Telephone:* (20) 7025-1818 (Office).

PRODI, Romano, L.L.B.; Italian politician and university professor; b. 9 Aug. 1939, Scandiano; s. of Mario Prodi and Enrica Prodi; m. Flavia Franzoni; two s.; ed Catholic Univ. of Milan, London School of Econs; Prof. of Econs and Industrial Policy, Univ. of Bologna 1971–99; Minister of Industry 1978–79; Chair. Scientific Cttee Econ. Research Inst. Nomisma, Bologna 1981–95; Chair. Istituto per le Ricostruzione Industriale (IRI) 1982–89, 1993–94; Prof. of Industrial Org. and Policy, Univ. of Bologna 1990–93; f. l'Olivo (coalition of centre-left parties) 1995; Pres. Council of Ministers (Prime Minister) 1996–98; Pres. European Comm. July 1999–; mem. Asscn di cultura e politica, Il Mulino, Bologna, Asscn Italiana degli Economisti, Rome; Hon. mem. Real Academia de Ciencias Morales y Políticas, Madrid; Hon. Fellow LSE; numerous hon. degrees. *Publications:* author of numerous scientific pubs with particular reference to questions of European industrial policies, public enterprises in Italy and comparative analysis of econ. systems. *Address:* European Commission, 200 rue de la Loi, 1049 Brussels, Belgium. *Telephone:* (2) 299-11-11. *Fax:* (2) 295-01-38. *Website:* europa.eu.int/comm/index_en.htm (Office).

PROFUMO, John Dennis, CBE; British fmr politician; b. 30 Jan. 1915; s. of the late Baron Albert Profumo, KC; m. Valerie Hobson 1954 (died 1998); one s.; ed Harrow, Brasenose Coll. Oxford; with 1st Northamptonshire Yeomanry 1939; Brig. Chief of Staff, UK Mission in Japan 1945; MP (Kettering Div.) 1940–45, (Stratford-on-Avon) 1950–63; Parl. Sec., Ministry of Transport and Civil Aviation 1952–57, Parl. Under-Sec. of State for the Colonies 1957–58, for Foreign Affairs 1958–59; Minister of State for Foreign Affairs 1959–60; Sec. of State for War 1960–63; Dir Provident Life Asscn of London 1975–, Deputy Chair. 1978–82; mem. Bd of Visitors, HM Prison, Grendon 1968–75; Chair. Toynbee Hall 1982–85, Pres. 1985–, Hon. Life Mem. 2001–; Hon. Fellow Queen Mary Coll., Univ. of London 2001–. *Leisure interests:* fishing, gardening, do-it-yourself.

PROKEŠ, Jozef, DSc; Slovak politician; b. 12 June 1950, Nitra; s. of Jozef Prokeš and Elena Manicová; m. 1979; one s. one d.; ed Komenský Univ., Bratislava; research student with Inst. of Physics, Slovak Acad. of Sciences, Bratislava 1973–82; worked for Heavy Current Electrotechnical Works, Čab 1982–85; research worker Inst. of Measurements, Slovak Acad. of Sciences, Bratislava 1985–89; co-f. Forum of Coordinating Cttees. of Workers in Slovakia 1989; Chair. Independent Trade Unions 1990; Chair. Trade Union of Research Workers of Slovak Acad. of Sciences 1990; Deputy to Slovak Nat. Council 1990–92; Chair. Slovak Nat. Party (SNP) 1991–92, Hon. Chair. 1992–; Vice-Pres. Slovak Nat. Council 1992–93; Deputy Premier of Slovak Govt 1993–94; Deputy to Nat. Council 1994–; Vice-Chair. Foreign Cttee of Nat. Council 1994–98; Head Slovak del. to CSCE 1993–94; mem. Slovak del. to WEU 1995. *Address:* National Council of the Slovak Republic, Mudroňova 1, 812 80 Bratislava, Slovakia (Office). *Telephone:* (7) 5934-1111 (Office). *E-mail:* k.badulin@nbrb.by.

PROKOPOVICH, Petr Petrovich; Belarus engineer and banker; b. 3 Nov. 1942, Rovno, Brest Region; s. of Petr Prokopovich and Evgeniya Prokopovich; m. Ludmila Prokopovich; one s. one d.; ed Dnepropetrovsk Eng and Construction Inst.; Dir-Gen. Brest Regional Planning and Construction Asscn 1976–96; mem. Supreme Soviet 1990–95; Deputy Head of Admin. of Pres. of Belarus 1996; First Deputy Prime Minister of Belarus 1996–98; Chair. Nat. Bank of Belarus 1998–; Order of Labour Red Banner, Order of Honour, Honoured Constructor of the USSR Award, Diploma of the Supreme Soviet of Belarus. *Publications:* various articles in Belorussian and foreign edns. *Address:* National Bank of Belarus, 20, F. Skorina Avenue, Minsk 220008, Belarus (Office). *Telephone:* 219-22-01 (Office). *Fax:* 227-48-79 (Office). *E-mail:* nbrb@nbrb.belpak.minsk.by (Office).

PROSSER, Sir Ian Maurice Gray, Kt, BComm, FCA; British business executive; b. 5 July 1943, Bath; s. of Maurice and Freda Prosser; m. Elizabeth Herman 1964; two d.; ed King Edward's School, Bath, Watford Grammar School and Univ. of Birmingham; with Cooper Bros (chartered accts) 1964–69; with Bass Charrington Ltd 1969–82, Financial Dir 1978; Vice-Chair. and Financial Dir Bass (now Six Continents) PLC 1982–84, Vice-Chair. and Group Man. Dir 1984–87, Chair. and CEO 1987–2000, Exec. Chair. 2000–; Pres. The Brewers' Soc. 1992–94; Dir Lloyds TSB Group PLC 1988–, BP (later BP Amoco now BP PLC) 1997– (Deputy Chair. 1999–), Smithkline Beecham PLC 1999–; Chair. Exec., World Travel and Tourism Council. *Leisure interests:*

bridge, gardening. *Address:* Six Continents PLC, 20 North Audley Street, London, W1Y 1WE, England. *Telephone:* (20) 7409-1919. *Fax:* (20) 7409-8506 (Office).

PROST, Alain Marie Pascal; French motor racing team owner and fmr racing driver; b. 24 Feb. 1955, Saint-Chamond; s. of André Prost and Marie-Rose Karatchian; m. Anne-Marie Prost; two s.; ed Coll. Sainte-Marie, Saint-Chamond; French and European Champion, Go-Kart Racing 1973, French Champion 1974–75; French and European Champion, Formula Three Racing 1979; joined Marlboro MacLaren Group 1980; winner French, Netherlands and Italian Grand Prix 1981; World Champion 1985, 1986, 1989, 1993; winner Brazilian, French, Mexican, Spanish and British Grand Prix 1990, South African, San Marino, Spanish, European, Canadian, French, British, German Grand Prix 1993; Silverstone Grand Prix 1993; Estoril Grand Prix; total 51 Grand Prix wins, 106 podium finishes; technical consultant to McLaren Mercedes 1995; founder and Pres. Prost Grand Prix Team 1997–2001; Officier, Légion d'honneur; Hon. OBE 1994; Trophée du champion automobile du siécle en Autriche 1999. *Publications:* Vive ma vie 1993. *Address:* Prost Grand Prix, 7 avenue Eugène Freyssinet, 78286 Guyancourt Cedex, France. *Telephone:* 1-39-30-11-07 (Office). *Fax:* 1-39-30-11-06 (Office).

PROT, Baudouin Daniel Claude; French banker; b. 24 May 1951, Paris; s. of André Prot and Marguerite Le Febvre; m. Viviane Abel 1981; one s. one d.; ed Inst. de Sainte-Croix, Neuilly, Ecole Saint-Louis des hautes études commerciales, Ecole nat. d'admin.; Inspecteur, Inspection générale des finances, Paris 1976; Deputy Dir Gen. Energy and Raw Materials, Ministry of Industry 1982–83; joined Banque Nat. de Paris (BNP) 1983, managerial positions depts. for Europe 1985–87, metropolitan networks 1987–92, France 1992–96, Deputy Dir-Gen. BNP 1992–96, Dir-Gen. 1996–; Chair. Carte bleue group 1991–97; Dir Accor, Pechiney, mem. Supervisory Cttee Pinault-Printemps-Redoute; Inspecteur générale des finances 1993; Chevalier Ordre Nat. du Mérite, Légion d'honneur. *Publications:* Armée-Nation, le Rendez-vous manqué 1975, Nationalisation 1977, Réduire l'impôt 1985, Dénationalisation 1986, La Jeunesse inégale 1987, Le Retour de capital 1990. *Leisure interests:* tennis, skiing, sailing. *Address:* BNP Paribas, 3 rue d'Autin, 75002 Paris (Office); 21 rue Monsieur, 75007 Paris, France (Home). *Telephone:* 1-40-14-59-11 (Office). *Fax:* 1-55-77-50-51 (Office). *E-mail:* baudouin.prot@bnpparibas.com (Office).

PROTHEROE, Alan Hackford, CBE, TD, DL; British journalist and broadcasting executive; b. 10 Jan. 1934, St David's, Wales; s. of Rev. B. P. Protheroe and R. C. M. Protheroe; m. Anne Miller 1956 (died 1999); two s.; ed Maesteg Grammar School, Glamorgan; Reporter, Glamorgan Gazette 1951–53; 2nd Lt, The Welch Regt 1954–56; Reporter, BBC Wales 1957–59, Industrial Corresp. 1959–64, Ed. News and Current Affairs 1964–70; Asst Ed. BBC TV News 1970–72, Deputy Ed. 1972–77, Ed. 1977–80; Asst Dir BBC News and Current Affairs 1980–82; Asst Dir-Gen. BBC 1982–87; Man. Dir The Services Sound and Vision Corpn 1987–94; Founder-mem. Asscn of British Eds, Chair. 1987; Dir Visnews Ltd 1982–87; Dir Defence Public Affairs Consultants Ltd 1987–; Dir Europac Group Ltd 1990– (Chair. 1990–2000), Chair. E Wessex Reserve Forces Asscn; mem. Inst. of Public Relations; mem. Man. Bd Royal British Legion; DL for Bucks.; Col TA 1991–96. *Publications:* contribs to journals on media and defence affairs. *Leisure interests:* travel, photography, rough golf. *Address:* Amberleigh House, 60 Chapman Lane, Flackwell Heath, Bucks., HP10 9BD, England. *Telephone:* (1628) 528492. *Fax:* (1628) 528492 (Office).

PROULX, Edna Ann (E. Annie), MA; American writer; b. 22 Aug. 1935, Norwich, Conn.; d. of George Napoleon Proulx and Lois Nellie Gill; m. 3rd James H. Lang 1969 (divorced 1990); three s. one d.; ed Sir George Williams (now Concordia) Univ., Montréal and Univ. of Vermont; freelance journalist, Vt 1975–87; f. Vershire Behind the Times newspaper, Vershire, Vt; short stories appeared in Blair & Ketchums Country Journal, Esquire, etc.; Vt Council Arts Fellowship 1989, Ucross Foundation Residency, Wyo. 1990, 1992; mem. PEN; Guggenheim Fellow 1993; active anti-illiteracy campaigner; Hon. DHumLitt (Maine) 1994; stories listed in Best American Short Stories 1983, 1987; Alumni Achievement Award, Univ. of Vt 1994, New York Public Library Literary Lion 1994, Dos Passos Prize for Literature 1996, American Acad. of Achievement Award 1998, Book Award, The New Yorker 2000, Amb. Book Award, English Speaking Union 2000. *Publications:* Heart Songs and Other Stories 1988, Postcards 1992 (PEN/Faulkner Award for Fiction 1993), The Shipping News 1993 (Chicago Tribune's Heartland Prize for Fiction, Irish Times Int. Fiction Prize, Nat. Book Award for Fiction (all 1993), Pulitzer Prize for Fiction 1994), Accordion Crimes 1996, Best American Short Stories of 1997 (Ed.), Brokeback Mountain 1998, Close Range: Wyoming Stories 1998, That Old Ace in the Hole 2002; numerous articles. *Leisure interests:* fly-fishing, canoeing, playing the fiddle. *Address:* PO Box 230, Centennial, WY 82055, USA. *Fax:* (307) 742-6159.

PROXMIRE, William, MA; American politician (retd); b. 11 Nov. 1915, Lake Forest, Ill.; s. of Theodore Stanley Proxmire and Adele (née Flanigan) Proxmire; m. Ellen Hodges; ed Yale and Harvard Univs.; with U.S. Army Intelligence Service 1941–46; State Assemblyman (Democrat) for Wisconsin 1951–52; Senator from Wisconsin 1957–89; Chair. Senate Banking Cttee 1975–81; Pres. Artcraft Press, Waterloo, Wisconsin 1954–57; Commentator NBC 1989–; Democrat. *Publications:* Can Small Business Survive?, Uncle Sam, Last of the Big Time Spenders, You Can Do It!, The Fleecing of America, Your Joy Ride to Health 1993.

PRUDNIKOV, Gen. Victor Alexeyevich; Russian army officer; b. 4 Feb. 1939, Rostov-on-Don; m.; two s.; ed Armavir Higher Mil. Aviation School of Pilots, Gagarin Mil. Aviation Acad., Mil. Acad. of Gen. Staff; pilot, instructor aviation regt 1959–65; Commdr of squadron, Regt Commdr, Deputy Div. Commdr 1968–75; Commdr Anti-Aircraft Defence Div. 1975–78; Deputy C-in-C 1978–81; First Deputy C-in-C 1981–83; Commdr Anti-Aircraft Defence Army 1983–89; C-in-C Moscow Mil. Command 1989–91; C-in-C Anti-Aircraft Defence Forces of Russia 1991–97; Head of Staff on Co-ordination of Mil. Co-operation CIS Cos 1998–2001. *Leisure interests:* tennis, swimming. *Address:* Ministry of Defence, Myasnitskaya str. 37, 103175 Moscow, Russia (Office). *Telephone:* (095) 296-18-00 (Office).

PRUEHER, Adm. Joseph W., M.S.; American diplomatist and naval officer; b. 25 Nov. 1942, Nashville, Tenn.; m. Suzanne Prueher; one s. one d.; ed Montgomery Bell Acad., US Naval Acad., Annapolis, Md, Naval War Coll., Newport, RI and George Washington Univ.; started naval career as Command Ensign, USN, advanced through grades to Adm., C-in-C US Pacific Command, Camp HM Smith, Hawaii 1996–99; Amb. to People's Repub. of China 1999–2001; mem. Bd of Dirs Merrill Lynch 2001–; multiple awards for combat flying as well as naval and jt service; has been decorated by govts. of Singapore, Thailand, Japan, Korea, Philippines, Indonesia and Australia. *Publications:* numerous articles on leadership, mil. readiness and Pacific region security issues. *Address:* c/o Department of State, 2201 C Street, NW, Washington, DC 20520, USA (Office). *Website:* www.ml.com (Office).

PRUNSKIENĖ, Kazimiera, D.ECON.SCI.; Lithuanian politician; b. 26 Feb. 1943, Shvenchioniu Region; d. of Ona Stankevičiene and Pranas Stankevičius; m. 1st Povilas Prunskus 1961; m. 2nd Algimantas Tarvydas 1990 (divorced); one s. two d.; ed Vilnius State Univ.; teacher, then Dean of Faculty, Vilnius State Univ. 1965–85; Deputy Dir Inst. of Econ. Agric. 1986–88; People's Deputy of the USSR 1989–90, mem. USSR Supreme Soviet 1989–90; Deputy Chair. Council of Ministers of Lithuania 1989–90, Chair. 1990–91; mem. Lithuanian Parl. 1990–92, 1996–; Pres. Lithuanian-European Inst. 1991–; Pres. pvt. consulting firm K. Prunskienė-Consulting 1993–; Founder and Pres. Lithuanian Women's Asscn (now Party) 1992–, Chair. 1995–; mem. CEPS Int. Advisory Council 1992–, Int. Cttee for Econ. Reform and Co-operation 1994–; Pres. Baltic Women's Basketball League 1994–; mem. Council of Women World Leaders 1997–; Order of Grand Duke of Lithuania Gediminas (2nd Degree) and Medal of the Order of Gediminas 2000, Medal of the Independence of Lithuania 2000, Medal of the Fed. Repub. of Germany, Order of Merit 2000, Grand Cross of Merit with Star 2001. *Publications:* Amber Lady's Confession 1991, Leben für Litauen 1992, Behind the Scenes 1992, Challenge to Dragon 1992, Price of Liberation 1993, Markt Balticum 1994, Transformation, Co-operation and Conversion 1996, Science and Technology Policy of the Baltic States and International Co-operation 1997, Intellectual Property Rights in Central and Eastern Europe: the Creation of Favourable Legal and Market Preconditions 1998. *Leisure interests:* sports, music, literature, knitting, cooking, walking in the forest. *Address:* Lithuanian-European Institute, Vilnius St 45-13, 2001 Vilnius (Office); Kriviu 53a-13, 2007 Vilnius, Lithuania (Home). *Telephone:* (2) 222-114, 222-834 (Office). *Fax:* (2) 221-955.

PRUSAK, Mikhail Mikhailovich, CAND.ECONS.; Ukrainian/Russian politician and economist; b. 23 Feb. 1960, Dzhurkov region, Ukraine; m.; one s. one d.; ed Higher Komsomol School, Acad. of National Economics; Sec. Novgorod regional Komsomol Cttee –1988; Dir Sovkhoz Trudovik Novgorod region 1988–91; People's Deputy, mem. USSR Supreme Soviet, mem. Interregional Deputies' Group 1989–91; Head of Admin. Velikiy Novgorod region 1991–93, 1995–99, Gov. of Velikiy Novgorod 1999–; mem. State Duma (Parl.) 1993–; mem. Presidium Political Council of People's Democratic Party; Vice-Pres. Parl. Ass. Council of Europe (PASE) Jan. 1999–; corresp. mem. St Petersburg Acad. of Eng. *Address:* Office of the Governor, Sofiyskaya pl. 1, 173005 Velikiy Novgorod, Russia (Office). *Telephone:* (81622) 13-12-02 (Office). *Fax:* (81622) 13-13-30 (Office). *E-mail:* infoserv@miac.natm.ru (Office).

PRYCE, Jonathan; British actor; b. 1 June 1947, North Wales; s. of Isaac Price and Margaret Ellen Price (née Williams); partner Kate Fahy; two s. one d.; ed Royal Acad. of Dramatic Art; Patron Friends United Network, Saving Faces; Tony Award for Comedians 1976, Olivier Award for Hamlet 1980, Olivier and Variety Club Awards for Miss Saigon 1991, also Tony and Drama Desk Awards, Best Actor, Cannes Film Festival 1995, Best Actor, Evening Standard Film Award 1996 for Carrington. *Stage appearances include:* Comedians, Nottingham Old Vic 1976, New York 1976, Hamlet, Royal Court Theatre, London 1980, The Caretaker, Nat. Theatre 1981, Accidental Death of an Anarchist, Broadway 1984, The Seagull, Queen's Theatre 1985, Macbeth, RSC 1986, Uncle Vanya 1988, Miss Saigon, Drury Lane 1989, New York 1991, Oliver!, London Palladium 1994, My Fair Lady, Nat. Theatre and Drury Lane, London 2001. *Television appearances in:* Roger Doesn't Live Here Anymore (series) 1981, Timon of Athens 1981, Martin Luther 1983, Praying Mantis 1983, Whose Line Is It Anyway? 1988, The Man from the Pru 1990, Selling Hitler 1991, Mr Wroe's Virgins 1993, Thicker than Water 1993. *Films include:* Something Wicked This Way Comes 1982, The Ploughman's Lunch 1983, Brazil 1985, The Doctor and the Devils 1986, Haunted Honeymoon 1986, Jumpin' Jack Flash 1987, Consuming Passions 1988, The Adventures of Baron Munchausen 1988, The Rachel Papers 1989, Glen Garry Glen Ross 1992, Barbarians at the Gate 1992, Great Moments in Aviation 1993, The Age of Innocence 1993, A Business Affair 1993, Deadly Advice 1994, Carrington

1995, Evita 1996, Tomorrow Never Dies 1997, Regeneration 1997, Ronin 1998, Stigmata 1999, Very Annie Mary 2001, Unconditional Love 2001, The Affair of the Necklace 2001, Bride of the Wind 2001. *Recordings:* Miss Saigon 1989, Nine–The Concert 1992, Under Milkwood 1992, Cabaret 1994, Oliver! 1995, Hey! Mr Producer 1998, My Fair Lady 2001. *Leisure interests:* painting, drawing. *Address:* c/o Julian Belfrage Assocs., 46 Albemarle Street, London, W1X 4PP, England; c/o U.T.A., 9560 Wilshire Blvd, Beverly Hills, CA 90212, USA.

PRYOR, David Hampton, LLB; American politician; b. 29 Aug. 1934, Camden, Ark.; s. of Edgar Pryor and Susan (née Newton) Pryor; m. Barbara Lunsford 1957; three s.; ed Univ. of Arkansas; admitted to Ark. Bar 1964; mem. Ark. House of Reps. 1961–66; served in Congress, House of Reps. 1966–72; Gov. of Arkansas 1974–79; Senator from Arkansas 1979–96; mem. American Bar Asscn, Ark. Bar Asscn; Fellow Inst. of Politics, School of Govt, Harvard Univ. 1999; Democrat. *Address:* 2701 Kavanaugh Boulevard, Suite 300, Little Rock, AR 72205, USA (Office).

PRYOR, Mark, BA, LLB; American politician and lawyer; b. 1963, Fayette-ville; s. of David Hampton Pryor (q.v.); ed Univ. of Arkansas; practised law with Wright, Lindsey & Jennings, Little Rock 1982–90; elected to Arkansas State House of Reps. (Democrat) for two terms 1990; Attorney-Gen. for Arkansas 1999–2003, Senator from Arkansas 2003–; served as campaign chair. in Arkansas for Vice-Pres. Al Gore 2000. *Address:* Office of the Senator from Arkansas, US Senate, Senate Buildings, Washington, D.C. 20150, USA (Office).

PRYOR, Richard; American actor and writer; b. 1 Dec. 1940, Peoria, Ill.; s. of Leroy Pryor and Gertrude (née Thomas) Pryor; two s. two d.; served with US Army 1958–60; owner Richard Pryor Enterprises Inc., LA 1975–; has written film scripts for: Blazing Saddles 1973, Lily 1974, Adios Amigos 1976, The Bingo Long Travelling All-Stars and Motor Kings 1976, Car Wash 1976, Silver Streak 1976, Greased Lightning 1977, Which Way is Up? 1977, Blue Collar 1978, Stir Crazy 1980; Emmy Award 1973, Grammy Award 1974, Kennedy Center Mark Twain Prize 1998. *Film appearances include:* Lady Sings the Blues 1972, Hit 1973, Wattstax 1973, Uptown Saturday Night 1974, Blue Collar 1978, California Suite 1978, The Wiz 1978, Richard Pryor Live in Concert 1979, Wholly Moses, In God We Trust, Bustin' Loose 1981, Some Kind of Hero 1982, Superman III 1983, The Toy 1984, Brewster's Millions 1985, Jo Jo Dancer Your Life is Calling (also wrote, produced and dir) 1986, Moving 1988, See No Evil, Hear No Evil 1989, Harlem Nights, Another You 1991, Lost Highway 1996, Mad Dog Time 1996. *Address:* c/o Jennifer Lee, Indigo Production, 4900 Valjean Avenue, Encino, CA 91436, USA (Office).

PSZONIAK, Wojciech Zygmunt; Polish actor; b. 2 May 1942, Lvov; m.; ed State High Theatre School, Cracow, Asst State High Theatre School, Cracow 1967–72, lecturer 1972–; prin. theatrical roles at Stary Theatre, Cracow 1968–72, Narodowy Theatre, Warsaw 1972–74, Powszechny Theatre, Warsaw 1974–80; presenter TV show Wojtek Pszoniak – pytania do siebie (Pszoniak – Questions to Himself) 1995–96; Prize of Ministry of Culture (2nd Class) 1975, Masters Award, Montréal Film Festival 1982; Gold Cross of Merit 1975, Kt's Cross, Order of Polonia Restituta 1997. *Films:* Wesele (The Wedding) 1973, Ziemia obiecana (The Promised Land) 1975, Austeria 1981, Danton 1982, Je hais les acteurs 1986, Les années-sandwiches 1987, Czerwona Wenecja (Red Venice) 1988, Korczak 1989. *Plays:* Poskromienie złośnicy (The Taming of the Shrew) 1969, Sen nocy letniej (A Midsummer Night's Dream) 1970, Wszystko dobre, co się dobrze kończy (All's Well That Ends Well) 1971, Biesy 1971, Makbet (Macbeth) 1973, Les gens déraisonnables sont en voie de disparition, Théâtre des Amandiers, Nanterre 1978, Zemsta (Revenge) 1980, Czekając na Godota (Waiting for Godot) 1989, Król Ubu (King Ubu) 1992, The Deep Blue Sea, Apollo Theatre, London 1993, Atelier, Théâtre Hébertot, Paris 1999, Pracownia krawiecka (Tailor's Shop – actor and dir) 2000, Kolacja dla głupca (Supper for Fools) 2001, La boutique au coin de la rue, Théâtre Montparnasse, Paris 2001. *Publication:* Pszoniak & Co. czyli Towarzystwo Dobrego Stołu 1993. *Leisure interests:* classical music, jazz, cooking.

PTASHNE, Mark Stephen, PhD; American professor of biochemistry; b. 5 June 1940, Chicago, Ill.; s. of Fred Ptashne and Mildred Ptashne; ed Reed Coll. and Harvard Univ.; Jr Fellow, Harvard Soc. of Fellows 1965–68; Lecturer, Dept of Biochem. and Molecular Biology, Harvard Univ. 1968–71, Prof. 1971–, Chair. Dept of Biochem. and Molecular Biology 1980–83; Herchel Smith Prof. of Molecular Biology 1993–; Guggenheim Fellow 1973–74; Fellow American Acad. of Arts and Sciences; mem. NAS; Feodor Lynen Lecturer 1988; Prix Charles-Léopold Mayer, Acad. des Sciences, Inst. de France (with W. Gilbert and E. Witkin) 1977; Eli Lilly Award 1975; shared Louisa Gross Horwitz Prize 1985; Gairdner Foundation Int. Award (with Charles Yanofsky) 1985; Cancer Research Foundation Award 1990. *Publications:* A Genetic Switch 1986, A Genetic Switch II 1992; 122 papers in scientific journals 1950–89. *Leisure interests:* classical music, opera. *Address:* Department of Biochemistry and Molecular Biology, Harvard University, 7 Divinity Avenue, Cambridge, MA 02138, USA. *Telephone:* (617) 495-2336.

PU HAIQING; Chinese politician; b. 1940, Sichuan Prov.; ed Chongqing Univ.; joined CCP 1973; Man. Chongqing Iron and Steel Co.; Vice-Gov. Sichuan Prov.; Mayor of Chongqing Municipality, Vice-Sec. CCP Chongqing Mun. Cttee 1997–; mem. 15th CCP Cen. Cttee 1997–. *Address:* Chongqing Municipal Government, Chongqing, People's Republic of China.

PU NAI-FU; Taiwanese author; b. Nanjing; m.; ed Beijing Russian-Language Jr Coll.; imprisoned for various periods in labour-reform camps during anti-intellectual campaigns in China; moved to Hong Kong, subsequently to Taiwan 1983. *Publications include:* Romance in the Arctic, The Woman in the Pagoda, Books Without Names (6 vols), The Scourge of the Sea, Red in Tooth and Claw.

PU SHAN, LLD; Chinese academic; b. 27 Nov. 1923, Beijing; m. Chen Xiuying 1951; ed Univ. of Shanghai, Univ. of Michigan, Harvard Univ., USA; Vice-Pres. Chinese Soc. of World Economy 1980–85, Pres. 1985–97, Dir Inst. of World Econs and Politics 1982–88; mem. Nat. Cttee, CPPCC 1988–98, mem. Standing Cttee 1993–98; Pres. Grad. School, Chinese Acad. of Social Sciences 1991–94; Hon. Pres. Chinese Soc. of World Economy 1997–. *Address:* Graduate School, Chinese Academy of Social Sciences, Beijing 100015 (Office); 24 Zhan Lan Road, Beijing 100037, People's Republic of China (Home). *Fax:* (10) 64362343 (Office).

PU TA-HAI; Taiwanese government official; b. 3 April 1922, Meihsien, Kwangtung; m.; one s. two d.; ed Chinese Mil. Acad., Chinese Army Command Gen. Staff Coll. and Chinese Armed Forces Staff Coll.; Section Chief (Col), Taiwan Peace Preservation H.Q. 1956–57; Dept Head (Col), Gen. H.Q., Chinese Army 1957–60; Dept Head (Maj.-Gen.), Personnel Div., Ministry of Nat. Defence 1963–68; Dept Head (Maj.-Gen.), Taiwan Garrison Gen. H.Q. 1968–72; Dept Head, Cen. Personnel Admin., Exec. Yuan 1972–78; Dir Dept of Personnel, Taipei City Govt 1978–81, Taiwan Provincial Govt 1981–84; Deputy Dir-Gen. Central Personnel Admin., Exec. Yuan 1984, Dir-Gen. 1984–93; Nat. Policy Adviser to the Pres. 1993–. *Leisure interests:* tennis, badminton. *Address:* Office of the Director-General, Central Personnel Administration, Executive Yuan, 109 Huai Ning Street, Taipei, Taiwan. *Telephone:* (2) 361-7072.

PUAPUA, Rt. Hon. Sir Tomasi, Kt, PC; Tuvaluan politician; b. 10 Sept. 1938; s. of Fitilau Puapua and Olive Puapua; m. Riana Tabokai 1971; two s. two d.; ed Fiji School of Medicine and Univ. of Otago, NZ; medical practitioner; Prime Minister of Tuvalu 1981–90, also Minister for Civil Service Admin., Local Govt and Minister for Foreign Affairs; Speaker of Parl. 1993–98; Gov. Gen. of Tuvalu 1998–. *Leisure interests:* athletics, rugby, tennis, volleyball, cricket, soccer, fishing, pig and poultry farming, gardening. *Address:* Government House, Vaiaku, Funafuti, Tuvalu (Office).

PUCK, Theodore Thomas, BS, PhD; American professor of medicine and biochemistry, biophysics and genetics; b. 24 Sept. 1916, Chicago, Ill.; s. of Joseph Puckowitz and Bessie Puckowitz; m. Mary R. Hill 1946; three d.; ed Univ. of Chicago; Univ. Fellow, Dept of Chem., Univ. of Chicago 1938–40, Research Assoc., Dept of Medicine 1941–45, Asst Prof. Depts of Medicine and Biochem. 1945–47; mem. Comm. on Airborne Infections, Army Epidemiological Bd, Office of Surgeon-Gen. 1944–46; Sr Fellow, Calif. Inst. of Tech., Pasadena 1947–48; Prof. and Chair. Dept of Biophysics, Univ. of Colo Medical Center 1948–67; Research Prof. of Biochem., Biophysics and Genetics, Univ. of Colo Medical Center 1967–86, Distinguished Prof. 1986–; Research Prof. of American Cancer Soc. 1966–; Prof. Dept of Medicine, Univ. of Colo Health Sciences Center 1981–, Distinguished Prof., Dept of Medicine, Univ. of Colo 1986–; Dir Eleanor Roosevelt Inst. for Cancer Research 1962–95, Sr Fellow 1995–; Fogarty Int. Scholar, NIH 1997–98; mem. NAS 1960–, Editorial Bd, Encyclopaedia Britannica 1980–87, Paideia Group; Fellow, American Acad. for Arts and Sciences 1967–; Lasker Award 1958, Borden Award 1959, Stearns Award, Univ. of Colo 1959, General Rose Memorial Hosp. Award 1960, Distinguished Service Award of Univ. of Chicago Med. Alumni Asscn 1969, Gross Horwitz Prize of Columbia Univ. in Cell Biology and Biochemistry 1973, Inst. of Med. 1974, Gordon Wilson Medal of American Clinical and Climatological Asscn 1977, Annual Award, Environmental Mutagen Soc. 1981, AAAS Award and Lectureship 1983, Heritage Foundation Scholar 1983, E. B. Wilson Medal of American Soc. for Cell Biology 1984, Bonfils–Stanton Award in Science 1984, ARCS Man of Science Award 1987, Hon. Award of Tissue Culture Asscn 1987, Who's Who Worldwide Award for Outstanding Achievement 1990, Porter Hosp. Medal 1992. *Publications:* The Mammalian Cell as a Micro-organism: Genetic and Biochemical Studies in Vitro 1972; many papers (some jointly) in the field of somatic cell genetics, also airborne infection, virus interaction with host cells, mammalian cell biochemical genetics, human cytogenetics, mammalian radiation biology and cancer. *Leisure interests:* skiing, hiking, travel, music. *Address:* Eleanor Roosevelt Institute for Cancer Research, 1899 Gaylord Street, Denver, CO 80206, USA (Office). *Telephone:* (303) 333-4515 (Office).

PUDDEPHATT, Andrew Charles, OBE, BA; British company director; b. 2 April 1950, Luton; s. of Andrew Ross Puddephatt and Margaret Deboo; two c.; ed Kingsbury School, Dunstable and Sidney Sussex Coll. Cambridge; Deputy Leader Hackney Council 1984–85, Leader 1986–89; Dir Nat. Council for Civil Liberties 1989–95; Dir Charter 88 1995–99; Exec. Dir Article 19. *Leisure interests:* music, cinema, walking. *Address:* c/o Article 19, Global Campaign for Freedom of Expression, Lancaster House, 33 Islington High Street, London, N1 9LH, England (Office). *Telephone:* (20) 7278-9292. *Fax:* (20) 7713-1356. *E-mail:* andrew@article19.org (Office). *Website:* www.article19.org (Office).

PUDDEPHATT, Richard John, PhD, FRS, FRSC; British/Canadian professor of chemistry; b. 10 Oct. 1943; s. of Harry Puddephatt and Ena Puddephatt; m. Alice Poulton 1969; one s. one d.; ed Univ. Coll. London; Teaching Postdoctoral Fellow Univ. of W. Ontario 1968–70, Prof. of Chemistry

1978–; lecturer Univ. of Liverpool 1970–77, Sr lecturer 1977–78; Nyholm Award 1997, CIC Medal 1998. *Publications include:* The Chemistry of Gold 1978, The Periodic Table of the Elements 1986. *Leisure interest:* gardening. *Address:* Department of Chemistry, University of Western Ontario, London, Ont., N6A 5B7, Canada (Office). *Telephone:* (519) 679-2111. *Fax:* (519) 661-3022.

PUENZO, Luis; Argentine film director; b. 24 Feb. 1949, Buenos Aires; worked as storyboard designer in advertising, becoming advertising dir; f. Cinemania 1974. *Films include:* Luces de mis zapatos (Lights of my Shoes) 1973, Cinco años de vida (Five Years of Life) 1975, The Official Story 1985 (Palme d'Or, Cannes, Acad. Award for Best Foreign Film 1986 and 47 other int. awards), Gringo viejo (Old Gringo) 1989. *Address:* c/o Instituto Nacional de Cinematografía, Lima 319, 1073 Buenos Aires, Argentina.

PUGACHEV, Sergey Victorovich; Russian politician; b. 4 Feb. 1963, Kostoma; m.; two c.; ed Leningrad State Univ.; credit inspector, Head of Div., mem. Bd of Dirs USSR Promstroibank 1985–90; mem. Bd of Dirs N Trade Bank 1990–92; Chair. Bd of Dirs Int. Industrial Bank (Mezhprombank) 1992–2002; mem. Bureau Russian Union of Businessmen and Entrepreneurs 2002–; mem. Council of Feds, Rep. of Govt, Tuva Repub. 2001–; mem. Cttee on Problems of Fed. and Regional Policy Council of Feds; mem. Russian Acad. of Eng. *Publications include:* Commercial Bank in Conditions of Free Market Relations Formation: Econ. and Financial Analysis 1998. *Address:* House of Government, Chuldum str. 18, 667000 Kyzyl, Russia (Office). *Telephone:* (839422) 11284 (Office). *Fax:* (839422) 11354 (Office). *E-mail:* council@gov.ru (Office).

PUGACHEVA, Alla Borisovna; Russian singer; b. 5 April 1949, Moscow; m. 2nd Filipp Kirkorov; one d.; ed M. Ippolitov-Ivanov Music High School, A. Lunacharsky State Inst. of Theatre Art; debut as soloist of Lipetsk vocal-instrumental group 1970; O Lundstrem Jazz orchestra 1971; soloist Veselye Rebyata Ensemble 1973–78; f. Song Theatre 1988; numerous prizes and awards including 3rd prize All-Union Contest Moscow, 1974; Grand Prix Int. Competition Golden Orpheus Bulgaria 1975, Int. Festival Sopot 1978; acted in films; several concert programmes; tours in USA, Germany, Switzerland, India, France, Italy and other countries; f. Theatre of Songs 1988, Alla Co. 1993, Alla Magazine 1993; USSR People's Artist, Ovation Prize 1994, State Prize of Russia 1995. *Repertoire includes:* numerous songs by popular Soviet composers such as R. Pauls, A. Muromtsev, A. Zatsepin and others, also songs of her own. *Address:* Tverskaya-Yamskaya str., Apt. 57, Moscow, Russia (Home). *Telephone:* (095) 250-95-78 (Home).

PUGIN, Nikolai Andreyevich; Russian industrialist; b. 30 June 1940; ed Gorky Polytechnic Inst.; worker, foreman at car factory 1958–75; chief engineer at gearbox factory 1975–81; Tech. Dir 1981–83, Gen. Dir of Gorky Automobile Works 1983–86; Minister of Automobile Industry 1986–88, of Automobile and Agricultural Machines Industry 1988–91; mem. Russian Eng Acad. 1991–; mem. Russian Acad. of Natural Science 1992–; Pres. ASM Holding Inc. (mfrs of motor vehicles and farm machinery in CIS) 1992–; Chair. Bd GAZ Co. (Nizhny Novgorod); Pres. Ind. Financial Group Nizhegorodskiye Automobili 1994–; Chair. Bd Dirs Autobank 1996–2002; mem. Nizhny Novgorod Regional Ass. 2002–. *Address:* ASM Holding, 21/5 Kuznetsk Most, 103895 Moscow; GAZ, Lenina prosp. 9, 603046, Nizhny Novgorod; Oblastnaya Duma, Kremlin, korp. 2, 603082 Nizhny Novgorod, Russia. *Telephone:* (095) 921-68-21; 924-53-85 (both Moscow); (8312) 56-10-70 (Nizhny Novgorod). *Fax:* (095) 924-39-00 (Moscow).

PUGOVKIN, Mikhail Ivanovich; Russian film actor; b. 13 July 1923, Rameshki, Yaroslav Region; s. of Ivan Pugovkin and Maria Pugovkina; m. 3rd Irina Medvedeva; one d.; ed Nemirovich-Danchenko School-Studio, Moscow Art Theatre; U.S.S.R. People's Artist. *Films include:* The Artamonov's Case, Wedding, Admiral Ushakov, Oleko Dundich, Wedding in Malinovka, May Stars, Land and People, A Girl with a Guitar, Ivan Vassilyevich Changes His Profession, Peasant. *Address:* Glinishchevsky per. 5/7, Apt. 23, 103009 Moscow, Russia (Home). *Telephone:* (095) 229-49-86 (Home).

PUIG, Lluis de Maria; Spanish politician and historian; b. 20 July 1945, Bascara, Gerona; m.; two c.; ed Autonomous Univ. of Barcelona, Ecole des Hautes Etudes de la Sorbonne, Paris; worked in anti-Franco opposition as active mem. of underground Catalan and socialist orgs.; Prof. of Contemporary History, Autonomous Univ. of Barcelona; Socialist mem. Cortes for Gerona 1979–; mem. Catalonian Socialist Party Bureau 1986–; Pres. Gerona Fed. of Socialist Party 1993–; mem. Council of Europe Ass. 1983–, Chair. Sub-Cttee on European Social Charter 1984–89, Vice-Pres. Ass. 1993–96; mem. Spanish del. to WEU Ass. 1990–, Vice-Chair. Socialist Group 1992–96, Defence Cttee 1992–94, Chair. Political Cttee 1994–96, mem. Presidential Cttee 1994–, Pres. WEU Ass. 1997–2000; Sec. Alexander Cirici Inst. for European Co-operation 1986–96, Pres. 1996–; Dr. hc (Ovidius Univ. of Constanta, Romania) 1998. *Publications:* several books on history of 19th and 20th century Catalonia, books and essays on Europe, articles on domestic and int. politics. *Address:* c/o Assembly of Western European Union, 43 avenue du Président Wilson, 75775 Paris Cedex 16, France.

PUISSOCHET, Jean-Pierre, LLD, PhD; French international judge and lawyer; b. 3 May 1936, Clermont-Ferrand; s. of René Puissochet and Hélène Puissochet (née Brengues); m. Eliane Millet 1973; one d.; ed Lycée du Parc, Lyon, Inst. for Political Studies, Lyon, School of Law, Lyon, Ecole Nat. d'Admin., Paris; Auditeur, Conseil d'Etat 1962, Maître des Requêtes 1968,

Conseiller 1985; Dir Legal Service, Council of EC 1968–70, Dir-Gen. 1970–73; Dir-Gen. Agence Nat. pour l'Emploi 1973–75; Dir Ministry of Industry and Research 1977–79; Dir of Legal Affairs, OECD 1979–85; Dir Int. Inst. of Public Admin. 1985–87; Legal Adviser, Dir of Legal Affairs, Ministry of Foreign Affairs 1987–94; Judge, Court of Justice of the European Communities 1994–; mem. Perm. Court of Arbitration, The Hague 1990–; Officier, Légion d'honneur, Commdr Ordre nat. du Mérite, Officier du Mérite agricole. *Publications:* The Enlargement of the EC 1974; numerous articles on Community and int. law. *Address:* Court of Justice of the European Communities, Plateau du Kirchberg, 2925 Luxembourg (Office); 15 rue Jean-Pierre Brasseur, 1258, Luxembourg, Luxembourg (Home). *Telephone:* 43-03-22-46 (Office). *Fax:* 43-03-20-00. *E-mail:* jean-pierre.puissochet@curia.eu.int (Office).

PUJATS, HE Cardinal Jānis; Latvian ecclesiastic; b. 14 Nov. 1930, Nautreni; ordained priest 1951; consecrated Bishop 1991; Archbishop of Riga; cr. Cardinal (secretly) 1998, (openly) 2001. *Address:* Metropolijas Kurija, Mazā Pils iela 2/a, 1050 Riga, Latvia (Office). *Telephone:* (2) 227-266 (Office). *Fax:* (2) 220-775 (Office).

PUJOL I SOLEY, Jordi, MD; Spanish politician, pharmacologist and businessman; b. 9 June 1930, Barcelona; s. of Florenci Pujol i Soley and Maria Pujol i Soley; m. Marta Ferrusola 1956; seven s.; ed Faculty of Medicine, Univ. of Barcelona; worked in pharmaceutical industry 1953–60; f. Banca Catalana group 1959, Man. Dir 1959–76; f. Convergència Democratica de Catalunya 1974; Councillor, provisional Generalitat 1977–80; mem. Congress, Madrid 1977, 1979; Head Convergència i Unió Parl. Group in Congress 1977–80; mem. Catalan Parl. 1980–; Pres. Generalitat de Catalunya 1980–2002; Vice-Pres. Ass. of European Regions 1988–92, Pres. 1992–96; Dr. hc (Brussels, Toulouse, Lyon, Rosario, Argentina). *Publications include:* Una política per Catalunya 1976, Construir Catalunya 1980, Als joves de Catalunya 1988, La Força serena i constructiva de Catalunya 1991, Pensar Europa 1993, Passió per Catalunya 1999. *Leisure interests:* reading, walking, cycling. *Address:* c/o Palau de la Generalitat, Plaça Sant Jaume s/n, Barcelona 2, Spain (Office).

PULATOV, Timur Iskhakovich; Uzbekistan writer; b. 1939, Bukhara; ed Bukhara Pedagogical Inst.; freelance writer 1974–; First Sec., Co-ordinator Exec. Bd Int. Soc. of Writers' Unions 1992–; Order, Friendship of Peoples for devt of lit. and art and strengthening of int. relations 1994. *Publications:* Other Populated Points, Properties, Passions of the Bukhara House, Tortoise Tarasi, Swimming Eurasia. *Address:* Moscow City Organization of Russian Writers' Union, B. Nikitskaya str. 50a/5, 121069 Moscow, Russia (Office). *Telephone:* (095) 202-87-83 (Office).

PULIKOVSKY, Lt-Gen. Konstantin Borisovich; Russian army officer and politician; b. 9 Feb. 1948, Ussuriysk, Primorsk Territory; ed M. Frunze Mil. Acad., Mil. Acad. of Gen. Staff; mil. posts to rank of Army Commdr 1972; took part in conflict in Chechnya 1994–96; Commdr group of Fed. forces in Chechen Repub. 1996, Deputy Commdr., N Caucasus Mil. District 1997–; leader Krasnodar Org. All-Russian Movt of veterans of local wars and mil. conflicts Boyevoye Bratstvo; Rep. of Russian Pres. to Far E Fed. Dist 2000–. *Publications include:* The Eastern Express: Through Russia With Kim Jong Il 2002. *Address:* Office of the Presidential Representative, Sheronova str. 22, 680030 Khabarovsk, Russia (Office). *Telephone:* (4212) 31-30-44 (Khabarovsk) (Office); (095) 206-73-52 (Moscow) (Office).

PULJIĆ, HE Cardinal Vinko; Bosnia and Herzegovina ecclesiastic; b. 8 Sept. 1945, Priječani, Banja Luka; s. of Ivan Puljić and Kaja Puljić (née Pletikosa); ed seminary of Šalata, Zagreb and at Đakovo; ordained priest Đakovo 1970; parish vicar Banja Luka, parish priest Sasina, then Ravska; pedagogue, Zmajević seminary, Zadar 1978–87; parish priest Bosanska Gradiška 1987–90; Vice-Rector Catholic Theological Seminary of Vrhbosnia, Sarajevo 1990; Archbishop of Vrhbosnia 1990–; cr. Cardinal 1994; travelled to many countries in Europe and N America to publicise the suffering caused by the war in Bosnia and Herzegovina and discuss possible solutions; Hon. Dr. Humanitarian Science (Grand Valley State Univ., Mich., USA) 1995; Hon. Dr. Pastoral Theology (Catholic Univ. Santa Maria in Apartade, Peru) 2001; Humanist of the Decade and Golden Diploma of Humanism, Int. League of Humanists, Sarajevo 1995. *Publications:* Suffering With Hope: Appeals, Addresses, Interviews 1995, Non cancellato l'uomo–Un grido di speranza da Sarajevo 1997, Per amore dell'uomo–Testimone di pace a Sarajevo 1999. *Address:* Nadbiskupski Ordinarijat, Kaptol 7, BH 71000 Sarajevo, Bosnia and Herzegovina.

PULLMAN, Bill; American actor; b. 1955, Hornell, NY; m. Tamara Pullman; three c.; ed Univ. of Massachusetts; fmr drama teacher, bldg contractor, dir of a theatre group; started acting in fringe theatres, New York; moved to LA. *Films include:* Ruthless People, A League of Their Own, Sommersby, Sleepless in Seattle, While You Were Sleeping, Caspar, Independence Day, Lost Highway 1997, The End of Violence 1997, The Thin Red Line 1998, Zero Effect 1998, A Man is Mostly Water 1999, History is Made at Night 1999, The Guilt 1999, Brokedown Place 1999, Lake Placid 1999, Coming To Light: Edward S. Curtis and the North American Indians (voice) 2000, Titan A.E. 2000, Numbers 2000. *Address:* c/o J. J. Harris, 9560 Wilshire Boulevard, Suite 500, Beverly Hills, CA 90212, USA.

PULLMAN, Philip, BA, FRSA; British author; b. 19 Oct. 1946, Norwich; m. Jude Speller 1970; two s.; ed Exeter Coll., Oxford; teacher in Oxford 1972–86; part-time lecturer Westminster Coll., Oxford 1986–96; BA/Book Data Author of the Year Award 2001, Booksellers' Asscn Author of the Year 2001, 2002,

British Book Awards Author of the Year Award 2002, Whitbread Book of the Year Award 2002. *Publications include:* The Ruby in the Smoke 1986, The Shadow in the North 1987, The Tiger in the Well 1990, The Broken Bridge 1992, The White Mercedes 1992, The Tin Princess 1994, Northern Lights (Carnegie Medal 1996, Guardian Children's Fiction Prize 1996, British Book Awards Children's Book of the Year 1996) 1995, The Golden Compass 1996, Spring-Heeled Jack, Puss in Books, The Subtle Knife 1997, Count Karlstein 1998, Clockwork 1998, I Was a Rat! 2000, The Amber Spyglass (British Book Awards WH Smith Children's Book of the Year 2000, Whitbread Children's Book of the Year Prize 2001, Whitbread Book of the Year Award 2001) 2000; contribs. to Times Educational Supplement, The Guardian. *Address:* c/o Caradoc King, A. P. Watt Ltd, 20 John Street, London, WC1N 2DR (Office); 24 Templar Road, Oxford, OX2 8LT, England (Home). *Telephone:* (20) 7405-6774 (Office). *Fax:* (20) 7831-2154 (Office).

PUNGOR, Ernő, PhD, DR.CHEM.SC.; Hungarian chemist; b. 30 Oct 1923, Vasszécsény; s. of József Pungor and Franciska Faller; m. 1st Erzsébet Lang 1950; m. 2nd Dr Tünde Horváth 1984; two s. one d.; ed Pázmány Univ., Budapest; Corresp. mem. Hung. Acad. of Sciences 1967, mem. 1976–; Asst Prof. Eötvös Univ., Budapest 1948–53, Assoc. Prof. 1953–62; Prof. Chemical Univ., Veszprém 1962–70; Dir Inst. for Gen. and Analytical Chemistry, Tech. Univ., Budapest 1970–90, now Prof. Emer.; Head Research Group for Tech. Analytical Chem. of Hungarian Acad. of Sciences 1970–93, Pres. Nat. Comm. for Tech. Devt 1990–94; Minister for Tech. Devt 1990–94; Gen. Dir Bay Zoltán Foundation for Applied Research 1994–2001; Pres. Asscn of Eds of European Chemical Journals 1977; mem. Int. Fed. of Scientific Eds Asscn 1981–87; Chair. Working Party of Analytical Chemists of Fed. of European Chemical Socs 1981–87; Chair. Analysis Div. of Hungarian Chemical. Soc.; Head Analysis Group, Hungarian Acad. of Sciences –2001; mem. IUPAC 1973, Chair. Hungarian Nat. Cttee for IUPAC 1985–; Vice-Pres. Electroanalytical Cttee 1985–87; mem. Scientific Advisory Bd of Org. for the Prohibition of Chemical Weapons, Scientific Advisory Bd of Hungarian Govt 1999; Pres. World Fed. of Hungarian Engineers and Architects 1991–95, mem. in perpetuity 1995–, mem. Hungarian Acad. of Sciences; Ed.-in-Chief Hungarian Journal of Chem. 1977–2002; developed new theory of absorption indicators; pioneering work in the field of ion-selective electrodes and in flow-through analytical techniques; Hon. mem. Czechoslovak Acad. Science Chemical Section 1966, Egyptian Pharmaceutical Soc. 1973, Austrian Analytical and Micro-analytical Soc. 1977, Chemical Soc. of Finland 1979, Analytical Chemical Soc. of Japan 1981, Finnish Tech. Soc. 1990, Royal Soc. 1992, Indian Acad. of Sciences 1993, Royal Soc. of Chemistry 1993; Hon. Prof., Agricultural Univ. of Lima 1973; Redwood Lecturer for English Soc. for Analytical Chemistry 1979; Dr hc (Tech. Univ. of Vienna), (Bucharest) 1993, (Tech. Univ. of Budapest) 1993 (Lomonosov Univ. Moscow) 1999, (Veszprém Univ. Hungary) 1999, (Babeş-Bolyai Univ.) 2000; Robert Boyle Gold Medal (Royal Soc.) 1986, Talanta Gold Medal 1987, Excellent Inventor Gold Medal 1987, Gold Medal of Hungarian Acad. of Science 1988, Gold Medal, Inst. of Analytical Chemists of Tech. Univ. of Vienna 1988; Hon. Prof. Árpád Acad., USA 1990, elected mem. Cen. European Hall of Fame for Eng Sciences and Tech. (ITI, USA) 1991; Eur. Ing. 1992; Fraunhofer Medal (Germany) 1993, Boyle Gold Medal, Royal Soc. of Analytical Chem., UK 1996, Hon. Medal, Fed. of European Chemical Socs 1997; Österreich-Ungarisch Corvinus Kreis Ehrenmitgliedschaft 1994, Grosse Deutsche Verdienstkreuz 1995, Officier, Ordre nat. du Mérite 1996, Decoration of Hungarian Repub. with Star 1998, Gold Medal, Arpád Acad., USA 1998, Prize of Hungarian Spiritual Heritage 1999, Pro Scientia Transsylvanica Medal 2000. *Leisure interest:* history. *Address:* Institute for General and Analytical Chemistry, Budapest Univ. of Technology and Economics, St Gellért tér 4, 1111 Budapest (Office); Bay Zoltán Foundation for Applied Research, Kondorfa u. 1, 1116 Budapest (Office); Meredek u. 4, 1112 Budapest, Hungary (Home). *Telephone:* 1-463-4054 (Univ. Inst.); 1-463-0502 (Bay Foundation). *Fax:* 1-463-3408 (Univ. Inst.); 1-463-0503 (Bay Foundation). *E-mail:* pungor@tki.aak.bme.hu (Office); pungor@bzaka.hu (Bay Foundation); pungor@axelero.hu (Home).

PURCELL, James Nelson, MPA; American international official; b. 16 July 1938, Nashville, Tenn.; s. of James N. Purcell Sr; m. Walda Primm 1961; two d.; ed Furman Univ., Syracuse Univ., New York; Budget Analyst, US Atomic Energy Comm. 1962–66; Man. Analyst, Agency for Int. Devt 1966–68; Deputy Dir Budget Preparation Staff, Office of Man. and Budget (OMB) 1968–72; Sr Examiner Int. Affairs Div. OMB 1972–74; Chief Justice, Treasury Br. OMB 1974–76; Chief Resources Programming and Man. Div., Bureau for Educ. and Cultural Affairs, Dept of State 1976–77; Deputy Budget Dir, Dept of State 1977–78; Exec. Dir Bureau of Admin., Dept of State 1978–79; Deputy Asst Sec., Programmes and Budget, Bureau for Refugee Programs, Dept of State 1979–82, Dir, Asst Sec. Bureau for Refugee Programmes 1982–87; Dir-Gen. Int. Org. for Migration (IOM) 1988–98; Int. Consultant 1998–; mem. American Soc. of Public Admin.; Distinguished Honor Award, State Dept. *Address:* c/o IOM, CP 71, 17 Route des Morillons, 1211 Geneva 19, Switzerland (Office); 5113 West Running Brook Road, Columbia, MD 21044, USA (Home). *E-mail:* ynpatcol@aol.com.

PURCELL, Philip James, MSc, MBA; American business executive; b. 5 Sept. 1943, Salt Lake City; m. Anne Marie McNamara 1964; seven s.; ed Univ. of Notre Dame, London School of Econs, Univ. of Chicago; Man. Dir consultants McKinsey & Co. Inc., Chicago 1967–78; Vice-Pres. Planning and Admin., Sears, Roebuck and Co., Chicago 1978–82; Pres., CEO then Chair., CEO, Dean Witter Discover & Co., New York 1982–97; Chair., CEO Morgan

Stanley, Dean Witter & Co., New York 1997– (now Morgan Stanley 2001–); Dir New York Stock Exchange 1991–96; Trustee Univ. of Notre Dame. *Address:* Morgan Stanley/Dean Witter & Co., 1585 Broadway, 39th Floor, New York, NY 10036, USA (Office).

PURDUM, Robert L., BS; American business executive; b. 1935, Wilmington, Ohio; m. Arlene Peterson; three s.; ed Purdue Univ.; served USN and Indiana Toll Road Comm. 1956–62; joined Armco Inc. 1962, Dist Eng, Metal Products Div. 1962–66, sales staff 1966–72, Dist Man. 1972–76, Gen. Man. 1976–78; Pres. Midwestern Steel Div. 1978–80, Area Vice-Pres. 1980–82, Group Vice-Pres., CEO Mfg Services Group 1982–86, Exec. Vice-Pres. and COO 1986, Pres. and COO 1986–90, Pres., CEO 1990–. *Leisure interests:* tennis, hunting, fishing, travel. *Address:* 26 Horizon Drive, Mendham, NJ 07945, USA (Home).

PURDY, James; American writer; b. 1923; ed Chicago and Spain; interpreter and other posts in Cuba, Mexico, Washington, DC; American Acad. of Arts and Letters Morton Dauwen Zabel Award for Fiction 1993, Oscar Williams and Gene Durwood Award for Poetry 1995. *Publications:* novels: Don't Call Me by My Right Name 1956, 63: Dream Palace 1956, Color of Darkness 1957, Malcolm 1959, The Nephew 1960, Cabot Wright Begins 1963, Eustace Chisholm and the Works 1967, Sleepers in Moon-Crowned Valleys (Part I Jeremy's Version 1970, Part II The House of the Solitary Maggot 1971), I Am Elijah Thrush 1972, In a Shallow Grave 1976, Narrow Rooms 1978, On Glory's Course 1983, Garments The Living Wear 1989, Out With the Stars 1992, Kitty Blue: A Fairytale 1993, Gertrude of Stony Island Avenue 1997; plays: Children is All 1962, A Day After the Fair 1977, How I Became a Shadow (eight plays) 1979, Proud Flesh 1980, Scrap of Paper 1981, The Berry-Picker 1981, Foment 1997; An Oyster is a Wealthy Beast (story and poems) 1967, Mr. Evening 1968 (story and poems), On the Rebound 1970 (story and poems), The Running Sun (poems) 1971, Sunshine is an Only Child (poems) 1973, Lessons and Complaints (poems) 1978, Mourners Below 1981, Dawn 1985, Don't Let the Snow Fall (poem) 1985, In the Hollow of His Hand 1986, The Candles of your Eyes (collected stories) 1987, Are You in the Winter Tree? 1987, The Brooklyn Branding Parlors (poems) 1987, The Room All to Itself (play) 1988, Garments the Living Wear 1989, Collected Poems 1990, Gertrude of Stony Island Avenue 1998, Moe's Villa and Other Stories (fiction) 2000; L.P. Recordings: 63: Dream Palace 1968, Eventide and Other Stories 1969. *Leisure interest:* walking in forests. *Address:* 236 Henry Street, Brooklyn, NY 11201, USA. *Telephone:* (718) 858-0015.

PURI, Om; Indian actor; BAFTA Award for East is East 2000. *Films include:* Jaane Bhi Do Yaaro 1983, Aaghat 1986, Mirch Masala 1986, Genesis 1986, Spices 1986, Dharavi 1992, In Custody 1993, Target 1995, Ghatak 1996, Brothers in Trouble 1996, Ghost and the Darkness 1996, Maachis 1997, My Son the Fanatic 1997, East is East 1999, Hera Pheri 2000, The Zookeeper 2001, Bollywood Calling 2001, Happy Now 2001, Indian 2001, The Mystic Masseur 2001, The Parole Officer 2001, Pitaah 2002. *Address:* 703, Trishul-2, Seven Bungalows, Andheri-W, Mumbai 61, India (Home). *Telephone:* 6342902 (Home).

PURPURA, Dominick Paul, MD; American professor of neuroscience; b. 2 April 1927, New York; s. of John R. Purpura and Rose Ruffino; m. Florence Williams 1948; three s. one d.; ed Columbia Univ. and Harvard Medical School; Chair. and Prof., Dept of Anatomy, Albert Einstein Coll. of Medicine 1967–74, Dept of Neuroscience 1974–82, Prof. and Chair. of Neuroscience 1974–82, Dean, Albert Einstein Coll. of Medicine 1984–; Dir Rose F. Kennedy Center for Research in Mental Retardation and Human Devt 1972–82; Dean, Stanford Univ. School of Medicine 1982–84; Pres. Soc. for Neuroscience 1982–83, Int. Brain Research Org. 1987–98, Vice-Pres. for Medical Affairs UNESCO 1961–; Fellow NY Acad. of Sciences; mem. Inst. of Medicine (NAS). *Publications:* numerous scientific papers. *Address:* Albert Einstein College of Medicine, Yeshiva University, Belfer Building, Room 312, 1300 Morris Park Avenue, Bronx, NY 10461, USA (Office). *Telephone:* (718) 430-2801. *Fax:* (718) 430-8822.

PURVANOV, Georgi, PhD; Bulgarian historian and politician; b. 28 June 1957, Sirishnik, Pernik Dist; m. Zorka Parvanova; two s.; ed Sofia Univ.; researcher 1981–91; joined Bulgarian Communist Party 1981 (became Bulgarian Socialist Party 1990), first party post 1991, Chair. 1996–2001; Pres. of Bulgaria 2002–. *Publications include:* numerous articles and essays. *Address:* Office of the President, 1000 Sofia, Bulgaria (Office). *Telephone:* (2) 923-93-33 . *E-mail:* press@president.bg. *Website:* www.president.bg.

PURVANOV, Georgi; Bulgarian politician and historian; b. 1957; m.; two c.; historian, has conducted research on the nat. question and history of social democracy in Bulgaria; mem. Narodno Sobraniye (Parl.) for Kurdjali (Southern Bulgaria) 1994–; Deputy Chair. Bulgarian Socialist Party (BSP), Chair. 1996–; Pres. of Bulgaria Jan. 2002–; fmr Chair. Parl. Group on Friendship between Bulgaria and Greece. *Address:* Office of the President, 2 Boulevard Knjaz Dondvkov, 1123 Sofia, Bulgaria (Office). *Telephone:* (2) 838-39 (Office). *Fax:* (2) 980-44-84 (Office). *E-mail:* president@president.bg (Office). *Website:* www.president.bg (Office).

PURVES, Sir William, Kt, CBE, DSO; British retd banker; b. 27 Dec. 1931, Kelso; s. of Andrew Purves and Ida Purves; m. 1st Diana T. Richardson 1958 (divorced 1988); two s. two d.; m. 2nd Rebecca Jane Lewellen 1989; ed Kelso High School; with Nat. Bank of Scotland, Kelso 1948–54; joined the Hongkong and Shanghai Banking Corpn 1954, Chief Accountant 1970–74, Man., Tokyo

1974–76, Sr Man. Overseas Operations 1976–78, Asst Gen. Man. Overseas Operations 1978–79, Gen. Man. Int. 1979–82, Exec. Dir 1982–84, Deputy Chair. 1984–86, Chair. and CEO 1986–92, Exec. Chair. HSBC Holdings PLC 1992–98; Pres. Int. Monetary Conf. 1992, mem. Exec. Council Hong Kong 1987–93; Chair. British Bank of the Middle East 1979–98, Midland Bank PLC 1994–97 (Dir 1987–98); Dir HBSC Americas Inc. 1984–88; Deputy Chair. (non-exec.) Alstom SA 1998–2003; Dir (non-exec.) Shell Transport and Trading Co. PLC 1993–2002, Trident Safeguards Ltd 1999–, World Shipping and Investment Ltd 1998–, Reuters Founders Share Co. Ltd 1998–, Scottish Medicine Ltd 1999–, Interpacific Holding Ltd 2000–; Chair. Hakluyt & Co. 2000–; Royal Hong Kong Jockey Club 1992–93; Fellow Chartered Inst. of Bankers; Trustee Gurkha Welfare Trust; Gov. Queenswood School; Hon. DUniv. (Stirling) 1987; Hon. DLaws (Sheffield) 1993; Hon. LLD (Nottingham) 1997; Hon. Dr Business Admin. (Hong Kong Polytechnic) 1993, (Strathclyde) 1996; Dr hc (Hong Kong) 1997, (Napier) 1998, (Hong Kong Open) 1998, (Manchester Science and Tech.) 2000; Grand Bauhimia Medal. *Leisure interests:* golf, rugby. *Address:* 100 Ebury Mews, London, SW1W 9NX, England. *Telephone:* (20) 7823-6775. *Fax:* (20) 7824-8351.

PURVIS, Stewart Peter, CBE, BA; British media executive and journalist; b. 28 Oct. 1947, Isleworth; s. of the late Peter Purvis and the late Lydia Purvis; m. Mary Presnail 1972 (divorced 1993); one d.; two s. with Jacqui Marson; ed Dulwich Coll., Exeter Univ.; fmr presenter Harlech TV; news trainee BBC 1969; Ind. TV News producer 1972, programme ed. News at Ten 1980, Ed. Channel 4 News 1983; Deputy Ed. Ind. TV News 1986, Ed. 1989, Ed.-in-Chief 1991, CEO 1995–; Pres. EuroNews 1997–; Dir Travel News Ltd 1995–, London News Radio 1996–; Deputy Chair. King's Cross Partnership (Dir 1996–); Dir (non-exec) Royal Marsden Nat. Health Service Trust; mem. council European Journalism Centre 1996–; Fellow Royal TV Soc.; recipient of two Royal TV Soc. Awards, BAFTA Award for Best News or Outside Broadcast 1987, 1988, Broadcasting Press Guild Award for Best News or Current Affairs Programme 1988. *Leisure interests:* being at home, keeping fit, yoga. *Address:* ITN Ltd., 200 Gray's Inn Road, London, WC1X 8XZ, England (Office). *Telephone:* (20) 7833-3000 (Office). *Fax:* (20) 7430-4305 (Office). *E-mail:* stewart.purvis@itn.co.uk (Office). *Website:* www.itn.co.uk (Office).

PUSTOVOITENKO, Valery Pavlovich, CAND.TECH.SC.; Ukrainian politician; b. 23 Feb. 1947, Adamivka, Nikolayev Region; m.; two c.; ed Dnipropetrovsk Inst. of Construction Eng; worked as mechanical eng.; head of trusts in Odessa and Dnipropetrovsk 1965–87; People's Deputy of Ukraine; Chair. Dnipropetrovsk City Soviet 1987–93; mem. Higher Econ. Council, Security Council 1997–; Head election campaign of Pres. Kuchma 1994; mem. Ukrainian Cabinet of Ministers 1994–97; Head Ukrainian Football Fed. 1996–; mem. People's Democratic Party of Ukraine, mem. Parl.; mem. Political Exec. Council 1996–; Prime Minister of Ukraine 1997–99; Minister of Transport 2000–02. *Address:* Government Offices, M. Hrushevskoga 12/2, 252008 Kiev, Ukraine. *Telephone:* (44) 226 2204.

PUTILIN, Nikolai Georgiyevich; Russian baritone; b. 1954; ed Krasnoyarsk Inst. of Arts; lessons with Nikola Nikolov in Bulgaria; started as singer of Variety Theatre; soloist of Syktyvkar Musical Theatre, Komi Repub. 1983–85; Kazan Opera Theatre 1985–92; Kirov (Mariinsky) Theatre in St Petersburg 1992–; Prizewinner Int. Chaliapin Competition 1989. *Repertoire includes:* over 40 leading roles toured Metropolitan Opera, La Scala, Teatro Comunale di Firenze, Covent Garden, Bolshoi Theatre and others. *Address:* Mariinsky Theatre, Teatralnaya pl. 1, St Petersburg, Russia (Office). *Telephone:* (812) 114-44-41 (Office).

PUTIN, Col Vladimir Vladimirovich, PhD; Russian politician; b. 7 Oct. 1952, Leningrad (now St Petersburg); m. Lyudmila Putina; two d.; ed Leningrad State Univ.; on staff KGB USSR, with First Chief Dept of KGB and in Germany 1975–90; adviser to Pro-rector Leningrad State Univ. 1990; adviser to Chair. of Leningrad City Exec. Cttee 1990–91; Chair. Cttee on Foreign Relations, St Petersburg Mayor's Office 1991–93; First Deputy Chair. St Petersburg Govt, Chair. Cttee on Foreign Relations 1994–96; Deputy Head, First Deputy Head, Admin. of Russian Presidency, Head, Main Control Dept 1997–98; Dir Fed. Security Service of Russian Fed. 1998–99; Sec. Security Council of Russia March–Aug. 1999; Chair. of Govt (Prime Minister) 1999; Acting Pres. of Russian Fed. 1999–2000, Pres. 2000–. *Address:* The Kremlin, Moscow, Russia. *Telephone:* (095) 205-55-04 (Office).

PUTNAM, Hilary, PhD; American university professor; b. 31 July 1926, Chicago, Ill.; s. of Samuel Putnam and Riva Sampson; m. 1st Erna Diesendruck 1948 (divorced 1962); one d.; m. 2nd Ruth A. Hall 1962; two s. one d.; ed Cen. High School of Philadelphia, Univ. of Pa, Harvard Univ. and Univ. of Calif. at Los Angeles; Asst Prof. of Philosophy, Princeton Univ. 1953–60, Assoc. Prof. 1960–61; Prof. of Philosophy of Science, MIT 1961–65; Prof. of Philosophy, Harvard Univ. 1965, Walter Beverly Pearson Prof. of Mathematical Logic and Modern Math. 1976–; Guggenheim Fellow 1960–61; Corresp. mem. British Acad.; many other fellowships; two hon. degrees. *Publications:* Meaning and the Moral Sciences 1978, Reason, Truth and History 1981, Philosophical Papers (3 Vols) 1975–83, The Many Faces of Realism 1987, Representation and Reality 1989, Realism with a Human Face 1990, Renewing Philosophy 1992. *Leisure interests:* hiking, cooking, languages. *Address:* Faculty of Arts and Sciences, Harvard University, Cam-

bridge, MA 02138 (Office); 116 Winchester Road, Arlington, MA 02174, USA (Home). *Telephone:* (617) 495-1000 (Office). *E-mail:* webmaster@harvard.odu (Office). *Website:* www.harvard.edu.

PUTTNAM, Baron (Life Peer), cr. 1997, of Queensgate in the Royal Borough of Kensington and Chelsea; **David Terence Puttnam,** Kt, CBE, FRGS, FRSA; British film producer and educationalist; b. 25 Feb. 1941, London; s. of Leonard Arthur and Marie Beatrix Puttnam; m. Patricia Mary Jones 1961; one s. one d.; ed Minchenden Grammar School, London; advertising 1958–66, photography 1966–68, film production 1968–2000; Chair. Enigma Productions Ltd Consultants 1999 1978–, Spectrum Strategy Consultants 1999–; Dir Nat. Film Finance Corpn 1980–85, Anglia TV Group 1982–99, Village Roadshow Corpn 1989–99, Survival Anglia 1989–, Chrysalis Group 1993–96; Chair., CEO Columbia Pictures, USA 1986–88; Pres. Council for Protection of Rural England 1985–92; Visiting Lecturer, Bristol Univ. 1984–86, Visiting Industrial Prof. 1986–96; Gov. and Lecturer LSE 1997–; Gov. Nat. Film and TV School 1974–, (Chair. 1988–96); Chair. Teaching Council 2000–02; mem. Governing Council Royal Photographic Soc., Bd Landscape Foundation; Trustee, Tate Gallery 1985–92, Science Museum, IPPR; Chancellor Univ. of Sunderland; Chair. Nat. Endowment for Science, Tech. and the Arts, Nat. Museum of Photography, Film and Television, Teaching Awards Trust; mem. Bd BECTA; Vice-Pres. BAFTA: mem. Educ. Standards Task Force 1997–2001, Arts Council Lottery Panel 1993–97; Trustee Royal Acad. of Arts; Trustee and Fellow World Econ. Forum; mem. Gov. Council for Nat. Coll. for School Leadership; Chair. Media and Culture Sector Advisory Group, QCA; Lay Canon Durham Cathedral; Hon. FCSD; Hon. degrees (Bristol, Keele, Leicester, Manchester, Leeds, Birmingham, Southampton, Bradford, Heriot Watt Edin., Westminster, Humberside, Sunderland, Cheltenham and Glos., Kent, Queens Belfast, London Guildhall Univs, North London, London (City), Royal Scottish Acad., Imperial Coll. London, Sheffield Hallam, American Int. Univ., Richmond, Nottingham, Winchester); Special Jury Prize for The Duellists, Cannes 1977, two Acad. Awards and four BAFTA Awards for Midnight Express 1978, four Acad. Awards (including Best Film), three BAFTA Awards (including Best Film) for Chariots of Fire 1981, three Acad. Awards and nine BAFTA Awards for The Killing Fields 1985; Michael Balcon Award for outstanding contrib. to the British Film Industry, BAFTA 1982; Palme d'Or (Cannes), one Acad. Award and three BAFTA Awards for The Mission 1987; Officier, Ordre des Arts et des Lettres 1986. *Films:* Bugsy Malone, The Duellists, Midnight Express, Chariots of Fire, Local Hero, The Killing Fields, Cal, The Mission 1985, Memphis Belle 1989, Meeting Venus 1990. *Publications:* Rural England: Our Countryside at the Crossroads 1998, Undeclared War: The Struggle to Control the World's Film Industry 1997. *Address:* Enigma Productions, 29A Tufton Street, London, SW1P 3QL, England. *Telephone:* (20) 7222-5757. *Fax:* (20) 7222-5858. *E-mail:* puttnam@enigma.co.uk (Office).

PUYANA, Rafael; Colombian harpsichordist; b. 14 Oct. 1931, Bogotá; s. of Ernesto Puyana and Alicia de Puyana; studied under Wanda Landowska; lives in Spain and Paris; Colombia's Amb. to UNESCO, Paris; Teacher of harpsichord Cursos Manuel de Falla, Granada and Summer Acad. Musica en Compostela, Santiago de Compostela 1976–; gives performances throughout the world; works written for and dedicated to him by several composers including Federico Mompou, Xavier Montsalvatge, Julian Orbón, Alain Louvier and Stephen Dodgson; appeared in two films about life of Domenico Scarlatti (BBC-TV and Televisión Española); Grand Prix du Disque (twice), Deutsche Schallplatten Preis for recording of works by François Couperin; Orden de Isabel la Católica (for his contrib. to study and performances of Spanish baroque and contemporary harpsichord music) 1996. *Leisure interest:* collecting 17th and 18th century keyboard instruments and Spanish and S. American colonial art. *Address:* 8 rue de Cirque, 75008 Paris, France; Hacienda La Chucua, Carrera 4 No 87-21, Santa Fe de Bogotá, Colombia.

PUYOL ANTOLIN, Rafael; Spanish university rector; b. 26 Feb. 1945, Telde, Las Palmas; m. Dolores Martínez-Ferrando; four c.; ed Universidad Complutense; Asst Prof. of Human Geography, Faculty of Geography and History, Universidad Complutense 1975–78, Assoc. Prof. 1978–82, Prof. 1982–, Rector of Univ. 1995–97; mem. editorial bds various journals; Pres. Population Group, Asociación de Geógrafos Españoles 1986–; Vice-Pres. Exec. Cttee Real Sociedad Geográfica. *Publications:* Emigración y desigualdades regionales en España 1979, Población y Espacio 1982, Población y recursos 1984, Población española 1988, Los grandes problemas demográficos 1993, La Unión Europea 1995. *Leisure interests:* music, reading. *Address:* C/Marbella, 50, 28034 Madrid, Spain (Home). *Telephone:* (91) 3720480 (Home). *Fax:* (91) 3943472.

PUZANOV, Col-Gen. Igor Yevgenyevich; Russian army officer; b. 31 Jan. 1947, Tyumen; ed Omsk Gen. Army Command School, M. V. Frunze Mil. Acad., Mil. Acad. of Gen. Staff; Commdr platoon Siberian Mil. Command –1976, Deputy Div. Commdr, then Commdr 1981–88; Deputy Regt Commdr, then Commdr Karpaty Mil. Command 1976–79; served in Afghanistan 1979–81; Head of Gen. Staff Baltic Mil. Command 1988–90; Army Commdr N Caucasian Mil. Command 1990–92; First Deputy Commdr Moscow Mil. Command 1992–2001, Statistics-Sec.; Deputy Minister of Defence March 2001–; Merited Mil. Specialist. *Address:* Ministry of Defence, Znamenka str. 19, 103160 Moscow, Russia (Office). *Telephone:* (095) 203-23-93 (Office).

PYAVKO, Vladislav Ivanovich; Russian tenor; b. 4 Feb. 1941, Krasnoyarsk; s. of Nina Piavko and step-s. of Nikolai Bakhin; m. Irina Arkhipova;

two s. two d.; ed State Inst. of Theatrical Art, Moscow; studied under S. Rebrikov, Moscow, R. Pastorino, La Scala, Milan; mem. CPSU 1978–89; soloist with Bolshoi Opera 1965–89, Berliner Staatsoper 1989–92; teacher of singing and dramatic art, State Inst. of Theatrical Art 1980–89, Dean of School 1983–89; producer at Mosfilm 1980–83; Vice-Pres. Int. Union of Musicians 1998–; has also sung at Teatro Colón, Buenos Aires, Teatro Comunale, Florence, Opéra la Bastille, Paris, Nat. and Smetana Operas, Prague, Metropolitan, New York, Kirov, St Petersburg and in many other houses; also at many int. festivals; Gold Medal in tenor section, Vervier Int. Competition 1969, Silver Medal, Tchaikovsky Int. Competition 1970, Gold Medal and Pietro Mascagni Silver Medal, Livorno 1984, Gold Plank of Cisternino, Italy 1993; People's Artist of USSR 1983, of Kyrgyzstan 1993 and other awards. *Major roles include:* Hermann in Queen of Spades, Andrei in Mazeppa, Dmitry and Shuisky in Boris Godunov, Andrei and Golitsin in Khovanshchina, Radames, Otello, Manrico in Trovatore, Cavaradossi in Tosca, Pinkerton in Madam Butterfly, Don José in Carmen, Turiddu in Cavalleria Rusticana, Guglielmo Ratcliff. *Recordings:* numerous recordings for leading int. labels including EMI, HMV, Philips, Chant du Monde, Columbia. *Leisure interests:* poetry, photography, cars. *Address:* Bryusov, per. 2/14, Apt. 27, 103009 Moscow, Russia. *Telephone:* (095) 229-43-07.

PYE, William Burns, ARCA, FRBS; British sculptor; b. 16 July 1938, London; s. of Sir David Pye and Virginia Pye; m. Susan Marsh 1963; one s. two d.; ed Charterhouse School, Wimbledon School of Art, Royal Coll. of Art; Visiting Prof., Calif. State Univ. 1975–76; kinetic sculpture Revolving Tower 1970; made film Reflections 1971; sculpture 'Zemran' 1971; introduction of tensioned cables with less emphasis on volume 1972; combined working on commissions with smaller work and installations 1972–75; water an integral element of sculptures since mid-70s; first visit to Far East for one-man show (retrospective) 1987; Slipstream and jetstream (water sculptures) commissioned by British Airports Authority, Gatwick Airport 1988; Balla Frois (100 ft long water sculpture) comm. for Glasgow Garden Festival 1988; Chalice water sculpture for 123 Buckingham Palace Rd, London 1990; cr. Water Wall and Portico for British Pavilion, Expo '92, Seville, Spain; Epidavros at Dolby Labs; Aventino at Mercury House, London; Cristos at St Christopher's Place; Downpour at British Embassy, Oman; Cascade at Market Square, Derby 1994; Confluence in Salisbury Square, Hertford 1994; Water Cone at Antony House, Cornwall for Nat. Trust 1996; bronze of Lord Hurd for Nat. Portrait Gallery 1996; Cader Idris at Cen. Square, Cardiff 1998; Prism for Cathay Pacific at Hong Kong Airport 1999; Aquarena Millennium Square, Bristol 2000; Scaladaqua Tonda, Nat. Botanical Garden of Wales 2000; Cornucopia at Millfield School; St John's Innovation Park, Cambridge; Millennium Fountain for Wilton House and Sunderland Winter Garden 2001; Hon. FRIBA 1993; Prix de Sculpture (Budapest) 1981, Vauxhall Mural Prize 1983, Peace Sculpture Prize 1984, ABSA award for best commission of new art in any medium 1988, Art at Work award for best site-specific comm. 1988, Royal Ueno Museum Award, Japan 1989. *Leisure interest:* playing the flute. *Address:* 43 Hambalt Road, London, SW4 9EQ; The Studio, 31 Bellevue Road, London, SW17 7EF, England. *Telephone:* (20) 8682-2727 (Studio). *Fax:* (20) 8682-3218.

PYETSUKH, Vyacheslav Alekseyevich; Russian writer; b. 18 Nov. 1946, Moscow; ed Moscow State Pedagogical Inst.; history teacher Moscow Pedagogical Inst.; work first published in Selskaya Molodezh magazine; freelance writer 1970s–. *Publications:* Alphabet 1983, New Times 1988, History of the Town of Glupov in New and Newest Times, New Moscow Philosophy 1989, Rommat, I and Others 1990, Cycles 1991, State Child 1997. *Address:* VAGRIUS Publishers, Troitskaya str. 7/1, building 2, 129090 Moscow, Russia (Office). *Telephone:* (095) 785-09-03 (Office).

PYM, Baron (Life Peer), cr. 1987, of Sandy in the County of Bedfordshire; **Francis Leslie Pym,** PC, MC, DL; British politician; b. 13 Feb. 1922, Abergavenny; s. of Leslie Ruthven Pym, MP and Iris Rosalind Orde; m. Valerie Fortune Daglish 1949; two s. two d.; ed Eton Coll. and Magdalene Coll.

Cambridge; served with 9th Queen's Royal Lancers (N African and Italian campaigns) 1942–46; mem. Liverpool Univ. Council 1949–53, Herefordshire Co. Council 1958–61; Hon. Fellow, Magdalene Coll.; MP for Cambridgeshire 1961–83; for Cambridgeshire SE 1983–87; Opposition Deputy Chief Whip 1967–70, Govt Chief Whip and Parl. Sec. to Treasury 1970–73; Sec. of State for Northern Ireland 1973–74; Opposition Spokesman for Agric. 1974–76, for House of Commons Affairs and Devolution 1976–78, for Foreign and Commonwealth Affairs 1978–79; Sec. of State for Defence 1979–81; Chancellor of Duchy of Lancaster, Paymaster-Gen. and Leader of the House of Commons Jan.–Sept. 1981; Lord Pres. of the Council and Leader of the House of Commons 1981–82; Sec. of State for Foreign and Commonwealth Affairs 1982–83; Dir Philip N. Christie 1990–93; Christie Brockbank Shipton Ltd 1994–99; Pres. Cambridge Univ. Conservative Asscn 1982–87, Atlantic Treaty Asscn 1985–88; Chair. English-Speaking Union of the Commonwealth 1987–92. *Publications:* The Politics of Consent 1984, Sentimental Journey–An Outline of Family History 1998. *Leisure interest:* gardens. *Address:* Everton Park, Sandy, Beds., SG19 2DE, England.

PYNCHON, Thomas, BA; American novelist; b. 8 May 1937, Glen Cove, NY; s. of Thomas R. Pynchon; ed Cornell Univ.; fmr editorial writer, Boeing Aircraft Co. *Publications include:* V (Faulkner prize for Best First Novel of 1963) 1963, The Crying of Lot 49 (Rosenthal Foundation Award 1967) 1966, Gravity's Rainbow (Nat. Book Award) 1973, Mortality and Mercy in Vienna 1976, Low-Lands 1978, Slow Learner (short stories) 1984, Vineland 1989, Deadly Sins 1994, Mason & Dixon 1996; contrib. short stories to various publs, including Saturday Evening Post. *Address:* c/o Penguin Books, 250 Madison Avenue, New York, NY 10016, USA.

PYNE, Natasha; British actress; b. 9 July 1946, Crawley, Sussex; d. of John Pyne and Iris Pyne; m. Paul Copley 1972; ed Hurlingham Comprehensive School, London; entered film industry 1961; mem. Young Vic Theatre Co., Exchange Co. and RSC, Manchester 1980–81; mem. BBC Radio Drama Co. 1985–87, 1994–95. *Stage plays include:* A Party for Bonzo (Soho Poly) 1985–87, Twelfth Night (Middle East and Africa Tour) 1989–90, Rafts and Dreams 1990, Alfie (UK Tour) 1992–93. *Films include:* The Idol, Taming of the Shrew, Breaking of Bumbo, One of Our Dinosaurs is Missing, Madhouse. *TV plays include:* Father Dear Father (series), Hamlet, Silas Marner; BBC Play for Today: A Brush with Mr Porter on the Road to Eldorado 1981, Van der Valk (Thames TV) 1990–91, The Bill (Thames TV series) 1991, 1993, 2001, 2003, Virtual Murder (BBC TV) 1992, McLibel! (Channel 4 drama-documentary) 1997, Cadfael III (TV film series) 1997. *Radio work includes:* On May-Day (BBC Radio 4 and BBC World Service) 1986, The Snow Queen 1994, Galileo 1995, Ben Hur (serial) 1995, Westway (BBC World Service serial) 1997–98, Young PC (BBC Radio 4 series) 1997, Westway (BBC World Service serial) 1998–2002, Westway (BBC World Service) 1999–2003, Mary Banter (BBC Radio 4) 2001. *Leisure interests:* cycling, reading, cooking, travel, photography, cats, SE Asia. *Address:* c/o Kate Feast Management, 10 Primrose Hill Studios, Fitzroy Road, London, NW1 8TR, England. *Telephone:* (20) 7586-5502. *Fax:* (20) 7586-9817.

PYNZENYK, Viktor Mikhailovich, DEcon; Ukrainian politician and economist; b. 15 April 1954, Smologovitsa; s. of Mikailo Vasilyevich Pynzenyk and Maria Ivanovna Pynzenyk; m. Maria Romanivna Pynzenyk; two s. one s.; ed Lviv State Univ.; Asst, then Docent, Sr Researcher, Prof., Chair. Lviv State Univ. 1975–92; People's Deputy of Ukraine (mem. Vakhovna Rada) 1991–2001; Deputy Chair. of Bd on Problems of Econ. Policy 1992; Minister of Economy 1992–93, Vice-Prime Minister 1992–97; Pres. Foundation of Support to Reforms 1993–; Chair. Council on Problems of Econ. Reforms 1994–; Chair. Nat. Council on Statistics 1995; Head State Comm. on Admin. Reform 1997–99; Head Reform and Order Party 1998–; Dir Inst. of Reforms; Hon. Prof. Nat. Univ. of Kiev-Mogilyansk Acad. 1996–. *Publications:* over 400 papers. *Leisure interests:* cards, music. *Address:* Verkhovna Rada Ukraini, M. Hrushevskogo str. 5, 01008 Kiev, Ukraine (Office). *Telephone:* (44) 291-75-04 (Office). *Fax:* (44) 293-72-59 (Office). *E-mail:* pinzenik@rada.kiev.ua (Office).

Q

QABOOS BIN SAID AS-SAID; Omani ruler; b. 18 Nov. 1940, Salalah; s. of the late HH Said bin Taimur; m. 1976; ed privately in UK, RMA, Sandhurst; 14th descendant of the ruling dynasty of Albusaid Family; Sultan of Oman (following deposition of his father) July 1970–, also Prime Minister, Minister of Foreign Affairs, Defence and Finance; Hon. KCMG. *Leisure interests:* reading, horse-riding, music. *Address:* Diwan of the Royal Court, P.O. Box 632, Muscat 113, Sultanate of Oman. *Telephone:* 738711. *Fax:* 739427. *Website:* www.diwan.gov.om (Office).

QADDAFI, Col Mu'ammar al- (see Gaddafi, Col Mu'ammar al-).

QADHAFI, Col Mu'ammar al- (see Gaddafi, Col Mu'ammar al-).

QANOONI, Younis; Afghanistan politician; b. 1957, Panjshir Valley; ed Kabul Univ., also studied in India and USA; joined mujahideen troops fighting against USSR occupation forces 1979–89; Jt Defence Minister 1993; co-f. Defence of the Motherland and United Nat. and Islamic Front for the Salvation of Afghanistan (Unifsa– Northern Alliance (NA)) 1996; political head of NA's main Jamiat-e-Islami party 2001–; Leader NA Del. to Future of Afghanistan Govt Talks, Bonn Nov. 2001; Minister of the Interior Afghan Interim Authority Dec. 2001–June 2002; Minister of Educ. 2002–. *Address:* Ministry of Education, Mohammad Jan Khan Wat, Kabul, Afghanistan (Office). *Telephone:* (93) 020200000.

QARASE, Laisenia, BCom; Fijian politician; b. 4 Feb. 1941; m.; four s. one d.; ed Ratu Kadavulevu School, Queen Victoria School, Suva Boys' Grammar School, Univ. of Auckland, NZ, British Co-operative Coll., UK, Auckland Tech. Inst.; exec. cadet, Fijian Affairs Bd 1959–66, financial adviser 1979–99; joined Civil Service 1967, Co-operative Officer 1, Co-operatives Dept 1967–68, Asst Registrar of Co-operatives 1969–70, Sr Asst Registrar 1971–72, Chief Asst Registrar 1973–75, Registrar 1976–78; Deputy Sec. of Finance 1978–79; Perm. Sec. for Commerce and Industry 1979–80; Sec. of the Public Service Comm. 1980–83; Prime Minister and Minister for Nat. Reconciliation and Unity July 2000– (resigned following Court of Appeal ruling that his Govt was illegal March 7th 2001, reappointed March 15th 2001); Founder and Leader United Fiji Party May 2001–; Man. Dir Fiji Devt Bank 1983–97, Merchant Bank of Fiji 1997–2000; Chair. South Pacific Fertilizers Ltd 1985–86, Fiji Post & Telecommunications Ltd 1990–91, Fiji TV Ltd 1994–98; Dir Fiji Int. Telecommunication Ltd (FINTEL) 1978–79, Foods Pacific Ltd 1985–86, Fiji Forest Industries Ltd 1988–97, Carlton Brewery (Fiji) Ltd 1989–99, Unit Trust of Fiji 1990–99, Voko Industries Ltd 1993–97, Air Pacific Ltd 1996–98, Colonial Advisory Council 1996–99; Chair. Mavanu Investments Ltd, Qalitu Enterprises Ltd; Dir Mualevu Tikina Holdings Ltd, Yatu Lau Co. Ltd. *Address:* Office of the Prime Minister, Government Building, PO Box 2353, Suva, Fiji (Office). *Telephone:* 211201 (Office). *Fax:* 306034 (Office). *E-mail:* pmsoffice@is.com.fj (Office). *Website:* www.fiji.gov.fj (Office).

QASEM, Subhi, PhD; Jordanian agriculturalist and politician; b. 1934, Palestine; ed Kansas State Univ., Univ. of Minnesota, USA; worked in Ministry of Agric.; fmr Prof. of Agric., Univ. of Jordan, Dean Faculty of Grad. Studies 1986, Founding Dean Faculties of Sciences, Agric. and Grad. Studies; Minister of Agric. 1991; consultant in scientific and tech. educ., research and devt, agric. policy and the environment; Fellow Islamic Acad. of Sciences; Medal of the Kawkab (Star) Award, Istiqlal (Independence) Medal. *Address:* PO Box 13300, Amman 11942 (Office); Villa No. 7, University District, Omas Abdul Rahim Street, Amman, Jordan (Home). *Telephone:* (6) 5346746 (Office); (6) 5155200 (Home). *Fax:* (6) 5346740 (Office). *E-mail:* ubcc@go.com.jo (Office).

QASIMI, HH Sheikh Saqr bin Muhammad al-, Ruler of Ras Al-Khaimah; b. 1920; Ruler of Emirate of Ras Al-Khaimah 1948–; Chair. Rulers' Council of Trucial States –1971; mem. Supreme Council of United Arab Emirates 1972–. *Address:* The Ruler's Palace, Ras Al-Khaimah, United Arab Emirates.

QASIMI, HH Sheikh Sultan bin Muhammad al-, Ruler of Sharjah, PhD; b. 1 July 1939; ed Cairo, Exeter and Durham Univs, UK; Minister of Educ., UAE 1972; Ruler of Sharjah 1972–; Chair. Sharjah Human Soc., Arab/African Symposium; mem. Arab Historians' Union; Fellow Durham Univ.; Hon. Fellow Centre for Middle Eastern and Islamic Studies 1992; Hon. LLD (Khartoum Univ., Sudan); Hon. DSc (Univ. of Agriculture, Faisalabad, Pakistan) 1983; Distinguished Personality Prize (Exeter Univ.) 1993. *Publications:* The Myth of Arab Piracy in the Gulf, The Division of the Omani Empire, The Occupation of Aden, French-Omani Relations, The Arabian Documents in the French Archives, The White Shaikh, The Rebellious Prince, The Return of Holako, Power Struggles and Trade in the Gulf, The Gulf in Historic Maps. *Leisure interest:* reading. *Address:* Ruler's Palace, Sharjah, United Arab Emirates.

QATAR, Emir of (see Thani, Sheikh Hamad bin Khalifa ath-).

QAZI, Ashraf Jehangir, MA; Pakistani diplomatist; b. 1942; with Foreign Service of Pakistan 1965–; Amb. to Germany 1990–91, to Russia 1991–94, to People's Repub. of China 1994–97, to USA 2000–; High Commr in India 1997–2001. *Address:* Embassy of Pakistan, 2815 Massachussetts Avenue, NW, Washington, DC 20008, USA (Office).

QAZI HUSSAIN AHMED, MSc; Pakistani politician; b. 1938, Dist of Now-shera, Northe-West Frontier Prov. (NWFP); s. of Qazi Muhammad Abdul Rab; m.; four c.; ed Islamic Coll., Peshwar; teacher; fmr Pres. Jamiat-e-Ulema-e-Hind for NWFP; mem. Jamaat-e-Islami Pakistan (JIP) 1970–, fmr Pres. Peshawar Br., Party Sec., Pres. for NWFP, Sec.-Gen. of JIP 1978–87, Chair. 1987–; mem. Senate of Pakistan 1986–96, resgnd in protest against corrupt political system, re-elected 2002–. *Leisure interest:* poetry. *Address:* Jamaat-e-Islami Pakistan, Mansoorah, Multan Road, Lahore 54570 (Office); Ziarat Kaka Sahib, Nowshera District, NWFP, Pakistan (Home). *Telephone:* (42) 7844605 (Office). *Fax:* (42) 5419504 (Office). *E-mail:* uroobah@pol.com.pk (Office). *Website:* www.jamaat.org.

QI GONG, (Aisin Giorro); Chinese calligrapher and professor; b. July 1912, Beijing; joined Jiu San Soc. 1956; fmrly lecturer, Assoc. Prof. Furen Univ.; Prof. Beijing Normal Univ.; Dir Nat. Cultural Relics Appraisal Cttee; Vice-Chair., Chair., Hon. Chair. Chinese Calligraphers' Asscn; mem. Standing Cttee of Jiu San Soc.; mem. Standing Cttee of 6th, 7th, 8th CPPCC 1983–98; Dir Cen. Research Inst. of Culture and History 1999–. *Publications:* Gudai Ziti Lun Gao (Manuscripts on the Style of Ancient Characters), Shi Wen Shenglü Lun Gao (Manuscripts on the Prosody of Poetry and Prose), Qi Gong Cong Gao (Collected Manuscripts of Qi Gong). *Address:* Beijing Normal University, 19 Xinjiekouwai Da Jie, Beijing 1000875, People's Republic of China. *Telephone:* (10) 62208305.

QI HUAIYUAN; Chinese diplomatist and state official; b. 1930, Echeng Co., Hubei Prov.; ed North China People's Univ., Harbin Foreign Languages Coll.; Vice-Minister of Foreign Affairs 1986, Dir Foreign Affairs Office of State Council 1991–98; mem. 14th CCP Cen. Cttee 1992–97; Pres. Chinese People's Asscn for Friendship with Foreign Countries (CPAFFC) 1994–, Vice-Chair. Foreign Affairs Cttee, 9th Nat. Cttee of CPPCC 1998–. *Address:* Chinese People's Association for Friendship with Foreign Countries, 1 Taijichang Dajie, Beijing 100740, People's Republic of China. *Telephone:* (10) 65125505.

QIAN GUANLIN; Chinese politician; b. Oct. 1946, Funing, Jiangsu Prov.; ed Shanghai Foreign Trade Inst.; joined CCP 1973; Dir Customs Head Office 1993–2001; Vice-Dir-Gen. State Gen. Admin. of Taxation 2001–; mem. CCP 14th Cen. Cttee for Discipline Inspection 1992–97; alt. mem. CCP 15th Cen. Cttee 1997–. *Address:* State General Administration of Taxation, Beijing, People's Republic of China.

QIAN GUOLIANG, Lt-Gen.; Chinese army officer; b. Wujiang, Jiangsu Prov.; PLA civilian work; rank of Commdr 1985, of Lt-Gen. 1994; alt. mem. Cen. Cttee 13th CCP Nat. Congress 1987–92, Cen. Cttee 14th CCP Nat. Congress 1992–97; Chief of Staff, Jinan Mil. Region 1994–96; Deputy Mil. Region Commdr 1996, Commdr 1996–; mem. 15th CCP Cen. Cttee 1998–. *Address:* c/o People's Liberation Army, Ministry of National Defence, Jing-shanqian Jie, Beijing, People's Republic of China.

QIAN LINGXI; Chinese university professor and civil engineer; b. 16 July 1916, Wuxi, Jiangsu; Pres. Dalian Univ. of Tech. 1981; Pres. Chinese Soc. of Theoretical and Applied Mechanics 1982–; mem. Chinese Acad. of Sciences 1955–, Congress Cttee and Gen. Ass. of Int. Union of Theoretical and Applied Mechanics 1985–, Founding Council of Int. Asscn for Computational Mechanics 1985–; Dept of Tech. Science, Acad. Sinica 1985–; Dr. hc (Univ. of Liège) 1987. *Address:* c/o Dalian University of Technology, Research Institute of Engineering Mechanics, Dalian, 116024 Liaoning, People's Republic of China.

QIAN , Liren; Chinese party official; b. 20 Aug. 1924, Jiaxing Co., Zhejiang Prov.; s. of Qian Xunyi and Hu Suxian; m. Zheng Yun 1952; one s. one d.; joined CCP 1940; Deputy Sec.-Gen. All-China Fed. of Democratic Youth 1953; Sec.-Gen. All-China Students' Fed. 1956; Dir Int. Liaison Dept Communist Youth League 1959–64; Vice-Chair. All-China Fed. of Youth 1962; Dept Dir Foreign Affairs Office, State Council of People's Repub. of China 1964–65; mem. Standing Council Chinese People's Asscn for Friendship with Foreign Coun-tries 1974–78; Amb. and Perm. Rep. UNESCO 1978–81; Deputy Dir Int. Liaison Dept, Cen. Cttee CCP 1982–83, Dir 1983–85; Pres. Remin Ribao (People's Daily) 1985–89; mem. CCP Cen. Cttee 1985–92, mem. Propaganda and Ideological Work Leading Group 1988–89; Hon. Pres. Newspaper Oper-ation and Man. Asscn 1988; mem. Standing Cttee 8th Nat. Cttee 1993–98; Chair. CPPCC Foreign Affairs Cttee 1995–98; Vice-Pres. Chinese Asscn for Int. Understanding 1995–. *Leisure interests:* reading, swimming. *Address:* c/o Chinese Association for International Understanding, 15 Wanshou Road, Beijing 100036, People's Republic of China. *Telephone:* (10) 68134132. *Fax:* (10) 68134181.

QIAN QICHEN; Chinese diplomatist and state official; b. Jan. 1928, Tiading Co., Shanghai; m. Zhou Hanqiong; one s. one d.; ed Shanghai Datung Middle School and in USSR; joined CCP 1942; Second Sec. Embassy, USSR 1955–62, Counsellor 1972–74; Amb. to Guinea and Guinea-Bissau 1974–76; Dir Infor-mation Dept, Ministry of Foreign Affairs 1977–82; Vice-Minister, Foreign

Affairs 1982–88, Minister 1988–98; alt. mem. 12th CCP Cen. Cttee 1982, mem. 1985, mem. 13th Cen. Cttee 1987–92, 14th Cen. Cttee 1992–97, Deputy Head Cen. Foreign Affairs Leading Group; mem. Politburo CCP 1992–; mem. 15th CCP Cen. Cttee 1997–; Leader Special Admin. Region Preparatory Cttee (to establish post-1997 govt in Hong Kong) 1993–97; Chinese Special Envoy, 2nd–11th Round Sino-Soviet Consultations 1983–87; Head of Chinese Del., First Round Sino-Soviet Border Talks 1987; Deputy Dir Comm. for Commemorating 40th Anniversary of UN 1985; Vice-Chair. Organizing Cttee for Int. Year of Peace 1985; State Councillor 1991–93; Vice-Premier of State Council 1993–. *Address:* State Council, Beijing, People's Republic of China.

QIAN RENYUAN, F.A.I.C.; Chinese chemist; b. 19 Sept. 1917, Changshu, Jiangsu; s. of Qian Nantie and Miao Lingfen; m. 1st Hu Miaozhen 1951 (divorced 1956); m. 2nd Ying Qicong 1961 (divorced 1994); one d.; m. 3rd Yu Yansheng 1996; ed Zhejiang Univ., Univ. of Wisconsin, USA; Assoc. Prof. Xiamen Univ. 1948–49, Zhejiang Univ. 1949–51; Prof. Inst. of Physical Chem. Acad. Sinica 1951–53, Inst. of Chem. 1956–; Deputy Dir, Inst. of Chem., Acad. Sinica 1977–81, Dir 1981–85; Pres. Chinese Chemical Soc. 1982–86, Exec. Pres. 1984–85; Chair. Polymer Div., Chinese Chemical Soc. 1986–94; mem. Chem. Div., Acad. Sinica 1980, Asia-Pacific Acad. of Materials 1999; Assoc. mem. IUPAC Comm. on Polymer Characterization & Properties 1985–97; Science Premium, (3rd class), Acad. Sinica 1956, Advanced Individual Award, Acad. Sinica 1977, Science Award Nat. Science Congress 1978, State Invention Award, (3rd class), State Comm. of Science and Tech. 1980, SINOPEC Science and Tech. Progress Award, (1st class) 1987, Acad. Sinica Natural Science Award (1st class) 1989, 1993, 1998, (2nd class) 1992, State Natural Science Award (2nd class) 1988, 1995, 1999, State Science & Tech. Progress Award (1st class) 1989, Qiushi Prize for Distinguished Scientists 1994, Int. Award, The Soc. of Polymer Science, Japan 1995. *Publications:* over 270 papers in Chinese and int. journals, over 50 reviews and book chapters, 4 books and 4 patents. *Leisure interest:* classical music. *Address:* Institute of Chemistry, Academia Sinica, P.O. Box 2709, Beijing 100080 (Office); Flat 304, Apt. Building #808, Zhong Guan Cun, Beijing 100080, People's Republic of China (Home). *Telephone:* (10) 82612514 (Office); (10) 62555505 (Home). *Fax:* (10) 62559373 (Office). *E-mail:* qianyu@infoc3.icas.ac.cn (Office).

QIAN SHUGEN, Gen.; Chinese army officer; b. Feb. 1939, Wuxi City, Jiangsu Prov.; ed Chongqing Artillery School, PLA Mil. Acad. and Univ. of Nat. Defence; mem. CCP 1956–; entered army 1954; Deputy Div. Commdr 47th Army 1981; Div. Commdr 139th Div. 1983; Deputy Army Commdr 47th Army 1984; Army Commdr 47th Group Army 1985; Chief of Staff, Lanzhou Mil. Region 1992; Deputy Political Commissar, Lanzhou Mil. Region 1993; rank of Lt-Gen. 1993; Asst to Chief of Gen. Staff 1994; Deputy Chief, PLA Gen. Staff 1995–; rank of Gen. 2000; alt. mem. 14th CCP Cen. Cttee 1992–97; mem. 15th CCP Cen. Cttee 1997–. *Address:* c/o Ministry of National Defence, Jingshanqian Jie, Beijing, People's Republic of China. *Telephone:* (10) 6370000.

QIAN WEICHANG, (Wei-zang Chien), MA, PhD; Chinese physicist and applied mathematician; b. 9 Oct. 1912, Wuxi, Jiangsu; s. of Prof. Chien Shen-Yi and Chien Wang Shui Ying; m. Kong Xiang-Ying 1939 (died 2001); one s. two d.; ed Nat. Tsing-Hua Univ. and Univ. of Toronto, Canada; Research Engineer Jet Propulsion Lab., Calif. Inst. of Tech., USA 1942–46; returned to China 1946; Prof. of Physics and Applied Maths. Qinghua Univ. Beijing 1946–83, Dean of Studies 1949–58, Vice-Pres. 1956–58; mem. Standing Cttee All China Fed. of Scientific Socs. 1950–58; mem. Standing Cttee, All China Democratic Youth League 1949–58; Head Mechanics Section, Inst. of Math., Acad. Sinica 1951–55; Vice-Dir Inst. of Mechanics; Dir Inst. of Automation 1955–58; mem. Acad. Sinica 1954–58, 1980–; mem. Polish Acad. of Sciences 1956–; mem. State Council Comm. for Scientific Planning 1956–58; Jiangsu Prov. Deputy to NCP 1954–58, 1975–78; labelled as rightist 1958; Pres. Shanghai Univ. of Tech. 1982, Shanghai Univ. 1994; Dir Shanghai Inst. of Applied Math. and Mechanics 1984–; Vice-Chair. CPPCC 6th Nat. Cttee, 7th Nat. Cttee 1987–93, 8th Nat. Cttee 1993–98, 9th Nat. Cttee 1998–; Chair. Science, Educ., Culture, Public Health and Sports Cttee; Vice-Chair. Chinese Democratic League, Cen. Cttee 1983–97, Hon. Chair. 1997–; mem. Draft Cttee Hong Kong Basic Law 1986–91; Vice-Chair. Draft Cttee Macao Basic Law 1988–93; Pres. (Exec.) Assocn for Peaceful Reunification Promotion 1988–; Pres. Soc. of Chinese Language Information Processing 1980–, Chinese Overseas Exchanges Assocn 1990–; Ed.-in-Chief, Applied Maths. and Mechanics (Chinese and English Edns.) 1980–; mem. Editorial Bd, Int. Journal of Eng Science (USA) 1982–, Advances in Applied Maths. (USA) 1984–, Journal of Thin-Walled Structure (USA) 1986–, Finite Elements in Analysis and Design (USA), Chinese Encyclopaedia 1983–; mem. Jt Chinese-U.S. Editorial Bd, Chinese Ed., Concise Encyclopaedia Britannica 1983–; Nat. Science Award 1955, 1982; Beijing Municipal Award for Discoveries 1974, Shanghai Municipal Award for Technological Discoveries 1985. *Publications:* Scientific Discoveries in Chinese History 1953, Theory of Elasticity 1956, Theory of Torsion for Elastic Columns 1956, Large Deflection of Circular Plates 1957, Variational Principles and Finite Elements Methods 1980, Generalized Variational Principles 1984, Mechanics of Penetration 1985 (Nat. Prize for Best Publ 1988), Green's Function and Variational Principles in the Problems of Electro-magnetic Fields and Waves 1989, Selected Works of Qian Wei-chang 1989, Applied Mathematics 1991, Foundation of Strength Computation in Electrical Machinery 1993; numerous articles for scientific papers on physics, applied maths. and mechanics. *Address:* 149 Yanchang

Road, Shanghai University, Shanghai 200072; Chinese People's Political Consultative Conference, National Committee, Beijing 100811, People's Republic of China. *Telephone:* (21) 56331245 (Shanghai). *Fax:* (21) 56333011 (Shanghai). *Website:* www.shu.edu.cn (Office).

QIAN XUESEN, PhD; Chinese scientist; b. 11 Dec. 1910, Shanghai; m. Jiang Ying 1947; one s. one d.; ed Jiaotong Univ. Shanghai, Calif. Inst. of Tech., USA; with MIT, USA 1935; Dir Rocket Section, US Nat. Defence Science Advisory Bd 1945–49; Prof., MIT 1946–49, Calif. Inst. of Tech. 1949–55; Dir China Inst. of Mechanics 1956; Pres. Dynamics Soc. 1956–63; Vice-Chair. Science and Tech. Comm. for Nat. Defence 1978–; mem. Dept for Math., Physics and Chem., Acad. of Sciences 1957–; mem. 9th CCP Cen. Cttee 1969–73, 10th 1973–74, 11th 1977–82, 12th 1982–85; Vice-Minister Comm. for Science, Tech. and Industry for Nat. Defence 1982–87, Sr Adviser 1987–; Pres. Dynamics Soc. 1957–82; Chair. China Asscn for Science and Tech. 1986–91, Hon. Chair. 1991–; Hon. Pres. Astronautics Soc. 1980–, Soc. of Systems Eng 1980–; Vice-Chair. Nat. Cttee 6th CPPCC 1986–88, 7th 1988–93, 8th 1993–98; Sr Fellow Chinese Acad. of Sciences and Chinese Acad. of Eng 1998–; Meritorious Service Medal (for devt of China's first atomic bomb, hydrogen bomb and satellite), CCP Cen. Cttee, State Council and Cen. Mil. Command 1999. *Address:* Chinese Academy of Sciences, 52 San Li He Road, Beijing 100864, People's Republic of China.

QIAN YI, MS; Chinese environmental scientist; b. 1936, Suzhou, Jiangsu Prov.; d. of Qian Mu; ed Tongji Univ., Shanghai, Tsinghua Univ.; Teaching Asst, Lecturer, Assoc. Prof. then Prof. Tsinghua Univ. 1959–; Dir State Key Jt Lab. of Environmental Simulation and Pollution Control; science consultant Environmental Protection Comm. of State Council; Vice-Chair., Gen. Cttee of ICSU; Vice-Chair. Eng and Environment Cttee of the World Fed. of Eng Orgs; mem. Standing Cttee 8th and 9th NPC 1993–; Nat. Science and Tech. Advancement Award (2nd Class); State Educ. Comm. Science and Tech. Advancement Award (1st Class) 1987. *Publications:* Modern Wastewater Treatment Technology; The Prevention and Control of Industrial Environmental Pollution; Water Pollution Volume of Environmental Engineering Handbook and nearly 100 research papers. *Address:* Department of Environmental Engineering, Tsinghua University, Beijing 100084, People's Republic of China (Office). *Telephone:* (10) 62585684 (Office). *Fax:* (10) 62595687 (Office). *E-mail:* denqy@tsinghua.edu.cn (Office).

QIAN YONGCHANG; Chinese politician; b. 1933, Shanghai City; joined CCP 1953; alt. mem. 12th Cen. Cttee CCP 1982–87, mem. 13th Cen. Cttee 1987–92; Vice-Minister of Communications 1982–84, Minister 1984–91; Chair. Bd of Dirs., Hong Kong China Merchants Group 1985–. *Address:* c/o Ministry of Communications, Beijing, People's Republic of China.

QIAN YUNLU; Chinese politician; b. Nov. 1944, Dawu, Hubei Prov.; ed Hubei Univ.; joined CCP 1965; Vice-Sec. CCP Hubei Prov. Cttee 1983–98; Sec. CCP Wuhan City Cttee 1991–98; Chair. Hubei Prov. People's Political Consultative Conf. 1998; Deputy Gov. of Guizhou Prov. 1998–99, Gov. 1999–2000; Sec. CCP Guizhou Prov. Cttee 2001–; alt. mem. CCP 14th and 15th Cen. Cttee 1992–. *Address:* Chinese Communist Party Guizhou Provincial Committee, Guiyang, Guizhou Province, People's Republic of China.

QIAN ZHENGYING; Chinese government official; b. 1923, Jiaxing Co., Zhejiang Prov.; m. Huang Xinbai; ed Dadong Univ., Shanghai; joined CCP 1941; Vice-Minister of Water Conservancy 1952–67; Minister of Water Conservancy and Electrical Power 1970–74, Minister 1974–88; Adviser to State Council 1981–82, mem. 1982–; Vice-Chair. CCP Nat. Comm., Chair. Women, Youth and Legal Affairs Cttee; Adviser to State Flood Control HQ 1988–; mem. 11th Cen. Cttee of CCP 1977–82, 12th Cen. Cttee 1982–87, 13th Cen. Cttee 1987–92; mem. 14th Cen. Cttee 1992–97; Vice-Chair. CPPCC 7th Nat. Cttee 1988–92, 8th 1993–98, 9th Nat. Cttee 1998–; Pres. Red Cross Soc. of China 1994–, China–India Friendship Asscn, China Award Foundation for Teachers of Middle and Primary Schools and Kindergartens; Gold Medal (Somalia). *Address:* National Committee of Chinese People's Political Consultative Conference, 23 Taipingqiao Street, Beijing, People's Republic of China.

QIAO SHI; Chinese party official; b. Dec. 1924, Dinghai Co., Zhejiang Prov.; m. Yu Wen; joined CCP 1940; Sec. CP br., Shanghai Middle School 1942; Deputy Sec. Shanghai Dist CP; Sec. Youth Cttee, Hangzhou CP 1950–; Dir Designing Inst. of Jiuquan Iron and Steel Co. 1960–63; Sec. Afro-Asian Solidarity Cttee 1965–Cultural Revolution; Deputy Dir Int. Liaison Dept, CCP Cen. Cttee 1978–82, Dir 1982–83; mem. 12th Cen. Cttee, CCP 1982, 13th Cen. Cttee 1985, 1987–92, 14th Cen. Cttee 1992–97; mem. Politburo 1985 and Standing Cttee of Politburo 1987–; Vice-Premier, State Council 1986–88; Alt. mem. Secr., Cen. Cttee 1982–85, mem. 1985; Dir Org. Dept, CCP Cen. Cttee 1984–85; Sec. Cen. Cttee of Political Science and Law 1985–87; Head Leading Group for Rectification of Party Style within Cen. Depts. 1986–; Sec. Cen. Comm. for Discipline Inspection 1987–93; mem. Politburo, Standing Cttee of Politburo, Secr. CPC Cen. Cttee 1989–92; Perm. mem. Politburo 14th Cen. Cttee 1992–97; Chair. Standing Cttee 8th NPC 1993–98. *Address:* c/o International Liaison Department, Central Committee, Communist Party, Beijing, People's Republic of China.

QIAO SHIGUANG; Chinese artist; b. 5 Feb. 1937, Guantao Co., Hebei Prov.; s. of Qiao Lu De and Wang Hao Ling; m. Luo Zhen Ru 1961; two d.; Prof. Cen. Acad. of Arts and Design; Founder-Chair. Chinese Soc. of Lacquer Painting 1990 (group exhbn Beijing 1990); Dir Chinese Artists Assn; Dir Int. Culture of Lacquer 1992–; Founder Korea-China Lacquer Art Exchange Exhbn, Seoul 1994; solo exhbns of lacquer paintings Tokyo 1989, 1990, 1994, Kyoto 1989, Japan 1990, Paris 1992, Anano 1993, China Art Gallery 1996, Seoul 1996. *Publications:* Selected Lacquer Paintings of Qiao Shiguang 1993, The Skill and Artistic Expression of Lacquer Painting 1995, Collection of Qiao Shiguang's Lacquer Paintings 1996. *Leisure interests:* calligraphy, writing poetry. *Address:* The Central Academy of Arts and Design, 34 Dong Huan Bei Lu, Beijing 100020 (Office); 3 602 Building, 6 Hong Miao Bei Li, Chao Yang District, Beijing 100025, People's Republic of China (Home).

QIN HUASUN; Chinese diplomatist; b. Sept. 1935, Jiangsu Prov.; Counsellor and Deputy Perm. Rep. to Office of UN and other int. orgs. Geneva 1984–87; Perm. Rep. Vienna 1987–90; Dir-Gen. Dept of Int. Orgs. and Confs. Ministry of Foreign Affairs 1990–93; Asst Minister of Foreign Affairs 1993–95; Perm. Rep. to UN 1995–97. *Address:* Ministry of Foreign Affairs, 225 Chaoyangmennei Dajie Dongsi, Beijing 100701, People's Republic of China.

QIN WENCAI; Chinese industrialist; b. Feb. 1925, Shanxi; s. of Qin Wanrong and Qin Wangshi; m. Zhang Huang 1950; one s. three d.; Vice-Minister, Minister of Petroleum Industry, Vice-Pres. Petroleum Corpn of People's Repub. of China 1979–82, China Enterprises Man. Assn 1991–; Pres. China Nat. Offshore Oil Corpn 1982–87; Chair. China Offshore Oil Service Co., Hong Kong 1985–; Chair. Consultative Cttee 1987–; Chair. Capital Entrepreneurs Club, now Consultant; Vice-Chair. China Corp. Union, China Entrepreneurs Assn 1991–. *Publications:* Facts About China National Offshore Oil Corporation, Oil People in the Chinese Petroleum Industry. *Leisure interests:* reading, sport. *Address:* P.O. Box 4705, No. 6, Dongzhimznwai Xiaojie, Chaoyang District, Beijing 100027 (Office); Apt. Sol, Bldg 7, Block 1, Liu Pu Kang, Xicheng District, Beijing, People's Republic of China (Home). *Telephone:* (10) 84521002 (Office); (10) 62025425 (Home). *Fax:* (10) 64602600 (Office). *E-mail:* quinwc@cnooc.com.cn (Office).

QIN YI; Chinese film actress; b. 2 Feb. 1922, Shanghai; mem. 6th CPPCC 1983–87, 7th 1987–92, 8th 1993–98; Outstanding Film Artist Prize 1992. *Films include:* Remote Love, Song of Youth, Fog is no Fog 1993 and others. *Address:* Shanghai Film Studio, 595 Caoxi North Road, Shanghai 200030, People's Republic of China.

QING XIAO; Chinese business executive; b. 1947; joined China Int. Trust and Investment Corpn (CITIC) 1986; served as Deputy Gen. Man., then Gen. Man. Business Dept, Pres. CITIC Devt Co. Ltd, Chair. CITIC Australia; Vice-Pres. CITIC 1994–95, Pres. 1995–. *Address:* China International Trust and Investment Corporation (CITIC), 6 Xianyuannan Lu, Chaoyang Qu, Beijing 100004, People's Republic of China. *Telephone:* 4660088. *Fax:* 4661186.

QIU BOJUN; Chinese business executive; b. 1964, Hebei Prov.; ed Univ. of Science and Tech. for Nat. Defence; developed the Chinese word processing system WPS; f. Kingsoft Corpn 1988, Dir 1988–. *Publications:* A WPS Course, WPS User Guide. *Address:* Kingsoft Corporation, Beijing, People's Republic of China (Office). *Telephone:* (10) 62524868 (Office).

QIU CHUNPU; Chinese business executive; b. 1930; joined CCP 1958; Chair. of Bd of Dirs., China Nat. Nonferrous Metals Industry Corpn 1993–. *Address:* China National Nonferrous Metals Industry Corporation, 9 Xizhang Hutong, Xicheng District, Beijing 100814, People's Republic of China.

QUADEN, Guy, PhD; Belgian central bank governor; b. 5 Aug. 1945, Liège; ed Univ. of Liège, Le Sorbonne, Paris, France; Asst Prof. of Econs Univ. of Liège 1978–; Pres. High Council for Econ. Affairs 1984–88; Exec. Dir Nat. Bank of Belgium 1988–99, Gov. 1999–; Belgian Govt Gen. Commr for the Euro 1996–99; Officier, Légion d'honneur. *Publications include:* Le budget de l'état belge 1980, Le crise des finances publiques 1984, L'économie belge dans la crise 1987, Politique économique 1991. *Leisure interests:* soccer, modern art. *Address:* Banque Nationale de Belgique/Nationale Bank van België, 14 boulevard de Berlaimont, 1000 Brussels, Belgium (Office). *Telephone:* (2) 221-20-96 (Office). *Fax:* (2) 221-32-10 (Office). *E-mail:* guy.quaden@nbb.be (Office). *Website:* www.nbb.be (Office).

QUADFLIEG, Will; German actor and director; b. 15 Sept. 1914, Oberhausen; s. of Franz Quadflieg and Maria Schütz; m. 1st Benita Vegesack 1940; five c.; m. 2nd Margaret Jacobs 1963; ed pvt. drama studies; first stage appearances in Giessen, Gera, Düsseldorf; with Volksbühne, Berlin 1937–40, Schiller-Theater, Berlin 1940–45, Schauspielhaus, Hamburg 1946–50; guest appearances at Zürich, Salzburg Festival, Ruhr Festival and Burgtheater, Vienna; tours in Germany, Austria and Switzerland; noted for recitation of works of classical and contemporary poets; maj. stage roles in works of Goethe, Schiller, Shakespeare, Ibsen, Strindberg, etc.; mem. Freie Akad. der Künste, Hamburg, Deutsche Akad. der Darstellenden Künste, Frankfurt; Grosser Hersfeld Preis 1980; Medaille für Kunst und Wissenschaft 1984, Lew Kapelew Friedenspreis 1999; Grosses Bundesverdienstkreuz. *Film appearances include:* Der Maulkorb, Der grosse Schatten, Lola Montez, Faust, Orest, Macbeth. *Publication:* Wir Spielen Immer 1976. *Leisure interest:* music. *Address:* 27711 Osterholz-Scharmbeck, Germany.

QUADRIO CURZIO, Alberto; Italian professor of economics; b. 25 Dec. 1937, Tirano-Valtellina; ed Faculty of Political Sciences, Catholic Univ., Milan, St John's Coll. Cambridge; Assoc. Prof. of Econs, Univ. of Cagliari 1965–68; Assoc. Prof. of Econs, Univ. of Bologna 1968–72, Prof. 1972–75, Chair., Faculty of Political Sciences 1974–75; Prof. of Econs, Catholic Univ., Milan 1976–, Dir Centre of Econ. Analysis 1977–, Chair. Faculty of Political Sciences 1989–; Dir, Economia Politica (quarterly review) 1984–; mem., Italian Nat. Research Council 1977–88; Pres. Italian Econs Assn 1995–98; Vice-Pres. Istituto Lombardo; mem. Consult Stato Città Vaticano, Accademia Naz. dei Lincei, Accademia di Scienze e Lettere; St Vincent Award 1984, W. Tobagi Award 1996, Cortina Ulisse Int. Award 1997, Italian Gold Medal for Contribs to Science and Culture 2000. *Publications:* about 300, including (since 1980) Rent, Income Distribution, Order of Efficiency and Rentability 1980, The Gold Problem: Economic Perspectives 1982, Planning Manpower Education and Economic Growth 1983, Sui Momenti costitutivi della Economia Politica (co-author) 1983–84, Technological Scarcity: an Essay on Production and Structural Change 1986, The Exchange-Production Duality and the Dynamics of Economic Knowledge (with R. Scazzieri) 1986, Industrial Raw Materials: a Multi-Country, Multi-Commodity Analysis (co-author) 1986, The agro-technological system towards 2000: a European perspective (co-ed. and co-author) 1988, Produzione ed efficienza con tecnologie globali (co-author) 1987, Le scarsita relative 1988, Rent, Distribution and Economic Structure (essays) 1990, Structural Rigidities and Dynamic Choice of Technologies (co-author) 1991, Issues on International Development and Solidarity 1992, On Economic Science: Its Tools and Economic Reality 1993, The Management of Municipal Solid Waste in Europe. Economic, Technological and Environmental Perspectives (co-ed.) 1994, Innovation, Resources and Economic Growth (co-ed. and co-author) 1994, Risorse, Tecnologie, Rendita (co-author) 1996, Noi, l'Economia e l'Europa 1996, Rent Resources, Technology (co-author) 1999, Il Made in Italy oltre il 2000 2000 La Società Italiana degli Economisti 2000, Profili della Costituzione Europea 2001, Sussidiarieta e Suiluppo Paradigmi per l'Europa e per l'Italia 2002. *Leisure interest:* skiing. *Address:* Facoltà di Scienze Politiche, Università Cattolica del Sacro Cuore, Largo Gemelli, 20123 Milan (Office); Via A. Saffi 31, 20123 Milan, Italy (Home). *Telephone:* (02) 72342474 (Office). *Fax:* (02) 72342475 (Office). *E-mail:* quadriocr@mi.unicatt.it (Office). *Website:* www.unicatt.it (Office).

QUAID, Dennis; American actor; b. 9 April 1954, Houston, Tex.; s. of William Rudy Quaid and Juanita B. Quaid; m. 2nd Meg Ryan (q.v.) 1991 (divorced); one s.; ed Univ. of Houston; appeared on stage in Houston before moving to Hollywood; appeared on stage in New York with brother, Randy Quaid, in True West; performs with rock band The Electrics; wrote songs for films The Night the Lights Went Out in Georgia, Tough Enough, The Big Easy. *Films:* September 30 1955, 1978, Crazy Mama, Our Winning Season, Seniors, Breaking Away, I Never Promised You a Rose Garden, Gorp, The Long Riders, All Night Long, Caveman, The Night the Lights Went Out in Georgia, Tough Enough, Jaws 3-D, The Right Stuff, Dreamscape, Enemy Mine, The Big Easy, Innerspace, Suspect, D.O.A., Everyone's All-American, Great Balls of Fire, Lie Down With Lions, Postcards From the Edge, Come and See the Paradise, A 22 Cent Romance, Wilder Napalu, Flesh and Bone, Wyatt Earp, Something To Talk About 1995, Dragonheart 1996, Criminal Element 1997, Going West 1997, Gang Related 1997, Savior 1997, Switchback 1997, The Parent Trap 1998, Any Given Sunday 1999, Frequency 2000, Far From Heaven 2002. *Television includes:* Bill: On His Own, Johnny Belinda, Amateur Night at the Dixie Bar and Grill, Everything That Rises.

QUAN SHUREN; Chinese party and government official; b. 1930, Xinmin Co., Liaoning Prov.; joined CCP 1949; Mayor of Fushun 1980–81; Sec. CCP Cttee, Fushun City 1981–82; Gov. of Liaoning 1983–86; Sec. 7th CCP Prov. Cttee, Liaoning 1983–85, Deputy Sec. 1985–86, Sec. 1986–93; Chair. Liaoning Prov. 8th People's Congress Standing Cttee 1993–; Alt. mem. 12th CCP Cen. Cttee 1985–87, mem. 13th Cen. Cttee 1987–92, mem. 14th Cen. Cttee 1992–97; Deputy to 6th NPC, to 8th NPC, Liaoning Prov. *Address:* Liaoning Provincial Committee, Shenyang, Liaoning Province, People's Republic of China.

QUAN ZHENGHUAN; Chinese mural artist, painter and university professor; b. 16 June 1932, Beijing; d. of Quan Liang-Su and Qin Xiao-Qing; m. Li Hua-Ji 1959; two d.; ed Cen. Acad. of Fine Arts, Beijing; Asst Lecturer Cen. Acad. of Fine Arts 1955–56, Cen. Acad. of Applied Arts 1956–59, Lecturer 1959–78, Asst Prof. 1978–87, Prof. and mem. Academic Cttee 1987–; mem. Standing Cttee Artists' Assn of China. *Murals include:* The Story of the White Snake (Beijing Int. Airport) 1979, Jin Wei filled the Ocean (Beijing Yian Jing Hotel), Dances of China (Beijing Opera House) 1984. *Leisure interests:* Beijing Opera, old movies of 1930–1940s, football. *Address:* Central Academy of Applied Arts, Beijing (Office); 3-601, 6/F Hongmiao Beili, 10025, Beijing, People's Republic of China. *Telephone:* (1) 5963912 (Office); (1) 5015522.

QUANT, Mary, OBE, F.S.I.A.; Welsh fashion, cosmetic and textile designer; b. 11 Feb. 1934, London; d. of Jack Quant and Mildred (née Jones) Quant; m. Alexander Plunket Greene 1957 (died 1990); one s.; ed Goldsmiths Coll. of Art, London; started career in Chelsea, London 1954; Dir Mary Quant Group of cos 1955–, Jt Chair. Mary Quant Ltd; Dir (non-exec.) House of Fraser 1997–; mem. Design Council 1971–74, UK-USA Bicentennial Liaison Cttee 1973, Advisory Council Victoria and Albert Museum 1976–78; retrospective exhbn of 1960s fashion, London Museum 1974; Sr Fellow, Royal Coll. of Art 1991;

Hon. Fellow Goldsmiths Coll., Univ. of London 1993; Hon. FRSA 1995; Sunday Times Int. Fashion Award, Rex Award (USA), Annual Design Medal, Soc. of Industrial Artists and Designers, Piavolo d'Oro (Italy), Royal Designer for Industry, Hall of Fame Award, British Fashion Council (for outstanding contrib. to British fashion) 1990; Dr hc (Winchester Coll. of Art) 2000. *Publications:* Quant by Quant 1966. Colour by Quant 1984, Quant on Make-up 1986, Mary Quant Classic Make-up and Beauty Book 1996. *Address:* Mary Quant Ltd, 3 Ives Street, London, SW3 2NE, England. *Telephone:* (20) 7584-8781. *Fax:* (20) 7589-9443.

QUARRACINO, HE Cardinal Antonio; Argentine ecclesiastic; b. 8 Aug. 1923, Salerno, Italy; ed San José Seminary, La Plata; ordained priest 1945; fmr Prof. Mercedes Diocese Seminary; fmr Sec. Mercedes Diocesan Curia; fmr ecclesiastical adviser to Diocesan Council of Catholic Youth Action; fmr Prof. of Theology Santa María de los Buenos Aires Pontifical Catholic Univ. of Argentina; Bishop of Nueve de Julio 1962–68, of Avellaneda 1968–85; Archbishop of La Plata 1985–90; Archbishop of Buenos Aires and Primate of Argentina 1990–98; cr. Cardinal June 1991; Sec.-Gen. Latin American Council of Bishops 1978, Pres. 1982–87; Pres. Argentinian Bishops' Conf. 1990–96; mem. Pontifical Council for the Promotion of Christian Unity, Pontifical Council for the Pastoral Care of Health Workers, Cardinals' Council for the Study of the Economy and Org. of the Holy See, Pontifical Comm. for Latin America; Hon. mem. Argentinian Acad. of Music 1995; Dr. hc (Catholic Univ. of Puerto Rico); Grand Cross of Belgrano Award 1995. *Address:* c/o Arzobispado Rivadavia 415, 1002 Buenos Aires, Argentina.

QUARRIE, Donald (Don); Jamaican athlete; b. 25 Feb. 1951, Kingston; ed Univ. of Southern Calif., USA; competed Olympic Games, Munich 1972, reaching semi-final of 200m; Montréal 1976, won gold medal at 200m and silver medal at 100m; Moscow 1980, won bronze medal at 200m; Los Angeles 1984, won silver medal 4×100m relay; competed Commonwealth Games, Edin. 1970, won gold medals at 100m, 200m and 4×100m relay; Christchurch 1974 won gold medals at 100m and 200m; Edmonton 1978 won gold medal at 100m; coach in Calif., runs sprint clinics in Calif. and around the world. *Address:* c/o PO Box 272, Kingston 5, Jamaica.

QUAYLE, James Danforth (Dan), BS, JD; American politician and international business consultant; b. 4 Feb. 1947, Indianapolis; s. of the late James C. Quayle and of Corinne (née Pulliam) Quayle; m. Marilyn Tucker 1972; two s. one d.; ed DePauw Univ., Greencastle, Ind., Indiana Univ.; served in Ind. Nat. Guard; court reporter Huntington Herald Press, Ind. 1965–69, Assoc. Publr and Gen. Man. 1974–76; mem. Consumer Protection Div., Office of Attorney-Gen., Ind. 1970–71; Admin. Asst to Gov. of Ind. 1971–73; Dir Ind. Inheritance Tax Div. 1973–74; admitted to Indiana bar 1974; teacher of business law Huntington Coll. 1975; mem. US House of Reps 1977–79; Senator for Indiana 1981–88; Vice-Pres. of USA 1989–93; Chair. Nat. Space Council 1989; with Circle Investors 1993–; Distinguished Visiting Prof. American Grad. School of Int. Man. 1997–99; f. J. D. Quayle & Co. 2000; mem. Huntington Bar Assscn; mem. Hoosier State Press Assscn; Chair. Council on Competitiveness; Republican. *Publications:* Standing Firm 1994, The American Family 1995, Worth Fighting For 1999. *Address:* Suite 1080, 2425 East Camelback Road, Phoenix, AZ 85016, USA (Office). *Telephone:* (602) 840-6750 (Office). *Fax:* (602) 840-6936 (Office). *E-mail:* lminter@quayleassoc.com (Office).

QUEFFÉLEC, Anne; French concert pianist; b. 17 Jan. 1948, Paris; d. of Henri Queffélec and Yvonne Pénau; m. Luc Dehaene 1983; two s.; ed Conservatoire National, Paris (First Prize for Piano 1965, for Chamber Music 1966); since 1968 has played all over Europe, Japan (seven tours), Israel, Africa, Canada and USA; has played with BBC Symphony, London Symphony, Royal Philharmonic, Bournemouth Symphony, Hallé, Scottish Chamber, City of Birmingham Symphony, Miami Symphony, NHK Tokyo, Tokyo Symphony orchestras, Nouvel orchestre philharmonique de Radio-France, Orchestre nat. de Radio-France, Orchestre de Strasbourg, Ensemble Intercontemporain, etc., under conductors including Zinman, Groves, Leppard, Marriner, Boulez, Semkow, Skrowaczewski, Eschenbach, Gardiner, Pritchard, Atherton, etc.; has played at numerous festivals including Strasbourg, Dijon, Besançon, La Roque-d'Anthéron, La Grange de Meslay, Bordeaux, Paris, King's Lynn, Bath, Cheltenham, London Proms; judge in several int. piano competitions; Masterclasses in France, England and Japan; Pres. Asscn des amis d'Henri Queffélec, Asscn musicale 'Ballades'; First Prize, Munich Int. Piano Competition 1968, Prizewinner, Leeds Int. Piano Competition 1969; Best Interpreter of the Year, Victoires de la Musique 1990; Chevalier Légion d'honneur 1998, Officier, Ordre du mérite 2001. *Recordings:* has made about 30 records for Erato-RCA, Virgin Classics and Mirare of music by Scarlatti, Chopin, Schubert, Fauré, Ravel (all his piano works), Debussy, Liszt, Hummel, Beethoven, Mendelssohn, Bach, Satie, complete piano works of Henri Dutilleux 1996 and Mozart and Haydn recitals. *Radio:* many appearances on BBC Radio 3, France Musique and Japanese radio. *Television:* many appearances on musical programmes but has also appeared on literary and religious programmes. *Leisure interests:* literature, cycling, theatre, friends, humour, art exhbns., children. *Address:* 15 avenue Corneille, 78600 Maisons-Laffitte, France. *Telephone:* 39-62-25-64. *Fax:* 39-62-25-64.

QUELCH, John Anthony, MA, MS, DBA, CIMgt, FRSA; British academic; b. 8 Aug. 1951, London; s. of Norman Quelch and Laura Sally Quelch (née Jones);

m. Joyce Ann Huntley 1978; ed Exeter Coll. Oxford, Wharton School, Univ. of Pennsylvania, Harvard Univ., USA; Asst Prof., Univ. of Western Ont., Canada 1977–79; Sebastian S. Kresge Prof. of Marketing, Harvard Univ. 1979–98; Dean London Business School 1998–2001; Sr Assoc. Dean and Lincoln Filene Prof. of Business Admin., Harvard Business School 2001–; Dir (non-exec.) WPP Group PLC, easyJet PLC; Fellow Int. Acad. of Man. 2000, Hon. Fellow Exeter Coll. Oxford 2002. *Publications:* Cases in Advertising and Promotion Management 1987, Global Marketing Management 1988, How to Market to Consumers 1989, Sales Promotion Management 1989, Marketing Management (vols 1–3) 1993. *Leisure interests:* squash, tennis. *Address:* Harvard Business School, Soldiers Field, Boston, MA 02163 (Office); 57 Baker Bridge Road, Lincoln, MA 01773, USA. *Telephone:* (617) 495-6325 (Office); (781) 259-0594 (Home). *Fax:* (617) 496-5637 (Office). *E-mail:* jquelch@hbs.edu (Office); jaquelch@yahoo.com (Home).

QUELER, Eve; American conductor; b. New York; ed Mannes Coll. of Music, New York, City Coll. of New York, piano with Isabella Vengerov, conducting with Carl Bamberger, Joseph Rosenstock, Walter Susskind and Igor Markevich; began as pianist, asst conductor New York City Opera 1958 and 1965–70; later became a conductor; guest-conducted Philadelphia, Cleveland, Montréal Symphony, New Philharmonia, Australian Opera, Opéra de Nice, Opera de Barcelona, San Diego Opera, Edmonton Symphony, Nat. Opera of Czechoslovakia, Hungarian State, Hungarian Operahaz, Hamburg Opera, Pretoria, Hamilton, Ont., Opei Bonn and various other orchestras; Music Dir and Conductor Opera Orchestra of New York 1968–; Dr hc (Russell Sage Coll., Colby Coll.); Chevalier des Arts et des Lettres, Musician of the Month, Musical American Magazine, Martha Baird Rockefeller Fund for Music Award. *Recordings:* Puccini's Edgar, Verdi's Aroldo, Massenet's Le Cid, Boito's Nerone, Strauss' Guntram, Wagner's Tristan und Isolde, Janacek's Jenufa. *Publications:* articles in Musical America and Orpheus magazines. *Leisure interests:* organic gardening, family, women's health issues. *Address:* c/o Alix Barthelmes, Manager Opera Orchestra, 239 W 72nd Street, New York, NY 10023, USA.

QUEYRANNE, Jean-Jack; French politician; b. Nov. 1945; s. of Maurice Queyranne and Jeanne Bonavent; First Deputy Mayor of Villeurbanne (Rhône) 1977–88; Parti Socialiste (PS) mem. Rhône Gen. Council 1979–90; Nat. Ass. Deputy (alt.) for Rhône 1981–93; mem. PS Steering Cttee, Deputy Nat. Sec. responsible for cultural policy 1983, for press and culture 1985, Party Spokesman 1985, Nat. Del. and Spokesman 1987, Nat. Sec. responsible for audiovisual policy 1988, mem. Nat. Council 1993–94; Mayor of Bron (Rhône) 1989–97, Deputy Mayor 1997–; Nat. Ass. Deputy for Rhône 1997–; Minister of State attached to Minister of the Interior, with responsibility for Overseas Depts. and Territories 1997–2000; Minister of Relations with Parliament 2000–02. *Leisure interests:* theatre, music, cinema. *Address:* c/o Ministry of Relations with Parliament, 69 rue de Varenne, 75000 Paris (Office); Mairie, Square Weingarten, 69500 Bron, France (Office).

QUIGLEY, Sir (William) George (Henry), Kt, C.B., PhD, CBIM, FIB; British banker; b. 26 Nov. 1929; s. of William G. C. Quigley and Sarah H. Martin; m. Moyra A. Munn 1971; ed Ballymena Acad. and Queen's Univ. Belfast; Asst Prin., Northern Ireland Civil Service 1955; Perm. Sec. Dept of Manpower Services, Northern Ireland 1974–76, Dept of Commerce 1976–79, Dept of Finance 1979–82, Dept of Finance and Personnel 1982–88; Deputy Chair. Ulster Bank, Ltd 1988–89, Chair. 1989–2001; Dir Irish-American Partnership 1989–; Chair. Short Brothers 1999–, (Dir 1989–), Nat. Westminster Bank 1990–99, Scottish Fee Support Review 1998–2000, NatWest Pension Fund 1998–; Chair. Inst. of Dirs. (Northern Ireland) 1990–94; Pres. Econ. and Social Research Inst. (Ireland) 1999–; Dir Ind. News & Media (UK) 2001–; mem. Dearing Cttee on Higher Educ. 1996–97; mem. Qualifications and Curriculum Authority 1997–99; Professorial Fellow, Queen's Univ. Belfast 1988–92; Hon. Fellow Inst. of Man. of Ireland; Hon. LLD (Queen's) 1996, DUniv (Ulster) 1998; Compaq Lifetime Achievement Award 1997. *Leisure interests:* historical research, reading, music, gardening. *Address:* Short Brothers PLC, Airport Road, Belfast, BT3 9DZ, Northern Ireland (Office). *Telephone:* (28) 9046-8408 (Office). *Fax:* (28) 9046-8430 (Office).

QUIGNARD, Pascal Charles Edmond, LicenFil; French writer; b. 23 April 1948, Verneuil-sur-Avre (Eure); s. of Jacques Quignard and Anne Quignard (née Bruneau); one s.; ed Lycée de Havre, Lycée de Sèvres and Faculté des Lettres de Nanterre; lecturer 1969–77; mem. Cttee of Lecturing 1977–94; Sec.-Gen. for Editorial Devt, Editions Gallimard; Pres. Int. Festival of Opera and Baroque Theatre, Château de Versailles 1990–94; Pres. Concert des Nations 1990–93; Chevalier, Légion d'honneur; Prix de la Société des gens de lettres for his collected works 1998, Grand prix du roman de la Ville de Paris 1998, Prix de la fondation Prince Pierre de Monaco for his collected works 2000. *Publications include:* L'être du balbutiement 1969, Alexandra de Lycophron 1971, La parole de la Délie 1974, Michel Deguy 1975, Echo 1975, Sang 1976, Le lecteur 1976, Hiems 1977, Sarx 1977, Inter aerias fagos 1977, Sur le défaut de terre 1979, Carus 1980, Le secret du domaine 1980, Petits traités (tome I à VIII) 1990, Les tablettes de buis d'Apronenia Avitia 1984, Le vœu de silence (essay) 1985, Une gêne technique à l'égard des fragments 1986, Ethelrude et Wolframm 1986, Le salon de Wurtemberg 1986, La leçon de musique 1987, Les escaliers de Chambord 1989, La raison 1990, Albucius 1990, Tous les matins du monde 1991, Georges de La Tour 1991, La Frontière 1992, Le nom sur le bout de la langue 1993, Le sexe et l'effroi 1994,

L'occupation américaine 1994, Rhétorique spéculative 1995, L'amour conjugal 1995, Les septante 1995, La haine de la musique 1996, Vie secrète 1998, Terrasse à Rome (Grand Prix du roman de l'Acad. française 2000) 2000, Albucius 2001, Les ombres errantes (Prix Goncourt 2002). *Address:* Editions Calmann-Lévy, 3 rue Auber, 75009 Paris, France (Office).

QUILÈS, Paul; French politician; b. 27 Jan. 1942, St Denis du Sig, Algeria; s. of René Quilès and Odette Tyrode; m. Josephe-Marie Bureau 1964; three d.; ed Ecole Polytechnique, Paris; engineer, Shell Française 1964–78; Socialist Deputy to Nat. Ass. 1978–83, 1986–88, 1993–; Mayor of Cordes-sur-Ciel (Tarn); Minister of Town Planning and Housing 1983–85 and Transport 1984–85, of Defence 1985–86, of Posts, Telecommunications and Space 1988–91, of Public Works, Housing, Transportation and Space Research 1991–92, of the Interior and Public Security 1992–93; Socialist Deputy to Nat. Ass. 1993–; Chair. Nat. Defence and Armed Forces Comm. 1997–2002; Mayor of Cordes-sur-Ciel 1995–; mem. Econ. and Social Council 1974–75. *Publications:* La Politique n'est pas ce que vous croyez 1985, Nous vivons une époque intéressante 1992, Les 577, Un parlement pour quoi faire 2001. *Address:* Assemblée nationale, 75355 Paris, France.

QUILLEY, Denis, OBE; British actor; b. 26 Dec. 1927, London; s. of Clifford Charles Quilley and Ada Stanley; m. Stella Chapman 1949; one s. two d.; ed Bancrofts School, Essex; worked as asst stage man., Birmingham repertory theatre; understudied Richard Burton in The Lady's Not for Burning; joined Nottingham Playhouse 1952; subsequently joined Nat. Theatre Co. *Musicals include:* Grab me a Gondola, Candide, West End 1959, Nat. Theatre 1999, Irma La Douce (New York and US tour), Robert and Elizabeth, The Boys from Syracuse, Sweeney Todd (SWET Award for Best Musical Actor), La Cage aux Folles. *Stage appearances include:* (at Royal Nat. Theatre) Coriolanus, Long Day's Journey, Richard II, School for Scandal, Front Page, Macbeth, The Cherry Orchard, Saturday Sunday Monday, The Tempest, White Devil, Troilus and Cressida, Money, Hamlet, The Merry Wives of Windsor, Humble Boy (and at Gielgud Theatre); (with RSC) Privates on Parade (SWET Award for Best Comedy Performance), A Patriot For Me; (with Peter Hall Co. at The Old Vic) King Lear, Waiting for Godot, Waste; (in West End) The Lady's Not For Burning, Deathtrap, Candida; (at Chichester Theatre) Antony and Cleopatra, Racing Demon. *Films include:* Murder on the Orient Express, Evil under the Sun, Privates on Parade, Life at the Top, Where the Spies Are, Anne of the Thousand Days, King David, Mr Johnson, A Dangerous Man 1991, Sparrow 1994. *Television appearances include:* The Desperate People (serial), The Little White God, Murder in the Cathedral, No. 10, Rhinestone Cowboy, Rich Tea and Sympathy 1991, The Marriage of Figaro 1994. *Leisure interests:* walking, writing, playing the piano, tennis. *Address:* c/o Bernard Hunter Associates, 13 Spencer Gardens, London, SW14 7AH, England. *Telephone:* (20) 8878-6308.

QUINLAN, Sir Michael Edward, GCB, MA; British civil servant and foundation executive; b. 11 Aug. 1930, Hampton; s. of the late Gerald Quinlan and Roseanne Quinlan; m. Mary Finlay 1965; two s. two d.; ed Wimbledon Coll. and Merton Coll. Oxford; civil servant 1954–92; Air Ministry 1954–64; Ministry of Defence 1964–70; Defence Counsellor, UK Del. to NATO 1970–73; Under-Sec. Cabinet Office 1974–77; Deputy Under-Sec. of State (Policy and Programmes), Ministry of Defence 1977–81; Deputy Sec. (Industry), Treasury 1981–82; Perm. Sec. Dept of Employment 1983–88; Perm. Under-Sec. of State, Ministry of Defence 1988–92; Dir Ditchley Foundation 1992–99; Dir Lloyds Bank 1992–95, Lloyds TSB Group 1996–98, Pilkington PLC 1992–99; Visiting Prof. King's Coll. London 1992–95, 2002–; Trustee Science Museum 1992–2001; Public Policy Scholar Woodrow Wilson Center 2000. *Publications:* Thinking About Nuclear Weapons 1997, European Defence Co-operation 2001; numerous articles on defence issues and public service issues. *Leisure interests:* cricket, music, golf. *Address:* 3 Adderbury Park, West Adderbury, Banbury, Oxon., OX17 3EN, England (Home). *Telephone:* (1295) 812951 (Home). *Fax:* (1295) 812951 (Home). *E-mail:* meq@adderbury03.fsnet.co.uk (Home).

QUINLAN, Mike, BS, MBA; American business executive; b. 9 Dec. 1944, Chicago; s. of Robert Joseph Quinlan and Kathryn (née Koerner) Quinlan; m. Marilyn DeLashmutt 1966; two s.; ed Loyola Univ.; part-time mailroom worker McDonald's 1963, Asst Buyer 1966, Pres. (USA) 1980–82, CEO 1987–98, Chair. 1989–97, Dir 1992–. *Leisure interest:* racquetball. *Address:* McDonald's Corporation, McDonald's Plaza, 1 Kroc Drive, Oakbrook, IL 60521, USA.

QUINN, Aidan; American actor; b. 8 March 1959, Chicago; worked with various theatre groups in Chicago before moving to New York; off-Broadway appearances in Sam Shepard's plays Fool for Love and A Lie of the Mind; appeared in Hamlet, Wisdom Bridge Theater, Chicago, numerous other plays; TV film: An Early Frost. *Films:* Reckless 1984, The Mission, All My Sons, Stakeout, Desperately Seeking Susan, Crusoe, The Handmaid's Tale, At Play in the Fields of the Lord, Avalon, Legends of the Fall, Mary Shelley's Frankenstein 1994, The Stars Fell on Henrietta 1994, Haunted 1994, Michael Collins 1996, Looking For Richard 1996, Commandments 1996, The Assignment 1997, Wings Against The Wind 1998, This is My Father 1998, Practical Magic 1998, Blue Vision 1998, The Imposters 1998, 50 Violins 1999, In Dreams 1999. *Stage appearances include:* Fool for Love 1983, A Streetcar

Named Desire (Theatre World Award) 1988, An Early Frost 1985, Lies of the Twins 1991, Two of Us 2000. *Address:* c/o Josh Lieberman, 9830 Wilshire Boulevard, Beverly Hills, CA 90212, USA.

QUINN, Andrea, BA; British conductor and music director; b. 22 Dec. 1964; m. Roderick Champ 1991; one s. two d.; ed Royal Acad. of Music, London, Nottingham Univ.; Music Dir London Philharmonic Youth Orchestra 1994–97, Royal Ballet 1998–2001; Music Dir New York City Ballet 2001–; has conducted London Symphony Orchestra, London Philharmonic, Philharmonia and other leading orchestras; operas and music theatre pieces conducted include Misper (Glyndebourne), Four Saints in Three Acts (ENO), Harrison Birtwistle's Pulse Shadows (UK tour). *Leisure interests:* art galleries, literature, horse riding, Italian. *Address:* New York City Ballet, New York State Theater, New York City, NY USA (Office). *Telephone:* (212) 870-5570 (Office); (20) 7272-4413. *Website:* www.nycballet.com (Office).

QUINN, Brian, CBE, MA(ECON.), PhD, F.I.B.S; British banker, economist and consultant; b. 18 Nov. 1936, Glasgow; s. of Thomas Quinn and Margaret Cairns; m. Mary Bradley 1961; two s. one d.; ed Glasgow, Manchester and Cornell Univs.; economist, African Dept IMF 1964–70; Rep. IMF, Sierra Leone 1966–68; joined Bank of England 1970, Econ. Div. 1970–74, Chief Cashier's Dept 1974–77, Head Information Div. 1977–82, Asst Dir 1982–88, Head of Banking Supervision 1986–88, Exec. Dir 1988–96, Acting Deputy Gov. 1995; Chair. Nomura Bank Int. PLC 1996–99; Vice-Chair. Celtic PLC 1996–2000, Chair. 2000–; Dir (non-exec.) Bankgesellschaft Berlin UK PLC 1996–2001, Britannic Asset Man. 1998–, Nomura Holdings Europe 1998–99; Man. Dir Brian Quinn Consultancy 1997–; Chair. Financial Markets Group, LSE 1996–2001; Consultant World Bank 1997–; Hon. MA. *Publications:* contribs. to books and journals. *Leisure interests:* fishing, golf, cycling, soccer. *Address:* Celtic Park, Kerrydale Street, Glasgow, G40 3RE, Scotland (Office); 14 Homewood Road, St Albans, Herts., AL1 4BH, England (Home). *Telephone:* (1727) 853900. *Fax:* (1727) 866646. *E-mail:* bqconns@aol.com.

QUINN, Ruairi, BArch, MRIAI, RIBA; Irish politician and architect; b. 2 April 1946, Dublin; s. of Malachi Quinn and Julia Quinn; m. 1st Nicola Underwood 1969 (divorced) one s. one d.; m. 2nd Liz Allman 1990; one s.; ed Blackrock Coll. and Univ. Coll., Dublin; School of Ekistics, Athens 1970–71; Architects' Dept Dublin Corpn 1971–73; Partner, Burke-Kennedy Doyle and Partner 1973–82; mem. Dublin Corpn 1974–77, 1981–82; mem. Seanad Éireann 1976–77, 1981–82; mem. Dáil Éireann 1977–81, 1982–; Minister of State, Dept of the Environment 1982–83; Minister for Labour and Minister for the Public Service 1983–87; Deputy Leader, Irish Labour Party 1989, Leader 1997–2002; Treas. Party of European Socialists 2000–; Dir of Elections for Pres. Mary Robinson (q.v.); Labour Spokesperson on Finance and Econ. Affairs 1990; Minister for Enterprise and Employment 1993–94, for Finance 1994–97. *Leisure interests:* athletics, reading. *Address:* Dáil Éireann, Kildare Street, Dublin 2 (Office); 23 Strand Road, Sandymount, Dublin 4, Ireland (Home). *Telephone:* (1) 6183434 (Office). *Fax:* (1) 6184153 (Office). *E-mail:* ruairi.quinn@oireachtas.irlgov.ie (Office).

QUIÑONES AMEZQUITA, Mario Rafael; Guatemalan lawyer and diplomatist; b. 4 June 1933, Quezaltenango; s. of the late Hector Quiñones and of Elisa de Quiñones; m. Yolanda de Quiñones 1963; two s. two d.; ed Univ. of San Carlos and Univ. of Rio Grande do Sul, Brazil; lawyer and notary with law firm of Viteri, Falla, Quiñones, Umaña, Orellana y Cáceres 1959–; Prof. of Law, Rafael Landívar Univ. 1962–, Dean Dept of Legal and Social Sciences 1974–82; Vice-Pres. of Landívar Univ. 1978–82, Pres. March–Oct. 1982; Perm. Rep. to UN 1982–84; Minister of Foreign Affairs 1986–87; Vice-Pres. N and Cen. American Region, Union of Latin Notaries 1978; Pres. Asscn of Lawyers and Notaries of Guatemala 1977; mem. Guatemalan Del. UN Comm. on Int. Trade Law 1974; Dr. hc (Univ. Rafael Landivar) 1998; Orden de Malta (Guatemala) and decorations from govts. of Spain, Peru, Germany, Argentina and Mexico. *Leisure interests:* reading, music. *Address:* 6A Calle 5-47, Zona 9 –3er. Nivel, Guatemala City 01009 (Office); 3A Ave. 13-81, Zona 14, Guatemala City, 01014 Guatemala. *Telephone:* (2) 331-1721 (Office); (2) 368-1449 (Home). *Fax:* (2) 337-0186 (Home).

QUINTANILLA SCHMIDT, Carlos, BSc; Salvadorean politician and lawyer; b. 5 Aug. 1953, San Miguel; m. Alexandra Rodríguez; two s.; ed José Matías Delgado Univ., San Salvador, American Univ., Washington, DC; partner in law firm Guandique, Segovia, Quintanilla 1981–; Prof. of Commercial Law José Matías Delgado Univ. 1985–, Dean School of Law 1986–92, Deputy Dean of Univ. 1992–; Legal Counsel to Alianza Republicana Nacionalista (ARENA) party 1988–97, mem. exec. body 1997–; Vice-Pres. of El Salvador 1999–. *Address:* Office of the Vice-President, Casa Presidencial, Barrio San Jacinto, San Salvador, El Salvador (Office).

QUINTON, Baron (Life Peer), cr. 1982, of Holywell in the City of Oxford and County of Oxfordshire; **Anthony Meredith Quinton,** FBA; British academic; b. 25 March 1925, Gillingham, Kent; s. of the late Richard Frith Quinton and Gwenllyan Letitia Quinton; m. Marcelle Wegier 1952; one s. one d.; ed Stowe School, Christ Church, Oxford; served in RAF, Flying Officer and Navigator 1943–46; Fellow, All Souls Coll., Oxford 1949–55, New Coll., Oxford 1955–78; Pres. Trinity Coll. Oxford 1978–87; Visiting Prof., Swarthmore Coll., Pa 1960, Stanford Univ., Calif. 1964, New School for Social Research, New York 1976–77, Brown Univ., RI; Dawes Hicks Lecturer, British Acad. 1971;

Gregynog Lecturer, Univ. of Wales Aberystwyth 1973; T. S. Eliot Lecturer, Univ. of Kent, Canterbury 1976; Robbins Lecturer, Univ. of Stirling 1988; R.M. Jones Lecturer, Queen's Univ. Belfast 1988; Tanner Lecturer, Univ. of Warsaw 1988; Pres., Aristotelian Soc. 1975–76, Soc. for Applied Philosophy 1988–91, Royal Inst. of Philosophy 1990–, Asscn of Ind. Libraries 1991–98, Friends of Wellcome Inst. 1992–98; Gov., Stowe School 1963–84, Chair. of Govs. 1969–75; Fellow, Winchester Coll. 1970–85; Del., Oxford Univ. Press 1970–76; mem. Arts Council 1979–81; mem. Bd of Eds. Encyclopaedia Britannica 1985–97; mem. Peacock Cttee; Chair. British Library 1985–90, Kennedy Memorial Trust 1990–97; Hon. Fellow Trinity Coll. Oxford 1989, New Coll. Oxford 1998. *Publications:* Political Philosophy (Ed.) 1967, The Nature of Things 1973, Utilitarian Ethics 1973, trans. of K. Ajdukiewicz's Problems and Theories of Philosophy (with H. Skolimowski) 1973, The Politics of Imperfection 1978, Francis Bacon 1980, Thoughts and Thinkers 1982, Hume 1998, From Wodehouse to Wittgenstein 1998. *Leisure interests:* sedentary pursuits. *Address:* A-11 Albany, Piccadilly, London, W1J 0AL, England; 825 Fifth Avenue, New York, NY 10021, USA. *Telephone:* (20) 7287-8686 (London); (212) 838-0800 (New York). *Fax:* (20) 7287-9525 (London).

QUINTON, Sir John Grand, Kt, MA, FCIB; British banker; b. 21 Dec. 1929; s. of William Grand and Norah May Quinton (née Nunn); m. Jean Margaret Chastney 1954; one s. one d.; ed Norwich School, St John's Coll. Cambridge; Asst Gen. Man. Barclays Bank Ltd 1968, Local Dir Nottingham Dist Barclays Bank Ltd 1969–71, Regional Gen. Man. 1971–75, Gen. Man. Barclays Bank Ltd and Dir Barclays Bank UK Ltd 1975–84, Dir Barclays Bank PLC and Sr Gen. Man. 1982–84, Deputy Chair. Barclays Bank PLC 1985–87, Chair. 1987–92; Chair. (non-exec.) Wimpey 1993–95; Chair. Motability Finance Ltd 1978–84, Gov. Motability 1985– (Hon. Treas. 1998–); Chair. Cttee of C.E.O.s., Cttee of London Clearing Bankers 1982–83; Chair. Office of the Banking Ombudsman 1987–92, Cttee of London and Scottish Bankers 1989–91; Dir (non-exec.) Norwich and Peterborough Bldg Soc. 1993–99 (Deputy Chair. 1996–99); Treas. Inst. of Bankers 1980–86; mem. City Capital Markets Cttee 1981–86; mem. NE Thames Regional Health Authority 1974–87; mem. Accounting Standards Cttee 1982–85; Gov. Royal Shakespeare Theatre 1986–2000; Pres. Chartered Inst. of Bankers 1989–90; Chair. Botanic Gardens Conservation Int. 1988–99; Chair. Football Asscn Premier League 1992–99, Metropolitan Police Cttee 1995–2000; mem. Metropolitan Police Authority 2000–; Trustee Royal Acad. 1987–93, Thrombosis Research Inst. 1993–2001. *Leisure interests:* gardening, music, golf. *Address:* Chenies Place, Chenies, Bucks., WD3 6EU, England.

QUIRK, Baron (Life Peer), cr. 1994, of Bloomsbury in the London Borough of Camden; **(Charles) Randolph Quirk,** Kt, CBE, PhD, DLitt, LLD, FBA; British university professor and official; b. 12 July 1920, Isle of Man; s. of the late Thomas and Amy Randolph Quirk; m. 1st Jean Williams 1946; two s.; m. 2nd Gabriele Stein 1984; ed Cronk y Voddy School, Douglas High School, Isle of Man, Univ. Coll. London; served in RAF 1940–45; Lecturer in English, Univ. Coll. London 1947–54; Commonwealth Fund Fellow, Yale Univ. and Univ. of Mich., USA 1951–52; Reader in English Language and Literature, Univ. of Durham 1954–58, Prof. of English Language 1958–60; Quain Prof. of English, Univ. Coll. London 1960–81; Dir Univ. of London Summer School of English 1962–67; Survey of English Usage 1959–83; mem. Senate, Univ. of London 1970–85 (Chair. Academic Council 1972–75), Court 1972–85; Vice-Chancellor, Univ. of London 1981–85; Pres. Inst. of Linguists 1983–86, British Acad. 1985–89, Coll. of Speech Therapists 1987–91; Gov. British Inst. of Recorded Sound, English-Speaking Union; Chair. Cttee of Enquiry into Speech Therapy Services, British Council English Cttee 1976–80, Hornby Educational Trust 1979–93; mem. BBC Archives Cttee 1975–79, British Council 1983–91; Trustee Wolfson Foundation 1987–; Lee Kwan Yew Fellow, Singapore 1985–86; Vice-Pres. Foundation of Science and Tech. 1986–90; mem. House of Lords Select Cttee on Science and Tech. 1999–2002; Fellow Queen Mary Coll. London, Univ. Coll. London, Imperial Coll. London, Academia Europaea, King's Coll. London; Foreign Fellow, Royal Belgian Acad. Sciences 1975, Royal Swedish Acad. 1986, Finnish Acad. of Sciences 1992, American Acad. of Arts and Sciences 1995; Hon. degrees (Lund, Uppsala, Poznań, Nijmegen, Paris, Liège, Helsinki, Prague, Reading, Leicester, Salford, London, Newcastle, Bath, Durham, Essex, Open Univ., Glasgow, Bar-Ilan, Brunel, Bucharest, Sheffield, Richmond Coll., Aston, Copenhagen); Hon. Fellow, Coll. of Speech Therapists, Inst. of Linguists; Hon. Master Gray's Inn Bench 1983; Jubilee Medal (Inst. of Linguists) 1973. *Publications:* The Concessive Relation in Old English Poetry 1954, Studies in Communication (with A. J. Ayer and others) 1955, An Old English Grammar (with C. L. Wrenn) 1955, Charles Dickens and Appropriate Language 1959, The Teaching of English (with A. H. Smith) 1959, The Study of the Mother-Tongue 1961, The Use of English (with supplements by A. C. Gimson and J. Warburg) 1962, Prosodic and Paralinguistic Features in English (with D. Crystal) 1964, A Common Language (with A. H. Marckwardt) 1964, Investigating Linguistic Acceptability (with J. Svartvik) 1966, Essays on the English Language–Medieval and Modern 1968, Elicitation Experiments in English (with S. Greenbaum) 1970, A Grammar of Contemporary English 1972 (with S. Greenbaum, G. Leech, J. Svartvik) 1972, The English Language and Images of Matter 1972, A University Grammar of English (with S. Greenbaum) 1973, The Linguist and the English Language 1974, Old English Literature: A Practical Introduction (with V. Adams, D. Davy) 1975, A Corpus of English Conversation 1980; contrib. to many others including Charles Dickens (ed. S. Wall) 1970, A New Companion to Shakespeare Studies 1971,

The State of the Language (with J. Svartvik) 1980, Style and Communication in the English Language 1982, A Comprehensive Grammar of the English Language (with S. Greenbaum, G. Leech and J. Svartvik) 1985, Words at Work: Lectures on Textual Structure 1986, English in Use (with Gabriele Stein) 1990, A Student's Grammar of the English Language (with S. Greenbaum) 1990, Grammatical and Lexical Variance in English 1995; papers in linguistic and literary journals. *Leisure interest:* music. *Address:* University College London, Gower Street, London, WC1E 6BT, England. *Telephone:* (20) 7219-2226 (Office). *Fax:* (20) 7916-2054 (Office).

QUIRK, James Patrick, AO, PhD, DSc, FAA; Australian agricultural scientist; b. 17 Dec. 1924, Sydney; s. of J. P. Quirk; m. Helen M. Sykes 1950; one s. one d.; ed Christian Brothers High School, Lewisham, St John's Coll., Univ. of Sydney and Univ. of London; Research Scientist, CSIRO Div. of Soils, Soil Physics Section 1947; CSIRO Sr Postgraduate Studentship, Physics Dept, Rothamsted Experimental Station, England 1950; Research Scientist, Sr Research Scientist, CSIRO 1952–56; Reader in Soil Science, Dept of Agricultural Chem., Waite Agricultural Research Inst., Univ. of Adelaide 1956–62; Carnegie Travelling Fellow, USA 1960; Foundation Prof. and Head, Dept of Soil Science and Plant Nutrition, Univ. of WA 1963–74, (Emer. Prof. 1974–), Dir Inst. of Agric. 1971–74, Dir, Waite Agricultural Research Inst. and Prof. 1974–89; Emer. Prof. and Hon. Research Fellow, Univ. of WA 1990–; Prof. Fellow, Dept Applied Math., ANU 1990–96, Hon. Prof. Fellow 1996–; Commonwealth Visiting Prof., Oxford Univ. 1967; Fellow Australian Acad. of Science (Sec. Biological Sciences 1990–94), Australian Inst. of Agricultural Science, Australian Acad. of Technological Sciences and Eng (mem. Council 1996–), American Soc. of Agronomy, Australian and NZ Asscn for the Advancement of Science; Hon. mem. Int. Union of Soil Science 1998; Brindley Lecturer (USA) 1992; Hon. DSc Agric. (Louvain, Belgium) 1978, (Melbourne) 1990, (Western Australia) 1991, (Sydney) 1997; Prescott Medal for Soil Science 1975, Medal of the Australian Inst. of Agricultural Science 1980, Farrer Memorial Medal 1982, Mueller Medal 1988, Distinguished Service Award (Soil Science Soc. of America) 1996. *Publications:* about 200 scientific publs. *Leisure interests:* reading, tennis. *Address:* Faculty of Agriculture, University of Western Australia, Nedlands 6009, Western Australia (Office); 70 Archdeacon Street, Nedlands 6009, Western Australia, Australia. *Telephone:* (8) 9386-5948 (Office). *Fax:* (8) 9380-2504.

QUIROGA RAMÍREZ, Jorge Fernando, BEng, MBA; Bolivian politician and engineer; b. 5 May 1960, Cochabamba; m. Virginia Gillum 1989; four c.; ed La Salle Coll., Santa Cruz de la Sierra, Texas A&M Univ. and St Edward's Univ., Austin, Tex.; with IBM, Austin, Tex. 1981–88; returned to Bolivia 1988; Econometrician, Mintec 1988; Vice-Pres. Banco Mercantil de Bolivia 1988; mem. Acción Democrática Nacionalista (ADN) 1988–, Deputy Leader 1995–; Under-Sec. for Public Investment and Int. Co-operation, Ministry of Planning 1989–90; Minister of Finance 1990–93; Gov. Cooperación Financiera de Inversiones –1993; Dir Andean Devt Corpn –1993; Nat. Sec. Política Social –1993; led electoral campaign of ADN 1993 then worked in pvt. sector; Vice-Pres. of Bolivia 1997–2001, Acting Pres. July–Aug. 2001, Pres. of Bolivia 2001–02; fmr Gov. IBRD and IMF. *Leisure interests:* football, basketball, mountain-climbing. *Address:* c/o Oficina del Presidente, Palacio de Gobierno, Plaza Murillo, La Paz, Bolivia (Office).

QURAISHI, Abdul Aziz Bin Said Al, MBA, FIBA; Saudi Arabian government official; b. 1930, Hail; s. of Zaid al-Quraishi and Sheikhah Abdul Aziz; m. Amal Abdul Aziz al-Turki 1965; one s. two d.; ed Univ. of Southern California, USA; Gen. Man. State Railways 1961–68; Pres. Gen. Personnel Bureau 1968–74; Minister of State 1971–74; Gov. Saudi Arabian Monetary Agency 1974–83; fmr Gov. for Saudi Arabia, IMF, Arab Monetary Fund; fmr Alt. Gov. for Saudi Arabia, Islamic Devt Bank; fmr mem. Bd of Dirs. Supreme Council for Petroleum and Mineral Affairs, Gen. Petroleum and Mineral Org.; Public Investment Fund, Pension Fund, Man. Dir Ali Zaid Al-Quraishi & Bros., Riyadh 1983–; fmr Chair. Nat. Saudi Shipping Co., Riyadh 1983; Vice-Chair. Saudi Int. Bank, London 1983–; mem. Int. Advisory Bd, Security Pacific Nat. Bank of LA 1983–; King Abdul Aziz Medal (Second Class), Order of Brilliant Star with Grand Cordon (Taiwan), Order of Diplomatic Merit, Gwan Ghwa Medal (Repub. of Korea), King Leopold Medal (Commdr Class), Belgium, Emperor of Japan Award, Order of Sacred Treasure (First Class) 1980. *Address:* Malaz, Riyadh (Office); P.O. Box 1848, Riyadh 11441, Saudi Arabia (Home).

QURASHI, Mazhar Mahmood, PhD, DSc; Pakistani science administrator and researcher; b. 8 Oct. 1925, Gujranwala; s. of Feroz-ud-din Qurashi; m.; four s. five d.; ed Punjab Univ., Manchester Univ.; fmr Sec.-Gen. Pakistan Acad. of Sciences; fmr Dir.-Gen. PCSIR Labs., Karachi; fmr Dir Nat. Science Council of Pakistan; fmr Prof. of Physics, Quaid-i-Azam Univ., Islamabad; Sec. Pakistan Asscn for History and Philosophy of Science 1986–; fmr mem. Pakistan Council of Scientific and Industrial Research; Fellow Islamic Acad. of Sciences, Pakistan Acad. of Sciences, Inst. of Physics, London; Open Gold Medal, Pakistan Acad. of Sciences 1972, Pakistani Pres. Sitara-i-Imtiaz Award 1991. *Publications:* 10 monographs; numerous research papers in scientific journals. *Leisure interest:* theoretical and experimental study of relation between science and Islam. *Address:* c/o Pakistan Academy of Sciences, Constitution Avenue, G-5, Islamabad (Office); House 34, Street 32,

F-7/1, Islamabad, Pakistan (Home). *Telephone:* (51) 9207789 (Office); (51) 2877644 (Home). *Fax:* (51) 9206770 (Office). *E-mail:* pasisb@yahoo.com (Office).

QURAY, Ahmad "Abu Ala"; Palestinian diplomatist; b. 1937, Abu Dis ; joined Fatah (largest political group within PLO) 1968, currently mem. Revolutionary Council Cen. Cttee; fmr Minister of Economy and Trade and Minister of Industry, Palestinian Authority; Chief Palestinian Negotiator Oslo Agreement 1993 and all subsequent Israeli–Palestinian talks including Taba, Cairo, Wye River; Deputy and Speaker Palestinian Legis. Council 1996–; mem. Palestinian Nat. Council; mem. Bd Palestinian Econ. Policy Research Inst., Peres Center for Peace; mem. Bd of Advisers Gleitsman Foundation; Norwegian Royal Order of Merit 1994, Seeds of Peace Foundation Award 1996, Gleitsman Foundation Int. Activist Award 1999. *Publications include:* Hanging Peace; numerous economic essays. *Address:* Palestinian Liberation Organization, Negotiations Affairs Department, POB 2245, Ramallah, Palestinian Autonomous Areas (Office). *Telephone:* (972) 2296-3741 (Office). *Fax:* (972) 2296-3740 (Office). *E-mail:* info@nsu-pal.org (Office). *Website:* www.nad-plo.org (Office).

QURESHI, Moeen Ahmad, MA, PhD; Pakistani economist and international official; b. 26 June 1930, Lahore; s. of Mohyeddin Ahmad Qureshi and Khursheed Jabin; m. Lilo Elizabeth Richter 1958; two s. two d.; ed Islamia Coll. and Govt Coll., Univ. of Punjab and Indiana Univ., USA; Social Science Consultant, Ford Foundation, Pakistan 1953; Hon. Lecturer, Univ. of Karachi 1953–54; Asst Chief, Planning Comm., Govt of Pakistan 1954–56, Deputy Chief 1956–58; Economist, IMF 1958–61, Div. Chief 1961–65, Adviser Africa Dept 1965–66, Resident Rep. Ghana 1966–68, Sr Adviser 1968–70; Econ. Adviser IFC 1970–74, Vice-Pres. 1974–77, Exec. Vice-Pres. 1977–81; Vice-Pres. Finance, World Bank 1979–80, Sr Vice-Pres. Finance 1980–87, Sr Vice-Pres. Operations 1987–91; Acting Prime Minister of Pakistan July–Oct. 1993. *Publications:* various articles in economic journals. *Leisure interests:* tennis, collecting antiques. *Address:* c/o Ministry of External Affairs, South Block, New Delhi 110 011, India (Office).

R

RÄÄTS, Jaan; Estonian composer; b. 15 Oct. 1932, Tartu; s. of Peeter Rääts and Linda Rääts; m. 1st Marianne Rääts 1958; m. 2nd Ebba Rääts 1983; three c.; ed Tallinn Conservatory (pupil of Heino Eller); mem. CPSU 1964–90; Music Dir Estonian TV 1966–74; Prof. Tallinn Conservatory 1978–; Chair. Estonian Composers' Union 1974–93; People's Artist of the Estonian SSR 1977. *Compositions include:* 10 symphonies, 18 concertos, 9 piano sonatas, 9 piano cycles. *Leisure interests:* technology, science. *Address:* c/o Estonian Composers' Union, A. Lauteri Street 7, 10145 Tallinn, Estonia. *Telephone:* 646-6536 (Office); 421-645 (Home).

RABAN, Jonathan, FRSL; British author and critic; b. 14 June 1942; s. of Rev. Peter J. C. P. Raban and Monica Sandison; m. 1st Caroline Cuthbert 1985 (divorced 1992); m. 2nd Jean Cara Lenihan 1992; one d.; ed Univ. of Hull; Lecturer in English and American Literature, Univ. Coll. of Wales, Aberystwyth 1965–67, Univ. of E Anglia 1967–69; professional writer 1969–; Heinemann Award, Royal Soc. of Literature and Thomas Cook Award for Old Glory 1982, Thomas Cook Award for Hunting Mister Heartbreak 1991, Nat. Book Critics Circle Award and PEN/West Creative Nonfiction Award for Bad Land 1997. *Publications:* The Technique of Modern Fiction 1969, Mark Twain: Huckleberry Finn 1969, The Society of the Poem 1971, Soft City 1973, Arabia Through the Looking Glass 1979, Old Glory 1981, Foreign Land 1985, Coasting 1986, For Love and Money 1987, God, Man & Mrs Thatcher 1989, Hunting Mister Heartbreak 1990, The Oxford Book of the Sea (Ed.) 1992, Bad Land: An American Romance 1996, Passage to Juneau 1999. *Leisure interest:* sailing. *Address:* c/o Gillon Aitken Associates, 29 Fernshaw Road, London, SW10 0TG, England.

RABASSA, Gregory, PhD; American professor of Romance languages; b. 9 March 1922, Yonkers, NY; s. of Miguel Rabassa and Clara Macfarland; m. 1st Roney Edelstein 1957 (divorced 1966); one d.; m. 2nd Clementine Christos 1966; one d.; ed Dartmouth Coll. and Columbia Univ.; mil. service 1942–45; Instructor in Spanish, Columbia Univ. 1947–52, Assoc. Instructor 1952–58, Asst Prof. 1958–63, Assoc. Prof. of Spanish and Portuguese 1963–68; Prof. of Romance Languages, Queens Coll., Flushing, NY 1968–86, Distinguished Prof. 1986–; Assoc. Ed. Odyssey Review 1961–64; mem. Renaissance Soc. of America, PEN Club and other professional asscns; Fulbright-Hays Fellow, Brazil 1965–66; Guggenheim Fellow 1988–89; Croce al Merito di Guerra (Italy), Order of San Carlos (Colombia), Gabriela Mistral Medal (Chile) 1996; Dr hc (Dartmouth Coll.) 1982; Nat. Book Award for trans. 1967, New York Gov.'s Arts Award 1985, Wheatland Translation Prize 1988, Literature Award, American Acad. and Inst. of Arts and Letters 1989, Sandrof Award (Nat. Book Critics Circle) 1993, New York Public Library Literary Lion Award 1993, Gregory Kolovakos Award, PEN 2001. *Publications:* O Negro na Ficção Brasileira 1965. *Address:* Department of Hispanic Languages and Literature, CUNY, Queens College, Flushing, NY 11367 (Office); 140 East 72nd Street, New York, NY 10021, USA. *Telephone:* (212) 439-6636.

RABBANI, Burhanuddin; Afghanistan politician and academic; b. 1940, Faiz Abad; ed Kabul Univ., Al Azhar Univ., Cairo; fmr lecturer in Islamic law Kabul Univ.; Pres. United Nat. and Islamic Front for the Salvation of Afghanistan (Unifsa) (also known as Northern Alliance); leader Jamiat-e-Islami (Islamic Soc. of Afghanistan) 1971–; left Afghanistan 1974; made armed raids against gov. of Mohammed Daoud from base in Pakistan; returned to Afghanistan 1992; elected Pres. of Afghanistan by Mujahideen Exec. Council 1992; forced to step down when Taliban occupied Kabul 1996; continued to be recognized as Pres. of Islamic State of Afghanistan by UN –2001. *Address:* Office of the President, Shar Rahi Sedarat, Kabul, Afghanistan (Office).

RABEE, Hayder K. Gafar, BA; Iraqi teacher of calligraphy; b. 22 Feb. 1962, Najaf; m. Ahalam A. Al-Zahawi 1986; two s. one d.; ed Inst. of Fine Arts; calligrapher, Baghdad TV 1982–88; worked as designer, newspapers and magazines 1989–91; teacher, Inst. of Fine Arts, Baghdad 1992–, Head, Calligraphy Dept (evening classes) 1995–; teacher of Arabic Calligraphy, Jordanian Calligraphers' Soc. 1998; Gen. Sec. Iraqi Calligraphers' Soc. 1998–99; mem. Iraqi Plastic Arts Soc. 1996–2002, Iraqi Union of Artists, Iraqi Soc. for Calligraphy Jordanian Calligraphers' Soc., Egyptian Calligraphers' Soc.; State Trophy for Plastic Arts and Calligraphy 1989, 1999, Gold Medal, 2nd World Festival 1992, Third World Festival 1993, Gold Medal for Creativity, Dar Es-Salaam 1st Nat. Festival 1993, Appreciation Prize, 4th Baghdad Nat. Festival 1998, Appreciation Prize in 5th Int. Competition for Calligraphy, Turkey 2001, a main prizewinner, Int. Meeting for Calligraphy of the Islam World, Tehran 2002. *Exhibition:* Breezes from Baghdad, Italy 2001. *Publication:* Proposed Alphabet Study for Arabic Calligraphy in Printing. *Leisure interest:* chess. *Address:* Department of Calligraphy, Institute of Fine Arts, Al-Mansur, Baghdad, Iraq.

RABEMANANJARA, Jacques; Malagasy writer and politician; b. c. 1913; mem. French Nat. Ass. as rep. for Madagascar 1946; initiated the Democratic Movt for the restoration of Malagasy independence in harmony with France; arrested during the Malagasy insurrection of 1947 and exiled in France; helped to inaugurate the review and publishing house Présence Africaine; winner of Le grand Prix de la Francophonie awarded by the Acad. Française 1988. *Publications:* (poems) Dieux malgaches, Rites millénaires, Antsa,

Lamba, Ode à Ranavalo, Antidote, Ordalies, (political works) Témoignage malgache et colonialisme, Nationalisme et problèmes malgaches, Premiers jalons pour une politique de la culture.

RABETAFIKA, Joseph Albert Blaise, LèsL, MA, MEd; Malagasy diplomatist; b. 3 Feb. 1932, Tananarive (now Antananarivo); m. Jeanne Razafintsalama 1956; one s. two d.; teacher in UK, France and Madagascar 1953–59; joined Ministry of Defence, France 1960; mem. Madagascar del. to independence negotiations with France 1960; Counsellor in charge of cultural affairs and information, Madagascar diplomatic mission, France 1960–63; Perm. Del. to UNESCO, Paris 1961–63; Head, del. to IBE Confs, Geneva 1961–63; mem. del. to UN Gen. Ass. 1962–69; Dir of Cabinet Foreign Ministry 1964–67; Consul-Gen., New York 1968; Perm. Rep. to UN 1969–93; Amb. to Canada 1970, to Cuba 1974; Vice-Pres. ECOSOC 1973; Chair. Group of 77 1973; Pres. UN Security Council 1985, 1986. *Leisure interests:* classical music, jazz, reading, violin playing.

RABIN, Oskar; Russian painter; b. 1928, Moscow; m. Valentina Kropovnitskaya; one s.; student of artist and teacher Yevgeny Kropovnitsky; worked in Riga 1946–48; thereafter student of Surikov Art Inst., Moscow; later expelled for unorthodox views; worked until 1958 as loader on railways and on construction sites, painting clandestinely; employed in arts and design centre 1958–67; f. Leonozovo group in Moscow; exhibited in 'Festival of Youth' Exhbn, Moscow 1957; forced to emigrate 1977; now lives in Paris. *Exhibitions:* one-man show Grosvenor Gallery, London 1965; two open-air exhbns in Cheremushki, outside Moscow and organized by s. (both exhbns officially bulldozed) 1974; 'Twenty Russian Artists', Moscow (Bee-keeping Pavilion, VDNKh) 1975; 'Unofficial Art in the Soviet Union', London 1977; other exhbns in FRG, Switzerland, Austria, France, Poland, USA (Chicago), Tbilisi, Denmark, Moscow. *Publication:* Memoirs: Three Lives 1986.

RABINOVITCH, B(enton) Seymour, PhD, FRS; Canadian professor of chemistry; b. 19 Feb. 1919, Montreal, PQ; s. of Samuel Rabinovitch and Rachel Shachter; m. 1st Marilyn Werby 1949 (deceased); m. 2nd Flora Reitman 1980; two s. two d. from 1st m.; ed McGill Univ.; Royal Soc. of Canada Research Fellow 1946–47; Milton Research Fellow, Harvard Univ. 1947–48; Asst Prof. Univ. of Washington, Seattle 1948–53, Assoc. Prof. 1953–57, Prof. Dept of Chem. 1957–85, Prof. Emer. 1985–; Fellow, American Acad. of Arts and Sciences, American Physics Soc.; mem. Silver Soc.; Guggenheim Fellowship 1961; Hon. Liveryman, Worshipful Co. of Goldsmiths, London 2000; Hon. DSc (Technion Univ., Haifa) 1991; Peter Debye Award, Michael Polyani Medal. *Publications:* Textbook of Physical Chemistry 1964, Antique Silver Servers 1991, Contemporary Silver 2000; Ed. Annual Reviews of Physical Chemistry 1975–85; 220 research papers. *Leisure interest:* silversmithing. *Address:* Department of Chemistry, Box 351700, University of Washington, Seattle, WA 98195 (Office); 12530 42nd Avenue, NE, Seattle, WA 98125, USA (Home).

RABINOWITZ, Harry, MBE; British composer and conductor; b. 26 March 1916, Johannesburg, S. Africa; s. of Israel Rabinowitz and Eva Rabinowitz (née Kirkel); m. 1st Lorna T. Anderson 1944 (divorced); one s. two d.; m. 2nd Mitzi Scott 2001; ed Athlone High School, Johannesburg and Guildhall School of Music, London; Conductor, BBC Radio 1953–60; Musical Dir BBC TV Light Entertainment 1960–68; Head of Music, London Weekend TV 1968–77; freelance composer and conductor 1977–; Music Dir (TV) Julia and Friends 1986, Paul Nicholas and Friends 1987, series New Faces 1987; has appeared with London Symphony and Royal Philharmonic Orchestras in UK and with the LA Philharmonic and Boston Pops Orchestras and Orchestra of St Luke's in USA; Musical Dir for world premieres of Cats and Song & Dance; Musical Dir (films) Chariots of Fire, Lord of the Flies, Camille Claudet, Shirley Valentine, La Baule-les Pins, La Fille des Collines, Eve of Destruction, Jesuit Joe, Jeanne, Putain du Roi, Ballad of the Sad Café, Howards End, The Remains of the Day, La Fille de d'Artagnan, Death and the Maiden, Jefferson in Paris, Secret Agent, Alien Empire (BBC TV), The Stupids, The English Patient, Tonka, Surviving Picasso, Wings of a Dove, My Story So Far, City of Angels, A Soldier's Daughter Never Cries, Cotton Mary, The Talented Mr Ripley, Place Vendome, F/X, The Golden Bowl, Possession, Le Divorce, Bon Voyage; has composed and conducted several TV scores including Reilly Ace of Spades, The Agatha Christie Hour, The Sign of Four; Freeman City of London 1995; awarded BASCA Gold Badge for Services to British Music 1985, Radio and TV Industries Award for Best TV Theme 1984, All-Music Gold Award 1991. *Leisure interests:* listening to others making music, edible fungi hunting, wine-tasting. *Address:* 11 Mead Road, Cranleigh, Surrey, GU6 7BG, England. *Telephone:* (1483) 278676. *Fax:* (1483) 278676. *E-mail:* mitziscott@aol.com (Office).

RABKIN, Mitchell T., MD; American physician and hospital administrator; b. 27 Nov. 1930, Boston, Mass.; s. of Morris A. Rabkin and Esther Quint Rabkin; m. Adrienne M. Najarian 1956; one s. one d.; ed Harvard Coll. and Harvard Medical School; trained in medicine, Mass. Gen. Hosp., Boston; U.S. Public Health Service, Nat. Inst. of Health, Bethesda, Md 1957–59; Chief Resident in Medicine, Mass. Gen. Hosp. 1962, medical staff 1963–66, Bd Consultation 1972–80, Hon. Physician 1981–; Gen. Dir Beth Israel Hosp., Boston 1966–80, Pres. 1980–96; Prof. of Medicine, Harvard Medical School 1983–, Pres. Medical Alumni Council 2000–; CEO CareGroup, Boston

1996–98; Distinguished Inst. Scholar, Inst. for Educ. and Research, Beth Israel Deaconess Medical Center, Boston 1998–; mem. NAS Inst. of Medicine; mem. Bd Dirs Duke Univ. Health System 1998–; mem. Bd of Trustees New York Univ. School of Medicine Foundation; Prin. Washington Advisory Group; Fellow AAAS, ACP; Hon. DSc (Brandeis), (Curry Coll., Milton, Mass.), (Mass. Coll. of Pharmacy) 1983, (Northeastern Univ.) 1994; Distinguished Service Award, American Hosp. Asscn 1999. *Address:* Carl J. Shapiro Institute for Education and Research at Harvard Medical School and Beth Israel Deaconess Medical Center, 330 Brookline Avenue, Boston, MA 02186, USA; 124 Canton Avenue, Milton, MA 02186, USA (Home). *Telephone:* (617) 667-9400 (Office); (617) 696-6614 (Home). *Fax:* (617) 667-9122 (Office); (617) 696-1008 (Home). *E-mail:* mrabkin@caregroup.harvard.edu (Office); mtrabkin@mindspring.com (Home). *Website:* www.bidmc.harvard.edu (Office).

RABUKA, Maj.-Gen. Sitiveni Ligamamada, OBE, MSc; Fijian politician and army officer; b. 13 Sept. 1948, Nakobo; s. of Kolinio E. V. Rabuka and Salote Lomaloma; m. Suluweti Camamaivuna Tuiloma 1975; one s. two d.; ed Provincial School Northern, Queen Victoria School, NZ Army schools, Indian Defence Services Staff Coll. and Australian Jt Services Staff Coll.; Sr Operational Plans Officer UNIFIL, Lebanon 1980–81; Chief of Staff, Fiji July–Dec. 1981; SO 1 Operations and Training, Fiji Army 1982–83, 1985–87; Commdr Fiji Bn, Sinai 1983–85; staged coup 14 May 1987; Adviser on Home Affairs and Head of Security May–Sept. 1987; staged second coup 25 Sept. 1987; declared Fiji a Repub. 7 Oct. 1987; Commdr and Head of Interim Mil. Govt of Fiji Sept.–Dec. 1987; Commdr Fiji Security Forces 1987–91; Minister for Home Affairs, Nat. Youth Service and Auxiliary Army Services 1987–90; Deputy Prime Minister 1991, Minister for Home Affairs 1991; Prime Minister of Fiji 1992–99, fmrly Minister for Home Affairs, Immigration, Fijian Affairs and Rural Devt and Foreign Affairs, fmrly with special responsibility for the Constitutional Review and the Agricultural, Landlords and Tenants Act; Commonwealth Rep. to Solomon Is. 1999; Pres. Fijian Political Party (FPP); OStJ.; Commdr, Légion d'honneur. *Publication:* No Other Way 1988. *Leisure interests:* golf, rugby. *Address:* c/o Office of the Prime Minister, Government Buildings, P.O. Box 2353, Suva, Fiji.

RAČAN, Ivica; Croatian politician and lawyer; b. 24 Feb. 1944, Ebersbach, Germany; ed Zagreb Univ.; research asst Inst. for Social Man., Zagreb; mem. Bd Cen. Cttee of SKY (Union of Communists of Yugoslavia) 1986–89; Chair. Cen. Cttee Croatian Union of Communists 1989–90; Chair. Social Democratic Party 1990–; elected to Croatian Parl. 1990–; Prime Minister of Croatia 2000–02. *Address:* c/o Government of the Republic of Croatia, trg Sv. Marka 2, 10000 Zagreb (Office); SDP, trg Iblerov 9, 10000 Zagreb, Croatia.

RACICOT, Marc F., BA, JD; American politician and lawyer; b. 24 July 1948, Thompson Falls, Mont.; s. of William E. Racicot and Patricia E. (Bentley) Racicot; m. Theresa J. Barber 1970; two s. three d.; ed Carroll Coll., Helena, Mont., Univ. of Montana; called to Bar, Mont. 1973; served US Army 1973–76, Chief Trial Counsel US Army, Kaiserslautern, Fed. Repub. of Germany 1975–76, resgnd 1976; Deputy Co. Attorney, Missoula (Mont.) Co. 1976–77; Asst Attorney-Gen. State of Mont. 1977–88, Attorney-Gen. 1988–93; Gov. of Montana 1993–2001; Partner Bracewell & Patterson, Washington 2001–; Chair. Republican Nat. Cttee 2003–. *Address:* Bracewell & Patterson, 2000 K Street, NW, Suite 500, Washington, DC 20006-1872 (Office); Republican National Committee, 310 First Street, SE, Washington, DC 20003, USA (Office). *Telephone:* (202) 828-5866 (B&P); (202) 863-8500 (RNC). *Fax:* (202) 857-2111 (B&P); (202) 863-8820 (RNC). *E-mail:* marc.racicot@bracepatt.com; info@rnc.org. *Website:* www.bracepatt.com; www.rnc.org.

RACIONERO GRAU, Luis; Spanish librarian, professor of economics and writer; b. 1940, Seu d'Urgell, Lleida; ed Univ. of Calif. at Berkeley, USA, Churchill Coll., Cambridge, UK; industrial engineer, Barcelona 1965; Prof. of MicroEcons, Faculty of Econ. Sciences and Urban Studies, School of Architecture, Barcelona; fmr Dir Spanish Coll., Paris; Dir-Gen. Biblioteca Nacional, Madrid 2001–. *Publications include:* Atenas de Pericles 1993, El Progreso Decadente (Espasa de Ensayo Prize 2001). *Address:* Biblioteca Nacional, Paseo de Recoletos 20, 28071 Madrid, Spain (Office). *Telephone:* (1) 5807870 (Office). *Fax:* (1) 5807876 (Office). *E-mail:* directorgeneral@bne.es (Office). *Website:* www.bne.es (Office).

RADCLIFFE, Paula, MBE; British athlete; b. 17 Dec. 1973, Northwich; d. of Peter Radcliffe and Pat Radcliffe; m. Gary Lough; ed Univ. of Loughborough; distance runner; World Jr Cross Country Champion 1992; started Sr career 1993; fifth place, 5,000m., Olympic Games 1996; won Fifth Avenue Mile, New York 1996, 1997; third place, Int. Asscn of Athletics Feds (IAAF) World Cross Challenge series 1997; fourth place, 5,000m., World Championships 1997; European Cross Country Champion 1998; second place, 10,000m., European Challenge 1998; silver medal, 10,000m. World Championships, 1999; fourth place, 10,000m. Olympic Games 2000; World Half Marathon Champion 2000, 2001; World Cross Country Champion 2002; gold medallist, 5,000m., Commonwealth Games 2002; gold medallist, 10,000m., European Championships 2002; won London Marathon 2002, 2003, Chicago Marathon 2002; Capt. GB's Women's Athletic Team 1998–; Hon. DLitt (De Montfort); British Female Athlete of the Year 1999, 2001 and 2002, IAAF World Female Athlete of the Year 2002, BBC Sports Personality of the Year 2002, Sunday Times Sportswoman of the Year 2002. *Leisure interests:* dining out, languages, reading, music, cinema. *Address:* c/o Bedford and County Athletics Club, 3 Regent Close, Bedford, MK41 7XG, England (Office).

RADCLIFFE, Father Timothy Peter Joseph, OP, MA; British ecclesiastic; b. 22 Aug. 1945, London; s. of Hugh Radcliffe and Marie-Therese Pereira; ed Downside School, Le Saulchoir, Paris and St John's Coll. Oxford; entered Dominican Order 1965; Chaplain to Imperial Coll.; Prior of Blackfriars, Oxford 1982–88; Chair. new Blackfriars 1983–88; Provincial of Prov. of England 1988–92; Pres. Conf. of Maj. Religious Superiors of England and Wales 1991–; Grand Chancellor, Pontifical Univ. of St Thomas (The Angelicum) 1992–2001, Univ. of Santo Tomas, Manila 1992–2001, Ecole Biblique, Jerusalem 1992–2001, Faculty of Theology, Fribourg, 1992–2001; Master, Order of Preachers 1992–2001; Hon. Citizen of Perpignan (France), Augusta (Italy) and Sepahua (Peru); Hon. Fellow, St John's Coll. Oxford; Hon. STD (Providence Coll. RI); Hon. LL.D (Barry Univ., Fla) 1996; Hon. DHumLitt (Ohio Dominican Coll.) 1996 (Dominican Univ., Chicago); Prix de Littérature Religieuse 2001, Prix Spiritualités d'aujourd'hui 2001. *Publications:* El Manantial de la Esperanza 1998, Sing a New Song: The Christian Vocation 1999, I Call You Friends 2001. *Leisure interests:* walking, reading long novels. *Address:* St Dominic's Priory, Southampton Road, London, NW5 4LB, England. *Telephone:* (20) 7482-9218. *Fax:* (20) 7482-9239. *E-mail:* timothy.radcliffe@english.op.org (Office).

RADDA, Sir George Karoly, Kt, CBE, MA, DPhil, FRS; British medical research director and professor of molecular cardiology; b. 9 June 1936, Gyor, Hungary; s. of Gyula Radda and Anna Bernolak; m. 1st Mary O'Brien 1961 (divorced 1995), two s. one d.; m. 2nd Sue Bailey 1995; ed Pannonhalma and Eötvös Univ., Budapest and Merton Coll. Oxford; Research Assoc., Univ. of Calif., USA 1962–63; Lecturer in Organic Chem., St John's Coll., Oxford Univ. 1963–64, Fellow and Tutor in Organic Chem., Merton Coll. 1964–84, Lecturer in Biochem, Oxford Univ. 1966–84, British Heart Foundation Prof. of Molecular Cardiology 1984–; Professorial Fellow, Merton Coll. 1984–, Head Dept of Biochem. 1991–96; Chair. MRC Cell. Bd 1988–92; mem. MRC Council 1988–92, Chief Exec. MRC (on leave from Oxford Univ.) 1996–; Chair. Nat. Cancer Research Inst. 2001–; mem. Council, Royal Soc. 1990–92, ICRF 1991–96; Ed. Biochemical and Biophysical Research Communications 1977–84; Man. Ed. Biochimica et Biophysica Acta 1977–, Chair. 1989–95; Founder mem. Oxford Enzyme Group 1970–87; Pres. Soc. for Magnetic Resonance in Medicine 1985–86; Fellow Int. Soc. of Magnetic Resonance in Medicine 1995; mem. European Molecular Biology Org. 1997–; Hon. Dir MRC Biochemical and Clinical Magnetic Resonance Unit 1988–96; Hon. FRCR 1985; Hon. Fellow American Heart Asscn and Citation for Int. Achievement 1987; Hon. FRCP 1997; Hon. DrMed (Berne) 1985, (London) 1991; Hon. DSc (Stirling) 1998; Colworth Medal, Biochemical Soc. 1969, CIBA Medal and Prize 1983, Feldberg Prize 1982, British Heart Foundation Prize and Gold Medal for cardiovascular research 1982, Gold Medal, Soc. for Magnetic Resonance in Medicine 1984, Buchanan Medal, Royal Soc. 1987, Rank Prize in Nutrition 1990. *Publications:* articles in books and scientific journals. *Leisure interests:* opera, jazz, swimming. *Address:* Medical Research Council, 20 Park Crescent, London, W1B 4AL, England. *Telephone:* (20) 7636-5422. *Fax:* (20) 7436-6179. *Website:* www.mrc.ac.uk (Office).

RADEBE, Jeffrey Thamsanqa (Jeff), LLB; South African politician; b. 18 Feb. 1953, Cato Manor; ed Isibonelo High School; joined Black Consciousness Movt 1970; co-founder Kwamashu Youth Org. 1972; articled clerk with A. J. Gumede & Phyllis Naidoo, E S. Mchunu & Co. 1976–77; with Radio Freedom 1977–78; Deputy Chief ANC Rep., Tanzania 1981; headed clandestine political Movt of ANC and South African Communist Party (SACP) 1986, Head Political Dept and Co-ordinator of 12-day hunger strike on Robben Island; arrested and sentenced to 10 years on Robben Island 1986, sentence reduced to 6 years, released 1990; Sec. interim leadership group of SACP 1990–91; Deputy Chair. ANC Southern Natal Region 1990–91, Chair. 1991–; Minister of Public Works, Govt of Nat. Unity 1994–99, of Public Enterprises 1999–; Hon. LLM (Leipzig Univ., Germany). *Address:* Ministry of Public Enterprises, Infotech Building 401, 1090 Arcadia Street, Hatfield, Pretoria 0083, South Africa (Office). *Fax:* (12) 3427226 (Office). *Telephone:* (12) 3427111 (Office). *Website:* www.dpe.gov.za.

RADER, Gen. Paul A., BA, BD, M.TH., D.MISS.; American religious leader; b. 14 March 1934, New York; s. of Lyell M. Rader and Gladys Mina Damon; m. Kay Fuller 1956; one s. two d.; ed Asbury Theological Seminary, Southern Baptist Theological Seminary, Salvation Army's School for Officers' Training, New York, Fuller Theological Seminary; mem. staff Salvation Army Training School, Seoul, Korea 1962–67, Vice-Prin. 1967–71, Training Prin., then Educ. Officer, then Asst Chief Sec. Salvation Army in Korea 1973–77, Chief Sec. with rank of Lt-Col 1977–84; Prin. School for Officers' Training, Suffern, New York 1984–87, Nat. Leader 1987–89; Chief Sec. USA Eastern Territory 1989; rank of Commr 1989; Commdr USA Western Territory 1989–94; Pres. The Salvation Army Calif. Corps 1989–94; rank of Gen. of The Salvation Army 1994–99; Pres. Asbury Coll. 2000–. *Address:* Salvation Army Headquarters, 101 Queen Victoria Street, London, EC4P 4EP, England (Office); Asbury College, 1 Macklem Drive, Wilmore, KY 40390, USA.

RADHAKISHUN, Pretaapnarain S. R.; Suriname politician; Vice-Pres. and Prime Minister of Suriname 1999–2000. *Address:* c/o Office of the Prime Minister, Paramaribo, Suriname (Office).

RADICE, Vittorio; Italian business executive; b. Como; m. Gemma Radice; two s.; studied architecture in Milan; mil. service; home furnishings buyer, Associated Merchandising Corpn; Buying Dir Habitat Int., then Man. Dir Habitat UK 1990–96; Man. Dir Selfridges PLC 1996–98, CEO 1998–2002;

Exec. Dir and Head of Home Furnishings, Marks and Spencer PLC 2003–; Dir (non-exec.) Nat. Gallery Co. Ltd, Abbey Nat. PLC, Shoppers Stop India. *Leisure interests:* travel, India, art, animals. *Address:* Marks and Spencer PLC, Michael House, Baker Street, London, W1U 8EP, England (Office). *Telephone:* (20) 7935-4422 (Office). *Fax:* (20) 7487-2679 (Office). *Website:* www.marksandspencer.com.

RADIŠIĆ, Zivko; Bosnia and Herzegovina (Serb) politician; Pres. and Chair. of the Presidency of Bosnia and Herzegovina Oct. 1998–June 1999, co-Pres. 1999–2001, Pres. 2001, Mem. of the Presidency 2002; Chair. Socialist Party of the Bosnian Serb Republic. *Address:* Office of the Presidency, 71000 Sarajevo, Musala 5, Bosnia and Herzegovina (Office). *Telephone:* (33) 664941 (Office). *Fax:* (33) 472491 (Office).

RADNER, Roy, PhD; American economist and applied mathematician; b. 29 June 1927, Chicago; s. of Ella Radner and Samuel Radner; m. 1st Virginia Honoski (died 1976); one s. three d. (one d. deceased); m. 2nd Charlotte V. Kuh 1978; ed Hyde Park High School, Chicago and Univ. of Chicago; served US army 1945–48; Research Assoc., Cowles Comm., Univ. of Chicago 1951–54, Asst Prof. 1954–55; Asst Prof. of Econs Yale Univ. 1955–57; Assoc. Prof. of Econs and Statistics, Univ. of Calif., Berkeley 1957–61, Prof. 1961–79, Chair. Dept of Econs 1965–69; Distinguished mem. tech. staff, AT&T Bell Labs 1979–95; Research Prof. of Econs New York Univ. 1983–95, Prof. of Econs and Information Systems 1995–96, L. N. Stern School Prof. of Business 1995–; Guggenheim Fellow 1961–62 and 1965–66; Overseas Fellow, Churchill Coll. Cambridge, UK 1969–70, 1989; Assoc. Ed. Journal of Econ. Theory 1968–, Games and Economic Behavior 1989–, Economic Theory 1990–, Review of Economic Design 1994–, Review of Accounting Studies 1994–; mem. NAS; Fellow American Acad. of Arts and Sciences, Econometric Soc. (Pres. 1973); Distinguished Fellow American Econ. Asscn, AAAS; Woytinsky Award, Univ. of Mich. 1998. *Publications:* Notes on the Theory of Economic Planning 1963, Optimal Replacement Policy (with others) 1967, Decision and Organization (co-ed.) 1972, Economic Theory of Teams (with J. Marschak) 1972, Demand and Supply in U.S. Higher Education (with L. S. Miller) 1975, Education as an Industry (co-ed.) 1976, Mathematicians in Academia (with C. V. Kuh) 1980, Information, Incentives and Economic Mechanisms (co-ed.) 1987, Perspectives on Deterrence 1989, Bargaining with Incomplete Information (co-ed.) 1992; and many articles. *Leisure interests:* music, hiking, cross-country skiing. *Address:* Stern School of Business, New York University, 44 W Fourth Street, KMC 8–87, New York, NY 10012 (Office); 3203 Davenport Street, NW, Washington, DC 20008, USA (Home). *Telephone:* (212) 998-0813 (Office). *Fax:* (212) 995-4228 (Office).

RADOS, Jozo; Croatian politician, academic and engineer; b. 3 Nov. 1956, Seonica, Tomislavgrad, Bosnia-Herzegovina; m.; three c.; ed Zagreb Univ.; Prof. of History and Electrical Eng Osijek and Dakovo 1983–1986; Devt Planner Rade Kondar Co., Zagreb 1986–90; engineer Zagreb Electric Bulb factory 1990–92; mem. House of Reps 1992–2000; mem. Zagreb City Ass. 1995–97; mem. Croatian Parl. Del. to Parl. Ass. of Council of Europe 1998–2000; Minister of Defence 2000–02; Homeland War Memorial Certificate. *Address:* c/o Ministry of Defence, Kardeljeva ploscad 24–26, 61000 Ljubljana, Slovenia (Office).

RADZINSKY, Edvard Stanislavovich; Russian dramatist; b. 23 Sept. 1936, Moscow; s. of Stanislav Radzinsky and Sofia Radzinsky; m. 2nd Yelena Timofeyevna Denisova (divorced); ed Inst. of History and Archival Science, Moscow. *Plays include:* My Dream is India 1960, You're All of Twenty-Two, you Old Men! 1962, One Hundred and Four Pages on Love 1964, Kolobashkin the Seducer 1967, Socrates 1977, Lunin 1980, I Stand at the Restaurant 1982, Theatre of the Time of Nero and Seneca 1984, Elderly Actress in the Role of Dostoevsky's Wife 1986, Sporting Scenes 1987, Our Decameron 1989. *Television:* author and narrator of TV series Mysteries of History 1997–. *Publications:* (novels): The Last of the Romanovs 1989, Our Decameron 1990; (non-fiction): The Last Tsar: The Life and Death of Nicholas II 1992, God Save and Restrain Russia 1993, Stalin 1996, Mysteries of History 1997, Mysteries of Love 1998, Fall of Gallant Century 1998, Rasputin 1999, The Theatrical Novel (memoirs) 1999; Collected Works (7 Vols) 1998–99. *Address:* Usiyevicha Street 8, Apt 98, 125319 Moscow, Russia.

RAE, Alexander Lindsay, CNZM, OBE, M.AGR.SC., PhD, FRSNZ; New Zealand professor of animal science; b. 3 Aug. 1923, Eltham; s. of Thomas Rae and Annie Rae; m. Fiona D. Thomas 1957 (died 1998); ed Massey Agricultural Coll. and Iowa State Univ.; Jr Lecturer in Sheep Husbandry, Massey Agricultural Coll. 1944-50; Prof. of Sheep Husbandry, Massey Univ. 1951–80, Prof. in Animal Science 1980–89, Prof. Emer. 1989–; Fellow NZ Inst. of Agricultural Science, Australian Asscn of Animal Breeding and Genetics; Trustee NZ Animal Breeding Trust 1991–; NZ Soc. of Animal Production McMeekan Memorial Award 1977, Sir Ernest Marsden Medal for Outstanding Service to Science 1982, Massey Univ. Award for Distinguished Service 1990. *Publications:* research papers on animal genetics and breeding in scientific journals. *Leisure interest:* fishing. *Address:* 16 Wallace Place, Palmerston North, New Zealand (Home). *Telephone:* (6) 357-8611 (Home).

RAE, Barbara, CBE, RA, RSA; British artist and lecturer; b. 10 Dec. 1943, Scotland; d. of James Rae and Mary Young; one s.; ed Edinburgh Coll. of Art; lecturer Glasgow School of Art 1975–96; Trustee British School, Rome 1997–2000, Hospitalfield House, Arbroath 1997–99; mem. Bd Royal Fine Art Comm. 1995–; Invited Artist, Royal Hibernian Acad., Dublin 1995, 1996, 2003; numerous group exhbns UK, USA, Germany, Netherlands, Spain;

works in public and pvt. collections including Scottish Nat. Gallery of Modern Art, Scottish Arts Council, Univs of Edin., Glasgow and York, Royal Bank of Scotland, Bank of England, TSB Group PLC, HRH the Duke of Edin.; mem. Royal Scottish Soc. of Painters in Watercolours, Royal Glasgow Inst. of the Fine Arts; Dr hc (Napier Univ., Edin.) 2000; several awards including Guthrie Award, RSA 1977, Sir William Gillies Travel Award 1983, Calouste Gulbenkian Printmaking Award 1983. *Leisure interest:* travel. *Address:* c/o Art First, 9 Cork Street, London, W1X 1PD, England; 11 Circus Lane, Edinburgh, EH3 6SU, Scotland (Home). *E-mail:* barbararaera@aol.com (Home).

RAE, Hon. Robert (Bob) Keith, OC, PC, BPhil; Canadian politician, lawyer and arbitrator; b. 2 Aug. 1948, Ottawa; s. of Saul Rae and Lois George; m. Arlene Perly 1980; three d.; ed public school in Washington, DC, Int. School of Geneva, Univ. of Toronto and Balliol Coll. Oxford; fmr volunteer, legal aid clinics in Toronto and Asst counsel for United Steelworkers of America and Union of Injured Workers; mem. Canadian Fed. Parl. 1978–82; Provincial Leader, New Democratic Party (NDP), Ont. 1982–96; mem. Ont. Provincial Legis. 1982–95; Premier of Ontario 1990–95; partner Goodman Phillips & Vineberg (now Goodmans LLP) 1996–; mem. Security Intelligence Review Cttee, numerous public and pvt. bds; Chair. Forum of Feds, Royal Conservatory of Music, Toronto Symphony Orchestra, Inst. for Research on Public Policy; Hon. LLD (Law Soc. of Upper Canada) 1998, (Toronto Univ.) 1999, (Assumption Univ.) 2001; Jerusalem Award 1996. *Publications:* From Protest to Power 1996, The Three Questions: Prosperity and the Public Good 1998. *Leisure interests:* tennis, golf, fishing, reading, music. *Address:* Goodmans LLP, 250 Yonge Street, Suite 2400, Toronto, Ont., M5B 2M6, Canada. *Telephone:* (416) 979-2211, ext. 6255. *Fax:* (416) 979-1234 (Office); (416) 604-2355 (Home). *E-mail:* brae@goodmans.ca (Office).

RAFELSON, Bob; American film director; b. 1933, New York. *Films directed include:* Head 1968, Five Easy Pieces 1970 (New York Film Critics Award), The King of Marvin Gardens 1972, Stay Hungry 1976, The Postman Always Rings Twice 1981, Black Widow 1987, Mountains of the Moon 1990, Man Trouble 1992, Wet 1993, Armed Response 1994, Blood and Wine 1997, Poodle Springs 1998.

RAFFARIN, Jean-Pierre; French politician; b. 3 Aug. 1948, Poitiers; s. of Jean Raffarin and Renée Michaud; m. Anne-Marie Perrier 1980; one d.; ed Lycée Henri IV, Poitiers, Faculté de Droit, Paris-Assas, Ecole Nat. d'Admin., and Ecole Supérieure de Commerce, Paris; Marketing Dept Cafés Jacques Vabre 1973–76; Adviser, Office of Minister of Labour 1976–81; Pres. Crédit Immobilier Rural de la Vienne 1978–95; lecturer, Inst. d'Etudes Politiques, Paris 1979–88; Dir-Gen. Bernard Krief Communication 1981–88; Gen. Del. Inst. Euro-92 1988–89; Nat. Del., Deputy Sec.-Gen. and mem. Political Bureau, Parti Républicain 1977–; City Councillor, Poitiers 1977–95; Conseiller Régional 1986–88; Pres. Conseil Régional, Poitou-Charentes 1988–; MEP 1989–95; Deputy Sec.-Gen. and Spokesman for Union pour la Démocratie Française 1993; Pres. Comm. Arc Atlantique 1994; Minister of Small and Medium-Sized Businesses, of Commerce and Craft Industry 1995–97; Sec.-Gen. U.D.F. 1995–; mem. Senate (for Vienne) 1995–; Deputy Mayor of Chasseneuil-du-Poitou 1995–2001; Vice-Pres. Démocratie Libérale 1997–; Pres. Asscn des régions de France 1998–2002; Prime Minister of France 2002–. *Publications:* La vie en jaune 1977, La publicité nerf de la communication 1983, L'avenir a ses racines 1986, Nous sommes tous les régionaux 1988, Pour une morale de l'action 1992, Le livre de l'Atlantique 1994, A New Governance 2002. *Leisure interests:* contemporary painting, regional literature. *Address:* Office of the Prime Minister, Hôtel Matignon, 57 rue de Varenne, 75008 Paris; Sénat, Palais du Luxembourg, 75291 Paris; 7 route de Saint-Georges, 86360 Chasseneuil-du-Poitou, France (Home). *Telephone:* 1-42-75-80-00. *Fax:* 1-42-75-75-04. *E-mail:* premier-ministre@premier-ministre.gouv.fr. *Website:* www.premier-ministre.gouv.fr.

RAFFENNE, Gen. Jean-Paul; French army officer; b. 1944; liaison officer, Fort Leavenworth, USA 1990–92; Deputy Defence Attaché, French Embassy, Washington 1994–96; Head French del. to EU Mil. Cttee 2001; Chief French liaison officer in unit directing Operation Enduring Freedom (mil. campaign in Afghanistan), Tampa, USA 2001; Head Direction du renseignement militaire (mil. intelligence agency) 2002–. *Address:* c/o Ministère de la Défense, 14 rue St Dominique, 75007 Paris, France.

RAFI, Brig.-Gen. Mohammed; Afghanistan politician; b. 1944, Kabul; ed Kabul Mil. Univ. and Mil. Acad. of the USSR; mem. People's Democratic Party of Afghanistan 1973, mem. Cen. Cttee 1978, Politburo 1981; fmr Minister of Public Works, Defence and Deputy Pres. of Revolutionary Council of Afghanistan; Deputy Chair. Council of Ministers and Minister of Defence 1986–88; Vice-Pres. of Afghanistan 1988–92; Order of the Red Banner.

RAFIQUE, Muhammad; Pakistan trade unionist; b. 3 Oct. 1942, Delhi, India; s.of Muhammad Umer; m.; three s. two d.; technician Karachi Water and Sewerage Bd 1971; currently man. of tech. affairs, water treatment plant; joined local union 1972; Treas. Nat. Trade Union Fed. (NTUF), Pres. 1999–; Pres. KMC United Workers Housing Soc.; Best Trade Unionist Award, NTUF-SINDH. *Leisure interest:* singing. *Address:* National Trade Union Federation Pakistan, Bharocha Bldg. 2-B/6, Commercial Area, Nazimabad No. 2, Karachi 74600, Pakistan (Office). *Telephone:* (21) 6622361 (Office). *Fax:* (21) 6622529 (Office). *E-mail:* ntuf@super.netpak.com (Office).

RAFSANJANI, Hojatoleslam Ali Akhbar Hashemi; Iranian politician; b. 1934, Rafsanjan; ed Qom; Speaker, Islamic Consultative Ass. 1980–89; MP

–2000; Deputy Chair. Council of Experts (f. to appoint eventual successor to Ayatollah Khomeini); mem. Islamic Repub. Party; Acting C-in-C of the Armed Forces 1988–89; Vice-Chair. Cttee to revise the Constitution 1989; Pres. of Iran 1989–97; Chair. Council to Determine the Expediency of the Islamic Order; fmr First Deputy Speaker Majlis-E-Khobregan. *Address:* c/o Islamic Republican Party, Dr Ali Shariati Avenue, Tehran, Iran.

RAFTER, Patrick; Australian tennis player; b. 28 Dec. 1972, Mount Isa, Queensland; s. of Jim Rafter and Jocelyn Rafter; pnr Lara Feltham; one s.; turned professional 1991; Grand Slam highlights: semi-finalist French Open 1997; winner US Open 1997, 1998; semi-finalist Wimbledon 1999, finalist 2000, 2001; semi-finalist Australian Open 2001; winner Australia Open Doubles title (with Jonas Bjorkman) 1999; sustained serious shoulder injury and took extended break from tennis following Australia's Davis Cup defeat in Dec. 2001; winner of 11 singles titles, 10 debut doubles titles at end Dec. 2002; announced retirement Jan. 2003; ATP Tour Newcomer of the Year 1993. *Leisure interests:* golf, fishing. *Address:* c/o SFX Sports Australia, PO Box 1235, North Sydney, NSW 2060, Australia (Office).

RAGHEB, Ali Abu; Jordanian politician; Head Financial and Econ. Affairs Cttee; mem. Nat. Ass.; Prime Minister of Jordan and Minister of Defence June 2000–. *Address:* Office of the Prime Minister, P.O. Box 80, 35216 Amman, Jordan (Office). *Telephone:* (6) 4641211 (Office). *Fax:* (6) 4687420 (Office). *E-mail:* pmic@pm.gov.jo (Office). *Website:* www.pm.gov.jo (Office).

RAGNEMALM, Hans, LLD; Swedish judge; b. 30 March 1940, Laholm; m. Vivi Ragnemalm 1961; Assoc. Prof. of Public Law, Univ. of Lund 1970–75; Prof. of Public Law, Univ. of Stockholm 1975–87, Dean, Faculty of Law 1984–87; Parl. Ombudsman 1987–92; Judge, Supreme Admin. Court 1992–94, Justice 1999–; Judge, Court of Justice of European Communities 1995–99; Alternate Mem. Court of Conciliation and Arbitration, OSCE. *Publications:* Appealability of Administrative Decisions 1970, Extraordinary Remedies in Administrative Procedure Law 1973, Elements of Administrative Procedure Law 1977, The Constitution of Sweden 1980, Administrative Justice in Sweden 1991; numerous other books and articles.

RAGON, Michel; French writer and lecturer; b. 24 June 1924, Marseille; s. of Aristide Ragon and Camille Sourisseau; m. Françoise Antoine 1968; worked in manual jobs from the age of 14; lived in Paris 1945–, bookseller on the Seine embankments 1954–64; art critic, architectural historian, novelist; Lecturer at l'Ecole Nat. Supérieure des Arts Décoratifs à Paris 1972–85; Chevalier, Ordre du Mérite, Légion d'honneur, Commdr des Arts et Lettres; Prix de l'Académie Française et de l'Académie d'Architecture. *Publications:* Histoire mondiale de l'architecture et l'urbanisme modernes 1971–78, L'homme et les villes 1975, L'espace de la mort 1981, L'art abstrait 1973–74, L'art pour quoi faire? 1971, 25 ans d'art vivant 1969, Histoire de la littérature prolétarienne en France 1974, L'accent de ma mère 1980, Ma soeur aux yeux d'Asie 1982, Les mouchoirs rouges de Cholet 1984, La louve de Mervent 1985, Le marin des sables 1988, La mémoire des vaincus 1990, Le Cocher du Boiroux 1992, Journal de l'Art Abstrait 1992, Le roman de Rabelais 1994, Les Coquelicots sont revenus 1996, Un si bel espoir 1999, Georges et Louise 2000, Un rossignol chantait 2001, Cinquante ans d'art vivant 2001, Un amour de Jeanne 2003. *Address:* 4 rue du Faubourg Poissonnière, 75010 Paris, France.

RAHIM, Q. A. M. A.; Bangladeshi diplomatist; b. 24 Dec. 1942, Naogaon; m.; two s.; ed Univ. of Dhaka; fmr Del. Bangladesh Missions to Tokyo, London, Doha, Islamabad, Washington, DC and UN; Dir of Secr. S. Asian Asscn for Regional Co-operation (SAARC) 1990–92, Sec.-Gen. Jan. 2002–; High Commr to Pakistan 1993–98, to Australia (concurrently accred to New Zealand and Fiji) 1998–99; Prin. Foreign Service Training Acad. 1999–2000; Sec. to the Govt 1999–2000; retd from govt service 2000; Officer on Special Duty (Sec.), Ministry of Foreign Affairs 2000–01. *Address:* South Asian Association for Regional Co-operation, POB 4222, Kathmandu, Nepal (Office). *Telephone:* (1) 221785 (Office). *Fax:* (1) 227033 (Office). *E-mail:* saarc@saarc-sec.org (Office). *Website:* www.saarc-sec.org (Office).

RAHMAN, A(llah) R(akha); Indian musician and composer; b. A. S. Dileep Kumar, 6 Jan. 1966, Madras; s. of the late R. K. Sekhar and of Kareema Begum; ed Padma Seshadri Bal Bhavan, Madras Christian Coll. and Trinity Coll. of Music, London; studied piano aged four; began musical career aged 11 as keyboard player; mem. local rock bands including Roots, Magic and Nemesis Avenue; began composing 1987; f. Panchathan Record Inn studio 1989; performances (keyboards) and recordings with many artists including Nusrat Fateh Ali Khan, Apache Indian, Zakir Hussein, Dr. L. Shankar, Talvin Singh, Dominic Miller, David Byrne and Michael Jackson (q.v.) (Friends of the World, Munich 2002); has created music for many TV and radio advertisements as well as scores for corp. videos and documentaries; fuses music of different traditions (Western classical, reggae, rock and Karnatic music); Padma Shree, Telega Purashkar Award 1992, 1993, 1994, Rajat Kamal Award for Best Music Dir, Nat. Film Awards, Filmfare Award every year 1992–2001, Cinema Express Award, Bommai Nagi Reddy Award, Sumu Award, Rajiv Gandhi Award. *Film soundtracks include:* Roja (numerous awards including Nat. Film Award, India 1992), Pudhiya Mugam, Gentleman, Kizhaku Seemaiyilae, Duet, Kadalan, Lagaan, Fiza, Taal (Screen Award), Earth, Dil Se, Fire, Bombay 1995, May, Madham, Indian, Muthu kadhal Dasam, Love Birds, Minsara Kanavu (Nat. Award for Best Music Direction 1997) and more than 30 others. *TV soundtracks include:* Vande Mataram (award-winning serial—Screen Award) 1997. *Musicals include:* Bombay Dreams (jtly with Don Black) 2002. *Albums include:* Deen Isai Malai

(Muslim devotional songs), Set Me Free (launch album of Malgudi Subha), Vande Mataram 1997, Jana Gana Mana 2000. *Leisure interest:* singing. *Address:* c/o The Really Useful Group, 22 Tower Street, London, WC2H 9TW, England (Office).

RAHMAN, Atta-Ur-, PhD, ScD; Pakistani professor of chemistry and politician; b. 20 Sept. 1942, Delhi, India; s. of Jameel-Ur-Rahman; m. Nargis Rahman; ed Karachi Univ., Cambridge Univ.; Lecturer in Chem., Karachi Univ. 1964–65, Asst Prof. 1969, Assoc. Prof. 1974–77, Prof. 1981; Commonwealth Scholar, King's Coll., Cambridge 1985–68; Fellow King's Coll., London 1969–73; Co-Dir HEJ Research Inst. of Chem. 1977–89, Dir 1990–; Chair. UNESCO/Scamap Network 1980; Minister for Science and Tech. 2000–02, for Educ. 2002; Chair. Higher Educ. Comm. 2002–; Founding Ed.-in-Chief Current Medicinal Chemistry; Pres. Chem. Soc. of Pakistan 1992; mem. American Chem. Soc.; Fellow Royal Soc. of Chem., Pakistan Acad. of Sciences 1980, Islamic Acad. of Sciences 1988, Uzbekistan Acad. of Sciences 1994; Tamgha-I-Imtiaz (Pakistan) 1987, Sitara-I-Imtiaz (Pakistan) 1989, Hilal-I-Imtiaz 1997, Nishan-I-Imtiaz 2002; Hon. ScD (Cambridge) 1987; Pakistan Acad. of Sciences Gold Medal 1977, 1995, Gold Medal Govt of Kuwait 1980, Open Gold Medal 1984, Scientist of the Year (Pakistan) 1985, FPCCI Prime, Pakistan 1985, Islamic Org. Prize for Science (Kuwait) 1987, First Kharazmi Prize (Iran) 1993, Fed. of Asian Chemical Socs Award, Japan 1997, TWAS Medal 1999, UNESCO Science Prize 1999, UNESCO Science Laureate, ECO Award 2000, ISESCO Award 2000 and other prizes and awards. *Publications:* has written or edited 63 books, mostly published in Europe, USA and Japan; 479 research papers in leading int. scientific journals. *Leisure interests:* cricket, table tennis. *Address:* Higher Education Commission, Sector H-9, Islamabad (Office); House No. 9, Ministers' Enclave, Islamabad, Pakistan (Home). *Telephone:* (51) 9290129 (Office); (51) 9290130 (Office); (21) 9202603 (Home). *Fax:* (51) 9290128 (Office); (51) 2823850 (Home). *E-mail:* chairman@hec.gov.pk (Office); attast@comsats.net.pk (Home). *Website:* www.hec.gov.pk (Office).

RAHMAN, Latifur, LLB, MA; Bangladeshi judge (retd); b. 1 March 1936, Jessore Town; s. of the late Khan Bahadur Lutfor Rahman; ed Jessore Zilla School, Dhaka Coll. and Dhaka Univ.; Lecturer in English Jagannath Coll. and Suhrawardy Coll., Dhaka; Advocate of the Dhaka High Court 1960; Advocate of the then Supreme Court of Pakistan 1965; Additional Judge, Supreme Court of Bangladesh, High Court Div. 1979, Permanent Judge 1981, Judge of the Appellate Div. 1990; Chief Justice of Bangladesh 2000–01; Chief Adviser of the Caretaker Govt of Bangladesh July–Oct. 2001; Head Interim Govt which conducted elections –2002; mem. Enquiry Comm. into train accident at Majukhan 1989; Chair. Enquiry Comm. into damage to aircraft and naval vessels in cyclone at Chittagong 1991. *Address:* Dhanmondi, Dhaka, Bangladesh (Office).

RAHMANI, Chérif; Algerian politician; b. 16 Jan. 1945, Ain Oussera; m.; four c.; ed Ecole Nat. d'Admin; Inspecteur Gen.; Sec. Gen. to the Ministry of the Interior; Minister of Youth and Sport 1988–89, of Equipment 1989–90, fmr Minister-del. to the Prime Minister in charge of the governorship of Algiers; currently Minister of Town Planning and the Environment. *Address:* Ministry of Town Planning and the Environment, c/o rue Docteur Saâdane, Algiers, Algeria (Office).

RAHMANI, Mawlawi Mohammed Arsala; Afghanistan politician; fmr Deputy Prime Minister; Minister of Religious Guidance, Endowment and the Haj; Prime Minister of Afghanistan 1994–95. *Address:* c/o Office of the Prime Minister, Shar Rahi Sedarat, Kabul, Afghanistan.

RAIDI; Chinese politician; b. 1938, Biru, northern Tibet; ed Cen. Nationalities Inst., Beijing; Sec. CCP Cttee, Nagu Region 1972; Sec. CCP Cttee, Tibet Autonomous Region 1975–77, Deputy Sec. (Exec.) 1977–; Chair. Peasants' Fed. of Tibet 1975; alt. mem. 11th CCP Cen. Cttee 1977–82; Vice-Chair. Revolutionary Cttee, Tibet Autonomous Region 1977–79; Vice-Chair. People's Congress of Tibet 1979–83, Chair. 1986; Chair. Tibet Autonomous Regional 6th People's Congress 1993–; Deputy Sec. CCP Tibet Autonomous Regional Cttee 1985–; 8th NPC Deputy, Tibet Autonomous Region; mem. 12th CCP Cen. Cttee 1982, 14th 1992–97, 15th 1997–2002. *Address:* Tibet Autonomous Region, Chinese Communist Party, Lhasa, Tibet, People's Republic of China.

RAIGETAL, Larry; Micronesian civil servant; b. 4 July 1968, Lamotrek Atoll; two d.; ed Oxford Univ., UK, Univ. of San Francisco, Calif., USA; Dean of Students, Xavier High School, Chuuk 1992–93; diplomatic functions 1993–2001; Chair. FSM Banking Bd 1998–; Chief of Manpower, Yap State Govt 2001–. *Leisure interest:* fishing. *Address:* Federated States of Micronesia Banking Board, P.O. Box 1187, Kolonia, Pohnpei, Eastern Caroline Islands, FM 96041 (Office); Box 254, Colonia Yap, 96943, Micronesia (Home). *Telephone:* 350-2182 (Office); 350-4557 (Home). *Fax:* 350-2571 (Office).

RAIKIN, Konstantin Arkadyevich; Russian actor and theatre director; b. 8 July 1950, Leningrad; s. of Arkady Raikin and Roma M. Joffe; m. Elena Butenko; one d.; ed M. Shchukin Theatre High School, Moscow; theatre Sovremennik 1971–81, debut in Valentin and Valentina; 38 roles including 15 leading, acted in plays of Shakespeare and Russian classics; actor State Theatre of Miniatures (renamed Theatre Satirikon 1987) under Arkady Raikin 1981–87, actor and Artistic Dir 1988–; Prize for Best Acting, Belgrade Festival 1990, People's Artist of Russia 1992, State Prize 1996, Gold Mask Prize 1996, Stanislavsky Prize 1998, Order of the Fatherland 2000. *Films:* Sensation is Anything 1971, Friends Among Strangers, Strangers Among

Friends 1972. *TV Films:* Truffaldino from Bergamo 1976, The Island of Dead Ships 1988, Shadow 1990, Failure Puaro 2002. *Stage appearances include:* Cyrano de Bergerac (Cyrano) 1992, The Magnanimous Cuckold (Bruno) 1994, Metamorphosis (Gregor Zamza) 1995, The Threepenny Opera (Mack the Knife) 1996, Jacques and His Master (Jacques) 1998, Hamlet (Hamlet) 1998, Double Bass 2000. *Plays directed include:* Mowgli 1990, Butterflies Are Free 1993, Romeo and Juliet 1995, The Chioggian Squabbles 1997, Quartet 1999, Chanticleer 2001. *Address:* Theatre Satirikon, Sheremetyevskaya str. 8, 129594 Moscow, Russia. *Telephone:* (095) 289-87-07 (Office). *Fax:* (095) 284-49-37 (Office). *E-mail:* theatre@satirikon.msk.ru (Office). *Website:* www .satirikon.ru (Office).

RAIKOV, Gennady Ivanovich; Russian politician and engineer; b. 8 Aug. 1939, Khabarovsk; m.; one s.; ed Omsk State Machine Construction Inst.; mechanical engineer, docent, Omsk State Machine-Construction Inst. 1956–63; lawyer Russian Acad. of Civil Service; engineer, Head of workshop, Deputy Chief Engineer, Branch Dir Omsk Machine Construction production corpn 1961–77; Chief Engineer, Dir-Gen. Tumen Motor Mfg plant 1977–90; Head of City Admin., Tumen City Soviet 1990–93; Deputy Chief Tumennefte-gazstroy Co. 1993, Deputy Dir-Gen. 1995–; Deputy Dir-Gen. Siberian Wood Co., Sweden 1993–95; mem. State Duma of Russian Fed. 1995–; Leader People's Deputy faction 2000–; mem. Duma Security Cttee; mem. Perm. Del. of Fed. Ass. of Russian Fed. to Ass. of WEU; Rep. of State Duma to Perm. Comm. of Parl. Ass. Union of Belarus and Russian Fed.; mem. Governmental Comm. of Russian Fed. for participation in APEC forum; Chair. People's Party of the Russian Fed. 2001–; Order Sign of Honour, Order of Red Banner of Labour, Order of October Revolution, Order for Service to Motherland (Fourth Degree), Order of Saint Sergei of Radonezh (Second Degree); several medals. *Leisure interest:* ice hockey. *Address:* State Duma, Okhotny Ryad 1, 103265 Moscow, Russia (Office). *Telephone:* (095) 292-87-01 (Office). *Fax:* (095) 292-87-15 (Office).

RAIMOND, Jean-Bernard; French diplomatist and politician; b. 6 Feb. 1926, Paris; s. of Henri Raimond and Alice Auberty; m. Monique Chabanel 1975; two d.; ed Ecole Normale Supérieure and Ecole Nat. d'Admin.; CNRS 1951–53; Dept of Political Affairs and Cen. Admin. of Ministry of Foreign Affairs 1956–66; Deputy Dir Europe 1967; Asst Dir Office of Minister of Foreign Affairs 1967; Tech. Counsellor, Office of Prime Minister 1968–69; Sec.-Gen. Presidency of the Repub. 1969–73; Amb. to Morocco 1973–77; Dir for N Africa and the Levant 1977–78; Dir Office of Minister of Foreign Affairs 1978; Dir-Gen. for Cultural Relations, Ministry of Foreign Affairs 1979–81; Amb. to Poland 1982–84, to USSR 1984–86; Minister of Foreign Affairs 1986–88; Amb. to Holy See, Rome 1988–91; Deputy to Nat. Ass. from Bouches-du-Rhône (RPR) 1993–; Amb. de France 1991; Adviser to the Pres. of the Servier Laboratory 1992–99; Pres. French-Russian Friendship Soc. (Sofarus), France–Italy Asscn; Officier, Légion d'honneur; Commdr, Ordre nat. du Mérite; Chevalier des Palmes Académiques; Order of Ouissan Alaouite (Morocco), Grand Cross, Order of Pius IX (Holy See). *Publications:* Le Quai d'Orsay à l'épreuve de la cohabitation 1989, Le choix de Gorbatchev 1992, Jean-Paul II, un pape au cœur de l'histoire 1999. *Address:* Assemblée Nationale, 75355 Paris Cedex 07 (Office); 12 rue des Poissonniers, 92200 Neuilly-sur-Seine, France (Home).

RAIMONDI, Ruggero; Monegasque bass opera singer and director; b. 3 Oct. 1941, Bologna, Italy; m. Isabel Maier 1987; operatic début in La Bohème, Spoleto Festival 1964; début at Metropolitan Opera, New York in Ernani 1970; other engagements include Don Giovanni, Le Nozze di Figaro, Faust, Attila, Don Carlos, Boris Godunov, Don Quichotte, Don Pasquale, Otello, Contes d'Hoffmann, Carmen, Il Viaggio a Rheims, Falstaff, I Vespri Siciliani, I Lombardi, L'Italiana in Algieri, Tosca, Assassinio nella Cattedrale; Commdr Ordre des Arts et Lettres, Kt Order of Malta, Grand Ufficiale della Repubblica Italiana, Citizen of Honour (Athens), Commdr Ordre du Mérite Culturel (Monaco). *Films:* Don Giovanni 1979, Six Characters in Search of an Author 1981, La Vie est un Roman 1982, Carmen 1983, Tosca 2001. *Opera productions include:* Don Giovanni, The Barber of Seville, Don Carlos. *Address:* 140 bis rue Lecourbe, 75015 Paris, France. *Telephone:* 1-45-33-61-59. *Fax:* 1-45-32-46-34.

RAINE, Craig Anthony, BA, BPhil; British writer; b. 3 Dec. 1944, Shildon, Co. Durham; s. of Norman Edward and Olive Marie Raine; m. Ann Pasternak Slater 1972; three s. one d.; ed Exeter Coll., Oxford; Lecturer, Exeter Coll., Oxford Univ. 1971–72, 1975–76, Lincoln Coll. 1974–75, Christ Church 1976–79; Books Ed. New Review 1977–78; Ed. Quarto 1979–80; Poetry Ed. New Statesman 1981; Poetry Ed. Faber and Faber Ltd 1981–91; Fellow in English, New Coll., Oxford 1991–; Ed. Areté 1999–; Kelus Prize 1979, Southern Arts Literature Award 1979, Cholmondeley Poetry Award 1983, Sunday Times Award for Literary Excellence 1998. *Publications:* The Onion, Memory 1978, A Martian Sends a Postcard Home 1979, A Free Translation 1981, Rich 1984, The Electrification of the Soviet Union (opera) 1986, A Choice of Kipling's Prose (ed.) 1987, The Prophetic Book 1988; '1953' (play) 1990, Haydn and the Valve Trumpet: Literary Essays 1990, Rudyard Kipling: Selected Poetry (ed.) 1992, History: The Home Movie 1994, Clay. Whereabouts Unknown 1996, New Writing 7 1998, A la recherche du temps perdu 1999, In Defence of T. S. Eliot: Literary Essays (Vol. 2) 2000, Collected Poems 1978–1999 2000, Rudyard Kipling: The Wish House and Other Stories (ed.) 2002. *Address:* c/o New College, Oxford, OX1 3BN, England.

RAINE, Kathleen Jessie, CBE, MA, FRSL; British poet; b. 1908; d. of late George Raine and Jessie Raine; m. Charles Madge (divorced, died 1996); one s. one d.; ed Girton Coll., Cambridge; Fellow, Girton Coll., Cambridge 1956; co-ed. Temenos (review) 1982–93; W. H. Smith Literary Award and other English and American poetry prizes and awards; Blake scholar; Hon. DLitt (Leicester) 1974, (Durham) 1979; Queens Medal for Poetry 1992; Commdr, Officier, Ordre des Arts et des Lettres. *Publications:* Stone and Flower 1943, Living in Time 1946, The Pythoness 1949, The Year One 1952, Collected Poems 1956, The Hollow Hill (poems) 1965, Blake and Tradition (Andrew Mellon Lectures) 1969, Selected Writings of Thomas Taylor the Platonist (with George Mills Harper) 1969, William Blake, Selected Poems 1970, The Lost Country (poems) 1971, On a Deserted Shore (poems) 1972, Faces of Day and Night 1973, Farewell Happy Fields (autobiog.) 1973, The Land Unknown (autobiog.) 1975, The Oval Portrait (verse) 1977, The Lion's Mouth (autobiog.) 1977, The Oracle in the Heart (poems) 1979, Collected Poems 1981, 2000, The Human Face of God 1982, The Presence (poems) 1988, Selected Poems 1988, Visages du Jour et de la Nuit 1989, India Seen Afar 1990, Golgonooza, City of the Imagination 1991, Living with Mystery (poems) 1992, Le Monde Vivant de l'Imagination 1998, W. B. Yeats and the Learning of the Imagination 1999; criticism: Defending Ancient Springs 1967, Yeats, the Tarot and the Golden Dawn 1973, Death in Life and Life in Death 1973, David Jones and the Actually Loved and Known 1978, From Blake to a Vision 1978, Blake and the New Age 1979, The Inner Journey of the Poet and other papers 1982, L'imagination créatrice de William Blake 1986, Yeats the Initiate 1986. *Address:* 47 Paultons Square, London, SW3 5DT, England.

RAINES, Franklin Delano, JD; American public servant and fmr investment banker; b. 14 Jan. 1949, Seattle; s. of Delano Thomas and Ida Mae (Fortson) Raines; m. Wendy Farrow 1982; three d.; ed Harvard Univ., Oxford Univ.; Assoc. Dir Seattle Model Cities Program 1972–73; Assoc. Preston, Thorgrimson, Ellis, Holman & Fletcher, Seattle 1976–77; Asst Dir White House Domestic Policy Staff, Washington, DC 1977–78, Assoc. Dir U.S. Office of Man. and Budget 1978–79, Dir 1996–98; Vice-Pres. Lazard Frères & Co., New York 1979–82, Sr Vice-Pres. 1983–84, Gen. Partner 1985–90, Ltd Partner 1990–91; Vice-Chair. Fed. Nat. Mortgage Asscn 1991–96; Chair., CEO Design Fannie Mae, Washington 1999–; mem. New York Stock Exchange (allied); mem. Bd Overseers Harvard Univ.; Trustee Univ. Puget Sound, German Marshall Fund of U.S., French-American Foundation, American Museum of Natural History and other bodies; Rhodes Scholar 1971. *Leisure interests:* running, tennis.

RAINES, Howell, MA; American journalist; ed Birmingham-Southern Coll. and Univ. of Alabama; journalist Birmingham Post-Herald 1964, Birmingham (Ala) News 1970; Political Ed. Atlanta Constitution 1971–76, St Petersburg (Fla) Times 1976–78; nat. corresp. in Atlanta, NY Times 1978, Atlanta bureau chief 1979–81, White House corresp. 1981–84, nat. political corresp. 1984, Deputy Washington Ed. 1985–87, London bureau chief 1987–88, Washington bureau chief 1988–93, editorial page ed. 1993–2001, Exec. Ed. 2001–; Pulitzer Prize for feature writing 1992. *Publications:* My Soul Is Rested 1977, Whiskey Man 1977, Fly Fishing Through the Midlife Crisis 1993. *Address:* The New York Times, 229 W. 43rd Street, New York, NY 10036, USA (Office). *Telephone:* (212) 556-1234 (Office). *Website:* www .nytimes.com (Office).

RAINIER III, His Serene Highness Prince Louis Henri Maxence Bertrand, Prince of Monaco; b. 31 May 1923; s. of the late Comte Pierre de Polignac and Princess Charlotte, Duchess of Valentinois; m. Grace Patricia Kelly 1956 (died 1982); one s. two d.; ed Summerfields School, Hastings (England), Montpellier Univ. and Ecole Libre des Sciences Politiques, Paris; Hereditary Prince of Monaco 1944; served in French army as Lt and Col 1944–45; succeeded his grandfather Prince Louis II 1949; f. Monaco Red Cross 1948, American Friends of Monaco 1952, Prix Rainier 1955; Grand Master, Ordre de St Charles de Monaco, Grand Croix, Légion d'honneur, Belgian, Swedish, Greek, Lebanese, Italian, Netherlands and San Marino orders. *Address:* Palais princier, BP 518, MC 98015, Monaco cedex.

RAIS, Amien; Indonesian politician; fmr teacher Gadjah Mada Univ., Jogjakarta; fmr Chair. Muhammadiyah (Muslim group); now Chair. People's Consultative Ass. (MPR); Gen. Chair. Nat. Mandate Party (PAN) 1998–. *Address:* Partai Amanat Nasional, c/o Dewan Perwakilan Rakyat, Jalan Gatot Subroto 16, Jakarta, Indonesia (Office).

RÄISÄNEN, Heikki Martti, MA, DTheol; Finnish professor of New Testament exegesis; b. 10 Dec. 1941, Helsinki; s. of Martti Olavi Räisänen and Saara Ilona Itkonen; m. Leena Marjatta Wright 1974; three s. one d.; ed Univ. of Helsinki; Lecturer in New Testament Exegesis, Univ. of Helsinki 1969–74, Acting Assoc. Prof. in Biblical Languages 1971–74, Prof. of New Testament Exegesis 1975–; Research Prof. Acad. of Finland 1984–94, 2001–; Dir Exegetical Inst., Univ. of Helsinki 1975–84, 1995–96, Vice-Dean of the Theological Faculty 1978–80, Dir Centre of Excellence 1994–; Chief Ed. Vartija 1989–2000; mem. Cttee Finnish Exegetical Soc. 1969–85, Chair. 1980–85; mem. Finnish Acad. of Sciences 1978–, Cttee Soc. for New Testament Studies 1986–89; Fulbright Visiting Scholar, Harvard 1970–71, Visiting Scholar, Cambridge Univ. 1978, Humboldt Visiting Scholar, Tübingen 1980–82; Edward Cadbury Lectures, Univ. of Birmingham 1996; Hon. DD (Edin.) 1990, (Uppsala) 2002. *Publications:* Die Mutter Jesu im Neuen Testament 1969, Das koranische Jesusbild 1971, The Idea of Divine Hardening 1972, Das 'Messiasgeheimnis' im Markusevangelium 1976, Paul and the Law 1983, The

Torah and Christ 1986, The 'Messianic Secret' in Mark's Gospel 1990, Beyond New Testament Theology 1990, Jesus, Paul and Torah 1992, Marcion, Muhammad and the Mahatma 1997, Neutestamentliche Theologie? 2000, Challenges to Biblical Interpretation 2001; numerous books in Finnish; numerous articles on early Christianity. *Leisure interest:* soccer. *Address:* Vantaanjänne 1 B 11, 01730 Vantaa, Finland. *Telephone:* (9) 898422. *E-mail:* heikki.raisanen@helsinki.fi.

RAISER, Konrad; German theologian and administrator; Study Sec. Comm. on Faith and Order, WCC 1969–73, Deputy Gen. Sec. WCC, Gen. Sec. 1992–2002; Prof. of Systematic Theology and Ecumenics, Univ. of the Ruhr, Bochum 1983–93; mem. Evangelical Church in Germany (EKD). *Address:* World Council of Churches, 150 route de Ferney, P.O. Box 2100, 1211 Geneva 2, Switzerland (Office). *Telephone:* (22) 7916111 (Office). *Fax:* (22) 7910361 (Office). *E-mail:* info@wcc-coe.org (Office). *Website:* www.wcc-coe.org (Office).

RAISMAN, John Michael, CBE, CBIM, MA; British business executive; b. 12 Feb. 1929, Lahore, India; s. of Sir Jeremy and Renee Mary (née Kelly) Raisman; m. Evelyn Anne Muirhead 1953; one s. three d.; ed Rugby School, Queen's Coll., Oxford; joined Shell Int. Petroleum Co. Ltd 1953, served in Brazil 1953–60; Gen. Man., Shell Panama 1960–62; Asst to Exploration and Production Co-ordinator, Shell Int. Petroleum, Maatschappij 1963–65; Gen. Man., Shell Co. of Turkey Ltd 1965–69; Pres. Shell Sekiyu KK 1970–73; Head of European Supply and Marketing, Shell Int. Petroleum 1974–77; Man. Dir, Shell UK Oil 1977–78; Deputy Chair. and C.E.O, Shell UK Ltd 1978–79, Chair. and CEO 1979–85; Chair. Shell Chemicals UK Ltd 1979–85; Dir Vickers 1981–90, Glaxo Holdings PLC 1982–90, Lloyds Bank 1985–95, Lloyds TSB 1996–98, Lloyds Merchant Bank Holdings 1985–87, Candover 1990–98, Tandem Computers 1991–97, British Biotech. 1993–98 (Chair. 1995–98); Deputy Chair. British Telecom 1987–91; mem. Pres.'s Cttee of Confed. of British Industry (CBI), Chair. Europe Cttee of CBI 1980–88; Chair. Council of Industry for Man. Educ. (CIME) 1981–85, Chair. Oil Industry Emergency Cttee (OIEC) 1981–85, Advisory Council, London Enterprise Agency 1979–85, Investment Bd Electra Candover Partners 1985–95, Electronics Industry EDC 1986–88, Business Forum of European Movement, Council for Industry and Higher Educ. 1991–96; Deputy Chair. Nat. Comm. on Educ. 1991–95; Gov. Nat. Inst. of Econ. and Social Research 1981–; mem. Governing Council of Business in the Community 1982–85; mem. Council, Inst. for Fiscal Studies 1982–92; mem. Royal Comm. on Environmental Pollution 1986–87; Chair. Bd Trustees RA 1986–96; Pro-Chancellor Aston Univ. 1987–93; Chair. British Empire and Commonwealth Museum Trust 2002–; Hon. DUniv (Stirling) 1983, Hon. LLD (Aberdeen) 1985, (Manchester) 1986, (UWE) 1994; Hon. DSc (Aston) 1992. *Leisure interests:* golf, travel, opera, theatre. *Address:* Netheravon House, Netheravon Road South, London, W4 2PY, England. *Telephone:* (20) 8994-3731. *Fax:* (20) 8742-1000.

RAITT, Bonnie Lynn; American blues singer and guitarist; b. 8 Nov. 1949, Burbank, Calif.; d. of John Raitt; ed Radcliffe Coll.; performer blues clubs, E Coast; concert tours UK 1976, 1977; numerous Grammy nominations. *Albums include:* Nick of Time 1989 (1990 Grammy Awards for rock—best vocal performance, female pop—best vocal performance, female album of the year), I'm in the Mood (with John Lee Hooker; 1990 Grammy Award for blues—best traditional record), Luck of the Draw 1991 (1992 Grammy Award for rock—best vocal performance, female, for best duet), Longing in their Hearts 1994 (Grammy Award for best pop album), Road Tested 1996, Fundamental 1998. *Singles include:* Something to Talk About (Grammy Award for best pop vocal performance, female 1992), Good Man, Good Woman (with Delbert McClinton). *Address:* P.O. Box 626, Los Angeles, CA 90078, USA.

RAJABOV, Safarali; Tajikistan politician; b. 2 Sept. 1955, Fayzabad Dist; m. 1976; two s. six d.; ed Dushanbe State Pedagogical Inst.; Dir Special Training Centre, Fayzabad Dist 1980–86; Tech. Coll. N2U, Fayzabad Dist 1986–90; Deputy of Tajikistan Supreme Soviet 1990–95; Sec., Deputy Chair., Chair. Cttee on Legislation and Human Rights 1990–95; Chair. Majlisi Oli (Parl.) of Tajikistan 1995–2000; Minister of Educ. 2000–; Dr hc (Tajik State Agrarian Univ.) 1998. *Publications:* Independence is Sacred 1997, Majlisi Oli 1998. *Address:* Ministry of Education, Nisor Mukhammad 13A, 734024 Dushanbe, Tajikistan. *Telephone:* (3772) 23-33-92. *Fax:* (3772) 22-92-81.

RAJNA, Thomas, DMus, ARCM; British composer and pianist; b. 21 Dec. 1928, Budapest; s. of the late Dr Nandor Rajna and Hella Eisen; m. Anthea Valentine Campion 1967; one s. two d.; ed Nat. Musical School, Budapest, Franz Liszt Acad. of Music, Budapest and Royal Coll. of Music, London; freelance composer, pianist and teacher, London 1951–63; Prof. of Piano, Guildhall School of Music 1963–70; Lecturer, Univ. of Surrey 1967–70; Sr Lecturer in Piano, Faculty of Music, Univ. of Cape Town 1970–89, Assoc. Prof. 1989–93; Fellow, Univ. of Cape Town 1981; Hon. DMus (Cape Town) 1985; Liszt Prize, Budapest 1947; Artes Award (SABC) 1981, UCT Book Award 1996, Cape Tercentenary Foundation Merit Award 1997. *Compositions include:* film and ballet music, orchestral and chamber music, two piano concertos, Harp Concerto 1990, Amarantha (opera in 7 scenes) 1991–94, Video Games (for orchestra) 1994, Rhapsody for clarinet and orchestra 1995, Fantasy for violin and orchestra 1996, Suite for violin and harp 1997, Stop All the Clocks (four songs on poems by W. H. Auden) 1998, The Creation – A Negro Sermon for unaccompanied choir 2000. *Recordings include:* works by Stravinsky, Messiaen, Scriabin, Granados, Liszt, Schumann, Dohnanyi and own compositions. *Publications:* Preludes for Piano, Music for Violin and Piano 1989–90, Dialogues for clarinet and piano, Concerto for harp and orchestra,

Suite for violin and piano. *Leisure interests:* chess, swimming. *Address:* 10 Wyndover Road, Claremont, Cape Town, West Cape 7708, South Africa. *Telephone:* (21) 671 3937. *Fax:* (21) 671 3937. *E-mail:* trajna@iafrica.com (Home). *Website:* www.cama.org.za/southafr/rajna (Home).

RAJOY, Mariano; Spanish politician; b. 1955, Santiago de Compostela; m.; one s.; ed Universidad de Santiago de Compostela; fmr Prof. of Law, Univ. of Santiago de Compostela; various positions Popular Party (PP), including Chair. Regional Council, later Deputy Chair. (Pontevedra), Chair. Local Council, mem. Perm. Cttee 1987, mem. Nat. Exec. 1989, Deputy Sec.-Gen. 1991–; Vice-Pres. Council of Galicia 1986–87; Nat. Deputy of Pontevedra; Minister of Public Admin 1996–99, of Educ. and Culture 1999–2000; First Deputy Prime Minister and Head of Prime Minister's Office 2000–01; First Deputy Prime Minister and Minister of the Interior 2001–02; First Deputy Prime Minister, Head of Prime Minister's Office and Govt Spokesperson July 2002–. *Address:* Office of the Deputy Prime Minister and Minister of the Interior, Ministry of the Interior, Paseo de la Castellana 5, 28071 Madrid, Spain (Office). *Telephone:* (91) 5371000 (Office). *Fax:* (91) 5371177 (Office). *Website:* www.mir.es (Office).

RAJU, B. Ramalinga, MBA; Indian business executive; ed Ohio and Harvard Univs, USA; Chair. Satyam Computer Services Ltd, Satyam Infoway Ltd and VisionCompass, Inc. 1987–, jt ventures include Satyam–GE Software Services Ltd, Satyam Venture Engineering Services Pvt. Ltd, Satyam Manufacturing Technologies Ltd, Satyam ideaEdge Technologies Pvt. Ltd, CA Satyam ASP Pvt. Ltd; f. several trusts and charities including Alambana, Naandi and the Byyrajju Foundation; Ernst & Young Entrepreneur of the Year Award 2000, Dataquest IT Man of the Year Award 2001, Asia Business Leader Award for Corp. Citizen of the Year, Hong Kong 2002. *Leisure interests:* reading, snooker. *Address:* Satyam Computer Services Ltd., Floor 1, Mayfair Centre, S P Road, Secunderabad 500003, Andhra Pradesh, India (Office). *Telephone:* (40) 7843222 (Office). *Fax:* (40) 7840058 (Office). *E-mail:* abhijit_roy@satyam.com (Office). *Website:* www.satyam.com (Office).

RAKE, Michael Derek Vaughan, FCA; British accountant; b. 17 Jan. 1948; s. of Derek Shannon Vaughan Rake and Rosamund Rake (née Barrett); m. 1st Julia Rake (née Cook) 1970; three s.; m. 2nd Caroline Rake (née Thomas) 1986; one s.; ed Wellington Coll.; with Turquands Barton Mayhew, London and Brussels 1968–74; accountant KPMG (Peat Marwick Mitchell Continental Europe), Brussels 1974, Pnr 1979–, Pnr in charge of Audit, Belgium and Luxembourg 1983–86, Sr Resident Pnr, ME 1986–89, Pnr London office 1989–, mem. UK Bd 1991–, Regional Man. Pnr, SE Region 1992–94, Chief Exec. London and SE Region 1994–96, COO, UK 1996–98, Sr Pnr, UK and Chair. UK Bd 1998–, Chair. KPMG Europe 1999–2002, Chair. KPMG Int. 2002–; Deputy Chair. BITC (Chair. Corp. Community Investment Leadership Team) 1998–; mem. Bd Prince of Wales Int. Business Leaders' Forum 1999–, Britain in Europe Business Leaders Group 2000–, CBI Pres.'s Cttee 2001–; Vice-Pres. RNIB 2003–, Reviseur d'Entreprise Luxembourg. *Leisure interests:* polo, skiing. *Address:* KPMG LLP, 8 Salisbury Square, London, EC4Y 8BB, England (Office). *Telephone:* (20) 7311-1000 (Office). *Fax:* (20) 7311-3311 (Office). *Website:* www.kpmg.co.uk (Office).

RAKHIMOV, Murtaza Gubaidullovich; Russian politician; b. 7 Feb. 1934, Tavakanovo, Bashkiria; s. of Gubaidulla Zufarovich Rakhimov and Galima Abdullovna Rakhimova; m. Luiza Galimovna Rakhimova; one s.; ed Ufa Oil Inst.; operator, then chief of oil rig, chief chemist, Chief Engineer, Dir Ufa Oil Processing Plant 1956–90; USSR People's Deputy 1990–92; Chair. Supreme Soviet Repub. of Bashkortostan 1990–93, Pres. 1993–; mem. Russian Council of Fed. (Parl.) 1996–2001. *Leisure interests:* sports, music, literature. *Address:* The Republic House, 46 Tukayev Street, 450101, Ufa, Bashkortostan, Russia. *Telephone:* (3472) 50-24-06. *Fax:* (3472) 50-01-75.

RAKHMANIN, Vladimir Olegovich; Russian diplomatist; b. 1958, Moscow; ed Moscow Inst. of Int. Relations; on staff USSR (later Russian) Ministry of Foreign Affairs 1980–; Deputy Dir First Asian Dept 1996–98; Dir Dept of Information and Press 1998–2000; Chief of Presidential Protocol Dept 2000–01; Amb. to Ireland 2002–. *Address:* Embassy of the Russian Federation, 184–186 Orwell Road, Rathgar, Dublin 14, Ireland. *Telephone:* (1) 4922048 (Office). *Fax:* (1) 4923525. *E-mail:* russiane@indigo.ie. *Website:* www.ireland.ru/embassy.

RAKHMONOV, Imamali Sharipovich, BEcons; Tajikistan politician; b. 5 Oct. 1952, Dangara, Kulyab Oblast; ed Tajik State Univ.; army service, USSR; worked as electrician, salesman, sec. trade union and CP cttees; Govt Sec.; Chair. of TU Cttee; Dir Dangarin Sovkhoz, Kulyab Oblast 1988–92; Sec. party org. in agric. enterprise; Chair. Kulyab Oblast Exec. Cttee 1992, Supreme Soviet (Majlisi Oli) of Tajikistan 1992–; Pres. of Tajikistan 1994–. *Address:* Office of the President, 734023 Dushanbe, pr. Rudaki 80 Tajikistan (Office). *Telephone:* (372) 21-04-18 (Office). *Fax:* (372) 21-18-37 (Office).

RAKOTOARIJAONA, Lt-Col Désiré; Malagasy politician and army officer; b. 1934; Minister of Finance Feb.–June 1975; mem. Supreme Revolutionary Council 1975–88; Prime Minister 1977–88; mem. Front Nat. pour la Défense de la Révolution Socialiste Malgache.

RAKOTOMAVO, Pascal; Malagasy politician and businessman; ed Higher School of Commerce, Lille, France; Minister of Finance and Economy 1982–89; Prime Minister of Madagascar 1997–98; Special Adviser to Pres. of Malagasy Repub. 1998–; Chair. Bd FIARO; Gov. of Antananarivo 2001–; Grand-Croix (Second Class), Nat. Order. *Leisure interests:* riding, travelling.

Address: c/o Fiaro, rue Jules Ranaivo, Ampefiloha, BP 725, 101 Antananarivo, Madagascar (Office). *Telephone:* (20) 2234260 (Office). *Fax:* (20) 2222147 (Office). *E-mail:* fiaromail@dts.mg (Office).

RAKOTONIAINA, Justin; Malagasy politician, teacher and diplomatist; b. 1933, Betsileo; fmr professor of Law, Univ. of Madagascar; Amb. to Algeria, also Accred to Tunisia and Guinea 1973–75; Minister of Nat. Educ. 1975–76; Prime Minister of Madagascar 1976–77; mem. Supreme Revolutionary Council.

RAKOTOVAHINY, Emmanuel; Malagasy politician; fmr Chair. Union nat. pour la démocratie et le développement (UNDD); fmr Minister of State for Rural Devt and Land Reform; Prime Minister of Madagascar 1995–96. *Address:* c/o Office of the Prime Minister, Antananarivo, Madagascar.

RAKOWSKI, Mieczysław Franciszek, DHist; Polish politician and journalist; b. 1 Dec. 1926, Kowalewko, Szubin district; m. 1st Wanda Wiłkomirska (q.v.) 1952 (separated); two s.; m. 2nd Elżbieta Kępińska; ed Higher School of Social Sciences, Cracow and Inst. of Social Sciences, Warsaw; worked at Cen. Cttee of Polish United Workers' Party (PZPR) 1949–52, 1955–57; Sub-ed., Polityka 1957, Ed.-in-Chief 1958–82; Chair. Gen. Bd, Polish Journalists' Asscn 1958–61; Deputy mem. Cen. Cttee, PZPR 1964–75, mem. 1975–90; Deputy to Sejm (Parl.) 1972–89, Deputy Chair. PZPR Sejm Deputies' Club 1980; Deputy Chair. Council of Ministers 1981–85; Chair. Cttee for Trade Unions of Council of Ministers 1981–85; Vice-Marshal (Deputy Speaker) of Sejm 1985–88; Chair. Socio-Econ. Council attached to Sejm 1985–88; mem. Political Bureau PZPR Cen. Cttee 1987–90; Sec. PZPR Cen. Cttee 1988–89; First Sec. PZPR Cen. Cttee 1989–90; Chair. Council of Ministers (Prime Minister) 1988–89; Ed.-in-Chief monthly Dziś, Przegląd społeczny 1990–; Presenter, TV programme Świat i Polityka (World and Politics); fmr Chair. Polish Yachting Union; Order of Banner of Labour 1st and 2nd Class, Gold Cross of Merit, State Prize 2nd Class 1976, Commdr's Cross with Star of Order of Polonia Restituta and other decorations. *Publications:* NRF z bliska (FRG from a Short Distance) 1958, New World 1959, Socjal demokratyczna Partia Niemiec w okresie powojennym 1949–54 (Social-Democratic Party of Germany in Post-war Period) 1960, Świat na zakręcie (The World in Turning) 1960, Zachód szuka ideologii (The West Looks for Ideology) 1961, Ameryka wielopiętrowa (Many-storied America), Klimaty w RFN (Climates of the FRG), Polityka Zagraniczna PRL (The Foreign Policy of the Polish People's Republic) 1974, Dymisja Kanclerza (Chancellor's Dismissal) 1975, Spełnione i niespełnione 1978, Przesilenie grudniowe (December Crisis) 1981, Partnerstwo (Partnership) 1982, Czas nadziei i rozczarowań (Time of Hopes and Disappointments), Vol. 1 1985, Vol. 2 1987, Ein schwieriger Dialog 1986, Jak to się stało 1992, Gorbachev: The First and the Last One 1993, People Wrote Letters to M.F. Rakowski: Years–People–Letters 1993, Es began in Polen 1995, Political Diaries (1958–62) 1998, Political Diaries (1963–66) 1999, Political Diaries (1967–68) 2000, Political Diaries (1969–72) 2001, Political Diaries (1973–75) 2002, Political Diaries (1976–78) 2002; co-author: The Polish Upswing 1971–75 1975. *Leisure interests:* joinery, angling, yachting. *Address:* Miesięcznik 'Dziś', ul. Poznańska 3, 00-680 Warsaw, Poland. *Telephone:* (22) 6210121.

RALLIS, George J., LLD; Greek politician and lawyer; b. 26 Dec. 1918; m. Helene Voultsos 1950; two d.; ed Athens Univ.; served Reconnaissance Groups 1940–41 and Tank Corps 1945–48; elected Deputy for Athens 1950–58, 1961–67, 1974–93; mem. Greek del. to European Council, Strasbourg 1953–58; Minister to Prime Minister's Office 1954–56, of Public Works and Communications 1956–58, of the Interior 1961–63, of Public Order April 1967; under house arrest April–May 1967, in prison and exile May–Sept. 1968; Minister to Prime Minister's Office and of Educ. 1974–77, for Co-ordination and Planning 1977–78, for Foreign Affairs 1978–80, Prime Minister of Greece 1980–81; mem. Popular Party 1950, Nat. Rally 1951, Nat. Radical Union 1956, New Democratic Party 1974–87, 1989–; Medal of Valour, War Cross with two bars, DSM and several foreign awards. *Publications:* John Rallis 1946, The Possibility of Increasing the Yield of Greek Agriculture 1952, Democracy and Communism 1959, The Truth about the Greek Politicians (in Greek) 1971, The Technique of Violence 1972, Hours of Responsibility 1983, George Theotoky: Prime Minister of Greece (biog.) 1986, Looking Back 1993, My Diary During the Dictatorship of the Colonels 1997. *Leisure interest:* golf. *Address:* 4 Kanari Street, 106 71 Athens, Greece. *Telephone:* (1) 3617340.

RALPH, Richard Peter, CMG, CVO, MSc; British diplomatist; b. 27 April 1946, London; s. of Peter Ralph and late Evelyn Marion Ralph; m. 1st Margaret Elisabeth Coulthurst 1970 (divorced 2001); one s. one d.; m. 2nd Jemma Victoria Elizabeth Marlor 2002; ed The King's School, Canterbury, Edin. Univ.; Embassy, Vientiane, Laos 1970–73, Lisbon, Portugal 1974–77; FCO 1977–81; High Comm., Harare, Zimbabwe 1981–84; FCO 1984–89; Embassy, Washington, DC 1989–93; Amb. to Latvia 1993–95; Gov. Falkland Islands 1996–99, concurrently Commr S Georgia and S Sandwich Islands; Amb. to Romania (also Accred to Moldova) 1999–2002, to Peru 2003–. *Leisure interests:* reading, music, art, motorcycling. *Address:* Embassy of the United Kingdom, Torre Parque, Piso 22, Avenida José Larco 1301, Miraflores, Lima 18, Peru (Office). *Telephone:* (1) 617-3000 (Office). *Fax:* (1) 617-3100 (Office). *E-mail:* richard.ralph@fco.gov.uk (Office). *Website:* www.britain.ro.

RALSTON, Gen. Joseph W.; American air force officer; b. 4 Nov. 1943, Hopkinsville, Ky; m. Diane Dougherty; two s. two d.; ed Miami Univ., Ohio, Cen. Michigan Univ., Army Command and Gen. Staff Coll., Nat. War Coll.,

Harvard Univ.; mem. reserve officer training program USAF 1965; Vice-Chair. of Jt Chiefs of Staff 1996–2000; concurrently Chair. Jt Requirements Oversight Council, Planning, Programming and Budgeting Systems; Vice-Chair. Defense Acquisition Bd; mem. Nat. Security Council Deputies Comm., Nuclear Weapons Council; Supreme Allied Commdr, Europe 2000–03; C-in-C, US European Command 2000–03; numerous mil. decorations including Defense Distinguished Service Medal (two awards), Distinguished Service Medal. *Address:* c/o NATO Allied Command Europe, Casteau, Belgium (Office).

RAMA, Carlos M., PhD; Uruguayan writer, lawyer, professor and editor; b. 26 Oct. 1921, Montevideo; s. of Manuel Rama and Carolina Facal; m. Judith Dellepiane 1943; one s. one d.; ed Univ. de la República and Univ. de Paris; Journalist 1940–48, 1972–; Exec. Sec. of Uruguayan Bar Asscn 1940–49; Prof. of Universal History in secondary schools 1944–48; Ed. Nuestro Tiempo 1954–56, Gacetilla Austral 1961–73; Prof. of Sociology and Social Research, Prof. of Contemporary History, Prof. of Theory and Methodology of History, Univ. de la República 1950–72; Prof. of Latin American History, Univ. Autónoma de Barcelona 1973–; Pres. PEN Club Latinoamericano en España; Sec. Gen. Grupo de Estudios Latinoamericanos de Barcelona; Commdr, Order of Liberation (Spain), Officier des Palmes académiques (France). *Publications:* La Historia y la Novela 1947, 1963, 1970, 1974, Las ideas socialistas en el siglo XIX 1947, 1949, 1963, 1967, 1976, Ensayo de Sociología Uruguaya 1956, Teoría de la Historia 1959, 1968, 1974, 1980, Las clases sociales en el Uruguay 1960, La Crisis española del siglo XX 1960, 1962, 1976, Itinerario español 1961, 1977, Revolución social y fascismo en el siglo XX 1962, Sociología del Uruguay 1965, 1973, Historia del movimiento obrero y social latinoamericano contemporáneo 1967, 1969, 1976, Los afrouruguayos 1967, 1968, 1969, 1970, Garibaldi y el Uruguay 1968, Uruguay en Crisis 1969, Sociología de América Latina 1970, 1977, Chile, mil días entre la revolución y el fascismo 1974, España, crónica entrañable 1973–77, 1978, Historia de América Latina 1978, Fascismo y anarquismo en la España contemporánea 1979. *Leisure interest:* gardening. *Address:* c/o Monte de Orsá 7, Vallvidrera, Barcelona 17, Spain.

RAMACHANDRAN, Cherubala Pathayapurayil, MSc, DR.MED.SCI., DAP&E, FIBiol, JSM; Malaysian professor and medical scientist; b. 3 June 1936, Kuala Lumpur; s. of KK Madhavan Nair and Kamalam M. Nair; m. Githa Priya Darshini 1966; one s. one d.; ed St John's Inst., Kuala Lumpur, Christian Coll., Madras, India, Univ. of London, UK, Univ. of Liverpool, UK, Tulane Univ., USA, Univ. of Tokyo, Japan; Wellcome Trust Research Scholar and Demonstrator in Medical Parasitology, Liverpool School of Tropical Medicine 1959–62, Research Fellow in Tropical Medicine Inst. for Medical Research, Kuala Lumpur 1962–63, Head Filariasis Research Div. 1967–70; Asst Prof. in Medical Parasitology Faculty of Medicine, Univ. of Malaysia, Kuala Lumpur 1963–67, Assoc. Prof. in Medical Parasitology and Head School of Biological Sciences University Sains Malaysia, Penang 1970–72, Prof. and Dean 1972–79; Sr Scientist Human Resource Devt Tropical Disease Research WHO, Geneva, Switzerland 1979–87, Man. Research and Devt Filariasis Research Programme, Tropical Disease Research, WHO, Switzerland 1987–92; Chief Filariasis Research and Control, WHO, Geneva 1992–96; Prof. of Clinical Parasitology, Universiti Putra, Malaysia 1996–; Fellow Liverpool School of Tropical Medicine, UK, Malaysian Scientific Asscn, Acad. of Medicine, Malaysia, Australian Coll. of Tropical Medicine, Indian Acad. of Sciences; fmr Pres. Malaysian Soc. of Parasitology and Tropical Medicine, mem. Council World Fed. of Parasitologists; Sandosham Medal (Malaysia) 1974; Mary Kingsley Medal for Tropical Medicine (UK) 1998, Darjah Setia Pangkuan Negeri (Malaysia) 1999. *Publications:* numerous scientific papers in learned journals. *Leisure interests:* squash, photography, music. *Address:* Apt-8A-4-4, Belvedere Bukit Tunku, 50480 Kuala Lumpur, Malaysia. *Telephone:* 89468491 (Office); 26987275 (Home). *Fax:* 26986152.

RAMADAN, Taha Yassin; Iraqi politician; Vice-Chair. Revolutionary Command Council –2003; Vice-Pres. of Iraq 1991–2003.

RAMADHANI, Rt Rev. John Acland, BA; Tanzanian ecclesiastic (retd); b. 1 Aug. 1932, Zanzibar; s. of Augustine Ramadhani and Mary Majaliwa; ed Dar es Salaam Univ., Queen's Coll. Birmingham and Univ. of Birmingham; Prin. St Andrew's Teacher Training Coll., Korogwe 1967–69; Warden, St Mark's Theological Coll., Dar es Salaam 1977–79; Bishop of Zanzibar and Tanga 1980–2000; Archbishop of the Prov. of Tanzania 1984–97; Bishop of Zanzibar 2001–02; Chair. Christian Council of Tanzania –2002. *Leisure interest:* reading. *Address:* Anglican Church of Tanzania, Diocese of Zanzibar, P.O. Box 5, Mkunazini, Zanzibar, Tanzania (Office). *Telephone:* (24) 2235348 (Office). *Fax:* (24) 2236772 (Office). *E-mail:* cathedral@zanzinet.com (Office).

RAMADORAI, S., BSc, BEng, MSc; Indian business executive; ed Delhi Univ., Indian Inst. of Science, Bangalore, Univ. of Calif. and MIT, USA; jr engineer Tata Consultancy Services (TCS) 1972, later set up TCS's operations in New York 1979, CEO TCS 1996–, Chair. Tata Technologies Ltd; Chair. CMC Ltd; Ind. Dir (non-exec.) Hindustan Lever Ltd 2002–; Asia Business Leader of the Year Award, Hong Kong 2002. *Address:* c/o Atul Takle, Vice-President Corporate Communications, Tata Consultancy Services, Air India Building, 11th Floor, Nariman Point, Mumbai 400021, India (Office). *Telephone:* (22) 2046026 (Office); (22) 2024827, ext. 269 (Office). *Fax:* (22) 2040711 (Office). *E-mail:* atul_takle@mumbai.tcs.co.in (Office). *Website:* www.tcs.com (Office).

RAMAHATRA, Maj.-Gen. Victor; Malagasy politician, army officer and international business consultant; b. Victor Ramahatra, 6 Sept. 1945, Antananarivo; s. of Pierre Longin Ramahatra and Marie Lucile Ratsimandresy; m. Nivonirina Rajoelson 1971; two s. one d.; ed Saint-Cyr Military Acad., France; officer in Corps of Engineers; mil. engineer; Prime Minister of Malagasy Repub. 1987–91; Gen. Man. locust plague control campaign 1998–2000; Special Adviser to Pres. of Malagasy Repub.; mem. Asscn des Ingénieurs Diplômés de l'Ecole Supérieure du Génie Militaire d'Angers, Asscn des Anciens Elèves de Saint-Cyr; Grand-Croix Ordre du Mérite (France) 1990, Officier Légion d'honneur (France) 2000, Grand Officier Ordre nat. du Mérite 2000. *Leisure interests:* reading, march/walking, swimming. *Address:* VR. 104P, Fenomanana, 101 Antananarivo, Madagascar (Home); P.O. Box 6004, 101 Antananarivo. *E-mail:* ramvictor@hotmail.com (Office); vicram@dts.mg (Home).

RAMALINGASWAMI, Vulimirl, MD, DPhil, DSc (Oxon)), FRCP, FRCPath, FRS; Indian medical scientist; b. 8 Aug. 1921, Srikakulam, Andhra Pradesh; s. of Vulimiri Gumpaswami and Vulimiri Sundaramma Gumpaswami; m. Kuppa Surya Prabha 1947; one s. one d.; ed Andhra Univ. and Univ. of Oxford, England; Pathologist for Indian Council of Medical Research at the Nutrition Research Labs, Coonor, South India 1947–54; Asst Sec. and Deputy Dir Indian Council of Medical Research 1954–57; Prof. of Pathology and Head of Dept, All-India Inst. of Medical Sciences, Ansari Nagar, New Delhi 1957–69, Dir and Prof. of Pathology 1969–79, now Prof. Emer.; Dir-Gen. Indian Council of Medical Research 1979–86; Pres. Indian Nat. Science Acad. 1979–80; Nat. Research Prof. 1995–; Jacobson Lecturer, Newcastle-upon-Tyne Univ. 1971, Jacques Parisot Lecturer, WHO 1975, Jawaharlal Nehru Memorial Lecturer 1975; Scholar-in-Residence, Fogarty Int. Center, Nat. Insts of Health, Bethesda, Md 1976; Pres. Indian Asscn for Advancement of Medical Educ. 1974–; Chair. Global Advisory Cttee on Medical Research, WHO 1982–86, Task Force on Health Research for Devt, Geneva 1991–92; Fellow, Indian Acad. of Medical Science, Royal Coll. Pathologists; Foreign Assoc., Nat. Acad. of Sciences, USA 1973–; Hon. Fellow, American Coll. of Physicians 1970–; DSc hc (Andhra Univ.) 1967; Hon. DrMed (Karolinska Inst.) 1974; Silver Jubilee Research Award, Medical Council of India 1974, Leon Bernard Foundation Award, WHO, Geneva 1976, J. C. Bose Medal, Indian Nat. Science Acad. 1977, Birla Award for Medical Research 1980; Padma Bhushan 1971. *Publications:* author and co-author of many papers, articles, lectures, monographs and books. *Leisure interests:* literature, music, sports. *Address:* Department of Pathology, AIIMS, New Delhi 110029 (Office); X-29 Hauz Khas, New Delhi 110016, India. *Telephone:* (11) 6593364 (Office); (11) 6856719. *Fax:* (11) 4622707.

RAMAPHOSA, Matamela Cyril, BProc; South African trade union leader and business executive; b. 17 Nov. 1952, Johannesburg; s. of Samuel Ramaphosa and Erdmuth Ramaphosa; m. Tshepo Motsepe; two s. two d.; ed Sekano-Ntoane High School, Soweto, Univ. of Turfloop and Univ. of S Africa; Chair. Univ. br. S African Students' Org. 1974; imprisoned under Section Six of Terrorism Act for 11 months, then for 6 months in 1976; returned to law studies and qualified 1981; apptd legal adviser, Council of Unions of S Africa; Gen. Sec. Nat. Union of Mineworkers 1982–91; Sec.-Gen. African National Congress (ANC) 1991–96; Visiting Prof. of Law, Stanford Univ. 1991; mem. Parl. 1994–96; Chair. of Constitutional Ass. 1994–96; Weapons Inspector N Ireland 2000; Deputy Exec. Chair. New Africa Investments Ltd 1996–99; with Nat. Empowerment Consortium 1996–; Chair. and CEO Molope Group 1999–2000; Chair. Rebserve Ltd 2000–; Dr hc (Univs of Natal, Port Elizabeth, Mass., Cape Town); Olaf Palme Prize (Sweden) 1987. *Address:* Rebserve Ltd, P.O. Box, 651 508, Benmore 2010, South Africa (Office). *Telephone:* (11) 2904200 (Office). *Fax:* (11) 7838883 (Office). *E-mail:* ramaphosac@rebserve.co .za (Office).

RAMATHLODI, Ngoako, LLM; South African politician; b. 21 Aug. 1955, Potgietersrus (Tauatswala); m. Mathuding Ouma Ramatlhodi; one s. one d.; fmr Chair. African Nat. Congress (ANC), Northern Prov.; Deputy Registrar (student affairs), Exec. Asst to Vice-Chancellor Univ. of the N; in exile 1979, Commdr Unkhonto weSizwe; Head Political and Mil. ANC Council, Zimbabwe 1986; Political Sec., Asst to Oliver Tambo and Nelson Mandela (q.v.) 1988–91; Premier of Northern Prov. 1994–2002, of Limpopo 2002–. *Publications:* History of the ANC, Charade of Social Emancipation and National Liberation, Ethnicity: How The ANC Must Govern. *Leisure interests:* music, reading, writing. *Address:* Premier of Limpopo's Office, Limpopo, South Africa (Office).

RAMBAUD, Patrick; French writer; b. 21 April 1946, Paris; s. of François Rambaud and Madeleine de Magondeau; m. Pham-thi Tieu Hong 1988; mil. service with French AF 1968–69; co-f. Actual magazine 1970–84; Prix Lamartine 1981. *Plays:* Fregoli (with Bernard Haller) (Théâtre nat. de Chaillot 1991. *Publications:* (as sole author) La Saignée 1970, Comme des rats 1980, Fric-Frac 1984, La Mort d'un ministre 1985, Comment se tuer sans en avoir l'air 1987, Virginie Q. 1988 (Prix de l'Insolent 1988), Bernard Pivot reçoit... 1989, Le Dernier voyage de San Marco 1990, Ubu Président ou L'Imposteur 1990, Les Mirobolantes aventures de Frégoli 1991, Mururoa mon amour 1996, Le Gros secret 1996, La Bataille 1997 (Prix du roman de l'Acad. Française 1997, Prix Goncourt 1997, Napoleonic Soc. of America Literary Award 2000), Les Aventures de Mai 1998, Il neigeait 2000 (Prix Ciné-Roman 2001); (with Michel-Antoine Burnier) Les Aventures communautaires de Wao-le-Laid 1973, Les Complots de la liberté: 1832 1976 (Prix Alexandre Dumas 1976), Parodies 1977, 1848 1977, Le Roland Barthes sans peine 1978, La Farce des choses et autres parodies 1982, Le Journalisme sans peine 1997; (with Jean-Marie Stoerkel) Frontière suisse 1986; (with Bernard Haller) Le

Visage parle 1988; (with Francis Szpiner) Les Carnets secrets d'Elena Ceaucescu 1990; (with André Balland) Oraisons funèbres des dignitaires politiques qui ont fait leur temps et feignent de l'ignorer 1996. *Leisure interests:* writing, cooking, walking. *Address:* c/o Editions Grasset, 61 rue des Saints-Pères, 75006 Paris, France. *Telephone:* 1-44-39-22-00.

RAMBERT, Charles Jean Julien, FRSA; French architect; b. 23 March 1924, Arrigny, Marne; s. of Jean Rambert; m. Françoise Coleda 1949; three s.; ed Lycée Pierre-Corneille, Rouen, Inst. Saint-Aspais, Melun and Ecole Nat. Supérieure des Beaux-Arts; Architect 1952–, Govt- registered architect 1953; Prof. of Construction and History of Art, Ecole de secrétariat technique du bâtiment 1957–82; Arbitrator-expert, Tribunal de Commerce 1960 and de Grande Instance, Versailles 1963, Cour d'Appel de Paris 1971–, Tribunal Administratif de Paris 1979–; Sec. Soc. of Registered Architects 1954–57, Sec.-Gen. 1957, 1st Vice-Pres. 1968; Ed.-in-Chief L'Architecture française 1964–75; Counsellor, Ordre des Architectes de Paris 1964, Treas. 1969, Pres. 1976–78; Pres. Cie des Experts-Architectes, Paris 1978; Asst Dir of Studies, Ecole Nat. Supérieure des Beaux Arts 1965, Prof. of History of Architecture 1969–89; mem. Union Franco-Britannique des Architectes 1969; Fellow, Royal Soc. of Arts 1971; mem. Acad. d'Architecture 1978, Vice-Pres. 1981; Chevalier, Légion d'honneur, Officier des Arts et Lettres 1967 and other awards. *Publications:* Constructions scolaires et universitaires 1955, L'habitat collectif, Problème urbain 1957, Maisons familiales de plaisance 1959, Magasins 1961, Histoire de l'architecture civile en France 1963, French adapatation of World Architecture 1964, Architecture des origines à nos jours 1968, (English trans. 1969), L'architecture française 1969, L'architecture occidentale 1974 (Audio-visual series), Architecture hispano-mauresque 1980, L'architecture américaine des XIXe et XXe siècles: Chicago, New York. *Leisure interests:* history of art, literature, painting.

RAMEL, Baron Stig, MA; Swedish administrator; b. 24 Feb. 1927, Lund; s. of Malte Ramel and Elsa née Nyström; m. Ann Marie Wachtmeister 1953; two s. two d.; ed studies in political science; attaché, Ministry of Foreign Affairs 1953; Swedish Embassy, Paris 1954–56; del. to OECD, Paris 1956–58; Swedish Embassy, Washington, DC 1958–60; Ministry of Foreign Affairs 1960–66; Vice-Pres. and Pres. Gen. Swedish Export Asscn 1966–72; Exec. Dir Nobel Foundation, Stockholm 1972–92, Chair. Fund 1992–94; mem. Royal Swedish Acad. of Sciences; hon. doctorates from Lund Univ., Karolinska Inst., Gustavus Adolphus Coll. and Loretto Heights Coll.; King Charles XVI Gustaf Medal; Chevalier Légion d'honneur, Commdr Order of Vasa Isabella Catholica and St Olav, White Rose of Finland. *Publications:* five books including autobiog. *Leisure interests:* literature, painting, skiing, orienteering. *Address:* Resedavägen 8, 170 74 Solna, Sweden (Home).

RAMGOOLAM, Hon. Navinchandra, LLB, LRCP; Mauritian politician, medical practitioner and barrister; b. 14 July 1947, Mauritius; s. of the late Sir Seewoosagur Ramgoolam (first Prime Minister of Mauritius) and Lady Sushill Ramgoolam; m. Veena Ramgoolam 1979; ed Royal Coll. of Surgeons, Dublin, London School of Econs and Inns of Court School of Law, London; called to the Bar, Inner Temple 1993; Leader, Mauritius Labour Party (MLP) 1991–, Pres. 1991–92; Leader of Opposition and mem. Nat. Ass. 1991–95; Prime Minister of Repub. of Mauritius 1995–2000, also Minister of Defence and Home Affairs, External Communications; mem. Int. Advisory Bd Center for Int. Devt, Harvard Univ. 1999–; Licentiate, Royal College of Surgeons in Ireland; Hon. Fellow London School of Econs 1998; Dr hc (Mauritius) 1998, (Aligarh Muslim Univ.) 1998. *Leisure interests:* reading, music, water skiing, chess. *Address:* Mauritius Labour Party, 7 Guy Rozemount Square, Port Louis, Mauritius (Office). *Telephone:* 212-6691. *E-mail:* labour@intnet.mu. *Website:* www.labour.intnet.mu.

RAMÍREZ DE RINCÓN, Marta Lucía; Colombian politician and lawyer; ed Javeriana Pontifical Univ., Univ. of the Andes and Harvard Univ., USA; fmr Prof., Univ. of the Andes; fmr Prof. of Foreign Trade, Faculty of Law, Javeriana Pontifical Univ.; Exec. Pres. Inversiones de Gases de Colombia SA, Federación Colombiana de Compañias Leasing, Nat. Asscn of Finance Insts, Financiera Mazda Crédito SA; fmr Vice-Minster of External Trade, Minister of External Trade 1998–2002; Amb. to France Feb.–Oct. 2002; Minister of Defence 2002–; Dir-Gen. Instituto de Comercio Exterior (INCOMEX); Fellow Center for Int. Affairs, Harvard Univ. *Publications include:* El Contrato de Descuento y la Apertura de Crédito Antecedentes y Perspectivas del Negocio Fiduciario en Colombia, Régimen Legal de las Compañías de Financiamiento Comercial, Los Avances del Proceso de Interación Andina entre 1990 y 1991, El Programa Especial de Cooperación de la CEE para los Países Andines. *Address:* Ministry of National Defence, Centro Administrativo Nacional, 2° Avda El Dorado, Santafé de Bogotá, DC, Colombia (Office). *Telephone:* (1) 220-4999 (Office); (1) 222-445 (Office). *Fax:* (1) 222-1874 (Office). *E-mail:* siden@ mindefensa.gov.co (Office). *Website:* www.mindefensa.gov.co (Office).

RAMÍREZ MERCADO, Sergio; Nicaraguan politician and author; b. 5 Aug. 1942, Masatepe, Masaya; s. of late Pedro Ramírez Gutiérrez and Luisa Mercado Gutiérrez; m. Gertrudis Guerrero Mayorga 1964; one s. two d.; ed Univ. Autónoma de Nicaragua; was active in revolutionary student movt and founding mem. of Frente Estudiantil Revolucionario 1962; mem. Cen. American Univ. Supreme Council (CSUCA), Costa Rica 1964, Pres. 1968; mem. Int. Comm. of FSLN (Sandinista Liberation Front) 1975; undertook tasks on diplomatic front, propaganda and int. work on behalf of FSLN leading to overthrow of regime 1979; mem. Junta of Nat. Reconstruction Govt 1979–; Vice-Pres. of Nicaragua 1984–90; minority leader, Speaker, Nat. Ass.

1990–94; Pres. Movimiento de Renovación Sandinista (MRS) 1994–; MRS pre-cand. for presidency 1996; Dr hc (Cen. Univ. of Ecuador); Bruno Kreisky Prize 1988, Alfaguara Prize (Madrid) 1998; Chevalier des Arts et des Lettres 1993. *Publications include:* Cuentos 1963, El cuento centroamericano 1974, Charles Atlas también muere 1976, El cuento nicaragüense 1976, Castigo divino 1988, Confesión de amor 1991, Clave de sol 1992, Cuentos 1994, Oficios compartidos 1994, Un baile de máscaras 1995, Margarita, Está Linda la Mar. *Leisure interests:* classical music, reading. *Address:* MRS, Tienda Katty lc. Abajo, Apdo. 24, Managua, Nicaragua. *Telephone:* (2) 78-0279. *Fax:* (2) 78-0268. *Website:* www.sergioramirez.org.ni (Office).

RAMÍREZ VÁZQUEZ, Pedro; Mexican architect; b. 16 April 1919, Mexico; s. of Dolores Vázquez and Max Ramírez; m. Olga Campuzano 1947 (died 1999); two s. two d.; ed Univ. Nacional Autónoma de México; Prof. of Design and City Planning, Nat. School of Architecture, Univ. Nacional Autónoma de México; Sec. of Human Settlements and Public Works of Mexican Govt 1976–82; Chair. Organizing Cttee, Games of XIX Olympiad; lecturer Autonomous Univ. of México 1984; Dir Inst. of Urban Devt and Ecology 1988; Dir of display design Nubia Museum, Egypt 1985; Pres. Soc. of Mexican Architects and Nat. Coll. of Architects of Mexico 1953–58; founding mem. Int. Acad. of Architecture, Sofia 1985; Hon. mem. Council of Socs. of Architects of Spain; Dr hc (Pratt Inst. New York) 1982; Gold Medal of the French Acad. of Architecture 1978, Grand Prix of Twelfth Milan Triennial for prefabricated rural school project, Gold Medal, Eighth São Paulo Biennial for Nat. Museum of Anthropology, Mexico City, Nat. Prize of the Arts 1972, European Museum of the Year Award for Olympic Museum Switzerland 1995, Aga Khan Award for Architecture, Museum Nubia, Syria 2001. *Major works include:* co-author of design for Nat. School of Medicine, Univ. City; plans for several cities in Mexico; numerous prefabricated schools in Mexico (also used in S. America, Europe and Asia); buildings in Mexico City; Secr. of Foreign Affairs, Aztec Stadium, Cía. Mexicana de Aviación, Omega Co. and Congress Bldg, Nat. Museum of Anthropology, Japanese Embassy; Guadeloupe Shrine for 10,000 persons; Cathedral of Villahermosa, Tabasco; Cultural Centre, Tijuana; Monument to Fray Antón de Montesinos, Dominican Repub.; Mexican pavilions at Brussels, Seattle and New York World Fairs; museums of Ciudad Juárez and Mexico City; Nat. Gallery of History and Nat. Gallery of Modern Art, Mexico City; Offices of Int. Olympic Cttee, Lausanne, Switzerland 1981; Olympic Museum Switzerland 1985; Cen. Library and Museum of Anthropology, Toluca, Mexico 1985; Museum of the Major Temple, Mexico City 1985; Chapel of the Virgin of Guadalupe, Vatican 1991; Amparo Museum, Puebla 1991; pavilions of Mexico and Int. Olympic Cttee, Seville 1992; Teotihuacán Museum 1994; Information Centres, Monclova and Saltillo 1994–96; Convention Centre, Mérida 1997. *Leisure interests:* industrial design and design of lead glass objects. *Address:* Avenida de las Fuentes 170, México 01900, DF, Mexico. *Telephone:* (55) 5595-4388. *E-mail:* pramirez@data.net.mx (Office).

RAMKALAWAN, Rev. Wavel John Charles, B.THEOL; Seychelles politician and theologian; b. 15 March 1961, Mahé; m.; two s.; ed Seychelles Coll.; founder and leader of Parti Seselwa 1991–94; mem. Nat. Ass. 1993–97; Leader of Seychelles Nat. Party; Leader of the Opposition 1998–. *Address:* Seychelles National Party, Arpent Vert, Mant Fleuri, P.O. Box 81, Victoria (Office); St Louis, Mahé, Seychelles (Home). *Telephone:* (248) 224124 (Office); (248) 266286 (Home). *Fax:* (248) 224124 (Office). *E-mail:* wavel24@hotmail.com (Office).

RAMLI, Rizal; Indonesian politician; Chief Econs Minister –2001; Minister of Finance 2001. *Address:* c/o Office of the Co-ordinating Minister for the Economy, Finance and Industry, Jalan Taman Suropati 2, Jakarta 10310, Indonesia (Office).

RAMO, Simon, BS, PhD; American engineering executive; b. 7 May 1913, Salt Lake City, Utah; s. of Benjamin and Clara (née Trestman) Ramo; m. Virginia May Smith 1937; two s.; ed Univ. of Utah and California Inst. of Tech.; with Gen. Electric Co., Schenectady 1936–46; Lecturer, Union Coll. 1941–46; Dir Research Electronics Dept, Guided Missiles Research and Devt, Vice-Pres. and Dir of Operations, Hughes Aircraft Co., Culver City 1946–53; Exec. Vice-Pres., Dir, Ramo-Wooldridge Corpn, LA 1953–58; Pres. Space Tech. Labs Div. Ramo-Wooldridge Corpn 1957–58; Scientific Dir USAF Ballistic Missiles Programme 1954–58; Dir TRW Inc. 1954–85, Exec. Vice-Pres. 1958–61, Vice-Chair. 1961–78, Chair. Exec. Cttee 1969–78, Chair. Scientific and Tech. Cttee 1978, Chair. TRW-Fujitsu Co. 1980–83; Research Assoc. Calif. Inst. of Tech. 1946, Visiting Prof. 1978–; Chair. Cen. for Study of American Experience, Univ. of Southern Calif. 1978–80; Faculty Fellow John F. Kennedy School of Govt, Harvard Univ. 1980–84; mem. White House Energy Research and Devt Advisory Council 1973–75; mem. U.S. State Dept Cttee on Science and Foreign Affairs 1973–75; Chair. President's Cttee on Science and Tech. 1976–77; mem. Advisory Council to Sec. of Commerce 1976–77; Chair. Aetna, Jacobs & Ramo Venture Capital 1987–90, Allenwood Ventures Inc. 1987–; Dir Union Bancorp Inc., Union Bank, Atlantic Richfield Co., US Chamber of Commerce; Trustee, Calif. Inst. of Tech., American Museum of Electricity; mem. advisory council Gen. Atomics Corpn 1988–; Aurora Capital Partners 1991–, Chartwell Investments 1992–; Consultant, President's Science Advisory Cttee; Adviser Axiom Venture Partners 1997–; Co-Chair., Bd of Overseers, Keck School of Medicine, Univ. of Calif. 1999–; Fellow, American Physical Soc., Inst. of Aeronautics and Astronautics, American Acad. of Arts and Sciences, AAAS, American Astronautical Soc., Inst. for the Advancement of Eng, Inst. of Electrical and Electronic Engineers; Founder mem. Nat. Acad. of Eng; mem. NAS 1973–, Int. Acad. of Astronautics, American Philosophical Soc., Sr Execs Advisory Council, Nat. Industrial Conf. Board, Advisory Council on Japan–US Econ. Relations, US Chamber of Commerce Council on Trends and Perspective; Hon. DSc, DEng, LLD; Presidential Medal of Freedom 1983, Pioneer Award, Int. Council on System Eng 1997, Lifetime Achievement Trophy, Smithsonian Inst. 1999, Distinguished Public Service Medal, NASA 1999 and numerous other awards. *Publications:* Fields and Waves in Modern Radio (with J. R. Whinnery) 1944, 1953, Introduction to Microwaves 1945, Fields and Waves in Communication Electronics (with J. R. Whinnery and Theodore Van Duzer) 1965, Cure for Chaos 1969, Century of Mismatch 1970, Extraordinary Tennis for the Ordinary Player 1970, The Islands of E, Cono and My 1973, The Business of Science 1988. *Leisure interests:* tennis, the violin. *Address:* 9200 W Sunset Boulevard, Suite 801, Los Angeles, CA 90069, USA.

RAMON, Haim, BA; Israeli politician and lawyer; b. 1950, Jaffa; s. of Asher Vishnia and Bina Vishnia; m. Prina Tenenbaum; one s. one d.; ed Tel-Aviv Univ.; Chair. Public Council for Youth Exchanges; Nat. Sec. Labour Party's Young Guard 1978–84; co-ordinator Finance Cttee-Labour Party 1984–88, Chair. Labour Party 1988–92; Minister of Health 1992–94, of the Interior 1995–96, 2000–01; mem. Foreign Affairs and Defence Cttee 2001–; Minister responsible for Jerusalem Affairs, Prime Minister's Office –2001; mem. Knesset 1983–; served on numerous cttees 1983–92 (Labour). *Address:* Knesset, Jerusalem, Israel (Office). *Telephone:* 3-6490033 (Office); 2-6753864. *Fax:* 3-6499055 (Office); 2-6753782.

RAMOS, Gen. Fidel; Philippine politician and army officer; b. 18 March 1928, Lingayen; s. of Narciso Ramos and Angela Valdez; m. Amelita Martinez; five d.; ed Nat. Univ. Manila, U.S. Mil. Acad. West Point and Univ. of Illinois; active service in Korea and Viet Nam; Deputy Chief of Staff 1981; Chief of Staff, Philippines Armed Forces 1986–98; Leader People's Power Party; Sec. of Nat. Defence 1988–98, Cand. for Pres. May 1992; Pres. of the Philippines 1992–98; numerous hon. degrees; Peace Prize Award, UNESCO 1997; Légion d'honneur 1987. *Address:* 37/F Urban Bank Plaza, Urban Avenue, Makati City (Office); 120 Maria Cristina Street, AAVA Muntinlupa City, Philippines (Home). *E-mail:* fvr@urbanbank.com; rpdeu@skyinet.net (Office).

RAMOS-HORTA, José, MA; Timor-Leste political activist; b. 26 Dec. 1949, Dili; s. of late Francisco Horta and of Natalina Ramos Filipe Horta; m. Ana Pessoa 1978 (divorced); one s.; ed Hague Acad. of Int. Law, Int. Inst. of Human Rights, Strasbourg, Columbia Univ., Antioch Univ.; journalist and broadcaster 1969–74; Minister for External Affairs and Information, Timor-Leste 1975; Perm. Rep. of FRETILIN to UN, NY 1976–89; Public Affairs and Media Dir Mozambican Embassy, Washington 1987–88; f., Dir, lecturer Diplomacy Training Programme, Univ. of NSW 1990–, Visiting Prof. 1996–; Special Rep. Nat. Council of Maubere Resistance 1991–; returned to Timor-Leste Dec. 1999; Vice-Pres. Nat. Council of Resistance 1999–; Sr Minister for Foreign Affairs and Co-operation 2000– (in Timor-Leste Transitional Admin. 2000–02); mem. Bd Timor-Leste Human Rights Centre, Melbourne; Sr Assoc. mem. St Antony's Coll., Oxford 1987–; received Unrepresented Nations and People's Org. Award 1996; shared Nobel Peace Prize 1996 (with Mgr Carlos Ximenes Belo, q.v.,); Order of Freedom (Portugal) 1996. *Publications:* Funu: the Unfinished Saga of E Timor 1987; articles in numerous publs worldwide. *Leisure interest:* tennis. *Address:* Ministry for Foreign Affairs, Dili, Timor-Leste; Rua São Lazaro 16, 1°, 1150 Lisbon, Portugal. *Telephone:* (1) 8863727. *Fax:* (1) 8863791.

RAMOS ROSA, António; Portuguese poet and literary critic; b. 17 Oct. 1924, Faro; m. Agripina Costa Marques 1962; one d.; Dir literary reviews Árvore 1951–53, Cassiopeia 1955, Cadernos do Meio-Dia 1958–60; Prize of Portuguese Centre of Int. Asscn of Literary Critics 1980, PEN Club's Poetry Prize 1980, Portuguese Asscn of Writers' Grand Prize 1989, Pessoa Prize 1988, Prize of Liège Poetry Biennial 1991, European Poet of the Decade (Collège de l'Europe) 1991, Jean Malrieux Prize (Marseille) 1992; Grand Oficial, Order of Santiago da Espada; Great Cross, Order of Infante Dom Henrique. *Publications:* numerous vols of poetry including Delta seguido de Pela Primeira Vez 1996, Nomes de Ninguém 1997, À Mesa do Vento seguido de As Espirais de Dioniso 1997, A Imobilidade Fulminante 1998; (essays): Poesia, Liberdade Livre 1962, A Poesia Moderna e a Interrogação do Real 1979, Incisões Oblíquas 1987, A Parede Azul 1991. *Address:* Av. Barbosa du Bocage, 3–5° E, 1000 Lisbon, Portugal. *Telephone:* (1) 7964183.

RAMPHAL, Sir Shridath Surendranath, GCMG, O.E., OM, ONZ, AC, QC, SC, LLM, FRSA; Guyanese international official, barrister and politician; b. 3 Oct. 1928, New Amsterdam; s. of James I. Ramphal and Grace Ramphal (née Abdool); m. Lois Winifred King 1951; two s. two d.; ed Queen's Coll., Georgetown, King's Coll., London, Harvard Law School; Crown Counsel, British Guiana 1953–54; Asst to Attorney-Gen. 1954–56; Legal Draftsman 1956–58; Solicitor-Gen. 1959–61; Legal Draftsman, West Indies 1958–59; Asst Attorney-Gen., West Indies 1961–62; Attorney-Gen., Guyana 1965–73; mem. Nat. Assembly 1965–75; Minister of State for External Affairs 1967–72, Minister of Foreign Affairs 1972–75, of Justice 1973–75; Commonwealth Sec.-Gen. 1975–90; Chancellor Univ. of Guyana 1988–92, Univ. of Warwick 1989–2001, Univ. of West Indies 1989–; Queen's Counsel 1965 and Sr Counsel, Guyana 1966; mem. Int. Comm. of Jurists, Ind. Comm. on Int. Devt Issues, Ind. Comm. on Disarmament and Security Issues, Ind. Comm. on Int. Humanitarian Issues, World Comm. on Environment and Devt, South Comm., Carnegie Comm. on Deadly Conflict, Bd of Govs Int. Devt Research Center, Canada, Exec. Cttee of Int. Inst. for Environment and Devt, Council of Int. Negotiation Network Carter Center, Georgia, USA 1991–97; Patron One World Broadcasting Trust; Chair. UN Cttee for Devt Planning 1984–87, West Indian Comm. 1990–92, Bd Int. Inst. for Democracy and Electoral Assistance (IDEA) 1995–2001, Advisory Cttee Future Generations Alliance Foundation 1995–97; Pres. World Conservation Union—IUCN 1990–93; Int. Steering Cttee Leadership for Environment and Devt Program Rockefeller Foundation 1991–98; Co-Chair. Comm. on Global Governance 1992–2000; Adviser to Sec.-Gen. of UNCED 1992; Chief Negotiator on Int. Econ. Issues for the Caribbean Region 1997–2001; Facilitator Belize–Guatemala Dispute 2000–02; John Simon Guggenheim Fellowship 1962; Hon. Bencher of Gray's Inn 1981; Fellow, King's Coll., London 1975, LSE 1979, RSA 1981, Magdalen Coll., Oxford 1982; Order of the Repub. (Egypt) 1973; Grand Cross, Order of the Sun (Peru) 1974; Grand Cross, Order of Merit (Ecuador) 1974, Order of Nishaan Izzuddeen (Maldives) 1989, Grand Commdr, Order of Niger 1990, Grand Commdr, Order of the Companion of Freedom (Zambia) 1990, Nishan-e-Quaid-i-Azam (Pakistan) 1990, Order of the Caribbean Community 1991, Commdr Order of the Golden Ark 1994; Hon. LLD (Panjab Univ.) 1975, (Southampton) 1976, (Univ. of The West Indies) 1978, (St Francis Xavier Univ., Halifax, Canada) 1978, (Aberdeen) 1979, (Cape Coast, Ghana) 1980, (London) 1981, (Benin, Nigeria) 1982, (Hull) 1983, (Yale) 1985, (Cambridge) 1985, (Warwick) 1988, (York Univ., Ont., Canada) 1988, (Malta) 1989, (Otago, NZ) 1990; Hon. DHL (Simmons Coll., Boston) 1982; Hon. DCL (Oxon.) 1982, (East Anglia) 1983, (Durham) 1985; Dr hc (Surrey) 1979, (Essex) 1980; Hon. DHumLitt (Duke Univ., USA) 1985; Hon. DLitt (Bradford) 1985, (Indira Gandhi Nat. Open Univ.) 1989; Hon. DSc (Cranfield Inst. of Tech.) 1987; Arden and Atkin Prize, Gray's Inn 1952, Int. Educ. Award (Richmond Coll., London) 1988, RSA Albert Medal 1988, Medal of Friendship, Cuba 2001, Pravasi Bharata Samman Award 2003. *Publications:* One World to Share: Selected Speeches of the Commonwealth Secretary-General 1975–79, Nkrumah and the Eighties (1980 Kwame Nkrumah Memorial Lectures), Sovereignty and Solidarity (1981 Callander Memorial Lectures), Some in Light and Some in Darkness: The Long Shadow of Slavery (Wilberforce Lecture) 1983, The Message not the Messenger (STC Communication Lecture) 1985, The Trampling of the Grass (Econ. Comm. for Africa Silver Jubilee Lecture) 1985, For the South, a Time to Think 1986, Making Human Society a Civilized State (Corbishley Memorial Lecture) 1987, Inseparable Humanity: An Anthology of Reflections of Shridath Ramphal 1988, An End to Otherness (six speeches) 1990, Our Country, The Planet 1992, No Island is an Island and contribs in journals of legal, political and int. affairs, including International and Comparative Law Quarterly, Caribbean Quarterly, Public Law, Guyana Journal, The Round Table, Royal Society of Arts Journal, Foreign Policy, Third World Quarterly, International Affairs. *Leisure interests:* photography, cooking. *Address:* 31 St. Mathew's Lodge, 50 Oakley Square, London, NW1 1NB, England (Home); 1 The Sutherlands, 188 Sutherland Avenue, London, W9 1HR. *Telephone:* (20) 7266-3409. *Fax:* (20) 7286-2302. *E-mail:* ssramphal@msn.com (Office).

RAMPHELE, Mamphela Aletta, MB, ChB, BCom, DPH, PhD; South African international organization official, university administrator and community health researcher; b. 28 Dec. 1947, Pietersburg; d. of Pitsi Eliphaz Ramphele and Rangoato Rahab Ramphele (née Mahlaela); two s.; ed Setotolwane High School, Pietersburg, Univ. of Natal; community health worker Black Community Programmes, Ktown 1975–77, Ithuseng Community Health Programme, Tzaneen 1978–84; Sr Researcher Dept Social Anthropology, Univ. of Cape Town 1986, Deputy Vice-Chancellor 1991–95, Vice-Chancellor 1996–2000; Man. Dir IBRD 2000–; Researcher and Consultant to Western Cape Hostel Dwellers' Asscn 1986–92; Dir (non-exec.) Anglo-American 1992–95, Old Mutual 1993–; Founder mem. Black Consciousness Movt 1969; mem. NAMDA 1985–; Hon. DHumLitt (Hunter Coll., New York) 1984; Hon. MD (Natal) 1989, (Sheffield) 1998; Dr. h.c. for Distinguished Career (Tufts Univ., Mass.) 1991; Hon. DSc (Univ. Coll., London) 1997; Hon. LLD (Princeton) 1997, (Brown Univ.) 1998, (Mich.) 1998; Dr hc (Inst. of Social Studies, Netherlands) 1997; Hon. DPhil (Univ. of Orange Free State); Barnard Medal of Distinction, Barnard Coll., New York 1991. *Publications:* Children on Frontline (UNICEF report) 1987, Uprooting Poverty: The South African Challenge (with David Philip) 1989 (Noma Award for publishing in Africa 1991), A Bed Called Home: Life in Migrant Labour Hostels of Cape Town (with David Philip) 1993, Mamphela Ramphele: A Life (with David Philip) 1995, Across Boundaries: The Journey of a South African Woman Leader 1996. *Leisure interests:* reading, walking. *Address:* IBRD, 1818 H Street, Washington, DC 20433 (Office); 4515 Foxhall Crescents, Washington, DC 20007, USA (Home). *Telephone:* (202) 473-2419 (Office). *Fax:* (202) 522-1638 (Office); (202) 625-7936 (Office). *E-mail:* mramphele@worldbank.org (Office). *Website:* www.worldbank.org (Office).

RAMPLING, Charlotte, OBE; British actress; b. 5 Feb. 1946, London; m. 2nd Jean-Michel Jarre 1978; two s. (one s. from previous marriage); one step-d.; film debut 1963; Chevalier Ordre des Arts et des Lettres 1986, César d'honneur 2001, Chevalier, Légion d'honneur 2002. *Films include:* The Knack 1963, Rotten to the Core, Georgy Girl, The Long Duel, Kidnapping, Three, The Damned 1969, Skibum, Corky 1970, 'Tis Pity She's a Whore, Henry VIII and His Six Wives 1971, Asylum 1972, The Night Porter, Giordano Bruno, Zardoz, Caravan to Vaccares 1973, The Flesh of the Orchid, Yuppi Du 1974–75, Farewell My Lovely, Foxtrot 1975, Sherlock Holmes in New York, Orca The Killer Whale, The Purple Taxi 1976, Stardust Memories 1980, The Verdict 1983, Viva la vie 1983, Beauty and Sadness 1984, He Died with His Eyes Open 1985, Max mon Amour, Max My Love 1985, Angel Heart 1987, Paris by Night 1988, Dead on Arrival 1989, Helmut Newton, Frames from the Edge, Hammers Over the Anvil 1991, Time is Money 1992, La marche de Radetzky (TV film) 1994, Asphalt Tango 1995, Wings of a Dove 1996, The Cherry Orchard 1998, Signs and Wonders, Aberdeen 1999, Fourth Angel, Under the Sand, Superstition 2000, See How They Run 2002; numerous TV plays. *Address:* c/o Artmédia, 20 ave. Rapp, 75007 Paris, France. *Telephone:* 1-43-17-33-00.

RAMQVIST, Lars Henry, PhD; Swedish business executive; b. 2 Nov. 1938, Grängesberg; s. of Henry Ramqvist and Alice Ramqvist; m. Barbro Pettersson 1962; one s. one d.; ed Univ. of Uppsala; Section Head, Stora Kopparberg AB 1962–65; with Axel Johnson Inst. 1965–80, Pres. 1975–80; joined L. M. Ericsson Telephone Co. as Vice-Pres. and head of Information Systems Div. 1980, Pres. and CEO 1990–98, Chair. 1998–, CEO 1999–, Pres. subsidiary RIFA AB 1984–86, Ericsson Radio AB 1988–90; Chair. AB Volvo 1999–, Skandia Insurance Co. Ltd 2000–; mem. Bd Swedish Eng Employers' Asscn, Asscn of Swedish Eng Industries and Fed. of Swedish Industries; mem. Prime Minister's Special Industry Advisory Cttee 1994–; mem. Royal Swedish Acad. of Science, Royal Swedish Acad. of Eng Sciences. *Address:* Telefonaktiebolaget L. M. Ericsson, 12625 Stockholm, Sweden. *Telephone:* (8) 719-46-02. *Fax:* (8) 744-35-74.

RAMSAMY, Pakereesamy (Prega), BA, MBA, PhD; Mauritian economist and international organization official; b. 1950, Rose Hill; m. Novia Ramsamy; two d.; with Preferential Trade Area for Eastern and Southern Africa, then Common Market for Eastern and Southern Africa for 14 years; Chief Economist, Southern African Devt Community 1997–, Deputy Exec. Sec. 1998–2000, Acting Exec. Sec. 2000, Exec. Sec. 2001–. *Address:* Southern African Development Community Bldg, Private Bag 0095, Gaborone (Office); Plot 16588, Gaborone, Botswana. *Telephone:* 351863 (Office). *Fax:* 372848 (Office). *E-mail:* sadsec@sadc.int. *Website:* www.sadc.int.

RAMSBOTHAM, Hon. Sir Peter (Edward), GCMG, GCVO, DL; British diplomatist and administrator; b. 8 Oct. 1919, London; s. of 1st Viscount Soulbury; m. 1st Frances Blomfield 1941 (died 1982); two s. one d.; m. 2nd Zaida Hall 1985; ed Eton Coll. and Magdalen Coll., Oxford; entered diplomatic service 1948; served in Political Div., Allied Control Comm., Berlin 1948–50; First Sec., Foreign Office 1950–53; Head of Chancery, UK del. to UN, New York 1953–57; Foreign Office 1957–62; Head of Chancery, British Embassy, Paris 1962–67; Foreign Office 1967–69; High Commr to Cyprus 1969–71; Amb. to Iran 1971–74, to USA 1974–77; Gov. and C-in-C of Bermuda 1977–80; Dir Commercial Union Assurance Co. 1980–90, Lloyds Bank Ltd 1980–90, Chair. Lloyds Bank Southern Region 1984–90; Chair. Ryder-Cheshire Foundation for the Relief of Suffering 1982–2000; World Memorial Fund for Disaster Relief 1992–96; KStJ 1976; DL Hants. 1992; Hon. Fellow Magdalen Coll., Oxford 1991; Hon. LLD (Akron Univ.) 1975, (William and Mary Coll.) 1975, (Maryland Univ.) 1976, (Yale Univ.) 1977; Croix de Guerre 1945. *Leisure interests:* gardening, fishing. *Address:* East Lane, Ovington, Alresford, Hants, SO24 0RA, England (Home). *Telephone:* (1962) 732515.

RAMSEY, Norman Foster, MA, PhD, DSc; American scientist; b. 27 Aug. 1915, Washington, DC; s. of Brigadier-Gen. and Mrs Norman F. Ramsey; m. 1st Elinor Stedman Jameson 1940 (died 1983); four d.; m. 2nd Ellie Welch 1985; ed Columbia, Harvard and Cambridge Univs; Assoc. Univ. of Illinois 1940–42; Asst Prof. Columbia Univ. 1942–46; Research Assoc. MIT Radiation Lab. 1940–43; Expert Consultant to Sec. of War 1942–45; Group Leader and Asscn Division Head, Los Alamos Lab. of Atomic Energy Project 1943–45; Chief Scientist of Atomic Energy Lab., Tinian 1945; Assoc. Prof. Columbia Univ. 1945–47; Head Physics Dept, Brookhaven Nat. Lab. 1946–47; Assoc. Prof. Harvard Univ. 1947–50; Dir Harvard Nuclear Lab. 1948–50 and 1952–53; Air Force Scientific Advisory Cttee 1947–55; Dept Defence Panel on Atomic Energy 1953–58; Prof. of Physics, Harvard Univ. 1950–66, Sr Fellow, Harvard Soc. Fellows 1970–; Higgins Prof. of Physics, Harvard Univ. 1966–86; Prof. Emer. 1986–; Scientific Adviser NATO 1958–59; Gen. Advisory Cttee, Atomic Energy Comm. 1960–72; Dir Varian Associates 1963–66; Pres. Univs Research Asscn 1966–81; Eastman Prof., Oxford Univ. 1973–74; Luce Prof. of Cosmology, Mount Holyoke Coll. 1982–83, Prof. of Physics, Univ. of Va 1983–84; Research Fellow, Jt Inst. Lab. Astrophysics, Univ. of Colo 1986–87; Distinguished Prof., Univ. of Chicago 1987–88; Prof., Williams Coll. 1989; Visiting Prof., Univ. of Mich. 1989–92; Vice-Pres. American Physical Soc. 1977 (Pres. 1978); Chair. Physics Div. American Asscn for Advancement of Science 1977; mem. NAS, American Acad. of Arts and Sciences, American Philosophical Soc., French Acad. of Sciences; Visiting Cttee Nat. Bureau of Standards 1982–; Trustee, Carnegie Endowment for Int. Peace 1962–85 and the Rockefeller Univ. 1976–90; Chair. Bd of Govs, American Inst. of Physics 1980–86; Hon. DSc (Case Western Reserve Univ.) 1968, (Middlebury Coll.) 1969, (Oxford) 1973, (Rockefeller) 1986, (Sussex) 1989, (Chicago, Houston) 1990, (Mich. 1993), (Philadelphia Coll. of Pharmacy and Science) 1995; Hon. DCL (Oxford) 1990; other hon. degrees; Presidential Order of Merit, Lawrence Award 1960, Davisson-Germer prize 1974, Award for Excellence in Science (Colombia Univ.) 1980, Medal of Honor of IEE 1984, Monie Ferst Prize 1985, Rabi Prize 1985, Karl Compton Award 1986, Rumford Premium 1985, Oersted Medal 1988, Nat. Medal of Science 1988, Nobel Prize in Physics (Jt) 1989, Pupin Medal 1992, Erice Science for Peace Prize 1992, Einstein Medal 1993, Vannevar Bush Award 1995, Alexander Hamilton Award 1995. *Publications:* Nuclear Moments 1953, Nuclear Two-Body Problems 1953, Molecular Beans 1955, 1985, Quick Calculus 1965, 1985, Spectroscopy with Coherent Radiation 1998; and numerous articles in the Physical Review.

Leisure interests: skiing, walking, sailing, swimming, tennis, reading, conversation, music. *Address:* Lyman Physics Laboratory, Harvard University, Cambridge, MA 02138; 24 Monmouth Court, Brookline, MA 02146, USA. *Telephone:* (617) 495-2864. *Fax:* (617) 496-5144.

RANARIDDH, Prince (see Norodom Ranariddh, Prince).

RANCHOD, Bhadra, BA, LLB, LLM, LLD; South African diplomatist and lawyer; b. 11 May 1944, Port Elizabeth; s. of Ghalloo Ranchod and Parvaty Ranchod; m. Vibha M. Desai 1980; two d.; ed Univs of Cape Town, Oslo and Leiden; Sr Lecturer, Dept of Pvt. Law, Univ. of Durban-Westville 1972, Prof. of Pvt. Law 1974, Dean, Faculty of Law 1976–79; Advocate of Supreme Court 1973–; mem. Bd of Govs S. African Broadcasting Corpn; mem. S African Law Comm.; mem. Human Sciences Research Council, numerous cttees and public bodies etc.; Visiting Scholar, Columbia Univ., New York 1980–81; Amb. and Head of S African Mission to European Communities 1986–92; Minister of Tourism 1993–94; Chair. Minister's Council in House of Dels 1993–94; MP 1994–96; Deputy Speaker, Nat. Ass. 1994–96; High Commr in Australia (also Accred to New Zealand and Fiji Islands) 1996–2001. *Publications:* Foundations of the South African Law of Defamation (thesis) 1972, Law and Justice in South Africa 1986; about 100 papers on human rights issues. *Leisure interests:* jogging, reading, travel. *Address:* c/o Ministry of Foreign Affairs, Union Buildings, East Wing, Government Avenue, Pretoria 0002, South Africa (Office).

RANDALL, Jeff William, BA; British journalist; b. 3 Oct. 1954, London; s. of Jeffrey Charles Randall and Grace Annie Randall (née Hawkridge); m. Susan Diane Fidler 1986; one d.; ed Royal Liberty Grammar School, Romford, Nottingham Univ., Univ. of Florida, USA; with Hawkins Publrs 1982–85; Asst Ed. Financial Weekly 1985–86; City Corresp. Sunday Telegraph 1986–88; Deputy City Ed. The Sunday Times 1988–89, City Ed. 1989–94, City and Business Ed. 1994–95, Asst Ed. and Sports Ed. 1996–97; Ed. Sunday Business 1997–2001; Business Ed. BBC 2001–; columnist Sunday Telegraph 2001–; Freelance contrib. Daily Telegraph, Euromoney, Sporting Life, Golf World; Dir Times Newspapers 1994–95; Deputy Chair. Financial Dynamics Ltd 1995–96; Dr hc (Anglia Polytechnic Univ.) 2001; Financial Journalist of the Year, FT-Analysis 1991, Business Journalist of the Year, London Press Club 2000. *Publications:* The Day That Shook the World (co-author). *Leisure interests:* golf, horse racing, football. *Address:* BBC Television Centre, Wood Lane, London, W12 7RJ, England (Office).

RANDLE, Sir Philip John, Kt, MA, PhD, MD, FRCP, FRS; British biochemist and medical practitioner; b. 16 July 1926, Nuneaton; s. of Alfred J. and Nora A. Randle; m. Elizabeth A. Harrison 1952; one s. (deceased) three d.; ed Sidney Sussex Coll., Cambridge and Univ. Coll. Medical School, London; house physician and house surgeon, Univ. Coll. Hosp. 1951; MRC Research worker, Dept of Biochem., Univ. of Cambridge 1952–55; Research Fellow, Sidney Sussex Coll. 1954–57; Lecturer in Biochem. Univ. of Cambridge 1955–64; Fellow and Dir of Medical Studies, Trinity Hall, Cambridge 1957–64; Prof. and Head of Dept of Biochem., Univ. of Bristol 1964–75; Prof. of Clinical Biochem. Univ. of Oxford and Fellow, Hertford Coll., Oxford 1975–93, Emer. Prof. and Emer. Fellow 1993–; Pres. Biochemical Soc. 1989–; Fellow Univ. Coll. London 1990; Hon. Fellow Trinity Hall 1988; Hon. DSc (Oxford Brookes) 1997; Minkowski Prize 1966, Ciba Medal 1984. *Publications:* numerous articles in scientific and medical journals. *Leisure interest:* travel, wherever and whenever possible. *Address:* 11 Fitzherbert Close, Iffley, Oxford, OX4 4EN, England; Department of Clinical Biochemistry, Radcliffe Infirmary, Oxford, OX2 6HE (Office). *Telephone:* (1865) 773115. *Fax:* (1865) 224000. *E-mail:* philip.randle@ndcb.ox.ac.uk (Office).

RANDT, Clark T., Jr, JD; American lawyer and diplomatist; m. Sarah A. Talcott; two s. one d.; ed Hotchkiss School, Yale Univ., Univ. of Mich. and Harvard Law School; with USAF Security Service 1968–72; China rep. Nat. Council for U.S.–China Trade 1974; First Sec. and Commercial Attaché, U.S. Embassy, Beijing 1982–84; fmr partner Shearman and Sterling (law firm), Hong Kong; Amb. to People's Repub. of China 2001–; mem. NY and Hong Kong Bars; fmr Gov. and First Vice-Pres. American Chamber of Commerce, Hong Kong; mem. American Bar Asscn, American Soc. of Int. Law, Hong Kong Law Soc. *Address:* Embassy of the USA, 3 Xiu Shui Bei Jie, Beijing 100600, People's Republic of China (Office). *Telephone:* (10) 65323831 (Office). *Fax:* (10) 65323178 (Office). *Website:* www.usembassy-china.org.cn (Office).

RANGARAJAN, Chakravarthi, PhD; Indian politician and academic; b. 5 Jan. 1932, Ariyalur; s. of B. R. Chakravarty and Rangam Chakravarty; m. Haripriya Chakravarty; one s. one d.; lecturer, Loyola Coll. Chennai 1954–58, Wharton School of Finance and Commerce, Pa Univ. 1963–64; reader Raj Univ. 1964–65; Prof. Indian Statistical Inst., New Delhi 1965–66; Visiting Assoc. Prof. New York Univ., 1966–68, Visiting Prof. 1972–73; Prof. IIM, Ahmedabad 1968–81; Deputy Gov. Reserve Bank of India 1982–91, Gov. 1992–97; Gov. of Andhra Pradesh 1997–; mem. Planning Comm., Indian Govt 1991–92; Pres. Indian Econ. Asscn 1982, 1994. *Publications:* Short-Term Investment Forecasting 1974, Principles of Macro-Economics 1979, Strategy for Industrial Development in the 80s 1982, Agricultural Growth and Industrial Performance in India 1982; and more than 40 papers. *Address:* Raj Bhavan, Hyderabad 500041, India (Office). *Telephone:* (40) 3313737 (Office); (40) 3310521.

RANGEL VALE, José Vicente; Venezuelan politician; b. 10 July 1929, Caracas; s. of José Vicente Rangel Cárdenas and Leonor Vale de Rangel; ed

Colegio La Salle, Barquismeto, Universidad de los Andes (ULA), Cen. Univ. of Venezuela (UCV), Univ. of Chile, Univs of Salamanca and Santiago de Compostela, Spain; joined Unión Republicana Democrática (URD) aged 16; fmr TV Presenter, Televen, Canal 10; fmr columnist El Universal, El Informadro, La Tarde, El Regional and Bohemia; Cand. in Presidential Elections 1973, 1978, 1983; elected Deputy to Congress for Estado Miranda; fmr Co-ordinator Movimento Independientes (with Hugo Chávez); Minister of Foreign Affairs 1999–2001, of Defence 2001–02; Vice-Pres. of Venezuela 2002–. *Publications include:* Tiempo de Verdades, Socialismo y Democracia, Expediente Negro, La Administración de La Justica en Venezuela. *Address:* Central Information Office of the Presidency, Torre Oeste, 18, Parque Central, Caracas 1010, Venezuela (Office). *Telephone:* (212) 572-7110 (Office). *Fax:* (212) 572-2675 (Office). *E-mail:* presidencia@venezuela.gov.ve. *Website:* www.venezuela.gov.ve.

RANIS, Gustav, PhD; American professor of economics; b. 24 Oct. 1929, Darmstadt, Germany; s. of Max Ranis and Bettina Goldschmidt; m. Ray Lee Finkelstein; two s. one d.; ed Brandeis Univ., Yale Univ.; Social Science Research Council Fellow (Japan) 1955–56; Jt Dir, Pakistan Inst. of Devt Econs, Karachi, Pakistan 1959–61; Assoc. Dir Econ. Growth Center, Yale Univ. 1961–65, Dir 1967–75; Assoc. Prof. of Econs, Yale Univ. 1961–64, Prof. of Econs 1964–82, Frank Altschul Prof. of Int. Econs 1982–; Dir Yale Center for Int. and Area Studies 1996–; Dir Yale-Pakistan Project 1970–71; Asst Admin. for Program and Policy, Agency for Int. Devt, Dept of State 1965–67, Consultant 1962–65, 1967–71, 1984–; Ford Foundation Faculty Fellow Colegio de Mexico, Mexico City 1971–72, Visiting Prof. Univ. de los Andes, Colombia 1976–77; Consultant UN FAO 1979–; Chief of Mission, ILO Comprehensive Employment Strategy Mission to the Philippines 1973, World Bank/CARICOM Project on Production and Investment Incentives in the Caribbean 1980–82; mem. Oversight Cttee Int. Conf. on Intellectual Property Rights, Nat. Research Council 1991–; mem. Editorial Advisory Bd Journal of Int. Devt 1995–, Oxford Devt Studies 1996–; mem. Bd of Trustees and Brandeis Chair. Acad. Affairs Cttee Brandeis Univ.; Fellow Inst. for Advanced Study, Berlin 1993–94; Dr hc Brandeis Univ. 1982. *Publications:* Development of Labor Surplus Economy: Theory and Policy (jtly) 1964, Growth with Equity: The Taiwan Case (jtly) 1979, Comparative Technology Choice in Development (jtly) 1988, Linkages in Developing Economics: A Philippine Study (jtly) 1990, The State of Development Economics, Science and Technology: Lessons for Development Policy (jtly) 1990, Taiwan: From Developing to Mature Economy (ed.) 1992, The Political Economy of Development Policy Change (jtly) 1992, Japan and the U.S. in the Developing World (ed.) 1997, Growth and Development from an Evolutionary Perspective (with John C. H. Fei) 1997, The Economics and Political Economy of Development in Taiwan into the 21st Century 1999, The Economics and Political Economy of Comparative Development into the 21st Century 1999. *Leisure interests:* tennis, squash, hiking. *Address:* Yale Center for International and Area Studies, 34 Hillhouse Avenue, P.O. Box 208206, New Haven, CT 06520-8206 (Office); 7 Mulberry Road, Woodbridge, CT 06525, USA (Home). *Telephone:* (203) 432-9368 (Office); (203) 397-2560 (Home). *Fax:* (203) 432-9383 (Office). *E-mail:* gustav.ranis@yale.edu (Office). *Website:* www.yale.edu/ycias (Office).

RANJEVA, Raymond, LLD; Malagasy lawyer and international official; b. 31 Aug. 1942, Antananarivo; m. Yvette Madeleine R. Rabetafika 1967; five c.; ed Univ. of Madagascar, Madagascar Nat. School of Admin., Univ. of Paris, France; trainee, Judicial Div., Conseil d'Etat, Paris; Civil Admin., Univ. of Madagascar 1966, Asst Lecturer 1966–72, Lecturer 1972, Dir Dept of Legal and Political Science 1973–82, Prof. 1981–91, Dean of Faculty of Law, Econs, Man. and Social Sciences 1982–88; Prof. Madagascar Mil. Acad., Madagascar School of Admin.; Dir Public Law and Political Science Study Centre; First Rector, Univ. of Antananarivo 1988–90; Man. Dir Jureco (econ., financial and legal databank for advisory and research bodies) 1986–90, Ed. Lettre mensuelle de Jureco 1986–88; Conciliator, IBRD Int. Centre for Settlement of Investment Disputes 1970–; Attorney to Mali, Border Dispute (Burkina Faso/ Mali); Consultant on transfer to the State of activities of Eau-Electricité de Madagascar and Electricité de France 1973; Judge Int. Court of Justice 1991–; Founder mem. Malagasy Human Rights Cttee 1971; mem. and Vice-Pres. Malagasy Acad. 1974, Pres. Ethics and Political Science section 1975–91; mem. Nat. Constitutional Cttee 1975; mem. Court of Arbitration for Sport 1995–; legal adviser to Catholic Bishops' Conf., Madagascar; mem. Governing Body of African Soc. of Int. and Comparative Law, French Soc. of Int. Law, Québec Soc. (Canada); Sec.-Gen. Malagasy Legal Studies Soc.; mem. Pontifical Comm. 'Justice et Paix' 2002–, Curatorium de l'Acad. de Droit Int. 2002–; Commdr Ordre Nat. Malgache of Madagascar, Chevalier Ordre de Mérite of Madagascar; Officier Ordre Nat. of Mali, Grand-Croix nat. malgache 2003. *Address:* International Court of Justice, Peace Palace, Carnegieplein 2, 2517 KJ The Hague, Netherlands (Office). *Telephone:* (70) 3022323 (Office). *Fax:* (70) 3649928 (Office). *E-mail:* information@icj-cij.org (Office).

RÁNKI, Dezső; Hungarian pianist; b. 8 Sept. 1951, Budapest; s. of József Ránki and Edith Jecsmen; m. Edit Klukon 1979; two c.; ed Ferenc Liszt Music Acad., Budapest (under Pál Kadosa); has given recitals and appeared with several leading orchestras throughout Europe, including Berlin Philharmonic, Concertgebouw and London Philharmonic; regular concert tours N America and Japan; four-hands piano recitals with Edit Klukon in many European cities 1982–; has taught piano at Budapest Music Acad. since 1973; First Prize, Int. Schumann Competition, Zwickau, GDR 1969, Grand Prix du Disque (Paris) 1972, Liszt Prize 2nd Degree 1973, Kossuth Prize 1978.

Leisure interests: gramophone records, sound tapes, books, gardening. *Address:* Caecilia, 29 rue de la Coulouvrenière 1204 Geneva, Switzerland (Agent); H-1112 Budapest, Ördögorom Lejtő 11/B, Hungary (Home). *Telephone:* (22) 8091526 (Agent, Switzerland) (Office); (1) 246-4403 (Home).

RANNEY, Helen M., MD, ScD; American physician (retd); b. 12 April 1920, Summer Hill, New York; d. of Arthur C. Ranney and Alesia (Toolan) Ranney; ed Barnard Coll. and Coll. of Physicians and Surgeons, Columbia Univ.; Asst Prof. of Clinical Medicine, Columbia Univ. 1958–60; Assoc. Prof. of Medicine, Albert Einstein Coll. of Medicine 1960–65, Prof. 1965–70; Prof. of Medicine, State Univ. of New York, Buffalo 1970–73; Prof. of Medicine, Dept of Medicine, Univ. of Calif., San Diego 1973–90, Prof. Emer. 1990–, Chair. 1973–86; Distinguished Physician, Department of Veterans' Affairs Medical Center, San Diego, Calif. 1986–91; consultant Alliance Pharmaceutical Corpn, San Diego 1991–; mem. NAS, Asscn of American Physicians, American Acad. of Arts and Sciences, American Soc. for Clinical Investigation, Inst. of Medicine; Kober Medal, Asscn of American Physicians 1996. *Publications:* papers in medical journals concerned with haemoglobin. *Address:* 6229 La Jolla Mesa Drive, La Jolla, CA 92037, USA (Home). *Telephone:* (858) 459-6768 (Home). *Fax:* (858) 459-6780 (Home). *E-mail:* hranney@ucsd.edu (Home).

RANQUE, Denis; French business executive; b. 7 Jan. 1952, Marseille; s. of Joseph Ranque and Charlotte Gassier; m. Monique Pfeiffer 1972; two s. three d.; fmrly with Industry Ministry; joined Thomson group as Head of Planning 1983, fmrly Dir-Gen. Thomson Tubes Electroniques, fmrly Pres., Man. Dir Thomson Sintra ASM, Pres. Thomson Marconi Sonar 1996–98, Head Thomson-CSF 1998–, Thales 1998–; Chevalier Légion d'honneur, Chevalier ordre nat. du Mérite. *Leisure interest:* music. *Address:* Thales, 173 boulevard Haussmann, 75415 Paris cedex 08 (Office); 27 avenue des Hubies, 92420 Vaucressan, France (Home). *E-mail:* denis.ranque@thalesgroup.com (Office).

RANTANEN, Juha Ilari, MSc, MBA; Finnish business executive; b. 25 Jan. 1952, Helsinki; m. Eija Jaaskelainen 1975; three s. one d.; ed Helsinki School of Econs, Int. Man. Inst., Geneva; Man., Internal Accounting, Neste Oy 1977–78, Planning Man. 1979–81, Exec. Vice-Pres., Gas 1986–89, Chemicals 1989–92, Chief Financial Officer 1992–94; Product Line Man., Covering Materials, Partek Oy 1981–84, Vice-Pres., Insulations 1984–86; CEO Borealis A/S 1994–97; Exec. Vice-Pres. Ahlstrom Corpn 1997–98, Pres., CEO 1998–. *Address:* Ahlstrom Corporation, PO Box 329, Etelaesplanadi 14, 00101 Helsinki, Finland (Office). *Telephone:* (10) 8884700 (Office). *Fax:* (10) 8884728 (Office). *E-mail:* juha.rantanen@ahlstrom.com (Office). *Website:* www .ahlstrom.com (Office).

RANTANEN, Paavo Ilmari, M.SC.POL.; Finnish diplomatist and business executive; b. 28 Feb. 1934, Jyväskylä; s. of Vilho Rantanen and Jenny Auer; m. Ritva Lehtinen 1956; two s. one d.; ed Univ. of Helsinki and Acad. for Int. Law, The Hague; entered Ministry of Foreign Affairs 1958; served Vienna, Belgrade and Paris 1958–71; Counsellor, Finnish Embassy, Brussels and Mission of Finland to EC, Brussels 1971–73; Counsellor, Deputy Chief of Special Mission of Finland to CSCE, Geneva 1973–74; Amb.-at-Large 1974–76; Ministry of Foreign Affairs 1976–81; Perm. Rep. of Finland, UN Orgs Geneva 1981–86; Amb. to USA 1986–88; mem. Exec. Bd Int. Relations and Trade Policy, Nokia Group 1988–95, April–Dec. 1995; Minister of Foreign Affairs Feb.–April 1995; Chair Finnish Inst. for Int. Trade 1996–; mem. numerous bds. *Address:* Confederation of Finnish Industry and Employers, Eteläranta 10, 00130 Helsinki (Office); Laivurinkatu 39 A 4, 00150 Helsinki, Finland (Home). *Telephone:* (9) 68681 (Office); (9) 6221285 (Home). *Fax:* (9) 68682316 (Office).

RANTZEN, Esther, OBE, MA; British television presenter, producer and writer; b. 22 June 1940; d. of Harry Rantzen and Katherine Rantzen; m. Desmond Wilcox 1977 (died 2000); one s. two d.; ed North London Collegiate School and Somerville Coll. Oxford; studio man. making dramatic sound effects, BBC Radio 1963; presenter, That's Life, BBC TV 1973–94, scriptwriter 1976–94; producer, The Big Time (documentary series) 1976; presenter, Esther Interviews . . . 1988, Hearts of Gold 1988, 1996, Drugwatch, Childwatch, The Lost Babies (also producer), Esther (talk show) 1994–, The Rantzen Report 1996–, That's Esther 1999–; mem. Nat. Consumer Council 1981–90, Health Educ. Authority 1989–95; Chair. ChildLine; Pres. Asscn of Youth with ME 1996–; numerous charitable activities; Hon. DLitt (South Bank Univ.) 2000; BBC TV Personality of 1975, Variety Club of GB; Richard Dimbleby Award, BAFTA 1988, Snowdon Award for Services to Disabled People 1996, Royal TV Soc. Hall of Fame Award 1997, Champion Community Legal Service 2000. *Publications:* Kill the Chocolate Biscuit (with D. Wilcox) 1981, Baby Love 1985, The Story of Ben Hardwick (with S. Woodward) 1985, Once Upon a Christmas 1996, Esther: The Autobiography 2001, A Secret Life 2003. *Leisure interests:* work and fantasy. *Address:* Billy Marsh Associates, 174–178 North Gower Street, London, NW1 2NB, England. *Telephone:* (20) 7388-6858.

RAO, Calyampudi Radhakrishna, MA, ScD, FNA, FRS; Indian statistician; b. 10 Sept. 1920, Hadagali, Mysore State; s. of C. D. Naidu and A. Laxmikanthamma; m. Bhargavi Rao 1948; one s. one d.; ed Andhra and Calcutta Univs; Research at Indian Statistical Inst. 1943–46, Cambridge Univ. 1946–48; Prof. and Head of Div. of Theoretical Research and Training 1949–64; Dir Research and Training School, Indian Statistical Inst. 1964–71, Sec. and Dir 1972–76, Jawaharlal Nehru Prof. 1976–84; Univ. Prof., Univ. of Pittsburgh 1979–88; Nat. Prof., India 1987–92; Eberly Prof. of Statistics, Pennsylvania State Univ. 1988–91, Prof. Emer. 1991–; Ed. Sankhya 1964–80, Journal of Multivariate Analysis 1988–92; Fellow, Inst. of Mathematical Statistics, USA, Pres. 1976–77; Treas. Int. Statistical Inst. 1961–65, Pres. 1977–79; Pres. Int. Biometric Soc. 1973–75; Pres. Forum for Interdisciplinary Math.; mem. NAS; Hon. Fellow, Royal Statistical Soc., American Acad. of Arts and Sciences; Fellow, American Statistical Asscn, Econometric Soc., Third World Acad. of Sciences; Hon. Prof. Univ. of San Marcos, Lima; Foreign mem. Lithuanian Acad. of Sciences; Hon. mem. Int. Statistical Inst., Inst. of Combinatorics and Applications; Hon. Foreign mem. American Acad. Arts and Sciences; Hon. Fellow, King's Coll., Cambridge Univ.; Hon. Life mem. Biometric Soc.; Hon. DSc (24 univs); Hon. DLitt (Delhi); Emanuel and Carol Parzen Prize for Statistical Innovation; Bhatnagar Memorial Award for Scientific Research; Padma Vibhushan; Guy Silver Medal Royal Statistical Soc., Meghnad Saha Medal, Nat. Science Acad., J. C. Bose Gold Medal, Wilks Memorial Medal, Calcutta Univ. Gold Medal, Mahalanobis Birth Centenary Gold Medal, Army Wilks Medal, Sankhyiki Bhushan, Pres.'s Nat. Medal for Science, USA 2002. *Publications include:* Advanced Statistical Methods in Biometric Research, Linear Statistical Inference and its Application, Generalized Inverse of Matrices and its Applications, Characterization Problems of Mathematical Statistics 1973, Estimation of Variance Components and its Applications (with J. Kleffe) 1988, Statistics and Truth 1989, Choquet Deny Type Functional Equations with Applications to Stochastic Models (with D. N Shanbhaq) 1994, Linear Models: Least Squares and Alternatives (with H. Toutenburg) 1995, Matrix Algebra and Its Applications to Statistics and Econometrics (with M. B. Rao) 1998; over 350 research papers in mathematical statistics. *Leisure interest:* writing humorous essays. *Address:* Department of Statistics, Pennsylvania State University, 326 Thomas Bldg, University Park, PA 16802 (Office); 826 West Aaron Drive, State College, PA 16803, USA (Home). *Telephone:* (814) 865-3194 (Office); (814) 234-6209 (Home). *Fax:* (814) 863-7114 (Office); (814) 234-0372 (Home). *E-mail:* crr1@ psu.edu (Office).

RAO, Chintamani Nagesa Ramachandra, DSc, PhD, FNA, FRS; Indian professor of chemistry; b. 30 June 1934, Bangalore; s. of H. Nagesa Rao; m. Indumati Rao 1960; one s. one d.; ed Mysore, Banaras and Purdue Univs; Lecturer, Indian Inst. of Science, Bangalore 1959–63; Prof. later Sr Prof., Indian Inst. of Tech., Kanpur 1963–77, Dean of Research and Devt 1969–72; Chair. Solid State and Structural Chem. Unit and Materials Research Lab., Indian Inst. of Science 1977–84, Dir of Inst. 1984–94; Albert Einstein Research Prof. and Pres. Jawaharlal Nehru Centre for Advanced Scientific Research 1994–99, Linus Pauling Research Prof. and Hon. Pres. 1999–; Visiting Prof. Purdue Univ., USA 1967–68, Oxford Univ. 1974–75; Prof. IISc, Bangalore; Fellow King's Coll. Cambridge Univ. 1983–84; Past Pres. IUPAC; fmr Chair. Science Advisory Council to Prime Minister of India; mem. editorial bds of 15 int. journals; Foreign mem. Serbian and Slovenian Acads. of Science, Yugoslavia, NAS, Russian, Czechoslovak and Polish Acads of Sciences, Pontifical Acad. of Sciences, American Acad. of Arts and Sciences, Royal Spanish Acad. of Sciences, French Acad. of Sciences, American Philosophical Soc., Materials Socs of Japan and Korea, Int. Acad. of Ceramics; Founding mem. Third World Acad. of Sciences; Corresp. mem. Brazilian Acad. of Sciences; Titular mem. European Acad. of Arts, Sciences and Humanities; Foreign mem. Academia Europaea; fmr Pres. Indian Acad. of Sciences; Past Pres. Indian Nat. Science Acad., St Catherine's Coll., Oxford 1974–75; American Chem. Soc. Centennial Foreign Fellow 1976; Jawaharlal Nehru Fellow, Indian Inst. of Tech.; Nehru Visiting Prof., Cambridge Univ.; Linnett Visiting Prof., Cambridge Univ. 1998; Blackett Lecturer, Royal Soc. 1991, NAS Int. Science Lecture, USA 1993, Hallim Distinguished Lecturer, Korean Acad. of Science and Tech. 1999; Hon. Foreign mem. Korean Acad. of Science and Tech.; Hon. mem. Japan Acad.; Hon. Fellow Royal Soc. of Chemistry 1989, Univ. of Wales, Cardiff 1997; Hon. DSc (Purdue Univ., USA), (Bordeaux) 1982, 1983, (Sri Venkateswara) 1984, (Roorkee) 1985, (Benares) 1986, (Osmania, Mangalore) 1986, (Manipur) 1987, (Anna, Mysore, Burdwan) 1988, (Wrocław) 1989, (Wales) 1994, (Notre Dame) 1996, (I.I.T., Bombay) 1997, (Russian Acad. of Sciences, Siberian Br.) 1999; Royal Soc. of Chem. Medal (London) 1981, Marlow Medal, Faraday Soc. 1967, Bhatnagar Award 1968, Padma Shri 1974, Fed. of Indian Chamber of Commerce and Industry Award for Physical Sciences 1977, Sir C. V. Raman Award 1978, S. N Bose Medal of Indian Nat. Science Acad. 1980, Jawaharlal Nehru Award 1988, Hevrovsky Gold Medal, Czechoslovakia 1989, CSIR Golden Jubilee Prize 1991, Sahabdeen Int. Award of Science, Sri Lanka 1994, Third World Acad. of Sciences Medal 1995, Albert Einstein Gold Medal, UNESCO 1996, Asutosh Mookerjee Medal 1996, Shatabdi Puraskar, Indian Scientific Congress 1999, Commdr Nat. Order of Lion, Senegal 1999, Centenary Lectureship and Medal, Royal Soc. of Chem. 2000, Hughes Medal, Royal Soc. 2000, Millennium Plaque of Honour, Indian Science Congress 2000; Padma Vibhushan 1984. *Publications:* Ultraviolet Visible Spectroscopy 1960, Chemical Applications of Infra-red Spectroscopy 1963, Spectroscopy in Inorganic Chemistry 1970, Modern Aspects of Solid State Chemistry 1970, Solid State Chemistry 1974, Educational Technology in Teaching of Chemistry 1975, Phase Transitions in Solids 1978, Preparation and Characterization of Materials 1981, The Metallic and Non-Metallic States of Matter 1985, New Directions in Solid State Chemistry 1986, Chemistry of Oxide Superconductors 1988, Chemical and Structural Aspects of High Temperature Oxide Superconductors 1988, Bismuth and Thallium Superconductors 1989, Chemistry of Advanced Materials 1992, Chemical Approaches to the Synthesis of Inorganic Materials 1994, Transition Metal Oxides 1995, Colossal Magnetoresistance 1998, Understanding Chemistry 1999; more than 1,000 original research papers. *Leisure* *interests:* gourmet cooking, general reading, music. *Address:* Jawaharlal Nehru Centre for Advanced Scientific Research, Jakkur P.O., Bangalore 560064 (Office); JNC President's House, Indian Institute of Science Campus, Bangalore 560012, India (Home). *Telephone:* (80) 8563075 (Office); (80) 3601410 (Home). *Fax:* (80) 8462760. *E-mail:* cnrrao@jncasr.ac.in (Office).

RAO, Raja; Indian writer; b. 21 July 1909; ed Nizam Coll., Hyderabad, Univs of Montpellier and Paris; Prof. of Philosophy, Univ. of Texas –1980, Prof. Emer. 1980–; Neustadt Int. Prize for Literature 1988. *Publications:* Kanthapura, Cow of the Barricades, The Serpent and The Rope, The Policeman and the Rose (short stories in French and English), The Cat and Shakespeare, Comrade Kirillov, The Chessmaster and his Moves 1988 (novels), On the Ganga Ghat (stories) 1989. *Address:* c/o Department of Philosophy, College of Humanities at Austin, University of Texas, Austin, TX 78712, USA.

RAO BIN; Chinese business executive; b. 1928, Jilin Prov. ed. Shanghai Univ.; joined CCP 1949; Vice-Minister of Machine Bldg 1960–82; Gen. Man., China Nat. Automotive Industry Corpn 1993–. *Address:* China National Automotive Industry Corporation, 12 Fuxing Menwai Street, Beijing 100860, People's Republic of China.

RAOULT, Eric, L. ÈS SC.ECON.; French politician; b. 19 June 1955, Paris; m. Béatrice Abollivier 1990; ed Inst. d'Etudes Politiques, Paris and Inst. Français de Presse; Parl. Asst to Claude Labbé; Town Councillor, Raincy 1977; Deputy Mayor of Raincy 1983–95, Mayor 1995–; mem. Cen. Cttee of RPR 1982–; Deputy to Nat. Ass. 1986–1995, Vice-Pres. 1993–95, 2002–; Regional Councillor, Ile de France 1992; Minister of Integration and the Fight against Exclusion May–Nov. 1995, Deputy Minister with responsibility for Urban Affairs and Integration 1995–97; Nat. Sec. with responsibility for elections 1998–99, with responsibility for Feds and Dom-Tom 1999–2002 (RPR). *Address:* Mairie, 93340 Le Raincy, France.

RÂPEANU, Valeriu; Romanian literary critic, historian and editor; b. 28 Sept. 1931, Ploiestiori, Prahova Co.; s. of Gheorghe and Anastasia Râpeanu; m. Sanda Marinescu 1956; one s.; ed Univ. of Bucharest; journalist 1954–69; Vice-Chair. of the Romanian Cttee of Radio and TV 1970–72; Dir Mihai Eminescu Publishing House, Bucharest 1972–90; Prof. Spinu Haret Univ., Bucharest; mem. Romanian Writers' Union; fmr mem. Cen. Cttee Romanian CP; mem. Int. Assoc. of Literary Critics. *Publications:* the monographs George Mihail-Zamfirescu 1958, Al. Vlahuţă 1964, Noi şi cei dinaintea noastră (Ourselves and Our Predecessors) 1966, Interferenţe spirituale (Spiritual Correspondences) 1970, Călător pe două continente (Traveller on Two Continents) 1970, Pe drumurile tradiţiei (Following Traditions) 1973, Interpretări si înţelesuri (Interpretations and Significances) 1975, Cultură si istorie (Culture and History), two Vols 1979, 1981; Tărâmul unde nu ajungi niciodată (The Land You Could Never Reach) 1982, Scriitori dintre cele două războaie (Writers between the two World Wars) 1986, La vie de l'histoire et l'histoire d'une vie 1989, N Iorga, Mincea Eliade, Nae Ionescu 1993, N Iorga 1994; Vols by Nicolae Iorga, Gh. Brătianu, Al. Kiriţescu, Cella Delavrancea, Marcel Mihalovici, I. G. Duca, Gh.I. Brătianu, George Enescu, C. Rădulescu-Motru, C. Brâncuşi; anthology of Romanian drama; essays on François Mauriac, Jean d'Ormesson, Marcel Proust, Aaron Copland, André Malraux, Jean Cocteau. *Leisure interests:* music, art. *Address:* Str. Mecet 21, Bucharest, Romania.

RAPHAEL (pseudonym of Rafael Martos); Spanish singer; b. Jaén; m. Natalia Figueroa 1972; two s. one d.; first prize winner at Salzburg Festival children's singing competition aged 9; subsequently won numerous other competitions; began professional career in Madrid nightclub 1960; first best-selling record Los Hombres Lloran También 1964; rep. of Spain, Eurovision Song Contest 1966, 1967; U.S. debut 1967; toured USSR 1968, Japan 1970, Australia 1971; Broadway debut 1974; celebrated 25th anniversary as professional singer with open-air concert at Bernabé Stadium, Madrid 1985; appearances in 16 feature films including Cuando Tú No Estás 1966, The Hobo 1968; has sold 220 million records; 250 Gold Discs, 21 Platinum Discs etc. *Address:* c/o Arie Kaduri Agency, Inc., 16125 NE 18th Avenue, North Miami Beach, FL 33162, USA.

RAPHAEL, Farid; Lebanese politician and banker; b. 28 Oct. 1933, Dlebta, Kesrouan; s. of Elie Raphael and Evelyne Khalife; m. Ilham Abdel Ahad 1970; one s. three d.; ed Univ. of St Joseph, Beirut, Univ. of Lyons, France; with Cie Algérienne de Crédit et de Banque, Beirut 1956–67; Founder and Gen. Man. Banque Libano-Française S.A.L. 1967–79, Chair. and Gen. Man. 1979–; Founder and Vice-Pres. Banque Libano-Française (France) SA (now Banque Française de l'Orient SA), Paris 1976–85, Chair. and Gen. Man. 1985–89, Adviser to BFO-France 1989–; Minister of Justice, Finance, Posts, Telephones and Telecommunications 1976–79. *Address:* Banque Libano-Française, B.P. 11-808, Immeuble Liberty Plaza, Hamra, Beirut (Office); Rue St Charles, Imm. Colette Eddé, Brazilia, Hazmieh, Beirut, Lebanon (Home). *Telephone:* (1) 340350. *Fax:* (1) 340355 (Office). *E-mail:* blf100@dm.net.lb (Office). *Website:* www.eblf.com (Office).

RAPHAEL, Frederic Michael, MA, FRSL; American writer; b. 14 Aug. 1931, Chicago, Ill.; s. of Cedric Michael Raphael and Irene Rose Mauser; m. Sylvia Betty Glatt 1955; two s. one d.; ed Charterhouse, St John's Coll., Cambridge; Lippincott Prize 1961, Prix Simone Genevors 2000; U.S. Acad. Award 1966, Royal TV Soc. Award 1976. *Publications:* novels: Obbligato 1956, The Earlsdon Way 1956, The Limits of Love 1960, Lindmann 1963, Orchestra and Beginners 1967, Like Men Betrayed 1970, April, June and November 1972,

California Time 1975, The Glittering Prizes 1976, Heaven and Earth 1985, After the War 1988, A Wild Surmise 1991, A Double Life 1993, Old Scores 1995, Coast to Coast 1998, All His Sons 1999; short stories: Sleeps Six 1979, Oxbridge Blues 1980, Think of England 1986, The Hidden I (illustrated by Sarah Raphael) 1990, The Latin Lover and Other Stories 1994, biography: Somerset Maugham and his World 1977, Byron 1982; essays: Cracks in the Ice 1979, Of Gods and Men (illustrated by Sarah Raphael) 1992, France, the Four Seasons 1994, The Necessity of Anti-Semitism 1997, Historicism and its Poverty 1998, Karl Popper 1998, Personal Terms 2001, The Benefits of Doubt 2002; translations: Catullus (with K. McLeish) 1978, The Oresteia of Aeschylus 1979, Aeschylus (complete plays, with K. McLeish) 1991, Euripides' Medea (with K. McLeish) 1994, Euripides: Hippolytus-Bacchae (with K. McLeish) 1997, Sophocles Aias (with K. McLeish) 1998, Bacchae 1999; screenplays: Nothing But the Best 1965, Darling 1966, Far from the Madding Crowd 1968, Two for the Road 1968, Richard's Things 1980, Oxbridge Blues 1984, After the War 1989, The Man in the Brooks Brothers Shirt (ACE award 1991), Armed Response 1995, Eyes Wide Shut 1998; plays: From the Greek 1979, The Daedalus Dimension (radio) 1982, The Thought of Lydia (radio) 1988, The Empty Jew (radio) 1993, Eyes Wide Open. *Leisure interests:* tennis, bridge. *Address:* c/o Deborah Rogers, Rogers, Coleridge & White, 20 Powis Mews, London, W11 1JN, England.

RAPLEY, C. G., PhD, FRAS; British geophysicist and astronomer; b. 8 April 1947, West Bromwich; s. of Ronald Rapley and Barbara Helen Rapley (née Stubbs); m. Norma Rapley; two d. (twins); ed King Edward's School, Bath, Jesus Coll. Oxford, Victoria Univ. of Manchester, Univ. Coll. London; Head of Remote Sensing, Mullard Space Science Lab., Univ. Coll. London 1982–94, Prof. of Remote Sensing 1991–97, Hon. Prof. 1998–; Exec. Dir Int. Geosphere-Biosphere Programme, Stockholm 1994–97; Dir British Antarctic Survey 1998–; Fellow St Edmund's Coll. Cambridge 1999–; mem. American Geophysical Union; Assoc. Fellow Remote Sensing and Photogrammetry Soc.; Hon. Prof. Univ. of E Anglia 1999–, Univ. Coll. London 1999–. *Publications:* over 120 articles and papers in professional scientific literature. *Leisure interests:* digital photography, jogging. *Address:* Director's Office, British Antarctic Survey, High Cross, Madingley Road, Cambridge, CB3 0ET (Office); Flat 3, 51 Bateman Street, Cambridge, CB2 1LR, England (Home). *Telephone:* (1223) 221524 (Office). *Fax:* (1223) 350456 (Office). *E-mail:* cgr@bas.ac.uk (Office); christopher.rapley@ntlworld.com (Home). *Website:* www.antarctica.ac.uk (Office).

RAPOSO, Mario; Portuguese politician; b. Jan. 1929, Coimbra; ed Univ. of Coimbra; Sub-Insp. for Social Assistance and Sec. to Minister of Finance, resgnd to practise law 1955; mem. Gen. Council, Ordem dos Advogados (Law Soc.) 1972–74, Chair. 1975–77; mem. Exec. Cttee First Nat. Congress of Lawyers 1972, Cttee for Judicial Reform, High Court of Justice 1974; Minister of Justice, Third Constitutional Govt; mem. Ass. of the Repub. 1978–79, for Social Democratic Party (PSD) Dec. 1979–; Minister of Justice 1980–81, 1985–87; mem. Council of State 1991–. *Address:* c/o PSD, Rua de São Caetano 9, 1296 Lisbon Codex, Portugal.

RAPOTA, Lt.-Gen. Grigory Alekseyevich; Russian security official and government official; b. 5 Feb. 1944, Moscow; m.; three c.; ed Moscow Bauman Higher School of Tech., Inst. of Intelligence Service; mem. First Chief Dept of KGB; served in USA and Finland; Deputy Dir Intelligence Service Russian Fed. 1994–98; Deputy Sec. Security Council April–Nov. 1998; Dir Gen. Rosvooruzheniye state co. 1998–99; First Deputy Minister of Econ. Devt and Trade 1999–2000; First Deputy Minister of Industry, Science and Tech. 2000–01. *Address:* c/o POB A-47, Miusskaya pl. 3, 125889 Moscow, Russia (Office).

RAPP, Bernard André, LenD; French journalist, producer and television presenter; b. 17 Feb. 1945, Paris; m. Gaëlle Bayssière 1996; one s. one d.; freelance journalist, Combat and Le Monde (dailies); Chief Writer Donneurs de sang de France et d'Outre-Mer (review) 1968; Founder Notre Epoque (review) 1968–71; Editorial Dir Les Informations (review) 1971–75; Chief Writer Conquêtes (review) 1975–76; Chief Reporter Antenne 2 (renamed France 2) 1976–81, London Corresp. 1981–83, Presenter of 8 o'clock News 1983–87, Producer-Presenter L'assiette anglaise 1987–89, Tranche de cake 1989–90, My télé is rich 1990, Caractères 1990–91, Le circle du cinéma 1997–98; Producer-Presenter France-Régions 3 (FR3) (renamed France 3 1992), Caractères 1991–92, Jamais sans mon livre 1993–94, Planète chaude 1993–94, Rapptout 1994, Les cinq continents 1994–95; Dir, Producer and Presenter Un Siècle d'écrivains (documentary series) 1995–; Columnist, Le Parisien 1986; Presenter, Découvertes (Europe 1) 1987–89, Les mots pour le dire (France-Inter) 1990; fmr Ed.-in-Chief Mystère Magazine; Chevalier, Ordre nat. du Mérite; Gold Medal for Best TV Presenter of Current Affairs 1987, for Best Journalist or Reporter 1988, for Best Artistic or Cultural Magazine for L'assiette anglaise 1989, Antenne de cristal 1988, Grand prix nat. de la culture 1999. *Films directed include:* Tiré à part (Prix du Scénario, Festival d'Arcachon 1996, Federico Fellini Prize, Festival de Cattolica 1997) 1997, Une affaire de goût (Grand prix, Festival du film policier de Cognac 2000) 2000. *Publications:* L'eau et les hommes (screenplay), Angleterre, Ecosse, Pays de Galles 1987, Quality: Objets d'en face 1988 (jtly), Le dictionnaire mondial des films (jtly) 1989. *Address:* France 3, 7 esplanade Henri de France, 75907 Paris cedex 15, France (Office).

RAPPENEAU, Jean-Paul; French film director and screenplay writer; b. 8 April 1932, Auxerre, Yonne; s. of Jean Rappeneau and Anne-Marie (Bornhauser) Rappeneau; m. Claude-Lise Cornély 1971; two s.; ed Lycée Jacques-Amyot, Auxerre, Faculté de droit, Paris; Asst Dir 1953–57; wrote screenplays for Signé Arsène Lupin 1959, Le Mariage (in La Française et l'Amour) 1959, Zazie dans le métro 1960, Vie privée 1961, Le Combat dans l'île 1961, L'Homme de Rio 1962; Chevalier Légion d'honneur, Officier Ordre Nat. du Mérite, Commdr des Arts et Lettres; 10 César Awards 1990 (including Best Dir, Best Picture), Golden Globe Award for best foreign film 1990, US Nat. Review Bd Best Foreign Film 1990, Grand Prix Nat. du Cinéma 1994. *Films directed include:* short films: La Maison sur la place, Chronique provinciale 1958; wrote and directed La Vie de château 1966 (Prix Louis-Delluc), Les Mariés de l'An Deux 1970, Le Sauvage 1975, Tout feu, tout flamme 1982; Dir and Jt adaptor Cyrano de Bergerac 1990, Le Hussard sur le toit 1995, Bon Voyage 2002. *Address:* c/o Artmédia, 20 avenue Rapp, 75007 Paris (Office); 24 rue Henri Barbusse, 75005 Paris, France.

RAPSON, Ralph, MArch; American architect; b. 13 Sept. 1914, Alma, Mich.; s. of Frank and Mable (née Nickols) Rapson; m. Mary Dolan; two s.; ed Alma (Mich.) Coll., Univ. of Mich. Coll. of Architecture and Cranbrook Acad. of Art; practising architect 1941–; f., now proprietor Ralph Rapson and Assocs; Head Dept of Architecture Chicago Inst. of Design 1942–46; Assoc. Prof. of Architecture MIT School of Architecture 1946–54 (leave of absence to execute designs in Europe for State Dept 1951–53); Prof. and Head of School of Architecture, Univ. of Minnesota 1954–84; Visiting Prof. Univ. of Va; mem. American Inst. of Architects, Int. Congress of Modern Architecture; Dir Walker Art Gallery; fmr Chair. Editorial Bd Northwest Architect; numerous awards include Parker Medal 1951, American Inst. of Architects Honor Award for US Embassy, Stockholm 1954, two Merit Awards 1955, Honour Award 1958. *Designs include:* projects for US Government, several churches and schools, commercial, industrial and residential bldgs, particularly US Embassy, Stockholm, US Embassy, Copenhagen, US Consulate, Le Havre, St Peter's Lutheran Church (Edinburgha, Minn.), Fargo (ND) Civic Center, St Paul (Minn.) Arts and Science Center, American Embassy, Beirut, Dr William G. Shepherd House, St Paul, Tyrone Guthrie Repertory Theatre, Minn. (Designs also executed for Embassies at Athens, The Hague and Oslo). *Address:* Ralph Rapson & Assocs., 409 Cedar Avenue, Minneapolis, MN 55454 (Office); 1 Seymour Avenue, Minneapolis, MN 55404, USA (Home).

RASHEED, Natheer al-; Jordanian business executive and civil servant; b. 19 June 1929, Salt; s. of Ahmad al-Rasheed and Sahah al-Hiary; m. Rabia al-Rasheed 1961; four s. one d.; ed mil. courses with British Army and Staff Coll.; Dir-Gen. Intelligence in Jordan 1969–73; Chief, Bd of Dirs Jordan Mines Phosphate Co. 1976; Senator 1989–; recipient of three medals. *Leisure interests:* horse-riding (polo), shooting. *Address:* PO Box 6583, Amman, Jordan. *Telephone:* (6) 893102/3 (Office); (6) 5523366 (Home). *Fax:* (6) 893117.

RASHID, Ahmed; Pakistani journalist and author; b. 1948, Rawalpindi; m.; three c.; ed Univ. of Cambridge, UK; currently Pakistan, Afghanistan and Cen. Asia Corresp. The Daily Telegraph, Far Eastern Economic Review; writes regularly for several Pakistani newspapers and magazines; broadcaster on TV and radio stations around the world, including BBC World Service, ABC Australia, Radio France Int. and German Radio; Nisar Osmani Award for Courage in Journalism. *Publications include:* The Resurgence of Central Asia: Islam or Nationalism, Fundamentalism Reborn: Afghanistan and the Taliban, Jihad: The Rise of Militant Islam in Central Asia. *Address:* The Daily Telegraph, 1 Canada Square, Canary Wharf, London, E14 5DT, England (Office). *Telephone:* (20) 7538-5000 (Office). *Fax:* (20) 7513-2506 (Office). *E-mail:* dtnews@telegraph.co.uk (Office). *Website:* www.telegraph.co.uk (Office).

RASHID, Hussain; Malaysian stockbroker and banker; fmrly with London Stock Exchange; est. own brokerage house 1983; est. Rashid Hussain group of financial services companies 1996, ceded control 1998; Chair. Exec. Cttee Khazanah Govt holding co. *Address:* c/o D.C.B. Bank Bhd., Menara T.R., 18th Floor, 161B Jalan Ampang, P.O. Box 10145, 50907 Kuala Lumpur, Malaysia. *Telephone:* (3) 2612444. *Fax:* (3) 2619541. *E-mail:* webmaster@moe.gov.sa (Office). *Website:* www.moe.gov.sa (Office).

RASHID, Muhammad ibn Ahmad ar-, PhD; Saudi Arabian politician and academic; b. 1944, Al-Majma'a; m.; five s. two d.; ed Imam Mohammed Bin Saud Islamic Univ., Riyadh, Univ. of Indiana, Univ. of Oklahoma; teacher Inst. of Religious Studies, Riyadh 1964–65; Grad. Asst Coll. of Shari'a and Islamic Studies, Makkah 1965–66; sent on mission to USA by King Abdulaziz Univ. 1966–72; Asst Prof. King Saud Univ. 1972–79, Assoc. Prof. 1979–89, Vice-Dean Coll. of Educ. 1974–76, Dean 1976–79; Dir-Gen. Arab Bureau of Educ. for Gulf States 1979–88; Founder of Arab Gulf States Univ. and Vice-Pres. of Founding Cttee 1979–88; Prof. of Educ. King Saud Univ. 1989–94; mem. Saudi Nat. Council 1994–95; Minister of Educ. 1995–; Distinguished Fulbright Fellow 1988–89, Distinguished Fellow World Council for Teacher Training 1989; Gold Medal of Merit (Arab League Educ. Cultural and Scientific Org.). *Publications:* numerous articles and research papers in professional journals. *Leisure interests:* walking, swimming, reading. *Address:* Ministry of Education, P.O. Box 3734, Airport Road, Riyadh 11481, Saudi Arabia. *Telephone:* (1) 402-9500. *Fax:* (1) 404-1391. *E-mail:* webmaster@moe.gov.

RASI, Satu Marjatta, LLB; Finnish diplomatist; b. 29 Nov. 1945, Punkalaidun; m.; ed Helsinki Univ.; Attaché Finnish Diplomatic Service 1970, Second Sec., London 1972–73; Paris 1974–76, Sec. of Section, Ministry of Foreign Affairs 1977; Counsellor Perm. Mission to the UN 1979; Counsellor,

Ministry of Foreign Affairs 1983–86, Dir UN Section, Political Dept 1986; Deputy Perm. Rep. to the UN 1987–91, Perm. Rep. 1999–; Chair. Security Council Cttee responsible for monitoring sanctions regime against Iraq 1990; Amb. to India (also Accred to Bangladesh, Sri Lanka, Nepal and Bhutan) 1991–95, Dir. Devt Co-operation, Ministry of Foreign Affairs 1995–98. *Address:* Permanent Mission of Finland to the United Nations, 866 United Nations Plaza, Suite 222, New York, NY 10017, USA (Office). *Telephone:* (212) 355-2100 (Office). *Fax:* (212) 759-6156 (Office). *E-mail:* finland@un.int. *Website:* www.un.int/finland.

RASI-ZADE, Artur Tair oglu; Azerbaijani politician and engineer; b. 26 Feb. 1935, Gyanja; m.; one d.; ed Azerbaijan Inst. of Industry; engineer, Deputy Dir Azerbaijan Inst. of Oil Machine Construction 1957–73, Dir 1977–78; chief engineer Trust Soyuzneftemash 1973–77; Deputy Head Azerbaijan State Planning Cttee 1978–81; Head of section Cen. Cttee of Azerbaijan CP 1981–86; First Deputy Prime Minister 1986–92; adviser Foundation of Econ. Reforms 1992–96; Asst to Pres. Aliyev Feb.–May 1996; First Deputy Prime Minister May–Nov. 1996; Prime Minister Nov. 1996–. *Address:* Council of Ministers, Lermontov str. 68, 370066 Baku, Azerbaijan. *Telephone:* (12) 980008.

RASMUSSEN, Anders Fogh; Danish politician; b. 26 Jan. 1953; m.; three c.; ed Econ. Univ. of Århus; Consultant to Danish Fed. of Crafts and Small Industries 1978–87; mem. Folketing (Parl.) 1978–, mem. Fiscal Affairs Cttee 1982–87, Vice-Chair. 1994–98; Vice-Chair. Housing Cttee 1981–86; Minister for Taxation 1987–92, also for Econ. Affairs 1990–92; Vice-Chair. Econ. and Political Affairs Cttee 1993–98; Prime Minister of Denmark 2001–; mem. Venstre (Liberal Party), Vice-Chair. Nat. Org. Venstre 1985–98, mem. Man. Cttee Parl. party 1984–87, 1992–2001, Spokesman for Venstre 1992–98, Vice-Chair. Foreign Policy Bd 1998–2001, Chair. Venstre 1998–; Grand Cross of the Portuguese Order of Merit 1992, Commdr (First Degree) of the Order of the Dannebrog 2002, Grand Cross of the German Order of Merit 2002; Danish Gold Medal of Merit 2002; Dr hc (George Washington Univ.) 2002. *Publications:* Oprør med skattesystemet 1979, Kampen om boligen 1982, Fra Socialstat til Minimalstat 1993. *Address:* Office of the Prime Minister, Christiansborg, Prins Jørgens Gård 11, 1218 Copenhagen K, Denmark (Office). *Telephone:* 33-92-33-00 (Office). *Fax:* 33-11-16-65 (Office). *E-mail:* stm@stm.dk (Office). *Website:* www.stm.dk (Office).

RASOLONDRAIBE, Gen. Jean Jacques; Malagasy army officer and politician; b. 28 May 1946; s. of Jean Lebo and Adèle Beky; m. Denise Mieah; two s. three d.; career in Madagascan Army, rising to rank of Général de Div.; fmr Minister of the Interior; apptd Prime Minister (interim—during period of disputed presidential elections) of Madagascar March–May 2002; Commdr Nat. Order of Merit, Légion d'honneur (France). *Address:* c/o Office of the Prime Minister, BP 248, Mahazoarivo, 101 Antananarivo, Madagascar (Office).

RASPUTIN, Valentin Grigoriyevich; Russian author; b. 15 March 1937, Ust-Uda (Irkutsk); ed Irkutsk Univ.; first works published 1961; elected People's Deputy 1989; mem. Presidential Council 1990–91; USSR State Prize 1977, 1987; Hero of Socialist Labour 1987. *Publications:* I Forgot to Ask Lyosha 1961, A Man of This World 1965, Bearskin for Sale 1966, Vasilii and Vasilisa 1967, Deadline 1970, Live and Remember, Stories, 1974, Parting with Matera 1976, Live and Love 1982, Fire 1985, Collected Works (2 vols) 1990, Siberia, Siberia 1991. *Address:* 5th Army Street 67, Apt 68, 664000 Irkutsk, Russia. *Telephone:* (3952) 4-71-00.

RASSADIN, Stanislav Borisovich; Russian literary critic; b. 4 March 1935, Moscow; s. of Boris Matveyevich Rassadin and Varvara Georgievna Rassadin; m. Alina Yegorovna Petukhova-Yakunina 1962; ed Moscow Univ. *Publications include:* Poetry of Recent Years 1961, Nikolai Nosov: A Bio-Critical Account 1961, Talk with the Reader: Essay on Literature 1962, The Role of the Reader 1965, Linden Alley 1966, Pushkin the Dramatist 1977, Fonvizin 1980, The Test with a Show: Poetry and Television 1984, Suppositions about Poetry 1988, The Genius and the Villainy or the Case of Sukhovo-Kobylin 1989, After the Flood 1990, I am Choosing Freedom 1990, Very Simple Mandelstam 1994, Russians (Russkiye, ili iz dvoryan v intelligenty) 1995, Bulat Okudzhava 1999. *Leisure interest:* work. *Address:* Kosygina Street 5, Apt. 335, 117334 Moscow, Russia. *Telephone:* (095) 137-81-84.

RATHBONE, Julian, BA; British writer; b. 10 Feb. 1935, London; s. of Christopher Fairrie Rathbone and Decima Doreen Frost; ed Claysmore School, Magdalene Coll., Cambridge; teacher of English, Ankara, London, W Sussex 1959–73; full-time writer 1973–; contrib. The Times, The New Statesman, Literary Review, The Guardian, The Independent, The Sunday Telegraph, The Times Literary Supplement; Swanage Int. Poetry Prize, Crime Writers Short Story Silver Dagger, Deutsche Krimi Preis. *Publications:* thirty novels, poetry, radio plays and screenplays, including: King Fisher Lives 1976, Joseph 1979, A Last Resort 1980, A Spy of the Old School 1982, Wellington's War 1984 (non-fiction), Nasty, Very 1984, Lying in State 1985, Intimacy 1995, Blame Hitler 1997, The Last English King 1997, Brandenburg Concerto 1998, Kings of Albion 2000, Homage 2001, A Very English Agent 2002. *Leisure interests:* music, painting, film, books. *Address:* Sea View, School Road, Thorney Hill, near Christchurch, Dorset, BH23 8DS, England. *Telephone:* (1425) 673313. *Fax:* (1425) 673313. *E-mail:* julesrathbone@supanet.com (Home).

RATHER, Dan, BA; American broadcaster and journalist; b. Oct. 1931, Wharton, Tex.; m. Jean Goebel; one s. one d.; ed Sam Houston State Coll., Univ. of Houston, Tex., S. Tex. School of Law; writer and sports commentator with KSAM-TV; taught journalism for one year at Houston Chronicle; with CBS 1962; with radio station KTRH, Houston for about four years; News and Current Affairs Dir CBS Houston TV affiliate KHOU-TV late 1950s; joined CBS News 1962; Chief London Bureau 1965–66; worked in Viet Nam; White House 1966; anchorman CBS Reports 1974–75; co-anchorman 60 Minutes CBS-TV 1975–81; anchorman Dan Rather Reporting CBS Radio Network 1977–; co-ed. show Who's Who CBS-TV 1977; anchorman Midwest desk CBS Nat. election night 1972–80; CBS Nat. Political Consultant 1964–; anchorman Man. Ed. CBS Evening News with Dan Rather 1981–, Co-anchorman 1993–; anchored numerous CBS News Special Programmes, including coverage of presidential campaigns in 1982 and 1984; as White House corresp. accompanied Pres. on numerous travels including visits to Middle East, USSR, People's Repub. of China; ten Emmy awards; numerous acad. honours; Distinguished Achievement for Broadcasting Award, Univ. of S. Calif. Journalism Alumni Asscn, Bob Considine Award 1983. *Publications:* The Palace Guard 1974 (with Gary Gates), The Camera Never Blinks Twice (with Mickey Herskowitz) 1977, I Remember (with Peter Wyden) 1991, The Camera Never Blinks Twice: The Further Adventures of a Television Journalist 1994. *Address:* CBS News, 524 West 57th Street, New York, NY 10019, USA (Office).

RATHKE, Most Rev. Heinrich Karl Martin Hans, DTheol; German ecclesiastic; b. 12 Dec. 1928, Mölln, Kreis Malchin; s. of Paul and Hedwig (née Steding) Rathke; m. Marianne Rusam 1955; six s. one d.; ed Univs of Kiel, Erlangen, Tübingen and Rostock; parish priest, Althof bei Bad Doberan 1954–55, Warnkenhagen, Mecklenburg 1955–62, Rostock Südstadt 1962–70; Priest in charge of community service and people's mission, Mecklenburg 1970–71; Bishop of the Evangelical-Lutheran Church of Mecklenburg 1971–84; Presiding Bishop of the United Evangelical Lutheran Church of the GDR 1977–81; Pastor in Crivitz/Mecklenburg 1984–91; Bishop and Pastor Emer. 1991–; Asst Bishop, Evangelical-Lutheran Church of Kazakhstan 1991–93; Hon. DTheol (Rostock) 1999. *Publication:* Ignatius von Antiochien und die Paulusbriefe 1967, Gemeinde heute und morgen 1979, Einstehen für Gemeinschaft in Christus 1980, Kirche unterwegs 1995, Predigthilfen (3 vols) 1998–2000, Märtyrer, Vorbilder für das Widerstehen 2002. *Address:* Schleifmühlenweg 11, 19061 Schwerin, Germany. *Telephone:* (385) 562887.

RATNAM, Mani; Indian film director and screenwriter; b. 1956, Madras; s. of 'Venus' Gopalrathnam; m. Suhasini Hassan; one s.; ed Madras Univ., Jamnalal Bajaj Inst., Mumbai; fmr man. consultant; worked for TVS Sudaram; f. Madras Talkies film production co. *Films include:* Pallavi Anu Palavi 1983, Mauna Ragam 1986, Nayakan 1987, Agni Nakshatram 1988, Gitanjali 1989, Anjali 1990, Roja 1992, Thiruda Thiruda 1993, Bombay 1994, Dalpati 1995, Chor Chor 1996, Iruvar 1996, Dil Se 1998, Alay Payuthe 2000, Kannathil Mutham Ittal (A Peck of the Cheek) 2002. *Address:* 1 Murrey Gate Road, Alwarpet, Chennai 600018, India (Office).

RATNER, Gerald Irving; British business executive; b. 1 Nov. 1949; s. of Leslie Ratner and Rachelle Ratner; m. 1st (divorced 1989); two d.; m. 2nd Moira Ratner; one s. one d.; ed Town and Country School, London; Man. Dir Ratners Group 1984, Chair. 1986–91, CEO 1986–92, Dir –1992; Dir (non-exec.) Norweb 1991; consultant Tobacco Dock 1993–; Dir Workshop Health and Fitness Club 1997–. *Leisure interests:* keeping fit, chess, art, cycling. *Address:* Hampton Lodge, Church Road, Bray, Berks., SL6 1UP, England.

RATSIRAHONANA, Norbert; Malagasy politician; Pres. Constitutional High Court –1996; Prime Minister of Madagascar 1996–97; Leader Ny asa vita no ifampitsara (AVI) party 1997–. *Address:* c/o Office of the Prime Minister, B.P. 248, Mahazoarivo, 101Antananarivo, Madagascar.

RATSIRAKA, Adm. Didier; Malagasy politician and naval officer; b. 4 Nov. 1936, Vatomandry; ed Coll. Saint Michel, Tananarive (now Antananarivo), Lycée Henri IV, Paris, Ecole Navale, Lanveoc-Poulmic (France), Ecole des Officiers 'Transmissions', Les Bormettes and Ecole Supérieure de Guerre Navale, Paris; had several naval postings 1963–70; Mil. Attaché, Paris 1970–72; Minister of Foreign Affairs 1972–75; Pres. Supreme Council of Revolution June 1975–; Prime Minister and Minister of Defence June–Dec. 1975; Pres. Democratic Repub. of Madagascar 1976–93 (relinquished exec. powers Aug. 1991), 1997–2002; Pres. Avant-garde de la révolution malgache 1976–, (renamed Association pour la renaissance de Madagascar 1997–), Front nat. pour la défense de la révolution socialiste malgache 1977–; Hon. Citizen, New Orleans, USA 1981. *Publications:* Stratégies pour l'an 2000. *Address:* c/o Présidence de la République, Antananarivo, Madagascar.

RATTANAKOSES, Gen. Mana; Thai politician; b. 16 Sept. 1925, Nakhon Phanom Muang Dist; s. of Luang Apibal Bancha; m. Pol Col Chalerm; four c.; ed Chulachomklao Royal Mil. Acad.; mil. career until 1986; MP for Nakhon Prov. 1986–; fmr Deputy Educ. Minister; Minister of Educ. 1988–90; Deputy Prime Minister Sept.–Dec. 1990; Co-Founder, Sec.-Gen. Rassadorn Party. *Address:* c/o Office of the Deputy Prime Minister, Rassadorn Party, Bangkok, Thailand.

RATTLE, Sir Simon, Kt, CBE; British conductor; b. 19 Jan. 1955, Liverpool; m. 1st Elise Ross 1980 (divorced 1995); two s.; m. 2nd Candace Allen 1996; ed Royal Acad. of Music; won John Player Int. Conducting Competition 1973; has conducted Bournemouth Symphony, Northern Sinfonia, London Philhar-

monic, London Sinfonietta, Berlin Philharmonic, LA Philharmonic, Stockholm Philharmonic, Vienna Philharmonic, Philadelphia Orchestra, Boston Symphony orchestras, etc.; début at Queen Elizabeth Hall, London 1974, Royal Festival Hall, London 1976, Royal Albert Hall, London 1976; Asst Conductor, BBC Symphony Orchestra 1977; Assoc. Conductor, Royal Liverpool Philharmonic Soc. 1977–80; Glyndebourne début 1977, Royal Opera, Covent Garden début 1990; Artistic Dir, London Choral Soc. 1979–84; Prin. Conductor and Artistic Adviser, City of Birmingham Symphony Orchestra (CBSO) 1980–90, Music Dir 1990–98; Artistic Dir South Bank summer music 1981–83; Jt Artistic Dir Aldeburgh Festival 1982–93; Prin. Guest Conductor, LA Philharmonic 1981–94, Rotterdam Philharmonic 1981–84; Prin. Guest Conductor Orchestra of the Age of Enlightenment 1992–; Chief Conductor and Artistic Dir Berlin Philharmonic Orchestra 2002–; more than 30 recordings with CBSO; Hon. DMus (Liverpool) 1991, (Leeds) 1993; Hon. Fellow St Anne's Coll. Oxford 1991; Edison Award (for recording of Shostakovich's Symphony no. 10) 1987, Grand Prix du Disque (Turangalîla Symphony) 1988, Grand Prix Caecilia (Turangalîla Symphony, Jazz Album) 1988, Gramophone Record of the Year Award (Mahler's Symphony no. 2) 1988, Gramophone Opera Award (Porgy and Bess) 1989, Int. Record Critics' Award (Porgy and Bess) 1990, Grand Prix de l'Acad. Charles Cros 1990, Gramophone Artist of the Year 1993, Montblanc de la Culture Award 1993, Toepfer Foundation Shakespeare Prize (Hamburg) 1996, Gramophone Award for Best Concerto recording (Szymanowski Violin Concertos Nos. 1 and 2), Albert Medal (RSA) 1997, Choc de l'Année Award (for recording of Brahms Piano Concerto op. 15) 1998, Outstanding Achievement Award, South Bank Show 1999, Diapason Recording of the Year Award (complete Beethoven Piano Concertos) 1999, Gramophone Award for Best Opera Recording (Szymanowski's King Roger) 2000, Gramophone Awards for Best Orchestral Recording and Record of the Year (Mahler's Symphony No. 10) 2000; Officier des Arts et des Lettres 1995. *Address:* Berlin Philharmonie Orchestra, Philharmonie, Matthäckirchstrasse 1, 14057 Berlin, Germany (Office); c/o Askonas Holt Ltd, Lonsdale Chambers, 27 Chancery Lane, London, WC2A 1PF, England. *Telephone:* (20) 7400-1700. *Fax:* (20) 7400-1799.

RATTNER, Steven Lawrence, AB; American financial executive; b. 5 July 1952, New York; s. of George Seymour Rattner and Selma Ann Silberman; m. P. Maureen White 1986; three s. one d.; ed Brown Univ.; Asst to James Reston, New York Times Corresp., Washington, New York and London 1974–82; Assoc. Vice-Pres. Lehman Brothers Kuhn Loeb, New York 1982–84; Assoc. Vice-Pres., Prin., Man. Dir then Head communications group Morgan Stanley and Co., New York 1984–89; Man. Dir then Head communications group Lazard Frères and Co. 1989–97, Deputy CEO and Deputy Chair. 1997–99; Man. Prin. Quadrangle Group LLC 2000–; Dir Falcon Cable Holding Group 1993–98; mem. Bd Dirs Cablevision, Global Energy Decisions, Pathfire, Inc., Publishing Group of America, MusicNet; mem. Man. Cttee Access Spectrum LLC; Dir New York Outward Bound Center 1990–2001, mem. Advisory Council 2001–; Harvey Baker Fellow, Brown Univ. 1974; Poynter Fellow Yale Univ. 1979; mem. Council on Foreign Relations; Assoc. mem. Royal Inst. for Int. Affairs; Trustee Brown Univ. 1987–93, 1994–2000 (Fellow 2000–), Educational Broadcasting Corpn 1990– (Vice-Chair. 1994–98, Chair. 1998–), Metropolitan Museum of Art 1996–, Brookings Inst. 1998–. *Publications:* contrib. to various news publs including New York Times, Wall Street Journal, Los Angeles Times, Newsweek and Financial Times. *Address:* 998 Fifth Avenue, New York, NY 10028, USA (Home).

RATUSHINSKAYA, Irina Borisovna; Russian poet; b. 4 March 1954; m. Igor Gerashchenko 1979; ed Odessa Pedagogical Inst.; teacher Odessa Pedagogical Inst. 1976–83; arrested with husband, Moscow 1981; lost job, arrested again, 17 Sept. 1982, convicted of 'subverting the Soviet regime' and sentenced 5 March 1983 to seven years' hard labour; strict regime prison camp Aug. 1983; released Sept. 1986; settled in UK 1986; f. Democracy and Independence Group April 1989–; poetry appeared in samizdat publs, West European Russian language journals, MusicNet; trans. in American and British press and in USSR 1989–. *Publications include:* Poems (trilingual text) 1984, No, I'm Not Afraid 1986, Off Limits (in Russian) 1986, I Shall Live to See It (in Russian) 1986, Grey Is the Colour of Hope 1989, In the Beginning 1990, The Odessans 1992, Fictions and Lies 1998. *Address:* c/o Vargius Publishing House, Kazakova str. 18, 107005 Moscow, Russia. *Telephone:* (095) 785-09-62.

RATZINGER, HE Cardinal Joseph Alois; German ecclesiastic; b. 16 April 1927, Marktl; s. of Joseph Ratzinger and Maria Peintner; ed Univ. of Munich; Chaplain 1951; Prof. of Theology, Freising 1958, Bonn 1959, Münster 1963, Tübingen 1966, Regensburg 1969; Archbishop 1977; cr. Cardinal 1977; Archbishop of Munich-Freising; Titular Bishop of Velletri-Segni; Chair. Bavarian Bishops' Conf.; Prefect, Sacred Congregation for the Doctrine of the Faith Nov. 1981–; Pres. Int. Theological Comm., Pontifical Biblical Comm.; Vice-Deacon, Collegio Cardinalizio Nov. 1998–; mem. Secr. Synod of Catholic Bishops 1983–; mem. Congregation for Public Worship 1985–; Dr hc (Navarra) 1998. *Publications:* books and articles on theological matters. *Address:* Palazzo del S. Uffizio II, 00193 Rome, Italy; Vatican City 00120. *Telephone:* (06) 69883357; (06) 69883296 (Vatican). *Fax:* (06) 69883409.

RAU, Johannes; German politician; b. 16 Jan. 1931, Wuppertal; s. of Ewald and Helene (Hartmann) Rau; m. Christina Delius 1982; one s. two d.; mem. North Rhine-Westphalian Diet 1958–98, Minister-Pres. North Rhine-Westphalian Land 1978–98; Chair. North Rhine-Westphalian Parl. Group Social Democratic Party (SPD) 1967–70, mem. Exec. Bd 1968–98, Chair. Dist Bd 1977–98, mem. Presidency 1978–98, Deputy Chair. 1982–98, Chair. Dist

–1998; Pres. Bundesrat 1982–83, 1994–95; Pres. of Germany 1999–; Lord Mayor, City of Wuppertal 1969–70; Minister of Science and Research, North Rhine-Westphalia 1970–78; Dr hc (Düsseldorf) 1985, (Open Univ. UK) 1986, (Haifa) 1986, (Theological Acad. Budapest of the Reformed Church, Hungary) 1987, (Fernuniversität, Ruhr-Universität Bochum, Ben Gurion Univ. of the Negev, Technion–Israel Inst. of Tech., Middle East Tech. Univ., Ankara); Leo Baeck Prize 1995, Kulturpreis Europa 1997, Leo Baeck Medal, Leo Baeck Inst., New York. *Publications:* Oberstufenreform und Gesamthochschule 1970 (co-author), Die neue Fernuniversität 1974, Friede als Ernstfall 2001, Geschichte in Portraits 2001, Dialog der Kulturen – Kultur des Dialogs 2002. *Leisure interests:* stamp-collecting, especially Israeli stamps, literature, art. *Address:* Office of the Federal President, 11010 Berlin, Schloss Bellevue (Office); Spreeweg 1, 10557 Berlin, Germany. *Telephone:* (30) 20000. *Fax:* (30) 20001999 (Office). *E-mail:* poststelle@bpra.bund.de (Office). *Website:* www .bundespraesident.de (Office).

RAUSCH, Jean-Marie Victor Alphonse; French politician; b. 24 Sept. 1929, Sarreguemines, Moselle; s. of Victor Rausch and Claire Hessemann; m. 2nd Nadine Haven 1980; two s. by first m.; ed Lycée de Sarreguemines and Ecole française de meunerie, Paris; Dir Moulin Rausch, Woippy 1953–76; Admin. Soc. Anonyme des Moulins Rausch, Woippy 1976–77; Pres. departmental milling syndicate 1967–81; Pres. Millers' Union of Moselle 1974–80; Conseiller-Gen. Metz III 1971, 1976, 1982–88, Pres. of Council 1979–82; Mayor of Metz 1971–; Pres. Lorraine Regional Council 1982–92; mem. Nat. Statistical Council 1979, Conseil Nat. du Crédit 1984; numerous other civic, public and professional appts; Minister of Foreign Trade 1988–91, of Foreign Trade and Tourism 1990–91, of Posts and Telecommunications 1991–92; Deputy Minister attached to Minister of Econ. and Finance in charge of Commerce and Labour April–Oct. 1992; Senator (Moselle) 1974–83, 1983–88, 1992–; Pres. Médiaville 1995–, Metz-interactive 1995–; Grand Prix de la littérature micro-informatique 1987. *Publication:* Le laminoir et la puce: la troisième génération industrielle 1987. *Leisure interests:* photography, skiing. *Address:* Sénat, Palais du Luxembourg, 75291 Paris cedex 06; Mairie de Metz, B.P. 21025, 57036 Metz Cedex (Office); 4 rue Chanoine Collin, 57000 Metz, France (Home). *Telephone:* (3) 87-55-51-50. *Fax:* (3) 87-74-73-80. *E-mail:* jmr@mairie-metz.fr (Office).

RAUSCHENBERG, Robert; American artist; b. 22 Oct. 1925, Port Arthur, Tex.; s. of Ernest and Dora Rauschenberg; m. Susan Weil 1950 (divorced 1952); one s.; ed Kansas City Art Inst., Acad. Julien, Paris, Black Mountain Coll., North Carolina and Art Students League, New York; travel in Italy and North Africa 1952–53; Designer of stage-sets and costumes for Merce Cunningham Dance Co. 1955–65, lighting for Cunningham Dance Co. 1961–65; costumes and sets for Paul Taylor Dance Co. 1957–59; Choreography in America 1962–; affiliated with Leo Castelli Gallery, New York City 1957–, Sonnabend Gallery, New York and Paris; works in Tate Gallery, London, Albright-Knox Gallery, Buffalo, Whitney Museum of American Art, New York City, Andrew Dickson White Museum, Cornell Univ., Museum of Modern Art, NY, Goucher Coll. Collection, Towson, Maryland, Cleveland Museum of Art, Cleveland, Ohio, Kunstsammlung, Noedheim, Westfalen, Germany, etc.; numerous one-man shows in USA and Europe; exhbn at Stedelijk Museum, Amsterdam 1968; travelling retrospective exhbn organized by Smithsonian Inst. Nat. Collection of Fine Art 1976–78, retrospective exhbn Staatliches Kunstmuseum, Berlin 1980, Kuala Lumpur Nat. Art Gallery 1990, LA Museum of Contemporary Art 1995–97, Guggenheim Museum 1998; mem. American Acad. and Inst. of Arts and Letters; First Prize Int. Exhbn of Prints, Gallery of Modern Art, Ljubljana 1963, Venice Biennale 1964, Corcoran Biennial Contemporary American Painters 1965, Grammy Award 1984. *Address:* Pace Wildenstein Gallery, 32 East 57th Street, New York, NY 10022, USA.

RAVALOMANANA, Marc; Malagasy politician and business executive; b. 1950; ed in Imerikasina and in Sweden; owns TIKO (dairy and oil producing co.); fmr Mayor of Antananarivo; following disputed victory in presidential elections Dec. 2001, declared himself Pres. of Madagascar Feb. 2002, High Constitutional Court ruled that he had won by an overall majority May 2002, Pres. of Madagascar 2002–; Vice-Pres. Protestant Church of Madagascar.

RAVEN, Peter Hamilton, PhD; American botanist, administrator and educator; b. 13 June 1936, Shanghai, China; s. of Walter Raven and Isabelle (née Breen) Raven; m. Tamra Engelhorn 1968; one s. three d.; ed Univ. of California, Berkeley and Univ. of California, L.A; Nat. Science Foundation Postdoctoral Fellow, British Museum, London 1960–61; Taxonomist, Rancho Santa Ana Botanical Garden, Claremont, Calif. 1961–62; Asst Prof., then Assoc. Prof. of Biological Sciences, Stanford Univ. 1962–71; Dir Mo. Botanical Garden 1971–, Engelmann Prof. of Botany, Washington Univ., St Louis, Mo. 1976–; Adjunct Prof. of Biology, Univ. of Mo., St Louis 1973–; Chair. Nat. Museum Services Bd 1984–88; mem. Nat. Geographic Soc. Comm. on Research and Exploration 1982, Governing Bd Nat. Research Council 1983–86, 1987–88, Bd World Wildlife Fund (USA) 1983–88, NAS Comm. on Human Rights 1984–87, Smithsonian Council 1985–90; Home Sec. NAS 1987–95; Pres. Org. for Tropical Studies 1985–88; Fellow, American Acad. of Arts and Sciences, Calif. Acad. of Sciences, AAAS, Linnean Soc. of London and John D. Raven and Catherine T. MacArthur Foundation Fellow, Univ. of Missouri 1985–90; Foreign mem. Royal Danish Acad. of Sciences and Letters, Royal Swedish Acad. of Sciences; several hon. degrees; Distinguished Service Award, American Inst. of Biological Sciences 1981; Int. Environmental Leadership Medal of UNEP 1982, Int. Prize in Biology, Japanese Govt, Pres.'s Conservation Achievement Award 1993, Field Museum of Natural History

Centennial Merit Award 1994; other awards and prizes. *Publications:* Papers on Evolution (with Ehrlich and Holm) 1969, Biology of Plants 1970, Principles of Tzeltal Plant Classification 1974, Biology 1985, Modern Aspects of Species (with K. Iwatsuki and W. J. Bock) 1986, Understanding Biology (with G. Johnson) 1988; more than 400 professional papers; Ed.: Coevolution of Animals and Plants 1975, Topics in Plant Population Biology 1979, Advances in Legume Systematics 1981, Biology (with G. B. Johnson) 1986, Understanding Biology 1988; contrib. to many other publs. *Leisure interests:* reading, collecting plants. *Address:* Missouri Botanical Garden, 4344 Shaw, Boulevard, St Louis, MO 63110, USA. *Telephone:* (314) 577-5111. *Fax:* (314) 577-9595.

RAVENSDALE, 3rd Baron, cr. 1911; Nicholas Mosley, MC; British writer; b. 25 June 1923; s. of the late Sir Oswald Mosley and of Lady Cynthia Curzon; m. 1st Rosemary Salmond 1947 (divorced 1974, died 1991); three s. one d.; m. 2nd Verity Bailey (née Raymond) 1974; one s.; ed Eton, Balliol Coll., Oxford. *Publications:* (novels) Accident 1964, Impossible Object 1968, Natalie, Natalia 1971, Catastrophe Practice 1979 (three plays and a short novel), Hopeful Monsters (Whitbread Book of the Year 1990), Children of Darkness and Light 1996, Inventing God 2003; (biographies) Rules of the Game: Sir Oswald and Lady Cynthia Mosley 1896–1933 1982, Beyond the Pale 1933–1980 1983, Efforts at Truth (autobiog.) 1994. *Address:* 2 Gloucester Crescent, London, NW1 7DS, England. *Telephone:* (20) 7485-4514.

RAVERA, Denis, LLM; Monegasque civil servant and sports official; b. 8 June 1948, Monaco; m.; one c.; joined Monaco Civil Service 1971, Sec. to Dept of Public Works and Social Affairs 1971–79, Chief Sec. 1979–84, Dir-Gen. 1984–91; Chef de Cabinet Minister of State 1991, Counsellor, Chargé du Cabinet 2000; Sec.-Gen. Féd. Monégasque de la Natation, Conféd. Mondiale des Sports de Boules; Vice-Pres. Bobsleigh Section, Monaco Sports Asscn; mem. Monaco Olympic Cttee; Officier, Légion d'honneur, Ordre de Saint-Charles; Médaille en vermeil de l'Educ. Physique et des Sports. *Address:* Ministère de l'Etat, Monte Carlo, Monaco.

RAVIER, Paul-Henri, LenD; French international organization official and civil servant; b. 9 Sept. 1948, Lyon; s. of the late Philibert André Ravier and of Roselyne Marie Bellon; m. Martine Caffin; one s.; ed Inst. d'Etudes Politiques, Ecole Nat. d'Admin.; joined Trade Dept, Ministry of the Economy and Finance, in charge of bilateral trade relations with SE Asia and Middle East, later Head of Trade Finance Policy Unit, Asst Dir responsible for man. of bilateral trade relations with Eastern Europe, Asia, the Pacific and the Middle East 1985–90, Deputy Sec. 1991–99; adviser on int. econ. issues to Prime Minister Raymond Barre 1980; Jt Deputy Head World Trade Org. 1999–2002; mem. Bd Agence Française de Développement 1993–99, SNECMA 1994–99, Pechiney 1993–97; Chevalier Ordre Nat. du Mérite 1993, Légion d'honneur 1998. *Leisure interests:* golf, skiing, mountain climbing, cooking, wine tasting. *Address:* 2 avenue Frédéric le Play, 75007 Paris, France (Home). *Telephone:* 1-45-55-42-46. *Fax:* 1-45-56-10-15 (Home). *E-mail:* phravier@noos.fr (Home).

RAVITCH, Diane, PhD; American historian; b. 1 July 1938, Houston, Tex.; d. of Walter Cracker and Ann Celia (née Katz) Silvers; m. Richard Ravitch 1960 (divorced 1986); three s. (one deceased); ed Wellesley Coll. and Columbia Univ.; Adjunct Asst Prof. of History and Educ. Teachers' Coll., Columbia Univ. 1975–78, Assoc. Prof. 1978–83, Adjunct Prof. 1983–91; Dir Woodrow Wilson Nat. Fellowship Foundation 1987–91; Chair. Educational Excellence Network 1988–91; Asst Sec. Office of Research and Improvement Dept of Educ., Washington 1991–93, Counsellor to Sec. of Educ. 1991–93; Visiting Fellow Brookings Inst. 1993–94, Brown Chair in Educ. Policy 1997–; Sr Research Scholar NY Univ. 1994–98, Research Prof. 1998–; Sr Fellow Progressive Policy Inst. 1998–; Adjunct Fellow Manhattan Inst. 1996–; Trustee New York Historical Soc. 1995–98, New York Council on the Humanities 1996–; mem numerous public policy bodies; Hon. DHumLitt (Williams Coll.) 1984, (Reed Coll.) 1985, (Amherst Coll.) 1986, (State Univ. of New York) 1988, (Ramopo Coll.) 1990, (St Joseph's Coll., NY) 1991; Hon. LHD (Middlebury Coll.) 1997, (Union Coll.) 1998. *Publications:* The Great School Wars: New York City 1805–1973 1974, The Revisionists Revised 1978, The Troubled Crusade: American Education 1945–1980 1983, The Schools We Deserve 1985, What Do Our 17-Year-Olds Know? (with Chester E. Finn, Jr) 1987, The American Reader (ed.) 1990, The Democracy Reader (ed. with Abigail Thernstrom) 1992, National Standards in American Education 1995, Debating the Future of American Education (ed.) 1995, Learning from the Past (ed. with Maris Vinovskis) 1995, New Schools for a New Century (ed. with Joseph Viteretti) 1997, Left Back 2000, City Schools (ed.) 2000; 300 articles and reviews. *Address:* New York University, 26 Washington Square East, New York, NY 10003, USA. *Telephone:* (212) 998-5146.

RAVONY, Francisque; Malagasy politician and barrister; fmr First Deputy Prime Minister, Transitional Govt; Prime Minister of Madagascar 1993–95, also fmr Minister of Finance and Budget; currently Minister of Defence; Leader Cttee for the Support of Democracy and Devt in Madagascar; Chair. Union des Forces Vives Démocratiques 1998–. *Address:* Ministry of Defence, BP 08, Ampahibe, 101 Antananarivo (Office); Union des Forces Vives Démocratiques, Antananarivo, Madagascar. *Telephone:* (20) 2222211 (Office). *Fax:* (20) 2235420 (Office).

RAWABDEH, Abd ar-Raouf ar-, BSc; Jordanian politician; b. 13 Feb. 1939, Es-Sarih, Irbid; m.; ed American Univ. of Beirut; Minister of Communications 1976–77, of Communications and Health 1977–78, of Health 1978–79, of

Public Works and Housing 1989–91, of Educ. and of State for Prime Minister's Affairs 1994–95; Vice-Pres. Nat. Consultative Council 1982–83 (mem. 1978–83; Chair. Bd of Dirs, Jordan Phosphate Mining Co. 1982–85; lecturer School of Pharmacy, Univ. of Jordan 1982–89; Mayor of Amman 1983–86, of Greater Amman 1987–89; Chair. Bd Dirs Amman Devt Corpn 1983–89; mem. of House of Reps 1989–; Sec.-Gen. Awakening Party (Al-Yakza) 1993–96; Deputy Prime Minister and Minister of Educ. 1995–96; Prime Minister and Minister of Defence 1999–2000; Deputy Sec.-Gen. Nat. Constitutional Party 1996–97; Vice-Chair. Bd of Trustees, Jordan Univ. of Science and Tech.; mem. Jordan Pharmaceutical Asscn 1962–, Royal Soc. for the Conservation of Nature 1994–; Jordan Al-Kawkab Medal (First Degree) 1976, Italian Medal of Honour (Sr Officer) 1983, German Medal of Merit 1984, Al-Nahda Medal (First Degree) 1999. *Publications:* An Outline of Pharmacology, Pharmacy, Democracy, Theory and Application, Education and the Future. *Address:* c/o Office of the Prime Minister, P.O. Box 80, Amman, Jordan (Office).

RAWI, Najih Mohamed Khalil el-, PhD; Iraqi civil engineer, educationalist and government official; b. 4 April 1935, Rawa; m.; one s. two d.; ed Univ. of Wales, Purdue Univ., Oklahoma State Univ.; instructor, Univ. of Baghdad 1967, Asst Prof. of Civil Eng 1971, Prof. 1980; Prof. Emer. 1990–; Dean Higher Inst. of Industrial Eng, Univ. of Baghdad 1968–69; Dean Coll. of Industry (now Tech. Univ.) 1969–70; mem. Bureau of Educ. Affairs, Revolutionary Command Council 1973–74, Council of Higher Educ. 1970–74, 1980–85; Deputy Minister of Municipalities 1974, of Public Works and Housing 1974–77; Minister of Industry and Minerals 1977–78; Vice-Pres. Iraqi Engineers Syndicate 1969–71; Pres. Iraqi Teachers Syndicate 1960–64, Iraqi–Soviet Friendship Soc. 1979–88, Nat. Cttee Tech. and Transfer 1984–89, Man and the Biosphere 1980–89, Int. Geological Correlation Programme 1980–89, Geophysics and Geodesy 1982–89, Council of Scientific Research 1980–89, Iraqi Acad. of Sciences 1996–2001 (mem. 1996–); Head Union of Arab Educators 1983–89; mem. Bd of Trustees, Al-Mustansiryah Univ. 1970–74, Arabian Gulf Univ. 1986–89, Teachers' Union Univ. Coll. 1990–96; mem. Iraq. Eng Soc. 1959, American Soc. of Civil Engineers 1967, Council of the World Fed. of Educators 1973–74, 1979–82; Founding Fellow Islamic Acad. of Sciences 1986; Corresp. mem. Syrian Acad. of Language, Damascus 2001. *Address:* Iraqi Academy of Sciences, Waziriya, A'Adamiah, Baghdad, Iraq (Office). *E-mail:* aos@uruklink.net (Office).

RAWIRI, Georges; Gabonese diplomatist and government official; b. 10 March 1932, Lambaréné; m.; two c.; ed Protestant school, Ngomo and Lycée Jean-Baptiste Dumas, Ales; Head Tech. Centre Garoua Radio Station 1957, Libreville Radio Station 1959; a founder of Radio Gabon 1959; Dir Radiodiffusion Gabonaise 1960, Radio-Télévision Gabonaise 1963; Counsellor for Foreign Affairs 1963; Minister of Information, Tourism, Posts and Telecommunications 1963–64; Minister of State and Amb. to France 1964–71, also Accred to Israel, Italy, Spain, UK, Malta 1965–71 and Switzerland 1967–71; Minister of State for Foreign Affairs and Co-operation 1971–74, of the Govt Office 1974–75, of Transport 1975–79, Civil Aviation 1975–78 and the Merchant Navy 1975–79, Asst to the Deputy Prime Minister 1978–79; Deputy Prime Minister and Minister of Transport 1980–83, First Deputy Prime Minister 1986, Minister for Transport and Public Relations 1983–86, First Deputy Prime Minister, Minister of Rail, Road and Inland Water Transport, Water and Forest Resources and Social Communications 1986–89, Fisheries, Food Resources and Nat. Parks 1989–90; now Pres. Senate; fmr Pres. Compagnie de Manutention et de Chalandage d'Owendo (COMACO); Grand Officer Ordre de l'Etoile Equatoriale and decorations from Mauritania, France, Malta and Côte d'Ivoire; Médaille d'Or des Arts, Sciences et Lettres; Grand Officier Ordre Int. du Bien Public. *Address:* The Senate, Libreville, Gabon (Office).

RAWLINGS, Flight-Lt Jerry; Ghanaian Head of State and air force officer; b. 22 June 1947, Accra; s. of John Rawlings and Madam Victoria Agbotui; m. Nana Konadu Agyeman; one s. three d.; ed Achimota School and Ghana Military Acad., Teshie; commissioned as Pilot Officer 1969, Flight-Lt 1978; arrested for leading mutiny of jr officers May 1979; leader mil. coup which overthrew Govt of Supreme Mil. Council June 1979; Chair. Armed Forces Revolutionary Council (Head of State) June–Sept. 1979; retd from armed forces Nov. 1979, from air force Sept. 1992; leader mil. coup which overthrew Govt of Dr Hilla Limann Dec. 1981; Head of State 1982–2001; Chief of the Defence Staff 1982–2001; Chair. Provisional Nat. Defence Council 1981–93; Pres. of Ghana 1993–2001. *Leisure interests:* boxing, deep-sea diving, swimming, horse riding, carpentry. *Address:* c/o P.O. Box 1627, Osu, Accra, Ghana.

RAWLINS, Surgeon-Vice-Adm. Sir John Stuart Pepys, KBE, FRCP, FFCM, FRAeS; British consultant; b. 12 May 1922, Amesbury, Wilts.; s. of Col Comdt. Stuart W. H. Rawlins and Dorothy P. Rawlins; m. Diana M. Freshney Colbeck 1944; one s. three d.; ed Wellington Coll., Univ. Coll., Oxford and St Bartholomew's Hosp., London; Surgeon-Lt RNVR 1947; Surgeon-Lt RN, RAF Inst. of Aviation Medicine 1951, RN Physiological Lab. 1957; Surgeon-Commdr RAF Inst. of Aviation Medicine 1961, HMS Ark Royal 1964, US Naval Medical Research Inst. 1967–70; Surgeon-Capt. 1969; Surgeon-Cdre, Dir of Health and Research (Naval) 1973; Surgeon-Rear-Adm. 1975; Dean of Naval Medicine and Medical Officer in charge of Inst. of Naval Medicine 1975–77; Acting Surgeon Vice-Adm. 1977; Medical Dir-Gen. (Navy) 1977–80; Hon. Physician to HM The Queen 1975–80; Dir Diving Unlimited Int. Ltd; Pres. Soc. for Underwater Tech. 1980–84; Chair. Deep Ocean Tech. Inc., Deep Ocean Eng Inc. 1982–90, Trident Underwater Systems Inc. 1986–, Gen. Offshore Corpn (UK) Ltd 1988–90, Europa Hosps Ltd; fmr consultant to Chemical Defence Establishment, Porton Down and British Airways PLC; designed first anti-G suit accepted in RN and RAF, first protective helmet for RN and RAF aircrew, designed and developed an aircraft underwater escape system; Hon. Research Fellow, Univ. of Lancaster, Univ. Coll., Oxford; CStJ; Hon. DTech, (Robert Gordon Univ.); numerous awards and medals including Royal Navy's Man of the Year 1964, Gilbert Blane Medal (Royal Coll. of Surgeons) 1971, Chadwick Naval Prize 1975, Nobel Award of Inst. of Explosive Engineers 1987, Acad. of Underwater Arts and Sciences NOGI Award 1996, Lowell Thomas Award, Explorers Club 2000. *Publications:* numerous papers in fields of aviation and diving medicine and underwater tech. *Leisure interests:* fishing, stalking, riding, judo. *Address:* Little Cross, Holne, Newton Abbot, South Devon, TQ13 7RS, England. *Telephone:* (1364) 631249. *Fax:* (1364) 631400. *E-mail:* john-rawlins@beeb.net.

RAWLINS, Peter Jonathan, MA, FCA, FRSA; British business executive and accountant; b. 30 April 1951, London; s. of Kenneth Raymond Ivan Rawlins and Constance Amande Malzy; m. 1st Louise Langton 1973 (divorced 1999); one s. one d.; m. 2nd Christina Conway 2000; one d.; ed St Edward's School and Keble Coll. Oxford; with Arthur Andersen & Co., Chartered Accountants, London 1972–85, partner 1983–85; seconded as Personal Asst to CEO and Deputy Chair. Lloyd's of London 1983–84; Dir Sturge Holdings PLC 1985–89, Man. Dir R. W. Sturge & Co. 1985–89, Dir Sturge Lloyd's Agencies Ltd 1986–89; Dir Wise Speke Holdings Ltd 1987–89; CEO The London Stock Exchange 1989–93; business strategy consultant 1994–; Man. Dir (Europe, Middle East and Africa) Siegel & Gale Ltd 1996–97; Dir Scala Business Solutions NV 1998–2000, Oyster Partners Ltd 2001–. *Leisure interests:* the performing arts, tennis, squash, shooting, travelling. *Address:* 70A Redcliffe Gardens, London, SW10 9HE, England. *Telephone:* (20) 7370-0666. *Fax:* (20) 7341-9691.

RAWLINSON OF EWELL, Baron (Life Peer), cr. 1978, of Ewell in the County of Surrey; **Peter Anthony Grayson Rawlinson,** Kt, PC, QC; British politician and lawyer; b. 26 June 1919, Birkenhead, Cheshire (now Merseyside); s. of Lt-Col A. R. Rawlinson and Ailsa Grayson Rawlinson; m. 1st Haidee Kavanagh 1940; three d.; m. 2nd Elaine Angela Dominguez 1954; two s. one d.; ed Downside and Christ's Coll., Cambridge; served in Irish Guards 1939–46; mentioned in despatches 1943; called to the Bar, Inner Temple 1946, Treas. 1984; mem. of Parl. 1955–78; Recorder of Salisbury 1961–62; Solicitor-Gen. 1962–64; mem. Bar Council 1966–68; Attorney-Gen. 1970–74; Attorney-Gen., Northern Ireland 1972–74; Leader Western Circuit 1975–82; mem. Senate, Inns of Court 1968; Chair. of the Bar 1975–76; Chair. of Senate, Inns of Court and Bar 1975–76, Pres. 1986–87; Recorder of Kingston-upon-Thames 1975–2001; Dir Daily Telegraph PLC 1985–2001; Conservative; Hon. mem. American Bar Asscn; Hon. Fellow, Christ's Coll., Cambridge, American Coll. of Trial Lawyers. *Publications:* War Poems and Poetry today 1943, Public Duty and Personal Faith: the example of Thomas More 1978, A Price Too High (autobiog.) 1989, The Jesuit Factor: A Personal Investigation 1990; novels: The Colombia Syndicate 1991, Hatred and Contempt 1992, His Brother's Keeper 1993, Indictment for Murder 1994, The Caverel Claim 1998, The Richmond Diary 2001. *Leisure interest:* painting. *Address:* Wardour Castle, Tisbury, Wilts., SP3 6RH, England. *Telephone:* (1747) 871900. *Fax:* (1747) 871611 (Home).

RAWNSLEY, Andrew Nicholas James, MA; British journalist, broadcaster and author; b. 5 Jan. 1962, Leeds; s. of Eric Rawnsley and Barbara Rawnsley (née Butler); m. Jane Leslie Hall 1990; three d.; ed Lawrence Sheriff Grammar School, Rugby, Rugby School, Sidney Sussex Coll. Cambridge; with BBC 1983–85, The Guardian 1985–93 (political columnist 1987–93); Assoc. Ed. and chief political columnist The Observer 1993–; Presenter Channel 4 TV series A Week in Politics 1989–97, ITV series The Agenda 1996–, Bye Bye Blues 1997, Blair's Year 1998, The Westminster Hour (radio) 1998–, The Unauthorized Biography of the United Kingdom (radio) 1999; Student Journalist of the Year 1983, Young Journalist of the Year 1987, Columnist of the Year, What the Papers Say Award 2000, Book of the Year Award, Channel 4/House Magazine Political Awards 2001. *Publication:* Servants of the People: The Inside Story of New Labour (Channel 4/Politico Book of the year 2001) 2000. *Leisure interests:* skiing, scuba diving, mah jong, books, cinema, food and wine. *Address:* The Observer, 119 Farringdon Road, London, EC1R 3ER, England. *Telephone:* (20) 7278-2332. *E-mail:* andrewrawnsley@observer.co.uk (Office). *Website:* www.observer.co.uk (Office).

RAWSON, Dame Jessica Mary, DBE, FBA; British archaeologist and college warden; b. 20 Jan. 1943; d. of Roger Quirk and Paula Quirk; m. John Rawson 1968; one d.; ed New Hall, Cambridge and Univ. of London; Asst Prin. Ministry of Health 1965–67; Asst Keeper II, Dept of Oriental Antiquities, British Museum 1967–71, Asst Keeper I 1971–76, Deputy Keeper 1976–87, Keeper 1987–94; Warden, Merton Coll. Oxford 1994–; Visiting Prof. Kunsthistorisches Inst. Heidelberg 1989, Univ. of Chicago 1994; Chair. Oriental Ceramic Soc. 1993–96; Vice-Chair. Bd of Govs, SOAS, London Univ. 1999–; mem. British Library Bd 1999–2003; Hon. DSc (St Andrews) 1997; Hon. DLitt (Sussex) 1998, (Royal Holloway, London) 1998, (Newcastle) 1999. *Publications:* Chinese Jade Throughout the Ages (with J. Ayers) 1975, Animals in Art 1977, Ancient China, Art and Archaeology 1980, Chinese Ornament: the lotus and the dragon 1984, Chinese Bronzes: art and ritual 1987, The Bella and P.P. Chiu Collection of Ancient Chinese Bronzes 1988, Western Zhou Ritual Bronzes from the Arthur M. Sackler Collections 1990, Ancient Chinese and Ordos Bronzes (with E. Bunker) 1990, The British Museum Book of Chinese Art (ed.) 1992, Chinese Jade from the Neolithic to the Qing 1995, The

Mysteries of Ancient China (ed.) 1996, Cosmological Systems and Sources of Art, Ornament and Design 2002. *Address:* Merton College, Oxford, OX1 4JD, England. *Telephone:* (1865) 276352. *Fax:* (1865) 276282.

RAY, Ajit Nath, MA; Indian judge; b. 29 Jan. 1912, Calcutta; s. of Sati Nath Ray and Kali Kumari Debi; m. Himani Mukherjee 1944; one s.; ed Presidency Coll., Calcutta, Oriel Coll., Oxford and Gray's Inn, London; fmrly practised as a barrister, Calcutta High Court; Judge, Calcutta High Court 1957–69; Judge, Supreme Court of India 1969–73, Chief Justice of India 1973–77; Pres. Int. Law Asscn 1974–76, Vice-Pres. 1977–, Vice-Pres. Ramakrishna Inst. of Culture 1981–; mem. Int. Permanent Court of Arbitration 1976–; Pres. Governing Body Presidency Coll., Calcutta 1957–69; Founder-Pres. Soc. for the Welfare of the Blind 1958–80; Treas. Asiatic Soc. 1961–63, Vice-Pres. 1963–65; mem. Karma Samiti Visva Bharati Santiniketan 1963–65, 1967–69, Life mem. 1969–; Hon. Fellow, Oriel Coll., Oxford. *Address:* 15 Panditia Place, Kolkata 700 029, India. *Telephone:* (33) 24541452.

RAY, Robert Francis, BA; Australian politician; b. 8 April 1947, Melbourne; m. Jane Ray; ed Rusden State Coll., Monash Univ.; fmr tech. school teacher; Senator from Victoria 1980–; mem. Australian Labor Party (ALP) Nat. Exec. 1983–98; Minister for Home Affairs and Deputy Man. of Govt Business in the Senate 1987–88, for Transport and Communications Jan.–Sept. 1988, for Immigration, Local Govt and Ethnic Affairs and Minister assisting Prime Minister for Multicultural Affairs 1988–90, for Defence 1990–96; Deputy Leader of Govt in Senate 1993–96. *Leisure interests:* films, billiards, tennis, watching Australian Rules football, golf and cricket. *Address:* Suite 3, Level 2, Illoura Plaza, 424 St Kilda Road, Melbourne, Vic. 3004, Australia.

RAY, Siddhartha Shankar, BA, LLB; Indian politician and lawyer; b. 20 Oct. 1920, Calcutta; s. of the late Sudhir Chandra Ray and Shrimati Aparna Devi (Das); m. Maya Bhattacharya 1947; ed Presidency Coll., Univ. Law Coll., Calcutta; called to the Bar, Inner Temple, London; Sr Advocate, Supreme Court 1969; corporate, commercial and constitutional lawyer; appeared in all Courts in India including the Supreme Court, the East Pakistan High Court, the Pakistan Supreme Court (Dhaka Circuit Bench) and Tribunal of Arbitration, Int. Chamber of Commerce, Paris; mem. West Bengal Legis. Ass. 1957–71, 1972–77, 1991–92; mem. Lok Sabha 1971–72, Jr Cen. Govt Counsel 1954–57; Minister of Law and Tribal Welfare, Govt of West Bengal 1957–58; Leader of the Opposition, West Bengal Ass. 1969–71, 1991–92; Cabinet Minister for Educ., Culture, Social Welfare and West Bengal Affairs, Govt of India 1971–72; Chief Minister of West Bengal 1972–77; Gov. of Punjab and Admin. of Chandigarh 1986–89; Amb. to USA 1992–96; High Commr in the Commonwealth of the Bahamas 1994–; Sec. Gen. Calcutta Univ. Law Coll. Union 1941–43; Under-Sec. Calcutta Univ. Inst. 1941–44; Univ. Blue in cricket, football and tennis; Individual Champion Athletics, Calcutta Univ. Law Coll. 1941, 1942; mem. Working Cttee Indian Nat. Congress, All India Congress Cttee, Congress Parl. Bd; Pres. Cricket Asscn of Bengal 1982–84; mem. Indian Nat. Trust for Art and Cultural Heritage; Trustee Jawaharlal Nehru Memorial Fund (mem. Exec. Cttee); Trustee Nehru Scholarship Trust for Cambridge Univ.; Hon. LLD (Drury Coll., Missouri) 1993. *Leisure interests:* reading, music and sports. *Address:* 2 Beltala Road, Kolkata 700026, India (Home). *Telephone:* (33) 4753465.

RAYES, Ghazi al; Kuwaiti diplomatist; b. 23 Aug. 1935; ed Univ. of Cairo, Egypt; Third Sec. Ministry of Foreign Affairs 1962; Kuwaiti Embassy, Washington and Beirut 1965–67; Chair. Int. Affairs Section, Ministry of Foreign Affairs 1967–70; Counsellor, Kuwaiti Embassy, Beirut 1970–73; Amb. to Bahrain 1974–80, to UK 1980–93, to People's Repub. of China 1993–97; Head, Follow-up and Co-ordination Office and Head, Protocol Dept, Ministry of Foreign Affairs 1997–. *Address:* c/o Ministry of Foreign Affairs, P.O. Box 3, 13001 Safat Gulf Street, Kuwait City, Kuwait.

RAYKHELHAUS, Iosif Leonidovich; Russian stage director; b. 12 June 1947, Odessa, Ukraine; m. Maria Khazina; two d.; ed Moscow Inst. of Theatre Arts; stage Dir Moscow Stanislavsky Theatre 1973; Founder and Artistic Dir School of Contemporary Play theatre 1989–; teacher All-Union Inst. of Cinematography 1997–; Prize of Moscow Festival of Chamber Productions Martenitsa 1991; Merited Worker of Arts 1993. *Productions include:* Salute, Don Juan!, A Man Came to a Woman, The Seagull. *Address:* Moscow Theatre School of Contemporary Play, Neglinnaya str. 29/14, 103031 Moscow, Russia (Office). *Telephone:* (095) 200-09-00 (Office). *Fax:* (095) 200-30-87 (Office).

RAYMOND, Lee R., PhD; American oil company executive; b. 13 Aug. 1938, Watertown, South Dakota; m. Charlene Raymond 1960; ed Univ. of Wisconsin, Univ. of Minnesota; various eng positions Exxon Corpn (now Exxon Mobil Corpn), Tulsa, Houston, New York and Caracas, Venezuela 1963–72; Man. Planning, Int. Co. Div., New York 1972–75; Pres. Exxon Nuclear Co. Div. 1979–81, Exec. Vice-Pres. Exxon Enterprises Inc. Div. 1981–83, Sr Vice-Pres. and Dir Exxon Corpn 1984–86, Pres. and Dir 1987–93, Chair. and CEO 1993–99, Chair., CEO and Pres. 1999–(2003); Vice-Pres. Lago Oil, Netherlands Antilles 1975–76, Pres. and Dir 1976–79; Pres. and Dir Esso Inter-American Inc., Coral Gables, Fla 1983–84, Sr Vice-Pres. and Dir 1984–; mem. Bd Dirs J. P. Morgan & Co. Inc., New York, Morgan Guaranty Trust Co. of New York, American Petroleum Inst.; mem. Bd Dirs Nat. Action Council for Minorities in Eng Inc., New York 1985–, New American Schools Devt Corpn 1991–, Project Shelter PRO-AM 1991–; mem. American Petroleum Inst. (mem. Bd Dirs 1987–), The Business Roundtable, American Council on Germany 1986–, British-N American Cttee 1985–, Visitors' Cttee Univ. of

Wis. Dept of Chem. Eng 1987–, Dallas Cttee on Foreign Relations 1988–, The Conf. Bd 1991–, Bd of Govs, Dallas Symphony Asscn. *Address:* Exxon Mobil, 5959 Las Colinas Boulevard, Irving, TX 75, USA (Office).

RAYMOND, Paul; British publisher, impresario and property owner; b. 15 Nov. 1925; one s. one d. (deceased); ed St Francis Xavier's Coll. Liverpool, Glossop Grammar School, Derbyshire; with RAF 1944–47; musician, impresario, night club propr; owner Raymond's Review Bar, numerous cen. London properties; Publr Mayfair, Men Only, Club Int., Men's World, Razzle, Escort, Model Directory; mem. Grand Order of Water Rats. *Address:* Paul Raymond Organization Ltd, 2 Archer Street, London, W1V 7HF, England. *Telephone:* (20) 734-9191. *Fax:* (20) 7734-5030.

RAYNAUD, Jean-Pierre; French sculptor; b. 20 April 1939, Courbevoie; s. of André Raynaud and Madeleine Dumay; ed Ecole d'Horticulture du Chesnay; first one-man exhbn Galerie Larcade, Paris 1965; numerous other one-man shows in France, Europe, USA, Japan, Israel; retrospective exhbns. The Menil Collection, Houston, Museum of Contemporary Art, Chicago and Int. Centre of Contemporary Art, Montreal 1991, CAPC, Bordeaux 1993, Paume 1998, Jérôme de Noirmont Gallery, Paris 2001; Grand Prix Nat. de Sculpture 1983; Prix Robert Giron, Palais des Beaux Arts, Brussels 1985; Grand Prix de Sculpture de la Ville de Paris 1986, Prix d'honneur de la Biennale de Venise 1993; Officier des Arts et des Lettres, Chevalier du Mérite, Légion d'honneur. *Work includes:* windows at Cistercian Abbey at Noirlac, Cher 1976–77, large sculpture in gardens of Fondation Cartier pour l'Art Contemporain, Jouy-en-Josas 1985, Autoportrait for City of Québec 1987, Container Zero, Pompidou Centre, Paris 1988, Carte du Ciel, Grande Arche, Paris La Défense 1989. *Address:* 12 avenue Rhin et Danube, 92250 La Garenne-Colombes, France.

RAYNE, Baron (Life Peer), cr. 1976, of Prince's Meadow in Greater London; **Max Rayne,** Kt; British company director; b. 8 Feb. 1918, London; s. of Phillip Rayne and Deborah Rayne; m. 1st Margaret Marco 1941 (divorced 1960); one s. two d.; m. 2nd Lady Jane Antonia Frances Vane-Tempest-Stewart 1965; two s. two d.; ed Cen. Foundation School and Univ. Coll.; Royal Air Force 1940–45; Chair. London Merchant Securities PLC 1960–2000, Life Pres. 2000–; Deputy Chair. British Lion Films 1967–72; Deputy Chair. First Leisure Corpn PLC 1984–92, Chair. 1992–95; Dir Housing Corpn (1974) Ltd 1974–78, Dir of other cos; Gov. St Thomas's Hospital 1962–74, Special Trustee 1974–92; Gov. Royal Ballet School 1966–79, Malvern Coll. 1966–, Centre for Environmental Studies 1967–73; mem. Gen. Council King Edward VII's Hospital Fund for London 1966–95; mem. Council St Thomas's Hospital Medical School 1965–82, Council of Govs, United Medical Schools of Guy's and St Thomas's Hospitals 1982–89; mem. RADA Council 1973–, South Bank Bd 1986–92; Chair. London Festival Ballet Trust 1967–75, Nat. Theatre Bd (now Royal Nat. Theatre Bd) 1971–88; f. Patron Rayne Foundation 1962–; f. mem. Motability 1979–96, Life Vice-Pres. 1996; Trustee Henry Moore Foundation 1988–; Hon. Vice-Pres. Jewish Care (fmrly Jewish Welfare Bd) 1966–; Vice-Pres. Yehudi Menuhin School 1987– (Gov. 1966–87); Hon. Fellow, Univ. Coll., London 1966, London School of Econs 1974, Darwin Coll., Cambridge 1966, Royal Coll. of Psychiatrists 1977, King's Coll. Hosp. Medical School 1980, Univ. Coll. Oxford 1982, King's Coll., London 1983, Westminster School 1989, Royal Coll. of Physicians 1992, UMDS, Guy's and St Thomas's 1992; Officier, Légion d'honneur 1987; Hon. LLD, (London) 1968. *Address:* 33 Robert Adam Street, London, W1U 3HR, England. *Telephone:* (20) 7935-3555. *Fax:* (20) 7935-3737.

RAYNES, Edward Peter, MA, PhD, FRS; British physicist; b. 4 July 1945, York; s. of Edward Gordon Raynes and Ethel Mary Raynes; m. Madeline Ord 1970; two s.; ed St Peter's School, York, Gonville and Caius Coll. and the Cavendish Lab., Cambridge; with Royal Signals and Radar Establishment, Malvern 1971–92, Deputy Chief Scientific Officer 1988–92; Chief Scientist Sharp Laboratories of Europe Ltd 1992–98, Dir of Research 1995–98; Visiting Prof., Dept of Eng Science, Univ. of Oxford 1996–98, Prof. of Optoelectronic Eng 1998–; Rank Opto-Electronic Prize 1980, Paterson Medal, Inst. of Physics 1986, Special Recognition Award, Soc. of Information Display 1987. *Publications:* numerous scientific publs and patents; The Physics, Chemistry and Applications of Liquid Crystals (Jt Ed.). *Leisure interests:* choral and solo singing. *Address:* Department of Engineering Science, University of Oxford, Parks Road, Oxford, OX1 3PJ, England. *Telephone:* (1865) 273024. *Fax:* (1865) 273905. *E-mail:* peter.raynes@eng.ox.ac.uk (Office).

RAYNSFORD, Rt Hon Nick (Wyvill Richard Nicolls), PC, MA; British politician; b. 28 Jan. 1945, Northampton; s. of the late Wyvill Raynsford and Patricia Raynsford (née Dunn); m. Anne Jelley 1968; three d.; ed Repton School, Sidney Sussex Coll. Cambridge, Chelsea School of Art and Design; mem. staff Soc. of Co-operative Dwellings (SCD), AC Nielen, Market Research; Dir SHAC, The London Housing Aid Centre 1976–86, Raynsford & Morris, Housing Consultants 1987–92; Councillor, London Borough of Hammersmith & Fulham 1971–75; MP for Fulham 1986–87, for Greenwich 1992–97, for Greenwich and Woolwich 1997–; mem. House of Commons Environment Select Cttee 1992–93; Front Bench Spokesperson for London 1993–94; Shadow Minister for Housing and Construction, Spokesperson for London 1994–97; Parl. Under-Sec. of State, Minister for London and Construction 1997–99; Minister of State for Housing, Planning and London July–Sept. 1999, for Housing and Planning 1999–2001, for Local Govt and the Regions 2001–; mem. Nat. Energy Foundation 1989–93. *Publication:* A Guide to Housing Benefits 1982. *Leisure interests:* walking, photography. *Address:*

House of Commons, London, SW1A 0AA, England (Office). *Telephone:* (20) 7219-2773 (Office). *Fax:* (20) 7219-2619 (Office). *E-mail:* raynsfordn@parliament.uk (Office).

RAZ, Joseph, DPhil, FBA; professor of the philosophy of law; b. 21 March 1939; ed Hebrew Univ. Jerusalem and Univ. of Oxford; lecturer, Faculty of Law and Dept of Philosophy, Hebrew Univ. 1967–71, Sr lecturer 1971–72; Fellow and Tutor in Law, Balliol Coll. Oxford 1972–85, also mem. sub-faculty of philosophy 1977–; Ed. (with Prof. A. M. Honoré), The Clarendon Law Series 1984–92; Prof. of Philosophy of Law, Univ. of Oxford and Fellow, Balliol Coll. 1985–; Visiting Prof., School of Law, Columbia Univ., New York 1995–2002; Prof., Columbia Law School 2002–; Foreign Hon. mem. American Acad. of Arts and Sciences; Dr hc (Katholieke Univ. Brussels) 1994. *Publications:* The Concept of a Legal System 1970, Practical Reason and Norms 1975, The Authority of Law 1979, The Morality of Freedom 1986, Ethics in the Public Domain 1994, Engaging Reason 2000, Value, Respect and Attachment 2001, The Practice of Value 2003. *Address:* Balliol College, Oxford, OX1 3BJ, England. *Telephone:* (1865) 277721. *Fax:* (1865) 277803.

RAZAFINDRATANDRA, HE Cardinal Armand Gaétan; Malagasy ecclesiastic; b. 7 Aug. 1925; ed Inst. Catholique de Paris; ordained priest 1954; parochial and teaching assignments; consecrated Bishop of Majunga 1978; Archbishop of Antananarivo 1994–; Pres. Bishops' Conf. of Madagascar; mem. Sec.-Gen.'s Special Council for Africa; Congregation for Evangelization of Peoples, Pontifical Council for the Laity; cr. Cardinal 1994; Cardinal-Priest, Basilica of Saint Sylvester and Saint Martin of the Hills, Rome 1994. *Address:* Archevêché, B.P. 3030, Andohalo, 101 Antananarivo, Madagascar. *Telephone:* (20) 2220726. *Fax:* (20) 22664181. *E-mail:* ecar.andohaolo@simicro.mg (Office).

RAZAK, Dato Sri Mohamad Najib bin tun Haj Abdul, BA; Malaysian politician; b. 23 July 1954, Kuala Lipis, Pahang; m. Tengku Puteri Zainah bint Tengku Iskandar; three c.; ed Univ. of Nottingham; Exec. Patronas 1974–78; Pengerusi Majuternak 1977–78; MP 1976–; Deputy Minister of Energy, Telecommunications and Posts 1978–80, of Educ. 1980–81, of Finance 1981–82; mem. State Ass. for Pakan constituency 1982; apptd Menteri Besar Pahang 1982; Minister of Culture, Youth and Sports 1986–87, of Youth and Sports 1987–90, of Defence 1990–95, 1999–, of Educ. 1995–99; mem. UMNO Supreme Council 1981–; Vice-Pres. UMNO Youth 1982–; Chair. Pahang Foundation 1982–86; Grand Order of Youth (Korea) 1988, Kt Grand Cross, First Class (Thailand), Bintang Yudha Dharma Utama (Indonesia) 1994, Distinguished Service Order (Singapore) 1994, DUBC (Thailand) 1995 Hon. Ph.D. 1990 Orang Kaya Indera Shahbandar 1976, Darjah Sultan Ahmad Shah 1978, Seri Indera Mahkota Pahang 1983, Darjah Kebesaran Seri Sultan Ahmad Shah 1985, Man of the Year Award, New Straits Times 1990, Panglima Bintang Sarawak 1990, Dato Paduka Mahkota Selangor 1992. *Address:* Ministry of Defence (Kementerian Pertahanan), Wisma Pertahanan, Jalan Padang Tembak, 50634 Kuala Lumpur, Malaysia (Office). *Telephone:* (3) 26921333 (Office). *Fax:* (3) 26914163 (Office). *E-mail:* cpa@mod.gov.my (Office). *Website:* www.mod.gov.my (Office).

RAZALEIGH HAMZAH, Tengku Tan Sri Datuk, PSM, S.P.M.K.; Malaysian politician and fmr company executive; b. c. 1936; s. of late Tengku Mohamed Hamzah bin Zainal Abidin (fmr Chief Minister of Kelantan); ed Queen's Univ., Belfast and Lincoln's Inn, London; Chair. of Kelantan Div. of United Malays' Nat. Org. (UMNO) in early 1960s; mem. Kelantan State Assembly for some years; Exec. Dir Bank Bumiputra 1963, Chair., Man. Dir 1970; Exec. Dir PERNAS 1971–74; Chair. Malaysian Nat. Insurance; led trade mission to Beijing 1971; a Vice-Pres. UMNO 1975; Pres. Assoc. Malay Chambers of Commerce until Oct. 1976; Chair. PETRONAS (Nat. Oil Co.) 1974–76; Minister of Finance 1976–84, of Trade and Industry 1984–87; Chair. IMF Meetings 1978, Asram Devt Bank 1977–, Islamic Devt Bank 1977.

RAZOV, Sergey Sergeyevich; Russian diplomatist and economist; b. 28 Jan. 1953, Sochi, Krasnodar Territory; m.; two c.; ed Moscow Inst. of Int. Relations; economist, Sr economist USSR Trade Mission to Repub. of China 1975–79; head of div., head of group Cen. CPSU Cttee 1979–90; Head Dept of Far East Countries and Indochina, USSR Ministry of Foreign Affairs 1990–92; Russian Amb. to Mongolia 1992–96; Dir Third Dept of CIS Countries, Russian Ministry of Foreign Affairs 1996–99; Amb. to Poland 1999–2002; Deputy Minister of Foreign Affairs 2003–. *Publications:* The People's Republic of China 1991, Foreign Policy of Open Doors of People's Republic of China 1985; articles and other publs. *Address:* Ministry of Foreign Affairs, Sadovaya-Sennaya 32/34, 121200, Moscow, Russia (Office). *Telephone:* (095) 244-91-45 (Office).

RE, HE Cardinal Giovanni Battista; Italian ecclesiastic; b. 30 Jan. 1934, Borno, Brescia; ordained priest 1957; Bishop 1987; Titular Archbishop of Vescovio; Asst Sec. of State, General Affairs; Prefect of Congregation for the Bishops; cr. Cardinal 2001. *Address:* Congregation for the Bishops, Palazzo delle Congregazioni, Piazza Pio XII 10, 00193 Rome, Italy (Office); Palazzina dell'Arciprete, 00120 Vatican City. *Telephone:* (06) 69884217 (Office); (06) 69883942. *Fax:* (06) 69885303 (Office). *E-mail:* vati07@cbishops.va (Office).

REA, Stephen James; Irish actor; b. 1949, Belfast, Northern Ireland; s. of James Rea and Jane (née Logue) Rea; m. Dolours Price 1983; two s.; ed Queen's Univ., Belfast; formed (with Brian Friel, q.v.) Field Day Theatre Co. 1980; Hon. DLitt (Univ. of Staffs.). *Stage appearances include:* The Shadow of a Gunman, The Cherry Orchard, Miss Julie, High Society, Endgame, The Freedom of the City, Translations, Communication Card, St Oscar, Boesman and Lena, Hightime and Riot Act, Double Cross, Pentecost, Making History, Someone Who'll Watch Over Me 1992 (Broadway, New York), Uncle Vanya 1995; at Nat. Theatre: Ashes to Ashes 1997, Playboy of the Western World, Comedians, The Shaughraun. *Directed:* Three Sisters, The Cure at Troy, Northern Star 1998. *Films include:* Angel 1982, Company of Wolves 1985, The Doctor and the Devils 1985, Loose Connections 1988, Life is Sweet 1991, The Crying Game 1992, Bad Behaviour 1993, Princess Caraboo 1994, Angie 1994, Interview with the Vampire 1994, Prêt-à-Porter 1994, All Men are Mortal 1994, Citizen X 1994, The Devil and the Deep Blue Sea 1994, Michael Collins 1995, Trojan Eddie 1995, A Further Gesture 1995, The Butcher Boy 1998, Guinevere 1999, The End of the Affair 2000, I Couldn't Read the Sky 2000. *TV appearances include:* Four Days in July, Lost Belongings, Scout, St Oscar, Not with a Bang, Hedda Gabler, Crime of the Century. *Address:* c/o Peters, Fraser & Dunlop Ltd, Drury House, 34-43 Russell Street, London, WC2B 5HA, England.

READ, Sir John Emms, Kt, FCA, FIB; British business executive (retd); b. 29 March 1918, Brighton; s. of William E Read and Daysie E (née Cooper) Read; m. Dorothy M. Berry 1942; two s.; ed Brighton, Hove and Sussex Grammar School and Admin. Staff Coll., Henley-on-Thames; Commdr Royal Navy 1939–46; Adm.'s Sec. to Asst Chief of Naval Staff, Admiralty 1942–45, Naval Sec., British Admiralty Tech. Mission, Ottawa 1945–46; Ford Motor Co. 1946–64, Dir of Sales 1961–64; Exec. Dir EMI Ltd 1965, Man. Dir 1966–69, CEO 1969–79, Deputy Chair. 1973–74, Chair. 1974–79; Deputy Chair. Thorn EMI Ltd 1979–80, Dir 1981–87; Chair. Trustee Savings Bank Cen. Bd 1980–88, Trustee Savings Banks (Holdings) Ltd 1980–86, TSB England and Wales 1983–86, TSB Group PLC 1986–88, (Dir TSB England and Wales PLC 1986–88), United Dominions Trust Ltd 1981–85; Dir Dunlop Holdings Ltd 1971–84, Thames Television Ltd 1973–88 (Deputy Chair. 1981–88), Capitol Industries-EMI Inc., USA 1970–83, Wonderworld PLC 1986–97, FI Group PLC 1989–94, Nat. Youth Film Foundation 1987–90, Cadmus Investment Man. Ltd 1993–98, Cafman Ltd (now Cafcash) 1994–2000, Cafinvest Ltd 1994–96; mem. P.O. Bd 1975–77, Royal Naval Film Corpn 1975–83, British Overseas Trade Bd 1976–79; Chair. Electronics Econ. Devt Comm. 1976–80, Armed Forces Pay Review Body 1976–83, Nat. Electronics Council 1977–80, Gov. Admin. Staff Coll., Henley 1974–92; mem. Council of CBI 1977–89, President's Cttee 1977–84, Chair. Finance Cttee 1978–84; Trustee, Westminster Abbey Trust 1978–87, Charity Aid Foundation 1985–98 (Pres. 1994–98), Crimestoppers Trust 1987–2001; Chair. Cttee of Man. Inst. of Neurology 1980–97, Brain Research Trust 1982–2001 (Pres. 2002–); Pres. Sussex Assen of Boys' Clubs 1982–97, Cheshire Homes, Seven Rivers, Essex 1979–85; Vice-Pres. Inst. of Bankers 1982–89; mem. Cttee of London and Scottish Bankers 1986–88; mem. Governing Body, British Postgraduate Medical Fed. 1982–96; Fellow, RSA 1975–90; Hon. Fellow Henley Man. Coll. 1993, Univ. Coll. London 1999; Companion, Inst. of Radio Engineers, Chartered Man. Inst.; Hon. DUniv (Surrey) 1987; Hon. DBA (Buckingham). *Leisure interests:* music, the arts, sport. *Address:* Flat 68, 15 Portman Square, London, W1H 6LL, England. *Telephone:* (20) 7935-7888.

READ, Piers Paul, MA, FRSL; British writer; b. 7 March 1941, Beaconsfield; s. of Herbert Edward Read and Margaret Ludwig; m. Emily Albertine Boothby 1967; two s. two d.; ed Ampleforth Coll., York and St John's Coll., Cambridge; Artist-in-Residence, Ford Foundation, W Berlin 1964; Sub-Ed. Times Literary Supplement, London 1965; Harkness Fellow Commonwealth Fund, New York 1967–68; Council mem. Inst. of Contemporary Arts (ICA), London 1971–75; Cttee of Man. Soc. of Authors, London 1973–76; mem. Literature Panel Arts Council, London 1975–77; Adjunct Prof. of Writing, Columbia Univ., New York 1980; Chair. Catholic Writers' Guild 1992–97; Bd mem. Aid to the Church in Need 1991–; Trustee Catholic Library 1997–; mem. Council Royal Soc. of Literature 2001; Sir Geoffrey Faber Memorial Prize, Somerset Maugham Award, Hawthornden Prize, Thomas More Award (USA), James Tait Black Memorial Prize. *Publications:* Game in Heaven with Tussy Marx 1966, The Junkers 1968, Monk Dawson 1969, The Professor's Daughter 1971, The Upstart 1973, Alive: The Story of the Andes Survivors 1974, Polonaise 1976, The Train Robbers 1978, A Married Man 1979, The Villa Golitsyn 1981, The Free Frenchman 1986, A Season in the West 1988, On the Third Day 1990, Ablaze: The Story of Chernobyl 1993, A Patriot in Berlin 1995, Knights of The Cross 1997, The Templars 1999, Alice in Exile 2001. *Leisure interest:* family life. *Address:* 50 Portland Road, London, W11 4LG, England. *Telephone:* (20) 7727-5719. *Fax:* (20) 7460-2499. *E-mail:* piersread@dial.pipex.com.

REAGAN, Nancy Davis (Anne Francis Robbins), BA; American fmr First Lady; b. 6 July 1921, New York; d. of Kenneth Robbins and Edith (née Luckett) Robbins, step-d. of Loyal Davis; m. Ronald Reagan (q.v.) 1952; one s. one d., one step-s. one step-d.; ed Smith Coll., Mass.; contract actress Metro-Goldwyn-Mayer 1949–56; fmr author syndicated column on prisoners-of-war and soldiers missing in action; civic worker active on behalf of Viet Nam war veterans, sr citizens, disabled children and drug victims; mem. Bd of Dirs Revlon Group Inc. 1989–; Hon. Nat. Chair. Aid to Adoption of Special Kids 1977; one of Ten Most Admired American Women, Good Housekeeping Magazine 1977, Woman of Year, LA Times 1977, perm. mem. Hall of Fame of Ten Best Dressed Women in US, Lifetime Achievement Award, Council of Fashion Designers of USA 1988, numerous awards for role in fight against drug abuse. *Films include:* The Next Voice You Hear 1950, Donovan's Brain

1953, Hellcats of the Navy 1957. *Publications:* Nancy 1980, To Love A Child (with Jane Wilkie), My Turn (memoirs) 1989. *Address:* 2121 Avenue of the Stars, 34th Floor, Los Angeles, CA 90067, USA.

REAGAN, Ronald Wilson; American politician and former actor; b. 6 Feb. 1911, Tampico, Ill.; s. of John Edward and Nelle (Wilson) Reagan; m. 1st Jane Wyman 1940 (divorced 1948); one s. one d. (deceased); m. 2nd Nancy (née Davis) Reagan 1952; one s. one d.; ed Northside High School, Dixon, Ill. and Eureka Coll., Eureka, Ill.; USAF 1942–46; Gov. of Calif. 1967–74; Pres. of USA 1981–89; Dir Nat. Review Bd 1989; Chair. Republican Govs Asscn 1969; fmr film actor and producer, radio sports announcer (at Des Moines, Iowa) and Ed., Cen. Broadcasting Co.; operated horse-breeding and cattle ranch; Player and Production Supervisor, Gen. Electric Theater TV for eight years; fmr Pres. Screen Actors Guild, Motion Picture Industry Council; mem. Bd of Dirs Cttee on Fundamental Educ., St John's Hosp. Cttee on Present Danger 1977–; Foreign Assoc. mem. Acad. des Sciences morales et politiques 1989; Republican; Dr hc (Notre Dame, Ind.) 1981, (Nat. Univ. of Ireland) 1984; Hon. Citizen of Berlin 1992; Hon. GCB; Grand Cordon, Supreme Order of the Chrysanthemum (Japan) 1989; numerous other awards including Presidential Medal of Freedom 1993, Matsunaga Medal of Peace 1993. *Films include:* Love is on the Air 1937, Accidents Will Happen 1938, Dark Victory 1939, Hell's Kitchen 1939, Brother Rat and a Baby 1940, Santa Fé Trail 1940, International Squadron 1941, Nine Lives are Not Enough 1941, King's Row 1941, Juke Girl 1942, Desperate Journey 1942, This is the Army 1943, Stallion Road 1947, That Hagen Girl 1947, The Voice of the Turtle 1947, Night unto Night 1948, John Loves Mary 1949, The Hasty Heart (Great Britain) 1949, Louisa 1950, Storm Warning 1951, Bedtime for Bonzo 1951, Hong Kong 1952, Prisoner of War 1954, Law and Order 1954, Tennessee's Partner 1955, Hellcats of the Navy 1957, The Killers 1964. *Publications:* Where's the Rest of Me? (autobiog.), reprinted as My Early Life 1981, Abortion and the Conscience of the Nation 1984, Speaking my Mind: Selected Speeches 1990, An American Life (autobiog.) 1990. *Address:* 11000 Wilshire Boulevard, 34th Floor, Los Angeles, CA 90067, USA (Office). *Telephone:* (213) 284-8940.

REARDON, Raymond (Ray), MBE; British snooker player; b. 8 Oct. 1932, Tredegar, Wales; s. of Benjamin Reardon and Cynthia Jenkins; m. 1st Susan Carter (divorced); one s. one d.; m. 2nd Carol Lovington 1987; ed Georgeton Secondary Modern School, Tredegar; Welsh Amateur Champion 1950–55; English Amateur Champion 1964; turned professional 1967; six times World Snooker Champion 1970–78; Benson & Hedges Masters Champion 1976; Welsh Champion 1977, 1981, 1983; Professional Players Champion 1982; retd 1992; active in running World Professional Billiards and Snooker Asscn; occasional appearances on BBC TV's Big Break show. *Publications:* Classic Snooker 1974, Ray Reardon (autobiog.) 1982. *Leisure interest:* golf.

REBE, Bernd Werner, DrIur; German university president; b. 5 Sept. 1939, Braunlage; s. of Werner Rebe and Liselotte Rebe; m. 1st Bärbel Bonewitz 1964 (died 1993); two s.; m. 2nd Katharina Ribe (née Becker) 1999; ed Univ. of Kiel, Freie Univ. Berlin and Univ. of Bielefeld; Prof. of Civil Law, Commercial Law, Competition Law and Corpn Law, Univ. of Hannover 1975, Vice-Pres. Univ. of Hannover 1979–81; Pres. Tech. Univ. of Braunschweig 1983–99, Prof. of Constitutional and Media Law 1999–; mem. Senate W German Rectors' Conf. 1988; Pres. Rectors' Conf. of Lower Saxony 1989; Hon. Citizen Otto-von-Guericke-Universität Magdeburg. *Publications:* Die Träger der Pressefreiheit nach dem Grundgesetz 1970, Privatrecht und Wirtschaftsordnung 1978, Arbeitslosigkeit—unser Sicherheit? 1983, Neue Technologien und die Entwicklung von Wirtschaft und Gesellschaft 1984, Verfassung und Verwaltung des Landes Niedersachsen 1986, Nutzen und Wahrheit: Triebkräfte der Wissenschaftsentwicklung 1991, Die Universität heute—Leitinstitution ohne Leitbild? 1991, Umweltverträgliches Wirtschaften—Wettbewerbsvorteile, Marktchancen, Wohlstandssicherung 1993, Denkerkundungen. Reden wider die Vordergründigkeit 1995, Die unvollendete Einheit. Bestandsaufnahme und Perspektiven für die Wirtschaft 1996, Vision und Verantwortung 1999, Humanität—Wandel—Utopie 2000. *Leisure interests:* swimming, skiing, tennis, history, politics. *Address:* Technical University of Braunschweig, Pockelsstrasse 14, 38106 Braunschweig (Office); Am Mühlenstieg 10, 38126 Braunschweig, Germany (Home). *Telephone:* (531) 3913133 (Office); (531) 8669292 (Home). *Fax:* (531) 3914577.

REBEK, Julius, Jr., PhD; American professor of chemistry; b. 11 April 1949, Beregszasz, Hungary; s. of Julius Rebek Sr and Eva Racz; m. (divorced); two d.; ed Univ. of Kansas and Mass. Inst. of Tech. (MIT); Asst Prof. Univ. of Calif. Los Angeles 1970–76; Assoc. Prof., then Prof. Univ. of Pittsburgh 1976–79; Prof. Dept of Chem. MIT 1989–96, Camille Dreyfus Prof. of Chem. 1991–; Dir Skaggs Inst. for Chemical Biology, Scripps Research Inst. 1996–; consultant to several cos; Sloan Fellow; Guggenheim Fellow; von Humboldt Fellow; Cope Scholar Award 1991, James Flack Norris Award in Physical Chem. 1997. *Publications:* 280 publs in scientific journals. *Leisure interest:* tennis. *Address:* Scripps Research Institute, 10550 North Torrey Pines Road, La Jolla, CA 92037 (Office); 2330 Calle del Oro, La Jolla, CA 92037, USA (Home). *Telephone:* (858) 784-2250. *E-mail:* jrebek@scripps.edu (Office). *Website:* www.scripps.edu/skaggs/rebek (Office).

REBEYROLLE, Paul; French artist; b. 3 Nov. 1926; ed Lycée Gay-Lussac, Limoges; exhbns at Salon des Indépendants, Salon d'Automne, Salon de Mai, Salon de la Jeune Peinture (France); Dir Salon de Mai; works in collections in England, Sweden, Belgium, USA, Poland, Italy, Japan, etc.; rep. at Dunn Int. Exhbn, London 1963; First Prize, La Jeune Peinture 1950, Fénéon Prize 1951, First Prize at French Section, Paris Biennale 1959.

REBUCK, Gail Ruth, CBE, BA, FRSA; British publishing executive; b. 10 Feb. 1952, London; d. of Gordon Rebuck and Mavis Rebuck; m. Philip Gould (q.v.) 1985; two d.; ed Lycée Français de Londres, Univ. of Sussex; Production Asst, Grisewood & Dempsey (children's book packager) 1975–76; Ed., later Publr Robert Nicholson Publs London Guidebooks 1976–79; Publr Hamlyn Paperbacks 1979–82; Founder Partner Century Publishing Co. 1982, Publishing Dir Non-Fiction 1982–85, Publr Century Hutchinson 1985–89, Chair. Random House Div., Random Century 1989–91, Chair. and Chief Exec. Random House UK Ltd (now Random House Group) 1991–; mem. COPUS 1995–97, Creative Industries Task Force 1997–2000; Non-Exec. Dir, Work Foundation 2001–; Trustee Inst. for Public Policy Research (IPPR) 1993–; mem. Court Univ. of Sussex 1997–; Council RCA 1999–. *Leisure interests:* reading, travel. *Address:* The Random House Group Ltd, 20 Vauxhall Bridge Road, London, SW1V 2SA, England (Office). *Telephone:* (20) 7840-8886. *Fax:* (20) 7233-6120. *E-mail:* grebuck@randomhouse.co.uk (Office). *Website:* www.randomhouse.co.uk.

RECHENDORFF, Torben; Danish politician; b. 1 April 1937; teacher and prin. at various schools, Frederiksberg and Hørsholm 1960–81; Sec.-Gen. Conservative People's Party 1981; Minister of Ecclesiastical Affairs 1988 and of Communications 1989–93; mem. Folketing (parl.) 1990–98; Leader Conservative People's Party 1993–95. *Address:* Conservative People's Party, Nyharu 4, P.O. Box 1515, 1020, Copenhagen K, Denmark.

REDFORD, Robert; American actor and director; b. 18 Aug. 1937, Santa Monica, Calif.; m. Lola Van Wegenen 1958 (divorced 1985); two d. one s.; ed Van Nuys High School, Univ. of Colorado, Pratt Inst. of Design, American Acad. of Dramatic Arts, NY; Founder and Pres. The Sundone Inst. 1981–; owner Sundance Ski Resort, Utah; Audubon Medal 1989, Dartmouth Film Soc. Award 1990, Screen Actors' Guild Award for Lifetime Achievement 1996, Hon. Acad. Award 2002. *Films include:* War Hunt 1961, Situation Hopeless But Not Serious 1965, Inside Daisy Clover 1965, The Chase 1965, This Property is Condemned 1966, Barefoot in the Park 1967, Tell Them Willie Boy is Here 1969, Butch Cassidy and the Sundance Kid 1969, Downhill Racer 1969, Little Fauss and Big Halsy 1970, Jeremiah Johnson 1972, The Candidate 1972, How to Steal a Diamond in Four Uneasy Lessons 1972, The Way We Were 1973, The Sting 1973, The Great Gatsby 1974, The Great Waldo Pepper 1974, Three Days of the Condor 1975, All the President's Men 1976, A Bridge Too Far 1977, The Electric Horseman 1980, Brubaker 1980, The Natural 1984, Out of Africa 1985, Legal Eagles 1986, Havana 1991; Dir Ordinary People 1980 (Acad. Award and Golden Globe Award for Best Dir 1981), Milagro Beanfield War 1988 (also producer), Promised Land (exec. producer) 1988, Sneakers 1992, A River Runs Through It (also Dir) 1992, Quiz Show (Dir) 1994, The River Wild 1995, Up Close and Personal 1996, The Horse Whisperer 1997, The Legend of Bagger Vance (also Dir, producer) 2000, How to Kill Your Neighbour's Dog (exec. producer) 2000, The Last Castle 2001, Spy Game 2001. *Address:* c/o David O'Conner Creative Artists Agency, 9830 Wilshire Boulevard, Beverly Hills, CA 90212, USA; 1223 Wilshire Boulevard, 412 Santa Monica, CA 90403 (Office).

REDGRAVE, Lynn; British actress; b. 8 March 1943, London; d. of the late Sir Michael Redgrave and of Rachel Kempson; sister of Vanessa Redgrave (q.v.); m. John Clark 1967; one s. two d.; ed Cen. School of Speech and Drama; Broadway debut in Black Comedy; other stage appearances include: My Fat Friend 1974, Mrs Warren's Profession, Knock Knock, Misalliance, St Joan, Twelfth Night (American Shakespeare Festival), Sister Mary Ignatius Explains It All for You, Aren't We All?, Sweet Sue, Les Liaisons Dangereuses; one-woman show Shakespeare for My Father (US and Canada tours, also in Melbourne and London 1996) 1993, Moon over Buffalo 1996, The Mandrake Root 2001, Noises Off 2001; numerous TV appearances. *Films:* Tom Jones, Girl With Green Eyes, Georgy Girl, The Deadly Affair, Smashing Time, The Virgin Soldiers, The Last of the Mobile Hot-Shots, Viva La Muerta Tua, Every Little Crook and Nanny, Everything You Always Wanted to Know About Sex, Don't Turn the Other Cheek, The National Health, The Happy Hooker, The Big Bus, Sunday Lovers, Morgan Stewart's Coming Home, Midnight, Getting It Right, Shine, Gods and Monsters, Strike, The Simian Line, Touched, The Annihilation of Fish, The Next Best Thing 2000, My Kingdom 2001, Unconditional Love 2001. *Leisure interests:* cooking, gardening, horse riding. *Address:* c/o John Clark, P.O. Box 1207, Topanga, CA 90290, USA. *Telephone:* (310) 455-1334. *Fax:* (310) 455-1032.

REDGRAVE, Sir Steven Geoffrey (Steve), Kt, CBE; British oarsman; b. 23 March 1962, Marlow, Bucks.; m. Elizabeth Ann Redgrave; one s. two d.; ed Marlow Comprehensive School; rep. UK at Jr World Championships 1979; rep. Marlow Rowing Club 1976–2000, Leander 1987–2000; stroke, British coxed four, gold medal winners, Los Angeles Olympic Games 1984; gold medals, single scull, coxless pair (with Andy Holmes) and coxed four, Commonwealth Games 1986, coxed pair (with Holmes), World Championships 1986; coxless pair gold medal and coxed pair silver medal (with Holmes), World Championships 1987; gold medal (with Holmes), coxless pair and bronze medal, coxed pair, Olympic Games, Seoul 1988; silver medal (with Simon Berrisford), coxless pairs, World Championships 1989; bronze medal, coxless pair (with Matthew Pinsent, q.v.) World Championships, Tasmania 1990; gold medal, coxless pair (with Pinsent), World Championships, Vienna 1991; gold medal, Olympic Games, Barcelona 1992; gold medal, World

Championships, Czech Repub. 1993; gold medal, Indianapolis, 1994; gold medal, Finland 1995; gold medal, Olympic Games, Atlanta 1996; gold medal, coxless four (with Pinsent, Foster, Cracknell), Aiguebelette 1997; gold medal, coxless four, Cologne 1998; gold medal, coxless four (with Pinsent, Coode, Cracknell), St Catherines 1999; gold medal, Olympic Games, Sydney 2000; holds record for most consecutive Olympic gold medals won in an endurance event (five); f. Sir Steve Redgrave Charitable Trust; Vice-Pres. SPARKS, SportsAid Southern; mem. Bd UK Sport Inst.; Steward Henley Royal Regatta; Celebrity Friend of the Royal Palace in support of local heritage; Patron to over 20 charities; Amb. for LifeScan and active in raising money for children's charities; Hon. Pres. Amateur Rowing Asscn; Hon. Vice-Pres. British Olympic Asscn, Diabetes UK; Hon. DCL (Durham) 1997; Hon. DSc (Bucks.) 2001, (Buckingham, Hull); Hon. DLitt (Open Univ., Oxford Brookes, Reading, Nottingham); Hon. DUniv (Buckingham Chiltern, Heriot-Watt); Hon. DTech (Loughborough); BBC Sports Personality of the Year 2000, British Sports Writers' Asscn Sportsman of the Year 2000, Laurens Lifetime Achievement Award 2001. *Publications:* Steven Redgrave's Complete Book of Rowing 1992, A Golden Age (autobiog.) 2000. *Leisure interest:* golf. *Address:* c/o Athole Still International Management Ltd, Foresters Hall, 25–27 Westow Street, London, SE19 3RY, England (Office). *Telephone:* (20) 8771-5271 (Office). *Fax:* (20) 8768-6600 (Office). *E-mail:* roxane@atholestill.co.uk (Office). *Website:* www.steveredgrave.com; www.redgravetrust.com.

REDGRAVE, Vanessa, CBE; British actress; b. 30 Jan. 1937; d. of the late Sir Michael Redgrave and of Rachel Kempson; sister of Lynn Redgrave (q.v.); m. the late Tony Richardson 1962 (divorced 1967, died 1991); two d.; one s. by Franco Reio; ed Queensgate School, London and Cen. School of Speech and Drama; actress 1957–; co-f. Moving Theatre 1974; mem. Workers' Revolutionary Party (Cand. for Moss Side 1979); Fellow BFI 1988; Dr hc (Mass.) 1990; Evening Standard Award, Best Actress 1961 and Variety Club Award 1961; Award for Best Actress, Cannes Film Festival 1966 for Morgan—A Suitable Case for Treatment; Award for Leading Actress, US Nat. Soc. of Film Critics and Best Actress Award, Film Critics' Guild (UK) for Isadora Duncan 1969; Acad. Award (Best Supporting Actress) for Julia 1978; Award (TV for Best Actress) for Playing for Time 1981; Laurence Olivier Award 1984. *Stage appearances include:* A Midsummer Night's Dream 1959, The Tiger and the Horse 1960, The Taming of the Shrew 1961, As You Like It 1961, Cymbeline 1962, The Seagull 1964, 1985, The Prime of Miss Jean Brodie 1966, Daniel Deronda 1969, Cato Street 1971, Threepenny Opera 1972, Twelfth Night 1972, Antony and Cleopatra 1973, 1986, Design for Living 1973, Macbeth 1975, Lady from the Sea 1976 and 1979 (Manchester), The Aspern Papers 1984, Ghosts 1986, A Touch of the Poet 1988, Orpheus Descending 1988, A Madhouse in Goa 1989, The Three Sisters 1990, Lettice and Lovage 1991, When She Danced 1991, Isadora 1991, Heartbreak House 1992, The Master Builder 1992, Maybe 1993, The Liberation of Skopje 1995, John Gabriel Borkman 1996, The Cherry Orchard 2000, The Tempest 2000; Dir and acted in Antony and Cleopatra, Houston, Tex. 1996, John Gabriel Borkman 1996, Song at Twilight 1999, Lady Windermere's Fan 2002. *Films include:* Morgan—A Suitable Case for Treatment 1965, Sailor from Gibraltar 1965, Camelot 1967, Blow Up 1967, Charge of the Light Brigade 1968, Isadora Duncan 1968, The Seagull 1968, A Quiet Place in the Country 1968, Dropout, The Trojan Women 1970, The Devils 1970, The Holiday 1971, Mary Queen of Scots 1971, Katherine Mansfield (BBC TV) 1973, Murder on the Orient Express 1974, Winter Rates 1974, 7% Solution 1975, Julia 1977, Agatha 1978, Yanks 1978, Bear Island 1979, Playing for Time (CBS TV) 1979, Playing for Time 1980, My Body My Child (ABC TV) 1981, Wagner 1982, The Bostonians 1983, Wetherby 1984, Prick Up Your Ears 1987, Comrades 1987, Consuming Passions 1988, King of the Wind 1989, Diceria dell'intore 1989, The Ballad of the Sad Cafe 1990, Howards End 1992, Breath of Life, The Wall, Sparrow, They, The House of the Spirits, Crime and Punishment, Mother's Boys, Little Odessa, A Month by the Lake 1996, Mission Impossible 1996, Looking for Richard 1997, Wilde 1997, Mrs Dalloway 1997, Bella Mafia (TV) 1997, Deep Impact 1998, Cradle Will Rock 2000; produced and narrated documentary film The Palestinians 1977. *Publications:* Pussies and Tigers 1963, An Autobiography 1991. *Leisure interest:* changing the status quo. *Address:* c/o Gavin Barker Associates, 2d Wimpole Street, London, W1M 7AA, England (Office).

REDGROVE, Peter William, FRSL; British author, poet and analytical psychologist; b. 2 Jan. 1932; s. of late Gordon James Redgrove and Nancy Lena Cestrilli-Bell; m. Penelope Shuttle; one d. (and two s. one d. by previous m.); ed Taunton School and Queens' Coll., Cambridge; scientific journalist and editor 1954–61; Visiting Poet, Buffalo Univ., New York 1961–62; Gregory Fellow in Poetry, Leeds Univ. 1962–65; Resident Author and Sr Lecturer in Complementary Studies, Falmouth School of Art 1966–83; O'Connor Prof. of Literature, Colgate Univ., New York 1974–75; Leverhulme Emer. Fellow 1985–87; Writer at large, N Cornwall Arts 1988; Hon. LittD (Sheffield); George Rylands' Verse-Speaking Prize 1954, Guardian Fiction Prize 1973; Fulbright Award 1961, Poetry Book Soc. Choices 1961, 1966, 1979, 1981, Arts Council Awards 1969, 1970, 1973, 1975, 1977, 1982, Prudence Farmer Poetry Award 1977, Cholmondeley Award 1985, Queen's Gold Medal for Poetry 1996, Authors' Foundation Grant 1998. *Radio plays include:* The God of Glass 1977 (Imperial Tobacco Award 1978), Martyr of the Hives 1980 (Giles Cooper Award 1981), Florent and the Tuxedo Millions 1982 (Prix Italia), The Sin Doctor 1983, Dracula in White 1984, The Scientists of the Strange 1984, Time for the Cat-Scene 1985, Trelamia 1986, Six Tales from Grimm 1987, Six Views to a Haunt 1992, An Inspector Named Horse 1995. *Publications:* novels: In the Country of the Skin 1973, The Terrors of Dr. Treviles 1974, The Glass Cottage (with Penelope Shuttle) 1976, The God of Glass 1979, The Sleep of the Great Hypnotist 1979, The Beekeepers 1980, The Facilitators, or, Madame Hole-in-the-Day 1982; The One Who Set Out to Study Fear 1989, From the Virgil Caverns 2002; short fiction: The Cyclopean Mistress 1993; psychology and sociology: The Wise Wound (with Penelope Shuttle) 1978, The Black Goddess and the Sixth Sense 1987, Alchemy for Women (with Penelope Shuttle) 1995; poetry: The Collector and Other Poems 1960, The Nature of Cold Weather 1961, At the White Monument 1963, The Force and Other Poems 1966, Penguin Modern Poets II 1968, Work in Progress 1969, Dr. Faust's Sea-Spiral Spirit and Other Poems 1972, Three Pieces for Voices 1972, The Hermaphrodite Album (with Penelope Shuttle) 1973, Sons of My Skin: Selected Poems 1975, From Every Chink of the Ark 1977, Ten Poems 1977, The Weddings at Nether Powers and Other New Poems 1979, The Apple-Broadcast 1981, The Working of Water 1984, The Man Named East 1985, The Mudlark Poems and Grand Buveur 1986, In the Hall of the Saurians 1987, The Moon Disposes 1987, Poems 1954–87 1989, The First Earthquake 1989, Dressed as for a Tarot Pack 1990, Under the Reservoir 1992, The Laborators 1993, My Father's Trapdoors 1994, Abyssophone 1995, Assembling a Ghost 1996, Orchard End 1997, What the Black Mirror Saw 1997, Selected Poems 1999, From the Virgil Caverns 2002. *Leisure interests:* work, photography, judo, yoga. *Address:* c/o David Higham Associates, 5–8 Lower John Street, Golden Square, London, W1R 4HA, England.

REDHEAD, Michael Logan Gonne, PhD, FBA; British academic; b. 30 Dec. 1929, London; s. of Robert Arthur Redhead and Christabel Lucy Gonne Browning; m. Jennifer Anne Hill 1964; three s.; ed Westminster School, Univ. Coll. London; Prof. of Philosophy of Physics, Chelsea Coll., London 1984–85, King's Coll. London 1985–87; Prof. of History and Philosophy of Science, Cambridge Univ. 1987–97; Fellow Wolfson Coll. Cambridge 1988–, Vice-Pres. 1992–96; Co-Dir Centre for Philosophy of Natural and Social Science, LSE 1998–, Centennial Prof. 1999–2002; Fellow King's Coll. London 2000; Tarner Lecturer, Trinity Coll. Cambridge 1991–94; Visiting Fellow All Souls Coll. Oxford 1995; Pres. British Soc. for Philosophy of Science 1989–91; Lakatos Award for Philosophy of Science 1988. *Publications:* Incompleteness, Non-locality and Realism 1987, From Physics to Metaphysics 1995. *Leisure interests:* poetry, music, tennis. *Address:* 34 Coniger Road, London, SW6 3TA, England. *Telephone:* (20) 7736-6767. *Fax:* (20) 7731-7627.

REDING, Viviane, PhD; Luxembourg politician; b. 27 April 1951, Esch-sur Alzette; m.; three c.; ed Sorbonne, Paris; journalist, Luxemburger Wort 1978–99; mem. Parl. 1979–89; communal councillor, City of Esch 1981–99; Pres. Luxembourg Union of Journalists 1986–98; Nat. Pres. Christian-Social Women 1988–93; MEP 1989–99; Pres. Cultural Affairs Cttee 1992–99; Vice-Pres. Parti Chrétien-Social 1995–99; Vice-Pres. Civil Liberties and Internal Affairs Cttee 1997–99; EU Commr for Educ. and Culture 1999–; mem. Benelux Parl., N Atlantic Ass. (Leader Christian Democrat/Conservative Group). *Address:* Commission of the European Communities, 200 rue de la Loi, 1049 Brussels, Belgium (Office). *Telephone:* (2) 298-16-00 (Office). *Fax:* (2) 299-92-01 (Office). *E-mail:* viviane.reding@cec.eu.int.

REDSTONE, Sumner Murray, LLB; American business executive and lawyer; b. 27 May 1923, Boston; s. of Michael Redstone and Belle (Ostrovsky) Redstone; m. Phyllis Redstone (divorced 2002); two c.; ed Harvard Univ.; called to Bar of Mass. 1947; Special Asst to US Attorney-Gen., Washington, DC 1948–51; partner, law firm of Ford, Bergson, Adams, Borkland & Redstone, Washington, DC 1951–54; Pres. and CEO Nat. Amusements Inc., Dedham, Mass. 1967–, Chair. Bd 1986–87; Chair. Bd, Viacom Inc., New York 1987–, CEO 1996–; Prof., Boston Univ. Law School 1982, 1985–86; Chair. Corp. Comm. on Education Tech. 1996–; mem. Corpn, New England Medical Center 1967–, Mass. Gen. Hosp.; Sponsor, Boston Museum of Science; mem. Bd of Dirs Boston Arts Festival, John F. Kennedy Library Foundation; mem. Nat. Asscn of Theatre Owners, Theatre Owners of America, Motion Picture Pioneers (mem. Bd of Dirs), Boston Bar Asscn, Mass. Bar Asscn; mem. Exec. Cttee Will Rogers Fund; mem. Bd of Overseers Boston Museum of Fine Arts; mem. Exec. Bd Combined Jewish Philanthropies; Army Commendation Medal, Legends in Leadership Award, Emory Univ. 1995, Lifetime Achievement Award American Cancer Society 1995, Trustees Award Nat. Acad. of TV Arts and Sciences 1997, Robert F. Kennedy Memorial Ripple of Hope Award 1998, Int. Radio and TV Gold Medal Award 1998, Nat. Conf. of Christians and Jews Humanitarian Award 1998, numerous other awards. *Publications:* A Passion to Win (autobiog.) 2001. *Address:* Viacom, 1515 Broadway, New York, NY 10027; 98 Baldpate Hill Road, Newton, MA 02159, USA (Home).

REDWOOD, Rt Hon John (Alan), PC, MA, DPhil; British politician; b. 15 June 1951, Dover, Kent; s. of William Charles Redwood and Amy Emma Champion; m. Gail Felicity Chippington 1974; one s. one d.; ed Kent Coll. Canterbury and Magdalen and St Antony's Colls Oxford; Fellow, All Souls Coll. Oxford 1972–85; Investment Adviser, Robert Fleming & Co. 1973–77; Dir (fmrly Man.) N. M. Rothschild & Sons 1977–87; Dir Norcros PLC 1985–89, Jt Deputy Chair. 1986–87, Chair. (non-exec.) 1987–89; Head, Prime Minister's Policy Unit 1983–85; MP for Wokingham 1987–; Parl. Under-Sec. of State, Dept of Trade & Industry 1989–90, Minister of State 1990–92, Minister of State, Dept of Environment 1992–93; Sec. of State for Wales 1993–95; unsuccessful cand. for leadership of Conservative Party 1995; Opposition Front Bench Spokesman on Trade and Industry 1997–99, on the Environment 1999–2000; Chair. Murray Financial Corpn 2002–; Dir (non-exec.) BNB Resources PLC, Mabey Securities; Visting Prof. Middx Univ. Business School;

Parliamentarian of the Year Awards 1987, 1995, 1997. *Publications:* Reason, Ridicule and Religion 1976, Public Enterprise in Crisis 1980, Value for Money Audits (with J. Hatch) 1981, Controlling Public Industries (with J. Hatch) 1982, Going for Broke 1984, Equity for Everyman 1986, Popular Capitalism 1989, The Global Marketplace 1994, The Single European Currency (with others) 1996, Our Currency, Our Country 1997, The Death of Britain? 1999, Stars and Strife 2001, Just Say No 2001, Third Way – Which Way 2002. *Leisure interests:* water sports, village cricket. *Address:* House of Commons, London, SW1A 0AA, England (Office). *Telephone:* (20) 7219-4205 (Office); (20) 7976-6603 (Home). *Fax:* (20) 7219-0377 (Office). *E-mail:* redwoodja@parliament.uk (Office). *Website:* www.epolitix.com (Office); www.wokinghamconservatives.com (Office).

REED, Bruce; American official; fmr aide to Pres. Clinton; Asst to Pres., Head Domestic Policy Council 1997–2001.

REED, Charles Bass, BS, MA, EdD; American university chancellor; b. 29 Sept. 1941, Harrisburg, Pa; s. of late Samuel Ross Reed and Elizabeth Johnson Reed; m. Catherine A. Sayers 1964; one s. one d.; ed George Washington Univ.; Asst Prof., then Assoc. Prof., George Washington Univ. 1963–70; Asst Dir, Nat. Performance-based Teacher Educ. Project 1970–71; Co-ordinator, Research and Devt in Teacher Educ., Fla Dept of Educ. 1971–72, Assoc. for Planning and Co-ordination 1972–74, Dir Office of Educational Planning, Budgeting and Evaluation 1974–79; Educ. Policy Co-ordinator, Exec. Office of Gov. Bob Graham 1979–80, Dir of Legis. Affairs 1980–81, Deputy Chief of Staff 1981–84, Chief of Staff 1984–85; Chancellor, State Univ. System of Fla 1985–98, Calif. State Univ. System 1998–, Bd Dirs Fla Progress Corpn, Capital Health Plan; Chair. Bd Dirs Regional Tech. Strategies Inc.; Fulbright 50th Anniversary Distinguished Fellow, Peru 1996; mem. Council on Foreign Relations; Dr hc (George Washington, Stetson and St Thomas Univs, Waynesburg Coll., Pa). *Address:* California State University, 401 Golden Shore, 6th Floor, Long Beach, CA 90802, USA. *E-mail:* creed@calstate.edu (Office).

REED, Ishmael Scott; American author; b. 22 Feb. 1938, Chattanooga; s. of Bennie S. Reed and Thelma Coleman; m. 1st Priscilla Rose 1960 (divorced 1970); two s.; m. 2nd Carla Blank; one d.; co-f. Reed, Cannon & Johnson Co.1973–; Assoc. ed., Calhoun House, Yale Univ. 1982–; co-ed., Quilt magazine 1981–; Guest Lecturer, Univ. of Calif. Berkeley 1968–; mem. usage panel, American Heritage Dictionary; Assoc. Ed. American Book Review; Exec. Producer Personal Problems (video soap opera); collaborator in multimedia Bicentennial mystery, The Lost State of Franklin (winner Poetry in Public Places contest 1975); Chair. Berkeley Arts Comm.; Advisory Chair. Co-ordinating Council of Literary Magazines; Pres. Before Columbus Foundation 1976–; Nat. Endowment for Arts Writing Fellow 1974; mem. authors Guild of America, PEN; Nat. Inst. of Arts and Letters Award 1975; Guggenheim Fellow 1975; Michaux Award 1978, ACLU Award 1978. *Publications:* novels: The Free-Lance Pallbearers 1967, Yellow Back Radio Broke Down 1969, Mumbo Jumbo 1972, The Last Days of Louisiana Red 1974, Flight to Canada 1976, The Terrible Twos 1982, Cab Calloway Stands in for the Moon 1986, Japanese By Spring 1993; several vols of poetry and essays. *Address:* c/o Penguin Putnam Inc., 375 Hudson Street, New York, NY 10014, USA.

REED, John Francis (Jack), BS, JD; American politician; b. 12 Nov. 1949, Providence, RI; s. of Joseph Reed and Mary Monahan; ed U.S. Mil. Acad. and Harvard Univ.; commissioned, 2nd Lt U.S. Army 1971, served with 82nd Airborne Div. 1973–77; Asst Prof. U.S. Mil. Acad. West Point, NY 1977–79; resgnd from Army 1979; called to Bar, DC 1982, Rhode Island 1983; Assoc. Sutherland, Asbill & Brennan, Washington 1982–83, Edwards & Angelli, Providence 1983–89; mem. Rhode Island Senate 1984–90; mem. 102–104th Congresses 1990–96; Senator from Rhode Island 1996–; Vice-Chair. NE-Midwest Congressional Coalition; Democrat. *Leisure interests:* reading, hiking. *Address:* United States Senate, 320 Hart Senate Office Building, Washington, DC 20510, USA.

REED, John Shepard, MS; American banker; b. 7 Feb. 1939, Chicago; m. 1st (divorced), four c.; m. 2nd Cindy McCarthy 1994; ed Washington and Jefferson Coll., MIT, Alfred P. Sloan School of Man., MIT; served with U.S. Army Eng Corps, Korea; fmr Trainee Goodyear Tire & Rubber; joined Citicorp/Citibank 1965, fmrly responsible for operating group, consumer business, fmr Sr Vice-Pres., Chair. and Chief Exec. 1984–98; named Jt Chair. and Chief Exec. of Citigroup (merger between Citicorp and Travelers Group) May 1998; Chair. Coalition of Service Industries, Services Policy Advisory Cttee to the U.S. Trade Rep.; Dir Philip Morris Inc., Monsanto Co.; mem. Business Council, Business Roundtable Policy Cttee; mem. Bd MIT, Bd Memorial Sloan-Kettering Cancer Center, Rand Corpn, Spencer Foundation, American Museum of Natural History. *Address:* Citigroup, 399 Park Avenue, New York, NY 10043, USA.

REED, Lou, BA; American musician; b. 2 March 1942, Brooklyn, New York; s. of Sidney Joseph Reed and Toby (Futterman) Reed; m. Sylvia Morales 1980; ed Syracuse Univ.; songwriter and recording artist 1965–; founder mem. Velvet Underground band 1966–70; toured with Andy Warhol's The Exploding Plastic Inevitable; poet; film actor; Rock and Roll Hall of Fame 1996; Commdr des Arts et des Lettres, Heroes Award 1997, American Master, PBS Documentary Series 1998. *Solo albums include:* Lou Reed 1972, Rock 'n' Roll Animal 1972, Berlin 1973, Sally Can't Dance 1974, Metal Machine Music 1975, Lou Reed Live 1975, Coney Island Baby 1976, Walk on the Wild Side 1977, Street Hassle 1978, Live, Take No Prisoners 1978, Vicious 1979, The

Bells 1979, Growing Up in Public 1980, Rock 'n' Roll Diary 1967–80, Blue Mask, Legendary Hearts 1983, New York 1989, Songs for Drella (with John Cale) 1990, Magic and Loss 1992, Set the Twilight Reeling 1996, Perfect Night Live in London 1998, Ecstasy 2000; several albums with Velvet Underground. *Publication:* Between Thought and Expression (selected lyrics) 1991, Pass Thru Fire 2000. *Address:* Sister Ray Enterprises, 584 Broadway, Room 609, New York, NY 10012, USA (Office).

REEDER, Franklin S., BA; American consultant and fmr government official; b. 25 Oct. 1940, Philadelphia, Pa; s. of late Simon Reeder and Hertha Strauss; m. Anna Marie Seroski 1962; one s. two d.; ed Univ. of Pennsylvania and George Washington Univ.; Treasury Dept 1961–64; Defense Dept 1964–70; Office of Man. and Budget, Exec. Office of Pres. of USA 1970–71, 1980–97, Dir 1995–97; Deputy Dir House Information System, U.S. House of Reps. 1971–80; consultant in information and governance; Chair. Computer Systems Security and Privacy Advisory Bd 2000–. *Leisure interests:* running, swimming, bicycling, watching baseball. *Address:* The Reeder Group, 3200 N Nottingham Street, Arlington, VA 22207, USA. *Telephone:* (703) 536-6635.

REES, Charles Wayne, CBE, DSc, FRSC, FRS; British professor of organic chemistry; b. 15 Oct. 1927, Cairo, Egypt; s. of Percival C. Rees and Daisy A. Beck; m. Patricia M. Francis 1953; three s.; ed Farnham Grammar School and Univ. Coll., Southampton; Lecturer in Organic Chem. Birkbeck Coll., London 1955–57, King's Coll., London 1957–63, Reader 1963–65; Prof. of Organic Chem. Univ. of Leicester 1965–69, Univ. of Liverpool 1969–78; Hofmann Prof. of Organic Chem., Imperial Coll., London 1978–93, Emer. Prof. 1993–; Visiting Prof., Univ. of Sunderland 1997–; Fellow King's Coll. London 1999; Tilden Lecturer, Royal Soc. of Chem. 1973–74, Pedler Lecturer 1984–85; August Wilhelm von Hofmann Lecturer, German Chem. Soc. 1985; Pres. Royal Soc. of Chem. 1992–94; Hon. DSc (Univ. of Leicester) 1994, (Univ. of Sunderland) 2000, (Univ. of London) 2003; Int. Award in Heterocyclic Chemistry 1995. *Publications:* some 400 research papers in scientific journals and 20 books. *Leisure interests:* music, wine, London, theatre. *Address:* Department of Chemistry, Imperial College London, London, SW7 2AZ, England (Office). *Telephone:* (20) 7594-5768. *Fax:* (20) 7594-5800. *E-mail:* c.rees@imperial.ac.uk (Office). *Website:* www.imperial.ac.uk (Office).

REES, Sir Dai (David Allan), Kt, PhD, DSc, FIBiol, FRSC, FRS; British scientist; b. 28 April 1936, Silloth; s. of James A. Rees and Elsie Bolam; m. Myfanwy Owen 1959; two s. one d.; ed Hawarden Grammar School, Clwyd and Univ. Coll. of N Wales, Bangor; Univ. of Edin. 1960, Asst Lecturer in Chem. 1961, Lecturer 1962–70, Section Man. 1970–72; Prin. Scientist Unilever Research, Colworth Lab. 1972–82; Assoc. Dir (part-time) MRC Unit for Cell Biophysics Kings Coll., London 1980–82; Dir Nat. Inst. for Medical Research 1982–87; Sec., then Chief Exec. MRC 1987–96, MRC scientist 1996–; Chair. European Medical Research Councils 1989–; Pres. European Science Foundation 1994–; Visiting Professorial Fellow, Univ. Coll., Cardiff 1972–77; Philips Lecture Royal Soc. 1984; mem. Royal Soc. Council 1985–87; Hon. DSc (Edin.) 1989, (Wales) 1991, (Stirling) 1995, (Leicester) 1997; Hon. FRCP 1986, FRCPE 1998; Hon. Fellow, King's Coll., London 1989, Univ. Coll. of N Wales 1988; Colworth Medal, Biochem. Soc. 1970; Carbohydrate Award, Chem. Soc. 1970. *Publications:* articles on carbohydrate biochem. and cell biology. *Leisure interests:* river cruising, reading, listening to music. *Address:* Ford Cottage, 1 High Street, Denford, Kettering, Northants. NN14 4EQ, England (Home). *E-mail:* drees@nimr.mrc.ac.uk.

REES, Sir Martin John, Kt, MA, PhD, FRS; British professor; b. 23 June 1942; s. of Reginald J. Rees and Joan Rees; m. Caroline Humphrey 1986; ed Shrewsbury School and Trinity Coll., Cambridge; Fellow, Jesus Coll., Cambridge 1967–69; Research Assoc. Calif. Inst. of Tech. 1967–68, 1971; mem. Inst. for Advanced Study, Princeton 1969–70, Prof. 1982–96; Visiting Prof. Harvard Univ. 1972, 1986–87; Prof. Univ. of Sussex 1972–73; Plumian Prof. of Astronomy and Experimental Philosophy, Univ. of Cambridge 1973–91, Royal Soc. Research Prof. 1992–; Astronomer Royal 1995–; Fellow, King's Coll., Cambridge 1969–72, 1973–; Visting Prof. Imperial Coll., London 2001–, Leicester Univ. 2001–; Dir Inst. of Astronomy 1977–82, 1987–91; Regents Fellow, Smithsonian Inst. 1984–88; mem. Council Royal Soc. 1983–85, 1993–95; Pres. Royal Astronomical Soc. 1992–94, British Asscn for the Advancement of Science 1994–95; Trustee British Museum 1996–2002, Inst. for Advanced Study, Princeton, USA 1998–2001, Nat. Endowment for Sciences, Tech. and Arts 1998, Kennedy Memorial Trust 1999, Inst. for Public Policy Research 2001; Foreign Assoc. NAS; mem. Academia Europaea 1989, Pontifical Acad. of Sciences 1990; Foreign mem. American Philosophical Soc., Royal Swedish Acad. of Science, Russian Acad. of Sciences, Norwegian Acad. of Arts and Science, Accad. Lincei (Rome), Royal Netherlands Acad.; Hon. Fellow Trinity Coll. and Jesus Coll., Cambridge, Indian Acad. of Sciences, Univ. of Wales, Cardiff 1998, Inst. of Physics 2001; Foreign Hon. mem. American Acad. of Arts and Sciences; Officier, Ordre des Arts et des Lettres; Hon. DSc (Sussex) 1990, (Leicester) 1993, (Copenhagen, Keele, Uppsala, Newcastle) 1995, (Toronto) 1997, (Durham) 1999, (Oxford) 2000; Heinemann Prize, American Inst. of Physics 1984, Gold Medal (Royal Astronomical Soc.) 1987, Guthrie Medal, Inst. of Physics 1989, Balzan Prize 1989, Robinson Prize for Cosmology 1990, Bruce Medal, Astronomical Soc. of Pacific 1993, Science Writing Award, American Inst. of Physics 1996, Bower Award (Franklin Inst.) 1998, Rossi Prize, American Astronomical Soc. 2000, Cosmology Prize of Gruber Foundation 2001. *Publications:* Perspectives in Astrophysical Cosmology 1995, Gravity's Fatal Attraction (with M. Begelman) 1995, Before the Beginning 1997, Just Six Numbers 1999, Our Cosmic Habitat 2001, Our Final

Century? 2003; edited books; articles and reviews in scientific journals and numerous gen. articles. *Address:* King's College, Cambridge, CB2 1ST, England. *Telephone:* (1223) 337548 (Office).

REES, Rt Hon Merlyn (see Merlyn-Rees, Baron).

REES, Roger; British actor; b. 5 May 1944, Aberystwyth, Wales; ed Camberwell and Slade Schools of Art; with RSC 1967–; Assoc. Dir Bristol Old Vic Theatre Co. 1986–. *Stage appearances include:* Hindle Wakes 1964, The Taming of the Shrew, Othello, Major Barbara, Macbeth, Twelfth Night, The Suicide, The Adventures of Nicholas Nickleby, Hapgood, Hamlet, Love's Labours Lost, The Real Thing, Double Double (also writer), Indiscretions, The End of the Day. *Film appearances include:* Star 80 1983, Keine Störung Bitte, Mountains of the Moon, If Looks Could Kill, Stop! Or My Mom Will Shoot, Robin Hood: Men in Tights 1993, Sudden Manhattan 1996, Titanic 1996, The Bumblebee Flies Away 1999, Double Platinum 1999, The Crossing 2000. *Television appearances include:* A Christmas Carol, Place of Peace, Under Western Eyes, Bouquet of Barbed Wire, Saigon: The Year of the Cat, Imaginary Friends, The Adventures of Nicholas Nickleby, The Comedy of Errors, Macbeth, The Voysey Inheritance, The Ebony Tower, The Finding, The Return of Sam McCloud, Charles & Diana: Unhappily Ever After, The Tower, The Possession of Michael D, Cheers, Singles, M.A.N.T.I.S.

REES-MOGG, Baron (Life Peer), cr. 1988, of Hinton Blewett in the County of Avon; **William Rees-Mogg,** Kt; British journalist; b. 14 July 1928, Bristol; s. of the late Edmund Fletcher and Beatrice Rees-Mogg (née Warren); m. Gillian Shakespeare Morris 1962; two s. three d.; ed Charterhouse and Balliol Coll., Oxford; Pres. Oxford Union 1951; Financial Times 1952–60, Chief Leader Writer 1955–60, Asst Ed. 1957–60; City Ed. Sunday Times 1960–61, Political and Econ. Ed. 1961–63, Deputy Ed. 1964–67; Ed. of The Times 1967–81, Dir The Times Ltd 1968–81; Vice-Chair. BBC 1981–86; Chair. Arts Council 1982–89; Chair. Broadcasting Standards Council 1988–93; mem. Exec. Bd Times Newspapers Ltd 1968–81, Dir 1978–81; Dir Gen. Electric Co. 1981–97; Chair. and Propr Pickering and Chatto Ltd (Publrs) 1983–; Chair. Sidgwick and Jackson 1985–89, Int. Business Communications PLC 1994–98; Dir M & G Group 1987, EFG Pvt. Bank and Trust Co. 1993–, Fleet Street Publications 1995–, Value Realization Trust PLC 1996–98, Nesmax Media, Inc., USA; columnist The Times 1992–; mem. Int. Cttee Pontifical Council for Culture 1983–87; Hon. LLD (Bath) 1977, (Leeds) 1992. *Publications:* The Reigning Error: the Crisis of World Inflation 1974, An Humbler Heaven 1977, How to Buy Rare Books 1985, Blood in the Streets (with James Dale Davidson) 1987, The Great Reckoning (with James Dale Davidson) 1992, Picnics on Vesuvius 1992, The Sovereign Individual (with James Dale Davidson) 1997. *Leisure interest:* collecting. *Address:* 17 Pall Mall, London, SW1Y 5LU, England. *Telephone:* (20) 7242-2241. *Fax:* (20) 7405-6216.

REESE, Colin Bernard, MA, PhD, ScD, FRS; British professor of organic chemistry; b. 29 July 1930, Plymouth; s. of the late Joseph Reese and Emily Reese; m. Susanne L. Bird 1968; one s. one d.; ed Dartington Hall School and Clare Coll., Cambridge; Research Fellow, Clare Coll. 1956–59, Harvard Univ. 1957–58; Official Fellow and Dir of Studies in Chem., Clare Coll. 1959–73; Demonstrator in Chem., Univ. of Cambridge 1959–63, Asst Dir of Research 1963–64, Univ. Lecturer in Chem. 1964–73; Daniell Prof. of Chem., King's Coll. London 1973–98, Fellow 1989, Prof. of Organic Chem. 1999–. *Publications:* scientific papers mainly in chemistry journals. *Address:* Department of Chemistry, King's College London, Strand, London, WC2R 2LS, England. *Telephone:* (20) 7848-2260 (Office). *Fax:* (20) 7848-1771 (Office). *E-mail:* colin.reese@kcl.ac.uk (Office).

REEVE, Sir Anthony, KCMG, KCVO, MA; British diplomatist (retd); b. 20 Oct. 1938, Wakefield; s. of Sidney Reeve and Dorothy Reeve (née Mitchell); m. 1st Pamela Margaret Angus 1964 (divorced 1988); one s. two d.; m. 2nd Susan Doull (née Collins) 1997; ed Queen Elizabeth Grammar School, Wakefield, Marling School, Stroud and Merton Coll., Oxford; joined Lever Bros and Assocs 1962–65; entered Diplomatic Service 1965; Middle East Centre for Arab Studies 1966–68; Asst Political Agent, Abu Dhabi 1968–70; First Sec. FCO 1970–73; First Sec., later Counsellor, Washington 1973–78; Head of Arms Control and Disarmament Dept FCO 1979–81; Counsellor, Cairo 1981–84; Head Southern Africa Dept, FCO 1984–86; Asst Under Sec. of State 1986–88; Amb. to Jordan 1988–91; Amb. to, later High Commr in, SA 1991–96; Chair. Foundation, SA 1998–2001; Dir (non-exec.) Barclays Pvt. Bank 1997–2001; Vice-Chair. Curzon Corpn 1998–. *Leisure interests:* music, golf. *Address:* Box Cottage, Horsley, Stroud, Glos., GL6 0QB, England. *Telephone:* (1453) 832891. *Fax:* (1453) 832608.

REEVE, Christopher, BA; American actor; b. 25 Sept. 1952, New York; one s. one d.; m. Dana Morosini; one s.; ed Cornell Univ., Juilliard School, New York; appeared on stage in New York in Street Smart 1986, The Winter's Tale 1989; and in more than 110 stage productions in USA and England. *Television appearances include:* Anna Karenina 1985, The Great Escape 1988, Rear Window 1998. *Films include:* Somewhere in Time, Superman, Superman 2, Deathtrap, Monsignor, Superman 3, The Bostonians, The Aviator, Superman 4, Street Smart 1988, Switching Channels 1988, Noises Off 1992, The Remains of the Day 1993, Morning Glory 1993, Speechless 1994, The Rhinehart Theory 1994, Village of the Damned 1995, A Step Toward Tomorrow 1996, Rear Window 1998. *Address:* c/o Scott Henderson, William Morris Agency, 151 El Camino Drive, Beverly Hills, CA 90212, USA.

REEVE, Michael David, MA, FBA; British professor of Latin; b. 11 Jan. 1943, Bolton, Lancs.; s. of Arthur Reeve and Edith Mary Barrett; m. Elizabeth Klingaman 1970 (divorced 1999); two s. one d.; partner Emma Gee; one s.; ed King Edward's School, Birmingham, Balliol Coll., Oxford; Harmsworth Sr Scholar, Merton Coll., Oxford 1964–65; Woodhouse Research Fellow, St John's Coll., Oxford 1965–66; Tutorial Fellow, Exeter Coll., Oxford 1966–84, Emer. Fellow 1984–; Kennedy Prof. of Latin and Fellow Pembroke Coll., Univ. of Cambridge 1984–; Visiting Prof. Univ. of Hamburg 1976, McMaster Univ. 1979, Univ. of Toronto 1982–83; Ed., Classical Quarterly 1981–86; Corresp. mem. Akad. der Wissenschaften, Göttingen 1990–; Foreign mem. Istituto Lombardo, Milan 1993–. *Publications:* Longus, Daphnis and Chloe 1982; contributions to Texts and Transmission 1983; Cicero, Pro Quinctio 1992; articles in European and American journals. *Leisure interests:* chess, music, gardening, mountain walking. *Address:* Pembroke College, Cambridge, CB2 1RF, England. *Fax:* (1223) 335409 (Office). *E-mail:* mdr1000@cam.ac.uk (Office).

REEVES, Christopher Reginald, CBIM; British merchant banker; b. 14 Jan. 1936, Cardiff; s. of Reginald Reeves and Dora Tucker; m. Stella Jane Whinney 1965; three s.; ed Malvern Coll.; served in Rifle Brigade, Kenya and Malaya 1955–58; Bank of England 1958–63; Hill Samuel & Co. Ltd 1963–67; joined Morgan Grenfell & Co. Ltd 1968, Dir 1970, Head of Banking Div. 1972, Deputy Chair. 1975–84, Chief Exec. 1980–84, Chair. and Group Chief Exec. 1984–87; Sr Adviser, Pres. Merrill Lynch Int. Ltd 1988, Vice-Chair. 1989–93, Chair. 1993–98, Deputy Chair. 1998–; Chair. Merrill Lynch Europe 1993–98, Merrill Lynch and Co. Inc. 1998–; Chair. MGM Assurance Group 1999–; Dir Cornhill Insurance (fmrly Allianz Int. Insurance Co. Ltd) 1983–, BICC PLC (now Balfour Beatty PLC) 1982–, Int. Freehold Properties SARL 1988–96, Andrew Weir and Co. Ltd 1982–92, Oman Int. Bank 1984–2001, India Fund 1989–, India Growth Fund 1989–, Austro-Hungary Fund 1990–95, Merrill Lynch Africa Ltd (fmrly Smith Borkum Hare (Pty) Ltd) 1996–99, DSP Merrill Lynch 1997–; mem. City Univ. Business School Council 1986–93, CBI Council 1998–2001; Gov. Dulwich Coll. Preparatory School 1977–; Treas. City Univ. 1992–. *Leisure interests:* sailing, shooting, skiing. *Address:* 64 Flood Street, London, SW3 5TE, England.

REEVES, Keanu; American actor; b. 2 Sept. 1964, Beirut, Lebanon; s. of Samuel Nowin Reeves and Patricia Reeves; ed Toronto High School for Performing Arts; training at Second City Workshop; Toronto stage debut in Wolf Boy; other stage appearances in For Adults Only, Romeo and Juliet; with rock band Dogstar 1996–. *Television films:* Letting Go 1985, Act of Vengeance 1986, Babes in Toyland 1986, Under the Influence 1986, Brotherhood of Justice 1986, Save the Planet (TV special) 1990. *Films:* Prodigal, Flying 1986, Youngblood 1986, River's Edge 1987, Permanent Record 1988, The Night Before 1988, The Prince of Pennsylvania 1988, Dangerous Liaisons 1988, 18 Again 1988, Bill and Ted's Excellent Adventure 1988, Parenthood 1989, I Love You to Death 1990, Tune In Tomorrow 1990, Bill and Ted's Bogus Journey 1991, Point Break 1991, My Own Private Idaho 1991, Bram Stoker's Dracula 1992, Much Ado About Nothing 1993, Even Cowgirls Get the Blues, Little Buddha 1993, Speed 1994, Johnny Mnemonic 1995, A Walk in the Clouds 1995, Chain Reaction, Feeling Minnesota, The Devil's Advocate 1996, The Last Time I Committed Suicide 1997, The Matrix 1998, The Replacements 2000, The Watcher 2000, The Gift 2000, Sweet November 2001, The Matrix: Reloaded 2003. *Address:* 581 North Crescent Heights Boulevard, Los Angeles, CA 90048 (Office); c/o Kevin Houvane, 9830 Wilshire Boulevard, Beverly Hills, CA 90212, USA.

REEVES, Marjorie Ethel, CBE, PhD, DLitt, FRHistS, FBA; British university teacher (retd); b. 17 July 1905, Bratton, Wilts.; d. of Robert John Reeves and Edith Sarah Reeves (née Whitaker); ed Trowbridge Girls' High School, Wilts., St Hugh's Coll. Oxford and Westfield Coll. London; History Mistress, Roan School for Girls, Greenwich, London 1927–29; History Lecturer, St Gabriel's Coll., London 1931–38; Tutor, later Fellow, St Anne's Coll. Oxford and Univ. Lecturer 1938–72, Vice-Prin. St Anne's Coll. 1948–68; Hon. Citizen of San Giovanni, Italy 1994; Hon. DLitt (Bath) 1992, (Queen Mary and Westfield Coll., London) 1998; Medlicott Medal 1993. *Publications:* The Influence of Prophecy in the Later Middle Ages 1969, The Figurae of Joachim of Fiore 1972, Joachim of Fiore and the Prophetic Future 1976, Sheepbell and Ploughshare 1978, Joachim of Fiore and the Myth of the Eternal Evangel in the Nineteenth Century (with Warwick Gould) 1987, Competence, Delight and the Common Good: reflections on the crisis in higher education 1988, The Diaries of Jeffrey Whitaker 1739–1741 (with J. Morrison) 1989, Prophetic Rome in the High Renaissance Period (ed.) 1992, Pursuing the Muses: A Study of Culture and Education from Two Collections of Family Papers 1700–1900 1996, Christian Thinking and Social Order, 1930 to the Present Day (ed. and contrib.) 1999, The Prophetic Sense of History in Medieval and Renaissance Europe 1999, Favourite Hymns: 2000 Years of Magnificat 2001; numerous books in the Then and There Series. *Leisure interests:* gardening, music. *Address:* 38 Norham Road, Oxford, OX2 6SQ, England. *Telephone:* (1865) 557039.

REEVES, Most Rev. Sir Paul Alfred, GCMG, GCVO, QSO, MA, LTh; New Zealand ecclesiastic, administrator and academic; b. Paul Alfred Reeves, 6 Dec. 1932, Wellington; s. of D'Arcy Lionel Reeves and Hilda Mary Reeves; m. Beverley Watkins 1959; three d.; ed Wellington Coll., Vic. Univ. of Wellington, St John's Theological Coll., Auckland and St Peter's Coll., Oxford; Deacon 1958; Priest 1960; Curate, Tokoroa, NZ 1958–59, St Mary the Virgin, Oxford 1959–61, Kirkley St Peter, Lowestoft 1961–63; Vicar, St Paul, Okato, NZ

1964–66; Lecturer in Church History St John's Coll., Auckland 1966–69; Dir of Christian Educ. Diocese of Auckland 1969–71; Bishop of Waiapu 1971–79, of Auckland 1979; Primate and Archbishop of New Zealand 1980–85; Gov.-Gen. of New Zealand 1985–90; Rep. of Anglican Church to UN 1991–93; Dean Te Rau Kahikatea Theological Coll., Auckland 1994–95; Prof. Auckland Univ. of Tech. 2000–; Chair. Environmental Council 1974–76; Deputy Leader Comm. of Observers S. African elections 1994; Leader Comm. of Observers Ghanaian elections 1996; Chair. Fijian Constitutional Review Comm. 1995–96; Visiting Prof. Univ. of Auckland 1997–2000; KStJ 1986; Hon. Fellow St Peter's Coll., Oxford 1980; Hon. DCL (Oxon.) 1985; Hon. LLD (Vic., NZ); Hon. DD (General, New York); Dr hc (Edin.) 1994; Companion of Order of Fiji 1999. *Leisure interests:* swimming, sailing, jogging. *Address:* Auckland University of Technology, Private Bag 92006, Auckland (Office); 16E Cathedral Place, Parnell, Auckland, New Zealand. *Telephone:* (9) 917-9672 (Office); (9) 302-2913. *Fax:* (9) 917-9983 (Office); (9) 309-9912 (Home). *E-mail:* paul .reeves@aut.ac.nz (Office); sirpaulreeves@hotmail.com (Home). *Website:* www.aut.ac.nz (Office).

REEVES, Saskia; British actress; b. London; d. of Peter Reeves; ed Guildhall School of Music and Drama, London; toured S. America, India and Europe with Cheek By Jowl theatre co. appearing in A Midsummer Night's Dream and The Man of Mode; subsequent stage appearances include: Metamorphosis (Mermaid), Who's Afraid of Virginia Woolf? (Young Vic), Measure for Measure (Young Vic), Separation (Hampstead Theatre), Smelling A Rat (Hampstead Theatre), Ice Cream (Royal Court), The Darker Face of the Earth; appeared in BBC TV In My Defence Series; other TV credits. *Films:* December Bride, Close My Eyes, The Butterfly Kiss, Much Ado About Nothing 1998.

REFALO, Michael A., BA(HONS), LLD; Maltese politician and lawyer; b. 25 Feb. 1936; s. of Edward Refalo; m. Blanche Smith; one s. three d.; ed St Aloysius Coll., Univ. of Malta; lawyer 1961; fmr Pres. of Students' Council; mem. Parl. 1971–; Parl. Sec. for Tourism 1987–94; Minister for Youth and the Arts 1994–95; Minister for Justice and the Arts 1995–96; Shadow Minister and Opposition Spokesman on Tourism 1996–98; Minister for Tourism 1998–; ed. for nine years of Sunday Nationalist Party newspaper; mem. Nationalist Party. *Publications:* editorials and articles in other newspapers. *Address:* Ministry of Tourism, Palazzo Spinola, St Julians, STJ 10, Malta. *Telephone:* 383847. *Fax:* 383834. *E-mail:* charles.micallef-st-john@magnet.mt.

REGAN, Donald Thomas, BA; American financial executive; b. 21 Dec. 1918, Cambridge, Mass.; s. of William F. Regan and Kathleen (née Ahern) Regan; m. Ann Gordon Buchanan 1942; two s. two d.; ed Harvard Univ.; US Marine Corps 1940–46, attaining rank of Lt.-Col; joined Merrill Lynch 1946, partner 1953; Vice-Pres. Merrill Lynch, Pierce, Fenner & Smith Inc. 1959, Exec. Vice-Pres. 1964, Chair. of Bd and Chief Exec. Officer 1971–81; Chair. of Bd and Chief Exec. Officer Merrill Lynch and Co. Inc. 1973–81; Pres. Regdon Assocs 1987–; Sec. of the US Treasury 1981–85, White House Chief of Staff 1985–87; Vice-Chair. Bd of Dirs of NYSE 1972–75; mem. Policy Cttee of Business Roundtable 1978–80; Trustee, Cttee for Econ. Devt 1978–80, Charles E Merrill Trust and Univ. of Pennsylvania; Hon. LLD (Hahnemann Medical Coll. and Hospital, Univ. of Penn., Tri-State Coll.); Commdr Légion d'honneur; Hon. LLD (Middlebury Coll.) 1999. *Publications:* A View from the Street 1972, For the Record: From Wall Street to Washington 1988. *Address:* Marketplace Center, 240 McLaws Circle, Suite 142, Williamsburg, VA 23185, USA. *Telephone:* (757) 220-5177. *Fax:* (757) 220-6270.

REGÁS, Rosa; Spanish writer; b. 1934, Barcelona; m.; five c.; ed Barcelona Univ.; with Seix Barral 1964-70, with Edhasa (both publrs); trans. for UN; f. La Gaya Ciencia; Premio Nadal for Azul 1994. *Publications include:* Memoria de Almator (novel) 1991, Azul (novel) 1993, La Canción de Dorotea (Planeta Prize) 2001.

REGESTER, Michael; British consultant; b. 8 April 1947, Godalming; s. of Hugh Regester and Monique Levrey; m. 1st Christine Regester 1969 (divorced 1993); two d.; m. 2nd Leanne Moscardi 1994 (divorced 2003); one s. one d.; ed St Peter's Coll., Guildford; Man. Public Affairs, Gulf Oil Corpn, Europe, W Africa and Middle East 1975–80; Co-Founder and Jt Man. Dir Traverse-Healy and Regester Ltd 1980–87; Man. Dir Charles Barker Traverse-Healy Ltd 1987–89; Man. Dir Regester PLC 1990–94; partner Regester Larkin 1994–. *Publications:* Crisis Management 1987, Investor Relations (with N. Ryder) 1990, Issues and Crisis Management (with J. Larkin) 1997. *Leisure interests:* sailing, golf, tennis, opera, cooking. *Address:* Regester Larkin Ltd, 16 Doughty Street, London, WC1N 2PL, England (Office). *Telephone:* (20) 7831-3839. *Fax:* (20) 7831-3632. *E-mail:* mregester@regesterlarkin.co.uk (Office).

REGGIANI, Serge; Italian-born French actor and singer; b. 2 May 1922, Reggio nell'Emilia; s. of Ferruccio Reggiani and Letizia Spagni; m. 1st Janine Darcey; one s. (deceased) one d.; m. 2nd Annie Noël (divorced); two s. one d.; m. 3rd Noelle Adam-Chaplin 2003; ed Conservatoire Nat. d'Art Dramatique; theatrical roles in Britannicus, Les parents terribles, Un homme comme les autres, Les trois mousquetaires, Les séquestrés d'Altona, etc.; Officier, Légion d'honneur, Ordre nat. du Mérite, Commdr, Ordre des Arts et des Lettres, Victoire d'honneur de la musique 1998. *Exhibition:* paintings, Vekava Gallery, Paris 1997. *Films include:* Le carrefour des enfants perdus, Les portes de la nuit, Manon, Les amants de Vérone, La ronde 1950, Casque d'or, Napoléon, Les salauds vont en enfer, Les misérables, Marie Octobre, La grande pagaille, La guerre continue, Tutti a casa, Le Doulos, Le guépard, Marie-Chantal contre le Docteur Kah, Les aventuriers, La 25e heure, La mafia fait sa loi, L'armée des ombres, Comptes à rebours, Touche pas à la

femme blanche 1974, Vincent, François, Paul . . . et les autres 1974, Le chat et la souris (Cat and Mouse) 1975, Une fille cousue de fil blanc 1977, L'empreinte des géants, Fantastica, La terrasse 1980, Mauvais sang 1986, L'Apiculture 1986, Ne réveillez pas un flic qui dort 1988, Coupe Franche 1989, Il y a des jours . . . et des lunes 1990, J'ai engagé un tueur 1991, De force avec d'autres 1993, Le petit garçon 1993, Saint-Cyr 2001. *Albums include:* Reggiani 91 1998, Nos quatre vérités 1998, 70 Balais 1998, Pour vous 1999, Les adieux différés 1999, Collection J. Canetti 1999 (Gold Record), Serge Reggiani l'Italien 1999, Elle Veut 2000, Le Zouave du Pont de l'Alma 2000, J't'aimerais 2000, Les Talents 2000, (tribute) Autour de Reggiani 2002. *Publications:* La question se pose 1990, Dernier courrier avant la nuit 1995. *Address:* Galerie Vekava, 8 rue de Charonne, 75011 Paris (Office); c/o Charley Marouani, 37 rue Marbeuf, 75008 Paris; c/o Artmédia, 10 avenue George V, 75008 Paris, France.

REGIS, John; British athlete; b. 13 Oct. 1966, Lewisham; s. of Antony Regis and Agnes Regis; winner, UK 200m 1985 (tie), 100m 1988, Amateur Athletics Asscn 200m 1986–87; UK record for 200m, World Championships 1987; World Championships bronze medallist 200m, silver medal, Olympic Games Seoul 1988, 300m indoor record holder Commonwealth Games 1990; silver medal 200m 1991, gold medal 4×100m relay 1991; gold medal 200m, 4×100m relay, 4×400m relay 1993; gold medal World Cup 1994, mem. British team Olympic Games, Atlanta 1996; retd 2000; mem. GB bobsleigh training team 2000–; f. Stellar Athletes Ltd (athletics man. team) 2001; coach UK Athletics sprint-relay team 2001–. *Leisure interests:* golf, tennis, martial arts. *Address:* c/o Belgrave Harriers Athletic Club, Batley Croft, 58 Harvest Road, Englefield Green, Surrey, England.

REGO, Paula; British artist; b. 26 Jan. 1935, Lisbon, Portugal; d. of José Figueiroa Rego and Maria de San José Paiva Figueiroa Rego; m. Victor Willing (died 1988); one s. two d.; ed St Julian's School, Carcavelos, Portugal, Slade School of Fine Art, University Coll. London; Assoc. Artist to Nat. Gallery 1990; Sr Fellow Royal Coll. of Art 1989; Dr hc (St Andrews), (Univ. of E Anglia), (Rhode Island School of Design, USA) 2000, (London Inst.) 2002. *Exhibitions:* one-person exhbns since 1979 in London, Lisbon, Amsterdam, Plymouth, Manchester, Bristol, Kendal, Dulwich Picture Gallery, London 1998, Yale USA; retrospective exhbns at Gulbenkian Foundation, Lisbon 1989, Serpentine Gallery, London 1989, 1992, Tate Gallery, Liverpool 1997, Centro Cultural de Belém, Lisbon 1997; included in many mixed exhbns in Paris, Rome, São Paulo, Tokyo, Madrid, Baden-Baden, New York, UK. *Television:* The South Bank Show 1992, Artsworld 'The Passion of Paula Rego' 2001, Paulo Rego (BBC Four) 2002. *Publications:* Monograph Phaidon 1992, 1997, Peter Pan (etchings) 1992, Nursery Rhymes (etchings) 1994, Pendle Witches (etchings) 1996, Children's Crusade (etchings) 1999, Monograph 2002. *Address:* c/o Marlborough Fine Art, 6 Albemarle Street, London, W1X 4BY, England. *Telephone:* (20) 7629-5161.

REGY, Claude, LLB; French theatre director; b. 1 May 1923, Nîmes; s. of Marcel Régy and Suzanne Picheral; ed Univs of Algiers, Lyons and Paris; dir plays by Marguerite Duras, Harold Pinter, James Saunders, Tom Stoppard, Edward Bond, David Storey 1960–70, by Nathalie Sarraute, Peter Handke, Botho Strauss 1970–80, by Maeterlinck, Wallace Stevens, Leslie Kaplan, Victor Slavkine 1980–90, by Gregory Motton, Henri Meschonnic, Charles Reznikoff, Jon Fosse, David Harrower 1990–2000; dir Ivanov (Chekhov) 1985, Huis-Clos (J. P. Sartre) 1990 (both at Comédie Française), Melancholia Théâtre (J. Fosse) 2001, 4.48 Psychose (S. Kane) 2002, Variations sur la mort (J. Fosse) 2003; dir operas Die Meistersinger (Wagner), Théâtre du Chatelet 1990, Jeanne d'Arc au Bûcher (Honegger), Opéra Bastille 1992, Carnet d'un Disparu (Janacek), Kunsten Festival des Arts, Festival d'Aix-en-Provence 2001; Artistic Dir Les Ateliers Contemporains 1976–; Officier des Arts et des Lettres; Grand Prix Nat. du Théâtre 1992, Grand Prix des Arts de la Scène de la Ville de Paris 1994. *Film:* Conversation avec Nathalie Sarraute 1989. *Publications:* Espaces Perdus 1991, L'Ordre des Morts 1999, L'Etat d'Incertitude 2002. *Leisure interest:* country house. *Address:* Les Ateliers contemporains, 68 rue J. J. Rousseau, 75001 Paris, France. *Telephone:* 1-48-87-95-10 (Office); 1-42-33-34-11 (Home).

REHME, Robert; American film producer; m.; two d.; ed Univ. of Cincinnati; Pres., CEO Avco Embassy Pictures 1978–81; Pres. worldwide distribution and marketing, Universal Pictures, then Pres. Theatrical Motion Picture Group 1981–83; Co-Chair., CEO New World Entertainment Inc. 1983–89; Co-founder, partner Neufeld/Rehme Productions 1989–; Pres. Acad. of Motion Picture Arts and Sciences 1996–; Chair. American Film Inst.'s Center for Advanced Film and TV Studies (CAFTS – AFI Conservatory), 2000–; mem. BAFTA. *Films:* (cinema) Patriot Games, Beverly Hills Cop 3, Clear and Present Danger; (TV) Gettysburg (TNT), Gridlock (NBC). *Address:* Academy of Motion Picture Arts and Sciences, 8949 Wilshire blvd, Beverly Hills, CA 90211, USA (Office). *Telephone:* (213) 856-7667 (Office).

REHN, Elisabeth, DSc; Finnish international official and politician; b. 6 April 1935; m. Ove Rehn 1955; one s. three d.; fmr leader Swedish People's Party in Parl.; fmr Minister of Defence, fmr Minister for Women's Equality; cand. in Finnish Presidential election 1994; MEP 1995–96; UN Special Rapporteur for Human Rights in fmr Yugoslavia 1995–98; Special Rep. of Sec.-Gen. of the UN in Bosnia and Herzegovina Jan. 1998–. *Leisure interests:* fine arts, sports, nature. *Address:* UNMIBH, O/SRSG, Geodetski Zavod, Mese Selimovica 69, 71210 Ilidza, Sarajevo, Bosnia and Herzegovina.

REHNQUIST, William H., LLB, MA; American judge; b. 1 Oct. 1924, Milwaukee, Wis.; s. of William Benjamin Rehnquist and Margery Peck Rehnquist; m. Natalie Cornell 1953; one s. two d.; ed Stanford and Harvard Univs; law clerk to US Supreme Court Justice R. H. Jackson 1952–53; pvt. practice, Evans, Kitchel and Jenckes, Phoenix, Ariz. 1953–57, Cunningham, Messenger, Carson & Elliott 1957–60, Powers & Rehnquist 1960–69; Asst Attorney-Gen., Office of Legal Counsel, Dept of Justice 1969–71; Assoc. Justice, Supreme Court of USA 1971–86, Chief Justice 1986–; Hon. Master of the Bench, Middle Temple, London 1986–; mem. American Bar Asscn, American Judicature Soc., etc. *Publications:* Grand Inquests 1992, All the Laws But One: Civil Liberties in Wartime 1998, All the Laws But One 1999, The Supreme Court: A History 2001. *Address:* Supreme Court of the United States, 1 First Street, NE, Washington, DC 20543, USA. *Telephone:* (202) 479-3000. *Fax:* (202) 479-3021.

REICH, Otto Juan; Cuban-American government official; b. 1945, Cuba; ed Univ. of N. Carolina, Georgetown Univ.; Lt, 3rd Civil Affairs Detachment, Panama Canal Zone, US Army 1967–69; Asst Admin. Econ. Assistance to Latin America and the Caribbean, US Agency for Int. Devt (USAID) 1981–83; Special Adviser to Sec. of State 1983–86; est. and Man. Office of Public Diplomacy for Latin America, the Caribbean and US Dept of State 1983–86; Amb. to Venezuela 1986–89; Alt. Rep. to UN Human Rights Comm., Geneva 1991–92; Asst Sec. of State for Western Hemisphere Affairs 2001–02, Special Envoy Nov. 2002–Jan. 2003; Presidential Special Envoy for Latin America, Nat. Security Council 2003–; Pnr, later Pres. Brock Group (consulting firm) 1989–2001; Dir Center for a Free Cuba, Washington DC; lobbyist numerous cos including Bacardi and Lockheed Martin; fmr Washington Dir Council of the Americas; fmr Community Devt Co-ordinator for City of Miami, FL; fmr Int. Rep. of FL Dept of Commerce; fmr staff asst US House of Reps; Meritorious Honour Award, Dept of State. *Address:* c/o Department of State, 2201 C Street, NW, Washington, DC 20520, USA (Office).

REICH, Robert Bernard, MA, JD; American politician and political economist; b. 24 June 1946, Scranton, Pa; s. of Edwin Saul and Mildred Dorf (Freshman) Reich; m. Clare Dalton 1973; two s.; ed Dartmouth Coll., Oxford Univ. (UK), Yale Univ.; Asst Solicitor-Gen., US Dept of Justice, Washington 1974–76; Dir of Policy Planning FTC, Washington 1976–81; mem. Faculty John F. Kennedy School of Govt, Harvard Univ. 1981–92; fmr Econ. Adviser to Pres. Bill Clinton; Sec. of Labor 1993–97; Prof. Brandeis Univ. Grad. School for Advanced Studies in Social Welfare 1997–; Chair. Biotechnology Section US Office Tech. Assessment, Washington 1990–91; Chair. Editorial Bd The American Prospect 1990–; mem. Bd of Dirs, Econ. Policy Inst., Washington; Contributing Ed. The New Republic, Washington 1982–93; Rhodes Scholar 1968. *Publications:* The Next American Frontier 1983, Tales of a New America 1987, The Power of Public Ideas (Co-author) 1987, The Work of Nations 1991, Putting People First 1997, Locked in the Cabinet 1997, The Future of Success 2001. *Address:* Brandeis University, 415 South Street, Waltham, MA 022454. *Telephone:* (781) 736-2000. *Fax:* (781) 736-8699. *Website:* www.brandeis.edu (Office).

REICH, Steve, MA; American composer; b. 3 Oct. 1936, New York; s. of Leonard Reich and June Carroll; m. Beryl Korot 1976; two s.; ed Cornell Univ., Juilliard School of Music, Mills Coll.; studied composition with Berio and Milhaud; also studied at the American Soc. for Eastern Arts and in Accra and Jerusalem; f. own ensemble 1966; Steve Reich and Musicians have completed numerous tours world-wide 1971–; his music performed by maj. orchestras and ensembles in United States and Europe; recipient of three Rockefeller Foundation Grants 1975–81 and a Guggenheim Fellowship; mem. American Acad. of Arts and Letters 1994–, Bavarian Acad. of Fine Arts 1999; Regent Lectureship, Univ. of Calif. at Berkeley 1999; Montgomery Fellowship, Dartmouth Coll.; Dr hc (Calif. Inst. of the Arts) 2000; Commdr des Arts et Lettres; award from the Koussevitzky Foundation 1981, Grammy Award for best contemporary composition (for Different Trains) 1990, (for Music for 18 Musicians) 1995; Schumann Prize, Columbia Univ. 2000. *Major works include:* Drumming 1971, The Desert Music 1984, Tehillim 1982, Eight Lines for Chamber Orchestra 1985, Music for 18 Musicians, Vermont Counterpoint, The Four Sections 1987, Different Trains 1988, The Cave (with Beryl Korot) 1993, City Life 1995, Proverb 1996. *Recordings include:* Come Out, Violin Phase, It's Gonna Rain, Four Organs, Drumming, Six Pianos, Music for Mallet Instruments, Voices and Organ, Music for a Large Ensemble, Octet and Variations for Winds, Strings and Keyboards, Music for 18 Musicians, The Desert Music, Electric Counterpoint, Different Trains, The Four Sections, Nagoya Marimbas, City Life, Proverb, Hindenburg (in collaboration with Beryl Korot). *Address:* c/o IMG Artists, 22 E 71st Street, New York, NY 10021, USA; c/o Boosey & Hawkes Inc., 35 East 21st Street, New York, NY 10010, USA.

REICH-RANICKI, Marcel; German author and literary critic; b. 2 June 1920, Wloclawek; s. of David Reich and Helene Auerbach; m. Teofila Langnas 1942; one s.; in Berlin 1929–38; deported to Poland 1938; publr, reader and literary critic, Warsaw until 1958; returned to Germany 1958; regular literary critic Die Zeit 1960–73; guest lecturer in US univs 1968–69; regular guest Prof. of Modern German Literature in Univs of Stockholm and Uppsala 1971–75; Man. Ed. Frankfurter Allgemeine Zeitung 1973–88; Hon. Prof. Univ. of Tübingen 1974–; DPhil hc (Univ. of Augsburg) 1992, (Univ. of Brandenburg) 1997, (Univ. of Düsseldorf) 2001, (Univ. of Utrecht) 2001; Heine-Plakette 1976, Ricarda Huch Prize 1981, Goethe-Plakette 1984, Thomas-Mann-Preis 1987, Ludwig-Börne-Preis 1995, Hess Kulturpreis 1999,

Goldenes Kamera 2000, Friedrich-Hölderin-Preis 2001. *Publications:* Deutsche Literatur in West und Ost 1963, Literarisches Leben in Deutschland 1965, Literatur der kleinen Schritte 1967, Lauter Verrisse 1970, Uber Ruhestörer-Juden in der deutschen Literatur 1973, Zur Literatur der DDR 1974, Nachprüfung, Aufsätze über deutsche Schriftsteller von gestern 1977, Entgegnung, Zur deutschen Literatur der siebziger Jahre 1979, Betrifft Goethe 1982, Lauter Lobreden 1985, Nichts als Literatur, Aufsätze und Anmerkungen 1985, Mehr als ein Dichter, Über Heinrich Böll 1986, Thomas Mann und die Seinen 1987, Herz, Ärzt und Literatur 1987, Thomas Bernhard, Aufsätze und Reden 1990, Max Frisch, Aufsätze 1991, Reden auf Hilde Spiel 1991, Ohne Rabatt—Über Literatur aus der DDR, Der doppelte Boden 1992, Günter Grass, Aufsätze 1992, Die Anwälte der Literatur 1994, Martin Walser 1994, Vladimir Nabokov 1995, Ungeheuer oben. Über Bertolt Brecht 1996, Der Fall Heine 1997, Sowie 'Mein Leben' 1999. *Leisure interests:* literature, theatre, music. *Address:* Frankfurter Allgemeine, Hellerhofstr. 2–4, 60327 Frankfurt am Main (Office); Gustav-Freytag-Strasse 36, 60320 Frankfurt am Main, Germany. *Fax:* (69) 75911623 (Office).

REICHARDT, Robert Heinrich, D. PHIL; Austrian/Swiss professor of sociology, social philosophy and methodology of the social sciences; b. 2 May 1927, Basel; s. of Heinrich Reichardt and Magdalena (née Bachlehner) Reichardt; m. Dr Isolde Dünhofen; ed Univ. of Basel; Research Assoc. Princeton Univ. 1960–61; Asst Inst. for Social Sciences, Univ. of Basel 1962–64; Dir Dept for Sociology, Inst. for Higher Studies, Vienna 1964–66; Prof. Univ. of Vienna 1966; Exec. Dir Inst. for Research on Socio-Econ. Devt, Austrian Acad. of Sciences 1977–84, Head Comm. for Sociology of Arts and Music 1990–; mem. Austrian Acad. of Sciences 1978–; Fellow Collegium Ramazzini Carpi, Italy 1990, Academia Artium et Scientiarum Europaea 1991; Co-operative Prize, Univ. of Basel 1960, Gold Medal of Honour, City of Vienna 1993. *Publications:* Die Schallplatte als kulturelles und ökon. Phänomen, Bedürfnisforschung im Dienste der Stadtplanung, Überleben wir den technischen Fortschritt (with others), Einführung in die Soziologie für Juristen. *Leisure interests:* composition, playing the piano.

REICHMANN, Paul; Canadian business executive; b. 1930, Vienna, Austria; s. of Samuel Reichmann and Renée Reichmann; moved to Toronto 1954; with brothers Ralph and Albert Reichmann formed Olympia & York Devts Ltd (business engaged mainly in real estate but with investments in Gulf Canada, The Consumers Gas Co., Abitibi-Price real estate); completed First Canadian Place, Toronto (five million sq. ft of offices) 1975; purchased eight office bldgs in Manhattan, New York 1976; completed cldg of World Financial Center (ten million sq. ft of offices) in New York 1986; responsible for concept and realization of Canary Wharf project in London's Docklands 1987; now Exec. Chair. Canary Wharf Group PLC; Chief Exec. of Reichmann Group of Cos, including Int. Property Corpn (with interests in real estate devt projects in Mexico); Trustee and Unitholder Retirement Residence Real Estate Investment Trust, CPL Long Term Care Real Estate Investment Trust, IPC US Income Commercial Real Estate Investment Trust. *Address:* c/o Canary Wharf Group PLC, 1 Canada Square, Canary Wharf, London, E14 5AB, England (Office). *Telephone:* (20) 7418-2244 (Office); (20) 7418-2000. *Fax:* (20) 7418-2085 (Office). *E-mail:* paul.reichmann@canarywharf.com (Office). *Website:* www.canarywharf.com (Office).

REICHSTUL, Henri Philippe; Brazilian oil industry executive; Vice-Pres. Banco Interamerican Express –1999; Pres. Petrobras 1999–. *Address:* Petrobras, Praca Pio X 119, Caixa Postal 809, Rio de Janeiro, Brazil (Office); Petróleo Brasileiro SA, Av. República do Chile 65, 20035-900 Rio de Janeiro, RJ. *Telephone:* (21) 534-4477. *Fax:* (21) 220-5052. *Website:* www.petrobras.com (Office).

REID, Allen (Alan) Forrest, AM, PhD, FAA, F.T.S.E.; Australian scientist; b. 26 March 1931, New Zealand; s. of V. C. Reid and L. E Reid; m. Prudence M. Little; two s. one d. two step-d.; ed Univ. of NZ, Christchurch, ANU, Canberra, Cornell Univ., New York; joined CSIRO 1959, research scientist 1972–82, Chief research scientist 1972–82, Chief Div. of Mineral Engineering 1982–84, Dir Inst. of Energy and Earth Resources 1984–87, Inst. of Minerals, Energy and Construction 1988–97; Chair. Australia Environmental Resources NL 1996–97, Dir 1997–; Chair. Man. Bd Australian Petroleum Co-operative Research Centre 1991–; Dir Australian Minerals and Energy Environmental Foundation 1991–; CSIRO Rivett Medal 1970. *Publications:* more than 80 scientific papers and six patents. *Leisure interests:* travel, art, gardening. *Address:* 178 Ward Street, North Adelaide, SA 5006, Australia.

REID, Chip, MBA; American business executive; b. 1948, Washington; four d.; ed Yale Univ., Harvard Univ.; corp. securities lawyer, Covington & Burling 1976, partner 1982, Head of Corp. and Securities Practice 1988; CEO Bacardi-Martini 1996–. *Leisure interests:* 1960s music, boating, cinema, golf. *Address:* Bacardi-Martini, 2100 Biscayne Boulevard, Miami, FL 33137, USA (Office). *Telephone:* (305) 573-8511 (Office).

REID, Harry, JD; American politician; b. 2 Dec. 1939, Searchlight, Nevada; s. of Harry Reid and Inez Reid; m. Landra Joy Gould; four s. one d.; ed Utah State Univ., George Washington Univ.; City Attorney, Henderson, Nev. 1964–66; Trustee, Southern Nev. Memorial Hosp. Bd 1967–69, Chair. Bd of Trustees 1968–69; mem. Nev. Ass. 1969–70; Lt-Gov. of Nev. 1970–74; Chair. Nev. Gaming Comm. 1977–81; Congressman, US House of Reps, Washington 1983–87; Senator from Nevada Jan. 1987–; mem. numerous senate cttees; mem. Bd of Dirs of American Cancer Soc., of Legal Aid Soc., of YMCA;

Democrat; Hon. LLD (Southern Utah State Coll.) 1984; Nat. Jewish Hosp., Humanitarian Award 1984. *Address:* US Senate, Washington, DC 20510, USA.

REID, Rt Hon John, PC, PhD; British politician; b. 8 May 1947, Bellshill, Lanarkshire; s. of the late Thomas Reid and Mary Reid; m. 1st Catherine McGowan (died 1998); two s.; m. 2nd Carine Adler 2002; ed St Patrick's Sr Secondary School, Coatbridge and Stirling Univ.; Scottish; Research Officer, Labour Party 1979–83; Political Adviser to Neil Kinnock (q.v) 1983–85; Organizer, Scottish Trade Unionists for Labour 1985–87; MP for Motherwell N 1987–97, for Hamilton N and Bellshill 1997–; Opposition Spokesman on Children 1989–90, on Defence 1990–97; Minister of State for Defence 1997–98; Minister for Transport 1998–99; Sec. of State for Scotland 1999–2000; Sec. of State for NI 2000–02; Chair. of the Labour Party and Minister without Portfolio 2002–03; Leader of the House of Commons and Pres. of the Privy Council 2003–; mem. Armed Forces Cttee and Reserved Forces Cttee 1996–97. *Leisure interests:* football, reading history, crossword puzzles. *Address:* House of Commons, London, SW1A 0AA, England (Office). *Telephone:* (1698) 454672 (Office). *Fax:* (1698) 424732 (Office).

REID, Sir Norman Robert, Kt, DLitt, DA; British art gallery director; b. 27 Dec. 1915, London; s. of Edward Reid and Blanche Drouet; m. Jean Lindsay Bertram 1941; one s. one d.; ed Wilson's Grammar School, London, Edinburgh Coll. of Art and Edinburgh Univ.; Maj. Argyll and Sutherland Highlanders 1939–46; Tate Gallery 1946–79, Dir 1964–79; Fellow, Int. Inst. for Conservation of Historic and Artistic Works, Sec.-Gen. 1963–65, Vice-Chair. 1966–79; Chair. British Council Fine Art Cttee 1968–76; Fellow Museums Asscn, Int. Inst. for Conservation of Historic and Artistic Works; paintings in Tate Gallery, London, Scottish Nat. Gallery of Modern Art and many pvt. collections; Officer, Order of Aztec Eagle (Mexico); Hon. DLitt (E Anglia Univ.) 1970. *Exhibitions:* one-man exhbn London 1991; collages exhibited at Tate Gallery 1995, RA Summer exhbns. *Leisure interests:* painting, gardening. *Address:* 50 Brabourne Rise, Park Langley, Beckenham, Kent, England (Home).

REID, Sir Robert Paul (Bob), Kt, MA; British businessman; b. 1 May 1934; m. Joan Mary Reid 1958; three s.; ed St Andrews Univ.; joined Shell 1956, Sarawak Oilfields 1956–59, Head of Personnel Nigeria 1959–67; Africa and S. Asia Regional Org. 1967–68, Personal Asst and Planning Adviser to Chair. Shell & BP Services, Kenya 1968–70, Man. Dir Nigeria 1970–74, Man. Dir Thailand 1974–78; Vice-Pres. Int. Aviation and Products Training 1978–80, Exec. Dir Downstream Oil, Shell Co. of Australia Int. Petroleum Co. 1984–90, Chair. and Chief Exec. Shell UK 1985–90; Chair. Foundation for Man. Educ. 1986–; Chair. British Railways Bd 1990–95, London Electricity PLC 1994–97, Sears PLC 1995–99, Rosyth 2000 1995–, Int. Petroleum Exchange 1999–; Deputy Gov. Bank of Scotland 1997–; Dir AVIS 1997–, Sun Life Assurance Co. of Canada 1997–, HBOS 2001–; Chancellor Robert Gordon Univ. 1993–; Hon. LLD (St Andrews) 1987, (Aberdeen) 1988, (Sheffield Hallam) 1995, (South Bank) 1995. *Leisure interest:* golf. *Address:* Bank of Scotland, 33 Old Broad Street, London, EC2N 1HP (Office); 24 Ashley Gardens, London, SW1P 1QD, England (Home). *Telephone:* (20) 7905-9581 (Office). *Fax:* (20) 7905-9509 (Office). *E-mail:* KathleenMurray@hbosplc.com (Office). *Website:* www .bankofscotland.co.uk (Office).

REID, Timothy Escott, MA, MLitt; Canadian investor, management consultant, educator and public servant; b. 21 Feb. 1936, Toronto, Ont.; s. of Escott Meredith Reid and Ruth (Herriot) Reid; m. Julyan Fancott 1962; one s. one d.; ed Univ. of Toronto, Yale Univ., Oxford Univ. (Rhodes Scholar), Harvard Graduate School of Business; Exec. Sec. Canadian Inst. of Public Affairs 1962–63; Asst to Pres., Asst Prof. of Econs, Research Assoc. for Public Policy, York Univ. 1963–72; mem. Legis. Ass., Ontario 1967–71; Prin. Admin., Manpower and Social Affairs, OECD, Paris 1972–74; joined Public Service of Canada 1974, subsequently Deputy Sec. Treasury Bd, Office of Comptroller-Gen. of Canada, Asst Deputy Minister, Dept of Regional Econ. Expansion, Exec. Dir Regional and Industrial Program Affairs, Dept of Regional Industrial Expansion, Asst Deputy Minister responsible for Tourism Canada 1984–85; Dir and mem. exec. Cttee Canada Mortgage and Housing Corpn 1980–82, Canadian Labour Market and Productivity Centre 1989 (Co-Chair. Bd of Dirs 1993–97); headed 18-nation OECD study visit to Japan 1984; Dean Faculty of Business and Prof. of Business Man., Ryerson Polytechnical Inst. 1985–89; Commr Ont. Securities Comm. 1987–89; Pres. Canadian Chamber of Commerce 1989–98, Pres. ReMan Canada Inc. 1998–; Venture Dir XPV Capital Corpn 2001–; mem. Bd of Dirs Canadian Exec. Service Org. 1991–95, VIA Rail Canada Corpn 2000–, Int. Volunteers 2001–; Consultant, US Nat. Science Foundation 1979–82; mem. Int. Trade Advisory Cttee (ITAC), Govt of Canada 1991–97; mem. Inst. of Corp. Dirs 1999–; Patron Canadian Inst. of Int. Affairs 1999–; mem. Canadian dels to 6th and 7th annual APEC Leaders Meetings 1995, 1996; 125 Anniversary Commemorative Medal, Canada 1992. *Publications:* Contemporary Canada: Reading in Economics 1969. *Leisure interests:* skiing, tennis, swimming, pilates. *Address:* XPV Capital Corporation, Suite 601, 44 Victoria Street, Toronto, Ont., M5C 2Y2 (Office); 210A Avenue Road, Unit 2, Ottawa, Ont., M5R 2J4, Canada (Home). *Telephone:* (416) 580-2584 (Office). *Fax:* (416) 864-0514 (Office). *E-mail:* tim .reid@xpvcapital.com (Office); timreid@interlog.com (Home). *Website:* www .xpvcapital.com (Office).

REIDY, Carolyn Kroll, PhD; American publishing executive; b. Carolyn Judith Kroll, 2 May 1949, Washington, DC; d. of Henry Kroll and Mildred Kroll; m. Stephen Kroll Reidy 1974; ed Middlebury Coll. Vt and Indiana Univ.; various positions, Random House, New York 1975–83; Dir of Subsidiary Rights, William Morrow & Co., New York 1983–85; Vice-Pres. Assoc. Publr, Vintage Books, Random House, New York 1985–87; Assoc. Publr, Random House (concurrent with Assoc. Publr and Publr of Vintage Books) 1987–88; Publr, Vintage Books 1987–88, Anchor Books, Doubleday, New York 1988; Pres. and Publr, Avon Books, New York 1988–92; Pres. and Publr, Simon and Schuster Trade Div. 1992–2001, Pres. Adult Publishing Div., Simon and Schuster 2001–; Dir NAMES Project 1994–98, New York Univ. Center for Publishing 1997–, Literacy Partners, Inc. 1999–; Matrix Award 2002. *Address:* Simon and Schuster, 1230 Avenue of the Americas, New York, NY 10020, USA (Office). *Telephone:* (212) 698-7323 (Office). *Fax:* (212) 698-7035 (Office). *E-mail:* carolyn.reidy@simonandschuster.com (Office). *Website:* simonsays.com (Office).

REIJNDERS, Lucas, PhD; Netherlands university professor; b. 4 Feb. 1946, Amsterdam; s. of C. Reijnders and C. M. Reijnders-Spillekom; one c.; ed Univ. of Amsterdam; Dir Environmental Inst. Univ. of Groningen 1974–80, mem. staff Nat. Environmental Office 1980–, Prof. of Environmental Science Univ. of Amsterdam 1988–; Prof. of Environmental Science Open Univ. 1999–; winner Gouden Ganzeveer 1990, Erewimpel ONRI 1992. *Publications:* Food in the Netherlands 1974, A Consumer Guide to Dutch Medicines 1980, Plea for a Sustainable Relation with the Environment 1984, Help the Environment 1991, Environmentally Improved Production and Products 1995, Agriculture in the Low Countries 1997, Travel Through the Ages 2000. *Leisure interest:* 19th-century literature. *Address:* Anna van den Vondelstraat 10, 1054 GZ Amsterdam, Netherlands. *Telephone:* (20) 5256269. *Fax:* (20) 5256272. *E-mail:* l.reijnders@frw.uva.nl (Office).

REILLY, (David) Nicholas (Nick), CBE, MA, FIMI; British business executive; b. 17 Dec. 1949, Anglesey, N Wales; s. of the late John Reilly and of Mona (née Glynne Jones) Reilly; m. Susan Haig 1976; one s. two d.; ed Harrow School, St Catharine's Coll. Cambridge; investment analyst 1971–74; joined Gen. Motors 1975, Finance Dir Moto Diesel Mexicana 1980–83, Supply Dir Vauxhall Motors 1984–87, Mfg Dir Vauxhall Ellesmere Port 1990–94, Vice-Pres. Quality Gen. Motors Europe 1994–96, Chair., Man. Dir Vauxhall Motors 1996–2001, Chair. (non-exec.) 2001, Vice-Pres. European Sales and Marketing, Gen. Motors Europe 2001, Pres. and CEO GM Daewoo 2002–; Vice-Pres. IBC 1987–90, Chair. IBC Vehicles 1996–; mem. Bd Saab GB 1996–; Chair. Chester, Ellesmere, Wirral Training and Enterprise Council 1990–94, Training Standards Council 1997–2001, Adult Learning Inspectorate 2001; Pres. Soc. of Motor Mfrs and Traders 2001–02. *Leisure interests:* skiing, swimming, sailing, golf, watching sports, music, opera, theatre. *Address:* Vauxhall Motors, Griffin House, Osborne Road, PO Box 3, Luton, Beds., LU1 3YT, England. *Telephone:* (1582) 427578.

REIN, Yevgeny Borisovich; Russian poet; b. 29 Dec. 1935, Leningrad; freelance poet published in samizdat magazine Sintaksis and émigré press abroad in magazines Grani, Kovcheg; participated in publication of almanac Metropol; literary debut in Russia 1984; teacher Moscow M. Gorky Inst. of Lit.; mem. Writers' Union 1987, Union of Moscow Writers 1992, Russian Pen-Centre; State Prize of Russian Fed. 1997. *Television:* Journeys with Iosif Brodsky 1995. *Publications:* numerous publs in magazines; collected verse: Names of Bridges 1984, Italian Boot 1996, Selected Verses and Poems 2001. *Address:* Russian Pen-Centre, Neglinnaya str. 18/1, building 2, Moscow, Russia (Office). *Telephone:* (095) 209-45-89 (Office). *Fax:* (095) 200-02-93 (Office). *E-mail:* info@vavilon.ru.

REINA IDIAQUEZ, Carlos Roberto; Honduran politician; b. 13 March 1926; m. Bessie Watson; one s. (deceased), three d.; ed Nat. Autonomous Univ. of Honduras, Univs of London, Cambridge and Paris (Sorbonne) and London Inst. of Int. Affairs; Court Judge, Tegucigalpa 1953; served Embassy of Honduras, Paris 1960–65; Deputy to Nat. Constituent Ass. 1965; Dir El Pueblo (official Liberal daily) 1966; Francisco Morazán Deputy for Nat. Congress 1971–77; Judge, Inter-American Court of Human Rights 1979; lecturer in Law, Nat. Autonomous Univ. of Honduras; regular lecturer at foreign univs; Pres. of Honduras 1994–98. *Publications:* El Reto Democrático en Centro America, Honduras: Realidad Nacional y Crisis. *Address:* c/o Office of the President, Casa Presidencial, 6a Avda 1a Calle, Tegucigalpa, Honduras.

REINER, Rob; American actor, writer and director; b. 6 March 1947, New York; s. of Carl Reiner and Estelle (née Lebost) Reiner; m. 1st Penny Marshall 1971 (divorced); m. 2nd Michele Singer 1989; ed Univ. of Calif. at Los Angeles; co-f. Castle Rock Entertainment; has appeared with comic improvisation groups The Session and The Committee; scriptwriter for Enter Laughing 1967, Halls of Anger 1970, Where's Poppa 1970, Summertree 1971, Fire Sale 1977, How Come Nobody's on Our Side 1977; directed: This is Spinal Tap 1984, The Sure Thing 1985, Stand By Me 1986, The Princess Bride 1987, Misery 1990; co-producer and dir When Harry Met Sally 1989, A Few Good Men 1992, North, The American President 1995, Ghosts of Mississippi 1996, The Story of Us 1999 (also actor), Loosely Based on a True Love Story 2003 (also actor). *Television appearances include:* All In The Family 1971–78, Free Country 1978, Thursday's Game 1974, More Than Friends 1978, Million Dollar Infield 1972. *Address:* c/o Castle Rock Entertainment, 335 North Maple Drive, Suite 135, Beverly Hills, CA 90210, USA.

REINHARD, Keith Leon; American advertising executive; b. 20 Jan. 1935, Berne, Ind.; s. of Herman Reinhard and Agnes Reinhard; m. Rose-Lee Simons

1976; two d.; four s. one d. by previous m.; ed public schools in Berne; commercial artist, Kling Studios, Chicago 1954–56; man. tech. communications Dept Magnavox Co., Fort Wayne, Ind. 1957–60; creative/account exec. Biddle Co., Bloomington, Ill. 1961–63; Exec. Vice-Pres., Dir Creative Services and Pres. Needham, Harper & Steers Inc., Chicago 1964; then Chair. and CEO Needham, Harper & Steers/U.S.A., Chicago; also Dir Needham, Harper & Steers Inc.; Chair. and CEO DDB Needham Worldwide Inc. New York 1986–, Chair., CEO 1989–. *Address:* DDB Needham Worldwide Inc., 437 Madison Avenue, New York, NY 10022, USA.

REINHARDT, Klaus, DR. PHIL.; German army officer; b. 15 Jan. 1941, Berlin; m. Heide-Ursula Reinhardt (née Bando) 1966; two s.; ed Univ. of Freiburg; joined army as officer cadet, Mountain Infantry; Commdr Mountain Infantry 1986–88; Commdr Army Führungsakademie 1990–93; Commdg Gen. III Corps. 1993–94; Gen.-Lieut., Commdr German Army, Koblenz 1994–96; Commdg Gen. of NATO Peace-keeping Unit in Kosovo (Kfor) 1999–2000; now Commdr NATO Forces, Heidelberg. *Publication:* Wende vor Moskau 1998. *Leisure interests:* classical music, skiing, mountaineering, travel. *Address:* Karthäuserhofweg 10, 56075 Koblenz, Germany. *Telephone:* (261) 55690.

REINO, Fernando, LicenDer; Portuguese diplomatist; b. Aug. 1929, Felgar, Moncorvo; s. of Abel Reino and Julia Janeiro Reino; m. Maria Gabriela Vaz Reino 1962; two d.; ed Univ. of Coimbra, Univ. of Strasbourg, NATO Defence Coll.; entered the Foreign Service 1958, Political and NATO Depts, Lisbon 1958–60, Portuguese del. to NATO, Paris 1960–61, Portuguese Embassy, Tokyo 1961–62, Chargé d'affaires titular, Antananarivo 1962–63, Consul-Gen. Cape Town 1963–66, Chargé d'affaires, Tunis 1966–71, Deputy Head of Mission to the EEC 1971–73; Dir Int. Econ. Org. Dept, Lisbon 1973–74; Head of Co-operation and Tech. Assistance Dept and Co-ordinator Nat. Decolonization Comm. 1974–75; Amb. to Norway and Iceland 1977–80, Head of Civilian Staff of the Pres. 1980–81; Perm. Rep. to the UN and other Int. Orgs, Geneva 1981–85; Amb. to Spain 1985–88; Perm. Rep. to UN 1989–92; Prof. Emer. Univ. of Coimbra; Chancellor, Nat. Orders. *Leisure interests:* writing, reading, music, golf, gardening. *Address:* Quinta do Rio Touro, Azoia, 2710 Sintra, Portugal. *Telephone:* 9292862. *Fax:* 9292360.

REINSHAGEN, Gerlind; German author; b. 4 May 1926, Königsberg; d. of Ekkehard Technau and Frieda Technau; m. 1949; ed studies in pharmacy; freelance author of novels, theatre and radio plays, screenplays, poetry, essays and criticism; mem. German PEN; mem. Deutsche Akad. der darstellenden Künste; Fördergabe Schillerpreis, Baden Württemberg 1974, Mühlheimer Dramatikerpreis 1977, Roswitha von Gandersheim Medaille 1984, Ludwig Mülheimes Preis 1993, Niedersächsischer Kunstpreis 1997, Niedersächsischer Staatspreis 1999. *Plays:* Doppelkopf 1968, Leben und Tod der Marilyn Monroe 1971, Himmel und Erde 1974, Sonntagskinder 1976, Frühlingsfest 1980, Eisenherz 1982, Die Clownin 1988, Feuerblume 1987, Tanz, Marie! 1989, Die fremde Tochter 1993, Die grüne Tür 1999. *Television:* Doppelkopf 1972, Himmel und Erde 1976, Sonntagskinder 1981. *Radio:* 12 radio plays. *Publications:* novels: Rovinato 1981, Die flüchtige Braut 1984, Zwölf Nächte 1989, Jäger am Rand der Nacht 1993, Am grossen Stern 1996, Göttergeschichte 2000; Gesammelte Stücke (collected pieces) 1986, Joint Venture 2003; contribs to theatrical journals and yearbooks etc. *Address:* Rheingaustrasse 2, 12161 Berlin, Germany. *Telephone:* (30) 8217171.

REISS, Timothy James, MA, PhD, FRSC; British/Canadian professor of literature; b. 14 May 1942, Stanmore, Middx; s. of James Martin Reiss and Joan Margaret Ping; m. 2nd Patricia J. Hilden 1988; two s. one d. from previous m.; ed Hardye's School, Dorchester, Manchester Univ., Sorbonne, Paris and Univ. of Illinois; Instructor to Asst Prof. Yale Univ. 1968–73; Assoc. Prof. Univ. de Montréal 1973–79, Prof. and Chair. of Comparative Literature 1979–84; Prof. of Comparative Literature, Modern Languages and Philosophy, Emory Univ. 1983–86, Samuel C. Dobbs Prof. of Comparative Literature and French 1986–87; Prof. and Chair. of Comparative Literature New York Univ. 1987–94, Prof. 1994–; Morse Fellow 1971–72; Canada Council Sr Fellowship 1977–78; SSHRC of Canada Sr Fellowship 1983–84; ACLS Fellow 1986–87; Guggenheim Fellowship 1990–91; Fellow Acad. of Literary Studies; several other awards and visiting professorships. *Publications:* Toward Dramatic Illusion 1971, Science, Language and the Perspective Mind (ed.) 1973, Tragedy and Truth 1980, De l'ouverture des disciplines (ed.) 1981, The Discourse of Modernism 1982, Tragique et tragédie dans la tradition occidentale (ed.) 1983, The Uncertainty of Analysis 1988, The Meaning of Literature 1992 (Forkosch Prize 1992), Sisyphus and Eldorado (ed.) 1997, Knowledge, Discovery and Imagination in Early Modern Europe 1997, For the Geography of a Soul (ed.) 2001, Against Autonomy: Global Dialectics of Cultural Exchange 2002, Mirages of the Selfs 2003; more than 100 essays and book chapters. *Address:* Department of Comparative Literature, New York University, 19 University Place, 3rd Floor, New York, NY 10003-4556 (Office); 1721 8th Street, Berkeley, CA 94710, USA (Home). *Telephone:* (212) 998-8795 (Office). *E-mail:* timothy.reiss@nyu.edu (Office).

REITER, Janusz; Polish diplomatist and international affairs scholar; b. 6 Aug. 1952, Kościerzyna; s. of Stanisław Reiter and Hilda Reiter; m. Hanna Reiter 1975; two d.; ed Warsaw Univ.; Foreign affairs commentator Życie Warszawy (daily) 1977–81 (dismissed during martial law); jt founder of Foundation for Int. Ventures and Centre for Int. Studies in Warsaw; mem. Dziekania Club of Political Thought; staff writer Przegląd Katolicki (weekly) 1984–89, daily Gazeta Wyborcza and Polish TV 1989–90, daily Rzeczpospo-

lita; Amb. to FRG 1990–95; Chair. of Bd and Dir Center for Int. Relations, Warsaw 1998–; co-founder Council for Foreign Policy; Co-Founder and mem. Bd Wissenschaftskolleg (Inst. for Advanced Studies), Berlin; mem. Landeshochschulrat of Brandenburg, Council on European Integration; Great Cross of Merit with the Star and Ribbon (Germany). *Publication:* Roads to Europe. *Leisure interests:* music, travelling, literature. *Address:* Fundacja Centrum Stosunków Międzynarodowych, ul. Flory 9, 00-586 Warsaw, Poland. *Telephone:* (22) 6465267. *E-mail:* reiter@csm.org.pl (Office). *Website:* www.csm.org.pl (Office).

REITH, Peter, BEcons, LLB; Australian company director, consultant and fmr politician; b. 15 July 1950, Melbourne; s. of A. C. Reith and E. V. Reith (née Sambell); m. Julie Treganowan 1971; four s.; ed Monash Univ.; Supreme Court 1975; worked as solicitor 1976–82; mem. Westernport Waterworks Trust and Cowes Sewerage Authority 1977–82; Councillor Shire of Phillip Island 1976–81, Pres. 1980–81; mem. various cttees and authorities; MP for Flinders 1982–83, 1984–2001; Deputy Leader of the Opposition 1990–93; Shadow Special Minister of State 1993, responsible for Mabo 1994; Shadow Minister for Defence Jan.–Sept. 1994, Shadow Minister with responsibility for Mabo Jan.–May 1994; Shadow Minister for Defence May–Sept. 1994; Shadow Minister for Foreign Affairs 1994–95, for Industrial Relations and Man. of Opposition Business in the House 1995–96; Minister for Industrial Relations and Leader of the House of Reps and Minister Assisting the Prime Minister for the Public Service 1996–97; Minister for Workplace Relations and Small Business and Leader of the House of Reps 1997–98, Minister for Employment, Workplace Relations and Small Business and Leader of the House of Reps 1998–2001; Minister for Defence 2001; mem. Assn of Christian Community Colls.; co-ordinator Free Legal Aid Services; Founding Sec., mem. Newhaven Coll. *Publication:* The Reith Papers. *Leisure interests:* golf, reading. *Address:* 1A Camperdown Street, Brighton East, Vic. 3187, Australia (Home). *E-mail:* peterreith@bigpond.com.au (Office).

REITMAN, Ivan, MusB; Canadian film director and producer; b. 27 Oct. 1946, Komarmo, Czechoslovakia; s. of Leslie Reitman and Clara R. Reitman; m. Genevieve Robert 1976; one s. two d.; ed McMaster Univ.; moved to Canada 1951; Hon. LLD (Toronto); Dir of the Year, Nat. Asscn of Theater Owners 1984, Canadian Genie Special Achievement Award 1985, Star on Hollywood Walk of Fame 1997. *Stage shows produced:* The Magic Show 1974, The National Lampoon Show 1975, Merlin 1983 (also Dir). *Films:* (Dir and exec. producer) Cannibal Girls 1973; (producer) They Came From Within 1975, Death Weekend 1977, Blackout 1978, National Lampoon's Animal House 1978 (People's Choice Award 1979), Heavy Metal 1981, Stop! Or My Mom Will Shoot 1992, Space Jam 1996, Private Parts 1996; (producer and dir) Foxy Lady 1971, Meatballs 1979, Stripes 1981, Ghostbusters 1984, Legal Eagles 1986, Twins 1988 (People's Choice Award 1989), Ghostbusters II 1989, Kindergarten Cop 1990, Dave 1993, Junior 1994, Father's Day 1996, Six Days/Seven Nights 1998, Doomsday Man 1999; (exec. producer) Rabid 1976, Spacehunter: Adventures in the Forbidden Zone 1983, Big Shots 1987, Casual Sex? 1988, Feds 1988, Beethoven 1992, Beethoven's 2nd 1993, Commandments 1996, Road Trip 2000. *TV series:* (producer and dir) Delta House 1978. *TV films:* (exec. producer) The Late Shift 1996; mem. Dirs Guild of America. *Address:* Building 489, 100 University City Plaza, Universal City, CA 91608 (Office); c/o CAA, 9830 Wilshire Boulevard, Beverly Hills, CA 90212, USA.

REITZ, Edgar; German film director; b. 1932. *Films include:* Mahlzeiten (appeared in UK as Lust for Love) 1966–67, Die Reise nach Wien 1973, Picnic 1975, Stunde Null 1976, Deutschland im Herbst (with others) 1977–78, Der Schneider von Ulm 1978, Heimat 1980–84, Die zweite Heimat 1991.

RELIGA, Zbigniew Eugeniusz, MD; Polish surgeon, cardiologist and politician; b. 16 Dec. 1938, Miedniewice; s. of Eugeniusz Religa and Zofia Religa; m. Anna Wajszczuk 1962; one s. one d.; ed Medical Acad., Warsaw; worked in Surgical Ward of Wolski Hosp., Warsaw 1966–80; worked in Cardiac Inst., Warsaw 1980–84, Head II Clinic 2000–, Dir Inst. 2001; Head of Cardiac Surgery Dept and Clinic, Silesian Med. Acad., Katowice 1984–, Prof. 1995–, Rector 1996–2000; inventor Polish mechanical heart-assistance devices, total artificial heart, biological heart valve; Chair. Non-Party Bloc in Support of Reforms (BBWR) 1993–95; Chair. Polish Republican Party 1995–98; Senator 1993–97, 2001–; mem. Conservative Peasant Party (SKL) 1998–; Dr hc (Lvov Medical Univ., Ukraine), (Medical Acad., Białystok), (Silesian Medical Acad.); numerous Polish and foreign awards including Great Cross Order of Polonia Restituta 1999. *Publications:* over 100, including books on cardiac surgery, transplantation and artificial hearts. *Leisure interest:* fishing. *Address:* Śląska Akademia Medyczna, ul. J. Poniatowskiego 15, 40-952 Katowice, Poland. *Telephone:* (32) 514964.

RELPH, Michael; British fmr film producer, writer, designer and director; b. 16 Feb. 1915, Broadstone, Dorset; s. of late George Relph and Deborah (née Nansen) Relph; m. 1st Doris Gosden 1938; one s.; m. 2nd Maria Barry 1949; one d.; fmr Assoc. Producer and Producer, Ealing; Founder/Dir. Allied Film Makers; Chair. Film Production Asscn of GB 1971–76, BFI Production Bd 1971–76; Producer mem. Cinematograph Films Council 1971–76; Exec. in charge of Production, Kendon Films 1979–80; Art Dir, Ealing on films Champagne Charley, Nicholas Nickleby, Dead of Night, Saraband for Dead Lovers; Hon. DLitt (De Montfort Univ.) 1998. *Films produced include:* The Captive Heart, Frieda, The Blue Lamp (Best British Film, British Film Acad. 1950), Kind Hearts and Coronets, The Square Ring, I Believe in You (co-author, screenplay), The Ship That Died of Shame, The Rainbow Jacket, The

Smallest Show on Earth, Sapphire (Best British Film Acad. 1959), League of Gentlemen, Victim, Man in the Moon (co-author, screenplay), Life For Ruth, The Mind Benders, A Place to Go, (author, screenplay), Woman of Straw (co-author, screenplay), Masquerade (co-author, screenplay), The Assassination Bureau (author, screenplay), The Man Who Haunted Himself (co-author), Scum, An Unsuitable Job for a Woman (co-producer), Heavenly Pursuits 1986, Mrs Warren's Profession (co-author, screenplay), Seven Against the West (screenplay with Fay Weldon), My Mother's Profession (screenplay), William Tell: the untold story; production consultant The Torrents of Spring 1989. *Films directed:* Davy, Rockets Galore, Desert Mice. *Address:* The Old Malthouse, 33 High Street, Selsey, West Sussex, PO20 0RB, England.

REMEDIOS, Alberto Telisforo, CBE; British opera singer; b. 27 Feb. 1935, Liverpool; s. of Albert Remedios and Ida Remedios; m. 1st Shirley Swindells 1958; one s.; m. 2nd Judith Hosken 1965; one s. one d.; studied with Edwin Francis, Liverpool; joined Sadler's Wells Opera Co. 1955; now sings regularly with English Nat. Opera and Royal Opera House, Covent Garden; has made numerous appearances in USA, Canada, Argentina, Germany, France and Spain and appeared in concert with maj. British orchestras; Queen's Prize, Royal Coll. of Music; First Prize, Int. Singing Competition, Sofia, Bulgaria; Sir Reginald Goodall Award Wagner Soc. 1995. *Recordings include:* Wagner's Der Ring des Nibelungen and Tippett's A Midsummer Marriage. *Leisure interests:* football, motoring, record collecting. *Address:* c/o Stuart Trotter, 21 Lanhill Road, London, W9 2BS, England. *Telephone:* (20) 7289-6315.

REMENGESAU, Tommy E., Jr, BS; Palauan politician; b. 28 Feb. 1956, Koror; s. of Thomas O. Remengesau, Sr and Ferista Esang Remengesau; m. Debbie Mineich; two s. two d.; ed Grand Valley State Univ., Mich., Michigan State Univ., Admin./Planner, Palau Bureau of Health Services 1980–81; Public Information Officer, Palau Legislature 1981–84; Senator, Nat. Congress 1984–92; Vice-Pres. and Minister of Admin. 1993–99, Pres. of Palau 2001–; rep. to IMF 1997–; twice Grand Champion All-Micronesia Fishing Derby. *Leisure interest:* fishing. *Address:* Office of the President, P.O. Box 100, Koror, PW 96940, Palau. *Telephone:* 488-2541. *Fax:* 488-1662. *E-mail:* roppresoffice@palaunet.com.

REMINGTON, Deborah Williams, BFA; American artist; b. 25 June 1935, Haddonfield, NJ; d. of Malcolm van Dyke Remington and Hazel Irwin Stewart; ed San Francisco Art Inst.; work in many public collections including Whitney Museum, New York, Pompidou Centre, Paris and Bibliothèque Nat., Paris; mem. Nat. Acad. of Design, New York; Nat. Endowment Fellowship 1979; Guggenheim Fellowship 1984; Pollock-Krasner Foundation Grant 1999; Hassam & Speicher Purchase Prize, American Acad. and Inst. of Arts and Letters 1988. *Exhibitions:* one-woman shows include Dilexi Gallery, San Francisco 1962, 1963, 1965, San Francisco Museum of Art 1964, Bykert Gallery, New York 1967, 1969, 1972, 1974, Galerie Darthea Speyer, Paris 1968, 1971, 1973, 1992, Pyramid Gallery, Washington, DC 1976, Zolla-Lieberman Gallery, Chicago 1976, Hamilton Gallery, New York 1977, Portland Center for Visual Arts, Portland, Ore. 1977, Ramon Osuna Gallery, Washington, DC 1983, Newport Harbor Art Museum, Calif. 1983, Oakland (Calif.) Museum of Art 1984, Adams Middleton Gallery, Dallas, Tex. 1984, Ianuzzi Gallery, Phoenix, Ariz. 1985, Jack Shainman Gallery, New York 1987, Shoshana Wayne Gallery, Los Angeles 1988, Mitchell Algus Gallery, New York 2001; participant in numerous group shows in USA, France, Switzerland, Portugal etc. *Leisure interests:* gardening/horticulture. *Address:* 309 West Broadway, New York, NY 10013, USA. *Telephone:* (212) 925-3037. *Fax:* (212) 925-3037 (Office).

REMNICK, David J., AB; American journalist and editor; b. 29 Oct. 1958, Hackensack, NJ; s. of Edward C. Remnick and Barbara (née Seigel) Remnick; m. Esther B. Fein; two s. one d.; ed Princeton Univ.; reporter The Washington Post 1982–91; staff writer The New Yorker 1992–, Ed.-in-Chief 1998–; Pulitzer Prize 1994; Livingston Award 1991; George Polk Award 1994; Helen Bernstein Award 1994. *Publications include:* Lenin's Tomb: The Last Days of the Soviet Empire 1993, Resurrection 1997, The Devil Problem 1997, King of the World 1998. *Address:* The New Yorker, Four Times Square, New York, NY 10036, U.S.A. (Office).

REMSPERGER, Hermann; German economist; b. 24 Dec. 1949, Flörsheim-Weilbach am Main; ed Johann Wolfgang Goethe-Universität; asst lecturer Johann Wolfgang Goethe-Universität 1973–78, visiting lecturer 1979–, Hon. Prof. 1990–; with BHF-Bank 1979–98, Head of Econs Section 1984–98; mem. Bd Deutsche Bundesbank 1998–, now Chief Economist; Chair. Research Council, Center for Financial Studies; mem. Exec. Bd German Econ. Asscn. *Publications:* numerous articles on financial and econ. matters. *Address:* Deutsche Bundesbank, 60431 Frankfurt am Main, Wilhelm-Epstein-Str. 14 (Office); 60006 Frankfurt am Main, Postfach 100602, Germany (Office). *Telephone:* (69) 95661 (Office). *Fax:* (69) 5601071 (Office).

REMY, Pierre-Jean (see Angrémy, Jean-Pierre).

REN JIANXIN; Chinese fmr chief justice; b. Aug. 1925, Fencheng (now Xiangfen) Co., Shanxi Prov.; ed Eng Coll., Beijing Univ.; joined CCP 1948; Sec., Secr. N China People's Govt 1948–49; Sec. Gen. Office, Cen. Comm. for Political Science and Law, Sec. Cen. Comm. for Legis. Affairs 1949–54; Sec. Legis. Affairs Bureau, State Council 1954–59; Section Leader, Division Chief, China Council for the Promotion of Int. Trade (CCPIT) 1959–71, Dir Legal Dept, CCPIT, lawyer 1971–81, Vice-Chair. CCPIT 1981–83; Vice-Pres. Supreme People's Court 1983–88, Pres. 1988–98; Sec.-Gen. Leading Group of Cen. Cttee for Political Science and Law 1989, Deputy Sec. and Sec.-Gen. Cen. Cttee 1990; Chair. Soc. of Chinese Judges 1994–; Hon. Chair China Law Soc. (fmr Vice-Pres.), China Foreign Econ. Trade and Arbitration Cttee, China Maritime Arbitration Cttee (fmr Chair.); Hon. Pres. China Int. Law Soc. (fmr Vice-Pres.); Dir China Training Centre for Sr Judges; Prof. (part-time) Beijing Univ.; mem. 13th CCP Cen. Cttee 1987–92, 14th CCP Cen. Cttee 1992–97, Sec. Secr. 14th CCP Cen. Cttee 1992; Sec. CCP Cen. Comm. for Political Science and Law 1992–98; Vice-Chair. 9th Nat. Cttee CPPCC 1998–. *Address:* National Committee of Chinese People's Political Consultative Conference, 23 Taipingqiao Street, Beijing, People's Republic of China.

REN MEIE, PhD; Chinese scientist and university professor; mem. Dept of Earth Sciences, Academia Sinica 1985–; Prof. at Geography Dept of Nanjing Univ. 1986–; Chair. of Asscn for Devt and Man. of Coastal Zones 1986–; Victoria Medal (Royal Soc. of Geography) 1986. *Address:* Geography Department, Nanjing University, Nanjing City, Jiangsu Province, People's Republic of China.

RENDELL, Edward Gene, BA, JD; American state official; b. 5 Jan. 1944, New York City; s. of Jesse T. Rendell and Emma Rendell (née Sloat); m. Marjorie Osterlund 1971; one s.; ed Univ. of Pa, Villanova Univ.; Asst Dist Attorney, Chief Homicide Unit, Phila 1968–74; Deputy Special Prosecutor, Phila 1976, Dist Attorney 1978–86; partner Ballard Spahr Andrews & Ingersoll, LLP; Mayor of Phila 1992–99; Gen. Chair. Democratic Nat. Cttee 1999–2001; Gov. of Pa 2003–; Lecturer of Law Univ. of Pa; mem. ABA, Pa Dist Attorneys' Asscn, Phila Bar Asscn, B'nai B'rith, United Jewish Org., Jewish War Vets; Man of the Year Award, VFW 1980, American Cancer League 1981, Distinguished Public Service Award, Pa. Co. Detectives' Asscn. *Address:* Office of the Governor, Room 225, Main Capitol Building, Harrisburg, PA 17120, USA (Office).

RENDELL OF BABERGH, Baroness (Life Peer), cr. 1997, of Aldeburgh in the County of Suffolk; **Ruth Barbara Rendell,** CBE, FRSL; British crime novelist; b. 17 Feb. 1930; d. of Arthur Grasemann and Ebba Kruse; m. Donald Rendell 1950 (divorced 1975), remarried 1977 (died 1999); one s.; ed Loughton County High School; Dr hc (Essex) 1990; Arts Council Nat. Book Award for Genre Fiction 1981, Sunday Times Award for Literary Excellence 1990 and other awards. *Publications include:* From Doon with Death 1964, A Judgment in Stone 1976, The Lake of Darkness 1980, An Unkindness of Ravens 1985, Live Flesh 1986, Heartstones 1987, Talking to Strange Men 1987, Wolf to the Slaughter 1987, The Veiled One 1988, A Warning to the Curious—The Ghost Stories of M. R. James 1988, The Bridesmaid 1989, Suffolk 1989, The Third Wexford Omnibus 1989, Mysterious 1990, Going Wrong 1990, The Strawberry Tree 1990, Walking on Water 1991, The Copper Peacock 1991, Kissing the Gunner's Daughter 1992, The Ruth Rendell Omnibus 1992, The Crocodile Bird 1993, The Third Ruth Rendell Omnibus 1994, No Night is too Long 1994, Simisola 1994, Blood Lines, Long and Short Stories 1995, The Babes in the Wood 2002; (ed.) The Reason Why: An Anthology of the Murderous Mind 1995, Harm Done 2000; (under pseudonym Barbara Vine) A Dark-Adapted Eye 1986, A Fatal Inversion 1987, The House of Stairs 1988, Gallowglass 1990, King Solomon's Carpet 1991, Asta's Book 1993, The Children of Men 1994, No Night Is Too Long 1994, The Keys to the Street 1996, The Brimstone Wedding 1996, The Chimney Sweeper's Boy 1998, A Sight For Sore Eyes 1998, Grasshopper 2000, Piranha to Scurfy and Other Stories 2000; several Vols of short stories. *Leisure interests:* reading, walking, opera. *Address:* 26 Cornwall Terrace Mews, London, NW1 5LL; House of Lords, London, SW1A 0PW, England.

RENDLE, Michael Russel, MA; British business executive; b. 20 Feb. 1931, Kuala Lumpur, Malaya; s. of the late H. C. R. Rendle; m. Heather Rinkel 1957; two s. two d.; ed Marlborough Coll. and New Coll., Oxford; joined Anglo-Iranian Oil Co. (now British Petroleum) 1954; served in UK, Trinidad, Aden; Man. Dir BP Trinidad 1967–70, BP Australia 1974–78; Dir BP Trading (London) 1978–81; Man. Dir BP Co. 1981–86; Chair. TBI PLC (fmrly Markheath PLC) 1991–94; Deputy Chair. Imperial Continental Gas Asscn 1986–87, British-Borneo Petroleum Syndicate 1986–2000, Tace PLC 1991; Dir Willis Faber PLC (now renamed Willis Group PLC) 1985–98, Petrofina SA 1986–87, FIM Ltd 1989– (Chair. 1992–); Campbell and Armstong PLC 1992–98 (Chair. 1996–98), OIS Int. Inspection PLC 1993–96 (Chair. 1995–96), M.D.U. Ltd 1998–2001; mem. Willis Pension Trustees 1985– (Chair. 1999–); mem. London Bd Westpac Banking Corpn 1978–89; mem. British Overseas Trade Bd 1984–86, INSEAD Int. Council and UK Advisory Bd 1984–86; Chair. UNICE Social Affairs Cttee 1984–87; mem. Marlborough Coll. Council 1987–95. *Leisure interests:* golf, music, various outdoor sports. *Address:* 10 Trinity Square, London, EC3P 3AX, England. *Telephone:* (20) 7481-7152. *Fax:* (20) 7481-7154.

RENÉ, (France) Albert; Seychelles politician and barrister; b. 16 Nov. 1935, Mahé; s. of Price René and Louisa Morgan; m. 1st Karen Handley 1956; one d.; m. 2nd Geva Adam 1975; one s.; m. 3rd Sarah Zarquani 1993; one d.; ed St Louis Coll., Victoria, Seychelles Coll., St Maurice, Switzerland, St Mary's Coll., Southampton, UK, King's Coll., London; called to Bar 1957; founder and Leader Seychelles People's United Party (later Seychelles People's Progressive Party) 1964–; MP 1965–; Minister of Works and Land Devt 1975–77; Prime Minister 1976–77; Pres. of Seychelles 1977–, also C-in-C, Minister of Econ. Devt and Housing 1977–78, of Internal Affairs and Finance 1977–79, of Finance 1977–78, of Youth and Community Devt 1978–80, of Finance and Industries 1981–89, of Planning and External Relations 1984–89, of Industry

1986–93, of Community Devt 1993, of Defence 1986–93, of Tourism 1988–89, now of Internal Affairs, Defence and Legal Affairs; Order of the Golden Ark 1982. *Leisure interests:* gardening, fishing. *Address:* Office of the President, State House, Victoria; Seychelles People's Progressive Front (SPPF), P.O. Box 91, Victoria, Seychelles. *Telephone:* 224455; 224391 (Office). *Fax:* 225351; 224200 (Office).

RENFREW OF KAIMSTHORN, Baron (Life Peer), cr. 1991, of Hurlet in the District of Renfrew; **Andrew Colin Renfrew,** PhD, ScD, FBA, FSA; British professor of archaeology; b. 25 July 1937, Stockton-on-Tees; s. of the late Archibald Renfrew and Helena D. Renfrew; m. Jane M. Ewbank 1965; two s. one d.; ed St Albans School, St John's Coll., Cambridge and British School of Archaeology, Athens; Lecturer in Prehistory and Archaeology, Univ. of Sheffield 1965–70, Sr Lecturer 1970–72, Reader in Prehistory and Archaeology 1972; Prof. of Archaeology and Head of Dept, Univ. of Southampton 1972–81; Disney Prof. of Archaeology Univ. of Cambridge 1981–, Dir McDonald Inst. for Archaeological Research 1990–; Fellow St John's Coll., Cambridge 1981–86; Master Jesus Coll., Cambridge 1986–97, Prof. Fellow 1997–; Hon. FSA (Scotland); Foreign Assoc. Nat. Acad. of Sciences, USA; Visiting Lecturer, Univ. of Calif. at Los Angeles 1967; Hon. LittD (Sheffield) 1990, (Southampton) 1995; Dr hc (Faculty of Letters, Univ. of Athens) 1991; Prix Int. Fyssen, Fondation Fyssen, Paris 1997, Language and Culture Prize, Univ. of Umeå, Sweden 1998; Rivers Memorial Medal, Huxley Memorial Medal, Royal Anthropological Inst. *Publications:* The Emergence of Civilization 1972, Before Civilization 1973, The Explanation of Culture Change (ed.) 1973, British Prehistory (ed.) 1974, Transformations: Mathematical Approaches to Culture Change 1979, Problems in European Prehistory 1979, An Island Polity 1982, Theory and Explanation in Archaeology (ed.) 1982, Approaches to Social Archaeology 1984, The Archaeology of Cult 1985, Peer, Polity Interaction and Socio-Political Change (ed.) 1986, Archaeology and Language: The Puzzle of Indo-European Origins 1987, The Idea of Prehistory 1988, The Cycladic Spirit 1991, The Archaeology of Mind (co-ed. with E. Zubrow) 1994, Loot, Legitimacy and Ownership 2000, Archaeogenetics (ed.) 2000. *Leisure interests:* contemporary arts, coins, travel. *Address:* McDonald Institute for Archaeological Research, Downing Street, Cambridge, CB2 3ER, England. *Telephone:* (1223) 333521. *Fax:* (1223) 333536.

RENNERT, Wolfgang; German conductor and music and opera director; b. 1 April 1922, Cologne; s. of Dr Alfred Rennert and Adelheid (née Nettesheim) Rennert; m. 1st Anny Schlemm 1957 (divorced 1968); m. 2nd Ulla Berkéwicz 1971 (divorced 1975); one s.; ed Mozarteum Salzburg; Chief Conductor and Deputy Dir of Music, Frankfurt 1953–67; Head of Opera, Staatstheater am Gärtnerplatz 1967–71; Dir of Music and Dir of Opera, Nat. Theatre, Mannheim 1980–85; Perm. Guest Conductor, State Opera, Berlin 1970–2000; Guest Conductor, Royal Opera, Copenhagen 1975–79; Prin. Guest Conductor, Semperoper, Dresden 1991–; Prin. Guest Conductor, Portuguese Symphony Orchestra, Lisbon 1998–2002; Guest Conductor Oper Frankfurt 2000–; guest appearances with Vienna State Opera, Munich and Hamburg Operas, Royal Opera House Covent Garden, San Francisco Opera, Dallas Opera, Salzburg Festival, Munich Festival and Venice, Rome and Palermo opera houses. *Address:* 12203 Berlin, Holbeinstrasse 58, Germany. *Telephone:* (30) 8333094.

RENNIE, Heughan Bassett (Hugh), CBE, BA, LLB, QC; New Zealand barrister, company director and fmr broadcasting executive; b. 7 April 1945, Wanganui; s. of the late W. S. N. Rennie and of Reta Rennie; m. 1st Caroline Jane Harding 1967 (died 1992); three s.; m. 2nd Penelope Jane Ryder-Lewis 1998; ed Wanganui Collegiate School, Victoria Univ., Wellington; part-time law clerk, Wanganui 1960–67, legal officer NZ Electricity, Wellington 1967–70; barrister and solicitor Macalister Mazengarb Parkin and Rose (later Macalister Mazengarb Perry Castle), Wellington 1970–91, partner 1972–, sr litigation partner 1982–, Chair. 1989–91; sole barrister, Wellington 1991–95; QC 1995–; Chair. Broadcasting Corpn of NZ (BCNZ) 1984–88; Chair. Govt Cttee on Restructuring BCNZ 1988, Ministerial Inquiry into Auckland Power Supply Failure 1998; Chair. Chatham Is. Enterprise Trust 1990–2001, Policy Cttee, Dictionary of NZ Biography 1991–2001, Royal NZ Ballet 1999–, The Marketplace Co. Ltd 1999–, Fourth Estate Group 1970–88; Dir United Broadcasters Ltd 1981–84, Roydhouse Publishing Ltd 1981–88, Fletcher Challenge Ltd 1992–99, BNZ Finance Ltd 1993–97, Bank of NZ 1997–; Ed. Wellington Dist Law Soc. newspaper 1973–84; mem. NZ Law Soc. cttees on professional advertising and public affairs 1981–84, NZ Council for Law Reporting 1983–87, Govt Advisory Cttee to statutory mans of Equiticorp 1989–; mem. Sir David Beattie Chair of Communications Trust Bd (VUW) 1986–90, Scientific Cttee, Nat. Heart Foundation 1988–94; NZ Gen. Counsel Medical Protection Soc. (UK) 1983–; Trustee Broadcasting History Project Trust Bd 1988–; NZ Medal 1990. *Leisure interests:* history, travel, writing, cycling, reading. *Address:* Harbour Chambers, 10th Floor, Equinox House, 111 The Terrace, Wellington (Office); 45 Grant Road, Thorndon, Wellington 1 (Home); PO Box 10-242, Wellington, New Zealand (Postal). *Telephone:* 499-2684 (Office); 472-9503 (Home). *Fax:* 499-2705 (Office); 472-9257 (Home). *E-mail:* hughrennie@legalchambers.co.nz (Office).

RENO, Janet, BA, LLB; American lawyer; b. 21 July 1938, Miami, Fla; d. of Henry Reno and Jane Wood; ed Cornell and Harvard Univs; admitted Fla Bar 1963; Assoc. Brigham & Brigham 1963–67; partner, Lewis & Reno 1967–71; Staff Dir Judiciary Comm. Fla House of Reps Tallahassee 1971–72; Admin. Asst State Attorney, 11th Judicial Circuit Fla, Miami 1973–76, State Attorney 1978–93; partner, Steel, Hector & Davis, Miami 1976–78; US Attorney-Gen. (first woman to occupy post) 1993–2001; mem. American Bar Assen, American Law Inst., American Judicature Soc.; Democrat; Women First Award, YWCA 1993, National Women's Hall of Fame 2000. *Address:* Department of Justice, 10th Street and Constitution Avenue, NW, Washington, DC 20530, USA. *Telephone:* (202) 633-2000. *Fax:* (202) 633-1678.

RENO, Jean; French actor; b. Juan Moreno Errere y Rimenes, 30 July 1948, Casablanca, Morocco. *Films:* Claire de femme 1979, Le Dernier combat 1984, Subway 1985, Signes Extérieurs de Richesse 1983, Notre Histoire 1984, I Love You 1986, The Big Blue 1988, La Femme Nikita 1990, L'homme au Masque d'Or 1990, L'Opération Corned Beef 1990, Loulou Graffiti 1991, (also wrote screenplay) Les Visiteurs (The Visitors) 1993, The Professional (Leon) 1994, French Kiss 1995, Beyond the Clouds 1995, Mission: Impossible 1996, For Roseanna 1997, Ronin 1998, Les visiteurs 2: Les couloirs du temps 1998, Godzilla 1998, Tripwire 1999, Just Visiting 2001, The Crimson Rivers (Les Rivières pourpres) 2001, Wasabi 2002, Rollerball 2002, The Quiet American 2002, Jet Lag (Décalage horaire) 2003. *Address:* Chez Les Films du Dauphin, 25 rue Yves-Toudic, 75010 Paris, France.

RENSCHLER, Andreas; German business executive; joined Daimler-Benz 1988, fmrly Asst to Chair., led projects in Latin America and developing 4-wheel drive vehicles, now Pres. Mercedes-Benz U.S. Int., Inc. *Address:* Mercedes-U.S. International Inc., P.O. Box 100, Tuscaloosa, AL 35403-0100, USA.

RENTCHNICK, Pierre, MD; Swiss physician and editor of medical publications; b. 17 July 1923, Geneva; s. of Jacques Rentchnick and Blanche (Spiegel) Rentchnick; m. Paule Adam 1948; one s.; ed Univs of Geneva and Paris; Ed.-in-Chief, Médecine et Hygiène, Geneva 1956–93, Recent Results in Cancer Research; Ed. Springer, Heidelberg and New York 1962–83, Bulletin de l'Union int. contre le cancer, Geneva 1962–80; f. Kiwanis-Club, Geneva 1966, Pres. 1976–77; f. Int. Soc. for Chemotherapy 1959; Fellow New York Acad. of Sciences, Medical Soc. of Prague, French Soc. of Pathology; Prix Littré (France) 1977. *Publications:* Esculape chez les Soviets 1954, Klinik und Therapie der Nebenwirkungen 1963, Esculape chez Mao 1973, Ces malades qui nous gouvernent 1976, Les orphelins mènent-ils le monde? 1978, Ces malades qui font l'histoire 1983, Ces nouveaux malades qui nous gouvernent 1988–96; numerous publs on antibiotics in infectious diseases, on ethical problems, euthanasia etc. *Leisure interests:* skiing, golf, swimming, art (Netzuke). *Address:* La Taupinière, Chemin Bouchattet 8, 1291 Commugny, Vaud, Switzerland. *Telephone:* (22) 7762264. *Fax:* (22) 7765047 (Home).

RENTON OF MOUNT HARRY, Baron (Life Peer), cr. 1997, of Offham in the County of East Sussex; **(Ronald) Tim(othy) Renton,** PC, MA; British politician, businessman and author; b. 28 May 1932, London; s. of R. K. D. Renton and Mrs Renton; m. Alice Fergusson 1960; two s. three d.; ed Eton Coll., Magdalen Coll., Oxford; joined C. Tennant Sons & Co. Ltd 1954, with Tennants subsidiaries in Canada 1957–62, Dir 1964–73, Man. Dir Tennant Trading Ltd 1964–73; Dir Silvermines Ltd 1967–84, Australia and New Zealand Banking Group 1967–76, J. H. Vavasseur & Co. Ltd 1971–74; mem. BBC Gen. Advisory Council 1982–84; contested (Conservative) Sheffield Park 1970; MP for Mid-Sussex 1974–97; Parl. Pvt. Sec. to Rt Hon John Biffen, MP 1979–81, to Rt Hon Geoffrey Howe, MP 1983–84; Parl. Under Sec. of State FCO 1984–85, Minister of State FCO 1985–87; Parl. Sec. to HM Treasury and Govt Chief Whip 1989–90, Minister for the Arts and for the Civil Service 1990–92; mem. Select Cttee on Nationalized Industries 1974–79, Vice-Chair. Conservative Parl. Trade Cttee 1974–79, Chair. Conservative Foreign and Commonwealth Council 1982–84; mem. Select Cttee on Nat. Heritage 1995–97; mem. House of Lords European Communities Cttee 1997–; Vice-Pres. Conservative Trade Unionists 1978–80, Pres. 1980–84; Chair. Outsider Art Archive 1995–2000, Sussex Downs Conservation Bd 1997–; Vice-Chair. British Council 1992–98; Dir (non-exec.) Fleming Continental European Investment Trust PLC, Chair. 1999–; Parl. Consultant Robert Fleming Holdings 1992–97; mem. Council Sussex Univ. 2000–; Fellow Industry and Parl. Trust 1977–79; mem. Advisory Bd, Know-How Fund for Cen. and Eastern Europe 1992–99; mem. APEX, Council Roedean School 1982– (Pres. 1998–), Devt Council, Parnham Trust, Criterion Theatre Trust; Trustee Mental Health Foundation 1985–89; Founding Pres. (with Mick Jagger) of Nat. Music Day 1992–97; Green Ribbon Political Award for Environmental Campaigning 2000, Bowland Award, Assen of Areas of Outstanding Natural Beauty 2000. *Publications:* The Dangerous Edge 1994, Hostage to Fortune 1997. *Leisure interests:* writing, gardening, mucking about in boats, listening to opera. *Address:* House of Lords, London, SW1A 0PW; Mount Harry House, Offham, Lewes, East Sussex, BN7 3QW, England. *Telephone:* (1273) 471450 (Office); (20) 7219-3308. *Fax:* (1273) 471450 (Office). *E-mail:* rentont@ parliament.uk (Office).

RENTZEPIS, Peter M., PhD; American professor of chemistry; b. 11 Dec. 1934, Kalamata, Greece; s. of Michael Rentzepis and Leuci Rentzepis; m. Alma Elizabeth Keenan; two s.; ed Denison, Syracuse and Cambridge Univ., mem. Tech. Staff Research Labs Gen. Electric Co., New York, then mem. Tech. Staff, Bell Labs, NJ, Head, Physical and Inorganic Chem. Research Dept; Presidential Chair. and Prof. of Chem. and Electrical and Computer Eng, Univ. of Calif., 1986–, Dir CX (IT) 2; Adjunct Prof. of Chem., Univ. of Pa, of Chem. and Biophysics, Yale Univ. 1980–; Visiting Prof., Rockefeller Univ., 1971, MIT –1975, of Chem. Univ. of Tel Aviv; mem. numerous academic cttees, editorial and advisory bds including US Army Cttee on Energetic Materials Research and Tech. 1982–83; Dir NATO Advanced Study Inst. 1984–; Chair. Bd Call/Recall Inc. 1996; mem. Bd of Dirs KRIKOS—Science and Tech. for Greece, Bd of Dirs The Quanex Corpn 1984; mem. NAS 1978, American Physical Soc., AAAS, etc.; mem. Nat. Acad. of Greece 1980; Hon. ScD (Denison) 1981, (Carnegie-Mellon) 1983; Hon. DPhil (Syracuse) 1980; American Chem. Soc. Peter Debye Prize in Physical Chemistry, American Physical Soc. Irving Lungmuize Prize in Chemical Physics, Scientist of the Year 1978, NY Acad. of Sciences Cressy Morison Award in Natural Sciences and other awards. *Publications:* more than 400 on lasers, photochemistry, picosecond spectroscopy; 68 patents. *Address:* Department of Chemistry, University of California, Irvine, CA 92697, USA (Office). *Telephone:* (949) 824-5934 (Office). *Fax:* (949) 824-2761 (Office). *E-mail:* PMRentze@uci-edu (Office).

RENWICK OF CLIFTON, Baron (Life Peer), cr. 1997, of Chelsea in the Royal Borough of Kensington and Chelsea; **Robin William Renwick,** KCMG, MA; British diplomatist and business executive; b. 13 Dec. 1937; s. of Richard Renwick and Clarice Renwick; m. Annie Colette Giudicelli 1965; one s. one d.; ed St Paul's School, Jesus Coll., Cambridge and Univ. of Paris (Sorbonne); army 1956–58; entered Foreign Service 1963; Dakar 1963–64; Foreign Office 1964–66; New Delhi 1966–69; Pvt. Sec. to Minister of State, Foreign and Commonwealth Office (FCO) 1970–72; First Sec., Paris 1972–76; Counsellor Cabinet Office 1976–78; Head Rhodesia Dept, FCO 1978–80; Political Adviser to Gov. of Rhodesia 1980; Visiting Fellow Center for Int. Affairs, Harvard 1980–81; Head of Chancery, Washington 1981–84; Asst Under-Sec. of State, FCO 1984–87; Amb. to S Africa 1987–91, to USA 1991–95; Chair. Save and Prosper 1996–98, Fluor Ltd 1996–; Dir Robert Fleming (Deputy Chair. Robert Fleming Holdings Ltd 1999–2001), Richemont, British Airways 1996–, BHP, Billiton, Fluor Corpn 1997–, S Africa Breweries 1999–, Harmony Gold 1999–; Trustee The Economist; Hon. LLD (Witwatersrand) 1991, (American Univ. in London) 1993; Hon. DLitt (Coll. of William and Mary) 1993. *Publication:* Economic Sanctions 1981, Fighting with Allies 1996, Unconventional Diplomacy in Southern Africa 1997. *Leisure interests:* tennis, fishing, islands. *Address:* House of Lords, Westminster, London, SW1A 0PW, England.

RENYI, Thomas A., BA, MBA; American business executive; b. 1946; ed Rutgers Univ.; Pres. Bank of New York Co. Inc. 1992–98, CEO 1997–, Chair. 1998–; Vice-Chair. Bank of New York 1992–94, Pres. 1994–, CEO 1996–, Chair. 1998–; Chair. New York Bankers Asscn, New York Clearing House; mem. Bd of Govs Rutgers Univ., Bd of Mans New York Botanical Garden, Bd of Trustees Bates Coll., Financial Services Roundtable. *Address:* Bank of New York, 1 Wall Street, New York, NY 10286, U.S.A. (Office). *Telephone:* (212) 495-1784 (Office). *Fax:* (212) 495-1398 (Office). *Website:* www.bankofny.com (Office).

REPIN, Vadim Valentinovich; Russian violinist; b. 31 Aug. 1971, Novosibirsk; s. of Viktor Antonovich Repin and Galina Georgievna Repina; m. Nato Gabunia (divorced); ed Novosibirsk Music School with Zakhar Bron; prize winner int. competitions: Veniawsky in Poznan 1982, Tibor Varga in Mion 1985, Queen Elizabeth in Brussels 1990; toured Europe since 1985; debut in London (Barbican) 1988, in USA 1990; lives in Germany. *Address:* c/o IMG Artists Europe, Media House, 3 Burlington Lane, London, W4 2TH, England (Office). *Telephone:* (20) 8233-5800 (Office). *Fax:* (20) 8233-5801 (Office).

REPŠE, Einars, BS; Latvian politician and banker; b. 9 Dec. 1961, Jelgava; s. of Aivars-Rihards Repše and Aldona Repše (née Krasauska); m. Diana Vagale 1988 (divorced); two s. one d.; ed Univ. of Latvia; engineer Latvian Acad. of Sciences 1986–90; mem. Parl. 1990–91; Gov. Bank of Latvia 1991–2000; Mayor of Rīga 2000; Prime Minister of Latvia Nov. 2002–; Founder and Chair. New Era (Jaunais laiks) party 2002–; Commdr Order of the Three Stars 1997. *Leisure interest:* aviation. *Address:* Office of the Cabinet of Ministers, Brīvības bulv. 36, Rīga 1050 (Office); Jaunais laiks, Jekaba Kazarmas, Torna iela 4-3B, Rīga 1050, Latvia. *Telephone:* (2) 708-2810 (Office). *Fax:* (2) 728-6598 (Office). *E-mail:* vk@mk.gov.lv (Office). *Website:* www.mk.gov.lv (Office).

RESCHER, Nicholas, PhD; American philosopher and author; b. 15 July 1928, Hagen, Germany; s. of Erwin Hans Rescher and Meta Anna Rescher; m. 1st Frances Short 1951 (divorced 1965); one d.; m. 2nd Dorothy Henle 1968; two s. one d.; ed Queens Coll., New York, Princeton Univ.; Assoc. Prof. of Philosophy, Lehigh Univ. 1957–61; Prof., Univ. of Pittsburgh 1961–, Dir Center for Philosophy of Science 1982–89; Consultant RAND Corpn 1954–66, Encyclopaedia Britannica 1963–64, North American Philosophical Publs 1980–; Ed. American Philosophical Quarterly 1964–94; Sec.-Gen. Int. Union of History and Philosophy of Science 1969–75; Pres. American Philosophical Asscn (Eastern Div.) 1989–90, American Catholic Philosophical Asscn 2003–04; mem. Academia Europea, Institut Int. de Philosophie, Académie Int. de Philosophie des Sciences; Guggenheim Fellow 1970–71; Hon. mem. Corpus Christi Coll. Oxford; visiting lectureships at Univs of Oxford, Munich, Konstanz, W Ontario and others; six hon. degrees; Alexander von Humboldt Prize 1983. *Publications:* more than 90 books including The Coherence Theory of Truth 1973, Methodological Pragmatism 1977, Scientific Progress 1978, The Limits of Science 1984, Ethical Idealism 1987, Rationality 1988, A System of Pragmatic Idealism (3 Vols) 1992–94, Pluralism 1993, Predicting the Future 1997, Paradoxes 2001; numerous articles in many areas of philosophy. *Leisure interests:* reading history and biography. *Address:* 1012 Cathedral of Learning, University of Pittsburgh, Pittsburgh, PA 15260 (Office); 5818 Aylesboro Avenue, Pittsburgh, PA 15217, USA. *Telephone:* (412) 624-5950 (Office); (412) 521-6768 (Home). *Fax:* (412) 383-7506. *E-mail:* rescher@pitt.edu (Office).

RESHETNIKOV, Fedor Grigorevich; Russian physical chemist; b. 25 Nov. 1919, Sumy, Ukraine; s. of Grigory Pavlovich Reshetnikov and Elisaveta Ivanovna Reshetnikova; m. Tatyana Frolovna Reshetnikova 1948; one d.; ed Moscow Inst. of Non-Ferrous Metals, Dzerzhinsky Artillery Acad.; engineer, metallurgy works, Kazakhstan 1942, Perm 1944–45; mem. CPSU 1947–91; scientific research work 1946–; Head Lab., First Deputy Dir, A. A. Bochvar All Union Scientific and Research Inst. of Inorganic Materials 1966–92, adviser 1992–; Corresp. mem. USSR (now Russian) Acad. of Sciences 1974–92, mem. 1992–; six Orders; USSR State Prize 1951, 1975, 1985, Khlopin Prize, Russian Acad. of Sciences. *Publication:* Development, Production and Operation of Nuclear Power Reactor Fuels and numerous articles on physical chem. and tech. of radioactive and rare metals, nuclear fuels and structural materials for nuclear reactor cases. *Leisure interests:* touring, fishing. *Address:* Scientific Research Institute of Inorganic Materials, Rogov Street 5, 123060 Moscow; Peschany Ln. 4, Apt. 310, 125252 Moscow, Russia (Home). *Telephone:* (095) 196-66-61 (Office); 198-26-80 (Home). *Fax:* (095) 196-65-91 (Office).

RESIN, Vladimir Iosifovich, PhD; Russian politician and civil engineer; b. 21 Feb. 1936, Minsk (now in Belarus); s. of Josif Resin and Rosa Ressina; m. 1958; one d.; ed Moscow Ore Inst.; worked in orgs of USSR Ministry of Coal Industry and Ministry of Ass. and Special Construction; Deputy, First Deputy, then Head, Moscow Dept of Eng and Construction 1974–; Head, Moscow Industrial Construction Dept 1985–; Chair. Moscow Construction Cttee 1989–91; Deputy Chair. Exec. Cttee, Moscow City Council 1989–91; Deputy Premier, Moscow City Govt 1991–92, First Deputy Premier 1992–; Head, Dept of Moscow Architecture, Construction, Devt and Reconstruction 1992–; Prof. Russian G. V. Plekhanov Econ. Acad., Moscow Int. Univ.; Corresp. mem. Russian Acad. of Architecture and Construction Sciences, Russian Eng Acad.; Sr Fellow, Inst. of Civil Engineers 2000; author of 30 inventions; awarded 21 State Prizes; other awards and distinctions include Distinguished Constructor of Russian Fed., Honoured Constructor of Moscow, Order of Russian Orthodox Church (four). *Publications:* Managing the Development of a Large City: A Systems Approach; and numerous other publs. *Leisure interest:* work. *Address:* Moscow City Government, Department of Moscow Architecture, Construction, Development and Reconstruction, Nikitsky per. 5, 103009 Moscow, Russia. *Telephone:* (095) 925-46-26; (095) 291-09-47. *Fax:* (095) 200-53-22; (095) 956-81-40.

RESNAIS, Alain; French film director; b. 3 June 1922, Vannes; s. of Pierre Resnais and Jeanne (née Gachet) Resnais; m. 1st Florence Malraux 1969; m. 2nd Sabine Azéma 1998; ed Institut des Hautes Etudes Cinématographiques, Paris; Special Prize (Cannes) for Mon Oncle d'Amerique 1980; Grand Prix du Cinéma 1986, Prix Louis-Delluc 1993, Prix Méliès 1994, Silver Bear for Lifetime Achievement, Berlin 1998; Légion d'honneur. *Short films directed (1948–59) include:* Van Gogh 1948, Guernica (with Robert Hessens) 1950, Les statues meurent aussi (with Chris Marker) 1952, Nuit et brouillard 1955. *Feature films include:* Hiroshima mon amour 1959, L'année dernière à Marienbad 1961, Muriel 1963, La guerre est finie 1966, Je t'aime, je t'aime 1968, Stavisky 1974, Providence 1977, Mon oncle d'Amérique 1980, La vie est un roman 1983, L'amour à mort 1984, Mélo 1986, I want to go home 1989, Smoking/No Smoking 1993 (César awards for best dir, best film), On connait la chanson 1998 (César Award for Best French Film). *Address:* c/o Intertalent, 5 rue Clément Marot, 75008 Paris (Office); 70 rue des Plantes, 75014 Paris, France (Home).

RESNIK, Regina; American opera singer (mezzo-soprano); b. 30 Aug. 1924; d. of Samuel Resnik and Ruth Resnik; m. 1st Harry W Davis 1947; one s.; m. 2nd Arbit Blatas 1975; ed Hunter Col, New York; opera début as Lady Macbeth, New Opera Co. 1942; Mexico City 1943; New York City Opera 1943–44; Metropolitan Opera 1944–1983; sang 80 roles, soprano and mezzo-soprano, became regular mem. Royal Opera, London, Vienna State Opera, Bayreuth, Salzburg, San Francisco, Chicago, La Scala, Milan, Paris, Buenos Aires, Berlin, Brussels, etc.; Stage Dir for maj. productions Hamburg, Venice, Sydney, Vancouver, Strasbourg, Warsaw, Lisbon, Madrid, Wiesbaden; appeared on Broadway in Cabaret 1987, in A Little Night Music 1990, New York City Opera, 50th anniversary celebrations Danny Kaye Playhouse; Trustee Hunter Foundation, Metropolitan Opera Guild Bd; Dr hc (Hunter) 1991; Lincoln Center and Vienna State Opera awards; Pres.'s Medal, Commdr des Arts et des Lettres, France. *Address:* American Guild of Musical Artists, 1727 Broadway, New York, NY 10019, USA.

RESTAD, Gudmund; Norwegian politician; b. 19 Dec. 1937, Smøla; s. of Ola Restad and Olga Marie Dalen; m. Britt Jorun Wollum 1959; three c.; ed officers' training school (anti-aircraft artillery), business school, police training school; sergeant at Ørland airport 1959–61, country police Ørland and Orkdal 1961–67; detective constable/inspector Crime Police Cttee 1967–73; training in police investigation in Denmark and Germany 1967; lecturer Nat. Police Training School 1973–75; sergeant in Smøla 1975–85; mem. Parl. 1985–2001; Chair. Local Council, Smøla 1980–85, mem., Chair., Deputy Chair. Nordmøre Interkommunale Kraftlag (Nordmøre Electricity Bd) 1982–91; mem. Bd Central Police Org. 1969–73, Møre og Romsdal Centre Party 1982–83, The Centre Party 1983–89; mem. Judiciary Cttee Storting (Parl.) 1985–89; mem., Deputy Chair. Finance Cttee 1989–97; Minister of Finance and Customs 1997–2000; Deputy Chair. Defence Cttee 2000–01. *Address:* Stortinget, 0026 Oslo, Norway.

RÉTORÉ, Guy; French theatre director; b. 7 April 1924; s. of Hervé Rétoré and Aline Henry; ed Univ. of Paris; Public Relations Dept, SNCF until 1955; Actor and Producer, Théâtre de Boulevard until 1955; formed "La Guilde" (theatrical company), Menilmontant, E. Paris 1954; opened Théâtre de Menilmontant 1958; Dir Maison de la Culture, Menilmontant 1962; Dir Théâtre de l'Est Parisien 1963– (also gives concerts, ballets, films and confs); Chevalier Légion d'honneur, Officier Ordre nat. du Mérite, Officier des Arts et des Lettres. *Plays produced include:* La fille du roi (Cosmos) 1955, Life and Death of King John 1956, Grenadiers de la reine (Farquhar, adapted by Cosmos) 1957, L'avare (Molière), Les caprices de Marianne (Musset), La fleur à la bouche (Pirandello), Le médecin malgré lui (Molière), Le manteau (Gogol, adapted by Cosmos) 1963, La Locandiera (Goldoni), Arden of Faversham 1964, Monsieur Alexandre (Cosmos) 1964, Macbeth (Shakespeare) 1964, Turcaret (Lesage) 1965, Measure for Measure (Shakespeare) 1965, Le voyage de Monsieur Perrichon (Labiche) 1965, Live Like Pigs (Arden), The Silver Tassie (O'Casey) 1966–67, Les 13 soleils de la rue St Blaise (A. Gatti), La machine (Jean Cosmos) 1968–69, Lorenzaccio (Musset), The Threepenny Opera (Brecht), Major Barbara (Shaw) 1969–70, Les ennemis (Gorki), L'âne de l'hospice (Arden) 1970–71, Sainte Jeanne des abattoirs (Brecht) 1971–72, Macbeth (Shakespeare) 1972–73, Androclès et le lion 1974–75, Coquin de coq (O'Casey) 1975–76, L'ôtage (Claudel) 1976–77, Le camp du drap d'or 1980, Fin de partie, tueur sans gage 1981, Le Chantier 1982, Clair d'usine 1983, 325000 francs 1984, Entre passions et prairie (Denise Bonal) 1987, Arturo Ui 1988, Clair de Terre 1989, Chacun pleure son Garabed 1991. *Address:* TEP, 159 avenue Gambetta, 75020 Paris, France. *Telephone:* 1-43-63-20-96.

REUBER, Grant Louis, OC, PhD, LLD, FRSC; Canadian economist; b. 23 Nov. 1927, Mildmay, Ont.; s. of Jacob Daniel Reuber and Gertrude Catherine Reuber; m. Margaret Louise Julia Summerhayes 1951 (deceased); three d.; ed Walkerton High School, Univ. of W Ontario, Harvard Univ., Sidney Sussex Coll., Cambridge; with Econ. Research Dept Bank of Canada 1950–52; Econ. and Int. Relations Div. Dept of Finance 1955–57, Deputy Minister of Finance Govt of Canada 1979–80; at Univ. of W Ontario 1957–78, Asst Prof. 1957–59, Assoc. Prof. 1959–62, Prof. Econ. Dept 1962–78, Dean of Social Science 1969–74, Acad. Vice-Pres. and Provost, mem. Bd of Govs 1974–78; Chair. Ont. Econ. Council 1973–78; Sr Vice-Pres. and Chief Economist Bank of Montreal 1978–79, Exec. Vice-Pres. 1980–81, Dir, Deputy Chair. and Deputy Chief Exec. 1981–83, Pres. 1983–87, Deputy Chair. 1987–90; Chancellor Univ. of Western Ont. 1988–93; Lecturer, Grad. School of Business, Univ. of Chicago 1992–93; Chair. Canada Deposit Insurance Corpn 1993–99 (Dir 1999–), Canada Merit Scholarship Foundation 1994–; Dir Hermitage Museum Foundation of Canada Inc. 2000–; Sr Adviser and Dir Sussex Circle; Gov. Royal Ont. Museum 2000–03; Pres. and Dir Ditchley Foundation of Canada 1989–; Sr Fellow C. D. Howe Inst. 2000–; Hon. LLD (Wilfred Laurier Univ.) 1983, (Simon Fraser Univ., Univ. of W Ont.) 1985, (McMaster Univ.) 1994. *Publications:* The Cost of Capital in Canada (with R. J. Wonnacott) 1961, (with R. E Caves): Canadian Economic Policy and the Impact of International Capital Flows 1970, Private Foreign Investment in Development 1973, Canada's Political Economy 1980. *Leisure interests:* tennis, reading. *Address:* Bank of Montreal, 302 Bay Street, Fourth Floor, Toronto, Ont., M5X 1A1 (Office); 90 Glen Edyth Drive, Toronto, Ont., M4V 2V9, Canada (Home). *Telephone:* (416) 867-3614 (Office); (416) 924-4971. *Fax:* (416) 867-4806 (Office); (416) 924-4784 (Home).

REUTERSWÄRD, Carl Fredrik; Swedish artist, writer and sculptor; b. 4 June 1934, Stockholm; s. of Wilhelm Reuterswärd and Thérèse Ingeström; m. 1st Anna Tesch 1958 (divorced 1968); two s. two d.; m. 2nd Mona Moller-Nielsen 1974; one s.; m. 3rd Tonie Lewenhaupt 1997; ed Ecole de Fernand Léger, Paris and Royal Coll. of Art, Stockholm; first artist to use lasers 1965; Prof. Royal Coll. of Art, Stockholm 1965–70; since 1952 active in drawing, painting, sculpture, holography, scenography, graphics, design and architectural comms; principal themes: Nonsens 1952–58; Cigars and Games 1958–63; Exercise 1958–64; Lazy Lasers and Holy Holos 1965–74; a trilogy: Kilroy (anybody) 1962–72, CAVIART (a somebody) 1972–82; works in public collections in Sweden, USA, Germany, France, England, Switzerland, Netherlands, Norway and Denmark, including National museum, Stockholm, Museum of Modern Art, New York, Städtische Kunsthalle, Düsseldorf, Musée National d'Art Moderne, Paris, Tate Gallery, London and Stedelijk Museum, Amsterdam; Non-Violence, bronze sculpture on perm. display in front of UN Bldg, New York, since 1988; Medal bestowed by King Carl Gustaf XVI; Lifetime Achievements Award 1997. *Exhibitions:* numerous solo exhbns in Sweden, Switzerland, England, Norway, Germany, Denmark, South Africa, USA; participant in numerous group exhbns. *Publications:* Kafka, Wahlstrom and Widstrand 1981, Caviart 1982, Making Faces 1984, Mes Autres Moi 1989. *Address:* 6 rue Montolieu, 1008 Bussigny/Lausanne, Switzerland. *Telephone:* (21) 7010514. *Fax:* (21) 7012675.

REVEL, Jean-François; French writer; b. 19 Jan. 1924, Marseilles; s. of Joseph Ricard and France Mathez; m. 2nd Claude Sarraute 1966; one s.; one s. one d. by first m.; two step-s.; ed Ecole Normale Supérieure and Sorbonne, Paris; teacher of philosophy and French literature, Institut Français, Mexico, later Florence 1952–56; teacher of Philosophy, Lille and Paris 1956–63; Literary Adviser Editions Julliard and Pauvert 1961–66, Editions Laffont 1966–77; Columnist L'Express 1966–81, Dir 1978–81; Ed. and Columnist Le Point magazine 1982; Columnist Europe 1 1989–92, Radio télévision Luxembourg (RTL) 1995–99; mem. Acad. Française; Chevalier, Légion d'honneur; Konrad Adenauer Prize 1986, Chateaubriand Prize 1988, J. J. Rousseau

Prize 1989, Prix du livre politique 1997. *Publications:* Histoire de Flore 1957, Pourquoi des philosophes? 1957, Pour l'Italie 1958, Le style du général 1959, Sur Proust 1960, La cabale des dévots 1962, En France 1965, Contrecensures 1966, Histoire de la philosophie occidentale Vol. I 1968, Vol. II 1970, Ni Marx ni Jésus 1970, Les idées de notre temps 1972, La tentation totalitaire 1976, Descartes inutile et incertain 1976, La nouvelle censure 1977, Un festin en paroles 1978, La grâce de l'état 1981, Comment les démocraties finissent 1983, Le rejet de l'état 1984, Une anthologie de la poésie française 1984, Le terrorisme contre la démocratie 1987, La connaissance inutile 1988, Le regain démocratique 1992, L'absolutisme inefficace 1992, Histoire de la philosophie occidentale, de Thalès à Kant 1994, Un festin en paroles 1995, Le voleur dans la maison vide, mémoires 1997, Le moine et le philosophe 1997, L'œil et la connaissance, Ecrits sur l'art 1998, Le siècle des ombres 1999, La grande parade 2000, Les plats de saison (Journal de l'an 2000) 2001, L'Obsession anti-américaine 2002. *Leisure interests:* riding, swimming. *Address:* 55 quai de Bourbon, 75004 Paris, France. *Telephone:* 1-43-54-65-87. *Fax:* 1-47-00-76-93.

REXRODT, Günter, Dr rer. pol; German politician; b. 12 Sept. 1941, Berlin; m. Ingrid Hoyermann 1983; one c.; ed Freie Univ. Berlin; Berliner Bank, Berlin 1961–62; Standard Elektrik Lorenz AG, Berlin 1963–64; Adviser on Industrial Man., Industrie- und Handelskammer, Berlin 1968–72; Dir Dept of Political Tech. 1972–74; mem. Man. Bd and Dir Industry Dept 1974–79; Dir Industry Dept Senator for Econs and Transport, Berlin Senate 1979–82; Sec. of State to Senator for Econs and Transport 1982–85; Senator for Finance, Berlin 1985–89; joined Citibank, New York April–Dec. 1989; Chair. Man. Bd Citibank AG, Frankfurt 1990–91; mem. Man. Bd Treuhandanstalt (agency responsible for privatization of state enterprises of fmr E Germany), Berlin 1991–93; Minister for the Economy 1993–98; mem. Bundestag (Parl.) 1994–; mem. FDP 1980–; Deputy Chair. Landesverband Berlin 1983–87, 1989–; mem. Bundesvorstand 1990–95; mem. Bd of Dirs WMP Eurcom AG 2000–. *Leisure interests:* astrophysics, sailing. *Address:* Platz der Republik, 11011 Berlin, Germany.

REYES LÓPEZ, Juan Francisco; Guatemalan politician and business executive; b. 10 July 1938; m.; three c.; ed John Carroll High School, Birmingham, Ala, USA, Escuela Militar del General de Armas Bernardo O'Higgins, Santiago de Chile, Universidad Rafael Landivar, Guatemala City; primary school teacher; army officer 1960–61; in pvt. business 1961–89; Pres. Comité Coordinador de Asociaciones Agrícolas, Comerciales, Industriales y Financieras (CACIF) 1979–80, Pres. 1980; Man. Instituto Guatemalteco de Seguridad Social 1982; mem. Frente Republicano Guatemalteco (FRG) party, mem. Nat. Exec. Cttee 1991–99; Deputy to Congreso (Parl.) 1990–94, Chair. Comm. on Foreign Relations 1990, mem. Comm. on Finance 1990–94, First Vice-Pres. Exec. Bd 1994; Vice-Pres. of Guatemala 2000–; Orden del General O'Higgins 1989, Orden de la Estrella Brillante 1995. *Address:* c/o Office of the President, Guatemala City, Guatemala (Office).

REYMAN, Leonid Dododjonovich; Russian politician and engineer; b. 12 July 1957, Leningrad (now St Petersburg); m.; one s. one d.; ed Leningrad Inst. of Electro-Tech. Communications; engineer, head of workshop Leningrad Telephone Exchange 1979–85; leading posts Leningrad City Telephone Network 1985–88, later Head, Chief Eng, Dir on int. relations, Dir on investments, First Deputy Dir.-Gen. Jt Stock co. Peterburgskaya Telefonnaya Set 1988–99; First Deputy Chair. State Cttee on Telecommunications Russian Fed. July–Aug. 1999; Chair. 1999–2000; Minister of Communications and Information Tech. Nov. 1999–. *Address:* Ministry of Communications and Information Technology, Tverskaya str. 7, 103375 Moscow, Russia (Office). *Telephone:* (095) 771-81-00 (Office). *Fax:* (095) 771-87-18 (Office). *E-mail:* office@minsvyaz.ru (Office). *Website:* www.minsvyaz.ru (Office).

REYNALDO, Jacinto; Dominican Republic politician; fmr Vice-Pres. Dominican Republic; Partido Reformista Social Cristiano (PRSC) Cand. for Presidency May 1996. *Address:* c/o Office of the Vice-President, Santo Domingo, Dominican Republic.

REYNDERS, Didier, LLB; Belgian politician; b. 6 Aug. 1958, Liège; ed Inst. St Jean Berchmans, Liège, Univ. of Liège; lawyer 1981–85; Gen. Man. Ministry of Wallonia Region 1985–88; Chair. Belgian Nat. Railway Co. (SNCB) 1986–91; Chef de Cabinet of Deputy Prime Minister, Minister of Justice and Inst. Reforms 1987–88; Chair. Nat. Airways Co. 1991–93; Vice-Chair. Parti Réformateur Libéral (PRL) 1992; Deputy, House of Reps 1992; Head PRL Group in Liège Council 1995, Chair. PRL-FDF (Front Démocratique des Francophones) Group 1995; Chair. Fed. Provinciale et d'Arrondissement de Liège of PRL 1995–; lecturer, Hautes Ecoles Commerciales, Liège; Minister of Finance 1999–; Chevalier, Ordre de Léopold 2000. *Address:* Ministry of Finance, Wetstraat 12, rue de la Loi, 1000 Brussels (Office); En Jonruelle 27, 4000 Liège, Belgium (Home). *Telephone:* (2) 233-81-11 (Office). *Fax:* (2) 233-80-03 (Office). *E-mail:* contact@didier-reynders.org (Office). *Website:* www.didier-reynders.org (Office).

REYNOLDS, Albert; Irish politician and businessman; b. 3 Nov. 1935, Rooskey, Co. Roscommon; m. Kathleen Coén; two s. five d.; ed Summerhill Coll., Sligo; fmr Chair. C & D Petfoods; mem. Longford County Council 1974–79; mem. Dáil 1977–; Minister for Posts and Telegraphs and Transport 1979–81; Minister for Industry and Energy March–Dec. 1982; Minister for Industry and Commerce 1987–88, for Finance and the Public Service 1988–89, of Finance 1989–91, Taoiseach 1992–94; Vice-Pres. Fianna Fáil 1983–92, Pres. 1992–94; Chair. Bula Resources 1999–2002, Longford Recreational Devt Centre; mem. Bd of Govs European Investment Bank; Gov. for Ireland, Bd of Govs World Bank, Int. Monetary Fund; Dir Jefferson Smurfit 1996–; Hon. LLD (Univ. Coll., Dublin) 1995. *Address:* Leinster House, Dáil Éireann, Kildare Street, Dublin 2 (Office); 18 Nilesbury Road, Ballsbridge, Dublin 4, Ireland (Home); Government Buildings, Upper Merrion Street, Dublin 2. *Telephone:* (1) 6183390 (Office); (1) 2603450 (Home). *Fax:* (1) 6184199 (Office); (1) 2603434.

REYNOLDS, Anna, FRAM; British opera and concert singer; b. 5 June 1931, Canterbury; d. of Paul Grey Reynolds and Vera Cicely Turner; ed Benenden School, Royal Acad. of Music; studied with Professoressa Debora Fambri, Rome; has appeared at many int. festivals including Spoleto, Edin., Aix-en-Provence, Salzburg Easter Festival, Vienna, Bayreuth, Tanglewood; has sung with leading orchestras all over the world including Chicago Symphony, New York Philharmonic, Berlin Philharmonic, London Symphony, etc.; has appeared in opera performances in New York Metropolitan, La Scala, Milan, Covent Garden, Bayreuth, Rome, Chicago Lyric Opera, Teatro Colón, Buenos Aires, Teatro Fenice, Venice and many others. *Leisure interests:* reading, piano, travel, world-wide correspondence. *Address:* Peesten 9, 95359 Kasendorf, Germany. *Telephone:* (9228) 1661. *Fax:* (9228) 8468 (Home). *E-mail:* jean .cox@t-online.de (Home).

REYNOLDS, Burt; American actor; b. 11 Feb. 1936, Waycross, Ga; s. of Burt Reynolds Sr; m. 1st Judy Carne (divorced 1965); m. 2nd Loni Anderson 1988 (divorced 1994); one adopted s.; ed Florida State Univ.; mem. Dirs Guild of America; Golden Globe for Best Supporting Actor for Boogie Nights 1997. *Stage appearances include:* Mister Roberts, Look, We've Come Through, The Rainmaker. *Films include:* Angel Baby 1961, Operation CIA 1965, Navajo Joe 1967, Impasse 1969, Skullduggery 1970, Deliverance 1972, Everything You've Always Wanted to Know about Sex But Were Afraid to Ask 1972, The Man Who Loved Cat Dancing 1973, Hustle 1975, Silent Movie 1976, Gator (also Dir) 1976, Nickelodeon 1976, Smokey and the Bandit 1977, Starting Over 1979, Cannonball Run 1981, Sharky's Machine (also Dir) 1981, City Heat 1984, Stick (also Dir) 1984, Rent A Cop 1987, Switching Channels 1988, Physical Evidence 1989, Breaking In 1989, B. L. Stryker 1989, Modern Love 1990, Alby's House of Bondage 1990, Cop and a Half 1993, Striptease 1996, Mad Dog Time 1996, Boogie Nights 1997, Raven 1997, Waterproof 1998, Mystery Alaska 1998, The Hunter's Moon 1998, Pups 1999, Big City Blues 2000, Mystery Alaska 2000, The Crew 2000, Tempted 2000, The Hermit of Amsterdam 2001. *Television appearances include:* Riverboat, Pony Express, Gunsmoke, Hawk, Dan August, B. L. Stryker, Evening Shade 1990–94, The Cherokee Kid 1996. *Publication:* My Life (autobiog.) 1994. *Address:* Jeffrey Lane & Associates, 8380 Melrose Avenue, Suite 206, Los Angeles, CA 90069, USA. *Website:* www.burtreynolds.com (Office).

REYNOLDS, Francis Martin Baillie, QC, DCL, FBA; British professor of law; b. 11 Nov. 1932, St Albans; s. of Eustace Baillie Reynolds and Emma Holmes; m. Susan Shillito 1965; two s. one d.; ed Winchester Coll. and Worcester Coll. Oxford; Bigelow Teaching Fellow, Univ. of Chicago 1957–58; lecturer, Worcester Coll. Oxford 1958–60, Fellow 1960–2000, Emer. Fellow 2000–; barrister, Inner Temple 1960, Hon. Bencher 1979; Reader in Law, Univ. of Oxford 1977, Prof. of Law 1992–2000, Emer. Prof. 2000–; Ed. The Law Quarterly Review 1987–; Visiting lecturer, Univ. of Auckland 1971, 1977; Visiting Prof. Nat. Univ. of Singapore 1984, 1986, 1988, 1990–92, 1994, 1996, 1997, 2000, 2003, Univ. Coll. London 1987–89, Univ. of Melbourne 1989, Monash Univ. 1989, Univ. of Otago 1993, Univ. of Sydney 1993, Univ. of Auckland 1995, Univ. of Hong Kong 2002; Titular mem. Comité Maritime Int.; Hon. QC; Hon. Prof. Int. Maritime Law Inst., Malta. *Publications:* Bowstead and Reynolds on Agency, 13th–17th edns. 1965–2001, Benjamin's Sale of Goods, 1st–6th edns (jtly) 1974–2002, English Private Law (jtly) 2000. *Leisure interests:* music, walking. *Address:* 61 Charlbury Road, Oxford, OX2 6UX, England. *Telephone:* (1865) 559323. *Fax:* (1865) 511894. *E-mail:* francis .reynolds@law.ox.ac.uk (Office and Home).

REYNOLDS, Matthew; Australian trade union official; b. 24 Oct. 1964, Hobart, Tasmania; public servant 1983–94; Tasmanian Br. Sec., Community and Public Sector Union (CPSU) 1995–99, Professional Div. Sec. 1999–, Nat. Pres. 1999–. *Address:* Community and Public Sector Union, Level 5, 191–199 Thomas Street, Haymarket, NSW 2000, Australia (Office). *E-mail:* matthew-reynolds@cpsu.org (Office). *Website:* www.cpsu.org.au (Office).

REYNOLDS, Sir Peter William John, Kt, CBE; British business executive; b. 10 Sept. 1929, Singapore; s. of Harry Reynolds and Gladys Reynolds; m. Barbara Anne Johnson 1955; two s.; ed Haileybury Coll.; with Unilever Ltd 1950–70, Trainee, Man. Dir, then Chair., Walls Ltd; Asst Group Man. Dir Ranks Hovis McDougall 1971, Group Man. Dir 1972–81, Chair. 1981–89, Deputy Chair. 1989–93; mem. Consultative Bd for Resources Devt in Agric. 1982–84; Deputy Chair. AvisEurope PLC 1988–; Dir of Industrial Devt Bd for Northern Ireland 1982–89, Guardian Royal Exchange Assurance PLC 1986–99; Chair. of Resources Cttee of Food and Drink Fed. 1983–86; Dir Boots Co. PLC 1986–, Guardian Royal Exchange PLC 1986–99, Avis Europe Ltd 1988–, Cilva Holdings PLC 1989–, Nationwide Anglia Bldg Soc. 1990–92; Chair., Pioneer Concrete (Holdings) 1990–99; mem. Peacock Cttee 1985–86; High Sheriff of Buckingham 1990–91. *Leisure interests:* beagling, riding (occasionally), watching rugby football, reading, gardening. *Address:* Rignall Farm, Rignall Road, Great Missenden, Bucks., HP16 9PE, England. *Telephone:* (1240) 64714.

REZA, (Evelyne Agnès) Yasmina; French dramatist, actress and comedian; b. 1 May 1955, Paris; d. of the late Jean Reza and of Nora (née Heltaï) Reza; one s. one d.; ed Lycée de St-Cloud, Paris Univ. X, Nanterre, Ecole Jacques Lecoq; Chevalier Ordre des Arts et des Lettres; Prix du jeune théâtre Beatrix Dussane-André Roussin de l'Acad. française 1991. *Stage appearances include:* Le Malade imaginaire 1977, Antigone 1977, Un Sang fort 1977, La Mort de Gaspard Hauser 1978, L'An Mil 1980, Le Piège de Méduse 1983, Le Veilleur de nuit 1986, Enorme changement de dernière minute 1989, La fausse suivante 1990. *Plays directed include:* Birds in the Night 1979, Marie la louve 1981. *Plays written include:* Conversations après un enterrement 1987 (Molière Award for Best Author, Prix des Talents nouveaux de la Soc. des auteurs et compositeurs dramatiques, Johnson Foundation prize), La Traversée de l'hiver 1989, La Métamorphose (adapted) 1988, Art 1994, L'Homme du Hasard, Trois Versions d'une vie 2000, Life X3 2000. *Screenplays written include:* Jusqu'à la nuit (also Dir) 1984, Le Goûter chez Niels 1986, A demain 1992. *Publication:* Hammerklavier 2000, Desolation (novel) 2002. *Address:* c/o Marta Andras (Marton Play), 14 rue des Sablons, 75116 Paris, France.

REZA, (Reza Deghati); Iranian photographer; b. 26 July 1952, Tabriz; ed Univs of Tabriz and Tehran; photographer with Agence France Presse during Iranian revolution 1978; corresp. with Newsweek, Iran 1978–81, with Time Magazine 1983–88; consultant to UN Humanitarian Programme, Afghanistan 1989–90; Reporter for UNICEF 1989–95, for Nat. Geographic Magazine 1990–95; photographs have appeared in numerous int. magazines, including Der Spiegel, Paris-Match, Le Nouvel Observateur, The Observer, El Pais, Oggi, Newsweek, Life, etc; regular corresp. for BBC Radio Persia and Radio France Int. Persia; fmr teacher Ecole d'Art, Paris, Univ. of Georgetown, Washington, DC. *Exhibitions:* Modern Art Museum, Tehran 1979, Iranian Kurdish Exhbn, La Mutualité, Paris 1981, Opening Exhbn, Kurdish Inst., Paris 1984; also group exhbns in many cities world-wide including Amsterdam 1983, Paris 1984, 1988, 1991, New York 1987, Karachi 1988, Havana 1994.

REZEK, Francisco, LLD, JSD; Brazilian judge and politician; b. 18 Jan. 1944, Cristina, Minas Gerais; ed Fed. Univ. of Minas Gerais, Sorbonne, Oxford Univ., Harvard Univ., The Hague Acad. of Int. Law; Attorney at the Repub., Supreme Court 1972–79; Prof. of Int. and Constitutional Law Univ. of Brasília 1971–, Chair. Law Dept 1974–76, Dean Faculty of Social Studies 1978–79; Prof. of Int. Law Rio Branco Inst. 1976–; Justice of Supreme Court 1983–90, 1992–97; Foreign Minister 1990–92; mem. Perm. Court of Arbitration 1987–; Judge Int. Court of Justice, The Hague Feb. 1997–. *Publications:* Droit des traités: particularités des actes constitutifs d'organisations internationales 1968, La conduite des relations internationales dans le droit constitutionnel latino-américain 1970, Reciprocity as a Basis of Extradition 1980, Direito dos Tratados 1984, Public International Law 1989. *Address:* International Court of Justice, Peace Palace, Carnegieplein 2, 2517 KJ The Hague, Netherlands (Office). *Telephone:* (70) 3022405 (Office); (70) 3264243 (Home). *Fax:* (70) 3022409 (Office). *E-mail:* f.rezek@icj-cij.org (Office); f_rezek@hotmail.com (Home).

REZNIK, Genry Markovich, CAND JUR.; Russian barrister; b. 11 May 1938, Leningrad; m. Larissa Yulianovna Reznik; one s.; ed Kazakhstan Univ., Moscow Inst. of Law; professional volleyball mem. USSR youth team; investigator Investigation Dept, Ministry of Internal Affairs Kazakh Repub.; barrister since 1985; Dir Inst. of Bar Int. Union of Advocates; mem. Moscow Helsinki Group 1989–; Chair. of Bd, Moscow City Collegium of Barristers; participated in 22 civil trials; f. Reznik, Gagarin and Partners. *Publications:* over 100 articles on criminal law. *Address:* Reznik, Gagarin and Partners, Schmidtovskiy pr. 3, 123100 Moscow, Russia (Office). *Telephone:* (095) 205-27-09 (Office).

RHALLYS, George J. (see Rallis, George J.).

RHINES, Peter Broomell, PhD; American oceanographer and atmospheric scientist; b. 23 July 1942, Hartford, Conn.; s. of Thomas B. Rhines and Olive S. Rhines; m. 1st Marie Lenos 1968 (divorced 1983); m. 2nd Linda Mattson Semtner 1984; one s.; ed Loomis School, MIT, Trinity Coll., Cambridge, England; Sloan Scholar, MIT 1960–63, NSF Fellow 1963–64; Marshall Scholar, Cambridge 1964–67; Asst Prof. of Oceanography MIT 1967–71; Research Scientist, Cambridge Univ. 1971–72; mem. Scientific Staff, Woods Hole Oceanographic Inst. 1972–84, Dir Center for Analysis of Marine Systems 1979–82, oceanographic research cruises 1972–2000; Prof. of Oceanography and Atmospheric Sciences, Univ. of Washington, Seattle 1984–; Guggenheim Fellow, Christ's Coll. Cambridge, England 1979–80; Natural Environment Research Council Visiting Fellow, UK 1983; Fellow American Geophysical Union, American Meteorological Soc., American Acad. of Arts and Sciences, Queen's Fellow in Marine Sciences, Australia; mem. NAS; de Florez Award, MIT 1963, Creativity Award, NSF 1996, Stommel Research Award, American Meteorological Soc. 1998. *Publications:* research papers on general circulation of the oceans, waves and climate; contrib. to films on oceanography for BBC and Public Broadcasting System, USA. *Leisure interests:* classical guitar, conversation and the out-of-doors. *Address:* School of Oceanography, University of Washington, Box 357940, Seattle, WA 98195 (Office); 5753 61st Avenue NE, Seattle, WA 98105, USA (Home). *Telephone:* (206) 522-5753 (Home).

RHOADS, James Berton, PhD; American archivist; b. 17 Sept. 1928, Sioux City, Iowa; s. of James H. Rhoads and Mary K. Rhoads; m. S. Angela Handy

1947; one s. two d.; ed Univ. of California (Berkeley) and the American Univ., Washington, DC; held various positions in the Nat. Archives 1952–65; Asst Archivist, Civil Archives 1965–66; Deputy Archivist of USA 1966–68; Archivist of USA 1968–79; Pres. Rhoads Assocs Int. 1980–84; Dir Graduate Program in Archives and Records Man., Western Washington Univ. 1984–94, Prof. of History 1987–94, Prof. Emer. 1994–, Dir Center for Pacific Northwest Studies 1994–97; mem. Cttee on Soviet-American Archival Co-operation 1986–91, Bd of Trustees Washington State Historical Soc. 1986–95, Washington State Historical Records Advisory Bd 1990–97, Acad. of Certified Archivists 1989– (Pres. 1992–94); Fellow, Soc. of American Archivists, Pres. 1974–75; Pres. Int. Council on Archives 1976–79; Vice-Pres. Intergovernmental Council on Gen. Information Program, UNESCO 1977–79 and mem. numerous other related orgs. *Publications:* numerous articles in professional journals. *Leisure interests:* reading, philately. *Address:* 3613 Illinois Lane, Bellingham, WA 98226, USA. *Telephone:* (360) 676-1235.

RHODES, Frank Harold Trevor, PhD; American geologist and university president; b. 29 Oct. 1926, Warwickshire, England; s. of Harold C. Rhodes and Gladys (Ford) Rhodes; m. Rosa Carlson 1952; four d.; ed Univ. of Birmingham; Post-doctoral Fellow, Fulbright Scholar, Univ. of Ill. 1950–51, Visiting Lecturer in Geology summers of 1951–52, Asst Prof., Univ. of Ill. 1954–55, Assoc. Prof. 1955–56, Dir Univ. of Ill. Field Station, Wyoming 1956; Lecturer in Geology, Univ. of Durham 1951–54; Prof. of Geology and Head Dept of Geology, Univ. of Wales, Swansea 1956–68, Dean Faculty of Science 1967–68; Prof. of Geology and Mineralogy, Coll. of Literature, Science and Arts, Univ. of Michigan 1968–77, Dean 1971–74, Vice-Pres. for Academic Affairs 1974–77; Pres. Cornell Univ. 1977–94, Prof. of Geology 1977–95, Pres. Emer. 1995–; Dir John Heinz III Center for Science, Econs and the Environment 1996–98; Vice-Pres. Dyson Charitable Trust 1996–98; Prin. Washington Advisory Group 1997–; Chair. The Atlantic Foundation 2000–; mem. Nat. Science Bd 1987–98 (Chair. 1994–96), American Philosophical Soc. (Pres. 1999–), Johnson Foundation Bd 2000–; Trustee Andrew W. Mellon 1984–99; Jefferson Lecturer, Univ. of Calif. Berkeley 1999; 33 hon. degrees; Bigsby Medal, Geological Soc. 1967, Higher Educ. Leadership Award, Comm. on Ind. Colls and Univs 1987, Justin Smith Morrill Award 1987, Clark Kerr Medal, Univ. of Calif. Berkeley 1995. *Publications:* The Evolution of Life 1962, Fossils 1963, Geology 1972, Evolution 1974, Language of the Earth 1981, (Ed.) Successful Fund Raising for Higher Education: The Advancement of Learning 1997; over 70 maj. scientific articles and monographs and some 60 articles on educ. *Address:* Cornell University, 3104 Snee Hall, Ithaca, NY 14853, USA. *Telephone:* (607) 255-6233 (Office).

RHODES, Richard L., BA; American writer; b. 4 July 1937, Kansas City, Kan.; s. of Arthur Rhodes and Georgia Collier Rhodes; m. Ginger Untrif 1993; two c. by previous m.; ed East High School, Kansas City, Mo.; Yale Univ.; Trustee Andrew Drumm Inst., Independence, Mo. 1990–, Fellowships: John Simon Guggenheim Memorial Foundation 1974–75, Nat. Endowment for the Arts 1978, Ford Foundation 1981–83, Alfred P. Sloan Foundation 1985, 1993, 1995, 2001, MacArthur Foundation Program on Peace and Int. Co-operation 1990–91; Hon. DHumLitt (Westminster Coll., Fulton, Mo.) 1988; Nat. Book Critics Circle Award for general non-fiction 1987, Nat. Book Award for non-fiction 1987, Pulitzer Prize for general non-fiction 1988 (all for The Making of the Atomic Bomb). *Publications:* (non-fiction) The Inland Ground: An Evocation of the American Middle West 1970, The Ozarks 1974, Looking for America: A Writer's Odyssey 1979, The Making of the Atomic Bomb 1987, Farm: A Year in the Life of an American Farmer 1989, A Hole in the World: An American Boyhood 1990, Making Love: An Erotic Odyssey 1992, Nuclear Renewal: Common Sense about Energy 1993, Dark Sun: The Making of the Hydrogen Bomb 1995, How To Write 1995, Trying To Get Some Dignity: Stories of Triumph Over Childhood Abuse (with Ginger Rhodes) 1996, Deadly Feasts: Tracking the Secrets of a Terrifying New Plague 1997, Visions of Technology 1999, Why They Kill 1999, Masters of Death 2001; (fiction) The Ungodly 1973, Holy Secrets 1978, The Last Safari 1980, Sons of Earth 1981. *Address:* c/o Janklow & Nesbit Assocs, 455 Park Avenue, New York, NY 10021, USA (Office). *Telephone:* (212) 421-1700 (Office).

RHODES, Zandra Lindsey, CBE, FCSD, FSIAD; British textile and fashion designer; b. 19 Sept. 1940, Chatham, Kent; d. of Albert James Rhodes and Beatrice Ellen (née Twigg); ed Medway Coll. of Art and Royal Coll. of Art; set up print factory and studio 1965; began producing dresses using own prints 1966; founder-partner and designer, Fulham Clothes Shop, London 1967–68; freelance designer, producing own collections for British and U.S. markets 1968–75; founder and Man. Dir (with Anne Knight and Ronnie Stirling) Zandra Rhodes (UK) Ltd and Zandra Rhodes (Shops) Ltd 1975–86; opened first shop in London 1975; Man. Dir all Zandra Rhodes Cos 1975–; other shops in Bloomingdale's, New York, Marshall Field's, Chicago, Seibu, Tokyo and Harrods, London; licences include: Wamsutta sheets and pillowcases (USA) 1976, Eve Stillman Lingerie (USA) 1977, CVP Designs, interior fabrics and settings (UK) 1977, Philip Hockley decorative furs (UK) 1986, Zandra Rhodes saris (India) 1987, Littlewoods catalogues (UK) for printed T-shirts and intasia sweaters 1988, Hilmet silk scarves and men's ties (UK) 1989, Bonnay perfume (UK) 1993, Coats Patons needlepoint (UK) 1993, Pologeorgis Furs (USA) 1996, Zandra Rhodes II handpainted ready-to-wear collection (Hong Kong) 1995, Grattons Catalogue sheets and duvets (UK) 1996; work has featured in numerous exhbns and is represented in many perm. collections including Victoria & Albert Museum, London, Metropolitan Museum of Art, New York, Smithsonian Inst. Washington and Museum of Applied Arts and

Sciences, Sydney; retrospectives in El Paso, Texas 1984, Columbus, Ohio 1987, Tokyo 1987, 1991, Athenaeum Library, La Jolla 1996, 2001, Phoenix 1997, San Diego 1998; water-colour exhbns in New York, LA, New Orleans 1989; f. Zandra Rhodes Museum of Fashion and Textiles, UK 1996; costume designs The Magic Flute, San Diego Opera 2001; Hon. Fellow, Kent Inst. of Art and Design 1992; Hon. DFA (Int. Fine Arts Coll., Miami) 1986; Dr hc (RCA) 1986; Hon. DD (CNAA) 1987, Hon. DLitt (Westminster) 2000; Designer of the Year, English Fashion Trade 1972, Royal Designer for Industry 1974, Emmy Award for Best Costume Designs in Romeo and Juliet on Ice, CBS TV 1984, Alpha Award, New Orleans 1985, 1991, Woman of Distinction Award, Northwood Inst., Dallas 1986, Observer Award as top UK Textile Designer 1990, Hall of Fame Award, British Fashion Council 1995. *Publications:* The Art of Zandra Rhodes 1984, The Zandra Rhodes Collection by Brother 1988. *Leisure interests:* travelling, drawing, gardening, cooking. *Address:* 79–85 Bermondsey Street, London, SE1 3XF, England. *Telephone:* (20) 7403-5333 (Office).

RHYS-JAMES, Shani, BA; British artist and painter; b. 2 May 1953, Australia; d. of Harold Marcus Rhys-James and Jeannie James-Money; m. Stephen West 1977; two s.; ed Parliament Hill Girls School, Loughborough Coll. of Art and Cen. St Martin's Coll. of Art and Design; regular exhbns with Martin Tinney, Cardiff 1991–99, Stephen Lacey, London; work in art collections of Nat. Museum of Wales, Newport Museum and Art Gallery Cyfartha Castle, Merthyr Tydfil, Usher Gallery, Arts Council of England, Gallery of Modern Art, Glasgow, Wolverhampton Art Gallery, Birmingham City Museum and Art Gallery, National Library of Wales; featured artist Carlow Festival 2000, Royal Cambrian Acad. Three-Person show 2001; mem. Royal Cambrian Acad. 1994; BBC Wales Visual Artist Award 1994, BP Nat. Portrait Award, Gold Medal for Fine Art Royal Nat. Eisteddfod, First Prize Hunting/Observer Prize and others. *Solo exhibitions include:* Blood Ties, Wrexham Arts Centre and touring 1993, Facing the Self, Oriel Mostyn and touring 1997, Stephen Lacey Gallery 2000, Martin Tinney 2002, Aberystwyth Art Centre 2004. *Group exhibitions include:* Disclosure(s), Oriel Mostyn and touring 1994, Reclaiming the Madonna, Usher Gallery, Lincoln and touring 1994, In the Looking Glass, Usher Gallery and touring 1996, Birmingham City Art Gallery Gas Hall 2000, Let's Panic Later, Kunstlerhaus, Dortmund. *Television includes:* Blood Ties 1993, Painting the Dragon 2000, The Little Picture 2000, Paintings from Paradise 2000. *Leisure interests:* piano, films, plays, books, writing poetry, restoring our Welsh farm. *Address:* Dolpebyll, Llangadfan, Welshpool, Powys, SY21 0PU, Wales. *Telephone:* (1938) 820469. *Fax:* (1938) 820469.

RIBAS REIG, Oscar, LLB; Andorran politician, industrialist and banker; b. 26 Oct. 1936, Sant Julia de Loria; m.; five c.; ed Univ. of Barcelona, Univ. of Fribourg, Switzerland; MP 1972–75, 1976–79, Head of Govt 1982–84, 1990–94.

RIBEIRO, Inacio; Brazilian fashion designer; m. Suzanne Clements 1992; ed Cen. St Martin's Coll. of Art and Design, London; fmrly designer, Brazil; design consultant in Brazil with wife 1991–93; f. Clements Ribeiro with wife, London 1993; first collection launched Oct. 1993, numerous collections since; first solo show London Fashion Week March 1995; fashion shows since in London, Paris, Brazil, Japan; consultant to cos in UK and Italy; winners Designer of the Year New Generation Category 1996. *Address:* c/o Beverley Cable PR, 11 St. Christopher's Place, London, W1U 1NG (Office); Clements Ribeiro Ltd, 413–419 Harrow Road, London, W9 3QJ, England. *Telephone:* (20) 8962-3060. *Fax:* (20) 8962-3061. *E-mail:* inacioribeiro@hotmail.com (Office).

RIBEIRO, João Ubaldo Osório Pimentel, LLB, MS; Brazilian writer and journalist; b. 23 Jan. 1941, Itaparica, Bahia; s. of Manoel Ribeiro and Maria Felipa Osório Pimentel Ribeiro; m. 1st Maria Beatriz Moreira Caldas 1962; m. 2nd Mônica Maria Roters 1971; m. 3rd Berenice de Carvalho Batella Ribeiro 1982; one s. three d.; ed Fed. Univ. of Bahia Law School and School of Admin. and Univ. of Southern California, USA; Reporter, Jornal da Bahia, Salvador 1958–59, City Ed. and Columnist 1960–63; Chief Ed. Tribuna da Bahia 1968–73; Columnist O Globo, Rio de Janeiro, O Estado de São Paulo, São Paulo; Editorial-writer Folha de São Paulo 1969–73; Prof. of Political Science, Fed. Univ. of Bahia 1965–71, Catholic Univ of Bahia 1967–71; mem. Brazilian Acad. of Letters; Jabuti Prize (Brazilian Book Chamber) 1971, 1984; Golfinho de Ouro (Govt of Rio) and many others. *Publications:* (novels) Setembro Não Tem Sentido 1968, Sargento Getúlio 1971, Vila Real 1980, Viva o Povo Brasileiro 1984, O Sorriso do Lagarto 1989, O Feitiço da Ilha do Pavão 1997, Miséria e Grandeza do Amor de Benedita 2000, Diário do Farol 2002 ; (short stories) Vencecavalo e o Outro Povo 1973, Livro de Histórias 1983; Ein Brasilianer in Berlin (autobiog.) 1994. *Leisure interests:* microscopy (protozoa), music (Bach), sports (soccer, fishing). *Address:* c/o Editora Nova Fronteira SA, Rua Bambina 25, 22251-050 Rio de Janeiro, R.J.; Rua General Urquiza, 147/401, 22431-040 Rio de Janeiro, R.J., Brazil (Home). *Telephone:* (21) 537-8770 (Office); 21) 239-8528 (Home). *Fax:* (21) 286-6755.

RIBERA, José António Moya; Portuguese diplomatist; b. 19 July 1946, Oporto; s. of António Ribera y Romero and Maria Margarida da Silva Pereira Moya; m. Maria Filomena Leite Pereira de Magalhães 1976; one s. one d.; ed Liceu Alexandre Herculano, Oporto and Univ. of Oporto; joined Ministry of Foreign Affairs 1972; Sec. The Hague 1976–78; Consul, Vigo, Spain 1978–81; Counsellor, Kinshasa 1981–85; Counsellor, Perm. Mission of Portugal at EC, Brussels 1985–89; Deputy Dir-Gen. for EC, Ministry of Foreign Affairs

1989–92; Rep. of Portugal at EC Intergovernmental Conf. for Political Union (Maastricht Treaty) 1990–92; Perm. Rep. of Portugal to UNESCO 1992–; Kt Commdr of Infante D. Henrique Order, Officer of Mil. Order of Cristo, Grand Cross, Order of Merit, decorations from Netherlands, Zaïre, Brazil. *Leisure interests:* history, genealogy. *Address:* Permanent Representative of Portugal to UNESCO, 7 place de Fontenoy, 75352 Paris cedex 07 (Office); ave Foch 41, 75016 Paris, France (Home). *Telephone:* 1-45-68-10-00 (Office); 1-44-05-01-06 (Home). *Fax:* 1-45-67-16-90. *Website:* www.unesco.org (Office).

RIBERHOLDT, Gunnar; Danish diplomatist; b. 7 Nov. 1933, Naestved; s. of Poul G. Riberholdt and Erna M. Andersen; one s. one d.; ed US univs and Univ. of Copenhagen; Ministry of Foreign Affairs 1958–62; Sec. of Embassy, Danish Perm. Mission to European Communities 1962–64, Deputy Head of Mission 1964–65; Head of Section, Ministry of Foreign Affairs 1965–69; Econ. Counsellor, Paris 1969–72; Dir Ministry of Foreign Affairs 1973–75; Dir-Gen. European Econ. Affairs 1975–77; Amb., Perm. Rep. of Denmark to European Communities (now EU) 1977–84, 1992–94; Amb. to France 1984–91; Amb., Personal Rep. of Minister for Foreign Affairs to Intergovernmental Confs on Political Union and on Econ. and Monetary Union 1991–92; Amb., Head Danish Del. to OECD 1991–92; Perm. Rep. to NATO 1995–99; Amb. to Italy (also accred to Cyprus, Malta and San Marino) 1999–. *Address:* Danish Embassy, Via dei Monti Parioli 50, 00197 Rome, Italy. *Telephone:* (06) 3200441. *Fax:* (06) 3610290. *E-mail:* ambadane@iol.it.

RICCI, Christina; American film actress; b. 12 Feb. 1980, Santa Monica, Calif.; d. of Ralph Ricci and Sarah Ricci; began acting career in commercials. *Films:* Mermaids 1990, The Hard Way 1991, The Addams Family 1991, The Cemetery Club 1993, Addams Family Values 1993, Casper 1995, Now and Then 1995, Gold Diggers: The Secret of Bear Mountain 1995, That Darn Cat 1996, Last of the High Kings 1996, Bastard Out of Carolina 1996, Ice Storm 1997, Little Red Riding Hood 1997, Fear and Loathing in Las Vegas 1998, Desert Blue 1998, Buffalo 66 1998, The Opposite of Sex 1998, Small Soldiers 1998, Pecker 1999, 200 Cigarettes 1999, Sleepy Hollow 1999, The Man Who Cried 2000. *Address:* c/o ICM, 8942 Wilshire Boulevard, Beverly Hills, CA 90211, USA.

RICCI, Nino, MA; Canadian writer; b. 23 Aug. 1959, Leamington; s. of Virginio Ricci and Amelia Ricci (née Ingratta); m. Erika de Vasconcelos 1997; ed York Univ., Toronto, Concordia Univ., Montreal; Pres. Canadian Centre, Int. PEN 1995–96; Gov.-Gen.'s Award 1990, Betty Trask Award 1991, Winifred Holtby Award 1991. *Publications:* (novels) Lives of the Saints 1990, In a Glass House 1993, Where She Has Gone 1997, Testament 2002. *Address:* c/o Anne McDermid & Associates, 92 Wilcocks Street, Toronto, Ont., M5S 1C8, Canada.

RICCI, Ruggiero; American violinist; b. 24 July 1918, San Francisco; s. of Pietro Ricci and Emma Bacigalupi; m. 1st Ruth Rink 1942; m. 2nd Valma Rodriguez 1957; m. 3rd Julia Whitehurst Clemenceau 1978; two s. three d.; ed under Louis Persinger, Mischel Piastro, Paul Stassévitch and Georg Kulenkampff; début with Manhattan Symphony Orchestra, New York 1929; first tour of Europe 1932; served USAF 1942–45; Prof. of Violin, Univ. of Mich. 1982–87; Mozarteum, Salzburg, Austria 1989–; now makes annual tours of USA and Europe; has made 13 tours of S. America, five tours of Australia, two tours of Japan and three tours of USSR; played the first performances of the violin concertos of Ginastera, Von Einem and Veerhoff; made first complete recording of Paganini caprices; specializes in violin solo literature; Cavaliere Order of Merit (Italy). *Address:* Johann-Wolf-str. 16A, Salzburg, Austria; Intermusica, Stephen Lumsden, 16 Duncan Terrace, London, N1 8BZ, England; c/o John Gingrich Management Inc., P.O. Box 1515, New York, NY 10023, USA. *Telephone:* (20) 7278-5455 (London). *Fax:* (20) 7278-8434 (London).

RICCIARDONE, Francis J.; American diplomatist; b. Boston, Mass.; ed Dartmouth Coll., NH; taught in int. schools Italy 1974–76, Iran 1976–78; entered Foreign Service 1978; served in Ankara and Adana, Turkey 1979–81; Special Asst to Dir Bureau of Intelligence and Research and research analyst for Turkey, Greece and Cyprus 1981–82; country officer for Iraq 1982–85; political officer, Cairo 1986–89; led Civilian Observer Unit, Multinat. Force and Observers, Sinai Desert 1989–91; Deputy Chief of Mission (desig.), Baghdad Embassy 1991–93; Political Adviser to multinat. relief operation, Northern Iraq 1993; Dir Office of Policy Co-ordination for Dir.-Gen. of Foreign Service and of Personnel 1993; Deputy Chief of Mission and Chargé d'Affaires, Ankara 1995; Sec. of State's Special Rep. for Transition in Iraq 1999–2001; Dir Task Force on the Coalition Against Terrorism, Dept of State 2001; Sr. Adviser to the Dir-Gen. of the Foreign Service 2001; Amb. to the Philippines and to Palau 2002–; Meritorious Honor Award 1984, Dir.-Gen.'s Award for Political Reporting 1988. *Address:* Embassy of the U.S.A., 1201 Roxas Boulevard, Metro Manila, Philippines (Office). *Telephone:* (2) 5231001 (Office). *Fax:* (2) 5224361 (Office). *E-mail:* manila1@pd.state.gov. *Website:* www.usembassy.state.gov/manila.

RICE, Condoleezza, PhD; American political adviser; b. 14 Nov. 1954, Birmingham, Ala; ed Univ. of Denver, Univ. of Notre Dame; teacher at Stanford Univ., Calif. 1981–2001, Provost 1993–99, currently Hoover Sr Fellow and Prof. of Political Science; Special Asst to Dir of Jt Chiefs of Staff 1986; Dir, then Sr Dir of Soviet and East European Affairs, Nat. Security Council 1989–91; Special Asst to Pres. for Nat. Security Affairs 1989–91; primary foreign policy adviser to presidential cand. George W. Bush 1999–2000; Asst to Pres. for Nat. Security Affairs and Nat. Security Advisor

2001–; mem. Bd of Dirs, Chevron Corpn, Charles Schwab Corpn, William and Flora Hewlett Foundation and numerous other bds; Sr Fellow, Inst. for Int. Studies, Stanford; Fellow, American Acad. of Arts and Sciences; Dr hc (Morehouse Coll.) 1991, (Univ. of Ala) 1994, (Univ. of Notre Dame) 1995. *Publications:* Uncertain Allegiance: The Soviet Union and the Czechoslovak Army 1984, The Gorbachev Era (co-author) 1986, Germany Unified and Europe Transformed (co-author) 1995; and numerous articles on Soviet and East European foreign and defence policy. *Address:* The White House, 1600 Pennsylvania Avenue, NW, Washington, DC 20504, USA (Office). *Telephone:* (202) 456-1414 (Office); (202) 456-2883.

RICE, Dorothy P., BA; American academic; b. 11 June 1922, Brooklyn, New York; d. of Gershon Pechman and Lena Schiff; m. John D. Rice 1943; three s.; ed Brooklyn Coll., New York, Univ. of Wisconsin; Dept of Labor 1941–42; War Production Bd 1942–44; Nat. War Labor Bd 1944–45; Nat. Wage Stabilization Bd 1945–47; Health Economist, Public Health Service 1947–49, Public Health Analyst 1960–62, 1964–65; Social Science Analyst, Social Security Admin. 1962–64, Chief, Health Insurance Research Branch 1965–72, Deputy Asst Commr Office of Research and Statistics 1972–76; Dir Nat. Center for Health Stats. Hyattsville, Md 1976–82; Prof.-in-Residence, Dept of Social and Behavioral Sciences, Inst. for Health and Aging, Univ. of Calif., San Francisco 1982–, Inst. for Health Policy Studies, Univ. of Calif., San Francisco 1982–94, Prof. Emer. 1994–; numerous honours and awards. *Publications:* more than 200 articles in professional journals. *Address:* Institute for Health and Aging, Department of Social and Behavioral Sciences—N631, School of Nursing, University of California, San Francisco, CA 94143-0646 (Office); 13895 Campus Drive, Oakland, CA 94605, USA (Home). *Telephone:* (415) 476-2771 (Office). *Fax:* (415) 502-5208 (Office). *E-mail:* rice@itsa.ucsf.edu (Office); drice39223@aol.com (Home). *Website:* nurseweb.ucsf.edu/iha (Office).

RICE, Jerry; American football player; b. 13 Oct. 1962, Starkville, Miss.; s. of Joe Nathan; m. Jacqui Rice; three c.; ed Crawford and Mississippi Valley State Coll.; Nat. Football League (NFL) football player; wide receiver; played with San Francisco 49ers for 16 years, then with Oakland Raiders for two years; records include most touchdowns (190) and most passes received (1,306) 1985–2001; only player in NFL history to catch three touchdown passes in two Super Bowl games; Sporting News NFL Player of the Year 1987, 1990, Sports Illustrated NFL Player of the Year 1986, 1987, 1990, 1993. *Leisure interest:* golf. *Address:* c/o The Oakland Raiders, 1220 Harbor Bay Parkway, Alameda, CA 94502 USA (Office). *Website:* www.jerryrice.net (Office).

RICE, Stuart Alan, BS, AM, PhD; American professor of chemistry; b. 6 Jan. 1932, New York City; s. of Laurence Harlan Rice and Helen Rayfield; m. 1st Marian Coopersmith 1952 (died 1994); two d.; m. 2nd Ruth O'Brien 1997; one s.; ed Brooklyn Coll. and Harvard Univ.; Asst Prof. Dept of Chem. and Inst. for the Study of Metals, Univ. of Chicago 1957–59, Assoc. Prof. Inst. for the Study of Metals (later James Franck Inst.) 1959–60, 1960–69, Louis Block Prof. of Chem. 1969, Louis Block Prof. of Physical Sciences 1969–, Chair. Dept of Chemistry 1971–77, Frank P. Hixon Distinguished Service Prof. 1977–, Dean, Div. of Physical Sciences, Univ. of Chicago 1981–95; mem. NAS, Nat. Science Bd 1980–; Foreign mem. Royal Danish Acad. of Science and Letters 1976; Alfred P. Sloan Fellow 1958–62, Guggenheim Fellow 1960–61, NSF Sr Postdoctoral Fellow and Visiting Prof. Univ. Libre de Bruxelles 1965–66; Nat. Insts of Health Special Research Fellow and Visiting Prof. H. C. Orsted Inst., Univ. of Copenhagen 1970–71; Fairchild Distinguished Scholar, Calif. Inst. of Tech. 1979; Fellow, American Acad. of Arts and Sciences; Newton-Abraham Prof., Oxford Univ. 1999–2000; Bourke Lecturer, Faraday Soc. 1964; Baker Lecturer, Cornell Univ. 1985–86; Centenary Lecturer, Royal Soc. of Chemistry 1986–87; John Howard Appleton Lecturer, Brown Univ. 1995; lecturer, numerous univs in USA and abroad; Hon. DSc (Brooklyn Coll., Notre Dame Coll.) 1982; A. Cressy Morrison Prize in Natural Sciences, New York Acad. of Sciences 1955, ACS Award in Pure Chem. 1962, Marlow Medal, Faraday Soc. 1963, Llewellyn John and Harriet Manchester Quantrell Award 1970, Leo Hendrik Baekeland Award 1971, Peter Debye ACS Prize 1985, Joel Henry Hildebrand Award, ACS, Centennial Medal, Harvard Univ. 1997, Nat. Medal of Science 1999, Hirschfelder Prize in Theoretical Chem. 2002–03. *Publications:* Poly-electrolyte Solutions (with Mitsuru Nagasawa) 1961, Statistical Mechanics of Simple Liquids (with Peter Gray) 1965, Physical Chemistry (with R. S. Berry and John Ross) 1980, Optical Control of Molecular Dynamics (with Meishan Zhao) 2000; and 600 papers on chemical physics in scientific journals. *Leisure interests:* reading, carpentry, collecting antique scientific instruments. *Address:* The James Franck Institute, The University of Chicago, 5640 Ellis Avenue, Chicago, IL 60637 (Office); 5517 S. Kimbark Avenue, Chicago, IL 60637, USA (Home). *Telephone:* (773) 702-7199 (Office); (773) 667-2679 (Home). *Fax:* (773) 702-5863 (Office); (773) 667-0454 (Home). *E-mail:* s-rice@uchicago.edu (Office).

RICE, Thomas Maurice, PhD, FRS; American/Irish theoretical physicist; b. 26 Jan. 1939, Dundalk, Ireland; s. of James Rice and Maureen Rice; m. Helen D. Spreiter 1966; one s. two d.; ed Univ. Coll. Dublin and Univ. of Cambridge; asst lecturer, Dept of Mathematical Physics, Univ. of Birmingham 1963–64; Research Assoc. Dept of Physics, Univ. of Calif. at San Diego, La Jolla 1964–66; Bell Laboratories, Murray Hill, NJ 1966–81; Prof. of Theoretical Physics, Eidgenössische Technische Hochschule (ETH), Zürich 1981–; mem. NAS; Hon. MRIA; Hewlett-Packard Europhysics Prize 1998, John Bardeen

Prize 2000. *Address:* Theoretische Physik, ETH-Hönggerberg, 8093 Zürich, Switzerland. *Telephone:* (1) 6332581. *Fax:* (1) 6331115 (Office). *E-mail:* rice@itp.phys.ethz.ch (Office).

RICE, Sir Tim(othy) Miles Bindon, Kt; British songwriter and broadcaster; b. 10 Nov. 1944, Amersham; s. of Hugh Gordon Rice and Joan Odette Rice; m. Jane Artereta McIntosh 1974 (died 1990); one s. one d.; ed Lancing Coll., with EMI Records 1966–68, Norrie Paramor Org. 1968–69; Founder and Dir GRRR Books Ltd 1978–, Pavilion Books Ltd 1981–97; Chair. Foundation for Sport and the Arts 1991–; mem. Main Cttee MCC 1992–94, 1995– (Pres. 2002–03). *Lyrics for musicals* (music by Andrew Lloyd Webber, q.v.): Joseph and the Amazing Technicolor Dreamcoat 1968, Jesus Christ Superstar 1970, Evita 1976, Blondel (music by Stephen Oliver) 1983, Chess (music by Benny Andersson and Bjorn Ulvaeus) 1984, Cricket (with A. L. Webber) 1986, Starmania 1989–90, Tycoon (with music by Michael Berger) 1992, Aladdin (film musical, music by Alan Menken) 1992, The Lion King (with music by Elton John) 1993, Beauty and the Beast 1994, The Road to El Dorado 1999; some lyrics for stage version of Beauty and the Beast (music by Alan Menken) 1994, Heathcliff (music by John Farrar) 1995, King David (music by Alan Menken) 1997, Aida (music by Elton John) 1998, El Dorado (music by Elton John) 1999; numerous awards including Golden Globe and Acad. Award for Can You Feel the Love Tonight (from The Lion King) 1995, for You Must Love Me (from film Evita) 1997. *Publications:* Evita (with Andrew Lloyd Webber) 1978, Joseph and the Amazing Technicolor Dreamcoat 1982; ed. Heartaches Cricketers' Almanack 1975–; over 20 books in the series Guinness Book of British Hit Singles, Albums etc. (with Jonathan Rice, Paul Gambaccini and Mike Read), Treasures of Lords 1989, Oh, What a Circus (autobiog.) 1995, The Complete Eurovision Song Contest Companion (jtly) 1998. *Leisure interests:* cricket, history of popular music, chickens. *Address:* c/o Lewis & Golden, 40 Queen Anne Street, London, W1M 0EL, England.

RICH, Adrienne, AB; American writer; b. 16 May 1929, Baltimore; d. of Arnold Rich and Helen Elizabeth Jones; m. Alfred Conrad (died 1970); three s.; ed Radcliffe Coll.; Teacher, New York Poetry Center 1966–67; Visiting Lecturer, Swarthmore Coll. 1967–69; Adjunct Prof., Columbia Univ. 1967–69; Lecturer, City Coll. of New York 1968–70, Instructor 1970–71, Asst Prof. of English 1971–72, 1974–75; Visiting Prof. of Creative Literature, Brandeis Univ. 1972–73; Prof. of English, Rutgers Univ. 1976–79; Prof.-at-Large, Cornell Univ. 1981–87; Lecturer and Visiting Prof, Scripps Coll. 1983, 1984; Prof. of English and Feminist Studies, Stanford Univ. 1986–93; Marjorie Kovler Visiting Lecturer, Univ. of Chicago 1989; Clark Lecturer, Trinity Coll., Cambridge 2002; Guggenheim Fellow 1952, 1961; MacArthur Fellowship 1994–99; Hon. LittD (Wheaton Coll.) 1967, (Smith Coll.) 1979, (Brandeis Univ.) 1987, (Wooster Coll.) 1989, (Harvard) 1990, (City Coll. of New York) 1990; Yale Series of Younger Poets Award 1951, Ridgely Torrence Memorial Award, Poetry Soc. of America 1955, Shelley Memorial Award 1971, Nat. Book Award 1974, Ruth Lilly Prize 1987, Brandeis Medal in Poetry 1987, Nat. Poetry Assocn Award 1989, LA Times Book Award 1992, Frost Silver Medal (Poetry Soc. of America) 1992, The Poets' Prize 1993, Acad. of American Poets, Fellowship 1993, Dorothea Tanning Award 1996, Lannan Foundation Literary Award for Lifetime Achievement 1999, Bollingen Prize for Poetry 2003. *Publications:* A Change of World 1951, The Diamond Cutters and Other Poems 1955, Snapshots of a Daughter-in-Law 1963, Necessities of Life 1962–65, 1965–68 1969, Leaflets, Poems 1965–68, The Will to Change 1971, Diving into the Wreck 1973, Of Woman Born: Motherhood as Experience and Institution 1976, On Lies, Secrets and Silence: Selected Prose 1966–78 1979, A Wild Patience Has Taken Me This Far: Poems 1978–81 1981, Blood, Bread and Poetry: Selected Prose 1979–85 1986, Your Native Land, Your Life 1986, Time's Power: Poems 1985–88 1989, An Atlas of the Difficult World: Poems 1988–91 1991, Collected Early Poems, 1950–1970 1993, What Is Found There: Notebooks on Poetry and Politics 1993, Dark Fields of the Republic: Poems 1991–95 1995, Midnight Salvage: Poems 1995–1998 1999, Arts of the Possible: Essays and Conversations 2001, Fox: Poems 1998–2000 2001, The Fact of a Doorframe: Poems 1950–2000 2002. *Address:* c/o W. W. Norton Co., 500 Fifth Avenue, New York, NY 10110, USA.

RICH, Alexander, MD; American molecular biologist; b. 15 Nov. 1924, Hartford, Conn.; s. of Max Rich and Bella Shub; m. Jane Erving King 1952; two s. two d.; ed Harvard Coll. and Harvard Medical School; served US Navy 1943–46; Research Fellow, Gates and Crellin Labs., Calif. Inst. of Tech. 1949–54; Chief of Section on Physical Chem., Nat. Inst. of Mental Health, Bethesda, Md 1954–58; visiting Scientist, Cavendish Lab., Cambridge, UK 1955–56; Assoc. Prof. of Biophysics, MIT 1958–61, Prof. 1961–, William Thompson Sedgwick Prof. of Biophysics 1974–; Fairchild Distinguished Scholar, Calif. Inst. of Tech., Pasadena 1976; Visiting Prof., Coll. de France, Paris 1987; Sr Consultant, Office of Science and Tech. Policy, Exec. Office of the Pres. 1977–81; Chair. Perm. Science Cttee, American Acad. of Arts and Sciences 1967–71, Basic Research Cttee of Nat. Science Bd 1978–82, Biotech. Programme of NAS Cttee on Scholarly Communication with the People's Republic of China 1986–93; Co-Chair. Scientific and Academic Advisory Cttee of Weizmann Inst. of Science, Israel 1987–93; mem. or fmr mem. numerous cttees etc., including Marine Biological Lab., Woods Hole, Mass., 1965–77, 1987–96, Advisory Bd NAS Acad. Forum 1975–82, Scientific Advisory Bd Stanford Synchrotron Radiation Project 1976–80, US–USSR Jt Comm. on Science and Tech. 1977–82, Council Pugwash Conferences on Science and World Affairs 1977–82, Bd of Dirs Medical Foundation, Boston, Mass. 1981–90, Governing Bd Nat. Research Council 1985–88, Cttee on USSR and

E Europe of Nat. Research Council 1986–92, Exec. Cttee, Council of NAS 1985–88, External Advisory Cttee of Center for Human Genome Studies, Los Alamos, NM 1989–97, Nat. Critical Technologies Panel of Office of Science and Tech. Policy, Washington, DC 1990–91; on editorial bds of numerous publs, including Journal of Molecular Evolution 1983–94, Proteins, Structure, Function and Genetics 1986–91, Genomics 1987–, Journal of Biotechnology 1987–92, EMBO Journal 1988–90; mem. American Chem. Soc. and other socs., NAS 1970– (mem. Exec. Cttee 1985–88), Pontifical Acad. of Sciences, The Vatican 1978, American Philosophical Soc. 1980; Sr mem. Inst. of Medicine, Washington, DC 1990; Fellow, Nat. Research Council 1949–51, American Acad. of Arts and Sciences 1959, Guggenheim Foundation 1963, AAAS 1965; Foreign mem. French Acad. of Sciences 1984; Assoc. mem. European Molecular Biology Org. 1984; Hon. mem. Japanese Biochemical Soc. 1986; Dr hc (Rio de Janeiro) 1981; Hon. PhD (Weizmann Inst.) 1992; Hons DSc (Eidgenössische Technische Hochschule, Zurich) 1993, (Freie Universität Berlin) 1996; Skylab Achievement Award, NASA 1974; Theodore von Karmen Award 1976, Presidential Award, New York Acad. of Sciences 1977, James R. Killian Faculty Achievement Award, (MIT) 1980, Jabotinsky Medal, New York 1980, Nat. Medal of Science, Washington, DC 1995, Linus Pauling Medal, American Chemical Soc. 1995, Merck Award, American Soc. for Biochem. and Molecular Biology, Washington 1998, Bower Award for Achievement in Science Franklin Inst. Pa 2000. *Publications:* Structural Chemistry and Molecular Biology (co-ed.) 1968; Primary and Tertiary Structure of Nucleic Acids and Cancer Research (co-ed.) 1982; more than 500 publications in the fields of molecular structure of nucleic acid components, nucleic acids and polynucleotides, physical chem. of nucleotides and polynucleotides, molecular structure of proteins, mechanism of protein synthesis, molecular biology of the nucleic acids, X-ray crystallography, origin of life. *Leisure interests:* ocean sailing in small boats, growing tomato plants, collecting fossils. *Address:* Department of Biology, Room 68-233, Massachusetts Institute of Technology, 77 Massachusetts Avenue, Cambridge, MA 02139 (Office); 2 Walnut Avenue, Cambridge, MA 02140, USA (Home). *Telephone:* (617) 253-4715 (Office); (617) 547-1637 (Home). *Fax:* (617) 253-8699 (Office).

RICH, Frank Hart, Jr, BA; American journalist; b. 2 June 1949, Washington, DC; s. of Frank Hart Rich and Helene Aaronson; m. 1st Gail Winston 1976; two s.; m. 2nd Alexandra Rachelle Witchel 1991; ed Harvard Univ.; Film Critic and Sr Ed. New Times Magazine 1973–75; Film Critic, New York Post 1975–77; Film and TV Critic, Time Magazine 1977–80; Chief Drama Critic, New York Times 1980–93, Op-Ed. Columnist 1994–; Assoc. Fellow Jonathan Edwards Coll., Yale Univ. 1998–. *Publications:* Hot Seat: Theater Criticism for the New York Times 1980–93 1998, Ghost Light 2000. *Address:* The New York Times, 229 West 43rd Street, New York, NY 10036, USA. *Telephone:* (212) 556-7414.

RICH, Patrick Jean Jacques; French/Swiss/Canadian business executive; b. 28 March 1931, Strasbourg; s. of late Henri Rich and Marguerite Rich; m. Louise Dionne 1961; two s. one d.; ed Univ. of Strasbourg and Harvard Univ.; worked for Alcan Aluminium Ltd in Guinea, France, UK, Argentina, Spain and Italy 1959–70, Area Gen. Man. for Latin America 1971–75, Exec. Vice-Pres. Europe, Latin America and Africa 1976–77, mem. Bd 1978–86; Exec. Vice-Pres. Alcan Aluminium Ltd and CEO Aluminium Co. of Canada 1978–81; Exec. Vice-Pres. Europe, Africa, Middle East and Chair. Alcan Aluminium SA 1978–86; CEO Société Générale de Surveillance Holding SA, Geneva 1987–89; Deputy Chair. BOC Group PLC 1990–91, Chief Exec. 1991–92, Chair. 1992–94 (non-exec. 1994) and Chief Exec. 1992–94; Chair. Royal Packaging Industries Van Leer, Netherlands 1988–95, IMEC Research Project 1999–; Trustee Bernard van Leer Foundation 1982–99; Gov. Van Leer Group Foundation 1982–99, Van Leer Jerusalem Inst. 1995–; Croix de la Valeur Militaire, Médaille Commémorative Combattants d'Algérie. *Leisure interests:* opera, walking, skiing, piano playing, reading, sailing. *Address:* Mandarin D, 3962 Crans Montana, Switzerland. *Telephone:* (27) 481-45-89. *Fax:* (27) 481-45-89.

RICHARD, Alain; French government official; b. 29 Aug. 1945, Paris; m. Elisabeth Couffignal 1988; one s. one d. and one s. by previous m.; ed Lycée Henri IV, Paris, Institut d'Etudes Politiques, Ecole Nat. d'Admin; Auditor, Conseil d'Etat 1971, Maître des requêtes 1978, Conseiller d'Etat 1993–95; Mayor, St Ouen l'Aumône 1977–97, 2001–; Deputy, Val d'Oise 1978–93, Senator 1995–97; Vice-Pres. Commission des lois 1981–86, Nat. Ass. 1987–88; Minister of Defence 1997–2001; Founder and Vice-Pres. Forum for Man. of Towns 1985–97; mem. Nat. Office, Parti Socialiste Unifié 1972–74; mem. Cttee Parti Socialiste 1979, Exec. Bd 1988; mem. Bd Inst. for Int. Relations 1991–97. *Address:* Mairie, 95310 St Ouen l'Aumône; 28 rue René Clair, 95310 St Ouen l'Aumône, France.

RICHARD, Alison Fettes, MA, PhD; British university vice-chancellor and professor of anthropology and environmental studies; b. Kent; ed Univs of Cambridge and London; joined faculty of Yale Univ., USA 1972, Dir of Grad. Studies 1980–86, Prof. of Anthropology 1986 (Dept Chair. 1986–90), Prof. of Environmental Studies, Yale School of Forestry and Environmental Studies 1990, Dir Yale Peabody Museum of Natural History 1991–94, Provost Yale Univ. 1994–2002; Vice-Chancellor Univ. of Cambridge, UK 2003–; mem. Bd Dirs Worldwide Fund for Nature 1995–, Liz Claiborne/Art Ortenberg Foundation. *Publications include:* Primates in Nature 1985, Behavioral Variation: Case Study of a Malagasy Lemur 1978; numerous articles in scientific journals. *Address:* Office of the Vice-Chancellor, University of Cambridge,

Cambridge, CB2 1TN, England (Office). *Telephone:* (1223) 332200 (Office). *E-mail:* webmaster@admin.cam.ac.uk (Office). *Website:* www.cam.ac.uk (Office).

RICHARD, Sir Cliff, Kt, OBE; British singer and actor; b. (as Harry Rodger Webb), 14 Oct. 1940, India; s. of Rodger and Dorothy Webb; ed Riversmead School, Cheshunt; first successful record Move It 1958; plays guitar; own television series on BBC and ITV; various repertory and variety seasons; Top Box Office Star of Great Britain 1962–63, 1963–64; awarded Gold Discs (for sales over a million each) for Living Doll, The Young Ones, Bachelor Boy, Lucky Lips, Congratulations, Power to All Our Friends, Devil Woman, We Don't Talk Anymore, Daddy's Home, Mistletoe and Wine; also 32 Silver Discs (for sales over 250,000) and a Platinum Disc (for sales over 600,000) for Millennium Prayer 1999; Ivor Novello Award for Outstanding Achievement 1989 and numerous other awards. *Films:* Serious Charge 1959, Expresso Bongo 1960, The Young Ones 1961, Summer Holiday 1962, Wonderful Life 1964, Finders Keepers 1966, Two a Penny 1968, His Land, Take Me High 1973. *Stage appearances:* musicals Time, Dominion Theatre, London 1986–87, Heathcliff, Hammersmith Apollo, London 1996–97. *Publications:* Questions 1970, The Way I See It 1972, The Way I See It Now 1975, Which One's Cliff? 1977, Happy Christmas from Cliff 1980, You, Me and Jesus 1983, Mine to Share 1984, Jesus, Me and You 1985, Single-Minded 1988, Mine Forever 1989, My Story: A Celebration of 40 Years in Showbusiness 1998. *Leisure interests:* tennis, vineyards in Portugal. *Address:* c/o P.O. Box 46C, Esher, Surrey, KT10 0RB, England. *Telephone:* (1372) 467752. *Fax:* (1372) 462352. *Website:* www.cliffrichard.org (Office).

RICHARD, Baron (Life Peer), cr. 1990, of Ammanford in the County of Dyfed; **Ivor Seward Richard,** PC, MA; British politician, lawyer and diplomatist; b. 30 May 1932, Cardiff; s. of Seward Thomas and Isabella Irene Richard; m. 1st Geraldine Moore 1956 (dissolved 1961); one s.; m. 2nd Alison Mary Imrie 1962 (dissolved 1984); one s. one d.; m. 3rd Janet Armstrong Jones 1989; one s.; ed Cheltenham Coll., Pembroke Coll., Oxford; called to the Bar 1955; MP for Barons Court 1964–74; Parl. Pvt. Sec. to Sec. of State for Defence 1966–69; Under-Sec. of State for Defence for Army 1969–70; Queen's Counsel 1971; Perm. Rep. to UN 1974–79; Commr of European Communities for Social Affairs, Employment, Education and Vocational Training Policy 1981–84; Leader of Opposition in the House of Lords 1992–97; Lord Privy Seal and Leader of the House of Lords, 1997–98; Chair. World Trade Centre Wales Ltd (Cardiff) 1985–97; Chair. Rhodesia Conf., Geneva 1976; Counsel to Chadbourne, Parke, Whiteside and Wolff, New York 1979–81; Labour; Hon. Fellow, Pembroke Coll. 1981–. *Publications:* Europe or the Open Sea 1971, We, the British 1983, Unfinished Business: Reforming the House of Lords 1998; and articles in various political journals. *Leisure interests:* playing piano, watching football, talking. *Address:* House of Lords, Westminster, London, SW1A 0PW, England.

RICHARD, Jean Barthélemy, DèsSc; French historian; b. 7 Feb. 1921, Kremlin-Bicêtre; s. of Pierre Richard and Amélie Grandchamp; m. Monique Rivoire 1944; three s. two d.; ed Ecole des Chartes, Ecole Française de Rome and Sorbonne, Paris; Asst archivist, Dijon 1943–55; Prof. Univ. of Dijon 1955–88, Dean, Faculté des Lettres 1968–71; mem. Acad. des Inscriptions, Inst. de France and other learned socs; Officier, Légion d'honneur, Commdr Ordre du Mérite, Commdr Palmes académiques; Gold Medal for Altaic Studies, Indiana Univ. *Publications:* The Latin Kingdom of Jerusalem 1953, Les ducs de Bourgogne 1954, L'Esprit de la Croisade 1969, La papauté et les missions d'Orient 1977, Histoire de la Bourgogne 1978, St Louis 1983, Le livre des remembrances de la secrète du royaume de Chypre 1983, Histoire des Croisades 1996; four vols in Variorum Reprints on Crusades and Oriental History 1976–92. *Leisure interests:* garden and forest activities. *Address:* 12 rue Pelletier de Chambure, 21000 Dijon; Les Billaudots, 71540 Igornay, France. *Telephone:* (3) 80-66-10-28; (3) 85-82-82-98.

RICHARD, Pierre, BEng; French business executive; b. 9 March 1941, Dijon; s. of Henri Richard and Marguerite Richard (née Genty); m. Aleth Sachot 1966; three c.; ed Univ. of Dijon and Univ. of Pennsylvania, USA; teacher, Inst. of Urbanism, Paris 1967–68; Asst Dir-Gen. Public Devt Corpn, new town of Cergy-Pontoise 1967–72; Tech. Adviser to Sec. of State for Housing 1972–74, to Gen. Secr. for the Pres. of the Rep. 1974–78; Dir Gen. for Local Communities, Ministry of the Interior 1978–82; Asst Dir-Gen. of Treasury, Dept of Local Devt 1983–93; Man. Dir Crédit Local de France (CLF) 1993–, Co-Chair. Dexia Group (after merger between CLF and Crédit Communal de Belgique) 1996–, Deputy Dir 1999–, Pres. Supervisory Bd Dexia Crédit Local de France 2000–; Pres. Group of Specialized Financial Insts 1991–93; Pres. Inst. of Decentralization 1993–95; Pres. Admin. Bd, Ecole Nat. des Ponts et Chaussées 1994–; Dir Municipal Bond Investors Assurance (MBIA) 1990–, Air France 1995–, Banque européenne d'investissement (Bei) 1994–, Le Monde 1995–; Chevalier Légion d'honneur, Officier Ordre nat. du Mérite. *Publications:* Les Communes françaises d'aujourd'hui, Le Temps des citoyens pour une démocratie décentralisée 1995. *Leisure interest:* horseriding. *Address:* Dexia, 7–11 quai André Citroën, 75901 Paris Cedex 15, France (Office). *E-mail:* pierre.richard@dexia.com (Office). *Website:* www.dexia.com (Office).

RICHARDS, Ann Willis, BA; American fmr state governor; b. 1 Sept. 1933, Waco, Tex.; d. of Cecil Willis and Ona Willis; m. David Richards (divorced); two s. two d.; ed Baylor Univ. and Univ. of Tex.; fmr schoolteacher; County Commr Travis County, Austin 1977–82; mem. Pres.'s Advisory Comm. on Women 1979; State Treas. State of Texas, Austin 1983–91; mem. State Banking Bd of Tex. 1982; Chair. Texas Depository Bd 1983; Sr Adviser Verner, Liipfert, Bernhard, McPherson & Hand, Austin 1995–2001; Sr Adviser Public Strategies Inc. 2001–; mem. various bds and cttees etc.; Gov. of Texas 1991–95; Democrat. *Address:* Public Strategies Inc., 98 San Jacinto Boulevard, Suite 900, Austin, TX 78701, USA (Office).

RICHARDS, Sir Francis Neville, Kt, KCMG, CVO, MA; British diplomatist; b. 18 Nov. 1945; s. of Sir Francis Brooks Richards; m. Gillian Bruce Nevill 1971; one s. one d.; ed Eton Coll. and King's Coll., Cambridge; with Royal Green Jackets 1967, served with UN Force in Cyprus (invalided 1969); joined FCO 1969, seconded to Moscow 1971; UK Del. to MBFR negotiations, Vienna 1973; FCO 1976–85 (Asst. Pvt. Sec. to Sec. of State 1981–82); Econ. and Commercial Counsellor, New Delhi 1985–88; FCO 1988–90 (Head S. Asian Dept); High Commr, Windhoek, Namibia 1990–92; Minister, Moscow 1992–95; Dir (Europe) FCO 1995–97; Deputy Under-Sec. of State, FCO 1997–98; Dir Govt Communications HQ (GCHQ) 1998–2003; Gov. and C.-in-C. of Gibraltar May 2003–. *Leisure interests:* walking, travelling, riding. *Address:* Office of the Governor, The Convent, Main Street, Gibraltar (Office). *Website:* www.gibraltar.gov.uk (Office).

RICHARDS, Frederic Middlebrook, PhD; American biochemist; b. 19 Aug. 1925, New York; s. of George and Marianna Richards; m. 1st Heidi Clark 1948 (divorced 1955); two d.; m. 2nd Sarah Wheatland 1959; one s.; ed Mass Inst. of Tech. and Harvard Univ.; Research Fellow, Physical Chem., Harvard Univ. 1952–53; Nat. Research Council Fellow, Carlsberg Lab., Denmark 1954; Nat. Science Foundation Fellow, Cambridge Univ., UK 1955; Asst Prof. of Biochemistry, Yale Univ. 1955–59, Assoc. Prof. 1959–62, Prof. 1963–89, Chair. Dept of Molecular Biology and Biophysics 1963–67, Dept of Molecular Biophysics and Biochemistry 1969–73, Henry Ford II Prof. of Molecular Biophysics 1967–89, Sterling Prof. of Molecular Biophysics 1989–91, Sterling Prof. Emer. 1991–; Sr Research Scientist Yale Univ.; mem. Council Int. Union of Pure and Applied Biophysics 1975–81; Dir Jane Coffin Childs Memorial Fund for Medical Research 1976–91, Bd Dirs 1997–; Corpn mem. Woods Hole Oceanographic Inst. 1977–83, 1985–91; mem. Scientific Bd Whitney Lab. for Experimental Marine Biology and Medicine 1979–84, Nat. Advisory Research Resources Council NIH 1983–87, Board of Trustees, Cold Spring Harbor Lab. 1986–91, Medical Advisory Bd, Howard Hughes Medical Inst. 1989–92, Donaghue Foundation for Medical Research 1991–92, NAS, American Acad. of Arts and Sciences, American Chem. Soc., American Soc. of Biological Chemistry (Pres. 1978–80), Biophysical Soc. (Pres. 1972–73), American Crystallographic Asscn, Conn. Acad. of Science and Eng Guggenheim Fellow 1967–68; Hon. DSc (New Haven) 1982; Pfizer-Paul Lewis Award 1965; Kaj Linderstrøm-Lang Prize 1978, Merck Award of American Soc. for Biochemistry and Molecular Biology 1988, Stein and Moore Award of Protein Soc. 1988, Biophysical Soc. Distinguished Service Award 2001. *Publications:* various original research articles in scientific journals in the general field of protein and enzyme chemistry. *Leisure interest:* sailing. *Address:* Department of Molecular Biophysics and Biochemistry, Yale University, P.O. Box 208114, 260 Whitney Avenue, New Haven, CT 06520 (Office); 69 Andrews Road, Guilford, CT 06437, USA. *Telephone:* (203) 432-5620 (Office); (203) 453-3361 (Home). *Fax:* (203) 453-4794 (Home).

RICHARDS, Sir Isaac Vivian Alexander ('Viv'), KGN, OBE; Antiguan cricketer; b. 7 March 1952, St John's, Antigua; s. of Malcolm Richards; m. Miriam Lewis; one s. one d.; ed Antigua Grammar School; right-hand batsman, off-break bowler, cover-point fielder; played for Leeward Islands 1971–91 (Capt. 1981–91), Somerset 1974–86, Queensland 1976–77, Glamorgan 1990–93; 121 Tests for W Indies 1974–91, 50 as Capt., scoring 8,540 runs (average 50.2) including 24 hundreds and holding 122 catches; scored record 1,710 runs in a calendar year (11 Tests in 1976); scored 36,212 first-class runs (114 hundreds, only W Indian to score 100 hundreds); toured England 1976, 1979 (World Cup), 1980, 1983 (World Cup), 1984, 1988 (as Capt.), 1991 (as Capt.); 187 limited-overs ints scoring 6,721 runs (11 hundreds including then record 189 not out v. England at Old Trafford 1984); Chair. Selectors, W Indies Cricket Bd 2002–; Dr hc (Exeter) 1986; Wisden Cricketer of the Year 1977; one of Wisden's Five Cricketers of the Century 2000; Cricket Hall of Fame 2001. *Publications:* (with David Foot) Viv Richards (autobiog.) 1982, Cricket Masterclass 1988, Hitting Across The Line (autobiog.) 1991, (with Bob Harris) Sir Vivian (autobiog.) 2000. *Leisure interests:* music, football, golf, tennis. *Address:* West Indies Cricket Board, PO Box 616, St John's, Antigua.

RICHARDS, Sir John (Charles Chisholm), KCB, KCVO; British military officer (retd); b. 21 Feb. 1927, Wallasey; s. of Charles Richards and Alice Milner; m. Audrey Hidson 1953; two s. one d.; ed Worksop Coll. Notts.; joined Royal Marines 1945; served in commando units and HM ships worldwide; Canadian Army Staff Coll. 1959–61; Naval Staff in Ministry of Defence 1963–64; Instructor Army Staff Coll. Camberley 1965–67; CO 42nd and 45th RM Commandos; Chief of Staff, British Defence Staff, Washington, DC and del. to UN 1972–74; Brig. Commdg 3rd Commando Brigade 1975–77; Maj.-Gen. 1977; Commdt-Gen. Royal Marines (with rank of Lt-Gen.) 1977–81; Rep. Col Commdt Royal Marines 1989–90; HM Marshal of the Diplomatic Corps 1982–92; Dir (non-exec.) DSC Communications (Europe) Ltd 1986–93, Andrew Ltd 1987–94; Extra Equerry to HM The Queen 1992; Freeman, City of London 1982; numerous foreign awards including decorations from FRG, France, Netherlands, Spain, Mexico, Italy, Norway, Senegal, UAE, Malawi,

Bahrain, Qatar and Oman. *Leisure interests:* golf, gardening, swimming, military history. *Address:* c/o NatWest Bank, 5 Market Place, Kingston-upon-Thames, KT1 1JX, England.

RICHARDS, Keith (Keith Richard); British musician and songwriter; b. 18 Dec. 1943, Dartford; s. of Bert Richards and Doris Richards; m. 1st Anita Pallenberg; two s. (one deceased) one d.; m. 2nd Patti Hansen 1983; two d.; ed Sidcup Art School; lead guitarist, vocalist with the Rolling Stones 1962–; composer (with Mick Jagger, q.v.) of numerous songs and albums 1964–, including: The Rolling Stones Now! 1964, Aftermath 1966, Flowers 1967, Beggars' Banquet 1968, Let it Bleed 1969, Sticky Fingers 1971, Hot Rocks 1972, Exile on Main Street 1972, Goat's Head Soup 1973, It's Only Rock and Roll 1974, Metamorphosis 1975, Black and Blue 1976, Some Girls, Emotional Rescue 1980, Tattoo You 1981, Still Life 1982, Under Cover 1983, Dirty Work 1986, Hail Hail Rock 'n' Roll 1987 (with Chuck Berry), Talk is Cheap (solo) 1988, Steel Wheels 1989, Flashpoint 1991, Voodoo Lounge 1994, Stripped 1995, Bridges to Babylon 1997, No Security 1999; Living Legend Award for Int. Rock, mem. Rock and Roll Hall of Fame 1989. *Films:* Sympathy for the Devil 1970, Gimme Shelter 1970, Ladies and Gentlemen, the Rolling Stones 1974, Let's Spend the Night Together 1983, Hail Hail Rock 'n' Roll 1987 (with Chuck Berry, Eric Clapton and Friends), Flashpoint 1991, Voodoo Lounge 1994. *Address:* c/o Jane Rose, Raindrop Services, 1776 Broadway, Suite 507, New York, NY 10019, USA.

RICHARDS, Peter, MA, MD, PhD, FRCP, FMedSci; British professor of medicine (retd.); b. 25 May 1936, London; s. of Dr William Richards and Barbara Taylor; m. 1st Anne Marie Larsen 1959 (divorced); one s. three d.; m. 2nd Carol Anne Seymour 1987; ed Monkton Combe School, Emmanuel Coll., Cambridge, St George's Hosp. Medical School and Royal Postgrad. Medical School; MRC Clinical Research Fellow and tutor in Medicine, Royal Postgrad. Medical School 1964–67; lecturer, St Mary's Hosp. Medical School 1967–70; Consultant Physician, NW Surrey Hosps 1970–73; Sr lecturer and Consultant Physician, St George's Hosp. and Medical School 1973–79; Dean, St Mary's Hosp. Medical School 1979–95; Prof. and Hon. Consultant Physician, St Mary's Hosp. 1979–95; Pro-Rector (Medicine), Imperial Coll. of Science, Tech. and Medicine, London 1988–95; Medical Dir and Consultant Physician, Northwick Park and St Mark's NHS Trust 1995–99; Pres. Hughes Hall, Cambridge 1998–; Medical Adviser to Parl. Health Service Commr 1999–2001; mem. Gen. Medical Council (GMC) 1994, Deputy Chair. GMC Professional Conduct Cttee 1999–2001; Chair. Fulbright Award, Univ. of Calif. San Francisco 1990; Hon. Fellow Emmanuel Coll., Cambridge 2002; Kt, Order of the White Rose of Finland 2001. *Publications:* The Medieval Leper 1977, Understanding Water, Electrolytes and Acid/Base Metabolism 1983, Learning Medicine 1983, Living Medicine 1990, Student's Guide to Entry to Medicine 1996, New Learning Medicine 1997; scientific papers on renal disease, metabolism, student selection and educ. *Leisure interests:* social history, music, cycling, mountain walking, Finland. *Address:* Hughes Hall, Cambridge, CB1 2EW, England. *Telephone:* (1223) 334890. *Fax:* (1223) 311179. *E-mail:* pr229@cam.ac.uk (Office).

RICHARDS, Sir Rex Edward, Kt, DSc, FRSC, FRS; British professor of chemistry and university administrator (retd); b. 28 Oct. 1922, Colyton, Devon; s. of H. W. and E. N. Richards; m. Eva Edith Vago 1948; two d.; ed Colyton Grammar School, Devon, St John's Coll., Oxford; Fellow of Lincoln Coll., Oxford 1947–64; Dr Lee's Prof. of Chem., Oxford 1964–70; Fellow of Exeter Coll., Oxford 1964–69; Warden Merton Coll., Oxford 1969–84; Vice-Chancellor Univ. of Oxford 1977–81; Chancellor Exeter Univ. 1982–98; Tilden Lecturer 1962; Research Fellow, Harvard Univ. 1955; Assoc. Fellow, Morse Coll., Yale 1974–79; Chair. Oxford Enzyme Group 1969–83; Dir Oxford Instruments Group 1982–91; Dir Leverhulme Trust 1985–93; Pres. Royal Soc. of Chem. 1990–92; mem. Chem. Soc. Council 1957, 1988, Faraday Soc. Council 1963, Royal Soc. Council 1973–75, Advisory Bd for Research Councils 1980–82, Advisory Council for Applied Research and Devt 1984–87; Dir IBM United Kingdom Holdings, IBM (UK) 1978–82; Chair. British Postgraduate Medical Fed. 1986–93, Nat. Gallery Trust 1995–99; Trustee of CIBA Foundation 1978–97, Nat. Heritage Memorial Fund 1979–84, Tate Gallery 1982–88, 1991–93, Nat. Gallery 1982–93, Henry Moore Foundation 1989– (Vice-Chair. 1993–94, Chair. 1994–2001); Commr Royal Comm. for Exhbn of 1851 1984–97; Foreign Assoc. Acad. des Sciences, Inst. de France 1995–; Hon. Fellow of St John's Coll. and Lincoln Coll., Oxford 1968, Merton Coll., Oxford 1984, Thames Polytechnic 1991; Hon. FRCP 1987; Hon. FBA 1990; Hon. FRAM 1991; Hon. DSc (East Anglia) 1971, (Exeter) 1975, (Leicester) 1978, (Salford) 1979, (Edin.) 1981, (Leeds) 1984, (Birmingham) 1993, (London) 1994, (Oxford Brookes) 1998, (Warwick) 1999; Hon. DLitt (Dundee) 1977, (Kent) 1987; Hon. ScD (Cambridge) 1987; Corday-Morgan Medal of Chemical Soc. 1954, Davy Medal, Royal Soc. 1976, Award in Theoretical Chem. and Spectroscopy, Chemical Soc. 1977, Epic Award 1982, Medal of Honour, Bonn Univ. 1983, Royal Medal, Royal Soc. 1986, Pres.'s Medal, Soc. of Chemical Industry 1991. *Publications:* numerous contribs to scientific journals. *Leisure interests:* painting and sculpture. *Address:* 13 Woodstock Close, Oxford, OX2 8DB, England (Home). *Telephone:* (1865) 513621. *E-mail:* rex.richards@merton.oxford.ac.uk (Home).

RICHARDS, Simon Paul, BA, LLB, M.ECON.; Dominican diplomatist and lawyer; b. 19 April 1937, Wesley; ed London Univ., Univ. of the West Indies and City Univ. of New York; Asst Master Dominica Grammar School 1958–60, Sr Master 1963–66; caseworker City of New York Dept of Social Services 1967–74; admitted to Bar of England and Wales 1975, of the State of NY 1977,

of US Dist Courts for Southern and Eastern Dists of NY 1978, of Dominica 1980; practised law in New York 1977–, currently a sr trial attorney in pvt. practice; Counsellor, Deputy Perm. Rep. and Chargé d'Affaires Perm. Mission of Dominica to the UN at various times 1982–95, Perm. Rep. 1995–. *Address:* Permanent Mission of Dominica to the United Nations, 800 Second Avenue, Suite 400H, New York, NY 10017, USA (Office). *Telephone:* (212) 949-0853 (Office). *Fax:* (212) 808-4975 (Office). *E-mail:* dominica@un.int (Office).

RICHARDSON, George Barclay, CBE, MA; British university administrator (retd); b. 19 Sept. 1924, London; s. of George Richardson and Christina Richardson; m. Isabel A. Chalk 1957 (dissolved 1999); two s.; ed Aberdeen Cen. Secondary School and other schools in Scotland, Aberdeen Univ. and Corpus Christi Coll. Oxford; Admiralty Scientific Research Dept 1944; Lt RNVR 1945; Intelligence Officer, HQ Intelligence Div. British Army of the Rhine 1946–47; Third Sec. HM Foreign Service 1949; student, Nuffield Coll. Oxford 1950; Fellow, St John's Coll. Oxford 1951–88; Univ. Reader in Econs, Univ. of Oxford 1969–73; Warden, Keble Coll. Oxford 1989–94; Pro-Vice-Chancellor, Univ. of Oxford 1988–94; Del. Oxford Univ. Pres. 1971–74, Sec. to Dels and Chief Exec. 1974–88; mem. Econ. Devt Cttee for Electrical Eng Industry 1964–73, Monopolies Comm. 1969–74, Royal Comm. on Environmental Pollution 1973–74; Econ. Adviser, UKAEA 1968–74; mem. Council, Publishers' Assocn 1981–87; Hon. DCL (Oxford); Hon. LLD (Aberdeen). *Publications:* Information and Investment 1960, 1991, Economic Theory 1964, The Economics of Imperfect Knowledge 1998; articles in academic journals. *Leisure interests:* reading, music, swimming. *Address:* 33 Belsyre Court, Observatory Street, Oxford, OX2 6HU, England. *Telephone:* (1865) 510113. *Fax:* (1865) 510113. *E-mail:* george.richardson@keble.oxford.ac.uk.

RICHARDSON, George Taylor, OC, BComm, LLD; Canadian business executive (retd); b. 22 Sept. 1924, Winnipeg, Manitoba; s. of the late James A. Richardson and Muriel Richardson (née Sprague); m. Tannis Maree Thorlakson 1948; two s. one d.; ed Grosvenor and Ravenscourt Schools, Winnipeg and Univ. of Manitoba; joined family firm of James Richardson & Sons, Ltd, Winnipeg 1946, Vice-Pres. 1954, Pres. 1966–93, Chair. 1993–2000, Hon. Chair. 2000–; Order of Manitoba 2000; Hon. LLD (Manitoba, Winnipeg). *Leisure interests:* hunting, helicopter flying. *Address:* James Richardson & Sons Ltd, Richardson Building, 1 Lombard Place, Winnipeg, Manitoba, R3B 0Y1 (Office); Briarmeade, PO Box 158, St Germain, Manitoba, R0G 2A0, Canada (Home). *Telephone:* (204) 934-5811 (Office); (204) 253-4221 (Home). *Fax:* (204) 944-8806 (Office); (204) 255-4208 (Home). *E-mail:* grichard@jrsl.ca (Office).

RICHARDSON, Graham; Australian politician, broadcaster and journalist; b. 27 Sept. 1949, Kogarah, Sydney; s. of Frederick James Richardson and Catherine Maud Richardson; m. Cheryl Gardener 1973; one s. one d.; ed Marist Brothers Coll., Kogarah; state organizer Australian Labor Party, NSW 1971–76, Gen. Sec. 1976–94, State Campaign Dir 1976; Vice-Pres. Nat. Labor Party 1976, Del. to Nat. Conf. 1977–94, convenor Nat. Industrial Platform Cttee; Senator for NSW 1983–94; Minister for the Environment and the Arts 1987–90, for Sports, Tourism and Territories 1988–90, for Social Security 1990, of Transport and Communications 1991–92, of Health 1993–94; political commentator on election coverage and journalist, The Nine Network 1994–; journalist, The Bulletin 1994–; fmr Chair. Senate Estimates Cttee 1986, Senate Select Cttee on TV Equalization; mem. several senate cttees and three ministerial cttees; mem. Bd Sydney Organizing Cttee for the Olympic Games 1996–. *Leisure interests:* golf, reading, skiing, tennis. *Address:* Macquarie Radio Network, Level 8, 368 Sussex Street, Sydney, NSW 2000 (Office); 24 Artarmon Road, Willoughby, NSW 2028, Australia.

RICHARDSON, Ian William, CBE, FRSAMD, D.DR.; British actor; b. 7 April 1934, Edinburgh; s. of John Richardson and Margaret (Drummond) Richardson; m. Maroussia Frank 1961; two s.; ed Tynecastle, Edin., Royal Scottish Acad. of Music and Drama, Glasgow Univ.; joined Birmingham Repertory Theatre Co. 1958, playing leading parts including Hamlet; joined RSC, Stratford and Aldwych 1960–75, tours with RSC to Europe, USA, USSR, Japan; James Bridie Gold Medal (R.S.A.M.D.); Drama Desk Award, New York, Royal Television Soc. Award 1981/82, 1991, Broadcasting Press Guild Award 1990; BAFTA Award 1991. *Stage appearances include:* Aragon (Merchant of Venice), Sir Andrew Aguecheek (Twelfth Night) 1960, Malatesti (Duchess of Malfi) 1960, Oberon (A Midsummer Night's Dream) 1961, Tranio (Taming of the Shrew) 1961, The Doctor (The Representative) 1963, Edmund (King Lear) 1964, Antipholus of Ephesus (Comedy of Errors) 1964, Herald and Marat (Marat/Sade) 1964, 1965, Ithamore (The Jew of Malta) 1964, Ford (Merry Wives of Windsor) 1964, 1966, 1969, Antipholus of Syracuse (Comedy of Errors) 1965, Chorus (Henry V) 1965, Vindice (The Revenger's Tragedy) 1965, 1969, Coriolanus 1966, Bertram (All's Well That Ends Well) 1966, Malcolm (Macbeth) 1966, Cassius (Julius Caesar) 1968, Pericles 1969, Angelo (Measure for Measure) 1970, Buckingham (Richard III) 1970, Proteus (Two Gentlemen of Verona) 1970, Prospero (The Tempest) 1970, Tom Wrench (Trelawny), Sadler's Wells 1971–72, Richard II/Bolingbroke (Richard II) 1973, Berowne (Love's Labour's Lost) 1973, Iachimo (Cymbeline) 1974, Shalimov (Summer Folk) 1974, Henry Higgins (My Fair Lady), Broadway 1974, Ford (Merry Wives of Windsor) 1975, Richard III 1975, Jack Tanner (Man and Superman), Shaw Festival Theatre, Niagara-on-the-Lake, Canada, The Government Inspector, Romeo and Juliet, Old Vic 1979, Lolita (New York) 1981, The Miser (Chichester) 1995, The Magistrate (Chichester and London) 1997, The Seven Ages of Man (Guildford) 1999. *Film appearances* *include:* The Darwin Adventure 1971, Man of la Mancha 1972, Marat/Sade, The Hound of the Baskervilles 1982, The Sign of Four 1982, Whoops Apocalypse 1986, The Fourth Protocol 1986, Asking for Trouble 1986, Burning Secret 1988, Rosencrantz and Guildenstern are Dead 1990, The Year of the Comet 1991, Words Upon the Window Pane 1993, Baps 1996, Dark City 1996, From Hell 2002. *TV appearances include:* Anthony Beavis (Eyeless in Gaza) 1971, Voyage Round My Father, Canterbury Tales, Danton's Death (BBC) 1977, Sorry (BBC) 1978, Ike: The War Years (ABC TV, USA) 1978, Tinker, Tailor, Soldier, Spy (BBC) 1979, Churchill and His Generals (BBC) 1979, Private Schulz (BBC) 1980, A Cotswold Death (BBC) 1981, The Woman in White (BBC serial) 1982, Underdog 1982, Salad Days 1982, Brass 1983, Mistral's Daughter, The Master of Ballantrae 1984, Six Centuries of Verse 1984, Nehru (Mountbatten: the Last Viceroy) 1985, Monsieur Quixote 1985, Star Quality 1985, Blunt 1986, Porterhouse Blue 1986, Devil's Disciple 1986, Troubles 1988, Pursuit (mini-series) 1988, Burning Secret 1988, The Winslow Boy 1989, Under a Dark Angel's Eye (HTV), Phantom of the Opera (mini-series), The Plot to Kill Hitler (mini-series), The Gravy Train (mini-series), King of the Wind 1989, House of Cards (BBC), The Gravy Train Goes East (mini-series) 1991, An Ungentlemanly Act 1992, To Play the King (BBC mini-series) 1993, Remember (US mini-series) 1993, Catherine the Great (mini-series) 1994, Savage Play (mini-series) 1994, The Final Cut (mini-series) 1995, The Canterville Ghost (Carlton TV) 1997, The Magician's House (BBC) 1999, Murder Rooms (BBC) 2000, Gormenghast (BBC) 2000, Murder Rooms II (BBC) 2001. *Publications:* Preface to Cymbeline 1976, Preface to The Merry Wives of Windsor 1988. *Leisure interests:* archaeology, music, books, cinematography, travel. *Address:* c/o London Management, 2–4 Noel Street, London, W1V 3RB, England. *Telephone:* (20) 7237-9000.

RICHARDSON, Joanna, MA, FRSL; British author; b. London; d. of the late Frederick Richardson and Charlotte Richardson (née Benjamin); ed The Downs School, Seaford, Sussex, St Anne's Coll., Oxford; mem. Council, RSL 1961–86; Chevalier, Ordre des Arts et des Lettres. *Radio:* numerous interviews, trans. of plays and novels, and feature programmes for Third Programme (now BBC Radio 3) and Home Service (now BBC Radio 4). *Publications:* Fanny Brawne: a biography 1952, Théophile Gautier: his Life and Times 1958, Edward FitzGerald 1960, The Pre-Eminent Victorian: A Study of Tennyson 1962, The Everlasting Spell: A Study of Keats and his Friends 1963, Introduction to Victor Hugo: Choses Vues 1964, George IV: A Portrait 1966, Princess Mathilde 1969, Verlaine 1971, Enid Starkie 1973, Stendhal: A Critical Biography 1974, Victor Hugo 1976, Zola 1978, Keats and his Circle: an album of portraits 1980, The Life and Letters of John Keats 1981, Letters from Lambeth: the Correspondence of the Reynolds Family with John Freeman Milward Dovaston 1808–1815, 1981, Colette 1983, Judith Gautier (Prix Goncourt de la Biographie 1989; first time award was made to a non-French author) 1987, Portrait of a Bonaparte: The Life and Times of Joseph-Napoleon Primoli 1851–1927 1987, Baudelaire 1994; FitzGerald: Selected Works 1962 (ed.), Essays by Divers Hands (ed.) 1964, Verlaine Poems (and trans.) 1974, Baudelaire Poems (ed. and trans.) 1975, Gautier, Mademoiselle de Maupin (ed. and trans.) 1981; has contributed to The Times, The Times Literary Supplement, Sunday Times, Spectator, New Statesman, New York Times Book Review, The Washington Post, French Studies, French Studies Bulletin, Modern Language Review, Keats-Shelley Memorial Bulletin, etc. *Leisure interest:* antique collecting. *Address:* c/o Curtis Brown Group, Haymarket House, 28–29 Haymarket, London, SW1Y 4SP, England. *Telephone:* (20) 7396-6600.

RICHARDSON, Joely; British actress; b. 1958, Lancs.; d. of the late Tony Richardson and of Vanessa Redgrave (q.v.); m. Tim Bevan 1992 (divorced); one d.; ed Lycée Français de Londres, St Paul's Girls' School, London, Pinellas Park High School, Fla, The Thacher School, Ojai, Calif. and Royal Acad. of Dramatic Art. *Plays include:* Steel Magnolias 1989, Lady Windermere's Fan 2002. *Films:* Wetherby 1985, Drowning by Numbers 1988, Shining Through 1991, Rebecca's Daughters 1992, Lochness 1994, Sister, My Sister 1995, 101 Dalmatians 1995, Believe Me 1995, Hollow Reed 1996, Event Horizon 1996, Wrestling with Alligators, Under Heaven, The Patriot 2000, Maybe Baby 2000, Return to Me 2000, The Affair of the Necklace 2001. *Television appearances include:* Body Contact, Behaving Badly 1989, Heading Home, Lady Chatterley's Lover 1993, The Tribe, Echo. *Address:* c/o ICM, Oxford House, 76 Oxford Street, London, W1N 0AX, England.

RICHARDSON, Baron (Life Peer), cr. 1979, of Lee in the County of Devon; **John Samuel Richardson,** Bt, Kt, LVO, MA, MD, FRCP; British consultant physician; b. 16 June 1910, Sheffield; s. of Major John Watson Richardson and Elizabeth Blakeney Roberts; m. Sybil Trist 1933; two d.; ed Charterhouse, Trinity Coll., Cambridge and St Thomas's Hospital Medical School; various appointments at St Thomas's Hosp. and Royal Postgraduate Medical School; with RAMC during Second World War; Consulting Physician at St Thomas's Hosp.; Consultant Physician to Metropolitan Police 1957–80, London Transport Bd 1964–80; Consultant Emer. to Army; Pres. Gen. Medical Council 1973–80; Chair. Council for Postgraduate Medical Educ. in England and Wales 1972–80, Armed Forces Medical Advisory Bd 1975; mem. Council Royal Coll. of Physicians; fmr Pres. Royal Soc. of Medicine, Int. Soc. for Internal Medicine, British Medical Asscn; Past-Master, Worshipful Soc. of Apothecaries of London; Perkins Fellowship 1939–40; Hon. Bencher, Gray's Inn 1974; C.StJ; Hon. Fellow, Trinity Coll., Cambridge, Hon. FRCP (Edin., Ireland), Hon. Fellow, Royal Coll. of Physicians and Surgeons (Glasgow), Royal Coll. of Psychiatrists, Royal Coll. of Surgeons of England, Royal Coll.

of Gen. Practitioners, Faculty of Community Medicine; Hon. DSc (Nat. Univ. of Ireland, Univ. of Hull); Hon. DCL (Newcastle); Hon. LLD (Nottingham, Liverpool); Hadden Prize and Bristowe Medal, St Thomas's Hosp. 1936, 1st De Lancy Law Prize (Royal Soc. of Medicine) 1978, Gold Medal BMA 1980, Guthrie Medal, RAMC 1980. *Publications:* The Practice of Medicine 1960, Connective Tissue Disorders 1963, Anticoagulant Prophylaxis and Treatment (jtly) 1965. *Leisure interest:* gardening. *Address:* Windcutter, Lee, North Devon, EX34 8LW, England. *Telephone:* (1271) 863198.

RICHARDSON, Keith, MA; British writer, administrator and fmr journalist; b. 14 June 1936, Wakefield, Yorks.; s. of Gilbert Richardson and Ellen Richardson; m. Sheila Carter 1958; three d.; ed Wakefield Grammar School, Univ. Coll. Oxford; feature writer, The Financial Times 1960–63; Industrial Ed. and European Corresp. The Sunday Times 1964–68, 1970–83; Production Man. GKN 1969–70; Head of Group Public Affairs, B.A.T. Industries 1983–88; Sec.-Gen. The European Round Table of Industrialists 1988–98. *Publications:* Monopolies and Mergers 1963, Do it the Hard Way 1971, Daggers in the Forum 1978, Reshaping Europe 1991, Beating the Crisis 1993, Europe Made Simple 1998. *Leisure interest:* mountaineering. *Address:* European Round Table, Avenue Jaspar 113, 1060 Brussels, Belgium. *Telephone:* (2) 534-31-00. *Fax:* (2) 534-73-48.

RICHARDSON, Miranda; British actress; b. 3 March 1958, Southport; d. of William Alan Richardson and Marian Georgina (née Townsend) Richardson; ed Old Vic Theatre School, Bristol. *Theatre appearances include:* Moving 1980–81, All My Sons, Who's Afraid of Virginia Woolf?, The Life of Einstein, A Lie of the Mind 1987, The Changeling, Mountain Language 1988, Etta Jenks, The Designated Mourner 1996, Aunt Dan and Lemon 1999. *Film appearances include:* Dance with a Stranger (debut 1985; Best Actress Award, Evening Standard), The Innocent, Empire of the Sun, The Mad Monkey, Eat the Rich, Twisted Obsession, The Bachelor 1992, Enchanted April 1992 (Golden Globe Award for Best Comedy Actress 1993), The Crying Game 1992, Damage (BAFTA Award for Best Supporting Actress 1993), Tom and Viv 1994, La Nuit et Le Moment 1994, Kansas City, Swann 1995, Evening Star 1996, The Designated Mourner 1996, The Apostle 1996, All For Love, Jacob Two Two and the Hooded Fang 1998, The Big Brass Ring 1998, Sleepy Hollow 1998–99, Get Carter 1999, Snow White 2001, The Hours 2001, Spider 2001, Rage on Placid Lake 2001, The Actors 2002, Falling Angels 2002. *Television appearances include:* The Hard Word, Sorrel and Son, A Woman of Substance, After Pilkington, Underworld, Death of the Heart, Blackadder II and III, Die Kinder (mini-series) 1990, Sweet as You Are (Royal TV Soc.'s Best Actress Award), Fatherland (Golden Globe Award), Saint X 1995, Magic Animals, Dance to the Music of Time 1997, The Scold's Bridle, Merlin 1997, Alice 1998, Ted and Ralph 1998. *Leisure interests:* gardening, junkshops, music, occasional art, reading, softball, walking. *Address:* c/o ICM, 76 Oxford Street, London, W1N 0AX, England.

RICHARDSON, Natasha Jane; British actress; b. 11 May 1963; d. of the late Tony Richardson and of Vanessa Redgrave (q.v.); m. 1st Robert Fox 1990 (divorced 1994); m. 2nd Liam Neeson (q.v.) 1994; two s.; ed Lycée Français de Londres, St Paul's Girls' School, Cen. School of Speech and Drama; Most Promising Newcomer Award 1986; Plays and Players Award 1986, 1990; Best Actress, Evening Standard Film Awards 1900; London Theatre Critics Award 1990. *Stage appearances include:* A Midsummer Night's Dream, Hamlet, The Seagull 1985, China 1986, High Society 1986, Anna Christie 1990, 1992, Cabaret (Tony Award) 1998, Closer 1999, The Lady from the Sea 2003. *Film appearances include:* Every Picture Tells a Story 1985, Gothic 1987, A Month in the Country 1987, Patty Hearst 1988, Fat Man and Little Boy 1989, The Handmaid's Tale 1990, The Comfort of Strangers 1990, The Favour, The Watch and The Very Big Fish 1992, Past Midnight 1994, Widow's Peak 1994, Nell 1994, The Parent Trap 1998, Waking up in Reno 2000, Blow Dry 2001, Maid in Manhattan 2003. *Television appearances include:* In a Secret State 1985, Ghosts 1986, Hostages 1992, Suddenly Last Summer 1993, Zelda 1993, Tales from the Crypt 1996, Haven 2000. *Address:* ICM Limited, Oxford House, 76 Oxford Street, London, W1N 0AX, England.

RICHARDSON, Peter Damian, PhD, FRS, ACGI, DIC; British mechanical engineer; b. 22 Aug. 1935, West Wickham; s. of the late Reginald W. Richardson and Marie S. Richardson; one d.; ed Imperial Coll. London, Brown Univ., USA; demonstrator Dept of Mechanical Eng, Imperial Coll. 1955–58; went to USA 1958; Visiting Lecturer Brown Univ. 1958–59, Research Assoc. 1959–60; Asst Prof. of Eng 1960–65, Assoc. Prof. 1965–68, Prof. 1968–84, Prof. of Eng and Physiology 1984–, Chair. Univ. Faculty 1987–; Chair. Exec. Cttee Center Biomedical Eng 1972–; Consultant to Industry US Govt Agencies; mem. American Soc. of Mechanical Eng, American Soc. of Artificial Internal Organs, European Soc. of Artificial Organs, Biomedical Eng Soc.; Founding Fellow American Inst. of Medical and Biological Eng; recipient of Sr Scientist Award Alexander Von Humboldt Foundation 1976, Laureate in Medicine, Ernst Jung Foundation 1987. *Publications:* Principles of Cell Adhesion 1995; contribs to many professional journals. *Address:* Box D, Brown University, Providence, RI 02912, USA. *Telephone:* (401) 863-2687.

RICHARDSON, Robert Coleman, PhD; American professor of physics and researcher; b. 26 June 1937, Washington, DC; s. of Robert Franklin Richardson and Lois (Price) Richardson; m. Betty Marilyn McCarthy 1962; two d.; ed Virginia Polytechnic Inst. and State Univ., Duke Univ.; served in U.S. Army 1959–60; Research Assoc. Cornell Univ., Ithaca, NY 1966–67, Asst Prof. 1968–71, Assoc. Prof. 1972–74, Prof. 1975–; Chair. Int. Union Pure and

Applied Physics Comm. (C-5) 1981–84; mem. Bd Assessment Nat. Bureau of Standards 1983–; mem. Editorial Bd Journal of Low Temperature Physics 1984–; Fellow AAAS, American Physical Soc.; mem. NAS; Guggenheim Fellow 1975, 1983; Simon Memorial Prize, British Physical Soc. 1976, Oliver E. Buckley Prize, American Physical Soc. 1981, shared Nobel Prize for Physics 1996. *Leisure interests:* photography, gardening. *Address:* Department of Physics, Cornell University, Clark Hall, Ithaca, NY 14853, USA.

RICHARDSON, Ruth, LLB; New Zealand politician, economic consultant and company director; b. 13 Dec. 1950, Wanganui; d. of Ross Pearce Richardson and Rita Joan Richardson; m. Andrew Evan Wright 1975; one s. one d.; ed Canterbury Univ., NZ; fmr Legal Adviser, Federated Farmers; Nat. Party MP for Selwyn 1981–94; Shadow Minister for Finance 1987; Minister of Finance 1990–93; consultant Ruth Richardson (NZ) Ltd 1994–; Dir Reserve Bank of NZ 1999–; Chair. Kula Fund 1997–, Jade Corpn 2000–; Dir Centre for Ind. Studies 1999–. *Publications:* Making a Difference 1995. *Leisure interests:* gardening, running, swimming. *Address:* RD5, Christchurch, New Zealand. *Telephone:* (3) 347-9146.

RICHARDSON, Sir Tom, KCMG, MA; British diplomatist; b. 6 Feb. 1941, Manchester; s. of Arthur Legh Turnour Richardson and Penelope Margaret Richardson (née Waithman); m. Alexandra Frazier Wasiqullah (née Ratcliff) 1979; ed Westminster School, Christ Church, Oxford; postings in Ghana, Tanzania, FCO, Milan, New York; Cen. Policy Review Staff 1980–81; Counsellor, Embassy, Rome 1982–86; Head Econ. Relations Dept, FCO 1986–89; Deputy Perm. Rep. to UN 1989–94; FCO 1994–96; Amb. to Italy 1996–2000; Chair. Governing Body, British Inst. of Florence 2003; mem. Council, British School of Rome 2002. *Leisure interests:* reading, music, walking, Italy. *Address:* 59 Hugh Street, London, S.W.1., England (Home).

RICHARDSON, William Blaine, MA; American diplomatist and politician; b. 15 Nov. 1947, Pasadena, Calif.; m. Barbara Flavin 1972; ed Tufts Univ., Fletcher School of Law and Diplomacy; staff mem. US House of Reps. 1971–72, Dept of State 1973–75, US Senate Foreign Relations Cttee 1975–78; Exec. Dir NM State Democratic Cttee 1978, Bernalillo Co. Democratic Cttee 1978; business exec. Santa Fe 1978–82; mem. (Democrat) 98th–103rd Congresses from 3rd Dist NM 1982–97; Perm. Rep. to UN 1997–98; Sec. of State for Energy 1998–2001; Sr Man. Dir Kissinger McLarty Assocs 2001–; Adjunct Prof. of Public Policy Harvard Univ. 2001–; Gov. of NM 2003–; mem. NATO 2000 Bd. *Address:* Office of the Governor, State Capitol, Room 400, Santa Fe, NM 87501, USA (Office). *Telephone:* (505) 476-2200. *Website:* www.governor.state.nm.us.

RICHARDSON, William Chase, MBA, PhD; American university administrator; b. 11 May 1940, Passaic, NJ; s. of Henry B. and Frances (Chase) Richardson; m. Nancy Freeland 1966; two d.; ed Trinity Coll., Hartford, Conn. and Univ. of Chicago; Research Assoc., Instr. Univ. of Chicago 1967–70; Asst Prof. Univ. of Washington, School of Public Health and Community Medicine 1971–73, Assoc. Prof. 1973–76, Prof. of Health Services 1976–84, Chair. Dept of Health Services 1973–76, Graduate Dean, Vice-Provost for Research, 1981–84; Exec. Vice-Pres., Provost and Prof. Dept of Family and Community Medicine, Pennsylvania State Univ. 1984–90; Pres. Johns Hopkins Univ. 1990–95; Prof. of Health Policy Man. 1990–95, Prof. Emer. 1995–; Pres. and CEO W.K. Kellogg Foundation Battle Creek, Mich. 1995–; mem. Inst. of Medicine, NAS; Fellow American Public Health Assocn; Kellogg Fellow; Trinity Whitlock Award; Mary H. Bachmeyer Award (Univ. of Chicago). *Publications:* articles in professional journals. *Address:* W.K. Kellogg Foundation, 1 Michigan Avenue E, Battle Creek, MI 49017, USA.

RICHARDSON OF DUNTISBOURNE, Baron (Life Peer), cr. 1983, of Duntisbourne in the County of Gloucestershire; **Gordon William Humphreys Richardson,** KG, PC, MBE; British banker; b. 25 Nov. 1915, London; s. of John Robert and Nellie Richardson (née Humphreys); m. Margaret Alison Sheppard 1941; one s. one d.; ed Nottingham High School and Gonville and Caius Coll., Cambridge; S. Notts. Hussars Yeomanry 1939, Staff Coll., Camberley 1941; called to the Bar, Gray's Inn 1947; mem. Bar Council 1951–55; Industrial and Commercial Finance Corpn Ltd 1955–57; Dir J. Henry Schroder and Co. 1957–62; Chair. J. Henry Schroder Wagg and Co. Ltd 1962–72; Chair. Schroders Ltd 1965–73, J. Henry Schroder Banking Corpn (USA) 1967–69, Schroders AG (Switzerland) 1967, Schroders Inc. (USA) 1969–73; Dir Bank of England 1967–73, Gov. 1973–83; Dir BIS 1973–93, Vice-Chair. 1985–88, 1991–93; Chair. Cttee on Turnover Taxation 1963–64; Vice-Chair. Legal and Gen. Assurance Soc. Ltd 1959–70, Lloyds Bank Ltd 1962–66; Vice-Chair. Chase Manhattan Int. Advisory Council 1996–2000; Dir Rolls-Royce (1971) Ltd 1971–73, ICI 1972–73; mem. Int. Advisory Bd Chemical Bank 1986–96, Chair. 1986–96; Chair. Morgan Stanley Int. Inc. 1986–96; mem. Co. Law Amendment Cttee 1959–62; mem. Court, London Univ. 1962–65; mem. Nat. Econ. Devt Council 1971–73, 1980–83; Chair. Industrial Devt Advisory Bd 1972–73, 'Group of Ten' 1982–83, 'Group of Thirty' 1985–91, Hon. Chair. 'Group of Thirty' 1991–; Dir Glyndebourne Arts Trust 1982–88, Royal Opera House 1983–88; Chair. Pilgrim Trust 1984–89; Hon. Master of Bench of Gray's Inn 1973; one of HM Lts for City of London 1974–; High Steward of Westminster Cathedral 1985–89; Deputy High Steward, Univ. of Cambridge 1982–; Deputy Lt for Glos. 1983; Hon. Fellow, Wolfson Coll. and Gonville and Caius Coll., Cambridge Univ.; Hon. DSc (The City Univ.) 1975, (Univ. of Aston in Birmingham) 1979, Hon. LLD (Cambridge) 1979, Hon. DCL

(East Anglia) 1984; Benjamin Franklin Medal (Royal Soc. of Arts) 1984. *Address:* 25 St. Anselm's Place, London, W1K 5AF, England. *Telephone:* (20) 7629-4448.

RICHIE, Lionel, B.S.(ECONS.); American singer, songwriter and musician; b. 20 June 1949, Tuskegee, AL; m. Diane Alexander 1996; ed Tuskegee Univ.; mem. The Commodores 1968–82; support tours with The Jackson 5 1973, The Rolling Stones 1975, The O'Jays 1976; solo artiste 1982–; concerts include: Closing Ceremony, Olympic Games, Los Angeles 1984, Live Aid, Phila 1985; ASCAP Songwriter Awards 1979, 1984–96, numerous American Music Awards 1979–, Grammy Awards include: Best Pop Vocal Performance 1982, Album of the Year 1985, Producer of the Year (shared) 1986; Lionel Richie Day, Los Angeles 1983, two Nat. Asscn for the Advancement of Colored People (NAACP) Image Awards 1983, NAACP Entertainer of the Year 1987, Acad. Award for Best Song 1986, Golden Globe Award for Best Song 1986. *Compositions include:* with The Commodores: Sweet Love 1975, Just To Be Close To You 1976, Easy 1977, Three Times A Lady (No. 1, USA and UK) 1979, Sail On 1980, Still (No. 1, USA) 1980, Oh No 1981; for Kenny Rogers: Lady (No. 1, USA) 1980; for Diana Ross: Missing You 1984; Solo hits: Endless Love, film theme duet with Diana Ross (No. 1, USA) 1981, Truly (No. 1, USA) 1982, All Night Long (No. 1, USA) 1983, Running With The Night 1984, Hello (No. 1, USA and UK) 1984, Stuck On You 1984, Penny Lover (jtly with Brenda Harvey) 1984, Say You Say Me (No. 1, USA) 1986, Dancing On The Ceiling 1987, Love Will Conquer All 1987, Ballerina Girl 1987, My Destiny 1992, Don't Wanna Lose You 1996; contrib. We Are The World (jtly with Michael Jackson), USA For Africa (No. 1 world-wide) 1985. *Albums include:* with The Commodores: Machine Gun 1974, Caught In The Act 1975, Movin' On 1975, Hot On The Tracks 1976, Commodores 1977, Commodores Live! 1977, Natural High 1978, Greatest Hits 1978, Midnight Magic 1979, Heroes 1980, In The Pocket 1981; solo: Lionel Richie 1982, Can't Slow Down 1983, Dancing On The Ceiling 1986, Back To Front 1992, Louder Than Words 1996, Time 1998, Encore 2002. *Address:* John Reid Management, 505 South Beverly Drive, Suite 1192, Beverly Hills, CA 90212, USA (Office).

RICHMOND, Sir Mark Henry, Kt, ScD, FRS; British academic; b. 1 Feb. 1931, Sydney, Australia; s. of Harold Sylvester Richmond and Dorothy Plaistowe Tegg; m. 1st Shirley Jean Townrow 1958 (divorced); one s. one d. (and one d. deceased); m. 2nd Sheila Travers 2000; ed Epsom Coll., Clare Coll., Univ. of Cambridge; mem. scientific staff, Medical Research Council 1958–65; Reader in Molecular Biology, Univ. of Edin. 1965–68; Prof. of Bacteriology, Univ. of Bristol 1968–81; Vice-Chancellor and Prof. of Molecular Bacteriology, Victoria Univ. of Manchester 1981–90; mem. Public Health Laboratory Service Bd 1976–85; Chair. Cttee of Vice-Chancellors and Prins of the UK 1987–89, Microbiological Food Safety Cttee 1989–90, Science and Eng Research Council 1990–94; Group Head of Research, Glaxo 1993–95, Science Adviser 1995–96; mem. staff School of Public Policy, Univ. Coll. London 1996–; mem. Int. Science Advisory Cttee, UNESCO 1996–2001; mem. and fmr mem. numerous bds; Robert Koch Award 1977. *Publications:* numerous scientific articles. *Leisure interests:* gardening, hill walking, opera. *Address:* School of Public Policy, University College London, 29–30 Tavistock Square, London, WC1H 9QU, England. *Telephone:* (20) 7679-4968.

RICHTER, Burton, PhD; American physicist; b. 22 March 1931, Brooklyn, New York; s. of Abraham Richter and Fannie (Pollack) Richter; m. Laurose Becker 1960; one s. one d.; ed Massachusetts Inst. of Technology; joined Stanford Univ. 1956–, Research Assoc. in Physics, High Energy Physics Lab., Stanford Univ. 1956–59; mem. group building first electron storage ring and conducting a colliding beam experiment extending validity of quantum electrodynamics; Asst Prof., Stanford Univ. 1959–63, Assoc. Prof. 1963–67, Prof. 1967–, Paul Pigott Prof. in Physical Sciences 1980–; worked at Stanford Linear Accelerator Center 1963–99, Tech. Dir 1982–84, Dir 1984–99, Dir Emer. 1999–; set up a group which built a high-energy electron positron machine (SPEAR) and has continued to develop new accelerator and detector techniques including most recently the SLAC linear collider; Pres. IUPAP; mem. Bd of Dirs Varian Assocs, Litel Instruments; sabbatical year at European Org. for Nuclear Research (CERN), Geneva 1975–76; Loeb Lecturer, Harvard Univ. 1974, DeShalit Lecturer, Weizmann Inst. 1975; mem. NAS 1977; Fellow, American Acad. of Arts and Sciences 1989, American Physical Soc. (Pres. 1994), AAAS; E. O. Lawrence Medal 1976, Nobel Prize for Physics (jtly with Samuel Ting, q.v.) for discovery of the heavy, long-lived 'psi' particle 1976. *Publications:* over 300 articles in various scientific journals 1963–89. *Address:* Stanford Linear Accelerator Center, P.O. Box 20450, Stanford, CA 94309, USA.

RICHTER, Gerhard; German artist; b. 9 Feb. 1932, Dresden; s. of Horst Richter and Hildegard Richter; m. 1st Marianne Richter (née Eufinger); m. 2nd Isa Richter (née Genzken) 1982; m. 3rd Sabine Richter (née Moritz) 1995; one s. two d.; ed Staatliche Kunstakademien Dresden and Düsseldorf; emigrated to West Germany 1961; Visiting Prof. Kunstakademie Hamburg 1967, Coll. of Art, Halifax, Canada 1978; Prof. Staatliche Kunstakademie Düsseldorf 1971–; mem. Akad. der Künste, Berlin; one-man shows in galleries and museums all over world 1964–; paintings in public collections in Berlin, Cologne, Basle, Paris, New York, Chicago, Toronto, London, etc.; mem. Acad. of Arts, Berlin; Kunstpreis Junger Westen 1966, Arnold Bode Preis 1982, Kokoschka Prize (Austria) 1985, Wolf Prize 1994–95, Venice Biennial Art Festival Jury Prize 1997, Nordrhein-Westfalen State Prize 2000. *Address:* Osterrietweg 22, 50996 Cologne, Germany.

RICHTER, Horst-Eberhard, MD, DPhil; German professor of psychological medicine; b. 28 April 1923, Berlin; s. of Otto Richter and Charlotte Richter; m. Bergrun Luckow 1947; one s. two d.; ed Berlin Univ.; Dir Advisory and Research Centre for Childhood Emotional Disturbances, Wedding Children's Hosp., Berlin 1952–62; Physician, Psychiatric Clinic, W Berlin Free Univ. 1955–62; Dir Berlin Psychoanalytic Inst. 1959–62; Chief of Dept of Psychosomatic Medicine, Univ. of Giessen, Fed. Repub. of Germany 1962–, Dir Centre for Psychosomatics 1973, now Hon. Dir; Dir Sigmund-Freud Inst Frankfurt am Main 1992–2002; mem. PEN, Germany; Research Prize, Swiss Soc. of Psychosomatic Medicine 1970; Theodor-Heuss Prize 1980, Goethe-Plakette der Stadt Frankfurt 2002. *Publications:* Eltern, Kind und Neurose 1963, Herzneurose (with D. Beckmann) 1969, Patient Familie 1970, Giessen-Test (with D. Beckmann) 1972, Die Gruppe 1972, Lernziel Solidarität 1974, The Family as Patient 1974, Flüchten oder Standhalten 1976, Der Gotteskomplex 1979, Alle redeten vom Frieden 1981, Sich der Krise stellen 1981, Zur Psychologie des Friedens 1982, Die Chance des Gewissens 1986, Leben statt Machen 1987, Die hohe Kunst der Korruption 1989, Russen und Deutsche 1990, Umgang mit Angst 1992, Wer nicht leiden will, muss hassen 1993, Psychoanalyse und Politik 1995, Als Einstein nicht mehr weiterwusste 1997, Wanderer zwischen den Fronten 2000, Das Ende der Egomanie 2002. *Address:* Friedrichstrasse 28, 35392 Giessen, Germany. *Telephone:* (641) 9945625. *Fax:* (641) 74350. *E-mail:* SFL-C.Schaefer@t-online.de (Office).

RICHTER PRADA, Gen. Pedro; Peruvian politician and army officer; fmr Chief of Staff of the Army, fmr Minister of the Interior; Chair. Jt Chiefs of Staff 1978–81; Prime Minister, Minister of War and C-in-C of Armed Forces of Peru 1978–80; Pres. Mokichi Okada Foundation, Peru 1981–. *Address:* c/o Oficina del Primer Ministro, Lima, Peru.

RICHTHOFEN, Hermann, Freiherr von, DJur; German diplomatist; b. 20 Nov. 1933, Breslau; s. of Herbert Freiherr von Richthofen and Gisela Freifrau von Richthofen (née Schoeller); m. Christa Gräfin von Schwerin 1966; one s. two d.; joined diplomatic service 1963; served Saigon and Djakarta; Head of Dept Perm. Rep. Office of FRG for GDR 1975–78; Dir German and Berlin Dept Ministry of Foreign Affairs 1978–80; Dir Working Party on German Policy, Fed. Chancellery 1980–86; Dir Gen. Legal Dept Ministry of Foreign Affairs 1986, Political Dept 1986–88; Amb. to UK 1988–93; Perm. Rep. to NATO 1993–98; Chair. Deutsch-Britische Gesellschaft, Berlin; Trustee and mem. Exec. Council 21st Century Trust, London; Rep. of Prime Minister of Brandenburg for Co-operation with Poland; Gov. Ditchley Foundation; Hon. Prof., Cen. Connecticut State Univ.; Officer's Cross Order of Kts of Malta, Commdr's Cross Order of Merit (Italy), Commdr, Légion d'honneur, Grand Officer's Cross Order of Infante D. Henrique (Portugal), Grand Cross Order of Merit (Luxemburg), Kt Commdr's Cross 2nd Class (Austria), Hon. GCVO, Grand Cross Order of Merit (Germany); Hon. LLD (Birmingham). *Leisure interests:* skiing, walking, swimming, literature, history, arts, music. *Address:* Beckerstr. 6A, 12157 Berlin, Germany.

RICKE, Kai-Uwe; German telecommunications executive; b. Oct. 1961, Krefeld; ed European Business School, Schloss Reichartshausen, Germany; began career as asst to Bd of Bertelsmann, Guetersloh, later Head of Sales and Marketing, Scandinavian Club (subsidiary); CEO Talkline and Talkline PS Phone Service, Elmshorn 1990–95, Chair. and CEO 1995–98; Chair. Bd Man. DeTeMobil Deutsche Telekom Mobilnet (now T-Mobile Deutschland) 1998–2000, Chair. T-Mobile Int. 2000–01, COO and mem. Bd Man. Deutsche Telekom AG 2001, Chair. Bd Man. and CEO Nov. 2002–. *Address:* Deutsche Telekom AG, Postfach 2000, 53105 Bonn, Germany (Office). *Telephone:* (228) 18188880 (Office). *Fax:* (228) 18171915 (Office). *Website:* www.telekom.de (Office).

RICKMAN, Alan; British actor; ed Chelsea Coll. of Art, Royal Coll. of Art and Royal Acad. of Dramatic Art (RADA); repertory theatre in Manchester, Leicester, Sheffield and Glasgow; spent two seasons with RSC at Stratford; later appeared at Bush Theatre, Hampstead and Royal Court Theatre; Time Out Award 1991, Evening Standard Film Actor of the Year 1991, BAFTA Award 1991, Golden Globe Award 1996, Emmy Award 1996, Variety Club Award 2002. *Stage appearances include:* Les Liaisons Dangereuses (RSC Stratford, London and Broadway), The Lucky Chance, The Seagull (Royal Court), Tango at the End of Winter (Edin. Festival and West End London) 1991, Hamlet (Riverside Studios) 1992, Antony and Cleopatra (Nat. Theatre) 1998, Private Lives (West End and Broadway) 2001–02. *Play directed:* The Winter Guest (W Yorkshire Playhouse and Almeida, London) 1995. *Radio includes:* The Seagull, A Good Man in Africa, A Trick to Catch the Old One. *Television appearances include:* The Barchester Chronicles 1982, Pity in History 1984, Revolutionary Witness, Spirit of Man 1989, Rasputin (USA) 1995. *Films include:* Die Hard 1988, The January Man 1989, Close My Eyes 1991, Truly, Madly, Deeply 1991, Closetland 1991, Robin Hood: Prince of Thieves 1991, Bob Roberts 1992, Mesmer 1993, An Awfully Big Adventure 1994, Sense and Sensibility 1995, Michael Collins 1996, Rasputin 1996, Dark Harbour 1997, The Judas Kiss 1997, Dogma 1998, Galaxy Quest 1999, Blow Dry 1999, Play 2000, The Search for John Gissing 2000, Harry Potter and the Philosopher's Stone 2001, Harry Potter and the Chamber of Secrets 2002, Love Actually 2003. *Film directed:* The Winter Guest 1997 (Best Film, Chicago Film Festival 1997). *Address:* c/o ICM, Oxford House, 76 Oxford Street, London, W1N 0AX, England.

RICKS, Christopher Bruce, FBA; British professor of humanities; b. 18 Sept. 1933; s. of James Bruce Ricks and Gabrielle Roszak; m. 1st Kirsten Jensen 1956 (dissolved); two s. two d.; m. 2nd Judith Aronson 1977; one s. two d.; ed King Alfred's School, Wantage, Oxon., Balliol Coll., Univ. of Oxford; 2nd Lt Green Howards 1952; Andrew Bradley Jr Research Fellow Balliol Coll. Univ. of Oxford 1957, Fellow Worcester Coll. 1958–68; Prof. of English Bristol Univ. 1968–75; Fellow Christ's Coll., Prof. of English Univ. of Cambridge 1975–86, King Edward VII Prof. of English Literature 1982–86; Prof. of English Boston Univ. 1986–98, Warren Prof. of the Humanities 1998–, Co-Dir Editorial Inst. 1999–; Visiting Prof. at Univs of Berkeley and Stanford 1965, Smith Coll. 1967, Harvard Univ. 1971, Wesleyan 1974, Brandeis 1977, 1981, 1984, USA; Vice-Pres. Tennyson Soc.; Fellow American Acad. of Arts and Sciences 1991; Hon. Fellow, Balliol Coll. 1989, Worcester Coll. 1990, Christ's Coll. Cambridge 1993; Hon. DLitt (Oxford) 1998; George Orwell Memorial Prize 1979; Beefeater Club Prize for Literature 1980. *Publications:* Milton's Grand Style 1963, The Poems of Tennyson (Ed.) 1969 (revised 1987), Tennyson 1972, Keats and Embarrassment 1974, The State of the Language (Ed. with Leonard Michaels) 1980, 1990, The Force of Poetry 1984, The New Oxford Book of Victorian Verse 1987 (Ed.), Collected Poems and Selected Prose of A. E. Housman (Ed.) 1988, T. S. Eliot and Prejudice 1988, Ed. (with William Vance) The Faber Book of America 1992, Beckett's Dying Words (Clarendon Lectures) 1993, Essays in Appreciation 1996, Inventions of the March Hare: Poems 1909–1917 by T. S. Eliot (Ed.) 1996, The Oxford Book of English Verse (Ed.) 1999, Reviewery 2002, Selected Poems of James Henry (Ed.) 2002, Allusion to the Poets 2002. *Address:* 39 Martin Street, Cambridge, MA 02138, USA; Lasborough Park, near Tetbury, Glos., GL8 8UF, England. *Telephone:* (617) 354-7887 (USA); (1666) 890252 (England).

RICKSON, Ian, BA; British director; ed Essex Univ., Goldsmiths' Coll., London Univ.; freelance Dir King's Head, The Gate, Chichester Festival Theatre; Special Projects Dir Young People's Theatre 1991–92; Assoc. Dir Royal Court Theatre 1993–98, Artistic Dir 1998–. *Plays:* Royal Court Theatre productions: Killers 1992, SAB 1992, Wildfire 1992, Ashes and Sand 1994, Some Voices 1994, Pale Horse 1995, Mojo 1995, The Lights 1996, The Weir 1997, Dublin Carol 2000, Mouth to Mouth 2001, Boy Gets Girl (Royal Court) 2001, The Night Heron 2002; other productions: Rinty (Group Theatre, Belfast) 1990, Who's Breaking (Battersea Arts Centre) 1990, First Strike (Soho Poly) 1990, Queer Fish (Battersea Arts Centre) 1991, Me and My Friend (Chichester Festival Theatre) 1992, The House of Yes (Gate Theatre) 1993, La Serva Padrona (Broomhill) 1993, Mojo (Chicago) 1996, The Day I Stood Still (Cottesloe Theatre) 1997. *Address:* c/o Curtis Brown Group, Haymarket House, 26-28 Haymarket, London, SW1Y 4SP, England (Office).

RICO, Francisco, PhD; Spanish professor of medieval literature; b. 28 April 1942, Barcelona; s. of late Cipriano Rico and María Manrique; m. Victoria Camps 1966; three s.; ed Univ. of Barcelona; Prof. of Medieval Literature, Autonomous Univ. of Barcelona 1971; Visiting Prof. The Johns Hopkins Univ. 1966–67, Princeton Univ. 1981, Scuola Normale Superiore di Pisa 1987; Gen. Dir Centre of Spanish Letters, Ministry of Culture 1985–86; Ed. Book Series: Letras e ideas, Filología, Biblioteca clásica; mem. Royal Spanish Acad. 1986–; Foreign mem. British Acad. 1992, Accademia dei Lincei 2000; Commdr Ordre des Palmes Académiques (France). *Publications:* El pequeño mundo del hombre 1970, The Spanish Picaresque Novel and the Point of View 1970, Vida u obra de Petrarca (Vol. 1) 1974, Historia y crítica de la literatura española (8 Vols) 1980–84, Breve biblioteca de autores españoles 1990, El sueño del humanismo (De Petrarca a Erasmo) 1993, Critical Edition of Cervantes' Don Quixote 1998. *Leisure interest:* contemporary literature. *Address:* Santa Teresa 38, 08190 St Cugat del Vallès, Barcelona; Apartado 1, Universidad Autónoma de Barcelona, 08193 Bellaterra-Barcelona, Spain. *Telephone:* (93) 674-07-08; 581-15-26. *E-mail:* informacio@uab.es (Office). *Website:* www.uab .es (Office).

RICÚPERO, Rubens; Brazilian international organization official, fmr diplomatist and politician; b. 1 March 1937, São Paulo; m. Marisa Parolari; four c.; Prof. of Theory of Int. Relations, Univ. of Brasília 1979–95; Prof. of History of Brazilian Diplomatic Relations, Rio Branco Inst. 1980–95; with Ministry of Foreign Relations 1981–93, Minister of the Environment and Amazonian Affairs 1993–94, of Finance March–Sept. 1994; Perm. Rep. to UN, Geneva 1987–91; Amb. to USA 1991–93, to Italy 1995; Sec.-Gen. of UNCTAD Sept. 1995–. *Address:* Office of the Secretary-General, UNCTAD, Palais des Nations, 1211 Geneva 10, Switzerland. *Telephone:* (22) 9071234. *Fax:* (22) 9070057. *E-mail:* ers@unctad.org (Office). *Website:* www.unctad.org (Office).

RIDDICK, Frank Adams, Jr., MD; American physician; b. 14 June 1929, Memphis; s. of Frank Adams Riddick Sr and Falba Crawford Riddick; m. Mary Belle Alston 1952; two s. one d.; ed Vanderbilt and Washington Univs; Staff Physician, Ochsner Clinic, New Orleans 1961–, Asst Medical Dir 1969–73, Assoc. Medical Dir 1973–75, Medical Dir 1975–92, Trustee, Alton Ochsner Medical Foundation 1973–, CEO 1991–; Clinical Prof. of Medicine, Tulane Univ., New Orleans 1977–; Chair. Council on Medical Educ., American Medical Asscn 1982–84, Council on Judicial and Ethical Affairs 1995–; mem. NAS Inst. of Medicine; Distinguished Physician Award, American Soc. of Internal Medicine 1980; Physician Exec. Award, American Coll. of Medical Group Admins 1984; Distinguished Alumnus Award, Vanderbilt Univ. School of Medicine 1988. *Publications:* 56 scientific papers. *Leisure interest:* travel. *Address:* Ochsner Clinic, 1516 Jefferson Highway, New Orleans, LA 70121; 1923 Octavia Street, New Orleans, LA 70115, USA (Home). *Telephone:* (504) 838-4001 (Office); (504) 897-1737 (Home).

RIDE, Sally, PhD; American astronaut and professor of physics; b. 26 May 1951, Los Angeles; d. of Dale Ride and Joyce Ride; m. Steven Hawley (divorced); ed Westlake High School, Los Angeles and Stanford Univ.; astronaut trainee, NASA 1978–79, astronaut 1979–87; on-orbit capsule communicator STS-2 mission, Johnson Space Center, NASA, Houston; on-orbit capsule communicator STS-3 mission NASA, mission specialist STS-7 1983; Scientific Fellow, Stanford Univ. 1987–89; Dir Calif. Space Inst., Univ. of Calif. at San Diego 1989–96, Prof. of Physics 1989–; Pres. Space Comm. 1999–2000; mem. Presidential Comm. on Space Shuttle 1986, Presidential Comm. of Advisers on Science and Tech. 1994–; mem. Bd of Dirs. Apple Computer Inc. 1988–90. *Publications:* To Space and Back (jtly.) 1986, Voyager: An Adventure to the Edge of the Solar System 1992, The Third Planet: Exploring the Earth from Space (jtly.) 1994, The Mystery of Mars 1999. *Address:* California Space Institute, 0426, University of California at San Diego, La Jolla, CA 92093, USA. *Telephone:* (619) 534-5827. *Fax:* (619) 822-1277.

RIDGE, Tom (Thomas Joseph), BA, JD; American politician and lawyer; b. 26 Aug. 1945, Munhall, Pa; m. Michele Moore 1979; one s. one d.; ed Harvard Univ. and Dickinson School of Law, Carlisle, Pa; admitted to Pa Bar 1972; practising lawyer, Erie, Pa 1972–82; Asst Dist Attorney, Erie, Pa 1979–82; mem. US House of Reps. 1983–95; Gov. of Pennsylvania 1995–2001; Dir Office of Homeland Security 2001–03, Sec. Dept of Homeland Security 2003–; mem. numerous cttees.; Republican; Bronze Star for Valor. *Address:* US Department of Homeland Security, Washington, DC 20528, USA (Office). *Website:* www.dhs.gov.

RIDLEY, Brian Kidd, PhD, FInstP, CPhys, FRS; British physicist; b. 2 March 1931, Newcastle upon Tyne; s. of Oliver Archbold Ridley and Lillian Beatrice Ridley; m. Sylvia Jean Ridley; one s. one d.; ed Yorebridge (Askrigg) and Gateshead Grammar Schools, Univ. of Durham; Research Physicist Mullard Research Labs. 1956–64; lecturer to Reader, Dept of Physics, Univ. of Essex 1964–86, Prof. 1986–91, Research Prof. 1991–; several visiting professorial appointments including Cornell, Stanford and Princeton Univs.; Paul Dirac Medal and Prize, Inst. of Physics 2001. *Publications:* Time, Space and Things, The Physical Environment 1979, Quantum Process in Semiconductors 1988, Electrons and Phonons in Semiconductor Multilayers 1997, On Science 2001. *Leisure interests:* piano, tennis. *Address:* Department of Electronic Systems Engineering, University of Essex, Colchester, CO4 3SQ, England (Office). *Telephone:* (1206) 872873 (Office). *Fax:* (1206) 872900 (Office).

RIEBER-MOHN, Georg Fredrik; Norwegian lawyer; b. 13 Aug. 1945, Lillehammer; m. Kari Nergaard 1967; two s. one d.; ed Univ. of Oslo; Deputy Gov. Western Prison Dist 1971–74; Asst Judge, Magistrates' Court of Stavanger 1975–76; Dist Attorney (Regional Head of Prosecutions) 1976–80; Gen. Dir Prison and Probation Service 1980–85; Judge, Appeal Court 1985–86; Gen. Dir of Public Prosecutions 1986–97 (resgnd); Justice Supreme Court of Norway. *Leisure interest:* salmon fishing. *Address:* Karl Johans Gate 12, Postbox 8002 DEP, 0030 Oslo 1 (Office); Nedre Hval Gård, 3525 Hallingby, Norway (Home). *Telephone:* 22-33-02-70 (Office).

RIEDLBAUCH, Václav; Czech composer; b. 1 April 1947, Dýšina; m.; two s.; ed Prague Conservatoire; lecturer, Prague Acad. of Performing Arts, Sr Lecturer, Sec. Dept of Composition 1984–; Chief Composer Nat. Theatre Opera 1987–89; Dir Gen. Czech Philharmonic Orchestra 2000–; Prof. Acad. of Performing Arts, Prague 2000–; Chair. Young Composers Section, Czech Composers' and Performing Artists' Union 1982–; compositions include Macbeth (for ballet), quartet for four saxophones, Vision (symphonic poem); Artist of Merit 1987. *Address:* Academy of Performing Arts, Malostranské nám. 12, 110 00 Prague 1 (Office); Revoluční 6, 110 00 Prague 1, Czech Republic (Home). *Telephone:* (2) 57533956 (Office); (2) 22310710 (Home). *Fax:* (2) 57530405 (Office).

RIEFENSTAHL, Leni; German film director, photographer and writer; b. 22 Aug. 1902, Berlin; d. of Alfred Riefenstahl and Bertha Riefenstahl; ed Kunstakademie, Berlin; solo dancer 1920s; acted in films 1920s and 1930s; directed first film 1932; Silver Medal Venice Biennale (for The Blue Light) 1932, Gold Medal 1937, 1938, Gold Medal German Art Dir Club 1975. *Films include:* The White Hell of Pitz Palu (actor) 1929, The Blue Light (actor/Dir) 1932, S.O.S. Iceberg (actor) 1933, Triumph of the Will (Dir, documentary of Nuremberg Rally) 1934, Olympische Spiele (Dir, documentary of Berlin Olympic Games) 1936, Tiefland 1945. *Publications:* The Last of the Nuba 1974, People of the Kau 1976, Coral Gardens 1978, Mein Afrika (photographs) 1982, Memoiren 1987, Wonders Under Water 1991, The Sieve of Time (autobiog.) 1992, Leni Riefenstahl: A Memoir 1994. *Address:* 82343 Pöcking, Germany.

RIESENHUBER, Heinz Friedrich, Dr rer. nat; German politician; b. 1 Dec. 1935, Frankfurt; s. of Karl Riesenhuber and Elisabeth (née Birkner) Riesenhuber; m. Beatrix Walter 1968; two s. two d.; ed Gymnasium in Frankfurt and Univs of Frankfurt and Munich; with Erzgesellschaft mbH, c/o Metall-gesellschaft, Frankfurt 1966–71; Tech. Man. Synthomer-Chemie GmbH, Frankfurt 1971–82; joined CDU 1961, Chair. Frankfurt Branch 1973–78; mem. Bundestag 1976–, Chair. Cttee on Econs and Tech.; Fed. Minister for Research and Technology 1982–93; Chair. and mem. of numerous supervisory bds. and advisory panels; Distinguished Service Cross, Commdr, Légion d'honneur and numerous other decorations; Dr hc (Weizmann Inst., Israel, Berg Acad., Poland, Surrey, Göttingen). *Publications:* Japan ist offen; articles in specialist journals. *Leisure interests:* reading, golf. *Address:* Bundestag,

Platz der Republik 1, 11011 Berlin, Germany. *Telephone:* (30) 22777381 (Office). *Fax:* (30) 22776381 (Office). *E-mail:* heinz.riesenhuber@bundestag.de (Office).

RIESS-PASSER, Susanne; Austrian politician and lawyer; b. 1960, Braunau; joined Freedom Party as Press Officer 1987, succeeded Jörg Haider (q.v.) as leader 2000–02; Vice-Chancellor and Minister for Public Affairs and Sports –2002. *Address:* Freiheitliche Partei Österreichs, Esslingasse 14–16, 1010 Vienna, Austria (Office). *Website:* www.fpoe.at (Office).

RIESTER, Walter; German politician and trade unionist; b. 27 Sept. 1943, Kaufbeuren; ed Labour Acad. Frankfurt; apprentice tiler 1957–60; tiler 1960–68; youth training officer German TU Fed. Baden-Württemberg Region 1970, Departmental Gen. Sec. for Youth Questions Stuttgart Region 1970–77; Admin. Sec. IG Metall Geislingen 1977–78, Second Deputy 1978–79, Sec. Dist HQ IG Metall Stuttgart 1980–88, Dist Man. 1988–93, Second Chair. IG Metall Germany 1993–98; Fed. Minister of Labour and Social Affairs 1998–2002; mem. (SPD) Bundestag (German Parl.) 2002–. *Address:* Deutscher Bundestag, Platz der Republik 1, 11011 Berlin, Germany (Office). *Telephone:* (30) 22772042 (Office). *Fax:* (30) 22776042 (Office). *E-mail:* walter.riester@bundestag.de (Office).

RIFBJERG, Klaus; Danish author; b. 15 Dec. 1931, Copenhagen; s. of Thorvald Rifbjerg and Lilly Nielsen; m. Inge Merete Gerner 1955; one s. two d.; ed Princeton Univ., USA and Univ. of Copenhagen; Literary Critic, Information 1955–57, Politiken 1959–65 (Copenhagen daily newspapers); Literary Dir Gyldendal Publrs 1984–92, mem. Bd of Dirs 1992–; Prof. of Aesthetics, Laererhøjskole, Copenhagen 1986; Grant of Honour from the Danish Dramatists 1966, Grant of Honour from the Danish Writers' Guild 1973; Dr hc (Lund) 1991, (Odense) 1996; Aarestrup Medal 1964, Danish Critics' Award 1965, Danish Acad. Award 1966, Golden Laurels 1967, Soren Gyldendal Award 1969, Nordic Council Award 1970, PH Prize 1979, Holberg Medal 1979, H. C. Andersen Prize 1988, Johannes V. Jensen Prize 1998, Prize for Nordic Writers, Swedish Acad. 1999, Danish Publicists' Award 2001, Danish Language Soc. Award 2001. *Publications include:* novels: Den Kroniske Uskyld 1958, Operaelsken 1966, Arkivet 1967, Lonni Og Karl 1968, Anna (Jeg) Anna 1970, Marts 1970 1970, Leif den Lykkelige JR. 1971, Til Spanien 1971, Lena Jorgensen, Klintevej 4, 2650 Hvidovre 1971, Brevet til Gerda 1972, R.R. 1972, Spinatfuglene 1973, Dilettanterne 1973, Du skal ikke vaere ked af det Amalia 1974, En hugorm i solen 1974, Vejen ad hvilken 1975, Tak for turen 1975, Kiks 1976, Twist 1976, Et Bortvendt Ansigt 1977, Tango 1978, Dobbeltgœnger 1978, Drengene 1978, Joker 1979, Voksdugshjertet 1979, Det sorte hul 1980, De hellige aber 1981, Maend og Kvinder 1982, Jus 1982, En omvej til Klostret 1983, Falsk Forår 1984, Borte tit 1986, Engel 1987, Rapsodi i blåt 1991; short stories: Og Andre Historier 1964, Rejsende 1969, Den Syende Jomfru 1972, Sommer 1974, Det. Svage Køn 1989; non-fiction: I Medgang Og Modgang 1970, Deres Majestæt! 1977; plays: Gris Pa Gaflen 1962, Hva Skal Vi Lave 1963, Udviklinger 1965, Hvad en Mand Har Brug For 1966, Voks 1968, Ar 1970, Narrene 1971, Svaret Blaeser i Vinden 1971, Det Korte af det lange 1976; poems: Livsfrisen 1979 and several other vols of poetry; twenty radio plays, essays, several film and TV scripts. *Address:* c/o Gyldendal Publishers, 3 Klareboderne, 1001 Copenhagen, Denmark.

RIFKIN, Joshua, BS, MFA; American musician; b. 22 April 1944, New York; s. of Harry H. Rifkin and Dorothy Helsh; m. Helen Palmer 1995; one d.; ed Juilliard School and New York, Göttingen and Princeton Univs.; Musical Adviser, Assoc. Dir Nonesuch Records 1963–75; Asst, Assoc. Prof. of Music, Brandeis Univ. 1970–82; Dir The Bach Ensemble 1978–; Visiting Prof. New York Univ. 1978, 1983, 2000, Yale Univ. 1982–83, Princeton Univ. 1988, Stanford Univ. 1989, King's Coll. London 1991, Univ. of Basel 1993, 1997, Ohio State Univ. 1994, Univ. of Dortmund 1996, Schola Cantorum Basiliensis 1997, 2001, Univ. of Munich 2000; Fellow, Inst. for Advanced Study, Berlin 1984–86; guest conductor English Chamber Orchestra, Los Angeles Chamber Orchestra, St Louis Symphony Orchestra, St Paul Chamber Orchestra, Scottish Chamber Orchestra, BBC Symphony Orchestra, Bayerische Staatsoper, numerous others; made several recordings of Rags by Scott Joplin, Bach's Mass in B minor 1982, Bach's Magnificat 1983, numerous Bach cantatas 1986–2001, Rags and Tangos 1990, Haydn Symphonies 1994, Silvestre Revueltas 1999; Dr hc (Univ. of Dortmund) 1999; Gramophone Award 1983. *Publications:* articles in musical journals and the New Grove Dictionary of Music and Musicians. *Leisure interests:* food and wine, cinema, his daughter. *Address:* 61 Dana Street, Cambridge, MA 0238, USA. *Telephone:* (617) 876-4017 (Office). *Fax:* (617) 441-5572 (Office). *E-mail:* jrifkin@compuserve.com.

RIFKIND, Rt. Hon. Sir Malcolm Leslie, KCMG, PC, QC, LLB, MSc; British politician; b. 21 June 1946; s. of late E. Rifkind; m. Edith Steinberg 1970; one s. one d.; ed George Watson's Coll. and Univ. of Edinburgh; lecturer, Univ. of Rhodesia 1967–68; called to Scottish Bar 1970; MP for Edin., Pentlands 1974–97; Parl. Under-Sec. of State, Scottish Office 1979–82, FCO 1982–83; Minister of State, FCO 1983–86; Sec. of State for Scotland 1986–90, for Transport 1990–92, for Defence 1992–95, for Foreign and Commonwealth Affairs 1995–97; Pres. Scottish Conservative and Unionist Party 1998–; Hon. Col 162 Movt Control Regt, Royal Logistic Corps (V); mem. Queen's Bodyguard for Scotland, Royal Co. of Archers; Conservative; Hon. LLD (Napier) 1998; Commdr Order of Merit (Poland). *Leisure interests:* walking, field sports, reading. *Address:* c/o Pentlands Conservatives, 20 Spylaw Street, Collinton, Edinburgh, EH13 0JX, Scotland (Office).

RIGBY, Jean Prescott, ARAM, ARCM, A.B.S.M.; British opera singer; b. Fleetwood, Lancs.; d. of Thomas Boulton Rigby and Margaret Annie Rigby; m. James Hayes 1987; three s.; ed Elmslie Girls' School, Blackpool, Birmingham School of Music, RAM and Opera Studio; studied piano and viola at Birmingham then singing at RAM with Patricia Clark, with whom she continues to study; Prin. Mezzo-Soprano, English Nat. Opera 1982–90, roles include Mercedes, Marina, Lucretia, Dorabella, Octavian, Penelope, Jocasta, Helen (King Priam), Rosina; début Covent Garden 1983, roles have included Tebaldo, Mercedes, Hippolyta, second Lady, Magic Flute and Olga, Eugene Onegin, Cenerentola, Nicklausse (Hoffman); Glyndebourne début 1984, sang Nancy in Albert Herring and Mercedes in Carmen 1985; American début 1993; TV appearances in Così fan tutte and film on Handel; videos of Xerxes, Rigoletto, Lucretia, Carmen, Albert Herring; also sings concert repertoire and has made recordings with Giuseppe Sinopoli; Hon. FRAM 1989; Hon. Assoc. Birmingham Conservatoire 1996; numerous prizes and scholarships at RAM including Countess of Munster, Leverhulme, Peter Stuyvesant, RSA scholarships and the Prin.'s Prize; Royal Overseas League and Young Artists' Competition 1981. *Leisure interests:* theatre, sport, British heritage. *Address:* c/o Askonas Holt, Lonsdale Chambers, 27 Chancery Lane, London, WC2A 1PF, England.

RIGBY, Peter William Jack, MA, PhD; British medical research scientist; b. 7 July 1947, Savernake; s. of Jack Rigby and Lorna Rigby; m. 1st Paula Webb 1971 (divorced 1983); m. 2nd Julia Maidment 1985; one s.; ed Lower School of John Lyon, Harrow and Jesus Coll. Cambridge; mem. scientific staff, MRC Lab. of Molecular Biology, Cambridge 1971–73; Helen Hay Whitney Foundation Research Fellow, Stanford Univ. Medical School 1973–76; lecturer, Sr lecturer in Biochem. Imperial Coll. London 1976–83; Reader in Tumour Virology, Univ. of London 1983–86; Head, Genes and Cellular Controls Group and Div. of Eukaryotic Molecular Genetics, MRC Nat. Inst. for Medical Research 1986–99; Chief Exec. Inst. of Cancer Research, Univ. of London 1999–; mem. Science Council, Celltech Therapeutics 1982–; European Ed. Cell 1984–97; mem. Scientific Advisory Bd Somatix Therapy Corpn 1989–97, KuDos Pharmaceuticals 1999–; Scientific Cttee Cancer Research Campaign 1983–88, 1996–99; Chair. Scientific Advisory Bd.: Proflix 1996–99, Hexagen Tech. Ltd 1996–99; Carter Medal, Clinical Genetics Soc. 1994. *Publications:* papers on molecular biology in scientific journals. *Leisure interests:* narrow boats, listening to music, sport. *Address:* Chester Beatty Laboratories, Institute of Cancer Research, 237 Fulham Road, London, SW3 6JB, England (Office). *Telephone:* (20) 7878-3824 (Office).

RIGG, Dame (Enid) Diana (Elizabeth), DBE; British actress; b. 20 July 1938, Doncaster, Yorks.; d. of Louis Rigg and Beryl (Helliwell) Rigg; m. 1st Menahem Gueffen 1973 (divorced 1976); m. 2nd Archibald Hugh Stirling 1982 (divorced 1993); one d.; ed Fulneck Girls' School, Pudsey, Yorks, R.A.D.A; professional début as Natella Abashwilli (The Caucasian Chalk Circle), York Festival 1957; repertory Chesterfield and Scarborough 1958; Chair. MacRobert Arts Centre, Univ. of Stirling, Chancellor Univ. of Stirling 1997–; Prof. of Theatre Studies, Oxford Univ. 1998–; Dir United British Artists 1982–; a Vice-Pres. Baby Life Support Systems (BLISS) 1984–; Visiting Prof. of Contemporary Theatre Oxford Univ. 1999; mem. Arts Council Cttee 1986; mem. British Museum Devt Fund, Asscn for Business Sponsorship of the Arts; Assoc. Artist of RSC, Stratford and Aldwych 1962–79; mem. Nat. Theatre 1972; Dr. hc (Stirling Univ.) 1988; Hon. DLitt (Leeds) 1992, (South Bank) 1996; Plays and Players Award for Best Actress (Phaedra Britannica 1975, Night and Day 1978), BAFTA Award for Best Actress in Mother Love 1990, Evening Standard Award for Best Actress (Medea 1993, Mother Courage and Her Children 1996, Who's Afraid of Virginia Woolf? 1996), Tony Award for Best Actress in Medea 1994, Special Award for The Avengers, BAFTA 2000. *Roles with RSC include:* Andromache (Troilus and Cressida), 2nd Ondine, Violanta and Princess Bertha (Ondine), Philippe Trincant (The Devils), Gwendolen (Becket), Bianca (The Taming of the Shrew), Madame de Tourvel (The Art of Seduction), Helena (A Midsummer Night's Dream), Adriana (Comedy of Errors), Cordelia (King Lear), Nurse Monika Stettler (The Physicists), Lady Macduff (Macbeth); toured Eastern Europe, USSR, USA in King Lear, Comedy of Errors 1964; Viola (Twelfth Night), Stratford 1966. *Roles there included:* Dottie Moore (Jumpers) 1972, Hippolita ('Tis Pity She's A Whore) 1972, Lady Macbeth (Macbeth) 1972, Célimène (The Misanthrope), Washington and New York 1973, 1975, The Governor's Wife (Phaedra Britannica) 1975; rejoined Nat. Theatre at the Lyttelton to play Ilona in The Guardsman 1978. *Other stage appearances include:* Heloise (Abelard and Heloise) London 1970, LA, New York 1971, Eliza Doolittle (Pygmalion) London 1974, Ruth Carson (Night and Day) London 1978, Colette, Seattle and Denver 1982, Hesione Hushabye (Heartbreak House) London 1983, Rita in Little Eyolf, London 1985, Cleopatra in Antony and Cleopatra, Chichester 1985, Wildfire, London 1986, Phyllis in Follies 1987, Love Letters, San Francisco 1990, Cleopatra in All for Love, London 1991, Berlin Bertie 1992, Medea 1993 (London and Broadway), Mother Courage and Her Children, London, 1995, Who's Afraid of Virginia Woolf?, London 1996–97, Phèdre 1998, Britannicus 1998, Humble Boy 2001. *Television appearances include:* Sentimental Agent 1963, A Comedy of Errors 1964, The Hothouse 1964, Emma Peel (The Avengers) 1965–67, Women Beware Women 1965, Married Alive 1970, Diana (U.S. series) 1973, In This House of Brede 1975, Three Piece Suite 1977, Clytemnestra in The Serpent Son 1979, The Marquise 1980, Hedda Gabler 1981, Rita Allmers in Little Eyolf 1982, Regan in King Lear 1983, Witness for the Prosecution 1983, Bleak House 1984, Host, Held in Trust, A Hazard of Hearts 1987, Worst Witch 1987, Unexplained Laughter 1989, Mother Love 1989, Host, Mystery! 1989 (USA), Zoya 1995, The Haunting of Helen Walker 1995, Moll Flanders 1996, Samson & Delilah 1996, Rebecca 1996 (Emmy Award for Best Supporting Actress 1997). *Films include:* A Midsummer Night's Dream 1969, The Assassination Bureau 1969, On Her Majesty's Secret Service 1969, Julius Caesar 1970, The Hospital 1971, Theatre of Blood 1973, A Little Night Music 1977, The Great Muppet Caper 1981, Evil under the Sun 1982, A Good Man in Africa 1993. *Publications:* No Turn Unstoned 1982, So To The Land 1994. *Leisure interests:* reading, writing, cooking, travel. *Address:* c/o ARG, 4 Great Portland Street, London, W1W 8PA, England (Office).

RIGGIO, Leonard; American business executive; b. 1941, NY; m. (divorced); two d.; ed Brooklyn Tech. High School, New York Univ.; fmrly with New York Univ. campus bookstore; opened Waverly Student Book Exchange 1965; acquired Barnes & Noble Bookstore 1971, Chair., CEO Barnes & Noble Inc. 1986–; Chair. of Bd, Prin. Beneficial Owner Software Etc. Stores, Mpls, MBS Textbook Exchange, Inc. *Address:* MBS Textbook Exchange Inc., 2711 West Ash Street, Columbia, MO 65205; c/o Barnes & Noble Inc., 122 5th Avenue, New York, NY 10011, USA.

RIGGS, Lorrin Andrews, AB, MA, PhD; American psychologist; b. 11 June 1912, Harput, Turkey; s. of Ernest Wilson Riggs and Alice Riggs (née Shepard); m. 1st Doris Robinson 1937 (died 1993); two s.; m. 2nd Caroline Cressman 1994; ed Dartmouth Coll. and Clark Univ.; NRC Fellow, Biological Sciences, Univ. of Pa 1936–37; Instructor Univ. of Vermont 1937–38, 1939–41; with Brown Univ. 1938–39, 1941–, Research Assoc., Research Psychologist Nat. Defense Research Cttee, Asst Prof., Assoc. Prof. 1938–51, Prof. of Psychology 1951–, L. Herbert Ballou Foundation Prof. of Psychology 1960–68, Edgar J. Marston Univ. Prof. of Psychology 1968–77, Prof. Emer. 1977–; Guggenheim Fellow, Univ. of Cambridge 1971–72; mem. American Psychological Asscn (Div. Pres. 1962–63), Eastern Psychological Asscn (Pres. 1975–76), AAAS (Chair. and Vice-Pres. Section 1 1964), Optical Soc. of America, NAS, American Physiological Soc., Int. Brain Research Org., Soc. for Neuroscience, Soc. of Experimental Psychologists, American Acad. of Arts and Sciences, Asscn for Research in Vision and Ophthalmology (Pres. 1977); William James Fellow, American Psychological Soc. 1989; Hon. DSc (Brown Univ.) 2001; Howard Crosby Warren Medal, Soc. of Experimental Psychologists 1957, Jonas S. Friedenwald Award, Asscn for Research in Ophthalmology 1966, Edgar D. Tillyer Award, Optical Soc. of America 1969, Charles F. Prentice Award, American Acad. of Optometry 1973, Distinguished Scientific Contribution Award, American Psychological Asscn 1974, Kenneth Craik Award, Cambridge Univ. 1979, Frederick Ives Medal, Optical Soc. of America 1982. *Publications:* numerous scientific articles on vision and physiological psychology. *Address:* 80 Lyme Road, Hanover, NH 03755, USA. *Telephone:* (603) 643-2342. *E-mail:* clriggs@bigplanet.com (Home).

RIIS, Povl, MD, DM, FRCP; Danish physician and editor; b. 28 Dec. 1925, Copenhagen; s. of Lars Otto Riis and Eva Elisabeth (née Erdmann) Riis; m. Else Harne 1954 (died 1997); one s. three d.; ed Univ. of Copenhagen; specialist in internal medicine 1960, gastroenterology 1963; Head of Medical Dept B, Gentofte Univ. Hosp. 1963–76; Prof. of Internal Medicine, Univ. of Copenhagen 1974–, Vice-Dean Faculty of Medicine 1979–82; Head of Gastroenterological Dept C, Herlev Co. Hosp. 1976–96; Asst Ed. Journal of the Danish Medical Asscn 1957–67, Chief Ed. 1967–90; Ed. Bibliothek for Laeger 1965–90, Danish Medical Bulletin 1968–90, Nordic Medicine 1984–91; mem. Bd, Danish Soc. for Internal Medicine 1962–67, Danish Anti-Cancer League 1970–75, Danish Soc. for Theoretical and Applied Therapy 1972–77, Int. Union against Cancer 1978–86; mem. Danish Medical Research Council 1968–74, Chair. 1972–74; mem. Danish Science Advisory Bd 1972–74, Co-Chair. 1974; mem. Nordic Scientific Co-ordination Cttee for Medicine 1968–72, Chair. 1970–72; Chair. Nordic Medical Publs Cttee 1970–72; Vice-Pres. European Science Foundation (ESF) 1974–77, mem. Exec. Council 1977–83; Chair. ESF Cttee on Genetic Manipulation 1975–77, Chair. ESF Liaison Cttee on Genetic Manipulation 1977–83; mem. Council for Int. Org. of Medical Sciences Advisory Cttee 1977; mem. Trustees Foundation of 1870 1976, Trier-Hansen Foundation 1977, Hartmann Prize Cttee 1986–2002, Buhl Olesen Foundation 1982, Madsen Foundation 1978, Jakobsen Foundation 1989, Brinch Foundation 1990–96; Chair. Danish Central Scientific-Ethical Cttee 1979–98, Nat. Medical Bd Danish Red Cross 1985–94, Int. Org. of Inflammatory Bowel Diseases 1986–89; mem. Nat. Cttee on Scientific Misconduct 1992–99; Danish Foreign Office del. Helsinki negotiations, Hamburg 1980; mem. Bd Danish Helsinki Cttee; mem. Nuffield Foundation Working Party on Ethics 1999–, Ethical Collegial Council, Danish Dental Asscn 2000–, Ethical Collegial Council, Danish Medical Asscn 2000–; mem. Medical Advisory Bd NetDoktor 1999–; Evaluator EU 1999–; Adviser Augustinus Foundation 1999; mem. Int. Cttee of Medical Journal Eds 1980–90, Editorial Bd, Acta Medicina Scandinavica, Journal Int. Medicine 1980, Ethics Bd, Danish Medical Asscn 1980–82, WHO European Advisory Cttee for Medical Research 1980–85, Scientific Bd, Danish Nat. Encyclopaedia 1991–2001, Editorial Bd JAMA 1994–; Chair. Nat. Medical Bd of Danish Red Cross; Chair. Nat. Center for First Aid and Health Promotion –1991, Age-Forum 1996–; Hon. mem. Icelandic Medical Asscn 1978, Danish Soc. of Gastroenterology 1995; Hon. MRCP (UK) 1991; Hon. DMed (Univ. of Odense) 1996, (Gothenburg); Alfred Benzon Prize, August Krogh Prize 1974, Christensen-Ceson Prize 1976, Klein-Prize 1980, Barfred-Pedersen Prize 1980, Hagedorn Prize 1983, Nordic Gastro Prize 1983, Nordic Language Prize in Medicine 1993, Danish Prize of Honour in Research Ethics 2003. *Pub-*

lications: Contributor: Handbook of Scientific Methodology (in Danish) 1971–, World Medical Asscn Helsinki Declaration 1975, We Shall All Die—but how? (in Danish) 1977; Author: Handbook of Internal Medicine (in Danish) 1968, Grenzen der Forschung 1980; Community and Ethics (in Danish) 1984, Medical Ethics (in Danish) 1985, Ethical Issues in Preventive Medicine 1985, Medical Science and the Advancement of World Health 1985, Bearing and Perspective 1988, The Appleton Consensus 1988, Face Death 1989, Ethics in Health Education 1990, The Future of Medical Journals 1991, Research on Man: Ethics and Law 1991, Scientific Misconduct—Good Scientific Practice 1992, Health Care in Europe after 1992 1992, A Better Health Service–but how? (in Danish), The Culture of General Education 1996, Drugs and Pharmacotherapy 1997, The Time That Followed (in Danish) 1998, Ethics and Clinical Medicine (in Danish) 1998, Can Our Nat Heritage Survive? (in Danish) 1999, Frailty in Aging (in Danish) 1999, Ethics and Evidence-based Pharmacotherapy 2000, Can We Not Do It A Little Better? 2000, In That We Believe 2001, Fraud and Misconduct in Biomedical Research 2001, The Ethics of Research Related to Health Care in Developing Countries 2002; 32 Age Forum publs 1996–2002; many articles in medical journals; lyrics to contemporary Danish compositions, trans. of lyrics. *Leisure interests:* tennis, music, mountain walking, botany. *Address:* Nerievej 7, 2900 Hellerup, Denmark (Home). *Telephone:* 39629688. *Fax:* 39629588.

RIKLIS, Meshulam, MBA; American business executive; b. 2 Dec. 1923, Istanbul, Turkey; s. of Pinhas Riklis and Betty (Guberer) Riklis; m. 1st Judith Stern 1944; one s. two d.; m. 2nd Pia Zadora 1977; one s. one d.; ed High School, Israel, Univ. of Mexico and Ohio State Univ.; Co-Dir Youth Activities and Mil. Training, Hertzlia High School, Tel Aviv 1942; went to U.S. 1947, naturalized 1955; Teacher of Hebrew, Talmud Torah School, Minneapolis 1951; Research Dept, Piper, Jaffray and Hopwood 1951–53, Sales Rep. 1953–56; Chair., CEO Rapid Electrotype Co., American Color-type Co. 1956–57; Pres. Rapid-American Corpn 1957–73, CEO 1957, Chair. 1958, Pres., CEO 1957–73, Chair., CEO 1973–76, Chair., Pres., CEO 1976–; Vice-Chair. McCrory Corpn 1960–69, Vice-Chair. Exec. Cttee and Dir 1970–, Chair. 1975–85; owner Riviera Hotel, Las Vegas. *Address:* Riklis Family Corporation, 2901 Las Vegas blvd, Las Vegas, NV 89109; McCrory Corpn, 1700 Broadway, Suite 1403, New York, NY 10019, USA.

RILEY, Bridget Louise, CH, CBE, ARCA; British artist; b. 24 April 1931, London; d. of John Fisher and the late Bessie Louise (née Gladstone) Riley; ed Cheltenham Ladies' Coll., Goldsmiths Coll. of Art and Royal Coll. of Art, London; first one-woman exhbn in London at Gallery One 1962, followed by others in England, America, Switzerland, Australia and Japan; has exhibited in group shows in Australia, Italy, France, Holland, Germany, Israel, America, Japan and Argentina; represented Great Britain at Biennale des Jeunes, Paris 1965, at Venice Biennale 1968; retrospective exhbn Europe and UK 1970–72; second retrospective exhbn touring America, Australia and Japan 1978–80; Arts Council Touring Exhbn 1984–85; paintings, drawings and prints in public collections in England, Ireland, Switzerland, Netherlands, Austria, Germany, Japan, Israel, America, Australia and New Zealand; founder mem. and fmr Dir SPACE Ltd; mem. RSA; Trustee, Nat. Gallery 1981–88; Hon. Dr of Letters (Manchester Univ.) 1976, (Exeter) 1997, Dr hc (Ulster) 1986, (Oxford) 1993, (Cambridge) 1995, (De Montfort) 1996. Hon. DLitt (Cambridge) 1995; AICA Critics Prize 1963; Prize in Open Section, John Moores Liverpool Exhbn 1963; Peter Stuyvesant Foundation Travel Bursary to USA 1964; Maj. Painting Prize, Venice Biennale 1968; Prize at Tokyo Print Biennale 1971; Gold Medal at Grafikk-bienniale, Fredrikstad, Norway 1980. *Address:* c/o Karsten Schubert, 47 Lexington Street, London, W1R 3LG, England (Office).

RILEY, Richard Wilson, LLB; American politician and lawyer; b. 2 Jan. 1933, Greenville, South Carolina; s. of E. P. and Martha Dixon Riley; m. Ann Yarborough 1957; three s. one d.; ed Greenville Sr High School, Furman Univ. and SC School of Law; Lt in US Navy; Legal Counsel to US Senate Cttee of Olin D. Johnston 1960; with family law firm 1961–62; mem. SC House of Reps 1962–66, SC Senate 1966–76; SC State Chair. for Jimmy Carter's Presidential Election Campaign 1976; Gov. of SC 1979–87; Personnel Dir for Bill Clinton's Transition Team 1991–92; Sec. of Educ. 1993–2001; Partner Nelson, Mullins, Riley & Scarborough 1987–93, 2001–; Distinguished Visiting Prof., Univ. of SC 2001–; several awards. *Address:* Nelson, Mullins, Riley & Scarborough, Suite 900, Poinsett Plaza, 104 South Main Street, Greenville, SC 29601, USA (Office).

RILEY, Robert, BA; American state official; b. 3 Oct. 1944, Ashland, Ala; m. Patsy Adams; one s. three d.; ed Clay Co. High School, Univ. of Ala; fmr propr of poultry and egg business, automobile dealership, trucking co. grocery store and pharmacy; mem. Ashland City Council 1972–76; mem. House of Reps, Ala 1996–2002, Asst Whip.; Gov. of Ala 2003–; mem. First Baptist Church, Masons, Shriners, Jaycees. *Address:* Office of the Governor, State Capitol, 600 Dexter Avenue, Suite N104, Montgomery, AL 36130, USA (Office).

RILEY, Saxon; British business executive; b. 1938; Cornhill Insurance Co. 1955–61; Scholfields 1961–64; Price Forbes, Johannesburg 1964–70; Dir Sedgwick Group PLC 1985, mem. Exec. Cttee 1988, Vice-Chair. 1990, Group Man. Dir, CEO 1992–, Chair. 1997–; Chair. Sedgwick Broking Services Ltd 1989; Dir Marsh and McLennan Cos Inc.; mem. Council of Lloyd's 1999–, Deputy Chair. Lloyds of London Jan.–Dec. 2000, Chair. 2001–02. *Address:* c/o Lloyds of London, 1 Lime Street, London, EC3M 7HA, England (Office); Sackville House, 143-152 Fenchurch Street, London, EC3M 6BN, England.

RILEY, Terence; American museum curator; ed Univ. of Notre Dame and Columbia Univ., New York; f. architectural practice with John Keenen; curator of 'Paul Nelson Filter of Reason' inaugural exhbn at Arthur Ross Architectural Galleries, Columbia Univ. 1989, Dir –1991; directed exhbns. on work of Iacov Chernikhov and restaging of Museum of Modern Art's (MoMA) first exhbn on architecture: 'Exhibition 15: The International Style and The Museum of Modern Art', New York; adjunct faculty mem. 1987–; joined MoMA 1991, Chief Curator of Architecture and Design 1992–, organized exhbns on the works of, amongst others, Frank Lloyd Wright, Rem Koolhaas 1994, Bernard Tschumi, Mies van der Rohe 2001; Instructor, Harvard Design School 2001–. *Publications include:* The Un-Private House (jtly with Glenn D. Lowry) 2002, MoMA QNS Box Set 2002; The Changing of the Avant-garde (Ed.) 2002. *Address:* The Museum of Modern Art, 11 West 53rd Street, New York, NY 10019, USA (Office). *Website:* www.moma.org (Office).

RILEY, Terry Mitchell, MA; American composer, pianist and raga singer; b. 24 June 1935, Colfax, Calif.; s. of Wilma Ridlofi and Charles Riley; m. Ann Yvonne Smith 1958; three c.; ed San Francisco State Univ. and Univ. of California and pvt. studies with Duane Hampton, Adolf Baller and Pandit Pran Nath; taught music composition and N Indian Raga at Mills Coll. 1971–83; freelance composer and performer 1961–; launched Minimal Music Movt with composition and first performance of In C 1964; John Simon Guggenheim Prize 1980. *Compositions include:* The Harp of New Albion for Solo Piano in Just Intonation, Salome Dances for Peace (string quartet), Cadenza on the Night Plain, Sunrise of the Planetary Dream Collector, Sri Camel, a Rainbow in Curved Air, In C, The Ten Voices of the Two Prophets, Persian Surgery Dervishes, Jade Palace (for large orchestra) 1989, June Buddhas 1991, The Sounds (concerto for string quartet and orchestra) 1991, The Saint Adolf Ring (chamber opera) 1992, Ritmos and Melos 1993, El Hombre (piano quintet) 1993, Ascension (solo guitar) 1993, The Heaven Ladder 1996, Three Requiem Quarters 1997, Autodreamographical Tales 1997. *Leisure interests:* music, gardens and orchards. *Address:* c/o ASCAP, ASCAP Building, 1 Lincoln Plaza, New York, NY 10023; 13699 Moonshine Road, Camptonville, CA 95922, USA. *Telephone:* (916) 288-3522. *Fax:* (916) 288-3468.

RILLING, Helmuth, DPhil, DTheol; German conductor, professor of music and church music director; b. 29 May 1933, Stuttgart; s. of Eugen Rilling and Hildegard Plieninger; m. Martina Greiner 1967; two d.; ed protestant theological seminars of Schöntal and Urach, Staatliche Hochschule für Musik, Stuttgart; studied organ with Fernando Germani, Conservatorio di Santa Cecilia, Rome and conducting with Leonard Bernstein, New York; organist and choirmaster, Gedächtniskirche, Stuttgart 1957–98; taught organ and conducting, Berliner Kirchenmusikschule, Berlin-Spandau and Dir. Spandauer Kantorei 1963–66; Prof. of Conducting, Staatliche Hochschule für Musik, Frankfurt 1966–85; taught at Ind. Univ., Bloomington, USA 1976–77; Dir Frankfurter Kantorei 1969–81; f. Summer Festival (now Oregon Bach Festival), Eugene, USA 1970–; Founder and Dir Gächinger Kantorei, Stuttgart 1954–, Figuralchor of the Gedächtniskirche, Stuttgart 1957–80, Bach-Collegium Stuttgart 1965–, Festival Choir and Orchestra 2001–, Sommer Acad. Johann Sebastian Bach Stuttgart 1979–99, Int. Bach Acad. Stuttgart 1981–, Bach Acad. Tokyo, Buenos Aires 1983, Santiago de Compostela, Spain, Prague, Cracow, Moscow, Budapest, Caracas; Chief Conductor, Real Filarmonía de Galicia, Santiago de Compostela, Spain 1996–2000; worldwide int. appearances with own ensembles and as guest conductor and guest prof.; regular co-operation with Israel Philharmonic Orchestra, The Cleveland Orchestra, Boston Symphony Orchestra, Minnesota Orchestra, LA Philharmonic, Toronto Symphony Orchestra, New York Philharmonic, Vienna Philharmonic Orchestra, Münchner Philharmoniker, Radio-Sinfonie-Orchester Munich; mem. Kungl. Musikaliska Akad. Stockholm 1993; Hon. DFA (Concordia Coll., USA) 1990; Dr hc (Univ. of Oregon) 1999; Distinguished Service Award (Univ. of Oregon) 1985, Harvard Glee Club Medal 1989, UNESCO/IMC Music Prize 1994, Theodor-Heuss Prize 1995, Int. Prize Compostela 1999, Grammy Award (Best Choral Performance) 2000. *Recordings:* all the sacred cantatas and oratorios of J. S. Bach 1985, complete recording of J. S. Bach's work 1998–2000 and many others. *Publications:* Johann Sebastian Bach, Matthäus-Passion, Einführung und Studienanleitung 1975, Johann Sebastian Bach's h-moll-Messe 1975. *Address:* Internationale Bachakademie Stuttgart, Johann-Sebastian-Bach-Platz (Hasenbergsteige 3), 70178 Stuttgart, Germany (Office). *Telephone:* (711) 6192113 (Office). *Fax:* (711) 6192123 (Office). *E-mail:* rita.rupp@bachakademie.de (Office). *Website:* www.bachakademie.de (Office).

RIMAWI, Fahd Namr ar-, BA; Jordanian journalist; b. 1942, Palestine; m.; two s. one d.; ed Cairo Univ., Egypt; Ed. Difa (newspaper) 1965–67; Ed. in Chief, Jordan News Agency 1968–70; Sec. Editorial Bd of Afkar (magazine) 1970–73; Dir Investigating Dept of Al-Raiue (newspaper) 1975–76; writer Al-Destour (newspaper) 1978–81; Political writer, Al-Raiue (newspaper) 1981–85; Corresp. al Talie'ah (magazine) Paris 1982–85; political writer 1985–94; Publr and Ed.-in-Chief Al Majd (weekly). *Publications:* Mawaweel Fi al Layl Al Taweel, short stories in Arabic 1982. *Address:* P.O. Box 926856, Amman 1111, Jordan. *Telephone:* (6) 5530553 (Office); (6) 5160615 (Home). *Fax:* (6) 553 0352.

RIMINGTON, Dame Stella, DCB, MA; British civil servant; b. 1935; m. John Rimington 1963; two d.; ed Nottingham High School for Girls, Edinburgh Univ.; Dir-Gen. Security Service 1992–96; Dir (non-exec.) Marks and Spencer 1997–, BG PLC 1997–2000, BG Group 2000–, G.K.R. Group (now Whitehead

Mann GKR) 1997–2001; Chair. Inst. of Cancer Research 1997–2001; Hon. Air Commodore 7006 (VR) Squadron Royal Auxiliary Air Force 1997–2001; Hon. LLB (Nottingham) 1995, (Exeter) 1996. *Publications:* Open Secret 2001. *Address:* P.O. Box 1604, London, SW1P 1XB, England.

RIMSEVICS, Ilmars, BA, MBA; Latvian central banker and economist; b. 30 April 1965, Riga; ed Riga High School No. 6, Riga Tech. Univ., St Lawrence Univ., USA and Clarkson Univ., USA; Deputy Chair. Econs Cttee, Popular Front of Latvia 1989–90; Man. Foreign Operations Dept and Head of Securities Dept Latvijas Zemes Banka 1990–92; Deputy Gov. Bank of Latvia 1992–2001, Chair. Exec. Bd 1992–, Gov. Dec. 2001–. *Address:* Bank of Latvia, 2A Valdemara Street, 1050 Riga, Latvia (Office). *Telephone:* (2) 7022-260 (Office). *Fax:* (2) 7022-268 (Office). *E-mail:* governor@bank.lv (Office). *Website:* www.bank.lv (Office).

RINDLER, Wolfgang, PhD; British university professor; b. 18 May 1924, Vienna; s. of Dr Ernst Rindler; m. 1st Phyllis Berla 1959 (died 1966); m. 2nd Linda Veret 1977; two s. one d.; ed Ruthin Grammar School, Liverpool Univ., Imperial Coll., London; asst lecturer Univ. of Liverpool 1947–49; lecturer Sir John Cass Coll., London 1949–56; Asst Prof. Cornell Univ., USA 1956–63; Assoc. and Full Prof. Southwest Center for Advanced Studies, Dallas, Texas 1963–69, Prof. Univ. of Texas at Dallas 1969–; Visiting Prof. Univ. of Vienna, Univ. of Rome, Max-Planck Inst. at Munich and Potsdam, King's Coll. London; Visiting Fellow Churchill Coll., Cambridge 1990; mem. Foreign Editorial Bd Rendiconti di Matematica 1984–; Assoc. Ed. American Journal of Physics 1988–91; Foreign mem. Acad. of Sciences of Turin, Italy 2000; Hon. mem. Austrian Acad. of Sciences 1998; Gold Medal of Honour, City of Vienna 1996. *Publications:* Special Relativity 1960, Essential Relativity 1969, Introduction to Special Relativity 1982, Spinors and Space-Time (with R. Penrose) Vol. I 1984, Vol. II 1986, Relativity: Special, General, and Cosmological 2001, numerous research and encyclopedia articles on special and gen. relativity and cosmology. *Address:* Physics Department, University of Texas at Dallas, Richardson, TX 75083-0688 (Office); 7110 Spring Valley Road, Dallas, TX 75254, USA (Home). *Telephone:* (972) 883-2880 (Office); (972) 387-9768 (Home). *E-mail:* rindler@utdallas.edu (Office).

RING, Wolfhard, Dr rer. nat; German business executive; b. 15 April 1930, Cologne; m. Karina Hellmann 1968; two s.; ed Univs of Göttingen and Karlsruhe; Research Asst Univ. of S. Carolina; Chemie-Konzern Hüls AG, Marl 1960, Dir of Research and Devt 1981, Exec. Vice-Pres. and mem. Bd Dirs. Hüls America Inc. 1985; mem. Bd Rütgerswerke AG 1989, Chair. Bd 1989–95; Visiting Prof. Univ. of Münster 1977–. *Leisure interests:* music, history, modern art.

RINPOCHE, Samdhong; Tibetan academic and politician; b. 5 Nov. 1939, Nagdug, Tibet; ed monastic studies, Univ. of Drepung, Tibet (rehoused in India after Chinese occupation), Monastery of Gyuto, Dalhousie, India; various positions in Tibetan colls in Simla, Darjeeling and Dalhousie, India; Vice-Pres. Congress of Tibetan Youth 1970–73; joined Cen. Inst. for High Tibetan Studies, Benares (now Varanasi), India 1971, apptd Dir 1988; mem. Standing Cttee Asscn of Indian Univs 1994–, Pres. 1998–; fmr Pres. Tibetan Parl. in Exile; elected Chair. Tibetan Govt in Exile 2001; Vice-Pres. Library of Tibetan Works and Files, Dharamsala, India; Adviser World Peace Univ., USA; mem. Cttee for Charter of Tibetans in Exile and Future Constitution of Tibet; mem. Bd Dirs Tibetan Schools, New Delhi, India; mem. Bd Dirs Asiatic Soc., Calcutta; mem. Bd Dirs Foundation for Universal Responsibility, New Delhi; mem. Directorate of Indian Council for Philosophical Research; mem. Directorate Krishnamurti Foundation, India; Advisory mem. Inst. of Asian Democracy, NY, USA. *Publications include:* numerous academic essays and newspaper articles. *Address:* c/o The Kashag, Exchange Tibetan Secretariat, POB Dharamsala 176215, Dist Kangra, H.P., India (Office).

RINTZLER, Marius Adrian; German opera and concert singer; b. 14 March 1932, Bucharest, Romania; m. Sanda Dragomir 1964; ed Acad. of Music, Bucharest; soloist with Bucharest Philharmonic 1959; début in opera in Bucharest as Don Basilio in Il Barbiere di Siviglia 1964; went to Germany 1966; leading bass at Düsseldorf's Deutsche Oper am Rhein 1968–; guest singer with major opera cos., including Metropolitan, San Francisco, Glyndebourne, Paris, Brussels, Munich; repertoire includes various roles in Richard Strauss' Rosenkavalier (Ochs), Capriccio (La Roche), Schweigsame Frau (Morosus), in Rossini's La Cenerentola (Don Magnifico), Il Barbiere (Bartolo), in Richard Wagner's Ring (Alberich), in Mozart's Don Giovanni (Leporello), Die Entführung (Osmin); appears with major symphony orchestras in Europe and USA, including Philharmonia (London), Berlin Philharmonic, Cleveland Symphony; also gives recitals, TV appearances in England, Germany and France; Kammersänger. *Address:* Friedingstrasse 18, 40625 Düsseldorf, Germany. *Telephone:* (211) 297083.

RIORDAN, Richard, JD; American politician and business executive; b. 1930, Flushing, NY; m. 1st Eugenia Riordan; six c. (two deceased); m. 2nd Jill Riordan; ed Univ. of Calif., Santa Clara, Princeton Univ., Univ. of Michigan; Mayor of LA 1993–2001; Co-founder LEARN 1991; mem. Republican Party. *Address:* c/o Los Angeles City Hall, 200 North Main Street, Room 800, Los Angeles, CA 90012, USA (Office).

RÍOS, Juan; Peruvian poet, dramatist, journalist and critic; b. 28 Sept. 1914, Barranco, Lima; s. of Rogelio Ríos and Victoria Rey (de Ríos); m. Rosa Saco 1946; one d.; Writers' Fellowship, UNESCO, Europe and Egypt 1960–61; mem. Academia Peruana de la Lengua Correspondiente a la Española; Nat.

Prize for Playwriting 1946, 1950, 1952, 1954, 1960; Nat. Poetry Prize 1948, 1953. *Publications:* Canción de Siempre 1941, Malstrom 1941, La Pintura Contemporánea en el Perú 1946, Teatro (I) 1961, Ayar Manko 1963, Primera Antología Poética 1982. *Address:* Bajada de Baños 109, Barranco, Lima 04, Peru. *Telephone:* (14) 671799.

RÍOS MONTT, Gen. Efraín; Guatemalan politician and army officer (retd); b. 1927; joined army 1943; defence posting, Washington, DC 1973; contested presidential election for Christian Democratic coalition 1974; Mil. Attaché, Madrid; fmr Commdr Honour Guard Brigade; Dir Mil. Acad.; installed as leader of mil. junta after coup March 1982; Minister of Nat. Defence March–Sept. 1982; Pres. of Guatemala, also C-in-C of the Army 1982–83; overthrown Aug. 1983; leader Frente Republicano Guatemalteco (F.R.G.); Pres. of Guatemalan Congress 1995–96, 2001–. *Address:* Frente Republicano Guatemalteco, 3a Calle 5-50, Zona 1, Guatemala City; Congreso Nacional, Guatemala City, Guatemala. *Telephone:* 238-0826 (FRG). *Website:* www.frg .com.gt (Office).

RIPA DI MEANA, Carlo; Italian politician and journalist; b. 15 Aug. 1929, Marina di Pietrasanta, Lucca; m. 1st Gae Aulenti (divorced); m. 2nd Marina Punturieri; journalist on Il Lavoro (weekly journal of the Confederazione Generale Italiana del Lavoro) and on L'Unità (Italian daily) 1950–53; co-f. and ran weekly Nuova Generazione 1953–56; co-f. and Ed. magazine Passato e Presente 1957; publisher's ed. for Feltrinelli and Rizzoli 1958–66; resgnd from Italian CP 1957, joined Italian Socialist Party (PSI) 1958; Sec.-Gen. Club Turati, Milan 1967–76; Regional Councillor, Lombardy, Leader, Socialist Party group in the Council 1970–82; mem. Bd La Scala Theatre, Milan 1970–74; Chair. Venice Biennale 1974–79; head of int. relations, Italian Socialist Party 1979–80; MEP 1979–; mem. Comm. of the European Communities (responsible for Citizen's Europe, information, culture and tourism) 1985–89, (responsible for communication) 1986–89, (responsible for environment, nuclear safety and civil protection) 1989–93; Minister for the Environment 1992–93, leader Green Party 1993–98 (left PSI); Chair. Istituto per la Cooperazione economica internazionale e i problemi dello sviluppo 1983–. *Publications:* Un viaggio in Viet Nam 1956, Dedicato a Raymond Roussel e alle sue impressioni d'Africa 1965, Il governo audiovisivo 1973. *Address:* European Parliament, Centre Européen, Plateau du Kirchberg, 2929 Luxembourg, Luxembourg.

RIPKEN, Calvin Edward (Cal), Jr; American professional baseball player; b. 24 Aug. 1960, Havre de Grace, Md; s. of the late Cal Ripken Sr; m. Kelly Ripken; one s. one d.; ed Aberdeen High School, Md; player minor league teams in Bluefield, Miami, Charlotte, Rochester 1978–81; player Baltimore Orioles 1978–2001; highest single season fielding percentage 1990; maj. league record for consecutive games played (breaking Lou Gehrig's record of 2,131 in 1995), 2,632 ending in 1998; 4,000 home runs, 3,000 hits (2000); retd 2001; f. The Kelly and Cal Ripken, Jr Foundation 1992; Rookie of the Year, Int. League 1981, Rookie of the Year, Baseball Writers Asscn, American League 1982, Silver Slugger Award 1983–86, 1989, 1991, 1993–94, Golden Glove Award 1991–92, Sportsman of the Year, Sports Illustrated 1995; numerous other awards. *Address:* c/o Baltimore Orioles, Oriole Park at Camden Yards, 333 West Camden Street, Baltimore, MD 21201, USA.

RIPPON, Angela; British broadcaster and journalist; b. 12 Oct. 1944, Plymouth, Devon; d. of John Rippon and Edna Rippon; m. Christopher Dare 1967 (divorced); ed Plymouth Selective School for Girls; Presenter and Reporter, BBC TV Plymouth 1966–69; Ed., Producer, Dir and Presenter, Westward TV (ITV) 1969–73; Reporter, BBC TV Nat. News 1973–75, Newsreader 1975–81; Founder and Presenter TV-am Feb.–April 1983; Arts Corresp. for WNETV (CBS), Boston, 1983; Reporter and Presenter BBC and ITV 1984–; Vice-Pres. Int. Club for Women in TV 1979–, British Red Cross, NCH Action for Children, Riding for the Disabled Asscn; Dir Nirex 1986–; Chair. English Nat., Ballet 2000–; Dr hc (American Int. Univ.) 1994; New York Film Festival Silver Medal 1973, Newsreader of the Year (TV and Radio Industries Club) 1975, 1976, 1977, TV Personality of the Year 1977, Emmy Award 1984 (Channel 7 Boston), Sony Radio Award 1990, New York Radio Silver Medal 1992, Royal TV Soc. Hall of Fame 1996, European Woman of Achievement 2002 and other awards. *Television appearances include:* Angela Rippon Meets (documentary), Antiques Roadshow, In the Country, Compere, Eurovision Song Contest 1976, The Morecombe and Wise Christmas Show 1976, 1977, Royal Wedding 1981, Masterteam (BBC) 1985, 1986, 1987, Come Dancing 1988–, What's My Line? 1988–, Healthcheck, Holiday Programme, Simply Money (Family Finance Channel) 2001–, Channel 5 News 2003–. *Radio series include:* Angela Rippon's Morning Report for LBC 1992, Angela Rippon's Drive Time Show, LBC 1993, The Health Show (BBC Radio 4), Friday Night with Angela Rippon (BBC Radio 2), LBC Arts Programme 2003–. *Publications:* Riding 1980, In the Country 1980, Mark Phillips—The Man and his Horses 1982, Victoria Plum (eight children's books) 1983, Angela Rippon's West Country 1982, Badminton: A Celebration 1987. *Leisure interests:* cooking, tennis, reading, theatre. *Address:* Knight Ayton, 114 St. Martin's Lane, London, WC2N 4AZ, England (Office). *Telephone:* (20) 7287-4405 (Office).

RISCHEL, Jørgen, MA, DPhil; Danish professor of linguistics and phonetics; b. 10 Aug. 1934, Kullerup; s. of Ejner Rischel and Gunnild Rischel; m. Anna-Grethe Rischel 1961; three d.; ed Univs of Copenhagen, Iceland and Oslo; lecturer in Danish, Univ. of Bergen, Norway 1960–61; Assoc. Ed. Norwegian-English Dictionary Project, Univ. of Wis. 1961–62; Asst Prof., later Assoc.

Prof. Univ. of Copenhagen 1963–78, Prof. of Linguistics 1978–81, Prof. of Phonetics 1981–98, Prof. Emer. 1998–; Visiting Prof. Univ. of Calif. 1978; research work in SE Asia 1982–; Co-Ed. Acta Linguistica Hafniensia to 1996; Mem. Bd Folia Linguistica and Int. Journal of American Linguistics; Dir Int. Critical Pali Dictionary project 1996–99; mem. Royal Danish Acad. of Sciences and Letters 1978–, Acad. Europaea 1989; mem. Danish Research Council for the Humanities 1988–90, Comm. for Scientific Research in Greenland 1990–99, Comité Int. Permanent de Linguistes 1990–; Gold Medal, Univ. of Copenhagen 1958; Kt, Order of Dannebrog. *Publications:* The Lepchas (with Halfdan Siiger) Vol. II 1967, Topics in West Greenlandic Phonology (Essay) 1974, Pioneers of Eskimo Grammar (with Knut Bergsland) 1987, Minor Mlabri — A Hunter-Gatherer Language of Northern Indochina 1995, Aspects of Danish Prosody (with Hans Basbøll) 1995, In Honour of Eli Fischer-Jørgensen (with Anna Grønnum) 2001; co-author of dictionaries of various languages and ed. of scientific publs works on the Faroe Islands. *Leisure interests:* enjoying the world's ethnic and cultural diversity. *Address:* Institute of General and Applied Linguistics, University of Copenhagen, 80 Njalsgade, 2300 Copenhagen S (Office); 57 Stenhøjgaardsvej, 3460 Birkerød, Denmark (Home). *Telephone:* 816803 (Home). *Fax:* 816808. *E-mail:* jr@cphling.dk (Office).

RISTE, Olav, DPhil; Norwegian historian; b. 11 April 1933, Volda; s. of Olav Riste and Bergliot Meidell; m. Ruth Pittman 1964; ed Univs of Oslo and Oxford; lecturer, Volda Gymnas 1963–64; Historian, Office of Mil. History (with leaves of absence) 1964–79, Dir 1979–80; Research Fellow, Charles Warren Center, Harvard Univ. 1967–68; Visiting Scholar, LSE 1971, 1986; Visiting Prof. Freie Univ. Berlin 1972–73; Dir Research Centre for Defence History (with leaves of absence) 1980–87; Adjunct Prof. of History, Univ. of Bergen 1980–2003, Univ. of Oslo 1998–2003; Guest Scholar, Woodrow Wilson Center, Washington, DC 1982; Dir Norwegian Inst. for Defence Studies 1988–95, Research Dir 1996–2003; Fellow, Norwegian Acad. of Science and Letters 1984. *Publications:* The Neutral Ally 1965, Norway and the Second World War (ed.) 1966, Norway 1940–45: The Resistance Movement 1970, London-regjeringa: Norge i krigsalliansen 1940–45 I-II 1973–79, Western Security: The Formative Years (ed.) 1985, Norge i Krig: Utefront 1987, Otto Ruge: Felttoget (ed.) 1989, Fredsgeneralen (ed.) 1995, "Strengt hemmelig." Norsk etterretningsteneste 1945–70 (with A. Moland) 1997, The Norwegian Intelligence Service 1945–1970 1999, Norway's Foreign Relations: A History 2001. *Leisure interests:* classical music, skiing. *Address:* Husarveien 18, 1396 Billingstad, Norway. *Telephone:* 66-84-63-05. *Fax:* 66-98-11-08 (Home). *E-mail:* oriste@c2i.net (Home).

RITBLAT, John Henry, F.S.V.A., FRICS; British business executive; b. 3 Oct. 1935; m. 1st Isabel Paja 1960 (died 1979); two s. one d.; m. 2nd Jill Rosemary (née Slotover) Zilkha 1986; ed Dulwich Coll., Coll. of Estate Management, London Univ.; Chair. and Man. Dir The British Land Co. PLC 1970–, Chair. and Chief Exec. The British Land Corpn 1991–; Founder and Chair. Conrad Ritblat & Co., Consultant Surveyors and Valuers 1958, Man. Dir 1970, Chair. Conrad Ritblat Group PLC 1993–; Chair. Milner Estates PLC 1997, Colliers Conrad Ritblat Erdman 2000–; Man. Dir Union Property Holdings (London) Ltd 1969, Crown Estates Paving Commn. 1969–; mem. Bd of Govs. Weizmann Inst. 1991–, London Business School 1991– (Hon. Fellow 2000); Dir and Gov. RAM 1998– (Deputy Chair. 1999–, Hon. Fellow 2000); mem. Council, Business in the Community 1987–, Prince of Wales' Royal Parks Tree Appeal Cttee 1987–, Patrons of British Art (Tate Gallery), Nat. Art. Collections Fund, British Library Bd 1995–; Pres. British Ski Fed. 1994–; Life Fellow Royal Soc. of Arts; Life mem. Royal Inst. of GB. *Leisure interests:* golf, skiing, real tennis, books, architecture. *Address:* 10 Cornwall Terrace, Regent's Park, London, NW1 4QP, England. *Telephone:* (20) 7486-4466. *Fax:* (20) 7935-5552.

RITCHIE, Guy; British film director; b. 1968, Hatfield, Herts.; s. of John Ritchie and Amber Mary Ritchie; m. Madonna Ciccone 2000; one step-d. one s.; ed Standbridge Earls; British Ind. Film Award 1998, London Film Critics' Circle Award 1999. *Films:* directed numerous eighties pop videos; Lock, Stock and Two Smoking Barrels 1998, Snatch 2000, What it Feels Like For a Girl 2001, Star, Swept Away 2002, Mean Machine (exec. producer) 2002. *Television:* The Hard Case 1995, Lock, Stock and Two Smoking Barrels. *Leisure interests:* karate, judo.

RITCHIE, Ian, CBE, RA, RIBA, FRSA, DIPL.ARCH.; British architect; b. 24 June 1947, Hove; s. of Christopher Ritchie and Mabel Long; m. Jocelyne van den Bossche 1972; one s.; ed Polytechnic of Central London; project architect Foster Assocs. 1972–79; in pvt. practice, France 1976–78; ind. consultant 1979–81; founder partner Chrysalis Architects 1979–81; co-founder Rice Francis Ritchie 1981, Dir 1981–87, Consultant 1987–89; Prin. Ian Ritchie Architects 1981–; comms. include: Eagle Rock House, Sussex, several projects for the Louvre, Paris, including work on the Louvre Pyramid and Sculpture Courts, pharmacy at Boves, France, cultural centre, Albert, France, planetarium, Greenwich, Ecology Gallery, Natural History Museum, London, office block, Stockley Business Park, three all-glass towers of Reina Sofía Museum of Modern Art, Madrid, glass hall, Leipzig Int. Exhbn Centre, Bermondsey Station, London Underground, electricity pylons, France, Royal Opera House Theatre, Tower Bridge, London, work on Nat. Museum of Science, Tech. and Ind., La Villette, Paris, Crystal Palace Concert Platform, White City redevt., Theatre Royal Production Centre, Plymouth, Scotland's Home of Tomorrow, Glasgow, Spire of Dublin Monument, 3rd Millennium Light Monument, Milan, Hawking Spacetime Centre, London, Hayward Gallery Exhbns., London; numerous exhbns; Chair. Touch the Earth 1988–2003, Royal Acad.

Collections and Library Cttee 2000–; Pres. Europan UK 1997–; Visiting Prof. Tech. Univ. Vienna 1994–95; Special Prof., Leeds Univ. School of Civil Eng 2001–; mem. Advisory Bd London Docklands Devt Corpn 1990–96, Council Steel Construction Inst. 1994–97, Advisory Bd City journal 1994–99, Research Cttee Nat. Maritime Museum 1995–97, Royal Fine Art Comm. 1995–99, CABE 1999–2001, UK Construction Foresight Panel 1996–98; Adviser, Natural History Museum 1991–95; Hon. DLitt (Westminster); numerous awards including Iritecna Prize for Europe (Italy) 1991, Eric Lyons Memorial Award for Housing in Europe 1992, Commonwealth Asscn of Architects Robert Matthews Award 1994, AIA Award 1997, Civic Trust Award 1997, RIBA Award, Stephen Lawrence Award 1998, RFAC Arts Building of the Year 1998, two Millennium Product Awards 1999, Silver Medal, Acad. d'Architecture 2000, RFAC Sports Building of the Year 2000, RIBA Award 2000, IABSE Int. Outstanding Structure Award 2000, Copper Building of the Year 2000, Regeneration of Scotland Supreme Award 2000, British Construction Industry Special Award 2000, two Civic Trust Awards 2002. *Exhibitions include:* Paris Biennale, Venice Biennale, Inst. of Contemporary Arts, London, Centre Pompidou, Paris, São Paulo Biennale, Aedes Berlin, Grassi Museum, Leipzig. *Films:* La cité en lumière (co-scripted/dir) 1986, Sandcastles (BBC) 1990. *Publications:* (Well) Connected Architecture 1994, The Biggest Glass Palace in the World 1997, Ian Ritchie. Tecnoecologie 1999. *Leisure interests:* art, swimming, reading, writing, film-making. *Address:* 110 Three Colt Street, London, E14 8AZ, England (Office). *Telephone:* (20) 7338-1100 (Office). *Fax:* (20) 7338-1199 (Office). *E-mail:* iritchie@ianritchiearchitects.co.uk (Office). *Website:* www.ianritchiearchitects.co.uk (Office).

RITCHIE, Ian Russell, MA; British television executive and barrister; b. 27 Nov. 1953, Leeds; s. of Hugh Ritchie and Sheelah Ritchie; m. Jill Middleton-Walker 1982; two s.; ed Leeds Grammar School, Trinity Coll. Oxford; Barrister (Middle Temple) 1976–77; Industrial Relations Adviser, Eng Employers' Fed. 1978–79; joined Granada TV 1980, Head Production Services 1987–88; Dir of Resources, Tyne-Tees TV 1988–91, Man. Dir 1991–93, Group Deputy Chief Exec. Yorkshire Tyne-Tees TV PLC 1993; Man. Dir Nottingham Studios, Cen. TV 1993–94; Man. Dir London News Network 1994–96; CEO, subsequently COO Channel 5 Broadcasting 1996–97; Man. Dir Russell Reynolds Assocs 1997–98; Chief Exec. Middle East Broadcasting Centre 1998–2000; CEO Assoc. Press TV News 2000–. *Leisure interests:* golf, tennis, theatre. *Address:* Associated Press Television News, The Interchange, Oval Road, Camden Lock, London, NW1 7DZ, England (Office). *Telephone:* (20) 7482-7440. *Fax:* (20) 7413-8355. *E-mail:* ian-ritchie@ap.org (Office).

RITCHIE, J. Murdoch, PhD, DSc, FRS, FInstP; British professor of pharmacology; b. 10 June 1925, Aberdeen, Scotland; s. of Alexander Farquharson and Agnes Jane Bremner; m. Brenda Rachel Bigland 1951; one s. one d.; ed Univs. of Aberdeen and London; Research Physicist in Radar at Telecommunications Research Establishment, Malvern 1944–46; Jr Lecturer in Physiology, Univ. Coll. London 1949–51; mem. of staff, Inst. for Medical Research, Mill Hill 1951–56; Asst Prof. of Pharmacology, Albert Einstein Coll. of Medicine, New York, USA 1956–57, Assoc. Prof. 1958–63, Prof. 1963–68; Prof. and Chair. Dept of Pharmacology, Yale Univ. School of Medicine, USA 1968–74, Dir Div. of Biological Sciences 1975–78, Eugene Higgins Prof. of Pharmacology 1968–; Fellow Univ. Coll. London; Hon. MA (Yale) 1968; Hon. DSc (Aberdeen) 1987; Van Dyke Memorial Award 1983. *Publications:* numerous scientific articles in Journal of Physiology, Proceedings of Royal Soc., Nature, Proceedings of NAS, USA. *Leisure interests:* chess, skiing and squash. *Address:* 47 Deepwood Drive, Hamden, CT 06517, USA. *Telephone:* (203) 785-4567 (Office); (203) 777-0420 (Home). *Fax:* (203) 737-2027 (Office).

RITCHIE, John Hindle, PhD, MBE; British architect; b. 4 June 1937, Delaval, Northumberland; s. of Charles Ritchie and Bertha Ritchie; m. Anne B. M. Leyland 1963; two d.; ed Univs. of Liverpool and Sheffield; research and devt architect 1963–74; environmental planner, Merseyside 1974–81; Devt Dir Merseyside Devt Corpn 1981–85, Chief Exec. and mem. Bd 1985–91, maj. projects included Liverpool Waterfront Redevt. 1981–91, Albert Dock Conservation (Civic Trust Jubilee Award 1981, European Gold Medal 1986), Liverpool Int. Garden Festival 1984; devt consultant 1991–; with Lord Chancellor's panel of inspectors 1994–; Gov. Liverpool Community Coll. 1995–. *Leisure interests:* urban and rural conservation. *E-mail:* jr1@btclick.com (Office).

RITHAUDDEEN AL-HAJ BIN TENGKU ISMAIL, Y.M. Tengku Ahmad; Malaysian politician and barrister; b. 24 Jan. 1932, Kota Bharu; s. of Y. M. Tengku Ismail and Y. M. Besar Zabidah Tengku abd Kadir; m. Y. M. Tengku Puan Sri Datin Noor Aini 1957; three s. two d.; ed Nottingham Univ. and Lincoln's Inn, UK; mem. of Royal family of Kelantan; Circuit Magistrate in Ipoh 1956–58, Pres. of Sessions Court 1958–60; Deputy Public Prosecutor and Fed. Counsel 1960–62; mem. Council of Advisers to Ruler of State of Kelantan (MPR), resgnd to enter pvt. practice; Chair. East Coast Bar Cttee of Malaya; Chair. Sri Nilam Co-operative Soc., Malaysia; mem. Malayan Council 1967, 1968, 1969, 1970; Sponsor, Adabi Foundation; Sponsor, Kelantan Youth; Adviser, Kesatria; Chair. Farmers' Org. Authority; Minister with Special Functions Assisting Prime Minister on Foreign Affairs 1973–75; mem. Supreme Council, United Malays' Nat. Org. 1975–; Minister for Foreign Affairs 1975–81, 1984–86, for Trade and Industry 1981–83, for Information 1986, of Defence 1986–90; Jt Chair. Malaysia-Thailand Devt Authority (Gas and Oil); Chair. Kinta Kellas Investments PLC 1990–, Idris Hydraulic (Malaysia) Berhad 1991–, Concrete Eng Products Berhad, Road Builder

(Malaysia) Holdings Berhad; Adviser, KPMG Peat Marwick Malaysia; Pro-Chancellor Nat. Univ. of Malaysia; Deputy Pres. Football Asscn of Malaysia. *Leisure interest:* golf. *Address:* Road Builder (M) Holdings Bhd., 5th Floor, 38 Jalan Dang Wangi, Kuala Lumpur, Malaysia. *Telephone:* (3) 2916888. *Fax:* (3) 2550230.

RITOÓK, Zsigmond; Hungarian professor of Latin; b. 28 Sept. 1929, Budapest; s. of Zsigmond Ritoók and Ilona (née Gaylhoffer) Ritoók; m. Ágnes (née Szalay) Ritoók; one s. two d.; ed Univ. of Budapest; teacher 1958–1970; research fellow, Centre of Classical Studies of Hungarian Acad. of Sciences 1970–86; Prof. of Latin, Univ. of Budapest 1986–99, Prof. Emer. 2000–; Corresp. mem. Acad. of Sciences 1990–93, mem. 1993–, Vice-Pres. Section of Linguistics and Hungarian Literary Scholarship 1990–96, Pres. 1996–99; mem. Academia Latinitati Fovendae, Rome 1984–, Academia Europaea, corresp. mem. Österreichische Akademie der Wissenschaften 1998–; Gen. Sec. Hungarian Soc. of Classical Studies 1980–1985, co-Pres. 1985–1991, Pres. 1991–1997.; Széchenyi Prize 2001. *Publications:* Everyday Life in Ancient Greece 1960, The Golden Age of Greek Culture (co-author) 1968, (enlarged) 1986, Theatre and Stadium 1968, Greek Singer of Tales 1973, Sources for the History of Greek Musical Aesthetics 1982 (all in Hungarian); c. 110 papers in Hungarian and foreign periodicals. *Address:* 1093 Budapest, Mátyás u. 20., Hungary (Home). *Telephone:* (1) 217-4033 (Home).

RITTER, Gerhard A., DPhil; German professor of modern history; b. 29 March 1929, Berlin; s. of Wilhelm Ritter and Martha (née Wietasch) Ritter; m. Gisela Kleinschmidt 1955; two s.; ed Arndt.-Oberschule, Berlin, Univ. of Tübingen, Free Univ., Berlin; research, Univ. of Oxford, England 1952–54; Asst Free Univ., Berlin 1954–61, Prof. of Political Science 1962–65; Prof. of Modern History, Univ. of Münster 1965–74; Prof. of Modern History, Univ. of Munich 1974–94, Prof. Emer. 1994–; fmr Guest Prof., Washington Univ., St Louis, Mo., Univ. of Oxford, Univ. of Calif. (Berkeley), Tel Aviv Univ.; mem. Senate and Main Cttee, Deutsche Forschungsgemeinschaft (German Research Soc.), Bonn 1973–76; Chair. Asscn of Historians of Germany 1976–80; mem. Bavarian Acad. of Sciences, Munich, Comm. for History of Parliamentarism and Political Parties, Historische Kommission, Berlin; Hon. Fellow St Antony's Coll., Oxford; Dr hc (Univ. Bielefeld) 1994, (Humboldt Univ., Berlin) 1999. *Publications:* Die Arbeiterbewegung im Wilhelminischen Reich 1959, Parlament und Demokratie in Grossbritannien 1972, Deutsche Sozialgeschichte 1870–1914 (with Jürgen Kocka) 1982, Arbeiterbewegung, Parteien und Parlamentarismus 1976, Die II. Internationale 1918/19. Protokolle, Memoranden, Berichte und Korrespondenzen 1980, Staat, Arbeiterschaft und Arbeiterbewegung in Deutschland 1980, Die deutschen Parteien 1830–1914 1985, Social Welfare in Germany and Britain 1986, Der Sozialstaat 1991, Wahlen in Deutschland 1946–91 (with M. Niehuss) 1991, Das Deutsche Kaiserreich 1871–1914 1992, Arbeiter im Deutschen Kaiserreich 1871–1914 (with Klaus Tenfelde) 1992, Grossforschung und Staat in Deutschland 1992, Der Umbruch von 1989/91 und die Geschichtswissenschaft 1995, Arbeiter, Arbeiterbewegung und soziale Ideen in Deutschland 1996, Soziale Frage und Sozialpolitik in Deutschland seit Beginn des 19. Jahrhunderts 1998, Über Deutschland, Die Bundesrepublik in der deutschen Geschichte 2000, Continuity and Change. Political and Social Developments in Germany after 1945 and 1989/90 2000. *Leisure interests:* sailing, tennis. *Address:* Windscheidstrasse 41, 10627 Berlin, Germany (Home). *Telephone:* (30) 31015794 (Home). *Fax:* (30) 31019614 (Home).

RITTER, Jorge Eduardo, PhD; Panamanian politician and diplomatist; b. 1950; m.; two c.; ed Pontificia Univ., Colombia; Clerk to Legis. Comm. 1973–77; Lecturer in Constitutional and Civil Law Univ. of Panama; fmr mem. Governing Council Inst. for Human Resources Training and Devt; Vice-Minister of Labour and Social Welfare 1977–78; Pvt. Sec. and Adviser to Pres. of Panama 1978–81; Minister of Foreign Affairs (desig.) 1981; teacher Nat. Political Training Coll. of the Guardia Nacional 1981; Minister of Interior and Justice 1981–82; Amb. to Colombia 1982–86; Perm. Rep. to UN 1986–88; Minister of Foreign Affairs 1988–89, 1998–99; Chair. Exec. Council Nat. Telecommunications Inst. 1981; Chair. Bd Civil Aviation Authority 1981–82; mem. Bd Banco Ganadero 1980–, Ritter, Días y Asociados 1982–, Banco Interoceánico de Panamá 1985–. *Address:* c/o Ministry of Foreign Affairs, Panamá 4, Panama.

RITTERMAN, Janet Elizabeth, DBE, PhD, MMus, FRNCM, FRSA; music college director; b. 1 Dec. 1941, Sydney, Australia; d. of Charles Eric Palmer and Laurie Helen Palmer; m. Gerrard Peter Ritterman 1970; ed North Sydney Girls' High School and New South Wales State Conservatorium of Music, Australia, Univ. of Durham and King's Coll. London, UK; pianist; accompanist, chamber music player; Sr Lecturer in Music, Middx Polytechnic 1975–79, Goldsmiths' Coll. Univ. of London 1980–87; Head of Music, Dartington Coll. of Arts 1987–90, Dean Academic Affairs 1988–90, Acting Prin. 1990–91, Prin. 1991–93; Visiting Prof. of Music Educ., Univ. of Plymouth 1993–; Dir Royal Coll. of Music 1993–; Chair. Assoc. Bd Royal Schools of Music (Publishing) Ltd 1993–, The Mendelssohn and Boise Foundations 1996–98, 2002–, Advisory Council, Arts Research Ltd 1997–; Fed. of British Conservatories 1998–; Vice-Pres. Nat. Asscn of Youth Orchestras 1993–; mem. Music Panel, Arts Council of England 1992–98, Council Royal Musical Asscn 1994– (Vice-Pres. 1998–), Bd English Nat. Opera 1996–, Exec. Cttee Inc. Soc. of Musicians 1996–99, Arts and Humanities Research Bd 1998– (Postgrad. Panel 1998–2002, Chair. Postgrad. Cttee 2002–), Steering Cttee, London Higher Educ. Consortium 1999–, Arts Council of England 2000–02, Dept for Educ. and Skills Advisory Group, Music and Dance Scheme 2000–, Council

of Goldsmith's Coll., Univ. of London 2002–, Arts and Humanities Research; Trustee, Countess of Munster Musical Trust 1993–, Prince Consort Foundation 1993–; Fellow Univ. Coll., Northampton 1997, Dartington Coll. of Arts 1997; Gov. Associated Bd Royal Schools of Music 1993–, Purcell School 1996–2000, Heythrop Coll. Univ. of London 1996–; Hon. RAM 1995; Hon. mem. Guildhall School of Music and Drama 2000; Hon. DUniv (Univ. of Cen. England) 1996. *Publications:* articles in learned journals, France, Germany, Australia and UK. *Leisure interests:* reading, theatre-going, country walking. *Address:* Royal College of Music, Prince Consort Road, London, SW7 2BS, England. *Telephone:* (20) 7591-4363 (Office). *Fax:* (20) 7591-4356 (Office). *E-mail:* jritterman@rcm.ac.uk (Office). *Website:* www.rcm.ac.uk (Office).

RITTNER, Luke Philip Hardwick; British arts administrator; b. 24 May 1947, Bath; s. of Stephen Rittner and Joane Rittner; m. Corinna Frances Edholm 1974; one d.; ed Blackfriars School, Laxton, City of Bath Tech. Coll., Dartington Coll. of Arts and London Acad. of Music and Dramatic Art; Asst Admin. Bath Festival 1968–71, Jt Admin. 1971–74, Admin. Dir 1974–76; Founder and Dir Asscn for Business Sponsorship of the Arts 1976–83; Sec.-Gen. Arts Council of Great Britain 1983–90; UK Cultural Dir Expo '92 1990–92; Chair. English Shakespeare Co. 1990–94; Dir Marketing and Communications, Sotheby's Europe 1992–99; Chief Exec. Royal Acad. of Dance 1999–; Chair. London Choral Soc. 1994–, Exec. Bd London Acad. of Music and Dramatic Art 1994–; Artistic Adviser to Spanish Arts Festival, London 1991–94; Gov. Urchfont Manor, Wiltshire Adult Educ. Centre 1982–83; mem. Music Panel, British Council 1979–83, Council Victoria and Albert Museum 1980–83, J. Sainsbury Arts Sponsorship Panel 1990–96, Olivier Awards Theatre Panel 1992, Council Almeida Theatre 1997–2001; non-exec. mem. Bd Carlton Television 1991–93; Trustee Bath Preservation Trust 1968–73, Theatre Royal, Bath 1979–82; Foundation Trustee Holburne Museum, Bath 1981–83. *Leisure interest:* the arts. *Address:* Royal Academy of Dance, 36 Battersea Square, London, SW11 3RA, England (Office).

RITZEN, Jozef, D. ECON.; Netherlands politician and economist; b. 3 Oct. 1945, Heerlen, Limburg Prov.; ed Univ. of Delft; Prof. of Educ. Econs, Nijmegen Univ. 1981–83; Prof. of Public Sector Econs, Erasmus Univ., Rotterdam 1983–89; sometime adviser to Minister of Social Affairs; Minister of Educ., Culture and Science 1989–99; Special Adviser to the Human Devt Network, IBRD (World Bank) 1998, Vice-Pres. for Devt Policy 1999–. *Address:* Office of the Vice-President for Reconstruction and Development, IBRD, 1818 H Street, NW, Washington, DC 20433, U.S.A. *Telephone:* (202) 477-1234. *Fax:* (202) 477-6391. *E-mail:* pic@worldbank.org. *Website:* www.worldbank.org.

RIVALDO; Brazilian footballer; b. Vito Barbosa Ferreira, 19 April 1972, Recife; played with Paulista, Santa Cruz 1989–91, Magi-Mirin 1992, Corinthians 1993, Palmeiras 1994–96, Deportivo La Coruña (Spain) (21 goals in 41 matches) 1996–97, FC Barcelona (Spain) 1997–; scored 5 goals for Brazil nat. team in World Cup 2002; FIFA World Player of the Year 1999, Ballon D'Or, Best Player in Europe (France) 1999. *Address:* Barcelona Club de Fútbol, Noucamp Aristides Maikol 12, Barcelona, Spain (Office). *Telephone:* (93) 4963 600 (Office). *Website:* www.fcbarcelona.es (Office).

RIVAS, Cándido Muatetema; Equatorial Guinean politician; fmr Sec. Gen. Partido Democrático de Guinea Ecuatorial; Prime Minister of Equatorial Guinea 2000–. *Address:* Office of the Prime Minister, Malabo, Equatorial Guinea (Office).

RIVAS-MIJARES, Gustavo, MSc, DrIng; Venezuelan environmental engineer; b. 7 Nov. 1922, Valencia; s. of J. A. Rivas-Montenegro and Amparo Mijares de Rivas; m. Ligia Cardenas 1946; four c.; ed Liceo Pedro Gual, Valencia, Univ. Central de Venezuela, Caracas and Univs. of Michigan and California (USA); Prof. of Sanitary Eng. Faculty of Eng. Univ. Central de Venezuela 1945–85, Dean, Grad. School 1973–76, Prof. Emer. 1985–; Pres. Nat. Acad. of Physics, Mathematics and Natural Science 1981–85; Dir Nat. Council of Scientific and Tech. Research 1969–72; fmr Dir Venezuela Inst. of Scientific Research; Pres. Superior Council, Universidad Simón Bolívar, Caracas, Venezuela 1988–91; Chair. Pan-American Eng Acad. 1998; Fellow mem. Third World Acad. of Sciences 1988; Foreign Assoc. Nat. Acad. of Eng, USA, Mexico, Spain; Nat. Science Prize, Venezuela 1986; several awards including Libertador Bolívar 1989. *Publications:* author and co-author of several books and 132 research papers. *Address:* Department of Sanitary Engineering, Faculty of Engineering, Universidad Central de Venezuela, Ciudad Universitaria, Los Changuaramos, Zona Postal 104, Caracas 1051 (Office). Urb. Santa Rosa de Lima, Calle C, Res. Jarama, Apt. 7–A, Caracas, Venezuela (Home). *Telephone:* (2) 991-7156 (Home). *Fax:* (2) 484-6611 (Office). *E-mail:* acfmn@ccs.internet.ve (Office).

RIVERA, Chita (Conchita del Rivero); American actress, singer and dancer; b. 23 Jan. 1933, Washington; d. of Pedro Julio Figuerva del Rivero; m. Anthony Mordente; ed American School of Ballet, New York; performs in nightclubs and cabarets around the world. *Stage appearances include:* Call Me Madam, Guys and Dolls, Can-Can, Seventh Heaven, Mister Wonderful, West Side Story, Father's Day, Bye Bye Birdie, Threepenny Opera, Flower Drum Song, Zorba, Sweet Charity, Born Yesterday, Jacques is Alive and Well and Living in Paris, Sondheim—A Musical Tribute, Kiss Me Kate, Ivanhoe, Chicago, Bring Back Birdie, Merlin, The Rink 1984 (Tony Award 1984), Jerry's Girl's 1985, Kiss of the Spider Woman 1993 (Tony Award for Best Actress in a Musical). *Television includes:* Kojak and the Marcus Nelson Murders 1973, The New Dick Van Dyke Show 1973–74, Kennedy Center

Tonight–Broadway to Washington!, Pippin 1982, The Mayflower Madam 1987. *Address:* c/o Gayle Nachlis, William Morris Agency, 1325 Avenue of the Americas, New York, NY 10019, USA.

RIVERA, Geraldo, BS, JD; American television correspondent; b. 4 July 1943, New York; s. of Cruz Allen Rivera and Lillian Friedman; m. 3rd Sheri Rivera (divorced 1984); m. 4th C. C. Dyer 1987; two s. two d.; ed Univ. of Arizona, Brooklyn Law School, Univ. of Pennsylvania; with Eyewitness News WABC-TV, New York 1970–75; reporter Good Morning America programme ABC-TV 1973–76; corresp. and host Good Night America programme 1975–77; corresp. and sr producer 20/20 Newsmagazine 1978–85; host syndicated talk show The Geraldo Rivera Show, New York 1987–98; host CNBC Rivera Life Show, N.J. 1994–, investigative show on cable CNBC Upfront Tonight, NJ 1998–2000, Travel Channel documentaries: Voyager – Sail to the Century, NBC –2001 Geraldo Rivera Specials; war reporter in Afghanistan, Somalia, Lebanon, Israel and Sudan 2001–02; ten Emmy Awards, three Peabody Awards, Kennedy Journalism Award 1973, 1975, Columbia DuPont Award and numerous other awards. *Publications:* Willowbrook 1972, Miguel 1972, Island of Contrasts 1974, A Special Kind of Courage 1976, Exposing Myself 1991. *Address:* NBC News, 30 Rockefeller Plaza, 2nd Floor, New York, NY 10019, USA (Office).

RIVERA CARRERA, HE Cardinal Norberto, DD; Mexican ecclesiastic; b. 6 June 1942, La Purísima; s. of Ramón Rivera Cháidez and Soledad Carrera de Rivera; ed Conciliary Seminary, Durango, Gregorian Univ., Rome; ordained priest 1966; Prof. of Ecclesiology, Univ. Pontificia de Mexico 1982; Bishop of Tehuacán 1985; Archbisop of Mexico City; Archbishop Primate of Mexico 1995–; cr. HE Cardinal Feb. 1998; mem. Cttee of Presidency of Papal Council for the Family 1993–; Apostolic Visitor for Diocesan and Religious Seminaries 1993–. *Address:* Curia Arzobispal, Aptdo. Postal 24-4-33, Durango #90, 5°, Col Rome, C.P. 06700 México, DF, Mexico. *Telephone:* (5) 208-3200. *Fax:* (5) 208-5350.

RIVETTE, Jacques; French film director; b. 1 March 1928, Rouen; s. of André Rivette and Andrée (née Amiard) Rivette; ed Lycée Corneille, Rouen; journalist and critic on Cahiers du Cinéma 1953–82; Asst to Jacques Becker and Jean Renoir 1954; Dir of Films 1956–; Dir La religieuse (theatre) 1963; Chevalier, Ordre nat. du Mérite; Grand Prix nat. 1981, Prix Friedrich Wilhelm Murnau for Outstanding Lifetime Achievement 1998. *Films:* Le coup du berger (Dir) 1956, Paris nous appartient (author and Dir) 1958–60, Suzanne Simenon, La Religieuse de Diderot 1966, L'Amour fou 1968, Out One: Spectre 1973, Céline et Julie vont en bateau 1974, Le vengeur, Duelle 1976, Le pont du Nord 1982, Merry-go-round 1983, Wuthering Heights 1984, L'amour par terre 1984, The Gang of Four (Berlin Film Award 1989) 1988, La Belle Noiseuse 1991, Jeanne La Pucelle 1993, Haut, Bas, Fragile 1994, Va Savoir 2001. *Address:* 20 boulevard de la Bastille, 75012 Paris, France.

RIVLIN, Alice Mitchell, MA, PhD; American economist and government official; b. 4 March 1931, Philadelphia; d. of Allan Mitchell and Georgianna Fales; m. 1st Lewis A. Rivlin 1955 (divorced 1977); two s. one d.; m. 2nd Sidney G. Winter 1989; ed Bryn Mawr Coll. and Radcliffe Coll.; mem. staff, Brookings Inst. Washington, DC 1957–66, 1969–75, 1983–93, Dir of Econ. Studies 1983–87; Dir Congressional Budget Office 1975–83; Prof. of Public Policy, George Mason Univ. 1992; Deputy Dir U.S. Office of Man. and Budget 1993–94, Dir 1994–96; Vice-Chair Fed. Reserve Bd 1996–99; Sr Fellow, Johnson Chair. Brookings Inst. 1999–; Chair. Dist of Columbia Financial Control Bd; mem. American Econ. Asscn (Nat. Pres. 1986); MacArthur Fellow 1983–88. *Publications:* The Role of the Federal Government in Financing Higher Education 1961, Microanalysis of Socioeconomic Systems (jtly.) 1961, Systematic Thinking for Social Action 1971, Economic Choices (jtly.) 1986, The Swedish Economy (jtly.) 1987, Caring for the Disabled Elderly: Who Will Pay? 1988, Reviving the American Dream 1992. *Address:* Brookings Institution, 1755 Massachusetts Avenue, Washington, DC 20036, USA (Office).

RIVLIN, Moshe; Israeli executive; b. 16 Jan. 1925, Jerusalem; s. of Yitzhak Rivlin and Esther Rivlin; m. Ruth Moav (Horbaty) 1960; two d.; ed Teachers' Seminary, Graduate Aluma Inst. for Jewish Studies, Mizrachi Teacher's Coll. and School for Political Science, Hebrew Univ., Jerusalem; Maj. in ZAHAL 1948–49; Consul in USA 1952–58; Dir, Information Dept, The Jewish Agency 1958–60, Sec.-Gen. 1960–66, Dir-Gen. and Head of Admin. and Public Relations Dept 1966–71; elected Dir-Gen. of reconstituted Jewish Agency 1971–77; Assoc. mem. Exec., World Zionist Org. 1971; Chair. Keren Kayemeth Le Israel 1977–; mem. Bd of Govs. Ben-Gurion Univ., Coll. for Public Admin., Jewish Telegraphic Agency; mem. Exec. Cttee Yad Ben-Zvi, mem. Council Yad Ben-Gurion; mem. Bd of Dirs. Jerusalem Post, Beit Hatfutzot, Hebrew Univ. *Address:* Keren Kayemeth Le Israel, P.O. Box 283, Jerusalem; 34 Hapalmach Street, Jerusalem, Israel (Home). *Telephone:* 2-6244023 (Office); 2-5635173 (Home).

RIVOYRE, Christine Berthe Claude Denis de, LèsL; French author and journalist; b. 29 Nov. 1921, Tarbes; d. of François Denis de Rivoyre and Madeleine (née Ballande) de Rivoyre; ed Inst. du Sacré Coeur, Bordeaux and Poitiers, Faculté des lettres, Paris and Univ. of Syracuse, USA; journalist Le Monde (daily) 1950–55; Literary Dir Marie-Claire (monthly magazine) 1955–65; mem. Haut Comité de la Langue française 1969–, Conseil Supérieur des Lettres, Prix Medicis Jury 1970–; Chevalier, Légion d'honneur, Chevalier des Arts et des Lettres; Prix Paul Morand (Académie française) 1984 and other awards. *Publications:* L'alouette au miroir 1956, La mandarine 1957, La tête en fleurs 1960, La glace à l'ananas 1962, Les sultans 1964, Le petit matin

1968, Le seigneur des chevaux (with A. Kalda) 1969, Fleur d'agonie 1970, Boy 1973, Le voyage à l'envers 1977, Belle alliance 1982, Reine-Mère 1985, Crépuscule taille unique 1989, Racontez-moi les flamboyants 1995, Le Petit matin 1998. *Address:* Editions Grasset, 61 rue des Saints-Pères, 75006 Paris (Office); Dichats Ha, Onesse-Laharie, 40110 Morcenx, France.

RIX, Timothy John, CBE, BA, CIMgt, FRSA, F.INST.D.; British publisher; b. 4 Jan. 1934, Maidenhead, Berks.; s. of late Howard T. Rix and of Marguerite Selman Rix; m. 1st Wendy E. Wright 1960 (dissolved 1967); m. 2nd Gillian Greenwood 1968; one s. two d.; ed Radley Coll., Clare Coll., Cambridge and Yale Univ.; joined Longmans Green & Co. Ltd 1958, Overseas Educ. Publr 1958–61, Publishing Man. Far East and SE Asia 1961–63, Head, English Language Teaching Publishing 1964–68, Div. Man. Dir 1968–72, Jt Man. Dir 1972–76, Chief Exec. Longman Group Ltd 1976–90, Chair. 1984–90; Chair. Addison-Wesley-Longman Group Ltd 1988–89; Chair. Pitman Examinations Inst. 1987–90; Dir Pearson Longman Ltd (now Pearson PLC) 1979–83, Goldcrest Television 1981–83, Yale Univ. Press Ltd, London 1984–, ECIC (Man.) Ltd 1990–92, Blackie & Son Ltd 1990–93, B.H. Blackwell Ltd 1991–95, Geddes and Grosset Ltd 1996–98, Jessica Kingsley Publrs Ltd 1997–, Frances Lincoln Ltd 1997–, Meditech Media Ltd 1997–, Scottish Book Source 1999–, Central European Univ. Press 1999–; Pres. Publrs' Asscn 1981–83; mem. British Library Bd 1986–96, British Council Bd 1988–97, Health Educ. Authority Bd 1995–99; Chair. Book Trust 1986–88, British Library Centre for the Book 1989–95, Book Marketing Ltd 1990–, Soc. of Bookmen 1990–92, British Library Publishing 1992–, Book Aid Int. 1994–, Bell Educational Trust 1994–2001, Nat. Book Cttee 1997–, Edin. Univ. Press 2001–; mem. Oxford Brookes Univ. Devt Cttee 1991–96, Finance Cttee, Oxford Univ. Press 1992–2002, Council, Ranfurly Library Services 1992–94, Advisory Council, Inst. of English Studies, London Univ. 2000–; Hon. Pres. Independent Publishers' Guild 1993–; Gov. English-Speaking Union 1998–. *Publications:* articles on publishing in trade journals. *Leisure interests:* reading, landscape, wine. *Address:* Top Flat, 27 Wolseley Road, London, N8 8RS, England. *Telephone:* (20) 8341-4160. *Fax:* (20) 8341-4160. *E-mail:* greenrix@atlas.co.uk (Home).

RIZA, Iqbal, MA; Pakistani international civil servant; b. 20 May 1934, India; s. of Sharif Alijan; m. 1959; two s.; ed Pakistan and USA; Pakistan Foreign Service 1958–77; served Spain, Germany, Sudan, UK, USA; Dir Foreign Service Acad. Lahore 1968–71; Deputy Chief of Mission, Washington, DC 1972–76; Chargé d'Affaires, Paris 1977; joined UN 1978; assigned to negotiations in Iran-Iraq war 1981–87; Dir UN Gen. Ass. 1988; Chief, UN Electoral Mission, Nicaragua 1988–90; Special Rep. of UN Sec.-Gen. in El Salvador 1991–93; Asst Sec.-Gen. for Peace-keeping Operations 1993–97, Under-Sec.-Gen., Chief of Staff in Exec. Office of Sec.-Gen. 1997–. *Leisure interests:* reading, music, riding. *Address:* Executive Office of the UN Secretary-General, United Nations Plaza, New York, NY 10017, USA.

RIZAYEV, Ramiz Gasangulu oglu, DR.CHEM.SC.; Azerbaijani diplomatist and chemist; b. 2 Nov. 1939, Nakhichevan; m.; one s. one d.; ed Azerbaijan State Univ.; Corresp. mem. Azerbaijan Acad. of Sciences 1983; Dir Inst. of Inorganic and Physical Chem. Azerbaijan Acad. of Sciences 1985–93; Plenipotentiary Rep., then Amb. of Azerbaijan to Russian Fed. 1993–; numerous inventions in the field of oil extraction and oil processing, of 36 patents in various cos.; mem. Scientific Council on Catalysis, Russian Acad. of Sciences; mem. Int. Acad. of Eng. Sciences 2000–; mem. Ed. Bd Neftekhimiya (journal); Honoured Engineer of Russian Fed. 2000. *Publications:* 250 scientific articles on problems of oil chem. and chemical catalysis. *Address:* Azerbaijan Embassy, Leontyevsky per. 16, 103009 Moscow, Russia. *Telephone:* (095) 229-16-49 (Office).

RIZZO, Alessandro Minuto; Italian international organization official; mem. staff Directorate of Cultural Affairs, Ministry of Foreign Affairs, Rome 1969–72; First Sec. Washington, DC 1972–75; Counsellor, Prague 1975–80; Head Eastern Europe Desk, Directorate for Econ. Affairs 1980–81, Head EEC External Relations Desk 1981–86; Minister Counsellor OECD, Paris 1986–92; Minister Plenipotentiary Jan. 1992; Diplomatic Counsellor of Minister for Budget and Econ. Planning 1992–96, of Minister for Co-ordination of European Policies (a.i.) 1995–96; Deputy Chief of Cabinet, Ministry of Foreign Affairs Jan.–Oct. 1996, Co-ordinator for EU Affairs 1996–97; Diplomatic Counsellor of Minister of Defence 1997–2000; Amb. to Cttee for Policy and Security of EU 2000–01; Deputy Sec.-Gen. NATO 2001–; Del. to Council, European Space Agency 1986–92; Chair. Admin. and Financial Cttee 1993–96; Chair. Ass. of Parties of Eutelsat 1989; mem. Man. Bd Italian Space Agency 1994–95; Chair. EU Cttee for Territorial Devt 1996. *Address:* NATO, blvd Léopold III, 1110 Brussels, Belgium (Office). *Telephone:* (2) 707-41-11 (Office). *Fax:* (2) 707-45-79 (Office). *E-mail:* nato-doc@hq.nato.int (Office). *Website:* www.nato.int (Office).

RIZZOLI, Angelo; Italian publisher; b. 12 Nov. 1943, Como; s. of Andrea and Lucia (née Solmi) Rizzoli; m. Eleonora Giorgi 1979; one c.; ed univ.; Pres. and Man. Ed. Rizzoli Editore 1978–; Pres. Cineriz Distributori Associati 1978–, Rizzoli Film 1978–. *Address:* Via Angelo Rizzoli 2, 20132 Milan, Italy (Office). *Telephone:* (02) 25841.

RO JAI-BONG; South Korean politician; b. Masan, S Gyeongsang Prov.; Chief Presidential Sec. March–Dec. 1990; Prime Minister Repub. of Korea 1990–91.

ROA BASTOS, Augusto; Paraguayan writer and journalist; b. 1917; ed Asunción; returned to Paraguay after 40 years in exile March 1989; awarded John Simon Guggenheim Memorial Foundation 1971. *Publications:* Poetry: El Ruiseñor y la Aurora 1936, El Naranjal Ardiente 1947–49; Novels: El Trueno entre las Hojas 1953, Hijo de Hombre 1960, El Baldío 1966, Los Pies sobre el Agua 1967, Madera Quemada 1967, Moriencia 1969, Cuerpo Presente y otros cuentos 1971, Yo el Supremo 1974, Los Congresos 1974, El Somnámbulo 1976; Screenplays: El Trueno entre las Hojas 1955, Hijo de Hombre 1960, Shunko 1960, Alias Gardelito 1963, Castigo al Traidor 1966, El Señor Presidente 1966, Don Segundo Sombra 1968.

ROA-KOURI, Raúl, BSc; Cuban diplomatist; b. 9 July 1936, Havana; s. of Raúl Roa and Ada Kouri; m. 1st 1960 (divorced); one d.; m. 2nd 1972 (divorced); one d.; m. 3rd 1975 (divorced); one d.; m. 4th Lillian Martino de Roa-Kouri 1996; ed Univ. of Havana, Columbia Univ., New York, USA; Deputy Perm. Rep. to UN 1959–60; Amb. to Czechoslovakia 1961–63, to Brazil 1963–64; Dir of Trade Policy, Ministry of Foreign Trade 1964–66; Dir-Gen. of Int. Dept Ministry for Food Industries 1967–70; Dir-Gen. of Nat. Cttee for Econ., Scientific and Tech. Co-operation 1971–72; Perm. Sec. CMEA Nat. Cttee for Econ. Scientific and Tech. Co-operation 1972–76; Sr Political Adviser to Vice-Pres. of Council of State in charge of Foreign Affairs 1976–78; Perm. Rep. to UN 1978–84; Vice-Minister of Foreign Affairs 1984; Amb. to UNESCO 1993–94; Amb. to France 1994–98; mem. Scientific Council, Higher Inst. for Int. Relations, Havana 2001–; Chair. Nat. Comm. for UNESCO 2000–; Orden de Mayo al Mérito, Gran Cruz, Argentina, Grand Officier, Ordre Nat. du Mérite, France, Order of Merit, First Degree, UAR; Enrique Hart Medal (Cuba), First Mención Género Testimonio Premio Casa de las Américas 2000. *Publications:* Bolero y otras Prosas 2000, En el Torrente 2003, Roa x Roa 2003. *Leisure interests:* music, literature, writing. *Address:* Cuban National Commission for UNESCO, Avenida Kohly No. 151, esq. a 32, Nuevo Vedado, Havana (Office); Calle 38 No. 508, Miramar, Playa, Havana, Cuba (Home). *Telephone:* (7) 8810088 (Office); (7) 532103 (Office). *Fax:* (7) 432104 (Office). *E-mail:* roa@cncu.minrex.gov.cu (Office); akouri@infomed.sld.cu (Home).

ROACH, Maxwell Lemuel; American jazz musician; b. 10 Jan. 1924, Elizabeth City, NC; s. of Alphonzo Roach and Cressie (née Saunders) Roach; m. 1st Mildred Wilkinson 1949 (divorced); one s. one d.; m. 2nd Abbey Lincoln 1962 (divorced); ed Manhattan School of Music, New England Conservatory of Music; Prof. of Music, Univ. of Massachusetts 1973–; specialized in percussion instruments, with Charlie Parker 1946–48, later with Thelonius Monk, Bud Powell, Dizzy Gillespie, etc.; Co-leader Max Roach-Clifford Brown Quintet 1954–56; appearances at Paris Jazz Festival 1949, Newport Jazz Festival 1972; composer and choreographer Freedom Now suite; mem. Jazz Artists Guild Inc.; Officier des Arts et des Lettres 1989; Hon. mem. American Acad. and Inst. of Arts and Letters; received Best Record of Year Award, Down Beat magazine 1956 and other awards.

ROBAINA GONZÁLEZ, Roberto, BEd; Cuban politician; b. 18 March 1956, Pinar del Río; m.; one s.; ed Pinar del Río Higher Pedagogical Inst.; Prof. of Mathematics 1978; Pres. Fed. of Univ. Students 1979; First Sec. Young Communist League, Plaza Municipality 1983, mem. Nat. Bureau of Young Communist League 1984–85, Second Sec. 1985–86, First Sec. 1986–93; Deputy for Consolación del Sur municipality Nat. Ass. of People's Power 1986–92, Deputy for Cerro municipality 1992–; mem. Council of State 1986–98; mem. Cen. Cttee of Communist Party of Cuba, Politburo of Cen. Cttee 1990; Minister of Foreign Affairs 1993–99; mem. Cuban Internationalist Mil. Contingent to Angola 1998. *Address:* c/o Ministry of Foreign Affairs, Calzada 360, esq. a G. Plaza de la Revolución, Havana, Cuba.

ROBB, Charles Spittal, B.B.A., JD; American politician and lawyer; b. 26 June 1939, Phoenix, Ariz.; s. of James Spittal Robb and Frances Howard (née Woolley) Robb; m. Lynda Bird Johnson (d. of late Pres. Lyndon B. Johnson) 1967; three d.; ed Cornell Univ., Univ. of Wisconsin and Univ. of Virginia; admitted to Va Bar 1973; law clerk to John D. Butzner, Jr, US Court of Appeals 1973–74; admitted to US Supreme Court Bar 1976; Attorney, Williams, Connolly and Califano 1974–77; Lt-Gov. of Va 1978–82, Gov. 1982–86; Senator from Virginia 1989–2001; Chair. Democratic Govs' Assocn 1984–85, Democratic Leadership Council 1986–88; Chair Educ. Comm. of the States, Educ. Sub-Cttee of the Nat. Govs Assocns' Standing Cttee on Human Resources; Chair. Southern Govs' Assocn 1984–85; Pres. Council of State Govts 1985–86; Partner, Hunton and Williams 1986–; Distinguished Prof. of Law and Public Policy, George Mason Univ. 2001–; mem. Bd various educational insts; mem. American, Va Bar Assocns, Va Trial Lawyers' Assocn; Bronze Star, Viet Nam Service Medal with four stars, Vietnamese Cross of Gallantry with Silver Star; Raven Award 1973; Seven Socs. Org. Award, Univ. of Va. *Address:* School of Law, George Mason University, Room 415, 3301 North Fairfax Drive, Arlington, VA 22201, USA (Office).

ROBB, Graham MacDonald, PhD, FRSL; British writer; b. 2 June 1958, Manchester; m. Margaret Hambrick 1986; ed Univ. of Oxford, Goldsmiths Coll., London and Vanderbilt Univ., Nashville, Tenn., USA; British Acad. Fellowship 1987–90; mem. Society of Authors; New York Times Book of the Year Award 1994, Whitbread Biog. of the Year Award 1997, R.S.L. Heinemann Award 1998. *Publications include:* Le Corsaire – Satan en Silhouette 1985, Baudelaire Lecteur de Balzac 1988, Scènes de la Vie de Bohème (ed.) 1988, Baudelaire (trans.) 1989, La Poésie de Baudelaire et la Poésie Française 1993, Balzac 1994, Unlocking Mallarmé 1996, Victor Hugo: A Biography

1998, Rimbaud 2000; Contribs to Times Literary Supplement, London Review of Books, New York Times, New York Review of Books. *Address:* 139 Hollow Way, Oxford, OX4 2NE, England (Home).

ROBB, Sir John Weddell, Kt; British business executive; b. 27 April 1936; s. of John Robb and Isabella Robb; m. Janet Teanby 1965; two s. one d.; ed Daniel Stewart's Coll. Edin.; Market Research Exec. H.J. Heinz 1952; Product Man. Assoc. Fisheries 1960; Marketing Exec. Young & Rubicam 1965; joined Beecham Group 1966, Man. Dir Beecham (Far East), Kuala Lumpur 1971, Vice-Pres. W Hemisphere Div. Beecham Products, USA 1974, Man. Dir Food and Drink Div., Beecham Products 1976, mem. Bd Beecham Group 1980, Chair. Food and Drink Div. 1980, Chair. Beecham Products 1984–85, Group Man. Dir 1985–88; Dir (non-exec.) Nat. Freight Corpn 1983– (Deputy Chair. (non-exec.) 1990–), Allied-Lyons PLC 1991–, De La Rue Co. 1993–, Unigate 1996–; Deputy Chief Exec. Wellcome PLC 1989–90, Chief Exec. 1990–95, Chair. 1994–95; Deputy Chair. Horserace Betting Levy Bd 1993–; Chair. British Energy PLC 1995–2001, Logitron Holdings PLC 1996–, Chair. Hewden Stuart PLC 1999–; Trustee Royal Botanic Garden, Edin. 1997–. *Leisure interests:* golf, gardening, racing. *Address:* c/o British Energy, 14/16 Cockspur Street, London, SW1Y 5BL, England (Office).

ROBBE-GRILLET, Alain; French writer, film-maker and agronomist; b. 18 Aug. 1922, Brest; s. of Gaston Robbe-Grillet and Yvonne Canu; m. Catherine Rstakian 1957; ed Lycée Buffon, Lycée St Louis and Inst. Nat. Agronomique, Paris; Chargé de Mission, Inst. Nat. de la Statistique 1945–48; Engineer Inst. des Fruits Tropicaux (Guinea, Morocco, Martinique and Guadeloupe) 1949–51; Literary Adviser Editions de Minuit 1955–85; teacher, New York Univ. 1972–97; Dir Centre for the Sociology of Literature, Univ. of Brussels 1980–88; Chevalier, Légion d'honneur; Officier Ordre nat. du mérite, des Arts et des Lettres; Prix Louis Delluc 1963; Premio Vittorio de Sica 2001. *Films:* L'année dernière à Marienbad 1961; films directed: l'immortelle 1963, Trans-Europ-Express 1967, L'homme qui ment 1968, L'Eden et après 1970, Glissements progressifs du plaisir 1974, Le jeu avec le feu 1975, La belle captive 1983, Un bruit qui rend fou 1995. *Publications:* Novels: Les gommes 1953, Le voyeur 1955, La jalousie 1957, Dans le labyrinthe 1959, La maison de rendez-vous 1965, Projet pour une révolution à New York 1970, Topologie d'une cité fantôme 1976, La belle captive 1977, Un régicide 1978, Souvenirs du triangle d'or 1978, Djinn 1981, Le miroir qui revient 1984, Angélique ou l'enchantement 1988, Les derniers jours de Corinthe 1994, La Reprise 2001; short stories: Instantanés 1962; essay: Pour un nouveau roman 1964, Le Voyageur 2001. *Leisure interest:* collection of cacti. *Address:* Editions de Minuit, 7 rue Bernard-Palissy, 75006 Paris (Office); 18 boulevard Maillot, 92200 Neuilly-sur-Seine, France (Home). *Telephone:* 1-47-22-31-22 (Home). *Fax:* 2-31-77-03-30 (Home).

RÖBBELEN, Gerhard Paul Karl, Dr rer. nat; German professor of plant breeding; b. 10 May 1929, Bremen; s. of Ernst Röbbelen and Henny Röbbelen; m. Christa Scherz 1957; two s. one d.; ed Univs. of Göttingen and Freiburg Br.; Asst Prof. Inst. of Agronomy and Plant Breeding, Univ. of Göttingen 1957–67, Prof. and Head Div. of Cytogenetics 1967–70, Dir of Inst. 1970–94, Dean Faculty of Agric. 1971–72, Prof. Emer. 1994–; Visiting Prof. Univ. of Mo., USA 1966–67; Ed. Plant Breeding 1976–2000; mem. German Soc. for Genetics (Pres. 1969–70, 1977–79), European Asscn for Research in Plant Breeding–EUCARPIA (Chair. Section for Oil and Protein Crops 1978–86, Pres. 1986–89), German Botanical Soc., Asscn for Applied Botany, Genetics Soc. of Canada, German Soc. Fat Research (Pres. 1989–92), German Soc. of Plant Breeding (Pres. 1991–96), Acad. of Sciences, Göttingen 1981, Acad. Leopoldina 1990; Order of Merit 1st Class (Germany) 2001; Hon. DAgric. (Kiel) 1976, (Halle/Saale) 1997, (Brno Czech Repub.) 2001; Norman Medal, German Soc. of Fat Science 1984, Chevreul Medal, Asscn Française pour l'Etude des Corps Gras 1989, Eminent Scientist Award, Paris 1999. *Publications:* over 300 articles on research into plant genetics and breeding. *Leisure interests:* music, mountain climbing, gardening. *Address:* 8 Von Sieboldstrasse, 37075 Göttingen (Office); 9 Tuckermannweg, 37085 Göttingen, Germany.

ROBBINS, Frederick Chapman, AB, BS, MD; American physician (retd); b. 25 Aug. 1916, Auburn, Ala; s. of William J. Robbins and Christine (Chapman) Robbins; m. Alice Havemeyer Northrop 1948; two d.; ed Univ. of Missouri and Harvard Medical School; served US Army 1942–46; Sr Fellow, Nat. Research Council 1948–50; Research Fellow, Harvard Medical School 1948–50; Instructor, Harvard Medical School 1950–51, Assoc. (Pediatrics) 1951–52; Assoc., Research Div. of Infectious Disease, Children's Medical Center, Boston 1950–52; Assoc. Physician and Assoc. Dir of Isolation Services, Children's Hosp., Boston 1950–52; Research Fellow, Boston Lying-in Hosp. 1950–52; Asst Children's Medical Service, Mass. Gen. Hosp., Boston 1950–52; Dir Dept of Pediatrics and Contagious Diseases, Cleveland Metropolitan Gen. Hosp. 1952–66; Prof. of Pediatrics, Case Western Reserve Univ. School of Medicine, Cleveland 1950–80, Dean 1966–80, Dean Emer. 1980–; Prof. Emer. 1987–; now Dir Center Adolescent Health, School of Medicine; Assoc. Pediatrician Univ. Hosps Cleveland 1952–66; Pres. Inst. of Medicine, NAS 1980–85; mem. Nat. Acad. of Sciences 1972, American Philosophical Soc. 1972, American Acad. of Arts and Sciences; Hon. DSc (John Carroll and Mo. Univs); Hon. LLD (New Mexico) 1968; Bronze Star 1945; First Mead Johnson Award (jtly) 1953; Nobel Prize for Physiology and Medicine (jtly) 1954; Medical Mutual Honor Award for 1969. *Publications:* various scientific papers related to virus and rickettsial diseases, especially 'Q' fever in the Mediterranean area and cultivation of poliomyelitis viruses in tissue culture.

Address: Case Western Reserve University, School of Medicine, 10900 Euclid Avenue, Cleveland, OH 44106 (Office); 2626 West Park Boulevard, Shaker Heights, OH 44120, USA (Home).

ROBBINS, Keith Gilbert, DPhil, DLitt, FRSE; British historian and university vice-chancellor; b. 9 April 1940, Bristol; s. of Gilbert Henry John Robbins and Edith Mary Robbins; m. Janet Carey Thomson 1963; three s. one d.; ed Bristol Grammar School, Magdalen Coll. Oxford, St Antony's Coll. Oxford; lecturer, Univ. of York 1963–71; Prof. of History Univ. Coll. of N Wales, Bangor 1971–79; Prof. of Modern History, Univ. of Glasgow 1980–91; Vice-Chancellor Univ. of Wales, Lampeter 1992–, Sr Vice-Chancellor Univ. of Wales 1995–2001; Pres. Historical Asscn 1988–91; Winston Churchill Travelling Fellow 1990. *Publications:* Munich 1938, 1968, Sir Edward Grey 1971, The Abolition of War... 1976, John Bright 1979, The Eclipse of a Great Power: Modern Britain 1870–1975 1983, 1870–1992 (2nd Edn) 1994, The First World War 1984, Nineteenth-Century Britain: Integration and Diversity 1988, Appeasement 1988, Blackwell Dictionary of Twentieth-Century British Political Life (ed.) 1990, Churchill 1992, History, Religion and Identity in Modern Britain 1993, Politicians, Diplomacy and War in Modern British History 1994, Bibliography of British History 1914–1989 1996, Great Britain: Identities, Institutions and the Idea of Britishness 1997, The World Since 1945: a Concise History 1998, The British Isles 1901–1951 2002. *Leisure interests:* walking, music. *Address:* University of Wales, Lampeter, Ceredigion, SA48 7ED (Office); Rhyd y Fran, Cribyn, Lampeter, Ceredigion, SA48 7NH, Wales (Home). *Telephone:* (1570) 424717 (Office); (1570) 470349 (Home). *Fax:* (1570) 421011 (Office). *E-mail:* k.robbins@lamp.ac.uk (Office); profkgr@clara.co.uk (Home).

ROBBINS, Tim, BA; American actor, director and screen writer; b. 16 Oct. 1958, New York; one s. with Susan Sarandon (q.v.); ed Univ. Coll. of Los Angeles; began career as mem. Theater for the New City; Founder and Artistic Dir The Actors' Gang 1981–. *Theatre:* (actor) Ubu Roi 1981; (dir) A Midsummer Night's Dream 1984, The Good Woman of Setzuan 1990; (co-writer with Adam Simon) Alagazam, After the Dog Wars, Violence: The Misadventures of Spike Spangle, Farmer, Carnage – A Comedy (rep. USA at Edin. Int. Festival, Scotland). *Films:* Bull Durham 1988, Cadillac Man, Jacob's Ladder, Five Corners, Tapeheads, Miss Firecracker, Eric the Viking, Jungle Fever, The Player, The Shawshank Redemption, Short Cuts, The Hudsucker Proxy, I.Q.; (actor, writer, dir) Bob Roberts; Dead Man Walking (writer, dir), Nothing to Lose (dir, actor), The Moviegoer, Arlington Road, The Cradle Will Rock, Austin Powers, Mission to Mars, High Fidelity, The Truth About Charlie. *Address:* c/o Elaine Goldsmith Thomas, ICM, 40 West 57th Street, New York, NY 10019, USA.

ROBBINS, Tom, BA; American author; b. 22 July 1936, Blowing Rock, NC; s. of George T. Robbins and Katherine d'Avalon Robbins; m. Terrie Lunden 1967 (divorced 1972); one s.; ed Virginia Commonwealth Univ. and Univ. of Washington; operated black market ring in S. Korea 1956–57; int. news Times-Dispatch, Richmond, Va 1959–62; art critic, The Seattle Times and contrib. to Artforum and Art in America etc. 1962–65; art critic, Seattle Magazine 1965–67. *Publications:* novels: Another Roadside Attraction 1971, Even Cowgirls Get the Blues 1976, Still Life With Woodpecker 1980, Jitterbug Perfume 1984, Skinny Legs and All 1990, Half Asleep in Frog Pajamas 1994, Fierce Invalids Home from Hot Climates 2000. *Leisure interests:* volleyball, white magick, psychedelic plants, art, pop culture and religions. *Address:* P.O. Box 338, La Conner, WA 98257, USA.

ROBERT, Jacques Frédéric, DenD; French professor of law; b. 29 Sept. 1928, Algiers, Algeria; s. of Frédéric Robert and Fanny Robert; m. Marie-Caroline de Bary 1958; two s. two d.; ed Lycée E. F. Gautier, Algiers, Univs. of Algiers and Paris, CNRS; Prof. of Law, Univs of Algiers 1956–60, Rabat, Morocco 1960–62, Grenoble 1962–65; Dir Maison franco-japonaise, Tokyo 1965–68; Prof. of Law, Univ. of Nanterre 1968–69, Univ. of Paris II 1969–; Contributor, Le Monde and La Croix 1970–; Dir Revue de droit public 1977–; Pres. Univ. of Paris II (Panthéon) 1979–85; Pres. of Centre français de Droit comparé 1989–; mem. Conseil Constitutionnel 1989–98; mem. Japan Acad. 1997; Officier, Légion d'honneur; Order of the Sacred Treasure (Japan); Officier, Ordre des Palmes académiques; Commdr, Ordre nat. du Mérite; Commdr, Order of Honour (Austria); Prix Paul Deschanel 1954. *Publications:* Les violations de la liberté individuelle 1954, La monarchie marocaine 1963, Le Japon 1970, Introduction à l'Esprit des Lois 1973, Libertés publiques 1988, L'Esprit de défense 1988, Libertés et droits fondamentaux (5th edn) 2002, Droits de l'homme et Libertés fondamentales (7th edn) 1999, Le juge constitutionnel, juge des libertés 1999, La Garde de la République 2000, Enjeux du siècle: nos libertés 2002. *Leisure interests:* music, photography, swimming. *Address:* Centre français de Droit comparé, 28 rue Saint-Guillaume, 75007 Paris (Office); 14 Villa Saint-Georges, 92160 Antony, France (Home). *Telephone:* 1-44-39-86-23 (Office); 1-46-66-12-32 (Home). *Fax:* 1-44-39-86-28 (Office); 1-46-66-12-13 (Home).

ROBERTO, Holden (see Holden, Roberto).

ROBERTS, Bernard, FRCM; British concert pianist; b. 23 July 1933, Manchester; s. of William Wright Roberts and Elsie Alberta Ingham; m. 1st Patricia May Russell 1955 (dissolved 1987); two s.; m. 2nd Caroline Ireland 1992; ed William Hulme's Grammar School, Manchester, Royal Coll. of Music, London; won Scholarship to RCM 1949; début as concert pianist, Wigmore Hall, London 1957; Piano Prof., RCM 1962–99; tutor, Chetham's School of Music, Manchester 1999–; numerous solo recitals and concerto performances,

chamber music player; Hon. DUniv (Brunel). *Recordings include:* Beethoven's 32 piano sonatas and Bach's 48 preludes and fugues. *Leisure interests:* philosophy, religion, model railways. *Address:* Uwchlaw'r Coed, Llanbedr, Gwynedd, LL45 2NA, Wales. *Telephone:* (1341) 241532.

ROBERTS, Bert, BS; British business executive; b. 1942; m.; ed Johns Hopkins Univ.; trained as electrical engineer; joined MCI (now WorldCom) 1972, CEO 1991–94, Chair. 1992–2002. *Address:* c/o WorldCom, 500 Clinton Center Drive, Clinton, MS 39056, USA.

ROBERTS, Brian Leon; American communications executive; b. 28 June 1959, Philadelphia; s. of Ralph J. Roberts and Suzanne F. Roberts; m. Aileen Kennedy 1985; one s. two d.; ed Univ. of Pennsylvania; Vice-Pres. Operations Comcast Cable Communications Inc. 1985–86, Exec. Vice-Pres. Comcast Corpn 1986–92, also mem. Bd Dirs, Pres. 1992– (acquired AT&T Broadband Dec. 2002); Vice-Chair. Walter Katz Foundation; mem. Bd Dirs Turner Broadcasting System, QVC Network, Viewer's Choice, Cable Labs, Cable TV Asscn. *Address:* Comcast Corporation, Floor 33, East Tower, 1500 Market Street, Philadelphia, PA 19102, USA.

ROBERTS, Chalmers McGeagh, AB; American journalist; b. 18 Nov. 1910; m. Lois Hall 1941; two s. one d.; ed Amherst Coll.; Reporter Washington Post, DC 1933–34, Associated Press, Pittsburgh Bureau 1934–35, Toledo News-Bee 1936–38, Japan Times, Tokyo 1938–39; Asst Man. Ed. Washington Daily News 1939–41; Sunday Ed. Washington Times-Herald 1941; Office of War Information, London and Washington 1941–43; U.S. Army Air Force 1943–46; Life magazine 1946–47; Washington Star 1947–49; Washington Post 1949–71, Chief Diplomatic corresp. 1954–71, contrib. columnist 1971–, San Diego Union contrib. columnist 1971–86; mem. American Newspaper Guild; Hon. DHumLitt 1963; Order of Merit, Fed. Repub. of Germany. *Publications:* Washington Past and Present 1950, Can We Meet the Russians Half Way? 1958, The Nuclear Years: the Arms Race and Arms Control, 1945–70 1970, The Washington Post: The First 100 Years 1971, First Rough Draft: a Journalist's Journal of Our Times 1973, In the Shadow of Power: The Story of the Washington Post 1989, How Did I Get Here So Fast? 1991. *Address:* 6699 MacArthur Boulevard, Bethesda, MD 20816-2247, USA (Office and Home). *Telephone:* (301) 229-2471.

ROBERTS, (Charles) Patrick; American politician; b. 20 April 1936, Topeka, Kan.; s. of Wes Roberts and Ruth Roberts (née Patrick); m. Franki Fann 1970; one s. two d.; ed Kansas State Univ.; with US Marine Corps 1958–62; Publr Litchfield Park, Arizona 1962–67; Admin. Asst to US Senator F. Carlson 1967–68, to US Congressman Keith Sebelius 1968–70; mem. 97th to 104th Congresses 1980–97; Senator from Kansas Jan. 1997–; Republican. *Address:* United States Senate, 302 Hart Senate Office Building, Washington, DC 20510, USA. *Telephone:* (202) 224-4774.

ROBERTS, Sir Denys Tudor Emil, KBE, QC, MA, BCL; British judge and administrator; b. 19 Jan. 1923, London; s. of William David Roberts and Dorothy Eliza Morrison; m. 1st B. Marsh 1949; one s. one d.; m. 2nd Fiona Alexander 1985; one s.; ed Aldenham School, Wadham Coll., Oxford and Lincoln's Inn; Captain, Royal Artillery 1943–46; English Bar 1950–53; Crown Counsel, Nyasaland (now Malawi) 1953–59; Attorney-Gen., Gibraltar 1960–62; Solicitor-Gen., Hong Kong 1962–66, Attorney-Gen. 1966–73, Colonial Sec. 1973–76, Chief Sec. 1976–78, Chief Justice Hong Kong and Brunei 1979–88, of Brunei 1988–; Pres. Court of Appeal for Bermuda 1988–94, Court of Final Appeal Hong Kong 1997–; Pres. MCC 1989–90; Hon. Bencher Lincoln's Inn and Court of Final Appeal, Hong Kong Special Admin. Region; Hon. Fellow Wadham Coll.; Seri Paduka Makhuta Brunei. *Publications:* eight books (including four novels) 1955–. *Leisure interests:* writing, cricket, tennis, walking. *Address:* Supreme Court, Bandar Seri Begawan, Brunei; Leithen Lodge, Innerleithen, Peeblesshire, EH44 6NW, Scotland. *Telephone:* (1896) 830297 (Scotland). *Fax:* (1896) 830726.

ROBERTS, Sir Derek Harry, Kt, CBE, BSc, FRS, FEng; British physicist, business executive, university provost and university president; b. 28 March 1932, Manchester; s. of Harry Roberts and Alice Roberts (née Storey); m. Winifred Short 1958; one s. one d.; ed Manchester Cen. High School and Manchester Univ.; Research Scientist, Plessey Co. 1953–67; Gen. Man. Plessey Semiconductors 1967–69; Dir Plessey Allen Clark Research Centre 1969–73; Man. Dir Plessey Microsystems Div. 1973–79; Dir of Research, The General Electric Co. PLC 1979–83, Tech. Dir 1983–85, Jt Deputy Man. Dir (Tech.) 1985–88, Dir 1988–; Visiting Prof. Univ. Coll., London 1979, Provost and Pres. 1989–99, 2002–; Pres. BAAS 1996–97, Sr Research Fellow School of Public Policy 1999–; Hon. DSc (Bath) 1982, (Loughborough) 1984, (City) 1985, (Lancaster) 1986, (Manchester) 1987, (Queens Univ., Belfast) 1990; Hon. DUniv (Open) 1984, (Salford), (Essex), (London) 1988. *Publications:* about 30 tech. papers in learned soc. journals. *Leisure interests:* gardening, reading. *Address:* Provost's Office, University College London, Gower Street, London, WC1E 6BT (Office); The Old Rectory, Maids Moreton, Buckingham, England (Home). *Telephone:* (20) 7679-7234 (Office); (1280) 813470 (Home). *Fax:* (20) 7388-5412 (Office). *E-mail:* provost@ucl.ac.uk (Office). *Website:* www .ucl.ac.uk (Office).

ROBERTS, Sir Gareth Gwyn, Kt, PhD, FRS; British professor of applied physics and university vice-chancellor; b. 16 May 1940, Wales; s. of Edwin Roberts and Meri Roberts; m. 1st Charlotte Standen 1962; two s. one d.; m. 2nd Carolyn Rich 1993; two step-d.; ed Univ. Coll. of N Wales, Bangor; Lecturer in Physics, Univ. of Wales 1963–66; research physicist, Xerox Corpn

USA 1966–68; Sr Lecturer, Reader and Prof. of Physics, Univ. of Ulster 1968–76; Prof. of Applied Physics and Head, Dept of Applied Physics and Electronics. Univ. of Durham 1976–85; Visiting Prof. of Electronic Eng, Dept of Eng Science Oxford Univ. 1985–95; Chief Scientist and Dir of Research, Thorn EMI PLC; Vice-Chancellor, Univ. of Sheffield 1991–2000; Chair. Medical Solutions PLC 2000–; Pres. Wolfson Coll. Oxford 2001–; Chair. Defence Scientific Advisory Council 1993–97, CVCP 1995–97; Pres. Inst. of Physics 1998–2000, Science Council 2000–; Dir Sheffield Health Authority 1996–2000; mem. Higher Educ. Funding Council for England 1997–, Univs. Superannuation Scheme Bd 1997–2001; Chair. Medical Solutions PLC 2001–; mem. Bd Retained Organs Comm. 2001–; Pres. Techniquest 2002–; Trustee Higher Educ. Policy Inst. 2002–, Oxford Philomusica Advisory Council; Dr hc (Univ. of Wales, Univ. of Sheffield, Univ. of West of England); Holweck Gold Medal and Prize, Inst. of Physics 1986. *Publications:* Insulating Films on Semiconductors 1979, Langmuir-Blodgett Films 1990; many publs and patents on physics of semiconductor devices and molecular electronics. *Leisure interests:* watching soccer, classical music, organizing 'town and gown' functions. *Address:* Wolfson College, Oxford, OX2 6UD, England (Office). *Telephone:* (1865) 274102 (Office). *Fax:* (1865) 2741365 (Office). *E-mail:* gareth .roberts@wolfson.ox.ac.uk (Office).

ROBERTS, Sir Ivor Anthony, KCMG, MA; British diplomatist; b. 24 Sept. 1946, Liverpool; s. of the late Leonard Moore Roberts and Rosa Maria Roberts (née Fusco); m. Elizabeth Bray Bernard Smith 1974; two s. one d.; ed St Mary's Coll., Crosby, Keble Coll., Oxford; entered diplomatic service 1968, with Middle East Centre for Arab Studies 1969, Third, then Second Sec. Paris 1970–73, Second, then First Sec. FCO 1973–78, First Sec. Canberra 1978–82, Deputy Head of News Dept FCO 1982–86, Head Security Co-ordination Dept FCO 1986–88, Minister and Deputy Head of Mission, Madrid 1989–93, Chargé d'affaires Belgrade 1994–96; Amb. to Yugoslavia 1996–97, to Ireland 1999–2003, to Italy 2003–; Fellow Inst. of Linguists 1991; Sr Assoc. Mem., St Antony's Coll., Oxford 1998–99; Hon. Fellow, Keble Coll., Oxford 2001. *Leisure interests:* opera, skiing, golf, photography. *Address:* British Embassy, Via XX Settembre 80A, 00187 Rome, Italy. *Telephone:* (06) 42202266 (Office). *Fax:* (06) 42202333 (Office). *E-mail:* ivor.roberts@fco.gov.uk (Office). *Website:* www.britain.it.

ROBERTS, John D., PhD; American chemist and educator; b. 8 June 1918, Los Angeles, Calif.; s. of Allen Andrew Roberts and Flora Dombrowski; m. Edith M. Johnson 1942; three s. one d.; ed Univ. of California at Los Angeles; Instructor Univ. of Calif. at Los Angeles; Nat. Research Fellow in Chem., Harvard Univ. 1945–46, Instructor 1946; Instructor MIT 1946–47, Asst Prof. 1947–50, Assoc. Prof. 1950–53; Guggenheim Fellow, Calif. Inst. of Technology 1952–53, Prof. of Organic Chem. 1953–72, Inst. Prof. of Chem. 1972–88, Prof. Emer. 1988–, lecturer 1988–, Chair. Div. of Chem. and Chemical Eng 1963–68, Acting Chair. 1972–73, Dean of the Faculty 1980–83, Vice-Pres. and Provost 1980–83; Visiting Prof. Ohio State Univ. 1952, Harvard Univ. 1959–60, Univ. of Munich 1962; Distinguished Visiting Prof. Univ. of Iowa 1967; Visiting Prof. Stanford Univ. 1973; Noyce Visiting Prof. of Science, Grinnell Coll. 2001; Distinguished Grad. Lecturer Scripps Research Inst. 1996; mem. NAS, Chair. Section of Chem. 1968–71, of Math. and Physical Sciences 1976–78, Class I 1977–79, Counsellor 1980–83; mem. American Philosophical Society 1974, Counsellor, Class I 1983–86; Dr hc (Munich); Hon. DSc (Temple Univ., Wales, Scripps Research Inst.); numerous awards, including Nat. Medal of Science 1990, Welch Award 1990, Arthur C. Cope Award 1994, NAS Award in Chemical Sciences 1999, Nakanishi Prize 2001. *Publications:* Nuclear Magnetic Resonance 1958, Spin-Spin Splitting in High Resolution Nuclear Magnetic Resonance Spectra 1961, Molecular Orbital Calculations 1961, Basic Principles of Organic Chemistry 1965, Modern Organic Chemistry 1967, Organic Chemistry, Methane to Macromolecules 1971, At the Right Place at the Right Time 1990, ABC's of FT NMR 2000; and numerous articles 1940–. *Leisure interests:* tennis, skiing, sailing, classical music, colour photography. *Address:* California Institute of Technology, Crellin Laboratory, Pasadena, CA 91125, USA. *Telephone:* (626) 395-6036.

ROBERTS, John Morris, CBE, DPhil; British historian; b. 14 April 1928, Bath, Somerset; s. of the late Edward Henry Roberts and Dorothy Julia Hallett; m. Judith Armitage 1964; one s. two d.; ed Taunton School, Keble Coll., Univ. of Oxford; nat. service 1949–50; Prize Fellow Magdalen Coll., Univ. of Oxford 1951–53, Tutorial Fellow Merton Coll. 1954–79, Warden 1984–94, Hon. Fellow 1994–; Vice-Chancellor Univ. of Southampton 1979–85; mem. Bd of Govs. BBC 1988–93; mem. Bd British Council 1991–98; Trustee Nat. Portrait Gallery 1984–98; Writer and Presenter BBC TV Series, The Triumph of the West 1985; Hon. Fellow, Merton and Keble Colls., Univ. of Oxford; Hon. DLitt (Southampton) 1987. *Publications:* Twentieth Century 1999, The New History of the World 2003; and other historical books and articles. *Leisure interest:* music. *Address:* c/o Merton College, Oxford, OX1 4JD, England.

ROBERTS, Julia; American actress; b. 28 Oct. 1967, Smyrna, Ga; m. 1st Lyle Lovett 1993 (divorced 1995); m. 2nd Daniel Moder 2002; ed high school; appeared in TV movie Baja Oklahoma; UNICEF Goodwill Amb. 1995. *Films:* Firehouse 1987, Satisfaction 1988, Mystic Pizza 1988, Blood Red 1989, Steel Magnolias (Golden Globe Award 1990) 1989, 3000, Flatliners 1990, Pretty Woman 1990, Sleeping with the Enemy 1991, Dying Young 1991, Batman, Hook 1991, The Player 1992, The Pelican Brief 1993, I Love Trouble 1994, Prêt à Porter 1994, Mary Reilly 1994, Something to Talk About 1996, Michael Collins 1996, Everyone Says I Love You 1996, My Best Friend's Wedding

1997, Conspiracy Theory 1997, Notting Hill 1998, Stepmom 1998, Runaway Bride 1999, Erin Brockovich 2000 (Acad. Award for Best Actress), The Mexican 2001, America's Sweethearts 2001, Ocean's Eleven 2001, Full Frontal 2002, Confessions of a Dangerous Mind 2003. *Address:* ICM, 8942 Wilshire Boulevard, Beverly Hills, CA 90211, USA.

ROBERTS, Kevin John; business executive; b. 20 Oct. 1949, Lancaster; s. of John Roberts and Jean Roberts (née Lambert); m. 1st Barbara Beckett; one d.; m. 2nd Rowena Joan Honeywill 1974; two s. one d.; Brand Man. Gillette Co., London 1972–74; Group Marketing Man., Procter & Gamble, Geneva 1975–82; Vice-Pres. Pepsico, Nicosia 1982–86; Pres. and CEO Pepsi Cola Canada, Toronto 1987–89; COO Lion Nathan, Auckland 1990–96; CEO Worldwide Saatchi & Saatchi, New York City 1997–. *Publication:* Peak Performance (co-author) 2000. *Leisure interests:* rugby football, tennis, art, travel, music. *Address:* Saatchi & Saatchi, 375 Hudson Street, New York, NY 10014, U.S.A. (Office).

ROBERTS, Matthew Vernon, MA Phil; Saint Lucian politician; b. 29 July 1954, Castries; ed Univ. of W. Indies, Jamaica, City Univ., London, UK; primary school teacher 1969–72; Asst Ed. The Voice newspaper 1972–80; fmr Public Relations Officer, Saint Lucia Tourist Bd; fmr Regional Communications Consultant, Caribbean Family Planning Affiliation; fmr Chief Information Officer Govt Information Service; Resident Tutor, School of Continuing Studies, Univ. of W. Indies; currently Speaker of House of Ass. *Address:* Office of the Speaker, House of Assembly, Parliament, Castries (Office); Clavier Ridgeway, Entrepot Summit, POB 927, Castries, Saint Lucia (Home). *Telephone:* 453-6647 (Office); 452-7282 (Home). *Fax:* 452-5451 (Office). *E-mail:* parliament@gosl.gov.lc (Office). *Website:* stlucia.gov.lc (Office).

ROBERTS, Michèle (Brigitte), MA (OXON), ALA, FRSL; British novelist and poet; b. 20 May 1949, Herts.; d. of Reginald Roberts and Monique Caulle; m. Jim Latter 1991; two step-s.; ed Convent Grammar School, Somerville Coll., Oxford and University Coll. London; British Council Librarian, Bangkok 1973–74; Poetry Ed. Spare Rib 1974, City Limits 1981–83; Visiting Fellow Univ. of E. Anglia 1992, Univ. of Nottingham Trent 1994; Visiting Prof. Univ. of Nottingham Trent 1996–2001; Prof. of Creative Writing, Univ. of E. Anglia 2002–; Chair. Literary Cttee British Council 1998–2002; mem. and Bd mem. PEN Club; Judge Booker Prize 2001; Chevalier des Arts et des Lettres 2001; Hon. MA (Nene) 1999; W. H. Smith Literary Award 1993. *Plays:* The Journeywoman 1988, Child-Lover 1995. *Television film:* The Heavenly Twins (Channel 4) 1993. *Publications include:* novels: A Piece of the Night 1978, The Visitation 1983, The Wild Girl 1984, The Book of Mrs Noah 1987, In the Red Kitchen 1990, Daughters of the House 1992, Flesh and Blood 1994, Impossible Saints 1997, Fair Exchange 1999, The Looking-Glass 2000, The Mistressclass 2003; (ed. jtly) Mind Readings 1996; Stories: During Mother's Absence 1993, Playing Sardines 2001; essays: Food, Sex and God 1998; poetry: The Mirror of the Mother 1986; plays: Psyche and the Hurricane 1991, Child Lover 1993, All the Selves I Was 1995; non-fiction: Food, Sex and God 1998. *Leisure interests:* reading, talking with friends, cooking, gardening, looking at art. *Address:* c/o Gillon Aitken, Gillon Aitken Associates, 29 Fernshaw Road, London, SW10 0TG, England.

ROBERTS, Richard John, PhD, FRS; British scientist; b. 6 Sept. 1943, Derby; s. of John Walter Roberts and Edna Wilhelmina Roberts; m. 1st Elizabeth Dyson 1965 (deceased); one s. one d.; m. 2nd Jean Tagliabue 1986; one s. one d.; ed Sheffield Univ.; researcher Harvard Univ. 1969–72; Sr. Staff Investigator Cold Spring Harbor Lab. Research Inst., Long Island 1972–86, Asst. Dir. for Research 1986–92; Research Dir New England Biolabs 1992–; Chair. NCI Bd. of Scientific Counselors 1996–2000; Chair. Scientific Advisory Bd. Celera 1998–, MultiGene Biotech 1998–; Chair. Steering Cttee. on Genetics and Biotech. ICSU 1998–; mem. Editorial Bd. Bioinformatics 1985–, Current Opinions in Chemical Biology 1997–; mem. Scientific Advisory Bd. Conservation Law Foundation 1998–, PubMed Central 2000–, Orchid Biosciences 2000–; mem. Bd. Albert Schweitzer Acad. of Medicine 1998–; Exec. Ed. Nucleic Acids Research 1987–; Patron Oxford Int. Biomedical Centre 1994–; Hon. MD (Uppsala) 1992, (Bath) 1994; Hon. DSc (Sheffield) 1994, (Derby) 1995; Nobel Prize in Physiology or Medicine (for the discovery of 'split genes') 1993; Golden Plate Award, American Acad. of Achievement 1994, Convocation Award, Sheffield Univ. 1994, Faye Robiner Award, Ross Univ. 1994. *Publications:* Nucleases (co-ed.) 1982, The Applications of Computers to Research on Nucleic Acids (co-ed.) 1982. *Leisure interest:* croquet. *Address:* New England Biolabs, 32 Tozer Road, Beverly, MA 01915, USA. *Telephone:* (978) 927-3382 (Office). *Fax:* (978) 921-1527 (Office). *E-mail:* roberts@neb.com (Office).

ROBERTSON, Geoffrey R., QC, BA, LLB, BCL; Australian judge and lawyer; b. 30 Sept. 1946, Sydney; s. of Francis Robertson and Bernice Beattie; m. Kathy Lette (q.v.) 1990; one s. one d.; ed Epping Boys' High School and Univs. of Sydney and Oxford; Rhodes scholar; solicitor, Allen, Allen & Hemsley 1970; called to bar, Middle Temple, London 1973; QC 1988; Visiting Prof. Univ. of NSW 1979, Univ. of Warwick 1981; leader, Amnesty missions to S Africa 1983–90; consultant on Human Rights to Govt of Australia 1984; Head, Doughty St Chambers 1990–; Counsel to Royal Comm. on gun-running to Colombian drug cartels 1991; Asst Recorder 1993–99, a Recorder 1999–; Master of Bench, Middle Temple 1997–; Chief Counsel Comm. on Admin. of Justice in Trinidad and Tobago 2000; Pres. UN Special Court for War Crimes in Sierra Leone 2002–; mem. Exec. Council Justice; Freedom of Information Award 1992. *Radio:* Chair. You the Jury, BBC Radio 4. *Plays:* The Trials of

Oz. BBC 1992. *TV series:* Hypotheticals, Granada TV, ABC and Channel 7 (Australia). *Publications:* Reluctant Judas 1976, Obscenity 1979, People Against the Press 1983, Geoffrey Robertson's Hypotheticals 1986, Does Dracula Have Aids? 1987, Freedom, The Individual and The Law 1989, The Justice Game 1998, Crimes Against Humanity 1999, Media Law (with A. Nicol) 2002. *Leisure interests:* tennis, opera, fishing. *Address:* Doughty Street Chambers, 11 Doughty Street, London, WC1N 2PL, England. *Telephone:* (20) 7404-1313. *Fax:* (20) 7404-2283. *Website:* www.doughtystreet.co.uk (Office).

ROBERTSON, Sir Lewis, Kt, CBE, FRSE; British industrialist and administrator; b. 28 Nov. 1922, Dundee, Scotland; s. of John Robertson and Margaret Robertson (née Arthur); m. Elspeth Badenoch 1950 (died 2001); two s. (and one s. deceased) one d.; ed Trinity Coll., Glenalmond and trained as accountant; RAF Intelligence 1942–46; worked in textile industry, Chair. and Man. Dir Scott & Robertson PLC 1946–70; Chief Exec. and Deputy Chair. Grampian Holdings PLC 1971–76; Deputy Chair. and Chief Exec. Scottish Devt Agency 1976–81; Dir Scottish & Newcastle Breweries PLC 1975–87, Whitman Int., SA, Geneva 1987–90, Edin. Income Trust 1989–99, Berkeley Hotel Co. 1995–97, Advanced Man. Programme Scotland 1996–2003; Chair. F.H. Lloyd Holdings PLC 1982–87, Triplex PLC 1983–87, Triplex Lloyd PLC 1987–90, Girobank Scotland 1984–90, Borthwicks PLC 1985–89, Lilley PLC 1986–93, Havelock Europa PLC 1989–92, Stakis PLC 1991–95, Postern Exec. Group Ltd 1991–96; Trustee (Exec. Cttee), Carnegie Trust for the Univs of Scotland 1963– (Chair. 1990–2003), Scottish Cancer Foundation 2000–, Foundation for Skin Research 2000–; mem. Monopolies and Mergers Comm. 1969–76, British Council (Chair. Scottish Advisory Cttee) 1978–87, Restrictive Practices Court 1983–96; mem. Council Royal Soc. of Edin. 1992, Treas. 1994–99; Hon. FRCSE 1999; Hon. LLD (Dundee) 1971, (Aberdeen) 1999; Hon. DBA (Napier) 1992; Hon. DUniv (Stirling) 1993, (Glasgow) 2003. *Leisure interests:* work, computer use, list-making, things Italian, music, literature. *Address:* 32 Saxe Coburg Place, Edinburgh, EH3 5BP, Scotland (Office). *Telephone:* (131) 332-5221. *Fax:* (131) 343-1840. *E-mail:* lr32scp@talk21.com (Home).

ROBERTSON, Pat (Marion Gordon Robertson), BA, MDiv; American theologian and broadcasting executive; b. 22 March 1930, Lexington, Va; s. of A. Willis Robertson and Gladys Churchill; m. Adelia Elmer; two s. two d.; ed Washington and Lee Univ., Yale Univ., New York Theology Seminary; founder, CEO Christian Broadcasting Network, Va Beach, Va 1960–; ordained Minister Southern Baptist Convention 1961–87; founder, Chancellor Regent Univ. (fmrly CBN Univ.) 1977–; founder, Chair. Operation Blessing Int. Relief and Devt Inc. 1978–, Int. Family Entertainment Inc. 1990–97, Asia Pacific Media Corpn 1993–; Chair. Starguide Digital Networks Inc. 1995–, Porchlight Entertainment Inc. 1995–; founder, Pres. Christian Coalition 1989–, American Center for Law and Justice 1990–; Cand. for Republican nomination for Pres. 1988; Dir United Va Bank, Norfolk; mem. Nat. Broadcasters (Dir 1973–); Knesset Medallion, Israel Pilgrimage Cttee, Faith and Freedom Award, Religious Heritage America, Bronze Halo Award, Southern Calif. Motion Picture Council, George Washington Honor Medal, Freedom Foundation at Valley Forge 1983. *Publications:* Shout it from the Housetops: The Story of the Founder of the Christian Broadcasting Network (jtly.) 1972, My Prayer for You 1977, The Secret Kingdom 1982, Answers to 200 of Life's Most Probing Questions 1984, Beyond Reason 1984, America's Dates with Destiny 1986, The Plan 1989, The New Millennium 1990, The New World Order 1991, The End of the Age 1995. *Address:* The Christian Broadcasting Network, 977 Centreville Turnpike, Virginia Beach, VA 23463, USA (Office).

ROBERTSON OF PORT ELLEN, Baron (Life Peer), cr. 1999, of Islay in Argyll and Bute; **George Islay MacNeill Robertson,** PC, MA, FRSA; British international official; b. 12 April 1946, Port Ellen, Isle of Islay, Argyll; s. of George P. Robertson and Marion Robertson; m. Sandra Wallace 1970; two s. one d.; ed Dunoon Grammar School and Univ. of Dundee; Research Asst Tayside Study 1968–69; Scottish Organizer, Gen. & Municipal Workers' Union 1969–78; MP for Hamilton 1978–97, for Hamilton South 1997–99; Parl. Pvt. Sec. to Sec. of State for Social Services 1979; Opposition Spokesman on Scottish Affairs 1979–80, on Defence 1980–81, on Foreign and Commonwealth Affairs 1981–93; Prin. Spokesman on European Affairs 1984–94; Shadow Spokesman for Scotland 1994–97; Sec. of State for Defence 1997–99; Sec.-Gen. of NATO 1999–(2003); Chair. Scottish Council of Labour Party 1977–78; Vice-Chair. Bd British Council 1985–94; Vice-Pres. Operation Raleigh (now Raleigh Int.) 1982–; mem. Bd Scottish Devt Agency 1975–78, Scottish Tourist Bd 1974–76; mem. Council, Nat. Trust for Scotland 1976–82, 1983–85; mem. Steering Cttee Königswinter Conf. 1983–92; mem. Council, Royal Inst. of Int. Affairs 1984–91, Jt Pres. 2001–; Gov. Ditchley Foundation 1989–; Elder Brother, Trinity House 2001–; Pres. Burns Club 2002–; Hon. Regimental Col London Scottish (Volunteers); Hon. LLD (Dundee, Bradford, Baku State Univ., Azerbaijan); Hon. DSc (Cranfield – Royal Mil. Coll. of Science); Commdr's Cross, Order of Merit (Germany), Grand Cross, Order of Star of Romania. *Leisure interests:* photography, golf, walking, family, reading. *Address:* NATO Headquarters, 1110 Brussels, Belgium (Office); House of Lords, London, SW1A 0PW, England. *Telephone:* (2) 707-49-17 (Office). *Fax:* (2) 707-46-66 (Office). *Website:* www.nato.int (Office).

ROBICHAUD, Hon. Louis Joseph, CC, PC, QC, BA; Canadian politician; b. 21 Oct. 1925, St Anthony, Kent County, NB; s. of Amédée Robichaud and Annie (née Richard) Robichaud; m. 1st Lorraine Savoie 1951 (died 1986); three s. one d.; m. 2nd Jacqueline Grignon 1998; ed Sacred Heart and Laval

Univs.; pvt. law practice 1951–60; mem. NB Legislature 1952–71, Leader of Opposition 1958–60, 1970–71; Premier of NB 1960–70, Attorney-Gen. 1960–65, Minister of Youth 1968–70; mem. Senate 1973–; mem. Liberal Party; numerous hon. degrees. *Address:* Senate of Canada, 475-S Centre Block, Ottawa, Ont., K1A 0A4 (Office); 1501–400 Stewart Street, Ottawa, Ont., K1N 6L2, Canada.

ROBINS, Lee Nelken, MA, PhD; American professor of social science; b. 29 Aug. 1922, New Orleans, La.; m. 1st Eli Robins 1946 (died 1994); four s.; m. 2nd Hugh Chaplin, MD 1998; ed Radcliffe Coll. and Harvard Univ.; Research Assoc. Prof. Dept of Psychiatry, Washington Univ., St Louis, Mo. 1962–66, Research Prof. of Sociology in Psychiatry 1966–68, Prof. of Sociology in Psychiatry 1968–91, Prof. Dept of Sociology 1969–91, Univ. Prof. of Social Science, Prof. of Social Science in Psychiatry 1991–2001, Prof. Emer. 2001–; NIMH Special Research Fellowship, Washington Univ. 1968–70; mem. Inst. of Medicine (NAS); Research Scientist Award 1970, 1990, Lifetime Achievement Award, American Public Health Asscn 1994, Special Presidential Commendation, American Psychiatric Asscn 1999, 2nd Century Award, Wash. Univ. 2000, Distinguished Scientific Contrib. Award, Soc. for Research into Child Devt 2003 and many other awards. *Publications include:* Deviant Children Grown Up: A Sociological and Psychiatric Study of Sociopathic Personality 1966, The Vietnam Drug User Returns 1974, Validity of Psychiatric Diagnosis 1989, Psychiatric Disorders in America 1991, Straight and Devious Pathways from Childhood to Adulthood 1990. *Address:* Washington University School of Medicine, Department of Psychiatry, St Louis, MO 63110, USA (Office). *Telephone:* (314) 362-2471 (Office); (314) 361-0204 (Home). *Fax:* (314) 362-2470 (Office); (314) 361-6010 (Home). *E-mail:* robins@psychiatry.wustl.edu (Office); lro6@aol.com (Home).

ROBINS, Sir Ralph Harry, Kt, BSc, FREng; British business executive; b. 16 June 1932, Heanor; s. of Leonard Haddon and Maud Lillian Robins; m. Patricia Maureen Grimes 1962; two d.; ed Imperial Coll., Univ. of London; Devt Engineer, Rolls-Royce 1955–66, Exec. Vice-Pres. Rolls-Royce Inc. 1971, Man. Dir Rolls-Royce Industrial and Marine Div. 1973, Commercial Dir Rolls-Royce Ltd 1978, Man. Dir Rolls-Royce PLC 1984–89, Deputy Chair. 1989–92 and Chief Exec. 1990–92, Chair. Rolls Royce 1992–; Chair. Defence Industries Council 1986–; Pres. Soc. of British Aerospace Cos. 1986–87, Deputy Pres. 1987–88; Dir (non-exec.) Standard Chartered 1988–, Schroders 1990–, Marks & Spencer 1992–2001, Cable & Wireless 1994– (Chair. (non-exec.) 1998–2003); mem. Council for Science and Tech. 1993–98; Fellow of Imperial Coll.; Hon. FRAeS; Hon. FIMechE 1996; Hon. DBA (Strathclyde) 1996; Hon. DEng (Sheffield) 2001; Commdr Order of Merit (Germany) 1996. *Leisure interests:* tennis, golf, music, classic cars. *Address:* Rolls-Royce PLC, 65 Buckingham Gate, London, SW1E 6AT, England. *Telephone:* (20) 7222-9020. *Fax:* (20) 7227-9185.

ROBINSON, Sir Albert Edward Phineas, Kt, MA; South African business executive (retd); b. 30 Dec. 1915, Durban; s. of Charles Phineas Robinson and Mabel Victoria Robinson; m. 1st Mary J. Bertish 1944 (died 1973); four d.; m. 2nd M. L. Royston-Pigott (née Barrett) 1975; ed Durban High School and Stellenbosch, LSE, Trinity Coll., Cambridge and Leiden Univs; Barrister-at-Law, Lincoln's Inn; Imperial Light Horse, N. Africa 1940–43; mem. Johannesburg City Council and Leader United Party in Council 1945–48; United Party MP, South African Parl. 1947–53; perm. resident in Southern Rhodesia (now Zimbabwe) 1953; dir of banks, building socs, several financial and industrial cos 1953–61; Chair. Cen. African Airways Corpn 1957–61; mem. Monckton Comm. 1960; High Commr, Fed. of Rhodesia and Nyasaland in the UK 1961–63; Dir E. Oppenheimer and Son Ltd 1963–2000; Deputy Chair. Gen. Mining and Finance Co. Ltd 1963–71; Chair. Johannesburg Consolidated Investment Corpn Ltd 1971–80, Rustenburg Platinum Mines Ltd 1971–80; Dir Anglo-American Corpn of South Africa Ltd 1965–88; Chancellor, Univ. of Bophuthatswana 1980–91; Hon. DCom. *Leisure interests:* music, people, conversation. *Address:* 43 St Mary Abbots Court, Warwick Gardens, London, W14 8RB, England.

ROBINSON, Anne Josephine; British journalist and broadcaster; b. 26 Sept. 1944; m. 1st Charles Wilson; one d.; m. 2nd John Penrose; ed Farnborough Hill Convent and Les Ambassadrices, Paris, France; reporter Daily Mail 1967–68, Sunday Times 1968–77, Women's Ed. Daily Mirror 1979–80, Asst Ed. 1980–93, columnist 1983–93; columnist Today 1993–95, The Times 1993–95, 1998–, The Sun 1995–97, Daily Express 1997–98; Hon. Fellow John Moores Univ. *Radio work includes:* Anne Robinson Show (Radio 2) 1988–93. *Television:* presenter (BBC) of Points of View 1987–88, Watchdog 1993–, Weekend Watchdog 1997–, Going for a Song 2000–, The Weakest Link 2000– (also USA 2001–). *Publication:* Memoirs of an Unfit Mother (autobiog.) 2001. *Address:* Penrose Media, 19 Victoria Grove, London W8 5RW, England (Office).

ROBINSON, Arthur Howard, MA, PhD; American cartographer and geographer; b. 5 Jan. 1915, Montreal, Canada; s. of James Howard Robinson and Elizabeth Peavey Robinson; m. 1st Mary Elizabeth Coffin 1938 (died 1992); one s. one d.; m. 2nd Martha Elizabeth Rodabaugh 1993; ed Saffron Walden Friends School, England, McGuffey High School, Oxford, Ohio., Miami, Wisconsin and Ohio State Univs; Sec. to a Dir Ohio Bd of Liquor Control 1936; Teaching Asst Geography, Univ. of Wis. 1936–38, Ohio State Univ. 1938–41; Chief, Map Div., Office of Strategic Services 1941–45 (mem. US Del. Cairo and Québec Allied Confs during Second World War); mil. service 1944–45 (promoted to maj.); Asst Prof., later Prof., Univ. of Wis. 1945–80, Prof. Emer.

1980–; Dir Univ. of Wis. Cartographic Laboratory 1966–73; Lawrence Martin Prof. of Cartography 1967–; mem. Bd of Dirs American Congress on Surveying and Mapping 1952–54, Bd of Dirs Cartography Div. 1966–69, 1970, Vice-Chair. 1970, Chair. 1971–72, Ed. American Cartographer 1973–76; mem. Council Asscn of American Geographers 1960–64, Vice-Pres. 1962–63, Pres. 1963–64; Corresp. mem. Comm. II (Tech. Terms), Int. Cartographic Asscn 1964–72, mem. Comm. on the History of Cartography 1976–, Chair. Cttee on Statutes 1976–84, Pres. 1972–76, Past Pres. 1976–80; Chair. Cttee on State Cartography 1974–79, 1981–82; mem. Gov.'s Cttee on State Mapping (Wis.) 1961–63; Co-Ed. Int. Yearbook of Cartography 1961–73; Fellow British Cartographic Soc. 1998; Hon. DLitt (Miami) 1966; Hon. DSc (Ohio State) 1984; numerous awards including Citation for Meritorious Contribs to Geography (Cartography), Asscn American Geographers 1953, American Congress on Surveying and Mapping (ACSM) Award for Meritorious Service to the Discipline of Cartography 1979, Carl Mannerfelt Medal, Int. Cartographic Asscn 1981, Presidential Citation for Outstanding Services to ACSM 1988, John Oliver LaGorce Medal, Nat. Geographical Soc. 1988, Silver Medal, British Cartographic Soc. 1991, O. M. Miller Medal, American Geographical Soc. 1998. *Publications:* numerous books and monographs and over 100 professional papers on maps and cartography including The Look of Maps 1952, Elements of Cartography 1953, Robinson Map Projection 1963, The Atlas of Wisconsin (with J. B. Culver) 1974, The Nature of Maps: Essays Toward and Understanding of Maps and Mapping (with B. Petchenik) 1976, Early Thematic Mapping in the History of Cartography 1982, Which Map is Best? 1986, Cartographical Innovations: An Historical International Handbook of Mapping Terms to 1900 (Co-Ed. with H. Wallis) 1987, Choosing a World Map 1988. *Address:* 7707 North Brookline Drive #302, Madison, WI 53719, USA. *Telephone:* (608) 662-0302.

ROBINSON, (Arthur Napoleon) Raymond, MA, LLB, SC; Trinidad and Tobago politician, barrister and economist; b. 16 Dec. 1926, Calder Hall; s. of James Andrew Robinson and Emily Isabella Robinson; m. Patricia Jean Rawlins 1961; one s. one d.; ed Bishop's High School, Tobago, London Univ., St John's Coll., Oxford and Inner Temple, London; MP West Indies 1958–61; Rep. of Trinidad and Tobago Council of Univ. of West Indies 1960–62; Minister of Finance and Gov. for Trinidad Bd of Govs. of IMF and IBRD 1961–67; Deputy Leader, People's Nat. Movt 1967–70; Minister of External Affairs 1967–68; Dir of the Foundation for the Establishment of an Int. Criminal Court 1971; Chair. Democratic Action Congress 1971–86; Rep. for Tobago East, House of Reps. 1976–80; Chair. Tobago House of Ass. 1980–86; Leader Nat. Alliance for Reconstruction 1986–91; Prime Minister of Trinidad and Tobago 1986–91, also Minister of the Economy; Minister Extraordinaire and Minister for Tobago Affairs; Adviser to the Prime Minister 1995–97; Pres. of Trinidad and Tobago 1997–2003; mem. UN Expert Group on Crime and the Abuse of Power 1979; Vice-Chair. Parliamentarians for Global Action 1993, Pres. 1995–96, Hon. Patron 1997–; Visiting Scholar, Harvard Univ. 1971; Chief of Ile Ife 1991; KStJ 1992; Hon. Fellow St John's Coll., Oxford 1989; Hon. LLD (West Indies); Studentship Prize, Inner Temple; Distinguished Int. Criminal Law Award 1977, Defender of Democracy Award, Parliamentarians for Global Action 1997 and numerous other honours and awards. *Publications:* The New Frontier and the New Africa 1961, Fiscal Reform in Trinidad and Tobago 1966, The Path of Progress 1967, The Teacher and Nationalism 1967, The Mechanics of Independence 1971, Caribbean Man 1986; and contributions to Encyclopaedia Britannica. *Leisure interests:* walking, swimming, travel, reading, modern music. *Address:* 21 Ellerslie Park, Maraval, Trinidad, Trinidad and Tobago (Home).

ROBINSON, Basil William, BLitt, MA, FBA, FSA; British museum curator (retd); b. 20 June 1912, London; s. of William Robinson and Rebecca Frances Mabel (née Gilbanks) Robinson; m. 1st Ailsa Mary Stewart 1945 (died 1954); m. 2nd Oriel Hermione Steel 1958; one s. one d.; ed Winton House, Winchester, Winchester Coll., Corpus Christi Coll., Oxford; taught at Holyrood School, Bognor Regis 1936–39; Asst Keeper Victoria & Albert Museum 1939; war service with Indian Army 1940–46; Deputy Keeper, Dept of Metalwork, Victoria & Albert Museum 1954–66, Keeper 1966–72, Keeper Emer. 1972–76; founder and Chair. Aldrich Catch Club 1954–; Consultant Sotheby's 1976–91; Pres. Royal Asiatic Soc. 1970–73; Uchiyama Memorial Prize (Japan) 1983, Ferdowsi Award (Iran) 2002. *Publications include:* Descriptive Catalogue of the Persian Paintings in the Bodleian Library 1958, Kuniyoshi 1961, Arts of the Japanese Sword 1961, Persian Miniature Paintings 1967, Persian Paintings in the India Office Library 1976, Persian Paintings in the John Rylands Library 1980, Kuniyoshi: The Warrior Prints 1982, The Aldrich Book of Catches 1989, Fifteenth-Century Persian Painting: Problems and Issues 1991, Collection Jean Pozzi 1992, Persian Paintings in the Collection of the Royal Asiatic Society 1998, The Persian Book of Kings 2002. *Leisure interests:* singing catches, cats. *Address:* 41 Redcliffe Gardens, London, SW10 9JH, England.

ROBINSON, (Francis) Alastair Lavie; British banker; b. 19 Sept. 1937, London; s. of late Stephen Robinson; m. Lavinia Napier 1961; two d.; ed Eton Coll.; Gen. Man. Mercantile Credit Co. 1971–78; Chair. Exec. Cttee then CEO and Pres. Barclays America Corpn, USA 1981–83; Regional Gen. Man. Barclays Bank Int. 1983–87; Dir Personnel, Barclays Bank PLC 1987–90, Exec. Dir 1990–96, Group Vice-Chair. 1992–96; Dir RMC PLC 1996–; Dir Marshall of Cambridge (Holdings) Ltd 1996–; Portman Bldg Soc. 1998–. *Leisure interests:* music, country pursuits, golf. *Address:* 24 Clarendon Street, London, SW1V 4RF, England.

ROBINSON, Geoffrey; British politician; b. 25 May 1938; s. of Robert Norman Robinson and Dorothy Jane Robinson (née Skelly); m. Marie Elena Giorgio 1967; one s. one d.; ed Emanuel School, Univ. of Cambridge, Yale Univ.; research Asst Labour Party 1965–68; Sr exec. Industrial Reorganization Corpn 1968–70; Financial Controller British Leyland 1971–72; Man. Dir Leyland Innocenti, Milan 1972–73; Chief Exec. Jaguar Cars 1973–75, Meriden Motor Cycle Workers' Co-operative 1978–80 (Dir 1980–82); MP for Coventry NW 1976–; HM Paymaster General 1997–98; Opposition Spokesman on Science 1982–83, on Regional Affairs and Industry 1983–86. Chair. TransTec PLC 1986–97; Dir W Midlands Enterprise Bd 1980–84; Labour. *Publications:* The Lencowen Naval Minister 1999, The Unconventional Minister (autobiog.) 2000. *Leisure interests:* reading, architecture, gardens. *Address:* c/o House of Commons, London, SW1A 0AA, England. *Telephone:* (20) 7219-3000.

ROBINSON, Gerrard Jude, FCMA; British business executive; b. 23 Oct. 1948; s. of Antony Robinson and Elizabeth Ann Robinson; m. 1st Maria Ann Borg 1970 (divorced 1990); one s. one d.; m. 2nd Heather Peta Leaman 1990; one s. one d.; ed St Mary's Coll., Castlehead; started work aged 16 as a cost clerk in a Matchbox toy factory; Works Accountant, Lesney Products 1970–74; Financial Controller, Lex Industrial Distribution and Hire 1974–80; Finance Dir Coca-Cola 1980–81, Sales and Marketing Dir 1981–83, Man. Dir 1983–84; Man. Dir Grand Metropolitan (GrandMet) Contract Services 1984–87; led a man. buy-out of GrandMet catering div. 1987; Chief Exec. Compass GP PLC 1987–91, Granada Group PLC 1991–95, Chair. 1995–2001; Chair. London Weekend Television 1994–96, ITN 1995–97, BSkyB 1995–98, Arts Council May 1998–, Allied Domecq March 2002–; Hon. D. Litt. (Ulster), Hon. D.Sc. (Econ.) (Queen's) 1999. *Leisure interests:* golf, opera, chess, skiing, reading, music. *Address:* Allied Domecq PLC, The Pavilions, Bridgwater Road, Bedminister Down, Bristol, BS13 8AR (Office); Arts Council of England, 14 Great Peter Street, London, SW1P 3NQ, England. *Telephone:* (117) 978-5000 (Office). *Fax:* (117) 978-5300 (Office). *Website:* www.allieddomecqplc.com (Office).

ROBINSON, James D., III, MBA; American business executive; b. 19 Nov. 1935, Atlanta, Ga; s. of James D. Robinson Jr and Josephine Crawford; m. 1st Bettye Bradley (divorced); one s. one d.; m. 2nd Linda Gosden 1984; ed Georgia Inst. of Tech., Harvard Graduate School of Business Admin.; Officer, U.S. Naval Supply Corps 1957–59; various depts. of Morgan Guaranty Trust Co. 1961–66, Asst Vice-Pres. and Staff Asst to Chair. and Pres. 1967–68; Gen. Partner, White, Weld & Co. 1968–70; Pres., CEO American Express Int. Banking Corpn 1970–73; Exec. Vice-Pres. American Express Co. 1970–75, Pres. 1975–77, Dir 1975–93, Chair. Bd 1977–93; Chair. American Express Credit Corpn 1973–75; Pres. J. D. Robinson Inc. 1993–; Chair., CEO RRE Investors 1994, Gen. Partner RRE Ventures GP II, LLC 1999–; Chair. Violy, Byorum and Partners Holdings, LLC 1996–; Dir The Coca-Cola Co., Bristol-Meyers Squibb Co., Novele Inc., First Data Corpn, Concur Technologies, Screaming Media, Clayson Interactive Group Inc.; Dir and Chair. Emer. New York City Partnership, Chamber of Commerce Inc.; Hon. Co.-Chair. Memorial Sloan-Kettering Cancer Center; mem. The Business Council, Council on Foreign Relations, U.S. Japan Business Council; Hon. mem. Bd of Trustees The Brookings Inst. *Address:* RRE Ventures, 126 East 56th Street, 22nd Floor, New York, NY 10022, USA (Office).

ROBINSON, John Harris, BSc, CEng, FREng, FIChemE; British business executive; b. 22 Dec. 1940; s. of Thomas Robinson and Florence Robinson; m. Doreen Alice Gardner 1963; one s. one d.; ed Woodhouse Grove School, Univ. of Birmingham; with ICI PLC 1962–65, Fisons PLC 1965–70, PA Consulting Group 1970–75, Woodhouse and Rixson 1975–79; Man. Dir Healthcare Div., Smith & Nephew PLC 1979–82, Dir 1982–89, Deputy CEO 1989–90, CEO 1990–97, Chair. 1997–99; Chair. Low & Bonar PLC 1997–2001, RJB Mining 1997–, George Wimpey PLC 1999– (Dir (non-exec.) 1998–), Railtrack June–Nov. 2001; Pres. (elect) Inst. of Man. 2001; Dir (non-exec.) Delta PLC 1993–; Chair. Healthcare Sector Group, Dept of Trade and Industry (DTI) 1996–, mem. Industrial Devt Advisory Bd 1998–; mem. Council, CBI 1991– (Chair. Tech. and Innovation Cttee 1998–); Chair. Council and Pro-Chancellor Univ. of Hull 1998–; mem. Cttee of Univ. Chairmen 1998–; Pres. Inst. Chemical Engineers 1999; FRSA 1992; Hon. DEng (Birmingham) 2000, DUniv (Bradford) 2000. *Leisure interests:* theatre, golf. *Address:* 35 Marsham Court, Marsham Street, London, SW1P 4JY, England (Office). *Telephone:* (20) 7834-6838 (Office).

ROBINSON, Kenneth Ernest, CBE, DLitt, LLD, FRHistS; British historian and university administrator; b. 9 March 1914, London; s. of late Ernest Robinson and Isabel Robinson; m. Stephanie Christine S. Wilson 1938 (died 1994); one s. one d.; ed Monoux Grammar School, Walthamstow, Hertford Coll., Oxford and London School of Econs; entered Colonial Office 1936; Asst Sec. 1946–48; Fellow of Nuffield Coll. 1948–57, Hon. Fellow 1984–; Reader in Commonwealth Govt, Oxford 1948–57; Leverhulme Research Fellow 1952–53; Reid Lecturer, Acadia Univ. 1963; part-time mem., Directing Staff, Civil Service Selection Bd 1951–56, Chair. Panel 1972–77; Prof. of Commonwealth Affairs and Dir of Inst. of Commonwealth Studies, Univ. of London 1957–65, Hon. Life mem. 1980–; Vice-Chancellor, Univ. of Hong Kong 1965–72; mem. Colonial Econ. Research Cttee 1949–62, Colonial Social Science Research Council 1958–62, Councils of Overseas Devt Inst. 1960–65, Int. African Inst. 1960–65, Royal Inst. of Int. Affairs 1962–65, African Studies Asscn of UK 1963–65, 1978–81, Asscn of Commonwealth Univs 1967–69, Royal Asiatic Soc. Hong Kong Br. 1965–69, Hong Kong Man. Asscn 1966–72,

Univ. of Cape Coast 1972–74, Inter-Univ. Council for Higher Educ. Overseas 1973–79, Royal Commonwealth Soc. 1974–87 (Vice-Pres. 1983), Royal African Soc. 1983–89, (Pres. 1989–95); Gov. LSE 1959–65; Ed. Journal of Commonwealth Political Studies 1961–65; Hallsworth Research Fellow, Manchester Univ. 1972–74; Callander Lecturer, Aberdeen Univ. 1979; Dir Survey of Resources for Commonwealth Studies, Univ. of London 1974–75; JP Hong Kong 1967–72; Corresp. mem. Acad. des Sciences d'Outre-Mer, Paris; Hon. LLD (Chinese Univ. of Hong Kong) 1969; Dr hc (Open Univ.) 1978; Special Commonwealth Award, Ministry of Overseas Devt 1965. *Publications:* Africa Today (co-author) 1955, Africa in the Modern World (co-author) 1955, Five Elections in Africa (with W J. M. Mackenzie) 1960, Essays in Imperial Government (with A. F. Madden) 1963, The Dilemmas of Trusteeship 1965, A Decade of the Commonwealth (with W. B. Hamilton and C. Goodwin) 1966, University Co-operation and Asian Development (co-author) 1967, L'Europe au XIXe et XXe siècles, Vol. VII (co-author) 1967, Experts in Africa (co-author) 1980, Perspectives in Imperialism and Decolonisation (Festschrift; ed. M. Twaddle) 1984, Decolonisation and the International Community 1993. *Address:* 52 The Cloisters, Pegasus Grange, Whitehouse Road, Oxford, OX1 4QQ, England. *Telephone:* (1865) 725517.

ROBINSON, Mary, LLM, DCL, SC, MRIA; Irish international civil servant and fmr head of state; b. 21 May 1944, Ballina, Co. Mayo; d. of Dr Aubrey Bourke and Dr Tessa O'Donnell; m. Nicholas Robinson 1970; two s. one d.; ed Mount Anville, Trinity Coll. Dublin, King's Inns, Dublin and Harvard Univ., USA; Barrister 1967, Sr Counsel 1980; called to English Bar (Middle Temple) 1973; Reid Prof. of Constitutional and Criminal Law, Trinity Coll. Dublin 1969–75, lecturer in European Community Law 1975–90; Founder and Dir Irish Centre for European Law 1988–90; Senator 1969–89; Pres. of Ireland 1990–97; UN High Commr for Human Rights and Under Sec.-Gen. 1997–2002; Chancellor Dublin Univ. 1998–; mem. Dublin City Council 1979–83; mem. New Ireland Forum 1983–84; mem. Irish Parl. Jt Cttee on EC Secondary Legislation 1973–89; mem. Vedel Cttee on Enlargement of European Parl., EC 1971–72, Saint-Geours Cttee on Energy Efficiency, EC 1978–79, Advisory Bd of Common Market Law Review 1976–90, Irish Parl. Jt Cttee on Marital Breakdown 1983–85, Editorial Bd of Irish Current Law Statutes Annotated 1984–90, Advisory Cttee of Interights, London 1984–90, Int. Comm. of Jurists, Geneva 1987–90, Cttee of Man., European Air Law Assn 1989–90, Scientific Council of European Review of Public Law 1989–90, Euro Avocats, Brussels 1989–90; Gen. Rapporteur, Human Rights at the Dawn of the 21st Century, Council of Europe, Strasbourg 1993; Pres. Cherish (Irish Assn of Single Parents) 1973–90; mem. American Philosophical Soc.; Hon. Bencher King's Inns, Dublin, Middle Temple, London; Hon. mem. NY Bar Assn, American Soc. of Int. Lawyers, Bar of Tanzania; Hon. Fellow Trinity Coll. Dublin, Inst. of Engineers of Ireland, Royal Coll. of Physicians in Ireland, Hertford Coll. Oxford, LSE, Royal Coll. of Psychiatrists, London, Royal Coll. of Surgeons, Ireland, Royal Coll. of Obstetricians and Gynaecologists, London; Dr hc (Nat. Univ. of Ireland, Cambridge, Brown, Liverpool, Dublin, Montpellier, St Andrews, Melbourne, Columbia, Nat. Univ. of Wales, Poznań, Toronto, Fordham, Queens Univ. Belfast, Northeastern Univ., Rennes, Coventry, Dublin City, Essex, Harvard, Leuven, London, Seoul, Univ. of Peace (Costa Rica), Uppsala, Yale, Basle, Nat. Univ. of Mongolia, A. Schweitzer Univ. Berne); Berkeley Medal, Univ. of Calif., Medal of Honour, Univ. of Coimbra, Medal of Honour, Ordem dos Advogados (Portugal), Gold Medal of Honour, Univ. of Salamanca, Andrés Bello Medal, Univ. of Chile, New Zealand Suffrage Centennial Medal, Freedom Prize, Max Schmidheiny Foundation (Switzerland), UNIFEM Award, Noel Foundation (USA), Marisa Bellisario Prize (Italy) 1991, European Media Prize (Netherlands) 1991, CARE Humanitarian Award (USA) 1993, Int. Human Rights Award, Int. League of Human Rights 1993, Liberal Int. Prize for Freedom 1993, Stephen P. Duggan Award (USA) 1994, Council of Europe North South Prize (Portugal) 1997, Collar of Hussein Bin Ali (Jordan) 1997, F. D. Roosevelt Four Freedoms Medal 1998, Erasmus Prize (Netherlands) 1999, Fulbright Prize (USA) 1999, Garrigues Walker Prize (Spain) 2000, William Butler Prize (USA) 2000, Indira Gandhi Peace Prize (India) 2000, Sydney Peace Prize. *Address:* Palais des Nations, United Nations, 1211 Geneva 10, Switzerland. *Telephone:* (22) 9171873. *Fax:* (22) 9170245. *E-mail:* scrt.hchr@unog.ch (Office). *Website:* www.unhchr.ch (Office).

ROBINSON, Peter David, MLA; British politician; b. 29 Dec. 1948, Belfast; s. of the late David McCrea Robinson and Sheila Robinson; m. Iris Collins, MP 1970; two s. one d.; ed Annadale Grammar School, Castlereagh Coll. of Further Educ.; fmr estate agent; Founding mem. Ulster Democratic Unionist Party (DUP) and mem. Cen. Exec. Cttee 1973– (Sec. 1974–79), Gen. Sec. DUP 1975–79, Deputy Leader 1980–87; MP for Belfast E, House of Commons 1979– (resgnd seat Dec. 1985 in protest against Anglo-Irish Agreement; re-elected Jan. 1986); mem. for Belfast E, NI Ass. 1982–86 (Chair. Environment Cttee 1982–86); mem. NI Select Cttee 1994–, Shipbuilding Group 1997–; mem. for Belfast E, NI Ass. 1998–2000 (Ass. suspended 11 Feb. 2000); DUP Spokesman on Constitutional Affairs; Minister for Regional Devt 1999–2000, 2001–; mem. Castlereagh Borough Council 1977, Alderman 1978, Deputy Mayor 1978, Mayor 1986; mem. NI Forum 1996–98, NI Sports Council; Democratic Unionist; Hon. Dir Voice Newspaper Ltd, Crown Publications. *Publications:* Ulster – The Facts 1982 (jtly); booklets: Give Me Liberty, Hands Off the UDR, IRA/Sinn Fein, The North Answers Back 1970, Capital Punishment for Capital Crime 1978, Ulster the Prey, Carson Man of Action, A War to Be Won, It's Londonderry, Self-inflicted 1981, Ulster in Peril 1981, Savagery and Suffering 1981, Their Cry Was "No Surrender" 1989, The Union Under Fire 1995, Victims. *Leisure interests:* breeding Japanese Koi, bowling, golf. *Address:* House of Commons, London, SW1A 0AA, England (Office); 51 Gransha Road, Dundonald, BT16 0HB; Strandtown Hall, 96 Belmont Avenue, Belfast, BT4 3DE, Northern Ireland (Office). *Telephone:* (20) 7219-3506 (Westminster) (Office); (28) 9047-3111 (Belfast) (Office). *Fax:* (20) 7219-5854 (Westminster) (Office); (28) 9047-1797 (Belfast) (Office). *E-mail:* peter.robinson@niassembly.gov.uk (Office); Probin1690@aol.com (Office).

ROBINSON, Raymond (see Robinson, Arthur Napoleon Raymond).

ROBLES, Marisa, HRCM, FRCM; British concert harpist; b. 4 May 1937, Madrid, Spain; d. of Cristóbal Robles and María Bonilla; m. 3rd David W. Bean 1985; two s. one d. from previous marriages; ed Madrid Royal Conservatoire of Music; Prof. of Harp, Madrid Royal Conservatoire of Music 1958–63; Harp Tutor, Nat. Youth Orchestra of GB 1964–85; Prof. of Harp, Royal Coll. of Music, London 1969–94; Artistic Dir World Harp Festival, Cardiff, Wales 1991, World Harp Festival II 1994; appearances as soloist with all maj. orchestras in GB and throughout the world, including New York Philharmonic; chamber music performances with Marisa Robles and Friends, Marisa Robles Harp Ensemble, Marisa Robles Trio and other chamber groups; solo recitals in Australia, Canada, Europe, Japan, NZ, S America and the USA; many TV appearances and radio performances; masterclasses in GB and abroad; four recordings of Mozart's Flute and Harp Concerto with James Galway (q.v.) and more than 20 other recordings. *Publications:* several harp pieces and arrangements. *Leisure interests:* theatre, indoor plants, nature in general, cooking, spending private time with family. *Address:* 38 Luttrell Avenue, London, SW15 6PE, England. *Telephone:* (20) 8785-2204.

ROBOZ, Zsuzsi, FRSA; British artist; b. 15 Aug. 1939, Budapest, Hungary; d. of Imre Roboz and Edith Grosz; m. A. T. (Teddy) Smith 1964; ed Royal Acad. of Arts, London; also studied with Pietro Annigoni, Florence; various commissions 1956–, including scenes back-stage at Windmill Theatre, London 1964, theatre card of ballet movements for Theatre Museum 1979, portrait of HRH Alice, Duchess of Gloucester 1981, portraits painted include Dame Ninette de Valois, Lord Olivier and Lucian Freud; rep. in perm. public collections at Tate Gallery, London, Nat. Portrait Gallery, London, Theatre Museum, London, Museum of Fine Arts, Budapest, Graves Art Gallery, Sheffield, Bradford Museum and City Art Galleries, St Andrew's Convent, London, Barnwell Church, Northants, New Scotland Yard, London, Durham Univ., St John's Coll., Cambridge, Royal Festival Hall, London, Pablo Casals Museum, Jamaica; also rep. in various pvt. collections; guest of honour Spring Festival, Budapest 1984. *Solo exhibitions include:* Walker Galleries, London 1958, André Weil Gallery, Paris 1960, 1968, O'Hana Gallery, London 1967, 1970, 1973, Hong Kong Arts Festival 1976, Curwen Gallery, London 1977, Victoria and Albert Museum, London 1978, Hamilton Gallery, London 1979, L'Horizon Gallery, Brussels 1980, Piccadilly Festival of Arts 1981, Vigado Gallery, Budapest 1988, Amsterdam Gallery, Lincoln Center, New York 1989, Business Design Centre, London 1993, Mall Galleries, London 1993, Roy Miles Gallery, London 1994, David Messum Gallery, London 1995, 1997, 1998, 2000, 2002. *Publications include:* Women and Men's Daughters 1970, Chichester 10, Portrait of a Decade 1975, British Ballet Today (with James Monahan) 1980, British Art Now (with Edward Lucie-Smith, q.v.) 1993, Twentieth Century Illusions 1998. *Leisure interests:* classical music, reading, swimming. *Address:* 6 Bryanston Court, George Street, London, W1H 7HA, England. *Telephone:* (20) 7723-6540. *Fax:* (20) 7724-6844 (Home).

ROBSON, Bobby (Robert William), CBE; British professional football manager and player; b. 18 Feb. 1933, Sacriston, Co. Durham; s. of Philip Robson and Lilian Robson; m. Elsie Mary Gray 1955; three s.; ed Waterhouses Secondary Modern, Co. Durham; player Fulham 1950–56, 1962–67, West Bromwich Albion 1956–62; 20 caps for England; Man. Vancouver FC 1967–68, Fulham 1968–69, Ipswich Town 1969–82 (won FA Cup 1978, UEFA Cup 1981), England nat. team 1982–90, PSV Eindhoven 1990–92, 1998 (won Dutch title twice), Sporting Lisbon 1993, Porto 1994–96 (won Portuguese title twice), Barcelona 1997–98 (won Spanish Cup, European Cup Winner's Cup), Newcastle United 1999–; Hon. MA (Univ. of E Anglia) 1997; Hon. DCL (Newcastle Univ.) 2003. *Publications:* Time on the Grass (autobiog.) 1982, So Near and Yet So Far: Bobby Robson's World Cup Diary 1986, Against the Odds 1990, My Autobiography: An Englishman Abroad 1998. *Leisure interests:* golf, gardening, reading, squash. *Address:* c/o Newcastle United FC, St James' Park, Newcastle upon Tyne, NE1 4ST, England (Office).

ROBSON, Bryan, OBE; British footballer; b. 11 Jan. 1957, Chester-le-Street; s. of Brian Robson and Maureen Lowther; m. Denise Robson 1979; one s. two d.; ed Birtley Lord Lawson Comprehensive; teams: West Bromwich Albion 1974–81; 1981–94 with Manchester United, F.A. Cup winners 1983, 1985, 1990; Euro Cup Winners' Cup 1991; winner of League Championship 1992–93, 1993–94; the only British captain to lead a side to 3 FA Cup wins; 90 caps (65 as capt.), scoring 26 int. goals; player, Man. Middlesbrough FC 1994–2001; Asst coach English nat. team 1994; Hon. BA (Salford) 1992, (Manchester) 1992. *Leisure interests:* golf, horse racing.

ROBSON, Sir (James) Gordon, Kt, CBE, MB, ChB, FRCA, FRCS, DSc; British professor of anaesthetics (retd); b. 18 March 1921, Stirling, Scotland; s. of James C. Robson and Freda E. Howard; m. 1st Martha G. Kennedy 1945 (died 1975); one s.; m. 2nd Jennifer Kilpatrick 1984; ed High School of Stirling and Univ. of Glasgow; Wellcome Research Prof. of Anaesthetics, McGill Univ., Montreal 1956–64; Dir and Prof. of Anaesthetics, Royal Postgraduate Medical School, Univ. of London 1964–86; Dean, Faculty of Anaesthetists, Royal Coll.

of Surgeons 1973–76; Vice-Pres. Royal Coll. of Surgeons 1977–79; Master, Hunterian Inst. 1982–88; Consultant Adviser in Anaesthetics to Dept of Health and Social Security 1975–84; Chair. Medical and Survival Cttee Royal Nat. Lifeboat Inst. 1988–91, mem. Cttee Man. 1988–, Vice-Pres. 1992–96, Life Vice-Pres. 1996–; Civilian Consultant to the Army in Anaesthetics 1982–88; Chair. Advisory Cttee on Distinction Awards 1984–94; Pres. Scottish Soc. of Anaesthetists 1985–86, Royal Soc. of Medicine 1986–88; Hon. FRCP (Canada) 1988; Hon. FRCPS (Glasgow) 1993; Hon. DSc (McGill) 1984, (Glasgow) 1991. *Publications:* numerous articles in learned journals on neurophysiology, anaesthesia, pain and central nervous system mechanisms of respiration. *Leisure interests:* music, opera, information tech. *Address:* Brendon, Lyndale, London, NW2 2NY, England. *Telephone:* (20) 7435-3762 (Home). *Fax:* (20) 7435-3762 (Home).

ROBUCHON, Joël; French chef and restaurateur; b. 7 April 1945, Poitiers; s. of Henri Robuchon and Julienne Douteau; m. Janine Pallix 1966; one s. one d.; ed Petit séminaire de Mauléon sur Sèvre; Apprenti 1960–63, Commis 1963–64, Chef de Partie 1965–69, Chef 1969–73, Chef de Cuisine 1974–78, Dir Hotel Nikko de Paris 1978–81, Propr and Chef, Restaurant Jamin, Paris 1981–93, Restaurant Laurent, Paris 1992–2001, Restaurant Joël Robuchon 1994–96, Man. Restaurant l'Astor, Paris 1996–, L'Atelier de Joël Robuchon, Paris 2003–; Man. Relais du Parc 1992; numerous demonstrations overseas; Compagnon du Tour de France des Devoirs Unis; Titular mem. Acad. Culinaire de France; Pres. du Salon SIREST 1998–2002, (Cuisine Section) Meilleurs Ouvriers de France Competition 1991–, Chaîne Thématique Gastronomique GOURMET TV 2002–; Conseiller de la marque 'Reflets de France' (Groupe Carrefour) 1996–; mem. Council, Ordre du Mérite Agricole 1998–; Head Editorial Cttee Larousse Gastronomique; Commdr dans l'Ordre du Mérite Agricole; Officier des Arts et des Lettres; Chevalier, Ordre Nat. du Mérite; Chevalier, Légion d'honneur; professional awards include: Prix Prosper Montagné 1969, Prix Pierre Taittinger 1970, Trophée National de l'Académie Culinaire de France 1972, Meilleur Ouvrier de France 1976, Lauréat du Prix Hachette 1985, Chef de l'Année 1987, Chef of the Century, Gault Millau Guidebook 1990, Int. Herald Tribune Best Restaurant in the World 1994, 3 Stars Michelin Guide; also some 15 gold, silver and bronze medals. *Television:* Cuisinez Comme un Grand Chef (TF1) 1996–99, Bon Appétit Bien Sûr (FRANCE 3) 2000–. *Publications:* Ma cuisine pour vous, Simply French, Le meilleur et le plus simple de Robouchon, Les dimanches de Joël Robuchon, Le meilleur et le plus simple de la pomme de terre, Recettes du terroir d'hier et d'aujourd'hui, Le carnet de route d'un compagnon cuisinier, L'atelier de Joël Robuchon, Le meilleur et le plus simple de la France, Cuisinez comme un grand chef (Grand Prix du Meilleur Ouvrage, Acad. Nat. de Cuisine 1999), Le meilleur et le plus simple pour maigrir, Bon appétit bien sûr (Best Book of Cuisine Award, 7th Salon Int. du Livre Gourmand de Périgueux 2002). *Leisure interest:* tennis. *Address:* Société de gestion culinaire, 67 boulevard du Général Martial Valin, 75015 Paris, France. *Telephone:* 1-53-78-20-30. *Fax:* 1-53-78-20-31.

ROCARD, Michel Louis Léon, LèsL; French politician; b. 23 Aug. 1930, Courbevoie; s. of Yves Rocard and Renée Favre; m. 2nd Michèle Legendre 1972 (divorced); two s.; one s. one d. from 1st m.; m. 3rd Sylvie Geoffroy-Emmanuelli; ed Lycée Louis-le-Grand, Paris, Univ. of Paris, Ecole Nat. d'Admin; Nat. Sec. Asscn des Etudiants socialistes, French Section of Workers' Int. (Socialist Party) 1955–56; Insp. des Finances 1958, Econ. and Financial Studies Service 1962, Head of Budget Div., Forecasting Office 1965, Insp. Gen. des Finances 1985; Sec.-Gen. Nat. Accounts and Budget Comm. 1965; Nat. Sec. Parti Socialiste Unifié (PSU) 1967–73; Cand. in first round of elections for presidency of French Repub. 1969; Deputy (Yvelines) to Nat. Ass. 1969–73, 1978–81; left PSU to join Parti Socialiste (PS) 1974, mem. Exec. Bureau 1975–81, 1986–, Nat. Sec. in charge of public sector 1975–79, First Sec. 1993–94; Mayor of Conflans-Sainte-Honorine 1977–94; Minister of State, Minister of Planning and Regional Devt 1981–83, of Agric. 1983–85; Prime Minister of France 1988–91; MP for Yvelines 1986–88; MEP 1994–; mem. Senate 1995–97; Chair. Cttee on Devt and Co-operation 1997–99, Employment and Social Affairs 1999–2001, Culture, Educ. and Youth Matters 2001–03; Grand-Croix, Ordre nat. du Mérite, Commdr du Mérite agricole, Grand Cross, Order of Christ (Portugal), Grand Officer, Order of the Tunisian Repub. and numerous other decorations. *Publications:* Le PSU et l'avenir socialiste de la France 1969, Des militants du PSU présentés par Michel Rocard 1971, Questions à l'Etat socialiste 1972, Un député, pourquoi faire? 1973, Le marché commun contre Europe (with B. Jaumont and D. Lenègre) 1973, L'inflation au cœur (with Jacques Gallus) 1975, Parler vrai 1979, A l'épreuve des faits: textes politiques (1979–85) 1986, Le cœur à l'ouvrage 1987, Un pays comme le nôtre, textes politiques 1986–89 1989, Les Moyens d'en sortir 1996, L'art de la paix (essay) 1998, Mes idées pour demain 2000, Pour une autre Afrique 2001, Entretiens 2001. *Leisure interests:* skiing, sailing, gliding. *Address:* 266 blvd Saint-Germain, 75007 Paris (Office); 5 rue de Coulmiers, 75014 Paris, France (Home); European Parliament, 97–113 rue Belliard, 1047 Brussels, Belgium. *Telephone:* 1-47-05-25-00 (Office). *Fax:* 1-45-51-42-04 (Office). *E-mail:* mrocard.paris@noos.fr (Office).

ROCCA, Costantino; Italian golfer; b. 4 Dec. 1956, Bergamo; m. Antonella Rocca 1981; one s. one d.; fmr factory worker and caddie; turned professional 1981; qualified for PGA European Tour through 1989 Challenge Tour; won Open V33 Da Grand Lyon and Peugeot Open de France; first Italian golfer to be mem. European Ryder Cup team 1993; mem. European Ryder Cup team 1995, 1997. *Leisure interests:* fishing, football.

ROCHA, John; Irish fashion designer; b. 1953, Hong Kong; ed London Coll. of Fashion; f. own fashion design co. 1980; started menswear line 1993, jeans line 1997; regular collections at all the major int. fashion shows; also designed interiors for hotels and office blocks including The Morrison Hotel, Dublin, glassware for Waterford Crystal; British Designer of the Year 1993. *Address:* John Rocha, 12–13 Temple Lane, Dublin 2, Ireland (Office). *Telephone:* (1) 6772011 (Office). *Fax:* (1) 6719979 (Office).

ROCHA, José Luis; Cape Verde international organization official; b. 1956, São Vicente; ed Univ. of Louvain, Belgium; joined Ministry of Planning and Co-operation 1981, Chief of Div. and Dir of Int. Co-operation Dept 1982–95; Amb. to Belgium and Luxembourg 1995–99; Perm. Rep. of Org. Int. de la Francophonie to EU 2000–. *Address:* 2 Place Sainctelette, 1080 Brussels, Belgium (Office). *Telephone:* (322) 420-54-60 (Office). *Fax:* (322) 426-20-02 (Office). *E-mail:* reper.bruxelles@francophonie.org (Office).

ROCHA VIEIRA, Lt-Gen. Vasco Joaquim, MA; Portuguese administrator and army officer; b. 16 Aug. 1939, Lagoa; s. of João da Silva Vieira and Maria Vieira Rocha e Vieira; m. Maria Leonor de Andrada Soares de Albergaria 1976; three s.; ed Tech. Univ. of Lisbon; Prof. Mil. Acad. Lisbon 1968–69; Army Staff course 1969–72; engineer Urbanization Dept Urban Council, Lisbon 1969–73; Sec. for Public Works and Communications, Govt of Macao 1974–75; Dir Engineers Branch, Portuguese Army 1975–76; Army Chief-of-Staff 1976–78; Mil. Rep. of Portugal, SHAPE, Mons, Belgium 1978–82; Army War Coll. course 1982–83; Nat. Defence course 1983–84; Prof. Army War Coll. Lisbon 1983–84; Deputy Dir Nat. Defence Inst. Lisbon 1984–86; Minister for Portuguese Autonomous Region of the Azores 1986–91; Gov. of Macao 1991–99; Grand Cross, Order of Prince Henry; Knight Commdr Mil. Order of Aviz; service medals; decorations from Brazil, France, Belgium, USA and Japan. *Leisure interests:* tennis, golf.

ROCHAS DA COSTA, Celestino; São Tomé e Príncipe politician; fmrly Minister of Labour, Educ. and Social Security; Prime Minister of São Tomé e Príncipe 1988–91; mem. Movimento de Libertação de São Tomé e Príncipe (MLSTP). *Address:* c/o Movimento de Libertacão de São Tomé e Príncipe, Riboque, Cidade Capital, São Tomé (Office); c/o Prime Minister's Office, São Tomé, São Tomé e Príncipe. *Telephone:* (12) 22253 (Office).

ROCHE, (Eamonn) Kevin; American architect; b. 14 June 1922, Dublin, Ireland; s. of Eamon Roche and Alice Roche (née Harding); m. Jane Tuohy 1963; two s. three d.; ed Nat. Univ. of Ireland and Illinois Inst. of Tech.; with Eero Saarinen & Assocs. 1950–66, Chief Designer 1954–66; Partner, Kevin Roche John Dinkeloo and Assocs 1966–; Pres. American Acad. of Arts and Letters 1994–97; Academician Nat. Inst. of Arts and Letters, American Acad. in Rome 1968–71; mem. Fine Arts Comm., Washington, DC, Acad. d'Architecture; Academician Nat. Acad. of Design; mem. Bd of Trustees, Woodrow Wilson Int. Center for Scholars, Smithsonian Inst. Accad. Nazionale di San Luca 1984; LLD hc (Ireland Nat. Council for Educational Awards); Brunner Award, Nat. Acad. of Arts and Letters 1965, Brandeis Univ. Creative Arts Award 1967, ASID 1976 Total Design Award, Acad. d'Architecture 1977 Grand Gold Medal, Pritzker Architecture Prize 1982, Gold Medal Award for Architecture, American Acad. of Arts and Letters 1990, Gold Medal AIA 1993, AIA Twenty-five Year Award 1995 and other awards. *Major works include:* IBM World Fair Pavilion, New York; Oakland Museum; Rochester Inst. of Tech.; Ford Foundation Headquarters, New York; Fine Arts Center, Univ. of Mass.; Power Center for the Performing Arts, Univ. of Mich.; Creative Arts Center, Wesleyan Univ., Middletown, Conn.; Coll. Life Insurance Co. of America Headquarters, Indianapolis; Master Plan, Galleries and Wings, Metropolitan Museum of Art, New York; Office Complex, UN Devt Corpn, New York; Denver Center for the Performing Arts, Denver, Colo; John Deere & Co., West Office Bldg, Moline, Ill.; Union Carbide Corpn World HQ, Conn.; General Foods Corpn HQ, Rye, NY; John Deere Insurance Co. Headquarters, Moline, Ill.; Bell Telephone Labs., Holmdel, NJ; Morgan Bank Headquarters, New York; Northern Telecom HQ, Atlanta, Ga; E. F. Hutton Headquarters, New York; Bouygues HQ, Paris; IBM Hudson Hills Computer Research Lab., New York; UNICEF HQ, New York; Leo Burnett Company HQ, Chicago; Corning Glass Works HQ, Corning, NY; Merck and Co. HQ, Readington, NJ; Dai Ichi-Seimei Norinchukin Bank HQ, Tokyo; The Jewish Museum, New York; Museum of Jewish Heritage Holocaust Memorial, New York; Nations Bank Plaza, Atlanta, Ga; Tata Cummins, India; Menara Maxis, Kuala Lumpur, Malaysia; Pontiac Marina Hotel and Office Bldg, Singapore; Total System Services Corpn HQ, Columbus, Ga; MIT Central Athletic Facility, Cambridge, Mass.; Shiodome Block B Devt, Tokyo; Research and Devt Facilities, Lucent Technologies, Lisle, Naperville, Ill., Denver, Co., Allentown, Pa, Nuremberg, Germany; New York Univ. Palladium Student Dormitory; New York Univ. Kimmel Center; Santander Cen. Hispano HQ, Madrid; Bouygues SA Holding Co. HQ, Paris; S.E.C. HQ, Washington, DC; Nat. Conf. Centre, Dublin, Ireland. *Address:* Kevin Roche John Dinkeloo and Associates, 20 Davis Street, P.O. Box 6127, Hamden, CT 06517, USA. *Telephone:* (203) 777-7251 (Office). *Fax:* (203) 777-2299 (Office). *E-mail:* kroche@krjda.com (Office).

ROCHEFORT, Jean; French actor; b. 29 April 1930, Paris; s. of Celestin Rochefort and Fernande Guillot; m. 3rd Françoise Vidal 1989; one s. one d.; two s. one d. from previous marriages; ed Conservatoire nat. d'art dramatique; Trophée Dussane 1970, César 1975 (for Que la fête commence), 1978 (for Best Actor of the Year, in Le Crabe-tambour), best actor awards Montreal 1982, Brussels 1982, Locarno 1984, César d'honneur 1999; Chevalier Légion d'honneur, Officier des Arts et des Lettres. *Films include:* 20,000 Leagues Under the Sea 1960, La Porteuse de pain 1964, Qui êtes-vous Polly Magoo? 1967, Les Dimanches de la vie 1967, Le Temps de mourir 1970, Céleste 1970, L'Œuf 1971, l'Héritier 1972, Le Fantôme de la liberté 1974, Un divorce heureux 1975, Isabelle devant le désir 1975, Que la fête commence 1975, Les Magiciens 1976, Un éléphant ça trompe énormément 1976, Le Crabe-tambour 1977, Chère inconnue 1980, Un étrange voyage 1981, l'Indiscrétion 1982, Le grand frère 1982, Un dimanche de flic 1983, L'Ami de Vincent 1983, Réveillon chez Bob, Frankenstein 90 1984, La Galette du roi 1986, Tandem 1987, Le Moustachu 1987, Je suis le seigneur du château 1989, Le Mari de la coiffeuse 1990, Le Château de ma mère 1990, Le Bal des casse-pieds 1992, La prochaine fois le feu 1993, Tombés du ciel 1994, Tom est tout seul 1995, Les grands ducs 1996, Ridicule 1996, Barracuda 1997, Le Vent en emporte autant 1999, Rembrandt 1999, Le Placard 2001. *Television:* Le Scénario défendu 1984, L'Enigme blanche 1985, Eleveur de chevaux. *Leisure interest:* riding. *Address:* c/o Artmédia, 20 avenue Rapp, 75007 Paris, France.

ROCHER, Guy, CC, OQ, PhD, FRSC; Canadian professor of sociology; b. 20 April 1924, Berthierville, PQ; s. of the late Barthélemy Rocher and Jeanne Magnan; m. 1st Suzanne Cloutier 1949; m. 2nd Claire-Emmanuèle Depocas 1985; four d.; ed Univ. of Montreal, Univ. Laval and Harvard Univ.; Asst Prof. Univ. Laval 1952–57, Assoc. Prof. 1957–60; Prof. of Sociology, Univ. of Montreal 1960–; Deputy Minister of Cultural Devt Govt of Québec 1977–79, of Social Devt 1981–82; mem. Royal Comm. on Educ. in Québec 1961–66; Vice-Pres. Canada Council of Arts 1969–74, Cttee on Univ. Research, Royal Soc. of Canada 1989–90; Pres. Radio-Québec 1979–81; mem. American Acad. of Arts and Sciences; Hon. LLD (Laval) 1996; Dr hc Sociology (Moncton) 1997, (Univ. of Québec at Montreal) 2002; Prix Marcel-Vincent (ACFAS) 1989, Prix Léon-Gérin (Québec Govt) 1995, Prix Molson 1997, Prix Esdras-Minville 1998; Outstanding Contrib. Award (Canadian Asscn Sociology and Anthropology) 1988, Médaille Pierre Chauveau (Royal Soc. of Canada) 1991, Prix William Dawson, Royal Soc. of Canada 1999. *Films:* subject of film by Anne-Marie Rocher: Guy Rocher, Sociologist as Protagonist. *Publications:* Introduction à la sociologie générale 1969, Talcott Parsons et la sociologie américaine, le Québec en mutation 1973, Ecole et société au Québec 1975, Entre les rêves et l'histoire 1989, Le Québec en jeu 1992, Entre droit et technique 1994, Etudes de sociologie du droit et de l'éthique 1996, Théories et emergence du droit 1998, May Weber, Rudolf Stammler et le matérialisme historique 2001, Le Droit à l'égalité 2001; and numerous articles on sociology, on sociology of law, of education and of health and on the evolution of Québec society. *Leisure interests:* tai-chi, skiing, swimming, concerts, reading. *Address:* Faculté de Droit, Université de Montreal, C.P. 6128, Succursale Centre-Ville, Montreal, QC, H3C 3J7 (Office); 4911 Chemin de la Côte-des-Neiges, Apt. 409, Montreal, QC, H3V 1H7, Canada (Home). *Telephone:* (514) 343-5993 (Office); (514) 344-0882 (Home). *Fax:* (514) 343-7508. *E-mail:* rocher@droit.umontreal.ca (Office).

ROCKBURNE, Dorothea; American artist; b. 18 Oct. 1934, Montreal, PQ, Canada; m. 1951 (divorced); one d.; ed Black Mountain Coll., NC, Ecole des Beaux-Arts, Montreal; participant in numerous group shows; work in many public collections including Whitney Museum, Museum of Modern Art, Metropolitan Museum of Art, artist-in-residence, American Acad. in Rome 1991; Guggenheim Museum, New York and Corcoran Gallery, Washington, DC; frescoes at Hilton Hotel, San Jose, Calif. 1992, Sony HQ, New York 1993, Edward T. Grignoux U.S. Courthouse, Portland, Maine 1996, Brooklyn Courthouse, New York 1996, UOFM, Mich. 1997; Guggenheim Fellow 1972; Nat. Endowment for the Arts 1974; Visiting Artist, Skowhegan School of Painting and Sculpture 1984; Avery Distinguished Prof. Bard Coll. Annandale-on-Hudson, NY 1986, mem. Dept of Art, American Acad. of Arts and Letters 2001; Art Inst. of Chicago Witowsky Painting Award 1972, Creative Arts Award, Brandeis Univ. 1985, Lifetime Achievement Award, American Acad. of Arts and Letters 1999. *Solo exhibitions include:* Bykert Gallery, New York 1970, 1972, 1973, Sonnabend Gallery, Paris 1971, Galleria Toselli, Milan 1972, 1974, 1983, Lisson Gallery, London 1973, Galleria Schema, Florence 1973, 1975, 1992, John Weber Gallery, New York 1976, 1978, Texas Gallery, Houston 1979, 1980, Museum of Modern Art, New York 1980, Xavier Fourcade, New York 1980, 1985, 1986, Arts Club of Chicago 1987, André Emmerich Gallery, New York 1988, 1989, 1991, 1992, 1994, Rose Museum, Brandeis Univ. (retrospective) 1989, Guild Hall Museum, East Hampton, NY 1995, Portland Museum of Art, Portland, Maine 1996, Rockefeller Foundation Center, Bellagio, Italy 1997, Ingrid Raab Gallery, Berlin 1997, Lawrence Rubin, Greenberg Van Doren Fine Art, New York 2000. *Leisure interests:* music, mathematics, theatre. *Address:* 140 Grand Street, New York, NY 10013, USA. *Telephone:* (212) 226-4471. *Fax:* (212) 925-0942. *E-mail:* octgrace@aol.com (Office). *Website:* www.dorothearockburne.com (Office).

ROCKEFELLER, David, BS, PhD; American banker; b. 12 June 1915, New York; s. of John Davison Rockefeller, Jr and Abby Greene (née Aldrich) Rockefeller; brother of Laurance; m. Margaret McGrath 1940 (died 1996); two s. four d.; ed Harvard Coll., London School of Econs, Univ. of Chicago; Sec. to Mayor Fiorello H. La Guardia, New York 1940–41; Asst Regional Dir U.S. Office of Defense, Health and Welfare Services 1941–42; served in U.S. Army (Capt.) 1942–45; Foreign Dept Chase Nat. Bank 1946–48, Second Vice-Pres. 1948–49, Vice-Pres. 1949–51, Sr Vice-Pres. 1951–55; Exec. Vice-Pres. Chase Manhattan Bank 1955–57, Vice-Chair. Bd 1957–61, Pres and Chair. Exec. Cttee 1961–69, CEO 1969–80, Chair. of Bd 1969–81, Chair. Chase Int. Investment Corpn 1961–81, Chase Int. Advisory Cttee 1980–99; Chair. Bd

Rockefeller Group Inc. 1981–95, Rockefeller Center Properties, Inc. 1996–, Rockefeller Center Properties Inc. Trust; Chair. Rockefeller Univ. 1950–75, Chair Exec. Cttee 1975–, Council on Foreign Relations 1970–85, Americas Soc. 1981–92, Rockefeller Brothers Fund Inc. 1981–87 and numerous other chairmanships; Trustee Rockefeller Family Fund, Carnegie Endowment for Int. Peace, Museum of Modern Art, Chicago Univ., etc.; Hon. LLD from 13 univs.; Hon. DEng (Colorado School of Mines) 1974, (Notre Dame Univ.) 1987; Hadrian Award (World Mathematics Fund) 1994, U.S. Presidential Medal of Freedom 1998; Grand-Croix, Légion d'honneur; numerous American and foreign awards. *Publications:* Unused Resources and Economic Waste 1940, Creative Management in Banking 1964. *Leisure interest:* sailing. *Address:* Chase Manhattan Bank, Room 5600, 30 Rockefeller Plaza, New York, NY 10112, USA.

ROCKEFELLER, James S.; American businessman; b. 8 June 1902, New York; s. of William G. and Elsie (Stillman) Rockefeller; m. Nancy Carnegie 1925; two s. two d.; ed Yale Univ.; worked with Brown Brothers & Co. 1924–30; joined Nat. City Bank of New York (now Citibank) 1930, Asst Cashier 1931, Asst Vice-Pres. 1933, Vice-Pres. 1940, Sr Vice-Pres. 1948, Exec. Vice-Pres. 1952, Pres. and Dir 1952–59, Chair. and Dir 1959–67; served with U.S. Army 1942–46; Pres. and Dir Indian Spring Land Co.; Vice-Pres. and Dir Indian Rock Corpn; mem. Bd of Overseers, Memorial Hosp. for Cancer and Allied Diseases, New York; Trustee of Estate of William Rockefeller, American Museum of Natural History; Hon. Dir NCR Corpn. *Leisure interests:* farming, shooting, fishing. *Address:* 425 Park Avenue, New York, NY 10022, USA.

ROCKEFELLER, John Davison, IV, BA; American politician; b. 18 June 1937, New York; s. of John Davison III and Blanchette F. (Hooker) Rockefeller; m. Sharon Percy 1967; three s. one d.; ed Harvard and Yale Univs. and Int. Christian Univ., Tokyo; mem. Nat. Advisory Council, Peace Corps 1961, Special Adviser to Dir 1962, Operations Officer in Charge of work in Philippines until 1963; Bureau of Far Eastern Affairs, U.S. State Dept 1963, later Asst to Asst Sec. of State for Far Eastern Affairs; consultant, President's Comm. on Juvenile Delinquency and Youth Crime 1964, White House Conf. on Balanced Growth and Econ. Devt 1978, Pres.'s Comm. on Coal 1978–80; field worker, Action for Appalachian Youth Program 1964; mem. W Va House of Dels. 1966–68; Sec. of State, W Va 1968–72; Pres. W Va Wesleyan Coll., Buckhannon 1973–75; Gov. of W Va 1977–85, Senator from W Va 1985–, Chair. Senate Steel Caucus, Bipartisan Cttee on Comprehensive Health Care; Republican. *Publications:* articles in magazines. *Address:* US Senate, 531 Hart Senate Building, Washington, DC 20510, USA.

ROCKEFELLER, Laurance Spelman, BA; American conservationist and business executive; b. 26 May 1910, New York; s. of John Davison Rockefeller Jr and Abby Greene (née Aldrich) Rockefeller; brother of David; m. Mary French 1934; one s. three d.; ed Princeton Univ., Harvard Law School; served in USNR 1942–45; Dir Eastern Airlines 1938–60, 1977–81, Advisory Dir 1981–87; Chair. Rockefeller Center 1953–56, 1958–66, Hudson River Valley Comm. 1965–66, New York Zoological Soc. 1970–75 (Hon. Chair. 1975–), Rockefeller Brothers Fund 1958–80 (Vice-Chair. 1980–82, Advisory Trustee 1982–85), Citizens' Advisory Cttee on Environmental Quality 1969–73 (mem. 1973–79); Pres. American Conservation Asscn 1958–80 (Chair. 1980–85, Hon. Chair. 1985–), Pres. Jackson Hole Preserve Inc. 1940–87, Chair. 1987–96, Chair. Emer. and Trustee 1997–; Commr Palisades Interstate Park Comm. 1970–77 (Commr Emer. 1978–); Dir Reader's Digest Asscn 1973–93; Trustee Emer., Princeton Univ.; Trustee Alfred P. Sloan Foundation 1960–82; Trustee Emer. Nat. Geographical Soc.; mem. Nat. Cancer Advisory Bd 1972–79, Memorial Sloan-Kettering Cancer Center (Chair. 1975–82, Hon. Chair. 1982–); Commdr, Ordre Royal du Lion (Belgium) 1950, Hon. OBE, Congressional Gold Medal and several American awards. *Address:* Room 5600, 30 Rockefeller Plaza, New York, NY 10112, USA.

ROCKLEY, 3rd Baron; James Hugh Cecil; British merchant banker; b. 5 April 1934, London; m. Sarah Cadogan 1958; one s. two d.; ed Eton Coll. and New Coll. Oxford; with Wood Gundy & Co., Canada 1957–62; joined Kleinwort Benson Ltd 1962, apptd. to Bd 1970, Head, Corp. Finance Div. 1983, Vice-Chair. 1985–93, Chair. 1993, Vice-Chair. Kleinwort Benson Group PLC 1988–93, Chair. 1993–96; Chair. Dartford River Crossing 1988–93, Kleinwort Devt Fund 1991–93, Midland Expressway 1992–93, Hall and Woodhouse 2001–; Dir, Equity and Law 1980–92, Christies Int. 1989–98, Cobham (fmrly FR Group) 1990–2002, Abbey Nat. 1990–99, Foreign and Colonial Investment Trust 1992–, Cadogan Group 1996–, Dusco (UK) 1996–2001. *Address:* Lytchett Heath, Poole, Dorset, BH16 6AE, England. *Telephone:* (1202) 622228.

ROCKWELL, John Sargent, PhD; American journalist, arts administrator, music critic and author; b. 16 Sept. 1940, Washington, DC; s. of Alvin John and Anne Hayward; m. Linda Mevorach; one d.; ed Harvard Univ., Univ. of Munich and Univ. of Calif. Berkeley; music and dance critic, Oakland (Calif.) Tribune 1969; Asst music and dance critic, Los Angeles Times 1970–72; freelance music critic, New York Times 1972–74; staff music critic 1974–91, Ed. Arts and Leisure section 1998–; European cultural corresp. and prin. classical recordings critic, New York Times, Paris 1992–94; Dir Lincoln Center Festival, Lincoln Center for the Performing Arts, New York 1994–98. *Publications:* All American Music: Composition in the Late 20th Century 1983, Sinatra: An American Classic 1984. *Address:* New York Times, 229 West 43rd Street, New York, NY 10036, USA.

RODAT, Robert; screenplay writer. *Film screenplays include:* Tall Tale 1994, Fly Away Home 1996, Saving Private Ryan 1998, The Patriot 2000. *Television:* TV screenplays include The Comrades of Summer 1992, The Ripper 1997.

RODDICK, Anita Lucia, OBE; British business executive; b. 23 Oct. 1942, Littlehampton; d. of Henry Perella and Gilda De Vita; m. Gordon Roddick 1970; two d.; ed Maude Allen Secondary Modern School for Girls, Newton Park Coll. of Educ., Bath; teacher of English and History, worked in library of Int. Herald Tribune, Paris and Women's Rights Dept of ILO, based at UN, Geneva, then owned and managed restaurant and hotel; opened first branch of The Body Shop, Brighton, Sussex 1976; The Body Shop Int. floated on Unlisted Securities Market 1984; Group Man. Dir The Body Shop Int. PLC –1994, CEO 1994–98, Jt Chair. 1998–2002, Dir (non-exec.), int. consultant 2002–; Trustee The Body Shop Foundation 1990–, New Acad. of Business 1996; Patron of various orgs.; Hon. Fellow, Bath Coll. of Higher Educ. 1994; Hon. DUniv (Sussex) 1988, (Open Univ.) 1995; Hon. LLD (Nottingham) 1990, (New England Coll.) 1991, (Victoria, Canada) 1995; Hon. DSc (Portsmouth) 1994; Hon. DBA (Kingston) 1996; Veuve Clicquot Business Woman of the Year 1984, British Asscn of Industrial Eds. Communicator of the Year 1988, Co. NatWest Retailer of the Year Award 1988, UN "Global 500" Environment Award 1989, Business Leader of Year, Nat. Asscn of Women Business Owners (USA) 1992, Botwinick Prize in Business Ethics 1994, Business Leadership Award, Univ. of Michigan 1994, First Annual Womanpower Award, Women's Business Devt Center 1995, USA Women's Center Leadership Award 1996, American Dream Award, Hunter Coll. 1996, Philanthropist of the Year, Inst. of Fundraising Managers 1996. *Publications:* Body and Soul (autobiog.) 1991, Business as Unusual 2000. *Leisure interests:* theatre, arts. *Address:* The Body Shop International, Watersmead, Littlehampton, West Sussex, BN17 6LS, England. *Telephone:* (1903) 731500. *Fax:* (1903) 726250. *E-mail:* info@bodyshop.co.uk (Office); www.bodyshop.co.uk (Office).

RODGER OF EARLSFERRY, Baron (Life Peer), cr. 1992, of Earlsferry in the District of North East Fife; **Alan Ferguson Rodger,** PC, QC, MA, LLD, DPhil, DCL, FBA, FRSE; British advocate and chief justice; b. 18 Sept. 1944; s. of Prof. Thomas Ferguson Rodger and Jean Margaret Smith Chalmers; ed Glasgow Univ., New Coll., Oxford; mem. Faculty of Advocates 1974, Clerk of Faculty 1976–79; Advocate Depute 1985–88; Home Advocate Depute 1986–88; Solicitor-Gen. for Scotland 1989–92; Lord Advocate 1992–95; Senator, Coll. of Justice in Scotland 1995–96; Lord Justice-Gen. of Scotland and Lord Pres. of the Court of Session 1996–2001; a Lord of Appeal in ordinary 2001–; Pres. Holdsworth Club 1998–99; mem. Mental Welfare Comm. for Scotland 1981–84, UK Del. to Comm. Consultative des Barreaux de la Communauté Européenne 1984–89, Acad. of European Pvt. Lawyers 1994–; Dyke Jr Res. Fellow, Balliol Coll., Oxford 1969–70; Fellow, New Coll., Oxford 1970–72; Maccabaean Lecturer, British Acad. 1991; Hon. Bencher, Lincoln's Inn 1992, Inn of Court of Northern Ireland 1998; Hon. mem. S.P.T.L. 1992; Hon. LLD (Aberdeen) 1999, (Edin.) 2001. *Publications:* Owners and Neighbours in Roman Law 1972, Gloag and Henderson's Introduction to the Law of Scotland (Asst Ed.) 1995. *Leisure interest:* walking. *Address:* Court of Session, Edinburgh, EH1 1RQ, Scotland (Office); House of Lords, London, SW1A 0PA, England. *Telephone:* (131) 240-6701 (Office).

RODGERS, Joan, CBE, BA; British soprano opera and concert singer; b. 4 Nov. 1956, Whitehaven, Cumbria; d. of late Thomas Rodgers and of Julia Rodgers; m. Paul Daniel (q.v.) 1988; two d.; ed Whitehaven Grammar School, Univ. of Liverpool and Royal Northern Coll. of Music, Manchester; first maj. professional engagement as Pamina (The Magic Flute), Aix-en-Provence Festival 1982; début at Metropolitan Opera House, New York, in same role 1995; other appearances include title role (Theodora) at Glyndebourne, The Governess (Turn of the Screw) for Royal Opera House, Blanche (Dialogues des Carmélites) for English Nat. Opera and in Amsterdam, Marschallin (Der Rosenkavalier) for Scottish Opera and title role (Alcina) for English Nat. Opera; regular appearances at Royal Opera House, English Nat. Opera, Glyndebourne, Promenade Concerts and with leading British and European cos; concert engagements in London, Europe and USA with conductors including Solti, Barenboim, Mehta, Rattle, Harnoncourt and Salonen; numerous recordings; Kathleen Ferrier Memorial Scholarship 1981; Royal Philharmonic Soc. Award as Singer of the Year 1997, Evening Standard Award for Outstanding Individual Performance in Opera 1997. *Leisure interests:* walking, cooking, talking. *Address:* c/o Ingpen and Williams Ltd, 26 Wadham Road, London, SW15 2LR, England.

RODGERS, John, MS, PhD; American professor of geology; b. 11 July 1914, Albany, NY; s. of Henry D. Rodgers and Louise W. Rodgers (née Allen) ; ed Albany Acad., Cornell and Yale Univs ; Dept of Geology, Cornell Univ. 1935–36, Instructor 1936–37; Field Geologist, US Geological Survey 1938–, in full time employment 1940–46; Scientific Consultant, US Army Corps. of Engineers 1944–46; Instructor, Yale Univ. 1946–47, Asst Prof. 1947–52, Assoc. Prof. 1952–59, Prof. 1959–62, Silliman Prof. of Geol. 1962–85, Emer. 1985–; Gen. Sec. Int. Comm. on Stratigraphy 1952–60; Sr Fellow, Nat. Science Foundation 1959–60; Commr Conn. Geol. and Nat. History Survey 1960–71; Visiting Lecturer, Coll. de France 1960; Exchange scholar Soviet Union 1967; Asst Ed. American Journal of Science 1948–54, Ed. 1954–95, Ed. Emer. 1995–; Hon. Prof. Inst. of Geology and Geophysics, Chinese Acad. of Sciences, Beijing 2000; mem. NAS, American Philosophical Soc.; Hon. mem. Geol. Soc. of London 1970; Pres. Conn. Acad. of Arts and Sciences 1969, Geol. Soc. of America 1970; Foreign mem., USSR (now Russian) Acad. of Sciences 1976; Foreign Corresp. mem. Acad. real de Ciencias y Artes, Barcelona 1976; John Simon Guggenheim Fellow (Australia) 1973–74; Hon. mem. Soc. Géologique de France 1973; Medal of Freedom, U.S. Army 1946, Penrose Medal (Geological Soc. of America) 1981, James Hall Medal (NY State Geological Survey) 1986, Prix Gaudry, Soc. Géologique de France 1987, Médaille Paul Fourmarier, Acad. Royale des Sciences, Lettres et Beaux Arts de Belgique 1987, Career Contrib. Award (Geological Soc. of America) 1989, William Clude DeVane Medal 1990. *Publications:* Principles of Stratigraphy (with C. Dunbar) 1957, The Tectonics of the Appalachians 1970, The Harmony of the World (record, with W. Ruff) 1979; many articles on geology. *Leisure interests:* music (piano), travel, reading (history, philosophy). *Address:* Department of Geology, Yale University, P.O. Box 208109, New Haven, CT 06520, USA. *Telephone:* (203) 432-3128.

RODGERS, Patricia Elaine Joan, MA, D.POL.SC.; Bahamian diplomatist; b. Nassau; ed School of St Helen & St Catherine, Abingdon, Univ. of Aberdeen, Graduate Inst. of Int. Relations, St Augustine, Trinidad, Inst. Universitaire des Hautes Etudes Int., Univ. of Geneva; Counsellor and Consul, Washington, DC 1978–83; Alt. Rep. to OAS 1982–83; Deputy High Commr (Acting High Commr) in Canada 1983–86, High Commr 1986–88; High Commr in UK (also Accred to France, Belgium and Germany) 1988–92; mem. Bahamas Del. to UN Conf. on Law of the Sea 1974, 1975, OAS Gen. Ass. 1982, Caribbean Co-ordinating Meeting (Head of Del.), OAS 1983, Canada/Commonwealth Caribbean Heads of Govt Meeting 1985, Commonwealth Heads of Govt Meeting Nassau 1985, Vancouver 1987; Adviser to Bahamas Del., Annual Gen. Meetings of World Bank and IMF 1978–82; mem. Commonwealth Observer Group, Gen. Elections Lesotho 1993; Perm. Sec., Ministry of Tourism 1995–. *Publications:* Mid-Ocean Archipelagos and International Law; A Study of the Progressive Development of International Law 1981. *Leisure interests:* folk art, theatre, gourmet cooking, gardening. *Address:* Ministry of Tourism, P.O.B. N-3701, Centre of Commerce, #1 Bay Street, Nassau, Bahamas. *Telephone:* 322-7500. *Fax:* 322-4041. *E-mail:* prodgers@bahamas.com (Office).

RODGERS OF QUARRY BANK, Baron (Life Peer), cr. 1992, of Kentish Town in the London Borough of Camden; **William Thomas Rodgers,** PC, MA; British politician and administrator; b. 28 Oct. 1928, Liverpool; s. of William Arthur Rodgers and Gertrude Helen Rodgers; m. Silvia Schulman 1955; three d.; ed Sudley Road Council School, Quarry Bank High School, Liverpool and Magdalen Coll., Oxford; Gen. Sec. Fabian Soc. 1953–60; Labour Cand. for Bristol West 1957; Borough Councillor, St Marylebone 1958–62; MP for Stockton-on-Tees 1962–74, for Stockton Div. of Teesside 1974–83; Parl. Under-Sec. of State, Dept of Econ. Affairs 1964–67, Foreign Office 1967–68; Leader, UK del. to Council of Europe and Ass. of WEU 1967–68; Minister of State, Bd of Trade 1968–69, Treasury 1969–70; Chair. Expenditure Cttee on Trade and Industry 1971–74; Minister of State, Ministry of Defence 1974–76; Sec. of State for Transport 1976–79; Opposition Spokesman for Defence 1979–80; left Labour Party March 1981; Co-founder Social Democratic Party March 1981, mem. Nat. Cttee 1982–87, Vice-Pres. 1982–87; Dir-Gen. RIBA 1987–94; Chair. Advertising Standards Authority 1995–2000; Leader Liberal Democratic Peers 1998–2001; Liberal Democrat. *Publications:* Hugh Gaitskell 1906–1963 (Ed.) 1964, The People Into Parliament (co-author) 1966, The Politics of Change 1982, Ed. and co-author Government and Industry 1986, Fourth Among Equals 2000. *Leisure interests:* reading, walking, cinema. *Address:* House of Lords, London, SW1A 0PW (Office); 43 North Road, London, N6 4BE, England. *Telephone:* (20) 7219-3607 (Office); (20) 8341-2434 (Home). *Fax:* (20) 7219-2377 (Office); (20) 8347-7133 (Home).

RODIER, Jean-Pierre; French business executive and mining engineer; b. 4 May 1947, Reims; s. of Pierre Rodier and Gabrielle Sayen; m. Michèle Foz 1969; ed Lycée de Saumur, Lycée de Pamiers, Lycée de Pierre-en-Fermat, Toulouse; Asst Sec.-Gen. Mines Directorate, Ministry of Industry 1975–78, Sec.-Gen. 1978; Head of Econs and Budget mission of Dir-Gen. of Energy and Raw Materials 1979; Head of Raw Material and Subsoil Dept 1981–83; tech. adviser to Prime Minister's Office 1983–84; Dir of Gen. Man. Penarroya mining and metallurgy Co. 1984–85, Asst Dir-Gen. 1985–86, Pres. and Dir Gen. 1986–88; Pres. Bd Dirs. Metaleurop 1988–91; Deputy Administrator Mining Union 1991–94; Pres. Asscn of Enterprise and Personnel 2001–; Pres. and Dir-Gen. Pechiney 1994–; Pres. Bd Dirs. Ecole nat. supérieure des techniques industrielles et des mines d'Alès 1992–95. *Address:* Société Pechiney, 7 Place du Chancelier Adenauer, 75218 Paris Cedex 16, France.

RODIN, Judith, PhD; American physician; b. 9 Sept. 1944, Philadelphia, Pa; d. of Morris Rodin and Sally (Winson) Seitz; m. 1st 1978; one s.; m. 2nd Paul Verkuil 1994; ed Univ. of Pennsylvania and Columbia Univ.; Nat. Science Foundation Postdoctoral Fellow, Univ. of Calif. 1971; Asst Prof. of Psychology, New York Univ. 1970–72; Asst Prof. Yale Univ. 1972–75, Assoc. Prof. 1975–79, Prof. of Psychology 1979–83, Dir of Grad. Studies 1982–89, Philip R. Allen Prof. of Psychology 1984–94, Prof. of Medicine and Psychiatry 1985–94, Chair. Dept of Psychology 1989–91, Dean Grad. School of Arts and Sciences 1991–92, Provost 1992–94; Prof. of Psychology, Medicine and Psychiatry, Univ. of Pa 1994–, Pres. Univ. of Pa 1994–; Chair. John D. & Catherine T. MacArthur Foundation Research Network on Determinants and Consequences of Health-Promoting and Health-Damaging Behavior 1983–93; Chair. Council of Pres.'s, Univs Research Asscn 1995–96; has served on numerous Bds of Dirs, including Int. Life Sciences Inst. 1993–, Aetna Life & Casualty Co. 1995–; has served as mem. of numerous professional cttees., including Pres. Clinton's Cttee of Advisors on Science and Tech. 1994–, Pa

Women's Forum 1995–; chief ed. Appetite 1979–92; has served on numerous editorial bds; mem. Bd of Trustees, Brookings Inst. 1995–; Fellow AAAS, American Acad. of Arts and Sciences; Hon. DHumLitt (New Haven) 1994, (Medical Coll. of Pa and Hahnemann Univ.) 1995; numerous awards and prizes, including 21st Century Award, Int. Alliance, Glass Ceiling Award, American Red Cross. *Publications:* author or co-author of 10 books on the relationship between psychological and biological processes in human health and behaviour; 100 articles in academic journals. *Leisure interests:* tennis, travel, reading. *Address:* University of Pennsylvania, Office of the President, 100 College Hall, Philadelphia, PA 19104, USA. *Telephone:* (215) 898-7221 (Office). *Fax:* (215) 898-9659.

RODINO, Peter Wallace, Jr; American politician; b. 7 June 1909, Newark, NJ; s. of Peter Rodino and Margaret (Gerard) Rodino; m. Marianna Stango 1941; one s. one d.; ed New Jersey Law School; admitted to NJ Bar 1938; mem. House of Reps for NJ 1948–74; Chair. House Judiciary Cttee 1973; Del. N Atlantic Ass. 1962–, Intergovernmental Cttee for European Migration 1962–72 (Chair. 1971–72); partner Rodino & Rodino, East Hanover, NJ 1989–; mem. Pres. Select Comm. on Western Hemisphere Immigration; Chair. Impeachment investigation of Pres. Richard Nixon 1973–74; 13 hon. degrees; Bronze Star, Kt, Order of the Crown (Italy), Grand Kt, Order of Merit (Italy) and numerous other awards and decorations.

RODIONOV, Gen. Igor Nikolayevich; Russian army officer (retd); b. 1 Dec. 1936, Kurakino, Penza Region; m.; one s.; ed Orel Tank Higher Mil. School, Mil. Acad. of Armoured Units, Mil. Acad. of Gen. Staff; Asst to Commdr, master sgt's student's co. Orel Tank Higher School 1965–67; in Group of Soviet Troops in Germany 1957–64; Commdr tank co., Deputy Commdr tank bn 1964–67; Deputy Commdr tank regt, Commdr Regt, Deputy Commdr, Commdr div. Carpathian Mil. Command 1970–78; Commdr Army corps Cen. Group of Troops 1980–83; Commdr 5th Army Far E. Mil. Command 1983–85; Commdr Army of Turkestan Mil. Command, participant of war in Afghanistan 1985–86; First Deputy Commdr Moscow Mil. Command 1986–88; Commdr Caucasian Mil. Command, involved in dispersal of demonstration in Tbilisi 1989; Chief Mil. Acad. of Gen. Staff 1989–96; Minister of Defence of Russian Fed., mem. Security Council and Defence Council 1996–97; discharged by Pres. Yeltsin; joined CP of Russian Fed. 1998; mem. State Duma (Parl.) (CP faction) 1999–. *Address:* State Duma, Okhotny Ryad 1, 103265 Moscow, Russia. *Telephone:* (095) 292-50-14.

RODIONOV, Piotr Ivanovich; Russian politician; b. 26 Jan. 1951, Przhevalsk, Kyrgyz SSR; m.; three c.; ed Leningrad Inst. of Vessel Construction, Leningrad Inst. of Finance and Econs, Higher School of Commerce, Acad. of Nat. Econs; with USSR Ministry of Gas Industry; chief technologist, Head of Div., with Lentransgas 1984–88; Dir-Gen. Lentransgas 1989–96; mem. Bd Dirs. Russian Jt Gazprom 1996–; rep. of Russian Govt to Gazprom 1996–, to United Energy System of Russia 1996–; Minister of Oil and Gas Industry 1996–97; mem. Govt Comm. for Operational Problems 1996–97; Chair. Bd of Dirs. Menatep St Petersburg Bank 1998–; First Deputy Chair. of Bd Gazprom 2001–; Hon. Worker of Gas Industry. *Address:* Gazprom, Nametkina str. 16, 117884 Moscow, Russia. *Telephone:* (095) 719-30-01.

RODMAN, Dennis Keith; American basketball player and actor; b. 13 May 1961, Trenton, NJ; s. of Shirley Rodman; m. 1st Annie Banks 1993 (divorced); m. 2nd Carmen Electra 1998 (divorced 1999); ed Cooke County Jr Coll., Southeastern Oklahoma State Univ.; with Detroit Pistons 1986–93; forward San Antonio Spurs 1993–95, Chicago Bulls 1995–99, LA Lakers March–April 1999; briefly with Dallas Mavericks before dropping out of League in 2000; NBA Defensive Player of the Year 1990, 1991; NBA Championship Team 1989–90, 1996, All-Defensive First Team 1989–93, All-Defense Second Team 1994; All-Star team 1990, 1992. *Film appearances:* include Cutaway, Simon Sez, Double Team. *Publications:* Bad as I Wanna Be 1997, Walk on the Wild Side 1997, Words From the Worm: An Unauthorized Trip Through the Mind of Dennis Rodman 1997. *Address:* LA Lakers, 3900 West Manchester Boulevard, Inglewood, CA 90306, USA.

RODOTÀ, Antonio, FRAeS; Italian aerospace engineer; b. 24 Dec. 1935, Cosenza; s. of Carlo Rodotà and Maria Cristofaro; m. Barbara Salvini 1965; one s. two d.; ed Univ. of Rome; Asst Lecturer in Radio Eng, Univ. of Rome 1959–61; joined SISPRE SpA 1959; Italian Del. to NATO, Paris 1965–66; Head Electronic Design Group, Selenia 1966–71, in charge of Eng, Radar and Systems Div. 1971–76, Head of Div. 1976–80; Dir-Gen. Compagnia Nazionale Satelliti (CNS) SpA 1980–83, Jt Man. Dir Selenia Spazio SpA 1983–90; Jt Man. Dir Alenia Spazio SpA (now Alenia Aerospazio) 1990–95, Man. Dir 1995–97, Chair. and Man. Dir Quadrics Supercomputer World Ltd (Jt venture between Alenia Spazio and Meiko Ltd) 1995–97; Dir-Gen. ESA 1997–; fmr mem. Bd of Dirs. Arianespace, Space Software Italia, Alelco, Marconi/Alenia Communication and Space System Loral. *Leisure interests:* skiing, tennis, classical music. *Address:* European Space Agency (ESA), 8–10 rue Mario Nikis, 75738 Paris Cédex 15, France (Office). *Telephone:* 1-53-69-76-54 (Office). *Fax:* 1-53-69-75-60 (Office). *E-mail:* antonio.rodota@esa.int (Office). *Website:* www.esa.int (Office).

RODRIGO, Nihal; Sri Lankan diplomatist and international organization official; Asst Lecturer, Univ. of Ceylon; with Foreign Service, including diplomatic missions to Australia, Germany, India, Switzerland and USA; Deputy Perm. Rep. to UN, New York, Perm. Rep., Geneva; Dir-Gen. for S. Asia, S. Asian Asscn for Regional Co-operation (SAARC), Sec.-Gen. 1999–2002; co-ordinated activities of Non-aligned Movt under Sri Lanka's

chairmanship 1976–79, del. to summit confs. 1976–, Chair. Political Cttee 1995; mem. Advisory Bd on Disarmament of UN Sec.-Gen.; mem. several presidential cttees., including Acquisition of Art Works for State Collections, Foreign Affairs, Human Rights and Information Strategy; mem. Man. Bd Bandaranaike Centre for Int. Studies. *Address:* c/o South Asian Association for Regional Co-operation, P.O. Box 4222, Kathmandu, Nepal (Office).

RODRIGUES, Christopher John, BA, MBA, FRSA; British business executive; b. 24 Oct. 1949; s. of Alfred John Rodrigues and Joyce Margaret Rodrigues (née Farron-Smith); m. Priscilla Purcell Young 1976; one s. one d.; ed Univ. of Cambridge, Harvard Univ.; fmr man. trainee Spillers; fmrly with McKinsey, American Express; fmr COO, fmr Chief Exec. Thomas Cook; Chief Exec. Bradford & Bingley Bldg Soc. (now Bradford and Bingley PLC) 1996–; Dir (non-exec.) Energis PLC 1997–, Financial Services Authority 1997–. *Leisure interests:* cooking, rowing, opera. *Address:* Bradford & Bingley PLC, Croft Road, Crossflatts, Bingley, W Yorks., BD16 2UA, England. *Telephone:* (1274) 554426. *Fax:* (1273) 569116. *Website:* www.bradford-bingley.co.uk (Office).

RODRIGUEZ, Narciso; American fashion designer; b. 27 Jan. 1961, New Jersey; ed Parsons School of Design, New York; Women's Designer Asst, Anne Klein under Donna Karan 1985–91, Women's ready-to-wear, Calvin Klein 1991–95; Women's and Men's Design Dir TSE, New York, Women's Creative Dir Cerruti, Paris 1995–97; Women's Design Dir Loewe, Spain 1997; Narciso Rodriguez signature collection presented Milan 1997; Best New Designer, VH1 Fashion Awards 1997, Perry Ellis Award, CFDA 1997, Hispanic Designers Moda Award 1997, New York Magazine Award 1997. *Address:* 50 Bond Street, 7th Floor, New York, NY 10012, USA (Office). *Telephone:* (212) 677-2989 (Office). *Fax:* (212) 677-2475 (Office).

RODRÍGUEZ ARAQUE, Ali; Venezuelan politician, lawyer and international organization official; ed Univ. Cen. de Venezuela, Univ. de los Andes; practised law; mem. Parl. 1983; mem. Nat. Council of Energy; Chair. Chamber of Deputies Comm. of Energy and Mines 1994–97; Vice-Chair., Bicameral Comm. of Energy and Mines; Senator 1999–; fmr Minister of Energy and Mines; Pres. of OPEC Conf. 2000, Sec.-Gen. 2001–02; Pres. Petróleos de Venezuela SA (PDVSA) 2002–. *Address:* PDVSA, Edif. Petróleos de Venezuela, Torre Este, Avenida Libertador, La Campiña, Apdo 169, Caracas 1010-A, Venezuela (Office). *Telephone:* (212) 708-4111 (Office). *Fax:* (212) 708-4661 (Office). *E-mail:* webmaster@pdvsa.com (Office). *Website:* www.pdvsa.com (Office).

RODRÍGUEZ ECHEVERÍA, Miguel Angel, PhD; Costa Rican head of state, economist and business executive; b. 9 Jan. 1940, San José; m.; ed Univ. de Costa Rica, Univ. of California, Berkeley; lecturer and economist Univ. of Costa Rica 1963; research Asst Univ. of Calif., Berkeley 1965–66; Dir of Planning Office and Presidential Adviser on Political Econs and Planning 1966–68; Dir Cen. Bank 1967–70; columnist for La Nación 1967–68; with Ministry of Planning 1968–69; Visiting Economist Univ. of Calif.; with Ministry of the Presidency 1970; exec. with Empacadora de Carne de Cartago and Abonos Superior SA 1970–71; Pres. Agrodinámica Int. SA and subsidiaries 1974–87; lecturer in Econs Univ. of Costa Rica and Univ. Autónoma de Centro América 1978; mem. of Counsel (legal and econ. advisers) 1982; mem. nat. political directorate Partido Unidad Social Cristiano 1984, mem. Exec. 1994; Dir Banco Agro Industrial y de Exportaciones SA 1986–87; gen. adviser Grupo Ganadero Int. de Costa Rica SA 1989–90; Deputy Legis. Ass. 1991–92; Vice-Pres. (for Cen. America), Christian Democratic Org. of Latin America 1991, Pres. 1995; Pres. of Costa Rica 1998–2002. *Publications:* El mito de la Racionalidad del Socialismo 1963, El Orden Jurídico de la Libertad 1967, Contributions to Economic Analysis. Production Economics: A Dual Approach to Theory and Applications 1978, Nuestra Crisis Financiera: Causas y Soluciones 1979, De las Ideas a la Acción 1988, Al Progreso por la Libertad 1989, Libertad y Solidaridad: Una Política Social para el Desarrollo Humano 1992, Una Revolución Moral: Democracia, Mercado y Bien Común 1992, Por una Vida Buena, Justa y Solidaria 1993; and numerous articles and contribs on econs. *Address:* c/o Ministry of the Presidency, 2010 Zapote, Apdo 520, San José, Costa Rica (Office).

RODRÍGUEZ GIAVARINI, Adalberto; Argentine politician and economist; ed Univ. of Buenos Aires; fmr Comptroller Gen. Trust of State Cos.; Pres. own macroecons. analysis co.; Chair. Microecons, Univ. of Buenos Aires 1972–78; Co-ordinator Postgrad. Studies in Econs, Univ. of Salvador 1980–83; Sec. of State for Budget, Ministry of Economy 1983–85, for Planning, Ministry of Defence 1986–89; elected mem. Chamber of Deputies 1995; Minister of Foreign Affairs, Int. Trade and Religion –2001; Visiting Prof. Univ. of Belgrano 1994; Prof. of Econs, School of Econs and Business Admin. 1995; mem. various academic insts and advisory bds; guest columnist maj. daily newspapers in Argentina and abroad. *Address:* c/o Ministry of Foreign Affairs, International Trade and Religion, Esmeralda 1212, 1061 Buenos Aires, Argentina (Office).

RODRÍGUEZ IGLESIAS, Gil Carlos, PhD; Spanish judge and professor of law; b. 26 May 1946, Gijón; m. Teresa Diez Gutiérrez 1972; two d.; ed Oviedo Univ. and Univ. Autónoma of Madrid; Asst Univs. of Oviedo, Freiburg, Autónoma of Madrid and Complutense of Madrid 1969–77; lecturer, Univ. Complutense of Madrid 1977–82, Prof. 1982–83; Prof. Univ. of Granada 1983–, Dir Dept of Int. Law 1983–86; Judge, Court of Justice of European Communities 1986–, Pres. 1994–; Hon. Bencher Gray's Inn 1995; Dr. hc (Turin) 1996, ('Babeş-Bolyai' Cluj-Napoca, Romania) 1996; Orden de Isabel la

Católica, Orden de San Raimundo de Peñafort. *Publications:* El régimen jurídico de los monopolios de Estado en la Comunidad Económica Europea 1976; articles and studies on EC law and int. law. *Address:* Court of Justice of the European Communities, Plateau du Kirchberg, Luxembourg 2925 Luxembourg. *Telephone:* 4303-1. *Fax:* 4303-6000. *Website:* www.curia.eu.int (Office).

RODRÍGUEZ LARA, Maj.-Gen. Guillermo; Ecuadorean army officer; b. 4 Nov. 1923; ed Quito Mil. Acad. and studied abroad; C-in-C of Army 1971; Pres. of Ecuador (following coup d'état) 1972–76.

RODRÍGUEZ MADARIAGA, HE Cardinal Oscar Andrés; Honduran ecclesiastic; b. 29 Dec. 1942, Tegucigalpa; ordained priest 1970; Bishop 1978; Archbishop of Tegucigalpa 1993–; cr. Cardinal 2001. *Address:* Conferencia Episcopal de Honduras, Los Lavreles, Comayagüela, Apdo 3121, Tegucigalpa, Honduras (Office). *Telephone:* 2370353 (Office); 2372366 (Home). *Fax:* 2222337 (Office).

RODRÍGUEZ MENDOZA, Miguel; Venezuelan international organization official; ed Cen. Univ. of Venezuela, Univ. of Manchester, Ecole des Hautes Etudes en Sciences Sociales; First Sec. Perm. Mission of Venezuela to UN 1978–81; Dir for Consultation and Co-ordination, Latin American Econ. System 1982–88; Special Adviser to Pres. on int. econ. affairs 1989–91; Minister of State, Pres. Inst. of Foreign Trade 1991–94; Pres. Comm. of Cartagena Agreement 1993; Chief Trade Adviser, OAS –1998; Visiting Scholar Georgetown Univ., Washington; Jt Deputy Dir-Gen. World Trade Org. 1999–2002. *Publications:* numerous articles in books and journals; has edited numerous books. *Address:* c/o World Trade Organization, 154 rue de Lausanne, 1211 Geneva 21, Switzerland (Office).

RODRIQUEZ, Isaias, PhD; Venezuelan lawyer, poet and politician; ed Univs. of Santa Maria and Zulia and Cen. Univ. of Venezuela; legal adviser to Ministry of Agric. 1969; consultant to Veterinary Asscn 1971–; Attorney-Gen.; Chief Attorney of Aragua 1990–91; Prof. of Univ. of Carabobo, Vice-Pres. of the Nat. Ass.; Vice-Pres. of Venezuela 1998–2000; regular columnist for El Siglo. *Publications:* (legal) New Labour Procedures 1987, Legal Stability in Labour Laws 1993; (poetry) Pozo de Cabrillas, Con las Aspas de Todos los Molinos, Los Tiempos de la Sed.; numerous articles. *Address:* Congreso Nacional, Caracas, Venezuela (Office).

ROEG, Nicolas Jack, CBE; British film director; b. 15 Aug. 1928, London; s. of Jack Nicolas Roeg and Mabel Roeg; m. 1st Susan Rennie Stephen 1957 (divorced); four s.; m. 2nd Theresa Russell (divorced); two s.; ed Mercers School; started in film industry as clapper-boy; Fellow BFI 1994; Hon. DLitt (Hull) 1995. *Principal films:* as cinematographer: The Caretaker 1963, The Masque of the Red Death, Nothing but the Best 1964, Fahrenheit 451 1966, Far from the Madding Crowd 1967, Petulia 1968; Dir: Performance (with Donald Cammell) 1968, Walkabout 1970, Don't Look Now 1972, The Man who Fell to Earth 1975, Bad Timing 1979, Eureka 1983, Insignificance 1984, Castaway 1985, Track 29 1987, Aria (Sequence) 1988, Cold Heaven 1989, The Witches 1989, Sweet Bird of Youth 1989, Without You I'm Nothing (exec. producer) 1990, Young Indy – Paris 1916 1991, Cold Heaven 1991, Heart of Darkness 1993, Two Deaths 1994, Full Body Massage 1995, Hotel Paradise 1995, Samson and Delilah 1996, The Sound of Claudia Schiffer 2001; co-writer film script for Night Train 2002. *Address:* c/o Luc Roeg Artists Independent Network, 32 Tavistock Street, London, WC2, England.

ROEHM, Carolyne, BFA; American fashion designer; b. 7 May 1951, Kirksville, Mo.; d. of Kenneth Smith and Elaine (Beaty) Bresee; m. 1st Axel Roehm 1978 (divorced 1981); m. 2nd Henry R. Kravis 1985; ed Washington Univ. St Louis; designed sportswear for Kellwood Co. New York; apprentice, Oscar de la Renta, Rome 1975–84; Pres. Carolyne Roehm Inc. (fashion design house) 1984–; Pres. Council of Fashion Designers of America 1989. *Leisure interests:* gardening, skiing, tennis, opera, playing the piano.

ROEM, Mohammad; Indonesian politician; b. 16 May 1908, Parakan, Kedu Central Java; s. of Dzoelkarnain Djojosasmito and Siti Tarbiyah; m. Markisah Dahlia 1932; one s. one d.; ed Law School, Batavia (now Jakarta); Solicitor in pvt. practice, Jakarta 1940–67; fmr leader of Islamic Youth Movement; Indonesian Minister of the Interior 1946–48; mem. del. in Dutch-Indonesian talks leading to Linggajati Agreement 1947, Renville Agreement 1948; Chair. Indonesian del. leading to Van Roijem-Roem Statements 1949; Deputy Chair. Round Table Conf. with Netherlands Govt 1949; first High Commr of Indonesia to the Netherlands 1950; Minister of Foreign Affairs 1950–51, of Home Affairs 1952–53; First Vice-Premier 1956–57; mem. Exec. Cttee Masjumi Party 1945–62, Third Deputy Chair. 1959; Pres. Islamic Univ., Medan 1953–62; detained 1962–66; founder-mem. Partai Muslimin Indonesia 1967, Chair. 1968–72; mem. World Muslim Congress 1975–; mem. Bd Dirs. Asian Conf. for Religion and Peace; Vice-Chair. Bd of Curators, Islamic Medical Faculty, Jakarta. *Publications:* Bunga Rampai Sejarah I (1972), II (1977). *Leisure interests:* swimming, horse-riding. *Address:* c/o Jalan Teuku Cik Ditiro 58, Jakarta Pusat, Indonesia. *Telephone:* 343393.

ROEMER, John E., PhD; American professor of economics; b. 1 Feb. 1945, Washington, DC; s. of Milton I. Roemer and Ruth Rosenbaum Roemer; m. Carla Natasha Muldavin 1968; two c.; ed Harvard Univ., Univ. of California, Berkeley; Asst Prof., Univ. of Calif., Davis 1974, Prof. of Econs 1981–; Elizabeth S. and A. Varick Stout Prof. of Political Science and Econs Yale Univ. 2000; Dir Program on Economy, Justice and Society 1988; Guggenheim Fellow; Fellow Econometric Soc.; Russell Sage Fellow. *Publications:* A Gen-

eral Theory of Exploitation and Class 1982, Free to Lose 1988, Egalitarian Perspectives 1994, A Future for Socialism 1994, Theories of Distributive Justice 1996, Equality of Opportunity 1998, Political Competition 2001. *Address:* Department of Political Science, Box 208301, Yale University, New Haven, CT 06520, USA. *Telephone:* (203) 432-5249. *Fax:* (203) 432-6196. *Website:* www.yale.edu (Office).

ROESKY, Herbert Walter, DrSc; German professor of inorganic chemistry; b. 6 Nov. 1935, Laukischken; s. of Otto Roesky and Lina Roesky; m. Christel Roesky 1964; two s.; ed Univ. of Göttingen; lecturer 1970, Prof. of Inorganic Chem., Univ. of Frankfurt 1971–80; Dir Inst. of Inorganic Chem., Univ. of Göttingen 1980–, Dean Dept of Chem. 1985–87; Visiting Prof. Univ. of Auburn, USA 1984, Tokyo Inst. of Tech. 1987; mem. Gesellschaft Deutscher Chemiker (Vice-Pres. 1995), American Chemical Soc., Chemical Soc., London, Gesellschaft Deutscher Naturforscher und Ärzte, Deutsche Bunsen-Gesellschaft für Physikalische Chemie, Göttinger Akad., Akad. Leopoldina, Austrian Acad. of Sciences, Russian Acad. of Sciences 1999; Foreign Assoc. Acad. des Sciences, France; mem. Selection Bd, Alexander von Humboldt-Stiftung 1973–84; numerous editorial bds; Wöhler Prize 1960, French Alexander von Humboldt Prize 1986, Leibniz Prize 1987; Alfred-Stock-Gedächtnispreis 1990, Georg Ernst Stahl Medal 1990; Manfred and Wolfgang Flad Prize 1994, Grand Prix Fondation de la maison de la chimie, Carus Prize 1998, Wilkinson Award 1999. *Publications:* more than 800 learned papers and articles. *Leisure interest:* antique collecting. *Address:* Institute of Inorganic Chemistry, University of Göttingen, Tammannstrasse 4, 37077 Göttingen, Germany. *Telephone:* (551) 393001. *Fax:* (551) 393373. *E-mail:* hroesky@gwdg.de (Office).

ROGACHEV, Igor Alekseevich, PhD; Russian diplomatist; b. 1 March 1932, Moscow; s. of Aleksey Petrovich Rogachev; m. Dioulber Rogacheva; one s. one d. (adopted); ed Moscow Inst. of Int. Relations 1955, USSR Ministry of Foreign Affairs; worked as interpreter in China 1956–58; joined diplomatic service 1958; Attaché, Embassy in China 1959–61; mem. Cen. Admin. U.S.S.R Ministry of Foreign Affairs 1961–65; First Sec. Embassy, USA 1965–69; Counsellor Embassy, China 1969–72; Deputy Head, Far Eastern Dept, Ministry of Foreign Affairs 1972–75, Head Asian Section, Dept of Planning of int. policies 1975–78, Head of South-East Asia Dept 1978–83, Head First Far East Div. 1983–86, Chief Dept of Socialist Countries of Asia 1986–87, Deputy-Minister of Foreign Affairs 1986–91; Head USSR del. Sino-Soviet talks on frontier issues 1987–91, int. talks on Cambodia 1988–91; Amb.-at-Large to People's Dem. Repub. of Korea 1992; Amb. to People's Repub. of China 1992–; Vice-Chair. Russian–Chinese Friendship Soc. 1992–; mem. Editorial Bd journal Far Eastern Affairs; Academician Int. Acad. of Information Processes and Tech.; Order of the Badge of Honour 1971, Order of Friendship of Peoples 1982, Order of Friendship 1996, Order of Honour 1999, Honoured Diplomatic Service Worker of Russian Fed. 2002; several medals. *Publications:* numerous articles and essays on Asian Pacific region. *Leisure interests:* playing the piano, tennis, reading, theatre. *Address:* Embassy of the Russian Federation in China, 4 Dongzhimen Beizhong Street, Beijing 100600, People's Republic of China. *Telephone:* (10) 65322051; (10) 65321381. *Fax:* (10) 65324851. *E-mail:* embassy@russia.org.cn (Office). *Website:* www.russia .org.cn (Office).

ROGÉ, Pascal; French pianist; b. 6 April 1951, Paris; two s.; ed Paris Conservatoire; début Paris 1969, London 1969; First Prize, Marguerite Long-Jacques Thibaud Int. Competition 1971; specialist in Ravel, Poulenc, Debussy, Satie; soloist with leading orchestras; exclusive recording contract with Decca, London. *Leisure interests:* reading, tennis, riding, golf. *Address:* Lorentz Concerts, 3 rue de la Boétie, 75008 Paris, France; 17 avenue des Cavaliers, 1224 Geneva, Switzerland.

ROGER OF TAIZÉ, Brother (Roger Louis Schutz-Marsauche); French/Swiss monk; b. 12 May 1915, Provence, Switzerland; s. of Charles Schutz and Amélie Marsauche; ed theological studies in Lausanne and Strasbourg; Founder and Prior of Taizé (int. ecumenical, monastic community) 1940–; arrived in Taizé 1940; lived there alone for two years sheltering Jews and political refugees; joined by the first brothers in 1942; there are now small fraternities of brothers living among the poor on every continent; attended Second Vatican Council 1962–65; launched Pilgrimage of Trust on Earth 1982; Dr hc (Catholic Theological Acad. of Warsaw) 1986; Hon. DD (Glasgow) 1991; Templeton Prize for Religion 1974; UNESCO Prize for Peace Educ. 1988, Robert Schuman Prize for his participation in construction of Europe 1992. *Publications:* The Sources of Taizé, Peace of Heart in All Things, The Wonder of a Love, with Mother Teresa of Calcutta: The Way of the Cross, Mary Mother of Reconciliations, Prayer: Seeking the Heart of God. *Address:* The Taizé Community, 71250 Cluny, France. *Telephone:* (3) 85-50-30-30. *Fax:* (3) 85-50-30-20. *E-mail:* community@taize.fr (Office). *Website:* www.taize.fr (Office).

ROGERS, Gen. Bernard William, MA; American army officer; b. 16 July 1921, Fairview, Kan.; s. of the late W. H. Rogers and Mrs Rogers; m. Ann Ellen Jones 1944; one s. two d.; ed Kansas State Coll., US Mil. Acad., Univ. of Oxford, US Army Command and Gen. Staff Coll., US Army War Coll.; Commdg Officer, Third Bn, Ninth Infantry Regt, Second Infantry Div., Korea 1952–53; Commdr, First Battle Group, 19th Infantry, 24th Infantry Div., Augsburg, FRG 1960–61; Exec. Officer to the Chair., Joint Chiefs of Staff, the Pentagon 1962–66; Asst Div. Commdr, First Infantry Div., Repub. of Viet Nam 1966–67; Commdt of Cadets, US Mil. Acad. 1967–69; Commdg Gen., Fifth Infantry Div., Fort Carson, Colo 1969–70; Chief of Legis. Liaison, Office of the US Sec. of the Army 1971–72; Deputy Chief of Staff for Personnel 1972–74; Commdg Gen., US Army Forces Command, Fort McPherson, Ga 1974–76; Chief of Staff, US Army 1976–79, Supreme Allied Commdr Europe, NATO 1979–87, Supreme Commdr-in-Chief US Forces Europe 1979–87; Rhodes Scholar 1947–50; Hon. Fellow Univ. Coll., Oxford; Hon. LLD (Akron, Boston); Hon. DCL (Oxford) 1983; Distinguished Grad. Award, US Mil. Acad. 1995, George C. Marshall Medal, Asscn of US Army 1999, DSC, Defense Distinguished Service Medal, DSM of Army, Navy and Air Force, Silver Star, Legion of Merit, Bronze Star, Air Medal. *Publications:* Cedar Falls-Junction City: a Turning Point 1974, NATO's Strategy: An Undervalued Currency 1985, The Realities of NATO Strategy 1985, NATO's Conventional Defense Improvements Initiative: A New Approach to an Old Challenge, NATO's 16 Nations 1986, Western Security and European Defense RUSI 1986, NATO and US National Security: Misperception Versus Reality 1987, Soldat und Technik 1987, Arms Control and NATO, The Council for Arms Control 1987, Arms Control: for NATO, the Name of the Game is Deterrence, Global Affairs 1987; contribs. to Atlantic Community Quarterly 1979, Foreign Affairs 1982, NATO Review 1982, 1984, RUSI 1982, Strategic Review, Nato's 16 Nations 1983, Géopolitique 1983, Europa Archiv 1984, Leaders Magazine 1984. *Leisure interests:* golf, reading. *Address:* 1467 Hampton Ridge Drive, McLean, VA 22101, USA. *Telephone:* (703) 448-0188.

ROGERS, Sir Frank Jarvis, Kt; British newspaper publisher; b. 24 Feb. 1920, Lawton, Cheshire; s. of Percy Rogers and Elsie Rogers; m. 1st Esma Sophia Holland 1949 (died 1998); two d.; m. 2nd Sheena Phillip 2001; ed Wolstanton Grammar School; journalist 1937–49; mil. service 1940–46; Gen. Man. Nigerian Daily Times 1949–52; Man. Argus, Melbourne 1952–55; Man. Dir Overseas Newspapers 1958–60; Dir Daily Mirror 1960–65; Man. Dir IPC 1965–70; Vice-Chair. Newspaper Publrs. Asscn 1968–69, Dir 1971–73, Chair. 1990–98; Chair. Nat. Newspapers Steering Group 1970–72; Dir EMAP (fmrly East Midland Allied Press) 1971–91, Chair. 1973–90; Adviser on Corp. Affairs The Plessey Co. Ltd 1973–81; Deputy Chair. Argyll Investments Ltd 1982–90; Exec. Dir 1986–, Deputy Chair. Daily Telegraph PLC 1986–95; Trustee Reuters Founders Share Co. 1989–, Chair. 1998–99. *Leisure interest:* motoring. *Address:* Greensleeves, Loudwater Drive, Loudwater, Rickmansworth, Herts., WD3 4HJ, England.

ROGERS, George Ernest, PhD, DSc, FAA; Australian professor of biochemistry; b. 27 Oct. 1927, Melbourne; s. of Percy Rogers and Bertha Beatrice (née Baxter) Rogers; m. 1st Alison Phoebe Rogers 1951 (divorced 1970); one s. two d.; m. 2nd Racheline Aladjem 1972; two d.; ed Caulfield Grammar School, Univ. of Melbourne and Trinity Coll., Cambridge, England; Research Scientist, Wool Research Unit, CSIRO 1951–53, Sr Research Scientist Div. of Protein Chem. 1957–62; Research Scientist, Univ. of Cambridge, England 1954–56; Reader in Biochem., Univ. of Adelaide 1963–77, Prof. of Biochem. 1978–92 and Chair. Dept of Biochem. 1988–92, Prof. Emer. of Biochem., Hon. Visiting Research Fellow 1993–; Visiting Fellow, Clare Hall, Cambridge, England 1970; Program Man. Premium Quality Wool CRC 1995–; Visiting Scientist, Univ. de Grenoble, France 1977; Guest Scientist, NIH, Bethesda, USA 1985; CSIRO studentship 1954–56; Bourse Scientifique de Haut Niveau 1977; mem. Australian Soc. of Biochemistry and Molecular Biology, New York Acad. of Sciences; Eleanor Roosevelt Int. Cancer Research Fellow 1985; Lemberg Medal, Australian Biochemical Soc. 1976. *Publications include:* The Keratins (jtly) 1972, The Biology of Wool and Hair (jtly) 1989; 150 publs in scientific journals on wool and hair growth, hair structure and sheep transgenesis. *Leisure interests:* family activities, swimming, golf, gardening. *Address:* Visiting Scientist, University of Adelaide, Sardi, 33 Flemington Street, Glenside, Adelaide, SA 5065 (Office); 1 Gandys Gully Road, Stonyfell, SA 5066, Australia (Home). *Telephone:* (8) 8207-7801 (Office); (8) 8332-4143 (Home). *E-mail:* rogers.george@saugov.sa.gov.au (Office); grogers@ozemail.net.au (Home).

ROGERS, Paul; British actor; b. 22 March 1917, Plympton, Devon; s. of Edwin Rogers and Dulcie Myrtle Rogers; m. 1st Jocelyn Wynne 1939 (divorced 1955); two s.; m. 2nd Rosalind Boxall 1955; two d.; ed Newton Abbot Grammar School, Devon and Michael Chekhov Theatre Studio; first stage appearance at Scala Theatre 1938; Stratford-on-Avon Shakespeare Memorial Theatre 1939; Royal Navy 1940–46; with Bristol Old Vic Co. 1947–49, London Old Vic 1949–53, 1955–56; Clarence Derwent Award 1952, Tony Award 1967. *Plays include:* The Merchant of Venice 1952, The Confidential Clerk 1953, Macbeth 1954, The Taming of the Shrew; toured Australia as Hamlet 1957; The Elder Statesman 1958, King Lear 1958, Mr. Fox of Venice 1959, The Merry Wives of Windsor 1959, A Winter's Tale 1959, One More River 1959, JB 61, Photo Finish 1962, The Seagull 1964, Season of Goodwill 1964, The Homecoming 1965, 1968, Timon of Athens (Stratford) 1965, The Government Inspector 1966, Henry IV (Stratford) 1966, Plaza Suite 1969, The Happy Apple 1970, Sleuth (London 1970, New York 1971), Othello (Old Vic) 1974, Heartbreak House (Nat. Theatre) 1975, The Marrying of Ann Leete (Aldwych) 1975, The Return of A. J. Raffles (Aldwych) 1975, The Zykovs (Aldwych) 1976, Volpone, The Madras House (Nat. Theatre) 1977, Half Life (Nat. Theatre), Eclipse (Royal Court Theatre) 1978, Merchant of Venice (Birmingham Repertory Co.) 1979, You Never Can Tell (Lyric, Hammersmith) 1979, The Dresser (New York) 1981–82, The Importance of Being Earnest (Nat. Theatre) 1982, A Kind of Alaska (Nat. Theatre) 1982, The Applecart (Haymarket) 1986, Danger: Memory! 1986 (Hampstead Theatre, Old Vic), King Lear 1989, Other People's Money (Lyric) 1990. *Films include:* A Midsummer Night's Dream 1968, The Looking-Glass War 1969, The Reckoning 1969, The Homecoming 1973, The

Abdication 1975, Mr. Quilp 1975. *Television films:* Porterhouse Blue 1986, Return of the Native 1993. *Leisure interests:* books, gardening. *Address:* 9 Hillside Gardens, Highgate, London, N6 5SU, England. *Telephone:* (20) 8340-2656.

ROGERS, Thomas Sydney, BA, JD; American communications executive and lawyer; b. 19 Aug. 1954, New Rochelle, NY; s. of Sydney Michael Rogers Jr and Alice Steinhardt; m. Sylvia Texon 1983; two s. one d.; ed Wesleyan Univ., Columbia Univ.; attorney with Wall St law firm 1979–81; called to New York Bar 1980; Sr Counsel U.S. House of Reps. Subcttee. on Telecommunications, Consumer Protection and Finance 1981–86; Vice-Pres. Policy Planning and Business Devt, NBC 1987–88; Pres. NBC Cable 1988–89, NBC Cable and Business Devt 1989–99; Exec. Vice-Pres. NBC 1992–99; Vice-Chair. NBC Internet 1999; Chair. and CEO Primedia Inc. 1999–; Pres., CEO Int. Council, Nat. Acad. of TV Arts and Sciences 1994–97, Chair. 1998–99; mem. New York State Bar Asscn, Int. Radio and TV Soc. *Address:* Primedia Inc., 745 Fifth Avenue, 23rd Floor, New York, NY 10151, U.S.A. (Office).

ROGERS OF RIVERSIDE, Baron (Life Peer), cr. 1996, of Chelsea in the Royal Borough of Kensington and Chelsea; **Richard George Rogers,** Kt, A.A.DIPL., M. ARCH., RA; British architect; b. 23 July 1933, Florence, Italy; s. of Nino Rogers and Dada Geiringer; m. 1st Su Brumwell 1961; three s.; m. 2nd Ruth Elias 1973; two s.; ed Architectural Asscn, London, Yale Univ.; Fulbright, Edward D. Stone and Yale Scholar; Chair. Richard Rogers Architects Ltd, London, Richard Rogers Japan KK, Tokyo, Architecture Foundation, Nat. Tenants Resource Centre, Govt Urban Task Force; Dir River Café Ltd; numerous exhbns, including Museum of Modern Art, NY and Royal Acad., London; Saarinen Prof. Yale Univ. 1985; has also taught at Architectural Asscn, London, at Cambridge, Princeton, Columbia, Harvard, Cornell, McGill and Aachen Univs and at UCLA; Vice-Chair. Arts Council of England 1994–97; mem. UN Architects' Cttee; Trustee Tate Gallery 1981–89 (Chair. 1984–88), London First 1993–98, UK Bd Médecins du Monde; Reith Lecturer 1995; winner of numerous int. competitions including Centre Pompidou, Paris 1971–77, Lloyd's HQ, London 1978; major int. work includes: masterplanning: Royal Docks, London 1984–86, Potsdamer Platz, Berlin 1991, Shanghai Pu Dong Financial Dist 1992, Greenwich Peninsula Masterplan 1997–98; airports and HQ bldgs: PA Tech., Cambridge 1975–83, PA Tech., Princeton, NJ, USA 1984, European Court of Human Rights, Strasbourg 1990–95, Marseille Airport 1992, Law Courts, Bordeaux, France 1992–98, VR Techno offices and lab., Gifu, Japan 1993–98, Channel 4 HQ 1994; current projects include: masterplanning of Heathrow Airport Terminal 5 1989–, Montevetro Housing, Battersea, London 1994–2000, ParcBIT Devt, Majorca 1994–, Lloyd's Register of Shipping HQ, London 1995–99, Daiwa Europe HQ, London 1995–99, New Millennium Experience, Greenwich, London 1996–99, masterplanning of Piana di Castello, Florence 1997–, new terminal for Barajas Airport, Madrid 1997–, Nat. Ass. for Wales 1998–, Law Courts, Antwerp 1999; Hon. FRIBA, FAIA 1986; Dr hc (Westminster) 1993, (RCA) 1994, (Bath) 1994, (South Bank) 1996; Hon. DLitt (Univ. Coll., London) 1997; Constructa Prize 1986, 1992, Eternit Int. Prize 1988; eleven RIBA awards 1969–, Royal Gold Medal RIBA 1985, Civic Trust Award 1987, Thomas Jefferson Memorial Foundation Medal in Architecture 1999, Praemium Imperiale Award 2000 and many other awards; Chevalier Légion d'honneur 1986. *Publications:* Richard Rogers and Architects 1985, A+U: Richard Rogers 1978–88 1988, Architecture: A Modern View 1990, A New London (with Mark Fisher) 1992, Reith Lecturer 1995, Cities for a Small Planet 1997, Richard Rogers The Complete Works (Vol. 1) 1999, Cities for a Small Country 2000. *Leisure interests:* friends, food, travel, art, architecture. *Address:* Thames Wharf, Rainville Road, London, W6 9HA, England. *Telephone:* (20) 7385-1235. *Fax:* (20) 7385-8409.

ROGERSON, Philip Graham; British business executive; b. 1 Jan. 1945, Manchester; s. of Henry Rogerson and Florence Rogerson; m. Susan Janet Kershaw 1968; one s. two d.; ed William Hulme's Grammar School, Manchester; with Dearden Harper, Miller & Co. Chartered Accountants 1962–67; with Hill Samuel & Co. Ltd 1967–69; with Thomas Tilling Ltd 1969–71; with Steetly Ltd 1971–72; with J.W. Chafer Ltd 1972–78; joined ICI 1978, Gen. Man. Finance 1989–92; Man. Dir Finance British Gas PLC 1992–94, Exec. Dir 1994–96, Deputy Chair. 1996–98; Deputy Chair. (non-exec.) Aggre-ko PLC 1997–98; Dir (non-exec.) Halifax Bldg Soc. (now Halifax PLC) 1995–98, Shandwick Int. PLC 1997–, LIMIT PLC 1997, Int. Public Relations 1997–98, Wates City of London Properties 1998–; Chair. (non-exec.) Pipeline Integrity Int. 1998–, British Biotech 1999–, Octopus Capital PLC 2000–, Copper Eye Ltd 2001–; Chair. Viridian Group PLC 1999– (Deputy Chair. 1998), Bertram Group Ltd 1999–; Project Telecom PLC 2000–; Trustee Changing Faces 1997–, School for Social Entrepreneurs 1997–. *Leisure interests:* golf, theatre, opera, ballet.

ROGGE, Jacques; Belgian international organization official and surgeon; b. 2 May 1942, Ghent; m.; two c.; fmr orthopaedic surgeon and sports medicine lecturer; participated as Olympic sailing competitor 1968, 1972, 1976; Pres. Belgian Nat. Olympic Cttee 1989–92; Pres. European Olympic Cttee 1989–2001, Chef de mission, two winter and three summer Olympic Games (Chief Co-ordinator, Olympic Games 2000, (2004)); mem. Int. Olympic Cttee (IOC) 1991–, Pres. 2001–. *Address:* International Olympic Committee, Château de Vidy, 1007 Lausanne, Switzerland (Office). *Telephone:* (21) 6216111 (Office). *Fax:* (21) 6216216 (Office). *Website:* www.olympic.org (Office).

ROGOFF, Ilan; Israeli concert pianist and conductor; b. 26 July 1943; s. of Boris Rogoff and Sofija Rogoff; m. Vesna Zorka Mimiça 1985; two d.; ed Israel Acad. of Music, Royal Conservatoire, Brussels, Mannes Coll., Juilliard School, New York; has played all over Israel, Europe, N. America, Latin America, S. Africa, Japan and Far East with Israel Philharmonic Orchestra and many other orchestras; plays mostly works by Romantic composers including Beethoven, Schumann, Brahms, Chopin, Liszt, César Franck, Rachmaninov, Tchaikovsky, Piazzolla; has performed twentieth-century and contemporary works including world premiere of concerti by John McCabe and by Ivan Erod; has performed with various chamber music groups including Enesco Quartet, Orpheus Quartet, Amati Trio, Festival Ensemble, Matrix Quintet, soloists of Vienna Chamber Orchestra and Vienna Philharmonic Orchestra; conducting début 1985, with Israel Philharmonic 1988; Music and Artistic Dir Sociedad Filarmónica de Mallorca 1992–93; radio performances and TV appearances in UK, Spain, Austria, Germany, Israel, Canada, USA, SA, Colombia, Ecuador, Venezuela and Argentina; lectures and recital/lectures, masterclasses; Trustee Tel-Aviv Museum, Misgav Ladach Hosp., Jerusalem; f. Ilan Rogoff Foundation, Colombia to provide medical care to children of poor families; various int. awards. *Recordings include:* works by Bach–Busoni, César Franck, Schumann, Schubert, Chopin, Beethoven and Liszt, Chopin in Mallorca, Chopin Concerti (version for piano and string quintet), Portraits by Schumann, transcriptions for piano solo of works by Astor Piazzolla. *Publications:* Transcriptions for Piano Solo of Works by Astor Piazzolla; articles on music published in Scherzo magazine (Madrid). *Leisure interests:* water sports, reading, visual arts, theatre, cinema and music research. *Address:* Estudio/Taller, Calle Bartomeu Fons 13, 07015 Palma de Mallorca, Spain. *Telephone:* (71) 707016. *Fax:* (71) 707703. *E-mail:* ilanrogoff@telefonica.net (Home). *Website:* www.infonegocio.com/ilanrogoff (Office).

ROGOFF, Kenneth S., PhD; American economist, international finance official and university professor; b. 22 March 1953, Rochester, NY; s. of Stanley Miron Rogoff and June Beatrice Rogoff; m. Natasha Lanre; one s. one d.; ed Yale Univ., Massachusetts Inst. of Tech., Cambridge, Mass.; economist with Fed. Reserve Bd 1980–84; Assoc. Prof., Univ. of Wis. 1985–88; Prof., Univ. of Calif. at Berkeley 1989–92; Charles and Marie Robertson Prof. of Public Policy, Princeton Univ. 1992–98; Prof. of Econs, Harvard Univ. 1998–; Chief Economist and Dir of Research, IMF 2001–; Fellow Econometric Soc. 1990–; Guggenheim Fellow 1998; mem. American Acad. of Arts and Sciences 2000–; Int. Grandmaster of Chess (World Chess Fed.) 1978–. *Publications:* Foundations of International Macroeconomics (with Maurice Obstfeld) 1996; contribs. to learned journals. *Leisure interests:* swimming, chess, cinema. *Address:* IMF, 700 19th Street, NW, Washington, DC 20431 (Office); 3723 Harrison Street, NW, Washington, DC 20015, USA (Home). *Telephone:* (202) 623-8977 (Office); (202) 363-4529 (Home). *Fax:* (212) 623-7271 (Office). *E-mail:* krogoff@imf.org (Office). *Website:* www.post.economics.harvard.edu./faculty/rogoff/rogoff.html.

ROGOV, Sergey Mikhailovich, DR.HIST.; Russian political scientist; b. 22 Oct. 1948, Moscow; m.; one s. one d.; ed Moscow State Inst. of Int. Relations; jr, sr researcher, head of sector Inst. of USA and Canada, Russian Acad. of Sciences 1976–84; Rep. of ISKAN to USSR Embassy, Washington, DC 1984–87; leading researcher, Head of div., Deputy Dir Inst. of USA and Canada, Russian Acad. of Sciences 1987–95, Acting Dir 1995–98, Dir 1998–; mem. Scientific Council at Ministry of Foreign Affairs, Russian Fed.; counsellor Cttee on Foreign Relations of State Duma; mem. Scientific Council of Security Council Russian Fed.; mem. Russian Acad. of Nat. Sciences; Corresp. mem. Russian Acad. of Sciences 2002–. *Publications:* 12 books on foreign policy of USSR and Russian Fed., Russian-American relationship, mil. aspects of foreign policy, problems of nat. security and over 250 scientific publs and articles. *Address:* Institute of USA and Canada, Russian Academy of Sciences, Khlebny per. 2/3, 121814 Moscow, Russia (Office). *Telephone:* (095) 291-11-66 (Office). *Fax:* (095) 954-33-20 (Office).

ROGOWSKI, Michael, Dr rer. pol; German business executive; b. 13 March 1939; ed Univ. of Lausanne, Technical Univ. of Karlsruhe; Man. Dir SISCO GmbH, Frankfurt 1973; joined J.M. Voith GmbH (later AG) as Dir of Personnel and Stock Man., Dir Propulsion Tech. Div. 1982–92, Man. Rep. 1986–, Chair. 1992–, Pres. Exec. Cttee 1997–, Chair. Supervisory Bd 2000–; mem. Presidency, Bund Deutscher Industrie (BDI), Vice-Pres. 1997–98, 2001–02, Pres. 2002–; mem. Pay Policy Council Gesamtmetall (Metal Workers' Union); mem. Bd Asscn of German Mechanical and Plant Engineers (VDMA) 1992–, Vice-Pres. 1993, Pres. 1996–98; mem. European Advisory Bd, Carlyle 2002–. *Address:* St Pöltener Str 43, P.O. Box 2000, 89522 Heidenheim, Germany (Office). *Telephone:* (7321) 370 (Office). *Fax:* (7321) 377000 (Office).

ROGOZHKIN, Aleksandr Vladimirovich; Russian scriptwriter; b. 3 Oct. 1950, Leningrad; ed Leningrad State Univ., All-Union Inst. of Cinematography; worked in TV cos. in Leningrad; cinema debut in 1980s; Cinema Festival of Youth Prize 1985, Alfred Bauer Prize, Berlin Festival 1989, Nika Prize 1989. *Films include:* For the Sake of a Few Lines, Golden Button, Miss Millionaire, Guard, Peculiarities of National Hunting, Peculiarities of National Fishing, Operation Happy New Year. *Address:* Gertsena str. 21, apt. 8, 191065 St Petersburg, Russia (Home). *Telephone:* (812) 311-76-81 (Home).

ROGOZIN, Dmitry Olegovich, CandPhil; Russian politician and journalist; b. 21 Dec. 1963, Moscow; s. of Oleg Konstantinovich Rogozin and Tamara Rogozina; m. Tatyana Serebryakova; one s.; ed Moscow State Univ.; worked in USSR Cttee of Youth Orgs; one of founders Research and Educ. Co. RAU Corp. 1986–90; one of Party of People's Freedom 1990; Pres. Asscn of Young Political Leaders of Russia Forum-90; f. Congress of Russian Communities 1993; active in nat. movt; took part in resurrection of numerous churches; mem. State Duma (faction Regions of Russia) 1997–; Chair. Cttee on Int. Affairs 2000–; Deputy Chair. Cttee on Nationalities, State Duma; Chief Negotiator with EU on problems of Kaliningrad Region. *Publications:* Russian Answer 1996 and other books and articles on Russian people and Russian Culture. *Leisure interests:* master of sports, handball. *Address:* State Duma, Okhotny Ryad, 1, 103265 Moscow, Russia (Office). *Telephone:* (095) 292-67-27 (Office); (095) 292-57-47 (Office). *Fax:* (095) 292-10-81 (Office).

ROH MOO-HYUN; South Korean politician; b. 1946, Kimhae, S. Kyonsang Prov.; m.; one s. one d.; ed Pusan Commercial High School; mil. service, rank of corporal; served as judge in Taejon Dist court 1977; practised as human rights lawyer 1978; elected lawmaker 1988; elected mem. ruling Millennium Democratic Party's (MDP) Supreme Council 2000–; Minister of Maritime Affairs and Fisheries 2000–01; Pres. of the Repub. of Korea 2003–. *Leisure interests:* mountain climbing and bowling. *Address:* Office of the President, Chong Wa Dae (The Blue House), 1, Sejong-no, Jongno-gu, Seoul (Office); Millennium Democratic Party, 14–31 Yeouido-dong, Yeongdeungpo-gu, Seoul, Republic of Korea. *Telephone:* (2) 770-0055 (Office); (2) 770-0055 (Office). *Fax:* (2) 770-0344 (Office); (2) 770-0344 (Office). *E-mail:* president@cwd.go.kr (Office); president@cwd.go.kr. *Website:* www.bluehouse.go.kr.1 (Office); www.cwd.go.kr (Office); www.knowhow.or.kr.

ROH TAE WOO; South Korean politician; b. 4 Dec. 1932, Daegu; m. Roh (née Kim) Ok Sook 1959; one s. one d.; ed Taegu Tech. School, Kyongbuk High School, Korean Mil. Acad., US Special Warfare School, Repub. of Korea War Coll.; served in Korean War 1950; Commanding Gen. 9th Special Forces Brigade 1974–79, 9th Infantry Div. Jan.–Dec. 1979, Commdr Capital Security Command 1979–80, Defence Security Command 1980–81, Four-Star Gen. 1981, retd from army July 1981; Minister of State for Nat. Security and Foreign Affairs 1981–82, Minister of Sports 1982, of Home Affairs 1982; Pres. Repub. of Korea 1988–93; mem. Nat. Ass. 1985; Chair. Democratic Justice Party 1985–87, Pres. 1987–90, Jt Pres. Democratic Liberal Party (DLP) 1990–92 (had to quit the ruling party by agreement); Pres. Seoul Olympic Organizing Cttee 1983, Korean Amateur Sports Asscn 1984, Korean Olympic Cttee 1984; arrested Nov. 1995, charged with aiding Dec. 1979 Coup Dec. 1995; also charged with taking bribes; convicted of mutiny and treason, sentenced to 22½ years' imprisonment Aug. 1996; numerous decorations. *Publications:* Widaehan pot'ougsaram ui shidae 1987, Korea: A Nation Transformed 1990. *Leisure interests:* tennis, swimming, golf, music, reading.

ROHATYN, Felix George; American investment banker and diplomatist; b. 29 May 1928, Vienna, Austria; s. of Alexander Rohatyn and Edith Rohatyn (née Knoll); m. 1st Jeannette Streit 1956; three s.; m. 2nd Elizabeth Fly 1979; ed Middlebury Coll., Vt; moved to USA 1942; joined Lazard Freres & Co. (investment bankers) 1948, Gen. Partner 1961–97; Amb. to France 1997–2000; Founder and Pres. Rohatyn Assocs LLC 2001– (Advisers to HSBC Holdings PLC 2002–); mem. Bd of Govs NY Stock Exchange 1968–72; Chair. Municipal Assistance Corpn (MAC) 1975–93, Aton Pharma Inc.; mem. Bd of Dirs Pfizer Co., Comcast Corpn, Fiat SpA, Suez, LVMH (Moet Hennessy Louis Vuitton), Publicis Groupe SA, Gen. Instrument Crown Cork and Seal; Trustee, Center for Strategic and Int. Studies; mem. Council on Foreign Relations; mem. American Acad. of Arts and Sciences; eight hon. degrees; Commdr, Légion d'honneur. *Publications:* The Twenty-Year Century: Essays on Economics and Public Finance 1983, Money Games: My Journey Through American Capitalism 1950–2000 2003. *Address:* Rohatyn Associates LLC, 30 Rockefeller Plaza, 50th Floor, New York, NY 10020 (Office); c/o Aton Pharma Inc., 777 Old Saw Mill, River Road, Tarrytown, NY 10591-6717, USA.

ROHDE, Helmut; German politician and journalist; b. 9 Nov. 1925, Hanover; m. 1st Hanna Müller 1950; one s.; m. 2nd Ruth Basenaü 1983; ed Acad. for Labour, Political Studies and Econs; journalist, German Press Agency; Press Officer, Ministry for Social Affairs, Lower Saxony; mem. Parl. (Bundestag) 1957–87; mem. European Parl. 1964–; Parl. State Sec. Fed. Ministry of Labour and Social Affairs 1969–74; Chair. SPD Working Group for Issues Concerning Employees 1973–84; Fed. Minister for Educ. and Science 1974–78; Deputy Chair. SPD, Bundestag 1979; Prof. Univ. of Hanover 1985–; Hon. Prof. (Univ. Bremen) 1994; Paul Klinger Prize 1974, Gold Medal, Asscn of War-Blinded, Grosses Bundesverdienstkreuz mit Stern und Schalterband 1995, Landesmedaille, Lower Saxony 1995. *Publications:* Sozialplanung – Theorie und Praxis der deutschen Sozialdemokratie, Gesellschaftspolitische Planung und Praxis, Für eine soziale Zukunft; and numerous articles on social and education policy. *Leisure interests:* modern art, music, modern jazz. *Address:* Sanddornweg 3, 53757 St Augustin, Germany. *Telephone:* (2241) 333593.

ROHMER, Eric (pseudonym of Maurice Henri Joseph Schérer); French film director; b. 21 March 1920, Tulle, Corrèze; s. of Désiré Schérer and Jeanne Monzat; m. Thérèse Barbet 1957; ed in Paris; school teacher and journalist until 1955; film critic of Revue du cinéma, Arts, Temps modernes, La Parisienne 1949–63; founder (with others) and fmr co-editor of La Gazette du cinéma (review); fmr co-editor of Cahiers du cinéma; co-dir Soc. des Films du Losange 1964–; made educational films for French TV 1964–70; Prix Max-Ophuls 1970 (for Ma nuit chez Maud); Prix Louis-Delluc 1971, Prix du Meilleur Film du Festival de Saint-Sébastien 1971, Prix Méliès 1971 (all for Le genou de Claire), Prix Special Soc. des Auteurs et Compositeurs 1982, Best

Dir Award, Berlin Film Festival 1983, Lifetime Achievement Golden Lion Award, Venice Film Festival 2001, Officier des Arts et des Lettres, Officier, Légion d'honneur. *Wrote and directed:* Présentation ou Charlotte et son steak 1951, Véronique et son cancre 1958, Le signe du lion (first feature) 1959, La boulangère de Monceau 1962, La carrière de Suzanne 1963, La collection-neuse 1966, Ma nuit chez Maud 1969, Le genou de Claire 1970, L'amour l'après-midi 1972, La Marquise d'O 1976, Percival le Gallois 1978, La Femme de l'Aviateur, Le Beau Mariage 1982, Pauline à la Plage 1982, Les Nuits de la pleine lune 1984, Le Rayon Vert 1985, Four Adventures of Reinette and Mirabelle 1987, My Girlfriend's Boyfriend 1988, A Tale of Springtime 1990, A Winter's Tale 1992, Tous les Matins du Monde 1992, L'Arbre, Le Maire et la Mediathèque 1993, Les Rendez-vous de Paris 1995, Conte d'été 1996, An Autumn Tale 1998, The Lady and the Duke 2001. *Publications:* Alfred Hitchcock, Charlie Chaplin 1973, Six contes moraux 1974, L'organisation de l'espace dans le "Faust" de Murnau 1977, The Taste for Beauty 1991. *Address:* Les Films du Losange, 22 avenue Pierre 1er de Serbie, 75116 Paris, France.

ROHOVIY, Vasyl Vasylyovich, CandEcons; Ukrainian politician and economist; b. 2 March 1953, Mirivka, Kiev region; s. of Vasyl Loginovich and Zinaida Mikhailivna Rohoviy; m. Svetlana Mikhailivna Rogovaya; one s.; ed Kiev Inst. of National Economics., Ukrainian Acad. of Sciences; engineer and economist Kiev Artem Production co. 1974–75, 1976–77; Sr mechanic Odessa Mil. Command 1975–76; Jr researcher Inst. of Econs, then Scientific Sec. Dept of Econs, Ukrainian Acad. of Sciences 1980–88; Chief Expert, Head of Sector, then Head of Div. Ukrainian Council of Ministers 1988–94; First Deputy Minister of Econs 1994–98, Minister 1998–99, 2000–01; First Deputy Head of Admin., Office of the Pres. 2000; Deputy Prime Minister for Econ. Policy 2001–02. *Address:* c/o Cabinet of Ministers, Hrushevskogo str. 12/2, 252008 Kiev, Ukraine (Office).

ROHR, Hans Christoph von, PhD; German business executive; b. 1 July 1938, Stettin; s. of Hansjoachim von Rohr; m.; two c.; ed Univs. of Heidelberg, Vienna, Bonn and Kiel and Princeton Univ.; joined Klöckner-Werke AG, Bremen; subsequently held leading position with Klöckner subsidiary in Argentina; worked for Fisser & von Doornum, Einden; mem. Bd Klöckner & Co. Duisburg 1984; Chair. Exec. Bd Klöckner-Werke AG 1991–95; Man. Chair. Industrial Investment Council GmbH 1997; Chair. (non-exec.) Baring Brothers (Germany) GmbH. *Address:* Semmelweisstrasse 34, 45470 Mülheim, Ruhr, Germany.

ROHRER, Heinrich, PhD; Swiss physicist; b. 3 June 1933, Buchs, St Gallen; m. Rose-Marie Egger 1961; two d.; ed Swiss Federal Inst. of Technology; postdoctoral fellow, Rutgers Univ., NJ 1961–63; with IBM Research Lab., Rüschlikon 1963–97; sabbatical, Univ. of Calif. Santa Barbara 1974–75; research appointments at CSIC, Madrid 1997–2001, RIKEN, Waco, Japan 1997–, Tohoku Univ., Sendai, Japan 1997–; mem. Swiss Acad. of Tech. Sciences 1998–; Foreign Assoc. NAS 1988–; Hon. mem. Swiss Physical Soc. 1990–, Swiss Asscn of Engineers and Architects 1991–; Hon. DSc (Rutgers Univ.) 1986; Dr hc (Marseille, Madrid) 1988, (Tsukuba, Japan) 1994, (Wolfgang Goethe Univ., Frankfurt) 1995, (Tohoku, Japan 2000; King Faisal Int. Prize for Science 1984, Hewlett Packard Europhysics Prize 1984, Nobel Prize for Physics (with Ernst Ruska and Gerd Binnig) for work in pioneering devt of electronic microscope 1986; Cresson Medal, Franklin Inst., Phila 1986; named to Nat. Inventors Hall of Fame 1994. *Address:* Rebbergstr. 9D, CH 8832, Wollerau, Switzerland. *Telephone:* (1) 7841572. *Fax:* (1) 7841379. *E-mail:* h.rohrer@gmx.net (Home).

ROITHOVÁ, Zuzana, DenM, MBA; Czech doctor and politician; b. 30 Jan. 1953, Prague; m.; one s.; ed Charles Univ., Prague, Wharton Univ., USA, Sheffield Hallam Univ., UK; radiologist Dist Hosp., Beroun 1978–79, Univ. Hosp. Motol, Prague 1979–85; radiologist Univ. Hosp. Kralovske Vinohadry, Prague 1985–90, Dir 1990–98; Vice-Chair. Hosp. Asscn of Czech Repub. 1991–98; Minister of Health Jan.–June 1998; Senator 1998–; Chair. Senate Cttee on Health Care and Social Policy 1998–; Pres. Czech Council of the European Movt 2000–01; Deputy Chair. KDU–CSL party 2001–. *Publications include:* papers in medical journals. *Leisure interests:* sport, mountaineering. *Address:* Senát PCR, Valdštejnské nám. 4, 11800 Prague 1, Czech Republic (Office). *Telephone:* (2) 57075153 (Office). *Fax:* (2) 57534510 (Office). *E-mail:* roithovaz@senat.cz (Office). *Website:* www.senat.cz (Office).

ROIZMAN, Bernard, ScD; American professor of virology; b. 17 April 1929, Romania; m. Betty Cohen 1950; two s.; ed Temple Univ., Phila, Johns Hopkins Univ., Baltimore; Instructor of Microbiology, Johns Hopkins Univ. 1956–57, Research Assoc. 1957–58, Asst Prof. 1958–65; Assoc. Prof. of Microbiology, Univ. of Chicago 1965–69, Prof. 1969–84, Prof. of Biophysics 1970–, Chair. Interdepartmental Cttee on Virology 1969–85, 1988–, Joseph Regenstein Prof. of Virology 1981–83, Joseph Regenstein Distinguished Service Prof. of Virology 1984–; Chair. Dept of Molecular Genetics and Cell Biology 1985–88; fmr of numerous specialist scientific pubns and mem. Editorial Bd Journal of Virology 1970–, Intervirology 1972–85, Virology 1976–78, 1983–; Ed.-in-Chief Infectious Agents and Diseases 1992–96; mem. or fmr mem. numerous grant review panels, int. panels, including Chair. Herpesvirus Study Group, Int. Cttee for Taxonomy of Viruses 1971–94, Chair. Bd of Dirs 1991–; Scientific Advisory Bd, Teikeo-Showa Univs Center 1983–; mem. Int. Microbial Genetics Comm., Int. Asscn of Microbiological Sciences 1979–86; numerous nat. panels on vaccines, cancers; Scholar in Cancer Research at American Cancer Soc., Inst. Pasteur (with Andre Lwoff), Paris 1961–62; Travelling Fellow Int. Agency for Research Against Cancer (with Dr Klein), Stockholm,

Sweden 1970; Fellow Japanese Soc. for Promotion of Science, American Acad. of Arts and Sciences, American Acad. of Microbiology; mem. NAS, Inst. of Medicine, American Asscn of Immunologists, Soc. for Experimental Biology and Medicine, American Soc. for Microbiology, for Biological Chemists, Soc. for Gen. Microbiology (UK), American Soc. for Virology, Chinese Acad. of Eng, Hungarian Acad. of Science; Hon. DHumLitt (Govs State Univ., Ill.) 1984; Hon. MD (Ferrara) 1991; Hon. DSc (Paris) 1997, (Valladolid, Spain) 2001; numerous awards including Bristol-Myers Squibb Award for Distinguished Achievement in Infectious Disease Research 1998. *Publications:* author or co-author of approx. 500 papers in scientific journals and books, Ed. or Co-Ed. of 12 books. *Address:* Viral Oncology Laboratories, University of Chicago, Marjorie B. Kouler Viral Oncology Laboratories, 910 East 58th Street, Chicago, IL 60637 (Office); 5555 South Everett Avenue, Chicago, IL 60637, USA (Home). *Telephone:* (773) 702-1898 (Office); (773) 493-2986 (Home). *Fax:* (773) 702-1631 (Office); (773) 493-9042 (Home).

ROJAS DE MORENO DÍAZ, María Eugenia; Colombian politician; b. 1934; d. of the late Gen. Gustavo Rojas Pinilla (Pres. of Colombia 1953–57); m. Samuel Moreno Díaz; two s.; fmr mem. of the Senate; Majority Leader, Bogotá City Council; Leader Alianza Nacional Popular (ANAPO) 1975–. *Address:* Alianza Nacional Popular (ANAPO), Carrera 18, No 33-95, Santa Fe de Bogotá, DC, Colombia. *Telephone:* (1) 287-7050 (Office). *Fax:* (1) 245-3138 (Office).

ROJAS PENSO, Juan Francisco; Venezuelan economist; b. 18 Sept. 1952; ed Andrés Bello Catholic Univ., Caracas and CENDES; Prof. Univ. Cen. de Venezuela and Univ. Simón Bolívar; Official, Council of Acuerdo de Cartagena (Cartagena Agreement, now Andean Community of Nations) 1977–79, 1982–85, Alt. Plenipotentiary Rep. and Dir Corporación Andina de Fomento 1985–87; Councillor (Econ. Affairs) to Colombia 1980–81; Dir-Gen. of Econ. Integration, Venezuelan Inst. of Foreign Trade 1985–87; Dir Commercial Policy Dept, Latin American Integration Asscn (LAIA) 1989–93, Deputy Sec.-Gen. 1993–99, Sec.-Gen. March 1999–; ind. consultant to various orgs. including Andean Community of Nations, OAS and Friedrich Ebert Foundation. *Address:* Latin American Integration Association, Cebollatí 1461, Casilla 577, 11000 Montevideo, Uruguay (Office). *Telephone:* (2) 4001121 (Office). *Fax:* (2) 4090649 (Office). *E-mail:* sgaladi@aladi.org (Office). *Website:* www.aladi.org (Office).

ROJAS RAMÍREZ, José Alejandro, PhD; Venezuelan politician and economist; b. 3 Sept. 1959; m.; one s.; ed Universidad Central de Venezuela, Inst. of Petroleum and Univ. of Paris II – Sorbonne, Paris, France; Sr Economist Office of Programming and Macroeconomic Analysis, IDB, Gov. (for Venezuela) IDB; mem. Bd of Dirs. Compañía de Energía Eléctrica del Estado Venezolano (CADAFE), Electrificación del Caroni (EDELCA) CA; Pres. Ass. of Fondo Latinoamericano de Reservas (FLAR), Consultant Council, Andean Community of Nations; Deputy Minister, then Minister of Finance; consultant several cos. and orgs.; Dir Quantitative Methods Dept, Universidad Central de Venezuela, mem. Postgrad. Scientific Cttee; Prof. of Econometrics and Math. Econs, Universidad Católica Andrés Bello, Caracas, of Operational Research, Instituto Politécnico de las Fuerzas Armadas, Caracas; mem. Colegio de Estadístico de Venezuela, Royal Econometric Soc., UK. *Publications:* numerous research papers. *Address:* c/o Ministry of Finance, Edificio Sede, Piso 11, Av. Urdaneta Esquina de Carmelitas, Caracas, Venezuela (Office).

ROJO, Luis Angel, PhD; Spanish economist; b. 6 May 1934, Madrid; s. of Luis Rojo and Luisa Duque de Rojo; m. Concepción de Castro 1958; two s. one d.; ed Univ. of Madrid and London School of Econs; economist, Research Dept Ministry of Commerce 1959–68; Asst Prof. Dept of Econ. Analysis, Faculty of Econs, Univ. of Madrid, 1959–65, Prof. of Econ. Analysis 1966–84; Gen. Dir of Research and Studies, Bank of Spain 1971–88, Deputy Gov. 1988, Gov. –2000; Monetary Policy Adviser to IMF 2002–; mem. Royal Acad. of Moral and Political Sciences; First Int. Prize "Rey Juan Carlos I" for Econs 1986. *Publications:* Keynes y el pensamiento macroeconómico actual 1965, El Nuevo Monetarismo 1971, Renta, precios y balanza de pagos 1975, Marx: Economía y sociedad (with V. Pérez Díaz) 1984, Keynes: su tiempo y el nuestro 1984. *Address:* International Monetary Fund, 700 19th Street, NW, Washington, DC 20431, USA; San Agustín 9, 28014 Madrid, Spain. *Telephone:* (202) 623-7300 (IMF); 5324947. *Fax:* (202) 623-6220 (IMF). *E-mail:* publicaffairs@imf.org. *Website:* www.imf.org.

ROKITA, Jan Maria, LLM; Polish politician and lawyer; b. 18 June 1959, Kraków; s. of Tadeusz Rokita and Adela Rokita; m. Nelli Arnold 1994; one d.; ed Jagiellonian Univ., Cracow, Pontifical Acad. of Theology, Kraków; fmr active mem. of Independent Students' Union (NZS), Chair. NZS Acad. Comm., Jagiellonian Univ. 1980–81; interned 1982; banned from practising law 1983–89; co-founder and participant Freedom and Peace Movt 1985–88; founder and mem. Intervention and Law-abidingness Comm. of Solidarity Trade Union 1986–89; mem. Civic Cttee attached to Lech Wałęsa (q.v.) 1988–90; organizer and Chair. Int. Conf. on Human Rights, Kraków 1988; political commentator in illegal bi-weekly Swit 1989–90; participant Round Table debates 1989; Deputy to Sejm (Parl.) 1989–, Deputy Chair. Civic Parl. Caucus 1989–90, Deputy Chair. Democratic Union Parl. Caucus 1991–96, Deputy Chair. Freedom Union Parl. Caucus 1996–97, mem. Solidarity Election Action Parl. Caucus 1997–; Deputy Chair. Citizens' Platform Parl. faction 2001–; Chair. Parl. Comm. for Admin. and Internal Affairs 1997–, mem. Extraordinary Parl. Comm. for Examining Laws Determining Competences of Organs of Public Admin. 1997–; Minister-Chief of Office of Council of Ministers 1992–93, Vice-Chair. 1997–, Chair. Little Poland Br. 1999–; mem. Conservative People's Party (SKL) 1997–, Chair. 1999–; POLCUL Foundation Award (Australia) 1988. *Publications:* political and historical journalism. *Leisure interests:* politics, music, architecture. *Address:* Sejm RP, ul. Wiejska 4/6/8, 00-902 Warsaw, Poland. *Telephone:* (22) 6942592. *Fax:* (22) 6942594.

RØKKE, Kjell Inge; Norwegian business executive; f. Resource Group Int., co. merged with Aker to form Aker RGI 1996, sole shareholder 2000–; Chair. Bd Aker Maritime –2001, Norway Seafoods, Aker Yards; Chair. Kvaerner ASA 2001–, co.merged with Aker Maritime 2001. *Address:* Kvaerner ASA, Prof. Kohtsvei 15, 1325 Lysaker, Norway (Office). *Telephone:* 67-51-30-00 (Office). *Fax:* 67-51-30-10 (Office). *Website:* www.kvaerner.com (Office).

ROLANDIS, Nikos A.; Cypriot politician, company executive and barrister; b. 10 Dec. 1934, Limassol; m. Lelia Aivaliotis; one s. two d.; ed Pancyprian Gymnasium Nicosia, Middle Temple, London; called to the bar, Middle Temple 1956; practised law in Cyprus for a short time then entered business; owner of industrial and commercial cos.; active in politics 1976–, founding mem. Democratic Group (now Democratic Party); f. Liberal Party 1986, Pres. 1986–96; Minister of Foreign Affairs 1978–83; mem. House of Reps. 1991–96; Vice-Pres. Liberal Int. 1994–99; Minister of Commerce, Industry and Tourism 1998–2003. *Address:* 13 Ayias Agapis, Strovolos, Nicosia, Cyprus (Home).

ROLFE JOHNSON, Anthony, CBE; British singer; b. 5 Nov. 1940, Tackley, Oxon.; m. Elisabeth Jones Evans; one s. two d. and two s. from previous m.; has appeared with all maj. UK opera cos. and with Netherlands Opera, Hamburg State Opera, Zürich Opera, at the Monnaie Theatre, Brussels, La Scala Milan, Metropolitan Opera New York and at Aix-en-Provence and Salzburg Festivals; concerts with all maj. UK orchestras and with Chicago Symphony, Boston Symphony, New York Philharmonic and Cleveland orchestras in USA. *Recordings include:* Acis and Galatea, Saul, Hercules, Jephtha, Alexander's Feast, Esther, Solomon, Semele, Messiah, J. S. Bach's St Matthew Passion and St John Passion, Peter Grimes, Samson, Oedipus Rex, Orfeo, War Requiem. *Roles include:* Fenton (Falstaff), Albert Herring, Don Ottavio (Don Giovanni), Tamino (Magic Flute), Essex (Gloriana), Ferrando (Così fan tutte), Male Chorus (Rape of Lucretia), Orfeo (Monteverdi's Orfeo), Jupiter (Semele) and Aschenbach (Death in Venice). *Address:* c/o Askonas Holt, Lonsdale Chambers, 27 Chancery Lane, London, WC2A 1PF, England.

ROLL OF IPSDEN, Baron (Life Peer), cr. 1977, of Ipsden in the County of Oxford; **Eric Roll,** KCMG, CB, PhD, BCom; British banker and former civil servant; b. 1 Dec. 1907, Austria; s. of Mathias Roll and Fany (Frendel) Roll; m. Winifred Taylor 1934 (died 1998); two d.; ed Univ. of Birmingham; Asst Lecturer, Univ. Coll., Hull 1930, Prof. of Econs and Commerce 1935–39; Special Fellow, Rockefeller Foundation 1939–41; Deputy mem., Combined Food Bd 1941–46; Asst Sec. Ministry of Food 1946–47, The Treasury 1947, Under-Sec. 1948–53; Chair. Econ. Cttee, OEEC 1948–53; Minister, UK del. to NATO 1952–53; Under-Sec. Ministry of Agric., Fisheries and Food 1953–57; Exec. Dir Int. Sugar Council 1957–59; Deputy Sec. Ministry of Agric., Fisheries and Food 1960–61; Deputy Leader, UK del. to EEC Brussels Conf. 1961–63; Econ. Minister and Head of UK Treasury del., Washington; Exec. Dir for UK, IMF, IBRD 1963–65; Perm. Under-Sec. of State, Dept of Econ. Affairs 1964–66; Chair. S. G. Warburg & Co. Ltd 1974–84, Jt Chair. 1984–87, Pres. S. G. Warburg Group PLC 1987–95; Sr Adviser, UBS Warburg Ltd 1995–; Chair. Mercury Securities 1974–84, Pres. 1984–87; Dir Bank of England 1968–77, Peugeot Talbot Motor Co. Ltd 1967–87; Chair. NEDC Cttee on Finance for Industry 1975–80; Chancellor, Southampton Univ. 1974–84; Hon. Chair. Book Devt Council; Hon. Fellow LSE 1997; Grosses Goldenes Ehrenzeichen mit Stern (Austria) 1979; Commdr First Class, Order of the Dannebrog (Denmark) 1981; Officier, Légion d'honneur 1984; Order of the Sacred Treasure (Japan) 1993; Grand Cross of the Order of Merit of the Repub. of Italy 2000; Hon. DSc (Hull, Birmingham), (City Univ., London) 2002; Hon. LLD (Southampton). *Publications:* An Early Experiment in Industrial Organization 1930, Spotlight on Germany 1933, About Money 1934, Elements of Economic Theory 1935, Organized Labour (co-author) 1938, The British Commonwealth at War (co-author) 1943, A History of Economic Thought 1954, The Combined Food Board 1957, The World after Keynes 1968, Uses and Abuses of Economics 1977, Crowded Hours 1985, Where Did We Go Wrong? 1995, Where Are We Going? 2000. *Leisure interests:* reading, music. *Address:* c/o UBS Warburg Ltd, 1 Finsbury Avenue, London, EC2M 2PP, England. *Telephone:* (20) 7568-2477 (Office). *Fax:* (20) 7568-0050 (Office). *E-mail:* lorderic.roll@ubsw.com (Office).

RÖLLER, Wolfgang, Dr rer. pol; German bank executive; b. 20 Oct. 1929, Uelsen, Lower Saxony; m.; three s.; ed Univs. of Berlin and Frankfurt; joined Dresdner Bank AG, Frankfurt Main, Deputy mem. Bd of Man. Dirs. 1971–73, Full mem. 1973–85, Chair. Man. Bd 1985–93, Chair. Supervisory Bd 1993–97; Chair. Supervisory Bd ABD Securities Corpn, New York, Metallgesellschaft AG, Deutscher Investment-Trust Gesellschaft für Wertpapieranlagen m.b.H., Frankfurt, Dresdnerbank Investment Man. Kapitalanlage G.m.b.H., Frankfurt, Heidelberger Zementwerke AG; mem. Supervisory Bd Allianz AG Holding, Munich, Daimler-Benz AG, Stuttgart, Degussa AG, Frankfurt, Henkel KGaA, Düsseldorf, Hoechst AG, Frankfurt; Fried. Krupp GmbH, Essen; Rheinisch-Westfälisches Elektrizitätswerk AG (fmr Chair. Super-

visory Bd), Essen; fmrly Chair. Deutsche Lufthansa AG, Cologne; mem other supervisory, advisory and man. bds. *Address:* c/o Dresdner Bank AG, Jürgen-Ponto-Platz 1, 60329 Frankfurt am Main, Germany.

ROLLINS, Ed; American politician; b. 1943, Vallejo, Calif.; ed Chico State Coll.; intern for Speaker of Calif. Ass.; Dean, Washington Univ. St Louis 1970; worked on numerous presidential election campaigns 1972; Republican. *Publication:* Bare Knuckles and Back Rooms: My Life in American Politics (with Tom DeFrank) 1996. *Address:* c/o Republican National Committee, 310 First Street, SE, Washington, DC 20003, USA.

ROLLINS, (Theodore Walter) Sonny; American jazz musician; b. 7 Sept. 1930, New York; s. of Walter Rollins and Valborg Solomon; m. 1st Dawn Finney 1956 (divorced); m. 2nd Lucille Pearson 1959; ed High School, New York; began rehearsing while in high school with Thelonious Monk; recorded with Bud Powell 1949; wrote standards 'Airegin' and 'Oleo' recorded with Miles Davis 1953; played and recorded with Clifford Brown/Max Roach 1955; recorded album Saxophone Colossus 1957, wrote and recorded Freedom Suite 1958; took sabbatical playing on a NY bridge 1959–61; scored and played music for film Alfie 1966; has appeared in Jazz Heritage series, Smithsonian Inst. and at Newport Jazz Festival; numerous concert tours in Europe, Far East; Guggenheim Fellow 1972; Dr hc (Bard Coll.) 1993, (Long Island Univ.) 1998, (Wesleyan Univ.) 1998, (New England Conservatory of Music) 2002; Hon. DFA (Duke Univ.) 1999; recipient of numerous awards for instrumental playing 1950s–. *Address:* R.R.9, G, Germantown, NY 12526, USA. *Telephone:* (518) 537-6112 (Office). *Fax:* (518) 537-4342 (Office).

ROMAHI, Seif al-Wady, PhD; Jordanian professor of diplomacy and consultant; b. 28 Dec. 1938, Muzera, Palestine; s. of Ahmed al-Hajj Abdul-Nabi; m. Zaka al-Masri 1971; one s. two d.; ed Lebanese State Univ., Univ. Coll. London, Southern Illinois Univ., USA and Univ. of Birmingham, UK; Area Educ. Supt, Ministry of Educ., Qatar 1960–64; Vice-Pres. Office of the Ruler of Abu Dhabi, Pres. UAE 1968–73; Rep. League of Arab States in USA 1970–72; Assoc. Prof. of Middle East Studies and Political Science, Southern Ill. Univ., USA 1971–72; Minister Plenipotentiary, Foreign Ministry, UAE 1973–91, set up UAE Embassies in Beijing, Tripoli, Tokyo and Seoul; Founder and Prof., Diplomatic Training Centre, UAE 1980–82; Co-founder and Chief Rep. Nat. Bank of Abu Dhabi in Japan 1982–86; Prof. of Int. Law, Diplomacy and Islamic Civilization, Int. Univ. of Japan, Sophia Univ., Tokyo; Founder, Gen. Man. Arab Int. Co. for Investment and Educ. 1988–91, Chair. 1990–94; founder Applied Science Univ., Amman, Jordan, Prof. of Diplomacy and Int. Law 1990–95; Co-Founder Islamic-American Univ. Coll., Chicago; planner Jordan Women's Univ. (now Petra Univ.), Zaitouneh Jordanian Univ., American Univ. of the Middle East in Jordan, Graduate Studies Univ. in Jordan, Middle East Acad. for Aviation, House of Euro-Arab Experts in Jordan 1992– (also Chair.); co-author Abu Dhabi Public Service Code; Co-Chair. Planning Cttee for British Univ. of Dubai; consultant for establishment of RAK British Univ., UAE 2002–; mem. Acad. of Islamic Research (India), Japanese Acad. of Middle East Studies, Middle East Studies Asscn of USA and Canada, Middle East Inst., Washington, DC, British Soc. for Middle East Studies, Japanese Assoc. for Middle Eastern Studies; Order of Independence (Jordan) 1979; Hon. PhD (World Univ.) 1985. *Publications:* Economics and Political Evolution in Arabian Gulf States 1973, The Palestinian Question and International Law 1979, Studies in International Law and Diplomatic Practice 1980, Arab Customs and Manners 1984; contribs. to professional and scientific journals. *Leisure interests:* calligraphy, travel, poetry, listening to music, painting, reading and research. *Address:* PO Box 851757, Sweifieh, Amman 11185, Jordan. *Telephone:* (6) 5513274 (Office); (6) 5537028 (Home). *Fax:* (6) 5514199 (Office); (6) 5528328 (Home). *E-mail:* seif@romahi.com (Office).

ROMAN, Petre, DTech, PhD; Romanian university professor and politician; b. 22 July 1946, Bucharest; s. of Valter Roman and Hortensia Roman; m. Mioara Georgescu; two d.; ed Petru Groza High School, Bucharest, Bucharest Polytechnic Inst. and Nat. Polytechnic Inst. of Toulouse; fmrly Prof. and Head of Dept Hydraulics Dept, Faculty of Hydroenergy, Bucharest Polytechnic Inst.; Prime Minister 1989–91; Pres. Democratic Party (fmrly Nat. Salvation Front) 1990–; mem. Parl. 1992–, Chair. Defence, Public Order and Nat. Security Cttee, Chamber of Deputies; Pres. of Senate; Special Rapporteur of North Atlantic Ass.; Deputy Prime Minister, Minister of Foreign Affairs 1999–2000; Traian Vuia Award, Romanian Acad. 1990; Great Cross of Merit, France; Star of Repub. of Ecuador; High Award of Repub. of Colombia. *Publications:* Introduction to the Physics of Fluid Pollution 1980, Fluid Mechanics 1989, Dynamic Hydrology 1990, Le Devoir de Liberté 1992, Romania incotro? 1995. *Leisure interests:* sports, hunting, reading, hiking. *Address:* c/o Ministry of Foreign Affairs, 14 Aleea Modrogan, Bucharest, Romania.

ROMANI, Roger; French politician; b. 25 Aug. 1934, Tunis, Tunisia; s. of Dominique Romani and Madeleine Santelli; m. Joelle Fortier 1971; began career with ORTF; various positions in pvt. offices of govt ministers 1967–71; Conseiller de Paris 1971–; Adviser, Office of Jacques Chirac (Minister of Agric. 1973, of Interior 1974, Prime Minister 1974–76); Deputy to Mayor of Paris 1977–; mem. Conseil Régional, Ile-de-France 1977; Senator for Paris 1977–93, Pres. RPR Group in Senate 1986–93; adviser to fmr Prime Minister Chirac 1986–88; Minister-Del. for Relations with Senate 1993–95; Minister for Relations with Parl. 1995–97; adviser to Pres. Chirac 1997–; Senator of Paris 2002–. *Address:* Présidence de la République, 55–57 rue du Faubourg Saint Honoré, 75008 Paris; Hôtel de Ville, 75196 Paris, France.

ROMANO, Sergio, LLD; Italian diplomatist and historian; b. 7 July 1929, Vicenza; s. of Romano Romano and Egle Bazzolo; m. Mary Anne Heinze 1954; two s. one d.; ed Liceo C. Beccaria, Milan, Univ. of Milan, Univ. of Chicago; foreign corresp. and film critic for Italian radio and newspapers, Paris, London and Vienna 1948–52; entered Italian Foreign Service 1954; Vice-Consul, Innsbruck, Austria 1955; Sec., Italian Embassy, London 1958–64; Pvt. Sec. to Minister of Foreign Affairs 1964; mem. Diplomatic Staff of the Pres. of the Repub. 1965–68; Counsellor (later Minister), Italian Embassy, Paris 1968–77; Dir-Gen. of Cultural Relations, Ministry of Foreign Affairs 1977–83; Guest Prof. Faculty of Political Sciences, Univ. of Florence 1981–83; Italian Perm. Rep. Atlantic Council, Brussels 1983–85, Amb. to USSR 1985–89; mem. Ateneo Veneto, Venice, Accad. Olimpica, Vicenza; Dr. hc (Inst. d'Etudes Politiques, Paris); Grand' Ufficiale of the Italian Order of Merit, Commdr Légion d'honneur, other European and Latin-American honours. *Publications:* Crispi, Progetto per una Dittatura 1973, 1986, La Quarta Sponda 1977, Histoire de l'Italie du Risorgimento à nos jours 1977, Italie 1979, Giuseppe Volpi, Industria e Finanza tra Giolitti e Mussolini 1979, La Francia dal 1870 ai nostri giorni 1981, Benedetto Croce, La Philosophie comme histoire de la Liberté (Ed.) 1983, La Lingua e il Tempo 1983, Giovanni Gentile, La Filosofia al Potere 1984, Florence, Toscane 1988, Giolitti, Lo Stile del Potere 1989, Disegni per una Esposizione 1989.

ROMANOV, Piotr Vasilyevich, D.TECH.SC.; Russian politician; b. 21 July 1943, Kansk, Krasnoyarsk territory; m.; three c.; ed Siberia Inst. of Tech.; engineer, then chief of workshop, Chief Engineer, Dir-Gen. Krasnoyarsky Production Unit of Mil. Chemical Enterprise Enisey 1967–96; mem. Russian Council of Fed. 1993; Co-Chair. Russian Nat. Sobor 1992–93, mem. Org. Cttee All-Russia Congress of Russian Communists, Co-Chair. Co-ordination Council All-Russia Congress of Russian Communists 1994–; mem. State Duma 1995–, now Deputy Chair.; Sec. Cen. Cttee CP of Russian Fed. 1997–; mem. Russian Acad. of Eng Sciences; Hero of Socialist Labour, Distinguished Chemist of Russian Fed., Order of Lenin, Sergei Radonezhsky Medal. *Publications:* I Am Piotr Romanov: About the Times and Myself 1995, With a Son's Care about Russia 1995, The Sovereign Cross 1997. *Leisure interests:* winter sports, gathering mushrooms and berries, gardening. *Address:* State Duma, Okhotny Ryad 1, 103265 Moscow (Office); pr. Mira 108, 660017 Krasnoyarsk, Russia. *Telephone:* (095) 292-18-10 (Office). *Fax:* (095) 292-40-58 (Office).

ROMASZEWSKI, Zbigniew, PhD; Polish politician; b. 2 Jan. 1940, Warsaw; m.; one d.; ed Warsaw Univ.; researcher Inst. of Physics, Polish Acad. of Sciences 1964–83; ed. Acta Physica Polonica, Inst. of Physics, Jagiellonian Univ., Cracow 1984–; participant relief action in support of repressed workers in Radom and Ursus 1976; mem. Defence Cttee of Workers (KOR) 1977–81, admin. Intervention Office; admin. Helsinki Watch Group 1979–80, ed. Madrid Report; mem. Solidarity Ind. Self-Governing Trade Union 1980–, Chair. Intervention and Law Observance Cttee 1980–81, mem. Bd Presidium Mazovia Br. and Nat. Cttee 1982; ran Solidarity (underground radio) 1982; imprisoned 1982–84; organizer of first Int. Human Rights Confs. in Cracow (illegal) 1988, Leningrad (USSR) 1990, Warsaw 1998; Senator 1989–; mem. Latin American Constitutional Lawyers Asscn 2001–; Aurora Award (Jt recipient with his wife) for achievement in the fields of human rights and democracy) 1987. *Leisure interest:* mountain trekking. *Address:* al. 3 Maja 5 m. 51, 00-401 Warsaw, Poland (Office). *Telephone:* (22) 6254749 (Office). *E-mail:* warsaw@humanrights.org.pl (Office). *Website:* www.romaszewski.pl (Office).

ROMER, Roy R., BS, LLB; American politician; b. 31 Oct. 1928, Garden City, Kan.; s. of Irving Rudolph and Margaret Elizabeth (née Snyder) Romer; m. Beatrice Miller 1952; five s. two d.; ed Colorado State Univ., Univ. of Colorado, Yale Univ.; farmed in Colo 1942–52; admitted to Colo Bar 1952; ind. practice, Denver 1955–66; mem. Colo House of Reps. 1958–62, Colo Senate 1962–66; Commr for Agric. for Colo 1975; State Treas. 1977–86; Gov. of Colorado 1987–98; owner Arapahoe Aviation Co., Colo Flying Acad., Geneva Basin Ski Area, Chain Farm Implement and Industrial Equipment Stores in Colo, Fla and Va; Gov. Small Business Council; mem. Agric. Advisory Cttee, Colo Bd of Agric., Colo Bar Asscn; Chair. Nat. Educ. Goals Panel, Democratic Govs.' Asscn 1991, Democratic Nat. Cttee 1997–. *Address:* P.O. Box 6949, Denver, CO 80206, USA (Office).

ROMERO, Edward L.; American diplomatist; m. Cayetana García; four c.; ed Los Angeles State Coll., Calif., Citrus Coll.; founder, Chair., CEO Advanced Sciences Inc.; Amb. to Spain 1998–2000; mem. President's Hispanic Advisory Cttee, U.S. Trade Reps. Services Policy Advisory Cttee; Nat. Hispanic Businessman of the Year (Hispanic Chamber of Commerce). *Address:* c/o Department of State, 2201 C Street, NW, Washington, DC 20520, USA (Office).

ROMERO, Pepe; American (naturalized) classical guitarist; b. 3 Aug. 1944, Málaga, Spain; s. of Celedonio Romero and Angelita (née Gallego) Romero; m. 1st Kristine Eddy 1965; m. 2nd Carissa Sugg 1987; one s. three d.; ed various music acads. in USA, including Music Acad. of the West; began career in Seville, Spain, as part of Romero Quartet 1951, re-formed in USA 1960; averages 200–250 concerts a year world-wide; recordings number more than 50 solos, plus others with the Romero Quartet and various orchestras; artist-

in-residence Univ. of Southern Calif. 1972, Univ. of Calif., San Diego 1984. *Publications:* Guitar Method, Guitar Transcriptions for 1, 2 and 4 guitars. *Leisure interests:* photography, chess.

ROMERO-BARCELÓ, Carlos Antonio, BA, LLB, JD; American politician, lawyer and real estate executive; b. 4 Sept. 1932, San Juan, Puerto Rico; s. of Antonio Romero-Moreno and Josefina Barceló-Bird; m. 1st; two s.; m. 2nd Kathleen Donnelly 1966; one s. one d.; ed Phillips Exeter Acad., NH, Yale Univ., Univ. of Puerto Rico; admitted to bar, San Juan, Puerto Rico 1956; Pres. Citizens for State 51 1965–67; Mayor of San Juan 1969–77; Pres. New Progressive Party 1974–86, Chair. 1989; Pres. Nat. League of Cities 1974–75; Gov. of Puerto Rico 1977–85; Chair. Southern Govs Conf. 1980–81; Resident Commr in Washington, DC 1993–2001; in pvt. practice 2001–; mem. Council on Foreign Affairs 1985–, Int. Platform Asscn 1985–; Hon. LLD (Univ. of Bridgeport, Conn.) 1977; James J. and Jane Hoey Award for Interracial Justice, Catholic Interracial Council of NY 1977; Special Gold Medal Award, Spanish Inst., New York 1979; US Attorney-General's Medal 1981. *Publications:* Statehood is for the Poor 1973, Statehood for Puerto Rico, Vital Speeches of the Day 1979, Puerto Rico, USA: The Case for Statehood, Foreign Affairs 1980, The Soviet Threat to the Americas, Vital Speeches of the Day 1981. *Leisure interests:* reading, horse riding, tennis, swimming, water sports, golf. *Address:* Centro de Seguros, Building 701, Ponce de León Avenue # 412, Miramar, PR 00907 (Office); PO Box 364351, San Juan, PR 00936, Puerto Rico. *Telephone:* (787) 724-0526; (787) 724-0511. *Fax:* (787) 724-0959 (Office). *E-mail:* rbarcelo@prtc.net (Office).

ROMERO KOLBECK, Gustavo, MA; Mexican economist and public official; b. 3 July 1923, Mexico City; s. of Gustavo and Ana María (de Romero) Kolbeck; m. Leonor Martínez 1950; one s. two d.; ed Nat. Univ. of Mexico, George Washington Univ. and Chicago Univ.; Prof. at Nat. School of Econs 1949, Nat. Univ. of Mexico 1966; Dir School of Econs Anahuac Univ. 1967–70; Economist Bank of Mexico 1944–45; Research Dept of Banco de Comercio 1946; Head of Dept of Econ. Studies, Banco Nacional de México 1949–54; Deputy Dir and Dir of Public Investments, Ministry of Programming and Budget 1954–62; Founder and Dir, Centre for Econ. Study of Pvt. Sector 1963–65; mem. Bd of Govs. CONCANACO 1967; Dir and Founder of journals Business Trends and Expansión 1967–69; Amb. to Japan 1971–73, to USSR 1982–83; Dir-Gen. Financiera Nacional Azucarera SA 1973, Nacional Financiera, SA 1974–76, Bank of Mexico 1976–82; Alt. Gov. World Bank 1974–76, IMF and IADB 1976–82; Dir-Gen. Banco Obrero, SA 1983; decorations from Japan, France, Fed. Repub. of Germany, Brazil and other countries. *Leisure interests:* swimming, reading. *Address:* Rubén Darío 45-2, Cd. Rincón del Bosque 11580, México DF, Mexico (Home).

ROMERO MENA, Gen. Carlos Humberto; Salvadorean army officer and politician; b. Chalatenango; s. of late José María Romero and Victoria Mena de Romero; m. Gloria Guerrero de Romero; two s. two d.; ed Capitán General Gerardo Barrios Mil. School, Escuela de Armas y Servicios, Escuela de Comando y Estado Mayor Manuel Enrique Araujo; Section Commd., Adjutant and Paymaster, Capt.-Gen. Gerardo Barrios Mil. School and other mil. bodies; Regt Commdr Cavalry; Second Officer 1st Infantry Regt; Sub-Dir Escuela de Armas y Servicios and Head Dept Personnel, Gen. Staff Armed Forces; Mil. Attaché to Embassy, Mexico; Head of Staff of Presidency of Repub.; Minister of Defence and Public Security; Pres. Cen. American Defense Council 1973–77; Pres. of Repub. of El Salvador 1977–79 (overthrown in coup); del. 7th Conf. of American Armies 1966, 2nd Conf. of Cen. American Defense Council 1960, 6th Conf. of American Intelligence Officials 1967; Partido de Conciliación Nacional.

ROMITI, Cesare, BEcons; Italian industrial executive; b. 24 June 1923, Rome; m. Luigina Gastaldi; two s.; joined Bombrini Parodi Delfino (BPD) Group 1947; Gen. Man. Finance and Co-ordination SNIA Viscosa 1968–70; Man. Dir and Gen. Man. Alitalia Airlines 1970–73, Italstat (IRI group) 1973–74; Head Corp. Finance Planning and Control Dept, Fiat SpA 1974–76, Man. Dir Fiat SpA and Vice-Chair. IHF 1976–96, Chair. 1996–98, Man. Dir Fiat Auto SpA 1989–90; Dir Mediobanca 1991; Chair. Rizzoli Corriere della Sera newspaper and publishing group 1998; Head RSC Editori 1998–; mem. Exec. Cttee Italian Stock Cos. Asscn, Bd Turin Industrial Asscn, Confindustria, Aspen Inst. Italia, Advisory Bd Deutsche Bank, Alcatel Alsthom, Council of Int. Advisers, Swiss Bank, Bd Int. Advisers, Westinghouse Electric SA; received 18-month suspended sentence and banned from holding corp.office April 1997, case on appeal; indicted on charges of corruption and bribery June 1998.

ROMNEY, Mitt (Robert W.), BA, JD, MBA; American state official; b. 12 March 1947, Detroit; s. of the late George Romney and of Lenore Romney; m. Ann Romney; five s.; ed Brigham Young Univ., Harvard Univ.; Vice-Pres. Bain & Co. 1978–84, f. Bain Capital 1984–99, CEO (interim) Bain & Co. 1990–92; CEO Salt Lake City Organizing Cttee 1999–2002; Gov. of Mass. 2003–. *Address:* Office of the Governor, State House, Room 360, Boston, MA 02133, USA (Office).

RONALDO; Brazilian footballer; b. Ronaldo Luiz Nazario de Lima, 22 Sept. 1976, Bento Ribeiro, Rio de Janeiro; s. of Nelio Nazario de Lima and Sonia Nazario de Lima; m.; teams: Social Ramos, Rio (at age 15) (12 games, 8 goals), São Cristóvão, Rio Second Div. (54 games, 36 goals), Cruzeiro, Brazil (60 games, 58 goals), PSV Eindhoven, Holland (58 games, 54 goals), Barcelona, Spain (49 games, 47 goals), Inter Milan 1997–2002 (90 games, 53 goals); transferred to Real Madrid after the World Cup 2002; Brazilian Nat. Team

1994– (29 int. caps, 18 goals); played for winning team World Cup 1994 (at age 17) and Copa America 1997 (Brazil); Spanish Cup and European Cup Winners' Cup (Barcelona) 1997; World Soccer Magazine World Player of the Year 1996, FIFA World Footballer of the Year 1996, 1997, 2002, European Footballer of the Year 1997, 2002. *Address:* c/o FC Real Madrid, Estadio Santiago Bernabeu, Paseo de la Castellana 104, Madrid, Spain. *Website:* www .realmadrid.com (Office); www.r9ronaldo.com (Home).

RONAY, Egon, LLD; British publisher and journalist; b. Pozsony, Hungary; m. 2nd Barbara Greenslade 1967; one s. (and two d. by previous marriage); ed School of Piarist Order, Budapest, Univ. of Budapest and Acad. of Commerce, Budapest; trained in kitchens of family catering firm and abroad; managed 5 restaurants within family firm; emigrated from Hungary 1946; Gen. Man. 2 restaurant complexes in London before opening own restaurant The Marquee 1952–55; gastronomic and good living columnist, Sunday Times 1986–91 and Sunday Express 1991, weekly columnist on eating out, food, wine and tourism, Daily Telegraph and later Sunday Telegraph 1954–60; weekly column, The Evening News 1968–74; Ed. Egon Ronay's Guide to Eating at the Airport 1992–94; mem. Acad. des Gastronomes (France) 1979; Founding Vice-Pres. Int. Acad. of Gastronomy; Founder and Pres. British Acad. of Gastronomes; Founder the Egon Ronay Guides 1957, Publr 1957–85; Médaille de la Ville de Paris 1983, Chevalier de l'Ordre du Mérite Agricole 1987. *Publications:* Egon Ronay's Guides 1957–84 annually, The Unforgettable Dishes of My Life 1989. *Address:* 37 Walton Street, London, SW3 2HT, England (Office). *Telephone:* (20) 7584-1384 (Office).

RONG GAOTANG; Chinese sports official; b. May 1912, Bazhou Co., Hebei Prov.; ed Tsinghua Univ.; joined CCP 1936; Sec. Communist Youth League Beijing Mun. Cttee 1949; Sec. Secr. Communist Youth League Cen. Cttee; Sec.-Gen. then Vice-Dir State Physical Culture and Sports Comm.; Vice-Pres. All-China Sports Fed; mem., Sec.-Gen. CCP Cen. Consultative Cttee; Vice-Pres. Soong Ching Ling foundation 1983–; Head Chinese Celebrities Asscn 1994–; mem. 5th CPPCC Standing Cttee. *Address:* All-China Sports Federation, Beijing, People's Republic of China.

RONG YIREN; Chinese financial company executive and government official; b. 1 May 1916, Wuxi, Jiangsu; s. of Rong Deshen; m. Yang Jinaqing 1936; five c.; ed St John's Univ., Shanghai; Man. Mow Sing Flour Mills, Wuxi 1937–55; Vice-Pres. Foh Sing Flour Mills, Shanghai 1947–55; Pres. Sung Sing Textile Printing and Dyeing Co., Shanghai 1950–55; Chair. and Pres. China Int. Trust and Investment Corpn (CITIC), Beijing 1979–82, Chair. 1983–93; Vice-Mayor Shanghai 1957–66; Vice-Minister, Ministry of Textile Industry 1959–66; mem. 2nd, 3rd, 4th, 5th Nat. Cttees of CPPCC; Vice-Chair. 7th Nat. Cttee; mem. 1st, 2nd, 3rd, 4th, 5th, 6th NPC; Vice-Chair. Nat. Cttee CPPCC 1978–83, Standing Cttee 6th, 7th NPC; Vice-Pres. of People's Repub. of China 1993–98; Vice-Chair. Soong Ching Ling Foundation, Beijing 1982–; Vice-Chair. then Chair. All-China Asscn of Industry and Commerce 1953–93; Hon. Chair. China Football Asscn 1984; Chair. Bd of Trustees Jinan Univ. Guangzhou 1985–; Chair. Bd of Dirs Jinan Univ. 1986–; Hon. Chair. Bd CITIC Industrial Bank 1987–; a Pres. China Council for Promoting Peaceful Reunification 1988–; Hon. Adviser, China Confucius Foundation 1992–. *Publications:* articles and speeches on China's devt and related matters. *Leisure interests:* walking, rose-gardening, spectator sports, including soccer. *Address:* c/o Office of the Vice-President, Great Hall of the People, Beijing, People's Republic of China.

RONTÓ, Györgyi; Hungarian biophysicist; b. 13 July 1934, Budapest; d. of György Rontó and Erzsébet Lanczkor; m. Dr. Dezső Holnapy 1961; two s.; ed Semmelweis Univ. of Medicine, Budapest; Prof. of Biophysics Semmelweis Univ. 1980–, Dir Semmelweis Univ. Inst. of Biophysics 1982–99; Head of Research Group for Biophysics of the Hungarian Acad. of Sciences 1982–; Gen. Sec. Hungarian Biophysical Soc. 1969–90, Vice-Pres. 1990–98; Vice-Pres. Asscn Int. de Photobiologie 1988–92; officer European Soc. for Photobiology; specialises in effects of environmental physical and chemical agents on nucleo-proteins; special interest in biological dosimetry of environmental and artificial UV radiations and in exo/astrobiology; Gold Ring, Semmelweis Univ. 1999. *Publications:* A biofizika alapjai (An Introduction to Biophysics) (co-author) 1981 (also English and German editions), Light in Biology and Medicine (Vol. 2) 1991; more than 140 articles. *Leisure interests:* arts, architecture, gardening. *Address:* 1444 Budapest, P.O. Box 263, Hungary. *Telephone:* (1) 266-6656. *E-mail:* ronto@puskin.sote.hu (Office).

ROOCROFT, Amanda, FRNCM; British opera singer; b. 9 Feb. 1966, Coppull; d. of Roger Roocroft and Valerie Roocroft (née Metcalfe); m. 2nd David Gowland 1999; two s.; ed Royal Northern Coll. of Music; appearances include Sophie in Der Rosenkavalier, Welsh Nat. Opera 1990, Pamina in The Magic Flute, Covent Garden 1991, 1993, Fiordiligi in Così fan tutte, Glyndebourne 1991, European tour with John Eliot Gardiner 1992, Bavarian State Opera 1993, 1994, Covent Garden 1995, Giulietta in I Capuleti e I Montecchi, Covent Garden 1993, Ginevra in Ariodante, English Nat. Opera 1993, Donna Elvira in Don Giovanni, Glyndebourne 1994, NY Metropolitan Opera 1997, Amelia in Simon Boccanegra, Bavarian State Opera 1995, Mimi in La Bohème, Covent Garden 1996, Countess in Marriage of Figaro, Bavarian State Opera 1997, NY Metropolitan Opera 1999, Cleopatra in Giulio Cesare, Covent Garden 1997, Desdemona in Otello, Bavarian State Opera 1999, Covent Garden 2001, Jenůfa, Glyndebourne 2000, Berlin 2002, Katya Kabanova, Glyndebourne 2000, Covent Garden 2000, Meistersinger, Royal Opera House 2002; début at BBC Promenade Concert and Edin. Festival 1993; regular

concert engagements and recitals; Fellow Univ. of Cen. Lancs. 1992; Hon. DMus (Univ. of Manchester) 2003; Kathleen Ferrier Prize 1988; Silver Medal, Worshipful Co. of Musicians 1988, Royal Philharmonic Soc./Charles Heidsieck Award 1990, Barclay Opera Award 2000. *Recordings include:* Amanda Roocroft (solo album) 1994, Mozart and his Contemporaries 1996, Vaughan Williams Serenade to Music (with Matthew Best) 1990, Così fan tutte (with John Eliot Gardiner) 1993, Schoenberg String Quartet No 2 (with Britten Quartet) 1994, Vaughan Williams Sea Symphony (with Andrew Davies), Mahler Symphony No. 4 (with Simon Rattle), Vaughan Williams Pastoral Symphony (with Bernard Haitink). *Television documentaries include:* The Girl from Coppall, The Debut (Granada TV), Hard Pressed for Signals (Channel 4), Jenufa (BBC Wales). *Leisure interests:* theatre, cinema, reading, cooking. *Address:* c/o Ingpen & Williams Ltd, 26 Wadham Road, London, SW15 2LR, England. *Telephone:* (20) 8874-3222. *Fax:* (20) 8877-3113.

ROOD, Johannes (Jon) Joseph Van, PhD, MD; Netherlands immunologist; b. 7 April 1926, The Hague; s. of Albert van Rood and Rientje Röell; m. Sacha Bsse. van Tuyll van Serooskerken 1957; one s. two d.; ed Univ. of Leiden; worked in bloodbanking 1952–; in charge of Bloodbank and foundation of Dept of Immunohaematology, Univ. Hosp., Leiden 1957; work in tissue typing 1958–; worked on antibody synthesis in Public Health Research Inst., New York 1962; lecturer in Immunohaematology, Univ. of Leiden 1965–, Prof. in Internal Medicine 1969–; Founder Eurotransplant 1967, Europdonor 1970. *Publications:* Leukocyte Antibodies in Sera of Pregnant Women 1958, Platelet Survival 1959, Erythrocyte Survival with DFP 32 1961, Leukocyte Groups, the Normal Lymphocyte Transfer Test and Homograft Sensitivity 1965, Platelet Transfusion 1965, The Relevance of Leukocyte Antigens 1967, A Proposal for International Co-operation: EUROTRANSPLANT 1967, Transplantation of Bone-marrow cells and Fetal Thymus in an Infant with Lymphonenic Immunological Deficiency 1969, The 4a and 4b Antigens: Do They or Don't They? 1970, Anti HL-A 2 Inhibitor in Normal Human Serum 1970, HL-A Identical Phenotypes and Genotypes in Unrelated Individuals 1970, HL-A and the Group Five System in Hodgkin's Disease 1971, The (Relative) Importance of HL-A Matching in Kidney Transplantation 1971, Simultaneous Detection of Two Cell Populations by Two Colour Fluorescence and Application to the Recognition of B Cell Determinants 1976, HLA-linked Control of Susceptibility to Tuberculoid Leprosy and Association with HLA-DR types 1978. *Leisure interest:* sailing. *Address:* Department of Immunohaematology, University Hospital, Leiden 2333AA, Netherlands. *Telephone:* (71) 5226187. *Fax:* (71) 5210457.

ROOKE, Sir Denis Eric, Kt, OM, CBE, BSc(Eng), FRS, F.R.ENG.; British engineer and business executive; b. 2 April 1924, London; s. of F. G. Rooke; m. Elizabeth Brenda Evans 1949; one d.; ed Westminster City School, Addey and Stanhope School, Univ. Coll., London; served with Royal Electrical and Mechanical Engineers in UK and India 1944–49; joined SE Gas Bd 1949, Asst Mechanical Engineer 1949, Deputy Man. of Works 1954, Devt Engineer 1959; seconded to N Thames Gas Bd 1957; mem. tech. team aboard Methane Pioneer 1959; Devt Engineer, Gas Council 1960 (name changed to British Gas Corpn 1973 and to British Gas PLC 1986), mem. for Production and Supply 1966–71, Deputy Chair. 1972–76, Chair. 1976–89; mem. Offshore Energy Tech. Bd 1975–78; mem. Nat. Econ. Devt Council (NEDC) 1976–80, UK Energy Comm. 1977–79; Pres. Inst. of Gas Engineers 1975–76; part-time mem. British Nat. Oil Corpn (BNOC) 1976–82; Pres. Welding Inst. 1981–83; Chair. Council for Nat. Academic Awards 1978–83; Trustee Science Museum 1988–95 (Chair. 1995); Commr Royal Comm. for the Exhbn of 1851 1983–2001; Pres. Royal Acad. of Eng 1986–91; Chancellor Loughborough Univ. 1989–2003; Fellow, Univ. Coll. London 1972; Master Worshipful Co. of Engineers 1985–86; Hon. Fellow Inst. of Chemical Engineers, Inst. of Gas Engineers, Inst. of Mechanical Engineers, Inst. of Energy, Inst. of Civil Engineers 1988, Inst. of Electrical Engineers 1988, City & Guilds of London Inst., Humberside Coll. of Higher Educ., Univ. of Plymouth 1991; Hon. Sr Fellow RCA 1991; Hon. DSc (Salford) 1978, (Leeds) 1980, (City Univ.) 1985, (Durham) 1986, (Cranfield Inst. of Tech.) 1987, (London) 1991, (Loughborough) 1994, (Cambridge) 2000; Hon. DTech (Council for Nat. Acad. Awards) 1986; Hon. LLD (Bath) 1987; Hon. DEng (Bradford) 1989, (Liverpool) 1994; Hon. DUniv (Surrey) 1990. *Publications:* numerous papers to learned socs. and professional asscns. *Leisure interests:* photography, listening to music. *Address:* 1 Great Cumberland Place, London, W1H 7AL (Office); 23 Hardy Road, Blackheath, London, SE3 7NS, England (Home). *Telephone:* (20) 7723-5173 (Office). *Fax:* (20) 7723-5985 (Office).

ROONEY, Mickey (Joe Yule, Jr); American actor; b. 23 Sept. 1920, Brooklyn; s. of Joe Yule and Nell Carter; m. 1st Ava Gardner 1942 (divorced 1943); m. 2nd Betty J. Rase 1944 (divorced 1949); two s.; m. 3rd Martha Vickers 1949 (divorced); m. 4th Elaine Mahnken (divorced 1958); m. 5th Barbara Thomason 1958; four c.; m. 6th Margie Lang 1966 (divorced 1967); m. 7th Carolyn Hockett (divorced); one s. and one adopted s.; m. 8th Jan Chamberlin 1978; two step s.; ed in Dayton Heights, Vine Street Grammar School and Pacific Mil. Acad.; served AUS, World War II; first appeared in vaudeville with parents; later appeared with Sid Gould; numerous TV programmes including series The Mickey Rooney Show; Special Acad. Award 1940; Tony Award for Best Musical Actor 1980. *Films include:* Judge Hardy's Children, Hold That Kiss, Lord Jeff, Love Finds Andy Hardy, Boystown, Stablemates, Out West With the Hardys, Huckleberry Finn, Andy Hardy Gets Spring Fever, Babes in Arms, Young Tom Edison, Judge Hardy and Son, Andy Hardy Meets Debutante, Strike Up the Band, Andy Hardy's Private Secretary, Men of Boystown, Life Begins for Andy Hardy, Babes on Broadway, A Yank at Eton, The Human Comedy, Andy Hardy's Blonde Trouble, Girl Crazy, Thousands Cheer, National Velvet, Ziegfeld Follies, The Strip, Sound Off, Off Limits, All Ashore, Light Case of Larceny, Drive a Crooked Road, Bridges at Toko-Ri, The Bold and Brave, Eddie, Private Lives of Adam and Eve, Comedian, The Grabbers, St Joseph Plays the Horses, Breakfast at Tiffany's, Somebody's Waiting, Requiem for a Heavyweight, Richard, Pulp, It's a Mad, Mad, Mad, Mad World, Everything's Ducky, The Secret Invasion, The Extraordinary Seaman, The Comic, The Cockeyed Cowboys of Calico County, Skidoo, B.J. Presents, That's Entertainment, The Domino Principle, Pete's Dragon, The Magic of Lassie, Black Stallion, Arabian Adventure, Erik the Viking, My Heroes Have Always Been Cowboys 1991, Little Nimo: Adventures in Slumberland (voice) 1992, Silent Night Deadly Night 5: The Toymaker, The Milky Life, Revenge of the Red Baron, That's Entertainment III, The Legend of O.B. Taggart 1995. *Stage appearances in:* Sugar Babies 1979, The Will Rogers Follies 1993. *Publications:* I.E. An Autobiography 1965, Life Is Too Short 1991, Search for Sunny Skies 1994, Sinbad: The Battle of the Dark Knights 1998, The First Day of May 1998, The Face on the Barroom Floor 1998, Babe: Pig in the City 1998. *Address:* P.O. Box 3186, Thousand Oaks, CA 91359, USA.

ROOSEN, Gustavo; Venezuelan politician and business executive; ed Andrés Bello Catholic Univ., Caracas, New York Univ., USA; Vice-Pres. Venezuelan Banking Asscn 1981–83; Pres. Caracas Chamber of Commerce 1986–88; Minister of Educ. 1989–92; Pres. Petróleos de Venezuela 1992–95; Pres. CANTV (CA Nacional Teléfonos de Venezuela) 1995–, CEO 2002–. *Address:* CANTV, Final Av. Libertador, Centro Nacional de Telecomunicaciones, Nuevo Edf. Administrativo, Planta Baja, Caracas, Venezuela (Office). *Telephone:* (212) 500-2371 (Office). *Fax:* (212) 500-3437 (Office). *E-mail:* agar2@cantv.com.ve (Office). *Website:* www.cantv.com.ve (Office).

ROOTS, Ott, PhD; Estonian environmental scientist; b. 9 May 1946, Tallinn; s. of Otto Roots and Ida (née Lass) Roots; m. Marika Voit; one s.; ed Tallinn Tech. Univ., Inst. of Chem., Estonian Acad. of Sciences; Engineer-Lt, Company Vice-Commdr, 537 Soviet Army Bldg Bn 1969–71; scientist Inst. of Zoology and Botany, Estonian Acad. of Sciences 1971–74, Baltic Sea Dept, Inst. of Thermo- and Electrophysics 1974–84; Chief Researcher Baltic Br., Inst. of Applied Geophysics 1984–90; Chief Researcher Water Protection Lab., Tallinn Tech. Univ. 1990–92; Sr Scientist Dept of Environmental Carcinogenesis, Inst. of Experimental and Clinical Medicine 1992–94; lecturer, Tallinn Tech. Univ. 1993, Helsinki Univ. 1995, Tallinn Pedagogical Univ. 1997; Monitoring Counsellor, Environment Information Centre, Ministry of the Environment 1993–2000, Councillor, Dept of Environmental Man. and Tech., Ministry of the Environment 2000–02; Monitoring Co-ordinator, Estonian Environmental Research Centre (EERC) 2000–; Del. Helsinki Comm. (HELCOM) (expert on persistent organic contaminants) 1974–, UN ECE ICP (expert on monitoring) 1994–; Coordinator Finnish-Estonian Training Project (environmental monitoring) 1996–; mem. Estonian Chemistry Soc. 1995–, Nat. Geographic Soc., Washington 1996–, New York Acad. of Sciences 1997–, Estonian Nature Fund 1998–, Estonia Chemicals Safety Comm. 2000–, Estonian Toxicological Comm., Ministry of Educ. 2001–, Steering Cttee on the Support Project of Chemicals Control in Estonia 2002–(05), Scientific Council of EERC; Bronze Medal, Environmental Protection Exhbn (Russia) 1982, honoured by Ministry of the Environment, Estonia, for work in environmental protection 1996. *Publications include:* Polychlorinated Biphenyls and Chlororganic Pesticides in the Ecosystem of the Baltic Sea 1992, Toxic Chlororganic Compounds in the Ecosystem of the Baltic Sea 1996, The Effect of Environmental Pollution on Human Health in the Baltic States 1999, Persistent Bioaccumulative and Toxic Chemicals in Central and Eastern European Countries (jtly) 2000; contrib. to publs for Estonian Environment Information Centre; more than 190 scientific articles in learned journals. *Leisure interests:* environmental protection, sport (especially basketball), music. *Address:* Estonian Environmental Research Centre, Marja Str. 4D, Tallinn 10617 (Office); Paekaare 46-64, 13613 Tallinn, Estonia (Home). *Telephone:* (2) 611-2964 (Office). *Fax:* (2) 611-2901 (Office). *E-mail:* ott@klab.envir.ee (Office); oliver .roots@neti.ee (Home). *Website:* www.envir.ee/eerc (Office).

ROP, Anton, MA; Slovenian politician and economist; b. 27 Dec. 1960, Ljubljana; ed Univ. of Ljubljana; Asst Dir Slovene Inst. for Macroeconomic Analysis and Devt 1985–92; State Sec. Ministry of Econ. Relations and Devt 1993; Minister of Labour, Family and Social Affairs 1996–2000, of Finance 2002–. *Address:* Ministry of Finance, Županciceva 3, 1502 Ljubljana, Slovenia (Office). *Telephone:* (1) 478-5248 (Office). *Fax:* (1) 478-5655 (Office). *Website:* www.gov.si/mf (Office).

ROPER, Warren Richard, MSc, PhD, FRS, FRSNZ, F.N.Z.I.C.; New Zealand professor of chemistry; b. 27 Nov. 1938, Nelson; s. of Robert J. Roper and Nancy L. Robinson; m. Judith D. C. Miller 1961; two s. one d.; ed Nelson Coll., Univ. of Canterbury and Univ. of N Carolina; lecturer, Univ. of Auckland 1966, Prof. of Chem. 1984–; Visiting Lecturer, Univ. of Bristol 1972; Visiting Prof. Univ. of Leeds 1983, Univ. of Rennes 1984, 1985, Stanford Univ. 1988; Centenary Lecturer, Royal Soc. of Chem. 1988; G.T. Seaborg Lecturer, Univ. of Calif., Berkeley 1995; Fellow Japan Soc. for Promotion of Science 1992; Visiting Prof., Univ. of Sydney 2001; Hon. DSc (Canterbury) 1999; Royal Soc. of Chem. Award in Organometallic Chem. 1983, I.C.I. Medal, NZ Inst. of Chem., 1984, Hector Medal, Royal Soc. of NZ 1991, Inorganic Chem. Award, Royal Australian Chemical Inst. 1992, Dweyr Medal, Univ. of NSW 2000. *Publications:* over 190 original papers and reviews in scientific journals.

Leisure interests: listening to music (especially opera), walking. *Address:* Department of Chemistry, The University of Auckland, Private Bag, Auckland (Office); 26 Beulah Road, Auckland 10, New Zealand (Home). *Telephone:* (9) 373-7999 (Office); (9) 478-6940 (Home).

RORTY, Richard McKay, PhD; American professor of humanities; b. 4 Oct. 1931, New York; s. of James Hancock Rorty and Winifred Raushenbush Rorty; m. 1st Amelie Oksenberg 1954 (divorced 1972); one s.; m. 2nd Mary Varney 1972; one s. one d.; ed Univ. of Chicago, Yale Univ.; taught at Yale and Wellesley Coll. 1956–61 (army service 1957–58); taught philosophy at Princeton 1961–82; Prof. Univ. of Va 1982–98; Prof. of Comparative Literature, Stanford Univ. 1998–; Pres., Eastern Div., American Philosophical Asscn; Fellow American Acad. of Arts and Sciences; MacArthur Fellow. *Publications:* Philosophy and the Mirror of Nature 1980, Consequences of Pragmatism 1982, Contingency, Irony and Solidarity 1989, Objectivity, Relativism and Truth 1991, Essays on Heidegger and Others 1991, Truth and Progress: Philosophical Papers 1998, Achieving our Country: Leftist Thought in Twentieth Century America 1998, Philosophy and Social Hope 1999. *Leisure interest:* bird watching. *Address:* Department of Comparative Literature, Stanford University, Stanford, CA 94305 (Office); 82 Peter Coutts Circle, Stanford, CA 94305, USA (Home). *Telephone:* (650) 723-2300 (Office); (650) 856-8048 (Home). *Website:* www.stanford.edu (Office).

ROS, Enrique Jorge, LLD; Argentine diplomatist; b. 16 July 1927; ed Univs of Buenos Aires and Paris; practised as lawyer 1949–54; joined Diplomatic Service 1954; Perm. Mission to OAS 1956–58, to UN 1959–63; Chargé d'Affaires, The Hague 1965–67; Embassy, London 1967–71; Head of Mission, Beijing 1973–75; Amb. to Israel 1976–77, to UN 1977–80; Dir-Gen. Foreign Policy Bureau, Ministry of Foreign Affairs 1980, Under-Sec. for Foreign Affairs 1980–82; Amb. to Spain 1982–84, to Japan 1984–89, to Viet Nam (non-resident) 1985–89; mem. Higher Council of Ambs of Ministry of Foreign Affairs 1990–; Chair. Bilateral Admin. Comm. of River Plate 1991; decorations from Bolivia, Brazil, Chile, Colombia, Ecuador, Paraguay, Peru, Venezuela, Japan. *Leisure interests:* reading, gardening. *Address:* Ministry of Foreign Affairs, International Trade and Worship, Esmeralda 1212, 1007 Buenos Aires, Argentina.

ROSATI, Dariusz Kajetan, DEcon; Polish professor of economics; b. 8 Aug. 1946, Radom; s. of Angelo Rosati and Wanda Pleszczyńska; m. Teresa Nowińska 1971; one s. one d.; ed Main School of Planning and Statistics; scientific researcher Main School of Planning and Statistics (now Warsaw School of Econs), Warsaw 1969–, Asst Prof. 1988, Prof. 1990–; with Citibank, New York 1978–79, Princeton Univ., NJ 1986–87; Dir Inst. of Econ. Situation and Foreign Trade Prices, Warsaw 1988–91; Head UN Section for Cen. and E Europe, Geneva 1991–95; Minister of Foreign Affairs 1995–97; mem. Council of Monetary Policy of Nat. Bank of Poland 1998–. *Publications:* Decision-Making 1977, Inflation 1989, Export Policies 1990, Polish Way to Market 1998; about 200 scientific articles. *Leisure interests:* sports, reading. *Address:* ul. Świętokrzyska 12, 00-919 Warsaw, Poland. *Telephone:* (22) 6532888. *E-mail:* drosati@bptnet.pl (Home).

ROSCITT, Richard R. (Rick); American telecommunications executive; fmr Pres. AT&T Business Services, then Pres. and CEO AT&T Solutions, fmr mem. Operations Group, AT&T; Chair. and CEO ADC Telecommunications 2001–. *Address:* ADC Telecommunications, P.O. Box 1101, Minneapolis, MN 55440-1101, USA (Office). *Website:* www.adc.com (Office).

ROSE, Sir Clive (Martin), GCMG, MA, FRSA, F.I.C.D.D.S.; British diplomatist (retd); b. 15 Sept. 1921, Banstead, Surrey; s. of the late Bishop Alfred Rose; m. Elisabeth MacKenzie Lewis 1946; two s. three d.; ed Marlborough Coll. and Christ Church, Oxford; Rifle Brigade (rank of Maj., mentioned in despatches), Europe, India, Iraq 1941–46; Commonwealth Relations Office 1948; High Comm. Madras 1948–49; Foreign Office 1950; served in Bonn, Montevideo, Paris, Washington and London 1950–73; Imperial Defence Coll. 1968; Amb. and Head of UK Del. to Mutual and Balanced Force Reduction talks, Vienna 1973–76; Deputy Sec. to Cabinet Office 1976–79; UK Perm. Rep. on N Atlantic Council 1979–82; Consultant to Control Risks Group Ltd 1983–95; Chair. Control Risks Information Services Ltd 1991–93 (Dir 1986–93); Pres. Emergency Planning Asscn 1987–93; mem. Advisory Bd Royal Coll. for Defence Studies 1985–92; Chair. Council Royal United Services Inst. 1983–86, Vice-Pres. 1986–93, Vice-Patron 1993–2001; Vice-Pres. Suffolk Preservation Soc. 1988– (Chair. 1985–88). *Publications:* Campaigns Against Western Defence: NATO's Adversaries and Critics 1985, The Soviet Propaganda Network: a Directory of Organisations Serving Soviet Foreign Policy 1988. *Leisure interests:* gardening, genealogy, conservation of buildings and countryside. *Address:* Chimney House, Lavenham, Suffolk, CO10 9QT, England. *Telephone:* (1787) 247699 (Home).

ROSE, Comte François Jean-Baptiste Hubert Edouard Marie de Tricornot de; French diplomatist (retd); b. 3 Nov. 1910; s. of Carlo de Tricornot de Rose and Madeleine Tavernier; m. Yvonne Daday 1933 (deceased); two d.; ed Ecole Libre des Sciences Politiques, Paris; Sec. French Embassy, London, UK 1937–40; liaison officer with Allied Forces in Tunisia 1943, Normandy, Belgium and Holland 1944; Sec. French Embassy, Italy 1945–46; mem. French del. to UN 1946–50; Minister-Counsellor, Spain 1952–56; Ministry of Foreign Affairs, Paris 1956–60; mem. Atomic Energy Comm. (Paris) 1950–64; Pres. European Nuclear Research Org. (CERN) 1958–60; Asst to Chief of Staff, Nat. Defence 1961–62; Amb. to Portugal 1964–69; Amb. and Perm. Rep. to NATO Council 1970–75; Vice-Pres. Council of Int. Inst. of Strategic Studies (London) 1980–2002; mem. Trilateral Comm. (European Group) 1976–90; Officier, Légion d'honneur, Commdr Ordre nat. du Mérite, Croix de Guerre. *Achievements:* Guiness Book of Records Award for playing 90 holes of golf (5 rounds) to celebrate his 90th birthday. *Publications:* La France et la défense de l'Europe 1976, European Security and France 1984, La paix. Pourquoi pas? (with J. D. Remond and Chantal Ruiz-Barthélémy) 1986, Defendre de la Défense 1989, La Troisième Guerre Mondiale n'a pas eu lieu, L'Alliance Atlantique et la Paix 1995. *Leisure interest:* golf. *Address:* 5 rue du Faubourg Saint-Honoré, 75008 Paris, France (Home). *Telephone:* 1-42-65-70-75 (Office); 1-42-65-70-60 (Home). *Fax:* 1-40-17-02-56 (Office).

ROSE, Gen. Sir (Hugh) Michael, KCB, CBE, DSO, QGM; British army officer; b. 5 Jan. 1940; s. of late Lt-Col Hugh Rose and of Barbara Allcard; m. Angela Shaw 1968; two s.; ed Cheltenham Coll., St Edmund Hall, Oxford and Royal Coll. of Defence Studies; commissioned, Gloucestershire Regt Territorial Army Volunteer Reserve 1959; RAF Volunteer Reserve 1962; Coldstream Guards 1964; served Germany, Aden, Malaysia, Gulf States, Dhofar, N Ireland, Falkland Islands; Brigade Major, 16 Para. Brigade 1973–75; CO 22 SAS Regt 1979–82; Command, 39 Infantry Brigade 1983–85; Commdt School of Infantry 1987–88; Dir Special Forces 1988–89; GOC NE Dist and Commdr 2nd Infantry Div. 1989–91; Commdt Staff Coll. 1991–93; Commdr UK Field Army and Insp.-Gen. of Territorial Army 1993–94; Commdr (UN Forces in) Bosnia-Herzegovina 1994–95; Adjutant Gen. 1995–97; Aide de Camp Gen. to the Queen 1995–97; Col Coldstream Guards 1999–2000; Dir Control Risks Group; Hon. DLitt (Nottingham) 1999. *Television:* presenter Power House 2000. *Publication:* Fighting for Peace 1998. *Leisure interests:* sailing, skiing. *Address:* c/o Regimental H.Q. Coldstream Guards, Wellington Barracks, Birdcage Walk, London, SW1E 6HQ, England.

ROSE, Richard, BA, DPhil, FBA; author, professor of public policy and consultant; b. 9 April 1933, St Louis, Mo.; s. of Charles Imse Rose and Mary Conely Rose; m. Rosemary J. Kenny 1956; two s. one d.; ed Clayton High School, Mo., Johns Hopkins Univ., LSE, Oxford; worked in political public relations, Miss. Valley 1954–55; Reporter St Louis Post-Dispatch 1955–57; Lecturer in Govt, Univ. of Manchester 1961–66; Prof. of Politics Strathclyde Univ. 1966–82, Prof. of Public Policy and Dir, Centre for the Study of Public Policy 1976–; Specialist Adviser, House of Commons Public Admin Cttee 2002–03; Consultant Psephologist, The Times, Ind. Television, Daily Telegraph, etc. 1964–; Sec. Cttee on Political Sociology, Int. Sociology Asscn 1970–85; Founding mem. European Consortium for Political Research 1970; mem. US/UK Fulbright Comm. 1971–75; Guggenheim Fellow 1974; Visiting scholar at various insts, Europe, USA, Hong Kong; mem. Home Office Working Party on Electoral Register 1975–77; Co-Founder British Politics Group 1974–; Convenor Work Group on UK Politics, Political Studies Asscn 1976–88; mem. Council Int. Political Science Asscn 1976–82; Tech. Consultant OECD, UNDP, World Bank, Council of Europe, Int. IDEA; Dir S.S.R.C. Research Programme, Growth of Govt 1982–86; Ed. Journal of Public Policy 1985–, Chair. 1981–85; Scientific Adviser, New Democracies Barometer, Paul Lazarsfeld Soc., Vienna 1991–; Convenor Global Barometer Survey Network 2001–; Hon. Vice-Pres. UK Political Studies Asscn; Hon. Fellow American Acad. of Arts and Sciences, Finnish Acad. of Science and Letters, Acad. of Learned Socs. in the Social Sciences 2000; AMEX Prize in Int. Econs 1992, Lasswell Prize for Lifetime Achievement, Policy Studies Org. 1999; Lifetime Achievement Award, UK Political Studies Asscn 1990. *Publications:* numerous books on politics and public policy including Elections Without Order, The Prime Minister in a Shrinking World, What is Europe?, Politics in England, Elections and World Order: Russia's Challenge to Vladimir Putin, Public Employment in Western Nations, Taxation by Political Inertia, Understanding Big Government, Do Parties Make a Difference?, Presidents and Prime Ministers, The Postmodern President, Voters Begin to Choose: Loyalties of Voters, International Almanac of Electoral History, Northern Ireland: Time of Choice, Ordinary People in Public Policy, Lesson-Drawing in Public Policy: Inheritance in Public Policy, How Russia Votes, Democracy and Its Alternatives, Understanding Post-Communist Societies, A Society Transformed: Hungary in Time-Space Perspective, International Encyclopedia of Elections; hundreds of papers in academic journals. *Leisure interests:* architecture, music, writing. *Address:* Centre for the Study of Public Policy, University of Strathclyde, Livingstone Tower, Richmond Street, Glasgow, G1 1XH (Office); Bennochy, 1 East Abercromby Street, Helensburgh, G84 7SP, Scotland (Home). *Telephone:* (141) 548-3217 (Office); (1436) 672164 (Home). *Fax:* (141) 552-4711 (Office); (1436) 673125 (Home). *Website:* www.cspp.strath.ac.uk (Office).

ROSE, Stuart Alan Ransom; British business executive; b. 17 March 1949; s. of Harry Ransom Rose and Margaret Ransom Rose; m. Jennifer Cook 1973; one s. one d.; ed St Joseph's Convent, Dar-es-Salaam and Bootham School, York; with Marks & Spencer PLC 1971–89, Commercial Exec. (Europe); CEO Multiples, Burton Group PLC 1989–97, Argos PLC 1998, Booker PLC 1998–2000, Iceland Group PLC 2000, Arcadia PLC 2000–02. *Address:* c/o Arcadia PLC, Colegrave House, 70 Berners Street, London, W1T 3NL, England (Office).

ROSEANNE; American actress; b. (Roseanne Barr), 3 Nov. 1952, Salt Lake City; d. of Jerry Barr and Helen Barr; m. 1st Bill Pentland 1974 (divorced 1989); m. 2nd Tom Arnold 1990 (divorced 1994); three c. (from previous m.); m. 3rd Ben Thomas 1994; one s.; fmr window dresser, cocktail waitress; worked as comic in bars and church coffeehouse, Denver; produced forum for

women performers Take Back the Mike, Univ. of Boulder, Colo; performer, The Comedy Store, L. A.; featured on TV special Funny and The Tonight Show; TV special, On Location: The Roseanne Barr Show 1987; star of TV series, Roseanne ABC 1988–97; host Roseanne Show 1998–; Emmy award (Outstanding Leading Actress in a Comedy Series) 1993. *Films:* She Devil 1989, Freddy's Dead 1991, Even Cowgirls Get the Blues 1994, Blue in the Face 1995, Unzipped 1995, Meet Wally Sparks 1997. *Television includes:* Roseanne Show 1998–, Get Bruce 1999. *Publications:* My Life as a Woman 1989, Roseanne: My Lives 1994. *Address:* c/o Full Moon and High Tide Productions, 4024 Radford Avenue, Dressing Room 916, Studio City, CA 91604, USA.

ROSELLE, David, PhD; American mathematician and university president; b. 30 May 1939, Vandergrift, Pa; s. of William Roselle and Suzanne Clever; m. Louise H. Dowling 1967; one s. one d.; ed West Chester State Coll. and Duke Univ.; Asst Prof. Univ. of Md 1965–68; Assoc. Prof., Prof. La State Univ. 1968–74; Prof. Va Polytechnic Inst. and State Univ. 1974–87, Dean, Grad. School 1979–81, Dean of Research and Grad. Studies 1981–83, Univ. Provost 1983–87; Pres. Univ. of Ky 1987–90, Univ. of Del. 1990–; numerous grants and honours. *Publications:* numerous mathematics articles in graph theory and combinatorics. *Leisure interests:* golf, reading, jogging. *Address:* Office of the President, University of Delaware, Newark, DE 19716; 47 Kent Way, Newark, DE 19711, USA. *Telephone:* (302) 831-2111 (Office); (302) 831-2721 (Home).

ROSEMAN, Saul, MS PhD; American biochemist; b. 9 March 1921, Brooklyn, NY; s. of Emil Roseman and Rose Roseman (née Markowitz); m. Martha Ozrowitz 1941; one s. two d.; ed City Coll. of New York and Univ. of Wisconsin; Instructor to Asst Prof., Univ. of Chicago 1948–53; Asst Prof. to Prof. of Biological Chem. and chemist, Rackham Arthritis Research Unit, Univ. of Mich. 1953–65; Prof. of Biology, Johns Hopkins Univ. 1965–, Chair. Dept of Biology 1969–73, 1988–90, Dir, McCollum-Pratt Inst. 1969–73, 1988–90; Ralph S. O'Connor Prof. of Biology; Consultant, Nat. Cystic Fibrosis Research Foundation. Nat. Science Foundation, American Cancer Soc., Hosp. for Sick Children, Toronto; Scientific Counsellor to Nat. Cancer Inst.; Counsellor to American Soc. of Biological Chemists; mem. Editorial Bd Journal of Biological Chemistry 1962–75, Journal of Lipid Research 1967–73, Journal of Membrane Biology 1969–80, Biochimica et Biophysica Acta 1971–75, Biochemistry 1976–80; Fellow American Acad. of Microbiology 1992; mem. American Soc. of Biological Chemists, American Acad. of Arts and Sciences, American Chemical Soc., Nat. Acad. of Sciences., AAAS, Biophysical Soc., American Asscn of Univ. Profs.; Lynch Lecturer, Univ. of Notre Dame 1989; Van Niel Lecturer, Stanford Univ. 1992; Hon. mem. Biochemical Soc. of Japan; Hon. MD (Univ. of Lund, Sweden) 1984; Sesquicentennial Award (Univ. of Mich.) 1967, 15th Annual T. Duckett Jones Memorial Award, Helen Hay Whitney Foundation 1973, Rosensteihl Award (Brandeis Univ.) 1974, Gairdner Foundation Int. Award 1981, Townsend Harris Medal, City Coll. of New York 1987, Special Award, 11th Int. Symposium on Glycoconjugates, Toronto, Canada 1991, Karl Meyer Award, Soc. of Complex Carbohydrates 1993. *Publications:* 233 original articles in scientific journals. *Leisure interests:* sailing, music, reading, athletics. *Address:* Department of Biology and McCollum-Pratt Institute, The Johns Hopkins University, MD 21218 (Office); 8206 Cranwood Court, Baltimore, MD 21208, USA (Home). *Telephone:* (410) 516-7333 (Office); (410) 486-7439 (Home). *E-mail:* roseman@jhu.edu (Office).

ROSEN, Charles, PhD; American pianist; b. 5 May 1927, New York City; s. of Irwin Rosen and Anita Gerber; ed Juilliard School of Music, Princeton Univ., Univ. of S. California; studied piano with Moriz Rosenthal and Hedwig Kanner-Rosenthal 1938–45; recital début, New York 1951; first complete recording of Debussy Etudes 1951; première of Double Concerto by Elliott Carter, New York 1961; has played recitals and as soloist with orchestras throughout America and Europe; has made over 35 recordings including Stravinsky: Movements with composer conducting 1962, Bach: Art of Fugue, Two Ricercares, Goldberg Variations 1971, Beethoven: Last Six Sonatas 1972, Boulez: Piano Music, Vol. I, Diabelli Variations, Beethoven Concerto No. 4, 1979, Schumann: The Revolutionary Masterpieces, Chopin: 24 Mazurkas 1991; Prof. of Music, State Univ. of NY 1972–90; Guggenheim Fellowship 1974; Messenger Lectures, Cornell Univ. 1975, Bloch Lectures, Univ. of Calif., Berkeley 1977, Gauss Seminars, Princeton Univ. 1978; Norton Prof. of Poetry, Harvard Univ. 1980–81; George Eastman Prof., Balliol Coll., Oxford 1987–88, Prof. of Music and Social Thought, Univ. of Chicago 1988–96; Nat. Book Award 1972; Edison Prize, Netherlands 1974; Dr. Mus. hc (Trinity Coll., Dublin 1976, Leeds Univ. 1976, Durham Univ.), Dr. h.c (Cambridge) 1992. *Publications:* The Classical Style: Haydn, Mozart, Beethoven 1971, Schoenberg 1975, Sonata Forms 1980, Romanticism and Realism (with Henri Zerner) 1984, The Musical Language of Elliott Carter 1985, Frontiers of Meaning 1994, The Romantic Generation 1995, Romantic Poets, Critics and other Madmen 1998, Critical Entertainment: Music Old and New 2000 and several articles. *Address:* c/o Owen/White Management, Top Floor, 59 Lands-downe Place, Hove, East Sussex, BN3 1FL, England.

ROSÉN, Haiim B., PhD; Israeli professor of linguistics and classics; b. 4 March 1922, Vienna, Austria; s. of late Georg Rosenrauch and Olga Gerstl; m. Hannah Steinitz 1953; one s.; ed schools in Vienna, Hebrew Univ., Jerusalem, Ecole Pratique des Hautes Etudes and Coll. de France, Paris; went to Palestine 1938; school-teacher, Tel Aviv 1944–49; mem. Faculty, Hebrew Univ. Jerusalem 1949–, Prof. of Gen. and Indo-European Linguistics 1968–, Head, Dept of Linguistics 1973–86; Prof. of Classics and Hebrew Linguistics, Tel Aviv Univ. 1961–91, Prof. Emer. 1991–; mem. Israeli Nat. Acad. of

Sciences and Humanities; Rep. of Israel, Perm. Int. Cttee of Linguists; visiting professorships at Univ. of Chicago, Univ. of Paris, Coll. de France, Univ. of Tübingen etc.; Israel State Prize in the Humanities 1978, Humboldt Research Award 1993. *Publications:* about 25 books including Ha-Ivrit Shelanu (Our Hebrew Language) 1955, East and West–Selected writings in linguistics, 3 Vols 1982–94, Herodoti Historiae edition in the Bibliotheca Teubneriana, 2 Vols 1987–97; about 200 articles on classical philology, general, Indo-European and Hebrew linguistics. *Address:* 13, Bruria, Jerusalem 93184, Israel. *Telephone:* 2-6784236.

ROSEN, Milton William, BS; American engineer and physicist; b. 25 July 1915, Philadelphia, Pa; s. of Abraham Rosen and Regina (Weiss) Rosen; m. Josephine Haar 1948; three d.; ed Univ. of Pennsylvania, Univ. of Pittsburgh and California Inst. of Tech.; Engineer Westinghouse Electric and Mfg Co. 1937–38; Engineer-physicist Naval Research Lab., Washington 1940–58, Scientific Officer Viking Rocket 1947–55, Head Rocket Devt Branch 1953–55, Tech. Dir Project Vanguard (earth satellite) 1955–58; engineer NASA 1958–74; Chief Rocket Vehicle Devt Programs 1958–59, Asst Dir Launch Vehicle Programs 1960–61, Dir Launch Vehicles and Propulsion 1961–63; Sr Scientist, Office of DOD and Interagency Affairs, NASA 1963–72; Deputy Assoc. Admin. for Space Science (Eng) 1972–74; Exec. Sec. Space Science Bd 1974–78; Exec. Sec. Cttee on Impacts of Stratospheric Change, Nat. Acad. of Sciences 1978–80, Cttee on Underground Coal Mine Safety 1980–83; Exec. Dir Space Applications Board 1983–85; Chair. Greater Washington Asscn of Unitarian Churches 1966–68; Study Leader, Inst. for Learning in Retirement, American Univ., Washington, DC 1987–; First James H. Wyld Award for the Application of Rocket Power 1954. *Publication:* The Viking Rocket Story 1955. *Leisure interests:* music, art collecting, rug making. *Address:* 5610 Alta Vista Road, Bethesda, MD 20817, USA. *Telephone:* (301) 530-1497.

ROSENAU, James N., AM, PhD; American academic; ed Bard Coll., Johns Hopkins, Princeton, Columbia and New York Univs; Instructor in Political Science, Douglass Coll., Rutgers Univ. 1949–54, Asst Prof. 1954–60, Assoc. Prof. 1960–62, Prof. 1962–70, Acting Chair. 1963–64, Faculty Fellow 1965–66, Chair. New Brunswick Dept of Political Science 1968–70; Research Assoc., Center for Int. Studies, Princeton Univ. 1960–70; Prof. of Political Science, Ohio State Univ. 1970–73; Dir Inst. for Transnational Studies, Univ. of Southern Calif. 1973–92, Prof. of Political Science and Int. Relations 1973–92, Dir School of Int. Relations 1976–79; Sr Fellow, Center for Int. and Strategic Affairs, Univ. of Calif. at LA 1979–92; Prof. of Int. Affairs and Political Science, George Washington Univ. 1992–; Visiting Prof. of Political Science, McGill Univ., Montréal 1990; Visiting Prof. of Int. Relations, UN Univ. for Peace, Costa Rica 1991; Co-Principal Investigator (with Ole R. Holsti), Foreign Policy Leadership Project, NSF 1979–81, 1983–85, 1988–89, 1992–94, 1997–99; Pres. Int. Studies Asscn 1984–85; mem. Transparency Int. Council on Governance Research 1995–; Guggenheim Fellowship 1987–88. *Publications include:* Turbulence in World Politics: A Theory of Change and Continuity 1990, Governance without Government 1991, The United Nations in a Turbulent World: Engulfed or Enlarged? 1992, Global Voices 1993, International Relations Theory 1993, Thinking Theory Thoroughly: Coherent Approaches to an Incoherent World (with Mary Durfee) 1995, Along the Domestic-Foreign Frontier: Exploring Governance in a Turbulent World 1997, Strange Power: Shaping the Parameters of International Relations and International Political Economy 2000, Information Technologies and Global Politics: The Changing Scope of Power and Governance 2002; author or ed. of more than 30 books, 140 articles and Kwangju: An Escalatory Spree (two-act play, produced at Odyssey Theater, Los Angeles 1991). *Address:* Elliot School of International Affairs, George Washington University, Gelman 709G, 2130 H Street, NW, Washington, DC 20052, USA (Office). *Telephone:* (202) 994-3060 (Office). *Fax:* (202) 994-0792 (Office). *E-mail:* jnr@gwu.edu (Office). *Website:* www.gwu.edu (Office).

ROSENBERG, Pierre Max; French curator; b. 13 April 1936, Paris; s. of Charles Rosenberg and Gertrude Rosenberg; m. 2nd Béatrice de Rothschild 1981; one d.; ed Lycée Charlemagne, Faculté de droit de Paris and Ecole du Louvre; Chief Curator Dept des Peintures, Musée du Louvre 1983, Inspecteur gén. des musées 1988, Conservateur gén. du Patrimoine 1990–94, Pres. and Dir 1994–2001; Curator Musée Nat. de l'Amitié et des Relations franco-américaines de Blérancourt 1981–93; mem. Acad. Française 1995; Chevalier Ordre des Arts et des Lettres, Ordre nat. du Mérite, Légion d'honneur. *Publications:* numerous works on 17th and 18th centuries. *Address:* 35 rue de Vaugirard, 75006 Paris, France (Home); Institut de France, 23 quai Conti, 75006 Paris.

ROSENBERG, Richard Morris; American banker; b. 21 April 1930, Fall River, Mass.; s. of Charles Rosenberg and Betty Peck; m. Barbara K. Cohen 1956; two s.; ed Suffolk and Golden Gate Univs; publicity Asst Crocker-Anglo Bank, San Francisco 1959–62; Banking Services Officer, Wells Fargo Bank 1962–65, Asst Vice-Pres. 1965–68, Marketing Dept 1968, Vice-Pres. Dir of Marketing 1969, Sr Vice-Pres. Marketing and Advertising Div. 1970–75, Exec. Vice-Pres. 1975, Vice-Chair. 1980–83; Vice-Chair. Crocker Nat. Corpn 1983–85; Pres. and COO Seafirst Corpn 1986–87; Dir, Pres. and COO Seattle-First Nat. Bank 1985–87; Vice-Chair. Bd Bank America Corpn San Francisco 1987–90; Chair. and CEO BankAmerica Corpn/Bank of America 1990–91, Chair. Bank America Corpn 1990–96; Dir Airborne Express, Northrop Grumman Corpn, Pacific Mutual Life Insurance Co., San Francisco Symphony, United Way; mem. State Bar of Calif.; Trustee, Calif. Inst. of Tech. *Leisure interests:* tennis, avid reader, history. *Address:* Bank Am

Corporation, Mail Code CA5-705-11-01, PO Box 37000 San Francisco, CA 94137, USA. *E-mail:* richard.rosenberg@bankofamerica.com (Office). *Website:* www.bankofamerica.com (Office).

ROSENBERG, Steven A., MD, PhD; American physician and immunologist; b. 2 Aug. 1940, New York; s. of Abraham Rosenberg and Harriet Wendroff; m. Alice R. O'Connell 1968; three d.; ed Bronx High School of Science and Johns Hopkins Univ.; Intern, Peter Bent Brigham Hosp. Boston 1963–64, Surgical Resident 1968–69, further surgical training 1972–74; Fellow in Immunology, Harvard Medical School 1969–70, Nat. Insts. of Health 1970–72; Chief of Surgery, Nat. Cancer Inst. Bethesda, Md 1974–; Prof. of Surgery, Uniformed Services Univ. of Health Sciences; mem. numerous professional socs.; Public Health Service Medal 1981. *Publications:* thirteen books and hundreds of articles in medical journals. *Address:* National Cancer Institute, 31 Center Drive, Building 10, Room 2042, Bethesda, MD 20892, USA.

ROSENNE, Shabtai, LLB, PhD; Israeli lawyer and diplomatist (retd); b. 24 Nov. 1917, London, England; s. of Harry Rowson and Vera Rowson; m. Esther Schultz 1940; two s.; ed London Univ. and Hebrew Univ. of Jerusalem; Advocate (Israel), Political Dept, Jewish Agency for Palestine 1946–48; Legal Adviser, Ministry of Foreign Affairs 1948–66; Deputy Perm. Rep. to UN 1967–71; Perm. Rep. to UN, Geneva 1971–74; Ministry of Foreign Affairs 1974–82; mem. Israeli del. to UN Gen. Assemblies 1948–83, Vice-Chair. Legal Cttee Gen. Assembly 1960; mem. Israeli del. to Armistice Negotiations with Egypt, Jordan, Lebanon and Syria 1949; mem. Israel del. to UN Conf. on Law of the Sea 1958, 1960, Chair. 1973, 1978–82; Chair. Israel del. to UN Conf. on Law of Treaties 1968, 1969, mem. other UN confs.; Govt Rep. before Int. Court of Justice in several cases; mem. Int. Law Comm. 1962–71, UN Comm. on Human Rights 1968–70; Visiting Prof., Bar Ilan Univ. 1976–; Arthur Goodhart Visiting Prof. of Legal Science, Cambridge 1985–86; Belle van Zuylen Visiting Prof., State Univ. of Utrecht 1986–87, Univ. of Amsterdam 1987; Visiting Scholar, Univ. of Va 1988–92; mem. Inst. of Int. Law 1963–, Rapporteur, Termination and Modification of Treaties 1965; Fellow Jewish Acad. of Arts and Sciences 1981; Hon. mem. American Soc. of Int. Law 1976; Israel Prize 1960, Certificate of Merit, American Soc. of Int. Law 1968, Manley O. Hudson Medal 1999. *Publications:* International Court of Justice 1957, The Time Factor in Jurisdiction of the International Court of Justice 1960, The Law of Treaties: Guide to the Vienna Convention 1970, Procedure in the International Court 1983, Practice and Methods of International Law 1984, Developments in the Law of Treaties 1945–86 1989, Documents on the International Court of Justice 1991, An International Law Miscellany 1993, The World Court: What It Is And How It Works 1995, The Law and Practice of the International Court 1920–1996 (4 vols) 1997, The United Nations Convention on the Law of the Sea 1982: A Commentary (7 vols) (Gen. Ed.) 1985–2003; numerous articles, mainly on law. *Leisure interests:* reading, music. *Address:* PO Box 3313, Jerusalem 91033, Israel. *Telephone:* 2-6524339. *Fax:* 2-6526401. *E-mail:* rosennes@netvision.net.il (Home).

ROSENSHINE, Allen Gilbert, BA; American advertising executive; b. 14 March 1939; s. of Aaron Rosenshine and Anna Zuckerman; m. Suzan Weston-Webb 1979; two s.; ed Columbia Coll.; copywriter, J.B. Rundle, New York 1962–65; copywriter, Batten, Barton, Durstine & Osborn, New York 1965, copy supervisor 1967, Vice-Pres. 1968, Assoc. Creative Dir 1970, Sr Vice-Pres. and Creative Dir 1975–77, Exec. Vice-Pres. 1977–80, Pres. 1980–82, CEO 1981–86, Chair. 1983–86; Pres. and CEO BBDO Int. New York 1984–86; Pres. and COO Omnicom Group, New York 1986–88; Chair. and CEO BBDO Worldwide, New York 1989–. *Address:* BBDO Worldwide, 1285 Avenue of the Americas, New York, NY 10019, USA.

ROSENTHAL, Abraham Michael; American journalist; b. 2 May 1922, Sault Ste. Marie, Ont., Canada; s. of Harry Rosenthal and Sarah (née Dickstein) Rosenthal; m. 1st Ann Marie Burke 1949; three s.; m. 2nd Shirley Lord 1987; with New York Times 1944–, UN Bureau 1946–54, New Delhi 1954–58, Warsaw 1958–59, Geneva 1959–61, Tokyo 1961–63, Metropolitan Ed. 1963–66, Asst Man. Ed. 1966–68, Assoc. Man. Ed. 1968–69, Man. Ed. 1969–77, Exec. Ed. 1977–86, Assoc. Ed. and columnist 1986–87, columnist 1986–99; columnist Daily News 2000–; syndicated columnist Daily News, Washington Times, etc.; Ed. at large, Ed. Consultant G.P. Putnam 1988–; Pulitzer Prize 1960, Nat. Press Foundation Award 1986, Light of Truth Award 1994. *Publications:* 38 Witnesses, One More Victim (co-author). *Address:* New York Daily News, 450 West 33rd Street, New York, NY 10001, USA (Office).

ROSENTHAL, Gert, MA; Guatemalan economist and international organization official; b. 11 Sept. 1935, Amsterdam, Netherlands; s. of Ludwig Rosenthal and Florence Rosenthal (née Koenigsberger); m. Margit Uhlmann; four d.; ed Amercian School of Guatemala, Univ. of California at Berkeley, Universidad de San Carlos de Guatemala; worked in pvt. sector 1959–67; economist, Nat. Planning Secr. 1960–64, Head Econ. Devt Div. 1965, Sec.-Gen. (rank of Minister) 1969–70, 1973–74; Officer in charge of external financing, Ministry of Finance 1966–67; Asst to Sec.-Gen., Secr. of Cen. American Common Market (SIECA) 1968, Project Dir UNCTAD project to promote SIECA, Guatemala City 1972–73; Prof. of Econ. Devt and Public Finance, Universidad Rafael Landívar, Guatemala 1969–74; Dir Sub-regional Office UN ECLA, Mexico 1974–85, Deputy Exec. Sec. UN ECLA, Santiago, Chile 1985–87, Exec. Sec. (rank of Under-Sec.-Gen. of UN) 1988–97; mem. Oversight Comm. of Guatemalan Peace Accords 1998; Perm. Rep. to

UN, New York Dec. 1998–; Hon. PhD (Universidad del Valle) 1996. *Publications:* numerous publs on devt issues 1960–. *Address:* Permanent Mission of Guatemala to the UN, 57 Park Avenue, New York, NY 10016, USA (Office); Calle de los Duelos #6, Antigua, Guatemala (Home). *Telephone:* (212) 679-4760 (Office); 832-3659 (Home). *Fax:* (212) 685-8741 (Office); 832-3666 (Home). *E-mail:* grosenthal@un.int (Office); grosenthal@guate.net (Home). *Website:* www.un.int/guatemala.

ROSENTHAL, Norman Leon, BA; British art curator; b. 8 Nov. 1944; s. of Paul Rosenthal and Kate Zucker; m. Manuela Beatriz Mena Marques 1989; two d.; ed Westminster City Grammar School, Univ. of Leicester; librarian Thomas Agnew & Sons 1966–68; Exhbns. Officer, Brighton Museum and Art Gallery 1970–71, Exhbn Organizer Inst. Contemporary Arts 1974–76, Exhbns. Sec. RA 1977–; organizer of many exhbns. including: Art into Society, I.C.A. 1974, A New Spirit in Painting, 1981, Zeitgeist, W Berlin 1982, German Art of the Twentieth Century and Staatsgalerie, Stuttgart 1985–86, Italian Art of the Twentieth Century, Royal Acad 1989, Metropolis, Berlin 1991, American Art in the Twentieth Century and Martin-Gropius Bau, Berlin 1993, Sensation 1997, Charlotte Salomon, RA 1998, Apocalypse RA 2000; TV and radio broadcasts on contemporary art; mem. Opera Bd, Royal Opera House 1995–99, Bd Palazzo Grassi, Venice 1995–; Hon. Fellow RCA 1987; Chevalier, Ordre des Arts et des Lettres 1987, Cavaliere Ufficiale, Order of Merit (Italy) 1992, Cross, Order of Merit (Germany) 1993. *Leisure interest:* music, especially opera. *Address:* The Royal Academy of Arts, Burlington House, Piccadilly, London, W1V 0DS, England. *Telephone:* (20) 7300-8000.

ROSENTHAL, Thomas Gabriel, MA; British publisher, critic and broadcaster; b. 16 July 1935; s. of late Erwin I. J. Rosenthal and Elisabeth Charlotte Marx; m. Ann Judith Warnford-Davis; two s.; ed Perse School, Cambridge and Pembroke Coll., Cambridge; served RA 1954–56; joined Thames and Hudson Ltd 1959, Man. Dir Thames and Hudson Int. 1966; joined Martin Secker and Warburg Ltd as Man. Dir 1971, Dir Heinemann Group of Publrs. 1972–84, Man. Dir William Heinemann Int. Ltd 1979–84, Chair. World's Work Ltd 1979–84, Heinemann Zsolnay Ltd 1979–84, Kaye and Ward Ltd 1980–84, William Heinemann, Australia and SA 1981–82, Pres. Heinemann Inc. 1981–84; Jt Man. Dir and Jt Chair. André Deutsch Ltd 1984, CEO 1987–96, Sole Man. Dir and Chair. 1987, Chair. 1984–98; Chair. Frew McKenzie (Antiquarian Booksellers) 1985–93, Bridgewater Press 1997–; Art Critic The Listener 1963–66; Chair. Soc. of Young Publrs. 1961–62; mem. Cambridge Univ. Appointments Bd 1967–71, Exec. Cttee Nat. Book League 1971–74, Cttee of Man. Amateur Dramatic Club, Cambridge (also Trustee), Council RCA 1982–87, Exec. Council Inst. of Contemporary Arts 1987–99 (Chair. 1996–99); Trustee Phoenix Trust; mem. Editorial Bd Logos 1989–93. *Publications:* Monograph on Jack B. Yeats 1964, Monograph on Ivon Hitchens (with Alan Bowness) 1973; A Reader's Guide to European Art History 1962, A Reader's Guide to Modern American Fiction 1963, Monograph on Arthur Boyd (with Ursula Hoff) 1986, The Art of Jack B. Yeats 1993, Sidney Nolan 2002; articles in journals and newspapers. *Leisure interests:* opera, pictures, bibliomania. *Address:* Flat 7, Huguenot House, 19 Oxendon Street, London, SW1Y 4EH, England. *Telephone:* (20) 7839-3589. *Fax:* (20) 7839-0651.

ROSENZWEIG, Mark Richard, PhD; American psychologist and neuroscientist; b. 12 Sept. 1922, Rochester, New York; s. of Jacob Rosenzweig and Pearl Grossman Rosenzweig; m. Janine S. A. Chappat 1947; one s. two d.; ed Univ. of Rochester and Harvard Univ.; served US Navy 1944–46; Asst Prof., Univ. of Calif., Berkeley 1951–56, Assoc. Prof. 1956–60, Prof. 1960–91, Prof. Emer. 1991–, Prof. of Grad. Studies 1994–; Assoc. Research Prof. Inst. of Basic Research in Science, Univ. of Calif. 1958–59, Research Prof. 1965–66; main area of interest: neural mechanisms of learning and memory formation; main findings: plastic anatomical and neurochemical responses of the nervous system of vertebrates to training and differential experience, specific neurochemical processes required for formation of the successive stages of memory, requirement of protein synthesis in brain for formation of long-term memory; Fellow AAAS, American Psychological Soc., American Psychological Asscn; Charter mem. Int. Brain Research Org., Soc. for Neuroscience; mem. NAS, American Physiological Soc., Société Française de Psychologie; mem. Exec. Cttee, Int. Union of Psychological Science, Vice-Pres. 1980–84, Pres. 1988–92, Past Pres. 1992–96, mem. U.S. Nat. Cttee 1985–96, Chair. 1985–88; mem. Int. Cttee on Social Science Information and Documentation 1972–80 (Pres. 1976–78); mem. Advisory Cttee for Int. Council of Scientific Unions (N.A.S.—N.R.C.) 1985–88; Ed. Annual Review of Psychology 1968–94; Dr hc (Université René Descartes, Sorbonne, Paris) 1980, (Université Louis Pasteur, Strasbourg) 1997; Distinguished Scientific Contrib. Award (American Psychological Asscn) 1982, Award for Distinguished Contributions to Int. Advancement of Psychology (American Psychological Asscn) 1997. *Publications:* Psychology: An introduction (with P. H. Mussen) 1973, Biologie de la Mémoire 1976, Neural mechanisms of learning and memory (Co-Ed. with E. L. Bennett) 1976, Physiological Psychology (with A. L. Leiman) 1982, 1989, Psychophysiology: Memory, motivation and event-related potentials in mental operations (Co-Ed. with R. Sinz) 1983, La recherche en psychologie scientifique (with D. Sinha) 1988, International Psychological Science: Progress, Problems and Prospects 1992, Biological Psychology (with A.L. Leiman and S. M. Breedlove) 1996, 1999, International Handbook of Psychology (Co-Ed.) 2000, History of the International Union of Psychological Science (co-author) 2000, Biological Psychology (with S. M. Breedlove and A. L. Leiman) 2001; book chapters and articles in scientific journals. *Address:* Department

of Psychology, 3210 Tolman Hall, University of California, Berkeley, CA 94720-1650, USA. *Telephone:* (510) 642-5292. *Fax:* (510) 642-5293. *E-mail:* memory@socrates.berkley.edu (Office).

ROSHAL, Leonid Mikhailovich, MD, DSc; Russian paediatrician; b. 27 April 1933, Livnya, Orel Region; s. of Mikhail Filippovich Roshal and Emilia Lazarevna Roshal; m. 1st; one s.; m. 2nd Veda Zuponcic; ed Moscow Medical Inst.; paediatrician and specialist, paediatric surgeon Moscow hosps 1957–61; jr, sr researcher, then sr research paediatric surgeon MONIKI Inst. 1961–81; Chief Urgent Surgery Clinic of Research Inst. of Paediatrics, USSR (now Russian) Acad. of Medical Sciences 1982–; Chair. Int. Task Force Cttee on Paediatric Disaster Medicine; mem. Exec. Cttee World Asscn for Emergency and Disaster Medicine, Exec. Cttee Russian Union of Paediatrics; Pres. Int. Charitable Fund for Children in Disasters and Wars; mem. Bd of Dirs Russian Asscn of Paediatric Surgery, British Asscn of Paediatric Surgeons, Georgian Acad. of Medical Sciences; organized and carried out rescue operations and rendered medical assistance following earthquakes and wars in many countries in Europe, Asia and America; took part in negotiations with terrorists taking hostages in Moscow theatre Sept. 2002, provided medical assistance to hostages and negotiated release of some children; elected Children's Doctor of the World by Moscow Journalists Community 1995; Order of Courage 2002; awarded title of National Hero 2002, Person of the Year (chosen by several Russian periodicals) 2002; numerous other awards. *Publications:* 7 books and more than 200 scientific articles on surgery and problems of children in catastrophes and wars. *Leisure interest:* music. *Address:* Children's Hospital, B. Polyanka str. 20, 103118 Moscow, Russia. *Telephone:* (095) 238-30-00 (Office); (095) 137-87-08 (Home). *Fax:* (095) 230-29-98. *E-mail:* roshal@lamport.ru.

ROSHCHEVSKY, Mikhail Pavlovich; Russian physiologist; b. 5 March 1933; m.; two d.; ed Ural State Univ.; jr, sr researcher, scientific sec. Ural Research Inst. of Agric. 1958–60; sr researcher Inst. of Biology Komi ASSR 1960–70; Deputy Chair. Presidium Scientific Cen. Komi ASSR 1970–83, Chair. 1983–; Dir Inst. of Physiology Komi Scientific Cen. Ural br. USSR Acad. of Sciences 1983–; Corresp. mem. USSR (now Russian) Acad. of Sciences 1987, mem. 1990; studies of ecological-physiological aspects of blood circulation, electrophysiology of heart, electrocardiology; mem. Dept of Physiology Russian Acad. of Sciences. *Publications:* books and scientific works. *Address:* Presidium of Komi Scientific Centre, Kommunisticheskaya str. 24, 167610 Syktyvkar, Komi Republic, Russia. *Telephone:* (82122) 42-16-08 (Office); 42-25-11 (Home).

ROSI, Francesco; Italian film director; b. 1922, Naples; apprenticed as asst to Antonioni and Visconti; Dir first feature, La Sfida (The Challenge) 1958. *Films:* Salvatore Giuliano, Hands Over the City, More than a Miracle, Just Another War, Lucky Luciano, The Mattei Affair, Three Brothers, Chronicle of a Death Foretold, To Forget Palermo.

ROSOMAN, Leonard Henry, OBE, RA, FSA; British artist and teacher; b. 27 Oct. 1913, London; s. of Henry Edward Rosoman and Lillian Blanche Rosoman (née Spencer); m. 1st Jocelyn Rickards 1963 (divorced 1968); m. 2nd Roxanne Wruble Levy 1994; ed Deacons School, Peterborough, Durham Univ., RA Schools and Cen. School of Art and Design, London; taught Reimann School, London 1937–39; Official War Artist to Admiralty 1943–45; taught Camberwell School of Art, London 1946–47; taught Edin. Coll. of Art 1947–56, Chelsea School of Art, London 1956–57, RCA, London 1957–78; freelance artist 1978–; designed and painted vaulted ceiling in Lambeth Palace Chapel, London; exhbns at Rowland Browse & Delbanco and Fine Art Soc., London, Lincoln Center and Touchstone Gallery, New York, State Univ. of New York at Albany, Oldham Art Gallery, David Paul Gallery, Chichester and Royal Acad. of Art; Winston Churchill Fellow 1966–67; Hon. ARCA; Hon. mem. Royal Scottish Soc. of Painters in Water Colours, Royal West of England Acad. *Leisure interests:* travel, bicycling. *Address:* 7 Pembroke Studios, Pembroke Gardens, London, W8 6HX, England. *Telephone:* (20) 7603-3638.

ROSS, André Louis Henry, LenD; French diplomatist; b. 13 March 1922, Calais; s. of René Ross and Yvonne Alexander; m. Thérèse Anne Guéroult 1951; ed Univ. of Paris and Ecole nat. d'admin; First Counsellor, Bangkok 1964–66; Amb. to Laos 1968–72, Zaïre 1972–78, India 1979–83, Japan 1983–85; Sec.-Gen. Ministry of Foreign Affairs 1985–87; Amb. of France 1985; Sr Adviser Indosuez Bank 1987–; mem. Council of French Museums 1988–96; mem. Comm. des archives diplomatiques 1988–; Pres. France-Amérique, Paris 1993–98; Chair. Foundation for Japanese Civilization, Tanaka Foundation 1991–98; Commdr, Légion d'honneur, Ordre nat. du Mérite. *Leisure interests:* the arts, history and mathematics. *Address:* Crédit Agricole Indosuez, 96 boulevard Haussmann, 75371 Paris cedex 08 (Office); 1 rue de Fleurus, 75006 Paris, France (Home). *Telephone:* 1-45 48 55 60.

ROSS, Dennis B., PhD; American diplomatist; ed Univ. of Calif. at Los Angeles; involved in American policy in Middle East since 1986, Dir Near East and S Asian Affairs, Nat. Security Council (during Reagan Admin), Policy Planning Office, State Dept 1988–92, Special Middle East Co-ordinator 1997–2001, helped achieve the 1995 Interim Agreement and brokered the Hebron Accord 1997; Distinguished Fellow and Counsellor, Washington Inst. Near East Policy; now. DHumLitt (Amherst Coll.) 2002. *Address:* Washington Institute for Near East Policy, 1828 L Street, NW, Suite 1050, Washington, DC 20036, USA. *Website:* www.washingtoninstitute.org.

ROSS, Diana; American singer and actress; b. 26 March 1944, Detroit; d. of Fred and Ernestine Ross; m. 1st Robert Ellis Silberstein 1971 (divorced 1976); three d.; m. 2nd Arne Naess 1985; one s.; fmr lead singer Diana Ross and the Supremes; solo singer 1970–; numerous records with Supremes and solo; TV specials; citation from Vice-Pres. Humphrey for efforts on behalf of Pres. Johnson's Youth Opportunity Programme; from Mrs. Martin Luther King and Rev. Abernathy for contrib. to Southern Christian Leadership Conf. cause; Billboard, Cash Box and Record World magazine awards as world's outstanding female singer; Grammy Award 1970; Female Entertainer of the Year, Nat. Asscn for the Advancement of Colored People 1970; Cue Award as Entertainer of the Year 1972; Golden Apple Award 1972; Gold Medal Award, Photoplay 1972; Antoinette Perry Award 1977; Golden Globe Award 1972. *Films include:* Lady Sings the Blues 1972, Mahogany 1975, The Wiz 1978. *Albums include:* I'm Still Waiting 1971, Touch Me In The Morning 1973, Why Do Fools Fall in Love? 1981, Eaten Alive 1984, Chain Reaction 1986, Workin' Overtime 1989, Surrender 1989, Ain't No Mountain High Enough 1989, The Forces Behind the Power 1991, The Remixes 1994, Take me Higher 1995, Gift of Love 1996, The Real Thing 1998, Every Day is a New Day 1999. *Publication:* Secrets of a Sparrow (autobiog.) 1993. *Address:* c/o Motown Records, Suite 825, 8th Avenue, New York 10019, U.S.A. (Office).

ROSS, Rt Hon Lord Donald MacArthur, PC, MA, LLB, FRSE; British judge (retd); b. 29 March 1927, Dundee; s. of John Ross and Jessie MacArthur Thomson; m. Dorothy M. Annand 1958; two d.; ed High School of Dundee and Univ. of Edin.; nat. service with Black Watch 1947–49; TA rank of Capt. 1949–58; Advocate 1952; QC (Scotland) 1964; Vice-Dean, Faculty of Advocates 1967–73, Dean 1973–76; Sheriff Prin. of Ayr and Bute 1972–73; Senator, Coll. of Justice, Scotland and Lord of Session 1977–97; Lord Justice Clerk of Scotland and Pres. of Second Div. of the Court of Session 1985–97; Chair. Judicial Studies Cttee for Scotland 1997–2001; mem. Parole Bd for Scotland 1997–2002; Deputy Chair. Boundary Comm. for Scotland 1977–85; mem. Scottish Cttee of Council on Tribunals 1970–76, Cttee on Privacy 1970; mem. Court of Heriot Watt Univ. 1978–90 (Chair. 1984–90); mem. Council Royal Soc. of Edin. 1997–99, Vice-Pres. 1999–2002; Lord High Commr to Gen. Ass. of Church of Scotland 1990, 1991; Hon. LLD (Edin.) 1987, (Dundee) 1991, (Abertay, Dundee) 1994, (Aberdeen) 1998; Hon. DUniv (Heriot Watt) 1988. *Publication:* contrib. to Stair Memorial Encyclopaedia of Scots Law. *Leisure interests:* gardening, walking, travelling. *Address:* 33 Lauder Road, Edinburgh, EH9 2JG, Scotland. *Telephone:* (131) 667-5731. *Fax:* (131) 667-7296. *E-mail:* rosd33@aol.com (Home).

ROSS, Ian Gordon, AO, MSc, PhD, FAA; Australian professor of chemistry; b. 5 July 1926, Sydney; s. of Gordon R. Ross and Isabella M. Jenkins; m. Viola Bartlett 1975; ed Univs. of Sydney and London; Research Assoc., Fla State Univ. 1953; Lecturer, then Reader in Physical Chem., Univ. of Sydney 1954–67, Prof. of Chem. 1968–90; Pro-Vice-Chancellor Australian Nat. Univ. 1975, 1989–90, Deputy Vice-Chancellor 1977–88; Chair. Australian Research Grants Cttee 1977–79, Inquiry into Govt Labs. 1982–83, Australian & New Zealand Asscn for the Advancement of Science 1984–86, Communication Research Inst. of Australia 1994–; Sec. for Science Policy, Australian Acad. of Science 1989–93; Dir Anutech Pty Ltd 1979–97; Hon. LLD; H. G. Smith Medal, Royal Australian Chem. Inst. 1972. *Publications:* scientific papers on theoretical chemistry and molecular spectroscopy. *Address:* 3 Highland Close, Queanbeyan, NSW 2620, Australia. *Telephone:* (2) 6297-3510. *Fax:* (2) 6299-6324.

ROSS, James Hood, BA; British business executive; b. 13 Sept. 1938, London; s. of Capt. T. D. Ross RN and Lettice Ferrier Hood; m. Sara B. V. Purcell 1964; one s. two d.; ed Sherborne School, Jesus Coll. Oxford and Manchester Business School; British Petroleum Co. PLC 1959–92, Gen. Man. BP Zaïre, Burundi and Rwanda, Gen. Man. BP Tanker Co., Gen. Man. Stolt-Nielsen (USA), Gen. Man. Corp. Planning BP, Chief Exec. BP Oil Int., Chair. and Chief Exec. BP America; Chief Exec. Cable & Wireless PLC 1992–95; Chair. Littlewoods Org. 1996–2002, Nat. Grid Group PLC 1999–; Dir (non-exec.) McGraw Hill Inc. 1988–, Schneider Electric 1996, Datacard Inc. 1997–; Trustee, The Cleveland Orchestra 1988–. *Leisure interests:* music, gardening, sailing. *Address:* 15 Marylebone Road, London, NW1 5JD, England. *Telephone:* (20) 7312-5721.

ROSS GOOBEY, Alastair, CBE, MA; British business executive; b. 6 Dec. 1945; s. of George Henry Ross Goobey and Gladys Edith Menzies; m. Sarah Georgina Mary Stille; one s. one d.; ed Marlborough Coll., Trinity Coll. Cambridge; with Kleinwort Benson 1968–72; with Hume Holdings Ltd 1972–77; Investment Man. Pension Fund, Courtaulds Ltd 1977–81; Dir Geoffrey Morley & Partners Ltd 1981–85; Special Adviser to Chancellor of Exchequer, HM Treasury 1986–87, 1991–92; Chief Investment Strategist, James Capel & Co. 1987–93; Chief Exec., Hermes Pensions Man. Ltd 1993–2001, Chair. Hermes Focus Asset Man. Ltd 2001–; Pres. Investment Property Forum 1995–; Chair. HM Treasury Pvt. Finance Panel 1996–97; Dir Scottish Life 1978–86, Cheltenham and Gloucester PLC 1989–91, 1992–97, TR Property Investment Trust PLC 1994–, John Wainwright & Co. Ltd 1994– (Chair. 1997–); mem. Pensions Law Review Cttee (Goode Cttee) 1992–93; nominated mem. Council of Lloyd's 1997–; Liveryman Gold and Silver Wyre Drawers' Co.; Charter Soc. Property Award 1999. *Radio:* panellist in series The Board Game, BBC Radio 4. *Publications:* The Money Moguls 1987, Bricks and Mortals 1992, Kluwer Handbook on Pensions (Jt Ed.) 1988. *Leisure interests:* music, cricket, writing, broadcasting. *Address:* Lloyds Chambers, 1

Portsoken Street, London, E1 8HZ, England (Office). *Telephone:* (20) 7702-0888 (Office). *Fax:* (20) 7702-9452 (Office). *E-mail:* a.ross.goobey@hermes.co.uk (Office). *Website:* www.hermes.co.uk (Office).

ROSSANT, Janet, PhD, FRS, FRSC; British/Canadian geneticist; b. 13 July 1950, Chatham; d. of Leslie Rossant and Doris Rossant; m. Alex Bain 1977; one s. one d.; ed St Hugh Coll., Oxford Univ., Darwin Coll., Cambridge Univ.; research fellow in Zoology, Oxford Univ. 1975–77; Asst Prof. of Biological Sciences, Brock Univ. 1977–81, Assoc. Prof. 1981–85; Assoc. Prof. of Molecular and Medical Genetics, Univ. of Toronto 1985–88, Prof. 1988–, Univ. Prof. 2001–, Sr Scientist Programme in Devt and Foetal Health, Samuel Lunenfeld Research Inst. 1985–, Co-Head 1998–; Pres. Soc. for Developmental Biology; mem. American and Canadian Socs. for Cell Biology; Gibb's Prize for Zoology, Oxford 1972, Beit Memorial Fellowship 1975, E. W. R. Steacie Memorial Fellowship 1983, Howard Hughes Int. Scholar 1991, MRC Distinguished Scientist 1996, McLaughlin Medal (Royal Soc. of Canada) 1998, NCIC/Eli Lilly Robert L. Noble Prize 2000. *Publications:* Experimental Approaches to Mammalian Embryonic Development (with R. A. Pedersen) 1986, Mouse Development (with P. P. L. Tam) 2001; over 200 articles in scientific journals. *Leisure interests:* running, cooking, theatre. *Address:* Samuel Lunenfeld Research Institute, Mount Sinai Hospital, 600 University Avenue, Room 884, Toronto, Ont., M5G 1X5, Canada (Office). *Telephone:* (416) 586-8267 (Office). *E-mail:* rossant@mshri.on.ca (Office).

ROSSEL, Eduard Ergartovich, CAND.TECH.SC; Russian politician; b. 8 Oct. 1937, Bor, Gorki region; m.; one d.; ed Sverdlovsk Ore Inst.; master construction site, head of construction trust Sreduralstroi; supervised construction of Krasnouralsk superphosphate factory, Nevyansk cement factory, Nizhny Tagil metallurgy plant; head Sverdlovsk regional exec. cttee, then Gov. Sverdlovsk Region 1991–93, tried to proclaim Ural Repub., discharged by Pres. Yeltsin, re-elected Head of Admin. and Gov. Sverdlovsk Region 1995–; mem. Russian Council of Fed. 1993–94, 1995–2001; Chair. Sverdlovsk regional Duma 1994–95; founder and Chair. Org. Preobrazhenie Otechestva; Pres. Asscn for Econ. Co-operation of Ural Region 1995–; mem. Bd Union of Russian Govs 1996; mem. Int. Acad. of Regional Devt and Co-operation; Order 'Decoration of Honour' 1975, 1980, Order for Achievement to Fatherland Fourth Degree 1996, Third Degree 2000; Lenin Centenary Anniversary Medal 'For Valiant Labour' 1970, Honoured Constructor of Russian Soviet Federal Socialist Repub. 1983. *Address:* Governor's Office, Oktyabrskaya pl. 1, 620031 Yekaterinburg, Russia. *Telephone:* (343) 70-54-68; (343) 70-54-73. *Fax:* (343) 70-54-72. *E-mail:* so@midural.ru (Office).

ROSSELLINI, Isabella; American actress and model; b. 18 June 1952, Rome; d. of Roberto Rossellini and Ingrid Bergman; m. 1st Martin Scorsese (q.v.) 1979 (divorced 1982); m. 2nd Jonathan Wiedemann (divorced); one d.; ed Acad. of Fashion and Costume, Rome; and New School for Social Research, New York; worked briefly as costume designer for father's films; went to New York 1972; worked as journalist for Italian TV; cover-girl for Vogue 1980; contract to model Lancôme cosmetics 1982–95; Vice-Pres. Lancaster Cosmetics GPs Marketing Dept 1995–. *Films include:* A Matter of Time 1976, White Nights 1985, Blue Velvet 1986, Tough Guys Don't Dance 1987, Siesta 1987, Zelly and Me, Cousins 1989, Wild at Heart 1990, The Siege of Venice 1991, Death Becomes Her, The Pickle, The Innocent, Fearless 1994, Wyatt Earp 1994, Immortal Beloved 1994, The Innocent 1995, The Funeral 1996, Big Night 1996, Crime of the Century 1996, Left Luggage 1998, The Imposters, The Real Blonde 1998, Don Quixote 2000.

ROSSELLÓ, Hon. Pedro, BS, MD, MPH; American politician and surgeon; b. 5 April 1944, San Juan, Puerto Rico; m. Irma Margarita Nevares; three s.; ed Notre Dame Univ., Yale Univ., Harvard Univ., Univ. of Puerto Rico; fmr paediatric surgeon, Prof. of Medicine; Dir of Health, City of San Juan 1985–87; cand. elections to Congress 1988; Chair. New Progressive Party 1991–99; Gov. of Puerto Rico 1993–2001; Pres. Council of State Govts 1998; Chair. Democratic Govs' Asscn, Southern Govs' Asscn 1998–2001, Southern Int. Trade Council 1998–99, Southern Tech. Council 1998–99, Southern Growth Policies Bd 1999–2000; mem. Advisory Council Welfare to Work Partnership, USA, Democratic Nat. Cttee, Nat. Advisory Bd of Initiative and Referendum Inst., Bd of Dirs US–Spain Council and other bodies; five times men's singles tennis champion, Puerto Rico; Hon. LLD (Notre Dame) 1995, (Mass.) 1995; Pres.'s Award, US Hispanic Chamber of Commerce 1996, LULAC 1998, Rolex Achievement Award 1999. *Address:* c/o Office of the Governor, La Fortaleza, San Juan, 00901, Puerto Rico.

ROSSI, Guido, LLM; Italian business executive and professor of law; b. 16 March 1931, Milan; ed Univ. of Pavia and Harvard Law School; fmr Prof. of Commercial Law, Univs. of Trieste, Venice and Pavia; fmr Prof. of Law, State Univ. of Milan; Chair. CONSOB (Italian cos. and stock exchange regulatory body) 1981–82; Senator, Repub. of Italy (tenth legislature); Chair. Montedison SpA, Milan 1993–95, Ferruzzi Finanziaria SpA 1993; Dir Eridiana Beghin-Say 1993–. *Publications include:* Trasparenza e Vergogna, La Società e La Borsa 1982, La Scalata del mercato 1986; several other books and numerous studies on subjects of corp. enterprises, the securities market and anti-trust legislation.

ROSSI, José Lucien André, DenD; French politician and lawyer; b. 18 June 1944, Ajaccio, Corsica; s. of Pierre Rossi and Emilie Leca; m. Denise Ferri 1968; two d.; ed Ecoles Sainte-Lucie and Castelvecchio, Lycée Fesch, Ajaccio, Faculté de Droit and Inst. d'Etudes Politiques, Paris; Asst Faculté de Droit, Paris 1969–73; served in pvt. office of Minister of Labour 1972, Minister of

Educ. 1972–74; Press Officer to Minister of Health 1974–75; Parl. Relations Officer to Minister of Labour 1975–78, to Minister of Educ. 1978; pvt. office of Pres. of Senate 1981–82; mem. Conseil Général, Corsica 1973–, Pres. 1985–98; Conseiller Régional, Corsica 1975–85; Deputy Mayor of Ajaccio 1983–90, 1995–; Pres. Corsica Tourism and Leisure Agency 1983–84; Pres. Regional Information Centre 1979–85; Deputy to Nat. Ass. 1988–94; Sec.-Gen. Parti Républicain 1989–91; Mayor of Grosseto-Prugna 1990–95; Vice-Pres. Union pour la Démocratie Française (UDF) group in Nat. Ass. 1993–94; Minister of Industry, Posts and Telecommunications and Foreign Trade 1994–95; Deputy to Nat. Ass. 1995–; Deputy Sec.-Gen. U.D.F. 1996–97; Titular Judge Higher Court of Justice 1997–; Pres. Démocratie Liberale Group, Nat. Ass. 1998–2000, Assemblée de Corse 1998–, Vice-Pres. Démocratie Libérale 2000–. *Publication:* Les Maires de grandes villes en France 1972. *Address:* Assemblée Nationale, 75355 Paris (Office); Assemblée de Corse, 22 cours Grandval, BP 277, 20187 Ajaccio cedex (Office); 461 boulevard Rive Sud, 20166 Porticcio, France (Home).

ROSSIER, William; Swiss economist and international organization official; b. 1942; ed Univ. of Lausanne; joined Foreign Econ. Service 1970; Head Secr., Conf. on Security and Co-operation in Europe, Geneva 1972–73; Deputy Head Div. for Gen. Foreign Econ. Questions, Berne 1973–76; Counsellor, Mission to the EC, Brussels 1976–80; with Fed. Office for External Econ. Affairs 1981–88, apptd. Head Div. in charge of Relations with Countries of Eastern Europe and the People's Repub. of China 1981, later Head Div. in Charge of Relations with Western Europe; fmrly involved in negotiations with GATT, OECD, UNCTAD; fmr Chair. EFTA, ECE, UNCTAD Trade and Devt Bd; Chair. World Trade Org. Gen. Council 1996; Perm. Rep. to EFTA, Sec.-Gen. 2000–. *Address:* European Free Trade Association, 74 rue de Trèves, 1040 Brussels, Belgium (Office). *Telephone:* (2) 286-17-11 (Office). *Fax:* (2) 286-17-50 (Office). *E-mail:* eftamailbox@secrbru.efta.be (Office). *Website:* www.efta.int (Office).

ROSSIN, Lawrence G., BA; American diplomatist; m. Debra J. McGowan; one s. one d.; ed Claremont Men's Coll., California, NATO Defence Coll., Rome, Massachusetts Inst. of Tech.; fmr Dir, Chief of Mission Authority and Overseas Staffing State Dept; fmr Counsellor for Political Affairs, The Hague and Port-au-Prince; fmr Peru Desk Officer; fmr Staff Asst to Secs of State for Inter-American Affairs; Dir Inter-American Affairs, Nat. Security Council 1993–94; Deputy Chief of Mission, Spain 1995–98; Dir Office S. Cen. European Affairs, Dept of State, led dels. to Rambouillet and Paris confs on Kosovo 1999, directed govt outreach to Kosovo Liberation Army (KLA); first Chief of Mission, Kosovo, opened and headed American Office, Pristina 1999–2000, responsible for all policy initiatives and collaboration with UN Interim Admin. in Kosovo and NATO Kosovo Force; Amb. to Croatia 2001–; State Dept Award for Valour, three Superior Hon. Awards, Meritorious Hon. Award. *Address:* American Embassy, 10000 Zagreb, Andrije Hebranga 2, Croatia (Office). *Telephone:* (1) 4555500 (Office). *Fax:* (1) 558585 (Office). *Website:* www.usembassy.hr (Office).

ROSSINOT, André, DenM; French politician and doctor; b. 22 May 1939, Briey, Meurthe-et-Moselle; s. of Lucien Rossinot and Jeanne Fondeur; m. 3rd Françoise Cordelier 1985; one s. one d.; three c. from previous marriages; ed Lycée Poincaré and Faculty of Medicine, Nancy; ear, nose and throat specialist in pvt. practice; Town Councillor, Nancy 1969–71; Mayor of Nancy 1983–; Vice-Pres. Greater Nancy Urban Council 1996–2001, Pres. 2001–; Deputy to Nat. Ass. (UDF) 1978–86, 1988–93, 1995–97; Pres. Parti Radical 1983–88, 1994–97, Hon. Pres. 1997–; Minister for Relations with Parliament 1986–88, of Civil Service 1993–95; Vice-Pres. Nat. Ass. 1988–89; Pres. Conf. Permanente des caisses de crédit municipal 1987–93; Nat. Vice-Pres. UDF 1983–90, 1994–; mem. Political Bureau Union pour la France 1990–, UDF 1991–2000; Vice-Pres. Asscn des Eco Maires 1990–; Pres. Nouveau Contrat Social 1992–, TGV 1994–99, Fed. nat. des agences d'urbanisme 1995–, Inst. nat. du génie urbain 1996–98 and founder Agence des villes 1998–, Asscn Seine-Moselle-Rhône 1999–; Sec-Gen. l'Association des maires des grandes villes de France (AMGVF) 2001–; Chevalier Légion d'honneur, Commdr. Order of Merit (Germany). *Publications include:* Stanislas, Le Roi philosophe 1999. *Leisure interests:* walking, tennis, fishing. *Address:* Hôtel de Ville, place Stanislas, 54000 Nancy, France. *Telephone:* (3) 83-85-30-00 (Office). *Fax:* (3) 83-32-90-96 (Office). *E-mail:* arossinot@mairie-nancy.fr (Office). *Website:* www.mairie-nancy.fr (Office).

ROST, Andrea; Hungarian operatic soprano; b. 1962, Budapest; d. of Ferenc Rost and Erzsébet Privoda; m. Miklós Harazdy 1985 (divorced); one s. one d.; ed Ferenc Liszt Acad. of Music, Budapest; operatic début, Budapest 1989; First Prize, Helsinki Competition 1989; La Scala début as Gilda in Rigoletto 1994; début, Metropolitan Opera, New York as Adina 1996; took part in Superconcert with José Carreras and Plácido Domingo, Budapest 1996; appeared as Elisabeth in Donizetti's opera, London 1997; début, Tokyo Opera, as Violetta 1998; took part in concert in memory of Lehár with José Carreras and Plácido Domingo, Bad Ischl, Austria 1998; has also appeared at Staatsoper, Vienna, Salzburg Festival, Opéra Bastille, Paris, Royal Opera House, Covent Garden and Chicago Opera; Ferenc Liszt Artistic Merit of Honour 1997, Nat. Artistic Merit of Honour 1999. *Address:* Budaörs, Nefelejes u. 27, 2040 Hungary. *Fax:* (23) 416-583 (Home). *E-mail:* arost@elender.hu (Home).

ROST, Yuri Mikhailovich; Russian photographer; b. 1 Feb. 1939, Kiev, Ukraine; s. of Arkadyevich Rost and Georgiyevna Rost; m. (divorced); columnist Komsomolskaya Pravda (newspaper) 1966–79; reviewer Literaturnaya Gazeta (newspaper) 1979–94; author TV programme Stables of Rost 1994–97; reviewer Obshchaya Gazeta (newspaper) 1993–; Prizes of Acad. of Free Press 1998, 1999; Tsarskoye Selo Artistic Prize 1999; Gilyarovsky Medal 1990; Triumph Prize. *Art exhibitions:* Strasbourg, Colmar, Prague, Tallinn, Tbilisi, Samara, Moscow. *Publications include:* People 1980, 10 Short Stories about Leningrad 1976, Everest 1983, My View 1988, Armenian Tragedy 1990; Birds (jtly); numerous essays. *Leisure interest:* collecting smoking pipes. *Address:* Makarenko str. 1/19, Apt. 21, 103062 Moscow, Russia (Home).

ROSTROPOVICH, Mstislav Leopoldovich; Russian cellist, conductor and pianist; b. 27 March 1927, Baku, Azerbaijan; s. of Leopold Rostropovich and Sofia Fedotova; m. Galina Vishnevskaya (q.v.) 1955; two d.; ed Moscow Conservatoire; cello début (USSR) 1940; numerous concert tours in USSR and abroad as soloist and cellist in trio with Emil Gilels and Leonid Kogan and later with David Oistrakh and Sviatoslav Richter and as pianist with Galina Vishnevskaya; début in USA as cellist 1955, as conductor 1975; Music Dir Nat. Symphony Orchestra (Washington, DC) 1977–94; Conductor Laureate 1991–; expelled from Soviet Union 1974, deprived of Soviet citizenship 1978, citizenship restored 1990; Joint Artistic Dir Aldeburgh Festival (UK) 1977–; Founder and Pres. Rencontres Musicales d'Evian festival (France); mem. Union of Soviet Composers 1950–78, 1989–; Prof. Moscow and Leningrad Conservatoires 1960–78; among composers who have written works for him are Prokofiev, Shostakovich, Miaskovsky, Khachaturian, Kabalevsky, Britten, Piston, Shchedrin, Schnittke, Bernstein, Penderecki; f. Int. Competition for Young Cellists; Hon. mem. Acad. of St Cecilia (Rome), Guildhall School of Music and Drama 1991, AAAS; Hon. FRAM; Commdr, Ordre des Arts et des Lettres, Légion d'honneur; Hon. KBE 1987; Hon. DMus (Oxford) 1980; hon. degrees (including Humanities, Law, Letters, Music) from over 20 univs; First Prize at All-Union Competition of Musicians 1945, Int. 'Cellist Competitions, Prague 1947, 1950, Budapest 1949, USSR State Prize 1951, People's Artist of the USSR, Lenin Prize 1964, Gold Medal, Royal Philharmonic Soc. (UK), Siemens Prize (FRG), Sonning Prize (Denmark), Albert Schweitzer Music Award 1985, Presidential Medal of Freedom 1987, Four Freedoms Award 1992, Kennedy Center Honor 1992, Freedom of Speech and Expression Award (Franklin Delano Roosevelt) 1992, Imperial Award 1993. *Address:* c/o National Symphony Orchestra, John F. Kennedy Center for the Performing Arts, Washington, DC 20566, USA; Gazetny per. 13, Apt. 79, 103009 Moscow, Russia. *Telephone:* (095) 229-04-96 (Moscow) (Home); 1-45-53-69-16 (Paris) (Home); (202) 785-8100 (USA).

RØSTVIG, Maren-Sofie, PhD; Norwegian professor of English literature; b. 27 March 1920, Melbo; d. of Olaf Røstvig and Sigrid Røstvig; ed Univ. of Oslo and Univ. of Calif. Los Angeles; imprisoned by Nazi regime 1943, subsequently released; joined Resistance Movt and published underground newspaper until end of World War II 1944–45; Reader in English Literature, Univ. of Oslo 1955–67, Prof. 1968–87, Sr Research Fellow 1988, retd 1990; mem. Norwegian Acad. of Science and Letters; Mil. Medal of Participation in World War II. *Publications:* The Happy Man. Studies in the Metamorphoses of a Classical Ideal 1600–1760 (two Vols) 1954–58, The Hidden Sense and Other Essays 1963, Fair Forms 1975, Configurations. A Topomorphical Approach to Renaissance Poetry 1994; contribs. to learned journals and collections of scholarly essays on English literature. *Address:* 14 Urb. Rosa de Piedras, Carretera de Coín, 29650 Mijas, Málaga, Spain. *Telephone:* (95) 2486938. *Fax:* (95) 2485125 (Home).

ROTAS, Nikiphoros Giorgos; Greek composer; b. 14 May 1929, Athens; s. of Vasilis Rotas and Katherini Giannakopoulos; m. Maria Paschalis 1956; one s. two d.; ed Theatriko Spoudastirio drama school, Conservatory of Athens and Music Acad. of Vienna; took part in nat. resistance against German Occupation 1941–44; since 1962 composer, teacher of music, lecturer, broadcaster and dir of music educ. in professional dance schools; mem. Greek Composers' Asscn, Greek Play Writers' and Composers' Asscn, Theatre Museum; award for The Song of the Creation, Vienna 1960, Abgangspreiz (Music Acad. of Vienna) 1961. *Compositions:* 80 works for all kinds of instrumental and/or vocal ensembles, including Acolouthia (for symphonic orchestra) 1959, String quartet No. 1 1959, Six piano preludes 1959, Orchesis (oratorio) 1962, Agamemnon (ballet) text by Aeschylus 1967, Odyssey (for baritone narrator, men's choir and symphonic orchestra) text by Homer 1979, Concerto for trumpet and orchestra 1981, Violin sonata 1981, Sonata for violin and piano No. 1 1986, No. 2 1994, Exodus (for seven instruments) 1987, Electra (for narrator and symphonic orchestra) 1988, Cello sonata 1989, duo for contrabass and piano 1990, Concerto for nine wind instruments 1994; electronic music: Antiphonia I 1967, Big Antiphonia 1973, Antiphonia III 1973; also about 40 works for theatre and music for cinema and TV. *Radio includes:* six series on music and musical instruments 1967–94: The Musical Instruments, Music, Works of Music, How We Listen to Music, Memories from the Future of Music (on music and civilization), Radio-Rays (on the music praxis of today). *Publications:* How We Listen to Music 1986, And the Music, Where Is It? 1994; articles in newspapers. *Address:* 15 Astydamantos Street, Athens 116 34, Greece (Home). *Telephone:* 7708322 (Office); 7211730 (Home). *E-mail:* rotas_ni@otenet.gr (Office). *Website:* users.otenet.gr/~rotas_ni (Office).

ROTBLAT, Sir Joseph, KCMG, CBE, MA, DSc, PhD, FInstP, FRS; British (b. Polish) physicist; b. 4 Nov. 1908, Warsaw; s. of the late Z. Rotblat; ed Univ. of Warsaw; Research Fellow, Radiological Lab. of Scientific Soc. of Warsaw 1933–39; Asst Dir of Atomic Physics, Inst. of Free Univ. of Poland 1937–39; Oliver Lodge Fellow, Univ. of Liverpool 1939–40, Lecturer, later Sr Lecturer,

Dept of Physics 1940–49, Dir of Research in Nuclear Physics 1945–49; Prof. of Physics, Univ. of London, at St Bartholomew's Hosp. Medical Coll. 1950–76, Emer. 1976–; Sec.-Gen. Pugwash Confs 1957–73, Pres. 1988–97; mem. WHO Man. Group; Ed. Physics in Medicine and Biology; Pres. Hosp. Physicists' Asscn, British Inst. of Radiology; Pres. Int. Youth Science Fortnight; mem. Polish Acad. of Sciences; Foreign mem. American Acad. of Arts and Sciences; Foreign mem. Czechoslovak Acad. of Sciences; Hon. Fellow UMIST, Queen Mary and Westfield Coll. 1996, Royal Soc. of Edin. 1998; Hon. DSc (Bradford) 1973, (Liverpool) 1989, (City Univ.) 1996, (Slovak Acad. of Sciences) 1996, (Univ. Coll. London) 2001; Dr hc (Univ. of Moscow); Bertrand Russell Soc. Award 1983, Albert Einstein Peace Prize 1992, Nobel Peace Prize 1995, Jamnalal Bajaj Peace Award 1999, Toda Peace Prize 2000; Order of Merit (Poland); Kt Commdr Order of Merit (Fed. Repub. of Germany); Copernicus Medal of Polish Acad. of Sciences 1996; Hon. Freeman, London Borough of Camden 1997. *Publications*: Atomic Energy, a Survey 1954, Atoms and the Universe 1956, Science and World Affairs 1962, Aspects of Medical Physics 1966, Pugwash 1967, Scientists in the Quest for Peace 1972, Nuclear Reactors: To Breed or Not to Breed? 1977, Nuclear Energy and Nuclear Weapon Proliferation 1979, Nuclear Radiation in Warfare 1981, Scientists, the Arms Race and Disarmament 1982, The Arms Race at a Time of Decision 1984, Nuclear Strategy and World Security 1985, World Peace and the Developing Countries 1986, Strategic Defence and the Future of the Arms Race 1987, Coexistence, Co-operation and Common Security 1988, Verification of Arms Reductions 1989, Global Problems and Common Security 1989, Nuclear Proliferation: Technical and Economic Aspects 1990, Building Global Security through Co-operation 1990, Towards a Secure World in the 21st Century 1991, Striving for Peace, Security and Development in the World 1992, A Nuclear-Weapon-Free World: Desirable? Feasible? 1993, A World at the Crossroads 1994, World Citizenship: Allegiance to Humanity 1996, Nuclear Weapons: The Road to Zero 1998. *Leisure interests*: travel, music. *Address*: 8 Asmara Road, London, NW2 3ST, England. *Telephone*: (20) 7435-1471.

ROTH, Daryl; American theatre producer; m. Steven Roth; ed New York Univ.; began career as interior designer; f. Daryl Roth Theater 1996; Bd mem. Lincoln Center Theater 1992–, Vineyard Theater 1994–. *Plays produced include*: Nick and Nora 1991, Twilight: Los Angeles 1992 1993, Three Tall Women 1994 (Pulitzer Prize), How I Learned to Drive 1998 (Pulitzer Prize), Wit 1999 (Pulitzer Prize), Snakebit, Villa Villa.

ROTH, Joe; American film executive and producer; b. 1948; fmrly production asst various commercials and films; fmrly lighting dir Pitched Players, also producer; co-f. Morgan Creek Productions 1987–89; Chair. Twentieth Century Fox Film Corpn 1989–92; f. Caravan Pictures 1992–94; Chair. Walt Disney Motion Pictures Group 1994–97, Walt Disney Studios, Burbank 1997–2000; f. Revolution Pictures 2000–; mem. Bd Dirs. Pixar Studios 2000–. *Films produced include*: Tunnelvision, Cracking Up, Americathon, Our Winning Season, The Final Terror, The Stone Boy, Where the River Runs Black, Bachelor Party, Off Beat, Streets of Gold (also Dir), Revenge of the Nerds (also Dir), Young Guns, Dead Ringers, Skin Deep, Major League, Renegades, Coupe de Ville (also Dir), Enemies: A Love Story; films for Caravan Pictures include Walt Disney's The Three Musketeers, Angie, Angels in the Outfield, I Love Trouble, A Low Down Dirty Shame, Houseguest, The Jerky Boys, Heavyweights, Tall Tale, While You Were Sleeping. *Address*: c/o Walt Disney Studio, 500 South Buena Vista Street, Room 606, Burbank, CA 91521, USA.

ROTH, John, MEng; Canadian communications executive; b. 6 Oct. 1942, Alberta; s. of Henry Roth and Sophia Brix; m. Margaret Anne Roth 1968; ed McGill Univ., Montreal; with RCA 1964–69; joined Nortel 1969, Head Wireless Div. 1991–93, Pres. Nortel N. America 1993–95, Group COO 1995–97, Chief Exec. 1997–2001. *Leisure interest*: making stained-glass windows. *Address*: Nortel Networks Corporation, 8200 Dixie Road, Suite 100, Brampton, Ont., L6T 5P6, Canada (Office).

ROTH, Klaus Friedrich, PhD, FRS; British mathematician; b. 29 Oct. 1925, Breslau, Germany; s. of the late Dr Franz Roth and Mathilde Roth (née Liebrecht); m. Dr Melek Khairy 1955 (died 2002); ed St Paul's School, London, Peterhouse, Cambridge and Univ. Coll., London; Asst Master Gordonstoun School 1945–46; postgraduate student Univ. Coll., London 1946–48; mem. Mathematics Dept Univ. Coll., London 1948–66 (title of Prof. in Univ. of London conferred 1961); Prof. of Pure Mathematics (Theory of Numbers), Imperial Coll., London 1966–88, Visiting Prof. 1988–96, Hon. Research Fellow Dept of Math., Univ. Coll., London 1996–; Visiting Lecturer, MIT 1956–57, Visiting Prof. 1965–66; Fellow Univ. Coll. London 1979, Imperial Coll. 1999; Foreign Hon. mem. AAAS 1966; Hon. Fellow Peterhouse, Cambridge 1989; Hon. FRSE 1993; Fields Medal (Int. Math. Union) 1958, De Morgan Medal (London Math. Soc.) 1983, Sylvester Medal (Royal Soc.) 1991. *Publications*: papers in journals of learned socs. *Leisure interests*: chess, cinema, ballroom dancing. *Address*: Colbost, 16A Drummond Road, Inverness IV2 4NB, Scotland (Home). *Telephone*: (1463) 712595.

ROTH, Sir Martin, Kt, MD, FRCP, FRCPsych, FRS; British psychiatrist; b. 6 Nov. 1917, Budapest, Hungary; s. of late Samuel Simon Roth and Regina Roth; m. Constance Heller 1945; three d.; ed Davenant Foundation School, St Mary's Hosp. Medical School, London and McGill Univ.; Dir of Clinical Research, Graylingwell Hosp. 1950–55; Visiting Asst Prof. McGill Univ. 1954; Prof. of Psychological Medicine, Univ. of Newcastle-upon-Tyne (fmrly

Durham Univ.) 1956–77; Prof. of Psychiatry, Univ. of Cambridge 1977–85, Prof. Emer. 1985–; Fellow Trinity Coll., Cambridge 1977–; Hon. Physician Royal Victoria Infirmary, Newcastle-upon-Tyne 1956–77; mem. Medical Research Council 1964–70, Chair. Grants Cttee 1968–70; Co-Ed. British Journal of Psychiatry 1968, Psychiatric Devts 1983–89; mem. Cen. Health Services Council, Standing Medical Advisory Cttee, Dept of Health and Social Security 1968–75; Visiting Prof. Swedish univs 1967; Mayne Guest Prof. Univ. of Queensland 1968; Visiting Prof. Univ. of Iowa 1976, Univ. of Indianapolis 1976; Pres. Section of Psychiatry, Royal Soc. of Medicine 1968–69; First Pres. Royal Coll. of Psychiatrists 1971–75; Corresp. mem. Deutsche Gesellschaft für Psychiatrie und Nervenheilkunde 1970; Adolf Meyer Lecturer, American Psychiatric Asscn 1971; Distinguished Fellow American Psychiatric Asscn 1972, Linacre Lecturer St John's Coll. Cambridge 1984; Hon. mem. Soc. Royale de Médecine Mentale de Belgique 1970, Canadian Psychiatric Asscn 1972; Hon. Fellow Australian and New Zealand Coll. of Psychiatrists 1974, Royal Coll. of Psychiatrists 1975, Alpha Omega Alpha Soc. 1998; Hon. ScD (Dublin) 1977; Hon. DSc (Indiana) 1993; Anna Monika Award 1977, Paul Hoch Award 1979, Gold Medal, Soc. of Biological Psychiatry 1980, Golden Florin, City of Venice 1979, Kesten Award (Univ. of S. Calif.) 1983, Sandoz Prize, Int. Gerontological Asscn 1985, Kraepelin Medal 1985, Max-Planck Inst., Munich, Salmon Medal, NY Acad. of Medicine 1988, Gold Medal, Int. Alzheimer's Soc. 1992, Camillo Golgi Award in Neuroscience, Italian Acad. of Neuroscience 1993, Lifetime Achievement Award, Soc. of Biological Psychiatry 1996. *Publications*: Clinical Psychiatry (with W.Mayer-Gross and Eliot Slater) 1954, Clinical Psychiatry (with E.Slater) 1977; Ed.: Psychiatry, Genetics and Pathography: A Tribute to Eliot Slater 1979, Psychiatry, Human Rights and the Law 1985, Alzheimer's Disease and Related Disorders (with Iversen), Reality of Mental Illness (with J. Kroll), CAMDEX-Cambridge Examination for Mental Disorders of the Elderly (with Mountjoy, Huppert and Tym) 1988, Handbook of Anxiety Vols I–V (Jt ed.) 1992. *Leisure interests*: literature, music, swimming. *Address*: Trinity College, Cambridge, CB2 1TQ, England. *Telephone*: (1223) 338400.

ROTH, Philip, MA; American writer; b. 19 March 1933, Newark, NJ; s. of Bess Finkel Roth and the late Herman Roth; m. 1st Margaret Martinson 1959 (died 1968); m. 2nd Claire Bloom 1990 (divorced 1994); ed Bucknell Univ. and Univ. of Chicago; in US Army 1955–56; Lecturer in English, Univ. of Chicago 1956–58; Visiting Lecturer, Univ. of Iowa Writers' Workshop 1960–62; Writer-in-Residence, Princeton Univ. 1962–64, Univ. of Pa 1967–80; Distinguished Prof. of Literature, Hunter Coll. 1989–92; Visiting Lecturer, State Univ. of NY, Stony Brook 1967, 1968; Houghton Mifflin Literary Fellow 1959; Guggenheim Fellowship Grant 1959–60, Rockefeller Grant 1965, Ford Foundation Grant 1966; mem. Nat. Inst. of Arts and Letters 1970–; Daroff Award of Jewish Book Council of America 1959, Award of Nat. Inst. of Arts and Letters 1959, Nat. Book Award for Fiction 1960, Nat. Book Critics' Circle Award (for The Counterlife) 1987, (for Patrimony) 1992, Nat. Arts Club's Medal of Honor for Literature 1991, PEN/Faulkner Fiction Award (for Operation Shylock) 1993, shared Karel Capek Prize 1994, Nat. Book Award for Fiction (for Sabbath's Theater) 1995, Pulitzer Prize (for American Pastoral) 1998, Ambassador Book Award of the English-Speaking Union (for I Married a Communist) 1998. *Publications*: Goodbye Columbus (novella and stories) 1959; novels: Letting Go 1962, When She Was Good 1967, Portnoy's Complaint 1969, Our Gang 1971, The Breast 1972, The Great American Novel 1973, My Life as a Man 1974, Reading Myself and Others (essays) 1975, The Professor of Desire 1977, The Ghost Writer 1979, A Philip Roth Reader 1980, Zuckerman Unbound 1981, The Anatomy Lesson 1983, The Prague Orgy 1985, Zuckerman Bound 1985, The Counterlife 1986, The Facts: A Novelist's Autobiography 1988, Deception 1990, Patrimony 1991, Operation Shylock 1993, Sabbath's Theater 1995, American Pastoral 1997, I Married a Communist 1998, The Human Stain 2000 (Prix Médicis Étranger 2002), The Dying Animal 2001, Shop Talk 2001. *Address*: c/o Wylie Agency, Inc., 250 W 57th Street, Suite 2114, New York, NY 10107, USA.

ROTH, Tim; British actor; b. 1961, Dulwich; ed Dick Sheppard Comprehensive School, Brixton and Camberwell Coll. of Art; began acting career with fringe groups including Glasgow Citizens Theatre, The Oval House and the Royal Court; appeared on London stage in Metamorphosis; numerous TV appearances. *Films*: The Hit, A World Apart, The Cook The Thief His Wife and Her Lover, Vincent & Theo, Rosencrantz and Guildenstern are Dead, Jumpin at the Boneyard, Reservoir Dogs, Bodies Rest and Motion, Pulp Fiction, Little Odessa, Rob Roy, Captives, Four Rooms, Hoodlums, Everyone Says I Love You, Liar, The War Zone (Dir), The Legend of 1900, Vatel. *Address*: Ilene Feldman Agency, 8730 West Sunset Boulevard, Suite 490, Los Angeles, CA 90069, USA (Office).

ROTH, William V., Jr, BA, MBA, LL.B; American politician; b. 22 July 1921, Great Falls, Mont.; s. of William V. and Clara Nelson Roth; m. Jane K. Richards 1965; one s. one d.; ed Univ. of Oregon and Harvard Univ.; admitted to Del. Bar and US Supreme Court; fmr Congressman from Delaware; mem. Republican Nat. Cttee 1961–64; Senator from Delaware 1971–2001; Chair. Senate Govt Affairs Cttee 1981; Pres. N. Atlantic Ass. 1996–98. *Address*: c/o U.S. Senate, 104 Hart Senate Office Building, Washington, DC 20510, USA.

ROTHENBERG, Alan I., JD; American lawyer; b. 10 April 1939; m. Georgina Rothenberg; three c.; ed Univ. of Mich.; admitted Calif. Bar 1964; partner Manatt Phelps Rothenberg & Phillips, LA 1968–90, Latham & Watkins, LA 1990–; Instructor in Sports Law, Univ. of S. Calif. 1969, 1976, 1984, Whittier

Coll. of Law 1980, 1984; Pres. LA Clippers Basketball Team 1982–89, US Soccer Fed., Chicago 1990–; mem. Soccer Comm. 1984 Olympic Games; mem. Equal Educ. Opportunities Comm. State of Calif. Bd of Educ. 1972–75; mem. Bd of Govs Nat. Basketball Asscn; Pres. Constitutional Rights Foundation 1987–90; Chair. Pres. CEO 1994 World Cup Organizing Cttee 1990–94; Founders and Chair. Major League Soccer 1994. *Address:* Latham & Watkins, 633 W 5th Street, Suite 4000, Los Angeles, CA 90071; Office of the President, US Soccer Federation, 1801–811 South Prairie Avenue, Chicago, IL 60616, USA.

ROTHENBERG, Susan, BFA; American artist; b. 20 Jan. 1945, Buffalo, New York; d. of Leonard Rothenberg and Adele Cohen; m. George Trakas 1971 (divorced 1976); one d.; ed Cornell and George Washington Univs. and Corcoran Museum School; has participated in numerous group exhbns. at Museum of Modern Art, Whitney Museum of American Art, Venice Biennale and galleries in Germany, Denmark, Spain, Finland etc.; work exhibited in several public collections in USA and Netherlands; Guggenheim Fellow 1980. *Solo exhibitions include:* Akron Art Museum 1981–82, Stedelijk Museum, Amsterdam 1982, San Francisco Museum of Art 1983, Carnegie Inst. Museum of Art, Pittsburgh 1984, LA County Museum of Art 1983, Inst. of Contemporary Art, Boston 1984, Aspen Center for the Visual Arts 1984, Willard Gallery 1976, 1977, 1979, 1981, 1983. *Address:* c/o Sperone Westwater, 142 Greene Street, New York, NY 10012, USA.

ROTHENBERGER, Anneliese; German opera singer (soprano) and painter; b. 19 June 1926, Mannheim; d. of Josef Rothenberger and Sophie Häffner; m. Gerd W.Dieberitz 1954 (deceased); ed Real- und Musikhochschule, Mannheim; début, Coblenz Theatre 1947; with State Opera Hamburg, Munich, Vienna 1958–70; guest singer at La Scala, Milan, Metropolitan Opera, New York and Salzburg, Glyndebourne and Munich Festivals, etc.; TV Special 1969–; several exhbns as painter, Germany and Switzerland; recital tours to Russia, Japan, Iceland, Germany; Distinguished Service Cross 1st Class, Great Cross. *Exhibitions include:* Haus Engelhardt, Mannheim, Alte Schule CH-8268 Salenstein, Schloss Mainan. *Films:* Oh, Rosalinda 1955, Der Rosenkavalier 1960. *Television:* many appearances on Zweites Deutsches Fernsehen. *Publication:* Melody of My Life 1973. *Leisure interests:* driving, books, painting, modelling, swimming. *Address:* Quellenhof, 8268 Salenstein am Untersee, Switzerland.

ROTHERMERE, 4th Viscount, cr. 1919, of Hemsted; **Jonathan Harold Esmond Vere Harmsworth,** BA; British newspaper publisher; b. 3 Dec. 1967, London; s. of the late 3rd Viscount Rothermere and Patricia Evelyn Beverley Brooks; m. Claudia Clemence 1993; one s. two d.; ed Gordonstoun School, Scotland, Kent School, Conn., USA, Duke Univ., USA; joined Mirror Group 1993; joined Northcliffe Newspapers Group Ltd 1995; Deputy Man. Dir, then Man. Dir Evening Standard 1997; Chair. Assoc. Newspapers Ltd 1998–; Chair. Assoc. New Media 1998, Daily Mail and Gen. Trust PLC 1998–; Pres. Newspaper Press Fund 1999–. *Leisure interests:* family, tennis, golf, riding. *Address:* Daily Mail and General Trust PLC, Room 602, Northcliffe House, 2 Derry Street, London, W8 5TT, England (Office). *Telephone:* (20) 7938-6613. *Fax:* (20) 7937-0043. *E-mail:* chairman@chairman.dmgt.co.uk (Office).

ROTHSCHILD, Baron David René James de; French banker; b. 15 Dec. 1942, New York; s. of Baron Guy de Rothschild (q.v.) and Baroness Alix Schey de Koromla; m. Olimpia Aldobrandini; ed Lycée Carnot, Paris and Inst. d'Etudes Politiques, Paris; Dir Société Le Nickel 1970–73; Dir-Gen. Cie du Nord 1973–78; Chair. Man. Bd Banque Rothschild 1978–82; Pres.-Dir-Gen. Paris-Orléans Man. 1982–84, Paris-Orléans Banque 1984–86; Chair. Rothschild & Cie Banque 1986–, Rothschild NA Inc. 1986–, Rothschild Canada 1990–; Chair. Man. Bd Saint-Honoré-Matignon (investment co.) 1986–94; Pres.-Dir-Gen. Francarep; Pres. Financière Viticole SA, Rothschild Europe; Dir Cie Financière Martin-Maurel, Imetal, Asscn française des entreprises privées (Afep), Rothschilds Continuation Ltd, etc.; Vice-Pres. Imetal 1989; Deputy Chair. N. M. Rothschild, London 1992–; Chair. N. M. Rothschild Corporate Finance 1996–; Pres. Fondation Rothschild. *Leisure interests:* golf, skiing, tennis. *Address:* 17 avenue Matignon, 75008 Paris (Office); 6 rue de Tournon, 75006 Paris, France (Home).

ROTHSCHILD, Edmund Leopold de, CBE, MA, TD; British merchant banker; b. 2 Jan. 1916, London; s. of Lionel N. de Rothschild and Marie-Louise (née Beer) de Rothschild; m. 1st Elizabeth E. Lentner 1948 (died 1980); two s. two d.; m. 2nd Anne Evelyn Harrison, JP 1982; ed Harrow, Trinity Coll. Cambridge; Maj. R.A. (T.A.), served in World War II; Deputy Chair. British Newfoundland Corpn Ltd 1963–69, Churchill Falls (Labrador) Corpn Ltd 1966–69; Dir Rothschild Continuation Ltd 1970–75 (Chair. 1970–75); Chair. AUR Hydropower Ltd 1980–91; Pres. Asscn of Jewish Ex-Servicemen and Women; Vice-Chair. Cen. British Fund for Jewish Relief and Rehabilitation; Vice-Pres. Queen's Nursing Inst., Trustee British Freedom from Hunger Campaign 1965–97; Vice-Pres. Council of Christians and Jews; f. Research Into Ageing; mem. Council Royal Nat. Pension Fund for Nurses –1996; Freeman, City of London; Order of the Sacred Treasure, 1st Class (Japan) 1973; Hon. LLD (Memorial Univ. of Newfoundland) 1961; Hon. DSc (Salford) 1983. *Publications:* Window on the World 1949, A Gilt-Edged Life – Memoir (autobiog.) 1998. *Leisure interests:* gardening, fishing, golf. *Address:* N.M. Rothschild & Sons Ltd, New Court, St Swithins Lane, London, EC4P 4DU; Exbury House, Exbury, nr Southampton, SO45 1AF, England. *Telephone:* (23) 8089-1203 (Office). *Fax:* (23) 8089-9940 (Office).

ROTHSCHILD, Baron Elie Robert de, FRSM; French banker; b. 29 May 1917, Paris; s. of Baron Robert and Nelly (née Beer) de Rothschild; m. Liliane Fould-Springer 1942; one s. two d.; ed Lycée Louis le Grand, Faculty of Law, Univ. de Paris; Pres. Rothschild Bank, Zürich, Assicurazioni Generali, Trieste and Venice; Officier, Légion d'honneur, Croix de guerre, Ufficiale Ordine al Merito della Repubblica Italiana. *Leisure interests:* breeding, gardening. *Address:* 32 Ormonde Gate, London, SW3 4HA, England.

ROTHSCHILD, Sir Evelyn de, Kt; British banker; b. 29 Aug. 1931, London; s. of the late Anthony Gustav de Rothschild; m. 1st Victoria Schott 1972 (dissolved 2000); two s. one d.; m. 2nd Lynn Forester 2000; ed Harrow, Trinity Coll., Cambridge; Chair. Economist Newspaper 1972–89, United Racecourses Ltd 1977–94, British Merchant Banking and Securities Houses Asscn (fmrly Accepting Houses Cttee) 1985–89; Chair. N. M. Rothschild & Sons Ltd 1976–. *Leisure interests:* art, racing. *Address:* N. M. Rothschild & Sons Ltd, New Court, St Swithin's Lane, London, EC4P 4DU, England. *Telephone:* (20) 7280-5302 (Office). *Fax:* (20) 7220-7108 (Office).

ROTHSCHILD, Baron Guy Edouard Alphonse Paul de; French banker; b. 21 May 1909, Paris; s. of the late Baron Edouard de Rothschild and Germaine de Rothschild (née Halphen); m. 1st Alix Schey de Koromla 1937 (divorced 1956); one s.; m. 2nd Baronne Marie-Hélène de Zuylen de Nyevelt van de Haar 1957 (deceased); one s.; ed Lycées Condorcet and Louis-le-Grand, Univ. de Paris; Pres. Compagnie du Nord (fmr Cie du chemin de fer du Nord) 1949, Dir, Exec. Pres. 1968; Pres., Dir-Gen. Soc. minière et métallurgique de Penarroya 1964–71; Pres., Dir-Gen. Banque Rothschild-Paris 1968–78; Pres., Dir-Gen. Imetal (fmr Soc. Le Nickel) 1971–79; Pres. Fonds juif unifié 1950–82; Officier, Légion d'honneur, Croix de guerre, Chevalier du mérite agricole. *Publications:* Contre bonne fortune (The Whims of Fortune, autobiog.) 1985, Mon ombre siamoise 1993, Le fantôme de Léa 1998, Les surprises de la fortune 2002. *Leisure interests:* breeding and racing horses, golf. *Address:* 17 avenue Matignon, 75008 Paris; Hôtel Lambert, 2 rue St Louis en l'Ile 75004, Paris, France.

ROTHSCHILD, 4th Baron, cr. 1885; **(Nathaniel Charles) Jacob Rothschild,** GBE, BA; British banker; b. 29 April 1936; s. of late 3rd Baron Rothschild; m. Serena Dunn 1961; one s. three d.; ed Eton Coll. and Christ Church, Oxford; Chair. St James's Place Capital PLC (fmrly J. Rothschild Holdings) 1971–96, Five Arrows 1980–, RIT Capital Partners, Bd of Trustees, Nat. Gallery 1985–91; Chair. Bd of Trustees Nat. Heritage Memorial Fund 1992–98; Pres. Inst. of Jewish Affairs 1992–; Chair. RIT Capital Partners; mem. Council, Royal Coll. of Art 1986–92 (Sr Fellow 1992); Commdr Order of Henry the Navigator (Portugal). *Address:* 14 St James's Place, London, SW1A 1NP, England. *Telephone:* (20) 7493-8111.

ROTTERMUND, Andrzej; Polish curator and art historian; b. 11 May 1941, Warsaw; s. of Julian and Zofia Lenart; m. Maria Reklewska 1963; one d.; ed ed. Warsaw Univ.; Prof. Inst. of Art, Polish Acad. of Sciences, Warsaw 1990; Dept Dir Nat. Museum, Warsaw 1975–83, The Royal Castle, Warsaw 1987–90 (Dir 1991–); Deputy Minister of Culture and Arts 1991; mem. Polish Acad. of Sciences, Polish Art Historians' Asscn 1987–91, Polish ICOM Cttee 1990–96; organized exhbns in Poland and abroad including Treasures of a Polish King, Dulwich Picture Gallery London 1992, Land of the Winged Horsemen. Art in Poland 1572–1764, USA 1999–2000, Thesauri Poloniae, Austria 2002; Silver Cross of Merit 1977; Meritorious Activist of Culture 1978; Kt's Cross, Order of Polonia Restituta 1988, Officer's Cross 1994, Commdr's Cross 1998; Cross of Merit (Germany) 1999; Ordre de la Couronne (Belgium) 2002; Officier, Légion d'honneur 2002, and other decorations. *Publications:* 100 books, articles and essays including Katalog rysunków architektonicznych ze zbiorów Muzeum Narodowego w Warszawie (The Catalogue of Architectural Drawings of the Nat. Museum in Warsaw) 1970, Klasycyzm w Polsce (Neoclassicism in Poland) 1984, Zamek Królewski – funkcje i treści rezydencji monarszej wieku Oświecenia (The Royal Castle in the Age of the Enlightenment – the Functions and Symbolic Meaning of the Monarch's Residence) 1988, J. N. L. Durand a polska architektura I połowy XIX wieku (J. N. L. Durand and the Polish Architecture of the First Half of the 19th Century) 1990, Warsaw 2000. *Leisure interests:* music, cinema. *Address:* Royal Castle, pl. Zamkowy 4, 00-277 Warsaw, Poland (Office). *Telephone:* (22) 6350808 (Office), (22) 6752150 (Office). *Fax:* (22) 6357260 (Office). *E-mail:* a .rottermund@zamek-krolewski.art.pl (Office). *Website:* www .zamek-krolewski.art.pl (Office).

ROUCH, Jean, PhD; French anthropologist and film-maker; b. 31 May 1917, Paris; s. of Jules Rouch and Lucienne, née Gain) Rouch; m. Jane Margaret George 1952 (deceased); started career as civil engineer, Head of Public Works Dept, Niger 1942; CO, Reconnaissance Section, Engineer Corps, First French Army 1944–45; made first ever canoe journey down Niger River from source to sea (with Jean Sauvy and Pierre Ponty) 1946–47; studied Songhay people of Niger and the Dogon of Mali; has made over 100 films, including Circoncision (Grand Prix, Festival du film maudit, Biarritz 1949), Les Maîtres Fous (Grand Prix, Venice Int. Film Festival 1957), Moi, un Noir (Prix Louis Delluc 1958), Chronique d'un Eté (with Edgar Morin; Prix international de la Critique, Cannes 1961) La Chasse au Lion à l'Arc (prizewinner, Venice Documentary Film Festival 1965), Le Vieil Anaï (Int. Critics' Prize, Venice 1980), Dionysos (Official choice, Venice Festival 1984), Boulevard d'Afrique (Official choice, Venice Festival 1987), Enigma 1986, Bac ou mariage 1988, Liberté, égalité, fraternité . . . et puis après 1990, Madame L'eau 1992, La Vache merveilleuse 1995, Moi fatigué debout, moi couché 1997; Dir of

Research, Cen. Nat. de la Recherche Scientifique, Paris 1966–86; Head of Int. Anthropological Film Cttee 1953–86; Gen. Sec. Cinémathèque Française 1985–86, Pres. 1987–91; Pres. CICT (UNESCO) 1991; Visiting Prof., Harvard Univ., USA (summer school) 1980–86; Hon. PhD (Leyden) 1980, (USC, LA) 1991; Officier, Légion d'honneur, Officier des Arts et des Lettres; Croix de guerre. *Publications:* four major vols about the Songhay people of the Niger river 1954–57. *Leisure interests:* swimming, bicycling, canoeing on African rivers, drawing and painting. *Address:* Musée de l'Homme, place du Trocadéro, 75116 Paris (Office); 168 boulevard du Montparnasse, 75014 Paris, France (Home). *Telephone:* 47-04-38-20 (Office); 43-35-48-62 (Home).

ROUCO VARELA, HE Cardinal Antonio María, LicenD, DCL; Spanish ecclesiastic; b. 20 Aug. 1936, Villalba; s. of Vicente Rouco and María Eugenia Varela; ordained priest 1959; taught at Mondoñedo Seminary, Lugo 1964–66, Univ. of Munich 1966–69, Univ. Pontificia de Salamanca 1969–76 (Vice-Rector 1972–76); Auxiliary Bishop of Santiago de Compostela 1976–84; Archbishop of Santiago de Compostela 1984–94, of Madrid 1994–; cr. Cardinal 1998; Gran. Canciller San Dámaso Faculty of Theology. *Publications:* Staat und Kirche im Spanien des XVI Jahrhunderts 1965, Sacramento e diritto: antinomia nella Chiesa (with E. Corecco) 1972. *Leisure interests:* music, reading. *Address:* Arzobispado, Calle San Justo 2, 28071 Madrid, Spain. *Telephone:* (91) 3665601. *Fax:* (91) 3667739.

ROUILLY, Jean, LenD; French television executive; b. 21 Dec. 1943, Villennes-sur-Seine; s. of Roger Rouilly and Nicole Antigna; m. Annyck Graton 1987; one s.; ed Lycées Jules Verne and Georges Clémenceau, Nantes, Faculté de Droit, Bordeaux and Inst. d'Etudes Politiques, Bordeaux; Asst to the Dir, Office de Radiodiffusion-Télévision Francaise, 1966–70, Admin. Documentary Programmes 1970–72, Gen. Man. to Del. Gen. of TV Production 1972–74; Sec.-Gen. Production, Antenne 2 1975–81, Asst Dir Finance 1981–85, Production Man. 1985–87, Dir-Gen. Programme Production 1987–90; Asst Dir-Gen. Antenne 2 1987–90; Dir Films A2 1981–87, Dir-Gen. 1987–90; Sec.-Gen. TV5 1983–85; Dir-Gen. Hachette Int. TV (now Europe Images Int.) 1990–, CEO 1999–. *Address:* Europe Images International, 25 rue François 1er, 75008 Paris (Office); 7 rue Edouard Laferrière, 92190 Meudon, France (Home). *Telephone:* 1-47-23-28-00 (Office). *Fax:* 1-47-23-28-10 (Office). *E-mail:* jean_rouilly@europeimages.com (Office). *Website:* www .europeimages.com (Office).

ROULEAU, Joseph-Alfred, OC; Canadian bass singer; b. 28 Feb. 1929, Matane, Québec; s. of Joseph-Alfred Rouleau and Florence Bouchard; m. 1st Barbara Whittaker 1952; one d.; m. 2nd Jill Renée Moreau; one s. one d.; ed Coll. Jean De Brebeuf, Montreal, Univ. of Montreal, Conservatoire of Music, Province of Québec; three years in Milan for singing studies; début in Montreal 1955, at Royal Opera House, Covent Garden 1957–, has sung over 40 roles at Covent Garden; guest artist at prin. opera houses all over the world; tours of Canada 1960, Australia (with Joan Sutherland) 1965, Russia 1966, 1969, Romania, S. Africa 1974, 1975, 1976; Paris Opera 1975, Metropolitan Opera, New York 1984, 1985, 1986, San Francisco 1986, 1987; Prof. of Voice, Univ. of Québec (UQAM) 1980, mem. Admin. Bd; mem. Bd Corpn of Montreal Opéra Co. 1980–; several awards including Prix Calixa-Lavallée 1967 (La Société St Jean Baptiste, Montreal), Silver Medal (Royal Opera House, Covent Garden) 1983, Felix Award for Best Classical Artist of the Year 1989, Prix du Québec pour les Arts d'interprétation 1990. *Recordings include:* Scenes from Anna Bolena, Ruddigore, Roméo et Juliette (Gounod); L'enfance du Christ (Berlioz), Semiramide, Boris Godunov, Renard (Stravinsky), F. Leclerc's Songs, Les habitués du rêve de Jacques Hêtu (song cycle) and recording of French operatic arias with Royal Opera House Orchestra. *Major roles include:* Boris Godunov (Boris Godunov), Philip II (Don Carlos), Basilio (Barber of Seville), Mephisto (Faust), Dosifei (Khovanshchina), Don Quixote (Don Quixote), Inquisitore (Don Carlos), Ramfis (Aida), Prince Gremin (Onegin), Father Lawrence (Roméo et Juliette). *Leisure interests:* tennis, golf, reading. *Address:* 32 Lakeshore Road, Beaconsfield, Que. H9W 4H3, Canada (Home). *Telephone:* (514) 697-9266.

ROUNDS, M. Michael; American state official; m. Jean Rounds; four c.; ed S. Dak. Univ.; partner Fischer, Rounds & Assocs. Inc.; fmr. Republican State Senator, S. Dak., fmr Senate Majority Leader; Gov. of S. Dak. 2003–; Guardian of Small Business, Nat. Fed. of Ind. Business 1992, 1998, Agent of the Year, S. Dak. Ind. Insurance Agents 1999, Special Award, S. Dak. Horsemen 2000. *Leisure interests:* flying, hunting, racquetball, camping, boating, family. *Address:* Office of the Governor, 500 East Capitol Avenue, Pierre, SD 57501, USA (Office).

ROURKE, Mickey (Philip Andre); American actor and boxer; b. 1956, New York; m. 1st Debra Feuer (divorced); m. 2nd Carre Otis; ed Actors' Studio, New York. *Film appearances include:* Fade to Black, 1941 1979, Heaven's Gate 1980, Body Heat 1981, Diner 1982, Eureka 1983, Rumblefish 1983, Rusty James 1983, The Pope of Greenwich Village 1984, 9½ Weeks 1984, Year of the Dragon 1985, Angel Heart 1986, A Prayer for the Dying 1986, Barfly 1987, Johnny Handsome 1989, Homeboy 1989, Francesco 1989, The Crew 1989, The Desperate Hours 1990, Wild Orchid 1990, On the Sport 1990, Harley Davidson and the Marlboro Man 1991, White Sands 1992, F.T.W., Fall Time, Double Time, Another 9½ Weeks, The Rainmaker 1997, Love in Paris 1997, Double Team 1997, Buffalo '66 1997, Thursday 1998, Shergar 1999, Shades 1999, Out in Fifty 1999, The Animal Factory 2000.

ROUSE, Irving, BS, PhD, D.F.L.; American professor of anthropology; b. 29 Aug. 1913, Rochester, NY; s. of B. Irving Rouse and Louise Bohachek; m. Mary Mikami 1939; two s.; ed Yale Univ.; Asst, then Assoc. Curator, Peabody Museum of Natural History, Yale Univ. 1938–62, Curator 1977–85, Curator Emer. 1985–, Instructor to Assoc. Prof. 1939–54, Prof. of Anthropology 1954–69, Charles J. MacCurdy Prof. of Anthropology, Yale Univ. 1969–84, Charles J. MacCurdy Prof. and Curator Emer. 1984–, Sr Research Scientist in Anthropology 1993–98, fmr Chair. Dept of Anthropology; Pres. Soc. for American Archaeology 1952–53, American Anthropology Asscn 1967–68, Asscn for Field Archaeology 1977–79; mem. American Acad. of Arts and Sciences, Nat. Acad. of Sciences, Royal Anthropological Inst., Soc. of Antiquaries of London; Dr hc (Centro de Estudios Avanzados de Puerto Rico y el Caribe); A. Cressy Morrison Prize in Natural Science 1948, Viking Fund Medal and Award in Anthropology 1960, Distinguished Service Award, American Anthropological Asscn 1984. *Publications:* Prehistory in Haiti 1939, Culture of the Ft. Liberté Region, Haiti 1941, Archaeology of the Maniabón Hills, Cuba 1942, A Survey of Indian River Archaeology, Florida 1951, Porto Rican Prehistory 1952, An Archaeological Chronology of Venezuela (with J. M. Cruxent) 1958, Venezuelan Archaeology (with J. M. Cruxent) 1963, Introduction to Prehistory 1972, Migrations in Prehistory 1986, The Tainos 1992. *Leisure interests:* singing, swimming. *Address:* 12 Ridgewood Terrace, North Haven, CT 06473, USA (Home). *Telephone:* (203) 432-3690 (Office); (203) 288-1485 (Home). *Fax:* (203) 432-3669. *E-mail:* bir@ aoi.com, Blrouse@aol.com (Home). *Website:* www.yale.edu (Office).

ROUSSEL, Paul Henri Michel; French business executive; b. 3 March 1954, Bayeux; s. of Jacques Roussel and Janine Piton; m. Jacqueline Claire Roussel 1975; one s. one d.; ed Lycée Malherbe, Caen; Head of Group, Havas Conseil 1976–80; Consumer Dir SNIP 4 1981–83; Consumer Dir Robert & Partners 1984–86; Commercial and Marketing Dir L'Equipe magazine 1986–89, Deputy Dir-Gen. 1990–92, Dir-Gen. 1993–; Deputy Dir-Gen. Groupe Amaury 1995–. *Leisure interests:* tennis, football, skiing. *Address:* L'Equipe, 4 rue Rouget de l'Isle, 92793 Issy-les-Moulineaux cedex 09, France. *Telephone:* 40-93-20-20. *Fax:* 40-93-20-08.

ROUSSELET, André Claude Lucien, L.EN D.; French business executive; b. 1 Oct. 1922, Nancy; s. of Marcel and Yvonne (née Brongniart) Rousselet; m. Catherine Roge (divorced); two s. one d.; ed Lycée Claude Bernard, Paris, Faculté de Droit, Paris and Ecole Libre des Sciences Politiques; Chef de Cabinet, Prefects of Ariège and L'Aube 1944; Sub-prefect of Condom 1946, Pointe-à-Pitre 1948, Issoudun 1935; Chef de Cabinet, Minister of the Interior 1954; Special Asst Office of Minister of Posts and Telecommunications 1955; Chef de Cabinet, Minister of Justice 1956; Dept of External Relations, Simca 1958; Pres.-Dir-Gen. Sociétés nouvelles des autoplaces G7 1962–67, 1972–; Deputé for Haute-Garonne 1967–68; Man. Galerie de France and Dir du Cabinet, Pres. of Repub. 1981–82; Pres.-Dir-Gen. Agence Havas 1982–86 (now Dir); mem. Comité stratégique de Havas 1987; Pres.-Dir-Gen. Canal Plus 1984–94; Pres. société éditrice de InfoMatin (Sodepresse) 1994–; Pres. Advisory Council Tonna Electronique 1990, Sodepresse 1995; Dir Information; Pres. Editorial Soc. Sodepresse; Dir Télévision le mensuel (Publ). *Leisure interests:* golf, tennis, painting, skiing. *Address:* 44 avenue Georges V, 75008 Paris; 28 rue Henri Barbusse, 92110 Clichy, France.

ROUSSELLE, Régis; French stockbroker; b. 25 Jan. 1948, Rheims; ed Ecole des Arts et Manufactures and Faculté des Sciences Econs; Chair. Finance Eng 1974–81; Stockbroker Meeschaert-Rousselle 1981–87, Chair. 1988–89; Chair. Soc. des Bourses Françaises 1988–90, Conseil des Bourses de Valeurs 1988–90; Coll. mem. Comm. des Opérations de Bourse 1988–90; Pres. Economics and Finance Professionals Group of Fmr. Students of Ecole centrale de Paris 1988–.

ROUSSELY, François, MEcons; French industrial executive; b. 9 Jan. 1945, Dordogne; ed Paris Inst. of Political Science, French Nat. School of Admin.; auditor, State Accounting Office 1978; sr civil servant, Ministry of Interior, Prin. Pvt. Sec. 1981–84; assigned to chair. of a parl. cttee, Assemblée Nat. 1986–89; Dir-Gen. Nat. Police (Ministry of Interior) 1989–91; Gen. Sec. for Admin. of Ministry of Defence 1991–94; Sec.-Gen. and mem. Exec. Cttee Soc. Nat. des Chemins de Fer (SNCF) 1997; Prin. Pvt. Sec. Ministry of Defence 1998; Chair. and CEO Electricité de France (EDF) 1998–; mem. Comité de l'Energie Atomique; mem. Bd Usinor, Framatome, Aérospatiale-Matra 1998; Officier Légion d'honneur, Officier Ordre nat. du Mérite. *Leisure interests:* jogging, classical music. *Address:* Electricité de France (EDF), 22–30 avenue de Wagram, 75008 Paris, France. *Telephone:* 1-40-42-70-70 (Office). *Fax:* 1-40-42-89-00. *E-mail:* francois.roussely@edf.fr (Office).

ROUSSIN, Michel, DLitt; French politician, civil servant and police officer; b. 3 May 1939, Rabat, Morocco; s. of Gabriel Roussin and Sylvia Tonieti; m. Annick Dussud 1966; two s.; ed St Joseph Coll., Avignon, Paris Univ.; artillery officer 1960–63; police officer 1963–90; responsible for Press Relations Directorate of Police and Mil. Justice 1969–72; Mil. Commdr Hotel Mâtignon 1972–76; Pvt. Sec. to Indre-et-Loire Prefect 1976–77, to Dir-Gen. of Foreign Documentation and Counter-Espionage (SDECE) 1977–81, to Mayor of Paris 1984–86, 1989, to Prime Minister 1986; with Ministry of Defence 1980–81; with Compagnie Gen. des Eaux 1981–83; Tech. Adviser at Mayor's Office 1983–84; Minister of Co-operation 1993–94; Deputy Mayor of Paris 1995–2001; Chair. SAE Int. 1997–99; Bd Dirs. Eiffage Group 1996–99, Saga Group 1997–, Défense nationale (journal) 1999–, Conseil économique et social 1999–; Vice-Pres. Afrique du groupe Bolloré 1999–, CNPF Int. 2000–; Officier Légion d'honneur, Croix de la Valeur militaire, Officier du Ouissam Alaouite.

Publication: Afrique majeure 1997. *Leisure interest:* swimming. *Address:* Groupe Bolloré, 31–32 quai de Dion Buton, 92811 Puteaux cedex (Office); c/o Hôtel de Ville, 75004 Paris, France.

ROUVILLOIS, Philippe André Marie; French government official; b. 29 Jan. 1935, Saumur; s. of Gen. Jean Rouvillois and Suzanne Hulot; m. Madeleine Brigol 1960; four s.; ed Lycée Fustel-de-Coulanges, Strasbourg, Lycée Louis-le-Grand, Faculté de Droit, Paris and Inst. d'Etudes Politiques, Paris; Insp. of Finance 1959; Office of Revenue 1964; Adviser, Pvt. Office of Minister of Econ. and Finance 1966–68; Deputy Dir Office of Revenue, Ministry of Econ. and Finance 1967, Head of Service 1969; Deputy Dir-Gen. of Revenue 1973, Dir-Gen. 1976; Insp.-Gen. of Finance 1982; Deputy Dir-Gen. SNCF 1983–87, Dir-Gen. 1987–88, Pres. Admin. Bd 1988; Gen. Man. and Pres. Admin. Council, Atomic Energy Comm. (CEA) 1989–95; Pres. CEA-Industrie 1989–92, 1993–99; Pres. Pasteur Inst. 1997–; Commdr Légion d'honneur, Croix de Valeur militaire. *Address:* Institut Pasteur, 25–28 rue du Docteur Roux, 75015 Paris (Office); Inspection générale des finances, 139 rue de Bercy, 75572 Paris, cedex 12 France.

ROUX, Albert Henri; French chef and restaurateur; b. 8 Oct. 1935, Semur-en-Brionnais; s. of the late Henri Roux and of Germaine Roux (née Triger); brother of Michel André Roux (q.v.); m. Monique Merle 1959; one s. one d.; ed Ecole Primaire, St Mandé; mil. service, Algeria; founder (with brother Michel Roux), Le Gavroche Restaurant, London 1967 (now owned jtly. with his son Michel Jr), The Waterside Inn, Bray 1972 (now owned solely by Michel Roux); opened 47 Park Street Hotel 1981; opened Le Poulbot, Le Gamin, Gavvers, Les Trois Plats and Rouxl Britannia (all as part of Roux Restaurants Ltd) 1969–87; commenced consultancy practice 1989; founder-mem. Acad. Culinaire de Grande Bretagne, Maître Cuisinier de France 1968; Hon. Prof. Bournemouth Univ. 1995–; Hon. DSc (Council for Nat. Academic Awards) 1987; Chevalier du Mérite Agricole. *Publications:* with Michel Roux: New Classic Cuisine 1983, The Roux Brothers on Pâtisserie 1986, The Roux Brothers on French Country Cooking 1989, Cooking for Two 1991. *Leisure interests:* fishing, racing. *Address:* Le Gavroche, 43 Upper Brook Street, London, W1Y 1PF, England (Office). *Telephone:* (20) 7408-0881 (Restaurant). *Fax:* (20) 7491-4387 (Restaurant).

ROUX, Bernard Georges Marie; French business executive; b. 15 Aug. 1934, St Raphaël (Var); s. of Edouard Roux and Juliette Boyer; m. 1st Chantel Bergerat; one s. one d.; m. 2nd Laurence Grand; one s. one d.; m. 3rd Roselyne Mainfroy 1983; three s.; ed École de Commerce, Faculté de Droit de Lyon; Commercial Dir Meunier Textiles 1959; Dir-Gen. Centrale voile ameublement (Groupe Rhodiaceta) 1963; joined Axe Publicité 1965, Dir 1967; f. Roux Séguéla agency with Jacques Séguéla 1969; Pres. Roux, Séguéla, Cayzac et Goudard 1991; f. RLC 1992– (changed to Opera-RLC 1993); Pres. and Dir-Gen. Gymnase Club 1997–99. *Leisure interests:* tennis, reading, cinema. *Address:* 8 square Chezy, 92200 Neuilly-sur-Seine, France.

ROUX, Jean-Louis, CC; Canadian official, theatre director, actor, author and senator; b. 18 May 1923, Montreal; s. of Louis Roux and Berthe Leclerc; m. Monique Oligny 1950; one s.; ed Coll. Sainte-Marie and Univ. de Montréal; mem. Les Compagnons de Saint Laurent theatrical co. 1939–42, Ludmilla Pitoëff theatrical co. 1942–46; mil. training 1942–46; founder, Théâtre d'Essai, Montreal 1951; Sec.-Gen., Théâtre du Nouveau Monde 1953–63 (co-founder 1950), Artistic Dir 1966–82; Dir-Gen. Nat. Theatre School of Canada 1982–87; has appeared in more than 200 roles (in both French and English) on stage (Montreal, Stratford, Paris), TV, cinema and radio and directed more than 50 theatrical productions; apptd to Senate 1994; Lt Gov. of Québec 1996; Chair. Canada Council for the Arts 1998; mem. Royal Soc. of Canada 1982–; Life Gov. Nat. Theatre School of Canada; Dr hc (Laval Univ.) 1988, (Univ. of Ottawa) 1995; Hon. LLD (Concordia Univ.) 1993; numerous awards and medals including Molson Award 1977, World Theatre Award 1985, Ordre de la Pléiade 1995, KStJ; Chevalier, Ordre Nat. du Québec 1989. *Leisure interests:* reading, chess, swimming, walking. *Address:* 4145 Blueridge Crescent, Apt. 2, Montreal, Québec, H3H 1S7, Canada. *Telephone:* (514) 937-2505.

ROUX, Michel André; French chef and restaurateur; b. 19 April 1941; s. of the late Henri Roux and of Germaine Roux (née Triger); brother of Albert Henri Roux (q.v.); m. 1st Françoise Marcelle Becquet (divorced 1979); one s. two d.; m. 2nd Robyn Margaret Joyce 1984; ed Ecole Primaire St Mandé, Brevet de Maîtrise; commis pâtissier and cuisinier British Embassy, Paris 1955–57; commis cook to Cécile de Rothschild 1957–59, Chef 1962–67; mil. service 1960–62; Propr Le Gavroche 1967, The Waterside Inn 1972, Le Gavroche (Mayfair) 1981; mem. Acad. Culinaire de France (UK Br.), Asscn Relais et Desserts, Asscn Relais et Châteaux; Chevalier, Ordre Nat. du Mérite 1987, Ordre des Arts et des Lettres 1990; Hon. OBE 2002; numerous other decorations; numerous culinary awards including Gold Medal Cuisiniers Français (Paris) 1972, Laureate Restaurateur of the Year 1985. *Publications:* New Classic Cuisine 1983, Roux Brothers on Pâtisserie 1986, At Home with the Roux Brothers 1987, French Traditional Country Cooking 1989, Cooking for Two 1991, Desserts, a Lifelong Passion 1994, Sauces 1996, Life is a Menu (autobiog.) 2000, Only the Best 2002. *Leisure interests:* shooting, skiing, walking. *Address:* The Waterside Inn, Ferry Road, Bray, Berks., SL6 2AT, England. *Telephone:* (1628) 771966. *Fax:* (1628) 789182. *E-mail:* michelroux@aol.com (Office). *Website:* www.waterside-inn.co.uk (Office).

ROVE, Karl; American consultant; b. 25 Dec. 1950, Denver; Chair. Coll. Republicans 1973, later Pres.; mem. George Bush, Sr's presidential campaign team 1980; f. Karl Rove & Co. consultancy 1981; Chief Strategist to George W. Bush 1993–; consultant to Gov. Bill Clements 1978, 1986, Tom Phillips, Texas Supreme Court 1988, U.S. Senators Phil. Gramm, Kay Bailey Hutchison and other right-wing politicians; teaches grad. students at Univ. of Texas. *Address:* c/o The White House Office, 1600 Pennsylvania Avenue, N.W., Washington, DC 20500, USA (Office).

ROVERSI, Paolo; Italian photographer; b. 25 Sept. 1947, Ravenna; fashion photographer since 1973, working for numerous int. magazines including British and Italian Vogue, Uomo Vogue and others; advertising for Georgio Armani, Cerruti 1881, Comme des Garçons, Christian Dior, Alberta Ferretti, Romeo Gigli and Yohji Yamamoto; Dir commercials. *Art exhibitions:* one-man exhbns include: Solomon Gallery, NY 1989, Tokyo 1990, Galerie Pvt. View, Paris 1992, Photo Gallery Int., Tokyo 1994, Hamilton Gallery, London 1994, Galerie Municipale du Château d'Eau, Toulouse 1994, Galerie 213, Paris 1998, Galleria Carla Sozzani, Milan 2000, Pace MacGill Gallery, New York 2002, Galerie Camera Obscura, Paris 2002; participant in numerous group shows. *Publications:* Una Donna 1989, Angeli 1993, Nudi 1999, Libretto 2000. *Address:* 9 rue Paul Fort, 75014 Paris, France (Office). *Telephone:* 1-45-40-40-49 (Office). *Fax:* 1-45-40-72-98 (Office). *E-mail:* italy@club-internet.fr (Office). *Website:* www.paoloroversi.com (Office).

ROWE, John W., MD; American physician and business executive; b. 1944; ed Univ. of Rochester; began career with residency in internal medicine, Beth Israel Hosp., Boston, later becoming Chief of Gerontology; Clinical and Research Fellow, Mass. Gen. Hosp.; Research Fellow and later Prof. of Medicine, Harvard Medical School (Founding Dir Div. on Aging); Pres. School of Medicine and Chief Exec. Mount Sinai NYU Health 1988–, also Prof. of Medicine and Geriatrics; mem. Bd, Pres. and Chief Exec. Aetna Inc. 2000–; fmr Dir MacArthur Foundation on Successful Aging; mem. Bd of Govs American Bd of Internal Medicine; fmr Pres. Gerontological Soc. of America; mem. Inst. of Medicine, Nat. Acad. of Sciences, Medicare Payment Advisory Comm.; numerous honours and awards. *Publications:* over 200 scientific publs on the aging process; Successful Aging (jt author) 1998. *Address:* Aetna Inc., 151 Farmington Avenue, Hartford CT 06156, USA (Office). *Telephone:* (860) 273-0123 (Office).

ROWE-HAM, Sir David (Kenneth), GBE, FCA; British accountant; b. 19 Dec. 1935; s. of the late Kenneth Henry Rowe-Ham and Muriel Phyllis Rowe-Ham; m. Sandra Celia Glover (née Nicholls); three s.; ed Dragon School, Charterhouse; mem. Stock Exchange 1964–84; Sr Partner, Smith Keen Cutler 1972–82; Dir W. Canning PLC 1981–86, Savoy Theatre Ltd 1986–98, Williams PLC 1992–2000, CLS Holdings PLC 1994–99, Chubb PLC 2000–; Regional Dir (London) Lloyds Bank PLC 1985–91; Pres. The Crown Agents Foundation 1996–2002; Chair. Advisory Panel, Guinness Flight Unit Trust Managers Ltd 1987–99; Consultant, Touche Ross & Co. 1984–93; Chair. Birmingham Municipal Bank 1970–72, Olayan Europe Ltd 1989–, Asset Trust PLC 1982–89, Brewin Dolphin Holdings PLC 1992–2003, Apta Healthcare PLC 1994–96, Coral Products PLC 1995–, Gradus Group PLC (Joint Chair.) 1995–97; Alderman, City of London 1976–, Lord Mayor of London 1986–87; Chair. Political Council, Jr Carlton Club 1977, Deputy Chair. Carlton Political Cttee 1977–79; Gov. Royal Shakespeare Co.; Trustee, Friends of D'Oyly Carte; Gov., Christ's Hosp.; KStJ 1986; Commdr Ordre du mérite 1984; Commdr Order of the Lion, Malawi 1985; Order of the Aztec Eagle (Class II), Mexico 1985; Order of King Abdul Aziz (Class I) 1987; Grand Officier du Wissam Alouite 1987, Order of Diego Losada of Caracas 1987; Hon. DLitt (City Univ.) 1986; Pedro Ernesto Medal, Rio de Janeiro 1987. *Leisure interest:* theatre. *Address:* 140 Piccadilly, London, W1J 7NS, England. *Telephone:* (20) 7245-4000 (Office). *Fax:* (20) 7245-4001 (Office).

ROWLAND, Frank Sherwood, PhD; American professor of chemistry; b. 28 June 1927, Delaware, Ohio; s. of Sidney A. Rowland and Margaret Lois Drake Rowland; m. Joan Lundberg 1952; one s. one d.; ed Chicago and Ohio Wesleyan Univs; Instructor in Chem., Princeton Univ. 1952–56; Asst to Prof., Kansas Univ. 1956–64; Prof., Univ. of Calif. Irvine 1964–, Daniel G. Aldrich Endowed Prof. of Chem. 1985–89, Bren Prof. of Chem. 1989–94, Bren Research Prof. 1994–; Guggenheim Fellow 1962, 1974; mem. American Acad. of Arts and Sciences 1977, NAS 1978– (Foreign Sec. 1994–), American Philosophical Soc. 1995, Inst. of Medicine 1995; Fellow AAAS (Pres. 1992, Chair. Bd Dirs. 1993); numerous lectureships and Cttee memberships; 16 hon. degrees; Tyler Prize in Ecology and Energy (now called World Prize for Environmental Achievement) 1983, Japan Prize in Environmental Science and Tech. 1989; Nobel Prize for Chem. 1995, Nevada Medal 1997; numerous other awards. *Publications:* about 380 articles in scientific journals. *Leisure interests:* athletics, opera. *Address:* 572 Rowland Hall, Department of Chemistry, University of California, Irvine, CA 92697 (Office); 4807 Dorchester Road, Corona del Mar, CA 92625, USA (Home). *Telephone:* (949) 824-6016 (Office); (949) 760-1333 (Home). *Fax:* (949) 824-2905 (Office). *E-mail:* rowland@uci.edu (Office).

ROWLAND, Sir (John) David, Kt, MA; British business executive; b. 10 Aug. 1933, London; s. of Cyril Arthur Rowland and Eileen Mary Rowland; m. 1st Giulia Powell 1957 (divorced 1991); one s. one d.; m. 2nd Diana L. Matthews 1991; ed Trinity College, Cambridge Univ.; joined Matthews Wrightson and Co. 1956, Dir 1965; Dir Matthews Wrightson Holdings 1972; Dir Project Fullemploy 1973–88; Deputy Chair. Stewart Wrightson Holdings PLC 1978–81, Chair. 1981–87; Vice-Pres. British Insurance and Investment Brokers Asscn 1980–; Chair. Westminster Insurance Agencies 1981–88; Dir Royal London Mutual Insurance Soc. 1985–86; Deputy Chair. Willis Faber

PLC 1987–88; Dir Fullemploy Group Ltd 1989–90; Chair. Sedgwick Group PLC 1989–92; Pres. Templecon Coll., Oxford 1998–; mem. Council, Lloyd's 1987–90, Chair. 1993–97; Trustee Somerset House Trust 1997–, NatWest Group 1998–2000; Chair. NatWest 1999–2000 (Jt Deputy Chair. 1998–99); mem. Templeton Coll.; Gov. Coll. of Insurance 1983–85, Chair. 1985; Gov. St Paul's Girls School, St Paul's School (also Deputy Chair.); Hon. Fellow Faculty of Actuaries; Hon. Fellow (Cardiff) 1999; Hon. MA (Oxford) 1993; Hon. DPhil (London Guildhall) 1996; Hon. DSc (City) 1997. *Leisure interests:* golf, running slowly, admiring his wife's garden. *Address:* 6 Danbury Street, London, N1 8JU; Giffords Hall, Wickhambrook, Newmarket, Suffolk, CB8 8PQ, England. *Telephone:* (1440) 820221 (Home).

ROWLAND, John Grosvenor; American state governor; b. 24 May 1957, Waterbury, Conn.; s. of the late Sherwood L. Rowland and of Florence M. Jackson; m. 1st Deborah Nebhan 1982; one s. two d.; m. 2nd Patricia Rowland 1994; ed Villanova Univ.; mem. Conn. House of Reps. 1980–84; mem. U.S. House of Reps. 1985–91; Gov. of Connecticut 1995–; Pres. Rowland Asscns.; mem. Bd Dirs. American Cancer Soc.; Republican; Malcolm Daldrige Award, Ella Grasso Award, Excellence in State Govt Award, Pres.'s Medallion for Public Service, Southern Conn. State Univ., Arts Leadership Award, Americans for the Arts and U.S. Conf. for Mayors. *Address:* Office of the Governor, State Capitol, 210 Capitol Avenue, Hartford, CT 06106 (Office); 990 Prospect Avenue, Hartford, CT 06105, USA (Home). *Telephone:* (860) 566-4840 (Office). *Fax:* (860) 524-7396 (Office). *Website:* www.state.ct.us/governor (Office).

ROWLANDS, Christopher John, MA, FCA, CBIM, FRSA; British business executive; b. 29 Aug. 1951, Leeds; s. of the late Wilfred John Rowlands and of Margaretta Rowlands (née Roberts); m. Alison Mary Kelly 1978; two d.; ed Roundhay School, Leeds, Gonville and Caius Coll., Cambridge; articled clerk Peat Marwick Mitchell 1973–75, Man. 1981, seconded as partner, Zambia 1981–83, Sr Man., London 1983–85; Controller Business Planning Asda Group PLC 1985–86, Div. Dir Group Finance 1986–88, Deputy Man. Dir and Finance Dir Property Devt and Investment 1988–92; Group Finance Dir HTV 1992–93, Chief Exec. 1993–97; Chief Exec. The TV Corpn 1998–2001; Dir (non-exec.) Access Plus PLC, ITouch PLC 2002–; mem. Council, Ind. TV Asscn Co. 1993–97. *Leisure interests:* family, theatre, church, reading, skiing, tennis, travel. *Address:* Buchan House, Northumberland Road, Bristol, BS6 7BB, England (Home). *Telephone:* (117) 924-528 (Home).

ROWLING, J. K. (Joanne Kathleen), OBE, BA; British writer; b. 31 July 1965, Chipping Sodbury; d. of Peter Rowling and Anne Rowling; m. 1st (divorced); one d.; m. 2nd Neil Murray 2001; one s.; ed Wyedean Comprehensive School, Exeter Univ., Moray House Teacher Training Coll.; writer; British Book Awards Children's Book of the Year 1999; Smarties Prize. *Publications:* Harry Potter and the Philosopher's Stone 1997, Harry Potter and the Chamber of Secrets 1998, Harry Potter and the Prisoner of Azkaban 1999, Harry Potter and the Goblet of Fire 2000, Quidditch Through the Ages 2001, Fantastic Beasts and Where to Find Them 2001, Harry Potter and the Order of the Phoenix 2003. *Address:* c/o Christopher Little Literary Agency, Ten Eel Brook Studios, 125 Moore Park Road, London, SW6 4PS, England. *Telephone:* (20) 7736-4455 (Office). *Fax:* (20) 7736-4490 (Office). *Website:* www .jkrowling.com (Office).

ROWLINSON, Sir John Shipley, F.R.ENG., FRS; British scientist and university professor; b. 12 May 1926, Handforth, Cheshire; s. of Frank Rowlinson and Winifred (née Jones) Rowlinson; m. Nancy Gaskell 1952; one s. one d.; ed Trinity Coll., Univ. of Oxford; Research Assoc., Univ. of Wis. 1950–51; Research Fellow, then Lecturer, then Sr Lecturer in Chem., Univ. of Manchester 1951–60; Prof. of Chemical Tech., Univ. of London 1961–73; Dr. Lee's Prof. of Chem., Univ. of Oxford 1974–93; Fellow Exeter Coll., Oxford 1974–; A.D. White Prof.-at-Large, Cornell Univ. 1990–96; Hoffman Lecturer, Gesellschaft Deutscher Chemiker 1980, Faraday Lecturer 1983, Lennard-Jones Lecturer 1985, Royal Soc. of Chem., Mary Upson Prof. of Eng, Cornell Univ. 1988; Physical Sec. and Vice-Pres. Royal Soc. 1994–99; Meldola Medal, Royal Inst. of Chem. 1954; Marlow Medal, Faraday Soc. 1956, Leverhulme Medal, Royal Soc. 1993. *Publications:* Liquids and Liquid Mixtures (jtly) 1982 (3rd edn), The Perfect Gas 1963, Thermodynamics for Chemical Engineers (jtly) 1975, Molecular Theory of Capillarity (jtly) 1982, J. D. van der Waals: On the Continuity of the Gaseous and Liquid States (ed.) 1988, Record of the Royal Society 1940–89 (jtly) 1992, Van der Waals and Molecular Science (jtly) 1996, Cohesion: A Scientific History of Intermolecular Forces 2002. *Leisure interest:* mountaineering. *Address:* Physical and Theoretical Chemistry Laboratory, South Parks Road, Oxford, OX1 3QZ (Office); 12 Pullens Field, Headington, Oxford, OX3 0BU, England (Home). *Telephone:* (1865) 275400 (Office); (1865) 767507 (Home). *Fax:* (1865) 275410. *E-mail:* john.rowlinson@ chem.ox.ac.uk (Office).

ROWNY, Lt-Gen. the Hon. Edward Leon, BCE, MA, MS, PhD; American army officer; b. 3 April 1917, Baltimore, Md; s. of Gracyan J. Rowny and Mary Ann (née Rodgers) Rowny; m. Mary Rita Leyko 1941; four s. one d.; 2nd Lt U.S. Army 1941; eventually Lt-Gen. 1970; in African campaign 1942, European and Middle Eastern Campaigns 1944–45; Korea 1950–52; Viet Nam 1962–63; Special Asst Tactical Mobility Dept of army 1963–75; Commdg Gen. 24th Infantry Div., Europe 1965–66; Deputy Chief of Staff Logistics, Europe 1968–69; Deputy Chief of Research and Devt 1969–70; Commdg Gen. Intelligence Corps, Korea, 1970–71; Deputy Chair. Mil. Comm. NATO 1971–73; Jt Chiefs of Staff rep. to SALT del., Geneva 1973–79; Chief Arms Control Negotiator 1981–85; Special Adviser to Pres. 1985–89; Special Counsellor to

State Dept 1989–90; Pres. Nat. War Coll. Alumni Asscn 1987–88; DSM, Silver Star with two oak leaf clusters, Legion of Merit with four oak clusters, Combat Infantry Badge with star. *Publication:* It Takes One to Tango 1992. *Address:* 1105 S. 23rd Road, Arlington, VA 22202, USA.

ROY, Arundhati; Indian writer and activist; b. 1960; m. 1st Gerard Da Cunha (divorced); m. 2nd Pradeep Krishen; ed Delhi School of Architecture; fmrly with Nat. Inst. of Urban Affairs; has written newspaper articles; judge, Cannes Film Festival 2000–; faced charges of inciting violence, attacking a court official and contempt of court for opposing Sardar Sarovar dam project in the Narmada valley 2001. *Publications:* In Which Annie Gives It Those Ones (screenplay), Electric Moon (screenplay), The God of Small Things (Booker Prize) 1997, The End of Imagination (essay) 1998, The Great Common Good (essay) 1999, The Cost of Living (collected essays), The Algebra of Infinite Justice (collected essays) 2002. *Address:* c/o India Ink Publishing Co. Pvt. Ltd, C-1, Soami Nagar, New Delhi 110 017, India.

ROYAL, HRH The Princess Anne Elizabeth Alice Louise, LG, GCVO; b. 15 Aug. 1950; d. of Queen Elizabeth II (q.v.) and Prince Philip, Duke of Edinburgh (q.v.); m. 1st Capt. Mark Anthony Peter Phillips 1973 (divorced 1992); one s., Peter Mark Andrew, b. 15 Nov. 1977, one d., Zara Anne Elizabeth, b. 15 May 1981; m. 2nd Commander Timothy Laurence, RN, MVO, 1992; ed Benenden School, Kent; Col-in-Chief, 14th/20th King's Hussars, Worcs. and Sherwood Foresters Regt (29th/45th Foot), Royal Regina Rifles, 8th Canadian Hussars (Princess Louise's), Royal Corps of Signals, The Canadian Armed Forces Communications and Electronics Branch, The Royal Australian Corps of Signals, The Royal Scots, Royal New Zealand Corps of Signals, King's Royal Hussars, Royal Logistics Corps; Royal New Zealand Nursing Corps, The Grey and Simcoe Foresters Militia; Chief Commdt, WRNS; Hon. Air Commodore, RAF Lyneham; Pres. WRNS Benevolent Trust, British Acad. of Film and TV Arts, Hunters' Improvement and Light Horse Breeding Soc., Save the Children Fund, Windsor Horse Trials, The Royal School for Daughters of Officers of the Royal Navy and Royal Marines (Haslemere), British Olympic Asscn, Council for Nat. Acad. Awards; Patron, Asscn of Wrens, Riding for the Disabled Asscn, Jersey Wildlife Preservation Fund, The Royal Corps of Signals Asscn, The Royal Corps of Signals Inst., Missions to Seamen, British Knitting and Clothing Export Council, The Army and Royal Artillery Hunter Trials, Gloucs. and North Avon Fed. of Young Farmers' Clubs, Royal Lymington Yacht Club, Royal Port Moresby Soc. for the Prevention of Cruelty to Animals, Horse of the Year Ball, Benenden Ball, British School of Osteopathy, Communications and Electronics Branch Inst., All England Women's Lacrosse Asscn, Home Farm Trust; Vice-Patron, British Show Jumping Asscn; Commdt-in-Chief, St John Ambulance and Nursing Cadets, Women's Transport Service; Freeman of the City of London, of the Fishmongers' Co., Master Warden Farriers' Co., Master and Hon. Liveryman, Carmen's Co., Hon. Liveryman Farriers' Co.; Yeoman, Saddlers' Co.; Life mem. Royal British Legion Women's Section, Royal Naval Saddle Club; mem. Island Sailing Club; Visitor, Felixstowe Coll.; official visits abroad to the 14th/20th King's Hussars in Fed. Repub of Germany 1969, 1975, to see the work of the Save the Children Fund in Kenya 1971, to the 2,500th anniversary celebrations of the Iranian monarchy 1971, to 14th/20th King's Hussars and to see the work of the Save the Children Fund, Hong Kong 1971, to SE Asia 1972, Munich 1972, Yugoslavia 1972, Ethiopia and the Sudan 1973, to visit Worcs. and Sherwood Foresters Regt in Berlin 1973, in Hereford, Fed. Repub. of Germany 1974, to Canada 1974, to Australia 1975, to USA 1977, to Fed. Repub. of Germany and Norway 1978, to Portugal, Fed. Repub. of Germany, Thailand, Gilbert Islands, New Zealand, Australia and the Bahamas, Canada 1979, to Royal Corps of Signals in Cyprus, France, Belgium and Fiji 1980, Royal Corps of Signals in Berlin, Nepal, Worcs. and 14th/20th King's Hussars in Fed. Repub. of Germany; USA, Canada and tour of Africa, North Yemen and Lebanon 1982, to France, Japan, Hong Kong, Singapore, Pakistan, Australia, Netherlands and BAOR 1983, USA, Africa, India, Bangladesh, Fed. Repub. of Germany, UAE 1984; Chancellor, Univ. of London 1981–; has accompanied the Queen and the Duke of Edinburgh on several State Visits; has taken part in numerous equestrian competitions including Montreal Olympics 1976, Horse of the Year Show, Wembley and Badminton Horse Trials; winner of Raleigh Trophy 1971 and Silver Medal in 1975 in Individual European Three Day Event; Hon. Freeman, Farmers' Co., Loriners' Co.; Hon. mem., British Equine Veterinary Asscn, Royal Yacht Squadron, Royal Thames Yacht Club, Minchinhampton Golf Club, Lloyds of London; Hon. Life mem. RNVR Officers' Asscn; Sportswoman of the Year, Sports Writers' Asscn, Daily Express, World of Sport, BBC Sports Personality 1971, Special BAFTA Award 1993. *Publication:* Riding Through My Life 1991. *Address:* Buckingham Palace, London, S.W.1, England.

ROYAL, Ségolène; French politician; b. 22 Sept. 1953, Dakar, Senegal; d. of Jacques Royal and Hélène Dehaye; m.; two s. two d.; ed Univs. of Nancy and Paris; Conseillère Gen. La Mothe Saint Héray (Deux-Sèvres); Deputy to Nat. Ass. 1988–92; Sec. Comm. for Production and Exchange, Nat. Ass.; mem. Nat. Cttee on Tourism; adviser on environment, town planning and social affairs to Pres. of Repub. 1982–88; Minister of the Environment 1992–93; Deputy to Nat. Ass. from Deux-Sèvres 1993–; practised law in Paris; Pres. Nat. Council of Socialist Group 1994–95; Deputy Minister of Educ. 1997–2000, of Family and Childhood 2000–01, of Family Childhood and Disabled Persons 2001–02. *Publications:* Le Printemps des Grands Parents, Le Ras-le-bol des Bébés

Zappeurs 1989, Pays, Paysans, Paysages 1993, La Vérité d'une femme 1996. *Address:* Assemblée Nationale, 75355 Paris; Parti socialiste, 10 rue de Solférino, 75333 Paris, France.

ROYER, Jean; French politician; b. 31 Oct. 1920, Nevers; s. of Léon-Antoine Royer and Odette Bourgoin; m. Lucienne Leux 1944; two s. two d.; ed Ecole primaire supérieure Paul-Louis-Courier, Tours and Univ. de Poitiers; teacher at Langeais 1945–48, at Sainte-Maure 1950–54, at Tours 1954–58; del. of RPF (Rassemblement du Peuple Français) 1947–51; Ind. Deputy to Nat. Ass. 1958–73, 1976–97; Mayor of Tours 1959–95; Councillor for Tours-ouest Dist 1961; Minister of Commerce, Trades and Crafts 1973–74, of Posts and Telecommunications March–May 1974; Presidential cand. 1974; Pres. Loire Basin Devt Org. 1984–95; Pres. 'République et Liberté' group, Assemblée Nationale.

ROYO SÁNCHEZ, Arístides, PhD; Panamanian politician and lawyer; b. 14 Aug. 1940, La Chorrera; s. of Roberto Royas and Gilma Sánchez; m. Adele Ruíz 1963; one s. two d.; ed Nat. Institute, Panama City, Univs. of Salamanca and Bologna; Gen. Sec. of the Gen. Solicitorship of the Repub. of Panama 1965–68; Prof. of Consular, Notarial and Mercantile Law, Univ. of Panama 1966–69, then Prof. of Criminal Law, research 1967–71; mem. Law Codification Comm. 1969; mem. drafting comms. for Penal Code 1970, Constitution 1972; mem. Legis. Comm. of Nat. Council of Legislation 1972–73; Gen. Sec. School of Lawyers of Panama 1973; mem. Morgan & Morgan (lawyers) 1968–; a negotiator of Torrijos-Carter Canal Treaties between Panama and USA 1977; mem. Org. Comm. of Democratic Revolutionary Party; Minister of Educ. 1973–78; Pres. of Panama 1978–82; Amb. to Spain 1982–85; hon. mem. Spanish Law Soc. 1979; Grand Cross, Alfonso X the Wise (Spain) 1977, Extraordinary Grand Cross, Vasco Núñez de Balboa (Panama) 1978; Grand Collar, Order of Manuel Amador Guerrero (Panama) 1978; Grand Collar, Order of Isabel la Católica (Spain) 1979; Grand Cross, Légion d'honneur 1979; Extraordinary Grand Cross, Order of Boyaca (Colombia) 1979; Dr. hc Univ. San Martín de Porres, Lima, Peru 1979. *Publications:* Philosophy of Law in Cathrein and Del Vecchio 1963, History of Spanish Commercial Code 1964, The Responsibility of the Carrier in Sea Shipping 1965, Extraterritoriality of the Panamanian Criminal Law 1967, Draft Criminal Code of Panama, The Participation of Labourers in the Utilities of Enterprises, Revolution or De Facto Government, Manager in the Enterprise 1970, Commentaries to the Law on Retiring Funds for Journalists 1971, The Technician and the Politician in Public Administration 1973, Popular Consultation of the Law 1972. *Leisure interests:* reading, writing, skiing, jogging. *Address:* Morgan and Morgan, P.O. Box 1824, Panama City 1, Panama. *Telephone:* (507) 63-8822 (Office).

ROZANOV, Yevgeny Grigoryevich; Russian architect; b. 8 Nov. 1925, Moscow; s. of Grigory Alexandrovich Rozanov and Anastasiya Nikolaevna Rozanova; m. Aida Ilyenkova 1952; one s.; ed Moscow Inst. of Architecture; mem. CPSU 1964–91; Dir of Mezentsev Inst. of Standard and Experimental Design of Culture and Sports Activities 1970–85; maj. bldgs designed in Essentuki, Vladivostok, Tashkent, Moscow (notably Dinamo Sports Centre); teacher of architecture at Moscow Architectural Inst. 1960–85, Prof. 1953–85; Chair. State Cttee on Architecture and Town Planning 1987–91; Sec. USSR Union of Architects 1981–92; People's Deputy of the USSR 1989–91; mem. USSR (now Russian) Acad. of Arts 1979; Pres. Int. Acad. of Architecture (Moscow br.) 1991–; Vice-Pres. Russian Acad. of Arts 1998–; mem. Russian Acad. of Architecture and Construction Sciences 1997, Acad. of Architecture, Paris 1998; Hon. mem. Acad. of Architecture of Ukraine 1995; Dr hc (Moscow Architectural Inst.) 2001; Khamza Uzbek State Prize 1969, 1970, Navoi Uzbek State Prize 1975, USSR State Prize 1975, 1980, First Prize in Borovitskaya Square Competition, Moscow 1997, People's Architect of USSR 1983. *Publication:* The Works of E. G. Rozanov 1995. *Leisure interests:* painting, drawing, sculpture, music. *Address:* International Academy of Architecture, 2nd Brestskaya Street 6, 125047 Moscow (Office); Kosygina Street 9, Apt. 74, Moscow, Russia (Home). *Telephone:* (095) 972-47-85 (Office); (095) 137-56-09 (Home). *Fax:* (095) 972-47-85.

ROZANOVA, Irina Yuryevna; Russian actress; b. 22 July 1961, Penza; ed Moscow Inst. of Theatre Arts; actress Moscow Mayakovsky Theatre 1985–96, Moscow Theatre on Malaya Bronnaya 1996–; Merited Actress of Russian Fed. *Films include:* Intergirl, Serf, Encore, Encore, Cynics, Gambrinus, End of the Operation Resident, Red Stone. *Theatre includes:* Illusion, King Lear, Wood-Goblin, Abyss, Idiot, Provincial Girl. *Address:* Moscow Theatre on Malaya Bronnaya, M. Bronnaya str. 4, 103104 Moscow, Russia (Office); B. Bronnaya str. 8, apt. 21, 103104 Moscow, Russia (Home). *Telephone:* (095) 290-40-83 (Office); (095) 202-23-42 (Home). *Fax:* (095) 125-74-32 (Home).

ROZARIO, Patricia; singer (soprano); b. 1960, Bombay, India; m. Mark Troop; one d.; ed Guildhall School of Music; concerts with Songmakers' Almanac, including tour to USA; solo recitals, South Bank, London and elsewhere; frequent performances of Bach, Handel, Mozart; Vaughan Williams' Serenade to Music, BBC Proms 1988; Schumann's Paradies und der Peri, Madrid with Gerd Albrecht; appearances at Bath and Edin. Festivals; season 1993–94 included Wexford Festival appearance, tour of Germany with BBC Nat. Orchestra of Wales/Otaka, Hong Kong Philharmonic, world premiere of Taverner's Apocalypse, BBC Proms; season 1994–95 included recital in Lebanon, Purcell Room with Nash Ensemble; sang Les illuminations at St John's Smith Square, London 1997; performed in Handel's Triumph of Time and Truth, BBC Proms 1999; British Song Prize, Barcelona, Maggie Teyte

Prize, Sängerforderungspreis, Salzburg Mozarteum, Guildhall School of Music Gold Medal, Asian Women of Achievement Arts and Culture Award 2002. *Operatic roles include:* Giulietta (Jommelli's La schiava liberata) for Netherlands Opera, Gluck's Euridice for Opera North, Mozart's Bastienne and Pamina for Kent Opera, Ilia on Glyndebourne tour, Ismene in Lyon production of Mithridate and Zerlina at Aix, Statue in Rameau's Pygmalion and Purcell's Belinda for Kent Opera; Florinda in Handel's Rodrigo at Innsbruck, Nero in L'incoronazione di Poppea and Massenet's Sophie; concert performance of Il re pastore, Queen Elizabeth Hall, London, world premiere of John Casken's Golem, as Miriam, Almeida Festival, London, Ismene at Wexford Festival 1989, cr. title role in premiere of Taverner's Mary of Egypt, Aldeburgh Festival 1992, season 1992–93 in Monteverdi's Il combattimento, ENO and Haydn's L'infedeltà delusa, Garsington Opera, Romilda in Serse, Brussels 1996. *Recordings include:* Mahler Symphony No. 4, London Symphony Orchestra, Songs of the Auvergne with John Pritchard (conductor), Haydn Stabat Mater with Trevor Pinnock (conductor), Golem (Gramophone Award 1991), Taverner: We Shall See Him As He Is, Mary of Egypt, To a Child Dancing in the Wind; Spanish Songs, Britten's Rape of Lucretia. *Address:* c/o Askonas Holt Ltd., Lonsdale Chambers, 27 Chancery Lane, London, WC2A 1PF, England (Office).

ROZES, Simone, LenD, DèsSc; French lawyer; b. 29 March 1920, Paris; d. of Léon Ludwig and Marcelle Cetre; m. Gabriel Rozes 1942; one s. one d.; ed Lycée de Sèvres, Lycée de St-Germain-en-Laye, Univ. of Paris, Ecole Libre des Sciences Politiques; trainee lawyer, Paris 1947–49; Surrogate Judge, Bourges 1949–50; Judge 1951–; attaché, Justice Dept 1951–58; Admin. Chief, Cabinet of the Minister of Justice 1958–62, Vice-Pres. Tribunal de Grande Instance de Paris 1969–73, Pres. 1975–81; Dir Reformatory Educ. 1973–76; mem. UN Crime Prevention and Control Cttee 1977; Advocate-Gen. European Court of Justice 1981–84; First Advocate Gen. 1982–84; Pres. Cour de Cassation (Chief Justice) 1984–88, Hon. Pres. 1989–; Int. and Nat. Arbitrator 1989–; Pres. Int. Soc. of Social Defence, fmr. Pres. Soc. of Comparative Law; Hon. Vice-Pres. Int. Asscn of Penal Law; Inst. Frederik R. Bull; mem. Bd Alliance Française, Vice-Pres. 1994–; Grand Officer, Légion d'honneur; Officier, Ordre nat. du Mérite; Médaille de l'Educ. Surveillée, Médaille de l'Admin. Pénitentiaire, Commdr Cross, Order of Merit (FRG); Hon. LLD (Edin.). *Publication:* Le Juge et l'avocat (jtly.) 1992. *Leisure interest:* travelling. *Address:* 34 rue Bayen, 75017 Paris, France. *Telephone:* 1-43-80-16-67. *Fax:* 1-47-63-42-90.

RÓŻEWICZ, Tadeusz; Polish poet and playwright; b. 9 Oct. 1921, Radomsko; ed Jagiellonian Univ., Kraków; fmr factory worker and teacher; mem. Art Acad. of Leipzig; Corresp. mem. Bavarian Acad. of Fine Arts 1982–, Acad. of Arts (GDR); Order of Banner of Labour (2nd class) 1977, Great Cross of Polonia Restituta Order 1996; Dr hc (Wrocław) 1991, (Silesian Univ., Katowice) 1999, (Jagiellonian Univ.) 2000, (Kraków) 2000, (Warsaw) 2001; State Prize for Poetry 1955, 1956, Literary Prize, City of Cracow 1959, Prize of Minister of Culture and Art 1962, State Prize 1st Class 1966, Austrian Nat. Prize for European Literature 1982, Prize of Minister of Foreign Affairs 1974, 1987, Golden Wreath Prize for Poetry (Yugoslavia) 1987, Władysław Reymont Literary Prize 1999; Home Army Cross, London 1956, Alfred Jurzykowski Foundation Award, New York 1966, Medal of 30th Anniversary of People's Poland 1974, Nike Literary Prize 2000. *Plays include:* Kartoteka (The Card Index), Grupa Laokoona (Laocoön's Group), Świadkowie albo nasza mała stabilizacja (The Witnesses), Akt przerywany (The Interrupted Act), Śmieszny staruszek (The Funny Man), Wyszedł z domu (Gone Out), Spaghetti i miecz (Spaghetti and the Sword), Maja córeczka (My Little Daughter), Stara kobieta wysiaduje (The Old Woman Broods), Na czworakach (On All Fours), Do piachu (Down to Sand), Białe małżeństwo (White Marriage), Odejście Głodomora (Starveling's Departure), Na powierzchni poematu i w środku: nowy wybór wierszy, Pułapka (The Trap), Próba rekonstrukcji, (Spread Card Index), Kartoteka rozrzucona (The Card Index Scattered). *Prose includes:* Tarcza z pajęczyny, Opowiadania wybrane (Selected Stories), Na powierzchni poematu (They Came to See a Poet) 1991, Płaskorzeźba (Bas-Relief) 1991, Nasz starszy brat 1992, Historia pięciu wierszy 1993. *Publications:* 15 vols of poetry including Niepokój (Faces of Anxiety), Czerwona rękawiczka (The Red Glove), Czas, który idzie (The Time Which Goes On), Równina (The Plain), Srebrny kłos (The Silver Ear), Rozmowa z księciem (Conversation with the Prince), Zielona róża (The Green Rose), Nic w płaszczu Prospera (Nothing in Prosper's Overcoat), Twarz (The Face), Duszyczka (A Little Soul), Poezje (Poetry) 1987, Słowo po słowie (Word by Word) 1994, Zawsze fragment (Always the Fragment) 1996, Zawsze fragment: Recycling (Always the Fragment: Recycling) 1999, Matka odchodzi (The Mother Goes) 2000, Nożyk profesora (The Professor's Knife) 2001, Szara strefa 2002. *Address:* ul. Januszowicka 13 m. 14, 53-135 Wrocław, Poland. *Telephone:* (71) 3677138.

ROZHDESTVENSKY, Gennadiy Nikolayevich; Russian conductor; b. 4 May 1931, Moscow; s. of Nikolai Anosov and Natalia Rozhdestvenskaya; m. Viktoria Postnikova; one s.; ed Moscow State Conservatoire; Asst Conductor, Bolshoi Theatre 1951, Conductor 1956–60, Prin. Conductor 1965–70, Artistic Dir 2000–01; Chief Conductor of USSR Radio and TV Symphony Orchestra 1961–74; Chief Conductor Stockholm Philharmonia 1974–77, 1992–95, Moscow Chamber Opera 1974–83; Founder, Artistic Dir, Chief Conductor, State Symphony Orchestra of Ministry of Culture 1983–92; Prin. Conductor BBC Symphony Orchestra 1978–82, Vienna Symphony Orchestra 1980–83; has been guest conductor of numerous orchestras throughout Europe, America and Asia; Prof. of Conducting, Moscow State Conservatoire 1965–; Hon. mem. Swedish Royal Acad. 1975; People's Artist of the RSFSR 1966,

People's Artist of the USSR 1976, Hero of Socialist Labour 1991, Lenin Prize 1970 and other awards. *Publications:* The Fingering of Conducting 1974, Thoughts about Music 1975; numerous articles. *Leisure interest:* music. *Address:* c/o Victor Hochhauser Ltd, 4 Oak Hill Way, London N.W.3, England. *Telephone:* (095) 299-58-71 (Moscow) (Home).

ROZHKOV, Pavel Alekseyevich; Russian politician and wrestler; b. 30 June 1957, Ramenskoye, Moscow region; ed Moscow Inst. of Physical Culture; metal worker Radipribor plant 1974–75; coach Urozhai classical wrestling team Moscow 1977–78; Jr researcher All-Union Research Inst. of Physical Culture, Moscow 1979–82; coach State Sports Cttee 1982–87; docent Cen. State Inst. of Physical Culture, Moscow 1992; Sr coach Olympic Greek-Roman wrestling team 1992–96; Dir-Gen. Olymp-Tour co., Moscow 1997–99; Deputy Minister of Physical Culture, Sports and Tourism 1999, First Deputy Minister 1999–2000; Chair. State Cttee on Physical Culture, Sports and Tourism 2000–02, First Deputy Chair. 2002–. *Address:* State Committee for Physical Culture, Sports and Tourism, Kazakova str. 18, 103064 Moscow, Russia (Office). *Telephone:* (095) 263-08-40 (Office). *Fax:* (095) 263-08-41 (Office).

ROZOV, Viktor Sergeevich; Russian dramatist; b. 21 Aug. 1913, Yaroslavl; s. of Sergey Rozov and Ekaterina Rozova; m. Nadezda Kozlova 1945; one s. one d.; ed M. Gorki Literary Inst.; worked initially as actor in Kostroma and Moscow; served in Red Army 1941–45; Prof. Literary Inst. 1967–; USSR State Prize 1967. *Works include:* Her Friends 1949, Pages from Life 1953, In Search of Joy 1957, Uneven Fight 1960, Before Supper 1962, The Immortals (made into film The Cranes are Flying) 1957, A Traditional Meeting 1967, From Evening till Noon 1970, How Things Stand 1973, The Little Hog 1978 (banned, then performed Moscow 1979), The Capercaillie's Nest 1979, The Hidden Spring 1989, At Home 1989. *Publications include:* The Journey in Different Directions (memoirs) 1987, Examining the Old Photographs (memoirs, Vol. 2) 1995, Hofmann 1996. *Leisure interest:* philately. *Address:* Chernyakhovskogo Str. 4, Apt. 28, 125319 Moscow, Russia. *Telephone:* (095) 151-15-28.

ROZOVSKY, Mark Grigorievich; Russian theatre director and scriptwriter; b. 3 April 1937, Petropavlovsk; ed Moscow Univ. Higher Scriptwriters' School; f. and managed 'Our Home' (amateur studio theatre) with fellow students of Moscow Univ. 1958–70; theatre officially disbanded 1970, revived in 1987 as professional co. U Nikitskikh Vorot; wrote 3 books on theatre, dir versions of Karamzin, Kafka, Dostoevsky and others in Leningrad, Moscow and Riga 1970–87; Chief Dir Moscow State Music Hall 1974–79; Dir Orpheus and Eurydice (rock-opera) 1975 and a musical adaptation of 'Strider' jtly with Georgii Tovstonogov, by L. N. Tolstoy for Gorky Theatre, Leningrad; Theatre of Nations Prize Hamburg and Avignon 1979. *Other productions include:* Amadeus (P. Shaffer) for Moscow Arts Theatre; libretto for opera about Mayakovsky; work for TV including documentary on Meyerhold, Triumphal Square 1984; works for Gorky Theatre, Leningrad and Theatre of Russian Drama, Riga, Latvia and his own Studio Theatre, Moscow; Romances with Oblomov, Alexandrinsky Theatre, St Petersburg 1992. *Address:* Theatre U Nikitskikh Vorot, Bolshaya Nikitskaya Str. 23/9, 103009 Moscow, Russia. *Telephone:* (095) 291-84-19.

RU XIN; Chinese philosopher; b. 1932, Wujiang Co., Jiangsu Prov.; joined CCP 1948; Deputy Dir of Philosophy Inst., Acad. of Social Sciences 1979–; Exec. Vice-Pres. Acad. of Social Sciences 1984–99; alt. mem. 14th CCP Cen. Cttee 1992–97; Vice-Chair. Academic Degrees Cttee, State Council 1995–98. *Address:* c/o Academy of Social Sciences, 5 Jianguomen Nei Da Jie, Beijing 100732, People's Republic of China.

RUAN CHONGWU; Chinese politician; b. 1933, Huai'an Co., Hebei Prov.; ed Moscow Auto-Eng Inst.; Deputy Dir Shanghai Materials Research Inst.; joined CCP 1952; Deputy Sec. Shanghai Municipal Scientific Workers' Asscn; Science and Tech. Counsellor, Chinese Embassy in Bonn 1978; Vice-Mayor Shanghai 1983–85; Sec. CCP, Shanghai Municipality 1983–85; mem. 12th CCP Cen. Cttee 1985–87, 13th Cen. Cttee 1987–92, 14th Cen. Cttee 1992–97; Minister of Public Security 1985–87; Vice-Minister Science and Tech. Comm., State Council 1987–89, of Labour 1989–93; Sec. CPC 2nd Hainan Provincial Cttee 1993; Gov. of Hainan 1993. *Address:* c/o Office of the Governor, Haikou City, Hainan Province, 570003, People's Republic of China.

RUBADIRI, David, PhD; Malawi diplomatist, academic and author; b. 19 July 1930, Luila; m.; nine c.; ed King's Coll., Oxford, Univ. of Bristol, Univ. Coll., Kampala; fmr Prin. Soche Hill Coll. (now part of Univ. of Malawi), fmr Acting Prov. Educ. Officer, Southern Prov.; Amb. to UN and USA 1963–65; various academic and admin. posts, Univ. of Makerere, Kampala 1965–76, Sr Lecturer Dept of Literature, Univ. of Nairobi 1976–84, Prof. and Head Dept of Languages and Literature and Social Science Educ., Univ. of Botswana 1984–95; Perm. Rep. to the UN 1995–2000; Visiting Prof. of English Literature, Northwestern Univ. 1972, Univ. of Ife 1978–80. *Publications:* literary books, poetry and plays. *Address:* c/o Ministry of Foreign Affairs and International Co-operation, POB 30315, Capital City, Lilongwe 3, Malawi.

RUBBIA, Carlo; Italian professor of physics; b. 31 March 1934, Gorizia; s. of Silvio Rubbia and Bice Rubbia; m. Marisa Rubbia; one s. one d.; ed high school, Pisa and Columbia and Rome Univs.; research physicist. CERN 1960, mem. Cttee CERN 1985, Dir-Gen. 1989; Prof. of Physics, Harvard Univ. 1972–88; mem. Papal Acad. of Science 1986–; Foreign mem. USSR Acad. of Sciences; mem. American Acad. of Arts and Sciences, Accademia dei Lincei, European Acad. of Sciences; Nobel Prize for Physics 1984, Leslie Prize for

Exceptional Achievements 1985, Jesolo d'Oro 1986. *Address:* c/o Organisation Européenne pour la Recherche Nucléaire (CERN), EP Division, 1211 Geneva 23, Switzerland.

RUBENS, Bernice Ruth, BA; British author; b. 26 July 1928, Cardiff; d. of Eli Reubens and Dorothy Reubens; m. Rudi Nassauer 1947; two d.; ed Cardiff High School for Girls and Univ. of Wales, Cardiff; author and Dir of documentary films on Third World subjects; Fellow Univ. Coll., Cardiff; Hon. DLit (Wales) 1991; Booker Prize 1970; American Blue Ribbon (documentary film) 1972. *Films:* Madame Cousatzka, I Sent a Letter to My Love. *Musical:* I Sent a Letter to My Love. *Play:* I Sent a Letter to My Love. *Television includes:* mini series of Mr Wakefield's Crusade (BBC 1) 1997. *Publications:* Set on Edge 1960, Madame Sontsatzka 1962, Mate in Three 1964, The Elected Member 1968, Sunday Best 1970, Go Tell the Lemming 1972, I Sent a Letter to my Love 1974, Ponsonby Post 1976, A Five-year Sentence 1978, Spring Sonata 1979, Birds of Passage 1980, Brothers 1982, Mr. Wakefield's Crusade 1985, Our Father 1987, Kingdom Come 1990, A Solitary Grief 1991, Mother Russia 1992, Autobiopsy 1993, Yesterday in the Back Lane (novel) 1995, The Waiting Game (novel) 1997, I, Dreyfus (novel) 1999, Milwaukee 2001, Nine Lives (novel) 2002, The Sergeant's Tale (novel) 2003. *Leisure interest:* playing 'cello. *Address:* 213 Goldhurst Terrace, London, NW6 3ER, England. *Telephone:* (20) 7625-4845.

RUBENSTEIN, Edward, MD; American professor of medicine; b. 5 Dec. 1924, Cincinnati; s. of Louis Rubenstein and Nettie Nathan; m. Nancy Ellen Millman 1954; three s.; ed Cincinnati Univ. Coll. of Medicine; Laboratory Asst, Dept of Physiology, Cincinnati Univ. 1947; Intern, then Jr Asst, then Sr Asst Resident in Medicine, Cincinnati Gen. Hosp. 1947–50, Medical Chief, Psychosomatic Service 1953–54; Research Fellow, May Inst., Cincinnati 1950; Chief of Medicine, USAF Hosp., March Airforce Base 1950–52; Sr Asst Resident in Medicine, Barnes Hosp., St Louis 1952–53; Chief, Clinical Physiology Unit, San Mateo Co. Gen. Hosp. 1955–63, Chief of Medicine 1960–70; Prof. of Medicine and Assoc. Dean of Postgraduate Medical Educ., Stanford Univ. School of Medicine 1971, now Emer; Ed.-in-Chief Scientific American 1978–94; founding Ed.-in-Chief Scientific American Medicine; mem. Inst. of Medicine of NAS; Master, American Coll. of Physicians; TV documentary Being Human 1979; research in synchrotron radiation; Fellow AAAS, Royal Soc. of Medicine; Kaiser Award, Albion Walter Hewlett Award 1993. *Publications:* Intensive Medical Care 1971, Handbook on Synchrotron Radiation Vol. 4 (Ed.), Introduction to Molecular Medicine (Ed.), Synchrotron Radiation in the Life Sciences (Ed.); numerous scientific papers. *Address:* Department of Medicine, Stanford Medical Centre, Stanford, CA 94305, USA. *Telephone:* (650) 343-2992 (Office). *Fax:* (650) 343-2992 (Office). *E-mail:* exr@leland.stanford.edu (Office).

RUBENSTEIN, Howard Joseph, LLB; American public relations executive; b. 3 Feb. 1932, New York; s. of Samuel Rubenstein and Ada Sall; m. Amy Forman 1959; three s.; ed Univ. of Pa, Harvard Univ. and St John's Law School; admitted New York State Bar 1960; Pres. Howard J. Rubenstein Assocs. Inc. (public relations consultants), New York 1954–; numerous civic and other public appointments including Co-Chair. Holocaust Comm. 1993–; Bd Dirs. Albert Einstein Coll. of Medicine 1997–; mem. Mayor's Business Advisory Council, New York 1996–, communications adviser Gov.'s Jerusalem 3000 Cttee 1996–; Bd Govs. Jewish County Relations Council 1999–; Hon. LLD (St John's Law School) 1990. *Address:* Howard J. Rubenstein Associates Inc., 1345 Avenue of the Americas, New York, NY 10105; 993 Fifth Ave, New York, NY 10028, USA (Home).

RUBIANO SÁENZ, H.E. Cardinal Pedro; Colombian ecclesiastic; b. 13 Sept. 1932, Cartago; ordained priest 1956; Bishop of Cúcuta 1971; Coadjutor of Cali 1983, Bishop of Cali 1985; Archbishop of Santafé de Bogotá 1994–; cr. Cardinal 2001. *Address:* Arzobispado, Carrera 7 N. 10–20, Santafé de Bogotá, DC1, Colombia (Office). *Telephone:* (1) 3345500 (Office). *Fax:* (1) 3347867 (Office).

RUBIK, Ernő; Hungarian inventor, architect and designer; b. 13 July 1944, Budapest; s. of Ernő Rubik Sr and Magdolna Szántó; m.; one s. two d.; ed Technical Univ. and Acad. of Applied Arts, Budapest; consecutively Asst Prof., then Assoc. Prof., Acad. of Applied Arts, Dir of Postgraduate Studies 1983–86; Hon. Prof. Acad. of Crafts and Design, Budapest 1987; inventor Rubik's Cube and other games and puzzles; Pres. Rubik Studio; Pres. Hungarian Acad. of Eng 1990–96; Labour Order of Merit Gold Medal of the Hungarian People's Repub., Toy of the Year award 1981–82 of UK, Fed. Repub. of Germany, Italy, Sweden, Finland, France, USA; State Prize 1983. *Publications:* co-author and ed. of A büvös kocka (The Magic Cube) 1981, Rubik's Magic 1986, Rubik's Cubic Compendium 1987. *Leisure interests:* swimming, skiing, sailing. *Address:* Rubik Studio, 1122 Budapest, Városmajor u. 74, Hungary. *Telephone:* 156-9533.

RUBIKS, Alfreds; Latvian politician; b. 1935, Daugavpils, Latvia; ed Riga Polytechnic; mem. CPSU 1958–91; started work as engineer at Riga Electro-Machinery Plant 1959–; Komsomol and party work; Sec. Latvian Komsomol Cen. Cttee; First Sec. of Leningradsky Region of Riga Regional CP Cttee 1976–82; Minister of Local Industry for Latvian SSR 1982–84; Chair. Exec. Cttee Riga City Council of People's Deputies 1984–90; First Sec. Cen. Cttee Latvian CP 1990–91; USSR People's Deputy 1989–91; mem. CPSU Cen. Cttee 1990–91; mem. CPSU Politburo July 1990–91; arrested by Latvian authorities Aug. 1991, accused of high treason; elected to Saeima (Parl.) 1993;

sentenced to 8 years' imprisonment 1995; released 1997; mem. Saeima 1998–; Chair. Socialist Party 1998–. *Address:* Saeima, Jecaba str. 11, 1811 Riga, Latvia.

RUBIN, The Hon. James P., BA, MIA; American politician; b. 1960, New York; ed Columbia Univ.; Research Dir Arms Control Asscn, Washington DC 1985–89, also consultant to Senate Foreign Relations Cttee on nuclear arms control issues; fmrly staff mem. U.S. Senate Foreign Relations Cttee, Sr Foreign Policy Adviser to Joseph R. Biden, Jr (q.v.); Sr Adviser and spokesman for U.S. Rep. to UN, Madeleine Albright 1993–96; Dir of Foreign Policy and spokesman Clinton/Gore presidential campaign Aug.–Nov. 1996; Sr Adviser to Sec. of State 1996–97; Asst Sec. of State for Public Affairs 1997–2000; public speaker, commentator, author, London 2000–; partner Brunswick 2001–; Visiting Prof. of Int. Relations LSE 2001–; Democrat; John Jay Award for Distinguished Professional Achievement (Columbia Coll.) 1998, Distinguished Service Award, Sec. of State 2000.

RUBIN, Louis Decimus, Jr, PhD; American writer, professor of English and publisher; b. 19 Nov. 1923, Charleston, SC; s. of Louis Decimus Rubin, Sr and Janet Weinstein Rubin; m. Eva Maryette Redfield 1951; two s.; ed High School of Charleston, Coll. of Charleston, Univ. of Richmond and Johns Hopkins Univ.; U.S. Army 1943–46; instructor in English Johns Hopkins Univ. 1948–54; Exec. Sec. American Studies Asscn 1954–56 (also fmr Vice-Pres.); Assoc. Ed. News Leader, Richmond, Va 1956–57; Assoc. Prof. of English, Hollins Coll., Prof., Chair. of Dept 1960–67, of English Univ. of NC 1967–73, Univ. Distinguished Prof. 1973-89, Prof. Emer. 1989–; Visiting Prof. La. State Univ., Univ. of Calif. at Santa Barbara, Harvard Univ.; lecturer, Aix-Marseille at Nice, Kyoto Summer American Studies Seminars; USICA, Austria, Germany; Ed. Southern Literary Studies Series, Louisiana State Univ. Press 1965–90; Co-Ed. Southern Literary Journal 1968–89; Editorial Dir Algonquin Books, Chapel Hill 1982–91; fmr Pres. Soc. for Study of Southern Literature; fmr Chair. American Literature Section, Modern Language Asscn; mem. SC Acad. of Authors, Fellowship of Southern Writers; Hon. DLitt (Richmond, Clemson, Coll. of Charleston, Univ. of the South, Univ. of NC, Ashville, Univ. of NC Chapel Hill). *Publications:* author: Thomas Wolfe: The Weather of His Youth 1955, No Place on Earth 1959, The Faraway Country 1964, The Golden Weather (novel) 1961, The Curious Death of the Novel 1967, The Teller in the Tale 1967, George W. Cable 1969, The Writer in the South 1972, William Elliott Shoots a Bear 1975, The Wary Fugitives 1978, Surfaces of a Diamond (novel) 1981, A Gallery of Southerners 1982, The Even-Tempered Angler 1984, The Edge of the Swamp: a study in the Literature and Society of the Old South 1989, The Mockingbird in the Gum Tree 1991, Small Craft Advisory 1991, The Heat of the Sun (novel) 1995, Babe Ruth's Ghost 1996, Seaports of the South 1998, A Memory of Trains 2000, An Honorable Estate 2001; editor: Southern Renascence 1953, Idea of an American Novel 1961, South 1961, Comic Imagination in American Literature 1973, The Literary South 1979, American South 1980, The History of Southern Literature 1985, An Apple for My Teacher 1986, Algonquin Literary Quiz Book 1990, A Writer's Companion 1995. *Leisure interests:* baseball, classical music, reading. *Address:* 702 Gimghoul Road, Chapel Hill, NC 27514, USA (Home).

RUBIN, Robert; American business executive, lawyer and government official; b. 29 Aug. 1938, New York; s. of Alexander Rubin and Sylvia (née Seiderman) Rubin; m. Judith L. Oxenberg 1963; two s.; ed Harvard Univ., London School of Econs, Yale Law School; lawyer Cleary, Gottlieb, Steen & Hamilton New York 1964–66; joined Goldman, Sachs 1966, Vice-Chair. & Co-COO 1987–90, Co-Chair. 1990–92; Chair. New York Host Cttee 1992 Democratic Convention; Asst to Pres. Clinton for Econ. Policy 1993–95; Sec. of Treasury Jan. 1995–99; Chair. Citigroup 1999–; Hon. DHumLitt (Yeshiva Univ.) 1996; Nat. Asscn of Christians and Jews Award 1977, Columbia Business School Award 1996, Euromoney Magazine's Finance Minister of the Year Award 1996, Medal for High Civic Service, Citizens' Budget Comm. 1997, Foreign Policy Asscn Medal 1998, Jefferson Award, American Inst. for Public Service 1998, Award of Merit, Yale Univ. 1998, Paul Tsongas Award 1998, Global Leadership Award, UN Asscn 1998. *Leisure interest:* fly fishing. *Address:* c/o Citigroup, 1 Court Square, Long Island City, NY 11120, USA.

RUBIN, Vera Cooper, PhD; American astronomer; b. 23 July 1928, Philadelphia; d. of Philip Cooper and Rose Applebaum Cooper; m. Robert J. Rubin 1948; three s. one d.; ed Vassar Coll., Cornell Univ., Georgetown Univ.; Research Assoc. to Asst Prof. Georgetown Univ. 1955–65; mem. Staff Dept of Terrestrial Magnetism, Carnegie Inst., Wash. 1965–; Distinguished Visiting Astronomer, Cerro Tololo Inter-American Observatory 1978, Chancellor's Distinguished Prof. of Astronomy Univ. of Calif., Berkeley 1981; Pres.'s Distinguished Visitor, Vassar Coll. 1987; B. Tinsley Visiting Prof., Univ. of Texas 1988; Oort Visiting Prof., Univ. of Leiden 1995; has observed at Kitt Peak Nat. Observatory, Lowell, Palomar, McDonald, Las Campanas, Chile Observatories; Chair. Nat. Comm. for Int. Astronomical Union 1998–2000; Assoc. Ed. Astronomical Journal 1972–77, Astrophysical Journal of Letters 1977–82; mem. Council American Astronomical Soc. 1977–80, Nat. Science Bd 1986–(2002); mem. Editorial Bd Science Magazine 1979–87; mem. Council Smithsonian Inst. 1979–85, Space Telescope Science Inst. 1990–92; Pres. Galaxy Comm. Int. Astronomical Union 1982–85; mem. NAS, American Acad. of Arts and Sciences, American Philosophical Soc., Pres's Cttee to select recipients of Nat. Medal of Science, Pontifical Acad. of Sciences; Jansky Lecture, Nat. Radio Astronomy Observatory 1994, Russel Lecturer, American Astronomical Soc. 1995; Hon. DSc (Creighton Univ.) 1978, (Harvard Univ.)

1988, (Yale Univ.) 1990, (Williams Coll.) 1993, (Univ. of Mich.) 1996, (Ohio State Univ.) 1998; Hon. DHL (Georgetown) 1997; Dickson Prize for Science, Carnegie Mellon Univ. 1994, Helen Hogg Prize, Canadian Astronomical Soc. 1997; Nat. Medal of Science 1993, Weizmann Women and Science Award 1996, Gold Medal Royal Astronomical Soc., London 1996, Canadian Astronomy Soc. Helen Hogg Prize 1997. *Publications:* Bright Galaxies, Dark Matters 1999; over 150 scientific papers on the dynamics of galaxies in specialist journals. *Leisure interests:* family, garden, hiking, travel. *Address:* Department of Terrestrial Magnetism, Carnegie Institution of Washington, 5241 Broad Branch Road, NW, Washington, DC 20015, USA.

RUBIN, William, PhD; American art historian and curator; b. 11 Aug. 1927, New York; ed Univ. of Paris, Columbia Univ.; Prof. of Art History Sarah Lawrence Coll. 1952–67, City Univ. of New York 1960–68; Adjunct Prof. Art History, Inst. of Fine Arts, New York Univ. 1968–; Chief Curator Painting and Sculpture, Museum of Modern Art, New York 1968, Dir Painting and Sculpture 1973–88, Dir Emer. 1988–; exhbns. arranged include: Dada, Surrealism and their Heritage 1968, New American Painting and Sculpture 1969, Stella 1970, Miró 1973, Picasso: A Retrospective 1980, Giorgio De Chirico 1982, Primitivism in 20th Century Art 1984, Frank Stella 1970–87 1987, Picasso and Braque: Pioneering Cubism 1989, Ad Reinhardt 1991; American Ed. Art Int. Magazine 1959–64; Trustee Sarah Lawrence Coll. 1980–86; Officier Légion d'honneur 1991, Officier des Arts et Lettres (Paris) 1979. *Publications:* Matta 1957, Modern Sacred Art and the Church of Assy 1961, Dada, Surrealism and their Heritage 1966, Dada and Surrealist Art 1969, Frank Stella 1970, Picasso in the Collection of the Museum of Modern Art 1973, The Paintings of Gerald Murphy 1974, Anthony Caro 1975, (with Carolyn Lanchner) André Masson 1976, Paris-New York: Situation de l'Art 1978; ed. (with Carolyn Lanchner) Cézanne: The Late Work 1977, Picasso: A Retrospective 1980, Giorgio De Chirico 1982, Picasso and Portraiture: Representation and Transformation 1996.

RUBINA, Dina Ilyinichna; Uzbekistan writer; b. 19 Sept. 1953, Tashkent; ed Tashkent State Conservatory; music teacher Tashkent Inst. of Culture 1977–90; literary debut in Yunost magazine 1971; emigrated to Israel 1990; Head Dept of Public and Cultural Relations, The Jewish Agency in Russia 1999–; Ed. Nasha Strana (Russian language newspaper); Ministry of Culture Award 1982, Arye Dulchin Award (Israel) 1990, Israel Writers' Union Award 1995. *Publications:* The Double-Barrelled Name (short stories) 1990, In Thy Gates 1994, An Intellectual Sat Down on the Road 1995, Here Comes the Messiah 1997, The Escort Angel 1998. *Address:* The Jewish Agency in Russia, Presnensky val 36A, 123557 Moscow, Russia (Office). *Telephone:* (095) 253-46-55 (Office); (095) 253-10-36 (Office). *Fax:* (095) 253-46-67 (Office). *E-mail:* dina@sohnut.ru (Office).

RUBINSTEIN, Amnon, PhD; Israeli politician, author and professor of law; b. 5 Sept. 1931, Tel. Aviv; s. of Aaron Rubinstein and Rachel (Vilozny) Rubinstein; m. Ronny Havatzeleth 1959; one s. one d.; ed Hebrew Univ., London School of Econs; mil. service Israeli Defence Forces; fmr Dean Faculty of Law and Prof. of Law, Tel Aviv Univ.; mem. Knesset (Parl.) 1977–; mem. Constitution Cttee; Minister of Communications 1984–87, of Energy and Infrastructure and Science and Tech. 1992–93, of Educ. and Culture 1993–96; Chair. Constitution Law and Justice Cttee of Knesset 1999–2001, State Audit Cttee of Knesset; Dr. hc (Bradford) 1968, (Hewbrew Union Coll., Jerusalem) 1969. *Publications:* Jurisdiction and Illegality 1965, The Zionist Dream Revisited 1985 (French trans. Le Rêve et l'histoire), The Constitutional Law of Israel (5th Edn) 1997, From Herzl to Rabin 1999. *Leisure interests:* music, drama, swimming. *Address:* 13 Yacov Street, Tel Aviv 69015, Israel. *Telephone:* 2-6753388 (Office); 3-6495454 (Home). *Fax:* 3-6753111 (Office); 2-6484851 (Home). *E-mail:* rubinstn@knesset.gov.il (Office); amnon_r@netvision.net.il (Home).

RUCKAUF, Carlos Federico; Argentine politician; b. 10 July 1944; m.; three c.; ed Nat. Univ. of Buenos Aires; Asst Sec. Insurance Union 1969–72; Labour Judge 1973–75; Sec. Trabajo de la Nación (Labour of the Nation) 1975–76; Pres. Partido Justicialista de Capital Federal (Fed. Justice Party) 1983, Vice-Pres. 1993, Pres. 1994; Senatorial Cand. 1983; Nat. Deputy 1987–89, 1991–93; Amb. to Italy, Malta and FAO 1989–91; Pres. Foreign Affairs Comm. 1991–93; Minister of the Interior 1993; apptd Vice-Pres. of Argentina 1995; Gov. Buenos Aires Prov. 1999–; Minister of Foreign Affairs 2002–; Kt of the Grand Cross, Order of Merit (Italy) 1995, Grand Cross, Order Bernardo O'Higgins (Chile) 1996, Medal of the Congress of Deputies (Spain) 1997, Commdr, Légion d'honneur (France) 1997, Alaoui Order (Morocco) 1998, Grand Cross, Ordem Nacional do Cruzeiro do Sul (Brazil) 1998, Special Grand Cross, Nat. Order of Merit (Paraguay) 1999. *Address:* Ministry of Foreign Affairs, International Trade and Worship, Esmeralda 1212, 1007 Buenos Aires, Argentina (Office). *Telephone:* (11) 4819-7000 (Office). *E-mail:* web@mrecic.gov.ar (Office). *Website:* www.mrecic.gov.ar (Office).

RUCKELSHAUS, William Doyle; American government official; b. 24 July 1932, Indianapolis, Ind.; s. of John K. and Marion (Doyle) Covington Ruckelshaus; m. Jill E. Strickland 1962; one s. four d.; ed Portsmouth Priory School, RI and Princeton and Harvard Univs; served with US Army 1953–55; admitted to Ind. Bar 1960; attorney with Ruckelshaus, Bobbit & O'Connor 1960–68; Partner Ruckelshaus, Beveridge, Fairbanks & Diamond (fmrly Ruckelshaus, Beveridge & Fairbanks), Sr Partner 1974–76; Deputy Attorney-Gen. Ind. 1960–65; Minority Attorney, Ind. State Senate 1965–67; mem. Ind. House of Reps 1967–69; Asst Attorney-Gen., US Civil Div., Dept of Justice

1969–70; Dir Environmental Protection Agency 1970–73; Acting Dir FBI 1973; Deputy Attorney-Gen. 1973; Sr Vice-Pres. Weyerhaeuser Co. 1976–83; Dir Environmental Protection Agency 1983–84; mem. firm Perkins Coie, Seattle 1985–88; Chair. CEO Browning-Ferris Industries Inc., Houston 1988–95; f., Prin. Madronea Investment Group 1996–; Chair. World Resources Inst. 1999–; fmr mem. Bd Dirs Cummins Engine Co., Inc., Peabody Int. Corpn, Church and Dwight Co. Inc., Nordstrom, Inc.; fmr Chair. Bd Geothermal Kinetics Inc., Trustees of Urban Inst.; mem. Bd American Paper Inst., Council on Foreign Relations, Twentieth Century Fund; Trustee, Pacific Science Center Foundation, Seattle Chamber of Commerce, The Conservation Foundation, Seattle Art Museum; mem. Public Interest Advisory Cttee Harvard Univ. Medical Project, Bd of Overseers, Harvard J.F.K. School of Govt, Bd of Regents, Seattle Univ., World Resource Inst. (Chair. 1998–); mem. several US bar asscns. Publication: Reapportionment – A Continuing Problem 1963. Leisure interests: tennis, fishing, reading. Address: Madronea Investment Group, 1000 2nd Avenue, Suite 3700, Seattle, WA 98104, USA.

RÜCKL, Jiří; Czech politician and business executive; b. 20 Oct. 1940, Prague; s. of Jiří Rückl and Věra Rückl; m. Jana Hrabánková; two d.; ed Econ. Univ., Prague; specialist positions in glassware 1961–90; Propr., Dir. Rückl Crystal 1992–; Dir., Ministry of Industry 1990–92; Councillor for Nižbor 1994–; Senator 1996–. Publications include: specialist papers about glass production. Address: Ruckl Crystal a.s., 26705 Nižbor 141 (Office); c/o Senát PCR, Valdštejnské nám. 4, 11800 Prague 1, 11800, Czech Republic (Office). Telephone: (3) 11696111 (Office). Fax: (3) 11693510 (Office). E-mail: rucklj@senat.cz (Office); ruckl@telecom.cz. Website: www.ruckl-crystal.com.

RUDD, Sir (Anthony) Nigel (Russell), Kt, DL, FCA; British business executive; b. 31 Dec. 1946; m. Lesley Elizabeth Rudd (née Hodgkinson) 1969; two s. one d.; ed Bemrose Grammar School, Derby; chartered accountant 1968; Divisional Finance Dir London & Northern Group 1970–77; Chair. C. Price & Son Ltd 1977–82; Chair. Williams Holdings (later Williams PLC) 1982–2000; Deputy Chair. Raine Industries 1992–94 (Chair. (non-exec.) 1986–92); Dir Pilkington PLC 1994, Chair. 1995–2002; Deputy Chair. Boots PLC 2002, Chair. 2003–; Chair. (non-exec.) Pendragon PLC 1989–, East Midlands Electricity 1994–97 (Dir 1990–97), Kidde 2000–; Dir (non-exec.) Williams Man. Services 1985–96, Westminster Securities 1987–96, Gartmore Value Investment 1989–93, Gartmore 1993–96, Derby Pride 1993–98, Mithras Investment Trust 1994–98, Barclays Bank 1996–; mem. European Round Table of Industrialists –2001, Council CBI 1999–; mem. Chartered Accountants' Co. DL Derbys 1996; Freeman, City of London; Hon. DTech (Loughborough) 1998; Hon. DUniv (Derby) 1998. Leisure interests: golf, skiing, theatre, field sports. Address: The Boots Company PLC, Nightingale House, 65 Curzon Street, London, W1Y 7PE, England (Office). Website: www.boots-plc.com (Office).

RUDDEN, Bernard (Anthony), LLD, DCL, FBA; British professor of law; b. 21 Aug. 1933, Carlisle; s. of John Rudden and Kathleen Rudden; m. Nancy Campbell 1957; three s. one d.; ed City of Norwich School and St John's Coll. Cambridge; Fellow and Tutor, Oriel Coll. Oxford 1965–79; Prof. of Comparative Law, Univ. of Oxford and Fellow, Brasenose Coll. Oxford 1979–99, Prof. Emer. 1999–; Hon. LLD (McGill) 1979. Publications: Soviet Insurance Law 1966, The New River 1985, Basic Community Cases 1987, Source-Book on French Law (co-author) 1991, Basic Community Law (co-author) 1996, Law of Property 2002. Address: 15 Redinnick Terrace, Penzance, Cornwall, TR18 4HR, England. Telephone: (1736) 360395.

RUDDLE, Francis Hugh, PhD; American professor of biology and human genetics; b. 19 Aug. 1929, West New York, NJ; s. of Thomas Hugh Ruddle and Mary Henley (Rodda); m. Nancy Marion Hartman 1964; two d.; ed Wayne State Univ., Detroit and Univ. of California, Berkeley; Research Assoc., Child Research Center of Mich., Detroit 1953–56; Nat. Insts. of Health Postdoctoral Fellow, Dept of Biochem., Univ. of Glasgow, Scotland 1960–61; Asst Prof., Yale Univ. 1961–67, Assoc. Prof. 1967–72, Prof. of Biology and Human Genetics 1972–, Chair. Dept of Biology 1977–83, 1988–, Ross Granville Harrison Prof. of Biology 1983–88, Sterling Prof. of Biology 1988–; Pres. American Soc. of Human Genetics 1985; Pres. American Soc. of Cell Biology 1986; Fellow A.A.A.S; mem. NAS, American Genetic Asscn, American Soc. of Biological Chemists, American Soc. of Zoologists, Genetics Soc. of America. Leisure interest: boating. Address: Department of Biology, Yale University, Kline Biology Tower, P.O. Box 6666, New Haven, CT 06511-8112, USA. Telephone: (203) 436-0418. Website: www.yale.edu (Office).

RUDDOCK, Joan Mary, BSc, ARCS; British politician; b. 28 Dec. 1943; d. of Ken Anthony and Eileen Anthony; m. Dr. Keith Ruddock 1963 (died 1996); ed Pontypool Grammar School for Girls and Imperial Coll. London; worked for Shelter (nat. campaign for the homeless) 1968–73; Dir Oxford Housing Aid Centre 1973–77; Special Programmes Officer with unemployed young people, Manpower Services Comm. 1977–79; Man., Reading Citizens Advice Bureau 1979–87; Chair. Campaign for Nuclear Disarmament (CND) 1981–85, Vice-Chair. 1985–86; MP for Lewisham Deptford 1987–; mem. Select Cttee on Televising House of Commons; mem. British Del., Council of Europe 1988–89; Shadow Spokesperson on Transport 1989–92, on Home Affairs 1992–94, on Environmental Protection 1994–; Parl. Under Sec. of State for Women 1997–98; Co-founder Women Say No to GMOs 1999; mem. Select Cttee on Modernization; Founder and Co-ordinator UK Women's Link with Afghan Women; Hon. Fellow Goldsmith's Coll., Univ. of London 1996, Laban Centre, London; Labour; Frank Cousins Peace Award 1984. Publications: CND Scrapbook 1987, The CND Story (contrib.) 1983, Voices for One World (contrib.) 1988. Leisure interests: gardening, music, art. Address: House of Commons, Westminster, London, SW1A 0AA, England. Telephone: (20) 7219-4513. Fax: (20) 7219-6045. E-mail: alexanderh@parliament.uk (Office). Website: www.joanruddock.org.uk (Office).

RUDDOCK, Hon. Philip M., BA, LLB; Australian politician and solicitor; b. 12 March 1943, Canberra; s. of the Hon. Max S. Ruddock; m. Heather Ruddock 1971; two d.; ed Barker Coll., Horsby, Sydney Univ.; Shadow Minister for ACT and Shadow Minister Assisting Opposition Leader on Public Service Matters 1983–84, Immigration and Ethnic Affairs 1984–85, 1989–93, Shadow Minister for Social Security and Sr Citizens 1993, mem. Shadow Cabinet 1996; Minister for Immigration and Multicultural Affairs 1996–2001, also Minister Assisting Prime Minister for Reconciliation 1998–2001, Minister for Immigration and Multicultural and Indigenous Affairs 2001–02; Minister Assisting the Prime Minister on Reconciliation 2002–. Leisure interests: jogging, bushwalking, gardening, opera, reading. Address: Parliament House, Canberra 2600, Australia (Office); Level 3, 20 George Street, Hornsby, NSW 2077. Telephone: (2) 6277-7860 (Office). Fax: (2) 6273-4144 (Office). E-mail: minister@immi.gov.au (Office). Website: www.immi.gov.au (Office).

RUDENSTINE, Neil Leon, PhD; American university administrator; b. 21 Jan. 1935, Ossining, New York; s. of Harry Rudenstine and Mae Rudenstine; m. Angelica Zander 1960; one s. two d.; ed Princeton Univ., Oxford Univ., Harvard Univ.; instructor. English Dept, Harvard Univ. 1964–66, Asst Prof. 1966–68, Prof. of English, Pres. Harvard Univ. 1991–2001; Assoc. Prof. of English, Princeton Univ. 1968–73, Dean of Students 1968–72, Prof. of English 1973–88, Dean of Coll. 1972–77, Provost 1977–88; Exec. Vice-Pres. Andrew W. Mellon Foundation, New York 1988–91; Hon. Fellow New Coll., Oxford Univ.; Fellow American Acad. of Arts and Sciences. Publications: Sidney's Poetic Development 1967, English Poetic Satire: Wyatt to Byron (with George Rousseau) 1972, In Pursuit of the PhD (with William G. Bowen) 1992. Address: 33 Elmwood Avenue, Cambridge, MA 02138 USA (Home); A.W. Mellon Foundation, 140 East 62nd Street, New York NY 10021 (Office).

RUDIN, Alexander Izraliyevich; Russian cellist and conductor; b. 25 Nov. 1960, Moscow; m. Rudina Olga Ryurikovna; two s.; ed Gnessin Music Inst., Moscow State Conservatory; has appeared as a soloist with numerous orchestras including Royal Philharmonic, Danish Radio, St Petersburg Philharmonic, Moscow Philharmonic, Austrian Symphony, Bolshoi Theatre; has worked as conductor with orchestras in Finland, Germany, Italy, Norway, Russia; has participated in festivals in Edin., Istanbul, Kuhmo, Vaasa; founder and artistic Dir Musica Viva Chamber Orchestra 1987; artistic Dir Int. Festival Music Ensembles; teacher Moscow State Conservatory; Visiting Prof. Sibelius Acad., Helsinki; winner of Concertino Prague 1973, J. S. Bach Competition, Leipzig 1976, Nat. Competition, Vilnius 1977. Address: Malaya Ostroumovskaya str. 1/10, Apt. 46, 107014 Moscow, Russia (Home). Telephone: (095) 268-15-77 (Home).

RUDIN, Scott; American film and theatre producer; b. 14 July 1958, New York; production asst, asst to theatre producers Kermit Bloomgarden and Robert Whitehead; Casting Dir, Producer with Edgar Scherick; Exec. Vice-Pres. Production 20th Century Fox 1984–86, Pres. Production 1986–87; f. Scott Rudin Productions 1990–. Films: He Makes Me Feel Like Dancing 1982 (Outstanding Children's Program Emmy Award 1982, Feature Documentary Acad. Award 1982), Mrs Soffel 1984, Flatliners 1990, Pacific Heights 1990, Regarding Henry 1991, Little Man Tate 1991, The Addams Family 1991, Sister Act 1992, Jennifer Eight 1992, Life With Mikey 1993, The Firm 1993, Searching for Bobby Fischer 1993, Sister Act 2 1993, Addams Family Values 1993, I.Q. 1994, Nobody's Fool 1994, Sabrina 1995, Clueless 1995, Up Close and Personal 1996, Ransom 1996, Marvin's Room 1996, The First Wives' Club 1996, In and Out 1997, Twilight 1998, The Truman Show 1998, A Civil Action 1998, Wonder Boys 1999, Rules of Engagement 1999, Brokeback Mountain 1999, Angela's Ashes 1999, Bringing Out the Dead 1999, Sleepy Hollow 1999, Shaft 2000, Rules of Engagement 2000, Zoolander 2001, The Royal Tenenbaums 2001, Iris: A Memoir of Iris Murdoch 2001, Orange County 2002, The Hours 2002, Changing Lanes 2002, Marci X 2003. Theatre: Passion 1994 (Tony Award Best Musical 1994), Indiscretions 1995, Hamlet 1995, Seven Guitars 1995, A Funny Thing Happened on the Way to the Forum 1996, Skylight 1997, On the Town (New York Shakespeare Festival) 1997, The Chairs 1998, The Judas Kiss 1998, Closer (London) 1998, Amy's View 1999, Wide Guys 1999, Copenhagen 1999 (Tony Award). Address: Scott Rudin Productions, 10th Floor, 120 West 45th Street, New York, NY 10036; c/o William Morris Agency, 151 El Camino Drive, Beverly Hills, CA 90212, USA.

RUDINI, Gen.; Indonesian army officer; b. 15 Dec. 1929, Malang, E. Java; s. of R. I. Poespohandojo and R. A. Koesbandijah; m. Oddyana Rudini 1959; one s. two d.; ed Breda Mil. Acad., Netherlands, reaching rank of Second Lt; Commdr Kostrad Infantry/Airborne Brigade 1972–73; Commdr Indonesian contingent of UN Peace-keeping Force in Middle East 1973–76; Commdr Kostrad Airborne Combat 1976–81; Commdr N. and Cen. Sulawesi Mil. Region, Manado 1981, later Commdr of Kostrad; Chief of Staff, Indonesian Army 1983–88; Minister of Home Affairs 1988–93, concurrently Chair. of the Election Cttee. Leisure interests: sport, music. Address: c/o Ministry of Home Affairs, Jalan Merdeka Utara 7, Jakarta Pusat, Indonesia.

RUDMAN, Michael P.; American publishing executive; b. 1950, New York; ed Michigan and New York Univs.; Pres. Nat. Learning Corpn, also CEO, Dir;

Pres. Delaney Books Inc., also CEO, Dir; Pres. Frank Merriwell Inc., also CEO, Dir; mem. Assen of American Publrs. *Address:* National Learning Corporation, 212 Michael Drive, Syosset, NY 11791, USA.

RUDMAN, Warren Bruce, LLB; American politician and lawyer; b. 18 May 1930, Boston, Mass.; s. of Edward G. Rudman and Theresa (née Levenson) Rudman; m. Shirley Wahl 1952; one s. two d.; ed Valley Forge Mil. Acad., Syracuse Univ., Boston Coll. Law School; rank of Capt. U.S. Army 1952–54; admitted to NH Bar, mem. law firm Stein, Rudman and Gormley 1960–69; Attorney-Gen. NH, Concord 1970–76; Partner Sheehan, Phinney, Bass and Green 1976–80; Fiscal Agent Gov. Walter Peterson's campaign 1968, Special Counsel to Gov. Peterson 1969–70; Republican Senator from NH 1980–92; co-founder Concord Coalition 1992–; Deputy Chair. Fed. Reserve Bank of Boston 1993; partner Paul, Weiss, Rifkind, Wharton and Garrison 1993–; Founder, Chair. Bd Trustees Daniel Webster Jr Coll., New England Aeronautical Inst. 1965–81; Sr Advisory Cttee, John F. Kennedy School of Govt, Harvard Univ.; Dir Chubb Corpn 1993–, Raytheon Corpn 1993–, Dreyfus Corpn 1993–; mem. American Legion, Sub-Cttee on Defense Co-operation of the North Atlantic Ass., Sec. of State's Advisory Panel on Overseas Security; Bronze Star. *Address:* Paul Weiss Rifkind Wharton & Garrison, 1615 L Street, NW, Suite 1300, Washington, DC 20036, USA (Office).

RUDZIŃSKI, Witold; Polish composer and musicologist; b. 14 March 1913, Siebież (now in Russia); s. of Henryk Rudziński and Maria Rudzińska; m. Nina Rewieńska 1958; one s. three d.; ed Wilno Univ. and Wilno Conservatoire and Gregorian Inst., Paris; Prof. Wilno Conservatoire 1939–42, Łódź Conservatoire 1945–47, Extraordinary Prof. 1964, Ordinary Prof. 1983; Dir Dept of Music, Ministry of Culture 1947–48; Ed. Muzyka 1951–54; Prof. State Higher School of Music, Warsaw 1957–83, Chief Dept of Theory of Music, Prof. Emer. 1983–; Pres. Warsaw Br. of Polish Composers Union 1963–69, 1977–83; Dr. hc (Acad. of Music, Warsaw) 1998; First Prize, Edward Grieg Competition 1965, Minister of Culture and Art Prize, 1st Class 1976, 1978, 1981, Prize of Chair. Council of Ministers 1984; Special Award, Monaco 1963; Officer and Commdr Cross, Order of Polonia Restituta. *Works include:* Piano Concerto, two Symphonies, Symphonic Suite, two String Quartets, two Sonatas for piano and violin, cantata, flute quartet, song cycle, chamber works for piano, flute, 'cello, woodwind and percussion instruments; Operas: Janko Muzykant 1951, Komendant Paryża (Commander of Paris) 1957, Odprawa posłów greckich (Dismissal of the Greek Envoys) 1962, Sulamita (Sulamith) 1964, Chłopi (The Peasants) 1972; opera for children: The Ring and the Rose 1982; music poem Dach świata (Roof of the World) for recitative and orchestra 1960; Gaude Mater Polonia for solo voice, choir, recitative and orchestra 1966; Lipce (oratorio), Hebraic songs, In the Circle of Psalms (oratorio) 1987, Litany for Holy Mother of Ostra Brama (Wilno) 1994, Kaszuby wedding songs for mixed choir, Passacaglia for violin, Divertimento rustico for orchestra and violin, Variations and fugue for solo percussion 1966, Triple Concerto for Trumpet, Two Cors, percussion and string orchestra 1998. *Publications:* 12 books include: Muzyka dla wszystkich (Music for Everybody) 1948, Studies in Musical Rhythm 1987; monographs on Moniuszko and Bartók. *Leisure interests:* history, biography, linguistics. *Address:* ul. Narbutta 50 m. 6, 02-541 Warsaw, Poland. *Telephone:* (22) 8493477.

RUELLE, David Pierre, PhD; French research mathematician and physicist; b. 20 Aug. 1935, Ghent, Belgium; s. of Pierre Ruelle and Marguerite de Jonge; m. Janine Lardinois 1960; one s. two d.; ed high school at Mons and Free Univ. of Brussels; Research Asst and Privatdozent, Eidgenössische Technische Hochschule, Zürich 1960–62; mem. Inst. for Advanced Study, Princeton 1962–64; Hon. Prof. Inst. des Hautes Etudes Scientifiques, Bures-sur-Yvette 1964–2000; mem. Acad. des Sciences 1985; mem. Acad. Europaea 1993; Foreign Assoc. NAS 2002–; Foreign Hon. mem. American Acad. of Arts and Sciences 1992; Chevalier, Légion d'honneur; Dannie Heineman Prize 1985, Boltzmann Medal 1986. *Publications:* Statistical Mechanics: Rigorous Results 1969, Thermodynamic Formalism 1978, Elements of Differentiable Dynamics and Bifurcation Theory 1989, Chance and Chaos 1991. *Address:* I.H.E.S., 91440 Bures-sur-Yvette (Office); 1 avenue Charles-Comar, 91440 Bures-sur-Yvette, France (Home). *Telephone:* 1-60-92-66-52 (Office); 1-69-07-61-52 (Home). *E-mail:* ruelle@ihes.fr (Office).

RUFIN, Jean-Christophe, MD; French writer and doctor; b. 28 June 1952, Bourges; s. of Marcel Rufin and Denise Bonneau; one s. two d.; ed Lycées Janson-de-Sailly and Claude Bernard, Paris, Pitié-Salpêtrière School of Medicine, Paris; Hosp. Intern, Paris 1975–81, Dir of Clinic 1981–83; Medical Dir Action Int. Contre la Faim (ACF) 1983–85; Chief of Mission of Sec. of State for Human Rights 1986–88; Cultural Attaché French Embassy in Brazil 1989–90; Vice-Pres. Médecins sans Frontières (MSF) 1991–93; Adviser to Minister of Defence 1993–95; Hospital Dr., Nanterre Hosp. 1994–95; Conference Dir Univ. de Paris-Nord 1993–95; Admin. French Red Cross 1995; Dir of Research Inst. des Relations Int. et Stratégiques (Iris) 1996, later Deputy Dir; Chevalier des Arts et des Lettres. *Publications:* Le Piège humanitaire 1986, L'Empire et les nouveaux barbares 1992, La Dictature libérale (Prix Jean-Jacques Rousseau) 1994, L'Aventure humanitaire 1994, L'Abyssin (Prix Goncourt, Prix Méditerranée) 1997, Sauver Ispahan 1998, Les Causes perdues (Prix Bergot, Prix Interallié) 1999, Rouge Brésil (Prix Goncourt) 2001. *Leisure interest:* music. *Address:* 73 rue du Cherche-Midi, 75006 Paris, France (Home). *E-mail:* jchrufin@club-internet.fr (Home).

RÚFUS, Milan; Slovak poet, literary historian and essayist; b. 10 Dec. 1928, Závazná Poruba; m.; one d.; ed Comenius Univ., Bratislava; at Inst. of Slovak Language and Literature Faculty of Philosophy Comenius Univ. 1952–89; Assoc. Prof., Lecturer in Slovak Language and Literature Inst. Universitario, Naples 1971–72; mem. Club of Ind. Writers of Slovakia; Hon. LittD (Bratislava); State Prize 1970, Slovak Nat. Prize 1982, World Congress of Slovaks Nat. Prize, Nat. Literature Prize 1996; Tomáš Garrigue Masaryk Order 1990, L'udovít Štúr Order (1st Class) 1993. *Publications:* Until We Have Matured 1956, Bells 1968, A Triptych 1969, People of the Mountains 1969, The Table of the Poor 1972, The Cradle 1972; A Boy is Drawing a Rainbow 1974, Music of Forms (accompanied by paintings of L. Fulla) 1977, Forest (accompanied by photographs of M. Martincek) 1978, Ode to Joy 1981, Severe Bread 1987, A Late Self-Portrait 1993, Reading from Destiny 1996, Dragonfly 1998, Simple One Until the Little Roots of its Hair 2000; for children: Book of Fairy Tales 1975, Saturday Evenings 1979, A Small Well 1985, Silent Fern 1990, Small Prayers 1990, Small Prayers for a Child 1995; essays: Man, Time and Work 1968, Four Epistles to People 1969, On Literature 1974, And What is a Poem 1978, Epistles Old and New 1997, Time of Shy Questions 2001. *Address:* Fialkové údolie 31, 811 01 Bratislava, Slovakia. *Telephone:* (7) 5441-2948.

RUGARLI, Giampaolo; Italian author; b. 5 Dec. 1932, Naples; s. of Mirko Rugarli and Rubina De Marco; m. Maria Pulci 1985; three c.; ed legal studies; bank dir since 1972; a dir of Cariplo 1981–85; contrib. Messaggero and Corriere della Sera and other reviews; Premio Bagutta Opera Prima 1987; Premio Capri 1990. *Publications:* Il Superlativo assoluto, La troga, Il nido di ghiaccio, Diario di un uomo a disagio, Andromeda e la notte, L'orrore che mi hai dato 1987, Una montagna australiana 1992, Per i pesci non è un problema 1992, I camini delle fate 1993, Il manuale del romanziere (The Novelist's Handbook) 1993, L'infinito, forse 1995, Una gardenia ni capilli 1997, Il bruno dei crepuscoli (Leopardi) 1998, La Viaggiatrici del tram numero 4 2001, Il Cavaliere e la vendita della saggiera 2002, La mia Milano 2003. *Leisure interest:* gardening. *Address:* Via Colle di Giano 62, Olevano Romano 00035, Italy. *Telephone:* (06) 9564518.

RUGGIERO, Renato; Italian diplomatist and investment banker; b. 9 April 1930, Naples; ed Univ. of Naples; entered Diplomatic Service 1955; served São Paulo, Moscow, Washington; Counsellor, Belgrade 1966; Counsellor for Social Affairs, Perm. Mission to European Communities 1969; Chef de Cabinet Pres. of Comm. of European Communities 1970–73, Dir-Gen. of Regional Policy 1973–77, Comm. Spokesperson 1977; Co-ordinator EEC Dept, Ministry of Foreign Affairs 1978; Diplomatic Counsellor of Pres. of Council 1979; Chef de Cabinet of Minister of Foreign Affairs 1979; Perm. Rep. to European Communities 1980–84; Dir-Gen. for Econ. Affairs, Ministry of Foreign Affairs 1984–85; Sec.-Gen. Ministry of Foreign Affairs 1985–87, Minister of Foreign Trade 1987–91; Dir-Gen. World Trade Org. 1995–99; Chair. ENI June–Sept. 1999; Vice-Chair. Schroder Salomon Smith Barney Int., Chair. Schroder Salomon Smith Barney Italy 2000; Minister of Foreign Affairs 2001–02; Personal Rep. of Pres. of Council, Econ. Summits Bonn 1978, Tokyo 1979, Venice 1980, London 1984, Bonn 1985, Tokyo 1986, Venice 1987; Pres. Exec. Cttee OECD; Kt, Grand Cross, Order of Merit and numerous other honours. *Address:* c/o Ministry of Foreign Affairs, Piazzale della Farnesina 1, 00194 Rome, Italy.

RUGOVA, Ibrahim, PhD; Serbia and Montenegro (Serbian/Kosovan) politician and writer; b. 2 Dec. 1944, Crnce, Kosovo; m. Fana Rugova; two s. one d.; ed Univ. of Pristina, Ecole Pratique des Hautes Etudes, Paris, France; fmr writer and ed. Albanian-language magazines and Pres. of the Writers of Kosovo; Pres. of self-proclaimed 'Repub. of Kosovo' 1992–2000; elected Pres. of Kosovo March 2002– (following UN-supervised elections in Nov. 2001); championed non-violent resistance to Yugoslav rule; as Chair. of Democratic League of Kosovo apptd. team to engage in peace talks with Fed. Govt August 2000; corresp. mem. Kosovo Acad. of Arts and Sciences 1996; PL-Fonden Prize for Peace and Freedom 1995, Sakharov Award 1998, Homo Homini Award 1998, Peace and Tolerance Award 1999. *Address:* Democratic League of Kosovo, Priština, Serbia and Montenegro (Office).

RÜHE, Volker; German politician; b. 25 Sept. 1942, Hamburg; m. Anne Rühe 1968; two s. one d.; ed Univ. of Hamburg; fmr teacher; mem. Hamburg City Council 1970–76; mem. Bundestag 1976–; Deputy Chair. CDU/CSU Parl. Group 1982–89, 1998–; Sec. Gen. CDU 1989–92, Deputy Party Leader 1998–; Minister of Defence 1992–98. *Address:* Deutscher Bundestag, Platz der Republik 1, 11011 Berlin, Germany (Office); CDU, 53113 Bonn. *Telephone:* (30) 22773610 (Office). *E-mail:* volker.ruehe@bundestag.de (Office).

RUIJGH, Cornelis Jord, DPhil; Netherlands professor of Greek; b. 28 Nov. 1930, Amsterdam; s. of Jord Ruijgh and Trijntje Swart; ed Univ. of Amsterdam and Ecole Pratique des Hautes Etudes, Paris; Asst in Greek Philology, Univ. of Amsterdam 1954–66, lecturer, Ancient Greek Language 1966–69, Prof. of Ancient Greek Language, Dialectology and Mycenology 1969–95; mem. Royal Netherlands Acad.; mem. Int. Perm. Cttee of Mycenaean Studies 1970–; Prix Zographos 1957; Michael Ventris Memorial Award 1968. *Publications:* L'élément achéen dans la langue épique, 1957, Etudes sur la grammaire et le vocabulaire du grec mycénien 1967, Autour de 'te épique' 1971, Scripta Minora I 1991, Scripta Minora II 1996 etc. *Leisure interest:* music. *Address:* Keizersgracht 800, 1017 ED Amsterdam, Netherlands. *Telephone:* (20) 6247995.

RUITENBERG, Elis Joost, PhD; Netherlands professor of immunology; b. 24 May 1937, Amersfoort; s. of E J. Ruitenberg and D. H. van Mechelen; m. Christiane Friederike Ambagtsheer 1963; three d.; ed Univ. of Utrecht;

veterinarian, Lab. Zoonoses, Nat. Inst. of Public Health, Bilthoven 1964–, Head Pathology Lab. 1970, Dir Div. of Immunology 1979, Vaccine Production 1980; Dir Div. of Microbiology and Immunology, Nat. Inst. of Public and Environmental Protection, Bilthoven 1984, Deputy Dir-Gen. 1986; Prof. of Veterinary Immunology, Univ. of Utrecht 1984–; Gen. and Scientific Dir Sanquin Blood Supply Foundation (CLB) 1989–; Chair. Netherlands-Vietnam Medical Cttee 1998–; Visiting Prof., Nat. School of Public Health, Madrid, Spain 1987; retd, mem. numerous advisory cttees including Advisory Council for Devt Research; mem. Royal Netherlands Acad. of Arts and Sciences; Schimmel Viruly Award 1976, Annual Award, Nat. Journal of Veterinary Medicine 1977, Award Medical Acad., Poznan, Poland, Kt, Order of Netherlands Lion 1986, Schornagel Award 1996. *Publications include:* Anisakiasis, Pathogenesis, Diagnosis and Prevention 1970, Preventive Screening of Adults (with D.A.T. Griffiths) 1987, Statistical Analysis and Mathematical Modelling of AIDS (with J.C. Jager) 1988, AIDS Impact Assessment Modelling and Scenario Analysis (with J.C. Jager) 1992; numerous articles on immunology, vaccinology, pathology and parasitology. *Leisure interests:* European languages, history, cycling.

RUIZ-GALLARDÓN JÍMENEZ, Alberto; Spanish politician and lawyer; b. 1963; Pres. Community of Madrid –(2003); mem. Partido Popular. *Address:* Presidencia del Gobierno de Madrid, Madrid, Spain (Office).

RUKAVISHNIKOV, Aleksander Yulianovich; Russian sculptor; b. 2 July 1950, Moscow; s. of Yulian Rukavishnikov and of Anagelina Filippova; m. Olga Mikhailovna Rukavishnikova; one s.; ed Surikov Moscow State Inst. of Arts; freelance artist; Prof. Surikov Inst.; mem. Presidium, Russian Acad. of Fine Arts; mem. Union of Artists; People's Artist of the Russian Federation. *Major works include:* portraits: Feofan Grek 1977, Sergey of Radonezh 1981, Dmitry Donskoy 1982, Aleksander Peresvet 1983, John Lennon 1982, Tamara Bykova 1983; Vladimir Vysotsky memorial; installation Intrusion 1988; Tatishchev monument, Togliatti 1997; Dostoyevsky statue 1997, Nikulin monument 2000. *Address:* Bolshaya Molchanovka str. 10, Moscow (Office); Granatny per. 11, Apt 30, 103001 Moscow, Russia (Home). *Telephone:* (095) 290-67-60 (Office); (095) 291-05-52 (Home). *Fax:* (095) 291-01-52 (Home).

RUKEYSER, Louis Richard, AB; American broadcaster, lecturer, columnist and author; b. 30 Jan. 1933, New York; s. of Merryle Stanley Rukeyser and Berenice Helene Simon; m. Alexandra Gill 1962; three d.; ed Princeton Univ.; reporter, Baltimore Sun Newspapers 1954–65, Chief Political Corresp. Evening Sun 1957–59, Chief London Bureau of The Sun 1959–63, Chief Asian Corresp. 1963–65; Sr Corresp. and Commentator ABC News 1965–73, Paris Corresp. 1965–66, Chief London Bureau 1966–68, Econ. Ed. and Commentator 1968–73; Presenter Wall St Week With Louis Rukeyser (PBS TV programme) 1970–2002, Louis Rukeyser's Wall Street (CNBC and public stations TV programme) 2002–; nationally syndicated econ. columnist McNaught Syndicate 1976–86, Tribune Media Services 1986–93; also lecturer; Ed.-in-Chief Louis Rukeyser's Wall Street 1992–, Louis Rukeyser's Mutual Funds 1994–; Hon. Litt. D. (NH Coll.) 1975; Hon. LLD (Moravian Coll.) 1978, (Mercy Coll.) 1984; Hon. DBA (Southeastern Mass. Univ.) 1979; Hon. LHD (Loyola Coll.) 1982, (Johns Hopkins Univ.) 1986, (American Univ.) 1991, Hon. Dr of Finance (Roger Williams Univ.) 1997; Overseas Press Club Award 1963, G. M. Loeb Award (Univ. of Conn.) 1972, George Washington Honor Medal Freedoms Foundation 1972, 1978, Janus Award for Excellence in Financial News Programming 1975, New York Financial Writers Asscn Award 1980, Free Enterprise Man of the Year Award, Texas A. and M. Univ. Centre for Educ. and Research in Free Enterprise 1987, Hero of Wall Street Award, Museum of American Financial History 1998, Malcolm S. Forbes Public Awareness Award for Excellence in Advancing Financial Understanding 2000. *Publications:* How to Make Money in Wall Street 1974, What's Ahead for the Economy: The Challenge and the Chance 1983, Louis Rukeyser's Business Almanac 1988, Louis Rukeyser's Book of Lists 1997, Right on the Money 1998. *Address:* 586 Round Hill Road, Greenwich, CT 06831, USA.

RUKINGAMA, Luc, PhD; Burundian politician and academic; b. 1952, Kiremba; m. Thérèse Niyonzima; two s. two d.; ed Sorbonne, Paris; MP; fmr Minister for Higher Educ., for Cooperation, for Foreign Affairs and Cooperation; Minister of Communication and Govt Spokesman 2000–01; Co-Pres. Union pour le Progrès National (UPRONA); presidential cand. 2001; univ. prof.; Chevalier Ordre des Palmes Académiques, Medaille de l'Unité Nationale, UNESCO Medal. *Publications:* Voyage au Congo d'André Gide ou la stéréotype au cœur de l'image, 1995; numerous articles. *Leisure interests:* reading, sport, music. *Address:* Office of the Leader, Union pour le Progrès National, P.O. Box 704, Bujumbura (Office); Avenue de Juillet no 4, Kiriri, P.O. Box 1810, Bujumbura, Burundi (Home). *Telephone:* 224666 (Office); 226561 (Home). *Fax:* 216318 (Office); (257) 226561 (Home). *E-mail:* minicom@cb.inf.com (Office).

RUML, Jan; Czech politician; b. 5 March 1953, Prague; m. Marie Ruml; two s.; ed grammar school, Prague, Univ. of Plzeň; stoker, woodcutter, hosp. technician, mechanic, bookseller, cattle-minder; signed Charter 77, Feb. 1977; freelance journalist 1977–79; mem. Cttee for Protection of the Unjustly Persecuted 1979–89; in custody, indicted for subversive activities 1981–82; co-f. of Lidové noviny (monthly samizdat) 1988–90; spokesman of Charter 77 1990; First Deputy Minister of Interior of CSFR 1990–91; Deputy Minister of Interior 1991–92; mem. Civic Democratic Party (ODS) 1992–97; Deputy to House of Nations, Fed. Ass. June–Dec. 1992; Minister of Interior of Czech Repub. 1992–97; mem. Interdepartmental Anti-drug Comm. 1993–97, Comm. for Prevention of Crime 1994–97; mem. of Parl. 1996–98, Senator 1998–, Vice-Pres. of Senate (Parl.) 2000–; Founder Freedom Union (US), Chair. 1998–99; Hon. Medal of the French Nat. Police 1992. *Films:* Hledání Pevného Bodu (Looking for a Stable Point). *Publication:* (with Jana Klusáková) What Was, Is and Will Be (in Czech). *Address:* Senate of the Czech Republic, Valdštejnské náměstí 17/4, 118 01 Prague 1, Czech Republic. *Telephone:* (2) 57072770 (Office). *Website:* www.senat.cz (Office).

RUMMEL, Reinhard Franz, DrIng; German professor of physical geodesy; b. 3 Dec. 1945, Landshut; m. Renate Schophaus 1970; one s. one d.; ed Hans Leinberger Gymnasium, Technische Univ. Munich and Technische Hochschule, Darmstadt; Research Assoc. Dept of Geodetic Science, Ohio State Univ., Columbus, Ohio 1974–76; scientist, German Geodetic Research Inst. and Bavarian Acad. of Science, Munich 1976–80; Prof. of Physical Geodesy, Faculty of Geodetic Eng Delft Univ. of Tech. 1980–; mem. Netherlands Acad. of Science; Speuerwerkpreis, KIVI, Netherlands 1987. *Publications:* Zur Behandlung von Zufallsfunktionen und -folgen in der physikalischen Geodäsie 1975, Geodesy's Contribution to Geophysics 1984, Satellite Gradiometry 1986, Encyclopedia of Earth System Science, Vol. II (on geodesy) 1992. *Address:* Delft University of Technology, Faculty of Geodesy, Thijsseweg 11, 2629 JA Delft, Netherlands. *Telephone:* (15) 785100. *Fax:* (15) 782348.

RUMSFELD, Donald H., BA; American fmr government official and business executive; b. 9 July 1932, Chicago; s. of George and Jeannette Rumsfeld (née Husted); m. Joyce Pierson 1954; one s. two d.; ed New Trier High School, Ill., Princeton Univ.; aviator, US Navy 1954–57; Admin. Asst, House of Reps 1957–59; investment broker, A. G. Becker & Co., Chicago 1960–62; mem. 88th–91st Congresses; Republican; Asst to Pres. and Dir Office of Econ. Opportunity 1969–70; Dir Econ. Stabilization Program, Counsellor to Pres. 1971–72; Amb. to NATO, Brussels 1973–74; White House Chief of Staff 1974–75; Sec. of Defense 1975–77, 2001–; mem. Cabinet 1969–73, 1974–77; Pres., CEO then Chair. G. D. Searle and Co., Skokie, Ill. 1977–85; Sr Adviser, William Blair and Co. 1985–90; Chair. and CEO General Instrument Corpn 1990–93; Chair. Gilead Sciences, Inc. 1997–2000; Pres. Special Middle East Envoy 1983–84; Chair. Eisenhower Exchange Fellowships 1986–93, US Ballistic Missile Threat Comm. 1998–99; mem. Presidential Advisory Cttee on Arms Control 1982–86, Nat. Econ. Comm. 1988–89, Trade Deficit Review Cttee, US Comm. to Assess Nat. Security, Space Man. and Org. 2000–; 11 hon. degrees; Presidential Medal of Freedom 1977, Woodrow Wilson Award 1985, Outstanding Pharmaceutical CEO 1980, Eisenhower Medal 1993 and other awards. *Leisure interests:* wrestling, skiing, squash, farming, collecting antique clocks. *Address:* 1000 Defense Pentagon, Washington, DC 20301-1000, USA. *Website:* www.defenselink.mil.

RUNDQUIST, Dmitri Vasilyevich; Russian geologist and mineralogist; b. 10 Aug. 1930; m.; two d.; ed Leningrad Inst. of Mines; jr, then sr researcher, Deputy Dir All-Union Research Inst. of Geology 1954–84; Dir Inst. of Geology and Geochronology Russian Acad. of Sciences 1984–90, Head of Lab. 1990–; Corresp. mem. USSR (now Russian) Acad. of Sciences 1984, mem. 1990, Acad.-Sec. Dept of Geology, Geophysics, Geochemistry and Mining Sciences 1996–2002; research in mineralogy, petrography, developed theory on laws of mineral deposit location; USSR State Prize; Merited Geologist of Russian Fed. *Publications include:* Greisen Deposits 1971, Zones of Endogenic Mineral Deposits 1975, Precambrian Geology 1988. *Address:* State Geological Museum, Morkhovaya 11, 103009 Moscow, Russia. *Telephone:* (095) 203-53-87.

RUPEL, Dimitrij, PhD; Slovenian politician and sociologist; b. 7 April 1946, Ljubljana; m.; ed Ljubljana Univ., Univ. of Essex, Brandeis Univ. (Mass., USA); worked as journalist in Yugoslav newspapers and magazines; was considered as dissident for criticism of Yugoslav Communist regime; Asst Prof. Ljubljana Univ. 1982–89, Prof. 1989–; lectured in Queen's Univ. (Canada) 1985, Cleveland State Univ. 1989; one of founders of Cultural-Political journal Nova Revija 1987; Founder and first Chair. Opposition Slovenian Democratic Party 1989; Minister of Foreign Affairs, mem. first elected Govt of Slovenia 1990, Chair. Cttee for Culture, Educ. and Sports; elected Mayor of Ljubljana 1992–97; Amb. to USA 1997–2000; Minister of Foreign Affairs 2000–. *Publications include:* Secret of the State 1992, The Disenchanted Slovenia 1993, Meetings and Partings 2001; plays for radio. *Address:* Ministry of Foreign Affairs, Presernova 25, 1000 Ljubljana, Slovenia (Office). *Telephone:* (1) 4782231 (Office). *Fax:* (1) 4782340 (Office). *E-mail:* info .mzz@gov.si (Office). *Website:* www.sigov.si/mzz (Office).

RUPÉREZ, Francisco Javier, LLB; Spanish diplomatist and politician; b. 24 April 1941, Madrid; m. Rakela Cerovic; two d.; ed El Pilar Coll., Univ. of Madrid; joined Diplomatic Service 1965, posts in Addis Ababa 1967–69, Warsaw 1969–72, Helsinki 1972–73; mem. Del. to CSCE, Helsinki 1972–73, to Int. Orgs., Geneva 1973–75; Chief of Staff of Under-Sec. of Foreign Affairs 1976; Chief of Staff of Ministry of Foreign Affairs 1976–77; mem. Exec. Cttee, Union of Democratic Center (UCD) 1977–82; MP for Cuenca 1979–82, 1986–89, for Madrid 1989–93, for Ciudad Real 1993–2000; Amb. and Head of Del. to Madrid Session of CSCE 1980–82; First Spanish Amb. to NATO 1982–83; Senator and Mem. Regional Parl. of Castilla La Mancha 1983–86; Vice-Pres. Democratic People's Party (PDP) 1983–87; Pres. Christian Democratic Party 1987–89; Vice-Pres. People's Party (PP) 1989–90, Spokesman in Parl. Defence Cttee 1989–91, mem. Exec. Cttee 1990–2000, Spokesman in Parl. Foreign Affairs Cttee 1991–96; Vice-Pres. NATO Parl. Ass. 1994–96,

Pres. Parl. Ass. 1998–2000; Pres. Parl. Ass. of OSCE 1996–98; Pres. Spanish Atlantic Asscn (AAE) 1996–2000; Pres. Foreign Affairs Cttee, House of Deputies 1996–2000; Pres. Christian-Democratic Int. (CDI) 1998–2000; Pres. Cttee on Defence, House of Deputies 2000; Amb. to USA 2000–; Pres. Foundation for Humanism and Democracy 1989–; Co-founder Cuadernos para el Diálogo (monthly political magazine) 1963–77; lectures regularly and directs courses at Int. Univ. Menéndez Pelayo, Univ. of Madrid and the Diplomatic School; Gran Cruz de la Orden de Isabel la Católica, Comendador de la Orden de Carlos III, Oficial de Isabel la Católica, Oficial de la Orden del Mérito Civil, Orden Bernardo O'Higgins (Chile), Gran Cruz de Vasco Núñez de Balboa (Panama), Grand Ordre de Léopold II (Belgium), Comendador con Placa de la Orden del Infante Don Enrique (Portugal), Kt Commdr of the Order of Alistical (Jordan), Kt Commdr of the Order of the Arab Kingdom of Egypt, Officier, Légion d'honneur (France). *Publications include:* Confessional State and Religious Liberty 1970, Europe Between Fear and Hope 1976, Spain in NATO 1986, First Book of Short Stories 1987, Kidnapped by ETA: Memoirs 1990; contribs to co-authored books and numerous articles in the Spanish press and specialized publs. *Address:* Embassy of Spain, 2375 Pennsylvania Avenue, NW, Washington, DC 20037, USA (Office). *Telephone:* (202) 452-0100 (Office). *Fax:* (202) 833-5670 (Office). *Website:* www.spainemb .org (Office).

RUPERT, Anthony Edward, MSc, FIAM; South African business executive; b. 4 Oct. 1916, Graaff-Reinet; s. of late John P. Rupert and Hester A. van Eeden; m. H. Goote 1941; two s. one d.; ed Volks High School, Graaff-Reinet, Pretoria Univ. and Univ. of SA; Lecturer in Chem., Pretoria Univ. 1939–41; Founder Rembrandt Group of Cos. (tobacco) 1948–; Founder and Pres. World Wide Fund for Nature, SA; Chair. Historical Homes of SA Ltd; Chair. Peace Parks Foundation 1997–; Fellow of the Int. Acad. of Man.; Life mem. South African Chemical Inst., South African Inst. of Man., South African Acad. for Arts and Science; Hon. Prof. in Business Admin. at Univ. of Pretoria 1964–83; mem. of Honour World Wild Fund for Nature; Decoration for Meritorious Service 1980; Commdr Order of Golden Ark.; Order for Meritorious Service (Class I) 1999; Hon. DSc (Pretoria); Hon. DComm (Stellenbosch); Hon. LLD (Univ. of Cape Town); Hon. DLit (Univ. of Natal). *Publications:* Progress through Partnership, Leaders on Leadership, Inflation – How to Curb Public Enemy Number One, Priorities for Coexistence. *Leisure interests:* research, conservation, art. *Address:* Millennia Park, PO Box 456, Stellenbosch 7599 (Office); 13 Thibault Street, Mostertsdrift, Stellenbosch, South Africa (Home). *Telephone:* (21) 8883320 (Office).

RUPP, George, PhD; American university president and professor of religion; b. 22 Sept. 1942, Summit, NJ; m. Nancy Katherine Farrar 1964; two d.; ed Univ. of Munich, Germany, Princeton Univ., Yale Divinity School, Univ. of Sri Lanka, Harvard Univ.; Faculty Fellow in Religion, Johnston Coll., Univ. of Redlands, Calif., 1971–73, Vice-Chancellor 1973–74; Asst Prof. of Theology, Divinity School, Harvard Univ. 1974–76, Assoc. Prof. of Theology and Chair. Dept of Theology 1976–77, Dean and John Lord O'Brian Prof. of Divinity 1979–85; Dean for Acad. Affairs and Prof. of Humanistic Studies, Univ. of Wis.-Green Bay 1977–79; Pres. and Prof. of Religious Studies, Rice Univ. 1985–93; Pres. and Prof. of Religion, Columbia Univ. 1993–2002; mem. Bd Asscn of American Univs, Inst. of Int. Educ., Nat. Asscn of Ind. Colls and Univs, The New York Partnership, YMCA of America and other orgs; Hon. DLitt (Columbia). *Publications:* Christologies and Cultures: Toward a Typology of Religious Worldviews 1974, Culture-Protestantism: German Liberal Theology at the Turn of the Twentieth Century 1977, Beyond Existentialism and Zen: Religion in a Pluralistic World 1979, Commitment and Community 1989; numerous book chapters and articles. *Address:* c/o Office of the President, Columbia University, New York, NY 10027, U.S.A. (Office).

RUPRECHT, William F.; American business executive; joined Sotheby's 1980, Man. Dir Sotheby's N. and S. America 1994–2000, Pres. and CEO Sotheby's Holdings, Inc. 2000–. *Address:* Sotheby's, 1334 York Avenue at 72nd Street, New York, NY 10021, USA (Office). *Telephone:* (212) 606-7000 (Office). *Fax:* (212) 606-7107 (Office). *Website:* www.sothebys.com (Office).

RUSBRIDGER, Alan, MA; British journalist; b. 29 Dec. 1953, Lusaka, Zambia; s. of G. H. Rusbridger and B. E. Rusbridger (née Wickham); m. Lindsay Mackie 1982; two d.; ed Cranleigh School, Magdalene Coll., Cambridge; reporter Cambridge Evening News 1976–79; reporter The Guardian 1979–82, diary ed. and feature writer 1982–86, special writer 1987–88, launch ed. Weekend Guardian 1988–89, Features Ed. 1989–93, Deputy Ed. 1993–95, Ed. 1995–; TV critic and feature writer The Observer 1986–, Exec. Ed. 1996–; Washington Corresp. London Daily News 1987; Chair. Photographer's Gallery 2001–; mem. Bd Guardian Newspapers Ltd 1994–, Guardian Media Group 1999–; mem. Scott Trust 1997–; Ed. of the Year, What the Papers Say Awards (Granada TV) 1996, Nat. Newspaper Ed., Newspaper Industry Awards 1996, Editor's Ed., Press Gazette 1997, Ed. of the Year, What The Papers Say Awards (Granada TV) 2001. *Television:* presenter of What the Papers Say (Granada TV) 1983–94, co-writer (with Ronan Bennett) of Fields of Gold (BBC TV) 2001. *Publications:* New World Order (ed.) 1991, Altered State (ed.) 1992, Guardian Year 1994. *Leisure interests:* golf, music, painting. *Address:* The Guardian, 119 Farringdon Road, London, EC1R 3ER, England. *Telephone:* (20) 7278-2332. *Fax:* (20) 7239-9997.

RUSCHA, Edward Joseph; American artist; b. 16 Dec. 1937, Omaha, Neb.; s. of Edward Joseph Ruscha and Dorothy Driscoll; m. Danna Knego 1967; one

s.; ed Chouinard Art Inst., LA; first one-man exhbn LA 1963; produced films Premium 1970, Miracle 1975; maj. exhbns, San Francisco Museum of Modern Art 1982, Musée St Pierre, Lyons, France 1985, Museum of Contemporary Art, Chicago 1988, Centre Georges Pompidou, Paris 1989, Serpentine Gallery, London 1990, Museum of Contemporary Art, LA 1990, Robert Miller Gallery, New York 1992, Thaddaeus Ropac, Salzburg, Austria 1992; first public comm., for Miami Dade Cultural Center's Main Library, Miami, Fla 1985; other comms. include Great Hall, Denver Cen. Library 1994–95, Auditorium Getty Center, Los Angeles 1997; represented in numerous perm. collections; Guggenheim Foundation Fellowship 1971; mem. American Acad. of Arts and Letters 2001. *Publications:* 12 books, including Twenty-six Gasoline Stations 1963, The Sunset Strip 1966. *Address:* 90 Gagosian Gallery, 980 Madison Avenue, New York, NY 10021, USA (Office).

RUSH, Geoffrey; Australian actor; b. 6 July 1951, Toowoomba, Queensland; s. of Roy Baden Rush and Merle Kiehne; m. Jane Menelaus 1988; one s. one d.; studied at Jacques Lecoq School of Mime, Paris, began professional career with Queensland Theatre Co. *Films include:* The Wedding 1980, Starstruck 1981, Twelfth Night 1985, Midday Crisis 1994, Dad and Dave on our Selection 1995, Shine (Acad. Award, BAFTA Award, Australian Film Inst. Award, Golden Globe Award, numerous other awards) 1995, Children of the Revolution 1996, Les Miserables 1997, Elizabeth 1998, Shakespeare in Love (BAFTA Award for Best Supporting Actor) 1998, The Magic Pudding 1999, Mystery Men 1999, House on Haunted Hill 1999, Quills 1999, Tailor of Panama 2000, Lantana 2001, Frida 2002. *Theatre includes:* Hamlet 1994, The Alchemist 1996, The Marriage of Figaro 1998, The Small Poppies 1999; also dir of numerous productions. *Television includes:* Menotti 1980–81, The Burning Piano 1992, Mercury 1995, Bonus Mileage 1996. *Address:* c/o Shanahan Management, P.O. Box 478, King's Cross, NSW 2011, Australia.

RUSHAYLO, Col.-Gen. Vladimir Borisovich; Russian politician; b. 28 July 1953, Tambov; m.; three c.; ed Omsk Higher School of Militia, USSR Ministry of Internal Affairs; militiaman 1972–76; investigator Moscow Dept of Internal Affairs 1976–88, later Head Moscow Dept of Internal Affairs; Head Dept for Struggle against Organized Crime 1988–93, 1998–99, Head Regional Dept for Struggle against Organized Crime 1993–96; Counsellor Council of Fed. 1996–98; Deputy Minister of Internal Affairs 1998–99, Minister 1999–2001; Sec. Security Council of Russia 2001–; mem. Presidium of Russian Govt, Security Council; Order of Sign of Honour, Order for Personal Courage and numerous other decorations. *Address:* Security Council of Russian Federation, Staraya pl. 4, 103132 Moscow, Russia (Office). *Telephone:* (095) 910-19-08, (095) 910-19-07 (Office).

RUSHDIE, (Ahmed) Salman, MA, FRSL; British writer; b. 19 June 1947, Bombay, India; s. of Anis Ahmed and Negin (née Butt) Rushdie; m. 1st Clarissa Luard 1976 (divorced 1987, died 1999); one s.; m. 2nd Marianne Wiggins 1988 (divorced 1993); one step-d.; m. 3rd Elizabeth West 1997; one s.; ed Cathedral and John Connon Boys' High School, Bombay, Rugby School, England, King's Coll., Cambridge; British citizen 1964; mem. Footlights revue, Univ. of Cambridge 1965–68; actor, fringe theatre, London 1968–69; advertising copywriter 1969–73; wrote first published novel Grimus 1973–74; part-time advertising copywriter while writing second novel 1976–80; mem. Int. PEN 1981–, Soc. of Authors 1983–, Exec. Cttee Nat. Book League 1983–, Council Inst. of Contemporary Arts 1985–, British Film Inst. Production Bd 1986–; Hon. Prof. MIT 1993; Hon. Spokesman Charter 88 1989; Exec. mem. Camden Cttee for Community Relations 1977–83; Hon. DLitt (Bard Coll.) 1995; Booker McConnell Prize for Fiction 1981, Colette Prize 1993, Booker of Bookers Award 1993; Arts Council Literature Bursary 1981, English Speaking Union Literary Award 1981, James Tait Black Memorial Book Prize 1981, Prix du Meilleur Livre Etranger for Shame 1984; Kurt Tucholsky Prize Sweden 1992, Prix Colette Switzerland 1993, Austrian State Prize for European Literature 1994, Whitbread Fiction Award 1996, British Book Awards Author of the Year 1996, London Int. Writers Award 2002. *Publications:* Grimus 1975, Midnight's Children 1981, Shame 1983, The Jaguar Smile: A Nicaraguan Journey 1987, The Satanic Verses 1988, Is Nothing Sacred (lecture) 1990, Haroun and the Sea of Stories (novel) 1990, Imaginary Homelands: Essays and Criticism 1981–91 1991, The Wizard of Oz 1992, East, West (short stories) 1994, The Moor's Last Sigh (novel) 1995, The Vintage Book of Indian Writing 1947–97 1997, The Ground Beneath Her Feet 1999, Fury 2001, Step Across the Line: Collected Non-Fiction 1992–2002 2002; articles for New York Times, Washington Post, The Times and Sunday Times. *Leisure interests:* films, chess, table tennis, involvement in politics, especially race relations. *Address:* c/o Wylie Agency (UK) Ltd, 4–8 Rodney Street, London, N1 9JH, England (Office).

RUSNOK, Jiří, DIP.ECON.ENG.; Czech politician and economist; b. 16 Oct. 1960, Ostrava-Vítkovice; m.; two c.; ed Univ. of Economics, Prague; various positions in state admin.; Econ. Adviser, Czech-Moravian Confed. of Trade Unions 1992–98; mem. Czech Social Democratic Party (CSDP) 1998–; Deputy Minister for Labour and Social Affairs 1998–2001; Minister of Finance 2001–02, of Industry and Trade 2002–; mem. World Bank Gov. Council 2001–02; mem. Bd of Govs. EBRD. *Leisure interests:* nature, history, botany. *Address:* Ministry of Industry and Trade, Na Františku 32, 110 15 Prague 1 (Office); Třída Politických vězňů 20, 110 00 Prague 1, Czech Republic. *Telephone:* (2) 24851111 (Office); (2) 24061111. *Fax:* (2) 24811089 (Office). *Website:* www.mpo.cz (Office); www.vlada.cz; www.psp.cz.

RUSSELL, Sir George, Kt, CBE, BA, FRSA, CBIM, FID; British business executive; b. 25 Oct. 1935; s. of William H. Russell and Frances A. Russell; m. Dorothy Brown 1959; three d.; ed Gateshead Grammar School, Durham Univ.; Vice-Pres. and Gen. Man. Welland Chemical Co. of Canada Ltd 1968, St Clair Chemical Co. Ltd 1968; Man. Dir Alcan UK Ltd 1976; Asst Man. Dir Alcan Aluminium (UK) Ltd 1977–81, Man. Dir 1981–82; Man. Dir and CEO British Alcan Aluminium 1982–86; Dir Alcan Aluminiumwerke GmbH, Frankfurt 1982–86, Alcan Aluminium Ltd 1987–2000; Group Chief Exec. Marley PLC 1986–89, Chair. 1989–93, CEO 1989–92, Chair. (non-exec.) 1993–97; Deputy Chair. Channel Four TV 1987–88; Chair. Ind. TV News (I.T.N.) 1988; Chair. Ind. Broadcasting Authority (IBA) 1989–90, Ind. Television Comm. (ITC) 1991–96; Chair. Camelot Group PLC 1995–2002; Chair. Luxfer Holdings Ltd 1976; Dir Northern Rock Building Soc. (now Northern Rock PLC) 1985–, 3i Group PLC 1992–2001 (Chair. non-exec. 1993–2001), Taylor Woodrow PLC 1992– (Deputy Chair. 2000–); Chair. Northern Devt Co. 1994–99; Deputy Chair. Granada PLC 2002–, Wildlife Wetlands Trust 2002–; Visiting Prof. Univ. of Newcastle-upon-Tyne 1978; mem. Northern Industrial Devt Bd 1977–80, Washington Devt Corpn 1978–80, IBA 1979–86, Civil Service Pay Research Unit 1980–81, Council CBI 1984–85, Widdicombe Cttee of Inquiry into Conduct of Local Authority Business 1985; Fellow Inst. of Industrial Mans.; Trustee Beamish Devt Trust 1985–90, Thomas Bewick Birthplace Trust; Hon. Fellow RIBA, Royal TV Soc.; Hon. DEng (Newcastle upon Tyne) 1985; Hon. DBA (Northumbria) 1992; Hon. LLD (Sunderland) 1995, (Durham) 1997. *Leisure interests:* tennis, badminton, bird watching. *Address:* Granada PLC, London Television Centre, Upper Ground, London, SE1 9LT, England (Office). *Telephone:* (20) 7261-8033 (Office). *Fax:* (20) 7620-1405 (Office).

RUSSELL, John, CBE, MA; British art critic; b. 22 Jan. 1919, Fleet, Hants.; s. of Isaac J. Russell and Harriet E. Russell (née Atkins); m. 1st Alexandrine Apponyi 1945 (divorced 1950); one d.; m. 2nd Vera Poliakoff 1956 (divorced 1971, died 1992); m. 3rd Rosamund Bernier 1975; ed St Paul's School, London, Magdalen Coll., Oxford; Hon. attaché Tate Gallery, London 1940; with Ministry of Information 1941, Intelligence Div. Admiralty 1942–46; mem. editorial staff Sunday Times 1946–74; moved to USA 1974; Art Critic New York Times 1974–, Chief Art Critic 1982–90; Hon. Fellow RA 1989; Officier des Arts et Lettres (France); Order of Merit (FRG); awarded Empire Grand Medal of Honour, Austria. *Exhibitions:* organized major exhbn of Vuillard (Montreal), Modigliani, Balthus, Lucian Freud, Pop Art Revisited (with Suzi Gablik) (all at Tate Gallery or Hayward Gallery, London). *Publications include:* Shakespeare's Country 1942, Switzerland 1950, Braque 1959, Erich Kleiber: A Memoir 1956, Paris 1960, Max Ernst 1967, Vuillard 1971, Francis Bacon 1971, Seurat 1965, Henry Moore 1968, The Meanings of Modern Art 1981, (revised 1990), Reading Russell 1989, London 1994, Matisse: Father and Son 1999; contrib. to numerous books. *Leisure interests:* Raimund, writing, reading. *Address:* 166 East 61st Street, New York, NY 10021, USA. *Telephone:* (212) 753-5280.

RUSSELL, Ken; British film director; b. 3 July 1927, Southampton; s. of Henry Russell and Ethel Smith; m. 1st Shirley Kingdam (divorced 1978); four s. one d.; m. 2nd Vivian Jolly 1984; one s. one d.; m. 3rd Hetty Baines 1992 (divorced 1997); one s.; ed Nautical Coll., Pangbourne; fmr actor and freelance magazine photographer; Hon. DLitt (Univ. Coll., Salford) 1994. *Films:* French Dressing 1964, Billion Dollar Brain 1967, Women in Love 1969, The Music Lovers 1970, The Devils 1971, The Boyfriend 1971, Savage Messiah 1972, Mahler 1973, Tommy 1974, Lisztomania 1975, Valentino 1977, Altered States 1981, Gothic 1986, Aria (segment) 1987, Salome's Last Dance 1988, The Lair of the White Worm 1988, The Rainbow 1989, Whore 1990, Prisoners of Honour 1991, Lion's Mouth 2000; acted in film The Russia House 1990. *Plays directed:* Rake's Progress (Stravinsky) 1982, Die Soldaten (Zimmerman) 1983; opera: Princess Ida 1992, Salome, Bonn 1993. *Television:* has directed the following documentaries: Elgar, Bartok, Debussy, Henri Rousseau, Isadora Duncan, Delius, Richard Strauss, Clouds of Glory, The Mystery of Dr. Martini, The Secret Life of Arnold Bax; series: Lady Chatterley's Lover. *Publications:* A British Picture: an Autobiography 1989, Altered States: The Autobiography of Ken Russell 1991, Fire Over England 1993, Mike and Gaby's Space Gospel 1999. *Leisure interests:* music, walking. *Address:* 16 Salisbury Place, London, W1H 1FH, England.

RUSSELL, Kurt von Vogel; American actor; b. 17 March 1951, Springfield, Mass.; s. of Bing Oliver and Louise Julia (Crone) Russell; m. Season Hubley 1979 (divorced); one s.; one s. by Goldie Hawn; lead role in TV series The Travels of Jamie McPheeters 1963–64; child actor in many Disney shows and films; professional baseball player 1971–73; numerous TV guest appearances; mem. Professional Baseball Players' Asscn, Stuntman's Asscn; recipient 5 acting awards, 10 baseball awards, 1 golf championship. *Films include:* It Happened at the World's Fair 1963, Unlawful Entry 1992, Captain Ron 1992, Tombstone 1993, Stargate 1994, Executive Decision 1996, Escape from LA 1996, Breakdown 1997, Soldier 1998, Vanilla Sky 2002. *Television series include:* Travels with Jamie McPheeters 1963–64, The New Land 1974, The Quest 1976. *Television films include:* Search for the Gods 1975, The Deadly Tower 1975, Christmas Miracle in Caulfield USA 1977, Elvis 1979, Amber Waves 1988. *Address:* Creative Artists' Agency, 9830 Wilshire Boulevard, Beverly Hills, CA 90212-1825, USA.

RUSSELL, Paul; British music industry executive; b. 3 July 1944, London; m. Elizabeth Russell; three s. two d.; ed Coll. of Law; fmrly band mem. Red Diamond; fmrly with law firm Balin & Co.; joined CBS 1973, fmrly Man. Dir,

Pres. Sony Music Europe 1993–; Chair. Sony Music Europe 1997–2000; Sr Vice-Pres. Sony Music Entertainment Inc. 2000–; Chair. Sony ATV Music Publishing 2000–, Chair. Sony ATV Music Publishing 2000–; co-f. Brit Awards; f. Platinum Europe Awards. *Leisure interests:* music, films, theatre, golf, swimming, all sports. *Address:* 550 Madison Avenue, New York, NY 10022-3211, USA (Office). *Telephone:* (212) 833-7500 (Office). *Fax:* (212) 833-7501 (Office). *E-mail:* paul_russell@sonymusic.com (Office).

RUSSELL, William Martin (Willy); British author; b. 23 Aug. 1947; s. of William Russell and Margery Russell; m. Ann Seagroatt 1969; one s. two d.; ed St Katharine's Coll. of Educ., Liverpool; ladies hairdresser 1963–69; teacher 1973–74; Fellow in Creative Writing, Manchester Polytechnic 1977–78; founder mem. and Dir Quintet Films; Hon. Dir Liverpool, Playhouse; work for theatre includes: Blind Scouse (3 short plays) 1971, When the Reds (adaptation) 1972, John, Paul, George, Ringo and Bert (musical) 1974, Breezeblock Park 1975, One for the Road 1976, Stags and Hens 1978, Educating Rita 1979, Blood Brothers (musical) 1983, Our Day Out (musical) 1983, Shirley Valentine 1986; screenplays include: Educating Rita 1981, Shirley Valentine 1988, Dancing through the Dark 1989; TV and radio plays; Hon. MA (Open Univ.) 1983; Hon.D.Lit. (Liverpool Univ.) 1990. *Publications:* Breezeblock Park 1978, One for the Road 1980, Educating Rita 1981, Our Day Out 1984, Stags and Hens 1985, Blood Brothers 1985, Shirley Valentine 1989, The Wrong Boy (novel) 2000; songs and poetry. *Leisure interests:* playing the guitar, composing songs, gardening, cooking. *Address:* c/o Casarotto Company Ltd, National House, 60–66 Wardour Street, London, W1V 3HP, England. *Telephone:* (20) 7287-4450.

RUSSELL BEALE, Simon, BA; British actor; b. 12 Jan. 1961, Penang, Malaya; s. of Lt-Gen. Sir Peter Beale and Lady Beale; ed Gonville and Caius Coll., Cambridge; Assoc. Artist of RSC 1986. *Theatre:* (Traverse Theatre, Edin.): Die House, Sandra/Manon, Points of Departure, The Death of Elias Sawney; (Lyceum, Edin.): Hamlet (Royal Court, London): Women Beware Women, The Duchess of Malfi, Volpone, Rosencranz and Guildenstern are Dead, Candide, Money 1999, Sommerfolk, Hamlet (Royal Nat. Theatre) 2000, Uncle Vanya (Olivier Award for Best Actor 2003; Donmar Warehouse, London) 2002. *RSC productions include:* The Winter's Tale, The Art of Success, Everyman in his Humour, The Fair Maid of the West, The Storm, Speculators, The Constant Couple, The Man of Mode, Restoration, Mary and Lizzie, Some Americans Abroad, Playing with Trains, Troilus and Cressida, Edward II (title role), Love's Labours Lost, The Seagull, Richard III (title role), The Tempest, King Lear, Ghosts, Othello. *Television includes:* A Very Peculiar Practice, Down Town Lagos, The Mushroom Picker, Dance to the Music of Time (Royal TV Soc. Award for Best Actor 1997), BAFTA Award for Best Actor 1998), The Double Life of Franz Schubert. *Films:* Orlando, Hamlet 1997, The Temptation of Franz Schubert 1997, An Ideal Husband 1999. *Leisure interests:* medieval history, music, history of religion.

RUSSELL-JOHNSTON, Baron (Life Peer), cr. 1997, of Minginish, in Highland; **David Russell Russell-Johnston,** Kt, MA; British politician; b. 28 July 1932; m. Joan Graham Menzies 1967; three s.; ed Portree High School, Edinburgh Univ.; history teacher, Liberton Secondary School, Edin. 1961–63; research Asst, Scottish Liberal Party 1963; MP for Inverness 1964–83, for Inverness, Nairn and Lochaber 1983–97; mem. Scottish Liberal Party Exec. 1961, Org. Cttee 1962, Vice-Chair. Scottish Liberal Party 1963–70, Chair. 1970–74, Leader 1974–88; Pres. Scottish Liberal Democrats 1988–94; Parl. Spokesman on numerous subjects including Foreign and Commonwealth Affairs 1970–75, 1979–85, 1987, 1988–89, European Affairs 1988–89, East-West Relations 1989–94, Cen. and Eastern Europe 1994; mem. European Parl. 1973–75, 1976–79, Vice-Pres. Political Cttee 1976–79; mem. Parl. Ass. of Council of Europe 1984–86, 1987–, Pres. 1999–; Leader, Council of Europe Liberal Democratic and Reformers' Group 1994; Pres. Council of Europe Sub-Cttee on Youth and Sport 1996; Chair. Cttee on Culture and Educ. 1996; mem. Ass. of WEU 1984–86, 1987–, Vice-Pres. Liberal Democratic and Reformers' Group 1992; Pres. WEU Parl. and Public Relations Cttee 1996; Trustee, Nat. Life Story Collection 1986–92. *Leisure interests:* reading, photography, shinty. *Address:* House of Lords, London, SW1A 0PW, England. *Telephone:* (20) 7219-5353 (Office).

RUSSO, Carlo; Italian judge and international official; b. 19 March 1920, Savona; s. of Giovanni Russo and Nilde Volta; m. Elena Neviani 1945; one d.; Deputy to Italian Parl. 1948–79; fmr Pres. Parl. Comm. of Chamber of Deputies; fmr Minister and Under-Sec. of State; Pres. Italian Comm. for Security and Cooperation in Europe 1980–; Judge, European Court of Human Rights 1981–; Cavaliere di Gran Croce della Repubblica Italiana, Ordine di San Gregorio di San Silvestro del Vaticano, Hon. GCMG, Grand Officier, Légion d'honneur; decorations from Germany and Malta. *Publications:* numerous articles on int. law in Italian and foreign reviews. *Leisure interest:* yachting. *Address:* Via Monti 213, 17100 Savona (Office); Corso Italia 13, 17100 Savona, Italy. *Telephone:* (019) 1814776 (Office); (019) 1824603 (Home); (019) 814776. *Fax:* (019) 814776 (Office).

RUSSO, René; American actress; b. 17 Feb. 1955, Calif.; d. of Shirley Russo; one d.; fmrly model Eileen Ford Agency. *Film appearances include:* Major League 1989, Mr Destiny, One Good Cop, Freejack, Lethal Weapon 3, In the Line of Fire, Outbreak, Get Shorty, Tin Cup, Ransom, Buddy, Lethal Weapon 4 1998, The Adventures of Rocky and Bullwinkle 1999, The Thomas Crown

Affair 1999, Showtime 2002, Big Trouble 2002. *Television appearance:* Sable (Series). *Address:* c/o Progressive Artists Agency, 400 South Beverly Drive, Suite 216, Beverly Hills, CA 90212, USA.

RUSSO JERVOLINO, Rosa; Italian politician; b. 1936, Naples; ed Univ. of Rome; worked in Research Dept CNEL 1961–68; joined Legis. Div. Ministry of the Budget 1969; mem. staff, subsequently Nat. Vice-Pres. Centro Italiano femminile 1969–78; mem. Nat. Exec. Women's Movt of Christian Democrat (DC) Party 1968–78, Pres. 1992–; Nat. Organizer DC Family Div. 1974–; Senator 1979–; Minister for Social Affairs 1989–92, of Educ. 1992–94; Chair. Parl. Supervisory Comm. of RAI (nat. TV and radio Corpn) 1985–. *Address:* Senato, Palazzio Madama, 00186 Rome, Italy.

RUSTIN, Jean; French artist; b. 3 March 1928, Moselle; s. of Georges Rustin and Andrée Carrat; m. Elsa Courand 1949; two s. (one deceased); ed Ecole Nationale Supérieure des Beaux Arts, Paris; works displayed at Musée d'Art Moderne, Paris and numerous other museums and centres in Europe and the USA; subject of books including Rustin by Edward Lucie-Smith 1991. *Exhibitions include:* one-man exhbns Galerie La Roue, Paris 1959–68, ARC (Musée d'Art Moderne, Ville de Paris) 1971, Galerie 9, Paris 1972–75, Tsuchya Gallery, Japan 1973, Maison des Arts, Creteil 1982, Galerie Isy Brachot 1981–86, European Fine Art Gallery, Maastricht 1991, Cooling Gallery, London 1992, Oberhausen, Germany 1994, Bergen Op Zoom, Netherlands 1994; numerous group exhbns including Foire Devand-Lineart, Belgium 1990, Galerie Marni Neerman, Bruges, Belgium 1986–, Fondation Veranneman, Belgium 2000, V. Frissiras Museum, Greece 2000, Halle St-Pierre, Paris 2001. *Publications:* Enfer = Rustin 1996, La quête de la figuration 1999. *Leisure interest:* the violin. *Address:* 110 rue Carnot, 93170 Bagnolet (Office); 167 avenue Gambetta, 75020 Paris, France; Fondation Rustin, Grote Goddaert 18, 2000 Antwerp, Belgium. *Telephone:* 1-43-61-08-98 (Paris); (3) 232-70-25 (Antwerp).

RUTHVEN, Kenneth Knowles, PhD; British professor of English; b. 26 May 1936; ed Univ. of Manchester; Asst Lecturer, Lecturer, Sr Lecturer Univ. of Canterbury, Christchurch, NZ 1961–72, Prof. of English 1972–79; Prof. of English, Univ. of Adelaide 1980–85, Univ. of Melbourne, Victoria, Australia 1985–99, Prof. Emer. 2000–; Visiting Prof. of English, Univ. of Adelaide 2002–. *Publications:* A Guide to Ezra Pound's Personae 1969, The Conceit 1969, Myth 1976, Critical Assumptions 1979, Feminist Literary Studies: An Introduction 1984, Ezra Pound as Literary Critic 1990, Beyond the Disciplines: The New Humanities (ed.) 1992, Nuclear Criticism 1993, Faking Literature 2001; Southern Review (Adelaide) (ed.) 1981–85, Interpretations series (gen.) 1993–96 (19 vols). *Address:* 27 Fairleys Road, Rostrevor 5073, South Australia, Australia (Home). *Telephone:* (8) 8336-6348 (Home). *E-mail:* kruthven@chariot.net.au (Home).

RUTKIEWICZ, Ignacy Mikołaj; Polish journalist; b. 15 April 1929, Vilna; s. of Józef Rutkiewicz and Maria Rutkiewicz (née Turkułł); m. Wilma Helena Koller 1961; two s.; ed Poznań Univ.; Ed., Ed.-in-Chief Wrocławski Tygodnik Katolicki (weekly) 1953–55; journalist, Zachodnia Agencja Prasowa (ZAP) 1957–66, Polska Agencja Interpress 1967–70; Ed. Odra (monthly) 1961–81, Ed.-in-Chief 1982–90, mem. Editorial Council 1991–; Co-founder, mem. Editorial Council Więź (monthly), Warsaw 1958–; Pres.-Ed.-in-Chief Polish Press Agency (PAP), Warsaw 1990–92, 1992–94; Adviser to Prime Minister, Warsaw 1994–95; TV journalist TV Centre of Training, Polish TV (TVP) 1994–96; Sec. TV Comm. for Ethics 1996–; Ed.-in-Chief Antena (weekly) 1998; Adviser to Minister of Culture and Arts 1998–99; Sr Ed. On-line News, TVP 1999–; Co-founder and Vice-Pres. Polish-German Asscn, Warsaw 1990–; Vice-Pres. Alliance Européenne des Agences de Presse, Zürich 1991–92; mem. Exec. Bd, Polish Journalists' Asscn (SDP) 1980–82, 1998–, Pres. 1993–95; mem. Council on Media and Information, Pres.'s Office 1993–95; mem. Euroatlantic Asscn 1995–; mem. Bd Press Centre for Cen. and Eastern Europe Foundation 1996–, Programme Bd Nat. Club of Friends of Lithuania 1996–, Programme Bd Polish Press Agency 1998–; Assoc. mem. Orbicom (int. network of UNESCO Chairs in Communications) 2000–; City of Wrocław Award 1963, B. Prus Award of SDP 1990, Phil epistémoni Award, Jagiellonian Univ., Crakow 1991; Order of Polonia Restituta 1981. *Publications:* author or co-author of more than 10 books, Transformation of Media and Journalism in Poland 1989–1996 (Co-Ed.). *Leisure interests:* literature, recent history, foreign languages, mountain trips, skiing. *Address:* Telewizyjna Agencja Informacyjna TVP SA, pl. Powstańców Warszawy 7, 00-999 Warsaw (Office); Al. Jerozolimskie 42/55, 00-024 Warsaw, Poland (Home). *Telephone:* (22) 5477082 (Office); (22) 8275813 (Home). *Fax:* (22) 5477964 (Office). *E-mail:* ignacy.rutkiewicz@waw.tvp.pl (Office); ignacyru@polbox.com (Home). *Website:* www.wiadomosci.tvp.pl (Office).

RUTSKOY, Maj.-Gen. Aleksandr Vladimirovich, CAND.ECON.SC.; Russian politician and military officer; b. 16 Sept. 1947, Proskurov, Kamenets Podolsk Region (now Khmelnitsky, Ukraine); s. of Vladimir Alexandrovich Rutskoy and Zinaida Iosifovna Rutskaya; m. 3rd Irina Rutskaya; three s. one d.; ed Higher Air Force Coll., Barnaul, Y. Gagarin Higher Air Force Acad., Acad. of Gen. Staff; fmr mem. CPSU (expelled 1991); Regimental Commdr, Afghan War 1985–86; Deputy Commdr Army Air Force 1988; RSFSR People's Deputy, mem. Supreme Soviet, mem. Presidium of Supreme Soviet 1990–91; Leader Communists for Democracy (renamed People's Party of Free Russia 1991, renamed Russian Social Democratic Party 1994); Vice-Pres. RSFSR (now Russia) 1991–93; Head Centre for the Operational Supervision of the Progress of Reforms 1991–93; Leader Civic Union coalition 1992–93; declared

Acting Pres. of Russia by Parl. Sept. 1993; arrested as one of organizers of failed coup d'état Oct. 1993; freed on amnesty Feb. 1994; Chair. Social-Patriotic Movt Derzhava 1994; Gov. of Kursk Region 1996–2000; mem. Council Europe Parl. 1996–2000; Pro-Rector Moscow State Sociological Univ. 2001–; Hero of Soviet Union 1988, Order of Lenin, seven Russian and Afghan orders; 15 medals. *Publications include:* Agrarian Reform in Russia 1992, Unknown Rutskoy 1994, About Us and Myself 1995, Finding Faith 1995, Lefortovo Protocols 1995, March Records 1995, Bloody Autumn 1996, Liberal Reforms – Strong Power 1996. *Leisure interests:* painting, gardening, designing, fishing. *Telephone:* (095) 292-66-98.

RUTT, Rev. Canon Cecil Richard, CBE, MA, DLitt; British ecclesiastic; b. 27 Aug. 1925, Langford, Beds.; s. of Cecil Rutt and Mary Hare Turner; m. Joan M. Ford 1969; ed Huntingdon Grammar School, Kelham Theological Coll. and Pembroke Coll., Cambridge; RNVR 1943–46; ordained 1951; curate St George's, Cambridge 1951–54; Church of England Mission to Korea 1954–74, consecrated Bishop 1966, Bishop of Taejon, Repub. of Korea 1968–74; Bishop of St Germans, Cornwall 1974–79; Bishop of Leicester 1979–90; Chair. Advisory Council for Relations of Bishops and Religious Communities 1980–90; joined Roman Catholic Church as a layman Sept. 1994; became priest 1995; mem. Anglican/Orthodox Jt Doctrinal Discussions 1983–89; Hon. Canon Diocese of Plymouth 2001; Bard of the Gorseth of Cornwall 1976, Chaplain 1993; Chaplain, Order of St John of Jerusalem 1978; Hon. Fellow Northumbrian Univs. E Asia Centre 1990–; Hon. DLitt (Confucian Univ., Seoul) 1974; Tasan Cultural Award (for writings on Korea) 1964, Order of Civil Merit, Peony Class (Korea) 1974. *Publications:* Korean Anglican Hymnal (ed.) 1961, Korean Works and Days 1964, P'ungnyu Han'guk (in Korean) 1965, An Anthology of Korean Sijo 1970, The Bamboo Grove 1971, James Scarth Gale and His History of the Korean People 1972, Virtuous Women 1974, A History of Hand Knitting 1987, The Book of Changes (Zhouyi): A Bronze Age Document 1996, Korea: A Cultural and Historical Dictionary (with Keith Pratt) 1999, The Martyrs of Korea 2002; contribs. to various Korean and liturgical publications. *Address:* 3 Marlborough Court, Falmouth, Cornwall, TR11 2QU, England. *Telephone:* (1326) 312276. *E-mail:* richard@ruttc.fsnet.co.uk (Home).

RUTTER, John Milford, DMus, MA; British composer and conductor; b. 24 Sept. 1945, London; m. JoAnne Redden 1980; two s. (one deceased) one step-d. ; ed Highgate School and Clare Coll., Cambridge; Dir of Music Clare Coll., Cambridge 1975–79, part-time lecturer in Music, Open Univ. 1975–87; Founder and Dir The Cambridge Singers 1981–; Hon. Fellow Westminster Choir Coll., Princeton, Hon. DMus (Lambeth) 1996. *Compositions include:* choral: The Falcon 1969, Gloria 1974, Bang! (opera for young people) 1975, The Piper of Hamelin (opera for young people) 1980, Requiem 1985, Magnificat 1990, numerous carols, anthems and songs; orchestral works and music for TV; and recorded original version of Fauré Requiem 1984. *Address:* Old Laceys, St John's Street, Duxford, Cambridge, CB2 4RA, England. *Telephone:* (1223) 832474. *Fax:* (1223) 836723.

RUTTER, Sir Michael Llewellyn, Kt, CBE, MD, FRCP, FRCPsych, FRS; British professor of child psychiatry; b. 15 Aug. 1933; s. of Llewellyn Charles Rutter and Winifred Olive Rutter; m. Marjorie Heys 1958; one s. two d.; ed Birmingham Univ. Medical School, training in paediatrics, neurology and internal medicine 1955–58; practised at Maudsley Hosp. 1958–61; Nuffield Medical Travelling Fellow, Albert Einstein Coll. of Medicine, New York 1961–62; scientist with MRC Social Psychology Research Unit 1962–65; Sr Lecturer, then Reader, Univ. of London Inst. of Psychiatry 1966–73, Prof. of Child Psychiatry 1973–98, Research Prof. 1998–; Dir MRC Research Centre for Social, Genetic and Developmental Psychiatry 1994–98; Hon. Dir MRC Child Psychiatry Unit 1984–98; Fellow Center for Advanced Study in Behavioral Sciences, Stanford Univ. 1979–80; guest lecturer at many insts in Britain and America; Pres. Soc. for Research in Child Devt 1999–2001 (Pres. elect 1997–99); Hon. Fellow British Psychological Soc. 1978, Hon. Fellow American Acad. of Pediatrics 1981, Royal Soc. of Medicine 1990; Hon. doctorates (Leiden) 1985, (Catholic Univ. of Leuven) 1990, (Birmingham) 1990, (Edin.) 1990, (Chicago) 1991, (Minnesota) 1993, (Jyväskylä) 1996, (Warwick) 1999–, (E. Anglia) 2000; numerous awards UK and USA. *Publications:* Children of Sick Parents 1966, (jtly) A Neuropsychiatric Study in Childhood 1970; (ed. jtly) Education, Health and Behaviour 1970; (ed.) Infantile Autism 1971, Maternal Deprivation Reassessed 1981; (ed. jtly) The Child with Delayed Speech 1972, Helping Troubled Children 1975, (jtly) Cycles of Disadvantage 1976; (ed. jtly) Child Psychiatry 1977, (2nd edn as Child and Adolescent Psychiatry 1985); (ed. jtly) Autism 1978, Changing Youth in a Changing Society 1979, (jtly) Fifteen Thousand Hours: Secondary Schools and Their Effect on Children 1979; (ed.) Scientific Foundations of Developmental Psychiatry 1981, A Measure of Our Values: Goals and Dilemmas in the Upbringing of Children 1983, (jtly) Lead versus Health 1983, (jtly) Juvenile Delinquency 1983; (ed.) Developmental Neuropsychiatry 1983; (ed. jtly) Stress, Coping and Development 1983; (ed. jtly) Depression and Young People 1986, Studies of Psychosocial Risk: The Power of Longitudinal Data (ed.) 1988, Parenting Breakdown: The Making and Breaking of Intergenerational Links (jtly) 1988, Straight and Devious Pathways from Childhood to Adulthood (ed. jtly) 1990, Biological Risk Factors for Psychosocial Disorders (ed. jtly) 1991, Developing Minds (jtly) 1993, Development Through Life: a handbook for clinicians (ed. jtly) 1994, Stress, Risk and Resilience in Children and Adolescents (ed. jtly) 1994, Psychological Disorders in Young

People 1995, Antisocial Behaviour by Young People (jtly) 1998. *Leisure interests:* fell walking, tennis, wine tasting, theatre. *Address:* 190 Court Lane, Dulwich, London, SE21 7ED, England.

RÜÜTEL, Arnold, PhD, DR.AGR.SC; Estonian politician and agronomist; b. 10 May 1928, Laimjala, Saaremaa Island; s. of Feodor Rüütel and Juuli Rüütel; m. Ingrid Rüütel (née Ruus) 1959; two d.; ed Jäneda Agric. Coll., Estonian Agricultural Acad.; Sr Agronomist, Saaremaa Dist, Estonian SSR 1949–50; mil. service 1950–55; teacher, Tartu School of Mechanization of Agric. 1955–57; Deputy Dir Estonian Inst. of Livestock-breeding and Veterinary Sciences 1957–63; mem. CPSU 1964–90; Dir of Tartu State Research Farm 1963–69; Rector Estonian Agric. Acad. 1969–77; Agricultural Sec. of Cen. Cttee of Estonian CP on Agric. Problems 1977–79; First Deputy Chair. Council of Ministers of Estonia 1979–83; Chair. Presidium of Supreme Soviet of Estonian SSR 1983–90, of Supreme Council of Repub. of Estonia 1990–92; Deputy Pres. of USSR Presidium of Supreme Soviet 1984–91; mem. Constitutional Ass. 1991–92; Founder, Chair. Inst. of Nat. Devt and Cooperation 1993–2001; Founder and Chair. Estonian Rural People's Party (Maarava) 1994–99, Estonian People's Union 1999–2000, Hon. Chair. 2000–01; mem. of State Ass. (Riigikogu) 1995–2001, Vice-Chair. 1995–97, Chair. ruling coalition's council 1995–99; Head Del. of Riigikogu to Baltic Ass. 1995–99, mem., alternately Chair. Presidium 1995–99; presidential cand. 1996; Pres. of the Repub. of Estonia Sept. 2001–; Chair. Estonian Soc. for Nature Protection 1981–88, Keep Estonian Sea Clean, Forselius (educational org.); Pres. Estonian Green Cross 1993–2001; mem. Tallinn City Council 1993–2001; Chair. Estonian Soc. for Nature Conservation 1981–88 (Hon. mem. 1989–), B. G. Forselius Soc. 1989–2002, Hon. Chair. 2002–, Movt 'Protect the Estonian Sea' 1993–2002 (Hon. Chair. 2002–); Pres. Estonian Nat. Org. of the Green Cross Int. 1993–2001; Hon. mem. Estonian Academic Agricultural Soc. 2002–, Int. Raoul Wallenberg Foundation 2002–; Collar of Order of Grand Cross of Terra Mariana (Estonia) 2001; Grand Cross Order of the White Rose with Collar (Finland) 2001; Grand Cross Order of the White Eagle (Poland) 2002; Grand Cross Royal Order of St Olaf (Norway) 2002; Grand Cross Order of Merit (Hungary) 2002; Dr hc (Bentley Coll.) 1991, (Estonian Agricultural Univ.) 1991, (Univ. of Helsinki) 2002, (Nat. Agricultural Univ. of Ukraine) 2002, (Univ. of Naples II) 2002; Rotary Foundation Distinguished Service Award 2002, Andres Bello Commemorative Medal 2002. *Publications:* Tuleviku taassünd (The Rebirth of the Future) (memoirs) 2001. *Leisure interests:* nature protection, sports. *Address:* Office of the President of the Republic of Estonia, Weizenbergi 39, 15050 Tallinn, Estonia (Office). *Telephone:* (2) 631-6202 (Office). *Fax:* (2) 631-6250 (Office). *E-mail:* sekretar@vpk.ee (Office).

RUYS, Anthony; Dutch business executive; b. 20 July 1947, Antwerp, Belgium; m. Melanie E. van Haaften; two s.; ed Univ. of Utrecht, Harvard Business School; marketing trainee Van den Bergh & Jurgens 1974–80; Marketing Dir Cogra Lever S.A. 1980–84, Chair. 1984–87; Chair. Van den Bergh Italy; mem. Bd Italian Unilever Cos 1987–89; Chair. Van den Bergh Netherlands; mem. Bd Dutch Unilever Cos 1989–92; Sr Regional Man. Food Exec., North European Region, Unilever NV 1992–93; mem. Exec. Bd Heineken NV 1993–96, Vice-Chair. 1996–2002, Chair. 2002–; Dir TRN, BAT Europe (Netherlands) BV, Rembrandt Foundation, Gtech Corpn, NH Hotels SA; mem. Supervisory Bd Robeco Groep NV, NH Hotels SA, Spain, Gtech Corpn, USA, Tourism Recreation Netherlands, Aiesec Netherlands; mem. Bd Netherlands Asscn for Int. Affairs, Int. Chamber of Commerce Netherlands, Veerstichting; mem. Nationaal Fonds Kunstbehoud. *Address:* Heineken NV, Tweede Weteringplantsoen 21, Postbus 28, 1000 AA Amsterdam, Netherlands (Office). *Telephone:* (20) 5239200 (Office). *Fax:* (20) 5239719 (Office). *E-mail:* a.ruys@heineken.com (Office). *Website:* www.heineken.com (Office).

RŮŽIČKA, Karel Zdeněk; Czech musician and composer; b. 20 June 1940, Prague; s. of Zdeněk Růžička and Vlasta Růžička; m. Marie-José; one s.; ed Conservatoire Prague; pianist Samafor Theatre, Prague 1960–66; mem. Prague Radio Big Band 1960–66; teacher Conservatoire J. Ježka, Prague 1966–69; imprisoned for political activities 1969; pianist, composer, arranger, conductor 1970–2000; f. Karel Růžička Jazz Quartet; has toured and performed in Canada, Poland, Cuba, France and Czech Repub.; has collaborated with Laco Deczi's Jazz Cellula septet, Czech–Polish Big Band, Veleband All-Stars and with numerous musicians including Rudolf Dasek (guitarist), Jarmo Sermila (trumpeter), Martial Solal (pianist), Wilson de Oliveira (saxophonist); Monte Carlo Int. Jazz Festival composition awards 1977 (Interlude), 1978 (Echoes), 1979 (Triste). *Recordings:* 10 albums and 100 compositions, including Fata Morgana, Going Home, Flight, Celebration Jazz Mass, Te Deum. *Leisure interests:* literature. *Address:* c/o Konzervatoř Jaroslava Ježka, Roškotova 4/1692, 14000 Prague 4 (Office); Devanská 1, 15200 Prague 5, Czech Republic (Home). *E-mail:* karuz@barr.cz.

RUZIMATOV, Farukh Sadulloyevich; Russian ballet dancer; b. 26 June 1963, Tashkent; ed Vaganova Acad. of Russian Ballet; with Mariinsky Theatre 1981–, soloist 1986–; guest dancer Bolshoi Theatre, Moscow; with American Ballet Theatre 1990–91; toured abroad; prize-winner int. competitions in Varna 1983, Paris 1984, Merited Artist of Russia and Tatarstan, Benoit de la Danse Prize. *Principal roles include:* Albert in Giselle, Siegfried in Swan Lake, Basil in Don Quixote, The Prince in The Nutcracker. *Address:* Mariinsky Theatre, Teatralnaya pl. 1, St Petersburg, Russia (Office). *Telephone:* (812) 315-57-42 (Office).

RWIGYEMA, Pierre Célestin; Rwandan politician; fmrly Minister of Primary and Secondary Educ.; Prime Minister of Rwanda 1995–2000; fmr Chair. Democratic Republican Movt (MDR). *Address:* c/o Office of the Prime Minister, Kigali, Rwanda.

RYABOV, Nikolai Timofeyevich; Russian politician and lawyer; b. 9 Dec. 1946, Salsk, Rostov Region; ed Rostov Univ.; mem. CPSU 1968–91; worked as tractor driver, engineer Salsk Agricultural Machine Factory 1966–72; taught in higher educ. school of Rostov Region 1973–90; People's Deputy of Russia 1990–93; mem. Supreme Soviet 1990–92, Chair. Sub-Cttee for legis. 1990–91; Chair. Council of Repubs. 1991–92, Deputy Chair. Supreme Soviet 1992–93; Deputy Chair. Constitutional Comm. 1991–93, Chair. Cen. Election Comm. of Russian Fed. 1993–96; Amb. to Czech Repub. 1996–2000, to Azerbaijan 2000–. *Address:* Embassy of the Russian Federation, Bakikhanova str. 17, 370133 Baku, Azerbaijan. *Telephone:* (12) 98-60-16. *Fax:* (12) 98-60-83. *E-mail:* embrus@azdata.net.

RYABOV, Vladimir Vladimirovich, PhD; Russian composer and pianist; b. b. 15 Sept. 1950, Chelyabinsk; m. 1st; one d.; m. 4th Ellen Levine; ed Moscow State Conservatory (expelled twice for non-conformist attitudes), Gnessin Pedagogical Inst. of Music (under Aram Khachaturyan), Leningrad State Conservatory; taught composition in Leningrad and Sverdlovsk conservatories 1977–81; Artistic and Repertoire Consultant, Moscow Symphony Orchestra 1993–; toured as pianist in Russia, Finland, USA, Germany, Austria, Hungary, Italy and Spain, performing standard repertoire and own compositions; mem. Int. Informatization Acad.; winner First S. Prokofiev Int. Composers' Competition 1991, Merited Artist of Russia 1995, Pushkin Gold Medal 1999. *Film:* The Life of Frederic Chopin (pianist) 1992. *Compositions include:* 4 symphonies (Nine Northern Tunes 1977, Pushkin 1980, Listen! 1981, In Memoriam of J. Brahms 1983), 5 string quarters, works for full and chamber orchestras, sonatas and other compositions for piano, violin, viola, organ, choir, song cycles on Russian poetry and English, American, Spanish and German poetry in Russian trans., transcriptions and paraphrases of classical music and folk songs; 6 cycles of sacred music 'European Cathedrals'; 7 cycles for different chamber ensembles, Norwegian Suite for symphony orchestra. *Leisure interests:* reading Russian poetry on stage, collecting illustrations of owls. *Address:* Novoyasenevsky pr. 14, kor. 2 Apt. 48, Moscow, Russia; Orisaarentie 6E, 00840 Helsinki, Finland. *Telephone:* (095) 143-97-13 (Moscow); (9) 6984059 (Helsinki) (Home). *Fax:* (9) 6988025 (Helsinki).

RYAN, Alan James, MA, DLitt, FBA; British professor of politics and author; b. 9 May 1940, London; s. of James W. Ryan and Ivy Ryan; m. Kathleen Alyson Lane 1971; one d.; ed Christ's Hospital and Balliol Coll. Oxford; Fellow, New Coll. Oxford 1969–; Reader in Politics, Univ. of Oxford 1978–88; Prof. of Politics, Princeton Univ. 1988–96, Mellon Fellow, Inst. for Advanced Study 1991–92; Warden, New Coll., Oxford 1996–; Visiting Prof., City Univ. of New York, Univ. of Texas, Calif., Witwatersrand Univ., Univ. of Cape Town; Visiting Fellow, Australian Nat. Univ.; de Carle Lecturer, Univ. of Otago; del. Oxford Univ. Press 1982–87; Almoner Christ's Hosp. 1998–. *Publications:* The Philosophy of John Stuart Mill 1970, The Philosophy of the Social Sciences 1970, J. S. Mill 1974, Property and Political Theory 1984, Property 1987, Russell: A Political Life 1988, John Dewey and the High Tide of American Liberalism 1995, Liberal Anxieties and Liberal Education 1998. *Leisure interests:* dinghy sailing, long train journeys. *Address:* Warden's Lodgings, New College, Oxford, OX1 3BN, England. *Telephone:* (1865) 279515 (Office). *Fax:* (1865) 724047 (Office). *E-mail:* alan.ryan@new.ox.ac.uk (Office). *Website:* new.ox.ac.uk (Office); users.ox.ac.uk/~newco499; users.ox.ac.uk/ajryan

RYAN, Arthur Frederick; American financial executive; b. 14 Sept. 1942, Brooklyn; s. of Arthur Ryan and Gertrude Wingert; m. Patricia Kelly; two s. two d.; ed Providence Coll.; Area Man. Data Corpn Washington, DC 1965–72; Project Man. Chase Manhattan Corpn and Bank, New York 1972–73, Second Vice-Pres. 1973–74, Vice-Pres. 1974–75, Operations Exec. 1978, Exec. Vice-Pres. 1982, later Vice-Chair., Pres. 1990–94; Chair. and CEO Prudential Insurance Co. of America 1994–; mem. American Bankers Asscn. *Address:* Prudential Insurance Company, 751 Broad Street, 24th Floor, Newark, NJ 07102, USA.

RYAN, George H., BS; American politician; b. 24 Feb. 1934, Maquoketa, Iowa; s. of Thomas J. Ryan and Jeanette (née Bowman) Ryan; m. Lura Lynn Lowe 1956; one s. five d.; ed Ferris State Coll.; fmrly with US Army, Korea; mem. Ill. House of Reps. 1973–82, minority leader 1977–80, Speaker 1981–82, Lt-Gov. of Ill. 1983–91, State Sec. 1991–99; Gov. of Illinois 1999–2003; Republican; numerous awards. *Address:* c/o Governor's Office, 207 State House, Springfield, IL 62706, USA.

RYAN, James M., MBE, JP, M.ED.; Cayman Islands government official; m.; one s. one d.; fmr teacher, Prin. Cayman Brac High School; Dist Commr 1980–92; Deputy Chief Sec. of the Cayman Islands 1992–94, Chief Sec. 1994–; First Official mem. Exec. Council and Legis. Ass. 1994–. *Address:* Office of the Chief Secretary, Government Administration Building, Elgin Avenue, George Town, Grand Cayman, Cayman Islands (Office).

RYAN, Meg; American actress; b. 19 Nov. 1961, Fairfield, Conn.; m. Dennis Quaid (q.v.) 1991 (divorced); one s.; ed Bethel High School and New York Univ.; fmrly appeared in TV commercials; TV appearances in As the World Turns, One of the Boys, Amy and the Angel, The Wild Side, Charles in Charge; owner of Prufrock Pictures. *Films:* Rich and Famous 1981, Amityville III-D,

Top Gun, Armed and Dangerous, Innerspace, D.O.A., Promised Land, The Presidio, When Harry Met Sally, Joe Versus the Volcano, The Doors, Prelude to a Kiss, Sleepless in Seattle, Flesh and Bone, Significant Other, When a Man Loves a Woman, I.Q., Paris Match, Restoration, French Kiss 1995, Two for the Road 1996, Courage Under Fire 1996, Addicted to Love 1997, City of Angels 1998, You've Got Mail 1998, Hanging Up 1999, Lost Souls 1999, Proof of Life 2000, Kate & Leopold 2001. *Address:* c/o Steve Dontanville, ICM, 8942 Wilshire Boulevard, Beverly Hills, CA 90211, USA.

RYAN, Richard, BA; Irish diplomatist; b. 1946, Dublin; m.; three c.; ed Oatlands Coll. and Univ. Coll., Dublin; joined Dept of Foreign Affairs 1973, First Sec. Perm. Mission of Ireland to EC 1980 (seconded to Comm. of EC 1982–83); Counsellor, London 1983, Minister-Counsellor (Political) 1988, Amb. to Repub. of Korea 1989, to Spain (also Accred to Algeria, Andorra and Tunisia) 1994–98, Perm. Rep. to UN 1998–. *Address:* Permanent Mission of Ireland to the United Nations, 1 Dag Hammarskjöld Plaza, 885 Second Avenue, 19th Floor, New York, NY 10017, USA (Office). *Telephone:* (212) 421-6934 (Office). *Fax:* (212) 752-4726 (Office). *E-mail:* ireland@un.int (Office).

RYAN, Thomas Anthony (Tony), LLD; Irish business executive; b. 2 Feb. 1936, Co. Tipperary; m.; three s.; ed Christian Brothers School, Thurles, Co. Tipperary, N Western Univ., Chicago; Aer Lingus 1956–75; f. GPA Group with Aer Lingus and Guinness Peat Group, Chair., CEO 1975–93; Chair. and CEO GE Capital Aviation Services 1994–, GE Aviation Services 1994–; Chair. (non-exec.) Ryanair 1995–98, Dir. 1996–; Dir (non-exec.) Bank of Ireland 1988, Trafalgar House 1989–; Consul for Mexico in Ireland; mem. Bd Govs. Nat. Gallery of Ireland, Europe Round Table, Nat. Univ. of Ireland 1987; Hon. mem. Limerick Univ. 1986; Hon. LLD (Trinity Coll., Dublin). *Leisure interests:* farming, the arts. *Address:* GE Capital Aviation Services, 201 High Ridge Road, Stamford, CT 06927, USA.

RYAZANOV, Eldar Aleksandrovich; Russian film director, writer and television broadcaster; b. 18 Nov. 1927, Samara; studied at VGIK under Pyriev, Kozintsev and Eisenstein; writes most of his own scripts (often together with playwright Emil Braginsky); Chevalier, Légion d'honneur; State Prize of USSR, State Prize of Russia, People's Artist of the USSR 1984, People's Artist of Russia. *Films include:* Voices of Spring 1955, Carnival Night 1956, The Girl without an Address 1957, How Robinson was Created 1961, The Hussar Ballad 1962, Let Me Make a Complaint 1964, Look out for the Cars 1966, The Zigzag of Success 1968, The Old Rascals 1971, The Amazing Adventures of Italians in Russia 1973, The Irony of Fate 1975, An Official Romance 1978, Garage 1979, Put in a Word for the Poor Hussar 1981, Railway Station for Two 1983, A Cruel Romance 1984, Forgotten Melody for Flute 1988, Dear Elena Sergeevna 1988, The Promised Heaven 1991 (Nika Prize 1992), The Prediction 1993, Hey, Fools! 1996, The Old Horses 2000, The Quiet Streams 2000, The Key of the Bedroom 2003; numerous TV productions, including interviews with Boris Yeltsin and Naina Yeltsin 1993. *Television:* The Paris Secrets (series), The Conversations on Fresh Air (series), The Woman's Summer (series). *Publication:* Not Summarizing (memoirs), Nostalgia (poems), The Prediction (novel), Irony of Fate, The Quiet Streams, Eldar TV or My Portrait's Gallery (memoirs) 2002. *Address:* Bolshoi Tishinski per. 12, Apt. 70, 123557 Moscow, Russia. *Telephone:* (095) 721-83-70; (095) 546-94-15. *Fax:* (095) 546-94-15 (Office).

RYBKIN, Ivan Petrovich, DR.POLIT.SCH., CAND.TECH.SC.; Russian politician; b. 20 Oct. 1946, Semigorovka, Voronezh Region; m.; two d.; ed Volgograd Inst. of Agric. Acad. of Social Sciences at Cen. Cttee CPSU; Sr engineer Kolkhoz Zavety Ilyicha Volgograd Region 1968–69; lecturer, Prof., Head of Chair, Deputy Dean, Volgograd Inst. of Agric. 1970–87; Sec. Party Cttee 1983–87, First Sec. CPSU Dist Cttee in Volgograd, Second Sec. Volgograd Regional Cttee CPSU 1987–91; Head of Div. Cen. Cttee CP of RSFSR 1991; People's Deputy of Russia 1990–93; one of founders and Co-Chair. faction Communists of Russia 1990–91; mem. Agrarian Party, concurrently one of founders of Socialist Party of Workers 1991–93; deputy to State Duma (Parl.) 1993–96, Chair. 1994–95; mem. Council on Personnel Policy of Pres. Yeltsin 1994–95, mem. Security Council 1994–96, Sec. 1996–98; head of group negotiating with Chechen leaders 1996–98; Deputy Prime Minister 1998; Plenipotentiary Rep. of Russian Pres. to CIS states 1998; Chair. Political Union Regions of Russia, concurrently of Election Bloc 1995–96; Chair. Political Consultative Council of Pres. of Russia 1999–2000; Prize for Contribution to Peace with Chechnya (Ichkeria) 1996. *Publications:* State Duma, Fifth Attempt, We are Doomed to Consensus, Russia and the World: The Way to Security; numerous articles. *Address:* Administration of the President, Staraya pl. 4, 103132, Moscow, Russia; Socialist Party, Novo-Basmannaya str. 14, bldg 1, 107078 Moscow, Russia. *Telephone:* (095) 925-35-81.

RYCHETSKY, Pavel, JU.DR.; Czech politician; b. 17 Aug. 1943, Prague; m.; three c.; ed Charles Univ.; Sr Lecturer and Asst Prof., Dept of Civil Law, Charles Univ. Law School, Prague 1966–70, compelled to leave for political reasons; worked as co. lawyer for Fortuna commercial agency, Mladá fronta publrs and for housing devt co-operative; mem. Communist party 1966–69; Co-Founder and signatory Charter 77; Co-Founder Civic Forum, Rep. Civic Forum Liberal Club and later of Civic Movt; Public Prosecutor-Gen. of Czech Repub. 1990; Deputy Prime Minister and Chair. Legis. Council of the then Czech and Slovak Fed. Repub. 1990; f. solicitor's practice 1992; Lecturer in Political Sciences, Prague School of Econs Faculty of Int. Relations 1992; joined Czech Social Democrat Party 1995; elected Senator for Strakonice Constituency No. 12, later Chair. Constitutional Law Cttee of the Senate; Deputy Prime Minister of Czech Repub. and Chair. Govt Legis. Council 1998–; Chair. Govt Council for Research and Devt 1998–2002, Govt Council for Roma Community Affairs 1998–2002, Govt Council for Ethnic Minorities 1998–2002; Minister of Justice 2000–01, 2002–; Chair. Czech Lawyers' Asscn 1990–92; Pres. Bd Trustees Pro-Bohemia Foundation 1992–98; Founder Práchensko Region Citizens' Endowment Fund. *Address:* Ministry of Justice, Vyšehradská 16, 128 10 Prague 2, Czech Republic (Office). *Telephone:* (2) 219977111 (Office). *Fax:* (2) 24919927 (Office). *E-mail:* msp@msp.justice.cz (Office). *Website:* www.justice.cz (Office).

RYCKMANS, Pierre, PhD; Belgian professor of Chinese studies and writer; b. 28 Sept. 1935, Brussels; m. Chang Han-fang; three s. one d.; ed Univ. of Louvain; fmr Prof. of Chinese Studies, Univ. of Sydney; mem. Académie Royale de Littérature Française (Brussels) 1991; Prix Stanislas-Julien (Institut de France), Prix Jean Walter (Acad. Française), The Independent (UK) Foreign Fiction Award 1992, Christina Stead Prize for Fiction (NSW) 1992, Prix Bernheim 1999, Prix Renaudot 2001, Prix Henri Gal (Acad. Française) 2001, etc.; Officer Ordre de Léopold, Commdr Ordre des Arts et des Lettres 1999. *Film:* The Emperor's New Clothes (Dir. Alan Taylor, Producer U. Pasolini) 2001, adapted from Simon Leys' The Death of Napoleon. *Publications:* (under pen-name Simon Leys) The Chairman's New Clothes: Mao and the Cultural Revolution 1977, Chinese Shadows 1977, The Burning Forest 1985, La Mort de Napoléon 1986 (English trans. 1991), Les Entretiens de Confucius 1989, L'humeur, l'honneur, l'horreur 1991, The Analects of Confucius 1996, Essais sur la Chine 1998, The View from the Bridge 1996, The Angel and the Octopus 1999, Protée et autres essais 2001. *Address:* 6 Bonwick Place, Garran, ACT 2605, Australia. *Fax:* (2) 6281-4887.

RYDER, Guy; British international trade union official; b. 3 Jan. 1956, Liverpool; ed Univ. of Cambridge; Asst, Int. Dept, Trade Union Congress (TUC) 1981–85; Sec. Industry Trade Section, Int. Fed. of Commercial, Clerical, Professional and Tech. Employees (FIET), Geneva, Switzerland 1985–88; Sec. Workers' Group, Int. Labour Org. (ILO) 1993–96, 1996–98, Sec. Worker's Group, Int. Labour Conf. 1994–98, Dir of Bureau for Workers' Activities, ILO 1998–99, Chief of Cabinet 1999–2001, Special Adviser to Dir-Gen. –2001; Asst Dir, then Dir ICFTU, Geneva 1988–98, Gen. Sec. Feb. 2002–. *Address:* ICFTU, 5 boulevard Roi Albert II, 1210 Brussels, Belgium (Office). *Telephone:* (2) 224-02-11 (Office). *Fax:* (2) 201-58-15 (Office). *E-mail:* internetpo@icftu.org (Office). *Website:* www.icftu.org (Office).

RYDER, Winona; American actress; b. 29 Oct. 1971, Winona, Minn.; d. of Michael Horowitz and Cynthia Istas; ed Petaluma Jr High School, San Francisco and acting classes at American Conservatory Theatre, San Francisco. *Films include:* Lucas 1986, Square Dance, Beetlejuice 1969, Heathers, Great Balls of Fire, Welcome Home Roxy, Carmichael, Edward Scissorhands, Mermaids, The Age of Innocence, Reality Bites, House of Spirits, Boys, Little Women, How to Make an American Quilt, The Crucible, Looking for Richard, Boys, Alien Resurrection, Girl Interrupted 1999, Lost Souls 2000, Autumn in New York 2000, Mr Deeds 2002.

RYDER OF WENSUM, Baron (Life Peer), cr. 1997, of Wensum in the County of Norfolk; **Richard Andrew Ryder,** OBE, PC, BA; British politician; b. 4 Feb. 1949; s. of Richard Stephen Ryder and Margaret MacKenzie; m. Caroline Mary Stephens 1981; one s. (deceased) one d.; ed Radley Coll., Magdalene Coll., Cambridge; journalist 1972–75; Political Sec. to Margaret Thatcher, Leader of the Opposition and Prime Minister 1975–81; MP for Mid-Norfolk 1983–97; Parl. Pvt. Sec. to Financial Sec. to the Treasury 1984, Parl. Pvt. Sec. to Foreign Sec. 1984–86; Govt Whip 1986–88; Parl. Sec. Ministry of Agric. 1988–89; Econ. Sec. to Treasury 1989–90; Paymaster Gen. 1990; Parl. Sec. to Treasury and Govt Chief Whip 1990–95; Chair. Eastern Counties Radio 1997–2001; Vice-Chair. BBC 2002–; dir of family businesses. *Address:* House of Lords, Westminster, London SW1A 0PW, England.

RYDIN, Bo, BSc; Swedish business executive; b. 7 May 1932; s. of Gunnar Rydin and Signe (née Höög) Rydin; m. 1st Monika Avréus 1955 (died 1992); m. 2nd Françoise Yon 1997; with Stockholms Enskilda Bank 1956–57; Marma-Långrör AB 1957–60; AB Gullhögens Bruk 1960, Pres. 1965–71; Pres. and CEO Svenska Cellulosa AB 1972–88, Chair. and CEO 1988–90, Chair. 1990–; Chair. Svenska Cellulosa AB, SCA, AB Industrivärden, Graningeverken, Skanska AB; Vice-Chair. Svenska Handelsbanken, mem. Bd SAS Ass. of Reps.; Vice-Chair. Volvo 1988–93; Chair. Fed. of Swedish Industries 1993–94; mem. Skandia 1983–93; mem. Royal Swedish Acad. of Eng Sciences, Royal Swedish Acad. of Agric. and Forestry; Hon. D.Econs., Hon. DTech; King's Medal 12th Dimension of Order of the Seraphim. *Leisure interests:* golf, hunting, opera. *Address:* AB Industrivärden, Storgatan 10, Box 5403, 114 84 Stockholm (Office); Karlavägen 3, 114 24 Stockholm, Sweden (Home).

RYKIEL, Sonia; French fashion designer; b. 25 May 1930, Paris; d. of Alfred Flis and Fanny Tesler; m.; one s. one d.; began designing rabbit-hair sweaters which est. her reputation 1963; opened own boutique, Paris 1968; opened further boutiques specializing in men's knitwear and household linens 1976, 1981; launched first perfume 7e Sens 1979; supervised renovation of Hotel Crillon, Paris 1982; first boutique opened New York 1983; launched first children's collection 1984; Vice-Pres. Chambre Syndicale du Prêt-à-Porter des Couturiers et des Créateurs de Mode, Paris 1982; launched Sonia Rykiel perfume 1997; Hon. Prof. China Textile Univ., Shanghai 1998; Award for Design Excellence (Costume Cttee, Chicago Historical Soc.); Officier Ordre des Arts et des Lettres 1993, Officier Légion d'honneur 1996. *Publications:* Et je la voudrais nue 1979, Célébration 1988, La collection 1989, Colette et la mode 1991, Collection terminée, collection interminable 1993, Tatiana Acacia (jtly.) 1993, Les lèvres rouges 1996, Sonia Rykiel (memoirs) 1997. *Address:* 175 boulevard Saint Germain, 75006 Paris, France. *Telephone:* 1-49-54-60-00. *Fax:* 1-49-54-60-96.

RYLANCE, Mark; British actor and director; b. 1960, Ashford, Kent; ed Royal Acad. of Dramatic Art and Chrysalis Theatre School, Balham; joined The Citizen's Theatre, Glasgow 1980; has since worked with RSC, Royal Nat. Theatre, Royal Opera House, Scottish Ballet, Shared Experience, Bush Theatre, Tricycle Theatre, London Theatre of Imagination, Contact Theatre, Oxford Playhouse, Project Theatre, Dublin, Mermaid Theatre, Royal Court, American Repertory Theatre, Boston, Theatre for a New Audience, New York, Pittsburgh Playhouse, Thelma Holte; now Assoc. actor, RSC; Artistic Dir Shakespeare's Globe, Phoebus Cart; recent work includes title role in Phoebus Cart's production of Macbeth (also Dir) and Proteus in The Two Gentlemen of Verona, Shakespeare's Globe's Prologue Season 1996, title role in Henry V in Shakespeare's Globe's opening season 1997, Bassanio in The Merchant of Venice and Hippolito in The Honest Whore, Shakespeare's Globe 1998, Cleopatra in Antony and Cleopatra, Shakespeare's Globe 1999, Life x3 2000, Twelfth Night, Shakespeare's Globe 2002; Olivier Award for Best Actor 1994. *Television appearances include:* The Grass Arena, Love Lies Bleeding, In Lambeth, Incident in Judea. *Films:* Prospero's Books, Angels and Insects, Institute Benjamenta, Hearts of Fire, Intimacy. *Address:* Shakespeare's Globe, 21 New Globe Walk, Bankside, London SE1 9DT, England. *Telephone:* (20) 7902-1400. *Fax:* (20) 7902-1420. *E-mail:* info@shakespearesglobe.com. *Website:* www.shakespeares-globe.org.

RYNNE, Etienne Andrew, MA, MRIA, FSA; Irish professor of archaeology; b. 11 Sept. 1932, Dublin; s. of Dr. Michael Rynne and Nathalie Fournier; m. Aideen Lucas 1967; four s. one d.; ed Terenure Coll., Dublin, Ecole des Roches, Verneuil-sur-Avre, France, Clongowes Wood Coll., Clane, Co. Kildare and Univ. Coll. Dublin; part-time Archaeological Asst, Nat. Museum of Ireland 1954–56, Asst, Irish Antiquities Div. 1957–66, Asst-Keeper 1966–67; lecturer in Celtic Archaeology, Univ. Coll., Galway 1967–78, Prof. of Archaeology 1978–; Hon. Curator Galway City Museum 1972–86; Pres. Royal Soc. of Antiquaries of Ireland 1985–89, Galway Archaeological & Historical Soc. 1989–95; Ed. North Munster Antiquarian Journal 1964–; mem. Royal Irish Acad.; Travelling Studentship Prize, Nat. Univ. of Ireland 1956. *Publications:* Ed. North Munster Studies 1967, Figures from the Past 1987; about 200 articles in learned journals. *Leisure interests:* archaeology (visiting ancient sites, museums etc.), art history, sport (boxing, athletics). *Address:* Department of Archaeology, University College, Galway, Ireland. *Telephone:* (91) 524411 (Office). *Fax:* (91) 525700 (Office).

RYRIE, Sir William Sinclair, KCB, MA, FRSA; British merchant banker and fmr civil servant; b. 10 Nov. 1928, Calcutta, India; s. of Rev. Dr Frank Ryrie and Mabel M. Ryrie; m. 1st Dorrit Klein 1953 (divorced 1969); two s. one d.; m. 2nd Christine G. Thomson 1969; one s.; ed Heriot's School, Edinburgh, Edinburgh Univ.; army service, Lt Intelligence Corps in Malaya 1951–53 (despatches 1953); joined Colonial Office as Asst Prin. 1953; seconded to Govt of Uganda 1956–58; Prin., UN Affairs, Colonial Office 1959–63; Prin., Balance of Payments Div. of HM Treasury 1963–66, Asst Sec. for Int. Monetary Affairs 1966–69; Prin. Pvt. Sec. to Chancellor of the Exchequer 1969–71; Under-Sec., Public Sector Group in Treasury 1971–75; Econ. Minister, Embassy in USA and Exec. Dir of IMF, IBRD, IDA, IFC 1975–79; Second Perm. Sec., Domestic Economy Sector, HM Treasury 1980–82; Perm. Sec. Overseas Devt Admin. 1982–84; Exec. Vice-Pres. and Chief Exec. Int. Finance Corpn, World Bank Group 1984–93; Exec. Dir Barings PLC 1994–95, Vice-Chair. ING Barings Holding Co. Ltd 1995–98; Chair. Baring Emerging Europe Trust 1994–2002; Deputy Chair. Commonwealth Devt Corpn 1994–98; Dir W S. Atkins Ltd 1994–2001, First NIS Regional Fund 1999–, Ashanti Goldfields Co. 1995–2000; mem. Group of Thirty 1992–2002; Council mem. Overseas Devt Inst. 1994–2000; Pres. Edin. Univ. Devt Trust 1994–99; Dir CARE UK 1993–2001. *Publication:* First World, Third World 1995. *Leisure interests:* walking, photography. *Address:* Hawkwood, Hawkwood Lane, Chislehurst, Kent, BR7 5PW, England. *Telephone:* (20) 8295-1853 (Home). *Fax:* (20) 8468-7495 (Office). *E-mail:* billryrie@btinternet.com (Home).

RYTKHEU, Yuriy Sergeyevich; Russian/Chukchi writer; b. 8 March 1930, Uellen, Chukotka N.O., Magadan Region; m. Galina Vinogradova 1949; two s. one d.; ed Leningrad Univ.; foremost Chukchi writer; works have been translated into Russian; started writing for the newspaper Soviet Chukotka 1947; mem. CPSU 1967–91; Grinzane Cavour Literary Prize 1983, Prix RFI (France) 2000. *Publications:* Short stories: Friends and Comrades, People of our Coast 1953, When the Snow Melts (novel) 1960, The Sorceress of Konerga 1960, The Saga of Chukotka 1960, Farewell to the Gods (short stories) 1961, Nunivak (tales) 1963, The Magic Gauntlet (novel) 1963, In the Vale of the Little Sunbeams (novel) 1963, The Walrus of Dissent (stories) 1964, Blue Foxes (stories) 1964, Wings are Becoming Stronger in Flight (novel) 1964, Bear Stew (verses) 1965, The Finest Ships 1967, Dream at the Onset of Mist 1969, Frost on the Threshold 1971, The Harpoon Thrower 1971, White Snows (novel) 1975, When the Whales Depart 1976, Contemporary Legends 1980, The Magic Numbers (novel) 1985, Island of Hope (novel) 1987, The Dream in

the Beginning of Mist (novel) 1988, Intercontinental Bridge 1989, The Journey to Youth or The Time of Red Cloudberries 1991, Unter dem Sternbild der Trauer 1997, Unna 1998, Im Spiegel des Vergessens (novel) 1999, Die Reise der Anna Odinzowa. *Address:* Suvorovsky Prosp. 56, Apt. 84, 193015 St Petersburg, Russia. *Telephone:* (812) 274-85-26. *Fax:* (812) 274-85-26. *E-mail:* uelcn@dux.ru (Office); teryky@yandex.ru (Office).

RYTTER, Jakob, LLD; Danish diplomatist; b. 17 Dec. 1932, Aarhus; s. of the late Ejnar I. J. Rytter and Ingeborg J. Rytter; m. Suzanne Engelsen 1963 (died 1986); two d.; ed Marselisborg Gymnasium, Aarhus, Lycée de Fontainebleau, Univ. of Aarhus, Institut d'Etudes Politiques, Paris; mil. service 1960; entered Danish Foreign Office 1961, Sec. of Embassy, Bonn 1963–66, Del. to UN Gen. Ass., New York 1966, 1968, First Sec. Tel-Aviv 1969–72, Counsellor Danish EC Representation, Brussels 1973–78, Dir EC Affairs, Danish Foreign Ministry 1978–83, Deputy Perm. Rep., Danish EC Representation 1983–86; Amb. to Israel 1986–89, 1992–96, Amb., Perm. Rep. to the EC, Brussels 1989–92; Amb. to the Netherlands 1996–2001 and Perm. Rep. to OPCW, The Hague 1998–2001; Chair. Admin. and Financial Council, European Schools 1977–78; Commdr (First Class) Order of Dannebrog 1998. *Address:* Ministry of Foreign Affairs, Copenhagen Asiatisk Plads 2, 1448 Copenhagen K (Office); Esplanaden 28, DK-1263 Copenhagen K, Denmark (Home). *Telephone:* 33-9-00-00 (Office); 33-33-97-98 (Home).

RYWIN, Lew; Polish film producer and business executive; b. 10 Nov. 1945, Niżne Alkiejewo; m. Eżbieta Sitek; one s.; ed Warsaw Univ.; Asst Inst. of Applied Linguistics, Warsaw Univ. 1969–70; Head Dept Orgmasz, Warsaw 1970–78; fmr Interpreter and Sec. Main Bureau of Co-operation with Foreign Countries, Polish Interpress Agency; Man. Poltel Commerce Bureau of Polish Radio and TV Cttee 1983–88, 1st Deputy Chair. 1988–91; Chair. Heritage Films 1991–97, Canal + Polska 1997–; Co-Founder and mem. Polish Interpreters' Asscn 1981–. *Films produced include:* Pierścionek z orłem w koronie (The Crowned-Eagle Ring) 1992, Schindler's List (Humanitas Prize, Jt recipient with co-producer 1994) 1993, Pułkownik Kwiatkowski (Colonel Kwiatkowski) 1994, Les Milles 1995, Tato (Dad) 1995, Wielki Tydzień (Holy Week) 1995, Matka swojej matki (Mother of Her Own Mother) 1996, Sara 1996, Ostatni rozdział (Last Chapter) 1997, 13 Posterunek (13 Police Station) 1997, Jakub kłamca (Jacob the Liar) 1998, Podróże (Travels) 1998, Złoto dezerterów (Deserter's Gold) 1998, Pan Tadeusz (Last Foray in Lithuania) 1998, The Pianist 2002. *Leisure interests:* tennis, fishing. *Address:* Heritage Films, ul. Marszałkowska 2/65, 00-581 Warsaw, Poland (Office). *Telephone:* (22) 6252553 (Office). *Fax:* (22) 6252601 (Office). *E-mail:* heritage@heritage .com.pl (Office).

RYZHKOV, Nikolai Ivanovich; Russian politician; b. 28 Sept. 1929, Donetsk; m. Lyudmila Sergeyevna Ryzhkova; one d.; ed S. M. Kirov Ural Polytechnic Inst.; mem. CPSU 1956–91; Chief Engineer 1965–70, Deputy Dir, later Dir S. Orzhonikidze Ural Factory of Heavy Machine Bldg 1970; Gen. Dir of Production Uralmash Factory 1971–75; First Deputy Minister of Heavy and Transport Machine Bldg 1975–79; mem. Cen. Cttee CPSU in charge of Heavy Industry 1981–90; mem. Politburo 1985–90; Chair. Council of Ministers 1985–90; First Deputy Chair. of Gosplan 1979–82; Head Econ. Affairs 1982–85; Deputy of the USSR Supreme Soviet 1974–89; People's Deputy of the USSR 1989–91; cand. for Pres. of Russia 1991; Chair. Bd Tveruniversalbank; 1993–95, Pres. Int. Public Union; leader pre-election bloc 'Power to People'; mem State Duma 1995–, Chair. deputies bloc Narodvlastiye 1996–; mem. Acad. of Social Sciences, Acad. of Tech. Sciences, Int. Eng Acad., Int. Acad. of Man.; Order of Lenin (twice), Order of Red Banner of Labour (twice) and other decorations; USSR State Prizes 1969, 1979. *Publication:* Perestroika: a series of betrayals. *Address:* State Duma, Okhotny Ryad 1, 103009, Moscow, Russia. *Telephone:* (095) 292-88-40. *Fax:* (095) 292-73-41.

RYZHKOV, Vladimir Aleksandrovich, DHist; Russian politician; b. 3 Sept. 1966, Altai Territory; ed Altai State Univ.; Deputy Head Altai Territory Soc. of Encouraging Perestroika 1988–90; Deputy Chair. Altai Territory Movt Democratic Russia 1990–91; Vice-Gov. Altai Territory; mem. State Duma (Parl.) 1993–; mem. Cttee on Fed. and Regional Policy 1994–95; Deputy Chair. faction Russia Our Home 1996–97, Chair. 1999–2000; First Deputy Chair. State Duma 1997–99, Ind. mem. 2000–. *Publications:* Chetvertaya respublika (The Fourth Republic in Russia) 1999; more than 80 articles on contemporary policy. *Address:* State Duma, Georgievsky per. 2, 103265 Moscow, Russia (Office). *Telephone:* (095) 292-07-01 (Office). *Fax:* (095) 292-15-63 (Office). *E-mail:* ryzhkov@duma.gov.ru (Office).

RYZHOV, Yuri Alexeevich, DTech; Russian politician and scientist; b. 28 Oct. 1930, Moscow; m.; two d.; ed Moscow Physical Tech. Inst.; mem. CPSU 1961–90; engineer 1954–60; Sr researcher Moscow Inst. of Aviation 1960–, Prof. 1970–, Prorector 1972–86, Rector 1986–91; mem. USSR (now Russian) Acad. of Sciences 1987; author of works on aerodynamics of high velocities; political activities since late 1980s; mem. of the Supreme Soviet of the USSR 1989–91; mem. Interregional Group of Deputies 1989–; Russian Amb. to France 1992–98; Pres. Int. Eng Univ. 1999–. *Leisure interest:* music. *Address:* International Engineering University, Leninsky prosp. 6, Moscow, Russia. *Telephone:* (095) 236-50-66 (Office); (095) 135-12-44 (Home).

S

SÁ, Angelo Calmon de; Brazilian politician and banker; b. 1 Nov. 1935, Salvador, Bahia; s. of Francisco de Sá and Maria dos Prazeres Calmon de Sá; m. Ana Maria Carvalho 1962; two s. two d.; ed Univ. Federal da Bahia; Sec. of Industry and Commerce, Bahia State 1967–70, Sec. of Finance 1970–71; Minister of Industry and Commerce 1977–79; Minister of Regional Devt 1992–93; Pres. Banco do Brasil SA 1974–77, mem. Bd of Dirs. 1987–; mem. Bd of Dirs. Banco Econômico SA 1977–, Pres. and CEO 1979–92, Chair. of Bd 1992–; Chair. Brazilian Cocoa Trade Comm. (Comcauba) 1980–; Dir Nordeste Química SA 1980–, American Express Int. Bank Ltd, New York 1982–, Associação de Exportadores Brasileiros 1982–; mem. Int. Advisory Council Wells Fargo Bank, San Francisco 1979–; mem. Nat. Monetary Council, representing pvt. sector 1979–86; Vice-Pres. Bahia Chamber of Commerce 1981–; Dir Brazilian Exporters' Asscn 1982–; Pres. Brazil section, Brazil-U.S. Business Council 1984–87, mem. Exec. Cttee 1987–; mem. Bd of Trustees, Eisenhower Exchange Fellowships Inc.; several Brazilian honours. *Publication:* study on the Bank of Brazil as an agent of Devt and a factor of nat. integration. *Leisure interests:* riding, tennis, golf. *Address:* Banco Econômico SA, Rua Miguel Calmon, 285, Edf. Goes Calmon, 11° andar, 40015 Salvador, Bahia, Brazil.

SAÁ, Adolfo Rodríguez; Argentine politician; b. 25 July 1947, San Luis; s. of Juan Rodríguez Saá and Lilia Ester Paez Montero; m.; five c.; ed Nat. Univ. of Buenos Aires; lawyer 1971–; Rep. of Partido Justicialista (PJ—Justice Party) 1971–83; Provincial Deputy and Pres. Justicialista Block 1973–76; Provincial Congressman 1976–85; Nat. Congressman (PJ) 1983–91; Nat. Councillor 1987–94; Conventional Nat. Component 1994; Pres. Partido Justicialista (San Luis Dist) 1985–95, Third Vice-Pres. Nat. Partido Justicialista 1996–2000; Gov. of San Luis Prov. 1983–2001; Interim Pres. of Argentina Dec. 2001–Jan. 2002. *Address:* c/o General Secretariat of the Presidency, Balcarce 50, 1064 Buenos Aires, Argentina (Office).

SAADAWI, Nawal al-, MD; Egyptian writer and medical practitioner; b. 27 Oct. 1931; m. Sherif Hetata 1964; one s. one d.; ed Cairo Univ.; novelist and writer 1956–; Dir-Gen. Ministry of Health 1965–72; psychiatrist 1974–; Pres. Arab Women's Solidarity Asscn; with UN Beirut, Lebanon and Ethiopia; Hon. DUniv (York) 1994; Short Story Award (Cairo) 1974, Franco-Arab Literary Award (Paris) 1982 and many other literary prizes. *Publications:* 30 books (novels, collections of short stories, memoirs, plays and studies on women in the Arab World), including Women and Sex 1971, The Hidden Face of Eve: Women in the Arab World, Woman at Point Zero, God Dies by the Nile, The Circling Song, The Fall of the Imam 1987, My Travels Around the World; 16 of her books translated into many languages. *Leisure interests:* swimming, walking.

SAAKIAN, Suren Mushegovich; Armenian politician; b. 1 Jan. 1958; m.; three c.; ed Yerevan State Univ.; researcher Chair. of Nuclear Physics, Yerevan State Univ. 1979–81; researcher Inst. of Physical Studies, Armenian SSR Acad. of Sciences 1981–88; Head of Div. Lazernaya Tekhnika 1988–90; Head of Dept Armenian Ministry of Higher Educ. 1990–91; Deputy Minister of Internal Affairs 1991; Minister of Armenian State Tax Service 1991–94; envoy to Russian Fed. 1994–96, Amb. 1999–; Rep. to Bd of Int. Econs Cttee 1996–99. *Address:* Embassy of Armenia, Armyanskii per. 2, 101000 Moscow, Russia (Office). *Telephone:* (095) 924-32-43 (Office).

SAATCHI, Charles; British advertising executive; b. 9 June 1943; s. of Nathan Saatchi and Daisy Saatchi; brother of Maurice Saatchi (q.v.); m. 1st Doris Lockhart 1973 (divorced 1990); m. 2nd Kay Saatchi 1990 (divorced 2001); one d.; ed Christ's Coll. Finchley; fmr jr copywriter, Benton & Bowles (US advertising agency), London; Assoc. Dir Collett Dickenson Pearce 1966–68; with Ross Cramer formed freelance consultancy, Cramer Saatchi, Dir 1968–70; Co-Founder (with Maurice Saatchi), of Saatchi and Saatchi (advertising agency) 1970, (Saatchi & Saatchi PLC 1984), Dir 1970–93, Pres. 1993–95; Co-Founder and partner M&C Saatchi Agency 1995–; f. The Saatchi Gallery 2003–. *Address:* 36 Golden Square, London, W1R 4EE, England (Office). *Telephone:* (20) 7543-4500.

SAATCHI, Baron (Life Peer), cr. 1996, of Staplefield in the County of West Sussex; **Maurice Saatchi,** BSc; British advertising executive; b. 21 June 1946; s. of Nathan Saatchi and Daisy Saatchi; brother of Charles Saatchi (q.v.); m. Josephine Hart 1984; one s.; one step-s.; ed London School of Econs; Co-Founder Saatchi & Saatchi Co. 1970; Chair. Saatchi & Saatchi Co. PLC 1984–94, Dir. –1994; Co-Founder and Partner M&C Saatchi Agency 1995–; Chair. Megalomedia PLC 1995–; Dir (non-exec.) Loot 1998–; Shadow Cabinet Office Minister 2001–; Gov. LSE 1996–, Trustee Victoria and Albert Museum 1988–96; mem. Council RCA1997–2000. *Publication:* The Science of Politics 2001. *Address:* 36 Golden Square, London, W1R 4EE, England (Office). *Telephone:* (20) 7543-4500 (Office).

SAAVEDRA, Gustavo Fernández; Bolivian politician and diplomatist; b. 1941, Cochabamba; m.; three c.; ed San Simon Univ.; Amb. of Bolivia 1968–69; Exec. Sec., Secr. of Integration, La Paz 1969–70; Head Legal Dept, Comm. on Cartagena, Lima, Peru 1970–76; Dir of Consultation and Latin American Co-ordination, Caracas, Venezuela 1976–77; Consulting Dir-Gen. Coprinco y Asociados Consultores 1977–78, Pres. 1979–80, 1982–83; Minister of Integration 1978, of Foreign Affairs 1979, 1984–85, 2001–02; Consultant to UNCTAD 1980–83, 1987–89, 1993–98; Rep. of Ministries of Industry and Foreign Affairs, Quito, Ecuador 1980–81, Geneva, Switzerland 1985–87;

Amb. to Brazil 1983–84; Exec. Dir Muller y Asociados Consultores 1987–89, Network of Advising and Man. SA 1993; Vice-Presidential Cand. 1989; Minister of the Presidency 1989–93; Co-ordinator Nat. Dialogue 1997; Rep. Andean Corpn of Promotion in Peru 1998–99; Gen. Consul of Bolivia in Chile 2000–01. *Address:* c/o Ministry of Foreign Affairs and Worship, Calle Ingavi, esq. Junin, La Paz, Bolivia (Office).

SABA, Elias, BLitt; Lebanese politician and economist; b. 1932, Lebanon; s. of Shukri Saba and Guilnar Abou Haidar; m. Hind Sabri Shurbagi 1960; five d.; ed American Univ. of Beirut and Univ. of Oxford; Econ. Adviser to Ministry of Finance and Petroleum, Kuwait and Kuwait Fund for Arab Econ. Devt 1961–62; Chair. Dept of Econs, American Univ. of Beirut 1963–67; Assoc. Prof. of Econs, American Univ. of Beirut 1967–69; Deputy Prime Minister of the Lebanon, Minister of Finance and of Defence 1970–72; Econ. and Financial Adviser to the Pres. 1972–73; Chair., Gen. Man. St Charles City Centre SARL 1974–; Vice-Chair. Banque du Crédit Populaire, Chair. Allied Bank, Beirut 1983; Chair., CEO The Associates, SARL 1981–; mem. Nat. Dialogue Cttee 1975. *Publication:* Postwar Developments in the Foreign Exchange Systems of Lebanon and Syria 1962. *Leisure interests:* hunting, vintage and classic cars. *Address:* P.O. Box 5292, Ayoub Centre, Ashrafieh, Beirut, Lebanon.

SABA, Shoichi, BEng, FIEEE; Japanese business executive; b. 28 Feb. 1919; s. of Wataru Saba and Sumie Saba; m. Fujiko Saito 1945 (deceased); two s. (one deceased) one d.; ed Tokyo Imperial Univ.; Pres. Toshiba Corpn 1980–86, Chair. 1986–87, Adviser 1987–; Dir ICI (UK) 1985–91 and numerous other bodies; Vice-Chair. Keidanren 1986–92, Vice-Chair. Bd of Councillors 1992–94, Advisor 1994–; Chair. Electronic Industries Asscn of Japan 1986–87, The Japan Inst. of Industrial Eng 1982–88, Japan Int. Devt Org. Ltd (JAIDO) 1989–94, Nat. Bd of Govs., Nat. Asscn, Boy Scouts of Nippon 1994–; Pres. Japanese Ind. Standards Cttee 1994–; mem. Public Review Bd, Andersen Worldwide SC (USA) 1991–98; Progress Prize (Inst. of Electrical Engineers of Japan) 1958; Blue Ribbon Medal (Govt of Japan) 1980, Commdr.'s Cross, Order of Merit (FRG) 1988, Hon. CBE (UK) 1989, Order of the Sacred Treasure (1st Class) 1990, Hon. KBE (UK) 1993. *Leisure interests:* golf, yachting. *Address:* c/o Toshiba Corpn, 1-1 Shibaura 1-chome, Minato-ku, Tokyo 105, Japan.

SABAH, Sheikh Jaber al-Ahmad as-, Amir of Kuwait; b. 1928, Kuwait; ed Almubarakiyyah School, Kuwait and private tutors; Gov. of Ahmadi and Oil areas 1949–59; Pres. Dept of Finance and Economy 1959; Minister of Finance, Industry and Commerce 1963, 1965; Prime Minister 1965–67; Crown Prince 1966–77; Amir Dec. 1977–, succeeding his uncle. *Address:* Sief Palace, Amiry Diwan, Kuwait (official residence).

SABAH, Sheikh Saad al-Abdullah as-Salim as-; Kuwaiti Crown Prince and politician; b. 1930, Kuwait; m. Sheikha Latifah Fahad al-Sabah; one s. four d.; ed Kuwait Govt schools and Hendon Coll., UK; Deputy Chief, Police and Public Security Dept 1959, Chief 1961; Minister of Interior 1961 and of Defence 1965; Crown Prince Jan. 1978–; Prime Minister Feb. 1978–; Ex-officio Chair. Supreme Defence Council, Supreme Petroleum Council, Civil Service Council, Supreme Housing Council. *Leisure interests:* fishing, gardening, photography. *Address:* Diwan of HH The Crown Prince and Prime Minister, P.O. Box 4, 13001 Safat, Kuwait City, Kuwait.

SABAH, Sheikh Sabah al-Ahmad al-Jaber as-; Kuwaiti politician; b. 1929; half-brother of the Amir of Kuwait; ed Mubarakiyyah Nat. School, Kuwait and privately; mem. Supreme Cttee 1955–62; Minister of Public Information and Guidance and of Social Affairs 1962–63, of Foreign Affairs 1963–91, acting Minister of Finance and Oil 1965, Minister of the Interior 1978; Deputy Prime Minister 1978–91; acting Minister of Information 1981–84; now First Deputy Prime Minister and Minister of Foreign Affairs. *Address:* Ministry of Foreign Affairs, P.O. Box 3, 13001 Safat, Gulf Street, Kuwait City, Kuwait. *Telephone:* 2425141. *Fax:* 2430559. *E-mail:* info@mofa .org (Office). *Website:* www.mofa.org (Office).

SABAH, Sheikh Salem Abd al-Aziz Sa'ud as-, BA(Econs); Kuwaiti central bank governor; b. 1 Nov. 1951; ed American Univ. of Beirut, Lebanon; Econ. Analyst Studies Section, Foreign Operations Dept, Cen. Bank of Kuwait 1977–78, Head 1978–80, Deputy Man. and Head of Investment and Studies Section 1980–84, Deputy Man. and Head of Inspection Section, Banking Supervision Dept March–Aug. 1984, Man. Banking Supervision Dept 1984–85, Exec. Dir for Banking Supervision and Monetary Policy 1985–86, Deputy Gov. Feb.–Sept. 1986, Gov. and Chair. Bd of Dirs 1986–; Chair. Bd of Dirs Inst. of Banking Studies; Alternate Gov. of the State of Kuwait, IMF and Arab Monetary Fund; mem. Higher Planning Council, Higher Petroleum Council, Bd of Dirs Kuwait Investment Authority, Higher Cttee for Econ. Devt and Reform (Chair. of Sub-Cttee); Gov. of the Year Award, Euromoney magazine 1988, Personality in Banking Management Award, Arab Research Center 1997. *Publications include:* Casting Light on the Monetary Policy and the Kuwaiti Economy 1988, Recent Issues of Central Bank Policy in Kuwait 1989, Prominent Landmarks in the Operation of the Central Bank of Kuwait 1995, Monetary Policy and the Role of the Central Bank of Kuwait: Current

Concerns and Future Prospects 1997. *Address:* Central Bank of Kuwait, P.O. Box 526, 13006 Safat, Abdullah as-Salem Street, Kuwait City, Kuwait (Office). *Telephone:* 2449200 (Office). *Fax:* 2402715 (Office). *E-mail:* cbk@cbk .gov.kw (Office). *Website:* www.cbk.gov.kw (Office).

SABAH, Sheikh Salim Sabah as-Salim as-; Kuwaiti diplomatist; b. 18 June 1937; s. of the late Sheikh Sabah al-Salim al-Sabah, Amir of Kuwait; ed Secondary School Kuwait, Gray's Inn, London and Christ Church, Oxford; joined Foreign Service 1963; fmr Head Political Dept Ministry of Foreign Affairs; Amb. to the UK 1965–70; also to Norway, Denmark and Sweden 1968–70; Amb. to USA 1970–75, also Accred to Canada; Minister of Social Affairs and Labour 1975–78, of Defence 1978–87, of the Interior 1987–91; Deputy Prime Minister and Minister of Foreign Affairs 1991 then Deputy Prime Minister and Minister of Defence. *Address:* Ministry of Defence, P.O. Box 1170, 13012 Safat, Kuwait City, Kuwait.

SABATIER, Robert; French writer; b. 17 Aug. 1923, Paris; s. of Pierre Sabatier and Marie Exbrayat; m. Christiane Lesparre 1957; fmr manual worker and factory exec.; produced journal La Cassette; mem. Académie Goncourt; Commdr, Légion d'honneur; Commdr Ordre nat. du Mérite, des Arts et des Lettres; Officier du Mérite agricole; Lauréat de la Soc. des gens de lettres 1961; Grand Prix de Poésie de l'Académie française 1969 for Les châteaux de millions d'années; Antonin-Artaud Prize and Prix Apollinaire for poems Les fêtes solaires. *Publications:* Alain et le nègre 1953, Le marchand de sable 1954, Le goût de la cendre 1955, Les fêtes solaires 1955, Boulevard 1956, Canard au sang 1958, St Vincent de Paul, Dédicace d'un navire 1959, La Sainte-Farce 1960, La mort du figuier 1962, Dessin sur un trottoir 1964, Les poisons délectables (poems) 1965, Le Chinois d'Afrique 1966, Dictionnaire de la mort 1967, Les châteaux de millions d'années (poems) 1969, Les allumettes suédoises 1969, Trois sucettes à la menthe 1972, Noisettes sauvages 1974, Histoire de la poésie française des origines à nos jours (8 Vols) 1975, Icare et autres poèmes 1976, Les enfants de l'été 1978, Les fillettes chantantes 1980, L'oiseau de demain 1981, Les années secrètes de la vie d'un homme 1984, David et Olivier 1986, Lecture (poetry) 1987, La souris verte 1990, Le livre de la déraison souriante 1991, Olivier et ses amis 1993, Ecriture (poems) 1993, Le cygne noir 1995, Le lit de la merveille 1997, Les masques et le miroir 1998, Le sourire aux lèvres 2000. *Address:* 64 boulevard Exelmans, 75016 Paris, France.

SÁBATO, Ernesto; Argentine writer; b. 24 June 1911, Rojas; m. Matilde Kusminsky-Richter; two s.; ed Univ. Nacional de la Plata; fmr Dir of Cultural Relations, Argentina; has lectured in the following univs.: Paris, Columbia, Berkeley, Madrid, Warsaw, Bucharest, Bonn, Milan, Pavia, Florence, etc.; Pres. Comisión Nacional sobre Desaparición de Personas (CONADEP) 1984; mem. The Club of Rome; Ribbon of Honour, Argentine Soc. of Letters; Prize of the Inst. of Foreign Relations (Stuttgart) 1973, Grand Prize of Argentine Writers' Soc. 1974, Prix Meilleur Livre Etranger for Abaddon el Exterminador (Paris) 1977; Chevalier, Ordre des Arts et des Lettres (France), Chevalier, Légion d'honneur 1978, Gran Cruz de la República Española, Gabriela Mistral Prize 1984, Cervantes Prize, Madrid 1984, Jerusalem Literary Prize 1989. *Publications:* Uno y el Universo 1945, Hombres y Engranajes 1951, Heterodoxia 1953, El escritor y sus fantasmas 1963, Tres Aproximaciones a la Literatura de Nuestro Tiempo 1969 (essays); El Túnel 1947, Sobre Héroes y Tumbas 1961, Abaddon el Exterminador 1976 (novel). *Address:* Langeri 3135, Santos Lugares, Argentina. *Telephone:* 757-1373.

SÁBATO, Jorge Federico, DJur; Argentine politician; b. 25 May 1938, La Plata; ed Univ. de Buenos Aires, Univ. of Paris; researcher, CNRS, Paris; researcher in Political Science; Prof. Faculties of Econs and Eng, Univ. de Buenos Aires; Expert UN and OAS projects in Brazil, Peru, Ecuador, Colombia and Venezuela; Sec. of State and Adviser to Pres. 1983–84; Sec. of State for Foreign Affairs 1984–85, Int. Relations and Culture 1985–87; Minister of Educ. and Justice 1987–89; holds numerous decorations, including Gran Cruz de la Orden del Mérito Civil (Spain) 1985, Gran Cruz, Orden de la República Italiana 1985, Gran Cruz, Orden del Mérito (FRG) 1987. *Publications:* various books and articles on science of politics.

SABATTANI, HE Cardinal Aurelio; Italian ecclesiastic; b. 18 Oct. 1912, Imola; ordained priest 1935; fmr Prelate of Loreto–1971; Prefect of Holy See's Supreme Tribunal 1983; cr. Cardinal 1983; fmr Archpriest Vatican Basilica, fmr Vicar-Gen. of His Holiness for the Vatican City, hon. mem. Pontifical Acad. *Address:* Palazzo del Tribunale, Piazza S. Marta, 00120 Vatican City. *Telephone:* (06) 69884615. *Fax:* (06) 69882520.

SABBAH, Michel; ecclesiastic; b. 1933, Nazareth; ed Patriarchate Seminary of Beit-Jala and in Beirut and Paris; ordained priest 1955; fmr Dir Gen. of Schools, Patriarchate of Jerusalem; priest, Misdar, nr Amman; Pres. Frères Univ. Bethlehem; Latin (Roman Catholic) Patriarch of Jerusalem 1988–; Pres. Bishops' Conf. for Arab Countries. *Address:* Office of the Latin Patriarch, P.O. Box 14152, 91141 Jerusalem, Israel. *Telephone:* 2-6282323 (Office). *Fax:* 2-6271652 (Office). *E-mail:* latinpat@actcom.co.il (Office). *Website:* www .lpj.org (Office).

SABHAVASU, Pramual; Thai politician; b. 29 Nov. 1927, Muang Dist, Ayutthaya; ed Ayutthaya Wittyalai and Wat Bovornnives Schools; Chat-Thai Party MP 1975–76, 1979–; Premier's Adviser 1976; Minister of Industry 1986, 1990–91; of Finance 1988–90; Deputy Prime Minister Sept.–Dec. 1990. *Address:* c/o Office of the Deputy Prime Minister, Bangkok, Thailand.

SABIRIN, Syahril, MBA, PhD; Indonesian banker; b. 14 Oct. 1943, Bukittinggi; m.; one s. one d.; ed Univ. Gazah Mada, Yogyakarta, Williams Coll., Williamstown, Mass., USA, Vanderbilt Univ., Nashville, Tenn., USA; mem. staff, Bank Indonesia 1969–93, mem. Bd 1988–93; Sr Financial Economist, World Bank, Washington, DC 1994–96; with Bank Indonesia 1997–, Gov. 1998–; sentenced to three years' imprisonment for role in misuse of state funds 2002. *Leisure interests:* travel, tennis. *Address:* Bank Indonesia, Jalan M.H. Thamrin 2, Jakarta 10002 (Office); Jalan Ikan Mas No. 96, Blok K, Cinere, Depok 16514, Indonesia (Home). *Telephone:* (21) 2310408 (Office); (21) 7535011 (Home). *Fax:* (21) 2311058 (Office); (21) 7549101 (Home). *E-mail:* sabirin@hotmail.com, humasbi@bi.go.id (Home). *Website:* www.bi.go .id (Office).

SABISTON, David Coston, Jr, MD; American professor of surgery; b. 4 Oct. 1924, Onslow County, NC; s. of David Coston and Marie (née Jackson) Sabiston; m. Agnes Barden 1955; three d.; ed Univ. of NC and Johns Hopkins Univ. School of Medicine; Intern, Asst Resident, Chief Resident in Surgery, Johns Hopkins Hospital 1947–53; Asst Prof., Assoc. Prof., Prof. of Surgery, Johns Hopkins Univ. School of Medicine 1953–64; Howard Hughes Investigator 1955–61; James Buchanan Duke Prof. of Surgery and Chair. of Dept, Duke Univ. Medical School 1964, Medial Center 1964–94, Chief of Staff 1994–96, Dir of Int. Programs 1996–; Fulbright Research Scholar, Univ. of Oxford 1961; Research Assoc. Hosp. for Sick Children, London 1961; mem. or fellow of numerous professional orgs; Hon. mem. Colombian Surgical Soc., German Soc. for Surgery, Japanese Coll. of Surgeons; Hon. FRCS, FRCSE, FRACS; Hon. Fellow, Asociación de Cirugía del Litoral Argentino, Brazilian Coll. of Surgeons, Royal Coll. of Physicians and Surgeons of Canada; several achievement awards. *Publications:* Gibbon's Surgery of the Chest (Co-Ed.) 1969, Textbook of Surgery (Ed.) 1972, Essentials of Surgery (Ed.). *Address:* Duke University Medical Center, P.O. Box 2600 MSRB, Durham, NC 27715 (Office); 1528 Pinecrest Road, Durham, NC 27705, USA (Home). *Telephone:* (919) 684-2831 (Office).

SABOURET, Yves Marie Georges; French civil servant; b. 15 April 1936, Paris; s. of Henri Sabouret and Colette (née Anthoine) Sabouret; m. 1st Anne de Caumont la Force 1965 (divorced); one s. two d.; m. 2nd Laurence Vilaine 1991; one d.; ed Ecole Nat. d'Admin.; Inspecteur des finances 1964–81; technical counsellor, Office of Minister of Supply and Housing 1968–69; Dir Office of Minister of Labour, Employment and Population 1969–72; Counsellor for Social and Cultural Affairs to Prime Minister Pierre Messmer 1972–74; Conseiller gén., Côtes du Nord (Canton de Matignon) 1973–92; Pres. Société de développement régional de la Bretagne 1977–2000; Vice-Pres., Société Matra 1979; Dir-Gen. Hachette 1981–90, Vice-Pres. 1981–90; Pres. Atlas Copco France 1990–; Co-Dir-Gen. La Cinq 1990; Dir-Gen. NMPP 1994–; Chevalier Légion d'honneur, Officier Ordre nat. du Mérite, Croix de la Valeur militaire. *Address:* NMPP, 52 rue Jacques Hillairet, 75012 Paris; 5 rue Mignard, 75116 Paris, France.

SABOURIN, Louis, LLL, PhD, FRSC; Canadian academic; b. 1 Dec. 1935, Québec City; s. of Rolland Sabourin and Valeda Caza; m. Agathe Lacerte 1959; one s. two d.; ed Univ. of Ottawa, Univ. of Paris, France, Institut d'Etudes Politiques de Paris, France, Columbia Univ., USA; Prof. Dir Dept of Political Science, Univ. of Ottawa, Dean of Faculty of Social Science; Founder and Dir Inst. of Int. Co-operation and Devt, Visiting Sr Research Fellow Jesus Coll., Oxford and Queen Elizabeth House, England 1974–75; Pres. OECD Devt Centre, Paris 1977–82; Prof. of Int. Econ. Orgs., Ecole Nationale d'Admin. Publique, Univ. of Québec 1983–; Dir Groupe d'Etude, de Recherche et de Formation Internationales 1983–; Visiting Prof. University of Paris (Sorbonne) 1982, Univ. of Notre Dame and Stanford Univ. 1992, Hanoi, Vietnam 2000; Founding mem. Asia-Pacific Foundation, Montreal Council of Foreign Relations; Pontifical Comm. on Justice and Peace; Pres. Soc. de Droit Int. Economique 1988; Legal Counselor Hudon, Gendron, Harris, Thomas 1989–; Ford Int. Fellow 1962, Canada Council Scholar 1963; mem. Pontifical Acad. of Social Sciences, Rome 1994; Chevalier Pléiade de la Francophonie 1988; Chevalier Légion d'honneur; Dr hc (Sorbonne, Paris) 1998. *Publications:* Le système politique du Canada 1969, Dualité culturelle dans les activités internationales du Canada 1970, Canadian Federalism and International Organizations 1971, Le Canada et le développement international 1972, Allier la théorie à la pratique: le développement de la Chine nouvelle 1973, International Economic Development: Theories, Methods and Prospects 1973, The Challenge of the Less Developed Countries 1981, La crise économique: contraintes et effets de l'interdépendance pour le Canada 1984, Passion d'être, désir d'avoir, le dilemme Québec-Canada dans un univers en mutation 1992, Les organisations économiques internationales 1994, The Social Dimensions of Globalization 2000; numerous articles. *Leisure interests:* music, travel, wine-tasting (Grand officier du Tastevin), skiing, tennis, cycling. *Address:* GERFI-ENAP, 4750 avenue Henri-Julien, Montreal, Québec H2T 3E5, Canada. *Telephone:* (514) 849-3989 (Office); (514) 735-4541 (Home). *Fax:* (514) 849-3369 (Office). *E-mail:* lsabourin@hotmail.com (Home).

SABRI, Naji, MA, PhD; Iraqi politician and journalist; b. 1951; Foreign Ed. and Man. Ed. al-Thawra Daily 1968–75; Lecturer in English, Coll. of Arts, Univ. of Baghdad 1969–75; Councillor at Iraqi Embassy, London 1975–80; Founder and Dir Iraqi Cultural Centre, London 1977–80; Founder and Ed.-in-Chief UR (journal of modern Arab arts) 1977–80; Dir-Gen. Dar al-Mamun House (trans. and publishing) 1980–90; Ed.-in-Chief Baghdad Observer 1980–98; Founder and Ed.-in-Chief Gilgamesh (journal of modern Iraqi arts) 1986–95; Vice-Pres. Iraqi Nat. Cttee of Educ., Science and Culture 1986–95;

Dir-Gen. of Foreign Information, Ministry of Information and Culture 1990–91, Deputy Minister of Information and Culture 1991–95, Adviser to Minister of Information and Culture 1997–98; lecturer, Coll. of Arts, Univ. of Mustansiriya 1995–99; Adviser, Presidential Office 1995–98; Amb. at Ministry of Foreign Affairs, Baghdad 1998; Amb. to Austria and Perm. Rep. to IAEA, UNIDO and UN Office, Vienna 1999–2001; Amb. (non-resident) to Slovakia 2000–01; Minister of State for Foreign Affairs April–Aug. 2001, Minister of Foreign Affairs 2001–03. *Publications include:* trans. into Arabic: The Genius of Show (Michael Holroyd), Aspects of Biography (André Maurois), Lectures on Literature (Vladimir Nabokov); several Iraqi political books into English; Iraq's Year Book (Ed.-in-Chief) 1988, 1990, 1995, 1998, 1999.

SABUROV, Yevgeny Fedorovich, D.ECON.SC.; Russian economist and poet; b. 13 Feb. 1946, Crimea; m. Tatiana Petrovna; three d.; ed Moscow State Univ.; researcher econ. inst. in Moscow –1990; Deputy Minister of Educ. of Russian Fed. 1990–91; project leader Programme of Econ. Reform in Russia April–Aug. 1991; Deputy Prime Minister, Minister of Econ. Aug.–Nov. 1991; Dir Cen. for Information and Social Tech. of Russian Govt 1991–94; Deputy Head of Govt of Repub. of Crimea Feb.–Oct. 1994; Prof. Acad. of Econs; Dir Investment Research Inst. 1995–; Chief Consultant, Menatep Bank 1995–; Chair. Bd of Guardians, Inst. for Urban Econs 1996–; Chair. Bd of Dirs. Confidential and Investment Bank 1999–2000, Deputy Chair. 2000–; mem. Acad. of Information, Acad. of Social Sciences; poetry published in Europe since 1970, in Russia since 1990. *Publications:* Gunpowder Conspiracy (poems) 1996, On the Edge of the Lake (selected poems); over 100 articles on problems of econ. reform in Russia; numerous verses in periodicals. *Address:* Confidential and Investment Bank, Sadovnicheskaya 84/3–7, 113035 Moscow, Russia. *Telephone:* (095) 958-24-26. *Fax:* (095) 958-24-28.

SACASA, Juan B.; Nicaraguan diplomatist; Amb. to UK July 2001–. *Address:* Embassy of Nicaragua, Suite 31, Vicarage House, 58–60 Kensington Church Street, London, W8 4DB, England (Office). *Telephone:* (20) 7938-2373 (Office). *Fax:* (20) 7937-0952 (Office).

SACHS, Jeffrey David, PhD; American professor of international trade; b. 5 Nov. 1954, Detroit, Mich.; s. of Theodore Sachs and Joan Sachs; m. Sonia Ehrlich; one s. two d.; ed Harvard Univ.; Research Assoc. Nat. Bureau of Econ. Research, Cambridge, Mass. 1980–85; Asst Prof. of Econs Harvard Univ. 1980–82, Assoc. Prof. 1982–83, Galen L. Stone Prof. of Int. Trade 1984–2001; Dir Harvard Inst. for Int. Devt 1995–2002, Center for Int. Devt –2002; Quetelet Prof. of Sustainable Devt and Prof. of Health Policy and Man. and Dir The Earth Inst., Columbia Univ. 2002–; adviser, Brookings Inst. Washington, DC 1982–; Special Advisor to UN Sec.-Gen. Kofi Annan on Millennium Devt Goals 2002–; Founder and Chair. Exec. Cttee Inst. of Econ. Analysis, Moscow 1993–; Chair. Comm. on Macroecons and Health, WHO 2000–01; Co-Chair. Advisory Bd The Global Competitiveness Report; mem. Int. Financial Insts Advisory Comm., US Congress 1999–2000; econ. adviser to various govts in Latin America, Eastern Europe, the fmr Soviet Union, Asia and Africa, Jubilee 2000 movt; fmr consultant to IMF, World Bank, OECD and UNDP; adviser to Pres. of Bolivia 1986–90; Fellow, World Econometric Soc.; Research Assoc. Nat. Bureau of Econ. Research; syndicated newspaper column appears in more than 50 countries; mem. American Acad. of Arts and Sciences, Harvard Soc. of Fellows, Brookings Panel of Economists, Bd of Advisers, Chinese Economists Soc.; f. Inst. for Econ. Analysis, Moscow; Distinguished Visiting Lecturer to LSE, Oxford Univ., Tel-Aviv, Jakarta, Yale Univ.; Commdr's Cross Order of Merit (Poland) 1999; Hon. PhD (St Gallen) 1990, (Universidad del Pacífico, Peru) 1997, (Lingnan Coll., Hong Kong) 1998, (Varna Econs Univ., Bulgaria) 2000, (Iona Coll., New York) 2000; Frank E. Seidman Award in Political Econ. 1991, Berhard Harms Prize (Germany) 2000. *Publications:* Economics of Worldwide Stagflation (with Michael Bruno) 1985, Developing Country Debt and the Economic Performance (Ed.) 1989, Global Linkages: Macroeconomic Interdependence and Cooperation in the World Economy (with Warwick McKibbin) 1991, Peru's Path to Recovery (with Carlos Paredes) 1991, Macroeconomics in the Global Economy (with Felipe Larrain) 1993, Poland's Jump to the Market Economy 1993, The Transition in Eastern Europe (with Olivier Blanchard and Kenneth Froot) 1994, Russia and the Market Economy (in Russian) 1995, Economic Reform and the Process of Global Integration (with A. Warner) 1995, The Collapse of the Mexican Peso: What Have We Learned? (jtly) 1995, Natural Resource Abundance and Economic Growth (with A. Warner) 1996, The Rule of Law and Economic Reform in Russia (co-ed.) 1997; more than 200 scholarly articles. *Leisure interests:* skiing, biking, watching ballet. *Address:* The Earth Institute at Columbia University, Lamont Hall 2-G, Lamont-Doherty Earth Observatory, 61 Route 9W, Palisades, NY 10964-8000, USA (Office). *Telephone:* (845) 365-8565 (Office). *Fax:* (845) 365-8164 (Office). *E-mail:* sachs@columbia.edu (Office). *Website:* www.earth.columbia.edu (Office).

SACHS, Leo, PhD, FRS; British/Israeli professor of biology; b. 14 Oct. 1924, Leipzig, Germany; s. of Elias Sachs and Louise Sachs; m. Pnina Salkind 1970; one s. three d.; ed City of London School, Univ. of Wales, Bangor, Trinity Coll., Cambridge; research scientist in genetics, John Innes Inst. 1951–52; research scientist Weizmann Inst. of Science, Rehovot, Israel 1952–, Assoc. Prof. 1960, est. Dept of Genetics and Virology 1960, Prof. 1962, Head Dept of Genetics 1962–89, Dean Faculty of Biology 1974–79, now Otto Meyerhof Prof. of Biology; mem. European Molecular Biology Org. 1965, Israel Acad. of Sciences and Humanities 1975; Foreign Assoc. NAS 1995–; Foreign mem. European Acad. 1998; Harvey Lecture, Rockefeller Univ., USA 1972; Hon. Fellow Univ.

of Wales 1999; Hon. Life mem. Int. Cytokine Soc. 2001–; Dr hc (Bordeaux) 1985; Hon. DMed (Lund) 1997; Israel Prize for Natural Sciences 1972, Rothschild Prize in Biological Sciences 1977, Wolf Prize in Medicine 1980, Bristol-Myers Award for Distinguished Achievement in Cancer Research 1983, Royal Soc. Wellcome Foundation Prize 1986, Sloan Prize, General Motors Cancer Research Foundation 1989, Warren Alpert Foundation Prize, Harvard Medical School, Mass. 1997, Emet Prize for Life Sciences 2002. *Publications:* papers in various scientific journals on blood cells, devt and cancer research. *Leisure interests:* music, museums. *Address:* Department of Molecular Genetics, Weizmann Institute of Science, Rehovot 76100, Israel. *Telephone:* 8-9344068. *Fax:* 8-9344108.

SACHTOURIS, Miltos; Greek poet; b. 1919, Athens; Greek National Literary Award 1962, 1987. *Publications include:* I Lismonimeni 1945, O Peripatos 1960, Ta Stigmata 1962, Poems 1945–71 1977, Ektoplasmata 1986. *Address:* 14 Mithimnis Street, 112 57 Athens, Greece.

SACIRBEY, Muhamed, JD, MBA; Bosnia and Herzegovina diplomatist and politician; b. 20 July 1956, Sarajevo; s. of Nedzib Sacirbey and Aziza Sacirbey; m. Susan Walter; ed Tulane Univ. and Columbia Univ. New York; admitted New York Bar 1981; attorney, Booth & Baron New York 1981–83; Financial Analyst, Vice-Pres. Standard Poor's Corpn New York 1983–85; Financial Investment Banking, Trepp & Co. New York 1985–87; Sr Vice-Pres. and Man. Dept of Investment Security Pacific Merchant Bank, New York 1987–91; Partner, Consultant, Princeton Finance, New York 1991–92; Perm. Mission of Repub. of Bosnia-Herzegovina to the UN, New York 1992–95; Minister of Foreign Affairs of Bosnia-Herzegovina 1995–96; Amb. to UN 1996–2000; int. arrest warrant issued for him by Interpol over allegations of misuse of govt funds; Man of the Year, Tulane Univ. (USA) 1996, Lifetime Achievement Award, Decapo Tolerance Foundation 1999. *Leisure interests:* athletic activities, reading. *Address:* c/o Ministry of Foreign Affairs, 71000 Sarajevo, Musala 2, Bosnia and Herzegovina.

SACKER, Ulrich, PhD; German cultural administrator; b. 16 March 1951, Luenen; s. of Erich and Dorothea Sacker; m. Christina Sacker; one s.; ed Univ. of Münster, Munich, Aix-en-Provence, France; mem. Bureau Int. de Documentation et de Liaison Franco-Allemandes, Paris; Prof. of French and Russian, Univ. of Bonn, Cologne; Commr Promotion of Germany Worldwide, Goethe-Institut HQ Munich, DirGoethe-Institut San Franciso, USA, Hong Kong, Inter Nationes, London 2000–, Regional Dir Inter Nationes UK and Ireland 2000–. *Address:* Goethe Institute, 50 Prince's Gate, Exhibition Road, London, SW7 2PH, England (Office). *Telephone:* (20) 7596-4048 (Office). *Fax:* (20) 7594-0211 (Office). *E-mail:* sacker@london.goethe.org (Office). *Website:* www.goethe.de/london (Office).

SACKS, Jonathan Henry, PhD; British rabbi; b. 8 March 1948, London; s. of the late Louis Sacks and of Louisa (née Frumkin) Sacks; m. Elaine Taylor 1970; one s. two d.; ed Christ's Coll. Finchley, Gonville & Caius Coll., Cambridge, New Coll., Oxford, London Univ., Jews' Coll., London and Yeshivat Etz Hayyim, London; Lecturer in Moral Philosophy, Middx Poly. 1971–73; Lecturer in Jewish Philosophy, Jews' Coll., London 1973–76, in Talmud and Jewish Philosophy 1976–82, Chief Rabbi Lord Jakobovits Prof. (first incumbent) in Modern Jewish Thought 1982–, Dir Rabbinic Faculty 1983–90, Prin. 1984–90, Chief Rabbi of the United Hebrew Congregations of the British Commonwealth of Nations 1991–; Assoc. Pres. Conf. of European Rabbis 2000–; Visiting Prof. of Philosophy Univ. of Essex 1989–90; currently Visiting Prof. of Philosophy Hebrew Univ., Jerusalem and of Theology and Religious Studies King's Coll., London; rabbi Golders Green Synagogue, London 1978–82, Marble Arch Synagogue, London 1983–90; Ed. Le'ela (journal) 1985–90; mem. CRAC; Presentation Fellow King's Coll., London 1993; Sherman Lecturer, Manchester Univ. 1989, Reith Lecturer 1990, Cook Lecturer 1997; Hon. Fellow Gonville and Caius Coll., Cambridge 1993; Hon. DD (Cantab.) 1993, (Archbishop of Canterbury) 2001; Dr hc (Middx Univ.) 1993, (Haifa Univ., Israel) 1996, (Yeshiva Univ., NY) 1997, (St Andrews Univ.) 1998; Hon. LLD (Univ. of Liverpool) 1997; Jerusalem Prize 1995. *Publications:* Torah Studies 1986, Tradition and Transition (essays) 1986, Traditional Alternatives 1989, Tradition in an Untraditional Age 1990, The Persistence of Faith (Reith Lecture) 1991, Orthodoxy Confronts Modernity (Ed.) 1991, Crisis and Covenant 1992, One People?: Tradition, Modernity and Jewish Unity 1993, Will We Have Jewish Grandchildren? 1994, Faith in the Future 1995, Community of Faith 1995, The Politics of Hope 1997, Morals and Markets 1999, Celebrating Life 2000, Radical Then Radical Now 2001, The Dignity of Difference: How To Avoid the Clash of Civilizations 2002, The Chief Rabbi's Hagadah 2003. *Leisure interests:* walking, music. *Address:* 735 High Road, London, N12 0US, England (Office). *Telephone:* (20) 8343-6301 (Office). *Fax:* (20) 8343-6310 (Office). *E-mail:* info@chiefrabbi.org (Office). *Website:* www.chiefrabbi.org (Office).

SACKS, Oliver Wolf, BM, B.CH.; British neurologist and writer; b. 9 July 1933, London; s. of Dr. Samuel Sacks and Dr. Muriel Elsie (Landau) Sacks; ed St Paul's School, London and Queen's Coll., Oxford; Resident, Univ. of Calif., LA 1962–65; Consultant Neurologist, Bronx State Hosp., New York 1965–91, Beth Abraham Hosp., Bronx 1965–, Headache Unit, Montefiore Hosp., Bronx 1966–68, several clinics and homes for the aged and chronically ill, New York 1966–; Consultant Neurologist and mem. Medical Advisory Bd, Gilles de la Tourette Syndrome Asscn, New York 1974–; Instructor in Neurology, Albert Einstein Coll. of Medicine, Bronx, New York 1966–75, Asst Clinical Prof. of Neurology 1975–78, Assoc. Clinical Prof. 1978–85, Clinical

Prof. 1985–; Fellow American Acad. of Arts and Letters 1996, New York Acad. of Sciences 1999; Hon. DHumLitt (Georgetown Univ.) 1990, (Staten Island Coll., CUNY) 1991; Hon. DSc (Tufts Univ.) 1991, (New York Medical Coll.) 1991, (Bard Coll.) 1992; Hon. DMedSc (Medical Coll. of Pennsylvania); Hawthornden Prize (for Awakenings) 1975, Felix Marti-Ibanez Book Award for Humanism in Medicine, Special Presidential Award, American Neurological Asscn. 1991, George S. Polk Award 1994, Mainichi Publishing Culture Award (Tokyo) for Best Natural Science Book (Seeing Voices) 1996 and many others. *Publications:* Migraine 1970, Awakenings 1973, A Leg to Stand On 1984, The Man Who Mistook His Wife For A Hat 1985, Seeing Voices: A Journey Into The World of the Deaf 1989, An Anthropologist on Mars 1995, The Island of the Colourblind 1996, Uncle Tungsten 2001, Oaxaca Journal 2002. *Address:* 2 Horatio Street, New York, NY 10014, USA. *Telephone:* (212) 633-8373. *Fax:* (212) 633-8928. *Website:* www.oliversacks.com (Office).

SADANAGA, Ryoichi, DSc; Japanese mineralogist and crystallographer; b. 25 June 1920, Osaka; m. Sakiko Iwata 1945; two d.; ed Univ. of Tokyo; Prof. of Mineralogy, Univ. of Tokyo 1959–81, Prof. Emer. 1981–; mem. Japan Acad. 1981–. *Publication:* Introduction to Crystallography 1986. *Address:* University of Tokyo, 7-3-1 Hongo, Bunkyo-ku, Tokyo 113-8654 (Office); 4-1-4, Suimeidai, Kawanishi-shi, Hyogo-Ken, 666-0116 Japan. *Telephone:* (3) 3812-2111 (Office); (727) 92-5100. *Fax:* (3) 5689-7344 (Office); (727) 92-5200. *E-mail:* kokusai@adm.u-tokyo.ac.jp (Office). *Website:* www.u-tokyo.ac.jp (Office).

SADCHIKOV, Nikolai Ivanovich; Russian diplomatist; b. 20 March 1946, Moscow; s. of Ivan Sadchikov and Ludmila Sadchikova; m. Olga Olegovna Sadchikova; one s. one d.; ed Moscow State Inst. of Int. Relations; Attaché Dept of Middle Asia, USSR Ministry of Foreign Affairs 1970–72; Third Sec. USSR Embassy, North Yemen 1972–76; Counsellor Dept of Int. Econ. Orgs, USSR Ministry of Foreign Affairs 1976–80; UN Secr. New York, 1980–83; Counsellor USSR Mission to UN, New York 1983–86; Counsellor Office of the Minister of Foreign Affairs 1986–90; Counsellor Russian Embassy, UK 1990–95; Deputy Dir Dept of Consular Affairs, Ministry of Foreign Affairs 1995–97; Consul-Gen. Embassy USA 1997–99; Dir Dept of Consular Affairs, Ministry of Foreign Affairs, Russian Fed. 1999–2001; Amb. to Sweden 2001–. *Leisure interests:* serious music, theatre, classical literature. *Address:* Embassy of Russian Federation, Gjowellsgatan 31, 11260 Stockholm, Sweden (Office). *Telephone:* (8) 13-04-41 (Office); (8) 13-04-44 (Office); (095) 252-61-45 (Moscow) (Home). *Fax:* (8) 618-27-03 (Office). *E-mail:* rusembsw@algonet.se.

SADDAM HUSSEIN, LLB; Iraqi politician; b. 28 April 1937, Tikrit, nr Baghdad; m. Sajida Khairalla 1963; two s. three d.; ed al-Karkh Secondary School, Baghdad, al-Qasr al-Aini Secondary School, Cairo, Cairo Univ. and al-Mustanseriya Univ., Baghdad; joined Arab Baath Socialist Party 1957; sentenced to death for attempted execution of Gen. Abdul Karim Qassim 1959; joined leadership of Cairo branch of Baath Party 1962; returned to Iraq following revolution 1963; mem. 4th Regional Congress and 6th Nat. Congress of Baath Party 1963; mem. Regional Leadership of Baath Party in Iraq following overthrow of Party rule 1963; mem. 7th Nat. Congress, Syria 1964; arrested for plotting overthrow of Abdul Salam Aref 1964; elected mem. Leadership by 8th Nat. Congress while still in prison 1965; Deputy Sec. Regional Leadership of Baath Party 1966–79, Sec. 1979–2003 played prominent role in July 1968 revolution; Acting Deputy Chair. Revolutionary Command Council 1968–69, Deputy Chair. 1969–79, Chair. 1979–2003; Pres. of Iraq 1979–2003, Prime Minister 1994–2003; Deputy Sec. Regional Leadership in 7th Regional Congress 1968; mem. Nat. Leadership of Party in 10th National Congress 1970; rank of Gen. 1976; forces invaded Iran Sept. 1980 initiating 1980–88 Iran-Iraq War; illegally invaded and annexed Kuwait Aug. 1990, forces defeated and forced to withdraw by UN-backed Allied Force under command of Gen. Norman Schwarzkopf (q.v.) Feb. 1991; USA led coalition forces in invasion of Iraq March–April 2003, Baath Party leadership overthrown, whereabouts of Saddam Hussein not known as at April 2003; Order of Rafidain, 1st Class 1976. *Publications:* Zazibah and the King (also adapted into musical), One Trench or Two, The Impregnable Fortress 2002, Men and the City (autobiog.) 2003.

SADIE, Stanley (John), CBE, MusB, MA, PhD; British writer on music; b. 30 Oct. 1930, Wembley; s. of David Sadie and Deborah Sadie (née Simons); m. 1st Adèle Bloom 1953 (died 1978); two s. one d.; m. 2nd Julie Anne McCornack Vertrees; one s. one d.; ed St Paul's School, London, Gonville and Caius Coll., Cambridge; Prof. Trinity Coll. of Music 1957–65; Music Critic, The Times 1964–81; Ed., The Musical Times 1967–87, New Grove Dictionary of Music and Musicians 1970–2001, Master Musicians series 1976–; Music Consultant to Man and Music (Granada TV series) 1984–90; broadcaster on musical subjects; Ed. of 18th-century music; Pres. Int. Musicological Soc. 1992–97; Chair. The Handel House Trust 1994–96, Pres. 1996–; mem. Critics' Circle, American Musicological Soc., Royal Musical Asscn (Pres. 1989–94); Hon. RAM 1982; Hon. FRCM 1994; Hon. Fellow Gonville and Caius Coll., Cambridge 2001; Hon. DLitt (Leicester) 1982. *Publications:* Handel 1962, The Pan Book of Opera/The Opera Guide (with A. Jacobs) 1964, Mozart 1966, Beethoven 1967, Handel 1968, Handel Concertos 1972, The New Grove Dictionary of Music and Musicians, 20 vols (Ed.) 1980, revised edn, 29 vols 2001, Mozart (The New Grove) 1982, The New Grove Dictionary of Musical Instruments, 3 vols (Ed.) 1984, The Cambridge Music Guide (with A. Latham) 1985, Mozart Symphonies 1986, The New Grove Dictionary of American Music, 4 vols (Co-Ed.) 1986, Handel Tercentenary Collection (Co-Ed.) 1987, The Grove Concise Dictionary of Music (Ed.) 1988, History of Opera (Ed.) 1989, Performance Practice, 2 vols (Co-Ed.) 1989, Man and Music, A Social History, 8 vols (Gen. Ed.) 1989–93, Music Printing and Publishing (Co-Ed.) 1990, The New Grove Dictionary of Opera, 4 vols (Ed.) 1992, Wolfgang Amadè Mozart: Essays on His Life and Work (Ed.) 1995, New Grove Book of Operas (Ed.) 1996; and contribs to various music periodicals and journals. *Leisure interests:* watching cricket, drinking (coffee, wine), bridge, family. *Address:* The Manor, Cossington, Somerset, TA7 8JR, England. *Telephone:* (1278) 723655. *Fax:* (1278) 723656. *E-mail:* s.sadie@ukgateway.net (Home).

SADIK, Nafis, MD; Pakistani international official and physician; b. 18 Aug. 1929, Jaunpur, India; d. of Iffat Ara and Mohammad Shoaib; m. Azhar Sadik 1954; one s. two d. and two adopted d.; ed Loretto Coll. Calcutta, Calcutta Medical Coll., Dow Medical Coll. Karachi and Johns Hopkins Univ.; Intern, Gynaecology and Obstetrics, City Hosp., Baltimore, Md 1952–54; civilian medical officer in charge of women's and children's wards in various Pakistani armed forces hosps. 1954–63; Resident, Physiology, Queen's Univ., Kingston, Ont. 1958; Head, Health Section, Planning Comm., on Health and Family Planning, Pakistan 1964; Dir of Planning and Training, Pakistan Cen. Family Planning Council 1966–68, Deputy Dir-Gen. 1968–70, Dir-Gen. 1970–71; Tech. Adviser, UN Population Fund (UNFPA) 1971–72, Chief, Programme Div. 1973–77, Asst Exec. Dir 1977–87, Exec. Dir UNFPA 1987–2000; currently UN Under-Sec.-Gen. and Special Adviser to Sec.-Gen.; Sec.-Gen. Int. Conf. on Population and Devt 1994, UN Special Envoy for HIV/AIDS in Asia May 2002–; Pres. Soc. for Int. Devt 1994–; Fellow ad eundem, Royal Coll. of Obstetricians and Gynaecologists; Hon. DHumLitt (Johns Hopkins) 1989, (Brown) 1993, (Duke) 1995; Hon. LLD (Wilfrid Laurier) 1995; Hon. DSc (Mich.) 1996, (Claremont) 1996; Bruno H. Schubert-Stiftung Prize 1995; Hugh Moore Award 1976, Women's Global Leadership Award 1994, Peace Award (UNA) 1994, Prince Mahidol Award 1995; Order of Merit, First Class (Egypt) 1994, Population Award, UN 2001. *Publications:* Population: National Family Planning Programme in Pakistan 1968, Population: The UNFPA Experience (ed.) 1984, Population Policies and Programmes: Lessons Learned from Two Decades of Experience 1991, Making a Difference: Twenty-five Years of UNFPA Experience 1994; articles in professional journals. *Leisure interests:* bridge, reading, theatre, travel. *Address:* 300 East 56th Street, 9J, New York, NY 10022, USA. *Telephone:* (212) 826-5025 (Home). *Fax:* (212) 758-1529 (Office). *E-mail:* sadik@unfpa.org (Office).

SADOVNICHY, Victor Antonovich, D.PHYS-MATH.SC.; Russian physicist; b. 3 April 1939, Krasnopavlovka, Kharkov Region; m.; three c.; ed Moscow Univ.; Asst, Docent, Deputy Dean Chair of Mechanics and Math., Moscow Univ. 1972–78, Prof., Prorector 1982–84, Head Chair of Math. Analysis, First Pro-Rector 1982–92, Rector 1992–; Corresp. mem. Russian Acad. of Sciences 1994, mem. 1997, mem. Presidium; Dir Inst. of Math. Problems of Complex Systems 1995–; Prof. Int. Acad. of Marketing; mem. Russian Acad. of Tech. Sciences; Sec.-Gen. Asscn of USSR Univs. 1987–91; Vice-Pres. Int. Acad. of Higher School 1992–; mem. Perm. Cttee, Pres. Conf. of Rectors of Europe; State and Lomonosov Prizes. *Address:* Moscow State University, 119899 Moscow, Russia. *Telephone:* (095) 939-27-29.

SADUR, Nina Nikolayevna; Russian writer and playwright; b. 15 Oct. 1950, Novosibirsk; d. of Nikolai Sadur; one d.; ed Moscow Inst. of Culture, Moscow M. Gorky Inst. of Literature; literary debut in Sibirskiye Ogni magazine; freelance writer; mem. USSR Writers' Union 1989. *Plays include:* Chardym, My Brother Chichikov, Weird Baba, Move Ahead. *Publications:* New Amazons (collected stories) 1991, Irons and Diamonds (short stories), German (novel). *Address:* Vagrius Publishers, Troitskaya str. 7/1, Bldg 2, 129090 Moscow, Russia (Office). *Telephone:* (095) 785-09-63 (Office).

SÆBØ, Magne, DTheol; Norwegian professor of Old Testament theology (retd); b. 23 Jan. 1929, Fjelberg; s. of Samson Sæbø and Malla Ølfaernes; m. Mona Uni Bjørnstad 1953; three s.; ed Free Faculty of Theology, Oslo and Univ. of Oslo; studied Old Testament and Semitic languages in Jerusalem, Kiel and Heidelberg; teacher of Biblical Hebrew, Univ. of Oslo 1961–70; Lecturer in Old Testament, Free Faculty of Theology (Church of Norway) 1969–70, Prof. 1970–99, Dean 1975–77, 1988–90, now Prof. Emer.; Ed.-in-Chief int. project on Hebrew Bible/Old Testament: The History of Its Interpretation I–III; Ed.-in-Chief Tidsskrift for Teologi og Kirke (Univ. Press), Oslo 1977–94; mem. Bd Norwegian Bible Soc. 1965–91, Chair. O.T. Trans. Cttee 1968–78, Gen. Trans. Cttee 1978–91; Chair. Norwegian Israel Mission 1978–87; mem. WCC Consultation on the Church and the Jewish People 1976–81; Chair. Lutheran European Comm. on the Church and the Jewish People, Hanover 1979–82; Pres. Int. Org. for the Study of Old Testament 1995–98; mem. Royal Soc. of Science and Letters, Trondheim, Norwegian Acad. of Science and Letters, Oslo, Nathan Söderblom Soc., Uppsala; received on 65th birthday Festschrift Text and Theology 1994; Kt 1st Class of Royal Norwegian Order of St Olav 1994; Fridtjof Nansen Award for Eminent Research 1995. *Publications:* Sacharja 9-14. Untersuchungen von Text und Form 1969, Gjennom alle tider 1978, Ordene og Ordet. Gammeltestamentlige studier 1979, Salomos ordsprak, Forkynneren, Høysangen, Klagesangene (Commentary) 1986, On the Way to Canon: Creative Tradition History in the Old Testament 1998; articles in int. journals and theology books. *Leisure interests:* biographies, stamp collecting, mountain walking. *Address:* The Free Faculty of Theology, P.O. Box 5144, Majorstua, N-0302 Oslo (Office); Lars Muhles vei 34, N-1338 Sandvika, Norway (Home). *Telephone:* 22-59-05-00 (Office); 67-54-38-06 (Home). *Fax:* 22-69-18-90 (Office); 67-54-38-06 (Home). *E-mail:* msabo@mf.no (Office); m-saebo@frisurf.no (Home).

SAEMALA, Francis Joseph, BA; Solomon Islands diplomatist and civil servant; b. 23 June 1944; m. Eve Mercy 1974; four s. one d.; ed Victoria Univ., Wellington, NZ; Head of Planning, Cen. Planning Office 1976; Sec. to Independence Timetable Talks del. and Jt Sec. to Constitutional Conf. in London 1977; Special Sec. to Chief Minister 1976, to Prime Minister 1978–81; Sec. to Leader of the Opposition 1981–82; Perm. Sec. Ministry of Foreign Affairs and Int. Trade 1982–83; Perm. Rep. to UN 1983–90; MP 1989–; Chair. Parl. Foreign Relations Cttee 1992–93, 1995; Chair. Solomon Islands Ports Authority Bd 1991–93; Deputy Prime Minister, Minister of Foreign Affairs 1993–94. *Publications:* Our Independent Solomon Islands, Solomon Islands in Politics in Melanesia. *Address:* Auki, Malaita Province, Solomon Islands.

SÁENZ ABAD, Alfredo; Spanish banker; b. Nov. 1942, Las Arenas, Basque Country; ed Univ. of Valladolid and Deusto Univ. Bilbao; mem. Bd Tubacex (Basque steel pipe producer) 1965–80; Dir of Planning, Banco de Vizcaya 1981; Man. Dir Banca Catalana 1983; Man. Dir Banco Bilbao Vizcaya 1988, First Vice-Pres. 1990; Pres. Banco Español de Crédito (Banesto) 1993–. *Address:* Banco Español de Crédito (Banesto), Gran vía de Hortaleza 3, 28043 Madrid, Spain. *Telephone:* (91) 3383100 (Office). *Fax:* (91) 3381883 (Office). *E-mail:* uninternac@banesto.es (Office). *Website:* www.banesto.es (Office).

SAFDIE, Moshe, OC, BArch, FRAIC; Canadian architect; b. 14 July 1938, Haifa; s. of Leon Safdie and Rachael Esses; m. 1st Nina Nusynowicz 1959 (divorced 1981); one s. one d.; m. 2nd Michal Ronnen 1981; two d.; ed McGill Univ. Montreal, Canada; with VanGinkel & Assocs., Montreal 1961–62; Louis I. Kahn, Philadelphia 1962–63; architect, planner Canadian Corpn for 1967 World Exhbn 1963–64; Moshe Safdie & Assocs., Montreal 1964–, Jerusalem 1970–, Moshe Safdie and Assocs. Inc., Boston 1978–, Toronto 1985–; Visiting Prof. McGill Univ. 1970–71; Davenport Prof. of Architecture, Yale Univ. 1971–72; Prof. of Architecture and Dir Desert Research Inst., Ben Gurion Univ., Israel 1975–78; Dir Urban Design Program of Harvard Univ. 1978–84; Ian Woodner (Studio) Prof. of Architecture and Urban Design, Grad. School of Design 1984–89; mem. Israel Inst. of Architects and Engineers, Royal Canadian Acad. of Arts; Fellow Royal Architectural Inst. Canada, mem. AIA Order of Architects of Que., Ont. Asscn Architects; Hon. FAIA 1996; Hon. LLD (McGill Univ.) 1982; Dr. hc (Laval Univ.) 1988; Hon. DFA (Univ. of Vic.) 1989; Hon. DEng (Tech. Univ. of Nova Scotia) 1996; Hon. DHumLitt (Brandeis Univ.); Lt-Gov. Gold Medal (Canada) 1961, Massey Medal for Architecture (Canada) 1967, Urban Design Concept Award (USA) 1980, Int. Design Award in Urban Design (USA) 1980, Rechter Prize for Architecture 1982, Mt. Scopius Award for Humanitarianism (Israel) 1987, Prix d'excellence in Architecture, Canada 1988, Gov. Gen.'s Medal for Architecture (Canada) 1992, Nentra Award for Professional Excellence 1995, Gold Medal (Australia) 1995. *Projects include:* Habitat '67, Montreal; Coldspring New Town, Baltimore; Mamilla Business District, Jerusalem; Musée de la Civilisation, Québec City; Hosh Dist Restoration, Jerusalem; Colegio Hebreo Maguen David, Mexico City; Nat. Gallery of Canada, Ottawa; Ardmore Habitat Apartments, Singapore; Ottawa City Hall; Ford Centre for the Performing Arts, Vancouver; Library Square, Vancouver; The Esplanade, Cambridge, Mass.; Musée des beaux arts de Montreal, Québec; Harvard Business School master plan and Morgan Hall, Boston; Hebrew Union Coll., Jerusalem; Skirball Museum and Cultural Center, LA, Calif.; Mamilla Hilton Hotel, Jerusalem; Rabin Center for Israeli Studies, Tel Aviv; Corrour Estate, Scotland; Exploration Place Science Center and Children's Museum, Wichita, Kan.; Ben Gurion Airport, Tel Aviv; Hebrew Coll. Newton Mass.; Peabody Essex Museum, Salem, Mass.; The Edge on Cairnhill condominiums, Singapore; Lester B. Pearson Airport, Toronto; Khalsa Heritage Memorial Complex, Punjab, India; Telfair Museum of Art, Savannah, Ga; Eleanor Roosevelt Coll., Univ. of Calif., San Diego; Nat. Health Museum, Washington, DC; Salt Lake City Public Library, Utah; Springfield Fed. Courthouse, Springfield, Mass.; Converse Network Systems Ltd, Tel Aviv; Alcohol, Tobacco and Firearms HQ, Washington, DC; Kansas City Performing Arts Center, Mo. *Publications:* Beyond Habitat 1970, The Japan Architect 1970, The Coldspring Presentation 1972, Horizon 1973, For Everyone a Garden 1974, Habitat Bill of Rights 1976, Form and Purpose 1982, The Harvard Jerusalem Studio: Urban Design for the Holy City 1986, Beyond Habitat by 20 years 1987, The Language and Medium of Architecture 1989, Jerusalem: The Future of the Past 1989, Moshe Safdie: Buildings and Projects 1967–1992 1996, The City After the Automobile 1997. *Address:* 100 Properzi Way, Somerville, MA 02143-3798, USA; 55 Port Street East, Mississauga, Ont., L5G 4P3, Canada; 4 Ha'emek, 7 Schlomo Street, Hamelech, Jerusalem 94106, Israel. *Telephone:* (617) 629-2100 (USA); (905) 891-8666 (Canada); 2-6251471 (Israel). *Fax:* (617) 629-2406 (USA) (Office); (416) 925-0406 (Canada) (Office); 2-6254679 (Israel) (Office). *E-mail:* safdieb@msafdie.com (USA) (Office); safdiej@msafdie.com (Israel) (Office). *Website:* www.msafdie.com (Office).

SAFIRE, William; American journalist and author; b. 17 Dec. 1929, New York; s. of Oliver C. Safir and Ida Panish; m. Helene Belmar Julius 1962; one s. one d.; ed Syracuse Univ.; journalist, New York Herald Tribune Syndicate 1949–51; Corresp. WNBC-WNBT, Europe and Middle East 1951, Radio and TV Producer, WNBC, New York 1954–55; Vice-Pres. Tex McCrary Inc. 1955–60; Pres. Safire Public Relations Inc. 1960–68; Special Asst to Pres. Nixon, Washington 1968–73; Columnist, New York Times, Washington 1973–; Chair. of Bd Charles A. Dana Foundation; mem. American Acad. of Arts and Sciences, Pulitzer Bd; Trustee Syracuse Univ.; Pulitzer Prize for Distinguished Commentary 1978. *Publications:* The Relations Explosion 1963, Plunging into Politics 1964, Safire's Political Dictionary 1968, Before the Fall 1975, Full Disclosure 1977, Safire's Washington 1980, On Language 1980, What's the Good Word? 1982, Good Advice (with Leonard Safir) 1982, I Stand Corrected 1984, Take My Word for It 1986, Freedom (novel) 1987, You Could Look It Up 1988, Words of Wisdom 1989, Language Maven Strikes Again 1990, Leadership (with Leonard Safir) 1990, Coming To Terms 1991, The First Dissident 1992, Good Advice on Writing (with Leonard Safir) 1992, Lend Me Your Ears 1992, Safire's New Political Dictionary 1993, Quote the Maven 1993, In Love With Norma Loquendi 1994, Sleeper Spy 1995, Watching My Language 1997, Spreading the Word 1999, Scandalmonger 2000, Let A Smile Be Your Umbrella 2002. *Address:* c/o New York Times, 1627 I Street, NW, Washington, DC 20006, USA.

SAFONOV, Col-Gen. Anatoly Yefimovich; Russian politician; b. 5 Oct. 1945, Krasnoyarsk; m. Galina Nikolayevna Safonova; one s. one d; ed Krasnoyarsk Polytechnic Inst., Higher KGB School, Minsk; Engineer, Expedition in Far N regions Chukotka, Krasnoyarsk 1969; KGB service 1970–, Head Counter-Espionage Dept 1983–87, Head, Territorial KGB 1988–92; First Deputy Dir, Fed. Service of Security, Russian Fed. 1994–97, Chair. Cttee on Security Problems of Union State of Russia and Belarus 1997; Peoples' Deputy of Russian Fed. 1990–93; Deputy Minister of Foreign Affairs 2002–; Corresp. mem. Int. Acad. of Information Tech.; Hon. Worker of Counter-espionage. *Address:* Ministry of Foreign Affairs, Smolenskaya-Sennaya pl. 32–34, 121200 Moscow, Russia (Office). *Telephone:* (095) 244-95-20 (Office). *Fax:* (095) 244-16-57 (Office). *E-mail:* safonov@mid.ru (Office).

SAFONOVA, Yelena Vsevolodovna; Russian actress; b. 14 June 1956, Leningrad; d. of Vsevolod Safonov; m.; ed All-Union Inst. of Cinematography, Leningrad Inst. of Theatre, Music and Cinema; actress Mosfilm Studio 1986–; David di Donatello Prize (Italy) for Best Role (Black Eyes) 1988. *Films include:* Return of Butterfly, Winter Cherries, Winter Cherries 2, Winter Cherries 3, Sofia Kovalevskaya, Secret of the Earth, Strange Call, Confrontation, Sleuth, Continuation of the Clan, Taxi Blues, Butterflies, Music for December, The President and His Woman, All Red. *Address:* Taganskaya pl. 31/22, Apt. 167, 109004 Moscow, Russia. *Telephone:* (095) 278-07-36.

SAGALAYEV, Eduard Mikhailovich; Russian journalist; b. 3 Oct. 1946, Samarkand; m.; one s. one d.; ed Samarkand Univ., Acad. of Social Sciences Cen. Cttee CPSU; Dir, Sr Ed. Cttee on TV and Radio Samarkand; on staff, Deputy Exec. Sec. Leninsky Put 1969–72; Exec. Sec. Komsomolets Uzbekistana Tashkent 1972–73; instructor Propaganda Div. Cen. Comsomol Cttee Moscow 1973–75; Deputy Ed.-in-Chief programs for youth, USSR Cen. TV 1975–80, Ed.-in-Chief 1980–88; Ed.-in-Chief Information section of Cen. TV 1988–90; Dir Gen. Studio Channel IY 1990; First Deputy Chair. All-Union State Radio and TV Corpn 1991–92; Dir Gen. TV Ostankino Jan.–July 1992; f. and Pres. TV-6, Moscow's first independent broadcasting co. 1992–96, 1997–; Chair. Russian TV and Broadcasting co. (RTR) 1996–97; now Chair. Bd of Dirs. and Pres. Moscow Ind. Broadcasting Corpn, Deputy Chair. Bd of Dirs. ORT (Channel 1); Co-Chair. Int. TV and Radio Broadcasting Policies Comm. 1990–97; Dir.-Gen. RTR Signal Co.; Chair. Bd of USSR Journalists' Union 1990–91; Chair. Confed. of Journalists' Unions of CIS 1992–97, Pres. Nat. Asscn of TV and Radio Producers of Russia 1995–; mem. Acad. of Russian TV 1995–; USSR State Prize 1978; Order of Friendship (twice). *Address:* National Association of TV Producers, Myasnitskaya str. 13/11, 101000 Moscow, Russia. *Telephone:* (095) 924-24-38. *Fax:* (095) 923-23-18.

SAGAN, Françoise (pseudonym of Françoise Quoirez); French writer; b. 21 June 1935, Cajarc; d. of Pierre Quoirez and Marie (née Laubard) Quoirez; m. 1st Guy Schoeller 1958 (divorced); m. 2nd Robert Westhoff 1962 (divorced); one s.; ed Couvent des Oiseaux and Couvent du Sacré Coeur, Paris; Prix des Critiques for Bonjour tristesse 1954. *Plays:* Château en Suède 1959, Les violons parfois... 1961, La robe mauve de valentine 1963, Bonheur, impair et passe 1964, Le cheval évanoui 1966, L'écharde 1966, Un piano dans l'herbe 1970, Zaphorie 1973, Le lit défait 1977, Pol Vandromme 1978, Il fait beau jour et nuit 1978, Le chien couchant 1980, Un orage immobile 1983, l'Excès contraire 1987. *Publications:* Bonjour tristesse 1954, Un certain sourire 1956, Dans un mois, dans un an 1957, Aimez-vous Brahms... 1959, La chamade 1965, Le garde du coeur 1968, Un peu de soleil dans l'eau froide 1969, Des bleus à l'âme 1972, Il est des parfums (with Guillaume Hanoteau) 1973, Les merveilleux nuages 1973, Un profil perdu 1974, Réponses 1975, Des yeux de soie 1976, La femme fardée, Musique de scène 1981, De guerre lasse 1985, Un sang d'aquarelle 1987, Dear Sarah Bernhardt 1988, Les Faux-Fuyants 1991, Répliques 1992... Et toute ma sympathie 1993, Evasion (novel) 1993, Un chagrin de passage 1994, Le miroir égaré 1996, Derrière l'épaule 1998; scenario for the ballet Le rendez-vous manqué (with Michel Magne); own film adaption of Dans un mois, dans un an; Dir Les fougères bleues (film) 1976. *Address:* Editions Juilliard, 24 avenue Marceau, 75008 Paris (Office); 14600 Honfleur, France.

SAGARRA, Eda, MA, DPhil, LittD, MRIA; Irish professor of German; b. 15 Aug. 1933, Dublin; d. of Kevin O'Shiel and Cecil Smiddy; m. Albert Sagarra i Zacarini 1961; one d.; ed Loreto Convent, Foxrock, Farnborough Hill Convent, Hants., England, Univ. Coll. Dublin and Univs of Freiburg, Zürich and Vienna; jr lecturer, lecturer, Univ. of Manchester 1958–68; Special Lecturer in German History 1968–75; Prof. of German, Trinity Coll. Dublin 1975–98, Dean of Visiting Students 1979–86, Prof. Emer. 1998–; Registrar Univ. of Dublin 1981–86, Pro-Chancellor 2000–; Chair. Irish Research Council for the Humanities and Social Sciences 2000–, Irish Research Council (Humanities/Social Sciences) 2000–, Salzburg Univ. Arts Faculty 2002–; mem. Council,

Royal Irish Acad. (Sec. 1993–2000), Nat. Council for Educational Awards 1991–96; mem. Standing Cttee for Humanities, European Science Foundation 1996–2002; mem. Germanistische Kommission of German Research Council 1982–90; mem. Bd Inst. of Germanic Studies of Univ. of London 1983–87; mem. Academia Europaea 1991–, Quality Review Group 1998–, Max Planck Inst., Quality Review Group, Swiss Research Council 2001–, Bd Giessen Univ., Germany; Bundesverdienstkreuz (Austria); Bundesverdienstkreuz (FRG); Goethe Medal 1990, Jacob and Wilhelm Grimm Prize 1995. *Publications:* Tradition and Revolution 1971, A Social History of Germany 1648–1914 1977, Theodor Fontane: Der Stechlin 1986, Literatur und Anthropologie um 1800 (Ed. with Jürgen Barkhoff) 1992, Companion to German Literature 1494 to the Present (with Peter Skrine) 1997, Germany in the 19th Century: History and Literature 2001; scientific bibliographies/review essays on German women writers; articles on legal, social and literary history of servants in Germany. *Leisure interests:* golf (county golfer 1969–75), ornithology, cooking, European politics. *Address:* 5066 Arts Building, Trinity College, Dublin 2 (Office); 30 Garville Avenue, Rathgar, Dublin 6, Ireland (Home). *Telephone:* (1) 6081373 (Office); (1) 4975967 (Home). *Fax:* (1) 6772694 (Office). *E-mail:* esagarra@irchss.ie (Office); esagarra@tcd.ie (Home).

SAGDEEV, Roald Zinnurovich, DSc; Russian physicist; b. 26 Dec. 1932, Moscow; m. Susan Eisenhower (grand-d. of the late Pres. Eisenhower) 1990; ed Moscow State Univ.; Research Worker, Inst. of Atomic Energy, USSR Acad. of Sciences 1956–61; Head of Lab., Inst. of Nuclear Physics, Siberian Dept, Acad. of Sciences 1961–70, Inst. of High Temperature Physics of USSR Acad. of Sciences 1970–73; Prof. Novosibirsk State Univ. 1964–73; Dir Inst. of Space Research 1973–88, Sr Researcher 1988–; Distinguished Prof. Univ. of Md, USA 1990–, Founder and Dir East-West Space Science Center 1992–; Corresp. mem. USSR (now Russian) Acad. of Sciences 1964, mem. 1968–; specialist on global warming, plasma physics, controllable thermonuclear synthesis, cosmic ray physics; mem. Council of Dirs. Int. Fund for Survival and Devt of Mankind 1988–; Head Scientific-Methodical Centre for Analytical Research, Inst. of Space Research 1988–; mem. NAS Swedish Royal Acad., Max Planck Soc.; USSR People's Deputy 1989–91; Order of October Revolution, Order of Red Banner and other decorations; Dr hc (Tech. Univ. Graz, Austria) 1984; Hero of Socialist Labour 1986; Lenin Prize 1984. *Address:* East-West Space Science Center, University of Maryland, College Park, MD 20742, USA. *Telephone:* (301) 985-7000. *E-mail:* rzs@ew1.umd.edu (Office).

SAGER, Dirk; German journalist; b. 13 Aug. 1940, Hamburg; m. Irene Dasbach-Sager; one s. one d.; fmrly with Radio RIAS Berlin; fmr corresp. ZDF TV, East Berlin, Washington DC, Chief of Moscow Office 1990–97, 1998–, of Brandenburg Office 1997–98. *Publication:* Betrogenes Rubland 1996. *Leisure interest:* reading. *Address:* Zweites Deutsches Fernsehen, August-Bebel-Strasse 15-16, 14482 Potsdam, Germany.

SAGET, Louis Joseph Edouard; French government official (retd); b. 27 April 1915, Paris; s. of Pierre Saget and Jeanne (née Barbare) Saget; m. Anne Vincens 1940; six c.; ed Lycée Janson-de-Sailly, Paris, Sorbonne; Mayor of Tananarive 1954–56; First Counsellor, French Embassy, Madagascar 1959–60; High Commr in Comoro Islands 1960–62; Commissaire aux Comptes, European Launcher Devt Org. 1963–66; Gov. of French Somaliland 1966–67; High Commr in Djibouti 1967–69; Conseiller maître à la Cour des Comptes 1970–84; Pres. Agence nat. pour l'amélioration de l'habitat 1971–78, Comm. de terminologie du ministère de la Défense 1973–87; Investigator, Comité central d'enquête sur le coût et le rendement des services publics 1974–84; mem. Electoral Comm. for French living abroad 1977–88, Cttee for Fiscal Matters, Customs and Exchange 1987–93; mem. town council of Méréville 1969–95; Officier Légion d'honneur, Commdr Ordre nat. du Mérite, Croix de guerre, Commdr de l'Etoile noire, Commdr de l'Ordre nat. Malgache, Grand Commdr of the Order of the Star of Ethiopia, Commdr de l'Etoile équatoriale de Gabon, Nat. Order of Upper Volta, Order of the Leopard of Zaire, Grand Officier Ordre du Croissant Vert des Comores. *Leisure interest:* nature. *Address:* 13 rue Cambon 75001 Paris (Office); 1 rue de Laborde, 91660 Méréville, France (Home).

SAGLIO, Jean-François; French mining engineer; b. 29 July 1936, Toulon; s. of Georges Saglio; m. Odile Bertrand 1968; two s. one d.; ed Ecole Polytechnique and Ecole Supérieure des Mines, Paris; Engineer, Govt Del. Algiers 1960–61; Mining Engineer, Mines de Metz 1961–66; Founder/Dir. Agence de Bassin Rhin-Meuse, Metz 1966–69; Adviser, Cabinet of Pres. of France 1969–73; Head, Perm. Secr. for Study of Water Problems of Paris 1971–73; Dir in charge of Pollution and Nuisance, Ministry of Environment 1973–78; Pres. Dir-Gen. Agence Foncière et Technique de la Région Parisienne 1979–81; Dir of Innovation and Valorization of Research, Elf Aquitaine, also Dir of New Projects 1981–84; Pres. Dir-Gen. INOVELF 1981–84; Asst Dir-Gen. Société Elf-France 1984; Asst Dir-Gen. Refineries and Distribution, Société Nat. Elf Aquitaine 1984; Dir-Gen. of Industry, Ministry of Industry, Posts & Telecommunications and Tourism 1987–88; Dir Soc. Roussel-Uclaf 1989–91; Vice-Pres. SCH Consultants; Pres. Admin. Council Rhin-Meuse 1992–97, ERSO 1993; Dir-Gen. CEA Industrie 1992–94; Pres. Dexter SA 1992–99, Inst. français de l'environnement 1995–98; Pres. BNFL SA 1996; mem. Conseil Général des Mines 1991–99; Officier, Légion d'honneur, Ordre nat. du Mérite; Croix de la Valeur militaire. *Address:* 143 rue de la Pompe, 75116 Paris, France (Home). *Telephone:* 1-45-53-05-44 (Home).

SAGUIER CABALLERO, Bernardino Hugo, PhD; Paraguayan diplomatist; b. 21 July 1935; m.; three c.; ed ed. Catholic Univ. of Asunción, Nat.

War Coll., Asunción; joined Foreign Ministry, held various posts as Sec. to Comms., etc. 1962–75, Pvt. Sec. to Minister of Foreign Affairs 1965–68, Chef de Cabinet 1968–70, Dir of Int. Orgs, Treaties and Instruments 1970–75, Dir responsible for binat. entity of Itaipu 1975–89, Under-Sec. of State for Foreign Affairs 1989–92; Perm. Rep. to the UN 1992–99; Head del. negotiations on Treaty of the Common Market of the Southern Cone (Mercosur), on Mercosur–US trade and investment agreement, mem. del. to sessions of UN Gen. Ass. and meetings of the OAS, the Rio Group, the River Plate Basin and the Latin American Free Trade and Integration Asscns; fmr Prof. Diplomatic Acad., Ministry of Foreign Affairs, lecturer at Catholic Univ., Asunción and Higher Police Coll., Asunción; decorations from China, Brazil, South Africa, Argentina, Spain, Ecuador, Chile and others. *Address:* c/o Ministry of Foreign Affairs, Juan E. O'Leary y Presidente Franco, Asunción, Paraguay. *Telephone:* (21) 49-4593 (Office). *Fax:* (21) 49-3910 (Office).

SAHABDEEN, Desamanya Abdul Majeed Mohamed, BA, PhD; Sri Lankan foundation president, entrepreneur, fmr civil servant and scholar; b. 19 May 1926, Gampola; s. of Abdul Majeed and Shaharwan Majeed; m. Ruchia Halida 1959; one s. one d.; ed Univ. of Ceylon; joined Ceylon Civil Service 1950, served as Sec., Dir, Commr, Chair. several maj. Govt orgs. until 1973; Visiting Head Dept of Western Philosophy, Univ. of Sri Lanka, Vidyodaya (now Sri Jayawardanapura) 1957–59; Chair. Majeedsons Group of Cos. 1973–, Muslim Law (Amendments) Cttee 1990; f. A.M.M. Sahabdeen Trust Foundation 1991, for Educ. and Social Devt; Mohamed Sahabdeen Int. Awards for Science, Literature and Human Devt est. by Act. of Parl. 1991; f. Mohamed Sahabdeen Inst. for Advanced Studies and Research in Pahamune 1997; mem. Presidential Comms. on Delimitation of Electoral Dists. 1988, Taxation 1989, Finance and Banking 1990, Industrialization 1990, Public Service Comm. 1989; mem. Press Council 1998; Vice-Patron Sri Lanka-India Friendship Soc. 1998; received Desamanya (highest civilian honour) 1992. *Publications:* several articles and books on philosophy and allied subjects, including Sufi Doctrine in Tamil Literature 1986, God and the Universe 1995, The Circle of Lives. *Leisure interests:* philosophy, classical music. *Address:* A.M.M. Sahabdeen Trust Foundation, 30/12 Bagatalle Road, Colombo 03, Sri Lanka. *Telephone:* (1) 502447; (1) 586327. *Fax:* (1) 505080; (1) 505081.

SAHADE, Jorge, PhD; Argentine astrophysicist; b. 23 Feb. 1915, Alta Gracia (Córdoba); s. of Nallib Jorge Sahade and María Kassab; m. 1st Myriam Stella Elkin Font 1948 (died 1974); one s. one d.; m. 2nd Adela Emilia Ringuelet 1975; ed Colegio de Monserrat, Córdoba, Univ. of Córdoba, Univ. of La Plata; Fellow Univ. of La Plata at Univ. of Chicago (Yerkes Observatory) 1943–46; Prof. Univ. of Córdoba 1948–55, Dir Córdoba Observatory 1953–55; Guggenheim Fellow Univ. of Calif., Berkeley 1955–57, Research Astronomer 1957–58, 1960; Prof. and Head Div., Univ. of La Plata Observatory 1958–71, in charge of two-m telescope project 1958–69, Dir Observatory 1968–69, Dean Faculty of Exact Sciences 1969; Dir Inst. of Astronomy and Space Physics, Buenos Aires 1971–74; Pres. Argentine Astronomical Asscn 1963–69; Pres. Comm. 29, Int. Astronomical Union (IAU) 1964–67, Vice-Pres. Exec. Cttee IAU 1967–73, Pres. 1985–88, Adviser 1988–91, Vice-Pres. Comm. 38 1988–91, Pres. 1991–94; Pres. Argentine Space Agency (CONAE) 1991–94; Emer. Researcher, CONICET 1995; Scientific Co-ordinator of Argentinian participation, Gemini Project 1996–2001; Chair. COSPAR Advisory Panel on Space Research in Developing Countries 1973–79, Pres. 1979–82; mem. Bd Dir Nat. Research Council 1969–73, 1996, Exec. Bd ICSU 1972–76, Gen. Cttee 1972–80, COSTED 1973–79; mem. Bd Dir Div. V, Int. Astronomical Union 1997–2003; Visiting Prof. at numerous univs: Indiana, Sussex, Mons, Collège de France, Int. School for Advanced Study (Trieste), San Marcos (Peru), Porto Alegre (Brazil); Visiting Astronomer Dominion Astrophysical Observatory, Victoria, BC, later Visiting Research Officer; Visiting Scientist Max-Planck Institut-für-Astrophysik, FRG, Cerro Tololo Interamerican Observatory, Chile, Trieste Observatory; Guest Investigator at numerous observatories; Assoc. Royal Astronomical Soc. 1970, COSPAR 1992; Founder-mem. Argentine Acad. of Aeronautical and Space Sciences 1989; mem. Buenos Aires Nat. Acad. of Sciences 2001–; Foreign, Corresp. mem. numerous acads; Hon. Prof. Univ. of San Marcos, Peru 1987; Hon. mem. Argentine Asscn of Friends of Astronomy 1970, Argentine Astronomical Asscn 1985; Dr hc (Córdoba) 1987, (San Juan) 1996; Golden Planetarium Award 1973, Konex Award 1983, Diploma of Recognition, World Cultural Council 1987; Asteroid (2605)=1974 QA named Sahade at the proposal of the discoverer 1986, Consagración Científica Medal 1988; IAU Symposium No. 151 dedicated to J. Sahade; CASLEO's 2.15m telescope named Jorge Sahade 1996; Conf. Room of Cen. American Suyapa Observatory, Nat. Autonomous Univ. of Honduras named after him 2000. *Publications:* books and 190 research papers in int. journals. *Leisure interests:* music, travel, walking. *Address:* Observatorio Astronómico, FCAG, Universidad Nacional de La Plata, B 1900 CGA-La Plata (Office); 53-448 (p. 11 #1), B 1900 BAV-La Plata, Argentina (Home). *Telephone:* (221) 423-6593/4 (Office); (221) 482-4639 (Home). *Fax:* (221) 423-6591 (Office). *E-mail:* sahade@fcaglp.unlp.edu.ar (Office). *Website:* www.fcaglp.unlp.ar (Office).

SAHE AL KAFAJE, Galib Nahe; Iraqi artist; b. 1932, Emara; m. 1967; three d.; ed Inst. of Fine Arts, Baghdad and Acad. of Fine Arts, Rome; Instructor Inst. of Fine Arts, Baghdad 1966, Acad. of Fine Arts, Baghdad 1969; work includes mural at Saddam Airport 1987, 130 graphics at Rashed Hotel, Baghdad; works in collection at Saddam Art Center and have been widely exhibited in European cities, New Delhi, Cairo etc.; several awards. *Leisure* *interest:* handicrafts in gold. *Address:* College of Fine Arts, University of Baghdad, P.O. Box 17635, Jadiriya, Baghdad (Office); Dawoody, Street 15 No 102, Baghdad, Iraq (Home). *Telephone:* 5423690.

SAHEL, El Mostafa, LenD; Moroccan politician; b. 5 May 1946, Ouled Frej, El Jadida; s. of Maati Sahel and Hajja Ghita; m. Farida Benmansour Nejjai 1972; two s.; ed Lycée Mohamed V, Casablanca, Univ. Mohamed V, Rabat and Univ. de Sorbonne, Paris; Insp. des Finances 1968–70; Financial Controller 1970–74; Head of Service of Working Budget 1974–81, Equipment Budget 1981–86; Dir of Budget 1986–91; Sec.-Gen. Ministry of Finance 1992–93; Dir-Gen. of Communal Equipment Funds 1993–; Minister of Ocean Fisheries, Admin. Affairs and Parl. Relations 1993–98, of the Interior 2002–; Ordre de Mérite, Ordre du Trône. *Leisure interest:* golf. *Address:* Ministry of the Interior, Quartier Administratif, Rabat, Morocco. *Telephone:* (3) 7761868. *Fax:* (3) 7762056.

SAHGAL, Nayantara; Indian writer; b. Nayantara Pandit, 10 May 1927, Allahabad; d. of Ranjit Sitaram Pandit and Vijaya Lakshmi Pandit; m. 1st Gautam Sahgal 1949 (divorced 1967); one s. two d.; m. 2nd E. N. Mangat Rai 1979; ed Wellesley Coll., USA; Scholar-in-Residence, holding creative writing seminar, Southern Methodist Univ., Dallas, Texas 1973, 1977; Adviser English Language Bd, Sahitya Akademi (Nat. Acad. of Letters), New Delhi; mem. Indian Del. to UN Gen. Ass. 1978; Vice-Pres. Nat. Exec., People's Union for Civil Liberties; Fellow, Radcliffe Inst. (Harvard Univ.) 1976, Wilson Int. Center for Scholars, Washington, DC 1981–82, Nat. Humanities Center, NC 1983–84; mem. jury Commonwealth Writers' Prize 1990, Chair. Eurasia Region 1991; Annie Besant Memorial Lecture (Banaras Hindu Univ.) 1992; Arthur Ravenscroft Memorial Lecture (Univ. of Leeds) 1993; Foreign Hon. mem. American Acad. Arts and Sciences 1990; Hon. DLitt (Leeds) 1997; Diploma of Honour, Int. Order of Volunteers for Peace, Salsomaggiore, Italy 1982, Sinclair Prize 1985, Doon Ratna Citizens' Council Prize 2002, Wellesley Coll. Alumni Achievement Award 2002. *Publications:* Prison and Chocolate Cake 1954, A Time to Be Happy 1958, From Fear Set Free 1962, This Time of Morning 1965, Storm in Chandigarh 1969, History of the Freedom Movement 1970, The Day in Shadow 1972, A Situation in New Delhi 1977, A Voice for Freedom 1977, Indira Gandhi's Emergence and Style 1978, Indira Gandhi: Her Road to Power 1982, Rich Like Us (Sinclair Prize 1985, Sahitya Akad. Award 1987) 1985, Plans for Departure 1985 (Commonwealth Writers' Prize 1987), Mistaken Identity 1988, Relationship: Extracts from a Correspondence 1994, Point of View 1997, Before Freedom: Nehru's Letters to His Sister 1909–47 (ed.) 2000, Lesser Breeds 2002. *Leisure interests:* walking, reading, music. *Address:* 181a Rajpur Road, Dehra Dun, 248009 Uttaranchal, India. *Telephone:* (135) 2734278.

SAHL, Mort(on) Lyon, BS; American comedian; b. 11 May 1927, Montreal, Canada; s. of Harry Sahl; m. 1st Sue Babior 1955 (divorced 1957); m. 2nd China Lee; one c.; ed Compton Jr Coll., Univ. of Southern California; Ed. Poop from the Group; magazine writing; many night club engagements; radio and TV performances, including Comedy News TV show, Steve Allen Show, Jack Paar Show, Eddie Fisher Show, Nightline, Wide Wide World; monologues on long-playing records; in Broadway revue, The Next President 1958; one-man show Broadway 1987. *Films include:* In Love and War 1958, All the Young Men 1960, Doctor, You've Got to be Kidding 1967, Nothing Lasts Forever 1984, (TV) Inside the Third Reich 1982. *Publication:* Heartland 1976.

SAHLIN, Mona; Swedish politician; b. 9 March 1957, Sollefteå; m. Bo Sahlin; three c.; ed Correspondence School, Swedish Cooperative Movt 1978–80; Sec. State Employees' Union 1980–82; Mem. Parl. (Riksdag) 1982–90; Minister of Employment 1990–91; Gen. Sec. Swedish Social Democratic Party 1992–94; Govt Rep. Bd of Swedish Sports Confed. 1983–90; Chair. Cttee on Working Hours 1982–90; mem. Bd Centre for Working Life 1982–90; Deputy Prime Minister and Minister with Special Responsibility for Equality Issues 1994–95; self-employed 1995–98; Minister, Ministry of Industry, Employment and Communications 1998–. *Address:* Ministry of Industry, Employment and Communications, 103 33 Stockholm, Sweden (Office). *Telephone:* (8) 405-39-91 (Office); (8) 718-06-28 (Home). *Fax:* (8) 405-39-99 (Office); (8) 718-48-77 (Home). *E-mail:* registrator@industry.ministry.se (Office).

SAHNOUN, Mohamed; Algerian diplomatist and United Nations official; Deputy Sec.-Gen. OAU (in charge of Political Affairs) 1964–73, League of Arab States (for Arab-African dialogue) 1973–75; Amb. to FRG, to France, to USA 1984–89, to Morocco 1989–1990; Perm. Rep. to the UN 1982–84; Sec. of the Maghreb Union 1989–90; Counsellor to the Pres. of Algeria for Foreign Affairs 1990–92; UN Special Rep. in Somalia 1992; OAU Special Rep. in the Congo 1993; with UN Special Envoy in Africa 1997–; fmr Special Adviser to Sec.-Gen. UN Conf. on Environment and Devt, UNCED; now Special Adviser to Culture of Peace Prog. UNESCO, Paris, War-Torn Societies Project UNRISD, Geneva; fmr Exec. Dir Earth Charter Project; fmr mem. World Comm. on Environment and Devt (Brundtland Comm.); mem. Bd Int. Inst. for Sustainable Devt (IISD), Winnipeg, Int. Council for Human Rights; Distinguished Fellow U.S. Inst. of Peace, Washington 1992–93; currently Pearson Fellow, Int. Devt Research Centre (IDRC), Ottawa, Canada. *Publications:* Somalia: The Missed Opportunities 1994, Managing Conflicts in the Post-Cold War Era 1996. *Address:* International Development Research Centre (IDRC), 250 Albert Street, P.O. Box 8500, Ottawa, Ont., K1G 3H9, Canada (Office); Department of Peace-keeping Operations, Room S-3727B, United Nations, New York

10017, USA (Office). *Telephone:* (613) 236-6163 (Office); (212) 963-9222 (New York) (Office). *Fax:* (212) 963-8079 (New York) (Office). *E-mail:* info@idrc.ca (Office). *Website:* www.idrc.ca (Office); www.un.org (Office).

SAIBOU, Brig. Ali; Niger politician and army officer; fmr Chief of Staff of Armed Forces; fmr Acting Head of State; Pres. Mouvement nat. pour une Société de développement (MNSD); Chair. of the Higher Council for Nat. Orientation (fmrly Conseil militaire Suprême) 1987; Pres. of the Council of Ministers 1987, Minister of Nat. Defence 1987–91, of Interior 1987–89 (stripped of exec. power Aug. 1991).

SAID, Edward W., MA, PhD; American university professor; b. 1 Nov. 1935, Jerusalem; s. of Wadie Said and Hilda Musa; m. Mariam Cortas 1970; one s. one d.; ed Victoria Coll., Cairo, Mt. Hermon School, Mass., Princeton and Harvard Univs; instructor in English, Columbia Univ. 1963–65, Asst Prof. of English and Comparative Literature 1967–69, Prof. 1969–77, Parr Prof. 1977–89, Old Dominion Foundation Prof. in Humanities, Columbia Univ. 1989–, Univ. Prof. 1992–; Visiting Prof. of Comparative Literature, Harvard Univ. 1974, of Humanities, Johns Hopkins Univ. 1979; Ed., Arab Studies Quarterly; Chair. Bd of Trustees, Inst. of Arab Studies; mem. Palestine Nat. Council, Council on Foreign Relations, New York, Acad. of Literary Studies, PEN Club, New York, American Acad. of Arts and Sciences; Fellow, Center for Advanced Study in Behavioral Science, Stanford 1975–76; Bowdoin Prize (Harvard Univ.); Lionel Trilling Award 1976, Spinoza Prize 1999, Morton Dauwen Zabel Award 2000 and numerous other awards for literature. *Publications:* Joseph Conrad and the Fiction of Autobiography, Beginnings: Intention and Method, Orientalism, The Question of Palestine, Literature and Society, Covering Islam 1981, The World, the Text and the Critic 1983, After the Last Sky 1986, Blaming the Victims 1988 (ed.), Musical Elaborations 1991, Culture and Imperialism 1993, Representations of the Intellectual 1994, Politics of Dispossession 1994, Ghazzah-Arihah: Salam Amriki 1994, Out of Place: A Memoir 1999, The End of the Peace Process: Oslo and After 2000, Reflections on Exile (essays) 2001. *Address:* Columbia University, Department of English, 602 Philosophy Hall, New York, NY 10027, USA. *Telephone:* (212) 854-1754. *Fax:* (212) 932-0418. *Website:* www.columbia.edu (Office).

SAID, Sayyid Faisal bin Ali as-; Omani diplomatist and politician; b. 1927, Muscat; attached to Ministry of Foreign Affairs, Muscat 1953–57; lived abroad 1957–70; Perm. Under-Sec. Ministry of Educ. 1970–72; Minister of Econ. Affairs 1972; Perm. Rep. to UN, Amb. to USA 1972–73; Minister of Educ. 1973–76, of Omani Heritage 1976–, of Culture 1979–. *Address:* Ministry of National Heritage and Culture, P.O. Box 668, Muscat 113, Oman. *Telephone:* 602555 (Office). *Fax:* 602735 (Office).

SAID, Wafic Rida; Saudi Arabian (b. Syrian) financier; b. 1939, Damascus; s. of Dr. Rida Said; m. Rosemary Thompson; one s. one d. (and one s. deceased); ed in Lebanon and at Inst. of Banking, London; began banking career at UBS Geneva 1962; f. TAG System Construction for design and construction projects in Saudi Arabia 1969; became Saudi Arabian citizen 1981; f. SIF-CORP Holdings (int. investment co.) 1981; f. Karim Rida Said Foundation (an English Charity) to alleviate poverty and suffering in the Middle East 1981; now Chair. of several pvt. cos. including Said Holdings Ltd and Sagitta Asset Man. (Bermuda) Ltd; mem. Oxford Univ. Court of Benefactors; Trustee Said Business School Foundation; Gov. RSC, London. *Leisure interests:* horse racing, collecting art and antiques. *Address:* c/o Royal Shakespeare Company, Barbican Theatre, London, E.C.2, England.

SAIER, Oskar, D.JUR.CAN.; German Roman Catholic ecclesiastic; b. 12 Aug. 1932, Wagensteig; s. of Adolf Saier and Berta Saier; ed Univs. of Freiburg, Tübingen and Munich; ordained 1957; Asst Kanonist. Inst. Univ. of Munich 1963; Dir Mayor Seminar St Peter, Black Forest 1970–77; Auxiliary Bishop in Freiburg 1972, Archbishop 1978–; Chair. Pastoral Comm. of German Conf. of Bishops 1979–98; mem. Vatican Congregation for the Clergy 1984–99; Second Chair. of German Conf. of Bishops 1987–99; Freeman of Buchenbach 1972, of St Peter, Black Forest 1977 and of Bethlehem, Palestine 1984; Order El Sol del Peru 1990, Grosses Bundesverdienstkreuz 1992, Verdienstmedaille des Landes Baden-Württemberg 1997. *Publication:* Communio in der Lehre des Zweiten Vatikanischen Konzils 1973. *Address:* Herrenstrasse 35, 79098 Freiburg, Germany. *Telephone:* 21881. *Fax:* (761) 2188230. *E-mail:* erzbischof@ordinariat-freiburg.de (Office). *Website:* www.erzbistum-freiburg .de (Home).

SAIF, Abdulla Hassan; Bahraini banker; b. 10 March 1945, Muharraq; ed Inst. of Cost and Man. Accountants, UK, IMF Inst. and other int. forums; apprentice, Bahrain Petroleum Co. 1957, served in all depts. –1971; Head of Finance and Admin. Civil Aviation Directorate 1971–74; Deputy Dir-Gen. Bahrain Monetary Agency 1974–77, Dir-Gen. 1977, fmr Gov.; Chair. Gulf Int. Bank BSC; now Minister of Finance and Nat. Economy; Chair. Specific Council for Training of Banking Sector; mem. Bd of Dirs Gulf Air Co., Org. for Social Insurance, Civil Service Pension Bd; Alt. Gov. IMF. *Address:* Ministry of Finance and National Economy, P.O. Box 333, Diplomatic Area, Manama, Bahrain (Office). *Telephone:* 530800 (Office). *Fax:* 532853 (Office). *Website:* www.mofne.gov.bh (Office).

SAIF AL-ISLAM, HRH Mohamed al-Badr, fmr Imam of the Yemen; b. 1927; ed Coll. for Higher Education, San'a (Yemen); Minister for Foreign Affairs 1955–61 and Minister of Defence and C-in-C 1955–62; succeeded to

Imamate on the death of his father, Imam Ahmed Sept. 1962; in hills, Yemen, leading Royalist Forces in civil war 1962–68; replaced by Imamate Council May 1968; in exile in Saudi Arabia 1968.

SAIFUDIN (see Seypidin).

SAIGH, Nassir M. Al-, DBA; Saudi Arabian business administrator; b. 10 Oct. 1942, Riyadh; s. of Mohammed Al-Saigh and Noura Al-Saigh; m. Azza J. Hammad 1989; ed Univ. of Kentucky, Lexington, Univ. of Indiana, Bloomington, King Saud Univ., Riyadh; Chair. Business Admin. Dept, King Saud Univ. 1980–83, Asst Prof., Faculty of Admin. Sciences 1979–80; Chief Ed., Arab Journal of Admin. 1983–; Dir-Gen. Arab Admin. Devt Org. 1983–. *Publications:* Administrative Reform in the Arab World: Readings 1986, Public Administration and Administrative Reform in the Arab World 1986. *Leisure interest:* reading.

SAIGNASON, Lt-Gen. Choummali; Laotian army officer and politician; mem. Nat. Ass.; Deputy Prime Minister and Minister of Nat. Defence –2001; Vice-Pres. of Laos March 2001–. *Address:* Office of the Vice-President, c/o Office of the President, Vientiane, Laos (Office). *Telephone:* (21) 214200 (Office). *Fax:* (21) 214208 (Office).

SAINSBURY, (Richard) Mark, DPhil, FBA; British professor of philosophy; b. 2 July 1943, London; s. of Richard Eric Sainsbury and Freda Margaret Horne; m. 1st Gillian McNeill Rind 1969 (separated 1982); one s. one d.; m. 2nd Victoria Goodman 2000; ed Sherborne School, Corpus Christi Coll., Oxford; Radcliffe Lecturer in Philosophy, Magdalen Coll., Oxford 1968–70; Lecturer in Philosophy, St Hilda's Coll., Oxford 1970–73, Radcliffe Lecturer in Philosophy, Brasenose Coll., Oxford 1973–75; Lecturer in Philosophy, Univ. of Essex 1975–78, Bedford Coll., Univ. of London 1978–84, King's Coll., London 1984–87, Reader 1987–89, Stebbing Prof. of Philosophy 1991–2003; Prof. of Philosophy, Univ. of Texas at Austin 2002–; Ed. Mind 1990–2000; Radcliffe Fellow 1987–88; Fellow King's Coll., London 1994, British Acad. 1998; Leverhulme Sr Research Fellow 2000–02. *Publications:* Russell 1979, Paradoxes 1988, Logical Forms 1991, Departing From Frege 2002. *Leisure interest:* baking bread. *Address:* Department of Philosophy, 1 University Station, University of Texas at Austin, Austin, TX 78712, USA. *Telephone:* (512) 417-5433. *E-mail:* marksainsbury@mail.utexas.edu (Office).

SAINSBURY OF PRESTON CANDOVER, Baron (Life Peer), cr. 1989, of Preston Candover in the County of Hampshire; **John Davan Sainsbury,** KG, MA; British business executive; b. 2 Nov. 1927, London; s. of the late A. J. (later Baron) Sainsbury; m. Anya Linden 1963; two s. one d.; ed Stowe School and Worcester Coll., Oxford; Dir J Sainsbury Ltd 1958–92, Vice-Chair. 1967–69, Chair., CEO 1969–92, Pres. 1992–; Chair. Anglo-Israel Asscn 2001–; Dir Royal Opera House, Covent Garden 1969–85 (Chair. 1987–91), The Economist 1972–80, Royal Opera House Trust 1974–84, 1987–97; Chair. Friends of Covent Garden 1969–81, Benesh Inst. of Chorology 1986–87, Dulwich Picture Gallery 1994–; Vice-Pres. Contemporary Arts Soc. 1984–; mem. Council, Retail Consortium 1975–79, Pres. 1993–97; mem. Nat. Cttee for Electoral Reform 1976–85; Jt Hon. Treas. European Mov. 1972–75; Fellow, Inst. of Grocery Distribution 1973; Hon. Fellow Worcester Coll., Oxford 1982; Gov. Royal Ballet School 1965–76, 1987–91, Royal Ballet 1987– (Chair. 1995–); Trustee Nat. Gallery 1976–83, Westminster Abbey Trust 1977–83, Tate Gallery 1982–83, Rhodes Trust 1984–98, Prince of Wales Inst. of Architecture 1992–96; Hon. Bencher, Inner Temple 1985; Hon. DSc (London) 1985; Hon. DLitt (South Bank) 1992; Albert Medal (RSA) 1989. *Address:* c/o J Sainsbury PLC, 33 Holborn, London, EC1N 2HT, England.

SAINSBURY OF TURVILLE, Baron (Life Peer), cr. 1997, in the County of Buckinghamshire; **David John Sainsbury,** MBA; British business executive; b. 24 Oct. 1940; s. of Sir Robert Sainsbury; m. Susan C. Reid 1973; three d.; ed King's Coll., Cambridge and Columbia Univ., NY; joined J Sainsbury 1963, Finance Dir 1973–90, Deputy Chair. J Sainsbury PLC 1988–92, Chair. and CEO 1992–98, Dir J Sainsbury USA Inc.; Parl. Under-Sec. of State for Science and Innovation 1998–; mem. Cttee of Review of Post Office (Carter Cttee) 1975–77; fmr Trustee, Social Democratic Party (SDP); mem. Gov. Body, London Business School 1985– (Chair. 1991–98); Visiting Fellow, Nuffield Coll., Oxford 1987–95; mem. IPPR Comm. 1995–97; Chair. Transition Bd, Univ. for Industry 1998–99; Hon. FREng 1994; Hon. LLD (Cambridge) 1997. *Publications:* Government and Industry: A New Partnership 1981, Wealth Creation and Jobs (with C. Smallwood) 1987. *Address:* House of Lords, Westminster, London, SW1A 0PW, England (Office).

ST AUBIN de TERAN, Lisa Gioconda, FRSL; British author; b. 2 Oct. 1953, London; d. of Jan Rynveld Carew and Joan Mary St Aubin; m. 1st Jaime Terán 1970 (divorced 1981); one d.; m. 2nd George Macbeth 1981 (divorced 1989, deceased); one s.; m. 3rd Robbie Duff-Scott 1989; one d.; ed James Allen's Girls' School, Dulwich; travelled widely in France and Italy 1969–71; managed sugar plantation in Venezuelan Andes 1971–78; moved to Italy 1983; fmr Vice-Pres. Umbria Film Festival, now Hon. Pres.; CEO Radiant Pictures 2002– (film production co.); Somerset Maugham Award, John Llewelyn Rhys Award, Eric Gregory Award for Poetry. *Screenplays:* The Slow Train to Milan (co-writer), The Hacienda, The Blessing, A Woman Called Solitude, The Moneymaker, The Orange Sicilian (co-writer, animated feature film). *Television:* wrote and presented documentaries Santos to Santa Cruz in Great Railway Journeys series (BBC) 1994, Great Railway Journeys of the World (BBC and PBS). *Radio:* adapted and read (for BBC) Off the Rails 1995, The Bay of Silence 1996. *Publications:* novels: Keepers of the House 1982, The

Slow Train to Milan 1983, The Tiger 1984, The Bay of Silence 1986, Black Idol 1987, Joanna 1990, Nocturne 1993, The Palace 1998; The High Place (poetry) 1985; The Marble Mountain (short stories) 1989; Distant Landscapes (novella) 1995; Off the Rails—A Memoir 1989, Venice: The Four Seasons 1992, A Valley in Italy 1994, The Hacienda; My Venezuelan Years 1997, Southpaw (short stories) 1999, Memory Maps (memoirs) 2001; ed. The Virago Book of Wanderlust and Dreams 1998. *Leisure interests:* travelling, medicinal plants, gardening, architecture, falconry, antiques, reading. *Address:* c/o Maggie Phillips, Ed Victor Ltd, 6 Bayley Street, Bedford Square, London, WC1B 3HB, England (Office); Radiant Pictures, 101 Vondelstraat, 1054 GM Amsterdam, Netherlands (Office). *Telephone:* (20) 7304-4100 (London) (Office). *Fax:* (20) 7304-4111 (London) (Office). *Website:* www.radiantpictures.com (Office).

ST JOHN, (Harold) Bernard, QC; Barbadian politician and lawyer (retd); b. 16 Aug. 1931, Christ Church; m. Stella Hope; one s. two d.; ed Boys' Foundation, Harrison Coll., Univ. of London, Inner Temple; called to Bar 1954; pvt. legal practice, Barbados and Eastern Caribbean 1954–; QC 1969; Legal Adviser to Southern Dist Council; Pres. Barbados Bar Asscn; mem. Senate 1964–66, 1971–76; mem. House of Ass. 1966–71, 1976–; Chair. Barbados Labour Party 1966–71; Leader of the Opposition 1970–71; Minister of Trade, Tourism and Industry 1976–86, also Deputy Prime Minister, Prime Minister and Minister of Finance 1985–86; Trustee, Barbados Labour Party 1986–; Chair. Caribbean Tourism Research Cen. 1977–79; Pres. ACP (African, Caribbean and Pacific) Council of Ministers 1979; Pres. Latin American Council of Ministers 1980. *Leisure interest:* fishing. *Address:* 3 Enterprise, Christchurch, Barbados (Home).

ST JOHN OF FAWSLEY, Baron (Life Peer), cr. 1987, of Preston in the County of Northampton; **Norman Antony Francis St John-Stevas,** PC, MA, BCL, PhD, FRSL; British politician, barrister, author and journalist; b. 18 May 1929; s. of the late Stephen Stevas and Kitty St John O'Connor; ed Ratcliffe, Fitzwilliam Coll., Cambridge, Christ Church, Oxford and Yale Univ.; Barrister, Middle Temple 1952; Lecturer, King's Coll., London 1953–56; Tutor in Jurisprudence, Christ Church, Oxford 1953–55, Merton Coll., Oxford 1955–57; Founder mem. Inst. of Higher European Studies, Bolzano 1955; Legal Adviser to Sir Alan Herbert's Cttee on Book Censorship 1954–59; Legal and Political Corresp., The Economist 1959–64; Conservative MP for Chelmsford 1964–87; Sec. Conservative Party Home Affairs Cttee 1969–72; mem. Fulbright Comm. 1961; Parl. Select Cttee Race Relations and Immigration 1970–72; Parl. Under-Sec. for Educ. and Science 1972–73; Minister of State for the Arts 1973–74; mem. Parl. Select Cttee on Race Relations and Immigration 1970–72, on Civil List 1971–83, on Foreign Affairs 1983–87; mem. Shadow Cabinet 1974–79, Shadow Leader of the House of Commons 1978–79, Opposition Spokesman on Educ. 1974–78, Science 1974–78 and the Arts 1974–79; Chancellor of the Duchy of Lancaster 1979–81; Leader of the House of Commons 1979–81; Minister for the Arts 1979–81; Vice-Chair. Cons. Parl. NI Cttee 1972–87; Vice-Chair. Cons. Group for Europe 1972–75; Chair. Royal Fine Art Comm. 1985–99; Master Emmanuel Coll., Cambridge 1991–96, Life Fellow 1996; Vice-Pres. Theatres Advisory Council 1983; Founder mem. Christian-Social Inst. of Culture, Rome 1969; mem. Council RADA 1983–88, Nat. Soc. for Dance 1983–, Nat. Youth Theatre 1983– (Patron 1984–), RCA 1985–; Trustee Royal Philharmonic Orch. 1985–88, Decorative Arts Soc. 1984–; Hon. Sec. Fed. of Conservative Students 1971–73; Ed. The Dublin (Wiseman Review) 1961; Romanes Lecturer, Oxford 1987; Hon. FRIBA; Hon. DD (Susquehanna, Pa) 1983; Hon. DLitt (Schiller) 1985, (Bristol) 1988; Hon. LLD (Leicester) 1991; Hon. DArts (De Montfort) 1996; Silver Jubilee Medal 1977; Kt Grand Cross, St Lazarus of Jerusalem 1963; Cavaliere Ordine al Merito della Repubblica (Italy) 1965, Commendatore 1978; Grand Bailiff Mil. and Hospitaller Order of St Lazarus of Jerusalem. *Publications:* Obscenity and the Law 1956, Walter Bagehot 1959, Life, Death and the Law 1961, The Right to Life 1963, Law and Morals 1964, The Literary Essays of Walter Bagehot 1965, The Historical Essays of Walter Bagehot 1968, The Agonising Choice 1971, The Political Essays of Walter Bagehot 1974, The Economic Works of Walter Bagehot 1978, Pope John Paul, His Travels and Mission 1982, The Two Cities 1984. *Leisure interests:* reading, talking, listening to music, travelling, walking, appearing on TV. *Address:* Emmanuel College, Cambridge, CB2 3AP (Office); 7 Brunswick Place, Regent's Park, London, NW1 4PS; The Old Rectory, Preston Capes, Daventry, Northants., NN11 6TE, England.

SAINT LAURENT, Yves (Henri Donat); French couturier; b. 1 Aug. 1936, Oran, Algeria; s. of Charles Mathieu Saint Laurent and Lucienne-Andrée Wilbaux; ed Lycée d'Oran; f. his couture house 1961; opened first Rive Gauche ready-to-wear boutique 1966; has also designed costumes for theatre, ballet and cinema; announced retirement Jan. 2002; Neiman-Marcus Award for fashions 1958, Oscar, Harper's Bazaar 1966, Int. Award of Council of Fashion Designers of America 1982, Best Fashion Designer Oscar 1985, Commdr., Légion d'honneur 2002, Council of Fashion Designers of America Award 1999, Lifetime Achievement Award 1999, Rosa d'Oro, Palmero 2001. *Exhibitions include:* Metropolitan Museum of Art, New York 1983, Beijing Museum of Fine Arts 1985, Musée des Arts de la Mode, Paris 1986, House of Painters of USSR 1986, Hermitage Museum Leningrad (now St Petersburg) 1987, Art Gallery of NSW Sydney 1987, Sezon Museum, Tokyo 1990, Espace Mode Méditerrannée, Marseille 1993. *Publications:* La Vilaine Lulu 1967. *Address:* 5 avenue Marceau, 75116 Paris, France.

SAITO, Gunzi, PhD; Japanese professor of chemistry; b. 10 March 1945, Otaru, Hokkaido; s. of Nenosuke Saito and Toyo Saito; m. Atsuko Nishikawa

1971; three s.; ed Otaru Choryo High School, Hokkaido Univ.; Postdoctoral Fellow, Emory Univ., Atlanta, Ga, USA 1973–74, Guelph Univ., Ont., Canada 1975–76; Welch Fellow Univ. of Tex., Dallas, USA 1977–78; Research Assoc., Inst. for Molecular Science, Okazaki 1979–84; Assoc. Prof., Inst. for Solid State Physics, Tokyo Univ. 1984–89; Prof., Dept of Chem., Faculty of Science, Kyoto Univ. 1989–; mem. Science Council, Ministry of Educ., Sport and Culture 1996–; Inoue Award 1988, Nishina Award 1988, Japan Surface Science Award 1991. *Publications:* The Physics and Chemistry of Organic Superconductors (Co-Ed.) 1990; more than 500 scientific articles on organic superconductors, organic metals and other organic functional materials. *Address:* 201 Kyodaitakatsukishukusha, 12-7 Hacchonawate-cho, Takatsuki City, Osaka, Japan (Home); Chemistry Division, Graduate School of Science, Kyoto University, Sakyo-ku, Kitashirakawa, Kyoto 606-8501, Japan. *Telephone:* (72) 683-8704 (Home); (75) 753-4035. *Fax:* (72) 683-8704 (Home); (75) 753-4000. *E-mail:* saito@kuchem.kyoto-u.ac.jp (Office). *Website:* www.kyoto-u.ac.jp (Office).

SAITO, Nobufusa, DSc; Japanese chemist; b. 28 Sept. 1916, Tokyo; m. Haruko Umeda 1944; one s. two d.; ed Tokyo Imperial Univ.; fmr Asst Prof., Kyushu and Seoul Univs., Prof. of Inorganic Chem., Tokyo Univ. 1956–65; Chief Researcher, Inst. of Physical and Chemical Research 1959–76; fmr Consultant to IAEA, Dir of Isotopes Div. 1963–65; Prof. Inorganic and Nuclear Chem., Tokyo Univ. 1965–77, Dir Radioisotope Centre 1970–77; Prof. Inorganic and Analytical Chem. Toho Univ. 1978–87, Dean, Faculty of Science 1979–82; Pres. Japan Chemical Analysis Centre 1990–96; Dir Japan Radioisotopes Asscn 1967–; Tech. Adviser, Japan Atomic Energy Research Inst. 1966–2000; mem. Chemical Soc. of Japan (Vice-Pres. 1976–78, Pres. 1981–82, Hon. mem. 1987–), ACS, Atomic Energy Soc. of Japan, Japan Soc. for Analytical Chem., Pres. 1979–80, Hon. mem. 1980–, Japan Soc. of Nuclear and Radiochemical Sciences (Hon. mem. 2000–); Royal Decoration of Second Order of Sacred Treasure 1987; Chem. Soc. of Japan Award 1974; Nat. Purple Ribbon Medal for Chemistry 1979. *Publication:* Analytical Chemistry (jtly) 2001. *Leisure interests:* music, travel. *Address:* 5-12-9, Koshigoe, Kamakura 248-0033, Japan. *Telephone:* (467) 31-3178. *Fax:* (467) 31-3178 (Home).

SAITO, Toshitsugu, BA, MBA; Japanese politician; m.; two c.; ed Sophia Univ. and Univ. of Washington; Pres. Japan Jr Chamber 1984; mem. House of Reps. for Shizuoka Prefecture, 5th Electoral Dist 1986–; Dir Youth Div., Party Org. HQ, Liberal Democratic Party 1991, Dir Communications Div., Policy Research Council 1995, Dir-Gen. Information Research Bureau 1996, Deputy Chair. Diet Affairs Cttee 1996, Acting Chair. Public Relations HQ 1999, Dir-Gen. Int. Bureau 2001–; Parl. Vice-Minister, Ministry of Posts and Telecommunications 1992; Chair. Standing Cttee on Commerce and Industry, House of Reps 1997, Standing Cttee on Local Admin 1999; Minister of State and Dir-Gen. of Defense Agency 2000–. *Address:* c/o Liberal Democratic Party (Jiyu-Minshuto), 1-11-23, Nagata-cho, Chiyoda-ku, Tokyo 100-8910, Japan (Office). *Telephone:* (3) 3581-6211 (Office). *E-mail:* koho@ldp.jimin.or.jp (Office). *Website:* www.jimin.jp (Office).

SAITOTI, George, PhD; Kenyan politician; ed Univ. of Warwick, UK; fmr Prof. of Math. and Chair. Dept of Math., Univ. of Nairobi; mem. E African Legis. Ass. 1974–77; Dir and Exec. Chair. Kenya Commercial Bank 1977–82; nominated MP 1983; Minister of Finance and Planning 1983–85, of Finance 1986–93, of Planning and Nat. Devt 1993–98; Vice-Pres. of Kenya 1989–97, 1999–2002, also Minister of Home Affairs 2001–02; Minister of Educ. 2003–; Chair. Annual Meetings Bd of Govs, IMF and World Bank Group 1990. *Address:* Ministry of Education, Jogoo House "B", Harambee Avenue, PO Box 30040, Nairobi, Kenya. *Telephone:* (20) 334411. *Website:* www.education.go.ke.

SAITOV, Oleg; Russian boxer; two-time Olympic welterweight champion; named Best Boxer of Sydney Olympic Games 2000. *Address:* c/o Russian Olympic Committee, Luzhnetskaya Nab. 8, 119992 Moscow, Russia (Office).

SAKAGUCHI, Chikara; Japanese politician; mem. House of Reps.; fmr Dir Finance Cttee; Chair. Komeito Policy Bd; Minister of Labour 1993–94, of Health, Labour and Welfare 2000–. *Address:* Ministry of Health, Labour and Welfare, 1-2-2 Kasumigaseki, Chiyoda-ku, Tokyo 100-8916, Japan (Office). *Telephone:* (3) 5253-1111 (Office); (3) 3501-2532. *E-mail:* www-admin@mhlw.go.jp (Office). *Website:* www.mhlw.go.jp.

SAKAIYA, Taichi (pseudonym of Kotaro Ikeguchi); Japanese politician, author and fmr civil servant; b. 1935; fmr civil servant at Ministry of Int. Trade and Industry; became full-time writer 1978; Dir-Gen. Econ. Planning Agency 1998–2000. *Publication:* Yudan 1975. *Address:* c/o Economic Planning Agency, 3-1-1, Kasumigaseki, Chiyoda-ku, Tokyo 100, Japan.

SAKAKI, Hiroyuki, MS, PhD; Japanese university professor; b. 6 Oct. 1944, Aichi; s. of Yone-ichiro Sakaki and Fumiko Sakaki; m. Mutsuko Sakaki 1973; one s. four d.; ed Univ. of Tokyo; Assoc. Prof. Inst. of Industrial Science, Univ. of Tokyo 1973; Visiting Scientist, IBM T.J. Watson Research Center (group of Dr. Leo Esaki) 1976–77; Prof. Inst. of Industrial Science, Univ. of Tokyo 1987–; Prof. Research Center for Advanced Science and Tech. Univ. of Tokyo 1988–; Dir for Quantum Wave Project (Japan's governmental project for Exploratory Research for Advanced Tech. (ERATO)) 1988–93; Dir for Japan-U.S. Jt Research Project on Quantum Transition 1994–98; IBM Science Prize 1989; Hattori-Hokoikai Prize 1990; Japan Applied Physics Soc. Prize 1983, 1990, Shimazu Science Prize. *Leisure interests:* listening to classical music, museum stroll for paintings. *Address:* Research Center for Advanced Science

and Technology, University of Tokyo, 4-6-1 Komaba, Tokyo 153 (Office); Institute of Industrial Science, University of Tokyo, 7-22-1 Roppongi, Tokyo 106 (Office); 1–41–5 Kagahara, Tsuzukiku, Yokohama 224, Japan (Home). *Telephone:* (3) 3401-7429 (Office); (3) 3481-4464 (Office); (45) 943-1539 (Home).

SAKAKIBARA, Eisuke, PhD; Japanese politician; ed Univs. of Tokyo and Michigan; fmrly lecturer Harvard Univ. and in Japan; with Ministry of Finance; Vice-Minister for Int. Affairs 1997–99; sentenced to a suspended two-year prison term for accepting bribes. *Publication:* Beyond Capitalism 1990. *Address:* c/o Ministry of Finance, 3-1-1, Kasumigaseki, Chiyoda-ku, Tokyo 100, Japan.

SAKAMOTO, Ryuichi; Japanese composer; b. 1952, Tokyo; m. Akiko Yano 1979; ed Shinjuku High School, Composition Dept, Tokyo Fine Arts Univ.; began composing at age of ten; mem. group Yellow Magic Orchestra 1978–83; solo albums include Thousand Knives 1978, Musical Encyclopaedia 1984; composed soundtrack for and starred in film Merry Christmas Mr Lawrence 1982, soundtrack for Wuthering Heights 1992.

SAKER, Ahmad, DEcon; Syrian diplomatist; b. 17 May 1938; s. of the late Mahmoud Saker and Hasina Saker; m. Layla Hassan; three s. one d.; ed Damascus Univ., Government Univ. of Moscow; postings in Czechoslovakia, Iran, India, Turkey, USSR 1966–75; Minister Plenipotentiary, Ministry of Foreign Affairs, Damascus; Lecturer in Political Economy, Damascus Higher Planning Inst. 1976–79, Perm. Mission to UN, Geneva 1980–85; Dir Americas Div., Ministry of Foreign Affairs 1985–88; Amb. Plenipotentiary and Extraordinary to Poland 1988–93; Dir Africa Dept, then Asia Dept, Ministry of Foreign Affairs 1993–95, Asia, Australia Dept 1995–. *Publications:* numerous articles on econ. and political affairs and human rights. *Leisure interests:* reading, sports (especially swimming), painting. *Address:* Adawi Inshaat Building 101, Apt. 10, Damascus, Syria. *Telephone:* 4442070; 4455848.

SAKMANN, Bert, BA, MD; German physician; b. 12 June 1942, Stuttgart; s. of Berthold Sakmann and Annemarie Schaeffer Sakmann; m. Dr Christiane Wulfert 1970; two s. one d.; ed Univ. of Tübingen, Univ. of Munich, Univ. Hosp., Munich, Univ. of Göttingen; Research Asst Max-Planck-Institut für Psychiatrie, Munich 1969–70; British Council Fellow Dept of Biophysics, Univ. Coll., London 1971–73; Research Asst Max-Planck-Institut für biophysikalische Chemie, Univ. of Göttingen 1974–79, Research Assoc. Membrane Biology Group 1979–82, Head Membrane Physiology Unit 1983–85, Dir 1985–87, Prof. Dept of Cell Physiology 1987–89; Dir Dept of Cell Physiology Max-Planck-Institut für medizinische Forschung, Heidelberg 1989–; Prof. of Physiology, Univ. of Heidelberg 1990–; Foreign mem. NAS 1993, Royal Soc., UK 1994; Hon. DSc (London) 1999; shared Nobel Prize for Medicine or Physiology 1991 for discoveries about single-ion channels in cells; numerous other awards, prizes and guest lectures. *Publications:* The Visual System: Neurophysiology, Biophysics and Their Clinical Applications 1972 (contrib.), Advances in Pharmacology and Therapeutics 1978 (contrib.), Single Channel Recording 1983 (jtly), Membrane Control of Cellular Activity 1986 (contrib.), Calcium and Ion Channel Modulation 1988 (contrib.), Neuromuscular Junction 1989 (contrib.), numerous articles. *Leisure interests:* music, reading, tennis, skiing. *Address:* Max-Planck-Institut für medizinische Forschung, Jahnstrasse 29, 69120 Heidelberg, Germany. *Telephone:* (6221) 486460 (Office). *Fax:* (6221) 486459 (Office).

SAKO, Soumana, BA, MPA; Malian politician, civil servant and international civil servant; b. 23 Dec. 1950, Nyamina; s. of Sayan Sako and Djeneba Traore; m. Cisse Toure; two s. two d.; ed Univ. of Pittsburgh, Pa, USA, Ecole Nationale d'Admin du Mali; Staff mem. Gen. Inspectorate, Office of the Pres. of Repub. of Mali 1974; Admin. and Finance Man., Operation Puits Project 1975–76; Staff mem. Ministry of Industrial Devt and Tourism 1981; Adviser Ministry of Foreign Affairs and Int. Co-operation 1981–82; Sr Adviser Ministry of Planning and Econ. Man. 1982–84; Dir of Sr Staff, Ministry of State-Owned Enterprises 1985–87; Minister of Finance and Commerce Feb.–Aug. 1987; Deputy Controller-Gen. Office of the Pres. 1988–89; UNDP official serving in Cen. African Repub. 1989–91; Sr Economist for Madagascar and Comoros Islands 1993–97; Prime Minister of Mali 1991–92; Prof. of Devt Econs and Public Finance, Univ. of Mali 1997–2000; int. consultant 1998–; Exec. Sec. African Capacity Bldg Foundation, Harare Jan. 2000–; AFGRAD Distinguished Alumnus 1992; Sennen Andriamirado Prize of Excellence 2000; Commdr Nat. Order of Mali 2000. *Publication:* Determinants of Public Policy—A Comparative Analysis of Public Expenditure Patterns in African States. *Leisure interests:* soccer, chess, gardening. *Address:* POB 1502, Harare (Office); The African Capacity Building Foundation, Intermarket Life Towers, 7th Floor, Corner Jason Moyo/Sam Nujoma Street, Harare, Zimbabwe; Villa f4 bis 48, Sema Gexco Bamako, Mali (Home); BP 433, Bamako, Mali. *Telephone:* (4) 702931 (Harare) (Office); 236196 (Bamako) (Home). *Fax:* 229748 (Bamako); (4) 702915 (Harare) (Office). *E-mail:* s.sako@acbf-pact.org (Office). *Website:* www.acbf-pact.org (Office).

SAKS, Gene; American actor and director; b. 8 Nov. 1921, New York; m. Beatrice Arthur (divorced); two s. one d.; ed Cornell Univ.; began acting career off-Broadway at Provincetown Playhouse and the Cherry LaneTheatre; appeared in Dog Beneath the Skin (Auden), Him (e. e. cummings), The Bourgeois Gentilhomme (Molière); Broadway appearances in Mr Roberts, South Pacific, Middle of the Night, The Tenth Man, A Shot in the Dark, Love and Libel, A Thousand Clowns; début as Dir on Broadway with Enter Laughing 1963; later Dir plays: Nobody Loves an Albatross, Half a Sixpence,

Generation, Mame, Same Time, Next Year, California Suite, I Love My Wife (Tony Award), Brighton Beach (Tony Award), Biloxi Blues 1985 (Tony Award), Broadway Bound 1986, A Month of Sundays 1987, Rumours 1988, Jake's Woman 1992, Lost in Yonkers (original Broadway stage production), Barrymore 1997. *Films directed:* Barefoot in the Park, The Odd Couple, Cactus Flower, Last of the Red Hot Lovers, Brighton Beach Memoirs, Mame, A Fine Romance. *Film appearances:* A Thousand Clowns, Prisoner of Second Avenue, Lovesick, The One and Only, The Goodbye People 1986, Brighton Beach Memoirs, Nobody's Fool 1994, IQ 1994, Deconstructing Harry. *Address:* c/o ICM, 40 West 80th Street, 1, New York, NY 10024, USA.

SALA, Marius, PhD; Romanian linguist; b. 8 Sept. 1932, Vaşcău, Bihor Co.; s. of Sabin Sala and Eleonora Tocoianu; m. Florica Sala 1958; one d.; ed Coll. of Philology, Bucharest Univ.; researcher, Inst. of Linguistics, Bucharest 1955–90, Deputy Dir 1990–94, Dir 1994–; Visiting Prof. Heidelberg 1971, Málaga 1968, 1970, 1973, 1979, Madrid 1978, 1981, 1987, Mexico City 1981, Cologne 1984, Frankfurt 1992, Oviedo 1994, Nancy 1999; Corresp. mem. Royal Acad. Spain 1978, Mexican Inst. of Culture 1981, Romanian Acad. 1993, Full mem. 2001, Acad. Nacional de Letras, Montevideo 1994–, Int. Cttee of Onomastic Studies 1969; mem. Int. Cttee of the Mediterranean Linguistic Atlas 1960; mem. Man. Junta of the Int. Assçn of Hispanists 1974–80; mem. Cttee Soc. of Romance Linguistics 1974–80, 1989–; mem. Perm. Int. Cttee of Linguists 1987–92; Prize of Romanian Acad. 1970; Prize of Mexican Acad. Centennial 1976. *Publications:* Contribuţii la fonetica istorică a limbii române (Contributions to the Historical Phonetics of the Romanian Language) 1970, Estudios sobre el judeo-español de Bucarest 1970, Phonétique et Phonologie du Judéo-Espagnol de Bucarest 1971, Le judéo-espagnol 1976, Contributions à la phonétique historique du roumain 1976, El léxico indígena del español americano, Apreciaciones sobre su vitalidad (co-author) 1977, El español de América, (Vol. 1), Léxico (co-author) 1982, Limbile lumii. Mică enciclopedie (The Languages of the World: A Concise Encyclopaedia) (co-author), 1981, Les langues du monde (Petite Encyclopédie) (co-author) 1984, Etimologia şi Limba Română (Etymology and the Romanian Language) (co-author) 1987, Vocabularul Reprezentativ Al Limbilor Romanice (The Representative Vocabulary of the Romance Languages) (co-author) 1988, El problema de las lenguas en contacto 1988, Enciclopedia Limbilor Romanice (Encyclopaedia of the Romance languages) (co-author) 1989, Unité des langues romanes 1996, Limba română, limbă romanică (Romanian Language, Romance Language) 1997, Limbi în contact (Languages in Contact) 1997, De la latină la română (From Latin to Romanian) 1998, Lenguas en contacto 1998, Introducere în etimologia limbii române (Introduction to the Etymology of Romanian) 1999, May We Introduce the Romanian Language to You? (co-author) 1999, Du latin au roumain 2000, Limbile Europei (The Language of Europe) (jtly.) 2001. *Leisure interests:* philately, cooking. *Address:* Institutul de Lingvistică, Calea 13 Septembrie 13, 79515 Bucharest, B.O. 42-37, Romania. *Telephone:* 4113698 (Office); 4103409 (Office); 7457564 (Home). *Fax:* 4103410 (Office). *E-mail:* inst@lingv.ro.

SALA-I-MARTÍN, Xavier, PhD; Spanish professor of economics; b. 17 June 1963, Barcelona; ed Univ. Autònoma, Barcelona, Harvard Univ.; Assoc. Prof. Yale Univ. 1990–95; fmrly Prof. Univ. Pompeu Fabra, Barcelona, Research Assoc. Nat. Bureau of Econ. Research, Cambridge, Mass.; Prof. of Econs, Columbia Univ. 1996–; consultant IMF 1992–, World Bank 1996–; NSF Award 1998; King Juan Carlos I Prize for Social Sciences 1998. *Publications include:* Apuntes de Crecimiento Económico 1994, Economic Growth 1995, over 40 scientific articles. *Address:* 420 West 118th Street, New York, NY 10027, USA. *Telephone:* (212) 854-1754. *Fax:* (212) 932-0418. *Website:* www .columbia.edu (Office).

SALAD HASAN, Abdulkasim; Somali politician; Minister of Industry, of Trade, of Labour, of Information and of the Interior 1973–1990; Pres. of Somalia Aug. 2000–. *Address:* Office of the President, People's Palace, Mogadishu, Somalia (Office). *Telephone:* (1) 723 (Office).

SALAKHITDINOV, Makhmud, DSc; Uzbekistan mathematician; b. 23 Nov. 1933, Namangan, Uzbek SSR; s. of Salahiddin Shamsuddinov and Zuhra Shamsuddinova; m. Muharram Rasulova 1955; three s. one d.; ed Cen. Asian State Univ., Asst Tashkent State Univ. 1958–59; Scientific Fellow, Chief of Section, Deputy Dir, Dir Inst. of Math. Uzbek SSR Acad. of Sciences 1959–85, Chief, Differential Equation Section 1974–; Vice-Pres. Uzbek SSR Acad. of Sciences 1984–85, Pres. 1988–94, Chair. Dept of Physical and Math. Sciences 1994–; Chief of Chair. (Jt) Tashkent State Univ. 1980–85; Minister of Higher and Secondary Specialized Educ. of Uzbek SSR 1985–88; Uzbekistan People's Deputy 1990–; Ed. papers of Uzbekistan Acad. of Sciences; Honoured Scientist of Uzbek SSR; Badge of Honour, Uzbek State Prize. *Publications:* Mixed-Complex Type Equation 1974, Ordinary Differential Equation 1982; contribs to professional publs. *Leisure interests:* walking, reading fiction. *Address:* 70 Gogol Street, Tashkent, Uzbekistan. *Telephone:* (712) 233-72-81. *Fax:* (712) 233-49-01.

SALAKHOV, Tair Teimur ogly; Azerbaijani/Russian painter; b. 29 Nov. 1928, Baku, Azerbaijan; m. Varvara Salakhova; three d.; ed Azerbaijan Azimzade Higher School of Fine Arts, Moscow State Inst. of Fine Arts; Docent, Prof. Azerbaijan State Inst. of Arts 1963–74; Chair. Exec. Bd Azerbaijan Union of Artists 1972–74; Head of Studio Moscow State Inst. of Fine Arts 1974–92; First Sec. Exec. Bd USSR Union of Artists 1973–91; mem. Exec. Bd USSR Acad. of Fine Arts, Sec. 1986–; author of numerous portraits, landscapes, theatre decorations; Vice-Pres. Russian Acad. of Arts; Corresp. mem. French

Acad. of Fine Arts 1986–, Real Academia San Fernando, Madrid –1998; Hon. Pres. Int. Asscn of Art, Paris; Hon. mem. Austrian Soc. of Fine Arts 1975, Acad. of Fine Arts, Kazakhstan, Acad. of Fine Arts, Kyrgyzstan; Hon. citizen Trenton, NJ, Santa Fe, NM and Billings, Mont.; Order of Istiglal of Azerbaijan 1998, Order of Za Zaslugi pered Otechestvom (3rd class) (Russia) 1998; Prize of Cen. Komsomol Cttee 1959, Akhundov Prize of Azerbaijan SSR 1964, USSR State Prize 1968, State Prize of Azerbaijan 1970 (for picture New Sea), Grekov's Gold Medal 1977, Hero of Socialist Labour 1989, People's Painter of Russia 1996–. *Exhibitions:* many in Europe, Asia, N. and S. America. *Address:* Russian Academy of Fine Arts, Prechistenka str. 21, 119034, Moscow, Russia (Office); 3 Mamedyarov lane, h.1 'Icheri Sheher', Baku, Azerbaijan (Home). *Telephone:* (095) 201-39-71. *Fax:* (095) 201-39-71.

SALAMA, Hussein Samir Abdul-Rahman, PH.D.; Egyptian professor of entomology and educationalist; b. 26 Jan. 1936, Gharbia; m.; two c.; ed Ain Shams Univ., Cairo Univ.; Research Asst, Entomology Research Unit, Nat. Research Centre (NRC) 1956–62, Researcher 1962–67, Assoc. Research Prof. 1967–73, Research Prof. of Entomology NRC 1973, Vice-Pres. NRC, Pres. 1988–92, Research Prof. Emer. 1996–; Pres. Research Council for Basic Sciences, Egyptian Acad. of Scientific Research and Tech., Nat. Cttee for Biological Sciences, Egyptian Inst. for Scientific Culture 1991, Int. Union of Biological Sciences; Vice-Pres. Entomological Soc. of Egypt; mem. Bd Egyptian Acad. of Sciences, African Acad. of Sciences; Post-Doctoral Fellow, Dept of Entomology, Univ. of Alberta 1963–65, Fellow Islamic Acad. of Sciences; State Prize for Biological Sciences 1973, Golden Medal of NRC 1981, Golden Medal of the Entomological Soc. of Egypt 1982, African Acad. of Sciences Prize for Agric. 1991 and numerous other awards. *Address:* National Research Centre, Al-Tahir Street, Dokki, Cairo, Egypt (Office). *Telephone:* (2) 701010 (Office). *Fax:* (2) 700931 (Office).

SALAMÉ, Riad, B.A.(ECON.); Lebanese banker; b. 17 July 1950, Beirut; s. of Toufic Salamé and Renée Salamé; ed Coll. Notre Dame de Jamhour, American Univ. of Beirut; Merrill Lynch, Beirut 1973–76, 1978–85, Paris 1976–78, Sr Vice-Pres. and Financial Counsellor, Paris 1985–93; Gov. Banque du Liban 1993–; Chevalier Légion d'honneur; Best Arab Banker Award, Euromoney 1996. *Address:* Banque du Liban, Hamra, Masraf Loubnan Street, P.O. Box 11-5544, Beirut, Lebanon. *Telephone:* (1) 750000. *Fax:* (1) 747600. *E-mail:* bdlg0@bdl.gov.lb (Office). *Website:* www.bdl.gov.lb (Office).

SALAMI, Alawi Salih as-, BA; Yemeni politician; b. 21 Dec. 1945, Radaa; ed Univ. of Baghdad, Iraq; Gen. Man. Financial and Admin. Affairs, Ministry of Educ. 1970–73; Gen. Man. Budget Office 1973–75; Deputy, Budget Div. 1975–86, with rank of Vice-Minister 1986; Minister of Finance 1986–94; Gov. Yemen Cen. Bank 1994–97; currently Deputy Prime Minister and Minister of Finance. *Address:* Ministry of Finance, San'a, Yemen (Office).

SALÁNKI, János, MD; Hungarian physician and biologist; b. 11 May 1929, Debrecen; m. Katalin Rózsa; two d.; ed Medical Univ. Debrecen., Lomonosov Univ. Moscow 1959; Dir Balaton Limnological Research Inst., Hungarian Acad. of Sciences, Tihany 1962–90, Research Prof. 1991–; Research Prof. Univ. of Veszprém 1998–; Titular Prof. Eötvös Loránd Univ. Budapest; Pres. Int. Union of Biological Sciences (IUBS) 1988–91, Hungarian National IUBS Cttee, Int. Soc. for Invertebrate Neurobiology (ISIN) 1989–95, Interdisciplinary Cttee for Bioindicators (IUBS); Chief Ed. Acta Biologica Hungarica; mem. Ed. Bd, Acta Physiologica Hungarica, Journal of Aquatic Ecosystem Stress and Recovery, Lakes and Reservoirs: Research and Man.; mem. Int. Lake Environment Cttee 1987–95; corresp. mem. Hungarian Acad. of Sciences 1976, mem. 1987–; Labour Order of Merit, Order of Merit for Hungary. *Publications:* Ed. 12 Vols on Neurobiology, 13 Vols on Environmental Biology and Hydrobiology, 261 papers. *Address:* P.O.B. 35, Balaton Limnological Research Institute of the Hungarian Academy of Sciences, 8237 Tihany (Home); 8237 Tihany, Váralja utca 18, Hungary. *Telephone:* (87) 448-244 (Office). *Fax:* (87) 448-006 (Office). *E-mail:* salanki@tres.blki.hu (Office).

SALAS COLLANTES, Javier; Spanish business executive; b. 1949; ed Faculty of Econs Univ. of Madrid; joined Instituto Nacional de Industria (INI) 1973, Chair. Oct. 1990–; Chair. Iberia 1993–95. *Leisure interest:* hill-trekking.

SALAYEV, Eldar Unis ogly, D.PHYS-MATH.SC.; Azerbaijani scientist and politician; b. 31 Dec. 1933, Nakhichevan City; s. of Yunis Sala oglu Salayev and Telly Tahir kizi Salayeva; m. Dilara Ashraf Guseynova; two s.; ed Azerbaijan Univ.; mem. CPSU 1963–91; Jr Researcher, Deputy Dir Inst. of Physics, Azerbaijan Acad. of Sciences 1956–73, Dir 1973–83; Corresp. mem. Acad. of Sciences of Azerbaijan 1980, mem. 1983, Pres. 1983–97; mem. Council on co-ordination of scientific activities of Acads of Sciences, Presidium of USSR Acad. of Sciences 1985–91; Chair. Repub. Council, Presidium of Acad. of Sciences of Azerbaijan; Ed.-in-Chief Doklady Akademii Nauk Azerbaijana; Deputy to USSR Supreme Soviet 1985–89; USSR People's Deputy 1989–91; Merited Worker of Arts of Azerbaijan. *Publications:* Dynamics and Statistics, Non-linear Effects on Layer Crystals, Type of Selenite Gallium 1993; more than 200 scientific publns in numerous journals. *Leisure interest:* sport. *Address:* Azerbaijan Academy of Sciences, İstiglaliyat str. 10, 370001 Baku, Azerbaijan. *Telephone:* (12) 923529.

SALCEDO-BASTARDO, José Luis; Venezuelan diplomatist and writer; b. 15 March 1926, Carúpano, Sucre; s. of Joaquín Salcedo-Arocha and Catalina (née Bastardo) Salcedo-Arocha; m. María Cecilia Avila Prieto 1968; four s.; ed Universidad Central de Venezuela, Univ. de Paris and London School of Econs; Teacher of Social Sciences 1945; Chief Ed. Revista Nacional de Cultura

1948–50; Asst Lecturer, Universidad Central de Venezuela 1949; Founder Rector, Univ. of Santa María, Caracas 1953; Senator for State of Sucre, mem. Senate Foreign Relations Cttee 1958; Amb. to Ecuador 1959–61, to Brazil 1961–63; Prof. of Sociology, Univ. Central de Venezuela 1964; Pres. Nat. Inst. of Culture and Fine Arts 1965–67; Vice-Pres., Supreme Electoral Council 1970–74; Amb. to France 1974–76, to UK 1984–87, to GDR 1987–90; Sec.-Gen. to Presidency 1976–77; Minister of State for Science, Tech. and Culture 1977–79; mem. Exec. Cttee Centre for Higher Int. Studies, Andean Univ. of Bolivia 1992–, Centre for Diplomatic and Strategic Studies, Paris 1992–, Comm. V (Educ., Culture, Science and Tech.) of Andean Parl. 1993–; Pres. Nat. Comm. for Bicentenary of Antonio José de Sucre 1993; several hon. doctorates. *Publications:* Por el Mundo Sociológico de Cecilio Acosta 1945, En Fuga hacia la Gloria 1947, Visión y Revisión de Bolívar 1957, Biografía de Don Egidio Montesinos 1957, Tesis para la Unión 1963, Bases de una Acción Cultural 1965, Historia Fundamental de Venezuela 1970, La Conciencia del Presente 1971, Carabobo: Nacionalidad e Historia 1972, Bolívar: Un Continente y un Destino 1972, El Primer Deber 1973, Despolitizar la Historia: una tarea para el desarrollo 1973, De la Historia y los Deberes 1975, Bolívar y San Martín 1975, Un Hombre Diáfano 1976, Crucible of Americanism (Miranda's London House) 1979, Concordancias Ideológicos y Literarias en Bolívar 1981, Andrés Bello Americano 1982, Reiteración Bolivariana 1983, Andrés Eloy Blanco para jóvenes 1983, Simón Bolívar, L'unico scopo e la libertá 1983, Simón Bolívar: La Esperanza del Universo 1983, Bolívar, el Nacer Constante 1986, Bolívar: las ideas y los pueblos 1994, El Hombre y los hombres 1994, Razón y Empeño de Unidad: Bolívar por América Latina 1999. *Leisure interest:* travelling abroad. *Address:* Apartado Postal 2777, Caracas, Venezuela (Home). *Telephone:* (2) 979-5575 (Home). *Fax:* (2) 979-5575 (Home). *E-mail:* fsalcedo@c-con.net.re (Office).

SALEH, Gen. Ali Abdullah; Yemeni politician and army officer; b. 1942, Beit al-Ahmer, Sanhan District; m.; several c.; entered mil. service 1958; participated in 1974 coup; Mil. Gov., Taiz Province until June 1978; mem. Provisional Presidential Council, Deputy C-in-C of Armed Forces June–July 1978; Pres. of Yemen Arab Repub. 1978–90, 1990–94, of Presidential Council of Repub. of Yemen 1990–94, of Repub. of Yemen 1994–; C-in-C of Armed Forces 1978–90; Sec.-Gen. People's Gen. Congress 1982; rank of Marshal 1997; Hon. M.Mil.Sc.; Nat. Republican Award. *Address:* Office of the President, San'a, Republic of Yemen.

SALEH, Ali Bin Saleh al-, BCom; Bahraini politician and official; b. 28 Dec. 1942; s. of Saleh Al Saleh; m. Afaf Radhi Salman Almousawi 1970; one s. two d.; ed Ain Shams Univ., Cairo; Dir of several public cos 1975–95; Minister of Commerce 1995–; Chair. Bahrain Promotions and Marketing Bd 1995–2000, Bahrain Convention and Exhbn Bureau, Bahrain Stock Exchange; Deputy Chair. Bahrain Chamber of Commerce and Industry 1975–93, Shura (Consultative Council) 1993–95; mem. Bd of Trustees Univ. of Bahrain 1985–95, Bahrain Centre for Studies and Research, Econ. Devt Bd. *Leisure interests:* reading, music, travel. *Address:* Ministry of Commerce, PO Box 5479, Diplomatic Area, Manama, Bahrain (Office). *Telephone:* 531531 (Office); 532121 (Office). *Fax:* 530469 (Office).

SALEH, Jaime Marcelino; Netherlands Antilles government official and judge; b. 20 April 1941, Bonaire; m. Marguerite Marie Halabi; two s. two d.; ed State Univ. of Utrecht; Deputy Public Prosecutor, Netherlands 1967–68, Curaçao 1968–74; attorney-at-law, Curaçao 1971–74; Deputy mem. High Court of the Netherlands Antilles 1974–76; Justice 1976–79; Chief Justice High Court of Justice of the Netherlands Antilles and Aruba 1979–90, Vice-Pres. Dutch Navy Mil. Court for the Netherlands Antilles 1978–79, Pres. Dutch Navy Mil. Court for the Netherlands Antilles and Aruba 1979–90; Gov.-Gen. of Netherlands Antilles 1990–2002; Order of Merit of Corps Consulaire 1989; Order of Libertador en el grado de Gran Cordón, Venezuela 1996; Order of Knighthood of the Dutch Lion; Royal Medal 1980, Almirate Luis Brion Naval Medal 1994. *Publications:* various works on law and politics, with particular reference to the Netherlands Antilles. *Address:* Franse Bloemweg 22, Willemstad, Curaçao, Netherlands Antilles (Home).

SALEK, Lt-Col Mustapha Ould; Mauritanian army officer and politician; ed Saumur Mil. Acad., France; Chief of Staff of Armed Forces 1968–69, March 1978; fmr Dir Société Nat. d'Import/Export (SONIMEX); Commdr Third Mil. Region 1977; Head of State and Chair. Mil. Cttee for Nat. Recovery (later for Nat. Salvation) 1978–79; sentenced to 10 years' imprisonment for plotting against Pres. Haidalla March 1982.

SALEM, Elie Adib, PhD; Lebanese politician and academic; b. 5 March 1930, Bterram Kurah; s. of Adib Salem and Lamia (née Malik) Salem; m. Phyllis Sell; two s. two d.; ed American Univ. of Beirut, Univ. of Cincinnati, USA, Johns Hopkins Univ., USA; Instructor in Public Admin., American Univ. of Beirut 1954–56, Assoc. Prof. of Political Studies and Public Admin. 1962–68, Asst Dean of Arts and Sciences 1966–68, Chair. Middle East Area Program and Prof. of Political Studies and Public Admin. 1969–74, Chair. Dept of Political Studies and Public Admin. 1972–74, Dean of Arts and Sciences 1974–82; Asst Prof. of Middle East Politics, School of Advanced Int. Studies, Johns Hopkins Univ. 1956–62; Visiting Prof. Dept of Govt and Research Scholar Int. Devt Research Center, Ind. Univ. 1968–69; Deputy Prime Minister and Minister of Foreign Affairs 1982–84; Adviser to Pres. on Foreign Affairs 1984–88; Founder and Pres. Lebanese Centre of Policy Studies 1988–; Pres. Univ. of Balamand 1993–. *Publications include:* The Arab Public Administrative Conference 1954, Political Theory and Institutions of the Khawarij 1956, Modernization without Revolution: Lebanon's Experience 1973, "Rusum Dar al-Khilafah al Abbasiyah" manuscript by Hlal al Sab' (translator) 1977, Violence and Diplomacy in Lebanon 1982–88 1994; articles in professional journals. *Leisure interests:* tennis, swimming, table tennis. *Address:* Université de Balamand, P.O. Box 100, Tripoli (Office); Sibnai, Baabda, Villa Salem, Beirut, Lebanon. *Telephone:* (3) 335683 (Office); (1) 468887. *Fax:* (6) 400742 (Office). *E-mail:* pr@balamand.edu.lb (Office). *Website:* www.balamand.edu.lb (Office).

SALGADO, Sebastião Ribeiro, Jr., PhD; Brazilian photographer; b. 8 Feb. 1944, Aimorés, Minas Gerais; m. Lélia Deluiz Wanick 1967; two s.; ed São Paulo Univ., Vanderbilt Univ., USA, Univ. of Paris; with Brazilian Ministry of Finance 1968–69; with Investment Dept, Int. Coffee Org., London 1971–73; photo-reporter, working in Europe, Africa (particularly covering drought in Sahel) and Latin America 1973–, with Sygma News Agency of Paris 1974, with Gamma Agency 1975–79, mem. Magnum Photos 1979–; numerous solo exhbns Europe, Brazil, Israel, China, Canada, Cuba, including L'Afrique des Colères 1977–78, Sahel – L'Homme en Détresse 1986, Other Americas 1986–90; many prizes, including Kodak/City of Paris Award for book Autres Amériques 1984, Oskar Barnack Prize, World Press Photos, the Netherlands, for work in Sahel 1985, Int. Center of Photography Photojournalist of the Year Award, New York 1986, 1988, Photographer of the Year Award, American Soc. of Magazine Photographers 1987, Olivier Rebbot Award, Overseas Press Club, New York 1987, King of Spain Award 1988, Erich Salomon Award, Germany 1988, Erna and Victor Hasselblad Award, Sweden 1989, Grand Prix Nationaux 1995. *Publications:* several books of photographs and exhbn catalogues, including Autres Amériques 1986, Sahel: L'Homme en Détresse 1986, Les Cheminots 1988, Sahel: El Fin del Camino 1988, Workers: An Archaeology of the Industrial Age 1993.

SALIJ, Jacek; Polish Roman Catholic ecclesiastic and professor of theology; b. 19 Aug. 1942, Budy; ed Acad. of Catholic Theology, Warsaw; ordained priest 1966; Asst Acad. of Catholic Theology (now Cardinal Stefan Wyszyński Univ.), Warsaw 1970–71, Asst Prof. 1971–90, Extraordinary Prof. 1990–99, Ordinary Prof. 2000–; Co-Founder Gaudium Vitae Movt 1979–; mem. Council of Educ. attached to the Pres. of Poland 1992–95, Main Council of Higher Educ. 1993–96; consultant to Educ. of Faith Comm. of Episcopate of Poland 1997–; mem. Polish Soc. of Philosophy 1982–, PEN Club 1989–. *Publications:* Modlitwa za świętych w liturgii rzymskiej 1974, Królestwo Boże w was jest 1980, Legendy dominikańskie (composition and translation) 1982, Rozpacz pokonana 1983, Rozmowy ze św. Augustynem 1985, Pytania nieobojętne 1986, Dekalog 1989, Wiara na co dzień 1994, Nadzieja poddawana próbom 1995, Nasze czasy są OK. 1997, Praca nad wiarą 1999. *Leisure interest:* cycling. *Address:* ul. Freta 10, 00-227 Warsaw, Poland (Office).

SALIM, Salim Ahmed; Tanzanian diplomatist; b. 23 Jan. 1942, Pemba Island, Zanzibar; m. Amne Salim; three c.; ed Lumumba Coll., Zanzibar, Univ. of Delhi and Columbia Univ., New York; Publicity Sec. of UMMA Party and Chief Ed. of its official organ Sauti ya UMMA 1963; Exec. Sec. United Front of Opposition Parties and Chief Ed. of its newspaper; Sec. Gen. All-Zanzibar Journalists Union 1963; Amb. to UAR 1964–65; High Commr to India 1965–68; Dir African and Middle East Affairs Div., Ministry of Foreign Affairs 1968–69; Amb. to People's Repub. of China and Democratic People's Repub. of Korea June–Dec. 1969; Perm. Rep. to UN 1970–80 (Pres. of Gen. Ass. 1979), also High Commr to Jamaica, accred to Guyana, Trinidad and Tobago, Barbados and Amb. to Cuba 1971–80; Chair. UN Special Cttee on Decolonization 1972–80; Minister of Foreign Affairs 1980–84, Prime Minister of Tanzania 1984–85, Deputy Prime Minister, Minister of Defence and Nat. Service 1986–89; Sec.-Gen. OAU 1989–2001; a fmr Vice-Pres. of Tanzania; Chair. UN Security Council Cttee on Sanctions against Rhodesia Jan.–Dec. 1975; fmr del. of Tanzania at UN Gen. Ass. and other int. confs; mem. Bd of Dirs South Centre 2002–(05); currently Pres. Julius K. Nyerere Foundation; Hon. LLD (Univ. of Philippines); Hon. DH (Univ. of Maiduguri, Nigeria) 1983; Hon. DCL (Univ. of Mauritius) 1991; Hon. Dr of Arts (Univ. of Khartoum, Sudan) 1995; Hon. PhD (Univ. of Bologna, Italy) 1996. *Address:* South Centre, 17–19 chemin du Champ d'Anier, 1209 Petit Saconnex, Geneva, Switzerland. *Telephone:* (22) 7918050. *Fax:* (22) 7988531. *E-mail:* south@southcentre.org. *Website:* www.southcentre.org.

SALINAS DE GORTARI, Carlos, PhD; Mexican politician; b. 1948, Mexico City; ed Nat. Univ. of Mexico and Harvard Univ.; Asst Prof. of Statistics, Nat. Univ. of Mexico 1970; Research Asst Harvard Univ. 1974; taught Public Finance and Fiscal Policy in Mexico 1976, 1978; Asst Dir of Public Finance, Ministry of Finance 1971–74, Head of Econ. Studies 1974–76, Asst Dir of Financial Planning 1978, Dir-Gen. 1978–79; Dir-Gen. of Econ. and Social Policy, Ministry of Programming and Budget 1979–81; Dir-Gen. Inst. of Political, Social and Econ. Studies 1981–82; Minister of Planning and Fed. Budget 1982–87; named as Pres. Cand. by Partido Revolucionario Institucional (PRI) 1987; Pres. of Mexico 1988–94. *Publications:* numerous articles and essays. *Address:* c/o Office of the President, Los Pinos, Puerta 1, Col San Miguel, Chapultepec, 11850 México, DF, Mexico.

SALINGER, J. D. (Jerome David); American author; b. 1 Jan. 1919, New York; s. of Sol Salinger and Miriam (née Jillich) Salinger; m. Claire Douglas 1953 (divorced 1976); one s. one d.; ed Manhattan public schools and a military coll.; travelled in Europe 1937–38; army service with 4th Infantry Div. (Staff Sergeant) 1942–46; mem. Légion d'honneur. *Publications include:* The Catcher in the Rye 1951, Franny and Zooey 1961, Raise High the Roof Beam,

Carpenters and Seymour—An Introduction 1963 (novels), For Esme with Love and Squalor 1953 (stories); numerous stories, mostly in the New Yorker 1948–, Hapworth 16, 1924 1997. *Address:* c/o Harold Ober Associates Inc., 425 Madison Avenue, New York, NY 10017, USA.

SALINGER, Pierre Emil George, BS; American journalist and politician; b. 14 June 1925, San Francisco; s. of the late Herbert Edgar Salinger and of Jehanne Bietry Carlson; m. 1st Renee Laboure 1947; two s. (one deceased) one d. (deceased); m. 2nd Nancy Brook Joy 1957; m. 3rd Nicole Helene Gillmann 1965 (divorced 1988); one s.; m. 4th Nicole Christine Beauvillain 1989; ed Univ. of San Francisco; San Francisco Chronicle 1942–55; USN Second World War; Press Officer, Calif., Stevenson for Pres. Campaign 1952, Richard Graves for Gov. (Calif.) 1954; West Coast Ed., Contributing Ed. Collier's Magazine 1955–56; Investigator, Senate Labor Rackets Cttee 1957–59; Press Sec. to Senator John F. Kennedy 1959–61, to Pres. John F. Kennedy 1961–63, to Pres. Lyndon Johnson 1963–64; US Senator from Calif. 1964–65; Dir Nat. Gen. Productions 1965; Vice-Pres. Nat. Gen. Corpn 1965, Continental Airlines 1965–68; Chair. Great America Man. and Research Co. Int. (Gramco) 1968–, Deputy Chair. Gramco (UK) Ltd 1970–71; Sr Vice-Pres. Amprop Inc. 1969; Roving Ed. L'Express, Paris 1973–78; roving reporter in Europe for ABC (TV) 1977–87 (Adviser on Foreign Affairs 1987–93); Bureau Chief, ABC News, Paris 1977–87; Chief Foreign Corresp. ABC News 1983–93; Sr Ed. Europe ABC News 1988–93, Int. Consultant to ABC News 1993–; Vice-Chair. Burson-Marsteller 1993–96; Dir Global Teleworks Corpn 1993–; ind. public relations consultant 1996–; lecturer at over 60 US univs and colls 1965–69; Trustee, Robert F. Kennedy Memorial Foundation, American Coll. in Paris (now American Univ. in Paris) 1973–88; Officier Légion d'honneur 1978. *Publications:* A Tribute to John F. Kennedy 1964, With Kennedy 1966, A Tribute to Robert F. Kennedy 1968, On Instructions of my Government (novel) 1971, Je suis un américain 1975, La France et le nouveau monde 1976, Venezuelan Notebooks 1978, America Held Hostage: The Secret Negotiations 1981, The Dossier (novel, with Leonard Gross) 1984, Above Paris (with Robert Cameron) 1984, Mortal Games (novel, with Leonard Gross) 1988, La Guerre du Golfe—Le Dossier Secret (with Eric Laurent) 1990, P.S. A Memoir 1995, John F. Kennedy, Commander in Chief 1997. *Address:* 3904 Hillandale Court, NW, Washington, DC 20007, USA. *Telephone:* (202) 337-6744. *Fax:* (202) 337-6746.

SALISBURY, David Murray, MA; British financial executive; b. 18 Feb. 1952; s. of Norman Salisbury and Isobel Sutherland Murray; m. Lynneth Mary Jones 1977; two d.; ed Harrow School, Trinity Coll., Oxford; joined J. Henry Schroder Wagg & Co. Ltd 1974, Chief Exec. Schroder Capital Man. Int. Inc. 1986–2001, Jt Chief Exec. Schroder Investment Man. Ltd 1995–97, Chair. 1997–2001; Dir Dimensional Fund Advisers Inc. 1991–96; Gov. Harrow School 1996–99. *Leisure interests:* tennis, skiing. *Address:* The Dutch House, West Green, Wintney, Hants. R627 8JN, England.

SALJE, Ekhard Karl Hermann, MA, PhD, FRS, FGS, FInstP; German professor of mineralogy and petrology; b. 26 Oct. 1946, Hanover; s. of Gerhard Salje and Hildegard Salje (née Drechsler); m. Elisabeth Démaret; one s. four d.; ed Univ. of Hanover, Cambridge Univ.; Prof. of Crystallography, Univ. of Hanover 1983–86; Lecturer in Mineral Physics, Cambridge Univ. 1986–92, Prof. 1992–94, Prof. of Mineralogy and Petrology 1994–, Head Dept of Earth Sciences 1998–; Pres. Clare Hall, Cambridge 2002–; Fellow Leopoldina (Germany); Werner Medal 1997, Schlumberger Medal 1997, Humboldt Research Prize 1999. *Publications:* over 300 scientific publs including book on phase transitions in ferroelastic and co-elastic crystals. *Leisure interests:* music, painting. *Address:* Department of Earth Sciences, University of Cambridge, Downing Street, Cambridge, CB2 3EQ (Office); The President's House, Clare Hall, Herschel Road, Cambridge, CB3 7AL, England (Home). *Telephone:* (1223) 333478 (Office). *E-mail:* es10002@esc.cam.ac.uk (Office); president@clarehall.cam.ac.uk (Home).

SALKIND, Ilya; film producer; b. 1947, Mexico; s. of Alexander Salkind; ed Univ. of London; Assoc. Producer, Cervantes, The Light at the Edge of the World, Spain, 1974. *Films include:* (with Alexander Salkind) Bluebeard, The Three Musketeers, The Four Musketeers, The Twist, The Prince and the Pauper, Superman, Superman 2, Superman 3, Supergirl, Santa Claus: The Movie, Christopher Columbus: The Discovery, Superboy (TV).

SALLAH, Ousman Ahmadou, BA; Gambian diplomatist; b. 26 July 1938, Kudang; s. of Ahmadou Jabel Sallah and Haddy Sallah; m. Ramou Sallah 1966; two s. two d.; ed Trinity Coll., Hartford, Conn., School of Int. Affairs, Columbia Univ., New York; Asst Sec., Prime Minister's Office 1967; Asst Sec. Ministry of External Affairs 1967–68, Deputy Perm. Sec. 1973–74; First Sec., Head of Chancery and Acting High Commr, London 1971; Amb. to Saudi Arabia (also Accred to Egypt, Iran, Kuwait, Qatar and UAE) 1974–79, to USA 1979–83; Perm. Rep. to UN 1979–83, 1987–94; Perm. Sec. Ministry of External Affairs and Head of Gambian Diplomatic Service 1982–; Hon. LLD (Trinity Coll., Hartford); Diploma in Int. Relations and Diplomacy from UNITAR. *Leisure interest:* tennis. *Address:* P.O. Box 667, Banjul, The Gambia. *Telephone:* 39-23-63 (Home).

SALLE, David, MFA; American artist; b. 1952, Okla; s. of Alvin S. Salle and Tillie D. Salle (née Brown); ed California Inst. of Arts; retrospective exhbn Museum of Contemporary Art, Chicago 1987; Guggenheim Fellow 1986. *One-man exhibitions include:* Project Inc., Cambridge, Mass. 1975, Foundation Corps de Garde, Groningen, Holland 1976, 1978, Artists Space, New York 1976, Foundation de Appel, Amsterdam 1977, The Kitchen, New York 1977, 1979, Mary Boone Gallery, New York 1981–83, Lucio Amelio Gallery, Naples

1981, Mario Diacono, Rome 1982, Anthony D'Offay Gallery, London 1982, Akira Ikeda Gallery, Tokyo 1983, Castelli Graphics, New York 1984, Gagosian Gallery, LA 1984, 1991, Tel Aviv Museum of Art 1989, Maria Diacono Gallery, Boston 1990, Castelli Graphics, New York 1990, Gagosian Gallery, New York 1991. *Group exhibitions include:* Serial Gallerie, Amsterdam 1977, Studio Cannaviello, Milan 1979, Grand Palais, Paris 1980, Nigel Greenwood Gallery, London 1981, Kunsthallen, Göteborg, Sweden 1981, New York Public Library 1982, Whitney Museum of American Art, New York 1982–83, Kassel 1982, Venice 1982, Stockholm 1983, Madrid 1983, São Paulo 1983, London (Tate Gallery) 1983, Pace Gallery 1983, Museo de Arte Contemporaneo de Monterrey, Mexico 1991.

SALLEH, Mohd Nor, PhD; Malaysian forester; b. 20 Oct. 1940, Kuala Pilah; s. of Mohammed Nor and Nyonya Nor; m. Habiba Alias 1966; two s. one d.; ed Univ. of Adelaide, Australia, Australian Forestry School, Canberra, ITC Delft, Netherlands; Deputy Conservator of Forests, Forest Dept Peninsular Malaysia 1965, Dir Forest Inventory 1971; Dir Forestry Research Inst., Kepong 1977–85; Dir Gen. Forest Resarch Inst. of Malaysia (FRIM) 1985–; Vice-Pres. Int. Union of Forest Research Orgs. (IUFRO) 1986–90, Pres. 1991; Pres. Malaysian Nature Soc. 1978–; Dr. hc (Nat. Univ. of Malaysia) 1992, (Aberdeen) 1993; K.M.N. 1981, D.S.N.S. 1989, Award of Third World Network of Scientific Orgs. for Public Understanding of Science 1991; Langkawi Environmental Award 1991, Nat. Science Award 1993. *Publications:* The Tropical Garden City 1990, The Malaysian Marine Heritage 1991, over 100 articles and contribs. to seminars, books and journals. *Leisure interests:* squash, badminton, reading, nature-oriented activities. *Address:* Forest Research Institute Malaysia, Kepong, 52109 Kuala Lumpur, Malaysia. *Telephone:* (3) 6342633. *Fax:* (3) 6367753.

SALLEO, Ferdinando, LLB; Italian diplomatist; b. 2 Oct. 1936, Messina; m.; two c.; ed Univ. of Rome; joined diplomatic service 1960, assigned to Directorate-Gen. for Political Affairs, Third Sec. in Paris 1963; Second Sec., Foreign Minister's Cabinet, Rome 1964; Counsellor in Prague 1969; Head of NATO Desk, Ministry of Foreign Affairs 1974–77; First Counsellor in Bonn 1977–82; Deputy Dir-Gen. for Devt Co-operation, Ministry of Foreign Affairs 1982–85; Special Envoy and Minister Plenipotentiary of First Class and Dir-Gen. 1985; Amb. to USSR (later Russian Fed.) 1989–95; Amb. to USA 1995–. *Address:* Embassy of Italy, 3000 Whitehaven Street, NW, Washington, DC 20008, USA (Office). *Telephone:* (202) 612-4400 (Office). *Fax:* (202) 518-2154 (Office). *E-mail:* stampa@itwash.org (Office). *Website:* www.italyemb.org (Office).

SALLINEN, Aulis Heikki; Finnish composer and professor of arts; b. 9 April 1935, Salmi; s. of Armas Rudolf Sallinen and Anna Malanen; m. 1st Pirkko Holvisola 1955 (died 1997); four s.; m. 2nd Maisa Lokka 1999; ed Sibelius Acad.; primary school teacher 1958–60; Man. Finnish Radio Orchestra 1960–69; Prof. of Arts Sibelius Acad. 1979–2000; Chair. TEOSTO; mem. Swedish Royal Music Acad. 1979; mem. Finnish Composers' Asscn, Sec., Chair.; mem. Bd Finnish Nat. Opera; Hon. DPhil (Turku) 1991, (Helsinki) 1994; Nordic Council Music Prize 1978, Wihuri Int. Sibelius Prize 1983. *Compositions include:* eight symphonies, violin concerto, cello concerto, flute concerto and other orchestral music, five string quartets and other chamber music; film score for The Iron Age 1983. *Operas include:* The Horseman 1975, The Red Line 1978, The King Goes Forth to France 1982, Kullervo 1988, The Palace 1993, King Lear 1999. *Address:* TEOSTO, Lauttasaarentie 1, 00200 Helsinki 20, Finland (Office).

SALMAN IBN ABDUL AZIZ, HRH Prince; Saudi Arabian politician; b. 13 Dec. 1936; s. of the late King Abdul Aziz ibn Saud; brother of HRH King Fahd; m.; Gov. of Riyadh 1962–; Chair. Bd Riyadh Water and Sanitary Drainage Authority and numerous other orgs.; active in Abdul Aziz Foundation. *Leisure interest:* reading. *Address:* Office of the Governor, Riyadh, Saudi Arabia.

SALMERÓN, Fernando; Mexican philosopher; b. 30 Oct. 1925, Córdoba, Veracruz; s. of Prof. Fernando A. Salmerón and Ana María Roíz de Salmerón; m. Alicia Castro V. 1952; four s. two d.; ed University of Veracruz, Nat. Autonomous Univ. of Mexico (UNAM), Albert Ludwig Univ., FRG; Dir Faculty of Philosophy, Univ. of Veracruz 1956–58, Rector 1961–63; Dir Inst. of Philosophical Investigations (UNAM) 1966–78, Investigator of Complete Time 1981–93, Investigator Emer. 1993–; Rector Iztapalapa Section, Metropolitan Autonomous Univ. 1978–79, Gen. Rector 1979–81; mem. El Colegio Nacional 1972–; Hon. Dr. Univ. of Veracruz, Investigador Nacional 1984, Prize of Nat. Univ. 1993, Nat. Prize for Social Sciences, History and Philosophy 1993. *Publications include:* Las Mocedades de Ortega y Gasset 1959, Cuestiones educativas y páginas sobre México 1962, La Filosofía y las actitudes morales 1971, Ética y análisis (ed.) 1985, Ortega y Gasset (ed.) 1984, Ensayos filosóficos 1988, Philosophie und Rechtstheorie in Mexico (co-ed.) 1989, Enseñanza y Filosofía 1991, Concepciones de la ética (co-ed.) 1992, Epistemología y cultura (co-ed.) 1993, La identidad personal y la colectiva (co-ed.) 1994, Los estudios cervantinos de José Gaos 1994. *Address:* El Colegio Nacional, Luis González Obregón 23, México 1, DF (Office); Congreso 70, Tlalpan, 1400 México DF, Mexico (Home). *Telephone:* 573-2165 (Home).

SALMON, Peter Andrew, BA; British broadcasting executive; b. 15 May 1956, Burnley; m.; three s.; ed Univ. of Warwick; fmr Dir of Programmes, Granada TV and Controller of Factual Programmes, Channel 4; fmr producer and Series Ed. BBC TV, later Head of Features, BBC Bristol, Controller, BBC One 1997–2000, Dir of BBC Sport 2000–. *Leisure interests:* cycling, football, tennis. *Address:* Room 5060, BBC TV Centre, Wood Lane, London, W12 7RJ, England (Office). *Telephone:* (20) 8225-8755 (Office). *Fax:* (20) 8576-7744 (Office). *E-mail:* peter.salmon@bbc.co.uk (Office).

SALMON, Robert; French journalist; b. 6 April 1918, Marseille; s. of Pierre Salmon and Madeleine Blum; m. Anne-Marie Jeanprost 1942; five c.; ed Lycée Louis le Grand, Ecole Normale Supérieure and at the Sorbonne; Founder Mouvement de Résistance Défense de la France; mem. Comité Parisien de Libération; Leader Paris Div., Mouvement de Libération Nationale; mem. Provisional Consultative Ass. 1944, First Constituent Ass. 1945; Founder Pres. and Dir Gen. France-Soir 1944; fmr Pres. Soc. France-Editions (Elle, Le Journal de Dimanche, Paris-Presse, etc.), Hon. Pres. 1976–; fmr Pres. Soc. de Publications Economiques (Réalités, Connaissance des Arts, Entreprise, etc.); Sec.-Gen. Féd. Nat. de la Presse 1951–77; Hon. Pres. French Cttee Int. Press Inst. 1973; mem. Admin. Council Fondation Nat. des Sciences Politiques 1973–93; Prof. Inst. d'Etudes Politiques, Univ. of Paris and Ecole Nat. d'Admin. 1967–88; mem. Haut Conseil de l'audiovisuel 1973–82; mem. Comm. de la République Française pour l'UNESCO 1979–; Commdr, Légion d'honneur, Croix de guerre, Rosette de la Résistance, Médaille des évadés. *Publications:* Le sentiment de l'existence chez Maine de Biran 1943, Notions élémentaires de psychologie 1947, L'organisation actuelle de la presse française 1955, Information et publicité 1956, L'information économique, clé de la prospérité 1963. *Leisure interests:* yachting, skiing, gardening. *Address:* 4 rue Berlioz, 75116 Paris, France.

SALMOND, Alexander Elliot Anderson, MA; Scottish politician; b. 31 Dec. 1954, Linlithgow; s. of Robert F. Salmond and Mary S. Milne; m. Moira McGlashan; ed Linlithgow Acad., St Andrews Univ.; Vice-Pres. Fed. of Student Nat. 1974–77, St Andrews Univ. Students' Rep. Council 1977–78, Founder mem. Scottish Nat. Party (SNP) 79 Group 1979; Asst Economist Dept of Agric. and Fisheries 1978–80; Economist Bank of Scotland 1980–87, MP for Banff and Buchan 1987–; mem. SNP Nat. Exec. Cttee 1981–82, 1983–, SNP Exec. Vice Convener for Publicity 1985–87, SNP Nat. Convener (Leader) 1990–2000; SNP Parl. Spokesperson on Constitution and Fishing 1997–99; Hon. Vice-Pres. Scottish Centre for Econ. and Social Research, mem. Scottish Parl. 1999–2001; Visiting Prof. of Econs, Strathclyde Univ. *Leisure interests:* golf, reading. *Address:* 17 Maiden Street, Peterhead, Aberdeenshire, AB42 1EE, Scotland (Office); House of Commons, London SW1A 0AA, England. *Telephone:* (1779) 470444 (Constituency Office). *Fax:* (1779) 474460 (Office). *Website:* www.snp.org.

SALOLAINEN, Pertti Edvard, MSc(Econ); Finnish diplomatist and politician; b. 19 Oct. 1940, Helsinki; s. of Edvard Paavali Salolainen and Ella Elisabeth Salolainen; m. Anja Sonninen 1964; one s. one d.; ed Helsinki School of Econs; TV journalist, Finnish Broadcasting Co. 1962–65, producer 1965–66, corresp. in London 1966–69, mem. Working Cttee, Supervisory Bd 1970–87; journalist, BBC, London 1966; Head of Dept Finnish Employers' Confed. 1969–89; mem. Parl. 1970–96; Minister for Foreign Trade 1987–95; Deputy Prime Minister 1991–95; Head, negotiating team for entry of Finland into EU 1993–95; Amb. to UK 1996–; Chair. Finance Cttee IPU 1982–87; Hon. Founder Worldwide Fund for Nature Finland 1972; mem. Supervisory Bd's Working Cttee Outokumpu Mining Co. 1979–91; mem. Supervisory Bd Suomi-Salama Insurance Co. 1980–91, Finnair 1995–2002; mem. Legal Cttee Nordic Council 1982–87; Freeman of City of London 1998; holds mil. rank of Maj.; several one-man exhbns of art and photographs in Finland, Germany and UK; Nat. Coalition Party (Leader 1991–94); Grand Cross of the Lion of Finland 1994, Grand Cross of the Nordstjerna Order (Sweden) 1996, Grand Cross of the FRG, Grand Cross of Hungary, Grand Cross of Austria, Medal of Merit, Finnish Defence Force 1997; Int. Conservation Award, Worldwide Fund for Nature, Gold Medal of Merit, Finnish Asscn for Nature Conservation. *Leisure interests:* nature conservation, photography, sports, tennis. *Address:* Finnish Embassy, 38 Chesham Place, London, SW1X 8HW, London, England. *Telephone:* (20) 7838-6200. *Fax:* (20) 7838-9500.

SALONEN, Esa-Pekka, FRCM; Finnish conductor and composer; b. 30 June 1958, Helsinki; ed Sibelius Acad., Helsinki; studied composition with Rautavaara and conducting with Panula; studied in Italy 1979–81; Prin. Guest Conductor, Philharmonia Orchestra 1984–94; Oslo Philharmonic Orchestra 1985–; Music Dir, LA Philharmonic Orchestra 1992–; Prin. Conductor Swedish Radio Symphony Orchestra 1985–95; Artistic Adviser New Stockholm Chamber Orchestra 1986; Artistic Dir Helsinki Festival 1995–96; Royal Philharmonic Soc. Opera Award 1995, Litteris et Artibus Medal (Sweden) 1996, Royal Philharmonic Soc. Conductor Award 1997, Officier Ordre des Arts et des Lettres (France). *Compositions:* orchestral: Concerto (for Alto Saxophone and Orchestra) 1980–81, Giro 1982–97; Chamber Music: YTA I (for alto flute) 1985, YTA II (for piano) 1985, YTA III (for cello) 1986, FLOOF (for soprano and chamber ensemble) 1990, Mimo II 1992, LA Variations 1996, Gambit 1998, Five Images after Sappho 1999, Mania 2000, Foreign Bodies 2001. *Address:* c/o Van Walsum Management Ltd, 4 Addison Bridge Place, London, W14 8XP, England. *Telephone:* (20) 7371-4343. *Fax:* (20) 7371-4344.

SALOUM, Nasir ibn Muhammad as-, PhD; Saudi Arabian engineer; b. 4 Nov. 1936, Medina; resident engineer, Ministry of Communications 1965; Head of Study Dept, Ministry of Communications 1965–68; Deputy Minister of Communications 1976–96, Minister 2000–; Minister of Transport 1991–2000; mem. Bd of Saudi Arabian Railways Authority. *Leisure interests:* reading, travel. *Address:* Ministry of Communications, Airport Road, Riyadh 11178, Saudi Arabia. *Telephone:* (1) 404-3000. *Fax:* (1) 403-1401.

SALPETER, Edwin E., MSc, PhD; American physicist, professor and astronomer; b. 3 Dec. 1924, Vienna, Austria; s. of Jakob L. Salpeter and Friedericke Salpeter; m. Miriam M. Mark 1950 (died 2000); two d.; ed Sydney Boys' High School, Australia and Univ. of Birmingham, England; Dept of Scientific and Industrial Research Fellow, Univ. of Birmingham, England 1948–49; Research Assoc., then Assoc. Prof., Cornell Univ., U.S. 1949–56, Prof. of Physics and Astrophysics 1956–71, J. G. White Distinguished Prof. of Physical Sciences 1971–; mem. Nat. Science Bd 1978–84; Visiting Prof. ANU 1954, Sydney Univ. 1960, Cambridge Univ. 1968; mem. NAS, American Acad. of Arts and Sciences, American Philosophical Soc., Deutsche Akad. Leopoldina; Foreign mem. Australian Acad. of Sciences, Royal Soc.; Hon. DSc (Sydney, Chicago, NSW and Case Western Reserve Univs.); Crafoord Laureate 1997; H.A. Bethe Prize, American Physics Soc. 1999. *Publications:* one book and over 300 scientific papers on quantum mechanics, plasma physics and theoretical astrophysics. *Leisure interests:* tennis, skiing, photography. *Address:* 612 Space Sciences, Cornell Univ., Ithaca, NY 14853 (Office); 116 Westbourne Lane, Ithaca, NY 14850, USA (Home). *Telephone:* (607) 255-4937.

SALTANOV, Aleksander Vladimirovich; Russian politician; b. 14 Feb. 1946, Moscow; m.; two s.; ed Moscow State Inst. of Int. Relations; attaché USSR Embassy, Kuwait 1970–74; attaché, Third then Second Sec., Dept of Near E and N Africa, Ministry of Foreign Affairs 1974–79, Counsellor, Head of Sector, then Head of Div. 1986–92, Dir of Dept 1999–2001; Consul then Gen., Consulate in Aleppo (Syria) 1979–83; First Sec. then Counsellor, USSR Embassy, Syria 1983–86; Amb. to Jordan 1992–98; Deputy Minister of Foreign Affairs 2001–. *Address:* Smolenskaya-Sennaya pl. 32–34, 121200 Moscow, Russia (Office). *Telephone:* (095) 244-47-15 (Office). *Fax:* (095) 244-92-39 (Office). *E-mail:* saltanov@mid.ru (Office).

SALTER, John Rotherham, MA, FCIM, FCIWM, FRGS, FRSA, ACIArG; British international business lawyer, solicitor and academic; b. 2 May 1932, London; s. of Herbert Salter and Nora Salter; m. Cynthia Brewer 1961; one s. two d.; ed Queen Elizabeth's School, Ashridge Coll., Lincoln Coll., Oxford and King's Coll. London; Lt RA 1951–53; partner, Denton Hall 1961–94, consultant 1994–99; Chair. Environmental Law Group 1994–98, Chair. Maj. Projects Group 1994–98; Vice-Chair. IBA Cttee of Energy and Natural Resources Law 1976–79, IBA Cttee on Int. Environmental Law 1979–82; Chair. North Sea Gas Gathering Consortium 1979–80; Chair. Section on Business Law, Int. Bar Asscn 1986–88; Chair. ABA Cttee on Int. Law 1993–95, Legal Issues Group of ISWA 1994–2000; Treas. Anglo-American Real Property Inst. 1985–86; Trustee, Petroleum Law Educ. Trust 1980–98, IBA Educ. Trust 1983–95; consultant, UNIDO 1983–84; Vice-Chair. ABA Cttee on Comparative Govt Law 1988–91; Chair. IBA Cttee on Oil and Gas Construction Law 1989–93; mem. Bd Int. Capital Markets Group 1987–89; mem. Law Soc.'s Planning Panel 1991–97; Legal Assoc., Royal Town Planning Inst. 1992–98; Chair. The Silver Soc. 1986–87, The Care Foundation 1994–2001, Hospice in the Weald 1994–2001, IBA Standing Cttee on UN and World Orgs. (UNWOC) 1995–2000, Murray Soc. 1996–98; Pres. The Wine Label Circle 1986–87; Dir John Ray Initiative 1997–; mem. Soc. of Chemical Industry, London Chapter of Lamda Alpha Int., Advisory Cttee on Integrated Environmental Man. by Distance Learning, Bath Univ., Scientific and Tech. Cttee, ISWA 1994–2000; Visiting Fellow Cranfield Univ. 1993–, mem. of Court 1995–, Visiting Prof. of Law 1997–, Chair. Legislation and Policy Unit 2000–; mem. Sr Common Room, Lincoln Coll., Oxford 1991–; mem. of Court Worshipful Co. of Fan-Makers 1997–; partner, John Salter & Associates 1999–; mem. Advisory Panel, US Inst. of Peace 2001–; Hon. mem. Bar of Madrid 1987–, ISWA 2000–, ICC (UK) 2000–, IBA 2001–; Freeman of London and of Glasgow; Hon. Fellow Centre for Petroleum and Mineral Law and Policy, Univ. of Dundee. *Television appearances:* The Law is Yours series. *Publications:* Planning Law for Industry (Jt) 1981, UK Onshore Oil and Gas Law 1986, Corporate Environmental Responsibility – Law and Practice 1992; contrib. to UK Oil and Gas Law 1984, Halsbury's Laws of England (Vol. 58) 1986, Law of the European Communities 1986, Vaughan's Law of the European Communities Service 1990, Environment and Planning Law 1991, Frontiers of Environmental Law 1991, Directors' Guide to Environmental Issues 1992, European Community Energy Law 1994, European Environmental Law 1994, How to Understand an Act of Parliament (with D. J. Gifford) 1996, Understanding the English Legal System (with D. J. Gifford) 1997, Sauce Labels (1750–1950) 2002; numerous articles in professional journals. *Leisure interests:* the arts, archaeology, sailing, tennis. *Address:* John Salter and Associates, 118 Oak Hill Road, Sevenoaks, Kent TN13 1NU (Office); Jumpers Hatch, Oak Hill Road, Sevenoaks, Kent, TN13 1NU, England (Home). *Telephone:* (1732) 460870 (Office); (1732) 458388 (Home). *Fax:* (870) 052-2008 (Office); (1732) 458388 (Home). *E-mail:* jrs@jumpershatch.demon.co.uk (Office); jrs@jumpershatch.demon.co.uk (Home).

SALTYKOV, Boris Georgievich, C.ECON.SC.; Russian politician and economist; b. 27 Dec. 1940, Moscow; s. of Georgy Saltykov and Evdokia M. Saltykova (née Pukaleva); m. Lubov N. Klochkova 1972; two d.; ed Moscow Inst. of Physics and Tech.; researcher, Head of lab., Head of Div. Cen. Inst. of Econ. and Math. USSR (now Russian) Acad. of Sciences 1967–86; Head of Div. Inst. of Econ. and Forecasting of Progress in Science and Tech. (now Forecasting of Econ.) USSR Acad. of Sciences 1986–91; Deputy Dir Analytical Centre USSR Acad. of Sciences 1991; Minister of Science, Higher School and Tech. Policy of Russian Fed. 1991–92; Deputy Prime Minister of Russian Fed. 1992–93; Minister of Science and Tech. Policy 1993–96; Pres. Russian House of Int. Science and Tech. Cooperation 1996–; mem. State Duma (Parl.) 1993–95; Chair. Russian Comm. for UNESCO 1992–97; Dir-Gen. Fed. State Unitary Co. Russian Technologies 1998–2000; Hon. Foreign mem. American Acad. of Arts and Letters 1999–. *Leisure interest:* cars. *Address:* Russian House of International Science and Technology Cooperation, Bryusov per. 11, 103009 Moscow (Office); Protochny per. 11, ap. 99, 121099 Moscow, Russia (Home). *Telephone:* (095) 229-58-40 (Office); (095) 241-44-03 (Home). *Fax:* (095) 200-32-77 (Office); (095) 229-59-01. *E-mail:* bsaltykov@osi.ru (Office).

SALVATICI, Nilo; Italian banker; b. 10 March 1922, Monticiano; s. of Arturo Salvatici and Serafina Mugelli; m. Dina Branconi 1946; two c.; served for 43 years with Bank Monte dei Paschi di Siena, retiring with title of Cen. Man.; fmr Chair. Monte Paschi Belgio, Brussels; fmr Dir Istituto Nazionale di Credito Agrario, Florence; Dir Istituto dell'Enciclopedia Italiana Treccani, Rome, Banksiel, Milan; Chair. Cassa di Risparmio di Prato; Grande Ufficiale della Repubblica Italiana. *Leisure interests:* numismatics, philately. *Address:* 93 Strada Terrensano e Belcaro, 53100 Siena, Italy. *Telephone:* (0577) 47074.

SALVETTI, Carlo; Italian physicist; b. 30 Dec. 1918, Milan; s. of Adriano Salvetti; m. Piera Pinto 1951; two d.; ed Univ. of Milan; fmr Prof. of Theoretical Physics, Univ. of Bari; Dir-Gen. Nuclear Study Centre, Ispra 1957–59; Dir Int. Atomic Energy Agency (IAEA) Research Div. 1959–62; Gov. for Italy to IAEA 1962–64, 1968–70, Chair. Bd of Govs IAEA 1963–64; Chair. European Atomic Energy Soc. 1967–68, mem. EAES Council 1963–72; Chair. Euratom Scientific and Technical Cttee 1969–70, mem. 1967–73; Chair. ENEA-OECD Steering Cttee 1969–73; Chair. ANS, Italian Section 1971–75; Prof. of Gen. Physics, Univ. of Milan; Vice Pres., Italian Nat. Cttee for Nuclear Energy (CNEN) 1964–81; Chair. Italian Forum for Nuclear Energy (FIEN) 1965–; Consultant to ENEA 1981–; mem. Bd of Moscow Int. Energy Club (MIEC); Chair. Italian Nuclear Soc. (SNI) 1975–79, 1991–; mem. Bd European Nuclear Soc. (ENS) 1975–, Chair. 1979–81, Hon. Fellow 1986–; mem. Consultative Cttee on Fusion (CCF) within Comm. of European Communities 1976–81; Fellow, American Nuclear Soc. 1970–. *Publications:* over 120 scientific and technical articles on nuclear physics, reactor theories and energy problems. *Leisure interests:* golf, painting. *Address:* Via Gramsci 38, 00197 Rome, Italy. *Telephone:* (06) 3200960.

SALZ, Anthony Michael Vaughan, LLB, FRSA; British lawyer; b. 30 June 1950, Tavistock, Devon; s. of Michael H. Salz and Veronica Edith Dorothea Elizabeth Salz (née Hall); m. Sally Ruth Hagger 1975; one s. two d.; ed Summerfields School, Oxford, Radley Coll. and Univ. of Exeter; Articled Clerk, Kenneth Brown Baker Baker 1972–74, Asst Solicitor 1974–75; Asst Solicitor, Freshfields 1975–77, seconded to Davis Polk & Wardwell, New York 1977–78, Solicitor, Freshfields 1978–80, Partner 1980–96, Sr Partner 1996–2000, Co-Sr Partner Freshfields Bruckhaus Deringer 2000–; mem. Tate Gallery Corp. Advisory Group 1997– (Chair. 1997–2002); mem. Business Action on Homelessness Exec. Forum, Business in the Community—BITC, Chair. BITC Cttee for Leadership in Educ.; Trustee Tate Foundation, Eden Project. *Publications include:* contribs to various legal books and journals. *Leisure interests:* fishing, soccer, sports, theatre, arts. *Address:* Freshfields Bruckhaus Deringer, 65 Fleet Street, London, EC4Y 1HS, England (Office). *Telephone:* (20) 7832-7028 (Office). *Fax:* (20) 7832-7392 (Office). *E-mail:* anthony.salz@freshfields.com (Office). *Website:* www.freshfields.com (Office).

SALZMAN, Pnina; Israeli pianist; b. 1923, Tel-Aviv; m. Igal Weissmann 1947; one d.; ed Ecole normale de musique and Conservatoire national de musique, Paris; gave first concert in Paris at age of twelve; since then has given concerts in Israel, Japan, USSR, South Africa, Australia, New Zealand, France, Britain, Belgium, Denmark, Sweden, Norway, Finland, USA, etc., under baton of Sir Malcolm Sargent, Charles Munch, Koussevitsky, etc.; over 300 concerts with Israeli orchestras and regular performances with orchestras all over the world; fmr Prof. of Piano, Tel-Aviv Univ. *Leisure interests:* gardening, painting, graphology. *Address:* 20 Dubnov Street, Tel-Aviv, Israel. *Telephone:* 3-261993.

SAMA, Koffi, DMV; Togolese politician; b. 1944, Amoutchou, Ogou Prefecture; m.; ed Lycée Bonnecarrère, Lomé and Ecole Nat. Vétérinaire de Toulouse, France; qualified as a vet 1972; Minister of Youth, Sport and Culture 1981–84; Dir-Gen. SOTOCO (Société Togolaise de Coton) 1990–96; fmr Minister of Health; Minister of Nat. Educ. and Research –2002; Prime Minister of Togo 2002–; Officier, Ordre de Mono, Grand Officier, Ordre du Mérite agricole. *Address:* Office of the Prime Minister, Lomé, Togo (Office). *Telephone:* 221-15-64 (Office). *Fax:* 221-20-40 (Office). *E-mail:* info@ republicoftogo.com (Office). *Website:* www.republicoftogo.com.

SAMADIKUN, Samaun, PhD; Indonesian professor of electronic engineering and administrator; b. 15 April 1931, Magetan; ed Stanford Univ., Queen Mary Coll., London; lecturer, Electrical Eng Dept, Bandung Inst. of Tech. 1957, Chair. 1964–67, Prof. of Electronics 1974, now Prof. of Electrical Eng; First Dir Inter-Univ. Centre for Microelectronics 1984–89, now Sr Researcher; Dir.-Gen. of Energy, Ministry of Mining and Energy 1978–83; Chair. Indonesian Inst. of Sciences 1989–95; mem. Indonesian Engineers Asscn; Fellow Islamic Acad. of Sciences, Indonesian Acad. of Sciences; Nat. Scientific Citation Medal 1978, Adhikara Rekayasa Award 1984, Mahaputra Utama Medal 1995, ASEAN Award 1998. *Address:* Institut Teknologi Bandung, Il. Tamansari 64, Bandung 40132, Indonesia. *Telephone:* (22) 2503147. *Fax:* (22) 431792. *E-mail:* webmaster@itb.ac.id (Office). *Website:* www.itb.ac.id (Office).

SAMAR, Sima, DMed; Afghanistan politician and physician; b. Feb. 1957, Ghazani; ed Kabul Univ.; exiled in Pakistan following Soviet invasion; Founder and Dir Shuhada (hosp. for Afghan women and children), Quetta, Pakistan 1989, founder of three medical clinics, four hosps. and girls' schools in rural Afghanistan (also providing medical training, literacy programmes and food aid), f. school for refugee girls in Quetta; mem. Women Living Under Muslim Law; political activist amd opponent of women's subjugation under Taliban regime; Vice-Chair. and Minister of Women's Affairs Afghan Interim Authority Dec. 2001–June 2002.

SAMARAKIS, Antonis; Greek author; b. 16 Aug. 1919, Athens; s. of Evripidis Samarakis and Adriani Pantelopoulos; m. Eleni Kourebanas 1963; ed Univ. of Athens; Chief of Emigration, Refugees and Technical Assistance Depts., Ministry of Labour 1935–40, 1944–63; active in resistance Movt during second World War; has served on many humanitarian missions in many parts of the world for ILO, UNHCR, ICEM and Council of Europe; Expert on social and labour problems (many African countries, chiefly Guinea) ILO 1968–69; denied a passport Oct. 1970; mem. PEN, Nat. Soc. of Authors; Officier, Ordre de Léopold II (Belgium); hon. citizen of San Francisco and New Orleans; Greek Nat. Book Award 1962, Greek Prize of the Twelve 1966, Grand Prix de la Littérature policière (France) 1970, Europalia Prize for Literature 1982. *Publications:* short stories: Wanted: Hope 1954, I Refuse 1961, The Jungle 1966, The Passport (in Nea Kimina 2) 1971; novels: Danger Signal 1959, The Flaw 1965; contrib. to The Child's Song (anthology of poems for children); works have been translated in 16 languages and frequently adapted for cinema and TV. *Leisure interest:* travel. *Address:* 59 Anagnostopoulou Street, 106 72 Athens, Greece. *Telephone:* (1) 3647444.

SAMARANCH TORELLO, Marqués de Samaranch Juan Antonio; Spanish diplomatist and international sports official; b. 17 July 1920, Barcelona; s. of Francisco Samaranch and Juana Torello; m. María Teresa Salisachs Rowe 1955 (died 2000); one s. one d.; ed German Coll., Higher Inst. of Business Studies, Barcelona; mem. Spanish Olympic Cttee 1954–, Pres. 1967–70; mem. IOC 1966, Vice-Pres. 1974–78, Pres. 1980–2001; Amb. to USSR (also accred to Mongolia) 1977–80; fmr Chair. La Caixa (Savings Bank), Pres. Int. Boat Show; Dr hc; Seoul Peace Prize 1990; Hon. Chair. La Caixa (Savings Bank); Hon. Pres. Int. Boat Show; numerous decorations from many countries. *Leisure interests:* philately, art. *Address:* Avda Pau Casals, 24, 08021 Barcelona, Spain (Home). *Fax:* (93) 4145931 (Office).

SAMARAS, Antonis C., B.A.(Econs), MBA; Greek politician; b. 23 May 1951, Athens; s. of Constantinos Samaras and Eleni Samaras; m. Georgia Kritikou 1990; one s. one d.; ed Amherst Coll., Harvard Business School, USA; MP for Messinia 1977–; Minister of Finance 1989, of Foreign Affairs 1989–90, 1990–92; Founder-Pres. Politiki Anixi Party (POLAN) 1993–. *Leisure interests:* tennis, swimming, music, poetry, reading. *Address:* Politiki Anixi (POLAN), Odos Aiolou 11, 105 55 Athens (Office); Patission 67, Athens 10434 (Office); 10 Mourouzi Street, Athens 10674, Greece. *Telephone:* (1) 3254355-9 (POLAN), (1) 8228435 (Office); (1) 7213014 (Home). *Fax:* (1) 3249429 (POLAN), (1) 3249621 (Office). *E-mail:* anixi@otenet.gr (Office). *Website:* www.politikianixi.gr (Office).

SAMARSKY, Aleksander Andreyevich; Russian mathematician; b. 19 Feb. 1919; m.; two d.; ed Moscow State Univ.; Asst, teacher, docent Moscow State Univ.; Head of Lab. Inst. of Applied Math., Dir Centre of Mathematical Modelling; Corresp. mem. USSR (now Russian) Acad. of Sciences 1966, mem. 1976; research in math. physics, theory of differential equations, theory of nonlinear processes, computational math., math. modelling; Chair. Nat. Council on Mathematical Modelling; Deputy Pres. Scientific Council on Mathematical Modelling; Ed. Mathematical Modelling journal; Hon. Dir Hemnitz Tech. Univ. (Germany); Hero of Socialist Labour, Lenin Prize, USSR State Prize. *Publications include:* 3 books and numerous articles in scientific journals. *Leisure interests:* geography, fiction. *Address:* Institute of Applied Mathematics, Russian Academy of Sciences, Miusskaya pl. 4, 125047 Moscow, Russia. *Telephone:* (095) 250-79-86 (Office).

SAMHAN, Mohammad Jasim, MA, M.SC.S.; United Arab Emirates diplomatist; b. 1950, Ras Al Khaimah; m.; four c.; ed Goddard Coll. and Syracuse Univ., USA; worked for Dept of Water and Electricity 1966–68, with Nat. Oil Co. 1972–74; joined diplomatic corps 1974, with Consulate in Karachi 1975, then with del. to UN, rank of Counsellor 1981, with Consulate in Bombay 1981, rank of Minister Plenipotentiary; Dir Dept of Int. Orgs. and Confs., Arab League 1982–84; Dept of Arab Homeland 1984–87, UAE Interests section Feb.–Nov. 1987; Perm. Rep. to Arab League 1988–90, also Amb. to Tunisia 1988–92; Perm. Rep. to the UN 1992–2001. *Address:* c/o Ministry of Foreign Affairs, P.O. Box 1, Abu Dhabi, United Arab Emirates.

SAMIOS, Nicholas Peter, PhD; American physicist; b. 15 March 1932, New York; s. of Peter Samios and Niki Samios; m. Mary Linakis 1958; two s. one d.; ed Columbia Coll., Columbia Univ., New York; Instructor, Dept of Physics, Columbia Univ. 1956–59, Adjunct Prof. 1970–; Asst Physicist Brookhaven Nat. Lab. Dept of Physics 1959–62, Assoc. Physicist 1962–64, Physicist 1964–68, Group Leader 1965–75, Sr Physicist 1968–, Chair. Div. of Particles and Fields 1975–76, Chair. PEP Experimental Program Cttee (of SLAC & LBL) 1976–78, Adjunct Prof., Stevens Inst. of Tech. 1969–75, Chair. Dept of Physics 1975–81, Deputy Dir 1981, Acting Dir 1982, Dir 1982–97; mem. Bd of Dirs. Stony Brook Foundation 1989, Adelphi 1989–97, Long Island Asscn 1990–97; fmr mem. or fmr chair. numerous specialist cttees. and bds.; Corresp. mem. Akademia Athenon 1994–; Fellow American Physical Soc.

1964, mem. Exec. Cttee 1976–77; Fellow American Acad. of Arts and Sciences; mem. NAS; E. O. Lawrence Memorial Award 1980, New York Acad. of Sciences Award in Physical and Math. Sciences 1980, AUI Distinguished Scientist 1992, W.K.H. Panofsky Prize 1993. *Address:* Brookhaven National Laboratory, Building 510, Upton, New York, NY 11973, USA. *Telephone:* (516) 344-4545.

SAMMUT, Salv; Maltese trade union official; b. 4 March 1947, Lija; m.; two s. one d.; ed Univ. of Malta; mem. Nat. Comm. for Health and Safety 1994, Bd Health and Safety Authority 2001; Vice-Pres. General Workers' Union 1999–2001, Pres. 2001–. *Publications include:* book of poetry. *Leisure interests:* reading, writing literature. *Address:* The General Workers' Union, Workers' Memorial Building, South Street, Valletta, VLT 11 (Office); The Quest, Maisonette 2, Block R, Mtarfa, RBT 10, Malta (Home). *Telephone:* 21244300 (Office); 21454903 (Home). *Fax:* 21234911 (Office). *E-mail:* ssammut@gwu.org.mt (Office); sammutsalv@hotmail.com (Home). *Website:* www.gwu.org.mt (Office).

SAMOILOVA, Tatyana Yevgeniyevna; Russian film actress; b. 4 May 1934, Leningrad; d. of Eugeniy V. Samoilov and Zinaida I. Levina-Samoilova; one s.; ed Shchukin Theatre School; Cannes Festival Palm Award for The Cranes are Flying 1958 and Special Prize for personal creative achievements in cinematography 1990; Merited Artist of the RSFSR; Order of the Badge of Honour. *Roles include:* Maria (The Mexican) 1955, Veronika (The Cranes Are Flying) 1957, Tanya (The Unsent Letter) 1960, Natasha (Leon Garros Looks for a Friend) 1960, Alba (Alba Regia) 1961, Sonia (They Went East) 1964, Anna (Anna Karenina) 1968; Yekaterina (A Long Way to a Short Day) 1972, Masha (Ocean) 1974, Maria (Jewels for the Dictatorship of the Proletariat) 1976. *Address:* Spiridonyevsky per. 8/11, 103104 Moscow, Russia. *Telephone:* (095) 254-34-68.

SAMPAIO, Jorge Fernando Branco de; Portuguese politician; b. 18 Sept. 1939; m. Maria José Ritta; one s. one d.; fmr Sec.-Gen. Socialist Party (PS); Mayor of Lisbon; Pres. of Portugal March 1996–. *Leisure interests:* music, golf. *Address:* Presidência da República, Palácio de Belém, 1300-004 Lisbon, Portugal. *Telephone:* (21) 3614600. *Fax:* (21) 3610570. *E-mail:* belem@presidenciarepublica.pt (Office). *Website:* www.presidenciarepublica.pt (Office).

SAMPEDRO, José Luis; Spanish economist and novelist; b. 1 Feb. 1917, Barcelona; s. of Luis Sampedro and Matilde Saez; m. Isabel Pellicer Iturrioz 1944; one d.; ed Madrid Univ.; Civil Service, Ministry of Finance 1935–50, 1957–62; Asst Prof. of Econ. Structure, Madrid Univ. 1947–55, Prof. 1955–69; Economist, Ministry of Commerce 1951–57; Adviser to Spanish Del. to UN 1956–58; Special Prof. of Econ. Sociology, Madrid Univ. 1962–65; Asst Gen. Dir Banco Exterior de España 1962–69; Visiting Prof. Univ. of Salford 1969–70, Univ. of Liverpool 1970–71; Econ. Adviser Customs Bureau, Ministry of Finance 1971–79; nominated mem. Senate 1977–79; Econ. Adviser Banco Exterior de España 1979–81; Vice-Pres. Fundación Banco Exterior de España 1981–84; Real Academia Española 1990; Spanish Nat. Award for new playwrights 1950; Gold Medal, Madrid City. *Publications:* Economics: Principles of Industrial Location 1954, Effects of European Economic Integration 1957, Economic Reality and Structural Analysis 1958, The European Future of Spain 1960, Regional Profiles of Spain 1964, Decisive Forces in World Economics 1967, Economic Structure 1969, Conscience of Underdevelopment 1973, Inflation Unabridged 1976; Fiction: Congreso en Estocolmo 1952, El Río que nos lleva 1962, El Caballo Desnudo 1970, Octubre, Octubre 1981, La Sonrisa Etrusca 1985, La Vieja Sirena 1990, Mar al Fondo 1993, Mientras la Tierra Gira 1993, Real Sitio 1993, La Estatua de Adolfo Espejo 1994, La Sombra de los Días 1994, Fronteras 1995, El Amante Lesbiano 2000, El Mercado y la Globalización 2002; plays: La Paloma de Cartón 1950, Un sitio para vivir 1956. *Leisure interest:* human communication. *Address:* Cea Bermúdez 51, 28003 Madrid, Spain. *Telephone:* (91) 5442860.

SAMPER, Armando; Colombian agricultural economist; b. 9 April 1920, Bogotá; s. of the late Daniel Samper Ortega and of Mayita Gnecco de Samper; m. Jean K. de Samper 1945; two s. two d.; ed Cornell Univ., USA; research and teaching posts in agricultural Econs, Colombia 1943–49; Inter-American Inst. of Agricultural Sciences of OAS, Turrialba, Costa Rica 1949–69, Head of Scientific Communications Service 1949–54, Dir of Regional Services 1955–60, Dir of Inst. 1960–69, Dir Emer. 1969–; Visiting Prof. Univ. of Chicago 1954–55; Minister of Agric. 1966–67, 1969–70; Agricultural Adviser, Banco de la República, Bogotá 1970–72; Chancellor Univ. de Bogotá 1971; FAO Asst Dir-Gen. for Latin American Affairs, Santiago, Chile 1972–74; Pres. Nat. Corpn for Forestry Research and Devt (CONIF), Bogotá 1975–77, Consultant Delsa Ltd 1978–92; Dir-Gen. Colombian Sugar Cane Research Centre 1978–90, Dir Emer. 1990–; consultant COLCIENCIAS 1990–91; mem. Bd Int. Centre of Tropical Agriculture 1967–76 (Chair. 1973–76, Chair. Emer. 1976–), Foundation for Higher Educ. 1978–95 (Chair. 1984–89), UN Science and Tech. Cttee 1981–83, Nat. Council of Science and Tech. 1982–86, Gimnasio Moderno 1989–, Oil Palm Research Center 1991–, Aquaculture Research Centre 1993–; Chair. Emer., Colombian Program for the Admin of Agric. Research 1990–; Vice-Chair. Bd Colombian Corpn for Agric. Research 1993–94; mem. Nat. Acad. Econ. Sciences 1984–. *Publications:* Importancia del Café en el Comercio Exterior de Colombia 1948, Desarrollo Institucional y Desarrollo Agrícola (3 Vols) 1969, El Cuatrenio de la Transformación Rural 1966–70, Los Estudios Microeconómicos en Colombia 1988, Evolución de la

Investigación en Caña de Azúcar en el Valle del Cauca 1930–79 1998. *Address:* Apartado Aéreo 100-286, Santa Fe de Bogotá, Colombia. *Telephone:* (1) 611-0941 (Office). *Fax:* (1) 616-4813.

SAMPERMANS, Françoise, LèsL; French business executive; b. 10 July 1947, Paris; d. of Jacques Durand and Jeannine Behot; one s. one d.; joined CIT-TRANSAC 1974; est. public relations service, Chapelle Darblay 1978; Head of Public Relations, Entreprise et Crédit 1981; Dir of Communications, Transmission, Group Thomson 1982; subsequently Deputy Dir, Dir of Communications, Alcatel CIT; Dir of Communications, Alcatel NV 1987, Alcatel Alsthom 1987; Dir-Gen. Générale Occidentale 1991–95; Dir in charge of communications section and assoc. services, Alcatel Alsthom; Pres. Dir-Gen. Groupe Express 1992–95; Vice-Pres. Québecor-Europe 1996–; Pres., Dir-Gen. Nouvel Economiste 1999–; Dir-Gen. Marianne and L'Evènement du Jeudi 1999–; Vice-Pres. Nouvelles Messageries de la Presse Parisienne; Chevalier Ordre des Arts et des Lettres. *Address:* 18 rue Charles Silvestri, 94300 Vincennes, France.

SAMPHAN, Khieu (see Khieu Samphan).

SAMPRAS, Pete; American tennis player; b. 12 Aug. 1971, Washington, DC; s. of Sam Sampras and Georgia Sampras; m. Brigette Wilson 2000; one s.; turned professional 1988; holds men's record for most Grand Slam singles titles (14 as at end 2002); US Open Champion 1990, 1993, 1995, 1996, 2002; Grand Slam Cup Winner 1990; IBM/ATP Tour World Championship–Frankfurt Winner 1991; US Pro-Indoor Winner 1992; Wimbledon Singles Champion 1993, 1994, 1995, 1997, 1998, 1999, 2000; European Community Championships Winner 1993, 1994; ranked No. 1 1993–98 (record); winner Australian Open 1994; RCA Championships 1996, ATP Tour World Championships, 1996, Australian Open 1997; winner San José Open 1997, Philadelphia Open 1997, Cincinnati Open 1997; Munich Open 1997, Paris Open 1997, Hanover Open 1997, Advanta Championship 1998; mem. US Davis Cup Team 1991, 1995; winner of 64 WTA Tour singles titles, 2 doubles titles and over 43 million dollars in prize money by end of 2002; Chair. ATP Tour Charities Programme 1992; f. Acres for Charity Fund; Jim Thorpe Tennis Player of the Year 1993, ATP Tour Player of the Year 1993–97, US Olympic Cttee Sportsman of the Year 1997. *Leisure interests:* golf, basketball, Formula 1 racing. *Address:* ATP Tour, 420 West 45th Street, New York, NY 10036, USA (Home). *Website:* www.petesampras.com (Office).

SAMPSON, Anthony (Terrell Seward), MA; British writer and journalist; b. 3 Aug. 1926, Billingham, Durham; s. of Michael Sampson and Phyllis (née Seward) Sampson; m. Sally Bentlif 1965; one s. one d.; ed Westminster School and Christ Church, Oxford; served with RN 1944–47; Sub Lt RDVR 1946; Ed. Drum magazine, Johannesburg 1951–55; Editorial Staff, The Observer 1955–66, Chief American Corresp. 1973–74, Ed. The Observer Colour Magazine 1965–66; Assoc. Prof. Univ. of Vincennes, Paris 1968–70; Contributing Ed. Newsweek 1977–; Chair. Soc. of Authors 1992–94; Editorial Adviser, Brandt Comm. 1979; Ed. The New Statesman 1979–83; Ed. The Sampson Letter 1984–86; Trustee Scott Trust 1993–96; Prix Int. de la Presse for The Seven Sisters 1976. *Publications:* Drum, a Venture into the New Africa 1956, The Treason Cage 1958, Commonsense about Africa 1960, (with S. Pienaar), Anatomy of Britain 1962, Anatomy of Britain Today 1965, South Africa: Two Views of Separate Development 1966, Macmillan: a Study in Ambiguity 1968, The New Anatomy of Britain 1971, The Sovereign State: the Secret History of ITT 1973, The Seven Sisters 1975, The Arms Bazaar 1977, The Money Lenders 1981, The Changing Anatomy of Britain 1982, Empires of the Sky 1984, The Oxford Book of Ages (with Sally Sampson) 1985, Black and Gold: Tycoons, Revolutionaries and Apartheid 1987, The Midas Touch 1989, The Essential Anatomy of Britain 1992, Company Man 1995, The Scholar Gypsy 1997, Mandela, the Authorised Biography 1999 (Heinemann Prize 2000, Robert F. Kennedy Book Award 2000, Marsh Biog. Prize 2001). *Leisure interest:* gardening. *Address:* 10 Hereford Mansions, Hereford Road, London W2 5BA; Quarry Garden, Wardour, nr Tisbury, Wiltshire, SP3 6RN, England. *Telephone:* (20) 7727-4188 (London); (1747) 870407 (Wiltshire). *Fax:* (20) 7221-5738 (Home).

SAMS, Jeremy Charles; British director, writer and composer; b. 12 Jan. 1957; s. of Eric Charles Sydney Sams and Enid Sams (née Tidmarsh); one s.; ed Whitgift School, Magdalene Coll., Cambridge, Guildhall School of Music. *Plays:* Dir The Wind in the Willows (Tokyo) 1993, 1995, (Old Vic) 1995, Neville's Island (Nottingham Playhouse and West End), Forty Years On (West Yorks. Playhouse), Maria Friedman by Special Arrangement (Donmar Warehouse and West End), Enjoy (Nottingham Playhouse), Wild Oats (Royal Nat. Theatre) 1995, Passion (West End) 1996, Marat/Sade (Royal Nat. Theatre) 1997, 2 Pianos 4 Hands (Birmingham Repertory and West End) 1999, Spend Spend Spend (Plymouth and West End) 1999–2000, (tour) 2001, Noises Off (Royal Nat. Theatre) 2000, (West End, Broadway and tour) 2001, What The Butler Saw (Theatre Royal Bath and tour) 2001, Benefactors (West End) 2002; translated A Fool and His Money: Time And The Room (Nottingham Playhouse), Les Parents Terribles/Indiscretions (Royal Nat. Theatre/Broadway), Mary Stuart, The Miser (Royal Nat. Theatre), The Park (RSC), Becket (West End), The Rehearsal (Almeida and West End), Saturday, Sunday and Monday (Chichester Festival Theatre), Leonce and Lena (Crucible Theatre, Sheffield); as adaptor: Chitty Chitty Bang Bang (West End); as lyricist: Amour (Broadway) 2002; as composer: Arcadia, The Rehearsal, Kean, Talking Heads, The Scarlet Pimpernel, The Wind in the Willows, Ghetto, Merry Wives of Windsor, Some Americans Abroad, Ring Round The Moon,

The Country Wife, Jumpers, Don Carlos, Edward II, As You Like It. *Music:* composed for the BBC: The Mother, Have Your Cake, Persuasion (BAFTA Award), Old Times, Uncle Vanya, Welcome Home Comrades, Nativity Blues, Down Town Lagos; translated (opera) The Ring (ENO 2001–(05), The Merry Widow (Royal Opera), Der Kuhhandel (Juilliard School, New York), The Threepenny Opera (lyrics) (Donmar Warehouse & ART, Boston), La Bohème, Marriage of Figaro, Macbeth, The Force of Destiny (ENO), The Magic Flute (ENO, Opera 80, Scottish Opera), Cendrillon (Welsh Nat. Opera), Orpheus in the Underworld (Opera North, D'Oyly Carte), L'Étoile, The Reluctant King (Opera North). *Address:* c/o The Agency, 24 Pottery Lane, London, W11 4LZ (Office); 8 Quernmore Road, London, N4 4QU, England (Home). *Telephone:* (20) 7727-1346 (Office); (20) 8341-6390 (Home). *Fax:* (20) 8341-6331 (Home).

SAMSONOWICZ, Henryk, PhD; Polish politician and historian; b. 23 Jan. 1930, Warsaw; m. Agnieszka Lechowska; one s. one d.; ed Warsaw Univ.; Staff mem. Warsaw Univ. 1950–, Asst, Sr Asst, Lecturer 1950–60, Asst Prof. 1960–69, Prof., History Inst. 1969–, Dean Dept of History 1969–74, Rector 1980–82; mem. Civic Cttee attached to Lech Wałęsa (q.v.), Chair. Science and Educ. Comm., Solidarity Trade Union 1988–89; Head Dept of Social Sciences, Polish Acad. of Sciences 2001–; participant Round Table plenary debates, mem. group for political reforms and team for science, educ. and tech. progress Feb.–April 1989; Minister of Nat. Educ. 1989–90; Deputy Head Scientific Research Cttee 1994–97; mem. Polish Historical Soc., Chair. Gen. Bd 1977–82, Soc. for Advancement and Propagation of Sciences 1980–, Academia Europaea 1992–94, Acad. des Belles Lettres, Polish Acad. of Sciences 1994–; Gold Cross (Hungary); Commdr's Cross, Order of Polonia Restituta; Gold Cross of Merit; Officier, Légion d'honneur; Dr hc (Duquesne Univ., USA, High School of Educ., Cracow, Nicolaus Copernicus Univ., Toruń, Marie Curie-Skłodowska Univ., Lublin); Nat. Educ. Comm. Medal. *Publications:* books include: Bürgerkapital in Danzig des XV Jh 1970, Złota jesień polskiego Średniowiecza (Golden Autumn of the Polish Middle Ages) 1971, Dzieje miast i Polsce (History of the Towns of Poland) 1984, Republic of Nobles 1990, Dziedzictwo Średniowiecza (Heritages of the Middle Ages) 1994, Miejsce Polski w Europie (Poland's Place in Europe) 1996, Europe – North-South 1999; numerous articles. *Address:* Instytut Historyczny Uniwersytetu Warszawskiego, ul. Krakowskie Przedmieście 26/28, 00-325 Warsaw (Office); ul. Wilcza 22 m. 5, 00-544 Warsaw, Poland (Home). *Telephone:* (22) 8261988 (Office); (22) 6214061 (Home). *Fax:* (22) 8261988 (Office).

SAMUELSON, Paul Anthony, PhD, LLD, DLitt, DSc, FAAS; American economist; b. 15 May 1915, Gary, Ind.; s. of Frank Samuelson and Ella Lipton; m. 1st Marion E. Crawford 1938 (died 1978); four s. (including triplets) two d.; m. 2nd Risha Eckaus 1981; ed Hyde Park High School Chicago, Univ. of Chicago and Harvard Univ.; Prof. of Econs at MIT 1940–65, Inst. Prof. 1966–85, Inst. Prof. Emer. 1986–, Gordon Y. Billard Fellow 1986, mem. Radiation Lab. Staff 1944–45; Visiting Prof. of Political Economy, New York Univ. 1987–; Consultant to Nat. Resources Planning Bd 1941–43, to War Production Bd 1945, to US Treasury 1945–52, 1961–74, to Rand Corpn 1949–75, to Council of Econ. Advisers 1960–68, to Fed. Reserve Bd 1965–, to Finance Cttee, NAS 1977–, to Loomis, Sayles & Co. Boston and to Burden Investors Services Inc.; Research Advisory Bd Cttee for Econ. Devt 1960; Advisory Bd to Pres. Eisenhower's Comm. on Nat. Goals 1960; Nat. Task Force on Econ. Educ. 1960–61; Special Comm. on Social Sciences of Nat. Science Foundation 1967–68; Comm. on Money and Credit; Econ. Adviser to Pres. Kennedy during election campaign; author of report to Pres. Kennedy on State of American Economy 1961; Assoc. Ed. Journal of Public Econs, Journal of Int. Econs, Journal of Nonlinear Analysis; NAS Guggenheim Fellow 1948–49; mem. American Acad. of Arts and Sciences, American Economic Asscn (Pres. 1961), Int. Econ. Asscn (Pres. 1965–68, Lifetime Hon. Pres.); Fellow American Philosophical Soc., Econometric Soc. (Council mem., Vice-Pres. 1950, Pres. 1951); Corresp. Fellow British Acad.; Corresp. mem. Leibniz-Akad. der Wissenschaften und der Literatur; numerous hon. degrees; numerous awards including Nobel Prize for Economic Science 1970, Albert Einstein Commemorative Award 1971, Alumni Medal, Univ. of Chicago 1983, Britannica Award 1989, Gold Scanno Prize, Naples 1990, Medal of Science 1996, John R. Commons Award 2000; MIT est. Paul A. Samuelson Professorship in Econs 1991. *Publications:* Foundations of Economic Analysis 1947, Economics 11 edns 1948–1980, 12th–17th edns (with William D. Norhaus) 1985–2001 (trans. into 40 languages), Readings in Economics (Ed.), 7 edns 1955–73, Linear Programming and Economic Analysis (jtly) 1958, 1987, Collected Scientific Papers, I and II 1966, III 1972, IV 1979, V 1986, Collected Scientific Papers of Paul A. Samuelson (Vols I–V) 1966–87; author and jt author of numerous articles on economics. *Leisure interest:* tennis. *Address:* Massachusetts Institute of Technology, Department of Economics E52-383, Cambridge, MA 02139 (Office); 94 Somerset Street, Belmont, MA 02478, USA (Home). *Telephone:* (617) 253-3368 (Office). *Fax:* (617) 253-0560 (Office).

SAMUELSON, Sir Sydney Wylie, Kt, CBE; British film commissioner (retd); b. 7 Dec. 1925, Paddington, London; s. of G. B. Samuelson and Marjorie Samuelson; m. Doris Magen 1949; three s.; ed Irene Avenue Council School, Lancing, Sussex; served RAF 1943–47; from age 14 career devoted to various aspects of British film industry; cinema projectionist 1939–42; Asst film 1943; Asst film cameraman, cameraman and Dir of documentary films 1947–59; f. co. to service film, TV etc. supplying technical equipment 1954; continued filming as technician on locations throughout the world until 1959; Chair. Samuelson Group PLC 1966–90, Pres. 1990–95, Sr. Consultant 1998–2000; first British Film Commr 1991–97; Perm. Trustee, BAFTA 1973–, Chair. Council 1973–76, Chair. Bd Man. 1976–, Fellow 1993; Chair. BAFTA-Shell UK Venture Cttee 1988-91; Hon. Pres. Brighton Jewish Film Festival; mem. Exec. Cttee Cinema and TV Veterans (Pres. 1980–81); mem. Council and Exec. Cttee Cinema & TV Benevolent Fund 1969–92 (Trustee 1982–90); Fellow BFI 1997; Gov. British Soc. of Cinematographers 1969–79, Chair. Scholarships' Trust 1999–; Patron BKSTS–The Moving Image Soc.; many other professional appts; Dr hc (Sheffield Hallam) 1996; Michael Balcon Award, BAFTA 1985; Award of Merit, Guild of Film Production Execs 1986, Lifetime Achievement Award, Birmingham Int. Film and TV Festival 1997. *Leisure interests:* collecting recorded film music, vintage motoring, veteran jogging. *Address:* 31 West Heath Avenue, London, NW11 7QJ, England (Home). *Telephone:* (20) 8455-6696 (Home). *Fax:* (20) 8458-1957 (Home). *E-mail:* sydneysam@compuserve.com (Home).

SAMUELSSON, Bengt Ingemar, DMS, MD; Swedish medical chemist; b. 21 May 1934, Halmstad; s. of Anders Samuelsson and Stina Nilsson; m. Inga Bergstein 1958; two c.; ed Karolinska Inst. Stockholm; Asst Prof. Karolinska Inst. 1961–66, Prof. of Medical and Physiological Chem. 1972–, Chair. Dept of Physiological Chem. 1973–83, Dean, Faculty of Medicine 1978–83, Rector 1983–95; Research Fellow, Harvard Univ. 1961–62; Prof. of Medical Chem. Royal Veterinary Coll. Stockholm 1967–72; mem. Nobel Cttee of Physiology or Medicine 1984–89, Chair. 1987–89; Chair. Nobel Foundation 1993–; mem. Research Advisory Bd Swedish Govt 1985–88, Nat. Comm. on Health Policy 1987–90, European Science and Tech. Ass. 1994–; Special Advisor to Commr for Research and Educ., EC 1995–; mem. Royal Swedish Acad. of Sciences; Foreign Assoc. NAS; Foreign mem. Royal Soc. (London), Mediterranean Acad. of Sciences, Acad. Europaea, French Acad. of Sciences, Spanish Soc. of Allergology and Clinical Immunology, Royal Nat. Acad. of Medicine (Spain), Int. Acad. of Sciences; Hon. Prof. Bethune Univ. of Medical Sciences, Changchun, China 1986; Hon. mem. Asscn of American Physicians, AAAS, Swedish Medical Asscn, American Soc. of Biological Chemists, Italian Pharmacology Soc., Acad. Nat. Medicina de Buenos Aires, Int. Soc. of Haematology; Hon. DSc (Chicago) 1978, (Illinois) 1983, (Louisiana State Univ.) 1993; Dr. hc (Rio de Janeiro) 1986, (Complutense Univ., Madrid) 1991, (Milan) 1993; Hon. DUniv (Buenos Aires) 1986; recipient of numerous honours and awards including Louisa Gross Horwitz Award 1975, Lasker Award 1977, Gairdner Foundation Award 1981, Nobel Prize in Physiology or Medicine 1982, Abraham White Science Achievement Award 1991, City of Medicine Award 1992, Maria Theresa Medal 1996. *Publications:* articles in professional journals. *Address:* Karolinska Institutet, Department of Medical Biochemistry and Biophysics, Solnavagen 1, 17177 Stockholm, Sweden. *Telephone:* (8) 728-76-00.

SAN GIACOMO, Laura; American actress; b. 11 Nov. 1962, New Jersey; m. Cameron Dye; ed Carnegie Mellon Univ., Pennsylvania; started career in regional theatre productions. *Theatre includes:* North Shore Fish, Beirut, The Love Talker, Italian American Reconciliation. *Films:* Sex, Lies and Videotape (New Generation Award, LA Film Critics' Asscn) 1989, Pretty Woman, Vital Signs, Quigley Down Under, Once Around, Under Suspicion, Where the Day Takes You, Nina Takes a Lover, Stuart Saves His Family, Eat Your Heart Out 1997, Suicide Kings 1997, Apocalypse 1997, With Friends Like These . . . 1998, Mom's on the Roof. *Television:* Miami Vice, Crime Story, Spenser: For Hire, The Equalizer, Just Shoot Me. *Address:* More Medavoy Management, 7920 West Sunset Boulevard, Suite 401, Los Angeles, CA 90046, USA.

SANBAR, Samir H., BBA; Lebanese international civil servant; b. 9 March 1934, Haifa; s. of Habib Sanbar and Georgette Khoury; ed American Univ. of Beirut; Deputy Ed. Al Howadeth, Al-Sayyad (Arab weeklies) and journalist with various Lebanese, Arab and int. media; Political Ed. Al-Usbu Al Araby (pan-Arab weekly), Beirut 1954–65; Information Officer of Special Rep. of Sec.-Gen. for UNYOM 1964; Special Asst to Personal Rep. of Sec.-Gen. of UNITAR 1965–70; Special Asst to Exec. Dir UNITAR 1970–73; accompanied UN Sec.-Gen. on all visits to Middle East 1973–87; Dir UN Information Centre, Beirut, Chief, Information Services of ECWA and Co-ordinator of UN public information activities in Gulf countries 1975–82; special assignment to assist Office of Sec.-Gen. in liaison and media functions during establishment of UNIFIL 1978–82; Chief UN Centres Services 1982–87; Dir UN Information Centres, Dept of Public Information 1987–93; Special Rep. of UN Sec.-Gen. to head UN mission to verify Referendum in Eritrea 1993; Asst Sec.-Gen. UN Dept of Public Information 1994–98; int. communications consultant. *Publication:* Hold on to Your Dreams; (short stories in Arabic): Characters From Ras Beirut, Aleikum Salam (Greetings). *Address:* 240 East 47th Street, New York, NY 10017, USA. *Telephone:* (212) 371-3302. *Fax:* (212) 371-3302.

SANBERK, Özdem; Turkish diplomatist (retd); b. 1 Aug. 1938, Ankara; s. of Halil Turgut Sanberk and Nimet Sanberk; m. Sumru Sanberk; one d.; ed Lycée de Galatasaray, Faculty of Law, Univ. of Istanbul; fmrly at Embassies in Bonn, Paris, Madrid; fmr Foreign Policy Adviser to Prime Minister Turgut Ozal; fmr Amb. to EU 1987–91, to UK 1995–2000; fmr Under-Sec. to Ministry of Foreign Affairs 1990–95; Dir Turkish Econ. and Social Studies Foundation 2000–; mem. Turkish–Armenian Reconciliation Comm., Turkish–Greek Forum; specialist on Turkish–EU relations, the Western Alliance, the Middle East second-track diplomacy and conflict resolution; broadcaster on domestic and foreign policy issues on radio and both Turkish and foreign TV; Comendador de la Orden de Mérito (Spain), Comendador de la Orden de Isabel la Católica (Spain); Verdienstmedaille des Verdienstordens (Germany). *Publications:* numerous articles in Turkish and int. newspapers. *Leisure interests:* reading, walking, music. *Address:* Turkish Economic and Social Studies Foundation, Bankalar Cad. No. 2, Minerva Han Kat 3, Karaköy, 80020

Istanbul, Turkey (Office). *Telephone:* (212) 2928903 (Office). *Fax:* (212) 2929046 (Office). *E-mail:* osanberk@tesev.org.tr (Office). *Website:* tesev.org.tr (Office).

SANCAR, M. Sitki, MSc; Turkish petroleum executive; b. 10 Aug. 1941, Gemlik; m. Ayse Sancar 1968; one s. one d.; ed Univs. of Istanbul and Tulsa, Okla; well site geologist, Turkish Petroleum Co. (TPAO) 1967–70, research geologist and Dist Man. 1974–79; Gen. Dir MTA-Mineral Research & Exploration Inst. of Turkey 1979–88; Deputy Under-Sec. Ministry of Energy 1988–93; Chair. and Gen. Man. TPAO 1993–99; Adviser to Ministry of Energy 1999–; mem. Asscn of Petroleum Geologists of Turkey; Hon. mem. Chamber of Petroleum Engineers of Turkey. *Publications:* several scientific papers. *Address:* Binses Sitesi, 4 Cad. 21, Ümitköy, 06530 Ankara, Turkey (Home). *Telephone:* (312) 2351095 (Home). *E-mail:* mssancar@tr.net (Home).

SÁNCHEZ DE LOZADA, Gonzalo; Bolivian politician; b. 1 July 1930; m. Ximena Iturralde Monje; one s. one d.; ed Univ. of Chicago; Founder and Man. Telecine Ltda (documentary and commercial film production) 1953–57; Founder and Gen. Man. Andean Geo-Services Ltd 1957–62; Founder and Pres. Compañía Minera del Sur (COMSUR) 1962–79, Pres. 1980–82; mem. Parl. 1979–80, 1982–85; Senator for Cochabamba and Pres. Senate 1985–86; Minister for Planning and Coordination 1986–88; Presidential cand. 1989; Leader, Movimiento Nacionalista Revolucionario (Histórico) (MNR) 1988–; Pres. of Bolivia 1993–97, 2002–. *Address:* Ministry of the Presidency, Palacio de Gobierno, Plaza Murillo, La Paz, Bolivia (Office). *Telephone:* (2) 237-1082 (Office). *Fax:* (2) 237-1388 (Office).

SÁNCHEZ GALÁN, Ignacio; Spanish industrial engineer; b. Sept. 1950, Salamanca; ed Eng Tech. School (ICAI), Madrid; Commercial Dir SE Acumulador Tudor SA, Operations Man., Man. Industrial Batteries Div., Pres. and CEO several cos in Grupo Tudor 1972–91; Gen. Man. and CEO ITP 1991–95; CEO Airtel Movil 1995–2001; Vice-Chair. and CEO Iberdrola 2001–; Chair. of APEX Inmobiliaria; mem. Bd Nutreco Holding BV, Page Iberica, GALP, Red Electrica de España, Bodegas Matarromera, Corporación IBV, Puleva Biotech and other cos. *Leisure interests:* hunting, horse riding. *Address:* Iberdrola, Cardenal Gardoqui 8, 48008 Bilbao, Spain (Office). *Telephone:* (4) 4794811 (Office). *Fax:* (4) 4705069 (Office). *Website:* www .iberdrola.es (Office).

SÁNCHEZ-VICARIO, Arantxa; Spanish tennis player; b. 18 Dec. 1971, Barcelona; d. of Emilio Sánchez and Marisa Vicario; most successful Spanish tennis player ever; turned professional in 1984 and won first professional title at Brussels 1988; winner French Open Women's title 1989, 1994, 1998, Int. Championships of Spain 1989, 1990, Virginia Slims Tournaments Newport 1991, Washington 1991, Canadian Open 1992, Australian Open Women's Doubles 1992, Mixed Doubles 1993, US Open 1994; named Int. Tennis Fed. World Champion 1994; silver medal (doubles), bronze medal (singles) 1992 Olympics; silver medal (singles), bronze medal (doubles) 1996 Olympics; Spanish Fed. Cup team 1986–98, 2000–01; winner of 14 Grand Slam titles, 96 WTA Tour titles and over 16 million dollars in prize money at retirement Nov. 2002; mem. Spanish Olympic Cttee 2001; Infiniti Commitment to Excellence Award 1992, Tennis Magazine Comeback Player of the Year 1998, Principe de Asturias Award (Spain) 1998, Int. Tennis Fed. Award of Excellence 2001. *Publication:* The Young Tennis Player: A Young Enthusiast's Guide to Tennis 1996. *Leisure interests:* soccer, water skiing, reading, horse riding, languages. *Address:* IMG, 1360 East 9th Street, Suite 100, Cleveland, OH 4414, USA (Office).

SÁNCHEZ-VILELLA, Roberto; Puerto Rican politician; b. 19 Feb. 1913, Mayaguez; s. of Luis Sánchez-Frasqueri and Angela Vilella-Vélez; one s. three d.; ed Ohio State Univ.; Sub-Commr of the Interior 1941–42; Dir Transportation Authority of Puerto Rico 1942–45; Special Asst to Pres. of Senate 1946–47; Resident Engineer Caribe Hilton Hotel 1947–48; Exec. Sec. to Govt 1949–51; Sec. of State 1952–64; Gov. Puerto Rico 1965–69; Prof. School of Public Admin. 1974–94, School of Laws, Univ. of Puerto Rico 1987–94; fmr Pres. People's Party; mem. Puerto Rico Coll. of Engineers, American Soc. of Public Administrators; Hon. LLD (Ohio State Univ.) 1966; Hon. DEng (Mayagüez Campus, Univ. of Puerto Rico) 1996; Hon. DJur (Rio Piedras Campus, Univ. of Puerto Rico) 1996. *Leisure interests:* reading, dominoes. *Address:* 414 Muñoz Rivera Avenue, Suite 7-A, Stop 31-1/2, Hato Rey, Puerto Rico 00918. *Telephone:* 753-9156.

SANCHO-ROF, Juan, D.CHEM.ENG.; Spanish businessman; b. 9 Feb. 1940, Madrid; m. Paloma Suils; two s. three d.; ed Universidad Complutense de Madrid and Instituto de Estudios Superiores de la Empresa, Barcelona; Technical–Commercial post Petronor SA (Petróleos del Norte) 1970–74, Deputy Gen. Man. 1976–85; Chair. and CEO Repsol Petróleo SA 1985, Pres. 1995–; now Pres. Petronor and Exec. Vice-Pres. Repsol SA. *Publications:* several technical works. *Address:* Petronor, Apartado 1418, 48080, Bilbao, Spain (Office); Paseo de la Castellana 180, 28046 Madrid, Spain. *Telephone:* (91) 3488116 (Office). *Fax:* (91) 3488793 (Office). *E-mail:* petronor@repsol.ypf .es (Office). *Website:* www.repsol-ypf.com (Office).

SANDAGE, Allan Rex, PhD, DSc; American astronomer; b. 18 June 1926, Iowa City; s. of Charles H. Sandage and Dorothy M. Briggs; m. Mary L. Connelly 1959; two s.; ed Univ. of Illinois and California Inst. of Tech.; staff mem. Mount Wilson and Palomar Observatories 1952–; Asst Astronomer Hale Observatories, Calif. 1952–56, Astronomer 1956–; Sr Research Astronomer Space Telescope Scientific Inst., NASA 1986–; Homewood Prof. of

Physics, Johns Hopkins Univ., Baltimore 1987–88; Visiting Astronomer, Univ. of Hawaii 1986; Visiting Lecturer, Harvard Univ. 1957; Consultant, NSF 1961–63; Assoc. Ed. Annual Review of Astronomy and Astrophysics 1990–; mem. Cttee on Science and Public Policy 1965; Philips Lecturer, Haverford Coll. 1968; Research Assoc. ANU 1968–69; Fulbright-Hayes Scholar 1972; Grubb-Parson Lecturer, Royal Astronomical Soc. 1992; mem. Royal and American Astronomical Socs.; numerous hon. degrees; Helen Warner Prize of American Astronomical Soc. 1960, Russell Prize 1973; Eddington Medal, Royal Astronomical Soc. (UK) 1963; Pope Pius XI Gold Medal, Pontifical Acad. of Sciences 1966; Gold Medal, Royal Astronomical Soc. (UK) 1967, Rittenhouse Medal 1968, Nat. Medal of Scientific Merit 1971, Elliott Gresson Medal, Franklin Inst. 1973, Gold Medal of Pacific Astronomical Soc. 1975, Craaford Prize, Swedish Acad. of Science 1991, Adion Medal, Observatoire de Nice 1991, Tomalla Gravity Prize, Swiss Physical Soc. 1992, Gruber Cosmology Prize 2000. *Publications:* numerous scientific papers and Hubble Atlas of Galaxies. *Leisure interests:* bread-making, gardening. *Address:* Carnegie Observatories, 813 Santa Barbara Street, Pasadena, CA 91101 (Office); 8319 Josard Road, San Gabriel, CA 91775, USA (Home). *Telephone:* (818) 285-5086 (Home).

SANDBERG, Baron (Life Peer), cr. 1997, of Passfield in the County of Hampshire; **Michael Graham Ruddock Sandberg,** Kt, CBE, FCIB, FRSA; British banker; b. 31 May 1927, Thames Ditton, Surrey; s. of the late Gerald Arthur Clifford Sandberg and Ethel Marion (née Ruddock) Sandberg; m. Carmel Mary Roseleen Donnelly 1954; two s. two d.; ed St Edward's School, Oxford; mil. service 1945–48, commissioned into 6th DCO Lancers, Indian Army, later 1st King's Dragoon Guards; joined Hongkong and Shanghai Banking Corpn 1949, Deputy Chair. 1973–77, Chair. 1977–86; Chair. British Bank of the Middle East 1980–86; Pres. Surrey County Cricket Club 1987–88; Vice-Pres. Chartered Inst. of Bankers 1984–87; JP Hong Kong 1972–86; Dir Int. Totalizator Systems Inc., New World Devt Ltd, Winsor Ind. Corpn; mem. of Exec. Council of Hong Kong 1978–86; Treasurer Univ. of Hong Kong 1977–86; Chair. of Stewards, Royal Hong Kong Jockey Club 1981–86, Hon. Steward 1986; Hon. LLD (Hong Kong) 1984, (Pepperdine) 1986; Freeman City of London; Liveryman Worshipful Co. of Clockmakers. *Publication:* The Sangberg Watch Collection 1998. *Leisure interests:* horse racing, cricket, bridge, horology. *Address:* House of Lords, London, SW1A 0PW (Office); Suite 9, 100 Piccadilly, London, W1V 9FN; Waterside, Passfield, Liphook, Hants., GU30 7RT, England (Home). *Telephone:* (1428) 751225 (Liphook) (Home); (20) 7629-2204 (Piccadilly).

SANDER, Michael Arthur, BSc; South African business executive; b. 2 Oct. 1941, Germiston; s. of Norman William Henry Sander and Nora McLaverty; m. Pamela Wendy Mills 1968; one s. one d.; ed Durban High School, Univ. of Natal; joined AECI Ltd as Overseas Industrial Bursar and seconded to ICI Heavy Organic Chemicals Div., Teeside, UK 1963–65; then returned to AECI Devt Dept and became involved in new project Devt; apptd. Gen. Man., Anikem (Pty) Ltd 1970; moved to subsidiary Co. Rand Carbide as Devt Man. 1977; Man. Dir AECI Chlor-Alkali and Plastics Ltd 1982, Chair. 1984; Exec. Dir AECI Ltd 1984, Man. Dir 1985–95, Chair. (non-exec.) 1994–97; Chair. Daewoo Electronics; Deputy Chair. Amic (Pty) Ltd, currently Dir of a number of AECI group subsidiary and assoc. cos. *Leisure interests:* shooting, fishing, photography, music. *Address:* P.O. Box 61587, Marshalltown 2107, South Africa.

SANDERLING, Kurt; German conductor; b. 19 Sept. 1912, Arys; m. 1st Nina Bobath 1941; m. 2nd Barbara Wagner 1963; three s.; Conductor Moscow Radio Symphony Orchestra 1936–41, Leningrad Philharmonic 1941–60, Chief Conductor Dresden State Orchestra 1964–67; Guest appearances at Prague, Warsaw, Salzburg and Vienna Festivals; with Leipzig Gewandhaus Orchestra, New Philharmonia Orchestra 1972–; conducted LA Philharmonic 1991; Chief Prof. of Conducting, Leningrad Conservatory; retd 2002; many awards and prizes (USSR and GDR). *Address:* c/o Norman McCann International Artists Ltd, The Coach House, 56 Lawrie Park Gardens, London, SE26 6YJ (Office); The Music Partnership Ltd, 41 Adelbert Terrace, London, SW8 7BH, England (Office); Am Iderfenngraben 47, 13156 Berlin, Germany. *Telephone:* 9167558. *Fax:* 9167558.

SANDERS, Donald Neil, AO, C.B., B.ECON.; Australian banker; b. 21 June 1927, Sydney; s. of L. G. and R. M. Sanders; m. Betty Elaine Constance 1952; four s. one d.; ed Wollongong High School, Univ. of Sydney; Commonwealth Bank of Australia 1943–60; Australian Treasury 1956; Bank of England 1960–61; with Reserve Bank of Australia 1961–87, Supt, Credit Policy Div. of Banking Dept 1964–66, Deputy Man. of Banking Dept 1966–67, of Research Dept 1967–70; Australian Embassy, Washington DC 1968; Chief Man. of Securities Markets Dept 1970–72, of Banking and Finance Dept 1972–74, Adviser and Chief Man. 1974–75, Deputy Gov. and Deputy Chair. of Bd 1975–87; Man. Dir Commonwealth Banking Corpn 1987–91; Man. Dir, CEO Commonwealth Bank of Australia 1991–92; Chair. H-G Ventures Ltd 1995–2000; Dir Lend Lease Corpn Ltd, MLC Ltd 1992–99, Queensland Investment Corpn 1992–98, Australian Chamber Orchestra Pty Ltd 1992–99. *Leisure interests:* golf, music. *Address:* 'Somerset', Taralga Road, via Goulburn, NSW 2580, Australia. *Telephone:* (2) 4840-2095. *Fax:* (2) 4840-2058 (Home).

SANDERS, Jeremy Keith Morris, PhD, ScD, FRS; British professor of chemistry; b. 3 May 1948, London; s. of Sidney Sanders and Sylvia Sanders (née Rutman); m. Louise Elliott 1972; one s. one d.; ed Wandsworth School,

Imperial Coll., London, Univ. of Cambridge; Research Assoc. in Pharmacology Stanford Univ. 1972–73; Demonstrator in Chemistry Univ. of Cambridge 1973–78, Lecturer 1978–92, Reader 1992–96, Prof. 1996–, Head Dept of Chemistry 2000–; Fellow Selwyn Coll., Cambridge 1976–; Pedler Lecturer, RSC 1996, Chair. Editorial Bd Chemical Soc. Reviews 2000–02; Pfizer Award 1984, 1988. *Publication:* Modern NMR Spectroscopy (with B. K. Hunter). *Address:* University Chemical Laboratory, Lensfield Road, Cambridge, CB2 1EW, England. *Telephone:* (1223) 336411. *Fax:* (1223) 336017. *E-mail:* jkms@ cam.ac.uk (Office). *Website:* www.ch.cam.ac.uk/cucl/staff/jkms.html (Office).

SANDERS, Sir Ronald Michael, Kt, KCMG, KCN, MA; Antigua and Barbuda diplomatist and international relations consultant; b. 26 Jan. 1948, Guyana; m. Susan Ramphal 1975; ed Sacred Heart RC School, Guyana and Boston Univ., USA, Univ. of Sussex; Man. Dir Guyana Broadcasting Service, Public Affairs Adviser to Prime Minister of Guyana 1973–76; Lecturer in Communications, Univ. of Guyana 1975–76; Consultant to Pres. of Caribbean Devt Bank, Barbados 1977–78; Special Adviser to the Minister of Foreign Affairs of Antigua and Barbuda 1978–82; Deputy Perm. Rep. of Antigua and Barbuda to the UN, New York 1982–83; Antigua and Barbuda Amb. Extraordinary and Plenipotentiary Accred to UNESCO 1983–87; Antigua and Barbuda High Commr in UK 1984–87, 1995– (also accred to FRG 1986–87, 1996–, to France 1996–), Chief Foreign Affairs Rep. with Ministerial Rank 1999–; Deputy Chair. Caribbean Financial Action Task Force 2002–; Pres. Caribbean Broadcasting Union 1975–76; Chair. Caribbean Sub-Group at UNESCO 1983–85; mem. Bd of Dirs. of Caribbean News Agency 1976–77; mem. Inter-Governmental Council of the Int. Programme for the Devt of Communications at UNESCO 1983–87; mem. Exec. Bd UNESCO 1985–87; Visiting Fellow, Oxford Univ. 1987–89; freelance broadcaster with BBC World Service 1987–89; Consultant (Int. Rels.) Atlantic Tele-Network, US Virgin Islands 1989–97; mem. Bd Dirs. Swiss American Nat. Bank of Antigua 1990–97, Guyana Telephone and Telegraph Co. 1991–97, Innovative Communications Inc., U.S. Virgin Is. 1998–. *Publications:* Broadcasting in Guyana 1978, Antigua and Barbuda: Transition, Trial, Triumph 1984, Inseparable Humanity: Anthology of Reflections of the Commonwealth Secretary-General (Ed.) 1988, Antigua Vision: Caribbean Reality, Perspectives of Prime Minister Lester Bird (Ed.) 2002; numerous articles on media ownership and control, communication and development and Antarctica. *Leisure interests:* reading, West Indian history, cinema. *Address:* Antigua and Barbuda High Commission, 15 Thayer Street, London, W1I 3JT, England (Office). *Telephone:* (20) 7486-7073 (Office). *Fax:* (20) 7486-9970 (Office). *E-mail:* antiguahc@msn.com (Office). *Website:* www.antigua-barbuda.com (Office).

SANDERSON, Bryan Kaye, CBE, BSc; British business executive; b. 14 Oct. 1940, Co. Durham; s. of Eric and Anne Sanderson; m. Sirkka Kärki 1966; one s. one d.; ed Dame Allan's School, LSE, UK, IMEDE Lausanne, Switzerland; VSO Peru 1962–64; joined British Petroleum (BP) 1964, Senior Rep. for South East Asia and China 1984–87, CEO BP Nutrition 1987–90, CEO BP Chemicals, then BP Amoco Chemicals 1990–97, mem. Bd BP 1992–2000; Dir (non-exec.) Corus (frmly British Steel) 1994–, Six Continents hotel group 2001–; Chair. (non-exec.) BUPA 2001–; Dir (non-exec.) Standard Chartered 2002–03, Chair. May 2003–; mem. Advisory Group to the Labour Party on Industrial Competition Policy 1997–98, DTI Advisory Group on Competitiveness 1998–, King's Fund Man. Cttee 1999–, DTI Co. Law Steering Group 1998–2001, DTI Industrial Devt Advisory Bd 2000–; Pres. CEFIC 1998–2000; Gov. LSE 1997–, Vice-Chair. Govs. 1998–; Chair. Sunderland Football Club PLC 1998–, Learning and Skills Council 2000–, Sunderland Urban Regeneration Co. 2001–; Hon. FIChemE 2002; Hon. DBA (Sunderland) 1998, (York) 1999. *Leisure interests:* reading, golf, walking, gardening. *Address:* Standard Chartered PLC, 1 Aldermanbury Square, London, EC2V 7SB England (Office). *Telephone:* (20) 7280-7500 (Office). *Fax:* (20) 7600-2546 (Office). *Website:* www .standardchartered.com (Office).

SANDERSON, Tessa, OBE; British athlete; b. 14 March 1956, St Elizabeth, Jamaica; ed Bilston Coll. of Further Educ.; silver medal for javelin Euro Championships 1978; gold medal Commonwealth Championships 1978, 1986, 1990; gold medal (Olympic record), Olympic Games, LA 1984; gold medal World Cup 1992; competed Olympic Games, Atlanta 1996; sports presenter Sky News 1989–92; Bd mem. English Sports Council 1998–; Vice-Chair. Sport England; Patron Disabled Olympics; Hon. Fellow Wolverhampton Polytechnic; Hon. BSc (Birmingham). *Publication:* My Life in Athletics (autobiog.) 1985. *Leisure interest:* cardiofunk (low impact aerobic exercise workout). *Address:* c/o Derek Evans, 68 Meadowbank Road, Kingsbury, London, N.W.9, England. *E-mail:* tessa@tprmplus.freeserve.co.uk (Office).

SANDIFORD, Rt Hon Sir Lloyd Erskine, PC, JP, MA(ECON.); Barbadian politician and educationalist; b. 24 March 1937; s. of the late Cyril G. Sandiford and of Eunice Sandiford; m. Angelita P. Ricketts 1963; one s. two d.; ed Coleridge-Parry Secondary School, Harrison Coll., Barbados, Univ. Coll. of the W Indies, Jamaica and Univ. of Manchester; Asst Master, Modern High School, Barbados 1956–57, Kingston Coll., Jamaica 1960–61; part-time Tutor and Lecturer, Univ. of the W Indies, Barbados 1963–65, Distinguished Fellow, Sir Arthur Lewis Inst. of Social and Econ. Studies, Univ. of the West Indies 1999–; Sr Grad. Master, Harrison Coll. 1964–66; Asst Tutor, Barbados Community Coll. 1976–86; mem. Barbados Senate 1967–71, MP for St Michael S. 1971–99; Personal Asst to Prime Minister 1966–67; Minister of Educ. 1967–71, of Educ., Youth Affairs, Community Devt and Sport 1971–75, of Health and Welfare 1975–76; Deputy Prime Minister and Minister of Educ.

and Culture 1986–87; Prime Minister of Barbados and Minister of Finance 1987–93, Prime Minister and Minister of Econ. Affairs and the Civil Service 1987–94, also of Defence; mem. Democratic Labour Party, Asst Sec., Gen. Sec., Pres. 1974–75; Founder, Acad of Politics; Pres. Sandiford Centre for Public Affairs; mem. Council of Freely Elected Presidents and Prime Ministers, Carter Center, Atlanta; Life mem. Barbados Cricket Asscn; Barbados Scholar 1956, Pres.'s Medal of Excellence, Bowie State Univ., Md, Order of the Liberator (Venezuela), Kt of St Andrew 2000. *Publications;* The Essence of Economics 1997, Caribbean Politics and Society 2000. *Leisure interests:* choral singing, reading, gardening, swimming, cricket. *Address:* Hillvista, Porters, St James, Barbados. *Telephone:* 422-3458 (Home). *Fax:* 422-0281 (Home). *E-mail:* lesandiford@canbsurf.com (Home).

SANDLE, Michael Leonard, FRBS, DFA; British artist; b. 18 May 1936, Weymouth, Dorset; s. of Charles E. Sandle and Dorothy G. Sandle (née Vernon) ; m. 1st Cynthia D. Koppel 1971 (divorced 1974); m. 2nd Demelza Spargo 1988; one s. one d.; ed Douglas High School, Isle of Man, Douglas School of Art and Tech. and Slade School of Fine Art; studied lithography, Atelier Patris, Paris 1960; began sculpture 1962; held various teaching posts in UK 1961–70 including Leicester and Coventry Colls of Art; resident in Canada 1970–73; Visiting Prof. Univ. of Calgary 1970–71; Visiting Assoc. Prof. Univ. of Victoria, BC 1972–73; Lecturer in Sculpture, Fachhochschule für Gestaltung, Pforzheim, FRG 1973–77, Prof. 1977–80; Prof. Akad. der Bildenden Künste, Karlsruhe 1980–99; resgnd from RA 1997; various exhbns in UK and internationally since 1957 including V. Biennale, Paris 1966, Documenta IV, Kassel 1968, Documenta VI 1977, Whitechapel Art Gallery, London 1988, Württembergischer Kunstverein, Stuttgart 1989, Ernst Múzeum, Budapest 1990; works in many public collections in UK, Germany, Australia, USA etc.; Nobutaka Shikanai Prize, 1st Rodin Grand Prize Exhbn, Japan 1986; Henry Hering Memorial Medal, Nat. Sculpture Soc. of America 1995. *Achievement:* designed architecture and executed sculpture for the Malta Siege Memorial, Grand Harbour, Valletta 1999–92; designed the Int. Memorial for Seafarers sited at the Int. Maritime Org's HQ, London 2001. *Address:* c/o Royal Society of British Sculptors, 108 Old Brompton Road, London, SW7 3RA, England. *Fax:* (1566) 773984 (Home).

SANDLER, Adam; American actor and screenwriter; b. 1964; ed New York Univ.; recorded album They're All Gonna Laugh at You! 1993; People's Choice Award 2000. *Albums:* They're All Gonna Laugh at You! 1993, Big Daddy 1999. *Films include:* Shakes the Clown, Coneheads, Mixed Nuts, Airheads, Billy Madison, Happy Gilmore, Bullet Proof, Guy Gets Kid 1998, The Wedding Singer 1998, The Water Boy 1998, Big Daddy 1999, Little Nicky 2000, Punch-Drunk Love 2002, Mr Deeds 2002, Anger Management 2003; actor, writer Saturday Night Live. *Television appearances include:* Saturday Night Live Mother's Day Special 1992, MTV Music Video Awards 1994, Saturday Night Live Presents Pres. Bill Clinton's All-Time Favorites 1994, The 37th Annual Grammy Awards 1995, The ESPY Awards 1996. *Screenplays:* (co-writer) Billy Madison, Happy Gilmore, The Water Boy. *Publications:* Little Nicky 2000. *Address:* Agency for Performing Arts, 888 7th Avenue, Suite 602, New York, NY 10106 (Office); c/o Ballstein-Grey, 9150 Wilshire Boulevard, Suite 350, Beverly Hills, CA 90212, USA.

SANDLER, Ron, MA, MBA; South African financial executive; b. 5 March 1952, Durban, South Africa; s. of Bernard M. Sandler and Carla Sandler; m. Susan Lee 1977; two s.; ed Queens' Coll. Cambridge, Stanford Univ., USA; ran LA office of Boston Consulting, USA, then London office of Booz Allen; f. own man. consultancy firm 1988; apptd. Chair. Quadrex Holdings 1990; joined Lloyd's of London 1994, Chief Exec. 1995–99, COO Nat. Westminster Bank PLC 1999–2000; Chair. Computacenter 2001–, Kyte Group–; Head, Inquiry into Long-term Savings 2001; Trustee Royal Opera House 1999–. *Address:* 5 Southside, Wimbledon, London, SW19 4TG, England. *Telephone:* (1707) 631602 (Office); (20) 8946-1179 (Home).

SANDMO, Agnar, DR.ECON.; Norwegian economist; b. 9 Jan. 1938, Tønsberg; m. Tone Sverdrup 1959; two s. one d.; ed Tønsberg Gymnasium and Norwegian School of Econs and Business Admin.; Grad. Fellow, Norwegian School of Econs and Business Admin. 1963–66, Asst Prof. of Econs 1966–71, Prof. 1971–, Vice-Rector 1985–87; Visiting Fellow, Catholic Univ. of Louvain 1969–70; Visiting Prof. Univ. of Essex 1975–76; mem. Petroleum Price Bd 1976–80 and several Govt bds and cttees on social science and gen. research policy; Fellow, Econometric Soc.; mem. Norwegian and Swedish Acads of Science; Pres. European Econ. Asscn 1990; Order of St Olav 1997; Dr hc (Univ. of Oslo) 1997; Research Council of Norway Prize for Outstanding Research 2002. *Publications:* articles and books on Econs and econ. policy. *Address:* Norwegian School of Economics and Business Administration, Helleveien 30, 5045 Bergen (Office); Øyjordsbotten 28A, 5038 Bergen, Norway (Home). *Telephone:* 55-95-92-76 (Office); 55-25-65-86 (Home). *E-mail:* agnar.sandmo@ nhh.no (Office).

SANDOVAL, Arturo; Cuban jazz trumpeter; b. 1949, Artemisa; m. Marianela Sandoval; one s.; ed Nat. School of Art; began trumpet playing aged 12 and made first public appearances in Cuba aged 13; played in group with Chucho Váldez until 1981; formed own group in 1981 and now undertakes annual maj. world tour; festival appearances at Tokyo, Newport, Montreux, Antibes, Chicago, the Hague and the Hollywood Bowl; several record albums.

SANDOVAL IÑÍGUEZ, HE Cardinal Juan; Mexican ecclesiastic; b. 28 March 1933, Yahualica, Jalisco; s. of Esteban Sandoval and María Guadalupe Iñiguez; ed Seminario Diocesano de Guadalajara, Pontifica Universidad

Gregoriana; ordained as a Catholic priest 1957; teacher Seminario de Guadalajara 1961, Prof. of Philosophy, Vice-Rector 1971, Rector 1980; Bishop's Coadjutor, Juárez 1988, Bishop of Juárez 1992; Archbishop of Guadalajara 1994; cr. Cardinal 1994; mem. IV Latin American Archbishop's Conf., Santo Domingo 1992. *Address:* Arzobispado, Liceo 17, Apdo. 1-331, 44100 Guadalajara, Mexico. *Telephone:* (3) 614-5504. *Fax:* (3) 658-2300.

SANDRE, Didier (Didier de Maffre); French actor; b. 17 Aug. 1946, Paris; s. of Pierre Maffre and Geneviève Gevril; one d.; m. 2nd Nada Strancar 1990; ed Lycée d'Enghien-les-Bains, Collège Estienne, Paris; stage roles include: Dom Juan, La Tempête, Le Conte d'hiver, Phèdre, L'Ecole des Femmes, Le Misanthrope, Tartuffe, Les Paravents, Fausse Suivante, Terre Etrangère, Martyr de Saint-Sébastien, Madame de Sade, Le Mariage de Figaro, Le Soulier de Satin, Ivanov, Le Chemin Solitaire, Partage de Midi, Dinner with Friends, Thomas Becket, Bérénice; Chevalier des Arts et des Lettres, Chevalier Ordre nat. du Mérite; Prix Syndicat de la Critique; Molière Prize for Best Actor 1996. *Films include:* Mensonge 1993, Train d'enfer, La Femme de ma vie, Petits arrangements avec les morts 1995, Conte d'Automne 1997, Le mystère Paul 2000. *Leisure interests:* piano, skiing, climbing. *Address:* c/o Agents Associés Guy Bonnet, 201 rue Faubourg St Honoré, 75008 Paris, France. *Telephone:* 1-42-56-04-57.

SANDSTRÖM, Sven, BA, MBA, PhD; Swedish banker and international finance official; ed Univ. of Stockholm, Stockholm School of Econs, Royal Inst. of Tech.; consultancy work 1966–68; Research Assoc. MIT and Harvard Business School, USA 1969–72; joined IBRD 1972, Project Analyst, Urban Projects Dept 1973, Deputy Div. Chief 1977, Div. Chief 1979, Div. Chief Urban Devt and Water Supply, S. Asia Projects 1986, Dir Southern Africa Dept 1987–90, Dir Office of the Pres. 1990–91, Man. Dir 1991–, Chair. Operation Cttee, Chair. Information and Knowledge Man. Council. *Address:* IBRD, 1818 H Street, N.W., Washington, DC 20433, USA (Office). *Telephone:* (202) 477-1234 (Office). *Fax:* (202) 477-6391 (Office). *E-mail:* pic@worldbank.org (Office). *Website:* www.worldbank.org (Office).

SANDURA, Wilson Runyararo, BA, LLB; Zimbabwean barrister; b. 29 July 1941, Shamva; s. of the late Fore Sandura and Gilliet Sandura; m. 1st Joyce Alexis Sandura 1972 (divorced 1976); m. 2nd Caroline Elizabeth Sandura 1985; two s. one d.; ed Mavuradonha Mission, Goromonzhi High School, Morehouse Coll., USA, London Univ., England; joined the Bar, Lincoln's Inn, England; pvt. practice as barrister 1973–80; Regional Magistrate 1980–82; Perm. Sec., Ministry of Justice 1982–83; Judge, High Court 1983–84, Judge Pres. 1984–97, 2000–, Supreme Court 1998–; Chair. several comms. 1985, 1989, 1990, 1991, 1995, 2000. *Leisure interest:* gardening. *Address:* Supreme Court, P.B. 870, Causeway, Harare, Zimbabwe. *Telephone:* 736 951. *E-mail:* supreme_court@gta.gov.zw (Office).

SANDVED, Arthur Olav, DPhil; Norwegian professor of English; b. 2 Feb. 1931, New York; s. of Ole Sandved and Ane Aarsland; m. Ruth Øgaard 1953; three d.; ed Univ. of Oslo; Lecturer in English Language, Univ. of Trondheim 1959–63, Univ. of Oslo 1963–71; Reader in English Philology, Univ. of Oslo 1971–74, Prof. of English Language 1974–96; mem. Norwegian Acad., Royal Norwegian Acad. Trondheim. *Publications:* Studies in the Language of Caxton's Malory and that of the Winchester Manuscript 1968, An Advanced English Grammar (with P. Christophersen) 1969, Introduction to Chaucerian English 1985, Vers fra Vest (anthology of Old English verse translated into Norwegian) 1987, Peter Plogmann (extracts from Piers Plowman translated into Norwegian) 1990, Paradise Lost (translated into Norwegian) 1993, trans. King Lear into Norwegian 1995, trans. the three parts of King Henry VI into Norwegian 1996, trans. Henry VIII into Norwegian 1997, Fra 'Kremmersprog' til Verdensspråk (history of English studies in Norway 1850–1943) 1998, trans. A History of Reading into Norwegian 1999, trans. Joseph Andrews into Norwegian 1999, trans. Revelation of Divine Love into Norwegian 2000, Fra 'Kremmersprog' til Verdensspråk, Vol. II (1945–57) 2002, trans. Canterbury Tales (extracts) into Norwegian 2002. *Address:* I. F. Gjerdrums vei 74, 1396 Billingstad, Norway. *Telephone:* 66-84-57-77.

SANÉ, Pierre Gabriel Michel, MSc, MBA; Senegalese administrator; b. 7 May 1948, Dakar; s. of Nicolas Sané and Thérèse Carvalho; m. Ndeye Coumba Sow 1981; one s. one d.; ed Lycée Van Vollenhoven, Dakar, Ecole Supérieure de Commerce de Bordeaux, France, Ecole Nouvelle d'Organisation Economique et Sociale, Paris, London School of Econs, UK, Carleton Univ., Ottawa, Canada; Vice-Pres. Fédération des Etudiants d'Afrique Noire en France 1971–72; auditor with audit firms in France 1973–77; Deputy Gen. Man. Société Sénégalaise Pharmaceutique (Senepharma) 1977–78; joined Int. Devt Research Centre (IDRC) 1978, various positions Ottawa, Nairobi and Dakar, to Regional Dir W and Cen. Africa, Dakar 1988–92; mem. Amnesty Int. 1988–, Sec.-Gen. 1992–2001; Asst Dir-Gen. UNESCO, Paris May 2001–; Pres. PANAF 92 1991–92, Founding mem. Int. Cttee; winner, Concours Nat. de Commercialisation, France 1972. *Publications:* papers and reports on African Devt, science and tech. and human rights research man. for (IDRC). *Leisure interests:* reading, travelling, music, museums, arts. *Address:* UNESCO, 1 rue Miollis, 75732 Paris Cedex 15, France. *Telephone:* 1-45-68-39-23. *Fax:* 1-45-68-57-20. *E-mail:* p.sane@unesco.org. *Website:* www.unesco.org.

SANEJOUAND, Jean Michel, D. EN L.; French painter; b. 18 July 1934, Lyon; s. of Henri Felix Sanejouand and Angêle Fardel; m. Michelle Bourgeois 1957; two s.; ed Institut d'études politiques, Faculté de Droit, Lyon; self-taught in art; worked as artist, Lyon 1955–59, Paris 1959–93, Vaulandry 1993–; 'charges-objets' (assemblage works) 1963–67, 'organisations d'espaces'

(environmental works) 1967–75, 'calligraphies d'humeurs' (calligraphic works on canvas) 1968–77, 'espaces-peintures' (painted and drawn works) 1978–86, black and white paintings 1987–93, sculptures 1988–, colour paintings 1993–96; 'sculptures-peintures' (paintings of sculptures) 1997–2002; retrospective exhbn Centre Georges Pompidou, Paris, 1995; Espaces critiques (imaginary landscapes organized with earlier works) 2002–. *Address:* Belle-Ville, 49150 Vaulandry, France. *Telephone:* (2) 41-82-88-71. *E-mail:* web-site@sanejouand.com (Office). *Website:* www.sanejouand .com (Office).

SANFORD, Marshall (Mark), B.A., MBA; American state official; b. 28 May 1960, Fort Lauderdale; m. Jenny Sullivan; four s.; ed Furman Univ., SC, Univ. of Va.; with Goldman Sachs –1988; with CRC Realty 1988–89; Prin. Southeastern Partners 1989–; Propr Norton & Sanford 1992–, Prin. 1993–95, 2001–03; Republican mem. US Congress, SC 1995–2001; Gov. of SC 2003–; Taxpayers' Best Friend Award, Nat. Taxpayers Union, Deficit Hawk Award, Concord Coalition Citizens Council, Taxpayer Hall of Fame, Taxpayers for Common Sense, Golden Bulldog Award, Watchdogs of the Treasury Inc., Spirit of Enterprise Award, US Chamber of Commerce, Congressional Youth Leadership Council Award. *Address:* Office of the Governor, POB 11829, Columbia , SC 29211, USA (Office).

SANGARE, Oumou; Malian singer and songwriter; b. 1968, Bamako; m. Ousmane Haidara; one c.; began singing aged five; first performance at Stade des Omnisports aged six; mem. Nat. Ensemble of Mali; mem. Djioliba percussion 1986–89; solo artiste with own backing group 1989–; regular concert tours in W Africa and Europe; first U.S. concert 1994; campaigner for women's rights; Performance of the Year 1993; numerous African Music Awards. *Recordings include:* Moussolou (Women) (Best Selling Album of the Year 1990) 1990, Ko Sira (Marriage Today) (European World Music Album of the Year 1993) 1993, Worotan 1996, Moussolou 1999, Ko Sira 2000; appears on African Blues 1998, Beloved 1998; also recordings with Ali Farka Touré, Trilok Gurtu. *Address:* Wim Westerweldt, World Circuit Records, 106 Cleveland Street, London, W1P 5DP, England (Office).

SANGER, David John, FRAM, FRCO, ARCM; British organist; b. 17 April 1947, London; s. of Stanley C. Sanger and Ethel L. F. Sanger; ed Eltham Coll., London and Royal Acad. of Music; studied organ in Paris with Marie-Claire Alain and later with Susi Jeans 1966–68; First Prize, Int. Organ Competition, St Albans 1969, since then has been freelance soloist and teacher of organ; has performed throughout Europe and in USA and Canada; Prof. of Organ, RAM 1983–89, Visiting Prof. of Organ 1989–; has recorded six organ symphonies of Louis Vierne and complete organ works of César Franck; First Prize, Int. Organ Competition, St. Albans 1969, Kiel 1972. *Publication:* Play the Organ (organ tutor for beginners) 1990. *Leisure interests:* fell-walking, racquet sports, swimming, gardening. *Address:* Old Wesleyan Chapel, Embleton, Cumbria, CA13 9YA, England. *Telephone:* (17687) 76628. *Fax:* (17687) 76628. *E-mail:* david.sanger@virgin.net (Home). *Website:* www.davidsanger.co.uk (Home).

SANGER, Frederick, OM, CH, CBE, PhD, FRS; British research biochemist; b. 13 Aug. 1918, Rendcomb, Glos.; s. of Frederick Sanger and Cicely Crewdson; m. Joan Howe 1940; two s. one d.; ed Bryanston School and St John's Coll., Cambridge; biochemical research at Cambridge 1940–; Beit Memorial Fellowship 1944–51; mem. Scientific Staff, Medical Research Council 1951–83; retd, Fellow, King's Coll., Cambridge 1954, Hon. Fellow 1983; Corresp. mem. Asociación Química de Argentina; mem. Acad. of Science of Argentina and Brazil, World Acad. of Arts and Science, Russell Cttee against Chemical Weapons 1981–; Foreign Assoc. NAS, French Acad. of Sciences; Hon. Foreign mem. American Acad. of Arts and Sciences 1958; Hon. mem. American Soc. of Biological Chemists, Japanese Biochemical Soc.; Hon. DSc (Leicester, Oxford, Strasbourg, Cambridge 1983); Corday-Morgan Medal and Prize, Chemical Soc. 1951, Nobel Prize for Chem. 1958 and (jtly) 1980, Alfred Benzon Prize 1966, Royal Medal (Royal Soc.) 1969, Hopkins Memorial Medal 1971, Gairdner Foundation Annual Award 1971, 1979, Hanbury Memorial Medal 1976, William Bate Hardy Prize 1976, Copley Medal 1977, G. W. Wheland Award 1978, Louisa Gross Horwitz Prize 1979, Albert Lasker Basic Medical Research Award, Columbia Univ. (with W. Gilbert, q.v.) 1979, Gold Medal, Royal Soc. of Medicine 1983. *Publications:* various papers on protein and nucleic acid structure and metabolism in scientific journals. *Leisure interests:* boating, gardening. *Address:* Far Leys, Fen Lane, Swaffham Bulbeck, Cambridge, CB5 0NJ, England (Home). *Telephone:* (1223) 811610.

SANGHELI, Andrei; Moldovan politician; b. 20 July 1944, Grinautsy; m.; one s.; ed Kishinev Agric. Inst., Kishinev Higher CP School; mem. CPSU 1967–91; agronomist, Deputy Dir, Dir of collective farms, Moldova 1971–75, Sec. Kamenka Regional CP Cttee 1975–79, Vice-Chair. Council of Collective Farms of Moldova 1979–80; Chair. Dondushansk Regional Exec. Cttee; First Sec. Regional CP Cttee 1980–86; First Deputy-Chair. Council of Ministers, Chair. State Agric.-Industrial Cttee 1986–89, First Deputy Prime Minister of Moldova; Minister of Agric. and Food 1990–92; Prime Minister of Moldova 1992–96; now works in agricultural business; Chair. Union of Agrarians 1997–. *Address:* House of Parliament, Prosp. 105, 277073 Chișinău, Moldova. *Telephone:* (3732) 23-30-92. *Fax:* (3732) 24-26-96.

SANGMA, Shri P. A., MA, LLB; Indian politician and lawyer; b. 1 Sept. 1947, Chapahati Village, West Garo Hills Dist; m. Soradini K. Sangma 1972; two s. two d.; ed Dalu High School, St Anthony's Coll. Shillong and Dibrugarh Univ.; mem. Lok Sabha 1977–79, 1980–84, 1985–89, 1991–; Deputy Minister,

Ministry of Industry 1980–82, Ministry of Commerce 1982–85; Minister of State for Commerce 1985–86, for Home Affairs 1986; Minister of State (Independent Charge) for Labour 1986–88; Chief Minister, Meghalaya State 1988–90; Minister of State (Independent Charge) for Coal 1991–95, also for Labour 1993–95; Minister of Information and Broadcasting 1995–96; Speaker Lok Sabha 1996–98; del. to various int. confs.; Founder mem. Nationalist Congress Party. *Leisure interests:* reading, discussion, music, indoor games. *Address:* 3A Aurangzeb Road, New Delhi 110011 (Home); Walbakgre, Tura P.O., West Garo Hills, Meghalaya, India (Home). *Telephone:* (11) 3017785.

SANGSTER, Robert Edmund; British racehorse owner; b. 23 May 1936; s. of the late Vernon Sangster; m. Susan Mary Dean; five s. one d.; ed Repton Coll.; Chair. Vernons Org. 1980–88, Sangster Group Ltd 1988–; owner of Derby winners The Minstrel 1977, Golden Fleece 1982; other winners include 2,000 Guineas: Lomond 1983, El Gran Señor 1984, Rodrigo de Triano 1992; 1,000 Guineas: Las Meninas 1994; King George VI and Queen Elizabeth Stakes: The Minstrel 1977; Ascot Gold Cup: Gildoran 1984, 1985; Irish Derby: The Minstrel 1977, Assert 1982, El Gran Señor 1984, Law Society 1985; Irish 2,000 Guineas: Jaazeiro 1978, King's Lake 1981, Sadlers Wells 1984, Prince of Birds 1988, Rodrigo de Triano 1992, Turtle Island 1994; Irish 1,000 Guineas: Lady Capulet 1977, Godetia 1979; Irish Oaks: Godetia 1979; Irish St Leger: Transworld 1997, Gonzales 1980, Leading Council 1985, Dark Lomond 1988; French Derby: Assert 1982, Caerleon 1983; French 2,000 Guineas: River Lady 1982; French 1,000 Guineas: Turncoat 1984; Prix de l'Arc de Triomphe: Alleged 1977, 1978, Detroit 1980; Breeder's Cup Mile: Royal Heroine 1984, Royal Academy 1990; Hollywood Derby: Royal Heroine 1983; Melbourne Cup: Beldale Ball 1980; Golden Slipper Stakes: Marauding 1987; Sydney Cup: Marooned 1986; now a citizen and resident of Barbados. *Leisure interests:* golf, boxing. *Address:* Janes Harbour, Sandy Lane, St James, Barbados. *Telephone:* (20) 7245-9229 (England) (Office). *Fax:* (20) 7235-7902 (England) (Office).

SANGUINETI, Edoardo; Italian writer; b. 9 Dec. 1930, Genoa; s. of Giovanni Sanguineti and Giuseppina Cocchi; m. Luciana Garabello 1954; three s. one d.; ed Univ. degli Studi, Turin; Prof. of Italian Literature, Univ. of Salerno 1968–74, Genoa 1974–2000; Town Councillor of Genoa 1976–81; mem. Chamber of Deputies 1979–83. *Publications:* Laborintus 1956, Opus metricum 1960, Interpretazione di Malebolge 1961, Tre studi danteschi 1961, Tra liberty e crepuscolarismo 1961, Alberto Moravia 1962, K. e altre cose 1962, Passaggio 1963, Capriccio italiano 1963, Triperuno 1964, Ideologia e linguaggio 1965, Il realismo di Dante 1966, Guido Gozzano 1966, Il Giuoco dell' Oca 1967, Le Baccanti di Euripide (trans.) 1968, Fedra di Seneca (trans.) 1969, T.A.T. 1969, Teatro 1969, Poesia Italiana del Novecento 1969, Il Giuoco del Satyricon 1970, Orlando Furioso (with L. Ronconi) 1970, Renga (with O. Paz, J. Roubaud, C. Tomlinson) 1971, Storie Naturali 1971, Wirrwarr 1972, Catamerone 1974, Le Troiane di Euripide (trans.) 1974, Giornalino 1976, Postkarten 1978, Le Coefore di Eschilo (trans.) 1978, Giornalino secondo 1979, Stracciafoglio 1980, Edipo tiranno di Sofocle (trans.) 1980, Scartabello 1981, Segnalibro 1982, Alfabeto apocalittico 1984, Scribilli 1985, Faust, un travestimento 1985, Novissimum Testamentum 1986, Smorfie 1986, La missione del critico 1987, Bisbidis 1987, Ghirigori 1988, Commedia dell'Inferno 1989, Lettura del Decameron 1989, Senzatitolo 1992, I Sette contro Tebe di Eschilo (trans.) 1992, Dante reazionario 1992, Gazzettini 1993, Per musica 1993, Satyricon di Petronio (trans.) 1993, Opere e introduzione critica 1993, Malebolge (with E. Baj) 1995, Libretto 1995, Per una critica dell'avanguardia poetica (with J. Burgos) 1995, Tracce (with M. Lucchesi) 1995, Minitarjetas 1996, Orlando Furioso, un travestimento ariostesco 1996, Corollario 1997, Il mio amore è come una febbre (with S. Liberovici) 1998, Cose 1999, Don Giovanni di Molière (trans.) 2000, Il chierico organico 2000, Verdi in Technicolor 2001, La Festa delle donne di Aristofane (trans.) 2001, Sei personaggi 2001, L'amore delle tre melarance 2001, L'orologio astronomico 2002, Il gatto lupesco 2002, Il cerchio di gesso del Caucaso di Brecht (trans.) 2003. *Address:* Via Pergolesi 20, 16159 Genoa, Italy (Home). *Telephone:* (10) 7452050 (Home).

SANGUINETTI CAIROLO, Julio María; Uruguayan politician and lawyer; b. 1936; m. Marta Canessa; one s. one d.; mem. Gen. Ass. 1962–73; Minister of Industry and Labour 1969–72, of Educ. and Culture 1972–73; then Pres. Comisión Nacional de Artes Plásticas and Pres. of UNESCO Comm. for promotion of books in Latin America; Pres. of Uruguay 1985–89, 1995–2000; Leader (Foro Batllista) Colorado Party 1989–94; Pres. Nat. Fine Arts Council. *Address:* c/o Office of the President, Casa de Gobierno, Edif. Libertad, Avda. Luis Alberto de Herrera 3350, esq. Avda José Pedro Varela, Montevideo, Uruguay.

SANKEY, John Anthony, CMG, PhD; British diplomatist (retd); b. 8 June 1930, London; m. Gwendoline Putman 1958; two s. two d.; ed Cardinal Vaughan School, Kensington, Peterhouse, Cambridge, NATO Defence Coll., Rome, Univ. of Leeds; Colonial Office 1953, UK Mission to UN, New York 1961, FCO 1964, Guyana 1968, Singapore 1971, Malta 1973, The Hague 1975, Special Counsellor for African Affairs, FCO 1980–82; High Commr in Tanzania 1982–85; Perm. Rep. to the UN in Geneva 1985–90; Sec.-Gen. Soc. of London Art Dealers 1991–96; Dir Int. Art and Antiques Loss Register 1993–96; Chair. Tanzania Devt Trust 1999–. *Leisure interest:* Victorian sculpture. *Address:* 108 Lancaster Gate, London, W2 3NW, England. *Telephone:* (20) 7723-2256.

SANT, Alfred, MSc, MBA, DBA; Maltese politician; b. 28 Feb. 1948; ed Univ. of Malta, Inst. Int. d'Admin Publique, Paris, Boston Univ. and Harvard Business School; Second Sec., First Sec. Malta Mission to European Communities, Brussels 1970–75; adviser on gen. and financial man. Ministry of Parastatal and People's Industries, Valletta 1977–78; Man. Dir Medina Consulting Group 1978–80; Exec. Deputy Chair. Malta Devt Corpn 1980–82; consultant to pvt. and public sectors 1982–; Chair. Metal Fond Ltd, Bottex Clothing 1982–84, First Clothing Cooperative 1983–87; lecturer, Man. Faculty, Univ. of Malta 1984–87; Adviser to Prime Minister on econ. and diplomatic affairs 1985–87; Chair. Dept of Information, Malta Labour Party 1982–92; Pres. Malta Labour Party 1984–88, Leader 1992–; mem. Parl. 1987–; Prime Minister of Malta 1996–98; Leader of the Opposition 1998–. *Publications:* articles in the press and professional publs. *Address:* Malta Labour Party, National Labour Centre, Mile End Road, Hamrun HMR 02, Malta. *Telephone:* 21249900. *Fax:* 21244204. *E-mail:* mlp@mlp.org.mt. *Website:* www.mlp.org.mt.

SANTANA, Carlos; Mexican musician; b. 20 July 1947, Autlán de Navarro; s. of José Santana; debut with the Santana Blues Band 1966; Woodstock Festival Aug. 1969; guitarist Santana Man. 1987–; Prin. Guts and Grace Records 1993; Santana Band first to earn CBS Record's Crystal Globe Award, multiple Best Pop-Rock Guitarist in Playboy Magazine's Readers' Poll, Grammy for Best Rock Instrumental Performance 1988, Recording Acad. (NARAS) tribute concert and induction into Hollywood Rock Walk, Billboard Magazine Century Award 1996, ten Bay Area Music Awards, BAMMY Hall of Fame, Chicano Music Awards Latino Music Legend of the Year 1997, Rock 'n' Roll Hall of Fame, Hollywood Walk of Fame 1998, also won nine Grammys Feb. 2000; numerous civic and humanitarian commendations. *Films:* Viva Santana 1988, Sacred Fire 1993, A History of Santana: The River Of Color And Sound 1997, A Supernatural Evening With Santana 2000. *Music:* 36 albums (8 platinum, 8 gold) including Santana 1969, Abraxas 1970, Santana III 1971, Greatest Hits 1974, Dance Of The Rainbow Serpent 1995, Live At The Fillmore 1997, Best of Santana 1998, Supernatural 1999; solo and collaborative projects include Live With Buddy Miles, Blues For Salvador 1987, Brothers, Mystic Man 1994; musical score for La Bamba. *Address:* Santana Management, P.O. Box 10348, San Rafael, CA 94912, USA (Office). *Website:* www.santana.com/carlos/bio.asp (Office).

SANTER, Jacques, D. EN D; Luxembourg politician; b. 18 May 1937, Wasserbillig; s. of Josef Santer and Marguerite Santer; m. Danièle Binot; two s.; ed Athénée de Luxembourg, Univs of Paris and Strasbourg and Inst. d'Etudes Politiques, Paris; advocate, Luxembourg Court of Appeal 1961–65; attaché, Office of Minister of Labour and Social Security 1963–65; Govt attaché 1965–66; Parl. Sec. Parti Chrétien-Social 1966–72, Sec.-Gen. 1972–74, Pres. 1974–82; Sec. of State for Cultural and Social Affairs 1972–74; mem. Chamber of Deputies 1974–79; Municipal Magistrate, City of Luxembourg 1976–79; Minister of Finance, of Labour and of Social Security 1979–84; Prime Minister, Minister of State and Minister of Finance 1984–89, Prime Minister, Minister of State, of Cultural Affairs and of the Treasury and Financial Affairs 1989–94; MEP 1975–79, 1999–, Vice-Pres. 1975–77; Pres. European Comm. 1994–99; Hon. LLD (Wales) 1998, (Miami Univ.), (Sacred Heart Univ., Ohio), (Univ. of Urbino, Italy), (Kyoto Univ., Japan) and others; Prize Prince d'Asturias (Spain) 1998, Robert Schuman Prize, Jean Monnet Medal (Lausanne, Switzerland) and others. *Leisure interests:* walking, swimming. *Address:* European Parliament, rue Wiertz, 1047 Brussels, Belgium (Office); 69 rue J.-P. Huberty, 1742 Luxembourg (Home). *Telephone:* (2) 284-57-37 (Office); 42-00-40 (Home). *Fax:* 26-43-09-99 (Home).

SANTER, Rt Rev Mark, MA, DD; British ecclesiastic; b. 29 Dec. 1936, Bristol; s. of Rev. Canon E. A. R. Santer and Phyllis C. Barlow; m. 1st Henriette Cornelia Weststrate 1964 (died 1994); m. 2nd Sabine Böhmig Bird 1997; s. two d.; ed Marlborough Coll., Queen's Coll. and Westcott House, Cambridge; Curate All Saints Cuddesdon 1963–67; Tutor Cuddesdon Coll., Oxford 1963–67; Dean and Fellow Clare Coll., Cambridge 1967–72; Asst Lecturer in Divinity, Univ. of Cambridge 1968–72; Principal Westcott House 1973–81; Area Bishop of Kensington 1981–87; Bishop of Birmingham 1987–2002; Co-Chair. Anglican/RC Int. Comm. 1983–99; Hon. Fellow Clare Coll., Cambridge 1987, Queen's Coll., Cambridge 1991; Hon. DD (Birmingham) 1998, (Lambeth) 1999; Hon. DUniv (Univ. of Cen. England) 2003. *Publications:* Documents in Early Christian Thought (with M. F. Wiles) 1975, Their Lord and Ours (Ed.) 1982. *Address:* 81 Clarence Road, Birmingham, B13 9UH, England.

SANTO CARVALHO, Evaristo do Spirito; São Tomé e Príncipe politician; Prime Minister of São Tomé e Príncipe July–Oct. 1994; mem. Partido de Convergência Democrática-Grupo de Reflexão (PCD-GR) (expelled from party July 1994). *Address:* c/o Office of the Prime Minister, São Tomé, São Tomé e Príncipe.

SANTORUM, Rick, MBA, JD; American politician; b. 10 May 1958, Winchester, Va; s. of Aldo Santorum and Catherine Dughi; m. Karen Garver 1990; two s. two d.; ed Pennsylvania State Univ., Pennsylvania State Coll., Univ. of Pittsburgh and Dickinson Law School; mem. Bar of Pa 1986; admin. Asst to State Senator Doyle Corman, Harrisburg, Pa 1981–86; Exec. Dir Local Govt Cttee Pa State Senate 1981–84, Transport Cttee 1984–86; Assoc. Attorney, Kirkpatrick and Lockhart, Pittsburgh 1986–90; mem. 102–103rd Congresses from 18th Pa Dist 1991–95; Senator from Pennsylvania 1995–; Republican. *Leisure interests:* golf, cross-country skiing, racquet sports. *Address:* Widener

Building, 1 South Penn Square, Suite 960, Philadelphia, PA 19107 (Office); U.S. Senate, 120 Russell Senate Office Bldg, Washington 20510; 127 Seminole Drive, Pittsburgh, PA 15228, USA (Home).

SANTOS CALDERÓN, Juan Manuel; Colombian politician; b. 19 Aug. 1951, Bogotá; m. María Clemencia Rodríguez; two s. one d.; ed Naval Acad. of Colombia, Univ. of Kansas, USA, London School of Econs, UK, Harvard Univ., USA; fmr leader Colombian Del. to Int. Coffee Org. negotiations, London; fmr journalist, Deputy Dir and Pres. Editorial Bd El Tiempo (daily); apptd. Minister of Foreign Trade 1991; elected Vice-Pres. 1993; Minister of Finance and Public Credit 2000–; Pres. UNCTAD 1992–96, UN ECLA 1997–99; fmr Vice-Pres. Press Freedom Comm. of Inter-American Press Soc.; Founder and Chair. Fundación Buengobierno; Fulbright and Neiman Fellowships, King of Spain Prize for journalism; Bernardo O'Higgins en el Grado de Comendador 1996, Gran Oficial de la Orden Nacional Francesca del Mérito 2001. *Publications:* several books including The Third Way, An Alternative for Colombia. *Address:* Ministry of Finance and Public Credit, Carrera 8A, No. 6-64, Of. 308, Santafé de Bogotá, DC (Office); Calle 76, No. 3-70 Apto., 800, Bogotá, DC, Colombia (Home). *Telephone:* (1) 350-1285/33 (Office); (1) 312-9791 (Home). *Fax:* (1) 350-9344 (Office); (1) 310-7382 (Home). *E-mail:* jmsantos@minhacienda.gov.co (Office). *Website:* www.minhacienda.gov.co (Office).

SANTOS SIMÃO, H.E. Leonardo; Mozambican politician and medical practitioner; b. 6 June 1953, Mandlakaze; s. of Antonio Santos Simão Sitoi and Amélia Muchanga; m. Josephine P. Simão; two s.; ed Liceu Salazar, Maputo, Eduardo Mondlane Univ., Univ. of London, UK, Boston Univ., USA; Dir, Centre of Dist Formation of Chicumbane, Gaza 1981–1982; Prov. Health Dir, Zambezia Prov. 1982–84; Dir, Provincial Hosp. of Quelimane, Zambezia Prov. 1984–88; Minister of Health 1988; apptd Prof. of Medicine, Eduardo Mondlane Univ. 1988; Minister of Foreign Affairs and Co-operation 1994–; mem. Cen. Cttee Frelimo Party; mem. Medical Asscn of Mozambique, Mozambique Asscn of Public Health; Chair. Nat. Mine Clearance Comm.; Great Cross, Order of Rio Branco (Brazil) 1996, Order of Good Hope, II Grade (South Africa) 1997, Great Cross, Order of Merit (Portugal) 1998. *Leisure interests:* music, reading, swimming. *Address:* Ministério dos Negócios Estrangeiros e Cooperação, Avda Julius Nyerere 4, Maputo, Mozambique (Office). *Telephone:* (1) 492258 (Office). *Fax:* (1) 491460 (Office). *E-mail:* lsimão@tropical.co.mz (Office); gabminec@zebra.uem.mz (Office). *Website:* www.mozambique.mz/governo/minec (Office).

SAOUMA, Edouard; Lebanese international official and agricultural engineer; b. 6 Nov. 1926, Beirut; m. Inès Forero; one s. two d.; ed St Joseph's Univ. School of Eng., Beirut, Ecole nat. Supérieure d'Agronomie, Montpellier, France; Dir Tel Amara Agricultural School 1952–53, Nat. Centre for Farm Mechanization 1954–55; Sec.-Gen. Nat. Fed. of Lebanese Agronomists 1955; Dir-Gen. Nat. Inst. for Agricultural Research 1957–62; mem. Governing Board, Nat. Grains Office 1960–62; Lebanese del. to FAO 1955–62, Deputy Regional Rep. for Asia and Far East 1962–65, mem. of Secr. 1963–, Dir Land and Water Devt Div. 1965–75, Dir-Gen. of FAO 1976–93; Minister of Agric., Fisheries and Forestry Oct.–Nov. 1970; Hon. Prof. of Agronomy, Agric. Univ. of Beijing; Accademico Corrispondente dell' Accademia Nazionale di Agricoltura (Italy); Dr. hc from 16 univs.; Order of the Cedar (Lebanon), Said Akl Prize (Lebanon); Chevalier du Mérite agricole (France), Grand Croix, Ordre nat. du Tchad, du Ghana, de la Haute Volta (Burkina Faso), Gran Cruz al Mérito Agrícola (Spain), Kt Commdr Order of Merit (Greece), Orden del Mérito Agrícola (Colombia), Gran Oficial del Orden de Vasco Núñez de Balboa (Panama), Orden al Mérito Agrícola (Peru), Order of Merit (Egypt, Mauritania), Grand Officier, Ordre de la République (Tunisia), Grand Officier, Ordre Nat. (Madagascar). *Publications:* technical Publs in agric. *Address:* P.O. Box H0210, Baabda, Lebanon.

SAPIN, Michel; French politician; b. 9 April 1952, Boulogne-Billancourt; m. Yolande Millan 1982; three c.; ed Ecole Normale Supérieure, Paris and Ecole Nat. d'Admin; joined Parti Socialiste 1975; elected Deputy to Nat. Ass. for Indre 1981–86, for Hauts-de-Seine 1986–91, Sec. 1983–84, Vice-Pres. 1984, Chair. of the Cttee for Law 1988–91; town councillor, Nanterre 1989–94; Minister Del. for Justice 1991–92; Minister of Economy Finances 1992–93, of Civil Service, of Admin. Reform 2000–02; Regional Councillor Ile de France 1992–94; mem. Council for Monetary Policy of Banque de France 1994–95; Mayor of Argenton-sur-Creuse 1995–; Gen. Councillor of Indre 1998–; Pres. Centre Regional Council 1998–2000, Vice-Pres. 2000–01; First Vice-Pres. Asscn of the Regions of France 1998–2000. *Address:* Mairie, 69 rue Auclert Descottes, 36200 Argenton-sur-Creuse; 7 rue Dupertuis, 36200 Argenton-sur-Creuse, France (Home). *Telephone:* (2) 54-24-12-50 (Office). *Fax:* (2) 54-24-01-08 (Office). *E-mail:* mairie_argenton_36@wanadoo.fr (Office).

SAPORTA, Marc, LLD; French writer; b. 20 March 1923; s. of Jaime Saporta and Simone Nahmias; m. 1st Denise Kleman 1949 (died 1966); m. 2nd Michèle Truchan 1972; three d.; ed Univs of Paris and Madrid; worked in Dept of Cultural Activities UNESCO 1948–53, Asst Ed. Informations et Documents 1954–71, Ed. 1971–78; Ed.-in-Chief Dept of Publs US Information Agency (Paris) 1978–84; Literary Critic L'Express 1954–71, La Quinzaine Littéraire 1966–71. *Radio:* 1917 La Relève 1967. *Publications:* Les lois de l'air 1953, La convention universelle du droit d'auteur de l'UNESCO 1952, Le grand défi: USA-URSS, I 1967, II 1968 (ed. and jt author), Histoire du roman américain 1970, La vie quotidienne contemporaine aux USA 1972, Go West 1976, William Faulkner (ed. and jt author) 1983, Henry James (ed. and jt author)

1983, I. B. Singer (ed. and jt author) 1984, Nathalie Sarraute (Ed. and jt author) 1984, Marguerite Duras (ed. and jt author) 1985, Vivre aux Etats-Unis 1986, André Breton ou le Surréalisme Même (ed. and co-author) 1988, Israel 1988, Les Erres du Faucon, une Psychobiographie de William Faulkner 1989, Le Roman américain 1997; novels: Le furet 1959, La distribution 1961, La quête 1961, Composition numéro un 1962, Les invités 1964. *Leisure interest:* ice-skating. *Address:* 9 rue Saint-Didier, 75116 Paris, France.

SARABHAI, Mrinalini; Indian dancer and choreographer; b. 11 May 1918, Madras; d. of Shri Swaminadhan and Smt. Ammu Swaminadhan; m. Dr. Vikram A. Sarabhai; one s. one d.; studied under Meenakshi Sundaram Pillai; Founder/Dir. Darpana Acad. of Performing Arts, Ahmedabad 1949; Chair. Handicrafts & Handloom Devt Corpn of Gujarat State; Chair. Friends of Trees, Gujarat State; mem. Sangeet Natak Acad., New Delhi; Hon. Consultant, Nat. Centre for Performing Arts, Bombay; Pres. Alliance Française; Exec. Cttee Int. Dance Council 1990; adviser to many arts and cultural insts. in India; Fellow Sangeet Natak Akademi 1994; Kerala Kalamandalam Fellowship 1995; Vishwa Gurjari Award 1984; Deshikothama Award (Vishwa Bharati Univ. Shantiniketan) 1987, Fellowship Award Kerala Acad. of Arts 1990, Honor Summus Award (Watumull Foundation) 1991, First Hall of Fame Award for lifelong service to dance 1991, Vijay Shri Award (Int. Friendship Soc. of India) 1991, Pandit Omkarnath Thakur Award (Gujarat Govt) 1991, Pres.'s Award of Padmabhushan 1992, Raseshwar Award 1992, Scroll of Honour for her work in dance and choreography 1995, Kalidas Samman Award 1996. *Publications:* Staging a Sanskrit Classic—Bhasa's Vision of Vasavadatta (with John D. Mitchell) 1992, one novel, textbook on Bharata Natyam, a book on various classical dance-dramas, children's books and articles in newspapers and journals. *Leisure interests:* reading, watching TV, writing, dancing, social work. *Address:* Darpana Academy of Performing Arts, Usmanpura, Ahmedabad 380013, Gujarat, India. *Telephone:* 445189.

SARAH, Peter John, OAM, BA, MPhil, LRAM, ARCM, AMusA, FRSA; Australian arts administrator; b. 7 Aug. 1946, W. Australia; s. of Rimmington V. Sarah and Jean Ada Price Sarah; ed Scotch Coll. Perth, Univ. of W. Australia and Univ. of London; Asst Dir (Touring and Devt), Western Australian Arts Council 1977–81; Gen. Man. Arts Council of S. Australia 1981–85; Dir Arts and Entertainment, Australian Bicentennial Authority 1985–89; Chief Exec. Contemporary Dance Trust 1990–94; Chief Exec. The Year of Opera and Music Theatre 1995–97; Gen. Man. Theatre Royal, Newcastle-upon-Tyne 1998–; Trustee Acad. of Indian Dance, Chair. 1995–2002; Dir The Touring Partnership 1998–, Daree Consortium (UK); mem. Cttee North East Chamber of Commerce 2000–. *Leisure interests:* sailing, architecture, France. *Address:* 10 Mall Chambers, Kensington Mall, London, W8 4DY, England.

SARAIVA GUERREIRO, Ramiro Elysio; Brazilian diplomatist; b. Salvador; s. of José Affonso Guerreiro and Esther Saraiva Guerreiro; m. Gloria Vallim Guerreiro 1947; one s. one d.; ed Univ. of Brazil and Rio Branco Inst. (Diplomatic Acad.); Foreign Service 1945; Brazilian Mission to UN 1946–69; Embassies, La Paz 1950–51, Washington, DC 1956–58; Minister-Counsellor, Montevideo 1966–67, Deputy Del. to Meeting of Chiefs of American States 1967; Del. Emergency Special Session of UN Gen. Ass. 1967; Asst Sec.-Gen. of Int. Orgs., Ministry of Foreign Affairs 1967–79; mem. del. to numerous UN Gen. Assemblies; Under Sec.-Gen. of External Policy 1969; Rep. at meetings of Comm. of Sea Bed and Ocean Floor 1969–72; Chief of Del. UN Conf. on Law of the Sea 1968–77, 26th Session of GATT 1970, Geneva 1970–74, Disarmament Cttee 1970–74, Chief of Section of Brazilian-German Cttee on Econ. Co-operation and Science and Tech. 1974, 1975, 1977; Amb. to France 1978–79; Minister of Foreign Affairs 1979–85; Chief of Dels. to 24th–28th UN Gen. Assemblies 1979–83; mem. Geographical Soc. (Rio de Janeiro), American Soc. of Int. Law, Brazilian Soc. of Air Law, Argentine Council for Int. Relations. *Leisure interests:* reading, golf. *Address:* c/o Ministério das Relações Exteriores, Esplanada dos Ministérios 70170, Brasília, DF, Brazil.

SARAIVA MARTINS, H.E. Cardinal José; Portuguese ecclesiastic; b. 6 Jan. 1932, Gagos, Guarda; ordained priest 1957; Bishop 1988; Titular Archbishop of Thuburnica; Prefect of the Congregation for the Causes of Saints; cr. Cardinal 2001. *Address:* Congregation for the Causes of Saints, Palazzo delle Congregazioni, Piazza Pio XII 10, 00193 Rome, Italy (Office). *Telephone:* (06) 69884247 (Office). *Fax:* (06) 69881935 (Office).

SARAMAGO, José; Portuguese author and poet; b. 16 Nov. 1922, Azinhaga; m. Pilar del Rio; one c.; Grinzane Cavour Prize, Mondello Prize, Flaiano Prize, Ind. Prize, Luís de Camões Prize, Nobel Prize for Literature 1998. *Publications include:* (novels) Manual de pintura e caligrafia 1976, Objecto quase 1978, Levantado do chão 1980, Memorial do convento 1982, O ano da morte de Ricardo Reis 1984, A jangada de pedra 1986, História do Cerco de Lisboa 1989, O Evangelho Segundo Jesus Cristo 1991, Eusaio sobre a Cegueira 1995; (poetry) Os poemas possíveis 1966, Provavelmente Alegria 1970, O ano de 1993 1975; (plays) A noite 1979, Que farei com este livro? 1980, A segunda vida de Francisco de Assis 1987, In Nomine Dei 1993; (opera libretto) Blimunda 1990, Divara 1993, All the Names 1999; (other writing) Deste mundo e do outro 1971, A bagagem do viajante 1973, O embargo 1973, Os opiniões que o DL teve 1974, Os apontamentos 1976, Viagem a Portugal 1981, Cadernos de Lanzarote 1994–96, O poeta perguntador (ed.) 1979. *Address:* Los Topes 3, 35572 Tias, Lanzarote, Canaries, Spain; Ray-Güde Mertin, 1 Friedrichstrasse, 61348 Bad Hamburg 1, Germany.

SARANDON, Susan Abigail; American actress; b. 4 Oct. 1946, New York; d. of Philip Tomalin and Lenora Criscione; m. Chris Sarandon 1967 (divorced

1979); one d. with Franco Amurri; two s. with Tim Robbins (q.v.); ed Catholic Univ. of America; numerous TV appearances. *Films include:* Joe 1970, Lady Liberty 1971, The Rocky Horror Picture Show 1974, Lovin' Molly 1974, The Great Waldo Pepper 1975, The Front Page 1976, Dragon Fly 1976, Walk Away Madden, The Other Side of Midnight 1977, The Last of the Cowboys 1977, Pretty Baby 1978, King of the Gypsies 1978, Loving Couples 1980, Atlantic City 1981, Tempest 1982, The Hunger 1983, Buddy System 1984, Compromising Positions 1985, The Witches of Eastwick 1987, Bull Durham 1988, Sweet Hearts Dance 1988, Married to the Mob, A Dry White Season 1989, The January Man 1989, White Palace, Thelma and Louise 1991, Light Sleeper 1991, Lorenzo's Oil, The Client, Little Women 1995, Safe Passage 1995, Dead Man Walking (Acad. Award for Best Actress 1996) 1996, James and the Giant Peach 1996, Illuminata 1998, Twilight 1998, Stepmom 1999, Anywhere But Here 1999, The Cradle Will Rock 1999, Rugrats in Paris 2000, Joe Gould's Secret 2000, Cats and Dogs 2001, Igby Goes Down 2002, The Banger Sisters 2003. *Stage appearances include:* A Coupla White Chicks Sittin' Around Talkin', An Evening with Richard Nixon, A Stroll in the Air, Albert's Bridge, Private Ear, Public Eye, Extremities. *Address:* c/o Samuel Cohen, ICM, 40 West 57th Street, New York, NY 10019, USA (Office).

SARASTE, Jukka-Pekka; Finnish conductor; b. 22 April 1956, Heinola; m. Marja-Lisa Ollila; three s. one d.; ed Sibelius Acad., Helsinki; debut with Helsinki Philharmonic 1980; Prin. Conductor and Music Dir Finnish Radio Symphony Orchestra 1987–2001; Music Dir Toronto Symphony Orchestra 1994–2001; Prin. Guest Conductor BBC Symphony Orchestra 2002–; has been guest conductor with Boston Symphony Orchestra, Cleveland Orchestra, San Francisco Orchestra, Frankfurt Radio Orchestra, NY Philharmonic Orchestra, London Philharmonic Orchestra, Orchestre Philharmonique de Radio France, BBC Symphony Orchestra, Munich Philharmonic Orchestra; has toured Japan, Hong Kong, Taiwan, Germany, USA, Canary Islands Festival; Artistic Adviser Finnish Chamber Orchestra. *Recordings include:* complete Sibelius symphonies 1995 (with Finnish Radio Symphony Orchestra) Mussorgsky (with Toronto Symphony Orchestra) Nielsen Symphonies 4, 5 (with Finnish Radio Symphony Orchestra), Romeo and Juliet Suite (Prokofiev). *Address:* c/o Van Walsum Management Ltd, 4 Addison Bridge Place, London, W14 8XP, England (Office). *Telephone:* (20) 7371-4343 (Office). *Fax:* (20) 7371-4344 (Office). *E-mail:* c/o nmcghee@vanwalsum.co.uk (Office). *Website:* www.vanwalsum.co.uk (Office).

SARBANES, Paul Spyros, BA, LLB; American politician and lawyer; b. 3 Feb. 1933, Salisbury, Md; s. of Spyros P. Sarbanes and Matina (née Tsigounis) Sarbanes; m. Christine Dunbar 1960; two s. one d.; ed Princeton Univ., Balliol Coll., Oxford, Harvard Law School; Rhodes Scholar, Balliol Coll., Oxford 1954–57; admitted to Maryland Bar 1960; Law Clerk to Circuit Judge 1960–61; Assoc., Piper and Marbury, Baltimore 1961–62; Admin. Asst to Chair. Council of Econ. Advisers 1962–63; Exec. Dir Charter Revision Comm., Baltimore 1963–64; Assoc., Venable, Baetjer & Howard, Baltimore 1965–70; mem. Md House of Dels 1967–71, US House of Reps 1971–76, Senator from Maryland 1977–; Chair. Cttee on Banking, Housing and Urban Affairs 2001–; Democrat. *Address:* United States Senate, 309 Hart Senate Building, Washington, DC 20510; Tower 1, Suite 1710, 100 South Charles Street, Baltimore, MD 21201, USA.

SARBANOV, Ulan Kytaibekovich, PhD; Kyrgyzstan banker; b. 28 May 1967, Bishkek; two s.; ed Novosibirsk State Univ., Moscow State Univ. of Man.; served in USSR Army 1985–87; researcher, Novosibirsk Inst. of Economy and Industry Org. of USSR 1991–93; Leading Engineer Information Science and Banking Computerization Div., Nat. Bank of the Kyrgyz Repub. 1993–94, Head Econ. Research and Analysis Div. of Econ. Dept 1994–97, Head Econ. Dept 1997, mem. Bd 1997–99, Acting Chair. 1999, Chair. 1999–; Anniversary Gold Coin 1998. *Publications:* Monetary Policy of Transition Economies (Kyrgyzstan) 2001, Psychological Mechanisms of Banking Management (co-author with V. I. Medvedev and A. A. Aldasheva) 2002. *Address:* National Bank of the Kyrgyz Republic, 101 Umetaliev Street, Bishkek 720040 (Office); 191 Toktogul Street, Flat 35, Bishkek, Kyrgyz Republic (Home); 101 Umetaliev Street, Bishkek 720040. *Telephone:* (312) 66-90-11 (Office); (312) 24-17-05 (Home). *Fax:* (312) 61-07-30 (Office). *E-mail:* mail@nbkr.kg (Office). *Website:* www.nbkr.kg (Office).

SARCINELLI, Mario; Italian banker and economist; b. 9 March 1934, Foggia; ed Univ. of Pavia, Univ. of Cambridge; joined Bank of Italy 1957, fmr Head Data Processing and Information Systems Dept, Cen. Man. for Banking Supervision 1976, Deputy Dir-Gen. 1976; Econ. Adviser to Italian Del. to UN 1960; Dir-Gen. Treasury 1982–91; Minister of Foreign Trade April–July 1987; Vice-Pres. EBRD 1991–94; Chair. Monetary Cttee 1989–90, Banca Nazionale del Lavoro SpA 1994–98; Chair. Diners Club Sim p.a. 1999–; alt. mem. EEC Cttee of Govs of Cen. Banks 1978–81, Bd Dirs BIS 1978–81; Officier Légion d'honneur, Cavaliere del Lavoro 1996. *Address:* c/o Diners Club, Lungotevere Flamiario 18, 00196 Rome, Italy.

SARFATI, Alain; French architect and town-planner; b. 23 March 1937, Meknès, Morocco; s. of Maurice Sarfati and Sarah Levy de Valencia; m. 1–; ed Lycée Poeymirau, Meknès, Lycée Laknal, Sceaux, École des Beaux Arts, Paris and Inst. d'Urbanisme, Univ. de Paris; town planner, Inst. d'Urbanisme, Paris region 1966; Founder of review A.M.C. and Atelier de Recherche et d'Études d'Aménagement (AREA) 1967; Prof. of Architecture, Nancy 1969; Prof. and Head of Dept Ecole des Beaux Arts, Paris-Conflans 1979–; architectural adviser, Ministère de l'Equipement, de l'Urbanisme, du Logement et des

Transports 1985–; Vice-Pres. of Construction Planning, Ministère de l'Equipement, du Logement des Transports et de la Mer 1988; mem. Consultative Cttee Centre Scientifique et Technique du Bâtiment 1990–; Vice-Pres. Ordre Nat. des Architectes 1992; work includes housing, schools, hosps., leisure centres and Centre des Archives du Monde du Travail, Roubaix 1993; Chevalier, Ordre du Mérite, Officier des Arts et des Lettres. *Leisure interests:* opera, cinema, art, golf, skiing. *Address:* 43 rue Maurice Ripoche, 75014 Paris (Office); 28 rue Barbet de Jouy, 75007 Paris (Office); 79 rue du Cherche-Midi, 75006 Paris, France (Home). *Telephone:* 45-50-34-10 (Office); 45-44-44-38 (Home). *E-mail:* sarfati.sarea@wanadoo.fr.

SARGENT, Wallace Leslie William, PhD, FRS, ARAS; British astronomer; b. 15 Feb. 1935, Elsham, Lincs.; s. of Leslie Sargent and Eleanor Sargent; m. Anneila I. Cassells 1964; two d.; ed Scunthorpe Tech. High School and Manchester Univ.; Research Fellow in Astronomy, Calif. Inst. of Tech. 1959–62; Sr Research Fellow, Royal Greenwich Observatory 1962–64; Asst Prof. of Physics, Univ. of Calif., San Diego 1964-66; Asst Prof. of Astronomy, Calif. Inst. of Tech. 1966–68, Assoc. Prof. 1968–71. Prof. 1971–81, Exec. Officer for Astronomy 1975–81, Ira S. Bowen Prof. of Astronomy 1981–, Dir Palomar Observatory 1997–2000; Fellow, American Acad. of Arts and Sciences; Alfred P. Sloan Foundation Fellow 1968–70; George Darwin Lecturer, Royal Astronomical Soc. 1987; Thomas Gold Lecturer, Cornell Univ. 1995; Sackler Lecturer, Harvard Univ. 1995; Sackler Lecturer, Univ. of Calif. Berkeley 1996; Henry Norris Russell Lecturer, American Astronomical Soc. 2001; Icko Iben Lecturer, Univ. of Illinois 2002; Helen B. Warner Prize, American Astronomical Soc. 1969, Dannie Heineman Prize, American Astronomical Soc. 1991, Bruce Gold Medal, Astronomical Soc. of the Pacific 1994. *Publications:* numerous papers in scientific journals. *Leisure interests:* reading, gardening, watching sports, oriental rugs. *Address:* Department of Astronomy 105–24, California Institute of Technology, Pasadena, CA 91125 (Office); 400 South Berkeley Avenue, Pasadena, CA 91107, USA (Home). *Telephone:* (626) 356-4055 (Office); (626) 795-6345 (Home). *Fax:* (626) 568-9352. *E-mail:* wws@astro.caltech.edu (Office).

SARGESON, Alan McLeod, PhD, FAA, FRS; Australian professor of inorganic chemistry; b. 13 Oct. 1930, Armidale, NSW; s. of Herbert L. Sargeson and Alice McLeod; m. Marietta Anders 1959; two s. two d.; ed Maitland Boys' High School and Univ. of Sydney; Lecturer, Dept of Chem., Univ. of Adelaide 1956–57; Research Fellow, John Curtin School of Medical Research, ANU 1958; Fellow, ANU 1960, Sr Fellow, Research School of Chem. 1967, Professorial Fellow 1968–78, Prof. 1978–96, Dean 1986–88, Prof. Emer. 1996–, Visiting Fellow 2001; Foreign mem. Royal Danish Acad. of Arts and Sciences, American Acad. of Arts and Sciences; Foreign Assoc. NAS, Royal Physiographic Soc., Lund; Hon. DSc (Sydney, Copenhagen, Bordeaux). *Leisure interests:* swimming, music, cycling, walking, literature. *Address:* 53 Dunstan Street, Curtin, ACT 2605 (Home); Research School of Chemistry, Australian National University, Canberra, ACT 0200, Australia. *Telephone:* (2) 6125-3160. *Fax:* (2) 6125-0750.

SARID, Yossi, MA; Israeli politician and journalist; b. 1940, Rehovot; m.; three c.; ed New School for Social Research, New York; served in Artillery Corps and as a mil. corresp.; Chair. Meretz Party and Leader of the Opposition; mem. Knesset 1974; served on Educ. and Culture Cttee 1974–77, House Cttee 1974–92, Immigration and Absorption Cttee 1996–99 and Foreign Affairs and Security Cttee 1972–92, 1996–99; Minister of Environment 1993–96, of Educ. 1999–2000. *Publications:* writes regular column for Ha'aretz newspaper, articles for local and int. press; anthology of poetry. *Address:* P.O. Box 20177, 30 Hamasger Street, Tel-Aviv 61201, Israel (Office). *Telephone:* 3-6360111 (Office). *Fax:* 3-5375107 (Office). *E-mail:* yossis@knesset.gov.il (Office). *Website:* www.meretz.org.il (Office).

SARIN, Arun, MS, MBA; American/Indian telecommunications executive; b. 1954, India; m.; two c.; ed Indian Inst. of Tech., Univ. of Calif.; fmr corp. developer, Pacific Telesis Group, San Francisco, Chief Financial Officer, Chief Strategy Officer, Pacific Bell, Vice-Pres., Gen. Man. San Francisco Bay Area Telephone Co. (div. of Pacific Bell); Sr Vice-Pres. of Corp. Strategy and Devt, AirTouch Communications (on demerger from Pacific Telesis), Pres. and CEO AirTouch Int., Pres. and CEO AirTouch Communications, CEO, USA and Asia Pacific region 1999–2000; CEO Infospace 2000–01, Accel-KKR Telecom, San Francisco 2001–03, Vodafone Group PLC 2003–; Dir. (non-exec.) Vodafone AirTouch PLC 2000–, Charles Schwab Corpn, Cisco Systems, Gap Inc. *Address:* Vodafone Corporate Communications, c/o Mike Caldwell, The Courtyard, 2–4 London Road, Newbury, Berkshire, RG14 1JX, England (Office). *Telephone:* (1635) 33251 (Office). *Website:* www.vodafone.com (Office).

ŠARINIĆ, Hrvoje; Croatian politician; b. 17 Feb. 1935, Rijeka; ed Inst. of Civil Eng, Zagreb Univ.; worked in France as head of construction co.; gen. rep. of French nuclear industry in France; Gen. Man. Yugoslav Co. CITRAM in Morocco; Head of Admin. to Pres. of Croatia 1991–92, 1993–2000; Prime Minister 1992; mem. Croatian Democratic Union (CDU).

ŠARKINAS, Reinoldijus; Lithuanian banker and economist; b. 16 July 1946, Toliūnų Village, Ukmergės; m.; two d.; ed Vilnius Univ.; Head Labour and Sales Div., Spindulys factory 1968–72; Deputy Head Bd of Planning and Finance, Head Financial Accounting Dept, Ministry of Educ. 1972–80; Finance Adviser, Ministry of Educ., Cuba 1980–82; Deputy Head, Head of Culture and Health Care Financing Bd, Dir Budget Dept, Ministry of Finance 1983–90; Deputy Minister, Ministry of Finance 1990–95, Minister 1995; mem. Bd Bank of Lithuania 1992–95, Chair. Bd, Gov. 1996–; Gov. for

Lithuania, IMF 1996–. *Address:* Bank of Lithuania, Gedimino pr. 6, Vilnius 2001, Lithuania (Office). *Telephone:* (2) 680-001 (Office). *Fax:* (2) 221-501 (Office). *E-mail:* bank_of_lithuania@lbank.lt (Office). *Website:* www.lbank.lt (Office).

SARKISIAN, Sos Artashesovich; Armenian actor; b. 24 Oct. 1929, Armenia; m. Nelli Martirosian; three d.; ed Yerevan Theatre Inst.; acted with Sundukian Theatre 1954–; acted in films 1960–; USSR People's Deputy 1989–91; Artistic Man. Hamazgain Theatre; People's Artist of Armenian SSR 1972, Armenian State Prize for work in the theatre 1979, People's Artist of USSR 1985, Mesrop Mastots Prize 1998. *Films:* Matenadaran Soliaris, The Boys of the Band, We and Our Mountains, Hegnar, Nahapet, Dzori, Miro and many others. *Plays:* King John, The Judge, Pepo, Othello, The Apple Garden; more than 40 plays. *Publications:* At This Side of the Curtain 1991, DIY Branches 1991, The Break Off 2000. *Address:* Amirian 26, Yerevan State Institute of Theatre and Cinema (Office); Terian 63 fl. 20, Yerevan, Armenia (Home); Sundukian Theatre, Abovyan Str. 35, Yerevan, Armenia. *Telephone:* 53-62-21 (Office); 58-26-60 (Home). *Fax:* 53-62-33 (Office). *E-mail:* Nit@EDU .am (Office).

SARKISOV, Aleksander Aleksandrovich, D.TECH.SC.; Russian aviation engineer; b. 19 May 1936; ed Ufa Inst. of Aviation; engineer, Ufa Experimental Construction Bureau SOYUZ, USSR Ministry of Aviation 1959–72; Deputy Chief Constructor, Deputy Dir 1972–83; Deputy Head, Chief Engineer, First Deputy Head, Dept of Experimental Construction of Aircraft Engines, Ministry of Aviation Industry 1984–86; Gen. Constructor, Dir Klimov factory 1988–91; Chair. Bd Dirs. MTA Corpn; Pres. Klimov Corpn; Chair. Jt Venture Pratt-Whitney-Klimov 1991–; Sr mem., American Inst. of Aviation and Astronautics; mem. Russian Acad. of Transport, Acad of Eng, Acad. of Aviation; Lenin Prize, Lawrence Prize, Prize of Zhukovsky Acad. of Transport 1994. *Achievements:* responsible for the modernization of numerous mil. aircraft and vehicles. *Leisure interests:* history, art, architecture.

SARKISOV, Ashot Arakelovich; Russian nuclear energy specialist; b. 30 Jan. 1924, Tashkent, USSR; s. of Arakel A. Sarkisov and Evgeniya B. Grigoryan; m. Nelli G. Sarkisov 1951; two s.; ed F. Dzerzhinsky Higher Marine Eng School, Leningrad Univ.; worked as engineer Baltic fleet; Chair. Higher Marine School, Sevastopol; Deputy Dir Naval Acad.; Chair. Scientific-Tech. Council of the Navy; Head of Dept, Inst. for Nuclear Safety; Chair. Expert Council on Navy and Shipbuilding; Chair. Panel of Experts, Int. Scientific and Eng Program on Radioactive Waste; Corresp. mem. USSR (now Russian) Acad. of Sciences 1981, Adviser, Nuclear Safety Inst. 1990–, mem. 1994; research in theory of dynamic processes and automatic protection of nuclear plants, problems of safety and security in nuclear energy; eight Orders of the USSR and of Russia; many medals. *Publications include:* Dynamics of Nuclear Power Plants of Submarines 1964, Nuclear Propulsion Power Plants 1968, Dynamic Regimes in the Operation of Nuclear Propulsion Power Plants 1971, Physics of Transitional Processes in Nuclear Reactors 1983, Nuclear Propulsion Power Plants and Steam Generators 1985, Thermo-Electric Generators with Nuclear Sources of Heat 1987, Physical Principles of Nuclear Steam-Productive Plants 1989, Nuclear Submarine Decommissioning and Related Problems 1996, Analysis of Risks Associated with Nuclear Submarine Decommissioning, Dismantling and Disposal 1999. *Leisure interests:* tennis, history of the navy. *Address:* Nuclear Safety Institute, Russian Academy of Sciences, B. Tulskaya str. 52, 113191 Moscow, Russia. *Telephone:* (095) 958-14-59 (Office); (095) 955-22-80 (Office). *Fax:* (095) 958-00-40. *E-mail:* sarkisov@ibrae.ac.ru (Office); sarkisov@ibrae.ac.ru (Home).

SARKISSIAN, Aram; Armenian politician; b. 2 Jan. 1961, Ararat; m.; three c.; ed Yerevan School of Arts, Yerevan Polytechnical Inst.; army service 1981–83; various positions with Araratstroytrust 1989–93; Asst Dir-Gen., then Deputy Dir-Gen. Araratcement 1993–98, Exec. Dir 1998–99; mem. Republican Party of Armenia, Yerkrapah Union of Volunteers; Prime Minister of Armenia 1999–2000; in pvt. business. *Address:* Republican Party of Armenia, Yerevan, Armenia (Office).

SARKISSIAN, Serge; Armenian politician; b. 1954, Stepanakert; m.; two c.; ed Yerevan State Univ.; turner, electronic factory, Yerevan 1975–79; Komsomol Sec., Head of Propaganda section City Cttee, Stepanakert 1979–88; Head Self-Defence Cttee, Karabakh 1988–93; Deputy in Nat. Ass. 1990–93; Minister of Defence 1993–95, 2000–, of Nat. Security 1995–96, 1999, of Internal Affairs and Nat. Security 1996–99; Chief Council of Nat. Security 1999–2000; Order of the Fighting Cross, Kt of the Golden Eagle Order. *Address:* Ministry of Defence, House of Government, Yerevan, Armenia (Office). *Telephone:* (12) 34-56-56 (Office).

SARKISYAN, Armen, CandPhys-MathSc; Armenian politician; b. 1953, Yerevan; m.; two s.; ed Yerevan State Univ.; docent Yerevan State Univ. 1979–84; researcher Cambridge Univ. UK 1984–85; lecturer Yerevan State Univ. 1985–90, Head Dept of Math. Modelling; Prof. London Univ. 1992–; apptd. Chargé d'affaires, then Amb. to UK 1992–2000; Amb., Doyen of Armenian Diplomatic Corps to Europe (also accred to Belgium, Netherlands, Vatican City, Luxembourg) 1993–96; Prime Minister 1996–97; mem. London Int. Inst. of Strategic Studies; Hon. Mem. Royal Soc. of Int. Relations and Cen. of Strategic Studies, Oxford Univ. *Publications:* author of numerous articles on politology, theoretical physics, astronomy and math. modelling. *Address:* c/o Ministry of Foreign Affairs, Government House 2, Republic Square 1, 375010 Yerevan, Armenia.

SARKISYAN, Fadey Tachatovich, DTechSci; Armenian politician and scientist; b. 18 Sept. 1923, Yerevan; s. of Tachat Sarkisyan and Maria Sarkisyan; m. Tatiana Roubenovna; one d.; ed Yerevan Polytechnical Inst. and Mil. Acad. of St Petersburg; mem. CPSU 1945–91; responsible for new techniques in devt and Scientific Centres of USSR Ministry of Defence 1945–63; Gen. Dir Yerevan Computer Research Inst. 1963–77; Chair. Council of Ministers of Armenian SSR 1977–89; Deputy to USSR Supreme Soviet 1979–89; Academician-Sec. Nat. Acad. of Sciences of Armenia 1989–93, Pres. 1993–; Dir Eurasia Centre, Univ. of Cambridge; mem. Nat. Ass. of Armenia 1974–99; State Prize of the USSR 1971, 1981, State Prize of the Ukraine 1986. *Publications:* more than 200 scientific articles. *Leisure interests:* new technologies, literature, music. *Address:* Armenian Academy of Sciences, 24 Marshal Baghramian Avenue, Yerevan 375019 (Office); 10/1 Zarobyan Street, Apt. 11, Yerevan 375019, Armenia (Home). *Telephone:* 527031 (Office); 527419 (Home). *Fax:* 584385 (Office); 584385. *E-mail:* fsark@sci.am (Office).

SARKÖZY de NAGY BOSCA, Nicholas Paul Stéphane; French politician, barrister and civil servant; b. 28 Jan. 1955, Paris; s. of Paul Sarközy de Nagy Bosca and Andrée Mallah; m. 1st Marie-Dominique Culioli 1982; two s.; m. 2nd Cecilia Ciganer-Albeniz 1996; one s.; ed Inst. of Political Studies, Paris, Paris Univ.; barrister Paris 1981–87; Assoc. Leibovici Claude Sarközy 1987; mem RPR Cen. Cttee 1977–, Nat. Del. 1978–79, Nat. Sec. 1988–90, Asst Sec.-Gen. 1990–93; Town Councillor Neuilly-sur-Seine 1977–83, Mayor 1983–; Pres. Nat. Cttee Jacques Chirac's Presidential Campaign 1981; Regional Councillor Ile-de-France 1983–88; (RPR) Deputy to Nat. Ass. from Hauts-de-Seine 1988–93, 1993–95, 1997–; Chief Spokesman RPR 1997–; Minister of the Budget 1993–94, of Communications 1994–95; Minister of the Interior and Security May 2002–; mem. RPR Political Office 1995–, Sec.-Gen. RPR 1998–99, Interim Pres. April–Oct. 1999, Pres. RPR Regional Cttee of Hauts-de-Seine 2000–; Leader RPR-DL List, European Elections June 1999. *Publications:* Georges Mandel, moine de la politique 1994, Au bout de la passion, l'équilibre (co-author) 1995, Libre 2001. *Leisure interests:* tennis, cycling. *Address:* Ministry of the Interior and Security, place Beauveau, 75008 Paris; Mairie, 96 Ave A. Peretti, 92200 Neuilly-sur-Seine, France. *Telephone:* 1-49-27-49-27 (Office). *Fax:* 1-43-59-89-50. *E-mail:* sirp@interieur.gouv.fr. *Website:* www.interieur.gouv.fr.

SARMADI, Morteza, BSc, MA; Iranian diplomatist; b. July 1954, Tehran; m. Fatima Hosseini 1982; four d.; ed Sharif Univ., Tehran; joined Ministry of Foreign Affairs 1981, Dir-Gen. of Press and Information 1982–89, Deputy Foreign Minister for Communication 1989–97, Deputy Foreign Minister for Europe and America 1997–; Amb. to UK 2000–; Sr Del. Iran-Iraq peace talks; Trustee, Islamic Thought Foundation, Islamic Repub. News Agency, Islamic High Council of Propagation Policy, Inst. for Political and Int. Studies. *Publications:* numerous political articles. *Leisure interests:* reading, writing, watching TV, spending time with family. *Address:* Embassy of Iran, 16 Prince's Gate, London SW7 1PT, England (Office). *Telephone:* (20) 7225-3000, ext. 206 (Office). *Fax:* (20) 7589-7103 (Office).

SARNE, Tanya, BA; British fashion designer; b. 15 Jan. 1945, London; d. of Jean-Claude Gordon and Daphne Tucar; m. Michael Sarne 1969 (divorced); one s. one d.; ed Sussex Univ.; worked as a model then as a teacher, then briefly in film production; travelled extensively throughout S. America and Europe; returned to England and set up co. importing Alpaca wool knitted garments influenced by traditional Inca designs which launched career in 1970s; introduced Scandinavian labels In Wear and Laize Adzer to UK; est. successful labels Miz 1978–83 and Ghost 1984–; British Apparel Export Award for Womenswear 1993, 1995. *Leisure interests:* cooking, tennis. *Address:* Ghost Ltd., The Chapel, 263 Kensal Road, London, W10 5DB, England. *Telephone:* (20) 8960-3121. *Fax:* (20) 8960-8374.

SARNEY, José; Brazilian politician; b. 1930; Asst to Maranhão State Gov. 1950; Maranhão State Rep. 1956, re-elected 1958, 1962; elected Gov. of Maranhão 1965; State Senator (Arena Party, now Partido Democrático Social (PDS)) 1970; Nat. Pres. Arena 1970; fmr Chair. PDS; mem. Partido Frente Liberal 1984, PMDD; Acting Pres. of Brazil March–April 1985, Pres. 1985–90; fmr Pres. of Senate; mem. Brazilian Acad. of Letters. *Publication:* Tales of Rain and Sunlight 1986. *Leisure interests:* literature, painting. *Address:* Senado Federal, Brasília; c/o Oficio do Presidente, Palácio do Planalto, Praça dos Tres Podêres, 70.150 Brasília, DF, Brazil.

SAROVIĆ, Mirko, LLB; Bosnia and Herzegovina/Serb politician; b. 16 Sept. 1956, Rogatica; m. Stojanka Sarović; two s.; ed Faculty of Law, Sarajevo Univ.; mem. Serb Democratic Party (SDP); mem. Nat. Ass., Repub. of Srpska, Bosnia and Herzegovina 1996–98; Vice-Pres. of Repub. of Srpska, Bosnia and Herzegovina 1998–2000, de facto Pres. 2000–02; Pres. of Bosnia and Herzegovina 2002–03; several honours, awards, prizes and decorations. *Leisure interest:* collecting old books. *Address:* c/o Office of the President, Musala 9, 71000 Sarajevo (Office); Lukavica b6, 71123 Serbs Sarajevo, Bosnia and Herzegovina (Home). *Fax:* (51) 312805 (Home).

SARPANEVA, Timo Tapani; Finnish artist and designer; b. 31 Oct. 1926, Helsinki; s. of Akseli Johannes Sarpaneva and Martta Sofia Karimo; m. 1st Ann-Mari Holmberg (divorced); m. 2nd Marfatta Svennerig; three s. one d.; ed Industrial Art Inst., Helsinki; Designer for A. Ahlström Oy, Iittala Glassworks 1950–; Teacher in Textile Printing and Design, Industrial Art Inst. Helsinki 1953–57; Artistic Dir Porin Puuvilla Cotton Mill 1955–66; AB Kinnasand Textile Mill, Sweden 1964–; Designer for Juhava Oy, Jughans AG, FRG, Opa Oy, Primo Oy, Rosenlew Oy, Roserthal AG, FRG, Villayhnymä;

invited by Brazilian Govt to lecture on and exhibit Finnish art glass 1958; Exhbn architect for Finnish industrial art exhbns. in most European countries, Japan and USA; architect for Finnish Section, Expo 1967, Montreal; pvt. exhbns. in Finland, Sweden, Norway, Denmark, Iceland, Netherlands, England, Germany, France, Italy, USA, Brazil, USSR, Australia; mem. Bd of Dirs. Asscn of Arts and Crafts, State Cttee of Design, Bd of Inst. of Industrial Design; numerous awards, including three Grand Prix at Milan Triennali; Hon. Dr. of Design, Royal Coll. of Art, London 1967; Commdr, Order of Lion of Finland.

SARRAJ, Eyad Rajab el, PhD; Palestinian human rights activist and psychiatrist; Founder and Medical Dir Gaza Community Mental Health Programme; Co-Founder and Commr.-Gen. Palestinian Independent Comm. for Citizens' Rights; arrested three times for criticism of Palestinian Nat. Authorities; mem. Int. Rehabilitation Centre for Torture Victims; mem. Co-ordinating Cttee Campaign Against Torture in the Middle East and N Africa; Martin Ennals Award for Human Rights Defenders 1998.

SARRAZIN, Jürgen; German banker; b. 21 March 1936, Freiberg; ed Univ. of Heidelberg; joined Dresdner Bank AG 1960, Sr Gen. Man. 1975, Man. Dir 1983, Chair. Bd Man. Dirs. 1993–98; Officier Légion d'honneur (France), Commdr Ordre Grand-Ducal de la Couronne de Chaine (Luxembourg). *Address:* c/o Dresdner Bank AG, 60301 Frankfurt am Main, Germany.

SARRE, Claude-Alain, DèsL; French industrialist and writer; b. 10 April 1928, Douai; s. of Henri Sarre and Claudine Vau; m. Simone Allien 1952; two s. one d.; ed Univ. de Lille, Inst. d'Etudes Politiques, Paris, Univ. d'Aix-Marseille; with Cie Air France; joined Soc. André Citroën 1955, Commercial Dir 1968, Chair., Man. Dir Soc. Automobiles Citroën and Soc. Commerciale Citroën 1968–70; joined Lainière de Roubaix-Prouvost Masurel SA 1970, Pres., Dir-Gen. 1972–77; Chair. Inst. de Devt industriel 1975–77; Dir Soc. Sommer-Allibert 1976; Pres. and Dir Gen. Nobel-Bozel 1978–82; Dir Conseil nat. du patronat français 1983–88; Pres. Council of Improvement, Magni; Chevalier, Légion d'honneur; Prix Mignet Académie d'Aix-en-Provence 1995, Prix de Beaujour, Académie de Marseille 1999. *Publications:* Vivre sa soumission 1997, Un procès de sorcière 1999, Les Panhard et Lavassor 2000, Le dossier-verité du Concorde 2002. *Address:* Le grand pin, La Crémade Nord, 13100 Le Tholonet, France. *Telephone:* 4-42-66-96-22 (Office). *E-mail:* casarre@aol.com (Home).

SARRE, Massamba, L. EN. D.; Senegalese diplomatist; b. 6 Oct. 1935, St Louis; m.; four c.; ed Law Colls. Dakar, Senegal and Grenoble, France; Asst Coll. of Law and Econ. Sciences, Dakar 1959; Asst Sec.-Gen. to Minister of Foreign Affairs 1960–62, Sec.-Gen. 1962–64, Cabinet Dir 1964–68; Amb. to Morocco 1968–72, to Iran (also accred to Turkey, Pakistan, Afghanistan, Bahrain and Qatar) 1972–79, to Tunisia 1979–80; Perm. Rep. to UN 1980–88; Amb. to France (also accred to Spain and Portugal) 1988–96; del. at numerous confs of UN, OAU, Non-Aligned Countries and Islamic Conf. *Address:* c/o Ministry of Foreign Affairs and Senegalese Abroad, 1 place de l' Indépendence, Dakar, Senegal.

SARTORIUS, Norman, MD, PhD, F.R.C.PSYCH.; German psychiatrist and psychologist; b. 28 Jan. 1935, Münster, Germany; m. Vera Pecikozić 1963; one d.; ed Univ. of Zagreb, Univ. of London; Consultant, Dept of Psychiatry, Univ. of Zagreb 1959–64; Research Fellow, Inst. of Psychiatry, Univ. of London 1964–65; WHO medical officer in psychiatric epidemiology 1967–68; Medical Officer in charge of Epidemiological and Social Psychiatry and Standardization of Psychiatric Diagnosis, Classification and Statistics, WHO 1969–73, Chief, Office of Mental Health 1974–76, Dir Div. of Mental Health 1976–93; Prof. Univ. of Zagreb, Univ. of Geneva, Univ. of Prague, St Louis Univ.; Corresp. mem. Royal Spanish Acad. of Medicine, Mexican Acad. of Medicine, Peruvian Acad. of Medicine; Hon. Fellow Royal Coll. of Psychiatrists, UK, Royal Australian and New Zealand Coll. of Psychiatrists; Hon. mem. of numerous professional and scientific orgs.; Hon. Dr.Med. (Umeå), (Prague); Hon. DSc (Bath); Rema Lapouse Medal. *Publications:* more than 250 articles, several books (author or ed.) on schizophrenia, transcultural psychiatry, mental health policy, scientific methodology. *Leisure interests:* chess, reading. *Address:* Hôpitaux Universitaires de Genève, Batiment Saleve, Chemin du Petit Bel Air 2, 1225 Geneva, Switzerland. *Telephone:* (22) 3055741 (Office). *Fax:* (22) 3055749 (Office). *E-mail:* norman.sartorius@hcuge .ch (Office).

SARTZETAKIS, Christos A., LLD; Greek fmr Head of State and lawyer; b. 6 April 1929, Salonika; m. Efi Argyriou; one d.; ed Salonika Univ. and Law Faculty, Paris (Sorbonne); called to Bar 1954; apptd. JP 1955, Judge of 1st Instance 1956; Investigating Magistrate in Lambrakis affair (which inspired Vasilis Vasilikos' novel Z, later made into film) 1963–64; postgrad. studies Paris 1965–67; mem. Société de Législation Comparée, Paris 1966–; fmr mem. Admin. Council Hellenic Humanistic Soc. recalled by junta and posted to Volos Court of Misdemeanours 1967–69; arrested and detained for 50 days on unspecified charges 1969; reinstated as an Appeal Judge 1974; Sr Appeal Judge, Nauplion 1981, Justice of Supreme Court 1982–85; Pres. of Greece 1985–90; mem. Société de Législation Comparée, Paris 1966–; fmr mem. Admin. Council Hellenic Humanistic Soc. *Address:* c/o Office of the President, Athens, Greece.

SARY IENG (see Ieng Sary).

SASSER, James Ralph, JD; American politician; b. 30 Sept. 1936, Memphis, Tenn.; s. of Joseph Ralph Sasser and Mary Nell (née Gray) Sasser; m. Mary

Ballantine Gorman 1962; one s. one d.; ed Vanderbilt Univ.; served U.S. Marine Corps Reserve 1958–65; partner, Goodpasture, Carpenter, Woods & Sasser, Nashville 1961–76; Chair. Tennessee Democratic State Cttee 1973–76; Senator from Tennessee 1977–95; Amb. to People's Repub. of China 1996–99; Foreign Policy Adviser to Vice-Pres. Al Gore 2000; J. B. and Maurice C. Shapiro Prof., Elliott School of Int. Affairs, George Washington Univ. 2000–; mem. ABA, UN Asscn. *Address:* Elliott School of International Affairs, George Washington University, 2013 G Street, NW, Washington, DC 20052 USA (Office). *Telephone:* (202) 994-6240. *Fax:* (202) 994-0335.

SASSOON, David; British fashion designer; b. 5 Oct. 1932, London; s. of George Sassoon and Victoria Gurgi; ed Chelsea Coll. of Art and Royal Coll. of Art; designer, Belinda Bellville 1958; first ready-to-wear collection 1963; Dir Belinda Bellville 1964; Licensee Vogue Butterick USA 1966 (became Bellville Sassoon 1970); Dir and sole shareholder Bellville Sassoon 1983–. *Leisure interests:* theatre, ballet. *Address:* Bellville Sassoon, 18 Culford Gardens, London, SW3 2ST, England. *Telephone:* (20) 7581-3500 (Office).

SASSOON, Vidal; hair stylist; b. 17 Jan. 1928, London; s. of Nathan Sassoon and Betty (Bellin) Sassoon; m. (divorced 1980); two s. two d.; ed New York Univ.; served with Palmach Israeli Army; cr. a form of hairstyling based on Bahaus and geometric forms; Founder and Chair. Vidal Sassoon Inc.; Pres. Vidal Sassoon Foundation; f. Vidal Sassoon Centre for the Study of Anti-Semitism and Related Bigotries at Hebrew Univ., Jerusalem; Fellow Hair Artists Int.; awards include French Ministry of Culture Award, Award for Services Rendered, Harvard Business School, Intercoiffure Award, Cartier, London 1978. *E-mail:* ukvidals.im@pg.com (Office). *Website:* www .vidalsassoon.com (Office).

SASSOU-NGUESSO, Gen. Denis; Republic of the Congo politician and army officer; b. 1943; mem. Council of State 1976–77; First Vice-Pres., Mil. Cttee of the Parti Congolais du Travail (PCT), co-ordinator of PCT activities 1977–79, concurrently Minister of Nat. Defence; Pres. of the Republic of the Congo 1979–92, Oct. 1997–; also fmr Minister of Defence and Security; Cand. Pres. Elections 1992; Pres. Cen. Cttee PCT; Leader Forces Démocratiques Unies (alliance of six parties including PCT) 1994–95. *Address:* Palais du Peuple, Brazzaville, Republic of the Congo. *E-mail:* collgros@altranet.fr (Office). *Website:* www.congo-site.com (Office).

SATARAWALA, Kershasp Tehmurasp, MA; Indian administrator and diplomatist; b. 15 Feb. 1916, Satara, Maharashtra; s. of Tehmurasp P. Satarawala and Meherbai H. Chhiber; m. Frainy Bilimoria 1947; three d.; ed Bilimoria High School, Panchagani, Wadia Coll., Poona, Govt Coll., Lahore and Staff Coll., Quetta; Fellow, Nuffield Foundation, London; in Indian Army during Second World War; Indian Admin. Service 1947–75; with Indian Airlines 1967–71, Man. Dir, later Chair.; Adviser to Govs. of Gujarat, Orissa, Jammu and Kashmir 1971–80; Special Sec. Foreign Trade Ministry, later Sec. Steel and Mines Ministry 1972–73; Sec.-Gen. Family Planning Asscn of India 1976–81; Chair. Gujarat Aromatics Ltd 1977–83; mem. Indian Wild Life Bd 1976–81, Nat. Cttee on Environmental Planning 1980–83, Minorities Comm. 1981–83; Vice-Chair. Organizing Cttee and Co-ordinator IX Asian Games, New Delhi 1982; Co-ordinator Non-aligned Summit Meeting, New Delhi 1983; Lt-Gov. of Goa, Daman and Diu and Admin., Dadra and Nagar Haveli 1983–84; Gov. of Punjab 1984–85; Amb. to Mexico, Guatemala and El Salvador 1985–88; Padma Bhushan Award 1983. *Publications:* Plan on Tourism and Civil Aviation for Gujarat 1972, Gir Lion Sanctuary 1972, Perspective Plan of Gujarat 1974–84; articles on industrial Devt, environment, etc. *Leisure interests:* classical music, trekking, golf. *Address:* 423 Kriti Apartments, Narangi Bagh Road, Pune 411001, India. *Telephone:* (20) 6123213.

SATO, Humitaka, PhD; Japanese astrophysicist; b. 23 March 1939, Yamagata; s. of Mokichi Sato and Kane Sato; m. Keiko Okazaki 1965; one s. one d.; ed Kyoto Univ.; Prof. of Astrophysics and Relativity, Kyoto Univ. 1974–, Dean Faculty of Sciences 1993; Dir Yukawa Inst. for Theoretical Physics 1976–80; Pres. Physical Soc. of Japan 1998–2000; Nishina Prize 1973; Purple Medal of Honour 1999. *Publications:* Black Holes 1976, Discovery of Big Bang 1983, Invitation to Cosmology 1988. *Address:* Department of Physics, Kyoto University, Yoshida-Honmachi, Jakyo-ku, Kyoto 606-8501, Japan. *Telephone:* (75) 753-3886. *E-mail:* sato@tap.scphys.kyoto-u.ac.jp (Office). *Website:* www .kyoto-u.ac.jp (Office).

SATO, Kazuo, PhD; Japanese/American professor of economics; b. 5 Jan. 1927, Sapporo, Japan; s. of Kinzo Sato and Naka Sato; m. Midori Sasayama 1961; one s. two d.; ed Hokkaido Univ., Yale Univ.; Research Asst Yale Univ. 1956–59, Asst Prof. Osaka Univ., Japan 1959–65; Econ. Affairs Officer, UN (New York) 1962–70; Prof. State Univ. of New York at Buffalo 1970–83, Leading Prof. 1978–83; Prof. Rutgers Univ. 1984–2000; Visiting Prof. MIT 1969–70, Univ. of Pittsburgh 1976, State Univ. of New York at Albany 1978, Columbia Univ. 1981–83, Yale Univ. 1985; Visiting Fellow Osaka Univ. 1987, Netherlands Inst. for Advanced Studies in the Humanities and Social Sciences 1988, Nagoya City Univ., Japan 1990. *Publications:* Production Functions and Aggregation 1975, Industry and Business in Japan 1980, The Anatomy of Japanese Business 1984, Macroeconomics 1989, The Japanese Economy: Primer 1996, The Transformation of the Japanese Economy 1999, Ed. Japanese Economic Studies 1972–. *Address:* 300 E 71, 15H, New York, NY 10021-5245, USA (Home). *Telephone:* (212) 737-9407 (Home).

SATO, Megumu; Japanese politician; b. 28 Feb. 1924; ed Kyoto Univ.; joined Ministry of Posts and Telecommunications; mem. House of Reps. 1969–; Parl. Vice-Minister for Home Affairs 1974–75, for Post and Telecommunications 1976, Minister 1984–85; Minister of Justice 1990–91; Dir-Gen. Nat. Land Agency May–June 1994; mem. Liberal Democratic Party. *Publication:* Ohshu Zakki Sekai no Tabi kara. *Leisure interests:* Go, sport.

SATO, Mitsuo; Japanese banker; b. 1 Feb. 1933, Gunma; m. (wife deceased); two s.; ed Univ. of Tokyo and Harvard Law School; entered Ministry of Finance 1955; Sr Deputy Dir Int. Taxation and Div. Tax Bureau, Ministry of Finance 1968–70; Sr Economist, Tax Policy Div. Fiscal Affairs Dept, IMF 1970–73; Dir Research Div. Tax Bureau, Ministry of Finance 1976–78; Dir Securities Cos. Div., Securities Bureau, Ministry of Finance 1978–79; Dir-Gen. Fukuoka Regional Tax Bureau, Nat. Tax Admin. Agency 1980–81; Deputy Dir-Gen. Customs and Tariff Bureau, Ministry of Finance 1981–83, Deputy Dir-Gen. Int. Finance Bureau 1983–84; mem. Policy Bd Bank of Japan 1984–85; Dir-Gen. Customs and Tariff Bureau, Ministry of Finance 1985–86; Man. Dir Tokyo Stock Exchange 1986–88, Sr Man. Dir 1988–91, Deputy Pres. 1991–93; Pres. and Chair. Bd of Dirs. Asian Devt Bank 1993–98. *Address:* c/o Asian Development Bank, 6 ADB Avenue, Mandaluyong City 0401, Metro Manila, Philippines. *Telephone:* (2) 632-4444. *Fax:* (2) 636-2444.

SATO, Moriyoshi; Japanese politician; b. 28 March 1922; ed Chuo Univ.; Pvt. Sec. to two Govt Ministers; mem. of House of Reps. 1969–; Parl. Vice-Minister for Transport 1975–76, for Nat. Land Agency 1976–77; Deputy Sec.-Gen. Liberal Democratic Party 1977–78, Vice-Chair. Policy Affairs Research Council; Minister of Agric. Forestry and Fisheries 1984–85; Dir-Gen. Nat. Land Agency, Minister of State Feb.–Dec. 1990; Dir-Gen. Hokkaido Devt Agency and Okinawa Devt Agency May–June 1994. *Leisure interest:* reading.

SATO, Ryuzo, PhD, DEcon; Japanese professor of economics; b. 5 July 1931, Akita-ken; m. Kishie Hayashi 1959; one s. one d.; ed Hitotsubashi Univ., Tokyo, Johns Hopkins University, Baltimore, Md, USA; Fulbright Scholar, Johns Hopkins Univ. 1957–62; Prof. of Econs Brown Univ. 1967–85; C. V. Starr Prof. of Econs New York Univ. 1985–, also Dir Japan–US Center, New York Univ. Stern School of Business; Adjunct Prof. of Public Policy, John F. Kennedy School of Govt Harvard Univ. 1983; Guggenheim Fellow; Ford Foundation Fellow; Yomiuri newspaper Rondan Prize, Nihon-Keizai newspaper Economics Award (Nikkei Prize). *Publications:* Theory of Technical Change and Economic Invariance 1981, Research and Productivity (with G. Suzawa) 1983, Growth Theory and Technical Change 1996, Production, Stability and Dynamic Invariance 1999. *Leisure interests:* skiing, music, gardening. *Address:* The Center for Japan–US Business and Economic Studies, 44 West Fourth Street, Suite 7-190, New York, NY 10012, USA (Office). *Telephone:* (212) 998-0750 (Office). *Fax:* (212) 995-4219 (Office). *E-mail:* rsato@stern.nyu.edu (Office).

SATOH, Yukio, BA; Japanese diplomatist; b. 6 Oct. 1939; m.; two c.; ed Tokyo and Edin. Univs.; entered Foreign Service 1963, with Ministry of Foreign Affairs, Tokyo, then Embassy, Washington, DC –1976, Dir Div. of Security Affairs, American Affairs Bureau, Ministry of Foreign Affairs 1976, Counsellor, London 1981–84, also Consul-Gen.; Asst Vice-Minister for Parl. Affairs, Ministry of Foreign Affairs 1987–88; Consul-Gen., Hong Kong 1988–90; Dir.-Gen. North American Affairs Bureau and Dir.-Gen. Information Analysis, Research and Planning Bureau, Ministry of Foreign Affairs 1990–94, Amb. to the Netherlands 1994–96, to Australia 1996–98; Perm. Rep. to the UN 1998–. *Address:* Permanent Mission of Japan to the United Nations, 866 United Nations Plaza, 2nd Floor, New York, NY 10017, USA (Office). *Telephone:* (212) 223-4300 (Office). *Fax:* (212) 751-1966 (Office). *E-mail:* jpnun@undp.org (Office).

SATTAR, Abdul, MA; Pakistani politician; b. 1931; m. Yasmine Sattar 1955; one s. two d.; ed Punjab Univ. and Fletcher School, USA; served in Pakistan Missions in Saudi Arabia, Sudan and the USA; Amb. of Pakistan to Austria 1975–78, to India 1978–82, 1990–92, to USSR 1988–90; Dir, then Dir-Gen. and Additional Sec. at Foreign Office, for Asia 1982–86; Foreign Sec., Islamabad 1986–88; Sr Del. to Geneva Talks on Afghanistan 1988; fmr Minister of Foreign Affairs; Distinguished Fellow, US Inst. of Peace, Washington, DC 1994; mem. Nat. Security Council. *Publications:* Pakistan in Perspective, 1947–97 (jtly); articles in learned journals on nuclear nonproliferation and regional studies. *Address:* House 7, College Road, F-7/3, Islamabad, Pakistan. *Telephone:* (51) 2270476.

SATTERFIELD, David M.; American diplomatist; ed Univ. of Maryland, Georgetown Univ.; served in Saudi Arabia, Tunisia, Lebanon and Syria; worked in Bureaus of Near Eastern Affairs, East Asian and Pacific Affairs and Intelligence and Research; Dir for Exec. Secretarial Staff and for Near East and South Asian Affairs, Nat. Security Council 1993–96; Amb. to Lebanon 1998–2001; several Dept individual and group Superior Honor Awards. *Address:* c/o Department of State, 2201 C Street, NW, Washington, DC 20520, USA (Office).

SA'UD, HRH Prince Sultan ibn Abd al-Aziz as-; Saudi Arabian politician; b. 1930; s. of the late King Abd al-Aziz as-Sa'ud; ed at court and abroad; Gov. of Riyadh 1947; Minister of Agric. 1954, of Transportation 1955; mem. most Saudi Dels. to Arab and Islamic Summit Confs, State visits and UN Gen. Ass. Sessions 1962–75; Vice-Pres. Supreme Cttee for Educ. Policy; Minister of Defence and Aviation and Insp. Gen. 1963, 1982–; Chair. Ministerial Cttee for Econ. Offset Program 1982–; Chair. Bd Saudia Airlines 1963–; Chair. Bd

General Enterprise of Mil. Industries; Pres. Supreme Council of Manpower 1980; Second Deputy Prime Minister 1982–; Chair. Bd of Gen. Enterprise of Mil. Industries 1985–; Chair. Bd for Nat. Comm. for Wildlife Conservation and Devt 1986–; Chair Supreme Council for Islamic Affairs 1994–; Supreme Pres. and Chair. Trustees Sultan bin Abdulaziz Charity Foundation 1995–; Chair. Ministerial Cttee on Environment 1995–; Vice-Pres. Supreme Econ. Council 2000–; Chair. High Comm. for Tourism 2000–; Order of Merit (First Class) from many countries. *Address:* Ministry of Defence and Aviation, P.O. Box 26731, Airport Road, Riyadh 11165, Saudi Arabia. *Telephone:* (1) 476-9000. *Fax:* (1) 405-5500.

SA'UD AL-FAISAL, HRH Prince, B.A.(Econs); Saudi Arabian politician and diplomatist; b. 1941, Riyadh; s. of the late King Faisal; ed Princeton Univ., USA; fmr Deputy Minister of Petroleum and Mineral Resources 1971–74; Minister of State for Foreign Affairs March–Oct. 1975, Minister of Foreign Affairs Oct. 1975–; leader del. to UN Gen. Ass. 1976; Special Envoy of HM King Khaled in diplomatic efforts to resolve Algerian–Moroccan conflict over Western Sahara and the civil war in Lebanon; mem. Saudi Arabian del. to Arab restricted Summit, Riyadh, Oct. 1976 and to full Summit Conf. of Arab League, Oct. 1976; Founding mem. King Faisal's Int. Charity Soc. *Leisure interest:* reading. *Address:* Ministry of Foreign Affairs, Nasseriya Street, Riyadh 11124, Saudi Arabia. *Telephone:* (1) 401-5000. *Fax:* (1) 403-0159. *Website:* www.mofa.gov.sa (Office).

SAUDARGAS, Algirdas; Lithuanian politician and biophysicist; b. 17 April 1948, Kaunas; m. Laima Saudargené; one s. one d.; ed Kaunas Inst. of Medicine; research Asst Inst. of Math. and Information Tech. Lithuanian Acad. of Sciences 1972–77; Sr Lecturer Lithuanian Acad. of Agric. 1977–82; researcher Kaunas Inst. of Medicine (now Acad.) 1982–90; Founder mem. Sajūdis Movt, Chair. Sajūdis Seimas (Parl.) Political Cttee 1988–90; elected to Supreme Soviet Repub. of Lithuania 1990; Minister of Foreign Affairs 1990–92, 1996–99; mem. official del. Repub. of Lithuania to negotiations with Soviet Union; mem. Seimas, Cttee on Foreign Affairs, mem. Seimas del. to European Parl. 1992–, Chair. Subcttee on European Affairs 1995–; Chair. Lithuanian Christian Democratic Party 1995– (mem. 1989–). *Leisure interest:* reading. *Address:* L. Stuokos-Gucevičiaus str. B/10, Apt. 3, Vilnius 2001, Lithuania (Home). *Telephone:* (2) 22-22-13 (Home).

SAUDEK, Jan; Czech photographer; b. 13 May 1935, Prague; s. of Gustav Saudek and Pavla Saudková; m. 1st Marie Geislerová 1958 (divorced 1973); m. 2nd Marie Šrámková 1974 (died 1993); two s. three d.; studied reproduction photography at graphic school; factory worker 1953–83; over 400 solo exhbns world-wide, over 300 jt exhbns; works include Man Holding New Born Child 1966, Artist's Father of the Cemetery 1972, Mother and Daughter 1979, Walkman 1984, Desire 1985, The Wedding 1990, The Deep Devotion 1994, Pretty Girl I Loved 1995, Joan of Arc 1998; exhbn of paintings, Prague 1997, 1998; Chevalier, Ordre des Arts et des Lettres 1990; Award for Platinum CD cover 'Soul Asylum' 1999. *Art exhibitions include:* Art Institute of Chicago 1976, Robert Koch Gallery, San Francisco, Calif. 1987, Jan Kesner Gallery LA, Calif. 1989, Musée Nat. d'Art Moderne, Centre Pompidou, Paris 1991, Ken Damy Museo, Brescia, Italy 1997, Kamel Mennour Gallery, Paris 1999, Louvre, Paris 2000. *Films include:* Jerôme du Missolz 1991, Jan Saudek – Czech Photographer (Documentary), Telewizja Wroslaw, Poland 1997. *Publications include:* Il Teatro de la Vita 1980, The World of Jan Saudek 1983, JanSaudek – 200 Photographs 1953–1986 1987, Life, Love, Death and Such Other Trifles 1992, Theatre of the Life 1992, The Letter 1995, Jubilations and Obsessions 1995, Album 1997, Jan Saudek... 1998, Love is a 4 Letter Word 1999, Single, Married, Divorced, Widower 1999, Realities 2002. *Leisure interests:* women, running long distances, painting, drinking. *Address:* Blodkova 6, 130 00 Prague 3, Czech Republic. *Telephone:* (2) 22711482; (2) 22726845. *Fax:* (2) 22711482; (2) 22726845 (Home). *E-mail:* jan@saudek.com (Office). *Website:* www.saudek.com (Office).

SAUDI ARABIA, King of (see Fahd ibn Abdul Aziz).

SAUER, Fernand Edmond; French international official, pharmacist and lawyer; b. 14 Dec. 1947, St Avold, Moselle; m. Pamela Sheppard; one s. two d.; ed Univs. of Strasbourg and Paris II; fmr hosp. pharmacist and pharmaceutical insp. French Ministry of Health; joined European Comm. Brussels, Head of Pharmaceuticals 1986; Exec. Dir European Agency for Evaluation of Medicinal Products (EMEA), London 1994–2000; Dir. for Public Health, European Comm. Luxembourg 2001–; Hon. Fellow School of Pharmacy, Univ. of London; Hon. mem. Royal Pharmaceutical Soc.; Chevalier Légion d'honneur (France), Order of Merit (France). *Address:* DG Sanco G – EUFO 4270, European Commission, rue Alcide de Gasperi, 2920 Luxembourg (Office). *Telephone:* 43-01-32-71-9 (Office). *Fax:* 43-01-34-51-1 (Office). *E-mail:* Fernand.Sauer@cec.eu.int (Office).

SAUER, Louis, FAIA; American architect and urban planner; b. 15 June 1928, Forest Park, Ill.; s. of Frank J. Sauer and Jeanne LaFazia; m. 1st Elizabeth Mason 1956; two c.; m. 2nd Perla Serfaty 1990; ed Univ. of Pennsylvania, Int. School of City Planning, Venice, Italy, Illinois Inst. of Tech.; Prin. Louis Sauer Assoc. Architects, Phila, Pa 1961–79; Prof. of Architecture, Univ. of Pa 1974–79, Carnegie-Mellon Univ., Pittsburgh, Pa 1979–85, Univ. of Colo 1985–89; Commr, Ville de Montreal Jacques Viger Comm. 1991–; Partner Archiris Inc., Pittsburgh 1981–84; Prin. Louis Sauer Architect, Boulder, Colo 1985–89; Dir of Urban Design, Daniel Arbour and Assocs, Montreal, Canada 1989–; fmr Consultant to USAID to advise govts of Lebanon, Egypt and Portugal on low-income housing devt; Nat. Endowment for the Arts Design Fellowships 1978; over 50 design and public service awards. *Work includes:* Water Plaza and high-rise housing, Cincinnati, renewal plan for Fells Point waterfront, public open-space landscape, pvt. housing and housing for the elderly, Baltimore, new town Devt for Golf Course Island, Reston, Va, Oaklands Mills Village Center, Columbia, Md, housing at Society Hill, Phila; work in Canada includes master-plans for Verdun Nuns Island 1991, Bois-Franc St-Laurent New Town 1992, Ville de Laval 1993, Angus C. P. Rail Rosemont Community 1993, Gatineu City Town Centre 1993, Ile Bizard Town Centre 1993. *Leisure interests:* gardening, fishing. *Address:* 3472 Marlowe Street, Montreal, Québec, H4A 3L7, Canada. *Telephone:* (514) 485-4616. *Fax:* (514) 939-1814.

SAUERLÄNDER, Willibald, DPhil; German art historian; b. 29 Feb. 1924, Waldsee; s. of Wilhelm Sauerländer and Anita Sauerländer-Busch; m. Brigitte Rückoldt 1957; one s.; ed Univ. of Munich; Visiting mem. Inst. for Advanced Study, Princeton 1961–62, 1973; Prof. of History of Art, Univ. of Freiburg Br. 1962–70; Dir Zentralinst. für Kunstgeschichte, Munich 1970–89; Visiting Prof. Inst. of Fine Arts, New York Univ. 1964–65, Collège de France, Paris 1981, Madison/Wis. Univ. 1982, Harvard 1984–85, Berkeley 1989; Mellon Lectures, Washington 1991, New York Univ. 1992; mem. Bayerische Akad. der Wissenschaften, Medieval Acad. of America, British Acad., Soc. Nat. des Antiquaires de France, Royal Soc. of Antiquaries, London, Kon. Acad. Voor Wetenschappen, Letteren en Schone Kunsten van Belgie, Acad. Europaea, Acad. des Inscriptions et Belles-Lettres, American Acad. of Art and Sciences; Dr hc (Pertezionto Suola Normale, Pisa, Italy). *Publications:* Die Kathedrale von Chartres 1954, Jean-Antoine Houdon: Voltaire 1963, Gotische Skulptur in Frankreich 1140-1270 1970, Das Königsportal in Chartres 1984, Das Jahrhundert der grossen Kathedralen 1990, Initiàlen 1996, Gegenwart der Kritik 1999, Cathedrals and their Sculptures 2000. *Leisure interests:* reading, travelling. *Address:* c/o Zentralinstitut für Kunstgeschichte, Meiserstrasse 10, 80333 Munich; Victoriastrasse II, 80803 Munich, Germany (Home). *Telephone:* (89) 5591546; (89) 390988 (Home).

SAUL, Hon. David John, JP, PhD; Bermudan politician (retd) and business consultant; b. 27 Nov. 1939, Bermuda; s. of John A. Saul and Sarah Elizabeth Saul; m. Christine Hall 1963; one s. one d.; ed Mt St Agnes Acad., Saltus Grammar School, Loughborough Coll. UK, Queen's and Toronto Univs, Canada; teacher 1962–67; consultant to Ont. Educ. Communications Authority 1970–72, to Bermuda Dept of Educ. 1972–73, Visiting Prof. Univ. of Toronto 1972; Perm. Sec. Ministry of Educ. 1972–76; Financial Sec. Ministry of Finance 1976–81; Chief Admin. Officer, Gibbons Co. 1981–84; Pres. Fidelity Int. Bermuda Ltd 1984–95, Bermuda Audubon Soc. 1998, Bermuda Debating Soc. 1998; Chair. Bermuda Council on Int. Affairs 1983–85; Dir Bermuda Monetary Authority 1986–88, 1997–99, London Bermuda Reins Co. Ltd, Bermuda Track and Field Asscn 1987–99, Fidelity Investments 1984–, Lombard Odier (Bermuda) Ltd 1989–, Odyssey Marine Exploration, Inc. 2001–; Trustee Bermuda Underwater Exploration Inst. 1992–99 (Life Trustee 1999); mem. House of Ass. 1989–97; Minister of Finance 1989–95; Prime Minister of Bermuda 1995–97; mem. Bermuda Defence Bd 1997–2001; Fellow, Explorers' Club. *Leisure interests:* scuba diving, fly-fishing, canoeing, oil painting, ocean cruising, exploration. *Address:* Rocky Ledge, 18 Devonshire Bay Road, DV 07, Bermuda. *Telephone:* 236-7338. *Fax:* 236-5087. *E-mail:* davidjsaul@aol.com (Home).

SAUL, Ralph Southey, BA, LLB; American stock exchange official, lawyer and insurance executive; b. 21 May 1922, Brooklyn, NY; s. of Walter Emerson and Helen Douglas; m. Bette Jane Bertschinger 1956; one s. one d.; ed Univ. of Chicago and Yale Law School; war service, USNR 1943–46; attached to American Embassy, Prague 1947–48; admitted to DC Bar 1951, to New York Bar 1952; Assoc., firm of Lyeth and Voorhees, New York City 1951–52; Asst Counsel to Gov. of New York State 1952–54; Staff Attorney, Radio Corpn of America 1954–58; with Securities and Exchange Comm. 1958–65, Dir Div. of Trading and Markets 1963–65; Vice-Pres. for Corporate Devt, Investors Diversified Services, Inc. 1965–66; Pres. American Stock Exchange 1966–71; Vice-Chair. First Boston Corpn 1971–74; Chair., CEO INA Corpn, Phila, 1975–81; Chair. CIGNA Corpn (fmrly Connecticut Gen. and INA Corpn) 1982–84, Peers and Co. 1985; mem. Bd of Dirs Sun Co. 1976, Certain Teed Corpn 1983, Drexel Burnham 1989–; mem. ABA, NY Stock Exchange (regulatory advisory cttee). *Leisure interest:* golf. *Address:* c/o Cigna Corporation, 1 Logan Square, P.O. Box 7716, 18th and Cherry Streets, Philadelphia, PA 19192, USA.

SAUMAREZ SMITH, Charles Robert, PhD, FSA; British museum administrator; b. 28 May 1954; s. of the late William Hanbury Saumarez Smith and of Alice Elizabeth Harness Saumarez Smith (née Raven); m. Romilly Le Quesne Savage 1979; two s.; ed King's Coll. Cambridge, Harvard Univ., USA; Christie's Resident Fellow in Applied Arts, Christ's Coll. Cambridge 1979–82; apptd. Asst Keeper Victoria & Albert (V&A) Museum 1982, with special responsibility for V&A/RCA MA course in History of Design, Head of Research 1990–94; Dir Nat. Portrait Gallery 1994–2002, Nat. Gallery 2002–; Slade Prof., Univ. of Oxford 2002; Chair. English Art Museum Dir's Conf.; mem. Advisory Council, Warburg Inst. 1997–, Inst. of Historical Research 1999–, Expert Panel for Museums, Libraries and Archives of the Heritage Lottery Fund; Hon. Fellow RCA 1991; Hon. FRIBA 2000; Hon. DLitt (Univ. of E Anglia) 2001. *Publications:* The Building of Castle Howard (Alice Davis Hitchcock Medallion) 1990, Eighteenth Century Decoration 1993, The

National Portrait Gallery 1997. *Address:* National Gallery, Trafalgar Square, London, WC2N 5DN, England (Office). *Telephone:* (20) 7747-2885 (Office). *Fax:* (20) 7747-2423 (Office). *Website:* www.nationalgallery.org.uk (Office).

SAUNDERS, Ernest Walter, MA, FInstM; British business executive; b. 21 Oct. 1935, Vienna, Austria; m. Carole A. Stephings 1963; two s. one d.; ed St Paul's School, London and Emmanuel Coll., Cambridge; Man. Dir Beecham Products Int., Dir Beecham Products 1966–73; Chair. European Div. Great Universal Stores 1973–77; Pres. Nestlé Nutrition SA and mem. Man. Cttee, Nestlé SA, Vevey, Switzerland 1977–81; Chief Exec. and Deputy Chair. Guinness PLC 1981–86, Chief Exec. and Chair. 1986–87; Chair. Arthur Guinness Son & Co. (GB) Ltd, 1982–87, Guinness Brewing Worldwide 1982–87, Guinness-Harp Corpn 1983–86, Martin Retail Group 1984–86, Distillers Co. Ltd 1986–87; charged with fraud in connection with illegal share dealings Oct. 1987, sentenced to five years' imprisonment on charges of conspiracy and theft Aug. 1990; sentence halved by Appeal Court May 1991; released from prison June 1991; European Court of Human Rights ruled trial was unfair Dec. 1996; now marketing consultant, lecturer; Pres. Stambridge Assocs. (now Stambridge Man.) 1992–; Dir Queens Park Rangers Football & Athletic Club 1983, Brewers' Soc. 1983; fmr Chair, CEO Arthur Bell & Sons PLC. *Leisure interests:* skiing, tennis, football.

SAUNDERS, Jennifer; British actress and writer; b. 6 July 1958; m. Adrian Edmonson; three d.; ed Cen. School of Speech and Drama, London; Hon. Rose, Montreux 2002. *Theatre:* An Evening with French and Saunders (nat. tour) 1989, Me and Mamie O'Rourke 1993, French and Saunders Live in 2000 (nat. tour) 2000. *Television series:* The Comic Strip Presents... 1990, Girls on Top, French and Saunders (5 series), Absolutely Fabulous 1994, 1995, 2001 (Emmy Award 1993), Ab Fab The Last Shout 1996, Let Them Eat Cake 1999, Mirrorball 2000. *Films include:* The Supergrass 1984, Muppet Treasure Island 1996, Maybe Baby 2000, Spice World the Movie. *Publications:* A Feast of French and Saunders (with Dawn French) 1992, Absolutely Fabulous: The Scripts 1993, Absolutely Fabulous 'Continuity' 2001. *Address:* c/o Peters, Fraser & Dunlop, Drury House, 34–43 Russell Street, London, WC2B 5HA, England.

SAUNDERS, Stuart John, MD, FRCP, FCPSA; South African physician; b. 28 Aug. 1931, Cape Town; s. of the late Albert Frederick Saunders and of Lilian Emily; m. 1st Noreen Merle Harrison 1956 (died 1983); one s. one d.; m. 2nd Anita Louw 1984; ed Christian Brothers Coll. and Univ. of Cape Town; Registrar in Pathology and Medicine, Groote Schuur Hosp. and Univ. of Cape Town 1955–58; Research Asst Royal Postgraduate Medical School, London 1959–60; Lecturer and Sr Lecturer, Groote Schuur Hosp. and Univ. of Cape Town 1961–70; Fellow in Medicine Harvard Medical School and Mass. Gen. Hosp. 1963–64; Prof. and Head of Medicine Dept Groote Schuur Hosp. and Univ. of Cape Town 1971–80; Deputy Principal for Planning, Univ. of Cape Town 1978–80, Vice-Chancellor and Prin. Univ. of Cape Town 1981–96; Past Pres. SA Inst. of Race Relations; Sr Adviser Andrew G. Mellon Foundation; Life Fellow (Univ. of Cape Town); Hon. mem. Faculty of Community Medicine; Hon. LLD (Aberdeen), (Sheffield), (Princeton); Hon. DSc (Toronto), (Cape Town). *Publications:* Access to and Quality in Higher Education: A Comparative Study 1992, Vice-Chancellor on a Tightrope 1999; numerous scientific publications particularly in the field of liver diseases. *Leisure interests:* reading, fishing. *Address:* 45 Belvedere Avenue, Oranjezicht, 8001 Cape Town, South Africa. *Telephone:* 453035. *Fax:* 4620047. *E-mail:* stuarts@ iafrica.com (Home).

SAUNIER-SEÏTE, Alice Louise, DèsSc; French politician and educator; b. 26 April 1925, Saint-Jean-le-Centenier; d. of Daniel-René and Marie-Louise (Lascombe) Saunier; m. 1st Elie-Jacques Picard 1947; two s.; m. 2nd Jérôme Seïté (deceased); ed Lycée de Tournon, Facultés des Lettres et des Sciences de Paris, Ecole nat. des langues orientales vivantes; Attachée, then Chargée de recherche, CNRS 1958–63; Lecturer in Geography, Faculté des Lettres, Rennes 1963–65, Prof. 1965–69; mem. Nat. Cttee for Scientific Research 1963–70; mem. Perm. Section CNRS 1967–70; Dir Collège littéraire universitaire, Brest 1966–68, Dean of Faculté des Lettres et Sciences Sociales 1968–69; Dir Inst. universitaire de technologie, Sceaux 1970–73; Prof. Univ. of Paris XI 1969–73, Vice-Pres. 1970–71; Rector, Acad. of Reims 1973–76; Sec. of State for Univs 1976–77, Minister of Univs 1978–81, of the Family and Women's Affairs 1981; Prof. of Geographic Org. of Space, Hon. Chair. Dept of Econs and Man., Conservatoire Nat. des Arts et Metiers 1981–94; Municipal Councillor, Manso 1971–83, Deputy Mayor 1977–83; mem. political bureau, Parti Républicain 1978–; Councillor, Paris 1983–; Vice-Pres. Nat. Movt of Local Reps. 1983–, Pres. 1990–98, Hon. Pres. 1998–; Founder-Pres. Fondation de la Mutuelle des Élus Loceaux 1991–98; Dir-Treas. Inst. Océanographique (Pres. 1996–98); Dir then Vice-Pres. Inst. de barrages-réservoirs du Bassin de la Seine 1983–2001; Dir Vieux Paris Comm.; mem. Jury, Prix Mémorial; Conseiller de Paris; Pres. Club des Explorateurs français; mem. Institut de France (Ancien Ministre) 1995–, Acad. des Sciences Morales et Politiques 1995; Assoc. mem. Institut d'Egypte, Acad. of Sciences, Iceland; Commdr Légion d'honneur; Grand Officier de l'Ordre nat. du Mérite; Commdr des Palmes académiques; Commdr Ordre des Arts et Lettres; decorations from Burkina Faso, Cameroon, Côte d'Ivoire, Egypt, Gabon, Greece, Indonesia, Iceland, Luxembourg, Portugal and Sweden; Médaille d'or de la jeunesse et des sports; Medal of CNRS; Medal of Société de géographie de Paris. *Publications:* Les vallées septentrionales de l'Oetztal 1963, Südföhn d'Innsbruck (contrib.) 1965, En première ligne 1982, Remettre l'état à sa place 1984, Une Europe à la carte 1985, Le cardinal de Tournon, le

Richelieu de François 1er (1997), Les Courtenay, destin d'une illustre famille bourguignonne 1998, Le Conte Boissy d'Anglas, conventionnel et pair de France (biog.) 2001. *Leisure interest:* fencing. *Address:* Institut de France, 23 quai de Conti, 75006, Paris (Office); 5 rue Visconti, 75006 Paris, France (Home). *Telephone:* 1-44-41-43-26. *Fax:* 1-44-41-43-27.

SAUR, Klaus Gerhard, DHumLitt; German publisher; b. 27 July 1941, Pullach; s. of Karl-Otto Saur and Veronika Saur; m. Lilo Stangel 1977; one s. one d.; ed High School, Icking and Commercial High School, Munich; Marketing Man. Vulkan-Verlag, Essen 1962; Publishing Man. KG Saur, Munich 1963, Publishing Dir 1966; Pres. KG Saur New York and KG Saur, London 1977; Man. Dir KG Saur Munich 1988–; Founder World Guide to Libraries, Publrs Int. Directory; mem. Bd F.A. Brockhaus Bibliographical Inst. (Mannheim); Chair. Bd Beltz Publishing and Printing Corpn; Vice-Pres. Goethe-Institut, Germany; Hon. Prof. Univ. of Glasgow, Humboldt-Univ. Berlin; Hon. Fellow, Tech. Univ. of Graz; Hon. mem. Austrian Library Asscn 1998, German Library Asscn; Senator hc (Ludwig Maximilians Univ., Munich) 1992, (Leipzig) 2001; Bundesverdienstkreuz der Bundesrepublik Deutschland, Officier Ordre des Arts et Lettres (France), Sächsischer Verdienstordern 2002, Bayerischer Verdienstordern 2002; Hon. DPhil (Marburg) 1985, (Ishevsk, Russia) 1997, (Pisa, Italy) 1998, (Simmons Coll., Mass.) 1992; Hon. Medal City of Munich 1988, Hon. Bene Merenti Medal, Bavarian Acad. of Sciences 1997, Helmut-Sontag Award, Asscn of German Libraries 1999. *Publications:* World Biographical Information System, Pressehandbuch für Exportwerbung, World Guide to Libraries. *Leisure interests:* special German exile literature 1933–45, int. politics, history of publishing and book trade. *Address:* KG Saur Verlag, Ortlerstrasse 8, 81373 Munich (Office); Beuerbergerstrasse 9, 81479 Munich, Germany (Home). *Telephone:* (89) 76902460 (Office); (89) 74979585 (Home). *Fax:* (89) 76902450 (Office); (89) 74994652 (Home). *E-mail:* k.saur@saur.de (Office). *Website:* www.saur.de (Office).

SAURA, Carlos; Spanish film director; b. 4 Jan. 1932, Huesca; m.; two c.; ed film school in Madrid; professional photographer 1949–; teacher Instituto de Investigaciones y Experiencias Cinematograficos, Madrid 1957–64, dismissed for political reasons. *Films include:* La Prima Angelica, La Caza (Silver Bear, Berlin Film Festival), Blood Wedding, Carmen (flamenco version), El Amor Brujo, El Dorado 1987, The Dark Night 1989, Dispara! 1993, Ay Carmela!, Sevillanas, Outrage, Flamenco, Taxi, Tango, Pajarico, Esa Luz!

SAUTTER, Christian; French economist and politician; b. 9 April 1940, Autun; s. of Yves Sautter and Huguette Duval; m. 1st Gisèle Jacquet (deceased); two d.; m. 2nd Catherine Cadou 1996; ed Ecole Polytechnique, Ecole nat. de la Statistique et de l'Administration Economique, Institut d'Etudes Politiques, Paris; economist, Inst. Nat. de la Statistique et des Etudes Economiques (INSEE) 1965–71; researcher, Japanese Planning Agency's Econ. Research Inst., Tokyo 1971–72; Head, Business Research Div., INSEE 1973–76, planning research Dept 1976–78; Dir Centre d'études prospectives et d'informations internationales (CEPII) 1979–81; Adviser on int. econ. questions to Presidency of Repub. 1981–82, Deputy Sec.-Gen. of Presidency 1982–85, 1988–91; Insp.-Gen. of Finance, Ministry of Finance 1985–88, 1993–; Prefect of Paris and Ile-de-France Region 1991–93; Minister of State attached to Minister for the Economy, Finance and Industry, with responsibility for the budget 1997–99, Minister of Finance 1999–2000; Adjunct Mayor of Paris, responsible for Econ. Devt, Finance and Employment 2001–; Pres. France-Active Foundation 2001–; Dir of Studies on Japanese Economy, Ecole des Hautes Etudes en Sciences Sociales 1975–; Chevalier Légion d'honneur, Officier Ordre nat. du Mérite. *Publications:* several publs on Japanese economy. *Address:* Hôtel de ville, 75196 Paris RP (Office); 1 rue de Turbigo, 75001 Paris, France. *E-mail:* chris-cat@imaginet.fr (Home).

SAVAGE, Francis Joseph, CMG, LVO, OBE; British administrator, diplomatist and consultant; b. 8 Feb. 1943, Preston; s. of Francis Fitzgerald Savage and Mona May Savage (née Parsons); m. Veronica Mary McAleenan 1966; two s.; ed St Stephen's Catholic School, Welling, N Kent Coll., Dartford; joined Foreign Office 1961, Embassy, Cairo 1967–70, Washington, DC 1971–73, Vice-Consul, Aden 1973–74, Foreign Office 1974–78, Consul, Düsseldorf 1978–82, Consul, Peking (now Beijing) 1982–86, First Sec., Lagos and Consul, Benin 1987–90; First Sec./Counsellor, Foreign Office 1990–93; Gov. of Montserrat 1993–97, The British Virgin Islands 1998–2002; adviser to FCO 2003–; freelance consultant 2003–; Patron Virgin Islands Search and Rescue (VISAR); mem. Bd Visar Trust 2002–; Kt, Order of St Gregory the Great 2002; Montserrat Badge of Honour 2000. *Leisure interests:* cricket, travel, volcano watching. *Address:* c/o Foreign and Commonwealth Office, King Charles Street, London, SW1A 2AH, England (Office); 19 Cleeve Park Gardens, Sidcup, Kent, DA14 4JL, England (Home). *Telephone:* (20) 8309-5061 (Home). *E-mail:* frank.savage@fco.gov.uk (Office); fjsavage@savagef.fsnet.co.uk (Home).

SAVARY, Jérôme; French theatre director and actor; b. 27 June 1942, Buenos Aires, Argentina; s. of Jacques Savary and Claire Hovelaque; one s. two d.; ed Collège Cévenol, Haute-Loire, les Arts-Déco, Paris; studied music Paris; moved to France 1947; became jazz musician New York 1961; returned to France; f. Compagnie Jérôme Savary 1965, subsequently called Grand Magic Circus, then Grand Magic Circus et ses animaux tristes 1968–; theatre Dir 1969–; Dir Centre Dramatique nat. du Languedoc-Roussillon, Béziers and Montpellier 1982–85; Dir Carrefour Européen, Théâtre-du 8e, Lyon 1985–; Dir Théâtre Nat. de Chaillot, Paris 1988–2000; Dir Opéra Comique,

Paris Oct. 2000–; Dir about 80 plays and shows in Europe, Brazil, Argentina, Canada, USA, Israel; several TV films of plays and operas and three films for cinema; Prix Dominique for Cyrano de Bergerac; Molière Award for best musical and 6 nominations 1997, Victoire de la Musique 1987 for best musical, for Cabaret; Best Dir for Cabaret Spain 1993; Chevalier Ordre des Arts et des Lettres, Chevalier Légion d'honneur; Grand Badge of Hon., Austria. *Publications:* La Vie privée d'un magicien ordinaire 1985, Ma vie commence à 20h30 1991, Magic Circus 1966–96, 30 ans d'aventures et d'amour 1996, Havana Blues 2000. *Address:* Opéra Comique, 5 rue Favart, 75002 Paris, France. *Telephone:* 1-42-44-45-40 (Office). *Fax:* 1-49-26-05-93 (Office). *E-mail:* mtarot@free.fr (Office). *Website:* www.opera-comique.com (Office).

SAVCHENKO, Arkadiy Markovich; Belarus opera singer (baritone); b. 6 April 1936, Vitebsk, Byelorussia; s. of Mark Iosifovich Savchenko and Marfa Stratonovna Savchenko; m. Glasova Serafima Semienovna 1977; two s.; ed Moscow Conservatoire; soloist with Byelorussian (now Belarus) Bolshoi Theatre 1960–; Faculty mem., Prof., Vocal Dept, Belarus Acad. of Music 1987–; People's Artist of USSR 1985. *Roles include:* Yevgeny in Tchaikovsky's Yevgeny Onegin, Kizgaylo in Smolsky's Ancient Legend, Telramund in Wagner's Lohengrin, Malatesta in Donizetti's Don Pasquale, Jermon in Verdi's Traviata, Valentin in Gounod's Faust, Rigoletto in Verdi's Rigoletto, Renato in Verdi's A Masked Ball, Zurga in Bizet's Pearl Fishers, Almaviva in Mozart's The Marriage of Figaro, Tomsky, Eletsky in Tchaikovsky's Queen of Spades, Gryaznoy in Rimsky-Korsakov's The Tsar's Bride, Don Giovanni in Mozart's Don Giovanni, Amonasro in Verdi's Aida, Di Luna in Verdi's Trovatore, Rodrigo in Verdi's Don Carlos, Sharpless in Puccini's Madame Butterfly, Escamillo in Bizet's Carmen, Figaro in Rossini's The Barber of Seville, Prince Igor in Borodin's Prince Igor, Bolkonsky in Prokofiev's Warand Peace, Alfio in Mascagni's Cavalleria Rusticana etc., Iago in Verdi's Otello, Robert in Tchaikovsky's Iolanta, Mizgir in Rimsky-Korsakov's Snowmaiden, Tonyo in Leoncavallo's Pagliacci. *Leisure interests:* gardening, fishing, reading. *Address:* Bolshoi Teatr, 1 Parizhskaya Kommuna Square, 220029 Minsk (Theatre); 8–358 Storozhovskaya Str., 220002 Minsk, Belarus (Home). *Telephone:* (17) 219-22-01 (Theatre); (17) 239-15-51 (Home). *Fax:* (17) 34-05-84.

SAVELYEVA, Lyudmila Mikhailovna; Russian actress; b. 24 Jan. 1942, Leningrad (now St Petersburg); ed Vaganova Ballet School, Leningrad; soloist, Kirorskiy (Mariinskiy) Theatre 1961–65; People's Artist of the RSFSR 1985. *Films include:* War and Peace (Natasha), by Bondarchuk 1966–67, The Sunflowers (de Sica) 1971, Flight 1971, The Headless Horseman 1973, The Seagull 1973, Yulia Vrevskaya 1978, The Hat 1982, The Fourth Year of War 1983, Success 1985, Another's Belaya and Ryaboy 1986, White Rose–Emblem of Grief, Red Rose–Emblem of Love 1989, The Mystery of Nardo 1999, The Tender Age 2001. *Theatre productions include:* The Price (Miller), M. Rozovsky theatre. *Address:* Tverskaya Str. 19, Apt. 76, 103050 Moscow, Russia. *Telephone:* (095) 299-99-34.

SAVI, Toomas, PhD; Estonian politician and physician; b. 30 Dec. 1942, Tartu; m. Kirsi Savi; two d.; ed Univ. of Tartu; Chief Physician USSR light athletics team, concurrently Sr Researcher Tartu State Univ. 1970–80; nat. team physician at Olympic Games in Munich 1972, Montreal 1976, Moscow 1980, Lillehammer 1994; Chief Physician Tartu Medical Centre of Physical Educ. 1973–93; worked as Asst Doctor Kuopio Univ. Hosp. and Kajaani Hosp., Finland 1991–92; mem. Tartu Town Council 1989–96, 1999–2000; Deputy Mayor of Tartu 1993–95; Speaker of Riigikogu (State Ass.) 1995–99, mem. 1999–, Chair. (Speaker) 1999–; Pres. Estonian Ski Asscn 1999–; mem. Estonian Olympic Team 1989–, Tartu Rotary Club 1993–, Estonian Reform Party 1994–, Bd of the Fit and Sound Estonia Movt 1994–, Estonian Soc. 2001–, Supervisory Bd of Tartu St Mary's Church Foundation 2003–; Grand Cross, Royal Norwegian Order of Merit 1998; Nat. Order of Merit (Malta) 2001; Grand Cross, Ordre nat. du Mérite (France) 2001; Commdr Grand Cross, Order of the Lion (Finland) 2002. *Address:* Riigikogu, Lossi plats 1A, 15165 Tallinn, Estonia (Office). *Telephone:* (2) 631-63-01 (Office). *Fax:* (2) 631-63-04 (Office). *E-mail:* toomas.savi@riigikogu.ee. *Website:* www.riigikogu.ee (Office).

SAVILL, Rosalind Joy, CBE, BA, FSA, FRSA; British curator; b. 12 May 1951, Hants.; d. of Dr Guy Savill and Lorna Williams; one d.; ed Wycombe Abbey School, Chatelard School, Montreux and Univ. of Leeds; Museum Asst, Ceramics Dept, Victoria & Albert Museum 1973–74; Museum Asst and Sr Asst, The Wallace Collection 1974–78, Asst to Dir 1978–92, Dir 1992–; mem. Arts Panel, Nat. Trust 1995–; Gov. Camden School for Girls 1996–; Leverhulme Scholar 1975; Getty Scholar 1985; Trustee Somerset House 1997–; mem. Art Advisory Cttee, NMGW 1998–; Trustee, Campaign for Museums 1999–; mem. Royal Mint Advisory Cttee; Pres., French Porcelain Soc. 1999–; Nat. Art Collections Fund Prize 1990. *Publications:* The Wallace Collection Catalogue of Sèvres Porcelain, 3 Vols 1988; articles, reviews, contribs to exhbn catalogues etc. *Leisure interests:* music, the countryside and gardens. *Address:* The Wallace Collection, Hertford House, Manchester Square, London, W1M 6BN, England. *Telephone:* (20) 7563-9500. *Fax:* (20) 7224-2155. *E-mail:* admin@wallace-collection.com (Office). *Website:* www .the-wallace-collection.com (Office).

SAVIN, Anatoliy Ivanovich, DTechSc; Russian specialist in radio analysis and systems analysis; b. 6 April 1920; ed Bauman Tech. Inst., Moscow; mem. CPSU 1944–91; fmrly employed as engineer and constructor; constructor with machine-bldg plant 1944–51; positions of responsibility on eng side of radio-tech. industry 1951–; Gen. Dir Scientific and Production Asscn Kometa 1973–98, Scientific Dir 1999–; Corresp. mem. Acad. of Sciences 1979, mem. 1984–, Prof. 1984; Academician Russian Acad. of Sciences; main research has been on complex radio-tech. automatized informational systems; inventor of cosmic radio-telescope KRT-10; Acad. of Sciences Raspletin Prize 1972, Lenin Prize 1972, Hero of Socialist Labour 1976, State Prizes 1946, 1949, 1951, 1981. *Address:* Kometa Association, Velozavodskaya Str. 5, 109280 Moscow, Russia. *Telephone:* (095) 275-15-33.

SAVOLA, Kai Kari; Finnish freelance theatre director; b. 30 Sept. 1931, Helsinki; s. of Tauno Savola and Hilppa Korpinen; m. Terttu Byckling 1958; two s. one d.; ed Helsinki Univ.; Admin. Dir Helsinki Student Theatre 1959–62; Man. Dir Finnish Drama Agency 1962–65; Literary Man. Helsinki City Theatre 1965–68; Dir-Gen. Tampere Workers' Theatre 1968–73; Dir Finnish Nat. Theatre 1973, Dir-Gen. 1974–92; stage direction of Finnish, English, Russian and Japanese drama; designed the two experimental stages of the Finnish Nat. Theatre (with Prof. Heikki Siren) 1976, 1987; Prof. hc; Commdr Order of White Rose of Finland. *Publications:* translations of English and German plays into Finnish. *Address:* Laivurinkatu 39 A 12, 00150 Helsinki, Finland. *Telephone:* (9) 636939. *Fax:* (9) 636939.

SAVÓN, Felix; Cuban boxer; b. 22 Sept. 1967, San Vicente; heavyweight boxer; six world amateur championships (1986, 1989, 1991, 1993, 1995, 1997); three consecutive Olympic championships (1992, 1996, 2000); announced retirement Jan. 2001, currently coach for Cuban nat. boxing team. *Address:* c/o Cuban Boxing Federation, Havana, Cuba (Office).

SAVOSTYANOV, Maj.-Gen. Yevgeny Vadimovich, CAND.TECH.SC.; Russian politician; b. 28 Feb. 1952, Moscow; m.; two s.; ed Moscow Mining Inst.; Jr researcher Inst. of Physics of the Earth USSR Acad. of Sciences 1975–77; researcher Inst. for Problems of Complex Use of Mineral Wealth USSR Acad. of Sciences 1975–90; Founder and Co-Chair. Club of Voters of Acad. of Sciences for election of Andrey Sakharov and other scientists as people's deputies from Acad. of Sciences; Asst to Chair. Moscow City Soviet, then Dir-Gen. Dept Moscow Mayor's Office 1990–91; mem. Co-ordination Council Movt Democratic Russia; mem. Org. Cttee of Democratic Reforms 1991; Deputy Dir Russian Fed. Service of Counterespionage, Head of Dept Moscow and Moscow Region 1991–94; Adviser to Chair. Russian Fed. of Ind. Trade Unions 1995–96; Deputy Head Admin. of Russian Presidency 1996–98; Vice-Pres. Moscow Petroleum Co. 1999–; Chair. Bd of Dirs Ke Mos Co. 2000–. *Address:* Moscow Petroleum Company, Miza Prosp. 222, 129128, Moscow, Russia (Office).

SAVOY, Guy; French chef and restaurateur; b. 24 July 1953, Nevers; m. Marie Danielle Amann 1975; one s. one d.; for three years Chef at La Barrière de Clichy, Paris; Propr Restaurant Guy Savoy, Paris 1980–, Restaurant Le Bistrot de l'Etoile Troyon 1989–, Restaurant Le Bistrot de l'Etoile-Niel 1989–, Restaurant Le Bistrot l'Etoile-Lauriston 1991, Restaurant La Butte Chaillot 1992, Les Bookinistes 1994, Le Cap Vernet, Paris 1995. *Publications:* Les Légumes gourmands 1985, La Gourmandise apprivoisée 1987, La Cuisine de mes bistrots 1998, 120 recettes comme à la maison 2000. *Leisure interest:* modern painting. *Address:* Restaurant Guy Savoy, 18 rue Troyon, 75017 Paris (Office); 101 boulevard Pereire, 75017 Paris, France (Home). *Telephone:* 43-80-40-61 (Office); (Bistrot de l'Étoile) 42-67-25-95.

SAVVINA, Iya Sergeyevna; Russian actress; b. 2 March 1936, Voronezh; ed Moscow State Univ.; played leading role in adaptation of Chekhov's The Lady with the Lap-dog 1960; acts in cinema and on stage with Mossovet Theatre, Moscow 1960–78, with Moscow Arts Theatre 1978–; USSR State Prize 1983; USSR People's Artist 1990. *Films include:* Lady with a Lapdog 1960, A Gentle Woman 1960, Asya's Happiness 1967 (State Prize 1990), Anna Karenina 1968, A Day in the Life of Dr. Kalinnikova 1974, A Lovers' Romance 1975, An Open Book, 1980, Garage 1980, Private Life 1983, Last, Last the Fascination... 1985, Mother and Son 1990, Lev Trotsky 1993; numerous stage roles in classical and contemporary works. *Address:* Bolshaya Gruzinskaya Str. 12, Apt. 43, 123242 Moscow, Russia. *Telephone:* (095) 254-97-39.

SAWA, Metropolitan Michał Hrycuniak, ThD; Polish ecclesiastic; b. 15 April 1938, Śniatycze; ed Christian Acad. of Theology, Warsaw, Univ. of Belgrade; teacher Orthodox Seminary, Warsaw 1962–, Rector Int. Section 1964–65; Rector Orthodox Theological Seminary, Jabłeczna 1970–79; Assoc. Prof. and Prof. Christian Acad. of Theology, Warsaw 1966–, Prof. of Theological Sciences 1990–; ordained deacon 1964; ordained priest 1966; Dir Chancellery of Metropolitan of Warsaw and All Poland 1966–70; Superior Monastery of St Onufrey at Jabłeczna 1970–79; ordained Bishop 1979, Bishop of Łódź and Poznań 1979–81, of Białystok and Gdańsk 1981–99; Archbishop 1987; Metropolitan of Warsaw and All Poland, Primate of the Polish Autocephalous Orthodox Church 1998–; Orthodox Ordinary of the Polish Armed Forces 1994–98, rank of Brig.-Gen. 1996; f. quarterly publs of Diocese of Białystok and Gdańsk and of Orthodox Ordinate of Polish Armed Forces; Dean and Prof. of the Chair of Orthodox Theology at the Univ. in Białystok 1999–; Ed.-in-Chief Kalendarz Polskiego Autokefalicznego Kościoła Prawosławnego, Elpis, Rocznik Teologiczny (annual), Cerkiewny Wiestnik (quarterly), Wiadomości Polskiego Autokefalicznego Kościoła Prawosławnego (monthly); Hon. Prof. of Theological Sciences; Dr hc (Thessaloniki Univ.), Greece. *Publication:* Prawosławne pojmowanie małżeństwa (The Orthodox Understanding of Marriage) 1994. *Address:* al. Solidarności 52, 03-402 Warsaw, Poland (Home). *Telephone:* (22) 6190886 (Home). *Fax:* (22) 6190886 (Home).

SAWALLISCH, Wolfgang; German conductor; b. 26 Aug 1923, Munich; m. Mechthild Schmid; ed Wittelsbacher Gymnasium, Munich; studied under Profs. Ruoff, Haas and Sachsse; mil. service 1942–46, POW in Italy; conductor Augsburg 1947–53; Musical Dir Aachen 1953–58, Wiesbaden 1958–60, Cologne Opera 1960–63; Conductor Hamburg Philharmonic Orchestra 1960–73, Hon. mem. 1973–; Prin. Conductor Vienna Symphony Orchestra 1960–70, Hon. mem. and Hon. Conductor 1980; Prof. Staatliche Hochschule für Musik, Cologne 1960–63; Musical Dir Bayerische Staatsoper Munich 1971–92; Prin. Conductor Bayerisches Staatsorchester –92; Perm. Conductor Teatro alla Scala, Milan; conducted at many Festivals; recordings in Germany, USA and Britain; Hon. Conductor NHK Symphony Orchestra, Tokyo 1967; Artistic Dir Suisse Romande Orchestra, Geneva 1973–80; Dir Bayerische Staatsoper, Munich 1982–92; Music Dir Philadelphia Orchestra 1993–; Dr. hc (Curtis Inst., Philadelphia), (Princeton Univ.); Accademico Onorario Santa Cecilia; Österreichisches Ehrenkreuz für Kunst und Wissenschaft, Bayerische Verdienstorden, Bruckner-Ring of Vienna Symphony Orchestra 1980, Grosses Bundesverdienstkreuz (mit Stern), Bayerische Maximiliansorden für Wissenschaft und Kunst 1984, Orden der aufgehenden Sonne am Halsband, Japan, Robert-Schumann-Preis 1994, Suntory Special Music Prize, Japan, Golden Baton Toscanini Teatro Scala, Milan; Chevalier Légion d'honneur, Commdr des Arts et des Lettres, Cavaliere di Gran Croce (Italy). *Publications:* Im Interesse der Deutlichkeit—Mein Leben mit der Musik 1988, Kontrapunkte 1993. *Address:* Hinterm Bichl 2, 83224 Grassau/Chiemsee, Germany; The Philadelphia Orchestra, 260 S. Broad Street, 16th Floor, Philadelphia, PA 19102, USA (Office). *Telephone:* (215) 893-1900 (Office); (49) 86412315. *Fax:* (215) 893-1948 (Office); (49) 86414501 (Home). *E-mail:* graphil@gmx.de (Home).

SAWCHUK, Arthur R., BSc; Canadian business executive; m. Mary Sawchuk; one s. one d.; ed Univ. of Manitoba; joined DuPont Eng group, Kingston, Ont. 1958; transferred to Montreal, holding managerial positions in Fibres Marketing 1967; Div. Man. Home Furnishings, Toronto 1974; Man. Corp. Planning and Devt 1981; Div. Man. Packaging 1984; Vice-Pres. and Gen. Man. Fibres and Intermediate Chemicals 1985; Sr Vice-Pres. and mem. Corp. Policy Advisory Council 1988; Pres., CEO, Dir DuPont Canada Inc. 1992–97; Chair. 1995–97; Chair. Manulife Financial 1998–; mem. Bd Dirs. Canadian Chemical Producers' Asscn, Avenor Inc., Mfrs Life Insurance Co., Ontario Hydro. *Address:* Manulife Financial, 200 Bloor Street East, Toronto, Ont., M4W 1E5, Canada.

SAWDY, Peter Bryan; British company executive; b. 17 Sept. 1931, London; s. of Alfred Eustace Leon and Beatrice (Lang) Sawdy; m. 1st Anne Stonor 1955 (divorced 1989, died 1995); two d.; m. 2nd Judith Mary Bowen 1989; ed Ampleforth Coll., London School of Econs (external); nat. service, commissioned Queen's Regt, also served Parachute Regt Egypt and Iraq 1951–53; Exec. Trainee, Brooke Bond Group 1953; Buying Exec., Brooke Bond Ceylon Ltd 1956, Chair. 1964; Dir Brooke Bond Group 1965; Dir Brooke Bond Liebig Ltd 1968, Man. Dir 1975–77; Group Chief Exec. Brooke Bond Group 1977–81, Deputy Chair., Group Chief Exec. 1981–85; Deputy Chair. Hogg Group 1992–94 (Dir 1986–); Dir Griffin Int. Ltd 1988–, Yule Catto PLC 1990–, Lazard Birla Indian Investment Fund PLC 1994–; Dir Costain Group 1979–, Chair. 1990–93; Deputy Chair. and Chief Exec. Brooke Bond Group 1981–85. *Leisure interests:* squash, golf, 20th-century literature, opera. *Address:* 20 Smith Terrace, London, SW3 4DH, England.

SAWYER, Amos; Liberian politician; fmrly installed as Leader of Interim Govt of Nat. Unity (by leaders of combined guerrilla forces which overthrew regime of fmr Pres. Samuel Doe 1990) Aug. 1990, inaugurated Nov. 1990; fmr leader Liberian People's Party (LPP).

SAXE-COBURG GOTHA, Simeon; Bulgarian politician and fmr King of Bulgaria; b. 1937; s. of the late King Boris and of Queen Joanna; m. Margarita Gómez y Acebo 1962; five c.; ed in England, Victoria Coll., Alexandria and Valley Forge Mil. Acad. Pa; proclaimed King of Bulgaria 1943; deposed 1946; sought refuge in Egypt in 1947; has since lived mainly in Spain; Constitutional Court ruled in 1998 that confiscation of royal property by Communist regime had been illegal; returned to Bulgaria 1996; f. Nat. Movt for King Simeon II 2001; Prime Minister of Bulgaria July 2001–. *Address:* Council of Ministers, 1000 Sofia, Boulevard Dondukov 1, Bulgaria. *Telephone:* (2) 940-27-70. *Fax:* (2) 980-20-56. *E-mail:* iprd@government.bg (Office). *Website:* www .government.bg (Office).

SAXENA, Girish Chandra, MA; Indian politician and fmr. police officer; b. 5 Jan. 1928, Agra; s. of Rama Kant; m. Rajni Kaul; two d.; joined Indian Police Service 1950, served as Chief of Police in numerous dists. in Uttar Pradesh, Head of Special Br., Intelligence Dept, Uttar Pradesh; served in Research and Analysis Wing, Govt of India, Head 1983–86; Adviser to Prime Minister 1986–88; Gov. of Jammu and Kashmir 1990–93, 1998–; mem. India Int. Centre, Foundation for Nat. Amity and Solidarity; Police Medal for Meritorious Services, Pres.'s Medal for Distinguished Services. *Address:* Raj Bhavan, Srinagar, Jammu and Kashmir (Office); C-4/4028, Vasant Kunj, New Delhi 110070, India (Home). *Telephone:* (194) 452208 (Office); (11) 6125498 (Home).

SAY, Rt Rev Richard David, KCVO, DD, DCL; British ecclesiastic; b. 4 Oct. 1914, London; s. of Commdr Richard Say, OBE, RDVR and Kathleen Mary Wildy; m. Irene Frances Rayner, OBE, JP, 1943; two s. (one deceased) two d.; ed Univ. Coll. School, Christ's Coll., Cambridge and Ridley Hall, Cambridge; Curate Croydon Parish Church 1939–43, St Martin-in-the-Fields 1943–50,

Gen. Sec., Church of England Youth Council 1944–47; Gen. Sec., British Council of Churches 1947–55; Rector of Hatfield and Domestic Chaplain to Marquess of Salisbury, KG 1955–61; Hon. Canon of St Albans 1957–61; Bishop of Rochester 1961–88; Asst Bishop of Canterbury 1988–; Church of England del. to World Council of Churches 1948, 1954 and 1961; Sub-Prelate of the Order of St John of Jerusalem; Chaplain to the Pilgrims of GB 1968–2002, Vice-Pres. 2001–; mem. House of Lords 1969–88; High Almoner to HM the Queen 1970–88; Deputy Pro-Chancellor, Univ. of Kent 1977–83, Pro-Chancellor 1983–93; Court of Ecclesiastical Causes Reserved 1984–92; Chair. Age Concern England 1986–89, Patron 1992–; Vice-Pres. UNA, GB and NI 1986–; Pres. Friends of Kent Churches 1988–; Hon. mem. Inst. of Royal Engineers 1986; Hon. Freeman Borough of Tonbridge and Malling 1987, Borough of Rochester Upon Medway 1988; Hon. DCL (Kent) 1987. *Publication:* Kent Pilgrim 1961–2001 in Rochester and Canterbury Dioceses 2001, The Royal Maundy – Past and Present 2002. *Leisure interests:* history, travel. *Address:* 23 Chequers Park, Wye, Ashford, Kent, TN25 5BB, England. *Telephone:* (1233) 812720.

SAYAVONG, Khammy; Laotian government official; b. 9 April 1944, Khai Village; m. Boun Ngiem; ed Inst. of Party Moscow, Russia; Head of Propaganda and Training Div., Vientiane Prov. 1992–95; Vice-Chair. Propaganda and Training Cen. Cttee 1996–98; Vice-Chair Cen. Control Cttee 1999–2000; Pres. People's Supreme Court 2001–. *Address:* Office of the President, People's Supreme Court, c/o Ministry of Justice, Ban Phonxay, Vientiane (Office); Sisavat Village, Chanthabouly District, Vientiane Municipality, Laos (Home). *Telephone:* (21) 412170 (Office); (21) 212355 (Home). *Fax:* (21) 451371 (Office). *E-mail:* lao99006@laotel.com (Office).

SAYED, Mostafa Amr El-, PhD, FAAS; American professor of chemistry; b. 8 May 1933, Zifta, Egypt; s. of Amr El-Sayed and Zakia Ahmed; m. Janice Jones 1957; three s. two d.; ed Ein Shams Univ., Cairo, Egypt, Florida State, Yale and Harvard Univs, Calif. Inst. of Tech.; Prof. Univ. of Calif., LA 1961–64; Ed.-in-Chief Journal of Physical Chem. 1980–; Julius Brown Prof. and Dir Laser Dynamics Lab., Ga Inst. of Tech. 1994–, Regents Prof. 2000–; Visiting Prof. American Univ. of Beirut 1968, Univ. of Paris 1976, 1991; Mem.-at-Large US Nat. Research Council Cttee for IUPAC 1987–91 (Chair. 1990–92); mem. Bd of Trustees Assoc. Univs Inc. 1988–91, Advisory Cttee NSF Chem. Div. 1990–93, American Acad. of Sciences 1980, Third World Acad. of Arts and Sciences 1984, NSF 2000; Alexander von Humboldt Sr Fellow Tech. Univ. of Munich 1982; Fellow American Acad. of Arts and Sciences 1986, American Physical Soc. 2000; Dr hc (Hebrew Univ.) 1993; Fresenius Nat. Award in Pure and Applied Chem. 1967, Alexander von Humboldt Sr US Scientist Award, 1982, King Faisal Int. Prize in Sciences (Chem.) 1990, Harris Award, Univ. of Nebraska 1995, and many other honours and awards. *Publications:* many articles in scientific journals. *Address:* Department of Chemistry and Biochemistry, Georgia Institute of Technology, Atlanta, GA 30332 (Office); 579 Westover Drive, Atlanta, GA 30305, USA (Home). *Telephone:* (404) 894-0292 (Office); (404) 352-0453 (Home). *Fax:* (404) 894-0294 (Office). *E-mail:* mostafa.el-sayed@chemistry .gatech.edu (Office). *Website:* www.chemistry.gatech.edu/faculty/elsayed/ el-sayed.html (Office).

SAYEED, Mufti Mohammed; Indian politician; b. 1936; joined Nat. Conf. party 1950, left to join Congress Party, then left to join Janata Dal, rejoined Congress Party, finally left to found his own People's Democratic Party 1999; fmr Minister of Home Affairs (India's first Muslim Home Minister); daughter kidnapped by Kashmiri militants 1989, released in exchange for militants; Chief Minister of Jammu and Kashmir Nov. 2002–. *Address:* Chief Minister's Secretariat, Jammu, Jammu and KashmirIndia (Office).

SAYEGH, Bishop Selim Wahban, PhD; Jordanian ecclesiastic; b. 1935, Jordan; s. of Wahban Sayigh; ed Lateran Univ., Rome; Pres. of the Latin Patriarchal Court, Jerusalem 1967–79; Rector of the Latin Patriarchal Seminary 1976–81; Titular Bishop of Aquae in Proconsulari, Vicar Gen. for Transjordan 1982–; Commdr of the Equestrian Order of the Holy Sepulchre of Jerusalem. *Publications:* Le Statu Quo des Lieux-Saints 1971, The Christian Family's Guidebook. *Leisure interests:* chess, table tennis, volley-ball, history, ecclesiastical law. *Address:* Latin Vicariate, P.O. Box 851379, Amman 11185, Jordan. *Telephone:* (6) 5929546. *Fax:* (6) 5920548. *E-mail:* proffice@joinnet.com.jo (Office).

SAYLES, John Thomas, BS; American writer, film director, actor and scriptwriter; b. 28 Sept. 1950, Schenectady; s. of Donald John Sayles and Mary (née Rausch) Sayles; ed Williams Coll. *Screenwriter for:* Piranha 1978, The Lady in Red 1979, Battle Beyond the Stars 1980, The Howling 1981, Alligator 1981, The Challenge 1982, The Perfect Match 1980. *Films include:* Baby It's You 1983, Return of the Secaucus Seven 1980 (LA Film Critics Award), Lianna 1983, The Brother from Another Planet 1984, Matewan (also screenwriter and actor) 1987, Eight Men Out 1989, City of Hope 1991, Malcolm X, Passion Fish (dir, screenwriter and actor), Matinee, My Life's in Turnaround 1994, The Secret of Roan Inish (dir, screenwriter) 1994, Lone Star (dir, screenwriter) 1996, Men With Guns (dir, screenwriter) 1998, Mimic, Limbo (dir, screenwriter and ed.) 1999. *Publications:* Pride of the Bimbos 1975, Union Dues 1979, Thinking in Pictures 1987, I-80 Nebraska, M.490-M.205 (O. Henry Award) 1975, Breed, Golden State (O. Henry Award) 1977, Hoop, The Anarchists' Convention 1979, New Hope for the Dead (play) 1981, Turnbuckle (play), Los Gusanos 1991. *Address:* c/o Stuart Robinson, Paradigm, 10100 Santa Monica Boulevard, Los Angeles, CA 90067, USA.

SCACCHI, Greta; actress; b. 18 Feb. 1960, Milan, Italy; one d. by Vincent D'Onofrio; one s. by Carlo Mantegazza; ed Bristol Old Vic Drama School. *Films:* Das Zweite Gesicht, Heat and Dust, Defence of the Realm, The Coca-Cola Kid, A Man in Love, Good Morning Babylon, White Mischief, Paura e Amore (Three Sisters), La Donna dell Luna, Presumed Innocent, Shattered, Fires Within, Turtle Beach, The Player, Salt on Our Skin, The Browning Version, Jefferson in Paris 1994, Country Life 1995, Emma 1996, The Serpent's Kiss 1997, The Red Violin 1998, Ladies Room 1999, The Manor 1999, Tom's Midnight Garden 2000, Looking for Alibrandi 2000, One of the Hollywood Ten 2000, Cotton Mary 2000, Festival in Cannes 2002, Baltic Storm 2003. *Television:* The Ebony Tower, Dr. Fischer of Geneva, Waterfront (Australia), Rasputin (Emmy Award 1996), The Odyssey (series) 1996, Macbeth 1998, The Farm (Australia) 2000, Daniel Deronda, Jeffrey Archer – The Truth 2002. *Theatre:* Cider with Rosie, In Times Like These, Airbase, Uncle Vanya 1988, A Doll's House, Miss Julie, Simpatico, Midsummer Night's Dream, Easy Virtue, The Guardsman 2000, Old Times 2000, The True-Life Fiction of Mata Hari 2002. *Address:* c/o Conway van Gelder, 3rd Floor, 18–12 Jermyn Street, London, SW1Y 6HP, England (Office).

SCAIFE, Brendan (Kevin Patrick), PhD, DScEng, MRIA, CEng, FIEI, FIEE, CPhys, FInstP; Irish electrical engineer; b. 19 May 1928, London; s. of James Scaife and Mary Kavanagh; m. Mary Manahan 1961; three s. one d.; ed Cardinal Vaughan Memorial School, London, Chelsea Polytechnic and Queen Mary Coll. London; GEC Research Labs, Wembley 1953–54; Scholar, School of Theoretical Physics, Dublin Inst. for Advanced Studies 1954–55; Inst. for Industrial Research and Standards, Dublin 1955–56; Electricity Supply Bd Dublin 1956; Coll. of Tech., Dublin 1956–61; Lecturer in Electronic Eng, Trinity Coll. Dublin 1961–66, Fellow 1964, Reader 1966, Assoc. Prof. 1967–72, Prof. of Eng Science 1972–86, Prof. of Electromagnetics 1986–88, Sr Fellow 1987–88, Fellow Emer. 1988–; Visiting Prof. Univ. of Salford 1969–82; Boyle Medal (Royal Dublin Soc.) 1992. *Publications:* Complex Permittivity (compiler) 1971, Studies in Numerical Analysis (ed.) 1974, Principles of Dielectrics (revised edn) 1998, The Mathematical Papers of Sir William Rowan Hamilton Vol. IV (ed.) 2000. *Address:* Department of Electronic and Electrical Engineering, Trinity College, Dublin 2 (Office); 6 Trimleston Avenue, Booterstown, Blackrock, Co. Dublin, Ireland (Home). *Telephone:* (1) 6081580 (Office); (1) 2693867 (Home). *Fax:* (1) 6772442 (Office). *E-mail:* bscaife@eircom.net (Home).

SCAJOLA, Claudio; Italian politician; b. 15 Jan. 1948, Imperia, Liguria; m.; two c.; mem. staff Inpdap; Chair. Unità Sanitaria Locale (USL) of Imperia 1980–83; Mayor of Imperia 1990–95; mem. Forza Italia party; mem. Chamber of Deputies 1996–; Minister of the Interior 2001–02; Chair. ANCI Liguria, Rivera Trasporti. *Address:* c/o Ministry of the Interior, Piazzale del Virinale, 00184 Rome, Italy (Office).

SCALES, John Tracey, OBE, FRCS, LRCP, CIMechE; British professor and medical practitioner; b. 2 July 1920, Colchester; s. of W. L. Scales and E. M. (née Tracey) Scales; m. Cecilia May Sparrow 1945 (deceased 1992); two d.; ed Haberdashers' Aske's School, London, King's Coll., London, Univs. of Glasgow and Birmingham, Charing Cross Hosp. Medical School; Capt. RAMC 1945–47; House Surgeon Royal Nat. Orthopaedic Hosp., Stanmore 1947–49, M.O. Plastics Research Unit 1949–50, Hon. Registrar/Sr Registrar 1950–57, Sr Lecturer Plastics Research Unit 1951–56, Reader in Biomedical Eng, Inst. of Orthopaedics 1968–74, Prof. 1974–87, Prof. Emer. 1987–; Medico-Legal Consultant 1995–; Visiting Prof. Biomedical Centre, Cranfield Univ. 1997–98; Hon. Consultant Royal Nat. Orthopaedic Hosp., Stanmore, Royal Orthopaedic Hosp., Birmingham 1968–97, Mount Vernon Hosp., Middx; Dir of Pressure Sore Prevention, RAFT Inst. of Plastic Surgery, Mount Vernon Hosp. 1988–97; Sr Companion Fellow British Orthopaedic Asscn 1993; Hon. mem. British Asscn Plastic Surgeons 1993; Hon. Adviser British Asscn of Plastic Surgeons 1993; Freeman City of London 1995; Hon. Fellow Biological Eng Soc. 1962; Commissioned Ky Col for contribs. to surgery, USA 1994; Thomas Henry Green Prize in Surgery, Robert Danis Prize, Brussels 1969, James Berrie Prize, Royal Coll. of Surgeons 1973, Donald Julies Groen Prize, Inst. of Mechanical Engineers 1988; S. G. Brown Award, Royal Coll. of Medicine 1974, Award for Applied Research in Biomaterials, Clemson Univ. (USA) 1974, A. A. Griffith Medal, Materials Science Club 1980, Jackson Burrows Medal, Royal Nat. Orthopaedic Hosp. and Inst. of Orthopaedics 1985. *Publications:* 176 articles and scientific papers. *Leisure interests:* cats, dogs, Goss china. *Address:* Fairbanks, Riverview Road, Pangbourne, Berks., RG8 7AU, England (Home). *Telephone:* (118) 984-3568 (Home). *Fax:* (118) 984-4945 (Home).

SCALES, Prunella Margaret Rumney, CBE; British actress; b. Sutton Abinger; d. of John Richardson Illingworth and Catherine Scales; m. Timothy West (q.v.) 1963; two s.; ed Moira House, Eastbourne, Old Vic Theatre School, London, Herbert Berghof Studio, New York; in repertory, Huddersfield, Salisbury, Oxford, Bristol Old Vic etc.; seasons at Stratford and Chichester 1967–68; numerous radio broadcasts, readings, poetry recitals, fringe productions; has directed plays at numerous theatres including Bristol Old Vic, Arts Theatre, Cambridge, Nottingham Playhouse, W Yorkshire Playhouse (Getting On); Pres. Council for the Protection of Rural England 1997–2002; Freeman of City of London 1990; Hon. DLitt (Bradford) 1995, (East Anglia) 1996. *Plays include:* The Promise 1967, Hay Fever 1968, The Wolf 1975, Make and Break 1980, An Evening with Queen Victoria 1980, The Merchant of Venice 1981, Quartermaine's Terms 1981, When We Are Married 1986, Single Spies (double bill) 1988, School for Scandal, Long Day's Journey into Night

(Nat. Theatre), Happy Days 1993, Staying On 1996, Some Singing Blood (Royal Court), The Mother Tongue, The Editing Process 1994, The Birthday Party 1999, The Cherry Orchard 2000, The External 2001, Too Far to Walk (King's Head) 2002. *Television includes:* Fawlty Towers (series) 1975, 1978, Mapp and Lucia (series) 1985–86, Absurd Person Singular 1985, What the Butler Saw 1987, After Henry (series) 1988–92, A Question of Attribution 1991, Signs and Wonders 1995, Breaking the Code 1995, Lord of Misrule 1995, Dalziel & Pascoe 1996, Breaking the Code 1997, Midsomer Murders 1999, Silent Witness 2000, Queen Victoria 2003. *Films include:* An Awfully Big Adventure 1994, Stiff Upper Lips 1997, The Ghost of Greville Lodge 1999. *Radio includes:* Smelling of Roses 2000, Ladies of Letters 2001. *Leisure interests:* gardening, crosswords, canal boat. *Address:* c/o Jeremy Conway, 18–21 Jermyn Street, London, SW1Y 6HP, England. *Telephone:* (20) 7287-0077 (Office). *Fax:* (20) 7287-1940 (Office).

SCALFARI, Eugenio, DIur; Italian editor; b. 6 April 1924, Civitavecchia; m. Simonetta de Benedetti 1959; two d.; contrib. Il Mondo, L'Europeo 1950–; Promoter Partito Radicale 1958, L'Espresso 1955–, Ed.-in-Chief 1963–68, Man. Dir 1970–75; Promoter La Repubblica 1976–, Ed.-in-Chief 1976–96, Dir 1988–; Deputy to Parl. 1968–72; Siena Award 1985, Journalist of the Year Award 1986. *Publications:* Rapporto sul Neocapitalismo Italiano, Il Potere Economico in URSS, L'Autunno della Repubblica, Razza Padrona, Interviste ai Potenti, L'Anno di Craxi, La Sera Andavamo in Via Veneto, Incontro con Io, La Morale Perduta, La Ruga Sulla Fronte. *Address:* c/o La Repubblica, Piazza dell'Indipendenza 11/B, 00185 Rome, Italy. *Telephone:* (06) 49821.

SCALFARO, Oscar Luigi; Italian politician and lawyer; b. 9 Sept. 1918, Novara; ed Università Cattolica del Sacro Cuore, Milan; elected Christian Democrat (DC) MP for Turin-Novara-Vercelli 1948; Sec. then Vice-Chair. Parl. Group and mem. Nat. Council of DC, mem. of DC Cen. Office during De Gasperi's leadership, Under-Sec. of State at Ministry of Labour and Social Security in Fanfani Govt, Under-Sec. in Ministry of Justice, Under-Sec. in Ministry of Interior 1959–62; Minister of Transport and Civil Aviation in Moro, Leone and Andreotti Govts, Minister of Educ. in second Andreotti Govt; Vice-Chair. House of Deputies; Minister of the Interior 1983–87; mem. House of Deputies Comm. for Foreign and Community Affairs; Pres. of Italy 1992–99.

SCALIA, Antonin, AB, LLB; American judge; b. 11 March 1936, Trenton, NJ; s. of S. Eugene Scalia and Catherine L. (Panaro) Scalia; m. Maureen McCarthy 1960; five s. four d.; ed Univ. of Fribourg, Switzerland and Harvard Univ.; called to Bar, Ohio 1962, Virginia 1970; Assoc. Jones, Day, Cockley & Reavis, Cleveland 1961–67; Assoc. Prof. Univ. of Va Law School 1967–70, Prof. 1970–74; Gen. Counsel Office of Telecommunications Policy, Exec. Office of President 1971–72; Chair. Admin. Conf. US, Washington 1972–74; Asst Attorney Gen., US Office of Legal Counsel, Justice Dept 1974–77; Prof. Law School, Univ. of Chicago 1977–82; Visiting Prof. Georgetown Law Center 1977, Stanford Law School 1980–81; Judge, US Court of Appeals (DC Circuit) 1982–86; Assoc. Justice, US Supreme Court 1986–; mem. numerous advisory councils etc; Hon. Master of the Bench, Inner Temple, London 1986. *Address:* U.S. Supreme Court, 1 First Street, NE, Washington, DC 20543, USA.

SCANLAN, John Oliver, MEng, PhD, DSc, MRIA, FIEE, FIEEE; Irish professor of electronic engineering; b. 20 Sept. 1937, Dublin; s. of John Scanlan and Hannah Scanlan; m. Ann Weadock 1961; ed St Mary's Coll., Dundalk, Univ. Coll. Dublin; Research Engineer, Mullard Research Labs., Surrey, UK 1959–63; lecturer, Univ. of Leeds, UK 1963–68, Prof. of Electronic Eng 1968–73; Prof. of Electronic Eng, Univ. Coll. Dublin 1973–; Sec. Royal Irish Acad. 1981–89, Pres. 1993–96; Dir Bord Telecom Eireann 1984–97. *Publications:* Analysis and Synthesis of Tunnel Diode Circuits 1966, Circuit Theory (Vols 1 and 2) 1970. *Leisure interests:* music, golf. *Address:* Department of Electronic and Electrical Engineering, Engineering Building, University College Dublin, Belfield, Dublin 4, Ireland. *Telephone:* (1) 7161909. *Fax:* (1) 2830921. *E-mail:* eleceng@ucd.ie (Office).

SCANLON, Baron (Life Peer), cr. 1979, of Davyhulme in the County of Greater Manchester; **Hugh Parr Scanlon;** British trade unionist (retd); b. 26 Oct. 1913, Australia; m. Nora Markey 1943; two d.; ed Stretford Elementary School, Nat. Council of Labour Colls; apprentice; instrument maker; Shop Steward, Convener Associated Electrical Industries, Trafford Park; Div. Organizer Amalgamated Eng Union, Manchester 1947–63, mem. Exec. Council AEU London 1963–67; Pres. Amalgamated Union of Engineering Workers (AUEW) 1967–78; fmr Vice-Pres., mem. Exec. Cttee Int. Metalworkers' Fed.; fmr mem. Nat. Econ. Devt Council (NEDC); fmr mem. Metrication Bd; fmr Pres. European Metalworkers' Fed.; Chair., Chief Exec. Eng Industry Training Bd 1975–82; mem. Advisory Council for Applied Research and Devt 1982–; mem. British Gas Corpn 1976–82, Govt Cttee of Inquiry into Teaching of Maths in Primary and Secondary Schools in England and Wales 1978–; Hon. DCL (Kent) 1988. *Leisure interests:* golf, swimming, gardening. *Address:* 23 Seven Stones Drive, Broadstairs, Kent, England. *Telephone:* (1843) 867064 (Home).

SCANNELL, Vernon, FRSL; British poet, author and broadcaster; b. 23 Jan. 1922; ed Leeds Univ.; served with Gordon Highlanders 1940–45; professional boxer 1946–47; various jobs including teacher, Hazelwood Prep. School 1955–62; Southern Arts Asscn Writing Fellowship 1975–76; Visiting Poet, Shrewsbury School 1978–79; Resident Poet, King's School, Canterbury 1979. *Publications:* (novels) The Fight 1953, A Lonely Game (for younger readers) 1979, Ring of Truth 1983, Feminine Endings 2000; (poetry) The Masks of Love 1960 (Heinemann Award), A Sense of Danger (Ed., with Ted Hughes and Patricia Beer) 1962; New Poems, a PEN anthology 1962; Walking Wounded: Poems 1962–65, 1968, Epithets of War: Poems 1965–69, 1969; Mastering the Craft (Poets Today Series) 1970, Pergamon Poets, No. 8 (with J. Silkin) 1970, Selected Poems 1971, The Winter Man: New Poems 1973, The Apple Raid and Other Poems 1974 (Cholmondeley Poetry Prize), The Loving Game 1975, New and Collected Poems 1950–80, 1980, Winterlude and Other Poems 1982, Funeral Games 1987, Soldiering On, Poems of Military Life 1989, A Time for Fires 1991, Collected Poems 1950–1993 1994, The Black and White Days 1996, Views and Distances 2000; (criticism) Not Without Glory: Poets of World War II 1976, How to Enjoy Poetry 1982, How to Enjoy Novels 1984; (autobiography) The Tiger and the Rose 1971, A Proper Gentleman 1977, Argument of Kings 1987, The Drums of Morning: Growing Up in the Thirties 1992; Sporting Literature: An Anthology 1987, The Clever Potato, Poems for Children 1988, Love Shouts and Whispers (poems for children) 1990, Travelling Light (for children) 1991. *Leisure interests:* listening to radio (mainly music), drink, boxing (as a spectator), films, reading. *Address:* 51 North Street, Otley, W Yorks., LS21 1AH, England. *Telephone:* (1943) 467176.

SCARAMUZZI, Franco; Italian agricultural scientist; b. 26 Dec. 1926, Ferrara; s. of Donato Scaramuzzi and Alberta Rovida; m. Maria Bianca Cancellieri 1955; one s. one d.; Prof. of Pomology, Univ. of Pisa 1959, Univ. of Florence 1969, now Prof. Emer.; Rector Magnificus, Univ. of Florence 1979–91; Pres. Int. Soc. of Horticultural Science 1986–90; Pres. Accademia dei Georgofili 1986–; mem. Soviet (now Russian) Acad. of Agricultural Sciences 1982–; Pres. Società di San Giovanni Battista 2001–; Hon. Pres. Italian Horticultural Soc. 1976–, Italian Acad. of Vine and Wine; Hon. mem. Rotary; Cavaliere di Gran Croce 1998; Dr hc (Bucharest); Gold Medal of the Minister of Education, 1983, Gold Medal of Univ. of Florence. *Publication:* Fruit Pomology. *Address:* Accademia dei Georgofili, Logge Uffizi Corti, 50122 Florence (Office); Viale Amendola 38, 50121 Florence, Italy (Home). *Telephone:* (55) 213360 (Office); (55) 2342825 (Home). *Fax:* (55) 2302754 (Office). *E-mail:* accademia@georgofili.it (Office). *Website:* www.georgofili.it (Office).

SCARDINO, Dame Marjorie Morris, DBE, JD, BA; American/British business executive; b. 25 Jan. 1947, Flagstaff, Arizona; d. of Robert Weldon Morris and Beth Lamb Morris; m. Albert James Scardino 1974; two s. one d.; ed Baylor Univ., Univ. of San Francisco; reporter and for the Associated Press; Partner, Brannen, Wessels and Searcy law firm 1975–85; Publr The Ga Gazette Co. 1978–85; Pres. The Economist Newspaper Group Inc. 1985–93; Chief Exec. The Economist Group 1993–97; CEO Pearson PLC 1997–; Dir (non-exec.) Nokia Corpn 2001–; mem. Bd Trustees Carter Center, Victoria and Albert Museum; Hon. Fellow London Business School, City and Guilds of London Inst.; Hon. LLD (Exeter); Hon. DHumLitt (New School Univ.); Dr hc (Heriot-Watt), (Brunel); Veuve Cliquot Businesswoman of the Year Award 1998. *Address:* Pearson PLC, 80 Strand, London, WC2R 0RL, England. *Telephone:* (20) 7010-2300. *Fax:* (20) 7010-6601 (Office). *E-mail:* marjorie.scardino@pearson.com (Office). *Website:* www.pearson.com (Office).

SCARF, Herbert Eli, PhD; American economist; b. 25 July 1930, Philadelphia, Pa; s. of Louis H. Scarf and Lena Elkman; m. Margaret Klein 1953; three d.; ed Temple Univ. and Princeton Univ.; employee of Rand Corpn, Santa Monica, Calif. 1954–57; Asst and Assoc. Prof., Dept of Statistics, Stanford Univ., Calif. 1957–63; Fellow, Center for Advanced Study in the Behavioral Sciences, Stanford, Calif. 1962–63; Prof. of Econs, Yale Univ. 1963–70, Stanley Resor Prof. of Econs 1970–78, Sterling Prof. of Econs 1979–; Dir Cowles Foundation for Research in Econs 1967–71, 1981–84, Dir Div. of Social Sciences 1971–72, 1973–74; Visiting Prof., Stanford Univ., Calif. 1977–78, Mathematical Sciences Research Inst. Spring 1986; Ford Foundation Sr Faculty Fellowship 1969–70; Fellow Econometric Soc., Pres. 1983; Fellow American Acad. of Arts and Sciences; mem. NAS, American Philosophical Soc.; Distinguished Fellow American Econ. Asscn 1991; Hon. LHD (Chicago) 1978; Lanchester Prize, (Operations Research Soc. of America) 1974, Von Neumann Medal 1983. *Publications:* Studies in the Mathematical Theory of Inventory and Production (with K. Arrow and S. Karlin) 1958, The Optimality of (S, s) Policies in the Dynamic Inventory Problem 1960, The Computation of Economic Equilibria (with Terje Hansen) 1973, Applied General Equilibrium Analysis (with John Shoven, eds.) 1984; articles in learned journals. *Leisure interests:* music, reading, hiking. *Address:* Yale University, Cowles Foundation for Research in Economics, P.O. Box 208281, New Haven, CT 06520-8281; 88 Blake Road, Hamden, CT 06517, USA (Home). *Telephone:* (203) 432-3693 (Office); (203) 776-9197 (Home). *E-mail:* herbert.scarf@yale.edu (Office). *Website:* www.yale.edu (Office).

SCARFE, Gerald A.; British cartoonist; b. 1 June 1936, London; m. Jane Asher; two s. one d.; has contributed cartoons to Punch 1960–, Private Eye 1961–, Daily Mail 1966–, The Sunday Times 1967–, Time 1967–; exhibited at Grosvenor Gallery (group exhbns.) 1969, 1970, Pavillion d'Humour, Montreal 1969, Expo 1970, Osaka 1970; animation and film directing BBC 1969–; consultant designer and character design for film Hercules 1997; Hon. Fellow London Inst. 2001; Hon. LLD (Liverpool) 2001; Zagreb Prize for BBC film Long Drawn Out Trip 1973, BAFTA Award for Scarfe on Scarfe 1987, Olivier Award for Absolute Turkey 1993. *Solo exhibitions include:* Waddell Gallery, New York 1968, 1970, Vincent Price Gallery, Chicago 1969, Grosvenor Gallery 1969, Nat. Portrait Gallery 1971, Royal Festival Hall 1983, Langton Gallery 1986, Chris Beetles Gallery 1989, Nat. Portrait Gallery 1998–99, Comic Art Gallery, Melbourne, Gerald Scarfe in Southwark 2000. *Television:* dir. and presenter Scarfe on Art, Scarfe on Sex, Scarfe on Class, Scarfe in

Paradise; subject of Scarfe and His Work with Disney (South Bank Special). *Theatre design:* Ubu Roi (Traverse Theatre) 1957, What the Butler Saw (Oxford Playhouse) 1980, No End of Blame (Royal Court, London) 1981, Orpheus in the Underworld (English ENO, Coliseum) 1985, Who's a Lucky Boy (Royal Exchange, Manchester) 1985, Born Again 1990, The Magic Flute (LA Opera) 1992, An Absolute Turkey 1993, Mind Millie for Me (Haymarket, London) 1996, Fantastic Mr. Fox (LA Opera) 1998, Peter and the Wolf (Holiday on Ice, Paris and world tour). *Publications:* Gerald Scarfe's People 1966, Indecent Exposure 1973, Expletive Deleted: The Life and Times of Richard Nixon 1974, Gerald Scarfe 1982, Father Kissmass and Mother Claus 1985, Scarfe by Scarfe (autobiog.) 1986, Gerald Scarfe's Seven Deadly Sins 1987, Line of Attack 1988, Scarfeland 1989, Scarfe on Stage 1992, Scarfe Face 1993, Hades: The Truth at Last 1997. *Leisure interests:* drawing, painting, sculpting. *Address:* c/o London Management, 2–4 Noel Street, London, W1V 3RB, England.

SCARGILL, Arthur; British trade unionist; b. 11 Jan. 1938, Worsborough, Yorks.; s. of the late Harold Scargill and of Alice Scargill; m. Anne Harper 1961; one d.; ed White Cross Secondary School; worked first in a factory, then Woolley Colliery 1955; mem. Barnsley Young Communist League 1955–62; mem. Nat. Union of Mineworkers (NUM) 1955–, NUM Br. Cttee 1960, Br. del. to NUM Yorks. Area Council 1964, mem. NUM Nat. Exec. 1972–, Pres. Yorks. NUM 1973–82, Pres. NUM 1981–2002, Hon. Pres. and Consultant July 2002–; Chair. NUM Int. Cttee; Pres. Int. Miners Org. 1985–; mem. Labour Party 1966–95; mem. TUC Gen. Council 1986–88; f. Socialist Labour Party 1996; contested Newport East 1997, Hartlepool 2001, Gen.-Sec. 1996–. *Address:* Socialist Labour Party, 9 Victoria Road, Barnsley, S. Yorks, S70 2BB (Office); National Union of Mineworkers, 2 Huddersfield Road, Barnsley, S. Yorks., S70 2LS, England. *Telephone:* (1226) 770957 (Office). *Fax:* (1226) 770957 (Office). *E-mail:* info@socialist-labour-party.org.uk (Office). *Website:* www.socialist-labour-party.org.uk (Office).

SCARLETT, John McLeod, CMG, OBE, MA; British civil servant, politician and diplomatist; b. 18 Aug. 1948, London; s. of the late James Henri Stuart Scarlett and of Clara Dunlop Scarlett (née Morton); m. Gwenda Mary Rachel Stilliard 1970; one s. three d. (and one s. deceased); ed Epsom Coll., Magdalen Coll., Oxford; with Secret Intelligence Service 1971–2001, FCO London 1971–73, 1977–84, 1988–91, 1994–2001 (Dir of Security and Public Affairs 1999–2001), Third Sec., Nairobi 1973–74; language student 1974–75; Second, later First Sec., Moscow 1976–77; First Sec., Paris 1984–88, Political Counsellor, Moscow 1991–94; Chair. Jt Intelligence Cttee and Intelligence and Security Dir, Cabinet Office 2001–. *Leisure interests:* history, medieval churches, family. *Address:* c/o Cabinet Office, 70 Whitehall, London, SW1A 2AS, England (Office). *Telephone:* (20) 7276-0360 (Office).

SCARMAN, Baron (Life Peer), cr. 1977, of Quatt in the County of Salop (Shropshire); **Leslie George Scarman,** Kt, PC, OBE, QC; British judge; b. 29 July 1911, London; s. of George Charles and Ida Irene Scarman; m. Ruth Clement Wright 1947; one s.; ed Radley Coll. and Oxford Univ.; Harmsworth Law Scholar, Middle Temple 1936; RAF (Volunteer Reserve) 1940–45; QC 1957; Judge, High Court of Justice, England 1961; Chair. Law Comm. for England and Wales 1965–72; Lord Justice of Appeal 1973–77, Lord of Appeal in Ordinary 1977–86 (retd); Chancellor of Univ. of Warwick 1981–89; Pres. Royal Inst. of Public Admin. 1981–89, Constitutional Reform Centre 1984–, Citizen Action Compensation Campaign 1988–; numerous hon. degrees include Hon. LLD (London, Warwick, Kent, Exeter, City of London, Cambridge, Wales); Hon. DCL (Oxford, Freiburg); Hon. DUniv (Brunel) 1987. *Publications:* Pattern of Law Reform 1967, English Law—the New Dimension 1974, Scarman Report on the Brixton Riots 1981. *Leisure interests:* music, walking, gardening, history. *Address:* House of Lords, London, SW1A 0PW, England. *Telephone:* (20) 7219-3000.

SCARONI, Paolo, MBA; Italian business executive; b. 28 Nov. 1946, Vicenza; m.; three c.; ed Univ. of Bocconi, Milan, Columbia Univ., NY, USA; staff mem. Chevron 1969–71; consultant McKinsey & Co. 1972–73; joined Saint Gobain Group 1973, various exec. positions including Financial Man. St German Italia, Gen. Man. Balzaretti & Modigliani SpA, Chair. Borma SpA and Air Industrie SpA –1978; Gen. Del. St Gobain Venezuela, Colombia, Ecuador and Peru, Caracas 1978–81; Gen. Del. St Gobain Italia 1981–84; Chair. St Gobain Flat Glass Div., Paris 1984; Chair. and Man. Dir St Gobain Vitrage SA; CEO Saint Gobain Group –2002; Chair. Fabbrica Pisana SpA, Vegla GmbH, Cristaleria Espanola SA, Saint Roch SA; Vice-Chair. and Man. Dir Techint 1985; Vice-Chair. Falck SpA 1986–88; Man. Dir SIV SpA 1993–95; Group CEO Pilkington PLC 1996; CEO Enel SpA May 2002–; Vice-Chair. Sadi SpA; mem. Exec. Cttee Confindustria; Pres. Unindustria Venice 2001–; mem. Exec. Bd BAE Systems, London, Alstom SA, Paris, Alliance UniChem. *Publication:* Professione manager 1985. *Leisure interests:* reading, skiing, golf, football. *Address:* Ente Nazionale per l'Energia Elettrica (Enel) SpA, Viale Regina Margherita 137, 00198 Rome, Italy (Office). *Telephone:* (06) 85091 (Office). *Fax:* (06) 85095617 (Office). *Website:* www.enel.it (Office).

SCAZZIERI, Roberto, M.LITT., DPhil, DR.SC.POL.; Italian professor of economics; b. 1 May 1950, Bologna; s. of Guerrino Scazzieri and Fosca Lambertini; m. Maria Cristina Bacchi 1983; one s.; ed Liceo Minghetti, Bologna, Univ. of Bologna, Univ. of Oxford, UK; Asst Lecturer, Univ. of Bologna 1974–79, Lecturer in Theory and Policy of Econ. Growth 1980–83, in Econ. Principles 1983–86, in Advanced Econ. Analysis 1985–87, Assoc. Prof. of Econs, Faculty of Political Sciences 1986–87, Full Prof. of Econs, Faculty of Econs and

Commerce and Dept of Econs 1990–; Prof. of Econs, Faculty of Statistics, Univ. of Padua 1987–90; Visiting Scholar, Dept of Applied Econs, Cambridge Univ. 1987, 1989, Research Assoc. 1992–93; Visiting Fellow Clare Hall 1992, Life mem. 1992; Visiting Fellow Gonville and Caius Coll. 1999, mem. 1999–, Centre for Research in the Arts, Social Sciences and Humanities (CRASSH),Univ. of Cambridge 2004; Resident Fellow Bologna Inst. of Advanced Study 1997, Scientific Dir 2000–; Visiting Prof. Univ. of Lugano, Switzerland 1997; Man. Ed. and Review Ed. Structural Change and Economic Dynamics; Assoc. Ed. Journal of Econ. Methodology; mem. Steering Cttee Bologna-Cambridge-Harvard Sr Seminars Network, Bologna Inst. for Advanced Study, Steering Cttee European Consortium of Humanities Centres and Insitutes (ECHCI) 2002–; mem. Man. Bd European Summer School in Structural Change and Econ. Dynamics (Selwyn Coll., Cambridge) 1995–; mem. Scientific Cttee Int. Centre for the History of Univs. and Science 1994, Scientific Cttee Centre for Research on Complex Automated Systems (CASy), Univ. of Bologna 2002–; mem. Man. Bd 'Federigo Enriques' Centre for Epistemology and History of Sciences, Univ. of Bologna 2001–; Foundation Fellow Kyoto Univ.; Rector's Del., Bologna-Clare Hall Fellowship 1993–; mem. Bologna Acad. of Sciences 1994; Bonaldo Stringher Prize Scholarship (Bank of Italy) 1974, St Vincent Prize for Econs 1985. *Publications:* Efficienza produttiva e livelli di attività 1981, Protagonisti del pensiero economico (jtly) 1977–82, Sui momenti costitutivi dell'economia politica 1983 (jtly), Foundations of Economics: Structures of Inquiry and Economic Theory 1986, The Economic Theory of Structure and Change 1990, A Theory of Production: Tasks, Processes and Technical Practices 1993, Production and Economic Dynamics 1996, Incommensurability and Translation. Kuhnian Perspectives on Scientific Communication and Theory Change 1999, Knowledge, Social Institutions and the Division of Labour 2001, Economics of Structural Change 2003; numerous articles. *Leisure interests:* reading and conversation, art, walking. *Address:* Università degli Studi di Bologna, Piazza Scaravilli 2, 40126 Bologna (Office); Via Garibaldi 5, 40124 Bologna, Italy (Home). *Telephone:* (051) 2098146 (Office); (051) 2098132 (Office); (051) 582789 (Home). *Fax:* (051) 2098040 (Office). *E-mail:* scazzieri@economia.unibo.it (Office). *Website:* www.economia.unibo.it (Office); www.isa.unibo.it (Office).

SCHABRAM, Hans, DPhil; German professor of medieval English; b. 27 Sept. 1928, Berlin; s. of Paul Schabram and Lucia Schabram; m. Candida Larisch 1956; two s. one d.; ed Univs. of Berlin and Cologne; Asst English Dept Univ. of Heidelberg 1957–63; Prof. of Medieval English Language and Literature Univ. of Giessen 1964–67, Univ. of Göttingen 1968–; mem. Akad. der Wissenschaften, Göttingen. *Publications:* 55 Publs on English Philology since 1956. *Address:* Seminar für Englische Philologie der Universität, Humboldtallee 13, 37073 Göttingen (Office); Heinz-Hilpert-Str. 6, 37085 Göttingen, Germany. *Telephone:* (551) 55444 (Home).

SCHACHMAN, Howard Kapnek, PhD; American biochemist and educator; b. 5 Dec. 1918, Philadelphia, Pa; s. of Morris H. Schachman and Rose Kapnek Schachman; m. Ethel H. Lazarus 1945; two s.; ed Mass. Inst. of Technology and Princeton Univ.; Fellow, Rockefeller Inst. for Medical Research, Princeton, NJ, 1947–48; Instructor (Biochem.), Univ. of Calif., Berkeley 1948–50, Asst Prof. 1950–54, Assoc. Prof. 1955–59, Prof. of Biochem. and Molecular Biology 1959–91, Prof. Emer. 1991–94, Prof. of Grad. School 1994–, Chair. Dept of Molecular Biology, Dir Virus Lab. 1969–76, NIH Ombudsman in Basic Sciences 1994–; Carl and Gerty Cori Lecturer, Washington Univ. School of Medicine, St Louis 1993; Faculty Research Lecturer, Univ. of Calif. at Berkeley 1994; Pres. American Soc. for Biochem. and Molecular Biology 1987–88, Chair. Public Affairs Cttee 1989–2000; mem. NAS 1968 (Chair. Biochem. Section 1990–93), AAAS, American Acad. of Arts and Sciences 1966; Foreign mem. Accad. Nazionale dei Lincei, Rome 1996; Scholar-in-Residence Fogarty Int. Center, NIH 1977–78; Pres. Fed. of American Socs. for Experimental Biology 1988–89; mem. Scientific Council and Scientific Advisory Bd of Stazione Zoologica Naples, Italy 1988–, Bd of Scientific Consultants of Memorial Sloan-Kettering Cancer Center 1988–97, Bd of Scientific Counselors Nat. Cancer Inst., Div. of Cancer Biology and Diagnosis 1989–92, Cttee on Scientific Freedom and Responsibility 1998–; Special Adviser to Dir of NIH and Ombudsman in the Basic Sciences 1994–; Burroughs Wellcome Fund Lecturer 1999; Hon. DSc (Northwestern Univ.) 1974; Hon. MD (Naples) 1990; Calif. Section Award, American Chemical Soc. 1958, E. H. Sargent & Co. Award for Chemical Instrumentation, ACS 1962, John Scott Award, City of Philadelphia 1964, Warren Triennial Prize, Mass. Gen. Hosp. 1965, Merck Award, American Soc. of Biological Chemists 1986, Alexander von Humboldt Award 1990, NAS Panel on Scientific Responsibility and the Conduct of Research 1990–92, Alberta Heritage Foundation for Medical Research Visiting Professorship, Univ. of Alberta 1996; Herbert A. Sober Award, American Soc. for Biochem. and Molecular Biology 1994, Public Service Award, FASEB 1994, Theodor Sredberg Award 1998, Scientific Freedom and Responsibility Award, AAAS 2001. *Publications:* Ultracentrifugation in Biochemistry 1959; articles. *Leisure interest:* sports. *Address:* Department of Molecular and Cell Biology, 229 Stanley Hall #3206, University of California, Berkeley, CA 94720-3206, USA. *Telephone:* (510) 642-7046.

SCHACHT, Henry Brewer, MBA; American business executive; b. 16 Oct. 1934, Erie, Pa; s. of Henry Schacht and Virginia Schacht; m. Nancy Godfrey 1960; one s. three d.; ed Yale and Harvard Univs; Investment Man. Irwin Man. Co. 1962–64; Vice-Pres. Finance, Subsidiaries and Int. Areas, Cummins Engine Co., Inc. 1964–69; Pres. Cummins Engine Co., Inc. 1969–77, Chair. 1977–95, CEO 1977–94; Chair., CEO Lucent Techs, Murray Hill, NJ 1995–98,

2000–; Dir AT&T, Chase Manhattan Corpn, Chase Manhattan Bank NA; mem. Business Council and Council of Foreign Relations; Trustee, Ford Foundation, Brookings Inst., Yale Univ., Business Enterprise Trust, Calver Educ. Foundation; Sr Mem. The Conf. Bd. *Address:* The Ford Foundation, 320 East 43rd Street, New York, NY 10017, USA (Office); Lucent Technologies, 600 Mountain Avenue, Murray Hill, NJ 07974.

SCHADEWALDT, Hans, DrMed; German professor emeritus of medical history; b. 7 May 1923, Kottbus; s. of Johannes Schadewaldt and Hedwig Schadewaldt; m. Lotte Schadewaldt 1943; four s.; ed Univs of Tübingen, Würzburg and Königsberg; Lecturer Univ. of Freiburg 1961–63; Prof. History of Medicine, Univ. of Düsseldorf 1963– (now Emer.), Dean, Faculty of Medicine 1976–77; mem. numerous int. medical socs.; mem. Rhine-Westfalian Acad. Arts and Sciences (Pres. 1990), Accad. Nazionale Virgiliana Mantova 2001–; Hon. Fellow Royal Soc. of Medicine; Dr hc (Szcecin); Officier Ordre du Mérite Culturel, Monaco; Officier Ordre des Palmes Académiques, Paris; Bundesverdienstkreuz, Commdr.'s Cross, Order of Merit; Sarton Medal, Sudhoff Medal, Langerhans Medal, Ernst von Bergmann Medal, Hansen Medal, Hahnemann Medal. *Films include:* History of Diabetes, Dance of Death, Trepanation in Kenya, Folklore Medicine in Kenya. *Television:* Sanfte Medizin (ARD) 1992–2001. *Publications:* Michelangelo und die Medizin seiner Zeit 1965, Die berühmten Ärzte 1966, Kunst und Medizin 1967, Der Medizinmann bei den Naturvölkern 1968, Geschichte der Allergie 1979–83, Die Chirurgie in der Kunst 1983, Das Herz, ein Rätsel für die antike und mittelalterliche Welt 1989, Betrachtungen zur Medizin in der bildenden Kunst 1990, 100 Jahre Pharmakologie bei Bayer 1890–1990 1990, Totentanz und Heilberufe 1993, Chronik der Medizin 1993, Die Seuchen kehren zurück 1994, Paul Ehrlich und die Anfänge der Chemotherapie 2001–02, Sieben Jahre Sanfte Medizin 2002. *Address:* Institute zum Geschichte der Medizin, Heinrich-Heine-Univeristät Düsseldorf, Moorenstr. 5, 40225 Düsseldorf (Office); Brehmstrasse 82, 40239 Düsseldorf, Germany (Home). *Telephone:* (211) 8114053 (Office); (211) 623163 (Home). *Fax:* (211) 8114053.

SCHAEFER, Henry Frederick, III, PhD, FAAS; American professor of chemistry and researcher; b. 8 June 1944, Grand Rapids, Mich.; s. of Henry Frederick Schaefer, Jr and Janice Christine Trost Schaefer; m. Karen Regine Rasmussen; three s. two d.; ed Massachusetts Inst. of Tech., Stanford Univ.; Prof. of Chem., Univ. of Calif., Berkeley 1969–87; Wilfred T. Doherty Prof. and Dir Inst. for Theoretical Chem., Univ. of Tex. 1979–80; Graham Perdue Prof. and Dir Center for Computational Quantum Chem., Univ. of Ga 1987–; Ed. Molecular Physics 1991–, Encyclopedia of Computational Chem. 1995–98; Pres. World Asscn of Theoretically Oriented Chemists 1996–; Alfred P. Sloan Research Fellow 1972–74; John Simon Guggenheim Fellow 1976–77; Fellow American Physical Soc. 1977; mem. Int. Acad. of Quantum Molecular Sciences; numerous lectureships including Albert Einstein Centennial Lecturer, Nat. Univ. of Mexico 1979, Lester P. Kuhn Lecturer, Johns Hopkins Univ. 1982, John Howard Appleton Lecturer, Brown Univ. 1985, J. A. Erskine Lecturer, Univ. of Canterbury, Christchurch, NZ 1986, John Lee Pratt Lecturer, Univ. of Va 1988, Guelph-Waterloo Distinguished Lecturer, Univ. of Guelph and Univ. of Waterloo, Ont., Canada 1991, John M. Templeton Lecturer, Case Western Reserve Univ. 1992, Herbert H. King Lecturer, Kansas State Univ. 1993, Francis A. Schaeffer Lectures, Washington Univ., St Louis 1994, Mary E. Kapp Lecture, Va Commonwealth Univ. 1996, Abbott Lectures, Univ. of ND 1997, C. S. Lewis Lecture, Univ. of Tenn. 1997, Joseph Frank McGregory Lecture, Colgate Univ. 1997, Kenneth S. Pitzer Lecture, Univ. of Calif. at Berkeley 1998, Donald F. Othmer Lectures in Chem., Tokyo 2000, Israel Pollak Lectures, Technion-Israel Inst. of Tech., Haifa 2001, Coochbehar Lectures, Indian Asscn for the Cultivation of Science, Kolkata 2001, Lise Meitner Lecture, Hebrew Univ., Jerusalem 2001, Oakley Vail Lecture, Wake Forest Univ. 2002; nine hon. degrees; ACS Award in Pure Chem. 1979, Leo Hendrik Baekeland Award (ACS) 1983; Annual Medal, World Asscn of Theoretical Organic Chemists 1990, Centenary Medal, RSC, London 1992, ACS Award in Theoretical Chem. 2003, ACS Ira Remson Award 2003. *Publications:* The Electronic Structure of Atoms and Molecules 1972, Modern Theoretical Chemistry 1977, Quantum Chemistry 1984, A New Dimension to Quantum Chemistry 1994; 900 publs in scientific journals. *Leisure interests:* Bible study, running, hiking. *Address:* Center for Computational Quantum Chemistry, University of Georgia, Athens, GA 30602, USA. *Telephone:* (706) 542-2067. *Fax:* (706) 542-0406.

SCHAEFER, William Donald, LLM, JD; American politician; b. 2 Nov. 1921, Baltimore; s. of William Henry Schaefer and Tululu Skipper; ed Baltimore Univ.; law practice, Baltimore 1943–; mem. Baltimore City Council 1955–67, Pres. 1967–71, Mayor 1971–86; Gov. of Maryland 1986–95, Comptroller 1999–; professional lecturer and William Donald Schaefer Chair, School of Public Affairs, Univ. of Md and Inst. for Policy Studies, Johns Hopkins Univ. 1996–; fmr Counsel Gordon, Feinblatt, Rothman, Hoffberger & Hollander; Democrat; numerous hon. degrees; numerous awards including: Jefferson Award 1979, Michael A. DiNunzio Award 1981, Distinguished Mayor Award, Nat. Urban Coalition 1982, Best Mayor in America, Esquire Magazine 1984, Commendation, Pres.'s Council on Physical Fitness and Sports 1988, Making Marylanders Safe Award, Marylanders Against Handgun Abuse 1991. *Address:* Louis L. Goldstein Treasures Building, Annapolis, MD 21404, USA. *Telephone:* (410) 240-7827. *Fax:* (410) 974-3808.

SCHAEFERS, Wolfgang Friedrich Wilhelm, DrIng; German business executive and engineer; b. 11 Dec. 1930, Oberhausen; s. of Friedrich Schaefers and Adele (née Verhufen) Schaefers; m. Christel Weingarten 1954; two s.; ed Rheinisch-Westfälische Technische Hochschule, Aachen; Works Man. with Mannesmann AG 1961–62; mem. Man. Bd Verein Deutscher Eisenhüttenleute 1962–64 (also currently); Technical Works Man. Rheinstahl Hüttenwerke AG 1964–69; mem. Man. Bd Rheinstahl AG (Thyssen Industrie AG from April 1976) 1969–75, Spokesman 1975–76, Chair. 1976–80; Chair. Supervisory Bd Thyssen Nordseewerke GmbH, Thyssen Schalker Verein GmbH, Thyssen Giesserei AG, Österreichische Salen-Kunststoffwerk GmbH; Chair. Advisory Bd Thyssen Industrie AG Henschel; Vice-Chair. Supervisory Bd Henschel Flugzeug-werke AG; mem. Supervisory Bd, Messerschmitt-Bölkow-Blohm GmbH, Munich; mem. Max-Planck-Gesellschaft zur Förderung der Wissenschaften eV Deutsch-Türkische Gesellschaft für Kultur, Wirtschaft und Handel eV and other socs; Special mem. South African Inst. of Foundrymen; Cttee or Bd positions with nine firms and asscns. in steel and other sectors. *Publications:* numerous publs on technical subjects, including steel production. *Leisure interests:* sailing, hunting.

SCHAEFFER, Bogusław, DPhil; Polish composer and playwright; b. 6 June 1929, Lwów (now Lvov, Ukraine); s. of Władysław Schaeffer and Julia Schaeffer; m. Mieczysława Hanuszewska 1953; one s.; ed State Higher School of Music (student of A. Malawski), Jagiellonian Univ., Cracow; wrote first dodecaphonic music for orchestra, Music for Strings: Nocturne 1953; Assoc. Prof. State Higher School of Music, Cracow 1963–, Extraordinary Prof. of Composition, Higher School of Music, Mozarteum, Salzburg 1986–89, Prof. 1989–; Chief Ed. Forum Musicum 1967–; leads Int. Summer Courses for New Composition in Salzburg and Schwaz (Austria) 1976–; Hon. mem. Int. Soc. for Contemporary Music 1998; Gold Cross of Merit 1969; Kt's Cross of Polonia Restituta Order 1972; numerous prizes include G. Fitelberg Prize 1959, 1960, 1964, A. Malawski Prize 1962, Minister of Culture and Arts Prize 1971, 1980, Union of Polish Composers Prize 1977, Alfred Jarzykowski Award 1999. *Main compositions:* Extrema, Tertium datur, Scultura, S'alto for alto saxophone, Collage and Form, Electronic Music, Visual Music, Heraclitiana, Missa Electronica, Jangwa, Missa Sinfonica, Piano Concerto, Maah, Sinfonia, Hommage à Guillaume for two cellos and piano 1995, Sinfonietta for 16 instruments 1996, Symphony in One Movement 1997, Enigma for Orchestra 1997, Four Psalms for choir and orchestra 1999, Musica Omogènea for 32 violins 1999, Si Gueris Miracula for soprano and orchestra 2000, Model XXI (wendepunkt) for piano 2000, De Profundiis for soprano and chamber orchestra 2000, Monophonie VIII for 24 violins 2000, Ave Maria for soprano and orchestra 2000, opera Liebesblicke, Mini opera, also film and theatre music, Miserere, Organ Concerto, 8 string quartets, Orchestral and Electronic Changes, Concerto for Violin, Piano and Orchestra, Symphony/ Concerto for 15 solo instrumentalists and orchestra, Heideggerriana, Winter Musik for horn and piano, Concerto for percussion, electronic media and orchestra. *Plays include:* Three Actors 1970, Darknesses 1980, Screenplay for Sins of Old Age 1985, The Actor 1990, Rehearsals 1990, Séance 1990, Tutam 1991, Rondo 1991, Together 1992, Toast 1991, Harvest 1993, Promotion 1993, Daybreak 1994, Multi 1994, Largo 1996, Stage Demon 1998, Alles 1998, Advertisement 1998, Farniente 1998, Chance 1999, Dwa Te (Two Te) 2000, Skala 2000; plays trans. into 16 languages. *Publications:* Nowa Muzyka. Problemy współczesnej techniki kompozytorskiej (New music. Problems of Contemporary Technique in Composing) 1958, Klasycy dodekafonii (Classics of Dodecaphonic Music) 1964, Leksykon kompozytorów XX wieku (Lexicon of 20th Century Composers) 1965, W kręgu nowej muzyki (In the Sphere of New Music) 1967, Mały informator muzyki XX wieku 1975, Introduction to Composition (in English) 1975, Historia muzyki (Story of Music) 1980, Kompozytorzy XX wieku (20th Century Composers) 1990, Trzy rozmowy (kompozytor, dramaturg, filozof) (Three Conversations: Composer, Playwright and Philosopher) 1992. *Leisure interests:* literature, theatre. *Address:* Osiedle Kolorowe 4, m. 6, 31-938 Cracow, Poland; St. Julienstrasse, 5020 Salzburg, Austria. *Telephone:* (12) 6441960 (Poland). *E-mail:* bsch@ceti.pl (Office).

SCHAFER, Edward, MBA; American state governor; b. 8 Aug. 1946, Bismarck, ND; s. of Harold Schafer and Marian Schafer; m. Nancy Jones; four c.; ed Univ. of N Dakota and Denver Univ.; quality control ensp. Gold Seal 1971–73, Vice-Pres. 1974, Chair. Man. Cttee 1975–78, Pres. 1978–85; Owner/ Dir H & S Distribution 1976–; Pres. Dakota Classics 1986–, TRIESCO Properties 1986–, Fish 'N Dakota 1990–94; Gov. of ND 1992–2000; Republican. *Address:* c/o Office of the Governor, 600 E Boulevard Avenue, Bismarck, ND 58505, USA.

SCHÄFER, Walter; German banker; b. 19 Dec. 1936, Lohra, Marburg; m. Edelgard Schäfer; two c.; ed Municipal Savings Banks and Banking System Training Inst., Bonn; qualified as Savings Banks Customer Counsellor; bank Br. Man. 1966; Deputy Exec. Pres. Hessian Savings Bank and Giro Asscn, Frankfurt 1974; mem. Bd of Man. Dirs. Hessische Landesbank Girozentrale, Frankfurt 1980; Chair. Man. Bd Landesbank Schleswig-Holstein, Kiel 1993–96, Landesbank Hessen-Thüringen Girozentrale, Frankfurt 1996–2001. *Address:* c/o Landesbank Hessen-Thüringen, Main Tower, Neue Mainzer strasse 52-58, 60311 Frankfurt (Office); Mannenweg 14, 6397 Karbenl, Germany (Home).

SCHAFF, Adam, PhD; Polish philosopher and sociologist; b. 10 March 1913, Lvov (now Lviv, Ukraine); s. of Maks Schaff and Ernestina Schaff (née Felix); m. 1st Anna Schaff 1935 (died 1975); one d.; m. 2nd Teresa Schaff 1976; ed Lvov Univ. and Ecole des Sciences Politiques et Economiques, Paris; scientific work in USSR 1940–45; Prof. Łódź Univ. 1945–48; Prof. of Philosophy, Warsaw Univ. 1948–70; Dir Polish United Workers' Party Inst. of Social

Sciences 1950–57; mem. Polish Acad. of Sciences (Chair. Philosophy Cttee 1951–68, Dir Inst. of Philosophy and Sociology 1957–68); Visiting Prof., Univ. of Vienna 1969–72, Hon. Prof. of Philosophy 1972–88; mem. Bulgarian Acad. of Sciences; mem. Polish Workers' Party 1944–48, Polish United Workers' Party (PZPR) 1948–84, 1989–90, (mem. Cen. Cttee 1959–68); mem. Exec. Cttee Int. Fed. of Philosophical Asscns; mem. of Int. Inst. of Philosophy, Paris; mem. Royal Acad. of Political and Moral Sciences, Madrid; Hon. Pres. Bd of Dirs of the European Centre for Social Sciences in Vienna; mem. Exec. Cttee, Club of Rome; Ed. Myśl Współczesna (Contemporary Thought) 1946–51, Myśl Filozoficzna (Philosophical Thought) 1951–56; Dr. hc (Mich. Univ., Ann Arbor) 1967, (Sorbonne) 1975, (Univ. de Nancy) 1982; State Prizes, 1st and 2nd Class, Commdr Cross of Polonia Restituta Order, Order of Banner of Labour (First Class), Nicolaus Copernicus Medal, Polish Acad. of Sciences. *Publications:* Pojęcie i słowo (Concept and Word) 1946, Wstęp do teorii marksizmu (Introduction to the Theory of Marxism) 1947, Narodziny i rozwój filozofii marksistowskiej (Birth and Development of Marxist Philosophy) 1949, Z zagadnień marksistowskiej teorii prawdy (Some Problems of the Marxist Theory of Truth) 1951, Obiektywny charakter praw historii (The Objective Character of Historical Laws) 1955, Wstęp do semantyki (Introduction to Semantics) 1960, Filozofia człowieka (A Philosophy of Man) 1962, Język i poznanie (Language and Cognition) 1963, Marksizm a jednostka ludzka (Marxism and the Human Individual) 1965, Szkice z filozofii języka (Essays in the Philosophy of Language) 1967, Historia i prawda (History and Truth) 1970, Gramatyka generatywna a koncepcja wrodzonych idei (Generative Grammar and Conception of Innate Ideas) 1972, Strukturalizm i marksizm (Structuralism and Marxism) 1975, Entfremdung als soziales Phänomen (Alienation as a Social Phenomenon) 1977, Stereotypen und das menschliche Handeln 1980, Die Kommunistische Bewegung am Scheideweg 1982, Polen Heute 1983, Wohin führt der Weg? 1985, Perspektiven des modernen Sozialismus 1988, Ökumenischer Humanismus 1992, Mi Siglo XX 1993, Noticias de un hombre con dudas 1997, Meditaciones sobre el socialismo 1997, Meditations 1998, Attempt to Recapitulate 1999. *Leisure interest:* tennis. *Address:* al. J. Ch. Szucha 2/4 m. 24, 00-582 Warsaw, Poland; Flossgasse 2/28, 1020 Vienna, Austria. *Telephone:* (22) 6281832 (Warsaw); (1) 212-92-39 (Vienna).

SCHAFFSTEIN, Friedrich, DJur; German professor of law; b. 28 July 1905, Göttingen; s. of Dr. Karl Schaffstein and Emma Barkhausen; ed Univs. of Innsbruck and Göttingen; teacher in criminal law Univ. of Göttingen 1927–33, Prof. of Criminal Law, Leipzig 1933–35, Univ. of Kiel 1935–41, Univ. of Strasbourg 1941–45, Verwaltungs-Akad. Lüneburg 1946–50; Prof. of Law (Criminal and Criminology) Univ. of Göttingen 1953–70, Prof. Emer. 1970–; mem. Akad. der Wissenschaften, Göttingen 1955. *Publications:* Die Entwicklung der allgemeiner Lehren vom Verbrechen im gemeinen Strafrecht 1930, Wilhelm von Humboldt 1952, Die Strafrechtswissenschaft im Zeitalter des Humanismus 1954, Jugendstrafrecht (9th Edn) 1987, Abhandlungen zur Strafrechtsgeschichte und Wissenschaftsgeschichte 1987. *Address:* c/o Stift am Klausberg, Habichtsweg 55, 37075 Göttingen, Germany. *Telephone:* (551) 2098529.

SCHALLER, George Beals, PhD; American zoologist; b. 26 May 1933, Berlin, Germany; s. of George Ludwig Schaller and Bettina (Byrd) Iwersen; m. Kay Suzanne Morgan 1957; two s.; ed Univ. of Alaska, Univ. of Wisconsin; Research Assoc., Johns Hopkins Univ., Baltimore 1963–66; research zoologist Wildlife Conservation Soc. 1966–, Dir Int. Conservation Programme 1972–88; Adjunct Assoc. Prof., Rockefeller Univ., New York 1966–; Adjunct Prof. Peking Univ., Beijing; Research Assoc. American Museum of Natural History; Fellow Guggenheim Foundation 1971; Hon. Dir Explorers' Club 1991; Int. Cosmos Prize, Japan 1996, Tyler Environmental Prize 1997; Gold Medal, World Wildlife Fund 1980; Order of Golden Ark, Netherlands 1978. *Publications:* The Mountain Gorilla 1963, The Year of the Gorilla 1964, The Deer and the Tiger 1967, The Serengeti Lion 1972 (Nat. Book Award 1973), Mountain Monarchs 1977, Stones of Silence 1980, The Giant Pandas of Wolong (co-author) 1985, The Last Panda 1993, Tibet's Hidden Wilderness 1997, Wildlife of the Tibetan Steppe 1998, Antelopes, Deer and Relatives (co-ed.) 2000. *Leisure interests:* photography, reading. *Address:* The Wildlife Conservation Society, Bronx Park, Bronx, New York, NY 10460, USA. *Telephone:* (718) 220-6807 (Office). *Fax:* (718) 364-4275 (Office). *E-mail:* asiaprogram@wcs.org (Office).

SCHALLY, Andrew Victor, PhD; American medical researcher; b. 30 Nov. 1926, Wilno, Poland (now Vilnius, Lithuania); s. of Casimir Peter and Maria (Lacka) Schally; m. 1st Margaret Rachel White; one s. one d.; m. 2nd Ana Maria de Medeiros-Comaru 1976; ed Bridge of Allan, Scotland, London Univ., McGill Univ., Montreal, Canada; Asst Prof. of Physiology and Asst Prof. of Biochem., Baylor Univ. Coll. of Medicine, Houston, Tex. 1957–62; Chief, Endocrine and Polypeptide Labs., Veterans Admin. Hosp., New Orleans, La. 1962–; Sr Medical Investigator, Veterans' Admin. 1973–99, Distinguished Medical Research Scientist, Veterans' Affairs Dept 1999–; Assoc. Prof. of Medicine, Tulane Univ. School of Medicine, New Orleans, La. 1962–67, Prof. of Medicine 1967–; mem. NAS, AAAS and numerous other socs and nat. academies; more than 20 hon. degrees; decorations from Ecuador and Venezuela; Charles Mickle Award 1974, Gairdner Foundation Award 1974, Edward T. Tyler Award 1975, Borden Award in the Medical Sciences (Asscn of American Medical Colls.) 1975, Lasker Award 1975, shared Nobel Prize for Physiology or Medicine with Roger Guillemin (q.v.) for discoveries concerning peptide hormones 1977, US Govt Distinguished Service Award 1978. *Pub-*

lications: more than 2,000 scientific papers, particularly concerning hormones and cancer. *Leisure interest:* swimming, soccer. *Address:* Veterans Administration Hospital, 1601 Perdido Street, New Orleans, LA 70112 (Office); 5025 Kawanee Avenue, Metairie, LA 70006, USA (Home). *Telephone:* (504) 589-5230 (Office). *Fax:* (504) 566-1625 (Office).

SCHAMA, Simon Michael, CBE, MA; British historian and author; b. 13 Feb. 1945, London; s. of the late Arthur Schama and of Gertrude Steinberg; m. Virginia Papaioannou 1983; one s. one d.; ed Christ's Coll., Cambridge; Fellow and Dir of Studies in History, Christ's Coll., Cambridge 1966–76; Fellow and Tutor in Modern History, Brasenose Coll., Oxford 1976–80; Prof. of History (Mellon Prof. of the Social Sciences), Harvard Univ. 1980; Prof. Columbia Univ. 1997–; art critic, New Yorker 1995–; Wolfson Prize 1977, Leo Gershoy Prize (American Historical Asscn) 1978, Nat. Cash Register Book Prize for Non-Fiction (for Citizens) 1990. *Television:* Rembrandt: The Public Eye and the Private Gaze (film for BBC) 1992, A History of Britain (series) 2000–01. *Publications:* Patriots and Liberators: Revolution in the Netherlands 1780–1813 1977, Two Rothschilds and the Land of Israel 1978–79, The Embarrassment of Riches: An Interpretation of Dutch Culture in the Golden Age 1987, Citizens: A Chronicle of the French Revolution 1989, Dead Certainties (Unwarranted Speculations) 1991, Landscape and Memory 1995, Rembrandt's Eyes 1999, A History of Britain Vol. I: At the Edge of the World? 3000 BC–AD 1603 2000, Vol. II: The British Wars 1603–1776 2001, Vol. III: The Fate of the Empire 1776–2001 2002. *Leisure interests:* wine, Dutch bulbs, children's fiction. *Address:* Center for European Studies, 27 Kirkland Street, Cambridge, MA 02138; Department of History, 522 Fairweather Hall, Columbia University, New York, NY 10027, USA. *Telephone:* (617) 495-4303 (Cambridge). *Website:* www.columbia.edu (Office).

SCHANBERG, Sydney Hillel, BA; American journalist; b. 17 Jan. 1934, Clinton, Mass.; s. of Louis Schanberg and Freda (née Feinberg) Schanberg; two d.; ed Harvard Univ.; joined New York Times 1959, reporter 1960, Bureau Chief, Albany, New York 1967–69, New Delhi, India 1969–73, SE Asia Corresp., Singapore 1973–75, City Ed. 1977–80, Columnist 1981–85; Assoc. Ed., Columnist Newsday newspaper, New York 1986–; numerous awards, including Page One Award for Reporting 1972, George Polk Memorial Award 1972, Overseas Press Club Award 1972, Bob Considine Memorial Award 1975, Pulitzer Prize 1975. *Address:* Newsday Inc., 2 Park Avenue, New York, NY 10016; 164 West 79th Street, Apt. 12-D, New York, NY 10024, USA.

SCHARP, Anders; Swedish business executive; b. 8 June 1934; ed Royal Inst. of Tech. Stockholm; joined AB Electrohelios 1960 (merged with AB Electrolux 1963), Exec. Vice-Pres. (Production and Research & Devt) 1974; Pres. AB Electrolux 1981, CEO 1986; Chair. SAAB-Scania 1990–95; Chair. Saab AB 1995–; Chair., CEO AB SKF 1992–; Chair. Incentive AB 1992–98; Chair. White Consolidated Industries 1993–98, fmrly CEO; mem. Bd Swedish Asscn of Metalworking Industries, Swedish Metal Trades Employers' Asscn, Swedish Employers' Confed., AB Investor. *Address:* SAAB AB, 581 88 Linköping, Sweden.

SCHARPING, Rudolf; German politician; b. 2 Dec. 1947, Niederelbert, Westerwald; m.; three c.; ed Univ. of Bonn; joined Social Democratic Party (SPD) 1966; State Chair. and Nat. Deputy Chair. Jusos (Young Socialists) 1966; mem. State Parl. of Rhineland-Palatinate 1975; Party Leader of SPD in Rhineland-Palatinate 1985; Leader of Opposition in Rhineland-Palatinate 1987; Minister-Pres. of Rhineland-Palatinate 1991–94; mem. Bundestag (German Parl.) 1994–; Leader, SPD 1993–95, Deputy Chair. 1995–, Chair. SPD Parl. Group, Leader of the Opposition 1994; Chair. Social Democratic Party of Europe 1995–2001; Minister of Defence 1998–2002. *Address:* Bundestag, Platz der Republik, 11011 Berlin, Germany (Office). *Telephone:* (30) 22771923 (Office), (30) 22776064 (Office). *E-mail:* rudolf.scharping@bundestag.de.

SCHATZ, Gottfried, PhD; Austrian professor of biochemistry; b. 18 Aug. 1936, Strem; s. of Andreas Schatz and Anna Schatz; m. Merete Bjorn Petersen 1962; three c.; ed Univ. of Graz; Asst Prof. Univ. of Vienna 1961–64; Postdoctoral Fellow, Public Health Research Inst. City of New York 1964–66; Assoc. Prof., Prof. Cornell Univ. 1968–74; Prof. of Biochem., Univ. of Basle 1974–; Pres. Swiss Science and Tech. Council 2000–; Dr hc (Bratislava) 1996, (Stockholm) 2000; Innitzer Prize 1967, Louis Jeantet Prize 1990, Prix Benoist 1993; Gairdner Award 1998; Hansen Gold Medal 1983; Sir Hans Krebs Medal 1985; Otto Warburg Medal 1988, E. B. Wilson Medal 2000. *Publications:* about 200 scientific pubs in biochemical journals. *Leisure interests:* music, jogging. *Address:* Unterer Rebbergweg 33, 4153 Reinach, Switzerland (Home). *Telephone:* (61) 7112795 (Office). *Fax:* (61) 7112448 (Office). *E-mail:* gottfried.schatz@unibas.ch (Office).

SCHATZMAN, Evry; French research scientist; b. 16 Sept. 1920, Neuilly; s. of Benjamin Schatzman and Cécile Kahn; four c.; ed Ecole Normale Supérieure; Research Assoc. CNRS 1945, Head of Research 1948; Prof. Univ. of Paris 1954; Dir of Research, CNRS 1976–89; mem. Acad. of Sciences 1985–; Prix Holweck 1976, Médaille d'Or, CNRS 1983; Chevalier, Légion d'honneur, Officier, Ordre nat. du Mérite. *Publications:* Astrophysique générale 1957, Structure de l'Univers 1968, Science et société 1971, Les Enfants d'Uranie 1986, Le Message du photon voyageur 1987, La science menacée 1989, L'expansion de l'Univers 1989, Les étoiles 1990, L'outil théorie 1992, The Stars 1993; more than 200 research papers, mainly on physical processes in astrophysics. *Address:* Observatoire de Meudon, 92195 Meudon cedex

(Office); Institut de France, 23 quai Canti, 75006 Paris; 11 rue de l'Eglise, Dompierre, 60420 Maignelay-Montigny, France (Home). *Telephone:* 1-45-07-78-73 (Office). *E-mail:* evry.schatzman@obspm.fr (Office).

SCHAUB, Alexander, D.J.; German civil servant; b. 14 June 1941, Duisburg; s. of Franz Schaub and Gertrud Stockert; m. Nicole Van der Meulen 1974; one s. two d.; ed Univs. of Freiburg, Lausanne, Cologne and Bonn and Coll. of Europe, Bruges; with Fed. Ministry of Econ. Affairs 1971; mem. Secr. of Ralf Dahrendorf 1973; mem. Secr. and Deputy Chef de Cabinet of Guido Brunner 1974–78; Deputy Chef de Cabinet Messrs Davignon and Burke 1980, of Pres. Gaston Thorn 1981; Chef de Cabinet of Willy de Clercq 1985–89; Dir DG External Relations and Trade Policy, EC 1989–90, Deputy Dir-Gen. DG Internal Market and Industrial Affairs 1990–93, Deputy Dir-Gen. DG Industry 1993–95, Dir-Gen. DG Competition 1995–; Grosses Silbernes Ehrenzeichen mit Stern (Austria). *Publications:* Die Anhörung des Europäischen Parlaments in Rechtsetzungsverfahren der EWG 1971, Food Quality in the Internal Market of 1993 1993, Gentechnik im Lebensmittelbereich—Die Politik der EG-Kommission 1994 and numerous contribs. to legal and professional journals, articles in newspapers etc. *Leisure interests:* tennis, skiing. *Address:* European Commission, 70 rue Joseph II, 1000 Brussels, Belgium. *Telephone:* (2) 295-23-87. *Fax:* (2) 295-01-28.

SCHÄUBLE, Wolfgang, DrIur; German politician and lawyer; b. 18 Sept. 1942, Freiburg; s. of Karl Schäuble and Gertrud (née Göhring) Schäuble; m. Ingeborg Hensle 1969; one s. three d.; ed Univs. of Freiburg and Hamburg; Regional Pres., Junge Union, S. Baden 1969–72; worked in admin. of taxes, Baden-Württemberg 1971–72; mem. Bundestag 1972–, Exec. Sec. CDU/CSU Parl. Group 1981–84; mem. parl., European Council 1975–84; Chair. CDU Cttee on Sport 1976–84; Regional Vice-Pres., CDU, S. Baden 1982–95, mem. Federal Exec. Cttee CDU; Minister with special responsibility and Head of Chancellery 1984–89, of Interior 1989–91; CDU Parl. Leader 1991–2000, Leader 1998–2000; legal practice in Offenburg 1978–84; Chair. Arbeitsgemeinschaft Europäischer Grenzregionen (AGEG) 1979–82; Grosses Bundesverdienstkreuz; Commdr, Ordre nat. du Mérite. *Publication:* Mitten im Leben 2002. *Leisure interests:* chess, music. *Address:* The Bundestag, Berlin, Germany.

SCHECKTER, Jody David; South African racing driver and business executive; b. 29 Jan. 1950, East London, nr Durban; m. Pam Bailey; one s.; raced karts from age of 11, graduated to motorcycles and racing cars; won SA Formula Ford Sunshine Series in 1970, competed in Britain from 1971; Formula One World Champion 1979, runner-up 1977, third 1974 and 1976; Grand Prix wins: 1974 Swedish (Tyrrell-Ford), 1974 British (Tyrrell-Ford), 1975 South African (Tyrrell-Ford), 1976 Swedish (Tyrrell-Ford), 1977 Argentine (Wolf-Ford), 1977 Monaco (Wolf-Ford), 1977 Canadian (Wolf-Ford), 1979 Belgian (Ferrari), 1979 Monaco (Ferrari), 1979 Italian (Ferrari); retd 1980, running a business in Atlanta, Ga. *Leisure interest:* keeping fit.

SCHEEL, Walter; German politician; b. 8 July 1919, Solingen; m. 1st Eva Kronenberg 1942 (died 1966); one s.; m. 2nd Dr. Mildred Wirtz 1969 (died 1985); one s. two d.; m. 3rd Barbara Wiese 1988; ed Reform-Gymnasium, Solingen; served German Air Force, World War II; fmr head of market research org.; mem. Landtag North Rhine-Westphalia 1950–53; mem. Bundestag 1953–74, Vice-Pres. 1967–69; Fed. Minister for Econ. Co-operation 1961–66; Chair. of Free Democrats 1968–74 (Hon. Chair. 1979); Vice-Chancellor, Minister of Foreign Affairs 1969–74; Pres. FRG 1974–79; mem. European Parl. 1958–61; Pres. Bilderberg Conf. –1985; Chair. German Council of European Movt 1980–85; Chair. Bd of Trustees, Friedrich Naumann Foundation 1979–90; Chair. Admin. Council, Germanic Nat. Museum, Nuremberg 1978, Cttee European Music Year 1983–86, Supervisory Bd, DEG-German Investment and Devt Co. 1980–, Directory for Thoroughbreds and Races 1981; Pres. Europa-Union Deutschland 1980–89; mem. Supervisory Bd ROBECO Group 1982–89, Supervisory Bd Thyssen AG 1980–, Supervisory Bd Thyssen Stahl AG 1983–; Hon. Pres. German Fed. of Artists; Theodor Heuss Prize 1971, Peace Prize (Kajima Inst., Tokyo) 1973; numerous hon. degrees and awards from Germany and abroad; Gold Medal, Fondation du Mérité Européen 1984, Grosses Bundesverdienstkreuz (special class). *Publications:* Konturen einer neuen Welt 1965, Schwierigkeiten, Ernüchterung und Chancen der Industrieländer 1965, Formeln deutscher Politik 1968, Warum Mitbestimmung und wie 1970, Die Freiburger Thesen der Liberalen (with K.-H. Flach and W Maihofer) 1972, Bundestagreden 1972, Reden und Interviews 1974–79, Vom Recht des anderen—Gedanken zur Freiheit 1977, Die Zukunft der Freiheit 1979, Nach 30 Jahren; Die Bundesrepublik Deutschland, Vergangenheit, Gegenwart, Zukunft 1979, Die andere deutsche Frage 1981, Wen Schmerzt noch Deutschlands Teilung? 1986. *Leisure interest:* modern art. *Address:* Flemingstrasse 107, 81925 Munich, Germany.

SCHEELE, Sir Nicholas Vernon, Kt, KCMG, BA; British business executive; b. 3 Jan. 1944, Essex; s. of Werner James Scheele and Norah Edith Scheele (née Gough); m. Rosamund Ann Jacobs 1967; two s. one d.; ed Durham Univ.; Purchasing, Supply, Procurement Ford of Britain 1966–78; Purchasing, Supply, Procurement Man. Ford of USA 1978–83, Dir Supply Policy and Planning 1983–85, Dir Body and Chassis Parts Purchasing 1985–88; Pres. Ford of Mexico 1988–91; mem. Supervisory Bd Ford Werke AG 1999–2001; Vice-Chair. Jaguar Cars Jan.–April 1992, Chair. and CEO 1992–99; Chair. Ford of Europe –2001, Vice-Pres. for N America, Ford Motor Co. 2001, COO and Pres. 2001–; Chair. Prince of Wales Business and Environment Cttee

1999–, Mfg Theme Group, Foresight 2020 1999–; mem. of Council Midlands Region Inst. of Dirs. 1994–99, of Exec. Cttee Soc. of Motor Mfrs and Traders; mem. Advisory Bd British American Chamber of Commerce 1995–99, Fulbright Comm., Coventry Univ. 1995–, Durham Univ. 1996–; five hon. doctorates. *Leisure interests:* reading, classical music, tennis, squash. *Address:* Ford of Europe, Ford Werke AG, Henry-Ford-Strasse 1, 50725 Cologne, Germany (Office); Ford Motor Company, 1 American Road, Dearborn, MI 48126, USA.

SCHEEPBOUWER, Ad (Adrianus Johannes); Netherlands telecommunications executive; b. 22 July 1954, Dordrecht; Pres. Air Freight Div. Pakhoed Holding NV (later Pandair Group) 1976–88; Man. Dir PTT Post 1988–98; mem. Bd of Man. Royal KPN NV (fmr holding co. of PTT Post and PTT Telecom) 1992–98, Chair. and CEO TPG 1998–2001, Royal KPN 2001–. *Address:* Royal KPN, Maanplein 55, 2516 CK The Hague, Netherlands (Office). *Telephone:* (70) 4510100 (Office). *Fax:* (70) 4510101 (Office). *E-mail:* ad.scheepbouwer@kpn.com (Office). *Website:* www.kpn.com (Office).

SCHEER, François, DES; French diplomatist (retd); b. 13 March 1934, Strasbourg; s. of Alfred Scheer and Edmée Lechten; m. 2nd Nicole Roubaud 1985; one s. one d.; one s. three d. from 1st m.; ed Faculty of Law, Univ. of Paris, Inst. d'Etudes Politiques de Paris, Ecole Nat. d'Admin Second Sec. Embassy, Algiers 1962–64; Direction des Affaires Economiques et Financières, Admin. Cen. 1964–67; Cultural Attaché Embassy, Tokyo 1967–71; Deputy Dir for Budget 1971, also for Financial Affairs 1972–76; Amb. to Mozambique and Swaziland 1976–77; Deputy Perm. Rep. to European Community 1977–79, Dir of Cabinet to the Pres. of the European Parl. 1979–81; Dir of Cabinet of Minister of Foreign Affairs 1981–84; Amb. to Algeria 1984–86; Amb. and Perm. Rep. for France to the EC 1986–88; Sec.-Gen. Ministry of Foreign Affairs 1988–92; Amb. Perm. Rep. to the EC (now EU) 1992–93; Amb. to FRG 1993–99; mem. Cttee for Atomic Energy 1988–92; Admin. Cie générale des matières nucléaires (Cogema) 1989–93; mem. Conseil d'Admin. Ecole Nat. d'Admin. 1991–95; Adviser to the Pres. of Cogema 1999–2001, to the Pres. Exec. Bd of Areva 2001–; Commdr Légion d'honneur; Commdr Ordre nat. du Mérite. *Address:* 27–29 rue le Peletier, 75433 Paris cedex 09 (Office); 22, rue Bobillot, 75013 Paris, France. *Telephone:* 1-44-83-71-73 (Office); 1-45-81-35-84. *Fax:* 1-44-83-25-37 (Office); 1-45-80-76-43. *E-mail:* francois.scheer@arevagroup.com (Office).

SCHEFFCZYK, HE Cardinal Leo, DTheol; German ecclesiastic and university professor; b. 21 Feb. 1920, Beuthen; s. of Alfred A. Scheffczyk and Hedwig Koscielny; ed Humanistisches Gymnasium Beuthen, Univ. of Breslau; war service, POW 1941–45; ordained priest 1947, chaplain 1947–48; Subregens Königstein Seminary 1948–51; Lecturer in Dogmatics, Univ. of Munich 1957–59, univ. teacher 1957–59, Univ. Prof. 1965–85; prelate 1978; cr. Cardinal 2001; Consultor Pontificio Consiglio per la Famiglia 1982; mem. Pontificia Acad. Mariana Internationalis 1973, Inst. der Görresgesellschaft für Interdisziplinäre Forschung 1974, Pontificia Acad. Theologica Romana 1977, Bayerische Akad. der Wissenschaften 1980; Hon. DTheol (Pamplona) 1994. *Publications:* numerous publs on theological topics. *Address:* St-Michaelstrasse 87, 81673 Munich, Germany (Home). *Telephone:* (89) 154731. *Fax:* (89) 151978.

SCHEFFLER, Israel, PhD; American philosopher and educator; b. 25 Nov. 1923, New York; s. of Leon Scheffler and Ethel Grünberg Scheffler; m. Rosalind Zuckerbrod 1949; one s. one d.; ed Brooklyn Coll., Jewish Theological Seminary and Univ. of Pennsylvania; mem. Faculty, Harvard Univ. 1952–, Prof. of Educ. 1961–62, Prof. of Educ. and Philosophy 1962–64, Victor S. Thomas Prof. of Educ. and Philosophy 1964–92, Prof. Emer. 1992–, Hon. Research Fellow in Cognitive Studies 1965–66, Co-Dir Research Center for Philosophy of Educ. 1983–, Dir 1999–; Fellow Center for Advanced Study in Behavioral Sciences, Palo Alto, Calif. 1972–73; Guggenheim Fellow 1958–59, 1972–73; Fellow American Acad. of Arts and Sciences; fmr Pres. Philosophy of Science Asscn; Hon. AM (Harvard Univ.) 1959; Hon. DHL (Jewish Theological Seminary) 1993; Alumni Award of Merit, Brooklyn Coll. 1967, Distinguished Service Medal, Teacher's Coll., Columbia 1980. *Achievements:* Founding mem. Nat. Acad. of Educ. 1965, Mead-Swing Lecturer, Oberlin Coll. 1965, Patten Foundation Lecturer, Indiana Univ. 1981. *Publications:* Philosophy and Education 1958, The Language of Education 1960, The Anatomy of Inquiry 1963, Conditions of Knowledge 1965, Science and Subjectivity 1967, Logic and Art (co-ed.) 1972, Reason and Teaching 1973, Four Pragmatists 1974, Beyond the Letter 1979, Of Human Potential 1985, Inquiries 1986, In Praise of the Cognitive Emotions 1991, Work, Education and Leadership (co-author) 1995, Teachers of My Youth 1995, Symbolic Worlds 1997. *Leisure interests:* reading, crosswords, travel. *Address:* Harvard University, Cambridge, MA 02138, USA (Office). *Telephone:* (617) 495-3569 (Office). *Fax:* (617) 495-5908 (Office). *E-mail:* israel_scheffler@harvard.edu (Office).

SCHEIBE, Erhard A. K., Dr rer. nat; German professor of philosophy (retd); b. 24 Sept. 1927, Berlin; s. of Albert Scheibe and Maria (née Heidenreich) Scheibe; m. Maria Elgert-Eggers 1958; two s. one d.; ed Berlin and Singen High Schools, Univ. of Göttingen; Asst Max Planck Inst. of Physics, Göttingen 1956–57; Asst and Lecturer Univ. of Hamburg 1957–64; Prof. of Philosophy, Univ. of Göttingen 1964–83, Univ. of Heidelberg 1983–92; mem. Acad. of Sciences, Göttingen, Acad. of Sciences and Literature, Mainz, Int. Acad. of Philosophy of Science, Brussels. *Publications:* Die kontingenten Aussagen in der Physik 1964, The Logical Analysis of Quantum Mechanics 1973, Die Reduktion physikalischer Theorien (Vol. 1) 1997, (Vol. 2) 1999, Between

Rationalism and Empiricism – Selected Papers in the Philosophy of Physics (ed. by B. Falkenburg) 2001. *Leisure interests:* music, art, literature. *Address:* Moorbirkenkamp 2A, 22391 Hamburg, Germany. *Telephone:* (40) 5368107.

SCHEIDER, Roy; American actor; b. 10 Nov. 1932, Orange, N.J.; ed Franklin and Marshall Coll.; mem. Lincoln Center Repertory Co., American Repertory Co.; stage appearances in 1960s at McCann Theater, Princeton, Boston Fine Art Festival, American Shakespeare Festival, Arena Stadium, Washington, DC; off-Broadway appearances in Sergeant Musgrave's Dance, The Alchemist; Obie Award for Performance in Stephen D 1968; League of New York Award for Most Distinguished Stage Performance for Pinter's Betrayal 1980. *Films include:* Paper Lion, Star, Stilleto, Puzzle of a Downfall Child, Klute 1971, The French Connection 1971, The Outside Man, The Seven-Ups, Sheila Levine is Dead and Living in New York, Jaws, Marathon Man, L'Attentat, Sorcerer, Last Embrace, Jaws II 1979, All that Jazz 1979, Still of the Night, Blue Thunder, 2010, The Men's Club, 52 Pick Up, Cohen and Tate, Night Game, The Crew, The Fourth Man, The Russia House, The Naked Lunch, Romeo is Bleeding, Covert Assassin, The Rainmaker, Silver Wolf, Falling Through, Time Lapse, Daybreak. *Television appearances include:* As Short a Name, Cell Without a Number, Assignment Munich, Jacobo Timerman, Tiger Town, Somebody Has to Shoot the Pictures.

SCHELL, Jozef Stephaan, PhD; Belgian professor of genetics; b. 20 July 1935, Antwerp; m. Elizabeth Frederick 1968; two s.; Prof. Inst. of Genetics, Rijksuniversiteit Ghent 1967–95; Prof. Collège de France, Paris 1994–; Dir Max-Planck-Inst. für Züchtungsforschung, Cologne 1978; mem. numerous scientific advisory councils etc.; mem. NAS, Deutsche Akad. der Naturforscher Leopoldina, Rheinisch-Westfälisch Akad. etc.; Foreign mem. Royal Swedish Acad.; Foreign Fellow, Indian Nat. Science Acad.; Dr. hc (Univ. Louis Pasteur) 1992, (Hebrew Univ.) 1994; numerous awards and prizes including Prix Francqui 1979, Mendel Medal (Akad. Leopoldina) 1985, Otto Bayer Prize 1985, Humboldt Prize 1985, Rank Prize for Nutrition 1987, IBM Prize 1987, Wolf Prize in Agriculture 1990, Australia Prize for Agric. and Environment 1990, Charles L. Mayer Prize (French Acad.) 1990, Hansen Gold Medal 1991, Max Planck Prize 1992, Wilhelm-Exner-Médaille 1995, Japan Prize 1996. *Publications:* articles in professional journals, book chapters. *Leisure interests:* tennis, sailing.

SCHELL, Maximilian; Swiss actor; b. 8 Dec. 1930, Vienna; s. of Hermann Ferdinand Schell and Margarete Noe von Nordberg; m. Natalya Andreichenko 1985; one d.; ed Humanistisches Gymnasium, Basel, Freies Gymnasium, Zürich and Univs. of Zürich, Basel and Munich; Corporal, Swiss Army 1948–49; various appearances on stage in Switzerland and Germany 1952–55; German début in Children, Mothers and a General 1955; American film début in Young Lions 1958, on Broadway stage in Interlock 1958; Dir. Volkstheater, Munich 1981–; Critics' Award (Broadway) 1958; New York Critics' Award 1961, 1978; Golden Globe Award 1961, 1974, 1993; Acad. Award 1961, 1970, 1971, 1978, 1985; Silver Award San Sebastian 1970, 1975; German Fed. Award 1971, 1979, 1980; Film Critics' Award, Chicago 1973; Golden Cup 1974; Bavarian Film Prize 1984. *Films include:* Judgment at Nuremberg 1961, Five Finger Exercise 1961, Reluctant Saint 1962, Condemned of Altona 1962, Topkapi 1964, Return from the Ashes 1965, Beyond the Mountains 1966, The Deadly Affair 1966, Counterpoint 1966, Krakatoa, East of Java 1967, The Castle 1968, First Love 1969, Pope Joan 1971, Paulina 1880 1971, The Pedestrian 1973, The Odessa File 1974, The Man in the Glass Booth 1975, Assassination 1975, Cross of Iron 1977, Julia 1977, Avalanche Express 1978, The Black Hole 1979, The Diary of Anne Frank 1980, The Chosen 1980, Les îles 1983, Phantom of the Opera 1983, Man Under Suspicion 1983, The Assisi Underground 1984, Peter the Great (TV mini-series) 1985, The Rosegarden 1989, The Freshman, Stalin (TV) 1992, Miss Rose White (TV), Labyrinth 1994, A Far Off Place 1993, Little Odessa 1995, Through Roses 1996, Left Luggage 1997, Telling Lies in America 1997, Deep Impact 1997, Fisimatenten 1998, Joan of Arc 1998; Producer, Dir First Love 1969, Tales from the Vienna Woods 1979, Dir and wrote screenplay End of the Game 1975. *Plays include:* Hamlet, Prince of Homburg, Mannerhouse, Don Carlos, Sappho (Durrell), A Patriot for Me, The Twins of Venice, Old Times, Everyman 1978/79/80; Dir All for the Best, A Patriot for Me, Hamlet, Pygmalion, La Traviata 1975, Tales from the Vienna Woods, Nat. Theatre 1977, The Undiscovered Country, Salzburg Festival 1979/80, Der Seidene Schuh, Salzburg Festival 1985. *Address:* c/o Image Management, Lucile-Grahn-Strasse 48, 81675 Munich; c/o Erna Baumbauer, Keplerstrasse 2, 81679 Munich, Germany. *Telephone:* (89) 478577.

SCHENKER, Joseph G., MD; Israeli physician; b. 20 Nov. 1933, Cracow, Poland; s. of the late Itzhak Schenker; m. Ekaterina Idels 1959; two s.; ed Herzlia High School, Tel Aviv and the Hebrew Univ. of Jerusalem; Exec. Chief of Teaching Obstetrics and Gynaecology, Hebrew Univ. Medical School 1977–84; Chair. Dept of Obstetrics and Gynaecology, Hadassah Univ. Hosp. 1978; Prof. Obstetrics and Gynaecology, Hebrew Univ. Jerusalem 1979–; Chair. Dept of Obstetrics and Gynaecology, Hadassah Univ. Hosp., Jerusalem; Pres. Israel Soc. of Obstetrics and Gynaecology 1984–92; Pres. Israel Medical Asscn, Jerusalem br. 1984–; Chair. of Directory, Bd Examination in Obstetrics and Gynaecology, State of Israel 1979–83, of Advisory Cttee 1979–86; Acting Chair. of Hadassah Org. of Heads of Depts. 1983–; Chair. Residency Programme, Medical Council 1987, of Cttee Licensing Physicians, Ministry of Health 1987; Pres. of Int. Soc. for Study of Pathophysiology 1983; Chair. European Residency Exchange Programme, Extended European Bd of Gynaecology and Obstetrics 1993– (Pres. of Bd 1994–), Cttee for European

Examination for Excellence in Gynaecology and Obstetrics 1993–, FIGO (Int. Fed. of Gynaecology and Obstetrics) Cttee for Study of Ethical Aspects of Human Reproduction 1994–; Pres. Int. Acad. of Human Reproduction 1996–; mem. Exec. Bd FIGO 1991–; Deputy Pres. and Sec. Israeli Soc. of Obstetrics and Gynaecology 1993–; Israel Medical Council 1985–, European Asscn of Gynaecology and Obstetrics; Founder mem. European Soc. of Human Reproduction, Int. Soc. of Gynaecological Endocrinology, Int. Soc. of Study of Pathophysiology of Pregnancy and other orgs; mem. exec. bds and cttees, hon. mem. or mem. numerous int. professional orgs; Hon. Fellow American Coll. of Obstetricians and Gynaecologists, Royal Coll. of Obstetricians and Gynaecologists and other int. orgs; mem. Editorial Bd Human Reproduction (Oxford), Int. Journal of Gynaecology and Obstetrics (USA), Int. Journal of Foeto-Maternal Medicine (Germany), European Journal of Obstetrics, Gynaecology and Reproductive Biology and several other journals; Award for Outstanding Contribution to the Field of Human Reproduction 1999. *Publications:* Ed. Recent Advances in Pathophysiological Conditions in Pregnancy 1984, The Intrauterine Life-Management and Therapy 1986, Female and Male Infertility 1997, Pregnancy and Delivery 1998, Textbook of Gynecology 2000; more than 500 articles in medical journals on obstetrics and gynaecology, new tech. in reproduction, ethical and legal aspects of IVF etc. *Leisure interests:* history, chess. *Address:* Department Obital Gyneocology, Hadassah Medical Center, P.O. Box 12000, Jerusalem 91120 (Office); 5 Mendele Street, Jerusalem 91147, Israel (Home). *Telephone:* 2-6777779 (Office); 2-637775 (Home). *Fax:* 2-6432445. *E-mail:* schenker@cc.huji.ac.il (Office).

SCHEPISI, Frederic Alan; Australian film writer, director and producer; b. 1939, Melbourne; s. of Frederic Thomas Schepisi and Loretto Ellen (née Hare) Schepisi; m. 1st Joan Mary Ford 1960; two s. two d.; m. 2nd Rhonda Elizabeth Finlayson 1973 (divorced 1983); two d.; m. 3rd Mary Rubin 1984; one s.; ed Assumption Coll., Kilmore, Victoria, Marist Brothers' Juniorate, Macedon, Victoria, Marcellin Coll., Melbourne; Carden Advertising, Melbourne, Press TV Production; Paton Advisory Service, Melbourne 1961–64; Victorian Man. Cinesound Productions, Melbourne 1964–66; Man. Dir, The Film House, Melbourne 1966–79, Chair. 1979–92; Chauvel Award 1994. *Films:* A Devil's Playground (also screenplay) 1975, The Chant of Jimmie Blacksmith 1978, Barbarosa 1981, Iceman 1983, Plenty 1985, Roxanne 1986, Evil Angels (Australian Film Inst. Award for Best Film 1989) (also known as A Cry in the Dark (Longford Award 1991)) 1990, The Russia House 1990, Mr. Baseball 1991, Six Degrees of Separation 1993, IQ 1994, Fierce Creatures 1997, That Eye the Sky (exec. producer), Last Orders (also screenplay) 2001, It Runs in the Family 2002. *Leisure interests:* tennis, swimming. *Address:* P.O. Box 743, South Yarra, Vic. 3141, Australia.

SCHERAGA, Harold A., PhD; American professor of chemistry; b. 18 Oct. 1921, Brooklyn, New York; s. of Samuel Scheraga and Etta Scheraga; m. Miriam Kurnow 1943; one s. two d.; ed City Coll. of New York and Duke Univ.; ACS Postdoctoral Fellow Harvard Medical School 1946–47; Instructor of Chem. Cornell Univ. 1947–50, Asst Prof. 1950–53, Assoc. Prof. 1953–58, Prof. 1958–92, Todd Prof. 1965–92, Todd Prof. Emer. 1992–; Chair. Chem. Dept 1960–67; Guggenheim Fellow and Fulbright Research Scholar Carlsberg Lab., Copenhagen 1956–57, Weizmann Inst., Rehovoth, Israel 1963; NIH Special Fellow Weizman Inst., Rehovoth, Israel 1970; Visiting Lecturer Wool Research Labs CSIRO, Australia 1959; Visiting Prof. Weizmann Inst., Rehovoth, Israel 1972–78, Japan Soc. for the Promotion of Science 1977; Regional Dir Nat. Foundation for Cancer Research 1982–; mem. NAS, American Acad. of Arts and Sciences; Vice-Chair. Cornell Section ACS 1954–55, Chair. 1955–56, Councillor 1959–62; mem. Advisory Panel in Molecular Biology NSF 1960–62; mem. Ed. Bd numerous scientific journals; mem. Biochem. Training Cttee, NIH 1963–65, Fogarty Scholar 1984, 1986, 1988, 1989, 1990, 1991; mem. Comm. on Molecular Biophysics Int. Union for Pure and Applied Biophysics 1967–69; mem. Comm. on Macromolecular Biophysics, Int. Union for Pure and Applied Biophysics 1969–75, Pres. 1972–75; mem. Comm. on Subcellular and Macromolecular Biophysics, Int. Union for Pure and Applied Biophysics 1975–81; mem. Exec. Comm. Div. of Biological Chem. ACS 1966–69; Vice-Chair. Div. of Biological Chem. ACS 1970, Chair. 1971; mem. Council Biophysical Soc. 1967–70; mem. Research Career Award Cttee NIH 1967–71; mem. Bd of Governors Weizmann Inst., Rehovoth, Israel 1970–97; Fellow Biophysical Soc. 1999; Welch Foundation Lecturer 1962; Harvey Lecturer 1968; Gallagher Lecturer 1968–69; Lemieux Lecturer 1973; Hill Lecturer 1976; Venable Lecturer 1981, Ramachandran Lecturer 2002; Hon. life mem. New York Acad. of Sciences 1985; Hon. mem. Hungarian Biophysical Soc. 1989; Hon. ScD (Duke Univ.) 1961, (Univ. of Rochester) 1988, (Univ. of San Luis) 1992, (Technion) 1993; ACS Eli Lilly Award in Biochem. 1957, Townsend Harris Medal CCNY 1970, Nichols Medal, NY Section, ACS 1974, City Coll. Chem. Alumni Scientific Achievement Award Medal 1977, ACS Kendall Award in Colloid Chem. 1978, Linderstrøm-Lang Medal 1983, Kowalski Medal 1983, Pauling Medal, ACS 1985, Mobil Award, ACS 1990, Repligen Award, ACS 1990, Stein and Moore Award, Protein Soc. 1995, ACS Award for Computers in Chemical and Pharmaceutical Research 1997, Hirschmann Award in Peptide Chem., ACS 1999. *Publications:* Protein Structure 1961, Theory of Helix-Coil Transitions in Biopolymers 1970; 1,100 articles; research on physical chem. of proteins and other macromolecules; structure of water; chem. of blood clotting and growth factors. *Leisure interests:* golf, skiing. *Address:* 212 Homestead Terrace, Ithaca, NY 14850, USA. *Telephone:* (607) 272-5155.

SCHERER, Frederic M., PhD; American professor of economics; b. 1 Aug. 1932, Ottawa, Ill.; s. of Walter K. Scherer and Margaret Lucey Scherer; m. Barbara Silbermann 1957; one s. two d.; mem. staff Princeton Univ. 1963–66 (Visiting Lecturer 2000–03), Univ. of Mich. 1966–72, Int. Inst. of Man. 1972–74, Northwestern Univ. 1976–82, Swarthmore Coll. 1982–89; Chief Economist U.S. Fed. Trade Comm. 1974–76; Aetna Prof. of Public Policy and Corp. Man., Harvard Univ. 1989–2000, Prof. Emer. 2000–; Co-Founder European Asscn for Research in Industrial Econs; pioneering work on theory of research and Devt strategy and timing; Lanchester Prize, Operations Research Soc. of America 1964, O'Melveny & Myers Centennial Research Prize 1989, Distinguished Fellow, Industrial Org. Soc. 1999, Antitrust Achievement Award, American Antitrust Inst. 2002. *Publications:* The Weapons Acquisition Process: Economic Incentives 1964, Industrial Market Structure and Economic Performance 1970, Innovation and Growth: Schumpeterian Perspectives 1984, Industry Structure, Strategy and Public Policy 1996, Quarter Notes and Bank Notes: The Economics of Music Composition in the 18th and 19th Centuries 2003. *Leisure interest:* 17th–19th century music. *Address:* 601 Rockbourne Mills Court, Wallingford, PA 19086, USA (Home). *Telephone:* (610) 872-2557 (Office and Home). *Fax:* (610) 872-2557. *E-mail:* -fmscherer@comcast.net (Office).

SCHERER, Peter Julian; New Zealand journalist; b. 15 Aug. 1937, Stratford; s. of Arnold F. Scherer and Constance M. White; m. Gaelyn P. Morgan 1964; one s. one d.; ed Browns Bay School and Takapuna Grammar School; joined New Zealand Herald 1955; mem. later Chief, Wellington Bureau 1960–71; Chair. Parl. Press Gallery 1965; leader-writer, Duty Ed., Business News Ed. 1973–76, Editorial Man. 1977–83, Asst Ed. 1977–85; Ed. New Zealand Herald 1985–96; Dir Community Newspapers Ltd 1972–73, Wilson & Horton Group 1989–96, NZ Press Asscn 1991–96; Chair. NZ Associated Press 1985–90, NZ section, Commonwealth Press Union (CPU) 1989–94; Chair. Planning Cttee., North Health Medical Workforce 1996–97; Councillor, CPU, London 1989–94; mem. NZ Press Council 1988–97, Communications and Media Law Asscn 1990–97; mem. Communications Advisory Council NZ Comm. for UNESCO 1989–94; mem. Bd of Control, Newspaper Publishers Asscn of NZ 1991–96; mem. NZ Nat. Cttee for Security Co-operation in Asia-Pacific 1994–96, NZ Div., Inst. of Dirs. 1989–96; other professional appts.; CPU Fellowship 1963; Cowan Prize 1959. *Leisure interests:* reading, tennis, gardening, fishing, golf. *Address:* Apartment C, 25 Ring Terrace, St Mary's Bay, Auckland 1001; 267 School Road, Tomarata, RD4 Wellsford 1242, New Zealand. *Telephone:* (9) 378-9184 (Auckland); (9) 431-5244 (Wellsford). *Fax:* (9) 431-5244 (Wellsford); (9) 378-9184 (Auckland). *E-mail:* gandpscherer@xtra.co.nz (Home).

SCHERMERS, Henry G., LLD; Netherlands professor of law; b. 27 Sept. 1928, Epe; s. of Petrus Schermers and Amelia M. Schermers Gooszen; m. Hotsche AC Tans 1957; one s. two d.; mil. service 1948–50; Int. Org. Dept, Ministry of Foreign Affairs 1953–56, Office of Legal Adviser 1956–63; Prof. of Law, Univ. of Amsterdam 1963–78, Univ. of Leiden 1978–; Dir Int. Course in European Integration 1965–81; Pres. Acad. Council Asser Inst., The Hague 1977–90; Ed. Common Market Law Review 1978–93; Visiting Prof. Univ. of Mich. 1968–69, 1994, Queen Mary Coll., London 1988; Dean Leiden Law School 1985–87; Jacques Delors Prof. of European Community Law, Univ. of Oxford 1996–97; mem. European Comm. of Human Rights 1981–96; mem. Inst. of Int. Law; Corresp. Fellow British Acad.; Commdr Order of Orange-Nassau; Kt Order of the Netherlands Lion, Officer, Crown of Belgium, Officier, Ordres des Palmes Académiques (France); Dr hc (Edinburgh, Osnabrück). *Publications:* International Institutional Law 1972, Judicial Protection in the European Communities 1976; articles collected in Opera Patris (7 vols) (3rd edn) 1995. *Leisure interests:* sports, youth, carpentry. *Address:* Hugo de Grootstraat 27, Leiden (Office); Schouwenhove 226, 2332 DV Leiden, Netherlands (Home). *Telephone:* (71) 5277746 (Office); (71) 5124294 (Home).

SCHERPENHUIJSEN ROM, Willem; Netherlands banker; b. 1936; fmr Chair. NMB Postbank; Chair. International Nederlande (formed by merger of NMB Postbank and Internationale Nederlande Groep in 1991) 1992–94. *Address:* c/o ING Bank NV, P.O. Box 1800, 1000 BV Amsterdam, Netherlands.

SCHEUCH, Erwin K., Dr rer. pol; German sociologist; b. 9 June 1928, Cologne; s. of Otto Wilhelm Scheuch and Cecilie Bauschert; m. Dr Ute Pulm 1985; two s.; ed Univ. of Conn., USA, Univs. of Frankfurt and Cologne; Research Asst UNESCO Inst. for Social Research, Cologne 1951–53, Inst. for Social Research, Univ. of Cologne 1953–58; Instructor Univ. of Cologne 1961; Lecturer in Social Relations, Harvard Univ. 1962–64; Prof. of Sociology, Univ. of Cologne 1965–93, Prof. Emer. 1993–; Visiting Prof. of Sociology, Berlin 1965, Inst. for Advanced Studies, Princeton 1973–74, Auckland Univ. 1977, Univ. of Penn. 1975, Collège de l'Europe, Bruges 1977, Stockholm Univ. 1979, Paris 1981, Canton 1996, Harbin 1996; Dir Cen. Archive for Empirical Social Research 1964–93, Inst. of Applied Social Research 1965–93 (Pres.); Chair. Kölner Gesellschaft für Sozialforschung 1990–, Pres. 2000–; Pres. Deutsche Gesellschaft für Kommunikationsforschung; Past Pres. Inst. Int. de Sociology; mem. Int. Acad. for Tourism Research, Academia Scientarium et Artium Europaea, PEN; Counsellor to Nestlé, The Social Affairs Unit (London), Visions in Leisure; Rockefeller Foundation Fellow, Columbia Univ., Univ. of Mich., Univ of Calif., Berkeley, Univ. of Chicago 1959–60; Bundesverdienstkreuz (First Class); Zeitschrift Liberal 1967, Gracian Kulturpreis 2001. *Publications:* Soziologie der Wahl 1965, Wiedertäufer der Wohlstandsgesellschaft 1969, Die alte Rechte und die Neue Linke 1970, Haschisch und LSD als Modedrogen 1973, Grundbegriffe der Soziologie (2nd Edn) 1975, Kulturintelligenz als Machtfaktor 1976, Wird die Bundesrepublik unregierbar? 1976, Das Forschungsinstitut 1978, Historical Social Research 1979, Datenzugang und Datenschutz 1981, Gesundheitspolitik zwischen Staat und Selbstverwaltung 1982, Empirische Sozialforschung in der modernen Gesellschaft 1983, Zwischen Wohlstand und Bankrott 1984, (with Ute Scheuch) China und Indien 1987 (with Gräf and Kühnel), Volkszählung, Volkszählungsprotest u. Bürgerverhalten 1989, Wie Deutsch Sind die Deutschen? (with Ute Scheuch) 1991, Perspectives des sciences sociales en Allemagne aujourd'hui 1991, Muss Sozialismus misslingen? 1991, Cliquen, Klüngel und Karrieren (with Ute Scheuch) 1992, Empirische Sozialforschung über Entwicklungsländer 1992, USA—ein maroder Gigant? Amerika besser verstehen (with Ute Scheuch) 1992, Bürokraten auf den Chefetagen (with Ute Scheuch) 1995, Quantitative Social Research in Germany and Japan (with Ch. Hayashi) 1996, Die neuen Inquisitoren (with G. Besier) 1999, Die Spendenaffäre. Parteien ausser Kontrolle (with Ute Scheuch) 2000, The Annals of the International Institute of Sociology. Societies, Corporations and the Nation State (with David Sciulli) 2000, Deutsche Pleiten (with Ute Scheuch) 2001/03, Manager im Großenwahn (with Ute Scheuch) 2003, Sozialer Wandel 2003. *Leisure interests:* modern literature, jazz, tennis. *Address:* Kölner Gesellschaft für Sozialforschung e.V., Liliencronstr. 6, 50931 Cologne-Lindenthal (Office); Hauptstr. 39C, 51143 Cologne, Germany (Home). *Telephone:* (221) 47694-62 (Office); (2203) 87638 (Home). *Fax:* (221) 47694-98 (Office); (2203) 87753 (Home). *E-mail:* scheuch@za.uni-koeln.de (Office); scheuch.partner@t-online.de (Home). *Website:* www.gesis.org/za (Office).

SCHEVILL, James E., BS; American professor of English, poet and playwright; b. 10 June 1920, Berkeley, Calif.; s. of Rudolph Schevill and Margaret Erwin Schevill; m. 1st Helen Shaner 1942; two d.; m. 2nd Margot Blum 1966; ed Harvard and Brown Univs.; with US Army 1942–46, rank of Capt.; teacher, Calif. Coll. of Arts and Crafts 1951–58, Pres. of Faculty Ass. 1956; San Francisco State Univ. 1959–68, Prof. of English 1968; Prof. of English, Brown Univ. 1969–85, Prof. Emer. 1985–; Pres. Rhode Island Playwrights' Theatre 1984; Co-Dir, Dir Creative Writing Program, Brown Univ. 1972–75; Dir The Poetry Centre, San Francisco State Univ. 1961–68; adaptor and translator (with A. Hall) of Bertolt Brecht's Galileo 1983; mem. Bd Trinity Square Repertory Co., Providence, Rhode Island 1975–82; Hon. MA (Browns) 1970; Hon. LHD (Rhode Island Coll.) 1986; numerous awards including Ford Foundation Grant in Theatre to work with Joan Littlewood's Theatre Workshop in London 1960–61, William Carlos Williams Award for The Stalingrad Elegies 1965, Guggenheim Fellowship in Poetry 1981, McKnight Fellowship in Playwriting 1984, Literary Award for Plays, American Acad. of Arts and Letters, New York 1991. *Plays:* High Sinners, Low Angels 1953, The Bloody Tenet 1957, Voices of Mass and Capital A 1962, The Black President and Other Plays 1965, Lovecraft's Follies 1969, Cathedral of Ice 1975, Wastepaper Theatre Anthology (co-ed) 1978, Collected Short Plays 1986, Oppenheimer's Chair 1985, Time of the Hand and the Eye 1986, Shadows of Memory 1989, Mother O or the Last American Mother 1990, The Garden on F Street (with Mary Gail) 1992, The Phantom of Life: A Melville Play 1993, 5 Plays 5 (collection of plays) 1993, Myth of the Docile Woman 1997, To Die Well 1999, Emperor Norton of the USA (opera libretto) 1999, With the Composer, Jerome Rosen. *Publications:* poetry: Tensions 1947, The American Fantasies 1951, The Right To Greet 1955, Selected Poems 1945–59 1959, Private Dooms and Public Destinations: Poems 1945–62 1962, The Stalingrad Elegies 1964, Release 1968, Violence and Glory: Poems 1962–68 1969, The Buddhist Car and Other Characters 1973, Pursuing Elegy 1974, The Mayan Poems 1978, Fire of Eyes: A Guatemalan Sequence 1979, The American Fantasies: Collected Poems 1945–81 1983, Performance Poems 1984, The Invisible Volcano 1985, Collected Poems, Vol. II, 1945–1986, Ambiguous Dancers of Fame 1987, Winter Channels 1994, The Complete American Fantasies 1996, New and Selected Poems 2000. *Other publications:* Sherwood Anderson: His Life and Work (biog.) 1951, The Roaring Market and the Silent Tomb (biog.) 1956, The Cid (trans.) 1961, Breakout: In Search of New Theatrical Environments 1973, The Arena of Ants (novel) 1976, Six Historians by Ferdinand Schevill (ed.) 1956, numerous readings 1960–, Bern Porter (A Personal Biography) 1993. *Address:* 1309 Oxford Street, Berkeley, CA 94709, USA (Home). *Telephone:* (510) 845-2802 (Home).

SCHICKEL, Richard, BS; American writer; b. 10 Feb. 1933, Milwaukee; s. of Edward J. Schickel and Helen (née Hendricks) Schickel; two d.; ed Univ. of Wisconsin; Ed. Look Magazine 1957–60, Show Magazine 1960–63; self-employed 1963–; Film Critic Life Magazine 1965–72, Time Magazine 1973–; Pres. Lorac Productions 1986–; Consultant Rockefeller Foundation 1965; Lecturer in History of Art, Yale Univ. 1972, 1976; Guggenheim Fellow 1964; mem. Nat. Soc. of Film Critics, NY Film Critics. *Publications:* The World of Carnegie Hall 1960, The Stars 1962, Movies: The History of an Art and an Institution 1964, The Gentle Knight 1964, The Disney Version 1968, The World of Goya 1968, Second Sight: Notes on Some Movies 1972, His Pictures in the Papers 1974, Harold Lloyd: The Shape of Laughter 1974, The Men Who Made the Movies 1975, The World of Tennis 1975, The Fairbanks Album 1975, Another I, Another You 1978, Singled Out 1981, Cary Grant: A Celebration 1984, D.W. Griffith: An American Life 1984, Intimate Strangers: The Culture of Celebrity 1985, James Cagney, A Celebration 1985, Striking Poses 1987, Schickel on Film 1989, Brando: A Life in Our Times 1991, Double Indemnity 1992; Co-Ed. Film 1967–68; Producer, Dir, Writer: (TV Specials) The Man Who Made the Movies 1973, Funny Business 1978, Into the Morning: Willa Cather's America 1978, The Horror Show 1979, James Cagney: That Yankee

Doodle Dandy 1981, From Star Wars to Jedi: The Making of a Saga 1983, Minnelli on Minnelli: Liza Remembers Vincent 1987, Gary Cooper: American Life, American Legend 1989, Myrna Loy: So Nice to Come Home To 1990, Barbara Stanwyck: Fire and Desire 1991, Eastwood & Co: Making Unforgiven 1992, Hollywood on Hollywood 1993, Elia Kazan: A Director's Journey 1995, Clint Eastwood: A Biography 1996, The Moviemakers 1996, Eastwood on Eastwood 1997, The Harryhausen Chronicles 1998, Matinee Idols: Reflections on the Movies 1999; Producer, Writer: TV Life Goes to the Movies 1976, SPFX 1980, Cary Grant, A Celebration 1989.

SCHIEFFER, Bob, BA; American broadcaster; b. Austin, Tex.; m. Patricia Penrose; two d.; ed Texas Christian Univ.; reporter Fort Worth Star-Telegram; news anchorman WBAP-TV, Dallas, with CBS 1969–, Pentagon Corresp. 1970–74, White House Corresp. 1974–79, Chief Washington Corresp. 1982–, anchorman CBS Sunday Night News 1973–74, Sunday Ed. CBS Evening News, then Sun. Ed. 1976–; now Moderator Face the Nation, CBS News; co-anchorman CBS Morning News 1985–, anchors Face the Nation, CBS News 1991–; participant CBS special reports including Peace and the Pentagon 1974, Watergate: The White House Transcripts 1974, The Mysterious Alert 1974, Ground Zero 1981; various awards. *Publication:* The Acting President (with Gary P. Gates) 1989. *Address:* c/o Face the Nation, CBS News, 2020 M Street, NW, Washington, DC 20036; c/o CBS News Weekend/Sunday News, 524 W 57th Street, New York, NY 10019, USA.

SCHIEFFER, Rudolf; German professor of history; b. 31 Jan. 1947, Mainz; s. of Theodor Schieffer and Annelise Schreibmayr; Research Assoc. DFG project, Spätantike Reichskonzilien 1971–75; Research Assoc. Monumenta Germaniae Historica, Munich 1975–80; Prof. of Medieval and Modern History, Univ. of Bonn 1980–94; Prof. of Medieval History, Univ. of Munich; Pres. Monumenta Germaniae Historica, Munich 1994–; Corresp. mem. Nordrhein-Westfäl. Acad. of Sciences, Austrian Acad.; mem. Bavarian Acad.; Corresp. Fellow Royal Historical Soc., Medieval Acad. of America. *Publications:* Die Entstehung von Domkapiteln in Deutschland 1976, Hinkmar v. Reims, De ordine palatii (with T. Gross) 1980, Die Entstehung des päpstlichen Investiturverbots für den deutschen König 1981, Die Karolinger 1992, Die Streitschriften Hinkmars v. Reims und Kinkmars v. Laon 2003. *Address:* Monumenta Germaniae Historica, Postfach 340223, 80099 Munich, Germany. *Telephone:* (89) 286382383. *Fax:* (89) 281419. *E-mail:* rudolf.schieffer@mgh.de.

SCHIFF, Andras; Hungarian concert pianist; b. 21 Dec. 1953, Budapest; s. of Odon Schiff and Klara Schiff (Csengeri); m. Yuuko Shiokawa 1987; ed Franz Liszt Acad. of Music, Budapest, with Prof. Pal Kadosa Gyorgy Kurtag and Ferenc Rados and privately with George Malcolm; recitals in London, New York, Paris, Vienna, Munich, Florence; concerts with New York Philharmonic, Chicago Symphony, Vienna Philharmonic, Concertgebouw, Orchestre de Paris, London Philharmonic, London Symphony, Philharmonia, Royal Philharmonic, Israel Philharmonic, Philadelphia, Washington Nat. Symphony; played at Salzburg, Edinburgh, Aldeburgh, Feldkirch Schubertiade, Lucerne and Tanglewood Festivals; recordings include Bach Goldberg Variations, Bach Partitas, Bach Piano Concertos, Mendelssohn Concertos 1 and 2, all the Schubert Sonatas, Schubert Trout Quintet, Schumann and Chopin 2, all the Mozart Concertos, Bach Two- and Three-part Inventions, Bach Well-Tempered Clavier, Beethoven Violin and Piano Sonatas with Sandor Vegh, Beethoven Piano Concertos, Bartok Piano Concertos, Tchaikovsky Piano Concerto, Bach English Suites, Bach French Suites, Lieder with Peter Schreier (q.v.), Robert Holl and Cecilia Bartoli, etc.; f. Musiktage Mondsee Festival 1989 (Artistic Dir 1989–98); f. own orchestra Cappella Andrea Barca 1999; Prizewinner at 1974 Tchaikovsky Competition in Moscow and Leeds Piano Competition 1975, Liszt Prize 1977, Premio della Accad. Chigiana, Siena 1987, Wiener Flotenuhr 1989, Bartok Prize 1991, Instrumentalist of the Year 1993, Royal Philharmonic Soc.'s Instrumentalist of the Year 1994, Claudio Arrau Memorial Medal 1994, Kossuth Prize 1996, Soning Prize (Copenhagen 1997). *Television:* The Wanderer – A Film About Schubert with Andras Schiff (BBC Omnibus, narrator), Chopin with Andras Schiff (BBC Omnibus, narrator). *Leisure interests:* literature, languages, soccer, theatre, cinema, art. *Address:* c/o Terry Harrison Artists Management, The Orchard, Market Street, Charlbury, Oxon., OX7 3PJ, England. *Telephone:* (1608) 810330. *Fax:* (1608) 811331. *E-mail:* artists@terryharrison.force9.co.uk (Office). *Website:* www.terryharrison.force9.co.uk (Office).

SCHIFF, Heinrich; Austrian cellist and conductor; b. 18 Nov. 1951, Gruunden; studied cello in Vienna with Tobias Kühne and André Navarra; London and Vienna debuts 1973; subsequently undertook extensive concert tours in Europe, Japan and USA appearing with maj. orchestras; interpreter of contemporary music including work of Lutosławski, Henze, Krenek and Penderecki and has given first performances of many new works; Artistic Dir Northern Sinfonia 1990–91; Prin. Guest Conductor, Deutsche Kammerphilharmonie 1990–92; Prin. Conductor, Musikkollegium, Winterthur and Copenhagen Philharmonic Orchestra 1995–; guest conductor of many int. orchestras. *Address:* Künstlersekretariat Astrid Schoerke, Mönckebergallee 41, 30453 Hannover, Germany. *Telephone:* (511) 401048. *Fax:* (511) 407435.

SCHIFFER, Claudia; German fmr fashion model; b. 25 Aug. 1970, Düsseldorf; m. Matthew Vaughn 2002; one s.; fashion model for Karl Lagerfeld 1990, model for Revlon 1992–96, Chanel –1997; has appeared on numerous covers for magazines and journals; designs calendars; appears on TV specials; has share in Fashion Café, New York 1995–; announced retirement from model-

ling 1998; mem. US Cttee UNICEF 1995–98. *Films include:* Richie Rich 1994, Pret-a-Porter 1994, The Blackout 1997, And She Was 1999, Friends and Lovers 1999, Black and White 2000, Chain of Fools 2000. *Publication:* Memories 1995.

SCHIFFRIN, Andre, MA; American publisher; b. 12 June 1935, Paris; s. of Jacques Schiffrin and Simone Heymann; m. Maria Elena de la Iglesia 1961; two d.; ed Yale Univ. and Univ. of Cambridge; with New American Library 1959–63; with Pantheon Books, New York 1962–90, Ed., Ed.-in-Chief, Man. Dir 1969–90; Publr Schocken Books (subsidiary of Pantheon Books Inc.) 1987–90; Pres. Fund for Ind. Publishing 1990–; Dir, Ed.-in-Chief The New Press, New York City 1990–; Visiting Fellow, Davenport Coll. 1977–79; Visiting Lecturer, Yale Univ. 1977, 1979; mem. Council Smithsonian Inst.; mem. Bd of Dirs. New York Council for Humanities; mem. Special Cttee American Centre, Paris 1994–; mem. Visting Cttee of Grad. Faculty The New York School 1995–; other professional appts. and affiliations; Hon. Fellow, Trumbull Coll. Yale Univ. *Publications:* L'Edition sans Editeurs 1999, The Business of Books 2000; contribs. to professional journals. *Address:* The New Press, 450 West 41st Street, New York, NY 10036 (Office); 250 West 94th Street, New York, NY 10025, USA (Home).

SCHIFRES, Michel Maurice René; French journalist; b. 1 May 1946, Orléans; s. of Jacques Schifres and Paulette Mauduit; m. Josiane Gasnier (divorced); two c.; ed Lycée du Mans, Lycée de Caen, Faculté des Lettres de Caen, Centre de Formation des Journalistes; journalist with Combat 1970–72, with Monde 1972–74; Head of Political Affairs Quotidien de Paris 1974–76; Asst Head of Political Affairs France-Soir 1976; Head of Political Affairs Journal du Dimanche 1977, Editorial Dir 1985–89; mem. Comm. on quality of radio and TV broadcasts 1977–79; Editorial Dir France-Soir 1989–92, Asst Dir-Gen.; Asst Editorial Dir Figaro 1992–98, Man. Ed. 1998–2000, Vice-Pres. Editorial Cttee 2000–; Chevalier, ordre nat. du Mérite. *Publications include:* La CFDT des militants 1972, D'une France à l'autre 1974, L'enaklatura 1987, L'Elysée de Mitterrand 1987, Villes de Chiens 1988, Un siècle d'écrivains: Jules Romains 1998 (TV), La désertion des énarques 1999. *Leisure interest:* antiques. *Address:* Le Figaro, 37 rue du Louvre, 75002, Paris (Office); 150 avenue Emile Zola, 75015 Paris, France (Home). *Telephone:* 1-42-21-29-73 (Office); 1-40-58-16-64 (Home). *Fax:* 1-42-21-63-82 (Office).

SCHILY, Otto; German politician and lawyer; b. 20 July 1932, Bochum; s. of Franz Schily; m. (divorced); two c.; ed Munich, Hamburg and Berlin Univs; mem. Bundestag 1983–86, 1987–89, 1990–, SPD 1990–; Deputy Chair. SPD 1994–; Minister of the Interior 1998–; mem. Presidium Neue Gesellschaft für bildende Kunst; Adviser, Humanist Union. *Address:* Ministry of the Interior, 10559 Berlin, Alt-Moabit 101 (Office); Oberanger 38, 80331 Munich, Germany. *Telephone:* (1888) 5810 (Office). *Fax:* (1888) 6815522 (Office). *E-mail:* poststelle@bmi.bund400.de (Office). *Website:* www.bmi.bund.de (Office).

SCHIMBERNI, Mario, BEcons; Italian industrial executive; b. 10 March 1923, Rome; s. of Tommaso Schimberni and Lina Ludovici; m. Angela Peppicelli; ed Rome Univ.; Lecturer in Industrial and Commercial Techniques, Rome Univ. 1946–54; various admin., financial and managerial posts with Bomprini Parodi Delfino 1954–64, Gen. Man. 1964–70, SNIA Viscosa 1970–72, Man. Dir 1972–75; Pres. Montefibre 1975–77; Deputy Chair. Montedison 1977–80, Chair. 1980–87; Chair. CEFIC 1982–84, META 1984–88, Erbamont 1983–88, Ausimont 1985–88; Deputy Chair. Himont 1983–88, Confindustria 1983–88; Special Commr Nat. Railway Authority 1988; Chair. Fincentro 1988–, Armando Curcio Ed. 1988.

SCHINZLER, Hans-Jürgen, DJur; German insurance executive; b. 12 Oct. 1940, Madrid, Spain; mem. Admin. Bd Municher Rückversicherungsgesellschaft, Munich, Chair. Bd 1993–; Deputy Chair. Allgemeine Kreditversicherung AG, Mainz, Allianzversicherung AG, Munich; Chair. Supervisory Bd ERGO Versicherungsgruppe AG, MR Beteiligungen AG; mem. Supervisory Bd Dresdner Bank AG, Hoechst AG. *Address:* Königinstrasse 107, 80802 Munich, Germany. *Telephone:* (89) 38913534.

SCHIRNER, Jochen; German business executive; b. 27 Feb. 1939, Berlin; s. of Karl Schirner and Inge Schirner; m. Marietheres Schirner 1962; two s. one d.; ed Univs. of Munich and Cologne; joined Rheinische Blattmetall AG (now VAW-Leichtmetall GmbH) 1963–, Head Business Man. Dept 1969, Dir 1974, Chair. Bd of Dirs 1986–98; mem. Bd Dirs of numerous cos. *Address:* Kiefernweg 16, 53639 Königswinter, Germany (Home).

SCHIRO, James J.; American business executive; m. Tomasina Schiro; two. c.; ed St John's Univ., Dartmouth Coll.; joined Price Waterhouse 1967, Chair. Mining Special Services Group 1979–88, Nat. Dir Mergers and Acquisitions Services 1988–91, Vice-Chair. and Man. Partner for New York Metropolitan Region 1991; apptd. to Council of Partners 1990, to Gen. Council 1992, Deputy Chair. World Exec. Group and World Bd 1993–, Chair. and Sr Partner Price Waterhouse 1995, CEO 1997; CEO Pricewaterhouse Coopers 1998–2001; COO Group Finance Zurich Financial Services; Treas. and mem. Exec. Cttee U.S. Council for Int. Business, mem. council World Econ. Forum; mem. British-North American Cttee, mem. Italian-American Foundation; Ellis Island Medal of Honor 1994, St John's Univ. Alumni Pietas Medal 1992, Avenue of the Americas Asscn's Gold Key Award 1992. *Address:* Zurich Financial Services, Media and Public Relations, 8022 Zurich, Switzerland (Office). *Telephone:* (1) 6252100 (Office). *Fax:* (1) 6252641 (Office). *Website:* www.zurich.com (Office).

SCHLAGMAN, Richard Edward, FRSA; British publisher; b. 11 Nov. 1953; s. of Jack Schlagman and the late Shirley Schlagman (née Goldston); ed Univ. Coll. School, Hampstead, Brunel Univ.; Co-Founder, Jt Chair., Man. Dir Interstate Electronics Ltd 1973–86; purchased Bush from Rank Org., renamed IEL Bush Radio Ltd 1981, floated on London Stock Exchange 1984, sold as Bush Radio PLC 1986; acquired Phaidon Press Ltd 1990, Chair. and Publr 1990–; mem. Exec. Cttee Patrons of New Art, Tate Gallery 1994–97, Royal Opera House Trust, Glyndebourne Festival Soc., Designers and Arts Dirs. Asscn of UK; patron Bayreuth, Salzburger Festspiele; Pres. Judd Foundation, MARFA, Texas 1999–. *Leisure interests:* music, art, architecture. *Address:* Phaidon Press Limited, Regent's Wharf, All Saints Street, London, N1 9PA, England. *Telephone:* (20) 7843-1100. *Fax:* (20) 7843-1212. *E-mail:* rschlagman@phaidon.com (Office).

SCHLESINGER, Arthur, Jr, AB; American writer and educator; b. 15 Oct. 1917, Columbus, Ohio; s. of the late Arthur Meier and Elizabeth Bancroft Schlesinger; m. 1st Marian Cannon 1940 (divorced 1970); two s. two d.; m. 2nd Alexandra Emmet 1971; one s.; ed Phillips Exeter Acad., Harvard Univ. and Peterhouse, Cambridge, England; Soc. of Fellows Harvard 1939–42; with Office of War Information 1942–43; Office of Strategic Services 1943–45; U.S. Army 1945; Assoc. Prof. of History, Harvard Univ. 1946–54, Prof. 1954–61; Special Asst to Pres. of USA 1961–64; Schweitzer Prof. of the Humanities, City Univ. of New York 1966–94; Consultant, Econ. Co-operation Admin. 1948, Mutual Security Admin. 1951–52; mem. Adlai Stevenson campaign staff 1952 and 1956; mem. American Historical Asscn, American Inst. of Arts and Letters (Pres. 1981–84, Chancellor 1984–87), Jury Cannes Film Festival 1964; Commdr Order of Orange-Nassau (Netherlands), Orden del Libertador (Venezuela), Order of St Michael and St George (UK) 2001; numerous hon. doctorates including Hon. DLitt (Oxon.) 1987; Hon. LLD (Harvard) 2001; Parkman Prize 1957, Pulitzer Prize for History 1946, for Biography 1966, Nat. Book Award 1966, Gold Medal, Nat. Inst. of Arts and Letters 1967, Fregene Prize for Literature 1983, U Thant Award for Int. Understanding 1998, Nat. Humanities Medal 1998. *Publications:* Orestes A. Brownson: A Pilgrim's Progress 1939, The Age of Jackson 1945, The Vital Center (English title The Politics of Freedom) 1949, The General and the President (with R. H. Rovere) 1951, The Age of Roosevelt: Vol. I The Crisis of the Old Order 1957, Vol. II The Coming of the New Deal 1958, Vol. III The Politics of Upheaval 1960, Kennedy or Nixon 1960, The Politics of Hope 1963, Paths of American Thought (ed. with Morton White) 1963, A Thousand Days: John F. Kennedy in the White House 1965, The Bitter Heritage: Vietnam and American Democracy 1941–1966 1967, The Crisis of Confidence 1969, History of American Presidential Elections (ed. with F. L. Israel) 1971, The Imperial Presidency 1973, Robert Kennedy and His Times 1978, Cycles of American History 1986, The Disuniting of America 1991, Running for President (ed.) 1994, A Life in the 20th Century: I. Innocent Beginnings 2000; articles in various magazines and newspapers. *Leisure interests:* tennis, movies, opera. *Address:* 455 E 51st Street, New York, NY 10022, USA (Office). *Telephone:* (212) 751-6898. *Fax:* (212) 688-8399 (Office).

SCHLESINGER, John Richard, CBE, FBA; British film and theatre director; b. 16 Feb. 1926, London; s. of Dr Bernard Schlesinger, OBE, FRCP and Winifred Henrietta Regensburg; ed Uppingham School and Balliol Coll., Oxford; early career as actor on TV and in films Singlehanded, Battle of the River Plate, Brothers in Law and numerous others; directed shorts for Tonight and Monitor (BBC); made films for BBC TV including part of The Valiant Years; joined Sapphire Films for Four Just Men; Assoc. Dir Nat. Theatre 1973–88; Shakespeare Prize (FVS Found., Hamburg) 1981. *Major films:* Terminus 1961 (Venice Golden Lion), A Kind of Loving 1962 (Berlin Golden Bear), Billy Liar 1963, Darling 1965 (New York Film Critics' Award), Far From the Madding Crowd 1967, Midnight Cowboy 1968 (Dir Guild of America Award, Acad. Award for Best Dir and British Film Acad. Award), Sunday Bloody Sunday 1970 (David Donatello Award, British Film Acad. Award), Olympic Marathon in Visions of Eight 1973, The Day of the Locust 1974, Marathon Man 1976, Yanks 1978, Honky Tonk Freeway 1980, The Falcon and the Snowman 1985, The Believers 1986, Madame Sousatzka 1988, Pacific Heights 1990, The Innocent 1992, Cold Comfort Farm 1994, Eye for an Eye 1995, Sweeney Todd 1997, The Next Best Thing 2000. *Plays and television drama:* No Why (John Whiting), Aldwych Theatre 1964, Timon of Athens, Royal Shakespeare Theatre, Stratford 1965, Days in the Trees, Aldwych 1966, I and Albert, Piccadilly Theatre 1972, Heartbreak House, Nat. Theatre 1975, Julius Caesar, Nat. Theatre 1977, True West, Nat. Theatre 1980, Separate Tables (for TV) 1982, An Englishman Abroad (BBC) 1983 (British Acad. Award, Barcelona Film Festival and Broadcasting Press Guild Award), A Question of Attribution (BBC TV) (British Acad. Award) 1991, Cold Comfort Farm (BBC TV) 1994, Sweeney Todd 1997. *Operas directed:* Les Contes d'Hoffmann, Royal Opera House, Covent Garden (Soc. of West End Theatres Award 1980), Der Rosenkavalier, Covent Garden 1984, Un Ballo in Maschera, Salzburg Festival 1989, Peter Grimes, La Scala, Milan and LA Opera 2000. *Leisure interests:* gardening, travel, music, antiques. *Address:* c/o Duncan Heath, ICM, Oxford House, 76 Oxford Street, London, W1R 1RB, England. *Telephone:* (20) 7636-6565.

SCHLINK, Bernhard, PhD, JD; German judge, professor of law and author; b. 1944, Bethel, nr Bielefeld; s. of the late Prof. Edmund Schlink; m. Hadwig Arnold (divorced); one s.; ed Free Univ., West Berlin, Heidelberg, Darmstadt and Bielefeld Univs.; Prof. of Constitutional and Admin. Law, Bonn Univ. 1981–91; Judge, Constitutional Law Court of North Rhein-Westphalia,

Munster 1987–; Prof., Wolfgang Goethe Univ., Frankfurt 1991–92; Prof. of Public Law and Legal Philosophy, Humboldt Univ., Berlin 1992–; fmr judge of Constitutional Court, Bonn; Visiting Prof. of Law, Benjamin Cardozo School of Law, Yeshiva Univ., New York 2003–; qualified as masseur in Calif.; began writing crime fiction in 1980s. *Publications include:* non-fiction: Weimar: A Jurisprudence of Crisis (co-author), several books on constitutional law, fundamental rights and the issue of separation of powers; fiction: crime trilogy (with Walter Popp): Selbs Justiz 1987, Selbs Betrug 1994, Selbs Mord 2001; The Reader (novel) 1995, The Gordian Knot (novel), Flights of Love (short stories) 2001. *Address:* c/o Benjamin N. Cardozo School of Law, Brookdale Center, 55 Fifth Avenue (12th Street), New York, NY 10003-4391, USA (Office). *Telephone:* (212) 790-0200 (Office). *E-mail:* bschlink@ymail.yu.edu (Office).

SCHLÖGL, Herwig, PhD; German international organization official; b. 1942; ed Univ. of Marburg; mem. German Perm. Representation to European Econ. Union, Brussels 1969–72; mem. staff Industrial Policy Div., Ministry of Econs 1972–76, Head Foreign Econ. Affairs Div. of Industry Dept 1980–84, Head Div. for Foreign Econ. Policy, Export Promotion 1984–96; Head Econs Dept German-American Chamber of Commerce, New York 1976–80; Deputy Dir-Gen. for Trade Policy, Bonn 1996–98; Deputy Sec.-Gen. OECD, Paris 1998–. *Publications:* books and articles on competition policy and trade issues. *Address:* Organisation for Economic Co-operation and Development, 2 rue André-Pascal, 75775 Paris cédex 16, France (Office). *Telephone:* 1-45-24-82-00 (Office). *Fax:* 1-45-24-85-00 (Office). *E-mail:* webmaster@oecd.org (Office). *Website:* www.oecd.org (Office).

SCHLÖNDORFF, Volker; German film director; b. 1939, Wiesbaden; m. Margarethe von Trotta (q.v.) 1991; has directed numerous cinema and TV films; mem. German PEN Centre; Prize of the Int. Film Critics, Cannes 1966, Konrad-Wolf-Prize 1997, Blue Angel Award for Best European Film 2000. *Films include:* Der junge Törless, Mord und Totschlag, Michael Kohlhaas, Der plötzliche Reichtum der armen Leute von Kombach, Baal, Die Moral der Ruth Halbfass, Strohfeuer, Die Ehegattin, Übernachtung in Tirol, Die verlorene Ehre der Katharina Blum, Die Blechtrommel (The Tin Drum) (Golden Palm of Cannes) 1979, Die Fälschung 1981, Circle of Deceit 1982, Eine Liebe von Swann (Swann in Love) 1984, Death of a Salesman 1985, The Handmaid's Tale 1989, Voyager 1991, The Ogre 1996, Palmetto 1997, Die Stille nach dem Schuss 2000.

SCHLUMPF, Leon; Swiss politician; b. 3 Feb. 1925, Felsberg, Canton Grisons; m. Trudi Rupp; three d.; ed Univ. of Zürich; pvt. practice as lawyer and notary, Chur 1951–65; mem. Grisons Cantonal Parl. 1955–74, Pres. 1964–65, Head, Cantonal Dept of Interior and Public Econ. 1966–74; mem. Nat. Council 1966–74; mem. Council of States 1974–; Controller of Prices, Swiss Confed. 1974–78; mem. Fed. Council 1979–87; Head of Fed. Dept of Transport, Communications and Energy 1979–87; Pres. of Switzerland Jan.–Dec. 1984; Swiss People's Party. *Address:* c/o Department of Transport, Communications and Energy, Berne, Switzerland.

SCHLÜTER, Poul Holmskov, LLB; Danish politician and lawyer; b. 3 April 1929, Tønder; s. of Johannes Schlüter; m. 1st Lisbeth Schlüter 1979 (died 1988); two s. one d.; m. 2nd Anne Marie Vessel Schlüter 1989; ed Univs of Aarhus and Copenhagen; barrister and Supreme Court Attorney; Leader of Conservative Youth Movt (KU) 1944, Nat. Leader 1951; Del. to Int. Congress of World Asscn of Youth 1951, 1954; Chair. Young Conservatives, mem. Exec. Cttee Conservative Party 1952–55, 1971, Nat. Chair. Jr Chamber 1961, Vice-Pres. Jr Chamber Int. 1962; mem. Folketing (Parl.) 1964–; Chair. Jt Danish Consultative Council on UN 1966–68; MP Foreign Affairs Cttee 1968, Chair. 1982; mem. Council of Europe 1971–74; fmr Chair. Conservative Party 1974; Chair. Danish Del. to Nordic Council and mem. Presiding Cttee 1978–79; Prime Minister of Denmark 1982–93; Dir Nat. Cleaning Group 1993–, Int. Service System (ISS). *Address:* c/o Prime Minister's Office, Christiansborg, Prins Jørgens Gaard 11, 1218 Copenhagen K, Denmark.

SCHMALENBACH, Werner, DPhil; German art museum director; b. 13 Sept. 1920, Göttingen; s. of Prof. Dr Herman Schmalenbach and Sala Schmalenbach (née Müntz); m. 1st Esther Grey (died 2001); two d.; m. 2nd Anna Schlüter 2001; ed Basle Grammar School and Univ. of Basle; organiser of exhbns, Gewerbemuseum, Basle 1945–55; Dir Kestner Gesellschaft, Hanover 1955–62; mem. working Cttee, 'Documenta II', Kassel 1959, 1964, 1968; German Commr, Venice Biennale 1960, São Paulo Biennale 1961, 1963, 1965; Dir Kunstsammlung Nordrhein-Westfalen, Düsseldorf (Museum of Modern Art) 1962–90, Sotheby's Int. Advisory Bd 1991–2000; Grosses Bundesverdienstkreuz; Officer, Nat. Order of Southern Cross (Brazil). *Publications:* Der Film 1947, Die Kunst Afrikas 1956, Julius Bissier 1963, Kurt Schwitters 1967, Antoni Tàpies 1974, Fernand Léger 1976, Eduardo Chillida 1977, Marc Chagall 1979, Emil Schumacher 1981, Joan Miró 1982, Paul Klee 1986, African Art from the Barbier-Mueller Collection (ed.) 1989, Amedeo Modigliani 1990, Die Lust auf das Bild 1996, Henri Rousseau 1997, Kunst! Reden Schreiben Streiten 2000. *Address:* Marktpl. 3, 40213 Düsseldorf (Office); Poststrasse 17, 40667 Meerbusch, Germany (Home). *Telephone:* (211) 322230 (Office); (2132) 77802 (Home). *Fax:* (211) 320743 (Office).

SCHMID, Hans Heinrich, DTheol; Swiss university rector (retd); b. 22 Oct. 1937, Zürich; s. of Gotthard Schmid and Erika Hug; m. Christa Nievergelt 1962; two s. two d.; ed Zürich and Göttingen Univs; Asst Prof. Univ. of Zürich 1967–69; Prof. for Old Testament, Kirchliche Hochschule Bethel/Bielefeld 1969–76, Univ. of Zürich 1976–88; Rector, Univ. of Zürich 1988–2000;

Goldenes Ehrenkreuz der Republik Österreich 1996; Hon. DTheol (Leipzig) 1991. *Publications include:* Altorientalische Welt in der alttestamentlichen Theologie (essays) 1974, Der sogennante Jahwist. Beobachtungen und Fragen zur Pentateuchforschung 1976. *Leisure interest:* conducting a chamber orchestra. *Address:* In der Halden 11, 8603 Schwerzenbach, Switzerland (Home). *Telephone:* (1) 8252533 (Home). *Fax:* (1) 8252517 (Home). *E-mail:* hhschmid@freesurf.ch (Home).

SCHMID, Rudi, MD, PhD; American (b. Swiss) professor of medicine; b. Rudolf Schmid, 2 May 1922, Glarus, Switzerland; s. of Rudolf Schmid and Bertha Schiesser; m. Sonja D. Wild 1949; one s. one d.; ed gymnasium, Zurich, Univ. of Zurich, Univ. of Minnesota; Intern in Internal Medicine Univ. of Calif., San Francisco 1948–49, Prof. of Medicine and Chief Gastroenterology Unit and Dir of Liver Center 1966–83, Dean School of Medicine 1983–89, Assoc. Dean for Int. Relations 1989–95, Prof. Emer. of Medicine (on recall) 1991–; Resident Internal Medicine, Univ. of Minn. 1949–52, Instructor in Medicine 1952–54; Research Fellow in Biochem. Columbia Univ. Coll. of Physicians and Surgeons 1954–55; Sr Investigator Nat. Insts of Health, Bethesda, Md 1955–57; Assoc. in Medicine Harvard Medical School, Thorndike Memorial Lab., Boston City Hosp. 1957–59, Asst Prof. of Medicine Harvard Medical School 1959–62; Prof. of Medicine Univ. of Chicago 1962–66; mem. numerous editorial bds; mem. Acad. Leopoldina (German Acad. of Natural Sciences) 1965, NAS 1974–, American Acad. of Arts and Sciences 1982–, Swiss Acad. of Medical Science 1994–, German American Acad. Council 1994–2000; Hon. Prof., Shanghai Second Medical Coll., People's Repub. of China (PRC) 1983, Peking Union Medical Coll., PRC 1990, Jillin Univ., PRC 1993; Hon. Ed.-in-Chief World Journal of Gastroenterology 1996–; Ludwig Aschoff Prize, Univ. of Freiburg 1981, Lucie-Bolt Prize, German Asscn for the Study of the Liver 1989, Gold Medal, Canadian Liver Asscn 1985, Friedenwald Medal, American Gastroenterological Asscn 1990. *Achievements:* mem. Swiss Nat. Ski Team (Downhill and Slalom) 1942–45; mountaineering: first ascent East Face of Zinal Rothorn (Zermatt) 1945, first ascent West Face of Mont Blanc, Chamonix 1946. *Publications:* over 200 scientific publs in the field of porphyrin, heme and bile pigment metabolism, liver function, liver disease, muscle and blood diseases. *Leisure interests:* travel, reading, music, skiing, mountain climbing, tennis. *Address:* University of California San Francisco, Box 0410, S-224, San Francisco CA 94143-0410 (Office); 211 Woodland Road, Kentfield, CA 94904, USA (Home). *Telephone:* (415) 476-6054 (Office); (415) 461-9698 (Home). *Fax:* (415) 476-0689 (Office); (415) 461-6998 (Home). *E-mail:* schmidr@medsch.ucsf.edu (Office); s.d.schmid@worldnet.att.net (Home).

SCHMIDBAUR, Hubert, Dr rer. nat; German professor of chemistry; b. 31 Dec. 1934, Landsberg/L; s. of Johann B. Schmidbaur and Katharina S. Ehelechner; m. Rose-Marie Fukas; one s. one d.; ed Univ. of Munich; Asst Prof., Univ. of Munich 1960–64; Assoc. Prof., Univ. of Marburg 1964–69; Prof., Univ. of Würzburg 1969–73; Prof. and Head of Dept, Tech. Univ. of Munich 1973–; Dean Faculty of Science 1983–; mem. Göttingen, Leopoldina, Bavarian and Finnish Acads., Senate, German Science Foundation; A. Stock Prize, German Chemical Soc., Wacker Silikon Preis, Bonner Chemie-preis, F. Kipping Award, ACS, Leibniz Award, German Science Foundation, Dwyer Medal, Bailar Medal, Bundesverdienstkreuz, Ludwig Mond Medal, Birch Medal. *Publications:* about 850, including books, monographs and scientific papers on inorganic, metalorganic and analytical chemistry. *Address:* Konigsberger Str. 36, 85748 Garching, Germany. *Telephone:* (89) 28913130. *Fax:* (89) 28913125. *E-mail:* h.schmidbaur@lrz.tum.de (Office). *Website:* hiris.anorg .chemie.tu-muenchen.de/ac3 (Office).

SCHMIDHUBER, Peter Michael; German international official; b. 15 Dec. 1931, Munich; one d.; ed Univ. of Munich; mem. Bavarian Christian Social Union Party (CSU) 1952–; served in Bavarian State Ministries of Finance and of Econ. Affairs and Transport 1961–72; lawyer in Munich 1972–; Hon. Munich City Councillor 1960–66; mem. Bundestag 1965–69, 1972–78; mem. Bavarian Landtag, Bavarian State Minister for Fed. Affairs and Proxy for Free State of Bavaria to Fed. Govt 1978–87; mem. Bundesrat 1978–87; mem. N Atlantic Ass. 1978–87; mem. European Comm. 1987–94, EC Commr for Budget and Financial Control 1989–95, for the Cohesion Fund 1993–95; Dir Bundesbank 1995–99; Bundesverdienstkreuz. *Address:* Wilhelm-Epstein-Strasse 14, 60341 Frankfurt am Main, Germany.

SCHMIDT, Andreas; German singer; b. 30 June 1960, Düsseldorf; m. Eva Grundhoff 1989; one s. one d.; studied piano, organ, conducting in Düsseldorf, singing in Düsseldorf and Berlin; youngest mem. of Deutsche Oper Berlin 1983; debut Hamburg State Opera 1985, Munich State Opera 1985, Covent Garden London 1986, Vienna State Opera 1988, Geneva Opera 1989, Salzburg Festival 1989, Aix-en-Provence Festival 1991, Metropolitan New York 1991, Edin. Festival 1991, Paris Bastille 1992, Paris Garnier 1993, Glyndebourne Festival 1994, State Opera Berlin 1995, Amsterdam Opera 1995, Bayreuth Festival 1996; has sung with maj. orchestras including Berlin, Geneva, Vienna, Munich, London, New York, Israel Philharmonic orchestras, Cincinnati, Cleveland Symphony orchestras, La Scala, Milan; 1st Prize Deutscher Musikwettbewerb, several German and int. awards and prizes. *Leisure interests:* fly-fishing, golf, literature, art. *Address:* c/o IMG Artists, Media House, 3 Burlington Lane, London, W4 2TH, England; Fossredder 51, 22359 Hamburg, Germany.

SCHMIDT, Benno C., Jr.; American university president; b. 20 March 1942, Washington; s. of the late Benno Charles Schmidt Sr and Martha Chastain; m. 2nd Helen Cutting Whitney 1980; one d. (one s. one d. by previous marriage); ed Yale Coll. and Yale Law School; Clerk to Chief Justice Earl Warren 1966–67; Dept of Justice 1967–69; mem. Faculty, Columbia Univ. Law School 1969–86, Dean 1984–86; Pres. and Prof. of Law, Yale Univ. 1986–92; Pres., CEO The Edison Project 1992–; Dir Nat. Humanities Center, Chapel Hill, NC 1985–; Hon. Master of Bench, Gray's Inn 1988. *Publications:* Freedom of the Press versus Public Access 1976, The Judiciary and Responsible Government 1910–1921 (with A. M. Bickel) 1984; papers on constitutional law, freedom of the press and first amendment issues.

SCHMIDT, Chauncey Everett, BS, MBA; American banker; b. 7 June 1931, Oxford, Ia; s. of Walter F. Schmidt and Vilda Saxton; m. Anne Garrett McWilliams 1954 (deceased); one s. two d.; ed U.S. Naval Acad., Harvard Graduate School of Business Admin.; with First Nat. Bank of Chicago 1959–75, Vice-Pres. 1965, Gen. Man., London 1966, Gen. Man. for Europe, Middle East and Africa 1968, Sr Vice-Pres. 1969–72, Exec. Vice-Pres. 1972, Vice-Chair. 1973, Pres. 1974–75; Chair. and CEO, Bank of Calif. 1976–; Chair., Pres., CEO BanCal Tri-State Corpn 1976–; Dir Amfac Ltd, Calif. Bankers Clearing House Asscn, Calif. Roundtable, Bay Area Council; Exec. Bd San Francisco Bay Area Council of Boy Scouts of America; Bd of Govs. San Francisco Symphony; mem. Fed. Advisory Council of Fed. Res. System, Advisory Council of Japan-U.S. Econ. Relations, SRI Int. Council, Int. Monetary Conf., American Bankers Asscn. *Address:* 525 Middlefield Road, Suite 140, Menlo Park, CA 94025 (Office); 40 Why Worry Farm, Woodside, CA 94062, USA (Home). *Telephone:* (650) 322-3000 (Office). *E-mail:* ceschmidt@ aol.com (Office).

SCHMIDT, Christian, PhD, D.SC.ECON.; French university professor; b. 20 July 1938, Neuilly-sur-Seine; s. of Paul Schmidt and Jeanne Loriot; m. Marie-Pierre de Cossè Brissac 1988; ed Facultés de Lettres, Droit, Sciences, Inst. d'Etudes Politiques, Paris, Inst. des Hautes Etudes de Défense Nationale, Acad. of Int. Law, The Hague; Research Asst Inst. of Applied Econ. Sciences Laboratoire Coll. de France 1964–67; Asst La Sorbonne 1967–70; Chargé de Mission Forecasting Admin. Ministry of Finances 1970–72; f. Dir Econ. Perspectives 1969–86; Asst Dir French Inst. of War Studies 1980–82; Pres. Charles Gide Asscn for the Study of Econ. Thought 1981–90; Consultant on Econ. Aspects of Disarmament UN 1980; Prof. of Econs Univ. of Paris IX (Paris Dauphine) 1983–; Pres., Founder Asscn française des économistes de défense 1981–, Int. Defence Econ. Asscn 1985–; Dir Lab. of Econs and Sociology of Defence Orgs. (LESOD) 1984–; Co-Dir (Research Group) CNRS 1990–; Chair. Scientific Council of European Soc. of Econ. Thought; mem. Council French Econs Asscn 2000–02, Societé d'Economie Politique 2000–; mem. various editorial bds; Croix de Chevalier, Légion d'honneur; Prix de L'institut (Acad. des Sciences Morales et Politiques) 1986, 1993. *Publications:* Conséquences Economiques et Sociales de la Course aux Armaments 1983, Essai sur l'Economie Ricardienne 1984, La Semantique Economique en Question 1985, Peace, Defence and Economic Analysis 1987, Penser la Guerre, Penser l'Economie 1991, Game Theory and International Relations 1994, Uncertainty and Economic Thought 1996, Game Theory and International Relations (co-ed.) 1996, The Rational Foundations of Economic Behaviour (co-ed.) 1996, La Theorie des Jeux: Essai d'Interpretation 2001, Game Theory and Economic Analysis 2002; numerous articles in learned journals. *Leisure interests:* theatre, opera. *Address:* Université de Paris-IX Dauphine, Place du Maréchal de Lattre de Tassigny, 75775 Paris cedex 16; 109 rue de Grenelle, 75007 Paris, France (Home). *Telephone:* 1-44-05-49-39 (Office); 1-45-51-01-78 (Home). *Fax:* 1-44-05-46-87 (Office); 1-45-51-22-70 (Home). *E-mail:* christian.schmidt@dauphine.fr (Office); schmidt@wanadoo.fr (Home).

SCHMIDT, Eric E., MS, PhD; American business executive; b. 1956, 1956; ed Univ. of California at Berkeley, Princeton Univ.; began career with Bell Labs and Zilog; mem. Research Staff Computer Science Lab., Xerox Palo Alto Research Center (PARC) –1983; Chief Tech. Officer and Corp. Exec. Officer Sun Microsystems 1983–97; Chair. and Chief Exec. Novell Inc. 1997–2001; Chair. Google Inc. Aug. 2001–, Volera Inc.; mem. Bd Siebel Systems Inc., Integrated Archive Systems, Tilion. *Address:* Google Inc., 2400 Bayshore Parkway, Mountain View, CA 94043, USA (Office). *Telephone:* (650) 330-0100 (Office). *Fax:* (650) 618-1499 (Office).

SCHMIDT, Helmut; German politician and economist; b. 23 Dec. 1918, Hamburg; s. of Gustav Schmidt and Ludovica Schmidt; m. Hannelore Glaser 1942; one d.; ed Lichtwarkschule and Univ. Hamburg; Man. Transport Admin. of State of Hamburg 1949–53; mem. Social Democrat Party 1946–; mem. Bundestag 1953–61, 1965–87; Chair. Social Democrat (SPD) Parl. Party in Bundestag 1967–69; Vice-Chair. SPD 1968–84; Senator (Minister) for Domestic Affairs in Hamburg 1961–65; Minister of Defence 1969–72, for Econ. and Finance July–Dec. 1972, of Finance 1972–74; Fed. Chancellor 1974–82; Publr Die Zeit 1983–; Hon. DCL (Oxford) 1979; Dr hc (Newberry Coll.) 1973, (Johns Hopkins) 1976, (Cambridge) 1976, (Harvard) 1979, (Sorbonne) 1981, (Louvain) 1984, (Georgetown) 1986, (Bergamo) 1989, (Tokyo) 1991, (Haifa) 2000, (Potsdam) 2000 and others; European Prize for Statesmanship (FUS Foundation) 1979, Nahum Goldmann Silver Medal 1980, Athinai Prize 1986. *Publications:* Defence or Retaliation 1962, Beiträge 1967, Strategie des Gleichgewichts 1969 (English edn 'Balance of Power' 1970), Kontinuität und Konzentration (2nd edn) 1976, Als Christ in der politischen Entscheidung 1976, Der Kurs heisst Frieden 1979, Pflicht zur Menschlichkeit 1981, Kunst im Kanzleramt 1982, Freiheit verantworten 1983, Die Weltwirtschaft ist unser Schicksal 1983, Eine Strategie für den Westen, (English edn)

A Grand Strategy for the West, (Adolphe Bentinck Prize 1986) 1986, Vom deutschen Stolz: Bekenntnisse zur Erfahrung von Kunst 1986, Menschen und Mächte 1987, (English edn) Men and Powers 1988, Die Deutschen und ihre Nachbarn 1990, Mit Augenmass und Weitblick 1990, Einfügen in die Gemeinschaft der Völker 1990, Kindheit und Jugend unter Hitler 1992, Ein Manifest – Weil das Land sich ändern muss (jtly) 1992, Handeln für Deutschland 1993, Jahr der Entscheidung 1994, Was wird aus Deutschland? 1994, Weggefährten 1996, Jahrhundertwende 1998, Allgemeine Erklärung der Menschenpflichten 1998, Globalisierung 1998, Auf der Suche nach einer öffentlichen Moral 1998, Die Selbstbehauptung Europas 2000, Hand aufs Herz 2002. *Address:* Bundeskanzler a.D., Deutscher Bundestag, Platz der Republik 1, 11011 Berlin, Germany. *Telephone:* (30) 22771580. *Fax:* (30) 22770571.

SCHMIDT, Klaus, PhD; German professor of economics; b. 16 June 1961, Koblenz; m. Monika Schnitzer; two d.; ed Univs. of Hamburg and Bonn; Visiting Asst Prof., MIT, Mass., USA 1992; Asst Prof. Univ. of Bonn 1993–95; Full Prof. of Econs Univ. of Munich 1995–; Visiting Prof. Stanford Univ. *Address:* Department of Economics, Universität München, Ludwigstr. 28, 80539 Munich, Germany (Office). *Telephone:* (89) 21803405 (Office). *Fax:* (89) 21803510 (Office). *E-mail:* klaus.schmidt@lrz.uni-muenchen.de (Office). *Website:* www.vwl.uni-muenchen.de/ls-schmidt (Office).

SCHMIDT, Maarten, PhD, ScD; Netherlands astronomer; b. 28 Dec. 1929, Groningen; s. of W. Schmidt and A. W. Haringhuizen; m. Cornelia J. Tom 1955; three d.; ed Univs of Groningen and Leiden; Scientific Officer Univ. of Leiden Observatory 1949–59; Carnegie Fellow Mt. Wilson Observatory, Pasadena 1956–58; Assoc. Prof. Calif. Inst. of Tech. 1959–64, Prof. of Astronomy 1964–96, Prof. Emer. 1996–; discovered large red shifts in spectra of quasi-stellar radio sources (quasars); Rumford Award, American Acad. of Arts and Sciences 1968, Royal Astronomy Soc. Gold Medal 1980, James Craig Watson Medal 1991. *Leisure interest:* classical music. *Address:* California Institute of Technology, 105 24 Robinson Laboratory, 1201 E California Boulevard, Pasadena, CA 91125, USA. *Telephone:* (626) 395-4204.

SCHMIDT, Ole; Danish conductor and composer; b. 14 July 1928, Copenhagen; s. of Hugo Schmidt and Erna S. P. Schmidt; m. Lizzie Rode Schmidt 1960; two d.; ed Royal Danish Acad. of Music, Copenhagen; conducting debut 1955; Conductor, Royal Theatre, Copenhagen 1959–65; Chief Conductor, Hamburg Symphony 1969–70; Conductor Danish Radio Concert Orchestra 1971–73; Chief Conductor and Artistic Dir Aarhus Symphony 1978–84; Perm. Guest Conductor, Royal Northern Coll. of Music, Manchester 1986–89; Chief Conductor and Artistic Dir The Toledo Symphony, Ohio 1989–; Carl Nielsen Legat 1975; Gramex Award 1975, H. C. Lumbye Award 1988. *Leisure interests:* writing, painting, gardening. *Address:* Mariot, Gazax et Bacarrisse, 32230 Marciac, France; Puggaardsgade 17, 1573 Copenhagen V, Denmark (Home).

SCHMIDT-JORTZIG, Edzard, DrIur; German politician; b. 8 Oct. 1941, Berlin; s. of Rear-Adm. Friedrich-Traugott Schmidt and Carla Freiin von Frydag; m. Marion von Arnim 1968; two d. two s.; Academic Counsellor and Prof., Münster 1977; Head Law Dept, Kiel Univ. 1982, Prof. of Public Law 1982–; Higher Admin. and Constitutional Court Judge, Lüneburg 1983–91, 1993–94; mem. Bundestag 1994–; Fed. Minister of Justice 1996–98; mem. FDP. *Publications:* Zur Verfassungsmässigkeit von Kreisumlagesätzen 1977, Kommunale Organisationshoheit 1979, Die Einrichtungsgarantien der Verfassung 1979, Kommunalrecht 1982, Gemeindliches Eigentum an Meereshäfen 1985, Reformüberlegungen für die Landessatzung Schleswig-Holstein 1988, Handbuch des Kommunalen Finanz und Haushaltsrechts (with J. Makswit) 1991, Staatsangehörigkeit im Wandel 1997, Wann ist der Mensch tot? 1999. *Address:* Faculty of Law, Christian-Albrechts University of Kiel, Olshausenstrasse 40, 24098 Kiel, Germany (Office). *Telephone:* (431) 8802125 (Office). *Fax:* (431) 8801689 (Office). *E-mail:* dekanat@law.uni-kiel.de (Office). *Website:* www.uni-kiel.de (Office).

SCHMIDT-ROHR, Ulrich, Dr rer. nat; German physicist; b. 25 May 1926, Frankfurt an der Oder; s. of Georg and Ruth Schmidt-Rohr; m. Helma Wernery 1963; four s. one d.; ed Friedrichsgymnasium, Frankfurt an der Oder, Technische Hochschule, Berlin and Brunswick and Univ. of Heidelberg; research Lab., OSRAM 1948–49; Asst, Univ. of Heidelberg 1950–53; FSSP Fellow, MIT 1954; Asst Max Planck Inst. for Medical Research 1955–58, Max Planck Inst. for Nuclear Physics 1958–61; Dir Inst. for Nuclear Physics, Kernforschungsanlage, Jülich 1962–65; Dir Max Planck Inst. for Nuclear Physics 1966–; Hon. Prof. Univ. of Heidelberg 1966. *Publications:* three books; papers on nuclear physics, accelerators and the history of nuclear physics in Germany. *Address:* Max Planck Institut für Kernphysik, Postfach 10 39 80, 69029 Heidelberg, Germany. *Telephone:* (6221) 516202204.

SCHMIED, Wieland; Austrian professor of art history; b. 5 Feb. 1929, Frankfurt am Main; m. Erika Schmied 1966; two d.; ed Univ. of Vienna; Dir Kestner-Gesellschaft, Hannover 1963–74; Dir Berliner Künstlerprogramm DAAD (Artists-in-Residence Programme) 1978–86; Prof. of Art History and Rector Acad. of Fine Arts, Munich 1986–94; Pres. Int. Summer Acad. of Fine Arts, Salzburg 1984–99; mem. Bayerische Akad. der Schönen Künste 1988– Pres. 1995–; Vienna City Prize for Essays 1984, Staatspreis for Essays, Vienna 1992, Friedrich Märker Award for Essays, Munich 1994, Theo Wormland Award, Munich 1997. *Publications:* monographs on Alfred Kubin 1967, Caspar David Friedrich 1975, 1992, 1999, Giorgio de Chirico 1982, 1989, 2001, Francis Bacon 1985, 1996, Ezra Pound 1994, 2000, 2002, Edward

Hopper 1995, Thomas Bernhards Häuser 1995, Max Weiler-Ein anderes Bild der Natur 1998; maj. catalogues on modern art. *Address:* Bayerische Akademie der Schönen Künste, Max Joseph Platz 3, 80539 Munich, Germany. *Telephone:* (89) 2900770 (Office). *Fax:* (89) 29007723 (Office). *E-mail:* bayerische-akademie@gmx.de.

SCHMITT, Harrison H., PhD; American fmr astronaut, politician and businessman; b. 3 July 1935, Santa Rita, NM; s. of Harrison A. Schmitt and Ethel Hagan Schmitt; m. Teresa Fitzgibbons 1985; ed Calif. Inst. of Technology, Univ. of Oslo, Norway and Harvard Univ.; Fulbright Fellowship 1957–58, Kennecott Fellowship in Geology 1958–59, Harvard Fellowship 1959–60, Harvard Travelling Fellowship 1960, Parker Travelling Fellowship 1961–62, NSF Postdoctoral Fellowship, Dept of Geological Sciences, Harvard 1963–64; has done geological work for Norwegian Geological Survey, Oslo, for US Geological Survey, NM and Montana and in Alaska 1955–56; with US Geological Survey Astrogeology Dept until 1965; Project Chief on photo and telescopic mapping of moon and planets; selected as scientist-astronaut by NASA June 1965; completed flight training 1966; Lunar Module pilot Apollo XVII Dec. 1972; Chief, Astronaut Office, Science and Applications, Johnson Space Center 1974; Asst Admin., Energy Programs, NASA, Washington, DC 1974–76; Senator from New Mexico 1977–83; Consultant 1983–; mem. Pres.'s Foreign Intelligence Advisory Bd 1984–85, Army Sciences Bd 1985–89, Army Research Lab. Tech. Review Bd 1993–; co-leader group to monitor Romanian Elections 1990; Chair., Pres. Annapolis Center 1994–; Adjunct Prof. Univ. of Wis. 1995–; Republican; Lovelace Award, NASA 1989, Gilbert Award, GSA 1989.

SCHMUDE, Jürgen; German politician and lawyer; b. 9 June 1936, Insterburg; m.; two c.; ed Göttingen, Berlin, Bonn, Cologne Univs.; practised law, Essen; mem. Social Democratic Party 1957–; various local party functions 1957–; mem. Town Council and Del. District Council, Moers 1964–71; mem. Bundestag 1969–94; Sec. of State to Fed. Minister of the Interior 1974–78; Fed. Minister of Educ. and Science 1978–81, of Justice 1981–82; Pres. Synod of Evangelical Churches (FRG) 1985–. *Address:* Am Jostenhof 2, 47441 Moers, Germany.

SCHNABEL, Julian, BFA; American painter and film director; b. 1951; ed Univ. of Houston; solo exhbns. Houston, New York, San Francisco, LA, Chicago, Düsseldorf, Zürich, Amsterdam, London, Paris, Rome, Tokyo etc.; numerous group exhbns. including Venice Biennale 1980, 1982, Royal Acad. London 1981, 64th Whitney Biennial 1987; Dir and wrote screenplay for film Build a Fort and Set It on Fire 1995, Dir film Basquiat 1996, Before Night Falls 2001. *Publication:* Nicknames of Maître D's and Other Excerpts From Life 1988. *Address:* Pace Gallery New York, 32 East 57th Street, New York, NY 10022, USA.

SCHNEBLI, Dolf, MArch; Swiss architect and planner; b. 27 Dec. 1928, Baden; s. of Robert Schnebli and Margret Heer; m. Jamileh Jahanguiri; one s. two d.; ed Swiss Fed. Inst. of Tech. (ETH), Zürich and Harvard Grad. School of Design; own architectural office 1958; partner, Ryser, Engeler, Meier 1971; Prof. ETH Zürich 1971, Prof. Emer.; Partner, Schnebli Ammann Ruchat 1990, Schnebli Ammann Menz SAM Architects; Pres. Schnebli Ammann Ruchat & Assocs. Architecture, Planning, Urban Design 1994; mem. Bd SAM Architects and Partner Inc. 1997–; Hon. mem. BDA; Hon. Prof. South China Univ. 1983; numerous first prizes in architecture competitions and other awards. *Publication:* SAM – Recent Buildings and Projects 1998. *Leisure interests:* visual arts, literature. *Address:* SAM Architects and Partner Inc., Hardturmstrasse 175, P.O. Box 48, 8037 Zürich (Office); Südstrasse 45, 8008 Zürich, Switzerland (Home). *Telephone:* (1) 4474343 (Office); (1) 3831430 (Home). *Fax:* (1) 4474340 (Office); (1) 3832737 (Home). *E-mail:* dschnebli@samarch.ch (Office). *Website:* www.samarch.ch (Office).

SCHNEEBELI, Christian; French oil executive; b. 1 Oct. 1938, Zürich, Switzerland; s. of Walter Schneebeli and Gertrud Maria Witschi; m. Elisabeth Duval 1966; one s. one d.; ed Ecole Polytechnique, Paris; joined Mobil Group 1962; man. positions in Benelux 1971–73, Japan 1973–77, Sweden 1977–80, France 1980–88; Area Exec. Europe 1988–92; Pres.-Dir-Gen. Mobil Oil Française 1993–. *Address:* Mobil Oil Française, Tour Septentrion, 92976 Paris La Défense cedex (Office); 46 rue Spontini, 75116 Paris, France (Home). *Telephone:* 1-41-45-45-22 (Office).

SCHNEIDER, Cynthia P., PhD; American diplomatist and professor of art history; b. 16 Aug. 1953, Pa; ed Harvard Univ., Oxford Univ.; Asst Curator of European Paintings, Museum of Fine Arts, Boston; Asst Prof. of Art History, Georgetown Univ. 1984–90, Assoc. Prof. 1990–; Amb. to Netherlands 1998–2001; Vice-Chair. Pres.'s Cttee on the Arts and Humanities; fmr mem. Bd of Dirs. Nat. Museum of Women in the Arts, Australian-American Leadership Dialogue. *Publications:* Rembrandt's Landscapes 1990, Rembrandt's Landscapes: Drawing and Prints 1990. *Address:* Georgetown University, 37th and O Streets, NW, Washington, DC 20057 (Office); 17201 Norwood Road, Sandy Spring, MO 20860, USA; c/o Department of State, 2201 C Street, NW, Washington, DC 20520. *Telephone:* (202) 687-5055 (Office).

SCHNEIDER, Dieter, Dr rer. pol; German professor of business administration; b. 2 April 1935, Striegau, Silesia; s. of Walter Schneider and Lina Schneider, née Wolff; m. Marlene Jakobs 1971; ed Univs of Frankfurt and Nuremberg; Prof., Univ. of Münster 1965, Univ. of Frankfurt am Main 1970, Univ. of Bochum 1973–2001; Dr. hc (Duisburg, Würzburg, Bayreuth) 1992, (Göttingen) 1995. *Publications:* Steuerbilanzen 1978, Grundzüge der Unternehmensbesteuerung 1990, Allgemeine Betriebswirtschaftslehre 1987, Investition, Finanzierung und Besteuerung 1992, Betriebswirtschaftslehre (Vol. 1) 1993, (Vol. 2) 1994, (Vol. 3) 1997, (Vol. 4) 2001. *Leisure interests:* classical and chamber music. *Address:* c/o Ruhr-Universität Bochum, Fakultät für Wirtschaftswissenschaft, Seminar für Angewandte Wirtschaftslehre V, Universitäts strasse 150, 44801 Bochum, Germany. *Telephone:* (234) 3222906.

SCHNEIDER, Manfred; German business executive; b. 21 Dec. 1938, Bremerhaven; m.; one d.; ed Univs. of Freiburg, Hamburg and Cologne; joined Bayer AG, Leverkusen 1966, Head Finance and Accounting Dept of subsidiary co. Duisburger Kupferhütte, later Chair. of Bd; returned to Bayer AG 1981, apptd. Head Regional Co-ordination, Corp. Auditing and Control 1984, mem. Bd of Man. 1987–2002, Chair. 1992–2002; mem. Supervisory Bd Daimler-Chrysler AG, Stuttgart (mem. Chair's Council 2001–), RWE Aktiengesellschaft, Essen, Allianz AG, Munich, Metro AG, Cologne; Pres. Chemical Industry Asscn (VCI). *Address:* c/o Bayer AG, 51368 Leverkusen, Germany.

SCHNEIDER, Oscar, D.JUR.UTR.; German politician; b. 3 June 1927, Altenheideck, Bavaria; s. of Josef Schneider; m. Josefine Kampfer 1961; two d.; ed Univs. of Erlangen and Würzburg; mem. Nuremberg City Council 1956–69; mem. Bundestag 1969–94; Chair. Bundestag Cttee on Regional Planning, Bldg and Urban Devt 1972-82; Minister for Regional Planning, Bldg and Urban Devt 1982–89; Pres. Curatorial Cttee German Historical Museum 1990–; CSU. *Publications:* three books.

SCHNITZER, Moshe, MA; Israeli diamond exporter; b. 21 Jan. 1921; m. Varda Reich 1946; one s. two d.; ed Balfour High School, Tel Aviv, Hebrew Univ. of Jerusalem; Chair. Asscn of Diamond Instructors 1943–46; Vice-Pres. Israel Diamond Exchange 1951–66, Pres. 1966–93, Hon. Pres. 1993–; Pres. Israel Exporters' Asscn of Diamonds 1962–; World Pres. Int. Fed. of Diamond Exchanges 1968–72, Hon. World Pres. 1993–; partner Diamond Export Enterprise 1953–; mem. Consulting Cttee to Minister of Commerce and Industry 1968–; Ed. The Diamond; Most Distinguished Exporter of Israel 1964. *Publication:* Diamond Book (in Hebrew) 1946. *Address:* Israel Diamond Exchange, 1 Jabotinsky Road, Ramat Gan 52520, P.O. Box 3025 (Office); Uri 4, Tel Aviv 64954, Israel (Home). *Telephone:* 3-5751188. *Fax:* 3-5752479.

SCHOCKEMÖHLE, Alwin; German show jumper (retd); b. 29 May 1937, Osterbrock, Kreis Meppen; s. of Aloys Schockemöhle and Josefa (née Borgerding) Schockemöhle; m. 2nd Rita Wiltfang; two s. one d.; two d. from previous m.; began riding 1946, in public events 1948; trained in mil. riding 1954–55; reserve for Mil. and Showjumping, Melbourne Olympics 1956; specialized in showjumping 1956–77; first Derby win, riding 'Bachus', Hamburg 1957; continually in int. showjumping events 1960–77; Showjumping Champion FRG (four times); second in European Championship (three times); European Champion riding 'Warwick' 1975, 1976; gold medal (Team Award) Rome Olympics 1960; gold medal (Individual Award) and silver medal (Team Award) riding 'Warwick' Montreal Olympics 1976. *Publication:* Sportkamerad Pferd (A Horse for Sports Companions). *Address:* 49453 Mühlen, Kreis Diepholz/Niedersachsen, Germany.

SCHOELLER, François; French engineer; b. 25 March 1934, Nancy; s. of Gustave Schoeller and Suzanne Woelflin; m. Colette Canonge 1960; three c.; ed Ecole Polytechnique and Ecole Nat. Supérieure des Télécommunications; Eng equatorial office of PTT, Brazzaville 1960–63; Chief Eng, Regional Man., Télécommunications de Strasbourg 1963–73; Operational Dir Télécommunications de Marseille 1973–75, Regional Dir Montpellier 1975–80, Regional Dir with grade of Engineer-Gen. 1980; Chair. TéléDiffusion de France 1983–86; Dir Higher Educ. in Telecommunication 1987–94; Pres. France Cables et Radio de México 1994–97; Project Man. France Telecom 1997–98; Man. Consultant, François Schoeller Conseil 1998–; Commdr Ordre nat. du Mérite; Officier, Légion d'honneur. *Publication:* Professional Ethics. *Address:* 6 rue Marietta Martin, 75016 Paris, France (Office). *Telephone:* 1-42-15-01-45 (Office). *Fax:* 1-42-15-07-16 (Office). *E-mail:* schoeller.conseil@wanadoo.fr (Office).

SCHOENDOERFFER, Pierre; French writer, scriptwriter and film director; b. 5 May 1928; m. Patricia Chauvel 1957; two s. one d.; served as able seaman on Swedish ship S.S. Anita Hans 1947–48; combat cameraman in French Expeditionary Corps, Indochina 1952–55, taken prisoner by Viet Minh; mem. Institut de France, Acad. des beaux arts 1988; Pres. Acad. de l'histoire et de l'image 2000; mem. Council, Musée de l'armée 1990, Haut Conseil de La mémoire combattante 1997–; Officier, Légion d'honneur; Officier, Ordre Nat. du Mérite; Croix de guerre (6 mentions); Chevalier des Palmes académiques; Officier des Arts et Lettres; Médaille militaire; Prix Vauban for literary and cinematographic work 1984. *Films:* La Passe du Diable (Pellman Award 1958, Award of City of Berlin 1958) 1957, Ramuntcho 1958, Pêcheurs d'Islande 1959, La 317ème Section (Platoon 317) (Award for Best Script, Cannes 1965) 1964, Objectif: 500 Millions 1966, Le Crabe Tambour (Grand Prix du Cinéma Français 1977, Prix Femina Belge 1978, 3 Césars 1978) 1977, L'Honneur d'un Capitaine (Grand Prix du Cinéma de l'Académie Française, Prix Leduc, Grand Prix de l'Académie du Cinéma) 1982, Dien Bien Phu 1992, La Haut 2002. *Documentaries:* Attention Hélicoptère (Gold Sun, Mil. Film Festival, Versailles) 1963, The Anderson Platoon (Oscar, USA 1968, Int. Emmy Award, USA 1968, Prix Italia 1967, Merit Award of Guild of TV Dirs. and Producers, UK 1967 and other awards) 1967, La Sentinelle du Matin 1976, Reminiscence (sequel to Anderson Platoon) 1989. *Publications:* La 317ème Section (Prix de l'Académie de Bretagne) 1963,

L'Adieu au Roi (Farewell to the King) (Prix Interallié) 1969, Le Crabe Tambour (The Paths of the Sea) (Grand Prix du Roman de l'Académie Française) 1976, Là Haut 1981, Dien Bien Phu, De la Bataille au Film 1992, L'Aile du Papillon 2003. *Address:* 3 bis rue de l'Alboni, 75016 Paris, France. *Telephone:* 1-40-50-06-41 (Paris).

SCHOLAR, Sir Michael Charles, KCB, PhD, ARCO; British civil servant and academic; b. 3 Jan. 1942, Merthyr Tydfil, Wales; s. of Richard Scholar and Blodwen Scholar (née Jones); m. Angela Sweet 1964; three s. one d. (deceased); ed St Olave's and St Saviour's Grammar School, St John's Coll., Cambridge, Univ. of Calif. at Berkeley, Harvard Univ.; worked at HM Treasury 1969–93; Sr Int. Man. Barclay's Bank 1979–81; Pvt. Sec. to Prime Minister 1981–83; Perm. Sec., Welsh Office 1993–96; Perm. Sec. Dept of Trade and Industry 1996–2001; Pres. St John's Coll., Oxford 2001–; Dir (non-exec.) Council of Man., Nat. Inst. of Econ. and Social Research 2001–, Legal and General Investment Man. 2002–; Hon. Fellowship Univ. of Wales (Aberystwyth), St John's Coll., Cambridge; Dr hc (Univ. of Glamorgan). *Leisure interests:* playing the organ and piano, opera, long-distance walking. *Address:* St John's College, Oxford, OX1 3JP (Office); St John's College, Oxford, OX1 3JP, England (Home). *Telephone:* (1865) 277419 (Office); (1865) 277424 (Home). *Fax:* (1865) 277482 (Office). *E-mail:* president@sjc.ox.ac.uk (Office). *Website:* www.sjc.ox.ac.uk (Office).

SCHOLES, Myron S., MBA, PhD; American professor of law and finance; b. 1941; ed McMaster Univ., Univ. of Chicago; instructor Univ. of Chicago Business School 1967–68; Asst Prof., MIT Man. School 1968–72, Assoc. Prof. 1972–73; Assoc. Prof. Univ. of Chicago 1973–75, Prof. 1975–79, Edward Eagle Brown Prof. of Finance 1979–82; Prof. of Law, Stanford Univ. 1983–, also Peter E. Buck Prof. of Finance; Man. Dir Salomon Bros 1991–93; Dir Center for Research in Security Prices, Univ. of Chicago 1975–81; Sr Research Fellow Hoover Inst, Stanford Univ. 1988–; Prin. Long-Term Capital Man. 1994–99; shared Nobel Prize for Econs 1997 for devising Black-Scholes Model for determining value of derivatives. *Address:* Graduate School of Business, Stanford University, Stanford, CA 94305, USA.

SCHOLEY, Sir David Gerald, Kt, FRSA, CBE; British banker; b. 28 June 1935, Chipstead, Surrey; s. of Dudley Scholey and Lois Scholey; m. Alexandra Drew 1960; one s. one d.; ed Wellington Coll. and Christ Church, Oxford; joined S. G. Warburg & Co. Ltd 1964, Dir 1967–, Deputy Chair. 1977–80, Joint Chair. 1980–87; Dir Mercury Securities PLC 1969, Deputy Chair. Mercury Securities PLC 1980–84, Chair. 1984–86; Chair. S. G. Warburg (now UBS Warburg) Group PLC 1985–95, fmr CEO July–Nov. 1995, Sr Adviser 1995–; Chair. Swiss Bank Corp. Int. Advisory Council 1995–97; Chair. Close Bros. Group PLC 1999–; Dir Orion Insurance Co. PLC 1963–67, Stewart Wrightson Holdings PLC 1972–81, Union Discount Co. of London Ltd 1976–81, Bank of England 1981–98, British Telecom PLC 1985–94, Chubb Corpn, USA 1991–, Gen. Electric Co. 1992–95, J Sainsbury PLC 1996–2000, Inst. européen d'admin des affaires (INSEAD) (Chair. UK Council 1992–97, Int. Council 1995–), Vodafone Group PLC 1998–, Anglo American PLC 1999–; Sr Adviser Int. Finance Corpn 1996–2002; mem. Export Guarantees Advisory Council 1970–75, Deputy Chair. 1974–75; Chair. Construction Exports Advisory Bd 1975–78; mem. Cttee on Finance for Industry, Nat. Econ. Devt Office 1980–87, Fitch Int. Advisory Cttee 2001–, Mitsubishi Int. Advisory Cttee 2001–, Sultanate of Oman Int. Advisory Cttee 2002–; Gov. Wellington Coll. 1977–89, 1996– (Vice-Pres. 1998–), BBC 1994–2000; Hon. Treasurer IISS 1984–90; Trustee Glyndebourne Arts Trust 1989–2002, Nat. Portrait Gallery (Chair. of the Trustees) 1992–; Hon. DLitt (Guildhall) 1993. *Address:* UBS Warburg, 1 Finsbury Avenue, London, EC2M 2PA, England. *Telephone:* (20) 7568-2400. *Fax:* (20) 7568-4225. *E-mail:* david.scholey@ubsw.com (Office). *Website:* www.ubswarburg.com (Office).

SCHOLEY, Sir Robert, Kt, CBE, DEng, FREng, FIM; British company executive and engineer; b. 8 Oct. 1921, Sheffield; s. of Harold Scholey and Eveline Scholey; m. Joan Methley 1946; two d.; ed King Edward VII School, Sheffield Univ.; joined United Steel Co. 1947, holding various eng and production posts within the org. until the nationalization of the steel industry; Dir Rotherham Div., Midland Group (British Steel Corpn) 1968, Dir Special Steels Div., Steelworks Group 1970, Man. Dir Operations 1972, Man. Dir Strip Mills Div. 1972–73, Chief Exec., mem. of Bd 1973–76, Deputy Chair. and Chief Exec. 1976–86, Chair. 1986–92; Pres. Eurofer 1985–90; Dir Eurotunnel 1987–94; Chair. Int. Iron and Steel Inst. 1989–90; Dir (non-exec.) Nat. Health Service Policy Bd 1989–92; mem. Higher Educ. Funding Council for England 1992–95; Pres. Inst. of Metals 1989–90; Chair. Close Bros 1999–; Hon. DEng (Sheffield) 1987; Hon. DSc (Teesside) 1995; British Inst. of Man. Gold Medal Award 1988, City Personality of the Year Award 1989. *Leisure interests:* history of the arts, reading, photography, caravanning, gardening.

SCHOLL, Andreas; German counter-tenor singer; b. 1967, Eltville; ed Schola Cantorum Basiliensis, Basel, Switzerland; mem. Kiedricher Chorbuben choir as child; soloist, Pueri Cantors Gathering, St Peter's Basilica, Rome 1981; debut int. recital at Théâtre de Grévin, Paris 1993; opera debut in Handel's Rodelinda, Glyndebourne Festival Opera, England 1998; performed at Belgian Royal Wedding Dec. 1999; teacher, Schola Cantorum Basiliensis, Basel 2000–; numerous int. tours and recitals, working with the world's leading Baroque conductors and ensembles; Conseil de l'Europe 1992, Foundation Claude Nicolas Ledoux 1992, Cannes Classical Award 1998, Artist of the Year, German Kultur Radio 1998, Belgian Musical Press Union Prize 1999. *Recordings include:* Handel's Messiah, Solomon, Italian Cantatas and Opera Arias, Bach's Christmas Oratorio, St Matthew Passion, St John Passion, Solo Cantatas for Alto and B Minor Mass, Vivaldi's Stabat Mater (Gramophone Award) 1996, Nisi Dominus (Edison Award) 2001, Monteverdi's L'Orfeo and 1610 Vespers, works by Pergolesi and Caldara; Heroes (Echo Classic Award) 1999, Wayfaring Stranger 2001. *Address:* c/o Harrison/Parrott Artists, 12 Penzance Place, London W1 4PA, England.

SCHÖLLKOPF, Ulrich, PhD; German professor of chemistry; b. 11 Oct. 1927, Ebersbach; m. Edith Jennewein 1957; two s. one d.; ed Univ. of Tübingen, Univ. of Calif., Los Angeles; Lecturer in Chem., Univ. of Heidelberg 1961–63; Assoc. Prof. Univ. of Göttingen 1964–68, Prof. 1968–; Ed. Liebigs Annalen der Chemie; mem. Cttee for the Dr. Paul-Janssen Prize, Akad. der Wissenschaften, Göttingen, Liebigs Denkmünze der GDCh; Award of the Japanese Soc. for the Promotion of Science. *Publications:* 250 articles in scientific journals. *Address:* Eichenweg 5, 37120 Bovenden, Germany (Home). *Telephone:* (551) 8925 (Home).

SCHOLTEN, Willem, BL; Netherlands politician; b. 1 June 1927, Deventer; s. of G. Scholten and W. H. (née Berends) Scholten; m. C. M. van der Eijk 1954; one s. one d.; ed Rijksbelastingacademie, Univ. of Amsterdam; Insp. of Taxes 1950–63; mem. Second Chamber, States-Gen. (Parl.) 1963–71; Sec. of State for Finance 1971–73; mem. European Parl. 1973–76; mem. Council of State 1976–78; Minister of Defence 1978–80; Vice-Pres. Council of State 1980–97; apptd. Minister of State 1997. *Address:* Koningsspil 87, 2265 VJ Leidschendam, Netherlands (Home). *Telephone:* (70) 3276785 (Home).

SCHOLZ, Rupert, DJur; German politician and fmr academic; b. 23 May 1937, Berlin; m.; ed Free Univ. of Berlin and Univ. of Heidelberg; taught law, Univs. of Berlin and Munich 1972–81; Senator for Justice, W Berlin 1981–88, for Fed. Affairs 1983–88; Minister of Defence 1988–90; mem. CDU 1983–; mem. Bundestag 1990–. *Address:* Bundestag, Platz der Republik 1, 11011 Berlin, Germany (Office). *Telephone:* (30) 2270 (Office). *Website:* www.bundestag.de.

SCHÖNBERG, Claude-Michel; French composer; b. 6 July 1944, France; s. of Adolphe Schönberg and Julie Nadás; one s. one d.; started in business as producer for EMI France and as pop song writer 1967–72; recording his own songs in France 1974–77; composed musicals La Révolution Française 1973, Les Misérables 1980–85, Miss Saigon 1989, Martin Guerre 1996; recipient of Tony, Grammy, Evening Standard and Laurence Olivier Awards, French 'Molière' and 'Victoires de la musique' for musicals. *Ballet:* Wuthering Heights with the Northern Ballet Theatre 2002. *Address:* c/o Cameron Mackintosh Limited, 1 Bedford Square, London, WC1B 3RA, England. *Telephone:* (20) 7637-8866.

SCHONBERG, Harold C.; American music critic; b. 29 Nov. 1915, New York, NY; s. of David and Minnie Schonberg; m. 1st Rosalyn Krokover 1942 (died 1973); m. 2nd Helene Cornell 1975; ed Brooklyn Coll. and New York Univ.; Assoc. Ed. American Music Lover 1938–42; Music Critic New York Sun 1946–50; Contributing Ed. and Record Columnist Musical Courier 1948–52; Music and Record Critic New York Times 1950–60, Sr Music Critic 1960–80, Cultural Corresp. 1980–85; columnist for The Gramophone (London) 1948–60; Contributing Ed. Int. Encyclopaedia of Music and Musicians; U.S. Army service 1942–46; Pulitzer Prize for Criticism 1971. *Publications:* The Guide to Long-Playing Records: Chamber and Solo Instrument Music 1955, The Collector's Chopin and Schumann 1959, The Great Pianists 1963, The Great Conductors 1967, Lives of the Great Composers 1970, Grandmasters of Chess 1973, Facing the Music 1981, The Glorious Ones: Classical Music's Legendary Performers 1985, Horowitz: His Life and Music 1992. *Leisure interests:* chess, golf, poker, backgammon. *Address:* 160 Riverside Drive, New York, NY 10024, USA (Office). *Fax:* (212) 813-8338 (Office).

SCHÖNBORN, HE Cardinal Christoph, OP; Austrian ecclesiastic; b. 22 Jan. 1945; ordained priest 1970; Bishop 1991; Coadjutor 1995; Archbishop of Vienna 1995–; cr. Cardinal 1998. *Address:* Wollzeile 2, 1010 Vienna, Austria. *Telephone:* (1) 515-52-0. *Fax:* (1) 515-52-37-28.

SCHÖNE, Albrecht, DPhil; German philologist; b. 17 July 1925, Barby; s. of Friedrich Schöne and Agnes Moeller; m. Dagmar Haver 1952; one s. one d.; ed Univs. of Freiburg, Basle, Göttingen and Münster; Extraordinary Prof. of German Literature, Univ. of Münster 1958; Prof. of German Philology, Univ. of Göttingen 1960–90, Prof. Emer. 1990–; Pres. Int. Asscn for Germanic Studies 1980–85; mem. Akad. der Wissenschaften, Göttingen, Deutsche Akad. für Sprache und Dichtung, Bayerische, Nordrhein-Westfäl. Akad. der Wissenschaften, Austrian and Netherlands Acads; Hon. mem. Modern Language Asscn of America; Foreign Hon. mem. American Acad. of Arts and Sciences; Officier, Ordre nat. du Mérite; Hon. DPhil; Hon. DTheol; several prizes. *Publications:* numerous books and articles on German literature and philology. *Leisure interests:* riding, hunting, painting. *Address:* University of Göttingen, Käte-Hamburger-Weg 13, 37073 Göttingen (Office); Grotefendstrasse 26, 37075 Göttingen, Germany (Home). *Telephone:* (551) 56449 (Home).

SCHOTTE, HE Cardinal Jan; Belgian ecclesiastic; b. 29 April 1928, Beveren-Waregem; s. of Marcel Schotte and Rhea Duhou; ed Sacred Heart Diocesan Coll., Waregem, Belgium, CICM Scholasticate, Scheut-Brussels and Katholieke Universiteit, Leuven; Asst Prof. Canon Law Catholic Univ., Leuven 1955–62; Rector IHM Seminary, Catholic Univ. of America, Washington DC 1963–66; Sec. Gen. Congregation Immaculate Heart of Mary, Rome 1967–72; Attaché for Int. Orgs. Secr. of State, Vatican 1972–80; Vice-Pres.

Pontifical Comm. for Justice and Peace 1980–85; Sec. Gen. Synod of Bishops 1985–; Titular Bishop of Silli 1984, Titular Archbishop 1985; cr. Cardinal 1994; mem. Pontifical Comm. for the Catechism of the Catholic Church 1986–92; Pres. Labour Office of Apostolic See, Vatican 1989–; mem. Pontifical Comm. for Latin America, Vatican 1989–, Congregation for Bishops 1985–; mem. Jt Working Group Holy See-WCC 1983–; mem. Interdicasterial Comm. on the Universal Catechism 1993–; mem. Congregation for Evangelization of Peoples 1994–; mem. Supreme Court Signatura Apostolica 1998–; mem. Final Court of Appeal, Vatican City State 1998; Special Envoy of the Pope, Taiwan 1996, St Louis, USA 1997, Siberia, Russia 2000; Officier, Légion d'honneur, Ordre Léopold II (Belgium), Kt Commdr Grand Cross, Order of Holy Sepulchre (USA). *Address:* Sinodo dei Vescovi, 00120 Vatican City State, Vatican City. *Telephone:* (06) 69884821. *Fax:* (06) 69883392.

SCHRADER, Paul Joseph, MA; American screenwriter and director; b. 22 July 1946, Grand Rapids, Mich.; m. 1st Jeannine Oppewall (divorced); m. 2nd Mary Beth Hurt 1983; ed Calvin Coll. and Univ. of Calif. at Los Angeles; film critic for LA Free Press magazine 1970–72; Ed. Cinema magazine 1970–; fmr Prof. Columbia Univ. *Screenplays:* Taxi Driver 1976, Obsession 1976, Raging Bull 1981, The Mosquito Coast 1986, Bringing Out the Dead; co-author: The Yazuka 1974, Rolling Thunder 1977, Old Boyfriends 1979; *Directed:* Bluecollar (also co-writer) 1978, Hardcore 1978, American Gigolo (also co-writer) 1979, Cat People 1982, Mishima (also co-writer) 1985, Patty Hearst 1989, The Comfort of Strangers 1990, Light Sleeper 1991 (also writer), Witch-hunt 1994, Touch 1997, Forever Mine (also writer), Dino. *Publication:* Transcendental Style in Film: Ozu, Bresson, Dreyer 1972. *Address:* 9696 Culva Blvd., Ste 203, Culver City, CA 90232, USA.

SCHREIER, Peter; German tenor and conductor; b. 29 July 1935, Meissen; ed Dresden Hochschule für Musik; sang with Dresden State Opera 1959–63; joined Berlin Staatsoper 1963; has appeared at Vienna State Opera, Salzburg Festival, La Scala, Milan, Sadler's Wells, London, Metropolitan Opera, New York and Teatro Colón, Buenos Aires; recital début London 1968; début as conductor 1969; has conducted recordings of several choral works by J. S. Bach, Mozart and Schubert; retd. as opera singer 1999 but continues to conduct. *Address:* c/o Norman McCann Ltd., The Coach House, 56 Lawrie Park Gardens, London, SE26 6XY (Office); c/o Askonas Holt, Lansdale Chambers, 27 Chancery Lane, London, WC2A 1PF, England (Office); Calberlastr. 13, 01326 Dresden, Germany.

SCHREYER, Rt Hon Edward Richard, PC, CC, C.M.M., CD, MA LLD; Canadian politician and diplomatist; b. 21 Dec. 1935, Beausejour, Manitoba; s. of John J. Schreyer and Elizabeth Gottfried; m. Lily Schulz 1960; two s. two d.; ed Cromwell Public School, Beausejour Collegiate, United Coll., St John's Coll. and Univ. of Manitoba; mem. for Brokenhead, Manitoba Legislature 1958, re-elected 1959, 1962; Prof. Political Science and Int. Relations, Univ. of Manitoba 1962–65; MP for Springfield Constituency 1965–68, for Selkirk 1968; Leader, Manitoba New Democratic Party 1969–78; Premier of Manitoba, Minister of Dominion-Provincial Relations 1969–77, Minister of Hydro 1971–77, of Finance 1972–74; Leader of the Opposition 1977–78; Gov.-Gen. of Canada 1979–84; High Commr to Australia, also Accred to Papua New Guinea and Solomon Islands 1984–88; Amb. to Vanuatu 1984–88; Distinguished Visiting Prof. Univ. of Winnipeg 1989–90, Simon Fraser Univ. 1991; Distinguished Fellow, Inst. of Integrated Energy Systems, Univ. of Victoria 1992–94, Dept of Geography, Univ. of BC 1995–96, Chair. Canadian Shield Foundation 1984–; Dir Perfect Pacific Investments 1989–, China Int. Trust and Investment Corpn (Canada) Ltd 1991–, Swan-E-Set Bay Resort and Country Club 1991–, Habitat for Humanity Canada 1992–, Sask. Energy Conservation and Devt Authority 1993–96, Alt. Fuel Systems Inc. (Calgary) 1994–, Cephalon Oil and Gas Resource Corp. (Calgary) 1994–95; Hon. Dir Sierra Legal Defence Fund 1991–; mem. Int. Asscn of Energy Econs, Churchill Econ. Advisory Cttee, Pacific Inst. of Deep Sea Tech.; Counsellor Canada West Foundation 1989–; Sr Adviser Summit Council for World Peace (World Peace Fed.), Washington DC 1991–; Hon. Adviser Canadian Foundation for the Preservation of Chinese Cultural and Historical Treasures 1994–; Hon. Patron John Diefenbaker Soc. 1991–; Hon. LLD (Manitoba) 1979, (Mount Allison) 1983, (McGill) 1984, (Simon Fraser) 1984, (Lakehead) 1985; Gov.-Gen. Vanier Award 1975. *Leisure interests:* reading, golf, sculpting, woodworking. *Address:* 250 Wellington Center, Unit 401, Winnipeg, Man. R3M 0B3, Canada. *Telephone:* (204) 989-7580. *Fax:* (204) 989-7581.

SCHREYER, Michaele, PhD; German politician; b. 9 Sept. 1951, Cologne; ed Univ. of Cologne; research asst, Inst. for Public Finances and Social Policy, Free Univ. of Berlin 1977–82; research asst and adviser for Green Caucus, Bundestag 1983–87; researcher, Inst. for Econ. Research 1987–88; Minister for Urban Devt and Environmental Protection in Senate of Berlin 1989–90; mem. State Parl., Berlin 1991–; mem. numerous co. bds; mem. Budget and Public Finance Cttee; Chair. Sub-Cttee on Funds for Public Housing 1995–97; Chair. Green Caucus, Berlin Parl. 1998–; lecturer, Dept of Social Sciences, Free Univ. of Berlin 1998–; mem. Bd Berlin br. of German Soc. for UN; EU Commr for Budget, Financial Control and Fraud Prevention 1999–. *Address:* Commission of the European Communities, 200 rue de la Loi, 1049 Brussels, Belgium (Office). *Telephone:* (2) 299-11-11 (Office). *Fax:* (2) 295-01-38 (Office). *Website:* europa.eu.int/comm/index-en.htm.

SCHREYER, William Allen, BA; American business executive; b. 13 Jan. 1928, Williamsport, Pa; s. of the late William Schreyer and Elizabeth Engel; m. Joan Legg 1953; one d.; ed Pennsylvania State Univ.; with Merrill Lynch

& Co., Inc. 1948–93, CEO Merrill Lynch & Co. 1984–92, Chair. 1985–93, Chair. Emer. 1993–; mem. Exec. Cttee, Bd of Dirs AEA Investors, Inc., Center for Strategic and Int. Studies, Washington, DC, Bd Trustees and Exec. Cttee Int. Councillor; Hon. DH; Distinguished Alumnus Award (Pa State Univ.). *Leisure interests:* tennis, reading, swimming. *Address:* Merrill Lynch & Co., Inc., 800 Scudders Mill Road, Plainsboro, NJ 08536 (Office); 117 Mercer Street, Princeton, NJ 08540, USA (Home). *Telephone:* (609) 282-1621. *Fax:* (609) 282-1222. *E-mail:* RARempe@NA2.US.ML.com.

SCHRIEFFER, John Robert, PhD; American professor of physics; b. 31 May 1931, Oak Park, Ill.; s. of John Henry Schrieffer and Louise Anderson; m. Anne Grete Thomson 1960; one s. two d.; ed Mass. Inst. of Technology and Univ. of Illinois; NSF Fellow, Univ. of Birmingham, UK and Univ. Inst. for Theoretical Physics, Copenhagen 1957–58; Asst Prof., Univ. of Chicago 1957–60, Univ. of Ill. 1959–60; Assoc. Prof., Univ. of Ill. 1960–62; Prof., Univ. of Pa 1962, Mary Amanda Wood Prof. of Physics 1964–79; Prof. of Physics, Univ. of Calif., Santa Barbara 1980–91, Essan Khashoggi Prof. of Physics 1985; Prof. Fla State Univ., Tallahassee 1992–; Chief Scientist Nat. High Magnetic Field Lab. 1992–; Vice-Pres. American Physical Soc. 1994–96, Pres. 1996; Univ. Eminent Scholar, Fla State Univ. System 1996; Dir Inst. for Theoretical Physics, Santa Barbara 1984–89; Andrew D. White Prof. Cornell Univ. 1969–75; mem. NAS, American Acad. Arts and Sciences, mem. American Philosophical Soc. 1974, mem. Royal Danish Acad. of Science and Letters; mem. Nat. Medal of Science Cttee1996–; Guggenheim Fellow 1967–68; Fellow American Physical Soc. (Pres. 1997); Dr hc (Geneva, Technische Hochschule, Munich, Univs of Pa, Ill., Cincinatti and Tel-Aviv); Buckley Prize 1968, Comstock Prize (NAS) 1968, Nobel Prize for Physics (with J. Bardeen and L. N. Cooper) 1972, John Ericsson Medal (American Soc. of Swedish Engineers) 1976, Alumni Achievement Award, Univ. of Ill. 1979, Nat. Medal of Science 1985, Superconductivity Award of Excellence (World Congress of Superconductivity) 1996. *Publication:* Theory of Superconductivity 1964. *Address:* NHMFL, Florida State University, 1800 E Paul Dirac Drive, Tallahassee, FL 32306, USA.

SCHROCK, Richard R., PhD; American professor of chemistry; b. 4 Jan. 1945, Berne, Indiana; m. Nancy F. Carlson 1971; two s.; ed Univ. of California, Riverside, Harvard Univ., Cambridge Univ., UK; Research Chemist, Cen. Research and Devt Dept, E.I. du Pont de Nemours & Co. 1972–75; Asst Prof. of Chem., MIT 1975–78, Assoc. Prof. 1978–80, Prof. 1980–89, Frederick G. Keyes Prof. of Chem. 1989–; Sherman T. Fairchild Scholar, Calif. Inst. of Tech. 1986, Science and Eng Research Council Visiting Fellow, Cambridge, UK 1991; ACS Award in Organometallic Chem. 1985 and Harrison Howe Award 1990, Inorganic Chem. Award 1996, Bailar Medal, Univ. of Ill. 1998, ACS Cope Scholar Award 2001, Royal Soc. of Chem. Sir Geoffrey Wilkinson Medal 2002. *Publications:* numerous papers in scientific journals. *Address:* Department of Chemistry, 6-331, Massachusetts Institute of Technology, 77 Massachusetts Avenue, Cambridge, MA 02139, USA. *Telephone:* (617) 253-1596.

SCHRODER, Baron Bruno Lionel, MBA; British business executive; b. 17 Jan. 1933; s. of the late Baron Bruno Schroder and Margaret Eleanor Phyllis (née Darell) Schroder; m. Patricia Leonie Mary Holt 1969; one d.; ed Eton, Univ. Coll., Oxford, Harvard Business School; Second Lt Life Guards 1951–53; joined Schroders PLC 1960, Dir 1963–, J. Henry Schroder & Co. Ltd 1966–, Schroders Inc. 1984–; Gov. English Nat. Ballet; mem. Exec. Cttee Air Squadron, Court of Assts. Worshipful Co. of Goldsmiths, Liveryman Guild of Air Pilots and Air Navigators; Queen Beatrix of Netherlands Wedding Medal. *Leisure interests:* flying, stalking, shooting. *Address:* Schroders PLC, 31 Gresham Street, London, EC2V 7QA, England. *Telephone:* (20) 7382-6000. *Fax:* (20) 7288-2006.

SCHRÖDER, Gerhard, LL.B.; German politician; b. 7 April 1944, Mossenburg, Lippe; s. of the late Fritz Schröder and of Erika Schröder; m. 1st Eva Schubach; m. 2nd Anna Taschenmacher; m. 3rd Hiltrud Hensen 1984; m. 4th Doris Köpf 1997; one d.; ed Univ. of Göttingen; apprentice as shop asst 1961; joined Social Democratic Party (SDP) 1963, Chair. 1999–; lawyer, Hanover 1976; Nat. Chair. of Young Socialists 1978–80; mem. Bundestag 1980–86; Leader of Opposition in State Parl. of Lower Saxony 1986; Minister-Pres. of Lower Saxony 1990–98; Chancellor of Germany 1998–; Mittelstandspreis 1997. *Address:* Bundeskanzleramt, Willy Brandt Strasse 1, 10557 Berlin, Germany. *Telephone:* (30) 40000. *Fax:* (30) 40001818. *E-mail:* bundeskanzler@bundeskanzler.de (Office). *Website:* www.bundeskanzler.de (Office).

SCHROEDER, Barbet; French film producer and director; b. 26 April 1941, Tehran, Iran; ed Sorbonne, Paris; worked as jazz tour operator Europe, photojournalist India, critic for Cahiers du Cinéma and L'Air de Paris 1958–63; Asst to Jean-Luc Godard on Les Carabiniers 1963; f. own production co. Les Films du Losange 1964; worked as actor and producer. *Films produced include:* The Collector, My Night at Maud's, Claire's Knee, Chloe in the Afternoon, Céline and Julie Go Boating, The Rites of Death, Perceval Le Gallois, Le Navire Night, Le Pont du Nord, Mauvaise Conduite, Une Sale Histoire. *Films directed include:* More, Sing-Song (documentary), La Vallée, General Idi Amin Dada (documentary), Maîtresse, Koko, the Talking Gorilla (documentary), Charles Bukowski (50 four-minute videos), Tricheurs, Barfly, Reversal of Fortune, Single White Female, Kiss of Death, Before and After (also producer), Desperate Measures, La Virgen de los Sicarios 2000.

SCHROEDER, Manfred Robert, Dr rer. nat; American physicist; b. 12 July 1926, Ahlen, North Rhine-Westphalia, Germany; s. of Karl Schroeder and Hertha Schroeder; m. Anny Menschik 1956; two s. one d.; ed Univ. of Göttingen; joined AT&T Bell Laboratories, Murray Hill 1954, Head of Acoustics Research Dept 1958–63, Dir of Acoustics, Speech and Mechanics Research 1963–69; Dir Drittes Physikalisches Inst., Univ. of Göttingen 1969–91, Univ. Prof. Emer. 1991–; Founder mem. Institut de Recherche et Coordination Acoustique/Musique, Centre Pompidou, Paris; mem. Nat. Acad. of Eng Washington, Göttingen Acad. of Sciences, Max-Planck Soc.; Fellow American Acad. of Arts and Sciences 1986, New York Acad. of Sciences 1993; holds 45 US Patents in speech and signal processing and other fields; Gold Medal, Audio Eng Soc. 1972, Baker Prize Award, Inst. of Electrical and Electronics Engineers, New York 1977, Sr Award, Acoustics, Speech and Signal Processing Soc. 1979, Lord Rayleigh Gold Medal, British Inst. of Acoustics, Gold Medal, Acoustical Soc. of America 1991, Niedersachsenpreis 1992, Helmholtz Medal, German Acoustical Soc. 1995. *Exhibitions:* Int. Computer Art Exhbn, Las Vegas (awarded First Prize) 1969. *Publications:* Speech and Speaker Recognition 1985, Fractals, Chaos, Power Laws: Minutes From an Infinite Paradise 1991, Number Theory in Science and Communication 1999, Computer Speech: Recognition, Compression, Synthesis 1999 and about 130 articles on acoustics, speech, hearing, microwaves, computer graphics. *Leisure interests:* languages, down-hill skiing, bicycling, photography, computer graphics. *Address:* Drittes Physikalisches Institut, Universität Göttingen, Bürgerstrasse 42-44, 37073 Göttingen; Rieswartenweg 8, 37077 Göttingen, Germany (Home). *Telephone:* (551) 21232 (Home); (551) 397713. *Fax:* (551) 397720. *E-mail:* mrs17@aol.com (Home). *Website:* www.physik3.gwdg.de/~mrs/ (Office).

SCHROEDER, Patricia Nell (Scott), JD; American administrator and politician; b. Patricia Nell Scott, 1940, Portland, Ore.; m. James W. Schroeder; one s. one d.; ed Univ. of Minnesota, Harvard Law School; mem. House of Reps. 1972–96, served on House Armed Services Cttee and several other cttees., Chair. House Select Cttee on Children, Youth and Families 1991–93; Prof., Woodrow Wilson School of Public and Int. Affairs, Princeton Univ. Jan.–June 1997; Pres. and CEO Asscn of American Publishers (AAP) 1997–; Leader New Century/New Solutions think-tank, Inst. for Civil Soc., Newton, Mass.; mem. Bd Marguerite Casey Foundation. *Publications:* Champion of the Great American Family 1989, 24 Years of House Work... and the Place is Still a Mess 1998. *Address:* Association of American Publishers Inc., 50 F Street, NW, Suite 400, Washington, DC 20001 (Office); 4102 Lester Court, Alexandria, VA 22311, USA (Home). *Telephone:* (202) 347-3375, ext. 543 (Office). *Fax:* (202) 347-3690 (Office). *Website:* publishers.org (Office).

SCHROEDER, Steven Alfred, MD; American professor of medicine; b. 26 July 1939, New York; s. of Arthur E. Schroeder; m. Sally Ross Schroeder 1967; two s.; ed El Cerrito High School, Stanford Univ., Harvard Univ.; Fellow, Harvard Community Health and Medical Care and Instructor Harvard Medical School 1970–71; Asst Prof. of Medicine and Health Care Sciences, later Assoc. Prof., The George Washington Univ. Medical Center 1971–76; Medical Dir The George Washington Univ. Health Plan 1971–76; Assoc. Prof. of Medicine, Univ. of Calif., San Francisco 1976–80, Prof. 1980–90, Chief, Div. of Gen. Internal Medicine 1980–90; Clinical Prof., Univ. of Medicine and Dentistry of NJ, Robert Wood Johnson Medical School 1991–; Pres. Robert Wood Johnson Foundation 1990–99, Pres. and CEO 1999–; Founding Chair. Int. Advisory Cttee of The Health Services, Ben-Gurion Univ. of the Negev, Israel 1996–; mem. Bd of Dirs American Legacy Foundation 2000–, Vice-Chair. 2001–; mem. Bd of Overseers, Harvard Coll. 2000–; mem. Editorial Bd New England Journal of Medicine 1994– Visiting Prof. Dept of Community Medicine, St Thomas's Hosp. Medical School, London 1982–83; numerous hon. degrees. *Publications:* more than 200 articles. *Leisure interests:* climbing, hiking, tennis, gardening, literature, history. *Address:* Robert Wood Johnson Foundation, College Road, P.O. Box 2316, Princeton, NJ 08543; 49 W Shore Drive, Pennington, NJ 08534, USA.

SCHUBARTH, Martin, DrIur; Swiss judge and professor of law; b. 9 June 1942, Basel; m. Musa Retschmedin 1944; one d.; ed Univ. of Basel; began practising as lawyer, Basel 1969; lecturer, Univ. of Basel 1973; apptd. Prof. Univ. of Bonn 1976, Univ. of Hanover 1980; Fed. Judge 1983–, Pres. Fed. Supreme Court 1999–2000, Pres. Criminal Court 1999–2002. *Publication:* Kommentar zum Schweizer Strafrecht 1982. *Address:* Office of the President, Schweizerisches Bundesgericht – Tribunal Fédéral, Mon Repos, 1000 Lausanne 14, Switzerland (Office). *Telephone:* (21) 3189111 (Office). *Fax:* (21) 3233700 (Office).

SCHUHL, Jean Jacques; French writer; Goncourt Prize for Literature 2000. *Publications:* Rose poussière 1972, Telex No. 1 1976, Ingrid Caven 2000. *Address:* c/o Editions Gallimard, 5 rue Sébastien Bottin, 75007 Paris, France (Office).

SCHULBERG, Budd, LLD; American novelist and scriptwriter; b. 27 March 1914, New York, NY; s. of Benjamin P. Schulberg and Adeline (Jaffe) Schulberg; m. 1st Virginia Ray 1936 (divorced 1942); one d.; m. 2nd Victoria Anderson 1943 (divorced 1964); two s.; m. 3rd Geraldine Brooks 1964 (died 1977); m. 4th Betsy Langman 1979; one s. one d.; ed Deerfield Acad. and Dartmouth Coll.; short-story writer and novelist 1936–; Screenwriter for Samuel Goldwyn, David O. Selznick and Walter Wanger, Hollywood, Calif. 1936–40; Lt US Navy 1943–46, assigned to Office of Strategic Service; taught writing courses and conducted workshops at various institutes in the US;

mem. Authors Guild, Dramatists Guild, American Civil Liberties Union, American Soc. Composers Authors and Publishers, Sphinx, Writers Guild of America East, Bd of Trustees, Humanitas Prize, Advisory Cttee on Black Participation John F. Kennedy Center for the Performing Arts; Founder and Dir. Watts Writers Workshop 1965–, Frederick Douglass Creative Arts Center, New York 1971–; numerous awards for writings, numerous humanitarian awards. *Publications:* novels: What Makes Sammy Run? 1941, The Harder They Fall 1947 (screen adaptation 1955), The Disenchanted 1950, Waterfront 1955, Sanctuary V 1969, Some Faces in the Crowd (short stories) 1953, From the Ashes: Voices of Watts (ed. and author of introduction) 1967, Loser and Still Champion: Muhammad Ali 1972, The Four Seasons of Success 1972, Swan Watch (with Geraldine Brooks) 1975, Everything That Moves 1980, Moving Pictures: Memories of a Hollywood Prince 1981, Writers in America 1983, Love, Action, Laughter and Other Sad Tales (short stories) 1990, Sparring with Hemingway: And Other Legends of the Fight Game 1995; plays, films: Winter Carnival (with F. Scott Fitzgerald) 1939, The Pharmacist's Mate 1951, On the Waterfront (Acad. Award and Screen Writers Guild Award for the screenplay) 1954, A Face in the Crowd (German Film Critics Award) 1957, Wind Across the Everglades 1958, The Disenchanted 1958, What Makes Sammy Run? (TV play 1959, stage 1964), Senor Discretion Himself (musical) 1985, A Table at Ciru's 1987, Joe Louis: For All Time (film documentary) 1988; stories and articles in numerous anthologies; contrib. to Newsday Syndicate, Esquire, Saturday Review, Life, Harper's, Playboy, Intellectual Digest, The New Republic, The New Yorker, The New York Times, Disenchanted (play) 1999, On the Waterfront 2001. *Leisure interests:* bird watching, boxing, fishing, Mexican archaeology, Black Arts movt. *Address:* Miriam Altshuler Literary Agency, RR # 1, Box 5, Old Post Road, Red Hook, NY 12571; c/o Mr. Freiberg, 2221 Pelham, Los Angeles, CA 90046, USA.

SCHULLER, Gunther; American composer and conductor; b. 22 Nov. 1925, New York; s. of Arthur E. Schuller and Elsie (Bernartz) Schuller; m. Marjorie Black 1948; two s.; ed St Thomas Choir School, New York, NY and Manhattan School of Music; Principal French horn, Cincinnati, Symphony Orchestra 1943–45, Metropolitan Opera Orchestra 1945–59; teacher, Manhattan School of Music 1950–63; Yale Univ. 1964–67; Head Composition Dept, Tanglewood 1963–84; Music Dir First Int. Jazz Festival, Washington 1962; active as conductor since mid-1960s with maj. orchestras in Europe and USA; reconstructed and orchestrated Der Gelbe Klang by De Hartmann/Kandinsky 1912; Pres. New England Conservatory of Music 1967–77; Pres. Nat. Music Council 1979–81; Artistic Dir Summer Activities, Boston Symphony Orchestra, Tanglewood, Berkshire Music Center 1969–84, Festival at Sandpoint 1985–98; Founder and Pres. Margun Music Inc. 1975, GM Records 1980; mem. American Acad. of Arts and Sciences, Nat. Inst. of Arts and Letters; Pulitzer Prize in Music 1999; Creative Arts Award, Brandeis Univ. 1960; Nat. Inst. Arts and Letters Award 1960; Guggenheim Grant 1962, 1963; ASCAP Deems Taylor Award 1970; Rogers and Hammerstein Award 1971; William Schuman Award, Columbia Univ. 1989; McArthur 'Genius' Award 1994; Max Rudolf Award 1998; Gold Medal American Acad. of Arts and Letters 1996, Order of Merit, Germany 1997; Hon. DMus (Ill. Univ.) 1966; (Northeastern Univ.) 1967, (Colby Coll.) 1969, (Ill. Univ.) 1970, (Williams Coll.) 1975, (Rutgers Univ.) 1980, (Oberlin Coll.) 1989, (Fla State Univ.) 1991. *Compositions include:* Symphony for Brass and Percussion 1950, Fantasy for Unaccompanied Cello 1951, Recitative and Rondo for Violin and Piano 1953, Dramatic Overture 1951, Music for Violin, Piano and Percussion 1957, String Quartet No. 1 1957, Woodwind Quintet 1958, Spectra 1958, Concertino for Jazz Quartet and Orchestra 1959, Seven Studies on Themes of Paul Klee 1959, Conversations 1960, Variants (ballet with choreography by Balanchine) 1961, Music for Brass Quintet 1960, String Quartet No. 2 1965, Symphony 1965, Sacred Cantata 1966, Gala Music (Concerto for Orchestra) 1966, The Visitation (opera commissioned by Hamburg State Opera) 1966, Movements for Flute and Strings, Six Renaissance Lyrics, Triplum I 1967, Shapes and Designs 1968, Fisherman and his Wife (opera) 1970, Capriccio Stravagante 1972, Tre Invenzioni 1972, Three Nocturnes 1973, Four Soundscapes 1974, Triplum II 1975, Violin Concerto 1976, Concerto No. 2 for Horn and Orchestra 1976, Diptych (for organ) 1976, Concerto No. 2 for Orchestra 1977, Concerto for Contrabasson and Orchestra 1978, Deaï (for three orchestras) 1978, Concerto for Trumpet and Orchestra 1979, Eine Kleine Posaunenmusik 1980, In Praise of Winds (symphony for large wind orchestra) 1981, Concerto No. 2 for Piano and Orchestra 1981, Symphony for Organ 1981, Concerto Quaternio 1983, On Light Wings (piano quartet) 1984, Farbenspiel (Concerto No. 3 for Orchestra) 1985, String Quartet No. 3 1986, Chimeric Images 1988, Concerto for String Quartet and Orchestra 1988, Concerto for Flute and Orchestra 1988, Horn Sonata 1988, On Winged Flight: A Divertimento for Band 1989, Chamber Symphony 1989, Impromptus and Cadenzas for Chamber Sextet 1990, Violin Concert No. 2 1991, Brass Quintet No. 2 1993, Reminiscences and Reflections 1993, The Past is the Present for Orchestra 1994, Sextet for Left-hand Piano and Woodwind Quintet 1994, Concerto for Organ and Orchestra 1994, Mondrian's Vision 1994, Blue Dawn into White Heat (concert band) 1995, An Ave Ascending 1996, River Reflections 1998, etc. *Publications:* Horn Technique 1962, Early Jazz, Its Roots and Musical Development, Vol. I 1968, Musings: The Musical Worlds of Gunther Schuller 1985, The Swing Era: The Development of Jazz 1930–45 1989, The Compleat Conductor 1997. *Address:* 167 Dudley Road, Newton Center, MA 02159, USA. *Telephone:* (617) 332-6398. *Fax:* (617) 969-1079 (Office).

SCHULTE, Dieter; German trades unionist; b. 13 Jan. 1940, Duisburg; m.; two c.; began career as blast furnace bricklayer, Thyssen; became active in trades union movt; Head of Deutscher Gewerkschaftsbund (Fed. of German Unions). *Address:* Deutscher Gewerkschaftsbund, Hans-Böckler-Str. 39, 40476 Düsseldorf, Germany; c/o Henriette-Herz-Platz 2, 10178 Berlin (Office).

SCHULTE-NOELLE, Henning; German banking executive; joined Allianz Group 1975, mem. Man. Bd Allianz Versicherung 1988–90, Allianz Leben 1988–90 (Chair. 1991), Chair. Allianz AG (now Allianz-Dresdner after acquisition of Dresdner Bank 2001) 1991–2002; Chair. Supervisory Bd Dresdner Bank AG 2001–. *Address:* c/o Allianz-Dresdner AG, Königinstrasse 28, 80802 Munich, Germany (Office).

SCHULTZ, Howard, BS; American business executive; b. 19 July 1953, Brooklyn, NY; m. Sheri Kersch Schultz; ones. one d.; ed Canarsie High School and Northern Michigan Univ.; began career as sales trainee for Xerox; Vice-Pres. of U.S. Sales, Hammerplast (subsidiary of Swedish-based Perstorp); joined Starbucks in Sales and Marketing Dept 1982, Chair. and CEO after buying out original owners 1987, Chief Global Strategist Starbucks Corpn; prin. owner Seattle SuperSonics (NBA) and Seattle Storm (WNBA). *Address:* Starbucks Coffee Company, P.O. Box 34067, Seattle, WA 98124-1067, USA (Office).

SCHULTZE, Charles Louis, PhD; American economist and government official; b. 12 Dec. 1924, Alexandria, Va; s. of Richard Lee Schultze and Nora Woolls (née Baggett) Schultze; m. Rita Irene Hertzog 1947; one s. five d.; ed Georgetown Univ. and Univ. of Maryland; Economist, Office of Price Stabilization 1951–52, Council of Econ. Advisers 1952–53, 1955–59; Assoc. Prof. of Econs, Indiana Univ. 1959–61; Assoc. Prof., Adjunct Prof. of Econs, Univ. of Md 1961–87; Asst Dir, Bureau of the Budget 1962–65, Dir 1965–68; Sr Fellow, Brookings Inst., Washington, DC 1968–76, 1981–87, 1991–96, Emer. 1997–; Dir Econ. Studies, Brookings Inst., Washington, DC 1987–90; Chair. Council of Econ. Advisers to Pres. 1977–81; Hon. Pres. American Econ. Asscn 1984. *Publications:* National Income Analysis 1964, The Politics and Economics of Public Spending 1969 (co-author), Setting National Priorities: The 1974 Budget, The Public Use of Private Interest 1977, Other Times, Other Places 1986, American Living Standards (co-ed. and co-author) 1988, Barriers to European Growth (co-ed. and co-author) 1989, An American Trade Strategy: Options for the 1990s (co-ed.) 1990, Memos to the President 1992. *Address:* Brookings Institution, 1775 Massachusetts Avenue, NW, Washington, DC 20036; 5520 33rd Street, NW, Washington, DC 20015, USA (Home).

SCHULZ, Ekkehard D., DrIng; German business executive; b. 24 July 1941, Bromberg, Westpreussen; m.; two c.; ed Clausthal Mining Acad., Clausthal Univ.; mem. scientific staff and Chief Engineer, Inst. for Gen. Metallurgy and Casting, Clausthal Univ. 1967–72; joined Thyssen Group 1972, Deputy Mem. (Production) Exec. Bd, Thyssen Stahl AG 1985, mem. (Production) 1986, (Tech.) 1988, Chair. 1991; mem. Exec. Bd, Thyssen AG 1991, Chair. 1998; Chair. Exec. Bd, ThyssenKrupp Stahl AG 1997, ThyssenKrupp AG 1999–, Thyssen Krupp Steel AG 1999–2001; Pres. EUROFER, Brussels; mem. supervisory bds./advisory councils, AXA Konzern AG, Commerzbank AG, Hapag Lloyd AG, MAN AG, RAG AG, RWE Plus AG, STRABAG AG; mem. int. advisory Bd, Salomon Smith Barney, New York; mem. Exec. Cttee and Bd, Wirtschaftsvereinigung Stahl und VDEh; mem. Advisory Council of BDI (Vice-Pres.); Hon. Prof. (Clausthal Univ.) 1999. *Address:* ThyssenKrupp AG, August-Thyssen-Strasse 1, 40211 Dusseldorf, Germany. *Telephone:* (211) 8240 (Office). *Fax:* (211) 82436000 (Office).

SCHUMACHER, Joel, BA; American film director; b. 29 Aug. 1939, NY; s. of Francis Schumacher and Marian Kantor; ed Parson School of Design, New York; began to work in fashion industry aged 15; later opened own boutique Paraphenalia; costume designer for Revlon in 1970s; also set and production designer; wrote screenplays Sparkle, Car Wash, The Wiz; also wrote and directed for TV. *Films include:* The Incredible Shrinking Woman, DC Cab (also screenplay), St Elmo's Fire (also screenplay), The Lost Boys, Cousins, Flatliners, Dying Young, Falling Down, The Client, Batman Forever, A Time to Kill, Batman and Robin, Eight Millimeter, Flawless (also screenplay and producer), Gossip, Tigerland, Phone Booth, Bad Company. *Address:* Joel Schumacher Productions, 400 Warner Boulevard, Burbank, CA 91522, USA (Office).

SCHUMACHER, Michael; German motor racing driver; b. 3 Jan. 1969, Hürth-Hermülheim; s. of Rolf Schumacher and the late Elizabeth Schumacher; m. Corinna Betsch 1995; two c.; began professional career 1983; 2nd place, Int. German Formula 3 Championship 1989; driver for Mercedes 1990; Int. German Champion, Formula 3 Championship 1990; European Formula 3 Champion 1990; World Champion, Formula 3, Macau and Fiji 1990; Formula 1 contestant since 1991; First Formula 1 victory, Belgium 1992; other Grand Prix wins include: Portuguese 1993, Brazilian 1994, 1995, 2000, 2002, Pacific (Aida) 1994, San Marino 1994, 2000, 2002, Monaco 1994, 1995, 1999, 2001, Canadian 1994, 1998, 2000, French 1994, 1995, Hungarian 1994, 1998, 2001, European (Jerez) 1994, (Nürburgring) 1995, 2000, 2001, Spanish 1995, 2001, 2002, Italian 1996, Japanese 1997, Australian 2000, 2001, 2002, Italian 2000, American 2000, Japanese 2000, Malaysian 2000, 2001, Austrian 2002; Third Place, World Motor Racing Championship 1992, Fourth Place 1993; Formula One World Champion 1994, 1995, 2000, 2001, 2002 (record five times, shared with Juan Manuel Fangio); 64 victories at end 2002. *Publications:* Formula For Success (with Derick Allsop) 1996, Michael Schumacher (biog. with Christopher Hilton) 2000. *Leisure interests:* football, tennis, swimming, skiing. *Address:* c/o Weber Management GmbH, Tränkestr. 11, 70597 Stuttgart, Germany. *Telephone:* (711) 726460. *Fax:* (711) 7264633. *Website:* www.mschumacher.com (Office).

SCHUMER, Charles Ellis, JD, BA; American politician; b. 23 Nov. 1950, Brooklyn, NY; s. of Abraham Schumer and Selma (née Rosen) Schumer; m. Iris Weinshall 1980; one d.; ed Harvard Univ.; called to Bar NY 1975; mem. staff US Senator Claiborne Pell 1973; Assoc. Paul, Weiss, Rifking, Wharton and Garrison 1974; mem. NY State Ass. 1975–80, Chair. Subcttee on City Man. and Governance 1977, Cttee on Oversight and Investigation 1979; mem. 97th–98th Congresses from 16th NY Dist 1981–85, 99th–105th Congresses from 10th (now 9th) NY Dist 1985–99, Senator from New York 1999–2001; Democrat. *Address:* c/o US Senate, 313 Hart Office Building, Washington, DC 20515, USA.

SCHÜSSEL, Wolfgang; Austrian politician; b. 7 June 1945, Vienna; m.; two c.; ed Vienna Univ.; Sec. Parl. Austrian People's Party (ÖVP) 1968, Chair. 1995–; Sec.-Gen. Austrian Econ. Fed. 1975–89; MP 1979; Leader ÖVP group of Econ. Fed. Parl. Dels. 1987; Minister of Econ. Affairs 1989–95; Vice-Chancellor of Austria and Minister of Foreign Affairs 1996–2000, Chancellor of Austria Feb. 2000–; Deputy Chair. Parl. Finance Cttee. *Publications:* several books on issues relating to democracy and economics. *Address:* Officer of the Federal Chancellor, 1014 Vienna, Ballhausplatz 2, Austria (Office). *Telephone:* (1) 531-15-0 (Office). *Fax:* (1) 535-03-380 (Office). *E-mail:* praesidium@bka.gv.at. *Website:* www.bka.gv.at (Office).

SCHUSTER, Rudolf; Slovak politician and diplomatist; b. 4 Jan. 1934, Košice; s. of Alojz Schuster and Mária Benediková; m. Irene Trojáková; two c.; ed Slovak Tech. Univ.; designer Regional Agric. Inst., Bratislava 1960; Asst Hydrology and Hydraulic Inst., Slovak Acad. of Sciences 1960–62; Dir Energetic Investment Dept and Tech. Dir E Slovak Steelworks 1963–74; Vice-Mayor of Košice 1975–83, Mayor 1983–86, 1994–99, Chair. E Slovak Region Nat. Cttee 1986–89; Chair. Nat. Council 1989–90; Amb. of Czech Repub. and Slovakia to Canada 1990–92; with Ministry of Foreign Affairs 1993–94; Pres. of Slovakia June 1999–; Order of Labour 1988, Pribina Cross, First Class 1998, Grand Cross of Merit with Collar (Malta) 1999; Dr hc (Tech. Univ. Košice) 1998, (Wuppertal) 1999; Merit Award for Peace and Democratic Achievement 2000 and numerous other decorations. *Publications:* Ultimatum 1997 and numerous books and screenplays. *Leisure interests:* documentaries, literature. *Address:* Office of the President, Hodžovo Namestie 1, P.O. Box 128, 810 00 Bratislava, Slovak Republic (Office). *Telephone:* (2) 52498945 (Office).

SCHÜTZ, Klaus; German politician and diplomatist; b. 17 Sept. 1926; m. Heidi Seeberger 1953; one s. one d.; ed Paulsen-Realgymnasium, Humboldt Univ. zu Berlin, Freie Univ. Berlin and Harvard Univ., USA; war service, seriously wounded 1944–45; Asst, Inst. für Politische Wissenschaften, Freie Univ., Berlin 1951–61; mem. City Ass. 1954–57, 1963–77; mem. Bundestag 1957–61; Liaison Senator between Berlin Senate and Bonn Govt 1961–66; mem. Bundesrat 1961–77, Pres. 1967–68; Under-Sec. Ministry of Foreign Affairs 1966–67; Governing Mayor of West Berlin 1967–77; Chair. Berlin Social Democratic Party 1968–77; Amb. to Israel 1977–81; Dir-Gen. Deutsche Welle 1981–87; Dir Landesanstalt für Rundfunk NRW, Düsseldorf 1987–93; Pres. Landesverband Berlin des Deutschen Roten Kreuzes 1996–. *Leisure interests:* books, baroque music. *Address:* 9 Konstanzerstrasse, 10707 Berlin, Germany. *Telephone:* (30) 8813617 (Home). *E-mail:* drschuetz@t-online.de (Home).

SCHÜTZEICHEL, Rudolf, DPhil; German professor of philology; b. 20 May 1927, Rahms; s. of Matthias Schützeichel and Gertrud Schützeichel; m. Margrit Britten 1955; two d.; ed Univ. of Mainz; Docent Univ. of Cologne 1960–63; Prof. of German Philology, Univ. of Groningen 1963–64, Univ. of Bonn 1964–69, Univ. of Münster 1969–; mem. Akad. Wissenschaften, Göttingen, Kgl. Akad., Göteborg; Hon. DPhil (Leipzig) 1992; Festschrift 1987 (Althochdeutsch 2 Bände Heidelberg); Officer Order of Orange-Nassau. *Publications:* Mundart, Urkundensprache und Schriftsprache 1974, Grundlagen d.w. Mitteldeutsch 1976, Das alem. Memento Mori 1967, Codex. Pal. lat. 52 1982, Mittelrh. Passionsspiel 1978, Gottschald Namenkunde 1982, Addenda und Corrigenda (I) 1982, (II) 1985, (III) 1991, Textgebundenheit 1981, Althochdeutsch. Wörterb. (5th Edn) 1995; Ed. various publs including BNF.NF. 1966–, Sprachwissenschaft 1976–, NOWELE 1983–, Die älteste Überlieferung von Williams Kommentar des Hohen Lìedes 2001. *Address:* Potstiege 16, 48161 Münster, Germany. *Telephone:* (251) 861345.

SCHUWIRTH, Lieut.-Gen. Klaus; German army officer; Commdr of German army's 4th Corps in Potsdam; Dir of Mil. Staff, EU Rapid Reaction Force 2001–. *Address:* c/o Ministry of Defence, Stauffenbergstr. 18, 10785 Berlin, Germany (Office). *Telephone:* (30) 200400 (Office). *Fax:* (30) 200-48333 (Office). *Website:* www.bundeswehr.de (Office).

SCHWAB, Charles R., BA(Econs), MBA; American business executive; b. 1937, Sacramento; m. Helen O'Neill; five c.; ed Stanford Univ., Stanford Grad. School of Business; f. The Charles Schwab Corpn, San Francisco 1971, now Chair. and Co-CEO; mem. Bd The Gap, Inc., Transamerica Corpn, AirTouch Communications, Siebel Systems, Inc.; Chair. Parent's Educational Resource Center, San Mateo; mem. Bd of Trustees, Stanford Univ.; mem. World Business Forum, CEO Org., San Francisco CEO Cttee on Jobs; mem. Bd and Treas. Nat. Park Foundation. *Publication:* How To Be Your Own Stockbroker 1984. *Address:* The Charles Schwab Corporation, 101 Montgomery Street, San Francisco, CA, USA (Office).

SCHWAETZER, Irmgard; German politician; b. 5 April 1942, Münster; m. Udo Philipp; ed Univs. of Passau, Münster and Bonn; worked in pharmaceutical industry in Germany and abroad 1971–80; mem. FDP 1975–, Gen. Sec. 1982–84, mem. Presidium 1982–, Deputy Chair. 1988–94, Chair. Work-Group on Youth, Family, Employment, Women and Health 1998–; mem. Bundestag 1980–; mem. Landesvorstand Nordrhein-Westfalen 1980–; Minister of State, Ministry of Foreign Affairs 1987–91; Chair., Nat. Union of Liberal Women 1990–95; Minister for Planning and Construction 1991–94; Regional Pres., Aachen 1997–. *Address:* Bundestag, Platz der Republik 1, 11011 Berlin, Germany (Office). *Telephone:* (30) 2270 (Office). *Website:* www .bundestag.de (Office).

SCHWALB LÓPEZ ALDANA, Fernando; Peruvian politician; b. 26 Aug. 1916, Lima; m. Carmen Rosa Tola de Schwalb 1950; two s. one d.; ed Pontifica Univ. Católica del Perú; entered Ministry of Foreign Affairs 1933; entered diplomatic service 1939; Second Sec., Washington, DC 1944–45, First Sec. 1945–48, Minister Counsellor 1948; pvt. law practice 1949–50, 1950–53, 1968–69; Alt. Exec. Dir IBRD 1950; Senator from Lima 1962 (prevented from taking office by coup d'état); Minister of Foreign Affairs 1963–65; Chair. Council of Ministers 1963–65; Chair. Peruvian Del. to Gen. Ass. of UN 1963; First Vice-Pres. 1980–84, Prime Minister of Peru 1983–84, Minister of Foreign Affairs 1983–84; Amb. to USA 1980–82; Pres. Banco Central de Reserva del Perú 1966–68; Rep. of Pres. to Bogotá Meeting of Presidents 1966; Banco de la República, Bogotá 1969; Consultant, Cen. Banking Service, IMF 1969–82; mem. Partido Acción Popular. *Publication:* El Contrato de la Florgreen y el Pago a la I.P.C. *Address:* c/o Oficina del Primer Ministro, Lima, Peru.

SCHWAN, Gesine Marianne, Dr rer. pol; German university professor; b. 22 May 1943, Berlin; d. of Hildegard Schneider (née Olejak) and Hans R. Schneider; m. Alexander Schwan 1969 (died 1989); one s. one d.; ed Lycée Français de Berlin, Free University of Berlin; Asst Prof. Dept of Political Sciences, Free Univ. of Berlin 1971–77, Prof. 1977–; Fellow Woodrow Wilson Int. Center for Scholars 1980–81; By-Fellow Robinson Coll., Cambridge, UK 1984; Pres. Europa-Univ. Viadrina 1999–; Verdienstkreuz (1st class). *Publications:* Leszek Kolakowski, Eine Philosophie der Freiheit nach Marx 1971, Die Gesellschaftskritik von Karl Marx 1974, Sozialdemokratie u. Marxismus (with Alexander Schwan) 1974, Sozialismus in der Demokratie; Eine Theorie Konsequent sozialdemokratischen Politik 1982, Der normative Horizont moderner Politik I und II (with Alexander Schwan) 1985, Politik und Schuld: Die zerstörerische Macht des Schweigens 1997; Jahrbuch für Politik (co-ed.) 1991–. *Leisure interests:* music, theatre, travelling. *Address:* Europa-Universität Viadrina, 15230 Frankfurt an der Oder, Grosse Scharmstrasse 59; Department of Political Science, Free University of Berlin, Ihnestrasse 21, 1000 Berlin 33 (Office); Teutonenstrasse 6, 14129 Berlin, Germany (Home). *Telephone:* (335) 55340 (Office), (30) 8382340 (Free Univ.) (Office), (30) 8038366 (Home). *Fax:* (335) 5534305 (Office). *E-mail:* presidents.office@ euv-frankfurt-o.de (Office). *Website:* www.euv-frankfurt-o.de (Office).

SCHWARTZ, Jacob T., PhD; American computer scientist; b. 9 Jan. 1930, New York; s. of Harry Schwartz and Hazel Schwartz; m. 1st Frances E. Allen 1972; two d.; m. 2nd Diana Robinson 1989; ed City Coll. of New York, Yale Univ.; Instructor, Computer Science Dept, Yale Univ. 1951–53, Asst Prof. 1953–56; Assoc. Prof. of Math. and Computer Science, New York Univ. 1957–58, Prof. 1958–; Chair. Computer Science Dept, Courant Inst. of Mathematical Sciences, New York Univ. 1969–77, now Dir; Assoc. Ed. Journal of Programming Languages; mem. Editorial Bd, Journal of Computer and System Sciences, Communications on Pure and Applied Math., Advances in Applied Math.; mem. NAS; mem. (fmr Chair.) Computer Science Bd, Nat. Research Council; Sloane Fellow 1961–62; Distinguished Lecturer, Univ. of Calif., Santa Barbara 1978, MIT 1980; Wilbur Cross Medal (Yale Univ.), Townsend Harris Medal (City Univ. of New York), Steele Prize (American Mathematical Soc.) 1981. *Publications:* Linear Operators (3 Vols) 1958–70, Matrices and Vectors for High Schools and Colleges 1961, Relativity in Illustrations 1962, Lectures on the Mathematical Method in Analytical Economics (2 Vols) 1962, W*Algebras 1967, Lie Groups: Lie Algebras 1967, Lectures on Nonlinear Functional Analysis 1968, Lectures on Differential Geometry and Topology 1969, Programming Languages and their Compilers 1969, On Programming: An Interim Report on the SETL Project 1973, Higher Level Programming 1981; numerous scientific papers. *Leisure interests:* history, music. *Address:* New York University, Courant Institute of Mathematical Sciences, 251 Mercer Street, New York, NY 10012, USA. *Telephone:* (212) 998-3375.

SCHWARTZ, Maxime; French administrator and scientist; b. 1 June 1940, Blois; ed Ecole Polytechnique; entered Inst. Pasteur 1963, Deputy Dir 1985–87, Dir-Gen. 1987–; also mem. of the Scientific Council of Inst. Pasteur and Head of the Dept of Molecular Biology. *Address:* L'Institut Pasteur, 25–28 rue du Dr. Roux, 75015 Paris, France.

SCHWARTZENBERG, Roger-Gérard, DenD; French politician and professor of law; b. 17 April 1943, Pau, Pyrénées-Atlantiques; s. of André Schwartzenberg and Simone Gutelman; ed Inst. d'Etudes Politiques, Paris; Prof. Univ. de Droit, d'économie et de sciences sociales de Paris II 1969–, Inst. d'Etudes Politiques 1972–83; Pres. Mouvement des Radicaux de Gauche

1981–83, Hon. Pres. 1983–; mem. European Parl. 1979–83; Sec. of State, Ministry of Educ. 1983–84; Sec. of State responsible for univs, Ministry of Educ. 1984–86; Deputy for Val de Marne to Nat. Ass. 1986–2000, 2002–; Sec. to Nat. Ass. 1988–92, 1993–97, Vice-Pres. Foreign Affairs Comm. 1992–2000; Mayor of Villeneuve-Saint-Georges 1989–95, 2001–; Deputy Judge High Court of Justice and Court of Justice of the Repub. 1993–97; Pres. Groupe parlementaire radical, citoyen et vert 1999–2000; Minister of Research 2000–02. *Publications:* books on political and legal topics including La Droite absolue 1981, La Politique mensonge 1998. *Leisure interest:* tennis. *Address:* Assemblée Nationale, 75355 Paris; Université de Droit de Paris, 12 Place du Panthéon, 75005 Paris, France.

SCHWARZ, Antoine, LenD; French administrator and business executive; b. 9 Aug. 1943, Paris; s. of Willy Schwarz and Elisabeth du Brusle de Rouvroy; m. Christine Coudreau 1974; two s. one d.; ed Inst. d'Etudes Politiques de Paris, Ecole Nat. d'Admin; Admin. to the Treasury, Ministry of the Economy and Finance 1971–74; Prin. Inst. d'Études Politiques 1972–74; Head Service Juridique et Technique de l'Information 1974; Head of Cabinet André Rossi 1975–76, Raymond Barre 1977; Dir Radio Monte-Carlo 1978–81, Editions Mondiales 1982–83; Counsellor Centre Nat. de la Cinématographie 1984–85; Pres. and Dir-Gen. Société Financière de Radiodiffusion (SOFIRAD) 1986–89; Pres. Sofica-valor 1988–89, Consultant 1990; Founder, Pres. Radiofina 1993; Pres. SFP-Productions 1994–99, Sportotal 2000–; Chevalier Ordre du Mérite. *Address:* Sportotal, 51 rue d'Amsterdam, 75008 Paris (Office); 20 square de la Motte-Piquet, 75015 Paris, France (Home).

SCHWARZ, Gerard; American conductor; b. 19 Aug. 1947, Weehawken, NJ; m. Jody Greitzer 1984; two s. two d.; ed Professional Children's School, Juilliard School; joined American Brass Quintet 1965; Music Dir Erick Hawkins Dance Co. 1966, Eliot Feld Dance Co. 1972; Co-Prin. Trumpet, New York Philharmonic 1973–74; Founding Music Dir Waterloo Festival 1975; Music Dir New York Chamber Symphony 1977–, LA Chamber Orchestra 1978–86; est. Music Today series, Merkin Concert Hall, New York 1981 (Music Dir 1988–89); Music Adviser Mostly Mozart Festival, Lincoln Center, New York 1982–84, Music Dir 1984–; Music Adviser Seattle Symphony 1983–84, Prin. Conductor 1984–85, Music Dir 1985–2001; Artistic Adviser Tokyu Bunkamura's Orchard Hall, Japan 1994–; Music Dir Royal Liverpool Philharmonic Orchestra Sept. 2001–; Guest Conductor, Cosmopolitan Symphony, Aspen Festival Chamber, Tokyo Philharmonic, Residentie, The Hague, St Louis Symphony, Kirov, St Petersburg, Royal Liverpool Philharmonic and Vancouver Symphony Orchestras, City of London Symphonia and London Mozart Players; has conducted many US orchestras and the Hong Kong Philharmonic, Jerusalem Symphony, Israeli Chamber and English Chamber Orchestras, London Symphony, Helsinki Philharmonic and Monte Carlo Philharmonic Orchestras, Ensemble Contemporain, Paris and Nat. Orchestra of Spain; operatic conducting début, Washington Opera 1982; has also conducted Seattle Opera 1986, San Francisco Opera 1991 and New Japan Philharmonic 1998; numerous recordings for Delos, Nonesuch, Angel and RCA labels; numerous TV appearances; Hon. DFA (Fairleigh Dickinson Univ., Seattle Univ.); Hon. DMus (Univ. of Puget Sound); named Conductor of the Year 1994 by Musical America Int. Directory of the Performing Arts; Ditson Conductor's Award, Columbia Univ. 1989; has received two Record of the Year Awards, one Mumms Ovation Award. *Address:* Royal Liverpool Philharmonic Orchestra, Philharmonic Hall, Hope Street, Liverpool, L1 9BP, England.

SCHWARZ, Harry Heinz, BA, LLB; South African politician, attorney and diplomatist; b. 13 May 1924, Cologne, Germany; s. of Fritz Schwarz and Alma Schwarz; m. Annette Louise Rudolph 1952; three s.; ed Univ. of Witwatersrand; with SA Air Force (seconded to RAF) during World War II; mem. Middle Temple; practised as attorney and advocate 1949–; Chief Exec. Merchant Bank 1969–74; mem. Johannesburg City Council 1951–57; mem. Transvaal Prov. Council 1958–74, Leader of Opposition 1960–74; MP 1974–91; Amb. to USA 1991–94; Sr Adviser to Hofmeyr Inc., Johannesburg fmr columnist Sunday Star; Hon. Col 15 Squadron (SA Air Force); Order of Meritorious Service; several hon. doctorates. *Publications:* Poverty Erodes Freedom and articles and book chapters on politics, law and economics. *Leisure interest:* writing. *Address:* 6 Sandown Valley Crescent, Sandton 2196 (Office); 5 Dukes End, 163 Buckingham Avenue, Craighall Park, Johannesburg 2196 (Home); P.O. Box 413063, Craighall 2024, South Africa. *Telephone:* (11) 2861116 (Office); (11) 4479879 (Home). *Fax:* (11) 7849976; (11) 7849976 (Office). *E-mail:* HarryS@hofmeyr.com (Office).

SCHWARZ-SCHILLING, Christian, DPhil; German politician; b. 19 Nov. 1930, Innsbruck, Austria; s. of Prof. Rheinhard Schwarz-Schilling and Duzsa Schwarz-Schilling; m. Marie Luise Jonen 1957; two d.; ed Univs. of Berlin and Munich; mem. Landtag, Hesse, FRG 1966–76; Sec.-Gen. Hesse CDU 1966–80, Deputy Chair. 1967–96; Chair. Coordinating Cttee for Media Policy CDU/CSU 1975–83; mem. Bundestag 1976–; Minister of Posts and Telecommunications 1982–92; Deputy Chair. CDU/CSU Fed. Medium and Small Business Asscn 1977–97; Pres. Exec. Cttee European Medium and Small Business Union 1979–82; Chair. Inquiries Cttee Bundestag New Information and Communication Technologies 1981–82; Pres. Dr. Schwarz-Schilling and Partner GmbH 1993–; Chair. Bundestag Subcttee. on Human Rights and Humanitarian Aid 1995–98, Deputy Chair. 1998–; Int. Mediator-Arbitrator for Fed. of Bosnia and Herzegovina 1996–98, also for Repub. Srpska 1997; Chair. Bd Prima Com AG, Mainz, 1999–, Mox Telecom AG Ratingen 1999–, 2Venture AG 2000–; Hon. DUniv (Bryant Coll., USA) 1997; Grosses Bun-

desverdienstkreuz mit Stern. *Publication:* Unsere Geschichte Schicksal oder zufall. *Leisure interests:* swimming, skiing, piano. *Address:* Dr. Schwarz-Schilling & Partner GmbH, Industriestrasse 35, 63654 Büdingen (Office); Am Dohlberg 10, 63654 Büdingen, Germany (Home). *Telephone:* (6042) 964440 (Office). *Fax:* (6042) 964432 (Office).

SCHWARZENEGGER, Arnold Alois, BA; American (b. Austrian) actor, author, businessman and fmr bodybuilder; b. 30 July 1947, Graz, Austria; s. of Gustav Schwarzenegger and Aurelia Schwarzenegger; m. Maria Owings Shriver 1985; two s. two d.; ed Univ. of Wisconsin-Superior; went to USA 1968, naturalized 1983; Nat. Weight Training Coach Special Olympics; Body-building Champion 1965–80; volunteer, prison rehabilitation programmes; Chair. Pres.'s Council on Physical Fitness and Sport 1990; Jr Mr Europe 1965, Best Built Man of Europe 1966, Mr Europe 1966, Mr International 1968, Mr Universe (amateur) 1969, and numerous other prizes. *Film appearances include:* Stay Hungry 1976 (Golden Globe Award), Pumping Iron 1977, The Jayne Mansfield Story 1980, Conan, the Barbarian 1982, Conan The Destroyer 1983, The Terminator 1984, Commando 1985, Raw Deal 1986, Predator 1987, Running Man 1987, Red Heat 1988, Twins 1989, Total Recall 1990, Kindergarten Cop 1990, Terminator II: Judgment Day 1991, Last Action Hero 1993, Dave (cameo) 1993, True Lies 1994, Junior 1994, Eraser 1996, Jingle All the Way 1996, Batman and Robin 1997, With Wings of Eagles 1997, End of Days 1999, The Sixth Day 2001, Collateral Damage 2002. *Publications:* Arnold: The Education of a Bodybuilder 1977, Arnold's Body-shaping for Women 1979, Arnold's Bodybuilding for Men 1981, Arnold's Encyclopedia of Modern Bodybuilding 1985, Arnold's Fitness for Kids (jtly) 1993. *Address:* PMK, Suite 200, 955 South Carillo Drive, Los Angeles, CA 90048, USA.

SCHWARZKOPF, Gen. H. Norman, BS; American army officer (retd); b. 22 Aug. 1934, Trenton, NJ; s. of H. Norman Schwarzkopf and Ruth Bowman; m. Brenda Holsinger 1968; one s. two d.; ed US Mil. Acad. and Univ. of Southern Calif.; 2nd Lt US Army 1956; Deputy Commdr 172nd Infantry Brigade, Fort Richardson, Alaska 1974–76; Commdr 1st Brigade, 9th Infantry Div. Fort Lewis, Wash. 1976–78; Deputy Dir Plans, US Pacific Command, Camp Smith, Hawaii 1978–80; Asst Div. Commdr 8th Infantry Div. (mechanized), US Army Europe, FRG 1980–82; Dir Mil. Personnel Man. Office of Deputy Chief of Staff for Personnel, Washington, DC 1982–83; Commdg Gen. 24th Infantry Div. (mechanized), Fort Stewart, Ga 1983–85; Deputy Commdr US Forces in Grenada Operation 1983; Asst Deputy Chief of Staff Operations, HQ, Dept of Army, Washington, DC 1985–86; Commdg Gen. I Corps, Fort Lewis, Wash. 1986–87; Deputy Chief of Staff for Operations and Plans, HQ, Dept of Army, Washington, DC 1987–88; C-in-C US Cen. Command, MacDill Air Force Base, Fla 1988–91; retd 1992; contrib. and analyst NBC News 1995–; Chair. Starbright Foundation 1995–; Commdr Allied Forces in War to liberate Kuwait after illegal invasion and annexation by Iraq (Operation Desert Storm) 1990–91; DSM, DFC, Silver Star with two oak leaf clusters, Legion of Merit, Bronze Star with three oak leaf clusters, Purple Heart with oak leaf cluster, Grand Officier Légion d'honneur 1991, Hon. Pvt. French Foreign Legion 1991, Distinguished Order of Kuwait 1991; Hon. KCB (UK) 1991, and numerous other awards. *Publication:* It Doesn't Take A Hero (autobiog.) (with Peter Petre) 1992. *Leisure interests:* hunting, fishing, skeet and trap-shooting. *Address:* 400 North Ashley Drive, Suite 3050, Tampa, FL 33602; c/o International Creative Management, 40 West 57th Street, New York, NY 10019, USA.

SCHWEBEL, Stephen Myron, BA, LLB; American judge, lawyer, arbitrator and mediator; b. 10 March 1929, New York; s. of Victor Schwebel and Pauline Pfeffer Schwebel; m. Louise I. N. Killander 1972; two d.; ed Harvard Coll., Univ. of Cambridge and Yale Law School; Attorney 1954–59; Asst Prof. of Law, Harvard Univ. 1959–61; Asst Legal Adviser, then Special Asst to Asst Sec. of State for Int. Org. Affairs 1961–67; Exec. Vice-Pres. and Exec. Dir American Soc. of Int. Law 1967–73; Consultant, then Counsellor on Int. Law, Dept of State 1967–74, Deputy Legal Adviser 1974–81; Prof. of Int. Law, then Edward B. Burling Prof. of Int. Law and Org., Johns Hopkins Univ., Washington 1967–81; Legal Adviser to US Del. and Alt. Rep. in 6th Cttee, UN Gen. Ass. 1961–65; Visiting Lecturer or Professor at Cambridge Univ. 1957, 1983, ANU 1969, Hague Acad. of Int. Law 1972, Inst. Univ. de hautes études int., Geneva 1980 and various American univs. 1987–; rep. in various cttees UN 1962–74; Assoc. Rep., Rep., Counsel or Deputy Agent in cases before Int. Court of Justice 1962–80; Judge Int. Court of Justice 1981–2000, Vice-Pres. 1994–97, Pres. 1997–2000; mem. Int. Law Comm. 1977–81; arbitrator or chair. in int. commercial arbitrations 1982–; mem. Tribunal in Eritrea-Yemen Arbitration 1997–99, Ethiopia-Eritrea Boundary Comm. 2000–; Pres. Admin. Tribunal, IMF 1994–, Southern Blue Fin Tuna Arbitration 2000; mem. Panels of Arbitrators and of Conciliators of the Int. Centre for the Settlement of Investment Disputes (ICSID) of the World Bank 2000–; mem. Bd of Eds, American Journal of Int. Law 1967–81, 1994–; mem. Council on Foreign Relations; mem. Inst. of Int. Law; mem. Bars of State of New York, Dist of Columbia, Supreme Court of the USA; Hon. Bencher, Gray's Inn 1998–; Gherini Prize, Yale Law School 1954; Medal of Merit, Yale Law School 1997. *Publications:* The Secretary-General of the United Nations 1952, The Effectiveness of International Decisions (ed.) 1971, International Arbitration: Three Salient Problems 1987, Justice in International Law 1994; author of some 150 articles in legal periodicals and the press on problems of international law and relations. *Leisure interests:* music, cycling. *Address:* 1501 K Street, NW, Washington, DC 20005 (Office); 1917 23rd Street, NW, Washington, DC 20008, USA (Home). *Telephone:* (202) 736-8328 (Office); (202) 232-3114 (Home). *Fax:* (202) 736-8709 (Office); (202) 797-9286 (Home). *E-mail:* judgeschwebel@aol.com (Office).

SCHWEIGER, Til; German actor, producer and director; b. 19 Dec. 1963, Freiburg, Germany; m. Dana Schweiger; four c.; ed acting acad., Cologne; Best Actor Award, Moscow Film Festival 1997. *Films include:* Manta Manta 1991, Ebbie's Bluff (Max Ophuls Prize for Best Actor) 1992, Der Bewegte Mann 1994, Maennerpension, Das Superweib, Brute 1996, Knocking on Heaven's Door 1996 (also producer and co-writer), Replacement Killers, Judas Kiss 1997, Der Eisbär (also producer), Der grosse Bagarozy 1998, Magicians 1999, Investigating Sex, Driven 2000, Was tun wenn's brennt 2000, Jetzt oder Nie (producer) 2000, Auf Herz und Nieren (producer) 2000, Joe and Max 2001, Tomb Raider 2 2002. *Address:* c/o Players Agentur Management GmbH, Sophienstr. 21, 10178 Berlin, Germany. *Telephone:* (30) 2851680 (Office). *Fax:* (30) 2851686 (Office). *E-mail:* mai@players.de (Office). *Website:* www.players.de.

SCHWEIKER, Mark, BSc, M. ADMIN.; American politician; b. 31 Jan. 1953, Bucks County, Pa; s. of John Schweiker and Mary Schweiker; m. Katherine Schweiker; two s. one d.; ed Bloomsberg Univ., Rider Univ.; began career with Merrill Lynch, moving on to McGraw-Hill; first elected to public office as Middletown Township Supervisor 1979; Bucks County Commr 1987–94; Lt-Gov. of Pa 1994–2001, Gov. Oct. 2001–; numerous awards including Bloomsburg Univ. Alumnus of the Year 1990, Pa Nature Conservancy Award for Outstanding Service to Conservation 1993, Tech. Council of Pa Advocate of the Year 1996, Pa Econ. League Commitment to Excellence in Local Govt Award 1998, Pa League of Cities Outstanding Public Service Award 1999. *Address:* 225 Main Capitol, Harrisburg, PA 17120, USA (Office). *Telephone:* (717) 787-2500 (Office). *Fax:* (717) 772-3155 (Office). *Website:* www.state.pa.us (Office).

SCHWEIKER, Richard Schultz, BA; American fmr politician and businessman; b. 1 June 1926, Norristown, Pa; s. of Malcolm A. Schweiker and Blanche Schultz; m. Claire Joan Coleman 1955; two s. three d.; ed Pennsylvania State Univ.; business exec. 1950–60; mem. US House of Reps. 1960–68; US Senator from Pa 1969–80; Sec. of Health and Human Services 1981–83; Pres. American Council of Life Insurance 1983–94; Chair. Partnership for Prevention 1991–97; mem. Bd of Dirs Tenet Healthcare Corpn 1984–, LabOne Inc. 1994–; Republican; ten hon. degrees and numerous awards. *Address:* 904 Lynton Place, McLean, VA 22102-2113, USA (Office).

SCHWEITZER, Louis, LenD; French business executive; b. 8 July 1942, Geneva, Switzerland; s. of Pierre-Paul Schweitzer and Catherine Hatt; m. Agnes Schmitz 1972; two d.; ed Inst. d'Etudes Politiques, Paris, Faculté de Droit, Paris and Ecole Nat. d'Admin; Insp. of Finance 1970–; special assignment, later Deputy Dir, Ministry of the Budget 1974–81; Dir du Cabinet to Minister of Budget 1981–83, of Industry and Research 1983, to Prime Minister 1984–86; Prof. Inst. d'Etudes Politiques de Paris 1982–86; Vice-Pres. for Finance and Planning Régie Renault 1986–90, Chief Finance Officer 1988–90, Exec. Vice-Pres. 1989–90, Pres. and COO 1990, Chair. and CEO 1992–; Admin., Soc. Générale 1989–93, UAP 1988–94, Inst. Pasteur 1988–94, Péchiney 1989–92, IFRI 1989–, Réunion des Musées Nat. 1990–96, Renault Véhicules Industriels 1992–2001, BNP 1993–, Roussel UCLAF 1994–97, Crédit Nat. (now Natexis) 1995–99, Philips 1997–, Volvo AB 2001–; Chair. Bd Dirs l'Ecole des mines de Nancy 1999–; Officer Légion d'honneur, Officier ordre nat. du Mérite . *Address:* Renault, 34 quai du Point du Jour, 92109 Boulogne-Billancourt Cedex (Office); 1 rue Dauphine, 75006 Paris, France (Home). *Telephone:* 1-41-04-56-94 (Office). *Fax:* 1-41-04-62-30 (Office). *E-mail:* louis.schweitzer@renault.com (Office).

SCHWERY, HE Cardinal Henri; Swiss ecclesiastic; b. 14 June 1932, St Léonard, Valais; s. of the late Camille Schwery and Marguerite Terroux; ed Lycée-Coll. de Sion, Valais, Faculty of Sciences, Univ. de Fribourg, Grand Séminaire de Sion and Pontificia Università Gregoriana, Rome; ordained priest 1957; teacher of science, math. and religious studies, Lycée-Coll. de Sion 1961–; Rector 1972–77; Dir Pensionnat de la Sitterie (Petit Séminaire) de Sion 1968–72; Diocesan Chaplain, Action Catholique de Jeunesse Etudiante 1958–66; Mil. Chaplain 1958–77; Bishop of Sion 1977–95, Bishop Emer. 1995–; cr. Cardinal 1991; Kt of the Grand Cross, Order of the Holy Sepulchre of Jerusalem. *Publications:* Un Synode extraordinaire 1986, Chemin de Croix, chemin de lumière, L'Année Mariale dans le diocèse de Sion 1987, Sentiers Pastoraux 1988, Sentiers épiscopaux – Regards sur nos familles (2 Vols) 1992, Magnificat (in collaboration) 1992, Chrétien au quotidien 1996. *Leisure interest:* spirituality. *Address:* Case postale 2334, CH 1950 Sion 2, Switzerland. *Telephone:* (27) 323-26-32. *Fax:* (27) 321-10-88.

SCHWIMMER, David, BS; American actor, writer and director; b. 12 Nov. 1966, New York; s. of Arthur Schwimmer and Arlene Schwimmer; ed Beverly Hills High School and Northwestern Univ., Chicago; Co-Founder Lookingglass Theater Co., Chicago 1988; mem. Bd Dirs Rape Foundation for Rape Treatment Center of Santa Monica. *Theatre includes:* (with Lookingglass Theater Co.): West, The Odyssey, Of One Blood, In the Eye of the Beholder, The Master and Margarita. *Theatre directed includes:* The Jungle (six Joseph Jefferson Awards), The Serpent, Alice in Wonderland (Edin. Festival, Scotland). *Films include:* Flight of the Intruder 1990, Crossing the Bridge 1992, Twenty Bucks 1993, The Waiter 1993, Wolf 1994, The Pallbearer 1996, Shooting the Moon (exec. producer) 1996, Apt Pupil 1998, Kissing a Fool (exec. producer) 1998, Six Days Seven Nights 1998, The Thin Pink Line 1998, All

the Rage 1999, Picking Up the Pieces 2000, Hotel 2001, Dogwater (also Dir). *Television includes:* The Wonder Years 1988, Monty 1993, NYPD Blue 1993, Friends 1994–, L.A. Law, The Single Guy (NBC), Happy Birthday Eilzabeth: A Celebration of Life 1997, Breast Men 1997, Since You've Been Gone (Dir) 1998, Band of Brothers (mini series) 2001, Uprising 2001; hosted Montreal's 13th Annual Just for Laughs Festival. *Leisure interests:* writing, playing softball and basketball. *Address:* c/o The Gersh Agency, P.O. Box 5617, Beverly Hills, CA 90210, USA (Office).

SCHWIMMER, Walter, LLD; Austrian politician, international organization official and lawyer; b. 16 June 1942, Vienna; s. of Walter Schwimmer and Johanna Schwimmer; m. Martina Schwimmer; two s.; ed Univ. of Vienna; mem. Nationalrat (Austrian Parl.) 1971–99, Chair. Parl. Cttee on Health 1989–94, on Justice 1995–96; Vice-Chair. Parl. Group, Austrian People's Party (ÖVP) 1986–94; mem. Council of Europe Parl. Ass. 1991–, Vice-Pres. Council of Europe 1996, Jan.–Sept. 1999, Sec.-Gen. Aug. 1999–; Chair. European People's Party Group – Christian Democrats 1996–99; Dir, Exec. Vice-Pres. Vienna Health Insurance Fund; Grosses Goldenes Ehrenzeichen der Republik Österreich; Grosses Silbernes Ehrenzeichen der Republik Österreich mit dem Stern; Grosses Silbernes Ehrenzeichen der Stadt Wien; Grand Cross of the Order of the Star of Romania; Commdr's Cross, Order of Grand Duke Gaudemes (Lithuania); Leopold-Kunschak Award 1975. *Publications:* Christian Trade Unions in Austria 1975, Social Consequences of Inflation 1988, A Union Goes Down in History 1993. *Leisure interests:* books, history, travelling, hiking. *Address:* Office of the Secretary General, Council of Europe, 67075 Strasbourg Cedex, France (Office). *Telephone:* (3) 88-41-20-50 (Office). *Fax:* (3) 88-41-27-99 (Office). *E-mail:* walter.schwimmer@coe.int (Office). *Website:* www.coe.int (Office).

SCHWYZER, Robert, DPhil; Swiss molecular biologist; b. 8 Dec. 1920, Zürich; s. of Robert Schwyzer and Rose Schätzle; m. Rose Nägeli 1948; two s. one d.; ed primary school, Nathan Hale, Minneapolis, USA, Canton High School (A), Zürich and Dept of Chemistry, Univ. of Zürich; Privatdozent, Univ. of Zürich 1951–59, Asst Prof. 1960–63; initiation of Polypeptide Research, Head of Polypeptide Research Group, Ciba Ltd, Basel 1952–63, Asst Man. 1960–63; Prof. and Head of Dept of Molecular Biology, Swiss Fed. Inst. of Tech., Zürich 1963–; Prof.-in-Res., Clinical Research Inst. of Montreal 1991–; Werner Award, Swiss Chemical Soc. 1957; Ruzicka Prize, Swiss Fed. Inst. of Tech. 1959; Otto Nägeli Award, Switzerland 1964; Vernon Stouffer Award, American Heart Asscn, Cleveland 1968; Ernesto Scoffone Award 1982; Alan E. Pierce Award, American Peptide Symposia 1985; Rudinger Gold Medal, European Peptide Symposia 1988. *Publications:* scientific papers on syntheses of biologically active polypeptides; structure activity relationships; relationships between structure and biophysical interactions with lipid-bilayer membranes; molecular mechanisms of opioid receptor selection by peptides, new principles governing receptor specificity. *Leisure interests:* mountain climbing, skiing, literature. *Address:* Institut für Molekularbiologie und Biophysik, Eidgenössische Technische Hochschule, Hartriegelstrasse 12, 8180 Bülach, Switzerland. *Telephone:* (1) 8607111.

SCHYGULLA, Hanna; German actress; b. 1943; has made nearly 40 films; Bundesverdienstkreuz Erster Klasse. *Stage appearances include:* Mother Courage 1979. *Films include:* Die Ehe der Maria Braun (Silberner Bär Berlinale) 1979, Die Dritte Generation 1979, Lili Marleen 1980, Die Fälschung 1981, La Nuit de Varennes 1982, Eine Liebe in Deutschland 1983, The Story of Piera 1983, Miss Arizona 1987, The Summer of Mr. Forbes, Dead Again 1991, The Merchant of Four Seasons 1998. *Television appearances include:* 8 Stunden sind kein Tag (series) 1972. *Leisure interests:* travel, painting. *Address:* 80802 Munich, Germany (Office).

SCLATER, John G., PhD, FRS; British professor of geophysics; b. 17 June 1940, Edinburgh, Scotland; s. of John G. Sclater and Margaret Bennett Glen; m. 1st Fredrica R. Sclater 1968 (divorced 1985), two s.; m. 2nd Paula Ann Edwards 1985 (divorced 1991); m. 3rd Naila G. Burchett 1992; ed Stonyhurst Coll., Edinburgh Univ. and Cambridge Univ.; Postdoctoral Research Geophysicist, Scripps Inst. of Oceanography 1965–67, Asst Research Geophysicist 1967–72; Assoc. Prof. MIT 1972–77, Prof. 1977–83; MIT Dir, Jt Program in Oceanography with the Woods Hole Oceanographic Inst. 1981–83; Assoc. Dir Inst. for Geophysics, Univ. of Texas at Austin, Prof., Dept of Geological Sciences and Shell Distinguished Chair. in Geophysics 1983–91; Prof. of Geophysics, Scripps Inst. of Oceanography, Univ. of Calif. (San Diego) 1991–; Fellow Geological Soc. of America, American mem. NAS Geophysical Union; Swiney Lecturer, Edin. Univ. 1976; Shell Distinguished Prof. 1984–89; Guggenheim Fellow 1998–99; Rosenstiel Award 1978; Bucher Medal, American Geophysical Union 1985. *Leisure interests:* running, swimming, golf. *Address:* GRD 0215, Scripps Institution of Oceanography, University of California at San Diego, La Jolla, CA 92093, USA (Office). *Telephone:* (619) 534-3051.

SCLATER, John Richard, CVO, MA, MBA; British business executive; b. 14 July 1940, Camborne; s. of Arthur Sclater and Alice Sclater (née Collett); m. 1st Nicola Mary Gloria Cropper 1967 (divorced); one s. one d. (deceased); m. 2nd Grizel Elizabeth Catherine Dawson MBE 1985; ed Charterhouse, Gonville and Caius Coll., Cambridge and Yale and Harvard Univs; Commonwealth Fellow 1962–64; Glyn, Mills & Co. 1964–70; Dir Williams, Glyn & Co. 1970–76; Man. Dir Nordic Bank 1976–85, Chair. 198–87; Dir Guinness Peat Group PLC 1985–87, Jt Deputy Chair. 1987; Dir and Deputy Chair. Guinness Mahon & Co. Ltd 1985–87, Chair. 1987; Chair. Foreign & Colonial (now

Graphite) Enterprise Trust PLC 1986–, Foreign & Colonial Ventures Advisers Ltd 1988–, Foreign & Colonial Ventures Ltd 1990–98, Berisford PLC 1990–2000 (Dir 1986–), Hill Samuel Bank Ltd 1992–96, (Dir 1990–96), Foreign & Colonial (now Graphite) Pvt. Equity Trust PLC 1994–2002, Finsbury Life Sciences Investment Trust PLC 1997–, Argent Group Europe Ltd 1998–; Pres. Equitable Life Assurance Soc. 1994–2001 (Dir 1985–2001); Deputy Chair. Yamaichi Int. (Europe) Ltd 1985–97, Union PLC 1986–96 (Dir 1981–, Chair. 1996), Grosvenor Group Holdings Ltd 2000–02 (Dir 1989–2002); Dir Berner Nicol & Co. Ltd 1968 (Chair. 2002–), James Cropper PLC 1972, Holker Estates Co. Ltd 1974, Foreign & Colonial Investment Trust PLC 1981–2002 (Chair. 1985–2002), Millennium & Copthorne Hotels PLC 1996–, Deva Group Ltd 1999–, Deva Holdings Ltd 1999–, Wates Group Ltd 1999–; Consultant RP&C Int. 1997–; First Church Estates Commr 1999–2001 (mem. Archbishops' Council and Gen. Synod, Church of England 1999–2001); Dir and Gov. Brambletye School 1976–; Trustee The Grosvenor Estate 1973–, Coll. of Arms Trust 1994–; mem. Council of Duchy of Lancaster 1987–2000, CBI City Advisory Group 1988–99; Gov. Int. Students House 1976–99; Freeman City of London 1993–; Liveryman Goldsmiths' Co. 1993–. *Leisure interest:* country pursuits. *Address:* 117 Eaton Square, London, SW1W 9AA (Office); Sutton Hall, Barcombe, Nr Lewes, E Sussex, BN8 5EB, England (Home). *Telephone:* (20) 7235-2223 (Office); (1273) 400450 (Home). *Fax:* (20) 7235-1228 (Office); (1273) 401086 (Home). *E-mail:* john.sclater@talk21.com (Office).

SCOFIDIO, Ricardo; American artist and professor of architecture; co-f. (with Elizabeth Diller, q.v., Diller & Scofidio (D + S), New York 1979, cr. installations and electronic media projects; Prof. of Architecture, The Cooper Union 1965–; Jt recipient (with Elizabeth Diller) fellowships from Graham Foundation for Advanced Study in the Fine Arts 1986, New York Foundation for the Arts 1986, 1987, 1989, Chicago Inst. for Architecture and Urbanism 1989, Tiffany Foundation Award for Emerging Artists 1990, Progressive Architecture Award (for Slow House) 1991, Chrysler Award for Achievement and Design 1997. *Art exhibitions:* group shows at Richard Anderson Gallery, New York 1992, 1993, Museum of Modern Art, New York 1993, New Museum, New York 1993, Sagacho Gallery, Tokyo 1997, Thomas Healy Gallery, New York 1998. *Publications:* (with Elizabeth Diller) Flesh 1995, Back to the Front: Tourisms of War. *Address:* School of Architecture, The Cooper Union for the Advancement of Science and Art, Cooper Square, New York, NY 10003-7120, USA (Office). *Telephone:* (212) 353-4000 (Office). *Website:* www.cooper .edu (Office).

SCOFIELD, Paul, CH, CBE; British actor; b. 21 Jan. 1922, Hurstpierpoint, Sussex; s. of Harry Scofield and Mary Scofield; m. Joy Parker 1943; one s. one d.; trained London Mask Theatre Drama School; Birmingham Repertory Theatre 1941 and 1943–46; Stratford-upon-Avon Shakespeare Memorial Theatre 1946–48; Arts Theatre 1946; Phoenix Theatre 1947; with H.M. Tennent 1949–56; Assoc. Dir Nat. Theatre 1970–71; Hon. LLD (Glasgow Univ.) Hon. DLit (Kent) 1973, (Sussex) 1985, (St Andrews) 1998; Oscar and New York Film Critics' Award, Moscow Film Festival and British Film Acad. Awards for (Film) A Man for All Seasons 1967, Shakespeare Prize, Hamburg 1972, Danish Film Acad. Award, Tony Award, Evening Standard Drama Award for John Gabriel Borkman 1996, Life Achievement Award American Film Inst. 1996, The Shakespeare Birthday Award 1999. *Theatre:* Chekhov's Seagull, Anouilh's Ring Round the Moon, Charles Morgan's The River Line, Richard II, Time Remembered, A Question of Fact, Hamlet (also in Moscow), Power and the Glory, Family Reunion, A Dead Secret, Expresso Bongo, The Complaisant Lover, A Man for all Seasons, Stratford Festival, Ont., Canada 1961, Coriolanus, Don Armado New York 1961–62, A Man for All Seasons London 1962–63, King Lear 1963 (E Europe, Helsinki, Moscow, New York 1964), Timon of Athens 1965, The Government Inspector London 1966, Staircase 1967, Macbeth 1968, The Hotel in Amsterdam 1968, Uncle Vanya 1970, The Captain of Köpenik 1971, Rules of the Game 1971, Savages 1973, The Tempest 1974, 1975, Dimetos 1976, Volpone 1977, The Madras House 1977, The Family 1978, Amadeus 1979, Othello 1980, Don Quixote 1982, A Midsummer Night's Dream 1982, I'm Not Rappaport 1986, Exclusive 1989, Heartbreak House 1992, John Gabriel Borkman (Royal Nat. Theatre) 1996. *Radio includes:* Billy Budd, Dr Iben's Ghosts, On the Train to Chemnitz, T. S. Eliot's The Waste Land and Four Quartets and many others. *Films:* The Train 1963, A Man for All Seasons 1967, King Lear 1970, Scorpio 1972, A Delicate Balance 1972, '1919', Anna Karenina 1984, When the Whales Came 1988, Henry V 1989, Hamlet 1991, Quiz Show 1993, The Little Riders 1995, The Crucible 1995. *Television:* The Ambassadors 1977, The Potting Shed 1981, If Winter Comes 1981, Song at Twilight 1982, Come into the Garden Maud 1982, A Kind of Alaska 1984, Summer Lightning 1985, Only Yesterday 1986, The Attic 1988, Utz 1991, Martin Chuzzlewit 1994. *Address:* The Gables, Balcombe, Sussex, RH17 6ND, England.

SCOGNAMIGLIO, Carlo, DEcon; Italian politician, economist and business consultant; b. 27 Nov. 1944, Varese; s. of Luigi Scognamiglio and Esther Scognamiglio (née Pasini); m. Cecilia Pirelli; one s. one d.; ed L. Bocconi Univ., Milan, London School of Econs; Asst Lecturer L. Bocconi Univ.; Asst Prof. of Finance, Univ. of Padua 1973–79; Asst Prof. of Industrial Econs Univ. L. Bocconi, Milan 1968–73; Prof. 1973; Prof. of Econs and Industrial Policy, Libera Università Int. degli Studi Sociali, Rome 1979–, Dean and Rector 1984–92; Liberal Party cand. in Milan constituency, elected to Senate 1992, Chair. European Affairs Cttee, mem. Budget Cttee, re-elected to Senate 1994; Pres. of Senate 1994–; Acting Pres. of Italy 1994–96; Pres. Rizzoli-Corriere

della Sera 1983–84, Vice-Pres. 1984–; Minister of Defence 1998–99; Co-Founder, Bocconi School of Business Admin. 1979; Pres. Aspen Inst. Italia 1995–; Acad. of France Award for Economics 1988. *Publications include:* The Stock Exchange 1973, Industrial Crises 1976, The White Book on PPSS 1981, The White Book on the Italian Financial Market 1982, Theory and Policy of Finance 1987, Industrial Economics 1987, Report to Minister of Treasury of Commission for Privatization of Industry 1990, The Liberal Project 1996. *Leisure interests:* economics, history. *Address:* Aspen Institute Italia, Via Carducci 2, 20123 Milan, Italy (Office). *Telephone:* (06) 67062835 (Office). *Fax:* (02) 866855 (Office). *E-mail:* c.scognamigliopasini@senato.it (Office).

SCOLA, Ettore; Italian director and screen writer; b. 10 May 1931, Trevico (Avellino); m. Gigliola Fantoni 1956; two d.; ed Univ. of Rome; studied law, then worked in journalism and radio; started scriptwriting 1952–; directed: Se permettete parliamo di donne 1964, La Congiuntura 1965, Thrilling 1965, L'arcidiavolo 1966, Riusciranno i nostri eroi a ritrovare l'amico misteriosamente scomparso in Africa? 1968, Il commissario Pepe 1969, Dramma della gelosia (tutti i particolari in cronaca) (Jealousy, Italian Style) 1970, Permette? Rocco Papaleo 1971, La più bella serata della mia vita 1972, Trevico—Torino...viaggio nel Fiat-nam 1973, C'eravamo tanto amati 1974, Brutti, sporchi e cattivi 1976 (Best Dir, Cannes Film Festival), Signore e signori buonanotte 1976, Una giornata particolare (A Special Day) 1977 (Special Jury Prizes, Cannes Film Festival), I nuovi mostri 1977, La terrazza 1979, Passione d'amore 1980, Il mondo nuovo 1982, Le bal 1983, Maccheroni 1985, La Famiglia (The Family) 1987, Splendor 1988, Che Orà È? 1989, Il Viaggio di Capitan Fracassa 1990, Mario, Maria e Mario 1992, Romanzo di un giovane povero 1995.

SCOLARI, Luiz Felipe; Brazilian football manager; b. 9 Nov. 1948, Passo Fundo-RS; Man. Club Gremio (three league titles, Brazilian Cup, Libertadores Cup); Man. Palmeiras (Libertadores Cup); Man. Brazilian Nat. Team 2001–02; led Brazil to a record fifth world championship in June 2002; resgnd July 2002; Man. Portuguese Nat. Team Nov. 2002–. *Address:* c/o Secretaria de Estado da Juventude e Desportos, Av. Brasília, 1° Andar, 1449-011 Lisbon, Portugal.

SCOON, Sir Paul, GCMG, GCVO, OBE; Grenadian public administrator; b. 4 July 1935; m. Esmai Monica Lumsden 1970; two step-s. one step-d.; ed Inst. of Educ., Leeds, Toronto Univ.; teacher Grenada Boys' Secondary School 1953–67, Chief Ed. Officer 1967–68; with Civil Service 1968, Vice-Pres. Civil Service Asscn 1968, Perm. Sec. 1969, Sec. to Cabinet 1970–72, Deputy Dir, Commonwealth Foundation 1973–78, Gov. Centre for Int. Briefing, Farnham Castle 1973–78, Gov.-Gen. of Grenada 1978–92; now Chair. Grenada Tourism Bd. *Leisure interests:* reading, tennis. *Address:* P.O. Box 180, St George's, Grenada. *Telephone:* 4402180.

SCORSESE, Martin, MA; American film director and writer; b. 17 Nov. 1942, Flushing, NY; s. of Charles Scorsese and Catherine (née Cappa) Scorsese; m. 1st Laraine Marie Brennan 1965; one d.; m. 2nd Julia Cameron (divorced); one d.; m. 3rd Isabella Rossellini (q.v.) 1979 (divorced 1983); m. 4th Barbara DeFina 1985; ed New York Univ.; Faculty Asst and Instructor, Film Dept, New York Univ. 1963–66; instructor 1968–70; Dir and writer of films: What's a Nice Girl Like You Doing in a Place Like This? 1963, It's Not Just You, Murray 1964, Who's That Knocking At My Door? 1968, The Big Shave 1968; Dir play The Act 1977–78; Dir and writer of documentaries; Supervising Ed. and Asst Dir Woodstock 1970; Assoc. Producer and Post-Production Supervisor Medicine Ball Caravan 1971, Box Car Bertha 1972; Edward J. Kingsley Foundation Award 1963, 1964; First Prize, Rosenthal Foundation Awards of Soc. of Cinematologists 1964; named Best Dir, Cannes Film Festival 1986; First Prize, Screen Producer's Guild 1965, Brown Univ. Film Festival 1965, shared Rosellini Prize 1990, Award American Museum of Moving Image 1996, Award for Preservation, Int. Fed. of Film Wards 2001etc. *Films directed include:* Mean Streets 1973, Alice Doesn't Live Here Any More 1974, Taxi Driver 1976, New York, New York 1977, King of Comedy 1981; actor and Dir The Last Waltz 1978; Dir Raging Bull 1980, After Hours 1985, The Color of Money 1986; Dir The Last Temptation of Christ 1988 (Courage in Filmmaking Award, LA Film Teachers Asscn 1989), Good Fellas 1989, Cape Fear 1991, The Age of Innocence 1993, Clockers 1994, Casino 1995, Kundun 1997, Bringing Out the Dead 1999, The Muse 1999, Gangs of New York (Golden Globe for Best Dir 2003) 2002; exec. producer: The Crew 1989, Naked in New York 1994, Grace of My Heart 1996; producer: The Grifters 1989, Naked in New York 1994, Casino 1996, Kundun 1998; co-producer Mad Dog and Glory 1993; acted in Cannonball 1976, Triple Play 1981, Dreams 1990. *Publications:* Scorsese on Scorsese 1989, The Age of Innocence: The Shooting Script (with Jay Cocks) 1996, Casino (with Nicholas Pileggi) 1996. *Address:* C/o Artists Management Group, 9465 Wilshire Boulevard, Suite 519, Los Angeles, CA 90212; Jeff Doolly Starr & Co., 350 Park Avenue, 9th Floor, New York, NY 10022, USA.

SCOTCHMER, Suzanne Andersen, PhD; American professor of economics and public policy; b. 23 Jan. 1950, Seattle; d. of Toivo Andersen and Margaret Andersen; ed Univ. of Washington, Univ. of California at Berkeley; Asst and Assoc. Prof. of Econs, Harvard Univ. 1980–86; Prof. of Econs and Public Policy, Univ. of Calif. at Berkeley 1986–; Sloan Fellowship, Olin Fellowship (Yale Univ.), Hoover Nat. Fellowship (Stanford Univ.). *Publications:* many articles on econs in professional journals including Econometrica and Science. *Address:* Goldman School of Public Policy and Department of Economics, University of California at Berkeley, 2607 Hearst Avenue, Berkeley, CA

94720-7320, USA (Office). *Telephone:* (510) 643-8562 (Office). *E-mail:* scotch@socrates.berkeley.edu (Office). *Website:* socrates.berkeley.edu/~scotch (Office).

SCOTT, Alastair Ian, PhD, FRSE, FRS; British professor of chemistry; b. 10 April 1928, Glasgow, Scotland; s. of William Scott and Nell (Newton) Scott; m. Elizabeth W Walters 1950; one s. one d.; ed Univ. of Glasgow; Lecturer in Organic Chem. Univ. of Glasgow 1957–62; Prof. Univ. of British Columbia, Vancouver 1962–65, Univ. of Sussex 1965–68, Yale Univ. 1968–77; Distinguished Prof. Texas A & M Univ. 1977–80, Davidson Prof. of Chemistry and Biochemistry 1982–2001, The Robert A. Welch Chair and D. H. R. Barton Prof. of Chem. 2001–; Prof. Dept of Chem. Univ. of Edinburgh 1980–82; mem. ACS, Royal Soc. of Chem. (RSC); Hon. mem. Pharmaceutical Soc. of Japan 1984; Hon. MA (Yale) 1968; Hon. DSc (Coimbra) 1990, (Univ. Pierre et Marie Curie, Paris) 1992; Corday Morgan Medal, RSC 1964, ACS Guenther Award 1975, ACS A. C. Cope Scholar Award 1992, Centenary Lecturer (RSC) 1994, Tetrahedron Prize 1995, RSC Award in Natural Product Chem. 1995, Robert A. Welch Award in Chemistry 2000, Royal Soc. of Edin. Queen's Royal Medal 2001, Royal Soc.'s (Davy Medal) 2001, Distinguished Texas Scientist of the Year, Texas Acad. of Science) 2002, ACS Nakanishi Prize 2003 and other awards. *Publications:* Interpretation of Ultraviolet Spectra of Natural Products 1964, Handbook of Naturally Occurring Compounds (co-author) 1972; articles in professional journals. *Leisure interests:* tennis, walking, reading. *Address:* Department of Chemistry, Texas A & M University, College Station, TX 77843, USA. *Telephone:* (979) 845-3243. *Fax:* (979) 845-5992. *E-mail:* aiscott@tamu.edu (Office).

SCOTT, Alexander Brian, DPhil, MRIA; British academic; b. 1 Dec. 1933, Bangor, N Ireland; s. of John Scott and Lil Scott; m. Margaret Byrne 1997; ed Foyle Coll. Londonderry, Queen's Univ. Belfast and Merton Coll. Oxford; temporary lecturer, Magee Univ. Coll. Londonderry 1957–58; Asst Dept of Western Manuscripts, Bodleian Library, Oxford 1958–62; Lecturer, Dept of Humanity, Aberdeen Univ. 1963–64; Lecturer, Dept of Latin, Queen's Univ. Belfast 1964, Reader in Late Latin 1971–92, Prof. of Late Latin 1992–94, Prof. Emer. 1995–. *Publications:* Hildeberti Cenomanensis Carmina Minora 1969, Malachy, a Life 1976, Expugnatio Hibernica, The Conquest of Ireland by Gerald of Wales 1978, Medieval Literary Theory and Criticism c.1100–1375 1988, Liudprand of Cremona 1992. *Leisure interest:* travelling by train, preferably in France. *Address:* 31 Valentia Road, Drumcondra, Dublin 9, Ireland (Home). *Telephone:* (1) 8372924 (Home).

SCOTT, Charles Thomas; British advertising executive; b. 22 Feb. 1949; with Binder Hamlyn 1967–72; Chief Accountant, ITEL Int. Corpn 1972–77; Controller, IMS Int. Inc. 1978–84, Chief Financial Officer 1985–89; Chief Financial Officer, Saatchi & Saatchi Co. (later Cordiant PLC, now Cordiant Communications Group PLC) PLC 1990–91, COO 1991–92, CEO 1993–95, Chair. 1995–, Bates Worldwide 1997. *Leisure interests:* golf, tennis. *Address:* Cordiant Communications Group PLC, 121–141 Westbourne Terrace, London, W2 6JR, England (Office).

SCOTT, (Harold) Lee, Jr, BBA; American business executive; b. 14 March 1949, Joplin, MO; s. of Harold Lee Scott and Avis Viola Scott (née Parsons); m. Linda Gale Aldridge 1969; two s.; ed Pitts. State Univ., Kansas; Br. Man. Yellow Freight System, Springdale, AR 1972–78; Man. Queen City Warehouse, Springfield, MO 1978–79; joined Wal-Mart Stores Inc., Bentonville, AR 1979, Dir of Transportation 1979–83, Vice-Pres. of Distribution, Sr Vice-Pres. of Logistics, Exec. Vice-Pres. of Logistics, mem. Exec. Cttee 1995–, Pres. and CEO Wal-mart Stores Div. 1996, then COO and Vice-Chair., Pres. and CEO 2000–; Dir Cooper Industries, Inc.; mem. Bd Dirs Pvt. Truck Council, Washington, DC 1985–86; mem. Republican party. *Leisure interests:* reading, quail hunting. *Address:* Wal-Mart Stores, Inc., Bentonville, AK 72716-8611 (Office); 611 Prairie Creek Road, Rogers, AR 72756-3019, USA (Home). *Website:* www.walmartstores.com (Office).

SCOTT, James, MSc, FRCP; British physician; b. 13 Sept. 1946, Ashby-de-la-Zouch; s. of Robert B. Scott and Iris O. Scott (née Hill); m. Diane M. Lowe 1976; two s. one d.; ed London Univ., London Hosp. Medical Coll.; house surgeon London Hosp. 1971–72; House Physician Hereford Co. Hosp. July–Dec. 1972; Sr House Officer Queen Elizabeth Hosp., Midland Centre for Neurosurgery and Neurology, Birmingham Jan.–Dec. 1973; Registrar Gen. Hosp., Birmingham Jan.–Dec. 1974, Royal Free Hosp., Academic Dept of Medicine 1975–76; Hon. Sr Registrar, MRC Research Fellow Hammersmith Hosp., Dept of Medicine 1976–80; Postdoctoral Fellow Univ. of Calif., Dept of Biochemistry and Biophysics 1980–83; Clinical Scientist; Head Div. of Molecular Medicine, MRC Research Centre 1983–91; Hon. Consultant Physician Northwick Park Hosp., Harrow 1983–91, Hammersmith Hosp. 1992–97; Prof., Chair. of Medicine Royal Postgrad. Medical School 1992–97; Hon. Dir MRC Molecular Medicine Group 1992–; Dir of Medicine Hammersmith Hosps. NHS Trust, Dir Div. of Medical Cardiology 1994–97; Prof of Medicine Imperial Coll. School of Medicine 1997–, Deputy Vice-Prin. for Research 1997–; European Ed. Arteriosclerosis, Thrombosis and Vascular Biology (Journal of American Heart Asscn); several prizes and awards include Graham Bull Prize (Royal Coll. of Physicians) 1989, Squibb Bristol Myers Award for Cardiovascular Research 1993, etc. *Publications:* numerous articles on molecular medicine, molecular genetics, atherosclerosis, RNA modification, RNA editing and gene expression. *Leisure interests:* family and friends, the twentieth-century novel, British impressionist and modern

painting, long distance running, swimming. *Address:* Department of Molecular Medicine, Imperial College School of Medicine, Hammersmith Hospital, Du Cane Road, W12 0NN, England.

SCOTT, Peter Denys John, MA, QC; British lawyer and arbitrator; b. 19 April 1935; s. of John Ernest Dudley Scott and Joan G. Steinberg; ed Monroe High School, Rochester, New York, USA, Balliol Coll., Oxford; called to Bar 1960, QC 1978; Chair. of Bar 1987 (Vice-Chair. 1985–86); Standing Counsel to Dir-Gen. of Fair Trading 1974–78, to Dept of Employment 1973–78; mem. Interception of Communications Tribunal 1986–, Lord Chancellor's Advisory Cttee on Legal Educ. and Conduct 1991–94; Chair. Inst. of Actuaries Appeal Bd 1995–; Judicial Chair. City Disputes Panel 1997–; Chair. Panel on Takeovers and Mergers 2000–; Harmsworth Scholar of Middle Temple; Bencher of Middle Temple; Chair. Kensington Housing Trust 1999–; Chair. Bd of Trustees, Nat. Gallery 2000–; mem. Investigatory Powers Tribunal 2000–. *Leisure interests:* gardening, theatre. *Address:* Fountain Court, Temple, London, EC4Y 9DH (Office); 4 Eldon Road, London, W8 5PU, England (Home). *Telephone:* (20) 7583-3335 (Office); (20) 7937-3301 (Home). *Fax:* (20) 7376-1169.

SCOTT, Sir Ridley, Kt; British film director; b. 30 Nov. 1937, South Shields; ed Royal Coll. of Art; Dir of numerous award-winning TV commercials since 1970; début as feature film Dir with The Duellists 1978; Hon. DLitt (Sunderland) 1998. *Other films include:* Alien, Blade Runner, Legend, Someone to Watch Over Me, Black Rain, Thelma and Louise, 1492: Conquest of Paradise 1992, White Squall 1995, G.I. Jane 1997, Gladiator (Acad. Award for Best Picture) 1999, Hannibal 2000, Black Hawk Down 2001, The Gathering Storm (TV—Emmy for Best Made-for-TV Film) 2002; co-producer The Browning Version 1994. *Address:* Scott Free, 42/44 Beak Street, London, W1R 3DA, England. *Telephone:* (20) 7437-3163. *Fax:* (20) 7734-4978.

SCOTT, Robert G.; American financial services executive; investment banker Morgan Stanley 1970–79, Managing Dir 1979–97, Head Capital Market Services, Corp. Finance, Investment Banking Div. –1997; Chief Financial Officer and Exec. Vice-Pres. Morgan Stanley Dean Witter 1997–2001, Pres. and COO 2001–. *Address:* Morgan Stanley Dean Witter, 1585 Broadway, New York, NY 10036, USA (Office). *Telephone:* (212) 761-4000 (Office). *Fax:* (212) 761-0086 (Office). *Website:* www.msdw.com (Office).

SCOTT, Timothy; British sculptor; b. 18 April 1937, Richmond, Surrey; s. of A. C. Scott and Dorothea Scott; m. Malkanthi Wirekoon 1958; two s. three d.; ed Lycée Jaccard, Lausanne, Architectural Asscn and St Martin's School of Art, London; worked at Atelier Le Corbusier-Wogenscky and others, Paris 1959–61; Sr Lecturer Canterbury Coll. of Art 1975–76; Head of Fine Art Dept, Birmingham Polytechnic 1976–78; Head Dept of Sculpture, St Martin's School of Art 1980–86; Prof. of Sculpture, Akad. der Bildenden Künste Nürnberg 1993–2002; numerous visiting lectureships in USA, Canada, Australia, Germany, UK, Chile. *One-man exhibitions:* (since 1964) Waddington, Kasmin Galleries, London, Rubin, Emmerich, Tibor de Nagy, Meredith Long Galleries, New York, Galerie Wentzel, Hamburg, David Mirvish, Toronto, Klonaridis, Toronto, Galerie Biederman, Munich, Galerie Ziegler, Zurich, Deutschland Funk, Cologne, Galerie In Fonte, Berlin, Galerie Tiergarten, Hanover, Deutsche Bank, Colombo, Galerie Winkelmann, Düsseldorf, Galerie Appel & Fertsch, Frankfurt, Galerie Fahlbusch, Mannheim, Thiessen-Krupp Stahl, Duisburg. *Retrospectives:* Whitechapel, London 1967, Museum of Modern Art, Oxford 1969, Corcoran Gallery of Art, Washington 1973, Museum of Fine Arts, Boston, USA 1972, Edmonton Art Gallery, Alberta 1976 (touring: Regina, Windsor, Toronto), Kunsthalle Bielefeld 1979–80 (touring: Lübeck, Duisburg, Ludwigshafen, Munich), Kettles Yard, Cambridge, Kunstverein Braunschweig 1988–89 (touring: Münster, Saarbrücken, Leverkusen, Regensburg). *Leisure interests:* music, architecture, travel, Sri Lanka, Indian culture, food. *Address:* Akademie der Bildenden Künste, Bingstrasse 60, Nuremberg 90480, Germany (Office); Keeper's Cottage, Troutsdale, N Yorkshire Moors, N Yorks., YO13 9PS England (Home); 'High House', 71 Gangawata Para Anniewatte, Kandy, Sri Lanka. *Telephone:* (911) 94040146 (Office); (1723) 859087 (N Yorks.); (8) 226913 (Sri Lanka). *Fax:* (911) 9404150 (Office).

SCOTT, Tony, MFA; British film director; b. 21 June 1944, Newcastle; m. Donna Wilson; ed Sunderland Coll. of Art, Leeds Coll. of Art, Royal Coll. of Art Film and TV Dept; Film Dir Totem Productions 1972–; Dir One of the Missing 1989 (Grand Prix, Mar Del Plata Festival, Argentina, Prix de la Télévision Suisse, Nyon, Second Prize, Esquire Film Festival, USA, Diploma of Merit, Melbourne); Asst Dir Dream Weaver 1967, The Movement Movement 1967; cameraman The Visit, Untitled, Compromise, Milian, Fat Man; worked for Derrick Knight & Alan King Assocs., Visual Dir and Cameraman, pop promotional films, Now Films Ltd, TV Cameraman, Seven Sisters 1968, Co-producer and actor, Don't Walk (promotional film), Asst Cameraman, Gulliver; Writer, Dir, Ed. Loving Memory 1969–70; Visual Dir and Cameraman, publicity film for Joe Egg; other films include Revenge, Top Gun, Beverley Hills Cop II, Days of Thunder, The Last Boy Scout, True Romance, Crimson Tide, The Fan, Enemy of the State, Spy Game; Dir Scott Free Enterprises Ltd; Dir of TV and cinema commercials for Ridley Scott and Assocs. *Address:* Totem Productions, 8009 Santa Monica Boulevard, Los Angeles, CA 90046, USA (Office); CAA, 9830 Wilshire Boulevard, Beverly Hills, CA 90212.

SCOTT, Walter, Jr, BS; American business executive; b. 1931; ed Colorado State Univ.; with Peter Kiewit Sons Inc., Omaha 1953–, Man. Cleveland Dist

1962–64, Vice-Pres. 1964, Exec. Vice-Pres. 1965–79, Chair. 1979–97, Pres., CEO 1979–97, Chair., Dir Level 3 Communications 1997, Chair. Emer. 1997–; Pres. Joslyn Art Museum, Omaha 1987–97. *Address:* Peter Kiewit Sons Inc., 1000 Kiewit Plaza, Omaha, NE 68131, USA (Office); Joslyn Art Museum, 2200 Dodge Street, Omaha NE 68102.

SCOTT, W(illiam) Richard, PhD; American sociologist and educator; b. 18 Dec. 1932, Parsons, Kan.; s. of Charles H. Scott and Hildegarde Hewit; m. Joy Lee Whitney 1955; three c.; ed Parsons Jr Coll., Kan., Univ. of Kansas, Univ. of Chicago; Asst Prof., Dept of Sociology, Stanford Univ. 1960–65, Assoc. Prof. 1965–69, Prof. 1969–99, Prof. Emer. 1999–, Chair. Dept of Sociology 1972–75, Dir Orgs. Research Training Program 1972–89; Dir Stanford Center for Orgs. Research 1988–96; Prof. by courtesy, Dept of Health Research and Policy, School of Medicine 1972– and of Educ., School of Educ. and of Organizational Behaviour, Graduate School of Business, Stanford Univ. 1977–; Sr Researcher, Nat. Center for Health Services Research, Dept of Health, Educ. and Welfare, Washington, DC 1975–76; Visiting Prof. Kellogg Grad. School of Man., Northwestern Univ. 1997, Hong Kong Univ. of Science and Tech. 2000; Sr Scholar, John Gordon Center 2002–; Ed. Annual Review of Sociology 1986–91; mem. Gov. Bd, Comm. on Social and Behavioral Sciences and Educ., NAS 1990–96; Woodrow Wilson Fellow 1954–55; Social Science Research Council Fellow 1958–59, Fellow Center for Advanced Study in the Behavioral Sciences 1989–90; Resident Fellow, Bellagio Center 2002; mem. Inst. of Medicine; Dr hc (Copenhagen Business School) 2000; Hon. DEcon (Helsinki School of Econs) 2001; Distinguished Scholar Award, Acad. of Man. 1988, Richard D. Irwin Award 1996. *Publications:* Metropolis and Region (with others) 1960, Formal Organizations (with P. M. Blau) 1962, Social Processes and Social Structures 1970, Evaluation and the Exercise of Authority (with S. M. Dornbusch) 1975, Organizations: Rational, Natural and Open Systems 1981, Organizational Environments (with J. W. Meyer) 1983, Hospital Structure and Performance (with A. Flood) 1987, Institutional Environments and Organizations: Structural Complexity and Individualism (with J. W. Meyer) 1994, Institutions and Organizations 1995, Institutional Change and Healthcare Organizations: From Professional Dominance to Managed Care (with others) 2000. *Leisure interests:* reading, tennis, cross-country skiing. *Address:* Stanford University Department of Sociology, Building 120, Stanford, CA 94305 (Office); 940 Lathrop Place, Stanford, CA 94305, USA (Home). *Telephone:* (650) 723-3959 (Office); (650) 857-1834 (Home). *Fax:* (650) 725-6471 (Office). *E-mail:* scottwr@stanford.edu (Office).

SCOTT BROWN, Denise, MArch, MCP, RIBA; American architect and urban planner; b. 3 Oct. 1931, Nkana, Zambia; d. of Simon Lakofski and Phyllis Hepker; m. 1st Robert Scott Brown 1955 (died 1959); m. 2nd Robert Venturi (q.v.) 1967; one s.; ed Kingsmead Coll. Johannesburg, Univ. of Witwatersrand, Architectural Asscn London and Univ. of Pennsylvania; Asst Prof. Univ. of Pa School of Fine Arts 1960–65; Assoc. Prof. Univ. of Calif. Los Angeles 1965–68; Venturi, Scott Brown & Assocs Inc., Philadelphia 1967–, Partner 1969–89, Prin. 1989–; Visiting Prof. Univ. of Calif. (Berkeley) 1965, Yale Univ. 1967–71, Univ. of Pa 1982–83; Eero Saarinen Visiting Critic, Yale Univ. 1987, Eliot Noyes Visiting Critic, Harvard Univ. 1990; mem. Advisory Bd, Carnegie Mellon Univ. Dept of Architecture 1992–, Bd of Overseers for Univ. Libraries, Univ. of Pa 1995–; numerous other academic and professional appts; Hon. DEng (Tech. Univ. of Nova Scotia) 1991; Hon. DHumLitt (Pratt Inst.) 1992; Hon. DFA (Univ. of Pa) 1994; Hon. DLit (Univ. of Nev.) 1998; President's Medal, Architectural League of NY 1986; Chicago Architecture Award 1987; Commendatore, Repub. of Italy 1987; Nat. Medal of Arts 1992, Philadelphia Award 1992, Benjamin Franklin Medal Award (RSA) 1993, ACSA–AIA Jt Award for Excellence in Architecture Educ., Topaz Medallion 1996, Giants of Design Award, House Beautiful Magazine 2000, Joseph Pennell Medal, Philadelphia Sketch Club 2000. *Publications:* Learning from Las Vegas (with R. Venturi and S. Izenour) 1977, A View from the Campidoglio: Selected Essays, 1953–84 (with R. Venturi) 1984, Urban Concepts 1990; articles in professional journals. *Leisure interests:* travelling, writing, teaching, lecturing. *Address:* Venturi, Scott Brown & Associates Inc., 4236 Main Street, Philadelphia, PA 19127, USA. *Telephone:* (215) 487-0400. *Fax:* (215) 487-2520.

SCOTT-JOYNT, Rt Rev Michael, MA; British ecclesiastic; b. 1943; m. Louise White 1965; two s. one d.; ed King's Coll. Cambridge and Cuddesdon Theological Coll.; ordained deacon 1967, priest 1968; Curate, Cuddesdon 1967–70; Tutor, Cuddesdon Coll. 1967–71, Chaplain 1971–72; Team Vicar, Newbury 1972–75; Priest-in-Charge, Caversfield 1975–79, Bicester 1975–79, Bucknell 1976–79; Rector, Bicester Area Team Ministry 1979–81; Rural Dean of Bicester and Islip 1976–81; Canon Residentiary of St Albans 1982–87; Dir of Ordinands and In-Service Training, Diocese of St Albans 1982–87; Bishop Suffragan of Stafford 1987–95; Bishop of Winchester 1995–. *Address:* Wolvesey, Winchester, Hants., SO23 9ND, England. *Telephone:* (1962) 854050. *Fax:* (1962) 842376.

SCOTT OF FOSCOTE, Baron (Life Peer), cr. 2000, of Foscote in the County of Buckinghamshire; **Richard Rashleigh Folliot Scott,** Kt, BA, LLB; British judge; b. 2 Oct. 1934, Dehra Dun, India; s. of the late Lt Col C. W. F. Scott and Katharine Scott (née Rashleigh); m. Rima E. Ripoll 1959; two s. two d.; ed Michaelhouse Coll. Natal, Univ. of Cape Town and Trinity Coll. Cambridge; called to Bar, Inner Temple 1959; practising barrister, Chancery Bar 1960–83; QC 1975; Attorney-Gen. to Duchy of Lancaster 1980–83; Bencher, Inner Temple 1981; Chair. of the Bar 1982–83 (Vice-Chair. 1981–82); High Court Judge, Chancery Div. 1983–91; Vice-Chancellor, County Palatine of

Lancaster 1987–91; a Lord Justice of Appeal 1991–94; Vice-Chancellor of the Supreme Court of Justice 1994–2000; Head of Civil Justice 1995–2000; Lord of Appeal in Ordinary 2000–; conducted inquiry into the sale of arms to Iraq 1992–96; Ed.-in-Chief Supreme Court Practice 1996–2001; Hon. mem. American Bar Assoc., Canadian Bar Assoc; Hon. LLD. (Birmingham) 1996, (Buckingham) 1999. *Publications:* Report of the Inquiry into the Export of Defence Equipment and Dual-Use Goods to Iraq and the Related Prosecutions; articles in legal journals. *Leisure interests:* equestrian activities, tennis, bridge. *Address:* Law Lords Corridor, House of Lords, London, SW1A 0PW, England. *Telephone:* (20) 7219-3117. *Fax:* (20) 7219-6156.

SCOTT-THOMAS, Kristin; British actress; b. 14 May 1960, Redruth; m. François Oliviennes; one s. one d.; ed Cen. School of Speech and Drama and Ecole Nat. des Arts et Technique de Théâtre, Paris; stage debut in Schnitzler's La Lune Déclinante Sur 4 ou 5 Personnes Qui Danse while student in Paris; has lived in France since age of 18. *Plays include:* La Terre Etrangère, Naive Hirondelles, Yes Peut-Etre, Bérénice, The Three Sisters. *Television includes:* L'Ami d'Enfance de Maigret, Blockhaus, Chameleon La Tricheuse, Sentimental Journey, The Tenth Man, Endless Game, Framed, Titmuss Regained, Look At It This Way, Body and Soul. *Films include:* Djamel et Juliette, L'Agent Troubé, La Méridienne, Under the Cherry Moon, A Handful of Dust, Force Majeure, Bille en Tête, The Bachelor, Bitter Moon, Four Weddings and a Funeral (BAFTA Award), Angels and Insects (Evening Standard Film Award), Richard III, The English Patient, Amour et Confusions, The Horse Whisperer, Random Hearts, Up at the Villa, Gosford Park, Life As a House, Petites Coupures 2003.

SCOTTO, Renata; Italian soprano; b. 24 Feb. 1935, Savona; m. Lorenzo Anselmi; ed under Ghirardini at Milan; joined La Scala Opera Company after début in La Traviata at Teatro Nuovo, Milan 1953; then studied under Merlino and Mercedes Llopart; roles in La Sonnambula, I Puritani, L'Elisir d'amore, Lucia di Lammermoor, Falstaff, La Bohème, Turandot, I Capuleti, Madame Butterfly, Tosca, Manon Lescaut, Otello, Rosenkavalier (Marschallin) 1992, La Voix Humaine 1993, Pirata 1993, etc. *Address:* 3 Stone Hallow Way, Armonk, NY 10504 (Office); c/o Robert Lombardo Associates, 61 W 62nd Street, Apt 6F, New York, NY 10023, USA; c/o La Scala, Via Filodrammatici 2, Milan, Italy.

SCOWCROFT, Lt-Gen. Brent, PhD; American government official and air force officer (retd); b. 19 March 1925, Odgen, Utah; s. of James Scowcroft and Lucile Balantyne Scowcroft; m. Marian Horner 1951 (died 1995); one d.; ed US Mil. Acad., West Point and Columbia Univ.; Operational and Admin. positions in US Air Force 1948–53; taught Russian history as Asst Prof., Dept of Social Sciences, US Mil. Acad., W Point 1953–57; Asst Air Attaché, US Embassy, Belgrade 1959–61; Assoc. Prof., Political Science Dept, US Air Force Acad., Colorado 1962–63, Prof., Head of Dept 1963–64; Plans and Operations Section, Air Force HQ, Washington 1964–66; various Nat. Security posts with Dept of Defense 1968–72; Mil. Asst to Pres., The White House 1972, Deputy Asst to Pres. for Nat. Security Affairs 1973–75, Asst to Pres. for Nat. Security Affairs 1975–77, 1989–93; Pres. Forum for Int. Policy 1993–; Pres. The Scowcroft Group 1994–; mem. Pres.'s Gen. Advisory Cttee on Arms Control 1977–81; Dir Atlantic Council, US Bd of Visitors US Air Force Acad. 1977–79, Council on Foreign Relations, Rand Corpn, Mitre Corpn; Vice-Chair. UNA/USA; Chair. Presidential Comm. on Strategic Forces 1983–89; mem. Cttee to Advise Dir of CIA 1995–; Chair. Pres.'s Foreign Intelligence Advisory Bd 2001–; mem. Cttee of Enquiry into Nat. Security Council 1986–87; Defense DSM, Air Force DSM (with two oak leaf clusters), Legion of Merit (with oak leaf cluster), Air Force Commendation Medal, Nat. Security Medal; Hon. KBE 1993. *Publication:* A World Transformed (with George Bush) 1998. *Address:* Apartment 500, 900 17th Street, NW, Washington, DC 20006, USA (Office).

SCRANTON, William Warren, AB, LLB; American politician and lawyer; b. 19 July 1917, Madison, Conn.; s. of Worthington Scranton and Marion Margery Warren Scranton; m. Mary Lowe Chamberlin 1942; three s. one d.; ed Hotchkiss School, Yale Univ. and Yale Univ. Law School; U.S. Army Air Force 1941–45; Pa Bar 1946; Assoc. O'Malley, Harris, Harris and Warren 1946–47; Vice-Pres. Int. Textbook Co., Scranton, Pa 1947–52, later Dir and mem. Exec. Cttee; Pres. Scranton-Lackawanna Trust Co. 1954–56; Chair. Bd and Dir Northeastern Pennsylvania Broadcasting Co. 1957–61; Special Asst to U.S. Sec. of State 1959–60; mem. U.S. House of Reps. 1961–63; Gov. of Pennsylvania 1963–67; Special Envoy to Middle East on behalf of Pres.-elect Nixon 1968; Chair. President's Commission on Campus Unrest 1970; Special Consultant to the Pres. 1974; Perm. Rep. to UN 1976–77; Chair of Bd Northeastern Bank of Pa 1974–76; Chair. UNA; official judge SE Wisconsin Scientific Fair, Milwaukee 1988–; Dir Cummins Engines Co., IBM Corpn, New York Times Co., Mobil Oil; Republican; numerous hon. degrees. *Leisure interests:* tennis, swimming, hiking. *Address:* Marquette University School of Dentistry, 604 N 16th Street, Milwaukee, Wis. 53233, USA.

SCREECH, Michael Andrew, MA, DLitt, FBA, FRSL; British clergyman and academic; b. 2 May 1926, Plymouth; s. of Richard John Screech MM and Nellie Screech (née Maunder); m. Anne Reeve 1956; three s.; ed Sutton High School, Plymouth and Univ. Coll. London; served Intelligence Corps, mainly Far East; Lecturer then Sr Lecturer, Birmingham Univ. 1951–60; Reader, then Prof. of French, Univ. of London 1960–71, Fielden Prof. of French Language and Literature 1971–84; Sr Research Fellow, All Souls Coll. Oxford 1984–93, Emer. 1993–, Fellow and Chaplain 2001–03; Extraordinary Fellow, Wolfson

Coll. Oxford 1993–2001, Hon. Fellow 2001–; ordained deacon 1993, priest 1994; Visiting Prof. London, Ont. 1964, Albany, NY 1969; Johnson Prof. Madison, Wis. 1979; Edmund Campion Lecturer, Regina, Sask. 1985, Dorothy Ford Wiley Prof. of Renaissance Culture, Chapel Hill, NC 1986; Prof. Collège de France 1989; Visiting Prof. Sorbonne 1990; Comité de Publ d'Humanisme et Renaissance 1965–; Corresp. mem. Soc. Historique et Archéologique de Geneva 1988, Institut de France: Acad. des Inscriptions et Belles Lettres, Paris 1999; Fellow Univ. Coll. London 1980; Ordre National du Mérite 1983, Chevalier, Légion d'honneur 1992; Hon. DLitt (Exeter) 1993; Hon. DTheol (Geneva) 1998; Médaille de la Ville de Tours. *Publications:* The Rabelaisian Marriage 1958, L'Evangélisme de Rabelais 1959, Le Tiers Livre de Pantagruel 1964, Les 52 Semaines de Lefèvre d'Etaples 1965, Les Regrets et Antiquités de Du Bellay 1966, Gargantua 1967, Marot Evangélique 1967, La Pantagrueline Prognostication 1975, Rabelais 1979, Ecstasy and the Praise of Folly 1981, 1988, Montaigne and Melancholy 1983, A New Rabelais Bibliography (with Stephen Rawles) 1987, Montaigne: An Apology for Raymond Sebond 1987, Montaigne: The Complete Essays 1991, Some Renaissance Studies 1992, Rabelais and the Challenge of the Gospel 1992, Clément Marot: A Renaissance Poet Discovers the Gospel 1993, The Doctrina et Politia Ecclesiae Anglicanae of Warden Mocket (ed.) 1995, Monumental Inscriptions in All Souls College, Oxford 1997, Laughter at the Foot of the Cross 1998, Montaigne's Copy of Lucretius 1998, 'Isaiah Berlin' in Armchair Athenians 2001. *Leisure interest:* walking. *Address:* All Souls College, Oxford, OX1 4AL (Office); 5 Swanston-field, Whitchurch-on-Thames, Reading, RG8 7HP, England (Home). *Telephone:* (1865) 279368 (Office); (118) 984-2513 (Home). *Fax:* (118) 984-2513 (Home). *E-mail:* michael.screech@all-souls.ox.ac.uk.

SCRIMSHAW, Nevin Stewart, PhD, MD, M.P.H., FAAS; American professor of nutrition; b. 20 Jan. 1918, Milwaukee, Wis.; s. of Stewart Scrimshaw and Harriet Scrimshaw (née Smith); m. Mary Ware Goodrich 1941; four s. one d.; ed Ohio Wesleyan Univ., Harvard Univ. and Univ. of Rochester; Consultant in Nutrition, Pan American Sanitary Bureau, Regional Office of the Americas, WHO 1948–49, Regional Adviser in Nutrition 1949–53; Dir Inst. of Nutrition of Cen. America and Panama (INCAP), Guatemala 1949–61, Consulting Dir 1961–65, Consultant 1965–; Adjunct Prof., Public Health Nutrition, Columbia Univ. 1959–61, Visiting Lecturer 1961–66; Visiting Lecturer on Tropical Public Health, Harvard Univ. 1968–85; Head, Dept of Nutrition and Food Science, MIT 1961–79, Inst. Prof. 1976–88, Inst. Prof. Emer. 1988–, Dir Clinical Research Center 1962–66, 1979–85, Principal Investigator 1962–86; Visiting Prof. Tufts Univ. 1987; Dir MIT/Harvard Int. Food and Nutrition Program 1979–88; Dir Int. Food and Nutrition Programme, UN Univ. 1976–97, Dir Devt Studies Div. 1986–87, Sr Adviser UN Univ. Food and Nutrition Programme 1998–; Pres. Int. Union of Nutritional Scientists 1978–81; John Boyd Orr Lecturer British Nutrition Soc.; Fellow American Acad. of Arts and Sciences; mem. NAS, Inst. of Medicine and numerous other nat. and foreign scientific socs and asscns; mem. numerous cttees and advisory panels to UN agencies and other orgs; Int. Award, Inst. of Food Technologists 1969, Goldberger Award in Clinical Nutrition, American Medical Asscn 1969, First James R. Killian Jr Faculty Achievement Award, MIT 1972, McCollum Award, American Soc. for Clinical Nutrition 1975, Conrad A. Elvehjem Award, American Inst. of Nutrition 1976, 1st Bolton L. Corson Medal, Franklin Inst. 1976, Medal of Honor, Fundación F. Cuenca Villoro 1978, Bristol Meyers Award 1988, World Food Prize 1991, McCollum Award, American Soc. of Nutritional Sciences 1999, etc. *Publications:* over 650 scientific articles and 22 books on various aspects of human and animal nutrition, nutrition and infection, agricultural and food chemistrychem. and public health. *Leisure interests* skiing, walking, gardening. *Address:* P.O. Box 330, Campton, NH 03223 (Office); 115 Sandwich Mount Farm, P.O. Box 330, Campton, NH 03223, USA (Home). *Telephone:* (603) 726-4200. *Fax:* (603) 726-4614. *E-mail:* nevin@cyberportal.net (Office).

SCRIPPS, Charles Edward; American newspaper publisher; b. 27 Jan. 1920, San Diego; s. of Robert Paine and Margaret Lou (née Culbertson) Scripps; m. 1st Louann Copeland 1941 (divorced 1947); m. 2nd Lois Anne MacKay 1949 (died 1990); two s. two d.; m. 3rd Mary Elizabeth Breslin 1993; ed William and Mary Coll. and Pomona Coll.; Reporter, Cleveland Press, Ohio 1941; Successor-Trustee, Edward W. Scripps Trust 1945, Chair. Bd of Trustees 1948–; Vice Pres., Dir E. W. Scripps Co. 1946–, Chair. of Bd 1953–, Chair. Exec. Cttee 1994–; Chair. Bd Scripps Howard, Inc. 1987–. *Address:* Scripps Howard, 312 Walnut Street, 28th Floor, Cincinnati, OH 45202, USA (Office).

SCRIVENER, Christiane; French international official; b. 1 Sept. 1925, Mulhouse; d. of Pierre Fries and Louise Fries; m. Pierre Scrivener 1944; one s. (deceased); ed Harvard Business School and Univ. of Paris; businesswoman involved since 1958 in org. of French tech. co-operation with more than 100 countries, Devt of int. tech. and industrial exchanges and promotion of French tech. abroad; State Sec. for Consumer Affairs 1976–78; MEP 1979–89; mem. Union pour la Démocratie (UDF); EEC Commr for Taxation and Customs Union and Consumers' Interests 1989–95; Pres. Ombudsman Société Générale 1996–, Plan Int. France 1997–; mem. Bd, Alliance Française 1995–97; Commdr Légion d'honneur; Grand-croix ordre de Leopold (Belgium); Grand-croix de Mérite (Luxembourg); Officier de Polonia Restituta (Poland). *Publications:* Le rôle et la responsabilité à l'égard du public 1978, L'Europe, une bataille pour l'avenir 1984, Histoires du petit Troll 1986. *Leisure interests:* skiing, music. *Address:* 21 Avenue Robert-Schuman, 92100 Boulogne-Billancourt, France.

SCRIVER, Charles Robert, CC, G.O.Q., MD, CM, FRS, FRSC, FAAS; Canadian professor of pediatrics, human genetics and biology; b. 7 Nov. 1930, Montreal; s. of Walter DeMoulpied and Jessie Marion Boyd; m. Esther Peirce 1956; two s. two d.; intern Royal Victoria Hosp. Montreal 1955–56, Resident 1956–57, Resident Montreal Children's Hosp. 1956–57, Chief Resident (Pediatrics) 1960–61, physician 1961–; Children's Medical Center, Boston, USA 1957–58; McLaughlin Travelling Fellow Univ. Coll. London, UK 1958–60; Asst Prof. of Pediatrics McGill Univ. 1961, Markle Scholar 1961–66, Assoc. Prof. 1965–69, Prof. of Pediatrics, Genetics and Biology 1969–, Co-Dir MRC Genetics Group 1972–95, Alva Prof. of Human Genetics 1994, now Alva Prof. Emer.; Assoc. Dir Canadian Genetic Diseases Network 1989–98; Pres. Canadian Soc. for Clinical Investigation 1974–75, Soc. for Pediatric Research 1975–76, American Soc. Human Genetics 1986, American Pediatric Soc. 1994–95; mem. Medical Advisory Bd./Scientific Advisory Bd Howard Hughes Medical Inst. 1981–88; Hon. DSc (Manitoba) 1992, (Glasgow, Montreal) 1993, (Utrecht) 1999, (Bristol) 2002; numerous awards and prizes including Allen Award, American Soc. of Human Genetics 1978, Gairdner Foundation Int. Award 1979, McLaughlin Medal, Royal Soc. of Canada 1981, Canadian Rutherford Lectureship, Royal Soc., London 1983, Ross Award, Canadian Pediatric Soc. 1990, Award of Excellence (Genetic Soc. of Canada) 1992, Prix du Québec 1995, Friesen Award 2001, Querci Prize (Italy) 2001, ASHG Award for Excellence in Human Genetics Educ. 2001. *Publications:* Amino Acid Metabolism and its Disorders (co-author) 1973, Garrod's Inborn Factors in Disease (co-author) 1989, Metabolic Basis of Inherited Disease (6th, 7th, 8th edns, Sr Ed.) (co-author) 1989–; author or co-author of more than 500 scientific articles. *Leisure interests:* literature, music, photography. *Address:* Montreal Children's Hospital, 2300 Tupper Street, Montreal, Que. H3H 1P3 (Office); 232 Strathearn Avenue, Montreal, Que. H4X 1Y2, Canada (Home). *Telephone:* (514) 934-4417 (Office). *Fax:* (514) 934-4329 (Office). *E-mail:* charles.scriver@mcgill.ca (Office).

SCRUTON, Roger; British philosopher and writer; b. 27 Feb. 1944, Buslingthorpe; s. of John Scruton and Beryl C. Haines; m. 1st Danielle Laffitte 1975 (divorced 1983); m. 2nd Sophie Jeffreys 1996; ed High Wycombe Royal Grammar School, Jesus Coll. Cambridge and Inner Temple, London; Fellow, Peterhouse, Cambridge 1969–71; Lecturer in Philosophy, Birkbeck Coll. London 1971–79, Reader 1979–86, Prof. of Aesthetics 1986–92; Prof. of Philosophy, Boston Univ. 1992–95; Founder and Dir The Claridge Press 1987–; Ed. The Salisbury Review 1982–2000. *Publications:* Art and Imagination 1974, The Aesthetics of Architecture 1979, The Meaning of Conservatism 1980, Fortnight's Anger 1981, A Dictionary of Political Thought 1982, Sexual Desire 1986, Francesca 1991, A Dove Descending 1991, Conservative Texts: An Anthology 1991, The Xanthippic Dialogues 1993, Modern Philosophy 1993, The Classical Vernacular 1994, Modern Philosophy 1996, An Intelligent Person's Guide to Philosophy 1997, The Aesthetics of Music 1997, Town and Country (co-ed.) 1998, An Intelligent Person's Guide To Modern Culture 1998, On Hunting 1999, England: An Elegy 2000, The West and the Rest: Globalization and the Terrorist Threat 2002. *Leisure interests:* music, literature, hunting. *Address:* Sunday Hill Farm, Brinkworth, Wilts., SN15 5AS, England.

SCUDAMORE, Peter, MBE; British jockey; b. 13 June 1958, Hereford; s. of Michael Scudamore and Mary Scudamore; m. Marilyn Scudamore 1980; two s.; fmr point-to-point and amateur jockey; worked in estate agency; professional Nat. Hunt jockey 1979–93; 1,678 winners (retd April 1993); seven times champion Nat. Hunt jockey inc. 1988–89 when he rode record 221 winners; Dir Chasing Promotions 1989–; racing journalist Daily Mail 1993–; Jt Pres. Jockeys' Asscn; in partnership with trainer Nigel Twiston-Davies; sports speaker with the Gordon Poole Entertainment Agency. *Publications:* A Share of Success (jtly) 1983, Scudamore on Steeplechasing (jtly), Scu: The Autobiography of a Champion 1993. *Leisure interests:* cricket, music, watching sport. *Fax:* (1451) 850995. *E-mail:* peter.scu@ic24.net.

SCULLY, Sean Paul, BA; American artist; b. 30 June 1945, Dublin; s. of John Anthony Scully and Holly Scully; m. Catherine Lee; ed Croydon Coll. of Art, Newcastle Univ., Harward Univ. with Fine Art Dept, Newcastle Univ. 1967–71; lecturer Harvard Univ. 1972–73; lecturer Chelsea School of Art and Goldsmiths School of Art, London 1973–75; lecturer Princeton Univ. 1978–83; lecturer in Painting Parsons School of Design, New York 1983–; one-man exhbns. in London, LA, New York, Berlin, Washington, etc. 1973–; exhibited at Carnegie Inst., Pittsburgh, Boston Museum of Fine Arts, Chicago Art Inst. 1987, Univ. Art Museum, Berkeley, Calif. 1987, Whitechapel Art Gallery, London 1989, Lenbachhaus, Munich 1989, Palacio Velázquez, Madrid 1989, Mary Boone Gallery, New York 1993, Fort Worth Museum of Modern Art 1993, Galerie Nat. de Jeu de Paume, Paris 1996; works in public collections in UK, USA, Australia, Germany, Ireland; Guggenheim Fellowship 1983; Stuyvesant Foundation Prize 1970, 1972 Prize, John Moores Liverpool Exhbn 8, 1974 Prize John Moores Liverpool Exhbn 9. *Address:* c/o Mayor Rowan Gallery, 31A Bruton Place, London, W1X 7AB, England (Office); c/o Diane Villani Editions, 211 Mulberry Street, New York, NY 10012, USA (Office).

SCULTHORPE, Peter Joshua, AO, OBE; Australian composer; b. 29 April 1929, Launceston, Tasmania; s. of Joshua Sculthorpe and Edna Moorhouse; ed Launceston Grammar School, Univ. of Melbourne and Wadham Coll., Oxford; lecturer, Sr Lecturer in Music, Univ. of Sydney 1963–68; Visiting Fellow, Yale Univ. 1965–67; Reader in Music, Univ. of Sydney 1968–91, Prof. in Musical Composition and Sydney Moss Lecturer in Music 1992–; Visiting Prof. of Music, Univ. of Sussex 1971–72; comms. from bodies including

Australian Broadcasting Comm., Birmingham Chamber Music Soc., Australian Elizabethan Theatre Trust, Australian Ballet, Musica Viva Australia, Australian Chamber Orchestra; Hon. DLitt (Tasmania, Sussex); Hon. DMus (Melbourne); Australian Council Composers' Award 1975–77, Australian Film Inst. Award 1980, Ted Albert Award 1993, Sir Bernard Heinze Award 1994, ABC Classic FM Listeners' Choice Award 1998 and numerous other awards. *Compositions published include:* The Loneliness of Bunjil 1954, Sonatina 1954, Irkanda I 1955, II 1959, III 1960, IV 1961, Ulterior Motifs, a musical farce and music for various revues 1957–59, Sonata for Viola and Percussion 1960, Theme and Journey's End (from film They Found a Cave) 1962, The Fifth Continent 1963, String Quartet No. 6 1965, No. 7 1966, No. 8 1969, No. 9 1975, No. 10 1983, No. 11 1990, Sun Music I 1965, Sun Music for Voices and Percussion 1966, Sun Music III 1967, IV 1967, Morning Song for the Christ Child 1966, Red Landscape 1966, Tabuh Tabuhan 1968, Autumn Song 1968, Sea Chant 1968, Sun Music II 1969, Orchestral Suite (from film The Age of Consent) 1968, Sun Music Ballet 1968, Love 200 for pop group and orchestra 1970, The Stars Turn 1970, Music for Japan 1970, Dream 1970, Night Pieces 1971, Landscape 1971, How The Stars Were Made 1971, Ketjak 1972, Koto Music I 1973, II 1976, Rites of Passage 1973, The Song of Tailitnama 1974, Postcard from Nourlangie to Clapham Common 1993, From Saibai 1993, Memento Mori for orchestra 1993, From Ubirr for string quartet and didgeridoo 1994; various works for radio, TV, theatre and film. *Leisure interests:* gardening, collecting Sung ceramics. *Address:* 91 Holdsworth Street, Woollahra, NSW 2025, Australia.

SCUTT, Der, FAIA; American architect and interior designer; b. 17 Oct. 1934, Reading, Pa; s. of George W. Scutt and Hazel Smith; m. Leena Liukkonen 1967; two c.; ed Pennsylvania State Univ., Yale Univ.; design partner Swanke Hayden Connell & Partners 1975–81; Prin. Der Scutt Architect, New York 1981–; mem. American Inst. of Architects, Bd of Govs NY Bldg Congress 1984–92 (Treasurer 1988), Bd of Trustees Chapin Soc. 1984–, Nat Maritime Historical Soc. 1991–, Ocean Liner Museum, New York 1994; numerous design awards. *Projects include:* One Astor Plaza and Minskoff Theatre, New York 1973, Equitable Life Assurance Data Center, Easton, Pa 1973, Creative Perfumery Center, Teaneck, NJ 1973, Grand Hyatt Hotel, New York 1980, 520 Madison Avenue, NY 1983, Continental Center Office Tower NY 1983, Trump Tower, NY 1983, US HQ Hong Kong Bank, NY 1985, office Bldg 625 Madison Avenue, NY 1988, IFF World HQ, NY 1994 and other office bldgs NY. *Address:* 44 West 28th Street, New York, NY 10001, USA.

SEAGA, Rt Hon Edward Philip George, BA, PC; Jamaican politician; b. 28 May 1930, Boston, Mass., USA; s. of Philip Seaga and Erna Seaga (née Maxwell); m. 1st Marie Elizabeth Constantine 1965 (divorced 1995); two s. one d.; m. 2nd Carla Frances Vendryes 1996; ed Wolmers Boys' School, Kingston and Harvard Univ.; Field Researcher with Inst. of Social and Econ. Research (Univ. of West Indies) on devt of child and revival spirit cults; nominated to Upper House, Legis. Council 1959; Asst Sec. to Jamaican Labour Party 1960, Sec. 1962; MP for Western Kingston 1962–; Minister of Devt and Social Welfare 1962–67, of Finance and Planning 1967–72; Leader of Jamaican Labour Party Nov. 1974–; Leader of Opposition 1974–80 1989; Prime Minister 1980–89; Minister of Finance and Planning, Information and Culture 1980–89, of Defence 1987–89; Chair. Premium Group 1989–; five Hon. LLD degrees from US univs; Dr Martin Luther King Humanitarian Award 1984, Enviromental Leadership Award, UNEP 1987 and other awards; decorations include Gold Mercury Int. Award (Venezuela) 1981, Grand Cross, Order of Merit (FRG) 1982. *Publications:* Development of the Child, Revival Spirit Cults, Faith Healing in Jamaica. *Leisure interests:* classical music, reading, hunting, sports, futurology. *Address:* 24–26 Grenada Crescent, New Kingston, Kingston 5, Jamaica, West Indies (Home); Jamaica Labour Party, 20 Belmont Road, Kingston 5 (Office). *Telephone:* 929-1183 (Office). *Fax:* 968-0873 (Office). *E-mail:* jlp@colis.com (Office). *Website:* www .thejlp.com (Office).

SEAGAL, Steven; American film actor and martial arts expert; b. 10 April 1951, Lansing, Mich.; m. 1st Miyako Fujitoni; one s. one d.; m. 2nd Kelly Le Brock; one s. two d.; moved to Japan aged 17 remaining there for 15 years; established martial arts acads. (dojo) in Japan and LA; CEO Steamroller Productions. *Films:* Above the Law 1988, Hard to Kill 1990, Marked for Death 1990, Out for Justice, Under Siege/On Deadly Ground (Dir) 1994, Under Siege 2 1995, The Glimmer Man, Executive Decision, Fire Down Below, The Patriot (also producer) 1998, Ticker 2001, Exit Wounds 2001, Half Past Dead 2002. *Website:* www.stevenseagal.com (Office).

SEAMAN, Christopher, MA, ARCM; British conductor; b. 7 March 1942, Faversham; s. of Albert Edward Seaman and Ethel Margery (née Chambers) Seaman; ed Canterbury Cathedral Choir School, The King's School, Canterbury, King's Coll., Cambridge; prin. timpanist London Philharmonic Orchestra 1964–68; Asst Conductor BBC Scottish Symphony Orchestra 1968–70; Chief Conductor 1971–77; Chief Conductor Northern Sinfonia Orchestra 1973–79; Prin. Conductor BBC Robert Mayer Concerts 1978–87; Conductor-in-Residence Baltimore Symphony Orchestra 1987–98; Chief Guest Conductor Utrecht Symphony Orchestra 1979–83; Music Dir Naples Philharmonic Orchestra, Florida 1993–, Rochester Philharmonic Orchestra, NY 1998–; appears as Guest Conductor world-wide and has appeared in USA, Germany, France, Holland, Belgium, Italy, Spain, Australia and all parts of the UK; Hon. FGSM 1972. *Leisure interests:* people, reading, shopping, theology. *Address:* 25 Westfield Drive, Glasgow, G52 2SG, Scotland.

SEAMAN, Rev. Sir Keith Douglas, KCVO, OBE, MA, LLB, DIP.HUM.; Australian state governor and ecclesiastic; b. 11 June 1920, McLaren Vale; s. of the late Eli Semmens Seaman and Ethel Maud Seaman; m. Joan Isabel Birbeck 1946; one s. one d.; ed Unley High School and Univ. of Adelaide; South Australia (SA) Public Service 1937–54; entered Methodist ministry 1954; Minister, Renmark 1954–58; Cen. Methodist Mission 1958–77; Dir 5KA, 5AU, 5RM Broadcasting Cos. 1960–77 (Chair. 1971–77); Sec. Christian TV Asscn SA 1959–73; mem. Exec. World Asscn of Christian Broadcasting 1963–70; RAAF Overseas HQ, London 1941–45, Flight Lt; Supt Adelaide Cen. Methodist Mission 1971–77; mem. Australian Govt Social Welfare Comm. 1973–76; Gov. of S. Australia 1977–82; KStJ. *Leisure interests:* gardening, reading. *Address:* 93 Rosetta Village, Victor Harbor, South Australia 5211, Australia. *Telephone:* (8) 85523535. *E-mail:* kds@ruralnet.net.au (Home).

SEAMANS, Robert Channing, Jr; American engineer, educator and government official (retd); b. 30 Oct. 1918, Salem, Mass.; s. of Robert Channing Seamans and Pauline (Bosson) Seamans; m. Eugenia Merrill 1942; three s. two d.; ed Harvard and Massachusetts Institute of Technology; MIT 1941–55, teaching and project man. positions, successively Asst then Assoc. Prof. Dept of Aeronautical Eng, also Chief Engineer Project Meteor 1950–53, Dir Flight Control Lab. 1953–55; Radio Corpn of America 1955–60, successively Man. Airborne Systems Lab., Chief Systems Engineer Airborne Systems Dept, Chief Engineer Missile Electronics and Control Div.; Assoc. Admin. and later Deputy Admin. NASA 1960–68, Consultant to Admin. 1968–69; Sec. of Air Force 1969–73; Visiting Prof. of Aeronautics and Astronautics and of Man., MIT 1968, Jerome Clarke Hunsaker Prof. 1968–69, Henry R. Luce Prof. of Environment and Public Policy 1977–84, Dean of Eng 1978–81, Sr Lecturer Dept of Aeronautics and Astronautics 1984–; mem. Nat. Acad. of Eng 1968–, Pres. 1973–74; Admin., Energy Research and Devt Admin. 1974–77; mem. Scientific Advisory Board, US AF 1957–62, Assoc. Adviser 1962–67; Nat. Del. to Advisory Group for Aerospace Research and Devt (NATO) 1966–69; fmr Trustee Nat. Geographic Soc.; fmr Dir Charles Stark Draper Lab. Inc., Combustion Eng Inc., Eli Lilly and Co., Johnny Appleseed's Inc., Aerospace Corpn, Putnam Funds; mem. numerous scientific and other orgs; Hon. DSc (Rollins Coll.) 1962, (New York Univ.) 1967; Hon. D. Eng (Norwich Acad.) 1971, (Notre Dame) 1974, (Rensselaer Polytech. Inst.) 1974; Hon. LLD (Univ. of Wyoming) 1975, (Thomas Coll.) 1980; Hon. Dr of Public Service (George Washington Univ.) 1975; Naval Ordnance Devt Award 1945; Lawrence Sperry Award, American Inst. of Aeronautics and Astronautics 1951; NASA Distinguished Service Medal 1965, 1969; General Thomas D. White USAF Space Trophy 1973; Dept of Defense Distinguished Public Service Medal 1973; Dept of Air Force Exceptional Civilian Award 1973, Nat. Soc. of Professional Engineers Achievement Award, Thomas D. White Nat. Defence Award 1980, Daniel Guggenheim Award 1996. *Publication:* Aiming at Targets (autobiog.). *Leisure interests:* tennis, sailing, skiing. *Address:* 675 Hale Street, Beverly Farms, MA 01915, USA.

SEARLE, John; American professor of philosophy; b. 1932, Denver, Colo; s. of George W. Searle and Hester Beck Searle; m. Dagmar Carboch 1958; two s.; ed Univ. of Wisconsin, Oxford Univ.; Prof. of Philosophy Univ. of California, Berkeley 1959–; Chair. Educ. TV series in Calif. 1960–74; involved with student radical Movt 1964; Advisor to Nixon Admin. on student unrest in Univs 1971, Reith Lecturer 1984; Rhodes Scholar 1952. *Publications:* Speech Acts 1969, The Campus War 1972, Expression and Meaning 1979, Intentionality 1983, Minds, Brains and Science 1984, The Foundations of Illocutionary Logic (with D. Vanderveken) 1985, The Rediscovery of the Mind 1992, (On) Searle on Conversation 1992, The Construction of Social Reality 1995, Mystery of Consciousness 1997, Mind, Language and Society 1998; contrib. to John Searle and his Critics; articles on artificial intelligence and philosophy. *Address:* Department of Philosophy, University of California, Berkeley, CA 94720, USA. *Telephone:* (510) 642-3173. *Fax:* (510) 642-5160.

SEARLE, Ronald, RDI, AGI, FRSA; British artist; b. 3 March 1920, Cambridge; s. of the late William James Searle and of Nellie (Hunt) Searle; m. 1st Kaye Webb (divorced 1967, died 1996); one s. one d.; m. 2nd Monica Koenig 1967; ed Central School, Cambridge and Cambridge School of Art; first drawings published 1935–39; served with Royal Engineers 1939–46; prisoner-of-war in Japanese camps 1942–45; contributor to nat. publs 1946; mem. Punch 'Table' 1956; special features artist Life magazine 1955, Holiday 1957, The New Yorker 1966–, Le Mande 1995–; Designer of medals for the French Mint 1974–, British Art Medal Soc. 1983–; work rep. in Victoria and Albert Museum, Imperial War Museum and British Museum (London), Bibliothèque Nationale, Paris and in several German and American museums; Royal Designer for Industry 1988; Venice, Edin., San Francisco and other film festival awards for film Energetically Yours; LA Art Dirs. Club Medal 1959, Philadelphia Art Dirs. Club Medal 1959, Nat. Cartoonists' Soc. Award 1959, 1960, Gold Medal, III Biennale, Tolentino, Italy 1965, Prix de la Critique Belge 1968, Grand Prix de l'Humour noir (France) 1971, Prix d'Humour, Festival d'Avignon 1971, Medal of French Circus 1971, Prix International 'Charles Huard' 1972, La Monnaie de Paris Medal 1974, Bundesrechtsanwaltskammer Award (Germany) 1998. *One-man exhibitions:* Leicester Galleries (London) 1950, 1954, 1957, Kraushaar Gallery (New York) 1959, Bianchini Gallery (New York) 1963, Kunsthalle (Bremen) 1965, in Paris 1964, 1967, 1968, 1969, 1970, 1971, Bibliothèque Nationale 1973, in Munich 1967, 1968, 1969, 1970, 1971, 1973, 1976, 1981, in London 1968, Neue Galerie Wien, Vienna 1985, 1988, Imperial War Museum 1986, Fitzwilliam Museum, Cambridge 1987, Wilhelm Busch Museum, Hanover 1996, Stadtmuseum,

Munich 1996, Galerie Martine Gossieaux, Paris 2000, etc. *Films designed:* designer of several films including John Gilpin, On the Twelfth Day, Energetically Yours, Germany 1960, Toulouse-Lautrec, Dick Deadeye, or Duty Done 1975; designed animation sequences for films Those Magnificent Men in their Flying Machines 1965, Monte-Carlo or Bust! 1969, Scrooge 1970, Dick Deadeye 1975. *Publications:* Forty Drawings 1946, John Gilpin 1952, Souls in Torment 1953, Rake's Progress 1955, Merry England 1956, Paris Sketchbook 1957, The St Trinian's Story (with Kaye Webb) 1959, USA For Beginners 1959, Russia for Beginners 1960, The Big City 1958 (all with Alex Atkinson), Refugees 1960 1960, Which Way Did He Go? 1961, Escape from the Amazon 1963, From Frozen North to Filthy Lucre 1964, Those Magnificent Men in their Flying Machines 1965, Haven't We Met Before Somewhere? (with Heinz Huber) 1966, Searle's Cats 1967, The Square Egg 1968, Hello—Where Did All the People Go? 1969, Secret Sketchbook 1970, The Second Coming of Toulouse-Lautrec 1970, The Addict 1971, More Cats 1975, Designs for Gilbert and Sullivan 1975, Paris! (with Irwin Shaw) 1977, Searle's Zodiac 1977, Ronald Searle (monograph) 1978, 1996, The King of Beasts 1980, The Big Fat Cat Book 1982, Illustrated Winespeak 1983, Ronald Searle in Perspective (monograph) 1984, Ronald Searle's Golden Oldies: 1941–1961, 1985, Something in the Cellar 1986, To the Kwai—and Back 1986, Ah Yes, I Remember It Well...: Paris 1961–1975 1987, Non-Sexist Dictionary 1988, Slightly Foxed—But Still Desirable 1989, Carnet de Croquis 1992, The Curse of St Trinian's 1993, Marquis de Sade Meets Goody Two-Shoes 1994, Ronald Searle dans le Monde 1998, etc. *Address:* The Sayle Literary Agency, Bickerton House, 25–27 Bickerton Road, London, N19 5JT, England; Eileen McMahon Agency, P.O. Box 1062, Bayonne, NJ 07002, USA. *Telephone:* (20) 7263-8681 (London); (201) 436-4362 (New York). *Fax:* (20) 7561-0529 (London); (201) 436-4363 (New York). *E-mail:* rcalder@sayleliteraryagency.com (Office); eileenmcmahon@earthlink.net (Office). *Website:* www.sayleliteraryagency.com (Office).

SEARS, Hon. Alfred M., BA, M.Phil., JD; Bahamian politician and lawyer; b. 13 Jan. 1953, Fort Charlotte; s. of Winifred Sears; m. Marion Bethel; three c.; ed Boys' Industrial School, St. Augustine Coll., Columbia Univ., USA, New York Law School, USA, Univ. of the West Indies, Jamaica; f. Interdenominational Christian Youth Asscn (ICYA); Lecturer in Caribbean Politics, Hunter Coll., Univ. of New York 1977–87; fmr Attorney, Civil Court of Manhattan, USA, Berthan Macaulay, Jamaica, Gibson & Co., The Bahamas; partner Sears & Co. law firm; currently Attorney-Gen. and Minister of Educ.; Head of Caribbean Financial Action Task Force (CFTAF) 2002–. *Address:* Office of the Attorney-General, P.O. Bldg., East Hill Street, P.O.B. N-3007, Nassau, The Bahamas (Office). *Telephone:* 322-1141 (Office). *Fax:* 322-4179 (Office).

SEATON, Michael John, PhD, FRS; British professor of physics; b. 16 Jan. 1923, Bristol; s. of Arthur William Robert Seaton and Helen Amelia Seaton (née Stone); m. 1st Olive May Singleton 1943 (died 1959); one s. one d.; m. 2nd Joy Clarice Balchin 1960; one s.; ed Wallington County School, Surrey, Univ. Coll., London; Asst Chemist British Industrial Solvents 1940–42; Navigator RAF 1942–46; student Univ. Coll., London 1946–50, Asst Lecturer 1950–52, Lecturer 1952–59, Reader 1959–63, Prof. 1963–88, Prof. Emer. 1988–; Chargé de Recherche, Inst. d'Astrophysique, Paris 1954–55; Fellow-Adjoint, Jt Inst. Lab. Astrophysics, Boulder, Colo 1963–; Sr Research Fellow, Science and Eng Research Council 1984–88; Pres. Royal Astronomical Soc. 1979–81; Foreign Assoc. NAS 1986; Hon. mem. American Astronomical Soc. 1983; Gold Medal, Royal Astronomical Soc. 1983, Guthrie Medal and Prize, Inst. of Physics 1984, Hughes Medal, Royal Soc. 1992. *Publications:* 280 papers in various journals on theoretical atomic physics and astronomy. *Address:* Chatsworth, Bwlch, Powys, LD3 7RQ, Wales. *Telephone:* (1874) 730652. *E-mail:* mjs@star.ucl.ac.uk (Home).

SEBASTIAN, Sir Cuthbert (Montraville), GCMG, OBE, BSc, MD, CM; Saint Christopher and Nevis Governor-General and doctor; b. 22 Oct. 1921; ed Mount Allison Univ., Dalhousie Univ., Canada; pharmacist and Lab. Technician, Cunningham Hosp., St Kitts 1942–43; RAF 1944–45; Capt. St Kitts Nevis Defence Force 1958–80; Medical Supt Cunningham Hosp. 1966, Joseph N. France Gen. Hosp. 1967–80; Chief Medical Officer Saint Christopher and Nevis 1980–83; pvt. medical practitioner 1983–95; Gov.-Gen. of Saint Christopher and Nevis 1996–. *Leisure interests:* farming, reading, dancing. *Address:* Government House, Basseterre (Office); 6 Cayon Street, Basseterre, St Kitts, Saint Christopher and Nevis, W Indies (Home). *Telephone:* 465-2315 (Office); 465-2344 (Home).

SEBASTIANI, HE Cardinal Sergio; Italian ecclesiastic; b. 11 April 1931, Montemonaco (Ascoli-Piceno); s. of Angelo Sebastiani and Lucia Valeri; ed Pontifical Gregorian Univ., Pontifical Lateran Univ., Pontifical Ecclesiastical Acad.; ordained priest 1956; Sec. of Apostolic Nunciature, Peru 1960; Sec. of Apostolic Nunciature, Brazil 1962; Uditore, Apostolic Nunciature, Chile 1966, Office Chief, Vatican Secr. of State, Counsellor Apostolic Nunciature in Paris, with special assignment to Council of Europe 1974; ordained Titular Archbishop of Cesarea in Mauritania; Apostolic Pro-Nuncio to Madagascar and Apostolic Del. to Réunion and Comoros 1976, Apostolic Nuncio to Turkey 1985; Sec.-Gen. Cen. Cttee of Great Jubilee Year 2000 1994; Pres. Pref. for Econ. Affairs of The Holy See 1997–; cr. Cardinal 2001; Commendadore Order of Merit, Italy, Nat. Order of Madagascar, Grand Cross Order O'Higgins, Chile. *Publications:* La Chiesa all'uomo del XX secolo, La Sapienza nell'Antico Testamento. *Address:* Prefecture for the Economic Affairs of the Holy See,

Palazzo delle Congregazioni, Largo del Colonnato 3, 00193 Rome (Office); Via Rusticucci 13, 00193 Rome, Italy (Home). *Telephone:* (06) 69884263 (Office). *Fax:* (06) 69885011 (Office).

SEBELIUS, Kathleen, MPA; American state official; m. Gary Sebelius; two s.; ed Univ. of Kansas; first woman employee Dept of Corrections, Kan. 1975–87; mem. House of Reps., Kan. 1987–94, mem. Ethics Comm.; Insurance Commr, Kan. 1994–2002; Gov. of Kan. 2003–; named amongst Top Ten Public Officials in America, Governing Magazine 2001. *Address:* Office of the Governor, State Capitol Building, 2nd Floor, Topeka, KS 66612, USA (Office). *Telephone:* (785) 296-3232 (Office). *Fax:* (785) 296-7973 (Office). *Website:* www.ink.org/public/governor (Office).

SEBRLE, Roman; Czech athlete; b. 26 Nov. 1974, Prague; m. Eva Sebrle; one c.; mem. Czech Olympic athletics team, Sydney 2000 (silver medal for decathlon); set new world record for decathlon (9,026 points), World Championships, Götziz, Austria May 2001; gold medals in heptathlon, European Indoor Championships March 2002, decathlon, European Championships Aug. 2002; Czech Athlete of the Year 2002. *Leisure interests:* computers, the Internet, football, sci-fi, music, spaghetti. *Address:* c/o Czech Olympic Committee, Benesovská 6, 10100 Prague 10, Czech Republic (Office). *Telephone:* (2) 71734734 (Office). *Fax:* (2) 71731318 (Office). *E-mail:* info@olympic.cz (Office).

SECHIN, Igor Ivanovich; Russian politician; b. 12 Sept. 1960, Leningrad; m.; one s.; ed Leningrad State Univ.; army service 1984–86; leading instructor Exec. Cttee, Dept of Foreign Econ. Relations, Leningrad Soviet 1988–91; Chief Expert, Asst to Head of Admin to First Vice-Mayor, Chair. Cttee on Foreign Relations, Office of Mayor of Leningrad 1991–96; Expert, Deputy Head of Div., Public Relations Dept, Dept of Foreign Affairs 1996–97; Head, Gen. Admin Dept, Advisor to Deputy Head then Head Chief Control Dept, Admin of the Russian Pres. 1998–99; Head, Secr. of First Deputy Chair., later Chair., Govt of Russian Fed. 1999–2000; Deputy Head, Admin of Pres. Putin 2000–. *Address:* Staraya pl. 4, 103132 Moscow, Russia (Office). *Telephone:* (095) 206-63-33 (Office); (095) 206-50-57 (Office). *Fax:* (095) 206-79-65 (Office). *Website:* www.gov.ru (Office).

SECK, Idrissa; Senegalese politician; mem. Parti démocratique sénégalais—PDS (Democratic Party), Deputy Sec.-Gen.; fmr Minister Without Portfolio; Sec. of State, Dir Office of the Pres. –2002; Prime Minister of Senegal Sept. 2002–. *Address:* Office of the Prime Minister, Building Administratif, Avenue Léopold Sédar Senghor, Dakar, Senegal (Office). *Telephone:* 823-10-88 (Office). *Fax:* 822-55-78 (Office).

SEDAKA, Neil; American singer and composer; b. 13 March 1939; s. of Mac Sedaka and Eleanor Appel; m. Leba M. Strassberg 1962; one s. one d.; ed Juilliard School of Music; solo performer world-wide 1959–; recipient of numerous gold records and recording industry awards. *Composed numerous popular songs including:* Breaking Up Is Hard to Do, Stupid Cupid, Calendar Girl, Oh! Carol, Stairway to Heaven, Happy Birthday Sweet Sixteen, Laughter in the Rain, Bad Blood, Love Will Keep Us Together, Lonely Night (Angel Face). *Recordings include:* In the Pocket, Sedaka's Back, The Hungry Years, Steppin' Out, A Song, All You Need Is The Music, Come See About Me, Greatest Hits 1988, Oh! Carol and Other Hits 1990, Timeless 1992. *Address:* c/o Neil Sedaka Music, 201 East 66th Street, Ste 3N, New York, NY 10021, USA.

SEDGWICK, (Ian) Peter; British business executive; b. 13 Oct. 1935; m. Verna Mary Sedgwick 1956; one s. one d.; with Nat. Provincial Bank 1952–59, Ottoman Bank Africa and Middle East 1959–69, J. Henry Schroder Wagg & Co. Ltd 1969–90; Dir Schroders Nominees Ltd 1981–95, CEO Schroder Investment Man. Ltd 1985–94, Dir Schroder Unit Trusts Ltd 1987–95, Group Man. Dir Investment Man. Schroders PLC 1987–95, Deputy Chair. (Chair. Desig.) 1995–2000, Chair. 2000–(03), CEO (interim) 2001, Dir (non-exec.) Schroder & Co. Inc. 1991–99, Chair. 1996–2000, Pres., CEO Schroders Inc. New York 1996–2000; Chair. Schroder All-Asia Fund 1991–99, Schroder UK Growth Fund 1994–; Pres. CEO Schroder US Holdings Inc. 1996–; Dir (non-exec.) Equitable Life Assurance Soc. 1991–2001, INVESCO City & Commercial Investment Trust PLC (fmrly New City & Commercial Trust PLC) 1992–. *Leisure interests:* golf, grandchildren, theatre. *Address:* c/o Schroders PLC, 31 Gresham Street, London, EC2V 7QA, England.

ŠEDIVÝ, Jaroslav, CSc, DPhil; Czech politician and diplomatist (retd.); b. 12 Nov. 1929, Prague; s. of Jaroslav Šedivý and Marie Šedivý; m. Marie Poslušná 1962; one s. one d.; ed Charles Univ., Prague; with Czech Acad. of Sciences 1954–57; scientist Inst. of Int. Policy and Econ. 1957–70; imprisoned on charges of subversion of the state 1970–71; worker, driver, window cleaner 1972–88; researcher Prognostic Inst., Prague 1989; adviser to Minister for Foreign Affairs 1989–90; Amb. to France 1990–95, to Belgium, Luxembourg and NATO 1995–97; Perm. Rep. to UNESCO 1993–95; Minister for Foreign Affairs 1997, Jan.–July 1998; Amb. to Switzerland 1998–2002; Adviser, Analysis Section, Ministry of Foreign Affairs 2002–; Grand Officier, Ordre de Mérite (France) 1994; Dr hc (J. F. Kennedy Univ., Buenos Aires) 1998. *Publications:* Policy and Relations 1969, Humiliated Revolution (published under pseudonym Y. Heřtová) 1978, Metternich contra Napoleon 1998, Palace Černín in the Year Zero 1997, Mystery and Sins of the Templars 1999, Decembrists: Anatomy of an Unsuccessful Coup 2000. *Address:* 14700 Prague 4, Podolské Nábřeží 14, Czech Republic (Home). *Telephone:* (2) 41431707. *Website:* www.mzv.cz (Home).

ŠEDIVÝ, Maj.-Gen. Jiří; Czech army officer; b. 3 Jan. 1953, Příbram; m.; two d.; ed Mil. High School, Mil. Univ. for Land Army, Mil. Acad., Brno; mem. CP 1975–89; various commands Czech Army 1975–96, including Commdr, Czech Unit, Implementation Force (IFOR), Bosnia 1996; Commdr Czech Land Army 1997–98, Chief of Gen. Staff 1998–2002; in pvt. sector 2002–; four Mil. Merit Awards; two Memorial Badges. *Leisure interests:* sport, music. *Address:* c/o Ministry of Defence, Tychonova 1, 160 00 Prague 6, Czech Republic. *Telephone:* (2) 33041111. *Website:* www.army.cz (Office).

SEDKI, Atef, DEcon; Egyptian politician; b. 1930; ed law school and the Sorbonne, Paris; Prof. of Gen. Finance, Cairo Univ. 1958–73; Cultural Attaché, Egyptian Embassy, Paris 1973–80; Pres. Govt Advisory Council Comm. for Economic and Financial Affairs 1980–85; Pres. Govt Audit Office 1985–86; Prime Minister of Egypt 1986–95; Minister of Int. Co-operation 1987–95. *Address:* c/o Office of the Prime Minister, Cairo, Egypt.

SEDNEY, Jules; Suriname politician; b. 28 Sept. 1922, Paramaribo; s. of Eugene Edwin Leonard Sedney and Marie Julia Linger; m. Ina Francis Waaldyk 1951 (divorced 1985); two s. two d.; one d. by A. Calor; ed Graaf van Zinzendorfschool, Mulo and Univ. of Amsterdam; fmr teacher; held sr post with Cen. Bank of Suriname 1956–58, Pres. 1980; Minister of Finance 1958–63; Dir Industrial Devt Corpn of Suriname and Nat. Devt Bank 1963; left Nationale Partij Suriname (NPS) and joined Progressieve Nationale Partij (PNP) 1967; Prime Minister and Minister of Gen. Affairs 1970–73; Prof. of Econs, Univ. of Suriname 1976–80; Chair. Nat. Planning Council 1980; fmr Dir Suriname Trade and Industry Asscn 1990–92; Chair. Monitoring Group Suriname Structural Adjustment Programme 1992–96, Tripartite Advisory Bd to Govt of Suriname 1994–98, Seniority Bd of Econ. Advisers to Pres. of the Repub. 1998–2000, Center for the Promotion and Protection of Democracy and Civil Soc. 1999; Gran Cordón Simón Bolívar (Venezuela), Groot-Officier Oranje Nassau (Netherlands), Kt, Nederlandse Leeuw (Netherlands). *Publications:* Growth Without Development 1978, To Choose and To Divide 1980, The Future of Our Past 1998. *Leisure interests:* bridge, golf. *Address:* Maystreet 34, Paramaribo, Suriname. *Telephone:* (597) 439114. *Fax:* (597) 421029.

SEELERT, Bob; American business executive; Gen. Man. Gen. Foods, 1966–86, Pres. Coffee and Int. Foods Div. 1986–89; Pres. and CEO Kayser-Roth (hosiery group) 1991–94; Pres. and CEO Topco American (grocery co.) 1989–91; Chief Exec. Cordiant Communications Group PLC (frmly. Saatchi & Saatchi, later Cordiant PLC) 1995–97; CEO Saatchi & Saatchi 1997–. *Address:* Cordiant PLC, 83–89 Whitfield Street, London, W1A 4XA, England (Office). *Telephone:* (20) 7436-4000 (London) (Office). *Fax:* (20) 7436-1998 (London) (Office).

SEGAL, Anthony Walter, MD, PhD, DSc, FMedSci, FRS, FRCP; British medical scientist and consultant physician; b. 24 Feb. 1944, Johannesburg, South Africa; s. of Cyril Segal and Doreen Segal (née Hayden); m. Barbara Miller 1966; three d.; ed Univs of Cape Town and London; Sr Clinical Fellow, Wellcome Trust 1979–86; Charles Dent Prof. of Medicine, Univ. Coll., London 1986–. *Leisure interests:* golf, sculpture, theatre, art. *Address:* Department of Medicine, University College London, 2nd Floor, Rayne Institute, 5 University Street, London, WC1E 6JJ (Office); 48B Regents Park Road, London, NW1 7SX, England (Home). *Telephone:* (20) 7679-6175 (Office); (20) 7586-8745 (Home). *Fax:* (20) 7679-6211 (Office).

SEGAL, George, BA; American film actor and producer; b. 13 Feb. 1934, New York, NY; s. of George Segal and Fanny Segal (née Bodkin); m. 1st Marion Sobol 1956 (divorced 1983); two d.; m. 2nd Linda Rogoff 1983 (deceased); m. 3rd Sonia Schulz; ed Manhasset Bay High School, Great Neck Junior High School, George School, Haverford Coll., Columbia Coll. *Films include:* The Young Doctors 1961, Act One 1962, The Longest Day 1962, Invitation to a Gunfighter 1964, The New Interns 1964, Ship of Fools 1965, King Rat 1965, Who's Afraid of Virginia Woolf? 1966, The Quiller Memorandum 1966, Bye Bye Braverman 1968, No Way to Treat a Lady 1968, The Bridge at Remagen 1969, She Couldn't Say No 1969, The Southern Star 1969, Loving 1970, Where's Poppa? 1970, The Owl and the Pussy Cat 1970, Born to Win 1972, The Hot Rock 1972, A Touch of Class (Golden Globe Award 1972) 1972, Blume in Love 1972, The Terminal Man 1973, California Split 1973, Blackbird 1974, Russian Roulette 1975, The Duchess and the Dirtwater Fox 1976, Fun with Dick and Jane 1976, Rollercoaster 1977, Who is Killing the Great Chefs of Europe? 1978, Lost and Found 1979, The Last Married Couple in America 1980, Stick 1983, The Endless Game (TV) 1989, Look Who's Talking 1990, The Clearing, For The Boys 1991, The Mirror has Two Faces 1996, Flirting with Disaster 1996, The Cable Guy 1996, The November Conspiracy 1997, Houdini 1998, The Linda McCartney Story 2000. *Play:* Art, New York 1999, West End, London 2001. *Television:* Just Shoot Me (NBC sitcom) 1996–. *Leisure interest:* banjo playing. *Address:* c/o Starr & Co., 350 Park Avenue, New York, NY 10022, USA.

SEGAL, Judah Benzion (Ben), MC, DPhil, FBA; British professor of semitic languages; b. 21 June 1912, Newcastle-upon-Tyne; s. of Prof. Moses Hirsch Segal and Hanna Leah; m. Leah Seidemann 1946; two d.; ed Magdalen Coll. School, Oxford, St Catharine's Coll., Cambridge and St John's Coll., Oxford; Deputy Asst Dir, Public Security, Anglo-Egyptian Sudan 1939–41; served in army in Middle East 1942–44; in charge of Arab Educ., Tripolitania, Libya 1945–46; Lecturer in Hebrew, Reader in Aramaic and Syriac, SOAS, Univ. of London 1947–60; Prof. of Semitic Languages, Univ. of London 1961–79, Prof. Emer. 1979–; Pres. Leo Baeck Coll., London (fmrly Prin.); Hon. Fellow SOAS; Freeman of City of Urfa, Turkey. *Publications:* The Diacritical Point and the Accents in Syriac 1953, The Hebrew Passover 1963, Edessa, the Blessed City 1970, Aramaic Texts from North Saqqara 1983, A History of the Jews of Cochin 1993, Aramaic and Mandaic Incantation Bowls in the British Museum 2000, Whisper Awhile 2000. *Leisure interests:* reading, meditation. *Address:* 17 Hillersdon Avenue, Edgware, Middx, HA8 7SG, England (Home). *Telephone:* (20) 8958-4993. *E-mail:* ben.segal@btopenworld.com (Home).

SEGAL, Ronald Michael, BA; South African/British author; b. 14 July 1932, Cape Town; s. of Leon and Mary Segal; m. Susan Wolff 1962; one s. two d.; ed Univ. of Cape Town and Trinity Coll., Cambridge; Dir Faculty and Cultural Studies Nat. Union of S African Students 1951–52; Pres. Univ. of Cape Town Council of Univ. Socs. 1951; won Philip Francis du Pont Fellowship to Univ. of Virginia (USA) 1955 but returned to S Africa to found Africa South (quarterly) 1956; helped launch economic boycott April 1959; banned by S African Govt from all meetings July 1959; in England with Africa South in Exile, April 1960–61; Gen. Ed. Penguin African Library 1961–84; Pluto Crime Fiction 1983–86; Hon. Sec. S African Freedom Asscn 1960–61; Convenor, Int. Conf. on Econ. Sanctions against S. Africa 1964, Int. Conf. on SW Africa 1966; Visiting Fellow, Center for Study of Democratic Insts., Santa Barbara 1973; Founding Chair. The Walton Soc. 1975–79, Pres. 1979–; Chair. Ruth First Memorial Trust 1983–. *Publications:* The Tokolosh (a fantasy) 1960, Political Africa: A Who's Who of Personalities and Parties 1961, African Profiles 1962, Into Exile 1963, Sanctions Against South Africa (Ed.) 1964, The Crisis of India 1965, The Race War 1966, South West Africa: Travesty of Trust (Ed.) 1967, America's Receding Future 1968, The Struggle Against History 1971, Whose Jerusalem? The Conflicts of Israel 1973, The Decline and Fall of the American Dollar 1974, The Tragedy of Leon Trotsky 1979, The State of the World Atlas 1981, The New State of the World Atlas 1984, The Book of Business, Money and Power 1987, The Black Diaspora 1995, Islam's Black Slaves 2001. *Leisure interest:* day-dreaming. *Address:* The Old Manor House, Manor Road, Walton-on-Thames, Surrey, England (Home). *Telephone:* (1932) 227766.

SEGAL, Uri; Israeli orchestral conductor; b. 7 March 1944, Jerusalem; s. of Alexander and Nehama Segal; m. Ilana Finkelstein 1966; one s. three d.; ed Rubin Acad., Jerusalem and Guildhall School of Music, London; debut with Seajillands Symphony Orchestra, Copenhagen 1969; Prin. Conductor Bournemouth Symphony Orchestra 1980–82, Philharmonia Hungarica 1981–85; Music Dir Chautauqua Festival (New York) 1990–; Founder/Chief Conductor Century Orchestra (Osaka) 1990–; orchestras conducted include Berlin Philharmonic, Stockholm Philharmonic, Concertgebouw, Orchestre de Paris, Vienna Symphony, Israel Philharmonic, London Symphony, London Philharmonic, Pittsburgh Symphony, Chicago Symphony and Houston Symphony; tours have included Austria, Switzerland, Spain, Italy, France, UK, Scandinavia and the Far East; recordings include Mahler Symphony No. 4 (with NZ Symphony Orchestra), music by Britten (Bournemouth Symphony), music by Stravinsky (Suisse Romande), concertos with Lupu, De Larrocha, Firkušný and Ashkenazy; First Prize Dimitri Mitropoulos Int. Competition, New York 1969. *Leisure interests:* reading, photography, cooking. *Address:* Terry Harrison Artists Management, The Orchard, Market Street, Charlburg, Oxon., OX7 3PY; c/o Olivia MA Artists' Management, 28 Sheffield Terrace, London, W8 7NA, England. *Telephone:* (20) 7221-3606. *Fax:* (20) 7221-3607.

SEGNI, Mario; Italian politician; Founder, fmr leader Democratic Alliance; fmr mem. Christian Democrat Party; mem. Camera dei Deputati. *Address:* Camera dei Deputati, Rome, Italy.

SEGUELA, Jacques Louis, ; French advertising executive; b. 23 Feb. 1934, Paris; s. of Louis Seguela and Simone Le Forestier; m. Sophie Vinson 1978; one s. four d.; ed Lycée de Perpignan, Faculté de Pharmacie de Montpellier; reporter, Paris Match 1960; with France Soir group's leisure magazines 1962; produced several TV programmes; joined Delpire 1964, then Axe; f. Roux Seguela Agency; f. Roux Seguela Cayzac & Goudard with Alain Cayzac and Jean Michel Goudard 1978; Vice-Pres. (Euro-RSCG) 1991–96; Vice-Pres. and Administrator Havas Advertising 1996–2001; Bleu comme bleu (restaurant), Paris 1995; Chevalier, Légion d'honneur, Chevalier des Arts et des Lettres; César winner. *Publications:* Terre en rond 1961 (Prix littérature sportive), Ne dites pas à ma mère que je suis dans la publicité, elle me croit pianiste dans un bordel 1979, Hollywood lave plus blanc 1982, Fils de pub 1984, Cache Cache Pub, Demain il sera tros star 1989, C'est gai la pub 1990, Vote au-dessus d'un nid de cocos 1992, Pub Story 1994, La parole de Dieu 1995, le Futur a de l'avenir 1996, 80 ans de publicité Citroën et toujours 20 ans 1999, Le Vertige des urnes 2000, Job Guide des métiers de demain 2001. *Address:* Havas Advertising, 84 rue de Villiers, 92300 Levallois-Perret, France.

SÉGUIN, Philippe Daniel Alain, LèsL; French politician; b. 21 April 1943, Tunis, Tunisia; s. of Robert Séguin and Denyse Danielle; m. 2nd Béatrice Bernascon; one d.; two s. one d. by first m.; ed Lycée Carnot, Tunis, Lycée de Draguignan, Ecole Normale d'Instituteurs, Var, Faculté des Lettres, Aix-en-Provence and Ecole Nationale d'Admin.; Auditor, Cour des Comptes 1970, Conseiller Référendaire 1977; Acad. de Nice 1971; Dir of Studies, Inst. d'Etudes Politiques, Aix-en-Provence 1970–74; Maître de Conferences, Inst. d'Etudes Politiques, Paris 1971–77; Prof. Centre de Formation Professionelle et de Perfectionnement 1971–73; Secr.-Gen. Presidency of the Repub. 1973–74; Asst to Dir of Physical Educ. and Sport 1974–75; Dir Office of Sec. of State responsible for relations with Parl. 1977; Chargé de mission, Office of Prime Minister 1977–78; Deputy to Nat. Ass. 1978–86, Vice-Pres. 1981–86; Mayor of Epinal 1983–97; Nat. Sec. RPR 1984–86, Pres. 1997–99, Pres. RPR

Conseil de Paris 2001–02; Minister of Social Affairs and Employment 1986–88; Deputy for Les Vosges 1988–; Pres. Nat. Ass. 1993–97, Parl. Floor Leader 1997–99; Pres. nat. tripartite comm., French Fed. of Football; Hon. DLitt (Loughborough Univ. of Tech.) 1987; Chevalier du Mérite Agricole. *Publications:* Réussir l'alternance 1985, La force de convaincre 1990, Louis Napoléon le Grand 1990, De l'Europe en général et de la France en particulier (jtly) 1992, Discours pour la France 1992, Demain, la France: tome I: La Priorité sociale (jty), Tome II: La Reconquête du Territoire 1993, Ce que j'ai dit 1993, Discours encore et toujours républicains 1994, Deux France (jtly) 1994, 240 dans un fauteuil 1995, C'est quoi La politique? (for children) 1999, Plus français que moi, tu meurs! (essay) 2000, Lettre ouverte à ceux qui veulent encore croire à Paris 2000. *Address:* Assemblée nationale, 75355 Paris, France.

SEGUY, Georges; French trade unionist; b. 16 March 1927, Toulouse; s. of André Seguy and Gabrielle Monfouga; m. Cécile Sédeillan 1949; two s. one d.; ed Armand-Leygues School, Toulouse; apprentice typographer 1942; mem. French CP 1942–, mem. Cen. Cttee 1954–, Political Bureau 1956–82; arrested by Gestapo and deported to Mauthausen Concentration Camp 1944; electrician, SNCF (French Railways) 1946; mem. Railway Workers' Union, Toulouse 1946–49; Sec. Fédération des cheminots CGT (Confédération Générale du Travail) 1949, Sec.-Gen. 1961–65; Sec. CGT 1965–67, Sec.-Gen. 1967–82; Pres. Inst. CGT d'Histoire Sociale 1982–; mem. Exec. Cttee Fédération syndicale mondiale 1970–83; Officier, Légion d'honneur; Order of the October Revolution 1982. *Publications:* Le mai de la CGT 1972, Lutter (autobiog.) 1975, Le 1er Mai les 100 printemps 1989, la Grève 1993. *Leisure interests:* shooting, fishing. *Address:* Institut CGT d'histoire sociale, 263 rue de Paris, 93516 Montreuil Cedex, France (Office).

SEHGAL, Amar Nath, MA; Indian sculptor and painter; b. 5 Feb. 1922, Campbellpur, West Pakistan; s. of Ram Asra Mal and Parmeshwari Devi; m. Shukla Dhawan 1954; two s.; ed Punjab Univ., Govt Coll., Lahore and New York Univ.; one-man exhbn New York 1950–51, Paris 1952, East Africa and India; Hon. Art Consultant to Ministry of Community Devt, Govt of India 1955–66; organized sculpture exhbns. in Belgrade 1964, Musée d'Art Moderne, Paris 1965, Pauls-kirche Frankfurt 1965, Haus am Lutzoplatz West Berlin 1966, Musées Royaux D'Art et Histoire, Brussels 1966, Musée Etat Luxembourg 1966, Wiener Secession, Vienna 1966, Flemish Acad. Arts 1967, Tokyo Int. Fair 1973, etc.; retrospective Exhbn Nat. Gallery of Modern Art, New Delhi 1972, City Hall, Ottawa 1975, Aerogolf, Luxembourg 1975, India House, New York 1976, Rathaus, Fransheim, FRG 1977, Frankfurt Airport 1977, Neustadt 1978, Brenners Park, Baden-Baden 1979, Luxembourg 1980; exhbns., Dubai, Abu Dhabi 1980, Jeddah 1981, Chaux de Fond (Switzerland) 1982, Cercle Munster, Luxembourg 1987, Berne 1988, New York 1991, London 1991, New Delhi 1992; participated in Sculpture Biennale, Musée Rodin, Paris 1966 and UNESCO Conf. on role of art in contemporary soc. 1974; org. Int. Children Art Workshop UNESCO, Paris 1979; est. The Creative Fund, charitable org.; Fellow Lalit Kala Akad. 1992; Sculpture Award, Lalit Kala Acad. 1957, President's Award, Lalit Kala Acad. 1958 (donated to Prime Minister Nehru during Chinese invasion), UN Peace Medal 1985. *Major works:* Voice of Africa (Ghana) 1959, A Cricketer 1961, Mahatma Gandhi, Amritsar, To Space Unknown (bronze; Moscow) 1963; commissioned to decorate Vidyan Bhawan (India's Int. Conferences Bldg) with bronze sculptural mural depicting rural life of India; bronze work Conquest of the Moon, White House Collection 1969; Anguished Cries (bronze) monument, W Berlin 1971; Gandhi monument, Luxembourg 1971; Monument to Aviation, New Delhi Airport, 1972; Rising Spirit, White House Collection 1978; The Crushing Burden, inaugurated 2nd World Population Conf., Mexico 1984; Victims of Torture, designed for UN; monument to Freedom Fighters of Namibia, Vienna 1986; Bust of Sam Nujoma, Nat. Gallery of Modern Art, New Delhi 1993; Int. Year of Peace sculpture, Head with Horns 1986; Captive, inaugurated at UN Conf. on sanctions against South Africa, Paris 1986; Nari, monument to Women, Int. Women's Day 1986; Flute Player (gift of children of India to UNICEF) 1986; monument to Nehru 1989; exhbn of gold sculptures Luxembourg 1990, The Captive, Palace of Human Rights, Geneva 1999 and Museum of Robben Island, SA 2001; works in Jerusalem, Vienna, Paris, West Berlin, Antwerp, Luxembourg, Connecticut, New Delhi. *Film:* film on life and work sponsored by UNESCO Int. Fund for the Promotion of Culture, with music by Yehudi Menuhin and Ravi Shankar. *Television appearance in:* films on life and works 1980, 1990, 2001. *Publications:* Arts and Aesthetics, Organising Exhibitions in Rural Areas, Der Innere Rhythmus (poems) 1975, Folio of Graphics 1981; folios of graphics with poetry in English, French, Arabic 1981–84, Folio on Ganesha 1991, Lonesome Journey, A Collection of Poems 1996, Awaiting a New Dawn 1997. *Leisure interests:* writing poetry, photography, cooking. *Address:* J-23 Jangpura Extension, New Delhi 110014, India; The Creative Fund, 1 Montée de Clausen, 1343 Luxembourg. *Telephone:* (11) 94319206 (India); (352) 47-02-20 (Luxembourg).

SEIDELMAN, Susan, MFA; American film director; b. 11 Dec. 1952, nr Philadelphia, Pa; ed Drexel Univ. and New York Univ. Film School; directing debut with And You Act Like One Too (Student Acad. Award, Acad. of Motion Picture Arts and Sciences); then Dir Deficit (short film funded by American Film Inst.) and Yours Truly, Andrea G. Stern, The Dutch Master; Hon. PhD (Drexel); Mary Pickford Award for Best Female Dir 2002. *Films:* Smithereens (Dir, producer, co-scriptwriter), Desperately Seeking Susan, Making Mr Right, Cookie, She-Devil, The Barefoot Executive 1995, Tales of Erotica, A Cooler Climate 1999, Gaudi Afternoon 2001. *Television:* directed several episodes of Sex and the City. *Leisure interests:* travel. *Address:* c/o Michael Shedler, 350 5th Avenue, New York, NY 10118 (Office); c/o Gary Pearl Pictures, 10956 Weyburn Avenue, Suite 200, Los Angeles, CA 90024, USA (Office). *Telephone:* stonehedge185@aol.com (Office).

SEIDLER, Harry, AC, OBE, MArch; Australian architect; b. 25 June 1923, Vienna, Austria; s. of Max Seidler and Rose Seidler; m. Penelope Evatt 1958; one s. one d.; ed Wasagymnasium, Vienna, Austria, Cambridge Tech. School, UK, Univ. of Manitoba, Canada, Harvard Univ. and Black Mountain Coll., USA; postgrad. work under Walter Gropius, Harvard Univ. 1946; study with painter Josef Albers, Black Mountain Coll. 1946; Chief Asst with Marcel Breuer, New York 1946–48; Prin. Architect, Harry Seidler and Assocs., Sydney, Australia 1948–; Thomas Jefferson Prof. of Architecture, Univ. of Va 1978; Visiting Prof. Harvard Univ. 1976–77, Univ. of NSW 1980; Univ. of Sydney 1984, 1996, 2001, Univ. of Tech., Sydney 1993, ETH, Zürich 1993; mem. Acad. d'Architecture, Paris 1982, Int Acad. of Architects, Sofia 1987; Life Fellow, Royal Australian Inst. of Architects 1970; Fellow Australia Acad. of Tech. Sciences 1979; Hon. mem. Israel Inst. of Architects and Town Planners 2001; Hon. FAIA 1966; Hon. LLD (Manitoba) 1988; Hon. DLitt (Univ. of Tech., Sydney) 1991; Hon. DSc (Univ. of NSW) 1999, (Sydney) 2000; Wilkinson Award 1965, 1966, 1967, 1999; Sir John Sulman Medal 1951, 1967, 1981, 1983, 1991, Civic Design Award 1967, 1981, 1992, Pan Pacific Citation of the AIA 1968, numerous RAIA awards including Gold Medal 1976, Special Jury Award 2000, Gold Medal, City of Vienna 1990, Royal Gold Medal, RIBA 1996; Cross of Honour (1st Class) for Art and Science, Austria 1996. *Major works:* Rose Seidler House 1949–51 (made a Historic Houses Trust museum 1988), flats and housing units in Australia, urban redevt. projects for McMahons Point 1957, city centre redevt. 'Australia Square', Sydney 1962–66, Commonwealth Trade Office Complex, Canberra 1970–72, High Rise Apartments, Acapulco 1970, MLC Center, Martin Place, Sydney 1972–75, Australian Embassy, Paris 1974–76, Hong Kong Club and Offices 1980–84, Grosvenor Place, Sydney 1982–88, Riverside Centre, Brisbane 1984–86, Capita Tower, Sydney 1984–89, Hilton Hotel, Brisbane 1984–86, Shell House, Melbourne 1985–89, Waverley Art Gallery, Melbourne 1988, QVI Tower, Perth 1987–91, Wohnpark Neue Donau (housing Devt, Vienna) 1993–(98), Horizon Apartments 1990-97. *Publications:* Houses, Interiors and Projects 1949–1954, Harry Seidler 1955–63, Architecture in the New World 1974, Australian Embassy, Paris 1979, Two Towers, Sydney 1980, Interment: The Diaries of Harry Seidler 1940–41 1986, Riverside Centre 1988, Harry Seidler: Four Decades of Architecture 1992, Harry Seidler—The Master Architect Series III 1997. *Leisure interests:* photography, architecture, skiing. *Address:* 2 Glen Street, Milsons Point, NSW 2061, Australia. *Telephone:* (2) 9922-1388 (Office); (2) 9498-5986 (Home). *Fax:* (2) 9957-2947. *E-mail:* hsa@seidler.net.au (Office). *Website:* www.seidler.net.au (Office).

SEIDMAN, L(ewis) William, LLB, MBA; American fmr government official, publisher and television broadcaster; b. 29 April 1921, Grand Rapids, Mich.; s. of Frank Seidman and Esther Lubetsky; m. Sarah Berry 1944; one s. five d.; ed Dartmouth Coll., Harvard Univ. and Univ. of Mich.; army service 1942–46; mem. Mich. Bar 1949, DC Bar 1977; Special Asst for Financial Affairs to Gov. of Mich. 1963–66; Nat. Man. Partner, Seidman & Seidman (certified public accountants) New York 1969–74; Asst for Econ. Affairs to Pres. Gerald Ford 1974–77; Dir Phelps Dodge Corpn New York 1977–82, Vice-Chair. 1980–82; Dean, Coll. of Business Admin. Ariz. State Univ. 1982–85; Chair. Fed. Deposit Insurance Corpn (FDIC) 1985–91; Chair. Detroit Fed. Reserve Bank, Chicago 1970; Co-Chair. White House Conf. on Productivity 1983–84; Chair. Resolution Trust Corpn 1989–91; Chief Commentator CNBC-TV 1991–; Publr Bank Director (magazine); Bronze Star Medal. *Address:* CNBC, 8th Floor, 1025 Connecticut Avenue, NW, Washington, DC 20036 (Office); 825 Audubon Drive, Bradenton, FL 34209, USA (Home). *Telephone:* (202) 530-0910 (Office). *Fax:* (202) 822-9551 (Office). *E-mail:* lws1025@aol.com (Office).

SEIFART, Angel Roberto; Paraguayan politician and lawyer; b. 12 Sept. 1941, Asunción; ed Nat. Univ. of Asunción; fiscal agent in commercial and civil law 1966–67; Judge of the First Instance 1968–74; mem. Court of Appeal (First Chamber) 1974–77; Pres. Judicial Magistrates Asscn 1974–75; Nat. Rep. Asociación Nacional Republicana (Partido Colorado) 1978–93, interim mem. Governing Bd 1981–87, titular mem. 1989–; Minister of State, Educ. and Culture 1990–91; Vice-Pres. of Paraguay 1993–98; mem. Man. Comm. of Rural Asscn of Paraguay 1983–89. *Address:* c/o Office of the Vice-President, Gral. Díaz, Calle Alberdi, Asunción, Paraguay.

SEIFERT, Werner G.; German (b. Swiss) finance executive; fmr partner McKinsey, then Swiss Re; now Chair. Man. Bd Deutsche Börse, CEO 1993–. *Address:* Deutsche Börse AG, 60313 Frankfurt a.M., Börsenplatz 4, Germany (Office). *Telephone:* (69) 21010 (Office). *Fax:* (69) 29977580 (Office).

SEIKE, Tomio; Japanese artist and photographer; b. 13 July 1943, Tokyo; m. Junko Seike; ed Sapporo Jr Coll., Japan Photographic Acad.; Asst Photographer, Japan 1970–74; moved to England 1974; freelance photographer, Tokyo. *Solo exhibitions include:* Zeit Foto Salon, Tokyo 1984, 1985, 1990; Gallery Seki, Nagoya 1985; Picture Photo Space, Osaka 1986, 1990, 1993; Hamiltons Gallery, London (UK) 1986, 1989, 1992, 1995; Comptoir de la Photographie, Paris (France) 1987; The Weston Gallery, Carmel (USA) 1989, 1993, 1995; Printz, Kyoto 1990; Galerie Reckerman, Koln (Germany) 1991, 1996; Galerie Agathe Gaillerd, Paris 1991; Blitz, Tokyo 1992; Kohji Ogura Gallery, Nagoya 1992, 1995, 2000; Gallery 292, NY (USA) 1993, 1998; Robert

Koch Gallery, San Francisco (USA) 1994; Galerie zur Stockerregg, Zurich (Switzerland) 1994; J. Jackson Fine Art, Atlanta (USA) 1995; Robert Klein Gallery, Boston (USA) 1995; Photo Gallery Int., Japan 1997, 2001; Exponera (Sweden) 1997; Galerie Camera Obscura, Paris 1998. *Publications include:* Portrait of Zoe, Paris, Waterscape 2003. *Address:* c/o Hamiltons Gallery, 13 Carlos Place, London, W1 2EU, England (Office). *Telephone:* (20) 7499-9494 (Office). *Fax:* (20) 7629-9919 (Office). *E-mail:* info@hamiltonsgallery.com (Office). *Website:* www.hamiltonsgallery.com (Office).

SEILLIÈRE de LABORDE, Ernest-Antoine; French business executive and fmr civil servant; b. 20 Dec. 1937, Neuilly-sur-Seine; s. of Jean Seillière de Laborde and Renée de Wendel; m. Antoinette Barbey 1971; two s. three d.; ed Ladycross Coll., Lycée Janson-de-Sailly, Faculty of Law, Paris, Nat. School of Admin.; attaché High Comm. of Algeria 1962; with Ministry of Information 1963, Sec. for Foreign Affairs 1966, mem. French del. at negotiations for EEC, Brussels and Gen. Agreement on Tariffs and Trade, Geneva 1966–69, Adviser on Foreign Affairs 1969, Adviser to the Prime Minister 1969–72, Tech. Adviser to Minister for Foreign Affairs 1972–73, Minister of Armed Forces 1973–74; lecturer Centre for Int. Affairs, Harvard Univ. 1975; Jt Dir-Gen. of Industrial Politics Marine-Wendel 1976, Pres. 1992–; Gen. Dir, Admin. CGIP 1978–87, Pres., Dir-Gen. 1987–; Vice-Pres. Carnaud SA (later CMB Packaging) 1984–91; Vice-Chair. Bd Cap Gemini 2000–; Vice-Pres. Fed. of Mechanical Industries 1985; fmrly Vice-Pres. Nat. Council of French Employers (CNPF), Pres. 1997–; Pres. MEDEF (French Business Confed.) 1997–; Officier Légion d'honneur, Officier Ordre nat. du Mérite. *Address:* Wendel Investissement, 89 rue Taitbout, 75009 Paris, France.

SEIN WIN, U; Myanma politician; s. of U Ba Lwin; cousin of Aung San Suu Kyi; leader New Democracy Party, banned by ruling State Law and Order Restoration Council (SLORC); Pres. of outlawed Nat. Coalition Govt of Union of Burma 1990.

SEINFELD, Jerry; American comedian; b. 29 April 1955, Brooklyn; s. of Kal Seinfeld and Betty Seinfeld; ed Queens Coll., NY; fmrly salesman; stand-up comedian 1976–; joke-writer Benson (TV series) 1980; actor Seinfeld (TV series) 1989–97, also co-writer, producer; Emmy Award Outstanding Comedy Series (for Seinfeld) 1993; American Comedy Award 1988, 1992. *Television includes:* The Ratings Game (film) 1984, The Seinfeld Chronicles 1990, I'm Telling You for the Last Time 1999. *Publication:* Sein Language 1993. *Leisure interests:* Zen, yoga.

SEIP, Anne-Lise, DPhil; Norwegian professor of modern history; b. 6 Nov. 1933, Bergen; d. of Edvin Thomassen and Birgit Thomassen; m. Jens Arup Seip 1960 (died 1992); one s. one d.; ed Univ. of Oslo; Sr Lecturer Inst. of Criminology and Penal Law, Univ. of Oslo 1974–75, Dept of History 1975–85, Prof. of Modern History 1985–; mem. Norwegian Acad. of Science, Det kongelige danske videnskabernes selskab. *Publications include:* Videnskap og virkelighet T.H. Asehehoug 1974, Eilert Sundt. 1983, Sosialhjelpstaten blir til 1984, Veier til velferdsstaten 1994, Norges historie, Vol.8 1830–70 1997; numerous articles. *Leisure interests:* books, music, gardening. *Address:* Gamle Drammensvei 144, 1363 Høvik (Home); Department of History, University of Oslo, P.O. Box 1008, Blindern, 0315 Oslo, Norway. *Telephone:* 22-85-68-78 (Office); 67-53-40-39 (Home). *E-mail:* informasjon@uio.no (Office). *Website:* www.uio.no (Office).

SEIPP, Walter, DJur; German banker and business executive; b. 13 Dec. 1925, Langen; m. 1954; two s.; ed Univ. of Frankfurt am Main; Jr Barrister 1950–53; with Deutsche Bank AG 1951–74 (Exec. Vice-Pres. 1970–74); mem. Man. Bd, Westdeutsche Landesbank Girozentrale 1974–77, Vice-Chair. 1978–81; Chair. Man. Bd, Commerzbank AG 1981–91; fmr Chair. Supervisory Bd, now Hon. Chair.; Chair. Supervisory Bd, Berliner Commerzbank AG, Rheinische Hypothekenbank AG, Frankfurt, Essen; Chair. Admin. Bd, Commerzbank Int. SA, Luxembourg, Commerzbank (Schweiz) AG, Zürich; Chair. Supervisory Bd Commerz Int. Capital Man. GmbH, Frankfurt; Chair. Bd of Dirs., Commerzbank Capital Markets Corpn, NY, Commerz-Securities (Japan) Co. Ltd, Commerzbank, SE Asia Ltd, Singapore; mem. Bd of Dirs, Int. Monetary Conf., Wash. (Pres. 1987–88), mem. Supervisory Bd, Bayer AG, Leverkusen, Daimler Benz AG, Stuttgart, Deutsche Shell AG, Hamburg, Vereinigte Industrie-Unternehmungen AG, Bonn, Linde AG Wiesbaden, Allianz Versicherungs AG, Munich, Hochtief AG, Essen, MAN AG, Munich, Thyssen AG, Duisburg; mem. Bd of Man. Dirs. Bundesverband deutscher Banken eV, Cologne; mem. advisory cttee of three cos.

SEITE, Berndt; German politician and veterinary surgeon; b. 22 April 1940, Hahnswalde, Silesia; m. Annemarie Seite 1964; two c.; ed Humboldt Univ. Berlin; mem. Synod of Lutheran Church in Mecklenburg and mem. Protestant WCC 1975–; initiated autumn anti-Govt demonstrations in fmr GDR (with Gottfried Timm) 1989; Co-Founder, New Forum 1989; mem. Christian Democratic Union (CDU) 1990–; Chair. Röbel Dist Council 1990; Gen. Sec. CDU Asscn in Mecklenburg-Western Pomerania 1991–92; Minister-Pres. of Mecklenburg-Western Pomerania 1992–98; mem. Landtag of Mecklenburg-Western Pomerania 1994–.

SEITERS, Rudolf; German politician; b. 13 Oct. 1937, Osnabrück; s. of Adolf Seiters and Josefine Gördel; m. Brigitte Kolata; three c.; ed Univ. of Münster; qualified as lawyer; joined Junge Union and Christian Democratic Party (CDU) 1958, Regional Chair. Junge Union, Osnabrück-Emsland 1963–65, Chair. CDU Land Asscn Hanover 1965–68, mem. Junge Union Fed. Exec. Cttee 1967–71, Sr Chair. CDU Land Asscn Lower Saxony 1968–70; Head

Econ. and Housing Dept, Office of Regierungspräsident (Regional Gov.), Osnabrück 1967–69; mem. Deutscher Bundestag 1969–; mem. CDU Fed. Exec. Cttee 1971–73; Parl. Party Man. CDU/CSU Parl. Party in Bundestag 1971–76, Sr Parl. Man. 1984–89; Parl. Party Man. 1982–84; Fed. Minister for Special Tasks and Head of Fed. Chancellery 1989–91, of the Interior 1991–93; Deputy Chair. CDU/Christian Social Union in Bundestag 1994–; Vice-Pres. Bundestag 1998–; Hon. Dr.rer.Pol.; Grosses Bundesverdienstkreuz mit Stern 1995, Grosses Silbernes Ehrenzeichen (Austria) 1995, Offizierskreuz der Ehrenlegion Frankreich 1996. *Publication:* Aussenpolitik im 21. Jahrhundert 1996. *Address:* Deutscher Bundestag, Platz der Republik, 11011 Berlin (Office); Spiekerooger Strasse 6, 26871 Papenburg, Germany. *Telephone:* (30) 22771366 (Office). *Fax:* (30) 22770167 (Office).

SEITZ, Frederick, AB, PhD; American physicist; b. 4 July 1911, San Francisco; s. of Frederick Seitz and Emily Seitz; m. Elizabeth K. Marshall 1935 (died 1992); ed Stanford and Princeton Univs; Instructor of Physics, Univ. of Rochester 1935–36, Asst Prof. 1936–37; on staff of Research Laboratory of Gen. Electric Co. 1937–39; Asst Prof., Univ. of Pa 1939–41; Assoc. Prof. 1941–42, Prof. and Head of Dept of Physics, Carnegie Inst. of Tech. 1942–49; Prof. Physics Univ. of Ill. 1949–57, Head of Dept 1957–64, Dean Graduate Coll. and Vice-Pres. of Research 1964–65; NATO Science Adviser 1959–60; Pres. Rockefeller Univ. 1968–78, Pres. Emer. 1978–; Pres. Richard Lounsbery Foundation, NY 1995–; mem. American Philosophical Soc., NAS (full-time Pres. 1962–69), American Physics Soc. 1961, American Acad. of Arts and Sciences, American Inst. of Physics; mem. numerous advisory cttees., including Advisory Group on Anticipated Advances in Science and Tech. (White House) 1970–76, NASA (SPAC) 1973– (Chair. 1976–77), Nat. Cancer Advisory Bd 1976–82; Chair. of Bd, John Simon Guggenheim Foundation 1976–83; Dir Texas Instruments 1971–82, Akzona Corpn 1973–82; mem. Bd of Trustees, Rockefeller Univ., Univ. Corpn for Atmospheric Research 1975–82, American Museum of Natural History 1975–, Ogden Corpn. 1977–; numerous hon. degrees; Nat. Medal of Science 1973, Joseph Henry Medal, Smithsonian Inst. 1997; Vannevar Bush Award 1983. *Publications:* The Modern Theory of Solids 1940, The Physics of Metals 1943, Solid State Physics 1955, The Science Matrix 1992, On the Frontier: My Life in Science 1994, Stalin's Captive: Nikolaus Riehl and the Soviet Race for the Bomb 1995. *Address:* Rockefeller University, 1230 York Avenue, New York, NY 10021, USA. *Telephone:* (212) 327-8423.

SEITZ, John N., BSc; American petroleum executive and geologist; ed Univ. of Pittsburgh, Rensselaer Polytechnic Inst. and Univ. of Pennsylvania; Sr Exploration Geologist, Anadarko Petroleum Corpn 1977–82, Chief Geologist 1982–83, Gen. Man. 1983–89, Vice-Pres. of Exploration and Production 1989–95, Sr Vice-Pres. of Exploration 1995–97, Exec. Vice-Pres. of Exploration and Production 1997–99, mem. Bd of Dirs. 1997–, Pres. and COO 1999–; mem. American Asscn of Petroleum Geologists, Geological Soc. of America, American Inst. of Professional Geologists, Houston Geological Soc., Soc. of Petroleum Engineers; mem. Advisory Bd Spindletop. *Address:* Anadarko Petroleum Corporation, 17001 Northchase Drive, Houston, TX 77060, USA (Office). *Website:* www.anadarko.com (Office).

SEITZ, Konrad, MA, DPhil; German diplomatist; b. 18 Jan. 1934, Munich; m. Eva Kautz 1965; Prof. of Classics, Univs of Marburg and Munich 1956–64; entered Foreign Office 1965; served in New Delhi 1968–72, UN Mission, New York 1972–75; main speech writer for Minister of Foreign Affairs 1975; Head, Policy Planning Staff, Foreign Office 1980–87; Amb. to India 1987–90; Co-Chair. Comm. Economy 2000, Baden-Württemberg 1992–93; Amb. to Italy 1992–95, to China 1995–99; Grosses Bundesverdienstkreuz. *Publications:* The Japanese-American Challenge: Germany's Hi-tech Industries Fight for Survival 1990, The Aimless Elites – Are the Germans Losing the Future? (with others), Europa—una Colonia Tecnológica? 1995, Race into the 21st Century – The Future of Europe Between America and Africa 1998, China—a World Power Comes Back 2000; contribs to foreign and econ. journals and newspapers. *Leisure interests:* history of ideas, literature, art, collecting Indian miniature paintings. *Address:* Dahlienweg 4, 53343 Wachtberg-Pech, Germany. *Telephone:* (228) 327811 (Home). *Fax:* (228) 9325154 (Home).

SEITZ, Hon. Raymond G. H.; American diplomatist and business executive; b. 8 Dec. 1940, Hawaii; m. Caroline Gordon Richardson; two s. one d.; ed Yale Univ.; joined Foreign Service 1966; served Montreal, Political Officer, Nairobi, Vice-Consul, Seychelles 1966–70; Prin. Officer, Bukavu, Zaire 1970–72; Secretariat Staff Washington 1972 then Dir of Staff; Special Asst to Dir-Gen. Foreign Service 1974; Political Officer, London 1975–79; Deputy Exec. Sec., Dept of State 1979–81, Sr Deputy Asst Sec. for Public Affairs 1981–82, Exec. Asst to Sec. Shultz 1982–84; Minister, US Embassy London 1984–89; Asst Sec. of State for European and Canadian Affairs 1989–91; Amb. to UK 1991–94; Vice-Chair. Lehman Bros. Int. (Europe) (now Lehman Bros Europe Ltd) 1996–; Dir Marconi 1994–, Cable and Wireless 1995–, BA 1995–, Rio Tinto 1996–, Pacific Century CyberWorks (PCCW) 1997–; Hon. DUniv (Herriot-Watt) 1994; Dr hc (Open Univ.) 1997. *Publication:* Over Here. *Address:* Lehman Brothers Europe Ltd, 1 Broadgate, London, EC2M 7HA, England.

SEKIYA, Katsutsugu; Japanese politician; ed Chuo Univ., Univ. of British Columbia, Canada; joined Japan Airlines 1963; sec. to a mem. of House of Reps. 1966; mem. LDP; mem. for Ehime, House of Reps. 1976; fmr Minister of Posts and Telecommunications, Chair. House of Reps. Transport Cttee; Minister of Construction 1998–99. *Address:* c/o Ministry of Construction, 2-1-3, Kasumigaseki, Chiyoda-ku, Tokyo 100, Japan.

SEKIZAWA, Tadashi, BEng; Japanese businessman; b. 6 Nov. 1931, Tokyo; m. Misako Sekizawa; two s.; ed Tokyo Univ.; joined Fujitsu Ltd 1954, Gen. Man. Switching Systems Group 1982–84, Bd Dir 1984–, Man. Dir 1986–88, Exec. Dir 1988–90, Pres. and Rep. Dir 1990–; Vice-Chair. Communication Industry Assen of Japan 1990–98, Chair. 1998–, Japan Electronic Industry Devt Assen 1990–. *Leisure interests:* literature, travel, motoring. *Address:* Fujitsu Ltd, 1-6-1 Marunouchi 1-chome, Chiyoda-ku, Tokyo 100, Japan. *Telephone:* (813) 3216-3211.

SELA, Michael, PhD; Israeli immunologist and chemist; b. 6 March 1924, Tomaszow, Poland; s. of Jakob Salomonowicz and Roza Salomonowicz; m. 1st Margalit Liebman 1948 (died 1975); two d.; m. 2nd Sara Kika 1976; one d.; ed Hebrew Univ., Jerusalem and Geneva Univ.; joined Weizmann Inst. of Science 1950, Head Dept of Chemical Immunology 1963–75, Vice-Pres. 1970–71, Dean Faculty of Biology 1970–73, mem. Bd of Govs 1970–, Pres. 1975–85, Deputy Chair. 1985–; W. Garfield Weston Prof. of Immunology 1966; Visiting Scientist, NIH, Bethesda 1956–57, 1960–61; Visiting Prof. Molecular Biology, Univ. of Calif., Berkeley 1967–68; Visiting Prof., Dept of Medicine, Tufts Univ. School of Medicine, Boston 1986–87; Inst. Prof. 1985; Fogarty Scholar-in-Residence, Fogarty Int. Center, Bethesda, Md 1973–74; mem. WHO Expert Advisory Panel of Immunology 1962–; Chair. Council, European Molecular Biology Org. 1975–79; Pres. Int. Union Immunological Socs. 1977–80; Chair. Scientific Advisory Cttee European Molecular Biology Lab. Heidelberg 1978–81; WHO Advisory Cttee on Medical Research 1979–82, WHO Special Programme for Research and Training in Tropical Diseases 1979–81; mem. Council Paul Ehrlich Foundation (Frankfurt) 1980–87; mem. Advisory Bd UCLAF, France 1980–92; Founding mem. Bd Dir Int. Foundation for Survival and Devt of Humanity, Moscow and Washington 1988–92; Nat. mem. Gen. Cttee Int. Council of Scientific Unions 1984–93; mem. Scientific Advisory Group of Experts, Programme for Vaccine Devt, WHO 1987–92; mem. Int. Guidance Panel, Israel Arts and Science Acad. 1987–; Vice-Pres. Assen Franco-Israélienne pour Recherche Scientifique et Technologique 1992–98; mem. Exec. Bd Int. Council of Human Duties, Trieste 1995–; mem. other int. bodies; serves on many editorial bds., including Exec. Advisory Bd of Dictionary for Science and Tech. 1989–, Ed. Acad. of the Int. J. Mol. Med. 1997, Int. Advisory Bd of Russian J. Immun. 2000, Int. Ed. Bd Reviews in Auto-immunity 2001, Cambridge Encyclopedia of the Life Sciences, Handbook of Biochemistry and Molecular Biology, Experimental and Clinical Immunogenetics, Receptor Biology Reviews, Encyclopedia of Human Biology, Encyclopedia of the Life Sciences; mem. Israel Acad. of Sciences and Humanities 1971, Pontifical Acad. of Sciences 1975, Deutsche Akad. der Naturforscher Leopoldina 1989; Foreign mem. Max-Planck Soc., Freiburg 1967, Russian Acad. of Sciences 1994, French Acad. of Sciences 1995; Foreign Assoc. NAS 1976, Italian Acad. of Sciences 1995, American Philosophical Soc. 1995; Fellow Polish Acad. of Arts and Sciences 1998; Hon. mem. American Soc. Biological Chemists 1968, American Assen of Immunologists 1973, Scandinavian Soc. for Immunology 1971, Harvey Soc. 1972, French Soc. for Immunology 1979, Chilean Soc. for Immunology 1981, Romanian Acad. 1991, Romanian Acad. of Medical Sciences 1991, Romanian Soc. for Immunology; Foreign Hon. mem. American Acad. Arts and Sciences 1971; Commdr's Cross of Order of Merit Award, FRG 1986; Officier, Légion d'honneur, 1987; Caballero, Order of San Carlos (Colombia) 1997; Dr hc (Bordeaux II) 1985, (Nat. Autonomous Univ. of Mexico) 1985, (Tufts Univ.) 1989, Colby Coll. 1989, (Univ. Louis Pasteur) 1990, (Hebrew Univ. of Jerusalem) 1995, (Tel-Aviv) 1999, (Ben Gurion Univ. of the Negev 2001; awarded NIH Lectureship 1973; Israel Prize Natural Sciences 1959, Rothschild Prize for Chem. 1968, Otto Warburg Medal, German Soc. of Biological Chem. 1968, Emil von Behring Prize, Phillipps Univ. 1972, Gairdner Int. Award, Toronto 1980, Prize, Inst. de la Vie Fondation Electricité de France, Lille 1984, Prix Jaubert, Faculty of Science, Univ. of Geneva 1986, Interbrew-Baillet Latour Health Prize 1997, Karl Landsteiner Medal, Toronto 1986, Albert Einstein Gold Medal 1995, Harnak Medal, Max-Planck-Soc. 1996, Wolf Prize in Medicine 1998. *Publications:* over 800 in immunology, biochemistry and molecular biology; Ed. The Antigens (7 Vols published). *Address:* Weizmann Institute of Science, Rehovot, 76100 Israel. *Telephone:* 8-9466969; 8-9471132 (Home). *Fax:* 8-9469713. *E-mail:* michael.sela@weizmann.ac.il (Office).

SELBORNE, 4th Earl, cr. 1882; John Roundell Palmer, KBE, FRS; British farmer; b. 24 March 1940; s. of the late Viscount Wolmer; m. Joanna van Antwerp James 1969; three s. one d.; ed Eton Coll., Christ Church, Oxford; Man. Dir Blackmoor Estate Ltd 1962–; Chair. Hops Marketing Bd 1978–82, Agricultural and Food Research Council 1983–89; Pres. Royal Agricultural Soc. of England 1987–88; Chair. Jt Nature Conservation Cttee 1991–97; Chair. House of Lords Select Cttee on Science and Tech. 1993–97; mem. Govt Panel on Sustainable Devt 1994–97; Chair. AMC 1994–2002, UK Chemical Stakeholder Forum 2000–; Dir Lloyds TSB Group 1995–; Chancellor Univ. of Southampton 1996–; Pres. Royal Geographical Soc. (with Inst. of British Geographers) 1997–2000; Vice-Pres. Royal Soc. for the Protection of Birds 1996–; elected Hereditary mem. House of Lords 1999–, Chair. Subcttee D (Agric. and Environment), House of Lords EU Select Cttee 1999–; Hon. LLD (Bristol) 1988; Hon. DSc (Cranfield) 1991, (Easr Anglia) 1996, (Southampton)

1996, (Birmingham) 2000; Massey-Ferguson Nat. Award for Services to UK Agric. 1990. *Address:* Temple Manor, Selborne, Alton, Hants, GU34 3LR, England. *Telephone:* (1420) 473646.

SELBY, Philip; British composer; b. 6 Feb. 1948; s. of George Selby and Sarah Selby (née Knott); m. Rosanna Burrai 1974; one s.; ed Manor Park Grammar School, Nuneaton, Royal Northern Coll. of Music; composition studies with G. Petrassi, C. Camilleri and Karlheinz Stockhausen; appeared as guitar soloist, Birmingham Town Hall 1966, Royal Albert Hall, London 1970, All-India Radio and TV, Pakistani TV, Youth Palace, Tehran, Istanbul Univ.; début as composer with first performance of From the Fountain of Youth (for guitar and chamber orch.), Leamington 1975; mem. British Acad. of Composers and Songwriters, Inc. Soc. of Musicians, Performing Right Soc.; Chevalier Ordre Souverain et Militaire de la Milice du Saint Sépulcre 1988. *Compositions include:* Suite for guitar 1965–67, Two Meditations for Piano 1972–74, Symphonic Dance for orchestra 1973, Fantasia for guitar 1974, Rhapsody for piano and orchestra 1975, Three Scottish Songs for voice and violin 1975, A Nature Meditation for violin and small orch., Guitar Concerto 1976–77, Suite for String Quartet 1977–78, Sonatina for piano 1978, Spirit of the Earth for flute 1978, Branch Touches Branch, pastorale 1979, Isa Upanishad (cantata sacra for double chorus and orchestra) 1979–87, Sonata for timpani 1980, Greek Suite for Oboe Solo 1981, Siddhartha (dance symphony) 1981–84, Logos for trumpet 1982, Ring Out Ye Bells (carol) 1988, Symphony of Sacred Images (for soprano and bass soli, double chorus and orchestra) 1986–92, Anthem for Gibraltar (unison voices and organ) 1994, Beatus Vir (motet) 1995, String Quartet No. 1 (Non Potho Reposare, Amore Coro) 1996–97, Autoritratto Vittorio Alfieri (for soprano, violin and guitar) 1998, Sonata Atma Brahma for Piano 1998–99, Fear no more the Heat of the Sun, madrigal 2001, Agape for solo violin 2001–02, Agape II for solo viola 2002. *Leisure interests:* reading, travel, the arts. *Address:* Hill Cottage, Via 1 Maggio 93, 00068 Rignano Flaminio, Rome, Italy. *Telephone:* (0761) 507945.

SELEŠ, Monica; American (born Yugoslav) tennis player; b. 2 Dec. 1973, Novi Sad, Yugoslavia (now Serbia and Montenegro); d. of the late Karolj Seleš and of Ester Seleš; moved to USA 1986; became US citizen March 1994; semi-finalist, French Open 1989; won French Open 1990, 1991, 1992; Virginia Slims Championships 1990, 1991, 1992; US Open 1991, 1992; Australian Open 1991, 1992, 1993, 1996; Canadian Open 1995, 1996; winner LA Open 1997, Canadian Open 1997, Tokyo Open 1997; quarter-finalist, Wimbledon Championships 1990; named youngest No. 1 ranked player in tennis history for women and men, at 17 years 3 months 9 days – Martina Hingis now holds the record; off court for over two years after being stabbed in the back by a spectator during a Hamburg quarter-final in 1993; 59 WTA Tour titles, 9 Grand Slam titles and over 14 million dollars in prize money at end of 2002; mem. winning US Fed. Cup team 1996, 1999, 2000; pnr in the All-Star Café; Ted Tinling Diamond Award 1990, Associated Press Athlete of the Year 1990–91, Tennis Magazine Comeback Player of the Year 1995, Flo Hyman Award 2000. *Publication:* Monica: From Fear to Victory 1996. *Leisure interests:* ice skating, horse riding, basketball, guitar, swimming, reading autobiographies. *Address:* c/o International Management Group, 1 Erieview Plaza, Cleveland, OH 44114, USA.

SELEZNEV, Gennadiy Nikolaevich; Russian politician; b. 6 Nov. 1947, Serov, Sverdlovsk Region; m. Irina Borisovna Selezneva 1978; one d.; ed Leningrad Univ. (by correspondence); mem. CPSU 1970–91, CP of Russian Fed. 1992–; work in komsomol 1968–74; Ed.-in-Chief Smena 1974–80, Komsomolskaya Pravda 1980–88, Uchitelskaya Gazeta (newspaper for teachers) 1988–91; First Deputy Ed., Ed.-in-Chief, Pravda 1991–93, dismissed then re-elected 1993; Ed.-in-Chief Pravda Rossii 1995–96; mem. State Duma (Parl.) 1993–, Deputy Chair. 1995–96, Chair. 1996– (re-elected 2000); Co-Chair. Interparl. Ass. of CIS; Chair. Parl. Union of Russia and Belarus 1997–; Founder, Chair. Rossiya (political movt) 2000–; expelled from CP 2002; mem. Security Council, Russian Fed.; Deputy Chair. Parl. Ass. of OSCE 1999–; mem. Int. Acad. of Information Russian Acad. of Social Sciences; Hon. Prof. Inst. of Youth, Heilutsiang Univ.; Order of Friendship of Peoples 1984, Order for Service to the Fatherland, Class II, 2000 and other state awards. *Publications:* All Power to Law 1997, Law, Power and Politics: National and Local Levels 1998; numerous articles on the state. *Leisure interests:* reading, swimming, riding. *Address:* c/o State Duma of the Federal Assembly of the Russian Federation, Okhotny Ryad 1, 103265 Moscow, Russia. *Telephone:* (095) 292-33-49 (Office); (095) 292-66-41 (Office). *Fax:* (095) 292-32-49 (Office). *Website:* www.seleznev.org (Office).

SELF, Colin Ernest, DFA; British artist; b. 17 July 1941, Rackheath; s. of Ernest Walter Self and Kathleen Augustine (née Bellamy) Self; m. 1st Margaret Ann Murrell 1963; m. 2nd Jessica Prendergast 1978; one s. two d.; ed Norwich Art School, Slade School of Fine Art, London Univ.; various one-man and group exhbns; Drawing Prize Biennale de Paris 1967, Giles Bequest Prize Bradford Biennale 1969, Tolly Cobbold Prize 1979. *Leisure interests:* nature study: in a constant perennial dreamy but acute way, un-academically, all music. *Address:* 31 St Andrew's Avenue, Thorpe, Norwich, Norfolk, NR7 0RG, England.

SELF, Will, MA; British author and cartoonist; b. 26 Sept. 1961; s. of Peter John Otter Self and Elaine Rosenbloom; m. 1st Katharine Sylvia Anthony Chancellor 1989 (divorced 1996); one s. one d.; m. 2nd Deborah Jane Orr 1997; one s.; ed Christ's Coll., Exeter Coll., Oxford; cartoon illustrations appeared in New Statesman and City Limits; Publishing Dir Cathedral Publishing

1988–90; Contributing Ed. London Evening Standard magazine 1993–95; columnist The Observer 1995–97, The Times 1997–99, Ind. on Sunday 2000–. *Publications:* short stories: Quantity Theory of Insanity 1991, Grey Area 1994, Tough Tough Toys for Tough Tough Boys 1998; novellas: Cock and Bull 1992, The Sweet Smell of Psychosis 1996; novels: My Idea of Fun 1993, Great Apes 1997, How the Dead Live 2000, Perfidious Man 2000, Feeding Frenzy 2001, Dorian 2002; Junk Mail (selected journalism) 1995, Sore Sites (collected journalism) 2000; collected cartoons 1985. *Leisure interest:* walking.

SELINGER, Benjamin Klaas, Dr rer. nat, DSc, FTSE, FRACI; Australian professor of chemistry and environmental consultant; b. 23 Jan. 1939, Sydney; s. of Herbert Selinger and Hilde Wittner; m. Veronica Hollander 1967; two s.; ed Sydney Boys High School, Univ. of Sydney, Tech. Univ. Stuttgart and Australian Nat. Univ. (ANU); Lecturer in Physical Chem. ANU 1966–71, Sr Lecturer 1971–78, Head, Dept of Chem. 1988–91, Prof. of Chem. 1992–, Prof. Emer. 1999–; Chair. Bd of Nat. Registration Authority for Agric. and Veterinary Chemicals 1993–97; mem. numerous Govt bodies, advisory cttees., etc.; various academic posts overseas; Deputy Chair ANZAAS 1994–96; Chair. Australian Science Festival Ltd 2001–; Fellow, Royal Australian Chem. Inst., Royal Inst. of GB, Australian Acad. of Tech. Sciences and Engs., Australian Acad. of Forensic Sciences; mem. Council Australian Consumers Asscn 2000–; consultant Versel Scientific Consulting; Columnist Canberra Times 1972–, Burke's Backyard magazine 2000–; Archibald Olle Prize 1979; Special Eureka Prize for Science Communication (ABC/Australian Museum) 1991; Alexander von Humboldt Fellow; ANZAAS Medallist 1993; many other awards and distinctions. *Film:* appeared in An Act of Necessity, Film Australia. *Radio:* Dial-a-Scientist, ABC. *Television:* has appeared in ABC World Series Debates on "Science Is a Health Hazard". *Publications:* Chemistry in the Market Place 1975–98 (5th edn), Thinking with Fourier 1992, Expert Evidence 1992, Why the Watermelon Will Not Ripen in Your Armpit 2000. *Leisure interests:* bushwalking, science museums, forensic chem. *Address:* Department of Chemistry, Bld. 33, Australian National University, Canberra, ACT 0200 (Office); 56 Brereton Street, Garran, Canberra, ACT 2605, Australia (Home). *Telephone:* (2) 6125-2929 (Office). *Fax:* (6) 6285-2832 (Home). *E-mail:* ben.selinger@anu.edu.au. *Website:* chemistry.anu.edu.au/staff/BKS/home.htm (Office).

SELIVON, Mykola Jedosovych, PhD; Ukrainian judge; b. 30 Oct. 1946, Shestovytsya, Chernigiv Region; one s. one d.; ed Faculty of Law, Kyiv Taras Shevchenko State Univ.; Research Fellow Inst. of State and Law, Acad. of Scinces of Ukraine 1973; apptd Sr Asst Govt Legal Group 1979, later Chief of Legal Dept; fmr Deputy Minister of Cabinet of Ministers, later First Deputy Minister –1996; Judge Constitutional Court of Ukraine 1996–99, Deputy Chair. 1999–2002, Chair. 2002–; Order for Service, Third Class; Distinguished Lawyer of Ukraine. *Leisure interests:* classical music, theatre, sport. *Address:* Constitutional Court, vul. Zhylianska 14, Kiev, Ukraine (Office). *Telephone:* (44) 253-84-88 (Office). *Fax:* (44) 227-20-01 (Office). *E-mail:* idep@ccu.gov.ua (Office). *Website:* www.ccu.gov.ua (Office).

SELLA, George John, Jr., BS, MBA; American business executive; b. 29 Sept. 1928, West New York, NJ; s. of George John Sella and Angelina Dominoni; m. Janet May Auf-der Heide 1955; two s. three d.; ed Princeton and Harvard Univs; joined American Cyanamid Co. 1954, Pres. Europe/Mideast/Africa Div. 1976–77, Corp. Vice-Pres. 1977, Vice-Chair. 1978, Pres. 1979–90, CEO 1983–, Chair. 1984–; mem. NAM, Soc. of Chem. Industry, Pharmaceutical Mfrs Asscn.

SELLA, Phillippe; French rugby player; b. 14 Feb. 1962, Tonneins; centre/wing rugby union player; 111 appearances with French nat. team 1982–1995, est. world record number of caps (yet to be surpassed as at Jan. 2003), scored 30 tries including one in every game of the 1986 Five Nations Championship; appeared in three World Cups, retd from nat. team 1995; with English club Saracens 1995–97; still involved in rugby, fmrly co-coach of Barbarians; currently involved in business ventures. *Address:* c/o Fédération Française de Rugby, 9 rue de Liège, 75009 Paris, France.

SELLARS, Peter, BA; American theatre and opera director; b. 27 Sept. 1957; ed Harvard Univ.; Dir Boston Shakespeare Co. 1983–84; Dir and Man. American Nat. Theater at J. F. Kennedy Center, Washington 1984–; Fellow MacArthur Foundation, Chicago 1983. *Productions include:* Nixon in China 1987, 2000, The Mikado, Orlando, The Marriage of Figaro, Don Giovanni, Così fan tutte 1984, Die Zauberflöte 1990, Ajax, Zangezi, Merchant of Venice (London) 1994, The Rake's Progress 1996, El Niño 2000. *Address:* American National Theater, Kennedy Center, Washington, DC 20566, USA.

SELLECK, Tom; American actor; b. 29 Jan. 1945, Detroit, Mich.; s. of Robert D. Selleck and Martha Selleck; m. 1st Jackie Ray (divorced 1982); one step-s.; m. 2nd Julie Mack 1987; one d.; ed Univ. of Southern Calif. *Films include:* Myra Breckenridge, Midway, Coma, Seven Minutes, High Road to China, Runaway, Lassiter, Three Men and a Baby, Her Alibi 1988, Quigley Down Under, An Innocent Man 1989, Three Men and a Little Lady 1991, Folks 1991, Mr Baseball 1991, Christopher Columbus: The Discovery 1992, In & Out, The Love Letter 1999, Running Mates 2000. *Television includes:* Returning Home, Bracken's World, The Young and the Restless, The Rockford Files, The Sacketts, played Thomas Magnum in Magnum PI, Divorce Wars, Countdown at the Super Bowl, Gypsy Warriors, Boston and Kilbride, The Concrete Cowboys, Murder She Wrote, The Silver Fox, The Closer (series) 1998–, Last Stand at Saber River, Friends, 1996, 2000, Ruby, Jean and Joe, Broken Trust (film) 1995, Washington Slept Here (film) 2000, Louis l'Amour's Crossroads

Trail (film) 2000. *Leisure interests:* volleyball (Hon. Capt. US Men's Volleyball Team for 1984 Olympic Games), outrigger canoe specialist. *Address:* c/o Esme Chandlee, 2967 Hollyridge Drive, Los Angeles, CA 90068, USA.

SELLERT, Wolfgang, DJur; German professor of law; b. 3 Nov. 1935, Berlin; s. of Horst-Günther Sellert and Else Kaiser; m. Dr Urte Wenger 1962; two d.; Asst in Dept for History of German Law, Univ. of Frankfurt 1965–72, Prof. 1972–77; Prof. History of German Law and Civil Law Georg-August Univ., Göttingen 1977–; Dir German-Chinese Inst. of Econ. Law, Univ. of Nanjing 1995–; mem. Akad. der Wissenschaften, Göttingen 1984–. *Publications:* Über die Zuständigkeitsabgrenzung von Reichshofrat und Reichskammergericht 1965, Prozessgrundsätze über Stilus Curiae am Reichshofrat 1973, Die Ordnungen des Reichshofrats 1980, Studien- u. Quellenbuch zur Geschichte der dt. Strafrechtspflege 1989, Recht u. Gerechtigkeit in der Kunst 1991. *Leisure interests:* collecting old manuscripts and baroque literature. *Address:* Konrad-Adenauer-Strasse 25, 37075 Göttingen, Germany. *Telephone:* (551) 23771. *Fax:* (551) 23771.

SELLICK, Phyllis, OBE, FRAM, FRCM; British concert pianist; b. 16 June 1911, Newbury Park, Essex; m. Cyril Smith 1937 (died 1974); one s. (deceased) one d.; ed Glenarm Coll., Ilford, Royal Acad. of Music and in Paris; Prof. RCM, London; Vice-Pres. Inc. Soc. of Musicians Centenary Year 1982–83; Malcolm Arnold, Bliss, Gordon Jacob, Tippett and Vaughan Williams have dedicated works to her; adjudicator of numerous important piano competitions, including BBC Young Musician of the Year and Leeds Int. Piano Competition. *Radio:* Talk on piano playing (Radio 3) 2001, Castaway on Desert Island Discs (Radio 4) 2002. *Leisure interests:* reading, Scrabble, bridge. *Address:* Beverley House, 29A Ranelagh Avenue, Barnes, London, SW13 0BN, England.

SELMER, Knut S., DJur; Norwegian professor of law; b. 7 Nov. 1924, Oslo; m. Elisabeth Schweigaard 1950; one s. one d.; ed Univ. of Oslo; Research Fellow, Univ. of Oslo 1953–58, Prof. of Insurance Law 1959–89; Sec. for revision of Norwegian Marine Insurance Conditions 1957–67; Chair. Public Comm. for revision of Norwegian Insurance Contracts Act 1973–87; Founder and Chair. Norwegian Research Center for Computers and Law 1970–86; Chair. Bd Norwegian Data Inspectorate 1980–96; Chair. Bd Norwegian Legal Information System, Lovdata 1980–89. *Publications:* The Survival of General Average 1958, A Decade of Computers and Law (with J. Bing) 1980, Forsikringsrett 1982; numerous articles on insurance law, tort law and computer law. *Address:* Krusesgate 11, 0263 Oslo 2, Norway.

SELTEN, Reinhard, D.PHIL.NAT.; German economist; b. 5 Oct. 1930, Breslau; s. of Adolf Selten and Käthe Luther; m. Elisabeth Langreiner 1959; ed Univ. of Frankfurt am Main; Prof. Freie Univ. Berlin 1969; Prof. Univ. of Bielefeld; Prof. of Econ. Theory, Univ. of Bonn 1984–96, Prof. Emer. 1996–; mem. Rheinisch-Westfalen Akad. der Wissenschaften; Fellow, Econometric Soc.; Foreign Hon. mem. American Acad. of Arts and Sciences; Dr hc (Bielefeld) 1989, (Frankfurt) 1991, (Graz) 1996, (E Anglia) 1996; shared Nobel Prize for Econs 1994; Nordrhein-Westfalen State Prize 2000. *Publications:* Preispolitik der Mehrproduktenunternehmung in der stat. Theorie 1970, General Equilibrium with Price Making Firms (with T. Marschak) 1974, Models of Strategic Rationality 1988, A General Theory of Equilibrium Selection in Games (with J. Harsanyi) 1988. *Address:* Laboratorium für Experimentelle Wirtschaftsforschung, Universität Bonn, 53113 Bonn, Germany. *Telephone:* (228) 739192. *Fax:* (228) 739193.

SEMAGO, Vladimir Vladimirovich; Russian politician; b. 10 Jan. 1947; m.; one s.; ed Moscow Inst. of Construction Eng, All-Union Acad. of Foreign Trade; with Mosoblstroi 1973–77; Deputy Dir-Gen., Solnechny 1977–81; accountant, tourist co., commerce Dept, State Cttee of Tourism 1981–83; Deputy Chair., Domodedovo Dist Consumers' Union 1983–86; Chief Engineer, State Cttee of Science and Tech. of USSR Council of Ministers 1986–87; Founder Jt Venture Moscow Commercial Club; co-f. Ecology and Energy Resources 1992; mem. CP of Russian Fed. 1993–98; mem. CP faction, later Regions of Russia faction; mem. State Duma 1993–98; Founder and leader New Left (political movt) 1999; mem. Cttee on Problems of Women, Family and Youth; Chair. Bd Dirs. Rosebusinesbank; mem. Presidium, Co-ordination Council Round Table of Russian Business; mem. People's Patriotic Union of Russia. *Leisure interests:* travelling, collecting modern paintings. *Address:* Noviye Leviye All-Russian Movement, Mira Prospect 108, 129626 Moscow, Russia. *Telephone:* (095) 287-18-02 (Office).

SEMEL, Terry, BS; American film company executive; b. 24 Feb. 1943, New York; s. of Ben Semel and Mildred (Wenig) Semel; m. Jane Bovingdon 1977; one s. two d.; ed Long Island Univ., City Coll. of New York; Domestic Sales Man. CBS Cinema Center Films, Studio City, Calif. 1970–72; Vice-Pres., Gen. Man. Walt Disney's Buena Vista, Burbank, Calif. 1972–75; Pres. W.B. Distribution Corpn, Burbank 1975–78; Exec. Vice-Pres., COO Warner Bros. Inc., Burbank 1979–80, Pres., COO 1980–96, Chair. CEO 1994–99; Chair., Co-CEO Warner Music Group Inc. 1995–99; Chair., CEO and Dir Yahoo! 2001–; Vice-Chair. San Diego Host Cttee for Republican Nat. Convention 1996; mem. Bd Dirs. Revlon, Polo Ralph Lauren Corpn, Guggenheim Museum. *Address:* Yahoo! 701 First Avenue, Sunnyvale, CA 94089, USA (Office). *Website:* www.yahoo.com (Office).

SEMENOV, Victor Aleksandrovich; Russian politician; b. 14 Jan. 1958, Novokuryanovo, Moscow Region; m.; one s. one d.; ed Moscow K. Timiryazev Acad. of Agric.; on state farm, later Agric. Co. Belaya Dacha 1980–85; instructor Agric. Dept, Lyubertsy Town CP Cttee 1987–88; Pres. and Dir-Gen.

Belaya Dacha 1989–98; Minister of Agric. and Food of Russian Fed. 1998–99; Deputy Chair. Agrarian Party 1999–; mem. State Duma (Otechestvo faction) 1999–. *Leisure interests:* gardening, fishing, hunting. *Address:* Agrarian Party, M. Kaluzhskaya str. 15, Bldg 5, 117071 Moscow, Russia. *Telephone:* (095) 958-21-75 (Party) (Office); (095) 292-89-01 (Duma) (Office).

SEMENOV, Gen. Vladimir Magomedovich; Russian army officer and politician; b. 8 June 1940, Khuzzuk, Karachayevo-Cherkessiya; ed Baku Higher All-Troops School, Frunze Mil. Acad., General Staff Acad.; mem. CPSU 1963–91; mem. Cen. Cttee 1990–91; Commdr of mil. units 1958–70, Head of staff, Commdr of Regt 1973, Head of staff, Deputy Commdr of Div. 1975, Commdr 1979, Commdr of army corps 1982–84, Commdr of army 1984–86, First Deputy Commdr, Commdr of troops of Baikal Command 1986–91; Deputy Minister of Defence of USSR, C-in-C of Land Troops 1991–92; Commdr of Land Troops of Russia 1992–97; Chief Adviser Ministry of Defence 1998–99; Pres. Karachayevo-Cherkessiya Repub. 1999–; USSR People's Deputy 1989–91. *Address:* House of Government, Komsomolskaya str. 23, 357100 Cherkessk, Russia (Office). *Telephone:* (87822) 5-4-11, 588-37 (Office). *Fax:* (87822) 529-80 (Office).

SEMENOV, Yuri Pavlovich; Russian mechanical engineer; b. 20 April 1935, Toropets, Kalinin region; m.; two d.; ed Dnepropetrovsk State Univ.; worked in rocket and space industry as engineer, head of group, Leading Designer 1967–72, Chief Designer 1972–78, Deputy Gen. Designer, Chief Designer 1978–81; First Deputy Gen. Designer, Chief Designer of BURAN Orbiter, Manned Spacecrafts and Stations 1981–89, Gen. Designer of ENERGIA Scientific and Production Assen (NPO ENERGIA) 1989–91, Dir Gen., Gen. Designer 1991–94; Gen. Designer and Pres. S. P. Korolev RSC ENERGIA 1994– (responsible for devt and operation of Buran reusable vehicle, devt, manufacture and operation of Soyuz, Progress-type vehicles, Salyut and Mir in-orbit complexes, rocket segment of the Sea Launch rocket and space complex-RSC, satellite systems based on YAMAL spacecraft of new generation communication satellites and devt of Russian segment of Int. Space Station and its main modules, devt and construction of the AURORA/ ONEGA RSC); mem. Int. Acad. of Astronautics 1986; Corresp. mem. USSR (now Russian) Acad. of Sciences 1987, mem. 2000–; Hero of Socialist Labour 1976, Lenin Prize 1978, USSR State Prize 1985, USSR Acad. of Sciences K. Tsyolkovsky Gold Medal 1987, Alan De Emil IAF State Prize 1991, State Prize of Russian Fed. 1999, François-Xavier Bagnoud Aeropace Prize 1999, RAS S. P. Korolev Gold Medal 2001 and others. *Publications:* more than 360 publs including S. P. Korolev Rocket and Space Corporation Energia 1946–96 1996, S. P. Korolev Rocket and Space Corporation ENERGIA at the Turn of Two Centuries 1996–2001 2001. *Leisure interests:* sports. *Address:* S. P. Korolev RSC Energia, Lenina str. 4A, 141070 Korolev, Moscow Region, Russia. *Telephone:* (095) 513-72-48 (Office). *Fax:* (095) 513-86-20, (095) 187-98-77 (Office). *E-mail:* post@rsce.ru (Office). *Website:* www.energia.ru (Office).

SEMENYAKA, Lyudmila Ivanovna; Russian ballerina; b. 16 Jan. 1952, Leningrad (St Petersburg); m. (divorced); one s.; ed Leningrad Choreographic School; danced with Kirov Ballet 1970–72; Prima Ballerina Bolshoi Theatre Co., Moscow 1972–96; has worked with English Nat. Ballet 1990–91 and Scottish Nat. Ballet; ballet teacher 1994–, with Moscow State Acad. of Choreography 1999–; mem. jury several int. ballet competitions; performed in Europe, USA and Argentina; winner Moscow Int. Ballet competition 1969, 1972, Varna 1972, Tokyo (First Prize and Gold Medal) 1976, Anna Pavlova Prize, Paris 1976, USSR State Prize 1977, USSR People's Artist 1986, Evening Standard Prize 1986. *Films:* Ludmila Semenyaka Danse, The Bolshoi Ballerina, Spartak, The Story Flower, Raymonda, The Nutcracker, Fantasy on the Theme of Casanova and others. *Roles include:* all of classical repertoire, debut in Odette/Odile, Swan Lake, Moscow; all of Y. Grigorovitch ballets: Frigia (Spartak), Anastasia (Ivan the Terrible), Katerina (Stony Flower) etc; roles in ballets by Balanchin, Petit, Lavrovsky, Vassilyev, Boccadoro, Ben Stivenson, May Murdmaa; has partnered Mikhail Bar- yshnikov, Vladimir Vassilyev, Ivek Mukhamedov, Farukh Ruzimatov etc. *Roles include:* Aurore (Eshpai's Angara), Giselle, Odette/Odile (Swan Lake), Anastasia (Ivan the Terrible), Katerina (Stone Flower). *Address:* Bolshoi Theatre, Teatralnaya ploshchad 1, Moscow, Russia. *Telephone:* (095) 253-87- 42 (Home). *Fax:* (095) 253-87-42 (Home). *Website:* www.bolshoi.ru (Office).

SEMENZA, Giorgio, DR.MED.; Swiss professor of biochemistry; b. 23 June 1928, Milan, Italy; s. of Prof. Carlo Semenza and Clementina Gerli; m. Berit Andersson 1958; three c.; ed Univ. of Milan; post-doctoral studies, Univ. of Uppsala 1955–56; Asst Lecturer, Lecturer, Dept of Biochem. Univ. of Zürich 1956–64, Asst Prof. 1964–69; Prof. of Gen. Physiology, Univ. of Milan 1967–69; Prof. of Biochem. Swiss Fed. Inst. of Tech., Zürich 1969–95, Chair. or Co.-Chair., Dean of School of Natural Sciences 1980–82; Prof. of Bio- chemistry, Univ. of Milan 1995–; Visiting Prof. at numerous foreign univs; Man. Ed. Fed. European Biochemical Soc. (FEBS) Letters 1985–99; mem. Editorial on Advisory Bd of a number of scientific journals; mem. Acad. Europaea Istituto Lombardo di Scienze a. Lettere, Milan 2000–; Hon. mem. Italian Soc. of Experimental Biology 1978, Spanish Soc. of Biochem. 1997; Hon. PhD (Univ. Autónoma de Madrid) 1985; Hon. MD (Univ. de Nice Sophia Antipolis, France) 1999, (Copenhagen) 1999; Int. Prize of Modern Nutrition 1975, Iorio-Rustichelli Prize 1985, European Pharmaceutical Industry Research Award 1988, Purkine Gold Medal, Prague 1988. *Publications:* 12 books; more than 250 publs in peer-reviewed journals. *Leisure interests:* literature, films, theatre. *Address:* Dipartimento di Chimica, Biochimica e Tecnologie per la Medicina, Università di Milano, Via Saldini 50, 20133

Milan, Italy; Swiss Institute of Technology, ETH-Zentrum, PO Box 35, 8092 Zürich, Switzerland. *E-mail:* semenza@bc.biol.ethz.ch (Office). *Website:* www .bc.biol.ethz.ch/professors/emeritus/semenza/semenza.html (Office).

SEMERDZHIEV, Col-Gen. Atanas; Bulgarian politician; b. 21 May 1924, Velingrad; ed Soviet mil. acads; mem. Bulgarian Communist Party 1943–90, Bulgarian Socialist Party 1990–; fmr guerrilla fighter and served in Patriotic War 1944–45; Chief of Gen. Staff of Bulgarian People's Army 1962–89; First Deputy Minister of Nat. Defence 1966–89; Minister of the Interior 1989–90; Vice-Pres. of Bulgaria 1990–91. *Address:* c/o Bulgarska Sotsialisticheska Partiya, Sofia, Positano Street 20. P.O. Box 382, Bulgaria.

SEMIGIN, Gennady Yuryevich, Dr rer. pol; Russian businessman and politician; b. 23 March 1964; ed Riga Higher Mil. Political School, Moscow Juridical Inst., Acad. of Finance; army service 1985–90; f. Centre of Econs and Russian AKROS 1990; f. Russian Group of Finance and Industry 1991; mem. Council on Business, Russian Presidency 1992–; mem. Exec. Bd Russian Union of Businessmen, Pres. Russian Group of Finance and Industry 1991–; f. Nat. Public Scientific Fund 1996; Pres. Congress of Russian Business Circles; mem. CP 1998; mem. State Duma (Agrarian faction) 1999–, Deputy Chair. 2000; mem. Comm. on Regulation of Labour and Social Relations, Russian Acad. of Social Sciences, Acad. of Political Sciences; corresp. mem. Acad. of Natural Sciences. *Publications:* Social Partnership in the Con- temporary World, Political Stability of Society, ed. New Philosophical Ency- clopedia (4 Vols). *Leisure interests:* swimming, tennis, running, classical music, boxing, history, philosophy, art, Econs. *Address:* State Duma, Okhotny Ryad 1, 103205 Moscow, Russia. *Telephone:* (095) 292-76-75; (095) 292-35-04 (Office).

SEMIKHVATOV, Mikhail Alexandrovich; Russian geologist; b. 21 Feb. 1932; m.; one s.; ed Moscow State Univ.; jr, sr researcher, head of lab. Inst. of Geology 1954–; Corresp. mem. USSR (now Russian) Acad. of Sciences 1990, mem. 1994; research in stratigraphy, paleontology; N Shatsky Prize. *Pub- lications include:* General Problems of the Proterozoic Stratigraphy in the USSR. *Leisure interest:* expeditions to Siberia. *Address:* Institute of Geology, Russian Academy of Sciences, Pyzhevsky per. 7, 109017 Moscow, Russia. *Telephone:* (095) 230-81-32 (Office).

SEMIZOROVA, Nina Lvovna; Russian ballerina; b. 15 Oct. 1956, Krivoi Rog; d. of Lev Alexandrovich Semizorov and Larisa Dmitrievna Semizorova; m. 1st Maris Liepa 1980; m. 2nd Mark Peretokin 1988; one d.; ed Kiev Choreographic School; danced with Shevchenko Theatre of Opera and Ballet, Kiev 1975–78, with Bolshoi, Moscow 1978–; many appearances abroad; First Prize, Int. Ballet Competition, Moscow 1977; Artist of Merit of Ukrainian SSR 1977, Honoured Artist of Russia 1987, Laureate of Moscow Komsomol 1987. *Roles include:* Odette/Odile, Lady Macbeth, Giselle, Don Quixote, Sleeping Beauty, La Bayadère, Spartacus, The Golden Age, Paquita, Raymonda, Les Sylphides. *Leisure interest:* reading. *Address:* 2 Zhukovskaya Street, Apt. 8, Moscow, Russia. *Telephone:* (095) 923-40-84 (Home). *Fax:* (095) 923-40-84 (Home).

SEMKOW, Jerzy (Georg), M.A.(MUS.); Polish conductor; b. 12 Oct. 1928, Radomsko; s. of Aleksander Semkow and Waleria Sienczak Semkow; ed Jagiellonian Univ., Cracow, State Higher School of Music (student of A. Malawski), Cracow and Leningrad Music Conservatoire; Asst Conductor, Leningrad Philharmonic Orch. 1954–56; Conductor, Bolshoi Opera and Ballet Theatre, Moscow 1956–58; Artistic Dir and Prin. Conductor, Warsaw Nat. Opera 1960–62; Perm. Conductor, Danish Royal Opera, Copenhagen 1965–68; Prin. Conductor Italian Radio and TV (RAI) Orchestra, Rome 1969–73; Conductor Cleveland Symphony Orchestra 1970–71; Musical Dir and Prin. Conductor St Louis Symphony Orchestra 1975–; Artistic Dir and Prin. Conductor, Rochester Philharmonic Orchestra, New York 1986–; Guest Conductor of London Philharmonic, New York Philharmonic, Chicago Sym- phony, Boston Symphony and many other leading European and American orchestras; engagements at Covent Garden, La Scala, Berlin, Vienna, Madrid, Paris, Rome, etc.; Commdr Cross, Order of Polonia Restituta, Ordre des Arts et des Lettres. *Recordings include:* Boris Godunov (Musorgski) with Polish Nat. Radio Symphony Orchestra, Kniaź (Borodin) with Group from Opera of Sofia, Symphony No. 3 and Symphonic Concerto No. 4 (Szyma- nowski), Symphony Nos 2 and 3 (Scriabin) with Nat. Philharmonic Symphony Orchestra, Warsaw. *Leisure interests:* reading, yachting. *Address:* c/o ICM Artists, 40 West 57th Street, New York, NY 10019, USA.

SEMPÉ, Jean-Jacques; French cartoonist; b. 17 Aug. 1932, Bordeaux; s. of Ulysse Sempé and Juliette Marson; one s. one d.; ed Ecole Communale à Bordeaux; work appears in L'Express magazine; has produced an album annually for 30 years; Officier des Arts et des Lettres. *Exhibition:* retro- spective Exhbn Pavillon des Arts, Les Halles, Paris 1991. *Publications include:* Rien n'est simple 1962, Tout se complique 1963, Sauve qui peut 1964, Monsieur Lambert 1965, La grande panique 1966, St Tropez 1968, Informa- tion-Consommation 1968, Des Hauts et des Bas 1970, Face á Face 1972, Bonjour Bonsoir 1974, L'Ascension Sociale de Mr Lambert 1975, Simple question d'equilibre 1977, Un léger décalage 1977, Les Musiciens 1979, Comme par hasard 1981, De bon matin 1983, Vaguement compétitif 1985, Luxe, calme et volupté 1987, Par Avion 1989, L'Histoire de Monsieur Sommer (with Patrick Süsskind) 1991, Ames Soeurs 1991, Insondables Mystères 1993, Raoul Taburin 1995, Les Musiciens 1996, Grands rêves 1997, Beau Temps 1999. *Address:* c/o Paris-Match, 63 avenue des Champs-Elysées, 75008 Paris, France; Editions Denoël, 9 rue du Cherche-Midi, 75006 Paris (Office).

SEMPLE, Sir John Laughlin, KCB, MA, BSc (ECON.); British civil servant (retd); b. 10 Aug. 1940, Belfast; s. of the late J. E. Semple and of Violet E. G. Semple; m. Maureen Anne Kerr 1970; two s. one d.; ed Campbell Coll., Belfast and Corpus Christi Coll., Cambridge; joined Home Civil Service, Ministry of Aviation 1961, transferred to NI Civil Service 1962, succession of posts relating to industrial training, financial planning, community relations, physical planning, Belfast Devt and housing policy, Perm. Sec. NI Dept of Finance and Personnel 1988–97, Head. NI Civil Service 1997–2000, (also Second Perm. Sec. NI Office 1998–99), Sec. to NI Exec. Cttee 1999–2000; mem. Consumer Council for Postal Services 2000–, Regional Chair. for NI 2000–. *Leisure interests:* golf, tennis, skiing, history. *Address:* Chamber of Commerce House, 22 Great Victoria Street, Belfast, BT2 7PU, Northern Ireland (Office). *Telephone:* (28) 9024-4113 (Office); (28) 9185-2594 (Home). *Fax:* (28) 9024-7024 (Office); (28) 9185-2351 (Home). *E-mail:* johnsemple@utvinternet.com (Home).

SEMPRÚN, Jorge; Spanish politician and writer; in exile in France following Spanish Civil War; fought in the French Resistance in World War II, captured by Nazis and sent to Buchenwald concentration camp; became leader of proscribed Spanish Communist Party, expelled as deviationist; Minister of Culture 1988–91; mem. Acad. Goncourt; Dr hc (Turin) 1990; Jerusalem Prize 1997. *Publications:* Le Grand Voyage (novel, in French), The Autobiography of Federico Sánchez (under pseudonym), Literature or Life 1998; screenplays for films: Z, La Guerre est finie.

SEMYNOCHENKO, Volodymr Petrovich, DMathSci; Ukrainian politician; b. 9 June 1950, Kiev; m.; two s.; ed Kharkov State Univ.; Dir-Gen. All-Union Scientific-Production co. Monocrystal-reaktiv (now Academic Concern Inst. of Monocrystals), Ukrainian Nat. Acad. of Sciences 1985–1996, Prof. 1988, Scientific Dir 1996–; mem. Verkhovna Rada (Parl.); Minister of Science and Tech. 1996–98; mem. Presidium Cabinet of Ministers 1996–98, 2001–; People's Deputy 1998; Deputy Prime Minister of Ukraine Aug.–Dec. 1999; Deputy Prime Minister for Humanitarian Issues 2001–02; Deputy Head Party of Regions 2001–; Head Nat. Foundation for Protection of Motherhood and Childhood; mem. Ukrainian Nat. Acad. of Sciences 1992; State Prize of Ukraine (twice), Int. Prize for Nuclear Physics. *Publications:* over 300 scientific publs and inventions, 10 patents, several books including About the Main, Ukraine: Science and Innovation Development, Energy and Life, Ecology and Future. *Address:* c/o Cabinet of Ministers, Hrushevskogo str. 12/2, 252008 Kiev, Ukraine (Office).

SEN, Amartya Kumar, PhD, FBA; Indian economist; b. 3 Nov. 1933, Santiniketan, Bengal; s. of the late Ashutosh Sen and of Amita Sen; m. 1st Nabaneeta Dev 1960 (divorced 1975); two d.; m. 2nd Eva Colorni 1978 (died 1985); one s. one d.; m. 3rd Emma Rothschild; ed Presidency Coll., Calcutta and Trinity Coll., Cambridge; Prof. of Econs, Jadavpur Univ., Calcutta 1956–58; Fellow, Trinity Coll., Cambridge 1957–63; Prof. of Econs, Univ. of Delhi 1963–71, Chair. Dept of Econs 1966–68; Hon. Dir Agricultural Econs Research Centre, Delhi 1966–68, 1969–71; Prof. of Econs LSE 1971–77, Oxford Univ. 1977–80; Drummond Prof. of Political Economy 1980–88; Lamont Univ. Prof., Harvard Univ. 1987–98, Prof. Emer. 1998–; Master Trinity Coll., Cambridge 1998–; Visiting Prof., Univ. of Calif., Berkeley 1964–65, Harvard Univ. 1968–69; Andrew D. White Prof.-at-Large Cornell Univ. 1978–84; Pres. Int. Econ. Asscn 1986–89; Fellow, Econometric Soc., Pres. 1984; Hon. Prof. Delhi Univ.; Foreign Hon. mem. American Acad. of Arts and Sciences; Hon. Fellow, Inst. of Social Studies, The Hague, Hon. Fellow LSE, Inst. of Devt Studies; Hon. DLitt (Univ. of Saskatchewan, Canada) 1979, (Visva-Bharati Univ., India) 1983, (Oxford) 1996; Hon. DUniv (Essex) 1984, (Caen) 1987; Hon. DSc (Bath) 1984, (Bologna) 1988; Dr. hc (Univ. Catholique de Louvain) 1989, (Padua) 1998; Senator Giovanni Agnelli Inst. Prize for Ethics 1989, Nobel Prize for Econs 1998, Hon. CH 2000, Grand Cross, Order of Scientific Merit (Brazil) 2000. *Publications:* Choice of Techniques: An Aspect of Planned Economic Development 1960, Growth Economics 1970, Collective Choice and Social Welfare 1970, On Economic Inequality 1973, Employment, Technology and Development 1975, Poverty and Famines 1981, Utilitarianism and Beyond (jtly with Bernard Williams) 1982, Choice, Welfare and Measurement 1982, Resources, Values and Development 1984, Commodities and Capabilities 1985, On Ethics and Economics 1987, The Standard of Living 1988, Hunger and Public Action (with Jean Drèze) 1989, Social Security in Developing Countries (jtly) 1991, Inequality Re-examined 1992, The Quality of Life (jtly) 1993, Development as Freedom 1999; articles in various journals in Econs, philosophy and political science. *Address:* Master's Lodge, Trinity College, Cambridge, CB2 1TQ, England.

SEN, Mrinal; Indian film director; b. 14 May 1923, Faridpur (now Bangladesh); s. of the late Dinesh Chandra Sen and Saraju Sen; m. Gita Shome 1953; one s.; started making films 1956, directed 24 feature films; mem. jury numerous int. film festivals; Chair. Gov. Council Film & TV Inst. of India 1983–85; Chair. Indian People's Human Rights Comm. 1987–90; Vice-Chair. Fed. of Film Socs. of India 1980–92, Cinéma et Liberté (Paris) 1992; Pres. Int. Fed. of Film Socs. 1991–; nominated mem. of Rajya Sabha (Upper House of Parl.); Padma Bhushan 1981; Hon. DLitt (Burdwan Univ.) 1981; Commdr Ordre des Arts et des Lettres 1985; numerous awards. *Films include:* The Dawn 1956, Wedding Day 1960, Up in the Clouds 1965, Two Brothers 1966, Bhuvan Shome 1968, Calcutta Trilogy—The Interview, Calcutta 71 and Guerrilla Fighter (Calcutta Trilogy 1971–73), Royal Hunt 1976, The Outsiders 1977, Man With an Axe 1978, And Quiet Rolls and Dawn 1979, In Search of Famine 1980, The Kaleidoscope 1982, The Case is Closed 1983, The

Ruins 1984, Genesis 1986, Suddenly One Day 1989, World Within, World Without 1991, Antareen. *Leisure interests:* reading, travelling, loafing about. *Address:* C-501, Talkatora Road, New Delhi 110 001 (Office); 4E, Motilal Nehru Road, Kolkata 700029, India (Home). *Telephone:* (11) 3351866 (Office); (22) 4754799 (Home).

SEN, Samar R., PhD; Indian economist; b. 29 June 1916, Noakhali; s. of the late Satya R. Sen and of Ashalata Sen; m. Anita Sen 1948; two s.; ed Calcutta Univ., Univ. of Dhaka and London School of Econs; taught Econs, Univ. of Dacca 1940–48; Deputy Econ. Adviser, Govt of India 1948–51; Econ. and Statistical Adviser, Ministry of Food and Agric., Govt of India 1951–58; Leader of Indian Agricultural Del. to USSR 1954; Chair. FAO Comm. on Commodity Problems 1956; mem. and sec. Indian Agricultural Del. to People's Repub. of China 1957; Jt Sec. (Plan Co-ordination and Admin.), Planning Comm. 1959–63; mem. UN Cttee on Int. Trade 1963; Adviser (Programme Admin.) and Additional Sec., Govt of India 1963–69; Adviser (Indicative World Plan) FAO 1967–68; Vice-Chair. Irrigation Comm., Govt of India 1969–70; mem. UN Cttee on Social Devt 1968, Advisory Bd, UNCTAD 1969–77; Pres. Int. Asscn of Agricultural Economists 1970–76; Amb. and Exec. Dir IBRD, IFC and IDA 1970–78; Chair. Int. Food Policy Research Inst., Washington, DC 1979, Govt of India Comm. on Cost of Production 1979, Cttee of Chairmen of Int. Agric. Research Centres of World Bank Group 1981–; Chair. Northern Bd, Reserve Bank of India 1982; Dir Reserve Bank of India 1983–; Dir Nat. Bank of Agric. and Rural Devt 1982–; mem. Comm. on Centre-State Relations, Govt of India 1983–87; has taken part in and led numerous Indian and int. agric. and Devt comms. and delegations; active participant in Gandhian non-violent Movt; mem. Int. Policy Council for Agric. and Trade 1989–; Hon. Fellow LSE, American Agricultural Econs Asscn; First Prize, Asia, World Essay Competition on Disarmament. *Publications:* Strategy for Agricultural Development, Economics of Sir James Stewart, Population and Food Supply, Planning Machinery in India, Growth and Instability in Indian Agriculture, Politics of Indian Economy, Decision Making and Agriculture, International Monetary and Financial System and Institutions, Restrictionism during the Great Depression in Indian Tea, Jute and Sugar Industries, Price Policy for the Plan, Economics of Oligopoly in Oligarchy, India's Political System: What Is To Be Done. *Leisure interests:* golf, travel, photography. *Address:* 41 Poorvi Marg, Vasant Vihar, New Delhi, 110057, India. *Telephone:* 381333 (Office); 675861.

SENDAK, Maurice Bernard, LHD; American illustrator and writer; b. 10 June 1928, New York; s. of Philip Sendak and Sadie (Schindler) Sendak; ed Art Students League, New York, Boston Univ.; writer and illustrator of children's books 1951–; Co-Founder, Artistic Dir The Night Kitchen 1990–; Hans Christian Andersen Illustrators Award 1970; Nat. Medal of Arts 1997. *Solo exhibitions include:* Gallery School of Visual Arts, New York 1964, Ashmolean Museum, Oxford 1975, American Cultural Center, Paris 1978. *Publications (writer and illustrator):* Kenny's Window 1956, Very Far Away 1957, The Sign on Rosie's Door 1960, The Nutshell Library 1963, Where the Wild Things Are (Caldecott Medal 1964) 1963, On Books and Pictures 1986, Caldecott and Co. (collection of reviews and articles) 1989, We Are All in the Dumps with Jack and Guy 1993. *Illustrator:* A Hole is to Dig 1952, A Very Special House 1954, I'll Be You and You Be Me 1954, Charlotte and the White Horse 1955, What Do You Say, Dear? 1959, The Moonjumpers 1960, Little Bear's Visit 1962, Schoolmaster Whackwell's Wonderful Sons 1962, Mr. Rabbit and the Lovely Present 1963, The Griffin and the Minor Canon 1963, Nikolenka's Childhood 1963, The Bat-Poet 1964, Lullabies and Night Songs 1965, Hector Protector and As I Went Over the Water 1965, Zlateh the Goat 1966, Higgelty Pigglety Pop, Or There Must Be More To Life 1967, In the Night Kitchen 1970, The Animal Family 1965, In The Night Kitchen Coloring Book 1971, Pictures by Maurice Sendak 1971, The Juniper Tree and Other Tales from Grimm 1973, Outside Over There 1981, The Love for Three Oranges (with Frank Corsaro) 1984, Nutcracker (with Ralph Manheim) 1984, The Cunning Little Vixen 1985, Dear Mili 1988, I Saw Esau 1992, The Ubiquitous Pig 1992; Writer, Dir and Lyricist for TV animated special Really Rosie 1975. *Stage designs:* The Magic Flute 1980, The Love for Three Oranges 1984, L'Enfant et les sortilèges 1987, The Cunning Little Vixen (for NY Opera) 1989, Idomeneo (opera) 1990. *Address:* c/o HarperCollins, Children's Division, 1350 Avenue of the Americas, New York, NY 10019, USA.

SENDERENS, Alain; French restaurateur; b. 2 Dec. 1939, Hyères; s. of René Senderens and Lucette Senderens (née Azan); m. Eventhia Senderens (née Pappadinas) 1974; one s.; ed Lycée de Vic-en Bigorre; Apprentice Chef Hôtel des Ambassadeurs, Lourdes 1957–59, La Tour d'Argent, Paris 1963; Sauce Cook Lucas Carton Restaurant 1964–65, Man. 1985–; Chief Sauce Cook and Fish Cook, Berkeley, Paris 1965–66, Chief Sauce Cook Orly Hilton Hotel, Paris 1966–68; Proprietor and Chef l'Archestrate, Paris 1968–85; Chair. Bd of Dirs, Auberge Franc Comtoise, Lucas Carton; Pres. Chambre Syndicale de la Haute Cuisine Française 1990–92, Conseil Nat. des Arts Culinaires 1990–98; Chevalier, Légion d'honneur; Officier des Arts et des Lettres, Ordre nat. du Mérite; Chevalier du Mérite Agricole, Ordre Nat. du Mérite en titre de l'Industrie 1986, Ordre des Palmes Académiques 1993; Médaille Vermeil de la Ville de Paris 1988. *Publications:* La Cuisine Réussie 1981, La Grande Cuisine à Petits Prix 1984, Figues sans barbarie 1991, Proust, la Cuisine retrouvée (jtly) 1991, Manger, c'est la santé (jtly) 1992, L'Atelier d'Alain Senderens 1997, Les Festins de Balthazar (jtly) 1997, Le vin et la table 1998. *Leisure interests:* classical music, contemporary art, reading. *Address:* Restaurant Lucas Carton, 9 place de la Madeleine, 75008 Paris (Office); 11 place de la Madeleine, 75008 Paris, France (Home). *Telephone:* 1-42-65-22-90 (Office). *Fax:* 1-42-65-06-23 (Office). *E-mail:* lucas.carton@lucascarton.com (Office). *Website:* www.lucascarton.com (Office).

SENDOV, Blagovest Hristov, PhD, DSc; Bulgarian mathematician; b. 8 Feb. 1932, Assenovgrad; s. of Christo and Marushka Sendov; m. 1st Lilia Georgieva 1958 (divorced 1982); two d.; m. 2nd Anna Marinova 1982; one s.; ed gymnasium in Assenovgrad, Sofia Univ., Moscow State Univ. and Imperial Coll., London; cleaner in Sofia 1949–52; teacher in Boboshevo and Elin Pelin 1956–58; Asst, Dept of Algebra, Univ. of Sofia 1958–60, Asst in Numerical Analysis and Computer Science 1960-63, Asst Prof. of Computer Sciences 1963–67, Prof. of Computer Science 1967, Dean, Faculty of Math. 1970–73, Rector 1973-79; mem. Parl. 1976–90, 1994–, Pres. of Parl. 1995–97, Vice-Pres. 1997–; Vice-Pres. Bulgarian Acad. of Sciences 1980–82, Vice-Pres. and Scientific Sec.-Gen. 1982–88, Dir Centre for Informatics and Computer Tech. 1985–90; Pres. 1988–91; Pres. Comm. of Science 1986–88; Hon. Pres. Int. Asscn of Univs. 1985–; Vice-Pres. Int. Fed. for Information Processing 1985–88, Pres. 1989–91; World Peace Council 1983–86, IIP—UNESCO 1986–90; Extraordinary Vice-Pres. ICSU 1990–93; mem. Exec. Cttee and Bd of Dirs, Int. Foundation for Survival and Devt of Humanity 1988–; two Orders of People's Repub. of Bulgaria and many others; Dr hc 1969, 1977; Dimitrov Prize for Science, Honoured Scientist 1984. *Publications:* Numerical Analysis, Old and New 1973, Hausdorff Approximation 1979, Averaged Moduli of Smoothness (monograph); textbooks and articles in learned journals. *Leisure interests:* tennis, travelling. *Address:* 5 Plachkoviza str., Sofia 1126, Bulgaria (Home); Narodno Sabranil, Sofia 1000 (Office). *Telephone:* (2) 981-00-82 (Office); (2) 62-60-83 (Home). *Fax:* (2) 980-36-36 (Office). *E-mail:* bsendov@nt14.parlament.bg (Office); bsendov@argo.bas.bg (Home).

SENGERA, Jürgen; German banking executive; b. 13 Feb. 1943, Schwerte, Westphalia; mem. Econ. Dept Westdeutsche Landesbank (WestLB) 1971–74, Deputy CEO Services Dept 1974–77, Head of EDP Dept and Exec. Vice-Pres. 1982, mem. Man. Bd 1984–2001, Chair. Sept. 2001–; Sr Vice-Pres. Corp. Planning Dept and Chair. Marketing Cttee Norddeutsche Landesbank 1977–82. *Address:* Westdeutsche Landesbank Girozentrale, Herzogstr. 15, 40217 Düsseldorf, Germany (Office). *Telephone:* (211) 826-01 (Office). *Fax:* (211) 826-6119 (Office). *Website:* www.westlb.de (Office).

SENGHAAS, Dieter, DPhil; German professor of social science; b. 27 Aug. 1940, Geislingen; m. Eva Knobloch 1968; one d.; ed Univs of Tübingen, Michigan and Frankfurt and Amherst Coll.; Research Fellow, Center for Int. Affairs, Harvard Univ. 1968–70; Research Dir, Peace Research Inst., Frankfurt (PRIF) 1971–78; Prof. of Int. Relations, Univ. of Frankfurt 1972–78; Prof. of Social Science, Univ. of Bremen 1978–; mem. several nat. and int. scientific orgs; Hon. PhD (Tübingen) 2000; Lentz Int. Peace Research Award 1987, Göttingen Peace Award 1999. *Publications:* Aggressivität und kollektive Gewalt 1972, Aufrüstung durch Rüstungskontrolle 1972, Gewalt-Konflikt-Frieden 1974, Weltwirtschaftsordnung und Entwicklungspolitik (5th edn) 1987, Abschreckung und Frieden (3rd edn) 1981, Rüstung und Militarismus (2nd edn) 1982, Von Europa lernen 1982, The European Experience 1985, Die Zukunft Europas 1986, Europas Entwicklung und die Dritte Welt 1986, Konfliktformationen im internationalen System 1988, Europa 2000: Ein Friedensplan 1990, Friedensprojekt Europa 1992, Wohin driftet die Welt 1994, Zivilisierung wider Willen 1998, Klaenge des Friedens 2001, The Clash within Civilizations 2001; ed. or co-ed. of 27 books related to political science, int. affairs, etc. *Leisure interest:* music. *Address:* University of Bremen, 28334 Bremen (Office); Freiligrathstrasse 6, 28211 Bremen, Germany (Home). *Telephone:* (421) 2182281 (Office); (421) 23-04-36 (Home). *Fax:* (421) 2187248 (Office); (421) 249169 (Home). *E-mail:* tmenge@uni-bremen.de (Office). *Website:* www.iniis.uni-bremen.de/mitarb/ds.htm (Office).

SENTAMU, Rt Rev. John Tucker Mugabi, LLB, MA, PhD, FRSA; Ugandan ecclesiastic; b. 1949; m. Margaret Sentamu; two c.; ed Makerere Univ., Cambridge Univ.; trained Barrister and Advocate of the High Court of Uganda; Asst Chaplain Selwyn Coll. Cambridge; ordained 1979; Chaplain Latchmere Remand Centre 1979–82; Curate St Andrew's Ham in Southwark 1979–82; Curate St Paul's, Herne Hill 1982–83; Priest-in-Charge Holy Trinity, Tulse Hill 1983–84; parish Priest St Matthias, Upper Tulse Hill 1983–84; mem. Gen. Synod 1985–96, mem. Standing, Policy and Appointments Cttees; mem. Archbishop's Comm. for Urban Priority Areas 1988–92; mem. Revision Cttee for the Ordination of Women to the Priesthood; Priest-in-Charge St. Saviour, Brixton Hill 1987–89; mem. Family Welfare Asscn 1989–; mem. Decade of Evangelism Steering Group; mem. Exec. Springboard; Prolocutor Convocation of Canterbury 1990–96; Chair. Cttee for Minority Ethnic Anglican Concerns 1990–99; Vicar of the joint benefice of Holy Trinity and St. Matthias, Tulse Hill 1994–96; Area Bishop of Stepney 1996–2002; Bishop of Birmingham Nov. 2002–; Adviser to the Stephen Lawrence Judicial Inquiry 1997–99; Gov. Univ. of North London 1998–2002; Pres. and Chair. London Marriage Guidance Council 2000–02; Chair. Review into the murder investigation of Damilola Taylor 2001–02; mem. Health Advisory Cttee HM Prisons, CTE Forum; Chair. NHS Haeomoglobinopathy Screening Programme, EC1 New Deal Devt Programme; Custodian Trustee London Diocesan Fund; Trustee, Tower Hamlets Summer Univ.; Chair. Islington Partnership; Freeman of the City of London 2000; Fellow Univ. Coll. Christ Church Canterbury; Fellow Queen Mary, Univ. of London. *Leisure interests:* music, cooking, reading, athletics, rugby, football. *Address:* Diocese of Birmingham, Church House, 175 Harborne Park Road, Harborne, Birmingham,

B17 0BH, England (Office). *Telephone:* (121) 426-0400 (Office). *E-mail:* bishop@birmingham.anglican.org (Office). *Website:* www.birmingham.anglican.org (Office).

SEPE, HE Cardinal Crescenzio; Italian ecclesiastic; b. 2 June 1943, Carinaro, Aversa; ordained priest 1967; Bishop 1992; Titular Archbishop of Grado; Sec.-Gen. Cttee of the Grand Jubilee of the Year 2000 and of the Presidential Council; Chair. "Peregrinatio ad Petri Sedem"; cr. Cardinal 2001. *Address:* Palazzo di Propaganda Fide, Piazza di Spagna 48, 00187 Rome (Office); Villa Betania, Via Urbans VIII 16, 00165 Rome, Italy (Home).

SEPÚLVEDA, Bernardo, LLB; Mexican politician; b. 14 Dec. 1941, Mexico City; s. of Bernardo Sepúlveda and Margarita Sepúlveda; m. Ana Yturbe 1970; three s.; ed Nat. Univ. of Mexico and Queen's Coll., Cambridge; fmrly taught int. law, El Colegio de México and Faculty of Political Science, Univ. of Mexico; Asst Dir of Juridical Affairs, Ministry of Presidency 1968–70; Dir-Gen. of Int. Financial Affairs, Ministry of Finance 1976–81; Int. Adviser, Minister of Programming and Budget 1981; Amb. to USA March–Dec. 1982; Sec. of Foreign Affairs 1982–88; Amb. to UK 1989–93; Foreign Affairs Advisor to Pres. of Mexico 1993–; Sec. Int. Affairs Institutional Revolutionary Party (PRI) 1981–82; Pres. to UN Sixth Comm. on Transnat. Corpns 1977–80; Hon. Fellow Queen's Coll., Cambridge 1991; Hon. GCMG. *Publications:* Foreign Investment in Mexico 1973, Transnational Corporations in Mexico 1974, A View of Contemporary Mexico 1979, Planning for Development 1981. *Address:* Rocas 185, México, DF 01900, Mexico. *Telephone:* (5) 652-0641. *Fax:* (5) 652-9739.

SEQUEIRA, Luis, PhD; American professor of plant pathology; b. 1 Sept. 1927, San José, Costa Rica; s. of Raul Sequeira and the late Dora Jenkins; m. Elisabeth Steinvorth 1954; one s. three d.; ed Harvard Univ.; Teaching Fellow, Harvard Univ. 1949–52; Parker Fellow, Harvard and Instituto Biológico, São Paulo, Brazil 1952–53; Plant Pathologist, Asst Dir, then Dir Coto Research Station, United Fruit Co., Costa Rica 1953–60; Research Assoc., NC State Univ., Raleigh, NC 1960–61; Assoc. Prof., then Prof., Dept of Plant Pathology, Univ. of Wis., Madison 1961–78, Prof., Depts of Bacteriology and Plant Pathology 1978–82, J. C. Walker Prof. 1982–; Consultant Agracetus, Madison 1982–93; Chief Scientist, Competitive Grants Office, USDA, Washington, DC 1987–88; research interests include physiology and biochem. of plant-parasite interactions, identification of genes for virulence in pathogens, particularly bacteria and breeding plants for disease resistance; Fellow American Phytopathological Soc. (Pres. 1985–86, Award of Distinction 1994), American Acad. of Microbiology; mem. NAS, Linnean Soc. of London; E. M. Stakman Award. *Publications:* approximately 250 publs in journals and covering plant pathology, bacteriology, biochem. and genetics. *Leisure interests:* classical music, cross-country skiing. *Address:* Department of Plant Pathology, University of Wisconsin, 1630 Linden Drive, Madison, WI 53706; 10 Appomattox Court, Madison, WI 53705, USA (Home). *Telephone:* (608) 262-3456 (Office); (608) 833-3440 (Home).

SERAGELDIN, Ismail, PhD; Egyptian international organization official; b. 1944, Guiza; m.; one s.; ed Cairo Univ., Harvard Univ.; fmr lecturer Cairo and Harvard Univs; fmr consultant in city and regional planning; with IBRD 1972–, Economist in Educ. and Human Resources 1972–76, Div. Chief for Tech. Assistance and Special Studies 1977–80, for Urban Projects in Europe, the Middle E and N Africa 1980–83, Dir for Programs in W Africa 1984–87, Co-Dir for Cen. and Occidental Africa 1987–89, Tech. Dir for Sub-Saharan Africa 1990–92, Vice-Pres. for Environmentally and Socially Sustainable Devt 1992–98, Co-Chair. Non Governmental Org.-Bank Cttee 1997–99, Vice-Pres. for Special Programs 1998–2000; Chair. Global Water Partnership 1996–2000, World Comm. for Water in the 21st Century 1998–2000; currently Dir Library of Alexandria and Distinguished Univ. Prof., Univ. of Wageningen, the Netherlands; Chair. and mem. of numerous advisory cttees.; Hon. DSc (Indian Agricultural Research Inst.) 1997, (Punjab Agricultural Univ.) 1998, (Tamil Nadu Veterinary and Animal Sciences Univ.) 1998, (Egerton Univ., Kenya) 1999 and numerous other hon. degrees. *Publications:* Nurturing Development 1995, Sustainability and the Wealth of Nations 1996, Architecture of Empowerment 1997, Rural Well-Being: From Vision to Action (jtly) 1997, The Modernity of Shakespeare 1998, Biotechnology and Biosafety (jtly) 1999, Very Special Places 1999, Promethean Science (jtly) 2000 and numerous other books and articles. *Address:* IBRD, 1818 H Street, NW, Washington, DC 20433, USA (Office). *Telephone:* (202) 477-1234 (Office). *Fax:* (202) 477-6391 (Office). *E-mail:* pic@worldbank.org (Office). *Website:* www.worldbank.org (Office).

SERAPHIN, Oliver; Dominican politician; b. 2 Aug. 1943; s. of Perry Seraphin and Theotil Seraphin; m. Virginia Rabess 1978; three s.; Prime Minister of Dominica and Minister for Foreign Affairs 1979–80; Leader Democratic Labour Party 1979–85, Deputy Leader Labour Party of Dominica 1985. *Leisure interests:* table-tennis, reading, music. *Address:* 44 Green's Lane, Goodwill, Dominica.

ŞERBAN, Andrei; Romanian stage director; b. 21 June 1943; s. of Gheorghe Şerban and Elpis Şerban; m.; two c.; ed Bucharest Theatrical and Cinematographic Art Inst.; int. scholarships: Ford 1970, Guggenheim 1976, Rockefeller 1980; has delivered numerous lectures; Gen. Man. Nat. Theatre of Romania 1990–93; Obie Awards; Tony Award, prizes at the Avignon, Belgrade and Shiraz festivals. *Productions include:* (in Romania) Ubu Roi 1966, Julius Caesar 1968, Jonah 1969, An Ancient Trilogy (Medea, The Trojan Women, Elektra) 1990; (in USA) Medea (Euripides) 1970, The Cherry Orchard 1972,

Fragments of a Trilogy (Medea, Elektra, The Trojan Women) 1974, As You Like It 1976, Uncle Vanya 1979, The Umbrellas of Cherbourg 1980, The Seagull 1981, Three Sisters 1983, The Miser 1988, Twelfth Night 1989, The King Stag 2001. *Opera productions include*: Eugene Onegin 1980, Turandot 1984, Norma 1985, Fidelio (Covent Garden) 1986, The Puritans (Paris Opera). *Address*: Teatrul Naţional, Bd N Bălcescu 2, Bucharest, Romania. *Telephone*: 614-56-92.

SERDENGEÇTİ, Süreyya, MA; Turkish central banker; ed Middle East Tech. Univ., Ankara, Vanderbilt Univ., Nashville, USA; mem. staff Foreign Debt Rescheduling Div., Cen. Bank of Turkey 1980–90, Int. Reserve Man. Div. 1990–92, Dir Open Market Operations Div. 1992–94, Asst Sec.-Gen. and Press Officer Cen. Bank 1994, Asst Gen. Dir Foreign Relations Dept 1994–96, Gen. Dir Markets Dept 1996–98, Vice-Gov. 1998–2001, Gov. 2001–. *Address*: Türkiye Cumhuriyet Merkez Bankası AS, İstiklal Caddesi 10 Ulu, s06100 Ankara, Turkey (Office). *Telephone*: (312) 3093137 (Office). *Fax*: (312) 3109121 (Office). *E-mail*: sureyya.serdengecti@tcmb.gov.tr (Office). *Website*: www.tcmb.gov.tr (Office).

SEREBRIER, José, MA; American conductor and composer; b. 3 Dec. 1938, Montevideo; s. of David Serebrier and Frida Serebrier (née Wasser); m. Carole Farley 1969; one d.; ed Univ. of Minn., Curtis Inst. of Music, Phila; started conducting at age of 12; went to USA 1956; studied composition with Aaron Copland and Vittorio Giannini, Curtis Inst., Phila 1956–58 and conducting with Antal Dorati and Pierre Monteux; guest conductor in USA, S America, Australia and Europe; Assoc. Conductor American Symphony Orchestra, with Leopold Stokowski 1962–68; conducted alongside Leopold Stokowski world première of Charles Ives' Fourth Symphony, Carnegie Hall, New York 1964; conducted first performance in Poland of Charles Ives' Fourth Symphony 1971 and premieres of over 100 works; Composer-in-Residence with Cleveland Orchestra 1968–70; Music Dir Cleveland Philharmonic Orchestra 1968–71; Artistic Dir Int. Festival of Americas, Miami 1984–, Miami Festival 1985– (also Founder); Nat. Endownment for Arts Comm. Award 1969, Ditson Award for Promotion of New Music, Columbia Univ. 1980, Deutsche Schallplatten Critics' Award 1991, UK Music Retailers' Asscn Award for Best Symphony Recording (Mendelssohn symphonies) 1991, Diapason d'Or Recording Award, France, Best Audiophile Recording (Scheherazade), Soundstage 2000. *Compositions*: Solo Violin Sonata 1954, Quartet for Saxophones 1955, Pequeña música (wind quintet) 1955, Symphony No. 1 1956, Momento psicológico (string orchestra) 1957, Solo Piano Sonata 1957, Suite canina (wind trio) 1957, Symphony for Percussion 1960, The Star Wagon (chamber orchestra) 1967, Nueve (double bass and orchestra) 1970, Colores mágicos (variations for harp and chamber orchestra) 1971, At Dusk, in Shadows (solo flute), Andante Cantabile (strings), Night Cry (brass), Dorothy and Carmine (flute and strings), George and Muriel (contrabass), Winter (violin concerto) 1995, Winterreise (for orchestra) 1999; composed music for several films; all compositions published and recorded; over 175 recordings to date. *Television includes*: int. TV broadcast of Gramm's Ceremony, LA 2002, conducting suite from Bernstein's West Side Story. *Publications*: orchestration of 14 songs by Edvard Grieg 2000, orchestrastion of Gerschwin's works 2002. *Leisure interests*: reading, swimming, football. *Address*: 20 Queensgate Gardens, London, SW7 5LZ, England. *Fax*: (212) 662-8073 (Office). *E-mail*: caspil23@aol.com (Office). *Website*: www.naxox.com (Office).

SERFATY, Abraham, DIP.ENG; Moroccan adviser, mining engineer and lecturer; b. 12 Jan. 1926, Casablanca; ed Ecole Nat. Supérieure des Mines, Paris; Dir Mining Research Operations Atlas Mountains 1949–50; arrested and imprisoned 1950; under house arrest in France 1952–56; with Mines du Maroc 1956; Head of Cabinet, Sec. of State for Industrial Production and Mines 1958; Dir of Mines and Geology 1959–60; Dir of Devt Research, Sherifian Office of Phosphates 1960–68; univ. lecturer 1962–63, 1964–65, 1968–72; arrested and tortured 1972; in hiding 1972–74; arrested, tortured and sentenced to life imprisonment 1977; released and exiled to France 1991; lecturer Univ. of Paris 1992–94; returned to Morocco as Adviser, Nat. Office of Petroleum Research and Devt 2000–. *Publications*: Lutte anti-sioniste et Révolution Arabe 1977, Ecrits de Prison sur la Palestine 1992. *Address*: c/o Ministry of the Economy and Finance, ave. Muhammad V, Rabat, Morocco (Office).

SERGEYEV, Marshal Igor Dmitrievich; Russian army officer (retd); b. 20 April 1938, Verkhny, Voroshilovgrad Region; m.; one s.; ed Nakhimov Black Sea Higher Navigation School, Military Eng Acad., Gen. Staff Acad.; with rocket troops since 1960, Head of staff of Regt 1971, Commdr of Regt 1973, Head of staff, Commdr of Div. 1975–80, Head of staff of Rocket Army 1980–83, Chief of operation div., Deputy Head of General Staff of Rocket Troops 1983–85, First Deputy then Deputy C-in-C of Rocket Troops 1989–92, C-in-C of strategic Rocket Troops 1992–97; Minister of Defence 1997–2001; Asst. to Pres. of Russia on Strategic Stability Issues 2001–. *Address*: Administration of the President, Staraya pl. 4, 103132 Moscow, Russia. *Telephone*: (095) 925-35-81 (Office).

SERGEYEV, Ivan Ivanovich; Russian civil servant and diplomatist; b. 7 Sept. 1941, Electrostal, Moscow Region; Deputy, First Deputy Chair., Exec. Cttee Moscow Regional Soviet 1978–83; Deputy, First Deputy Head, Dept on Problems of Diplomatic Corps USSR (now Russian) Ministry of Foreign Affairs 1983–97; Deputy Minister of Foreign Affairs 1997–; Deputy Chair. Bd

Black Sea Bank for Trade and Devt 1998–; State Prize of Russia 2002. *Address*: Ministry of Foreign Affairs, Smolenskaya-Sennaya 32/34, Moscow, Russia. *Telephone*: (095) 244-37-53 (Office). *Website*: www.mid.ru.

SERGEYEV, Victor Mikhailovich, CAND.MATH.SCI., DHist; Russian mathematician and political scientist; b. 22 April 1944, Moscow; m. Marina Alekseyevna Sergeyeva; one s.; ed Moscow Inst. of Energy, Moscow State Univ.; Sr Researcher All-Union Research Inst. of Meteorological Service, USSR State Cttee of Standards 1975–78, Problem Lab. of System Analysis, Moscow State Inst. of Int. Relations 1978–86, Prof. of Comparative Politics and Dir Centre for Int. Research 1998–; Head of Lab. Inst. of USA and Canada, USSR (now Russian) Acad. of Sciences 1986–90; Deputy Dir Analytical Centre on Scientific and Industrial Policy, Ministry of Science and Tech. 1998–; mem. Russian Acad. of Nat. Sciences, Asscn of Political Studies, Kant Soc., Russian Asscn of Artificial Intellect, Exec. Bd Centre of Philosophy, Psychology and Sociology of Religion; Hon. mem. Leeds Univ. (UK). *Publications*: numerous scientific works published in Russia and abroad on political and religious culture, cognitive studies etc., including The Wild East 1998, Limits of Rationality 1998. *Leisure interest*: foreign languages. *Address*: Centre for International Research, State Institute of International Relations, Vernadskogo prosp. 76, 117454 Moscow, Russia (Office). *Telephone*: (095) 434-20-44 (Office). *Fax*: (095) 434-20-44 (Office). *E-mail*: tsmi@mgimo.ru (Office); av205@comtv.ru (Home).

SERICHE DOUGAN, Angel Serafín; Equatorial Guinean politician; Prime Minister of Equatorial Guinea 1996–2001. *Address*: c/o Office of the Prime Minister, Malabo, Equatorial Guinea.

SERJEANT, Graham Roger, CMG, MD, FRCP; British medical research scientist; b. 26 Oct. 1938, Bristol; s. of Ewart E. Serjeant and Violet E. Serjeant; m. Beryl E. King 1965; ed Sibford School, Banbury, Bootham School, York, Clare Coll., Cambridge, London Hosp. Medical School and Makerere Coll. Kampala; House Physician, London Hosp. 1963–64, Royal United Hosp. Bath 1965–66, Hammersmith Hosp. London 1966; Registrar, Univ. Hosp. of the West Indies 1966–67; Wellcome Research Fellow, Dept of Medicine, Univ. Hosp. of the West Indies 1967–71; Visiting Prof. Dep. of Biochem., Univ. of Tenn. 1971; mem. scientific staff, MRC Abnormal Haemoglobin Unit, Cambridge 1971–72, Epidemiology Research Unit, Jamaica 1972–74; Dir MRC Labs., Jamaica 1974–99; Prof. of Epidemiology, Faculty of Medicine, Univ. of the West Indies 1981–99, Prof. Emer. 1999–; Visiting Prof. London School of Hygiene and Tropical Medicine 1999, Guy's, King's and St Thomas' Combined Medical School, London 1999; Hon. Fellow, Royal Coll. of Physicians, Edin. 1998; Hon. Prof. Dept of Public Health, Guy's Hosp., London 1999; Hon. Commdr Order of Distinction (Jamaica) 1996; Vice-Chancellor's Award for Excellence 1999. *Publications*: The Clinical Features of Sickle Cell Disease 1974, Sickle Cell Disease 1992 (2nd Edn); more than 400 papers on sickle cell disease in medical journals. *Leisure interests* squash, music. *Address*: 14 Milverton Crescent, Kingston 6, Jamaica. *Telephone*: 970-0077 (Office); 927 2300 (Home). *Fax*: 970-0074 (Office). *E-mail*: grserjeant@cwjamaica.com (Office and Home).

SERKIN, Peter Adolf; American concert pianist; b. 24 July 1947, New York; s. of Rudolf Serkin and Irene Busch; ed Curtis Inst. of Music; début, New York 1959; Dr hc (New England Conservatory) 2001; Premio Accademia Musicale Chigian Siena 1983. *Performances*: concert appearances in recital and with orchestras world-wide including Philadelphia, Cleveland, New York, Chicago, Berlin, London, Zürich, Paris and Japan; has premiered works composed for him by Knussen, Takemitsu, Lieberson, Berio; has given benefit performances to aid hunger and war victims. *Address*: Kirshbaum Demler and Associates, Inc., 711 West End Avenue, 5KN, New York, NY 10025, USA (Office). *Telephone*: (212) 222-4843 (Office). *Fax*: (212) 222-7321 (Office). *E-mail*: skirsh711@aol.com (Office). *Website*: www.skassoc.com (Home).

SEROTA, Sir Nicholas Andrew, Kt, MA; British art gallery director; b. 27 April 1946; s. of Stanley Serota and Baroness Serota; m. 1st Angela M. Beveridge 1973 (divorced 1995); two d.; m. 2nd Teresa Gleadowe 1997; ed Haberdashers' Aske's School, Hampstead and Elstree, Christ's Coll., Cambridge and Courtauld Inst. of Art; Regional Art Officer and Exhbn Organizer, Arts Council of GB 1970–73; Dir Museum of Modern Art, Oxford 1973–76; Dir Whitechapel Art Gallery 1976–88; Dir The Tate Gallery, London 1988–; Chair. British Council Visual Arts Advisory Cttee 1992–98 (mem. 1976–98); Sr Fellow Royal Coll. of Art 1996; Trustee Public Art Devt Trust 1983–87, Architecture Foundation 1991–99, The Little Sparta Trust 1995–; Commr Comm. for Architecture and the Built Environment 1999–; Hon. Fellow, Queen Mary and Westfield Coll., Univ. of London 1988, RIBA1992, Goldsmiths Coll., Univ. of London (1994); Hon. DArts (City of London Polytechnic) 1990; Hon. DLitt (Plymouth) 1993, (Keele) 1994, (South Bank) 1996, (Exeter) 2000; Hon. DUniv (Surrey) 1997. *Publication*: Experience or Interpretation: The Dilemma of Museums of Modern Art 1997. *Address*: Millbank, London, SW1P 4RG, England (Office). *Telephone*: (20) 7887-8000 (Office). *Fax*: (20) 7887-8007 (Office). *Website*: www.tate.org.uk (Office).

SERRA, José; Brazilian politician and professor of economics; b. 19 March 1942, São Paulo; m. Monica Serra; ed Univ. of São Paulo, CEPAL-ILPES, Santiago, Chile, Univ. of Chile and Cornell Univ., USA; Leader Nat. Students' Union 1963–64; forced to flee to Chile for opposing Brazil's fmr mil. regime in early 1970s, in exile for 14 years; Prof. of Econs, Univ. of Chile 1968–73; Prof., Univ. of Campinas; Sec. for Economy and Planning, São Paulo 1983–86; Co-Founder and mem. Brazilian Social Democratic Party (PSDB) 1988;

elected Fed. Deputy for São Paulo 1986–94; elected Senator 1994–95, 2002–; Minister of Planning 1995–96; Minister of Health 1998–2002; Presidential Cand. 2002; mem. Inst. for Advanced Study, Princeton Univ., USA 1976–78. *Address:* c/o Partido da Social Democracia Brasileira (PSDB), SCN Quadra 4, Bloco B, Torre C, 3° Andar, Sala 303/B, Centro Empresarial Varig, 70714-900 Brasília, DFBrazil (Office).

SERRA, Richard, MFA; American sculptor; b. 2 Nov. 1939, San Francisco, Calif.; ed Univ. of Calif. (Berkeley and Santa Barbara) and Yale Univ.; frequent exhbns. at Leo Castelli Gallery, New York since 1970; works in many perm. collections including Whitney Museum of Modern Art, Guggenheim Museum, Museum of Modern Art (New York), Art Gallery of Ontario, Stedelijk Museum Amsterdam; Skohegan School Medal 1975. *Solo exhibitions include:* Richard Hines Gallery, Seattle 1979, Venice Biennale 1981, Akira Ikeda Gallery, Nagoya, Japan 1982, Margo Levin Gallery 1984, Visual Arts Museum 1985, Bonnefantenmuseum, Maastricht 1990, Pace Gallery 1992. *Publications:* Weight and Measure 1992, Writings/Interviews 1994. *Address:* 173 Duane Street, New York, NY 10013, USA.

SERRA RAMONEDA, Antoni, PhD; Spanish fmr university rector and economist; b. 20 July 1933, Barcelona; s. of Antoni Serra Riera and Enriqueta Ramoneda Ruis; m. Margarita de la Figuera Buñuel 1958; one s. two d.; ed Lycée Français, Barcelona and Univ. Complutense de Madrid; Sec. Faculty of Econ. Sciences, Univ. of Barcelona 1960–64; Sec.-Gen. Univ. Autónoma de Barcelona 1960–72, Dir Inst. of Educ. Sciences 1977–78, Rector 1980–85; Pres. Comisión de Control Caja de Pensiones para la Vejez y de Ahorros 1979–82, Sec.-Gen. 1982–84; Pres. Caja de Ahorros de Cataluña 1984. *Publications:* Libro Blanco sobre los efectos para Cataluña del ingreso de España en la CEE, La industria textil algodonera y el Mercado Común Europeo, Sistema Económico y Empresa. *Address:* Pl. Bonanova 5, Barcelona 08022, Spain (Home). *Telephone:* (93) 2478101 (Home).

SERRA REXACH, Eduardo, LLB; Spanish business executive, fmr politician and museum administrator; b. 19 Dec. 1946, Madrid; m. 1st; one s.; m. 2nd Luz del Camino Municio; ed Complutense Univ., Madrid; began career as state lawyer; mem. staff Ministry of Educ. and Industry–1982; Sec. of State for Defence 1982–84, Minister of Defence 1984–87, 1996–2000; Chair. Telettra 1986; Vice-Chair. Cubiertas y MZOV 1989–91, Chair. 1991; Chair. Peugeot Spain 1992, Airtel 1994–96; Chair. UBS Warburg Spanish. Div. 2000–; Chair. Bd of Trustees, Prado Museum, Madrid 2000–; Pres. Foundation for Assistance Against Drug Addiction 1996–. *Address:* Museo del Prado, Ruiz de Alarcon 23, 28014 Madrid, Spain (Office). *Telephone:* (91) 3302800 (Office). *Fax:* (91) 33028556 (Office). *Website:* museo.nacional@prado.mcu.es (Office).

SERRA SERRA, Narcís, DEcon; Spanish politician; b. 30 May 1943, Barcelona; ed Barcelona Univ. and London School of Econs; Prof. of Econ. Theory Autonomous Univ. of Barcelona 1976–77; mem. Convergència Socialista de Catalunya 1974–, Minister of Public Works in Catalan Autonomous Govt 1977–79; Mayor of Barcelona 1979; Minister of Defence in Spanish Govt 1982–91, Deputy Prime Minister 1991–95; Gen. Sec. Catalan Socialist Party 1996–2000; Pres. CIDOB Foundation, Rafael Campalans Foundation; Hon. Fellow LSE 1991. *Address:* Fundació CIDOB, Elisabets 12, 08001 Barcelona, Spain. *Telephone:* (93) 3180807. *Fax:* (93) 3022118. *E-mail:* nserra@cidob.org (Office). *Website:* www.psc.es, www.cidob.org (Office).

SERRANO ELIAS, Jorge; Guatemalan politician and businessman; fmr Pres. Advisory Council of State 1982–83; Pres. of Guatemala 1991–93.

SERRAULT, Michel Lucien; French actor and singer; b. 24 Jan. 1928, Brunoy, Seine-et-Oise; s. of Robert Serrault and Adeline Foulon; m. Juanita Peyron 1958; two d. (one deceased); ed Petit Séminaire de Conflans and Centre du Spectacle de la rue Blanche, Paris; numerous film and TV appearances; Officier, Légion d'honneur, Commdr des Arts et des Lettres. *Recent films include:* On ne meurt que deux fois (Prix George Chamara 1986), La Cage aux folles III, Mon beau-frère a tué ma soeur 1986, Le Miraculé 1987, Ennemis intimes 1988, En toute innocence 1988, Bonjour l'angoisse 1988, Ne réveillez pas un flic qui dort 1988, Comédie d'amour 1989, Le Docteur Petiot 1989, Joyeux Noël, Bonne année 1989, Docteur Petiot 1990, La Vieille qui marchait dans la mer 1991, Ville à vendre 1992, Vieille Canaille 1992, Bonsoir 1994, Le Bonheur est dans le pré 1995, Nelly et M. Arnand 1995 (César Award for Best Actor, Pierre Belan Prize for Best Male Leading Role), Artemisia 1997, Rien ne va plus 1997, Le Comédien 1997, Les enfants du marais 1999, Le Monde de Marty 2000, Le Libertin 2000, Les Acteurs 2000, Belphégor: Le Fantôme du Louvre 2001. *Stage appearances include:* L'Ami de la famille, Pour avoir Adrienne, Le Train pour Venise, Sacré Léonard, Quand épousez-vous ma femme?, Monsieur Dodd 1965, Opération Lagrelèche 1966, Gugusse 1968, Le Vision voyageur et les Bonshommes 1970, Le Tombeur 1972, La Cage aux folles 1973, L'Avare 1986, Knock 1992. *Publication:* Le Cri de la Carotte 1995. *Leisure interest:* trumpet. *Address:* Agents Associés-Guy Bonnet, 201 rue du Faubourg Saint-Honoré, 75008 Paris (Office); 34 boulevard de Château, 92200 Neuilly-sur-Seine, France (Home).

SERRE, Jean-Pierre, DèsSc; French mathematician; b. 15 Sept. 1926, Bages; s. of Jean Serre and Adèle Serre; m. Josiane Heulot 1948; one d.; ed Lycée de Nîmes and Ecole Normale Supérieure; Prof. of Algebra and Geometry, Coll. de France 1956–94, now Hon. Prof.; mem. Acads of Sciences of France, Sweden, USA, Netherlands; Hon. FRS (UK); Commdr, Légion d'honneur, Grand Officier, Ordre nat. du Mérite; Fields Medal, Int. Congress of Math. 1954, Prix Balzan 1985, shared Wolf Prize 2000, Médaille d'Or, CNRS 1987. *Publications:* Homologie singulière des espaces fibrés 1951, Faisceaux algébriques cohérents 1955, Groupes algébriques et corps de classes 1959, Corps Locaux 1962, Cohomologie galoisienne 1964, Abelian *l*-adic representations 1968, Cours d'arithmétique 1970, Représentations linéaires des groupes finis 1971, Arbres, amalgames, SL2 1977, Lectures on the Mordell-Weil Theorem 1989, Topics in Galois Theory 1992, Collected Papers 1949–1998, 4 vols, Local Algebra 2000. *Address:* Collège de France, place M. Bertholet, 75005 Paris (Office); 6 avenue de Montespan, 75116 Paris, France (Home). *Telephone:* 1-44-27-17-90 (Office); 1-45-53-35-63 (Home). *Fax:* 1-44-27-17-04 (Office). *E-mail:* serre@dmi.ens.fr (Office).

SERREAU, Coline; French film director; d. of Jean-Marie Serreau; has acted in several stage plays including Lapin, lapin in Paris; wrote and acted in Bertuccelli's On s'est trompé d'histoire d'amour 1973; directed Oedipus the King for Italian TV; f. trapeze school in Canada. *Films include:* Mais qu'est-ce qu'elles veulent? (documentary) 1975, Pourquoi pas! 1976, Qu'est-ce qu'on attend pour être heureux! 1982, Trois hommes et un couffin (Three Men and a Cradle) 1985, Romuald et Juliette 1989.

SERRIN, James B., PhD, FAAS; American professor of mathematics; b. 1 Nov. 1926, Chicago, Ill.; s. of Helen Wingate Serrin and James B. Serrin; m. Barbara West 1952; three d.; ed Western Michigan Coll. and Indiana Univ.; MIT 1952–54; Univ. of Minn. 1955–, Chair. 1964–65, Regents Prof. of Math. 1968–; Fellow, American Acad. of Arts and Sciences; mem. NAS, Finnish Acad. of Science, Soc. for Natural Philosophy (Pres. 1969–70); Hon. DSc (Sussex, Ferrara, Padua); G. D. Birkhoff Award, American Math. Soc. *Publications:* Mathematical Principles of Fluid Dynamics 1958, New Perspectives on Thermodynamics 1985, The Problem of Dirichlet for Quasilinear Elliptic Differential Equations 1969. *Address:* Department of Mathematics, University of Minnesota, Minneapolis, MN 55455 (Office); 4422 Dupont Avenue South, Minneapolis, MN 55409, USA (Home). *Telephone:* (612) 624-9530 (Office). *Fax:* (612) 626-2017.

SERVAN-SCHREIBER, Jean-Claude, LenD; French media executive and newspaperman; b. 11 April 1918, Paris; s. of the late Robert Servan-Schreiber and Suzanne Crémieux; m. 1st Christiane Laroche 1947 (divorced); m. 2nd Jacqueline Guix de Pinos 1955 (divorced); two s. three d.; m. 3rd Paule Guinet 1983 (divorced); ed Exeter Coll., Oxford and Sorbonne; served World War II in Flanders 1940, in Resistance 1941–42, in N Africa 1943, France 1944, Germany 1945; with Les Echos 1946–65, Gen. Man. 1957, Dir 1963–65; Deputy for Paris, Nat. Ass. 1965–67; Asst Sec.-Gen. UNR-UDT 1965; Pres. Rassemblement français pour Israël 1967; Dir-Gen. Régie française de publicité 1968–78; mem. Haut Conseil de l'audiovisuel 1973–81; Pres. Groupe Européen des Régisseurs de Publicité Télévisée 1975–78; mem. Conseil politique, RPR 1977–81; Conseiller du Groupe de Presse L'Expansion 1980–93; Special Adviser Mitsubishi Electric (Europe) 1992–2000; Pres. Inst. Arthur Vernes (Medical and Surgical Center) 1993–; Commdr, Légion d'honneur; Médaille mil.; Commdr Ordre nat. du Mérite; Croix de guerre; Croix du Combattant volontaire de la Résistance; Legion of Merit (USA), etc. *Address:* 147 bis rue d'Alésia, 75014 Paris, France. *Telephone:* 1-45-39-96-11. *Fax:* 1-45-39-48-96. *Website:* jcss@noos.fr (Home).

SERVAN-SCHREIBER, Jean-Jacques; French politician, economist and writer; b. 13 Feb. 1924, Paris; s. of Emile Servan-Schreiber and Denise (née Bresard) Servan-Schreiber; four s.; ed Ecole Polytechnique, Paris; joined the Free French Forces of Gen. de Gaulle as fighter pilot 1943 (trained USAF); Foreign Affairs Ed. Le Monde 1948–53; Founder L'Express 1953, Ed. 1953–70; elected and re-elected Pres. Radical Party 1970–79; elected and re-elected Deputy for Nancy 1970–79 and Pres. Region of Lorraine 1975–78; Minister of Reform 1974; Pres. World Centre for Computer Literacy 1981–85; Prof. of Strategic Thinking, Chair. Int. Cttee Carnegie Mellon Univ., Pittsburgh 1985–; Croix de la Valeur mil. *Publications:* Lieutenant en Algérie 1957, Le défi Américain 1967, Le manifeste radical 1970, Le pouvoir régional 1971, Le défi mondial 1981, Le choix des juifs 1988, Passions 1991, Les Fossoyeurs 1993. *Address:* 37 avenue du Roule, 92200 Neuilly-sur-Seine, France.

SERVATIUS, Bernhard, DJur; German lawyer; b. 14 April 1932, Magdeburg; s. of Rudolf Servatius and Maria Servatius; m. Ingeborg Servatius 1985; ed Univs of Fribourg, Hamburg and other univs; lawyer 1959–, now Sr Partner, Dr. Servatius & Partner (legal firm); Sole Partner, Treubesitz GmbH, Hamburg (trust co.); legal adviser to Axel Springer and Springer Publishing Group 1970; Chair. Supervisory Bd Rheinische Merkur GmbH; Chief Rep. of Axel Springer and Acting Chair. of Man. Admin. Verlagshaus Axel Springer 1984; Chair. Supervisory Bd Axel Springer Verlag 1985–; Prof. Hochschule für Musik und Darstellende Kunst 1985–; many other professional and public appts; Hon. DPhil; Bundesverdienstkreuz Erste Klasse. *Address:* Axel Springer Verlag AG, Axel-Springer Strasse 65, 10888 Berlin, Germany. *Telephone:* (30) 259172401 (Office). *Fax:* (30) 259172403 (Office).

ŠEŠELJ, Vojislav, DJur; Serbia and Montenegro (Serbian) politician; b. 11 Nov. 1954, Sarajevo; s. of Nicola Šešelj and Danica Šešelj (née Misita); m. Jadranka Pavlović; two s.; ed Sarajevo Univ.; Docent Sarajevo Univ. 1981–84; Prof. Pristina Univ. 1991–, was persecuted by authorities for nationalistic activities, arrested and sentenced to 8 years' imprisonment 1984, released after 22 months; later was arrested twice 1990, 1994–95; Head of Cetniks (royalists) Movt 1989; Founder and Leader Serbian Radical Party 1990; supported war against Croatia 1991; cand. for presidency of Serbia 1997;

Deputy Prime Minister 1997–2001; worked and lectured in European countries, USA, Canada; indicted by the Int. Criminal Tribunal for the fmr Yugoslavia (ICTY) for crimes against humanity and war crimes Feb. 2003. *Publications:* over 50 books including Political Essence of Militarism and Fascism 1979, Dusk of Illusions 1986, Democracy and Dogma 1987, Debrozovisation of Public Mentality 1990, Destruction of Serbian National Being 1992, Actual Political Challenges 1993, Are We Threatened with Slobotomia 1994, Selected Works 1994. *Address:* Serbian Radical Party, Ohridska str. 1, 11000 Belgrade, Serbia and Montenegro. *Telephone:* (11) 457745 (Home).

SESSIONS, Jefferson Beauregard, III, BA, JD; American politician; b. 24 Dec. 1946, Hybart, Ala; s. of Jefferson Beauregard Sessions and Abbie Sessions (née Powe); m. Mary Montgomery Blackshear 1969; one s. two d.; ed Huntingdon Coll., Montgomery and Univ. of Alabama; admitted to Alabama Bar 1973; Assoc., Guin, Bouldin & Porch, Russellville, Ala 1973–75; Asst US Attorney, US Dept of Justice, Mobile, Ala 1975–77, US Attorney 1981–93; Assoc. Partner Stockman & Bedsole Attorneys, Mobile 1977–81; Partner Stockman, Bedsole & Sessions 1993–94; Attorney-Gen. for Ala 1996; Senator from Ala 1997–; mem. US Attorney-Gen.'s Advisory Cttee 1987–89, Vice-Chair. 1989; mem. Environment and Public Works Cttee, Judiciary Cttee; mem. Bd Trustees, Exec. Cttee Mobile Bay Area Partnership for Youth 1981–; Chair. Advisory Bd Ashland Place United Methodist Church, Mobile 1982; First Vice-Pres. Mobile Lions Club 1993–94; Capt. US Army Reserves 1975–85; mem. ABA, Ala Bar Asscn., Mobile Bar Asscn; US Attorney-Gen.'s Award for significant achievements in the war against drug-trafficking 1992. *Address:* Office of the Senator from Alabama, 493 Senate Russell Office Building, Washington, DC 20510-0001 (Office); 1119 Hillcrest, Xing E, Mobile, AL 36695-4505, USA (Home).

SESSIONS, William S., JD; American government official and judge; b. 27 May 1930, Fort Smith, Ark.; s. of Will A. Sessions and Edith A. Steele; m. Alice June Lewis 1952; three s. one d.; ed Baylor Univ.; called to Texas Bar 1959; Partner, McGregor & Sessions, Waco, Tex. 1959–61; Assoc. Tirey, McLaughlin, Gorin & Tirey, Waco 1961–63; Partner, Haley, Fulbright, Winniford, Sessions & Bice, Waco 1963–69; Chief, Govt Operations Section, Criminal Div. Dept of Justice 1969–71; US Attorney, US Dist Court (Western Dist) Texas, San Antonio 1971–74; US Dist Judge 1974–80, Chief US Dist Judge 1980–87; Dir Fed. Bureau of Investigation (FBI) 1987–93; Partner, Sessions & Sessions, LC 1995–2000, Holland & Knight, LC 2000–; mem. numerous cttees and subcttees; mem. ABA; mem. Bd of Trustees, Nat. Environmental Educ. and Training Foundation Inc. 2001–; Hon. Dir Martin Luther King Jr Fed. Holiday Comm. 1991–93, 1994–; numerous awards. *Publications:* articles in professional journals. *Leisure interests:* climbing, hiking, canoeing. *Address:* Holland & Knight, Suite 100, 2099 Pennsylvania Avenue, NW, Washington, DC 20006; 112 East Pecan, 29th Floor, San Antonio, TX 78205, USA. *Telephone:* (210) 229-3000 (Office). *Fax:* (210) 229-1194 (Office), (202) 955-5564. *E-mail:* wss@sessionslaw.com, wsession@hklaw.com (Office).

SETCH, Terry, DFA; British artist and teacher; b. 11 March 1936, Lewisham, London; s. of Frank Setch and Florence Skeggs; m. Dianne Shaw 1967; one d.; ed Sutton and Cheam School of Art and Slade School of Fine Art; Lecturer, Foundation Dept, Leicester Coll. of Art 1960–64; Sr Lecturer in Fine Art, Cardiff Coll. of Art 1964–2001, in Art History Hayward Gallery, London 1987; works in Tate Gallery and other collections; comm.: mural for restaurant, Nat. Museum of Wales 1993; broadcasts: (BBC TV) Statements 1990, (BBC TV) Wales Arts Awards 1993, (HTV) A Word in Your Eye 1997, (BBC TV) Catalyst 1997, (BBC Radio) Culture Vultures 1997; mem. Royal W of England Acad. 2002–; Welsh Arts Council Painting Award 1971, Welsh Arts Council Major Artist Award 1978, John Moores Exhbn (Third Prize) 1985, Athena Awards (shortlist prizewinner) 1988. *TV includes:* Statements, BBC 2 Wales 1990, A Word in Your Eye, HTV Wales 1997, Catalyst, BBC 1 Wales 1997, Painting the Dragon, BBC Wales 2000. *Radio:* Art Work: Terry Setch, BBC Radio 3 2000. *Exhibitions include:* Inner Image, Grabowski Gallery, London 1964, Structure 66, Welsh Arts Council, Cardiff 1966, Young Britain ICA Exhbn toured to New York and Los Angeles 1967, John Moores 6, Walker Art Gallery, Liverpool 1967, Multiples, Whitechapel Art Gallery, London 1971, Artist in Nat. Parks, Victoria and Albert Museum, London 1988–89, Images of Paradise, Survival Int. 1989, Tree of Life, South Bank Centre, London 1989–90, Shared Earth (Anglo-Soviet landscapes) (tour) 1991–92, Innovation and Tradition: Recent Painting in Britain, Tate Gallery, London 1993, Royal Acad. of Arts Summer Exhbn 1993, 1995, 1996, Disclosures, tour Wales 1995, Nat. Museum of Wales, Cardiff and Barcelona 1996, Contemporary British Landscape, Flowers East, London 1999, Node 5×5, Northern Gallery for Contemporary Art, Sunderland 1999, Painting the Dragon, Nat. Museums and Galleries of Wales Cardiff 2000, Welsh Artists Talking, Nat. Museums and Galleries of Wales, Cardiff 2000, Broken Ground, Tate Britain 2003; solo exhbns in Cardiff, Penarth, London 1992, Edin. 1993, Fishguard, London, 1995, Penarth 1997, Cardiff 2000, Retrospective exhbn shown in Bristol RWA, Cardiff, Swansea, Glynn Vivian Art Gallery 2001, Collins Gallery, Glasgow, Wrexham Arts Centre 2002. *Publications:* New Work by Terry Setch 1992, Terry Setch: a Retrospective 2001. *Address:* 111 Plymouth Road, Penarth, Vale of Glamorgan, CF64 5DF, Wales. *Telephone:* (29) 2071-2113 (Home). *Fax:* (29) 2071-2113 (Home). *E-mail:* setch@terrysetch.co.uk (Home). *Website:* www.terrysetch.co.uk (Home).

SETCHELL, David Lloyd, MA, FCA; British chartered accountant; b. 16 April 1937, Anston, Yorks.; s. of Raymond Setchell and Phyllis Jane Lloyd; m.

Muriel Mary Davies 1962; one s. one d.; ed Woodhouse Grammar School and Jesus Coll., Cambridge; Peat Marwick 1960–64; Shawinigan Ltd 1964–71; Vice-Pres. Gulf Oil Chemicals (Europe) 1971–82; Man. Dir Gulf Oil (GB) Ltd 1982–98; Pres. Inst. of Petroleum 1996–98, Oil Industries Club 1993–95; Council mem. Univ. of Gloucester 1994–, Chair. 2002–; Gov. Cheltenham Coll. 1998–; Dir Cheltenham Arts Festivals 1994–, RAF Personnel and Training Command Bd. *Leisure interests:* golf, music, theatre. *Address:* South Hayes, Sandy Lane Road, Cheltenham, Glos., GL53 9DE, England. *Telephone:* (1242) 571390.

SETH, Vikram, CBE, PhD; Indian author; b. 1952, Calcutta; s. of Premnath Seth and Leila Seth; ed Doon School, India, Tonbridge School, UK, Corpus Christi Coll., Oxford, Stanford Univ., USA; Hon. Fellow Corpus Christi Coll., Oxford 1994; W.H. Smith Literary Prize 1994, Commonwealth Writers' Prize 1994; Chevalier des Arts et des Lettres 2001. *Publications:* The Golden Gate: A Novel in Verse, From Heaven Lake: Travels Through Sinkiang and Tibet, A Suitable Boy (novel) 1993, Arion and the Dolphin (libretto) 1994, Beastly Tales (animal fables) 1994, An Equal Music (novel) 1999; several vols of poetry. *Leisure interests:* Chinese calligraphy, music, swimming. *Address:* c/o Curtis Brown (Giles Gordon), 37 Queensferry Street, Edinburgh, EH2 4QS, Scotland. *Telephone:* (131) 225-1286 (Office). *Fax:* (131) 225-1290 (Office).

SETHNESS, Charles Olin, AB, MBA; American government official, financial executive, university administrator and investment banker; b. 24 Feb. 1941, Evanston, Ill.; s. of C. Olin Sethness and Alison Louise Burge; ed New Trier High School, Princeton Univ. and Harvard Business School; Sr Credit Analyst, American Nat. Bank and Trust Co. of Chicago 1963–64; Research Asst Harvard Business School 1966–67; with Morgan Stanley & Co. 1967–73, 1975–81; Vice-Pres. 1972–73, Man. Dir 1975–81; Man. Morgan & Cie Int. SA, Paris 1971–73; Exec. Dir World Bank Group and Special Asst to Sec. of Treasury 1973–75; Assoc. Dean for External Relations, Harvard Business School, Boston 1981–85; Asst Sec. of the Treasury for Domestic Finance 1985–88; Dir Capital Markets Dept Int. Finance Corpn 1988–89; Chief Financial Officer Inter-American Devt Bank 1990–; Alexander Hamilton Medal, US Treasury Dept 1988. *Leisure interests:* Washington Inst. of Foreign Affairs, Washington Recorder Soc. *Address:* 7411 Hallcrest Drive, McLean, VA 22102, USA (Home); 1300 New York Avenue NW, Washington, DC 20577 (Office). *Telephone:* (202) 623-2201 (Office); (703) 356-0778 (Home). *Fax:* (202) 623-2350 (Office). *E-mail:* charlesse@iadb.org (Office); chucksethness@aol.com (Home). *Website:* www.iadb.org (Office).

SEVAN, Benon V., MA; Cypriot international organization official; b. 18 Dec. 1937; m.; one d.; ed Melkonian Educational Inst. and Columbia Coll. and School of Int. and Public Affairs, Columbia Univ., New York, USA; joined UN 1965; with Dept of Public Information 1965–66; with Secr. of Special Cttee on Decolonization 1966–68; served UN in W Irian (Irian Jaya), Indonesia 1968–72; with Secr. of UN Econ. and Social Council 1973–88; Dir and Sr Political Adviser to Rep. of Sec.-Gen. on Settlement of Situation relating to Afghanistan 1988–89; Personal Rep. of Sec.-Gen. in Afghanistan and Pakistan 1989–92; Rep. of Sec.-Gen. on Implementation of Geneva Accords on Afghanistan 1990–92; Dir Office for Co-ordination of UN Humanitarian and Econ. Assistance Programmes in Afghanistan 1991–92; Asst Sec.-Gen. Dept of Political Affairs 1992–94; Asst Sec.-Gen. for Conf. and Support Services 1994–97; Asst Sec.-Gen. Office of Security Co-ordination 1994–2002; Exec. Dir Office of Iraq Programme 1997–. *Address:* Office of the Iraq Programme, UN, United Nations Plaza, New York, NY 10017, USA (Office).

SEVERIN, (Giles) Tim, MA, DLitt; British traveller and author; b. 25 Sept. 1940; s. of Maurice Watkins and Inge Severin; m. Dorothy Virginia Sherman 1966 (divorced 1979); one d.; ed Tonbridge School, Keble Coll., Oxford; Commonwealth Fellow, USA 1964–66; expeditions: led motorcycle team along Marco Polo's route 1961, canoe and launch down River Mississippi 1965, Brendan Voyage from W Ireland to N America 1977, Sindbad Voyage from Oman to China 1980–81, Jason Voyage from Greece to Soviet Georgia 1984, Ulysses Voyage, Troy to Ithaca 1985, Crusade: on horseback from Belgium to Jerusalem 1987–88, Travels on horseback in Mongolia 1990, China Voyage: bamboo sailing raft Hong Kong-Japan-Pacific 1993, Spice Islands Voyage in Moluccas, E Indonesia 1996, Pacific travels in search of Moby Dick 1998, Latin America travels seeking Robinson Crusoe sources 2000; Hon. DLitt (Dublin) 1997. *Publications:* Tracking Marco Polo 1964, Explorers of the Mississippi 1967, The Golden Antilles 1970, The African Adventure 1973, Vanishing Primitive Man 1973, The Oriental Adventure 1976, The Brendan Voyage 1978, The Sindbad Voyage 1982, The Jason Voyage 1984, The Ulysses Voyage 1987, Crusader 1989, In Search of Genghis Khan 1991, The China Voyage 1994, The Spice Islands Voyage 1997, In Search of Moby Dick 1999, Seeking Robinson Crusoe 2002. *Address:* Inchy Bridge, Timoleague, Co. Cork, Ireland. *Telephone:* (23) 46127. *Fax:* (23) 46233. *E-mail:* timsev@eircom.net (Home). *Website:* www.timseverin.net (Home).

SEVERINO, Rodolfo Certeza, Jr, MA; Philippine diplomatist; b. 22 April 1936, Manila; m. Rowena V. Romero; ed Ateneo de Manila Univ., Johns Hopkins Univ. School of Advanced Int. Studies, Washington, DC; Assoc. Ed. Manor Press Inc. 1956–59, Philippine Inst. 1957–59, Marketing Horizons 1961–64; with Operation Brotherhood, Laos 1959–61; special Asst to Senator Raul S. Manglapus, Philippine Senate 1961–64; information Asst UN Information Centre, Manila 1964–65; Third, then Second and First Sec. Embassy, Washington, DC 1967–74; special Asst to Under-Sec. of Foreign Affairs 1974–76, Under-Sec. 1992–97; Chargé d'Affaires Embassy, Beijing 1976–78;

Consul-Gen., Houston, Texas 1979–86; Asst Sec. for Asian and Pacific Affairs 1986–88; Amb. to Malaysia 1988–92; Sec.-Gen. ASEAN 1997–2003; adviser to Cambodian Govt Jan.–June 2002; holds teaching post at Asian Inst. of Man., Manila 2003–; Order of Sikatuna, rank of Datu (Philippines) 1997; Royal Award (Cambodia) 2002. *Publications include:* ASEAN Faces the Future 2001. *Address:* c/o Department of Foreign Affairs, DFA Building, 2330 Roxas Boulevard, Pasay City, Metro Manila 12110, The Philippines.

SEVÓN, Leif, LLM; Finnish judge; b. 31 Oct. 1941, Helsingfors; s. of Enzio Sevón and Ulla Sevón; m. (divorced); one s. one d.; ed Univ. of Helsinki; Asst Univ. of Helsinki 1966–71, Asst Prof. 1971–74; Counsellor of Legislation, Ministry of Justice 1973–78; Sr Judge, Chamber Pres. City Court of Helsinki 1979–80; Dir of Legislation, Ministry of Justice 1980–86, Dir-Gen. Dept of Legislation 1986–91; Judge, Supreme Court of Justice 1991; Counsellor, Dept of Trade, Ministry of Foreign Affairs 1991–92; Pres. EFTA Court 1994; Judge, Court of Justice of European Communities 1995–2002; Pres. Supreme Court of Finland 2002–; Hon. LLD (Stockholm) 1999, (Helsinki) 2000. *Publications:* books, articles and translations. *Address:* The Supreme Court of Finland, Pohjoisesplanadi 3, 00170 Helsinki, Finland (Office). *Telephone:* (9) 12381 (Office).

SEVOSTYANOV, Grigory Nikolayevich; Russian historian; b. 5 April 1916; m.; one s.; ed Novocherkassk Polytech. Inst.; teacher Novocherkassk Polytech. Inst. 1940–41; Asst Deputy Chair. Govt Belorussian SSR 1944–45; Attaché Ministry of Foreign Affairs 1947; Jr, Sr researcher, head of div. Inst. of History USSR Acad. of Sciences 1950–68; head of div., head of Dept Inst. of Comprehensive History USSR Acad. of Sciences 1968–88; chief researcher 1988–; mem. USSR (now Russian) Acad. of Sciences 1987; research in history of America and int. relations, problems of history of World War II, workers' movt in USA; USSR State Prize. *Publications:* Policy of Great States in the Far East on the eve of World War II 1961, USA and France in wartime 1939–45: History of International Relations 1974, History of USA 1983–87; and other books and articles. *Address:* Institute of Comprehensive History, Russian Academy of Sciences, Leninsky pr. 32A, 117334 Moscow, Russia. *Telephone:* (095) 938-19-11 (Office); (095) 928-86-07 (Home).

SEWARD, George Chester, LLB; American lawyer; b. 4 Aug. 1910, Omaha, Neb.; s. of George F. Seward and Ada L. Rugh; m. Carroll F. McKay 1936 (died 1991); two s. two d.; ed Male High School, Louisville, Ky and Univ. of Virginia; with Shearman & Sterling, New York 1936–53, Seward & Kissel (renamed Seward & Kissel LLP), New York, Washington DC 1953–; Dir Witherbee Sherman Corpn 1952–66 (Pres. 1964–66), Howmet Corpn 1955–75, Chas. P. Young Co. 1965–72, Howmedica, Inc. 1970–72; Trustee Benson Iron Ore Trust 1969–80; Founder and Hon. Pres. Business Law Section of Int. Bar Asscn; Hon. Life Pres. and life mem. Council of Int. Bar Asscn; Chair. Cttee on Corporate Laws of ABA 1952–58, American Bar Foundation Cttee on Model Business Corpn Acts 1956–65, Banking Cttee of ABA 1960–61; life mem. Council of Section of Business Law of ABA (Chair. 1958–59); mem. House of Dels., ABA 1959, 1963–74, Jt Cttee on Continuing Legal Educ. of the American Law Inst. and ABA 1965–76, Univ. of Va Arts and Sciences Council 1984–93 (Pres. 1991–93), NY Stock Exchange Legal Advisory Cttee 1984–87; Fellow American Bar Foundation; mem. American Law Inst., Asscn of Bar of City of New York, NY State, Ky, Va and DC Bar Asscns; Trustee Edwin Gould Foundation for Children 1955–96, The Nature Conservancy Eastern Long Island, NY 1975–88, NY Genealogical and Biographical Soc.; George Seward Lecture series sponsored by Int. Bar Asscn, London (Hon. Life Pres.). *Publications:* Basic Corporate Practice, Seward and Related Families, co-author Model Business Corporation Act Annotated; ed. We Remember Carroll. *Address:* Seward & Kissel LLP, 1 Battery Park Plaza, New York, NY 10004 (Office); 48 Greenacres Avenue, Scarsdale, NY 10583, USA (Home); International Bar Association, 271 Regent Street, London, W1R 7PA, England. *Telephone:* (212) 574-1200 (Office).

SEWELL, Brian; British art historian and critic; art critic for Evening Standard; British Press Awards Critic of the Year 1988, Arts Journalist of the Year 1994, Hawthornden Prize for Art Criticism 1995. *Publications:* South from Ephesus 1988, The Reviews that Caused the Rumpus 1994, An Alphabet of Villains 1995. *Address:* The Evening Standard, Northcliffe House, 2 Derry Street, London, W8 5EE, England. *Telephone:* (20) 7938-6000. *Fax:* (20) 7937-2648.

SEWELL, Rufus Frederick; British actor; b. 29 Oct. 1967; s. of the late Bill Sewell; London Critics Circle Best Newcomer 1992, Broadway Theatre World Award 1995. *Stage appearances include:* Royal Hunt of the Sun, Comedians, The Lost Domain, Peter and the Captain, Pride and Prejudice, The Government Inspector, The Seagull, As You Like It, Making it Better, Arcadia, Translations, Rat in the Skull, Macbeth, Luther. *Television appearances include:* The Last Romantics, Gone to Seed, Middlemarch, Dirty Something, Citizen Locke, Cold Comfort Farm, Henry IV. *Film appearances include:* Twenty-One, Dirty Weekend, A Man of No Importance, Carrington, Victory, Hamlet, The Woodlanders, The Honest Courtesan, Martha Meet Frank, Daniel and Laurence, Illuminata, Dark City, Bless the Child, A Knight's Tale, The Extremists. *Address:* c/o Julian Belfrage Associates, 46 Albemarle Street, London, W1X 4PP, England. *Telephone:* (20) 7491-4400. *Fax:* (20) 7493-5460.

SEWERYN, Andrzej; Polish actor and theatre director; b. 25 April 1946, Heilbronn; m.; two s. one d.; ed State Higher School of Drama, Warsaw; actor Athenaeum Theatre, Warsaw 1968–82, Peter Brooks Group 1984–88, perm. mem. Comédie Française, Paris 1993–; co-operation with film, TV and radio;

mem. SPATiF (Asscn of Polish Theatre and Film Actors) 1969–82; Chevalier des Arts et des Lettes 1995, Kt's Cross, Order of Polonia Restituta 1997, Ordre Nat. du Mérite 1999; Prize Berlin Int. Film Festival for Conductor 1979, Best Actor, French Film Awards for Unpleasant Man 1996, Prize of Le Syndicat professionnel de la Critique dramatique et musicale de France 1996, Polish TV Award, Polish Film Festival, Gdansk 2000. *Films:* Zenon in The Border 1977, Rościszewski in Without Anaesthetic 1978, Ksiądz in The Brute 1979, Kung-fu 1979, Conductor 1979, Mahabharata 1988, French Revolution 1989, Schindler's List 1994, Journey to the East 1994, Total Eclipse 1995, Unpleasant Man 1996, With Fire and Sword 1998, Billboard 1998, The Last Foray in Lithuania 1999, Primate 2000, Revenge 2002. *Theatre:* (actor) leading roles in Don Carlos, Peer Gynt, Don Juan; (dir) Le Mariage forcé by Molière, Comédie Française 1999, Le Mal court by Jacques Audiberti, Comédie Française 2000, Tartuffe 2002. *Television:* Kliefhorn in Polish Roads (TV series) 1977, Marek in On the Silver Globe 1976–79 (TV series), Bukacki in Połaniecki's Family 1977 (TV series), Roman in Roman and Magda 1979 (TV series); numerous other roles on TV. *Address:* Comédie Française, Place Colette, 75001 Paris, France. *Telephone:* 1-44-58-14-00. *Fax:* 1-44-58-14-50.

SEXTON, John, MA, JD; American university president and lawyer; b. 1944, Brooklyn; m. Lisa Goldberg; one s. one d.; ed Fordham Coll., Fordham Univ., Harvard Law School; Law Clerk, US Court of Appeals and US Supreme Court 1979–81; joined Law Faculty, New York Univ. (NYU) 1981, Dean 1988–, later Benjamin Butler Prof. of Law, Pres. NYU May 2002–; fmr Pres. American Asscn of Law Schools; Fellow, American Acad. of Arts and Sciences. *Publications:* Redefining the Supreme Court's Role: A Theory of Managing the Federal Court System; Procedure: Cases and Materials (jtly). *Address:* Office of the President, New York University, 70 Washington Square South, New York, NY 10012, USA (Office). *Telephone:* (212) 998-2345 (Office). *Fax:* (212) 995-3679 (Office). *Website:* www.nyu.edu (Office).

SEXWALE, (Gabriel) Tokyo; South African politician; b. 5 March 1953; s. of Frank Sexwale; m. Judy Sexwale; three c.; imprisoned for 13 years on Robben Island for guerrilla activities; mem. ANC Mil. Wing; Chair. ANC, Witwatersrand Region, Transvaal Prov.; Premier Pretoria-Witwatersrand-Vereeniging Prov. (now Gauteng) 1994–97; mem ANC Nat. Exec. Cttee 1991–. *Address:* Private Bag X61, Marshalltown 2107, South Africa.

SEYBOU, Brig. Ali; Niger fmr Head of State and army officer; fmr army chief of staff; mem. Supreme Mil. Council; Pres. of Niger 1987–93. *Address:* c/o Office of the President, Niamey, Niger.

SEYDOUX FORNIER de CLAUSONNE, Jérôme; French business executive; b. 21 Sept. 1934, Paris; s. of René Seydoux Fornier de Clausonne and Geneviève Schlumberger; m. 1st (divorced); three s. one d.; m. 2nd Sophie Desserteaux-Bessis 1988; one s.; ed Lycées Montaigne, Louis-le-Grand and Buffon; Financial Analyst Istel, Lepercq and Co. Inc. NY 1962–63; sleeping partner Bank of Neuflize, Schlumberger, Mallet 1964, Partner 1966, mem. Bd Dirs. 1969–70; admin. Schlumberger Ltd 1969, Exec. Vice Pres. 1970, Dir Gen. 1975–76; admin. Compagnie Deutsch 1964–, Danone (fmrly BSN) 1973–; Pres. Pricel 1976; Pres. Chargeurs 1980–96, now Vice-Pres., Dir-Gen.; Pres. Admin. Council of France 5 1986; Pres., Dir-Gen. Pathé Palace (fmrly Pathé Cinema) 1991–2000, later Pres., Dir-Gen. Pathé, Vice-Pres. Supervisory Cttee 2000; Vice-Pres. Advisory Bd, Mont-Blanc Co. 2000–; Chair. BSkyB 1998–99; owner Libération newspaper. *Leisure interests:* skiing, golf. *Address:* Pathé, 5 rue François 1er, 75008 Paris, France.

SEYDOUX FORNIER de CLAUSONNE, Nicolas Pierre, LenD, L. EN SC.ECON.; French business executive; b. 16 July 1939, Paris; s. of René Seydoux Fornier de Clausonne and Geneviève Schlumberger; m. Anne-Marie Cahen-Salvador 1964; two c.; ed Lycée Buffon, Faculté de Droit, Paris, New York Business School and Inst. d'Etudes Politiques, Paris; Head of legal service, Cie Int. pour l'Informatique, Paris 1967–70; Financial Analyst, Morgan, Stanley & Co. Inc. New York 1970–71, Morgan & Cie Int. SA Paris 1971–74; Vice-Pres.-Dir-Gen. Société Gaumont 1974, Pres.-Dir-Gen. 1975–; Pres. Féd. Nat. des Distributeurs de Films 1988–2001, Bureau de liaison des industries cinématographiques (BLIC) 2000; Officier Légion d'honneur. *Leisure interests:* vintage cars, skiing. *Address:* Gaumont, 30 avenue Charles de Gaulle, 92200 Neuilly-sur-Seine (Office); 5 place du Palais-Bourbon, 75007 Paris, France (Home).

SEYMOUR, Lynn, CBE; Canadian ballet dancer; b. 8 March 1939, Wainwright, Alberta; d. of E. V. Springett; m. 1st Colin Jones 1963 (divorced 1974); three s.; m. 2nd Philip Pace 1974; m. 3rd Vanya Hackel 1983 (divorced 1988); ed Royal Ballet School; graduated into Royal Ballet 1957; promoted to Soloist rank 1958, to Prin. 1958; joined Deutsche Oper, Berlin 1966; Guest Artist, Royal Ballet 1970–78; Artistic Dir of Ballet Bayerische Staatsoper 1979–80; Guest Artist with other cos. incl. Alvin Ailey; Evening Standard Drama Award 1977. *Ballets:* The Burrow 1958, Swan Lake 1958, Giselle 1958, The Invitation 1960, The Two Pigeons 1961, Symphony 1963, Romeo and Juliet 1964, Anastasia 1966, Dances at a Gathering, The Concert, The Seven Deadly Sins, Flowers 1972, Shukumei, The Four Seasons 1975, Side Show, Rituals 1975, Manon Lescaut 1976, A Month in the Country 1976, Mayerling 1978, Manon 1978, Choreography for Rashomon 1976, The Court of Love 1977, Intimate Letters 1978, Mae and Polly, Boreas, Tattooed Lady, Wolfy, the Ballet Rambert 1987. *Publication:* Lynn: Leaps and Boundaries (autobiog. with Paul Gardner) 1984.

SEYPIDIN AZE; Chinese politician; b. 1916, Artush, Xinjiang; ed Cen. Asia Univ., Moscow; Leader of Uighur Uprisings 1933, 1944; participant in armed rebellion and establishment of E Turkestan Repub. 1944; Minister of Educ., E Turkistan Repub. 1945; Deputy Chair. Xinjiang Uighur People's Govt 1949–54, Chair. 1955–68; Deputy Commdr Xinjiang Uighur Mil. Region, PLA 1949; Second Sec. CCP Xinjiang Uighur 1956–68; Alt. mem. 8th Cen. Cttee of CCP 1956; Pres. Xinjiang Uighur Univ. 1964; Vice-Chair. Xinjiang Uighur Revolutionary Cttee 1968, Chair. 1972–78; mem. 9th Cen. Cttee of CCP 1969; Second Sec. CCP Xinjiang Uighur 1971, First Sec. 1973–78; Alt. mem. Politburo, 10th Cen. Cttee of CCP 1973, 1975–78; First Political Commissar Xinjiang Uighur Mil. Region, PLA 1974–78; Chair. Presidium NPC 1975; Alt. mem. Politburo, 11th Cen. Cttee of CCP 1976; Exec. Chair. Presidium 5th NPC; Vice-Chair. Cttee 5th NPC 1978–83; Vice-Chair. Standing Cttee 6th NPC 1983–88, 7th NPC 1988; Exec. Chair. Presidium 6th NPC 1986–88, 7th NPC 1988; Pres. China-Pakistan Friendship Assçn; Hon. Chair. China Society for Study of Uygur History and Culture; Hon. Pres. Minority Writers' Soc. 1985–, Minority Literature Foundation 1986; mem. 12th CCP Cen. Cttee 1982–87, 13th Cen. Cttee 1987–92, Presidium of 14th CCP Nat. Congress 1992–97; Vice-Chair. 8th Nat. Cttee CPPCC 1993–98. *Address:* 19 Xi Jiaomin Xiang, Xicheng District, People's Republic of China.

SEZER, Ahmet Necdet, BA; Turkish head of state and lawyer; b. 13 Sept. 1941, Afyon; m.; three c.; ed Univ. of Ankara; mil. service Land Forces Acad.; judge, Ankara, then Dicle; Supervisory Judge High Court of Appeal, Ankara; mem. High Court of Appeal 1983, Constitutional Court 1988–2000, Chief Justice 1998–2000; Pres. of Turkey May 2000–. *Address:* Office of the President, Cumhurbaşkanlığı, Köşku, Çankaya, Ankara, Turkey. *Telephone:* (312) 4685030. *Fax:* (312) 4271330. *E-mail:* cankaya@tccb.gov.tr (Office). *Website:* www.cankaya.gov.tr (Office).

SEZGIN, Ismet; Turkish politician; b. 1928, Aydln; m.; two c.; ed Izmir School of Economy and Trade; Founder-mem. True Path Party (DYP); deputy from Aydın 1961–80; fmr Minister of Youth and Sports and of Finance; Minister of the Interior 1991–93, of Nat. Defence and Deputy Prime Minister 1997–98.

SFAR, Rachid; Tunisian politician; b. 11 Sept. 1933, Mahdia; ed Lycée des Garçons, Sfax, Inst. de Hautes Etudes, Tunis and Ecole Nat. des Impôts, Paris; Inspector of Taxes 1960; Dir-Gen. Régie Nat. des Tabacs et Allumettes (RNTA) 1965; Dir of Taxation, Ministry of Finance 1969; Sec.-Gen. Ministry of Educ. 1971–73, Ministry of Finance 1973–77; Minister of Mines and Energy 1977–78, of Defence 1978–80, of Health 1980–83, of Nat. Economy 1983–86, of Finance and Economy April–July 1986; Prime Minister 1986–87; Deputy to Nat. Ass. 1979–; Pres. Chamber of Deputies 1988; mem. Cen. Cttee and Politburo, Parti Socialiste Destourien 1979–; Amb. to EEC 1989–92; Grand Cordon, Ordre de l'Indépendance; Grand Officier, Ordre de la République. *Address:* 278 avenue de Tervuren, 1150 Brussels, Belgium. *Telephone:* (2) 771-73-95.

SGORLON, Carlo Pietro Antonio, PhD; Italian novelist and journalist; b. 26 July 1930, Cassacco, Udine; s. of Antonio Sgorlon and Livia Sgorlon; m. Edda Agarinis 1961; ed Liceo Classico di Udine, Univs of Pisa and Munich; secondary school teacher 1953–79; journalist 1969–; Cavaliere di Gran Croce della Repubblica; Accademico pontificio; Enna Prize 1968, Rapallo Prize 1968, Supercampiello Prizes 1973 and 1983, Vallombrosa Prize 1983, Soroptomist Prize 1983, Strega Prize 1985, Hemingway Prize 1987, Palme D'Oro Prize 1988, Nonino Prize 1989, Campano D'Oro Prize 1989, Fiuggi Prize 1989, Un Libro per l'Avvenire Prize 1989, Tascabile S. Benedetto del Tronto Prize 1989, Napoli Prize 1989, Latina Prize 1989, Isola d'Elba Prize 1997, Ennio Flaiano Prize 1997, Rhegium Prize 1997, S. Vidal (Venice) 1999, Libraio Prize (Padua) Fregene Prize 2001, Frontino Prize 2001. *Publications:* Kafka narratore 1961, La Poltrona 1968, Elsa Morante 1972, Il Trono di Legno 1973, Regina di Saba 1975, Gli dei torneranno 1977, La Luna Color Ametista 1978, La Carrozza di Rame 1979, La Contrada 1981, La Conchiglia di Anataj 1983, L'Armata dei Fiumi Perduti 1985, Sette Veli 1986, L'Ultima Valle 1987, Il Caldèras 1988, I Racconti della Terra di Canaan 1989, La Fontana di Lorena 1990, Il Patriarcato della Luna 1991, La Foiba Grande 1992, Il Guaritore 1993, Il Regno dell'Uomo 1994. Il Costruttore 1995, La Malga di Sîr 1997, Il Processo di Tolosa 1998, Il Filo di Seta 1999, La Tredicesima Notte 2001, L'Uomo di Praga 2003. *Leisure interests:* painting, carpentry, walking. *Address:* Via Micesio 15, Udine CAP 33100, Italy. *Telephone:* (0432) 294140. *Fax:* (0432) 294140.

SGOUROS, Dimitris; Greek concert pianist; b. 30 Aug. 1969, Athens; s. of Sotirios Sgouros and Marianthi Sgouros; ed Univ. of Athens, Athens Conservatory of Music, Univ. of Maryland, USA, St. Peter's Coll., Oxford and RAM, London; debut (aged 7) Piraeus 1977; numerous concerts in Europe since 1980; solo piano recital (aged 11) to audience of 4,000 at Hirrodus of Atticus Theatre of Athens 1981; first US appearance (aged 12), with Nat. Symphony Orchestra of Washington, Carnegie Hall, New York 1982; appeared at Prague Spring Festival with Sir Charles Mackeras and the Czech Philharmonic Orchestra playing Beethoven's Piano Concerto No. 4 1986; played twelve different piano concertos in six nights with Singapore Symphony Orchestra, Sgouros Festival, Singapore 1990; has played in all the major cities and concert houses and on all the major radio and TV stations around the world; repertoire of 45 piano concertos; Acad. of Athens Award 1982, LA 1984, Gold Medal, Athens Conservatory 1984, Leonardo da Vinci Int. Prize and other prizes. *Recordings include:* works by Schumann, Brahms, Rachmaninov, Tchaikovsky, Liszt, Mozart and Chopin with the Berlin Philharmonic, London Philharmonic and Sofia Philharmonic Orchestras and the Radio Orchestra of Slovenia. *Leisure interests:* mathematics, conducting opera, languages. *Address:* Sahturi 25, 18535 Piraeus (Office); Tompazi 28, 18537 Piraeus, Greece (Home). *Telephone:* (1) 8959778. *Fax:* (1) 8956477 (Home); (1) 4538737. *E-mail:* info@sgouros-pianist.com (Office). *Website:* www.sgouros-pianist.com, www.sgourosmp3.com (Office).

SHAATH, Nabil A., DJur, DEcon; Palestinian politician, diplomatist, consultant and academic; b. 1938, Safad; ed Univ. of Pa Wharton School of Business, USA; fmr Business School Prof., taught Finance and Econs, Univ. of Pa, USA 1961–65, academic positions at Univs of Cairo, Alexandria and Beirut; consultant to several Arab govts, in Org. of Shuaiab industrial zone, Kuwait, power sector in Saudi Arabia, public transportation in Gulf Area; est. Eng and Man. Inst. and Arab Centre for Admin. Devt in Beirut, Cairo and 14 brs in other Arab countries training thousands of mans; mem. Fatah Cen. Cttee, del. to Middle E Peace Conf., Madrid 1991; mem. PLO–Israel peace negotiations, Oslo, Norway and Washington, DC; First Head of PLO Del. to UN, Adviser to Yasser Arafat, wrote his speech to UN Gen. Ass. 1974; Palestinian Authority Minister of Planning and Int. Co-operation 1994–; elected to Palestinian Legis. Council, Rep. of Khan Younis, Gaza Strip 1996–; Rep. of Palestine to world media confs, including World Econ. Forum. *Address:* Ministry of Planning and International Co-operation, Ramallah, Palestinian Autonomous Areas (Office). *Telephone:* 2-5747045 (Office). *Fax:* 2-5747046 (Office). *E-mail:* mopic@gov.ps (Office). *Website:* www.mopic.gov .ps (Office).

SHABANGU, Albert H. N., MA; Swazi politician and teacher; b. 23 March 1944, Hlathikhulu; s. of Lovela Shabangu and Mlambile Alice Shabangu (née Mamba); m. Minah Nomsa Dlamini 1976; two s. two d.; ed Univ. of Leeds, William Pitcher Coll.; teacher, then head teacher 1971–91; MP 1991–, also Minister, fmrly responsible for Transport and Communications, Labour and Public Service, Econ. Planning and Devt, Minister for Foreign Affairs and Trade 1998–2001, of Housing and Urban Devt 2001–; Pres. Swaziland Nat. Assçn of Teachers 1972–91; Chief Counsellor Order of King Sobhuza II. *Leisure interests:* athletics, soccer, boxing, choral music. *Address:* c/o Ministry of Housing and Urban Development, P.O. Box 1832, Mbabane, Swaziland. *Telephone:* 4041739. *Fax:* 4045290. *E-mail:* minhouse@realnet.co.sz. *Website:* www.housing.gov.sz.

SHABDURASULOV, Igor Vladimirovich; Russian civil servant; b. 3 Oct. 1957, Tashkent; m.; three c.; ed Moscow State Univ.; Head, UNESCO Project Great Silk Way, Russian Acad. of Sciences 1983–86; on staff Div. of Science, Culture and Educ., Russian Govt; mem., Admin. of Russian Presidency, then Head, Dept of Culture, Russian Govt 1993–94; Head, Dept of Culture and Information, Russian Govt 1994–98; Deputy Head, Admin. of Russian Presidency, Head Group of Speech Writers April–Sept. 1998; Dir-Gen. Russian Public TV 1998–99; Deputy Head Admin. of Russian Presidency 1999–2000; Pres. Triumph Fund 2000–; Chair. Bd of Dirs TV-6 Co. March–May 2001. *Address:* Triumph Fund, Povarskaya str. 8/1, 102069 Moscow, Russia. *Telephone:* (095) 916-54-96 (Office).

SHAFAREVICH, Igor Rostislavovich, DR.PHYS.-MATH.SC.; Russian mathematician; b. 3 June 1923, Zhitomir; m.; two c.; ed Moscow Univ.; Research Officer Moscow Math. Inst. 1943–44; staff mem. Faculty of Mechanics and Math., Moscow Univ. 1944–52; Prof. Moscow Univ. 1953–75 (dismissed for dissident activities); lecturer, Head of Dept, V. Steklov Math. Inst. 1960–; Corresp. mem. USSR (now Russian) Acad. of Sciences 1958, mem. 1991; mem. Bd Moscow Math. Soc. 1964, Pres. 1970–74; mem. USSR Human Rights Cttee; mem. Political Council, Nat. Salvation Front 1992; Hon. mem. US Acad. of Sciences, Acad. Leopoldina, American Acad. of Arts and Sciences, Royal Soc., London; Dr hc (Paris); Lenin Prize 1959, Heinemann Prize, Göttingen Acad. of Sciences 1975. *Publications include:* Has Russia a Future? and 'Socialism' in Solzhenitsyn's From Under the Rubble, Socialism as a Phenomenon in Global History 1977, Russophobia 1990. *Address:* c/o V. Steklov Mathematical Institute, Ul. Gubkina 8, 117966 Moscow, Russia. *Telephone:* (095) 135-25-49 (Office); (095) 135-13-47 (Home).

SHAFEI, Col Hussein Mahmoud El–; Egyptian politician and army officer; b. 8 Feb. 1918, Tanta; s. of Mahmoud El-Shafei; m. Magda Gabr 1948; two s. one d.; ed Mil. Coll., Cairo; commissioned as 2nd Lt 1938; took part in Palestine hostilities 1948; graduated from Staff Officers' Coll. 1953 and apptd Officer-in-Charge Cavalry Corps; Minister of War and Marine 1954, of Social Affairs (Egypt) 1954–58; Minister of Labour and Social Affairs, UAR 1958–61; Vice-Pres. of UAR and Minister of Social Affairs and Waqfs 1961–62; mem. Presidency Council 1962–64; Vice-Pres. of UAR (Egypt) 1964–67, 1970–75; Vice-Pres. and Minister of Religious Institutions (Waqfs) 1967–70; Pres. Egyptian del. to OAU Summit Conf. 1973–74; participated in preparing constitution of fed. between Egypt, Syria and Libya. *Leisure interests:* riding, tennis, swimming, drawing.

SHAFFER, Sir Peter Levin, Kt, CBE, FRSL; British playwright; b. 15 May 1926, Liverpool; s. of Jack Shaffer and Reka Shaffer (née Fredman); ed St Paul's School, London and Trinity Coll., Cambridge; with Acquisitions Dept New York Library 1951; returned to England 1954; with Symphonic Music Dept Boosey and Hawkes 1954; Literary Critic, Truth 1956–57, Music Critic Time and Tide 1957; playwright 1957–; Cameron Mackintosh Prof. of Contemporary Theatre, St Catherine's Coll. Oxford 1994–95; mem. European Acad., Yuste 1998–; Hon. DLitt (Bath) 1992, (St Andrews) 1999; New York Drama Critics Circle Award 1959–60 (Five Finger Exercise); Antoinette Perry

Award for Best Play and NY Drama Critics Circle Award 1975 (Equus) and 1981 (Amadeus); Evening Standard Drama Award 1957 (Five Finger Exercise) and 1980 (Amadeus), London Drama Critics Award; Acad. Award for Best Screenplay (Amadeus) 1984; Hamburg Shakespeare Prize 1987; Best Comedy, Evening Standard Award for Lettice and Lovage 1988. *Plays:* Five Finger Exercise, London 1958, New York 1939 (film 1962), The Private Ear and The Public Eye, London 1962, USA 1963, The Royal Hunt of the Sun London 1964, New York 1964, Black Comedy, London 1965, New York 1967, White Lies, New York 1967 (revised as The White Liars, London 1968 and as White Liars, London 1976), The Battle of Shrivings 1970, Equus, London 1973, New York 1974, Amadeus, London 1979, New York 1980, Yonadab 1985, Lettice and Lovage, London 1987, New York 1990, The Gift of the Gorgon 1992; also performed on stage, Chichester, Guildford, Malvern 1996. *Television:* several TV plays including The Salt Land 1955, Balance of Terror. *Film screenplays:* The Royal Hunt of the Sun 1965, Equus 1977, Amadeus 1984 (all adaptations of his plays). *Radio play:* Whom Do I Have the Honour of Addressing? 1989. *Leisure interests:* architecture, walking, music. *Address:* c/o MLR (Patricia MacNaughton), Douglas House, 16–18 Douglas Street, London, SW1P 4PB, England. *Telephone:* (20) 7834-4646 (Office); (212) 873-9786 (USA) (Home).

SHAFIE, Tan Sri Haji Mohammed Ghazali, P.M.N., S.S.A.P., S.I.M.P., S.P.D.K.; Malaysian politician; b. 22 March 1922, Kuala Lipis; m. Puan Sri Khatijah binti Abdul Majid; two s.; ed Raffles Coll., Singapore, Univ. Coll. of Wales; fmr civil servant; assigned to Office of Commr for Malaya, London; later Commr for Fed. of Malaya, New Delhi; Deputy Sec. for External Affairs 1957, Acting Perm. Sec. 1959; Senator 1970–72; Minister with Special Functions 1970–72, also of Information 1971–72; mem. Parl. 1972–; Minister of Home Affairs 1973–81, of Foreign Affairs 1981–84; Govt Special Envoy 1984; Chair. Paremba; Visiting Prof., Nat. Univ. of Singapore. *Address:* 15 Jalan Ampang Hilir, 55000 Kuala Lumpur, Malaysia. *Telephone:* 4562463.

SHAFIQ, Mohammad Musa, MA; Afghanistan politician; b. 1924, Kabul; ed Ghazi High School, Al Azhar Univ., Cairo and Columbia Univ., USA; joined Ministry of Justice 1957, later became Dir Legis. Dept; also taught at Faculty of Law and Political Science, Kabul Univ.; Partner, pvt. law firm, Kabul 1961; Deputy Minister of Justice 1963–66; Adviser, Ministry of Foreign Affairs 1966–68; Amb. to Egypt, also Accred to Lebanon, Sudan and Ghana 1968–71; Minister of Foreign Affairs 1971–73; Prime Minister 1972–73 (deposed by mil. coup); in detention 1973–75.

SHAGARI, Alhaji Shehu Usman Aliu; Nigerian fmr Head of State and educationist; b. 25 Feb. 1925, Shagari; m.; eight s. ten d.; ed Middle School, Sokoto, Barewa Coll., Kaduna, Teacher Training Coll., Zaria; Science Teacher, Sokoto Middle School 1945–50; Headmaster, Argungu Sr Primary School 1951–52; Sr Visiting Teacher, Sokoto Prov. 1953–58; mem. Fed. Parl. 1954–58; Parl. Sec. to the Prime Minister 1958–59; Fed. Minister of Econ. Devt 1959–60, of Establishments 1960–62, of Internal Affairs 1962–65, of Works 1965–66; Sec. Sokoto Prov. Educ. Devt Fund 1966–68; State Commr for Educ., Sokoto Prov. 1968–70; Fed. Commr for Econ. Devt and Reconstruction 1970–71, for Finance 1971–75; fmr Chair. Peugeot Automobile Nigeria Ltd; mem. Constituent Ass. 1977–83; Presidential candidate for the Nat. Party of Nigeria (NPN) 1979; Pres. of Nigeria and C-in-C of the Armed Forces 1979–83 (deposed by mil. coup), also Minister of Defence 1982–83; under house arrest 1983–86, banned from holding public office and from political activity Aug. 1986; confined to Shagari Village 1986–88; granted unrestricted freedom 1988; Hon. LLD (Ahmadu Bello Univ.) 1976; Grand Commdr Order of the Niger 1993. *Publications:* Wakar Nigeria (poem), Shehu Usman Dan-Fodio: Ideas and Ideals of his Leadership. *Address:* 6A Okoll'e Eboh Street, Ikoyi, Lagos, Nigeria.

SHAH, Amir; Afghanistan journalist and photographer; b. 1958, Kabul; journalist 1989–; Corresp. and Photographer, Afghanistan Bureau, Associated Press (American press agency) 1999–. *Address:* c/o Afghanistan Bureau, Associated Press, International Headquarters, JD Rockefeller Plaza, New York, NY 10020, USA (Office).

SHAH, Ayesha; British international banker; risk analyst and man. Citicorp Investment Bank 1980s; Exec. Dir and Jt Head of Swaps, Nomura Int. 1986–93; joined EBRD as consultant 1993, Head of Funding 1995–1999, Deputy Treas. and Head of Funding EBRD 1999–2002, Treas. and Acting Head of Investments-Credit 2002–; Business Woman of the Year, Asian Women of Achievement Awards 2002. *Address:* European Bank for Reconstruction and Development, One Exchange Square, 175 Bishopsgate, London, EC2A 2EH, England (Office). *Telephone:* (20) 7338-6000 (Office); *Fax:* (20) 7338-6100 (Office). *Website:* www.ebrd.com (Office).

SHAH, Eddy (Selim Jehane); British newspaper publisher; b. 1944, Cambridge; s. of Moochool Shah and Hazel Strange; m. Jennifer Shah; two s. one d.; ed several schools including Gordonstoun; worked as Asst Stage Man. in Repertory Theatre; also worked in TV and later as space salesman for free newspaper once published by Manchester Evening News; launched Sale and Altrincham Messenger freesheet in 1974, Stockport Messenger 1977, also Propr of Bury Messenger; launched Today newspaper 1986, Chair., CEO 1986–88; launched The Post Oct. 1988 (folded Dec. 1988). *Publications:* Ring of Red Roses (novel) 1991, The Lucy Ghosts 1992, Manchester Blue (novel) 1992, Fallen Angels (novel) 1994. *Leisure interest:* golf.

SHAH, Prakash, LLB, MCom; Indian diplomatist; b. 4 July 1939, Bombay; s. of H. Patel; m. Veenu Lall; two d.; joined Indian Foreign Service 1961; Third Sec. EEC 1962–64; Second Sec. Washington, DC 1964–67; Ministry of External Affairs 1967–69; Ministry of Finance 1969–71; First Sec., Petroleum Counsellor, Embassies, Iran and Gulf States 1971–75; Dir Ministry of Petroleum 1975–77; Dir Indian Petrochemicals Ltd, Petrofils Co-operatives Ltd 1976–77; Dir./Jt. Sec. Ministry of External Affairs 1977–78; Jt Sec. to Prime Minister 1978–80; High Commr in Malaysia and Brunei 1980–83; Amb. to Venezuela and Consul-Gen. to Netherlands Antilles 1983–85; Jt Sec. Ministry of External Affairs 1985–88, Additional Sec. 1989–90; Dir Kudremakh Iron Ore Ltd 1986; Amb. and Perm. Rep. to UN, Geneva 1991–92; Amb. to Japan 1992–95; Perm. Rep. to UN, New York 1995–97; del. to numerous int. confs etc. *Publications:* articles in professional journals. *Leisure interests:* cricket, tennis, golf, bridge. *Address:* c/o Ministry of External Affairs, S. Block, New Delhi, 110 011, India.

SHAH, Saira; British/Afghanistan journalist; b. 1965; freelance journalist in Afghanistan, covering guerrilla war against Soviet invasion 1986–89, in Baghdad, Iraq, covering Gulf War 1990–91; journalist with Channel Four News. *Television documentary films:* Beneath the Veil (Int. Documentary Asscn. Courage under Fire Award) 2001, Unholy War 2001. *Address:* c/o Michael Joseph, Penguin UK, 80 Strand, London, WC2R 0RL, England (Office).

SHAHA, Rishikesh; Nepalese politician and diplomatist; b. 1925, Tansen, Palpain Prov.; s. of Raja Tarak Bahadur Shaha and Madan Dibeshwari; m. Siddhanta Rajyalakshmi 1946; one s.; ed Patna Univ. and Allahabad Univ., India; Lecturer in English and Nepalese Literature, Tri-Chandra Coll. 1945–48; Opposition Leader, First Advisory Ass. 1952; Gen. Sec., Nepalese Congress 1953–55; Perm. Rep. (with rank of Amb.) to UN 1956–60; Amb. to USA 1958–60; Chair. UN Int. Comm. investigating death of Dag Hammarskjöld 1961; Minister of Finance, Planning and Economic Affairs 1961–62, of Foreign Affairs July–Sept. 1962; Amb.-at-Large 1962–63; Chair. Standing Cttee, Council of State 1963–64; Visiting Prof. East-West Center, Univ. of Hawaii 1965–66; MP 1967–70; solitary confinement 1969–70; Visiting Prof., School of Int. Studies of Jawaharlal Nehru Univ. 1971; Regent's Prof., Univ. of Calif., Berkeley 1971–72; returned to Nepal, arrested Dec. 1974; Fellow, Woodrow Wilson Int. Center for Scholars, Washington, DC 1976–77; returned to Nepal, arrested May 1977, released 1989; campaigned for restoration of multi-party democracy before 1980 referendum; Alumni Fellow, East-West Centre 1984; Pres. Human Rights Org. of Nepal 1988–; honoured by Human Rights Watch and Asia Watch for work as Human Rights Monitor 1989. *Publications:* Nepal and the World 1954, Heroes and Builders of Nepal (in UK) 1965, An Introduction to Nepal 1975, Nepali Politics—Retrospect and Prospect (in UK) 1975, Essays in the Practice of Government in Nepal (in India) 1982, Future of South Asia (in India) 1986, Modern Nepal: A Political History (1769–1955) 1990, Politics in Nepal 1980–1990 1990, Three Decades and Two Kings—End of Nepal's Partyless Monarchic Rule 1990, Ancient and Medieval Nepal 1991. *Leisure interests:* reading, writing, big game hunting. *Address:* Shri Nivas, Chandol, Kathmandu, Nepal. *Telephone:* (1) 411766.

SHAHABUDDEEN, Mohamed, SC, PhD, LLD; Guyanese international judge; b. 7 Oct. 1931; s. of Sheikh Abdul and Jamillah Hamid; m. Bebe Sairah 1955; two s. one d.; ed Univ. of London and Hague Acad. of Int. Law; called to the Bar, Middle Temple, London 1954; pvt. legal practice 1954–59; magistrate 1959; Crown Counsel 1959–62; Solicitor-Gen. (with rank of Justice of Appeal from 1971) 1962–73; Attorney-Gen. 1973–88; Minister of Justice and sometimes Acting Foreign Minister 1978–88; Vice-Pres. of Guyana 1983–88; Judge Int. Court of Justice 1988–97; Judge, Appeals Chamber, UN Int. Criminal Tribunal for Rwanda 1997–; Vice-Pres. Int. Tribunal for fmr. Yugoslavia 1997–99; Chair. Legal Practitioners' Disciplinary Cttee, Advisory Council on the Prerogative of Mercy; mem. Guyana del. to numerous int. confs.; hon. Bencher of the Middle Temple; HQ mem. Int. Law Asscn; mem. Soc. Française pour le droit int., Advisory Bd European Journal of Int. Law, Bd of Electors of Whewell Professorship of Int. Law of Cambridge Univ., Inst. de Droit int. (first Vice-Pres. 1999–2001), Int. Acad. of Comparative Law; Hon. mem. American Soc. of Int. Law; Order of Excellence, Order of Roraima, Cacique's Crown of Honour. *Publications:* several books and articles. *Address:* International Criminal Tribunal, Churchillplein 1, 2517 JW, The Hague, Netherlands (Office). *E-mail:* public@un.org (Office). *Website:* www.un.ictr.org (Office).

SHAHAL, Moshe; Israeli politician and lawyer; b. 1934, Iraq; m.; two c.; ed Haifa Univ., Tel Aviv Univ.; mil. service Israeli Defence Forces; mem. Seventh Knesset (Parl.) –1974, mem. Finance Cttee, mem. Econ. Cttee, mem. Labour Cttee; mem. Eighth Knesset 1974–77, mem. Finance Cttee, mem. Constitution, Law and Justice Cttee; mem. Tenth Knesset 1983; Deputy Speaker, mem. Knesset Cttee, mem. Constitution, Law and Justice Cttee; Minister of Energy and Infrastructure 1984–90, 1993–94, 1994–95; of Police and Communications 1992–93, of Internal Security 1993–96; mem. 14th Knesset 1996–98; fmr Chair. Israeli Consumers' Council; fmr Perm. Observer to European Council; fmr Perm. Rep. to Inter-Parl. Union. *Publication:* A New Agenda 1992. *Address:* c/o The Knesset, Jerusalem, Israel; 6 Ben Zakai Street, Tel Aviv 65203 (Home). *Telephone:* 3-5666886 (Office). *Fax:* 3-5662555 (Office). *E-mail:* shachezr@internet-zahav.net (Office).

SHAHEEN, C. Jeanne, BA, MSc; American state governor; b. 28 Jan. 1947, St Charles, Mo.; m. William H. Shaheen; three c.; ed Univs of Shippensburg and Mississippi; mem. NH Senate; Gov. of New Hampshire 1997–2003; Democrat. *Address:* c/o Office of the Governor, 107 N Main Street, Room 208, Concord, NH 03301, USA.

SHAHRUDI, Ayatollah Sayed Mahmoud Hashemi; Iranian jurist; b. Aug. 1948, Najaf, Iraq; s. of the late Ayatollah Seyed Ali Housseini Shahrudi; ed Alavi School, Iraq; jailed under Bathist regime of Iraq 1974; returned to Iran 1979; teacher of Islamic jurisprudence and methodology Qum School of Theology 1979–, mem. Supreme Man. Council, Vice-Chair. Asscn of Instructors; est. Inst. of Encyclopedia of Islamic Jurisprudence; currently Head of the Judiciary, Islamic Repub. of Iran; jurist mem. Council of Guardians; mem. Ass. of Experts. *Publications include:* Islamic Criminal Law (discretionary punishments), The Book of Khoms (religious tax) I, II, Hire, Sale, Dormant Partnership, Co-Partnership, Agricultural and Cultivation Partnership etc, Discourses in Islamic Methodology. *Address:* c/o Ministry of Justice, Panzdah-e-Khordad Square, Tehran, Iran.

SHAHRYAR, Ishaq, BSc, MA; Afghanistan diplomatist and scientist; b. 1936, Kabul; m. Hafizah Shahryar; two c.; awarded scholarship to study chemistry in USA 1956, remained in exile; Founder and Pres. Solec Int. Co. 1975–96; Founder and Pres. Solar-Utility Co. Inc. 1996–; Amb. to USA April 2002–. *Address:* Diplomatic Representation of Afghanistan in the USA (Chancery), 2341 Wyoming Avenue, NW, Washington, DC 20008, USA (Office). *Telephone:* (202) 234-3770 (Office). *Fax:* (202) 328-3516 (Office).

SHAIKH RASHID AHMED, MA, LLB; Pakistani politician; b. 6 Nov. 1950, Balra Bazar, Rawalpindi; ed Polytech. Coll., Rawalpindi, Gordon Coll., Punjab Univ.; mem. (Ind.) Nat. Ass.; fmr Minister for Labour and Manpower, for Industries and Production, for Culture and Sports, for Tourism and Investment; Minister of Information and Media Devt 2002–; imprisoned in fight for democracy; participated in Geneva Accords, Moscow Conf.; Head of Gulf War Monitoring Programme; Rep. of Pakistan to UN and numerous int. confs. *Publications include:* Farzand-I -Pakistan, Suboatta Hai. *Address:* Ministry of Information and Media Development, c/o Aiwan-e-Sadr, Islamabad, Pakistan.

SHAIMIYEV, Mintimer Sharipovich; Russian/Tatar politician; b. 20 Jan. 1937, Anyakovo, Aktanyshski Region, Tatarstan; s. of Sharip Shaimiev and Naghima Safioullina; m. Sakina Shaimieva; two s.; ed Kazan Inst. of Agric.; Engineer, Chief Engineer Service and Repair Station, Mouslyumovski Dist, Tatar ASSR 1959–62; Man. Selkhoztekhnika Regional Asscn, Tatar ASSR 1962–67; Instructor, Deputy Chief of Agricultural Dept, Tatar Regional Cttee of CPSU, Tatar ASSR 1967–69; Minister of Land Improvement and Water Man., Tatar ASSR 1969–83; First Deputy Chair. Council of Ministers, Tatar ASSR 1983, Chair. 1985–89; Sec. Tatar Regional Cttee of CPSU 1983–85, First Sec. 1989–90; Chair. Supreme Soviet, Tatar ASSR 1990–91; Pres. of Tatarstan 1991–; f. All Russia political movt 1999; mem. Acad. of Tech. Sciences; Hon. mem. Presidium, Int. Parl. of World Confed. of Knights (under auspices of UN); Hon. mem. Int. Acad. of Informatization; Hon. Prof. Moscow State Inst. of Int. Relations; Order of Lenin 1966, Order of Red Banner of Labour 1971, Order of Oct. Revolution 1976, Order of Friendship of Peoples 1987, Order for Services to the Fatherland, Grade II 1997; Silver Avitsenna Medal, UNESCO 2001. *Leisure interests:* chess, gardening, skiing. *Address:* Office of the President, respublika Tatarstan, 420014 Kazan, Kremlin, Russia. *Telephone:* (8432) 92-74-66 (Office). *Fax:* (8432) 92-70-88. *E-mail:* secretariat@tatar.ru (Office). *Website:* www.tatar.ru/president/english (Office).

SHAKAA, Riyadh al, BA; Jordanian politician and lawyer; b. 1941, Nablus; ed Univ. of Cairo; Lawyer and mem. Jordanian Bar Asscn; mem. Lower House of Parl. for Nablus 1985–; Minister of Justice 1985–89 and –1998. *Address:* c/o Ministry of Justice, P.O. Box 6040, Amman, Jordan.

SHAKAR, Karim Ebrahim al-, BA; Bahraini diplomatist; b. 23 Dec. 1945, Manama; m. Fatima Al-Mansouri 1979; three d.; ed Univ. of New Delhi; joined Ministry of Foreign Affairs 1970; mem. Perm. Mission to the UN, rising to rank of Second Sec. 1972–76; apptd Chief Foreign Affairs and Int. Org., Bahrain 1977; Perm. Rep. to the UN Office, Geneva and Consul-Gen., Switzerland 1982–87; apptd Amb. (non-resident) to FRG and Austria 1984; apptd Perm Rep. to the UN Office, Vienna 1982, Perm. Rep. (non-resident) 1984; Perm Rep. to the UN 1987–90; Amb. to UK 1990–95, Amb. (non-resident) to Ireland, Denmark and the Netherlands 1992–95; Dir Int. Directorate at Ministry of Foreign Affairs, Bahrain 1995–2001; Amb. to People's Repub. of China (also accred to Malaysia, the Philippines and Thailand) 2001–; Shaikh Isa Bin Salman Al-Khalifa Medal of Merit 2001. *Leisure interests:* reading, travelling. *Address:* No. 312 & 313, 3rd Floor, Beijing Lufthansa Centre Office, 50 Liangmaqiao Road, Chaoyang District, 100016 Beijing (Office); Delux House No. A2107 Gahood Villa, Xibaixingzhuang, Shunyi District, Beijing, People's Republic of China (Home); c/o Ministry of Foreign Affairs, P.O. Box 547, Government House, Government Road, Manama, Bahrain. *Telephone:* (10) 64635580 (Office); (10) 80466384 (Home). *Fax:* (10) 84517212 (Office); (10) 80464318 (Home). *E-mail:* karim_alshakar@hotmail.com (Office); karim_alshakar@yahoo.com (Office).

SHAKED, Shaul, PhD; Israeli professor of Iranian studies and comparative religion; b. 8 Feb. 1933, Debrecen, Hungary; m. Miriam Schächter 1960; one s. two d.; ed Hebrew Univ. Jerusalem and SOAS, Univ. of London; Asst Lecturer, SOAS 1964–65, Lecturer 1964–65; Lecturer, Assoc. Prof., Prof. Hebrew Univ. Jerusalem 1965–, Chair. Dept of Indian, Iranian and Armenian

Studies 1971–72, 1974–75, Chair. Dept of Comparative Religion 1972–74, 1977–79; Chair. Ben Zvi Inst. for Study of Jewish Communities in the East 1975–79, Inst. of Asian and African Studies 1981–85; Fellow, Israel Acad. of Sciences and Humanities; Visiting Prof. Univ. of Calif. at Berkeley 1969–70, Columbia and New York Univs 1980–81, Univ. of Heidelberg 1987–88; Visiting Fellow Wolfson Coll., Cambridge, NIAS, The Netherlands; Pres. Int. Academic Union 2001–04; Hon. Fellow Univ. Coll. London 1995; Israel Prize in Linguistics 2000. *Publications include:* A tentative bibliography of Geniza documents 1964, Amulets and Magic Bowls (with J. Naveh) 1985, Dualism in Transformation 1994, From Zoroastrian Iran to Islam 1995, Magische Texte aus der Kairoer Geniza (with P. Schäfer) (3 vols) 1994–99; articles and book chapters. *Address:* Institute of Asian and African Studies, The Hebrew University, Mount Scopus, Jerusalem 91905, Israel (Office). *Telephone:* 2-6416005 (Home). *Fax:* 2-6446273 (Home). *E-mail:* shaul.shaked@huji.ac.il (Home).

SHAKER, Mohamed Ibrahim, LLB, D. ÈS SC.POL.; Egyptian diplomatist; b. 16 Oct. 1933, Cairo; m. Mona El Kony 1960; one s. one d.; ed Cairo Univ., Inst. of Int. Studies, Univ. of Geneva, Switzerland; Rep. of Dir-Gen. of IAEA to UN, New York 1982–83; Deputy Perm. Rep. of Egypt to UN, New York 1984–86; Amb. to Austria, Perm. Rep. to UN in Vienna, Gov. on IAEA Bd of Govs., Perm. Rep. to UNIDO 1986–88; Amb. to UK 1988–97; fmr mem. Core Group, Programme for Promoting Nuclear Non-proliferation (PPNN) 1987–97, UN Sec.-Gen.'s Advisory Bd on Disarmament Matters 1993–98 (Chair. 1995); Chair. Egyptian Council for Foreign Affairs 1999–; Order of the Republic (Second Grade) 1976, Order of Merit (First Grade) 1983. *Publications:* The Nuclear Non-Proliferation Treaty: Origin and Implementation, 1959–1979 1980; several articles and contribs to books on nuclear energy and nuclear non-proliferation. *Leisure interests:* tennis, music. *Address:* 120 Mohie Eldin Abou Elezz, Mohandeseen, Guizeh, Cairo (Office); 9 Aziz Osman Street, Zamalek, Cairo, Egypt (Home). *Telephone:* (2) 3378242 (Office); (2) 7359593 (Cairo) (Home). *Fax:* (2) 7603552 (Office); (2) 7359593 (Home). *E-mail:* moshaker@ecfa-egypt.org (Office). *Website:* www.ecfa-egypt.org (Office).

SHAKESPEARE, Frank; American diplomatist and fmr radio and television executive; b. 9 April 1925, New York; s. of Frank J. Shakespeare, Sr and Frances Hughes Shakespeare; m. Deborah Ann Spaeth Shakespeare 1954; one s. two d.; ed Holy Cross Coll., Worcester, Mass.; Liberty Mutual Insurance Co., Washington, DC 1947–49; Procter and Gamble Co. 1949–50; Radio Station WOR, New York 1950, CBS 1950; Gen. Man. WXIX-TV, Milwaukee, Wis. 1957–59; Vice-Pres. and Gen. Man. WCBS-TV, New York 1959–63; Vice-Pres and Asst to Pres. CBS-TV Network 1963–65; Exec. Vice-Pres. CBS-TV Stations 1965–67; Pres. CBS Television Service Div. 1967–69; Dir US Information Agency 1969–73; Exec. Vice-Pres. Westinghouse Electric Co. 1973–75; Pres. RKO Gen. 1975–83, Vice-Chair. 1983–85; Chair. Bd Radio Free Europe/Radio Liberty Inc. 1982–85; Amb. to Portugal 1985–86, to the Holy See 1986–89; Dir Heritage Foundation 1989–; Kt Grand Cross with Palm, Order of the Holy Sepulchre and other honours; nine hon. degrees. *Address:* 303 Coast Boulevard, La Jolla, CA 92037, USA. *Telephone:* (858) 459-8640.

SHAKHNAZAROV, Karen Georgyevich; Russian film director; b. 8 July 1952, Krasnodar; s. of Georgy Shakhnazarov and Anna Shakhnazarova; m. Darya Igorevna Mayorova 1972; two s. one d.; ed All-Union Inst. of Cinematography; Asst Film Dir Mosfilm Studio 1973–75; on staff Mosfilm 1976–; Artistic Dir VI Creative Union 1987; Chair. Bd of Dirs. Courier Studio at Mosfilm 1991–, Pres., Dir-Gen. Mosfilm Concern 1998–; Boris Polevoy Prize 1982, Special Prize of the Jury (Grenoble) 1984, Silver Medal of Int. Film Festival, Lodz 1984, Diplomas of Int. Film Festivals in London, Chicago, Belgrade for We Are from Jazz 1984, Prize of Int. Film Festival in Moscow for Courier 1986, Comsomol Prize 1986, Brothers Vassilyev State Prize 1988, Grand Prix of Int. Film Festival in Belgrade for The Tsar-Murderer 1991, Special Prize of Karlovy Vary Film Festival for Day of Full Moon 1998, Merited Worker of Arts of Russia. *Film scripts:* debut as scriptwriter Ladies Invite Partners 1981. *Films include:* God Souls 1980, We Are from Jazz 1983, Winter Evening in Gagry 1985, Courier 1986, Town Zero 1989, Tsar-Murderer 1991, Dreams 1993, American Daughter 1995, Day of Full Moon 1998, Poisons or the World History of Poisoning 2001. *Leisure interests:* swimming, driving. *Address:* Mosfilmovskaya str. 1, 119858, Moscow, Russia (Office). *Telephone:* (095) 143-91-00 (Office).

SHAKHRAY, Sergey Mikhailovich, LLD; Russian politician; b. 30 April 1956, Simferopol; s. of Mikhail A. Shakray and Zoya A. Shakray; m. Tatyana Shakhray 1985; two s. one d.; ed Rostov State Univ.; Head of Law. Moscow State Univ.; People's Deputy of Russia 1990–92; Chair. of the Legis. Cttee of Russian Supreme Soviet 1990; State Councillor on legal issues of Russian Fed. 1991–92; Vice-Prime Minister of Russia 1991–92, 1993, 1994–95; Chair. State Cttee for nat. problems; Founder and Chair. Party of Russian Unity and Consent (PRES) 1993–; Head interim admin. in zone of emergency situation in N Ossetia and Ingushetia 1992–93; mem. State Duma (Parl.) 1993; Minister for Nationalities and Nat. Problems 1994–95; Deputy Head of Pres. Yeltsin's Admin., Pres.'s Rep. at Constitutional Court 1996–98; Deputy Chair. Political Consultative Council of Pres. Yeltsin; adviser to Prime Minister 1998–; Prof. Moscow Inst. of Int. Relations 1999–; Deputy Head of Accountant Chamber Admin. 2001–. *Leisure interests:* fishing, bicycling, badminton, Russian baths. *Address:* Accountant Chamber of Russian Federation, Zubovskaya str. 2, 121901 Moscow, Russia. *Telephone:* (095) 914-05-09.

SHAKIRA, (Shakira Isabel Mebarak Ripoll); Colombian singer and songwriter; b. 2 Feb. 1977, Barranquilla; wrote her first song aged 8; at age of 13 signed recording contract with Sony Music Colombia 1990; Grammy Award for Best Female Vocal Performance 2000; two Latin Grammys. *Albums include:* Magia (Magic) 1991, Peligro (Danger) 1993, Pies Descalzos (Bare Feet) 1996, ¿Dónde están los ladrones? (Where Are the Thieves?) 1998, Laundry Service (first album in English) 2002. *Television:* El Oasis (Colombian TV drama). *Address:* c/o Sony Discos Inc., 2190 NW 89 Place, Miami, FL 33172, USA (Office); c/o Epic, 131 avenue Wagram, 75017 Paris, France (Office). *Website:* www.shakira.com (Office).

SHAKUROV, Sergey Kayumovich; Russian actor; b. 1 Jan. 1942, Moscow; ed Theatre School of Cen. Children's Theatre; with K. Stanislavsky Drama Theatre 1978–88; acted in several other theatres; USSR State Prize 1980; prizes of All-Union Film Festivals for Best Actor 1988, 1991; People's Actor of Russia 1991. *Stage roles include:* Ivanov (Chekhov), Hamlet and others. *Films include:* Their Own Among Strangers, A Stranger Among His Own 1974, 100 Days after Childhood 1975, The Taste of Bread 1979, Portrait of the Artist's Wife 1982, Recipe of Her Youthfulness 1984, Visit to Minotaurus 1987, Dogs' Feast 1991, Squadron 1992, Hagy-Trager 1993, Declaration of Love 1995, Cranberries in Sugar 1995, Armaviz 1998. *Address:* Bibliotechnaya str. 27, Apt. 94, 109544 Moscow, Russia (Home). *Telephone:* (095) 270-15-32 (Home).

SHALALA, Donna Edna, PhD; American professor of political science; b. 14 Feb. 1941, Cleveland, Ohio; d. of James A. Shalala and Edna Smith; ed Western Coll. and Syracuse Univ.; Volunteer, Peace Corps, Iran 1962–64; Asst to Dir Metropolitan Studies Program, Syracuse Univ. 1965–69; Instr., Asst to Dean, Maxwell Grad. School, Syracuse Univ. 1969–70; Asst Prof. of Political Science, Bernard Baruch Coll., City Univ. New York 1970–72; Assoc. Prof. of Politics and Educ. Teachers' Coll. Columbia Univ. 1972–79; Asst Sec. for Policy Devt and Research, Dept of Housing and Urban Devt Washington 1977–80; Prof. of Political Science and Pres. Hunter Coll. City Univ. New York 1980–88; Prof. of Political Science, Chancellor, Univ. of Wis. Madison 1988–92; Sec. of Health and Human Services 1993–2001; Pres. Univ. of Miami 2001–; Dir Inst. of Int. Econs 1981–93, Ditchley Foundation 1981–93; mem. Nat. Acad. of Arts and Sciences, American Soc. for Public Admin.; 24 hon. degrees. *Publications:* Neighborhood Governance 1971, The City and the Constitution 1972, The Property Tax and the Voters 1973, The Decentralization Approach 1974. *Leisure interests:* tennis, mountain-climbing, reading, spectator sports. *Address:* Office of the President, University of Miami, 230 Ashe Building, Coral Gables, FL 33146, U.S.A. (Office). *Telephone:* (305) 284-2211 (Office).

SHALIKASHVILI, Gen. John; American army officer (retd); b. 27 June 1936, Warsaw, Poland; s. of Dimitri Shalikashvili and Maria (Ruediger) Shalikashvili; m. 1st Gunhild Bartsch 1963 (died 1965); m. 2nd Joan Zimpelman 1966; one s.; ed Bradley Univ., Naval War Coll., US Army War Coll., George Washington Univ.; entered US army active duty 1958; various troop and staff assignments Alaska, USA, FRG, Viet Nam, Repub. of Korea 1959–75; Commdr 1st Bn, 84th Field Artillery, 9th Infantry Div., Fort Lewis, Washington 1975–77; Deputy Chief of Staff for Operations, S European Task Force, Vicenza, Italy 1978–79; Commdr Div. Artillery 1st Armored Div. US Army, Nürnberg, FRG 1979–81; Chief, Politico-Mil. Div., later Deputy Dir, Strategy, Plans and Policy, ODCSOPS, the Army Staff, Washington, DC 1981–84; rank of Brig.-Gen. 1983; Asst Div. Commdr 1st Armored Div. US Army, Nürnberg, FRG 1984–86; Dir of Strategy, Plans, Policy, ODCSOPS, the Army Staff, Washington, DC 1986–87; rank of Maj.-Gen. 1986; Commdg Gen. 9th Infantry Div. Fort Lewis, Washington 1987–89; rank of Lt-Gen. 1989; Deputy C-in-C US Army Europe, Heidelberg, FRG 1989–91; Asst to Chair. Jt Chiefs of Staff, Washington, DC 1991–92; rank of Gen. 1992; Supreme Allied Commdr Europe and C-in-C US European Command 1992–93; Chair. Jt Chiefs of Staff 1993–97; Adviser to Pentagon 2000–; mem. Bd Govs of American Red Cross, Asscn of US Army, Field Artillery Assn, Retd Officers Asscn, Council on Foreign Relations, American Acad. of Achievement, Bradley Univ. Bd of Trustees; Hon. LLD (Univ. of Md, Bradley Univ.); numerous awards and decorations, including Mil. Order of the Carabao. *Address:* The Pentagon, Washington, DC 20301, USA.

SHALOM, Silvan, MA, LLB, CPA; Israeli politician and journalist; b. 1958, Tunisia; m.; five c.; ed Tel-Aviv Univ., Ben Gurion Univ.; rank of Sergeant during mil. service; mem. Knesset 1992–; Deputy Minister of Defence 1997, Minister of Science and Tech. 1998, of Finance and Deputy Prime Minister 2001–03; Minister of Foreign Affairs 2003–; Chair. Bd of Dirs Israel Electric Co., Dir-Gen. Ministry of Energy and Infrastructure; Deputy Chair. Public Council for Youth Exchange; mem. Exec. of the Broadcasting Authority; Adviser to Ministers of Finance, Econ., Planning and Justice; Israel Airport Authority, Dir Sun d'Or Int. Airlines. *Publications:* numerous articles on the Israeli press. *Address:* Ministry of Foreign Affairs, Hakirya, Romema, Jerusalem 91950, Israel (Office). *Telephone:* 2-5303111 (Office). *Fax:* 2-5303367 (Office). *E-mail:* sshalom@knesset.gov.il (Office); sar@mfa.gov.il (Office). *Website:* www.mfa.gov.il (Office).

SHAMANOV, Lt-Gen. Vladimir Anatolyevich; Russian army officer and politician; b. 15 Feb. 1957, Barnaul, Altai territory; m.; one s. one d.; ed Ryazan Higher Military School of Paratroopers, M. Frunze Military Acad. of General Army, Military Acad. of General Staff; Commdr of artillery platoon, Pskov region 1978–85, Bn Commdr 1985–87; Deputy Regt Commdr Kishinev,

Moldova 1990–91; Regt Commdr Kirovabad, Azerbaijan 1991–93, Regt moved to Ulyanovsk 1994; Head of Staff Novorossiysk div. 1994–95, transferred to Chechnya as Commdr operation group; Deputy Commdr army group, Ministry of Defence 1995–96; Head of Staff 20th Gen. Troops Army, Voronezh 1998–99; Commdr 58th Army N Caucasus Mil. Command 1999, W Direction of United Group of Fed. Forces 1999; participated in Devt and realization of Operation Hunting for Wolves, Grozny, Chechnya 2000; Commdr 58th Army 2000; Gov. Ulyanovsk Region 2000–; Hon. Citizen of Makhachkala, Dagestan; Hero of Russia 1999. *Address:* Office of the Administration, Lenina pl. 1, 423700 Ulyanovsk, Russia (Office). *Telephone:* (8422) 41-20-78 (Office). *Fax:* (8422) 31–27–65 (Office). *Website:* www.admobl.mv.ru.

SHAMASK, Ronaldus; Netherlands fashion designer; b. 24 Nov. 1945, Amsterdam; self-educated in design; window-dresser for dept store in Melbourne, Australia 1959; fashion illustrator, The Times and The Observer newspapers, London 1967–68; set and costume designer, Company of Man (multi-media artists' org.) Buffalo, NY 1968–71; subsequently undertook design and clothing comms. for pvt. clients in New York; founder-partner with Murrray Moss, Moss Shamask, New York 1978–; opened Moss boutique, Madison Avenue, New York and presented first collection 1979; costume designer, Lucinda Childs Dance Co. premiere of Available Light, Next Wave Fall Festival, Brooklyn Acad. of Music 1983; work exhibited at Hayden Gallery, MIT 1982 and in perm. collection of Smithsonian Inst.; Coty Fashion Award 1981; Fil d'Or, Conf. Int. du Lin 1982.

SHAMGAR, Meir; Israeli judge; b. 13 Aug. 1925, Danzig (now Gdańsk, Poland); s. of Eliezer Sterenberg and Dina Sterenberg; m. Geula Shamgar 1955 (deceased); two s. one d.; ed Balfour Coll. Tel-Aviv, Hebrew Univ. and Govt Law School, Jerusalem and London Univ.; Israeli army achieving rank of Brig.-Gen. 1948–68; Mil. Advocate-Gen. 1961–68; Legal Adviser, Ministry of Defence April–Aug. 1968; Attorney-Gen. of Israel 1968–75; Justice, Supreme Court 1975, Deputy Chief Justice 1982, Pres. of Supreme Court (Chief Justice of Israel) 1983–95; Chair. Comm. of Inquiry into Judiciary in Mil. Justice 1977, into Hebron Massacre 1994, into Murder of Prime Minister Yitzhak Rabin 1995, into Appointment and Powers and Duties of Attorney-Gen. of Israel 1999, into Pollution on Kishon River, into Cancer Cases in Naval Commands 2001; mem. Perm. Court of Arbitration, The Hague; mem. Council Open Univ. of Israel, World Jurist Assen (Peace Through Law); Distinguished Fellow Open Univ. of Israel 1993; Hon. Fellow Open Univ. of Israel; Dr hc (Weizman Inst.) 1987, (Hebrew Univ. Jerusalem) 1990, (Ben Gurion Univ., Beer-Sheva) 1996, (Tel Aviv Univ.) 1997, (Bar Ilan Univ.) 1998; Israel Prize for Special Service to Society and State 1996, Ben Gurion Prize 1998. *Publications:* The Military Government of the Territories Administered by Israel 1967–80: The Legal Aspects 1982; numerous articles and essays in legal publs. *Address:* Kiriat Ben Gurion, Rehov Shaare Mishpat 1, Jerusalem 91909 (Office); 12 Shahar Street, Jerusalem 96263, Israel (Home). *Telephone:* 2-6759730 (Office); 2-6526130 (Home). *Fax:* 2-6759609 (Office); 2-6518957 (Home).

SHAMI, Misbah-Ud-Din, PhD; Pakistani professor of chemistry and administrator; b. 1 Oct. 1930, Jalandhar, India; m.; four c.; ed Punjab Univ., Washington State Univ.; Prof. Punjab Univ. 1970, Dean, Faculty of Natural Sciences, Eng and Pharmacy 1973, Pro-Vice-Chancellor 1974–76; mem. Univs. Grants Comm. 1976–80; Chair. Pakistan Science Foundation 1980–90; Ed. Pakistan Journal of Science 1972–79; Postdoctoral Fellowship, Royal Soc. 1969; mem. and fmr Pres. Pakistan Asscn for the Advancement of Science, Pakistan Asscn of Scientists and Scientific Professions, Past-Pres. Scientific Soc. of Pakistan; Founding Fellow Islamic Acad. of Sciences, mem. Council 1994–99; Fellow Pakistan Acad. of Sciences, Fellow and Past-Pres. Pakistan Inst. of Chemical Engineers; Iqbal Centenary Commemorative Medal 1974, Nat. Award of the Pakistan Talent Forum 1987, UNESCO Kalinga Prize 1990, Sitara-Imtiaz 1990. *Address:* Islamic Academy of Sciences, P.O. Box 830036, Amman, Jordan (Office). *Telephone:* 5522104 (Office). *Fax:* 5511803 (Office).

SHAMIR, Yitzhak; Israeli politician; b. Yitzhak Yernitsky, 15 Oct. 1915, Ruzinoy, Poland; m.; one s. one d.; ed Hebrew Secondary School, Białystok, Warsaw Univ. and Hebrew Univ.; emigrated to Palestine 1935; mem. Irgun Zvai Leumi (Jewish Mil. Org.) 1937, then a founder and Leader of Lohamei Herut Yisrael 1940–48; arrested by British Mandatory Authority 1941, 1946 (exiled to Eritrea); given political asylum in France, returned to Israel 1948; retd from political activity until 1955; sr post Civil Service 1955–65; Man. Dir several business concerns 1965–; mem. Herut Movt 1970–, Chair. Exec. Cttee 1975–92; mem. Knesset 1973–96, Speaker 1977–80; Minister of Foreign Affairs 1980–83, Prime Minister of Israel 1983–84, 1986–92; also fmr Minister of Labour and Social Affairs; Deputy Prime Minister 1984–86, Minister of Foreign Affairs 1984–86; Acting Minister of the Interior 1987–88; Dr hc (Hebrew Union Coll., LA Jewish Inst. of Religion) 1991. *Publication:* Summing Up (memoirs) 1992. *Address:* Beit Amot Mishpat, 8 Shaul Hamelech Boulevard, Tel Aviv 64733, Israel.

SHAMLAN, Ali Abdullah Al-, PhD; Kuwaiti professor of geology and administrator; b. 8 March 1945, Kuwait; m.; ed Kuwait Univ.; demonstrator, Kuwait Univ. 1967, Asst Prof. 1973, Assoc. Prof. 1978, Prof. 1985–; Chair. Geology Dept, Kuwait Univ. 1975–78, Asst Dean 1978–82, Dean Faculty of Science 1982–; Dir-Gen. Kuwait Foundation for the Advancement of Sciences; Chair. Science Coll. Council of Kuwait; fmr Minister of Higher Educ.; mem. Higher Cttee for the Evaluation of the Educational System; mem. Kuwait

Univ. Council 1986–, American Soc. of Petroleum Geologists, Soc. of Econ. Palaeontologists and Mineralogists; Fellow Islamic Acad. of Sciences. *Address:* University of Kuwait, P.O. Box 5969, 13060 Safat, Kuwait City, Kuwait (Office). *Telephone:* 4811188 (Office).

SHAMSIE, Kamila, BA, MFA; Pakistani writer; b. 1973, Karachi; d. of Muneeza Shamsie; ed Hamilton Coll., New York, and Univ. of Mass., Amherst, USA; currently teaches creative writing at Hamilton Coll. *Publications include:* In the City by the Sea (Prime Minister's Award for Literature, Pakistan 1999) 1998, Salt and Saffron (Orange's list of 21 Writers for the 21st century) 2000, Kartography 2002. *Address:* c/o Victoria Hobbs, AM Heath & Co. Ltd., 79 St. Martin's Lane, London, WC2N 4RE, England (Office); c/o Hamilton College, 198 College Hill Road, Clinton, NY 13323, USA (Office). *E-mail:* kshamsie@hamilton.edu (Office).

SHAMSUL-ISLAM, Ahmad, MSc, PhD; Bangladeshi professor of plant genetics; b. 1 Jan. 1926; ed Presidency Coll., Calcutta, Manchester Univ.; research in genetics, plant breeding and tissue-culture 1955–; postdoctoral research work at Cornell, Calif. and Nottingham Univs.; lecturer, Univ. of Texas, Austin; Founder Ed. Sind Univ. Research Journal, Pakistan Journal of Botany, Dar-es-Salaam Univ. Scientific Research Journal, Bangladesh Journal of Botany; fmr Sec.-Gen. Bangladesh Asscn for the Advancement of Science; mem. Indian and Japanese Socs of Genetic and Plant Breeding; Fellow Islamic Acad. of Sciences; Hon. DSc; President's Gold Medal (Bangladesh). *Address:* 11901 Swearingen Drive, 1/78 Austin, TX 78758, U.S.A. (Office). *E-mail:* islam@utxsvs.cc.utexas.edu (Office); aislam24@yahoo.com (Office).

SHAMUZAFAROV, Anvar Shamukhamedovich; Russian politician and architect; b. 10 Nov. 1952; m.; one s.; ed Tashkent Polytech. Inst.; architect, then Sr architect Tashkent Research Inst. of USSR State Cttee on Construction 1974–85; worked in Armenia after earthquake in town restoration projects 1985–88; Chief Expert, Deputy Head of Dept, then Head of Dept Russian State Cttee on Construction, Ministry of Construction 1991–96, Statistics-Sec., Deputy Minister 1996–98; First Deputy Minister of Land Construction 1998–; consultant World Bank on problems of financing and reform 1992–98; Chair. Observation Bd Agency of Ipotech Credits (Jt stock co.) 1998–99; Chair. State Cttee on Construction – Gosstroi Rossii 1999–; Friendship of Peoples Order. *Address:* Gosstroi Rossii, Stroitelei str. 8, korp. 2, 117987 Moscow, Russia (Office). *Telephone:* (095) 930-17-55 (Office). *Fax:* (095) 938-22-02 (Office).

SHAN KUO-HSI, HE Cardinal Paul, SJ; Taiwanese ecclesiastic; b. 2 Dec. 1923, Puyang; s. of John Shan Cheng-Yin and Maria Teresa Shan Tsung Auo; ordained priest 1955; Bishop 1980; transferred to Kaohsiung 1991; cr. Cardinal 1998. *Address:* Bishop's House, 125 Szu-wei 3rd Road, Kaohsiung 80203, Taiwan.

SHANG FULIN; Chinese banker; b. 1951; Asst to Gov. People's Bank of China 1994–96, Deputy Gov. 1996–2001, Head of Monetary Policy Cttee 1997, Del. to BIS 1998; Gov. Agricultural Bank of China 2001–03; Chair. China Securities Regulatory Comm. (CSRC) Jan. 2003–. *Address:* China Securities Regulatory Commission (CSRC), 16 Jin Yang Plaza, Jin Rong Dajie, Xicheng District, Beijing 100032, People's Republic of China (Office). *Telephone:* (10) 66211283 (Office). *E-mail:* enadmin@ml.csrc.gov.cn (Office); crscweb@publicf.bta.net.cn (Office). *Website:* www.csrc.gov.cn (Office).

SHANGE, Ntozake, MA; American playwright and poet; b. 18 Oct. 1948, Trenton, NJ; d. of Paul Williams and Eloise Williams; m. David Murray 1977 (divorced); one c.; ed Barnard Coll. and Univ. of S Calif.; mem. Faculty, Sonoma State Univ. 1973–75, Mills Coll. 1975, City Coll. of New York 1975, Douglass Coll. 1978; author and actress in For Colored Girls Who Have Considered Suicide/When the Rainbow is Enuf (play) 1976, Where the Mississippi Meets the Amazon (play) 1977; author and Dir A Photograph: A Study in Cruelty 1979; Dir The Mighty Gents 1979; performing mem. Sounds in Motion Dance Co.; author, An Evening with Diana Ross: The Big Event 1977; Guggenheim Fellow 1981; mem. Nat. Acad. of TV Arts and Sciences, Acad. of American Poets, PEN America etc.; recipient of numerous drama and poetry awards. *Publications include:* plays: Melissa and Smith 1976, From Okra to Greens 1978, Spell #7 1979, Black and White Two Dimensional Planes 1979, Boogie Woogie Landscapes 1980, Mouths 1981, A Photograph: Lovers in Motion 1981, Three Views of Mt. Fuji 1987; novels: Sassafrass, Cypress and Indigo 1976, Betsey Brown 1985, The Love Space Demands 1991, I Live in Music 1994; poetry: Natural Disasters and Other Festive Occasions 1977, Nappy Edges 1978, Three Pieces 1981, A Daughter's Geography 1983, From Okra to Greens 1984; essays, short stories, non-fiction, adaptations; contribs to magazines and anthologies. *Address:* c/o St Martin's Press, 175 Fifth Avenue, New York, NY 10010, USA.

SHANKAR, Ramsewak; Suriname fmr Head of State and economist; fmr Agric. Minister; Pres. of Suriname 1988–90 (overthrown in coup); fmr Head of Armed Forces, fmr Chair. Council of State and Security Comm.

SHANKAR, Ravi; Indian sitar player and composer; b. 7 April 1920; m. Sukanya Rajan 1989; two d. (one s. deceased); pupil of Ustad Allauddin Khan 1938; fmr Dir of Music All-India Radio and Founder of the Nat. Orchestra; Founder Kinnara School of Music, Bombay 1962, Kinnara School of Music, Los Angeles 1967; Visiting Lecturer Univ. of Calif. 1965; appeared in film, Raga 1974; elected to Rajya Sabha (Upper House) 1986; Fellow Sangeet Natak Akademi 1977; numerous hon. degrees; Silver Bear of Berlin 1966;

Award of Indian Nat. Acad. for Music, Dance and Drama 1962; Award of Padma Bhushan 1967, Padma Vibhushan 1981, Deshikottam 1981, Int. Music Council UNESCO Award 1975, Ramon Magsaysay Award 1992, Praemium Imperiale 1997, Polar Music Prize 1998, Bharat Ratna (Jewel of India) Award 1999; Hon. KBE 2001. *Film Scores:* Pather Panchali, The Flute and the Arrow, Nava Rasa Ranga, Charly, Gandhi, etc. *Compositions include:* Concerto for Sitar No. 1 1971, No. 2 1981, Raga Jogeshwari 1981, Homage to Mahatma Gandhi 1981, Ghanashyam (opera) 1989. *Performances include:* concert tours in Europe, USA and the East. *Recordings:* has recorded traditional and experimental music in India, UK and USA. *Publications:* My Music, My Life 1968, Rag Anurag (Bengali), Ravi: The Autobiography of Ravi Shankar (with others) 1995. *Address:* c/o Sulivan Sweetland, 28 Albion Street, London, W2 2AX, England.

SHANKARANAND, B., BA, L.L.B.; Indian politician; b. 19 Oct. 1925, Chikodi, Belgaum Dist, Karnataka; s. of Bururao Talwar; m. Kamaladevi Shankaranand; two s. six d.; ed Govt Law Coll., Bombay and R.L. Law Coll., Belgaum; fmrly associated with Republican Party of India and PSP; mem. Lok Sabha 1967–70, 1971–79, 1980–96; Gen. Sec. Congress Party in Parl. 1969–71, mem. Exec. Cttee; Deputy Minister of Parl. Affairs 1971–77; Minister of Health, Educ. and Family Welfare Jan.–Oct. 1980, of Health and Family Welfare 1980–84, of Irrigation and Power Jan.–Sept. 1985, of Law and Justice and Water Resources 1988–89, of Law and Justice July–Nov. 1989, of Petroleum and Natural Gas 1991–93, of Health and Family Welfare 1993–94; mem. numerous cttees; Del. to UNCTAD 1968, UN Gen. Ass. 1969. *Leisure interests:* cricket, football. *Address:* 8 Tees January Marg, New Delhi 110001, India. *Telephone:* 3011307.

SHANKARDASS, Raghuvansh Kumar Prithvinath, MA, LLM; Indian lawyer; b. 9 June 1930, Nairobi, Kenya; s. of P. N. Shankardass and Pushpavati Shankardass; m. Ramma Handoo 1955; ed Trinity Coll., Cambridge, Lincoln's Inn, London; Gen. Sec. Bar Asscn of India 1975–85, Vice-Pres. 1985–; Asst Sec.-Gen. Int. Bar Asscn 1980–82, Vice-Pres. 1984–86, Pres. 1986–88; Gen. Sec. Indian Law Foundation 1975–1991, Pres. 1991–; Chair. Panel of Commrs UN Compensation Comm. 1996–; Fellow American Bar Foundation 1997; Ed. The Indian Advocate 1990–; Pres. Cambridge Univ. Majlis 1953; Trustee India Foundation for the Arts 1994–2000, Talwar Research Foundation 1996, Nurul Hasan Educational and Research Foundation 1998–; Hon. OBE 1996. *Leisure interests:* golf, music, reading, travel. *Address:* 87 Lawyer's Chambers, Supreme Court of India, New Delhi 110 001 (Office); B-12 Maharani Bagh, New Delhi 110 065, India (Home). *Telephone:* (11) 3383703 (Office); (11) 6830636 (Home). *Fax:* (11) 6848104.

SHANKS, Ian Alexander, PhD, FIEE, F.R.ENG., FRSA, FRSE, FRS; British scientist; b. 22 June 1948, Glasgow; s. of Alexander Shanks and Isabella A. Beaton; m. Janice Coulter 1971; one d.; ed Dumbarton Acad., Univ. of Glasgow and Portsmouth Polytechnic; Projects Man. Scottish Colorfoto Labs. Ltd Alexandria 1970–72; Jr Research Fellow, Royal Signals and Radar Establishment, Malvern, later Sr Scientific Officer, Prin. Scientific Officer 1973–82; Sr Scientist, later Prin. Scientist/Sr. Man. Unilever Research, Sharnbrook, Beds. 1982–86; Divisional Science Adviser 1994–2000, Vice-Pres. Eng Sciences 2001, Vice-Pres. Physical and Eng Sciences 2001–; Chief Scientist, Thorn EMI PLC 1986; Visiting Prof. of Electrical and Electronic Eng Univ. of Glasgow 1985–; mem. Optoelectronics Cttee The Rank Prize Fund.; fmr mem. Science Consultative Group, BBC; fmr mem. Council and Vice-Pres. Royal Soc.; fmr mem. Advisory Bd for Research Councils, Office of Public Service and Science; Chair. Inter-Agency Cttee for Marine Science and Technology 1991–93; Hon. DEng (Glasgow); Paterson Medal and Prize, Inst. of Physics 1984. *Publications:* 40 research papers and over 75 patents mainly on liquid crystals, displays and biosensors. *Leisure interests:* music, collecting antique pocket watches, scientific instruments and art deco figures. *Address:* Unilever Research Laboratory, Colworth House, Sharnbrook, Bedford, MK44 1LQ (Office); Kings Close, 11 Main Road, Biddenham, Bedford, MK40 4BB, England (Home). *Telephone:* (1234) 328773 (Home); (1234) 222993 (Office). *Fax:* (1234) 222161 (Office). *E-mail:* ian.shanks@unilever.com (Office).

SHANNON, Richard Thomas, PhD; New Zealand/British professor of modern history; b. 10 June 1931, Suva, Fiji; s. of Edward Arthur Shannon and Grace Shannon (née McLeod); ed Mount Albert Grammar School, Auckland, NZ, Auckland Univ. Coll., Gonville and Caius Coll., Cambridge; Lecturer and Sr Lecturer in History, Univ. Coll. Auckland 1955–57, 1961–62; Lecturer in English History, Univ. of E Anglia, Norwich, UK 1963–65, Sr Lecturer 1965–71, Reader 1971–79; Prof. of Modern History, Univ. of Wales, Swansea 1979–97, Head History Dept 1982–88, Dean Faculty of Arts 1985–88, Prof. Emer. 1997–; Visiting Fellow Peterhouse, Cambridge 1988–89; Leverhulme Sr Research Fellowship 1988–90. *Publications:* Gladstone and the Bulgarian Agitation, 1876 1963, The Crisis of Imperialism, 1865–1915 1974, Gladstone, Vol. I 1809–1865 1982, The Age of Disraeli 1868–1881 1992, The Age of Salisbury, 1881–1902 1996, Gladstone Vol. II 1865–1898 1999, A Press Free and Responsible. Self-regulation and the Press Complaints Commission, 1991–2001 2001. *Leisure interest:* mid-Wales borders. *Address:* Flat A, 86 Portland Place, London, W1B 1NU, England; Old School House, Cascob, Presteigne, Powys, LD8 2NT, Wales. *Telephone:* (20) 7436-0214 (London).

SHANNON, Robert William Ernest, CBE, PhD, DTech; British engineer; b. 10 Oct. 1937, Belfast, Northern Ireland; s. of Robert Albert Ernest Shannon and Letitia Shannon; m. Annabelle McWatters 1959; one s. one d.; ed Belfast Tech. High School, The Queen's Univ. Belfast; Research Fellow The Queen's

Univ. Belfast 1966–70, Professional Fellow 1996–; Research and Devt, British Gas 1970–83, Dir On Line Inspection Centre 1983–89, HQ Dir of Eng Research 1989–91, Group Dir of Devt 1991–93, Dir of Special Projects, British Gas Global 1993–95; Consultant 1995–; Bd mem. Industrial Research and Tech. Unit, NI 1995–; mem. Exec. Bd The European Prize Charitable Trust; Pres. Institution of Gas Engineers 1993–94, Institution of Mechanical Engineers 1996–; Chair. NIGC/IRTU Foresight Steering Cttee 1996–, Cen. TC54 Harmonization Cttee 1997–, IMechE Research and Tech. Cttee 1998– and Council Awards Cttee, Royal Acad. of Eng Int. Cttee 1998–, Inst. of Gas Engineers Research and Tech. Cttee 1998–, Northern Ireland Science Park Foundation Ltd 1999–; Fellow, Vice-Pres. Royal Acad. of Eng, Professorial Fellowship 1996; Fellow Irish Acad. of Eng; Hon. DSc; Hon. DTech; MacRobert Award, Inst. of Gas Engineers Gold Medal, Royal Soc. Mullard Medal. *Publications:* Experience with On-Line Inspection 1981; over 50 scientific Publs. *Leisure interests:* reading, gardening, walking. *Address:* Northern Ireland Science Park Foundation, Queen's Road, Queen's Island, Belfast, BT3 9DT, Northern Ireland (Office); Lindisfarne, 16 Friths Drive, Reigate, Surrey, RH2 0DS, England. *Telephone:* (1737) 223559. *Fax:* (1737) 223559. *E-mail:* ernest.shannon@btinternet.com, ernest_shannon@compuserve.com (Home).

SHANTSEV, Valery Pavlinovich; Russian politician; b. 1947, Susanino Kostroma Region; m.; one s. one d.; ed Moscow Aviation School, Moscow Inst. of Radiotech., Electronics and Automation, Acad. of Nat. Econs; asst to master factory Salut 1968–75; instructor Perov Dist CP Cttee, Deputy Head Machine Construction Dept Moscow City CP Cttee 1975–85; Chair. Exec. Cttee Perov Dist Soviet, First Sec. Perov Dist CP Cttee, Chair. Perov Dist Soviet of People's Deputies 1985–90; Sec. Moscow City CP Cttee 1990–91; Deputy of Perovo District Council of People's Deputies 1983–93; Deputy of Moscow Soviet 1987–93; Commercial Dir Hockey Club Dynamo 1991–94; Prefect of S Admin. Dist of Moscow 1994–96; Vice-Mayor of Moscow, First Deputy Prime Minister, Moscow Govt and Head of Social Complex 1996–99; Vice-Mayor of Moscow, First Deputy Prime Minister, Moscow Govt and Head of Econ. Policy and Devt Complex 1999–2001; Vice-Mayor of Moscow and Head of Econ. Policy and Devt Complex 2001–. *Address:* Office of the Mayor, Tverskaya str. 13, 103032 Moscow, Russia (Office). *Telephone:* (095) 292-08-81, (095) 290-73-74 (Office). *Fax:* (095) 230-28-69 (Office).

SHAO HUAZE; Chinese journalist, army officer and government official; b. June 1933, Chun'an Co., Zhejiang Prov.; ed PLA Political Cadres' School No 2, Chinese People's Univ.; joined PLA 1951; joined CCP 1957; Ed. Jiefangjun Ribao (PLA Daily) 1964; Vice-Dir Jiefangjun Ribao 1981; Dir Propaganda Dept PLA Gen. Political Dept 1985; rank of Maj. Gen. 1988; Ed.-in-Chief Renmin Ribao (People's Daily) 1989, Dir 1992–2000; Chair. All-China Journalists' Asscn 1996–, re-elected 2000; mem. Standing Cttee CPPCC 2001–. *Address:* People's Daily, 2 Jin Tai Xi Lu, Beijing, People's Republic of China.

SHAO QIHUI; Chinese administrator and engineer; b. 1934, Wuxi City, Jiangsu Prov.; joined CCP 1953; Gov. of Heilongjiang Prov. 1989–93; mem. 14th CCP Cen. Cttee 1992–; a Vice-Minister, Ministry of Machine-Bldg Industry 1994–98; Dir State Admin. of Machine Bldg Industry 1998–99. *Address:* c/o State Administration of Machine Building Industry, 46 Sanlihe Lu, Xichen Qu, Beijing, People's Republic of China.

SHAPAR, Howard Kamber, BA, JD; American international official; b. 6 Nov. 1923, Boston, Mass.; m. Henriette Albertine Emilie van Gerrevink 1977; two s. one d.; ed Amherst Coll., Yale Univ.; Chief Counsel US Atomic Energy Comm.'s Idaho Operations Office 1956–62; Asst Gen. Counsel for Licensing and Regulation, US Atomic Energy Comm. 1962–76; Exec. Legal Dir US Nuclear Regulatory Comm. 1976–82; Dir-Gen. OECD Nuclear Energy Agency, Paris 1982–88; Counsel to Shaw, Pittman, Potts and Trowbridge 1988–98; Past Pres. Int. Nuclear Law Asscn; mem. Bars of State of New Mexico, Court of Appeals for Dist of Columbia, Dist of Columbia Bar Asscn, US Supreme Court; Distinguished Service Award, US Nuclear Regulatory Comm. 1980; Presidential Award of Meritorious Exec. 1981. *Publications:* articles in legal journals and periodicals; papers on atomic energy law. *Address:* 4610 Langdrum Lane, Chevy Chase, MD 20815, USA. *Telephone:* (301) 986-5217. *E-mail:* hshapar@bigfoot.com (Office).

SHAPIRO, Ascher H(erman), SB, ScD; American mechanical engineering educator and consultant; b. 20 May 1916, New York City; s. of Bernard Shapiro and Jennie (Kaplan) Shapiro; m. 1st Sylvia Helen Charm 1939; m. 2nd Regina Julia Lee 1961; m. 3rd Kathleen Larke Crawford 1985; one s. two d.; ed Massachusetts Inst. of Tech.; mem. Teaching Faculty MIT 1938–, Ford Prof. of Eng 1962–75, Chair. of Faculty 1964–65, Head of Dept of Mechanical Eng 1965–74, Inst. Prof. 1975–86, Inst. Prof. Sr Lecturer 1986–; Visiting Prof., Cambridge Univ. 1955–56; Founder and Chair. Nat. Cttee for Fluid Mechanics Films 1962–; mem. USAF Scientific Advisory Bd 1964–66; Councillor, American Acad. of Arts and Sciences 1966–69; mem. Editorial Bd Journal Applied Mech. 1955–56, Editorial Cttee Annual Review of Fluid Mech. 1967–71, Editorial Bd MIT Press 1977–87, Chair. 1982–87; Consultant to Govt and Industry in propulsion, compressors and turbines, fluid dynamics, bioeng, fluid machinery, industrial centrifuges; patentee: fluid metering equipment, combustion chamber, propulsion apparatus and gas turbines, magnetic disc storage devices, vacuum pump, low density wind tunnels, recipe-conversion calculator, centrifuge apparatus (ten); mem. Bd of Govs, Israel Inst. of Tech.; Fellow, American Acad. of Arts and Sciences, ASME, AIAA, American Inst. of Medical and Biomedical Eng; mem. NAS, Nat. Acad. of Eng; Hon. mem. ASME Int.; Hon. DSc (Salford, UK) 1978, (Technion-Israel

Inst. of Tech.) 1985; Naval Ordnance Devt Award 1945, Joint Certificate for Outstanding Contribution, War and Navy Depts. 1947, Richards Memorial Award of ASME 1960, Worcester Reed Warner Medal of ASME 1965, Lamme Medal of American Soc. for Eng Educ. 1977, Townsend Harris Medal (Coll. of the City of New York) 1978, Fluids Eng Award (ASME) 1981, J. P. Den Hartog Distinguished Educator Award of MIT 1984, Daniel C. Drucker Medal (ASME) 1999. *Publications:* The Dynamics and Thermodynamics of Compressible Fluid Flow Vol. I 1953, Vol. II 1954, Physical Measurements in Gas Dynamics and Combustion (Contrib. to) 1954, Shape and Flow: The Fluid Dynamics of Drag 1961, Handbook of Fluid Dynamics (contrib. to) 1961; and numerous tech. articles in fields of thermodynamics, propulsion, gas dynamics, fluid mechanics, biomedical Eng; educational films (The Fluid Dynamics of Drag 1958, Vorticity 1961, Pressure Fields and Fluid Acceleration 1964); 39 videotape lecture series, Fluid Dynamics (with text notes) 1984. *Address:* Mechanical Engineering Department, Room 3-262, Massachusetts Institute of Technology, 77 Massachusetts Avenue, Cambridge, MA 02139; 111 Perkins Street, Jamaica Plain, MA 02174, USA (Home). *Telephone:* (617) 253-4337 (Office); (617) 522-4418 (Home). *Fax:* (617) 971-9345. *E-mail:* aschers@ao.com (Home).

SHAPIRO, Bernard, OC; Canadian (b. American) academic administrator and public servant; b. 8 June 1935, Montreal; s. of Maxwell Shapiro and Mary Tafler; twin brother of Harold T. Shapiro (q.v.); m. Phyllis Schwartz 1957; one s. one d.; ed McGill Univ., Harvard Univ., USA; Deputy Minister of Educ. Ont. Prov. 1986–89, of Skills Devt 1988–89; Deputy Sec. of Cabinet, Ont. 1989–90, Deputy Minister and Sec., Man. Bd 1990–91, of Colls and Univs 1991–93; Prof. of Educ. and Public Policy, Univ. of Toronto 1992–94; Prin. and Vice-Chancellor McGill Univ. 1994–(2003); Hon. LLD (McGill) 1988, (Toronto) 1994, (Ottawa) 1995, (Yeshiva) 1996, (Montreal) 1998, (Edin.) 2000, (Glasgow) 2001, (Bishop's) 2001. *Address:* McGill University, James Administration Building, Room 506, 845 Sherbrooke Street West, Montreal, Qué. H3A 2T5, Canada. *Telephone:* (514) 398-4180. *Fax:* (514) 398-4768. *E-mail:* shapiro@ums1.Ian.mcgill.ca (Office). *Website:* www.mcgill.ca (Office).

SHAPIRO, Harold Tafler, PhD; American university president and professor of economics; b. 8 June 1935, Montreal, Canada; s. of Maxwell Shapiro and Mary Tafler; twin brother of Bernard Shapiro (q.v.); m. Vivian Shapiro; four d.; ed McGill Univ. and Princeton Univ. Grad. School; Asst Prof. of Econs Univ. of Mich. 1964, Assoc. Prof. 1967, Prof. 1970, Vice-Pres. for Academic Affairs 1977, Pres. 1980–88; Pres. Princeton Univ. 1988–2001, Pres. Emer. 2001–, Prof. of Econs and Public Affairs 1988–; mem. Conf. Bd Inc., Bretton Woods Cttee; mem. Pres.'s Council of Advisors on Science and Tech. 1990–92; Chair. Nat. Bioethics Advisory Comm. 1996–; Dir Dow Chemical Co., Nat. Bureau of Econ. Research; mem. Inst. of Medicine of NAS, American Philosophical Soc.; mem. Bd of Overseers, Robert Wood Johnson Medical Center, Bd of Trustees Educational Testing Service 1994–2000, Univ. Corpn for Advanced Internet Devt 2000–; Fellow American Acad. of Arts and Sciences; Trustee, Alfred P. Sloan Foundation, Univ. of Pa Medical Center, Univs Research Asscn, Educational Testing Service. *Address:* c/o Office of the President, Princeton University, 1 Nassau Hall, Princeton, NJ 08544, USA. *Website:* www.princeton.edu (Office).

SHAPIRO, Irwin I., PhD, FAAS; American physicist; b. 29 Oct. 1929, New York; s. of Esther Feinberg and Samuel Shapiro; m. Marian Helen Kaplun 1959; one s. one d.; ed Cornell and Harvard Univs; mem. staff., MIT Lincoln Lab. 1954–70, Prof. of Geophysics and Physics 1967–80; Redman Lecturer, McMaster Univ. 1969; Sherman Fairchild Distinguished Scholar, Calif. Inst. of Tech. 1974; Schlumberger Prof., MIT 1980–85, Prof. Emer. 1985–; Sr Scientist Smithsonian Astrophysical Observatory 1982–; Paine Prof. of Practical Astronomy and Prof. of Physics, Harvard Univ. 1982–97, Timken Univ. Prof. 1997–; Dir Harvard-Smithsonian Center for Astrophysics 1983– (Chair. of Bd 1980–81); John C. Lindsay Lecturer, NASA Goddard Space Flight Center 1986; current research is on radio and radar techniques applied to astrometry, astrophysics, geophysics, planetary physics and tests of theories of gravitation; mem. Editorial Bd Celestial Mechanics 1969–75, Annals of Physics 1977–82; Assoc. Ed. Icarus 1969–75; Fellow American Geophysical Union, American Physical Soc.; mem. Int. Astronomical Union, NAS 1974, American Acad. of Arts and Sciences 1969, American Astronomical Soc., American Philosophical Soc. 1998; mem. Radio Science Teams, Mariner Venus–Mercury, Viking and Pioneer–Venus Missions 1970–79, Space Science Bd (NAS) 1977–80, NSF Astronomy Advisory Cttee 1983–86, Task Group on Astronomy and Astrophysics of Nat. Research Council Space Science Bd Study 'Major Directions for Space Science: 1995–2015' 1984–86, Tech. Oversight Cttee of Nat. Earth Orientation Service 1986–, NASA Advisory Council 1987–90; Chair. NASA Astrophysics Subcttee 1988–92, mem. 1992–96; Albert A. Michelson Medal of Franklin Inst. 1975, Benjamin Apthorp Gould Prize of NAS 1979, John Simon Guggenheim Fellowship 1982, New York Acad. of Sciences Award in Physical and Math. Sciences 1982, Dannie Heineman Award of American Astronomical Soc. 1983, Whitten Medal (American Geophysical Union) 1991, Bowie Medal (American Geophysical Union) 1993, Einstein Medal 1994, Gerard Kuiper Award 1997, Secretary's Gold Medal for Exceptional Service, Smithsonian Inst. 1999. *Publications:* over 350 including Prediction of Ballistic Missile Trajectories from Radar Observations 1958; Ed. of trans. of Mathematical Foundations of Quantum Statistics (Khinchin) 1960; numerous scientific articles, tech. reports and text books for students. *Address:* Harvard-Smithsonian Center for Astrophysics, 60 Garden Street, Cambridge, MA 02138 (Office); 17

Lantern Lane, Lexington, MA 02421, USA (Home). *Telephone:* (617) 495-7100 (Office). *Fax:* (617) 495-7105 (Office). *E-mail:* ishapiro@cfa.harvard.edu (Office). *Website:* cfa-www.harvard.edu (Office).

SHAPIRO, Joel, MA; American sculptor; b. 27 Sept. 1941, New York; s. of Dr Joseph Shapiro and Dr Anna Shapiro; m. Ellen Phelan; one d.; ed NY Univ.; teacher Princeton Univ. 1974–75, 1975–76, School of Visual Arts 1977–82; group exhbns England, USA, Australia, Germany, Holland 1969–89; Nat. Endowment for the Arts 1975; mem. American Acad. of Arts and Letters, Swedish Royal Acad. of Art; Brandeis Award 1984, Skowhegan Medal for Sculpture 1986. *Solo exhibitions include:* Paula Cooper Gallery, New York 1970–89, Whitney Museum of Art, New York, Stedelijk Museum, Amsterdam 1985, Hirshorn Museum and Sculpture Garden, Washington, DC 1987, Hans Strelow, Dusseldorf 1988, Toledo Museum of Art 1989, Waddington Gallery, London 1989, Baltimore Art Museum 1990, Center for Fine Arts, Miami 1991, Des Moines Art Center 1991, Pace Gallery, New York 1993, Gallery Seomi, Seoul 1994, Galerie Aronowitsch, Stockholm 1995, Karsten Greve, Paris 1995, Pace Gallery, New York. 1995, Walker Art Center/Minneapolis Sculpture Garden 1995, Nelson-Atkins Museum of Art/Kansas City Sculpture Park 1996, Pace Wildenstein Gallery, New York 1996, Addison Gallery, Mass. 1997, Haus der Kunst, Munich 1997, Galerie Jamileh Weber, Zurich 1997, American Acad. in Rome 1999, Yorkshire Sculpture Park, Wakefield 1999, Nat. Gallery, Ottawa 1999–2000, Galerie Daniel Templon, Paris 2001, Metropolitan Museum of Art, New York 2001, Pace Wildenstein Gallery, New York 2003. *Television:* Art'è (RAI, Rome) 1999, Il Telegiornale dell'Arte (Telemarket, Rome) 1999. *Address:* c/o Pace Wildenstein, 32 East 57th Street, New York, NY 10022, USA. *Telephone:* (212) 421-3292 (Pace Wildenstein). *Fax:* (212) 421-0835 (Pace Wildenstein).

SHAPIRO, Robert Leslie, BS, JD; American lawyer; b. 2 Sept. 1942, Plainfield, NJ; ed Univ. of Calif. at Los Angeles, Loyola Univ. Law School; called to Bar, Calif. 1969, US Court of Appeals 1972, US Dist Court Calif. 1982; Deputy Dist Attorney LA 1969–72; sole practice 1972–87; counsel Bushkin, Gaims, Gaines, Jonas 1987–88; with Christensen, White, Miller, Fink & Jacobs 1988–95; partner Christensen, Miller, Fink, Jacobs, Glaser, Weil & Shapiro 1995–; f. Trial Lawyers for Public Justice 1982; mem. Nat. Asscn of Criminal Defence Lawyers, Calif. Attorneys for Criminal Justice, Bar Asscn; American Jurisprudence Award, Bancroft Whitney 1969; Best Criminal Defence Lawyer, Bar Asscn 1993. *Publications:* Search for Justice 1996, Misconception 2001. *Address:* 2121 Avenue of the Stars, Floor 19, Los Angeles, CA 90067, USA.

SHAPLEY, Lloyd Stowell, PhD; American professor of mathematics and economics; b. 2 June 1923, Cambridge, Mass.; s. of Harlow Shapley and Martha Betz; m. Marian Ludolph 1955 (died 1997); two s.; ed Belmont Hill School, Phillips Exeter Acad., Harvard and Princeton Univs; served in US Army Air Corps in meteorology and cryptanalysis 1943–45; research mathematician, Rand Corpn 1948–49, 1954–81; visiting appointments at Calif. Inst. of Tech. 1955–56, Indian Statistical Inst. 1979, Hebrew Univ. of Jerusalem 1979–80, Catholic Univ. of Louvain, Belgium 1982, Nat. Univ. of Defence Tech., China 1987; intermittent teaching, Rand Graduate Inst. 1970; Prof. of Math. and Econs UCLA 1981–; main research interest: theory of games; Fellow, Econometric Soc., American Acad. of Arts and Sciences; mem. NAS; Hon. PhD (Hebrew Univ. of Jerusalem) 1986; Bronze Star, US Army 1943; Von Neumann Theory Prize, ORSA/TIMS 1981. *Publications:* Geometry of Moment Spaces (with S. Karlin) 1953, Values of Non-Atomic Games (with R. Aumann) 1974. *Leisure interest:* Kriegsspiel. *Address:* Department of Mathematics and Department of Economics, University of California at Los Angeles, Los Angeles, CA 90024, USA. *Telephone:* (213) 825-4418.

SHAPOSHNIKOV, Air Marshal Yevgeny Ivanovich; Russian air force officer and politician; b. 3 Feb. 1942, Bolshoy Log, Rostov region; s. of Ivan Sevastinovich Shaposhnikov and Klavdia Stepanova Shaposhnikova; m. Zemfira Nikolayevna Shaposhnikova 1980; one s. two d.; ed Kharkov Higher Aviation School, Y. Gagarin Aviation Acad., Gen. Staff Acad.; served Soviet Army 1959–; Head Soviet Air Force in Germany 1987–88; First Deputy Commdr All-Union Soviet Air Force 1988–, Commdr 1990–91; Minister of Defence and Head Soviet Armed Forces Aug.–Dec. 1991; C-in-C of the Armed Forces of the CIS 1991–93; Sec. of Security Council, resgnd 1993; rep. of Pres. Yeltsin in Rosvooruzhenie (state-owned armaments exports co.); Gen. Dir Aeroflot 1995–97; Asst to Pres. of Russian Fed. 1997–; mem. Bd Democratic Reforms Movt 1993–98. *Leisure interests:* literature, theatre, tennis. *Address:* Administration of the President, Staraya pl. 4, 103132, Moscow, Russia. *Telephone:* (095) 910-12-46. *Fax:* (095) 206-89-01.

SHAPOVALYANTS, Andrei Georgiyevich; Russian economist; b. 23 Feb. 1952, Moscow; m.; two d.; ed Moscow Plekhanov Inst. of Nat. Econs; researcher, Inst. Elektronika, Main Computation Centre, USSR State Planning Cttee, Head of Div., USSR State Planning Cttee 1969–90; Head, Div. of Financial-Credit Policy, USSR Ministry of Econs and Prognosis 1991; Deputy, First Deputy Minister of Econs and Finance of Russian Fed. 1991–93; Acting Minister of Econs and Finance, First Deputy Minister 1993–98, Minister of Econs 1998–99; mem. Presidium, Russian Govt 1998–; Man. Black Sea Bank of Trade and Devt 1999–; Pres. Bd of Dirs KAMAZ co. 1999–; Dir.-Gen. Centre of Reconstruction and Devt of Enterprises 2001–. *Address:* Centre of Reconstruction and Development of Enterprises, Ozerkovski per 12, 113184 Moscow, Russia. *Telephone:* (095) 251-82-26 (Office).

SHARANSKY, Natan; Israeli (b. Soviet) politician, human rights activist and computer scientist; b. 20 Jan. 1948, Donetsk, USSR (now Ukraine); s. of the late Ida Milgrom; m. Natalya (now Avital) Stiglitz 1974; a leading spokesman for Jewish emigration Movt in USSR; arrested by Soviet authorities for dissident activities 1977; received 13-year prison sentence on charges of treason 1978; following worldwide campaign, Soviet authorities released him in exchange for eastern spies held in West and he took up residence in Israel Feb. 1986; Visiting Prof. Brandeis Univ., Waltham, Mass.; currently Leader Israel B'Aliyah Party; Minister of Trade and Industry 1996–99, of the Interior 1999–2000; US Congressional Medal of Honor 1986. *Publication:* Fear No Evil 1988. *Address:* The Knesset, Jerusalem 91061, Israel (Office). *Telephone:* 2-6701411 (Office). *Fax:* 2-6701628 (Office).

SHARER, Kevin, BEng, MBA; American business executive; ed US Naval Acad., Annapolis and Univ. of Pittsburgh; fmr Consultant, McKinsey & Co.; fmr Exec. Gen. Electric Corpn; Exec. Vice-Pres. and Pres. of Business Markets Div., MCI Communications Corpn –1992; Pres., COO and mem. Bd of Dirs Amgen 1992–2000, CEO 2000–, Chair. 2001–; Chair. Bd of Trustees, LA Co. Museum of Natural History; mem. Bd of Dirs. UNOCAL Corpn. *Address:* Amgen Corporation, Amgen Center, Thousand Oaks, CA 91320-1977, USA (Office). *Website:* www.amgen.com (Office).

SHARIF, Ihab ash-, PhD; Egyptian diplomatist; b. 1 Jan. 1954, Cairo; s. of Salaheldin ash-Sharif; m. Asmaa Hussein; two d.; ed Univ. of Paris (Sorbonne), Univ. of Paris XI, France; Diplomatic Attaché, Cen. African Repub. 1981–85; Asst to Minister of State for Foreign Affairs 1985–88; First Sec., Paris 1988–92; Counsellor, Damascus 1994–98; Plenipotentiary Minister, then Head of Mission and Chargé d'affaires, Egyptian Embassy, Tel-Aviv 1999–; Order of Merit, Germany 1999. *Publications:* photographic travel books about 22 countries, including Europe, Myth and Reality 1997, India, Secret and Keys, Germany Today, France, A Country of Djinns and Angels. *Leisure interests:* sport, reading, driving. *Address:* Embassy of Egypt, 54 Rehov Street, Tel-Aviv 62744, Israel (Office). *Telephone:* 3-5464151 (Office); 2-4833668 (Home). *Fax:* 3-5441615 (Office). *E-mail:* ihabelsherif@hotmail.com (Home). *Website:* www.bosatalrih.com (Home).

SHARIF, Muhammad Safwat esh-; Egyptian politician; b. 1933, Cairo; ed Mil. Acad., Inst. of Strategic Studies; with Presidency of the Repub. 1957–74; Dir Gen., local information, State Information Dept 1975, Dir of Foreign Information Service, State Information Dept; mem. Arab Information Cttee 1975; Sec. Ministry of Information 1977; Chair. Information Authority 1978; mem. of the Media Cttee 1979; mem. constituent Cttee Nat. Democratic Party; Chief, Council of TV and Radio Trustees 1980; Minister of Information 1982–. *Address:* Ministry of Information, Radio and TV Bldg, Corniche en Nil, Cairo, Egypt. *Telephone:* (2) 5748984 (Office). *Fax:* (2) 5748981 (Office). *E-mail:* rtu@idsc.gov.eg (Office).

SHARIF, Omar (Michael Chalhoub); Egyptian actor; b. 10 April 1932, Cairo; s. of Claire Saada and Joseph Chalhoub; m. 1st Faten Hamama 1955 (divorced 1967); one s.; m. 2nd 1973; ed Victoria Coll., Cairo; Salesman, lumber-import firm; made first film The Blazing Sun 1953; starred in 24 Egyptian films and two French co-production films during following five years; commenced int. film career with Lawrence of Arabia; appeared in play The Sleeping Prince, England 1983. *Films include:* Lawrence of Arabia, The Fall of the Roman Empire, Behold a Pale Horse, Genghis Khan, The Yellow Rolls-Royce, Doctor Zhivago, Night of the Generals, Mackenna's Gold, Funny Girl, Cinderella-Italian Style, Mayerling, The Appointment, Che, The Last Valley, The Horsemen, The Burglars, The Island, The Tamarind Seed, Juggernaut, Funny Lady, Ace Up My Sleeve, Crime and Passion, Bloodline, Green Ice, Top Secret, Peter the Great (TV), The Possessed, Mountains of the Moon, Michaelangelo and Me, Drums of Fire, Le Guignol, The Puppet, The Rainbow Thief, 588 rue Paradis, Gulliver's Travels (TV), Heaven Before I Die, The 13th Warrior, Mysteries of Egypt. *Publication:* The Eternal Male (autobiog.) 1978. *Leisure interests:* bridge and horse racing. *Address:* c/o Ames Cushing, William Morris Agency, 151 South El Camino Drive, Beverly Hills, CA 90212, USA.

SHARIR, Abraham; Israeli politician and lawyer; b. 1932, Tel Aviv; m.; four c.; ed Hebrew Univ., Jerusalem; mil. service with Israeli Air Force; mem. Ninth Knesset (Parl.) –1981, mem. Finance Cttee, Chair. Likud Faction; mem. Tenth Knesset; Minister of Tourism 1981, 1984–86, of Tourism and Justice 1986–88; mem. High Court of Labour Relations, of Govt Cttee on Pensions; Likud Party. *Address:* c/o Ministry of Tourism, P.O. Box 1018, Jerusalem, Israel.

SHARMA, Arun Kumar, DSc, FNA, F.A.SC., F.N.A.SC.; Indian botanist; b. 31 Dec. 1924, Calcutta (now Kolkata); s. of the late Charu Chandra Sharma and of Shovamoyee Sharma; m. Archana Mookerjea 1955; ed Univ. of Calcutta; Research Scholar, Botanical Survey of India 1946–48; Asst Lecturer, Univ. of Calcutta 1948–52, Lecturer 1952–62, Reader 1962–69, Prof. and Head, Dept of Botany 1969–80, Programme Coordinator, Centre of Advanced Study, Dept of Botany 1980–90; Pres. Indian Nat. Science Acad. 1983–84, Golden Jubilee Prof. 1985–90, Hon. Prof. 1990–; Gen. Pres. Indian Science Congress Asscn 1981; Founding Pres. Fed. of Asian Scientific Acads. and Socs. 1984–; Fellow Third World Acad. of Sciences; S. S. Bhatnagar Award in Biology – CSIR 1967, Padma Bhushan, Om Prakash Bhasin Foundation Award 1993, First J. C. Bose Memorial Prize 1994, G. M. Modi Research Award 1994, Centenary Award in Biology 1999, M. N. Saha Memorial Award (Indian Nat. Science Acad.) 1999 and numerous other awards. *Publications:* Chromosome Techniques: Theory and Practice (with Archana Sharma) 1980, Chromosome in Evolution of Eukaryotic Groups, Vols I and II (with Archana Sharma) 1983, Chromosome Techniques—a manual (with Archana Sharma) 1994, Plant Chromosomes: analysis, manipulation and engineering (with Archana Sharma) 1999, Chromosome Painting (with A. Sharma) 2002; book chapters, articles in journals etc. *Leisure interests:* photography, bird-watching. *Address:* Centre of Advanced Study (Cell and Chromosome Research), Department of Botany, University of Calcutta, 35 Ballygunge Circular Road, Kolkata 700 019 (Office); Flat No. 2F2, 18/3 Gariahat Road, Kolkata, 700 019, India (Home). *Telephone:* (33) 24754681 (Office); (33) 24405802 (Home). *Fax:* (33) 24764419; (33) 24741042. *E-mail:* nuclaks@cal2.vsnl.net.in (Home).

SHARMA, Dwarka Prasad, MCom, LLB, PhD; Indian university vice-chancellor (retd); b. 28 Oct. 1933, Umreth; s. of Shri B. L. Sharma; m. Chandra Prabha Sharma 1963; three c.; Chair. and Dean Faculty of Commerce and Man. Sri Krishnadevaraya Univ., Anantapur 1974–89, Bhopal Univ. (renamed Barkatullah Univ.) 1989–91; Rector (Pro-Vice-Chancellor) Barkatullah Univ. 1991–93; Dir C. Rajagopalachari Inst. of Man. 1989–93; Regional Co-ordinator AIMS; Chair., Bhopal Br., IIMM; Visiting Prof. at several Indian and foreign univs; Best Teacher Award Govt of Andhra Pradesh 1982. *Publications:* Rural Economy of India 1976, Rural Banking in India 1981, Company Law and Secretarial Practice 1984, numerous research publs. *Leisure interests:* reading, writing. *Address:* 4/9B, Saketnagar, Bhopal, MP, 462024, India. *Telephone:* (755) 582802.

SHARMAN, Baron (Life Peer), cr. 1999, of Redlynch in the County of Wiltshire; **Colin Morven Sharman,** OBE, FCA, CIMgt; British chartered accountant; b. 19 Feb. 1943; s. of Col Terence John Sharman and Audrey Emmiline Newman; m. Angela M. Timmins 1966; one s. one d.; ed Bishops Wordsworth School, Salisbury; qualified as accountant with Woolgar Hennel & Co. 1965; joined Peat Marwick Mitchell 1966 (later KPMG Peat Marwick, now KPMG), Man. Frankfurt Office 1970–72, The Hague Office 1972–81 (Partner 1973, Partner-in-Charge 1975), London Office 1981–, Sr Partner Nat. Marketing and Industry Groups 1987–90, Sr Man. Consultancy Partner 1989–91, Sr Regional Partner, London and SE 1990–93, Sr Partner 1994–98, Chair. KPMG Int. 1997–99; Deputy Chair. Aegis PLC 1999–2000, Chair. 2000–; Chair. BG Group PLC; Dir Reed Elsevier 2002–; Deputy Chair. (non-exec.) Securicor 2003, Chair. (non-exec.) (Nov. 2003–); mem. Industrial Soc. *Publication:* Living Culture 2001. *Leisure interests:* food and wine, sailing, opera. *Address:* House of Lords, London, SW1A 0IW, England (Office).

SHARON, Maj.-Gen. Ariel; Israeli politician and army officer (retd); b. 1928; m.; two s.; active in Hagana since early youth; Instructor, Jewish Police units 1947; Platoon Commdr Alexandroni Brigade; Regimental Intelligence Officer 1948; Co. Commdr 1949; Commdr Brigade Reconnaissance Unit 1949–50; Intelligence Officer, Cen. Command and Northern Command 1951–52; studies at Hebrew Univ. 1952–53; in charge of Unit 101, on numerous reprisal operations until 1957, Commdr Paratroopers Brigade, Sinai Campaign 1956; studies Staff Coll., Camberley, UK 1957–58; Training Commdr, Gen. Staff 1958; Commdr Infantry School 1958–69; Commdr Armoured Brigade 1962; Head of Staff, Northern Command 1964; Head, Training Dept of Defence Forces 1966; Head Brigade Group during Six-Day War 1967; resigned from Army July 1973; recalled as Commdr Cen. Section of Sinai Front during Yom Kippur War Oct. 1973, forged bridgehead across Suez Canal; Founder mem. Likud Front 1973; mem. Knesset (Parl.) 1973–74, 1977–; Adviser to Prime Minister 1975–77; Minister of Agric. in charge of Settlements 1977–81, of Defence 1981–83, without Portfolio 1983–84, of Trade and Industry 1984–90, of Construction and Housing 1990–92, of Foreign Affairs and Nat. Infrastructure 1996–99; Prime Minister of Israel March 2001–, also Minister of Immigrant Absorption; mem. Ministerial Defence Cttee 1990–92; Chair. Cabinet Cttee to oversee Jewish immigration from USSR 1991–96; Leader Likud Party 1999–. *Publication:* Warrior (autobiog.) 1989. *Address:* Likud Party, 38 Rehov King George, Tel-Aviv 61231; Office of the Prime Minister, P.O. Box 187, 3 Rehov Kaplan, Kiryat Ben-Gurion, Jerusalem 91919, Israel (Office). *Telephone:* 2-6705511 (Office); 3-5630666. *Fax:* 2-6512531 (Office); 3-5282901. *E-mail:* doar@pmo.gov.il (Office). *Website:* www.pmo.gov.il, www.likud.org.il (Office).

SHARP, Hon. John Randall; Australian politician (retd) and company director; b. 15 Dec. 1954, Sydney; s. of J. K. Sharp; m. Victoria Sharp 1986; two s. one d.; ed The King's School, NSW, Orange Agricultural Coll.; farmer; mem. House of Reps. for Gilmore, NSW 1984–93; MP (Nat. Party of Australia) for Hume, NSW 1993–; Shadow Minister for Tourism and Sport 1988, for Tourism, Sport and Youth Affairs 1988–89, for Land Transport and Shipping 1989–90, for Shipping and Waterfront Reform 1990–93, for Transport 1993–96; Minister for Transport and Regional Devt 1996–97; Deputy Man. of Opposition Business in the House 1990–94; Exec. Dir Linfox 1999–2001, Corp. adviser 1999–2001; Dir John McEwan House, Australian Aerospace 2002–, French-Australian Chamber of Commerce and Industry; Fellow Chartered Inst. of Transport; Hon. Sec. Nat. Party of Australia. *Leisure interests:* rugby union, scuba diving, skiing, tennis, aviation. *Address:* Gibraltar Park, Mittagong Road, Bowral, NSW 2576, Australia. *Telephone:* (2) 4862-5226 (Office); (2) 4862-5226 (Home). *Fax:* (2) 4862-5214 (Office); (2) 4862-5214 (Home). *E-mail:* sharp@hinet.net.au (Home).

SHARP, Phillip Allen, PhD, FAAS; American professor of biology and academic administrator; b. 6 June 1944, Falmouth, KY; s. of Joseph W. Sharp and Katherin A. Sharp; m. Ann H. Holcombe 1964; three d.; ed Union Coll., Ky, Univ. of Illinois, California Inst. of Tech. and Cold Spring Harbor, New York; Research Asst, Dept of Chem., Univ. of Ill. 1966–69; Postdoctoral Fellow, Lab. of Prof. Norman Davidson, Calif. Inst. of Tech. 1969–71, Cold Spring Harbor Lab. 1971–72, Sr Research Investigator 1972–74; Assoc. Prof., Center for Cancer Research and Dept of Biology, MIT 1974–79, Prof. 1979–99, Inst. Prof. 1999–; Assoc. Dir Center for Cancer Research 1982–85, Dir 1985–91, Head of Dept of Biology 1991–99; Founding Dir The McGovern Inst. for Brain Research 2000–; Co-founder, Chair. Scientific Bd, mem. Bd of Dirs. Biogen, Inc.; Chair. Gen. Motors Cancer Research Foundation Awards Ass. 1994–, Scientific Advisory Cttee Dana-Farber Cancer Inst. 1996; mem. Cttee on Science, Eng and Public Policy 1992–95, Gen. Motors Cancer Research Foundation Advisory Council 1993–, Pres.'s Advisory Council on Science and Tech. 1991–97, Nat. Cancer Advisory Bd, NIH (Presidential appointment) 1996, Scientific Bd of Advisors, Van Andel Inst. 1996–, Scientific Cttee Ludwig Inst. for Cancer Research 1998–, Bd of Scientific Govs. Scripps Research Inst. 1999–; mem. and Trustee Alfred P. Sloan Foundation 1995–; mem. NAS, NAS Inst. of Medicine, American Acad. of Arts and Sciences, American Philosophical Soc.; Dr hc (Union Coll., Ky, Univ. of Buenos Aires); Hon. DSc (Univ. of Ky, Univ. of Tel-Aviv, Thomas More Coll., Ky, Glasgow Univ., Albright Coll., Pa); Hon. MD (Uppsala Univ.); Howard Ricketts Award, Eli Lilly Award, NAS US Steel Foundation Award, Gen. Motors Research Foundation Alfred P. Sloan, Jr Prize for Cancer Research, Gairdner Foundation Int. Award, New York Acad. of Sciences Award in Biological and Medical Sciences, Louisa Gross Horwitz Prize, Albert Lasker Basic Medical Research Award, Dickson Prize (Univ. of Pittsburgh), shared Nobel Prize for Medicine 1993, Benjamin Franklin Medal, American Philosophical Soc. 1999, Walter Prize, Museum of Science, Boston. *Publications:* numerous papers in scientific journals. *Leisure interests:* family, reading, sports. *Address:* Center for Cancer Research, Room E17-529B, Massachusetts Institute of Technology, 40 Ames Street, Cambridge, MA 02139 (Office); 36 Fairmont Avenue, Newton, MA 02458, USA (Home). *Telephone:* (617) 253-6421 (Office). *Fax:* (617) 253-3867 (Office). *E-mail:* sharppa@mit.edu (Office).

SHARP, Robert Phillip, PhD; American geologist; b. 24 June 1911, Calif.; s. of Julian Hebner Sharp and Alice Darling; m. Jean Prescott Todd 1938; one s. one d. (both adopted); ed Oxnard Union High School, Calif., California Inst. of Tech., Harvard Univ.; Asst Prof., Univ. of Ill. 1938–43; Capt., USAAF 1943–46; Prof. of Univ. of Minn. 1946–47; Prof., Calif. Inst. of Tech. 1947–79, Robert P. Sharp Emer. Prof. of Geology 1979–, Chair. Div. of Geological Sciences 1952–68; mem. NAS; Kirk Bryan Award, Penrose Medal, Geological Soc. of America, NASA Exceptional Scientific Achievement Medal, Nat. Medal of Science 1989, Charles P. Daly Medal, American Geographical Soc. 1990, G. K. Gilbert Award and Distinguished Career Award, Geological Soc. of America 1996. *Publications:* Living Ice: Understanding Glaciers and Glaciation 1989, Geology Underfoot in Death Valley and Owens Valley 1997, 100 papers on geomorphology, glaciers, glaciation, dunes and related subjects in scientific journals and several books. *Leisure interests:* fly-fishing, snorkelling, skiing. *Address:* Division of Geological and Planetary Sciences, California Institute of Technology, Pasadena, 1200 E California Blvd., CA 91106 (Office); 1901 Gibraltar Road, Santa Barbara, CA 93105, USA (Home). *Telephone:* (626) 395-6124 (Office); (805) 962-6675 (Home). *Fax:* (818) 568-0935.

SHARPE, Kevin Michael, MA, DPhil, FRHistS; British historian and critic; b. 26 Jan. 1949, Kent; s. of Thomas H. Sharpe and Nell D. Sharpe; ed Sir Joseph Williamson's Mathematical School, Rochester and St Catherine's Coll., Oxford; Sr Scholar, St Catherine's Coll., Oxford 1971–74; Fellow, Oriel Coll., Oxford 1974–78; Lecturer, Christ Church, Oxford 1976–78; Lecturer in Early Modern History, Univ. of Southampton 1978–89, Reader 1989–, Prof. of History, School of Research and Grad. Studies and Dir of Research 1994–2001; Prof. of Renaissance Studies, Univ. of Warwick 2001–; Visiting Fellow, Inst. for Advanced Study, Princeton 1981; Huntington Library, San Marino, Calif. 1982 (Fletcher Jones Research Prof. 2001–02); Visiting Prof. Stanford Univ. Humanities Center 1985–86; Visiting Fellow, Humanities Centre, ANU 1990; Visiting Prof., Calif. Inst. of Tech. 1992–93, Mellon Prof. 2001–02; Visiting Fellow St Catherine's Coll., Oxford 1996; Adviser to British Art Galleries Project, Victoria and Albert Museum, Lely Exhbn and Conf., Yale Center for British Art and NPG; Fulbright Fellow 1981; ANU Fellowship 1989; Avery Sr Research Fellowship, Huntington Library 1992, Fletcher Jones Sr Fellowship 2001–02; Alexander Von Humboldt Fellowship 2001; Fellow English Asscn 2002; Wolfson Award 1980, , . *Radio:* In Our Time, Nightwaves. *Publications:* Faction and Parliament 1978, Sir Robert Cotton, 1586–1631: History and Politics in Early Modern England 1979, Faction and Parliament: Essays on Early Stuart England (Ed.) 1985, Criticism and Compliment: The Politics of Literature in the England of Charles I (Royal Historical Soc. Whitfield Prize 1988) 1987, Politics of Discourse: The Literature and History of Seventeenth Century England (Co-Ed.) 1987, Politics and Ideas in Early Stuart England 1989, The Personal Rule of Charles I 1992, Culture and Politics in Early Stuart England (Co-Ed.) 1994, Refiguring Revolutions: Aesthetics and Politics from the English Revolution to the Romantic Revolution (Co-Ed.) 1998, Reading Revolutions (Soc. for History of Authorship, Readership and Publishing Prize 2001) 2000, Remapping Early Modern England 2000, Reading, Society, and Politics in Early Modern England (Co-Ed.) 2003; articles and reviews in The Sunday Times, The Independent, Times Literary Supplement, Spectator, History Today and other journals. *Leisure interests:* cycling, travel, conversation. *Address:* Department of English, University of Warwick, Coventry, CV4 7AL (Office);

8 Bertie Terrace, Warwick Place, Leamington Spa, CV32 5DZ; 97 Livingstone Road, Portswood, Southampton, SO17 1BY, England. *Telephone:* (24) 7652-3322 (Office); (23) 8055-3303 (Southampton) (Home); (1926) 435606 (Leamington Spa) (Home). *E-mail:* k.sharpe@warwick.ac.uk (Office). *Website:* www.warwick.ac.uk (Office).

SHARPE, Tom (Thomas Ridley), MA; British novelist; b. 30 March 1928, London; s. of Rev. George Coverdale Sharpe and Grace Egerton Sharpe; m. Nancy Anne Looper 1969; three d.; ed Lancing Coll., Pembroke Coll., Univ. of Cambridge; Social Worker 1952; Teacher 1952–56; Photographer 1956–61; Lecturer in History at Cambridge Coll. of Arts and Tech. 1963–71; full-time novelist 1971–. *Publications:* Riotous Assembly 1971, Indecent Exposure 1973, Porterhouse Blue 1974, Blott on the Landscape 1975, Wilt 1976, The Great Pursuit 1977, The Throwback 1978, The Wilt Alternative 1979, Ancestral Vices 1980, Vintage Stuff 1982, Wilt on High 1984, Grantchester Grind 1995, The Midden 1996. *Leisure interests:* photography, gardening. *Address:* 38 Tunwells Lane, Great Shelford, Cambridge, CB2 5LJ, England.

SHARPE, William Forsyth, PhD; American economist; b. 16 June 1934, Cambridge, Mass.; s. of Russell Thornley Sharpe and Evelyn Forsyth (Jillson) Maloy; m. 1st Roberta Ruth Branton 1954 (divorced 1986); one s. one d.; m. 2nd Kathryn Dorothy Peck 1986; one step-s. one step-d.; ed Univ. of California, Los Angeles; economist, Rand Corpn 1957–61; Asst Prof. of Econs, Univ. of Washington 1961–63, Assoc. Prof. 1963–67, Prof. 1967–68; Prof., Univ. of Calif., Irvine 1968–70; Timken Prof. of Finance, Stanford Univ. 1970–89, Prof. Emer. 1989–92; Pres. William F. Sharpe Assocs. 1986–92; Prof. of Finance Stanford Univ. 1993–95, STANCO 25 Prof. of Finance 1995–99, Prof. Emer. 1999–; Chair. Financial Engines Inc. 1996–; Hon. DHumLitt (De Paul Univ.) 1997; Graham and Dodd Award 1972, 1973, 1986, 1988, Nicholas Molodovsky Award 1989, Nobel Prize for Econ. Sciences 1990; UCLA Medal 1998. *Publications:* Economics of Computers 1969, Portfolio Theory and Capital Markets 1970, Fundamentals of Investments 1989, Investments. *Leisure interests:* sailing, all kinds of music. *Address:* Graduate School of Business, Stanford University, Stanford, CA 94305, USA (Office). *E-mail:* wtsharpe@stanford.edu (Office).

SHARPLESS, K(arl) Barry, BA, PhD; American chemist; b. 28 April 1941, Philadelphia; s. of Dr E. Dallett Sharpless and Evelyn Anderson Sharpless; m. Jan Sharpless; two s. one d.; ed Dartmouth Coll., New Hampshire, Stanford Univ., Harvard Univ.; mem. Chem. Faculty, MIT 1970–77, 1980–90, Arthur C. Cope Prof. 1987–90; mem. Chem. Faculty, Stanford Univ. 1977–80; W. M. Keck Prof. of Chem., The Scripps Research Inst. (TSRI), La Jolla, Calif. 1990–, Skaggs Inst. for Chemical Biology, TSRI 1996–; mem AAAS 1984, American Acad. of Arts and Sciences 1984, NAS 1985; numerous fellowships including A. P. Sloan Foundation Fellow 1973, Camille and Henry Dreyfus Foundation Fellow 1973, Simon Guggenheim Foundation Fellow 1987; numerous hon. degrees; Hon. mem. RSC 1998; Dr hc (Dartmouth Coll.) 1995, (Royal Inst. of Tech., Stockholm) 1995, (Tech. Univ., Munich) 1995, (Catholic Univ. of Louvain) 1996, (Wesleyan Univ.) 1999, (Hong Kong Christian Univ.) 2002; NAS Prize 1985, ten prizes from the ACS including Arthur C. Cope Scholar 1986, and Award 1992, San Diego Scientist of the Year 1992, Roger Adams Award in Organic Chem. 1997; Janssen Prize 1986, Prelog Medal, ETH, Zürich 1988, Sammet Award, Goethe Univ., Frankfurt 1988, Chemical Pioneer Award (American Inst. of Chemists) 1988, Scheele Medal (Swedish Acad. of Pharma Sciences) 1991, Tetrahedron Prize 1993, King Faisal Prize for Science (Saudi Arabia) 1995, Microbial Chem. Award, Kitasato Inst., Tokyo 1997, Harvey Science and Tech. Prize, Israel Inst. of Tech. 1998, Hon. Prize, Royal Soc. (UK) 1998, Organic Reactions Catalysis Soc. Richard Rylander Award 2000, NAS Chemical Sciences Award 2000, Chirality Medal, Italian Chemical Soc. 2000, Nobel Prize in Chemistry 2001 (jt recipient), Benjamin Franklin Medal Medal, Philadelphia 2001, Wolf Prize in Science (Israel) 2001, Rhône-Poulence Medal (UK) 2001, John Scott Prize and Medal, Philadelphia 2001. *Publications:* more than 300 publs in learned journals and 20 patents. *Address:* The Scripps Research Institute, 10550 North Torrey Pines Road, La Jolla, CA 92037, USA (Office). *Telephone:* (858) 784-7505 (Office). *Fax:* (858) 784-7562 (Office). *E-mail:* sharples@scripps.edu (Office). *Website:* www.scripps.edu (Office).

SHARQI, HH Sheikh Hamad bin Muhammad ash–, Ruler of Fujairah; b. 25 Sept. 1948; ed Mons Mil. Acad., Hendon Police Coll.; Minister of Agric. and Fisheries, UAE Fed. Cabinet 1971; Ruler of Fujairah 1974–; mem. Supreme Council 1974–. *Address:* Emiri Court, P.O. Box 1, Fujairah, United Arab Emirates.

SHATKIN, Aaron Jeffrey, PhD, FAAS; American scientist; b. 18 July 1934, RI; s. of Morris Shatkin and Doris Shatkin; m. Joan Arlene Lynch 1957; one s.; ed Bowdoin Coll. and Rockefeller Univ.; Research Chemist NIH, Bethesda, Md 1961–68; Visiting Scientist Salk Inst., La Jolla, Calif. 1968–69; mem. Roche Inst. of Molecular Biology, Nutley, NJ 1968–86, Head Lab. of Molecular Biology 1977–83, Head Dept of Cell Biology 1983–86; Univ. Prof. of Molecular Biology, Rutgers Univ. 1986–; Prof. of Molecular Genetics and Microbiology, R. W. Johnson Medical School 1986–; Adjunct Prof. Rockefeller Univ. 1978–87, Princeton Univ. 1984–87; Dir and Prof., New Jersey Center for Advanced Biotechnology and Medicine 1986–; Visiting Prof. Georgetown Univ. Medical School, Washington, DC 1968; Instructor Cold Spring Harbor Lab. 1972, 1973, 1974, Univ. of Puerto Rico 1978, 1980; Ed.-in-Chief Molecular and Cellular Biology 1980–90; mem. NAS 1981–, American Acad. of Arts and Sciences 1997, several editorial bds; Fellow American Acad. of Micro-

biology 1992; Hon. DSc (Bowdoin Coll.) 1979; U.S. Steel Award in Molecular Biology 1977, NJ Pride Award in Science 1989, Thomas Alva Edison Science Award 1991. *Publications:* more than 200 publs in scientific journals including original reports and review articles. *Leisure interests:* travel, birds, running. *Address:* Center for Advanced Biotechnology and Medicine, 679 Hoes Lane, Piscataway, NJ 08854 (Office); 1381 Rahway Road, Scotch Plains, NJ 07076, USA (Home). *Telephone:* (732) 235-5311 (Office). *Fax:* (732) 235-5318. *E-mail:* shatkin@cabm. rutgers. edu (Office).

SHATNER, William, BA; American actor and film director; b. 22 March 1931, Montreal, Que., Canada; s. of Joseph Shatner and Anne Shatner; m. 1st Gloria Rand 1956 (divorced 1969); m. 2nd Marcy Lafferty 1973 (divorced 1996); m. 3rd Nerine Kidd 1997 (died 1999); three d.; m. 4th Elizabeth Martin 2001; ed McGill Univ.; appeared, Montreal Playhouse 1952, 1953; juvenile roles, Canadian Repertory Theatre, Ottawa 1952–53, 1953–54; appeared Shakespeare Festival, Stratford, Ont. 1954–56; Broadway appearances include: Tamburlaine the Great 1956, The World of Suzie Wong 1958, A Shot in the Dark 1961 Founder, Presenter Hollywood Charity Horse Show, Los Angeles 1991–; CEO C.O.R.E. Digital Pictures, Inc., Toronto 1994–. *Films include:* The Brothers Karamazov 1957, The Explosive Generation 1961, Judgment at Nuremberg 1961, The Intruder 1962, The Outrage 1964, Dead of Night 1974, The Devil's Rain 1975, Star Trek 1979, The Kidnapping of the President 1979, Star Trek: The Wrath of Khan 1982, Star Trek III: The Search for Spock 1984, Star Trek IV: The Voyage Home 1986, Star Trek V: The Final Frontier (also Dir) 1989, Star Trek VI: The Undiscovered Country 1991, National Lampoon's Loaded Weapon 1993, Star Trek: Generations 1994, Ashes of Eden 1995, Star Trek: Avenger 1997, Tek Net 1997, Free Enterprise 1999, Miss Congeniality 2000, Groom Lake (also Dir and co-writer) 2002. *TV appearances include:* Star Trek, TekWar (also exec. producer and dir. of two episodes) T.J. Hooker, Land of the Free, The Fresh Prince of Bel-Air, Cosby, Third Rock from the Sun. *Publications include:* TekWar 1989, Star Trek Memories (jtly) 1993, Star Trek Movie Memories 1994, Ashes of Eden (jtly) 1995, Man O' War 1996, Tek Kill 1996, The Return 1996, Avenger 1997, Delta Search: Quest For Tomorrow 1997, Delta Search: In Alien Hands 1998, Step into Chaos 1999, Dark Victory 1999, Step Into Chaos 1999, Get a Life (jtly) 1999, The Preserver 2000, Spectre 2000. *Leisure interests:* tennis, yoga, skiing, riding, horse breeding, scuba diving, parasailing. *Address:* c/o Melis Productions Inc., 760 North La Cienega Boulevard, Los Angeles, CA 90069, USA. *Telephone:* (818) 509-2290. *Fax:* (818) 509-2299. *Website:* williamshatner.com.

SHATROV, (Marshak) Mikhail Filippovich; Russian dramatist and scriptwriter; b. 3 April 1932; s. of Filipp Semenovich and Cecilia Alexandrovna Marshak; m. Julia Vladimirovna Chernyshova; two d.; ed Moscow Mining Inst.; Pres. and Chair. of Bd of Dirs. Zao Moskva-Krasnye Kholmy Co. 1994–; Head of Drama, Theatre, Cinema and TV, Ministry of Culture of the Russian Fed. 2002–; began writing plays in 1955; USSR State Prize 1983. *Plays include:* In the Name of Revolution 1957, The Peace of Brest Litovsk 1962, The Sixth of July 1963, Przevalsky's Horse 1972, The Dictatorship of Conscience 1986, Further... Further... Further 1988. *Film screenplays include:* Two Lines of Tiny Handwriting 1981, Tehran-43 1981, Maybe (for Vanessa Redgrave) 1993. *Publications:* February (novel) 1988, Maybe 1993. *Address:* Serafimovich str. 2, Apt. 349, 109072 Moscow, Russia. *Telephone:* (095) 961-2230 (Office); (095) 959-31-68.

SHAW, Bernard Leslie, PhD, FRS; British professor of chemistry; b. 28 March 1930, Springhead, Yorks.; s. of Tom Shaw and Vera Shaw; m. Mary Elizabeth Neild 1951; two s.; ed Hulme Grammar School, Oldham and Manchester Univ.; Sr DSIR Fellow, Torry Research Station, Aberdeen 1953–55; Research Scientist, ICI Ltd 1956–61; Lecturer, School of Chem., Univ. of Leeds 1962–65, Reader 1965–71, Prof. 1971–94, Research Prof. 1995–; Visiting Prof. Univ. of Western Ont., Carnegie Mellon Univ. 1969, ANU 1983, Univ. of Auckland 1986, Univ. of Strasbourg 1993; mem. Science and Eng Research Council Chem. Cttee 1975–78, 1981–84; Tilden Lecturer, Chemical Soc. 1975, Liversidge Lecturer RSC 1987–88; Chemical Soc. Award in Transition Metal Chem. 1975, Ludwig Mond Lecturer and Prizewinner RSC 1992–93, Sir Edward Frankland Lecturer and Prizewinner 1995. *Publications:* Inorganic Hydrides, Organo-Transition Metal Compounds and Related Aspects of Homogeneous Catalysis and about 400 research papers; several patents. *Leisure interests:* walking, pottery, gardening, tennis. *Address:* School of Chemistry, University of Leeds, Leeds, LS2 9JT (Office); 14 Monkbridge Road, Leeds, West Yorks., LS6 4DX, England (Home). *Telephone:* (113) 343-6402 (Office); (113) 275-5895 (Home). *Fax:* (113) 343-6565 (Office). *E-mail:* B.L.Shaw@Chem.Leeds.ac.uk (Office). *Website:* www.leeds.ac.uk (Office).

SHAW, Colin Don, CBE, MA; British fmr broadcasting executive, writer and lecturer; b. 2 Nov. 1928, Liverpool; s. of Rupert M. Shaw and Enid F. Shaw (née Smith); m. Elizabeth A. Bowker 1955; one s. two d.; ed Liverpool Coll., St Peter's Hall, Oxford, Inner Temple; served with RAF 1947–49; joined BBC as radio drama producer 1953–57, variety of posts 1957–69, Sec. to Bd 1969–71, Chief Sec. 1972–77; Dir of TV IBA 1977–83; Dir Programme Planning Secr. Ind. Cos. TV Asscn 1983–87; Dir Broadcasting Standards Council 1988–96; mem. Arts Council of GB 1978–80; Gov. English Speaking Union of GB 1976–83; Trustee Int. Inst. of Communications 1983–89; Hon. Visiting Prof. Univ. of Manchester 1996–99. *Publications:* Deciding What We Watch 1999, several radio plays and a stage play for children. *Leisure interests:* travel, reading, theatre. *Address:* Lesters, Little Ickford, Aylesbury, Bucks., HP18 9HS, England. *Telephone:* (1844) 339225. *Fax:* (1844) 338351.

SHAW, Fiona, BA, FRSA; Irish actress; b. Fiona Wilson, 10 July 1958, Cork; d. of Dr. Denis Joseph Wilson and Mary Teresa Flynn; ed Univ. Coll. Cork, Royal Acad. of Dramatic Art (R.A.D.A.); debut in Love's Labours Lost; stage appearances include Julia in The Rivals, Nat. Theatre, Mary Shelley in Howard Brenton's Bloody Poetry, Hampstead; joined RSC 1985; appeared with RSC as Celia in As You Like It, Tatyana in Gorky's Philistines, Madame des Volonges in Les Liaisons Dangereuses, Beatrice in Much Ado About Nothing, Portia in The Merchant of Venice, Kate in The Taming of the Shrew, Mistress Carol in James Shirley's Hyde Park and as Sophocles's Electra; appeared as Rosalind in As You Like It, Old Vic 1990, as Shen Te/Shui Ta in Brecht's The Good Person of Sichuan, Nat. Theatre 1990 (Olivier Award for Best Actress 1990, London Critics' Award for Best Actress 1990), in Hedda Gabler, Abbey Theatre, Dublin and West End 1991 (London Critics' Award 1992), in Beckett's Footfalls, West End 1994, as Richard II in Richard II and in The Waste Land 1996, The Prime of Miss Jean Brodie, Royal Nat. Theatre 1998, Widower's Houses 1999, Medea, Abbey Theatre, Dublin 2000, West End 2001, The Power Book, Nat. Theatre 2002; Hon. Prof. of Drama, Trinity Coll. Dublin; Hon. LLD (Nat. Univ. of Ireland) 1998; Hon. DUniv (Open Univ.) 1999; Hon. D.Litt (Trinity Coll. Dublin) 2001; Tree Prize (R.A.D.A.) 1982; Ronson Award (R.A.D.A.) 1982, Olivier Award, Evening Standard Award for Machinal 1995, Evening Standard Award for Best Actress 2001, Bancroft Gold Medal (R.A.D.A.); Officier des Arts et des Lettres 2001; Hon. OBE 2002. *Films include:* My Left Foot, Mountains of the Moon, Three Men and a Little Lady 1990, Super Mario Brothers 1992, Undercover Blues 1993, The Waste Land 1995, Persuasion 1995, Jane Eyre 1996, The Avengers 1997, The Butcher's Boy 1997, Anna Karenina 1997, The Last September 1999, The Triumph of Love 2000, Harry Potter and The Philosopher's Stone 2001, Dr. Sleep 2001, Harry Potter and The Chamber of Secrets 2002. *Radio includes:* Transfiguration 2000, Aiding and Abetting 2000. *TV includes:* Gormenghast, BBC 1999, Mind Games 2000, The Sweetest Thing 2002. *Leisure interests:* opera, running, snorkling. *Address:* c/o ICM, Oxford House, 76 Oxford Street, London, W1N 0AX, England; Eglantine, Montenotte, Cork, Ireland.

SHAW, Sir Neil McGowan, Kt; Canadian business executive; b. 31 May 1929, Montreal; s. of Harold LeRoy Shaw and Fabiola Shaw (née McGowan); m. 1st Frances Audrey Robinson 1952 (divorced 1980); two s. three d.; m. 2nd Elizabeth Fern Mudge 1985; ed Knowlton High School, Lower Canada Coll.; Trust Officer Crown Trust Co. 1947–54; with Canada Dominion Sugar (now Redpath Industries) 1954–98, Merchandising Man. 1954–66, Vice-Pres. 1967–72, Pres. 1972–80, Vice-Chair. 1981–98; Group Man. Dir Tate and Lyle PLC, England 1980–86, Chair. 1986–93, CEO 1986–92, Exec. Chair. 1992–94; Redpath Div. Industries Ltd 1972–98 (Vice-Chair. 1981–98); fmrly Chair. Tate and Lyle Holdings Ltd, England, Tate and Lyle Industries Ltd, England, Tate and Lyle Inc., New York; Dir Tunnel Refineries Ltd, England, United Biscuits (Holdings) PLC 1988–97, G.R. Amylum N.V., Brussels, Americare Corpn Alcantara, Lisbon, Canadian Imperial Bank of Commerce, Toronto 1986–2000, A.E. Staley Manufacturing Co., Ill. 1991–98, M & G Investment Income Trust PLC 1991–95; Dir Inst. of Dirs 1986–; Chair. World Sugar Research Org. 1994–96 (Dir 1982–97), Foundation and Friends of Royal Botanic Gardens, Kew 1994– (Trustee 1990–), Anglo-Canadian Support Group CARE 1989–, Business in the Community 1991–95; Gov. Montreal Gen. Hosp., Reddy Memorial Hosp., World Food and Agro Forum 1988–96; mem. Canadian Memorial Foundation 1989–, Council of Advisers to Premier of Québec 1987–, Advisory Council Prince's Youth Business Trust 1990–, London Enterprise Agency 1986–, Food Asscn 1989–, Listed Cos. Advisory Cttee 1991–, British N American Cttee 1991–; Chair. and Dir CAPOCO Ltd (Theatre Royal Windsor) 1991–, The Atkins Restaurant Co. Ltd 1993–; Dir United World Coll. of Atlantic 1997–2000; Hon. LLD (E London) 1997. *Leisure interests:* sailing, skiing, golf. *Address:* Titness Park, Mill Lane, Sunninghill, Ascot, Berks., SL5 7RU, England (Home).

SHAW, Sir Run Run, Kt, CBE; British business executive; b. 14 Oct. 1907, Shanghai, China; s. of the late Shao Hang-yin and Wang Shun-xiang; m. 1st Lily Wang Mee-chun 1932 (deceased); two s. two d.; m. 2nd Lee Manglan 1997; ed in China; Founder and Chair. Shaw Group of Cos. 1959–; Chair. Shaw Foundation HK Ltd 1973–; Pres. Hong Kong Red Cross Soc. 1972–, Hong Kong Arts Festival 1974–88, Bd of Govs. Hong Kong Arts Centre 1978–88, Television Broadcasts Ltd, TVE (Holdings) Ltd 1980–; mem. Council, The Chinese Univ. of Hong Kong 1977–92; Chair. Bd of Trustees, United Coll., Chinese Univ. of Hong Kong 1983–92; Local Adviser on Hong Kong for People's Repub. of China 1992–; mem. Preparatory Cttee, Hong Kong Special Admin. Region (SAR) 1995–98; Founder, Shaw Coll. Chinese Univ. of Hong Kong 1986; hon. degrees from Univ. of Hong Kong, Chinese Univ. of Hong Kong, Univs. of E Asia (Macau), Sussex, New York at Stony Brook, City Polytechnic of Hong Kong, Hong Kong Baptist Coll., Hong Kong Polytechnic, Pepperdine Univ.; Queen's Badge, Red Cross 1982; Commdr Order of Crown of Belgium; Chevalier Légion d'honneur. *Leisure interests:* shadow-boxing, golf. *Address:* Shaw House, Lot 220, Clear Water Bay Road, Kowloon, Hong Kong Special Administrative Region, People's Republic of China. *Telephone:* 27198371.

SHAW, Vernon Lorden; Dominican head of state and civil servant; b. 13 May 1930; m.; four c.; ed Dominica Grammar School, Trinity Coll., Oxford; various appts. Treasury and Customs Dept, Post Office, Cen. Housing and Planning Authority, Audit Dept, Cen. Housing and Planning Authority 1948–62; Admin. Asst Ministry of Trade and Production 1962–65, Asst Sec. 1965–67; Perm. Sec. Ministry of Educ. and Health 1967, Ministry of External Affairs 1967–71; Chief Establishment Officer 1971–77; Sec. to Cabinet 1977–78 and Amb.-at-Large and Inspector of Missions 1978–90 (retd from public service); temporary resident tutor, Univ. of W Indies School of Continuing Studies 1991–93; Chair. Dominica Broadcasting Corpn 1993–95, Public Service Bd of Appeal 1993–98; Pres. of Dominica 1998–; mem. Inst. of Admin. Accounting; Assoc. mem. BIM; Dominica Award of Honour, Sisserou Award of Honour. *Address:* Morne Bruce, Roseau (Office); 8 Churchill Lane, Goodwill, Dominica (Home). *Telephone:* 448-2054 (Office); 448-2361 (Home). *Fax:* 449-8366 (Office). *E-mail:* presidentoffice@cwdom.dm (Office); shawe@cwdom.dm (Home).

SHAW YU-MING, PhD; Taiwanese public servant and academic; b. 3 Nov. 1938, Harbin; m. Shirley Shiow-jyu Lu; one s. one d.; ed Nat. Chengchi Univ., Tufts Univ. and Univ. of Chicago, USA; Asst Prof. of History, Newberry Coll., SC 1967–68, 1972–73; Assoc. Prof. of History, Univ. of Notre Dame, Ind. 1973–82; held various research posts in Asian studies in USA; Dir Asia and World Inst., Taiwan 1983–84; Dean, Graduate School of Int. Law and Diplomacy, Nat. Chengchi Univ. 1984–, Dir Inst. of Int. Relations 1984–87, 1994–; Dir-Gen. Govt Information Office and Govt spokesman 1987–91; Prof. of History, Nat. Chengchi Univ. 1991–; Pres. Cultural Foundation of the United Daily News Group 1992–; awards from American Council of Learned Socs., Asia Foundation, Inst. of Chinese Culture, USA and others. *Publications include:* China and Christianity 1979, Problems in Twentieth Century Chinese Christianity 1980, Twentieth Century Sino-American Relations 1980, History and Politics in Modern China 1982, International Politics and China's Future 1987, Beyond the Economic Miracle 1988, An American Missionary in China: John Leighton Stuart and Chinese-American Relations 1993. *Address:* 64 Wan Shou Road, Taipei, Taiwan.

SHAWA, Lol Mohammed; Chadian politician and fmr resistance leader; b. 15 June 1939, Mao (Kanem); s. of Mohammed Shawa and Amy Shawa; m. Fatimé Adouly Lol 1970; four s. two d.; ed Int. Inst. of Public Admin. and Inst. for the Study of Int. Relations, Paris; Leader of Mouvement populaire pour la libération du Tchad (the Third Army) 1979; Prime Minister and Head of State April–Aug. 1979; studied in Paris 1979–82; Minister of Transport 1982–85. *Address:* B.P. 1104, N'Djamena, Chad.

SHAWCROSS, Baron (Life Peer), cr. 1959, of Friston; **Hartley William Shawcross,** Kt, PC, GBE, QC, LLD; British jurist, politician and businessman; b. 4 Feb. 1902, Giessen, Germany; s. of John Shawcross and Hilda Shawcross; m. 1st Rosita Alberta Shyvers 1924 (died 1943); m. 2nd Joan Winifred Mather (died 1974); two s. one d.; ed Dulwich Coll. and abroad; called to Bar 1925; Sr Law Lecturer Liverpool Univ. 1927–34; Deputy Regional Commr SE Region 1941; Regional Commr NW Region 1942–45; Recorder of Salford 1941–45; Chair. Catering Wages Comm. 1943–45; Asst Chair. E Sussex Quarter Sessions 1941; Labour MP for St Helens 1945–58; Attorney-Gen. 1945–51; Pres. Bd of Trade April–Nov. 1951; Judge of Int. Court of Arbitration, The Hague; Chair. Royal Comm. on the Press 1961–62; Chair. British Medical Research Council 1962–65; Chair. "Justice" (British branch of Int. Comm. of Jurists) 1956–73; Chief Prosecutor, Nuremberg Trials 1945–46; UK del. UN 1945–49; withdrew from Labour Party 1958, joined SDP 1983; mem. Monckton Comm. 1959–60 (resgnd); Pres. Rainer Foundation until 1972; Chair. Int. Chamber of Commerce Special Comm. of Eminent Persons on Ethical Practices; Chair. Dominion Lincoln Assurance Co. Ltd, Thames Television Co. Ltd 1969–74, Upjohn and Co. Ltd to 1977, City of London Panel on Takeovers and Mergers 1969–80, Press Council 1974–78, London and Continental Bankers 1974–80; Dir Shell Transport and Trading Co. Ltd until 1973, EMI Ltd until 1980, European Enterprises Devt Co. SA (Luxembourg), Times Newspapers Ltd 1967–74, Ranks, Hovis Macdougall Ltd until 1977 (consultant 1977–94), Caffyns Ltd (Deputy Chair., until 1994), Morgan et Cie SA, Morgan et Cie International SA until 1976, The Observer 1981–93; Special Adviser to J.P. Morgan 1968–94; mem. Court of London Univ. until 1978; Sussex Univ. Exec. Council, Pro-Chancellor 1962–65, Chancellor 1965–85; mem. Int. Cttee of Jurists, Bd of Trustees, American Univ. of Beirut until 1975, Council of Int. Chambers of Commerce; Hon. mem. New York and American Bar Asscns.; Hon. FRCOG 1979, Royal Coll. of Surgeons 1981; Hon. D.Litt. (Loughborough) 1980; Hon. LLD (Columbia, Bristol, Michigan, Lehigh, Liverpool, Hull Univs.); Hon. DCL (New Brunswick Univ. and London). *Publication:* Life Sentence: The Memoirs of Hartley Shawcross 1995. *Address:* Friston Place, East Dean, Nr. Eastbourne, E Sussex, BN20 0AH, England. *Telephone:* (20) 7325-5127 (Office).

SHAWCROSS, William; British journalist; b. 28 May 1946, Sussex; s. of Baron Shawcross; m. 1st Marina Warner 1972 (divorced 1980); one s.; m. 2nd Michal Levin 1981 (divorced); one d.; m. Olga Forte 1993; ed Eton, Univ. Coll., Oxford; freelance journalist in Czechoslovakia 1968–69; Corresp. for The Sunday Times, London, 1969–72; Chair. Article 19, Int. Centre on Censorship 1986–96; mem. Bd Int. Crisis Group 1995–; mem. Council of Disasters Emergency Cttee 1998–. *Publications:* Dubcek 1970, Crime and Compromise: Janos Kadar and the Politics of Hungary Since Revolution 1974, Sideshow: Kissinger, Nixon and the Destruction of Cambodia 1979, Quality of Mercy: Cambodia, The Holocaust and the Modern Conscience 1985, The Shah's Last Ride 1989, Murdoch 1992, Cambodia's New Deal 1994, Deliver Us from Evil 2000. *Leisure interests:* sailing, walking. *Address:* c/o Green & Heaton Ltd, 37 Goldhawk Road, London, W12; Friston Place, East Dean, E Sussex, BN20 0AH, England. *Telephone:* (20) 7289-8089 (London). *E-mail:* williamshawcross@compuserve.com (Office).

SHAWN, Wallace, BA; American actor; b. 12 Nov. 1943, New York; s. of William Shawn and Cecille Lyon; brother-in-law of Jamaica Kincaid (q.v.); ed Harvard Univ., Magdalen Coll., Oxford Univ. *Films include:* My Dinner with André, Manhattan 1979, The Princess Bride, The Moderns, Scenes from the Class Struggle in Beverly Hills, We're No Angels, Shadows and Fog, Mom and Dad Save the World, Nickel and Dime, The Cemetery Club, Unbecoming Age, The Meteor Man, Vanya on 42nd Street, Mrs Parker and the Vicious Circle, Clueless 1995, Canadian Bacon, Toy Story (voice) 1995, The Wife 1995, House Arrest 1996, All Dogs Go To Heaven II (voice), Critical Care 1997, My Favorite Martian 1999, Toy Story 2 (voice) 1999, The Prime Gig 2000, Blonde 2001, The Curse of the Jade Scorpion 2002. *Stage appearances include:* My Dinner with André, A Thought in Three Parts, Marie and Bruce 1979, Aunt Dan and Lemon 1985, The Fever 1991. *Address:* William Morris Agency, 151 South El Camino Drive, Beverly Hills, CA 90212, USA.

SHAYE, Robert Kenneth; American cinema executive; b. 4 March 1939, Detroit, Mich.; s. of Max Shaye and Dorothy Shaye; m. Eva G. Lindsten 1970; two c.; ed Univ. of Michigan, Columbia Univ.; first prize Soc. of Cinematologists' Rosenthal Competition for best film directed by American under 25; wrote, produced, directed and ed. short films and TV commercials, including award-winning shorts, Image and On Fighting Witches; f. New Line Cinema Corpn 1967, Chair. and CEO. *Films:* (producer and exec. producer) Stunts, XTRO, Alone in the Dark, The First Time, Polyester, Critters, Quiet Cool, My Demon Lover, A Nightmare on Elm Street (Parts 1–6), The Hidden, Stranded, Critters 2, Hairspray, Heart Condition, Book of Love (Dir) Wes Craven's New Nightmare (also actor), Frequency, Lord of the Rings. *Television:* Freddy's Nightmare: The Series (exec. producer). *Leisure interest:* cooking. *Address:* New Line Cinema, 116 North Robertson Boulevard, Suite 200, Los Angeles, CA 90048, USA (Office).

SHAZLY, Lt-Gen. Saad Mohamed el-Husseiny el-, M.POL.SC.; Egyptian army officer and diplomatist; b. 1 April 1922, Cairo; s. of Mohamed el-Husseiny el-Shazly and Tafida Ibrahim el-Shazly; m. Zeinat Mohamed Metwally 1942; ed Khedive Ismail Secondary School, Cairo, Cairo Univ., Mil. Coll. and in USSR; Officer of the Guards 1943–48; Platoon Commdr Arab–Israeli War 1948; Commdr of Parachute School 1954–56; Commdr of Parachute Battalion 1956–58; Commdr UAR Contingent, UN, Congo 1960–61; Defence Attaché, London 1961–63; Brigade Commdr in Yemen Civil War 1965–66; Commdr Shazly Task Force Group, Egyptian–Israeli War 1967; Commdr of Special Forces, Paratroopers and Rangers 1967–69; Commdr Red Sea District 1970–71; Chief of Staff of Egyptian Armed Forces 1971–73; Amb. to UK 1974–75, to Portugal 1975–78; Founder and Sec.-Gen. Nat. Front Party 1980; Chief Ed. Algabha, Alger 1980–; mem. Int. Inst. for Strategic Studies; mem. Bd of Dirs. Islamic Inst. of Defence Tech.; holder of 23 decorations including Mil. Medal of Courage 1949, Médaille de Congo 1961, Medal of Yemen 1966, Medal of Distinguished Mil. Duty 1972, Order of the Repub. (1st Class) 1974, Honour Star 1974, Syrian Honour Star (Knight) 1974, Palestinian Honour Star 1974. *Publications:* How an Infantry Division Can Cross a Water Barrier 1973, Fonética Arabe Com Letras Portuguesas 1978, Kuraanunn Kariim 1978, The Crossing of the Suez 1980, Four Years in the Diplomatic Service 1983, Arab Military Option 1984, The Eighth Crusade 1990; contributes to numerous journals. *Leisure interests:* gliding, shooting, fencing, golf, camping, chess.

SHCHAPOV, Yaroslav Nikolayevich; Russian historian; b. 6 May 1928, Moscow; s. of Nikolai Mikhailovich Shchapov and Eugenia Nikolayevna Shchapova (née Dobrobozhenko); m. Yulia Leonidovna Schcapova (née Sinelnikova) 1954; one s.; ed Moscow State Univ.; Sr, Chief Librarian V. Lenin State Library 1952–57; Jr, Sr, Leading, Chief Researcher Inst. of History of USSR, USSR Acad. of Sciences 1957–90; Head Centre of Church and Religious History, Inst. of Russian History, Russian Acad. of Sciences 1990–99, Councillor 1999–; Corresp. mem. USSR (now Russian) Acad. of Sciences 1987; Pres. Russian Soc. of Historians and Archivists 1990–96; Dir County Estate Schapovo Municipal Museum, Podolsk 1998–; Chair. Scientific Council Role of Religion in History 1998–2001; mem. Russian Ass. of the Nobility, Vice-Pres. Russian Shchapovo Soc.; research in history of old Russia, law, social relations, religion, culture, old Russian manuscripts, Russian-Byzantine relations, Russian Orthodox Church; Hon. mem. Russian Palestine Soc.; Order of Friendship of the Peoples 1988, Church Order St Sergius of Radonezh (Second Class) 1997, Order of Honour 1998; B. Grekov Prize. *Publications:* Byzantine and South Slavic Legal Heritage in Russia of 11th–13th Centuries 1978, State and Church in Early Russia 10th–13th Centuries 1989 (published in USA 1993), Russian Orthodox Church and the Communist State (Documents from Secret Archives) 1996, Reference Books for the Researcher in Russian History 1998, Historical Country Estates in South Moscow District; more than 300 articles. *Leisure interests:* family history. *Address:* Institute of Russian History, Russian Academy of Sciences, D. Ulyanov str. 19, 117036 Moscow, Russia. *Telephone:* (095) 126-26-65 (Office); (095) 438-22-89 (Home). *Fax:* (095) 126-39-55 (Office); (095) 438-22-89 (Home). *E-mail:* y_schapov@mail.ru (Home).

SHCHEDRIN, Rodion Konstantinovich; Russian composer; b. 16 Dec. 1932, Moscow; s. of Konstantin Mikhailovich Shchedrin and Konkordia Ivanovna Shchedrin; m. Maya Plisetskaya 1958; ed Moscow Conservatoire; Chair. RSFSR (now Russian) Union of Composers 1973–90; USSR People's Deputy 1989–91; mem. Acad. of Fine Arts, Berlin, Bavarian Acad. of Fine Arts; Hon. mem. American Liszt Soc., Int. Music Council; Lenin Prize, USSR and Russian State Prizes, Russian Union of Composers Prize, Shostakovich

Prize, Beethoven Soc. Prize. *Compositions include:* operas: Not Only Love 1961, Dead Souls (operatic scenes in three acts) 1976, Lolita (after V. Nabokov) 1994; ballets: Humpbacked Horse 1960, Carmen Suite 1967, Anna Karenina 1972, The Seagull 1980, Lady with a Lapdog 1985; for orchestra: three symphonies 1958, 1965, 2000, 5 concertos for orchestra 1963, 1968, 1988, 1989, 1998; Self-Portrait 1984, Stykhira 1988, Old Russian Circus Music 1989; 5 concertos for piano and orchestra 1954, 1966, 1973, 1992, 1999, Concerto for cello and orchestra 1994, Concerto for trumpet and orchestra 1995, Concerto dolce for viola and string orchestra 1997; Chamber Suite 1961, Poetoria 1974, Musical Offering for organ and nine soloists 1983, The Sealed Angel (Russian Liturgy) 1988, Nina and the Twelve Months (musical) 1988, Piano Terzetto 1996, Concerto Cantabile (for violin and strings) 1997, Preludium for 9th Symphony by Beethoven 1999, Lolita-serenade 2001, Dialogue with Shostakovich 2001, The Enchanted Wanderer (concert opera) 2002, Tanja-Katya 2002, My Age, My Wild Beast 2003; works for chamber orchestra, string trio, piano, violin, organ and cello and song cycles, music for theatre and cinema. *Leisure interests:* jogging, fishing, water-skiing, wind surfing. *Address:* Theresienstrasse 23, 80333 Munich, Germany (Home); 25/9, Tverskaya St, apt. 31, 103050 Moscow, Russia (Home). *Telephone:* (89) 285834 (Munich); (095) 299-72-39 (Moscow). *Fax:* (89) 282057 (Munich).

SHCHERBAKOV, Vladimir Ivanovich, DEconSC.; Russian politician and business executive; b. 5 Dec. 1949, Novo-Sysoyevka, Primorsky territory; s. of Ivan Shcherbakov and Elena Shcherbakova; m. Natalia Chesnokova; one s.; ed Togliatti Polytech. Inst., Higher Comsomol School; engineer-mechanic; mem. CPSU 1970–91; party work in Togliatti 1971–74; engineer, controller, Chief Planning and Econ. Dept, Volga Motor Car Plant 1970–82; Deputy Dir-Gen., Dir Econ. and Planning Dept, Kama Big Lorries Plant 1982–85; Chief Machine Bldg and Metal Trade Plant Dept, USSR State Cttee for Labour and Social Affairs 1985–88; First Deputy Chief Nat. Economy Man. Dept, USSR Council of Ministers 1988–89; Minister of Labour and Social Affairs 1989–91; Deputy Prime Minister, later First Deputy Prime Minister, Minister of Economy and Planning of the USSR March–Aug. 1991; Pres. Interprivatization Fund 1991–; Chair. Bd of Dirs Avtotor Group of Cos 1995–; Chair. Russian United Industrial Party 1995–97; mem. Admin. Bureau, Vice-Pres. Russian Union of Mfrs and Entrepreneurs 1996; Vice-Pres. Free Econ. Soc. of Russia 1997–; mem. Russian Acad. of Natural Sciences. *Publications include:* about 50 monographs and articles, concerning Big Economic Complexes: Mechanism of Management, Industrial Labour and its Remuneration, New Mechanisms of Labour Remuneration, etc. *Leisure interests:* hunting, sports. *Address:* Interprivatization Fund, Solyanka 3, Bldg 3, 109028 Moscow, Russia. *Telephone:* (095) 924-60-61. *Fax:* (095) 923-14-11. *E-mail:* scherbakov@avtotor.ru (Office).

SHEA, Jamie, PhD; British international organization official; b. 1953; ed Sussex Univ., Lincoln Coll., Oxford; joined NATO as minute-taker 1981, later Sr Planning Officer and Speechwriter to Sec.-Gen.; Deputy Dir of Information and Press 1993–2000, Dir 2000–; Prof. of Int. Relations, American Univ. and Michigan State Univ.; European Communicator of the Year 1999. *Address:* NATO, 1110 Brussels, Belgium (Office). *Telephone:* (2) 707-44-13 (Office). *Fax:* (2) 707-45-79 (Office). *Website:* www.nato.int.

SHEARER, Alan, OBE; British footballer; b. 13 Aug. 1970, Gosforth, Newcastle upon Tyne; s. of Alan Shearer and Anne Shearer; m. Lainya Shearer; one s. two d.; coached as a child at Wallsend Boys' Club; striker; played for Southampton 1987–92, Blackburn Rovers 1992–96, becoming the only player in English football ever to score 30 or more goals in three consecutive seasons; signed by Newcastle United for then world record transfer fee of £15 million 1996, now Capt.; played for England 1992–2000 (63 caps, 30 goals), Capt. 1996–2000; Premiership all-time leading scorer; first player to score 200 Premiership goals and first to score 100 League goals for two different clubs; Football Writers' Asscn Footballer of the Year 1994, (Football Asscn) Hall of Fame 1998. *Leisure interest:* golf. *Address:* Newcastle United Football Club, St James' Park, Newcastle upon Tyne, NE1 4ST England. *Telephone:* (191) 201-8400.

SHEARER, Rt Hon Hugh Lawson; Jamaican politician; b. 18 May 1923, Martha Brae, Trelawny; ed St Simon's Coll.; journalist Jamaica Worker 1941–47; mem. Kingston and St Andrew Corpn 1947–51; mem. House of Reps. 1955–59; mem. Legis. Council (now Senate) 1961–66; Minister without Portfolio and Leader of Govt Business in the Senate 1962–67; Deputy Leader Jamaica Labour Party 1967–74; Jamaican del. to UN 1962–72; Prime Minister, Minister of Defence and Minister of External Affairs 1967–72; Leader of the Opposition 1972–74; MP for South-East Clarendon 1976–; Deputy Prime Minister and Minister of Foreign Affairs 1980–89, Minister of Foreign Trade 1980–86, of Industry 1986–89; Island Supervisor, Bustamante Industrial Trade Union 1953, Vice-Pres. 1960–79, Pres. 1979–; Chair. Jt Trade Unions Research Devt Centre 1992–; Pres. Jamaica Confed. of Trade Unions 1994–; Hon. LLD (Howard Univ.) 1968, (Univ. College of the West Indies, Jamaica) 1994; Order of Jamaica 1990. *Address:* Bustamante Industrial Trade Union, 98 Duke Street, Kingston, Jamaica. *Telephone:* 922-2443. *Fax:* 967-0120.

SHEARER, Moira; British ballet dancer, actress and writer; b. 17 Jan. 1926, Dunfermline; d. of Harold King; m. Ludovic Kennedy (q.v.) 1950; one s. three d.; ed Bearsden Acad.; trained Mayfair School; debut with Int. Ballet 1941; joined Sadler's Wells 1942; fmrly performed with Old Vic Theatre, Bristol Old Vic Theatre; Dir Border TV 1977–82; mem. BBC Gen. Advisory Council

1970–77, Scottish Arts Council 1971–73; fmrly touring lecturer on ballet. *Stage performances (ballet and plays) include:* Sleeping Beauty 1946, Cinderella 1948, Carmen 1950, Ballet Imperial 1950, A Midsummer Night's Dream 1954, I Am a Camera 1955, Man of Distinction 1957, The Cherry Orchard 1977, Hay Fever 1978, A Simple Man 1987, The Aspern Papers 1994. *Film appearances include:* The Red Shoes 1948, Tales of Hoffman 1950, Story of Three Loves 1952, The Man Who Loved Redheads 1954, Peeping Tom 1960, Black Tights 1961. *Publications include:* Balletmaster: A Dancer's View of George Balanchine 1986, Ellen Terry (biog.) 1998.

SHEARING, George Albert, OBE; British jazz pianist and composer; b. 13 Aug. 1919, London; s. of James Philip Shearing and Ellen Amelia Shearing (née Brightman); m. 1st Beatrice Bayes 1941 (divorced); one d.; m. 2nd Eleanor Geffert 1984; ed Linden Lodge School for the Blind, London; f. and performed with George Shearing Quintet 1949–67; has also led other jazz ensembles; composed many popular songs, including Lullaby of Birdland 1952; many recordings 1939–; mem. Bd Guide Dogs for the Blind, Hadley School for the Blind, Nat. Braille Press; Hon. DMus (Westminster Coll.) 1975, (Hamilton Coll.) 1994; Golden Plate Award, American Acad. of Achievement 1968, Helen Keller Achievement Award 1995. *Address:* c/o Joan Shulman, 103 Avenue Road, Suite 301, Toronto, Ont., M5R 2GR, Canada.

SHEARMAN, John Kinder Gowran, MA, PhD, FBA; British professor of history of art; b. 24 June 1931, Aldershot; s. of Brig. C. E. G. Shearman and Evelyn W. Shearman; m. 1st Jane D. Smith 1957 (deceased); one s. three d.; m. 2nd Deirdre Roskill 1983; m. 3rd Kathryn Brush 1998; ed Felsted School, Courtauld Inst.; Lecturer to Prof., Courtauld Inst., Univ. of London 1957–79, Deputy Dir 1974–78; Dept of Art and Archaeology, Princeton Univ., USA 1979–87, Chair. 1979–85, Class of 1926 Prof. 1986–87; Prof. of Fine Art, Harvard Univ. 1987–93, Chair. 1990–93, William Dorr Boardman Prof. 1988–94, Adams Univ. Prof. 1994–; mem. Accademia del Disegno, Florence, Accademia di San Luca, Rome, American Acad. of Arts and Sciences, Accademia Raffaello, Urbino; Serena Medal, British Acad. *Publications:* Andrea del Sarto 1965, Mannerism 1967, Raphael's Cartoons 1972, Catalogue, Earlier Italian Paintings in the Royal Collection 1983, Funzione e Illusione 1983, Only Connect... 1992, Raphael in Early Modern Sources 2002. *Leisure interests:* sailing, music, travel. *Address:* Sackler Museum, Harvard University, Cambridge, MA 02138 (Office); 3 Clement Circle, Cambridge, MA 02138, USA. *Telephone:* (617) 876-9548 (Home); (617) 495-9154 (Office). *Fax:* (617) 876-9548 (Home).

SHEBBEARE, Thomas Andrew (Tom), KCVO, BA; British charity administrator; b. 25 Jan. 1952; s. of the late Robert Austin Shebbeare and Frances Dare Graham; m. Cynthia Jane Cottrell 1976; one s. one d.; ed Malvern Coll., Univ. of Exeter; with World Univ. Service 1973–75; Gen. Sec. British Youth Council 1975–80; Admin. Council of Europe 1980–85; Exec. Dir European Youth Foundation 1985–88; Exec. Dir Prince's Trust 1988–99, CEO 1999–; Dir Royal Jubilee Trusts 1998–; Dir Inst. for Citizenship Studies 1991–2000, Gifts in Kind 1996–, Skills Festival Co. Ltd. 1998–; Trustee Nations Inst. for Citizenship Studies Trust (SA) 1995–; mem. Council Queen's Coll. 1999–. *Leisure interests:* family, cooking, food and drink. *Address:* 18 Park Square East, London, NW1 4LH, England. *Telephone:* (20) 7543-1234 (Office). *Fax:* (20) 7543-1200 (Office). *E-mail:* tom@shebbeare.freeserve.co.uk (Home). *Website:* www.princes-trust.org.uk (Office).

SHEED, Wilfrid John Joseph, MA; American author; b. 27 Dec. 1930, London, England; s. of Francis Joseph Sheed and Maisie (Ward) Sheed; m. 1st Maria Bullitt Dartington 1957 (divorced); three c.; m. 2nd Miriam Ungerer; one s. two d.; ed Lincoln Coll., Oxford Univ.; film reviewer Jubilee magazine 1959–61, Assoc. Ed. 1959–66; drama critic and fmr book Commonweal magazine, New York; film critic Esquire magazine 1967–69; Visiting Prof. Princeton Univ. 1970–71; columnist NY Times 1971–; judge and mem. editorial Bd Book of the Month Club 1972–88; Guggenheim Fellow 1971–72; mem. P.E.N. Club. *Publications include:* A Middle Class Education 1961, The Hack 1963, Square's Progress 1965, Office Politics 1966, The Blacking Factory 1968, Max Jamison 1970, The Morning After 1971, People Will Always Be Kind 1973, Three Mobs: Labor, Church and Mafia 1974, Transatlantic Blues 1978, The Good Word 1979, Clare Boothe Luce 1982, Frank and Maisie 1985, The Boys of Winter 1987, Baseball and Lesser Sports 1991, My Life as a Fan 1993, In Love with Daylight 1995; ed. of G.K. Chesterton's Essays and Poems 1957, 16 Short Novels 1986; contributes articles to popular magazines. *Address:* Sag Harbor, New York, NY 11963, USA.

SHEEHAN, Neil, AB; American journalist and author; b. 27 Oct. 1936, Holyoke, Mass.; s. of Cornelius Sheehan and Mary O'Shea; m. Susan Margulies 1965; two d.; ed Harvard Univ.; Viet Nam Bureau Chief, UPI Saigon 1962–64; reporter, New York Times, New York, Jakarta, Saigon, Washington, DC 1964–72; Guggenheim Fellow 1973–74; Adlai Stevenson Fellow 1973–75; Fellow, Lehrman Inst. 1975–76; Rockefeller Foundation Fellow 1976–77; Fellow, Woodrow Wilson Center for Int. Scholars 1979–80; mem. Soc. of American Historians, American Acad. of Achievement; Hon. LittD (Columbia Coll., Chicago) 1972; Hon. LHD (American Int. Coll.) 1990, (Lowell Univ.) 1991; recipient of numerous awards for journalism; Nat. Book Award 1988, J.F. Kennedy Award 1989, Pulitzer Prize for non-fiction 1989. *Publications:* The Arnheiter Affair 1972, A Bright Shining Lie: John Paul Vann and America in Viet Nam (chosen by The Modern Library as one of 100 Best Works of Non-Fiction in 20th Century 1999) 1988, After the War Was Over: Hanoi

and Saigon 1992; contrib. to The Pentagon Papers 1971; articles and book reviews for popular magazines. *Address:* 4505 Klingle Street, NW, Washington, DC 20016, USA (Home).

SHEEHY, Sir Patrick, Kt; British business executive (retd); b. 2 Sept. 1930; s. of Sir John Francis Sheehy and Jean Sheehy (née Newton); m. Jill Patricia Tindall 1964; one s. one d.; ed Ampleforth Coll., Irish Guards 1948–50; joined British-American Tobacco Co. 1950, first appointment, Nigeria, Ghana 1951, Regional Sales Man., Nigeria 1953, Ethiopian Tobacco Monopoly 1954, Marketing Dir, Jamaica 1957, Gen. Man., Barbados 1961, Netherlands 1967; Dir British-American Tobacco 1970–82, mem. Chair.'s Policy Cttee and Chair. Tobacco Div. Bd 1975; Deputy Chair. BAT Industries 1976–81, Vice-Chair. 1981–82, Chair. 1982–95; Chair. BAT Financial Services 1985–90, Barder Marsh (now Marlborough) 1995–; Dir Eagle Star Holdings 1984–87, British Petroleum 1984–98, The Spectator (1828) Ltd 1988–, Cluff Resources 1992–96, Celtic Football Club 1996–; Dir (non-exec.) Pvt. Bank and Trust Co. 1996–; Chair. Council of Int. Advisors Swiss Bank Corpn 1985–, UK Home Office Inquiry into Police Responsibilities and Rewards 1992–93; CEO Rainbow 1993–; Dir Asda Property Holdings 1994–, currently Chair. (non-exec.); mem. Pres.'s Cttee, CBI 1986–; mem. Trade Policy Research Centre 1984–89, Action Cttee for Europe 1985–; mem. CBI Task Force on Urban Regeneration; Chevalier, Légion d'honneur. *Leisure interests:* golf, reading. *Address:* 11 Eldon Road, London, W8 5PU, England. *Telephone:* (20) 7937-6250.

SHEEN, Charlie; American actor; b. (Carlos Estevez), 3 Sept. 1965, New York; s. of Martin Sheen (q.v.) and Janet Sheen (née Templeton); b. of Emilio Estevez; m. Donna Peele 1995 (divorced 1996); ed Santa Monica High School; TV debut in The Execution of Private Slovik; cinema debut in Apocalypse Now; pleaded no contest to charge of assault on girlfriend, given one year's suspended sentence, two years' probation, 300 hours' community service and fined 1997. *Films include:* Grizzly II: The Predator, The Red Dawn, Lucas, Platoon, The Wraith, Day Off, Young Guns, Wall Street, Eight Men Out, Major League, Backtrack, Men at Work, Courage Mountain, Navy Seals, The Rookie, Stockade (Dir), Secret Society, Hot Shots, Dead Fall, The Three Musketeers, The Chase, Major League II 1994, Terminal Velocity 1994, The Shadow Conspiracy 1995, Shockwave 1995, All Dogs Go To Heaven II (voice), The Arrival 1996, Money Talks 1997, No Code of Conduct 1998, Free Money 1998, Letter From Death Row 1998, Being John Malkovich 1999, Cared X, Good Advice 2000, Lisa Picard is Famous 2001. *Television includes:* Silence of the Heart (film), The Boys Next Door (film), Spin City (Globe for Best Actor 2002). *Leisure interests:* baseball, music, film-making. *Address:* c/o Jeffrey Ballard Public Relations, 4814 Lemara Avenue, Sherman Oaks, CA 91403, USA.

SHEEN, Martin; American actor; b. Ramon Estevez, 3 Aug. 1940, Dayton, Ohio; s. of Francisco Estevez and Mary Ann Phelan; m. Janet Templeton 1961; three s. one d.; worked as shipping clerk, American Express Co., New York; Hon. Mayor of Malibu 1989–. *Stage appearances:* The Connection (début, New York and European tour), Never Live Over A Pretzel Factory, The Subject Was Roses, The Crucible. *Films:* The Incident, Catch-22, Rage, Badlands, Apocalypse Now, Enigma, Gandhi, The King of Prussia, That Championship Season, Man, Woman and Child, The Dead Zone, Final Countdown, Loophole, Wall Street, Nightbreaker, Da 1988, Personal Choice 1989, Cadence (also Dir) 1990, Judgement in Berlin 1990, Limited Time, The Maid 1990, Cadence (also Dir), Hear No Evil, Hot Shots Part Deux (cameo), Gettysburg 1993, Trigger Fast, Hits!, Fortunes of War, Sacred Cargo, The Break, Dillinger & Capone, Captain Nuke and the Bomber Boys, Ghost Brigade, The Cradle Will Rock, Dead Presidents, Dorothy Day, Gospa, The American President, The War At Home, Spawn, Storm 1999, Monument Avenue, Free Money, Lost & Found 1999, Apocalypse New Redux 2001, Catch Me If You Can 2003. *Television appearances include:* The Defenders, East Side/West Side, My Three Sons, Mod Squad, Cannon, That Certain Summer, Missiles of October, The Last Survivors, Blind Ambition, Shattered Spirits, Nightbreaker, The Last P.O.W.?, Roswell, The West Wing (Golden Satellite Award 2000, Golden Globe Award 2000) 1999–. *Address:* c/o Jeff Ballard, 4814 Lemara Avenue, Sherman Oaks, CA 91403, USA.

SHEEN CHING-JING; Taiwanese business executive and property developer; b. 1947, Nanjing, China; moved with family to Taiwan 1947; joined Sea Snake Gang (triads) 1962; in prison 1966–69; mil. service 1969–71; worked on cargo ships 1971–73; Govt clerk 1974; est. co. to buy and sell textile quotas; f. Core Pacific property co. 1985, Core Pacific Securities 1988; negotiated merger between Core Pacific Securities and Yuanta 2000.

SHEIKH, Abdullah ibn Muhammad ibn Ibrahim ash-, PhD; Saudi Arabian politician; b. 1949; ed Shari'ah College, Imam Muhammad bin Saud Univ. and Al-Azhar Univ., Cairo; Dean, Imam Muhammad bin Saud Univ., 1975; Asst Prof., 1988; Minister of Justice 1992–. *Address:* Ministry of Justice, University Street, Riyadh 11137, Saudi Arabia. *Telephone:* (1) 405-7777.

SHEINWALD, Sir Nigel, KCMG; British diplomatist; b. 26 June 1953, London; s. of Leonard Sheinwald and Joyce Sheinwald; m. Julia Dunne; three s.; ed Harrow Co. Boys' School, Balliol Coll., Oxford; joined Diplomatic Service 1976–, Japanese Desk 1976–77; Embassy, Moscow 1978–79; mem. Lancaster House Conf. team on Zimbabwe 1979–80; Head of Anglo-Soviet Section FCO 1981–83; Washington Embassy 1983–87; Deputy Head of Policy Planning Staff FCO 1987–89, Press Sec. and Head of News Dept 1995–98, Dir EU Div. 1998–2000; Head of Political and Institutional Section, UK's Perm. Representation to the EU 1993–95, Amb. and Perm. Rep. to EU 2000–03; Foreign Policy Adviser to the Prime Minister 2003–; involved in Maastricht negotiations and co-ordinated UK Presidency of the EU 1989–92. *Address:* c/o Foreign and Commonwealth Office, King Charles Street, London, SW1A 2AH, England (Office). *E-mail:* nigel.sheinwald@fco.gov.uk.

SHELBY, Richard Craig, AB, LLB; American politician; b. 6 May 1934, Birmingham, Ala; s. of O. H. Shelby and Alice L. Skinner; m. Annette Nevin 1960; two s.; ed Alabama Univ.; Law Clerk, Supreme Court of Ala 1961–62; law practice, Tuscaloosa, Ala 1963–79; Prosecutor, City of Tuscaloosa 1964–70; US Magistrate, Northern Dist of Ala 1966–70; Special Asst Attorney-Gen., State of Ala 1969–70; Pres. Tuscaloosa Co. Mental Health Asscn 1969–70; mem. Ala State Senate 1970–78; mem. 96th–99th Congresses, 7th Ala Dist 1979–87; Senator from Alabama 1987–; Chair. Senate Banking Cttee 2003–; fmr mem. Exec. Cttee Ala State Democratic Party; joined Republican Party 1994; mem. ABA; Democrat. *Address:* US Senate, 110 Hart Senate Building, Washington, DC 20510 (Office); 1414 High Forest Drive, North Tuscaloosa, AL 35406, USA (Home).

SHELDON, Sidney; American author; b. 11 Feb. 1917, Chicago, Ill.; s. of Otto Sheldon and Natalie Marcus; m. 1st Jorja Curtright 1951 (died 1985); one d.; m. 2nd Alexandra Kostoff 1989; ed Northwestern Univ.; served U.S.AAF World War II; fmr reader, Universal and 20th Century Fox Studios; Acad. Award (Oscar) for screenplay, The Bachelor and the Bobby Soxer 1947; Writers Guild of America Screen Awards for Easter Parade 1948, Annie Get Your Gun 1950; Tony Award for Redhead 1959; listed in Guinness Book of the Records as Most Translated Author 1997. *Films:* screenplays including: Billy Rose's Jumbo, The Bachelor and the Bobby Soxer 1947, Easter Parade, Annie Get Your Gun, Dream Wife (also Dir), Buster Keaton Story (also Dir). *Theatre:* Roman Candle, Jackpot, Dream with Music, Alice in Arms, Redhead. *Television:* creator, writer and producer, Nancy, The Patty Duke Show, I Dream of Jeannie; creator, Hart to Hart (TV) show. *Publications:* novels: The Naked Face 1970, The Other Side of Midnight 1975, A Stranger in the Mirror 1976, Bloodline 1977, Rage of Angels 1980, Master of the Game 1982, If Tomorrow Comes 1985, Windmills of the Gods 1987, Memories of Midnight 1991, The Doomsday Conspiracy 1991, The Stars Shine Down 1992, Nothing Lasts Forever 1994, Morning, Noon and Night 1995, The Best Laid Plans 1997, Tell Me Your Dreams 1998, The Sky is Falling 2000. *Address:* c/o William Morrow & Co., 1350 Avenue of the Americas, New York, NY 10019, USA.

SHELDRICK, George Michael, MA, PhD, FRS; British professor of chemistry; b. 17 Nov. 1942, Huddersfield; s. of George Sheldrick and Elizabeth Sheldrick; m. Katherine E. Herford 1968; two s. two d.; ed Huddersfield New Coll. and Jesus Coll., Cambridge; Fellow, Jesus Coll., Cambridge and Univ. Demonstrator/Lecturer, Cambridge Univ. 1966–78; Prof. of Structural Chem., Univ. of Göttingen 1978–; author of widely used computer programme for crystal structure determination (SHELX); mem. Akad. der Wissenschaften zu Göttingen 1989; Leibniz Prize, Deutsche Forschungsgemeinschaft 1987, Patterson Prize, American Crystallographic Asscn 1993; Meldola Medal, RSC 1970, Corday-Morgan Medal, RSC 1978, Award for Structural Chem., RSC 1981, Carl-Hermann Medal, Deutsche Gesellschaft für Kristallographie 1999; mineral Sheldrickite named after him 1996. *Publications:* around 750 scientific papers. *Leisure interests:* chess, tennis. *Address:* c/o Department of Inorganic Chemistry, University of Göttingen, Tammannstr. 4, 37077 Göttingen, Germany. *Telephone:* (551) 393021 (Office). *Fax:* (551) 392582 (Office). *E-mail:* gsheldr@shelx.uni-ac.gwdg.de (Office). *Website:* shelx.uni-ac.gwdg.de (Office).

SHELLEY, Howard Gordon; British concert pianist and conductor; b. 9 March 1950, London; s. of Frederick Gordon Shelley and Anne Taylor; m. Hilary MacNamara 1975; one s. one step-s.; professional début Wigmore Hall, London 1971; regular soloist with all London and provincial British orchestras; regular tours to USA and Canada, Australia, Hong Kong and Europe; three piano concertos written for him (Cowie, Chapple, Dickinson); conducting début with London Symphony Orchestra 1985; Assoc. Conductor, London Mozart Players 1990–92, Prin. Guest Conductor 1992–98; Music Dir, Prin. Conductor Uppsala Chamber Orchestra, Sweden 2001–03; opera conducting debut 2002; current engagements as conductor or soloist; Hon. FRCM 1993; Dannreuther Concerto Prize 1971. *Repertoire:* from Mozart through Liszt to Gershwin; first pianist to perform in concert complete solo piano works of Rachmaninov 1983. *Recordings include:* the complete solo piano music of Rachmaninov (9 vols) and complete Rachmaninov song-cycle (3 vols), Chopin Preludes, Sonatas, Scherzi, Impromptus, Schumann Carnival, Kinderszenen, Hummel solo piano works, complete piano concertos of Rachmininov, piano concertos of British composers, Alwyn, Carwithen, Dickinson, Ferguson, Rubbra, Tippett and Vaughan Williams, piano concertos and rhapsodies for piano and orchestra of Gershwin, piano concertos of Balakirev, Korngold (Left Hand), Liapounov, Hindemith's Four Temperaments, Szymanowski's Symphony No. 4 and Messiaen's Turangalila; conducting from the keyboard Shelley has recorded the Mendelssohn piano concertos (3 vols) and Mozart piano concertos Nos. 9, 12, 13, 14, 17, 19, 20–24, 27 (6 vols); Hummel piano concertos (3 vols), Cramer piano concertos (1 vol.), Moscheles piano concertos (1 vol.); conducting the Royal Philharmonic Orchestra he has recorded Mozart symphonies 35 and 38 and Schubert symphonies 3 and 5 and with Tasmanian Symphony Orchestra Reinecke symphonies 2 and 3. *Television:* Documentary on Ravel with Tasmanian Symphony Orchestra (Australian Broadcasting Co.) featured Shelley as presenter, conductor and pianist (Gold Medal for Best Arts Biog., 40th New York Festival Awards);

documentary on Rachmaninov by Hessische Rundfunk (Channel 4). *Address:* c/o Caroline Baird Artists, Pinkhill House, Eynsham, Oxon., OX29 4DA; 38 Cholmeley Park, London, N6 5ER, England. *Telephone:* (1865) 882771 (Office). *Fax:* (1865) 882771 (Office).

SHELOV-KOVEDYAYEV, Fedor Vadimovich; Russian politician; b. 15 June 1956, Moscow; m.; two c.; ed Moscow State Univ.; researcher Inst. of History of USSR (now Russian) Acad. of Sciences; mem. Club of Moscow Intellectuals Moskovskaya Tribuna 1989–91; RSFSR People's Deputy; mem. Cttee on Human Rights, Supreme Soviet 1990–93; mem. State Duma 1993–95; mem. Constitutional Comm. on Regional Policy and Co-operation; mem. Parl. Block Coalition of Reforms; First Deputy Minister of Foreign Affairs 1991–92; mem. Political Council, Democratic Choice of Russia Party 1993–96; Co-Chair., Int. Russian Club; Vice-Pres. Expert Fund of Social Research (ELF). *Publications:* History of the Bosphorus from 6th to 14th Century BC and over 90 scientific works. *Address:* International Russian Club, Ogareva str. 5, 103009 Moscow, Russia.

SHELTON, Gen. Henry Hugh, MSc; American army officer; b. 2 Jan. 1942, Tarboro, NC; s. of the late Hugh Shelton and Sarah Shelton (née Laughlin); m. Carolyn L. Johnson; three s.; ed NC State Univ., Auburn Univ., Harvard Univ., Air Command and Staff Coll., Nat. War Coll.; commissioned into Infantry 1963; served in mainland USA, Hawaii, 2 tours of Vietnam; fmrly Commdr 3rd Bn 60th Infantry Div., Fort Lewis, Wash., Asst Chief of Staff for Operations 9th Infantry Div., Commdr 1st Brigade 82nd Airborne Div., Fort Bragg, NC, Chief of Staff 10th Mountain Div., Fort Drum, NY; rank of Brig.-Gen. 1987; Deputy Dir for Operations, Nat. Mil. Command CTR, Jt Staff Operations Directorate 1987–89; Asst Div. Cmmdr. for Operations 101st Airborne Div. (Air Assault) (including during Operations Desert Shield and Desert Storm 1990–91) 1989–91; rank of Maj.-Gen. 1991; Commdr 82nd Airborne Div., Fort Bragg, NC 1991–93; rank of Lt-Gen. 1993; Commdr XVIIIth and Fort Bragg Airborne Corps. 1993, Commdr Jt Task Force for Operation Restore Democracy, Haiti 1994; rank of Gen. 1996; C-in-C US Special Operations Command 1996–97; Chair. Jt Chiefs of Staff 1997–2001; recipient Defense DSM (with 2 oak leaf clusters) 1989, 1994, 1997, DSM 1994, Legion of Merit (with oak leaf cluster) 1985, 1991, Bronze Star Medal (with V device, 3 oak leaf clusters) 1968, 1969, 1991, Purple Heart 1967 and numerous other decorations. *Leisure interests:* jogging, woodworking, reading and playing guitar. *Address:* c/o Dianne Clark, M.I.C. Industries, Inc., 11911 Freedom Drive, Reston, VA 20190, USA (Office). *Telephone:* (703) 318-1900 (Office). *Fax:* (703) 318-9321 (Office).

SHELTON, William E., EdD; American university president; b. 6 Sept. 1944, Batesville, Miss.; s. of Loyd Shelton and Merle Shelton; m. Sharon Nordengreen Shelton 1965; one s.; ed Univ. of Mississippi and Memphis State Univ., Tenn.; high school teacher, Olive Br., Miss. 1967–68; elementary school Prin., Oakland, Tenn. 1968–70; Admin./Instr. NW Miss. Jr Coll. Senatobia 1970–75; Vice-Pres. Henderson State Univ. Arkadelphia, Ark. 1975–83; Vice-Pres. Kent State Univ., Ohio 1983–89; Pres. Eastern Mich. Univ. 1989–. *Leisure interests:* golf, flying. *Address:* Office of the President, Eastern Michigan University, 202 Welch Hall, Ypsilanti, MI 48197, USA. *Telephone:* (313) 487-1849. *Fax:* (313) 487-7140.

SHELTON-COLBY, Sally, MA; American international organization official; b. 29 Aug. 1944, San Antonio; ed Univ. of Missouri, Johns Hopkins School of Advanced Int. Studies, Institut des Sciences Politiques, Paris; fmr Deputy Asst Sec. of State for Inter-American Affairs; fmr mem. U.S. Perm. Mission to UN, New York; Amb. to Grenada, Barbados and other Caribbean nations 1979–81; Sr Fellow and Adjunct Prof., Georgetown Univ. Center for Latin American Studies; Asst Admin. for Global Problems, U.S. Agency for Int. Devt 1994–99; Deputy Sec.-Gen. OECD 1999–; fmr Vice-Pres. Bankers Trust Co., New York; fmr Dir Valero Energy Corpn, Baring Brother & Co. Ltd's Puma Fund; adviser to several multinat. corpns. on int. trade and investment strategies; mem. Council on Foreign Relations; fmr Co-Ed. Global Assessment (econ. journal); Fulbright Scholar. *Address:* Organisation for Economic Co-operation and Development, 2 rue André-Pascal, 75775 Paris, cédex 16, France (Office). *Telephone:* 1-45-24-82-00 (Office). *Fax:* 1-45-24-85-00 (Office). *E-mail:* webmaster@oecd.org (Office). *Website:* www.oecd.org (Office).

SHEMYAKIN, Mikhail Mikhailovich; Russian sculptor and painter; b. (Kardanov), 1943, Moscow; ed Inst. of Painting, Sculpture and Architecture, Leningrad (now St Petersburg); one-man exhbn Leningrad 1962; arrested for dissident activities, interned in lunatic asylums; emigrated in 1971; lived in Paris 1971–81; living in USA 1981–; f. Foundation for Helping Soviet Veterans of the War in Afghanistan 1989; visited Russia frequently after citizenship was restored 1990; created Peter the Great Memorial in St Petersburg; mem. European Acad. of Arts, New York Acad. of Sciences and Arts; Dr hc (San Francisco); State Prize 1993, Pres. of Russia Prize 1995. *Exhibitions:* one man exhbns. in America, Europe and Russia.

SHEMYAKIN, Yevgeniy Ivanovich, DTechSC.; Russian mining specialist; b. 9 Dec. 1929, Novosibirsk; s. of I. Shemyakin and Ella Shemyakina; m. L. T. Petrova 1952; one s. one d.; ed Leningrad Univ.; Sr research Asst at USSR Acad. of Sciences Inst. of Chemico-Physics 1955–60; head of lab. of USSR Acad. of Sciences Inst. of Theoretical and Applied Mechanics 1960–70; Prof. Novosibirsk State Univ. 1963–87, Chair. of Elasticity 1967–87; Acting Dir of USSR Acad. of Sciences Inst. of Mining (Siberian Div.) 1970–72, Dir 1972–87; Chair. Supreme State Cttee of Attestation, Moscow; Prin. Consultant, Russian Acad. of Sciences Inst. of Dynamics of Geospheres 1987–92;

Prof. Moscow State Univ. 1987–, Chair. of Wave and Gas Dynamics 1988–; Vice-Pres. of Presidium of Siberian Div. of Acad. of Sciences 1980–85; Chair. Russian Acad. of Sciences Scientific Council on Underground Space and Underground Construction 1994–; mem. of USSR (now Russian) Acad. of Sciences 1984, Royal Swedish Soc. of Engineers 1987, Czech Acad. of Science, Slovak Acad. of Science, Int. Soc. for Rock Mechanics (Vice-Pres. 1988–92), Int. Mining Congress; mem. CPSU 1963–91; mem. of several scientific editorial bds.; USSR State Prize 1984. *Publications:* author and co-author of more than 200 scientific and technical papers. *Leisure interests:* ancient history, old underground constructions. *Address:* Department of Mechanics and Mathematics, Moscow Lomonosov State University, Vorobyevy Gory, 119899 Moscow, Russia (Office). *Telephone:* (095) 939-37-54 (Office); (095) 332-62-63 (Home). *Fax:* (095) 939-49-95.

SHEN, James C. H., MA; Taiwanese diplomatist; b. 15 June 1909; m. Winifred Wei; one s. two d.; ed Yenching Univ., Beijing, Univ. of Missouri, USA; Ed. Cen. News Agency, Nanjing 1936–37; Chief Editorial Section, Int. Dept, Ministry of Information, Chongqing 1938–43; Dir Pacific Coast Bureau, Ministry of Information 1943–47; Dir of Int. Dept, Govt Information Office 1947–48, Sec. to Pres. of Repub. of China, Taipei 1956–59; Dir of Information Dept, Ministry of Foreign Affairs, Taipei 1959–61, Dir-Gen. 1961–66; Amb. to Australia 1966–68; Vice-Minister of Foreign Affairs 1968–71; Amb. to USA 1971–79; Nat. Policy Adviser to the Pres. 1979–; Ed. China News, Taipei 1983–85, Asian Cultural Quarterly; Faculty-Alumni Gold Medal (Univ. of Missouri) 1972. *Publication:* The US and Free China—How the US Sold Out Its Ally, My Earlier Years. *Address:* 7th Floor, 11 Lansui Bldg, Garden City, Hsintien, Taipei Co., Taiwan.

SHEN BEIZHANG; Chinese businessman; b. Jan. 1929, Cixi Co., Zhejiang Prov.; ed Jiaotong Univ. Shanghai; Chair. Shanghai Overseas Corpn 1990–; Chair. and Gen. Man., Shanghai Int. Group Corpn 1991–; mem. 8th CPPCC 1993–.

SHEN DALI; Chinese writer, historian and translator; b. 4 Sept. 1938, Yanan; s. of the late Shen Xu and Song Ying; m. Dong Chun 1993; one s. one d.; ed Beijing Foreign Languages Univ.; Prof. titulaire, French Dept Beijing Foreign Languages Univ. 1957–; trans. at UNESCO, Paris 1979–81, réviseur 1985–; visiting scholar in France 1990–91; Prof. Univ. of Montreal, Canada 1994; Prof. INALCO, Paris 1995; Prés. du Jury "Grands Reportages," FIPA 1996; del. to Cultural Comm. CIO, Lausanne, Switzerland 1997; mem. Chinese Writers' Assscn; mem. Editorial Cttee Revue des Deux Mondes (France) 1999; awarded title 'Membre d'honneur' by L'Association des Amis de la Commune de Paris, 1981; Chevalier, Ordre des Arts et des Lettres 1991, Croix de vermeil du Mérite et Dévouement français 1996. *Translations include:* Le Temps des cerises, Montserrat, Selected Poems of Eugene Pottier (additional transls.): Les Fleurs jumelles (play) 1982, L'Epreuve (novel) 1985, Les Trésors de la cité interdite 1986, Poésies choisies de la Commune de Paris 1986, l'Internationale, la Marseillaise, Le Chant du départ, N'a qu'un oeil, La paix du ménage, Le Vésuve, Les Couteaux, Les Yeux de demain, La Vraie Dame au camélias, Byron et les femmes 2002, Bruges la morte 2002. *Publications:* The Children of Yenan (novel, also in French and Italian) 1985, Les Fleurs du rêve (poetry) 1986, Les Lys rouges (novel) 1987, La Flûte des Titans 1987, The Humble Violet, The Meteor, Le rêve dans le pavillon d'azur, Le temps des cigales, Le Tableau de Paris (prose) 1989, L'Etoile filante (novel) 1993, (augmented edn) 1995, Voyage en Europe et en Amérique du Nord 1996, Les Amants du lac 1996 (film), Henri Matisse 2001, Chagall 2001 (both in Italian, French and English). *Leisure interest:* music. *Address:* French Department, Beijing Foreign Languages University, Beijing 100089; Bat N 49-1-4, Dongdaqiaolu, Beijing 100020, People's Republic of China (Home). *Telephone:* (10) 65007458. *Fax:* (10) 68414003.

SHEN DAREN; Chinese party official; b. 1928, Wuxian Co., Jiangsu Prov.; joined CCP 1954; Deputy Sec. Jiangsu Prov. CCP Cttee 1983–86; Sec. Changzhou Municipal CCP Cttee; Sec. Ningxia Hui Autonomous Regional Cttee 1987–89; Sec. Jiangsu Prov. CP 1989, NPC Deputy, Chair. Standing Cttee of 8th People's Congress 1993–; mem. CCP 13th Cen. Cttee 1987–92, 14th Cen. Cttee 1992–. *Address:* Jiangsu Provincial Communist Party, Nanjing City, Jiangsu, People's Republic of China.

SHEN GUOFANG; Chinese engineer; b. 15 Nov. 1933, Jiashan, Zhejiang Prov.; ed Leningrad Forestry Inst., USSR 1956; Prof. Beijing Forestry Univ.; Fellow Chinese Acad. of Eng. 1995–; Vice-Pres. Chinese Acad. of Eng 1998–. *Publication:* Silviculture. *Address:* Beijing Forestry University, Xiaozhaang, Haidan District, Beijing 100083, People's Republic of China (Office). *Telephone:* (10) 62338279 (Office). *Fax:* (10) 62335071 (Office). *E-mail:* shengf@public.bta.net.cn (Office).

SHEN PENG; Chinese calligrapher; b. 1931, Jiangyin, Jiangsu Prov.; Assoc. Ed.-in-Chief People's Fine Arts Press; Vice-Chair. Chinese Calligraphers Asscn, Chair. 2000–. *Publications:* Selected Calligraphic Works of Shen Peng; Shen Peng's Poems; Calligraphy of the Song, Jin and Yuan Dynasties in the Collected Works of Chinese Art; Mi Fu's Calligraphic Art. *Address:* People's Fine Arts Press, Beijing, People's Republic of China (Office).

SHEN RONG; Chinese writer; b. Oct. 1936, Hubei; perm. mem. Chinese Writers' Asscn 1985–; Perm. mem. China PEN 1986–; mem. Chinese Int. Exchange Asscn 1990–. *Publications:* Forever Green (novel), No Way Out,

Light and Dark, A Middle-aged Woman. *Address:* Chinese Writers' Association, 15 Nongzhanguan Nanli, Chaoyang District, Beijing, People's Republic of China.

SHENG HUAREN; Chinese politician; b. 1935, Xieyang Co., Jiangsu Prov.; joined CCP 1954; Dir Planning Dept of Ministry of Chemical Industry; Vice-Gen. Man. China Petrochemical Works Corp. 1983, then Gen. Man.; mem. 15th CCP Cen. Cttee 1997–; Minister of State Econ. and Trade Comm. 1998–2000; mem. Standing Cttee of NPC 2001. *Address:* Standing Committee, National People's Congress, Tiananmen, Beijing 100053, People's Republic of China.

SHENG ZHONGGUO; Chinese violinist; b. 1941, Chongqing, Sichuan Prov.; ed Moscow Acad. of Music, USSR; fmrly instructor Cen. Acad. of Music; solo performer (1st Class) Cen. Orchestra; prize at Int. Chaikovski Violin Competition 1962; 1st Prize for Musical Instruments at Competitive Performance by Troupes and Insts. (Ministry of Culture) 1981. *Music:* many albums including Butterfly Lovers. *Address:* Central Orchestra, Beijing, People's Republic of China (Office).

SHENGELAIA, Eldar; Georgian film director; b. 26 Jan. 1933, Georgia; s. of Nikolai Shengelaia and Nato Vachnadze; brother of Georgiy Nikolayevich Shengelaia (q.v.); m. 1st Ariadna Shengelaia (Shprink) 1957 (divorced 1980); two d.; m. 2nd Nelly Davlianidze 1981; one d.; ed Moscow Inst. of Cinematography; Dir at Mosfilm 1958–59, at Kartuli Pilmi film studio, Georgia 1960–; mem. CPSU 1966–90; Chair. Georgian Film-makers' Union 1976–; fmr sec. USSR Film-makers' Union; teacher, Tbilisi Theatre Inst., Tbilisi State Univ., Head of Film and TV Dept; Deputy, Supreme Soviet of Georgian SSR 1980–85, 1986–90, mem. Presidium 1989–90; elected to Supreme Soviet of Georgian Repub. (representing Democratic Centre) 1990–91; People's Deputy of USSR, USSR Supreme Soviet 1989–91; mem. State Council, Georgia, Parl. Repub. of Georgia 1992–; mem. Georgian Parl. 1995–, now Deputy Chair.; Chair. Cultural Comm.; People's Artist of Georgia 1979, USSR Prize 1985, People's Artist of USSR 1987; numerous other prizes. *Films include:* The Legend of the Ice Heart 1957, The Snow Fairy Tale 1958, White Caravan 1963, Mikela 1965, An Extraordinary Exhibition 1968, The Screwballs 1974, Stepmother of Samanishvili 1978, Blue Mountains or an Improbable Event 1984, Tbilisi 9 April Chronicles 1989, Express Information 1994. *Address:* c/o Georgian Film-makers' Union, Kakabadze Street 2, 380008 Tbilisi (Office); Ioseliani Street 37, Flat 58, 380091 Tbilisi, Georgia (Home). *Telephone:* (32) 99-75-18 (Office); (32) 99-80-80 (Home).

SHENGELAIA, Georgiy Nikolayevich; Georgian film director and actor; b. 11 May 1937, Tbilisi; s. of Nicolai Shengelaia and Nato Vachnadze; brother of Eldar Shengelaia (q.v.); m. 1st Sofiko Chiaureli 1957 (divorced); m. 2nd Ketevan Ninya 1985; three s.; ed Moscow Inst. of Cinematography; freelance artist; mem. Parl., Deputy Chair. 2000; Georgian State Prize 1980. *Films include:* Alaverdoba 1960, He Did Not Want to Kill 1966, Pirosmani 1969, Melodies of Veriysky Suburb 1973, Come into the Grape Valley 1977, The Girl with the Sewing-Machine 1980, Journey of the Young Composer 1985, Kchareba An Gogi 1987, Death of Orpheus 1996, Georgian Grapes 1999. *Roles include:* Dato (Our Yard), Georgi (Otar's Widow), Gela (The Tale About a Girl). *Address:* Kekelidze Street 16, Apt. 12, 380009 Tbilisi, Georgia. *Telephone:* (32) 22-64-11. *Fax:* (32) 99-07-54, 93-50-97.

SHENIN, Col Oleg Semyonovich; Russian politician; b. 22 July 1937, Vladimirskaya, Volgograd Dist; s. of Semyon Sidorovich Shenin and Angelina Nikolaevna Shenina; m. Tamara Aleksandrovna Shenina 1955; one s. two d.; ed Krasnoyarsk Tech. College for Mining, Tomsk Eng Inst. and CPSU Cen. Cttee Acad. of Social Sciences; mem. CPSU 1962–91; from works foreman to trust man. at construction sites in Krasnoyarsk Dist 1955–74; party work 1974–91; First Sec. Achinsk City Cttee, Second Sec. Khakassk Dist Cttee (obkom), Sec. Krasnoyarsk Dist Cttee, First Sec. Khakassk Dist Cttee (obkom) 1974–87; First Sec. Krasnoyarsk Dist Cttee 1987–90; elected USSR People's Deputy 1989; Chair. Krasnoyarsk Dist Council of People's Deputies 1990–91; fmr mem. CPSU Cen. Cttee; mem. Political Bureau, Sec. Cen. Cttee 1990–91; arrested Aug. 1991 for alleged participation in attempted coup d'état; charged with conspiracy Jan. 1992, released Oct. 1992; on trial 1993, released on amnesty 1994; Chair. Union of Communist Parties (SCP-CPSU) 1993–, Int. Comm. for Union and Brotherhood of Peoples 1997–; First Sec. Cen. Cttee CPSU 2000–; mem. Russian Fed. of Natural Sciences. *Leisure interests:* sport, reading, family. *Address:* Union of Communist Parties, Novaya sq. 14, 103132 Moscow, Russia (Office); Per Plotnikov 13 Kv. 24, Moscow, Russia (Home). *Telephone:* (095) 278-96-33. *Fax:* (095) 278-31-39. *E-mail:* shenin@cea.ru (Office). *Website:* www.cea.ru/shenin (Office).

SHENNAN, Joseph Hugh, PhD, FRHistS, FRSA; British professor of history; b. 13 March 1933, Liverpool; s. of Hugh Cringle Shennan and Mary Catherine Jones; m. Margaret King Price 1958; three s.; ed St Edward's Coll. Liverpool, Univ. of Liverpool and Corpus Christi Coll. Cambridge; Asst Lecturer, Lecturer in History, Univ. of Liverpool 1960–65; Lecturer, Sr Lecturer, Reader in History, Lancaster Univ. 1965–74, Prof. of European Studies 1974–79, Prof. of European History 1979–, Pro-Vice-Chancellor (Academic) 1985–93, Deputy Vice-Chancellor 1993–98; Sr Research Scholar (Visiting Fellow) Corpus Christi Coll. Cambridge 1984–85; Founding Ed. European Studies Review (now European History Quarterly) 1970–79. *Publications:* The Parlement of Paris 1968, Government and Society in France 1461–1661 1969, The Origins of the Modern European State 1450–1725 1974, Philippe, Duke of Orleans: Regent of France, 1715–1723 1979, France Before the

Revolution 1983, Liberty and Order in Early Modern Europe: The Subject and the State, 1650–1800 1986, Louis XIV 1986, International Relations in Europe, 1689–1789 1995. *Leisure interests:* golf, the 18th century, watching Liverpool Football Club. *Address:* Bull Beck House, Four Acres, Brookhouse, Lancaster, LA2 9JW, England (Home). *Telephone:* (1524) 770517. *Fax:* (1524) 771846 (Office). *E-mail:* j.shennan@lancaster.ac.uk (Home).

SHENOUDA III, Anba, BA, BD; Egyptian ecclesiastic; b. 3 Aug. 1923; ed Cairo Univ. and Coptic Orthodox Theological Coll.; theological teacher and writer; fmr Bishop and Prof. of Theology, Orthodox Clerical Coll., Cairo; 1st Chair., Asscn of Theological Colls. in the Near East; 117th Pope of Alexandria and Patriarch of the See of St Mark of Egypt, the Near East and All Africa (Coptic Orthodox Church) 1971–81, 1985; removed from post by Pres. Sadat and banished to desert monastery Wadi Natroun Sept. 1981, released Jan. 1985. *Address:* Coptic Orthodox Patriarchate, St Mark Cathedral, P.O. Box 9035, Anba Ruess, 222 Ramses Street, Abbasiya, Cairo, Egypt.

SHEPARD, Sam; American playwright and actor; b. 5 Nov. 1943, Fort Sheriden, Ill.; s. of Samuel Shepard Rogers and Jane Schook Rogers; m. O-Lan Johnson Dark 1969 (divorced); one s.; one s. one d. with Jessica Lange (q.v.); ed Duarte High School, Mount San Antonio Jr Coll. *Television appearances include:* Lily Dale 1996, Purgatory 1999, Hamlet 2000. *Plays include:* Cowboys—Rock Garden (double bill), Chicago—Icarus' Mother—Red Cross (triple bill; 1966, Obie Award), La Turista (1967 Obie Award), Forensic and the Navigators (1968 Obie Award), Melodrama Play, Tooth of Crime (1973 Obie Award), Back Dog Beast Bait, Operation Sidewinder, 4-H Club, The Unseen Hand, Mad Dog Blues, Shaved Splits, Rock Garden (included in Oh! Calcutta!), Curse of the Starving Class (1978 Obie Award), True West, Fool for Love, A Lie of the Mind, Simpatico. *Film appearances include:* Days of Heaven, Frances, The Right Stuff, Country, Crimes of the Heart, Baby Boom, Defenceless 1989, Voyager, Thunderheart 1992, The Pelican Brief 1994, Safe Passage 1995, The Good Old Boys 1995, Curtain Call 1997, The Only Thrill 1997, Snow Falling on Cedars 1999, One Kill 2000, Shot in the Heart 2001, Swordfish 2001, The Pledge 2001. *Screenplay:* Paris, Texas (Palme d'Or, Cannes Film Festival 1984), Far North (also Dir) 1989, Silent Tongue (also Dir), Snow Falling on Cedars, Hamlet, Curtain Call. *Publications:* A Murder of Crows 1996 (novel), Cruising Paradise (short stories) 1996. *Address:* ICM, 8942 Wilshire Boulevard, Beverly Hills CA 90211, USA.

SHEPARD, Stephen Benjamin; American journalist; b. 20 July 1939, New York; s. of William Shepard and Ruth Shepard (née Tanner); m. Lynn Povich 1979; one s. one d.; ed City Coll., NY, Columbia Univ.; reporter, writer Business Week 1966–75, Exec. Ed. 1982–84, Ed.-in-Chief 1984–; Asst Prof., Dir Walter Bagehot Fellowship Program in econs and business journalism, Columbia Univ. 1975–76; Sr Ed. Newsweek 1976–81; Ed. Saturday Review 1981–82; mem. American Soc. of Magazine Eds. (Vice-Pres. 1990–92, Pres. 1992–94), Council on Foreign Relations, Century Asscn; Lifetime Achievement Award, Gerald Coeb Foudation 1999, Henry Johnson Fisher Award, Magazine Publisher of America 2000. *Address:* Business Week, McGraw Hill Inc., 43rd Floor, 1221 Avenue of the Americas, New York, NY 10020 (Office); 322 Central Park West, New York, NY 10025, USA (Home).

SHEPHARD, Rt Hon Gillian Patricia, PC, MA; British politician; b. 22 Jan. 1940; d. of Reginald Watts and Bertha Watts; m. Thomas Shephard 1975; two step-s.; ed North Walsham High School for Girls, St Hilda's Coll., Oxford; Educ. Officer and Schools Inspector 1963–75; lecturer Cambridge Univ. Extra-Mural Bd 1965–87; Councillor Norfolk Co. Council 1977–89 (Chair. Social Services Cttee 1978–83, Educ. Cttee 1983–85); Chair. W Norfolk and Wisbech Health Authority 1981–85, Norwich Health Authority 1985–87; MP for S.W. Norfolk 1987–97, for Norfolk S.W. 1997–; Co-Chair. Women's Nat. Comm. 1990–91; Parl. Pvt. Sec. to Econ. Sec. to the Treasury 1988–89; Parl. Under-Sec. of State Dept of Social Security 1989–90; Minister of State (Treasury) 1990–92; Sec. of State for Employment 1992–93, for Agric., Fisheries and Food 1993–94, for Educ. 1994–95, for Educ. and Employment 1995–97; Shadow Leader of House of Commons and Shadow Chancellor of Duchy of Lancaster 1997–99; Opposition Spokesman on Environment, Transport and the Regions 1998–99; Deputy Chair. Conservative Party 1991–92; Vice-Pres. Hansard Soc. 1997–; mem. Council Univ. of Oxford 2000–; Hon. Fellow St Hilda's Coll. 1991. *Publication:* Shephard's Watch 2000. *Leisure interests:* music, gardening, France. *Address:* House of Commons, London, SW1A 0AA, England. *Telephone:* (1366) 385072.

SHEPHERD, Cybill; American actress; b. 18 Feb. 1950, Memphis, Tenn.; d. of William Jennings Shepherd and Patty Shobe Micci; m. 1st David Ford 1978 (divorced); one d.; m. 2nd Bruce Oppenheim 1987; twin s.; fmr magazine cover girl; eight years of commercials for L'Oréal Préférence; film debut in The Last Picture Show 1971; Emmy Award for series Moonlighting 1985. *Films include:* The Heartbreak Kid 1973, Daisy Miller 1974, At Long Last Love 1975, Taxi Driver 1976, Special Delivery 1976, Silver Bears 1977, The Lady Vanishes 1978, Earthright 1980, The Return 1986, Chances Are 1988, Texasville 1990, Alice 1990, Once Upon A Crime 1992, Married to It 1993; numerous TV films. *Plays include:* A Shot in the Dark 1977, Vanities 1981, The Muse 1999, Marine Life 2000. *Television includes:* The Yellow Rose 1983–84, Moonlighting 1985–89, Cybill 1994–98. *Publication:* Cybill Disobedience 2000. *Website:* www.cybill.com (Office).

SHEPPARD OF DIDGEMERE, Baron (Life Peer), cr. 1994, of Roydon in the County of Essex; **Allen John George Sheppard,** KCVO, BSc; British company director; b. 25 Dec. 1932, London; s. of John Baggott Sheppard and Lily Sheppard (née Palmer); m. 1st Peggy Damaris (née Jones) 1959 (divorced 1980); m. 2nd Mary Stewart 1980; ed Ilford Co. School, London School of Econs; with Ford 1958–68, Chrysler 1968–71, British Leyland 1971–75, Grand Metropolitan 1975–96, CEO 1986–93, Chair. 1987–96; Pres. London First 1992–, Chair. 2002–, Group Trust PLC 1994–2001, McBride PLC 1995–, GB Railways PLC 1996–, Unipart 1996–; Vice-Pres. Brewers' Soc. 1987–; Chair. Bd of Trustees, Prince's Youth Business Trust 1990–94, Advisory Bd, British American Chamber of Commerce 1991–94; Chair. Business in the Community 1994–97; Gov. LSE 1989–; Dir High Point Rendel 1997–, One Click HP PLC, Wyne PLC 2000–, Transware PLC 2001–; Dir (non-exec.) Bowater PLC 1994–95; Chancellor Middx Univ. 2000–; Hon. LLD (South Bank Univ.) 1994; Dr hc (Westminster) 1998, (Middx) 1999, (LSE) 2001. *Publications:* Your Business Matters 1958, Maximum Leadership 1995, various articles in professional journals. *Leisure interests:* reading, gardens, red setter dogs. *Address:* House of Lords, London, SW1A 0PW, England.

SHEPPARD OF LIVERPOOL, Baron (Life Peer), cr. 1998, of West Kirby in the County of Merseyside; **Rt Rev David Stuart Sheppard,** MA; British ecclesiastic (retd) and fmr test cricketer; b. 6 March 1929, Reigate, Surrey; s. of the late Stuart Sheppard and Barbara Sheppard; m. Grace Isaac 1957; one d.; ed Sherborne School, Trinity Hall, Cambridge and Ridley Hall Theological Coll. Cambridge; Asst Curate, St Mary's Islington 1955–57; Warden, Mayflower Family Centre, Canning Town 1957–69; Bishop Suffragan of Woolwich 1969–75; Bishop of Liverpool 1975–97; Vice-Chair. Archbishop of Canterbury's Comm. on Urban Priority Areas 1983–85; Chair. BBC and IBA Cen. Religious Advisory Cttee 1989–92, Gen. Synod Bd for Social Responsibility 1991–96, Churches' Enquiry into Unemployment and the Future of Work 1995–97; played cricket for Cambridge 1950–52 (Capt. 1952), Sussex 1947–62 (Capt. 1953), England 22 times 1950–63 (Capt. 1954); Pres. Sussex Co. Cricket Club 2001–03; Hon. LLD (Liverpool Univ.) 1983; Hon. DTech (Liverpool Polytechnic) 1987; Hon. DD (Cambridge Univ.) 1990, (Exeter) 1998, (Birmingham) 1999, (Univ. of Wales) 2000; Hon. DUniv (Open Univ.) 1999; Wisden Cricketer of the Year 1953. *Publications:* Parson's Pitch 1964, Built as a City 1974, Bias to the Poor 1983, The Other Britain (Dimbleby Lecture) 1984; (with Archbishop Worlock): Better Together 1988, With Christ in the Wilderness 1990, With Hope in Our Hearts 1994; Steps Along Hope Street 2002. *Leisure interests:* relaxing at home, following cricket, painting, gardening, cooking, singing in a choir. *Address:* 11 Melloncroft Drive, West Kirby, Wirral, CH8 2JA, England.

SHER, Sir Antony, Kt, KBE; British actor, artist and author; b. 14 June 1949, Cape Town, South Africa; ed Webber Douglas Acad. of Dramatic Art; numerous appearances at Liverpool Everyman, Nottingham Playhouse, Royal Court Theatre, Nat. Theatre, RSC (RSC Assoc. Artist 1982–) and in West End; Hon. DLitt (Liverpool) 1998; Best Actor Awards from Drama Magazine and The Evening Standard Awards, for performance as Richard III (RSC) 1985, Olivier Award for Best Actor, Soc. of West End Theatres, for performances as Richard III, as Arnold in Torch Song Trilogy 1985, for Stanley 1997, Best Actor Award, Martini TMA Awards, for performance as Titus Andronicus 1996, Peter Sellers Evening Standard Film Award for performance as Disraeli in Mrs. Brown 1998. *Plays include:* John, Paul, Ringo and Bert (Lyric Theatre), Teeth 'n' Smiles, Cloud Nine, A Prayer for My Daughter (Royal Court Theatre), Goosepimples (Hampstead and Garrick Theatres), King Lear, Tartuffe, Richard III, Merchant of Venice, The Revenger's Tragedy, Hello and Goodbye, Singer, Tamburlaine the Great, Travesties, Cyrano de Bergerac, The Winter's Tale, Macbeth (RSC), The Roman Actor, The Malcontent, Torch Song Trilogy (Albery Theatre), True West, Arturo Ui, Uncle Vanya, Titus Andronicus (Royal Nat. Theatre), Stanley (Royal Nat. Theatre, Circle in the Square Theater, New York), Mahler's Conversion (Aldwych Theatre), ID (Almeida Theatre) 2003, The Malcontent (Gielgud). *Films:* Shadey, The Young Poisoner's Handbook, Alive and Kicking, Mrs. Brown, Shakespeare in Love. *Television appearances include:* The History Man, Collision Course, The Land of Dreams, Genghis Cohn, Moonstone, Hornblower, Macbeth, The Jury. *Publications:* Year of the King 1986, Middlepost 1988, Characters (paintings and drawings) 1989, Changing Step (screenplay) 1989, The Indoor Boy 1991, Cheap Lives 1995, Woza Shakespeare! (co-written with Gregory Doran) 1996, The Feast 1998, Beside Myself (autobiog.) 2001. *Address:* c/o ICM, Oxford House, 76 Oxford Street, London, W1N 0AX, England (Office). *Telephone:* (20) 7636-6565.

SHERIF, Osama ash-, BA; Jordanian publisher; b. June 1960, Jerusalem; s. of Mahmoud El-Sherif and Aida El-Sherif; m. Ghada Yasser Amr 1984; one s. one d.; ed Univ. of Missouri; Chief Ed. The Jerusalem Star 1985–88; Pres. Info-Media, Jordan 1989–; Publr, Chief Ed. and weekly columnist, The Star, Jordan 1990–; Publr Arabian Communications & Publishing (ACP) 1994–, BYTE Middle East 1994–, Al Tiqaniyyah Wal 'Amal 1995–. *Leisure interests:* novel and short-story writing, travel, photography, horse riding. *Address:* The Star, P.O. Box 591, University Street, Amman 11118, Jordan. *Telephone:* (6) 5664153. *Fax:* (6) 5667170. *E-mail:* star@addustour.com.jo (Office). *Website:* star.arabia.com (Office).

SHERIMKULOV, Megetkan; Kyrgyzstan politician and diplomatist; b. 17 Nov. 1939, Tchapaevo (Kyrgyzia); m.; three d.; ed Kyrgyz Univ., Moscow Univ.; mem. CPSU 1962–91; lecturer Kyrgyz Univ., Prof. 1995–; Prof. Centre of Strategic Studies and Political Sciences Kyrgyz Nat. Univ. 1998–; instructor Div. of Science, Cen. Cttee CP of Kyrgyzia 1971–73; Sec. Party Cttee, Kyrgyz Univ. 1973–76; Sec. Issyk-Kul Regional CP Cttee 1976–80; Head Div. of Propaganda, Cen. Cttee CP, Kyrgyz SSR 1986–90; Chair.

Supreme Soviet (now Uluk Kenesh) of Repub. of Kyrgyzstan 1990–94; cand. for Presidency of Kyrgyzstan 1995; Amb. to Turkey 1996–2002. *Address:* Embassy of Kyrgyzstan, Çayhane S, 24, Gaziosmanpaşa, Ankara, Turkey (Office). *Telephone:* (312) 4468408 (Office). *Fax:* (312) 4468413 (Office).

SHERMAN, Sir Alfred, Kt, BSc, FRSA; British journalist and public affairs adviser; b. 11 Nov. 1919; s. of Jacob Vladimir Sherman and Eva Sherman (née Goldental); m. 1st Zahava Levin 1958 (died 1993); one s.; m. 2nd Angela Valentina Martins 2001; ed Hackney Downs County Secondary School, London and LSE; served in Int. Brigade, Spanish Civil War 1937–38 and in field security and occupied enemy territory admin., war of 1939–45; leader writer, Jewish Chronicle; various positions on Daily Telegraph 1965–86, leader writer 1977–86; Public Affairs Adviser in pvt. practice as Interthought; Co-Founder Centre for Policy Studies 1974, Dir of Studies –1984; Adviser to Radovan Karadžić 1993–94; Consultant, Nat. Bus Co.; mem. economic advisory staff, Israeli Govt in 1950s; Councillor, RBK&C 1971–78; Chair. Lord Byron Foundation for Balkan Studies; Order of Njegoŝ (First Class) from Radovan Karadžić. *Publications:* Local Government Reorganisation and Industry 1970, Councils, Councillors and Public Relations 1973, Local Government Reorganization and the Salary Bill 1974, Waste in Wandsworth (with D. Mallam) 1976, Crisis Calls for a Minister for Denationalization 1980, The Scott Report 1981, Communism and Arab Nationalism: A Reappraisal, Capitalism and Liberty, Our Complacent Satirists, Political Violence in Britain; contribs. to newspapers and periodicals, including The Guardian, The Independent and the Spectator. *Address:* 14 Malvern Court, Onslow Square, London, SW7 3HU, England (Home). *Telephone:* (20) 7581-4075 (Home). *E-mail:* shermania@aol.com (Office).

SHERMAN, Cindy, BA; American artist; b. 1954, Glen Ridge, NJ; ed State Univ. Coll., Buffalo; numerous solo exhbns. Buffalo, Houston, New York, Genoa, Paris, Amsterdam, Tokyo etc.; numerous group exhbns. Buffalo, New York, Chicago, Washington, London, Paris, Venice Biennale 1982, Documenta 7, Kassel 1982 etc.; work in perm. collections including Museum of Fine Arts, Houston, Museum Boymans-van Beuningen, Rotterdam, Museum of Modern Art, New York, Tate Gallery, London, Centre Pompidou, Paris, Stedelijk Museum, Amsterdam, Metropolitan Museum of Art, New York, San Francisco Museum of Modern Art. *Address:* c/o Metro Pictures, 519 W 24th Street, New York, NY 10011, USA.

SHERMAN, Martin; American playwright; b. New Jersey; ed Boston Univ. *Plays include:* Cracks, Bent, A Madhouse in Goa, When She Danced, Some Sunny Day. *Films include:* The Clothes in the Wardrobe (The Summer House in USA), Indian Summer.

SHERRIN, Edward George (Ned), CBE, MA; British director, writer and presenter; b. 18 Feb. 1931, Low Ham, Somerset; s. of Thomas Adam Sherrin and Dorothy Finch Sherrin (née Drewett); ed Sexey's School, Bruton, Exeter Coll., Oxford, Gray's Inn; Producer ATV 1955–58, BBC 1958–65; film producer 1965–75; theatre Dir 1972–; Olivier Award for the Ratepayers' Iolanthe 1984. *Films produced:* The Virgin Soldiers 1968, The National Health 1972. *Theatre:* directed and narrated Side by Side by Sondheim, London 1976–77, NY 1977–78; directed and co-adapted The Ratepayers' Iolanthe, London 1984; directed Mr. and Mrs. Nobody 1987, Jeffrey Bernard is Unwell 1989 (Australia 1992), Same Old Moon, Bookends 1990, Our Song 1992, A Passionate Woman 1994, Salad Days (revival tour) 1995, (Vaudeville Theatre) 1996, Good Grief 1998, A Saint She Aint 1999. *Radio:* presenter Loose Ends (BBC Radio 4) 1985–, Counterpoint (BBC Radio 4) 1985–. *Television:* created That Was The Week That Was (satire programme) 1961. *Publications:* (with Caryl Brahms) Cindy-Ella or I Gotta Shoe 1962, Rappel 1910 1964, Benbow Was His Name 1967, Ooh la! la! 1973, After You M. Feydeau 1975; A Small Thing Like an Earthquake 1983, Cutting Edge 1984, Too Dirty for the Windmill 1985; (with Neil Shand) 1956 and All That 1986, Loose Neds 1990; Ned Sherrin's Theatrical Anecdotes 1991, Ned Sherrin in His Anecdotage 1993, The Oxford Dictionary of Humorous Quotations 1994, Scratch an Actor (novel) 1996, Sherrin's Year (diary) 1996. *Leisure interests:* theatre, cricket. *Address:* 4 Cornwall Mansions, Ashburnham Road, London, SW10 0PE. *Telephone:* (20) 7352-7662.

SHERRINGTON, David, MA, PhD, FInstP, FRS; British professor of physics; b. 29 Oct. 1941, Blackpool; s. of the late James A. Sherrington and Elfreda Cameron; m. Margaret Gee-Clough 1966; one s. one d.; ed St Mary's Coll. Middlesbrough and Univ. of Manchester; Asst Lecturer in Theoretical Physics, Univ. of Manchester 1964–67, Lecturer (on leave) 1967–69; Asst Research Physicist, Univ. of Calif. at San Diego 1967–69; Lecturer in Solid State Physics, Imperial Coll. London 1969–74, Reader 1974–83, Prof. of Physics 1983–89; Cadre Supérieur, Inst. Laue Langevin, Grenoble 1977–79; Wykeham Prof. of Physics and Head of Theoretical Physics, Univ. of Oxford 1989–; Ulam Scholar, Los Alamos Nat. Lab., USA 1995–96; Fellow, American Physical Soc., New Coll. Oxford 1989–; Bakerian Lecture, Royal Soc. 2001. *Publications:* articles in scientific journals, co-ed. of 7 books. *Leisure interests:* travel, wine, theatre, walking, skiing. *Address:* Dept of Theoretical Physics, 1 Keble Road, Oxford, OX1 3NP (Office); 53 Cumnor Hill, Oxford, OX2 9EY, England (Home). *Telephone:* (1865) 273952 (Office); (1865) 862057 (Home). *Fax:* (1865) 273947 (Office). *E-mail:* d.sherrington@physics.ox.ac.uk (Office).

SHERSTYUK, Col.-Gen. Vladislav Petrovich, CAND.TECH.SC.; Russian security official; b. 16 Oct. 1940, Novoplastunovskaya, Krasnodar Region; m.; one s.; ed Moscow State Univ., Higher KGV School; with KGB 1966–; Head Dept of Radioelectronic Espionage Telecommunications, Fed. Agency of Govt

Telecommunications and Information 1995–98, Deputy Dir-Gen. 1998, Dir-Gen. 1998–99; First Deputy Sec. Council of Security May 1999–; Dir Fed. Agency of Govt Communications and Information (FAPSI) 2001–; USSR State Prize 1978, State Prize of Russian Fed. 1996, Order of Labour Red Banner 1975, Red Star 1988, Order for Service to Motherland 1996 and numerous other decorations. *Address:* FAPSI, B. Kiselny per. 4, 103031, Moscow, Russia (Office). *Telephone:* (095) 224-37-37.

SHERWOOD, James Blair, BEcons; American shipping entrepreneur; b. 8 Aug. 1933; s. of William Earl Sherwood and Florence Balph Sherwood; m. Shirley Angela Masser Cross 1977; two step s.; ed Yale Univ.; Lt USNR 1955–58; Man. French Ports, later Asst Gen. Freight Traffic. Man., U.S. Lines Co. 1959–62; Gen. Man. Container Transport Int. Inc. 1963–64; Founder and Pres. Sea Containers Group 1965–; Chair. Orient-Express Hotels 1987–, GE Senco SRL 1998–, Neptune Maritime Ltd 1999–; with Mark Birley est. Harry's Bar Club, London 1979; restored and brought into service Venice Simplon-Orient-Express 1982; Trustee Solomon R. Guggenheim Foundation 1989–. *Publication:* James Sherwood's Discriminating Guide to London 1975. *Leisure interests:* skiing, tennis, sailing. *Address:* Hinton Manor, Hinton Waldrist, Oxon. SN7 8SA, England (Home). *Telephone:* (1865) 820260 (Home).

SHESHINSKI, Eytan, PhD; Israeli university professor; b. 29 June 1937, Haifa; s. of Alice Sheshinski and Baruch Sheshinski; m. Ruth H. Sheshinski 1960; four d.; ed Hebrew Univ. Jerusalem, MIT, USA; Asst Prof. Harvard Univ. 1966–67; Lecturer, then Assoc. Prof., later Prof. of Econs Hebrew Univ., Jerusalem 1967–; Visiting Prof. Harvard Univ., Stanford Univ., MIT, Columbia Univ.; Chair. Bd Koor Industries 1990–, Khevrat Ha'Ovdim 1989–92; Sir Isaac Wolfson Prof. of Public Finance; Fellow Econometric Soc., mem. Royal Swedish Acad. of Sciences, American Acad. of Arts and Sciences. *Publications:* The Optimal Linear Income Tax (Review of Econ. Studies 1972), Inflation and Costs of Price Adjustment (Review of Econ. Studies 1977), Optimum Pricing, Inflation and the Costs of Price Adjustments (ed.) 1993. *Leisure interests:* tennis, hiking. *Address:* Hebrew University of Jerusalem, Mount Scopus, 91 905 Jerusalem, Israel (Office); 4 Kaufman Street, Tel Aviv 68012, Israel. *Telephone:* (2) 5882111; (2) 5105681. *Fax:* (2) 5322545 (Office); (2) 5195353.

SHESTAKOV, Sergey Vasilyevich; Russian biologist; b. 23 Nov. 1934, Leningrad; s. of Vasily Ivanovich Shestakov and Ludmila Shestakova; m. Galina A. Grigorieva 1964; one s.; ed Moscow State Univ.; on staff Moscow State Univ. 1957–; Dir Int. Biotech. Centre; Dir N. Vavilov Inst. of Gen. Genetics, Russian Acad. of Sciences 1988–91; Corresp. mem. Russian Acad. of Sciences 1987, mem. 2000; Chair. Scientific Council on Genetics; mem. Russian Biotech. Acad., Int. Acad. of Science, New York Acad. of Sciences; Visiting Prof. Mich. State Univ., USA 1992; Fulbright-Hays Fellowship 1975; UNESCO Fellowship Award 1985; research in molecular biology and genetics of microorganisms, genomics, radiation genetics; discovery of genetic transformation in cyanobacteria; 7 patented inventions in biotechnology; Hon. Prof. (Wales) 2000; USSR State Prize 1988, Lomonosov Prize 1995, Hon. Distinguished Scientist of Russian Fed. 1995, N. Vavilov Gold Medal 1997. *Publications:* on molecular genetics of DNA repair and recombination, photosynthesis, nitrogen-fixation, resistance to stresses. *Leisure interest:* sports. *Address:* Department of Genetics, Moscow State University, 119899 Moscow, Russia (Office). *Telephone:* (095) 939-35-12 (Office). *Fax:* (095) 939-35-12 (Office).

SHESTAKOVA, Tatyana Borisovna; Russian actress; b. 23 Oct. 1948, Leningrad; d. of Boris Shestakov and Aleksandra Shestakova; m. Lev Dodin 1972; ed Leningrad Theatre Inst.; Leningrad Theatre for Children 1972–75; Leningrad Comedy Theatre 1975–80; Bolshoi Drama Theatre 1980–83; Maly Drama Theatre 1983–; has also played for Moscow Arts Theatre; toured abroad 1983, 1987–2001; USSR State Prize 1986, RSFSR Merited Artist 1987, National 'Triumph' Prize 1992. *Film:* Mother Go and See 1986. *Theatre roles include:* Liza (The House) 1980, Sonya (Uncle Vanya) 1982, She (The Meek One) 1985, Anfisa (Brothers and Sisters) 1986, Anna (Stars of the Morning Sky) 1987, Lebyadkina (The Possessed), Lubov Andreevna (The Cherry Orchard) 1994, Dame Elegant (Roberto Zucco) 1994, Katya and Ivanova (Claustrophobia) 1994, Anna Petrovna (Play Without a Name) 1997, Sonya (Chevengur) 2000, Arcadina (The Seagull) 2001. *Leisure interests:* travelling, books, music. *Address:* Maly Drama Theatre, Rubinstein Str. 18, St Petersburg; Michurinskaya St. 1-140, St. Petersburg, Russia (Home). *Telephone:* (812) 113-21-08 (Office). *Fax:* (812) 113-33-66 (Office); (812) 113-33-66. *E-mail:* mdt@sp.wplus.net (Office).

SHETREET, Shimon; Israeli politician and professor of law; b. 1946, Morocco; ed Hebrew Univ., Chicago Univ.; Sec. Council for Public Justice; Chair. Cttee on Broadcasting Authority Law; Chair. Int. Conf. on Legal Matters; Chair. Bd Dirs. Afro-Asian Inst. of the Histadrut; Prof. of Law, Hebrew Univ. 1973–; Minister of Economy, Science and Tech. 1992–95, of Religious Affairs 1995–96; now Sr Deputy Mayor of Jerusalem; mem. Knesset 1988; served on numerous cttees. 1988–92, including the Landau Comm. on the Israeli Court System, the Council for Admin. Courts, plenum of the Israel Broadcasting Authority 1984–87; Dir Leumi Bank; Labour; Ethics Prize 1994. *Publications:* numerous books including The Good Land Between Power and Religion, Judges on Trial 1976, Justice in Israel 1994, Women in Law 1998; and articles on legal matters. *Address:* Hebrew University of Jerusalem,

Mount Scopus, Jerusalem 91905, Israel (Office). *Telephone:* 2-5882534 (Office). *Fax:* 2-5883042 (Office); 2-5864503 (Home). *E-mail:* mshetree@mscc .huji.ac.il (Office). *Website:* mishpatim.mscc.huji.ac.il (Office).

SHEVARDNADZE, Eduard; Georgian politician; b. 25 Jan. 1928, Mamati Lanchkhutsky Dist, Georgia; s. of Ambrosi Shevardnadze and Sophio Pateish-vili; m. Nanuli Tsagareishvili 1950; one s. one d.; ed Party School of the Cen. Cttee, CP of Georgia and Kutaisi Pedagogical Inst.; mem. CPSU 1948–91; Komsomol and party work 1946–56; Second Sec. 1956–57, First Sec. Komsomol in Georgia 1957–61; First Sec. Mtskheti raion 1961–63, Pervomaisky raion, Tbilisi, CP of Georgia 1963–64; First Deputy Minister 1964–65, Minister of Public Order (renamed Ministry of Internal Affairs 1968) 1965–72; First Sec. Tbilisi City Cttee of Cen. Cttee, CP of Georgia 1972; mem. Cen. Cttee, CP of Georgia 1958–64, 1966–91, mem. Politburo 1972–91, First Sec. 1972–85; mem. Cen. Cttee of CPSU 1976–91, Cand. mem. Politburo 1978–85, mem. 1985–90; Deputy to USSR Supreme Soviet 1978–; mem. Political Consultative Council 1991; Minister of Foreign Affairs 1985–90, Nov.–Dec. 1991; Head Soviet Foreign Policy Asscn 1991–92; mem. Presidential Council 1990–91; Founder mem. Bd Democratic Reform Movt 1991; Chair. Georgian State Council March–Oct. 1992; Chair. Parl. of Georgia and Head of State 1992–95, elected Pres. of Georgia Nov. 1995–, re-elected April 2000; Hon. GCMG 2000; various decorations; Dr hc numerous univs. *Publications:* My Choice 1991, The Future Belongs to Freedom 1991, The Great Silk Road 1999. *Address:* Office of the President, Rustaveli 29, 300002 Tbilisi, Georgia (Office). *Telephone:* (32) 99-74-75 (Office). *Fax:* (32) 99-96-30 (Office). *E-mail:* office@presidpress.gov.ge (Office).

SHEVCHENKO, Col.-Gen. Yuri Leonidovich, DMed; Russian politician and physician; b. 7 April 1947, Yakutsk; m.; two c.; ed Leningrad Acad. of Mil. Medicine; teacher, then Prof., then Head of Chair. Leningrad Mil. Acad. of Medicine 1980–92, Head of Acad. 1992–99; Chief Cardiosurgeon St Petersburg and Leningrad Region, Head Regional Centre of Cardiac Surgery 1992–99; Minister of Public Health 1999–; Vice-Pres. Russian Acad. of Natural Sciences; Vice-Pres. Peter's Acad. of Sciences and Arts; mem. Bd F. Lang Scientific Soc. of Cardiologists; Corresp. mem. Russian Acad. of Medical Sciences. *Publications:* over 300 articles. *Address:* Ministry of Health, 101431 Moscow, Rakhmanovskii per. 3, Russia (Office). *Telephone:* (095) 927-28-48 (Office). *Fax:* (095) 921-01-95 (Office).

SHEYNIS, Viktor Leonidovich, DrSc; Russian politician and economist; b. 16 Feb. 1931, Kiev; s. of Leonid M. Sheynis and Liah O. Kimelfeld; m. Alla K. Nazimova 1953; ed Leningrad Univ.; history teacher in secondary school 1953–56; manual worker Kirov factory, Leningrad 1958–64; teacher at Leningrad Univ. 1966–75; on staff as researcher at Inst. of World Economy and Int. Relations (IMEMO) 1975–92, Chief Research Fellow 2000–; one of the authors of Russian Constitution and electoral laws 1993–99; People's Deputy 1990–93; mem. Supreme Soviet of Russia 1991–93; Co-Founder Consent in Name of Progress faction 1992–93; mem. Council of Reps of 'Democratic Russia' Movt 1990–93, Yabloko Movt 1993–2001, Yabloko Party 2002–, Political Bureau and Fed. Council; mem. State Duma (Parl.) 1993–99; mem. Cttee on Legislation and Reform of the Judicial System; Imre Nagy Medal (Hungary) 1993. *Publications:* over 250 including Developing Nations at the Turn of the Millennium 1987, Capitalism, Socialism and Economic Mechanism of Present-day Production 1989, Die Präsidentenwahlen in Russland: Ergebnisse und Perspektiven, Osteuropa 1996, O caminho histórico da Revolução de Outubro visto sob a prisma de 1997 1997, Il tormentato cammino della Constituzione russa 1998, Wie Russland gewaklt hat. Osteuropa 2000. *Leisure interests:* tourism, cinematography, reading. *Address:* Institute of World Economy and International Relations, Profsoyuznaya str. 23, 117859 Moscow (Office); Vavilova str. 91, corp. 1, apt. 41, 117335 Moscow, Russia (Home). *Telephone:* (095) 128-08-83 (Office); (095) 132-73-15 (Home). *Fax:* (095) 292-93-79 (Office). *E-mail:* nazimova@mtu-net.ru (Home).

SHI DAZHEN; Chinese government official and engineer; b. 1932, Wuxi City, Jiangsu Prov.; ed Shandong Inst. of Tech. 1955; joined CCP 1978; alt. mem. 13th Cen. Cttee CCP 1988–92, 14th Cen. Cttee CCP 1992–97; Vice-Minister of Energy and Resources 1988–93, Minister of Electric Power Industry 1993–98; Vice-Chair. Econ. Cttee 9th Nat. Cttee of CPPCC 1998–. *Address:* National Committee of Chinese People's Political Consultative Conference, 23 Taipingqiao Street, Beijing, People's Republic of China.

SHI GUANGSHENG; Chinese politician; b. Sept. 1939, Changli, Hebei Prov.; ed Beijing Foreign Trade Inst.; joined CCP 1965; clerk, Deputy Section Dir then Vice-Gen. Man. of China Metals and Minerals Import and Export Corpn; Special Commr Ministry of Foreign Econ. Relations and Trade, Shanghai; Dir Import and Export Dept of Ministry of Foreign Trade, then Asst Minister of Foreign Trade 1965–93; Vice-Minister of Foreign Trade and Econ. Co-operation 1993–98, Minister 1998–. *Address:* Ministry of Foreign Trade and Economic Co-operation, 2 Dongchangan Jie, Dongcheng Qu, Beijing 100731, People's Republic of China.

SHI JILIANG; Chinese banker; Pres. Agricultural Bank of China –2000; Deputy Gov. People's Bank of China 2001–. *Address:* People's Bank of China, 32 Chengfang Jie, Xicheng Qu, Beijing 100800, People's Republic of China (Office). *Telephone:* (10) 66194114 (Office). *Fax:* (10) 66015346 (Office). *E-mail:* master@pbc.gov.cn (Office). *Website:* www.pbc.gov.cn (Office).

SHI JIUYONG, MA; Chinese lawyer and professor of law; b. 9 Oct. 1926, Zhejiang; m. Zhang Guoying 1956; one s.; ed St John's Univ. Shanghai and

Columbia Univ. New York; Asst Research Fellow, Inst. of Int. Relations, Beijing 1956–58; Sr Lecturer, Assoc. Prof. of Int. Law, Foreign Affairs Coll. Beijing 1958–64; Research Fellow in Int. Law, Inst. of Int. Law, Beijing 1964–73, Head of Int. Studies, Beijing 1973–80; Prof. of Int. Law, Foreign Affairs Coll. Beijing 1984–93, Foreign Econ. Law Training Centre of Ministry of Justice; Legal Adviser, Ministry of Foreign Affairs 1980–93, Chinese Centre of Legal Consultancy, Office of Chinese Sr Rep. Sino-British Jt Liaison Group (on question of Hong Kong) 1985–93; Adviser to Chinese Soc. of Int. Law, Inst. of Hong Kong Law of Chinese Law Soc.; mem. American Soc. of Int. Law, mem. Standing Cttee Beijing Cttee of CPCC 1988–93, mem. 8th Nat. Cttee 1993; mem. Int. Law Comm. (ILC) 1987–93, Chair. 1990; a Judge, Int. Court of Justice 1994–, Vice-Pres. 2000–03, Pres. 2003–(06); mem. Advisory Bd, The Global Community Yearbook of Int. Law and Jurisprudence.; legal adviser to Chinese dels. at numerous int. onfs etc.; Hon. Prof. Eastern China Univ. of Political Science and Law 2001–. *Publications:* numerous publs on int. law. *Leisure interest:* classical music. *Address:* International Court of Justice, Peace Palace, Carnegieplein 2, 2517 KJ The Hague, Netherlands (Office).

SHI LAIHE; Chinese farmer; b. 1930, Xinxiang, Henan Prov.; joined CCP 1949; Sec. CCP Liuzhuang Village br., Qiliying, Xinxiang Co. 1952–; founder of one of the first people's communes in China; mem. Standing Cttee of 5th, 6th, 7th NPC 1978–93. *Address:* Liuzhuang Village, Qiliying, Xinxiang County, Henan Province, People's Republic of China (Office).

SHI MING; Taiwanese political activist; m. (divorced); ed Waseda Univ., Tokyo; guerrilla fighter in NE China after graduation; joined Communist Party and worked in underground movt; resigned 1949; returned to Taiwan but fled following his involvement in unsuccessful plot to assassinate Gen. Chiang Kai-shek; lived in Japan 1952–93; returned to Taiwan 1993. *Publication:* 400 Years of Taiwan History 1962.

SHI QINGYUN; Chinese scientist; b. Aug. 1936, Hechuan, Sichuan Prov.; ed Peking Univ.; lecturer, Prof. Peking Univ. 1957–; initiator of visual database research in China; Fellow, Chinese Acad. of Sciences; Dir Nat. Audio-Visual Information Processing Lab. *Address:* Peking University, 5 Yiheynan Road, Hai Dian, Beijing 100871, People's Republic of China (Office). *Telephone:* (10) 62752114 (Office). *Fax:* (10) 62751207 (Office). *Website:* www.pku.edu.cn (Office).

SHI TIESHENG; Chinese writer; b. 1951, Beijing; graduated from middle school 1967; paralysed while working in countryside; Nat. Best Short Story Award 1983, 1984. *Publications:* The Professor of Law and His Wife, Half Hour Lunch Break, Brothers, My Far Away Qingpingwan, I and the Temple of Earth, Granny's Stars. *Address:* China Federation of Art and Literature, Beijing, People's Republic of China.

SHI XIUSHI; Chinese politician; b. July 1942, Shangqiu, Henan Prov.; ed Beijing Architecture Industry Inst.; joined CCP 1978; technician Building Material Science Research Inst. 1964; Dir, Second Sec. Bureau of the State Council –1996; Vice-Sec. Gen. State Council 1996–2000; Vice-Gov. of Guizhou, Acting Gov., Gov. Jan. 2001–; Vice-Sec. Guizhou Prov. Cttee 2000–. *Address:* Guizhou Provincial People's Government, Guiyang 550004, Guizhou Province, People's Republic of China (Office). *Telephone:* (851) 6827562 (Office). *E-mail:* admin@gzgov.gov.cn. *Website:* www.gzgov.gov.cn (Office).

SHI YUNSHEN, Adm.; Chinese naval officer; b. Jan. 1940, Fushun City, Liaoning Prov.; ed PLA Air Force Aviation School and PLA Navy Acad.; joined PLA 1956; mem. CCP 1960–; pilot, squadron leader, deputy group Commdr and deputy Regt Commdr Naval Aviation 1962–70; Deputy Commdr Naval Fleet Aviation 1976–81; Div. Commdr Naval Aviation 1981–83; Commdr Naval Fleet Aviation 1983–90; Deputy Commdr PLA Naval Aviation Dept 1990–92; Deputy Commdr PLA Navy 1992–97, Commdr 1997–; rank of Adm. 2000; rep. 13th Nat. Congress of CCP 1987; mem. 15th CCP Cen. Cttee 1997–. *Address:* c/o Ministry of National Defence, Jingshanqian Jie, Beijing, People's Republic of China. *Telephone:* (1) 6370000.

SHI ZHONGCI; Chinese computer scientist; b. Dec. 1933, Ningpo Co., Zhejiang Prov.; Dir Computer Centre, Acad. of Sciences 1988–; mem. Chinese Sciences Acad. 1992–. *Address:* Computer Centre, Zhong Guan Cun, Beijing 100080, People's Republic of China.

SHI ZONGYUAN; Chinese politician; b. July 1946, Baoding, Hebei Prov.; ed Northwest Ethnic Inst.; joined CCP 1979; fmrly clerk in various Govt offices in Hezheng Co., Gansu Prov.; Vice-Magistrate and then Magistrate Hezheng Co. 1981–84; Vice-Chief Magistrate Linxia Hui Autonomous Pref., Gansu Prov., Vice-Sec. and then Sec. CCP Linxia Hui Autonomous Pref. Cttee 1984–93; Dir Propaganda Dept of CCP Gansu Prov. Cttee 1993–98; Dir Propaganda Dept of CCP Jilin Prov. Cttee, also Vice-Sec. CCP 1998–2000; Dir Press and Publications Admin. and Dir State Bureau of Copyrights 2000–; alt. mem. 14th CCP Cen. Cttee 1992–97, alt. mem. 15th CCP Cen. Cttee 1997–. *Address:* Press and Publications Administration, Beijing, People's Republic of China (Office).

SHIEH, Samuel C.; Taiwanese banker and academic; ed Univ. of Minnesota; fmr Prof.; Gov. Cen. Bank of China 1989–94; Nat. Policy Adviser to Pres. 1994–. *Address:* c/o Office of the Governor, Central Bank of China, 2 Roosevelt Road, Sec. 1, Taipei 10757, Taiwan.

SHIELDS, Brooke Christa Camille, BA; American actress and model; b. 31 May 1965, New York; d. of Francis Shields and Teri Schmon; m. Andre Agassi

1997 (divorced 1999); m. Chris Henchy 2001; ed Princeton Univ.; began modelling of Ivory Soap commercials 1966, later for Calvin Klein jeans and Colgate toothpaste commercials; appeared on Broadway in Grease 1994–95. *Films:* Alice, Sweet Alice 1975, Pretty Baby 1977, King of the Gypsies 1978, Wanda Nevada 1978, Just You and Me Kid 1978, Blue Lagoon 1979, Endless Love 1980, Sahara 1983, Brenda Starr 1986, Backstreet Strays 1989, Brenda Starr, An American Love, Seventh Floor 1993, Running Wild 1993, Freaked 1993, Freeway 1997, Way of the Gun 2000, This Weekend 2000, Black and White 2000, What Makes a Family 2001. *Television films:* The Prince of Central Park 1997, After the Fall, Wet Gold. *Television appearances include:* The Tonight Show, Bob Hope specials, The Diamond Trap 1988, Friends.

SHIELDS, Carol Ann, CC, MA; Canadian/American author and university professor; b. Carol Warner, 2 June 1935, Oak Park, Ill., USA; d. of Robert Warner and Inez Warner; m. Donald Hugh Shields 1957; one s. four d.; ed Hanover Coll. and Univ. of Ottawa; Lecturer Univ. of Ottawa 1976–77, Writer-in-Residence 1989; Lecturer Univ. of BC 1978–79; Prof. Univ. of Man. 1980–2000, Emer. 2000–; Writer-in-Residence, Univ. of Winnipeg 1987; Chancellor Univ. of Winnipeg 1996–2000; mem. Canada Council, Royal Soc. of Canada; Guggenheim Fellow 1999–2000; 14 hon. degrees Univs of Ottawa, Winnipeg, BC, Toronto, Western Ont., Queen's Univ., Hanover Coll., Concordia, Carleton, Lakehead, Wilfrid Laurier, Victoria, Calgary, Manitoba; prizes and awards include Marian Engel Award 1990, Gov.-Gen.'s Award 1993, Pulitzer Prize 1995, 1999, Orange Prize 1998, Citizen of the Year, Winnipeg 2000, Order of Manitoba 2001, Charles Taylor Prize 2002, Queen Elizabeth Golden Jubilee Medal 2002. *Plays:* Departures and Arrivals, Anniversary – A Comedy (with David Williamson), Thirteen Hands – Fashion, Power, Guilt and the Charities of Families (with Catherine Shields), A Celibate Season (with Blanche Howard), Unless (with Sara Shields) 2002. *Publications:* Others 1972, Intersect 1974, Small Ceremonies 1976, The Box Garden 1977, Happenstance 1980, A Fairly Conventional Woman 1982, Various Miracles (short stories) 1985, Swann: A Mystery 1987, The Orange Fish 1989, Departure and Arrivals 1990, Coming to Canada 1992, The Republic of Love 1992, Thirteen Hands 1993, The Stone Diaries 1993, Various Miracles 1994, The Box Garden 1995, Larry's Party 1997, A Celibate Season (with Blanche Howard) 1999, Dressing Up for the Carnival 2000, Dropped Threads (with Marjorie Anderson) 2000, Jane Austen 2001, Unless 2002; contribs to numerous Canadian magazines and journals. *Leisure interests:* theatre, France. *Address:* 990 Terrace Avenue, Victoria, B.C., V8S 3V3, Canada. *Telephone:* (250) 519-0604 (Home). *Fax:* (250) 519-0603 (Office). *E-mail:* shieldscarol@shawa.ca (Office); shieldscarol@hotmail.com.

SHIELDS, Hon. Margaret Kerslake, QSO, BA, MP; New Zealand politician; b. 18 Dec. 1941, Wellington; d. of Ernest Blake Porter and Dorothy Bessie Porter (née Levy); m. Patrick John Shields 1960; two d.; ed Victoria Univ., Wellington; researcher Consumers' Inst. and Dept of Statistics; MP for Kapiti 1981–; Minister of Customs and of Consumer Affairs 1984–87, of Women's Affairs, Consumer Affairs and Statistics 1987–88, 1989–90, of Customs 1988–89, Assoc. Minister of Educ. 1989–90; mem. Wellington Regional Council 1995–, Deputy Chair. 1998–2001, Chair.; Vice-Pres. Local Govt New Zealand; co-founder, Pres. and Nat. Sec. of Soc. for Research on Women; Dir UN Int. Research and Training Inst. for the Advancement of Women (INSTRAW) 1991–94; co-convenor of Second UN Women's Convention 1975; mem. Wellington Hosp. Bd 1977–80, Complaints Review Tribunal of NZ Human Rights Comm. 1994–, Council of Vic. Univ. of Wellington 1996–99; Deputy Chair. Hutt Valley Dist Health Bd 2000–01; Chair. Plenary Session Int. Conf. of Women Mayors and Elected Councillors, Phitsanulok, Thailand 2001; Govt Del. to UN Int. Women's Year Conf. Mexico 1975, participated in IPU Conf. Seoul 1983, speaker IPU Conf. Geneva 1989; Labour. *Leisure interests:* hiking, gardening, music, drama. *Address:* Greater Wellington Regional Council, 142–146 Wakefield St., Wellington (Office); 23 Haunui Road, Pukera Bay, Porirua, New Zealand (Home). *Telephone:* (4) 802-0346 (Office); (4) 239-9949 (Home); (4) 239-9949. *Fax:* (4) 239-9084 (Home); (4) 239-9084. *E-mail:* margaret.shields@gw.govt.nz (Office); marg.shields@xtra.co.nz (Home).

SHIELDS, Sir Robert, Kt, MD, ChB, FRCS, FRCSE; British surgeon and professor of surgery; b. 8 Nov. 1930, Paisley, Scotland; s. of Robert Alexander Shields and Isobel Dougall Shields (née Reid); m. Grace Marianne Swinburn 1957; one s. two d; ed John Neilson Inst., Paisley, Univ. of Glasgow; House Officer posts at Western Infirmary, Glasgow 1953–54; served RAMC 1954–56, RAMC (TA), Surgeon Specialist 1956–61; Lecturer, Univ. of Glasgow 1960–63; Sr Lecturer, then Reader in Surgery, Welsh Nat. School of Medicine 1963–69; Prof. of Surgery, Univ. of Liverpool 1969–96; Dean Faculty of Medicine, Univ. of Liverpool 1980–84; Pres. Royal Coll. of Surgeons, Edinburgh 1994–97; mem. Gen. Medical Council 1982, MRC 1987–91; Deputy Lt of Merseyside 1991; Hon. Consultant Surgeon, Liverpool Health Authority 1969–96; Hon. Fellow American Coll. of Surgeons 1990; Hon. FCS (SA); Hon. FHKCS; Hon. FFRCSI; Hon. FRCS (Glasgow); Hon. FRCPE; Hon. FRACS; Hon. Fellow Acad. of Medicine Singapore, Japanese Council for Medical Training 2001; Hon. DSc (Wales) 1990; Moynihan Medal, Asscn of Surgeons of GB and Ireland 1965, Bellahouston Medal (Univ. of Glasgow) 1966. *Publications:* Surgical Emergencies II 1979, Textbook of Surgery 1983, Gastro-Intestinal Emergencies 1991. *Leisure interests:* sailing, walking. *Address:* Strathmore, 81 Meols Drive, West Kirby, Wirral, CH48 5DF,

England (Home); Ardlaraig, Tayvallich, Lochgilphead, Argyll, PA31 8PJ, Scotland. *Telephone:* (151) 632-3588 (Home). *Fax:* (151) 632-5613 (Home). *E-mail:* r.shields@rcsed.ac.uk (Home).

SHIER, Jonathan, B.CON., LLB; Australian broadcasting executive; b. 18 Oct. 1947; s. of Frank Shier and Mary Shier; m. Susan Crossland Pugsley 1993; ed Geelong Grammar School, Monash Univ.; fmr Pres. Vic. Young Liberals, State Pres., Vic. Ministerial Pvt. Sec. to Attorney-Gen. 1973–76; Head Australian Broadcasting Corpn 2000. *Address:* Australian Broadcasting Corporation, 700 Harris Street, Ultimo, P.O. Box 9994, Sydney, NSW 2007, Australia (Office). *Telephone:* (2) 9333-1500 (Office). *Fax:* (2) 9333-2003 (Office).

SHIGEHARA, Kumiharu, BL; Japanese economist; b. 5 Feb. 1939, Maebashi; s. of Seizaburo Shigehara and Rutsu Tanabe; m. Akiko Yoshizawa 1965; one s. one d.; ed Maebashi High School, Univ. of Tokyo and Univ. of Poitiers; economist, Bank of Japan 1962–70; admin. OECD 1970–71, Prin. Admin. 1971–72, Head, Monetary Div. 1972–74; Councillor for Policy Planning, Bank of Japan 1974–76, Man. Int. Affairs 1976–80; Deputy Dir Gen. Econs Branch, OECD 1980–82; Gen. Man. Bank of Japan 1983–87; Dir Gen. Econs Branch, OECD 1987–89; Dir-Gen. Inst. for Monetary and Econ. Studies and Chief Economist, Bank of Japan 1989–92; Head, Econs Dept and Chief Economist, OECD 1992–97, Deputy Sec.-Gen. 1997–99; Special Adviser Int. Friendship Exchange Council 2001; Head Int. Econ. Policy Studies Group 2002–; Hon. PhD; Dr. hchc (Liège) 1998; Hozumi Special Award, Univ. of Tokyo 1960. *Publications:* The Role of Monetary Policy in Demand Management (co-author) 1975, Europe After 1992 1991, The Problems of Inflation in the 1990s (ed.) 1992, Evolving International Trade and Monetary Regimes 1992, Causes of Declining Growth in Industrialised Countries 1992, Price Stabilization in the 1990s 1993, Long-term Tendencies in Budget Deficits and Debt 1995, The Options regarding the Concept of a Monetary Policy Strategy 1996, Monetary and Economic Policy: Then and Now 1998, Causes and Implications of East Asian Financial Crises 1998, International Aspects of Competition Policy 1999, Monetary Policy and Economic Performance 2001, Looking for Models in Pursuit of Economic Prosperity 2002. *Leisure interests:* golf, tennis, hiking. *Address:* 4-7-11-802, Setagaya-ku, Tokyo (Office); 4-7-11-1104 Seta, Setagaya-ku, Tokyo, Japan. *Telephone:* (3) 3709-7969. *E-mail:* office.shigehara@online.fr (Office).

SHIH, Stan; Taiwanese business executive; b. 18 Dec. 1944, Taiwan; m. Carolyn Yeh; two s. one d.; ed Nat. Chiao Tung Univ.; with Unitron Industrial Corpn 1971–72, Qualitron Industrial Corpn 1972–76; Chair. and CEO The Acer Group (electronics co.); title of Dato (Malaysia) 1994. *Publications:* more than 100 articles on man., marketing etc. *Address:* Acer Inc., 21/F, 88 Hsintaiwuh Road, Sec. 1, Hsih Chih Cheng, Taipei, Taiwan (Office). *Telephone:* (2) 26961234 (Office). *Fax:* (2) 25455308 (Office).

SHIH CHI-YANG, LLM, DJur; Taiwanese politician; b. 5 May 1935, Taichung City; m. Jeanne Tchong-Koei Li 1968; ed Nat. Taiwan Univ. and Univ. of Heidelberg; Asst Dept of Law, Nat. Taiwan Univ. 1959–62, Assoc. Prof. 1967–71, Prof. (part-time) 1971–84; Research Asst Inst. of Int. Relations, Nat. Chengchi Univ. 1967–69, Research Fellow 1969–71; Deputy Dir 5th Section, Cen. Cttee, Kuomintang 1969–72, Deputy Dir Dept of Youth Activities 1972–76; Admin. Vice-Minister, Ministry of Educ. 1976–79; Political Vice-Minister, Ministry of Educ. 1979–80, Ministry of Justice 1980–84; Minister of Justice 1984–88; Vice-Premier 1988–93; Sec.-Gen. Nat. Security Council 1993–94; Pres. Judicial Yuan 1994–. *Address:* Judicial Yuan, 124 Chungching S. Road, Sec. 1, Taipei, Taiwan. *Telephone:* (2) 3618577.

SHIH MING-TEH; Taiwanese politician; m. Linda Gail Arrigo; fmr political prisoner in Taiwan; Leader, Taiwan Democratic Progressive Party (DPP) 1993; mem. Taiwan Legis. Council. *Address:* Room 601, 10 Tsingtao E Road, Taipei, Taiwan.

SHIHAB, Hussain, MSc; Maldivian diplomatist; b. 1949; m.; six c.; ed Kuban Agric. Inst., Russia; Under-Sec. Ministry of Home Affairs and Social Services 1975, Ministry of Agric. 1976–78; Man. TV Maldives 1978–81, Deputy Dir, then Dir 1985; Dir of Environmental Affairs, Ministry of Home Affairs and Social Services 1986–88, Dir of Environmental Affairs, Ministry of Planning and the Environment 1988–93, Deputy Minister 1993–95, July–Sept. 1998, Dir South Asia Co-operative Environment Programme (SACEP) 1995–98; Perm. Rep. to the UN 1998–; del. to numerous UN meetings on the environment, including Conf. on Environment and Devt 1992 and Global Conf. on the Sustainable Devt of Small Island Developing States 1994; formulated Maldives' first nat. environment action plan. *Publications:* papers on the environment and sustainable Devt presented at int. confs. *Address:* Permanent Mission of Maldives to the United Nations, 800 Second Avenue, Suite 400E, New York, NY 10017, USA (Office). *Telephone:* (212) 599-6195 (Office). *Fax:* (212) 661-6405 (Office). *E-mail:* maldives@un.int (Office). *Website:* www.un .int/maldives (Office).

SHIKHMURADOV, Boris Orazovich; Turkmenistan politician and diplomatist; b. 1949, Ashgabat; m. Tatiana Shikhmurazova; one s.; ed Moscow State Univ., Diplomatic Acad.; journalist, diplomatist Press Agency Novosti and USSR Ministry of Foreign Affairs 1971–72; responsible positions in missions abroad, then on staff USSR Ministry of Foreign Affairs 1983–86; worked in USSR Embs to Pakistan, India, missions to Turkey, Afghanistan, USA, China, Singapore; apptd Deputy, then First Deputy Minister of Foreign Affairs of Turkmenistan May 1992; Deputy Chair. Cabinet of Ministers of

Turkmenistan 1992–; Minister of Foreign Affairs 1995–2000; Amb. to People's Repub. of China March–Nov. 2001; emigrated to Moscow Oct. 2001, returned to Ashgabat Dec. 2002, arrested and sentenced to life imprisonment on charges of conspiracy to organize assassination of Pres. Niyazov. *Address:* Ministry of Foreign Affairs, Ashgabat, Turkmenistan. *Telephone:* (3632) 35-66-88 (Office). *Fax:* (3632) 25-35-83 (Office).

SHILLER, Robert James, BA, SM, PhD; American; b. 29 March 1946, Detroit, Michigan; ed Univ. of Michigan, Mass. Inst. of Tech.; Asst Prof. of Econs, Univ. of Minn. 1972–74; Assoc. Prof. of Econs, Univ. of Pa 1974–80; Research Fellow Nat. Bureau of Econs Research, Cambridge, Mass. 1980–81; Visiting Prof. MIT 1981–82; Stanley B. Resor Prof. of Econs, Yale Univ. 1982–; Co-Founder Case Shiller Weiss Inc., Cambridge, Mass. 1991; research in behavioural finance and behavioural macroecons at Nat. Bureau of Econ. Research; Guggenheim Fellowship 1991, Paul Samuelson Award 1996, Commonfund Prize 2000. *Publications:* Market Volatility 1989, Macro Markets: Creating Institutions for Managing Society's Largest Economic Risks 1993, Irrational Exuberance 2000. *Address:* Cowles Foundation, Yale University, PO Box 208281, New Haven, CT 06511, USA (Office). *Telephone:* (203) 432-3708 (Office). *Fax:* (203) 432-6167 (Office). *E-mail:* robert.shiller@yale.edu (Office). *Website:* www.econ.yale.edu/~shiller/ (Office).

SHILOV, Aleksandr Maksovich; Russian artist; b. 6 Oct. 1943, Moscow; s. of Ludmila Sergeevna Pazhenova; ed V. I. Surikov Inst. of Fine Arts, Moscow; painted series of portraits of contemporary village people, social and political leaders, astronauts, intellectuals and the clergy, also present-day social phenomena, genre paintings, landscapes and still lifes; f. Moscow State A. Shilov Picture Gallery 1997, now Art Dir; mem. Acad. of Social Sciences 1997–, Council for Culture and Art 1999–; Corresp. mem. Russian Acad. of Arts 1997–, mem. 2001; Order for Services to the Motherland (Fourth Degree) 1997; Lenin Komsomol Prize 1977, People's Artist of RSFSR 1981, People's Artist of USSR 1985; asteroid named after him 1992. *Exhibitions include:* Moscow, St Petersburg and other Russian cities 1978–96, France 1981, FRG 1983, Portugal 1984, Canada 1987, Japan 1988, Kuwait and UAE 1990. *Address:* Romanov per. 3, Apt. 71, 103009 Moscow, Russia. *Telephone:* (095) 203-42-08. *Fax:* (095) 203-69-75 (Office).

SHILTON, Peter Leslie, MBE; British footballer; b. 18 Sept. 1949, Leicester; s. of Les Shilton and May Shilton; m. Sue Shilton 1970; ed King Richard III School, Leicester; played for English Youth side; played for Leicester City 1966–74, Stoke City 1974–77, Nottingham Forest 1977–82, Southampton 1982–87, Derby Co. 1987–92, Plymouth Argyle 1992–94, Bolton 1995, Leyton Orient 1996–97; Man. Plymouth Argyle FC 1992–95; became first England goalkeeper to win more than 100 caps at European Championships 1988; record English league appearances (1,005); record English cap holder (125), conceding only 80 goals. *Address:* Hubbards Cottage, Bentley Lane, Maxstoke, nr Coleshill, B46 2QR, England.

SHIMADA, Masao, LLD; Japanese university chancellor (retd); b. 29 Sept. 1915, Tokyo; m. Tsumae Shimada 1945; ed Univs. of Tokyo and Beijing; mem. Inst. of Oriental Culture, Tokyo Univ. 1941–47; Prof. Meiji Univ. 1947–84, Chancellor 1984–92, Prof. Emer. 1992–. *Publications:* Study on Social History of Liao 1951, Study on the Constitution of Liao 1954, Study of Official Systems of Liao 1978, Study on the History of Liao Dynasty 1979, Compilation of Modern Codes at the Late Ch'ing Period 1980, Study of the Northern Eurasian Legal System 1981, Study of the Special Laws for Mongolia in the Ch'ing Dynasty 1982, Studies on the Mongolian Laws 1986, History of Liao 1991, Studies in the Effectiveness of the Ch'ing Mongol Laws 1992, North Asian Legal History 1995, Preliminary Study of Shisha Code 2003. *Address:* No. 601, Mansion-Ichigaya, 82, Ichigaya Yakuoji, Shinjuku, Tokyo, Japan. *Telephone:* (3) 3268-0290.

SHIMELL, William; British opera singer; b. 23 Sept. 1952, Ilford, Essex; s. of W. Shimell and F. E. Shimell; m. Olga Slavka 1996; ed Westminster Abbey Choir School, St Edward's School, Oxford, Guildhall School of Music and Drama, Nat. Opera Studio, London; best known for interpretations of Don Giovanni, Count Almaviva (Marriage of Figaro) and Don Alfonso (Così fan Tutte), which he has sung in opera houses world-wide including La Scala, Milan, Metropolitan Opera House, New York, Paris Opéra, Rome Opera, Vienna Staatsoper, Covent Garden; Assoc. Guildhall School of Music and Drama; numerous recordings. *Leisure interests:* sailing, cooking. *Address:* c/o IMG Artists, Lovell, 616 Chiswick High Road, London, W4 5RX, England. *Telephone:* (20) 8747-9977. *Fax:* (20) 8742-8758.

SHIMIZU, Kayoko; Japanese politician; mem. House of Councillors; Chair. House of Councillor's Cttee on Educ.; Parl. Vice-Minister for Labour; Dir.-Gen. Environment Agency 1999–2000. *Address:* c/o Environment Agency, 1-2-2 Kasumigaseki, Chiyoda-ku, Tokyo 100-0013, Japan (Office).

SHIMOGAICHI, Yoichi; Japanese business executive; b. 26 Aug. 1934; two s.; ed Univ. of Tokyo; joined NKK Corpn 1958, Gen. Man. Sales Co-ordination, Export and Corp. Planning Depts. 1981–86, mem. Bd of Dirs., Gen. Man. Corp. Planning Dept 1987, Man. Dir 1989, Sr Man. Dir, Deputy Dir Steel Div. 1991, Exec. Vice-Pres., Exec. Dir Steel Div. 1994–, Exec. Vice-Pres. 1997, Pres. 1997–, Pres., CEO 2000–02, Chair. of Bd 2002–; exec. mem. Bd of Dirs. Japan Fed. of Econ. Orgs. 1997–; mem. Export and Import Transaction Council 1996–98, Coal Mining Council 1997–; Dir Japan Iron and Steel Fed. 1997–. *Address:* NKK Corporation, 1-1-2 Marunouchi, Chiyoda-ku, Tokyo 100-8202, Japan.

SHINEFIELD, Henry Robert, BA, MD; American pediatrician; b. 11 Oct. 1925, Paterson, NJ; s. of Louis Shinefield and Sarah (Kaplan) Shinefield; m. Jacqueline Walker 1983; one s. three d.; ed Columbia Univ.; Asst Resident Pediatrician New York Hosp. (Cornell) 1950–51, Pediatrician Outpatients 1953–59, Instructor in Pediatrics 1959–60, Asst Prof. 1960–64, Assoc. Prof. 1964–65; Chief of Pediatrics, Kaiser-Permanente Medical Center, San Francisco 1965–89, Chief Emer. 1989–; Co-Dir Kaiser Permanente Pediatric Vaccine Study Center, Calif.; Assoc. Clinical Prof. of Pediatrics, Univ. of Calif. 1966–68, Clinical Prof. of Pediatrics 1968–, Clinical Prof. of Dermatology 1970–; mem. Inst. of Medicine, NAS 1980, American Bd of Pediatrics; Fellow American Acad. of Pediatrics. *Leisure interests:* skiing, tennis, travel. *Address:* Kaiser Permanente, 4131 Geary Boulevard, San Francisco, CA 94118 (Office); 2705 Larkin Street, San Francisco, CA 94109, USA (Home). *Telephone:* (415) 202-3597 (Office); (415) 771-5372 (Home). *E-mail:* henry .shinefield@kp.org (Office).

SHINOZAKI, Akihiko, LLB; Japanese business executive; b. 8 Nov. 1927, Hokkaido; s. of Hikoshiro Shinozaki and Katsuno Shinozaki; m. Tetsuko Inoue 1954; one s. two d.; ed Tokyo Univ.; joined Sumitomo Metal Mining Co., Ltd 1952, Dir 1979–83, Man. Dir 1983–87, Sr Man. Dir 1987–88, Pres. 1988–95, Chair. 1995, Exec. Adviser 1998–; Exec. Dir Japan Fed. of Employers' Asscns. 1989–; Trustee, Japan Asscn of Corporate Execs. 1988–, Japan Mining Industry Asscn 1990– (Pres. 1993–94); Chair. Keidanren Cttee on Energy and Resources 1996–; Blue Ribbon Medal 1992. *Leisure interests:* appreciating paintings, golf. *Address:* Sumitomo Metal Mining Co. Ltd, 11-3 Shimbashi 5-chome, Minato-ku, Tokyo 105, Japan. *Telephone:* (3) 3436-7744.

SHIOKAWA, Masajuro; Japanese politician; b. 1922; from Osaka, House of Reps.; fmr Minister of Transport, of Educ., Chair. Cttee on Commerce and Industry; Minister of Home Affairs 1991–92, of Finance 2001–; mem. Liberal-Democratic Party (LDP), fmr Deputy Chair. Gen. Council, Deputy Sec.-Gen. LDP. *Address:* Ministry of Finance, 3-1-1 Kasumigaseki, Chiyoda-ku, Tokyo 100-8940, Japan (Office). *Telephone:* (3) 3581-4111 (Office). *Fax:* (3) 5251-2667 (Office). *E-mail:* info@mof.go.jp (Office). *Website:* www.mof.go.jp (Office).

SHIPLEY, Rt. Hon. Jennifer Mary (Jenny), PC; New Zealand politician; b. 4 Feb. 1952; m. Burton Shipley 1973; one s. one d.; fmr primary school teacher; farmer 1973–88; joined Nat. Party 1975; fmr Malvern Co. Councillor; MP for Ashburton (now Rakaia) 1987–; Minister of Social Welfare 1990–93 and of Women's Affairs 1990–98, of Health 1993–96, of State Services 1996–97, also of State Owned Enterprises, of Transport, of Accident Rehabilitation and Compensation Insurance, Minister Responsible for Radio New Zealand; Minister in Charge of NZ Security Intelligence Service 1997–2000; Prime Minister of NZ 1997–99; Leader of the Opposition 1999–2001. *Leisure interests:* family, gardening. *Address:* New Zealand National Party, 14th Floor, Willbank House 57 Willis Street, P.O. Box 1155, Wellington 60015 (Office); Parliament Buildings, Wellington, New Zealand. *Telephone:* (4) 472-5211 (Office). (4) 471-9838. *Fax:* (4) 478-1622 (Office). (4) 472-2075. *E-mail:* hq@national.org.nz (Office). *Website:* www.national.org.nz (Office).

SHIPLEY, Walter Vincent, BS; American banker (retd); b. 2 Nov. 1935, Newark, NJ; s. of L. Parks and Emily (née Herzog) Shipley; m. Judith Ann Lyman 1957; one s. four d.; ed Williams Coll., New York Univ.; with Chemical Bank 1956–96, Exec. Vice-Pres. Int. Div., New York 1978–79, Sr Exec. Vice-Pres. –1981, Pres. 1982–83, Chair. Bd 1983–92, Pres., COO 1992–93, Chair., CEO 1994–96; Chair. Chase Manhattan Banking Co. 1996–99, CEO 1996–99 (created after merger of Chomzal Banking Corpn with Chase Manhattan Corpn); retd 2000; Dir Champion Int. Corpn, NYNEX Corpn, Atlantic Corpn, Exxon Corpn; mem. Bd Dirs. Japan Soc., Lincoln Center for the Performing Arts Inc., NY City Partnership Inc., NY Chamber of Commerce and Industry, Goodwill Industries of Greater NY Inc., United Way of Tri-State; mem. The Business Council, Business Roundtable, Council for Foreign Relations, Pilgrims of U.S., English-Speaking Union; mem. Bd of Trustees, Cen. Park Conservancy. *Address:* c/o JP Morgan Chase & Co., 270 Park Avenue, New York, NY 10017, USA.

SHIPUK, Paviel Uladzimiravich; Belarus politician; b. 5 Aug. 1946, Opol, Brest Region; s. of the late Vladimir Shipuk and Anastasiya Shipuk; three brothers; one sister; m.; two d.; ed Belarus Polytech. Inst.; Sr Engineer, Dir Gomel Lomonosov Glass factory 1972–87; Dir, Pres. Gomelsteklo 1987–94; Chair. Gomel Exec. Cttee 1994–97; after dissolution of Parl. elected Chair. Council of Repub. Nat. Ass. 1997–2000; mem. Belarus Acad. of Engineers; 37 innovations in tech. and Eng; Order of Fatherland, Grade 3 1997. *Leisure Interests:* history of weapons, volleyball. *Address:* c/o 220016, Krasnoarmeiskaya str. 4, Minsk, Belarus (Office). *E-mail:* cr@soverp.gov.by (Office).

SHIRAISHI, Takashi, PhD; Japanese professor of economics; b. 1921, Tokyo; m. Toshiko Shiraishi; one d.; ed Keio Univ., Harvard Business School; Lecturer Keio Univ. 1947–49, Asst Prof. 1949–58, Prof. 1958–86, Vice-Pres. 1965–77, Dean, Faculty of Business and Commerce 1975–77, Prof. Emer. 1986–; Prin. Keio High School 1964–65; Dean Faculty of Social Sciences, Kyorin Univ. 1984–92; Dir Japan Soc. of Int. Econs 1974–; Dir and Pres. Union of Nat. Econ. Asscns. in Japan 1975–90; mem. Int. Exchange Program Cttee of Japan Soc. for the Promotion of Science 1982–84; mem. Exec. Cttee, Int. Econ. Asscn 1984–89. *Publications:* Economic Development and Direct Investment 1978, History of Economic Growth and Policy of Japan since the Second World War 1983, Japan's Trade Policies 1989, Reformation of World Economy and Japan 1991, History of Japan's Machine Export 1992, New Age of Asia and Japan 1993, Foreign Exchange Rates and the Japanese Economy 1996. *Address:* 1-19-10, Jiyugaoka, Meguroku, Tokyo, Japan. *Telephone:* (3) 3717-7118.

SHIRAKAWA, Hideki, PhD; Japanese scientist; b. 1936; ed Tokyo Inst. of Tech.; pioneered work on conductive polymers; Prof. Inst. of Materials Science, Univ. of Tsukuba; Nobel Prize for Chemistry (Jt recipient) 2000. *Address:* Institute of Materials Science, University of Tsukuba, Sakura-mura, Ibaraki 305, Japan (Office). *Telephone:* (298) 53-2111 (Office). *Fax:* (298) 53-6012 (Office). *E-mail:* hideki@ims.tsukuba.ac.jp (Office). *Website:* www.tsukuba.ac.jp (Office).

SHIRAYANAGI, HE Cardinal Peter Seiichi, DCnL; Japanese ecclesiastic; b. 17 June 1928, Tokyo; s. of Peter Hisazo Shirayanagi and Maria Kura Shirayanagi; ed Gyosei Stella Maris School, Major Seminary, Tokyo, Sophia Univ., Urban Univ., Rome; ordained priest 1954; Sec. Archbishop's House 1954–66, in Rome 1957–60; Auxiliary Bishop of Tokyo 1966; Coadjutor with right of succession 1969; Archbishop of Tokyo 1970–2000; cr. Cardinal 1994; Vice-Pres. Bishops' Conf. of Japan 1975, Pres. 1983–92; Pres. Episcopal Comm. for Social Action 1975. *Leisure interest:* piano. *Address:* Shinjukuku, Shimoochiai 3-2-11-301, Tokyo 161-0033, Japan. *Telephone:* (3) 5988-7817. *Fax:* (3) 5988-7818. *E-mail:* pshira@nifty.com.

SHIRIASHI, Kazuko; Japanese poet; b. 1931, Vancouver, BC; m.; one d.; mem. VOU avant-garde literary group 1948–53; with Kazuo Ono has mounted series of poetry/dance productions. *Publications:* poetic works include Seasons of Sacred Lust (in English) 1978.

SHIRKOV, Dmitrii Vasilevich, PhD; Russian physicist; b. 3 March 1928, Moscow; s. of Vasili Shirkov and Elizaveta Makushina; m. Svetlana Rastopchina 1950; two s. one d.; ed Moscow State Univ., Kurchatov, Steklov Math. Inst., Moscow; attached to Steklov Math. Inst. of Acad. of Sciences, in Moscow 1950–58 and Jt Inst. for Nuclear Research, Dubna 1958–60, 1971–; worked at Inst. of Math., Siberian Div. of Acad. of Sciences, Novosibirsk 1960–70; Prof., Univ. of Novosibirsk 1963–69; Nobel Guest Prof., Lund Univ., Sweden 1970–71; Prof., Moscow State Univ. 1972–; Corresp. mem. USSR (now Russian) Acad. of Sciences 1960, mem. 1994; Foreign mem. Saxonian Acad. of Sciences; Hon. Dir Bogolivbov Lab. at Joint Inst. for Nuclear Research; Lenin Prize 1984; USSR State Prize 1984. *Publications:* co-author: Introduction to the Theory of Quantized Fields 1957, A New Method in the Theory of Superconductivity 1958, Dispersion Theories of Strong Interactions at Low Energies 1967, Quantum Fields 1980, Theory of Particle Interactions 1986; numerous published papers mainly on the theory of elementary particles. *Leisure interests:* tourism, skiing. *Address:* Bogolivbov Laboratory of Theoretical Physics, Joint Institute for Nuclear Research, Joliot Curie str. 6, 141980 Dubna, Moscow Region, Russia. *Telephone:* (9621) 65088 (Office); (9621) 62262 (Home). *Fax:* (9621) 65084 (Office). *E-mail:* shirkovd@thsun1.jinr.ru (Office).

SHIRLEY, Donna, BS; American aeronautical engineer; b. 1941, Wynnewood, Okla; m. (divorced); one d.; ed Univ. of Oklahoma, Norman, Univ. of Southern California; specifications writer, McDonnell Aircraft, St Louis, Mo. 1963; joined NASA Jet Propulsion Lab. 1966; mission analyst for Mariner Venus-Mercury Expedition 1970; project engineer, Cassini Mission 1992; Man. Mars Exploration Project 1994–, now Dir; NASA Group Achievement Awards. *Publication:* Managing Martians (memoir) 1998. *Leisure interests:* acting, painting, playing the guitar, sailing.

SHIRLEY, George; American tenor; b. 18 April 1934, Indianapolis, Ind.; s. of Irving E Shirley and Daisy Shirley (née Bell); m. Gladys Lee Ishop 1956; one s. one d.; ed Wayne State Univ.; debuts with Metropolitan Opera, New York Opera, Festival of Two Worlds (Spoleto, Italy), Santa Fé Opera 1961, Teatro Colón, Buenos Aires 1965, La Scala, Milan 1965, Glyndebourne Festival 1966, Royal Opera, Covent Garden, Scottish Opera 1967, Vienna Festival 1972, San Francisco Opera 1977, Chicago Lyric Opera 1977, Théâtre Municipal d'Angers 1979, Edin. Festival 1979, Nat. Opera Ebony, Philadelphia 1980, Spoleto Festival, Charleston, SC 1980, Tulsa Opera, Okla 1980, Ottawa Festival 1981, Deutsche Oper 1983, Guelph Spring Festival 1983, Bregenz Festival, Austria 1998; Prof. of Voice, Univ. of Md 1980–87; Prof. of Music, Univ. of Mich. 1987–; Joseph Edgar Maddy Distinguished Univ. Prof. of Music 1992–; Hon. H.D.H. (Wilberforce Univ.); Hon. LLD (Montclair State Coll.); Hon. DFA (Lake Forest Coll.); Hon. DHumLitt (Northern Iowa) 1997; Nat. Arts Club Award 1960, Concorso di Musica e Danza (Italy) 1960; Distinguished Scholar-Teacher Award, Univ. of Md 1985–86. *Leisure interests:* tennis, sketching and cartoons, writing. *Address:* c/o Ann Summers International, Box 188, Station A, Toronto M5W 1B2, Canada; University of Michigan School of Music, Ann Arbor, MI 48109, USA. *Telephone:* (416) 362-1422 (Canada); (734) 665-7821 (Mich.). *Fax:* (734) 763-5097 (Office). *E-mail:* gis@umich.edu (Office); geotenor@netscape.net (Home).

SHIRLEY-QUIRK, John, CBE, BSc; British concert and opera singer and teacher; b. 28 Aug. 1931, Liverpool; s. of Joseph Stanley and Amelia Shirley-Quirk; m. 1st Dr. Patricia Hastie 1952 (died 1981); one s. one d.; m. 2nd Sara Watkins 1981 (died 1997); one s. two d. (one d. died 2001); ed Holt School, Liverpool and Liverpool Univ.; Flying Officer, RAF (Educ. Br.) 1952–55; Asst Lecturer, Acton Tech. Coll. 1956–60; Vicar Choral, St Paul's Cathedral 1960–61; professional singer 1961–; mem. Voice Faculty, Peabody Conservatory, Johns Hopkins Univ., Baltimore, USA 1992–; mem. Voice Dept, Coll. of Fine Arts, Carnegie-Mellon Univ., Pittsburgh, Pa 1994–98; many

recordings and first performances, notably works of Benjamin Britten and Michael Tippett; Hon. RAM 1972; Hon. DMus (Liverpool) 1976; Hon. DUniv (Brunel) 1981. *TV appearances include:* Carmen, The Marriage of Figaro, Billy Budd, Messiah, Owen Wingrave, Death in Venice. *Leisure interests:* clocks, canals, trees. *Address:* 6062 Red Clover Lane, Clarksville, MD 21029, USA. *Telephone:* (410) 531-1315 (Home). *Fax:* (410) 531-3335 (Home). *E-mail:* jssq@peabody.jhu.edu (Home).

SHIRVINDT, Alexander Anatolyevich; Russian actor; b. 19 July 1934, Moscow; m. Natalya Belousova; one s.; ed Shchukin School of Theatre Art; actor Moscow Theatre of Lenin's Comsomol 1957–70, actor Moscow Acad. Theatre of Satire 1957–, Artistic Dir 2000–; teacher Shchukin School of Theatre Art; mem. Union of Cinematographers; People's Artist of Russia 1989. *Films include:* Cossack Chieftain Kodr, Come Tomorrow, Major Vikhr, Facts of the Passed Day, Winter Evening in Gagry, Blackmailer, Once Again About Love, Crankies, A Station for Two, Irony of the Fate, Three in a Boat Not to Mention a Dog, Imaginary Invalid. *Stage appearances include:* Trigorin (The Seagull), Dobchinsky (The Government Inspector), King Louis (Bondage of Hypocrites), Akhmed Ryza (Crank), Count Almaviva (The Marriage of Figaro), Press Secretary (Burden of Decisions), Molchalin (Misfortune from Intellect), Nehrish (Red Horse with Small Bells), President of the Reportage (Bug). *Plays produced include:* Small Comedies of a Big House, Melancholy, Shut Up, Wake Up and Sing; two-man variety shows with M. Derzhavin. *Leisure interest:* fishing. *Address:* Moscow Academic Theatre of Satire, Triumfalnaya pl. 2, 103050 Moscow (Office); Kotelnicheskaya nab. 1/15, korp. A, Apt. 50, 109240 Moscow, Russia (Home). *Telephone:* (095) 299-63-05 (Office); (095) 916-49-82 (Home).

SHIVAS, Mark, MA; British film and television producer; b. 24 April 1938, London; s. of James Dallas Shivas and Winifred Alice Lighton Shivas (née Bristow); ed Whitgift School, Merton Coll. Oxford; Asst Ed. Movie Magazine 1962–64; freelance journalist; joined Granada TV 1964, Dir, Producer 1965–68; Producer of Drama, BBC TV 1969–79, Head of Drama 1988–93, Head of Films 1993–97; Creative Dir Southern Pictures 1979–81. *Television productions include:* The Six Wives of Henry VIII (BAFTA Awards, Prix Italia), The Evacuees (BAFTA and Emmy Awards), Casanova, The Glittering Prizes, Rogue Male, Professional Foul (BAFTA Award), Telford's Change, On Giant's Shoulders (Emmy Award), The Price, What If It's Raining?, The Storyteller (Emmy Award), Talking Heads 2, Telling Tales. *Feature films include:* Moonlighting 1982, A Private Function 1984, The Witches 1988, Truly, Madly, Deeply 1991, Enchanted April 1991, The Snapper 1993, Priest 1995, Small Faces 1996, Jude 1996, Regeneration 1997, Hideous Kinky 1998. *Publications:* articles in art journals. *Leisure interests:* Italy, gardens, swimming, cycling, moviegoing. *Address:* Perpetual Motion Pictures Ltd., 1st Floor, 74 Margaret Street, London, W1W 8SU (Office); 38 Gloucester Mews, London, W2 3HE, England. *Telephone:* (20) 7436-0548 (Office); (20) 7723-4678 (Home). *Fax:* (20) 7436-0316 (Office); (20) 7262-1415 (Home). *E-mail:* markshivas@hotmail.com (Office).

SHIVY, Sylvia Massey; American record producer; producer Zoo Records; worked with Johnny Cash, Cowboy Mouth, Cyclefly, The Deadlights, Deftones, Dig, Econoline Crush, Firewater, Glueleg, Green Jelly, Greta, Horsehead, Insolence, Luscious Jackson, Lollipop Lust Kill, Loudermilk, Love & Rockets, Lustra, Machines of Loving Grace, Oingo Boing, Powerman 5000, Artist formerly known as Prince, Red Hot Chili Peppers, R.E.M., Seigmen, Sevendust, Skunk Anansie, System Of A Down, Tallman, Tom Petty and the Heartbreakers, Tool, Toyshop, Virgos; f. RadioStar Studios. *Address:* Radio-Star Studios, Weed Palace Theater, 180 Main Street, Weed, CA 96094, USA (Office). *E-mail:* sylvia@radiostarstudios.com (Office). *Website:* www.radiostarstudios.com (Office).

SHKOLNIK, Vladimir Sergeyevich; Kazakhstan politician and scientist; b. 17 Feb. 1949, Serpukhov, Moscow Region; m.; two c.; ed Moscow Inst. of Physics and Math.; mem. Kazakhstan Acad. of Sciences; various posts from engineer to Deputy Dir Mangistauz Energy Complex 1973–92; Dir-Gen. Agency of Atomic Energy Repub. of Kazakhstan 1992–94; Minister of Science and New Tech. 1994–96; Minister of Science 1996–; Pres. Kazakhstan Acad. of Sciences 1996–; Deputy Prime Minister, Minister of Energy and Mineral Resources 1999–. *Address:* Mira prosp. 11, Astana, Kazakhstan (Office). *Telephone:* (3172) 33-71-64; (3172) 33-71-33 (Office).

SHMAKOV, Mikhail Viktorovich; Russian trade union leader; b. 12 Aug. 1949, Moscow; m.; one s.; ed Bauman Moscow Higher Tech. School; engineer in defence industry factories 1972–75, 1977–86; army service 1975–77; Head Moscow Trade Union of Workers of Defence Industry 1986–90; Chair. Moscow City Council of Trade Unions later transformed into Moscow Fed. of Trade Unions 1990–; Chair. Fed. of Ind. Trade Unions (FNPR) 1993–, re-elected 2001; mem. Organizational Cttee Otechestvo Movt. *Leisure interest:* sports. *Address:* Federation of Independent Trade Unions, Leninsky pr. 42, 117119 Moscow, Russia (Office). *Telephone:* (095) 938-86-52 (Office).

SHMAROV, Valery Nikolayevich, PhD; Ukrainian politician; b. 14 Aug. 1945, Zholobi, Vinnitsa; m. Olga Viktorivna Shmarova; one s. one d.; ed Kiev Coll. of Radioelectronics, Kiev State Univ.; radio equipment mechanic, Head of lab., Kiev Radiozavod 1966–72; head of lab., chief of div., chief of workshop, chief of Dept 1973–87; Dir Zhulyany Machine Construction Factory 1987–92; First Deputy Dir-Gen. Nat. Space Agency of Ukraine 1992–93; Deputy Prime Minister on problems of mil.-industrial complex 1993–94; Deputy Prime Minister and Minister of Defence 1994–96; Pres. Asscn of State Aviation

Industry Ukraviaprom (Asscn of Aviation Enterprises of Ukraine) 1996–2001; mem. Verhovna Rada (Parl.) 1998–; Dir-Gen. State co. for export and import of mil. equipment and arms 2002–; Prof. Kiev Int. Univ. of Civil Aviation; mem. Cttee for Nat. Security and Defence 1998–; mem. Ukrainian Tech. Acad. *Leisure Interests:* history, literature, swimming. *Address:* Bastionna str. 9, 01014 Kiev, Ukraine (Office). *Telephone:* (44) 294-81-00 (Office); (44) 294-88-49 (Home). *Fax:* (44) 294-81-47 (Office). *E-mail:* avia@iptelecom .net.ua (Office).

SHMELEV, Geliy Ivanovich; Russian economist; b. 11 June 1927; m. (wife deceased); ed Rostov State Univ.; head of div. Rostov Inst. of Railway Eng 1952–54; Sr teacher Black Sea Inst. of Mechanization and Electrification of Agric. 1954–59; Sr teacher, docent Lipetsk br. Moscow Inst. of Steel and Alloys 1962–70; Sr researcher Inst. of Econ. USSR Acad. of Sciences 1970–72; head of div. Inst. of Int. Econ. and Political Studies USSR Acad. of Sciences; Sr researcher Inst. of Econs Russian Acad. of Sciences 1998; Corresp. mem. USSR (now Russian) Acad. of Sciences and Russian Acad. of Agric. Sciences 1990; research in agrarian policy and econ., social problems of the village. *Publications:* Distribution and Usage of Labour in the Collective Farms 1964, Subsidiary Smallholding and its relations with Public Production 1971, Subsidiary Smallholding: Possibilities and Prospects 1983, Social and Economic Problems to Develop Agriculture in Socialist European Countries 1996, A Reform in American and Russian Scientists' Eyes 1996. *Address:* Institute of Economics, Russian Academy of Sciences, Nakhimovsky prosp. 32, 117 28 Moscow, Russia. *Telephone:* (095) 332-45-54 (Office).

SHMELYEV, Nikolai Petrovich, DEconSC.; Russian economist and author; b. 18 June 1936, Moscow; s. of Petr Shmelyev and Maria Shmelyeva; m. Gulia Shmelyeva 1965; one d.; ed Moscow Univ.; mem. CPSU 1962–91; researcher Inst. Econ. USSR Acad. of Sciences 1958–61; Prof., Head of Dept, Inst. of Econ. of World Socialist System (IEMSS), USSR Acad. of Sciences 1961–68, 1970–82; Sr scientific researcher, Inst. of USA and Canada 1982–92; Sr Researcher, Head CIS-Europe Dept, Russian Acad. of Sciences Inst. of Europe 1992–, Dir 2000–; researcher, Slavic Research Centre, Hokkaido Univ., Japan 1995; USSR People's Deputy 1989–91; Corresp. mem. Russian Acad. of Sciences 1994–, mem. 2000–; lecturer, Stockholm Inst. of Econ. of East European Countries 1992; lecturer, Middlebury Coll. Vt, USA 1993. *Publications:* books and articles on econ. problems, World Economic Tendencies, Progress and Contradictions 1987, Advances and Debts 1989, The Turning Point 1990; novels and stories include Pashkov House 1987, Performance for Mr. Prime Minister 1988, Pirosmani 1988, Silvestr 1991, V Puti Ya Zanemog 1995, Bezumnaya Greta 1995, Curriculum Vitae (o sebe) 2001. *Leisure interests:* books, travelling. *Address:* Institute of Europe, Mokhovaya 11/3, 101999 Moscow (Office); 3-d Frunzenskaya 7, Apt. 61, 119270 Moscow, Russia (Home). *Telephone:* (095) 203-41-87 (Office); (095) 242-13-06 (Home). *Fax:* (095) 200-42-98.

SHOCHAT, Avraham; Israeli politician and construction engineer; b. 1936, Tel Aviv; paratrooper Israel Defence Forces; Br. Dir Solel Boneh (Histadrut construction company); co-f. City of Arad; Mayor of Arad 1967–89; Chair. Citizens' Cttee Arad, Devt Towns Council, Econ. Cttee, Finance Cttee; Deputy Chair. Union of Local Authorities; Minister of Finance 1992–96, also of Energy; mem. Knesset 1988–; Dir Israel Aircraft Industries; mem. Labour Party. *Address:* c/o The Knesset, Jerusalem, Israel.

SHOCK, Sir Maurice, Kt, MA; British academic; b. 15 April 1926; s. of Alfred Shock and Ellen Shock; m. Dorothy Donald 1947 (died 1998); one s. three d.; ed King Edward's School, Birmingham and Balliol and St Antony's Colls. Oxford; served Intelligence Corps. 1945–48; Lecturer in Politics, Christ Church and Trinity Coll. Oxford 1955–56; Fellow and Praelector in Politics, Univ. Coll. Oxford 1956–77; Estates Bursar 1959–74; Vice-Chancellor, Univ. of Leicester 1977–87; Rector, Lincoln Coll. Oxford 1987–94, Hon. Fellow 1995; Chair. Nuffield Provincial Hosps. Trust 1988–; mem. Franks Comm. of Inquiry into Univ. of Oxford 1964–66; Hebdomadal Council, Oxford Univ. 1969–75; Chair. Univ. Authorities Panel 1980–85, Rand Health Bd of Advisors 1999–; Hon. FRCP 1989; Hon. LLD (Leicester) 1987. *Publications:* The Liberal Tradition; articles on politics and recent history. *Leisure interests:* gardening, theatre. *Address:* 4 Cunliffe Close, Oxford, OX2 7BL, England.

SHOEMAKER, Sydney, PhD; American professor of philosophy; b. 29 Sept. 1931, Boise, Idaho; s. of Roy Hopkins Shoemaker and Sarah Anderson Shoemaker; m. Molly McDonald 1960; one s.; ed Reed Coll., Edinburgh Univ., Cornell Univ.; instructor, Ohio State Univ. 1957–60; Santayana Fellow, Harvard Univ. 1960–61; Asst then Assoc. Prof., Cornell Univ. 1961–67, Prof. 1970–, Susan Linn Sage Prof. 1978–; Assoc. Prof. Rockefeller Univ. 1967–70; ed. The Philosophical Review, many terms 1964–; Gen. Ed. Cambridge Studies in Philosophy 1982–90; Vice-Pres. Eastern Div. American Philosophical Asscn 1992–93, Pres. 1993–94; John Locke Lecturer, Oxford Univ. 1972; Josiah Royce Lecturer, Brown Univ. 1993; Fulbright Scholar 1953–54, Fellow Center for Advanced Study in Behavioral Sciences 1973–74, Nat. Endowment for the Humanities Fellowship 1980–81, Guggenheim Fellow and Fellow at Nat. Humanities Center 1987–88; mem. American Acad. of Arts and Sciences, American Philosophical Asscn. *Publications:* Self-Knowledge and Self-Identity 1963, Identity, Cause and Mind 1984, Personal Identity (with Richard Swinburne) 1984, The First Person Perspective 1996. *Leisure interests:* music, reading, gardening. *Address:* The Sage School of Philosophy, 218 Goldwin Smith Hall, Cornell University, Ithaca, NY 14850 (Office); 104 Northway

Road, Ithaca, NY 14850, USA (Home). *Telephone:* (609) 257-7382 (Office); (607) 257-7382 (Home). *Fax:* (609) 255-8177 (Office). *Website:* www.cornell .edu (Office).

SHOEMAKER, Willie (William Lee); American jockey; b. 19 Aug. 1931, Fabens, Tex.; s. of Bebe Shoemaker and Ruby (née Call) Shoemaker; m. Cynthia Barnes 1978; one d.; jockey since 1949; Winner Ky Derby 1955, 1959, 1965, 1986, Belmont Stakes 1957, 1959, 1962, 1967, 1985, Preakness Stakes 1963, 1967; has won more than 1,009 Stakes races; first jockey to have 8,000 wins and to win over 100 million dollars in prize money; retd 1990 with 8,833 wins; trainer 1990–97; paralysed from neck down after car crash 1991; Hon. Chair. Paralysis Project. *Publications:* Mind Over Body – The Willie Shoemaker Story; Stalking Horse (mystery novel co-authored with Dick Lochte). *Address:* 2545 Fairfield Place, San Marino, CA 91108, USA.

SHOEMATE, C. Richard, MBA; American business executive; b. 10 Dec. 1939, LaHarpe, Ill.; s. of Richard Osborne Shoemate and Mary Jane (née Gillette) Shoemate; m. Nancy Lee Gordon 1962; three s.; ed Western Ill. Univ. and Univ. of Chicago; Comptroller Corn Products Unit, CPC Int. 1972–74, Plant Man. 1974–76, Vice-Pres. Operations 1976–81; Corpn Vice-Pres. CPC Int. 1983–88, Pres. 1988–98, Chair., CEO 1990–98; Chair., Pres., CEO Bestfoods (fmrly CPC Int.) 1998–; Pres. Canada Starch Co. 1981–83, mem., Bd of Dirs. 1981–88; Bd of Dirs. Corn Refiners Asscn 1985–88. *Address:* Unilever Bestfoods, 700 Sylvan Avenue, Englewood Cliffs, NJ 07632, USA (Office).

SHOENBERG, David, MBE, PhD, FRS; British physicist (retd); b. 4 Jan. 1911, St Petersburg, Russia; s. of Sir Isaac Shoenberg and Esther Shoenberg (née Aisenstein); m. Catherine Félicitée Fischmann 1940; one s. two d.; ed Latymer Upper School, London and Trinity Coll. Cambridge; Exhbn of 1851 Sr Student 1936–39; Research in Low Temperature Physics 1932–; in charge of Royal Soc. Mond. Lab. 1947–73; Lecturer in Physics 1944–52, Reader 1952–73, UNESCO Adviser on Low Temperature Physics, Nat. Physical Lab. of India 1953–54; Prof. of Physics Cambridge Univ. and Head of Low Temperature Physics Group, Cavendish Lab. 1973–78, Prof. Emer. 1978–; Life Fellow Gonville and Caius Coll. Cambridge; Guthrie Lecturer 1966, Rutherford Memorial Lecturer (India and Sri Lanka) 1980, Krishnan Memorial Lecturer 1988; Hon. Foreign mem. American Acad. of Arts and Sciences; Hon. Fellow Trinity Coll., Camridge 2002; Dr hc (Lausanne) 1973; Fritz London Award for Low Temperature Physics 1964, Hughes Medal, Royal Soc. 1995. *Publications:* Superconductivity 1938, 1952, Magnetism 1949, Magnetic Oscillations in Metals 1984, Kapitza in Cambridge and Moscow (co-ed.) 1990; scientific papers on low temperature physics and magnetism. *Address:* c/o Cavendish Laboratory, Madingley Road, Cambridge, CB3 0HE (Office); 2 Long Road, Cambridge, CB2 2PS, England (Home). *Telephone:* (1223) 337389 (Office).

SHOGO, Watanabe; Japanese executive; b. 31 Aug. 1915; m. Murako Tajima 1943; two s. one d.; ed Tokyo Univ.; with the Industrial Bank of Japan Ltd 1938–62; Man. Dir Nikko Securities Co. 1962, Sr Man. Dir 1963, Vice-Pres. 1966, Pres. 1970–91, Chair. 1973–; Pres. Nikko Research Centre Ltd 1970–88, Japan Fund Inc. 1973– (Vice-Chair. 1974–), Dir Pvt. Investment Co. for Asia (PICA) 1975–, Tokyo Stock Exchange 1973–; Exec. Dir Japan Fed. of Employers' Asscn 1970; Trustee, Japan Cttee for Econ. Devt 1971–; Man. Dir Fed. of Econ. Orgs. (Keidanren) 1970–; Pres. Bond Underwriters Asscn of Japan 1972–73; mem. Trilateral Comm. 1973–; Chair. Securities Dealers Asscn of Japan 1975–; mem. Securities and Exchange Council 1976–, Financial System Council 1976–, Taxation System Council of Govt. *Leisure interest:* oil painting. *Address:* Nikko Securities Company Ltd, 3-1, Marunouchi 3-chome, Chiyoda-ku, Tokyo (Office); 6-2, Eifuku 3-chome, Suginami-ku, Tokyo, Japan (Home). *Telephone:* (3) 283-2211 (Office); (3) 328-4205 (Home).

SHOIGU, Col-Gen. Sergey Kuzhugetovich; Russian politician; b. 21 May 1955, Chadan, Tuva ASSR; m.; two d.; ed Krasnoyarsk Polytech. Inst.; engineer, Sr master construction trust in Krasnoyarsk 1977–78; man. construction trusts Achinskamulinstroi, Cayantyazhstroi, Abakanvagonstroi 1979–88; Second Sec. Abakan City CP Cttee, insp. CP Cttee Krasnoyarsk Territory 1989–90; Deputy Chair. State Cttee on Architecture and Construction RSFSR 1990–91; Chair. State Cttee of Russian Fed. on Civil Defence, Emergencies and Natural Disasters 1991–94; Minister of Civil Defence, Emergencies and Clean-up Operations 1994–; Deputy Prime Minister Jan.–May 2000; mem. Security Council of Russia; a founder and leader pre-election bloc (then party) Yedinstvo (Unity) 1999–; mem. State Duma 1999; Co-Chair.of Yedinstvo and Otechestvo Party union; Hero of Russian Fed. 1999. *Leisure interests:* singing, playing guitar. *Address:* Ministry of Civil Defence, Emergencies and Clean-up Operations, Teatralny proezd 3, 103012, Moscow, Russia (Office). *Telephone:* (095) 926-39-01; (095) 924-19-46 (Office). *E-mail:* pressa@emercom.gov.ru. *Website:* www.emercom.gov.ru.

SHOKHIN, Aleksandr Nikolayevich, DR.EC.SC.; Russian politician; b. 25 Nov. 1951, Savinskoye, Arkhangelsk Region; m. Tatyana Valentinovna Shokhina; one s. one d.; ed Moscow Univ.; on staff Inst. of Econ., State Planning Cttee, Inst. of Labour, State Cttee of Labour 1974–82; researcher, Cen. Econ.-Math. Inst. and Inst. for Industrial Prognostics, USSR Acad. of Sciences 1982–87; adviser, Head of Dept of Int. Econ. Relations, Ministry of Foreign Affairs 1987–91; Dir Inst. of Employment Problems May–Aug. 1991; Russian Minister of Labour Aug.–Nov. 1991; Deputy Chair. of Russian Govt 1991–94; Minister of Labour and Employment 1991–92, of Foreign Econ. Relations 1992–93, of Econs 1994; Man. for Russia, IMF and IBRD 1992–94;

mem. Bd State Specialized Export-Import Bank 1995–; Pres. Higher School of Econs 1995–; mem. Bd Russian Party of Unity and Consent 1993–95; Co-ordinator pre-election Union 'Our Home Russia' 1995, Chair. 1997–98; mem. State Duma (Parl.) 1993–97, First Deputy Chair. 1996–97; Deputy Prime Minister Sept. 1998 (resgnd); Chair. Interdepartmental Comm. of Security Council for Econ. Security 1998–99; Ind. mem. 1999–, Chair. Cttee of Credit Org. and Financial markets. *Publications:* several books including Social Problems of Perestroika 1989, Consumer's Market 1989, Interactive of Powers in the Legislative Process 1997; over 200 scientific articles. *Address:* State Duma, Okhotny Ryad 1, 103009 Moscow, Russia. *Telephone:* (095) 292-83-01. *Fax:* (095) 292-83-00.

SHOKIN, Yuri Ivanovich; Russian mathematician; b. 9 July 1943, Kansk; m. 1968; two d.; ed Novosibirsk State Univ.; Sr researcher, head of lab. Computers Cen. Siberian br. USSR Acad. of Sciences 1969–76, head of lab. Inst. Theoretical and Applied Mechanics Siberian br. 1976–83, Dir Computers Cen. Siberian br. in Krasnoyarsk 1983–90; Dir Inst. of Computational Tech. Siberian br. Russian Acad. of Sciences 1990–, Gen. Scientific Sec. Siberian br. 1992–97, Gen. Dir United Inst. of Informatics 1997–; Dir Technopark Novosibirsk 1998–; corresp. mem. USSR (now Russian) Acad. of Sciences 1984, mem. 1994; research in computational math., numerical methods of mech., applied math., informatics; Order of Merit 1982, Order of Friendship 1999. *Publications:* Interval Analysis 1981, Numerical Modelling of Tsunami Waves 1983, Method of Differential Approximation: Application in Gas Dynamics 1985, Methods of Interval Analysis 1986, Fortran 90 for the Fortran Programmer 1995, numerous scientific articles. *Address:* Lavrentyev av. 6, 630090 Novosibirsk 90 (Office); Voevodskogo 10, 630090 Novosibirsk 90, Russia (Home). *Telephone:* (3832) 34-11-50 (Office). *Fax:* (3832) 34-13-42 (Office). *E-mail:* shokin@ict.nsc.ru (Office). *Website:* www.ict.nsc.ru/eng/shokin (Office).

SHONEKAN, Chief Ernest Adegunle Oladeinde, LLB; Nigerian administrative official and lawyer; b. 9 May 1936, Lagos; m. Beatrice Oyelayo Oyebola 1965; two s. three d.; ed Church Missionary Soc. (CMS) Boys' School, Lagos, CMS Grammar School, Lagos and Univ. of London; legal Asst UAC of Nigeria Ltd 1964–67, Asst legal adviser 1967–73, deputy legal adviser 1974–75, legal adviser 1975–78, Dir 1976, Chair. 1980–; Gen. Man. Bordpak Premier Packaging Co. 1978–79; Chair. Transitional Council of Nigeria Jan.–Aug. 1993; Pres. of Nigeria and Head of Interim Govt Aug.–Nov. 1993. *Address:* UAC of Nigeria Ltd, P.O. Box 9, Lagos (Office); 12 Alexander Avenue, Ikoyi, Lagos, Nigeria (Home). *Telephone:* 661091 (Office); 681437 (Home).

SHOOMBE, Pachukoni; Namibian politician; b. 12 Dec. 1936, Okadiva, Oshana Region; m.; five c.; ed Okahao Training Coll., UN Inst. for Namibia, Lusaka, Zambia; teacher 1958–74; Prin. Oshigambo Girls' School 1960–63; mem. SWAPO 1963–, joined mil. arm abroad 1974, elected mem. SWAPO Women's Council Cen. Cttee and Exec. Cttee 1980, SWAPO Cen. Cttee 1982, 1991; rep. SWAPO as Exec. Sec. for Information and Publicity, Pan-African Women's Org., Algeria and Angola 1985–89; apptd. Election Deputy Commr for Northern Region, Oshakati 1989; mem. Constitutional Ass. 1989, Nat. Ass. 1990–; Chair. Nat. Ass. Select Cttee on Human Resources; mem. Cttee on Standing Rules and Orders, Public Accounts Cttee; SWAPO Sec. for Finance 1991–; mem. nat. group of IPU; UNESCO Int. Award for work in SWAPO refugee camps 1980–85. *Leisure interests:* fighting against the oppression of women, reading, cooking, baking. *Address:* P.O. Box 1971, Windhoek, Namibia. *Fax:* 232368.

SHOR, Peter, BS, PhD; American mathematician; b. 14 Aug. 1959, New York; ed California Inst. of Technology, MIT; Post-doctoral Fellow, Mathematical Sciences Research Inst., Berkeley, Calif. 1985; mathematician AT&T Bell Labs., Florham Park, NJ 1986–; specialises in algorithms, quantum computing and quantum information theory; Nevanlinna Award 1998, MacArthur Fellowship 1999. *Publications:* frequent contribs. to professional journals. *Address:* AT&T Labs Research, 180 Park Avenue, Room C237, Florham Park, NJ 07932-1004, USA (Office). *Telephone:* (973) 360-8443 (Office). *Fax:* (973) 360-8178 (Office). *Website:* www.research.att.com (Office).

SHORE, Howard; Canadian film score composer; b. 18 Oct. 1946, Toronto; f. band Lighthouse; Musical Dir Saturday Night Live TV comedy show 1970s; began composing film music 1978; has collaborated on many films by David Cronenberg; composed title music for Late Night with Conan O'Brien TV show. *Film scores include:* I Miss You, Hugs and Kisses 1978, The Brood 1979, Scanners 1980, Videodrome 1983, Nothing Lasts Forever 1984, After Hours 1985, Fire with Fire 1986, The Fly 1986, Heaven 1987, Nadine 1987, Dead Ringers 1988, Big 1988, Signs of Life 1989, She-Devil 1989, The Local Stigmatic 1989, An Innocent Man 1989, Made in Milan 1990, The Lemon Sisters 1990, Naked Lunch 1991, The Silence of the Lambs 1991, A Kiss Before Dying 1991, Prelude to a Kiss 1992, Single White Female 1992, Philadelphia 1993, Mrs. Doubtfire 1993, Guilty as Sin 1993, Sliver 1993, M. Butterfly 1993, Nobody's Fool 1994, The Client 1994, Ed Wood (Los Angeles Film Critics' Asscn Award) 1994, Se7en 1995, Moonlight and Valentino 1995, White Man's Burden 1995, Before and After 1996, The Truth About Cats and Dogs 1996, Striptease 1996, Looking for Richard 1996, Crash 1996, That Thing You Do! 1996, The Game 1997, Cop Land 1997, Gloria 1999, Existenz 1999, Dogma 1999, Analyze This 1999, The Yards 2000, High Fidelity 2000, Esther Kahn 2000, The Cell 2000, Camera 2000, The Score 2001, The Lord of the Rings: The Fellowship of the Ring (Acad. Award for Best Original Score 2002, Grammy award for Best Soundtrack) 2001, Spider 2002, Panic Room

2002, The Lord of the Rings: The Two Towers 2002, The Lord of the Rings: The Return of the King 2003. *Address:* c/o Gorfaine/Schwartz, 13245 Riverside Drive, #450, Sherman Oaks, CA 91423, USA (Office).

SHORT, Rt Hon Clare, PC, BA; British politician; b. 15 Feb. 1946, Birmingham; d. of Frank Short and Joan Short; m. 1st 1964 (divorced 1974); one s.; m. 2nd Alex Lyon 1981 (died 1993); ed Keele and Leeds Univs; with Home Office 1970–75; Dir All Faith for One Race 1976–78, Youthaid and Unemployment Unit 1979–83; MP for Birmingham Ladywood 1983–; Shadow Employment Spokesperson 1985–89, Social Security Spokesperson 1989–91, Environment Protection Spokesperson 1992–93, Spokesperson for Women 1993–95; Shadow Sec. of State for Transport 1995–96, for Overseas Devt 1996–97; Sec. of State for Int. Devt 1997–2003; Chair. All Party Group on Race Relations 1985–86, Nat. Exec. Cttee (NEC) Women's Cttee 1993–97; Vice-Pres. Socialist Int. Women 1992–97; mem. Select Cttee on Home Affairs 1983–95, NEC of Labour Party 1988–98; mem. UNISON. *Leisure interests:* books, family, swimming. *Address:* House of Commons, London, SW1A 0AA, England (Office).

SHORT, Rt Hon Edward Watson (see Glenamara, Baron).

SHORT, Nigel; British chess player; b. 1 June 1965, Leigh, Lancs.; s. of David Short and Jean Gaskell; m. Rea Karageorgiou 1987; one s. one d.; ed Bolton School, Leigh Coll.; at age of 12 beat Jonathan Penrose in British championship; Int. Master 1980, Grandmaster 1984; British Champion 1984, 1987, 1998, English Champion 1991; Pres. Grandmasters' Asscn 1992; defeated Anatoly Karpov 1992; defeated by Kasparov 1993; chess columnist, The Daily Telegraph 1991, The Sunday Telegraph 1996–; stripped of int. ratings by World Chess Fed. June 1993, reinstated 1994; resgnd from Fédération Internationale des Echecs (FIDE) and formed Professional Chess Asscn (PCA) with Garry Kasparov 1993, left PCA 1995; ranked 17th in world by FIDE Jan. 2003; Hon. Fellow Bolton Inst. 1993–; now lives in Athens and Messina; Hon. MBE 1999. *Publication:* Learn Chess with Nigel Short 1993. *Leisure interests:* guitar playing, cricket, olive farming, swimming. *Address:* c/o The Sunday Telegraph, 1 Canada Square, London, E14 5DT, England. *E-mail:* ndshort@hotmail.com (Home).

SHORT, Roger Valentine, ScD, FAA, FRS, FRSE, F.R.C.V.S., FRCOG, FAAS, FRCPE, F.R.A.N.Z.O.G.; British professor of reproductive biology; b. 31 July 1930, Weybridge; s. of F.A. Short and M.C. Short; m. 1st Dr. Mary Bowen Wilson 1958 (divorced 1981); one s. three d.; m. 2nd Dr. Marilyn Bernice Renfree 1982; two d.; ed Sherborne School, Univs. of Bristol, Wisconsin and Cambridge; mem. ARC Unit of Reproductive Physiology and Biochem., Cambridge 1956–72; Lecturer, then Reader Dept of Veterinary Clinical Studies, Cambridge 1961–72; Dir MRC Unit of Reproductive Biology, Edinburgh, Scotland 1972–82; Prof. of Reproductive Biology, Monash Univ., Australia 1982–95; Wexler Professorial Fellow, Dept of Perinatal Medicine, Univ. of Melbourne 1996–; holder of patents for use of melatonin to control jet lag 1983, 1986, 1987; Chair. Bd of Dirs. Family Health Int., N.C. 1985–90 (mem. Bd 1983–97); Fellow, Magdalene Coll., Cambridge 1961–72; Fellow American Acad. of Arts and Sciences; Hon. Prof., Univ. of Edin. 1976–82; Hon. DSc (Guelph, Bristol). *Publications include:* Reproduction in Mammals, Vols 1–8 (with C.R. Austin) 1972–86, Contraceptives of the Future 1976, Ever Since Adam and Eve: The Evolution of Human Sexuality (with M. Potts) 1999; contrib. to numerous scientific journals. *Leisure interests:* gardening, wildlife, history of biology. *Address:* 18 Gwingana Crescent, Glen Waverley, Vic. 3150, Australia (Home); Department of Obstetrics and Gynaecology, Royal Women's Hospital, University of Melbourne, 132 Grattan Street, Vic. 3053 (Office). *Telephone:* (3) 9344-2635 (Office). *Fax:* (3) 9347-2472 (Office). *E-mail:* r.short@unimelb.edu.au (Office).

SHORTER, Wayne, BA; American musician; b. 25 Aug. 1933, Newark; ed New York Univ.; played saxophone with Art Blakey 1959–63, Miles Davis 1964–70, Weather Report 1970–86, Miles Davis Tribute Band 1992; served U.S. Army 1956–58; winner numerous Down Beat Magazine Awards, Best Soprano Sax 1984, 1985. *Solo albums include:* Native Dancer, Soothsayer, Etcetera 1981, Atlantis 1986, Phantom Navigator 1987, Joy Rider 1988, Native Dancer 1990, The All Seeing Eye 1994. *Address:* c/o Blue Note Records, 1750 Vine Street, Los Angeles, CA 90028, USA.

SHOSTAKOVICH, Maksim Dmitriyevich; American conductor; b. 10 May 1938, Leningrad, USSR (now St Petersburg, Russia); s. of the late Dmitriy Shostakovich; m. 1st; one s.; m. 2nd Marina Tisie 1989; one s. one d.; ed Cen. Music School, Moscow Conservatory; studied conducting under Rabinovich, Gauk, Rozhdestvensky (q.v.); Asst Conductor, Moscow Symphony Orchestra; Conductor, State Academic Symphony Orchestra; piano debut age 19 in father's Second Piano Concerto; Prin. Conductor and Artistic Dir USSR Radio and TV Symphony Orchestra; requested and granted political asylum in USA while on tour with USSR Radio and TV Symphony Orchestra, Nuremberg April 1981; conducted Nat. Symphony Orchestra, Capitol steps, Washington, DC, USA May 1981; Prin. Guest Conductor Hong Kong Philharmonic 1982–; Music Dir New Orleans Symphony Orchestra 1986–91; Hon. Music Dir Louisiana Philharmonic Orchestra 1993–94. *Performances:* Touring Western Europe with USSR Radio and TV Symphony Orchestra, Japan, USA 1971–81; has conducted all maj. N American orchestras and many in Europe, Asia, S America; conducted premiere of father's 15th Symphony and recorded virtually all father's symphonies in USSR; has performed with leading soloists, incl. Emil Gilels, Oistrakh, Rostropovich. *Address:* c/o Columbia Artists Management, Inc., 165 West 57th Street, New York, NY 10019 (Office); PO Box 273, Jordanville, NY 13361, USA.

SHOWALTER, Elaine, MA, PhD; American academic and literary critic; b. 21 Jan. 1941, Cambridge, Mass.; d. of Paul Cottler and Violet (Rottenberg) Cottler; m. English Showalter 1963; one s. one d.; ed Bryn Mawr Coll., Brandeis Univ.; Teaching Asst Dept of English, Univ. of Calif. 1964–66, teaching posts in Dept, later Assoc. Prof. 1967–78; Prof. of English Rutgers Univ. 1978–; Avalon Foundation Prof. of Humanities, Princeton Univ., NJ 1987–; Visiting Prof. of English and Women's Studies, Univ. of Del. 1976–77; Visiting Prof. School of Criticism and Theory, Dartmouth Coll. 1986; Guggenheim Fellow 1977–78; Rockefeller Humanities Fellow 1981–83; fmr Visiting Prof. at several univs. abroad; numerous TV and radio appearances; mem. Modern Language Asscn; Howard Behrman Humanities Award (Princeton Univ.) 1989. *Publications:* A Literature of Their Own 1977, The Female Malady 1985, Sexual Anarchy 1990, Sister's Choice 1991, Hysteria Beyond Freud (Jt author) 1993, Hystories 1997; also ed. of several feminist Publs and writer of numerous articles and reviews. *Address:* Princeton University, Department of English, Princeton, NJ 08544-0001, USA.

SHPAK, Col-Gen. Georgy Ivanovich, CAND.PED.SC.; army officer; b. 6 Sept. 1943, Osipovichi, Mogilev Region, Ukraine; m.; one s. (deceased) one d.; ed M. Frunze Mil. Acad., Mil. Acad. of Gen. Staff; Commdr paratroopers' Regt, head of staff, deputy Commdr paratroopers' div., Commdr of div. 1978–88; Deputy Commdr of Army Odessa Mil. Command 1988–89; Army Commdr, First Deputy Commdr Turkestan Mil. Command 1989–92; First Deputy Commdr Volga Mil. Command; Commdr Paratrooper Forces of Russian Army 1996–; three orders, ten medals. *Leisure interests:* countryside, fishing. *Address:* Ministry of Defence of Russian Federation, Znamenka str. 19, 103160 Moscow, Russia (Office). *Telephone:* (095) 296-18-00 (Office).

SHPEK, Roman Vasilyevich; Ukrainian economist; b. 10 Nov. 1954, Broshniv, Ivano-Frankovska Region; m. Mariya Romanivna Shpek; one s. one d.; ed Lvov Inst. of Wood Tech., Int. Inst. of Man., Delaver Univ.; engineer, chief of warehouse Wood Enterprise Osmoloda Ivano-Frankovsk Region 1976–78; Chief Engineer, Dir Verkhovinsk Wood Enterprise 1978–85; Dir Vorokhta Wood Enterprise 1985–89; Deputy Minister of Wood Industry Ukrainian SSR 1989–91; Deputy Chair. Ukrainian State Cttee on Wood Processing Industry 1991–92; Minister of Property Privatization and Production Demonopolization March–Nov. 1992; First Deputy Minister of Econs of Ukraine 1991–93, Minister 1995–96, Deputy Prime Minister 1995–96; Chair. Nat. Agency for Reconstruction and Devt; People's Deputy 1994; mem. Verkhovna Rada 1996–; Ukrainian Rep. UNDP Exec. Bd 1996–; with Nat. Agency for Devt and European Integration 1998–. *Address:* Verkhovna Rada, M. Hrushevskoho str. 5, 252019 Kiev, Ukraine.

SHREVE, Susan Richards, MA; American author; b. 2 May 1939, Toledo, Ohio; d. of Robert Richards and Helen Richards; m. 1st Porter Shreve (divorced 1987); m. 2nd Timothy Seldes 1987; two s. two d.; ed Univs. of Pennsylvania and Virginia; Prof. of English Literature, George Mason Univ., Fairfax, Va 1976–; Visiting Prof., Columbia Univ., New York 1982–; Princeton Univ., NJ 1991, 1992, 1993; Pres. PEN/Faulkner Foundation 1985–; producer The American Voice for TV 1986–; Essayist, MacNeil/Lehrer Newshour; Guggenheim Fellowship; NEA Fellowship in Fiction. *Publications:* novels: A Fortunate Madness 1974, A Woman Like That 1977, Children of Power 1979, Miracle Play 1981, Dreaming of Heroes 1984, Queen of Hearts 1987, A Country of Strangers 1989, Daughters of the New World 1992, The Train Home 1993, Skin Deep, Women and Race 1995, The Visiting Physician 1995, Outside the Law 1997, How We Want to Live (ed. jtly) 1998, Plum and Jaggers 2000; also several children's books including Jonah, The Whale 1997, Ghost Cats 1999, The End of Amanda, The Good 2000. *Address:* 3319 Newark Street, NW, Washington, DC 20008, USA.

SHRIVER, Duward F., PhD; American professor of chemistry; b. 20 Nov. 1934, Glendale, Calif.; s. of D. L. Shriver and J. S. Shriver; m. Shirley A. Clark 1957; two s.; ed Univ. of California, Berkeley, Univ. of Michigan; instructor, Northwestern Univ., Evanston, Ill. 1961–62, Asst Prof. 1962–67, Assoc. Prof. 1967–71, Prof. 1971–78, Morrison Prof. of Chem. 1988–, Chair. Chem. Dept 1992–95; Alfred P. Sloan Research Fellow 1967–69; Guggenheim Fellow 1983–84, mem. Inorganic Syntheses Inc. 1974–, Pres. 1982–85; ACS Award for Distinguished Service in Inorganic Chem. 1987, Materials Research Soc. Medal 1990. *Publications:* five books, including Inorganic Chemistry (jtly.) 1990; 295 scientific papers. *Address:* Department of Chemistry, Northwestern University, 2145 Sheridan Road, Evanston, IL 60208 (Office); 1100 Colfax Street, Evanston, IL 60201, USA (Home). *Telephone:* (847) 491-5655. *Fax:* (847) 491-7713. *E-mail:* shriver@chem.nwu.edu (Office).

SHRIVER, (Robert) Sargent, Jr, AB, LLD; American public servant and politician; b. 9 Nov. 1915, Westminster, Md; s. of Robert Sargent and Hilda Shriver; m. Eunice Kennedy 1953; four s. one d.; ed Yale Univ.; admitted to NY Bar 1941; served USN (Lt Commdr) 1941–45; Asst Ed. Newsweek 1945–46; Adviser The Joseph P. Kennedy, Jr Foundation 1955–; Asst Gen. Man. The Merchandise Mart 1948–61; mem. Chicago Bd of Educ. 1955–60, Pres. 1956–60; Dir The Peace Corps 1961–66, Office of Econ. Opportunity 1964–68; Special Asst to the Pres. 1964–68; Amb. to France 1968–70; Democratic Vice-Presidential Cand. 1972; Partner, Fried, Frank, Harris, Shriver & Jacobson 1971–86; of counsel 1986–; mem. American Comm. on East-West Accord 1978–, Americans for SALT 1979–; Dir The Arms Control

Asscn 1983–; Pres. Special Olympics Int. 1986–90, CEO and Chair. 1990–96, Chair. Bd 1996–; official of numerous educational bodies; Hon. LLD; Hon. LHD; Hon. DCL, etc. from numerous univs.; Golden Heart Presidential Award (Philippines), Médaille de Vermeil (City of Paris), US Presidential Medal of Freedom 1994, Equal Justice Award and many other nat. awards. *Publication:* Point of the Lance 1964. *Address:* Special Olympics International, 1325 "G" Street, NW, Suite 500, Washington, DC 20005, USA. *Telephone:* (202) 628-3630. *Fax:* (202) 347-3460.

SHTAUBER, Zvi Meir, PhD; Israeli diplomatist; b. 15 July 1947; s. of Yisrael Shtauber and Jaffa Shtauber; m. Nitza Rousso; two s. one d.; ed Harvard Business School, Fletcher School of Law and Diplomacy, Tufts Univ., USA; with Israel Defence Forces—IDF 1970–95, Head of Strategic Planning Div. 1995, retd from mil. career (with rank of Brig.-Gen.) 1995; Vice-Pres., Ben-Gurion Univ. of the Negev 1996–99; Foreign Policy Adviser to Prime Minister Ehud Barak 1999–2000; Amb. to UK 2001–. *Address:* Embassy of Israel, 2 Palace Green, Kensington, London, W8 4QB, England (Office). *Telephone:* (20) 7957-9500 (Office). *Fax:* (20) 7957-9601 (Office). *E-mail:* amb-assist@ london.mfa.gov.il (Office). *Website:* www.israel-embassy.org.uk/london (Office).

SHU HUIGUO; Chinese politician and agronomist; b. July 1938, Jing'an Co., Jiangxi Prov.; ed Zhejiang Agricultural Coll.; joined CCP 1980; Dir Dept of Agric., Animal Husbandry and Fishery, Jiangxi Prov.; Vice-Gov. Jiangxi Prov. 1991–; Vice-Sec. CCP Jiangxi Provincial Cttee 1995, Sec. 1997–2001; Vice-Minister of Personnel 2001–; mem. 15th CCP Cen. Cttee 1997–, now Chair. *Address:* Ministry of Personnel, 12 Hepingli Central Street, Beijing 100716, People's Republic of China. *Telephone:* (1) 84201114 (Office). *E-mail:* webmaster@mail.molss.gov.cn (Office). *Website:* www.mop.gov.cn (Office).

SHU SHENGYOU; Chinese politician; b. Dec. 1936, Yushan Co., Jiangxi Prov.; joined CCP 1959; Mayor Jingdezhen City; Vice-Gov. Jiangxi Prov. 1991, Gov. 1996–2001; Vice-Sec. CCP Jiangxi Provincial Cttee 1995–2001; mem. Standing Cttee of NPPCC 2001; mem. 15th CCP Cen. Cttee 1997–. *Address:* c/o Jiangxi Provincial Government, Nanchang, Jiangxi Province, People's Republic of China.

SHU TING, GONG SHUTING; Chinese poet; b. Gong Peiyu, 18 May 1952, Shima, Zhangzhou City, Fujian Prov.; m. Chen Zhongyi; mem. Writers' Asscn Fujian 1983–, Vice-Chair. 1985–, Council of Writers' Asscn of China 1985–. *Publications:* Shuangweichuan 1982, Shu Ting Shuqing Shixuan 1984, Poesiealbum Shu Ting 1989, Selected Poems of Seven Chinese Poets 1993. *Address:* 13 Zhonghua Road, Gulangyu, Xiamen City, Fujian Province, 361002, People's Republic of China.

SHUE, Elisabeth; American actress; b. 6 Oct. 1963, Wilmington; d. of James Shue and Anne Wells; m. Davis Guggenheim 1994 (divorced 1996); one s.; ed Wellesley Coll., Harvard Univ.; studied with Sylvie Leigh, Showcase Theater; appeared in Broadway plays including Some Americans Abroad, Birth and After Birth. *Films include:* The Karate Kid 1984, Link 1986, Adventures in Babysitting 1987, Cocktail 1988, Body Wars 1989, Back to the Future Part II 1989, Part III 1990, Soapdish 1991, The Marrying Man 1991, Twenty Bucks 1993, Heart and Souls 1993, Radio Inside 1994, Blind Justice 1994, The Underneath 1995, Leaving Las Vegas 1995, The Trigger Effect 1996, The Saint 1996, Palmetto 1997, Deconstructing Harry 1997, Cousin Bette 1997, Molly 1998, Hollow Man 2000, Amy and Isabelle 2001. *Television films include:* Charles and Diana, Double Switch 1987, Hale the Hero 1992, Blind Justice 1994. *Television series:* Call to Glory 1984. *Address:* c/o Creative Arts Agency, 9830 Wilshire Boulevard, Beverly Hills, CA 90212, USA.

SHUKLA, Vidya Charan, BA; Indian politician; b. 2 Aug. 1929, Raipur; s. of Ravi Shanker and Bhawani Shukla; m. Sarala Devi 1951; three d.; ed Morris Coll. and Univ. Coll. of Law, Nagpur; mem., Lok Sabha 1957–62, 1962–67, 1967–70, 1971–77; Deputy Minister of Communications and Parl. Affairs Jan.–Feb. 1966; Deputy Minister for Home Affairs 1966–67; Minister of State in Ministry of Home Affairs 1967–70; Minister of Revenue and Expenditure in Ministry of Finance 1970–71, Minister of Defence Production 1971–74, Minister of Planning 1974–75, for Information and Broadcasting 1975–77, for Civil Supplies 1980–81, for Foreign Affairs 1990–91, for Water Resources and Parl. Affairs 1991–96; Pres. Special Organising Cttee, 9th Asian Games, Delhi; Pres. All-India Council of Sports 1981–83; Chair. Nat. Insts. of Physical Educ. and Sports 1981–85; Pres. Indian Olympic Asscn 1984–88; expelled from Congress (I) Party 1987; f. Jan Monha (People's Front) 1987. *Leisure interests:* hunting, tracking and photography. *Address:* Radheshyam Bhavan, Krishak Nagar, Raipur, Chattisgarh; 502, Taj Apartments, 2 Ring Road, Near Safderjung Hospital, New Delhi, India. *Telephone:* (771) 423841 (Raipur); (11) 6196738 (New Delhi).

SHUKRI, Ibrahim; Egyptian politician; b. 22 Sept. 1916; joined Misr al-Fatat (Young Egypt) Party 1935; shot in Cairo strike 1935; managed family estate, Sharbeen; Sec.-Gen. Misr al-Fatat 1946; elected Vice-Pres., then Pres. Socialist Party (fmrly Misr al-Fatat) 1947–53; mem. for Kahaliyya, People's Ass. 1949–52; imprisoned for opposing the monarchy 1952, released after revolution 1952; returned to estate; joined Arab Socialist Union on its formation 1962, elected to Exec. Cttee 1964; re-elected mem. for Kahaliyya 1964–68; Pres. Farmers' Union and Sec. Professional Asscn 1965–66; Gov. Wadi al-Gadeed 1968–76; elected to People's Ass. 1976; Minister of Agric. and Agrarian Reform 1977–98, of Land Improvement May–Oct. 1978; Chair.

Socialist Labour Party 1978–99; fmrly Man. Ed. Al-Sha'b (party newspaper); Leader of the Opposition, People's Ass. 1979–86. *Address:* c/o Socialist Labour Party, 12 Sharia Awali el-Ahd, Cairo, Egypt.

SHULMAN, Alexandra; British journalist; b. 13 Nov. 1957, London; d. of Milton Shulman and Drusilla Beyfus; m. Paul Spike 1994; one s.; ed St Paul's Girls' School and Univ. of Sussex; Sec. Over-21 magazine; Writer and Commissioning Ed., later Features Ed. Tatler 1982–87; Ed. Women's Page, Sunday Telegraph 1987, later Deputy Ed. 7 Days current affairs photo/reportage; Features Ed. Vogue 1988; Ed. GQ 1990; Ed. Vogue 1992–; Trustee Nat. Portrait Gallery, London 1999–. *Address:* Condé Nast Publications, Vogue House, Hanover Square, London, W1R 0AD, England (Office). *Telephone:* (20) 7499-9080.

SHULMAN, Lawrence Edward, MD, PhD, FACP; American biomedical research administrator and rheumatologist; b. 25 July 1919, Boston, Mass.; s. of David Herman Shulman and Belle (Tishler) Shulman; m. 1st Pauline K. Flint 1946, m. 2nd Reni Trudinger 1959; one s. two d.; ed Harvard and Yale Univs; Research Assoc. John B. Pierce Foundation, New Haven, Conn. 1942–45; Intern, Resident and Fellow in Internal Medicine, Johns Hopkins Hospital and Univ. 1949–53; Dir Connective Tissue Div. Johns Hopkins Univ. Medical School 1955–75; Assoc. Prof. of Medicine, Johns Hopkins Univ. 1964–; Assoc. Dir for Arthritis, Musculosceletal and Skin Diseases, NIH 1976–82, Dir 1982–86; Dir Nat. Inst. of Arthritis and Musculoskeletal and Skin Diseases 1986–94, Dir Emer. 1994–; NIH Emissary for Clinical Research 1994–; several awards. *Publications:* over 100 scientific publications. *Leisure interests:* music, politics. *Address:* 6302 Swords Way, Bethesda, MD 20817, USA.

SHULMAN, Robert Gerson, MA, PhD; American biophysicist; b. 3 March 1924, New York; s. of Joshua S. Shulman and Freda (Lipshay) Shulman; m. 1st Saralee Deutsch 1952 (died 1983); three s.; m. 2nd Stephanie S. Spangler 1986; ed Columbia Univ.; Research Assoc. Columbia Univ. Radiation Lab., New York 1949; AEC Fellow in Chem. Calif. Inst. of Tech. 1949–50; Head, Semiconductor Research Section, Hughes Aircraft Co. Culver City, Calif. 1950–53; mem. tech. staff, Bell Labs., Murray Hill, NJ 1953–66, Head, Biophysics Research Dept 1966–79; Prof. of Molecular Biophysics and Biochem., Yale Univ. 1979–94, Dir Div. of Biological Sciences 1979–94, Sterling Prof. of Biophysics and Biochem. 1994–, Emissary for Clinical Research 1995–; numerous visiting professorships, lectureships etc.; mem. NAS, Inst. of Medicine; Guggenheim Fellow, Cambridge 1961–62. *Address:* Yale University MR Center, Department of Molecular Biophysics and Biochemistry, P.O. Box 208024, New Haven, CT 06520, USA (Office); (203) 432-1333 (Home). *E-mail:* robert.shulman@yale.edu (Office). *Website:* www.yale.edu (Office).

SHULTZ, George Pratt, BA, PhD; American politician, economist and educator; b. 13 Dec. 1920, New York; s. of Birl E. Shultz and Margaret Lennox Pratt Shultz; m. 1st Helena M. O'Brien 1946; two s. three d.; m. 2nd Charlotte Mailliard Swig 1997; ed Princeton Univ. and MIT; Assoc. Prof. of Industrial Relations, MIT 1955–57; Sr Staff Economist, President's Council of Econ. Advisers 1955–56; Prof. of Industrial Relations, Grad. School of Business, Univ. of Chicago 1957–68, Dean, Grad. School of Business 1962–68; Pres. Industrial Research Assocn 1968; US Sec. of Labor 1969–70; Dir Office of Man. and Budget, Exec. Office of the Pres. 1970–72; US Sec. of Treasury 1972–74; Chair. Council on Econ. Policy 1973–74; Sec. of State 1982–89; Exec. Vice-Pres. Bechtel Corpn 1974–75, Pres. 1975–77, Vice-Chair. 1977–81, Pres. Bechtel Group Inc. 1981–82; Prof. of Man. and Public Policy, Grad. School of Business, Stanford Univ. 1974–82, of Int. Economy 1989–91, Prof. Emer. 1991–; Chair. JP Morgan Chase Int. Council, Advisory Council Inst. of Int. Studies, Stanford, Govs'. Econ. Policy Advisory Bd, Calif.; mem. Bd GM Corpn Advisory Council, Bechtel Group Inc., Charles Schwab & Co.; Chair. Pres. Reagan's Econ. Policy Advisory Bd 1981–82; mem. Bd of Trustees, Center for Advancement of Study in the Behavioral Sciences, Stanford, Calif.; mem. Gilead Sciences Bd, Infrastructure World, Unext.com Bd; Distinguished Fellow, Hoover Inst., Stanford Univ. 1989–; Thomas W. and Susan B. Ford Distinguished Fellow, Hoover Inst. 2001–; Jefferson Award 1989, Presidential Medal of Freedom 1989, Grand Gordon, Order of the Rising Sun 1989, Seoul Peace Prize 1992, Eisenhower Medal 2001, Reagan Distinguished American Award 2002, Ralph J. Bunche Award for Diplomatic Excellence 2002. *Publications include:* Pressures on Wage Decisions, Labor Problems,The Dynamics of a Labor Market, Management Organization and the Computer, Strategies for the Displaced Worker, Guidelines, Informal Controls and the Market Place, Workers and Wages in the Urban Labor Market, Leaders and Followers in an Age of Ambiguity, Economic Policy beyond the Headlines (jtly), Turmoil and Triumph: My Years as Secretary of State 1993. *Leisure interests:* golf, tennis. *Address:* Hoover Institution, Stanford, CA 94305-6010, USA. *Telephone:* (650) 725-3492. *Fax:* (650) 723-5441.

SHULTZ, Mikhail Mikhailovich, PhD; Russian chemist; b. 1 July 1919, Petrograd (now St Petersburh); m. Nina Dimitrievna Paromova 1944; two s.; ed Leningrad State Univ.; served in Second World War 1941–45; Asst Prof. Leningrad State Univ. 1950–53, Assoc. Prof. 1953–65, Full Prof. 1965, Head of Lab. Research Inst. of Chem. 1965–72, Dean Chem. Dept 1967–72; Dir I. Grebenshchikov Inst. of Silicate Chem. USSR (now Russian) Acad. of Sciences 1972–; mem. USSR (now Russian) Acad. of Sciences 1979–; research in physical chem., thermodynamics of heterogeneous systems, chem. and elec-

trochem. of glass; Chair. Scientific Council for New Non-Metallic Inorganic Materials 1990–; Vice-Pres. Soc. of Ceramics 1991–; Deputy Academician-Sec. Dept of Physics, Chem. and Tech. of Inorganic Materials, Russian Acad. of Sciences 1991–; Ed. Soviet Journal of Glass Physics and Chem. 1975–90; mem. editorial bds Cement and Concrete Research 1976–94, Revue de Chimie Minérale 1981–87; Hero of Socialist Labour 1991; Patriotic War Orders (2nd Class) 1945, 1995; Orders of Labour, Red Banner 1971, 1975; Order of Lenin 1979, 1991; USSR State Prizes 1973, 1986, Hammer and Sickle Gold Medal 1991. *Publications include:* Dependence of Electrode Properties of Glass on their Structure 1963, Contemporary Ideas Concerning the Structure of Glasses and their Properties 1988; numerous articles in scientific journals. *Leisure interests:* painting, photography, gardening. *Address:* I. Grebenshchikov Institute of Silicate Chemistry, Russian Academy of Sciences, Odoevskogo str., 24 Korp. 2, St Petersburg 199155, Russia (Office). *Telephone:* (812) 350-65-16 (Office). *Fax:* (812) 218-54-01 (Office); (812) 553-72-72 (Home).

SHUMAKOV, Valery Ivanovich, MD, PhD; Russian surgeon and transplantologist; b. 9 Nov. 1931, Moscow; s. of Ivan Shumakov and Nataly Shumakova; m. Nataly Shumakova 1960; one s. one d.; ed Sechenov First Medical Inst.; worked as surgeon, Head of Lab. of Assisted Circulation and Artificial Heart, Head of Dept of Transplantology and Artificial Organs, Inst. of Clinical and Experimental Surgery of USSR (now Russian) Ministry of Public Health 1956–74; Dir Russian Research Inst. of transplantology and artificial organs 1974–; Head Dept of Physics of Living Systems, Moscow Inst. of Physics and Tech.; carried out the first heart, liver, pancreas and spleen transplants in clinical practice in Russia; carried out the first implantations of artificial cardiac ventricle and artificial heart in Russia; mem. Russian Acad. of Medical Sciences 1988, Russian Acad. of Sciences 1993, Russian Acad. of Medical and Tech. Sciences 1993; Chair. Scientific Council on Transplantology and Artificial Organs, Presidium of Acad. of Medical Sciences; Ed. journal Transplantology and Artificial Organs; mem. admin. of Russian Soc. of Cardiovascular Surgeons; mem. of numerous European and int. scientific socs; USSR State Prize, 1971; Meritorious Inventor of Russian Fed. 1978; Hero of Socialist Labour 1990. *Publications:* 18 monographs, 70 patents and more than 350 scientific works in the field of surgery. *Leisure interests:* swimming, literature. *Address:* Research Institute of Transplantology and Artificial Organs, Shchukinskaya ul. 1, 123436 Moscow, Russia (Office). *Telephone:* (095) 196-18-03 (Office). *Fax:* (095) 943-00-08 (Office).

SHUMEIKO, Vladimir Filippovich, C.TECH.SC., DEcon; Russian politician, economist and manager; b. 10 Feb. 1945, Rostov Don; m.; two d.; ed Krasnodar Polytech. Inst.; worked in factories as foreman, engineer, chief engineer, Dir-Gen. Concern Krasnodar Factory of Measuring Instruments –1991; People's Deputy of Russia 1990–92; Vice-Chair. Supreme Soviet of Russia 1991–92, First Deputy Prime Minister of Russia 1992–93; Pres. Confed. of Entrepreneurs' Unions of Russia 1992–93; mem. Council of Fed. (Upper House of Parl.) 1993–96, Chair. 1994–96; Founder and Chair. Reforms-New Course Movt 1996–; lecturer Acad. of Border Service; Chair. Bd Dirs Interregional Auction and Stock Corpn 1998–; Chair. Bd of Dirs Moskva Bank 2002–. *Publication:* Russian Reforms and Federalism 1995, Pelmeny po Protocoly 2001. *Leisure interests:* fishing, woodworking, collecting small bells. *Address:* Reforms-New Course, Novi Arbat 19, Moscow; Moskva Bank, Bolshoi Znamenski per. 6, bldg 9, 121019 Moscow, Russia. *Telephone:* (095) 203-33-47 (Movt); (095) 777-97-97 (Bank). *Fax:* (095) 916-72-07 (Bank). *E-mail:* office@moscow-bank.ru.

SHUSHKIEVICH, Stanislau Stanislavavich, DSc; Belarus politician; b. 15 Dec. 1934, Minsk; m. Irina Kuzminichna Shushkevich; one s. one d.; ed Belarus Univ.; CPSU 1967–91; researcher, Inst. of Physics, Belarus Acad. of Sciences 1959–60; engineer Minsk Radio Plant 1960–61; Chief Engineer, Head of Section Belarus Univ. 1961–67; Prof. Minsk Radiotechnical Inst. 1967–69; Head of Chair., Belarus Univ. 1969–86, Pro-Rector 1986–90; involvement in politics 1989– (as critic of Govt negligence in aftermath of Chernobyl accident); mem. Supreme Soviet (backed by opposition Belarus Popular Front) 1990–91; Chair. Supreme Soviet 1991–94, mem. –1996; Dir Centre of Political and Econ. Studies, European Humanitarian Inst. 1994–; mem. Civil Action faction; Cand. in presidential elections 1994; one of leaders of opposition; Corresp. mem. Belarus Acad. of Sciences; Belarus State Prize, Council of Ministers Prize. *Publications:* Belarus – Self-Identification and Statehood; more than 60 articles and papers on problems of nuclear electronics and political problems.

SHUVALOV, Igor Ivanovich; Russian politician and lawyer; b. 4 Jan. 1967, Bilibino, Magadan Region, Russia; m.; one s. two d.; ed Moscow State Univ.; Research Inst. EKOS, Moscow 1984–85; army service 1985–87; attaché Ministry of Foreign Affairs, Russian Fed. 1993; Sr legal adviser Stock co. (ALM) Consulting Moscow 1993–95; Dir Advocates' Bureau (ALM) 1995–97; Head Dept of State Cttee on Man. of State Property Russian Fed. 1997–98; Deputy Minister of State Property 1998; Chair. Russian Foundation of Fed. Property 1998–2000; Head of Presidential Admin. and Minister Without Portfolio 2000–. *Address:* Government of Russian Federation, Krasnopresnenskaya nab. 2, 103247 Moscow, Russia (Office). *Telephone:* (095) 205-60-05 (Office).

SHVYDKOI, Mikhail Yefimovich, PhD, DFA; Russian theatre scholar and politician; b. 5 Sept. 1940, Kyrgyzia; m. Marina Shvydkaya; two s.; ed Moscow Lunacharsky Inst. of Theatre Art; reviewer Radio Co., Ed.-in-Chief magazine Theatr 1973–90; Ed.-in-Chief Publrs Co. Kultura, Russian Fed. Ministry of Culture 1990–93; Deputy Minister of Culture 1993–97; Prof. of Foreign

Theatre, Acad. of Humanitarian Sciences; commentator on cultural problems Russian TV; Deputy Chair. Russian TV and Radio Co., Ed.-in-Chief Cultura TV Channel 1997–98; Chair. All-Russian State Radio and TV Holding 1998–2000; Minister of Culture 2000–; Chair. Nat. Comm. World Decade of Culture at UNESCO, Vice-Pres. Cttee on Communications Int. Inst. of Theatre at UNESCO; Govt Award of the Russian Fed. for Literature and Art 1999; numerous awards, prizes and decorations from France, Poland and Russian Fed. *Television:* broadcaster on Cultural Revolution (Cultura TV channel) 2002–. *Publications:* Dramatic Composition: Theatre and Life, Secrets of Lonely Comedians, Sketches on Foreign Theatre of the Late 20th Century; numerous articles on history and contemporary state of theatre in Russian and foreign periodicals. *Address:* Ministry of Culture, Kitaygorodsky Proyezd 7, 103074 Moscow, Russia (Office). *Telephone:* (095) 925-06-08 (Office). *Fax:* (095) 925-91-58 (Office).

SHWAYRI, Ramzi; Lebanese chef; b. Beirut; m. Tanya Jamous; ed Univ. of Lyon; son of Greek Orthodox parents; studied econs and law in France; Lebanon's first TV chef, live programmes three times weekly on Future Television; Pres. Al-Kafaàt Foundation (f. by his father—gives training in vocational skills to handicapped or troubled young people). *Publication:* Chef Ramzi. *Address:* Al-Kafaàt Foundation, PO Box 47, Hadath, Lebanon (Office). *Telephone:* (961) 1879301 (Office). *Fax:* (961) 1879307 (Office). *E-mail:* fondation@al-kafaat.org (Office). *Website:* www.al-kafaat.org (Office).

SHYAMALAN, Manoj Nelliyattu; Indian film director, writer, actor and producer; b. 6 Aug. 1970, Pondicherry, Tamil-Nadu Prov. *Films:* Praying with Anger (Dir, actor, producer) 1992, Wide Awake (writer, Dir) 1998, The Sixth Sense (writer, Dir, actor) 1999, Stuart Little (screenplay) 1999, Unbreakable (writer, Dir, actor and producer) 2000, Sings (Dir, producer) 2001.

SIAGURU, Sir Anthony, KBE; Papua New Guinea fmr government minister and international public servant; b. 4 Nov. 1946, Wewak, East Sepik Prov.; s. of Anthony Khaisir and Maria Krakemoine; m. Mina Isikini 1972; three s.; ed Papua New Guinea and Harvard Univs.; Sec. Dept of Foreign Affairs and Trade 1975–80; MP 1982–87, Minister of Public Service, of Youth and Devt 1982–85; Foundation Chair. S. Pacific Games 1988–90; Deputy Sec.-Gen. (Political) Commonwealth Secr. 1990–95; Chair. Port Moresby Stock Exchange 1998–, Pacific Rim Plantations, PNG Centre for Commercial Disputes, PNG Chapter of Transparency Int.; Dir Kula Fund, Lihir Gold, Steamships Trading, PEACE Foundation of Melanesia and Red Shield Appeal; columnist PNG Post Courier 1996–; fmr mem. Bd of Man. Inst. of Commonwealth Studies; Hon. Corresp. Sec. Royal Over-Seas League, fmr mem. Cen. Council; mem. Royal Commonwealth Soc. *Publications include:* The United States' Dilemma 1983, The Red Orchestra 1987, Ethics of Public Decision-making 1987; numerous articles on nat. and int. affairs. *Leisure interests:* tennis, fishing, gardening. *Address:* P.O. Box 5917, Boroko, NCD, Papua New Guinea. *Telephone:* 3092000. *Fax:* 3092099.

SIALE BILEKA, Silvestre; Equatorial Guinean politician; fmr Minister of Justice and Religion; Prime Minister and Head of Govt of Equatorial Guinea 1991–93, 1993–95; Minister of Foreign Affairs and Francophone Affairs 1991–92; Pres. Supreme Tribunal; mem. Partido Democrático de Guinea Ecuatorial (PDGE). *Address:* Supreme Tribunal, Halabo, Equatorial Guinea (Office).

SIANKO, Uladzimir Liavonavich; Belarus diplomatist; b. 5 Aug. 1946; ed Moscow State Inst. of Int. Relations, Diplomatic Acad.; diplomatic service 1973–; with USSR Embassy, Poland 1973–79, Second Sec. 1981–85, First Sec. 1988–91; Third Sec. Fourth European Div. USSR Ministry of Foreign Affairs 1979–81; First Sec. Dept of Socialist Countries, USSR Ministry of Foreign Affairs 1987–88; Deputy Minister of Foreign Affairs 1991–92, Minister 1994–97; Amb. to UK 1994–97, to France (also accred to Spain, Portugal and Rep. to UNESCO) 1998–. *Address:* Embassy of Belarus, 38 boulevard Suchet, 75016 Paris, France (Office). *Telephone:* 1-44-14-69-79. *Fax:* 1-44-14-69-70.

SIAZON, Domingo L., BA, BSc, MPA; Philippine politician and international civil servant; b. 1939, Aparri, Cagayan; m.; ed Ateneo de Manila Univ., Tokyo Univ., Japan, Harvard Univ., USA; interpreter and trans., then Attaché and Third Sec. and Vice-Consul, Embassy in Tokyo 1964–68; Acting Resident Rep. to IAEA, Alt. Perm. Rep. to UNIDO, Third, Second, then First Sec., Embassy in Berne 1968–73; First Sec. and Consul-Gen., Embassy in Vienna, then Amb. to Austria, also Perm. Rep. to IAEA, UNIDO and UN at Vienna 1973–85; Dir-Gen. UNIDO 1985–93; Minister of Foreign Affairs 1995–2000; Amb. to Japan 2002–. *Address:* Embassy of the Philippines, 5-15-5 Roppongi, Minato-ku, Tokyo 106-8537, Japan. *Telephone:* (3) 3406-4243. *E-mail:* phpjp@gol.com. *Website:* www.rptokyo.org.

SIBBETT, Wilson, CBE, PhD, FRS, FRSE; British physicist; b. 15 March 1948, Portglenone, Co. Antrim; s. of John Sibbett and Margaret Sibbett (née McLeister); m. Barbara Anne Browne 1979; three d.; ed Ballymena Tech. Coll., Queen's Univ. Belfast, Imperial Coll.; Post-doctoral Research Fellow, Imperial Coll., London, later Lecturer and Reader in Physics; Prof. of Natural Philosophy, Univ. of St Andrews 1985–; Chair. Scottish Science Advisory Cttee 2002–; Fellow Optical Soc. of America 1998; Schardin Gold Medal 1978, Boys Medal and Prize 1993, Rank Prize for Optoelectronics 1997, Royal Soc. Rumford Medal 2000. *Publications:* approx. 300 papers published in scientific journals. *Leisure interests:* golf, DIY, gardening. *Address:* School of Physics and Astronomy, University of St. Andrews, North Haugh, St Andrews, Fife,

KY16 9SS (Office); 1 Lawhead Road East, St Andrews, Fife, KY16 9ND, Scotland (Home). *Telephone:* (1334) 463100 (Office); (1334) 472778 (Home). *Fax:* (1334) 463104 (Office). *E-mail:* ws@st-andrews.ac.uk (Office).

SIBLEY, Dame Antoinette, DBE; British ballerina; b. 27 Feb. 1939, Bromley, Kent; d. of Edward G. Sibley and Winifred Smith; m. 1st Michael Somes 1964 (divorced 1973, died 1994); m. 2nd Panton Corbett 1974; one s. one d.; joined the Royal Ballet 1956, Soloist 1959, Prin. Ballerina 1960–; made film The Turning Point 1978; Vice-Pres. Royal Acad. of Dance 1989–91, Pres. 1991–. *Ballets* leading roles in: Swan Lake, Sleeping Beauty, Coppelia, The Nutcracker, La Fille Mal Gardée, Romeo and Juliet, Jabez and the Devil (cr. role of Mary), The Dream (cr. Titania), Jazz Calendar (cr. Friday's Child), Enigma Variations (cr. Dorabella), Thais (cr. Thais), Triad (cr. the Girl), Manon (cr. Manon), Soupirs (cr. pas de deux), Symphonic Variations, Daphnis and Chloe, Varii Capricci, The Good-Humoured Ladies, A Month in the Country, L'Invitation au Voyage. *Publications:* Sibley and Dowell 1976, Antoinette Sibley 1981, Reflections of a Ballerina 1985. *Leisure interests:* doing nothing, opera, cinema, reading. *Address:* c/o Royal Academy of Dance, 36 Battersea Square, London, SW11 3RA, England (Office).

SIBOMANA, Adrien; Burundian politician; fmr Deputy Speaker Nat. Ass.; fmr Gov. Muramvya Prov.; Vice-Pres. Comm. on Nat. Unity; Prime Minister 1988–94, also fmr Minister of Planning.

SICILIANO, Enzo, PhD; Italian novelist, playwright and journalist; b. 27 May 1934, Rome; s. of Natale Siciliano and Giuseppina Jenzi; m. Flaminia Petrucci 1963; two s.; literary critic, La Stampa, Turin 1969–77; Jt Ed., with Alberto Moravia and Francesca Sanvitale, Nuovi Argomenti 1972–; Literary Critic, Corriere della Sera, Milan 1977–; Theatre Critic, Epoca, Milan 1982–85; Literary Critic, L'Espresso, Rome 1985–; Premio Viareggio 1981. *Publications:* Racconti ambigui 1963, Autobiografia letteraria 1971, Rosa (pazza e disperata) 1973, La notte matrigna 1975, Puccini 1977, Vita di Pasolini 1978, La voce di Otello 1982, Diamante 1984, La Letteratura Italiana (Vols 1, 2, 3) 1986, 1987, 1988, Cuore e fantasmi 1990, Carta Blu 1992. *Address:* Nuovi Argomenti, via Sicilia 136, 00187 Rome (Office); via Caroncini 53, 00197 Rome, Italy (Home). *Telephone:* (06) 47497376 (Office).

SICKINGHE, Jonkheer Feyo Onno Joost, LLD; Netherlands business executive (retd); b. 1 May 1926, The Hague; s. of Jonkheer D. W. Sickinghe and Jonkvrouwe W. J. M. E. Radermacher Schorer; m. M. C. van Eeghen 1952; two s. two d.; ed Univ. of Utrecht; solicitor 1952–55; various functions within Stork NV 1955–63; Man. Dir Koninklijke Machinefabriek Stork NV 1963–69; Pres. Bd of Man. and CEO Stork NV 1969–89; fmr Chair. Foundation Amsterdam Promotion, French Chamber of Commerce and Ind. in the Netherlands; mem. numerous Supervisory Bds including Stork NV, FMO, Pechiney Int., DNB (Dutch Cen. Bank), Hagemeyer NV, ABN Amro Bank, Kahn Shipping BV; Commdr Order of Oranje Nassau; Officier Légion d'honneur. *Leisure interests:* sailing, theatre. *Address:* Oud Blaricumerweg 7, Naarden, Netherlands. *Telephone:* (35) 6943728 (Office). *Fax:* (35) 6945725 (Office).

SIDDHI SAVETSILA, Air Chief Marshal; Thai politician and air force officer; b. 7 Jan. 1919, Bangkok; s. of Phraya Wanapruksapijarn and Khunying Wanapruksapijarn; m. Khunying Thida Savetsila 1952; two s. two d.; ed Chulalongkorn Univ. and MIT; fmr pilot officer, Royal Thai Air Force and Adviser to Royal Thai Air Force; mem. Nat. Ass. 1973, Nat. Reform Council 1976; Minister, Prime Minister's Office 1979–80, Second Kriangsak Govt; Sec.-Gen. Nat. Security Council 1975–80; Minister of Foreign Affairs 1980–90; MP 1983–90; Leader Social Action Party 1986–90; Deputy Prime Minister 1986; Special ADC to HM the King 1986; Hon. LLD (Philippines) 1983, (Nat. Univ. Singapore) 1985; numerous decorations. *Leisure interests:* reading, exercise. *Address:* c/o Ministry of Foreign Affairs, Saranrom Palace, Bangkok 10200, Thailand. *Telephone:* 225-6312.

SIDHWA, Bapsi; Pakistani writer and Professor of English and Creative Writing; b. 11 Aug. 1939, Karachi; d. of Peshotan Bhandara and of Tehmina Bhandara; m. Nasher Rustam Sidhwa; two d. one s.; ed Kinnaird Coll. for Women, Lahore; self published first novel The Crow Eaters 1978; Asst Prof. Creative Writing Programme Univ. of Houston, Texas, USA 1985; Bunting Fellowship Radcliffe Coll., Harvard Univ. 1986; Asst Prof. Writing Div., Columbia Univ., New York 1989; Visiting Scholar Rockefeller Foundation Centre, Bellagio, Italy 1991; Prof. of English and Writer-in-Residence Mount Holyoake Coll., S. Hadley, Mass. 1997; Fannie Hurst Writer-in-Residence Brandeis Univ., Mass. 1998–99; Postcolonial Teaching Fellowship Southampton Univ., UK 2001; Chair. Commonwealth Writers Prize' 1993; mem. Advisory Cttee to Prime Minister Benazir Bhutto on Women's Devt –1996, Punjab Rep., Asian Women's Conf., Alma Ata; Sec. Destitute Women's and Children's Home, Lahore; Sitara-I-Imtiaz 1991, Lila Wallace Reader's Digest Award 1993, Nat. Award for English Literature, Pakistan Acad. of Letters 1991, Patras Bokhari Award for Literature 1992, Excellence in Literature Award, Zoroastrian Congress 2002. *Publications include:* The Crow Eaters 1978 (commercially published 1980), The Bride 1982, Ice-Candy-Man (Notable Book of the Year, New York Times 1991), Cracking India 1991 (film 1999), An American Brat 1993, Bapsi Sidhwa Omnibus 2001; numerous short stories and reviews. *Leisure interest:* reading. *Address:* c/o 5442 Cheena Drive, Houston, TX 77096, USA (Office); c/o Oxford University Press, Banglore Town, Shahrah-e-Faisal, Karachi, Pakistan. *Telephone:* (713) 282-0811 (USA); (21) 45290259. *Fax:* (713) 283-6405 (USA).

SIDIBÉ, Mandé; Malian politician and economist; b. 1939; economist IMF, Cen. Bank of W African States; Econ. Adviser to Pres. Alpha Oumar Konare –2000; Prime Minister of Mali and Minister of Integration 2000–02. *Address:* c/o Office of the Prime Minister, quartier du Fleuve, B.P. 790, Bamako, Mali (Office).

SIDIMÉ, Lamine; Guinean politician; fmr Pres. of Supreme Court; Prime Minister of Guinea, Co-ordinator of Govt Affairs Jan. 1999–. *Address:* Office of the Prime Minister, Cité des Nations, Conakry, Guinea (Office). *Telephone:* 41-52-83 (Office). *Fax:* 41-52-82 (Office).

SIDKI, Aziz, BEng, MA, PhD; Egyptian politician; b. 1 July 1920, Cairo; ed Cairo Univ., Univ. of Oregon and Harvard Univ.; taught Cairo Univ.; Tech. Counsellor to the President 1953; Ministry for Industry 1956–63, Deputy Prime Minister and Minister for Industry and Mineral Wealth 1964–65; Minister for Industry, Petroleum and Mineral Wealth 1968–71; Deputy Prime Minister 1971–72; Prime Minister 1972–73; Acting Gen. Sec. Arab Socialist Union 1971–73; Personal Asst to Pres. Sadat 1973–75; fmr Amb. to France; has participated in various int. confs. on industrial affairs. *Address:* c/o The Presidency, Cairo, Egypt.

SIDLIN, Murray, MM; American conductor; b. 6 May 1940, Baltimore, Md; ed Academia Chigiana, Siena, Cornell Univ.; Asst Conductor, Baltimore Symphony Orchestra 1971–73; Dir of Maryland Ballet Co. 1971–73; Prin. Conductor Baltimore Chamber Players 1971–73; Resident Conductor Nat. Symphony Orchestra under Dorati 1973–77, Wolf Trap American Univ. Music Acad. 1974; Host and Conductor Children's TV series Music is… 1977; Music Dir Tulsa Philharmonic Orchestra 1978–80; Music Dir Hew Haven Symphony 1977–88, Long Beach Symphony 1980–88, Resident Conductor Aspen Music Festival 1978–93; Resident Conductor Oregon Symphony Orchestra 1994–; Guest Conductor with numerous orchestras in N America, also performances in Europe and at the Festival Casals in Puerto Rico; Carnegie Hall début 1975; winner of Baltimore Symphony Orchestra Young Conductor's Competition 1962. *Address:* c/o Oregon Symphony Orchestra, 711 South West Adler, Suite 200, Portland, OR 97205; Shaw Concerts Inc., 3436 Springhill Road, Lafayette, CA 94549, USA.

SIDOROV, Vasily Sergeyevich; Russian diplomatist; b. 2 Jan. 1945, Moscow; m.; three c.; ed Moscow Inst. of Int. Relations; on staff Ministry of Foreign Affairs 1967–; Amb. to Greece; Deputy Head Dept of Int. Orgs. 1990–91; Deputy, First Deputy Perm. Rep. of Russia to UN 1991–95, Deputy Minister of Foreign Affairs 1995–98; Perm. Rep. to UN in Geneva 1998–2001; Head Russian del. to UN Comm. on Human Rights 1999–2001; on staff Ministry of Foreign Affairs 2001–, Russian Rep. to Conf. on Disarmament in den Haag, Geneva. *Address:* Ministry of Foreign Affairs, Smolenskaya-Sennaya 32/34, Moscow, Russia (Office).

SIDOROV, Veniamin Aleksandrovich; Russian physicist; b. 19 Oct. 1930, Babarino, Suzdal Dist, Vladimir Region; s. of Alexandr Mikhailovich Sidorov and Maria Vasilievna Sidorova; m. 1st Gendlina Larisa Semenovna 1962; one s. one d.; m. 2nd Lupashina Irina Sergeevna 1975; one s.; ed Moscow State Univ.; attached to Inst. of Atomic Energy, then Budker Inst. of Nuclear Physics, Siberian Div. of USSR (now Russian) Acad. of Sciences 1962–, Deputy Dir of Inst. 1977–2001, Scientific Adviser and mem. of Inst. Directorate 2001–; Corresp. mem. USSR (now Russian) Acad. of Sciences 1968–; Lenin Prize 1967, USSR Council of Ministers Prize 1985, USSR State Prize 1989. *Publications:* numerous works, mainly on colliding beam experiments in elementary particle physics. *Address:* Institute of Nuclear Physics, Siberian Division of Russian Academy of Sciences, Lavrentiev prospect 11, 630090 Novosibirsk (Office); Maltseva 10, 630090 Novosibirsk, Russia (Home). *Telephone:* (3832) 34-10-31 (Office); (3832) 30-09-10 (Home). *Fax:* (3832) 34-21-63. *E-mail:* sidorov@inp.nsk.su (Office).

SIDOROV, Yevgeniy Yurievich, DSc; Russian politician and literary critic; b. 11 Feb. 1938, Sverdlovsk (now Ekaterinburg); s. of Yuri Sidorov and Natalia Sidorova; m. Vera Indurskaya 1972; two s.; ed Moscow State Univ., Acad. of Social Sciences of the Cen. Cttee of CPSU; mem. CPSU 1962–92; Head of Dept Moskovski Komsomolets 1962–65, Literaturnaya Gazeta 1965–67, Yunost 1967–72; maj. works devoted to the analysis of Russian contemporary literature; Prof., Pro-rector of Moscow Gorky Literary Inst. 1978, Rector 1987–92; Minister of Culture of Russia 1994–97; mem. State Duma (Parl.) 1993–95; Perm. Rep. to UNESCO 1998–2003; Vice-Pres. European Union of Writers, Scientists, Artists; several nat. and int. literary prizes including Mediterranium Golden Oliva (Palermo, Italy) 1991. *Publications:* On the Stylistic Variety of Soviet Prose, Time to Write, On the Way to Synthesis, Yevgeniy Yevtushenko, The Flow of Poetry Days, Pages and Fates; articles on cinema and theatre. *Leisure interests:* friends, chess, travelling. *Address:* c/o Permanent Delegation of Russia to UNESCO, 1 rue Miollis, 75015 Paris.

SIDQI, Atif; Egyptian politician and fmr professor of law; fmr Prof. Cairo Univ. Law School; fmr adviser on econ. affairs; to Vice-Pres. Mubarak; mem. Shura; fmr Cultural Attaché, Embassy, Paris; Head Cen. Auditing Agency 1981–86; Prime Minister of Egypt 1986–96, also fmr Minister of Int. Co-operation; mem. Nat. Democratic Party. *Address:* c/o Office of the Prime Minister, Cairo, Egypt.

SIEBERT, Horst, PhD; German economist; b. 20 March 1938, Neuwied; s. of Fritz Siebert and Anna Heini; m. Christa Causemann 1965; ed Univ. of Cologne, Wesleyan Univ., Conn., Univ. of Münster; Asst Prof. of Econs Texas A & M Univ.; Prof. of Econs and Chair. of Econs and Int. Trade, Univ. of Mannheim 1969–84; Prof. of Econs and Chair. of Int. Econs Univ. of Konstanz 1984–89; Chair. of Theoretical Econs and Pres. Inst. of World Econs Univ. of Kiel 1989–; mem. Council of Govt Econ. Advisers 1990–, Group of Econ. Analysis of EC; Dr. h.c. (Ghent) 2000); Karl Bräuer Prize 1999, Ludwig Erhard Prize for Wirtschaftspublizistik 1999. *Publications:* Aussenwirtschaft 2000, Economics of the Environment: Theory and Policy 1998, Arbeitslos ohne Ende? Strategien für mehr Beschäftigung 1998, The World Economy 1999, Der Kobra-Effekt. Wie man Irrwege der Wirtschaftspolitik vermeidet 2001. *Address:* Institute of World Economics, University of Kiel, Düsternbrooker Weg 120, 24105 Kiel, Germany. *Telephone:* (431) 8814236. *Fax:* (431) 8814501. *E-mail:* hsiebert@ifw.uni-kiel.de (Office). *Website:* www.uni-kiel.de/ifw/staff/siebert.htm.

SIEGBAHN, Kai Manne Börje, BSc, DPhil; Swedish physicist; b. 20 April 1918, Lund; s. of Dr. Manne Siegbahn (winner of 1924 Nobel Prize for Physics) and of Karin (née Högbom) Siegbahn; m. Anna-Brita Rhedin 1944; three s.; ed Univ. of Uppsala, Univ. of Stockholm; Prof. of Physics, Royal Inst. of Tech., Stockholm 1951–54, Univ. of Uppsala 1954–84; Prof. Papal Acad. of Science 1996–; mem. Royal Swedish Acad. of Science, Royal Swedish Acad. of Eng Sciences, Royal Soc. of Science, Royal Acad. of Arts and Science of Uppsala, Royal Physiographical Soc. of Lund, Societas Scientiarum Fennica, Norwegian Acad. of Science, Royal Norwegian Soc. of Sciences and Letters, Papal Acad. of Science 1986–; Pres. IUPAP; Hon. mem. American Acad. of Arts and Sciences, Comité Int. des Poids et Mesures, Paris; Hon. DSc (Durham) 1972, (Basel) 1980, (Liège) 1980, (Upsala Coll., NJ) 1982, (Sussex) 1983; Lindblom Prize 1945, Björkén Prize 1955, 1977, Jt winner of Nobel Prize for Physics 1981 for work on atomic spectroscopy; Celsius Medal 1962, Sixten Heyman Award 1971, Harrison Howe Award 1973, Maurice F. Hasler Award 1975, Charles Frederick Chandler Medal 1976, Torbern Bergman Medal 1979, Pittsburgh Award of Spectroscopy 1982, Röntgen Medal 1985, Finggi Award 1986, Humboldt Award 1986, Premo Castiglione Di Sicilia 1990. *Publications:* Beta- and Gamma-Ray Spectroscopy 1955, Alpha-, Beta- and Gamma-Ray Spectroscopy 1965, ESCA-Atomic Molecular and Solid Structure Studied by Means of Electron Spectroscopy 1967, ESCA Applied to Free Molecules 1969, Some Current Problems in Electron Spectroscopy 1983 and 450 scientific papers. *Leisure interests:* music, skiing, tennis. *Address:* c/o Institute of Physics, University of Uppsala, Box 530, 751 21 Uppsala, Sweden (Office). *Telephone:* (18) 146963 (Office).

SIEGEL, Ira Theodore, MBA; American publishing executive; b. 23 Sept. 1944, New York City; s. of David A. Siegel and Rose Minsky; m. Sharon R. Sacks 1965; three d.; ed New York and Long Island Univs; Business Man. Buttenheim Publishing Co., New York 1965–72; Corp. Vice-Pres. (research) Cahners Publishing Co. (Div. Reed Publishing Co. USA, Boston) 1972–86; Pres. R.R. Bowker Publishing Co. (Div. Reed Publishing, USA, New York) 1986–91, Martindale-Hubbell Div. NJ 1990–91, Reed Reference Publishing 1991–95, Pres., CEO 1993–95; Pres., CEO Lexis-Nexis 1995–97; Pres. edata.com (now seisint) 1999–. *Address:* 16589 Senterra Drive, Delray Beach, FL 33484, USA. *Telephone:* (561) 999-4400 (Office), (561) 499-6457 (Home). *Fax:* (561) 999-4692 (Office). *E-mail:* ira@edata.com (Office).

SIEGELMAN, Don Eugene, JD; American politician; b. 24 Feb. 1946, Mobil, Ala; m. Lori Allen; one s. one d.; ed Univs. of Alabama, Georgetown and Oxford; called to Bar Ala 1972; Sec. of State of Ala 1979–87, Attorney-Gen. 1987–94, Lt-Gov. 1996–99, Gov. of Alabama 1999–2003; Democrat. *Address:* c/o Office of the Governor, State Capitol, 600 Dexter Avenue, Suite N104, Montgomery, AL 36130, USA (Office).

SIEMIĄTKOWSKI, Zbigniew, DH; Polish politician; b. 8 Oct. 1957, Ciechanów; m.; one d.; ed Warsaw Univ.; Sr Asst Warsaw Univ. 1981–; Deputy to Sejm (Parl.) 1991–; mem. Comm. for Nat. and Ethnic Minorities; mem. Comm. of Justice; mem. Polish United Workers' Party (PZPR) 1978–90; mem. Social Democracy of Polish Repub. (SDRP) 1990–99; Minister of Internal Affairs 1996; mem. Council of Ministers 1997; mem. Democratic Left Alliance 1999–; Sec. of State in Chancellery of Prime Minister 2001–; Acting Head Office of State Protection 2001–. *Leisure interest:* family, tourism. *Address:* Sejm RP, ul. Wiejska 4/6/8, 00-902 Warsaw, Poland. *Telephone:* (22) 6211820.

SIEVERTS, Thomas C. W., DIPL.ING.; German architect and town planner; b. 8 June 1934, Hamburg; s. of Rudolf Sieverts and Elisabeth Sieverts (née Ronnefeldt); m. Heide Pawelzick 1966; one s. two d.; ed in Stuttgart, Liverpool and Berlin; with Kossak and Zimmermann f. Freie Plannungsgruppe Berlin 1965; Prof. of Town Planning Dept of Architecture, Hochschule der Künste, Berlin 1967–70; Guest Prof., Grad. School of Design, Harvard Univ. 1970–71; Prof. of Town Planning, Dept of Architecture, Tech. Hochschule, Darmstadt 1971–99; Prof. Emer.; Special Prof. of Urban Design, Inst. of Planning Studies, Univ. of Nottingham 1978–88; in practice as architect and town planner, Bonn 1978–; Fellow Inst. for Advanced Study, Berlin 1995–96; mem. Scientific Advisory Council World Exhbn, 'Expo 2000', Hanover 1989–99, Sächsische Akad. der Künste; Deubau Prize (Essen) 1969, Verdienstzeichen in Gold (Vienna) 1988, Bauherren Prize 1992, Deutsche Städtebau Prize 1993. *Buildings:* town planning consultant to the City of Vienna, planning Danubia area 1973–78, the Gürtel area 1984–88; Dir of Int. Bldg Exhbn Emscher Park (Ruhr) 1989–94. *Publications:* Zwischenstadt 1997, Fünfzig Jahre Städtebau – Reflektion und Praxis 2001; many contribs to periodicals and books. *Leisure interest:* drawing. *Address:* Buschstrasse 20, 53113 Bonn, Germany. *Telephone:* (228) 218706 (Office). *Fax:* (228) 217101. *E-mail:* skat@skat-architecten.de. *Website:* www.skat-architecten.de (Office).

SIEW, Vincent C.; Taiwanese politician; b. 3 Jan. 1939, Chiayi City, Taiwan; m.; three d.; ed Nat. Chengchi Univ., Georgetown Univ.; Vice-Consul, Kuala Lumpur, Malaysia 1966–69, Consul 1969–72; Section Chief Asia Pacific Affairs Dept, Ministry of Foreign Affairs 1972; Deputy Dir 4th Dept Bd of Foreign Trade, Ministry of Econ. Affairs 1972–74, Dir 1974–77, Deputy Dir-Gen. Bd of Foreign Trade 1977–82, Dir-Gen. 1982–88; Vice-Chair. Council for Econ. Planning and Devt, Exec. Yuan 1988–89; Dir-Gen. Dept of Organizational Affairs, Kuomintang Cen. Cttee; Minister of Econ. Affairs 1990–93; Minister of State, Chair. Council for Econ. Planning and Devt, Exec. Yuan 1993–94; Minister of State, Chair. Mainland Affairs Council, Exec. Yuan 1994–95; legislator 1996–97; Premier of Taiwan 1997–2000; Eisenhower Fellow, USA 1985. *Address:* Kuomintang, 53 Jen Ai Road, Sec. 3, Taipei, Taiwan.

SIFIC, Mokdad; Algerian politician; fmr civil servant; fmr Minister of Public Works; Prime Minister of Algeria 1994–96.

SIGALOVA, Alla Mikhailovna; Russian choreographer and ballet dancer; b. 28 Feb. 1958, Volgograd; d. of Stalov Mikhail Petrovich and Viogina Tamara Aleksandrovna; m. Kozak Roman Yefimovich; one s. one d.; ed Leningrad Vaganova School of Choreography, Russian Acad. of Theatre Arts; teacher Russian Acad. of Theatre Arts 1983–87; choreographer Theatre Satirikon 1987–89; Artistic Dir Theatre Ind. Troupe of Alla Sigalova 1989–97, Choreography Theatre of Alla Sigalova 2001–; choreographer of New Year TV shows for ORT and NTV channels 1996–99. *Dance:* Othello 1990, Queen of Spades 1991, Salomea 1991. *Productions choreographed include:* Moscow Mayakovsky Theatre: Diary of an Ordinary Girl 1984, Bed-Bug 1986; Moscow Satirikon Theatre: Serving Girls 1988; Moscow Mossoviet Theatre: Banana 1994. *Address:* Russian Academy of Theatre Arts, Kislovsky per. 6, Moscow (Office); Prechistenka str. 25/13, apt. 10, Moscow, Russia (Home). *Telephone:* (095) 202-12-36 (Office); (095) 201-44-36 (Home). *Fax:* (095) 201-44-36 (Home). *E-mail:* asigalova@mail.ru (Home).

SIGCAU, Princess Stella, BA; South African politician; b. 1937; d. of Botha Sigcau (fmr Pres. of Transkei); m. Ronald Tshabalala 1962 (deceased); two c.; ed Univ. of Fort Hare; MP for Lusikisiki, Transkei Parl. 1968; Minister of the Interior, Public Works and Energy, Educ. and Post and Telecommunications –1976, of Interior Affairs 1976–81, Post and Telecommunications, Transkei 1981–87; Leader Transkei Nat. Independence Party 1987; Prime Minister of Transkei 1987 (ousted in a coup); Del. for Cape Traditional Leaders at Multiparty Negotiation Process, World Trade Center 1994; Chair. ANC Women's League, Transkei; mem. ANC Women's League Nat. Exec. Council; Minister for Public Enterprises, Govt of Nat. Unity 1994–99, of Public Works 1999–. *Leisure interests:* reading, farming. *Address:* Ministry of Public Works, Central Government Building, Corner Bosman and Vermeulen Streets, Pretoria 0002, South Africa (Office). *Telephone:* (12) 3241510 (Office). *Fax:* (12) 3256380 (Office). *E-mail:* imochaliban@pwdmail.pwv.gov.za (Office). *Website:* www.publicworks.gov.za (Office).

SIGUA, Tengiz Ippolitovich, D.TECH.S.; Georgian politician; b. 9 Nov. 1934, Lentekhi; s. of Ipolite Sigua and Lidia Schavdia; m. Nina Iwania 1975; one d.; ed Georgian Polytechnical Inst.; engineer and Dir Metallurgy Inst. Georgian Acad. of Sciences 1962–90, now mem. Georgian Acad. of Sciences; fmr Leading mem. Round Table—Free Georgia Alliance, Chair. All-Georgia Rustaveli Soc.; apptd. Head of Govt by Zviad Gamsakhurdia, Nov. 1990; resigned Aug. 1991 and joined the opposition; mem. State Council March–Oct. 1992; mem. Supreme Soviet 1992–95; apptd. Prime Minister by Mil. Council 1992–93 (resgnd), now in Parl. Opposition; Vice-Pres. Georgian Rustaveli Soc. 1989, Pres. 1992–93. *Leisure interests:* sport, art. *Address:* Phanaskerteli str. 16, Apt. 31, 380094 Tbilisi, Georgia (Home).

SIGURDSSON, Jón, M.SC.ECON.; Icelandic politician and economist; b. 17 April 1941, Ísafjörður; s. of Sigurdur Gudmundsson and Kristin Gudjona; m. Laufey Thorbjarnardóttir; four c.; ed Akureyri Coll., Univ. of Stockholm and London School of Econs; Econ. Inst. of Iceland 1964–71 (Dir Econ. Research 1970–71); Chief Econ. Research Div. Econ. Devt Inst. 1972–74; Man. Dir Nat. Econ. Inst. and Econ. Adviser to Govt 1974–80, 1983–86; Exec. Dir for Nordic Countries IMF 1980–83, Alt. Gov. IMF for Iceland 1974–87; Assoc. Jt IBRD/IMF Devt Cttee 1974–80; IBRD Gov. for Iceland 1987–; EBRD Gov. for Iceland 1991–; mem. Althing (SDP) 1987–; Minister of Justice and Ecclesiastical Affairs 1987–88, of Commerce 1987–93, of Industry 1988–93, of Nordic Co-operation 1988–89; Chair. OECD Council of Ministers 1989, Nordic Council of Ministers 1989; mem. Salaries Arbitration Court 1970–80; Rep. for Iceland Econ. and Devt Review Cttee OECD 1970–80, 1983–86; Gov. and Chair. Bd of Dirs, Cen. Bank of Iceland 1993–94; Pres. and CEO Nordic Investment Bank 1994– (mem. Bd 1976–87, Chair. 1984–86). *Address:* c/o Nordic Investment Bank, Fabianinkatu 34, P.O. Box 249, 00171-Helsinki, Finland. *Telephone:* (9) 18001. *Fax:* (9) 1800492.

SIGURDSSON, Niels P.; Icelandic diplomatist (retd); b. 1926, Reykjavik; s. of Sigurdur B. Sigurdsson and Karitas Einarsdóttir; m. Olafia Rafnsdóttir; two s. one d.; ed Univ. of Iceland; joined Diplomatic Service 1952; First Sec. Paris Embassy 1956–60; Deputy Perm. Rep. to NATO and OECD 1957–60; Dir Int. Policy Div. Ministry of Foreign Affairs, Reykjavik 1961; Del. to the UN Gen. Ass. 1965; Amb. and Perm. Rep. of Iceland to N Atlantic Council; Amb. to Belgium and the EEC 1968; Amb. to UK 1971–76, to FRG 1976–78, to Holy See 1977–95, Amb.-at-Large 1979–84, to Norway 1985–89; Chair.

Icelandic Del. to Madrid Conf. 1980–83; with Ministry of Foreign Affairs 1990–96. *Leisure interests:* swimming, riding. *Address:* Naustabryggja 55, Reykjavik 110, Iceland.

SIHANOUK, King (Norodom) (see (Norodom) Sihanouk, King).

SIIMANN, Mart; Estonian politician; b. 1946, Killingi-Nomme; m.; two c.; ed Tartu State Univ.; psychologist, Deputy Head Lab. of Scientific Org. of Work and Man. 1971–75; Sr research Asst Tartu State Univ. 1975–82; broadcaster, Deputy Dir-Gen., Ed.-in-Chief Estonian TV 1982–87; Dir-Gen. Estonian Radio 1987–89; Dir-General Estonian TV 1989–92; Man. Dir commercial TV station ReklamTV 1992–95; mem. Riigikogu (Parl.), Chair. Coalition Party Faction, mem. Constitutional Cttee 1995–98; Chair. Coalition Party 1997–99; Prime Minister of Estonia 1997–99; mem. Riigikugu 1998–. *Leisure interests:* sport, literature, fishing, philosophy. *Address:* c/o Riigikugu, Lossi Plats 1A, Tallinn 0100, Estonia (Office).

SILAJDŽIĆ, Haris, PhD; Bosnia and Herzegovina politician; b. 1945, Sarajevo; m.; one s.; ed Benghazi Univ., Libya; teacher, Prof. Priština Univ. –1990; Minister of Foreign Affairs Repub. of Bosnia and Herzegovina 1990–93; Prime Minister 1993–96; Chair. Movt for Bosnia and Herzegovina; Co-Chair. newly formed Govt of Bosnia and Herzegovina 1996–2000. *Publications:* several books and papers on int. relations, including relations between USA and Albania, 6 books and over 100 papers on Eng in USA, mainly on thermal and fluid Eng; three scientific journals. *Address:* c/o Council of Ministers, 71000 Sarajevo, Bosnia and Herzegovina (Office).

SILAPA-ARCHA, Banharn, LLM; Thai politician; b. 20 July 1932; s. of Sengkim and Sai-eng sae Ba; ed Ramkhamhaeng Univ.; elected to Suphan Buri Municipal Council 1973; Co-Founder Chart Thai Party 1975, Sec.-Gen. 1976, Party Leader 1994–; mem. Legis. Ass. 1973–; Deputy Minister of Industry 1976; Minister of Agric. 1980; Senator 1986; Minister of Communications 1986, of Industry 1989, of Finance 1990, of Interior 1990–91, of Communications 1992; Leader of Opposition 1992–95; Prime Minister 1995–96, also Minister of the Interior. *Address:* Chart Thai Party, House of Representatives, Bangkok, Thailand. *Telephone:* (2) 282-7054 (Office). *Website:* www.chartthai.or.th (Office).

SILAS, Cecil Jesse, BS; American business executive; b. 15 April 1932, Miami; s. of David Edward Silas and Hilda Videll Silas (née Carver); m. Theodosea Hejda 1965; three s. one d.; ed Miami Sr High School, Georgia Inst. of Tech.; joined Phillips Petroleum Co. 1953–; Pres. Phillips Petroleum Co. Europe-Africa, Brussels and London 1968–74; Man. Dir NRG Europe-Africa, London 1974–76; Vice-Pres. Gas and Gas Liquids, NRG, Bartlesville, Okla 1976–78; Sr Vice-Pres. Natural Resources Group, Bartlesville 1978–80, Exec. Vice-Pres. 1980–82; Pres. and COO (also Dir and Chair. Exec. Cttee) Phillips Petroleum Co. 1982–85, Chair. and CEO 1985–94; Chair. Bd American Petroleum Inst. –1993, Bd U.S. Chamber of Commerce; mem. Bd of Dirs Halliburton Co.; Dir Ethics Resource Centre; Commdr, Royal Order of St Olav, Norway 1976. *Leisure interests:* golf, fishing, hunting. *Address:* 2400 Terrace Drive, Bartlesville, OK 74004, USA (Home). *Telephone:* (918) 333-8577 (Home).

SILAYEV, Ivan Stepanovich; Russian politician; b. 21 Oct. 1930; m.; two c.; ed Kazan Aviation Inst.; mem. CPSU 1959–91; foreman, shop Supt, deputy chief engineer, chief engineer, plant Dir in Gorky 1954–74; Deputy Minister of Aircraft Industry of USSR 1974–77, First Deputy Minister 1977–80, Minister 1981–85; Minister of Machine Tool and Instrument-Making Industry of USSR 1980–81; mem. of CPSU Cen. Cttee 1981–91; Deputy Pres. Council of Ministers of the USSR 1985–89; Pres. Council of Ministers of the RSFSR 1989–91; Pres. Inter-Republican Econ. Cttee of the USSR 1991; Russian Perm. Rep. to EC (now EU) 1992–94; Pres. Bd of Dirs Ecology of Russia Consortium 1995–; Chair. Bd Moscow Interregional Commercial Bank 1996–, Int. Union of Mechanical Engineers 1997–; Deputy to USSR Supreme Soviet 1981–89; Hero of Socialist Labour 1975; Lenin Prize 1972. *Address:* International Union of Mechanical Engineers, Bolskaya Dmitrovka 5, Moscow, Russia (Office). *Telephone:* (095) 203-06-08.

SILBER, John Robert, PhD, LHD, LLD EdD, LittD, FRSA; American professor of philosophy and university administrator; b. 15 Aug. 1926, San Antonio, Tex.; s. of Paul G. Silber and Jewell Joslin; m. Kathryn Underwood 1947; one s. (deceased) six d.; ed Trinity, Northwestern and Yale Univs; Instructor in Philosophy, Yale Univ. 1952–55; Asst Prof., Univ. of Texas 1955–59, Assoc. Prof. 1959–62, Prof. of Philosophy 1962–70, Chair. Dept of Philosophy 1962–67, Chair. Comparative Studies Program 1967, Univ. Prof. of Arts and Letters 1967–70, Dean, Coll. of Arts and Sciences 1967–70; Univ. Prof. and Prof. of Philosophy and Law, Boston Univ. 1971–, Prof. of Int. Relations 1996–, Pres. 1971–96, Chancellor 1996–; mem. Bd of Dirs Americans for Medical Progress 1992–, Chair. 1994–95, mem. Exec. Cttee 1995–; mem. Bd of Dirs Northeast Savings Bank 1988–95, US Surgical Corpn 1994–98, Mutual of America Institutional Funds Inc. 1996–; Vice-Chair. US Strategic Inst.; Chair. Mass. Bd of Educ. 1996–99; mem. Bd of Dirs Nat. Humanities Faculty 1968–72, Exec. Bd, Nat. Humanities Inst. 1975–78, Bd of Dirs New England Holocaust Memorial Cttee; mem. Bd of Trustees Boston Univ. 1971–, Coll. of St Scholastica 1973–85, Univ. of Denver 1985–89, Adelphi Univ. 1989–97; mem. Pres.'s Advisory Bd, Radio Broadcasting to Cuba 1985–92; Pres. Southwestern Philosophy Soc. 1966–67; Fulbright Research Fellow 1959–60; Guggenheim Fellow 1963–64; Wilbur Lucius Cross Medal, Yale Univ. 1971, Ehrenmedaille, Univ. of Heidelberg 1986. *Publications:* The

Ethical Significance of Kant's "Religion" 1960, Democracy: Its Counterfeits and Its Promise 1967, The Tuition Dilemma 1978, Straight Shooting: What's Wrong with America and How to Fix It 1989, Ist Amerika zu Retten? 1992; Ed. Kant's "Religion Within the Limits of Reason Alone" 1960, Works in Continental Philosophy 1967; Assoc. Ed. Kant-Studien 1968–87, From Thebes to Auschwitz 1998, The Betrayal of Liberalism 1999; syndicated weekly column; articles in nat. press and philosophical journals. *Address:* Office of the Chancellor, Boston University, 147 Bay State Road, Boston, MA 02215, USA (Office). *Telephone:* (617) 353-4300 (Office). *Fax:* (617) 353-9674.

SILBERMAN, Laurence Hirsch, LLB; American lawyer, banker and diplomatist; b. 12 Oct. 1935, York, Pa; s. of William Silberman and Anna Hirsch; m. Rosalie Gaull 1957; one s. two d.; ed Dartmouth Coll., Harvard Law School; with Moore, Torkildson & Rice, Quinn & Moore, law firm 1961–64; partner Moore, Silberman & Schulze 1964–67; lawyer Nat. Labor Relations Bd 1967–69; solicitor, Labor Dept 1969–70, Under-Sec. for Labor Affairs 1970–73; Partner Steptoe & Johnson 1973–74; Deputy Attorney-Gen., Dept of Justice 1974–75; Amb. to Yugoslavia 1975–77 (withdrawn); Man. Partner Morrison and Foerster (Washington, DC) 1978–79, 1983–85; Exec. Vice-Pres. Legal and Govt Affairs Div., Crocker Nat. Bank 1979–83; Sr Fellow, American Enterprise Inst. for Public Policy Research, Washington, DC 1977–78, Visiting Fellow 1978–85; Vice-Chair. Advisory Council on Gen. Govt, Republican Nat. Comm. 1977–80; mem. US Gen. Advisory Cttee on Arms Control and Disarmament 1981–85; Assoc. Prof. of Admin. Law Georgetown Univ., Washington 1987–94, 1999–2001, New York Univ. 1995–96, Harvard 1998; US Circuit Judge 1985–. *Address:* US Court of Appeals, DC Circuit, US Courthouse, Washington, DC 20001, USA.

SILBERSTON, (Zangwill) Aubrey, CBE, MA; British professor of economics; b. 26 Jan. 1922, London; s. of Louis Silberston and Polly Silberston (née Kern); m. 1st Dorothy Marion Nicholls 1945 (divorced); m. 2nd Michèle Ledić 1985; one s. (one d. deceased); ed Hackney Downs School, London, Jesus Coll. Cambridge; Economist, Courtaulds Ltd 1946–50; Research Fellow St Catharine's Coll. Cambridge 1950–53, Univ. Lecturer in Econs, Cambridge 1951–71, Fellow St John's Coll. 1958–71, Chair. Faculty Bd of Econs and Politics 1966–70; Official Fellow in Econs, Nuffield Coll. Oxford 1971–78, Dean 1972–78; Prof. of Econs Imperial Coll. London 1978–87, Sr Research Fellow, Business School 1987–; mem. Monopolies Comm. 1965–68, Bd British Steel Corpn 1967–76, Royal Comm. on the Press 1974–77, Restrictive Practices Court 1986–92, Royal Comm. on Environmental Pollution 1986–96; Sec.-Gen. Royal Econ. Soc. 1979–92, Vice-Pres. 1992–; Pres. Confed. of European Econ. Asscns. 1988–90, Vice-Pres. 1990–92; Sr. Adviser, London Economics 1992–. *Publications:* Education and Training for Industrial Management 1955, The Motor Industry 1959, Economic Impact of the Patent System 1973, The Multi-Fibre Arrangement and the UK Economy 1984, The Future of the Multi-Fibre Arrangement 1989, Technology and Economic Progress (Ed.) 1989, Environmental Economics (Ed.) 1995, Beyond the Multifibre Arrangement 1995, The Changing Industrial Map of Europe 1996; articles in Economic Journal, Oxford Economic Papers etc. *Leisure interests:* opera, ballet. *Address:* 53 Prince's Gate, London, SW7 2PG, England. *Telephone:* (20) 7594-9354. *Fax:* (20) 7594-9353.

SILGUY, Yves-Thibault Christian Marie de; French diplomatist; b. 22 July 1948, Rennes; s. of Raymond de Silguy and Claude de Pompery; m. Jacqueline de Montillet de Grenaud; one s. one d.; ed Inst. Saint-Martin, Faculté de Droit et des Sciences Economiques, Rennes, Univ. de Paris I, Inst. d'Etudes Politiques de Paris and Ecole Nat. d'Admin; entered Ministry of Foreign Affairs 1976; Deputy Chef de Cabinet to François-Xavier Ortoli, Vice-Pres. of EC Comm. 1981–85; Second Counsellor, Washington, DC 1985–86; Adviser on European Questions and Int. Econs, Office of Prime Minister Chirac 1986–88; Dir of Int. Affairs, Usinor-Sacilor 1990–93; Adviser on European Affairs to Prime Minister Balladur 1993–94; Commr for Economic and Monetary Union, EC 1995–99; mem. Man. Bd Suez Lyonnaise des eaux 2000–, Dir-Gen. in charge of Int. Affairs, Inst. of Relations and Resources 2001–; Pres. Algeria Cttee Mouvement des entreprises de France (MEDEF) 2000–; Chevalier, Légion d'honneur, Officier du Mérite agricole, Officier des Arts et des Lettres. *Publications:* Le Syndrome du diplodocus 1996, L'Euro 1998, L'Economie, fil d'Ariane de l'Europe 2000. *Leisure interests:* sailing, hunting, tennis. *Address:* Ministry of Foreign Affairs, Service de la Valise, 37 quai d'Orsay, 75007 Paris (Office); Suez, 16 rue de la Ville-l'Evêque, 1 rue d'Astorg, 75008 Paris, France (Office). *E-mail:* ydesilguy@suez.fr (Office).

SILJA, Anja; German opera singer; b. 17 April 1940, Berlin; m. Christoph von Dohnanyi; one s. two d.; began career at age of ten; first opera engagement in Brunswick 1956; sang at Bayreuth Festival 1960–70, debut with Senta; appeared at major opera houses in Europe and USA, including festivals at Glyndebourne, Salzburg and Aix-en-Provence; repertoire includes Queen of the Night (Die Zauberflöte), Salome, Lulu, Fidelio, Elektra, Turandot, Ariadne, Isolde, Brünnhilde, Zerbinetta, Konstanze, Fiordiligi, Leonore, Santuzza, The Four Ladies (Les Contes d'Hoffmann), Katerina (Lady Macbeth of Mtsensk), Desdemona, Renata (Fiery Angel), Cassandra, Medea, Marie (Wozzeck), Hana Glawari (The Merry Widow); recent appearances as Herodias, Klytämnestra, Amma, Geschwitz, Jokaste, Emilia Marty, Kostelnicka, Mère Marie (Dialogues des Carmélites), The Seven Deady Sins, Erwartung, Pierrot Lunaire; many recordings and videos; debut as opera producer in Brussels with Lohengrin; subject of biog.: Sehnsucht nach dem Unerreichbaren; Kammersängerin; Bundesverdienstkveuz 1988. *Leisure interests:* driving, decorating, tennis, ice-skating, gardening. *Address:* c/o Artists Management, Rütistrasse 52, 8044 Zürich-Gockhausen, Switzerland. *Telephone:* (1) 8218957. *Fax:* (1) 8210127. *E-mail:* schuetz@artistsman.com.

SILLARD, Yves; French aerospace engineer; b. 5 Jan. 1936, Coutances, Manche; s. of Roger Sillard and Madeleine (Guerrand) Sillard; m. 1st Annick Legrand 1966 (divorced); m. 2nd Hélène Benech-Badiou 1982 (divorced); m. 3rd Martine Gautry 1999; ed Ecole Massillon, Ecole Polytechnique, Ecole nat. Supérieure de l'Aéronautique; Test. Eng and then Head of Colomb-Béchard unit of Centre d'Essais en Vol 1960–62, Tech. Dir of Cazeaux annex 1963–64; Head of Concorde Programme at Secrétariat général à l'Aviation civile 1965; Head of Div. setting up French Guiana Space Centre, Kourou 1966–68; Tech. Dir and then Dir Space Centre, Kourou 1968–72; Dir of Launchers, Centre Nat. des Etudes Spatiales 1973–76, Man. Dir 1976–82; Chair. and Man. Dir Centre nat. pour l'exploitation des océans 1982–; Chair. Conseil d'administration de l'institut français de recherche pour l'exploitation de la mer 1985–89; French Nat. Co-ordinator for EUREKA Programme 1986–89; Gen. Del., Armaments 1989–93; mem. Atomic Energy Cttee 1989–93; Chair., Man. Dir Cogepag 1993–, Défence conseil international (DCI) 1993–97; Asst Sec. Gen. for Scientific Affairs and Environment, NATO 1998–2001; Vice-Chair. Nat. Acad. for Aeronautics and Space; mem. Scientific Council for Defence; Commdr, Légion d'honneur, Chevalier, Ordre nat. du Mérite, Médaille de l'Aéronautique, Commdr Merit (FRG). *Address:* 8 rue de la Forge, 17800 Brives sur Charente, France. *Telephone:* (5) 46-95-01-56 (Home). *E-mail:* ysillard@cdub.internet.fr (Home).

SILLITOE, Alan; British author; b. 4 March 1928, Nottingham; s. of Christopher Sillitoe and Sabina Burton; m. Ruth Fainlight 1959; one s. one d.; ed elementary school, Radford, Nottingham; worked in various factories, Nottingham 1942–45; air traffic control Asst 1945–46; served as wireless operator, RAF, Malaya 1946–49; lived six years in France and Spain; Visiting Prof. of English, DeMontfort Univ., Leicester 1993–97; Fellow, Royal Geographical Soc., Royal Inst. of Navigation; Hon. Fellow, Manchester Polytechnic, De Montfort Univ. 1998; Dr hc (Nottingham Polytechnic) 1990, (Nottingham Univ.) 1994; Hawthornden Prize 1960. *Film screenplays:* Saturday Night and Sunday Morning, The Loneliness of the Long Distance Runner, The Ragman's Daughter, Counterpoint. *Publications:* (novels) Saturday Night and Sunday Morning 1958, The General 1960, Key to the Door 1961, The Death of William Posters 1965, A Tree on Fire 1967, A Start in Life 1970, Travels in Nihilon 1971, Raw Material 1972, The Flame of Life 1974, The Widower's Son 1976, The Storyteller 1979, Her Victory 1982, The Lost Flying Boat 1983, Down From The Hill 1984, Life Goes On 1985, Out of the Whirlpool 1987, The Open Door 1989, Last Loves 1990, Leonard's War: A Love Story 1991, Snowstop 1993, Alligator Playground 1997, The Broken Chariot 1998, The German Numbers Woman 1999, Birthday 2001; (stories) The Loneliness of the Long Distance Runner 1959, The Ragman's Daughter 1963, Guzman, Go Home 1968, Men, Women and Children 1973, The Second Chance 1981, The Far Side of the Street 1988, Collected Stories 1995; (essays) Mountains and Caverns 1975, The Mentality of the Picaresque Hero 1993; (poems) The Rats and Other Poems 1960, A Falling Out of Love 1964, Love in the Environs of Voronezh 1968, Barbarians and Other Poems 1974, Storm and Other Poems 1974, Snow on the North Side of Lucifer 1979, Sun Before Departure 1984, Tides and Stone Walls (with Victor Bowley) 1986, Collected Poems 1993; (travel) Road to Volgograd 1964, Leading the Blind: A Century of guide book travel 1815–1914 1995, The Saxon Shore Way (with Fay Godwin) 1983, Nottinghamshire (with David Sillitoe) 1986; (plays) Three Plays 1978; All Citizens are Soldiers 1969 (trans. of Lope de Vega play Fuenteovejuna, with Ruth Fainlight); (children's books) The City Adventures of Marmalade Jim 1967, Big John and the Stars 1977, The Incredible Fencing Fleas 1978, Marmalade Jim on the Farm 1980, Marmalade Jim and the Fox 1985, Alligator Playground 1998; (autobiog.) Life Without Armour 1995. *Leisure interests:* geography, navigation, radio communications, travel. *Address:* 14 Ladbroke Terrace, London, W11 3PG, England.

SILLS, Beverly; American coloratura soprano; b. Belle Silverman, 25 May 1929, Brooklyn, New York; d. of the late Morris Silverman and of Sonia Bahn; m. Peter Bulkeley Greenough 1956; one s. one d. three step-c.; ed pupil of Estelle Liebling; debut at San Francisco Opera as Helen of Troy in Mefistofele 1953, at New York City Opera as Rosalinda in Die Fledermaus 1955; with New York City Opera 1955–80, Gen. Dir 1979–88, Pres. New York City Opera Bd 1989–90, Man. Dir Metropolitan Opera, New York 1991–94; Chair. Lincoln Center 1994–2002; debut at the Vienna State Opera as Queen of the Night (The Magic Flute) 1967, at La Scala, Milan in The Siege of Corinth 1969, at Royal Opera House, Covent Garden in title role of Lucia di Lammermoor 1970, Metropolitan Opera, New York as Pamira in Siege of Corinth 1975; other best known roles include Cleopatra (Julius Caesar), Queen Elizabeth I (Roberto Devereux), all three heroines in The Tales of Hoffmann, Manon (Manon), Violetta (La Traviata), Marie (Daughter of the Regiment), Rosina (Barber of Seville); title roles in Anna Bolena and Maria Stuarda, Norma, Lucrezia Borgia; recordings for Columbia, RCA, Angel, ABC–Audio Treasury, Universal Classics; has appeared at most of the maj. opera houses of Europe and Latin America and given numerous recitals with leading orchestras throughout USA; retd 1980; Dir Warner Communications Inc., New York 1982–, American Express, Macy's; host Live from Lincoln Center (TV series) 1998; Presidential Medal of Freedom, Kennedy Center Honor Award, Heinz Award 1995, other awards; Chevalier des Arts et des Lettres. *Publications:*

Bubbles: A Self-Portrait 1976, Beverly (autobiog.) 1987. *Address:* c/o Vincent and Farrell Associates, 157 West Street, Suite 502, New York, NY 10019, USA.

SILUNGWE, Hon. Mr. Justice Annel Musenga, LLM; Zambian judge; b. 10 Jan. 1936, Mbala; s. of Solo Musenga Silungwe and Janet Nakafunda Silungwe; m. Abigail Nanyangwe Silungwe 1960; one s. four d.; ed Univs. of Zambia and London, Inner Temple, London; Resident Magistrate 1967, Sr Resident Magistrate (Class II) 1968, (Class I) 1970; Judge of the High Court 1971; nominated MP and apptd. Minister of Legal Affairs and Attorney-Gen. 1973; State Counsel 1974; Chief Justice 1975–92; Judge, Court of Appeal, Seychelles 1992–; Judge of High Court and Acting Judge of Supreme Court, Namibia 1999–; Dir Justice Training Centre, Ministry of Justice, Namibia 1994–99; Chair. Judicial Services Comm. 1975–92, Council of Legal Educ. 1975–92, Council of Law Reporting 1975–92; Rotary Int. Award for Community Service 1989. *Leisure interests:* music, golf, photography. *Address:* High Court, Private Bag 13179, Windhoek, Namibia. *Telephone:* (61) 2277927 (Office); (61) 242705 (Home). *Fax:* (61) 221686 (Office); (61) 242705 (Home).

SILVA-CALDERÓN, Alvaro; Venezuelan international organization executive; b. 9 June 1929, Teresén, Monagas State; m. Judith Pérez; one s. one d.; ed Universidad Cen. de Venezuela; Lecturer, Dept of Mining and Hydrocarbons Law, Law School, Universidad Cen. de Venezuela, now Prof. Emer.; mem. advisory team of Juan Pablo Pérez Alfonso; fmr mem. Regional Legislature, Monagas State; fmr mem. Nat. Congress, Pres. Int. Treaties Subcttee and mem. Energy and Mines Cttee; Minister of Energy and Mines 2000–02; Sec.-Gen. OPEC July 2002–; fmr External Dir Bd Petróleos de Venezuela, SA; fmr Dir Supreme Electoral Council of Venezuela; fmr Chief Legal Advisor to Ministry of Energy and Mines (also Dir.-Gen. and Vice-Minister of Mines); fmr columnist for El Globo nat. daily newspaper; mem. and del. Venezuelan Chapter at World Oil Congress; mem. Nat. Energy Council; Order Francisco de Miranda (First Class), Order Juan Pablo Pérez Alfonso (First Class), Merit Order Ambrosio Plaza (First Class), Order Sol de Carabobo (Chief Official), Order Farten de Bie Faire (Portugal), Merit Order Honor y Gloria (Portugal); OPEC Second Summit Dip. *Address:* OPEC, Obere Donaustrasse 93, 1020 Vienna, Austria (Office). *Telephone:* (1) 211-12-279 (Office). *Fax:* (1) 214-98-27 (Office). *E-mail:* info@opec.org (Office). *Website:* www.opec.org (Office).

SILVA DE LIMA, Maria Osmarina (Marina); Brazilian politician; b. 8 Feb. 1958, Amazon; ed Fed. Univ., Acre; fmr rubber tapper; teacher of history, Centro Educucional e Cultural Meta, Rio Branco 1985, Complexo Escolar de Ensino Médio, Rio Branco 1985–87, Fed. Univ., Acre 1986; co-f. ind. rubber tapping trade union Movt, organized 'empates' (peaceful demonstrations) against deforestation; elected councillor, Rio Branco 1988–89; mem. Brazilian Workers' Party; State Rep. 1990–94, Senator 1995–2002; Minister of the Environment 2003–; mem. Centre of Amazonian Workers (CTA); Nat. Homage, Bahia Legis. Ass. 1995, Citizen Paulistana, Municipal Chamber of Sao Paulo 1995, Municipal Legis. Medal, Municipal Chamber of Bela Horizonte 1995, Goldman Environmental Prize for Latin America 1996, Woman of the Year, MS Magazine, USA 1997. *Address:* Ministry of the Environment, SAIN, Av. L4 Norte, Edificio Sede Terreo, 70800 Brasília, DF, Brazil (Office). *Telephone:* (61) 226-8221 (Office). *Fax:* (61) 322-1058 (Office). *Website:* www .mma.gov.br (Office).

SILVEIRA GODINHO, José António da; Portuguese fmr politician, economist and business executive; b. 16 Oct. 1943, Lisbon; s. of Raul Catarino Godinho and Angela da Silveira Godinho; m. Isabel Maria Canhoto Segura de Faria 1972; three s.; ed Lisbon Tech. Univ.; Sr Vice-Pres. Banco de Portugal 1975–79; mem. Man. Bd Banco Pinto & Sotto Mayor 1979–82; Sec. of State for Finance 1980–81; mem. Exec. Bd Banco Espírito Santo 1982–93; Sec. of State for Nat. Defence 1986–87; Minister of Internal Affairs 1987–90; Amb. to OECD 1993–96; mem. Bd of Dir Espírito Santo, Ca. de Seguros SA 1996–, AdvanceCare, SA 1999–; mem. Gen. Council Asscn. of Portuguese Economists 1999–. *Leisure interests:* reading, travelling, music, sport. *Address:* Rua de Buenos Aires, 43-3°, 1200–623 Lisbon, Portugal. *Telephone:* (21) 353-4449 (Office); (21) 390-5236 (Home). *Fax:* (21) 350-3575 (Office). *E-mail:* sgodinho@ tranquilidade.pt (Office).

SILVER, Casey; American film company executive; began career as screenwriter; Asst to Adrian Lyne (q.v.); fmr Vice-Pres. Production, Sr Vice-Pres. Production TriStar Pictures, Dir of Devt and Production Simpson-Bruckheimer; joined Universal Pictures as Exec. Vice-Pres. Production 1987, Pres. 1989, Pres. Universal Pictures 1994, Chair. 1995–. *Address:* Universal Pictures, 100 Universal City Plaza, Universal City, CA 91608, USA.

SILVER, Joan Micklin, BA; American film and theatre director and scriptwriter; b. 24 May 1935, Omaha, Neb.; d. of Maurice Micklin and Doris Shoshone; m. Raphael Silver 1956; three d.; ed Sarah Lawrence Coll.; began career as writer for educational films; original screenplay for Limbo purchased by Universal Pictures; commissioned by Learning Corpn of America to write and direct short narrative film The Immigrant Experience 1972 and wrote and dir two children's films for same co.; Dir plays: Album and Maybe I'm Doing it Wrong; also Dir for TV. *Films include:* Hester Street (dir and screenplay), Bernice Bobs Her Hair (dir and screenplay), Between the Lines (dir), On the Yard (producer), Head Over Heels (dir and screenplay, retitled Chilly Scenes of Winter), Crossing Delancey (dir), Loverboy (dir), Big Girls Don't Cry... They Get Even (dir), In the Presence of Mine Enemies (dir) 1996, Fish in the Bathtub 1997, Invisible Child (dir) 1998, Charms for the Easy Life (dir) 2002, Hunger Point 2003. *Radio:* Great Jewish Short Stories from

Eastern Europe and Beyond (dir) 1995. *Address:* Silverfilm Productions Inc., 510 Park Avenue, Suite 9B, New York, NY 10022-1105, USA. *Telephone:* (642) 282-0312. *Fax:* (212) 421-8254. *E-mail:* jmicksil@aol.com (Office).

SILVER, Joel; American film producer; b. 14 July 1952, South Orange, NJ; ed New York Univ.; fmrly Asst to Lawrence Gordon, Pres. Lawrence Gordon Productions; producer, Vice-Pres. Universal Pictures; appeared in film Who Framed Roger Rabbit 1988. *Films:* The Warrior 1979, Xanadu 1980, 48 Hours 1982, Jekyll & Hyde... Together Again 1982, Streets of Fire 1984, Brewster's Millions 1985, Weird Science 1985, Commando 1985, Jumpin' Jack Flash 1986, Lethal Weapon 1986, Predator 1987, Action Jackson 1988, Die Hard 1988, Lethal Weapon 2 1989, Roadhouse 1989, Ford Fairlane 1990, Die Hard 2 1990, Predator 2 1990, Hudson Hawk 1991, Ricochet 1991, The Last Boy Scout 1991, Lethal Weapon 3 1992, Demolition Man 1993, The Hudsucker Proxy, Richie Rich 1994, Demon Knight 1994, Assassins 1995, Fair Game 1995, Executive Decision 1996, Conspiracy Theory, Father's Day, Lethal Weapon 4 1998, Romeo Must Die 1999, Made Men 1999, The Matrix 1999, The House on Haunted Hill 1999. *Television:* Tales from the Crypt, Two Fisted Tales, Parker Can, W.E.I.R.D. World. *Address:* Silver Pictures, c/o Warner Bros Pictures, 4000 Warner Boulevard, Building 90, Burbank, CA 91522-0001, USA.

SILVERMAN, Bernard Walter, PhD, ScD, B.TH., FRS; British professor of statistics; b. 22 Feb. 1952; s. of Elias Silverman and Helen Silverman; m. Rowena Fowler 1985; one s.; ed City of London School, Jesus Coll., Cambridge; Research Fellow Jesus Coll., Cambridge 1975–77; Calculator Devt Man. Sinclair Radionics 1976–77; Weir Fellow Univ. Coll., Oxford 1977–78, also Jr lecturer Oxford Univ.; lecturer, then Reader, Prof. of Statistics Univ. of Bath 1978–93, Head School of Mathematical Sciences 1988–91; Prof. of Statistics Univ. of Bristol 1993–99, Henry Overton Wills Prof. of Mathematics 1999–; Chartered Statistician; Pres. Inst. of Mathematical Statistics 2000–01; Provost Inst. for Advanced Studies 2000–; Ordained Deacon (Church of England) 1999–, priest 2000–; various awards from learned socs. for statistical research, UK and USA. *Publications include:* Density Estimation for Statistics and Data Analysis 1986, Nonparametric Regression and Generalized Linear Models (with P. J. Green) 1994, Functional Data Analysis (with J.O. Ramsay) 1997; numerous papers in learned journals. *Leisure interests:* church, opera, theatre, family, talking. *Address:* School of Mathematics, University of Bristol, University Walk, Bristol, BS8 1TW (Office); Institute for Advanced Studies, University of Bristol, Royal Fort House, Bristol, BS8 1UJ, England (Office). *Telephone:* (117) 928-9171 (Office). *E-mail:* b.w.silverman@ bristol.ac.uk (Office). *Website:* www.stats.bris.ac.uk.bernard, www.stats.bris .ac.uk/~bernard (Office).

SILVERMAN, Fred, MA; American broadcasting executive; b. 13 Sept. 1937, New York; m. Cathy Kihn; one s. one d.; ed Syracuse Univ., Ohio State Univ.; with WGN-TV Chicago; exec. position WP1X-TV New York; Dir Daytime Programmes CBS-TV New York, Vice-Pres. Programmes 1970–75; Pres. ABC Entertainment 1975–78; Pres. NBC 1978–81; ind. film producer 1981–; Pres. The Fred Silverman Co. 1986–.

SILVERMAN, Henry Richard, LLB; American business executive and lawyer; b. 2 Aug. 1940, New York; s. of Herbert Silverman and Roslyn (née Moskowitz) Silverman; m. 1st Susan H. Herson 1965 (divorced 1977); two d.; m. 2nd Nancy Ann Kraner 1978; one d.; ed Hackley School, Tarrytown, NY, Williams Coll., Philadelphia and New York Univs; with USNR 1965–73; called to Bar NY 1965; with U.S. Tax Court 1965; with U.S. Court of Appeals 1965; law practice 1965–66; with White, Weld & Co. 1966; gen. partner Oppenheimer & Co. 1966–70; Pres., CEO ITI Corpn 1970–72; f., Pres. Trans-York Securities Corpn 1972; CEO Vavasseur America Ltd 1974–75; Gen. Partner Brisbane Partners 1976–77; Prin. various investment groups 1977–, Silverman Energy Co. 1977–, NBC Channel 20 1977–83, ABC Channel 9 1977–81, Delta Queen Steamboat 1977–86, also Dir; Pres., CEO Reliance Capital Corpn (subsidiary Reliance Group Holdings Inc.) 1982–, Sr Vice-Pres. Business Devt Reliance Group Holdings Inc. 1982–90; Gen. Partner Blackstone Group 1990–91; Chair., CEO HFS Inc. 1990–; Dir NY Univ. Hosp. 1987–. *Leisure interest:* tennis. *Address:* Cendant Corporation, 9 West 57th Street, Floor 37, New York, NY 10019, USA (Office).

SILVERMAN, Marcia, MEconSc; American business executive; one s.; ed Univ. of Pennsylvania; fmr employee Nat. Labour Relations Bd; worked in Public Relations Div., J. Walter Thompson 1978–81; joined Washington office, Ogilvy & Mather Public Affairs 1981, Head of Washington Office 1990–2000; Pres. of the Americas, Ogilvy Public Relations Worldwide 2000–02, CEO Aug.2002–. *Address:* Ogilvy Public Relations Worldwide, 909 Third Avenue, New York, NY 10022, USA (Office). *Telephone:* 212-880-5200 (Office). *Fax:* 212-697-8250 (Office). *E-mail:* silverman.marcia@ogilvypr.com (Office). *Website:* www.ogilvypr.com (Office).

SILVERSTONE, Alicia; American actress; b. 4 Oct. 1976, Calif.; stage debut in play Carol's Eve at Met Theatre, LA; starred in three Aerosmith videos including Cryin'; formed own production co. First Kiss Productions. *Films:* The Crush 1993, The Babysitter 1995, True Crime 1995, Le Nouveau Monde 1995, Hideaway 1995, Clueless 1995, Batman and Robin 1997, Excess Baggage (also producer) 1997, Free Money 1998, Love's Labour's Lost 1999, Blast from the Past 1999. *Television:* Torch Song 1993, Shattered Dreams 1993, The Cool and the Crazy 1994, The Wonder Years 1997. *Address:* c/o

Premiere Artists Agency, Suite 510, 8899 Beverly Boulevard, Los Angeles, CA 90048; First Kiss Productions, c/o Columbia Pictures, 10202 Washington Boulevard, Culver City, CA 90232, USA.

SILVESTRINI, HE Cardinal Achille; Italian ecclesiastic; b. 25 Oct. 1923, Brisighella; ordained Catholic priest 1946, elected Archbishop of Novaliciana, Mauritania 1979, consecrated bishop 1979; Sec. Council for Public Affairs of the Church 1979; cr. Cardinal 1988 with title of St Benedict Outside the Gate of St Paul; Prefect of the Supreme Tribunal of the Apostolic Signatura 1988–91; Prefect of the Congregation for the Eastern Churches 1991– and Grand Chancellor of the Pontifical Eastern Inst.; mem. Congregations for the Doctrine of the Faith, for the Oriental Churches, for the Causes of the Saints, for the Bishops, for the Evangelization of Peoples, for Catholic Educ.; mem. Pontificial Councils for the Interpretation of Legislative Texts, for Inter-Religious Dialogue. *Address:* Congregation for the Eastern Churches, Palazzo del Bramante, Via della Conciliazione 34, 00193 Rome, Italy. *Telephone:* (06) 69884282. *Fax:* (06) 69884300.

SILVESTROV, Valentin Vasilyevich; Ukrainian composer; b. 30 Sept. 1937, Kiev; ed Kiev State Conservatory (pupil of B. Lyatoshinsky); author of compositions performed in USSR and many countries of Europe and in USA; S. Koussevitsky Prize (USA) 1967, Prize of Gaudeamus Soc. (Netherlands) 1970. *Compositions include:* 5 symphonies for large symphony orchestra 1963–82, Symphony for baritone with orchestra Echo Momentum on verses of A. Pushkin 1987, string quartets 1978, 1988, Dedication – symphony for violin and orchestra 1991, Mertamusica for piano and orchestra 1992, numerous chamber ensembles, piano pieces, vocal cycles, choruses. *Address:* Entuziastov str. 35/1, Apt. 49, 252147 Kiev, Ukraine (Home). *Telephone:* (44) 517-04-47 (Home).

SIM WONG HOO; Singaporean business executive; ed Ngee Ann Polytechnic; f. Creative Technology Ltd, Singapore 1981; f. Creative Labs., USA; launched Sound Blaster PC card 1989, Sound Blaster Pro 1991; Chair. Technopreneurship 21 Pvt. Sector Cttee. *Publication:* Chaotic Thoughts from the Old Millennium. *Address:* Creative Technology Ltd, 31 International Business Park, Creative Resource, Singapore 609921, Singapore (Office).

SIMAI, Mihály; Hungarian economist; b. 4 April 1930, Budapest; s. of Mátyás Simai and Jolán Rosenberg; m. Vera Bence 1953; one d.; Prof. of Int. Econs and Nat. Business, Univ. of Econs, Budapest 1971–, Dir of Grad. Studies in Int. Bus. and Strategy 1987–, in Int. Relations 1991–; Deputy Dir of Research, Inst. for World Econs, Budapest 1973–87; mem. Hungarian Acad. of Sciences 1979–; Pres. Hungarian UN Ass., Hungarian Nat. Cttee for UNICEF 1981–; Hon. Pres. World Fed. of UN Ass. 1982–; Chair. Council UN Univ. 1990–92; Vice-Pres. Int. Studies Asscn 1988–; fmr Pres. Ed. Cttee Acta Oeconomica; Dir Hungarian Acad. of Sciences Inst. of World Econs 1987–91; Dir UN Univ. World Inst. for Devt Econs Research 1993–96; mem. Governing Council, Nat. Studies Asscn 1984–, Governing Bd Karl Polanyi Inst. 1988–, Advisory Bd for UN TNCs 1990–, Editorial Bd Environmental Econs 1991–, Advisory Bd Global Governance 1993–; Peace Fellow US Inst. for Peace 1991–92; Labour Order of Merit (Golden Degree), Order of the Star of Hungary (Golden Degree), Order of the Flag of the Hungarian Repub. 1990. *Publications:* Capital Export in the Contemporary Capitalist System 1962, The World Economic System of Capitalism, 1965, View from the 26th Floor 1969, Joint Ventures with Foreign Partners 1971, The United States before the 200th Anniversary 1974, Planning and Plan Implementation in the Developing Countries 1975, The United Nations and the Global Problems 1977, Interdependence and Conflicts in the World Economy 1981, Economic Decolonization and the Developing Countries 1981, The United Nations Today and Tomorrow 1985, Power, Technology and the World Economy of the 1990s 1990, Foreign Direct Investments in Hungary 1991, The Future of Global Governance: Managing Risk and Change in the International System 1994, International Business Policy 1997, The Ages of Global Transformations 2001; numerous articles on int. econ. and political issues. *Leisure interests:* hiking, skiing. *Address:* Institute for World Economics, Hungarian Academy of Sciences, 1014 Budapest, Országház utca 30, Hungary (Office). *Telephone:* (1) 224-6762 (Office). *Fax:* (1) 224-6765 (Office).

SIMATUPANG, Lt-Gen. Tahi Bonar; Indonesian international church official and retd army officer; b. 28 Jan. 1920, Sidikalang; s. of the late Simon Mangaraja Soaduon and of Mina Boru Sibuea; m. Sumarti Budiardjo 1949; two s. one d.; ed Mil. Acad.; Dir of Org., Gen. Staff of Indonesian Nat. Army 1945–48; Deputy Chief of Staff, Armed Forces of Repub. of Indonesia 1948–49, Acting Chief of Staff 1949–51, Chief of Staff 1951–54; Mil. Adviser to Govt of Indonesia 1954–59; retd from mil. service 1959; Pres. Council of Churches in Indonesia 1967, Christian Conf. in Asia 1973–77; mem. Presidium World Council of Churches 1975–83; mem. Supreme Advisory Council, Republic of Indonesia 1973–78; Hon. DHumLitt (Tulsa) 1969. *Publications:* Pioneer in War, Pioneer in Peace (Role of the Armed Forces in Indonesia) 1954, Report from Banaran—Experiences During the People's War 1959, Christian Task in Revolution 1966, National Resilience in the New Situation in Southeast Asia 1980, From Revolution to Development 1984, Christian Faith and Pancasile (the Indonesian State Ideology) 1984, Hope, Fear and Determination 1985, Christian Presence in War, Revolution and Development 1986, Indonesia: Leadership and National Security Perceptions 1987. *Leisure interest:* reading. *Address:* Jalan Diponegoro 55, Jakarta, Indonesia. *Telephone:* 337800.

SIMBOMANA, Adrien; Burundian politician; b. 9 April 1953, Bukeye, Muramvya; fmr Deputy Speaker Nat. Ass.; Gov. of Muramvya Prov. –1988; MP 1993–; fmr Vice-Pres. of Comm. on Nat. Unity; Prime Minister of Burundi 1988–92; fmr Minister of Planning; Highest Nat. Unity 1992. *Leisure interests:* music, sport (basketball). *Address:* PO Box 2251, Vugizo, Bujumbura, Burundi. *Telephone:* 910345 (Office); 212798 (Home). *E-mail:* sobugea@cbinf .com (Office).

SIMEÓN NEGRÍN, Rosa Elena; Cuban politician and virologist; b. 17 June 1943, Havana; m.; one d.; ed Marianao High School and Univ. of Havana; Chief, Dept of Virology, Nat. Center of Scientific Research (CENIC) 1968–73, Chief, Microbiological Div. 1974–76; Prof. School of Veterinary Medicine 1969–73, Nat. Hosp. and Nat. Center of Scientific Investigations 1975, Nat. Inst. of Veterinary Medicine 1977–78, 1981; Dir Nat. Center of Agric. Health (CENSA) 1985; Pres. Acad. of Sciences of Cuba 1985–94; Minister of Science, Tech. and the Environment 1994–; many other professional appointments; awards and decorations from Cuba, Czechoslovakia and France. *Publications:* articles in professional journals. *Address:* Ministry of Science, Technology and the Environment, Capitolio Nacional, 10200 Havana, Cuba. *Telephone:* (7) 62-8631. *Fax:* (7) 93-8654.

SIMHON, Shalom, BA; Israeli politician and social worker; b. 1956; m.; two c.; ed Univ. of Haifa; served in Israel Defence Forces; Exec. Dir Youth Section, Moshav Movt 1985–91, Chair. Social Dept 1991–93, Pension Fund 1993–2001; Sec.-Gen. Moshad Movt 1993–2001; mem. Knesset (Labor Party) 1996–; Chair. Agric. Cttee 1996; mem. Econ. Cttee and Finance Cttee 1996–2002; Chair. Finance Cttee 2000; Minister of Agric. and Rural Devt 2001–; Sec.-Gen. Agricultural Centre 1997–2001; fmr Chair. Bd of Tnuva. *Address:* Ministry of Agriculture and Rural Development, P.O. Box 30, Beit Dagan, Tel-Aviv 50200, Israel (Office). *Telephone:* 3-9485800 (Office). *Fax:* 3-9485835 (Office). *E-mail:* sar@moag.gov.il (Office).

SIMIC, Charles; American poet; b. 9 May 1938, Belgrade, Yugoslavia; s. of George Simic and Helen Matijevich; m. Helen Dubin; one s. one d.; ed Oak Park High School, Chicago, Univ. of Chicago and New York Univ.; arrived in USA 1954; army service 1961–64; worked for Chicago Sun-Times as proofreader; later business Man. Aperture Magazine 1966–69; Prof. of English, Calif. State Univ., Hayward 1970–73; Lecturer in American Literature Univ. of NH 1973–; first vol. of poems published 1967; PEN Int. Award for Translation 1970, 1980, Pulitzer Prize for Poetry for The World Doesn't End (prose poems) 1990. *Publications include:* poems: What the Grass Says 1967, White 1972, Biography and a Lament 1976, Austerities 1982, Selected Poems 1985, Unending Blues 1986, The World Doesn't End 1989, The Book of Gods and Devils 1990, Hotel Insomnia 1992, A Wedding in Hell 1994, Walking the Black Cat 1996, Jackstraws 1999, Night Picnic 2001; prose: The Uncertain Certainty 1985, Wonderful Words, Silent Truth 1990, The Unemployed Fortune Teller 1994, Orphan Factory 1997, A Fly in the Soup 2000. *Address:* P.O. Box 192, Stafford, NH 03884, USA; Department of English, University of New Hampshire, P.O. Box 192, Durham, NH 0382.

SIMION, Eugen Ioan, PhD; Romanian literary critic; b. 25 May 1933, Chiojdeanca, Prahova County; s. of Dragomir Simion and Sultana Simion; m. Adriana Manea 1957; one d.; ed Faculty of Philology, Bucharest Univ.; researcher Romanian Acad. 1957–62; Ed. Gazeta literară 1962–68; Asst Lecturer, Bucharest Univ. 1964, Assoc. Prof. 1971, Prof. of Romanian Literature 1990–; Visiting Prof. Sorbonne, Paris 1970–73; Dir Caiete critice (cultural review) 1991–; mem. Bd Romanian Writers' Union; mem. Romanian Acad. 1991, Vice-Pres. 1994, Pres. 1998–; mem. Academia Europaea, London 1992; Vice-Pres. Intergovernmental Cttee for the World Decade for Cultural Devt–UNESCO 1992; mem. Int. Union of Literary Critics; prizes of the Romanian Writers' Union; Prize of the Romanian Acad. *Publications include:* Eminescu's Fiction 1964, Trends in Today's Literature 1965, E Lovinescu the Sceptic Spirit 1971, The Romanian Writers Today Vol. I 1974, Vol. II 1976, Vol. III 1983, Vol. IV 1989; A Time to Live, a Time to Confess (Paris Diary), The Morning of Poets 1980, Defying Rhetoric 1985, Mercutio's Death 1993, Talking to Petru Dumitriu 1994, Mircea Eliade, A Spirit Amplitude 1995, The Return of the Author 1996, Critical Fragments I–III 1998–99. *Address:* Romanian Academy, Calea Victoriei 725, Bucharest (Office); Dr. Lister 8, Bucharest, Romania (Home). *Telephone:* (1) 3122760 (Office); (1) 4109748 (Home). *Fax:* (1) 3120209 (Office); (1) 3365855 (Home). *E-mail:* esimion@acad .ro (Office); mdc@rnc.ro (Home).

SIMITIS, Constantine (Costas), DJur; Greek politician and lawyer; b. 23 June 1936, Athens; s. of George Simitis and Fani Cristopoulou; m. Daphne Arkadiou; two c.; ed Univ. of Marburg and London School of Econs; Supreme Court lawyer 1961–; taught in W German univs. 1971–75; Prof. of Commercial Law, Univ. of Athens 1977; active in politics 1965–; mem. Nat. Council of Panhellenic Liberation Movt (PAK) during colonels' dictatorship, mem. Pasok 1974–, mem. Cen. Cttee of Pasok, Pres. 1996–; mem. Parl. 1985–; Minister of Agric. 1981–85, of Nat. Economy 1985–87, of Educ. and Religious Affairs 1989–90, of Industry, Energy, Tech. and Trade 1993–95; Prime Minister of Greece 1996–. *Publications:* several books and numerous articles in Greek and German on legal and econ. matters. *Address:* Herodou Atticou 19, Maximos Mansion, 10674 Athens, Greece. *Telephone:* (1) 3385242. *Fax:* (1) 7241776. *E-mail:* mail@primeminister.gr (Office). *Website:* www .primeminister.gr (Office).

ŠIMKO, Ivan, Ing.Econ., DIur; Slovak politician; b. 1 Jan. 1955, Bratislava; m.; four c.; ed Univ. of Econs, Bratislava, Comenius Univ., Bratislava; mem. staff

Inst. for Planning, Bratislava 1978–79; mem. staff Dept of Chief Architect, Bratislava 1979–89; Adviser to Deputy Prime Minister 1990; mem. Parl. 1990–; Vice-Chair. Legis. Council 1992; Minister of Justice 1992; Deputy Prime Minister 1994; mem. Nat. Council for the Slovak Repub. 1994–; Minister of the Interior 2001–02; Minister of Defence 2002–; mem. Nat. Council Cttee for Constitutional Law. *Leisure interests:* sport, literature. *Address:* Ministry of Defence, Kutuzovova 8, 832 47 Bratislava, Czech Republic (Office). *Telephone:* (2) 44258861 (Office). *Fax:* (2) 44258904 (Office). *Website:* www.mod.gov.sk (Office).

SIMMEN, Jeannot, PD, DrPhil; Swiss art critic and curator; b. 14 Sept. 1946, Zürich; s. of Georges Simmen and Clara Brüngger; m. Dr Brigit Blass 1988; two d.; ed Univ. of Zürich, Free Univ. of Berlin; exhbn projects include: Licht: Objekt/Medium, Telematic, Net-Modern-Navigation; Prof., Univs of Wuppertal, Kassel, Essen 1990–; Curator Schwerelos (exhbn), Grosse Orangerie, Charlottenburg Palace, Berlin 1991–92, Die Macht des Alters – Strategien der Meisterschaft (exhbn), Kronprinzen-Palais, Berlin 1998; Dir media future project Ars Digitalis, Acad. of Fine Arts, Berlin 1996; Design-Preis Schweiz 01 für 'Interaction Design', Design Center Langenthal, Switzerland. *Publications:* Kunst – Ideal oder Augenschein 1980, Der Fahrstuhl 1983, Vertigo 1990, Schwerelos 1991, Vertikal 1994, Kasimir Malewitsch 1998, 1999, Kidai Shôran (CD) 2000, Telematik 2002, LED 2003. *Leisure interests:* art and the media. *Address:* Goethe-Strasse 45, 0-4163 Berlin, Germany. *Telephone:* (30) 80907145. *Fax:* (30) 80907146.

SIMMONDS, Rt. Hon. Kennedy Alphonse, PC; Saint Christopher and Nevis politician; b. 12 April 1936; s. of the late Arthur Simmonds and of Bronte Clarke; m. Mary Camella Matthew 1976; three s. two d.; ed Basse-Terre Boys' School, St Kitts-Nevis Grammar School and Univ. of the West Indies; Intern, Kingston Public Hosp., Jamaica 1963; Registrar in Internal Medicine, Princess Margaret Hosp., Bahamas 1966–68; Resident in Anaesthesiology, Pittsburgh 1968–69; medical practice in St Kitts and Anguilla 1964–66, in St Kitts 1969–80; Founder mem. People's Action Movt 1965, Pres. 1976, unsuccessfully contested elections 1966, 1971, 1975; elected to Parl. 1979; Premier 1980–83; Minister of Home and External Affairs, Trade, Devt and Industry 1980–84, of Finance, Home and Foreign Affairs 1984–95; Prime Minister 1983–95; Fellow American Coll. of Anaesthesiologists. *Leisure interests:* cricket, tennis, football. *Address:* P.O. Box 167, Earle Morne Development, Basse-Terre, St Kitts, West Indies.

SIMMONS, David, BA, M.ED.; Australian politician; b. 7 Nov. 1947, Broken Hill, NSW; m. Kaye Simmons; one s. one d.; ed Univ. of New England, NSW; Head Social Science Dept, Bathurst High School, NSW; Alderman, Bathurst City Council 1978–83; MP for Calare, NSW 1983–96; mem. House of Reps. Cttee on Finance and Public Admin. 1985–89; Minister for Defence, Science and Personnel 1989–90, for Arts, Tourism and Territories 1990–91, for Local Govt and Family Support 1991–93; Chair. House of Reps. Cttee on Banking, Fin. and Public Admin. 1994; Exec. Dir Hunter Regional Tourism Org. 1996–97; Gen. Man. Newcastle Regional Chamber of Commerce 1997–98. *Leisure interests:* golf, stamp collecting, arts, travel. *Address:* Newcastle and Hunter Business Chamber, 475 Hunter Street, Newcastle, NSW 2302, Australia. *Telephone:* (2) 4925-0498 (Office); (2) 4926-2097 (Home). *Fax:* (2) 4929-3540 (Office). *E-mail:* simmond@asol.net (Office); dsimmons@ldl.com .au (Home). *Website:* nhbusinesschamber.com.au (Office).

SIMMONS, Hardwick (Wick), AB, MBA; American business executive; b. 1940; m. Sloan T. Miller; five c.; ed Harvard Univ., Harvard Business School; with US Marine Corps Reserve 1960–66; Financial Adviser Hayden Stone 1966–69, Vice-Pres. Data Processing and Communications Div. 1969–70, Man. Boston office 1970–73, Exec. Vice-Pres. for Shearson Hayden Stone Retail Sales and Admin. 1973–77, Sr Exec. Vice-Pres. for Marketing and Sales, Shearson/American Express 1977, Pres. Pvt. Client Group, Shearson Lehman Brothers, Inc. –1991; Pres. and CEO Prudential Securities, Inc. 1991–2001; CEO Feb. Nasdaq 2001–; Dir NY City Partnership and Chamber of Commerce, Inc.; mem. Bd Nat. Acad. Foundation; mem. and fmr Chair. Securities Industry Asscn; fmr Dir Chicago Bd Options Exchange; mem. and fmr Pres. Bond Club of New York, Inc.; mem. NY City Public/Pvt. Initiatives (PPI) Bd; mem. Harvard Univ. John Kay Fairbank Center for E Asian Research; Trustee and Devt Cttee mem. S Street Seaport Museum; Pres. Bd of Trustees Groton School, Mass.; Trustee Rippowan Cisqua School, Mt. Kisco, NY. *Address:* Nasdaq Stock Market Inc., 2500 Sand Hill Road, Suite 220, Menlo Park, CA 94025, USA (Office). *Website:* www.nasdaq.com (Office).

SIMMONS, Jean, OBE; British actress; b. 31 Jan. 1929, London; d. of Charles Simmons and Winifred Ada Simmons (née Loveland); m. 1st Stewart Granger 1950 (divorced 1960); one d.; m. 2nd Richard Brooks 1960 (divorced 1977, died 1992); one d.; ed Orange Hill School, Burnt Oak, London; in films from 1943; stage appearance, Philadelphia and on tour in A Little Night Music 1974–75; appeared in TV series The Dain Curse 1978, Down at the Hydro 1982; BFI Fellowship 1994; Homage Award (Cannes Film Festival) 1988, Lake Como Italian Film Award 1989; Commdr des Arts et Lettres 1990. *Films include:* Great Expectations 1946, Black Narcissus 1946, Hamlet 1948, Adam and Evelyne 1949, So Long at the Fair 1950, Young Bess 1953, The Robe 1953, The Actress 1953, Guys and Dolls 1956, The Big Country 1958, Home Before Dark 1958, Elmer Gantry 1960, Spartacus 1960, The Grass is Greener 1961, All the Way Home 1963, Life at the Top 1965, Tough Night in Jericho 1967, Divorce American Style 1967, The Happy Ending 1969, Dominique 1979, The Thornbirds (TV) 1982 (Emmy Award), The Dawning 1988, Great Expectations (TV)

1989, People Like Us (TV) 1990, December Flower (TV), How To Make an American Quilt. *Address:* 1145 Gayley Avenue, Suite 303, Los Angeles, CA 90024, USA.

SIMMONS, Richard D., AB, LLB; American newspaper publisher; b. 30 Dec. 1934, Cambridge, Mass.; m. Mary DeWitt Bleecker 1961; two s.; ed Harvard and Columbia Univs; admitted to New York Bar; Assoc. Satterlee, Warfield & Stephens 1958–62; Gen. Counsel Giannini Science Corpn 1962–64; Vice-Pres. and Gen. Counsel Southeastern Publishing Service Corpn 1964–69; Counsel Dun & Bradstreet Inc., New York 1969–70, Vice-Pres. and Gen. Counsel 1970–72; Pres. Moody's Investors Service 1973–76, Dun & Bradstreet Inc. 1975–76; Exec. Vice-Pres. Dun & Bradstreet Corpn, New York 1976–78, Dir and Vice-Chair. Bd 1979–81; Pres. and COO The Washington Post Co. 1981–91, now Dir; Pres. Int. Herald Tribune 1989–96; Dir Washington Post Co. *Address:* 105 N Washington Street, Suite 202, Alexandria, VA 22314, USA.

SIMMONS, Robert Malcolm, PhD, FRS; British professor of biophysics; b. 23 Jan. 1938, London; s. of Stanley Laurence Simmons and Marjorie Simmons (née Amys); m. Mary Ann (Anna) Ross 1967; one s. one d.; ed King's Coll. London, Royal Inst., Univ. Coll. London; lecturer Univ. Coll., London Univ. 1967–81; MRC Staff Scientist King's Coll., Univ. of London 1981–83, Prof. of Biophysics 1983–, Dir Randall Inst. 1995–99, Randall Centre 1999–2001, Prof. Emer. 2002–. *Publication:* Muscular Contraction 1992. *Leisure interests:* music, fishing. *Address:* The Randall Centre, New Hunts House, King's College, London, SE1 1UL, England. *E-mail:* robert.simmons@kcl.ac.uk (Office).

SIMMONS, Ruth J., PhD; American university president; b. 3 July 1945, Grapeland, Tex.; two c.; ed Dillard Univ., New Orleans, Harvard Univ.; Asst Prof. of French Univ. of New Orleans, Asst Dean Coll. of Liberal Arts –1977; Visiting Assoc. Prof. of Pan-African Studies, Acting Dir Int. Programmes, Calif. State Univ., Northridge 1977–79; Asst, then Assoc. Dean of Grad. Studies, Univ. of S. Calif. 1979–83; Dir Afro-American Studies Princeton Univ., Assoc. Dean 1983, Vice-Provost 1992–95; Provost Spelman Coll., Atlanta 1990–91; Pres. Smith Coll. 1995–2001, Brown Univ. 2001–, also Albert D. Mead Prof. of Cognitive and Linguistic Sciences; nine hon. doctorates, numerous awards including Danforth Fellowship, Fulbright Fellowship. *Address:* Office of the President, Brown University, Providence, RI 02912, USA (Office). *Telephone:* (401) 863-1000 (Office). *Website:* www.brown .edu (Office).

SIMMS, David John, PhD, MRIA; Irish professor of mathematics; b. 13 Jan. 1933, Sankeshwar, India; s. of John Gerald Simms and Eileen Mary Simms (née Goold-Verschoyle); m. Anngret Erichson 1965; three s.; ed Berkhamsted School, Trinity Coll., Dublin and Peterhouse, Cambridge, England; Asst in Math., Univ. of Glasgow 1958–60, Lecturer in Math. 1960–64; Instructor in Math., Princeton Univ., NJ 1962–63; Lecturer in Math., Univ. of Dublin 1964–73, Assoc. Prof. 1973–; Visiting Prof. Univ. of Bonn 1966–67, 1972–73, 1978–80; Fellow Trinity Coll., Dublin 1972–2002, Sr Fellow 2002–03; mem. Royal Irish Acad. 1978–, Vice-Pres. 1983–84, 1987–88, 1995–96; Gold Medal in Math., Univ. of Dublin 1955. *Publications include:* Lie Groups and Quantum Mechanics 1968, Lectures on Geometric Quantization (with N. M. Woodhouse) 1974. *Address:* Trinity College, Dublin 2, Ireland. *Telephone:* (1) 6081944.

SIMMS, Sir Neville Ian, Kt, BSc, MEng, F.R.ENG., FRSA, FICE; British business executive and civil engineer; b. 11 Sept. 1944, Glasgow; s. of the late Arthur Neville Simms and of Anne Davidson Simms (née McCulloch); ed Queen Elizabeth Grammar School, Crediton, Univs. of Newcastle-upon-Tyne and Glasgow; structural engineer Ove Arup and Partners 1966–69; joined Tarmac PLC 1970, Chief Exec. Tarmac Construction Ltd 1988–92, Group Chief Exec. Tarmac PLC 1992–99, (Deputy Chair. 1994–99); Chair. Carillion PLC 1999–; Dir Bank of England 1995–2002; Chair. BITC West Midlands 1998–2001, Int. Power PLC 2000–; Chair. (non-exec.) Courtaulds 1994–98, Pvt. Finance Panel Ltd 1994–99, Nat. Power 1998–2000; mem. New Deal Task Force 1999–2001; Gov. Stafford Grammar School 1997–, Ashridge Man. Coll. 2000–; Fellow Chartered Inst. of Bldg; Hon. DTech (Wolverhampton) 1997; Dr hc (Edin.) 2000; Hon. DEng (Glasgow) 2001; Pres.'s Medal, Chartered Inst. of Bldg 1995; Princess of Wales Ambassador Award 2001. *Publications:* Building Towards 2001; numerous speeches and articles on industry-related topics. *Address:* Carillion PLC, 24 Birch Street, Wolverhampton, WV1 4HY, England. *Telephone:* (1902) 422431. *Fax:* (1902) 316709.

SIMON, Claude; French writer; b. 10 Oct. 1913, Tananarive, Madagascar; s. of Antoine Simon and Suzanne Simon (née Denamiel); ed Collège Stanislas, Paris; Prix de l'Express for La Route des Flandres 1960; Prix Médicis for Histoire 1967; Nobel Prize for Literature 1985; Grand Croix, Ordre nat. du Mérite. *Publications:* Le Tricheur 1945, La corde raide 1947, Gulliver 1952, Le Sacre du printemps 1954, Le Vent 1957, L'herbe 1958, La Route des Flandres 1960, Le Palace 1962, Femmes 1966, Histoire 1967, La Bataille de Pharsale 1969, Orion aveugle 1970, Les Corps conducteurs 1971, Tryptyque 1973, Leçon de choses 1975, Les Géorgiques 1981, La Chevelure de Bérénice 1985, Discours de Stockholm 1986, L'Invitation 1988, Album d'un amateur 1988, L'Acacia 1989, Photographies 1992, Le Jardin des plantes 1997, Le Tramway 2001. *Address:* Editions de Minuit, 7 rue Bernard-Palissy, 75006 Paris; place Vieille, Salses, 66600 Rivesaltes, France.

SIMON, Herbert A., PhD; American social scientist; b. 15 June 1916, Milwaukee, Wis.; s. of Arthur Simon and Edna Merkel Simon; m. Dorothea Pye 1937; one s. two d.; ed Univ. of Chicago; Research Asst, Univ. of Chicago 1936–38; Staff mem. Int. City Managers' Asscn 1938–39; Dir of Admin. Measurement Studies, Bureau of Public Admin. Univ. of Calif. at Berkeley 1939–42; Asst Prof., later Prof., Ill. Inst. of Tech. 1942–49, Chair. of Dept 1946–49; Prof. of Admin., Carnegie-Mellon Univ. 1949–65, Richard King Mellon Prof. of Computer Sciences and Psychology 1965–; Chair. Bd of Dirs. Social Science Research Council 1961–66, Div. of Behavioral Sciences of Nat. Research Council 1968–70; Ford Lecturer, New York Univ. 1960, Vanuxem Lecturer, Princeton Univ. 1961, William James Lecturer, Harvard Univ. 1963, Harris Lecturer, Northwestern Univ. 1967, Compton Lecturer, MIT 1968, Katz-Newcomb Lecturer, Univ. of Michigan 1976, Hovland Lecturer, Yale Univ. 1976, Gaither Lecturer, Univ. of Calif. (Berkeley) 1980, Camp Lecturer, Stanford Univ. 1982, Lecturer, Univ. of Calif. (Los Angeles) 1983, Univ. of Michigan 1983; mem. President's Science Advisory Cttee 1968–72, Nat. Acad. of Sciences, American Philosophical Soc., Bd of Trustees, Carnegie-Mellon Univ. 1972–93, Emer. Trustee 1993–; Distinguished Fellow, American Econ. Asscn 1976; Foreign mem. Yugoslav Acad. of Sciences, Chinese Acad. of Sciences, Russian Acad. of Sciences; Hon. Prof., Tianjin Univ., Beijing Univ.; Hon. mem. Inst. of Electrical and Electronic Engineers, Inst. of Psychology, Chinese Acad. of Sciences; Hon. DSc (Yale, Case Inst. of Tech., Marquette, Columbia, Gustavus Adolphus, Duquesne, Mich. Technological, Carnegie Mellon); Hon. LLD (Chicago, McGill, Mich., Pittsburgh, Harvard); Hon. Fil.D. (Lund); Hon. DPhil (Paul Valery Univ. of Montpellier); Hon. D.Econ.Sc. (Erasmus); Hon. DHumLitt; Hon. DSc (Illinois Inst. Tech.); Hon. Dr.rer.Pol. (Pavia); Dr. hc (Univ. of Rome), Univ. of Buenos Aires; Distinguished Scientific Contributions Award, American Psychological Asscn 1969, A.M. Turing Award, Asscn for Computing Machinery 1975, Nobel Prize for Econs 1978, Procter Prize 1980, James Madison Award, American Political Science Asscn 1984, Nat. Medal of Science 1986, Von Neumann Theory Prize 1988, Award for Research Excellence, Int. Jt Conf. on Artificial Intelligence 1995, Dwight Waldo Award, American Soc. for Public Admin. 1995, John M. Gans Award, American Psychology Soc. 2000. *Publications:* Administrative Behavior 1947, Public Administration 1950, Models of Man 1957, Organizations 1958, The Shape of Automation 1960, The Sciences of the Artificial 1969, Human Problem-Solving 1972, Models of Discovery 1977, Models of Thought, Vol. I 1979, Vol. II 1989, Models of Bounded Rationality (3 Vols) 1982, Vol. III 1997, Reason in Human Affairs 1983, Protocol Analysis 1984, Scientific Discovery 1987, Models of my Life 1991, An Empirically Based Microeconomics 1997. *Leisure interests:* hiking, music. *Address:* Department of Psychology, Carnegie-Mellon University, Schenley Park, Pittsburgh, PA 15213, USA. *Telephone:* (412) 268-2787.

SIMON, Josette, OBE; British actress; d. of Charles Simon and Eileen Petty; m. Mark Padmore 1996; ed Cen. School of Speech Training and Dramatic Art; appeared in TV series Blake's 7; joined RSC; Hon. MA (Leicester) 1995; appeared as Isabella in Measure for Measure 1988, as Maggie in Arthur Miller's After the Fall, Nat. Theatre, in The White Devil, Nat. Theatre 1991, as Ellida Wangel in Ibsen's The Lady from the Sea, Lyric Theatre, Hammersmith 1994, The Taming of the Shrew, Leicester 1995, The Maids, Donmar Warehouse 1997, Titania in A Midsummer Night's Dream 1999, several concert performances. *Films include:* Cry Freedom, Milk and Honey (Best Actress Atlantic Film Festival 1988, Paris Film Festival 1990), A Child From the South, Bitter Harvest, Bridge of Time. *TV includes:* Henry IV, Parts 1 and 2, Bodyguards, Kavanagh QC. *Leisure interests:* cinema, gardening, travel, learning languages. *Address:* c/o Conway van Gelder Ltd, 18–21 Jermyn Street, London, SW1Y 6HP, England. *Telephone:* (20) 7287-0077. *Fax:* (20) 7287-1940.

SIMON, Neil; American playwright; b. 4 July 1927, New York; s. of Irving Simon and Mamie Simon; m. 1st Joan Baim 1953 (deceased); two d.; m. 2nd Marsha Mason 1973 (divorced); m. 3rd Diane Lander 1987; one d.; ed New York Univ.; wrote for various TV programmes, including The Tallulah Bankhead Show 1951, The Phil Silvers Show 1958–59, NBC Special, The Trouble with People 1972; Hon. DHumLitt (Hofstra Univ.) 1981, (Williams Coll.) 1984; Evening Standard Award 1967, Writers' Guild Screen Award for The Odd Couple 1969, Writers' Guild Laurel Award 1979, American Comedy Award for Lifetime Achievement 1989, Pulitzer Prize for Lost in Yonkers 1991. *Plays:* Come Blow Your Horn 1961, Little Me (musical) 1962, Barefoot in the Park 1963, The Odd Couple 1965, Sweet Charity (musical) 1966, The Star-Spangled Girl 1966, Plaza Suite 1968, Promises, Promises (musical) 1968, Last of the Red Hot Lovers 1969, The Gingerbread Lady 1970, The Prisoner of Second Avenue 1971, The Sunshine Boys 1972, The Good Doctor 1973, God's Favorite 1974, California Suite 1976, Chapter Two 1977, They're Playing Our Song 1979, I Ought to be in Pictures 1980, Fools 1981, Little Me (revised version) 1982, Brighton Beach Memoirs 1983, Biloxi Blues 1985, The Odd Couple Female Version 1985, Broadway Bound 1986, Rumors 1988, Lost in Yonkers 1991, Jake's Women 1992, The Goodbye Girl (musical) 1993, Laughter on the 23rd Floor 1993, London Suite 1995. *Screenplays:* After the Fox 1966, Barefoot in the Park 1967, The Odd Couple 1968, The Out-of-Towners 1970, Plaza Suite 1971, The Last of the Red Hot Lovers 1972, The Heartbreak Kid 1973, The Prisoner of Second Avenue 1975, The Sunshine Boys 1975, Murder By Death 1976, The Goodbye Girl 1977, The Cheap Detective 1978, California Suite 1978, Chapter Two 1979, Seems Like Old Times 1980, Only When I Laugh 1981, I Ought to Be in Pictures 1982, Max Dugan Returns 1983, Lonely Guy (adaptation) 1984, The Slugger's Wife 1984,

Brighton Beach Memoirs 1986, Biloxi Blues 1988, The Marrying Man 1991, Broadway Bound (TV film) 1992, Lost in Yonkers 1993, Jake's Women (TV film) 1996, London Suite (TV film) 1996; other motion pictures adapted from stage plays: Come Blow Your Horn 1963, Sweet Charity 1969, The Star-Spangled Girl 1971; mem. Dramatists Guild, Writers' Guild of America; many awards including Emmy Award 1957, 1959; Antoinette Perry (Tony) Awards for The Odd Couple 1965, Biloxi Blues 1985 (Best Play), Lost in Yonkers 1991 (Best Play). *Publications:* Rewrites: A Memoir 1996; individual plays. *Address:* c/o Albert DaSilva, 502 Park Avenue, New York, NY 10022, USA.

SIMON, Paul; American politician, educationalist and writer; b. 29 Nov. 1928, Eugene, Ore.; s. of Martin Paul Simon and Ruth Simon (née Troemel); m. 1st Jeanne Hurley 1960 (died 2000); one s. one d.; m. 2nd Patricia Derge 2001; ed Univ. of Oregon, Dana Coll., Blair, Neb.; publisher Troy (Ill.) Tribune 1948–66 and weeklies; mem. Ill. House of Reps. 1955–63, Ill. Senate 1963–69, Lt Gov. Ill. 1969–73; Fellow John F. Kennedy Inst. of Politics, Harvard 1972–73; Prof. of Public Affairs Reporting Sangamon State Univ., Springfield 1973; mem. 94th–98th Congresses, Ill.; U.S. Senator from Illinois 1985–97; Dir of Public Policy, Southern Ill. Univ. 1997–; mem. Bd of Dirs. Dana Coll.; Democrat; holds 55 hon. degrees; recipient American Political Science Asscn Award 1957. *Publications:* Lovejoy: Martyr to Freedom 1964, Lincoln's Preparation for Greatness 1965, A Hungry World 1966, Protestant-Catholic Marriages Can Succeed (with Jeanne Hurley Simon) 1967, (with Arthur Simon) The Politics of World Hunger 1973, You Want to Change the World, So Change It 1971, The Tongue-Tied American 1980, The Once and Future Democrats 1982, The Glass House, Politics and Morality in the Nation's Capitol 1984, Beginnings 1986, Let's Put America Back to Work 1986, Winners and Losers 1989, Advice and Consent 1992, Freedom's Champion: Elijah Lovejoy 1994, We Can Do Better 1994, Tapped Out 1998. *Address:* Southern Illinois University, Public Policy Institute, Carbondale, IL 62901, USA.

SIMON, Paul F., BA; American composer and musician; b. 13 Oct. 1941, Newark; s. of Louis Simon and Belle Simon; m. 1st Peggy Harper; one s.; m. 2nd Carrie Fisher 1983 (divorced); m. 3rd Edie Brickell 1992; two s. one d.; ed Queens Coll., Brooklyn Law School; fmrly mem. singing duo Simon and Garfunkel (q.v.) 1964–71; solo performer 1972–; Hon. DMus (Berklee Coll.) 1986, (Yale) 1996, (Queens Coll.) 1997; numerous Grammy Awards and one Emmy Award; The Kennedy Center Honors Paul Simon 2002. *Songs with Garfunkel include:* The Sound of Silence, Dangling Conversation, Homeward Bound, I Am a Rock, At the Zoo, 7 O'Clock News, 59th Street Bridge Song, Scarborough Fair, Mrs. Robinson, The Boxer, Bridge Over Troubled Water. *Albums with Garfunkel:* Wednesday Morning 3 AM 1964, Sounds of Silence 1966, Parsley, Sage, Rosemary and Thyme 1966, The Graduate 1968, Bookends 1968, Bridge Over Troubled Water 1970, The Concert in Central Park 1982, Simon & Garfunkel's Greatest Hits 1972, Breakaway 1975, Waterpark 1978. *Solo albums include:* Paul Simon 1972, There Goes Rhymin' Simon 1973, Live Rhymin' 1975, Still Crazy After All These Years 1975, Greatest Hits, etc. 1977, One-Trick Pony 1980, Hearts and Bones 1983; Graceland 1986, Negotiations and Love Songs 1988; Paul Simon: Solo 1990, Rhythm of the Saints 1990, Paul Simon's Concert in the Park 1991, You're the One 2000; wrote score, author screenplay One-Trick Pony; co-wrote musical The Capeman 1997; appeared in film Annie Hall 1977; Grammy Award for Mrs Robinson (song), Bridge Over Troubled Water (album), The Graduate (soundtrack), Still Crazy After All These Years (album), Graceland (album) 1986; Emmy Award for NBC Paul Simon Special, Born at the Right Time tour, S. Africa 1992; series with Art Garfunkel, Paramount 1993. *Television appearances include:* Paul Simon Special 1987, several episodes of Saturday Night Live, NBC. *Publications:* At the Zoo 1991, The Capeman (play) 1998. *Address:* c/o C. Vaughn Hazell, Paul Simon Music, Suite 500, 1619 Broadway, New York, NY 10019 USA (Office).

SIMON OF HIGHBURY, Baron (Life Peer), cr 1997, of Canonbury in the London Borough of Islington; **David Alec Gwyn Simon,** Kt, CBE, MA, MBA; British business executive; b. 24 July 1939, London; s. of the late Roger Simon and of Barbara Hudd; m. 1st Hanne Mohn 1964; two s.; m. 2nd Sarah Smith 1992; ed Gonville and Caius Coll., Cambridge; joined B.P. 1961, Marketing Dir, Holland 1972–75, Marketing Co-ordinator, European Region 1975–80, Marketing Dir, Oil UK 1980–82, Man. Dir, Oil Int. Ltd 1982–85, Man. Dir B.P. Co. PLC 1986–95, Deputy Chair. 1990–95, Group Chief Exec. 1992–95, Chair. 1995–97; Dir Bank of England 1995–97; Minister of State Responsible for Trade and Competitiveness in Europe (attached to Dept of Trade and Industry and Treasury) 1997–99, Adviser, Cabinet Office 1999–; Dir (advisory) Unilever 2000–, LEK 2000–, Morgan Stanley Europe –, SUEZ 2001–, Fortis 2001–; Chair. Trustee Bd Cambridge Univ.; Trustee Hertz Foundation; Hon. DEcon (Hull) 1993; Dr. hc (Univ. of N London) 1995; Hon. LLD (Bath) 1998; Commdr Order of Leopold (Belgium). *Leisure interests:* golf, books, music. *Address:* House of Lords, Westminster, London, SW1A 0PW, England.

SIMONDS-GOODING, Anthony James Joseph; British business executive; b. 10 Sept. 1937, Dublin; s. of Maj. and Mrs. Hamilton Simonds-Gooding; m. 1st Fiona Menzies 1961 (divorced 1982); three s. two d. (one s. deceased); m. 2nd Marjorie A. Pennock 1982, one step-s.; ed Ampleforth Coll. and Britannia Royal Naval Coll. Dartmouth; served RN 1953–59; with Unilever 1960–73; Marketing Dir Whitbread & Co., PLC 1973, subsequently Man. Dir (UK), latterly Group Man. Dir until 1985; Chair. and Chief Exec. Saatchi PLC 1985–87; Chief Exec. British Satellite Broadcasting 1987–90, Chair. 1993–; Chair. S.P. Lintas 1994–95, Ammirati Puris Lintas 1994–96; Chair.

Designers and Art Dirs. Asscn 1992–2001; Dir ICA Devt Cttee 1992–94, Cancer Relief Macmillan Fund 1992–, Robinsons PLC 1993–, Brixton Prison 1994–97, Community Hosps. Group PLC 1995–2000, Interbrand Newell & Sorrell 1996–98, Clark & Taylor 1996–99, Blick PLC 1997–, Kunick PLC 1997–, CLK MPL 1999–, Rainbow Children's Trust 2001–, Sea Cadets Asscn 2001, OMG PLC 2002–. *Leisure interests:* oil painting, walking, opera, travel, tennis. *Address:* Burchetts Brook, Holmbury St Mary, Surrey, RH5 6NA, England. *Telephone:* (1306) 621266 (Home). *Fax:* (1306) 621482 (Office). *E-mail:* anthony@simonds-gooding.net (Office).

SIMONET, Henri François, DenD, D. ÈS SC.; Belgian politician; b. 10 May 1931, Brussels; m. Marie-Louise Angenent 1960; one s. one d.; ed Univ. Libre de Bruxelles and Columbia Univ., USA; Asst, Univ. Libre de Bruxelles 1956–58, now Prof.; Financial Adviser, Inst. National d'Etudes pour le Développement du Bas-Congo 1958–59; Legal Adviser, Comm. of Brussels Stock Exchange 1959–60; Deputy Dir Office of Econ. Programming 1961; Dir of Cabinet of Ministry of Econ. Affairs and Power 1961–65; Dir of Cabinet of Deputy Prime Minister responsible for Co-ordination of Econ. Policy 1965; Mayor of Anderlecht 1966–84; MP for Brussels 1966–84, 1985–92; Minister of Econ. Affairs 1972–73; mem., Vice-Pres. Comm. of the European Communities 1973–77; Minister of Foreign Affairs 1977–80; Sec. of State for Brussels Econ. Affairs 1977–79; Financial Consultant and Corp. Dir. *Publications:* various books and articles on economics, financial and political topics. *Address:* 34 avenue Franklin Roosevelt, 1050 Brussels, Belgium.

SIMONETTA; Italian fashion designer; b. Duchess Colonna di Cesarò; d. of Duke Giovanni Colonna di Cesarò and Countess Barbara Antonelli; m. 1st Count Galeazzo Visconti di Modrone 1944; one d.; m. 2nd Alberto Fabiani (fashion designer) 1952; one s.; separated Feb. 1970 and has taken back her maiden name of Duchess Colonna di Cesarò; opened fashion Atelier, Rome 1946; transferred fashion business to Paris 1962; Philadelphia Fashion Group Award 1953, Davison Paxon Award, Atlanta 1959, Fashion Oscar from Filene's of Boston 1960; after five consecutive years in list of world's best dressed women is in "Hall of Fame"; Hon. Citizen of Austin, New Orleans and Las Vegas. *Publication:* A Snob in the Kitchen 1967.

SIMONIA, Nodari Aleksandrovich, CAND.ECON.SC., D.HIST; Russian political economist; b. 30 Jan. 1932, Tbilisi, Georgia; m.; one d.; ed Moscow Inst. of Int. Relations; Corresp. mem., Russian Acad. of Sciences 1990, mem. 1997– Acad. Sec. Dept of Int. Relations, Jr researcher, Sr researcher, Prof. Head of Sector, Head of Div., Deputy Dir, Inst. of Oriental Studies 1955–86; Deputy Dir, Inst. of World Econ. and Int. Relations 1986–2000, Dir 2000–; Prof. Centre of Slavic Studies Hokkaido Univ.; main research in comparative studies: Russia and developing cos.; mem. Presidium, Russian Acad. of Sciences, Scientific Council Ministry of Foreign Affairs, European Acad. of Sciences, Arts and Literature. *Publications:* Over 250 scientific works, including 16 books and articles and papers on the Devt of capitalism in modern Russia. *Address:* IMEMO, Profsoyuznaya str. 23, 117997 Moscow, GSP-7, Russia. *Telephone:* (095) 120-84-50 (Office); (095) 434-15-68 (Home).

SIMONIS, HE Cardinal Adrianus J.; Netherlands ecclesiastic; b. 26 Nov. 1931, Lisse, Rotterdam; ordained 1957; consecrated Bishop of Rotterdam 1971; Archbishop of Utrecht 1983–; cr. Cardinal 1985; currently Pres. Netherlands Bishops' Conf.; mem. Congregations for Insts. of Consecrated Life and for Societies of Apostolic Life, for Catholic Educ., Pontifical Council for the Promotion of Christian Unity. *Address:* Nederlandse Bisschoppenconferentie, Biltstraat 121, P.O. Box 13049, 3507 LA Utrecht; Aartsbisdom, B.P. 14019, Maliebaan 40, 3508 SB Utrecht, Netherlands. *Telephone:* (30) 2338030; 2334244 (Bishop Conf.). *Fax:* (30) 2311962; 2332103 (Bishop Conf.). *E-mail:* secrbk@rkk.nl (Office). *Website:* www.de-oase.nl (Office); www.omroep.nl/rkk (Office).

SIMONIS, Heide, MA; German politician; b. (Steinhardt), 4 July 1943, Bonn; d. of Dr Horst Steinhardt and Sophia Brück; m. Prof. Udo E. Simonis 1967; tutor in German, Univ. of Zambia 1967–69, Goethe Inst. and Nat. TV and Radio Service, Tokyo 1970–72; mem. Bundestag 1976–88; Minister of Finance, Schleswig-Holstein 1988–93, Minister-Pres. 1993–; mem. Social Democratic Party (SPD). *Leisure interests:* music, literature. *Address:* Düsternbrooker Weg 70, 24105 Kiel; Klosterufer 2, 24582 Bordesholm, Germany. *Telephone:* (431) 9882000. *Fax:* (431) 9881960. *E-mail:* heide.simonis@stk.landsh.de.

SIMONOV, Aleksey Kirillovich; Russian film director and human rights activist; b. 8 Aug. 1939, Moscow; s. of writer and poet Konstantin Simonov; m.; two s.; ed Inst. of Oriental Languages at Moscow State Univ.; lab., Inst. of Permafrost Studies 1956–58; translator, USSR State Cttee for Int. Econ. Relations in Indonesia 1963–64; Ed., Khudozhestennaya Literatura 1964–67; film Dir EKRAN TV Studio 1970–91; lecturer All-Russian Inst. of Cinematography 1991–93; Sec. USSR Union of Cinematographists 1991; f. Konf 1991; Co.-Chair. Licence Cttee of Russian Fed. 1992–93; mem. Movt of Democratic Reforms 1991–93; mem. Public Chamber of Russian Presidency; a founder Movt for Mil. Reform 1995; Pres. Glasnost Defence Foundation 1991–; mem. Editorial Bd, Sovyetsky Ekran (magazine) 1988–92, Rossia (weekly) 1992–96; mem. Moscow Helsinki Group; Founder Dassier on Censorship (quarterly) 1997–, Law and Practice (monthly) 1995–; Moscow Int. Press Club 1997. *Films:* directed over 20 feature films and documentaries including Team 1985. *Publications:* Private Collection 1999 (prose); numerous articles in newspapers and magazines Yunost, Ogonyok, Moskva; translator of English plays, Indonesian and African poetry. *Leisure interest:* collecting

turtles. *Address:* Zubovski blvd. 4, apt. 432, 119121 Moscow (Office); Leningradski prosp. 60-A, apt. 2, Moscow, Russia (Home). *Telephone:* (095) 201-44-20 (Office); (095) 152-18-39 (Home). *Fax:* (095) 201-49-47 (Office). *E-mail:* maria@gdf.ru (Office).

SIMONOV, Mikhail Petrovich; Russian design engineer and academic; b. 1929, Rostov-on-Don; m.; one s. one d.; ed Kazan Inst. of Aviation; teacher, Prof., Head of Dept Kazan Inst. of Aviation –1959; Founder and Head Construction Bureau of Sports Aviation 1959–69; Deputy Chief Constructor, Chief Constructor, First Deputy Constructor Gen. P. Sukhoy Special Construction Bureau 1969–76; Deputy Minister of Aviation Industry 1979–83; Constructor Gen., Dir-Gen. P. Sukhoy Special Construction Bureau 1983–99; mem. Council on Industrial Policy and Business at Russian Govt 1994–; mem. Int. and Russian Acad. of Eng; took part in Devt of supersonic bombers, fighters-interceptors, low-flying attack aircraft and tactical bombers; Hero of Russia 1999, Lenin's Prize; several orders and medals. *Address:* P. Sukhoy Special Construction Bureau, Polikarpova str. 23A, 125284 Moscow, Russia (Office). *Telephone:* (095) 241- 01-24 (Office).

SIMONOV, Pavel Vasilyevich; Russian neurophysiologist and psychophysiologist; b. 20 April 1926, Leningrad (now St Petersburg); s. of Vasily Simonov and Maria Stankevich; m. Olga Simonova 1948; one s. one d.; ed Mil. Medical Acad., Leningrad; Scientific Worker, subsequently Head, Experimental Lab., Cen. Mil. Hosp., Moscow 1951–61; Sr Scientific Worker, subsequently Dir, Inst. of Higher Nervous Activity and Neurophysiology, USSR (now Russian) Acad. of Sciences 1961–; Corresp. mem. USSR (now Russian) Acad. of Sciences 1981, mem. 1987, Academician-Sec. Dept of Physiology 1988–96; Pavlov Prize, USSR Acad. of Sciences 1981, USSR State Prize 1987. *Publications:* Higher Nervous Activity of Man: Motivational-Emotional Aspects 1975, The Emotional Brain 1986, The Motivated Brain 1991, Temperament, Character, Personality 1991, The Creative Brain 1993. *Leisure interests:* neurophysiology and psychophysiology of motivations and emotions. *Address:* Russian Academy of Sciences, Institute of Higher Nervous Activity and Neurophysiology, Butlerov Street 5A, 117865 Moscow, Russia. *Telephone:* (095) 334-70-00 (Office); 332-68-86 (Home). *Fax:* (095) 338-85-00.

SIMONS, Elwyn LaVerne, MA, PhD, DPhil; American professor of anthropology and anatomy; b. 14 July 1930, Lawrence, Kan.; s. of Verne Franklin Simons and Verna Irene (Cuddeback) Simons; m. 1st Mary Hoyt Fitch 1964; one s.; m. 2nd Friderun A. Ankel 1972; one s. one d.; ed Rice, Princeton and Oxford Univs.; Lecturer in Geology, Princeton Univ. 1958–59; Asst Prof. of Zoology, Univ. of Pennsylvania 1959–61; Visiting Assoc. Prof. of Geology and Curator of Vertebrate Paleontology, Yale Univ. 1960–61, Assoc. Prof. and Head Curator 1961–65; Prof. of Geology and Curator in Charge, Div. of Vertebrate Paleontology, Peabody Museum 1965–77; Prof. of Anthropology and Anatomy, Duke Univ., 1977–82, James B. Duke Prof. 1982–, Prof. of Zoology and Dir Duke Primate Center 1977–91, Scientific Dir 1991–; mem. Exec. Cttee, Center for Tropical Conservation 1991–; mem. Steering Cttee, Madagascar Fauna Group 1990–; has directed over 70 expeditions to Wyoming, Iran, India and Madagascar and 29 to the Egyptian Fayum in search of fossil primates and associated fauna; discovered Gigantopithecus in India, discovered and named Aegyptopithecus, Catapithecus, Arsinoea and Proteopithecus in Egypt; mem. NAS, American Philosophical Soc.; Hon. MA (Yale) 1967; Hon. DSc (Oxford) 1996; numerous awards including Annandale Medal, Asiatic Soc. of Calcutta, Charles R. Darwin Award, Asscn of Physical Anthropology 2000; Hon. Citizen Fayum Prov., Egypt; Chevalier Ordre. Nat., Madagascar. *Publications:* 262 scientific articles, abstracts and books. *Leisure interests:* drawing and painting, folk singing, genealogy. *Address:* Duke University Primate Center, 3705 Erwin Road, Durham, NC 27706 USA (Office). *Telephone:* (919) 684-2535 (Office). *Fax:* (919) 490-5394. *E-mail:* esimons@acpub.duke.edu (Office).

SIMONYI, András, PhD; Hungarian diplomatist, economist and consultant; b. 16 May 1952, Budapest; s. of Denes Simonyi and Maria Balazs; m. Nada Pejak; one s. one d.; ed Karl Marx Univ. of Econs (now Budapest Univ.); worked in 1980s with different orgs in field of youth exchange, particularly promoting East-West contacts, including programmes with American Council of Political Leaders; mem. staff Foreign Relations Dept, Socialist Workers Party 1984–89; Head of Nordic Dept, Ministry of Foreign Affairs 1989–91; Deputy Chief of Mission Embassy of Hungary, The Hague 1991–92, Hungarian Mission to the EC and NATO, Brussels 1992–95; Head Hungarian NATO Liaison Office, Brussels 1995–99; Perm. Rep. to NATO Council (first Hungarian Perm. Rep) 1999–2001, rep. on North Atlantic Council during Kosovo campaign; Amb. to USA 2002–; ran own consulting co. Dansion Ltd 2001–02. *Publications include:* numerous articles on the accession process to NATO, trans-Atlantic relations and European security and the war on terror. *Leisure interests:* blues music (plays electric guitar). *Address:* Embassy of Hungary, 3910 Shoemaker Street, NW, Washington, DC 20008 (Office); 2950 Spring of Freedom Street, NW, Washington, DC 20008, USA (Home). *Telephone:* (202) 362-3284 (Office). *Fax:* (202) 966-8135 (Office). *E-mail:* ambassador@huembwas.org (Office). *Website:* www.huembwas.org (Office).

SIMPSON, Alan Kooi, BS, JD; American politician and lawyer; b. 2 Sept. 1931, Cody, Wyo.; s. of Milward Lee Simpson and Lorna (née Kooi) Simpson; m. Ann Schroll 1954; two s. one d.; ed Univ. of Wyoming; called to Wyo. Bar 1958, US Supreme Court 1964; Asst Attorney Gen. Wyo. State 1959; Attorney for Cody 1959–69; Partner Simpson, Kepler, Simpson & Cozzens, Cody 1959–78; Shareholder Burg. Simpson, Elderedge, Hersh & Jardine; mem.

Wyo. House of Reps. 1964–77, US Senate from Wyoming 1978–97, Asst Majority Leader 1985–87, Asst Minority Leader 1987–97; Visiting Lecturer, Lambard Chair., Shorenstein Center, Harvard Univ. 1997; Trustee Buffalo Bill Historical Center, Cody, Gottsche Foundation Rehabilitation Center; mem. Wyo. Bar Asscn, American Bar Asscn, Asscn of Trial Lawyers of America; Hon. LLD (Calif. Western School of Law) 1983, (Colo Coll.) 1986, (Notre Dame Univ.) 1987; Hon. JD (Rocky Mountain Coll.) 1996, (Wyo.) 1999; recipient Centennial Alum Award (Wyo. Univ.) 1987, Thomas Jefferson Award in Law, Univ. of Va 1998. *Address:* Burg, Simpson, Eldredge, Hersh & Jardino, 1135 14th Street, P.O. Box 490, Cody, WY 82414; Kennedy School of Government, 79 JFK Street, Cambridge, MA 02138, U.S.A.

SIMPSON, (Alfred William) Brian, QC, JP, MA, DCL, FBA; British professor of law; b. 17 Aug. 1931, Kendal; s. of Rev. B. W. Simpson and M. E. Simpson; m. 1st Kathleen Seston 1954 (divorced 1968); one s. one d.; m. 2nd Caroline E. A. Brown 1969; one s. two d.; ed Oakham School, Rutland and Queen's Coll., Oxford; Jr Research Fellow, St Edmund Hall, Oxford 1954–55; Fellow Lincoln Coll., Oxford 1955–73, Jr Proctor 1967–68; Dean Faculty of Law, Univ. of Ghana 1968–69; Prof. of Law, Univ. of Kent 1973–85, Prof. Emer. 1985–; Prof. of Law, Univ. of Chicago, USA 1983–86; Charles F. and Edith J. Clyne Prof. of Law, Univ. of Mich. 1987–; Goodhart Visiting Prof., Univ. of Cambridge, UK 1993–94; Fellow American Acad. of Arts and Sciences; Barrister-at-law, Gray's Inn. *Publications:* A History of the Common Law of Contract 1975, Cannibalism and the Common Law 1984, A Biographical Dictionary of the Common Law (Ed.) 1984, A History of the Land Law 1986, Legal Theory and Legal History 1987, Invitation to Law 1988, In the Highest Degree Odious: Detention Without Trial in Wartime Britain 1992, Leading Cases in the Common Law 1995, Human Rights and the End of Empire. Britain and the Genesis of the European Convention 2001. *Leisure interest:* sailing. *Address:* University of Michigan Law School, Hutchins Hall, Ann Arbor, MI 48109-1215, USA; 3 The Butchery, Sandwich, Kent, CT13 9DL; 17 Dalkeith Road, London, SE21 8LT, England. *Telephone:* (734) 763-0413 (USA); (1304) 612783 (Kent, England), (20) 8761-3767 (London, England). *Fax:* (734) 763-9375 (USA). *E-mail:* bsimpson@umich.edu (Office); bsimpson@umich.edu (Home).

SIMPSON, Derek, BSc; British trade unionist; b. Sheffield; m. (divorced, recently reunited); three c.; apprenticeship at age of 15 in local Eng firm; became involved in union work and attended Eng union's youth conf.; shop steward, then convenor, later Sheffield Dist sec. 1981; Amicus union official in Derby –2002; Gen. Sec. Eng Section, Amicus (after merger of Amalgamated Electrical and Eng Union—AEEU with Manufacturing, Science and Finance Union—MSF 2002) July 2002–; mem. Labour Party; fmr mem. Communist Party. *Leisure interests:* chess, computers, listening to music. *Address:* Amicus-AEEU, Hayes Court, West Common Road, Hayes, Bromley, Kent, BR2 7AU, England (Office). *Telephone:* (20) 8462-7755 (Office). *Fax:* (20 8315-8234 (Office). *Website:* www.aeeu.org.uk (Office).

SIMPSON, Joanne (Gerould), PhD; American meteorologist; b. 23 March 1923, Boston, Mass.; d. of Russell Gerould and Virginia Vaughan; m. 1st Victor Starr 1944; m. 2nd William Malkus 1948; two s. one d.; m. 3rd Robert Simpson 1965; ed Univ. of Chicago; instructor, later Asst Prof., New York Univ., Univ. of Chicago, Ill. Inst. of Tech. 1943–51; meteorologist, Woods Hole Oceanographic Inst. 1951–60; Prof. of Meteorology, Univ. of Calif. at LA 1960–64; Dir Experimental Meteorology Lab., NOAA, Coral Gables, Fla 1965–74; Prof. of Environmental Sciences, Univ. of Va 1974–76, William W. Corcoran Prof. 1976–81; Affiliate Prof. of Atmospheric Science, Colo State Univ. 1980–; Head, Severe Storms Branch, Goddard Lab. for Atmospheres, Goddard Space Flight Center, NASA 1979–88, Chief Scientist for Meteorology 1988–; Goddard Sr Fellow, NASA 1989–94; Study Scientist for Tropical Rainfall Measuring Mission, Goddard Space Flight Center 1986–89, Project Scientist 1986–98; mem. Bd on Geophysical and Environmental Data 1993–96, on Atmospheric Sciences and Climate 1991–93; Guggenheim Fellow 1954; Fellow American Meteorological Soc. 1968 (Pres. 1989, Hon. mem. 1995); mem. Nat. Acad. of Eng, American Geophysical Union (Fellow 1994), The Oceanography Soc.; Hon. mem. Royal Meteorological Soc. 1999–; Hon. DSc (State Univ. of New York) 1991; NASA Exceptional Scientific Achievement Medal 1982, Meisinger Award 1962 and Rossby Research Medal 1983, American Meteorological Soc., NASA Nordberg Award 1994, NASA Outstanding Leadership Medal 1998, Charles E. Anderson Award 2001 and numerous other prizes and awards. *Publications:* more than 190 papers on tropical meteorology, tropical cloud systems and modelling, tropical storms and tropical rain measurement from space. *Leisure interests:* sailing, reading, travel. *Address:* 540 North Street, SW, Washington, DC 20024, USA (Home); NASA/GSFC, Center for Earth Sciences, Greenbelt, MD 20771. *Telephone:* (301) 614-6310. *Fax:* (301) 614-5484. *E-mail:* simpson@agnes.gsfc.nasa.gov (Office).

SIMPSON, John Cody Fidler-, CBE, MA, FRGS; British broadcaster and writer; b. 9 Aug. 1944, Cleveleys; s. of Roy Fidler-Simpson and Joyce Leila Vivien Cody; m. 1st Diane Petteys 1965 (divorced 1996); two d.; m. 2nd Adèle Krüger 1996; ed St Paul's School, London, Magdalene Coll. Cambridge; joined BBC 1966, Foreign Corresp. in Dublin, Brussels, Johannesburg 1972–78, Diplomatic Corresp., BBC TV 1978–80, Political Ed. 1980–81, Diplomatic Ed. 1982–88, Foreign Affairs Ed. (now World Affairs Ed.) 1988–; Contributing Ed. The Spectator 1991–95; columnist, Sunday Telegraph 1995–; Hon. Fellow Magdalene Coll. Cambridge; Hon. DLitt (De Montfort) 1995, (Univ. of E Anglia) 1998; Dr hc (Nottingham) 2000; Golden Nymph Award Cannes 1979, BAFTA Reporter of the Year 1991, 2001, Royal TV Soc. Dimbleby Award 1991, Peabody Award 1998, Emmy Award (for coverage of the fall of Kabul) 2002, Bayeux War Correspondents' Prize 2002, Int. Emmy Award, New York 2002. *Publications:* The Best of Granta 1966, The Disappeared 1985, Behind Iranian Lines 1988, Despatches from the Barricades 1990, From the House of War 1991, The Darkness Crumbles 1992, In the Forests of the Night 1993, Lifting the Veil: Life in Revolutionary Iran 1995, The Oxford Book of Exile 1995, Strange Places, Questionable People (autobiog.) 1998, A Mad World, My Masters 2000, News from No Man's Land: Reporting the World 2002. *Leisure interests:* travel, scuba diving, book collecting. *Address:* c/o BBC World Affairs Unit, Television Centre, Wood Lane, London, W12 7RJ, England. *Telephone:* (20) 8743-8000. *Fax:* (20) 8743-7591.

SIMPSON, Louis Aston Marantz, PhD CD; American writer and teacher; b. 27 March 1923, Jamaica, West Indies; s. of Aston Simpson and Rosalind (Marantz) Simpson; m. 1st Jeanne Rogers 1949 (divorced 1954); one s.; m. 2nd Dorothy Roochvarg 1955 (divorced 1979); one s. one d.; m. 3rd Miriam Bachner (née Butensky) 1985 (divorced 1998); ed Munro Coll., Jamaica, Columbia Univ., New York; Assoc. Ed. Bobbs-Merrill Publishing Co., New York 1950–55; Instructor, Asst Prof. Columbia Univ. 1955–59; Prof. Univ. of Calif. at Berkeley 1959–67; Prof. State Univ. of New York at Stony Brook 1967–91, Distinguished Prof. 1991–; Hon. DHL (Eastern Mich. Univ.) 1977; Hon. DL (Hampden-Sydney Coll.) 1991; Pulitzer Prize for Poetry 1964, Columbia Univ. Medal for Excellence 1965, Elmer Holmes Bobst Award for Poetry 1987, Harold Morton Landon Award for Translation 1997. *Publications:* poetry: The Arrivistes: Poems 1940–49 1949, Good News of Death and Other Poems 1955, The New Poets of England and America (ed.) 1957, A Dream of Governors 1959, At the End of the Open Road 1963, Selected Poems 1965, Adventures of the Letter I 1971, Searching for the Ox 1976, Caviare at the Funeral 1980, People Live Here: Selected Poems 1949–83; The Best Hour of the Night 1983; Collected Poems 1988, In the Room We Share 1990, There You Are 1995, Nombres et poussière 1996 Modern Poets of France (translation) 1997, Kaviar pä begravningen 1998; prose: James Hogg: A Critical Study 1962, Riverside Drive 1962, An Introduction to Poetry (ed.) 1967, North of Jamaica 1971, Three on the Tower: The Lives and Works of Ezra Pound, T. S. Eliot and William Carlos Williams 1975, A Revolution in Taste 1978, A Company of Poets 1981, The Character of the Poet 1986, Selected Prose 1989, Ships Going Into the Blue 1994, The King My Father's Wreck 1995. *Leisure interests:* dogs, fishing. *Address:* P.O. Box 119, Setauket, NY 11733, USA (Home).

SIMPSON, Norman Frederick; British playwright; b. 29 Jan. 1919, London; s. of George Frederick Simpson; m. Joyce Bartlett 1944; one d.; ed Emanuel School, London and Birkbeck Coll., Univ. of London; teacher in adult educ. until 1963; full-time playwright 1963–. *Publications:* plays: A Resounding Tinkle 1958, The Hole 1958, One Way Pendulum (also film) 1959, The Form 1961, The Cresta Run 1965, Some Tall Tinkles 1968; co-author Diamonds for Breakfast (film) 1968, Was He Anyone? 1973; novel: Harry Bleachbaker 1976. *Leisure interests:* reading, walking.

SIMPSON, O. J. (Orenthal James); American fmr professional football player, actor and sports commentator; b. 9 July 1947, San Francisco; s. of Jimmie Simpson and Eunice Durton; m. 1st Marguerite Whitley 1967 (divorced); one s. one d.; m. 2nd Nicole Brown 1985 (divorced 1992, died 1994); two s.; ed Univ. of S Calif. and City Coll. San Francisco; mem. world record 440 yard relay team (38.6 sec.) 1967; Downtown Athletic Club 1968; Halfback, Buffalo Bills 1969–78, San Francisco 49'ers 1978–79; American Football League All-Star Team 1970, ProBowl Team 1972–76; sports commentator, ABC Sports 1979–86; analyst, ABC Monday Night Football broadcasts 1984–85; co-host, NFL Live on NBC 1990; has appeared in several TV films; acquitted of two charges of murder Oct. 1995; civil suit trial began Sept. 1996, found responsible for deaths of Nicole Brown Simpson and Ronald Goldman by a civil jury Feb. 1997, ordered to pay $8.5 million in compensatory damages and to pay $25 million in punitive damages to victims' families (case on appeal); recipient of various football awards. *Films include:* The Towering Inferno 1974, Killer Force 1976, The Cassandra Crossing 1977, Capricorn One 1978, Firepower 1979, Hambone & Hillie 1984, The Naked Gun 1988, The Naked Gun $2^1/_2$: The Smell of Fear 1991, The Naked Gun $33^1/_3$: The Final Insult 1994. *Publication:* I Want to Tell You 1995. *Address:* c/o O.J. Simpson Enterprises, 11661 San Vicente Boulevard, Suite 632, Los Angeles, CA 90049, U.S.A.

SIMPSON, Patricia Ann, PhD, FRS; British research scientist; b. 9 Dec. 1945; d. of James Simpson and Peggy Simpson; ed Univ. of Southampton, Univ. Pierre et Marie Curie, Paris; ind. researcher CGM, Gif sur Yvette 1975–80; Research Dir CNRS Strasbourg 1981–2000; Wellcome Trust Prin. Fellow, Dept of Zoology, Univ. of Cambridge 2000–, Prof. of Comparative Embryology 2002–; Silver Medal, CNRS, France 1993. *Publication:* The Notch Receptors 1994. *Leisure interests:* woodwork, boating, hiking, travel. *Address:* Department of Zoology, Downing Street, Cambridge, CB2 3EJ (Office); 25 Temple End, Great Wilbraham, Cambs., CB1 5JF, England (Home). *Telephone:* (1223) 336669 (Office); (1223) 880664 (Home). *Fax:* (1223) 336676 (Office). *E-mail:* pas49@cam.ac.uk (Office).

SIMPSON OF DUNKELD, Baron (Life Peer), cr. 1997, of Denkeld in Perth and Kinross; **Rt. Hon. George Simpson;** British business executive; b. 2 July 1942; s. of William Simpson and Eliza Jane (née Wilkie) Simpson; m. Eva Chalmers 1963; one s. one d.; ed Morgan Acad., Dundee, Dundee Inst. of Technology; Sr Accountant Scottish Gas 1964–68; Cen. Audit Man. British Leyland 1969–73, Financial Controller, Leyland Truck and Bus Div. 1973–76,

Dir of Accounting, Leyland Cars 1976–78, Finance and Systems Dir, Leyland Trucks 1978–80; Man. Dir Coventry Climax Ltd 1980–83, Freight Rover Ltd 1983–86; CEO Leyland DAF 1986–88; Man. Dir, Rover Group 1989–91, Chair. 1991–94, CEO 1991–92; Dir BAe 1990–94, Deputy CEO 1992–94; Chair. Ballast Nedam Construction Ltd 1992–94, Arlington Securities 1993–94; CEO Lucas Industries PLC 1994–96; Man. Dir Marconi PLC (fmrly GEC PLC) 1996–99, CEO 1999–2001; mem. Supervisory Bd and Dir (non-exec.) Pilkington PLC 1992–99, Northern Venture Capital 1992–, Pro Share 1992–4, ICI PLC 1995–2001, Nestlé SA 1999–; mem. Exec. Cttee SMMT 1986– (Vice-Pres. 1986–95, Pres. 1995–96); Industrial Prof. Warwick Univ. 1991–; Hon. Fellow London Business School. *Leisure interest:* golf. *Address:* House of Lords, London, SW1A 0PW, England (Office).

SIMS, Geoffrey Donald, OBE, MSc, PhD, ARCS, DIC, FIEE, FCGI, F.R.ENG.; British fmr university vice-chancellor; b. 13 Dec. 1926, London; s. of Albert Sims and Jessie Sims; m. Pamela Richings 1949; one s. two d.; ed Wembley County Grammar School and Imperial Coll. London; Research Physicist, GEC, Wembley 1948–54; Sr Scientific Officer, UKAEA, Harwell 1954–56; Lecturer, Sr Lecturer, Dept of Electrical Eng Univ. Coll. London 1956–63; Prof. and Head of Dept of Electronics, Univ. of Southampton 1963–74, Dean of Faculty 1967–70, Sr Deputy Vice-Chancellor 1970–72; Vice-Chancellor, Univ. of Sheffield 1974–90; Chair. Council for Educ. in the Commonwealth 1991–96; Chair. Sheffield Church Burgess Educ. Foundation 1991–, Sheffield Church Burgesses Trust 1984– (Chair. 1987, 1999); Hon. Fellow Sheffield City Polytechnic 1989; Hon. DSc (Southampton) 1979, (Huddersfield) 2001; Hon. ScD (Allegheny) 1989; Hon. DScEng (Belfast) 1990; Hon. LLD (Dundee) 1990, (Sheffield) 1991; Symons Medal (Asscn of Commonwealth Univs) 1991. *Publications:* Microwave Tubes and Semiconductor Devices (with I. M. Stephenson) 1963, Variational Techniques in Electromagnetism (translation) 1965; numerous papers on microwaves, electronics and education. *Leisure interests:* golf, music, travel. *Address:* Ingleside, 70 Whirlow Lane, Sheffield, S11 9QF, England. *Telephone:* (114) 236-6196. *Fax:* (114) 236-6196. *E-mail:* geoffreydsims@blueyonder.co.uk (Home).

SIMSON, Wilhelm, PhD; German business executive; b. 16 Aug. 1938, Cologne; m.; ed Univ. of Munich; with Diamalt AG, Munich 1968; man. responsible for automobile paints, ICI, Lacke-Farben, Hilden 1971, mem. Bd of Man. 1978, Chair. 1982; Visiting Dir, ICI Paints, UK 1984, Exec. Dir, Paints Div. 1987–89; mem. Bd of Man., SKW Trostberg AG 1989–91, Chair. and Personnel Dir 1991–98; Chair. Bd of Man., VIAG AG, Munich 1998–; Chair. Supervisory Bd, Bayernwerk AG, Th. Goldschmidt AG; mem. Supervisory Bd, RAG AG; Pres. German Paint-makers Asscn 1982–86, Asscn of the Chemical Industry (Bavaria Section) 1993–; Trustee, Chemical Industry Fund 1992–97; mem. Bd of Dirs., Fed. of German Chemical Industry 1997–, Chair. Cttee for Trade Policy 1998–; Hon. Prof. of Tech. Chem., Ludwig-Maximilians-Univ., Munich 1998. *Address:* c/o VIAG AG, Nymphenburger Strasse 37, 80335 Munich, Germany. *Telephone:* (89) 250020 (Office). *Fax:* (89) 250025555 (Office). *Website:* www.viag.com (Office).

SIN, HE Cardinal Jaime L., B.SC.ED., DD; Philippine ecclesiastic; b. 31 Aug. 1928, New Washington, Aklan; s. of Juan Sin and Maxima Reyes Lachica de Sin; ed New Washington Elementary School, St Vincent Ferrer Seminary; ordained Roman Catholic priest 1954; missionary priest 1954–57; First Rector, St Pius X Seminary, Roxas City 1957–67; Domestic Prelate to Pope John XXIII 1960; Auxiliary Bishop of Jaro, Iloilo 1967; Archbishop of Jaro 1972, of Manila 1974–; cr. Cardinal 1976; Chair. Comm. on Seminaries and Priestly Vocations 1969–73, Comm. on Clergy 1974–77; mem. Pontifical Comm. on Social Communications 1975–; mem. Admin. Council, Catholic Bishops' Conf. of the Philippines (CBCP) 1968–72, Vice-Pres. CBCP 1970–74; Perm. mem. of the Synod of Bishops in Rome 1977–; mem. Pontifical Comm. on the Evangelization of Peoples 1978; mem. Sacred Congregation for Catholic Educ. 1978; mem. Secr. for Non-Christians 1978; now mem. Congregations for the Clergy, for Divine Worship and the Discipline of the Sacraments, for Insts. of Consecrated Life and for Socs. of Apostolic Life; Royal Acad. of Spanish Language 1978; Pres. Catholic Bishops' Conf. of the Philippines 1978, 1980; Hon. LLD 1975; (Angeles Univ.) 1978; Hon. DHL 1975; Hon. DST (Santo Tomas Univ. Manila) 1977; Hon. DHumLitt (Univ. of Iloilo City) 1980; Hon. DPhil (Manila) 1980, (Fu Jen Univ. Taipei) 1980; Dr. hc (Yale) 1986; over 100 citations; Distinguished Son of Iloilo Award 1974, Honoured Don of Capiz Award 1976, Outstanding Aklanon Award 1979, Grand Cross, Knights of the Holy Sepulchre of Jerusalem 1976, Distinguished Son of Manila 1976, Rajah Soliman Award for Distinguished Citizenry 1976, Gran Cruz de Isabel la Católica of the King of Spain 1977, Outstanding Citizen Award for Religion, Manila 1979, Bailiff Grand Cross of Honour and Devotion, Sovereign Military Order of Malta, Rome 1979. *Publications:* Ratio Fundamentalis for Philippine Seminaries 1972, The Revolution of Love 1972, The Church Above Political Systems 1973, A Song of Salvation 1974, Unity in Diversity 1974, La Iglesia Renueva Sus Medios de Evangelicación y Adapta a la Idiosincracia de los Pueblos 1978, The Future of Catholicism in Asia 1978, Christian Basis of Human Rights 1978, Separation, Not Isolation 1978, Slaughter of the Innocents '79, 1979, Discipline, Discipleship and Discerning Service, The Making of "Men for Others" 1980; over 200 papers, articles in periodicals. *Leisure interests:* music: Bach, Chopin, Wagner, Strauss; reading, writing. *Address:* Arzobispado, 121 Arzobispo Street, Intramuros, P.O. Box 132, 1099 Metro Manila, Philippines. *Telephone:* (2) 5277631. *Fax:* (2) 5273955. *E-mail:* aocmanila@yahoo.com (Office). *Website:* www.geocities.com/aocmanila (Office).

SINAISKY, Vassily Serafimovich; Russian conductor; b. 20 April 1947, Abez, Komi Autonomous Repub., Russia; m. Tamara Grigoryevna Sinayskaya; one s.; ed Leningrad State Conservatory; Artistic Dir and Chief Conductor Novosibirsk State Symphony 1971–73; Latvian State Symphony 1975–89; Moscow State Philharmonic Orchestra 1991–96; State Symphony Orchestra of Russia 2000–02; Prin. Guest Conductor BBC Philharmonic 1996–; worked with Orchestre Nat. de France, Berlin Philharmonic Orchestra, Orchestre Philharmonic du Luxembourg, Royal Scottish Nat. Orchestra and Finnish Radio Symphony; Golden Medal and 1st Prize Karayan Competition, Berlin 1973; People's Artist of Latvia 1981. *Address:* Chayanova str. 10, apt. 21, Moscow, Russia (Home). *Telephone:* (095) 250-31-28 (Moscow) (Home).

SINAY, Yakov Grigoryevich, D.PHYS.MATH.SC.; Russian physicist; b. 21 Sept. 1935; m.; one s.; ed Moscow State Univ.; Jr, Sr Researcher, Prof. Moscow State Univ. 1960–71; Sr, Chief Researcher L. Landau Inst. for Theoretical Physics USSR Acad. of Sciences 1971–; Prof. Princeton Univ., USA 1993–; mem. USSR (now Russian) Acad. of Sciences 1991; research in ergodic theory of dynamic systems, math. problems of statistical physics and probability theory; mem. Ed. Bd Uspekhi Matematicheskyh nauk, Ed. Bd Theoretical and Math. Physics, Russian Acad. of Natural Sciences; Foreign mem. American Acad. of Arts and Sciences; Hon. mem. St Petersburg Math. Soc., American Acad. of Science and Art in Boston; shared Wolf Prize 1997, Heinemann Prize of American Math. Soc., Boltzmann Prize, P. M. Dirac Medal. *Publications include:* Dynamic Systems with Elastic Mappings 1970, Math. Theory of Phase Transitions 1981; numerous articles in scientific journals. *Address:* L. Landau Institute for Theoretical Physics, Russian Academy of Sciences, Kosygin str. 2, 117940 Moscow, Russia; Department of Mathematics, Princeton University, Princeton, NJ 08544, USA. *Telephone:* (095) 137-32-44 (Moscow). *E-mail:* sinai@math.princeton.edu.

SINCLAIR, Charles James Francis, BA, FCA; British business executive; b. 4 April 1948; s. of Sir George Sinclair and the late Lady Sinclair; m. Nicola Bayliss 1974; two s.; ed Winchester Coll. and Magdalen Coll. Oxford; Voluntary Service Overseas, Zambia 1966–67; Deardon Farrow, chartered accountants 1970–75; Associated Newspapers Holdings Ltd 1975, Man. Dir 1988; Group Chief Exec. Daily Mail and Gen. Trust plc 1988–; Dir (non-exec.) Euromoney Institutional Investor PLC 1985–, Schroders plc 1990–, Reuters Group PLC 1994–. *Leisure interests:* opera, fishing, skiing. *Address:* Daily Mail and General Trust plc, Northcliffe House, 2 Derry Street, London, W8 5TT, England. *Telephone:* (20) 7938-6000. *Fax:* (20) 7938-3909.

SINCLAIR, Sir Clive Marles, Kt; British inventor and business executive; b. 30 July 1940, London; s. of the late George William Carter Sinclair and of Thora Edith Ella (née Marles) Sinclair; m. Ann Trevor-Briscoe 1962 (divorced 1985); two s. one d.; ed St George's Coll., Weybridge; Ed. Bernards Publrs. Ltd 1958–61; Chair. Sinclair Radionics Ltd 1962–79, Sinclair Research Ltd 1979–, Sinclair Browne Ltd 1981–85, Cambridge Computer 1986–90; Chair. British Mensa 1980–98; Visiting Fellow, Robinson Coll., Cambridge 1982–85; Visiting Prof. Imperial Coll., London 1984–92; Dir Shaye Communications Ltd 1986–91, Anamartic Ltd; Hon. Pres. British Mensa 2001–; Hon. Fellow Imperial Coll., London 1984; Hon. DSc (Bath) 1983, (Warwick, Heriot Watt) 1983, (UMIST) 1984; Royal Soc. Mullard Award 1984. *Publications:* Practical Transistor Receivers 1959, British Semiconductor Survey 1963. *Leisure interests:* music, poetry, mathematics, science, poker. *Address:* Sinclair Research Ltd, FlatA, 1–3 Spring Gardens, Trafalgar Square, London, SW1A 2BB, England (Office). *Telephone:* (20) 7839-6868 (Office); (20) 7839-7744 (Home). *Fax:* (20) 7839-6622 (Office). *E-mail:* sinclair.research@btinternet.com (Office). *Website:* www.sinclair.research.co.uk (Office).

SINCLAIR, Rt Hon Ian McCahon, AC, PC, BA, LLB; Australian comsultant, lawyer, farmer and fmr politician; b. June 1929, Sydney; s. of George Sinclair and Hazel Sinclair; m. 1st Margaret Tarrant 1956 (died 1967); one s. two d.; m. 2nd Rosemary Edna Fenton 1970; one s.; ed Knox Grammar School, Wahroonga and Sydney Univ.; barrister 1952–; mem. Legis. Council in NSW Parl. 1961–63, House of Reps. 1963–98; Minister for Social Services 1965–68; Minister Assisting Minister for Trade and Industry 1966–71; Minister for Shipping and Transport 1968–71, for Primary Industry 1971–72; Deputy Leader Country Party (now Nat. Party) 1971–84, Fed. Parl. Leader 1984–89, Party Spokesman on Defence, Foreign Affairs, Law and Agric. 1973–75, Opposition Spokesman on Agric., Leader of Opposition in House of Reps. 1974–75; Minister for Agric. and Northern Australia Nov.–Dec. 1975, for Primary Industry 1975–79, for Communications 1980–82, for Defence 1982–83; Leader of Govt in House of Reps. 1975–82; Leader of Opposition in House of Reps. 1983–87, Opposition Spokesman for Defence 1983–87, for Trade and Resources 1987–89; Shadow Special Minister of State 1994; mem. Jt Cttee of Foreign Affairs, Defence and Trade 1991–98, Chair. 1996–98; Speaker, House of Reps., Fed. Parl. 1998; Adjunct Prof. of Political Science, Univ. of New England 2000–; Man. Dir Sinclair Pastoral Co. 1953–, Grazier 1953–; Dir Farmers' and Graziers' Co-operative Co. Ltd 1962–65; Chair. Australian Rural Summit 1999, Australia Taiwan Business Council 2000–, Foundation for Rural and Regional Renewal 2000–, CRC for Sheep 2001–, Good Beginnings Australia; Pres. Austcare 2000–; Nat. Party; Hon. DUniv (Univ. of New England). *Leisure interests:* squash, surfing, walking. *Address:* PO Box 27, Cundletown, NSW 2430; Mulberry Farm, Dumaresq Island, NSW 2430, Australia (Home). *Telephone:* (2) 65538276 (Home). *Fax:* (2) 65538358 (Home). *E-mail:* iansinclair@ozemail.com.au (Home).

SINCLAIR OYANEDER, Lt-Gen. Santiago; Chilean army officer and politician; b. 29 Dec. 1927, Santiago; m. Doris Manley Ramirez; three s. one d.; ed Cavalry School, Acad. of War; Sec. of Studies, Mil. School 1963; Adjutant, Army C-in-C 1966; Head of Army Public Relations 1967; mem. UN Observers Group, Suez Canal 1968; Lecturer, Acad. of War 1970, Vice-Dir 1973; Commdr 2nd Cazadores Cavalry Regt 1973; Mil. Attaché, Chilean Embassy, Repub. of Korea 1975; Sec., Deputy C-in-C of Army 1976; Dir of Army Operations 1977; Chief Min. of Presidential Staff 1979; Head Pres.'s Consultative Cttee 1982–; Deputy C-in-C of Army 1985; Senator, Nat. Congress 1990–98; numerous mil. decorations. *Address:* P.O. Box 1732, Santiago, Chile. *Telephone:* 232-5148. *Fax:* 232-5148.

SINDEN, Sir Donald Alfred, Kt, CBE, FRSA; British actor and author; b. 9 Oct. 1923, Plymouth; s. of Alfred E. Sinden and Mabel A. Sinden (née Fuller); m. Diana Mahony 1948; two s.; entered theatrical profession with Charles F. Smith's Co., Mobile Entertainments Southern Area 1942; with Leicester Repertory Co. 1945; with Memorial Theatre Co., Stratford-upon-Avon 1946–47; with Old Vic and Bristol Old Vic 1948; with Bristol Old Vic 1950; film actor before returning to theatre 1952–60; Chair. British Theatre Museum Assen 1971–77, Theatre Museum Advisory Council 1973–80; Pres. Fed. of Playgoers Socs. 1968–93, Royal Theatrical Fund 1983–; Vice-Pres. London Appreciation Soc. 1960–; Assoc. Artist, RSC 1967–; mem. Council, British Actors Equity Assen 1966–77 (Trustee 1988–), Council, RSA 1972, Advisory Council, V. & A. Museum 1973–80, Arts Council Drama Panel 1973–77, Leicestershire Educ. Arts Cttee 1974–, BBC Archives Advisory Cttee 1975–78, Council, London Acad. of Music and Dramatic Art 1976–, Kent and E Sussex Regional Cttee, Nat. Trust 1978–82, Arts Council 1982–86; Drama Desk Award (for London Assurance) 1974, Variety Club of GB Stage Actor of 1976 (for King Lear), Evening Standard Drama Award Best Actor (for King Lear) 1977. *Films:* appeared in 23 films including The Cruel Sea, Doctor in the House 1952–60. *Stage appearances include:* The Heiress 1949–50, Red Letter Day 1951, Odd Man In 1957, Peter Pan 1960, Guilty Party 1961, as Richard Plantagenet in Henry VI (The Wars of the Roses), as Price in Eh!, etc. (RSC) 1963–64, British Council tour of S. America in Dear Liar and Happy Days 1965, There's a Girl in My Soup 1966, as Lord Foppington in The Relapse (RSC) 1967, Not Now Darling 1968, as Malvolio, Henry VIII 1969, as Sir Harcourt Courtly in London Assurance 1972 (toured USA 1974), In Praise of Love 1973, as Stockmann in An Enemy of the People 1975, Habeas Corpus (USA) 1975, as Benedick in Much Ado About Nothing, King Lear (RSC) 1976–77, Shut Your Eyes and Think of England 1977, Othello (RSC) 1979–80, Present Laughter 1981, Uncle Vanya 1982, The School for Scandal 1983 (European tour 1984), Ariadne auf Naxos 1983, Two into One 1984, The Scarlet Pimpernel 1985, Major Barbara 1988, Over My Dead Body 1989, Oscar Wilde 1990, Out of Order 1990 (Australian tour 1992), Venus Observed 1991, She Stoops to Conquer 1993, Hamlet 1994, That Good Night 1996, Quartet 1999, The Hollow Crown (tour to Australia and NZ 2002–03); Dir The Importance of Being Earnest 1987. *Radio includes:* Doctor Gideon Fell (series). *Television series include:* Our Man from St Marks, Two's Company, Discovering English Churches, Never the Twain, Judge John Deed. *Publications:* A Touch of the Memoirs 1982, Laughter in the Second Act 1985, The Everyman Book of Theatrical Anecdotes (ed.) 1987, The English Country Church 1988, Famous Last Words (ed.) 1994. *Leisure interests:* theatrical history, architecture, ecclesiology, genealogy, serendipity. *Address:* Rats Castle, TN30 7HX, England.

SINDIKUBWABO, Théodore; Rwandan politician; fmr Speaker of Nat. Devt Council; Pres. of Rwanda April–July 1994 (after death of fmr Pres. Habyarimana which led to civil war); accused by UN Tribunal of participation in genocide 1995.

SINFELT, John Henry, PhD; American chemist; b. 18 Feb. 1931, Munson, Pa; s. of Henry Gustave Sinfelt and June Lillian McDonald; m. Muriel Jean Vadersen 1956; one s.; ed Pennsylvania State Univ. and Univ. of Illinois; Scientist Exxon Research and Eng Co. 1954–, Sr Research Assoc. 1968–72, Scientific Adviser 1972–79, Sr Scientific Adviser 1979–96, Sr Scientific Adviser Emer. 1996–; Consulting Prof. Dept of Chemical Eng, Stanford Univ. 1996–; active in catalysis research, formulated and developed the concept of bimetallic clusters as catalysts, applied the concept in petroleum refining for production of lead-free petrol; mem. NAS, American Philosophical Soc., Nat. Acad. of Eng; Fellow American Acad. of Arts and Sciences; Hon. ScD (Univ. of Ill.) 1981; Nat. Medal of Science 1979, Perkin Medal in Chem. 1984, NAS Award for the Industrial Application of Science 1996 and many other awards and prizes. *Publications:* Bimetallic Catalysts: Discoveries, Concepts and Applications 1983; 180 articles in scientific journals; 45 patents. *Address:* P.O. Box 364, Oldwick, NJ 08858, USA (Home). *Telephone:* (908) 439-3603 (Home). *Fax:* (908) 730-3301.

SINGER, Sir Hans Wolfgang, Kt, PhD; British development economist; b. 29 Nov. 1910, Elberfeld, Germany; s. of Heinrich Singer and Antonia Spier; m. Ilse Lina Plaut 1934; one s. (and one s. deceased); ed Univs of Bonn and Cambridge; researcher, Pilgrim Trust Unemployment Enquiry 1936–38; Asst Lecturer, Univ. of Manchester 1938–44; economist, Ministry of Town and Country Planning 1945–46; lecturer, Univ. of Glasgow 1946–47; UN Secr. New York 1947–69; Professorial Fellow, Inst. of Devt Studies, Univ. of Sussex 1969–, Prof. Emer. 1980–; consultant to developing countries and int. orgs. etc.; Hon. DLitt (Univ. Nacional del Litoral Santa Fé, Argentina, Sussex, Glasgow, Lisbon, Innsbruck, Kent); Frances Wood Memorial Prize. *Publications include:* International Development: Growth and Change 1964, Food Aid: The Challenge and the Opportunity (with Jennings and Wood), 1987, Rich and Poor Countries (with J. Ansari), The Foreign Aid Business (with K. Raffer) 1996; articles in professional journals. *Leisure interests:* chess, music. *Address:* The Institute of Development Studies, University of Sussex, Brighton, East Sussex, BN1 9RE (Office); 18 The Vale, Ovingdean, Brighton, East Sussex, BN2 7AB, England (Home). *Telephone:* (1273) 678279 (Office); (1273) 303567 (Home). *Fax:* (1273) 621202.

SINGER, Isadore Manuel, PhD; American mathematician; b. 3 May 1924, Detroit, Mich.; s. of Simon Singer and Freda Rose; m. Sheila Ruff 1961; five c.; ed Univs. of Michigan and Chicago; C.L.E. Moore Instructor at MIT 1950–52; Asst Prof. Univ. of Calif. (Los Angeles) 1952–54; Visiting Asst Prof. Columbia Univ. 1954–55; Visiting mem. Inst. for Advanced Study, Princeton 1955–56; Asst Prof. MIT 1956, Assoc. Prof. 1958, Prof. of Math. 1959, Norbert Wiener Prof. of Math. 1970–79; Visiting Prof. of Math., Univ. of Calif., Berkeley 1977–79, Prof. 1979–83; Miller Prof. Univ. of Calif., Berkeley 1982–83; John D. MacArthur Prof. of Math., MIT 1983–, Inst. Prof. 1987–; mem. NAS, American Math. Soc., Math. Assen of America, American Acad. of Arts and Sciences, American Philosophical Soc., American Physical Soc.; Sloan Fellow 1959–62, Guggenheim Fellow 1968–69, 1975–76; Bôcher Memorial Prize 1969, 1975–76, Nat. Medal of Science 1985, Wigner Prize, Int. Congress of Mathematicians 1989. *Publications:* Lecture Notes on Elementary Topology and Geometry; author of research articles in functional analysis, differential geometry and topology. *Leisure interests:* literature, hiking, tennis. *Address:* Department of Mathematics, Massachusetts Institute of Technology, Room 2-387, 77 Massachusetts Avenue, Cambridge, MA 02139, USA. *Telephone:* (617) 253-1000. *Fax:* (617) 253-8000. *Website:* web.mit.edu (Office).

SINGER, Maxine, PhD; American biochemist; b. 15 Feb. 1931, New York; d. of Hyman Frank and Henrietta Perlowitz Frank; m. Daniel M. Singer 1952; one s. three d.; ed Swarthmore Coll. and Yale Univ.; Research Chemist, Enzymes and Cellular Biochemistry Section, Nat. Inst. of Arthritis and Metabolic Diseases, NIH, Bethesda, Md 1958–74, Chief, Nucleic Acid Enzymology Section, Lab. of Biochemistry, Div. of Cancer Biology and Diagnosis, Nat. Cancer Inst. 1974–79, Chief, Lab. of Biochem. 1979–87, research chemist 1987–88, Scientist Emer. 1988–; Pres. Carnegie Inst., Wash. 1988–; Visiting Scientist, Dept of Genetics, Weizmann Inst. of Science, Rehovot, Israel 1971–72; Dir Foundation for Advanced Educ. in Sciences 1972–78, 1985–86; mem. Yale Corpn 1975–90; Chair. Smithsonian Council 1992–94 (mem. 1990–94); Chair. Comm. on the Future of the Smithsonian 1994–96; mem. Editorial Bd Journal of Biological Chem. 1968–74, Science 1972–82; Chair. Editorial Bd Proceedings of NAS 1985–88; Scientific Council Int. Inst. of Genetics and Biophysics, Naples 1982–86, Bd of Govs. of Weizmann Inst., Human Genome Org. 1989–, Cttee on Science, Eng and Public Policy, NAS 1989–91, Int. Advisory Bd, Chulabhorn Research Inst. 1990–; mem. Bd Dirs. Johnson & Johnson; mem. NAS, American Soc. of Biological Chemists, American Soc. of Microbiologists, ACS, American Acad. of Arts and Sciences, Inst. of Medicine of NAS, American Philosophical Soc., New York Acad. of Sciences; Trustee Wesleyan Univ., Middletown, Conn. 1972–75, Whitehead Inst. 1985–94; Hon. DSc (Wesleyan Univ.) 1977, (Swarthmore Coll.) 1978, (Univ. of Md) 1985, (Brandeis Univ.) 1988, (Radcliffe Coll.) 1990, (Williams Coll.) 1990, (Franklin and Marshall Coll.) 1991, (George Washington Univ.) 1992, (New York Univ.) 1992, (Lehigh Univ.) 1992, (Dartmouth) 1993, (Yale) 1994, (Harvard) 1994; Dir.'s Award, Nat. Insts. of Health 1977, Nat. Medal of Science 1992 and other awards. *Publications:* molecular biology textbooks (with Paul Berg), Why Aren't Black Holes Black? (with Robert Hazen) and numerous articles in major scientific journals. *Leisure interests:* scuba diving, cooking, literature. *Address:* Carnegie Institution of Washington, 1530 P St, NW, Washington, DC 20005 (Office); 5410 39th Street, NW, Washington, DC 20015, USA (Home). *Telephone:* (202) 387-6404. *Fax:* (202) 462-7395 (Office). *Website:* www.carnegieinstitution.org.

SINGER, Peter Albert David, MA, BPhil; Australian philosopher and author; b. 6 July 1946, Melbourne; s. of Ernest Singer and Cora Oppenheim; m. Renata Diamond 1968; three d.; ed Scotch Coll., Univ. of Melbourne and Univ. Coll. Oxford; Radcliffe Lecturer, Univ. Coll. Oxford 1971–73; Visiting Asst Prof. Dept of Philosophy, New York Univ. 1973–74; Sr Lecturer, Dept of Philosophy, La Trobe Univ. 1975–76; Prof. Dept of Philosophy, Monash Univ. 1977–99, Dir Centre for Human Bioethics 1981–91, Deputy Dir 1992–99; DeCamp Prof. of Bioethics, Princeton Univ., NJ, USA 1999–; various visiting positions in USA, Canada and Italy. *Publications:* numerous books and articles, including Animal Liberation 1975, Practical Ethics 1979, How Are We to Live? 1993, Rethinking Life and Death 1994, Ethics into Action 1998, A Darwinian Left 1999, Writings on an Ethical Life 2000, One World 2002, Pushing Time Away 2003. *Leisure interests:* bushwalking, reading, swimming. *Address:* University Center for Human Values, Princeton, NJ 08544, USA. *E-mail:* psinger@princeton.edu (Office).

SINGH, Bhishma Narain, BA; Indian politician; b. 13 July 1933, Palamau, Bihar; m. Ram Kumari Devi 1950; two s. two d.; ed Takeya High School, Sasaram, Bihar and Banaras Hindu Univ.; active Congress worker 1953–; mem. All Indian Congress Cttee; mem. Bihar Legis. Ass. 1967–69, 1969–72, 1972–76; Minister, State Gov. of Bihar 1971, 1972–73, 1973–74; mem. Rajya Sabha 1976, 1982, Deputy Chief Whip, Congress Parl. Party 1977, later Chief Whip; Minister of Parl. Affairs 1980–83, of Communications Jan.–March 1980, of Works and Housing, Labour, Supply and Food and Civil Supplies 1980–83; Gov. of Assam and Meghalaya 1983–89, of Sikkim 1985–86, of

Arunachal Pradesh 1987, of Tamil Nadu 1991–93; Deputy Chair. Cen. Cooperative Bank, Daltonganj 1964; Dir Bihar State Co-operative Mktg. Union 1967; Chair. Bihar State Co-operative Housing Construction Finance Soc. 1974–75, Bihar State Credit and Investment Corpn 1974. *Leisure interests:* horse riding, marksmanship, music, dance and drama, especially tribal folk dances. *Address:* Hamid Ganj, P.O. Daitonganj, Palamau District, Bihar, India.

SINGH, Bipin; Indian dancer and choreographer; b. 23 Aug. 1918, Vill-Singari-Cachar; s. of Laikhomsana Singha and Indubala Devi; m. 1st Manorama Sinha; m. 2nd Kalavati Devi; five s. three d.; Manipuri dance teacher, Calcutta 1936; joined Madam Menaka Troup 1938, toured India and abroad; Dir dance dramas, Bombay 1943; collected and recorded the oral traditions of Manipuri dance and music; toured world with routines; f. Manipuri Nartanalaya in Bombay, Manipur and Calcutta 1972. *Publications:* Vaisnav Sangeet Damodar (ed.) 1985, Panchamsarsanhita and Sangeet Damodar (ed.) 1986. *Leisure interests:* walking, listening to news. *Address:* Manipuri Nartanalaya, 15A Bipin Pal Road, Kolkata 700026, India. *Telephone:* 465922.

SINGH, Buta; Indian politician; b. 21 March 1934, Jalandhar Punjab; s. of Sardar Bir Singh; ed Lyallpur Khalsa Coll., Jalandhar and Guru Nanak Khalsa Coll., Bombay; elected to Lok Sabha 1962, 1967, 1971, 1980, 1984, 1999; Union Deputy Minister for Railways 1974–76, for Commerce 1976–77; Minister of State in Ministry of Shipping and Transport 1980–81; Minister of Supply and Rehabilitation 1981–82, of Sport 1982–83, Cabinet Minister in charge of several ministries 1983–84, Minister of Agric. 1984–86, of Home Affairs 1986–89, of Civil Supplies, Consumer Affairs and Public Distribution 1995–96, of Communications 1998; mem. Planning Comm. 1985, Gen. Sec. Indian Nat. Congress 1978–80; Pres. Amateur Athletic Fed. of India 1976–84. *Address:* 9 Lodi Estate, New Delhi 110003, India. *Telephone:* (11) 4699797.

SINGH, Chaudhary Randhir, MA, LLB; Indian politician; b. 1 July 1924, Bayanpur, Haryana; s. of the late Chaudhary Chandgi Ram and Chhoti Devi; m. Vijay Lakshmi Chaudhary 1939; four s. three d.; ed St Stephen's Coll., Delhi, Univ. of Delhi; fmr mem. Parl. (Lok Sabha), All India Congress Cttee, several Parl. Cttees., Exec. Congress Party in Parl.; mem. Nat. Comm. on Agric. 1970–76; Chair. Agric. Prices Comm., Govt of India 1976–79, 1980–83, 1987–89; Gov. Sikkim 1996–; Chair. or mem. numerous Govt working groups on land reform and agricultural Devt issues; fmrly Chair. Punjab Praja Socialist Party, mem. Nat. Exec. of Punjab Praha Socialist Party of India, Sec.-Gen. United Front of Opposition Parties Punjab, Chair. AICC Land Reforms Panel, Sr Vice-Chair. and Sec.-Gen. Farmers' Parl. Forum of India; active in social work in Haryana; recipient of numerous awards for work on behalf of peasant families and minority groups. *Publications:* 18 books on agricultural Devt and problems of rural peoples. *Leisure interests:* listening to and reading Urdu poetry, especially by Md Iqbal and Ghalib, folk songs and dances. *Address:* Office of Governor, Raj Bhavan, Gangtok 737103, Sikkim, India. *Telephone:* (3592) 22400 (Office); (3592) 23049 (Home). *Fax:* (3592) 22742.

SINGH, Digvijay, BEng; Indian politician; b. 28 Feb. 1947, Indore; s. of Balbhadra Singh; elected to Ass. 1977, 1980; Gen. Sec. Madhya Pradesh Youth Congress 1978–79; fmr Minister of State for Agric., Arjun Singh Ministry, later Cabinet Minister for Irrigation; elected to Lok Sabha 1991; Pres. Madhya Pradesh Congress Cttee 1980, Council 1984, 1992; Chief Minister Madhya Pradesh 1993–98, 1998–. *Address:* Chief Minister's Secretariat, Ballabh Bhavan, Bhopal (Office); 1 Shamla Hill, Bhopal, India (Home). *Telephone:* (755) 551581 (Office); (755) 540500 (Home). *Fax:* (755) 551781.

SINGH, Gopal, PhD; Indian politician, poet and writer; b. 29 Nov. 1919, Serai Niamat Khan, NW Frontier Prov.; s. of Atma Singh and Nanaki Devi; m. 1950; one d.; nominated MP 1962–68; Amb. to Bulgaria and Caribbean countries 1970–76; Chair. High Power Comm. of Minorities, Scheduled Castes, Scheduled Tribes and other Weaker Sections 1980–84; Gov. Goa, Daman and Diu 1984, of Nagaland 1989; has lectured at univs. in UK, USA, Thailand, Egypt, Iran and India; fmr Sec.-Gen. Indian Council for Africa; Chair. Presidium, World Punjabi Congress; many awards and decorations. *Publications:* first free-verse English translation of the Sikh Scripture; five books of Punjabi verse; A History of the Sikh People 1469–1978, The Religion of the Sikhs, A History of Punjabi Literature; The Unstruck Melody (poetry), The Man Who Never Died (poetry); collection of short stories, children's books, an English-Punjabi lexicon, several biogs. and books of literary criticism. *Leisure interests:* reading, walking.

SINGH, Jaswant, BA, BSc; Indian politician and army officer; b. 3 Jan. 1938, Jasol, Rajasthan; s. of the late Thakur Sardar Singhji and of Kunwar Baisa; m. Sheetal Kumari 1963; two s.; ed Mayo Coll., Ajmer, Jt Services Wing, Clement Town, Dehradun, Indian Mil. Acad., Dehradun; commissioned Cen. India Horse 1957; resgnd his comm. and elected to Rajya Sabha 1980; Minister of Finance 1996, 2002–; Deputy Chair., Planning Comm. 1998–99; Minister of External Affairs 1999, 2001–02; Minister of Electronics Feb.–Oct. 1999, of Surface Transport Aug.–Oct. 1999; Chair. Consultative Cttee for the Ministry of External Affairs 2000–01; Leader of the House, Rajya Sabha 1999–. *Publications:* National Security – An Outline of Our Concerns 1996, Shauryo Tejo 1997, Defending India 1999; numerous articles on int. affairs, security and Devt issues to Indian and foreign magazines, newspapers and journals. *Leisure interests:* horses, equestrian sports, reading, music, golf,

chess. *Address:* Ministry of Finance, North Block, New Delhi 110 001, India. *Telephone:* (11) 3012611. *Fax:* (11) 3012477. *E-mail:* jsdea@finance.delhi.nic .in. *Website:* www.finmin.nic.in.

SINGH, Karan, MA, PhD; Indian politician; b. 9 March 1931, Cannes, France; s. of Lt-Gen. HH Maharaja Sir Hari Singh, GCSI, GCIE, GCVO and Maharani Tara Devi, CI; m. Princess Yasho Rajya Lakshmi of Nepal 1950; two s. one d.; ed Doon School, Univ. of Jammu and Kashmir and Delhi Univ.; appointed Regent of Jammu and Kashmir 1949; elected Sadar-i-Riyasat (Head of State) by Jammu and Kashmir Legis. Ass. Nov. 1952, recognized by Pres. of India and assumed office 17 Nov. 1952, re-elected 1957 and 1962, Gov. 1965–67; Union Minister for Tourism and Civil Aviation 1967–73, for Health and Family Planning 1973–75, 1976–77, for Educ. 1979–80; re-elected mem. of Parl. 1977, 1980; mem. Upper House of Parl.; Amb. to USA 1989–91; Vice-Pres. Indian Council for Cultural Relations; Pres. Delhi Music Soc.; led Indian Del. to World Population Conf., Bucharest; Vice-Pres. World Health Ass. 1975–76; fmr Chancellor Jammu and Kashmir Univ., Banaras Hindu Univ.; fmr Sec. Jawaharlal Nehru Memorial Fund; fmr Chair. Indian Bd for Wild Life, Life Trustee of the India Int. Centre; Hon. Maj.-Gen. Indian Army; Hon. Col Jammu and Kashmir Regt 1962; Dr. hc (Aligarh Muslim Univ.) 1963, (Banaras Hindu Univ., Soka Univ., Tokyo). *Publications:* Prophet of Indian Nationalism: The Political Thought of Sri Aurobindo Ghosh 1893–1910 1963, Heir Apparent 1983, One Man's World 1986, Religions of India, Humanity at the Crossroads 1988, Autobiography 1989, Essays on Hinduism 1990; and several books on political science, philosophical essays, travelogues, trans. of Dogra-Pahari folksongs and poems in English. *Leisure interests:* reading, writing, music. *Address:* 3 Nyaya Marg, Chanakyapuri, New Delhi 110021, India. *Telephone:* (11) 6115291; (11) 6111744. *Fax:* (11) 6873171. *E-mail:* karansingh@karansingh.com (Home). *Website:* www.karansingh.com (Home).

SINGH, Khushwant, LLB; Indian author; b. Feb. 1915; m. Kaval Malik; one s. one d.; ed Government Coll., Lahore, King's Coll. and Inner Temple, London; practised High Court, Lahore 1939–47; joined Indian Ministry of External Affairs 1947; Press Attaché, Canada and then Public Relations Officer, London 1948–51; Ministry of Information and Broadcasting; edited Yojana; Dept of Mass Communication, UNESCO 1954–56; commissioned by Rockefeller Foundation and Muslim Univ., Aligarh, to write a history of the Sikhs 1958; MP 1980–; Ed.-in-Chief The Hindustan Times, New Delhi 1980–83; Visiting Lecturer Hawaii, Oxford, Princeton, Rochester, Swarthmore; numerous TV and radio appearances; Ed. The Illustrated Weekly of India 1969–78; Grove Press Award; Mohan Singh Award; Padma Bhushan 1974. *Publications:* Mark of Vishnu 1949, The Sikhs 1951, Train to Pakistan 1954, Sacred Writings of the Sikhs 1960, I Shall Not Hear the Nightingale 1961, Umrao Jan Ada—Courtesan of Lucknow (trans.) 1961, History of the Sikhs (1769–1839) Vol. I 1962, Ranjit Singh: Maharaja of the Punjab 1962, Fall of the Sikh Kingdom 1962, The Skeleton (trans.) 1963, Land of the Five Rivers (trans.) 1964, History of the Sikhs (1839–Present Day) Vol. II 1965, Khushwant Singh's India 1969, Indira Gandhi Returns 1979, Editor's Page 1980, Iqbal's Dialogue with Allah (trans.) 1981, Punjab Tragedy (with Kuldip Nayar) 1984, Roots of Dissent 1992 and others. *Leisure interest:* bird watching. *Address:* 49E Sujan Singh Park, New Delhi 110003, India. *Telephone:* (11) 4620159.

SINGH, Sukhmander, MS, PhD; American professor of civil engineering; b. 15 Sept. 1939, Lambi; s. of Mahla Singh and Jangir Kaur; m. Charanjit Kaur 1967; one s. one d.; ed Punjabi Univ., Patiala, Punjab, Indian Inst. of Tech., Delhi, Univ. of Ottawa and Carleton Univ., Ottawa, Canada, Rice Univ., Houston, Tex., Univ. of Calif., Berkeley; Assoc. Lecturer, Indian Inst. of Tech., Delhi, India 1966–67; Teaching Asst, Univ. of Ottawa 1967–68; Visiting Lecturer, Univ. of Alaska, Anchorage 1975, San Jose State Univ., Calif. 1978; Assoc. Prof. of Civil Eng, Calif. State Univ., LA, Calif. 1983–86; Assoc. Prof. of Civil Eng, Santa Clara Univ., Calif. 1986–90, Chair. Dept of Civil Eng and Chair. Eng Mechanics 1990–; professional work as engineer with John V. Lowney & Assocs., Palo Alto, Calif. 1969, Dames & Moore, San Francisco, London, Houston, Anchorage and Seattle offices 1969–83, as Consultant 1983–; Consultant with Purcell, Rhoades and Assocs., Hayward, Calif. 1987–, with Calpine/Kaiser 1989–; mem. numerous cttees. on soil dynamics and geotechnical Eng; research on liquefaction of silts and geotechnology of cold regions. *Publications:* numerous scientific papers. *Leisure interests:* reading, hiking, volleyball playing. *Address:* Department of Civil Engineering, Santa Clara University, Santa Clara, CA 95053, USA. *Telephone:* (408) 554-6869.

SINGH, Vijay; Fijian golfer; b. 22 Feb. 1963, Lautoka; m. Ardena Seth; one c.; ed Univ. of N Carolina; turned professional 1982, joined PGA Tour 1983; PGA Tour victories: Buick Classic 1993, Phoenix Open 1993, Buick Classic 1995, Memorial Tournament 1997, Buick Open 1997, PGA Championship 1998, Sprint Int. 1998, Honda Classic 1999, Masters Tournament 2000, Shell Houston Open 2002, PGA Championship 2002; int. victories: Malaysian PGA Championship 1984, Nigerian Open 1988, Swedish PGA 1988, Volvo Open di Firenze 1989, Ivory Coast Open 1989, Nigerian Open 1989, Zimbabwe Open 1989, El Bosque Open 1990, King Hassan Trophy, Morocco 1991, Turespaña Masters Open de Andalucía 1992, Malaysian Open 1992, Volvo German Open 1992, Bells Cup 1993, Scandinavian Masters 1994, Trophée Lancôme 1994, Passport Open 1995, South African Open 1997, Toyota World Match Play Championship 1997, Johnnie Walker Taiwan Open 2000, Singapore Masters 2001, Malaysian Open 2001. *Leisure interests:* snooker, cricket, rugby, soccer, James Bond movies.

SINGH, Vishwanath Pratap, LLB; Indian politician; b. 25 June 1931, Allahabad; s. of Raja Bahadur Ram Gopal Singh; m. Sita Kumari 1955; two s.; ed Poona and Allahabad Univs; Pres. Students Union, Udai Pratap Coll., Varanasi 1947–48; mem. Exec. Body, Allahabad Univ. 1969–71; mem. Legis. Ass., Uttar Pradesh 1969–71; Whip, Congress Legis. Party 1970–71; mem. Lok Sabha 1971–77, 1988–94, Rajya Sabha 1983–94; Union Deputy Minister for Commerce 1974–76, Union State Minister for Commerce 1976–77, 1983; Minister of Finance 1984–86, of Defence 1986–87; Prime Minister of India 1989–90; Chief Minister of Uttar Pradesh 1980–82, mem. Legis. Council 1980–81, Legis. Ass. 1981–83, Pres. Uttar Pradesh 1980–82, mem. Legis. Council 1980–81, Legis. Ass. 1981–83, Pres. Uttar Pradesh Congress Cttee 1984; Additional Charge of Dept of Supply 1983; expelled from Congress (1) Party 1987; Founder and Leader Jan Morcha Party 1987; Leader Janata Dal Party 1988–91 (resgnd); Pres. Samajwadi Janata Dal (Coalition) 1988–90. *Leisure interests:* painting, photography. *Address:* 1 Teen Murti Marg, New Delhi 110001; 4 Ashok Road, Allahabad, India. *Telephone:* (11) 3018288 (New Delhi).

SINGH, W. Nipamacha, M.A.; Indian politician; b. March 1930; s. of W. Gokulchand Singh; m. Longjam Ningol Maipak Devi; began career as teacher 1960; entered active politics as mem. Indian Nat. Congress 1971; Speaker Manipur Ass. 1995–97; Chief Minister of Manipur 1997–2000, 2000–01. *Address:* c/o Chief Minister's Bungalow, Imphal 795001, India (Office).

SINGHVI, Laxmi Mall, LLD, SJD; Indian diplomatist and jurist; b. 9 Nov. 1931, Jodhpur; s. of Dashrathmal Singhvi and Akal Kaur Singhvi; m. Kamla Singhvi 1957; one s. one d.; ed Jodhpur, Allahabad, Harvard and Cornell Univs.; Dir Indian Law Inst. 1957–58; Sr Standing Counsel for Govt of India and State of Uttar Pradesh; Sr Advocate, Supreme Court of India 1967–; independent mem. for Jodhpur, Lok Sabha 1962–67; mem. of Rajya Sabha (Parl.) 1998–; mem. Perm. Court of Arbitration, The Hague 2000–, Comm. of Inquiry into Admin. of Justice in Trinidad and Tobago 2000–; Dir Benett Coleman & Co. Ltd (owners of the Times of India Publications) and Punjab Nat. Bank Ltd; Founder and Chair. Inst. of Constitutional and Parl. Studies 1964; Chair. Commonwealth Legal Educ. Assn 1972–77; Chair. Nat. Legal Aid Asscn of India; Chair. Nat. Fed. of UNESCO Asscns in India 1974–; Chair. Indian Nat. Cttee for Abolition of Death Penalty 1977–, Govt of India Cttee on Local Self Govt 1986–87, Nat. High-Level Cttee on Persons of Indian Origin and Non-resident Indians (with rank of Cabinet Minister in Cen. Govt) 2000–; fmr Pres., now Pres. Emer. Supreme Court of India Bar Asscn, Pres. Asian Human Rights Conf. 1985, Indian Human Rights Trust, Indian Centre for the Independence of Judges and Lawyers; mem. UN Sub-Comm. on Protection of Minorities, UN Working Group for Protection of All Persons under any Form of Imprisonment or Detention; Chair. Samachar Bharati news agency; Life Trustee India Int. Centre, Pres. 1988–; Chair. Nat. Task Force on Child Labour 1989; Pres. Indian Centre for the Rights of the Child; Chief Justice Mehrchant Centennial Oration 1989; Pres. Authors Guild of India, Indira Gandhi Nat. Centre for Arts 2000–, Centre for Contemporary Culture; High Commr in UK 1991–97; Chair. Prava Mandals for Jamna Lal Bajaj and Jnan Peeth Awards; Co-Chair. Bharatiya Vidya Bhavan Int.; Trustee Jnanpith Awards; delivered C. D. Deshmukh Memorial Oration 1988; Jawaharlal Nehru Memorial Centennial Oration; Hon. Tagore Law Prof. (Calcutta) 1973; Hon. Prof. of Law (Delhi, Andhra, Calcutta); Hon. Bencher and Master, Middle Temple, London 1987–; Hon. Patron, Commonwealth Legal Educ. Assoc., London; Hon. LLD (Jabalpur Univ.) 1983, (Banaras Hindu Univ.) 1984, (Westminster) 1996, (London) 1997, (Luton) 1997; U Thant Peace Award, Padma Bhushan Award 1998, Award for Humanism Jury G. D. Birle Int. Centre 1988. *Publications:* Jain Temples in India and Around the World 2002, A Diplomatic Sojourn 2002, Democracy and the Rule of Law 2002, Towards Global Togetherness 2002, Bharat Aur Hamara Samaya, Towards a New Global Order, A Tale of Three Cities, Freedom on Trial, The Evening Sun (poems in Hindi);. *Leisure interests:* performing arts, poetry, gardening. *Address:* 18 Willington Crescent, New Delhi 110001, India (Home); Kamalalaya, B-8, South Extension Part II, New Delhi 110049. *Telephone:* (11) 3792424; (11) 3012121; (11) 3014646. *Fax:* (11) 3794466. *E-mail:* lsinghvi@del13.vsnl.net.in; lsinghvi@sansad.nic.in.

SINGLETON, William Dean; American newspaper proprietor; b. 1 Aug. 1951, Tex.; s. of the late William Hyde Singleton and of Florence E. Myrick Singleton; m. Adrienne Casale 1983; two s. one d.; Pres. Gloucester Co. Times, NJ.; Vice-Chair., Pres., CEO MediaNews Group, Inc. 1988–; Pres., Chair. The Houston Post 1988–95, The Denver Post; Vice-Chair. 27 daily newspapers and 55 non-daily publications including Houston Post, Denver Post, with daily circulation in excess of 1.1 million in 10 states. *Leisure interest:* skiing. *Address:* Media News Group, 1560 Broadway, Suite 1450, Denver, CO 80202, USA.

SINGSON, Gabriel, LLM; Philippine banker; b. 18 March 1929, Lingayen, Pangasinan; m. Moonyeen Retizos; two s. one d.; ed Pangasinan Provincial High School, Ateneo de Manila and Univ. of Michigan Law School, Ann Arbor; Assoc. Attorney, Law Office of Justice Jose Bengzon 1952–55; Prof. of Commercial Law and Civil Law, Ateneo de Manila Law School 1956–72; Legal and Evaluation Officer, Cen. Bank 1955–60, Tech. Asst Monetary Bd 1960–62, Asst to Deputy Gov. 1963–66, 1968–70; Legal Officer, Asian Devt Bank 1967–68; Asst to Gov. (with rank of Dir), Cen. Bank 1970–73, Special Asst to Gov. 1973–74, Gen. Counsel 1974–75, Deputy Gov. and Gen. Counsel 1975–80, Sr Deputy Gov. 1980–92; Pres. Philippine Nat. Bank 1992–93; Chair. Monetary Bd and Gov. Bangko Sentral ng Pilipinas 1993–98; Chair.

PR Holdings Inc. (holding co. of Philippine Air Lines); Vice-Chair. Philippine Air Lines. *Publications:* articles on Asian Devt Bank, foreign loans, foreign investments and foreign exchange regulations. *Leisure interest:* golf. *Address:* 28 Polk Street, Greenhills, San Juan, Metro Manila, Philippines (Home).

SINHA, Lieut.-Gen. Shreenivas Kumar, BA; Indian army officer; b. 7 Jan. 1926, Gaya; s. of M. K. Sinha and Radha Sinha; m. Premini Sinha; one s. three d.; commissioned 1944, transferred to 5 Gorkha Rifles after Independence, fmr. Col of Regt (5GR); fmr instructor Infantry School, Mhow and Defence Services Staff Coll., Wellington; fmr Dir of Mil. Intelligence and Deputy Adjutant-Gen.; fmr Adjutant-Gen., Army HQ; Gen. Officer C-in-C, W Command 1981–82; Vice-Chief of Army Staff 1983; Amb. to Nepal 1990; Gov. of Assam 1997–; Sec. Del. to UN Comm. for India and Pakistan for Kashmir 1949; Leader Del. UN Conf. on Application of Human Rights to Warfare 1972; Hon. Aide-de-Camp to Pres. of India 1979; PVSM. *Publications:* Operation Rescue, Of Matters Military, Pataliputra, Past to Present, A Soldier Recalls, Veer Kuer Singh. *Leisure interests:* golf. *Address:* Raj Bhavan, Guwahati, India (Office). *Telephone:* (361) 540500 (Office); (361) 540250 (Home). *Fax:* (361) 540310 (Office).

SINHA, Yashwant, MA; Indian politician, teacher and civil servant; b. 6 Nov. 1937, Patna, Bihar; m. Nilima Sinha 1961; two s. one d.; ed Patna Coll., Patna Univ. Bihar; Lecturer in Political Science, Patna Univ. 1958–60; joined I.A.S. 1960; Deputy Comm. Santhal Paraganas; Chair. Drafting Cttee of the UNCTAD Conf. on Shipping, Geneva; Consul-Gen. of India, Frankfurt; Prin. Sec. to Chief Minister, Bihar; Jt Sec. to Govt of India, Ministry of Shipping and Transport; retd from I.A.S. and joined Janata Party 1984, Gen. Sec. 1986–88; mem. Rajya Sabha 1988, mem. Cttee on Petitions 1989; joined Janata Dal (Samajwadi) after split in Janata Dal 1990; Minister of Finance 1998–99, 2001–02, of External Affairs 2002–; mem. Lok Sabha 1998–; mem. Parl. Pay Cttee 1998–99. *Leisure interests:* reading, travelling, listening to music, watching films. *Address:* Ministry of External Affairs, South Block, New Delhi, 110 011 (Office); Jasol House, Paotabarea, Jodhpur (Home); Vill. Hupad, Post-Morangi, Demotandh, Thana Muffassil, Hazaribagh (Bihar), India (Home). *Telephone:* (11) 3012380. *Website:* www.meadev.nic.in (Office).

SINISCALCO, Domenico, LLB, PhD; Italian economist and writer; b. 15 July 1954, Turin; m.; two s.; ed Univ. of Turin, Univ. of Cambridge; Prof. of Econs Univ. of Turin 1990–; Dir-Gen. Treasury, Rome Oct. 2001–; Dir ENI Oct. 2001–; fmr teaching posts at LUISS (Rome), Univ. of Cagliari, Johns Hopkins Univ. (USA), Univ. of Cambridge (UK), Univ. Catholique de Louvain (Belgium); Dir ENI Enrico Mattei Foundation 1989–2001; Adviser Querini Stampalia Foundation, IRI Foundation; fmr mem. Bd of Dirs several listed cos.; columnist Il Sole 24 Ore –2001; mem. Steering Cttee journals Equilibri, Mercato, Concorrenza and Regole; mem. Royal Swedish Acad. of Sciences, Beijer Inst. *Publications:* over 90 publs on privatization, environmental econs and industrial econs. *Address:* c/o Ministry of the Treasury and of the Budget, Via XX Settembre 97, 00187 Rome, Italy (Office).

SINIVASAN, Marimutu; Indonesian business executive; b. 1937, Medan, N Sumatra; began career as English teacher, later clerk in British firm; set up textile trading business (later Texmaco Group, conglomerate of 20 cos) late 1950s, Chair. Texmaco Group; nominated by Pres. Suharto to People's Consultative Ass. 1997. *Address:* Polysinda Eka Perkasa Tbk (Pt), Suite 1000, 10/Flr, Sentra Mulia Building, J1 HR Rasuna Said Kav. X-6, Jakarta, Indonesia (Office). *Telephone:* (267) 431-971 (Office). *Fax:* (267) 431-975 (Office).

SINN, Hans-Werner, Dr rer. pol; German economist; b. 7 March 1948, Brake, Westphalia; m. Gerlinde Sinn (née Zoubek) 1971; two s. one d.; ed Helmsholtz-Gymnasium, Bielefeld, Univ. of Münster, Univ. of Mannheim; lecturer Univ. of Münster 1972–74, Univ. of Mannheim 1974–78, Sr Lecturer 1979–83, Assoc. Prof. 1983–84; Visiting Asst Prof. Univ. of Western Ont. 1978–79; Prof. of Econs and Insurance Univ. of Munich 1984–94; Dir Centre for Econ. Studies 1991–; Prof. of Econs and Public Finance 1994–; Chair. Verein für Socialpolitik (German Econ. Asscn) 1997–2000; Pres. Ifo Inst. for Econ. Research 1999–; Hon. Dr rer. pol; Verdienstkreuz (Germany) 1999, Medal of Univ. of Helsinki. *Publications:* Economic Decisions under Uncertainty 1980, Capital Income Taxation and Resource Allocation 1985, Jumpstart: the Economic Unification of Germany 1991, The German State Banks—Global Players in the International Financial Markets 1999, The New Systems Competition 2002; numerous articles on public finance and other subjects. *Leisure interest:* photography. *Address:* Ifo Institute, Poschingerstr. 5, 81679, Munich; (Office); Centre for Economic Studies, University of Munich, Schackstr. 4, 80539 Munich, Germany (Office). *Telephone:* (89) 92241276 (Office); (89) 21802748 (Office). *Fax:* (89) 92241901 (Office); (89) 397303 (Office). *E-mail:* sinn@ifo.de (Office).

SINNOTT, Kevin, MA; British artist; b. 4 Dec. 1947, Bridgend, Wales; s. of Myles Vincent Sinnott and Honora Burke; m. Susan Forward 1969; three s. one d.; ed St. Robert's School, Royal Coll. of Art; teacher Canterbury Coll. of Art 1981–88, St Martin's School of Art, London 1981–93; solo exhbns. at Bernard Jacobson Gallery 1986, 1988, 1990, Bernard Jacobson, New York 1987, 1989, Flowers East 1992, 1994, 1996, 1998, Flowers West, Los Angeles 1999, Caldwell/Snyder, New York 2000; work in numerous public collections (including Arts Council of GB, British Museum, British Council, Nat. Museum of Wales, Metropolitan Museum of Art, New York). *Art exhibition:* Calder/Snyder, San Francisco 2001, Martin Tinney, Cardiff 2001, 2003, Calder/Snyder, New York 2002. *Leisure interests:* cinema, books, walks, opera. *Address:* Tyr Santes Fair, Pont-y-Rhyl, Bridgend, CF32 8LJ, Wales. *Telephone:* (1656) 871854 (Home). *Fax:* (1656) 871854 (Home). *E-mail:* kevin@kevinsinnott.co.uk (Home). *Website:* www.kevinsinnott.co.uk (Home).

SINOWATZ, Fred; Austrian politician; b. 5 Feb. 1929, Neufeld an der Leitha, Burgenland; m. Hermine Sinowatz 1954; one s. one d.; ed Univ. of Vienna; joined Burgenland provincial Govt service 1953; mem. Burgenland Prov. Legis. 1961–71, Pres. 1964; Party Sec. Burgenland Austrian Socialist Party (SPÖ) Org. 1961–78, Deputy Chair. 1978, Chair. –1988; mem. Nat. Exec. SPÖ 1981, Chair. 1983–88; mem. Nationalrat 1971; Fed. Minister of Educ. and Arts 1971–83; Fed. Vice-Chancellor 1981, Chancellor 1983–86. *Address:* Loewelstrasse 18, 1010 Vienna, Austria.

SINSHEIMER, Robert Louis, SB, SM, PhD; American biologist; b. 5 Feb. 1920, Washington, DC; s. of Allen Sinsheimer and Rose Davidson Sinsheimer; m. 1st Flora Joan Hirsch 1943 (divorced 1972); one s. two d.; m. 2nd Kathleen Mae Reynolds 1972 (divorced 1980); m. 3rd Karen B. Keeton 1981; ed MIT; Research Assoc., Biology, MIT 1948–49; Assoc. Prof. of Biophysics, Iowa State Coll. 1949–55, Prof. 1955–57; Prof. of Biophysics, Calif. Inst. of Tech. 1957–77, Chair. Div. of Biology 1968–77, Visiting Prof. of Biology 1987–88; Prof. Dept of Biological Sciences, Univ. of Calif. at Santa Barbara 1988–90, Prof. Emer. 1990–; Chancellor, Univ. of Calif. at Santa Cruz 1977–87; mem. NAS, mem. Council 1970–73; Pres. Biophysical Soc. 1970–71; Chair. Bd of Ed., NAS Proceedings 1972–80; Calif. Scientist of the Year Award 1968, Beijerinck Medal of the Royal Netherlands Acad. of Sciences 1969, Univ. of Calif. Presidential Medal 2001. *Publications:* The Strands of Life (memoirs) 1994; more than 250 scientific papers 1946–. *Leisure interests:* travel, hiking and photography. *Address:* MCD Biology, University of California at Santa Barbara, Santa Barbara, CA 93106 (Office); 4606 Via Cavente, Santa Barbara, CA 93110, USA (Home). *Telephone:* (805) 893-8038 (Office); (805) 683-2247 (Home). *Fax:* (805) 893-4724 (Office). *E-mail:* sinsheim@lifesci.ucsb.edu (Office).

SINT, Marjanne; Netherlands public servant; b. 24 July 1949, Amsterdam; ed Univ. of Amsterdam and IMEDE Business School; mem. staff, Ministry of Econ. Affairs 1974–77, Ministry of Culture, Health and Social Affairs 1977–79; Econ. Ed., Intermediair 1979–80, Chief Ed. 1980–81; Publisher, VNU Business Publs 1981–87; Pres. Dutch Labour Party (PvdA) 1987–91; mem. staff Ministry of Interior 1991–95; Chief Exec. City of Amsterdam 1995–; currently Sec.-Gen., Ministry of Housing, Spatial Planning and the Environment. *Publications:* Tussen wal en schip, etnische minderheden in Nederland 1980, Economen over crisis 1982. *Leisure interests:* literature, poetry, music, modern art and architecture. *Address:* Ministry of Housing, Spatial Planning and the Environment, Rijnstraat 8, POB 20951, 2500 EZ The Hague, Netherlands. *Telephone:* (70) 3393939 (Office). *Website:* www.minvrom.nl.

SINYAVSKAYA, Tamara Ilyinichna; Russian opera singer (mezzo-soprano); b. 6 July 1943, Moscow; m. Muslim Magovaev 1974; ed Moscow Music Coll. and State Theatre Art Inst.; soloist with Bolshoi Theatre 1964–; studied at La Scala, Milan 1973–74; First Prize Int. Singing Competition, Sofia 1968, Grand Prix Int. Singing Competition, Belgium 1969, First Prize at Int. Tchaikovsky Competition, Moscow 1970, People's Artist of RSFSR 1976, People's Artist of USSR 1982. *Opera roles include:* Olga in Tchaikovsky's Eugene Onegin, Carmen, Blanche and Frosya in Prokofiev's Gambler and Semyon Kotko, Vanya in Glinka's A Life for the Tsar, Ratmir in Glinka's Ruslan and Lyudmila, Lyubasha in Rimsky-Korsakov's The Tsar's Bride, Varvara in Not Love Alone, Carmen. *Address:* c/o Bolshoi Theatre, Teatralnaya Pl. 1, Moscow, Russia.

SIPHANDONE, Gen. Khamtay; Laotian politician and army officer; b. 8 Feb. 1924, Houa Khong Village, Champassak Prov.; mil. officer 1947–48, rep. of Lao Itsala 1948, mem. Front Cen. Cttee 1950–52, Chair. Control Cttee 1952–54; Gen. Staff mem. Pathet Lao 1955–56, Head Cen. Cttee 1957–59, propaganda and training officer 1959–60, mem. Cen. Cttee 1957, C-in-C 1960, mem. Politburo 1972; mem. Lao People's Revolutionary Party (LPRP) 1972, Leader Nov. 1992–; mem. Secr. LPRP 1982; Deputy Prime Minister and Minister of Nat. Defence 1975–91; Prime Minister of Laos 1991–98; fmr Supreme Commdr Lao People's Army; Pres. of Laos Feb. 1998–. *Address:* Office of the President, Vientiane, Laos. *Telephone:* (21) 214200 (Office). *Fax:* (21) 214208 (Office).

SIPINEN, Arto Kalevi; Finnish architect; b. 20 April 1936, Helsinki; s. of Veikko Emil Sipinen and Tuovi Maria Heino; m. 2nd Sinikka Rossi 1986; one s. one d.; ed Helsinki Univ. of Tech.; worked with Alvar Aalto 1959–61, Viljo Revell 1961–63; own architectural practice 1963–; lecturer, Helsinki Univ. of Tech. 1964–67, Acting Prof. of Architecture 1991–92; mem. SAFA community planning Dept Bd 1964–66; Chair. SAFA competition Cttee 1964–66; SAFA competition judge 1965–; work includes Imatra City Hall 1970, Jyväskylä Univ. Library and Admin. Bldg 1974, Music and Art Bldg 1976, Raisio City Hall 1981, Imatra Cultural Centre 1986, Mikkeli Concert Hall 1988, Espoo Cultural Centre 1989, Lahti Main Library 1990, Tammela Town Hall 1991, Mäntsälä Town Hall 1992, Kuusamo Cultural Centre 1995 and planning projects in Helsinki city centre; more than 40 prizes in architectural competitions; other awards include SL Pro Finlandia Medal 1990, Concrete Structure of the Year Prize 1990, Prof. 1995, State Award for Architecture 1999. *Address:* Arkkitehtitoimisto Arto Sipinen Oy, Pahurinpolku 1, 021120

Espoo (Office); Munkkiniemenranta 39, 00330 Helsinki, Finland (Home). *Telephone:* 4520080. *Fax:* 45200820. *E-mail:* sipinen@sci.fi (Office). *Website:* sci.fi/~skywalk/sipinen/arto.htm (Office).

SIRAT, René-Samuel; French rabbi; b. 13 Nov. 1930, Bône (now Annaba), Algeria; s. of Ichoua Sirat and Oureida Atlan; m. 1st Colette Salamon 1952; one s. two d.; m. 2nd Nicole Holzman 1978; ed Lycée St Augustin, Bône, Univs. of Strasbourg, Paris (Sorbonne) and Jerusalem, Ecole Nat. des Langues Orientales (ENLOV); Rabbi, Toulouse 1952–55; Chaplain, Jeunesse juive 1955–63; Prof. Emer., Institut Nat. des Langues et Civilisations orientales (INALCO, fmrly ENLOV), Dir of Hebrew Studies 1965–96; Prof., Ecole Rabbinique de France 1965–70, 1977–80; Insp.-Gen. of Hebrew, Ministry of Educ. 1972–80; Pres. Hebrew Examining Bd, Certificate of Professional Aptitude and Higher Studies 1973–78; Dir Centre de Documentation et Recherches des Etudes Juives modernes et contemporaines 1974–; Pres. Hebrew Examining Bd, Agrégation 1978–80; Dir Ecole Hautes Etudes de Judaïsme 1985–; Pres. Centre Universitaire Rachi, Troyes 1989; Chief Rabbi of France 1981–87; Chief Rabbi, Consistoire Central 1988; Pres. Conseil Perm. de la Conférence des Rabbins européens 1989–; Pres. Académie Hillel 1989–, Inst. des connaissances des religions du livre 1996–; Dr. hc (Yeshiva Univ., USA) 1985; Chevalier, Légion d'honneur, Commdr, Ordre nat. du Mérite, Officier des Palmes Académiques, Prix de Jérusalem, Commdr des Arts et des Lettres. *Publications:* Omer Hasikha (co-ed.) 1973, Mélanges A. Neher (co-ed.) 1974, Mélanges Vajda 1974–80 (co-ed.), La joie austère 1990, La tendresse de Dieu 1996. *Address:* 51 rue de Rochechouart, 75009 Paris, France.

SIREN, Heikki; Finnish architect; b. 5 Oct. 1918, Helsinki; s. of Prof. J. S. Siren and Sirkka Siren; m. Kaija Siren 1944 (died 2001); two s. two d.; started pvt. practice with Kaija Siren, Siren Architects Ltd 1949–; mem. Finnish Acad. of Tech. Sciences 1971–; Foreign mem. Académie d'Architecture, Paris 1983; Hon. FAIA; Hon. mem. Finnish Architects' Asscn (SAFA) 1992; Hon. Citation and Medal São Paulo Biennal 1957, Medal São Paulo Biennal 1961, Hon. Citation 'Auguste Perret', Union Int. des Architectes 1965; Prof. hc 1970; Officier Ordre nat. du Mérite 1971, SLK (Finland) 1974, Grand Silver Order of Austria 1977; Hon. DTech 1982; Camillo Sitte Prize, Vienna 1979, Grande Médaille d'Or d'Académie d'Architecture, Paris 1980, Architectural Prize of the State of Finland 1980, Grand Golden Order of the City of Vienna 1982, Prize of Finnish Cultural Foundation 1984, Cultural Prize of City of Helsinki 1988. *Major works include:* Little Stage of Nat. Theatre, Helsinki 1954, Concert House, Lahti 1954, Chapel in Otaniemi 1957, Church in Orivesi 1960, Office Buildings, Helsinki 1965, Housing Area in Boussy St Antoine, Paris 1970, "Round Bank" Kop, Helsinki, schools, sports centres, offices, industrial bldgs., housing, holiday centres, etc., Brucknerhaus Concert Hall, Linz, Austria 1974, Golf complex, Karuizawa, Japan 1974, Golf Club, Onuma, Hokkaido, Japan 1976, Reichsbrücke, Vienna, Austria, Conference Palace, Baghdad, Iraq. *Publication:* Kaija and Heikki Siren, Architects 1978. *Leisure interests:* boat planning, music. *Address:* Tiirasaarentie 35, 00200 Helsinki 20, Finland. *Telephone:* 6811680 (Office).

SISCO, Joseph John, PhD; American government official; b. 31 Oct. 1919; m. Jean Churchill Head 1946; two d.; ed Knox Coll. and Univ. of Chicago; US Army 1941–45; CIA 1950–51; Dept of State 1951–76, Officer-in-Charge, UN Political Affairs 1951–58; Deputy Dir Office of UN Political and Security Affairs 1958–60, Dir 1960–62; Deputy Asst Sec. 1962–65; Asst Sec. of State for Int. Org. Affairs, Dept of State 1965–69; Asst Sec. State, Middle East-S Asia 1969–74; Under-Sec. of State for Political Affairs 1974–76; mem. US dels to UN Gen. Ass. 1952–68; Pres. American Univ. in Washington 1976–80, Chancellor 1980–81; Foreign Affairs Analyst, Castle TV news; partner Sisco Assocs., Man. Consultants, Washington 1981–; Dir Geico, Raytheon, Gilette, Tenneco, InterPublic Group Inc.; Rockefeller Public Service Award 1971. *Address:* 5335 Wisconsin Avenue, NW, Washington, DC 20015 (Office); 5630 Wisconsin Avenue, Chevy Chase, MD 20815, USA (Home).

SISSOKO, Cheick Oumar, BA; Malian politician and film maker; b. 1945, San Dist, Bamako; ed Ecole nat. de cinématographie Louis Lumière, Ecole des hautes études en sciences sociales; began career in Mali Civil Service; Minister of Culture 2002–; Asst Dir-Gen., later Dir-Gen. Centre nat. de la production cinématographique; f. Kora Films (producers' Assn); Pres. Kayira (ind. radio station). *Films include:* Nyamanton ou la leçon des ordures 1987, Finzan 1991, Guimba le tyran, une époque (Grand Prize, Fespaco Festival, Ouagadougou 1995) 1993, La Genèse 1999, Battu 2000. *Documentaries include:* Africa is Moving 1992, Etre jeune à Bamako (Youth in Mali) 1992, Building a Nation – Eritrea 1996, Malnutrition in the Sahel Region 1997. *Radio includes:* L'Afrique en question (producer, weekly programme for Kayira). *Address:* Ministry of Culture, Korofina, BP 4075, Bamako, Mali (Office). *Telephone:* 24-66-63 (Office). *Fax:* 24-57-27 (Office). *E-mail:* info@culture.gov.ml (Office). *Website:* www.culture.gov.ml (Office).

SISSON, Charles Hubert, CH, DLitt, FRSL; British writer; b. 22 April 1914, Bristol; s. of R.P. Sisson and E.M. Sisson (née Worlock); m. Nora Gilbertson 1937; two d.; ed Univ. of Bristol, postgraduate studies in Berlin and Paris; various posts in Ministry of Labour, later Dept of Employment 1936–, Under-Sec. 1962–73; served in army, in the ranks 1942–45; Simon Sr Research Fellow, Univ. of Manchester 1956–57; Jt Ed. PN Review (fmrly Poetry Nation) 1976–84; Hon. DLitt (Bristol) 1980. *Publications:* An Asiatic Romance 1953, Versions and Perversions of Heine 1955, The Spirit of British Administration 1959, The London Zoo (poems) 1961, Christopher Homm 1965, Art and Action

1965, Numbers (poems) 1965, Catullus (trans.) 1966, Metamorphoses (poems) 1968, English Poetry 1900–1950 1971, The Case of Walter Bagehot 1972, In the Trojan Ditch (collected poems and selected trans.) 1974, The Poetic Art 1975, Lucretius (trans.) 1976, Anchises (poems) 1976, David Hume 1976, The Avoidance of Literature (collected essays) 1978, Some Tales of La Fontaine (trans.) 1979, Exactions (poems) 1980, The Divine Comedy of Dante (trans.) 1980, Philip Mairet: Autobiographical and Other Papers (ed.) 1981, Selected Poems 1981, Anglican Essays 1983, The Song of Roland (trans.) 1983, The Regrets of Joachim du Bellay (trans.) 1984, Collected Poems 1984, The Aeneid (trans.) 1986, Britannicus, Phaedra, Athalia of Racine (trans.) 1987, God Bless Karl Marx (poems) 1987, On the Look-Out (autobiog.) 1989, In Two Minds: Guesses at Other Writers 1990, Antidotes (poems) 1991, English Perspectives: Essays on Liberty and Government 1992, Is There a Church of England? 1993, What and Who (poems) 1994, Poems: Selected 1995, Collected Translations 1996, Collected Poems 1998. *Leisure interests:* gardening and washing-up. *Address:* Moorfield Cottage, The Hill, Langport, Somerset, TA10 9PU, England. *Telephone:* (1458) 250845.

SISSONS, Peter George, MA; British television presenter; b. 17 July 1942, Liverpool; s. of the late George Sissons and Elsie Evans; m. Sylvia Bennett 1965; two s. one d.; ed Liverpool Inst. High School for Boys and Univ. Coll. Oxford; grad. trainee, Independent TV News 1964, gen. reporter 1967, industrial corresp. 1970, industrial ed. 1972–78; presenter, News at One 1978–82, Channel Four News 1982–89; presenter, BBC TV news 1989– (6 O'Clock News 1989–94, 9 O'Clock News 1994–2000, 10 O'Clock News 2000–03, BBC News 24 2003–), Chair. BBC TV Question Time 1989–93; Hon. Fellow Liverpool John Moores Univ. 1997; Hon. LLD (Liverpool); Broadcasting Press Guild Award 1984, Royal Television Soc. Judges' Award 1988, Television and Radio Industries Club Newscaster of the Year 2000. *Address:* c/o BBC Television Centre, Wood Lane, London, W12 7RJ, England.

SISULU, Albertina Nontsikelelo; South African politician; b. 1919, Tsomo, Transkei; m. Walter Max Ulyate Sisulu 1944; five c.; trained as a nurse, Johannesburg NE Hosp.; joined Fed. of S. African Women 1954, Pres. 1984; mem. Women's League, African Nat. Congress (ANC) 1948, Deputy Pres. 1991, mem. Nat. Exec. Cttee of ANC 1991–; ANC MP 1994–; participated in women's protest against introduction of Women's Pass; under continual banning orders (including house arrest) 1964–82; Transvaal Pres. United Democratic Front (UDF) 1983–91; tried and sentenced to 4 years' imprisonment for furthering aims of ANC 1984, successful appeal 1987; elected to Nat. Council, Women's Congress, UDF 1987; Leader UDF Del. to USA and to England July 1989; Pres. World Peace Council 1993. *Address:* P.O. Box 61884, Marshalltown 2107, South Africa.

SISULU, Sheila Violet Makate; South African diplomatist and educationist; d.-in-law of Walter Max Ulyate Sisulu and Albertina Nontsikelelo Sisulu (q.v.); m. Mlungisi Sisulu; two s. one d.; various Sr positions, South African Comm. for Higher Educ. 1978–88; Educ. Co-ordinator, African Bursary Fund, South African Council of Churches 1988–91; Dir Jt Enrichment Project 1991–94; Special Adviser, Ministry of Educ. 1994–97; Consul-Gen., South African Consulate-Gen., New York 1997–99; Amb. to USA 1999–; mem. ANC Nat. Educ. Cttee, USA–South Africa Leadership Training Program, Community Bank Foundation; Council mem. Univ. of Witwatersrand; Trustee, Equal Opportunity Foundation, Women's Devt Foundation, Women's Devt Bank, South African Broadcasting Corpn. *Address:* Embassy of South Africa, 3051 Massachusetts Avenue, NW, Washington, DC 20008, USA (Office). *Fax:* (202) 265-1607 (Office). *E-mail:* safrica@southafrica.net (Office).

SITKOVETSKY, Dmitry; American violinist; b. 27 Sept. 1954, Baku, USSR (now Azerbaijan); s. of Julian Sitkovetsky and Bella Davidovich; m. Susan Roberts; ed Moscow Conservatory, The Juilliard School of Music; début with Berlin Philharmonic 1980; appearances with Vienna Symphony, Orchestre de Paris and the Amsterdam, Rotterdam, Munich and Royal Philharmonics in Europe and the Chicago, Cincinnati, Detroit, Montreal and Toronto Symphonies in North America, Carnegie Hall début 1986; Artistic Dir Kuhmo Festival, Finland 1983–; First Prize Fritz Kreisler Competition, Vienna 1979, Avery Fisher Career Grant 1983.

SITRUK, Joseph; French rabbi; b. 16 Oct. 1944, Tunis; m. Danielle Azoulay 1965; nine c.; ed Seminary rue Vauquelin, Paris; Asst to Rabbi Max Warsharski, Lower Rhine region 1970–75; Rabbi, Marseilles 1975–87; Chief Rabbi of France 1987–; mem. Nat. Cttee of Human Rights; Pres. Conf. of European Rabbis 2000; Chevalier, Ordre Nat. du Mérite, Officier, Légion d'honneur 2001. *Publications:* Chemin faisant 1999, Dix Commandements 2000. *Address:* Consistoire Central Union des Communautés Juives de France, 19 rue Saint Georges, 75009 Paris, France. *Telephone:* 1-49-70-88-00. *Fax:* 1-42-81-03-66.

SIVAN, Amiram; Israeli business executive; b. 1938, Israel; m. Aliza Sivan 1960; two s. one d.; ed Hebrew Univ., Jerusalem; Econ. Research Dept of State Revenue Authority 1962–65, Co-ordinator of social budgets, Budget Dept 1965–69, Deputy Dir of Budgets 1969–73; Dir Gen. of Nat. Insurance Inst. 1974–76; Dir Gen. of Ministry of Finance 1976–79; Chair. Bd of Dirs. and CEO of TEUS (Devt Areas Industrialization Ltd) 1980–86; Chair. Bd of Man. and CEO Bank Hapoalim BM 1986–2000. *Leisure interest:* music. *Address:* c/o Bank Hapoalim, P.O. Box 27, 50 Rothschild Blvd., Tel Aviv 66883 (Office); 33 Mishol Ha'ya'ara, Ramot 02, Jerusalem, Israel (Home).

SIWIEC, Marek Maciej; Polish politician and journalist; b. 13 March 1955, Piekary Śląskie; m.; one s. one d.; ed Acad. of Mining and Metallurgy, Kraków; Asst Acad. of Mining and Metallurgy, Kraków 1980–82; trainee Gas and Fuel Corpn of Victoria, Australia 1981–82; Ed.-in-Chief 'Student' (weekly) 1985–87, ITD (weekly) 1987–90, Trybuna (daily) 1990–91; mem. Nat. Broadcasting Council 1993–96; Sec. of State in Chancellery of Pres. of Poland 1996–, Head Nat. Security Bureau, Nat. Security Adviser to the Pres. of Poland 1997–; Deputy to Sejm (Parl.) 1991–97; mem. Polish del. to Parl. Ass., Council of Europe; mem. Polish United Workers' Party (PZPR); mem. Social Democracy of Polish Repub. (SdRP) 1990–93, presidium of Head Council 1991–93. *Leisure interests:* jogging, cycling, tennis. *Address:* Biuro Bezpieczeństwa Narodowego, Al. Ujazdowskie 5, 00-902 Warsaw, Poland (Office). *Telephone:* (22) 695-18-00 (Office). *Fax:* (22) 695-18-01 (Office). *Website:* www.bbn.gov.pl (Office).

SIZA, Alvaro (Joaquim de Meio); Portuguese architect; b. 25 June 1935, Matosinhos; m. Maria Antonia Marinho Leite 1962 (died 1973); two c.; ed Univ. of Porto; in pvt. practice 1954–; lecturer, Univ. of Porto 1966–69, Prof. of Construction 1976–; Gold Medal (Alvar Aalto Foundation) 1988, Gold Medal (Colegios de Arquitectos, Spain) 1988, Pritzker Architecture Prize 1992, Berlage Prize 1994, Gubbio Prize 1994, Nara World Architecture Exhbn Gold Medal 1995, Imperial Prize (Japan Arts Asscn) 1998. *Works include:* Beires House, Póvoa de Varzim 1973–76, Quinta da Malagueira Social Housing, Evora 1977–, Sclesisches Tor Housing Complex, Berlin 1980–84, Duarte House, Ovar 1981–85, João de Deus Kindergarten, Penafiel 1984–91, Figueiredo House, Gondomar 1985–94, School of Architecture, Univ. of Porto 1986–89, Galician Centre of Contemporary Art, Santiago de Compostela 1988–94, Meteorological Centre, Barcelona 1989–92. *Address:* Faculdade de Arquitectura, Universidade do Porto, Rua do Gólgota 215, 4150-755 Porto, Portugal (Office). *Telephone:* (226) 057100 (Office). *Fax:* (226) 057199 (Office). *Website:* www.arq.up.pt (Office).

SIZOVA, Alla Ivanovna; Russian ballet dancer; b. 22 Sept. 1939, Moscow; d. of Ivan Sizov and Ekaterina Sizova; m. Mikhail Serebrennikov 1965; one s.; ed Leningrad School of Ballet; joined Leningrad Kirov Theatre of Opera and Ballet 1958–; a frequent partner of Mikhail Baryshnikov; teacher A. Vagnova Choreography School 1987–91, Universal Ballet School 1991–; Gold Medals Youth Festival, Vienna 1959, 1st Int. Ballet Contest, Varna; Anna Pavlova Diploma, Paris 1964, People's Artist of the RSFSR 1983. *Major roles include:* Masha (Nutcracker), Mirta (Giselle), Pas de trois (Le Corsaire), Katerina (Stone Flower), Waltz and Mazurka (Chopiniana), Pas de trois (Swan Lake), Aurora (Sleeping Beauty), Maria (Fountain of Bakhchisarai), Juliet (Romeo and Juliet), Cinderella (Cinderella), Kitri (Don Quixote), Girl (Leningrad Symphony). *Address:* Universal Ballet School, 4301 Harewood Road, NE, Washington, DC 20017, USA.

SJAASTAD, Anders Christian, PhD; Norwegian politician; b. 21 Feb. 1942, Oslo; s. of Andreas Sjaastad and Ingrid Sjaastad; m. Torill Oftedal Sjaastad 1969 (died 2000); one d.; ed Univ. of Oslo; Pres. Norwegian Students' Asscn, Univ. of Oslo 1967; Research Asst, Inst. of Political Science, Univ. of Oslo 1968–70; Research Assoc. at Norwegian Inst. of Int. Affairs 1970–81, Dir of Information 1973–81, Dir European Studies 1998–; mem. Høyre (Conservative Party), Vice-Chair. Oslo Høyre 1977–88, Chair. 1996–2000; Deputy mem. Storting (Parl.) 1981–85, 1997–2001; mem. Storting (Parl.) 1985–97; Minister of Defence 1981–86; Pres. European Movt in Norway 1989–92; Chair. Defence and Security Cttee (North Atlantic Ass.) 1994–97; Vice-Chair. Standing Cttee on Justice (Stortinget) 1993–97; mem. Norwegian Nat. Defence Comm. 1974–78, Norwegian Cttee on Arms Control and Disarmament 1976–81, 2002–, N Atlantic Ass. 1989–97. *Publications:* Departmental Decision Making (co-author) 1972, Politikk og Sikkerhet i Norskehavsområdet (with J. K. Skogan) 1975, Norsk Utenrikspolitisk Arbok (ed.) 1975, Deterrence and Defence in the North (co-ed. and contrib.) 1985, Arms Control in a Multipolar World (contrib.) 1996. *Address:* Norwegian Institute of International Affairs, P.O. Box 8159, Oslo, Norway.

SKALICKÝ, Jiří; Czech politician; b. 26 April 1956, Kolín; m.; three s. one d.; ed Coll. of Advanced Chemical Tech., Prague; research worker with Astrid (state enterprise), Prague 1981–90; mem. Civic Democratic Alliance (CDA) 1990–98, Deputy Chair. 1990–92; Deputy to House of Nations, Fed. Ass. of ČSFR 1990–92; mem. Plan and Budget Cttee, House of Nations, Fed. Ass. 1990–92; Minister for Nat. Property Admin. and Privatization 1992–96, for the Environment 1996–98; Chair. Presidium of Nat. Property Fund 1992–96; Deputy Chair. Civic Democratic Alliance 1995–97, Chair. 1997–98, Vice-Premier 1997; Senator 1998–. *Address:* Unie Svobody, Legerova 72, 120 00 Prague 2, Czech Republic; Senate of the Czech Republic, Valdštejnské nám. 10/65, 11800 Prague 1 (Office). *Telephone:* (2) 57071111 (Office). *E-mail:* skalickyj@senat.cz (Office). *Website:* www.senat.cz (Office).

SKÁRMETA, Antonio; Chilean writer and diplomatist; b. 1940; novelist and playwright; Amb. to Germany 2000–01. *Radio:* Voy y Vuelo 2000. *Publications:* Soné que la nieve ardía 1975, Ardiente paciencia (made into film Il Postino) 1985, Match Ball 1989. *Address:* c/o Ministry of Foreign Affairs, Catedral 1158, Santiago, Chile (Office).

SKARSGÅRD, J. Stellan; Swedish actor; b. 13 June 1951, Göteborg; s. of J. Skarsgård and Gudrun Skarsgård; m. My Günther 1976; five s. one d.; with Royal Dramatic Theatre, Stockholm 1972–87; Best Actor, Berlin Film Festival 1982; twice Best Film Actor in Sweden; Best Actor, Rouen Film Festival 1988, 1992, Best Actor, Chicago Film Festival 1991, Jury's Special Prize, San

Sebastián Film Festival 1995, European Film Award. *Films include:* Simple Minded Murderer 1982, Serpent's Way 1986, Hip Hip Hurrah 1987, The Unbearable Lightness of Being 1988, Good Evening Mr Wallenberg 1990, The Ox 1992, Wind 1992, The Slingshot 1993, Zero Kelvin 1994, Breaking the Waves 1995, Insomnia 1997, Amistad 1997, Good Will Hunting 1997, Ronin 1998, Deep Blue Sea 1998, Passion of Mind 1999; for TV: Hamlet 1984.

SKARZYNSKI, Henryk, MD; Polish medical scientist; b. 3 Jan. 1954, Rosochate Koscielne; s. of Józef Skarzynski and Janina Skarzynska; ; m. Bozena Bruska; two s.; ed Warsaw Medical Univ.; researcher, Oto-rhino-laryngology Clinic, Warsaw Medical Univ. 1979–2000, Head Ward 1986–96; Dir Diagnostic Treatment Rehabilitation Centre for the Deaf and Hearing-Impaired 1993–95; Dir Inst. of Physiology and Pathology of Hearing 1996–; Head of Otology Clinic, Warsaw 1999–; Head of Audiology and Phoniatrics Dept, Acad. of Music, Warsaw 2002–; mem. American Acad. of Audiology 1994–, Collegium of Oto-Rhino-Laryngologicum Amicitiae Sacrum 1994–, New York Acad. of Sciences 1995–, American Tinnitus Asscn 1995–, Int. Evoked Response Audiometry Study Group 1997–, European Acad. of Otology and Neuro-Otology 1998–; Hon. mem. Slovak Asscn of Otolaryngology and Head and Neck Surgery 1998–; Hon. Prof. Audiology and Speech Therapy Dept, Brigham Young Univ., USA 1998–99; Prize of the Prime Minister 2000, Prize of the Minister of Health and Social Welfare 2000, 2001; Prof. Jan Miodonski Award 1983, Stockholm Challenge Award 2000, Gold Medal of the Acad. of Polish Success 2001, Gold Medal, Brussels Eureka 2002. pioneer work in developing first Polish Programme for the Treatment of Hearing Disorders, Cochlear and Brainstem Implants Programme. *Publications include:* co-author: Urazy kosci skroniowej (Damages of the Temporal Bone) 1999, Anatomia topograficzna kosci skroniowej dla potrzeb otochirurgii (Topographical Anatomy of the Temporal Bone for Otosurgery) 2000, Technika komputerowa w audiologii, foniatrii i logopedii (Informatic Techniques in Audiology Phoniatrics and Speech and Language Therapy) 2002, Objawy laryngologiczne w rzadkich zespolach chorobowych (Laryngological Symptoms in Rare Diseases) 2002; monographs: Kryteria kwalifikacji do zabiegów wszczepiania implantów slimakowych i program rehabilitacji calkowitej utraty sluchu u dzieci 1994, Implant nadziei. Nowe szanse dla osób nieslyszacych. Pytania i odpowiedzi (Implant of Hope. New Chances for the Hearing Impaired. Questions and Answers) 1994. *Leisure interests:* football, breeding doves. *Address:* The Institute of the Physiology and Pathology of Hearing, ul. Pstrowskiego 1, 01-943 Warsaw, Poland (Office). *Telephone:* (22) 8356670 (Office). *Fax:* (22) 8355214 (Office). *E-mail:* sekretariat@ifps.org.pl (Office). *Website:* www.ifps.org.pl (Office).

SKATE, William (Bill) Jack; Papua New Guinea politician; b. 1953, Baimuru Dist, Gulf Prov.; m.; three c.; ed Univ. of Tech., Lae; fmr Gen. Man. P.S.A. Savings and Loans Soc., Nat. Capital Dist Comm.; fmr Govt adviser; MP 1992–95, 1997–; Speaker of Parl. 1992–94; Deputy Leader of Opposition 1994–95; Gov., Nat. Capital Dist 1995–97; Prime Minister of Papua New Guinea 1997–99; Pres. and Founder PNG First Party 1998–2000; Leader People's Nat. Congress (PNC) 2000–. *Address:* People's National Congress, c/o National Parliament, Port Moresby (Office); c/o Office of the Prime Minister, P.O. Box 6605, Boroko, N.C.D., Papua New Guinea.

SKATOV, Nikolai Nikolayevich, DLit; Russian linguist; b. 2 May 1931; m.; one d.; ed Kostroma State Pedagogical Inst.; Sr teacher, Acting Head, Chair of Literature, Kostroma State Pedagogical Inst. 1956–62; Sr teacher, Sr researcher, docent, Prof., Head Dept of Literature, Leningrad State Pedagogical Inst. 1962–; Chair., Comm. on Literature and Educ., Russian Acad. of Sciences; Deputy Chair., Comm. on Russian Literature, Presidium Russian Acad. of Sciences; Ed.-in-Chief Russkaya Literature (magazine); corresp. mem. Russian Acad. of Sciences 1997–; Dir Inst. of Russian Literature (Pushkin House) 1987–. *Publications:* 12 books and over 200 scientific works. *Address:* Institute of Russian Literature, Makarova nab. 4, 199034 St Petersburg, Russia (Office). *Telephone:* (812) 218-19-01 (Office); (812) 311-49-58 (Home).

SKEAT, Theodore Cressy, BA; British papyrologist; b. 15 Feb. 1907, St Albans, Herts.; s. of Walter William Skeat and Theodora Duckworth; m. Olive Martin 1942 (died 1992); one s.; ed Whitgift School, Christ's Coll., Cambridge and British School of Archaeology, Athens; Assistant Keeper, Dept of Manuscripts, British Museum 1931–48, Deputy Keeper 1948–61, Keeper 1961–72; Cromer Greek Prize 1932. *Publications:* Fragments of an Unknown Gospel (with H. I. Bell) 1935, Scribes and Correctors of the Codex Sinaiticus (with H. J. M. Milne) 1938, The Reigns of the Ptolemies 1954, Papyri from Panopolis 1964, Catalogue of Greek Papyri in the British Museum, Vol. VII 1974, The Birth of the Codex (with C. H. Roberts) 1983, The Reign of Augustus in Egypt 1993, The Codex Sinaiticus, the Codex Vaticans and Constantine 1999. *Address:* 12 Berkeley Court, 31/33 Gordon Road, London, W5 2AE, England.

SKEHEL, Sir John James, Kt, PhD, FRS; British research scientist; b. 27 Jan. 1941, Blackburn, Lancs.; s. of Joseph Skehel and Ann Skehel; m. Anita Varley 1962; two s.; ed St Mary's Coll. Blackburn, Univ. Coll. of Wales, Aberystwyth and UMIST; Postdoctoral Fellow, Marischal Coll. Aberdeen 1965–68; Fellow, Helen Hay Whitney Foundation 1968–71; mem. Scientific Staff, Nat. Inst. for Medical Research 1971–, Dir 1987–; Dir World Influenza Centre 1975–93; Hon. Prof. of Virology, Glasgow Univ. 1997–; Feldberg Prize 1986; Koch Prize 1987; Prix Louis Jeantet de Médecine 1988; ICN Int. Prize in Virology 1993. *Publications:* articles in scientific journals. *Address:* The National Institute for Medical Research, The Ridgeway, Mill Hill, London,

NW7 1AA (Office); 49 Homewood Road, St Albans, Herts., AL1 4BG, England (Home). *Telephone:* (20) 8959-3666 (Office); (1727) 860603 (Home). *Fax:* (20) 8913-8525 (Office). *E-mail:* mbrenna@nimr.ac.uk (Office). *Website:* www.nimr.mrc.ac.uk (Office).

ŠKELE, Andris; Latvian politician; b. 16 Jan. 1958, Aluksne District; m. Dzintra Škele; two c.; ed Latvian Acad. of Agric.; Head of Sector, Sr research Asst, Deputy Dir Research Assoc. Inst. of Latvian Agricultural Mechanization and Electrification 1981–90; First Deputy Minister of Agric. 1990–93; mem. Saeima (Parl.) 1998–, Prime Minister of Latvia 1995–97, 1999–2000; Founder and Chair. Tautas Partija (People's Party) 1998–; mem. several Parl. Comms; Chair. several bds of holding cos. *Address:* Tautas Partija, Dzir navu iela 68, Riga, Latvia. *Telephone:* 728-6441. *Fax:* 728-6405. *E-mail:* koord1@tautas.lv. *Website:* www.tautaspartija.lv.

SKHIRI, Neji; Tunisian banker; b. 15 Feb. 1934, Monastir; m. Slimane Nebiha 1962; one s. three d.; ed Univ. of Tunis, Centre for Educ. of Bankers, Paris; Gen. Man. Cen. Bank of Tunisia 1958–80; Deputy Chair., Chair. Banque du Sud 1980–84; Deputy Chair. Union of Arab Banks 1980–89, Chair. 1989–92; Chair. Soc. Tunisienne de banque 1984–87, Union Int. de Banques 1987–89, Banque du Maghreb Arab 1989–91, Banque Tunisio-Qatari d'investissement 1991–95, NSK Finances 1996–, Tunisian-Italian Chamber of Commerce and Industry; Mayor of Monastir 1985–90; Officer Order of the Repub.; Kt Order of Independence. *Leisure interests:* science and literature. *Address:* 3 rue Hamidi, Menzah I, 1004 Tunis, Tunisia. *Telephone:* 751-584. *Fax:* 232-363.

SKIDELSKY, Baron (Life Peer), cr. 1991, of Tilton in the County of East Sussex; **Robert Jacob Alexander Skidelsky,** MA, DPhil, FBA, FRHistS, FRSL; British professor of political economy; b. 25 April 1939; s. of the late Boris Skidelsky and Galia Sapelkin; m. Augusta Hope 1970; two s. one d.; ed Brighton Coll. and Jesus Coll. Oxford; Research Fellow, Nuffield Coll. Oxford 1965; Assoc. Prof. Johns Hopkins Univ., USA 1970; Prof. of Political Economy Univ. of Warwick 1990–; Chair. Social Market Foundation; Chair. Hands Off Reading Campaign 1994–97; Conservative Front Bench Spokesman on Culture, Media and Sport 1997–98, on Treasury Affairs 1998–99; mem. Lord Chancellor's Advisory Council on Public Records 1988–93; mem. Schools Examination and Assessment Council 1992–93; mem. Bd Manhattan Inst. 1994–, Moscow School of Political Studies 1999–, Janus Capital Group Inc. 2001–; Gov. Brighton Coll. 1998–; Hon. DLitt (Buckingham) 1997; Wolfson History Prize 1993, Duff Cooper Prize 2000, Lionel Gelber Prize 2001, Council on Foreign Relations Prize 2002, James Tait Black Memorial Prize 2002. *Publications:* Politicians and the Slump 1967, English Progressive Schools 1970, Oswald Mosley 1975, John Maynard Keynes, Vol. 1 1983, Vol. 2 1992, Vol. 3 2000, Interests and Obsessions 1993, The World After Communism 1995, The Politics of Economic Reform 1998. *Leisure interests:* music, tennis. *Address:* Tilton House, Firle, East Sussex, BN8 6LL, England. *Telephone:* (20) 7219-8721 (Office); (1323) 811570. *Fax:* (1323) 811017. *E-mail:* skidelskyr@parliament.uk (Home).

SKILBECK, Malcolm, MA, PhD, FAASS; Australian educational researcher and consultant; b. 22 Sept. 1932, Northam, WA; s. of Charles Harrison Skilbeck and Elsie Muriel Nash Skilbeck; m. Dr Helen Connell 1984; one s. four d.; ed Sydney Univ., Univ. of Ill. and Univ. of London; Prof. and Dean of Educ., Univ. of Ulster 1971–75; Foundation Dir, Australian Curriculum Devt Centre 1975–81; Dir of Studies, Schools Council for Curriculum and Examinations for England and Wales 1981–83; Prof. of Curriculum Studies, Univ. of London, Inst. of Educ. 1981–85; Vice-Chancellor and Prin. Deakin Univ. 1986–91; Deputy Dir for Educ., Directorate of Educ., Employment, Labour and Social Affairs, OECD 1991–97; Consultant to OECD, UNESCO, nat. govts., British Council, Australian Int. Devt Assistance Bureau; Hon. DLitt. *Publications:* Culture and the Classroom 1976, A Core Curriculum for the Common School 1982, School Based Curriculum Development 1984, Evaluating the Curriculum for the Eighties 1984, Curriculum Reform 1990, The Vocational Quest 1994, Redefining Tertiary Education 1998, Access and Equity in Higher Education 2000, The University Challenged 2002. *Leisure interests:* gardens, books, art, travel. *Address:* PO Box 278, Drysdale, Vic. 3222, Australia. *Telephone:* 3525-33340. *Fax:* 3525-33340; 3525-33340 (Office). *E-mail:* skilbeck.connell@deakin.edu.au (Office).

SKINNER, Quentin Robert Duthie, MA, FBA; British professor of modern history; b. 26 Nov. 1940, Oldham; s. of Alexander Skinner and Winifred Skinner (née Duthie); m. 2nd Susan James 1979; one s. one d.; ed Bedford School, Gonville and Caius Coll., Cambridge; Fellow Christ's Coll., Cambridge 1962–, Vice-Master 1997–99; Lecturer in History, Univ. of Cambridge 1967–78, Prof. of Political Science 1978–96; Regius Prof. of Modern History, Univ. of Cambridge 1996–, Pro-Vice-Chancellor 1999; mem. Inst. of Advanced Study, Princeton, NJ 1974–75, 1976–79; Foreign mem. American Philosophical Soc. 1997; Hon. Fellow Gonville and Caius Coll., Cambridge 1997; Hon. Foreign mem. American Acad. of Arts and Sciences 1986; mem. Academia Europaea 1989; Hon. DLitt (Chicago, E Anglia) 1992, (Helsinki) 1997, (Oxford) 2000; Wolfson Literary Award 1979. *Publications:* The Foundations of Modern Political Thought, Vol. I The Renaissance 1978, Vol. II The Age of Reformation 1978, Machiavelli 1981, Philosophy in History (ed. jtly. and contrib.) 1984, The Return of Grand Theory in the Human Sciences (ed. and contrib.) 1985, The Cambridge History of Renaissance Philosophy (ed. jtly. and contrib.) 1988, Machiavelli: The Prince (ed. and introduction) 1988, Meaning and Context: Quentin Skinner and His Critics (ed. James Tully)

1988, Machiavelli and Republicanism (ed. jtly. and contrib.) 1990, Political Discourse in Early-modern Britain (ed. jtly. and contrib.) 1993, Milton and Republicanism (ed. jtly.) 1995, Reason and Rhetoric in the Philosophy of Hobbes 1996, Liberty before Liberalism 1998, Visions of Politics, Vol. I Regarding Method 2002, Vol. II Renaissance Virtues 2002, Vol. III Hobbes and Civil Science 2002. *Address:* Faculty of History, University of Cambridge, West Road, Cambridge, CB3 9EF, England (Home). *Telephone:* (1223) 333345.

SKOK, Vladimir Ivanovich; Ukrainian physiologist; b. 4 June 1932, Kiev; m.; one d.; ed Kiev State Univ.; Sr researcher Kiev State Univ., Inst. of Physiology 1956–62; Head of div. A. Bogomolets Inst. of Physiology 1962–; Prof. of Physiology 1977; mem. Ukrainian Acad. of Sciences 1979, Acad.-Sec. Dept of Biochem., Physiology and Theoretical Med. 1974–78, 1981–88, Vice-Pres. 1988–93; mem. USSR (now Russian) Acad. of Sciences 1987, Ukrainian Pedagogic Acad. 1992 and Polish Acad. of Sciences 1994; main research in physiology, biophysics and pharmacology of automatic nervous system; Vice-Pres. I. Pavlov Physiological Soc.; I. Sechenov Prize 1970, USSR State Prize 1981. *Publications include:* Physiology of Autonomic Ganglia 1973, Neuro-Muscular Physiology 1986, Neuronal Acetylcholine Receptors, London 1989, Natural Activity of Autonomic Ganglia 1989; and numerous articles. *Leisure interest:* fishing. *Address:* Institute of Physiology, Bogomoletz str. 4, 01024 Kiev, Ukraine. *Telephone:* (44) 253-01-58 (Office); (44) 235-23-68 (Home). *Fax:* (44) 256-20-00 (Office). *E-mail:* skok@serv.biph.kiev.ua (Office).

SKOKOV, Yuri Vladimirovich, C.TECH.SC.; Russian politician; b. 16 June 1938, Vladivostok; ed Leningrad Electrotech. Inst.; mem. CPSU 1967–91; researcher, Deputy Dir Kalinin Research Inst. of Electric Sources USSR Ministry of Defence 1969–75, Dir 1975–76; Deputy Dir-Gen. Research Production Union Quant 1977–86, Dir 1986–90; USSR People's Deputy 1989–91; People's Deputy of Russian Fed. 1990–; Chair. Bd of Concern Quantemp 1988–90, First Deputy Chair. Council of Ministers of RSFSR 1990–91; Econ. Counsellor to Pres. of Russia 1990–91; Sec. Council on Problems of Fed. and Territories 1991–92; Sec. Security Council 1992–93; Head Fed. of Community Producers of Russian Fed. 1994–; Chair. Bd Centre for Int. and Inter-regional Econ. Problems 1994; Chair. Bd Congress of Russian Communities 1995–99; f. AMBI-Bank 1998; Dir-Gen. Scientific Production Union Kvant-Co-operation 2000. *Address:* Federation of Commodity Producers, Novy Arbat 15, Office 1318, 121019 Moscow, Russia. *Telephone:* (095) 203-06-08.

SKOL, Michael, BA; American diplomatist; b. 15 Oct. 1942, Chicago, Ill.; s. of Ted Skol and Rebecca Skol; m. Claudia Serwer 1973; ed Yale Univ., Univ. of the Americas, Mexico City; joined U.S. Foreign Service 1965; served in Buenos Aires, Saigon, Santo Domingo, Naples, Rome, San José and Bogotá (Deputy Chief of Mission) and as Desk Officer for Costa Rica, Paraguay and Uruguay; Deputy Dir for Policy Planning and Dir Andean Affairs, State Dept Bureau of Inter-American Affairs; Deputy Asst Sec. of State for S. America, 1988–90; Amb. to Venezuela 1990–93; Prin. Deputy Asst Sec. Latin American/Caribbean Dept of State 1993–95; Founding Chair. U.S.-Colombia Business Partnership 1996–99; Sr Vice-Pres. Diplomatic Resolutions Inc., Washington, DC 1996–97; Pres. Skol and Assocs. Inc., Washington DC 1998–; Sr Man. Dir for Latin America, DSFX, Washington DC 1998–; Pres. Skol Ospina & Serna 2000–; Order of the Liberator (Venezuela) 1993, Order of Nat. Merit (Paraguay) 1995. *Television includes:* Co-creator and first Co-host 'Choque de Opiniones', CNN Spanish TV network 1997. *Address:* Skol and Associates Inc., 33 East 33rd Street, 4th Floor, New York, NY 10019 (Office); 400 East 54th St, Apt. 17B, New York, NY 10022 USA (Home). *Telephone:* (212) 935-4040 (Office). *Fax:* (212) 935-4046 (Office). *E-mail:* mskol@dsfx.com (Office).

ŠKOLČ, Jožef; Slovenian politician; b. 19 Aug. 1960, Breginj; ed Ljubljana Univ.; active in Socialist Youth League of Slovenia (ZSMS) 1979–84; mem. of Pres. Republican Conf. of Socialist Youth League (RKZSMS) 1984–, Pres. 1988–92; leader of movt for pluralism and democratization; Chair. Cttee for Constitution 1990; mem. first elected Parl. and Leader of ZSMS Deputies' Club (later Liberal Democratic Party) 1990–94; Co-ordinator of Liberal Democracy of Slovenia; Pres. Nat. Ass. of Slovenian Repub. 1994–96; Minister of Culture 1997–99; mem. Nat. Ass. 2000–, Chair. Comm. for Mandates and Elections 2000–. *Address:* National Assembly, Šubičeva str. 4, 1000 Ljubljana, Slovenia (Office).

SKOLIMOWSKI, Jerzy; Polish film director and artist; b. 5 May 1938, Warsaw; m. Joanna Szczerbic; ed Warsaw Univ. and State Superior Film School, Łódź; wrote scripts for Wajda's Innocent Sorcerers, Polanski's Knife in the Water and Łomnicki's Poślizg; Dir, designer, author, ed., actor Rysopis 1964; author, Dir, actor, Walkover 1965; author, Dir, Barrier 1966; Dir Le Départ 1967; author, Dir, actor Hands Up 1967; Dir Adventures of Gerard 1969; Grand Prix for Barrier Int. Film Festival, Bergamo 1966, Silver Palm for Scream, Cannes Film Festival 1978, British Film Award (for Moonlighting) 1982, Special Prize, Venice Film Festival 1985. *Group exhbns. include:* World Contemporary Art Exhbn, Civic Center Los Angeles, Time Capsules, Warsaw, Cracow, Venice 2001. *Films:* Rysopis (Identification Marks: None) 1964, Walkover 1965, Bariera (Barrier) 1966, Le Départ 1967, Ręce do góry (Hands Up) 1967, Dialogue 20-40-60 1968, Adventures of Gerard 1969, The Deep End 1971, King, Queen, Knave 1972, Lady Frankenstein (or Terminus) 1976, The Shout 1978, Moonlighting 1982, Success is the Best Revenge 1984, The Lightship 1985, Torrents of Spring 1988, Before and After Death 1990, 30 Door Key, The Hollow Men. *Publications:* Poetry: Gdzieś

blisko siebie (Somewhere Close to Oneself); Play: Ktoś się utopił (Somebody Got Drowned). *Address:* c/o Film Polski, ul. Mazowiecka 6/8, 00-048 Warsaw, Poland.

SKOMOROKHA, Viktor Yegorovich; Ukrainian judge; b. 1941, Matrosove Village, Solonyansk Dist, Dnipropetrovsk Region; m. Liudmyla Vasylivna; one s. one d.; ed Kharkiv Law Inst. (now Yaroslav Mudry Nat. Law Acad. of Ukraine); Judge, Krasny Luch Municipal Court, Luhansk Region 1967–70; mem. Luhansk Municipal Court 1970–76; Judge, Supreme Court of Ukraine 1976–96; Judge, Constitutional Court of Ukraine 1996–, Chair. 1999–; Veteran of Work Medal 1983, Distinguished Lawyer of Ukraine 1995. *Publications:* publs on Ukrainian constitutional issues, human rights and admin. reform. *Leisure interests:* history books, poetry, gardening. *Address:* Constitutional Court, vul. Zhylianska 14, Kiev, Ukraine (Office). *Telephone:* (44) 253-84-88 (Office). *Fax:* (44) 253-93-77 (Office). *Website:* www.ccu.gov.ua (Office).

SKOTHEIM, Robert Allen, PhD; American administrator; b. 31 Jan. 1933, Seattle, Wash.; s. of Sivert O. Skotheim and Marjorie F. (née Allen) Skotheim; m. Nadine Vail 1953; one s. two d.; ed Wash. Univ.; instructor to Prof. of History, Wash. Univ., Wayne State Univ., UCLA, Colo Univ. 1962–72; Provost, Faculty Dean Hobart and William Smith Colls. 1972–75; Pres. Whitman Coll. 1975–88; Dir Huntington Library, Art Collections, Botanical Gardens 1988–90, Pres. 1990–2001; Guggenheim Memorial Fellowship 1967–68; numerous hon. degrees. *Publications:* American Intellectual Histories and Historians 1966, co-ed. Historical Scholarship in the United States and Other Essays 1967; ed. The Historian and the Climate of Opinion 1969, Totalitarianism and American Social Thought 1971, co-ed. American Social Thought: Sources and Interpretations (two Vols) 1972. *Address:* The Huntington Library, Art Collections and Botanical Gardens, 1151 Oxford Road, San Marino, CA 91108 (Office); 1650 Orlando Road, San Marino, CA 91108 (Home); 2120 Place Road, Port Angeles, WA 98362, USA (Home). *Telephone:* (626) 405-2115 (Office). *Fax:* (626) 405-2289. *E-mail:* rskotheim@huntingdon.org (Office).

SKOTNIKOV, Leonid Alekseyevich; Russian diplomatist; b. 26 March 1951, Kalinin; m.; one s.; ed Moscow State Inst. of Int. Relations; mem. staff Consular Dept Ministry of Foreign Affairs 1974–77; attaché Perm. Mission to the UN 1977–81; mem. staff Legal Dept, Ministry of Foreign Affairs 1981–91, Dir 1991–92, 1998–2001; Amb. to the Netherlands 1992–98; Amb. and Perm. Rep. to UN Office and other Int. Orgs in Geneva, the Disarmament Conf. 2001–; Order of Friendship 2002. *Address:* Permanent Mission of the Russian Federation, 15 Avenue de la Paix, 1202 Geneva, Switzerland (Office). *Telephone:* (22) 7331870 (Office). *Fax:* (22) 7344044 (Office). *E-mail:* mission-russian@ties.itu.net.

SKOU, Jens Christian, MD; Danish professor of biophysics; b. 8 Oct. 1918, Lemvig; s. of Magnus Martinus Skou and Ane Margrethe Skou; m. Ellen Margrethe Nielsen 1948; two d.; ed Univ. of Copenhagen; clinical appointments in surgery and orthopaedics 1944–47; Asst Prof. Inst. of Physiology, Univ. of Aarhus 1947, Assoc. Prof. 1954, Prof. and Chair. of Dept 1963, Prof. of Biophysics 1978–88, Prof. Emer. 1988–; mem. Royal Danish Acad. of Sciences, Deutsche Akad. der Naturforscher, Leopoldina, European Molecular Biology Org.; Foreign Assoc. NAS, Academia Europaea, Int. Acad. of Humanism; Hon. mem. Japanese Biochemical Soc., American Physiological Soc., American Acad. of Arts and Sciences; Hon. DrMed (Copenhagen) 1986; Leo Prize 1959, Novo Prize 1964, Consul Carlsen Prize 1973, Anders Retzius Gold Medal 1977, Erik K. Fernström's Nordic Prize 1985, shared Nobel Prize for Chemistry 1997 (for study of energy in cells). *Publications:* scientific papers on the mechanism of action of local anaesthetics 1946–57; scientific Publs on structure and function of the Na, K-pump, the transport system in the cell membrane responsible for the exchange of cations across membranes 1957–. *Leisure interests:* classical music, yachting, skiing. *Address:* Institute of Biophysics, Ole Worms Allé 185, Universitetsparken, 8000 Aarhus C. (Office); Rislundvej 9, Risskov, 8240, Denmark. *Telephone:* 89-42-29-50 (Office); 86-17-79-18. *Fax:* 86-12-95-99. *E-mail:* jcs@biophys.au.dk (Office). *Website:* www.biophys.au.dk (Office).

SKOURAS, Thanos, PhD, FBIM; Greek professor of economics; b. 21 Dec. 1943, Athens; s. of Spyros D. Skouras and Ismini Xanthopoulos; m. 1st Gella Varnava 1966 (divorced 1987); two s.; m. 2nd Savina Ioannides 1998; ed Athens Coll., King's Coll., Durham Univ. and London School of Econs, UK; Asst Lecturer, Lecturer, Sr Lecturer, Middlesex Polytechnic at Enfield, UK 1967–73; Prin. Lecturer and Head Econs Div., Thames Polytechnic 1974–77; Head Dept of Applied Econ. Studies, NE London Polytechnic (now Univ. of E London) 1978–86; Prof., Athens Univ. of Econs and Business 1986–, Deputy Chair. Econs Dept 1987–89, Vice-Rector 1989–92, Pres. Research Centre 1989–92; fmr Visiting Lecturer, Architectural Asscn School, London, Cambridge Univ., CEMI Beijing, Fudan Univ. Shanghai, Katholieke Univ. Leuven; Adviser to Deputy Minister of Nat. Economy, Athens; mem. Council of Econ. Advisers 1986–88; Ed. The Thames Papers in Political Economy 1974–86, The British Review of Econ. Issues 1976–85; Assoc. Ed. Greek Econ. Review 1985–90; mem. Editorial Bd Int. Review of Applied Econs 1993–; Councillor Royal Econ. Soc., London 1982–86; mem. Governing Council Greek Centre of Planning and Econ. Research 1987–88; Chair. Cttee for Financing of Major Infrastructure Projects 1988; Council mem. Euro-China Research Asscn for Man. 1989–92; mem. Supreme Disciplinary Council, Econ. Chamber of Greece 1990–92; Consultant intra muros European Comm. DG XVI

1992–94; Chair. Bd Abax Stockbroking 1991–94; mem. Bd Ergose 1996–97, Commercial Bank 1997, Greek Econ. Soc. 1998–99, Hellenic Centre for European Studies 2001–; Hon. Research Fellow Polytech. of E London 1986–91. *Publications:* Land and its Taxation in Recent Economic Theory 1977, Post-Keynesian Economic Theory (co-ed.) 1985, The Greek Economy: Economic Policy for the 1990s (ed.) 1991, Production or Importation of Advanced Technology Manufactures? – The Case of Telecommunications Equipment (co-author) 1993, Economic Priorities on the Threshold of the 21st Century (co-ed.) 2000; about 60 articles in professional journals. *Address:* Athens University of Economics and Business, 76 Patission Street, 104 34 Athens (Office); 8 Chlois Street, 145 62 Athens, Greece. *Telephone:* 8203651 (Office). *Fax:* 8082543.

SKOVHUS, Bo; Danish opera singer; b. 22 May 1962, Ikast; s. of Freddy Jorgensen and Birthe Skovhus; one d.; ed Music Acad., Århus, Royal Music Acad. and Opera School, Copenhagen, and in New York; début in Don Giovanni, Vienna Volksoper 1988, début as Silvio, Pagliacci Vienna Staatsoper 1991; regular guest singer with all maj. orchestras and opera cos including Metropolitan, New York, San Francisco, Houston, Munich State Opera, Hamburg State Opera, Berlin, Cologne, Covent Garden, Dresden, etc.; many recitals in Europe, USA and Japan; numerous lieder recitals with Helmut Deutsch, Stefan Vladar, Yefim Bronfman, Lief Ove Andsnes,Christoph Eschenbach and Daniel Barenboim; repertoire includes Don Giovanni, Almaviva (La Nozze di Figaro), Guglielmo (Così fan Tutte), Wolfram (Tannhauser), Olivier (Capriccio), Barber (Schweigsame Frau), Wozzeck, Hamlet, Billy Budd, Eugene Onegin, Yeletsky (Pique Dame), Danilo (Lustige Witwe), Eisenstein (Die Fledermaus); Kammersänger (Austria) 1997. *Recordings include:* Don Giovanni (twice), Le Nozze di Figaro, The Merry Widow, Britten's War Requiem, Carmina Burana, Fidelio, Das Lied von der Erde, Wozzeck, Mirror of Perfection (Blackford), I Pagliacci, Der Waffenschmied (Lortzing), Maskarade (Nielsen), Venus (Schoek), Die Schöne Müllerin, Schwanengesang (Schubert), Dichterliebe (Schumann), Liederkreis Op. 24 (Schumann), Eichendorff Lieder (Wolf), Faust (Spohr), Oberon (Weber), Die Orchesterlieder (Strauss), Lyrische Sinfonie (Zemlinsky) (twice), Lieder (Zemlinski) and recording of arias by Britten, Gounod, Korngold, Verdi, Wagner, Thomas, Massenet and Tschaikowsky. *Address:* Balmer und Dixon Management AG, Kreuzstr. 82, 8032, Zürich, Switzerland. *Telephone:* (43) 2448644. *Fax:* (43) 2448649. *E-mail:* balmer@badix.ch. *Website:* www.badix .ch (Office).

SKRINSKY, Aleksandr Nikolayevich, DSc; Russian physicist; b. 15 Jan. 1936, Orenburg; s. of Nikolay Alexandrovich Skrinsky and Galina Stepanovna Skrinskaya; m. Lydia Borisovna Golovanova; one s. one d.; ed Moscow State Univ.; Research Worker, Inst. of Nuclear Physics, Siberian Dept, USSR (now Russian) Acad. of Sciences, Head of Laboratory 1959–, Deputy Dir 1971–77, Dir of Inst. 1977–; Prof. Novosibirsk Univ. 1967–85; Corresp. mem. USSR (now Russian) Acad. of Sciences 1968–70, mem. 1970, Academician-Sec. Nuclear Physics Dept 1988–2002; mem. Int. Cttee for Future Accelerators (ICFA) 1983–90 (Chair. 1990–93), CERN Scientific Policy Cttee 1985–91; Lenin Prize 1967, USSR State Prize 1989. *Publications:* more than 200 scientific works in the field of accelerator physics and technology, elementary particle physics. *Leisure interests:* ski-running, swimming, music. *Address:* Russian Academy of Sciences, Department of Physics, Leninsky prosp. 32A, 117334 Moscow, Russia. *Telephone:* (095) 938-07-53. *Fax:* (095) 938-54-24.

SKROWACZEWSKI, Stanisław; Polish conductor and composer; b. 3 Oct. 1923, Lwów (now in Ukraine); s. of Paweł Skrowaczewski and Zofia Skrowaczewska (née Karszniewicz); m. Krystyna Jarosz 1956; two s. one d.; ed Lwów Conservatoire and State Higher School of Music, Cracow; Conductor, Wrocław Philharmonic Orchestra 1946–47; further composition studies with Nadia Boulanger and P. Klecki, Paris 1947–49; Artistic Dir and First Conductor, Silesian Philharmonic Orchestra, Katowice 1949–54; First Conductor, Cracow Philharmonic Orchestra 1955–56; Dir Nat. Philharmonic Orchestra, Warsaw 1957–59; Musical Dir Minnesota Orchestra 1960–79; tours in Europe, N and S America, Israel, Japan, Australia; Prin. Conductor and Musical Adviser, Hallé Orchestra 1984–91; Musical Adviser St Paul Chamber Orchestra 1986–88, Milwauke Symphony 1992–94; Commdr Cross of Polonia Restituta Order; Hon. DHL (Hamline Univ., St Paul, Minnesota) 1961; Hon. DMus (Macalester Coll., St Paul, Minn.) 1977; Dr hc (Univ. of Minnesota) 1979; Second Prize for 'Overture 1947', Szymanowski Competition, Warsaw 1947, Second Prize, Int. Competition for String Quartet, Liège, Belgium 1953, State Prize (3rd Class) 1956, First Prize, Int. Conductor's Competition, Rome 1956, Conductor's Award of Columbia Univ., New York 1973, Third Prize, Kennedy Center Friedheim Award Competition (for Ricercari Notturni) 1978; 5 ASCAP Awards for imagination programming with Minneapolis Symphony 1961–79, Gold Medal, Bruckner-Mahler Soc. 1999. *Compositions include:* Symphony for String Orchestra, three other symphonies, Muzyka Nocą (Music by Night, suite of nocturnes), four string quartets, two overtures, Cantique des Cantiques (voice and orch.), Prelude, Fugue, Post-Ludium (orch.), English Horn Concerto 1969, Ricercari Notturni (orchestral), Clarinet Concerto, Violin Concerto 1985, Fanfare for Orchestra 1987, Sextet 1988, String Trio 1990, Triple Concerto 1992, Chamber Concerto 1993, Passacaglia Immaginaria 1995, Musica a quattro 1998, Concerto for Orchestra 1999, Trio for piano, clarinet and bassoon, six piano sonatas; also music for opera, ballet, film and theatre; recordings for Mercury, Philips,

Angel, RCA Victor, IMP, Erato, Arte Nova, Vox, Albany. *Leisure interests:* alpinism, skiing, books, film, theatre. *Address:* PO Box 700, Wayzata, MN 55391, USA. *Fax:* (763) 473-7384.

SKUBISZEWSKI, Krzysztof Jan, LLD; Polish politician and lawyer; b. 8 Oct. 1926, Poznań; s. of Ludwik Skubiszewski and Aniela Skubiszewska (née Leitgeber); ed Poznań Univ., Univ. de Nancy and Harvard Univ.; mem. Staff, Poznań Univ. (renamed Adam Mickiewicz Univ.) 1948–73, Voluntary Asst, Jr Asst, Lecturer 1948–56, Asst Prof. 1956–61, Dozent, Dept of Int. Law 1961–73, Pro-Dean Law Faculty 1961–63; Prof. Inst. of State and Law, Polish Acad. of Sciences, Warsaw 1973–96; Minister of Foreign Affairs 1989–93; Pres. Iran–U.S. Claims Tribunal, International Court of Justice The Hague 1994–; Judge ad hoc Int. Court of Justice 1994–; mem. Curatorium, Hague Acad. of Int. Law 1994–, Bureau, Court of Conciliation and Arbitration, OSCE, Geneva 1995–2000; Chair., Council for Foreign Policy 1996–, Dutch–French Arbitration Tribunal 2000–; Visiting Scholar, School of Int. Affairs, Columbia Univ., New York 1963–64, Prof. invité, Geneva Univ. 1971, 1979; Visiting Fellow, All Souls College, Oxford 1971–72; Curator, Student Asscn of UN Friends, Poznań 1960–73; mem. Poznań Friends of Learning Soc. 1951–, West Inst. in Poznań 1961–, Inst. de Droit Int. 1971–, Polish Group of Int. Law Asscn 1971–, American Soc. of Int. Law, Oxford Soc., Soc. Française pour le Droit Int.; mem. Legal Sciences Cttee, Polish Acad. of Sciences 1981–; Corresp. mem. Polish Acad. of Sciences, Warsaw 1989–, Inst. de France 1995–; mem. Polish Acad. of Arts and Sciences, Cracow 1994–; mem. Primatial Social Council 1981–84, Consultative Council attached to Chair. of Council of State 1986–89; Hon. Prof. (Bucharest); Hon. Bencher, Gray's Inn 1990; Grand Cross of Polonia Restituta; Order of the White Eagle; Grand Officier Légion d'honneur and other decorations; Dr hc (Ghent, Turin, Liège, Mainz, Geneva); Alexander von Humboldt Foundation Award 1984, R. Schuman Gold Medal 2000. *Publications:* Pieniądz na terytorium okupowanym 1960, Uchwały prawotwórcze organizacji międzynarodowych 1965, Zachodnia granica Polski 1969, Individual Rights and the State in Foreign Affairs (co-author) 1977, Resolutions of the General Assembly of the United Nations 1985, Polityka zagraniczna i odzyskanie niepodległości 1997; over 110 articles on int. law and int. relations. *Address:* Iran–United States Claims Tribunal, Parkweg 13, 2585 JH The Hague (Office); Parkweg, 3B, 2585 JG The Hague, Netherlands (Home). *Telephone:* (70) 3520064 (Office); (70) 3585195 (Home). *Fax:* (70) 3502456 (Office). *E-mail:* Urmila@xs4all.nl.

SKULACHEV, Vladimir Petrovich; Russian biologist; b. 21 Feb. 1935, Moscow; s. of Petr Stepanovich Skulachev and Nadezhda Aronovna Skulacheva; m. Severina Inna Isaakovna; four s. one d.; ed Moscow State Univ.; jr researcher, Head of Div., Head of Lab. Moscow State Univ.; Dir A. Belozersky Inst. of Physico-Chemical Biology, Dean Faculty of Bioeng Bioinformatics; Corresp. mem. USSR (now Russian) Acad. of Sciences 1974, mem. 1990–; research in biochem., bioenergetics, investigation of molecular mechanisms of energy transformation in membranes of bacteria, mitochondria and chloroplasts; USSR State Prize. *Publications:* Energy Accumulation in Cells 1969, Energy Transformation in Biomembranes 1972, Membranes Bioenergies 1988; numerous other books and articles. *Leisure interests:* badminton, skiing. *Address:* A. N. Belozersky Institute of Physico-Chemical Biology, Moscow State University, 119992 Moscow, Russia. *Telephone:* (095) 939-55-30 (Office); (095) 939-01-47 (Home). *Fax:* (095) 939-03-38. *E-mail:* skulach@belozersky.msu.ru.

SKURATOV, Yuri Ilyich, DJur; Russian lawyer and civil servant; b. 3 July 1952, Ulan-Ude; s. of Ilya I. Skuratov and Raisa G. Skuratova; m. Elena D. Besedina 1976; one s. one d.; ed Sverdlovsk Inst. of Law; teacher, Dean Sverdlovsk Inst. of Law 1977–89; Deputy Head Div. on legis. initiatives and legal issues, CPSU Cen. Cttee 1989–91; Sr Consultant Russian Ministry of Security 1991–92; Dir Research Inst. of Problems of Justice, Gen. Prosecutor's Office of Russia 1993–95; Gen. Prosecutor 1995–; dismissed by Pres. Yeltsin, but reinstated by Council of Fed.; dismissed again 1999. *Publications:* over 90 scientific works on problems of civil and criminal law. *Leisure interests:* chess, swimming.

ŠKVORECKÝ, Josef, PhD; Czech/Canadian writer and translator; b. 29 Sept. 1924, Náchod; m. Zdena Salivarová; ed Charles Univ., Prague; worked as teacher, Secondary Social School; ed. World Literature (journal); Chair. Editorial Bd of journal The Flame –1968; emigrated to Canada 1968; Co-Founder (with Zdena Škvorecky) of Sixty-Eight Publishers, Toronto, which, up to 1990, published 216 titles by authors banned in Czechoslovakia; Prof. of English and American Literature, Toronto Univ. 1969–90, Prof. Emer. 1990–; mem. Bd of Consultants to President Havel 1990–91; f. Literary Acad. Josef Škvorecky, Czech Rep. 2000; lives in Canada; Hon. Citizen of Prague 1990; Order of the White Lion (3rd Grade) Czechoslovakia 1990; Dr hc (Masaryk Univ., Brno) 1991; State Prize for Literature Czech Repub. 1999, Pangea Foundation Prize Czech Repub. 2001. *Publications:* Cowards (novel) 1958, The Legend of Emoeke (story) 1963, Bass-saxophone (story) 1965, Ideas of a Reader of Detective Stories, The Seven-Armed Candlestick, End of the Nylon Age (story) 1968, The Little Lion (novel), The Tank Battalion (novel) 1969, The Miracle Game (novel) 1972, Priest Knox's Sins, The Clean Season, A Stop to Lieutenant Borůvka (novel) 1972, Lieutenant Borůvka Is Coming Back, Tale of An Engineer of Human Souls (novel) 1977, Scherzo Capriccioso (novel) 1984, Sadness of Lieutenant Borůvka (novel) 1988, Voice from America, Bitter Jazz (dramatized stories) 1990, Texas Bride (novel) 1993, Two Murders in My Double Life (novel) 1996, Short Meeting with Murder (co-author with wife) 1999, Life and Work 1999; 5 full-length film screenplays.

SKWEYIYA, Zola Sidney Themba, LLD; South African politician and civil servant; b. 14 April 1942, Cape Town; s. of Winnie Skweyiya; one c.; ed Lovedale High School, Univ. of Fort Hare; mem. ANC 1956, mil. training, Lusaka 1965; Chief ANC Rep. at OAU, Addis Ababa 1980–85, ANC Rep. UN Comm. on Human Rights 1984–93; f. ANC Legal and Constitutional Dept 1985, Head 1985–94; mem. ANC Nat. Exec. Cttee 1991–; Minister of Public Services and Admin., Govt of Nat. Unity 1994–99, of Welfare and Population Devt. 1999–2000, of Social Devt 2000–; Chair., Trustee Nat. Children's Rights Comm. 1990–; Trustee SA Legal Defence Fund 1991–. *Leisure interests:* listening to jazz and classical music, reading. *Address:* Ministry of Social Development, Hallmark Building, Vermeulen Street, Pretoria 0002, South Africa (Office). *Telephone:* (12) 3284600 (Office). *Fax:* (12) 3257071 (Office). *E-mail:* welso57@welspta.pwv.gov.sa (Office). *Website:* www.welfare.gov.za (Office).

SKYRMS, Brian, PhD; American professor of philosophy; b. 11 March 1938, Pittsburgh, Pa; s. of Frederick John Skyrms and Marie Margaret Skyrms (née Schlipf); m. Pauline Jenkins 1972; two s.; ed Lehigh Univ., Univ. of Pittsburgh; Asst Prof., Calif. State Univ., Northridge 1964–65, Univ. of Del. 1965–66; Visiting Asst Prof., Univ. of Mich. 1966–67; Asst Prof. then Assoc. Prof., Univ. of Ill., Chicago 1967–70, Prof. 1970–80; Prof. of Philosophy, Univ. of Calif., Irvine 1980–97, Distinguished Prof. of Philosophy and Prof. of Econs 1997–, Dir Program in History and Philosophy of Science; UCI Distinguished Prof. of Social Sciences 1998–; mem. Governing Bd American Philosophical Asscn 1987–90, Philosophy of Science Asscn 1990–91, Pres.-elect 2003–; mem. several editorial bds including American Philosophical Quarterly and Philosophy of Science; Ed. Cambridge Studies in Probability, Induction and Decision Theory; Fellow Center for Advanced Study in the Behavioral Sciences 1993–94, American Acad. of Arts and Sciences 1994, NAS 1999; Guggenheim Fellow 1987–88; numerous science fellowships; Univ. of Calif. Pres.'s Research in the Humanities 1993–94; Pres. Pacific Div. American Philosophical Asscn 2000–01; Lakatos Prize 1999. *Publications:* Choice and Chance: An Introduction to Inductive Logic 1966, Causal Necessity 1980, Pragmatics and Empiricism 1984, The Dynamics of Rational Deliberation 1990, Evolution of the Social Contract 1996; ed. or co-ed. seven books; numerous articles in learned journals. *Address:* School of Social Sciences, 3151 Social Science Plaza, University of California at Irvine, Irvine, CA 92697-5100, USA (Office). *Telephone:* (949) 824-6495 (Office). *Fax:* (949) 824-8388 (Office). *E-mail:* bskyrms@uci.edu (Office).

SLABBERT, Frederik van Zyl, DPhil; South African politician; b. 2 March 1940, Pretoria; m. 1st Mana Jordaan; one s. one d.; m. 2nd Jane Stephens 1984; ed Pietersburg High School, Univs of Witwatersrand and Stellenbosch; Lecturer in Sociology, Univ. of Stellenbosch 1964–68, Sr Lecturer 1970–71; Sr Lecturer and Acting Head, Dept of Sociology, Rhodes Univ., Grahamstown 1969, Univ. of Cape Town 1972–73; Prof. and Head Dept of Sociology, Univ. of Witwatersrand 1973–74; Visiting Prof. WBS Business School 1988–; MP for Rondebosch 1974–86; Nat. Leader Progressive Fed. Party and Leader of the Opposition 1979–86; Chair. Cen. Witwatersrand Metropolitan Chamber 1991–94; Co-Chair. Task Group for Local Govt Elections 1994–; co-f. Inst. for Democratic Alternatives 1988–; Dir Adcorp Holdings 1996–. *Publications:* South Africa's Options; Strategies for Sharing Power (with David Welsh) 1979, The Last White Parliament 1986, The System and The Struggle 1989, The Quest for Democracy: South Africa in Transition 1992 and various articles on SA politics. *Leisure interests:* squash, tennis, swimming. *Address:* P.O. Box 98, Witwatersrand 2050, South Africa. *Telephone:* (11) 6436641.

SLACK, Paul Alexander, DPhil, FBA; British historian; b. 23 Jan. 1943, Bradford; s. of Isaac Slack and Helen Slack (née Firth); m. Diana Gillian Manby 1965; two d.; ed Bradford Grammar School, St John's Coll., Oxford; Jr Research Fellow Balliol Coll., Oxford 1966–69; Lecturer in History, York Univ. 1969–72; Fellow and Tutor in Modern History, Exeter Coll. 1973–96, Reader in Modern History, Univ. of Oxford 1990–96, Chair. Gen. Bd of Faculties 1995–96, Prin. Linacre Coll. 1996–, Prof. of Early Modern Social History, Oxford Univ. 1999–, Pro-Vice-Chancellor 1997–2000, Pro-Vice-Chancellor (Academic Services) 2000–03. *Publications:* The Impact of Plague in Tudor and Stuart England 1985, Poverty and Policy in Tudor and Stuart England 1988, The English Poor Law 1531–1782 1990, From Reformation to Improvement: Public Welfare in Early Modern England 1999. *Leisure interests:* opera, fell-walking. *Address:* Linacre College, Oxford, OX1 3JA, England. *Telephone:* (1865) 271650. *Fax:* (1865) 271668.

SLADE, Rt Hon Sir Christopher John, Kt; British judge (retd); b. 2 June 1927, London; s. of the late George Penkivil Slade, KC and Mary A.A. Slade; m. Jane G.A. Buckley 1958; one s. three d.; ed Eton Coll. and New Coll., Oxford; called to Bar 1951, QC 1965; in practice at Chancery Bar 1951–75; Judge, High Court of Justice, Chancery Div. 1975–82; Judge of Restrictive Practices Court 1980–82, Pres. 1981–82; Lord Justice of Appeal 1982–91; mem. Gen. Council of Bar 1958–62, 1965–69; mem. Senate of Four Inns of Court 1966–69; Bencher, Lincoln's Inn 1973; mem. Lord Chancellor's Legal Educ. Cttee 1969–71; Treas., Lincoln's Inn 1994. *Leisure interests:* multifarious. *Address:* 16 Elthiron Road, London, SW6 4BN, England. *Telephone:* (20) 7731-0938.

SLADE, Tuiloma Neroni, LLB; Samoan diplomatist and lawyer; b. 8 April 1941; m.; one d.; ed Hague Acad. of Int. Law; qualified as solicitor and barrister, law practice Wellington, NZ 1967–68; legal counsel Office of Attorney-Gen., Wellington 1969–73; Parl. Counsel 1973–75; Attorney-Gen. of Western Samoa 1976–82, also Chief Justice for periods between 1980–82; Asst Dir Legal Div. Commonwealth Secr., London 1983–93; Perm. Rep. to the UN 1993–; Head Del. UN Conf. on the Law of the Sea 1973–76; Chair. first S. Pacific Law Conf. 1986; legal consultant S. Pacific Forum Fisheries Agency 1989; UNITAR Fellowship Hague Acad. of Int. Law and UN Legal Office. *Address:* Permanent Mission of Samoa to the United Nations, 800 Second Avenue, Suite 400D, New York, NY 10017, USA (Office). *Telephone:* (212) 599-6196 (Office). *Fax:* (212) 599-0797 (Office). *E-mail:* samoa@un.int (Office). *Website:* www.un.org (Office).

SLANEY, Sir Geoffrey, KBE, MSc, ChM, FRCS; British professor of surgery; b. 19 Sept. 1922, West Hallam; s. of Richard Slaney and Gladys L. Slaney; m. Josephine M. Davy 1956; one s. two d.; ed Univs of Birmingham, London and Illinois; House Surgeon and Surgical Registrar, Gen. Hosp., Birmingham 1947–48; Capt. RAMC 1948–50; Surgical Registrar, Coventry, London and Hackney Hosps 1950–53; Surgical Registrar, Lecturer in Surgery and Surgical Research Fellow, Queen Elizabeth Hosp., Birmingham 1953–59; Hunterian Prof. Royal Coll. of Surgeons 1961–62; Prof. of Surgery, Univ. of Birmingham 1966–87; Barling Prof., Head Dept of Surgery, Queen Elizabeth Hosp., Birmingham 1971–86, now Emer.; Pres. Royal Coll. of Surgeons of England 1982–86, James IV Asscn Surgeons 1984–87, Int. Surgical Group 1985–86, Vascular Surgical Soc. 1974–75; Chair. Asscn Profs. of Surgery 1979–81, Confed. of Royal Colls and Faculties in the UK 1984–86; Fellow, Asscn of Surgeons of GB and Ireland, American Surgical Asscn; Hon. Consulting Surgeon, United Birmingham Hosps and Regional Hosp. Bd 1959–, Royal Prince Alfred Hosp., Sydney 1981–; Hon. Consulting Surgeon Emer., City of London and Hackney Health Authority 1983–; Hon. FRCSI, FRACS, FCSSL, FACS, FRCSC, FCSSA, FRCA; Jacksonian Prize and Medal (Royal Coll. of Surgeons) 1959, Pybus Memorial Medal 1978, Miles Memorial Medal 1984, Vanderbilt Univ. Medal 1987, Brooke Medal, Ileostomy Asscn of GB and Ireland 1990. *Publications:* Metabolic derangements in gastrointestinal surgery (with B. N. Brooke) 1967, Cancer of the Large Bowel (co-author) 1991; numerous contribs to medical and surgical journals. *Leisure interests:* family, fishing. *Address:* Hill Crest, Collins Green, Knightwick, Worcester, WR6 5PT, England. *Telephone:* (1886) 822024.

SLAOUI, Driss; Moroccan diplomatist, professor and business executive; b. 12 Dec. 1926; m.; two c.; studied law in Grenoble and Paris; Under-Sec. of State for the Interior 1958; Sec. of State for Commerce, Industry and the Merchant Marine 1959; various ministerial posts 1960–68; Dir-Gen. Royal Cabinet 1962 and 1969–71; Counsellor to King of Morocco Oct. 1977–; Perm. Rep. to the UN 1974–76, 1986–90; Sec.-Gen. Org. of Countries Signatories of the Charter of Casablanca 1961; Gov. of Bank of Morocco 1964; Dir-Gen. Nat. Investment Soc. 1978–; Prof. in Faculty of Law at Rabat 1971–. *Address:* c/o Ministry of Foreign Affairs, Avenue Franklin Roosevelt, Rabat, Morocco.

SLATER, Christian; American actor; b. 18 Aug. 1969, New York; s. of Michael Hawkins and Mary Jo Slater; m. Ryan Haddon 2000; one s.; appeared at age of seven in TV series One Life to Live; professional stage début at age of nine in touring production of The Music Man; sentenced to 90 days imprisonment for two counts of battery and one of being under the influence of cocaine 1998. *Stage appearances include:* Macbeth, David Copperfield, Merlin, Landscape of the Body, Side Man. *Films include:* The Name of the Rose, Tucker: The Man and his Dream, Heathers, The Legend of Billie Jean, Cry Wolf, Tales from the Darkside: The Movie, Gleaming the Cube, The Wizard, Pump up the Volume, Young Guns II, Robin Hood: Prince of Thieves, Kuffs, Mobsters, Where the Day Takes You, Untamed Heart, True Romance, Murder in the First, Untitled, Jimmy Hollywood, Interview with a Vampire, Bed of Roses, Hard Rain, Broken Arrow, Austin Powers: International Man of Mystery, The Flood, Very Bad Things (also exec.-producer), The Contender 2001.

SLATER, James Derrick, FCA; British company director and author; b. 13 March 1929, Wirral, Cheshire; s. of Hubert Slater and Jessica Slater; m. Helen Wyndham Goodwyn 1965; two s. two d.; ed Preston Manor County School; Dir A.E.C. Ltd 1959; Deputy Sales Dir Leyland Motor Corpn 1963; acquired with associates, H. Lotery and Co., Ltd, which was then renamed Slater, Walker Securities Ltd and apptd. Chair. and Man. Dir 1964–72, Chair., CEO 1972–75; Dir BLMC 1969–75; Chair. Salar Properties Ltd 1983; f. BioProjects 2000, Exec. Chair. BioProjects Int. 2002–; Parentcare 1988. *Publications:* Return to Go (autobiog.) 1977; on investment: The Zulu Principle 1992, Investment Made Easy 1994, Pep Up Your Wealth 1994, Beyond the Zulu Principle 1996, How to Became a Millionaire 2000; childrens books: Goldenrod, Goldenrod and the Kidnappers, Grasshopper and the Unwise Owl, The Boy Who Saved Earth, A. Mazing Monsters, Grasshopper and the Pickle Factory 1979, Roger the Robot Series 1980. *Leisure interests:* chess, backgammon, bridge, salmon fishing.

SLATER, Adm. Sir Jock (John) Cunningham Kirkwood, GCB, LVO, DL; British naval officer; b. 27 March 1938, Edinburgh, Scotland; s. of James K. Slater and M. C. B. Slater (née Bramwell); m. Ann Frances Scott 1972; two s.; ed Edinburgh Acad., Sedbergh School, Royal Naval Coll. Dartmouth; Lt HMS Soberton 1965; Lt Commdr, Equerry to HM The Queen 1968–71; Commdr HMS Jupiter 1972–73; Capt. HMS Kent 1976–77; with Royal Coll. of Defence Studies 1978; Capt. HMS Illustrious 1981–83; Capt. School of Maritime Operations, HMS Dryad 1983–85; Rear Adm., Asst Chief of Defence Staff 1985–87; Flag Officer Scotland, NI, Naval Base Commdr Rosyth 1987–89; Vice-Adm., Chief of Fleet Support 1989–91; Adm., C-in-C of Fleet,

Allied C-in-C Channel and Eastern Atlantic 1991–92; Vice-Chief of Defence Staff 1993–95, Chief of Naval Staff and First Sea Lord 1995–98; Gov. Sedbergh School; Dir Vosper Thornycroft Holdings; Dir and Sr Mil. Adviser to Lockheed Martin (UK) Ltd; Consultant to Bristow Helicopters; Ltd; Deputy Chair. RNLI; Chair. Imperial War Museum, RN Club 1765–1785, White Ensign Asscn; Freeman of the City of London; Liveryman of the Shipwrights Co.; Elder Brother, Trinity House; Commdr Legion of Merit (USA); DL Hants.; Hon. DSc (Cranfield); Sword of Honour and The Queen's Telescope (BRNC Dartmouth) 1958, Cheetham Hill Memorial Prize (HMS Dryad) 1966. *Achievements:* mem. Nat. Youth Orchestra 1955. *Leisure interests:* outdoor. *Address:* c/o Naval Secretary, Victory Building, HM Naval Base, Portsmouth, PO1 3LS, England.

SLATER, Joseph Elliott, BA, LLB; American administrator; b. 17 Aug. 1922, Salt Lake City, Utah; m. Annelore Kremser 1947; two d.; ed Univ. of California; Naval Reserve Officer, Mil. Govt Planning Officer, Berlin, London and Paris 1943–46; US Sec. of Econ. Directorate, Allied Control Comm. for Germany; Asst US Sec. of Allied Control Council Econ. and Financial Affairs 1945–48; mem. UN Affairs Planning Staff, Dept of State, Washington 1949; Sec.-Gen. Allied High Comm. for Germany, Bonn 1949–52; Exec. Sec. Office of US Special Rep. in Europe, US Sec. to NATO and mem. US Del. to OEEC 1952; Chief Economist, Creole Petroleum Corpn, Caracas 1954–57; Sec. to President's Comm. on Foreign Assistance 1959; Assoc. Dir, Int. Affairs Program, Program Officer (Office of Int. Relations), Ford Foundation 1957–67; Asst Man. Dir Devt Loan Fund 1960–61 and Deputy Asst Sec. of State for Educ. and Cultural Affairs 1961–62; Pres. Salk Inst. 1967–72, Pres. Emer.Trustee and Special Fellow; Pres. Aspen Inst. for Humanistic Studies 1969–86, Pres. Emer., Trustee, Sr Fellow 1986–; Pres. Anderson Foundation 1969–72; Chair. John J. McCloy Int. Center 1986–; mem. Council on Foreign Relations, New York, UN Policy Studies Group, Dir AMIDEAST, Center for Public Resources; Trustee, Acad. for Educ. Devt, Int. Inst. for Environmental Affairs, American Council on Germany, Carnegie Hall, Eisenhower Exchange Fellowships; Trustee Lovelace Medical Foundation 1993–; mem. of Bd Volvo N America; Hon. LLD (Univ. of Denver, Colorado Coll., Kyung Hee Univ., Korea, Univ. of NH); Commdr's Cross, German Order of Merit. *Address:* 870 UN Plaza, New York, NY 10017, USA (Home); 155 Hill Street, Apartment 6, Southampton, NY 11968 (Summer address).

SLATER, Rodney E., BS, JD; American politician and administrator; b. 23 Feb. 1955, Tutwyler, Miss.; m. Cassandra Wilkins; one c.; ed Eastern Michigan Univ., Univ. of Arkansas; Asst Attorney-Gen., Ark. 1980–82; Special Asst to Gov. of Ark. for community and minority affairs 1983–85, Exec. Asst for econ. and community programs 1985–87, Dir Intergovernmental Relations Ark. State Univ. 1987–93; Admin. Fed. Highway Admin. Dept of Transportation, Washington, DC 1993–97; Sec. of Transportation 1997–2001; Ark. Liaison Martin Luther King Jr Fed. Holiday Comm. 1983–87; Partner Patton Boggs 2001–; mem. Ark. Sesquicentennial Comm. 1986, Ark. State Highway and Transportation Comm. 1987–93, Chair. 1992–93; Pres. W. Harold Flowers Law Soc. 1985–92; Sec., Treasurer Ark. Bar Asscn 1989–93; Deputy Campaign Man., Sr Travelling Adviser Clinton for Pres. Campaign 1992; Deputy to Chair. Clinton/Gore Transition Team 1992–93; mem. Bd of Dirs Africane 2001–, Jt Center for Political and Econ. Studies 2001–. *Address:* Paton Boggs, 2550 M Street, NW, Washington, DC 20037, USA (Office).

SLATKIN, Leonard; American conductor; b. 1 Sept. 1944, LA; s. of Felix Slatkin and Eleanor Aller; m. Linda Hohenfeld 1986; ed Indiana Univ., Los Angeles City Coll., Juilliard School; studied violin, piano, viola, composition, conducting; Founder, Music Dir and Conductor St Louis Symphony Youth Orchestra 1979–80, 1980–81; Guest Conductor, orchestras in most countries; Asst Conductor Youth Symphony of New York, Carnegie Hall 1966, Juilliard Opera, Theater and Dance Dept 1967, St Louis Symphony Orchestra 1968–71, Assoc. Conductor 1971–74, Music Dir and Conductor 1979–96; Music Dir Nat. Symphony Orchestra, Washington DC 1996–2001; Prin. Conductor BBC Symphony Orchestra 2000–; Prin. Guest Conductor Minn. Orchestra 1974–, summer artistic Dir 1979–80; Music Dir New Orleans Philharmonic Symphony Orchestra 1977–78; five hon. degrees; two Grammy Awards. *Address:* BBC Symphony Orchestra, Maida Vale Studios, Delaware Road, London, W9 2LG, England (Office). *Telephone:* (20) 7765-5751 (Office).

SLATYER, Ralph Owen, AC, AO, DSc, FRS, FAA; Australian research scientist; b. 16 April 1929, Melbourne; s. of Thomas H. Slatyer and Jean Slatyer; m. June H. Wade 1953; one s. two d.; ed Univ. of Western Australia; Research Scientist, later Chief Research Scientist, CSIRO Div. of Land Research 1951–67; Prof. of Biology Research School of Biological Sciences, ANU 1967, Dir Research School of Biological Sciences 1984–89; Amb. to UNESCO, Paris 1978–81; Chair. (part-time) World Heritage Cttee 1981–83, Australian Nat. Comm. for UNESCO, Australian Science and Tech. Council, Canberra 1982–87; Chief Scientist, Dept of Prime Minister and Cabinet, Canberra 1989–92; Chair. (part-time) Co-operative Research Centre for Rainforest Ecology 1992–, ANU Centre for Visiting UNESCO Fellows 1997–; Chair. Australian Foundation for Science 1992–94; Visiting Fellow, Inst. of Advanced Studies, ANU 1994–; Foreign mem. Korea Acad. of Science and Tech. 1996; Foreign Assoc. American Nat. Acad. of Sciences; Fellow Australian Acad. of Technological Sciences and Eng.; Hon. DSc (Western Australia, Queensland, Duke Univ., Charles Sturt Univ.); Edgeworth David Medal, Royal Soc. of NSW 1968; Australian Medal of Agric. Science 1968, Medal of Australia and NZ Asscn for the Advancement of Science 1991, Clunies Ross Medal for Lifetime Contrib. to Science and Tech. *Publications include:* Practical Micro-climatology (jtly with I.C. McIlroy) 1961, Plant-Water Relationships 1967, Man and the New Biology 1970; ed. of several books and author of numerous scientific publs. *Leisure interests:* bush-walking, cycling, golf. *Address:* Research School of Biological Sciences, Australian National University, Canberra, ACT 0200 (Office); 54 Musgrave Street, Yarralumla, ACT 2600, Australia (Home). *Telephone:* (612) 6125-5041 (Office); (612) 6285-1728 (Home). *Fax:* (612) 6125-5095 (Office); (612) 6185-1738 (Home). *E-mail:* ralph.slatyer@anu.edu.au (Office).

SLAVITT, David Rytman, MA; American author; b. 23 March 1935, White Plains, NY; s. of Samuel Slavitt and Adele Slavitt; m. 1st Lynn Meyer 1956 (divorced 1977); two s. one d.; m. 2nd Janet Lee Abrahm 1978; ed Yale and Columbia Univs; writer, assoc. ed., movie Newsweek 1958–65; Visiting Lecturer, Univ. of Md 1977; Visiting Assoc. Prof. Temple Univ. 1978–80; Lecturer in English and Comparative Literature, Columbia Univ. 1985–86; teacher of creative writing, Rutgers Univ. 1987; Lecturer in English, Univ. of Pa 1991–97, Bennington Coll. 2000–; Assoc. Fellow, Trumbull Coll. Yale Univ.; has lectured widely at U.S. univs. and other academic insts.; Nat. Endowment for Arts Fellowship in Translation 1988; Nat. Acad. and Insts. of Arts and Letters Award 1989; Rockefeller Foundation Artist's Residence, Bellagio 1989. *Publications:* novels: Rochelle, or Virtue Rewarded 1967, Feel Free 1968, Anagrams 1970, ABCD 1972, The Outer Mongolian 1973, The Killing of the King 1974, King of Hearts 1976, Jo Stern 1978, Cold Comfort 1980, Ringer 1982, Alice at 80 1984, The Agent 1986, The Hussar 1987, Salazar Blinks 1988, Lives of the Saints 1990, Turkish Delights 1993, The Cliff 1994, Get Thee to a Nunnery 1999; seven novels under pseudonyms; short stories: Short Stories Are Not Real Life 1991; poetry: Suits for the Dead 1961, The Carnivore 1965, Day Sailing 1968, Child's Play 1972, Vital Signs: New and Selected Poems 1975, Rounding the Horn 1978, Dozens 1981, Big Nose 1983, The Walls of Thebes 1986, Equinox 1989, Eight Longer Poems 1990, Crossroads 1994, A Gift 1996, Epic and Epigram 1997, PS3569.L3 1998; non-fiction: Understanding Social Psychology 1976, Physicians Observed 1987, Virgil 1991; plays: King Saul 1967, The Cardinal Sins 1969; screenplays, translations, book reviews, articles in journals and magazines etc.

SLEEP, Wayne, OBE; British dancer, actor and choreographer; b. 17 July 1948, Plymouth; ed Royal Ballet School (Leverhulme Scholar); joined Royal Ballet 1966, Soloist 1970, Prin. 1973; roles in: Giselle, Dancers at a Gathering, The Nutcracker, Romeo and Juliet, The Grand Tour, Elite Syncopations, Swan Lake, The Four Seasons, Les Patineurs, Petroushka (title role), Cinderella, The Dream, Pineapple Poll, Mam'zelle Angot, 4th Symphony, La Fille Mal Gardée, A Month in the Country, A Good Night's Sleep, Coppelia; also roles in operas: A Midsummer Night's Dream, Aida; choreography and lead role, The Point: co-starred in Song and Dance 1982, 1990, Cabaret 1986; f. own co., DASH 1980; dancer and Jt choreographer, Bits and Pieces 1989; numerous TV appearances including series The Hot Shoe Show 1983, 1984; Show Business Personality of the Year 1983. *Films include:* The Virgin Soldiers, The First Great Train Robbery, The Tales of Beatrix Potter. *Theatre include:* Ariel in the Tempest, title role in Pinocchio, Genie in Aladdin, Soldier in The Soldier's Tale, Truffaldino in the Servant of Two Masters, Mr Mistoffelees in Cats. *Publications:* Variations on Wayne Sleep 1983, Precious Little Sleep (autobiog.) 1996. *Leisure interest:* entertaining. *Address:* c/o Nick Thomas Artists, Event House, Queen Margaret's Road, Scarborough, YO11 2SA; 22 Queensberry Mews West, London, SW7 2DY, England. *Telephone:* (1723) 500038.

ŠLEŽEVIČIUS, Adolfas; Lithuanian politician; b. 1948, Mirziskes, Šiauliai Region; ed Acad. of Nat. Econ., USSR Council of Ministers; Sr engineer-constructor, chief mechanic, chief engineer Kaunas dairy factory 1971–77; Vice-Minister of Dairy and Meat Industry of Lithuania 1977–81; Chair. dairy production enterprise Pienocentras 1989–90; Vice-Minister of Agric. 1990–91; Pres. Lithuanian-Norwegian Joint Venture C. Olsen-Baltic 1991–93; Pres. Lithuanian Dairy Producers Asscn 1992–; Prime Minister of Lithuania 1993–96, resgnd following corruption scandals; consultant to pvt. cos.

SLICHTER, Charles Pence, BA, MA, PhD, FAAS; American professor of physics; b. 21 Jan. 1924, Ithaca, NY; s. of Sumner Huber Slichter and Ada Pence Slichter; m. 1st Gertrude Thayer Almy 1952 (divorced 1977); three s. one d.; m. 2nd Anne FitzGerald 1980; two s.; ed Browne and Nichols School, Cambridge, Mass. and Harvard Univ.; Instructor, Univ. of Ill. 1949–51, Asst Prof. of Physics 1951–54, Assoc. Prof. 1954–55, Prof. of Physics 1955–97, mem. Center for Advanced Study, Univ. of Ill. 1968–, Prof. of Chem. 1986–97, Center for Advanced Study Prof. Emer. of Physics and Chem. 1997–, Research Prof. of Physics 1997–; mem. Bd of Dirs. Polaroid Corpn 1975–97; Morris Loeb Lecturer, Harvard Univ. 1961; mem. President's Science Advisory Cttee 1965–69, Cttee on the Nat. Medal of Science 1969–74, President's Cttee on Science and Tech. 1976; Alfred Sloan Fellow 1957–63; mem. Corpn of Harvard Univ. 1970–95; mem. Comm. on Physical Sciences, Math. and Applications, Nat. Research Council 1993–96; Fellow American Physical Soc.; mem. NAS, American Acad. of Arts and Sciences, American Philosophical Soc., Nat. Science Bd 1975–84; mem. Int. Soc. of Magnetic Resonance (ISMAR), Vice-Pres. 1983–86, Pres. 1987–90; Fellow Int. EPR Soc. 1998; Hon. mem. Corpn, Woods Hole Oceanographic Inst.; Hon. DSc (Univ. of Waterloo) 1993; Hon. LLD (Harvard) 1996; Langmuir Prize of American Physical Soc. 1969, ISMAR Award 1986, Comstock Prize (NAS) 1993, Buckley Prize of American Physical Soc. 1996 and other awards. *Publications:* Principles of Magnetic Resonance 1963, 1978, 1989, 1990; articles on solid state physics, chemical physics and magnetic resonance. *Address:* Department of Physics, Univ. of Illinois at Urbana-Champaign, 1110 W Green Street, Urbana, IL 61801 (Office); 61 Chestnut Court, Champaign, IL 61822, USA (Home). *Telephone:* (217) 333-3834 (Office); (217) 352-8255 (Home). *Fax:* (217) 244-7559 (Office).

SLIPMAN, Sue, OBE, BA; British consumer representative; b. 3 Aug. 1949; d. of Mark Slipman and Doris Barham; one s.; ed Stockwell Manor Comprehensive School, Univs of Wales, Leeds and London; Sec. and Nat. Pres. Nat. Union of Students 1975–78; mem. Advisory Council for Adult and Continuing Educ. 1978–79; area officer Nat. Union of Public Employees 1979–85; Dir Nat. Council for One Parent Families 1985–95; Dir London Training and Enterprise Council 1995–96; Dir Gas Consumer Council 1996–98; Dir for Social Responsibility, Camelot Group PLC 1998–, Bd mem., Dir Social Relations and Compliance 2000–; Chair. Women for Social Democracy 1983–86, Advice Guidance and Counselling Lead Body 1992–, Better Regulation Task Force 1997–2001; Deputy Chair. Corp. Responsibility Group 2002; Dir (non-exec.) Thames Water Utilities Ltd. *Publications include:* Helping Ourselves to Power: A Handbook for Women on the Skills of Public Life 1986, Helping One-Parent Families to Work 1988, Maintenance: A System to Benefit Children 1989, Making Maintenance Pay 1990. *Address:* Camelot Group PLC, 20 Cockspur Street, London, SW1Y 5BL, England (Office). *Telephone:* (20) 7839-6051 (Office). *Fax:* (20) 7839-6053 (Office).

SLISKA, Lubov Konstantinovna; Russian politician and lawyer; b. 15 Oct. 1953, Saratov; m.; ed Saratov Inst. of Law; lawyer Soyuzpechat Saratov 1977–89; on staff regional trade Cttee of heavy machine construction industry workers 1992–96; Perm. Rep. of Govt in Regional Duma, Deputy Chair. Regional Govt 1996–2000; mem. State Duma Russia (Yedinstvo Movt List) 1999; Deputy Chair. (Speaker) of State Duma 2000–; Order for Service to Motherland; Hon. PhD. *Leisure interests:* countryside, fishing. *Address:* State Duma, Okhotny Ryad 1, 103265 Moscow, Russia (Office). *Telephone:* (095) 292-55-52 (Office). *Fax:* (095) 292-86-00 (Office). *E-mail:* sliska@duma.gov.ru (Office).

SLIVA, Anatoly Yakovlevich, CAND.JUR.; Russian politician; b. 10 Feb. 1940, Slavgorod, Belarus; m.; ed Moscow State Univ.; teacher, dean All-Union Juridical Inst. by correspondence; Sr scientific consultant, Deputy Head of Div. of local soviets, USSR Supreme Soviet 1988–92; Deputy Head State Law Dept at Russian Presidency, concurrently Head Div. on Interaction with Organs of Representative and Exec. Power 1992–94; Official Rep. of Russian Pres. on legal problems to Supreme Soviet Russian Fed. 1992; mem. State Duma, Chair. Cttee on problems of local man. 1993–95; Rep. of Russian Pres. to Council of Fed. 1996–98; Justice Constitutional Court of Russian Fed. 1998. *Address:* Constitutional Court, Ilyinka str. 21, 103132, Moscow, Russia. *Telephone:* (095) 206-92-25.

SLOMAN, Sir Albert Edward, Kt, CBE, MA, DPhil; British university administrator; b. 14 Feb. 1921, Launceston, Cornwall; s. of Albert Sloman, CC and L.F. Brewer; m. Marie B. Bergeron 1948; three d.; ed Launceston Coll. and Wadham Coll., Oxford; lecturer, Univ. of Calif. (Berkeley) 1946–47; Reader in Spanish, Univ. of Dublin 1947–53; Fellow, Trinity Coll., Dublin 1950–53; Prof. of Spanish, Univ. of Liverpool 1953–62; Vice-Chancellor, Univ. of Essex 1962–87; Pres. Conf. of European Rectors and Vice-Chancellors 1969–74; Vice-Pres. Int. Asscn of Univs 1970–75; Chair. Cttee of Vice-Chancellors and Principals 1981–83; Chair. Bd of Govs. Centre for Information on Language Teaching and Research 1979–86; Chair. British Acad. Studentship Selection Cttee (Humanities) 1965–87, Overseas Research Students Fees Support Scheme 1980–87, Univs Council for Adult and Continuing Educ. 1984–87, Selection Cttee Commonwealth Scholarships Comm. 1986–94; Chair. Int. Bd United World Colls 1988–93; Vice-Chair. Council of Asscn of Commonwealth Univs 1984–87; mem. Econ. and Social Cttee EEC 1973–82, Cttee for Int. Co-operation in Higher Educ. 1981–88 (Chair. 1985–88), Cttee of Man., British Inst. in Paris 1982–96, Bd of Govs Univ. of Guyana 1966–92; Inspection of Ruskin Coll., Oxford 1986–87; Pres. Penzance Library 1990–96; Dir Close Bros. Bessa Cos 1992–98; Dr hc (Nice) 1974, (Essex) 1988, (Liverpool) 1989. *Publications:* The Sources of Calderón's El Príncipe Constante 1950, The Dramatic Craftsmanship of Calderón 1958, Calderón, La Vida Es Sueño (Ed.) 1960, Bulletin of Hispanic Studies (ed.) 1953–62, A University in the Making 1964. *Leisure interest:* travel. *Address:* 19 Inglis Road, Colchester, Essex, CO3 3HU, England. *Telephone:* (20) 7225-0972 (Office); (1206) 547270 (Home).

SLONIMSKI, Piotr, DSc, MD; French/Polish biologist; b. 9 Nov. 1922, Warsaw, Poland; s. of Piotr Slonimski; m. Hanna Kulagowska 1951 (deceased); one d.; ed Lycée Stephane Batory, underground Univ. of Warsaw, Jagiellonian Univ. of Cracow and Faculté des Sciences, Paris; Polish underground army 1939–45; Asst Univ. of Cracow 1945–47; Attaché, CNRS 1947, Chargé 1952, Maître 1956, Dir 1962; Prof. of Genetics, Faculté des Sciences and Univ. P. et M. Curie 1965–91, Prof. Emer. 1992–; Dir Centre de Génétique Moléculaire, CNRS 1971–91, Hon. Dir CNRS, Gif-sur-Yvette br. 1992–; Dir-Gen. Groupement de Recherches et d'Etudes sur les Genomes (GREG) 1993–96; Visiting Prof. Univs of Calif., Chicago and Louvain; mem. Acad. des Sciences (Inst. de France), Bavarian, Polish and Belgian Acads., Academia Europaea, American Acad. of Arts and Sciences etc.; Chevalier, Légion d'honneur, Mil. Cross (Poland), Officier, Ordre Nat. du Mérite, Commdr with Star of Merit of the Repub. (Poland); Dr hc (Wrocław, Louvain, Warsaw, Bratislava); CNRS Gold Medal 1985, Hansen Gold Medal 1987, G. J. Mendel Hon. Medal 2001 and other awards. *Publications:* scientific publs on cellular respiration, genetics and biogenesis of mitochondria, structure and function

of genes. *Leisure interest:* mushroom hunting. *Address:* Le Haut Chantemesle, 72150 Courdemanche, France (Home); Centre de Génétique Moléculaire du CNRS, avenue de la Terrasse, 91190 Gif-sur-Yvette Cedex; Institut de France, 23 quai Conti, 75006 Paris. *E-mail:* slonimski@cgm.cnrs-gif.fr (Office).

SLONIMSKY, Sergey Mikhailovich, PhD; Russian composer, pianist and musicologist; b. 12 Aug. 1932, Leningrad (now St Petersburg); s. of Mikhail Slonimsky and Ida Kaplan; m. Raisa Zankisova; one s. one d.; ed Leningrad Conservatoire; teacher of composition at Leningrad (now St Petersburg) Conservatoire 1958–, Prof. 1976–; RSFSR People's Artist 1987; RSFSR State (Glinka) Prize 1983. *Works include:* Virineya (opera) 1967, The Master and Margarita (opera) 1970–72, Icarus (ballet) 1971, Mary Stuart (opera) 1980, Hamlet (opera) 1991, Ivan the Terrible (opera) 1994, 10 symphonies 1958–95, 24 preludes and fugues for piano 1993–94. *Publication:* musicological study of Prokofiev's symphonies 1964. *Leisure interest:* telling funny stories. *Address:* St Petersburg Conservatoire of Music, Teatralnaya ploshchad, St Petersburg; 9 Kanal Griboedova, Apt. 97, 191186 St Petersburg, Russia. *Telephone:* 311-85-85.

SLOVES, Marvin, BA; American advertising agency executive; b. 22 April 1933, New York; s. of John H. Sloves and Evelyn S. (Wishan) Sloves; ed Brandeis Univ. and Oriental Inst., Univ. of Chicago; Staff Researcher, Leo Burnett Co., Chicago 1962; Dir of Research, Earle Ludgin Co., Chicago 1963–64; Account Exec. Ted Bates Co., New York 1965–67; Pres. and CEO, Scali, McCabe, Sloves, Inc., New York 1967–81, Chair. and CEO 1981–93; Vice-Chair. The Lowe Group 1993–95; Co-Chair. Lowe & Partners/Scali, McCabe, Sloves 1995–99. *Leisure interests:* boxing, memorabilia collecting. *Address:* P.O. Box 1745, Santa Fe, NM 87504, USA.

SLYNN OF HADLEY, Baron (Life Peer), cr. 1992, of Egginton in the County of Bedfordshire; **Gordon Slynn,** Kt, PC, QC, MA, LLB; British lawyer; b. 17 Feb. 1930; s. of John Slynn and Edith Slynn; m. Odile M.H. Boutin 1962; ed Sandbach School, Goldsmith's Coll. and Trinity Coll., Cambridge; called to Bar, Gray's Inn 1956, Bencher 1970, Vice-Treas. 1987, Treas. 1988; QC 1974; Jr Counsel, Ministry of Labour 1967–68, Treasury (Common Law) 1968–74; Leading Counsel to Treasury 1974–76; Recorder of Hereford 1971, a Recorder and Hon. Recorder 1972–76; Judge, High Court of Justice, Queen's Bench Div. 1976–81; Pres. Employment Appeal Tribunal 1978–81; Chief Steward and Hereford 1978– (Freedom of the City 1996); Advocate-Gen., Court of Justice of the European Communities 1981–88, Judge 1988–92, a Lord of Appeal in Ordinary 1992–; Lecturer in Air Law, LSE 1958–61; Visiting Prof. in Law, Univ. of Durham 1981–88, Cornell 1983 (Irvine Lecturer 1984), Kings Coll. London 1985–90, Univ. of Tech., Sydney 1990–, Nat. Univ. of India, Bangalore 1992–; Hon. Vice-Pres. Union Int. des Avocats 1976–; Vice-Chair. Exec. Council Int. Law Asscn 1986–88, Chair. 1988–; Gov. Sadlers Wells 1988–95; Chair. Govs. Mill Hill School 1989–95; Chair. Bd Acad. of Ancient Music; Hon. mem. Canadian Bar Asscn, Georgia Trial Lawyers' Asscn, Fla Defense Lawyers Asscn, Indian Soc. of Int. Law, Fellow Int. Soc. of Barristers (USA); Hon. Fellow, Univ. Coll. at Buckingham 1981, Trinity Coll. Cambridge 2001; Hon. LLD (Birmingham) 1983, (Buckingham) 1983, (Exeter) 1985, (Univ. of Tech., Sydney) 1991, (Staffordshire) 1994, (City Univ.) 1995, (Pondicherry) 1997, (Kingston) 1997; Hon. Decanus legis (Mercer) 1986; Hon. DCL (Durham) 1989; Hon. D.Univ. (Essex) 2001; Grand Croix ordre de Mérite Luxembourg 1998. *Publications:* contributions to Halsbury's Laws of England and Atkins' Court Forms. *Leisure interests:* music, travel. *Address:* House of Lords, Westminster, London, SW1A 0PW, England.

SMALE, John G., BS; American business executive; b. 1 Aug. 1927, Listowel, Ont., Canada; s. of Vera G. Gray and Peter J. Smale; m. Phyllis Anne Weaver 1950; two s. two d.; ed Miami Univ. (Ohio); worked for Vick Chemical Co., New York 1949–50; with Bio-Research Inc., New York 1950–52; with Procter and Gamble Co. 1952, Dir 1972, Pres. 1974–86, CEO 1981–90, Chair. 1986–90; Dir Gen. Motors Corpn, Detroit 1992–95, Chair. Exec. Comm. of Bd 1996–2000, Exec. Cttee Gen. Motors Corpn Detroit 1996–2000 (also Bd Dirs); retd 2000; Hon. LLD (Kenyon Coll.) 1974, (Miami Univ.) 1979, Hon. DSc (DePauw Univ.) 1983; Hon. D.Iur (St Augustine's Coll.) 1985.

SMALLMAN, Raymond Edward, CBE, PhD, DSc, FRS, F.R.ENG., FIM; British professor of metallurgy and materials science; b. 4 Aug. 1929, Wolverhampton; s. of David Smallman and Edith French; m. Joan D. Faulkner 1952; one s. one d.; ed Rugeley Grammar School and Univ. of Birmingham; Sr Scientific Officer, AERE Harwell 1953–58; Lecturer, Dept of Physical Metallurgy, Univ. of Birmingham 1958–63, Sr Lecturer 1963–64, Prof. of Physical Metallurgy 1964–69, Head, Dept of Physical Metallurgy and Science of Materials 1969–81, Feeney Prof. and Head, Dept of Metallurgy and Materials 1969–88, Prof. of Metallurgy and Materials 1988–93, Hon. Prof. 1993–2001, Prof. Emer. 2001–; Deputy Dean, Faculty of Science and Eng 1981–84, Dean 1984–85, Dean of Eng 1985–87, Vice-Prin. Univ. of Birmingham 1987–92; Pres. Birmingham Metallurgical Asscn 1972–73; Vice-Pres. Metals Soc. 1980–84; Vice-Pres. Fed. of European Materials Socs. 1992–94, Pres. 1994–96; Council mem., Science and Eng Research Council 1992–94, (Materials Comm. 1988–91); mem. Council Inst. of Materials (Chair. Int. Affairs Cttee 1993–97), Vice-Pres. 1995–99; Visiting Prof. Univ. of Pa 1961, Stanford Univ. 1962, NSW 1974, Cape Town 1976, Hong Kong 1990–; Van Horn Distinguished Lecturer, CASE Western Reserve Univ. 1978; Distinguished Lecturer, Hong Kong Univ. 1999; Warden Birmingham Assay Office 1994–98, Guardian 1997–2000; mem. Lunar Soc. 1991–99; Hon. Foreign mem. China

Ordnance Soc., Metal Science Soc. Czech Repub.; Hon. DSc (Wales) 1990, (Novi Sad) 1990, (Cranfield) 2001; Sir George Beilby Gold Medal, Inst. of Metals and Chem Soc. 1969, Rosenhain Medal Inst. of Metals 1972, Elegant Work Prize, Metals Soc. 1979, Platinum Medal, Inst. of Metals 1989. *Publications:* Modern Physical Metallurgy 1961, Modern Metallography (jtly) 1968, Structure of Metals and Alloys (jtly) 1969, Defect Analysis in Electron Microscopy (jtly) 1975, Metals and Materials: Science, Processes and Applications (jtly) 1994, Modern Physical Metallurgy and Materials Engineering (jtly) 1999; over 300 scientific papers on relationship of microstructure of materials and properties in learned journals. *Leisure interests:* writing, travel, friendly golf, bridge, gardening. *Address:* Department of Metallurgy and Materials, School of Engineering, University of Birmingham, Edgbaston, Birmingham, B15 2TT (Office); 59 Woodthorne Road South, Tettenhall, Wolverhampton, WV6 8SN, England (Home). *Telephone:* (121) 414-5223 (Office); (1902) 752545 (Home). *Fax:* (121) 414-7368 (Office); (1902) 752545 (Home). *E-mail:* r.e.smallman@bham.ac.uk (Office); ray.smallman@btopenworld.com (Home).

SMART, John Jamieson Carswell, AC, MA, BPhil, FAHA; Australian professor of philosophy; b. 16 Sept. 1920, Cambridge, England; s. of William M. Smart and Isabel M. Carswell; m. 1st Janet Paine 1956 (died 1967); one s. one d.; m. 2nd Elizabeth Warner 1968; ed King's Coll. Choir School, Cambridge, The Leys School, Cambridge, Univ. of Glasgow and Queen's Coll. Oxford; served in Royal Signals 1940–45; Jr Research Fellow, Corpus Christi Coll. Oxford 1948–50; Hughes Prof. of Philosophy, Univ. of Adelaide 1950–72, Prof. Emer. 1972–; Reader in Philosophy, La Trobe Univ. 1974–76; Prof. of Philosophy, Research School of Social Sciences, ANU 1976–85, Prof. Emer. 1986–; Fellow, Center for Advanced Study in the Behavioral Sciences, Stanford, USA 1979; Visiting Prof. Princeton 1957, Harvard 1963, Yale 1964, Stanford 1982, Univ. of Ala at Birmingham 1990; G. D. Young Lecturer, Univ. of Adelaide 1987; Hon. Fellow Corpus Christi Coll. Oxford 1991; Hon. Research Fellow, Monash Univ. 2002; Hon. DLitt (St Andrew's) 1983, (La Trobe) 1992, (Glasgow) 2001. *Publications:* An Outline of a System of Utilitarian Ethics 1961, Philosophy and Scientific Realism 1963, Between Science and Philosophy 1968, Ethics, Persuasion and Truth 1984, Essays Metaphysical and Moral 1987, Our Place In the Universe 1989, Atheism and Theism (with J. J. Haldane) 1996. *Leisure interest:* walking. *Address:* 159 Cumberland View, Whalley Drive, Wheelers Hill, Vic. 3150, Australia (Home). *Telephone:* (3) 9795-8075.

SMART, (Roderick) Ninian, MA, BPhil; British professor of religious studies; b. 6 May 1927, Cambridge; s. of William Marshall Smart and Isabel Macquarrie Carswell; m. Libushka Bariffaldi 1954; two s. two d.; ed Glasgow Acad. and Oxford Univ.; army service, Intelligence Corps. 1945–48, rank of Capt. 1947; Lecturer in Philosophy Univ. Coll., Wales 1952–56, in History and Philosophy of Religion King's Coll., London 1956–61; H.G. Wood Prof. of Theology Birmingham Univ. 1961–67; Founding Prof. of Religious Studies Lancaster Univ. 1967–82, Hon. Prof. 1982–86; Prof. of Religious Studies Univ. of Calif., Santa Barbara 1976– (Prof. Emer. 1999–), J.F. Rowny Prof. of Religious Studies 1988–; editorial consultant BBC TV series The Long Search 1974–77; Pres. American Acad. of Religion 2000; Visiting Lecturer Yale Univ. 1955–56, Banaras Hindu Univ. 1960; Visiting Prof. in Philosophy and History, Univ. of Wis. 1965, of Religious Studies, Princeton Univ. 1971, Univ. of Otago 1971, Univ. of Queensland 1980, 1985, Univ. of Cape Town 1982, Harvard Univ. 1989, Univ. of Hong Kong 1989; Gifford Lecturer Edinburgh Univ. 1979–80; Hon. Fellow Queen's Coll. Oxford 1999–; Hon. DHL (Loyola Chicago) 1968; Hon. DLitt (Glasgow) 1984, (Kelaniya Univ., Sri Lanka) 1990, (Lancaster) 1995, (Middx) 1996; Hon. DUniv (Stirling) 1986, (Middx). *Publications:* Reasons and Faiths 1958, Doctrine and Argument in Indian Philosophy 1964, Philosophers and Religious Truth 1964, The Philosophy of Religion 1968, The Religious Experience of Mankind 1969, The Phenomenon of Religion 1973, The Science of Religion and the Sociology of Knowledge 1974, Beyond Ideology 1981, Concept and Empathy 1986, Religion and the Western Mind 1987, World Religions 1989, Christian Systematic Theology in a World Context (with Steven Konstantine) 1991, Buddhism and Christianity: Rivals and Allies 1993, The Religions of Asia 1993, Religions of the West 1993, Religion and Nationalism 1994, Choosing a Faith 1995, The Dimensions of the Sacred 1996, Lights of Asia: The Buddha and Christ 1997, Reflections in the Mirror of Religion 1997, World Philosophies 1999. *Leisure interests:* painting, poetry, cricket and tennis. *Address:* Department of Religious Studies, Univ. of California at Santa Barbara, CA 93106, USA; Religious Studies, University of Lancaster, LA1 4YG, England. *Telephone:* (1524) 65201 (Lancaster); (805) 968-7419 (Santa Barbara).

SMART, Stephen Bruce, Jr., AB, SM; American fmr government official and business executive; b. 7 Feb. 1923, New York; s. of Stephen Bruce Smart and Beatrice Cobb; m. Edith Minturn Merrill 1949; one s. three d.; ed Harvard Coll. and Mass. Inst. of Tech.; US Army 1943–46, 1951–53; Sales Engineer, Permutit Co., New York 1947–51; joined Continental Group (fmrly Continental Can Co.) 1951, various sales and gen. man. posts 1951–62, Vice-Pres. Cen. Div. 1962–65, Marketing and Corpn Planning 1965–68, Exec. Vice-Pres. Paper Operations 1969–73, Vice-Chair. 1973–75, Pres. and COO 1975–81; Chair. and CEO Continental Group 1981–85; Under-Sec. for Int. Trade US Dept of Commerce 1985–88; Consultant, Dept of State, Washington 1988; Sr Fellow, World Resources Inst. 1989–95; Dir World Resources Inst. 1993–2001, League of Conservation Voters 1995. *Publications:* Ed. Beyond Compliance: A New Industry View of the Environment 1992, Indian Summer – A Memoir

1999. *Leisure interests:* fishing, sailing, American decorative arts. *Address:* 20561 Trappe Road, Upperville, VA 20184, USA (Home). *Telephone:* (540) 554-8302 (Home).

SMARTH, Rosny; Haitian politician and agricultural economist; Prime Minister of Haiti 1996–97. *Address:* c/o Office of the Prime Minister, Palais National, Port-au-Prince, Haiti.

SMIDT, Kristian, PhD; Norwegian professor of English Literature; b. 20 Nov. 1916, Sandefjord; s. of Bishop Johannes Smidt and Jofrid Smidt (née Grimstvedt); m. 1st Aagot Karner 1940 (divorced 1973); m. 2nd Anne Oulie-Hansen 1973; one s. two d.; ed Aske's Hatcham, London, Univ. of Oslo; Reader in English Literature Univ. of Oslo 1953–55, Prof. 1955–85, Prof. Emer. 1985–, Dir British Inst. 1955–73; Rockefeller Fellowship, Princeton Univ. 1951–52; Folger Shakespeare Library Fellowship, Washington DC 1960–61; Visiting Fellowship Clare College, Cambridge Univ. 1984; mem. Norwegian Acad. of Science and Letters, Vetenskaps-societen, Lund, Sweden, Norwegian Acad. of Language and Literature; Hon. OBE 1985; Nansen Award 1994. *Publications:* James Joyce and the Cultic Use of Fiction 1959, Poetry and Belief in the Work of T.S. Eliot 1961, Unconformities in Shakespeare's Plays (4 Vols) 1982–93, Shakespeare i norsk oversettelse 1994, Den mangfoldige Shakespeare 2000, The Importance of Recognition and Other Essays on T.S. Eliot 2001; Ed. Shakespeare's Richard III: Parallel Texts 1969; Ibsen Translated 1999. *Address:* Solveien 137, 1167 Oslo, Norway. *Telephone:* 22-28-86-42.

SMILEY, Jane Graves, MFA, PhD; American writer and university professor; b. 26 Sept. 1949, Los Angeles; d. of James La Verne Smiley and Frances (Graves) Nuelle; m. 1st John Whiston 1970 (divorced); m. 2nd William Silag 1978 (divorced); two d.; m. 3rd Stephen M. Mortensen 1987; one s.; ed Vassar Coll. and Univ. of Iowa; Asst Prof. Iowa State Univ. Ames 1981–84, Assoc. Prof. 1984–89, Prof. 1989–90, Distinguished Prof. 1992–96; Visiting Prof. Univ. of Iowa 1981, 1987; Pulitzer Prize for Fiction 1992; Nat. Book Critics Circle Award 1992 and other awards and prizes. *Publications:* Barn Blind 1980, At Paradise Gate 1981, Duplicate Keys 1984, The Age of Grief 1987, The Greenlanders 1988, Ordinary Love and Goodwill 1989, A Thousand Acres 1991, Moo: A Novel 1995, The All-True Travels and Adventures of Lidie Newton 1998. *Leisure interests:* cooking, swimming, playing piano, quilting. *Address:* c/o Molly Friedrick, Department of English, 708 3rd Avenue, Floor 23, New York, NY 10017, USA (Office).

SMIRNOV, Andrei Sergeyevich; Russian actor, film director and scriptwriter; b. 12 March 1941, Moscow; ed All Union State Inst. of Cinematography; numerous prizes at int. film festivals. *Films:* Dir: Hey, Anybody! (with B. Yashin) 1962, An Inch of Land (with B. Yashin) 1964, A Little Joke (TV film with B. Yashin) 1966, Somebody Else's Pain (TV film) 1966, Jacqueline Francois Sings (TV film) 1966, Angel 1987, Belorussian Railway Station 1970, Fall 1974, By Trust and Truth 1993, Unwillful Striptease 1983; Actor: Following, Chernov, Dreams of an Idiot, Mania of Giselle, Dairy of His Wife (Ivan Bunin); Script writer: Autumn, Sentimental Journey, My Dear Relatives. *Plays directed:* Late Supper (Moscow Art Theatre) 1994, Turgenev's Month in a Village (Comedy Francaise) 1997. *Publications include:* plays: Autumn, Sentimental Journey; My Dear Relative. *Address:* Suvirivski blvd 8, Apt 121019 Moscow, Russia (Office). *Telephone:* (095) 299-34-93 (Office).

SMIRNOV, Igor Nikolaevich, D.ECON.SC.; Russian politician; b. 1941, Petropavlovsk-Kamchatsky; m.; two s.; ed Zaporozhie Machine Construction Inst.; mem. CPSU 1963–90; engineer, chief engineer, chief of shop; Deputy Dir Novo-Kahovsk Electromash plant; Dir Tiraspol Electromash plant 1975–87; Dir Tiraspol Jt Trade Union 1989–91, Chair. City Soviet and Tiraspol City Exec. Cttee 1990–91; Pres. Self-Declared Pridniestrovskaya Repub. (expelled from CPSU for separatism 1990) 1990–; People's Deputy of Moldova 1990–92; Academician of Ukranian Economical-Cybernetics Acad.; mem. Int. Acad. of Informatization; Order of Republic, Medal, Order of Prince Daniyl of Moscow, Order of Sergei Radonejski, Russian Acad. of Sciences, Order of World Distributing Univ., Cross for Faith and Motherland (3rd Degree), Cross for Defence of Pridnestroive, Cross for Service to the Cossacks, Order of Lenin, Star of Hero; Medal for Labour Prowess. *Publications:* Human Beings, Science and Technical Progress in a Century of Information 2000, In Favour of the Republic 2000. *Leisure interest:* hunting. *Address:* Mira str. 50 Tiraspol (Office); K. Marksa str. 120/15, Tiraspol, Pridnestrovskaya Republic (Home); House of Government, Tiraspol, Pridnestrovskaya Republic, Moldova.

SMIRNOV, Igor Pavlovich, D.PHIL.SC.; Russian literary scholar; b. 19 May 1941, Leningrad (now St Petersburg); s. of Valentina Lomakina and Pavel Smirnov; m. Johanna Renate Döring 1979; ed Leningrad Univ.; Research Assoc. Leningrad Inst. of Russian Literature; left USSR 1981; Prof. Univ. of Konstanz, Germany; Vjazemski Prize 1998, Andrey Bely Prize 2000. *Publications include:* Meaning in Art and the Evolution of Poetic Systems 1977, Diachronic Transformations of Literary Genres and Motifs 1981, Essays on the History of the Typology of Culture (with Johanna Smirnov) 1982, The Emergence of the Inter-text 1985, Towards a Theory of Literature 1987, Being and Creating 1990, On Old Russian Culture, Russian National Specificity and the Logic of History 1991, Psychohistory of Russian Literature from Romanticism to the Present Day 1995, A Novel of Secrets – Dr. Zhivago 1996, Homo homini philosophus 1999, Megahistory 2000. *Address:* Department of Russian, University of Konstanz, 78457 Konstanz, 159; Kornblumenweg 14,

78465 Konstanz, Germany. *Telephone:* (7531) 882448 (Office); (7531) 43583 (Home). *Fax:* (7531) 4852 (Office). *E-mail:* igor.smirnov@uni-konstanz.de (Office).

SMIRNOV, Stanislav Alekseyevich, DEcon SC.; Russian business executive; b. 18 April 1954, Mashok, Vladimir Region; m.; two c.; ed Moscow Inst. of Motor Car Transport; Sec. Moscow City Comsomol Cttee 1982–85, First Sec. 1985–89; Sec., Second Sec. Cen. Comsomol Cttee 1989–90; Peoples' Deputy of Russian Fed.; mem. Supreme Soviet; Chair. Comm. on Problems of Youth 1990–93; expelled from CPSU 1991; mem. of Presidium, Fed. of Mfrs of Russia; mem. Council on Industrial Policy and Business of Russian Presidency; mem. Co-ordination Council Round Table of Russian Business 1994; Corresp. mem. Russian Acad. of Sciences 1997–; Pres. Russian Chamber of Commerce and Industry 1991–2001; Prof. of Sociology, State Tech. Univ. GTU–MADI 2000–. *Publications:* over 100 scientific works. *Address:* State Technical University, Avtomotornaya str. 2, 125438 Moscow, Russia. *Telephone:* (095) 155-03-71 (Office). *E-mail:* info@madi.ru.

SMIRNOV, Vitaly Georgiyevich; Russian sports official; b. 14 Feb. 1935, Khabarovsk; m. Irina Aleksandrovna Smirnova; three s.; ed Cen. State Inst. of Physical Culture; instructor, Head Div. of Sports Moscow Comsomol Cttee 1958–60; First Sec. Kuntzevo Regional Comsomol Cttee; Moscow Region 1960; Chair. Moscow Regional Council, Union of Sports Socs. and Orgs. 1960–62; Second Sec., First Sec. Moscow Regional Comsomol Cttee 1962–68; First Sec. City Cttee of CPSU 1968–70; Deputy Chair., First Deputy Chair. USSR Cttee of Sports and Physical Culture 1970–75; First Deputy Chair. Org. Cttee of Olympic Games 1980 in Moscow 1975–81; Chair. State Cttee on Sports and Physical Culture of Russian Fed. 1981–90; Chair. USSR Olympic Cttee 1990–92; Pres. Olympic Cttee of Russia 1992–2001, Hon. Pres. 2001–; mem. IOC 1971–, Vice-Pres. 2001–; mem. Acad. of Creativity 1994–, Int. Acad. of Informatization, Peter's Acad. of Sciences and Arts. *Publications:* numerous articles and papers on the devt of sports in Russia and the Olympic movt. *Leisure interests:* hunting, fishing, tennis. *Address:* Luzhnetskaya emb. 8, 119992 Moscow, Russia. *Telephone:* (095) 725-45-01 (Office). *Fax:* (095) 248-36-11 (Office).

SMIRNOV, Vladimir Nikolaevich; Russian biochemist; b. 17 May 1937, Cheliabinsk; m. 1st Valeriana Kreier 1956 (divorced 1973), m. 2nd Galina Chernonsova 1976; one s.; ed Leningrad Univ.; mem. CPSU 1976–91; postgraduate 1959–64; Jr, Sr Research Fellow at USSR Acad. of Med. Science Inst. of Medical Radiology 1964–68; Head of Biochemical Section, Ministry of Health 1968–72; Corresp. mem. of USSR (now Russian) Acad. of Sciences 1981; Prof. of Biological Science 1977; Head of Lab. at All-Union Scientific Centre for Cardiology (br. of USSR (now Russian) Acad. of Medical Science) 1973–76, Dir 1976–82; Dir of Inst. of Experimental Cardiography of Acad. of Medical Sciences 1982–; Corresp. mem., then mem. Acad. of Medical Sciences 1984–; USSR State Prize 1978. *Publications:* works on molecular biology, biochem. of the heart, cellular and molecular athero- and trombogenesis. *Leisure interests:* hunting, fishing. *Address:* Institute of Experimental Cardiology, Cardiology Research Centre, 3rd Cherepkovskaya 15A, 112552 Moscow, Russia. *Telephone:* (095) 415-00-35 (Office); (095) 203-84-83 (Home). *Fax:* (095) 415-29-62.

SMITH, Andrew David; British politician; b. 1 Feb. 1951; m.; one step-s.; ed Reading Grammar School and St John's Coll. Oxford; joined Labour Party 1973; mem. Oxford City Council 1976–87; MP for Oxford East 1987–; Opposition Spokesman on Higher Educ. 1988–92, on Treasury and Econ. Affairs 1992–94; Shadow Chief Sec. to HM Treasury 1994–96; Shadow Transport Sec. 1996–97; Minister of State, Dept for Educ. and Employment 1997–99; Chief Sec. to HM Treasury 1999–2002; Sec. of State for Work and Pensions 2002–; Chair. Bd Oxford Brookes Univ. (fmrly Oxford Polytechnic) 1987–93. *Address:* Department for Work and Pensions, Richmond House, 79 Whitehall, London, SW1A 2NS (Office); 4 Flaxfield Road, Blackbird Leys, Oxford, OX4 5QD, England (Home). *Telephone:* (20) 7238-0800 (Office). *Website:* www.dwp.gov.uk (Office).

SMITH, Anthony David, CBE, MA; British administrator; b. 14 March 1938; s. of Henry Smith and Esther Smith; ed Brasenose Coll., Oxford; Current Affairs Producer, BBC 1960–71; Fellow, St Antony's Coll., Oxford 1971–76; Dir British Film Inst. 1979–88; Pres. Magdalen Coll., Oxford 1988–; mem. Bd of Dirs Channel Four TV 1980–84; mem. Acton Soc. Trust 1978–90; Chair. Writers and Scholars Educational Trust (Index on Censorship) 1989–99; mem. Arts Council 1990–94; Hon. Fellow Brasenose Coll. 1994. *Publications:* The Shadow in the Cave: The Broadcaster, The Audience and the State 1973, British Broadcasting 1974, The British Press since the War 1976, Subsidies and the Press in Europe 1977, The Politics of Information 1978, Television and Political Life 1979, The Newspaper: An International History 1979, Newspapers and Democracy 1980, Goodbye Gutenberg – The Newspaper Revolution of the 1980s, The Geopolitics of Information 1980, The Age of the Behemoths 1991, From Books to Bytes 1993, The Oxford Illustrated History of Television 1995, Software for the Self: Culture and Technology 1996. *Address:* Magdalen College, Oxford, OX1 4AU; Albany, Piccadilly, London, W1V 9RP, England. *Telephone:* (1865) 276000 (Oxford).

SMITH, Bernard William, PhD; Australian academic; b. 3 Oct. 1916, Sydney; s. of Charles Smith and Rose Anne Tierney; m. 1st Kate Challis 1941 (died 1989); one s. one d.; m. 2nd Margaret Forster 1995; ed Univ. of Sydney, Warburg Inst., London and ANU, Canberra; school teacher NSW 1935–44, Educ. Officer, Art Gallery, NSW 1944–52; lecturer, Sr Lecturer Univ. of Melbourne 1955–63, Reader 1964–66; Art Critic The Age, Melbourne 1963–66; Prof. of Contemporary Art and Dir Power Inst. of Fine Arts, Univ. of Sydney 1967–77, Sr Assoc., Dept of Fine Arts 1977–; Assoc. Prof. Dept Fine Arts, Classical Studies and Archaeology, Univ. of Melbourne 1994–; Pres. Australian Acad of Fine Arts 1977–80; Chevalier, Ordre des Arts et des Lettres. *Publications:* Place, Taste and Tradition 1945, European Vision and the South Pacific 1960, Australian Painting 1962, The Boy Adeodatus 1985, The Art of Captain Cook's Voyages (jt author) 1985–87, The Death of the Artist as Hero 1988, The Critic as Advocate 1989, Imagining the Pacific 1992, Noel Counihan 1994, Poems 1938–1993 1996, Modernism's History 1998, A Pavane for Another Time 2002. *Leisure interests:* swimming, walking, reading. *Address:* 168 Nicholson Street, Fitzroy, Vic. 3065, Australia. *Telephone:* (3) 9419-7470. *Fax:* (3) 9419-8092.

SMITH, Brian (see Smith, Sir E. Brian).

SMITH, Brian (see Smith, Sir (Norman) Brian).

SMITH, Carsten, DJur; Norwegian judge (retd); b. 13 July 1932, Oslo; s. of Oscar Smith and Julie Høyer; m. Lucy Dahl 1958; three d.; ed Univ. of Oslo; attorney 1956; Deputy Judge 1960; Asst Prof. Univ. of Oslo 1957, Assoc. Prof. 1960, Prof. of Law 1964–91, Dir Inst. of Pvt. Law 1972–73, Dean, Faculty of Law 1977–79; Temporary Supreme Court Justice 1987, 1989–90; Chief Justice, Supreme Court of Norway 1991–2002; mem. Norwegian Acad. of Science and Letters, Pres. 1991; mem. and chair. numerous public cttees.cttees for preparation of legislation and org. of research and educ. etc.; recipient of several orders, hon. degrees and awards. *Publications include:* Law of Torts and Social Security (co-author) 1953, Law of Guarantees (Vols I–III) 1963–81, State Practice and Legal Theory 1978, Banking Law and State Regulations 1980, Contemporary Legal Reasoning 1992, The Law and the Life 1996; other books and articles in fields of int. law, constitutional law, admin. law and pvt. law. *Address:* Høyesterett, PO Box 8016 Dep, 0030 Oslo, Norway. *Telephone:* 22-03-59-05. *Fax:* 22-33-23-55.

SMITH, Rt Hon Chris(topher) Robert, PC, MP, PhD; British politician; b. 24 July 1951; s. of Colin Smith and Gladys Smith (née Luscombe); ed George Watson's Coll., Edinburgh, Pembroke Coll., Cambridge, Harvard Univ. (Kennedy Scholar 1975–76); Devt Sec. Shaftesbury Soc. Housing Asscn 1977–80; Devt Co-ordinator Soc. for Co-operative Dwellings 1980–83; Councillor London Borough of Islington 1978–83, Chief Whip 1978–79, Chair. Housing Cttee 1981–83; Labour MP for Islington S. and Finsbury 1983–; Opposition Spokesman on Treasury and Econ. Affairs 1987–92; Principal Opposition Spokesman on Environmental Protection 1992–94, on Nat. Heritage 1994–95, on Social Security 1995–96, on Health 1996–97; Sec. of State for Culture, Media and Sport 1997–2001; Chair. Labour Campaign for Criminal Justice 1985–88, Tribune Group of MPs 1988–89; Pres. Socialist Environment and Resources Asscn 1992–; mem. Exec. Fabian Soc. 1990–97; mem. Bd Shelter 1986–92, Royal Nat. Theatre 2001–; mem. Cttee on Standards in Public Life 2001–; Chair. Wordsworth Trust 2001–, Classic FM Consumer Panel 2001–; Visiting Prof. London Inst. 2002–; Sr Assoc. Judge Inst. in Man. Studies, Univ. of Cambridge 2001–. *Publication:* Creative Britain 1998. *Leisure interests:* mountaineering, literature, theatre, music. *Address:* House of Commons, London, SW1A 0AA, England.

SMITH, Sir David Cecil, Kt, FRS, FRSE; British academic; b. 21 May 1930, Port Talbot; s. of William Smith and Elva Smith; m. Lesley Mutch 1965; two s. one d.; ed Colston's School, Bristol, St Paul's School, London and Queen's Coll.; Browne Research Fellow, Queen's Coll. Oxford 1956–59; Harkness Fellow, Univ. of Calif. Berkeley 1959–60; Univ. Lecturer, Dept of Agric. Science, Univ. of Oxford 1960–74; Fellow and Tutor, Wadham Coll. Oxford 1964–74; Melville Wills Prof. of Botany, Univ. of Bristol 1974–80; Sibthorpian Prof. of Rural Econ. Univ. of Oxford 1980–87; Prin. and Vice-Chancellor, Univ. of Edin. 1987–94; Pres. Wolfson Coll., Oxford 1994–2000; Commdr Order of Merit (Italy), Commdr Order of Merit (Poland); Hon. DSc (Aberdeen) 1990, (Edin.) 1994 and numerous other hon. degrees. *Publication:* Biology of Symbiosis (with A. E. Douglas) 1987. *Leisure interest:* writing. *Address:* 13 Abbotsford Park, Edin., EH10 5DZ, Scotland. *Telephone:* (131) 446-0230. *Fax:* (131) 446-0230. *E-mail:* david.smith@wolfson.ox.ac.uk (Home).

SMITH, Delia, OBE, FRTS; British cookery writer and broadcaster; b. 18 June 1941; m. Michael Wynn Jones; creator and presenter of several TV series; cookery writer Evening Standard newspaper 1972–85; columnist Radio Times; Consultant Food Ed. Sainsbury's Magazine; Dir Norwich City Football Club; announced retirement from TV and book career Jan. 2003; Hon. Fellow St Mary's Coll., Univ. of Surrey 1996; Hon. Fellow John Moores Univ., Liverpool 2000; Dr hc (Nottingham Univ.) 1996, (Univ. of East Anglia) 1999; Special Award, Andre Simon Memorial Fund 1994. *Publications:* How to Cheat at Cooking 1971, Country Fare 1973, Recipes from Country Inns and Restaurants 1973, Family Fare: Book 1 1973, Book 2 1974, Evening Standard Cookbook 1974, Country Recipes from Look East (regional TV programme) 1975, More Country Recipes from Look East 1976, Frugal Food 1976, Book of Cakes 1977, Recipes from Look East 1977, Food for Our Times 1978, Cookery Course: Part 1 1978, Part 2 1979, Part 3 1981, The Complete Cookery Course 1982, A Feast for Lent 1983, A Feast for Advent 1983, One is Fun 1985, Food Aid Cookery Book (ed.) 1986, A Journey into God 1988, Delia Smith's Christmas 1990, Delia Smith's Summer Collection 1993, Delia Smith's Winter Collection 1995, Delia's Red Nose Collection 1997, How to Cook: Book 1 1998, How to Cook: Book 2 1999, How to Cook Book 3 2001, Delia's Chocolate Collection 2001, Delia's Vegetarian Collection 2002. *Address:* c/o Deborah

Owen Limited, 78 Narrow Street, Limehouse, London, E14 8BP, England. *Telephone:* (20) 7987-5119. *Fax:* (20) 7538-4004. *E-mail:* do@deborahowen.co .uk (Office).

SMITH, Sir E. Brian, Kt, MA, PhD, DSc, FRSC; British scientist and university vice-chancellor (retd); b. 10 Oct. 1933, Mold, North Wales; s. of S. Eric Smith and Dilys Olwen Hughes; m. 1st Margaret Barr 1957 (divorced 1978); two s. one d.; m. 2nd Regina Arvidson Ball 1983; two step-d.; ed Alun Grammar School, Mold, Wirral Grammar School, Univ. of Liverpool; Fellow St Catherine's Coll. Oxford and Lecturer in Physical Chem., Oxford Univ. 1960–88; Master St Catherine's Coll. 1988–93; Vice-Chancellor Cardiff Univ. 1993–2001; Dir ISIS Innovation Network 1988–97, Cardiff Int. Festival of Musical Theatre 2001; mem. Bd Welsh Devt Agency 1998–2001, Wales European Centre 2001–, Higher Educ. Funding Council for Wales 2002–. *Publications:* Virial Coefficients of Pure Gases and Mixtures 1969, Basic Chemical Themodynamics 1973, Intermolecular Forces 1981, Forces Between Molecules 1986; papers in scientific journals. *Leisure interest:* mountaineering. *Address:* c/o Cardiff University, Park Place, Main Building, Cardiff, CF10 3AT, Wales (Office). *Website:* www.cf.ac.uk (Office).

SMITH, Edwin, PhD, FRS; British engineer; b. 28 July 1931, Staveley, Derbyshire; s. of the late Albert Edwin Smith and Sarah Ann Smith (née Toft); m. Patricia Georgina Gale 1958; ed Chesterfield Grammar School, Nottingham and Sheffield Univs.; mem. staff Assoc. Electrical Industries Research Lab., Aldermaston 1955–61, Cen. Electrical Generating Bd Research Lab., Leatherhead 1961–68; Prof. of Metallurgy, Manchester Univ. 1968–88, Dean of Science 1983–85, Pro-Vice-Chancellor 1985–88, Prof. Emer. and Consultant 1988–. *Publications:* numerous publs in tech. journals. *Leisure interests:* sport (ran 14 marathons; personal best 2 hrs 47 mins. 1958). *Address:* Materials Science Centre, University of Manchester Institute of Science and Technology, University of Manchester, Grosvenor Street, Manchester, M1 7HS, England (Office). *Telephone:* (161) 200-3556 (Office). *Fax:* (161) 200-3586 (Office).

SMITH, Elizabeth Jean, MA; British broadcasting executive and international official; b. 15 Aug. 1936, Ajmer, India; d. of Sir Robert Hay and Lady Hay; m. Geoffrey Smith 1960; one s. one d.; ed Univ. of Edinburgh; producer, Radio News, BBC 1960; Asst Head, Cen. Talks and Features, BBC World Service 1980, Head, Current Affairs 1984, Controller, English Programmes 1987–94; Sec.-Gen. Commonwealth Broadcasting Asscn 1994–; Fellow, Radio Acad. *Publication:* as Elizabeth Hay: Sambo Sahib. *Address:* Commonwealth Broadcasting Association, 17 Fleet Street, London, EC4Y 1AA, England. *Telephone:* (20) 7583-5550. *Fax:* (20) 7583-5549. *E-mail:* elizabeth@cba.org.uk (Office).

SMITH, Emil L., BS, PhD; American biochemist and biophysicist; b. 5 July 1911, New York City; s. of Abraham and Esther Smith; m. Esther Press 1934; two s.; ed Columbia, Cambridge and Yale Univs; Instructor, Columbia Univ. 1936–38; Fellow, Rockefeller Inst. 1940–42; Sr Biochemist and Biophysicist, E. R. Squibb & Sons 1942–46; Assoc. Prof. and Prof., Univ. of Utah 1946–63; Prof. and Chair. Dept of Biological Chem., Univ. of Calif., LA 1963–79, Prof. Emer. 1979–; Foreign mem. Russian Acad. of Sciences; mem. NAS, American Acad. of Arts and Sciences, American Philosophical Soc., etc.; Guggenheim Fellow (Cambridge and Yale) 1938–40; Stein-Moore Award (Protein Soc.) 1987. *Publications:* Principles of Biochemistry (co-author) 1954; many articles on biochem. and biophysics. *Leisure interests:* music, literature, art. *Address:* Department of Biological Chemistry, University of California, School of Medicine, Los Angeles, CA 90095-1737, USA. *Telephone:* (310) 825-6494 (Office). *Fax:* (310) 206-5272 (Office).

SMITH, Francis Barrymore, PhD, FAHA; Australian historian; b. 16 May 1932, Hughesdale; s. of Francis John Smith and Bertha Smith; m. Ann Stokes 1965; two s. two d.; ed Univ. of Melbourne and Cambridge Univ.; Lecturer in History, Univ. of Melbourne 1962–66; Prof. Fellow in History, Inst. of Advanced Studies, ANU 1974–94, Hancock Prof. of History 1995–98; Ed. Historical Studies 1963–67; Pres. Australian Historical Asscn 1978–80. *Publications:* Making of the Second Reform Bill 1966, Radical Artisan: William James Linton 1973, The People's Health 1830–1910 1979, Florence Nightingale: Reputation and Power 1982, Retreat of Tuberculosis 1987, 'Agent Orange': The Australian Aftermath 1994, G.G. Achilli versus J. H. Newman 2000. *Address:* Division of Historical Studies, Institute of Advanced Studies, Australian National University, Canberra 0200, Australia. *Telephone:* (2) 6125-2358. *Fax:* (2) 6125-3969 (Office).

SMITH, Sir Francis Graham (See Graham-Smith, Sir Francis).

SMITH, Frank Thomas, DPhil, FRS; British professor of applied mathematics; b. 24 Feb. 1948, Bournemouth; s. of Leslie Maxwell Smith and Catherine Matilda Smith; m. Valerie Sheila Hearn 1972; three d.; ed Bournemouth School, Jesus Coll. Oxford, Univ. Coll. London; Research Fellow, Southampton Univ. 1972–73; Lecturer in Math., Reader then Prof., Imperial Coll. London 1973–84; Goldsmid Prof. of Applied Math., Univ. Coll. London 1984–; Visiting Prof. Univ. of Western Ont., Canada 1978–79, Ohio State Univ. 1990. *Publications:* Boundary-Layer Separation (co-ed.); numerous scientific papers, mostly on theoretical and computational fluid dynamics, industrial and biomedical applications and math. modelling. *Address:* Mathematics Department, University College, Gower Street, London, WC1E 6BT (Office); 9 Woodham Park Road, Woodham, Addlestone, Surrey, KT15 3ST, England (Home). *Telephone:* (20) 7679-2837 (Office); (1932) 352394 (Home).

SMITH, George David William, MA, DPhil, FRS, FRSA, FIM, FInstP, CEng, CPhys; British professor of metallurgy and materials science; b. 28 March 1943, Aldershot; s. of George Alfred William Smith and Grace Violet Hannah Dayton Smith; m. Josephine Ann Halford 1968; two s.; ed Corpus Christi Coll., Univ. of Oxford; SRC Research Fellow, Dept of Materials, Univ. of Oxford 1968–70, Research Fellow 1970–75, Sr Research Fellow 1975–77, Lecturer 1977–92, George Kelley Reader in Metallurgy 1992–96, Prof. of Materials Science 1996–, Head of Dept 2000–; Man. Dir Kindbrisk Ltd (renamed Oxford Nano-science Ltd 2000) 1987–2002, Chair. 2002–; mem. Council Inst. of Materials 1998– (Vice-Pres. 2002), UK Materials Foresight Panel 1998–, Council Inst. of Materials, Minerals and Mining 2003–, Council Royal Soc. 2003–04; Fellow, Trinity Coll., Oxford 1991–, St Cross Coll., Oxford 1977–91, Fellow Emer. 1991–; Freeman of the Armourers' and Brasiers' Company; Freeman of the City of London 1999; Beilby Medal and Prize 1985, Rosenhain Medal and Prize 1991. *Publications:* Atom Probe Microanalysis (with M. K. Miller) 1989, Atom Probe Field Ion Microscopy (co-author) 1996; numerous contribs. to scientific journals. *Leisure interests:* walking, fishing, bird watching, travel. *Address:* Department of Materials, Oxford University, Parks Road, Oxford, OX1 3PH, England (Office). *Telephone:* (1865) 273737 (Office). *Fax:* (1865) 273738 (Office). *E-mail:* george.smith@materials.ox.ac .uk.

SMITH, Hon. Godfrey, BL; Belizean politician and lawyer; ed Univ. of the W Indies; Assoc. Attorney Barrow & Williams, Belize City 1994–97; Sec.-Gen. People's United Party, Belize City 1997–98; Chief of Staff Office of the Prime Minister 1998–99; Attorney-Gen. and Minister of Information 1999–; lecturer, Univ. Coll. Belize. *Publications include:* Belize Law Report (ed.), Prectical Guide to Gross Receipt Tax. *Address:* Office of the Attorney General, Belmopan, Belize (Office). *Telephone:* (8) 22110/22504 (Office). *Fax:* (8) 22110/ 22504 (Office). *E-mail:* atgenmin@btl.net (Office). *Website:* www.belize.gov.bz (Office).

SMITH, Gordon Harold, BA, JD; American politician; b. 25 May 1952, Pendleton, Ore.; s. of Milan Dale Smith and Jessica Smith (née Udall); m. Sharon Lankford; two s. one d.; ed Brigham Young Univ. and Southwestern Univ.; law clerk to Justice H. Vern Payne, New Mexico Supreme Court; pvt. practice Ariz.; owner Smith Frozen Foods; mem. Ore. State Senate 1992–95, Pres. 1995–96; Senator from Ore. 1997–; mem. Budget Cttee; Chair. SubCttee on Water and Power; mem. SubCttee on Forests and Public Land Man., SubCttee on Energy Rescheduling, Devt, Production and Regulation; mem. Energy and Natural Resources Cttee; Chair. SubCttee on European Affairs; mem. SubCttee on nr Eastern and S Asian Affairs; mem. Foreign Relations Cttee; mem. SubCttee on E Asian and Pacific Affairs. *Address:* Office of the Senator from Oregon, 404 Russell Senate Office Building, Washington, DC 20510-3704, USA (Office).

SMITH, Gordon Scott, PhD; Canadian diplomatist, professor and consultant; b. 19 July 1941, Montreal, Que.; s. of the late G. Meredith Smith and Helen Scott; m. Lise G. Lacroix; three s. one d.; ed Lower Canada Coll. Montreal, McGill Univ., Univ. of Chicago and MIT; joined Defence Research Bd 1966; transferred to Dept of External Affairs 1967; mem. Canadian Del. to NATO 1968–70; Special Adviser to Minister of Nat. Defence 1970–72; joined Privy Council Office 1972; Deputy Sec. to Cabinet (Plans) 1978–79; Deputy Under-Sec. Dept of External Affairs 1979; Assoc. Sec. to Cabinet, Privy Council Office 1980–81; Sec. Ministry of State for Social Devt 1981–84; Assoc. Sec. to Cabinet and Deputy Clerk of Privy Council 1984; Deputy Minister for Political Affairs, Dept of External Affairs 1985; Amb. and Perm. Rep. of Canada to NATO 1985–90; Sec. to the Cabinet for Fed.-Provincial Relations, Govt of Canada 1990–91; Amb. to the EC 1991–94; Deputy Minister of Foreign Affairs 1994–97; Chair. Int. Devt Research Centre; Dir. Centre for Global Studies, Univ. of Vic., Pres. Gordon Smith Int. *Publication:* Altered States. *Leisure interests:* squash, tennis, sailing, skiing, antiques. *Address:* 2027 Runnymede Avenue, Victoria, BC V8S 2V5, Canada. *Telephone:* (250) 595-8622. *Fax:* (250) 595-8682. *E-mail:* gordonssmith@shaw.ca (Office).

SMITH, Hamilton O., MD; American university professor and research scientist; b. 23 Aug. 1931, New York City; s. of Tommie Harkey and Bunnie Othanel Smith; m. Elizabeth Anne Bolton 1957; four s. one d.; ed Univ. of Illinois, Univ. of California at Berkeley, Johns Hopkins Univ. School of Medicine, Baltimore, Md; Internship, Barnes Hosp., St Louis, Mo. 1956–57; Lt in USNR, Sr Medical Officer 1957–59; Resident, Henry Ford Hosp., Detroit, Mich. 1960–62; Postdoctoral Fellow, Dept of Human Genetics, Univ. of Mich. 1962–64, Research Assoc. 1964–67; Asst Prof. of Microbiology, Johns Hopkins Univ. School of Medicine 1967–69, Assoc. Prof. 1969–73, Prof. of Microbiology 1973–81, Prof. of Molecular Biology & Genetics 1981–; sabbatical year with Inst. für Molekular-Biologie, Zürich Univ. 1975–76; Guggenheim Fellow 1975–76; shared Nobel Prize for Physiology and Medicine 1978 with Prof. Werner Arber, and Dr. Daniel Nathans for work on restriction enzymes; mem. NAS 1980, AAAS. *Leisure interests:* piano, classical music. *Address:* Department of Molecular Biology, Johns Hopkins University School of Medicine, 720 Rutland Avenue, Baltimore, MD 21205 (Office); 8222 Carrbridge Circle, Baltimore, MD 21204, USA (Home). *Telephone:* (301) 955-3650 (Office); (301) 821-5409 (Home).

SMITH, Hans J., BSc, S.M.P.; South African business executive; b. 15 Jan. 1941, Krugersdorp; s. of the late Hendrik C. Smith and Johanna Smith; m. Lydia Minnaar 1969; two d.; ed Kensington High School, Univ. of Pretoria,

Univ. of the Witwatersrand, Univ. of SA and Harvard Univ.; with Gold Fields of SA 1965–70; Sr Investment Analyst, Gencor 1970, Asst Gen. Man. Buffalo Fluorspar Mine 1972, Gen. Man. Msuali Asbestos 1973, Operations Man. Chrome Div. Corp. HQ 1974, Man. Dir Zululand Titanium 1978; Tech. Dir Octha Diamonds 1981; rejoined Gencor as Man. Strategic Planning, Corporate Mining Div. 1985, Sr Man. Marketing, Coal Div. 1985; Chief Consultant, Safety and Health, Genmin 1988; Man. Dir Trans-Natal Coal Corpn Ltd 1988; Man. Dir Samancor Ltd 1989; Chief Exec. New Business, Group Co. Gencor 1993; Chief Exec. and Man. Dir Iscor Ltd 1993, Exec. Chair. 1995; Hon. DEcon (Univ. of Transkei) 1998; Communicator of the Year Award 1996, Great Silver Medal of Honour (Austria) 1996. *Leisure interests:* tennis, golf, jogging, scuba diving, underwater photography. *Address:* Iscor Ltd, PO Box 450, Pretoria 0001, South Africa. *Telephone:* (12) 3074127. *Fax:* (12) 3074238. *E-mail:* hanss@hq.iscorltd.co.za (Office); hanss@iscorltd.co.za (Home).

SMITH, Harvey (see Smith, (Robert) Harvey).

SMITH, Henry Sidney, MA, FBA, DLit; British professor of Egyptology; b. 14 June 1928, London; s. of Sidney Smith and Mary W. Smith (née Parker); m. Hazel Flory Leeper 1961 (died 1991); ed Merchant Taylors School, Sandy Lodge, Middx and Christ's Coll., Cambridge; Asst Lecturer in Egyptology, Faculty of Oriental Studies, Cambridge 1954–59, Lecturer 1959–63; Wallis Budge Fellow in Egyptology, Christ's Coll., Cambridge 1955–63; Field Dir Egypt Exploration Soc. Archaeological Survey of Nubia, Epigraphist at Nubian sites 1959–65; Reader in Egyptian Archaeology, Univ. Coll. London 1963–70, Edwards Prof. of Egyptology 1970–86, Prof. Emer. 1986–; Prin. Epigraphist and Site Supervisor, Egypt Exploration Soc., Saqqara, Egypt 1964–70, Field Dir, Sacred Animal Necropolis 1971–76, Anubieton 1976–81, Dir Memphis Project in Egypt 1981–88; Corresp. mem. Deutsches Archäologisches Institut; Medallist, Collège de France, Paris 1984. *Publications:* Preliminary Reports of the EES Archaeological Survey of Egyptian Nubia 1961, A Visit to Ancient Egypt: Memphis and Saqqara, c. 600–30 BC 1974, The Fortress of Buhen, II: The Inscriptions 1976, I: The Archaeological Report (with W. B. Emery and A. Millard) 1979, Saqqara Demotic Papyri I (with W. J. Tait) 1984, The Anubieton at Saqqara, Vols I and II (with D. G. Jeffreys and Lisa L. Giddy) 1988, 1992, The Sculpture from the Sacred Animal Necropolis at North Saqqara 1964–76 (with Elizabeth Anne Hastings) 1997; excavation reports, text publications and historical articles in int. journals. *Leisure interests:* varied. *Address:* Ailwyn House, High Street, Upwood, Huntingdon, Cambridgeshire, PE17 1QE, England (Home). *Telephone:* (1487) 812196 (Home).

SMITH, Ian Douglas; Zimbabwean politician; b. 8 April 1919; m. Janet Watt (died 1994); two s. one d.; ed Chaplin School, Gwelo, S. Rhodesia (now Gweru, Zimbabwe) and Rhodes Univ., Grahamstown, S. Africa; RAF 1941–46; farmer; MP S. Rhodesia Legis. Ass. 1948–53, Parl. of Fed. of Rhodesia and Nyasaland 1953–61; fmr Chief Whip United Fed. Party, resgnd 1961; Foundation mem. and Vice-Pres. Rhodesian Front (renamed Republican Front 1981) 1962, Pres. 1964–87; Deputy Prime Minister and Minister of Treasury S. Rhodesia 1962–64; Prime Minister of Rhodesia 1964–79, proclaimed Rhodesia's Unilateral Declaration of Independence, Nov. 1965; Minister without Portfolio in Bishop Muzorewa's Govt 1979; mem. Transitional Exec. Council to prepare for transfer of power in Rhodesia 1978–79; MP for Republican Front (now Conservative Alliance of Zimbabwe) 1980–88, suspended from Parl. 1987–88; Independence Decoration 1970, Grand Commdr, Order of the Legion of Merit 1979. *Address:* Gwenoro Farm, Shurugwi; 3 Phillips Avenue, Belgravia, Harare, Zimbabwe.

SMITH, Ian William Murison, PhD, FRS, FRSC; British professor of chemistry; b. 15 June 1937, Leeds; s. of William Murison Smith and Margaret Moir Smith; m. Susan Morrish 1961; two s. two d.; ed Giggleswick School, Christ's Coll., Cambridge; Fellow Christ's Coll., Cambridge 1963–85, Demonstrator in Physical Chem., Cambridge Univ., 1966–71, Lecturer Physical Chem. 1971–85, Tutor Christ's Coll., Cambridge 1968–76, Dir of Studies 1972–85; Prof. of Chemistry, Univ. of Birmingham 1985–91, Head School of Chem. 1989–93, Mason Prof. of Chem. 1991, now Prof. Emer.; Millar Research Professorship, U.C. Berkeley 1996; Stauffer Lectureship, Univ. Southern Calif. 2000; Fellowship Jt Inst. for Lab. Astrophysics, Univ. Colo 2000; Pres. Faraday Div. RSC 2001–02; RSC Liveside Lecturer 2002, Wilhelm Jost Memorial Lectures, Germany 2003; Tilden Medal and Lectureship, RSC, Special Award for Reaction Kinetics, RSC, Polanyi Medal 1990, EU Descartes Prize 2000. *Publications:* Kinetics and Dynamics of Elementary Gas Reactions 1980; (ed.) Modern Gas Kinetics 1987; more than 250 contrib. to scientific journals. *Leisure interests:* occasional golf, even more occasional tennis, theatre, walking, gardening under supervision. *Address:* School of Chemistry, University of Birmingham, Edgbaston, Birmingham, B15 2TT (Office); 36 Grantchester Road, Cambridge, Cambs., CB3 9ED, England (Home). *Telephone:* (121) 414-4422 (Office). *Fax:* (121) 414-4426 (Office). *E-mail:* i.w.m.smith@bham.ac.uk (Office).

SMITH, Ivor, MA, RIBA; British architect; b. 27 Jan. 1926, Leigh-on-Sea, Essex; s. of H. S. Smith and F. E. Smith; m. Audrey Lawrence 1947; one s. three d.; ed Bartlett School of Architecture, Univ. Coll. London, Cambridge Univ. School of Architecture, Architectural Asscn School of Architecture, London; City Architects Dept, Sheffield 1951–61; in pvt. architectural practice 1961–87; Prof., Univ. Coll. Dublin 1969–73, Bristol Univ. 1975–82, Heriot Watt Univ. 1982–90; Educational Consultant, The Caribbean School of Architecture 1998–2001; Hon. LLD. *Leisure interests:* walking, drawing.

Address: The Station Officer's House, Prawle Point, Kingsbridge, Devon, TQ7 2BX, England. *Telephone:* (1548) 511432. *Fax:* (1548) 511432. *E-mail:* ivor@prawle.co.uk (Home).

SMITH, Jack; British artist; b. 18 June 1928, Sheffield; s. of John Edward Smith and Laura Smith; m. Susan Craigie Halkett 1956; ed Sheffield Coll. of Art, St Martin's School of Art and Royal Coll. of Art; 1st Prize, John Moores, Liverpool 1957; Nat. Prize, Guggenheim Int. 1960. *One-man exhibitions:* Beaux Arts Gallery 1952–54, 1956, 1958, Catherine Viviano, New York 1958, 1962–63, Whitechapel Gallery, London 1959, Matthiesen Gallery, London 1960–63, Midland Group Gallery, Nottingham 1961, Grosvenor Gallery, London 1965, Marlborough Fine Art, London 1968, Gothenberg Museum, Sweden 1968, Whitechapel Gallery, London 1971, Redfern Gallery, London 1974, 1976, 1977, Fischer Fine Art, London 1981–83, Angela Flowers Gallery, London 1990, 1991, 1992, 1996, 2000; sets and costumes for Ballet Rambert's Carmen Arcadiae Mechanicae Perpetuum 1985, Royal Ballet's Pursuit 1987; subject of biog. by Norbert Lynton: Jack Smith – A Painter in Pursuit of Marvels 2000. *Address:* 29 Seafield Road, Hove, Sussex, BN3 2TP, England. *Telephone:* (1273) 738312.

SMITH, Hon. James H.; Bahamain politican and banker; fmr Chair. Bahamas Devt Bank; Perm. Sec., Sec. for Revenue, Ministry of Finance –1986; Gov. Cen. Bank of the Bahamas 1987–97; Amb. for Trade, Chief Negotiator, Free Trade Area of the Americas discussions 1997–2002; Minister of State for Finance 2002–; fmr Chair. Bahamas Maritime Museum. *Address:* Ministry of Finance, Cecil V. Wallace Centre, West Bay Street, P.O.B. N-3017, Nassau, The Bahamas (Office). *Telephone:* 327-1530 (Office). *Fax:* 327-1618 (Office).

SMITH, James Herbert, CBE, M.A.(ECON.); Bahamian banker; b. 26 Oct. 1947, Nassau; s. of the late Bertram A. Smith and Rosalie B. Smith; m. Portia M. Campbell 1973 (deceased); two s. one d.; ed Ryerson Polytechnical Coll., Toronto and Univs. of Windsor and Alberta, Canada; Deputy Perm. Sec. Ministry of Econ. Affairs 1977–79; Under-Sec. Cabinet Office 1980–84; Sec. for Revenue, Ministry of Finance 1984–85, Perm. Sec. 1985–86; fmr Chair. Bahamas Devt Bank; Gov. Cen. Bank of the Bahamas 1987–97; Deputy Chair. Bahamas Mortgage Corpn 1990–; Chair. Paradise Island Bridge Authority 1991–; Amb. for Trade and Investment 1997–; Bahamas Maritime Authority 1995, Chair. Sentinel Bank and Trust Ltd 2000–. *Leisure interests:* reading, golf, swimming. *Address:* P.O. Box CB 10973, Nassau (Office); Goodman's Bay Corporate Centre, P.O. Box CB12407, Nassau, Bahamas (Home); Bahamas Maritime Authority, Bahamas House, 10 Chesterfield Street, London, W1X 8AH, England. *Telephone:* (242) 502-7091 (Office); (242) 327-3213 (Home). *E-mail:* jsmith@sentinelbahamas.com (Office); jpz8451@hotmail.com (Home). *Website:* www.sentinelbahamas.com (Office).

SMITH, Jean Kennedy, BA; American diplomatist and foundation executive; b. 20 Feb. 1928, Massachusetts; d. of Rose (Fitzgerald) Kennedy and Joseph P. Kennedy; m. Stephen E. Smith 1956 (died 1990); two s. two d.; ed Manhattanville Coll., Purchase, NY; mem. Bd trustees Joseph P. Kennedy Jr Foundation 1964–, John F. Kennedy Center for the Performing Arts 1964– (Chair. Educ. Cttee 1964–74 and f. center's children's programmes); fmr mem. Bd IRC; f. Very Special Arts (int. programme for people with disabilities) 1974; Amb. to Ireland 1993–98; Hon. Irish Citizen; several hon. degrees; Jefferson Award for Outstanding Public Service, American Inst. for Public Service, Margaret Mead Humanitarian Award, Council of Cerebral Palsy Auxiliaries, Irish American of the Year Award, Irish America Magazine 1995, Rotary One Int. Award, Rotary Club of Chicago 1997, Terence Cardinal Cooke Humanitarian Award 1997, Hadassch Volunteer of the Year Award 2003. *Publication:* Chronicles of Courage: Very Special Artists 1993. *Leisure interests:* the arts, tennis, golf, sailing, reading. *Address:* 4 Sutton Place, New York, NY 10022, USA. *Telephone:* (212) 758-3610. *Fax:* (212) 813-1871.

SMITH, Jennifer M.; Bermudan politician; b. 14 Oct. 1947; d. of the late Eugene O. Smith and of Lillian E. Smith; began career as journalist; reporter Bermuda Recorder 1970–74, Ed. 1974; on staff of Fame magazine, later Ed.; joined ZBM Radio and TV; art teacher at Sr Training School (attached to Bermuda Prison Service) for eight years; represented Bermuda as an artist at CARIFESTA in Jamaica; last Exhbn in 1996; contested St George's N seat for Progressive Labour Party (PLP) in House of Ass. elections 1972, 1976, 1980; mem Senate 1980–; Shadow Minister for Educ.; mem. House of Ass. (PLP) 1989, 1993, 1998–; Leader of PLP 1996–; Prime Minister of Bermuda 1998–; Outstanding Woman in Journalism Award 1972 and several other awards. *Leisure interests:* painting, dancing, reading, working with young people, writing, collecting match-book covers and first day stamp covers. *Address:* The Cabinet Office, 105 Front Street, Hamilton HM12, Bermuda (Office). *Telephone:* 292-5501 (Office). *Fax:* 292-0304 (Office). *E-mail:* premier@gov.bm (Office).

SMITH, John Francis, Jr (Jack), MBA; American business executive; b. 6 April 1938, Worcester, Mass.; s. of John Francis Smith, Sr and Eleanor C. Sullivan; m. 1st Marie Roberta Halloway 1962 (divorced); two s.; m. 2nd Lydia G. Sigrist 1988; one step-d.; ed Boston and Massachusetts Univs; Divisional Man., Gen. Motors Corpn, Framingham, Mass. 1961–73, Asst Treas., New York 1973–80, Comptroller, Detroit 1980–81, Dir Worldwide Planning 1981–84, Pres. and Gen. Man., Gen. Motors Canada, Oshawa 1984–86, Vice-Pres. Gen. Motors Corpn and Pres. Gen. Motors Europe 1986–88, Exec. Vice-Pres. Int. Operations, Gen. Motors Corpn, Detroit 1988–90, Vice-Chair. 1990, Pres. Gen. Motors 1992–2003, COO April–Nov. 1992, also Chair., CEO, Chair. 1996–2000, Chair. Bd 1996–2003; mem. Bd Govs Jr Achievement Canada,

Ltd 1984; Bd Dirs Procter & Gamble; mem. Bd of Detroit Renaissance. *Address:* Globe Headquarters, Renaissance, PO Box 100, 100 Renaissance Center, Detroit, MI 48625, USA.

SMITH, Ley, BA; American business executive; b. 1934; ed Univ. of Western Ont.; joined Upjohn Co. 1958, now Pres. and COO.

SMITH, Dame Maggie Natalie, DBE; British actress; b. 28 Dec. 1934, Ilford, Essex; d. of Nathaniel Smith and Margaret Little; m. 1st Robert Stephens 1967 (divorced 1975, died 1995); m. 2nd Beverley Cross 1975 (died 1998); ed Oxford High School for Girls; first appeared with Oxford Univ. Dramatic Soc. (OUDS) in Twelfth Night 1952; appeared in revue New Faces NY 1956, Share My Lettuce 1957, The Stepmother 1958; with Old Vic Co. 1959–60 playing in The Double Dealer, As You Like It, Richard II, The Merry Wives of Windsor, What Every Woman Knows; other appearances include Rhinoceros 1960, Strip the Willow 1960, The Rehearsal 1961, The Private Ear and The Public Eye 1962, Mary, Mary 1963; with Nat. Theatre played in The Recruiting Officer 1963, Othello (Desdemona) 1964, The Master Builder 1964, Hay Fever 1964, Much Ado About Nothing 1965, Miss Julie 1965, A Bond Honoured 1966, The Beaux' Stratagem 1970, Hedda Gabler 1970, Three Sisters, Design for Living (Los Angeles) 1971, Private Lives London 1972, USA 1974–75, Peter Pan 1973, Snap 1974; played 1976, 1977, 1978 and 1980 seasons, Stratford, Ont., Canada, Night and Day 1979, Virginia, London 1981, The Way of the World, Chichester Festival and London 1984–85, Interpreters, London 1985, The Infernal Machine 1986, Coming in to Land 1987, Lettice and Lovage, London 1987, New York 1990, The Importance of Being Earnest 1993, Three Tall Women 1994–95, Talking Heads 1996, A Delicate Balance 1997, The Lady in the Van 1999, The Breath of Life 2002; Dir United British Artists 1992–; Hon. DLit (St Andrew's, Leicester) 1982, (Cambridge) 1993; Hon. DLitt (Bath) 1986; Evening Standard Best Actress Award 1962, 1970, 1982, 1985, 1994; Variety Club Actress of the Year 1963; LA Critics Award Best Actress 1970; Variety Club Award Best Stage Actress 1972 (plays); Acad. Award for Best Actress 1969, for Best Supporting Actress 1979; Best Actress Award from Soc. of Film and Television Arts (UK) 1969; Best Actress Award from Film Critics' Guild (USA) 1969 (films), BAFTA Award for Best Actress 1984, 1987, 1989, BAFTA Award for Lifetime Achievement 1992, BAFTA Award for Best Supporting Actress (for Tea with Mussolini); Tony Award 1990; Shakespeare Prize, FVS Foundation, Hamburg 1991. *Films include:* The V.I.P.s 1963, The Pumpkin Eater 1964, Young Cassidy 1965, Othello 1966, The Honey Pot 1967, Hot Millions 1968, The Prime of Miss Jean Brodie 1969, Travels with My Aunt 1972, Love and Pain and the Whole Damn Thing 1973, Murder by Death 1975, Death on the Nile 1978, California Suite 1978, Quartet 1980, Clash of the Titans 1981, Evil under the Sun 1982, Ménage à Trois 1982, The Missionary 1982, A Private Function 1984, A Room with a View 1986, The Lonely Passion of Judith Hearn 1987, Paris by Night 1988, Hook 1991, The Secret Garden 1993, Richard III 1995, First Wives Club 1996, Washington Square 1998, Tea with Mussolini 1999, The Last September 2000, Harry Potter and The Philosopher's Stone 2001, Gosford Park 2002, Harry Potter and the Chamber of Secrets 2002. *Television includes:* All the King's Men 1999, David Copperfield 1999. *Leisure interest:* reading. *Address:* c/o Write on Cue, 29 Whitcomb Street, London, WC2H 7EP, England. *Telephone:* (20) 7839-3040.

SMITH, Martin Cruz, BA; American writer; b. 3 Nov. 1942, Reading, Pa; s. of John Smith and Louise Lopez; m. Emily Arnold 1968; one s. two d.; ed Univ. of Pennsylvania; Golden Dagger Award, Crime Writers' Asscn 1981. *Publications:* Gorky Park 1981, Stallion Gate 1986, Polar Star 1989, Red Square 1992, Rose 1996, Tokyo Station (US edn: December 6) 2002.

SMITH, Michael, TD; Irish politician and fmr farmer; b. Nov. 1940, Roscrea, Co. Tipperary; m. Mary T. Ryan; one s. six d.; ed Univ. Coll. Cork; mem. Irish Farmers' Asscn 1969–; mem. Tipperary North Riding County Council 1967–88, Chair. 1986–87; mem. Dáil 1969–73, 1977–82; Minister of State, Dept of Agric. 1980–81; Senator, Agric. Panel 1982–83, Culture and Educ. Panel 1983–87; Minister of State, Dept of Energy 1987–88; Minister for Energy 1988–89; Minister of State, Dept of Industry and Commerce 1989–91; Minister for the Environment 1992–94, for Defence 1997–; Fianna Fáil. *Address:* Department of Defence, Infirmary Road, Dublin 7 (Office); Lismackin, Roscrea, Co. Tipperary, Ireland (Home). *Telephone:* (1) 8042000 (Office); (505) 43157 (Home). *Fax:* (1) 8042805 (Office).

SMITH, Sir (Norman) Brian, Kt, CBE, MSc, PhD, C.INST.M., FCIM; British business executive; b. 10 Sept. 1928, Monton; s. of the late Vincent Smith and Louise Smith; m. Phyllis Crossley 1955; one s. one d. (and one s. deceased); ed Sir John Deanes Grammar School, Northwich and Univ. of Manchester; joined ICI 1954, Deputy Chair. Fibres Div. 1972, Chair. Fibres Div. 1975–78, Dir ICI 1978–85, Chair. ICI Americas 1981–85; Deputy Chair. Metal Box PLC (now MB Group PLC) 1985–86, Chair. 1986–89; Dir Lister & Co. 1985–94 (Deputy Chair. 1990–91, Chair. 1991–94), Davy Corpn 1986–91; Pres. British Textile Confed. 1977–79; mem. British Overseas Trade Bd 1980–81, 1983–87; Chair. Priorities Bd for R&D into Agric. and Food 1987–92; Dir Cable and Wireless PLC 1988–95 (Chair. 1995–97, 1998–2000), Yorkshire Chemicals 1990–91, Mercury Communications 1990–93, Berisford Int. PLC 1990–96, Oxford Diocesan Bd of Finance 1990–, John Cabot CTC Bristol Trust 1997–98; Chair. BAA PLC 1991–98, Heatherwood & Wexham Park Hosps. Trust 1991–97, Standing Conf. on Schools' Science and Tech. 1992–96, Hydron Ltd 1994–2000, Hong Kong Telecommunications 1995–97, Dir (non-exec.) 1997–98; Fellow Textile Inst. *Leisure interests:* sailing, tennis, gardening.

SMITH, Sir Paul Brierley, Kt, CBE; British fashion designer and retailer; b. 5 July 1946, Nottingham; s. of the late Harold B. Smith and Marjorie Smith; ed Beeston Fields School, Nottingham; first Paul Smith Shop opened, Nottingham 1970, others in London 1979, 1982, 1983, 1987, 1998, 2001, New York 1987, first Paul Smith franchise shop in Hong Kong 1990, flagship store Tokyo, Japan 1991 (now over 200 shops in Japan) first Milan shop 2001, first stand-alone accessories shop, London 2001, shop at London Heathrow Terminal 3 2002; first Paul Smith Collection Show, Paris 1976; launched childrenswear collection 1991, toiletries range 1986, Paul Smith for Women 1994; designed limited edn Mini 1998; launched fragrances range for men and women 2000, two fragrances 'Paul Smith Extreme' 2002, collection of furniture with Cappellini 2002; designed collection of rugs for The Rug Company 2002–03; launched collection of Swiss-made watches 2003, collection of writing instruments 2003; Royal Designer for Industry RCA 1991; Hon. M.Des. (Nottingham Polytechnic) 1991; Queen's Award for Industry 1995. *Address:* Paul Smith Ltd, 40/44 Floral Street, Covent Garden, London, WC2E 9DG, England. *Telephone:* (20) 7836-7828. *Fax:* (20) 7379-0241.

SMITH, Peter J., CBE; British diplomatist; b. 1942, London; ed St Dunstan's Coll., London; joined Diplomatic Service 1964, postings in Saigon, Paris, New York, Mexico, London, Mauritius, Montreal, served as liaison officer with Buckingham Palace; fmr Dir of Trade and Investment, Consulate-Gen., Toronto; Amb. to Madagascar 1993–96, concurrently to The Comoros; High Commr in Lesotho 1996–99; Gov. of the Cayman Islands 1999–; Paul Harris Fellow Int. Rotary Club, Maseru 1997. *Address:* Government Administration Building, Elgin Avenue, George Town, Grand Cayman, Cayman Islands (Office).

SMITH, Richard, CBE; British artist; b. 1931, Letchworth, Herts.; m. Betsy Scherman; two s.; ed Luton School of Art, St Albans School of Art and Royal Coll. of Art; lived in New York 1959–61, 1963–65; teacher St Martin's School of Art, London 1961–63; Artist-in-Residence, Univ. of Virginia 1967; Grand Prix São Paulo Bienal 1967; one-man exhbns. at the Kasmin Gallery 1963, 1967, Whitechapel Gallery 1966; participated in the Pittsburgh Int. 1961, New Shapes in Colour, Amsterdam, Berne and Stuttgart 1966–67 and in exhbns. at Guggenheim Museum, Tate Gallery, etc.; works represented in Tate Gallery, Stuyvesant Foundation, Contemporary Art Soc., the Ulster Museum, Belfast, the Walker Art Centre, etc.

SMITH, Richard John, AM, BA, LLB; Australian diplomatist; b. 14 Dec. 1934, Tamworth, NSW; s. of C. A. Smith and T. A. O'Halloran; m. Janet Campbell 1958; two s. two d.; ed Sydney High School, Sydney Univ.; teacher, London 1958–59; solicitor NSW 1959–61; Foreign Affairs trainee 1961, First Sec., Washington 1967–70, Deputy Perm. Rep. Australian Mission to the U.N., Geneva 1972–74, Asst Sec. Int. Legal Branch 1974–75; Amb. to Israel 1975–77; First Asst Sec. Legal and Treaties Div. 1977–81, Man. and Foreign Service Div. 1981–83, Acting Deputy Sec. Dept of Foreign Affairs 1983–85; Amb. to Thailand 1985–88, to the Philippines 1994–96; Deputy Sec. Dept of Foreign Affairs and Trade, Canberra 1988–90; High Commr in UK 1991–94; Dir Gen. Office of Nat. Assessments, Canberra 1996–98. *Leisure interests:* walking, reading, travel. *Address:* Office of National Assessments, P.O. Box E436, Queen Victoria Terrace, Canberra, ACT 2600, Australia.

SMITH, Robert Clinton, BA; American politician; b. 30 March 1941; s. of Donald Smith and Margaret Eldridge; m. Mary Jo Hutchinson 1966; two s. one d.; ed Lafayette Coll. and Long Beach State Univ.; owner/Man. Yankee Pedlar Realtors, Wolfeboro, NH 1975–85; mem. 99th Congress from 1st District of NH 1985–91; Senator from New Hampshire 1990–2002; fmr Chair. Cttee on Environment and Public Works, Cttee on Armed Services, Cttee on the Judiciary, Select Cttee on Ethics; Republican. *Address:* c/o US Senate, 307 Dirksen Senate Office, Washington, DC 20510, USA.

SMITH, (Robert) Harvey; British show jumper and farmer; b. 29 Dec. 1938; m. 1st Irene Shuttleworth (divorced 1986); two s.; m. 2nd Susan Dye 1987; winner of numerous int. show jumping competitions including John Player Trophy (7 times), King George V Gold Cup, British Jumping Derby (4 times); Grand Prix and Prix des Nations wins in UK, Ireland, Europe and USA; participated in Olympic Games 1968, 1972; BBC TV commentator, Olympic Games, LA 1984; after-dinner speaker. *Publications:* Show Jumping with Harvey Smith 1979, Bedside Jumping 1985.

SMITH, Sir Roland, Kt, BA, PH.D.(ECON.); British business executive and professor; b. 1 Oct. 1928; s. of the late Joshua Smith and of Hannah Smith; m. Joan Shaw 1954; ed Univs. of Birmingham and Manchester; flying officer RAF 1953; Asst Dir Footwear Mfrs Fed. 1955; Lecturer in Econs, Univ. of Liverpool 1960, Dir Business School 1963; part-time Prof. of Marketing, Univ. of Manchester 1966–88, Prof. Emer. 1988–; Chair. Temple Bar Investment Trust Ltd 1980–99, House of Fraser 1981–86 (Deputy Chair. 1980–81), Readicut Int. 1984–96 (Deputy Chair. 1982–84), Hepworth PLC 1986–97, Phoenix Properties and Finance 1986–87, Kingston Oil and Gas 1987–91, British Aerospace 1987–92, P & P PLC 1988–97; Chair. Manchester United Football Club 1991–2002; Hon. Visiting Prof. UMIST 1988–, Chancellor 1996–; Chair. (non-exec.) Senior Eng Ltd 1973–92; Dir (non-exec.) Bank of England 1991–96; Hon. DSc (Cranfield Inst. of Tech.) 1989. *Leisure interest:* walking.

SMITH, Roland Hedley, CMG, BA; British diplomatist; b. 11 April 1943, Sheffield; s. of Alan Hedley Smith and Elizabeth Louise Smith; m. Katherine Jane Lawrence 1971; two d.; ed King Edward VII School, Sheffield, Keble Coll.

Oxford; joined Diplomatic Service 1967; Second Sec. Moscow 1969–71; Second, later First Sec., UK Del. to NATO, Brussels 1971–74; at FCO, London 1974–78; First Sec. and Cultural Attaché, Moscow 1978–80; at FCO 1980–83; mem. staff Int. Inst. for Strategic Studies 1983–84; Political Adviser, British Mil. Govt, Berlin 1984–88; at FCO 1988–92; Minister, UK Del. to NATO, Brussels 1992–95; Dir Int. Security, FCO 1995–98; Amb. to Ukraine 1999–2002. *Leisure interests:* music, especially choral singing, football (Sheffield United), trams. *Address:* St Ethelburga's Centre for Reconciliation and Peace, 78 Bishopsgate, London, EC2N 4AG, England (Office). *Telephone:* (20) 7496-1610 (Home). *Fax:* (20) 7638-1440 (Office). *E-mail:* roland.smith@stethelburgas.org (Office). *Website:* www.stethelburgas.org (Office).

SMITH, Gen. Sir Rupert (Anthony), Kt, KCB, DSO, OBE, QGM; British army officer; b. 13 Dec. 1943; with Parachute Regt 1964; Deputy Commdt. Staff Col, Camberley 1989–90; Commdr 1st Armoured Div. BAOR, Gulf 1990–92; Asst Chief of Defence Staff (Operations) 1992–94; Commdr UN Protection Force Bosnia-Herzegovina 1995; GOC and Dir of Mil. Operations, NI 1996–98; Deputy Supreme Allied Commdr Europe 1998–2002; Aide-de-Camp Gen. to the Queen 2000–02. *Address:* c/o RHQ The Parachute Regiment, Aldershot, Hants., GU11 2BU, England (Office).

SMITH, Vernon L., MA, PhD, FAAS; American economist and professor of economics; b. 1 Jan. 1927, Wichita; m. Candace Smith; ed Calif. Inst. of Tech., Univ. of Kansas and Harvard Univ.; Instructor in Econs Univ. of Kansas 1951–52; Economist, Harvard Econs Research Project 1954–55; mem. Man. Sciences Research Group, Purdue Univ. 1955–56, Asst Prof. 1956–58, Assoc. Prof. 1958–61, Prof. 1961–67, Krannert Outstanding Professorship 1964–67; Research Consultant Rand Corpn 1957–59; Contrib. Ed. Business Scope 1957–62; Visiting Prof. Stanford Univ. 1961–62; Prof. of Econs Brown Univ. 1967–68; Prof. of Econs Univ. of Mass. 1968–75; Visiting Prof. Univ. of Southern Calif. and Calif. Inst. of Tech. 1974–75; Prof. of Econs Univ. of Ariz. 1975–2001, Regents Prof. of Econs 1988–2001, McClelland Prof. of Econs 1998–; Research Dir Econ. Science Lab. 1986–2001; Prof. of Econs and Law George Mason Univ. (GMU), Arlington, Va 2001–, Dir and Research Scholar, Interdisciplinary Center for Econ. Science 2001–, Research Fellow Mercatus Center 2001–; Fellow Econometric Soc. 1988–, American Acad. of Arts and Sciences 1991; Distinguished Fellow American Econ. Asscn 1992; mem. Editorial Bd American Econ. Review 1969–72, The Cato Journal, Journal of Economic Behavior and Organization (Assoc. Ed. 1985–), Journal of Risk and Uncertainty, Science 1988–91, Economic Theory, Economic Design 1994–, Games and Economic Behavior, Journal of Economic Methodology 1995–; mem. NAS 1995–; mem. Acad. Advisory Council, Inst. of Econ. Affairs, UK 1993–; Pres. Public Choice Soc. 1988–90, Econ. Science Asscn (Founding Pres. 1986–87), Western Econ. Asscn 1990–91, Asscn for Pvt. Enterprise Educ. 1997, Int. Foundation for Research in Experimental Econs 1997; fmr Ford Foundation Faculty Research Fellow, Fellow Center for Advanced Study in the Behavioral Sciences 1972–73, Sherman Fairchild Distinguished Scholar, Calif. Inst. of Tech. 1973–74; Blue Ribbon Panel Mem. Nat. Electricity Rehabilitation Council 1997; consultant on privatization of electric power in Australia and NZ and participated in numerous pvt. and public discussions on energy deregulation in the USA; Hon. Dr.Man. (Purdue) 1989; Andersen Consulting Prof. of the Year 1993, Asscn for Pvt. Enterprise Educ. Adam Smith Award 1995, Distinguished Alumni Award, Calif. Inst. of Tech. 1996, Nobel Prize for Econs 2002. *Publications include:* Economics: An Analytical Approach (jtly. with K. Davidson and J. Wiley) 1958, Investment and Production 1961, Economics of Natural and Environmental Resources 1977, Papers in Experimental Economics (collected works) 1991, Experiments in Decision, Organization and Exchange 1993, Bargaining and Market Behavior: Essays in Experimental Economics (collected works) 2000; Research in Experimental Economics, Vols. 1–3 (Ed.) 1979, 1982, 1985; Schools of Economic Thought: Experimental Economics (Ed.) 1990; over 200 articles on capital theory, finance, natural resource Econs and experimental Econs. *Address:* Department of Economics, Interdisciplinary Center for Economic Science, George Mason University, 4400 University Blvd., MSN 1B2, Fairfax, VA 22030, USA (Office). *Telephone:* (703) 993-4850 (Office). *Fax:* (703) 993-4851 (Office). *E-mail:* vsmith2@gmu.edu (Office).

SMITH, Wilbur Addison, BComm; British author; b. 9 Jan. 1933, Zambia; m. 1st Danielle Antoinette Smith 1971 (died 1999); two s. one d.; m. 2nd Mokhiniso Rakhimova 2000; ed Michaelhouse, Natal and Rhodes Univ.; business exec. 1954–58; factory owner 1958–64; professional author 1961–. *Publications:* When the Lion Feeds 1964, The Dark of the Sun 1965, The Sound of Thunder 1966, Shout at the Devil 1968, Gold Mine 1970, The Diamond Hunters 1971, The Sunbird 1972, Eagle in the Sky 1974, The Eye of the Tiger 1975, Cry Wolf 1976, A Sparrow Falls 1977, Hungry as the Sea 1978, Wild Justice 1979, A Falcon Flies 1980, Men of Men 1981, The Angels Weep 1982, The Leopard Hunts in Darkness 1984, The Burning Shore 1985, Power of the Sword 1986, Rage 1987, A Time to Die 1989, Golden Fox 1990, Elephant Song 1991, River God 1993, The Seventh Scroll 1995, Birds of Prey 1997, Monsoon 1999, Warlock 2001, Blue Horizon 2003. *Leisure interests:* fishing, wildlife, skiing, wing shooting. *Address:* c/o Charles Pick Consultancy, 21 Dagmar Terrace, London, N1 2BN, England.

SMITH, Will; American actor and singer; b. Willard Christopher Smith II, 25 Sept. 1968, Philadelphia; s. of Willard Smith Sr and Caroline Smith; m. 1st Sheree Zampino 1992 (divorced); one s.; m. 2nd Jada Pinkett 1997; one s. one d.; ed Overbrook High School, Winfield, Pa. *Television series:* The Fresh Prince of Bel Air 1990–. *Films include:* Where the Day Takes You 1992, Made in America 1993, Six Degrees of Separation 1993, Bad Boys 1995, Independence Day 1996, Men in Black 1997, Enemy of the State 1998, Wild Wild West 1999, Men in Black: Alien Attack 2002, Legend of Bagger Vance 2000, Ali 2002. *Albums include:* (as The Fresh Prince with DJ Jazzy Jeff) And in This Corner. . . 1989, Homebase 1991, Rock the House 1991, He's the DJ, I'm the Rapper 1988, Code Red 1993, Big Willie Style 1997, Willennium 1999, Born to Reign 2002. *Singles include:* Just One of Those Days 1987, Girls Ain't Nothing But Trouble 1988, Brand New Funk 1988, A Nightmare On My Street 1988, Jazzy's Groove 1989, I Think I Can Beat Mike Tyson 1989, The Things That U Do 1991, Summertime 1991, Ring My Bell 1991, I'm Looking for the One 1993, Boom! Shake the Room 1993, Men in Black, Wild Wild West. *Address:* c/o Ken Stovicz, Creative Artists Agency, 9830 Wilshire Boulevard, Beverly Hills, CA 90212, USA.

SMITH OF CLIFTON, Baron (Life Peer), cr. 1997, of Mountsandel in the County of Londonderry; **Trevor Arthur Smith,** Kt, BSc(Econs), LLD, FRHistS, FRSA, CIMgt; British university vice-chancellor (retd); b. 14 June 1937, London; s. of the late Arthur J. Smith and Vera G. Cross; m. 1st Brenda Eustace 1960 (divorced 1973); two s.; m. 2nd Julia Bullock 1979; one d.; ed London School of Econs; schoolteacher, London 1958–59; Asst Lecturer in Politics, Univ. of Exeter 1959–60; Research Officer, Acton Soc. Trust 1960–62; Lecturer in Politics, Univ. of Hull 1962–67; Lecturer, Queen Mary Coll. London 1967, Sr Lecturer, Head Dept 1972–85, Dean of Social Studies 1979–82, Prof. of Politics 1983–91, Pro-Prin. 1985–87, Sr Pro-Prin. 1987–89, Sr Vice-Prin., Queen Mary & Westfield Coll. 1989–91; Vice-Chancellor, Univ. of Ulster 1991–99 and Hon. Prof.; Visiting Prof. Univ. of York 1999–, Univ. of Portsmouth 2000–01; Dir Joseph Rowntree Reform Trust Ltd 1975– (Chair. 1987–99); Chair. Political Studies Asscn UK 1988–89, Vice-Pres. 1989–91, Pres. 1991–93; Dir Job Ownership Ltd 1978–85, New Society Ltd 1986–88, Statesman and Nation Publishing Co. Ltd 1988–90, Bell Educ. Trust Ltd 1988–93, Gerald Duckworth Ltd 1990–95; Deputy Pres. Inst. for Citizenship 1991–01; Dir Irish Peace Inst. 1992–99; Pres. Belfast Civic Trust 1995–99; mem. Admin. Bd Int. Asscn of Univs 1995–96, Editorial Bd Government and Opposition journal 1995–, Bd A Taste of Ulster 1996–99; mem. N Yorks Health Authority 2000–02; Academician Coll. of Learned Socs in the Social Sciences 2000; Liberal Democrat Spokesman on NI 2000–; Chair. Lords Select Cttee on Animals in Scientific Procedures 2001–02; Trustee Stoke Asscn 2002–; Hon. mem. of Senate (Fachhochschule Augsburg) 1994; Hon. Fellow Queen Mary London 2003; Hon. LLD (Dublin) 1992, (Hull) 1993, (Belfast) 1995, (Nat. Univ. of Ireland) 1996; Hon. DHL (Alabama) 1998; Hon. DLitt (Ulster) 2002. *Publications:* Training Managers (with M. Argyle) 1962, Town Councillors (with A. M. Rees) 1964, Town and County Hall 1966, Anti-Politics 1972, The Politics of the Corporate Economy 1979, The Fixers (with Alison Young) 1996; contributed to numerous other Publs. *Leisure interest:* watercolour painting. *Address:* House of Lords, London, SW1A 0PW, England (Office). *Telephone:* (20) 7219-5353 (Office). *Fax:* (20) 7219-5979 (Office); (1347) 824109 (Home). *E-mail:* smitht@parliament.uk (Office); sirtas@jrrt.org.uk (Home).

SMITHERS, Sir Peter Henry Berry Otway, Kt, DPhil(Oxon.); British politician and international civil servant (retd.); b. 9 Dec. 1913, Moor Allerton, Yorks.; s. of the late Lt-Col H. Otway Smithers, JP and Ethel M. M. Berry; m. Dorothy Jean Sayman 1943; two d.; ed Harrow School and Magdalen Coll., Oxford; called to Bar, Inner Temple 1936, joined Lincoln's Inn 1937; Naval Service 1939–45; MP 1950–64; Parl. Pvt. Sec. to Minister of State for Colonies 1952–56, to Sec. of State for Colonies 1956–59; Vice-Chair. Conservative Parl. Foreign Affairs Cttee 1958–62; Parl. Under-Sec. of State, Foreign Office 1962–64; mem. UK Del. to UN Gen. Ass. 1960–63, Consultative Ass., Council of Europe 1952–56, 1960; Vice-Pres. European Ass. of Local Authorities 1959–62; Sec.-Gen. Council of Europe 1964–69; Sr Fellow UNITAR, New York 1969–73; Gen. Rapporteur, European Conf. of Parliamentarians and Scientists 1971–76; 22 one-man exhbns of photography in UK, USA, France and Italy 1984–; Hon. Fellow Royal Horticultural Soc. 1996; Hon. Citizen of Vico Morcote 1994; Chevalier, Légion d'honneur; Orden Mexicana de la Aguila Azteca; Hon. DrJur (Zürich) 1970; Humboldt Gold Medal (for int. work on conservation of nature and natural resources) 1970, Veitch Memorial Medal (Royal Horticultural Soc.) 1994 and 8 Royal Horticultural Soc. Gold Medals for Photography of Plants 1981–92, Medal of Honour of the Parl. Ass., Strasbourg 1984, Gardening Book of the Year Award 1995, Herbert Medal, Int. Bulb Soc. 1997, Royal Horticultural Soc. Lyttel Cup for Lily Breeding 2001, Schulthess Prize for Best Plants and Garden in Switzerland. *Publications:* Life of Joseph Addison 1954, Adventures of a Gardener 1995. *Leisure interests:* horticulture, on line. *Address:* 6921 Vico Morcote, Switzerland. *Telephone:* (91) 9961973. *Fax:* (91) 9962504 (Home). *E-mail:* ps@vico.to (Home).

SMITHIES, Oliver, DPhil; American (b. British) biomedical scientist; b. 23 June 1925, Halifax; m. Nobuyo Maeda; ed Univ. of Oxford; Postdoctoral Fellowship, Univ. of Wis. at Madison 1951–53, Asst Prof., later Prof. Genetics and Medical Genetics 1960–63, Leon J. Cole Prof. 1971–80, Hilldale Prof. 1980–88; Excellence Prof. of Pathology and Lab. Medicine, Univ. of NC at Chapel Hill 1988–; Pres. Genetics Soc. of America; Foreign mem. Royal Soc. 1998; Hon. DSc (Chicago); Gairdner Foundation Int. Award 1990, 1993; Bristol-Myers Squibb Award for Distinguished Achievement in Cardiovascular/Metabolic Disease Research; CIBA Award for Hypertension Research 1996; Jt recipient of American Heart Foundation Research Achievement Award for Distinguished Research in the Biomedical Sciences 1998; Int.

Okamoto Award, Japan Vascular Disease Research Foundation 2000; Albert Lasker Award for Basic Medical Research 2001. *Publications:* over 240 publs. *Address:* Department of Pathology and Laboratory Medicine, University of North Carolina at Chapel Hill, Chapel Hill, NC 27599, USA (Office). *Telephone:* (919) 966-6913 (Office).

SMOLENSKY, Aleksander Pavlovich; Russian businessman and banker; b. 6 July 1954, Moscow; m.; one s.; ed Djambue Geol.-Tech. Inst.; worked on enterprises of Moscow communal econ. 1974–87; many times persecuted by authorities for pvt. enterprising activities, was arrested 1981–82; deprived of the right to take responsible posts 1987; leader Construction-Assembly Co-operative, Moscow 1987–89; f. and Pres. Stolychny Bank (now Stolychny Savings Bank) 1991–; Chair. Bd Agroprombank 1996–, United SSB-Agro Bank 1997–99; Chair. Bd Dirs. Soyuz Bank 2000–; Order of Friendship of Peoples 1994.

SMOUT, Thomas Christopher, CBE, MA, PhD, FRSE, FBA, FSA (SCOT.); British historian; b. 19 Dec. 1933, Birmingham; s. of Sir Arthur J. G. Smout and Lady Smout (Hilda Smout, née Follows); m. Anne-Marie Schøning 1959; one s. one d.; ed Leys School, Cambridge, Clare Coll. Cambridge; joined staff Edinburgh Univ. 1959, Prof. of Econ. History 1970–79; Prof. of Scottish History, Univ. of St Andrews 1980–91, Prof. Emer. 1991–; Dir St John's House Inst. for Advanced Historical Studies, Univ. of St Andrews 1992–97, Inst. for Environmental History, Univ. of St Andrews 1992–2000; Visiting Prof. Univ. of Strathclyde 1991–95, Univ. of Dundee 1993–, Univ. of Stirling 1997–, Univ. of York 1998–99; Deputy Chair. Scottish Nat. Heritage 1992–97, mem. Bd 1992–98; Historiographer Royal in Scotland 1993–; mem. Bd Royal Comm. Ancient and Historical Monuments of Scotland 1986–2000, Nature Conservancy Council (Scotland) 1991–92, Royal Comm. on Historical Manuscripts 1999–2003; Trustee Woodland Trust 1998–; Chair. Scottish Coastal Archeological and Paleoenvironmental Trust (SCAPE) 2001–; Hon. Fellow Trinity Coll. Dublin 1994–; Dr hc (Queen's Univ., Belfast) 1995, (Edin.) 1996, (St Andrews) 1999, (Glasgow) 2001, (Stirling) 2002. *Publications:* Scottish Trade on the Eve of the Union 1963, History of the Scottish People, 1560–1830 1969, State of the Scottish Working Class in 1843 (with Ian Levitt) 1979, Scottish Population History from the 17th Century to the 1930s (with M. W. Flinn) 1976, Century of the Scottish People, 1830–1950 1986, Scottish Voices (with S. Wood) 1990, Prices, Food and Wages in Scotland (with A. Gibson) 1995, Nature Contested 2000, People and Woods in Scotland (ed.) 2002. *Leisure interests:* birdwatching and other natural history, conservation, architecture. *Address:* Chesterhill, Shore Road, Anstruther, Fife, KY10 3DZ, Scotland. *Telephone:* (1333) 310330. *Fax:* (1333) 311193. *E-mail:* tcs1@st-andrews.ac.uk.

SMURFIT, Anthony P. J.; Irish business executive; s. of Michael Smurfit; mem. Bd Jefferson Smurfit Group, Chief Exec. Smurfit France 1996, later Deputy Chief Exec. Smurfit Europe, then Chief Exec. Smurfit Europe, Group COO 2002–; Dir Irish Nat. Stud Co. *Address:* Jefferson Smurfit Group, Beech Hill, Clonskeagh, Dublin 4, Ireland. *Telephone:* (1) 202-7000. *Fax:* (1) 269-4481. *Website:* www.smurfit.ie.

SMURFIT, Michael, Jr, MBA; Irish business executive; s. of Michael Smurfit; ed Michael Smurfit Grad. School of Business, Univ. Coll. Dublin; fmr Vice-Pres. World Purchasing, Jefferson Smurfit Group, Pres. and Chief Exec., Smurfit Packaging Corpn and Smurfit Paperboard Inc. 1996–. *Address:* Smurfit Packaging Corporation, 8182 Maryland, Clayton, MO 63105, USA. *Telephone:* (314) 746-1203.

SMURFIT, Michael William Joseph; Irish business executive; b. 1936; m. 1st Norma Treisman (divorced); two s. two d.; m. 2nd Birgitta Beimark; two s.; joined Jefferson Smurfit & Sons Ltd 1955; f. Jefferson Smurfit Packaging Ltd (Lancashire) 1961; rejoined Jefferson Smurfit Group, Dir 1964, Jt Man. Dir 1967, Deputy Chair. 1979; Chair. and CEO Jefferson Smurfit Group PLC, Dublin 1977–2002, Chair. 2002–; Chair. Jefferson Smurfit Corpn & Container Corpn of America; Dir numerous Jefferson Smurfit subsidiaries and assocs.; fmr Chair. Telecom Eireann; Hon. LLD (Trinity Coll. Dublin), (Univ. of Scranton, Pa). *Address:* Jefferson Smurfit Group PLC, Beech Hill, Clonskeagh, Dublin 4, Ireland. *Telephone:* (1) 269-6622. *Fax:* (1) 269-4481. *Website:* www.smurfit.ie.

SMYTH, Craig Hugh, AB, MFA, PhD; American art historian and educationist; b. 28 July 1915, New York; s. of George Hugh Smyth and Lucy Salome Humeston; m. Barbara Linforth 1941; one s. one d.; ed Hotchkiss School, Princeton Univ.; Research Asst Nat. Gallery of Art, Wash., DC 1941–42; served in U.S.N.R. 1942–46; Officer-in-Charge, Dir Cen. Art Collecting Point, Munich 1945–46; Lecturer Frick Collection, New York 1946–50; Asst Prof. of Fine Arts, Inst. of Fine Arts, New York Univ. 1950–53, Assoc. Prof. 1953–57, Prof. 1957–73, Acting Dir 1951–53, Dir 1953–73; Visiting Scholar, Inst. for Advanced Study, Princeton 1971, 1983, 1985, Bibliotheca Hertziana, Rome 1972, 1973; Prof. of Fine Arts, Harvard Univ. 1973–85, Prof. Emer. 1985–; Kress Prof. Center for Advanced Study in the Visual Arts, Nat. Gallery of Art, Washington 1987-88; Dir Harvard Univ. Center of Italian Renaissance Studies, Florence 1973–85; mem. American Acad. of Arts and Sciences 1978, Inst. for Advanced Study, Princeton 1978, American Philosophical Soc. 1979; Chair. Advisory Cttee for the Getty Center for Advanced Study 1982–99, Comm. for the Conf. celebrating the 400th Anniversary of the Uffizi Gallery 1981–82; mem. Accad. Fiorentina delle Arti del Disegno 1978; Accad. di San Luca 1995; Alt. mem. Comité Int. d'Histoire d'Art 1970–83, mem. 1985–88; Trustee, The Burlington Magazine 1987–; Hon. Trustee, Metropolitan Museum of Art; Chevalier Légion d'honneur. *Publications:* Mannerism and Maniera 1963, revised Edn 1992, Bronzino as Draughtsman 1971, Michelangelo Architect (with H.A. Milton) 1988, Repatriation of Art from the Collecting Point in Munich after World War II 1988; ed. Michelangelo Drawings Nat. Gallery of Art 1992, series of articles on Michelangelo and St Peter's (with H. A. Millon) 1969–, articles on relations between Venice and Florence in painting and sculpture during 15th and 16th centuries 1979; ed. and contrib. to The Early Years of Art History in the United States: Notes and Essays on Departments, Teaching and Scholars 1993, The Early Years of Art History in The United States (with Peter M. Lukehart) 1994. *Leisure interests:* reading the classics, music. *Address:* P.O. Box 539, Cresskill, NJ 07626, USA. *Telephone:* (201) 568-5262.

SNEGUR, Mircea, DR.AGRI.SC.; Moldovan politician; b. 17 Jan. 1940, V. Trifăneşti, Soroca Dist; s. of Ion Snegur and Ana Snegur; m. Georgeta Snegur 1960; one s. one d.; ed Rishinev Inst. of Agric.; mem. CPSU 1964–90; work as agronomist, man. state and collective farms 1961–68, Chair. of Experimental Station 1968–73, Chief of Section Ministry of Agric. 1973–78; Dir-Gen. Research Production Asscn "Selektsia", Balts 1978–81; Sec. CP Cttee, Yedinetsky Dist 1981–85; Sec. Cen. Cttee of CP of Moldavia 1985–89, Chair. Presidium of Supreme Soviet of Moldavia 1989–90; Pres. of Moldova 1990–96; Chair. Party of Resurrection and Accord (later Democratic Convention) 1995–2001; mem. of Parl. 1998, Constant Bureau of Parl. 1998–; Hon. Chair. Liberal Party 2002–; Order of the Repub. *Publications:* more than 100 articles on phytotechnical matters and the application of scientific procedures to production. *Leisure interests:* billiards, history and detective fiction, sports programmes. *Address:* 62A Puschin str. Chsinev, Moldova. *Telephone:* 54-85-27 (Office). *Fax:* 54-85-28 (Office).

SNEH, Ephraim; Israeli politician, physician and army officer; b. 1944, Tel-Aviv; m.; two c.; ed Hebrew Univ. of Jerusalem; Research Fellow, Walter Reed Army Medical Center; rank of Brig.-Gen., army service includes Medical Officer of Paratroops Brigade 1972–74; Chief Medical Officer of the Paratroops and Infantry Corps 1974–78; Commdr of the Medical Teams during the Entebbe Rescue Operation 1976; Commdr of an IDF elite unit 1978–80; Chief Medical Officer IDF Northern Command 1980–81; Commdr of Security Zone in S. Lebanon 1981–82; Head of the Civil Admin. of the West Bank 1985–87; mem. Knesset (Parl.) 1992– (Labor Party); Minister of Health 1994, of Transportation 2001–; Deputy Minister of Defence 1999. *Address:* Ministry of Transportation, Klal Building, 97 Jaffav Street, Jerusalem 91000, Israel (Office). *Telephone:* 2-6228211 (Office). *Fax:* 2-6228693 (Office). *E-mail:* pniot@mot.gov.il (Office). *Website:* www.mot.gov.il (Office).

SNELL, Esmond Emerson, BA, MA, PhD; American professor of biochemistry (retd); b. 22 Sept. 1914, Salt Lake City, Utah; s. of Heber C. Snell and Hedwig Ludwig; m. Mary Caroline Terrill 1941; two s. one d. (and one s. deceased); ed Brigham Young Univ. and Univ. of Wis.; Asst Prof. of Chem., Univ. of Texas 1941–42, Assoc. Prof. 1943–45, Prof. 1951–56, Assoc. Dir Clayton Foundation, Biochemical Inst. of Univ. of Texas 1954–56; Assoc. Prof. of Biochem., Univ. of Wis. 1945–47, Prof. 1947–51; Prof. of Biochem., Univ. of Calif. at Berkeley 1956–76, Chair. Dept of Biochem. 1956–62; Prof. and Chair. Dept of Microbiology, Univ. of Texas at Austin 1976–80, Ashbel Smith Prof. of Chemistry and Microbiology 1980–90, Emer. Prof. 1990–; Ed. Annual Review of Biochemistry 1962–64, 1968–83; Walker-Ames Visiting Prof. of Biochem., Univ. of Wash., Seattle 1953; Guggenheim Fellow, Univs. of Cambridge, Copenhagen and Zürich 1954–55, Max-Planck Inst. für Zellchemie, Munich 1962–63, Rockefeller Univ., New York, Hebrew Univ., Jerusalem and Univs. of Freiburg and Würzburg, Germany 1970; mem. Editorial Bd, American Chemical Soc. 1948–58, Biological Chem. 1949–59, Biochemical and Biophysical Research Communications 1970–85, Biofactors 1988–91; mem. NAS, American Soc. of Biological Chemists (Pres. 1961–62), American Acad. of Arts and Sciences; Hon. DSc (Wisconsin) 1982; Eli Lilly Award in Bacteriology and Immunology 1945, Meade-Johnson Vitamin B Complex Award 1946, Osborn Mendel Award, American Inst. of Nutrition 1951, Kenneth A. Spencer Award in Agricultural Chem. (American Chemical Soc.) 1973, US Sr Scientist Award, Humboldt Fund 1978, W. C. Rose Award (American Soc. of Biological Chemists) 1985. *Publications:* over 300 research papers in scientific journals, including Journal of Biological Chemistry, Journal of Bacteriology, Biochemistry, Proc. of NAS, Journal of American Chemical Soc.; Biochemical Preparations, Vol. III (Ed.) 1953, Methods in Enzymology (Contrib.) 1957, 1967, Comprehensive Biochemistry (Contrib.) 1963, 1964, 1971, International Union of Biochemistry Symposium Series, Vol. 30 1963, Vol. 35 1968 (Co-Ed.), Annual Review of Biochemistry (Vols 38 to 52) (Ed.). *Leisure interests:* travel, gardening. *Address:* Department of Microbiology, University of Texas at Austin, Austin, TX 78712; 5001 Greystone Drive, Austin, TX 78731, USA. *Telephone:* (512) 345-9633 (Home); (512) 471-5543. *Fax:* (512) 471-7088. *E-mail:* esnell@aol.com. (Home).

SNELLGROVE, David Llewelyn, LittD, PhD, FBA; British professor of Tibetan and author; b. 29 June 1920, Portsmouth; s. of Lt-Commdr Clifford Snellgrove, R.N. and Eleanor M. Snellgrove; ed Christ's Hospital, Horsham, Southampton Univ. and Queen's Coll. Cambridge; war service in India until 1946; Lecturer in Tibetan, SOAS, Univ. of London 1950–60, Reader in Tibetan, Univ. of London 1960–74, Prof. of Tibetan 1974–82, Prof. Emer. 1982–; has undertaken numerous expeditions to India and the Himalayas; Co-founder, Inst. of Tibetan Studies (now Inst. of Buddhist Studies), Tring, Herts. 1966, fmr Chair. of Trustees; numerous overseas visits as visiting Prof. or consultant; expeditions in Indonesia 1987–94, in Cambodia 1995–; Rockefeller Grant 1961–64; Leverhulme Grant 1978–81. *Publications:* Buddhist Himalaya 1957, Himalayan Pilgrimage 1961, The Hevajra Tantra (2 Vols) 1959, The Nine Ways of Bon 1967, Four Lamas of Dolpo (2 Vols) 1967, A Cultural History of Tibet (with H. E. Richardson) 1968, The Cultural Heritage of Ladakh (with T. Skorupski) (2 Vols) 1979–80, Indo-Tibetan Buddhism, Indian Buddhists and their Tibetan Successors 1986, Asian Commitment 2000, Khmer Civilization and Angkor 2001; Gen. Ed. and maj. contrib. The Image of the Buddha 1978. *Address:* Via Matteo Gay 26/7, 10066 Torre Pellice, Italy; Villa Bantay Chah, Krom 11, no. 0718, Siem Reap, Cambodia.

SNIDER, Stacey, JD; American film executive; m.; two c.; ed Univ. of Pennsylvania, Univ. of California at Los Angeles; began career in post room, Triad Agency, later Asst; Asst, Simpson-Bruckheimer Productions; joined Guber-Peters Entertainment Co. (GPEC) as Dir of Devt 1986, becoming Exec. Vice Pres.; Production Pres. TriStar Pictures 1992–1996; Co-Pres. of Production, Universal Pictures 1996–98, Head of Production April–Nov. 1998, Pres. of Production 1998–, Chair. Universal Pictures 1999–. *Address:* Universal Pictures, 100 Universal City Plaza, Universal City, CA 91608-1002, USA (Office). *Website:* www.universalpictures.com (Office).

SNIPES, Wesley; American actor and producer; b. 31 July 1962, Orlando; one s.; ed High School for the Performing Arts, New York and State Univ. of New York, Purchase; fmr telephone repair man, New York; appeared in Martin Scorsese's video Bad 1987; Co-founder Struttin Street Stuff puppet theatre mid-1980s; ACE Award for Best Actor for Vietnam War Stories (TV) 1989, Best Actor for One Night Stand, Venice Film Festival. *Films:* Wildcats, Streets of Gold, Major League, Mo Better Blues 1990, Jungle Fever 1991, New Jack City, White Men Can't Jump, Demolition Man., Boiling Point, Sugar Hill, Drop Zone, To Wong Foo, Thanks for Everything, Julie Newmar 1995, The Money Train, Waiting to Exhale, The Fan 1996, One Night Stand, Murder at 1600, Blade (also producer) 1997, U.S. Marshals 1998, Down in the Delta (also producer) 1998, The Art of War 2000, Blade 2 2002. *Broadway stage appearances:* Boys of Winter, Execution of Justice, Death and King's Horsemen. *Address:* Amen Ra Films, 301 N Canon Drive, Beverly Hills, CA 90210, USA (Office).

SNODGRASS, Anthony McElrea, DPhil, FBA, FSA; British professor of archaeology; b. 7 July 1934, London; s. of Maj. W. M. Snodgrass and Kathleen M. Snodgrass; m. 1st Ann Vaughan 1959 (divorced 1978); three d.; m. 2nd Annemarie Künzl 1983; one s.; ed Marlborough Coll. and Worcester Coll., Oxford; nat. service RAF 1953–55; Lecturer in Classical Archaeology, Univ. of Edin. 1961–68, Reader 1968–75, Prof. 1975–76; Laurence Prof. of Classical Archaeology, Univ. of Cambridge 1976–2001; Sather Prof. in Classics, Univ. of Calif. at Berkeley 1984–85; Geddes-Harrower Prof. Univ. of Aberdeen 1995–96; Fellow, Clare Coll. Cambridge 1977–; Vice-Pres. British Acad. 1990–92; mem. Humanities Research Bd 1994–95; Chair. British Cttee for the Restitution of the Parthenon Marbles 2002–; Hon. Fellow Worcester Coll., Oxford 2000. *Publications:* Early Greek Armour and Weapons 1964, Arms and Armour of the Greeks 1967, The Dark Age of Greece 1971, Archaeology and the Rise of the Greek State 1977, Archaic Greece: the Age of Experiment 1980, An Archaeology of Greece 1987, Homer and the Artists 1998. *Leisure interests:* mountaineering, skiing. *Address:* Museum of Classical Archaeology, Sidgwick Avenue, Cambridge, CB3 9DA; Clare College, Cambridge, CB2 1TL, England. *Telephone:* (1223) 335960 (Museum).

SNODGRASS, W. D., MA, MFA; American poet, critic and teacher; b. 5 Jan. 1926, Wilkinsburg, Pa; s. of Bruce DeWitt Snodgrass and Helen J. Murchie; m. 1st Lila Jean Hank 1946 (divorced 1953); one d.; m. 2nd Janice Marie Wilson 1954 (divorced 1966); one s. one step-d.; m. 3rd Camille Rykowski 1967 (divorced 1977); m. 4th Kathleen Brown 1985; ed State Univ. of Iowa; Instructor, English Dept, Cornell Univ., Ithaca 1955–57, Univ. of Rochester 1957–58; Prof. English Dept, Wayne State Univ. 1959–68; Prof. English and Speech, Syracuse Univ. 1968–76; Distinguished Prof. of Creative Writing and Contemporary Poetry, Univ. of Delaware 1979–94; Visiting Prof., Old Dominion Univ., Norfolk, Va 1978; Leader, Poetry Workshop, Morehead, Kentucky 1955, Yellow Springs, Ohio 1958, 1959; mem. Nat. Inst. of Arts and Letters 1972, Acad. American Poets 1973; Guggenheim Fellow 1972–73; Pulitzer Prize for Poetry 1960, Guinness Prize for Poetry 1961, Coll. of William and Mary Bicentennial Medal 1976, Acad. of American Poets' Harold Morton Landon Trans. Award 1999 and other awards. *Publications:* Heart's Needle 1959, After Experience 1968, In Radical Pursuit (critical essays) 1975, The Führer Bunker (poems) 1977, Six Troubadour Songs (trans. with music) 1977, Traditional Hungarian Songs (trans. with music) 1978, If Birds Build with your Hair 1979, The Boy Made of Meat 1983, Six Minnesinger Songs (trans. with music) 1983, Magda Goebbels (poems) 1983, D.D. Byrde Callyng Jennie Wrenn (poem) 1984, The Four Seasons 1984, Remains 1985, The Death of Cock Robin 1987, Selected Poems, 1957–1987 1987, W. D.'s Midnight Carnival 1989, Autumn Variations 1990, Snow Songs 1992, Each in His Season 1993, The Führer Bunker: The Complete Cycle 1995, Selected Translations (poems and songs) 1998, After-Images (autobiographical sketches) 1999, De/Compositions: One Hundred and One Good Poems Gone Wrong (criticism) 2001, To Sound Like Yourself: Essays on Poetry (criticism) 2002. *Leisure interests:* translating medieval music to be sung, playing the lute, wood-carving, owl-watching. *Address:* 3061 Hughes Road, Erieville, NY 13061, USA (Home).

SNOOK, Hans; German business executive; m. Etta Lai Yee Lau; worked in hotel industry and in real estate sales in Canada; joined Young Generation paging group, Hong Kong 1984; co. bought by Hutchinson Whampoa 1986; Chief Exec. Orange 1994–2001; Chair. (non-exec.) Carphone Warehouse 2002–. *Address:* c/o The Carphone Warehouse PLC, Support Centre, North Acton Business Park, Waters Farm Road, London, W3 6RS, England (Office). *Website:* www1.carphonewarehouse.com (Home).

SNOUSSI, Ahmed, PhD; Moroccan diplomatist; b. 22 April 1929, Meknès; m. Farida Snoussi; three c.; ed Faculté de Droit, Univ. de Paris and Inst. des Hautes Etudes Politiques; Dir of Public Information, Govt of Morocco and ed. various Publs on foreign affairs 1958–60; Sec.-Gen. Ministry of Tourism, Information and Fine Arts 1963; Minister of Information 1967–71 (Moroccan Commr-Gen. Expo '67, Montréal); Amb. of Kingdom of Morocco to Nigeria 1965, to Cameroon 1966, to Tunisia 1971, to Algeria 1973, to Mauritania and Envoy of the King to Heads of State 1978–79; Head Moroccan del. UN Security Council 1992–94; Amb. and Perm. Rep. to UN 1997–2001; fmr Chair. Exec. Bd Somathon Tuna Fishing and Packing Corpn, Lafarge Maroc Group; fmr Pres. Cinouca Corpn, Asscn of Deep Sea Fishing Fleets, Nat. Producers Asscn. *Address:* c/o Ministry of Foreign Affairs and Co-operation, ave Franklin Roosevelt, Rabat, Morocco (Office).

SNOW, John W., LLB, PhD; American politician, lawyer and business executive; b. 2 Aug. 1939, Toledo, Ohio; ed Kenyon Coll., Univ. of Toledo, Univ. of Virginia, George Washington Univ.; Asst Prof. of Econs, Univ. of Maryland 1965–67; with Wheeler & Wheeler law firm, Washington, DC 1967–72; Asst Gen. Counsel, U.S. Dept of Transportation 1972–73; Adjunct Prof. of Law, George Washington Univ. Law School 1972–75; Deputy Asst Sec. for Policy, Plans and Int. Affairs 1973–74; Asst Sec. for Govt Affairs, U.S. Dept of Transportation 1974–75, Deputy Undersec. 1975–76; Admin., Nat. Highway Traffic Safety Admin. 1976–77; Visiting Prof. of Econs, Univ. of Virginia, American Enterprise Inst. 1977; Vice-Pres. of Govt Affairs, Chessie System Inc. (later part of CSX Corpn) 1977–80; Sr Vice-Pres. Corp. Services, CSX Corpn Richmond 1980–84; Exec. Vice-Pres. 1984–85, COO 1988–89, Pres. 1988–2001, CEO 1989–2003, Chair. 1991–2003; Sec. of the Treasury 2003–; Co-Chair. Nat. Comm. on Financial Inst. Reform, Recovery and Enforcement 1992–93; Chair. Business Roundtable 1995–96, now mem.; mem. Bd Sapient Corpn, Verizon, Johnson & Johnson, U.S. Steel, Asscn of American Railroads, Carmax, Bd of Trustees John Hopkins Univ., The Business Council, Virginia Business Council, Nat. Coal Council; Co-Chair. Conf. Bd Blue-Ribbon Comm. on Public Trust and Pvt. Enterprise; Chair. Kennedy Center Corp. Fund Bd; Hon. LLD (Kenyon Coll.) 1993; Marco Polo Award, U.S.–China Foundation for Int. Exchanges 2001. *Address:* Department of the Treasury, 1500 Pennsylvania Avenue, NW, Washington, DC 20220, USA (Office). *Telephone:* (20) 622-2970 (Office). *Fax:* (20) 622-0073 (Office). *Website:* www.ustreas.gov (Office).

SNOW, Jonathan George (Jon); British television journalist; b. 28 Sept. 1947; s. of the late Rt Rev George Snow and Joan Snow; partner Madeleine Colvin; two d.; ed St Edward's School, Oxford, Univ. of Liverpool; Voluntary Service Overseas, Uganda 1967–68; Co-ordinator New Horizon Youth Centre, London 1970–73 (Chair. 1986–); journalist, Independent Radio News, LBC 1973–76; reporter, ITN 1977–83, Washington Corresp. 1983–86, Diplomatic Ed. 1986–89; presenter, Channel Four News 1989–; Visiting Prof. of Broadcast Journalism, Nottingham Trent Univ. 1992–2001, Univ. of Stirling 2002–; Chair. New Horizon Youth Centre 1986–, Prison Reform Trust 1992–96, Media Trust 1995–; Trustee Noel Buxton Trust 1992–, Stephen Lawrence Trust, Nat. Gallery 1999–, Tate Gallery 1999–; Chancellor Oxford Brookes Univ. 2001–; Hon. DLitt (Nottingham Trent) 1994; Monte Carlo Golden Nymph Award, for Eritrea air attack reporting 1979, TV Reporter of the Year, for Afghanistan, Iran and Iraq reporting, Royal Television Soc. (RTS) 1980, Valiant for Truth Award, for El Salvador reporting 1982, Int. Award, for El Salvador reporting, RTS 1982, Home News Award, for Kegworth air crash reporting, RTS 1989, RTS Presenter of the Year 1994. *Publications:* Atlas of Today 1987, Sons and Mothers 1996. *Address:* Channel Four News, ITN, 200 Gray's Inn Road, London, WC1X 8HB, England. *Telephone:* (20) 7430-4237. *Fax:* (20) 7430-4607. *E-mail:* jon.snow@itn.co.uk (Office).

SNOW, Peter John; British television presenter, reporter and author; b. 20 April 1938, Dublin, Ireland; s. of Brig. John F. Snow, C.B.E. and Peggy Pringle; m. 1st Alison Carter 1964 (divorced 1975); one s. one d.; m. 2nd Ann Macmillan 1976; one s. two d.; ed Wellington Coll. and Balliol Coll. Oxford; Second Lt Somerset Light Infantry 1956–58; newscaster and reporter, ITN 1962–79, diplomatic and defence corresp. 1966–79; presenter, BBC Newsnight 1979–97, Tomorrow's World 1997–2001, BBC Election Programmes 1983–, BBC Radio 4 Mastermind 1998–2000, Radio 4 Random Edition 1998–, Radio 4 Masterteam 2001–; Judges' Award, Royal TV Soc. 1998. *Publications:* Leila's Hijack War (jtly) 1970, Hussein: A Biography 1972. *Leisure interests:* sailing, skiing, model railways, photography. *Address:* c/o BBC TV Centre, Wood Lane, London, W12 7RJ, England. *Telephone:* (20) 8752-4646. *E-mail:* peter.snow@bbc.co.uk (Office).

SNOWDON, 1st Earl of, cr. 1961, Baron Armstrong-Jones, cr. 1999; **Antony Charles Robert Armstrong-Jones**, GCVO, FRSA, R.D.I.; British photographer; b. 7 March 1930, London; s. of the late Ronald Owen Lloyd Armstrong-Jones, MBE, QC, DL and the Countess of Rosse; m. 1st HRH The Princess Margaret 1960 (divorced 1978, died 2002); one s. one d.; m. 2nd Lucy Lindsay-Hogg 1979; one d.; ed Eton Coll. and Jesus Coll. Cambridge; Consultant, Council of Industrial Design 1962–89; in charge of design of Investiture of HRH the Prince of Wales, Caernarfon 1969; Editorial Adviser, Design Magazine 1961–87; Artistic Adviser to The Sunday Times and Sunday Times

Publs Ltd 1962–90; photographer Telegraph Magazine 1990–96; Constable of Caernarfon Castle 1963–; Sits as Lord Armstrong-Jones in the House of Lords 1999–; Pres. Civic Trust for Wales, Contemporary Art Soc. for Wales, Welsh Theatre Co.; Vice–Pres. Univ. of Bristol Photographic Soc.; Sr Fellow, Royal Coll. of Art 1986, Provost 1995–; Fellow, Inst. of British Photographers, British Inst. of Professional Photography, Chartered Soc. of Designers, Royal Photographic Soc., Royal Soc. of Arts, Manchester Coll. of Art and Design; mem. Faculty Royal Designers for Industry; Hon. mem. North Wales Soc. of Architects, South Wales Inst. of Architects; Chair. Snowdon Report on Integrating the Disabled 1972; mem. Council, Nat. Fund for Research for the Crippled Child; Founder Snowdon Award Scheme for Disabled Students 1980; Pres. (England) Int. Year of Disabled People 1981; Patron British Disabled Water Ski Asscn; mem. The Prince of Wales Advisory Group on Disability 1983; Metropolitan Union of YMCAs, British Water Ski Fed., Welsh Nat. Rowing Club, Circle of Guide Dog Owners; designed Snowdon Aviary, London Zoo 1965 (Listed Grade II 1998), Chairmobile 1972; Dr. hc (Bradford) 1989; LLD (Bath) 1989; Dr. hc (Portsmouth) 1993; Art Dirs. Club of New York Certificate of Merit 1969, Soc. of Publication Designers Certificate of Merit 1970, The Wilson Hicks Certificate of Merit for Photocommunication 1971, Soc. of Publication Designers' Award of Excellence 1973, Design and Art Dirs. Award 1978, Royal Photographic Soc. Hood Award 1979, Silver Progress Medal, Royal Photographic Soc. 1986. Television documentaries: Don't Count the Candles (six awards, including two Emmys) 1968, Love of a Kind 1970, Born to be Small 1971, Happy being Happy 1973, Mary Kingsley 1975, Burke and Wills 1975, Peter, Tina and Steve 1977, Snowdon on Camera (presenter) (BAFTA nomination) 1981. Exhibitions: Photocall, London 1958, Assignments, Cologne, London, Brussels 1974, USA, Canada, Japan, Australia, Denmark, France, Holland, Serendipity, Brighton, Bradford 1989, Bath 1990, Snowdon on Stage 1996, A Retrospective, Nat. Portrait Gallery London 2000. Publications: London 1958, Malta (in collaboration with Sacheverell Sitwell) 1958, Private View (with John Russell and Bryan Robertson) 1965, Assignments 1972, A View of Venice (with Derek Hart) 1972, Inchcape Review 1977, Pride of the Shires (jointly) 1979, Personal View 1979, Tasmania Essay 1981, Sittings: 1979–83 1983, Israel: A First View 1986, My Wales (with Viscount Tonypandy) 1986, Stills 1983–87, 1987, Public Appearances 1987–1991 1991, Wild Flowers 1995, Snowdon on Stage 1996, Wild Fruit 1997, London Sight Unseen by Snowdon 1999, Photographs by Snowdon: A Retrospective 2000. Leisure interests: photography, gardening. Address: 22 Launceston Place, London, W8 5RL, England. Telephone: (20) 7937-1524.

SNOWE, Olympia J., BA; American politician; b. 21 Feb. 1947, Augusta, Maine; d. of George Bouchles and Georgia Bouchles; m. John McKernan 1969; ed Univ. of Maine; mem. Maine House of Reps. 1973–76, Maine Senate 1976–78; mem. 96th–103rd Congresses from 2nd Maine Dist 1979–95; Deputy Republican Whip; Senator from Maine Jan. 1995–; Counsel to Asst Majority Leader 1997; Hon. LLD (Husson Coll.) 1981, (Maine) 1982, (Bowdoin Coll.) 1985, (Suffolk) 1994, (Colby Coll.) 1996, (Bates Coll.) 1998; numerous awards and distinctions. Address: U.S. Senate, 154 Russell Senate Building, Washington, DC 20510, USA. E-mail: olympic@snowe.senate.gov (Office).

SNOWMAN, (Michael) Nicholas, MA; British music administrator; b. 18 March 1944, London; s. of Kenneth Snowman and the late Sallie Snowman (née Moghilevkine); m. Margo Michelle Rouard 1983; one s.; ed Hall School and Highgate School, London, Magdalene Coll. Cambridge; Asst to Head of Music Staff, Glyndebourne Festival 1967–69; Co-founder and Gen. Man. London Sinfonietta 1968–72; Admin. Music Theatre Ensemble 1968–71; Artistic Dir Institut de Recherche et de Coordination Acoustique/Musique (IRCAM), Centre d'Art et de la Culture Georges Pompidou 1972–86; Co-founder and Artistic Adviser Ensemble InterContemporain 1975–92, mem. Bd 1992–, Vice-Chair. 1998–; mem. Music Cttee Venice Biennale 1979–86; Artistic Dir Projects in 1980, 1981, 1983, Festival d'Automne de Paris; Programme Consultant Cité de la Musique, La Villette, Paris 1991–92; Gen. Dir (Arts) South Bank Centre, London 1986–92, Chief Exec. 1992–98; Gen. Dir Glyndebourne Opera 1998–2000, Opera Nat. du Rhin 2002–; Co-Chair. Wartski; mem. British Section, Franco-British Council 1995–; Trustee New Berlioz Edn 1996–; Gov. Royal Acad. of Music 1998–; Nat. Opera Studio 1998–; Chevalier Ordre nat. du Mérite, Officier Ordre des Arts et des Lettres, Polish Order of Cultural Merit. Publications: The Best of Granta (Co-Ed.) 1967, The Contemporary Composers (Series Ed.) 1982–; papers and articles on music, cultural policy and France. Leisure interests: films, eating, spy novels. Address: c/o Wartski, 14 Grafton Street, London, W1X 4DE, England. E-mail: wartski@wartski.com. Website: www.wartski.com.

SNYDER, Allan Whitenack, DSc, FAA, FTS, FRS; American/Australian optical scientist; b. 28 Nov. 1940; s. of E. H. Snyder and Zelda Cotton; ed Cen. High School, Pa State Univ., MIT, Harvard Univ. and Univ. Coll. London, UK; Greenland Ice Cap Communications Project 1961; Consultant, Gen. Telecommunications and Electricity Research Lab. 1963–67, British Post Office and Standard Telecommunications Lab. 1968–70; Sr Research Fellow, later Prof. Fellow, ANU 1971–79, Chair. Optical Physics and Visual Sciences Inst. for Advanced Studies 1978–, Head Applied Math. 1979–82, Founder and Head Optical Sciences Centre 1983–, Foundation Dir Centre for the Mind 1997, Peter Karmel Professorial Chair of Science and the Mind 1998–; Aniv Prof. of Science and the Mind, Univ. of Sydney 2000–; Nat. Science Foundation Fellowship, Dept of Applied Physics, Yale Univ. Medical School, USA 1970–71; Guggenheim Fellow 1977, Foundation Fellow, Nat. Vision Research

Inst. of Australia 1983, Royal Soc. Quest Research Fellow, Cambridge Univ., England 1987; 150th Anniversary Chair of Science and the Mind, Sydney Univ.; Assoc. Ed. Journal of Optical Soc. of America 1981–83; Clifford Patterson Lecturer, Royal Soc. 2001; Research Medal, Royal Soc. of Vic. 1974, Thomas Rankin Lyle Medal, Australian Acad. of Science 1985, Edgeworth David Medal, Royal Soc. of NSW, Sutherland Memorial Medal, Australian Acad. of Technological Sciences 1991, CSIRO Research Medal 1995, Harrie Massey Medal and Prize, British Inst. of Physics 1996, Arthur E. Mills Oration and Medal, RACP 1966, Int. Australia Prize 1997, Marconi Int. Fellowship and Prize 2001. Publications include: Photoreceptors Optics (jtly) 1975, Optical Waveguide Sciences (jtly) 1983, Optical Waveguide Theory (jtly) 1983, What Makes a Champion! (ed.). Leisure interests: art, thought and mind. Address: Centre for Mind, Institute of Advanced Studies, Australian National University, Canberra, ACT 0200, Australia (Office). Telephone: (2) 6125-2626, 9351-8531 (Office). Fax: (2) 6125-5184, 9351-8534 (Office). E-mail: allan@centreforthemind.com (Office). Website: www.centreforthemind.com (Office).

SNYDER, Richard E.; American publisher; b. 6 April 1933, New York; s. of Jack Snyder and Molly Rothman; m. 1st Otilie Freund 1963 (divorced); one s. one d.; m. 2nd Laura Yorke 1992; two s; ed Tufts Univ., Medford; sales rep. Simon & Schuster 1961, Vice-Pres. Marketing 1966–69, Vice-Pres. Trade Books 1969–73, Exec. Vice-Pres. Trade and Educ. Admin. 1973–75, Pres. and COO 1975–78, Pres. and CEO 1978–86, Chair. and CEO 1986–94, consultant 1994–95; Chair., CEO Golden Books Family Entertainment 1996–; Chair. PEN, NY Area 1988; Dir Reliance Group Holdings, Children's Blood Foundation; Trustee NY Presbyterian Hosp.; Founder-mem. Nat. Book Foundation, Nat. Book Awards; mem. Council on Foreign Relations, Wildlife Conservation Soc., Econ. Club of NY. Address: Golden Books Family Entertainment Inc., 888 7th Avenue, Floor 40, New York, NY 10106, USA.

SO, Augusto Ussumane; Guinea-Bissau politician; ed in USA; Minister, Ministry of Econs and Finance 2002–; Pres. Asscn of Guineans, Bissau. Address: Ministry of the Economy and Finance, CP 67, Avda. 3 de Agosto, Bissau, Guinea-Bissau (Office). Telephone: 215193 (Office). Fax: 214586 (Office).

SOARES, Mário Alberto Nobre Lopes, LèsL, DenD; Portuguese politician, lawyer and historian; b. 7 Dec. 1924, Lisbon; s. of João Lopes Soares and Elisa Nobre Soares; m. Maria Barroso Soares 1949; one s. one d.; ed Univ. of Lisbon, Faculty of Law, Sorbonne, Paris; active opponent to Salazar's dictatorship; deported to São Tomé March–Nov. 1968; rep. of Portuguese socialists at various European socialist congresses and 11th Congress of Socialist Int., Eastbourne, UK 1969; Portuguese rep. Int. League of Human Rights; imprisoned 12 times on political grounds; in exile in Paris 1970–74, returned to Portugal after coup April 1974; f. Partido Socialista 1973, Sec.-Gen. 1973–86; Vice-Pres. Socialist Int. 1976–86, Hon. Pres. 1986–; Minister of Foreign Affairs 1974–75; in charge of negotiations leading to independence of Portuguese colonies; Minister without Portfolio March–Aug. 1975; Deputy, Constituent Ass. 1975, Legis. Ass. 1976; mem. Council of State; Prime Minister of Portugal for three periods 1976–85; initiated negotiations in 1977 leading to Portugal joining the European Community, as Prime Minister signed Treaty of Accession June 1985; Pres. of Portugal 1986–96; Pres. Ind. World Comm. on the Oceans 1995–, Portugal Africa Foundation 1997–, European Movt 1997, Steering Cttee World Water Contract, Cttee of Experts; Founder and Pres. Soares Foundation 1991–; fmr Pres. Council of Europe; State Councillor; Corresp. mem. Academia Brasileira de Letras; Dr hc (Rennes, Hankuk, Lancaster, São Paulo, Brown, Salamanca, Princeton, Bologna, Turin, Sorbonne, Univ. Libre Bruxelles, Oxon., Leicester); Joseph Lemaire Prize 1975, Int. Prize of Human Rights 1977, Robert Schuman Prize 1987; numerous Portuguese and foreign decorations. Publications: As ideias político-sociais de Teófilo Braga 1950, Escritos Políticos 1969, Portugal's Struggle for Liberty 1972, Destruir o Sistema, Construir uma Vida Nova 1973, Caminho Difícil, do Salazarismo ao Caetanismo 1973, Escritos do Exílio 1975, Liberdade para Portugal (with Willy Brandt and Bruno Kreisky) 1975, Portugal, quelle Révolution? 1976, O Futuro será o Socialismo Democrático 1979, Resposta Socialista para o Mundo em Crise 1983, Persistir 1983, A Árvore e a Floresta 1985, Intervenções Vols I–VI 1987–92, Vols VII–VIII 1994, Moderador e Árbitro 1995; contribs. to República, Seara Nova, Ibéria (New York) etc. Leisure interests: books and collecting contemporary Portuguese paintings. Address: Rua Dr João Soares, 2-3, 1600 Lisbon, Portugal (Home).

SOARES ALVES, Francisco José, MA; Portuguese archaeologist; b. 18 April 1942, Lisbon; s. of José Augusto Ferreira Alves and Margaret Hellen Libbie Mason Soares; m. (divorced); ed D. João de Castro High School, Lisbon, Univ. of Paris, DEA—Inst. d'Art et d'Archéologie, Paris; Dir archaeological campus, Braga (Bracara Augusta) 1976–80; Dir Portuguese Dept of Archaeology 1980–82; Dir Nat. Museum of Archaeology 1980–96; Dir of underwater archaeology on the site of "L'Océan" (French flagship sunk in 1759) 1984–. Leisure interest: diving. Address: c/o Museu Nacional de Arqueologia e Etnologia, Praça do Império, 1400 Lisbon, Portugal.

SOBEL, Clifford M.; American diplomatist; ed New York Univ.; f. Norcrown Bank of Roseland, NJ, mem. Bd 1985–91; Chair. Net2Phone; Co-Chair. ADIR; Chair and Pres. SJJ Investment Corpn, CMS Realty Co.; mem. US Govt Industry Sector Int. Trade Bd 1987–89, US Holocaust Memorial Council 1994–98; Amb. to the Netherlands 2001–; mem. Bd Lexington Inst.; fmr

Chair. Bd of Overseers, Alexis de Tocqueville Inst.; mem. Advisory Bd Empower America, Bd Business Execs. for Nat. Security. *Address:* Embassy of the USA, Lange Voorhout 102, 2514 EJ The Hague, The Netherlands (Office). *Telephone:* (70) 3109209 (Office). *Fax:* (70) 3614688 (Office). *Website:* www.usemb.nl (Office).

SOBEL, Dava; American writer; b. 1948; m. Arthur Klein (separated); two c.; fmr science reporter New York Times; reported for several journals including Audubon, Discover, Life, The New Yorker; fmr Contributing Ed. Harvard Magazine; has lectured at The Smithsonian Inst., The Explorers Club, NASA Goddard Space Flight Center, Folger Shakespeare Library, Los Angeles Public Library, NY Public Library, Royal Geographical Soc. (London); numerous radio and TV appearances; Fellow, American Geographical Soc. *Publications:* Explorations: Italy's Golden Age of Science 1979, Food for Zero G 1979, So That Others May Live 1979, Time Capsule 1979, The Arts: Books 1983, The Birth of a Station 1983, Death Sentences 1983, Longitude (several awards including Harold D. Vursell Memorial Award, UK Book of the Year, Prix Faubert du Coton, Premio del Mare Circeo) 1995, Galileo's Daughter 1999. *Address:* c/o Walker & Company, 435 Hudson Street, New York, NY 10014, USA (Office).

SOBERS, Sir Garfield (Gary) St Aubrun, Kt; Barbadian cricketer; b. 28 July 1936, St Michael; s. of Thelma Sobers and Shamont Sobers; m. Prudence Kirby 1969 (divorced 1985); two s. one d.; ed Bay St School, Barbados; left-hand batsman, left-arm bowler, using all kinds of bowling; outstanding all-rounder; teams: Barbados 1952–74 (Capt. 1965–71), S Australia 1961–64, Notts. 1968–74 (Capt. 1968–71, 1973); 93 Tests for W Indies 1953–74, 39 as Capt., scoring 8,032 runs (average 57.7) with 26 hundreds, including record 365 not out (record 1958–94), taking 235 wickets (average 34.0) and holding 109 catches; scored 28,315 runs (86 hundreds), took 1,043 wickets and held 407 catches in first-class cricket; hit 6 sixes in an over, Notts. v. Glamorgan at Swansea 1968; toured England 1957, 1963, 1966, 1969, 1973; Special Consultant Barbados Tourism Authority 1980; Hon. Life mem. MCC 1981; Order of the Caribbean Community 1998; Wisden Cricketer of the Year 1964, Barbados National Hero 1998. *Publications:* Cricket Advance 1965, Cricket Crusader 1966, King Cricket 1967 (with J. S. Barker), Cricket in the Sun (with J. S. Barker) 1967, Bonaventure and the Flashing Blade 1967, Sobers: Twenty Years at the Top 1988, Sobers: The Changing Face of Cricket (with Ivo Tennant) 1995. *Leisure interest:* golf. *Address:* 23 Highgate Gardens, St Michael, Barbados (Home); Barbados Tourism Authority, PO Box 242, Harbour Road, Bridgetown (Office). *Telephone:* 427-2623 (Office). *Fax:* 426-4080 (Office).

SOBOTKA, Bohuslav, BLL; Czech lawyer and politician; b. 23 Oct. 1971, Telnice nr Brno; ed Masaryk Univ., Brno; mem. Czech Social Democrats—CSSD 1989–, Chair. Deputies Club 2001–02; mem. Parl. 1996–2002; mem. Mandate (Proxy) and Immunity Cttee 1996–98; Chair. SubCttee for Financial and Capital Markets, Budget Cttee 1998–2001; mem. Municipal Council of Slavkov, nr Brno 1998–; Chair. Interim Comm. for Pension Reform 2001; Minister of Finance 2002–. *Leisure interests:* history, literature, science fiction, film, travel. *Address:* Úrad vlády ČR, Nábreží Edvarda Beneše 4, 11801 Prague, Czech Republic (Office). *Telephone:* (2) 24002111 (Office). *Website:* www.vlady.cz (Office).

SOBOTKA, Přemysl, DenM; Czech doctor and politician; b. 18 May 1944, Mladá Boleslav; s. of Zdeněk Sobotka and Eliška Sobotka; ed Charles Univ., Prague; physician 1968–; councillor Liberec 1990–96; Chief Physician Hosp. Liberec 1990–98; Senator, Vice-Chair.of Senate 1996–2002. *Publications:* papers in medical journals. *Leisure interests:* tennis, volleyball, travel. *Address:* Senát PČR, Valdštejnské nám. 4, 11801 Prague 1 (Office); Nezvaolova 658, 46016 Liberec, Czech Republic (Home). *Telephone:* (2) 57072331 (Office); (6) 02348371 (Home). *Fax:* (2) 57534509 (Office). *E-mail:* sobotkap@senat.cz. *Website:* www.mfcr.cz (Office).

SOBYANIN, Sergei Semenovich; Russian politician; b. 21 June 1958, Nyaksumvol, Khanty-Mansiysk Autonomous Dist; m.; one d.; ed Kostroma State Inst. of Tech.; with Chelyabinsk Pipe Mfg plant; Head of Admin. Kogalym 1991–93; First Deputy Head Khanty-Mansiysk Autonomous Dist 1993–94; Deputy, then Chair. Regional Duma; mem. Council of Fed. Ass. Russian Fed.; Chair. Duma Khanty-Mansiysk Autonomous Dist; Rep. of Russian Pres. in Ural Fed. Dist 2000–01; Gov. of Tyumen Region 2001–. *Address:* Office of the Governor, Vodoprovodnaya str. 45, 625004 Tyumen, Russia (Office). *Telephone:* (3452) 36-77-20 (Office). *Fax:* (3452) 39-32-05 (Office).

SODANO, HE Cardinal Angelo, STD, JCD; Italian ecclesiastic; b. 23 Nov. 1927, Isola d'Asti; s. of Hon. Giovanni Sodano and Delfina Brignolo; ed Pontifical Gregorian Univ. Rome, Pontifical Lateran Univ. Rome and Pontifical Ecclesiastical Acad. Rome; Sec. Apostolic Nunciatures in Ecuador, Uruguay and Chile 1961–68; official, Council for Public Affairs of Church, Vatican City State 1968–77; Apostolic Nuncio, Chile 1978–88; Sec. Council for Public Affairs of the Church 1988–89; Sec. for Relations with States of Secr. of State 1989–90; Pro-Sec. of State to His Holiness Pope John Paul II 1990–91; cr. Cardinal 1991, Sec. of State 1991–; Titular Bishop of Albano; mem. Congregations for the Doctrine of the Faith, for the Bishops, Pontifical Comm. for Vatican City State; other appts.; numerous honours and awards. *Address:* Office of the Secretary of State, Palazzo Apostolico Vaticano, 00120 Vatican City State, Italy. *Telephone:* (06) 69883913. *Fax:* (06) 69885255.

SODEN, Michael; Irish banking executive; b. 1947, Dublin; CEO Citicorp Investment Bank, Canada 1983–85; joined Security Pacific Hoare Govett 1985, CEO 1989–94; Gen. Man. Treasury and Wholesale Banking (Europe), Nat. Australia Bank, Melbourne 1994–2000, Exec. Gen. Man., Global Business and Personal Financial Services 2000–01; Group CEO Bank of Ireland June 2001–. *Address:* Bank of Ireland Group, Lower Baggott Street, Dublin 2, Ireland (Office). *Telephone:* (1) 6615933 (Office). *Fax:* (1) 6615193 (Office). *E-mail:* customer.care@ho.boi.ie (Office). *Website:* www.bankofireland.ie (Office).

SODERBERG, Nancy E., BA; American government official; b. 13 March 1958, San Turce, Puerto Rico; d. of Lars Olof Soderberg and Nancy (née MacGilvrey) Soderberg; ed Vanderbilt Univ., Georgetown Univ.; budget and reports analyst, Bank of New England, Boston 1980–82; Research Asst Brookings Inst., Washington, DC 1982–83; Research Asst, U.S. Agency for Int. Devt, Washington 1983; Del. Selection Asst, Mondale-Ferraro Cttee, Washington 1983, Foreign Policy Adviser 1984; Deputy Issues Dir, Foreign Policy, Dukakis for Pres. Cttee, Boston 1988; Foreign Policy Adviser to Senator Edward Kennedy, Washington 1985–88, 1989–92; Foreign Policy Dir Clinton/Gore Transition, Little Rock 1992–93; Special Asst to Pres. for Nat. Security Affairs, Staff Dir Nat. Security Council, Washington 1993–95, Deputy Asst to Pres. for Nat. Security Affairs 1995–2001; Alt. Rep. to UN with rank of Amb. 1997–2001; Vice-Pres. (Multilateral Affairs), Int. Crisis Group, New York 2001–; mem. Council for Foreign Relations. *Address:* International Crisis Group, 400 Madison Avenue, Suite 11C, New York, NY 10017, USA. *Telephone:* (212) 813-0820 (Office). *Fax:* (212) 813-0825 (Office). *E-mail:* icgny@crisisweb.org. *Website:* www.intl-crisis-group.org.

SODERBERGH, Steven; American film director; b. 14 Jan. 1963, Atlanta; s. of Peter Andrew Soderbergh and Mary Ann Bernard; m. Elizabeth Jeanne Brantley 1989 (divorced 1994); ed high school and animation course at Louisiana State Univ.; aged 15 made short film Janitor; briefly ed. Games People Play (TV show); made short film Rapid Eye Movement while working as coin-changer in video arcade; produced video for Showtime for their album 90125 (Grammy nomination); author, screenplay for Sex, Lies and Videotape, Nightwatch 1998; producer or exec. producer of numerous films. *Films:* Sex, Lies and Videotape 1989 (Cannes Palme d'Or 1989), Kafka 1991, The Last Ship 1991, King of the Hill 1993, The Underneath 1996, Schizopolis 1996, Out of Sight 1998; exec. producer Suture 1994, The Daytrippers 1996, writer Mimic 1997, Nightwatch 1998, The Limey 1999, Erin Brockovich 1999, Traffic (Acad. Award for Best Dir) 2000, Ocean's Eleven 2001, Solaris 2002.

SÖDERSTROM, Elisabeth Anna; Swedish soprano opera singer; b. 7 May 1927, Stockholm; m. Sverker Olow 1950; three s.; studied singing under Andrejewa de Skilonz and Opera School, Stockholm; engaged at Royal Opera Stockholm 1950–; appearances at Salzburg 1955, Glyndebourne 1957, 1959, 1961, 1963, 1964, 1979, Metropolitan Opera, New York 1959, 1960, 1962, 1963, 1983, 1984, 1986, 1987, 1999; frequent concert and TV appearances in Europe and USA; toured USSR 1966; Artistic Dir Drottningholm Court Theatre 1993–97; mem. Royal Acad. of Music; Hon. CBE, Hon. RAM, Hon. Prof. 1996; Singer of the Court (Sweden) 1959; Prize for Best Acting, Royal Swedish Acad. 1965, "Litteris et Artibus" award 1969; Stelle della Solidarietà dell'Italia, Commdr of the Order of Vasa 1973, Commdr des Arts et des Lettres 1986; Ingmar Bergman Award 1988. *Recordings include:* complete Rachmaninov songs with Vladimir Ashkenazy, Janáček's operas Katya Kabanova, Jenufa and the Makropoulos Case conducted by Sir Charles Mackerras. *Roles include:* Fiordiligi (Così fan tutte), Countess and Susanna (Figaro), Countess (Capriccio), Christine (Intermezzo); sang three leading roles in Der Rosenkavalier 1959. *Publications:* I Min Tonart 1978, Sjung ut Elisabeth 1986. *Leisure interests:* sailing, literature, embroidery. *Address:* Drottningholms Slottsteater, Box 15417, 10465 Stockholm (Office); Hersbyvägen 19, 18142 Lidingo, Sweden. *Telephone:* (8) 765-22-89 (Home). *Fax:* (8) 566-931-01.

SODNOM, Dumaagiyn; Mongolian politician; b. 1933; ed School of Finance and Econs, Ulaanbaatar, Higher School of Finance and Econs, USSR; Expert, Ministry of Finance 1950–54, Dir of Dept in Ministry 1958–63; Minister of Finance 1963–69; First Deputy Chair. State Planning Comm. with rank of Minister 1969–72, Chair. State Planning Comm. 1972–74; Deputy Chair. Council of Ministers 1974–84, Chair. 1984–90 (resgnd); mem. Cen. Cttee Mongolian People's Revolutionary Party (MPRP) 1966, mem. Political Bureau 1984–90; Deputy, Great People's Hural (Ass.) 1966–90; Dir State Oil Co. 1990–92; Counsellor to the Prime Minister 1992–. *Address:* c/o Office of the Prime Minister, Ulan Bator, Mongolia.

SOEHARTO (see **SUHARTO**).

SOFAER, Abraham David, LLD; American lawyer; b. 6 May 1938, Bombay, India; m. Marian Bea Scheuer 1977; five s. one d.; ed Yeshiva Coll. and New York Univ.; called to New York Bar 1965; law clerk, US Court of Appeals 1965–66, to Hon. William J. Brennan, Jr, US Supreme Court 1966–67; Asst US Attorney, South Dist, New York 1967–69; Prof. of Law, Columbia Univ. 1969–79; Judge, US Dist Court for South Dist, New York 1979–85; Legal Adviser, State Dept, Washington, DC 1985–90; partner Hughes Hubbard and Reed 1991–94; George P. Shultz Distinguished Scholar, Sr Fellow, Hoover Inst. 1994–; Prof. of Law (by Courtesy), Stanford Univ., Calif. 1996–. *Publications:* War, Foreign Affairs and Constitutional Power: The Origins 1976; articles in legal journals. *Address:* The Hoover Institution, Stanford University, Stanford, CA 94305 (Office); 1200 Bryant Street, Palo Alto, CA 94301, USA (Home). *Telephone:* (650) 725-3763 (Office). *Fax:* (650) 723-2103 (Office). *E-mail:* sofaer@hoover.stanford.edu (Office).

SOGAVARE, Manasseh; Solomon Islands politician; Leader People's Progressive Party (PPP); Prime Minister of the Solomon Islands 2000–01. *Address:* c/o Office of the Prime Minister, P.O. Box G1, Honiara, Solomon Islands (Office).

SOGLO, Nicéphore, BA; Benin politician; b. 29 Nov. 1934, Lomé, Togo; ed Univ. of Paris (Sorbonne) and Ecole nat. d'admin., Paris, France; fmr Inspector-Gen. of Finances, Tech. Adviser, Finance Ministry; Head Finance Dept 1963; fmr Chair. Nat. Monetary Comm., other financial insts.; Gov. IMF 1964; Prime Minister of Benin 1990–91, Pres. of Benin 1991–96; Leader Parti de la Renaissance de Benin (renamed La Renaissance du Bénin), now Hon. Pres. *Address:* c/o Office of the President, P.O. Box 1288, Cotonou, Benin.

SOHLMAN, Staffan A.R., BA; Swedish diplomatist; b. 21 Jan. 1937, Rome, Italy; s. of Rolf R. Sohlman and Zinaida Jarotskaja; m. Åsa Maria Carnerud 1961; one s. one d.; ed Sigtuna Humanistiska Laroverk, Washington and Lee Univ., Stockholm and Lund Univs.; Nat. Inst. for Econ. Research 1962–65; Ministry of Finance 1965–68; mem. Swedish Del. to OECD 1968–70; Ministry for Foreign Affairs, Dept for Devt Co-operation 1970–75, Head Multilateral Dept 1972, Project Leader Secr. for Futures Studies 1975–77, Head Transport Div. 1977–78; Deputy Dir-Gen. Nat. Bd of Trade 1978–84; Head Multilateral Dept of Ministry for Foreign Affairs Trade Dept 1984–88; Co-ordinator for Econ. Co-operation with Cen. and Eastern Europe, Ministry for Foreign Affairs 1989–90; Dir Cen. Bank 1989; Amb., Perm. Rep. Swedish Del. to OECD 1991–95, Acting Sec.-Gen. OECD Oct.–Nov. 1994; Chair OECD Steel Cttee 1986–88, OECD Liaison Cttee with Council of Europe 1992, OECD Council Working Party on Shipbldg. 1993–95, Wassenaar Arrangement on Export Control for Conventional Arms and Dual-Use Goods and Technolgies 1996–99; Amb. and Insp. Gen. of Mil. Equipment, Ministry for Foreign Affairs 1995, Amb. and Insp. Gen., Head Nat. Inspectorate of Strategic Products 1996; Amb. and Defence Co-ordinator, Ministry of Defence 2000–. *Publications:* Swedish Exports and Imports 1965–70, Resources, Society and the Future 1980. *Leisure interests:* music, art, architecture, literature. *Address:* Ministry of Defence, 10333, Stockholm (Office); Hornsgatan 51, 118 49 Stockholm, Sweden (Home). *Telephone:* (8) 405-27-17 (Office); (8) 668-53-81 (Home). *E-mail:* staffan.sohlman@defence.ministry.se (Office).

SOISSON, Jean-Pierre Henri Robert, LenD; French politician; b. 9 Nov. 1934, Auxerre; s. of Jacques Soisson and Denise (née Silve) Soisson; m. Catherine Lacaisse 1961; two s.; ed Lycée Jacques-Amyot, Auxerre, Faculté de Droit, Paris, Ecole nationale d'administration; Auditor, Audit Office 1961; with del. to Algeria 1961–62; Lecturer, Institute d'Études Politiques de Paris 1962–68; tech. adviser to Sec.-Gen. of Merchant Navy 1964–65, to Sec. of State for Information, later for Foreign Affairs 1966–67, to Minister of Agric. 1967–68; Conseiller référendaire, Audit Office 1968; Deputy to Nat. Assembly for Yonne 1968–78; Deputy Sec.-Gen. Fédération nationale des républicains indépendants 1969–75, Vice-Pres. 1975–78; fmr Sec.-Gen. Parti Republicain; Co. Councillor, Auxerre sud-ouest 1970–76, Mayor 1971–98, Deputy Mayor 1998–; Pres. Caisse d'Aide à l'équipement des collectivités locales 1973–74; fmr Pres. parl. group for rural Devt; Sec. of State for Univs. 1974–76, for Professional Training 1976, to Minister of the Quality of Life (Youth and Sport) 1976–78; Minister for Youth, Sport and Leisure 1978–81, of Labour, Employment and Professional Training 1988–91, of State for the Civil Service and Admin. Reform 1991–92, of Agric. and Forests 1992–93; Conseiller Général for Canton of Auxerre Sud-Ouest 1982–88; Vice-Pres. Regional Council for Bourgogne 1983–92; 1st Vice-Pres., Yonne 1982–88 (Deputy 1993–); Pres. (du Conseil régional de Bourgogne 1992–93, 1998–; Pres. Comm. de surveillance de La Caisse des dépots et consignations; Sec.-Gen. United France 1991, Mouvement des Réformateurs 1992–; Croix de la valeur militaire; Commdr du Mérite agricole, des Palmes académiques et des Arts et Lettres; Grand Cross, German Order of Merit; Officer of various foreign orders. *Publications:* Le Piège (with Bernard Stasi and Olivier Stirn) 1973, La victoire sur l'hiver 1978, L'enjeu de la formation professionnelle 1987, Mémoires d'ouverture 1990, Politique en jachère 1992, #3, Voyage en Norvège 1995, Charles le Téméraire 1997, Charles Quint 2000, Marguerite, princesse de Baugogne 2002. *Leisure interests:* tennis, skiing. *Address:* Assemblée Nationale, 75355 Paris; Conseil Réginal de Bourgogne, 17 Boulevard de la Trémouille, B.P. 1602-21035, Dijon Cedex (Office); 2 place Robillard-89000 Auxerre, France (Home).

SOKOLOFF, Louis, MD; American research scientist; b. 14 Oct. 1921, Philadelphia; s. of Morris Sokoloff and Goldie Sokoloff; m. Betty Jane Kaiser 1947; one s. one d.; ed Univ. of Pennsylvania; Research Fellow, Instructor and Assoc. in Physiology and Pharmacology, Graduate School of Medicine, Univ. of Pa 1949–53; Assoc. Chief, Section on Cerebral Metabolism, Lab. of Neurochemistry, Nat. Inst. of Mental Health, Bethesda, Md 1953–56, Chief, Section on Cerebral Metabolism, Lab. of Clinical Science 1956–57, Chief 1957–68, Chief Lab. of Cerebral Metabolism 1968–; Sr mem. Inst. of Medicine, NAS 1997–; Hon. DSc (Glasgow) 1989; Dr hc (Philipps Univ. of Marburg) 1990; Hon. ScD (Georgetown) 1992, (Mich. State) 1993; Hon. MD (Rome) 1992; F. O. Schmitt Medal in Neuroscience 1980, Albert Lasker Clinical Medical Research Award 1981, Karl Spencer Lashley Award 1987, Distinguished Grad. Award, Univ. of Pa 1987, NAS Award in Neuroscience 1988, Cerebrovascular Disorder Research Promotion Award, Georg Charles de Hevesy

Nuclear Medicine Pioneer Award 1988, Mihara 1988, Ralph Gerard Award of Soc. of Neuroscience 1996. *Publications:* The Action of Drugs on the Cerebral Circulation (Pharmacological Review 11) 1959, The [14C] Deoxyglucose Method for the Measurement of Local Cerebral Glucose Utilization: Theory, Procedure and Normal Values in the Conscious and Anaesthetized Albino Rat (J. of Neurochem, Vol. 28) 1977, The Relationship Between Function and Energy Metabolism: Its Use in the Localization of Functional Activity in the Nervous System (Neurosciences Research Program Bulletin 19 (2)) 1981, Metabolic Probes of Central Nervous System Activity in Experimental Animals and Man (Magnes Lecture Series, Vol. I) 1984. *Leisure interests:* music, tennis, literature, history. *Address:* Laboratory of Cerebral Metabolism, National Institute of Mental Health, Building 36, Room 1A05, 36 Convent Drive, MSC 4030, Bethesda, MD 20892, USA. *Telephone:* (301) 496-1371. *Fax:* (301) 480-1668 (Office). *E-mail:* louis@shiloh.nimh.nih.gov.

SOKOLOV, Aleksandr (Sasha) Vsevolodovich; Russian writer; b. 6 Nov. 1943, Ottawa, Canada; s. of Vsevolod Sokolov and Lidia Sokolova; m. 2nd Johanna Steindl 1975; one s.; one d. from previous m.; ed Moscow Univ.; left USSR 1975 for Austria, USA, Canada, France, Greece; returned to USSR 1989 (first emigré writer to do so); now lives in Moscow, retaining Canadian citzenship; works published in USSR 1989–. *Publications include:* School for Fools 1976, Entre Chien et Loup 1979, Palisandriia 1985. *Address:* c/o Ardis Publishers, Ann Arbor, MI, USA.

SOKOLOV, Boris Sergeyevich; Russian palaeontologist and geologist; b. 9 April 1914, Vyshny Volochek, Tver Region; ed Leningrad State Univ.; Laboratory State Asst, Asst Lecturer, Leningrad (now St Petersburg) State Univ. 1937–41, Lecturer 1945–60, Prof. 1964–; Chief of Geological search party, Sr Research Worker, Head of Dept, All-Union Oil Research Geological Inst. 1943–60; Head of Dept, Inst. of Geology and Geophysics, Siberian Dept of USSR (now Russian) Acad. of Sciences 1960–78; Scientific Head of Lab., Moscow Palaeontological Inst. 1979–; Vice-Pres. Int. Palaeontological Asscn 1972–; Pres. All-Union Palaeontological Soc. of USSR (now Russian) Acad. of Sciences 1974–; mem. USSR (now Russian) Acad. of Sciences 1975, Acad. Sec., section of Geology, Geophysics and Geochemistry and mem. of Presidium of USSR (now Russian) Acad. of Sciences 1975–91, Councillor to Pres. 1991–; mem. French, Bulgarian and Chinese Geological Socs.; Corresp. mem. USSR (now Russian) Acad. of Sciences 1958–68, mem. 1968–; Hon. mem. Swedish Geological Soc. 1968–, Czechoslovak Acad. of Sciences; Hero of Socialist Labour 1984; Order of Lenin (twice) and other decorations; Lenin Prize 1967. *Publications:* works on biosphere of the Earth etc. *Address:* Palaeontological Institute, Profsoyuznaya str. 113, 117 647 Moscow, Russia. *Telephone:* (095) 339-95-66 (Office); (095) 146-84-44 (Home).

SOKOLOV, Grigory Lipmanovich; Russian pianist; b. 18 April 1950, Leningrad (now St Petersburg); ed Leningrad Conservatory (pupil of Moisey Halfin); Second Prize, All-Union Competition of Musicians 1965, First Prize, Int. Tchaikovsky Competition 1966; numerous concert appearances in Europe since late 1960s; Prof. Leningrad (St Petersburg) Conservatory 1975–; People's Artist of Russia 1988. *Address:* World Management for the Arts, 253 Fifth Avenue, Fifth Floor, New York, NY 10016, USA. *Telephone:* (812) 296-44-02 (St Petersburg, Russia).

SOKOLOV, Maksim Yur'yevich; Russian journalist; b. 1959, Moscow; m.; ed Moscow State Univ.; worked as programmer in All-Union Centre of Transport, USSR State Cttee on Science and Tech. 1981–83; All-Union Research Inst. of Patent Information 1983–84; All-Union Research Inst. for Man. of Coal Industry 1985–87; Research Inst. of Gen. Plan of Moscow 1988–89; journalist since late 1980s; contrib. Commersant (weekly) 1989–97; political observer, Izvestiya 1998–; publs in newspapers Nezavisimaya Gazeta, Atmoda, Segodnya, magazines Vek XX i Mir, Oktyabr, Soviet Analyst (UK); broadcaster Russian Public TV Co. ORT; commentator, TV programmes; special corresp., Soviet analyst; Gang 94 Journalism prize; Medal for the Defence of Free Russia 1991. *Leisure interests:* travelling, cooking, reading fiction, mushroom hunting. *Address:* Izvestiya, Tverskaya str. 18, 103791 Moscow, Russia. *Telephone:* (095) 299-21-22 (Office).

SOKOMANU, George; Ni-Vanuatu politician; b. George Kalkoa, 13 Jan. 1937, Vanuatu; m. Leitak Matautava 1960; four s. one d.; fmr Deputy Chief Minister and Minister of the Interior of New Hebrides; Pres. of Vanuatu 1980–88; arrested Dec. 1988; sentenced to six years' imprisonment March 1989, released April 1989; Sec.-Gen. South Pacific Comm. 1992–95; Deputy Prime Minister, Minister of Home Affairs, Local Govt, Police and Defence 1994–95. *Address:* Mele Village, P.O. Box 1319, Port Vilan, Vanuatu.

SOKUROV, Alexander Nikolayevich; Russian film director; b. 14 June 1951, Irkutsk; ed Gorky (now Nizhny Novgorod) Univ., All-Union Inst. of Cinematography; worked in Gorky (now Nizhny Novgorod) TV, Lenfilm Studio, directed feature and documentary films; Founder and Dir Experimental School of Young Cinema Vanguard; various prizes at int. film festivals. *Films include:* A Solitary Voice of a Man (Bronze Leopard, Locarno Int. Festival 1978), Mournful Callousness, Days of Eclipse (FIPRESSI Prize—Montreal Int. Festival), A Sonata for Hitler, Second Round, Elegy (about F. Shalyapin), Moscow Elegy (dedicated to A. Tarkovsky) Soviet Elegy, Russian Elegy, The Quiet Pages, The Spiritual Voices (Sony Prize, Locarno Int. Festival 1995), Oriental Elegy (Grand Prix Oberhausen Festival 1996), Mother and Son (prizes at Int. Festivals of Berlin, Moscow 1997), The Knot:

Solzhenitsyn 1998, Moloch 1999, Sonata for Hitler 2000, Calf 2001, Russian Ark 2003. *Address:* Smolenskaya nab. 4, Apt. 222, 199048 St Petersburg, Russia.

SOLANA MADARIAGA, Javier, PhD; Spanish politician and international organization official; b. 14 July 1942, Madrid; brother of Luis Solana Madariaga; m. Concepción Giménez; two c.; ed Colegio del Pilar, Universidad Complutense de Madrid; joined Spanish Socialist Party 1964; won Fulbright scholarship to study physical sciences in USA until 1968; Asst to Prof. Nicolas Cabrera, Univ. of Va 1968–71, then at Universidad Autónoma de Madrid (where contract was cancelled for political reasons); mem. Exec., Federación Socialista Madrileña and Federación de Trabajadores de la Enseñanza, Unión General de Trabajadores; Prof. of Solid State Physics, Universidad Complutense de Madrid 1977; mem. Congress of Deputies for Madrid; mem. Fed. Exec. Comm., Partido Socialista Obrero Español, fmr Press Sec. and Sec. for Research and Programmes; Minister of Culture 1982–88; Govt Spokesman 1985–88; Minister of Educ. and Science 1988–92, of Foreign Affairs 1992–95; Sec.-Gen. NATO 1995–99, responsible for NATO Defence and Foreign Policy 1999–; Sec.-Gen. and High Rep. for Common Foreign and Security Policy, Council of the EU 1999–; Sec.-Gen. WEU 1999–; mem. Spanish Chapter of Club of Rome; Hon. KCMG 1999. *Publications:* over 30 Publs in field of solid-state physics. *Address:* Council of the European Union, rue de la Loi 175, 1048 Brussels, Belgium (Office).

SOLBES MIRA, Pedro, D.POL.SCI.; Spanish politician; b. 31 August 1942, Pinoso, Alicante; m.; three c.; ed Univ. of Madrid, Inst. of European Studies of Free Univ., Brussels; Sub-Del. and Regional Del. of Commerce in Valencia 1968–73, Commercial Counsellor to Spain's Perm. Representation to the EC 1973–78, Special Adviser to Minister for Relations with the EC 1978–79; Dir Gen. Commercial Policy, Ministry of Econs and Trade 1979–82; Gen. Sec. Ministry of Econs. and Finance 1982–85; Sec. of State for Relations with the EC 1985; Minister of Agric., Fisheries and Food 1991–93, of Economy and Finance 1993–96; European Commr for Econ. and Monetary Affairs 1999–. *Address:* Rue de la Loi 200, 1049 Brussels, Belgium.

SOLBRIG, Otto Thomas, PhD; American professor of biology; b. 21 Dec. 1930, Buenos Aires, Argentina; s. of Hans Solbrig and Rose Muggleworth; m. Dorothy Crosswhite 1969; one s. one d.; ed Colegio Nacional de Mar de La Plata, Univ. Nacional de La Plata and Univ. of Calif. at Berkeley; Research Asst Univ. of La Plata 1951–54; Teaching Fellow, Univ. of Calif. at Berkeley 1956–58; Asst then Assoc. Curator, Gray Herbarium, Harvard Univ. 1960–66, Dir 1963–78; Assoc. Prof., Prof. Univ. of Mich. Ann Arbor 1966–69; Bussey Prof. of Biology Harvard Univ. 1969–; numerous professional appts. and affiliations etc.; Fellow, American Acad. of Arts and Sciences; Fellow, AAAS; Guggenheim Fellow 1975–76; Hon. MA (Harvard) 1969; Cooley Prize 1961; Congressional Antarctic Medal 1967; Willdenow Medal, Berlin Botanical Gardens 1979; Extraordinary Prof. hc (Univ. of La Plata) 1991; Distinguished Prof. hc (Univ. of Buenos Aires) 1994. *Publications:* author or co-author of 16 books and more than 210 articles and chapters in books on plant population biology, cytology, ecology, evolution and taxonomy. *Leisure interest:* sailing. *Address:* Department of Organismic and Evolutionary Biology, Harvard University, 22 Divinity Avenue, Cambridge, MA 02138, USA. *Telephone:* (617) 495-4302. *Fax:* (617) 495-9484.

SOLE TURA, Jordi, D.LAW.; Spanish politician; b. 23 May 1930, Mollet del Vallés, Barcelona; ed Cen. Univ. of Barcelona; Prof. of Constitutional Law Cen. Univ. of Barcelona 1982–; mem. United Catalonian Socialist Party (PSUC) 1956–64; Founder Bandera Roja 1970 (rejoined PSUC 1974); mem. Central Cttee Spanish CP; Deputy PSUC for Barcelona and Spokesman and Vice-Pres. Parl. Communist Group 1977–, mem. Perm. Deputation of Congress; Deputy PSC-PSOE for Barcelona and Pres. Constitutional Comm. of Congress 1989–; Minister of Culture 1991–93; Pres. Foreign Affairs Comm. of Congress 1993–96; Senator 2000–; mem. Ass. Council of Europe; mem. WEU; mem. group of Deputies who drafted the Spanish Constitution of 1978; Order of Isabel la Católica, Order of Carlos III, Order of Constitutional Merit. *Publications:* several books including Introduction to the Spanish Political Regime, Constitutions and Constitutional Periods in Spain, International Politics and Class Conflicts. *Leisure interests:* sports cross-country skiing, mountaineering, opera, books, movies. *Address:* The Senate, Plaza de la Marina Española 8, 28013, Madrid (Office); Pedró de la Creu, 21, ático 0803Y Barcelona, Spain (Home). *Telephone:* (1) 5381298 (Office). *Fax:* (3) 2803545 (Home). *E-mail:* jotec@intercom.es (Home).

SOLERI, Paolo, D.ARCH.; American architect and urban planner; b. 21 June 1919, Turin, Italy; m. Corolyn Woods 1949 (died 1982); two d.; ed Turin Polytechnic, Frank Lloyd Wright Fellowship, Taliesin, Ariz.; went to USA 1947 to study; returned to Italy 1949; commissioned to design and build ceramics factory, Ceramica Artistica Solimene; resident in USA 1955–; Pres. Cosanti Foundation (for research into urban planning); Prin. Paolo Soleri Assocs. Inc., Architects; developing Arcosanti as an Urban Lab. in Cen. Ariz. 1970–; exhbns of work have appeared in over 70 public and private museums, colls and univs, USA; exhbns at Corcoran Gallery Washington DC 1970, NY Acad. of Sciences 1989–90; Distinguished Visiting Lecturer, Coll. of Architecture, Ariz. State Univ.; Gold Medal, World Biennale of Architecture, Sofia, Bulgaria 1981; Gold Medal, American Inst. of Architects; Hon. Dr. (Dickinson Coll., Carlisle, Pa, Moore Coll. of Art, Phila, Ariz. State Univ.); Utopis Award 1989. *Publications:* Sketchbooks of Paolo Soleri 1970, Arcology: City in the Image of Man 1970, Matter becoming Spirit 1971, Fragments 1981, Omega

Seed 1981, Arcosanti: an Urban Laboratory? 1983, Paolo Soleri's Earth Casting (with Scott M. Davis) 1984, Space for Peace 1984, Technology and Cosmogenesis 1986. *Address:* Cosanti Foundation, 6433 East Doubletree Ranch Road, Scottsdale, AZ 85253; Arcosanti HC 74, PO Box 4136, Mayer, AZ 86333, USA. *Telephone:* (480) 948-6145 (Cosanti); (620) 632-7135 (Arcosanti).

SOLH, Rashid; Lebanese politician and lawyer; b. 1926, Beirut; ed Coll. des Frères des Ecoles Chrétiennes, Coll. Al Makassed, Faculty of Law, Beirut; successively Judge, Pres. of the Labour Arbitration Council, Examining Magistrate, Attorney-Gen. of the Charéi Tribunal; Ind. mem. Chamber of Deputies for Beirut 1964, 1972; Prime Minister 1974–75, May–Oct. 1992. *Address:* Chambre des Députés, Place de l'Etoile, Beirut, Lebanon.

SOLIMAN, Mohammed Sidky; Egyptian politician and engineer; b. 1919; ed Fuad I Univ., Cairo; studied Eng and mil. science; Col in Egyptian Army –1962; Minister of Aswan High Dam 1962–66; Prime Minister 1966–67; Deputy Prime Minister and Minister of Industry, Electricity and the Aswan Dam June 1967–70, 1971; recipient Order of Lenin.

SOLIMAN, Soliman Metwalli; Egyptian politician; b. 25 Oct. 1927, Menofia; one s. three d.; ed Cairo Univ.; engineer, Ministry of Irrigation; engineer, Corps of Engineers; Gov. Bani-Suef 1976, Menofia 1977; Minister of State for Parl. Affairs, Minister for Local Governorates 1978; Minister of Transport, Communications and Maritime Transportation 1980, of Transport and Communications –1999. *Address:* c/o Ministry of Transport, Sharia Qasr el-Eini, Cairo, Egypt.

SOLIS PALMA, Manuel; Panamanian politician; Minister of Educ. 1984–88; Prime Minister of Panama 1988–89; First Vice-Pres. of Panama 1988–89; Minister in Charge of the Presidency of the Repub. 1988–89.

SOLLERS, Philippe (pseudonym of Philippe Joyaux); French author; b. 28 Nov. 1936, Bordeaux; s. of Octave Joyaux and Marcelle Molinié; m. Julia Kristeva 1967; one s.; ed Lycées Montesquieu and Montaigne, Bordeaux and Ecole Sainte-Geneviève, Versailles; Dir L'Infini (review) 1983–; mem. reading Cttee Editions Gallimard 1990–, Asscn of French Museums 1998–; Chevalier Légion d'honneur; Officier, Ordre nat. du Mérite, des Arts et des Lettres; Prix Médicis 1961, Grand Prix du Roman de la Ville de Paris 1988, Prix Paul-Morand (Académie française) 1992. *Publications:* Une Curieuse Solitude 1958, Le Parc 1961, Drame 1965, Nombres, Logiques 1968, Lois 1972, H 1973, Paradis, Vision à New York 1981, Femmes 1983, Portrait du joueur 1985, Théorie des exceptions 1986, Paradis 2 1986, Le Coeur absolu 1987, Les Surprises de Fragonard 1987, Les Folies françaises 1988, De Kooning, vite 1988, Le Lys d'or 1989, Carnet de nuit 1989, La Fête à Venise 1991, Improvisations 1991, Le Secret 1993, Venise Éternelle 1993, La Guerre du Goût 1994, Femmes, Mythologies (jtly) 1994, Les Passions de Francis Bacon 1996, Sade contre l'Etre Suprême 1996, Picasso, le héros 1996, Studio 1997, Casanova, l'admirable (Prix Elsa-Morante 1999) 1998, L'Année du Tigre, Journal de l'année 1998, 1999, L'Oeil de Proust, les dessins de Marcel Proust 1999, Passion fixe 2000, La Divine Comédie 2000, Eloge de L'Infini 2001, L'Etoile des amants 2002. *Address:* L'Infini, 5 rue Sébastien-Bottin, 75007 Paris, France (Office).

SOLOMIN, Yuri Mefod'yevich; Russian actor and theatre director; b. 18 June 1935, Chita; s. of Mefody Solomin and Zinaida Ryabtseva; m. Olga Nikolayevna Solomina; one d.; ed Shchepkin Higher School of Theatre Art; actor Maly Drama Theatre 1959–; Artistic Dir 1988–; teacher, then Prof. Shchepkin Theatre Coll. 1960–; Minister of Culture of Russian Fed. 1990–92; Pres. Asscn of Russian Drama Theatres; mem. Int. Acad. of Creative Arts; corresp. mem. Russian Acad. of Educ.; master-classes in USA, Japan, S Korea; Order For Service to Motherland, Order Friendship of Peoples, Order of Russian Orthodox Church, Order for Contrib. to Int. Culture (Japan), Int. K. S. Stanislavsky Prize; State Prize of Russian Fed., Prize Golden Aries, A. D. Popov Gold Medal, USSR Peoples' Artist, People's Artist of Russia and Kyrghyzia. *Film roles include:* Sleepless Night, Adjutant of His Highness, Dersu Ursala, Blockade, Ordinary Miracle, Dreams of Russia, There was Evening, There was Morning, Walking Through the Torments (serial), The Bat. *Plays include:* Inspector, Tsar Fedor Ioannovich, The Deep, Uncle Vanya, Cyrano de Bergerac, Seagull, Lady Windermere's Fan, Alive Corps. *Plays produced:* Forest (produced in Bulgaria and Russia), Perfidy and Love. *Leisure interest:* dogs and cats. *Address:* State Academic Maly Theatre of Russia, Teatralnaya pl. 1/6, Moscow, Russia (Office). *Telephone:* (095) 925-98-68 (Office). *Fax:* (095) 925-54-36 (Office); (095) 921-03-50 (Office). *E-mail:* theatre@maly.ru (Office). *Website:* www.maly.ru (Office).

SOLOMON, Anthony Morton, MA, PhD; American economist and banker; b. 27 Dec. 1919, Arlington, NJ; s. of Jacob Solomon and Edna Solomon (née Yudin); m. Constance Beverly Kaufman 1950 (deceased); one s. one d.; ed Univ. of Chicago, Harvard Univ.; mem. American Financial Mission to Iran 1942–46; Securities Analyst, Bache & Co. 1950–51; Publr Nat. Industrial Directory, Mexico 1951–53; Pres. Rosa Blanca Products Corpn, Mexico 1953–61; Lecturer, Harvard Business School 1961–63; Chair. Agency for Int. Devt (AID) Mission to Bolivia 1963; Chair., as Special Consultant to Pres. Kennedy on U.S. Trust Territory, Pacific Islands 1963; Deputy Asst Sec. of State for Latin America and Deputy Asst AID 1963–65; Asst Sec. of State for Econ. Affairs 1965–69; Pres. Int. Investment Corpn for Yugoslavia, London 1969–72; Adviser to Chair., Ways and Means Cttee, House of Reps. 1972–73; Under-Sec. for Monetary Affairs, Treasury Dept 1977–80; Pres. and CEO New York Federal Reserve Bank 1980–84; Chair. S. W. Warburg (USA) and parent Bd Dir London 1985–90; Adviser The Blackstone Group; Chair. Exec. Cttee Inst. for Int. Econs; Dir Alexandria Real Estate Equities, Urban America; Chevalier, Légion d'honneur and other decorations; Alexander Hamilton Medal, US Treasury. *Exhibitions:* Collections of Ancient Chinese Sculptures at Fogg Museum, Harvard and Asia Soc., New York. *Leisure interests:* sculpture, ancient Chinese ceramics. *Address:* 535 Park Avenue, New York, NY 10021, USA (Office).

SOLOMON, Arthur Kaskel, PhD, DPhil, ScD; American professor of biophysics; b. 26 Nov. 1912, Pittsburgh, Pa; s. of Mark K. Solomon and Hortense Nattans; m. Mariot Fraser Matthews 1972; one s. one d. from previous m.; ed Univs. of Princeton, Harvard and Cambridge; Research Fellow, Cavendish Lab., Cambridge 1937–39; Research Assoc., Physics and Chem., Harvard Univ. 1939–41; Research Fellow, Biological Chem., Harvard Medical School 1940–42, Asst Prof. of Physiological Chem. 1946–57, Assoc. Prof. Biophysics 1957–68, Prof. Biophysics 1968–82, Prof. Emer. 1982–; Chair. Comm. on Higher Degrees in Biophysics, Harvard 1959–80; Council on the Arts, Harvard 1973–76; Sec.-Gen. Int. Union for Pure and Applied Biophysics 1961–72; mem. Exec. Cttee, Int. Council of Scientific Unions (ICSU) 1966–72; mem. U.S. Nat. Comm. for UNESCO 1969–74; Science Policy Adviser to Thai Govt 1969–72; mem. Editorial Bd Journal of General Physiology 1958–88; mem. Bd of Int. Orgs. and Programs, NAS 1973–80; Chair. ICSU-UNESCO Distinguished Fellowship Cttee 1982–85; Chair. 1977–79; mem. American Chem. Soc., American Physiology Soc., Biophysics Soc., Gen. Physiology; Pres. Read's Inc. 1961–77; mem. U.S. Del to Gen. Ass. of UNESCO, Paris 1978; U.S. Del. to 17th Gen. Ass. ICSU Athens 1978; Fellow American Acad. of Arts and Sciences, AAAS; Trustee, Inst. of Contemporary Art, Boston 1946–76, Pres. 1965–71; Overseer, Museum of Fine Arts, Boston 1978–84; mem. Collectors Cttee, Nat. Gallery of Art, Washington, DC 1985–87; Order Andres Bello, Venezuela 1974. *Publications:* Why Smash Atoms 1940 and over four hundred scientific articles. *Leisure interests:* art, travel. *Address:* Biophysical Laboratory, Harvard Medical School, 221 Longwood Avenue, Boston, MA 02115 (Office); 27 Craigie Street, Cambridge, MA 02138, USA (Home). *Telephone:* (617) 432-5488 (Office); (617) 876-0149 (Home).

SOLOMON, David H., MD; American professor of medicine; b. 7 March 1923, Cambridge, Mass.; s. of Frank Solomon and Rose Roud Solomon; m. Ronda Markson 1946; two d.; ed Brown Univ. and Harvard Medical School; Medical House Officer, Peter Bent Brigham Hospital 1946–47; Research Fellow in Medicine, Peter Bent Brigham Hospital and Harvard Medical School 1947–48; Sr Asst Surgeon, U.S. Public Health Service and Investigator, Gerontology Section, Nat. Heart Inst. 1948–50; Sr Asst Resident Physician, Peter Bent Brigham Hospital 1950–51; Fellow in Endocrinology, New England Center Hospital 1951–52; Instr. School of Medicine, Univ. of Calif. at Los Angeles (UCLA) 1952–54, Asst Prof. 1954–60, Assoc. Prof. 1960–66, Prof. of Medicine 1966, Chief of Medicine (Harbor-UCLA Medical Center) 1966–71, Chair. Dept of Medicine 1971–81, Assoc. Dir Multicampus Div. of Geriatric Medicine 1982–89, Dir UCLA Center on Aging 1991–96, Prof. Emer. UCLA 1993–; Consultant, Wadsworth Hosp., LA 1952–, Sepulveda Hosp. 1971–, RAND Corpn 1997–; several awards including John Phillips Memorial Award, American Coll. of Physicians 2002. *Publications:* co-author of three books, author of 202 scientific papers, 44 book chapters, 11 review articles and 122 published abstracts. *Leisure interests:* golf, running, reading, hiking, bridge. *Address:* 2103 Ridge Drive, Los Angeles, CA 90049, USA (Home). *Telephone:* (310) 471-6346 (Office); (310) 471-5256 (Home). *Fax:* (310) 471-6346 (Office); (310) 471-6346 (Home). *E-mail:* d.solomon4@verizon.net (Office); d.solomon4@verizon.net (Home).

SOLOMON, Edward I., PhD; American chemist; b. 20 Oct. 1946, New York; s. of Mordecai L. Solomon and Sally S. Solomon; m. Darlene J. Spira 1984; one s. one d.; ed Rensselaer Polytechnic Inst., Tory, New York, Princeton Univ.; Research Assoc., Princeton Univ., NJ 1972–73; Postdoctoral Fellow H.C. Ørsted Inst. 1973–74, Calif. Inst. of Tech. 1974–75; Asst Prof. MIT 1975–79, Assoc. Prof. 1979–81, Prof. 1981–82; Prof., Stanford Univ. 1982–, Spaght Prof. of Chem. 1991–; Invited Prof., Univ. of Paris, Tokyo Inst. of Tech., Tata Inst. India, Xiamen Univ. China, La Plata Univ. Argentina; First Glen Seaborg and other lectureships; Fellow AAAS, American Acad. of Arts and Sciences; Sloan Fellowship, NIH Merit Award., Japan Soc. for Promotion of Science Invitation Fellow, Dean's Award for Distinguished Teaching, Westinghouse Foundation Nat. Talent Search award, Remsen Award 1994. *Publications:* three books; over 320 papers in scientific journals. *Leisure interests:* tennis, running, gourmet dining, int. travel. *Address:* Department of Chemistry, Stanford University, Roth Way, Stanford, CA 94305, USA. *Telephone:* (650) 723-4694. *Fax:* (650) 725-0259. *Website:* www.stanford.edu (Office).

SOLOMON, Sir Harry, Kt; British business executive; b. 20 March 1937, Middlesbrough; s. of Jacob Solomon and Belle Solomon; m. Judith D. Manuel 1962; one s. two d.; ed St Alban's School and Law Soc. School of Law; qualified solicitor 1960; in pvt. practice 1960–75; Man. Dir Hillsdown Holdings PLC 1975–84, Jt Chair. 1984–87, Chair. 1987–93, Dir (non-exec.) 1993–97; Chair. Harveys Holdings PLC 1994–2000; Dir Princedale Group PLC 1993–; Dir (non-exec.) Charterhouse European Holding Ltd 1993–, Frogmore Estates PLC 1993–, U.S. Industries Inc. 1995–; fmr Dir Maple Leaf Foods Inc.; Hon. FRCP. *Leisure interests:* jogging, tennis, theatre, collector of historical autographed letters. *Address:* Hillsdown House, 32 Hampstead High Street, London, NW3 1QD, England.

SOLOMON, Yonty, BMus, FRCM; British/South African concert pianist; b. 6 May 1938, Cape Town; s. of David and Chaze Riva Solomon; ed Univ. of Cape Town; studied with Dame Myra Hess in London, Guido Agosti in Rome, Charles Rosen (q.v.) in USA; Concert début in Wigmore Hall, London 1963; recitals and concertos in UK, Italy, Netherlands, USA, Canada, Romania, South Africa; gave first performances of works dedicated to him by Richard Rodney Bennett, Wilfred Mellers, Merilaainen, Wilfred Josephs; given solo performing rights to composer Kaikhosru Sorabji 1976–77 for all his works; panel of judges of Royal Overseas League Commonwealth Music Competition 1974–; many TV and radio engagements; many recitals devoted to Charles Ives, J. S. Bach (The Well-Tempered Klavier and Klavierübung), Janáček, Boulez, Granados, Albéniz and much rarely performed piano music; first performance of unpublished scores by K. S. Sorabji 1978; Prof. of Piano, Royal Coll. of Music, London 1978–; Visiting Artist-in-Residence, Nottingham Univ. 1980–; Master classes in piano and chamber music at Int. Musicians Seminar (Cornwall) 1982; Leverhulme (Royal Coll. of Music) Project 1999; Scholarships from Univ. of Cape Town; Hon. mem. Royal Philharmonic Soc.; Hon. R.C.M. (London) 1982; Harriet Cohen Beethoven Medal 1962, Commonwealth Award. *Publications:* Schumann Symposium 1973, Bach's "48", Analysis and Historical Survey 1972. *Leisure interests:* collecting botanical books, growing camellias, meditation. *Address:* 56 Canonbury Park North, London, N1 2JT, England. *Telephone:* (20) 7226-8123. *Fax:* (20) 7226-8123. *E-mail:* yonty.solomon@btinternet.com (Home).

SOLOMOS, Alexis; Greek stage director (retd) and author; b. 9 Aug. 1918, Athens; s. of John Solomos and Aspasia Eliopoulos; m. Catherine Spathis 1953; two d.; ed Athens Univ., Athens Nat. Theatre Dramatic School, London Royal Acad. of Dramatic Art, Yale Univ., Piscator New School; stage Dir in USA and UK; stage Dir Athens Nat. Theatre 1950–80; Founder and Dir Proscinio Theatre 1964; Dir Festival of Greek Classical Theatre, Ypsilanti, Mich., USA 1965–66; Prof. Athens Nat. Dramatic School; Asst Man. Dir Hellenic Broadcasting Foundation; Deputy Dir Greek TV 1978; Dir Athens Nat. Theatre 1980, 1991, Athens TV; Hon. Prof. Univ. of Athens; four prizes for best author and Dir from Mayor of Athens and Greek Acad. *Plays:* directed a total of 160 plays in London, New York and at Nat. Theatre, Athens, including works by Aeschylus, Sophocles, Euripides and Aristophanes; two of his own plays produced in Athens at the Epidaurus Ancient Theatre. *Radio:* many programmes about the history of theatre art. *Publications include:* Living Aristophanes 1961, Saint Bacchus 1964, The Age of Theatre 1973, My Good Thalia 1984, Theatrical Dictionary 1989, Euripides 1995, Cinema Century 2000; trans. of more than 30 foreign plays into Greek. *Leisure interests:* travel, crosswords, cats. *Address:* 13 Fokilidou Street, 106 73 Athens, Greece. *Telephone:* 3626730; 3626677.

SOLOVYEV, Gleb Mikhailovich, PhD, DMS; Russian surgeon; b. 9 Sept. 1928, Moscow; m. Albine Dmetrevne 1951; one d.; ed First Medical Inst. Moscow; mem. CPSU 1950–91; postgraduate studies 1952–55; attached to Acad. of Medical Sciences 1955–60; Dir Cardiac Surgery Lab., Research Inst. of Clinical and Experimental Surgery 1960–69, Deputy Dir 1963–69; Dir of Inst. for Organ and Tissue Transplants, Acad. of Medical Sciences 1969–; Dir Clinic of Cardiac Surgery, Prof. Sechenov Moscow Medical Acad. 1974–80, Head of Dept of Cardiovascular Surgery 1980–, of Surgery 1990–; mem. Russian Acad. of Medical Sciences 1995, Int. Soc. of Cardiac Surgeons; State Prize (for part in developing kidney transplants) 1971 and numerous other prizes. *Publications:* over 400 works on problems of cardiac surgery and transplantology including 23 books. *Address:* Medical Academy City Hospital, Kolomensky pr. 4, 115446 Moscow; Gagarinsky per. 24, 935, Moscow, Russia (Home). *Telephone:* (095) 118-62-00 (Office); (095) 241-81-22 (Home); (095) 118-56-65. *E-mail:* esaranov@mail.ru (Office).

SOLOVYEV, Sergey Aleksandrovich; Russian film director and scriptwriter; b. 25 Aug. 1944, Kem, Karelia; m. Tatyana Drubich (divorced); ed All-Union Inst. of Cinematography with Leningrad TV 1960–69; film dir Mosfilm Studio 1969–, artistic Dir Krug Film Union 1987–; Sec. USSR Union of Cinematographers 1986–90; Chair. Moscow Union of Cinematographers 1990–97; Co-Chair. Russian Union of Cinematographers 1990–92; Prof. All-Russian Inst. of Cinematography; debut as scriptwriter Look into the Face 1966, as film dir Family Happiness; worked as stage dir in Maly Theatre (Uncle Vanya) and Taganka Theatre (The Seagull). *Films include:* Yegor Bulychev and Others 1971, Station Inspector 1972, A Hundred Days After Childhood 1975 (Silver Bear, Berlin, Prize of All-Union Festival, Tunes of A White Night 1977), Rescuer 1980, Direct Heir 1982, Strange, White and Speckled 1986, Assa 1987, Black Rose: an Emblem of Sadness, Red Rose: an Emblem of Love 1989, The House Under the Starry Sky 1991, Three Sisters 1994, The Tender Age 2001. *Address:* Akademika Pilyugina str. 8, korp. 1, Apt. 330, 117393 Moscow, Russia (Home). *Telephone:* (095) 132-36-95 (Home).

SOLOW, Robert Merton, PhD; American economist; b. 23 Aug. 1924, Brooklyn, NY; s. of Milton Solow and Hannah Solow; m. Barbara Lewis 1945; two s. one d.; ed Harvard Univ.; Asst Prof. of Statistics, Mass. Inst. of Technology 1950–53, Assoc. Prof. of Econs 1954–57, Prof. of Econs 1958–73, Inst. Prof. 1973–95, Inst. Prof. Emer. 1995–; W. Edwards Deming Prof., New York Univ. 1996; Sr Economist, Council of Econ. Advisers 1961–62; Marshall Lecturer, Cambridge Univ. 1963–64; De Vries Lecturer, Rotterdam 1963, Wicksell Lecturer, Stockholm 1964; Eastman Visiting Prof., Oxford Univ. 1968–69; Killian Prize Lecturer, MIT 1978; Geary Lecturer, Dublin 1980; Overseas Fellow, Churchill Coll., Cambridge 1984; Mitsui Lecturer, Birmingham 1985; Nobel Memorial Lecture, Stockholm 1987 and numerous others in int. academic insts.; mem. Nat. Comm. on Tech., Automation and Econ. Progress 1964–65, Presidential Comm. on Income Maintenance 1968–69; mem. Bd of Dirs Fed. Reserve Bank of Boston 1975–81, Chair. 1979–81; Fellow, Center for Advanced Study in Behavioral Sciences 1957–58, Trustee 1982–95; Vice-Pres. American Econ. Asscn 1968, Pres. 1979, Vice-Pres. AAAS 1970; Pres. Econometric Soc. 1964; Trustee Woods Hole Oceanographic Inst. 1988–, Alfred P. Sloan Foundation 1992–, Resources for the Future 1994–96, Urban Inst. 1994–, German Marshall Fund of US 1994–; Pres. Int. Econ. Asscn 1999–2002; mem. Nat. Science Bd 1995–2000; Fellow American Acad. of Arts and Sciences, mem. of Council, NAS 1977–80, mem. 1972–; Corresp. mem. British Acad.; mem. American Philosophical Soc.; Fellow Acad. dei Lincei (Rome); Foundation Fellow Russell Sage Foundation 2000–; Orden pour le mérite, Germany 1995; Hon. LLD (Chicago) 1967, (Lehigh) 1977, (Brown) 1972, (Wesleyan) 1982; Hon. LittD (Williams Coll.) 1974; Dr hc (Paris) 1975, (Geneva) 1982, (Conservatoire Nat. des Arts et Métiers, Paris) 1994; Hon. DLitt (Warwick) 1976, (Colgate) 1990, (Glasgow) 1992, (Harvard) 1992; Hon. ScD (Tulane) 1983; Hon. DScS (Yale) 1986, (Univ. of Mass., Boston) 1989, (Helsinki) 1990, (Boston Coll.) 1990, (Chile) 1992, (Rutgers Univ.) 1994; Hon. DSc in Business Admin. (Bryant Coll.) 1988; Hon. DEng (Colorado School of Mines) 1996; David A. Wells Prize, Harvard Univ. 1951, John Bates Clark Medal, American Econ. Asscn 1961, Killian Award, MIT 1977, Seidman Award in Political Econ. 1983, Nobel Prize for Econs 1987, Nat. Medal of Science 2000. *Publications:* Linear Programming and Economic Analysis 1958, Capital Theory and the Rate of Return 1963, Sources of Unemployment in the United States 1964, Price Expectations and the Behavior of the Price Level 1970, Growth Theory: An Exposition 1970, The Labor Market as a Social Institution 1989, Learning from "Learning by Doing" 1994, A Critical Essay On Modern Macroeconomic Theory (with Frank Hahn) 1995. *Leisure interest:* sailing. *Address:* Department of Economics, Massachusetts Institute of Technology E52-383, Cambridge, MA 02139; 528 Lewis Wharf, Boston, MA 02110, USA (Home). *Telephone:* (617) 253-5268; (617) 227-4436. *Fax:* (617) 253-0560 (Office).

SOLT, Pál; Hungarian judge; b. 3 Oct. 1937, Szentendre; m.; one c.; ed Univ. of Eötvös Lóránd, Budapest; Asst Court Clerk, Cen. Dist Court of Pest 1960–63, Judge 1964–66; Head, Secr. of Supreme Court of Justice 1966–71, Judge 1980–87, Chair. Panel 1987–89, Pres. Supreme Court of Justice 1990–; Asst, Legal Dept, Secr. of Ministry of Finance 1971–80; mem. Constitutional Court 1989–; Pres. Nat. Council of Justice 1997–; Hon. LLD (San Beda Coll. of Law, Manila) 2001. *Address:* Supreme Court, Markó u. 16, 1055 Budapest, Hungary (Office). *Telephone:* (1) 269-2646 (Office). *Fax:* (1) 269-2818 (Office).

SOLVAY, Jacques Ernest; Belgian business executive; b. 4 Dec. 1920, Ixelles; s. of Ernest-John Solvay and Marie Graux; m. Marie-Claude Boulin 1949; one s. three d.; ed Univ. of Brussels; joined Solvay Cie 1950, mem. Bd 1955, Chair. 1971; Dir Société Générale de Banque 1965–; Chair. Soltex Polymer Corpn 1974–; Hon. Pres. Fédération des Industries Chimiques de Belgique; Pres. Belgo-British Union; mem. European Advisory Council, Tenneco Inc. 1986–; Chevalier de l'Ordre de Leopold; Hon. KBE. *Leisure interest:* orchid growing. *Address:* c/o Solvay Cie SA, rue de Prince Albert 33, 1050 Brussels, Belgium.

SOLYMAR, László, MA, PhD, FRS, FIEE; British engineer; b. 24 Jan. 1930, Budapest, Hungary; s. of Pál Solymar and Aranka Gold; m. Marianne Klopfer 1955; two d.; ed Tech. Univ., Budapest, Hungarian Acad. of Sciences; lecturer Tech. Univ., Budapest 1952–53; research engineer Research Inst. for Telecommunications, Budapest 1953–56, Standard Telecommunications Labs. Ltd, Harlow, Essex 1956–65; lecturer Dept of Eng Science, Univ. of Oxford 1966–86, Fellow Brasenose Coll. 1966–86, Donald Pollock Reader in Eng Science 1986–92, Fellow Hertford Coll. 1986–, Prof. of Applied Electromagnetism 1992–97, Leverhulme Emer. Fellow 1997–2001; Visiting Prof. Physics Lab., Ecole Normale Supérieure, Univ. of Paris 1965–66, Tech. Univ. of Denmark 1972–73, Dept of Physics, Univ. of Osnabrück 1987, Optical Inst., Tech. Univ., Berlin 1990, Dept of Materials, Autonomous Univ. of Madrid 1993, 1995, Tech. Univ., Budapest 1994; Faraday Medal, IEE 1992. *Three plays for radio:* Anaxagoras; Archimedes; Hypatia (with John Wain). *Publications:* various research and text books and papers in learned journals; a book on the history of communications. *Leisure interests:* history, bridge, chess, swimming. *Address:* 62 Hurst Rise Road, Oxford, OX2 9HQ (Home); Department of Engineering Science, University of Oxford, Parks Road, Oxford, OX1 3PJ, England. *Telephone:* (1865) 273110. *Fax:* (1865) 273905. *E-mail:* laszlo.solymar@eng.ox.ac.uk (Office).

SOLYMOSI, Zoltan; Hungarian ballet dancer; b. 1967, Budapest; ed Ballet Acad. Budapest; joined Dutch Nat. Ballet as Prin. Dancer 1986, Munich Staatsoper 1989, La Scala Milan 1990; int. guest appearances; first appearance with Royal Ballet, London in Swan Lake, Metropolitan Opera House, New York 1991; full-time Artist of the Royal Ballet 1992–96, of English Nat. Ballet 1996; Resident Guest, London City Ballet 1996. *Repertoire includes:* prin. roles in maj. classical ballets, various works by Balanchine, works by Hungarian and Dutch choreographers, MacMillan and Ashton.

SOLYOM, Janos Paul; Hungarian/Swedish concert pianist and conductor; b. 26 Oct. 1938, Budapest; s. of Dr. I. Solyom and M. Weill; m. Camilla Lundberg 1987; ed Franz Liszt Acad. of Music, Budapest; pvt. studies with Ilona Kabos in London and with Nadia Boulanger in Paris; int. concert career 1958–; mem. Royal Swedish Acad. of Music; Royal Swedish Medal for Outstanding Artistic Merit 'Litteris et Artibus'. *Leisure interests:* architecture, hypnotherapy. *Address:* Norr Mälarstrand 54, VII 112 20 Stockholm, Sweden. *Telephone:* (8) 652-42-72. *Fax:* (8) 652-42-72. *E-mail:* janos.solyom@swipnet.se (Home). *Website:* www.solyom.se (Home).

SÓLYOM, László, LLD; Hungarian judge; b. 3 Jan. 1942, Pécs; m. Erzsébet Nagy; one s. one d.; ed Univ. of Pécs, Friedrich Schiller Univ., Jena, Hungarian Acad. of Sciences; Lecturer in Civil Law Univ. of Jena 1966–69; Research Fellow Hungarian Acad. of Sciences 1969–82; Prof. of Law Univ. of Budapest 1982–, Catholic Univ. of Budapest 1996–, Univ. of Cologne 1999–2000; Pres. Constitutional Court 1990–98; legal adviser to environmental groups and other civic movts 1982–89; mem. Int. Comm. of Jurists, Geneva 1994–2001, scientific council, Wissenschaftskolleg zu Berlin Inst. for Advanced Study, Berlin 1995–2001, European Comm. for Democracy Through Law (The Venice Comm.) 1998–; Corresp. mem. Hungarian Acad. of Sciences; Grand Cross of Merit with Star of the German Fed. Repub. 1998, Grand Cross of Merit of the Repub. of Hungary 1999; Hon. DJur (Cologne) 1999; Humboldt Research Award 1998. *Publications:* The Decline of Civil Law Liability 1980, Die Persönlichkeitsrechte: Eine vergleichend-historische Studie über ihre Grundlagen 1984, Verfassungsgerichtsbarkeit in Ungarn: Analysen und Entscheidungssammlung 1990–93 (with Georg Brunner) 1995, Constitutional Judiciary in a New Democracy: the Hungarian Constitutional Court (with Georg Brunner) 2000, The Beginnings of Constitutional Justice in Hungary (in Hungarian) 2001, The Role of Constitutional Courts in the Transition to Democracy, 18(1) Int. Sociology 2003. *Address:* Pázmány Péter Catholic University, Szentkirályi u. 28–30, 1088, Hungary. *E-mail:* lasolyom@axelero.hu (Home).

SOLZHENITSYN, Aleksandr Isayevich; Russian writer; b. 11 Dec. 1918, Kislovodsk; m. 1st Natalya Reshetovskaya (separated 1970); m. 2nd Natalya Svetlova; three s.; ed Rostov Univ. and Correspondence Course in Literature, Moscow History and Literature Inst.; joined Army 1941, attended artillery school, commissioned 1942, served at front as Commdr of Artillery Battery and twice decorated for bravery; sentenced to eight years in a forced labour camp 1945–53; contracted, later cured of cancer; in exile in Siberia 1953–57; officially rehabilitated 1957; taught mathematics at secondary school, Ryazan; expelled from Writers' Union of USSR Nov. 1969; expelled from USSR Feb. 1974, lived in Vt, USA; ended exile as treason charges dropped 1991; returned to Russia, citizenship restored 1994; hosted A Meeting with Solzhenitsyn 1995; mem. American Acad. of Arts and Sciences 1969–, Russian Acad. of Sciences 1997–; Hon. US Citizen 1974; Hon. Fellow, Hoover Inst. on War, Revolution and Peace 1975; Prix du Meilleur Livre Etranger (France) for The First Circle and Cancer Ward 1969, Nobel Prize for Literature 1970, Templeton Prize 1983. *Publications:* One Day in the Life of Ivan Denisovich 1962 (film 1971), Matryona's Home and An Incident at Krechetovka Station 1963 (short stories), For the Good of the Cause 1964 (short story), The First Circle (publ USA and UK 1968), Cancer Ward (USA and UK 1968), The Easter Procession (short story), The Love Girl and the Innocent (play, UK) 1969, Collected Works (6 vols) 1969, 1970, Stories and Prose Poems 1971, August 1914 1971, The Gulag Archipelago Vol. I 1973, Vol. II 1974, Vol. III 1976, Letter to Soviet Leaders 1974, Peace and Aggression 1974, Quiet Flows the Don: The Enigma of a Novel 1974, Candle in the Wind (play), The Oak and the Calf: Sketches of Literary Life in the Soviet Union 1975, The Nobel Prize Lecture 1975, Lenin in Zürich 1975, Détente (with others) 1976, Prussian Nights (poem trans. by Robert Conquest) 1977, Collected Works 1978–, Victory Celebrations, Prisoners (play) 1983, October 1916 1985, The Red Wheel, Live Not by Lies (essay) 1988, August 1914 (second version) 1989, Rebuilding Russia 1990, The Russian Question at the End of the 20th Century 1994, Invisible Allies (addendum to The Oak and the Calf) 1995, November 1916, Russia in Collapse 1998, Two Hundred Years Together (Jews in Russia) (2 vols) 2001–02. *Address:* PO Box 121, Cavendish, VT 05142, USA. *Telephone:* (095) 229-86-39 (Moscow).

SOMARE, Rt. Hon. Sir Michael Thomas, PC, CH, GCMG; Papua New Guinea politician; b. 9 April 1936, Rabaul, East New Britain Prov.; s. of Sana Ludwig Somare and Painari Betha; m. Veronica Bula Kaiap 1965; three s. two d.; ed Sogeri Secondary School, Admin. Coll.; teacher various schools 1956–64; Asst Area Educ. Officer, Madang 1962–63; Broadcasts Officer, Dept of Information and Extension Services, Wewak 1963–66, radio broadcaster and journalist 1966–67; mem. House of Ass. for East Sepik Regional 1968–; Parl. Leader Pangu Party 1968–88; Deputy Chair. Exec. Council 1972–73, Chair. 1973–75; Chief Minister Papua New Guinea 1974–75, Prime Minister 1975–80, 1982–85; Minister for Nat. Resources 1976–77, for Public Service Comm. and Nat. Planning 1977–80; Acting Minister for Police 1978–80; Leader of the Opposition 1980–82; Minister of Foreign Affairs 1988–94, 2000–01, also of Bougainville Affairs 2000–01; Gov. E Sepik Prov. 1995–; Chair. Bd of Trustees, P.N.G.; mem. Second Select Cttee on Constitutional Devt 1968–72, Australian Broadcasting Comm. Advisory Cttee; six hon. degrees; Ancient Order of Sikatuna, Title of Rajah (Philippines) 1976, Queen's Silver Jubilee Medal 1977, Pacific Man of the Year Award 1983, Grand Cross of Equestrian Order of St Gregory the Great 1993. *Publication:* Sana: An Autobiography. *Leisure interests:* reading, golf, soccer, cricket, fishing. *Address:* House of Assembly, Waigani, NCO (Office); Karan, Murik Lakes, East Sepik, Papua New Guinea (Home).

SOMAVÍA, Juan O.; Chilean diplomatist; m.; two c.; ed Catholic Univ. of Chile, Univ. of Paris; various posts in Ministry of Foreign Relations; Founder and Exec. Dir Latin American Inst. for Transnat. Studies, Mexico; Co-ordinator Third World Forum; mem. Bd of Dirs. and Vice-Pres. for Latin

America of Inter-Press Service 1976–87; Sec.-Gen. South American Peace Comm. 1987; Pres. Int. Comm. of Chilean opposition No Campaign for Referendum 1988–89; Perm. Rep. to UN, New York 1990–98; Dir-Gen. ILO 1998–; fmr consultant to GATT and UNDP; mem. Bd of Dirs. Int. Foundation for Devt Alternatives, mem. MacBride Comm. on communication problems; Leonidas Proaño Prize, Latin American Human Rights Asscn for contrib. to peace and regional security. *Address:* International Labour Organization, 4 route des Morillons, 1211 Geneva 22, Switzerland. *Telephone:* (22) 7996111 (Office). *Fax:* (22) 7988685 (Office). *Website:* www.ilo.org (Office).

SOMERS, Daryl; Australian television presenter; b. 6 Aug. 1951; m. Julie da Costa 1985; professional vocalist and drummer; first TV appearance on New Faces, GTV 9, Melbourne 1968; debut as TV host on weekday children's show Cartoon Corner 1971 (ran till 1977), later same year became host of Hey Hey It's Saturday; Chief Exec. Somers Carroll Pty Ltd, owner of Hey Hey 1971–99; 29 Logie Awards and numerous other awards. *Television appearances:* (host) Hey Hey It's Saturday, Daryl Somers Show, own Tonight show, Bandstand, Ossie Ostrich Video Show, Family Feud (game show), Blankety Blanks (game show), the King of Pop Awards, numerous other Tonight and variety shows (producer) The Russell Gilbert Show 1998, 1999, Gonged But Not Forgotten 1998, 1999; live singing performances with Melbourne Symphony Orchestra, concerts, pantomimes and sporting events. *Address:* PO Box 921, Hawthorn 3122, Australia. *Telephone:* (3) 9818-7766 (Office). *Fax:* (3) 9815-2066 (Office).

SOMLYÓ, György; Hungarian poet, novelist, critic and translator of poetry; b. 28 Nov. 1920, Balatonboglár; s. of Zoltán Somlyó and Margit Bolgár; m. (divorced 1986); one s.; ed Budapest Univ. and the Sorbonne, Paris; Lecturer in Modern Poetry Budapest Univ. 1975–78; Ed. Arion 1966–87; organizer Int. Meeting of Poets, Budapest 1966, 1970; corresp. PO&SIE poetry magazine, Paris 1976–; mem. Széchenyi Hungarian Acad. of Arts and Letters; corresp. mem. Académie Mallarmé, Paris 1977–; József Attila prize (four times), Tibor Déry Prize 1987, Kassák Prize, Soros Foundation 1991, Gabriela Mistral Memorial Medal (Chile) 1996, Kossuth Prize 1997; Officier, Ordre des Arts et Lettres (France) 1984, Order of Flag of Hungarian Repub. 1990. *Translations:* Szélrózsa I/III (Compass Card) 1973, Az utazás (The Journey), French Poetry from Baudelaire to our days 1984. *Publications include:* Collected Works: Vol. 1: A költészet vérszerzödése (The Blood Covenant of Poetry) 1977, Vols 2, 3: Collected Poems 1978, Vol. 4: Másutt (Elsewhere) 1979, Vol. 5: Szerelöszönyeg (Catwalk) 1981, Vol. 6: Megiratlan könyvek (Unwritten Books) 1982, Vol. 7: Miért hal meg az ember? (Why the Man Dies?) 1984, Philoktetész sebe (Philoctetes' Wound) 1980, Árnyjáték (Shadow Play) 1977, Rámpa (Ramp) 1984, Picasso 1981, Parisiens (poems in French) 1987, A Költészet ötödik évada (The Fifth Season of Poetry) 1988, Ami rajtam tul van (What's Beyond Me) 1988, Városok (Cities: essays) 1990, Palimpszeszt (poems) 1990, Párizsi Kettös (Duo in Paris) 1991, Nem titok (No Secret: poems) 1992, Az elvitathatatlan hely (The Evident Place, essays) 1994, A Negyedik Szoba (The Fourth Room Poems) 1994, Énekek Eneke (Song of Songs) 1994, Törésvonlak (Breaklines) poems (1997), Paul Valéry Füzetek (notebooks) 1997, Sebéskés (Wound and Knife) (selected poems 1976–97) 1998, From Philoctetes to Arion (collected essays) 2000, Collected Poems 2001, Önéletrajzaimból (autobiog.) 2001; Ed. 1001 Sonnets of World Literature (anthology) 1991. *Address:* Irinyi J. u. 39, 1111 Budapest, Hungary. *Telephone:* (1) 386-09-54.

SOMMARUGA, Cornelio, LLD; Swiss diplomatist; b. 29 Dec. 1932, Rome, Italy; s. of Carlo Sommaruga and Anna-Maria Valagussa; m. Ornella Marzorati 1957; two s. four d.; ed Rome, Paris, Univ. of Zürich; bank trainee, Zürich 1957–59; joined Diplomatic Service 1960; Attaché, Swiss Embassy, The Hague 1961; Sec. Swiss Embassy, Bonn 1962–64, Rome 1965–68; Deputy Head of Del. to EFTA, GATT and UNCTAD, Geneva 1969–73; Asst Sec.-Gen. EFTA July 1973–75; Minister plenipotentiary, Div. of Commerce, Fed. Dept of Public Economy, Berne 1976, Amb. 1977; del. Fed. Council for Trade Agreements 1980–84; State Sec. for External Econ. Affairs 1984–86; Pres. ICRC 1987–99; Pres., UN Econ. Comm. for Europe 1977–78; Pres. Caux-Initiative of Change Foundation 2000; Chair. Bd J. P. Morgan (Suisse) SA, Geneva 2000–, Geneva Int. Centre for Humanitarian Demining 2000, Karl Popper Foundation 2000; mem. of Panel on UN Peace Operations, Int. Comm. on Intervention and State Sovereignty; Hon. mem. ICRC 2000; Commdr Légion d'honneur; several other state honours from Italy, Belgium, The Holy See, Luxembourg, Lithuania, Iceland, Sweden; Hon. MD; Dr hc (Fribourg) 1985, (Braga) 1990, (Nice-Sophia Antipolis, Seoul Nat. Univ.) 1992; (Bologna) 1991, (Geneva) 1997, (Webster, St Louis) 1998; North-South Prize of the Council of Europe 2001; numerous awards from Red Cross Socs. *Address:* 16 chemin des Crêts-de-Champel, 1206 Geneva, Switzerland (Office). *Telephone:* (22) 3474552 (Home). *Fax:* (22) 3474555 (Home). *E-mail:* cornelio .sommaruga@bluewin.ch (Home); c.sommaruga@gichd.ch (Office).

SOMMER, Elke; German actress; b. 5 Nov. 1940, Berlin; d. of Friedrich Schletz and Renate Schletz; m. Joe Hyams (twice); Wolf Walther 1993; first film, L'Amico del Giaguaro 1958; since then has made more than 70 films including The Prize, The Victors, Shot in the Dark, The Oscar, Himmelsheim, Neat and Tidy, Severed Ties, own TV show (PBS), Painting with Elke 1985; Golden Globe Award 1965, Jefferson Award, Merit of Achievement Award 1990. *Leisure interests:* riding, art. *Address:* 91080 Marloffstein, Germany; 540 N Beverly Glen Boulevard W, Los Angeles, CA 90024, USA. *Telephone:* (9131) 53660 (Germany); (310) 724-8990 (U.S.A). *Fax:* (9131) 536699 (Germany); (310) 724-8993 (USA).

SOMMER, Ron; German business executive; b. 1949, Haifa, Israel; ed in Vienna; began career with Nixdorf Group in New York, Paris and Paderborn, Germany; Man. Sony Deutschland 1980, Chair. 1986; Pres., CEO Sony USA 1990; Pres., CEO Sony Europe 1993; CEO Deutsche Telekom AG 1995–2002. *Address:* c/o Deutsche Telekom AG, Friedrich-Ebert-Allee 140, 53113 Bonn, Germany (Office).

SOMMER, Theo, DPhil; German journalist; b. 10 June 1930, Constance; s. of Theo Sommer and Else Sommer; m. 1st Elda Tsilenis 1952; two s.; m. 2nd Heide Grenz 1976; two s.; m. 3rd Sabine Grewe 1989; one d.; ed Univ of Tübingen, Chicago and Harvard Univs; Local Ed. Schwäbisch-Gmünd 1952–54; Foreign Ed. Die Zeit 1958, Deputy Ed. 1968, Ed.-in-Chief 1973–92, Publr 1992–, Ed.-at-Large 2000–; Lecturer in Int. Relations, Univ. of Hamburg 1967–70; Chief of Planning Staff, Ministry of Defence 1969–70; mem. Deutsche Gesellschaft für Auswärtige Politik; mem. Council IISS 1963–76, 1978–87, German Armed Forces Structure Comm. 1970–72, Int. Comm. on the Balkans 1995–96, Ind. Int. Comm. on the Balkans 1999–2000; Deputy Chair. Comm. on the Future on the Bundeswehr 1999–2000; Chair. Comm. Investigating Effects of DU Ammunitions, Radar and Asbestos on German Armed Forces 2002; mem. Indo-German Consultative Group 1992– (Co-Chair. 1996–), German-Japanese Dialogue Forum 1993–; mem. Bd Deutsche Welthungerhilfe 1992–, Max-Bauer Preis 1992–, German-Turkish Foundation 1998–; mem. German Foreign Policy Asscn, IISS, Königswinter Conf., Advisory Council, Mil. History Inst.; Contributing Ed. Newsweek Int. 1968–90; regular contrib. to American, British, Japanese and Korean publs; commentator German TV, radio and moderator of monthly programmes;; Hon. mem. Asscn of Anciens, NATO Defense Coll. 1971, Trilateral Comm. 1993; Fed. Order of Merit (First Class) 1998, Gold Honor Cross, German Armed Forces 2002; Hon. LLD (Univ. of Maryland, USA) 1982; Theoder-Wolf Prize 1966, Int. Communications Award, People's Repub. of China 1991, Columbus Prize 1993. *Publications:* Deutschland und Japan zwischen den Mächten (Germany and Japan Between the Powers) 1935–40 1962, Vom Antikominternpakt zum Dreimächtepakt 1962, Reise in ein fernes Land 1964, Ed. Denken an Deutschland 1966, Ed. Schweden-Report 1974, Die chinesische Karte (The Chinese Card) 1979, Allianz in Umbruch (Alliance in Disarray) 1982, Blick zurück in die Zukunft (Look Back into the Future) 1984, Reise ins andere Deutschland (Journey to the Other Germany) 1986, Europa im 21. Jahrhundert 1989, Geschichte der Bonner Republik 1949–99 1999, Der Zukunft entgegen (Toward the Future) 1999, Phoenix Europe. The European Union: Its Progress, Problems and Prospects 2000. *Address:* Die Zeit, Pressehaus, Speersort 1, 20079 Hamburg (Office); 17 Zabelweg, 22359 Hamburg, Germany (Home). *Telephone:* (40) 3280240 (Office); (40) 6037300 (Home). *Fax:* (40) 3280407 (Office); (40) 6030044 (Home). *E-mail:* sommer@zeit.de (Office); tsommer01@aol.com (Home). *Website:* www.zeit.de (Office).

SOMOGYI, Peter, PhD, FRS; Hungarian professor of neurobiology; ed Loránd Eötvös Univ., Budapest; research training in neurocytology and neuroanatomy at Semmelweis Univ. of Medicine, Budapest, in biochemistry and immunocytochemistry at the Univ. of Oxford, UK; postdoctoral fellowship at Flinders Medical Centre, South Australia; has trained research students since 1978; Assoc., later Co-Dir Anatomical Neuropharmacology Unit, MRC, Oxford, 1995–98, Dir 1998–; Prof. of Neurobiology, Oxford Univ. 1996–; Moruzzi Memorial Lecturer, European Neuroscience Asscn 1990; Hon. PhD (Attila József Univ. of Szeged) 1990; Krieg Cortical Kudos, Cortical Discoverer Prize of the Cajal Club 1991, Yngve Zotterman Prize, Swedish Physiological Soc. 1995. *Address:* Medical Research Council Anatomical Neuropharmacology Unit, Mansfield Road, Oxford, OX1 3TH, England (Office). *Telephone:* (1865) 271865 (Office). *Fax:* (1865) 271647 (Office). *E-mail:* peter.somogyi@ pharm.ox.ac.uk (Office). *Website:* mrcanu.pharm.ox.ac.uk (Office).

SOMOL, Miroslav, DJur, PhD; Czech diplomatist and civil servant; b. 1 July 1952; ed Charles Univ., Prague, Inst. of State and Law of Czechoslovak Acad. of Sciences; joined Fed. Ministry of Trade 1975, Head of Govt Del. to meetings of UN Conf. of Trade and GATT; apptd Dir-Gen. Trade Policy 1992, responsible for trade agreements between fmr Czechoslovakia and EU; Acting Deputy Minister Czech Ministry for Industry and Trade, Deputy Minister for Multilateral Policy 2000–, responsible for relations with EU, OECD and other int. econ. orgs; Commercial Attaché to Embassy in Damascus, Syria 1989–92; Amb. and Perm. Rep. to UN and other int. orgs, Geneva; elected Chair. UN Comm. on Human Rights 1997; Pres. of Econ. Comm. for Europe (ECE). *Address:* Ministry for Industry and Trade, Na Františku 32, 110 15 Prague 1, Czech Republic (Office). *Telephone:* (2) 4851111 (Office). *Fax:* (2) 24811089 (Office). *E-mail:* mpo@mpo.cz (Office). *Website:* www.mpo.cz (Office).

SOMORJAI, Gabor Arpad, PhD, FAAS; American professor of chemistry; b. 4 May 1935, Budapest, Hungary; s. of Charles Somorjai and Livia Ormos; m. Judith Kaldor 1957; one s. one d.; ed Univ. of Tech. Sciences, Budapest, Univ. of Calif. at Berkeley; mem. Research Staff IBM, New York 1960–64; at Faculty of Dept of Chem., Univ. of Calif. at Berkeley 1964–, Asst Prof. 1964–67, Assoc. Prof. 1967–72, Prof. 1972–; Faculty Sr Scientist, Materials Science Div. and Dir Surface Science and Catalysis Program, Lawrence Berkeley Lab., Berkeley, Calif. 1964–; numerous awards and visiting professorships in USA and UK including Visiting Fellow Emmanuel Coll., Univ. of Cambridge 1969; Centenary Lecturer Royal Soc. of Chem., UK 1983; Hinshelwood Lecturer, Univ. of Oxford 1994; Linnett Lecturer, Univ. of Cambridge 1994; mem. NAS 1979–, ACS, American Physical Soc., American Acad. of Arts and Sciences 1983; Hon. mem. Hungarian Acad. of Sciences 1990; Dr hc (Tech. Univ., Budapest) 1989, (Univ. Pierre et Marie Curie) 1990, (Univ. Libre de Bruxelles) 1992, (Ferrara) 1998, Józse Attila Univ., Hungary) 1999 (Royal Inst. of Tech., Stockholm) 2000, (Manchester) 2001; Emmett Award American Catalysis Soc. 1977, ACS Colloid and Surface Chem. Award 1981, ACS Peter Debye Award 1989, ACS Adamson Surface Chemistry Award 1994, Von Hippel Award, Materials Research Soc. 1997, Wolf Prize 1998, ACS Catalysis Award 2000, Pauling Medal, Hungarian Acad. of Sciences 2000, Nat. Medal of Science 2002, Cotton Award 2003. *Publications:* Principles of Surface Chemistry 1972, Chemistry in Two Dimensions 1981, Introduction to Surface Chemistry and Catalysis 1994, serves editorial bds of numerous scientific publs, more than 900 publs in major scientific journals. *Leisure interests:* swimming, walking. *Address:* Department of Chemistry, University of California, Berkeley, Berkeley, CA 94720-1460 (Office); 665 San Luis Road, Berkeley, CA 94707, USA (Home). *Telephone:* (510) 642-4053 (Office). *Fax:* (510) 643-9668 (Office). *E-mail:* somorjai@socrates.berkeley.edu (Home).

SON, Masayoshi; Japanese business executive; ed Univ. of California; started by importing used video games from Japan (to USA); co-developed pocket electronic translator bought by Sharp; f. Softbank (Japan's largest software distributor); retailer of personal computer games, Japan. *Address:* 24-1, Nihonbash, Hakozakicho, Chuo-ku, Tokyo 103-8501, Japan.

SONDECKIS, Saulius; Lithuanian conductor; b. 11 Oct. 1928, Šiauliai; s. of Jackus Sondeckis and Rozalija Sondeckienė; m. Silvija Sondeckienė; three s.; ed Lithuanian Conservatory as violinist, Moscow State Conservatory; f., conductor and artistic Dir Lithuanian Chamber orchestra; tours fmr USSR and Europe 1960–; teacher Vilnius M. Čiurlionis School of Arts 1955–85, f. Youth Orchestra; f. and Artistic Dir St Petersburg Camerata Chamber Orchestra (now Orchestra of Hermitage Museum) 1989–; Prof. Vilnius Conservatory 1957–, Chair. Strings Dept 1959–87; Prof. St Petersburg Conservatory 1989–91; f. (with G. Kremer) Kremerata Baltica Chamber Orchestra 1996; Chief Conductor Patras Orchestra, Greece; conducted various European, U.S. and Japanese orchestras; worked together with Rostropovich and many other distinguished soloists; first performance of chamber music by Alfred Schnittke, Sergey Slonimsky, Arvo Pärt, contemporary Lithuanian composers; Lithuanian Grand Duke First and Fifth Order of Gediminas Cavalier; winner of Gold Medal at Herbert von Karajan Stiftung Competition in Berlin 1976, USSR People's Artist 1980, Lithuanian State Prize 1971, USSR State Prize 1987, State Prize of Lithuanian Govt 1998. *Address:* Čiurlionio 28, Vilnius, Lithuania. *Telephone:* (2) 33-15-57. *Fax:* (2) 62-36-46 (Home).

SONDHEIM, Stephen Joshua; American song writer; b. 22 March 1930, New York City; s. of Herbert Sondheim and Janet Fox; ed George School, Newtown, Pa, Williams Coll., Williamstown, Mass., private instruction; Pres. Dramatists' Guild 1973–81, Council mem. 1981–; Visiting Prof. of Drama and Musical Theatre, Oxford Univ. Jan.–June 1990; mem. American Acad. and Inst. of Arts and Letters 1983–; television: Topper (co-author) 1953, Evening Primrose (music and lyrics) 1967; lyrics: West Side Story 1957, Gypsy 1959, Do I Hear a Waltz? 1965, Candide 1974; music and lyrics: A Funny Thing Happened on the Way to the Forum 1962, Anyone Can Whistle 1964, Company 1970, Follies 1971, A Little Night Music 1973, The Frogs 1974, Pacific Overtures 1976, Sweeney Todd 1978, Merrily We Roll Along 1981, Sunday in the Park with George 1984, Into the Woods (Drama Critic's Circle Award 1988) 1986, Follies 1987, Assassins 1991, Passion 1994; anthologies: Side by Side by Sondheim 1977, Marry Me a Little 1980, You're Gonna Love Tomorrow 1983, Putting It Together 1993; screenplay: (with Anthony Perkins) The Last of Sheila 1973, Birdcage 1996, Getting Away Murder 1996; film scores: Stavisky 1975, Reds 1981, Dick Tracy 1989; Antoinette Perry Awards for Company 1971, Follies 1972, A Little Night Music 1973, Sweeney Todd 1979; Drama Critics' Awards 1971, 1972, 1973, 1976, 1979; Evening Standard Drama Award 1996; Grammy Awards 1984, 1986; Nat. Medal of Arts 1997, Praemium Imperial 2000. *Address:* c/o Flora Roberts, 157 West 57th Street, New York, NY 10019, USA.

SONG BAORUI; Chinese politician; b. Dec. 1937, Shunyi Co., Beijing; ed Qinghua Univ.; joined CCP 1958; fmr Deputy Dir, Chief Engineer China Welding Rod Plant, Dir China Welding Rod Plant Inst. 1975–82; Man. China Welding Materials Manufacture Co. 1982–83; Deputy Sec. then Sec. CCP Zigong City Cttee 1983–86; fmr mem. Standing Cttee CCP Sichuan Prov. Cttee; Chair. Sichuan Prov. Comm. for Restructuring the Economy 1986–89, Exec. Deputy Sec. CCP Sichuan Prov. Cttee 1989–99; Gov. of Sichuan Prov. 1996–99; alt. mem. 14th CCP Cen. Cttee; Deputy 8th NPC; mem. 15th CCP Cen. Cttee 1997–99. *Address:* c/o People's Government of Sichuan, Chengdu, Sichuan Province, People's Republic of China.

SONG DEFU; Chinese party and government official; b. 1946, Yanshan Co., Hebei Prov.; joined PLA and CCP 1965; First Sec. of Secr. Communist Youth League of China 1985–93; Minister of Personnel 1993–2000; Party Group Sec., Ministry of Personnel; Head Nat. Leading Group for Placement of Demobilized Army Officers 1993–2000; Sec. CCP Fujian Prov. Cttee 2001–; mem. 13th CCP Cen. Cttee 1987–92, 14th CCP Cen. Cttee 1992–97, 15th CCP Cen. Cttee 1997–. *Address:* c/o Chinese Communist Party, Fujian Provincial Committee, Fuzhou, Fujian Province, People's Republic of China.

SONG FATANG; Chinese politician; b. Dec. 1940, Tancheng, Shandong Prov.; ed Qufu Teachers' Univ.; joind CCP 1961; Vice-Sec. CCP Taian Co. Cttee, Vice-Sec. then Sec. CCP Taian Municipal Cttee, Mayor of Taian 1979–89; Vice-Gov. Shandong Prov. 1989–99; Vice-Sec. CCP Shandong Provincial Cttee 1994–99; mem. 15th CCP Cen. Cttee 1997–; Deputy Gov., then

Gov. Heilongjiang Prov. 2000–. *Address:* Office of the Governor, Heilongjiang Provincial People's Government, Harbin, Heilongjiang Province, People's Republic of China (Office).

SONG JIAN, DSc; Chinese state official; b. 29 Dec. 1931, Rongcheng Co., Shandong Prov.; s. of the late Song Zengjin and Jiang Yuxian; m. Wang Yusheng 1961; one s. one d.; ed Harbin Tech. Univ., Beijing Foreign Languages Inst., Bauman Eng Inst. Moscow; Dir and Head, Lab. of Cybernetics, Inst. of Math., Acad. Sinica 1960–70; Dir Guided Missile Control Lab., 7th Ministry of Machine Bldg Industry 1962–70; Head, Chief Scientist, Space Science Div., Acad. of Space Tech. 1971–78, Vice-Pres., Deputy Science Dir, Acad. of Space Tech. 1978–81; Vice-Minister and Chief Eng Scientist, Ministry of Astronautics 1981–84; Research Prof., Beijing Inst. of Information and Control 1983–; Chair. State Science & Tech. Comm. 1984–98; mem. Chinese Acad. of Sciences 1991–; State Councillor 1986–98; Visiting Prof. MIT, Harvard, Univ. of Minn. 1980; Vice-Pres. China Soc. of Demographic Science 1982–86; Assoc. Chief Ed. System & Control Letters 1983–85; Chief Ed. Automatic Control & System Eng, Encyclopaedia of China 1983–; mem. Ed. Bd Encyclopaedia of China 1984–; Council mem. Int. Fed. of Automatic Control 1984–87; Vice-Pres. China System Eng Soc. 1985–87; mem. Chinese Acad. of Eng 1994–, Pres. 1998–2002; Vice-Chair. Chinese People's Political Consultative Conf. 1998–; Pres. China-Japan Friendship Asscn 1998–; Foreign mem. Russian Acad. of Sciences 1994, Royal Swedish Acad. of Eng Sciences 1994, Nat. Acad. of Eng, USA 2000, Argentine Acad. of Eng 2001, Yugoslav Acad. of Eng 2002; Corresp. mem. Nat. Acad. of Eng of Mexico 1985; Prof. Qinghua Univ., Fudan Univ., Harbin Univ. of Tech. 1986–; Hon. Distinguished Visiting Prof. Washington Univ. 1986–; Hon. DHumLitt (Houston) 1996; numerous nat. and int. awards. *Publications:* Reference Frames in Space Flight 1963, Engineering Cybernetics (co-author) 1980, China's Population: Problems and Prospects 1981, Recent Development in Control Theory and Its Applications 1984, Population Projections and Control 1981, Population Control Theory 1985, Population Control in China: Theory and Applications 1985, Population System Control 1988, Science and Technology and Social System 1988; numerous articles. *Leisure interest:* swimming. *Address:* National Committee of Chinese People's Political Consultative Conference, 23 Taipingqiao Street, Beijing, People's Republic of China.

SONG PING; Chinese party official; b. 1917, Juxian Co., Shandong Prov.; ed Inst. Marxism-Leninism, Yan'an; joined CCP 1937; Vice-Minister, Labour 1953; Vice-Chair. State Planning Comm. 1957–63; Sec. CCP Gansu and Vice-Chair. Gansu Revolutionary Cttee 1972, First Sec. CCP Gansu, Chair. Gansu Revolutionary Cttee, Second Political Commissar, PLA Lanzhou Mil. Region and First Political Commissar Gansu Mil. District, PLA 1977–80; mem. 11th Cen. Cttee CCP 1977; First Vice-Chair. State Planning Comm. 1981–83; Minister in charge of State Planning Comm. 1983–87; mem. 12th Cen. Cttee CCP 1982–87, Political Bureau 1987–92, 13th Cen. Cttee, mem. Standing Cttee 1989–92; Chair. Family Planning Asscn 1990–; Hon. Pres. Chinese Asscn for Promotion of the Population Culture; Deputy Sec.-Gen., First Session of the 7th NPC March 1988; Deputy Dir Leading Group for Co-ordinating Nat. Scientific Work 1983; State Councillor 1983–88; Vice-Chair. Environmental Protection Cttee State Council 1984–87, Nat. Agric. Zoning Cttee 1983–; Deputy Head Leading Group for Scientific Work, State Council 1983–92; Head Leading Group for Econ. Information Man., State Council 1986–92; Head Org. Dept Cen. Cttee CCP 1988–90; visited Pakistan 1991; mem. Presidium 14th CCP Nat. Congress Oct. 1992; Hon. Dir-in-Chief China Welfare Fund for the Handicapped; Hon. Adviser "Happiness Project" Org. *Address:* Central Committee of CCP, Zhang Nan Hai, Beijing, People's Republic of China.

SONG QINGWEI, Gen.; Chinese army officer and party official; b. 1929, Lingxian Co., Shandong Prov.; joined CCP 1945; Political Commissar of PLA Jinan Mil. Area Command 1987–95; rank of Lt-Gen. 1988, of Gen. 1994; mem. 14th CCP Cen. Cttee 1992–97; Vice-Chair. Foreign Affairs Cttee 9th NPC 1998–. *Address:* c/o Standing Committee of National People's Congress, Beijing, People's Republic of China.

SONG RENQIONG; Chinese politician; b. 1903, Hunan Prov.; m.; two s. four d.; ed Huangpu Mil. Acad.; joined CCP 1926, on Long March 1934–35; Alt. mem. 7th Cen. Cttee CCP 1945; Cadre in SW China 1949–54; Minister of 3rd Ministry of Machine Building 1954, 2nd Ministry of Machine Building 1959–60, 7th Ministry of Machine Building 1977–79; mem. 8th Cen. Cttee CCP 1956, First Sec. NE Bureau 1961–67; Dir Org. Dept CCP 1979–; Chair. Credentials Cttee 5th NPC 1980–83; mem. Secr. 11th Cen. Cttee CCP; mem. Politburo 12th Cen. Cttee CCP 1982–85, Chair. Credentials Cttee; Vice-Chair. Cen. Advisory Comm. 1985, 1987; Adviser Cen. Party Consolidation Guidance Comm. 1983–92; mem. Presidium 14th CCP Nat. Congress Oct. 1992; Hon. Pres. Volleyball Asscn. *Address:* Zhongnandai, Beijing, People's Republic of China.

SONG RUIXIANG; Chinese politician; b. 1939, Jintan Co., Jiangsu Prov.; joined CCP 1959; Gov. of Qinghai Prov. 1988–93; Minister of Geology and Mineral Resources 1993–98, Party Group Sec. Ministry of Geology and Mineral Resources; Chair. Nat. Mineral Reserves Comm. 1995–96; Vice-Chair. Nat. Mineral Resources Cttee 1996–98; Vice-Dir State Gen. Admin. of Environment Protection 1998–2002; Dir China Seismological Bureau 2002–; mem. 15th CCP Cen. Cttee 1997–. *Address:* China Seismological Bureau, Beijing, People's Republic of China.

SONG ZHAOSU; Chinese politician; b. March 1941, Nanyang, He'nan Prov.; ed Zhengzhou Univ.; joined CCP 1965; Vice-Sec. CCP He'nan Prov. Cttee 1993–98; Deputy Gov. Gansu Prov. 1998–99, Gov. 1999–2001; Sec. CCP Gansu Prov. Cttee 2001–; alt. mem. CCP 15th Cen. Cttee 1997–. *Address:* Gansu Provincial People's Government, Lanzhou, Gansu Province, People's Republic of China.

SONN, Franklin Abraham; South African diplomatist; b. 11 Oct. 1939, Vosburg Dist; s. of Pieter (Pat) Sonn and Magdalene Klein; m.; two c.; ed UNISA and Univ. of W Cape; fmr Rector, Peninsula Technikon; fmr Chair. Comm. of Technikon Prins., Chair. W Cape Foundation for Community Work, Mobil Foundation of S Africa, Inst. for Distance Educ.; Chair. Bd Trustees, Die Suid-Afrikaan Magazine, Nat. Educ. and Training Forum 1994–; Vice-Chair. Urban Found.; Dir Metropolitan M-Net 1994–; mem. Bd Corp. Africa; Vice-Pres. Jt Council of Teachers Asscn of S Africa; numerous other public appts.; Amb. to USA 1995–98. *Publications include:* A Decade of Struggle 1986; numerous papers and official documents. *Leisure interests:* reading, walking, mountaineering, squash. *Address:* c/o Ministry of Foreign Affairs, Union Buildings, East Wing, Government Avenue, Pretoria 0002, South Africa.

SONNENFELD, Barry; American cinematographer and film director; b. 1 April 1953, New York. *Films include:* (cinematographer) Blood Simple 1984, Compromising Positions 1985, Three O'Clock High 1987, Raising Arizona 1987, Throw Momma from the Train 1987, Big 1988, When Harry Met Sally . . . 1989, Miller's Crossing 1990, Misery 1990, (Dir) The Addams Family 1991, Addams Family Values 1993, Get Shorty 1995, Men in Black 1997, Wild Wild West 1999, Chippendales 2000; (Dir, co-producer) For Love or Money 1993. *Television:* Out of Step 1984 (Emmy Award for best cinematography 1984), Fantasy Island 1998, Secret Agent Man 2000, The Crew 2000. *Address:* c/o Fred Specktor, CAA, 9830 Wilshire Boulevard, Beverly Hills, CA 90212; United Talent Agency, 9560 Wilshire Boulevard, Beverly Hills, CA 90212, USA.

SONNENFELDT, Helmut, MA; American international business consultant and fmr government official; b. 13 Sept. 1926, Berlin, Germany; s. of Dr. Walther H. Sonnenfeldt and Dr. Gertrud L. Sonnenfeldt; m. Marjorie Hecht 1953; two s. one d.; ed Univ. of Manchester, Johns Hopkins Univ.; went to USA 1944; mem. Counterintelligence Corps, US Army, Pacific and European Theaters; with Dept of State 1952–69, Policy Officer, US Disarmament Admin. 1960–61, Dir Office of Research and Analysis for the USSR and E Europe 1966–69; Sr Staff mem. for Europe and East–West Relations, Nat. Security Council 1969–74; Counselor of Dept of State 1974–77; Lecturer on Soviet Affairs, Johns Hopkins Univ. School of Advanced Int. Studies 1957–69; Trustee, Johns Hopkins Univ. 1974–; Visiting Scholar, School of Advanced Int. Studies, Johns Hopkins Univ. 1977–78; Guest Scholar, Brookings Inst., Washington, DC 1978–; Consultant Washington Center for Foreign Policy Research; Gov. and Dir UN Asscn of USA 1980; Dir Atlantic Council of USA 1978–; mem. IISS, London 1977–99, (mem. Exec. Cttee 1986–98), Council of Foreign Relations, Royal Inst. of Int. Affairs, London, Int. Advisory Council, Credit-Anstalt-Bankverein, Vienna 1993–98, Defense Policy Bd 2001–; Editorial Bd Politique Internationale (Paris) 1978–, Foreign Policy 1980–; Govt rep. to numerous confs and meetings abroad; consultant to int. investments firms and banks. *Publications:* Soviet Policy in the 1980s 1985, articles on int. issues in American and European journals. *Leisure interests:* tennis, music, reading biography. *Address:* Brookings Institution, 1775 Massachusetts Ave, NW, Washington, DC 20036; 5600 Wisconsin Avenue, #1505, Chevy Chase, MD 20815, USA. *Telephone:* (202) 797-6028. *Fax:* (202) 797-6004. *E-mail:* hsonnenfeldt@brookings.edu (Office).

SONTAG, Susan, MA; American author and film director; b. 16 Jan. 1933; m. Philip Rieff 1950 (divorced 1958); one s.; ed Univ. of Chicago and Harvard Univ.; mem. American Inst. of Arts and Letters, American Acad. of Arts and Sciences, PEN (Pres. American Centre 1987–89); Guggenheim Fellow 1966, 1975, Rockefeller Foundation Fellow 1965, 1974; Commdr, Ordre des Arts et des Lettres (France) 1999; recipient Ingram Merrill Foundation Award in Literature in the Field of American Letters 1976, Creative Arts Award, Brandeis Univ. 1976, Arts and Letters Award, American Acad. of Arts and Letters 1976, Nat. Book Critics Circle Prize 1978, MacArthur Fellowship 1990–95, Elmer Holmes Bobst Award 1991, Nat. Book Award for Fiction 2000, Jerusalem Prize 2001. *Films include:* Duet for Cannibals 1969, Brother Carl 1971, Promised Lands 1974, Unguided Tour 1983; Dir Waiting for Godot, Sarajevo 1993. *Publications:* The Benefactor (novel) 1963, Death Kit (novel) 1967, Against Interpretation (essays) 1966, Styles of Radical Will 1969, On Photography 1977, Illness as Metaphor 1978, I, Etcetera (stories) 1978, Under the Sign of Saturn 1980, A Susan Sontag Reader (anthology) 1982, A Barthes Reader (introduction) 1982, AIDS and Its Metaphors 1989, The Way We Live Now 1991, The Volcano Lover (novel) 1992, Alice in Bed (play) 1993, Under the Sign of Saturn (poetry) 1996, In America 2000, Women (with Annie Liebowitz) 2000, Where the Stress Falls 2001, Regarding the Pain of Others 2003. *Address:* c/o The Wylie Agency, 250 West 57th Street, Suite 2114, New York, NY 10107, USA (Office).

SOONG, James Chu-yul, PhD; Taiwanese politician; b. 16 March 1942, Hunan; m. Viola Chen; one s. one d.; ed Nat. Chengchi Univ., Taipei, Univ. of California, Berkeley, Catholic Univ. of America, Georgetown Univ., Washington DC; Sec. Exec. Yuan, Taiwan 1974–77; Deputy Dir-Gen. Govt Information Office 1977–79; Assoc. Prof., Nat. Taiwan Univ. 1975–79; Research Fellow, Inst. of Int. Relations, Nat. Chengchi Univ. 1974–; Personal Sec. to the Pres. 1978–89; Dir-Gen. Govt Information Office, Govt Spokesman 1979–84; mem. Cen. Cttee Kuomintang 1981–, Dir-Gen. Dept of Cultural Affairs, Kuomintang 1984–87; Deputy Sec.-Gen., Cen. Cttee Kuomintang 1987–89, Sec.-Gen. 1989–93; mem. Cen. Standing Cttee 1988–; Gov., Taiwan Provincial Govt 1993–98; Presidential Cand. (Ind.) 2000; Man. Dir China TV Co. 1984–93, Taiwan TV Enterprise 1984–93; Chair. Hua-hsia Investment Corpn; Distinguished Visiting Fellow Inst. of East Asian Studies, Univ. of Calif. 1999; Eisenhower Fellowship 1982; several decorations. *Publications:* A Manual for Academic Writers, How to Write Academic Papers, Politics and Public Opinions in the United States, Keep Free China Free.

SOPE, Barak; Ni-Vanuatu politician and diplomatist; leading mem. Vanuaaku Pati (VP), Roving Amb.; mem. govts. 1980–87; defected from VP, f. Melanesian Progressive Party (MPP) 1987, Chair. 1987–; mem. coalition govts. 1993–96; Prime Minister of Vanuatu 1999–2001; Opposition Leader 2001–. *Address:* Melanesian Progressive Pati (MPP), P.O. Box 39, Port Vila, Vanuatu (Office). *Telephone:* 23485 (Office). *Fax:* 23315 (Office).

SOPHUSSON, Fridrik; Icelandic politician and business executive; b. 18 Oct. 1943, Reykjavik; m. Dr. Sigridur Duna Kristmundsdottir 1990; one d. (and five c. from first m.); ed Reykjavik Higher Secondary Grammar School and Univ. of Iceland; lawyer, part-time teacher Hlídaskóli School, Reykjavik 1963–67; Man. Icelandic Man. Asscn 1972–78; mem. Radio Council Icelandic State Broadcasting Service 1975–78; Nat. Research Council and Exec. Cttee of State Hosps. 1984–87; Cen. Cttee Independence Party 1969–77, 1981–99, Vice-Chair. 1981–89, 1991–99; Pres. Independence Party's Youth Fed. 1973–77; MP for Reykjavik 1978–98; Minister of Industry and Energy 1987–88, of Finance 1991–98; mem. Bd of Dirs Nat. Bank of Iceland 1990–92, Icelandic Church Aid 1990–92, Enex 2001–, Pharmaco 2002–, Samorka (Fed. of Electricity and Waterworks) 2001–, Icelandic Int. Chamber of Commerce 2001–, Nordel 2001–, Icelandic Chamber of Commerce 2002–; Man. Dir Landsvirkjun (Nat. Power Co.) 1999–. *Address:* Landsvirkjun, Haaleitisbraut 68, 103 Reykjavik, Iceland. *Telephone:* 5159000 (Office). *Fax:* 5159007 (Office). *E-mail:* fridrik@lv.is (Office). *Website:* www.lv.is (Office).

SORABJI, Richard Rustom Kharsedji, CBE, BPhil, MA, FBA; British professor emeritus of philosophy; b. 8 Nov. 1934, Brighton; s. of late Prof. Richard Kakushru Sorabji and Mary Katherine Sorabji (née Monkhouse); m. Margaret Anne Catherine Taster 1958; one s. two d.; ed Charterhouse, Pembroke Coll., Oxford Univ.; Assoc. Prof. Sage School of Philosophy, Cornell Univ. 1962–69; King's Coll. 1970–, Prof. of Ancient Philosophy 1981–2000, British Acad./Wolfson Research Prof. 1996–99, Designer, First Dir King's Coll. Centre for Philosophical Studies 1989–91; Gresham Prof. of Rhetoric and mem. Sr Common Room, Pembroke Coll. 2000–03; Supernumerary Fellow, Wolfson Coll. 1996–; Ranieri Distinguished Visiting Scholar, New York Univ. 2000–03; Adjunct Prof., Philosophy Dept, Univ. of Texas at Austin 2000–; Pres. Aristotelian Soc. 1985–86; founder, organizer int. project to translate the ancient commentators on Aristotle in 50 Vols 1985–; Dir Inst. of Classical Studies, London Univ. 1991–96; Foreign Hon. mem. American Acad. of Arts and Sciences 1997. *Publications:* Aristotle on Memory 1972, Necessity, Cause and Blame 1980, Time, Creation and the Continuum 1983, Matter, Space and Motion 1988, Animal Minds and Human Morals 1993, Emotion and Peace of Mind 2001; ed. numerous Vols on commentators on Aristotle. *Leisure interests:* archaeology, architecture. *Address:* Wolfson College, Oxford, OX1 4LJ, England. *Telephone:* (1865) 274100. *Fax:* (1865) 274125.

SØRENSEN, Bengt Algot, DPhil; Danish professor emeritus of German literature; b. 24 Nov. 1927, Aarhus; s. of Christian Sørensen and Selma Mellquist; m. Agnes M. Pedersen 1954; one s. two d.; ed Århus, Hamburg and Tübingen Univs; Lecturer in Scandinavian Languages and Literature, Bonn, Germany 1955–60; Lecturer in German Literature, Århus Univ. 1962–66; Prof. of German Literature, Odense Univ. 1966–97, Prof. Emer. 1997–; Visiting Prof. Univ. of Calif. at Irvine 1980, Univ. of Kiel 1983; Pres. Danish Research Council for the Humanities 1971–73; mem. Exec. Council European Science Foundation 1983–89; Vice-Pres. IVG (Int. Vereinigung der Germanistik) 1995–2000; mem. Royal Danish Acad. 1978–, Göttinger Akad. der Wissenschaften 1996–; Gold Medal, Univ. of Århus 1953. *Publications:* Symbol und Symbolismus 1963, Allegorie und Symbol 1972, Herrschaft und Zärtlichkeit 1984, Jens Peter Jacobsen 1990, Geschichte der deutschen Literatur Bd I, II 1997, Funde und Forschungen. Ausgewählte Essays 1997; numerous articles about Danish and German literature. *Leisure interests:* fishing, gardening. *Address:* University of Odense, 5230 Odense M (Office); Frederiksberg Alle 100, 1820 Frederiksberg, Denmark (Home). *Telephone:* 65-50-32-16 (Office); 66-17-64-99 (Home). *Fax:* 65-93-16-64.

SÓRENSEN, Jórgen Haugen; Danish sculptor; ed Coll. of Art and Design, Copenhagen; began as apprentice plasterer and potter; exhbns. at Museum of Modern Art New York, Yorks. Sculpture Park; works in collections in Denmark, England, Italy, Slovenia, Turkey, Olympic Sculpture Park, Seoul; Dir film JHS late 1960s; Prix de la Critique for JHS (Paris Biennale) 1963.

SORENSEN, Theodore Chaikin, B.S.L., LLB; American government official and lawyer; b. 8 May 1928, Lincoln, Nebraska; s. of Christian A. Sorensen and Annis Chaikin; m. Gillian Martin 1969; one d.; three s. from previous m.; ed Univ. of Nebraska; Attorney, Fed. Security Agency 1951–52; Staff Researcher, Joint Cttee on Railroad Retirement 1952–53; Asst to Senator John F. Kennedy 1953–61; Special Counsel to Presidents Kennedy and Johnson 1961–64; with law firm Paul, Weiss, Rifkind, Wharton & Garrison,

New York 1966–; Ed.-at-Large Saturday Review 1966–69; mem. Advisory Cttee for Trade Negotiations March 1979–81; Chair. Task Force on Political Action Cttees.; mem. Task Force on Foreign Policy 1986, Int. Trade Round Table 1986, Democratic Nat. Cttee 1981–82, Comm. on White House Fellows 1996–; Dir The Twentieth-Century Fund 1984– (Chair. 1994–99), Council on Foreign Relations 1993–, Nat. Democratic Inst. for Int. Affairs 1993–99, Cen. Asian-American Enterprise Fund 1995–99; Chair. U.S.-Japanese Program Cttee of Japan Soc. 1990; Trustee The New York Acad. of Medicine 1991–97; Democrat. *Publications:* Decision-Making in The White House 1963, Kennedy 1964, The Kennedy Legacy 1970, Watchmen in the Night: Presidential Accountability After Watergate 1975, A Different Kind of Presidency 1984, A Widening Atlantic? Domestic Change and Foreign Policy (co-author Ralf Dahrendorf) 1986, Let the World go Forth: The Speeches, Statements and Writings of John F. Kennedy (Ed.) 1988, Why I Am a Democrat 1996. *Address:* c/o Paul, Weiss, Rifkind, Wharton and Garrison, Room 200, 1285 Avenue of the Americas, New York, NY 10019, USA (Office). *Telephone:* (212) 373-3000.

SORENSTAM, Annika; Swedish golfer; b. 9 Oct. 1970, Stockholm; m. David Esch; ed Univ. of Arizona, USA; World Amateur Champion 1992; champion in USA (three wins including US Women's Open) and Europe (two wins) 1995; winner World Championship, Repub. of Korea, Australian Masters 1995; other victories include Rite LPGA Classic 1998, JAL Big Apple Classic 1998, SAFECO Classic 1998, Michelob Light Classic 1999, Welch's Circle, K Championships 2000, 2001, Firstar LPGA Classic 2000, Evian Masters 2000, 2002, Cisco World Ladies' Match Play 2001, Samsung World Championship 2002; first woman to shoot 59 in an LPGA Tour tournament 2001; first woman to win 10 million dollars in golf prize money; lives in Nevada, USA; Rookie of the Year 1993, Sports Personality of the Year, Sweden 1995, Vare Trophy Award 1998. *Leisure interests:* sports, music, cooking. *Address:* LPGA, 100 International Golf Drive, Daytona Beach, FL 32124, USA (Office).

SORHAINDO, Crispin; Dominican politician; b. 23 May 1931, Vieille Case; s. of Clive Sorhaindo and Rosa Frederick; m. Ruby Etheldreda Allport 1956; two s. four d.; Speaker House of Ass. –1993; fmr Sr Official Caribbean Devt Bank (CDB); Pres. of Dominica 1993–98. *Leisure interests:* reading, gardening. *Address:* Morne Prosper, P.O. Box 572, Roseau, Dominica. *Telephone:* 448-8787. *Fax:* 449-8920.

SOROKIN, Vladimir Georgiyevich; Russian writer and painter; b. 7 Aug. 1955, Bykovo, Moscow Region; m. Sorokina Irina Igorevna; two d.; ed Moscow Gubkin Inst. of Oil and Gas Industry; worked as artistic Smena 1979–80; freelance 1980–; was not published in USSR until 1987; mem. Union of Russian Writers, Union of Graphic Artists of Russia, Russian PEN Centre; scholarship of Deutsche Akademische Austauschung Dienst 1992. *Publications include:* The Queue (novel) 1985, Thirteenth Love of Marina (novel) 1993, Obelisk (short stories) 1994, The Hearts of the Four 1994 (novel), The Norm (selected texts) 1994, A Novel 1994, Blue Lard 1999. *Leisure interests:* chess, cooking. *Address:* Proyezd Odoyevskogo 7, korp. 5, Apt. 621, Moscow, Russia (Home). *Telephone:* (095) 422-67-39 (Home).

SOROS, George; Hungarian investment banker and philanthropist; b. 12 Aug. 1930, Budapest; ed London School of Econs; moved to England 1947; much influenced by work of philosopher Karl Popper; with Singer & Friedlander (merchant bankers), London; moved to Wall Street, New York 1956; set up pvt. mutual fund, Quantum Fund, registered in Curaçao 1969; since 1991 has created other funds, Quasar Int., Quota, Quantum Emerging Growth Fund (merged with Quantum Fund to form Quantum Endowment Fund 2000), Quantum Realty Trust; Pres. and Chair. Soros Fund Man. LLC, New York 1973–; philanthropist since 1979, provided funds to help black students attend Cape Town Univ., SA; set up Open Soc. Fund (currently Chair. Open Soc. Inst.) 1979, Soros Foundations, Cen. European Univ., Budapest 1992; f. Global Power Investments 1994; Dr hc (New School for Social Research, Univ. of Oxford, Budapest Univ. of Econs, Yale Univ.); Laurea hc (Univ. of Bologna) 1995. *Publication:* The Alchemy of Finance 1987, Opening the Soviet System 1990, Underwriting Democracy 1991, Soros on Soros: Staying Ahead of the Curve (jtly) 1995, The Crisis of Global Capitalism: Open Society Engendered 1998, Open Society: Reforming Global Capitalism 2000, George Soros on Globalization 2002; numerous essays on politics, society and econs in major int. newspapers and magazines. *Address:* Soros Fund Management, 888 7th Avenue, 3300 New York, NY 10106, USA.

SOROUR, Ahmed Fathi, BSc, MA, PhD; Egyptian politician and academic; b. 9 July 1932, Cairo; s. of Motafa Kamel Sorour and Fatma Ali Hassan; m. Zeinab El-Housseiny; one s. two d.; ed Cairo Univ., Univ. of Michigan; Deputy Attorney Gen. 1953–59; Prof. of Criminal Law, Cairo Univ. 1959–, Head of Dept 1978–83, Dean of Faculty of Law 1983–85, Vice-Pres. Cairo Univ. 1985–86; Minister of Educ. 1986–90; Speaker People's Ass. 1990–; Pres. Union of African Parls. 1990–91; Pres. Inter-parl. Union 1994–97; Pres. Arab Parl. Union 1998–2000; Pres. Union of Islamic Parls. 2000–; Sciences and Art Medal 1964, 1983, Highest Homala Decoration of Alawi Throne, Morocco 1987, Ordre de la Pleiade, Assemblée Internationale des Parlementaires des Francophones 1992; Highest Distinction Award in Social Sciences 1993. *Publications:* Theory of Nullity 1959, Offences Against Public Interest 1963, Penal Law (parts I and II) 1980, Criminal Procedures Law 1993, Constitutional Legality and Human Rights 1995, Constitutional Protection of Rights and Liberties 2000, Criminal Constitutional Law 2001. *Address:* 11583 Maglis Al-Shaab, Cairo, Egypt (Office). *Telephone:* (2) 7943130 (Office). *Fax:* (2) 7943116 (Office).

SORRELL, John William, CBE, FCSD, FRSA; British designer; b. 28 Feb. 1945, London; s. of the late John William Sorrell and of Elizabeth Jane Sorrell (née Taylor); m. Frances Mary Newell (q.v.) 1974; two s. one d.; ed Hornsey Coll. of Art; designer, Maine Wolff & Partners 1964; partner Goodwin Sorrell 1964–71; Design Man. Wolff Olins 1971–76; Founder and Co-Chair. Newell and Sorrell 1976–97, Chair. Newell and Sorrell (now Interbrand Newell and Sorrell) 1983–2000; Vice-Pres. Chartered Soc. of Designers 1989–92; Chair. DBA 1990–92, Design Council 1994–2000; mem. British Rail Architecture and Design Panel 1991–93, RSA Design Advisory Group 1991–93, D & AD Strategic Planning Soc., Inst. of Design, New Millennium Experience Co. Creative Review Group 1998–2000 (and 'Godparent' for Identity Zone), Panel 2000, Dept of Trade & Industry's Encouraging Competitiveness Working Party 1998; Co-Founder the Sorroll Foundation 1999–; Gov. Design Dimension 1991–93; Chair. NHS London Design Advisory Group 2000–; Co-Chair. British Abroad Task Force 2000–; Hon. mem. Romanian Design Centre; Hon. D. Design (De Montfort) 1997, Dr. hc (London Inst.) 1999; R.S.A.'s Bicentenary Medal 1998. *Publications:* Secret of Design Effectiveness 1995, Utopian Nights 1996, Utopian Papers 1996–. *Leisure interests:* arboriculture, Arsenal Football Club, art, film. *Address:* The Lawns, 16 South Grove, London, N6 6BJ, England (Office).

SORRELL, Sir Martin Stuart, Kt, MA, MBA; British advertising executive; b. 14 Feb. 1945, London; s. of the late Jack Sorrell and of Sally Sorrell; m. Sandra Finestone 1971; three s.; ed Haberdashers' Aske's School, Christ's Coll. Cambridge and Harvard Business School, USA; consultant, Glendinning Assocs, Westport, Conn. 1968–69; Vice-Pres. Mark McCormack Org. 1970–74; Dir James Gulliver Assocs. 1975–77; Group Financial Dir Saatchi and Saatchi Co. PLC 1977–84; Founder and Group Chief Exec. WPP Group PLC 1986–; Dir Storehouse PLC 1994–97; Dir (non-exec.) Colefax and Fowler Group PLC 1997–; mem. Advisory Bd Int. Grad. School of Man., Univ. of Navarra 1989–, Judge Inst. for Man. Studies, Univ. of Cambridge 1990–, IBM 1997–, Advisory Bd, ATP 2001–; mem. Bd Dirs of Assocs, Harvard Business School 1998–, Bd Dean's Advisors 1998–; Dir (non-exec.) Colefax & Fowler; FCO Amb. for British Business 1997–99, mem. Panel 2000 2000–; mem. Council for Excellence in Man. and Leadership; Corp. Advisory Group, Tate Gallery 2000–, Bd Nat. Assen of Securities Dealers Automated Quotation System (NASDAQ) 2001–, Advisory Bd IESE, Spain, Dean's Advisory Council, Boston Univ., Bd Indian School of Business; Deputy Chair. and Gov. London Business School 1990–; Trustee Cambridge Foundation, Royal Coll. of Art Foundation; Patron Cambridge Alumni in Man., Queen Charlotte's Appeal at Hammersmith Hosp.; Hon. DBA (London Guildhall Univ.) 2001. *Leisure interests:* family, skiing, cricket. *Address:* WPP Group PLC, 27 Farm Street, London, W1J 5RJ, England. *Telephone:* (20) 7408-2204 (Office). *Fax:* (20) 7493-6819 (Office).

SORSA, (Taisto) Kalevi, M.SC.S.; Finnish politician and business executive; b. 21 Dec. 1930, Keuruu; s. of Kaarlo O. Sorsa and Elsa S. Sorsa (née Leinonen); m. Elli Irene Lääkäri 1953; ed Univ. of Tampere; Chief Ed., Vihuri 1954–56; Literary Ed. Tammi (publishing house) 1956–59; Programme Asst/Specialist UNESCO 1959–65; Sec.-Gen. of Finnish UNESCO Cttee 1965–69; Deputy Dir Ministry of Educ. 1967–69; Sec.-Gen. Social Democratic Party 1969–75, Pres. 1975–87; mem. Parl. 1970–91; Minister Foreign Affairs Feb.–Sept. 1972, 1975–76, 1979–82; Prime Minister 1972–75, 1977–79, 1982–87; Deputy Prime Minister and Minister of Foreign Affairs 1987–89; Speaker of Parl. 1989–91; mem. Man. Bd, Bank of Finland 1991–96; Chair. Foreign Affairs Cttee 1970–72, 1977, 1979–82, Socialist Int. Study Group on Disarmament 1978–80, Socialist Int. Advisory Council 1980–96, Vice-Pres. 1980–96; Chair. Bd of Admin. Finnair 1981–94, Chair. Bd of Finnair 1994–97; Nat. Defence Council 1982–87, Soviet-Finnish Comm. on Econ. Co-operation 1983–89; Dir Bank of Finland until 1996 (retd); Commdr Grand Cross Order of the White Rose of Finland; Grand Cross, Order of Orange-Nassau; Grand Cross, Order of the Icelandic Falcon; Great Golden Decoration with Ribbon, Order of Merit of Austria; Grand Cross of the Order of Merit, People's Repub. of Poland; Grand Cross, Order of the North Star of Sweden; Grand Star, Order of the Star of Friendship between Peoples (GDR); Grand Cross, Order of San Marino; Grand Cross, Order of Merit of the Repub. of Senegal; Grand Cross, Order of Dannebrog (Denmark); Order of the Banner of Hungary (Second Class); Grand Cross of the Order of Merit (FRG); Grand Cross, Order of the Southern Cross (Brazil); Grand Cross, Order of the Star (Jordan); Grand Cross, Order of Isabella The Catholic (Spain); Order of Trishakti-Patta (First Class), Nepal; Hon. KCMG; Dr hc (Tampere). *Publications:* seven books of essays and memoirs. *Leisure interests:* the arts, social and international questions, outdoor life. *Address:* Hakaniemenranta 16D, 00530 Helsinki, Finland. *Telephone:* 7734363. *Fax:* 7536118. *E-mail:* kalevi .sorsa@kolumbus.fi (Home).

SORVINO, Mira, AB; American actress; b. 28 Sept. 1968; d. of Paul Sorvino; ed Harvard Univ.; Acad. Award Best Supporting Actress (for Mighty Aphrodite). *Film appearances include:* Amongst Friends 1993 (also assoc. producer), The Second Greatest Story Ever Told 1993, Quiz Show 1994, Parallel Lives 1994, Barcelona 1994, Tarantella 1995, Sweet Nothing 1995, Mighty Aphrodite 1995, The Dutch Master 1995, Blue in the Face 1995, Beautiful Girls 1996, Norma Jean and Marilyn 1996, Jake's Women 1996, Romy and Michele's High School Reunion 1997, The Replacement Killers 1997, Mimic 1997, Summer of Sam 1999, At First Sight 1999, Joan of Arc: The Virgin

Warrior 2000. *Television includes:* The Great Gatsby 2000. *Address:* c/o Michelle Stern, The William Morris Agency, 1325 Avenue of the Americas, New York, NY 10019, USA.

SOSA PIETRI, Andrés; Venezuelan business executive; b. 1943, Caracas; ed Univ. Católica Andrés Bello and Harvard Univ., USA; fmr legal consultant, petrochemical sector; later ran group of cos. manufacturing valves and other specialized products for petroleum industry; served briefly as ind. Senator representing MAS (Venezuela's Socialist Party) in 1970s; Chair. Petróleos de Venezuela, SA (PDVSA) 1991. *Address:* c/o Petróleos de Venezuela SA, Torre Este, Avda Liberator, La Campiña, Apdo 169, Caracas 1010-A, Venezuela.

SOSKOVETS, Oleg Nikolayevich; Russian politician; b. 11 May 1949, Taldy-Kurgan, Kazakh SSR (now Kazakhstan); m. Evgenia Valentinovna Soskovets; one s. one d.; ed High School of Karaganda Metallurgic Plant; mem. CPSU 1972–91; rolling mill operator, foreman, chief of workshop Karaganda Metallurgic plant 1971–84; chief engineer, Deputy Dir 1984–87, Dir 1987–88, Dir Gen. 1988–91; USSR People's Deputy 1989–91; USSR Minister of Metallurgy April–Nov. 1991; Pres. Roschermet 1992; First Deputy Prime Minister of Kazakhstan, Minister of Industry 1992; Chair. Cttee on Metallurgy of Russian Fed. 1992–96; First Deputy Prime Minister of Russia 1993–96; Founder, Chair. of Bd and Pres. Asscn of Finance-Industrial Groups 1996–. *Publications:* more than 100 works on problems of metallurgic production.

SOTIN, Hans; German opera and concert singer; b. 10 Sept. 1939, Dortmund; m. Regina Elsner 1964; three c.; ed Dortmund Musikhochschule; with Opera House, Essen 1962–64; State Opera, Hamburg 1964–, State Opera, Vienna 1970–; perm. mem. Bayreuth Festival 1971–; guest appearances worldwide; pvt. singing teacher; Forderpreis des Landes, Friedrich Oberdörfer Preis, Kammersänger. *Recordings include:* Tannhäuser, Aida, Fidelio, Salome, Così fan tutte, Die Walküre, Parisfal, Paukenmesse. *Address:* c/o Askonas Holt Ltd, Lonsdale Chambers, 27 Chancery Lane, London, WC2A 1PF, England; 2106 Bendestorf, Schulheide 10, Germany. *Telephone:* (4183) 6614.

SOTKILAVA, Zurab Lavrentievich; Georgian tenor; b. 12 March 1937, Sukhumi; m.; two d.; ed Tbilisi Polytech. Inst., Tbilisi Conservatory; professional football-player in Dynamo, Tbilisi; soloist Tbilisi Opera Theatre 1965–74; Prof. Tbilisi Conservatory 1976–88; with Bolshoi Theatre 1974–; toured with Bolshoi and independently in Europe and America; Hon. Academician Boston Acad. of Arts; People's Artist of USSR and Georgia; Grand Prize Gold Orpheus Festival (Bulgaria) 1986, Second Prize Int. Tchaikovsky Competition (1970), Grand Priz Barcelona Competition 1970. *Operatic roles include:* Vodemon (Iolanthe), Absalom (Absalom and Eteri), Cavaradossi (Tosca), Richard (Un Ballo in Maschera), Manrico (Il Trovatore), Radames (Aida), José (Carmen), Otello and others. *Address:* Bolshoi Theatre, Teatralnaya pl. 1, Moscow, Russia. *Telephone:* (095) 244-07-31 (Home).

SOTO, Jesús-Rafael; Venezuelan artist; b. 5 June 1923, Ciudad Bolívar; ed School of Fine Arts, Caracas; Dir, School of Fine Arts, Maracaibo, Venezuela 1947–50; in Paris since 1950; early exponent of "optical art"; various films made on works in field of kinetic art and vibrations since 1958; one-man exhbns. at Caracas 1949, 1957, 1961, Paris 1956, 1959, 1962, 1965, 1967, 1969, 1970, 1979, Brussels 1957, Essen 1961, Antwerp 1962, Stuttgart 1964, New York 1965, 1966, 1971, 1974, 1996, Retrospective Exhbn, Signals, London 1965, Galerie Hermanns, Munich 1989, Galeria Theo, Madrid 1990, 1992, Khan Gallery, New York 1994 and others; represented in perm. collections including: Tate Gallery, London, Museum of Fine Arts, Caracas, Albright-Knox Art Gallery, Buffalo, Cali Inst. of Fine Arts, Cali, Colombia, Stedelijk Museum, Amsterdam, Museum of Contemporary Arts, São Paulo, Moderna Museet, Stockholm, Kaiser Foundation, Córdoba, Argentina, Palace of Fine Arts, Brussels, Kröller-Müller Museum, Otterloo, Holland, Museum of Modern Art, Jerusalem; numerous prizes including Wolf Prize, São Paulo Bienal 1963, David Bright Foundation Prize, Venice Biennale 1964, Picasso Medal 1981, 1990, other awards and prizes, several hon. degrees. *Major works include:* sculpture for garden of School of Architecture, Univ. City of Caracas, two murals and sculpture for Venezuelan pavilion, Brussels Exhbn 1958. *Address:* 10 rue Villehardouin, 75003 Paris, France.

SOTOMAYOR, Antonio, FRSA; Bolivian painter; b. 1904, Chulumani; s. of Carmen Celina Meza and Juan Sotomayor; m. Grace La Mora Andrews 1926; ed La Paz School of Applied Arts; awarded first prize of Nat. Exposition of Painting 1921; Award of Honor (City and County of San Francisco) 1978. *Works include:* El Crucifijo, Copacabana, Lavanderas, Funeral Aimara, Alacitas, Madre, Rezando Reposo, Historical Murals Palace Hotel and Sharon Building, San Francisco, Murals at Sonoma Mission Inn, Calif., Mural El Tigero, Hillsborough, Calif.; murals Peruvian Pavilion and terra cotta fountain Pacific Area, Theme Building, Golden Gate, Int. Exposition 1939–40, Murals, San Francisco; Art Faculty, Mills Coll. and Calif. School of Fine Arts; Mural Altarpiece, St Augustine Church, Pleasanton, Calif., Glass Mosaic Façade, Hillsdale Methodist Church, Calif.; Mural, Matson Navigation Co., San Francisco, Calif.; Murals, Grace Cathedral, San Francisco, Calif.; backdrop for San Francisco Civic Auditorium Concerts; Altarpiece, Church of St Francis, Nuevo Progreso, Guatemala; Mural, Peruvian Embassy, Washington, DC; Chapel Altarpiece, La Casa de los Pobres, Tihuana, Mexico. *Publications:* Pinturas interpretativas de indígenas de Bolivia 1929, Pinturas con motivos mejicanos 1930, Khasa Goes to the Fiesta 1967, Balloons 1972. *Leisure interests:* music, travel. *Address:* 3 Le Roy Place, San Francisco, CA 94109, USA. *Telephone:* (415) 673-6193.

SOTOMAYOR, Javier; Cuban athlete; b. 13 Oct. 1967, Limonar; m. María del Carmen García; first man to jump over eight feet; set world indoor record (7ft. 11.5in.) 1989 and world outdoor record (8ft. 0.5in.) 1993, both still stand as at end Dec. 2002; has cleared above 2.30m. in 227 events; Olympic gold medallist 1992, silver 2000; World Championships gold medallist 1993, 1997, silver 1991, 1995; achieved best height Pan-Amerian Games, Winnipeg 1999; disqualified after failing cocaine test and prevented from competing again until Aug. 2000 by Int. Asscn of Athletics Feds. (IAAF); finished 5th in World Indoor Championships March 2001; retd Oct. 2001; voted Best Cuban Athlete of the Century.

SOTTSASS, Ettore; Italian architect; b. 1917, Innsbruck, Austria; ed Turin Polytechnic; f. architectural and design co. 1947; design consultant Olivetti 1958–; co.-f. Memphis Group 1981; co.-f. Sottsass Associati 1981; with Zanotta 1981; Dr. hc RCA; Officer Ordre des Arts et des Lettres 1992, Brooklyn Museum Award 1996, Oribe Award (Japan) 1997. *Recent projects include:* architectural designs for Milan Airport, housing estates in Belgium, China, Hong Kong and town planning for Seoul. *Exhibitions include:* Italy, The New Domestic Landscape, Museum of Modern Art, New York, Biennale, Venice 1976. *Publications:* articles for Domus and Casabella magazines. *Address:* Via Melone 2, 20121 Milan, Italy (Office). *Telephone:* 3624981 (Office). *Fax:* 362451038 (Office).

SOULAGES, Pierre; French painter; b. 24 Dec. 1919, Rodez; m. Colette Llaurens 1942; ed Lycée de Rodez; exhibited abstract painting since 1947 in Salon des Surindépendants, Salon de Mai et Réalités Nouvelles; exhibited in int. festivals including Biennales of Venice and São Paulo and the itinerary of the Guggenheim Collection, the Carnegie Inst., Pittsburgh, The New Decade at the Museum of Modern Art, New York, Tate Gallery, London, etc.; also décors for theatres and ballet; and lithographs and engravings. Works in Museums of Modern Art, Paris and NY, Tate Gallery, London, Guggenheim Museum, NY, Phillips Gallery, Washington, Museum of Modern Art, Rio de Janeiro, museums in many American cities, in Europe, Australia and Japan; retrospective solo exhbns. Hanover, Essen, The Hague, Zürich 1960–61, Ljubljana 1961, MIT 1962, Copenhagen Glyptothek 1963, Fine Arts Museum, Houston 1966, Musée Nat. d'Art Moderne, Paris 1967; Carnegie Inst., Pittsburgh, Albright Knox Art Gallery, Buffalo, Musée de Québec, Musée d'Art Contemporain, Montréal 1968, Oslo, Aalborg, Neuchâtel, Charleroi 1973, Musée Dynamique, Dakar 1974, Gulbenkian Foundation, Lisbon, Museo de arte contemporáneo, Madrid, Musée Fabre, Montpellier, Museo de Arte Moderno, Mexico City 1975, Museu de Arte Moderna, Rio de Janeiro, Museo de Arte Moderno, Caracas 1976, Museu de Arte Contemporâneo, São Paulo 1976, Centre Georges Pompidou, Paris 1979, Musée du Parc de la Boverie, Liège 1980, Kunstlerhaus, Salzburg 1980, Kunstbygning, Århus; Kunstpavillon, Esbjerg; Palais de Charlottenborg, Copenhagen 1982; Musée d'Unterlinden, Colmar 1983; Museum Seibu, Tokyo 1984; Pulchri Studio, The Hague 1985, Galerie de France 1986, Museum Fridecianum, Kassel, IVAM, Valencia, Musée des Beaux-Arts, Nantes 1989, Galleries Tollarno, Melbourne 1989, Galerie Fandos, Valencia, Galerie Pauli, Lausanne 1990, Museum Moderner Kunst, Vienna 1991, Nat. Museum of Contemporary Art, Seoul, Nat. Palace of Fine Arts, Beijing, Nat. Museum of Fine Arts, Taiwan 1993, Musée d'art moderne de la Ville de Paris 1996, Fine Arts Museum, Montréal 1996, Museu de Arte, São Paulo 1996, Deichtorhallen, Hamburg 1997, Centro de Exposiciones y Congresos, Saragossa 1997, Sala Cultural Rioja, Logroño 1998, Kunstmuseum, Berne 1999, Musée Fabre, Montpelier 1999, Les Abattoirs, Toulouse 2000, The Hermitage, St Petersburg 2001, Galerie Tretiakof, Moscow 2001; Hon. mem. American Acad. of Arts and Letters; Commdr Légion d'honneur, des Arts et des Lettres, Grand Officier, ordre nat. du Mérite; Grand Prix, Tokyo Biennale 1957, Carnegie Prize, Pittsburgh, USA 1964, Grand Prix des Arts de la Ville de Paris 1975, Rembrandt Prize, Germany, 1976, Prix Nat. de Peinture, Paris 1986, Praemium Imperiale, Tokyo 1992. *Solo exhibitions include:* Lydia Conti Gallery, Paris 1949, Birch Gallery, Copenhagen 1951, Stangl Gallery, Munich 1952, Kootz Gallery, New York 1954–65, Gimpel Gallery, London 1955–67, Galerie de France, Paris 1956–92, Knoedler Gallery 1968, Galerie Protée, Toulouse 1972, Galerie Rieder, Munich 1987–99, Galerie Jade, Colmar 1991, Galerie H. Strelow, Düsseldorf 1997, Galerie A. Pauli, Lausanne 1990–2000, Galerie Karsten Frère, Paris 2002. *Address:* 18 rue des Trois-Portes, 75005 Paris, France. *Website:* pierre-soulages.com (Office).

SOULEZ-LARIVIÈRE, Daniel Joseph; French lawyer and writer; b. 19 March 1942, Angers (Maine-et-Loire); s. of Furcy Soulez-Larivière and Suzanne Soulez-Larivière (née Larivière); m. Mathilde-Mahaut Nobecourt 1988; one s. (and one s. with Michèle Abbaye); ed Lycée Janson-de-Sailly, Collège Stanislas, Paris, Garden City High School, New York, USA and Faculty of Law, Paris; lawyer in Paris 1965–; Chargé de mission, Ministry of Equipment and Housing 1966–67; Second Sec. Conférence du stage 1969; mem. Conseil de l'Ordre 1988–90; mem. Consultative Comm. for the Revision of the Constitution 1992–93; mem. Advisory Bd Centre de prospective de la gendarmerie; Municipal Counsellor for Chambellay 1995–; mem. Soc. of French Jurists; Chevalier, Ordre nat. du Mérite. *Publications include:* L'avocature 1982, Les juges dans la balance 1987, La réforme des professions juridiques et judiciaires, vingt propositions 1988, Justice pour la justice 1990, Du cirque médiatico-judiciaire et des moyens d'en sortir 1993, Paroles d'avocat 1994, Grand soir pour la justice 1997, Dans l'engrenage de la justice 1998, Lettres à un jeune avocat 1999, La justice à l'épreuve (jtly with Jean-

Marie Coulon) 2002. *Leisure interest:* hunting. *Address:* 2 avenue de la Grande Armée, 75017 Paris (Office); 6 rue des Fougères, 92140 Clamart (Home); le Prieuré, 49220 Chambellay, France (Home).

SOULIOTI, Stella; Cypriot politician and lawyer; b. 13 Feb. 1920, Limassol; d. of Panayiotis Cacoyannis and Angeliki Cacoyannis; sister of Michael Cacoyannis; m. Demetrios Souliotis 1949; one d.; ed Cyprus, Egypt and Gray's Inn, London; joined Women's Auxiliary Air Force, Nicosia and served in Middle East 1943–46; called to the Bar, London 1951; law practice, Limassol 1952–60; Minister of Justice 1960–70, concurrently Minister of Health 1964–66; Law Commr 1971–84; Attorney-Gen. 1984–88; Co-ordinator of Foreign Aid to Cyprus Refugees 1974–; Adviser to Pres. of Cyprus on Cyprus Problem 1976–; Chair. Cyprus Overseas Relief Fund 1977–82; Visiting Fellow Wolfson Coll. Cambridge 1982–83; Pres. Cyprus Red Cross 1981–, Cyprus Scholarship Board 1962–; Chair. Cyprus Town and Country Planning Cttee 1967–70; Vice-Pres. Cyprus Anti-Cancer Soc. 1971–; Trustee Cambridge Commonwealth Scholarship Trust for Cyprus 1983–; mem. Exec. Bd UNESCO 1987–91; Hon. Vice-Pres. Int. Fed. of Women Lawyers 1967–; Hon. LLD (Nottingham) 1972. *Leisure interests:* reading, writing, music, theatre. *Address:* P.O. Box 24102, 1701 Nicosia, Cyprus. *Telephone:* 22666955.

SOUMAKIS, Stavros Aristidi; Greek politician and medical practitioner; b. 18 Sept. 1951, Piraeus; m. Alexandra Papadopoulou; one d.; ed Athens Univ. Medical School; practised as doctor in various hosps., Piraeus 1979–86, as obstetrician and gynaecologist, Helena maternity clinic –1993; Founder-mem. Panhellenic Socialist Students' Movt, Panhellenic Fighting Movt 1969; mem. Panhellenic Socialist Movt (PASOK) 1974–; elected Town Councillor, Piraeus 1982, 1986; elected an MP for Piraeus 1993; Minister of Merchant Marine 1996–2000; mem. Cen. Cttee PASOK, Sec. Econ. Section, mem. Health Cttee; Chair. Admin. Bd Metaxa Hosp., Piraeus 1983–87; Sec. Doctors' Professional Syndicate. *Address:* c/o Ministry of Merchant Marine, Odos Grigoriou Lambraki 150, 186 18 Piraeus, Greece (Office).

SOUSA, Manuel Inocêncio; Cape Verde politician; b. 1951; fmr Minister of the Communities; Minister of Foreign Affairs, Co-operation and Communities 2001–02; Sr Minister of Infrastructure and Transport 2002–. *Address:* Ministry of Infrastructure and Transport, Ponta Belém, Praia, Santiago, Cape Verde (Office). *Telephone:* 61-56-99 (Office). *Fax:* 61-48-22 (Office).

SOUSA, Maria das Neves Ceita Baptista de; São Tomé e Príncipe politician and economist; b. 1958; two c.; ed Univ. of the East, Santiago de Cuba, Cuba; fmr economist World Bank and UNICEF; mem. Movimento Democrático das Forças para a Mudança–Partido de Convergência Democrática (Democratic Movement of Forces for Change–Party for Democratic Convergence); Minister of Trade, Industry and Tourism and Minister of the Economy –2002; Prime Minister of São Tomé e Príncipe (first woman premier in W Africa) Oct. 2002–. *Address:* Office of the Prime Minister, Rua do Município, CP 302, São Tomé, São Tomé e Príncipe (Office). *Telephone:* (12) 23913 (Office). *Fax:* (12) 24679 (Office).

SOUSA FRANCO, António L. P. de, PhD; Portuguese politician and professor of law; b. 21 Sept. 1942, Lisbon; s. of António de Sousa Franco and Maria de Jesus Pacheco; m. Maria Matilde Pessoa Figueiredo de Sousa Franco 1983; one d.; ed Univ. of Lisbon; Univ. Prof. Schools of Law, Lisbon, Coimbra and Portuguese Catholic Univs; Dean, Schools of Law, Univ. of Lisbon 1979–85, Portuguese Catholic Univ. 1989–95; Man. SACOR (oil-refining enterprise) 1968–72, Nat. Petrochemical Co. 1972–74, Caixa Geral Depósitos e Previdência 1974–75; mem. Parl. 1976–79, 1980–81; mem. Parl. Ass. for NATO 1978–79; Sec. of State for Treasury 1976; Minister of Finance 1979, 1995–99; Pres. Portuguese Court of Auditors 1986–95; Pres. PSD-Social Democratic Party 1977–78; mem. Acad. of Sciences; numerous professional appointments and affiliations; Grã Cruz da Ordem Militar de Cristo; decorations from Italy and Brazil; five academic awards. *Publications:* over 1,000 Publs on politics, Econs, finance etc. *Leisure interests:* history studies, travel, reading, tennis. *Address:* Rua de S. Bernardo 38, R/c Dto, 1200 Lisbon, Portugal (Home).

SOUTER, Brian; British business executive; b. 1954; s. of Iain Souter and Catherine Souter; m. Elizabeth McGoldrick 1988; two s. one d.; ed Dundee Univ., Univ. of Strathclyde; fmrly trainee accountant; f. Stagecoach Selkent bus co. with sister Ann Gloag (q.v.); Chair. Stagecoach Holdings 1980–2002, CEO 2002–. *Address:* Stagecoach Holdings PLC, 10 Dunkeld Road, Perth, PH1 5TW, Scotland (Office). *Telephone:* (1738) 442-111 (Office). *Fax:* (1738) 643-648 (Office). *E-mail:* info@stagecoachgroup.com (Office). *Website:* www .stagecoachplc.com (Office).

SOUTER, David Hackett, BA, LLB; American judge; b. 17 Sept. 1939, Melrose, Mass.; s. of Joseph A. Souter and Helen A. Hackett; ed Harvard Univ. and Univ. of Oxford, UK; admitted NH Bar; Assoc. Orr & Reno, Concord 1966–68; Asst Attorney-Gen. NH 1968–71, Deputy Attorney-Gen. 1971–76, Attorney-Gen. 1976–78; Assoc. Justice, NH Superior Court 1978–83, NH Supreme Court 1983–90; Assoc. Justice US Supreme Court 1990–; mem. American Bar Asscn, NH Bar Asscn. *Address:* US Supreme Court, Supreme Court Building, 1 First Street, NE, Washington, DC 20543, USA.

SOUTHALL, Ivan Francis, AM, DFC; Australian author; b. 8 June 1921, Melbourne; s. of Francis Southall and Rachel Southall (née Voutier); m. 1st Joyce Blackburn 1945 (divorced); one s. three d.; m. 2nd Susan W. Stanton 1976; ed Box Hill Grammar School; RAAF 1942–47; self-employed writer 1947–; Whitall Poetry and Literature Lecturer, Library of Congress 1973;

May Hill Arbuthnot Honor Lecturer 1974; Emer. Fellowship, Australia Council 1993; State Library of Vic. Retrospective exhbn, 'Southall A to Z' 1998; Australian Children's Book of the Year Award 1966, 1968, 1971, 1976, Australian Picture Book of the Year Award 1969, Carnegie Medal 1972, Nat. Children's Book Award 1986, The Phoenix Award 2003. *Publications:* over 60 works translated into 22 languages including They Shall Not Pass Unseen 1956, Softly Tread the Brave 1960, Hills End 1962, Ash Road 1965, To the Wild Sky 1967, The Fox Hole 1967, Let the Balloon Go 1968, Bread and Honey 1970, Josh 1971, Fly West 1974, Matt and Jo 1974, What About Tomorrow 1976, King of the Sticks 1979, The Golden Goose 1981, The Long Night Watch 1983, A City out of Sight 1984, Christmas in the Tree 1985, Rachel 1986, Blackbird 1988, The Mysterious World of Marcus Leadbeater 1990, Ziggurat 1997. *Leisure interests:* house and garden. *Address:* PO Box 1698, Healesville, Vic. 3777, Australia.

SOUTHAM, Gordon Hamilton, OC; Canadian civil servant (retd); b. 19 Dec. 1916, Ottawa; s. of Wilson Mills Southam and Henrietta Alberta Southam (née Cargill); m. 1st Jacqueline Lambert-David 1940 (divorced 1968); three s. one d.; m. 2nd Gro Mortensen 1968 (divorced 1978); one s. one d.; m. 3rd Marion Tantot 1981; ed Ashbury Coll., Trinity Coll., Toronto and Christ Church, Oxford; Officer, Second World War, British and Canadian Armies 1939–45; Reporter The Times, London 1945–46; Editorial Writer Ottawa Citizen 1946–47; joined Dept of External Affairs 1948; Second Sec., Stockholm 1949–53, Ottawa 1953–59; Chargé d'affaires, Warsaw 1959–60, Amb. 1960–62; Head Information Div., Dept of External Affairs 1962–64; Dir Southam Inc. 1964–87; Founder and Co-ordinator, Nat. Arts Centre 1964–67, Dir-Gen. 1967–77; Chair. Festival Canada Cttee 1978–79, Nat. Theatre School, Montréal 1979–81; Founder and Pres. Canadian Mediterranean Inst. 1980–86, Chair. 1986–92, Hon. Fellow 1992–; Chair. Rideau Canal Museum, Smiths Falls 1984–92, Hon. Chair. 1992–; Chair. Official Residences Council 1985–93; Chancellor Univ. of King's Coll. 1988–96; Co-Chair. Task Force on Mil. History Museums 1990–91; Founder and Vice-Pres. (France) Canadian Battle of Normandy Foundation 1991–98, Vice-Pres. 1998–; Founder and Pres. Valiant Nine Foundation 2001–; Hon. LLD (Univ. of Trent, Carleton Univ.) 1978, Hon. DCL (King's Coll.), Hon. D.Univ. (Ottawa); Cultural Merit Award, Poland. *Leisure interests:* the arts, reading. *Address:* 280 Thorold Road, Ottawa, Ont., K1M 0K2 (winter); P.O. Box 126, Portland, Ont. K0G 1V0, Canada (summer). *Telephone:* (613) 272-3606 (summer); (613) 747-8370 (winter) (Home). *Fax:* (613) 747-4616 (winter) (Home); (613) 272-3655 (summer). *E-mail:* calmofmind@rogers.com (Home).

SOUTHGATE, Sir Colin, Kt; British business executive; b. 24 July 1938, New Malden, Surrey; s. of Cyril Alfred Southgate and Edith Isabelle Southgate; m. Sally Southgate 1962; two s. two d.; ed City of London School; began career with NPI; later worked in computers with ICT then ICL; launched own firm Software Sciences 1970; business sold to Thorn EMI 1982; Dir Thorn EMI 1984, Man. Dir 1985, Chief Exec. 1987, Chair. 1989–99; Chair. Thorn PLC 1996–, Royal Opera House 1998–2003, Nettrain 2001–; Dir (non-exec.) Bank of England 1991–99, PowerGen 1990–96 (Chair. 1993–96), Terence Chapman Group 1997–99 (Chair. 1999–); Deputy Pres. CBI 1995–96; Trustee Nat. Gallery 1998–; Gov. The Man. Coll., Henley 1991–97; mem. World Business Council for Sustainable Devt 1994–96. *Address:* c/o Royal Opera House, Covent Garden, London, WC2E 9DD, England.

SOUTHWOOD, Sir (Thomas) Richard Edmund, Kt, DSc, PhD, ARCS, FRS; British professor of zoology; b. 20 June 1931, Kent; s. of Edmund W. Southwood and Ada Mary Southwood (née Regg); m. Alison Langley (Harden) 1955; two s.; ed Gravesend Grammar School and Imperial Coll., Univ. of London; ARC Research Scholar, Rothamsted Experimental Station 1952–55; Research Asst and Lecturer, Zoology Dept, Imperial Coll. 1955–64; Visiting Prof., Escuela Nacional de Agricultura, Mexico 1964; Visiting Prof., Dept of Entomology, Univ. of Calif. at Berkeley 1964–65; Reader in Insect Ecology, Univ. of London 1964–67, Prof. of Zoology and Applied Entomology 1967–79; Linacre Prof. of Zoology, Univ. of Oxford 1979–93; Fellow of Merton Coll., Oxford 1979–; Pro-Vice-Chancellor Univ. of Oxford 1987–89, 1993–98, Vice-Chancellor 1989–93; A. D. White Prof.-at-Large, Cornell Univ., USA 1985–91; Chair. Environmental Sciences Policy Dept, Central European Univ. (Budapest) 1991–95; Fellow of Imperial Coll. London 1984; Fellow of Eton Coll. 1993–2001; Dean of Royal Coll. of Science 1971-72; Trustee British Museum (Natural History) 1974–83, Chair. 1980–83; Mem. Royal Comm. on Environmental Pollution 1974–85, Chair. 1981–85; Pres. British Ecological Soc. 1976–78, Hon. mem. 1988; Vice Pres. Royal Soc. 1982–84; Chair. Nat. Radiological Protection Bd 1985–94; Dir (non-exec.) Glaxo-Wellcome PLC 1992–99; Chair. UK Round Table on Sustainable Devt 1995–99; Rhodes Trustee 1985– (Chair. 1999–); East Malling Trustee 1986–98; Lawes Trustee 1987–; mem. Academia Europaea, Pontifical Acad. of Sciences; Foreign mem. Norwegian Acad. of Science and Letters, Royal Netherlands Acad. of Arts and Sciences, Hungarian Acad. of Sciences; Foreign Assoc. NAS (USA); Fellow Entomological Soc. of America; Hon. Foreign mem. American Acad. of Arts and Sciences; Hon. mem. Ecological Soc. of America; Hon. Fellow Westminster Coll. 1995, Royal Coll. of Radiologists, Kellogg and Mansfield Colls, Oxford; Hon. FRCP; Cavaliere Ufficiale (Italy); Ordem Merito (II) (Portugal); DL (Oxfordshire); Hon. DSc (Griffith Univ., East Anglia, McGill, Warwick, Liverpool, Durham, Sussex, Vic.); Hon. LLD (London), (Brookes, Bristol); Hon. FilDr (Lund, Sweden); Scientific Medal, Zoological Soc., Linnean Medal. *Publications:* Land and Water Bugs of the British Isles 1959, Life of the Wayside and Woodland 1963, Ecological Methods 1966, 1978, 2000, Insects on Plants (with D. R. Strong and J. H. Lawton) 1984, Insects and the Plant Surfaces (with B. Juniper) 1986, Radiation and Health (with R. R. Jones) 1987, The Treatment and Handling of Wastes (with A. D. Bradshaw and F. Warner) 1992, The Story of Life 2003. *Leisure interests:* natural history, gardening, reading. *Address:* Merton College, Oxford, OX1 4JD; Department of Zoology, University of Oxford, South Parks Road, Oxford, OX1 3PS, England (Office).

SOVERN, Michael Ira, BA, LLB; American professor of law and university president; b. 1 Dec. 1931, New York; m. 2nd Eleanor Lean 1963 (divorced 1974); m. 3rd Joan Wit 1974 (died 1993); m. 4th Patricia Walsh 1995; two s. one d. from first m.; one d. from second m.; ed Columbia Coll., Columbia School of Law; called to the Bar 1956; mem. Faculty, Columbia Law School 1957–, Prof. of Law 1960–, Dean, Law School 1970–79, Chancellor Kent Prof. in Law 1977–, Univ. Provost 1979–80, Pres. 1980–93; Chair. Japan Soc. 1993–, American Acad., Rome 1993–; nat. advisory council Freedom Forum Media Studies Center 1993–, Sotheby's 2000–; Pres. Schubert Foundation 1996–; Dir Chemical Bank 1981–96, AT & T, GNY Insurance Group, Orion Pictures Corpn, Asian Cultural Corpn, other appointments; Fellow, American Acad. of Arts and Sciences; mem. American Law Inst.; Hon. DPhil (Tel-Aviv), Hon. LL.D (Columbia) 1980, Commendatore, Order of Merit (Italy) 1991, Alexander Hamilton Medal, Columbia Coll. 1993, Ctizens Union Civic Leadership Award. *Publications:* Legal Restraints on Racial Discrimination in Employment 1966, Law and Poverty 1969. *Address:* School of Law, Columbia University, 435 W 116th Street, New York, NY 10027, USA. *Website:* www .columbia.edu (Office).

SOW, Abdoulaye Sékou; Malian politician; b. 1931; fmr Dir Nat. Admin. School (ENA), Bamako; arrested by regime of Pres. Traore during 1970s; later Dir of Nat. Tourism Office; tech. adviser to various Govt ministries; contributed to drafting of Mali's new constitution; Minister of State responsible for Defence until 1993; Prime Minister of Mali 1993. *Address:* c/o Office of the Prime Minister, Bamako, Mali.

SOW, Ahmedou Mostapha; Senegalese professor of medicine and doctor; b. 5 May 1931, Saint Louis; m.; ten c.; ed Ecole Normale W. Ponty, Dakar, Dakar Univ.; studied medicine in Paris and Sarajevo; Asst Lecturer in Histology and Embryology, Dakar Univ. 1963–66, Prof. of Medicine 1976, Prof. Emer. 1988–; Head Physician, Diabetic Centre, Dakar, Head Internal Medicine 1978–97; Dir urban centre for non-transmissible chronic diseases; Consultant to OAU on Blood and Liver Diseases, to WHO on the Elderly and Diabetes; Fellow Islamic Acad. of Sciences; Officer Palmes Académiques Sénégalaises, Chevalier Ordre nat. du Lion, Commdr Ordre du Mérite, Senegal Commdr Ordre des Palmes académiques, Commdr Ordre nat. du Mérite (France), Distinction Prize in Medicine 1962. *Address:* Islamic Academy of Sciences, P.O. Box 830036, Amman, Jordan (Office). *Telephone:* 5522104 (Office). *Fax:* 5511803 (Office).

SOWRY, Hon. Roger; New Zealand politician; b. 1958, Palmerston North; m.; four c.; ed Victoria Univ. of Wellington; fmr Distribution Man., R. Hannah & Co.; Nat. Party MP 1990–; apptd. Jr Whip, then Sr Govt Whip 1993–96; Minister of Social Welfare, Minister in Charge of War Pensions, Assoc. Minister of Health 1996–98 and Minister in Charge of Social Services, Work, Income, Welfare, Housing, Employment and Leader of the House 1998–2000; mem. Transport and Industrial Relations Select Cttee 2002–; Deputy Divisional Chair. Wellington Young Nationals 1979–80, Electorate Chair. Pencarrow 1982–86, Divisional Councillor 1989–96, Deputy Chair. Wellington Div. 1988–90, Wellington Rep. on NZ Nat. Exec. 1989–90; Deputy Leader Nat. Party 2001–. *Address:* Parliament Buildings, Wellington, New Zealand (Office). *Telephone:* (4) 471-9999 (Office). *Fax:* (4) 472-2075 (Office); (4) 298-3832 (Home). *E-mail:* royer.sowry@national.org.nz (Office); sowry@kapiti.co .nz (Home). *Website:* www.national.org.nz (Office).

SOYINKA, Wole, BA; Nigerian playwright and lecturer; b. 13 July 1934, Abeokuta; s. of Ayo Soyinka and Eniola Soyinka; m.; four c.; ed Univ. of Ibadan, Nigeria and Univ. of Leeds, England; worked at Royal Court Theatre, London; Research Fellow in Drama, Univ. of Ibadan 1960–61; Lecturer in English, Univ. of Ife 1962–63; Sr Lecturer in English, Univ. of Lagos 1965–67; political prisoner 1967–69; Artistic Dir and Head Dept of Theatre Arts, Univ. of Ibadan 1969–72; Research Prof. in Dramatic Literature, Univ. of Ife 1972, Prof. of Comparative Literature and Head of Dept of Dramatic Arts 1976–85; passport seized Sept. 1994, living in France; charged with treason March 1997 in absentia; Ed. Ch'Indaba (fmrly Transition) Accra; Artistic Dir Orisun Theatre, 1960 Masks; Literary Ed. Orisun Acting Editions; Pres. Int. Theatre Inst. 1986–; Fellow, Churchill Coll. Cambridge 1973–74; mem. American Acad. of Arts and Letters; Fellow, Ghana Asscn of Writers, Pan-African Writers Asscn; Chair. Nigeria Road Safety Comm. 1988–91; Hon. DLitt (Leeds) 1973, (Yale) 1981, (Morehouse), (Paul Valéry), (Bayreuth), (Ibadan), (Harvard); Hon. DScS (Edin.) 1977; Prisoner of Conscience Award, Amnesty Int., Jock Campbell-New Statesman Literary Award 1969; Nobel Prize for Literature 1986; George Benson Medal, RSL 1990, Writers Guild Lifetime Achievement Award 1996 and numerous other awards; Commdr Légion d'honneur, Commdr Fed. Republic of Nigeria 1986, Commdr Order of Merit (Italy) 1990. *Publications:* plays: The Lion and the Jewel 1959, The Swamp Dwellers 1959, A Dance of the Forests 1960, The Trials of Brother Jero 1961, The Strong Breed 1962, The Road 1964, Kongi's Harvest 1965, Madmen and Specialists 1971, Before the Blackout 1971, Jero's Metamorphosis 1973, Camwood on the Leaves 1973, The Bacchae of Euripides 1974, Death and the King's Horsemen 1975, Opera Wonyosi 1978, From Zia, with Love 1991, A Scourge of Hyacinths (radio play) 1992, The Beatification of Area Boy 1995; novels: The Interpreters 1964, The Forest of a Thousand Daemons (trans.), Season of Anomy 1973; non-fiction: The Man Died (prison memoirs) 1972, Isara: A voyage round Essay 1990, Continuity and Amnesia 1991; poetry: Idanre and Other Poems 1967, A Shuttle in the Crypt 1972, Poems of Black Africa (ed.) 1975, Ogun Abibiman 1977, Mandela's Earth and Other Poems 1988; lectures: Myth, Literature and the African World 1972, Aké, The Years of Childhood (autobiog.) 1982, Art, Dialogue and Outrage 1988, Ibadan: The Pentelemes Years (memoir) 1994, The Open Sore of a Continent, A Personal Narrative of the Nigerian Crisis 1996, The Burden of Memory, The Muse of Forgiveness 1999. *Address:* c/o P.O. Box 935, Abeokuta, Ogun State, Nigeria.

SPACEK, Mary Elizabeth (Sissy); American actress; b. 25 Dec. 1949, Quitman, Tex.; d. of Edwin A. Spacek and Virginia Spacek; m. Jack Fisk 1974; two d.; ed Lee Strasberg Theater Inst. *Films:* Prime Cut 1972, Ginger in the Morning 1972, Badlands 1974, Carrie 1976, Three Women 1977, Welcome to LA 1977, Heart Beat 1980, Coal Miner's Daughter 1980, Raggedy Man 1981, Missing 1982, The River 1984, Marie 1985, Violets are Blue 1986, Crimes of the Heart 1986, 'night Mother 1986, JFK 1991, The Long Walk Home, The Plastic Nightmare, Hard Promises 1992, Trading Mom 1994, The Grass Harp 1995, Streets of Laredo 1995, If These Walls Could Talk 1996, Affliction 1998, Blast From the Past 1999. *Television:* The Girls of Huntington House 1973, The Migrants 1973, Katherine 1975, Verna, USO Girl 1978, A Private Matter 1992, A Place for Annie 1994, The Good Old Boys 1995; Best Actress (Nat. Soc. Film Critics) for Carrie 1976, Best Supporting Actress (New York Film Critics) for Three Women 1977, Best Actress (New York and Los Angeles Film Critics, Foreign Press Asscn, Nat. Soc. Film Critics) 1980; Album of the Year Award (Country Music Asscn) for Coal Miner's Daughter 1980, In the Bedroom (Golden Globe for Best Actress 2002) 2001. *Address:* c/o Steve Tellez, CAA, 9830 Wilshire Boulevard, Beverly Hills, CA 90212, USA.

SPACEY, Kevin; American actor; b. 26 July 1959, S Orange, NJ; ed Chatsworth High School, LA, Juilliard Drama School, NY; stage début in Henry IV, Part I; Broadway début in Ghosts 1982; other theatre appearances include: Hurlyburly 1985, Long Day's Journey into Night, London 1986, Yonkers, NY (received Tony award), The Iceman Cometh, London 1998; mem. Bd of Trustees, Old Vic, London, Artistic Dir 2003–. *Films:* Working Girl 1988, See No Evil, Hear No Evil 1989, Dad 1989, Henry and June 1990, Glengarry Glen Ross 1992, Consenting Adults 1992, Hostile Hostages 1994, Outbreak 1995, The Usual Suspects 1995, Seven 1995, Looking for Richard 1996, A Time to Kill 1996, LA Confidential 1997, Midnight in the Garden of Good and Evil 1997, American Beauty 1999 (Acad. Award for Best Actor), Ordinary Decent Criminal, Pay it Forward 2000, The Shipping News 2001, K-PAX 2001, The Life of David Gale 2003; Dir Albino Alligator 1997. *Address:* William Morris Agency, 151 South El Camino Drive, Beverly Hills, CA 90212, USA.

SPADER, James; American actor; b. 7 Feb. 1960, Boston; ed Phillips Acad. *Films include:* Endless Love 1981, The New Kids 1985, Pretty in Pink 1986, Baby Boom 1987, Less Than Zero 1987, Mannequin 1987, Jack's Back 1988, The Rachel Papers 1989, Sex, Lies and Videotape 1989, Bad Influence 1990, The Music of Chance 1993, Dream Lover 1994, Wolf 1994, Stargate 1994, Two Days in the Valley 1996, Crash 1997, Keys to Tulsa 1997, Critical Care 1997, Curtain Call 1998, Supernova 1998, Slow Burn 1999, Curtain Call 1999. *Address:* c/o ICM, 8942 Wilshire Boulevard, Beverly Hills, CA 90211, USA.

SPALDING, D. Brian, ScD, PhD, FIMechE, FInstF, FRS, FEng; British professor of heat transfer and business executive; b. 9 Jan. 1923, New Malden, Surrey; s. of Harold Spalding and Kathleen Spalding; m. 1st Eda Ilse-Lotte Goericke; two s. two d.; m. 2nd Colleen King; two s.; ed King's Coll. School, Wimbledon, The Queen's Coll. Oxford and Pembroke Coll. Cambridge; Bataafsche Petroleum Matschapij 1944–45; Ministry of Supply 1945–47; ICI Research Fellow at Cambridge Univ. 1948–50, Demonstrator in Eng 1950–54; Reader in Applied Heat, Imperial Coll. of Science and Tech., London 1954–58, Prof. of Heat Transfer 1958–88, Prof. Emer. 1988–, Head of Computational Fluid Dynamics Unit 1981–88; Man. Dir Conduction Heat and Mass Transfer Ltd 1970–75, Concentration, Heat and Momentum Ltd 1975–; Chair. CHAM of N America Ltd 1977–91; mem. Royal Norwegian Soc.; Bernard Lewis Combustion Medal 1982, Medaille d'Or 1980. *Publications:* Numerical Prediction of Flow, Heat Transfer Turbulence and Combustion (selected works) 1983, Heat Exchanger Design Handbook (jtly.) 1982, Combustion and Mass Transfer 1979, GENMIX: A General Computer Program 1978, Mathematical Models of Turbulence (jtly.) 1972, Heat and Mass Transfer in Recirculating Flows (Co-Author) 1967, Convective Mass Transfer (Co-Author) 1963, Engineering Thermodynamics (Co-Author) 1958, Some Fundamentals of Combustion 1955, Innocents of the Latter Day (fiction) 1996; numerous scientific papers. *Leisure interests:* music, poetry reading. *Address:* Concentration, Heat and Momentum Ltd (CHAM), Bakery House, 40 High Street, Wimbledon, SW19 5AU, England. *Telephone:* (20) 8947-7651. *Fax:* (20) 8879-3497.

SPALL, Timothy, OBE, FRSA; British actor; b. 27 Feb. 1957, London; s. of Joseph Spall and Sylvia Spall; m.; one s. two d.; ed Battersea Co. Comprehensive, Kingsway and Princeton Coll. of Further Ed., RADA, London. *Television:* The Brylcream Boys 1978, Auf Wiedersehen Pet 1983, 1985, Roots 1993, Frank Stubbs Promotes 1994, 1995, Outside Edge 1994, 1995, Neville's Island 1997, Our Mutual Friend 1997, Shooting the Past 1999, The Thing About Vince 2000, Vacuuming Completely Nude in Paradise 2001, Perfect

Strangers 2001, Auf Wiedersehen Pet (third series) 2002. *Plays:* Merry Wives of Windsor, Nicholas Nickleby, The Three Sisters, The Knight of the Burning Pestle (RSC 1978–81), St Joan 1985, Mandragola 1985, Le Bourgeois Gentilhomme 1993, A Midsummer Night's Dream 1994 (Royal Nat. Theatre), This is a Chair 1996 (Royal Court). *Films include:* Quadrophenia 1978, Gothic 1986, The Sheltering Sky 1989, Life is Sweet 1990, Secrets and Lies 1996, The Wisdom of Crocodiles 1998, Still Crazy 1998, Topsy Turvy 1999, Clandestine Marriage 1999, Love's Labour's Lost 2000, Intimacy 2001, Lucky Break 2001, Rock Star 2001, Vanilla Sky 2001, All or Nothing 2002. *Leisure interests:* boating, drinking fine wines, reading. *Address:* c/o Markham & Froggatt, 4 Windmill Street, London, W1P 1HF, England (Office). *Telephone:* (20) 7636-4412 (Office). *Fax:* (20) 8699-1657 (Office).

SPANGENBERG, Christa; German publisher; b. 1928, Munich; d. of Edgar J. Jung and Minni Jung; m. Berthold Spangenberg 1946 (died 1986); two s.; ed music and language studies; honorary work for Börsenverein des Deutschen Buchhandels; lecturer, Univ. of Munich 1987–; Founder Int. Youth Library Foundation, Munich 1996–; Kulturpreis der Bayrischen Landesstifteung 1999 and other awards. *Publications:* Elly Petersens praktisches Gartenlexikon, Praktisches Balkon- und Zimmerpflanzen-lexikon, Grüne Uhr, Garten Uhr, ABC für Kleine Gärtner. *Leisure interests:* gardening, music. *Address:* Bäumlstrasse 6, 80638 Munich, Germany. *Telephone:* 17-14-23. *Fax:* 17-14-23.

SPARGO, Peter Ernest, F.R.S.S.AF.; South African educator; b. 7 June 1937, Johannesburg; s. of Alfred Hugh Spargo and Lilias McCall (née Fisher) Spargo; m. Celia Rosamunde Key 1964; four d.; ed Jeppe High School, Univ. of the Witwatersrand, Johannesburg and Magdalene Coll. Cambridge, UK; Science Teacher Jeppe High School, Johannesburg 1961–63; Lecturer in Science Educ. Johannesburg Coll. of Educ. 1964–71; Science Educ. Planner, Pretoria 1972–75; School of Educ., Univ. of Cape Town 1976–97, Dir Science Educ. Unit 1980–97, Hon. Research Assoc., Dept of Chem. 1999–; Nat. Chair. SA Asscn of Teachers of Physical Science 1975–82; Trustee and Dir S. African Science Educ. Project 1977–; Educ. Consultant to Shell Oil Co. (SA) 1977–89, Rössing Uranium Co. (Namibia) 1982–90; Nat. Pres. Fed. of Science and Math. Teachers Asscns. of SA 1977–79, 1984–85; Gen. Sec. Royal Soc. of S. Africa 1986–89; Hon. Nat. Pres. S. African Spelaeological Asscn 1996–; Medal of Honour (Fed. of Science and Math. Teachers Asscns. of SA) 1981. *Publications:* numerous Publs in the fields of science education, history of science and history of physics and chemistry, author of science textbooks. *Leisure interests:* walking, reading, gardening. *Address:* P.O. Box 211, Rondebosch 7701; Department of Chemistry, University of Cape Town, Rondebosch 7700 (Office); 10 Lochiel Road, Rondebosch, Cape Town, South Africa (Home). *Telephone:* (21) 6864289 (Home). *Fax:* (21) 6503342 (Office). *E-mail:* peter@spargo.wcape.school.za (Home).

SPARK, Dame Muriel Sarah, DBE, CLit, FRSE; British author; b. 1 Feb. 1918, Edinburgh; d. of Bernard Camberg and Sarah Elizabeth Maud Uezzell; m. S. O. Spark 1937 (divorced); one s.; ed James Gillespie's High School for Girls, Edinburgh, Heriot-Watt Coll.; Foreign Office 1944–45; Ed. The Poetry Review and Gen. Sec. Poetry Soc., London 1947–49; Hon. mem. American Acad. of Arts and Letters 1978, Scottish PEN; Commdr Ordre des Arts et Lettres 1996; Hon. DLitt (Strathclyde) 1971, (Edin.) 1989, (Aberdeen) 1995, (St Andrews) 1998, (Oxford) 1999, (London) 2001; D. Univ. (Heriot-Watt) 1995; The Observer Story Prize 1951, Italia Prize 1962, James Tait Black Memorial Prize 1965, Ingersoll Prize (USA), T. S. Eliot Award 1992, David Cohen British Literature Prize 1997, Int. PEN Gold Pen Award 1998, Boccaccio Prize 2002. *Plays:* Doctors of Philosophy 1963. *Radio plays:* The Interview, The Dry River Bed, The Danger Zone, The Party Through the Wall. *Publications:* Child of Light: A Reassessment of Mary Wollstonecraft Shelley 1951, The Fanfarlo and Other Verse 1952, John Masefield (a critical study) 1953, The Comforters 1957, Robinson 1958, The Go-Away Bird and Other Stories 1958, Memento Mori 1959 (play 1964; BBC TV 1992), The Bachelors (also TV play) 1960, The Ballad of Peckham Rye 1960, The Prime of Miss Jean Brodie 1961 (play 1966, film 1969, TV 1978), Voices at Play 1961, The Girls of Slender Means (also TV play) 1963, The Mandelbaum Gate 1965, Collected Stories I. 1967, Collected Poems I. 1967, The Public Image 1968, The Very Fine Clock (juvenile) 1968, The Driver's Seat 1970 (film 1974), Not to Disturb 1971, The Hothouse by The East River 1973, The Abbess of Crewe 1974 (film Nasty Habits 1977), The Takeover 1976, Territorial Rights 1979, Loitering with Intent 1981, Bang-Bang You're Dead (stories) 1982, Going Up to Sotheby's (poems) 1982, The Only Problem 1984, The Stories of Muriel Spark 1985, Mary Shelley 1987, 1992, A Far Cry from Kensington 1988, Symposium 1990, Curriculum Vitae (autobiog.) 1992, The Essence of the Brontës 1993, The French Window and The Small Telephone (juvenile) 1993, Omnibus I 1993, Omnibus II 1994, The Portobello Road (stories) 1995, The Hanging Judge (stories) 1995, Reality and Dreams 1996, Omnibus III 1996, Harper and Wilton 1996, Omnibus IV 1997, Aiding and Abetting (novel) 2000, The Complete Short Stories 2001. *Leisure interest:* travel. *Address:* c/o David Higham Assocs. Ltd, 5–8 Lower John Street, Golden Square, London, W1R 4HA, England. *Telephone:* (20) 7437-7888 (Office). *Fax:* (20) 7437-1072 (Office). *Website:* murielspark.com (Office).

SPARKS, Robert Stephen John, PhD, FRS; British professor of geology and volcanologist; b. 15 May 1949, Harpenden, Herts.; s. of Kenneth Grenfell Sparks and Ruth Joan Rugman; m. Ann Elizabeth Talbot 1971; two s.; ed Imperial Coll. London; Fellow of Royal Comm. of Exhbn of 1851, Lancaster Univ. 1974–76; NATO Post-doctoral Fellow, Univ. of Rhode Island, USA 1976–78; Lecturer, Univ. of Cambridge 1978–89, Fellow Trinity Hall, Cambridge 1980–89; Prof. of Geology, Bristol Univ. 1989–, Channing Willis Prof. of Geology 1990–; Chief Scientist Montserrat Volcano Observatory 1997–99; Prof. of Earth Sciences, Nat. Environment Research Council 1998–; Pres. Geological Soc. of London 1994–96; Pres. Int. Asscn of Volcanology and Chem. of Earth's Interior 1999–; Fellow American Geophysics Union 1998; Hon. DSc (Lancaster) 2000; Dr hc (Univ. Blaise Pascal) 1999; Bakerian Lecture of Royal Soc. 2000; Bigsby Medal, Geological Soc. of London, Murchison Medal, Geological Soc. of London 1998, Arthur Day Medal, Geology Soc. of America 2000, Royal Soc. Wolfson Merit Award 2002. *Publications:* Volcanic Plumes 1997 and more than 240 scientific articles and papers on volcanology (especially physics of volcanic eruptions), fluid mechanics, petrology and other geological topics. *Leisure interests:* music, tennis, football, squash, travel, family. *Address:* Department of Earth Sciences, Bristol University, Bristol, BS8 1RJ (Office); Walnut Cottage, 19 Brinsea Road, Congresbury, Bristol, BS49 5JF, England (Home). *Telephone:* (1179) 545419 (Office); (1934) 834306 (Home). *E-mail:* steve.sparks@bristol.ac.uk (Office).

SPASSKII, Nikolai Nikolayevich, D.POL.SC.; Russian diplomatist; b. 1961, Sevastopol; s. of Nikolay Spasskiy and Rimma Spasskiy; ed Moscow Inst. of Int. Relations; with USSR (later Russian) Ministry of Foreign Affairs 1983–; Deputy Head, First Deputy, Dept of N America 1992–94; Dir 1994–97; mem. Advisory Council, Ministry of Foreign Affairs 1995; Amb. to Italy (also accred. to San Marino) 1997–. *Publication:* La Fine del Mondo e Altri Racconti Romani 1999, Il Complotto 2000. *Leisure interests:* art, travel. *Address:* Russian Embassy, Via Gaeta 5, 00185 Rome, Italy. *Telephone:* (06) 4941680 (Office). *Fax:* (06) 491031 (Office). *E-mail:* ambrus@flashnet.it (Office); nicholas.sp@flashnet.it (Home). *Website:* www.ambrussia.it (Office).

SPASSKY, Boris Vasiliyevich; French/Russian chess-player and journalist; b. 30 Jan. 1937, Leningrad (now St Petersburg); m. 1st Marina Shcherbacheva; m. 2nd; m. 3rd; ed Faculty of Journalism, Leningrad State Univ.; in Leningrad Section of Voluntary Sport Soc., Trud 1959–61; Trainer, Leningrad Section of Voluntary Sport Soc., Locomotiv 1964–79; played in numerous individual and command int. chess tournaments; USSR Grandmaster, Int. Grandmaster and World Chess Student Champion 1956, USSR Chess Champion 1962, World Chess Champion 1969–72 (when lost to Bobby Fischer); left USSR 1976; lost against Bobby Fischer in Yugoslavia 1992; now lives in Paris; works as a chess journalist; involved with World Chess Network; Hon. Pres. Kilkenny Chess Club, Ireland; several decorations including Honoured Master of the Sport 1965. *Website:* www.worldchessnetwork.com.

SPASSKY, Igor Dmitriyevich, DR.TECH.SC.; Russian engineer and professor; b. 2 Aug. 1926, Moscow Region; m.; two c.; ed Dzerdjinsky Higher Mil. School of Marine Eng; service in Black Sea marine forces 1949–50; worked in enterprises of Ministry of Vessel Construction, Leningrad (now St Petersburg) 1950–; Head of Sector, Deputy Chief Constructor, Chief Engineer, Head of CDB ME Rubin 1974–, Gen Constructor 1983–; USSR Peoples' Deputy 1990–91; mem. USSR (now Russian) Acad. of Sciences 1987–; Hero of Socialist Labour, Order of Lenin, Orders of October Revolution, Red Banner of Labour; 16 medals; Lenin Prize 1965, USSR State Prize 1984. *Publications:* numerous scientific works on designing atomic submarines, tech. of machine construction, construction mechanics, reliability and special energetics. *Leisure interest:* fishing. *Address:* Central Design Bureau for Marine Engineering "Rubin", Marata str. 90, 191119 St. Petersburg, Russia (Office). *Telephone:* (812) 113-51-32 (Office); (812) 388-82-65 (Home).

SPÄTH, Lothar; German politician; b. 16 Nov. 1937, Sigmaringen; s. of Friedrich Späth and Helene Späth (née Lillich); m. Ursula Heinle 1962; one s. one d.; ed Gymnasium, Heilbronn, State School of Man., Stuttgart; mem. Landtag 1968–91; Chair. CDU group in Stuttgart Landtag 1972–78, Hon. Leader 1991–; Rep. of CDU for Baden-Württemberg 1977–91; Sec. of Interior Feb.–Aug. 1978, Minister-Pres. of Baden-Württemberg 1978–91; Pres. Bundesrat 1985–86; Chair. Jenoptik AG, Jena 1991–; Royal Norwegian Consul-Gen. of Thuringia and Saxony-Anhalt 1992–; Dr hc (Karlsruhe) 1984, (Pecs). *Publications:* Wende in die Zukunft 1985, 1992– Der Traum von Europa 1989, Natur und Wirtschaft 1992, Sind die Deutschen noch zu retten? 1993, Countdown für Deutschland 1995, Blühende Phantasien und harte Realitäten 1997, Die zweite Wende 1998, Die Stunde der Politik 1999, Jenseits von Brüssel 2001. *Leisure interests:* modern painting and graphics, card games, tennis. *Address:* Carl-Zeiss-Str. 1, 07743 Jena, Germany. *Telephone:* (3641) 650. *Fax:* (3641) 652483.

SPAULDING, Winston, QC; Jamaican fmr politician and lawyer; b. 26 Aug. 1939; m.; five c.; called to the Bar, Inner Temple, London 1966; worked briefly in Jamaican and British civil service and practised law in the Bahamas; subsequently established legal practice in Jamaica; fmr mem. Nat. Exec. People's Nat. Party; Deputy Leader Jamaica Labour Party 1977–83; Senator and Opposition Spokesman on Security and Justice 1977–80; MP for Cen. St James 1980–83 and for SE St Andrew 1983–89; Minister of Nat. Security and Justice and Attorney-Gen. 1980–86; Chair. Defence Bd 1980–86, Legislation Cttee 1980–86, Statute Law Commrs. under the Law Revision Act 1980–86; mem. Council of Legal Educ. 1980–86; Founder mem. Jamaica Council for Human Rights; Founder and First Chair. Human Rights Bureau of Jamaica Labour Party; as Minister of Justice initiated review of Gun Court Act which included abolition of mandatory life sentence; as Minister of Security initiated establishment of Police Staff Coll. *Address:* 21 Balmoral Avenue, Kingston 10, Jamaica (Office). *Telephone:* 9298601. *Fax:* 9296196.

SPAVENTA, Luigi; Italian professor of economics; b. 5 March 1934, Rome; s. of Renato Spaventa and Lydia de Novellis; m. Margaret Royce 1962; three c.; ed Univ. of Rome and King's Coll., Cambridge; Prof. of Econ. Policy, Univ. of Palermo 1963–64; Prof. of Econs Univ. of Perugia 1964–70, Univ. of Rome 1970–; mem. Italian Parl. (on leave from univ.) 1976–83; Visiting Fellow, All Souls' Coll., Oxford 1968–69; Visiting scholar, IMF 1984; Luigi Einaudi Prof. Cornell Univ. 1989; Minister of the Budget 1993–94; Chair. of Bd Finanza & Futuro SpA, Banca Monte dei Paschi di Siena SpA 1997–98; Chair. Consob (Securities Comm.) 1998–2003; Fellow, Centre for Econ. Policy Research; Kt Grand Cross Order of Merit (Italy). *Publications:* essays and articles in specialized journals. *Address:* Via GB De Rossi 29, 00161 Rome, Italy (Home). *Telephone:* (06) 8477445 (Office); (06) 44238191 (Home). *Fax:* (06) 8477212 (Office); (06) 44236225 (Home).

SPEAKES, Larry Melvin; American public relations executive; b. 13 Sept. 1939, Cleveland, Miss.; s. of Harry Speakes and Ethlyn Fincher; m. Laura Crawford 1968; two s. one d.; ed Univ. of Mississippi; news Oxford (Miss.) Eagle 1961–62, Bolivar Commercial, Cleveland 1962–63; Man. Ed. Bolivar Commercial 1965–66; Gen. Man. Progress Publs Leland, Miss. 1966–68; Ed. Leland Progress, Hollandale Herald, Bolivar Co. Democrat, Sunflower Co. News; Press Sec. to Senator for Mississippi 1968–74; Staff Asst Exec. Office of Pres. of USA March–May 1974, Press Asst to Special Counsel to Pres. May–Aug. 1974; Asst to White House Press Sec. 1974–76, Asst Press Sec. to Pres. 1976–77; Press Sec. to Gerald R. Ford 1977; Vice-Pres. Hill & Knowlton, Inc., Washington 1977–81; Prin. Deputy Press Sec. and Asst to Pres. of USA 1981–87; Sr Vice-Pres. Merrill Lynch & Co., Inc., New York 1987–88; corp. communications consultant and lecturer on politics and the presidency 1988–91; Vice-Pres., Communications, Northern Telecom Ltd, Washington and Toronto 1991–93; Senior Vice-Pres. Corp. and Legis. Affairs, U.S. Postal Service 1994–98; Sr Adviser to Postmaster Gen. 1998–; LittD hc (Ind. Cen. Univ.); Presidential Citizens' Medal 1987 and several achievement awards. *Publication:* Speaking Out (biog.) 1988.

SPEAR, Laurinda Hope, MA, FAIA; American architect; b. 23 Aug. 1951, Rochester, Minn.; d. of Harold Spear; m. Bernardo Fort-Brescia 1976; five s. one d.; ed Columbia and Brown Univs.; founding prin., Arquitectonica; faculty mem. in charge of design studio, Univ. of Miami School of Architecture; lecturer to professional, civil and academic groups; numerous exhbns. throughout USA and Europe including Paris Biennale 1982, Inst. of Contemporary Art, Philadelphia 1986, Buenos Aires Biennale 1987, Inst. Français d'Architecture, Paris 1988, Centrum voor Architectuur en Stedebouw, Brussels 1991, Gallery MA, Tokyo 1993, Philips Arena, Atlanta 1999, Miami Int. Airport; various architectural awards. *Major projects include:* low-income housing, high-rise condominiums, residential additions and renovations, office towers, medical office bldgs., retail complexes and hotels in USA, France, Luxembourg and Peru, Festival Walk, Hong Kong 1998. *Address:* Arquitectonica, 550 Brickell Avenue, Suite 200, Miami, FL 33131, USA.

SPEARMAN, Thomas David, PhD, MRIA; Irish professor of natural philosophy and university vice-provost; b. 25 March 1937, Dublin; s. of Thomas Spearman and Elizabeth Leadbeater; m. Juanita Smale 1961; one s. two d.; ed Greenlanes and Mountjoy Schools, Dublin, Trinity Coll. Dublin and St John's Coll. Cambridge; Research Fellow, Univ. Coll. London 1960–61; Research Assoc. Univ. of Ill. 1962–64; Lecturer in Theoretical Physics, Univ. of Durham 1964–66; Univ. Prof. of Natural Philosophy, Trinity Coll. Dublin 1966–97, Fellow 1969–94, Senior Fellow 1994–97 (Fellow Emer. 1997–), Bursar 1974–77, Vice-Provost 1991–97; Prof. Associé, Univ. of Montpellier 1985–; Chair. Trustee Savings Bank, Dublin 1989–92; mem. Council, European Physical Soc. 1979–82; mem. European Space Science Cttee 1984–89; Vice-Pres. European Science Foundation 1983–89; Treas. Royal Irish Acad. 1980–88; Treas. Academia Europaea 1989–2000; mem. European Science and Tech. Ass. 1994–98; Pres. Royal Irish Acad. 1999–2002; mem. Bd Nat. Gallery of Ireland 1999–2002; mem. Governing Council European Science Foundation 2000–02. *Publications:* Elementary Particle Theory (with A. D. Martin) 1970; numerous papers and articles on aspects of elementary particle physics, inverse problems and history of science. *Leisure interests:* walking, gardening, reading, listening to music, looking at pictures. *Address:* House No. 25, Trinity College, Dublin 2 (Office); St Elmo, Marlborough Road, Glenageary, Co. Dublin, Ireland (Home). *Telephone:* (1) 6082360 (Office). *E-mail:* david.spearman@tcd.ie (Office).

SPEARS, Britney (Jean); American singer; b. 2 Dec. 1981, Kentwood, LA; winner of several MTV Video Music Awards 1999, Best Female Pop Vocal Performance 2000. *Recordings include:* Singles: Baby One More Time (No. 1 in UK and USA) 1999, Sometimes 1999, (You Drive Me) Crazy 1999, Born to Make You Happy (No. 1 in UK 2000), From The Bottom of Broken My Heart 2000, Oops! I Did It Again (No. 1 in UK) 2000, Lucky 2000, Stronger 2000, Don't Let Me Be The Last To Know 2001, I'm A Slave For You 2001, Overprotected 2002, I'm Not a Girl Not Yet A Woman 2002, I Love Rock 'n' Roll 2002; Albums: Baby One More Time 1999; Oops! I Did It Again 2000, Britney 2001 (first three albums debut at No. 1). *Film:* Crossroads 2002. *Address:* The Official Britney Spears International Fan Club, CS 9712, Bellingham, WA 98227, USA (Office). *Website:* www.britneyspears.com (Office).

SPECTER, Arlen; American politician; b. 12 Feb. 1930, Wichita, Kan.; s. of Harry Specter and Lillie Shanin Specter; m. Joan Lois Levy 1953; two s.; ed Univ. of Oklahoma, Univ. of Pennsylvania, Yale Univ.; served USAF 1951–53;

Asst Dist Attorney, Phila, Pa 1959–63, Dist Attorney 1966–74; Asst Counsel, Warren Comm., Washington, DC 1964; Special Asst Attorney-Gen., Pa Dept of Justice 1964–65; Del. Republican Nat. Convention 1968, 1972, Alt. Del. 1976; Senator from Pennsylvania (Republican) 1981–, Chair. Select Cttee on Intelligence, Special Cttee on Ageing and Veterans Affairs; mem. Nat. Advisory Cttee on Peace Corps 1969–; Lecturer in Law, Univ. of Pa Law School 1969–72, Temple Univ. Law School 1972–76; mem. White House Conf. on Youth 1971, Gov. Justice Comm., Regional Planning Council, Nat. Advisory Comm. on Criminal Justice Standards and Goals, Criminal Rules Cttee of Pa Supreme Court and Judicial Council of Phila; mem. American, Pa and Phila Bar Asscns., Nat. Council on Alcoholism; Hon. LL.B (Phila Coll. of Textiles and Science) 1968; Sons of Italy Award, Alessandroni Lodge. *Publications:* articles in law reviews. *Address:* U.S. Senate, 711 Senate Hart Building, Washington, DC 20510, USA.

SPEDDING, Sir Colin Raymond William, Kt, CBE, MSc, PhD, DSc, CBiol, F.I.HORT., F.R.A.S.E., F.R.AG.S.; British university professor; b. 22 March 1925, Cannock; s. of Robert Spedding and Ilynn Spedding; m. Betty N. George 1952 (died 1988); two s. (one deceased) one d.; ed London Univ. (external); Allen & Hanbury 1947; Grassland Research Inst. 1949–75, Deputy Dir 1972–75; Visiting, then part-time Prof. of Agric. Systems, Univ. of Reading 1970–75, Prof. 1975–90, Prof. Emer.; Head, Dept of Agric. and Horticulture 1975–83, Dean, Faculty of Agric. and Food 1983–86, Dir Centre for Agricultural Strategy 1981–90, Pro-Vice-Chancellor 1986–90; Pres. Inst. of Biology 1992–94; Chair. UK Register of Organic Food Standards 1987–99, Farm Animal Welfare Council 1988–98, Apple and Pear Research Council 1989–97, Council of Science and Tech. Insts (now The Science Council) 1994–2000; Deputy Chair. People's Dispensary for Sick Animals (PDSA) 1996–; Vice-Pres. Inst. of Biology 1997–2000 (now Hon. Fellow), Royal Soc. for Prevention of Cruelty to Animals 2002–; Advisory Dir World Soc. for the Protection of Animals 1998–; Adviser Companion Animal Welfare Council 1999–; Chair. Assured Chicken Productions Ltd 2000–, numerous other professional and public appointments; Hon. Assoc. Royal Coll. of Veterinary Surgeons; Hon. DSc (Reading); George Hedley Memorial Award 1971; Hawkesbury Centenary Medal of Honour, Univ. of W Sydney, Victory Medal, Central Veterinary Soc. 2000 and other honours and distinctions. *Publications:* 13 books and about 200 scientific papers. *Address:* Vine Cottage, Orchard Road, Hurst, Reading, RG10 0SD, England. *Telephone:* (118) 934-1771. *Fax:* (118) 934-2997.

SPEIGHT, George; Fijian business executive; s. of Sam Speight; worked in Australia and USA; returned to Fiji 1996; computer salesman; fmr Man. Dir Heath (Fiji) Ltd; fmr Chair. Fiji Pine Ltd and Fiji Hardwood Corpn Ltd; led armed coup against Govt May 2000, took Prime Minister Mahendra Chaudhry and cabinet hostage and declared constitution dissolved; cabinet mems. subsequently released and Speight and other coup leaders arrested; charged with treason May 2001.

SPEKREIJSE, Henk; Netherlands professor of visual systems analysis; b. 4 Nov. 1940, Rijssen; m. Y.J.M. van der Heijden; two d.; ed Tech. Univ. Delft and Univ. of Amsterdam; Prof. of Visual Systems Analysis, Netherlands Ophthalmic Research Inst., Lab. of Medical Physics and Informatics 1977–; Dir of Neuroresearch Netherlands Ophthalmic Research Inst. 1985–95; mem. Royal Netherlands Acad. of Arts and Sciences 1985–; AKZO Award 1985. *Publications:* Analysis of EEG responses in man, evoked by sine wave modulated light 1966, Spatial Contrast (with L. H. van der Tweel) 1977, Visual Pathways, Electrophysiology and Pathology (with P. A. Apkarian) 1981, Systems Approach in Vision (with D. Regan and D. M. Shapley) 1986, Brain Topography, Vol. No. 2 (with B. W van Dijk and F. H. Lopes da Vega) 1992. *Address:* Voorstraat 11, 1394 CS Nederhorst den Berg, Netherlands (Home). *Telephone:* (20) 5664584. *Fax:* (20) 6916521.

SPELLING, Aaron, BA; American television producer and writer; b. 22 April 1923, Dallas, Tex.; s. of David Spelling and Pearl Wall; m. Carole Gene Marer 1968; one s. one d.; ed Univ. de Paris (Sorbonne), Southern Methodist Univ.; served USAAF 1942–45; Co-owner Thomas-Spelling Productions 1969–72; Co-Pres. Spelling-Goldberg Productions 1972–76; Pres. Aaron Spelling Productions Inc., Los Angeles 1977–86, Chair. and CEO 1986–; mem. Bd of Dirs. American Film Inst.; mem. Writers' Guild of America, Producers' Guild of America, The Caucus, Hollywood Radio and TV Soc., Hollywood TV Acad. of Arts and Sciences; producer of numerous TV programmes, including Dynasty, The Colbys, Love Boat, Hotel, Beverly Hills 90210, Melrose Place, Sunset Beach, Pacific Palisades and over 110 Movies of the Week for American Broadcasting Corpn; films produced include Mr. Mom, 'Night, Mother, Surrender, Cross My Heart, Soapdish; author of numerous TV plays and films; Bronze Star Medal; Purple Heart with oak leaf cluster; Eugene O'Neill Award 1947, 1948; Nat. Asscn for Advancement of Colored People Image Award 1970, 1971, 1973, 1975; Man of the Year Award (Publicists' Guild of America) 1971; B'nai B'rith Man of the Year Award 1985, N.A.A.C.P. Humanitarian of the Year 1983. *Publication:* Aaron Spelling: A Prime Time Life 1996. *Address:* Spelling Entertainment Group, 5700 Wilshire Boulevard, Floor 5, Los Angeles, CA 90036, USA.

SPENCE, A. Michael, MA, PhD; American economist; ed Princeton Univ., Oxford Univ., UK, Harvard Univ.; Assoc. Prof. Harvard Univ. 1973–75, Chair. Advisory Cttee on Shareholder Responsibility 1978–79, Prof. 1979–86, Chair. Project in Industry and Competitive Analysis 1980–85, Chair. Business Econs PhD Program 1981–83, Chair. Dept of Econs 1983–84, Dean of Faculty

1984–90; Philip H. Knight Prof. Stanford Univ. 1990–2000, Dean 1990–99, Prof. Emer. 2000–; Dir Gen. Mills, Inc., Nike, Inc., Siebel Systems, Inc., Exult, Inc., Blue Martini Software, Torstar, ITI Educ.; mem. American Econ. Asscn; Fellow AAAS, Econometric Soc.; Nobel Prize in Econs 2001 (Jt recipient); numerous other awards and prizes. *Address:* Stanford Business School, 518 Memorial Way, Stanford University, Stanford, CA 94305-5015, USA (Office). *Telephone:* (650) 723-2146 (Office).

SPENCE, Jonathan Dermot, PhD; American professor of history; b. 11 Aug. 1936, Surrey, England; s. of Dermot Spence and Muriel Crailsham; m. 1st Helen Alexander 1962 (divorced 1993); two s.; m. 2nd Chin Annping 1993; ed Univ. of Cambridge, UK and Yale Univ.; Asst Prof. of History, Yale Univ. 1966–71, Prof. 1971–; Visiting Prof. Univ. of Beijing 1987; mem. Bd of Govs. Yale Univ. Press 1988–; mem. American Acad. of Arts and Sciences, American Philosophical Soc.; Guggenheim Fellow 1979–80; MacArthur Fellow 1987–92; Hon. LHD (Knox Coll.) 1984, (New Haven) 1989; Hon. LittD (Wheeling Coll.) 1985, (Chinese Univ. of Hong Kong) 1996, (Gettysburg) Coll. 1996, (Union Coll.) 2000, (Beloit Coll.) 2000, (Conn. Coll.) 2000; Vursell Prize, American Acad. and Inst. of Arts and Letters 1983, Comisso Prize (Italy) 1987; Gelber Literary Prize (Canada) 1991. *Publications:* Ts'Ao Yin and The K'Ang-Hsi Emperor 1966, To Change China 1969, Emperor of China 1974, The Death of Woman Wang 1978, The Gate of Heavenly Peace 1981, The Memory Palace of Matteo Ricci 1984, The Question of Hu 1988, The Search for Modern China 1990, Chinese Roundabout 1992, God's Chinese Son 1996, The Chan's Great Continent 1998, Mao Zedong 1999, The Chan's Great Continent 1998, Mao Zedong 1999. *Address:* Department of History, Yale University, P.O. Box 208324, New Haven, CT 06520 (Office); 691 Forest Road, New Haven, CT 06515, USA (Home). *Telephone:* (203) 432-1333 (Office). *Website:* www.yale.edu (Office).

SPENCER, Baldwin; Antiguan politician and trade unionist; b. 8 Oct. 1948; m.; one s. one d.; Leader United Progressive Party and Leader of the Opposition. *Leisure interests:* football, cricket, basketball, listening to steel band music, reading, dancing. *Address:* United Progressive Party, Nevis Street, St. John's (Office); Cooks Estate, St John's, Antigua (Home). *Telephone:* 562-1049 (Office); 461-4657 (Home); 462-1818. *Fax:* 462-5937 (Office); 562-1065 (Home). *E-mail:* upp@candw.ag (Office). *Website:* www.uppantigua .com (Office).

SPENCER, Elizabeth, MA; American author; b. 1921, Carollton, Miss.; d. of James L. Spencer and Mary James McCain; m. John A. B. Rusher 1956 (died 1998); ed Belhaven Coll. and Vanderbilt Univ.; Writer-in-residence, Univ. of N Carolina 1969, Hollins Coll. 1973, Concordia Univ. 1977–78, Adjunct Prof. 1981–86; Visiting Prof. Univ. of NC, Chapel Hill 1986–92; Vice-Chancellor Fellowship of Southern Writers 1993–97; mem. American Acad. of Arts and Letters; Guggenheim Foundation Fellow 1953; Hon. LittD (Southwestern Univ., Memphis) 1968, (Concordia Univ.) 1987, (Univ. of the South) 1992, (Univ. of NC) 1998, (Belhaven Coll.) 1999; Rosenthal Foundation Award, American Acad. of Arts and Letters 1957; McGraw-Hill Fiction Award 1960, Award of Merit for short story, American Acad. of Arts and Letters 1983, Salem Award for Literature 1992, Dos Passos Award for Fiction 1992, NC Gov.'s Award for Literature 1994, Fortner Award for Literature 1998, Mississippi State Library Asscn Award for Non-fiction 1999, Thomas Wolfe Award, Univ. of NC 2002, NC Hall of Fame 2002, William Faulkner Award for Literary Excellence 2002. *Publications:* Fire in the Morning 1948, This Crooked Way 1952, The Voice at the Back Door 1956, The Light in the Piazza 1960 (film MGM 1962), Knights and Dragons 1965, No Place for an Angel 1967, Ship Island and other stories 1968, The Snare 1972, The Stories of Elizabeth Spencer 1981, Marilee 1981, The Salt Line 1984, Jack of Diamonds and Other Stories 1988, For Lease or Sale (play) 1989, On the Gulf 1991, The Night Travellers 1991, Landscapes of the Heart (memoir) 1998, The Southern Woman: New and Selected Fiction 2001; short stories in magazines and collections. *Leisure interests:* movies, theatre, travel. *Address:* 402 Longleaf Drive, Chapel Hill, NC 27517, USA (Home). *Telephone:* (919) 929-2115. *E-mail:* elizabeth0222@earthlink.net (Home). *Website:* www .elizabethspencerwriter.com (Home).

SPENCER, John; British snooker player; b. 18 June 1935, Radcliffe, Lancs.; s. of William Spencer and Anne Spencer (née Bleakley); m. Margot Anni Sawbridge 1969; ed Stand Grammar School; Chair. World Professional Billiards and Snooker Asscn Ltd 1990–96; World Professional Snooker Champion in 1969, 1970, 1977; retd 1992; TV snooker commentator. *Publication:* Spencer on Snooker. *Leisure interest:* golf. *Address:* 17 Knowles Street, Radcliffe, Lancs., M26 4DN, England. *Telephone:* (161) 725-9656. *Fax:* (161) 725-9650.

SPERBER, Dan; French social sciences researcher; b. 20 June 1942, Cagnes; s. of the late Manes Sperber; ed Sorbonne, Oxford Univ., UK; researcher CNRS 1965–; Dir 1983–; Co-f. EURO-EDU Asscn LSE, Van Leer Inst., Jerusalem, Inst. for Advanced Study, Princeton Univ., Univ. of Michigan Duxx School, Monterrey, Univ. of Hong Kong; Rivers Memorial Medal (Royal Anthropological Inst.) 1991. *Publications:* Rethinking Symbolism 1975, On Anthropological Knowledge 1982, Relevance: Communication and Cognition (with Deirdre Wilson) 1986, Explaining Culture 1996. *Address:* CNRS, 3 rue Michel-Ange, 75794 Paris, France. *Website:* www.dan.sperber.com (Office).

SPERLICH, Peter Werner, PhD; American political scientist and legal consultant; b. 27 June 1934, Breslau, Germany (now Wrocław, Poland); s. of Max Otto and Anneliese Gertrud (née Greulich) Sperlich; ed Minnesota State Univ. at Mankato, Univ. of Mich.; arrived in USA 1956, naturalized 1961;

faculty mem. Univ. of Calif. at Berkeley 1963–, Prof., Law School 1963–, Prof. of Political Science 1980–; consultant, court and law firms; Social Science Research Council Fellow 1966, Ford Foundation Fellow 1968; mem. American Legal Studies Asscn, Law and Soc. Asscn, Nat. Asscn for Dispute Resolution, Int. Soc. of Political Psychology, Soc. for Psychological Study of Social Issues, American, Int. and Western Political Science Asscns., Conf. Group on German Politics; research on law and politics in USA, Germany, Austria, Denmark, the Netherlands, Switzerland, the UK, Canada, Mexico, the USSR, Japan, Thailand, Hong Kong. *Achievements:* work cited by US Supreme Court and various state courts. *Publications:* Conflict and Harmony in Human Affairs 1971, Single Family Defaults and Foreclosures 1975, Trade Rules and Industry Practices 1976, Over-the-Counter Drug Advertisements 1977, Residing in a Mobile Home 1977, An Evaluation of the Emergency School Aid Act Nonprofit Organization 1978, Rotten Foundations – The Conceptual Basis of the Marxist-Leninist Regimes of East Germany and Other Countries of the Soviet Bloc 2002; also numerous articles. *Address:* University of California, 210 Barrows Hall, Berkeley, CA 94720 (Office); 35503 Vista del Luna, Rancho Mirage, CA 92270, USA (Home). *Telephone:* (760) 770-0899 (Home).

SPERO, Nancy, BFA; American artist; b. 24 Aug. 1926, Cleveland, Ohio; d. of Henry Spero and Polly Spero; m. Leon Golub 1951; three s.; ed Chicago Art Inst., Atelier André l'Hôte, École des Beaux Arts, Paris; Hon. DFA (Chicago) 1991. *Solo exhibitions include:* Everson Museum of Art (Syracuse, NY) 1987, Rhona Hoffman Gallery (Chicago) 1988, Museum of Contemporary Art (Los Angeles) 1988, Le Grand Halle de la Villette (Paris) 1989, S. L. Simpson Gallery (Toronto) 1989, Josh Baer Gallery (New York) 1989, 1991, Haus am Walsee (Berlin) 1990, Honolulu Acad. of Arts 1990, Gallery Hibell (Tokyo) 1990, Anthony Reynolds Gallery (London) 1990, Galleria Stefani Miscetti (Rome) 1991, Künstlerhaus Salzburg 1991, Barbara Gross Galerie (Munich) 1991, Galerie Raymond Bollag (Zürich) 1991, Jürgen Becker Galerie (Hamburg) 1991, Museum of Modern Art (New York) 1992, The American Center (Paris) 1994, Hiroshima City Museum of Contemporary Art (Hiroshima, Japan) 1996, Miami Univ. (Oxford, Ohio) 2000. *Joint exhibitions include:* Whitney Museum of American Art (New York) 1993, Museum of Modern Art (New York) 1995. *Permanent installations include:* R. C. Harris Water Filtration Plant (Toronto) 1988, Well Woman Centre and exterior mural (Londonderry) 1990, Inst. of Contemporary Art (Philadelphia) 1991, Von der Heydt Museum (Wuppertal) 1991, Círculo de Bellas Artes (Madrid) 1991; also rep. in many collections including Art Gallery of Ont. (Toronto), Australian Nat. Gallery, Centro Cultural (Mexico), Museum of Fine Arts (Hanoi), Ulmer Museum (Germany), Musée des Beaux-Arts de Montréal; CAPS Fellow NY State Council on the Arts 1976–77. *Address:* 530 La Guardia Place, New York, NY 10012, USA.

SPETH, James Gustave, BA, BLitt, LLB; American international organization administrator; b. 4 March 1942, Orangeburg, SC; s. of James Gustave and Amelia St Clair Albergotti; m. Caroline Cameron Council 1964; two s. one d.; ed Yale Univ. and Oxford Univ., UK; barrister, Washington 1969, Clerk, Supreme Court 1969–70; Sr Staff Attorney Nat. Resources Defence Council, Washington 1977–79, mem. Bd Dirs. 1981–82; Chair. Council for Environmental Quality 1977–79; Prof. of Law Georgetown Univ. 1981–82; Pres. and Founder World Resources Inst. 1982–93; joined UNDP 1982, Admin. 1993–99; Dean and Prof. Yale School of Forestry and Environment Studies, Yale Univ. 1999–; several awards. *Address:* 88 Mulberry Farms Road, Guilford, CT 06437, USA (Home). *E-mail:* gus.speth@yale.edu (Office).

ŠPIDLA, Vladimír, PhD; Czech politician; b. 22 April 1951, Prague; s. of Václav Špidla and Dagmar Špidla; m. 1st; two s.; m. 2nd Viktorie Spidla; one d. one s.; ed Charles Univ., Prague; fmr archaeologist, worker at historical monuments, sawmill, dairy and livestock industry; Vice-Pres. for Education, Health Service, Social Affairs and Culture, Dist Cttee, Jindřichův Hradec 1990–91; Dir Labour Office, Jindřichův Hradec 1991–96; mem. Chamber of Deputies 1996–; Deputy Prime Minister and Minister of Labour and Social Affairs 1998–2002; Prime Minister of the Czech Repub. 2002–; Founding mem. Czech Social Democratic Party (CSSD) Br. in S. Bohemia 1989, joined party leadership 1992, Vice-Chair. CSSD 1997–2001, Chair. 2001–. *Leisure interests:* jogging, poetry. *Address:* Office of the Government of the Czech Republic, nábř. E. Beneše 4, 118 01 Prague 1, Czech Republic (Office). *Telephone:* (2) 24002111 (Office). *Fax:* (2) 24810231 (Office). *E-mail:* www@ vlada.cz (Office). *Website:* www.vlada.cz (Office).

SPIELBERG, Steven, BA; American film director; b. 18 Dec. 1947, Cincinnati, Ohio; s. of Arnold Spielberg and Leah (née Posner) Spielberg; m. 1st Amy Irving (q.v.) 1985 (divorced 1989); two s.; m. 2nd Kate Capshaw; two d. (one adopted); ed Calif. State Coll., Long Beach; won film contest with war film Escape to Nowhere 1961; Dir episodes of TV series, including Night Gallery, Marcus Welby, MD, Columbo; directed 20-minute short Amblin'; Dir TV films Duel 1971, Something Evil 1972; Dirs Guild of America Award Fellowship 1986; co-f. Dreamworks SKG 1995–; f. Starbright Foundation; Dr hc (Univ. of S Calif.) 1994; Hon. DLitt (Sussex) 1997; Irving G. Thalberg Award 1987, Golden Lion Award (Venice Film Festival) 1993, BAFTA Award 1994, Acad. Award for Schindler's List 1994, David Lean (BAFTA); John Huston Award for Artists Rights 1995, James Smithson Bicentennial Medal 1999, Lifetime Achievement Award, Dir's Guild of America 1999, Britannia Award 2000; Grosses Bundesverdienstkreuz 1998; Hon. KBE. *Films directed:* The Sugarland Express 1974, Jaws 1975, Close Encounters of the Third Kind 1977, 1941 1979, Raiders of the Lost Ark 1981, E.T. (The Extra Terrestrial) 1982, Indiana

Jones and the Temple of Doom 1984, The Color Purple (also produced) 1985, Empire of the Sun 1988; I Wanna Hold Your Hand (produced) 1978, Poltergeist (co-wrote and produced) 1982, Gremlins (produced) 1984, Young Sherlock Holmes 1985 (exec. producer), Back to the Future (co-exec. producer), The Goonies (writer and exec. producer) 1986, Batteries Not Included (exec. producer) 1986, The Money Pit (co-produced) 1986, An American Tail (co-exec. producer) 1986, Always 1989, Gremlins II (exec. producer), Dad (exec. producer), Joe versus the Volcano (exec. producer), Hook 1991, Cape Fear (co-exec. producer) 1992, Jurassic Park 1992, Schindler's List 1993 (Acad. Award for Best Dir), Casper (producer) 1995, Some Mother's Son 1996, Twister 1996 (exec. producer); The Lost World: Jurassic Park 1997, Amistad 1997, Deep Impact 1998, Saving Private Ryan 1998 (Acad. Award for Best Dir), The Last Days (documentary) 1999, AI: Artificial Intelligence 2001, Minority Report 2002, Catch Me If You Can 2003. *Television includes:* Band of Brothers (series) 2000, Semper Fi 2000, Taken 2002. *Publication:* Close Encounters of the Third Kind (with Patrick Mann). *Address:* CAA, 9830 Wilshire Boulevard, Beverly Hills, CA 90212, USA.

SPIELMANN, Alphonse, DenD; Luxembourg judge; b. 23 May 1931, Brattert; m. Catherine Hildgen 1961; three s.; ed Faculté de Droit and Inst. de Criminologie, Univ. of Paris and Centre Universitaire de Luxembourg; Attorney-Gen., Grand Duchy of Luxembourg; Judge, European Court of Human Rights 1985–98; numerous int. activities. *Publications:* Liberté d'expression ou censure? 1982, La Convention européenne des droits de l'homme et le droit luxembourgeois 1991. *Leisure interest:* history of the Second World War. *Address:* 12 Côte d'Eich, 1450 (Office); 108 rue des Muguets, 2167 Luxembourg, Luxembourg (Home).

SPIELVOGEL, Carl, BA; American advertising executive; b. 27 Dec. 1928, New York City; s. of Joseph Spielvogel and Sadie (née Tellerman) Spielvogel; m. Barbara Lee Diamonstein 1981; two s. one d.; ed Baruch Coll.; reporter, columnist, New York Times 1950–60; with McCann Erickson, Inc., Interpublic Group of Cos., Inc., New York City 1960–74; Vice-Chair., Chair. Exec. Cttee and Dir Interpublic Group of Cos., Inc. 1974–80; Chair. and CEO Backer & Spielvogel Inc. 1980–87, Backer Spielvogel Bates Worldwide Inc. New York 1987–94; Chair., CEO United Auto Group 1994–97, Consultant –2000; Dir Manhattan Industries, Franklin Corpn, NY Philharmonic, Data Broadcasting Corpn –2000, 2001–; Chair. Cttee Div., WNET-Public Broadcasting, Business Cttee, Metropolitan Museum of Art; Amb. to the Slovak Repub. 2000–01. *Address:* Data Broadcasting Corporation, 22 Crosby Drive, Bedford, MA 01730, USA (Office).

SPIERS, Ronald Ian, BA, MA; American diplomatist; b. 9 July 1925, Orange, NJ; s. of Thomas Hoskins Spiers and Blanca Spiers (née De Pothier); m. Patience Baker 1949; one s. three d.; ed Dartmouth Coll., Princeton Univ.; USN 1943–46; mem. U.S. Del. to UN 1955–58; Dir Disarmament Affairs, State Dept, Washington 1958–62, NATO Affairs 1962–66; Political Counsellor, US Embassy in London 1966–69, Minister 1974–77; Asst Sec. of State for Political-Mil. Affairs 1969–73; Amb. to the Bahamas 1973–74, to Turkey 1977–80; Asst Sec. for Intelligence and Research, Dept of State 1980–81; Amb. to Pakistan 1981–83; Under-Sec. for Man., Dept of State 1983–89; Under-Sec.-Gen. for Political and Gen. Ass. Affairs and Secr. Services, UN, New York 1989–92; consultant to State Dept 1992–; mem. Council on Foreign Relations; Fellow Nat. Acad. of Public Admin., American Acad. of Diplomacy; Presidential Distinguished Service Award 1984. *Leisure interests:* gardening, furniture making, classical music, opera. *Address:* 1320 Middletown Road, S. Londonderry, VT 05155, USA. *Telephone:* (802) 824-6482 (Home). *E-mail:* embassy@sover.net (Home).

SPIES von BÜLLESHEIM, Freiherr Adolf Wilhelm, DJur; German business executive, politician, lawyer and farmer; b. 4 June 1929, Hückelhoven; s. of Egon Freiherr von Büllesheim and Maria Freiin von Oer; m. Maria Gräfin von Mirbach-Harff 1961; one s. four d.; ed Univs. of Bonn and Munich; solicitor, Düsseldorf and Mönchengladbach 1960–; farmer on family estate in Hückelhoven 1961–; Mayor of Hückelhoven 1969–73; mem. Bundestag 1972–87; mem. WEU 1977–87, Council of Europe 1977–87; Chair. Eschweiler Bergwerks Verein AG, Herzogenrath 1987–; mem. Bd of several cos.; Bundesverdienstkreuz, Commdr Ordre de Mérite (Luxembourg) 1989. *Leisure interests:* hunting, skiing. *Address:* Haus Hall bei Ratheim, 41836 Hückelhoven, Germany. *Telephone:* (2433) 5066.

SPINETTA, Jean-Cyril, LLB, BSc; French airline executive; b. 4 Oct. 1943, Paris; s. of Adrien Spinetta and Antoinette Brignole; m. Nicole Spinetta (née Ricquebourg); two s. two d.; ed Institut d'études politiques and Ecole Nationale d'administration, Paris; entered French civil service 1972, Head Investments and Planning Dept, Ministry of Educ. 1972–76; Head Information Dept, Office of the Prime Minister 1981–83, Chief of Staff for Michel Delebarre 1984–90; successively Minister of Labour and Vocational Training, Minister of Social Affairs and Employment and Minister of Planning and Devt, Housing and Transport; joined Air Inter 1990, Pres. and CEO 1990–93; advisory posts to Pres. of France (including industrial matters) 1993–95; Admin. in charge of Public Service 1995–96; joined staff of Edith Cresson, European Commr for Science, Research and Educ. 1996–97; Chair. and CEO Air France 1997–; Dir Centre nat. d'études spatiales 1999–; Pres. Assćn European Airlines (AEA) 2001–; Chair. Scientific Council, Inst. of Public Admin. and Econ. Devt 2002–; Chevalier Légion d'honneur, Ordre nat. du Mérite, Officier des Palmes Académiques. *Address:* Groupe Air France, 45 rue

de Paris, 95747 Roissy CDG Cedex (Office); 7 rue Pierre-Nicole, 75005 Paris, France. *Telephone:* 1-41-56-78-00 (Office); 1-43-25-01-95 (Home). *Fax:* 1-41-56-61-59 (Office).

SPIRIDONOV, Yurii Alekseyevich, CAND.TECH.SC.; Russian politician; b. 1 Nov. 1938, Poltava, Omsk Region; m.; one d.; ed Sverdlovsk Mining Inst., Higher CP School at Cen. Cttee CPSU; engineer mine, Gorny Magadan Region 1961–69; master, head of section, chief engineer, Dir Yager oil mine Komi Autonomous Repub. 1969–75; party functionary different posts in Ukhta City CP Cttee 1975–85; Second Sec., First Sec. Komi Regional CP Cttee 1985–89; USSR Peoples' Deputy 1989–92; Chair. Supreme Soviet Komi Autonomous Repub. 1990–94; Chair. of Komi Repub. Govt, Head of Repub. 1994–2001; mem. Russian Council of Fed. 1993–2001; Peoples' Deputy of Komi Autonomous Repub.; mem. Russian Acad. of Natural Sciences, Acad. of Mining Sciences. *Address:* c/o House of Government, Kommunisticheskaya str. 9, 167010 Syktyvkar, Komi Republic, Russia (Office).

SPIRIN, Aleksandr Sergeyevich, PhD, DSc; Russian biochemist and molecular biologist; b. 4 Sept. 1931, Kaliningrad (now Korolev), Moscow Region; s. of Sergey Stepanovitch Spirin and Elena Abramovna Spirina (née Kalabekova); m. Tatiana Nikolayevna Fokina; ed Moscow State Univ.; mem. staff, Bakh Inst. of Biochem. 1958–62, Head of Lab. 1962–73; Prof. Moscow State Univ. 1964–92, Prof. Emer. 1992–, Prof. and Chair of Molecular Biology 1973–; Head of Lab. of Protein Synthesis, Inst. of Protein Research 1967–, Dir Inst. 1967–2001; Corresp. mem. USSR (now Russian) Acad. of Sciences 1966–70, mem. 1970–, mem. Presidium 1988–2001, Adviser Presidium 2001–; Chair. Bd Pushchino Scientific Centre 1990–2000; mem. Deutsche Akad. der Naturforscher Leopoldina 1974, Czechoslovak Acad. of Sciences 1988, Academia Europaea 1990, European Molecular Biology Org. 1991, Royal Physiographic Soc. (Lund) 1996, American Philosophical Soc. 1997; Order of Lenin and other decorations; Dr hc (Univ. of Granada) 1972, (Univ. of Toulouse) 1999; Sir Hans Krebs Medal 1969, Lenin Prize 1976, State Prize of the USSR for Science 1988, Ovchinnikov Prize, Russian Acad. of Science 1992, Karpinskij Prize of FVS for Achievements in Science (Hamburg) 1992, State Prize of Russian Fed. for Science 2000, Belozersky Prize, Russian Acad. of Sciences 2000, Big Gold Lomonosov Medal of the Russian Acad. of Sciences 2001. *Publications:* Macromolecular Structure of Ribonucleic Acids 1964, The Ribosome 1969, Ribosome Structure and Protein Biosynthesis 1986, Ribosomes 1999, Cell-Free Translation Systems (ed.) 2002. *Leisure interests:* hunting, breeding cats. *Address:* Institute of Protein Research, Russian Academy of Sciences, 142290 Pushchino, Moscow Region (Office); Zelinsky str. 38/8, Apt. 65, 119334 Moscow, Russia (Home). *Telephone:* (095) 924-04-93 (Office); (8277) 73-08-30 (Office); (095) 137-39-20 (Home). *Fax:* (095) 924-04-93 (Office). *E-mail:* spirin@vega.protres.ru (Office).

SPIROIU, Lt-Gen. Niculae; Romanian politician; b. 6 July 1936, Bucharest; s. of Constantin Spiroiu and Paulina Spiroiu; m. 1963 (wife died 1991); one s. one d.; ed Tech. Mil. Acad.; scientific researcher with the Centre of Studies and Tests for Tanks and Autos Deputy Chief and Tech. Dept Chief; State Sec. and Head of the Army Supply Dept; Minister of Nat. Defence 1992–94; Counsellor Minister to UN 1994–. *Leisure interests:* reading, symphonic music, motor cycling, motoring.

SPITAELS, Guy; Belgian politician; ed Catholic Univ. of Louvain; Prof. of Econs Univ. of Brussels; joined Socialist Party (French-speaking) 1961; Chef de Cabinet to Prime Minister Edmond Leburton 1973; Vice-Premier 1979–81; Leader of Socialist Party (French-speaking) 1981–92, Wallonia Regional Govt (PS-PSC coalition) 1992–94; Chair. Confed. of European Socialist Parties 1989. *Address:* Parti Socialiste, Maison du PS, 13 boulevard de l'Empereur, 1000 Brussels, Belgium.

SPITAL, Hermann Josef Silvester, DTheol; German ecclesiastic; b. 31 Dec. 1925, Münster; ed Gymnasium Paulinum, Münster and theological studies in Münster; ordained 1952; Generalvikar, Münster 1973; consecrated bishop 1980; Bishop of Trier 1981–2001; Dr hc 1996. *Publication:* Der Taufritus in den deutschen Ritualien 1968. *Address:* Sieh um Dich 2, 54290 Trier, Germany. *Telephone:* 0651-44441.

SPITERI, Lino, MA, DIP. SOC. STUD.; Maltese politician and journalist; b. 21 Sept. 1938, Qormi; s. of the late Emanuel Spiteri and of Pauline Spiteri (née Calleja); m. Vivienne Azzopardi 1964; two s. two d.; ed Lyceum, Plater Coll. and St Peter's Coll. Oxford; teacher 1956–57; Clerk UK Mil. Establishment 1957–62; Deputy Ed. Il-Helsien (daily) 1962–64, It-Torca (weekly) 1964–66; Ed. Malta News 1967–68; Research Officer Malta Chamber of Commerce 1968–70; with Cen. Bank of Malta as Sr Research Officer, then Asst Head of Research 1971, Head of Research 1972, Deputy Gov. and Chair. Bd of Dirs. 1974–81; Minister of Finance 1981–83, of Econ. Planning and Trade 1983–87; Opposition Spokesman on Econs and Finance 1989–96; Chair. Public Accounts Cttee 1995–96, Co-Chair, Malta-EU Jt Parl. Cttee 1996–98; Minister for Econ. Affairs and Finance 1996–97; mem. Malta Labour Party Gen. Exec. 1958–66; Gen. Sec. Labour League of Youth 1961–62; MP 1962–66; Malta Corresp. for Observer, Observer Foreign News Service, Guardian 1967–71; mem. Malta Broadcasting Authority 1968–70; mem. Comm. on Higher Educ. 1977–79; Chair. Students Selection Bd 1978–79; Pres. Qormi Football Club 1977–79; columnist, Sunday Times of Malta and others. *Publications:* Studies: The Development of Tourism in Malta 1968, The Development of Industry in Malta 1969; Fiction and poetry: Tad-Demm u L-Laham (short stories) 1968, Hala taz-Zghozija (short stories) 1970, Anatomija (short stories) 1978, Iz-Zewgt Ihbieb (short stories) 1979, Stqarrija (verses)

1979, Il-Halliel (short stories) 1979, Rivoluzzjoni do minore (novel) 1980, Jien Nimxi Wahdi (verses) 1987, Mal-Hmura tas-silla (short stories) 1993, Fejn Jixrob Il-Qasab fis-sajf (short stories) 1996, Stejjer ghal Valentina (short stories) 1997, Ghaliex ix-Xewk (verses) 1998, Honourable People (short stories), Moods and Angles (collected articles) 1998. *Leisure interests:* listening to other people's views, reading, writing. *Address:* "Aurora", Triq Il-Linja, H'Attard, BZN 05, Malta. *Telephone:* 21435089. *E-mail:* lspiteri@onvol.net (Home).

SPITZ, Lewis, MB, ChB, PhD, FRCS, FRCSE; British paediatric surgeon and university professor; b. 25 Aug. 1939, Pretoria, S. Africa; s. of Woolf Spitz and Selma Spitz; m.; one s. one d.; ed Univs of Pretoria and Witwatersrand; Consultant Paediatric Surgeon, Sheffield 1974–79; Nuffield Prof. of Paediatric Surgery, Inst. of Child Health, Univ. Coll. London 1979–; Consultant Paediatric Surgeon, Great Ormond St Hosp. for Children, London 1979–; Hunterian Prof., Royal Coll. of Surgeons (England) 2001–02; Fellow Royal Coll. of Paediatrics and Child Health,; Hon. Fellow American Acad. of Pediatrics; Hon. MD (Sheffield). *Publication:* Pediatric Surgery (co-ed. with A. G. Coran) 1995. *Address:* Paediatric Surgery, Great Ormond Street Hospital for Children, Great Ormond Street, London, WC1N 3JH (Office); 78 Wood Vale, London, N10 3DN, England (Home). *Telephone:* (20) 7829-8691 (Office); (20) 8444-9985 (Home). *Fax:* (20) 7404-6181 (Office); (20) 8883-6417 (Home). *E-mail:* L.Spitz@ich.ucl.ac.uk (Office).

SPITZ, Mark (Andrew); American swimmer; b. 10 Feb. 1950, Modesto, Calif.; s. of Arnold Spitz; m. Suzy Weiner; two s.; ed Indiana Univ.; won two gold medals in the team relay races (4×100m and 4×200m), Olympic Games, Mexico City 1968; became first athlete to win seven gold medals in a single Olympic Games, Munich 1972, in the 100m and 200m freestyle, 100m and 200m butterfly and as a team mem. of the 4×100m relay, 4×200m relay and 4×100m medley relay (all world records); unsuccessful comeback 1991; corporate spokesman, TV broadcaster, real-estate co. owner; mem. Int. Swimming Hall of Fame Selection Cttee; promotional work for US Olympic Cttee; World Swimmer of the Year 1969, 1971, 1972, James E. Sullivan Award (for America's Outstanding Amateur Athlete) 1971, Associated Press Male Athlete of the Year 1972, Athlete of the Century (Water Sports) 1999; mem. Laurens World Sports Acad. *Leisure interests:* sailing, travel.

SPITZER, Eliot; American lawyer; m. Silda Spitzer; three d.; ed Princeton Univ. and Harvard Law School; Asst Dist. Attorney, Manhattan 1986–92; fmr clerk to U.S. Dist Court judge, Chief of Labor Racketeering Unit; worked at Skadden, Arps, Slate, Meagher & Flom; fmr Partner Constantine & Partners; fmr Assoc. Paul Weiss, Rifkind, Wharton & Garrison; Attorney-Gen. for New York State 1999–; fmr Ed. Harvard Law Review. *Leisure interest:* community service. *Address:* Executive Office of the Attorney General, The Capitol, Albany, NY 12224-0341, USA (Office). *Telephone:* (518) 474-7330 (Office). *Website:* www.oag.state.ny.us (Office).

SPIVAKOV, Vladimir Teodorovich; Russian violinist and conductor; b. 12 Sept. 1944, Ufa, Bashkiria; m. Satinik Saakyants; three d.; ed Moscow State Conservatory, postgrad. with Yury Yankelevich; studied violin since age of six years with B. Kroger in Leningrad; prize winner several int. competitions including Tchaikovsky, Moscow; Founder and Conductor Chamber Orchestra Virtuosi of Moscow 1979–; f. and Artistic Dir Music Festival in Colmar, France 1988–; Artistic Dir and Chief Conductor Russian Nat. Symphony Orchestra 1999–; USSR State Prize 1989, USSR People's Artist 1990, Triumph Prize. *Leisure interest:* collecting paintings. *Address:* Columbia Artists Management, 165 West 57th Street, New York, NY 10019, USA; Vspolny per. 17, Apt. 14, Moscow, Russia. *Telephone:* (095) 290-23-24 (Moscow); 1-45-25-50-85 (Paris). *Fax:* 1-45-25-04-60 (Paris).

SPOHR, Arnold Theodore, OC; Canadian ballet director, teacher and choreographer; b. 26 Dec. 1927, Rhein, Canada; ed St John's High School and Winnipeg Teachers' Coll.; Piano Teacher 1946–51; Prin. Dancer Royal Winnipeg Ballet 1947–54; CBC Television Choreographer and performer 1955–57; Choreographer Rainbow Stage 1957–60; Artistic Dir Royal Winnipeg Ballet 1958–88; Dir-Teacher Royal Winnipeg Ballet School 1958–88, Artistic Dir Emer. 1988–; Dir Nelson School of Fine Arts Dance Dept 1964–67; Artistic Dir Dance Dept Banff School of Fine Arts 1967–81; mem. Bd of Dirs. Canadian Theatre Centre; Hon. LLD (Univ. of Manitoba) 1970, many awards including Molson Prize, Canada Council 1970, Centennial Medal, Gov. of Canada 1967, Royal Bank Award 1987. *Choreography:* Ballet Premier 1950, Intermed 1951, E Minor 1959, Hansel and Gretel 1960 and 18 musicals for Rainbow State. *Leisure interests:* sports, piano, travel-research for study of every type of dancing. *Address:* Canada's Royal Winnipeg Ballet, 380 Graham Avenue, Winnipeg, Man., R3C 4K2, Canada.

SPONG, Rt Rev John Shelby, AB, MDiv; American ecclesiastic; b. 16 June 1931, Charlotte, NC; s. of John Shelby Spong and Doolie Griffith Spong; m. 1st Joan Lydia Ketner 1952 (died 1988); three d.; m. 2nd Christine Mary Bridger 1990; ed Univ. of North Carolina, Chapel Hill, Virginia Theological Seminary, Alexandria, Va; Rector St Joseph's, Durham, NC 1955–57, Calvary Church, Tarboro, NC 1957–65, St John's Church, Lynchburg, Va 1965–69, St Paul's Church, Richmond, Va 1969–76, Bishop, Diocese of Newark, NJ 1976–2000; Pres. NJ Council of Churches; Quatercentenary Fellow, Emmanuel Coll. Cambridge, UK 1992; William Belden Noble Lecturer, Harvard Univ. 2000; Visiting Lecturer, Univ. of The Pucapé, Stockton, Calif. 2003; columnist for Beliefnet.com 1999–2000, AgoraMedia 2002–; has appeared on all major talk shows in USA, subject of major story by 60 Minutes (CBS),

extensive TV appearances in Canada, UK and Australia; Hon. DD (Va Theological Seminary), (St Paul's Coll.); Hon. DHL (Muhlenberg Coll.); Quatercentenary Scholar, Emmanuel Coll., Cambridge, UK 1992, David Frederick Strauss Award, Jesus Seminar 1999, Humanist of the Year, New York City 1999. *Radio:* Play by Play sportscaster in Jackson and Lynchburg, Va 1960–65. *Publications:* Honest Prayer 1973, This Hebrew Lord 1974, 1988, Dialogue: In Search of Jewish-Christian Understanding 1975, Christpower 1975, Life Approaches Death: A Dialogue on Medical Ethics 1976, The Living Commandments 1977, The Easter Moment 1980, Into the Whirlwind 1983, Beyond Moralism 1986, Consciousness and Survival 1987, Living in Sin? 1988, Rescuing the Bible from Fundamentalism 1991, Born of a Woman 1992, Resurrection: Myth or Reality? 1994, Liberating the Gospels: Reading the Bible with Jewish Eyes 1996, Why Christianity Must Change or Die: A Bishop Speaks to Believers in Exile 1998, Here I Stand: My Struggle for a Christianity of Integrity, Love and Equality 2000, A New Christianity for a New World 2001. *Address:* 24 Puddingstone Road, Morris Plains, NJ 07950, USA (Home).

SPONHEIM, Lars, MSc; Norwegian politician; b. 23 May 1957, Halden; m.; three c.; Consultant 1981–84; teacher Statens Gartnerskule Hjeltnes 1984–88, Prin. 1992–; mem. local council Ulvik Municipality 1984–95, Mayor 1988–91; mem. County Council, Hordalund Co. 1992–93; Dir of Agric., Ulvik and Granvin Municipalities 1993; mem. Parl. for Hordaland Co. to Storting (Parl.) 1993–, mem. Parl. Finance Cttee; Leader Liberal Party 1996–; Minister of Trade and Industry 1997–2000; mem. Parl. Foreign Cttee 2000–. *Address:* Venstre, Møllergt 16, 0179 Oslo, Norway. *Telephone:* 22-40-45-50 (Office). *Fax:* 22-40-45-51 (Office). *E-mail:* lars.sponheim@stortinget.no (Office); lars@venstre.no (Office). *Website:* www.venstre.no (Office).

SPORBORG, Christopher Henry, CBE; British banker; b. 17 April 1939; s. of the late Henry Nathan Sporborg and of Mary Rowlands; m. Lucinda Jane Hanbury 1961; two s. two d.; ed Rugby School, Emmanuel Coll. Cambridge; served as officer, Coldstream Guards; joined Hambros Bank 1962, Dir 1970, Exec. Dir Corp. Finance Dept 1975, Deputy Chair. 1983–95; Chair. Hambro Countrywide (now Countrywide Assured Group PLC) 1986–; Vice-Chair. Hambros PLC 1986–90, Deputy Chair. 1990–98; Dir various Hambro Group Cos.; Chair. Atlas Copco (UK) Holdings Ltd, Hambros Insurance Services Group 1993–; mem. Horserace Totalisator Bd 1993–96; Finance Steward, Jockey Club; Chair. Racecourse Holdings Trust 1998–; Dir Getty Images Inc. 1996–, Lindsey Morden Ltd 1999–; Steward Jockey Club 2001–. *Leisure interests:* riding, racing. *Address:* Brooms Farm, Upwick Green, Albury, Ware, Herts., SG11 2JX, England. *Telephone:* (1279) 771444.

SPOTTISWOODE, Clare Mary Joan, CBE, MA, M.PHIL.; British business executive; b. 20 March 1953, Lancs.; d. of Robert Spottiswoode and Charlotte Nuttall; m. Oliver Richards 1977; one s. three d.; ed Cheltenham Ladies' Coll., Clare Coll. Cambridge and Yale Univ., USA; economist, HM Treasury 1977–80; sole proprietor, import business, Spottiswoode Trading 1980–84; Chair. and Man. Dir Spottiswoode & Spottiswoode Ltd (micro-computer software house) 1984–90; also held several non-exec. directorships, taught at London Business School and acted as software consultant; Dir-Gen. of Gas Supply (Ofgas) 1993–98; Sr Vice-Pres. European Water 1998–; mem. Man. Group PA Consulting Group 1999–; Dir (non-exec.) Booker PLC; Dir (non-exec.) British Energy 2001–; Gov. Nat. Inst. of Econ. and Social Research; mem. Inst. of Man. Bd of Companions; Hon. Dr. Soc. Sci. (Brunel) 1997. *Publications:* Quill 1984, Abacus 1984. *Leisure interests:* children, theatre, gardening. *Address:* PA Consultancy, 123 Buckingham Palace Road, London, S.W.1, England (Office).

SPRATT, Sir Greville Douglas, GBE, TD, JP, DL, DLitt, FRSA, FRGS; British business executive; b. 1 May 1927, Westcliff-on-Sea; s. of Hugh D. Spratt and Sheelah I. Stace; m. Sheila F. Wade 1954 (died 2002); three d.; ed Leighton Park, Charterhouse and Sandhurst; served Coldstream Guards 1945–46; Commissioned Oxfordshire and Bucks Light Infantry 1946; seconded to Arab Legion 1946–48; joined HAC Infantry Bn 1950, CO 1962–65, Regimental Col 1966–70, mem. Court of Assistants 1960–70 and 1978–95; ADC to HM The Queen 1973–78; Lloyd's of London 1948–61, Underwriting Mem. 1950–; Man. Dir J. & N. Wade group 1972–76; Liveryman, Ironmongers' Co. 1977–, Master 1995–96; Alderman, Castle Baynard Ward 1978–95; Sheriff of City of London 1984–85; Lord Mayor of London 1987–88; Chancellor, City Univ. 1987–88; Dir Williams Lea Group, Craigie Taylor Int. Ltd; Chair. Forest Mere Ltd, Charterhouse Enterprises Ltd. 1992–95, Action Research for the Crippled Child 1989–99; Claremont and Kingsmead Underwriting Agency 1994–99; Regional Chair. Nat. Westminster Bank 1992–93; Vice-Pres. British Red Cross 1993–, Greater London TAVRA 1994–; holder of numerous civic, educational and charitable positions; Trustee Chichester Theatre and Cathedral; Hon. Col London Army Cadet Force 1983–98, Queen's Fusiliers 1988–92, London Regt 1992–95; Légion d'honneur, Ordre nat. du Mérite (France); Commdr Order of Lion (Malawi), Order of Aztec Eagle (Mexico), Order of Olav (Norway), Order of Merit (Senegal); KStJ; Hon. DLitt (City Univ.) 1988. *Leisure interests:* tennis, music, mil. history, stamp, coin and bank-note collecting. *Address:* W Kingsley Place, Kingsley Green, W Sussex, GU27 3LR, England. *Telephone:* (1428) 644367. *Fax:* (1428) 641405.

SPRIGGE, Timothy Lauro Squire, PhD, FRSE; British university professor; b. 14 Jan. 1932, London; s. of Cecil Sprigge and Katriona Sprigge; m. Giglia Gordon 1959; one s. two d.; ed Gonville and Caius Coll. Cambridge; Lecturer in Philosophy, Univ. Coll. London 1961–63, Univ. of Sussex 1963–70, Reader in Philosophy 1970–79; Prof. of Logic and Metaphysics, Univ. of Edin. 1979–89, Prof. Emer. 1989–, Endowment Fellow 1989–98, Hon. Fellow 1998–. *Publications:* Correspondence of Jeremy Bentham, Vols 1 and 2 (Ed.) 1968, Facts, Words and Beliefs 1968, Santayana: An Examination of his Philosophy 1974, The Vindication of Absolute Idealism 1983, Theories of Existence 1984, The Rational Foundations of Ethics 1987, James and Bradley: American Truth and British Reality 1993. *Leisure interests:* Five Hundred, Pinochle, Victorian novels, backgammon. *Address:* Philosophy Department, David Hume Tower, University of Edinburgh, George Square, Edinburgh, EH8 9JX (Office); 31A Raeburn Place, Edinburgh, EH4 1HU, Scotland (Home). *Telephone:* (131) 667-1011 (Office); (131) 315-2443 (Home). *E-mail:* sprigge@holyrood.ed.ac.uk (Office).

SPRING, Richard (Dick), BA, BL; Irish politician; b. 29 Aug. 1950, Tralee, Co. Kerry; s. of Dan Spring and Anna Laide; m. Kristi Lee Hutcheson 1977; two s. one d.; ed Mount St Joseph Coll., Roscrea, Co. Tipperary, Trinity Coll. Dublin, King's Inns, Dublin; mem. Dáil Éireann (House of Reps.) for Kerry North 1981–; Leader of Labour Party 1982–97; Tanaiste (Deputy Prime Minister) 1982–87 and Minister for the Environment 1982–83, for Energy 1983–87, Tanaiste and Minister for Foreign Affairs 1993–97; fmr Irish rugby union int.; Assos. Fellow Kennedy School of Govt, Harvard Univ. 1998–; Fellow Salzburg Seminar 1998; Dr. hc (Hartwick Coll., NY) 1998, (Misericordia Coll., Pa) 1999. *Leisure interests:* sport, reading, golf, swimming. *Address:* Dunroamin, Leinster House, Dublin 2; Cloonanorig, Tralee, Co. Kerry, Ireland (Home). *Telephone:* (66) 7125337 (Home); (1) 6183957.

SPRINGS, Alice (pseudonym of June Browne); Australian photographer; b. June 1923, Melbourne; m. Helmut Newton (q.v.) 1948; fmrly professional actress; professional photographer 1970–; clients have included Jean-Louis David, Fashion Magazine Dépêche Mode, Elle, Marie-Claire, Vogue, Vogue Homme, Nova, Mode Int., Absolu, London Cosmoplitan; contrib. to Egoiste, Vanity Fair, Interview, Passion, Stern, Decoration Internationale, Tatler, Photo, Les Cahiers de l'Energumène. *Solo exhibitions include:* Canon Gallery, Amsterdam 1978, Canon Gallery, Geneva 1980, Duc et Camroux, Paris 1980, David Heath Gallery, Atlanta 1982, Yuen Lui Gallery, Seattle 1982, Olympus Gallery, London 1983, Galerie de France, Paris 1983, Musée Cheret, Nice 1984, Musée Sainte Croix, Poitiers 1985, Documenta Gallery, Turin 1985, Centre Culturel, Orleans 1985, Centre Culturel et Artistique, Arbusson 1986, Espace Photographique de la Ville de Paris/Paris Audiovisuel 1986, Fotoform, Frankfurt am Main 1987, Gerfiollet, Amsterdam 1988, Olympus Galerie, Hamburg 1988, Nat. Portrait Gallery, London 1988, Musée d'Art Moderne, Paris 1988, Museo Contemporáneo, Mexico City 1990, Rheinisches Landesmuseum, Bonn 1991/92, 'Arrêt sur l'image', Bordeaux 1993, Galerie im alten Rathaus am Markt, Wittlich 1993, Hochschule für Graphik und Buchkunst, Leipzig 1993, FORUM, Bremen 1993. *Group exhibitions include:* Photokina, Cologne 1976, Photographers' Gallery, London 1979, G. Ray Hawkins, LA 1981, Grey Art Gallery, NY 1981, Paris Audiovisuel, French Photographers, Museum of Modern Art, Bratislava 1991, Teatro Circo (courtesy of Paris Audiovisuel), Braga 1992. *Catalogues:* Alice Springs Portraits, Musée Sainte Croix, Poitiers 1985, Espace Photo, Paris 1986, Musée d'Art Moderne de la Ville de Paris 1988, Centro Cultural Arte Contemporaneo, Mexico City 1991, Rheinisches Landesmuseum, Bonn 1991/92. *Film:* TV documentary 'Helmut by June' for Canal Plus 1995. *Publications:* Alice Springs Portraits 1983, 1986, 1991.

SPRINGSTEEN, Bruce; American singer and songwriter; b. 23 Sept. 1949, Freehold, NJ; s. of Douglas Springsteen and Adele Springsteen; m. 1st Julianne Phillips 1985 (divorced 1988); m. 2nd Patti Scialfa; one s. one d.; attended community coll.; performed in New York and NJ nightclubs; signed with Columbia Records 1972; first LP record Greetings from Asbury Park, New Jersey 1973; tours of USA and Europe with E-Street Band 1974–92; Golden Record Award 1975 (for Born to Run), Grammy Award, Best Male Vocalist 1984, 1987; Acad. Award for Best Original Song in a Film 1994, MTV Best Video from a Film Award 1994 (for Philadelphia). *Albums include:* The Wild, The Innocent and the E-Street Shuffle 1974, Born to Run 1975, Darkness on the Edge of Town 1978, The River 1981, Nebraska 1982, Born in the USA (25 million copies sold 1992) 1984, Bruce Springsteen and the E Street Band Live 1975–85 1986, Tunnel of Love 1987, Chimes of Freedom 1988, Human Touch 1992, Lucky Town 1992, Bruce Springsteen Greatest Hits 1995, The Ghost of Tom Joad 1995, Bruce Springsteen Plugged 1997, 18 Tracks 1998, The Rising (Grammy Award for Best Rock Album 2003) 2002. *Address:* c/o Premier Talent Agency, 3 East 54th Street, New York, NY 10022, USA.

SPRINKEL, Beryl Wayne, PhD; American economist and fmr government official; b. 20 Nov. 1923, Richmond, Mo.; s. of Clarence Sprinkel and Emma Sprinkel (née Schooley); m. 1st Esther Pollard (deceased); m. 2nd Barbara Angus Pipher (deceased); two s.; m. 3rd Lory Reid (née Kiefer) 1993; ed NW Missouri State Univ., Univs. of Missouri, Oregon and Chicago; served with U.S. army 1943–45; Instructor in Econs and Finance, Univ. of Missouri, Columbia 1948–49, Univ. of Chicago 1950–52; with Harris Trust and Savings Bank, Chicago 1952–81, Vice-Pres., economist 1960–68, Dir Research 1968–81, Exec. Vice-Pres. 1974–81; Under-Sec. for Monetary Affairs, Dept of the Treasury 1981–85; Chair. Pres.'s Council of Econ. Advisors 1985–89; mem. Pres.'s Cabinet 1987–89; Consulting Economist 1989–; Pres. Homewood-Flossmoor (Ill.) Community High School 1959–60; seven hon. degrees; Distinguished Alumnus Award (Chicago Univ.), Distinguished Service Award (Northwest Mo. State Univ.); Alexander Hamilton (U.S. Treasury)

1985; Distinguished Alumnus Award (Univ. of Missouri) 2001. *Publications:* Money and Stock Prices 1964, Money and Markets—A Monetarist View 1971, Winning with Money (co-author) 1977. *Leisure interests:* reading, writing, golf, tennis, fishing, travel. *Address:* 20140 St Andrew's Drive, Olympia Fields, IL 60461; 16625 Waters Edge, CT 101, Ft. Myers, FL 33908, USA. *Telephone:* (708) 481-9384 (Ill.); (941) 482-7593 (Fla). *Fax:* (708) 503-4430 (Ill.) (Home); (941) 482-7098 (Fla) (Home). *E-mail:* sprinkel@aol.com. (Home).

SQUIRE, Air Chief Marshal Sir Peter (Ted), GCB, DFC, AFC, DSc, FRAeS; British air force officer; b. 7 Oct. 1945; s. of the late Wing Commdr Frank Squire and Margaret Pascoe Squire (née Trump); m. Carolyn Joynson 1970; three s.; ed King's School, Bruton; with 20 Squadron, Singapore 1968–70, 4 FTS, Anglesey 1970–73, 3 (F) Squadron, Germany 1975–78; OC1 (F) Squadron 1981–83; Personal Staff Officer to Air Officer Commanding-in-Chief, Strike Command 1984–86; Station Commdr RAF Cottesmore 1986–88; Dir Air Offensive 1989–91; SASO, RAF Strike Command 1991–93; Air Officer Commdg No. 1 Group 1993–94; ACAS 1994–96, DCDS (Programmes and Personnel), Ministry of Defence 1996–99; Air Officer Commanding-in-Chief, Strike Command and Commdr Allied Air Forces Northwestern Europe 1999–2000; Air Aide-de-Camp to Queen 1999–; Chief of the Air Staff 2000–03; Gov. King's School, Bruton. *Leisure interests:* golf, cricket. *Address:* c/o National Westminster Bank, 5 South Street, Wincanton, Somerset, BA9 9DJ, England (Office).

SREDIN, Vasily Dmitriyevich; Russian diplomatist; b. 1948; ed Moscow State Inst. of Int. Relations; with USSR Ministry of Foreign Affairs, diplomatic posts abroad 1972–; Counsellor-Envoy, Embassy of USSR (now Russia), Canada 1990–96; Deputy Head, N America Dept, Ministry of Foreign Affairs 1996–97, Acting Dir 1997–; State-Sec., Deputy Minister of Foreign Affairs 1998–2001, Special Rep. of Russian Govt to UNESCO Exec. Cttee 1999–2001. *Address:* c/o Ministry of Foreign Affairs, Smolenskaya-Sennaya pl. 32/34, 121200 Moscow, Russia.

SRINIVASAN, Krishnan, MA; Indian diplomatist and writer; b. 15 Feb. 1937, Madras; s. of the late Capt. C. Srinivasan and Rukmani Chari; m. Brinda Srinivasan 1975; one s.; ed Bedford School, Christ Church, Oxford; Chargé d'affaires, Libya 1969–71; High Commr in Zambia (also accred to Botswana) 1974–77, in Nigeria (also accred to Benin and Cameroon) 1980–82, in Bangladesh 1989–92; Amb. to Netherlands 1986–89; Perm. Sec. Foreign Ministry 1992–94, Foreign Sec. 1994–95; Deputy Sec.-Gen. (Political) Commonwealth 1995–2002; Visiting Fellow, Wolfson Coll., Cambridge, Centre of Int. Studies, Cambridge; Sr Research Fellow, Inst. of Commonwealth Studies, Univ. of London; Hon. mem. Christ Church Sr Common Room; Hind Ratna (India) 2001. *Publications:* several novels, short stories and articles on int. affairs. *Leisure interests:* reading, writing, watching sports. *Address:* Flat 8, Courtleigh, 126 Earls Court Road, London, W8 6QL, England. *Telephone:* (20) 7370-0339. *E-mail:* ksrinivasanuk@yahoo.co.uk (Office).

SRIVASTAVA, Oudh Narain, MA; Indian governor and police officer; b. 15 April 1935, Bhopal; s. of R. P. Srivastava and Chanderbhagya Srivastava; m. Nini Srivastava; one s. one d.; various roles in Madhya Pradesh 1960–64; Commdt 14th Bn Madhya Pradesh S.A.F. 1964–67; Asst Insp.-Gen. of Police, Nagaland 1968–73, Tikamgarh and Satna 1973–75; Asst Dir, Deputy Dir I.B. 1975–82; Deputy Dir I.B. Gauhati, Jt Dir Calcutta and Shillong 1982–88; Special Dir I.B. HQ 1988–93; Gov. of Manipur 1994–2001; mem. Indian Int. Centre, India Habitat Centre; Indian Police Medal, Pres.'s Police Medal 1986, Padma Shri 1991. *Address:* c/o Raj Bhavan, Imphal 795001, India (Office).

SSEMOGERERE, Paul Kawanga, DipEd, MPA; Ugandan politician; b. 11 Feb. 1932, Bumangi Ssese Islands, Kalangala Dist; s. of Yozefu Kapere and Maria Lwiza Nakirya; m. Dr. Germina N. Ssemogerere; one s. four d.; ed St Mary's Coll., Kisubu, Makerere Univ. and Syracuse Univ., USA; teacher 1959–60; Leader Democratic Party (DP); fmr Leader of Opposition in Nat. Ass.; Minister of Internal Affairs 1986–88, Second Deputy Prime Minister and Minister of Foreign Affairs 1988–94, of the Public Service 1994, of Regional Co-operation 1989; Chair. OAU Council of Ministers 1993–94; Pres. Democratic Party; Cand. in 1996 Presidential elections; mem. Bd of Migration Policy Group 1999–; Hon. LHD (Alleghony Coll., USA) 1989. *Publications:* two book chapters on democracy and human rights in Africa. *Leisure interests:* seminars on politics and economics, eco-tourism, human rights advocacy, farming. *Address:* Democratic Party, P.O. Box 7098, Kampala (Office); 401 Streicher Road, Cathedral Lubaga-Kampala, P.O. Box 548, Kampala, Uganda (Home). *Telephone:* (41) 344155 (Home). *E-mail:* ssemo2@africaonline.com (Home).

STAAB, Heinz A., Dr rer. nat, DrMed; German professor of chemistry; b. 26 March 1926, Darmstadt; m. Dr. Ruth Müller 1953; one s. one d.; ed Univs. of Marburg, Tübingen and Heidelberg; research assoc., Max Planck Inst., Heidelberg 1953–59; Asst Prof. of Chem., Univ. of Heidelberg 1956–61, Assoc. Prof. 1961–62, Prof. 1963–; Dir Inst. of Organic Chem., Univ. of Heidelberg 1964–74; Dir Max Planck Inst. for Medical Research 1974–; Pres. Max Planck Soc. for the Advancement of Science, Munich 1984–90; mem. German Science Council 1976–79; Senator, Deutsche Forschungsgemeinschaft 1976–82 and 1984–90; mem. Bd of Govs. Weizmann Inst. of Science, Israel 1977–; Pres. Gesellschaft Deutscher Naturforscher und Ärzte 1981–82; Pres. German Chem. Soc. 1984–85; mem. Heidelberg Acad. of Sciences (Pres. 1994–96), Acad. Leopoldina, Academia Europaea; Corresp. mem. Austrian Acad. 1988, Bavarian Acad. 1991; Hon. Prof. Chinese Acad. of Sciences 1992; Foreign mem. Russian Acad. of Sciences 1994; Hon. mem. Senate Max-Planck Soc.

1990, German Chem. Soc. 1998; Hon. Fellow Indian Acad. of Sciences 1988; Hon. PhD (Weizmann Inst. of Science) 1984; Adolf von Baeyer Award (German Chem. Soc.) 1979. *Publications:* Einführung in die theoretische organische Chemie 1959 (translations), Azolides in Organic Synthesis and Biochemistry (co-author); about 370/400 publications in professional journals. *Leisure interests:* travel, history, classical music. *Address:* Max-Planck Society, Heidelberg (Office); Johnstrassee 29, Munich; Schlosswolfsbrunnenweg 43, 69118 Heidelberg, Germany. *Telephone:* (6221) 486421 (Office); (6221) 803330 (Home). *Fax:* (6221) 486219 (Office).

STAATS, Elmer Boyd, PhD; American economist and government official; b. 6 June 1914, Richfield, Kansas; s. of Wesley F. Staats and Maude (née Goodall) Staats; m. Margaret S. Rich 1940; one s. two d.; ed McPherson Coll. and Univs. of Kansas and Minnesota; Research Asst, Kansas Legis. Council 1936; mem. Staff, Public Admin. Service, Chicago 1937–38; Fellow, Brookings Inst. 1938–39; Staff mem. Bureau of the Budget 1939–47, Asst to Dir 1947, Asst Dir (Legis. Reference) 1947–49, Exec. Asst Dir 1949–50, Asst Dir 1958–59, Deputy Dir 1950–53, 1959–66; Research Dir, Marshall Field & Co., Chicago 1953; Exec. Officer Operations Co-ordinating Bd, Nat. Security Council 1953–58; Comptroller Gen. of the United States 1966–81; mem. Bd of Dirs of several corpns; mem. numerous public orgs including Pres. American Soc. for Public Admin. 1961–62; Pres. Harry S. Truman Scholarship Foundation 1981–84, Chair. Bd of Trustees 1984–; Chair. Govt Procurement Round Table 1984–; mem. Bd of Dirs of American Acad. of Political and Social Science 1966, Bd of Govs Int. Org. of Supreme Audit Insts 1969–81, Visiting Cttee John F. Kennedy School of Govt, Harvard Univ. 1974–80, Visiting Cttee, Graduate School of Man., Univ. of Calif. at LA 1976–85, Visiting Cttee to the Cttee in Public Policy Studies, Univ. of Chicago 1976–; President's Comm. on Budget Concepts 1967–68; mem. Bd of Govs Int. Center on Election Law and Admin. 1985–87; Dir George C. Marshall Foundation 1984–; mem. Bd of Visitors, Nat. Defense Univ. 1981–90; Trustee, Cttee for Econ. Devt 1981–, Nat. Planning Asscn 1981–; Hon. mem. Soc. of Mfg Engineers 1978–; Hon. Life mem. Municipal Finance Officers Asscn of USA and Canada 1980; Dr Publ Service (George Washington Univ.) 1971, Dr Admin. (Univ. of S Dak.) 1973, Hon. Certified Internal Auditor (Inst. of Internal Auditors) 1973; Hon. LLD (McPherson Coll.) 1966, (Duke Univ.) 1975, (Nova Univ.) 1976, (Lycoming Coll.) 1982, (Univ. of Penn.); Hon. DHumLitt (Ohio State Univ.) 1982; Rockefeller Public Service Award 1961; Productivity Award, American Productivity Cen. 1980; Medal of Honor AICPA 1980, Presidential Citizens Medal 1981, Accounting Hall of Fame 1981, Inst. of Internal Auditors Thurston Award 1988 and other medals and awards. *Publication:* Personnel Standards in the Social Security Program 1939. *Address:* Harry S. Truman Scholarship Foundation, 712 Jackson Place, NW, Washington, DC 20006; 5011 Overlook Road, NW, Washington, DC 20016, USA. *Telephone:* (202) 395-3530 (Office).

STABENOW, Deborah Ann, BS, M.S.W.; American politician; b. 29 April 1950, Gladwin, Mich.; d. of Robert Lee Greer and Anna Merle Greer (née Hallmark); one s. one d.; ed ed. Michigan State Univ.; with Special Services, Lansing School Dist 1972–73; Co. Commr Ingham Co., Mason, Mich. 1975–78; State Rep. for Mich., Lansing 1979–2002; mem. Agric. Cttee, Science Cttee 105th–106th Congress from 8th Mich. Dist; Senator from Mich. 2003–; Founder Ingham Co. Women's Comm.; Co-Founder Council Against Domestic Assault; mem. Democratic Business and Professional Club, Mich. Democratic Women's Political Caucus, Grance United Methodist Church (fmr lay preacher, Chair. Social Concerns Task Force, Sunday School Music teacher), Lansing Boys' Club, Professional Advisory Cttee Lansing Parents Without Partners, Advisory Cttee Center for Handicapped Affairs, Mich. Council Family and Divorce Mediation Advisory Bd, Nat. Council for Childrens' Rights, Big Brothers/Big Sisters Greater Lansing Advisory Bd, Mich. Child Study Asscn Bd. Advisers, Mich. Women's Campaign Fund; mem. Nat. Asscn for the Advancement of Colored People (NAACP), Lansing Regional Chamber of Commerce; awards include Service to Children Award, Council for Prevention of Child Abuse and Neglect 1983, Outstanding Leadership Award, Nat. Council of Community Mental Health Centers 1983, Snyder-Kok Award, Mental Health Asscn Mich., Awareness Leader of the Year Award, Awareness Communications Team Developmentally Disabled 1984, Communicator of the Year Award, Woman in Communications 1984, Lawmaker of the Year Award, Nat. Child Support Enforcement Asscn 1985, Distinguished Service Award, Lansing Jaycees 1985, Distinguished Service in Govt Award, Retarded Citizens of Mich. 1986. *Address:* Office of the Senator from Michigan, U.S. Senate Buildings, Washington, DC 20510 (Office); 2709 South Deerfield Avenue, Lansing, MI 48911-1783, USA (Home).

STABREIT, Immo Friedrich Helmut, DJur; German diplomatist (retd); b. 24 Jan. 1933, Rathenow/Havel; s. of Kurt Stabreit and Johanna Maria Stabreit (née Groeger); m. Barbara Philippi 1962; two s. one d.; ed Princeton Univ., Free Univ. of Berlin and Univ. of Heidelberg; jr law clerk 1957–61; Financial Dept ECSC, Luxembourg 1959; entered foreign service 1962; served Moscow 1962–63, 1966–71, Soviet clerk, Ministry of Foreign Affairs 1964–66, 1971–74; Fellow, Center for Int. Affairs, Harvard Univ. 1974–75; Head, Consumer Producer Relations Div. Int. Energy Agency, Paris 1975–78; European Corresp., Ministry of Foreign Affairs 1978–83; Fed. Chancellery 1983–87; Amb. to South Africa 1987–92, to USA 1992–95, to France 1995–98; Exec. Vice-Pres. German Soc. for Foreign Affairs 1998–2002; business con-

sultant. *Leisure interests:* sport, reading. *Address:* Wundt Str. 18, 14059 Berlin-Charlottenburg, Germany. *Telephone:* 25798160 (Home). *Fax:* 25798160 (Home).

STADEN, Berndt von; German diplomatist; b. 24 June 1919, Rostock; s. of Richard von Staden and Camilla von Voigt; m. Wendelgard von Neurath 1961; two s. one d.; ed Bonn and Hamburg Univs.; mil. service 1940–45; Jr Barrister 1948–51; with Foreign Ministry 1951–86; served Brussels 1953–55; Dir Soviet Affairs Desk, Bonn 1955–58; Staff mem. EEC Comm., Brussels, Head of Office of Pres. of Comm. 1958–63; Counsellor, Embassy, Washington 1963–68; Deputy Asst State Sec., Foreign Office 1968–70, Asst State Sec., Head of Political Dept 1970–73; Amb. to USA 1973–79; Head of Dept for Foreign Relations and Security, Fed. Chancery 1979–81; State Sec. Foreign Office 1981–83; Co-ordinator for German-American Co-operation 1982–86; Prof. of Diplomacy, Georgetown Univ., Washington, DC 1985, 1988, 1990; Order of Merit (FRG), Order of Terra Mariana, First Class (Estonia). *Publications:* Erinnerungen aus der Vorzeit: Eine Jugend im Baltikum 1919–1939 1999, Ende und Anfang: Errinerungen 1939–1963 2001. *Leisure interests:* music, horse-riding. *Address:* Leinfelderhof, 71665 Vaihingen, Germany. *Telephone:* (7042) 5440. *Fax:* (7042) 98994.

STADLER, Sergey Valentinovich; Russian violinist and conductor; b. 20 May 1962, Leningrad, (now St Petersburg); s. of Valentin Raymundovich Stadler and Margarita Petrovna Stadler; m. Ilza Liepa (divorced); ed Leningrad State Conservatory, studied with Mikhail Vaiman, Boris Gutnikov in Leningrad Conservatory, with Leonid Kogan, Viktor Tretyakov in Moscow State Conservatory; prize winner several int. competitions; tours Europe and USA since 1976; first performed music by Russian composers Rodion Shchedrin, Sergey Slonimsky, Boris Tishchenko and others; taught in Leningrad State Conservatory 1984–88; began conducting 1996. *Address:* Kaiserstrasse 43, Munich, Germany. *Telephone:* (89) 337005 (Munich); (812) 164-34-51 (St Petersburg); (095) 207-38-33 (Moscow).

STADTMAN, Earl R., PhD; American biochemist; b. 15 Nov. 1919, Carrizozo, NM; s. of Walter W. Stadtman and Minnie Ethyl Stadtman; m. Thressa Campbell Stadtman (q.v.) 1943; ed Univ. of California; Research Asst Dept of Food Technology, Univ. of Calif. 1943–46, Research Asst, Div. of Plant Nutrition 1948–49; Atomic Energy Comm. Fellow, Biochemical Research Lab., Mass. Gen. Hospital 1949–50; Chemist (Biochem.) GS-15-Lab. for Cellular Physiology and Metabolism Nat. Insts. of Health (NIH) 1950–58, Chief of Enzyme Section, Lab. of Cellular Physiology and Metabolism, NIH 1958–, Chief, Lab. of Biochem., Nat. Heart Inst., NIH 1962–94; mem. NAS, American Acad. of Arts and Sciences, US Cttee for Int. Union of Biochem. (mem. Council 1977–80), Exec. Cttee 1982–85, Council of American Soc. of Biological Chemists (Pres. 1982–83); Hon. DSc (Mich.) 1987; Hon. PhD (Weizmann Inst. of Science, Rehovot, Israel) 1988; Paul Lewis Award in Enzyme Chem. 1952, Washington Acad. of Sciences Annual Award in Biological Chem. 1957, Superior Service Award of Dept of Health, Educ. and Welfare 1968, Distinguished Service Award 1970, Hillebrand Award of American Chemical Soc. 1969, Award in Microbiology, NAS 1970, Nat. Medal of Science 1980, Meritorious Rank Award, Sr Exec. Service 1981, Presidential Rank Award, Distinguished Sr Exec. 1982, ASBC-Merck Award in Biochem. 1983, Welch Foundation Award in Chem. 1991, Research Award American Aging Asscn 1992, Paul Glen Award American Gerontology Soc. 1993. *Publications:* numerous scientific articles 1953–. *Leisure interests:* gardening, bowling, badminton, travelling. *Address:* National Heart and Lung Institute, 9000 Rockville Pike, Bethesda, MD 20814 (Office); 16907 Redland Road, Derwood, MD 20855, USA (Home). *Telephone:* (301) 869-1747.

STADTMAN, Thressa Campbell (Terry), PhD; American biochemist; b. 12 Feb. 1920, Sterling, New York; d. of Earl Campbell and Bessie (née Waldron) Campbell; m. Earl R. Stadtman (q.v.) 1943; ed Cornell Univ. and Univ. of California (Berkeley); Research Assoc., Univ. of Calif. (Berkeley) 1942–47; Research Assoc., Harvard Medical School, Boston 1949–50; Biochemist, Nat. Heart, Lung and Blood Inst., Nat. Insts. of Health 1950–, Section Head, Lab. of Biochemistry 1974–; Ed.-in-Chief Bio Factors (IUB-sponsored journal) 1987–; Senior Exec. Service 1988–; Pres. Int. Soc. of Vitamins and Related Bio Factors 1995; Helen Haye Whitney Fellow, Oxford Univ., England 1954–55; Rockefeller Foundation Grantee, Univ. of Munich, Fed. Repub. of Germany 1959–60; mem. NAS, American Acad. of Arts and Sciences, Burroughs-Welcome Fund Toxicology Advisory Cttee 1994–97; Hillebrand Award, Chemical Soc. of Washington 1979, Rose Award, American Soc. of Biological Chemists 1987, Klaus Schwarz Medal 1988, Public Health Service Special Recognition Award 1991, L'Oréal-UNESCO Women in Science Lifetime Achievement Award 2000, Gabriel Bertrand Award, Fed. of European Socs of Trace Elements and Minerals 2001. *Publications:* original research papers in fields of Methane Biosynthesis, Amino Acid Metabolism, Vitamin B12 biochemistry, selenium biochemistry. *Leisure interests:* travel, gardening, skiing. *Address:* National Institutes of Health, Building 50, Room 2120, Bethesda, MD 20892 (Office); 16907 Redland Road, Derwood, MD 20855, USA (Home). *Telephone:* (301) 496-3002 (Office); (301) 869-1747 (Home). *Fax:* (301) 496-0599 (Office). *E-mail:* tcstadtman@nih.gov (Office).

STAFFORD, Godfrey Harry, CBE, MA, MSc, PhD, FRS; British physicist; b. 15 April 1920, Sheffield; s. of Henry Stafford and Sarah Stafford; m. Helen Goldthorp 1950; one s. twin d.; ed Rondebosch Boys' High School, Univ. of Cape Town, Gonville and Caius Coll. Cambridge; South African Naval Forces 1941–46; AERE, Harwell 1949–51; Head of Biophysics Subdivision, Council for Scientific and Industrial Research, Pretoria 1951–54; Cyclotron Group, AERE 1954–57; Head of Proton Linear Accelerator Group, Rutherford Laboratory 1957, Head of High Energy Physics Div. 1963, Deputy Dir 1966, Dir 1969–79; Dir of Atlas and Rutherford Laboratory 1975–79, Dir-Gen. 1979–81; UK Del. IUPAP Comm. on Particles and Fields 1975–81; Vice-Pres. Inst. of Physics Meetings Cttee 1976–79; Chair. CERN Scientific Policy Cttee 1978–81; Master of St Cross Coll. Oxford 1979–87; Pres. European Physical Soc. 1984–86, Inst. of Physics 1986–88; Visiting Fellow St Cross Coll. 1971–79, Hon. Fellow 1987; Vice-Pres. European Physical Soc. 1982; Gov. Westminster Coll.; Ebden Scholar, Univ. of Cape Town; Hon. Scientist Rutherford Appleton Lab. 1986; Hon. DSc (Birmingham) 1980; Glazebrook Prize and Medal, Inst. of Physics 1981. *Publications:* papers and articles in learned journals on biophysics, nuclear physics and high energy physics. *Leisure interests:* music, foreign travel, walking. *Address:* Ferry Cottage, North Hinksey Village, Oxford, OX2 0NA, England. *Telephone:* (1865) 247621 (Home).

STAFFORD, HE Cardinal James Francis; American ecclesiastic; b. 26 July 1932, Baltimore; s. of F. Emmett Stafford and Mary Dorothy Stafford; ordained priest 1957; Bishop 1976; Archbishop Emer. of Denver 1996; Pres. Pontifical Council for the Laity 1998–; cr. Cardinal Feb. 1998. *Address:* 1300 South Steele Street, Denver, CO 80210, USA (Office); Pontifio Cansiglio per i Laici, San Calisto, 00120 Vatican City. *E-mail:* jfstafford@Laity.va (Office).

STAFFORD, John Rogers, AB, JD; American business executive and lawyer; b. 24 Oct. 1937, Harrisburg, Pa; s. of Paul Henry Stafford and Gladys Lee Sharp; m. Inge Paul 1959; four d.; ed Montgomery Blair High School, Dickinson Coll., George Washington Univ. Law School; Assoc., Steptoe and Johnson 1962–66; Gen. Attorney, Hoffman-LaRoche 1966–67, Group Attorney 1967–70; Gen. Counsel, American Home Products Corpn 1970–74, Vice-Pres. 1974–77, Sr Vice-Pres. 1977–80, Exec. Vice-Pres. 1980–81, Pres. 1981–2001, Chair., Pres. and CEO 1986–2001, Chair. 2001–; Dir Mfrs Hanover Corpn, Metropolitan Life Insurance Co., Cen. Park Conservancy, Pharmaceutical Mfrs Asscn, Project Hope, American Paralysis Asscn, numerous other orgs.; mem. Bd of Trustees U.S. Council for Int. Business; mem. American Bar Asscn, Dist of Columbia Bar Asscn; Order of the Coif; Outstanding Achievement Alumnus Award 1981. *Leisure interests:* boating, golf. *Address:* American Home Products Corporation, 5 Giralda Farms, Madison, NJ 07940, USA.

STAFFORD-CLARK, Max; British theatre director; b. 17 March 1941; s. of David Stafford-Clark and Dorothy Stafford-Clark; m. 1st Carole Hayman 1971; m. 2nd Ann Pennington 1981; one d.; ed Felsted School, Riverdale Country Day School, New York and Trinity Coll. Dublin; Artistic Dir Traverse Theatre, Edin. 1968–70; Dir Traverse Workshop Co. 1970–74; Founder and Artistic Dir Joint Stock Theatre Group 1974–79, English Stage Co. at Royal Court Theatre 1979–93; Founder and Artistic Dir Out of Joint Theatre Co. 1993–; Visiting Prof. Royal Holloway and Bedford Coll., Univ. of London 1993–94; Maisie Glass Prof. Univ. of Sheffield 1995–96; Visiting Prof. Univ. of Herts. 1999–; Hon. Fellow Rose Bruford Coll. 1996; Hon. D.Litt (Oxford Brookes) 2000, (Herts.) 2000. *Principal productions:* Fanshen, Top Girls, Tom and Viv, Rat in the Skull, Serious Money, Our Country's Good, The Steward of Christendom, Shopping And Fucking, Blue Heart, Drummers, Some Explicit Polaroids, Rita Sue and Bob Too/A State Affair, A Laughing Matter. *Publication:* Letters to George 1989. *Address:* 7 Gloucester Crescent, London, NW1 7DS, England.

STALLKAMP, Thomas; American business executive; b. 1946; fmrly Vice-Pres. for Procurement and Supply Chrysler Corpn, Pres. 1998–99. *Address:* c/o Chrysler Corporation, 1200 Chrysler Drive, 415-03-05 Highland Park, Michigan, MI 48288, USA.

STALLONE, Sylvester Enzio; American actor and film director; b. 6 July 1946, New York; s. of Frank Stallone and Jacqueline Labofish; m. 1st Sasha Czach 1974 (divorced); two s.; m. 2nd Brigitte Nielsen 1985 (divorced 1987); m. 3rd Jennifer Flavin 1997; two d.; ed American Coll. of Switzerland, Univ. of Miami; has had many jobs including usher, bouncer, horse trainer, store detective, physical educ. teacher; now actor, producer and Dir of own films; f. White Eagle Co.; Dir Carolco Pictures Inc. 1987–; mem. Screen Actors Guild, Writers Guild, Dirs. Guild; Hon. mem. Stuntmans' Asscn; Acad. Award for best film 1976, Golden Circle Award for best film 1976, Donatello Award 1976, Christopher Religious Award 1976; Officier Ordre des Arts et des Lettres. *Film appearances include:* Lords of Flatbush 1973, Capone 1974, Rocky 1976, F.I.S.T. 1978, Paradise Alley 1978, Rocky II 1979, Nighthawks 1980, Escape to Victory 1980, Rocky III 1981, First Blood, Rambo 1984, Rocky IV 1985, Cobra 1986, Over the Top 1986, Rambo II 1986, Rambo III 1988, Lock Up 1989, Set Up 1990, Tango and Cash 1990, Rocky V 1990, Isobar 1991, Stop or My Mom Will Shoot 1991, Oscar 1991, Cliffhanger 1992, Demolition Man 1993, Judge Dredd 1994, The Specialist 1994, Assassins 1995, Firestorm 1996, Daylight 1996, Cop Land 1997, An Alan Smithee Film: Burn Hollywood Burn 1998, Get Carter 2000; producer, Dir film Staying Alive 1983. *Publications:* Paradise Alley 1977, The Rocky Scrapbook 1997. *Address:* William Morris Agency, 151 El Camino Drive, Beverly Hills, CA 90212, USA.

STALS, Christian Lodewyk, DComm; South African central banker; b. 13 March 1935; s. of Petrus J. Stals and Lilian Barnard; m. Hester Barnard 1958; three s. one d.; ed Afrikaans Hoër, Germiston and Univ. of Pretoria Extra-mural Div.; joined South African Reserve Bank 1955, Gen. Man. 1975, Deputy Gov. 1976, Sr Deputy Gov. 1981; Dir-Gen. Dept of Finance 1985; Special Econ.

Adviser to Minister of Finance 1989; Gov. South African Reserve Bank 1989–99; Chancellor, Univ. of Pretoria 1997–; State President's Decoration for Distinguished Service. *Leisure interest:* golf. *Address:* Office of the Chancellor, Univerity of Pretoria, Pretoria 0002, South Africa (Office). *Telephone:* (12) 420-4111 (Office). *Fax:* (12) 362-5168.

STAMP, Gavin Mark, PhD, FSA; British architectural historian and writer; b. 15 March 1948, Bromley, Kent; s. of Barry Hartnell Stamp and Norah Clare Stamp (née Rich); m. Alexandra Artley 1982; two d.; ed Dulwich Coll., London, Gonville and Caius Coll., Cambridge; freelance writer and teacher until 1990; Lecturer, Mackintosh School of Architecture, Glasgow School of Art 1990–99, Sr Lecturer and Hon. Reader 1999–; Chair. The Twentieth Century Soc. (fmrly The Thirties Soc.) 1983–; Founder and Chair. Alexander Thomson Soc. 1991–; Hon. FRIAS 1994; Hon. FRIBA 1998. *Publications:* Robert Weir Schultz and his work for Marquesses of Bute 1981, The Great Perspectivists 1982, The Changing Metropolis 1984, The English House 1860–1914 1986, Telephone Boxes 1989, Greek Thomson (co-ed.) 1994, Alexander 'Greek' Thomson 1999, Edwin Lutyens' Country Houses 2001, An Architect of Promise: George Gilbert Scott Junior and the Late Gothic Revival 2002, Lutyens Abroad (co-ed.) 2002. *Address:* 1 Moray Place, Strathbungo, Glasgow, G41 2AQ, Scotland. *E-mail:* g.stamp@gsa.ac.uk (Office); gavin.stamp@ btopenworld.com (Home).

STAMP, Terence; British actor; b. 22 July 1938, London; s. of Thomas Stamp and Ethel Esther Perrott; ed Webber–Douglas Dramatic Acad.; theatre work before film debut in Billy Budd 1962; Hon. Dr of Arts (Univ. of East London) 1993. *Other films include:* Term of Trial 1962, The Collector 1965, Modesty Blaise 1966, Far From the Madding Crowd 1967, Poor Cow 1967, Blue 1968, Theorem 1968, Tales of Mystery 1968, The Mind of Mr. Soames 1969, A Season in Hell 1971, Hu-man 1975, The Divine Creature 1976, Striptease 1977, Meetings With Remarkable Men 1978, Superman 1978, Superman II 1979, Death in the Vatican 1980, The Bloody Chamber 1982, The Hit 1984, Link 1985, Legal Eagles 1986, The Sicilian 1986, Wall Street 1988, Alien Nation 1988, Young Guns 1988, Prince of Shadows 1991, The Real McCoy 1992, The Adventures of Priscilla Queen of the Desert 1994, Bliss 1995, Limited Edition 1995, Mindbender, Love Walked In 1996, Kiss the Sky 1997, The Limey 1999, Bow Finger 1999, Red Planet 2000. *Theatre:* Dracula, The Lady from the Sea. *Publications:* Stamp Album (memoirs, Vol. 1) 1988, Coming Attractions (memoirs, Vol. 2) 1988, Double Feature (memoirs, Vol. 3) 1989, The Night (novel) 1992, Stamp Collection Cookbook (jtly) 1997. *Address:* c/o Markham and Froggatt, 4 Windmill Street, London, W1P 1HF, England.

STANBURY, Hon. Robert Douglas George, PC, QC, BA, LLB, FID; Canadian executive, lawyer and fmr politician; b. 26 Oct. 1929, Exeter, Ont.; s. of James George Stuart Stanbury and Elizabeth Jean Stanbury (née Hardy); m. Miriam Voelker 1952; two s. two d.; ed Exeter and St Catharines public schools, St Catharines Coll. Inst., Univ. of Western Ontario, Osgoode Hall Law School and York Univ.; Account Exec. Public & Industrial Relations Ltd., Toronto 1950–51; Pres. Canadian Univ. Liberal Fed. 1954; Partner Holling-worth & Stanbury, Barristers and Solicitors, Toronto 1955–65; mem. North York Bd of Educ. 1961–64, Vice-Chair. 1962, Chair. 1963–64; mem. Metropolitan School Bd, Toronto 1963–64 and Metropolitan Toronto Planning Bd 1963; MP 1965–77; Chair. House of Commons Standing Cttee on Broad-casting, Films and Assistance to the Arts 1966–68; Parl. Sec. to Sec. of State of Canada 1968–69; Minister without Portfolio responsible for Citizenship 1969–71, for Information Canada 1970–71; Minister of Communications 1971–72, of Nat. Revenue 1972–74; Queen's Counsel 1974–; Del. to UN Gen. Assembly 1974, 1975, 1976, to UNESCO Conf., Paris 1969, UN Conf. on Crime, Kyoto 1970, UN Conf. on Apartheid, Lagos 1977, Inter-American Devt Bank meeting, Kingston 1977; Chair. Canadian Group IPU 1974–77; Founding Chair. Canadian Parl. Helsinki Group 1977; Pres. Hamilton Foundation 1982–83; Vice-Pres. Gen. Counsel and Dir, Firestone Canada Inc. 1977–83, Chair. and CEO 1983–85; Counsel Inch Easterbrook & Shaker 1986–2000; Dir Art Gallery of Hamilton (Vice-Pres. 1982–86, Pres. 1986–87), mem. Bd of Govs. 1988–, Dir Art Gallery of Hamilton Foundation 1996–; Dir Hamilton and Dist Chamber of Commerce 1980–85 (Pres. 1983–84), Dayton Tire Canada Ltd 1977–85, Canadian Chamber of Commerce 1982–86, Chedoke-McMaster Hospitals 1983–92, (Vice-Chair. 1987–89), Workers' Compensation Bd of Ont. 1985–88, 1991–94 (Vice-Chair. 1991–94); mem. Canadian Broadcast Standards Council (Ont.) 1990– (Vice-Chair. 1996–99, Chair. 1991–), Nunavut Arbitration Bd 1994–, Advisory Council, Grad. School of Journalism, Univ. of W Ont. 1994–97; Pres. Inst. of Corporate Dirs. in Canada 1987–88; Chair. McMaster Univ. Business Advisory Council 1987–88, Employers' Council on Workers' Compensation 1996–98, Employers' Council of Ont. 1998–2000; Pres. and CEO Canadian Council for Native Business 1989–91; Conflict of Interest Commr, Territory of Nunavut 2000–01, Integrity Commr of Nunavut 2001–; mem. Law Soc. of Upper Canada, Canadian Council of Administrative Tribunals, Int. Comm. of Jurists, UNA in Canada; Fellow Inst. of Dirs. 1985–; Canadian Centennial Medal 1967, Queen's Silver Jubilee Medal 1977, Confederation Medal 1993, Meredith Medal 1994, Queen's Golden Jubilee Medal 2002. *Address:* 607 Edgewater Crescent, Burlington, Ont., L7T 3L8, Canada (Home). *Telephone:* (905) 637-6576 (Office); (905) 632-9394 (Home). *Fax:* (905) 637-6576 (Office). *E-mail:* rstanbury@assembly.nu.ca (Office); robert.stanbury@sympatico.ca (Home). *Website:* www.integritycom.nu.ca (Office).

STANCLIFFE, Rt Rev David Staffurth, MA; British ecclesiastic; b. 1 Oct. 1942, Devizes, Wilts.; s. of the late Very Rev. Michael Stancliffe and Barbara

Tatlow; m. Sarah Smith 1965; one s. two d.; ed Westminster School, Trinity Coll. Oxford and Cuddesdon Theological Coll.; ordained deacon 1967, priest 1968; Asst Curate, St Bartholomew's, Armley, Leeds 1967–70; Chaplain, Clifton Coll. Bristol 1970–77; Canon Residentiary, Portsmouth Cathedral 1977–82, also Dir of Ordinands and Lay Ministry Adviser, Diocese of Portsmouth 1977–82; Vicar, St Thomas of Canterbury, Portsmouth and Provost of Portsmouth 1982–93; Bishop of Salisbury 1993–; mem. Gen. Synod 1985–, Liturgical Comm. 1986– (Chair. 1993–), Cathedral's Fabric Comm. 1991–; Pres. Council, Marlborough Coll. 1994–; Fellow Royal School of Church Music; Hon. DLitt (Portsmouth) 1993. *Publications include:* Liturgy for a New Century 1990 (contrib.), The Identity of Anglican Worship 1991, Enriching the Christian Year 1992, Celebrating Common Prayer—Pocket Version 1994, The Sense of the Sacramental 1995, New Soundings 1997 (contrib.), Flagships of the Spirit 1998 (contrib.). *Leisure interests:* old music, travel, Italy. *Address:* South Canonry, 71 The Close, Salisbury, Wilts., SP1 2ER, England. *Telephone:* (1722) 334031. *Fax:* (1722) 413112 (Office). *E-mail:* dsarum@salisbury .anglican.org (Office).

STANCZYK, Janusz, PH.D; Polish diplomatist; m.; two c.; ed Jagiellonian Univ., St Louis and Michigan Univs., Inst. of Legal Sciences, Polish Acad. of Sciences; Dir Legal and Treaties Dept, Foreign Ministry, Poland 1992–95, Dir Gen. for Legal Affairs 1995–97, Under-Sec. of State for Legal and Econ. Affairs and for relations with int. orgs. (also responsible for ministry contact with nat. parl.) 1997–2000; mem. Del. UN Gen. Ass. 1992–96, 1998–2000; Perm. Rep. to UN 2000–. *Address:* Permanent Mission of Poland to the United Nations, 9th East 66th Street, New York, NY 10021, USA (Office). *Telephone:* (212) 744-2506 (Office). *Fax:* (212) 517-6771 (Office). *E-mail:* poland@un.int (Office). *Website:* www.un.int/poland.

STANIER, Field Marshal Sir John Wilfred, GCB, MBE, DL; British army officer; b. 6 Oct. 1925, Essex; s. of the late Harold Allan and Penelope Rose (née Price) Stanier; m. Cicely Constance Lambert 1955; four d.; ed Marlborough Coll., Merton Coll., Oxford, Imperial Defence Coll., Staff Coll.; commissioned into 7th Queen's Own Hussars 1946; served N Italy, Germany and Hong Kong; commanded Royal Scots Greys 1966–68, 20 Armoured Brigade 1969–70; G.O.C. 1st Armoured Div. 1973–75; Commdt Staff Coll., Camberley 1975–78; Vice-Chief of Gen. Staff 1978–80; C-in-C UK Land Forces 1981–82; Chief of Gen. Staff 1982–85; rank of Field Marshal 1985; ADC to the Queen 1981–85; Chair. Royal United Services Inst. for Defence Studies 1986–89; Col Royal Scots Dragoon Guards 1979–85; Col Commdt Royal Armoured Corps 1982–85; Constable of the Tower of London 1990–96; Chair. Control Risks (GS) Ltd 1985–96; mem. Council Marlborough Coll. 1984–96; DL Hants. 1986. *Publication:* War and the Media (with Miles Hudson) 1997. *Leisure interests:* fishing, sailing. *Address:* The Old Farmhouse, Hazeley Bottom, Hook, Hants., RG27 8LU, England (Home). *Telephone:* (1252) 842341 (Home). *E-mail:* johnw.stanier@virgin.net (Office); john .stanier@amserve.net (Home).

STANISHEV, Sergey; Bulgarian politician; b. 5 May 1966; ed Moscow State Univ.; Leader Bulgarian Socialist Party. *Address:* Bulgarska Sotsialisticheska Partiya (BSP), Positano St 20, POB 382, Sofia, Bulgaria (Office). *Telephone:* (2) 9810559 (Office). *Fax:* (2) 9810559 (Office). *E-mail:* bsp@bsp.bg (Office). *Website:* www.bsg.bg (Office).

STANISLAUS, Lamuel A., BSc, DDS; Grenadian diplomatist and oral surgeon; b. 22 April 1921, Petite Martinique; m.; five c.; ed Howard Univ., USA; Asst teacher Petite Martinique RC School and St Patrick's RC School 1939–41; statistical clerk Harbour and Wharves Dept, Port-of-Spain, Trinidad 1941–45; dental practice, New York 1956–; Perm. Rep. to the UN 1985–; Founding mem. Grenada Nat. Party; mem. New Nat. Party, Mayor of New York's Advisory Council; Hon. DHumLitt (Univ. of St George's). *Leisure interests:* swimming, public speaking, reading, writing. *Address:* Permanent Mission of Grenada to the United Nations, 800 Second Avenue, Suite 400K, New York, NY 10017, USA (Office). *Telephone:* (212) 599-0301 (Office); (718) 282-9150 (Home). *Fax:* (212) 599-1540 (Office); (718) 282-9150 (Home). *E-mail:* grenada@un.int (Office).

STANKEVICH, Sergey Borisovich, CAND.HIST.SCI.; Russian politician; b. 20 Feb. 1945, Shchelkovo, Moscow region; m.; one d.; ed Moscow State Pedagogical Inst.; teacher Moscow Inst. of Oil and Gas, then sociologist Moscow Inst. of Nat. Econs 1977–80; Sr Researcher Inst. of World History, USSR (now Russian) Acad. of Sciences 1980–90; mem. Org. Cttee, Coordination Cttee Moscow People's Front 1988; mem. Interregional Deputies Group 1989; mem., co-ordinator Pre-Election Block Democratic Russia 1990; First Deputy Chair. Moscow Exec. Cttee 1990–92; active in election campaign of Boris Yeltsin (q.v.) May–June 1991, presidential adviser 1992–93; mem. State Duma (Parl.) 1993; charged with accepting bribes 1995, left Russia, sought by Interpol 1995, arrested by Warsaw police after Russian extradition request but released and given political émigré status, later cleared of charges; elected Chair. Party of Democratic Russia 2001; joined Union of Right Forces 2001; lives in Poland.

STANKEVIČIUS, Česlovas Vytautas; Lithuanian politician, engineer and dilomatist; b. 27 Feb. 1937, Vilkaviskis Region; s. of Jonas Stankevičius and Uršulė Dubickaitė; m. Jadvyga Litvinaitė 1962; two s.; ed Kaunas Polytech. Inst.; engineer, Chief of Design, Chief Engineer, Kaunas Inst. of Urban Planning and Designing 1965–89; Chair. Kaunas Bd Sajūdis Movt 1989–90; elected Deputy and Vice-Pres. of Supreme Council, Repub. of Lithuania; signatory to March 11th Act on Re-establishment of Independence; Head

official del. in negotiations with Russia 1990–93; Head Lithuanian Parl. del. to N Atlantic Ass. 1991–92; mem. Seimas, Parl. Group of Christian Democrats 1996–2000; Minister of Defence 1996–2000; Amb. to Norway 2001–(05); co-author projects on nat. security and defence concept of Lithuania 1996, Law on Defence Org. 1997, Lithuanian defence strategy 2000; Order of Gediminas 2000. *Publications:* Enhancing Security of Lithuania and Other Baltic States in 1992–94 (monograph), Negotiations with Russia on Troop Withdrawal 2002. *Leisure interests:* the arts. *Address:* Embassy of Lithuania, Gimle Terrasse 6, 0244 Oslo, Norway (Office). *Telephone:* 22558150 (Office). *Fax:* 22556730 (Office). *E-mail:* litauens@online.no (Office). *Website:* www .amb.urm.lt/norvegija (Office).

STANLEY, Eric Gerald, PhD, FBA; British academic; b. 19 Oct. 1923; m. Mary Bateman, MD, FRCP 1959; one d.; ed Queen Elizabeth's Grammar School, Blackburn, Univ. Coll. Oxford; Lecturer in English Language and Literature, Univ. of Birmingham 1951–62; Reader in English Language and Literature, Univ. of London, Queen Mary Coll. 1962–64, Prof. 1964–75; Prof. of English, Yale Univ. 1975–76; Rawlinson and Bosworth Prof. of Anglo-Saxon, Univ. of Oxford and Fellow Pembroke Coll. Oxford 1977–91, Prof. Emer. 1991–; mem. Mediaeval Acad. of America 1975–; Corresp. mem. Fryske Akad. 1991–, Bavarian Acad. of Sciences 1994–; Sir Israel Gollancz Memorial Lecturer, The British Acad. 1984. *Publications:* books and academic articles, some of them in A Collection of Papers with Emphasis on Old English Literature 1987, In the Foreground: Beowulf 1994, Die angelsächsische Rechtspflege und wie man sie später aufgefasst hat 1999, Imagining the Anglo-Saxon Past 2000. *Leisure interest:* travel. *Address:* Pembroke College, Oxford, OX1 1DW, England.

STANLEY, Julian Cecil, Jr, BS, EdD; American professor of psychology; b. 9 July 1918, Macon, Ga; s. of Julian C. Stanley and Ethel May Cheney Stanley; m. 1st Rose Roberta Sanders 1946 (died 1978); one d.; m. 2nd Barbara Sprague Kerr 1980 (died 2001); m. 3rd Dorothy Lee Fahey 2002; ed Georgia Southern Univ. and Harvard Univ.; postdoctoral studies at Univs. of Mich., Chicago, six NZ univs (Fulbright Lecturer), Catholic Univ. of Louvain, Belgium (Fulbright Act Research Scholar), Center for Advanced Study in the Behavioral Sciences, Stanford Univ., Calif.; taught science and math. in high school, Atlanta, Ga 1937–42; Instructor in Psychology, Newton (Mass.) Jr Coll. 1946–48; Instructor in Educ., Harvard Univ. 1948–49; Assoc. Prof. of Educational Psychology, George Peabody Coll. for Teachers 1949–53; Assoc. Prof. of Educ., Univ. of Wis. 1953–57, Prof. 1957–62, Prof. of Educational Psychology 1962–67, Chair. Dept 1962–64, Dir Lab. of Experimental Design 1961–67; Prof. of Educ. and Psychology, Johns Hopkins Univ. 1967–71, Prof. of Psychology 1971–99, Prof. Emer. 1999–, Dir of Study of Mathematically Precocious Youth 1971–99; fmr Pres. American Educational Asscn and other nat. asscns.; Fellow AAAS, American Statistical Asscn, American Psychological Asscn, American Psychological Soc.; Hon. DEE (Univ. of N Texas); Hon. DHumLitt (State Univ. of W Ga); Lifetime Achievement Award 1997, George Miller Award, American Psychological Soc. 1998. *Publications:* author, co-author or ed. of 13 books and more than 500 articles, book chapters and reviews; books (co-author) include Experimental and Quasi-Experimental Designs for Research 1966, Mathematical Talent 1974, The Gifted and the Creative 1977, Educating the Gifted 1979, Academic Precocity 1983. *Leisure interests:* cinema, hiking, travelling. *Address:* Center for Talented Youth (CTY), Johns Hopkins University, 2701 North Charles Street, Baltimore, MD 21218, USA. *Telephone:* (410) 516-6179. *Fax:* (410) 964-8439. *E-mail:* jstanley@jhu.edu (Office).

STANNARD, Robert William, CMG, BCom(NZ); New Zealand business executive; b. 16 Sept. 1926, Gisborne; s. of William C. Stannard and Clara Stannard; m. Shirley M. Sparkes 1956; one s. (deceased) two d.; ed Horowhenua Coll., Levin and Victoria Univ., Wellington; J. L. Arcus & Sons (chartered accountants), Wellington 1944–49; Peat, Marwick, Mitchell & Co. (chartered accountants), London and Singapore 1949–53; partner, Bowden, Bass & Cox (now KPMG), Wellington 1954–87; Statutory Man. Cornish Group 1974–90, Public Service Investment Soc. 1979–87; mem. Nat. Parks Centennial Comm. 1983–88; Chair. Databank Systems Ltd 1985–93, NZ Fishing Industry Bd 1988–93, Nat. Australia Bank (NZ) Ltd 1991–92, Overseas Investment Comm. 1978–97, Milburn NZ Ltd 1987–97, Trustees Executors 1991–2000, Bank of NZ 1993–96; Dir Fiordland Travel Ltd 1973–97, Tower Trust Ltd (Local Bd) 1991–2002, Commercial Fisheries Services Ltd 1998–, Tower Safe Ltd 1999–2002; Distinguished Fellow NZ Inst. of Dirs. 2000; Rotary Paul Harris Fellow 1998; Trustee Chatham Islands Enterprise Trust 1991–94; NZ 1990 Medal. *Leisure interests:* lawn bowls, mountain tramping, travel. *Address:* c/o KPMG, 135 Victoria Street, Wellington (Office); P.O. Box 996, Wellington (Office); 36, Spencer Street, Crofton Downs, Wellington 6004, New Zealand. *Telephone:* (4) 382-8800 (Office); (4) 479-3057 (Home). *Fax:* (4) 802-1225 (Office).

STANSFIELD SMITH, Sir Colin, Kt, CBE, MA, DIP.ARCH., ARIBA; British architect; b. 1 Oct. 1932, Manchester; s. of Stansfield Smith and Mary Simpson; m. Angela Jean Earnshaw 1961; one s. one d.; ed William Hulmes Grammar School, Manchester and Cambridge Univ. School of Architecture; London County Council (Schools Div.) 1958–60; Sr Asst then Assoc. Partner, Emberton Frank & Tardrew (architects) 1960–65; partner, Emberton Tardrew & Partners 1965–71; Deputy County Architect, Cheshire County Council 1971–73; County Architect, Hampshire County Council 1973–92, Consultant Co. Architect 1992–; Prof. of Architectural Design Studies, Portsmouth Univ. (fmrly Polytech.) School of Architecture 1990–; RIBA Gold Medal

1991. *Publications:* Hampshire Architecture 1974–84 1985, Schools of Thought, Hampshire Architecture 1974–91; articles in Architects' Journal and Architectural Review. *Leisure interests:* golf, painting. *Address:* Three Minsters House, 76 High Street, Winchester, Hants., SO23 8UL (Office); 8 Christchurch Road, Winchester, Hants., SO23 9SR, England (Home). *Telephone:* (1962) 847800 (Office); (1962) 851970.

STANTON, Frank (Nicholas), PhD; American administrator; b. 20 March 1908, Muskegon, Mich.; s. of Frank Cooper Stanton and Helen Josephine Schmidt; m. Ruth Stephenson 1931 (died 1992); ed Ohio Wesleyan Univ., Ohio State Univ.; Dir CBS Inc. 1945–78, Pres. 1946–71, Vice-Chair. 1971–73; Chair. American Red Cross 1973–79, Vice-Pres. League of Red Cross Socs., Geneva; Licensed Psychologist, NY; Diplomate, American Bd of Professional Psychology; Dir New York Life Insurance Co. 1956–81, Atlantic Richfield Co. 1973–81, Pan American World Airways Inc. 1967–81, American Electric Power Co. Inc. 1969–80, New Perspective Fund, Inc., Interpublic Group of Cos. Inc., EuroPacific Growth Fund, Capital Income Builder Fund, Capital World Growth and Income Fund, Sony Music Entertainment Inc., Museum of TV and Radio; Chair. Broadcast Int.; Trustee American Crafts Council 1957–75, Inst. for Architecture and Urban Studies 1970–75, Rockefeller Foundation 1961–73, The Rand Corpn 1956–78, The Observer (London) 1976–85, Int. Herald Tribune 1983–91; Chair. Carnegie Inst. of Washington; Founding Chair. and Trustee, Center for Advanced Study in the Behavioural Sciences 1953–71; Chair. U.S. Advisory Comm. on Information 1964–73; Co-Founder, Office of Radio Research, Princeton Univ. 1937; Chair., Panel on Int. Information, Educ. and Cultural Relations, Georgetown Univ. 1974–75; Dir-Trustee, Educational Broadcasting Corpn, Int. Design Conf. in Aspen, Lincoln Center Inst., etc.; Dir Recorded Anthology of American Music Inc., Lincoln Center for the Performing Arts 1960, Business Cttee for the Arts 1967–77, Chair. 1972–74, Municipal Art Soc. of New York 1974–77; mem. The Business Council 1956–, NY Council on the Arts 1965–70, Nat. Portrait Gallery Comm. 1977–, Bd of Overseers Harvard 1978–84, Pres.'s Cttee on the Arts and the Humanities 1983–91; Fellow, AAAS, American Psychological Asscn, American Acad. of Arts and Sciences, New York Acad. of Science; mem. Architectural League of NY, Council on Foreign Relations Inc., Inst. of Electrical and Electronic Engineers, Nat. Acad. of TV Arts and Sciences (elected to Hall of Fame 1986), Radio-TV News Dirs. Asscn, Int. Radio and TV Soc.; numerous medals, awards and hon. degrees. *Publications:* Students' Guide—The Study of Psychology (co-author) 1935, Radio Research 1941, Radio Research 1942–43, Communications Research 1948–49 (co-ed.), International Information, Education and Cultural Relations—Recommendations for the Future 1975. *Address:* 25 West 52nd Street, New York, NY 10019, USA (Office). *Fax:* (212) 765-4620.

STANZEL, Franz Karl, DPhil; Austrian professor of English (retd); b. 4 Aug. 1923, Molln; s. of Franz Stanzel and Luise Stanzel; m. Ina v. Navarini 1962; one d.; ed Univ. of Graz and Harvard Univ., USA; Lecturer in English, Univ. of Graz 1949–50, 1951–57; Asst Prof. Univ. of Göttingen 1957–59; Prof. Univ. of Erlangen 1959–62; Prof. of English, Univ. of Graz 1962–96, Prof. Emer. 1993–, Dean, Faculty of Arts and Sciences 1967–68, Head Dept of English 1962–78; mem. Austrian Acad.; Dr hc (Fribourg). *Publications include:* Typische Erzählsituationen im Roman 1955, Typische Formen des Romans 1964, Narrative Situations in the Novel 1969, Der literarische Aspekt unserer Vorstellungen vom Charakter fremder Völker 1974, Theorie des Erzählens 1979, A Theory of Narrative 1984, Englische und deutsche Kriegsdichtung, Sprachkunst 1987, Intimate Enemies (ed.) 1993, Europäer: Ein imagologischer Essay 1997, Europäischer Völkerspiegel (ed.) 1999, Unterweg Erzähltheorie für Leser 2002. *Leisure interests:* cross-country skiing, gardening, travel. *Address:* Karl-Franzens-Universität Graz, Universitäts-platz 3, 8010 Graz; Am Blumenhang 31/5, 8010 Graz, Austria. *Telephone:* (316) 47-55-56. *Fax:* (316) 47-55-56. *E-mail:* franzkarl.stanzel@kfunigraz.ac.at.

STAPLE, George Warren, C.B., QC; British lawyer; b. 13 Sept. 1940, Bristol; s. of Kenneth Staple and Betty Staple; m. Olivia Lowry 1968; two s. two d.; ed Haileybury; Assoc. Condon & Forsyth, New York 1963; admitted solicitor 1964; partner, Clifford-Turner, later Clifford Chance 1967–92, 1997–2001, consultant to Clifford Chance 2001–; Dir Serious Fraud Office 1992–97; Legal Assessor, Disciplinary Cttee Stock Exchange 1978–92; Dept of Trade & Industry Insp. Consolidated Goldfields 1986, Aldermanbury Trust 1988; a Chair. Authorization and Disciplinary Tribunals of Securities Asscn 1987–91, Securities and Futures Authority 1991–92; mem. Commercial Court Cttee 1977–92; mem. Council, Law Soc. 1986–2000; mem. Law Advisory Cttee of British Council 1998–2001; mem. Sr Salaries Review Body 2000–; Chair. Review Bd for Govt Contracts 2002–; Gov. London Guildhall Univ. 1982–94; Fellow Chartered Inst. of Arbitrators 1986, Soc. for Advanced Legal Studies 1997; Hon. Bencher Inner Temple 2000. *Leisure interests:* cricket, hill walking, gardening. *Address:* Clifford Chance, 200 Aldersgate Street, London, EC1A 4JJ, England. *Telephone:* (20) 7600-1000. *Fax:* (20) 7600-5555. *Website:* www.cliffordchance.com (Office).

STAPLETON, Nigel John, MA; British business executive; b. 1 Nov. 1946, London; s. of Frederick E J. Stapleton and Katie M. Tyson; m. Johanna Molhoek 1982; one s. one d.; ed Univ. of Cambridge; internal auditor, Unilever Ltd 1968–70; Group Man. Internal Audit, Unilever Ltd 1970–73, Sr Auditor 1973–75; Corp. Planning Man. BOCM Silcock 1975–77, Devt Dir 1977–80; Commercial mem. N American office, Unilever PLC 1980–83; Vice-Pres. Finance, Unilever US Inc. 1983–86; Finance Dir Reed Int. PLC, London 1986–96, Deputy Chair. 1994–97, Chair. 1997–99, CEO 1999; Chair. UNIQ PLC 2001–; Deputy Chair., Chief Financial Officer, Reed Elsevier 1994–97, Co-Chair. 1996–98; Chair. Veronis, Suhler Int. Ltd 1999–2002; Dir (non-exec.) GEC 1997–99, Marconi PLC 1999–, Axa UK PLC 2000–, London Stock Exchange PLC 2001–, Reliance Security PLC 2002–; Chair. (non-exec.) Cordiant 2003–. *Leisure interests:* gardening, classical music, opera, food and wine. *Address:* UNIQ PLC, No. 1 Chalfont Park, Gerrards Cross, Bucks., SL9 0UN, England (Office). *Telephone:* (1753) 276050 (Office). *Fax:* (1753) 276052 (Office). *E-mail:* nigel.stapleton@uniqplc.com (Office); nigel.stapleton@btinternet.com (Home). *Website:* www.uniqplc.com (Office).

STARCK, Christian, DrIur; German professor of law and judge; b. 9 Jan. 1937, Breslau; s. of Walter Starck and Ruth Hubrich; m. Brigitte Edelmann 1965; one s. two d.; ed Univs. of Kiel, Freiburg and Würzburg; clerk, Fed. Constitutional Court 1964–67; Govt official 1968–69; lecturer, Univ. of Würzburg 1969–71; Prof. of Public Law, Univ. of Göttingen 1971–; Rector, Univ. of Göttingen 1976–77; Judge, Constitutional Court of Lower Saxony 1991–; Ed. Studien und Materialen zur Verfassungsgerichtsbarkeit 1973–; co-Ed. Juristenzeitung 1978–, Staatswissenschaften und Staatspraxis 1990–98, Beiträge zum ausländischen und vergleichenden öffentlichen Recht 1989–, Zeitschrift für Staats- und Europawissenschaften 2003–; mem. TV Bd Zweites Deutsches Fernsehen 1978–92; mem. Asscn of German Profs. of Public Law 1969– (Exec. Cttee 1988, 1989, Pres. 1998, 1999), Exec. Cttee Int. Asscn of Constitutional Law 1981–, Exec. Cttee German Asscn of Comparative Law 1985–; Visiting Prof. Paris I (Panthéon-Sorbonne) 1987; mem. Acad. of Sciences of Göttingen 1982–; Fellow Inst. for Advanced Study, Berlin 1990–91. *Publications include:* Der Gesetzesbegriff des Grundgesetzes 1970, Rundfunkfreiheit als Organisationsproblem 1973, Das Bundesverfassungsgericht im politischen Prozess 1976; Bundesverfassungsgericht und Grundgesetz (2 vols) (Ed.) 1976, Vom Grund des Grundgesetzes 1979, El Concepto de Ley en la Constitución Alemana 1979, La Constitution, cadre et mesure du droit 1994, Praxis der Verfassungsauslegung 1994, Die Verfassungen der neuen deutschen Länder 1994, Der demokratische Verfassungsstaat 1995, Constitutionalism, Universalism and Democracy – A Comparative Analysis (Ed.) 1999, Das Bonner Grundgesetz Kommentar, 4th edn, Vol. I 1999, Vol. II 2000, Vol. III 2001, Freiheit und Institutionen 2002. *Leisure interests:* architecture, literature, walking. *Address:* Platz der Göttinger Sieben 6, 37073 Göttingen (Office); Schlegelweg 10, 37075 Göttingen, Germany (Home). *Telephone:* (551) 397412 (Office). *Fax:* (551) 397414 (Office). *E-mail:* cstarck@gdwg.de (Office).

STARCK, Philippe-Patrick; French designer; b. 18 Jan. 1949, Paris; s. of André Starck and Jacqueline Lanourisse; m. 1st Brigitte Laurent 1977 (deceased); two c.; m. 2nd Nori Vaccari-Starck; ed Institution Notre-Dame de Sainte-Croix, Neuilly-sur-Seine, Ecole Nissim de Camondo, Paris; f. Starck Products 1979; Interior architecture: La Main-Bleue 1976, Les Bains-Douches 1978, pvt. apartments in Elysée Palace 1982, Le Café Costes 1984, La Cigale, Paris 1987, restaurants, housing and offices in Tokyo 1986–88, Royalton Hotel, New York 1988, Paramount Hotel, New York 1990, Teatriz Restaurant, Madrid 1990, Groningen Museum 1994, Peninsula Restaurant, Hong Kong 1994, Delano Hotel, Miami 1995, Theatron Restaurant, Mexico 1995, Mondrian Hotel, LA 1996, Asia de Cuba Restaurant, New York 1997, St Martin's Hotel, London 1999, Mikli glasses shop, Paris 1999, Restaurant BON, Paris 2000, Sanderson Hotel, London 2000, Hudson Hotel, New York 2000, Clift Hotel, San Francisco 2001, Miramar Hotel, Santa Barbara (in progress); architecture includes knife factory, Laguiole 1988, Nani Nani Bldg, Tokyo 1989, bldgs. in USA, Japan, France, Spain, Ecole Nat. des Arts Décoratifs, Paris 1995, air traffic control tower for Bordeaux Airport 1997, incineration plant, Paris/Vitry (2004); cr. furniture for Pres. of the Repub. 1982, for French, Italian, Spanish, Japanese and Swiss cos.; designed boats for Bénéteau, vases for Daum, luggage for Vuitton, toothbrush for Fluocaril, urban furniture for Jean-Claude Decaux, Olympic Flame 1992, children's toys, Aprilia scooters, etc.; Worldwide Artistic Dir Thomson Consumer Electronics Group 1993–96; Artistic Dir Eurostar train 2001; Prof., Domus Acad., Milan, Italy, Ecole des Arts Décoratifs de Paris; Artistic Dir Int. Design Yearbook; exhbns. at Georges Pompidou Museum and Decorative Arts Museum, Paris, Villa Medici, Italy, Deutsches Museum, Munich, Kunstmuseum, Düsseldorf, Museum of Modern Art, Kyoto, Japan, Design Museum, London and in Switzerland and USA; Vanity Case Exhbn travelling around the world; numerous prizes, including Oscar du Luminaire 1980, three 1st prizes at Neocon, Chicago 1986, Delta de Plata, Barcelona 1986, Platinum Circle Award, Chicago 1987, Grand prix nat. de la Création Industrielle 1988; three awards for hotels in USA 1990, 1991, one for Hotel Paramount 1992, Disseny Barcelona 1995, Design-Zentrum Nordrhein Westfalen Award (Germany) for Duraint bathroom design 1995, Harvard Excellence in Design Award 1997; Commdr des Arts et des Lettres 1998; Chevalier Légion d'honneur 2000, Prath Inst. Black Alumni Award 2001. *Leisure interest:* sailing. *Address:* Starck-Ubik, 27 rue Pierre Poli, 92130 Issy les Moulineaux, France; 18/20 rue de Faubourg du Temple, 75010 Paris, France. *Telephone:* 1-48-07-54-54 (Office); 1-41-08-82-82. *Fax:* 1-48-07-54-64 (Office); 1-41-08-96-65. *E-mail:* starck@starckdesign.com (Office).

STARFIELD, Barbara, MD, MPh; American physician; b. 18 Dec. 1932; d. of Martin Starfield and Eva Starfield (née Illions); m. Neil A. Holtzman 1955; three s. one d.; ed Swarthmore Coll., State Univ. of New York, The Johns Hopkins Univ.; teaching Asst (anatomy), Downstate Med. Center, New York 1955–57; intern. and resident in Pediatrics, Johns Hopkins Univ. Hosp. 1959–62, Dir, Pediatric Medical Care Clinic 1963–66; Dir Pediatric Clinical

Scholars Program, Johns Hopkins Univ. 1971–76, Asst Prof., Assoc. Prof. 1967–76, Prof. and Div. Head, Health Policy, The Johns Hopkins Univ. School of Hygiene and Public Health 1976–94, Dir Primary Care Policy center 1996–; Univ. Distinguished Prof., Johns Hopkins Univ. 1994–; mem. Nat. Advisory Council for Health Care Policy, Research and Evaluation, US Dept of Health and Human Services 1990–93, Nat. Cttee Vital and Health Statistics (USDHHS) 1994–; mem. Inst. of Medicine, NAS; Hon. Fellow Royal Coll. of Gen. Practitioners (UK) 2000; Dave Luckman Memorial Award 1958, Career Devt Award 1970–75, Armstrong Award (Ambulatory Pediatric Asscn) 1983, Annual Research Award (Ambulatory Pediatric Asscn) 1990, Pew Primary Care Achievement Award 1994, Martha May Eliot Award (APHA) 1994, Maurice Wood Award for Lifetime Contrib. to Primary Care Research 2000. *Publications:* Effectiveness of Medical Care 1985, Primary Care: Concept, Evaluation and Policy 1992, Primary Care: Balancing Health Needs, Services and Technology 1998; over 150 scientific articles. *Address:* The Johns Hopkins Univ. School of Hygiene and Public Health, 624 N Broadway, Baltimore, MD 21205, USA. *Telephone:* (410) 955-9725. *Fax:* (410) 614-9046.

STARK, Hon. Nathan J., BS, JD; American lawyer; b. 9 Nov. 1920, Minn.; s. of Harold and Anna Stark; m. Lucile Seidler 1943; three s. one d.; ed U.S. Merchant Marine Acad. and Illinois Inst. of Tech., Chicago Kent Coll. of Law; Man., Vice-Pres. Rival Mfg Co. 1952–58; Partner, Downey, Abrams, Stark & Sullivan, law firm 1958–59; Sr Vice-Pres. Hallmark Cards Inc. 1959–74; Pres., Chair. of Bd, Crown Center Redevt. Corpn 1970–74; Sr Vice-Chancellor, Health Sciences, Univ. of Pittsburgh, also Prof. of Health Services Admin. 1974–84; Under-Sec., U.S. Dept of Health and Human Services 1979–80; Sr Vice-Chancellor Emer., Univ. of Pittsburgh 1984–, Vice-Pres. Univ. Health Center 1981–; partner, law firm of Kominers, Fort, Schlefer & Boyer 1984–92; mem. Bd Dirs., Allegheny Foundation 1980–, Curry Foundation 1986–, Health Enterprise Int. 1990–, Accreditation Council for Continual Medical Educ. 1991; Pres. Nat. Acad. of Social Insurance, CEO 1992–95; mem. Nat. Bd of Medical Examiners, NAS Inst. of Medicine 1973–; Hon. mem. American Hosp. Asscn; Hon. Fellow, American Coll. of Hosp. Admins, American Acad. of Pediatrics; Hon. LLD (Park Coll.) (Univ. of Missouri); Hon. DHumLitt (Scholl Coll. of Podiatric Medicine, Hahneman Univ.); Chancellor Medals, Univs of Pittsburgh and Mo. at Kansas City; numerous awards including Citation of a Layman for Distinguished Service, American Medical Asscn. *Publications:* numerous papers on health admin. and contribs. to professional journals. *Address:* 4000 Cathedral Avenue, N.W., Washington, DC 20016, USA. *Telephone:* (202) 452-8097 (Office); (202) 965-1516 (Home).

STARK, Ray; American film producer; m. Fran Stark; ed Rutgers Univ.; talent agent, Famous Artist Agency until 1957; co-founder, Seven Arts Production Co. 1957; ind. film producer 1966–; Thalberg Award, Acad. of Motion Picture Arts and Sciences 1980. *Films include:* The World of Suzie Wong 1960, The Night of the Iguana 1964, Reflections in a Golden Eye 1967, Funny Girl 1968, The Owl and the Pussycat 1970, Fat City 1972, The Way We Were 1973, Funny Lady 1975, The Sunshine Boys 1975, Murder By Death 1976, Smokey and the Bandit 1977, The Goodbye Girl 1978, The Cheap Detective 1978, California Suite 1978, Chapter Two 1979, The Electric Horseman 1979, Seems Like Old Times 1980, Annie 1981, Nothing in Common 1986, Peggy Sue Got Married 1986, The Secret of My Success 1987, Biloxi Blues 1988, Steel Magnolias 1989, Barbarians at the Gate 1993 (TV), Mr Jones, To Gillian on Her 37th Birthday 1996, Harriet the Spy 1996, Random Hearts 1998. *Address:* 1990 S. Bundy Drive, Suite 200, Los Angeles, CA 90025, USA. *Telephone:* (310) 274-5702 (Office).

STARKER, Janos; American cellist and educator; b. 5 July 1924, Budapest, Hungary; s. of Margit Starker and Sandor Starker; m. 1st Eva Uranyi 1944 (divorced); one d.; m. 2nd Rae Busch 1960; one d.; ed Franz Liszt Acad. of Music, Budapest; solo cellist, Budapest Opera House and Philharmonic Orchestra 1945–46; solo cellist Dallas Symphony Orchestra 1948–49, Metropolitan Opera Orchestra 1949–53, Chicago Symphony Orchestra 1953–58; Resident cellist, Indiana Univ. 1958–, Prof. of Music 1961, now Distinguished Prof. of Cello; inventor of Starker bridge for orchestral string instruments; worldwide concert tours; Hon. mem. American Fed. of Musicians, Royal Acad. of London 1981, Indiana Acad. of Arts and Sciences, American Acad. of Arts and Sciences; Hon. DMus (Chicago Conservatory) 1961, (Cornell Coll.) 1978, (East West Univ.) 1982, (Williams Coll.) 1983, (Lawrence Univ.) 1990; Grand Prix du Disque 1948, George Washington Award 1972, Sanford Fellowship Award, Yale 1974, Herzl Award 1978, Ed Press Award 1983, Kodály Commemorative Medallion, New York 1983, Arturo Toscanini Award 1986, Indiana Univ. Tracy Sonneborn Award 1986, Indiana Govs. Award 1995, Medal of Paris 1995, Chevalier Ordre des Arts et des Lettres 1997, Grammy Award 1998, Indiana Univ. Pres.'s Medal for Excellence 1999, Pres. of Hungary's Gold Medal 1999. *Recordings:* over 120 titles. *Publications:* Method 1964, Bach Suites 1971, Concerto Cadenzas, Schubert-Starker Sonatina, Bottermund-Starker Variations, Beethoven Sonatas, Beethoven Variations, Dvořák Concerto; numerous magazine articles, essays and record cover notes. *Leisure interests:* writing, swimming. *Address:* c/o Colbert Artists, 111 West 57th Street, New York, NY 10019 (Office); Department of Music, Indiana University, Bloomington, IN 47401, USA. *E-mail:* starker@indiana.edu (Home).

STARKEY, David, PhD, FSA, FRHistS; British historian; b. 3 Jan. 1945, Kendal; s. of Robert Starkey and Elsie Lyon; ed Kendal Grammar School, Fitzwilliam Coll. Cambridge; Research Fellow Fitzwilliam Coll. Cambridge 1970–72, Visiting Fellow 1998–2001, Bye-Fellow 2001; Lecturer in History,

Dept of Int. History, LSE 1972–98; Visiting Vernon Prof. of Biography, Dartmouth Coll., NH, USA 1987, 1989; British Council Specialist Visitor Australia 1989; contribs. to various newspapers; panellist Moral Maze (BBC Radio 4), presenter weekend show Talk Radio 1995–98; presenter/writer This Land of England (Channel 4 TV) 1985, Henry VIII (Channel 4 TV) 1998, Elizabeth (Channel 4 TV) 2000, Six Wives of Henry VIII (Channel 4 TV) 2001; mem. Editorial Bd History Today 1980–, Commemorative Plaques Working Group, English Heritage 1993–; Pres. Soc. for Court Studies 1995–; Patron Tory Group for Homosexual Equality 1994–; Historical Adviser to Henry VIII Exhbn, Nat. Maritime Museum, Greenwich 1991; Hon. Assoc. Rationalist Press Asscn 1995–; Fellow Royal Historical Soc. 1984, Soc. of Antiquaries of London 1994; Freeman Worshipful Co. of Barbers 1992, Medlicott Medal 2001. *Publications:* This Land of England (with David Souden) 1985, The Reign of Henry VIII: Personalities and Politics 1985–86, Revolution Reassessed: Revisions in the History of Tudor Government and Administration (ed. with Christopher Coleman) 1986, The English Court from the Wars of the Roses to the Civil War (ed.) 1987, Rivals in Power: the Lives and Letters of the Great Tudor Dynasties (ed.) 1990, Henry VIII: A European Court in England 1991, The Inventory of Henry VIII, vol. 1 (with Philip Ward) 1998, Elizabeth: Apprenticeship 2000 (W.H. Smith Award for Biog./Autobiog. 2001); numerous articles in learned journals. *Leisure interests:* decorating, gardening. *Address:* Fitzwilliam College, Cambridge, CB3 0DG (Office); 49 Hamilton Park West, London, N5 1AE, England.

STARKOV, Vladislav Andreyevich; Russian journalist; b. 28 Feb. 1940, Tomsk; s. of Andrei Nikolayevich Starkov and Maria Mikhailovna Starkova; m. Yulia Fedorovna Kuznetsova; one d.; ed Rostov State Univ.; researcher and computer engineer USSR Meteorology Centre 1962–73; corresp. Radio Moscow 1973–76; Znaniye Publishing House 1976–79; ed. Mezhdunarodnye Otnosheniya (journal) 1979–80; Ed.-in-Chief Argumenty i Fakty (weekly) 1980–; Head Argumenty i Fakty Publrs. 1995–; RSFSR People's Deputy 1990–93. *Leisure interests:* reading fiction, swimming. *Address:* AiF, Myasnitskaya str. 42, 101000 Moscow, Russia. *Telephone:* (095) 921-02-34 (Office). *Fax:* (095) 925-61-82 (Office). *E-mail:* into@aif.ru (Office). *Website:* www.aif.ru (Office).

STAROBINSKI, Jean, PhD, MD; Swiss academic; b. 17 Nov. 1920, Geneva; s. of Aron Starobinski and Szayndla Frydman; m. Jaqueline H. Sirman 1954; three s.; ed Univs. of Geneva and Lausanne; Asst Prof. Johns Hopkins Univ. 1953–56, Prof. of French Literature, History of Ideas 1958–85; Pres. Rencontres Int. de Geneva 1965–; mem. Acad. Lincei, British Acad., American Acad. of Arts and Sciences, Deutsche Akad.; Assoc. mem. Acad. des Sciences Morales et Politiques (France); Hon. degrees from Univs. of Lille 1973, Brussels, Lausanne 1979, Chicago 1986, Columbia (New York) 1987, Montréal 1988, Strasbourg 1988, Neuchâtel 1990, Nantes 1992, Oslo 1994, Urbino 1995, Cluj 1995, ETH, Zürich 1998; Balzan Prize 1984, Monaco Prize 1988; Officier, Légion d'honneur. *Publications:* Rousseau 1958, The Invention of Liberty 1964, Words Upon Words 1971, 1789: The Emblems of Reason 1973, Montaigne In Motion 1983, Le Remède dans le Mal 1989, La Mélancolie au Miroir 1989, Largesse 1994., Action et Réaction 1999. *Leisure interest:* music. *Address:* 12 Rue de Candolle, 1205 Geneva, Switzerland. *Telephone:* (22) 3209864.

STARODUBOV, Vladimir Ivanovich; Russian politician and surgeon; b. 17 May 1950, Kosobrodsk, Kurgan Region; m.; two d.; ed Sverdlovsk State Medical Inst.; surgeon, Head, Surgery Dept, Nizhny Tagil Hosp., Sverdlovsk Region 1973–77; Asst, Chair of Surgery, Sverdlovsk State Inst. of Medicine 1977–80; Chief, Sverdlovsk town clinic 1980–81; instructor, Sverdlovsk Regional CP Cttee 1981–87; Deputy Head, Sverdlovsk Regional Dept of Public Health 1987–88; First Deputy Head, Main Dept of Public Health, Sverdlovsk, Regional Soviet 1988–89; Head, Main Dept of Treatment and Prophylactics, Ministry of Public Health RSFSR 1989–90; Deputy Minister of Public Health Russian Fed. 1990–94; Head, Prof., Chair of Econs of Man., Russian Medical Univ. 1994–96; Deputy Minister of Public Health and Medical Industry 1996–98, Minister of Public Health 1998–99; Russian Rep. WHO 1999–2001; Prof. Russian State Medical Univ. 1999–. *Address:* RGMU, Ostrovityanova Str. 1, 117573 Moscow, Russia. *Telephone:* (095) 434-31-74.

STARODUBTSEV, Vasily Aleksandrovich, PhD; Russian politician; b. 25 Dec. 1931, Volovchik, Lipetsk Region; one s. one d.; ed Nat. Agric. Inst. of the USSR; machinist of mining machines 1955–64; Chair. Lenin Kolkhoz 1964–97; Chair. Council of Kolkhozes of the Russian Fed. 1986; USSR People's Deputy 1989–91; Chair. Agrarian Union of Russia 1990; Chair. Peasants' Union of the USSR 1990; mem. Cen. Cttee Communist Party of the Soviet Union 1990–91; mem. State Cttee for Nat. Emergency; Bd Agric. Party 1993; Gov. of Tula Region 1997–; mem. Council of Fed. 1997–2001; mem. Cen. Cttee of the CP of the Russian Fed. 1997–; mem. Presidium of the Coordination Council of the Popular Patriotic Union; mem. Int. Acad. of Information Process and Technologies; Corresp. mem. Acad. of Agric. Sciences; Order of the Sign of Honour 1965, Order of October Revolution 1971, Order of Lenin 1973, 1976, 1980, Hero of Socialist Labour 1976, USSR State Prize 1979, Appreciation of Pres. of Russian Fed. 2001, Diploma of Honour, Govt of Russian Fed. 2001. *Publications:* more than 50 scientific works. *Leisure interest:* chess. *Address:* pl. Lenina 2, 300600 Tula, Russia. *Telephone:* (872) 27-84-36 (Office). *Fax:* (872) 20-63-26 (Office). *E-mail:* doksvyaz@adm.tula.ru (Office). *Website:* www.starodubtsev.tula.ru (Office).

STAROSTENKO, Vladimir Ivanovich; Russian government official; b. 2 Sept. 1948, Tatarsk, Novosibirsk Region; m.; ed Tomsk Higher School of Railway Transport, Novosibirsk Inst. of Railway Eng; mem. of station staff Tatarskaya W Siberian railway 1966–79, station man. 1970–75, inspector Omsk Div. 1975–80, station man. Karbyshevo 1980–83, Head Div. of Cargo, then Head Div. of Transportation, Omsk Div. 1983–88, First Deputy Head Omsk Div. 1988–90, Head Novosibirsk Div. 1990–95, Deputy Head W Siberian Railway 1995–96, Head 1997–99, Sept. 1999–; Head Kemerovo Railway 1996–97; Minister of Railways May–Sept. 1999; Head West Siberian Railway 1999–. Address: c/o Ministry of Railways, 107174 Moscow, ul. Novobasmannaya 2, Russia (Office).

STAROVOITOV, Gen. Aleksander Vladimirovich, DTechSc; Russian communications engineer; b. 18 Oct. 1940, Balashov, Saratov Region; m.; one s.; ed Penza Polytech. Inst., Higher Courses of Gen. Staff; engineer, deputy head of workshop, Sr engineer, Head of lab., Head of div., Prof., Deputy Dir, Dir-Gen., Kristall, Dir Penza Research Electrotech. Inst. 1962–86; Deputy Head, Dept of Govt Telecommunications 1986–91; Chair. Cttee on Govt Telecommunications of Pres. Gorbachev 1991; Dir-Gen. Fed. Agency of Govt Telecommunications and Information of Pres. Yeltsin 1991–98; Chair. Co-ordination Council of CIS on Security of System of Govt Telecommunications; Constructor-Gen. of Integrated State System of Confidential Telecommunications of Russia; mem., Vice-Pres. Acad. of Eng Sciences; mem., Vice-Pres. Acad. of Electrotechnical Sciences; mem. Acad. of Cryptography. Publications: over 150 articles and papers on problems of communications; several patents. Address: c/o FAPSI, Bolshoi Kiselny per. 4, 103031 Moscow, Russia.

STAROWIEYSKI, Franciszek; Polish surrealist painter and poster designer; b. 8 July 1930, Bratkówka; ed Acad. of Fine Arts, Cracow and Warsaw; Prof. European Acad. of Art 1993–; Visiting Prof. Berliner Hochschule der Künste, W Berlin 1980; about 300 film and theatre posters and about 2000 paintings and drawings, film and theatre scenography; works in many museums and pvt. collections in Poland and abroad; presenter own TV shows on art; mem. Union of Polish Artists and Designers, Int. Graphic Asscn (Gawędy o sztuce) 1996–99; prizewinner all main int. poster festivals. Exhibitions: many one-man exhbns. including Museum of Modern Art, Houston, Tex. 1975, Museum of Modern Art, Seibul, Tokyo 1976, Museum of Modern Art, New York 1985 and in Poland, France, Italy and Switzerland; works shown at São Paulo Biennale 1973, Poster Biennale, Warsaw 1972, 1978, Int. Poster Film Exhbn, Cannes 1974, Annual Key Award Exhbn, Los Angeles 1978; Venice Biennale 1986. Leisure interest: collecting Baroque art. Address: ul. Bernardyńska 23 m. 75, 02-901 Warsaw, Poland (Home). Telephone: (22) 8403894 (Home).

STARR, Kenneth Winston, MA; American lawyer; b. 21 July 1946, Vernon, Texas; s. of W.D. Starr and Vannie M. (née Trimble) Starr; m. Alice J. Mendell 1970; one s. two d.; ed George Washington, Brown and Duke Univs.; law clerk Court of Appeals (5th Circuit), Miami 1973–74, Supreme Court 1975–77; assoc. Gibson, Dunn & Crutcher, LA 1974–75, assoc. partner 1977–81; counsellor to Attorney-Gen.; Justice Dept, Washington DC 1981–83, Solicitor Gen. 1989–93; judge Court of Appeals (DC Circuit) 1983; partner Kirkland & Ellis, Washington DC 1993–94; ind. counsel for Whitewater Investigation as well as any collateral matters arising out of any investigation of such matters including obstruction of justice or false statements 1994–; mem. several law orgs. Publications: contrib. articles to legal journals. Address: Kirkland and Ellis, 655 15th Street, Suite 1200, Washington, DC 2005, USA.

STARR, Ringo (Richard Starkey), MBE; British entertainer; b. 7 July 1940, Dingle, Liverpool; m. 1st Maureen Cox 1965 (divorced 1975); two s. one d.; m. 2nd Barbara Bach 1981; ed Dingle Vale Secondary Modern School; plays drums; fmrly an apprentice engineer; played with Rory Storme's Hurricanes 1959–62; joined The Beatles Aug. 1962; appeared with The Beatles in the following activities: performances in Hamburg 1962; toured Scotland, Sweden, UK 1963, Paris, Denmark, Hong Kong, Australia, NZ, USA, Canada 1964, France, Italy, Spain, USA 1965, Canada, Spain, Philippines, USA 1966; attended Transcendental Meditation Course at Maharishi's Acad., Rishikesh, India Feb. 1968; formed Apple Corps Ltd, parent org. of The Beatles Group of Companies 1968; following break-up of group 1970, now records solo. Television: narrator of Thomas the Tank Engine (childrens' programme) 1980s. Recordings by the Beatles include: Please, Please Me 1963, With the Beatles 1963, A Hard Day's Night 1964, Beatles for Sale 1965, Help! 1965, Rubber Soul 1966, Revolver 1966, Sergeant Pepper's Lonely Hearts Club Band 1967, The Beatles (White Album) 1968, Yellow Submarine 1969, Abbey Road 1969, Let It Be 1970, Anthology I 1995, Anthology II 1996. Films by The Beatles: A Hard Day's Night 1964, Help! 1965, Yellow Submarine (animated colour cartoon film) 1968, Let it Be 1970; TV film Magical Mystery Tour 1967. Individual appearances in films: Candy 1968, The Magic Christian 1969, 200 Motels 1971, Blindman 1971, That'll be the Day 1973, Born to Boogie (also directed and produced) 1974, Son of Dracula (also produced) 1975, Lisztomania 1975, Ringo Stars 1976, Caveman 1981, The Cooler 1982, Give My Regards to Broad Street 1984. Address: c/o Mercury Records, 825 8th Avenue, New York, NY 10019, USA.

STARSKI, Allan Mieczysław; Polish film maker; b. 1 Jan. 1943, Warsaw; m.; ed Fine Art Acad., Warsaw; mem. Acad. of Motion Picture Arts and Sciences, Polish Film Asscn; Gdańsk Film Festival Award 1979, Los Angeles Critics' Asscn Award, Polish Film Award for Polish Eagles 2000. Films include: The Shadow Line 1976, Man of Marble 1977, The Young Ladies of

Wilko 1979, The Conductor 1979, Man of Iron 1981, Danton 1982, Eine Liebe in Deutschland 1983, Escape From Sobibor 1986, Korczak 1990, Europa, Europa 1990, Daens 1992, Schindler's List (Acad. Award 1994) 1993, Washington Square 1997, Love Stories 1997, The Last Foray in Lithuania 1999, The Body 2000, The Pianist 2002. Leisure interests: cinema, ice skating.

STARZEWSKI, Tomasz; Polish fashion designer; b. 1961; ed St Martin's School of Art, London; collections shown around the world as part of the British Collections, a group he f. in 1987; opened House of Tomasz Starzewski, London 1991.

STASI, Bernard, LenD; French politician; b. 4 July 1930, Reims; s. of Mario Stasi and Mercédès Stasi (née Camps); m. Danièle Beaugier 1979; ed Institut d'Etudes Politiques, Paris and Ecole Nat. d'Admin; attached to the Cabinet of the Pres. of the Nat. Assembly 1955; served in army 1955–57; Civil Admin., Ministry of Interior 1959; Chef de Cabinet to the Prefect of Algiers 1959–60; Head of Section, Directorate-Gen. of Political Affairs and Territorial Admin., Ministry of Interior 1960–62; Tech. Adviser, Cabinet of the Sec. of State for Youth and Sports 1963–65; Directeur de Cabinet to the Sec. of Overseas Depts. 1966–68; Deputy for Marne, Nat. Ass. 1968–73, 1978–93; mem. European Parl. 1994–98; charged with missions to Israel, GB, Cuba and Chile; Mayor of Epernay 1970–77, 1983–; Médiateur de la République (Ombudsman) 1998–; Vice-Pres. Centre Démocratie et Progrès 1969–75, Centre des Démocrates Sociaux 1976–84 (first Vice-Pres. 1984); Minister for Overseas Depts and Territories 1973–74; Fed. Sec. Féd. des Réformateurs 1975–; mem. Regional Council of Champagne-Ardenne 1976–88, Pres. 1981–88; Pres. Fédération française de course d'orientation 1970–88; Pres. Nat. Council for Regional Econs and Productivity 1986–88; Founder, Groupe d'études parlementaires pour l'aménagement rural 1970; Vice-Pres. Co-operative and Devt Comm., Christian Democrat Int. 1993–; Sec.-Gen. Asscn. of Ombudsmen and Mediators of French-speaking Communities 1998–; mem. Bd of Dirs Association des Maires de France; mem. various municipal orgs; Chevalier, Légion d'honneur, Chevalier Ordre nat. du Mérite, Chevalier du Mérite agricole, Chevalier Ordre des Palmes académiques, Grand' Croix de l'Ordre du Croissant vert et de l'Etoile d'Anjouan (Comoros) and other awards. Publication: Le Piège (with J. P. Soisson and O. Stirn) 1973, Vie associative et démocratie nouvelle 1978, L'Immigration: une chance pour la France 1984, La Politique au coeur 1993. Leisure interests: football, tennis, sailing. Address: Médiature, 53 avenue d'Iéna, 75016 Paris (Office); Hôtel de Ville, 51200 Epernay; 22 rue de Tocqueville, 75017 Paris, France (Home). Telephone: 1-45-02-72-72 (Paris).

STASSE, François; French civil servant and economist; b. 11 Jan. 1948, Neuilly-sur-Seine; s. of Roger Stasse and Christiane (née Deveaux) Stasse; m. Nathalie Duhamel 1978; ed Inst. of Political Studies, Paris; with Ministry of Industry 1972–73; joined Gen. Bd of Planning 1974, Dir Commr.'s Office 1979–81; Tech. Adviser to Pres. of Rep. on Econs and Finance 1981–84; Counsel Council of State 1984, Sr mem. 1996; Dir State Hosp. Paris 1989–93; mem. consultative Cttee on future of state medical provision 1998–; Dir-Gen. Bibliothèque nationale de France 1998–2001. Publications include: La Morale de l'histoire 1994. Address: Conseil d'État, place du Palais Royal, 75100 Paris.

STASSINOPOULOS, Michael; Greek politician, university professor and judge; b. 27 July 1903, Calamata; s. of Demetrios Stassinopoulos and Catherine Scopetou; m. Stamatia Ritsoni 1942; one d.; ed Athens Univ.; Lecturer in Admin. Law, Athens Univ. 1937–68; Prof. Admin. Law, High School of Political Sciences, Athens 1939–68, Dean 1951–58; State Council Adviser 1943–58; Political Adviser to Dodecanese Gov. 1947; Chair. Cttee for the Civil Servants Code 1948; Minister of the Press and subsequently Minister of Labour 1952; Chair. Hellenic Nat. Broadcasting Inst. Admin. Bd 1953; Chair. Nat. Opera Admin. Bd 1953–63; Minister of the Press 1958; Vice-Pres. State Council 1963, Pres. 1966–69; MP Nov.–Dec. 1974; Pres. of Greece 1974–75; Judge ad hoc, Int. Court of Justice, The Hague 1976–78; mem. Acad. of Athens 1968, Pres. 1978; Chief Justice until 1974; Dr. hc (Univ. of Bordeaux) 1957, (Univ. of Paris) 1974, Order of St George (First Class). Publications: The States' Civil Responsibility 1949, Administrative Acts Law 1950 (in French), Civil Service Laws 1951, Administrative Disputes Laws 1953, Principles of Administrative Law 1954, Principles of Public Finance 1956, Traité des actes administratifs (in French), Poems 1949, The Land of the Blue Lakes 1950, Harmonia (poems) 1956, Thought and Life (essays) 1970, The Wolf's Law (essays) 1972, Le droit de la défense (in French) 1977, Political History of Greece 1978, Two Seasons (poems) 1979. Leisure interests: poetry, cinema, gardening. Address: Taygetou Street 7, 154 52 Psichicon, Athens, Greece. Telephone: 6713197.

STAUDINGER, Ulrich; German publisher; b. 30 May 1935, Berlin; s. of Wilhelm Staudinger and Elfriede Poth; m. Irmengard Ehrenwirth 1960 (died 1989); one s. two d.; ed Volksschule and Realgymnasium; publishing training 1954–57; Lingenbrinck Barsortiment, Hamburg 1957–58; Publicity and Sales, Ensslin & Laiblin, Jugendbuchverlag, Reutlingen 1958–59; Production, Carl Hanser Verlag, Munich 1959–60; Dawson & Sons, London 1960; Franz Ehrenwirth Verlag, Munich 1960; partner, Ehrenwirth Verlag, Munich 1964; responsible for purchase of Franz Schneekluth Verlag KG, Darmstadt by Ehrenwirth Verlag 1967 and following purchase of all parts of Franz Schneekluth Verlag the cos. were amalgamated into a single firm in 1976;

purchased parts of Philosophia Verlag GmbH, Düsseldorf 1978; various professional appointments. *Address:* Asgardstrasse 34, 8000 Munich 81, Germany (Home). *Telephone:* (89) 98-63-67 (Home).

STAUNTON, Imelda Mary Philomena Bernadette; British actress; b. 9 Jan. 1956; d. of Joseph Staunton and Bridie McNicholas; m. Jim Carter 1983; one d.; ed La Sainte Union Convent, Highgate, London, RADA; repertory Exeter, Nottingham, York 1976–81; Olivier Award 1985, 1990, Screen Actors' Guild Award 1999. *Stage appearances include:* Guys and Dolls 1982, 1996, Beggar's Opera 1985, She Stoops to Conquer, Chorus of Disapproval 1985 (Olivier Award, Best Supporting Actress), The Corn is Green 1985, Fair Maid of the West 1986, Wizard of Oz 1986, Uncle Vanya 1988, Into the Woods 1990, Phoenix 1990 (Olivier Award, Best Actress in a Musical), Life x 3 2000. *Television appearances include:* The Singing Detective 1986, Yellowbacks 1990, Sleeping Life, Roots, Up the Garden Path 1990, Antonia and Jane, David Copperfield 1999, Victoria Wood Xmas Special 2000, Murder 2001, Cambridge Spies 2002, Strange 2002. *Film appearances include:* Comrades 1987, Peter's Friends 1992, Much Ado About Nothing 1993, Deadly Advice 1994, Sense and Sensibility, Twelfth Night, Remember Me 1996, Shakespeare in Love 1998, Another Life 1999, Rat 1999, Crush 2000, Bright Young Things 2002, Virgin of Liverpool 2002, Blackball 2002, Family Business 2002. *Address:* c/o ARG, 4 Great Portland Street, London, W1W 4PA, England.

STAVROPOULOS, William S., PhD; American chemical company executive; b. 12 May 1939, Bridgehampton; m. Linda Stavropoulos; one s. one d.; ed Fordham Univ., Univ. of Washington; research chemist, Pharmaceutical Research Div., Dow Chemical Co. 1967, Diagnostics Product Research Div. 1970, Research Man. 1973, Diagnostic Products Business Man. 1976, Business Man. for polyolefins 1977, Dir of Marketing, Dow USA Plastics Dept 1979, Commercial Vice-Pres. Dow Latin America 1980, Pres. 1984, Commercial Vice-Pres. Dow USA, Basics and Hydrocarbons 1985, Group Vice-Pres. 1987, Pres. Dow USA 1990, Vice-Pres. The Dow Chemical Co. 1990, Dir 1990–, Sr Vice-Pres. 1991, Pres., COO 1993–95, Pres., CEO 1995–2000, 2002–, Chair. 2002–; mem. Bd of Dirs Dow Corning Corpn 1991, Marion Merrell Dow Inc. 1992, Dowell Schlumberger 1992, Chemical Bank; Trustees Midland Community Center and other bodies. *Address:* The Dow Chemical Company, 2030 Willard H. Dow Centre, Midland, MI 48674, USA. *Website:* www.dow.com.

STCHIN GOWA; Chinese actress; b. 2 Nov. 1949, Guangzhou City; with Inner Mongolia Song and Dance Ensemble 1965–79; film actress, First August Film Studio 1981–; winner Golden Rooster Award, Hundred Flowers. *Films include:* Luotuo Xiangzi 1981 (Best Actress Award in China 1982), Fleeting Time 1984 (Best Actress Award in Hong Kong), Xianghun Girl 1992 (Best Film in Berlin Film Festival). *Address:* Room 307, Building 2, Panjiapo Hutong, Beijing 100020, People's Republic of China.

STEAD, Christian Karlson (C. K.), CBE, MA, PhD, LittD, FRSL; New Zealand writer and professor of English (retd); b. 17 Oct. 1932, Auckland; s. of James Walter Ambrose Stead and Olive Ethel Stead (née Karlson); m. Kathleen Elizabeth Roberts 1955; one s. two d.; ed Mt. Albert Grammar School, Auckland Univ. Coll. and Auckland Teachers' Coll., Univ. of Bristol; Lecturer in English, Univ. of New England, NSW, Australia 1956–57; Michael Hiatt Baker Scholar Univ. of Bristol 1957–59; Lecturer, Sr Lecturer, Assoc. Prof. Univ. of Auckland 1960–67, Prof. of English 1967–86, Prof. Emer. 1986–; writer 1986–; Nuffield Fellow, Univ. of London 1965, Hon. Fellow 1977, Sr Visiting Fellow St John's Coll. Oxford 1996–97; Hon. DLitt (Bristol) 2001; Katherine Mansfield Prize 1960, New Zealand Book Award for Poetry 1972, 1986, New Zealand Book Award for Fiction 1985, 1995. *Publications:* fiction: Smith's Dream (also film) 1972, Crossing the Bar 1973, Geographies 1983, All Visitors Ashore 1984, The Death of the Body 1986, Sister Hollywood 1989, The End of the Century at the End of the World 1992, Talking about O'Dwyer 2000; poetry: Paris – A Poem 1984, Between (Poems) 1989, Straw into Gold: Poems New and Selected 1997, The Right Thing 2000, Dog: Poems 2002; short story collections; non-fiction: Pound, Yeats, Eliot, and the Modernist Movement 1986, The New Poetic: Yeats to Eliot 1964, In the Glass Case: Essays on New Zealand Literature 1982, Answering to the Language: Essays on Modern Writers 1990, Werner Forman's New Zealand 1994, Kin of Place: Essays on Twenty New Zealand Writers 2002, The Secret History of Modernism 2002; Ed.: New Zealand Short Stories 1974, Shakespeare's Measure for Measure 1971, Letters and Journals of Katherine Mansfield 1977, Collected Stories (New Zealand Fiction) 1981, The Faber Book of Contemporary South Pacific Stories 1994. *Leisure interests:* music, politics. *Address:* 37 Tohunga Crescent, Parnell, Auckland, 1001, New Zealand. *Telephone:* (649) 379-9420. *Fax:* (649) 379-9420.

STEAD, Rev. (George) Christopher, LittD, FBA; British professor of divinity (retd); b. 9 April 1913, Wimbledon; s. of Francis B. Stead CBE and Rachel E. Stead (née Bell); m. D. Elizabeth Odom 1958; two s. one d.; ed Marlborough Coll., King's Coll. Cambridge, New Coll. Oxford and Cuddesdon Coll. Oxford; ordained 1938; Curate, St John's Newcastle-upon-Tyne 1939; Fellow and Lecturer in Divinity, King's Coll. Cambridge 1938–48; Asst Master, Eton Coll. 1940–44; Fellow and Chaplain, Keble Coll. Oxford 1949–71; Ely Prof. of Divinity, Cambridge and Canon Residentiary of Ely Cathedral 1971–80, Canon Emer. 1981–; Fellow, King's Coll. Cambridge 1971–85, Professorial Fellow 1971–80; Emer. Fellow, Keble Coll. Oxford 1981–; Pitt Scholar, Univ. of Cambridge 1934. *Publications:* Divine Substance 1977, Substance and Illusion in the Christian Fathers 1985, Philosophie und

Theologie I, Alte Kirche 1990, Philosophy in Christian Antiquity 1994, A Filosofia na antiguedade Cristã 1998, Doctrine and Philosophy in Early Christianity: Arius, Athanasius, Augustine 2000, The Birth of the Steam Locomotive 2002; contrib. to books, encyclopaedias, journals, etc. *Leisure interests:* walking, sailing, music, industrial archaeology. *Address:* 13 Station Road, Haddenham, Ely, Cambs., CB6 3XD, England. *Telephone:* (1353) 740575.

STEADMAN, Alison, OBE; British actress; b. 26 Aug. 1946, Liverpool; d. of the late George Percival Steadman and Margorie Evans; m. Mike Leigh (q.v.); two s.; ed drama school, Loughton, Essex; began career in repertory theatre in Lincoln, Bolton, Liverpool, Worcester and Nottingham; Hon. MA (Univ. of E London); Evening Standard Best Actress Award 1977, Olivier Award for Best Actress 1993. *Films:* Champions, Number One, P'Tang Kipperbang, A Private Function, Wilt, Shirley Valentine, Life is Sweet, Blame It On the Bellboy, Topsy-Turvy 1999, Happy Now. *Stage appearances include:* Sandy in The Prime of Miss Jean Brodie, Beverley in Abigail's Party, Mae-Sister Woman in Cat on a Hot Tin Roof, Nat. Theatre (NT) 1988, Mari Hoff in The Rise and Fall of Little Voice, NT, David Edgar's Maydays, RSC, Tartuffe, RSC, Joking Apart, Kafka's Dick, Royal Court, Marvin's Room 1993, The Plotters of Cabbage Patch Corner, The Provok'd Wife, Old Vic 1997, When We Are Married, Chichester and Savoy Theatres, The Memory of Water, Vaudeville Theatre, Entertaining Mr Sloane, Arts Theatre, Bette in Cousin Bette. *Television appearances include:* Z Cars, Hard Labour, Abigail's Party, Nuts in May, The Singing Detective, Virtuoso, Newshounds, The Short and Curlies, Gone to Seed, Selling Hitler, Pride and Prejudice, The Wimbledon Poisoner, Karaoke, No Bananas, The Missing Postman, Let Them Eat Cake, Fat Friends, The Cappuccino Years. *Address:* c/o Peters, Fraser and Dunlop, The Chambers, Chelsea Harbour, London, SW10 0XF, England. *Telephone:* (20) 7352-4446. *Fax:* (20) 7352-7356.

STEADMAN, Ralph Idris; British cartoonist, writer and illustrator; b. 15 May 1936; s. of Raphael Steadman and Gwendoline Steadman; m. 1st Sheila Thwaite 1959 (divorced 1971); two s. two d.; m. 2nd Anna Deverson 1972; one d.; ed London School of Printing and Graphic Arts; with de Havilland Aircraft Co. 1952; Cartoonist Kemsley (Thomson) Newspapers 1956–59; freelance for Punch, Private Eye, Daily Telegraph during 1960s; political cartoonist New Statesman 1978–80; retrospective exhbns.: Nat. Theatre 1977, Royal Festival Hall 1984, Wilhelm Busch Museum, Hanover 1988, One on One Gallery, Denver 1997, Warrington Museum 1998, William Havu Gallery, Denver 2000; designed set of stamps Halley's Comet 1986; artist-in-residence, Leviathan (series of films, BBC2) 1999; designer of set and costumes, The Crucible, Royal Ballet 2000; Hon. D.Litt. (Kent) 1995; Designers and Art Dirs. Asscn Gold Award 1977, Silver Award 1977. *Written and illustrated:* Sigmund Freud 1979, A Leg in the Wind and Other Canine Curses 1982, That's My Dad 1986, The Big I Am 1988, No Room to Swing a Cat 1989, Near the Bone 1990, Tales of Weirrd 1990, Still Life with Bottle, Whisky According to Ralph Steadman 1994, Jones of Colorado 1998, Gonzo: The Art 1998, little.com 2000. *Illustrator:* many books from 1961, including Friendship 1990 (in aid of John McCarthy), Adrian Mitchell, Heart on the Left, Poems 1953–84 1997, Roald Dahl, The Mildenhall Treasure 1999, Doodaa: The Balletic Art of Gavin Twinge 2002. *Publications:* Jelly Book 1968, Still Life with Raspberry: collected drawings 1969, The Little Red Computer 1970, Dogs Bodies 1971, Bumper to Bumper Book 1973, Two Donkeys and the Bridge 1974, Flowers for the Moon 1974, The Watchdog and the Lazy Dog 1974, America: drawings 1975, America: collected drawings 1977 (r.e. Scar Strangled Banger 1987), I, Leonardo 1983, Between the Eyes 1984, Paranoids 1986, The Grapes of Ralph 1992, Teddy Where Are You? 1994. *Leisure interests:* gardening, sheep husbandry, fishing, guitar, trumpet.

STEEDS, John Wickham, PhD, FRS, FInstP; British professor of physics; b. 9 Feb. 1940, London; s. of John Henry William Steeds and Ethel Amelia Steeds, (née Tyler); m. Diana Mary Kettlewell 1969; two d.; ed Haberdashers' Aske's School, Univ. Coll. London, Cambridge Univ.; Mullard Research Fellow, Selwyn Coll. Cambridge 1964–67; Lecturer, Physics Dept, Univ. of Bristol 1967–77, Reader 1977–85, Prof. of Electron Microscopy 1985–, Head of Dept 2001–, Henry Overton Wills Prof. 2002–; fmr mem. Council European Pole Univ. of Lille; Chair., Emersons Innovations Ltd; Holweck Medal (Soc. Française de Physique and Inst. of Physics) 1996. *Publications:* Introduction to Anistropic Elasticity Theory of Dislocations 1973, Electron Diffraction of Phases in Alloys (with J. F. Mansfield) 1984, Thin Film Diamond (co-ed.) 1994. *Leisure interest:* tennis. *Address:* Physics Department, University of Bristol, Bristol, BS8 1TL (Office); 21 Canynge Square, Clifton, Bristol, BS8 3LA, England (Home). *Telephone:* (117) 928-8730 (Office); (117) 973-2183 (Home).

STEEL, Danielle (Danielle Fernande Schüelein-Steel); American writer; b. 14 Aug. 1950, New York; d. of John Steel and Norma (née Stone) Schüelein-Steel; m. 2nd Bill Toth 1977; m. 3rd John A. Traina Jr; four s. five d.; ed Lycée Français, Parsons School of Design, New York, Univ. of New York; worked as public relations and advertising exec., Manhattan, New York; published first novel 1973, then wrote advertising copy and poems for women's magazines; wrote first bestseller, The Promise 1979. *Publications:* Going Home 1973, Passion's Promise 1977, Now and Forever 1978, Season of Passion 1978, The Promise 1979, Summer's End 1980, To Love Again 1981, Palomino 1981, Loving 1981, Remembrance 1981, A Perfect Stranger 1982, Once in a Lifetime 1982, Crossings 1982, Thurston House 1983, Full Circle 1984, Having a Baby (Contrib., non-fiction) 1984, Family Album 1985,

Wanderlust 1986, Fine Things 1987, Kaleidoscope 1987, Zoya 1988, Star 1989, Daddy 1989, Heartbeat 1991, Message from Nam 1991, No Greater Love 1991, Jewels 1992, Mixed Blessings 1992, Vanished 1993, Accident 1994, The Gift 1994, Wings 1995, Lightning 1995, Five Days in Paris 1995, Malice 1995, Silent Honor 1996, The Ranch 1996, The Ghost 1997, Special Delivery 1997, His Bright Light 1998, The Ranch 1998, The Long Road Home 1998, The Klone and I 1998, Mirror Image 1998, Bittersweet 1999, The Wedding 2000, The House on Hope Street 2000, Journey 2000, Leap Faith 2001, The Kiss 2001, The Cottage 2002, Lone Eagle 2001, Answered Prayers 2002, Dating Game 2003; eight children's books, one book of poetry. *Leisure interest:* my children. *Address:* c/o Dell Publishing, 1540 Broadway, New York, NY 10036 (Office); P.O. Box 1637, New York, NY 10156, USA (Home).

STEEL, Sir David (Edward Charles), Kt, DSO, MC, TD; British company director; b. 29 Nov. 1916, London; s. of the late Gerald Arthur Steel, C.B.; m. Ann Price 1956 (died 1997); one s. two d.; ed Rugby School and Univ. Coll. Oxford; Officer, Q.R. Lancers, serving in France, the Middle East, N Africa and Italy 1940–45; admitted as Solicitor 1948; worked for Linklaters and Paines 1948–50; in Legal Dept, British Petroleum Co. Ltd 1950–56; Pres. British Petroleum (N America) Ltd 1959–61, Regional Co-ordinator, Western Hemisphere, B.P. Co. Ltd 1961–62; Man. Dir Kuwait Oil Co. Ltd 1962–65, Dir 1965–; a Man. Dir British Petroleum Co. Ltd 1965–72, Deputy Chair. 1972–75, Chair. 1975–81; Chair. B.P. Oil 1976–77; Dir Bank of England 1978–84, Kleinwort, Benson, Lonsdale 1985–92; Trustee, The Economist 1979–95; Chair. Wellcome Trust 1982–89; Deputy Chair. Governing Body, Rugby School 1982, Chair. 1984–88; Pres. London Chamber of Commerce and Industry 1982–85; Hon. Fellow, Univ. Coll. Oxford 1982; Hon. DCL (City) 1983. *Address:* 22 Hill Street, London, W1X 7FU (Office); Flat 6, 55 Onslow Square, London, SW7 3LR, England. *Telephone:* (20) 7496-5821 (Office); (20) 7581-0746 (Home).

STEEL OF AIKWOOD, Baron (Life Peer), cr. 1997, of Ettrick Forest in the Scottish Borders; **David Martin Scott Steel**, KBE, PC, MA, LLB; Scottish politician, journalist and broadcaster; b. 31 March 1938, Kirkcaldy; s. of Very Rev. Dr David Steel; m. Judith Mary MacGregor 1962; two s. one d.; ed Prince of Wales School, Nairobi, Kenya, George Watson's Coll. and Edinburgh Univ.; Pres. Edin. Univ. Liberals 1959; mem. Students' Rep. Council 1960; Asst Sec., Scottish Liberal Party 1962–64; MP for Roxburgh, Selkirk and Peebles 1965–83, for Tweeddale, Ettrick and Lauderdale 1983–97; Scottish Liberal Whip 1967–70; Liberal Chief Whip 1970–75; Leader of Liberal Party 1976–88; Co-Founder Social and Liberal Democrats 1988; Vice-Pres. Liberal Int. 1978–93, Pres. 1994–96; mem. Parl. del. to UN Gen. Ass. 1967; fmr Liberal spokesman on Commonwealth Affairs; Sponsor, Pvt. Member's Bill to reform law on abortion 1966–67; Pres. Anti-Apartheid Movt of UK 1966–69; Chair. Shelter, Scotland 1969–73, Countryside Movt 1995–97; BBC TV Interviewer in Scotland 1964–65; Presenter of weekly religious programme for Scottish TV 1966–67, for Granada 1969, for BBC 1971–76; Dir Border TV 1991–99; Rector Univ. of Edin. 1982–85; MSP 1999–, Presiding Officer of Scottish Parl. 1999–2003; Chubb Fellow, Yale Univ., USA 1987; DL Ettrick and Lauderdale and Roxburghshire; Freedom of Tweeddale 1989, of Ettrick and Lauderdale 1990; Dr hc (Stirling) 1991, (Heriot Watt) 1996; Hon. DLitt (Buckingham) 1994; Hon. LLD (Edin.) 1997, (Strathclyde) 2000, (Aberdeen) 2001; Hon. DUniv (The Open Univ.) 2001; Bronze Medal London-Cape Town Rally 1998. *Publications:* Boost for the Borders 1964, No Entry 1969, A House Divided 1980, Border Country 1985, Partners in One Nation 1985, The Time Has Come (with David Owen) 1987, Mary Stuart's Scotland (with Judy Steel) 1987, Against Goliath (autobiog.) 1989. *Leisure interests:* angling, classic cars. *Address:* House of Lords, London, SW1A 0PW; Aikwood Tower, Ettrick Bridge, Selkirkshire, Scotland (Home). *Telephone:* (20) 7219-4433 (Office).

STEELE, John Hyslop, DSc, FRS, FRSE, FAAS; British scientist; b. 15 Nov. 1926, Edinburgh; s. of Adam Steele and Annie Hyslop Steele; m. Margaret Evelyn Travis 1956; one s.; ed George Watson's Boys' Coll., Edinburgh, Univ. Coll., Univ. of London; Marine Lab., Aberdeen, Scotland 1951–77, Marine Scientist 1951–66, Sr Prin. Scientific Officer 1966–73, Dir Dept 1973–77; Dir Woods Hole Oceanographic Inst., Mass. 1977–89, Pres. 1986–91, Pres. Emer. 1991–; Dir Exxon Corpn 1989–97; Trustee Robert Wood Johnson Foundation 1990–2001; mem. Nat. Geographic Soc. Cttee Research and Exploration 1987–2000; Fellow American Acad. of Arts and Sciences 1980; Hon. Prof. Univ. of Aberdeen 1993–; Hon. DSc (Aberdeen) 2001; Agassiz Medal (NAS) 1973. *Publications:* Structure of Marine Ecosystems 1974, over 100 articles in oceanographic and ecological journals. *Leisure interest:* sailing, golf. *Address:* Woods Hole Oceanographic Institution, Woods Hole, MA 02543, USA. *Telephone:* (508) 289-2220. *Fax:* (508) 457-2184. *E-mail:* jsteele@whoi .edu (Office).

STEELE, Tommy, OBE; British actor and singer; b. Thomas Hicks, 17 Dec. 1936, Bermondsey, London; s. of Thomas Walter Hicks and Elizabeth Ellen Bennett; m. Ann Donoughue 1960; one d.; ed Bacon's School for Boys, Bermondsey; entered Merchant Navy 1952; first stage appearance Empire Theatre, Sunderland 1956, London début 1957; roles include Buttons (Cinderella) London 1958/59, Tony Lumpkin (She Stoops to Conquer) 1960, Arthur Kipps (Half A Sixpence) 1963/64, New York 1965/66, Truffaldino (The Servant of Two Masters) 1968, title role in Hans Andersen, London 1974/75, 1977/78, 1981, Don Lockwood (Singin' in the Rain), London 1983–85, 1989 (also dir), Some Like it Hot 1991 (also dir), What a Show! 1995; film debut in Kill Me Tomorrow 1956; sculpted tribute to the Beatles' Eleanor Rigby 1982; Hon. DLitt (South Bank) 1998. *Films include:* The Tommy Steele Story, The Duke Wore Jeans 1957, Tommy the Toreador 1959, Light Up the Sky 1963, Its All Happening 1966, The Happiest Millionaire 1967, Half A Sixpence, Finian's Rainbow 1968, Where's Jack 1971; TV début in Off the Record 1956, cabaret début, Caesar's Palace, Las Vegas 1974; composed and recorded musical autobiog. My Life, My Song 1974. *Live performances:* An Evening with Tommy Steele 1979, Tommy Steele in Concert 1998; Quincy's Quest (TV) 1979. *Publications:* Hans Andersen (co-author, stage version), Quincy 1981, The Final Run 1983. *Leisure interests:* squash, painting, sculpture. *Address:* c/o Laurie Mansfield, International Artistes, 4th Floor, 193–197 High Holborn, London, WC1V 7BD, England. *Telephone:* (20) 7025-0600. *Fax:* (20) 7404-9865.

STEELE-PERKINS, Christopher Horace, BSc; British photographer; b. 28 July 1947, Burma; s. of Alfred Steele-Perkins and Mary Lloyd; m. 1st Jacqueline de Gier 1984 (divorced 1999); two s.; m. 2nd Miyako Yamada 1999; ed Christ's Hospital, Horsham, Sussex, Univ. of Newcastle; mem. Exit Group, London 1974–82; Assoc. Viva Agency, Paris 1976–79; mem. Photography Cttee, Arts Council of GB 1977–79; mem. Magnum Photos 1983–, Pres. 1996–98; Visiting Prof., Mushishino Art Univ., Tokyo 2000; World Press Oskar Barnack 1988, Tom Hopkinson Award for Photo-journalism 1988, Robert Capa Gold Medal 1989, Cooperative Award, One World Award (both for film Dying for Publicity) 1994, Naçion-Premier Photojournalism Award, World Press Daily Life First 2000. *Exhibitions:* Afghanistan (Wales and London) 2000, Fuji (Midland Arts Centre and Impressions, York) 2002, Teds (292 New York) 2003. *Television films:* Dying for Publicity 1993, Afghan Taliban 1995. *Publications:* The Teds 1979, About 70 Photographs 1980, Survival Programmes 1982, Beirut: Frontline Story 1982, The Pleasure Principle 1989, St Thomas' Hospital 1992, Afghanistan 2000, Fuji 2002. *Leisure interests:* boxing, chess, photography, film, music, literature. *Address:* Magnum Photos, 5 Old Street, London, EC1V 9HL (Office); 49, St Francis Road, London, SE22 8DE, England. *Telephone:* (20) 7490-1771 (Office); (20) 8693-1114.

STEENBURGEN, Mary; American film actress; b. 8 Feb. 1953, Newport, Ariz.; m. 1st Malcolm McDowell 1980 (divorced); one s. one d.; m. 2nd Ted Danson (q.v.) 1995; ed Neighborhood Playhouse. *Films include:* Goin' South 1978, Time After Time 1979, Melvin and Howard 1980 (Acad. Award for Best Supporting Actress), Ragtime 1981, A Midsummer Night's Sex Comedy 1982, Romantic Comedy 1983, Cross Creek 1983, Sanford Meisner—The Theatre's Best Kept Secret 1984, One Magic Christmas 1985, Dead of Winter 1987, End of the Line 1987 (also exec. producer), The Whales of August 1987, The Attic: The Hiding of Anne Frank 1988, Parenthood 1989, Back to the Future Part III 1989, Miss Firecracker 1989, The Long Walk Home 1990, The Butcher's Wife 1991, What's Eating Gilbert Grape 1993, Philadelphia 1993, Pontiac Moon 1994, Clifford 1994, It Runs in the Family 1994, My Family, Powder, The Grass Harp, Nixon, About Sarah 1995, Trumpet of the Swan 1999, Picnic (TV) 2000. *Theatre appearances include:* Holiday (Old Vic, London) 1987, Candida (Broadway) 1993. *Address:* c/o Ames Cushing, William Morris Agency Inc., 151 S. El Camino Drive, Beverly Hills, CA 90212, USA.

STEENSBERG, Axel, DPhil; Danish academic; b. 1 June 1906, Sinding; s. of Jens Steensberg and Maren Steensberg; m. Frida Sillesen 1934 (died 1964); two s. one d.; working farmer until 1928; Asst to Gudmund Hatt surveying prehistoric fields and excavating villages of the Iron Age 1934–37; Head, Third Dept Nat. Museum 1946–59; Chair. Int. Secr. for Research on History of Agricultural Implements 1954–; Prof. of Material Culture, Copenhagen 1959–70; consultant, UNESCO, S. Pacific 1970–71; Ed. Tools and Tillage 1968–; Patron Techniques et Culture 1982–; excavations of deserted Danish villages 1937–82; research in Papua New Guinea, 1968, 1971, 1975, 1983; Hon. Vice-Pres. Medieval Settlement Research Group, Cambridge, UK; Hon. mem. Gustav Acad. Uppsala, Asscn Int. des Musées d'Agriculture, Ethnographic Soc. Budapest; Dr. Agr. hc; Culture Prize (Nordic Agrarian Cttee) 1993. *Publications include:* Ancient Harvesting Implements 1943, Atlas of Borup Fields 1968, Store Valby I-III 1974, Draved, an experiment in Stone Age agriculture, burning, sowing and harvesting 1979, New Guinea Gardens 1980, Borup A.D. 700-1400 I-II 1983, Man the Manipulator 1986, Hard Grains, Irrigation, Numerals and Script in the Rise of Civilizations 1989, Danish Peasant Furniture I–II 1989 (with Grith Lerche), Fire Clearance Husbandry: Traditional Techniques Throughout the World 1993.

STEENSGAARD, Niels Palle, DPhil; Danish academic; b. 7 March 1932, Rødovre; s. of Knud Steensgaard and Kirstine (née Knop) Steensgaard; m. Illa Frilis 1954; two d.; ed Univ. of Copenhagen, SOAS, London; Assoc. Prof. Inst. of History, Univ. of Copenhagen 1962, Dean, Faculty of Humanities 1974–76, Prof. 1977–; mem. Danish Research Council for the Humanities 1980–88, Chair. 1985–87; mem. Nordic Cttee Humanities Research Councils 1983–88, Chair. 1985–87; Danish Rep., Standing Cttee for the Humanities, European Science Foundation 1983–88; mem. Swedish Council for Research in the Humanities and Social Sciences 1992–96; Chair. Nat. Cttee of Danish Historians 1989; mem. Royal Danish Acad. of Sciences and Letters 1982, Acad. Europaea 1989, Royal Historical Soc. 1997. *Publications:* The Asian Trade Revolution of the Seventeenth Century 1973, Verden På Opdagelsernes tid 1984, Verdensmarked og kulturmøter 1985. *Leisure interests:* losing my way in large books or towns. *Address:* Faculty of Humanities, Københavns Universitet, Njalsgade 80, 2300 Copenhagen (Office); Lemnosvej 19, Copenhagen 2300 S, Denmark (Home). *Telephone:* 35-32-80-60 (Office). *Fax:* 35-32-80-52 (Office). *E-mail:* hum-fak@fak.hum.ku.dk (Office). *Website:* www.hum .ku.dk (Office).

ŞTEFĂNESCU, I. Ştefan, PhD; Romanian historian; b. 24 May 1929, Goicea, Dolj Co.; s. of Ion Ştefănescu and Dumitra Ştefănescu; m. Teodora Ştefănescu 1958; one s. one d.; ed Coll. of History, Bucharest Univ. Lomonosov Univ. Moscow; researcher in history 1951–65; Head Romanian Medieval History Dept of the N Iorga Inst. of History of the Romanian Acad. 1965–66, Deputy Dir 1966–70, Dir 1970–90; Dean of the Coll. of History and Philosophy, Bucharest Univ. 1977–85; mem. Romanian Acad. of Social and Political Sciences 1970–90; corresp. mem. Romanian Academy 1974, mem. 1992; mem. Romanian Soc. for Historical Sciences (on main Bd), Int. Comm. for Hist. of State Ass., Comm. int. des études slaves; Vice-Chair. of the Nat. Cttee of Historical Sciences; Chair. of the Dept of History and Archaeology, Romanian Acad. of Social and Political Sciences 1970–90; mem. European Acad. of History 1981–; Deputy Nat. Ass. 1975–80, 1985–90; Order of Scientific Merit 1966, Star of the Repub. 1971; Prize of the Romanian Acad. 1967. *Works include:* The History of the Romanian People 1970, Medieval Wallachia from Basarab I the Founder until Michael the Brave, 1970, History of Dobrudja, Vol. III (with I. Barnea) 1971, Demography – a Dimension of History 1974, Encyclopedia of Romanian Historiography 1978, The Romanian Nation 1984, The Beginnings of Romanian Principalities 1991, The Romanian Principalities in the 14th–16th Centuries 1992, Romania's Economic History (co-author) 1994, History of the Romanians in the 17th Century 1996, Romania: Historical-Geographic Atlas (co-author) 1996, The Illustrated History of Craiova (co-author) 1996, The Romanian Principalities in the Eighteenth Century 1998, Studies of Economic History and History of Economic Thought (co-author) 1998, A History of the Romanians (Medieval History), Vol. III (co-author), Vol. IV (Ed.) 2001. *Address:* 125 Calea Victoriei, 71102 Bucharest (Office); 214 Calea Victoriei, Apt. 44, 71104 Bucharest, Romania (Home). *Telephone:* (1) 2128640 (Office); (1) 6593932. *Fax:* (1) 3120209 (Office).

STEFANIUK, Franciszek Jerzy; Polish politician and farmer; b. 4 June 1944, Drelów, Biała Podlaska Prov.; m.; five c.; ed Economic Tech. School, Międzyrzec Podlaski; manages own farm; Chair. Cooperative of Agricultural Circles, Drelów 1978–82; mem. United Peasant Party (ZSL) 1963–89, Polish Peasants' Party (PSL) 1989–, Chair. Party Commune Cttee, Drelów 1982–89; Chair. Party Voivodship Cttee, Biała Podlaska 1990–98, Vice-Chair. Bd Supreme Exec. Cttee 1992–97, Chair. Supervisory Bd PSL 2000–; Deputy to Sejm (Parl.) 1989–; Deputy Chair. PSL Parl. Caucus 1991–93; Vice-Marshal (deputy Speaker) Sejm 1997–2001. *Leisure interests:* folklore, folk poetry, bee-keeping. *Address:* Kancelaria Sejmu RP, ul. Wiejska 4/6/8, 00-902 Warsaw, Poland. *Telephone:* (22) 6942321.

ŠTEFKA, Maj.-Gen. Pavel; Czech army general; b. 15 Sept. 1954, Ruda nad Modravou; s. of Ludevít Štefka and Irena Štefka; m. Jirina; three d.; ed Mil. Coll., Vyskov, Mil. Acad., Warsaw, European Business School, Prague and American Nat. War Coll., Washington DC, USA; Chief of Staff of motorized bn., then Deputy Chief of Staff of motorized Regt, E Mil. Dist; Chief of Staff, later Commdr of motorized Regt, Bratislava; Chief of Operations in an armoured div.; tutor Mil. Acad. Brno 1991–94; Commdr 6th Mechanized Brigade, Brno 1994; Deputy Commdr 2nd Army Corps and Chief of Staff HQ Ground Forces, Olomouc 1994–98; Chief of Operations Section of the Gen. Staff, Army of the Czech Repub. 1998–99, Chief of the Gen. Staff Dec. 2002–; Cross of Merit of Minister of Defence (Czech Republic), Medal for Service to the Nation, NATO Medal for Service for Peace and Freedom; Commemorative Medal of Minister of Defence (Slovakia); Silver Medal of Polish Army; Commemorative Medal of Auxiliary Tech. Bns; Hon. Remembrance Badge of Fifty Years of NATO. *Leisure interests:* sport, film, travel. *Address:* c/o Ministry of Defence, Tychonova 1, 16001 Prague 6, Czech Republic (Office). *Telephone:* (2) 33041111 (Office). *Fax:* (2) 3116238 (Office). *E-mail:* stefkap@ army.cz (Office). *Website:* www.army.cz (Office).

STEGER, Joseph A., PhD; American university president; b. 17 Feb. 1937, Philadelphia, Pa; s. of Joseph A. Steger and Georgianna Kirby; m. Carol R. Steger 1977; one s. one d.; ed Gettysburg Coll. and Kansas State Univ.; Sr Research Analyst, Prudential Insurance Co. 1964–66; Asst Prof., Assoc. Prof. Dept of Psychology, State Univ. of New York 1966–71; Prof. School of Man. Rensselaer Polytechnic Inst. 1971–74, Dean, School of Man. 1974–79, Dean and Vice-Pres. for Admin. and Budget 1977–78, Dean and Acting Provost 1978–79; Dir Organizational Devt and Human Resources, Colt Industries Inc. 1979–82; Sr Vice-Pres. and Provost, Univ. of Cincinnati 1982–84, Pres. 1984–. *Publication:* Readings in Statistics for the Behavioral Scientist 1971. *Leisure interests:* sailing, golf. *Address:* Office of the President, University of Cincinnati, P.O. Box 210063, Cincinnati, OH 45221-0063, USA. *Telephone:* (513) 556-2201.

STEGER, Norbert; Austrian politician and lawyer; b. 6 March 1944, Vienna; s. of Karl Steger and Anna Steger; m. Margarete Steger 1970; ed Univ. of Vienna; started pvt. law office, Vienna 1975; mem. FPÖ (Austrian Freedom Party) Fed. Exec. 1974, Deputy Chair. 1978, Chair. 1980; mem. Nationalrat 1979–; Vice-Chancellor and Fed. Minister of Commerce, Trade and Industry 1983–86. *Leisure interests:* music, skiing, basketball.

STEHELIN, Dominique Jean Bernard, PhD; French research scientist; b. 4 Sept. 1943, Thoisy; s. of Robert Stehelin and Berthe Zimmermann; m. Liliane Fachan 1969 (divorced 1975); one d.; ed Lycée Fustel, Strasbourg and Univ. Louis Pasteur, Strasbourg; Perm. Researcher, sponsored by CNRS, at Louis Pasteur Univ. 1969–71; Post-doctoral studies at Institut de la Recherche Scientifique sur le Cancer with Dr. A. Lwoff, Villejuif 1970–71; Visiting Scientist with J. M. Bishop at Univ. of Calif. Medical Center, San Francisco, USA 1972–75; Head of Molecular Oncology Research Unit, Institut Pasteur, Lille 1979–84, Prof. 1984–; Dir of Research CNRS 1985–, CNRS Inst. of Biology, Lille 1996–; corresp. Acad. of Sciences 1990–; mem. American Soc. of Microbiology, European Molecular Biology Org., Editorial Bd Oncogene; Grand Prix, Académie des Sciences 1975; Louis Jeantet Award (Medicine), Geneva 1987 and four other awards; Chevalier de l'Ordre nat. du Mérite, Officier, Légion d'honneur. *Publications:* more than 170 int. Publs on cancer research (cancer genes, retrovirus, angiogenesis). *Leisure interests:* skiing, diving, music. *Address:* CNRS Institut de Biologie, 1 rue Calmette, 59019 Lille (Office); 7 allée du Trianon, 59650 Villeneuve d'Ascq, France (Home). *Telephone:* (3) 20-87-79-78 (Office); (3) 20-91-38-94 (Home). *E-mail:* dominique .stehelin@ibl.fr (Office).

STEICHEN, René, DenD; Luxembourg politician and business executive; b. 27 Nov. 1942; m.; three c.; ed Lycée Classique, Diekirch, Cours Supérieurs, Luxembourg, Faculties of Law, Aix-en-Provence and Paris and Inst. d'Etudes Politiques, Paris; lawyer, Diekirch 1969–84; mem. Diekirch Town Council 1969, Mayor 1974–84; Christian Social Deputy in Parl. 1979; Sec. of State for Agric. and Viticulture 1984, of Agric., Viticulture and Rural Devt and Minister-Del. for Cultural Research and Scientific Research 1989–93; Commr for Agric. and Rural Devt, EC 1993–95; Chair. Soc. Européenne des Satellites 1996–2000, SES Global 2001–. *Address:* SES Global SA, Château de Betzdorf, L-6815 Betzdorf, Luxembourg (Office).

STEIDLE, Otto; German architect and professor of architecture; b. 16 March 1943, Munich; ed Acad. of Art, Munich; f. Muhr & Steidle Architects Co., Munich 1966, Steidle & Partner Architects Co. 1969; co-f. State Devt Planning Group (SEP) 1974; f. planning group 'Bauten für den Elementar- und Primarbereich' 1976; Prof. of Design and Functional Planning Univ. of Kassel 1979–81; Prof. of Design and Construction Tech. Univ. of Berlin 1981–90; est. architecture class Int. Summer Acad., Salzburg 1986; Guest Prof. MIT, Mass. 1991, Berlage Inst., Amsterdam 1991; Prof. of Architecture Acad. of Fine Arts, Munich 1991–, Rector 1993–95; mem. Acad. of Arts 1994–, Acad. of Fine Arts 1995–; DEBAU Prize, Essen 1981. *Architectural Designs include:* Elementa, Nürnberg 1974, Int. Centre of the Sciences, Berlin 1983, BUGA 'Green Houses', Berlin 1985, Volpinstrasse Integrated Houses, Munich 1987, Gruner & Jahr Publishing House, Hamburg 1990, Pilotengasse Housing Estate, Vienna 1991, University of Ulm 1992, Kreuzgassenviertel, Nürnberg 1992. *Current Projects include:* Townhouse, Munich 1997–, Bavaria 8, Munich 1998–, IVG Media Bridge, Munich 1998–, MK5 Wohnturm, Munich 1998–, Alfred Wegener Inst., Bremerhaven 2000–, WA5, Munich 2001–. *Publications:* Architectural (co-author) 1993, Structures for Living Zürich 1994, Universität Ulm 1995, Architektur und Kunst – Das neue Haus der T-Mobil in Bonn 1996, Wacker-Haus München 1998. *Address:* Steidle & Partner Architects, Genterstrasse 13, 80805 Munich, Germany (Office). *Telephone:* (89) 3609070 (Office). *Fax:* (89) 36107906 (Office). *E-mail:* architekten@ steidle-partner.de (Office). *Website:* www.steidle-partner.de (Office).

STEIN, Cyril; British business executive; b. 20 Feb. 1928; s. of the late Jack Stein and Rebecca Selner; m. Betty Young 1949; two s. one d.; Chair. and Jt Man. Dir Ladbroke Group PLC 1966–93, Dir (non-exec.) –1994; Chair. St James's Club Ltd 1995–.

STEIN, Elias M., MA, PhD; American professor of mathematics; b. 13 Jan. 1931, Antwerp, Belgium; s. of Elkan Stein and Chana Goldman Stein; m. Elly Intrator 1959; one s. one d.; ed Univ. of Chicago; Instructor MIT 1956–58; Asst Prof. Univ. of Chicago 1958–61, Assoc. Prof. 1961–63; mem. Inst. for Advanced Study, Princeton 1962–63, 1984–85; Prof. Princeton Univ. 1963–, Chair. of Dept of Math. 1968–70, 1985–87; Guggenheim Fellow 1976–77, 1984–85; mem. American Acad. of Arts and Sciences, NAS, American Mathematical Soc.; A.M.S. Steele Prize 1984, Shock Prize 1993. *Publications:* Singular Integrals and Differentiability Properties of Functions 1970, Topics in Harmonic Analysis Related to the Littlewood-Paley Theory 1970, Introduction to Fourier Analysis on Euclidean Spaces (with G. Weiss) 1971. *Address:* Department of Mathematics, Princeton University, Fine Hall, Washington Road, Princeton, NJ 08544 (Office); 132 Dodds Lane, Princeton, NJ 08544, USA (Home). *Telephone:* (609) 452-3497 (Office); (609) 924-9335 (Home). *Website:* www.princeton.edu (Office).

STEIN, Peter Gonville, FBA; British professor of law; b. 29 May 1926, Liverpool; s. of Walter O. Stein and Effie D. Walker; m. 1st Janet Chamberlain 1953, three d.; m. 2nd Anne Howard 1978; one step-s.; ed Liverpool Coll., Gonville and Caius Coll. Cambridge and Univ. of Pavia, Italy; served RN 1944–47; admitted solicitor 1951; Prof. of Jurisprudence, Univ. of Aberdeen 1956–68; Regius Prof. of Civil Law, Univ. of Cambridge 1968–93, now Prof. Emer., Fellow of Queens' Coll. Cambridge 1968–; mem. Univ. Grants Cttee 1971–76; JP, Cambridge 1970–; Fellow, Winchester Coll. 1976–91; Pres. Soc. of Public Teachers of Law 1980–81; mem. US–UK Educational Comm. 1985–91; Fellow Academia Europaea 1989; Foreign Fellow, Accad. Nazionale dei Lincei, Accad. di Scienze Morali e Politiche di Napoli, Accad. degli Intronati di Siena, Kon. Akad. v. Wetenschappen, Brussels; Hon. Fellow, Gonville and Caius Coll. Cambridge; Hon. QC 1993; Hon. DrJur (Göttingen) 1980; Dott.Giur. hc (Ferrara) 1990, (Perugia) 2001; Hon. LLD (Aberdeen) 2000; Dr hc (Paris II) 2001. *Publications:* Regulae Iuris: from juristic rules to legal maxims 1966, Legal Values in Western Society (with J. Shand) 1974, Legal Evolution 1980, Legal Institutions 1984, The Character and Influence of the Roman Civil Law: essays 1988, The Teaching of Roman Law in England around 1200 (with F. de Zulueta) 1990, Notaries Public in England since the

Reformation (ed. and contrib.) 1991, Römisches Recht und Europa 1996, Roman Law in European History 1999. *Leisure interest:* gardening. *Address:* Queens' College, Cambridge, CB3 9ET; Wimpole Cottage, 36 Wimpole Road, Great Eversden, Cambridge, CB3 7HR, England (Home). *Telephone:* (1223) 262349 (Home). *Fax:* (1223) 335522 (Office). *E-mail:* gonville@waitrose.com (Home).

STEINBERG, Donald K., M.ECON., MA; American diplomatist; b. 25 March 1953, Los Angeles; s. of Warren Linnington and Beatrice Blass; ed Reed Coll., Portland, Ore., Toronto and Columbia Univs; joined Foreign Service, rising to rank of Minister-Counselor; postings in Brazil, Malaysia, Mauritius and Cen. African Repub.; acting Chief Textile Negotiator, Office of US Trade Rep. 1988–89; first Dir House Task Force on Trade and Competitiveness 1989, Sr Policy Adviser for Foreign Affairs and Defense to Leader of House of Reps 1989–90; Officer-in-Charge and Counselor for Econ. and Commercial Affairs, US Embassy, Pretoria 1990–93; Deputy Press Sec. for Nat. Security Affairs, White House 1993; Special Asst to fmr Pres. Clinton for W African Affairs and Sr Dir for African Affairs, Sr Dir for Public Affairs, Nat. Security Council; Amb. to Angola 1995–98; Special Haiti Coordinator, Dept of State 1999–2001, Special Rep. of Pres. and Sec. of State for Global Humanitarian Demining 1998–, Deputy Asst Sec. of State for Population, Refugees and Migration 2000–01, Prin. Deputy Dir. for Policy Planning 2001–; Presidential Fellowship and fellowships from American Political Science Asscn, Toronto Univ., Uma Chapman Fox Foundation and US Dept of State; Presidential Meritorious Honor Award 1994, Hough Award for Excellence in Print, three Superior Honor Awards, US Dept of State. *Publications;* many publns on US trade policies, Africa, landmines and the role of Congress in foreign affairs. *Address:* Department of State, Room 7311, Washington, DC 20520, USA (Office). *Telephone:* (202) 647-6575 (Office). *Fax:* (202) 366-5580 (Office). *Website:* www.dot.gov (Office).

STEINBERG, Leo, PhD; American educationalist and historian; b. 9 July 1920, Moscow, USSR; ed Slade School of Art, Univ. of London, Inst. of Fine Arts, New York Univ.; Prof. of Art History Hunter Coll. & Grad. Center, City Univ., New York 1961–75, Univ. of Pa 1975–91, Prof. Emer. 1991–; Norton Visiting Prof., Harvard Univ. 1995–96; Fellow American Acad. of Arts and Sciences 1978, Univ. Coll. London 1979, MacArthur Foundation 1986; mem. Coll. of Art Asscn; Dr hc Phila Coll. of Art 1981, Parsons School of Design 1986, Mass. Coll. of Art 1987, Bowdoin Coll. 1995; Mather Award for Art Criticism 1956, 1984, Award in Literature, American Acad. and Inst. of Arts and Letters 1983. *Publications:* Other Criteria 1972, Michelangelo's Last Paintings 1975, Borromini's San Carlo alle Quattro Fontane 1977, The Sexuality of Christ in Renaissance Art and in Modern Oblivion 1983, Leonardo's Incessant Last Supper 2001; articles on the history of art in various journals. *Address:* 165 West 66th Street, New York, NY 10023, USA (Home).

STEINBERGER, Jack, PhD; American physicist; b. 25 May 1921, Germany; s. of Ludwig Steinberger and Bertha (née May) Steinberger; m. 1st Joan Beauregard 1943; m. 2nd Cynthia Eve Alff 1961; three s. one d.; ed Univ. of Chicago; Visiting mem. Inst. of Advanced Study, Princeton 1948–49; Research Asst, Univ. of Calif. at Berkeley 1949–50; Prof. Columbia Univ., New York 1950–71, Higgins Prof. 1967–71; Staff mem. Centre Européen pour la Recherche Nucléaire 1968–; mem. NAS 1967–, Heidelberg Acad. of Sciences 1967–, American Acad. of Arts and Sciences 1969–, Acad. Nat. dei Lincei 1997; Hon. Prof., Heidelberg 1968; Hon. DLitt (Glasgow) 1990; Dr hc (IU Inst. of Tech.), (Dortmund), (Columbia), (Barcelona), (Univ. Blaise Pascal); Nobel Prize in Physics (jtly) 1988; Pres.'s Science Medal, US 1988, Mateuzzi Medal, Società Italiana delle Scienze 1991. *Publications:* Muon Decay 1949, Pi Zero Meson 1950, Spin of Pion 1951, Parity of Pion 1954, 1959, Σ° Hyperon 1957, Properties of 'Strange Particles' 1957–64, Two Neutrinos 1962, CP Violating Effects in K° Decay 1966–74, High Energy Neutrino Physics 1975–83, Preparation of Lep Detector 1981, 3 Families of Matter 1989, Electroweak physics experiments 1989–97. *Leisure interests:* mountaineering, flute, cruising. *Address:* CERN, Geneva 23; 25 chemin des Merles, 1213 Onex, Geneva, Switzerland (Home). *Telephone:* 7934612 (Home).

STEINBRÜCK, Peer; German politician; b. 10 Jan. 1947, Hamburg; m.; three c.; ed Christian-Albrechts-Univ. zu Kiel; worked for Fed. Ministry of Planning 1974–76, Fed. Ministry of Research and Tech. 1976–77, Personal Asst to Minister 1977; mem. SPD party; Chief of Staff for Minister-Pres., State of Nordrhein-Westfalen 1986–90; State Sec., Ministry of Natural Conservation, Environmental Protection and Regional Devt, State of Schleswig-Holstein 1990–92, State Sec., Ministry of Econs, Tech. and Transport 1992–93, State Minister of Econs, Tech. and Transport 1993–98; State Minister of Econs, Small Businesses, Tech. and Transport, State of Nordrhein-Westfalen 1998–2000, State Finance Minister 2000–02, Minister-Pres. 2002–. *Address:* Staatskanzlei des Landes Nordrhein-Westfalen, Stadttor 1, 40190 Düsseldorf, Germany (Office). *Telephone:* (211) 837-01 (Office). *Fax:* (211) 837-1150 (Office). *E-mail:* postselle@stk.nrw.de (Office). *Website:* www.nrw.de (Office).

STEINEM, Gloria, BA; American writer, journalist and feminist activist; b. 25 March 1934, Toledo; d. of Leo Steinem and Ruth (née Nuneviller) Steinem; m. David Bale 2000; ed Smith Coll.; Chester Bowles Asian Fellow, India 1957–58; Co-Dir, Dir Ind. Research Service, Cambridge, Mass. and New York 1959–60; editorial Asst, contributing, ed., freelance writer various nat. and New York Publs 1960–; Co-Founder New York Magazine, contrib. 1968–72, Ms Magazine 1972 (Ed. 1971–87, columnist 1980–87, consulting ed. 1987–);

feminist lecturer 1969–; active various civil rights and peace campaigns including United Farmworkers, Vietnam War Tax Protest, Cttee for the Legal Defense of Angela Davis and political campaigns of Adlai Stevenson, Robert Kennedy, Eugene McCarthy, Shirley Chisholm, George McGovern; Co-Founder and Chair Bd Women's Action Alliance 1970–; Convenor, mem. Nat. Advisory Cttee Nat. Women's Political Caucus 1971–; Co-Founder, Pres. Bd Dirs Ms Foundation for Women 1972–; founding mem. Coalition of Labor Union Women; Woodrow Wilson Int. Center for Scholars Fellow 1977; Penney-Missouri Journalism Award 1970, Ohio Gov.'s Award for Journalism 1972, named Woman of the Year, McCall's Magazine 1972. *Publications:* The Thousand Indias 1957, The Beach Book 1963, Outrageous Acts and Everyday Rebellions 1983, Marilyn 1986, Revolution From Within: A Book of Self-Esteem 1992, Moving Beyond Words 1994; contribs to various anthologies. *Address:* c/o Ms Magazine, 20 Exchange Place, 22nd Floor, New York, NY 10005, USA. *Telephone:* (212) 509-2092 ext. 203 (Office). *Fax:* (212) 425-1247 (Office).

STEINER, George, DPhil, FBA, FRSL; writer and scholar; b. 23 April 1929, Paris, France; s. of Dr and Mrs F. G. Steiner; m. Zara Shakow 1955; one s. one d.; ed Univs. of Paris and Chicago, Harvard Univ. and Balliol Coll. Oxford; Editorial staff The Economist, London 1952–56; Fellow, Inst. for Advanced Study, Princeton 1956–58; Gauss Lecturer, Princeton Univ. 1959–60; Fellow and Dir of English Studies, Churchill Coll. Cambridge 1961–69, Extraordinary Fellow 1969–, Pensioner Fellow 1996–; Albert Schweitzer Visiting Prof., New York Univ. 1966–67; Visiting Prof. Yale Univ. 1970–71; Prof. of English and Comparative Literature, Univ. of Geneva 1974–94, Prof. Emer. 1994–; Visiting Prof., Collège de France 1992; First Lord Weidenfeld Visiting Prof. of Comparative Literature Oxford Univ. 1994–95; Charles Eliot Norton Prof. of Poetry, Harvard Univ. 2001–02; Pres. The English Asscn 1975–76; Corresp. mem. German Acad., Harvard Club, NY; Hon. mem. American Acad. of Arts and Sciences 1989; delivered Massey Lectures 1974, Ransom Memorial Lectures 1976, F. D. Maurice Lectures, Univ. of London 1984; Leslie Stephen Lecturer, Cambridge Univ. 1985; W. P. Ker Lecturer, Univ. of Glasgow 1986; Robertson Lecturer, Courtauld Inst., London 1985; Page-Barbour Lectures, Univ. of Va 1987; Gifford Lectures 1990; Priestley Lectures, Univ. of Toronto 1995; Hon. Fellow, Balliol Coll., Oxford, St Anne's Coll., Oxford; Chevalier, Légion d'honneur, Commdr Ordre des Arts et des lettres 2001; Hon. DLitt (East Anglia) 1976, (Louvain) 1979, (Bristol) 1989, (Glasgow, Liège) 1990, (Ulster) 1993, (Kenyon Coll., USA) 1995, (Trinity Coll. Dublin) 1995, (Rome) 1998, (Sorbonne) 1998, (Salamanca) 2002; O. Henry Award 1958, Jewish Chronicle Book Award 1968, Zabel Prize of Nat. Inst. of Arts and Letters 1970, Le Prix du Souvenir 1974, King Albert Medal of the Royal Belgian Acad. 1982, Prince of Asturias Prize 2001, 2002. *Publications:* Tolstoy or Dostoevsky 1959, The Death of Tragedy 1961, Anno Domini: Three Stories 1964, Language and Silence 1967, Extraterritorial 1971, In Bluebeard's Castle 1971, The Sporting Scene: White Knights in Reykjavik 1973, Fields of Force 1974, A Nostalgia for the Absolute (Massey Lectures) 1974, After Babel 1975, Heidegger 1978, On Difficulty and Other Essays 1978, The Portage of A.H. to San Cristobal 1981; Ed. Penguin Book of Modern Verse Translation 1967, Antigones 1984, George Steiner: A Reader 1984, Real Presences: Is there anything in what we say? 1989, Proofs and Three Parables 1992, No Passion Spent 1996, The Deeps of the Sea 1996, Errata: An Examined Life 1998, Grammers of Creation 2001. *Leisure interests:* chess, music, mountain walking. *Address:* 32 Barrow Road, Cambridge, England.

STEINER, Michael; German diplomatist and government policy adviser; b. 1949, Munich; ed Munich Univ. Law School; joined Diplomatic Service 1981, served at Perm. Mission to UN, New York, in Embassy in Prague and later Amb. to Czech Repub.; Head of Office of German Humanitarian Aid, Zagreb, Croatia 1991–92; Head of Foreign Office Special Task Force for Peace Efforts in Bosnia and Herzegovina; Nat. Rep. at Int. Contact Group on the Balkans; Contrib. Dayton Peace Talks 1995; Prin. Deputy High Rep. in Sarajevo; apptd Foreign Policy and Security Adviser to Chancellor 1998; Special Rep. for Kosovo and Head of UN Interim Admin. Mission in Kosovo (UNMIK) Jan. 2002–. *Address:* UNMIK, Department of Peace-keeping Operations, Room S-3727-B, United Nations, New York, NY 10017, USA (Office). *Telephone:* (212) 963-8077 (Office). *Fax:* (212) 963-9222 (Office). *Website:* www.un.org/Depts/dpko (Office).

STEINHOFF, Janusz Wojciech, DTech; Polish politician; b. 24 Sept. 1946, Gliwice; m.; one d.; ed Silesian Tech. Univ., Gliwice; with Coal Industry Construction and Mechanization Plants, Gliwice 1974–75; Mining Dept Silesian Tech. Univ., Gliwice 1976–89, 1994–97; Chair. Higher Mining Office 1990–94; adviser State Hard Coal Agency 1994–95; Vice-Chair. Regional Chamber of Commerce, Katowice 1996–97; Minister of the Economy 1997–2001, also Deputy Prime Minister; Co-Founder Solidarity Trade Union, Silesian Tech. Univ. 1980; underground Solidarity activist during martial law 1981–89; Solidarity expert on mining and protection of the environment during Round Table debates, 1989; Deputy to Sejm (Parl.) 1989–93, 1997–2001; mem. Presidium Citizens Parl. Caucus (OKP) 1989–91; mem. Solidarity Election Action (AWS) Parl. Caucus 1997–2001; author AWS programme for restructuring the mining sector; Co-Founder and Vice-Leader Christian Democratic Party.

STEINKÜHLER, Franz; German trade union executive; b. 20 May 1937, Würzburg; m.; one c.; trained as toolmaker and became Chief of Production Planning 1951–60; joined IG Metall 1951, mem. Youth Group 1952, Chair. Youth Del. 1953, numerous local exec. positions 1953–63, Sec. Regional Exec.

Bd, Stuttgart 1963–72, Dir Stuttgart Region 1972–83, Vice-Pres. IG Metall 1983–86, Pres. 1986–93; Pres. Int. Metalworkers' Fed. June 1987; mem. SPD 1951–, Vice-Pres. in Baden-Württemberg 1975–83, mem. Programme Cttee of Exec. Bd 1984; Workers' Rep. VW-AG, Wolfsburg Mannesmann AG, Supervisory Bd, Daimler Benz AG Supervisory Bd –1993, Thyssen AG; Deputy Chair. Supervisory Bd Volkswagen AG; mem. State Tribunal of Baden-Württemberg 1983; Hon. Senator Univ. of Konstanz 1983. *Address:* c/o IG Metall, 60329 Frankfurt, Germany.

STEINNES, Eiliv, DPhil; Norwegian professor of environmental science; b. 21 Sept. 1938, Elverum; s. of Eirik Steinnes and Aslaug Steinnes; m. Randi Surdal 1962; three d.; ed Univ. of Oslo; scientist, Norwegian Inst. for Atomic Energy 1964–68, Research leader 1969–79; Prof. of Environmental Science, Univ. of Trondheim Coll. of Arts and Science (now Norwegian Univ. of Science and Tech.) 1980–, Rector 1984–90; mem. Norwegian Acad. of Tech. Sciences, Norwegian Acad. of Science and Letters (Oslo), Royal Norwegian Soc. of Science and Letters (Trondheim); Hon. Prof. Univ. of Iasi, Romania 2000; Hevesy Medal 2001. *Publications:* two books and more than 500 scientific papers. *Leisure interests:* outdoor life, in particular cross-country skiing and mountain tours. *Address:* Department of Chemistry, Norwegian University of Science and Technology, 7491 Trondheim (Office); Sloreåsen 17A, 1257 Oslo, Norway (Home). *Telephone:* 73-59-62-37 (Office); 22-75-43-20 (Home). *Fax:* 73-55-08-77. *E-mail:* eiliv.steinnes@chem.ntnu.no (Office).

STELLE, Kellogg Sheffield, PhD, FInstP; American physicist; b. 11 March 1948, Washington, DC; s. of Charles C. Stelle and Jane E. Kellogg; ed Phillips Acad. Andover, Mass., Harvard Coll. and Brandeis Univ.; field observer, Bartol Research Foundation, South Pole, Antarctica 1970–72; Lecturer in Math. King's Coll. London 1977–78; Research Fellow, Imperial Coll. London 1978–80, Advanced Fellow 1982–87, Lecturer in Physics 1987–88, Reader 1988–95, Prof. 1995–; mem. Inst. for Advanced Study, Princeton, NJ 1986; Scientific Assoc. CERN, Geneva 1980–81, 1987, 1997–98; Programme Dir Institut Henri Poincaré, Paris 2000–01; Ed. Classical and Quantum Gravity 1984–93; mem. American Physical Soc., Fed. of American Scientists, AAAS. *Publications:* numerous articles in scientific journals. *Address:* The Blackett Laboratory, Imperial College, Prince Consort Road, London, SW7 2BW, England.

STEMPLOWSKI, Ryszard Maria, LLM, PhD; Polish diplomatist, lawyer and historian; b. 25 March 1939, Wygoda; s. of Kazimierz Stemplowski and Eugenia Białecka; m. Irena Zasłona 1975; two d.; ed Tech. Lycée, Bydgoszcz, Dept of Ecological Eng, Wrocław Univ. of Tech., Dept of Law, Wrocław Univ., Inst. of History, Polish Acad. of Sciences, Warsaw; Research Fellow, Inst. of History Polish Acad. of Sciences 1973–90; Chief, Chancellery of Sejm (Parl.) 1990–93; Amb. to UK 1994–99; Dir Inst. of Foreign Affairs 1999–; Ed. Polish Diplomatic Review 2000–; mem. Polish History Soc. 1975–, Sec.-Gen. 1976–78; Co-Founder and mem. Polish Soc. of Studies of Latin America 1978–; Visiting Fellow St Antony's Coll. Oxford, 1974; A. von Humboldt Research Fellow, Univ. of Cologne 1981–82. *Publications:* Dependence and Defiance: Argentina and the Rivalries among the USA, Germany and the UK 1930–46 1975, Economic Nationalism in East Central Europe and South America 1918–39 (co-author) 1990, The Slavic Settlers in Misiones 1898–1947 (co-author) 1992, State Socialism in Real Capitalism: Chile in the Year 1932 1996. *Leisure interests:* music, astrophysics. *Address:* Polski Instytut Spraw Miedzynarodowych, ul. Warecka 1A, 00-950 Warsaw, Poland (Office). *Telephone:* (22) 8268939 (Office). *Fax:* (22) 8268882 (Office). *E-mail:* pism@pism.pl (Office).

STENBÄCK, Pär Olav Mikael, MA; Finnish international administrator and fmr politician; b. 12 Aug. 1941, Porvoo (Borgå); s. of Arne Mikael Stenbäck and Rakel (née Granholm) Stenbäck; m. Liv Sissel Lund 1970; two s.; ed Helsinki Univ.; Ed. with Finnish Broadcasting Co. 1962–68; Chair. Svensk Ungdom (youth org. of Swedish People's Party of Finland) 1967–70; mem. Parl. 1970–85; Chair. Swedish People's Party 1977–85; Minister of Educ. 1979–82, of Foreign Affairs 1982–83; Man. Dir Hanaholmen Swedish-Finnish Culture Centre 1974–85; Sec.-Gen. Finnish Red Cross 1985–88, Pres. 1996–99; Sec.-Gen. Int. Fed. (fmrly League) of Red Cross and Red Crescent Socs., Geneva 1988–92, mem. Finance Comm. 1997–2002; Sec.-Gen. Nordic Council of Ministers, Copenhagen 1992–96; Pres. Foundation for Swedish Culture in Finland 1996–2002; Chair. Norwegian-Swedish Comm. preparing new Reindeer Grazing Convention 1998–2001; Vice-Pres. for Europe, Int. Youth Foundation, USA 1996–; Chair. Finnish Children and Youth Foundation 2001–; mem. Exec. Bd Int. Crisis Group 1995–; Sr Adviser Council on Women World Leaders (Harvard Univ.) 1997–; mem. Bd Mehiläinen Private Hosp. Corpn 2001–, Deutsche Kinder- und Jugendstiftung 2001–; numerous other professional appointments; Hon. Minister (Finland); Grand Cross, Royal Order of Northern Star (Sweden), Grand Cross of the Falcon (Iceland), Grand Cross St Olav (Norway), Grand Cross of Dannebrog (Denmark), Commdr of the Order of the Lion, Order of the White Rose (Finland), Grand Cross of Santa Miranda (Venezuela) and numerous other foreign decorations; Dr hc (Petrozavodsk State Univ.) 2000. *Leisure interests:* literature, fishing, history. *Address:* Finnish Children and Youth Foundation, Georgsgatan 29 A 3, 00100 Helsinki, Finland (Office). *Telephone:* (9) 61821211 (Office). *Fax:* (9) 61821200 (Office); 4128725. *E-mail:* pst@slns.org (Office); parstenback@ framtidsprojektet.nu (Home). *Website:* www.slns.org (Office).

STENFLO, Jan Olof, MS, PhD; Swedish astronomer; b. 10 Nov. 1942; s. of Carl Stenflo and Signe Röden; m. Joyce E. Tucker 1971; two s.; ed Univ. of Lund; Asst Prof. Univ. of Lund 1969–75; Research Scientist, Swedish Natural Science Research Council 1975–80; Prof. of Astronomy, Eidgenössische Technische Hochschule (ETH), Zürich and Univ. of Zürich 1980–; Dir Inst. of Astronomy, ETH 1980–; Pres. LEST Foundation 1983–97; mem. Royal Swedish Acad. of Sciences, Norwegian Acad. of Science and Letters, Royal Physiographic Soc. Lund; Edlund Prize, Royal Swedish Acad. of Sciences 1974. *Publications:* Solar Magnetic Fields 1994; more than 200 scientific papers on astronomy in int. journals. *Leisure interests:* classical music, mountain hiking, skiing. *Address:* Institute of Astronomy, ETH-Zentrum, 8092 Zürich (Office); Haldeweg 4, 5436 Würenlos, Switzerland (Home). *Telephone:* (1) 6323804 (Office); (56) 4242886. *E-mail:* stenflo@astro.phys .ethz.ch (Office). *Website:* www.astro.phys.ethz.ch (Office).

STENLUND, Bengt Gustav Verner, DTech; Finnish professor of polymer technology (retd); b. 17 Aug. 1939, Kristinestad; s. of Gustav Stenlund and Linda Hofman; m. Kerstin Ottosson 1964; one s.; Research Assoc. The Finnish Pulp and Paper Research Inst. 1965–77; Acting Prof. of Polymer Tech., Åbo Akad. 1977–79, Prof. 1979–2002, Dean. Faculty of Chemical Eng 1982–85, Vice-Rector 1985–88, Rector 1988–97; mem. Research Council of Tech. Finnish Acad. of Sciences 1983–85, Chair. and Bd mem. 1986–88; Chair. Finnish Rectors' Council 1990–92; Chair. LC Working Group on EC Research Policy 1993–95; Chair. Steering Group, Baltic Univ. Programme 1995–98; Head of Lab. of Polymer Tech. 1997–2002; mem. Scientific Del. of Finnish Chemical Industry 1985–90; mem. Bd Nordic Foundation of Tech. 1987–90; mem. Steering Cttee Finnish Centres of Expertise 1996–98; mem. Bd CRE 1994–98; mem. European Science and Tech. Asscn 1994–97; mem. Finnish Acad. of Eng, Finnish Soc. of Science and Letters, Royal Swedish Acad. of Eng, ACS 1997–2001, Japanese Inst. of Finland 1997–2002, European Univ. Evaluation Team 1998–; Chair. Swedish Acad. of Eng of Finland 2002–; Hon. DTech (Karlstad) 2000. *Publications:* Gel Chromatography of Lignosulfonates 1970; about 50 Publs about natural and synthetic polymers. *Leisure interests:* art, skiing, sailing, cycling. *Address:* Peltolantie 6 B 61, 20700 Åbo (Home); Åbo Akademi University, Biskopsgatan 8, 20500 Åbo, Finland. *Telephone:* (2) 2154230. *Fax:* (2) 2154866. *E-mail:* bengt.stenlund@abo.fi (Office).

STENT, Gunther Siegmund, PhD; American professor of molecular biology; b. Günter Stensch, 28 March 1924, Berlin, Germany; m. Inga Loftsdottir 1951; one s.; ed Hyde Park School, Chicago and Univ. of Illinois; Research Asst U.S. War Production Bd, Synthetic Rubber Research Programme 1944–48; Document Analyst, Field Intelligence Agency, Occupied Germany 1946–47; Merck Postdoctoral Fellow Calif. Inst. of Tech. 1948–50; American Cancer Soc. Postdoctoral Fellow Univ. of Copenhagen and Inst. Pasteur, Paris 1950–52; Asst Research Biochemist Univ. of Calif. at Berkeley 1952–56, Assoc. Prof. of Bacteriology 1956–59, Prof. of Molecular Biology 1959–94, Prof. Emer 1994–, Chair. Molecular Biology and Dir Virus Lab. 1980–86, Chair. Molecular and Cell Biology 1987–92; Natural Science Foundation Sr Fellow Univs. of Kyoto and Cambridge 1960–61; Guggenheim Fellow Harvard Medical School 1969–70; mem. NAS, American Acad. of Arts and Sciences, American Philosophical Soc.; External mem. Max Planck Inst. for Molecular Genetics, Berlin 1966–; Fellow, Inst. for Advanced Studies, Berlin 1985–90; Fogarty Scholar, NIH 1990–91; Hon. DSc (York, Toronto Univs.) 1984. *Publications:* Molecular Biology of Bacterial Viruses 1963, Phage and the Origins of Molecular Biology 1966, The Coming of the Golden Age 1969, Molecular Genetics 1970, Function and Formation of Neural Systems 1977, Paradoxes of Progress 1978, Morality as a Biological Phenomenon 1978, Shinri to Satori 1981, Nazis, Women and Molecular Biology 1998. *Leisure interest:* car repairs. *Address:* Molecular and Cell Biology, University of California, Berkeley, CA 94720; 145 Purdue Avenue, Kensington, CA 94708, USA (Home). *Telephone:* (510) 642-5214 (Office); (510) 526-7576 (Home). *Fax:* (510) 643-6791 (Office). *E-mail:* Stent@uclink4.berkeley.edu (Office).

STEPANKOV, Valentin Georgievich; Russian lawyer; b. 17 Sept. 1951, Perm; s. of Georgii Vassilyevich Stepankov and Antonina Andreyevna Klopova; m. 2nd Irina Vasilevna Martynova 2000; one s. from first m.; ed Perm State Univ.; investigator, Office of Public Prosecutor, Sverdlovsk Dist 1975–76, Perm Region 1976–77; Public Prosecutor of town of Gubakh Perm Region 1977–81; instructor Div. of Regional Cttee of CPSU 1981–83; Public Prosecutor of Perm 1983–87; Deputy-Dir Investigation Dept Office of Public Prosecutor of the USSR 1987–88; Public Prosecutor of Khabarovsk Region 1986–90; First Deputy Public Prosecutor of RSFSR 1990–91; Procurator-Gen. of Russia 1991–93; Deputy Head of Admin., Perm Region 1994–96; mem. State Duma (Parl.) 1996–99; Deputy Rep. of Russian Pres. to Privolzhsky Fed. Dist 2000–; mem. Bd of Dirs Permskiye Motory (Perm Engines) 1999–2000; Honoured Lawyer of Russian Fed. 2001–. *Publications:* monograph on Kremlin conspiracy and numerous articles. *Leisure interests:* painting, reading, walks in the forest. *Address:* Kremlin Korp 1, 603082 Nizhni Novorod, Russia (Office). *Telephone:* (831-2) 31-46-58; (095) 776-26-48 (Home). *E-mail:* v.g.stepankov@mtu-net.ru (Home).

STEPANOV, Victor Nikolayevich, C.PHIL.SC; Karelian politician; b. 27 Jan. 1947, Vidlitsa; ed Karelia State Pedagogical Inst., Higher CP School in Leningrad, Higher Political School of CP Czechoslovakia; worked as carpenter in lumber factory, then Dir village club 1962–66; mem. CPSU 1969–91; took number of posts in Komsomol and CP orgs. 1966–87; Head of Div. Karelian Regional CPSU Cttee 1987–88; mem. Cen. CPSU Cttee 1988–89; mem. Cen. Cttee and Politburo RSFSR CP 1990–91; Chair. Presidium Supreme Soviet Karelian Autonomous SSR 1990–; Chair. Supreme Soviet

1993; mem. Union of Communists of Karelia 1992–; People's Deputy of Russia 1989–91; mem. Russian Council of Fed. (Parl.) 1993–98; Chair. Karelian Govt 1995–98; Head Man. Dept Union of Russia and Belarus 1999–.

STEPASHIN, Col-Gen. Sergey Vadimovich, LLD; Russian security official; b. 2 March 1952, Port Arthur; m.; one s.; ed Higher Political Coll., USSR Ministry of Internal Affairs, Mil. Acad., Financial Acad. under Russian Fed. Govt; mem. staff USSR Ministry of Foreign Affairs 1973–80; Lecturer, Higher Political Coll., Leningrad 1981–90; Prof., Russian Fed. State Counsellor of Justice; Deputy to RSFSR Supreme Soviet 1989–93; after attempted coup Aug. 1991 Head Cttee on Defence and Security of the Russian Fed. Supreme Soviet; author programme of reorganization of state security system; Chief Leningrad Federal Security Agency; Admin. and Deputy Chair. Russian Fed. Federal Security Agency (fmrly KGB) 1991–92; Dir Fed. Service of Counterespionage 1994–95; Head of Admin., Chief of Govt 1995–97; Minister of Justice 1997–98, of Internal Affairs 1998–99; First Deputy Chair. of Govt April–May 1999, Chair. of Govt (Prime Minister) May–Aug. 1999; Chair. Exec. Council of Russia and Belarus Union May–Aug. 1999; joined Yabloko Movt 1999; mem. State Duma (Parl.) 1999–2000; Chair. Accountant Chamber of Russian Fed. 2000–; Order 'For Merits Before Fatherland', Third Degree; Order of Fortitude. *Publication:* Personal and Social Security (Political and Legal Issues) 1994. *Leisure interests:* sports, literature, theatre. *Address:* Accountant Chamber of the Russian Federation, Zubovskaya St. 2, 119992 Moscow, Russia. *Telephone:* (095) 914-05-09 (Office). *Fax:* (095) 914-09-52 (Office). *E-mail:* info@ach.gov.ru (Office). *Website:* www.ach.gov.ru (Office).

STEPHANOPOULOS, George Robert, AB; American federal official; b. 10 Feb. 1961, Fall River, Mass.; s. of Robert Stephanopoulos and Nikki C. Stephanopoulos; ed Univs. of Columbia and Oxford; fmrly admin. Asst to Edward Feighan, Washington; Deputy Communications Dir Dukakis-Bentsen Campaign 1988; fmrly Exec. Floor Man., later House Majority leader; Sr Adviser to Pres. of USA 1993–96; fmrly Communications Dir Clinton-Gore Campaign; Communications Dir The White House 1997–2001; Visiting Prof. of Political Science, School of Int. and Public Affairs, Columbia Univ. 2001–; contrib. ABC News, ABC Newsweek 1997–; Medal of Excellence, Columbia Univ. 1993. *Publication:* All Too Human 1999. *Address:* 47 West 66th Street, 6th Floor, New York, NY 10023, USA.

STEPHANOPOULOS, Konstantinos; Greek politician and lawyer; b. 1926, Patras; s. of Demetrius Stephanopoulos and Vrisiis Stephanopoulos; m. Eugenia El. Stounopoulou 1959; two s. one d.; ed Univ. of Athens; pvt. law practice 1954–74; mem. Parl.for Achaia (Nat. Radical Union) 1964, (New Democracy) 1974, 1977, 1981, 1985, (Democratic Renewal) 1989; Under-Sec. of Commerce July–Nov. 1974; Minister of the Interior 1974–76, of Social Services 1976–77; in Prime Minister's Office 1977–81; Pres. of Greece 1995–; Parl. Rep., New Democracy Party 1981–85, Pres. Party of Democratic Renewal 1985–94. *Publications:* The National Interest and Security Policy (co-author) 1995, Nouvelles Etudes d'Histoire, Vol. IX (co-author) 1995. *Address:* Office of the President, Odeos Vas. Georgiou 7, 106 74 Athens, Greece (Office). *Telephone:* (1) 7283111 (Office). *Fax:* (1) 7248938 (Office).

STEPHEN, Rt Hon Sir Ninian Martin, KG, AK, GCMG, GCVO, KBE; Australian lawyer and international official; b. 15 June 1923, Oxford, England; s. of the late Frederick Stephen and Barbara (née Cruickshank) Stephen; m. Valery Mary Sinclair 1949; five d.; ed George Watson's School, Edinburgh Acad., St Paul's School, London, Chillon Coll., Switzerland, Scotch Coll., Melbourne, Melbourne Univ.; served World War II, Australian Army; admitted as barrister and solicitor, Victoria 1949; QC 1966; Judge, Supreme Court, Victoria 1970; Justice, High Court, Australia 1972–82; Gov.-Gen. of Australia 1982–89; Chair. Nat. Library of Australia 1989–94; Amb. for the Environment 1989–92; Chair. Strand Two, Northern Ireland Talks 1992, UN Group of Experts on Cambodia, Australian Citizenship Council; Judge, Int. Criminal Tribunals for Yugoslavia 1993–97, for Rwanda 1995–97; mem. Ethics Comm. Int. Olympic Cttee 2000–; Chair. ILO High Level Team to Myanmar 2001; Hon. Bencher Gray's Inn 1981; KStJ 1982; Commdr Légion d'honneur 1993. *Address:* Flat 13/1, 193 Domain Road, South Yarra, Victoria, Australia. *Telephone:* (3) 9820-2787.

STEPHENS, Olin James II; American naval architect and yacht designer (retd); b. 13 April 1908, New York City; s. of Roderick Stephens and Marguerite Dulon; m. Florence Reynolds 1930; two s.; ed MIT; Partner, Sparkman & Stephens 1928; design agent USN 1939–; Chief Designer, Vice-Pres. and Dir, Sparkman & Stephens Inc. 1929–64, Chief Designer, Pres. and Dir 1964–78, Chair and Dir Jan. 1979–85, Dir Emer. 1987; Chair. Int. Tech. Cttee of Offshore Racing Council 1967–74, 1977–79, Councillor of honour 1979; Chair. of Research Cttee of Offshore Racing Council 1980; mem. Jt Cttee of Soc. of Naval Architects and US Yacht Racing Union on Yacht Capsize 1980–85; mem. Royal Designers for Industry, London; some yachts designed: Dorade 1930, Stormy Weather 1934, (with W. Starling Burgess) Ranger 1937, Vim, Goose, Bolero 1938, Finisterre 1954, Columbia 1958, Constellation 1964, Intrepid 1967, Morning Cloud 1969, 1971, 1973, 1975, Courageous 1974, Flyer 1977, Freedom 1979; Hon. mem. and Fellow, Soc. of Naval Architects and Marine Engineers; Hon. MS (Stevens Inst. of Tech.) 1945; Hon. MA (Brown Univ.) 1959; Hon. DSc (Webb Inst.) 2000; Dr hc Istituto Universitario di Architettura di Venezia, Italy 1991; David W. Taylor Medal (Soc. of Naval Architects and Engineers) 1954, Beppe Crole Award, Int. Yacht Racing Union 1992, Gibbs Brothers Medal (NAS) 1993. *Publication:* All This and Sailing Too

(autobiog.) 2000. *Leisure interest:* computer studies. *Address:* Sparkman & Stephens Inc., 529 Fifth Avenue, New York, NY 10017 (Office); 80 Lyme Road, Apt 160, Kendal at Hanover, Hanover, NH 03755, USA (Home).

STEPHENS, Toby; British actor. *RSC performances include:* Measure for Measure, Coriolanus in Coriolanus (Sir John Gielgud Award for Best Actor 1994, Ian Charlson Award 1995), Young Beamish in Unfinished Business, Wallenstein, Bertram in All's Well That Ends Well, Pompey in Anthony and Cleopatra. *Other stage appearances include:* Ring around the Moon, Lincoln Center Theater, NY, Britannicus, Phedre, Almedia & Brooklyn Acad., NY, A Streetcar Named Desire, The Haymarket, Damis in Tartuffe, Playhouse Theatre. *Films include:* Eugene Onegin, Sunset Heights, Photographic Fairies, Cousin Bette, Twelfth Night, Orlando, Die Another Day 2002. *Television includes:* Tenant of Wildfell Hall (BBC), A View from the Bridge, Oliver in Camomile Lawn, The Great Gatsby. *Address:* c/o ICM, Oxford House, 76 Oxford Street, London, W1N 0AX, England. *Telephone:* (20) 7636-6565. *Fax:* (20) 7223-0101.

STEPHENSON, Hugh; British journalist and professor; b. 18 July 1938, Simla, India; s. of the late Sir Hugh Stephenson and Lady Stephenson; m. 1st Auriol Stevens 1962 (divorced 1987); two s. one d.; m. 2nd Diana Eden 1990; ed New Coll. Oxford, Univ. of California at Berkeley; served diplomatic service, London and Bonn 1964–68; with The Times, London 1969–81, Ed., The Times Business News 1971–81; Ed. The New Statesman 1982–86; Prof. of Journalism, The City Univ. 1986–; Dir History Today Ltd 1981–. *Publications:* The Coming Clash 1972, Mrs. Thatcher's First Year 1980, Claret and Chips 1982, Libel and the Media (with others) 1997. *Address:* Department of Journalism, City University, Northampton Square, London, EC1V 0HB, England.

STEPIN, Vyacheslav Semenovich; Russian philosopher; b. 19 Aug. 1934, Bryansk; s. of Semen Nikolaievich Stepin and Antonina Grigorievna (née Petrova) Stepina; m. Tatiana Ivanovna Vagranova 1957; ed Belorussia State Univ.; Prof., Chair.; Dir Inst. of History of Natural Sciences and Tech. 1987–88; Dir Inst. of Philosophy 1988–; Corresp. mem. USSR (now Russian) Acad. of Sciences 1987, mem. 1994; research in theory of cognition, philosophy of science and tech., history of science; Vice-Pres. Philosophy Soc., Pres. Asscn For Humanitarian Dialogue; Hon. mem. Acad. of Sciences and Educ., Karlsruhe, Germany. *Publications include:* Contemporary Positivism and Science 1963, Practical Nature of Cognition and Methodical Problems of Contemporary Physics 1970, Methods of Scientific Cognition 1974, Scientific Revolutions in Dynamics of Culture 1987, Philosophical Anthropology and Philosophy of Science 1992, Scientific Picture of the World in the Culture of Technogenic Civilization 1994, Philosophy of Science and Technics 1995, Age of Changes and Scenarios of the Future 1996. *Address:* Institute of Philosophy, Russian Academy of Sciences, Volkhonka str. 14, 119842 Moscow (Office); DM Ulianov str. 3, Ap. 130, Moscow, Russia (Home). *Telephone:* (095) 203-95-69 (Office). *Fax:* (095) 200-32-50.

STERLING, Michael John Howard, PhD, DEng, F.R.ENG., FIEE, F.INST.M.C., FRSA; British professor of engineering and university vice-chancellor; b. 9 Feb. 1946, Paddock Wood, Kent; s. of Richard Howard Sterling and Joan Valeria Sterling, née Skinner; m. Wendy Karla Anstead 1969; two s.; ed Hampton Grammar School, Middx, Univ. of Sheffield; student apprentice, AEI 1964–68; GEC Research Engineer 1968–71; Lecturer in Control Eng, Univ. of Sheffield 1971–78, Sr Lecturer 1978–80; Prof. of Eng, Univ. of Durham 1980–90; Vice-Chancellor and Prin., Brunel Univ. 1990–2001; Vice-Chancellor, Birmingham Univ. 2001–; mem. Council IEE 1991–93, Vice-Pres. 1997–2001, Deputy Pres. 2001–02, Pres. 2002–03; Chair. OCEPS Ltd 1990–, Higher Educ. Statistics Agency 1990–, Higher Educ. Funding Council Steering Cttee on Performance Indicators 1992–95 (mem. Quality Assessment Cttee 1992–95), WASMACS Ltd 1994–, MidMAN 2001; Dir COBUILD Ltd 2001–, UCAS 2001–, Universitas 21 2001–; mem. Science & Eng Research Council Eng Bd 1989–92, Electricity Research Council 1987–89, Royal Acad. of Eng Standing Cttee for Educ., Training and Competence to Practise 1993–97, Cttee 2 for Int. Co-operation in Higher Educ., British Council 1991–96, AWM Broadband Steering Group 2002–, Bd WMHEA 2001–; Fellow Inst. of Measurement and Control (Pres. 1988, Council mem. 1983–91); Pres. Elmhurst School for Dance 2002–; Trustee Barber Inst. of Fine Art 2001–; Gov. Burnham Grammar School 1990–, Hampton School 1991– (Chair. of Govs 1997–); Liveryman Worshipful Co. of Engineers 1998; Freeman City of London 1996; Hon. DEng (Sheffield) 1995; Hon. DUniv (Tashkent, Uzbekistan) 1999; Dr hc (West Bohemia, Czech Repub.) 2001; Inst. of Measurement and Control ICI Prize 1980, IEE Hartree Premium 1985, Commemorative Medal 2000. *Publications:* Power Systems Control 1978; over 200 tech. papers and book contribs. *Leisure interests:* gardening, DIY, computers, model eng. *Address:* Vice-Chancellor's Office, Birmingham University, Edgbaston, Birmingham, B15 2TT, England (Office). *Telephone:* (121) 414-3344 (Office). *Fax:* (121) 414-3971 (Office). *Website:* www.bham.ac.uk (Office).

STERLING OF PLAISTOW, Baron (Life Peer), cr. 1990; **Jeffrey Maurice Sterling,** Kt, GCVO, CBE; British business executive; b. 27 Dec. 1934, London; s. of Harry Sterling and Alice Sterling; m. Dorothy Ann Smith 1985; one d.; ed Reigate Grammar School, Preston Manor County School and Guildhall School of Music, London; Paul Schweder & Co. (Stock Exchange) 1955-57; G. Eberstadt & Co. 1957–62; Financial Dir General Guarantee Corpn 1962–64; Man. Dir Gula Investments Ltd 1964–69; Chair. Sterling Guarantee Trust PLC 1969–85 (merged with P&O 1985), P&O Steam Navigation Co. 1983–,

P&O Asia 1992–, P&O Princess Cruises 2000–03; Special Adviser to Sec. of State for Industry 1982–83, to Sec. of State for Trade and Industry 1983–90; mem. British Airways Bd 1979–82; mem. Exec., World Org. for Rehabilitation by Training Union 1966–, Chair. Org. Cttee 1969–73, Chair. ORT Tech. Services 1974–, Vice-Pres. British ORT 1978–; Pres. Gen. Council of British Shipping 1990–91, EC Shipowners' Asscns 1992–94; Deputy Chair. and Hon. Treasurer London Celebrations Cttee Queen's Silver Jubilee 1975–83; Chair. Young Vic Co. 1975–83; Vice-Chair. and Chair. of Exec. Motability 1977–94, Chair. 1994–; Chair. of the Govs. Royal Ballet School 1983–99; Chair. Queen's Golden Jubilee Weekend Trust 2001–02; Fellow, ISVA 1995; Gov. Royal Ballet 1986–99; Hon. Capt. RNR 1991–; Elder Brother Trinity House 1991; Hon mem. Royal Inst. of Chartered Surveyors 1993; Freeman City of London; Hon. Fellow Inst. of Marine Engineers 1991, Inst. of Chartered Shipbrokers 1992, Royal Inst. of Chartered Shipbrokers 1992, Royal Inst. of Naval Architects 1997; KStJ 1998; Hon. DBA (Nottingham Trent) 1995; Hon. DCL (Durham) 1996. *Leisure interests:* music, swimming, tennis. *Address:* The Peninsular and Oriental Steam Navigation Company, 79 Pall Mall, London, SW1Y 5EJ, England. *Telephone:* (20) 7930-4343 (Office). *Fax:* (20) 7930-8572 (Office).

STERN, Ernest, MA, PhD; American international official; b. 25 Aug. 1933, Frankfurt, Germany; s. of Henry Stern; m. Zina Gold 1957; ed Queens Coll., New York and Fletcher School of Law and Diplomacy; Economist, US Dept of Commerce 1957–59; Program Economist, US Agency for Int. Devt (USAID) 1959–63; Instructor, Middle East Tech. Univ. 1960–61; Economist, Office of Pakistan Affairs, USAID 1963–64, Officer in Charge of Pakistan Affairs 1964–64, Asst Dir for Devt Policy USAID India 1965–67, Deputy Dir USAID Pakistan 1967–68, Deputy Staff Dir Comm. on Int. Devt (Pearson Comm.) 1968–69; Lecturer, Woodrow Wilson School of Public and Int. Affairs, Princeton 1971; Sr Staff mem. Council on Int. Econ. Policy, White House 1971; joined IBRD (World Bank) 1972, various posts including Deputy Chair. Econ. Cttee, Sr Adviser on Devt Policy, Dir Devt Policy, then Vice-Pres. S Asia until 1978; Vice-Pres. Operations, World Bank July 1978–, Sr Vice-Pres., Operations 1980–87, Sr Vice-Pres., Finance 1987, Man. Dir 1991–95; mem. Bd Advisors Inst. for Int. Econs, Washington DC; mem. Bd of Overseers, Int. Center for Econ. Growth, Calif., Bd of Dir Center for Global Devt; William A. Jump Memorial Foundation Meritorious Award 1964, 1966.

STERN, Fritz, PhD; American historian and professor; b. 2 Feb. 1926, Breslau, Germany; s. of Rudolf A. Stern and Catherine B. Stern; m. 1st Margaret J. Bassett 1947 (divorced 1992); one s. one d.; m. 2nd Elisabeth Niebuhr Sifton 1996; ed Bentley School, New York, Columbia Univ.; Lecturer and Instructor Columbia Univ. 1946–51; Acting Asst Prof. Cornell Univ. 1951–53; Asst Prof. Columbia Univ. 1953–57, Assoc. Prof. 1957–63, Full Prof. 1963–67, Seth Low Prof. 1967–92, Univ. Prof. 1992–96, Univ. Prof. Emer. 1997–, Provost 1980–83; Visiting Prof. Free Univ. of Berlin 1954, Yale Univ. 1963, Fondation Nationale des Sciences Politiques, Paris 1979; Perm. Visiting Prof. Konstanz Univ. 1966–; Consultant US State Dept 1966–67; Guggenheim Fellowship 1969–70; mem. OECD team on German Educ. 1971–72; Netherlands Inst. for Advanced Study 1972–73; Trustee German Marshall Fund 1981–99, Aspen Inst. Berlin 1983–2000; Sr Adviser, US Embassy, Bonn 1993–94; mem. American Acad. of Arts and Sciences 1969–, Trilateral Comm. 1983–90, American Philosophical Soc. 1988, German-American Academic Council 1993–97; Corresp. mem. Deutsche Akad. für Dichtung und Sprache 1988; Senator, Deutsche Nationalstiftung 1993–; Orden pour le Mérite (Germany) 1994; Hon. DLitt (Oxford) 1985; Hon. LLD (New School for Social Research, New York) 1997, (Columbia Univ.) 1998, (Wrocław) 2002; Lionel Trilling Book Award 1977, Lucas Prize (Tübingen) 1984, Kulturpreis Schlesien (Wrocław) 1996, Peace Prize of the German Book Trade 1999, Alexander-von-Humboldt Research Prize 1999, Bruno Snell Medal, Univ. of Hamburg 2002. *Publications:* The Politics of Cultural Despair: A Study in the Rise of the Germanic Ideology 1961, Gold and Iron: Bismarck, Bleichroeder and the Building of the German Empire 1977, The Failure of Illiberalism: Essays in the Political Culture of Modern Germany 1972, Dreams and Delusions: The Drama of German History 1987; ed. The Varieties of History from Voltaire to the Present 1956, Der Nationalsozialismus als Versuchung, in Reflexionen Finsterer Zeit 1984, Verspielte Grösse: Essays zur deutschen Geschichte 1996, Das Feine Schweigen: Historische Essays 1999, Einstein's German World 1999, Grandeurs et Defaillances de l'Allemagne du XXème Siècle 2001. *Leisure interests:* reading, hiking, cross-country skiing. *Address:* 15 Claremont Avenue, New York, NY 10027, USA. *Telephone:* (212) 666-2891 (Home). *Fax:* (212) 316-0370 (Home). *E-mail:* fs20@columbia.edu (Home).

STERN, Howard Allan, BA; American broadcaster and journalist; b. 1954, Roosevelt, NY; s. of Ben Stern and Ray Stern; m. Alison Berns 1978; three d.; ed Boston Univ.; disc jockey for WRNW, Briarcliff Manor, NY 1976–78, WCCC, Hartford, Conn. 1978–79, WWWW, Detroit 1979–80, WWDC, Washington 1980–82, WNBC, New York 1982–85, WXRK, New York 1985– and numerous other stations 1986–, The Howard Stern Radio Show 1998–; Libertarian Cand. for Gov. of NY State 1994. *TV includes:* The Howard Stern Show (WOR-TV) 1990–92, The Howard Stern Interview 1992–93, The Howard Stern Show (E!) 1994–. *Recordings include:* 50 Ways to Rank Your Mother 1982, Crucified by the FCC 1991. *Publications:* Private Parts 1993, Miss America 1995. *Address:* The Howard Stern Show WXRK-FM, 401 West 57th Street, New York, NY 10019 (Office); c/o Don Buchwald & Associates, 10 East 44th Street, New York, NY 10017, USA (Office).

STERN, Jacques, MSc; French business executive; b. 21 March 1932, Paris; m. Janine Riemer 1956; three s.; ed Ecole Polytechnique, Ecole Nationale supérieure de l'Aéronautique, Harvard Univ., USA; in charge of Devt of air defence computer system, French Air Force 1958–64; Founder and Pres. Société d'Etudes des Systèmes d'Automation (SESA) 1964; apptd. Chair. and CEO Bull 1982, Chair. Honeywell Bull Inc. 1987, Hon. Pres. Bull 1989–; Founder, Pres. Sycomore 1989–; Founder and consultant Stern Systèmes d'information 1998; Founder and Pres. Synesys 1998–; mem. Acad. of Tech.; Officier, Ordre nat. du Mérite; Chevalier, Légion d'honneur. *Publications:* several tech. books. *Address:* Stern Systèmes d'Information, Ile Saint Germain, 12 boulevard des Iles, 92130 Issy-les-Moulineaux, France (Office). *Telephone:* 1-41-23-09-42 (Office). *Fax:* 1-41-23-09-49 (Office). *E-mail:* jacques@stern-si.fr (Office).

STERN, Klaus, DrIur; German professor of law and judge; b. 11 Jan. 1932, Nuremberg; m. Helga Stern 1976; ed Humanistisches Gymnasium, Nuremberg and Univs. of Erlangen and Munich; Dozent, Univ. of Munich 1961; Prof. Berlin Univ. 1962; Prof. and Dir Inst. für öffentliches Recht und Verwaltungslehre, Univ. of Cologne 1966–, Rector 1971–73, Pro-Rector 1973–75; Head of Studies Verwaltungs- und Wirtschaftsakademie Düsseldorf 1966–; Judge, Constitutional Court, Nordrhein-Westfalen 1976–2000; mem. Rheinland-Westfälische Akademie der Wissenschaften 1978–; Grosses Bundesverdienstkreuz 1989, Austrian Ehrenkreuz for Science and Art 1997, Verdienstorden (N.R.W.) 2000. *Publications:* Staatsrecht der Bundesrepublik Deutschland (4 Vols); many other books and articles on constitutional and admin. law. *Address:* Universität Cologne, Institut für öffentliches Recht und Verwaltungslehre, Albertus-Magnus-Platz, 50931 Cologne, Germany.

STERN, Nicholas H., PhD; British economist; b. 1946, London; m. Susan Stern; three c.; ed Latymer Upper School, Peterhouse Coll., Univ. of Cambridge; academic Oxford Univ., Warwick Univ., LSE, Sorbonne, MIT; Chief Economist EBRD 1993–99, Sr Vice-Pres. and Chief Economist, World Bank 2000–. *Publications:* Palanpur: The Economy of an Indian Village (with C. J. Bliss) 1982, The Theory and Practice of Tax Reform in Developing Countries (with E. Ahmad) 1991, A Strategy for Development 2002. *Leisure interests:* reading, travelling, watching Wimbledon football club. *Address:* World Bank, 1818 H Street, NW, Washington, DC 20433, USA (Office). *Telephone:* (202) 473-3774 (Office). *Fax:* (202) 522-0906 (Office). *E-mail:* Nstern@worldbank .org (Office). *Website:* www.worldbank.org (Office).

STERN, Robert Arthur Morton, BA, MArch, FAIA; American architect and educator; b. 23 May 1939, New York; s. of Sidney Stern and Sonya (née Cohen) Stern; m. Lynn G. Solinger 1966 (divorced 1977); one s.; ed Columbia and Yale Univs.; Program Dir Architectural League New York 1965–66; designer, Richard Meier, architect, New York 1966; consultant Small Parks Program, Dept of Parks, New York 1966–70; urban designer, Housing and Devt Admin. New York 1967–70; partner Robert AM Stern & John S. Hagmann, Architects, New York 1969–77, Prin. Robert AM Stern Architects 1977–89, Prin. Partner 1989–; lecturer to Prof. of Architecture, Columbia Univ. 1970–72, Prof. 1982–; Acting Dir Historical Preservation Program 1991–; mem. Bd of Regents American Architecture Foundation 1989–91, Bd of Dirs Chicago Inst. for Architecture and Urbanism 1990–93, Bd of Dirs. Preservation League of NY, Exec. Cttee, Architectural League of New York 1977– (Pres. 1980–93); Dir (non-exec.) Walt Disney Co. –2003; numerous awards including AIA Nat. Honor awards 1980, 1985, 1990. *Publications include:* New Directions in American Architecture 1969, The House that Bob Built 1991, The American Houses of Robert A. M. Stern 1991, New York 1960 (with Thomas Mellins and David Fishman) 1995. *Address:* 460 West 34th Street, 18th Floor, New York, NY 10001 (Office); 177 East 77th Street, New York, NY 10021, USA (Home). *Telephone:* (212) 967-5100 (Office).

STERNBERG, Sir Sigmund, Kt, FRSA, JP; British business executive; b. 2 June 1921, Budapest, Hungary; s. of the late Abraham Sternberg and Elizabeth Sternberg; m. Hazel Everett Jones 1970; one s. one d. and one s. and one d. from a previous marriage; Chair. Martin Slowe Estates Ltd 1971–; Deputy Chair. Labour Finance and Industry Group 1972–93; Sr Vice-Pres. Royal Coll. of Speech and Language Therapists 1995–; Life Pres. Sternberg Centre for Judaism 1996–; Founder Three Faiths Forum (Christians, Muslims and Jews Dialogue Group) 1997; Pres. Reform Synagogues of GB 1998–; Life mem. Magistrates' Asscn 1965; mem. Bd of Deputies of British Jews, John Templeton Foundation 1998–; Paul Harris Fellow Rotary Foundation of Rotary Int. 1989; Gov. Hebrew Univ. of Jerusalem; Patron Int. Council of Christians and Jews; Freeman, City of London; Vice-Pres. Labour Finance and Industry Group; DUniv (Essex) 1996, (Open Univ.) 1998, (Hebrew Union Coll., Cincinnati) 2000; Rotary Int. Award of Honour 1998, Templeton Prize 1998; Order of the Gold Star (Hungary) 1990, Commdr's Cross, Order of Merit (Germany) 1993, Commdr, Order of Honour (Greece) 1996, Commdr, Royal Order of Polar Star (Sweden) 1997, Wilhelm Leuschner Medal, Wiesbaden 1998, Commdr's Cross with Star (Poland) 1999, Order of Commendatore (Italy) 1999, Václav Havel Memorial Medal (Ukraine) 2001, Commdr, Order of Merit (Portugal) 2000 and numerous other decorations. *Leisure interests:* golf, swimming. *Address:* 80 East End Road, London, N3 2SY, England (Office). *Fax:* (20) 7485-4512 (Office).

STERZINSKY, HE Cardinal Georg Maximilian; German ecclesiastic; b. 9 Feb. 1936, Warlack, Warmia; ordained priest 1960; elected Bishop of Berlin 1989, consecrated 1989; cr. Cardinal 1991; Archbishop of Berlin 1994–; mem. Congregation for Catholic Educ., Pontifical Council for the Pastoral Care of

Migrants and Itinerant People. *Address:* Wundstrasse 48–50, 14057 Berlin (Office); Erzbischöfl. Ordinariat, Postfach 15 60, 14005 Berlin, Germany. *Telephone:* (30) 326840. *Fax:* (30) 32684276.

STEVEN, Stewart Gustav; British journalist; b. 30 Sept. 1935, Hamburg, Germany; s. of Rudolph Steven and Trude Steven; m. Inka Sobieniewska 1965; one s.; ed Mayfield Coll., Sussex; political reporter, Cen. Press Features 1961–63; political corresp., Western Daily Press 1963–64; political reporter, Daily Express 1964–65, Diplomatic Corresp. 1965–67, Foreign Ed. 1967–72; Asst Ed. Daily Mail 1972–74, Assoc. Ed. 1974–82; Ed. Mail on Sunday 1982–92, columnist 1996–; Dir Associated Newspapers Holdings Ltd 1989–95; Ed. Evening Standard 1992–95; Chair. Liberty Publishing & Media Ltd 1996–97; Chair. Equity Theatre Comm. 1995–96, Nat. Campaign for the Arts 1996–; mem. Bd Better English Campaign 1995–97, Thames Advisory Group 1995–97, London Film Comm. 1996–99; Hon. perpetual student Bart's Hosp. 1993. *Publications:* Operation Splinter Factor 1974, The Spymasters of Israel 1976, The Poles 1982. *Address:* 20 Woodstock Road, Chiswick, London, W4 1UE, England. *Telephone:* (20) 8995-5212. *Fax:* (20) 8742-3626.

STEVENS, Sir Jocelyn Edward Greville, Kt, CVO, FRSA; British publisher; b. 14 Feb. 1932, London; s. of Major C.G.B. Stewart-Stevens and Betty Hulton; m. Jane Armyne Sheffield 1956 (dissolved 1979); one s. two d. (one s. deceased); ed Eton Coll., Cambridge Univ.; mil. service Rifle Brigade 1950–52; journalist Hulton Press 1955–56; Chair. and Man. Dir Stevens Press Ltd, Ed. Queen Magazine 1957–68; Personal Asst to Chair. Beaverbrook Newspapers 1968, Dir 1971–81, Man. Dir 1974–77; Man. Dir Evening Standard Co. Ltd 1969–72, Daily Express 1972–74; Deputy Chair. and Man. Dir Express Newspapers 1974–81; Ed. and Publr The Magazine 1982–84; Dir Centaur Communications 1982–84; Gov. Imperial Coll. of Science, Tech. and Medicine 1985–92, Winchester School of Art 1986–89; Rector and Vice-Provost RCA 1984–92; Chair. The Silver Trust 1990–93, English Heritage 1992–2000; Deputy Chair. Independent TV Comm. 1991–96; Dir (non-exec.) The TV Corpn 1996, Asprey & Co. –2002, Garrard & Co. –2002; Pres. The Cheyne Walk Trust 1989–93; Chair. The Phoenix Trust; Trustee Eureka! The Children's Museum 1990–2000; Hon. DLitt (Loughborough) 1989, (Buckingham) 1998; Hon. FCSD 1990, Sr Fellow RCA 1990. *Leisure interest:* skiing. *Address:* 14 Cheyne Walk, London, SW3 5RA, England. *Telephone:* (20) 7351-1141. *Fax:* (20) 7351-7963.

STEVENS, Sir John, Kt, M.PHIL., LLB, CIMgt, FRSA, DL; British police officer; b. 21 Oct. 1942; s. of C. J. Stevens and S. Stevens; m.; two s. one d.; ed St. Lawrence Coll., Ramsgate, Leicester Univ., Southampton Univ.; joined Metropolitan Police 1963, Deputy Commr 1998–99, Commr Feb. 2000–; Asst Chief Constable of Hants. Constabulary 1986–89, Deputy Chief Constable of Cambs. Constabulary 1989–91; Chief Constable of Northumbria 1991–96; HM Inspector of Constabulary 1996–98; has chaired numerous enquiries; Adviser Forensic Science Service; Visiting Prof. Cambridge Univ. 1984–85, City Univ., New York 1984–85; Head Stevens Enquiry N Ireland 1989–; Visiting Lecturer Int. Crime Prevention Centre, Canada 1998; Adviser to Prime Minister of Romania 2002–; patron various charities in Romania and London; Hon. Fellow Wolfson Coll. Cambridge 2000; DL Greater London 2001; KStJ 2002; Hon. LLD (Leicester) 2000; Hon. DCL (Northumbria) 2001; Queen's Police Medal 1992. *Leisure interests:* flying, rugby, walking, cricket, charity work. *Address:* New Scotland Yard, Broadway, London, SW1H 0BG, England (Office). *Telephone:* (20) 7230-1212 (Office).

STEVENS, John Paul, JD; American judge; b. 20 April 1920, Chicago, Ill.; s. of Ernest James Stevens and Elizabeth Street; m. 1st Elizabeth Jane Sheeren 1942; one s. three d.; m. 2nd Maryan Mulholland Simon 1979; ed Univ. of Chicago, Northwestern Univ. School of Law; served USN (Bronze Star Medal) 1942–45; Co-Ed. of Law Review at Northwestern Univ. School of Law 1947; Law Clerk to Supreme Court Justice Wiley Rutledge 1947; worked with Poppenhusen, Johnston, Thompson and Raymond law practice 1948–51, 1952; Partner, Rothschild, Stevens, Barry and Myers 1952–70; Circuit Judge, Seventh Circuit Court of Appeals 1970–75; Assoc. Justice, U.S. Supreme Court Dec. 1975–; Assoc. Counsel, Monopoly Power Sub-Cttee of House of Reps. Judiciary Cttee 1951; mem. Attorney Gen.'s Nat. Cttee on Antitrust Laws 1953–55; part-time teacher, Northwestern Univ. School of Law, later Univ. of Chicago Law School 1952–56; admitted to Ill. Bar 1949, to U.S. Supreme Court 1954; mem. American Law Inst. *Publications:* numerous articles on commercial monopoly affairs. *Address:* United States Supreme Court, Building One, 1 First Street, NE, Washington, DC 20543, USA.

STEVENS, Robert Bocking, MA, DCL, LLM; lawyer and academic; b. 8 June 1933; s. of John S. Stevens and Enid Dorothy Bocking Stevens; m. 1st Rosemary Wallace 1961 (divorced 1983); m. 2nd Katherine Booth 1985; one s. two d.; ed Keble Coll. Oxford and Yale Univ.; mem. Essex Court Chambers, Lincoln's Inn Fields 1965–, Midland Circuit 1962–76; Asst Prof. of Law, Yale Univ. 1959–61, Assoc. Prof. 1961–65, Prof. 1965–76, Fellow, Jonathan Edwards Coll. 1963–76; Prof. of Law and Adjunct Prof. of History, Tulane Univ. 1976–78, Provost 1976–78; Pres. Haverford Coll. 1978–87; Prof. of History, Univ. of Calif. Santa Cruz 1987–93, Chancellor 1987–91; Counsel, Covington & Burling (Washington, DC), London 1991–; mem. Council, Justice (UK Br.), Int. Comm. of Jurists 1992–98; Master, Pembroke Coll. Oxford 1993–2001; Chair. Sulgrave Manor (Home of Washington Family) Bd 2002–; numerous other academic and legal appts. etc.; Bencher Gray's Inn 1999; Hon. Fellow Keble Coll. Oxford 1983, Pembroke Coll. Oxford 2001; four hon. degrees. *Publications include:* Law and Politics: The House of Lords as a

Judicial Body 1800–1976 1978, The American Law School: Legal Education in America 1850–1980 1983, The Independence of the Judiciary: The View from the Lord Chancellor's Office 1993; co-author and ed. of other books on law, history and welfare; articles and monographs. *Leisure interests:* politics, history, talking, claret. *Address:* Covington & Burling, Leconfield House, Curzon Street, London, W1Y 8AS; Millbank, Northleach, Cheltenham, GL54 3HJ, England (Home). *Telephone:* (20) 7495-5655 (London); (1451) 860060 (Glos.). *Fax:* (1451) 860060 (Glos.); (20) 7495-3101 (London). *E-mail:* rbstevens@cov.com (Office); rbstevens33@hotmail.com (Home).

STEVENS, Rosemary Anne, PhD; American university professor; b. 18 March 1935, Bourne, England; d. of William E. Wallace and Mary A. Wallace; m. 1st Robert B. Stevens 1961 (divorced 1983); one s. one d.; m. 2nd Jack D. Barchas 1994; ed Oxford and Manchester Univs, UK and Yale Univ., USA; trained in hosp. admin. and worked as hosp. admin. Nat. Health Service, UK; mem. Faculty, Prof. of Public Health, Prof. in Inst. of Policy Studies, Yale Univ., USA 1962–76; Prof., Dept of Health Systems Man. (Chair. 1977-78) and Adjunct Prof. of Political Science, Tulane Univ. 1976–79; Prof. of History and Sociology of Science, Univ. of Pa 1979–, Chair. 1980–83, 1986–91; UPS Foundation Prof. in Social Sciences 1990–91, Dean, Thomas S. Gates Prof. 1991–96; Stanley I. Sheerr Prof. 1997–; mem. Inst. of Medicine of NAS; Fellow American Acad. of Arts and Sciences; (Northeastern OH Univ. Coll. of Medicine) 1995; Dr hc (Hahnemann Univ., Philadelphia) 1988, (Medical Coll. of Pa) 1992, (Rutgers) 1995, Rockefeller Humanities Award 1983–84, Guggenheim Award 1984–85, Baxter Foundation Prize for Health Services Research 1990; James A. Hamilton Book Award 1990, Welch Medal 1990, ABMS Special Award 1990. *Publications:* Medical Practice in Modern England 1966, American Medicine and the Public Interest 1971, Foreign Trained Physicians and American Medicine 1972, Welfare Medicine in America 1974, The Alien Doctors: Foreign Medical Graduates in American Hospitals 1978, In Sickness and in Wealth: American Hospitals in the Twentieth Century 1989; various articles. *Leisure interests:* painting, reading, flea markets. *Address:* 324 Logan Hall, University of Pennsylvania, 249 South 36th Street, Philadelphia, PA 19104 (Office); 1900 Rittenhouse Square, # 18A, Philadelphia, PA 19103, USA (Home). *Telephone:* (215) 898-8400. *Fax:* (215) 573-2231. *E-mail:* rstevens@sas.upenn.edu (Home).

STEVENS, Theodore Fulton, BA, LLB; American politician and lawyer; b. 18 Nov. 1923, Indianapolis, Ind.; s. of George A. Stevens and Gertrude Stevens (née Chancellor); m. 1st Ann Cherrington 1952 (died 1978); three s. two d.; m. 2nd Catherine Chandler 1980; one d.; ed High School, Redondo Beach, Calif., Univ. of Calif. at LA and Harvard Law School; US Attorney, Fairbanks, Alaska 1953–56; Legis. Counsel, Dept of Interior, Washington, DC 1956–58; Asst to Sec. of Interior 1958–60; Solicitor of Interior Dept 1960; pvt. law practice, Anchorage, Alaska 1961–68; Senator from Alaska 1968–; Asst Minority Leader US Senate 1977–80, Asst Majority Leader 1981–85; US Senate del. to Canadian–US Interparl. Conf., to British–US Interparl. Conf.; Admin. Co-Chair. Senate Appropriations Cttee 1997–2001, Pres. Pro Tempore 2003–; mem. Senate Commerce Cttee, Senate Governmental Affairs Cttee, Senate Rules Cttee; Republican. *Address:* US Senate, 522 Hart Senate Office Building, Washington, DC 20510 (Office); PO Box 100879, Anchorage, AK 99510, USA (Home). *Telephone:* (202) 224-3004 (Office).

STEVENS OF LUDGATE, Baron (Life Peer), cr. 1987, of Ludgate in the City of London; **David Robert Stevens,** MA; British business executive; b. 26 May 1936; s. of (Arthur) Edwin Stevens; m. 1st Patricia Rose (divorced 1971); one s. one d.; m. 2nd Melissa Milicevich 1977 (died 1989); m. 3rd Meriza Giori 1990; ed Stowe School and Sidney Sussex Coll. Cambridge; man. trainee, Elliott Automation 1959; Dir Hill Samuel Securities 1959–68, Drayton Group 1968–74; Chair. City & Foreign (now Alexander Proudfoot PLC) 1976–95, Drayton Far East 1976–93, English & Int. 1976–79, Consolidated Venture (fmrly Montagu Boston) 1979–93, Drayton Consolidated 1980–92, Drayton Japan 1980–93, Econ. Devt Cttee for Civil Eng 1984–86; Dir United News & Media PLC (fmrly United Newspapers PLC) 1974–99, Chair. 1981–99; CEO INVESCO MIM 1980–87, Deputy Chair. 1987–89; Chair. 1989–93; Chair. MIM Britannia Ltd (fmrly Montagu Investment Man. Ltd) 1980–92 (CEO 1980–87), Express Newspapers 1985–99, PNC Telecom (fmrly. Personal Number Co.) 1998–. *Leisure interests:* golf, gardening. *Address:* c/o Ludgate House, 245 Blackfriars Road, SE1 9UY; House of Lords, London, SW1A 0PW, England.

STEVENSON, Hon. Adlai E., III; American politician, lawyer and investment banker; b. 10 Oct. 1930, Chicago, Ill.; s. of the late Adlai Stevenson II (fmr Gov. of Illinois, presidential candidate and Amb. to UN); great-grandson of Adlai E. Stevenson (Vice-Pres. of USA 1893–97); m. Nancy L. Anderson 1955; two s. two d.; ed Milton Acad., Mass. and Harvard Univ.; law clerk to a justice of Ill. Supreme Court 1957; joined Chicago law firm of Mayer, Brown and Platt 1958–66, partner 1966–67, 1981–83, of Counsel 1983–91; elected to Ill. House of Reps. 1964; State Treas. of Ill. 1966–70; Senator from Illinois 1970–81; Democratic Cand. for Gov. of Ill. 1982, 1986; Chair. SC&M Int. Ltd 1991–95, Pres. 1995–98, Chair. 1998–; Democrat; Order of the Sacred Treasure, Gold and Silver Stars (Japan); numerous awards, hon. degrees and directorships. *Address:* 20 North Clark Street, Suite 750, Chicago, IL 60602 (Office); 4302 South Blandings Road, Hanover, IL 61041, USA (Home). *Telephone:* (773) 281-3578. *Fax:* (773) 281-4812.

STEVENSON, Juliet, CBE; British actress; b. 30 Oct. 1956; d. of Michael Guy Stevens and Virginia Ruth Marshall; one s. one d. two step-s.; ed Hurst Lodge

School, Berks., St Catherine's School, Surrey, Royal Acad. of Dramatic Art; with RSC (now assoc. artist), Royal Nat. Theatre, Royal Court Theatre, film, TV, radio, audiobooks; Bancroft Gold Medal, Royal Acad. of Dramatic Arts 1977, Time Out Award for Best Actress 1991, Evening Standard Film Award for Best Actress 1992, Lawrence Olivier Theatre Award for Best Actress 1992. *Plays include:* Midsummer Night's Dream, Henry IV Parts 1 and 2, Measure for Measure, As You Like It, Troilus and Cressida, Les Liaisons Dangereuses, Not I, Footfalls Money, The Witch of Edmonton, Breaking the Silence (all for RSC), Burn This (West End), Death and the Maiden (Royal Court and West End) (Olivier Award 1992), Duchess of Malfi (Greenwich Theatre and West End); Yerma, Hedda Gabler, The Caucasian Chalk Circle, Private Lives (Nat. Theatre), Other Worlds, The Country (Royal Court). *Films include:* Drowning by Numbers, Ladder of Swords, Truly Madly Deeply, The Trial, The Secret Rapture, Emma, The Search for John Gissing, Who Dealt?, Beckett's Play, Bend It Like Beckham, Food of Love. *Radio includes:* To the Lighthouse, Volcano, Albertina, House of Correction, Hang Up, Cigarettes and Chocolate, A Little Like Drowning, Victory. *Television includes:* The Road From Coorain, Play (Beckett), Trial by Fire, Cider with Rosie, Stone Scissors Paper, The Politician's Wife, Nora in A Doll's House, Life Story, Antigone, The March, Maybury, Thomas and Ruth, Aimée, The Mallens, Living With Dinosaurs; wrote and fronted a BBC documentary Great Journeys. *Publications:* Clamorous Voices (jtly.) 1988, Shall I See You Again? (jtly), Players of Shakespeare (jtly.). *Leisure interests:* piano, travelling, gardening, reading, tennis. *Address:* c/o Markham and Froggatt Ltd, Julian House, 4 Windmill Street, London, W1P 1HF, England.

STEVENSON, Robert Wilfrid, MA, FCCA; British public affairs consultant; b. 19 April 1947, Lochalsh; s. of James Stevenson and Elizabeth Macrae; m. 1st Jennifer Grace Antonio 1972 (divorced 1979); m. 2nd Elizabeth Ann Minogue 1991; one s. two d.; ed Edinburgh Acad. and Univ. Coll., Oxford; Research Officer Univ. of Edinburgh Students Asscn 1970–74; Sec. and Acad. Registrar, Napier Polytechnic, Edinburgh 1974–87; Deputy Dir BFI 1987–88, Dir 1988–97; Dir The Smith Inst. 1997–. *Leisure interests:* cinema, hill walking, squash. *Address:* Missenden House, Little Missenden, Amersham, Bucks., HP7 0RD, England. *Telephone:* (1494) 890689. *Fax:* (1494) 868127. *E-mail:* wilf_stevenson@btconnect.com (Office); wilfstevenson@msn.com (Home).

STEVENSON OF CODDENHAM, Baron (Life Peer), cr. 1999, of Coddenham in the County of Suffolk; **Henry Dennistoun Stevenson,** Kt, CBE; British business consultant; b. 19 July 1945, Edinburgh; s. of Alexander James Stevenson and Sylvia Florence Stevenson (née Ingleby); m. Charlotte Susan Stevenson (née Vanneck); four s.; ed Glenalmond School and King's Coll., Cambridge; Dir Pearson Employee Share Trustees Ltd, Chair. Pearson PLC 1997–; Chair. Halifax PLC 2000–01, Chair. HBOS 2001– (bank formed after merger of Halifax and Bank of Scotland); Chair. Trustees of the Tate Gallery 1988–98 (Trustee 1998–, Sinfonia 21 1989–99, GPA Group PLC (now Aer Fi) 1993–2000, Aldeburgh Productions 2000–; mem. Bd of Dirs Manpower Inc. 1988–, J. Rothschild Assurance PLC 1991–97, J. Rothschild Holdings PLC 1991–97, English Partnerships 1993–99, British Sky Broadcasting Group PLC 1994–2000, British Council 1996–2003, Lazard Bros. & Co. Ltd 1997–2000, St James's Place Capital PLC 1997–2002; Dir Cloaca Maxima Ltd 1996–, Saxton Bampfylde Int. PLC 1996–98, Economist Newspapers Ltd 1998–, Glynebourne Productions Ltd 1998–; Chair. Lords Appointments Comm. 2000–; mem. Take Over Panel 1992–2000; Gov. LSE 1996–2002; Chancellor London Inst. 2000–. *Publication:* Information and Communications Technology in UK Schools (The Stevenson Report) 1997. *Address:* House of Lords, London, SW1A 0PW, England.

STEVER, Horton Guyford, PhD; American scientist and company director; b. 24 Oct. 1916, Corning, NY; s. of Ralph Raymond Stever and Alma Matt; m. Louise Risley Floyd 1946; two s. two d.; ed Colgate Univ. and California Inst. of Tech.; mem. Staff Radiation Lab. and Instructor, Officers' Radar School, MIT 1941–42; Science Liaison Officer, London Mission, Office of Scientific Research and Devt 1942–45; Asst Prof. of Aeronautical Eng Mass. Inst. of Tech. 1946–51, Assoc. Prof. 1951–56, Prof. 1956–65; Chief Scientist, USAF 1955–56; Assoc. Dean of Eng, Mass. Inst. of Tech. 1956–59, Head Depts of Mechanical Eng Naval Architecture and Marine Eng 1961–65; Pres. Carnegie-Mellon Univ. 1965–72; Chair. USAF Scientific Advisory Bd 1962–69, Aeronautics and Space Eng Bd 1967–69, Foreign Sec. 1984–88; mem. Exec. Cttee Defense Science Bd, Dept of Defense 1962–69; mem. Panel on Science and Tech. US House of Reps Comm. on Science and Tech., 1959–72, Science and Tech. Adviser to Pres. 1976–77; Science Consultant, Corp. Trustee 1977–; Trustee, Colgate Univ. 1962–72; Sarah Mellon Scaife Foundation 1965–72, Shady Side Acad. 1967–72, Univ. Research Asscn 1977– (Pres. 1982–84); Dir Fisher Scientific Co. 1965–72, Koppers Co. 1965–72, System Devt Corpn 1965–70, United Aircraft Corpn 1966–72, TRW 1977–88, Saudi Arabian Nat. Center for Science and Tech. 1978–80; Schering Plough 1980–89, Goodyear 1981–86; mem. Nat. Acad. of Eng, Nat. Science Bd 1970–72; Dir Nat. Science Foundation 1972–76; Science Adviser to Pres. of USA and Chair. Fed. Council for Science and Tech., Exec. Cttee Nat. Science Bd, Energy R & D Advisory Council; US Chair. US-USSR Jt Comm. on Scientific and Tech. Co-operation 1973–77; mem. Carnegie Comm. on Science, Tech. and Govt 1988–93; mem. NAS 1973–; Foreign mem. Royal Acad. of Eng 1989–, Japan Acad. of Eng 1989–; mem. US-Japan Cttee on Scientific Co-operation, Fed. Council on the Arts and Humanities, Nat. Council on Educational Research and many other Govt bodies; 18 hon. degrees; President's Certificate of Merit 1948, Excep-

tional Civilian Service Award, USAF 1956, Scott Gold Medal of American Ordnance Asscn 1960, Alumni Distinguished Service Award Calif. Inst. of Tech. 1966, Distinguished Public Service Medal, Dept of Defense 1969, Nat. Medal of Science 1991, Vannevar Bush Award 1997; Commdr, Order of Merit, Poland 1976, Distinguished Public Service Medal, NASA 1988, Arthur M. Bueche Award, Nat. Acad. of Eng 1999. *Publications:* Flight (with J. J. Haggerty) 1965, In War and Peace: My Life in Science and Technology 2002. *Leisure interests:* skiing, fishing, golf, hiking. *Address:* 588 Russell Avenue, Gaithersburg, MD 20877, USA. *Telephone:* (301) 216-5689.

STEWART, Alec James, MBE; British cricketer; b. 8 April 1963, Merton, London; s. of Michael James Stewart (fmr Surrey Capt. and Test player) and Sheila Stewart; m. Lynn Blades 1991; one s. one d.; ed Tiffin Boys' School, Kingston upon Thames; right-hand opening batsman; wicket-keeper; Surrey 1981– (Capt. 1992–97); 126 Tests for England 1989–90 to 2 Jan. 2003, 14 as Capt., scoring 8,187 runs (average 40.13) including 15 hundreds; scored 25,438 first-class runs (48 hundreds) to end of 2002; held 11 catches, equalling world first-class record, for Surrey v. Leicestershire, Leicester, 19–22 Aug. 1989; toured Australia 1990–91, 1994–95 and 1998–99 (Capt.); 161 limited-overs ints to 7 Jan. 2003; overtook record (118) of Graham Gooch to become England's most-capped cricketer, Lords July 2002; Wisden Cricketer of the Year 1993. *Publication:* Alec Stewart: A Captain's Diary (jtly) 1999. *Leisure interests:* soccer (Chelsea), spending time with his family. *Address:* c/o Surrey County Cricket Club, Kennington Oval, London, SE11 5SS, England.

STEWART, Sir Brian John, Kt, CBE, MSc, CA; British brewery executive; b. 9 April 1945, Stirling, Scotland; s. of Ian M. Stewart and Christina McIntyre; m. Seonaid Duncan 1971; two s. one d.; ed Perth Acad., Edinburgh Univ.; joined Scottish & Newcastle Breweries (now Scottish and Newcastle PLC) 1976, Corp. Devt Dir 1985–88, Group Finance Dir 1988–91, Group Chief Exec. 1991–2000, Deputy Chair. 1997–2000, Exec. Chair. 2000–03, Chair. (non-exec.) 2003–; Dir (non-exec.) Booker 1993–99; Dir (non-exec.) Standard Life Assurance Co. 1993–, Chair. (non-exec.) 2003–. *Leisure interests:* skiing, golf. *Address:* Scottish & Newcastle PLC, 33 Ellersly Road, Edinburgh, EH12 6HX, Scotland (Office). *Telephone:* (131) 528-2000 (Office). *Fax:* (131) 528-2300 (Office). *Website:* www.scottishnewcastle.com (Office).

STEWART, Dave; British pop musician; b. 1952, Sunderland; m. 1st Pam Stewart (divorced); m. 2nd Siobhan Fahey 1988; two s.; formed band Longdancer and entered recording contract with Elton John's Rocket label 1973; later formed band The Tourists which reached No. 1 in charts with remake of I Only Want To Be With You 1979; The Tourists disbanded 1980; formed group Eurythmics with Annie Lennox in 1980s (disbanded 1989, reformed); produces records, shoots short films, writes soundtracks for films (including Disney film The Ref), directs films, produces computer-enhanced films and collects art; has produced records and written songs for Mick Jagger, Bob Dylan, Tom Hall, etc.; Hon. DMus (Westminster) 1998. *Film directed:* Honest 2000. *Albums include:* (with Eurythmics) Sweet Dreams, Touch, Revenge, Savage, We Too Are One 1989, Peace 1999 (solo), Greetings from the Gutter. *Website:* www.davestewart.com (Office).

STEWART, Jane, BSc; Canadian politician; b. 1955, St George, Ont.; d. of Bob Nixon; two s.; ed Trent Univ.; worked in area of human resources for many cos. in Canada and USA including Imperial Oil; MP for Brant 1993–; Minister of Nat. Revenue 1996–97, of Indian Affairs and Northern Devt 1997–99, of Human Resources Devt 1999–; Chair. Nat. Liberal Caucus 1994–96. *Address:* Human Resources Development, 140 Promenade du Portage, Phase IV, Hull, Quebec, K1A 0J9, Canada (Office). *Telephone:* (819) 994-2482 (Office).

STEWART, Sir John Young (Jackie), Kt, KBE; British racing driver; b. 11 June 1939, Milton, Scotland; s. of the late Robert Paul Stewart and Jean Clark Young; m. Helen McGregor 1962; two s.; ed Dumbarton Acad.; first raced 1961; competed in 4 meetings driving for Barry Filer, Glasgow 1961–62; drove for Ecurie Ecosse and Barry Filer, winning 14 out of 23 starts 1963, 28 wins out of 53 starts 1964; drove Formula 1 for British Racing Motors (BRM) 1965–67, for Ken Tyrrell 1968–73; has won Australian, New Zealand, Swedish, Mediterranean, Japanese and many other non-championship major int. motor races; set new world record by winning his 26th World Championship Grand Prix (Zandvoort) 1973, 27th (Nürburgring) 1973; third in World Championship 1965, 2nd in 1968 and 1972, World Champion 1969, 1971, 1973; retd 1973; involved with son, Paul, in operation of Stewart Grand Prix, a Formula One team cr. 1996, sold out to the Ford Motor Co. who have run the operation as Jaguar Racing from start of 2000 season; Chair. and CEO Jaguar Racing 1999–Jan. 2000; Pres. British Racing Drivers Club; Hon. Dr Aut. Eng (Lawrence Inst. of Tech., USA) 1986; Dr hc (Glasgow Caledonian) 1993; Hon. DEng (Heriot-Watt Univ.) 1996; British Automobile Racing Club Gold Medal 1971, 1973, Daily Express Sportsman of the Year 1971, 1973, BBC Sports Personality of the Year 1973, Scottish Sportsman of the Year 1973, US Sportsman of the Year 1973, Segrave Trophy 1973. *Film:* Weekend of a Champion 1972. *Publications:* World Champion (with Eric Dymock) 1970, Faster! (with Peter Manso) 1972, On the Road 1983, Jackie Stewart's Principles of Performance Driving 1986, The Jackie Stewart Book of Shooting 1991. *Leisure interests:* shooting (clay pigeon champion), golf, tennis. *Address:* Clayton House, Butlers Cross, Ellesborough, Bucks., HP17 0UR, England (Office). *Telephone:* (1296) 620913 (Office). *Fax:* (1296) 620049 (Office).

STEWART, Martha Kostyra, BA; American editor and author; b. Jersey City, NJ; d. of Edward Kostyra and Martha (née Ruszkowski) Kostyra; m. Andy Stewart 1961 (divorced 1990); one s.; ed Barnard Univ.; fmr model, stockbroker, caterer; owner, Ed.-in-Chief Martha Stewart Living magazine 1990–; Chair., CEO Martha Stewart Living Omnimedia 1997–; also appears in cooking feature on Today Show; mem. Bd NY Stock Exchange June–Oct. 2002; under investigation for alleged insider trading June 2002–. *Publications include:* (with Elizabeth Hawes) Entertaining 1982, Weddings 1987; (as sole author) Martha Stewart's Hors d'Oeuvres: The Creation and Presentation of Fabulous Finger Food 1984, Martha Stewart's Pies and Tarts 1985, Martha Stewart's Quick Cook Menus 1988, The Wedding Planner 1988, Martha Stewart's Gardening: Month by Month 1991, Martha Stewart's New Old House; Restoration, Renovation, Decoration 1992, Martha Stewart's Christmas 1993, Martha Stewart's Menus for Entertaining 1994, Holidays 1994. *Address:* Martha Stewart Inc., 19 Newton Toke, Suite 6, Westport, CT 06880; c/o Susan Magrino Agency, 40 West 57th Street, 31st Floor, New York, NY 10019; 10 Saugatuck Avenue, Westport, CT 06880, USA (Home).

STEWART, Patrick; British actor; b. 13 July 1940, Mirfield, W Yorks.; s. of Alfred Stewart and Gladys Stewart; m. 1st Sheila Falconer 1966; one s. one d.; m. 2nd Wendy Neuss 2002; ed Bristol Old Vic Theatre School; began career as junior reporter on local newspaper; acting experience with various repertory cos.; joined Royal Shakespeare Co. (RSC) 1966, Assoc. Artist 1967–87; Founding Dir ACTER (A Centre for Theatre Educ. and Research); Dir Flying Freehold Productions, Paramount Studios, LA 1998–. *Films:* Hedda, Excalibur, Dune, Lady Jane, Gunmen, Robin Hood – Men in Tights, LA Story, Jeffrey, Star Trek: First Contact, Conspiracy Theory, Dad Savage, Masterminds, Star Trek: Insurrection 1999, X-Men 2000, Moby Dick, Star Trek: Nemesis 2002, X-Men: X2 2003. *Theatre includes:* Antony and Cleopatra (Olivier Award, Soc. of West End Theatre Award) 1979, Henry IV 1984, Who's Afraid of Virginia Woolf (London Fringe Award) 1987, A Christmas Carol (Drama Desk Award, Olivier Award 1992) 1988–1996, The Tempest 1995, Othello 1997, The Ride Down Mount Morgan 1998. *Television:* Star Trek: The Next Generation, The Mozart Inquest, Maybury, I Claudius, Tinker, Tailor, Soldier, Spy, Smiley's People. *Music:* narrative on Peter and the Wolf (Grammy Award) 1996. *Address:* c/o International Creative Management Inc., 8942 Wilshire Boulevard, Beverly Hills, CA 90211, USA (Office). *Telephone:* (310) 550-4000 (Office). *Fax:* (310) 550-4100 (Office).

STEWART, Robert W., OC, MSc, PhD, FRSC, FRS; Canadian oceanographer; b. 21 Aug. 1923, Smoky Lake, Alberta; m. 1st V. Brande 1948 (divorced 1972); three s. one d.; m. 2nd Anne-Marie Robert 1973; one s. one d.; ed Queen's Univ., Kingston, Ont., Cambridge Univ.; research scientist, Canadian Defence Research Bd, Victoria, BC 1950–61; Prof. of Physics and Oceanography, Univ. of British Columbia, Vancouver 1961–70, Hon. Prof. 1971–; Dir-Gen., Pacific Region, Ocean and Aquatic Sciences, Dept of the Environment, Victoria, BC 1970; Asst Deputy Minister, Science and Tech., Ministry of Educ., Science and Tech. 1979, Deputy Minister, Ministry of Univs., Science and Communications, Victoria, BC 1979–84; Pres. Alberta Research Council 1984–87; Dir Centre for Earth and Ocean Research, Univ. of Vic. 1987–89, Adjunct Prof. 1989–; Hon. Prof. of Science Univ. of Alberta 1985–; Visiting Prof., Dalhousie Univ. 1960–61, Harvard Univ. 1964, Pa State Univ. 1964, Cambridge Univ. 1967–68; mem. Jt Organzing Cttee, Global Atmospheric Research Programme 1967–80, Vice-Chair. 1968–72, Chair. 1972–76; mem. Council, American Meteorological Soc. 1977–81; mem. Cttee on Climate Change and the Ocean 1978–89, Chair. 1983–87; Vice-Chair. Science Cttee Int. Geosphere-Biosphere Programme 1990–94; Science Officer Int. Council of Scientific Unions, Paris; IMO Lecturer 1975; Hon. DSc (McGill) 1972. LLD (Dalhousie) 1974; Patterson Medal, Canadian Meteorological Soc. 1973, Sverdrup Gold Medal, American Meteorological Soc. 1976. *Publications:* approx. 60 Publs on turbulence, oceanography and meteorology. *Address:* 4249 Thornhill Crescent, Victoria, BC, V8W 3G6, Canada (Home); School of Earth and Ocean Studies, University of Victoria, P.O. Box 1700, Victoria, BC, V8W 2Y2.

STEWART, Rod (Roderick David); British pop singer; b. 10 Jan. 1945, London; m. 1st Alana Collins 1979 (divorced 1984); one s. one d.; d. with Kelly Emberg; m. 2nd Rachel Hunter 1990; one d.; singer with Jeff Beck Group 1968–69, Faces 1969–75; Rock Star of the Year, Rolling Stone Magazine 1971; British Rock and Pop Award for Lifetime Achievement 1992. *Solo albums include:* Rod Stewart, Gasoline Alley, Every Picture Tells a Story, Never a Dull Moment, A Night on the Town, Atlantic Crossing, Smiler, Footloose and Fancy Free, Blondes Have More Fun, Foolish Behaviour, Body Wishes, Out of Order, Vagabond Heart, The Best of Rod Stewart (compilation) 1993, It Had To Be You: The Great American Songbook 2002. *Address:* c/o Warner Music, 28 Kensington Church Street, London, W8 4EP, England. *Telephone:* (20) 7937-8844.

STEWART, S. Jay, BS, MBA; American business executive; b. 18 Sept. 1938; s. of Virgil Harvey Stewart and Lena Rivers Repair; m. Judith Daniels 1961; one s. two d.; ed West Virginia Univ. and Univ. of Cincinnati; Eng marketing and Mfg, Monsanto Corpn 1961–73; Dir of Devt, Dir of Marketing, Gen. Man. Ventron Div., Thiokol Corpn 1973–79, Pres. Dynachem Div. 1979–82, Group Vice-Pres. for Chemicals 1982; Pres. Thiokol Chemical Div., Morton Thiokol, Inc. 1982–83, Group Vice-Pres. Chemicals 1983–86, Pres., COO and Dir 1986–89; Pres., COO and Dir Morton Int. Inc. 1986–94, Chair. CEO 1994–; Advisory Bd Nat. Foundation for History of Chem. 1991–; mem. American Chemical Soc., American Inst. of Chemical Engs., Commercial Devt Asscn. *Address:* Morton International Inc., 100 N Riverside Plaza, Chicago, IL 60606, USA.

STEWART, Thomas, MusB; American opera singer; b. 29 Aug. 1928, San Saba, Tex.; s. of Thomas James Stewart and Gladys Naomi (Reavis) Stewart; m. Evelyn Lear (q.v.) 1955; one s. one d.; ed Baylor Univ., Juilliard School of Music, Hochschule für Musik, Berlin; joined Berlin Opera 1958; first performance at Bayreuth Festival 1960; has performed at Metropolitan Opera, New York, Royal Opera House, Covent Garden, London, La Scala, Milan, Vienna State Opera, Grand Opera, Paris, Bavarian State Opera, San Francisco Opera, Chicago Opera, Hamburg Opera; appears with all maj. orchestras of the world; gives recitals internationally with Evelyn Lear; Fellow, American Univ. 1967; Artistic Adviser Vocal Arts Soc. 1995; Hon. mem. Advisory Bd George London Foundation for Singers, NY 1994; numerous honours, awards and prizes including Richard Wagner Medal 1963, Berlin Kammersänger 1963; Grammy Awards 1969, 1971. *Major roles include:* Hans Sachs (The Mastersingers of Nuremberg), Falstaff, Wotan (The Ring cycle), The Flying Dutchman, Scarpia (Tosca), Iago (Otello), Golaud (Pelléas et Mélisande), Amfortas (Parsifal). *Leisure interests:* theatre, tennis, golf. *Address:* Thomlyn Artists Inc., 3413 Olandwood Court, Ste. 203, Olney, MD 20832, USA.

STEWARTBY, Baron (Life Peer), cr. 1992, of Portmoak in the District of Perth and Kinross; **Bernard Harold Ian Halley Stewartby,** PC, LittD, FBA, FRSE; British banker and politician; b. Stewart, 10 Aug. 1935, London; s. of the late Prof. H. C. Stewart and Dorothy Stewart (née Lowen); m. Deborah Charlotte Buchan 1966; one s. two d.; ed Haileybury Coll. and Jesus Coll., Cambridge; Lt-Commdr RNR; Brown Shipley & Co. Ltd 1960–82; Conservative MP for Hitchin/N Herts. 1974–92; Econ. Sec. to the Treasury 1983–87; Minister of State for the Armed Forces 1987–88, for Northern Ireland 1988–89; Chair. Throgmorton Trust PLC 1990–; Dir Financial Services Authority 1993–97; Deputy Chair. Standard Chartered PLC 1993–; Deputy Chair. Amlin PLC 1995–; Chair. Treasure Valuation Cttee 1996–2001; Hon. Fellow Jesus Coll., Cambridge 1994; Medallist Royal Numismatic Soc. 1996, Royal Naval and Royal Marine Forces Reserve Decoration. *Publications:* The Scottish Coinage 1955, Coinage in Tenth-Century England 1989. *Leisure interests:* archaeology, tennis. *Address:* Standard Chartered PLC, 1 Aldermanbury Square, London, EC2V 7SB, England (Office); Broughton Green, Broughton, Peeblesshire, ML12 6HQ, Scotland (Home).

STEYN, Hon. Jan Hendrik, BA, BLL; South African lawyer; b. 4 March 1928, Cape Town; s. of H.P.M. Steyn and Zerilda Steyn; ed Jan van Riebeeck School, Univ. of Stellenbosch; began practising as lawyer, Cape Town 1950, took Silk 1963, apptd. Justice of Supreme Court, Cape Prov. Div. 1964, retd 1981; apptd. First Exec. Dir The Urban Foundation 1977 (on leave of absence from Supreme Court), now Hon. Chair.; Chair. Independent Devt Trust 1990–94, SA Media Council 1989–; Judge Court of Appeal, Lesotho 1992–, Botswana 1994–; Acting Judge of Cape Supreme Court; Jt Ombudsman to Life Assurance Industry 1996; Chair. Bd of Investigation into Saldanha Steel Project 1995, Comm. of Enquiry into Remuneration of Election Reps.; Dir First Nat. Bank, Anglo-American Corpn, Barlow Rand Ltd, Metropolitan Life of SA Ltd; Founder The Inst. of Criminology, Univ. of Cape Town; Trustee numerous charitable orgs.; four hon. degrees; Businessman of the Year Award, SA Inst. of Housing 1984, Paul Harris Fellowship Award, Rotary Int., Harvard Business School Business Statesman Award 1985. *Publications:* Crime and Punishment in South Africa (Jt Ed.); numerous Publs on crime and its control. *Leisure interest:* golf. *Address:* Court of Appeal, Maseru, Lesotho.

STEYN, Baron (Life Peer), cr. 1995, of Swafield in the County of Norfolk; **Johan Van Zyl Steyn,** Kt, PC, QC, MA; British judge; b. 15 Aug. 1932, Stellenbosch, South Africa; s. of Van Zyl Steyn and Janet Steyn (née Blignaut); m. Susan Leonore Lewis; two s. two d. by previous m.; one step-s. one step-d.; ed Jan van Riebeeck School, Cape Town, S. Africa, Univ. of Stellenbosch, S. Africa, Univ. Coll. Oxford; began practising at S. African Bar 1958; Sr Counsel of Supreme Court of SA 1970; settled in UK; began practising at English Bar 1973, Bencher, Lincoln's Inn 1985, QC 1979; a Presiding Judge, Northern Circuit 1989–91; Judge of the High Court 1985–91; a Lord Justice of Appeal 1992–95, a Lord of Appeal in Ordinary 1995–; mem. Supreme Court Rule Cttee 1985–89; Chair. Race Relations Cttee of the Bar 1987–88; mem. Lord Chancellor's Advisory Cttee on Legal Educ. and Conduct 1994–96; Pres. British Insurance Law Asscn 1992–94; Hon. Fellow Univ. Coll. Oxford 1995; Hon. mem. American Law Inst.; Hon. LLD (Queen Mary and Westfield Coll., London) 1997, (Univ. of East Anglia) 1997. *Address:* House of Lords, Westminster, London, SW1A 0PW, England. *Telephone:* (20) 7219-0793 (Office). *Fax:* (20) 7219-6156 (Office). *E-mail:* mundeng@parliament.uk (Office).

STICH, Michael; German tennis player; b. 18 Oct. 1968, Pinneberg; m. Jessica Stockmann 1992; Nat. Jr Champion 1986; turned professional 1988; semi-finalist, French Open 1990; mem. W German Davis Cup Team 1990; won first professional title, Memphis 1990; winner, Men's Singles Championship, Wimbledon 1991; Men's Doubles (with John McEnroe, q.v., 1992; won ATP World Championship 1993; retd 1997; won 28 professional titles and over 12 million dollars in prize money; UN Amb. 1999–; German Davis Cup team Capt. Oct. 2001–Sept. 2002. *Address:* Ernst-Barlach-Strasse 44, 2200 Elmshorn, Germany.

STICH, Otto, DEcon; Swiss politician; b. 10 Jan. 1927, Dornach, Canton Solothurn; m.; two c.; ed Basle; teacher –1971; mem. Dornach Accounts Audit Comm. 1953; Communal Councillor and part-time Mayor of Dornach 1953–65; Prefect of Dornach-Thierstein 1961–70; mem. Nat. Council (Fed.

Parl.) 1963–83, mem. External Trade Cttee 1965–71 (Chair. 1969–71), Finance Cttee 1971–77, 1982–83, Econ. Affairs Cttee 1978–81, fmr mem. other cttees.; Fed. Councillor Dec. 1983–, Head Fed. Dept of Finance 1984–95, Vice-Pres. Fed. Council 1987, Pres. of Swiss Confed. Jan.–Dec. 1988, Jan.–Dec. 1994; Chair. of Ministers, IMF Group of 10; joined Swiss SDP 1947, Chair. Solothurn cantonal party 1968–72, mem. Man. Cttee of Swiss SDP 1970–75, Vice-Chair. parl. party 1980; Chair. Trade Union Group of Asscn of Staffs of Pvt. Transport Firms and Swiss Railwaymen's Asscn; Man. Cen. Personnel Dept, Co-op Switzerland 1971–80, Deputy Dir and Head of Personnel and Training Dept 1980.

STICH, Stephen Peter, PhD; American professor of philosophy and cognitive science; b. 9 May 1943, New York; s. of Samuel J. Stich and Sylvia L. Stich; m. Judith Ann Gagnon 1971; one s. one d.; ed Univ. of Pennsylvania, Princeton Univ.; mem. staff Univs. of Mich. 1968–78, Md 1978–86, Calif. at San Diego 1986–89; Prof. of Philosophy and Cognitive Science, Rutgers Univ., 1989–, Bd of Govs Prof. 1998–, Dir Research Group on Evolution and Higher Cognition; Adjunct Prof., City Univ. of New York Grad. Center 1994–97; Pres. Soc. for Philosophy and Psychology 1982–83; Fulbright Sr Research Scholar 1978–79; Fellow, Center for Advanced Study in the Behavioral Sciences 1983–84; Visiting Fellow, Research School of Social Sciences, Australian Nat. Univ. 1992; Erskine Fellow, Canterbury Univ., Christchurch, NZ 1996. *Publications:* From Folk Psychology to Cognitive Science 1983, The Fragmentation of Reason 1990, Philosophy and Connectionist Theory (Co-author) 1991, Deconstructing The Mind 1996, Mindreading 2003. *Address:* Department of Philosophy, Davison Hall, Douglass Campus, Rutgers University, New Brunswick, NJ 08901 (Office); 55 Liberty Street, Apt. 8-A, New York, NY 10005, USA (Home). *Telephone:* (732) 932-9091. *Fax:* (212) 571-4838 (Office); (732) 932-8617. *E-mail:* stich@ruccs.rutgers.edu (Office). *Website:* ruccs .rutgers.edu/archivefolder/research%20group/research.html (Office); www .rci.rutgers.edu/~stich/ (Home).

STICHT, J. Paul; American business executive (retd); b. 3 Oct. 1917, Clairton, Pa; s. of Joseph P. and Adah M. Sticht; m. A. Ferne Cozad 1940; two s.; ed Grove City Coll. and Univ. of Pittsburgh Graduate School; started as shipping clerk, U.S. Steel Co. 1939, industrial engineer 1941–44; Air Transport Command, TWA airlines div. 1944–48; Vice-Pres. Campbell Soup Co. 1949–57, Int. Pres. 1957–60; Exec. Vice-Pres. Federated Dept Stores 1960–65, Vice-Chair. 1965–67, Pres. 1967–72; Chair Exec. Cttee and Dir R. J. Reynolds Industries Inc. 1972–73, Pres., COO and Dir 1973–78, Pres., CEO and Dir 1978–79, Chair. 1979–84, CEO 1979–83; Acting Chair. R. J. R. Nabisco March–Oct. 1987, Feb. 1989, CEO 1989; Pres. Castle Springs Inc., Winston Salem 1992–; fmr Chair. Caribbean/Latin American Action; fmr Chair. Nat. Chamber Foundation; fmr Dir Textron Inc., Chrysler Corpn; fmr Sr mem. The Conference Bd Inc.; Visitor, Wake Forest Univ. School of Medicine, Fuqua School of Business of Duke Univ.; Chair. of Trustees, Grove City Coll. *Leisure interests:* golf, boating, fishing. *Address:* Castle Springs Inc., 119 Brookstown Avenue, Winston Salem, NC 27101 (Office); 11732 Lake House Court, North Palm Beach, FL, USA (Home).

STICKLER, HE Cardinal Alfons, S.D.B.; Austrian ecclesiastic; b. 23 Aug. 1910, Neunkirchen, Vienna; ordained 1937; consecrated Archbishop (Titular See of Volsinium) 1983; cr. Cardinal 1985; fmr Chief Vatican Librarian and Archivist; Priest of S. Giorgio di Velabro. *Address:* Piazza del S. Uffizio 11, 00193 Rome, Italy. *Telephone:* (06) 6988-3325.

STIGLITZ, Joseph Eugene, PhD, FBA; American professor of economics; b. 9 Feb. 1943, Gary, Ind.; s. of Nathaniel D. Stiglitz and Charlotte Fishman; m. Jane Hannaway 1978; two s. two d.; ed Amherst Coll., Mass. Inst. of Tech. and Univ. of Cambridge (Fulbright Scholar); Prof. of Econs Cowles Foundation, Yale Univ. 1970–74; Visiting Fellow, St Catherine's Coll. Oxford 1973–74; Prof. of Econs Stanford Univ. 1974–76, 1988–2001, Joan Kenney Prof. of Econs 1992–2001; Oskar Morgenstern Distinguished Fellow, Inst. of Advanced Studies, Princeton 1978–79; Drummond Prof. of Political Econ. Univ. of Oxford 1976–79; Prof. of Econs Princeton Univ. 1979–88; Prof. of Econs, Columbia Business School, Columbia Univ. 2001–; mem. Pres.'s Council of Econ. Advisers 1993–95, Chair. 1995–97; Special Adviser to Pres. of World Bank, Sr Vice-Pres. and Chief Economist 1995–2000; Special Adviser, Bell Communications Research, numerous consultancies in public and pvt. sector, editorial Bd memberships etc.; Sr Fellow Brookings Inst. 2000–; Fellow American Acad. of Arts and Sciences, NAS, Econometric Soc., American Philosophical Soc., Inst. for Policy Research (Sr Fellow 1991–93); Guggenheim Fellow 1969–70; Hon. DHL (Amherst Coll.) 1974; Dr. hc (Univ. of Leuven), (Ben Gurion Univ.); John Bates Clark Award, American Econ. Asscn 1979; Int. Prize, Lincei, Rome 1988; UAP Scientific Prize, Paris 1989; Nobel Prize for Econs (Jt recipient) 2001. *Publications include:* Globalization and its Discontents, Economics of the Public Sector 2000, Principles of Economics 1997, Rethinking the East Asia Miracle (co-ed.) 2001; other books and more than 300 papers in learned journals. *Address:* Brookings Institute, 1775 Massachusetts Avenue NW, Washington DC, 20036, USA (Office).

STIGWOOD, Robert Colin; Australian business executive; b. 16 April 1934, Adelaide; s. of Gordon Stigwood and Gwendolyn Stigwood (née Burrows); ed Sacred Heart Coll., Adelaide; est. Robert Stigwood Orgn. (RSO) 1967; formed RSO Records 1973; founder, Music for UNICEF; TV Producer in England and USA of The Entertainer and The Prime of Miss Jean Brodie; Chair. of Bd Stigwood group of cos.; Key to cities of Los Angeles and Adelaide; Tony Award

1980 for Evita; Int. Producer of the Year, ABC Interstate Theatres Inc. *Producer of films:* Jesus Christ Superstar, Bugsy Malone, Gallipoli, Tommy, Saturday Night Fever, Grease, Sergeant Pepper's Lonely Hearts Club Band, Moment by Moment, Times Square, The Fan, Grease 2, Staying Alive, Evita. *Producer of stage musicals:* Hair, Oh! Calcutta, The Dirtiest Show in Town, Pippin, Jesus Christ Superstar, Evita, Grease (London) 1993, Saturday Night Fever. *Leisure interests:* tennis, swimming, sailing, reading. *Address:* c/o Robert Stigwood Organization, Barton Manor, East Cowes, Isle of Wight, PO32 6LB, England.

STIHL, Hans Peter; German business executive; b. 18 April 1932, Stuttgart; s. of Andreas Stihl and Maria Giersch; m.; ed Technische Hochschule, Stuttgart; Chair. and partner, Andreas Stihl Fabrik; Pres. Deutsche Industrie und Handelstag, Bonn 1988–2000, Hon. Pres. 2001–; Vice-Pres. Inst. of German Economy, Cologne 1983–88, Treas. 1983–88; Pres. IHK Stuttgart 1990–2001, Hon. Pres. 2001–; mem. Man. Bd Verein Deutscher Maschinen- und Anlagenbau (VDMA) until 1988; numerous other business and professional appointments. *Address:* Badstrasse 115, 71336 Waiblingen, Germany.

STILL, Ray; American oboist; b. 12 March 1920, Elwood, Ind.; s. of Roy R. Still and Lillian Taylor; m. Mary Powell Brock 1940; two s. two d.; ed Juilliard School of Music and privately under Phillip Memoli and Robert Bloom; oboist, Kansas City Philharmonic Orchestra 1939–41; mil. service 1941–46; Buffalo Philharmonic Orchestra 1947–49; Prof. of Oboe and mem. Baltimore Symphony 1949–53; solo oboist, Chicago Symphony Orchestra 1953–93; Prof. of Oboe, Northwestern Univ. 1960–; Conductor, Stratford Music Festival, Canada 1964–69; mem. of a Quintet for 100th anniversary of Yamaha Co., recordings, Tour of Japan, judge int. oboe competition, Japan 1988; has undertaken coaching of many symphony orchestra wind and brass sections; judges oboe competitions in New York, Toulon, Munich, Toronto and Japan. *Recordings include:* Oboe Quartettes (with Perlman, Zuckermann, Harrel) and Mozart Oboe Concerto with Chicago Symphony Orchestra, conducted by Claudio Abbado, Ray Still – A Chicago Legend – Baroque Oboe Sonatas. *Leisure interests:* collecting classical comedy films, listening to great jazz artists of '20s, '30s and '40s, records of great lieder singers. *Address:* c/o Chicago Symphony Orchestra, 220 South Michigan Avenue, Chicago, IL 60604; 585 West Hawthorne Place, Chicago, IL 60657, USA.

STILLER, Ben; American actor and film director; b. 30 Nov. 1965, New York; s. of Jerry Stiller and Ann Meara; m.; one d.; ed Univ. of California at Los Angeles. *Films:* Empire of the Sun 1988, Reality Bites (also Dir) 1994, Happy Gilmore 1996, Flirting with Disaster 1996, The Cable Guy (also Dir) 1996, Zero Effect 1998, Your Friends and Neighbors 1998, There's Something About Mary 1998, Permanent Midnight 1998, Mystery Men 1999, Black and White 1999, Meet the Parents 2000, Keeping the Faith 2000, Zoolander (also Dir) 2001, The Royal Tenenbaums 2001. *Television:* The Ben Stiller Show (Emmy Award) 1990–93. *Address:* c/o United Talent Agency, 9560 Wilshire Boulevard, Suite 500, Beverly Hills, CA 90212, USA (Office).

STILWELL, Richard Dale, MUS.B.; American baritone; b. 6 May 1942, St Louis; s. of Otho John Clifton and Tressie (née Parrish) Stilwell; m. 1st Elizabeth Louise Jencks 1967 (divorced); m. 2nd Kerry M. McCarthy 1983; ed Anderson Coll., Univ. of Indiana; with Metropolitan Opera Co., New York 1970–; appearances in maj. roles Washington Opera Soc., Marseilles Opera Co., Santa Fe Opera, San Francisco Opera Co., Paris Opera Co., La Scala, Covent Garden, Hamburg State Opera, Glyndebourne Opera Festival, Van. Opera Co., Chicago Opera Co., Tanglewood Festival, Israel Philharmonic, Boston Symphony, LA Philharmonic, etc.; soloist with Nat. Symphony, Washington, Chicago Symphony, American Symphony, Carnegie Hall, Boston Symphony, LA Philharmonic, etc.; mem. American Guild Musical Artists; Nat. Soc. of Arts and Letters award 1963, Fisher Foundation award Metropolitan Opera Auditions 1965. *Address:* c/o Columbia Artists Management, Arbib Division, 165 W 57th Street, New York, NY 10019, USA.

STING; British singer, bass-player, songwriter and actor; b. Gordon Matthew Sumner, 2 Oct. 1951, Northumberland; m. 1st Frances Tomelty (divorced 1984); five c.; m. 2nd Trudie Styler 1992; ed Warwick Univ.; fmr primary school teacher, Cramlington, Newcastle; singer, bass-player and songwriter for The Police (rock group) 1977–86; has undertaken maj. tours in UK, Europe and USA; Stage debut in The Threepenny Opera 1989; Hon. DMus (Northumbria) 1992; Ivor Novello Award for Best Song 'They Dance Alone' 1989, four songwriting awards (BMI) 1998; Brit Award for Outstanding Contrib. to Music 2002; Emmy Award for Best Performance (Sting in Tuscany... All This Time) 2002. *Film appearances include:* Brimstone and Treacle 1984, Quadrophenia, The Bride of Frankenstein, Plenty, Dune 1985, The Adventures of Baron von Munchausen 1989, Stormy Monday 1989, Rosencrantz and Guildenstern are Dead, Resident Alien, The Music Tells You, The Grotesque, Mercury Falling 1996. *Albums include:* (with Police) Regatta De Blanc, Ghost in the Machine, Synchronicity, (solo) Dream of the Blue Turtles, The Soul Cages, Ten Summoner's Tales. *Singles include:* Nothing Like the Sun 1987, The Soul Cages 1991, Englishman in New York, After the Rain has Gone 2000. *Publication:* Jungle Stories: The Fight for the Amazon 1989. *Address:* Kathryn Shenker Associates, 12th Floor, 1776 Broadway, New York, NY 10019, USA (Office); c/o Publicity Department, Polydor Records, 72 Black Lane, London, W6, England. *Telephone:* (20) 8910-4800.

STIPE, Michael; American rock musician; b. 4 Jan. 1960, Decatur, Ga; ed Univ. of Georgia; lead singer and song writer R.E.M. band 1980–; owner C-

OO (film co.); numerous awards. *Albums include:* (for IRS): Murmur 1982–83, Document; (for Warner): Green 1988, Out of Time 1991, Automatic for the People 1992, Monster 1994, New Adventures in Hi-Fi 1996, Up 1998. *Address:* R.E.M., PO Box 8032, Athens, GA 30603 (Office); c/o Warner Bros. Records, 3300 Warner Boulevard, Burbank, CA 91505, USA.

STIRLING, Sir Angus Duncan Aeneas, Kt, CBIM, FRSA; British arts administrator; b. 10 Dec. 1933, London; s. of late Duncan Alexander Stirling and of Lady Marjorie Stirling; m. Armyne Morar Helen Schofield 1959; one s. two d.; ed Eton Coll., Trinity Coll. Cambridge, London Univ.; mem. staff Christie, Manson & Woods Ltd 1954–57, Lazard Bros. and Co. Ltd 1957–66; Asst Dir Paul Mellon Foundation for British Art 1966–69, Jt Dir 1969–70; Deputy Sec.-Gen. Arts Council of GB 1971–79; Deputy Dir-Gen. The Nat. Trust 1979–83, Dir-Gen. 1983–95; Sr Policy Adviser Nat. Heritage Memorial Fund 1996–97; Dir Royal Opera House, Covent Garden 1979–96, Chair. 1991–96, Chair. Friends of Covent Garden 1981–91, Deputy Chair. Royal Ballet Bd 1988–91; Chair. Greenwich Foundation for the Royal Naval Coll. 1996–, Policy Cttee, Council for Protection of Rural England (CPRE) 1996–2001, Jt Nature Conservation Cttee 1997–2002; mem. Crafts Council 1980–85, Council of Man. Byam Shaw School of Art 1965–89, Man. Cttee Courtauld Inst. of Art 1981–83, 2002–, Advisory Cttee London Symphony Orchestra 1979–, Bd of Govs Live Music Now 1982–89, Council Royal School of Church Music 1996–98, Fabric Advisory Cttee, Wells Cathedral 2001–; Trustee The Theatres Trust 1983–91, Heritage of London Trust 1983–95, Samuel Courtauld Trust 1984–, World Monuments Fund UK 1996–, Stowe House Preservation Trust 1998–. *Leisure interests:* music, travel, walking. *Address:* 25 Ladbroke Grove, London, W11 3AY, England. *Telephone:* (20) 8269-4750 (Office).

STIRN, Olivier, LenD; French politician; b. 24 Feb. 1936, Boulogne-Billancourt; s. of Alexandre Stirn and Geneviève Dreyfus; m. Evelyn Toledano 1989; one s. one d. (and two s. from previous m.); ed Univ. of Paris, Institut de Sciences Politiques; Deputy for Calvados 1968–86 (Gen. Councillor 1994–), for Manche 1986–88; Councillor Gen., Mayor of Vire 1971–; Sec. of State for Parl. Relations 1973, for Overseas Territories 1974–78, for Foreign Affairs 1978–81, for Defence 1980–81; Minister Del. for Overseas Territories May–June 1988, Minister Del. attached to Minister of Industry and Territorial Devt 1988–89, to Minister of Industry, Territorial Devt and Tourism (with special responsibility for Tourism) 1989–90; Amb. to Council of Europe, Strasbourg 1991–93; Business Consultant 1993–; Pres. EOS Conseil Int. 1998–; Int. Adviser Rothschilds 1998–; Chevalier Légion d'honneur and many foreign decorations. *Publications:* Le piège (with Bernard Stasi and J. P. Soisson) 1973, Une certaine idée du centre 1985, Tourisme: chance pour l'économie, risque pour les sociétés? *Leisure interests:* tennis, golf, history. *Address:* 14 Avenue Pierre 1er de Serbie, 75116 Paris, France (Office). *Telephone:* 1-47-20-41-57 (Office); 1-47-20-41-93 (Office). *Fax:* 1-47-20-41-93 (Office). *E-mail:* olivier.stirn.eos@libertysurf.fr (Office).

STIRRUP, Air Marshall Sir Graham Eric (Jock), KCB, AFC, FRAeS; British air force officer; b. 4 Dec. 1949; s. of William Hamilton Stirrup and Jacqueline Brenda Stirrup (née Coulson); m. Mary Alexandra Elliot 1976; one s.; ed Merchant Taylors' School, Northwood, RAF Coll., Cranwell, Jt Service Defence Coll., Royal Coll. of Defence Studies; Qualified Flying Instructor 1971–73; Loan Service, Sultan of Oman's Air Force 1973–75; Fighter Reconnaissance Pilot 1976–78; Exchange Pilot USAF 1978–81; Flight Commdr 1982–84; Officer Commdr No. II (Army Co-operation), Squadron 1985–87; Dir Air Force Plans and Programmes, Ministry of Defence 1994–97; Air Officer Commdr No 1 Group 1997–98; Asst Chief of Air Staff 1998–2000; Deputy C-in-C, Stike Commdr, Commdr NATO Combined Air Operations Centre 9 and Dir European Air Group 2000–02; Deputy Chief of Defence Staff (Equipment Capability) 2002–03; Chief of Air Staff 2003–. *Leisure interests:* golf, music, theatre, history. *Address:* c/o Ministry of Defence, Main Building, Whitehall, London, SW1A 2HB, England (Office).

STITZER, H. Todd; American business executive; m. Marenda Stitzer; two c.; ed Harvard Univ., Univ. of Columbia; Asst Gen. Counsel Cadbury Schweppes Beverages N America 1983, Vice-Pres. and Gen. Counsel, Worldwide Beverages Stream 1988, Group Devt Dir responsible for Strategic Planning and External Devt, UK 1991–93, Vice-Pres. Marketing and Strategic Planning N America 1993–95, COO N America 1995–97; Pres. and CEO Dr Pepper/Seven Up 1997–2000; Chief Strategy Officer Cadbury Schweppes 2000–02, Deputy CEO 2002–03, CEO May 2003–. *Address:* Cadbury Schweppes PLC, 25 Berkeley Square, London, W1J 6HB, England (Office). *Telephone:* (20) 7409-1313 (Office). *Fax:* (20) 7830-5200 (Office). *Website:* www.cadburyschweppes.com (Office).

STOCKHAUSEN, Karlheinz; German composer; b. 22 Aug. 1928, Mödrath bei Cologne; s. of Simon Stockhausen and Gertrud Stupp; m. 1st Doris Andreae 1951; one s. three d.; m. 2nd Mary Bauermeister 1967; one s. one d.; ed Cologne Nat. Music Conservatory, Univs. of Cologne and Bonn; worked with Olivier Messiaen and with the "Musique Concrète" Group in Paris 1952–53; with Westdeutscher Rundfunk Electronic Music Studio, Cologne 1953–, Artistic Dir 1963–77; first composition of purely electronic music (Studie 1 for sinewaves) 1953; Co-ed. Die Reihe (Universal Edn) 1954–59; lecturer at the Int. Summer School for New Music, Darmstadt 1955–74; concert tours throughout the world since 1958; Founder and Artistic Dir Cologne Courses for New Music 1963–68; f. ensemble for live electronic music 1964–; Int. World Fair Expo 70, Osaka; Prof. of Composition Staatliche Hochschule für Musik, Cologne 1971–77; Stockhausen annual courses for composers and interpreters of music, Kürten 1998–; mem. Royal Swedish Acad., Akademie der Künste, Berlin, American Acad. and Inst. of Arts and Letters and others; Hon. mem. Royal Acad. of Music, London; Bundesverdienstkreuz (1st Class), Commdr, Ordre des Arts et des Lettres (France) 1985; Hon. PhD (Freie Univ. Berlin) 1966; many prizes including Preis der deutschen Schallplattenkritik 1964, Grand Prix du Disque 1968, Diapason d'Or 1983, UNESCO Picasso Medal 1992, Polar Music Prize 2001. *Compositions:* 296 works including Chöre für Doris 1950, Drei Lieder (alto voice and chamber orchestra) 1950, Choral (chorus) 1950, Sonatine (violin and piano) 1951, Kreuzspiel 1951, Formel (orchestra) 1951, Etude (musique concrète) 1952, Schlagtrio 1952, Spiel (orchestra) 1952, Punkte (orchestra) 1952 (new version 1962), Klavierstücke I-IV 1952–53, Kontra-Punkte (ten instruments) 1952–53, Elektronische Studien 1953–54, Klavierstücke V-X 1954–61, Zeitmasze (five woodwind) 1955–56, Gruppen (three orchestras) 1955–57, Klavierstück XI 1956, Gesang der Jünglinge (electronic) 1955–56, Zyklus (percussionist) 1959, Refrain (three players) 1959, Carré (four orchestras and four choruses) 1959–60, Kontakte (piano, percussion and/or electronic sounds) 1959–60, Originale (musical theatre) 1961, Momente (soprano, four choral groups and 13 instrumentalists) 1962–64, Plus Minus 1963, Mikrophonie 1 (tam-tam, two microphones, two filters and potentiometers) 1964, Mixtur (orchestra, four sine-generators and ring-modulators) 1964, Mikrophonie II (choir, Hammond organ and four ring-modulators) 1965, Stop (orchestra) 1965, Telemusik (electronic music) 1966, Solo (melodic instrument and feedback) 1966, Adieu (wind quintet) 1966, Hymnen (electronic and concrete music with or without soloists) 1966–67, Prozession (tam-tam, viola, electronium, piano, filters and potentiometers) 1967, Ensemble (process planning) 1967, Kurzwellen (six players) 1968, Stimmung (six vocalists) 1968, Aus den sieben Tagen (fifteen compositions of intuitive music) 1968, Musik für ein Haus (process planning) 1968, Spiral (soloist with short-wave receiver) 1968, Dr. K-Sextett 1969, Fresco (four orchestral groups) 1969, Hymnen Dritte Region (electronic music with orchestra) 1969, Pole (two players/singers) 1970, Expo (three players/singers) 1970, Mantra (two pianists) 1970, Sternklang (park music for 5 groups instrumentalists/singers), Trans (orchestra) 1971, Für kommende Zeiten (17 texts of intuitive music) 1968–70, Alphabet for Liège (13 musical pictures for soloists and duos) 1972, 'Am Himmel wandre ich' (12 American Indian songs) 1972, Ylem (19 or more players) 1972, 'Atmen gibt das Leben' (choir with orchestra or tape) 1974, Inori (Adorations for soloists and orchestra) 1973–74, Herbstmusik (4 players) 1974, Musik im Bauch (six percussionists and music boxes) 1975, Tierkreis (12 melodies of the star-signs) 1975, Harlekin (clarinet) 1975, The Little Harlequin (clarinet) 1975, Sirius (electronic music and trumpet, bass-clarinet, soprano and bass) 1975–77, Amour (5 pieces for clarinet or flute) 1976, Jubiläum (for orchestra) 1977, In Freundschaft 1977, Licht, die sieben Tage der Woche (for solo voices/instruments, dancers, choir, orchestra, ballet, electronic and concrete music) 1977–, an operatic cycle that includes Donnerstag aus Licht 1981, Samstag aus Licht 1984, Montag aus Licht 1988, Dienstag aus Licht 1991, Freitag aus Licht 1996, Mittwoch aus Licht 1998 and other scenes for a combination of forces, Sonntag aus Licht Lichter – Wasser (for soprano, tenor and orchestra with synthesizer) 1999, Engel-Prozessionen for choir a capella 2002, Hoch-Zeiten for choir and orchestra 2003; over 100 records; from 1991 a complete CD edn of all his works was being released. *Publications:* Texte zur Musik (10 vols) 1952–62, 1963–70, 1970–77, 1977–84, 1984–91, Stockhausen on Music – Lectures and Interviews 1989, Towards a Cosmic Music 1990. *Address:* Kettenberg 15, 51515 Kürten (Office); Stockhausen-Verlag, 51515 Kürten, Germany. *Telephone:* (2268) 1813 (Office). *Fax:* (2268) 1813 (Office). *Website:* www.stockhausen.org (Office).

STOCKMAN, David Allen, BA; American politician and administrator; b. 10 Nov. 1946, Fort Hood, Tex.; s. of Allen Stockman and Carol (Bartz) Stockman; m. Jennifer Blei 1983; two d.; ed Michigan State Univ., East Lansing and Harvard Univ. Divinity School; Special Asst to Congressman John Anderson 1970–73; Exec. Dir Republican Conf., House of Reps. 1972–75; mem. House of Reps. from 4th Dist of Mich. 1977–79, mem. Interstate and Foreign Commerce Cttee, Admin. Cttee; Chair. Republican Econ. Policy Task Force 1977–81; Dir U.S. Office of Man. and Budget 1981–85; with Salomon Bros. 1985–88; Sr Man. Dir The Blackstone Group 1988–99; Man. Partner Stockman and Co. 1988–; f. Heartland Industrial Partners 1999–; mem. Nat. Comm. on Air Quality 1978; Jefferson Award 1981. *Publication:* The Triumph of Politics: Why the Reagan Revolution Failed 1986. *Address:* Heartland Industrial Partners, 320 Park Avenue, Floor 33, New York, NY 10022, USA (Office).

STOCKTON, 2nd Earl of; **Alexander Daniel Alan Macmillan,** FBIM, FRSA; British publisher, farmer and politician; b. 10 Oct. 1943, Oswestry; s. of the late Maurice Victor Macmillan (Viscount Macmillan of Ovenden) and of Dame Katherine Macmillan (Viscountess Macmillan of Ovenden), DBE; grandson of the late 1st Earl of Stockton (fmrly, as Harold Macmillan, Prime Minister of UK 1957–63); m. 1st Hélène Birgitte Hamilton 1970 (divorced 1991); one s. two d.; m. 2nd Miranda Elizabeth Louise Nuttall 1995; ed Eton Coll. and Paris and Strathclyde Univs; Sub.-Ed. Glasgow Herald 1963–65; Reporter, Daily Telegraph 1965–67, Foreign Corresp. 1967–68, Chief European Corresp., Sunday Telegraph 1968–70; Dir Birch Grove Estates Ltd 1969–86, Chair. 1983–89; Dir Macmillan and Co. Ltd 1970–76, Deputy Chair. 1976–80, Chair. 1984–90, Pres. 1990–; Chair. Macmillan Publrs. Ltd 1980–90 (Pres. 1990–), St Martin's Press, New York 1983–88 (Dir 1974–90), Sidgwick and Jackson 1989–90; mem. European Parl. for SW of England 1999–; Chair. Cen. London

Training & Enterprise Council 1990–95; Dir Book Trade Benevolent Soc. 1976–88, Chair. Bookrest Appeal 1978–86; Dir United British Artists Ltd 1984–90 (Chair. 1985–90); mem. Lindemann Fellowship Cttee 1979– (Chair. 1983–), British Inst. of Man. 1981–, Council of Publrs. Asscn 1985–88, Carlton Club Political Cttee 1975–88 (Chair. 1984); Gov. Archbishop Tenison's School 1979–86, Merchant Taylor's School 1980–82, 1990–, English Speaking Union 1980–84, 1986–93; Liveryman Worshipful Co. of Merchant Taylors 1972, Court Asst 1987, of Stationers 1973, Master 1991–92; Hon. DLitt (De Montfort) 1993, (Westminster) 1995; Hon. DUniv (Strathclyde) 1993. *Leisure interests:* shooting, fishing, aviation. *Address:* European Parliament, ASP 8E107, Rue Wiertz, 1047 Brussels, Belgium (Office); Porters South, 4–6 Crinan Street, London, N1 9XW (Office); Hayne Manor, Stowford, Okehampton, Devon, EX20 4DB, England (Home). *Telephone:* (2) 284-76-83 (Brussels) (Office); (20) 7833-4000 (Porters) (Office); (1566) 783563 (Home); (20) 7881-8000. *Fax:* (2) 284-96-83 (Brussels) (Office); (1566) 783568 (Home); (20) 7881-8001. *E-mail:* estockton@europarl.eu.int (Office); l.ferguson@macmillan.uk (Home). *Website:* www.alexstockton.com (Office).

STOFILE, Rev. Makhenkesi Arnold, MA, M.THEOL.; South African lecturer in theology; b. 27 Dec. 1944, Winterburg, Adelaide Dist, East Cape; s. of Simon Stofile and Miriam Stofile; m. Nambita Stofile 1977; one s. (deceased) two d.; ed Univ. of Fort Hare; worked as a farm labourer and machine operator; joined ANC 1970; active in student politics, sport and church matters; arrested and sentenced to 11 years' imprisonment 1986; later returned to Fort Hare as a lecturer in religious studies; MP 1994; Govt Chief Whip 1994–96; Premier of Eastern Cape 1997–. *Dancing:* (with wife) Ballroom Dancing Champions for Black South African Univs. *Leisure interests:* rugby, boxing. *Address:* Office of the Premier, Bisho, Eastern Cape Province (Office); 143 Queens Road, King Williams Town, 5600, South Africa (Home). *Telephone:* (40) 6092207 (Office). *Fax:* (40) 6351166 (Office). *E-mail:* premier@otpmlegl.ecape.gov.za (Office). *Website:* www.ecprov.gov.za (Office).

STOIBER, Edmund, DJur; German politician and lawyer; b. 28 Sept. 1941, Oberaudorf; m. Karin Stoiber; three c.; ed Univ. of Munich and Hochschule für Politische Wissenschaft; personal counsellor to Bavarian State Minister for Devt 1972–74, Dir of Ministerial Office 1974; entered Bavarian Parl. 1974; admitted solicitor 1978; Gen. Sec. Christian Social Union (CSU) 1978–83; Campaign Man. for Franz Josef Strauss, Fed. Elections 1980; State Sec. and Dir Bavarian State Chancellery 1982–86, State Minister and Dir 1986–88; Bavarian State Minister for Internal Affairs 1988–93, Minister-Pres. of Bavaria 1993–; Chair. CSU 1999–; Cand. in Chancellery elections 2002; mem. Bd Bayern Munich (football team); Bayerischer Verdienstorden. *Publications:* Politik aus Bayern 1976, Der Hausfriedensbruch im Licht akt. Probleme 1984. *Leisure interests:* skiing, football. *Address:* Christlich-Soziale Union (CSU), Nymphenburger str. 64, 80335 Munich, Germany. *Telephone:* (89) 1243215. *Fax:* (89) 1243216. *E-mail:* edmund.stoiber@csu-bayern.de (Office). *Website:* www.csu.de (Office).

STOICHEFF, Boris Peter, OC, PhD, FRS, FRSC; Canadian professor of physics; b. 1 June 1924, Bitol, Yugoslavia (now Macedonia); s. of Peter Stoicheff and Vasilka Stoicheff (née Tonna); m. Lillian Joan Ambridge 1954; one s.; ed Jarvis Collegiate Inst., Toronto, Canada and Univ. of Toronto; Postdoctoral Fellow, Physics, Nat. Research Council, Ottawa 1951–53, Research Officer 1953–64; Visiting Scientist, MIT, USA 1963–64; Prof. of Physics, Univ. of Toronto 1964–89, Univ. Prof. 1977–89, Prof. Emer. 1989–; Chair., Eng Science 1972–77; I.W. Killam Scholar 1977–79; Visiting Scientist, Stanford Univ., USA 1978; Exec. Dir, Ont. Laser and Lightwave Research Centre 1988–91; UK and Canada Rutherford Lecturer 1989; professional interests include lasers, atomic and molecular spectroscopy and structure, light scattering and two-photon processes, nonlinear optics and generation of ultraviolet radiation; determined structures of many molecules by light scattering and discovered inverse Raman effect and stimulated Brillouin scattering (or the generation of sound by light); mem. Gov. Council of Nat. Research Council, Ottawa 1977–83; Pres. Optical Soc. of America 1976, Canadian Asscn of Physicists 1983; Vice-Pres. IUPAP 1993–96; Co-Foreign Sec., Royal Soc. of Canada 1995–2000; Hon. Foreign mem. American Acad. of Arts and Sciences 1989; Hon. Fellow, Indian Acad. of Sciences, Macedonian Acad. of Sciences and Arts, Hon. DSc (Skopje) 1982, (York Univ., Canada) 1982, (Univ. of Windsor, Canada) 1989, (Toronto) 1994; Medal of Achievement in Physics, Canadian Asscn of Physicists 1974, William F. Meggers Medal 1981, Frederic Ives Medal, Optical Soc. of America 1983, Henry Marshall Tory Medal, Royal Soc. of Canada 1989, Distinguished Service Award, Optical Soc. of America 2002. *Publications:* over 180 scientific Publs in int. journals. *Leisure interests:* travel, art, music. *Address:* Department of Physics, University of Toronto, Toronto, Ont., M5S 1A7 (Office); 66 Collier Street, Apt. 6B, Toronto, Ont., M4W 1L9, Canada (Home). *Telephone:* (416) 978-2948 (Office); (416) 923-9622 (Home). *Fax:* (416) 978-2537 (Office).

STOKER, Sir Michael George Parke, Kt, CBE, MA, MD, FRS, FRSE, FRCP; British medical researcher; b. 4 July 1918, Taunton, Somerset; s. of S. P. Stoker and D. Stoker (née Nazer); m. Veronica Mary English 1942; three s. two d.; ed Sidney Sussex Coll., Cambridge and St Thomas's Hosp., London; Capt. RAMC 1942–47; lecturer in Pathology, Univ. of Cambridge 1947–58, Fellow of Clare Coll., Cambridge 1948–58; Prof. of Virology, Univ. of Glasgow 1959–68; Dir Imperial Cancer Research Fund Labs., London 1968–79; Visiting Prof., Univ. Coll., London 1968–79; Fellow Clare Hall, Cambridge 1978, Pres. 1980–87; Foreign Sec., Vice-Pres. Royal Soc. 1976–81; mem. Gen. Cttee Int. Council of Scientific Unions 1977–82, Scientific Cttee, Ludwig Inst. for Cancer Research 1985–91; Chair. Governing Body Strangeways Research Lab. 1981–93; Foreign mem. Czech. Acad. of Sciences; Hon. Foreign mem. American Acad. of Arts and Sciences; Hon. DSc (Glasgow) 1982; Mendel Gold Medal 1984. *Publications:* over 150 articles and reviews on virology, oncology and cell biology. *Leisure interest:* painting. *Address:* 3 Barrington House, Southacre Drive, Cambridge, CB2 2TY, England.

STOKER, Richard, JP, FRAM, ARCM; British composer, author, poet and painter; b. 8 Nov. 1938; s. of late Capt. Bower Morrell Stoker and of Winifred Harling; m. 1st Jacqueline Margaret Trelfer (divorced 1985); m. 2nd Dr. Gillian Patricia Watson 1986; ed Breadalbane House School, Castleford, Huddersfield School of Music and School of Art, Royal Acad. of Music; studied with Sir Lennox Berkeley at RAM and Nadia Boulanger in Paris (Mendelssohn Scholar 1962); Prof. of Composition RAM 1963–86 (tutor 1970–80); Composition teacher St Paul's School 1972–74, Magdalene Coll., Cambridge 1974–76; APC Assoc. Prof. of Composition 1984–; Ed. Composer Magazine 1969–80; mem. Composers' Guild 1962– (mem. Exec. Cttee 1969–80), RAM Guild Cttee 1994– (Hon. Treas. 1995–); mem. European-Atlantic Group 1993–, Byron Soc. 1993–, Magistrates' Asscn 1995–, English and Int. PEN 1996–; mem. and Treas. Steering Cttee Lewisham Arts Festival 1990, 1992; two exhbns. (as artist); Founder-mem. Atlantic Council 1993, Creative Rights Alliance 2001–; Nat. Library of Poetry (USA) Ed.'s Choice Award 1995, 1996, 1997; American Biographical Inst. Man of the Year Award 1997; numerous awards for music 1950–. *Works include:* Johnson Preserv'd (opera), three string quartets, three piano trios, Organ Symphony, Piano Concerto, Piano Variations, two piano sonatas, A York Suite, Partita for Mandolin and Harp, two overtures, Benedictus, three violin sonatas, Sonatina for Guitar, Organ Partita, Three Improvisations, Kristallnacht Monody, Songs of Love and Loss, Music that Brings Sweet Sleep, Four Shakespeare Songs, Four Yeats Songs, Aspects of Flight, Make Me a Willow Cabin, Canticle of the Rose, A Chinese Canticle (Szuma Chien), Ecce Homo, Proverbs, O Be Joyful, A Landscape of Truth, Zodiac Variations, Regency Suite, A Poet's Notebook; recordings of Sonatina for clavichord and piano, Eric Parkin's Eight Piano Works, Four Piano Duos and Five Song Cycles, etc.; music for film and stage includes: Troilus and Cressida, Portrait of a Town, Garden Party, My Friend–My Enemy; compositions on the Internet. *Publications:* Portrait of a Town 1974, Words Without Music 1974, Strolling Players 1978, Open Window–Open Door 1985, Tanglewood 1990, Between the Lines 1991, Diva 1992, Collected Short Stories 1993, Thomas Armstrong—A Celebration 1998, Turn Back the Clock 1998, poems in numerous anthologies. *Leisure interests:* squash, skiing, tennis, swimming. *Address:* c/o Ricordi & Co. (London) Ltd, 210 New King's Road, London, SW6 4NZ, England. *Telephone:* (20) 7371-7501. *Fax:* (20) 7371-7270. *E-mail:* gps5@tutor.open.ac.uk (Office).

STOKES, Baron (Life Peer), cr. 1969, of Leyland in the County Palatine of Lancaster; **Donald Gresham Stokes,** Kt, TD, DL, F.R.ENG., FIMechE, FICE; British engineer and business executive; b. 22 March 1914, London; s. of Harry Potts Stokes; m. 1st Laura Lamb 1939 (died 1995); one s.; m. 2nd Patricia Pascall 2000; ed Blundell's School and Harris Inst. of Tech., Preston; student engineer Leyland Motors 1930–33; Tech. Asst 1933–39; mil. service 1939–45; Export Man. Leyland Motors 1946–50, Gen. Sales and Service Man. 1950, Dir 1954; Man. Dir Leyland Motors Corpn 1963, Chair. 1967; Man. Dir British Leyland Motors Corpn 1968–73, Chair. 1968–75, Chief Exec. 1973–75, Pres. British Leyland Ltd 1975–80, Consultant 1980–81; fmr Chair. British Leyland UK Ltd, NV Leyland Industries Belgium SA, NV British Leyland (Belgium) SA, British Leyland Motors Inc. USA; Chair. British Arabian Advisory Co. Ltd 1977–85, Two Counties Radio Ltd 1979–84 (Pres. 1984–90, Chair. 1990–94); Chair. Jack Barclay Ltd and Jack Barclay (Service) Ltd 1980–90; fmr Dir British Leyland Motor Corpn of Australia Ltd, Leyland Motor Corpn of S. Africa Ltd, NZ Motor Corpn, Ashok Leyland Ltd India, Ennore Foundries Ltd India, British Leyland Motors Canada Inc., Automóviles de Turismo Hispano Ingleses SA, Metalúrgica de Santa Ana, British Leyland France SA, Leyland Motor Corpn (Malawi) Ltd; Dir Nat. Westminster Bank Ltd 1969–81, OPUS Public Relations Ltd 1979–85, Scottish and Universal Investments Ltd 1980–92, The Dutton-Forshaw Motor Group Ltd 1980–90 (Chair. 1981–90), KBH Communications Ltd 1985 (Chair. 1987–96), Beherman Auto-Transports N.V. 1982–89, The Dovercourt Motor Co. 1982–90, GWR Group PLC 1990–94; Vice-Pres. Empresa Nacional de Autocamiones SA (Spain) 1969–73; mem. Council of Soc. of Motor Mfrs and Traders 1953, Vice-Pres. 1961, Pres. 1962, Deputy Pres. 1963; mem. Worshipful Co. of Carmen 1964, North West Econ. Planning Council 1967–70, EDC for the Motor Mfg Industry 1967, Nat. Advisory Council for the Motor Mfg Industry 1967; Vice-Pres. Eng Employers Fed. 1967–75, Inst. of Motor Industry 1967; Vice-Pres. UMIST 1968, Pres. 1972; Deputy Lt for the Lancashire County Palatine 1968; Deputy Chair. Ind. Reorganization Corpn 1968–71; Vice-Pres. IMechE 1971, Pres. 1972; Cdre Royal Motor Yacht Club, Poole 1979–81; Fellow, Inst. of Road Transport Engineers 1968, Pres. 1982–84; Fellow Royal Acad. of Eng; Hon. Fellow, Keble Coll., Oxford 1968; Officier, Ordre de la Couronne (Belgium); Commdr, Ordre de Léopold II (Belgium) 1972; Hon. LLD (Lancaster Univ.); Hon. DTech (Loughborough); Hon. DSc (Southampton and Salford); UK Marketing Award 1964. *Leisure interest:* yachting. *Address:* 2 Branksome Cliff, Westminster Road, Poole, Dorset, BH13 6JW, England.

STOKES, Kerry Matthew, AO, FAIM; Australian business and broadcasting executive; b. 13 Sept. 1940, Vic.; s. of M. P. Stokes; m. Peta Toppano; two s.; ed St George's Christian Boys Coll., WA Tech. Coll.; Dir, mem. Sydney Dance

Co. 1980; Chair. Australian Capital Equity Pty Ltd (Dir 1981–), Austrim Ltd, Golden West Network (TV), Westrac Equipment Pty Ltd; Chair. Canberra Theatre Trust 1981–86, Dir 1989–91; fmr Dir V.A. Holdings Ltd; Chair. Art Gallery Foundation, WA 1989–91; Chair. The Fed. Capital Press Pty Ltd (Canberra Times), Seven Network Ltd 1995–, Exec. Chair. Seven Network Ltd 1999–; Chair. Corp. Gifts Cttee SCITECH 1987–89, Dir 1989–91; Pres. Appeal Campaign for Inst. for Child Health Research; founder, mem. council Nat. Gallery of Australia, Chair. 1996–; Citizen of the Year Award 1994. *Publications:* Boyer Lectures (Advance Australia Where) 1994. *Leisure interests:* photography, sailing, scuba diving. *Address:* Seven Network Ltd, 14th Floor, 1 Pacific Highway, N Sydney, NSW 2060; c/o Australian Capital Equity Pty Ltd, Level 3, 30 Kings Park Road, West Perth, WA 6005, Australia.

STOL, Marten; Netherlands university professor; b. 10 Nov. 1940, Oldekerk; m. Rose C. van Wyngaarden 1968; one s. one d.; ed Gymnasium, Middelburg and State Univ. Leiden; Research Assoc. State Univ. Leiden 1968–70, Asst Prof. 1970–82; Research Assoc. Chicago Assyrian Dictionary, Oriental Inst., Univ. of Chicago 1973–74; Prof. of Akkadian (Assyriology), Ugaritic and History of Ancient Near East, Free Univ. Amsterdam 1983–; Gen. Sec. Soc. Ex Oriente Lux 1973–99; mem. Royal Netherlands Acad.; Hon. mem. American Oriental Soc. 1999. *Publications:* Studies in Old Babylonian History 1976, On Trees, Mountains and Millstones in the Ancient Near East 1979, Letters from Yale 1981, Letters from Collections in Philadelphia, Chicago and Berkeley 1986, Epilepsy in Babylonia 1993, Langs 's Heeren wegen 1997, Birth in Babylonia and the Bible 2000. *Address:* Heivlinder 27, 2317 JS Leiden, Netherlands.

STOLER, Andrew L., BS, MBA; American international organization official; ed George Washington Univ., Georgetown Univ.'s School of Foreign Service; with Office of Int. Trade Policy, Dept of Commerce 1975–79; Dir for Canada, Australia and New Zealand, U.S. Trade Rep. Office 1980–81, MTN Codes Co-ordinator, Geneva 1982–87, Deputy Asst U.S. Trade Rep. for Europe and Mediterranean, Washington 1988–89, Deputy Chief of Mission, Geneva 1989–99 (concurrently Deputy Perm. Rep. to World Trade Org.); Deputy Dir-Gen. World Trade Org. 1999–2002. *Address:* c/o World Trade Organization, 154 rue de Lausanne, 1211 Geneva 21, Switzerland (Office).

STOLL, Jean-François; French civil servant; b. 19 Jan. 1950, Isle-Adam; m. Noëlle Nicolas 1976; four c.; ed Inst. of Political Studies, Paris, Nat. School of Admin.; joined Ministry of Econ., Commercial Attaché Indonesia 1982–84, Tech. Adviser 1982–86, Commercial Adviser Mexico 1987–90, Tech. Adviser 1990–93, Head Service for Promotion of External Trade 1993, Dir External Econ. Relations 1998, Dir-Gen. Econ. and Trade Dept 2001–; Dir Electricité de France (EDF) 1999–; Chevalier Ordre Nat. du Mérite. *Address:* Ministry of the Economy, Finance and Industry, 139 rue de Bercy, 75572 Paris Cédex 12; 6 rue d'Ulm, 75005 Paris, France (Home). *Telephone:* 1-40-04-04-04. *Fax:* 1-43-43-75-97.

STOLLEY, Paul David, MD, M.P.H.; American professor of medicine; b. 17 June 1937, Pawling, New York; s. of Herman Stolley and Rosalie Chertock; m. Jo Ann Goldenberg 1959; one s. two d.; ed Lafayette Coll., Cornell Univ. Medical School and Johns Hopkins School of Public Health; medical officer, U.S. Public Health Service 1964–67; Asst and Assoc. Prof. of Epidemiology, Johns Hopkins School of Public Health 1968–76; Herbert C. Rorer Prof. of Medical Science, Univ. of Pa School of Medicine 1976–90; Prof. and Chair. Dept of Epidemiology, Univ. of Md 1991–; fmr mem. Editorial Bd New England Journal, Milbank Quarterly; fmr Assoc. Ed. Clinical Pharmacology and Therapeutics; Pres. American Coll. of Epidemiology 1987–88; mem. Inst. of Medicine, NAS, Soc. for Epidemiologic Research (Pres. 1984), Int. Epidemiology Asscn (fmr Treas.), Johns Hopkins Soc. of Scholars, Science Advisory Cttee to Fed. Drugs. Admin. Commr 1993; Hon. MA (Pennsylvania) 1976. *Publications:* Case Control Studies (co-author) 1982, Foundations of Epidemiology (co-author) 1994, Epidemiology 1994, Investigating Disease Patterns 1995 (received American Medical Writers Asscn Award 1996) and numerous articles on epidemiological subjects. *Leisure interests:* classical music, history, literature. *Address:* University of Maryland School of Medicine, 660 W Redwood Street, Baltimore, MD 21201; 6424 Brass Knob, Columbia, MD 21044, USA (Home). *Telephone:* (410) 997-9567 (Home). *Fax:* (410) 997-9574 (Home).

STOLOJAN, Theodor, PhD, DEcon; Romanian politician and economist; b. 24 Oct. 1943, Tîrgoviste; s. of Theodor Stolojan and Nadejda Stolojan; m. Elena Stolojan; one s. one d.; ed Acad. of Econ. Studies, Coll. of Finances, Credit and Accountancy, Bucharest; worked as economist, Ministry of the Food Industry 1966–72; first as economist and then as Chief of Division, State Budget Dept, Ministry of Finance 1972–82, then Deputy Dir, Dir of Dept Foreign Currencies and Int. Financial Relations 1982–87, Gen. Insp. Dept of State Revenues 1988–89, First Deputy Minister of Finance 1989–90, Minister of Finance 1990–91; Pres. of Nat. Agency of Privatization –1991; Prime Minister of Romania 1991–92; economist, later Sr Economist, IBRD 1992–98; Pres. Tofan Corporated Finance 1999–2000; Partner Strategic Consulting Ltd; Prof. Transylvanian Univ., Braşov. *Publications:* Integration and European Fiscal Policy 2002; numerous studies. *Leisure interests:* skiing, travelling in mountains, jogging. *Address:* Aurel Vlaicu 42-44, Apt. 3, Sector 2, Bucharest, Romania. *Telephone:* (1) 3124343.

STOLPE, Manfred; German politician; b. 16 May 1936, Stettin, Germany (now Szczecin, Poland); m. Ingrid Ehrhardt; one d.; legal studies in Jena and Berlin; formerly in charge of organizational work of Protestant Church in East

Germany; Consistorial Pres. Berlin-Brandenburg Church 1982–90; active in human rights movt; joined Social Democratic Party (SPD) 1990; Minister-Pres. of Brandenburg 1990–2002; Fed. Minister of Transport, Building and Housing 2002–; Dr hc; Carlo-Schmid Prize 1991. *Address:* Ministry of Transport, Building and Housing, Invaliedenstr. 44, 10115 Berlin, Germany. *Telephone:* (30) 20082000. *Fax:* (30) 20082019. *E-mail:* buergerinfo@bmvbw .bund.de. *Website:* www.bmvbw.bund.de.

STOLTE, Dieter; German television administrator and professor; b. 18 Sept. 1934, Cologne; ed Univs. of Tübingen and Mainz; Head of Science Dept, Saarländischer Rundfunk 1961–62; Personal adviser to Dir-Gen. of Zweites Deutsches Fernsehen (ZDF) 1962, Controller, Programme Planning Dept 1967, Programming Dir 1976–82, Dir-Gen. ZDF March 1982–; Dir and Deputy Dir Gen., Südwestfunk 1973; Prof. Univ. of Music and Presentation Arts, Hamburg 1980–; mem. Admin. Council, German Press Agency (dpa), Hamburg, European Broadcasting Union (EBU); Chair. Admin. Council TransTel, Cologne; Chair. Bd Dirs. DeutschlandRadio, Cologne; mem. Int. Broadcast Inst., London; mem. Council, Nat. Acad. of TV Arts, New York; Int. Acad. of Arts and Sciences, New York; Int. Emmy Directorate Award 1997; Bundesverdienstkreuz, Officer's Cross, Golden Order of Merit (Austria), Bavarian Order of Merit, Hon. Citizen of State of Tenn., USA; Köckritz Prize 1999, Verdienstorden, Berlin 1999, Robert Geissendorfer Prize 2001. *Publications:* ed. and co-author of several books on programme concepts and function of television, etc.; several essays on subjects relating to the philosophy of culture and the science of communication. *Address:* ZDF-Strasse, 55100 Mainz (Office); Essenheimerstrasse, P.O. Box 40 40, 6500 Mainz, Germany (Home). *Telephone:* (6131) 702000.

STOLTENBERG, Jens; Norwegian politician; b. 16 March 1959, Oslo; m. Ingrid Schulerud; two c.; journalist, Arbeiderbladet (nat. daily) 1979–81; information sec., Oslo Labour Party 1981; exec. officer, Statistics Norway 1989–90; Lecturer in Econs, Univ. of Oslo 1989–90; mem. Cen. Bd, Labour Youth League (AUF) 1979–89, Leader, AUF 1985–89; Vice-Pres. Int. Union of Socialist Youth 1985–89; mem. Cen. Bd, Labour Party 1985–, Deputy Leader 1992–; Leader, Oslo Labour Party 1990–92; mem. Storting (Parl.) for Oslo 1993–; State Sec., Ministry of Environment 1990–91; Minister of Trade and Energy 1993–96; Minister of Finance 1996–97; Prime Minister of Norway 2000–01; mem. Storting Standing Cttee on Social Affairs 1991–93; Leader, Storting Standing Cttee on Oil and Energy Affairs 1997–2000; mem. Defence Comm. 1990–92. *Address:* c/o Office of the Prime Minister, Akersgatan 42, P.O. Box 8001 Dep., 0030 Oslo, Norway.

STOLTENBERG, Thorvald; Norwegian politician and diplomatist; b. 8 July 1931, Oslo; s. of Emil Stoltenberg and Ingeborg Stoltenberg; m. Karin Stoltenberg 1957; one s. two d.; joined Foreign Service 1959; served in San Francisco, Belgrade, Lagos and Foreign Ministry; Int. Sec. Norwegian Fed. of Trade Unions 1970–71; Under-Sec. of State, Foreign Ministry 1971–72, 1976–79; Under-Sec. of State, Ministry of Defence 1973–74, Ministry of Commerce 1974–76; Minister of Defence 1979–81, of Foreign Affairs 1987–89, 1990–93; Amb. to UN, New York 1989–90; UN High Commr for Refugees 1989–90; Special Rep. for UN Sec.-Gen. in fmr Yugoslavia 1993–94; Co-Chair. Steering Cttee, Int. Conf. on the Fmr Yugoslavia 1993–96; Amb. to Denmark 1996–99; Pres. Norwegian Red Cross; Chair. Bd of Int. Inst. for Democracy and Electoral Assistance. *Address:* Norwegian Red Cross, PO Box 1, Groenland, 0133 Oslo, Norway (Office). *Telephone:* 22-05-40-00 (Office). *Fax:* 22-05-40-40 (Office).

STONE, Francis Gordon Albert, CBE, ScD, FRS; British professor of chemistry; b. 19 May 1925, Exeter; s. of Sidney Charles Stone and Florence Stone; m. Judith M. Hislop 1956; three s.; ed Christ's Coll., Univ. of Cambridge; Fulbright Scholarship, Univ. of Southern Calif. 1952–54; Instructor and Asst Prof., Harvard Univ. 1954–62; Reader, Queen Mary Coll., Univ. of London 1962–63; Head, Dept of Inorganic Chem. and Prof., Univ. of Bristol 1963–90, Prof. Emer. 1990–; Robert A. Welch Distinguished Prof. of Chem. Baylor Univ., Texas 1990–; Visiting Prof., numerous univs.; Pres. Dalton Div., Royal Soc. of Chem. 1981–83; Guggenheim Fellow 1961; Sr Visiting Fellow, Australian Acad. of Sciences 1966; mem. Council, Royal Soc. of Chem. 1968–70, 1981–83, Chem. Cttee, Science and Eng Research Council 1971–74, 1982–85; mem. Council of Royal Soc. 1986–88 (Vice-Pres. 1987–88); Hon. DSc (Exeter, Waterloo) 1992, (Durham, Salford) 1993, (Zaragoza) 1994; Royal Soc. of Chem. Medals for Organometallic Chem. 1972, Transition Metal Chem. 1979, Chugaev Medal and Diploma, Kurnakov Inst., USSR Acad. of Sciences 1978; ACS Award in Inorganic Chem. 1985, Davy Medal of Royal Soc. 1989. *Publications:* over 700 articles in scientific journals and books; Advances in Organometallic Chemistry, Vols 1–47 (Ed.); Comprehensive Organometallic Chemistry, Vols 1–9 (Co-Ed.) 1982, Comprehensive Organometallic Chemistry II, Vols 1–13 (Co-Ed.) 1995. *Leisure interest:* travel. *Address:* 60 Coombe Lane, Bristol, BS9 2AY, England; 88 Hackberry Avenue, Waco, TX 76706, USA. *Telephone:* (117) 968-6107 (England); (254) 752-3617 (USA).

STONE, John O., BA, BSc; Australian politician, financial executive, public servant and columnist; b. 31 Jan. 1929, Perth; s. of Horace Stone and Eva Stone (née Hunt); m. Nancy Hardwick 1954; four s. one d.; ed Univ. of Western Australia and New Coll., Oxford; Rhodes Scholar 1951; Asst to Australian Treasury Rep. in London 1954–56, Australian Treasury Rep. in London 1958–61; in Research and Information Div., Gen. Financial and Econ. Policy Branch, Dept of Treasury, Canberra 1956–57, in Home Finance Div. 1961–62, Asst Sec. Econ. and Financial Surveys Div. 1962–66; Exec. Dir for Australia,

New Zealand and S. Africa, Int. Monetary Fund (IMF) and IBRD—World Bank 1967–70; First Asst Sec., Revenue, Loans and Investment Div., Treasury 1971; Sec. Australian Loan Council, Sec. Australian Nat. Debt Comm. 1971; Deputy Sec. (Econ.) Treasury 1971–76, Deputy Sec. Treasury 1976–78, Sec. 1979–84; Visiting Prof. Centre of Policy Studies, Monash Univ., Melbourne 1984; Consultant, Potter Partners, Stockbrokers 1985–87; weekly columnist Melbourne Herald, Sydney Morning Herald 1985–87, The Australian 1987–89, Sunday Telegraph 1989, The Australian Financial Review 1990–98, Adelaide Review 1998–; Dir Sperry (Australia) Ltd 1985–87, Peko-Wallsend Ltd 1986–87; Chair. J. T. Campbell & Co. Ltd 1994–96; Senator for Queensland 1987–90; mem. Defence Efficiency Review 1996–97; Leader of Nat. Party in the Senate, Shadow Minister for Finance; Sr Fellow, Inst. of Public Affairs, Melbourne 1985–87, 1990–95; James Webb Medley Prize, Oxford Univ. 1953. *Publication:* Upholding the Australian Constitution, Proceedings of the Samuel Griffith Society, Vols 1–14 1992– (Ed. and Publr). *Leisure interests:* reading, wine and food. *Address:* 17 Fitzsimmons Avenue, NSW 2066, Australia. *Telephone:* (2) 9428-1311. *Fax:* (2) 9420-0063 (Home). *E-mail:* j_o_stone@bigpond.com (Home).

STONE, Norman, MA; British historian; b. 8 March 1941, Glasgow; s. of late Norman Stone and Mary Robertson Stone (née Pettigrew); m. 1st Marie-Nicole Aubry 1966 (dissolved 1977); two s.; m. 2nd Christine Booker (née Verity) 1982; one s.; ed Glasgow Acad. and Gonville & Caius Coll., Cambridge; research student, Christ's Coll., Cambridge attached to Austrian and Hungarian insts. 1962–65; Research Fellow, Gonville & Caius Coll. 1965–67; Asst Lecturer, Faculty of History, Univ. of Cambridge 1967–72, lecturer in History (Russian) 1973–84; Fellow, Jesus Coll., Cambridge and Dir of Studies in History 1971–79; Fellow, Trinity Coll., Cambridge 1979–84; Prof. of Modern History, Univ. of Oxford and Fellow, Worcester Coll., Oxford 1984–97; Prof. of Int. Relations, Bilkent Univ., Ankara 1997–; Wolfson Prize 1976, Order of Merit (Poland) 1993. *Publications:* The Eastern Front 1914–17 1976, Hitler 1980, Europe Transformed 1878–1919 1982, Czechoslovakia: Crossroads and Crises (Ed.) 1989, The Other Russia (with Michael Glenny) 1990, articles in the press. *Leisure interests:* music, Eastern Europe, languages, Turkey. *Address:* Bilkent University, 06533 Bilkent, Ankara, Turkey (Office); 22 St Margaret's Road, Oxford, OX2 6RX England (Home). *Telephone:* (1865) 439481 (Oxford). *Fax:* (312) 2664326 (Ankara).

STONE, Oliver, BFA; American film director and screenwriter; b. 15 Sept. 1946, New York; s. of Louis Stone and Jacqueline Goddet; m. 1st Najwa Sarkis (divorced); m. 2nd Elizabeth Stone (divorced); ed Yale Univ. and New York Univ. Film School; Teacher, Cholon, Vietnam 1965–66; U.S. Merchant Marine 1966, U.S. Army, Vietnam 1967–68; Taxi Driver, New York 1971. Wrote screenplay for films Midnight Express (Acad. Award for best screenplay adapted from another medium) 1978, Conan the Barbarian (co-wrote) 1982, Scarface 1983. Directed and wrote films: Seizure 1973, The Hand 1981, Year of the Dragon (with Michael Cimino) 1985, Salvador (co-wrote) 1986, Platoon (Acad. Awards for Best Film, Best Dir) 1986, Wall Street 1987, Talk Radio (co-wrote) 1988, Born on the Fourth of July 1989 (Acad. Award for Best Dir 1990), No One Here Gets Out Alive 1990, The Doors 1991, JFK 1991, Heaven and Earth 1993, Natural Born Killers 1994, Nixon 1995, A Child's Night Dream 1997, U-Turn 1998, Saviour 1998; producer Reversal of Fortune, Iron Maze, South Central, Zebrahead, Wild Palms (TV series) 1993, New Age 1994, The People vs Larry Flynt, Any Given Sunday 2000, Comandante (documentary) 2003; exec. producer Killer: A Journal of Murder 1995, Indictment: The McMartin Preschool 1995. *Address:* Ixtlan, 201 Santa Monica Boulevard, Santa Monica, CA 90401, USA (Office).

STONE, Roger, B.S.(ECON.); American business executive; b. 16 Feb. 1935, Chicago, Ill.; s. of Marvin Stone and Anita Masover; m. Susan Kessert 1955; three d.; ed Wharton School of Finance, Univ. of Pennsylvania; joined Stone Container Corpn 1957, Vice-Pres. Gen. Man. Container Div. 1970–75, Pres. and COO 1975–79, Pres., CEO 1979–98, Chair. 1983–98, Pres., CEO Smurfit Stone Container Corpn 1998–; mem. Bd Dirs. Morton Int., McDonalds Corpn, Option Care Inc.; mem. Advisory Council for Econ. Devt. *Leisure interest:* golf. *Address:* Smurfit Stone Container Corporation, 150 North Michigan Avenue, Chicago, IL 60601-7568, USA. *Telephone:* (312) 346-6600.

STONE, Sharon; American actress; b. 10 March 1958, Meadville, Pa; m. 1st Michael Greenburg 1984 (divorced 1987); m. 2nd Phil Bronstein 1998; one adopted s.; ed high school in Pennsylvania and Edinboro Coll.; film debut in Star Dust Memories; Chevalier, Ordre des Arts et des Lettres. *Films include:* Above the Law, Action Jackson, King Solomon's Mines, Allan Quatermain and the Lost City of Gold, Irreconcilable Differences, Deadly Blessing, Personal Choice, Basic Instinct, Diary of a Hit Man, Where Sleeping Dogs Lie, Sliver, Intersection, The Specialist, The Quick and the Dead, Casino, Last Dance, Diabolique 1996, Sphere, The Mighty 1999, The Muse 1999, Simpatico 1999. *Television appearances include:* Bay City Blues (series), Tears in the Rain (film), War and Remembrance (mini-series), Calendar Girl Murders (film), The Vegas Strip Wars (film). *Address:* c/o Guy McElwaine, P.O. Box 7304, North Hollywood, CA 91603, USA.

STONECIPHER, Harry Curtis, BS; American aircraft industry executive; b. May 1936, Scott Co., Tenn.; ed Tenn. Polytech. Inst.; with GE 1960–61, 1962–86, Martin Aircraft Co. 1961–62; Exec. Vice-Pres. Sundstrand Corpn 1987, Pres. and COO 1987–88, Pres. and CEO 1988–94, Chair. 1991–94, also fmr mem. Bd Dirs.; Pres. and CEO McDonnell-Douglas Corpn, St Louis 1994–97; Pres. and CEO Boeing Co., Seattle 1997–, Pres., CEO and COO

Boeing Corpn 1997–; mem. Bd Dirs. Milacron, Inc.; Fellow Royal Aeronautical Soc.; John R. Allison Award 1996, Rear Adm. John J. Bergen Leadership Medal Nay League 1996. *Address:* Boeing Co. Mail Stop 10–26, Seattle, WA 98124-2207, USA (Office). *Website:* www.boeing.com.

STOPFORD, Michael, MA; British international civil servant; b. 22 June 1953, London; s. of Edward Stopford and Patricia Carrick; ed Oxford Univ.; fmr mem. HM Diplomatic Service, UK Perm. Mission to UN, New York, Second Sec. and Press Attaché, Embassy in Vienna; Assoc. then Second Officer, Exec. Office of Sec.-Gen. of UN 1979–83, Special Projects Officer, Dept of Public Information 1983–87, Chef de Cabinet to Dir-Gen., UN Office in Geneva and Under-Sec.-Gen. for Human Rights 1987–91, Chef de Cabinet to Exec. Del. of Sec.-Gen. for Inter-Agency Humanitarian Programme in Iraq, Kuwait and Iraq–Turkey and Iraq–Iran border areas 1991–92, with Dept for Humanitarian Affairs 1992, Special Asst to Under-Sec.-Gen. for Public Information, Dept of Public Information, UN, New York 1992, Dir UN Information Center, Washington, DC, 1992–95; Chief of Media and Public Relations, Int. Financial Corpn 1996–97; Sr Asst to Pres. for Int. Affairs, American Univ., Washington, DC 1997–. *Address:* American University, 4400 Massachusetts Avenue, NW, Washington, DC 20016, USA (Office). *E-mail:* mjs@american.edu (Office).

STOPPARD, Sir Tom, Kt, OM, CBE, FRSL; British writer; b. Thomas Straussler, 3 July 1937, Zlin, Czechoslovakia; s. of the late Dr Eugene Straussler and Martha Straussler; step-s. of Kenneth Stoppard; m. 1st Jose Ingle 1965 (divorced 1972); two s.; m. 2nd Dr. Miriam Moore-Robinson 1972 (divorced 1992); two s.; ed Pocklington Grammar School, Yorks.; Journalist, Bristol 1954–60; freelance journalist, London 1960–64; mem. Cttee of the Free World 1981–; mem. Royal Nat. Theatre Bd 1989–; Hon. MLitt (Bristol, Brunel Univs.); Hon. LittD (Leeds Univ.) 1979, (Sussex) 1980, (Warwick) 1981, (London) 1982; Dr hc (Kenyon Coll.) 1984, (York) 1984; John Whiting Award, Arts Council 1967, Italia Prize (radio drama) 1968, New York Drama Critics Best Play Award 1968, Antoinette Perry Award 1968, 1976, Evening Standard Awards 1967, 1972, 1974, 1978, 1982, 1993, 1997. *Publications:* plays: Rosencrantz and Guildenstern are Dead 1967, The Real Inspector Hound 1968, Enter a Free Man 1968, After Magritte 1970, Dogg's Our Pet 1972, Jumpers 1972, Travesties 1975, Dirty Linen 1976, New-Found-Land 1976, Every Good Boy Deserves Favour (with music by André Previn, q.v., 1978, Night and Day 1978, Dogg's Hamlet, Cahoots Macbeth 1979, Undiscovered Country 1980, On the Razzle 1981, The Real Thing 1982, Rough Crossing 1984, Dalliance (adaption of Schnitzler's Liebelei) 1986, Hapgood 1988, Arcadia 1993 (Evening Standard Award for Best Play), Indian Ink 1995, The Invention of Love 1997, The Seagull (trans. 1997), The Coast of Utopia (trilogy: Part One: Voyage, Part Two: Shipwreck, Part Three: Salvage) 2002; radio plays: The Dissolution of Dominic Boot 1964, M is for Moon Among Other Things 1964, Albert's Bridge 1967, If You're Glad I'll be Frank 1968, Where Are They Now? 1970, Artist Descending a Staircase 1972, The Dog It Was That Died 1983, In the Native State 1991; short stories: Introduction 2 1963; novel: Lord Malquist and Mr. Moon 1966; screenplays: The Romantic Englishwoman (co-author) 1975, Despair 1977; film scripts: The Human Factor 1979, Brazil (with Terry Gilliam, q.v., and Charles McKeown) 1984, Empire of the Sun 1987, Rosencrantz and Guildenstern are Dead 1989 (also Dir), Russia House 1989, Billy Bathgate 1990, Shakespeare in Love (jtly) 1998 (Jt winner Acad. Award Best Original Screenplay 1999, Enigma 2001); television plays: Professional Foul 1977, Squaring the Circle 1984, The Television Plays 1965–84 1993; radio: The Plays for Radio 1964–91, 1994. *Address:* c/o Peters, Fraser & Dunlop Ltd, Drury House, 34–43 Russell Street, London, WC2B 5HA, England.

STORARO, Vittorio; Italian cinematographer; b. 24 June 1940, Rome; ed Centro Sperimentale; started with shorts then moved to feature length films. *Films include:* Giovinezza, Giovinezza 1968, Delitto al Circolo del Tennis, La Strategia del Rango 1969, Il Conformista, L'Eneide 1970, Addio Fratello Crudele 1971, Giornata Nera per l'Ariete 1971, Orlando Furioso 1971, Last Tango in Paris 1972, Bleu Gang. . ., Malizia 1972, Giordano Bruno 1973, Le Orme 1974, Novecento 1974, Scandalo 1975, Agatha, La Luna 1978, Apocalypse Now 1979, Reds (Acad. Award 1981) 1979, Tarzan, the Ape Man 1980, One from the Heart 1981, Wagner 1982, Ladyhawke 1983, The Last Emperor 1984, Tucker: The Man and His Dream, New York Stories (Life Without Zoe), Dick Tracy, The Sheltering Sky, Tosca, Little Buddha, Roma!, Imago Urbis, Flamenco, Taxi, Tango (Cannes Film Festival Award 1998), Bulworth.

STORCH, Marcus, MSc; Swedish business executive; b. 28 July 1942, Stockholm; s. of Hilel Storch and Anna Storch; m. Gunilla Berglund 1972; one d.; ed Royal Inst. of Tech., Stockholm; Dept Head, Welding 1968–72; Pres. Welding Div. AGA AB 1972–75, Pres. Gas Div. 1975–81, Exec. Vice-Pres. AGA AB 1978–81, Pres. and CEO 1981–96; Vice-Chair. Nobel Foundation 1999–, A. Johnson AB, AXFOOD AB; mem. Bd NCC AB, Dagens Industri AB, Acta Oncologica Foundation, AB Stockholm Exchange; Hon. MD. *Address:* Grevgatan 65, 114 59 Stockholm, Sweden. *Telephone:* (8) 661-71-95.

STOREY, David Malcolm; British author and playwright; b. 13 July 1933, Wakefield, Yorkshire; s. of Frank Richmond Storey and Lily (née Cartwright) Storey; m. Barbara Hamilton 1956; two s. two d.; ed Wakefield Grammar School, Wakefield Coll. of Art and Slade School of Art; Fellow, Univ. Coll. London 1974. *Publications:* novels: This Sporting Life (Macmillan Award) 1960, Flight into Camden (John Llewellyn Rhys Memorial Prize 1961, Somerset Maugham Award 1963) 1960, Radcliffe 1963, Pasmore (Faber

Memorial Prize 1972) 1972, A Temporary Life 1973, Saville (Booker Prize 1976) 1976, A Prodigal Child 1982, Present Times 1984; plays: The Restoration of Arnold Middleton (Evening Standard Award 1967), In Celebration 1969 (also film), The Contractor (New York Critics' Prize 1974) 1969, Home (Evening Standard Award, New York Critics' Prize) 1970, The Changing Room (New York Critics' Prize) 1971, Cromwell 1973, The Farm 1973, Life Class 1974, Night 1976, Mother's Day 1976, Sisters 1978, Dreams of Leaving 1979, Early Days 1980, The March on Russia 1989, Stages 1992; poems: Storey's Lives: Poems 1951–1991 1992, A Serious Man 1998. *Address:* c/o Jonathan Cape Ltd, Random Century House, 20 Vauxhall Bridge Road, London, SW1V 2SA, England.

STORK, Gilbert, PhD; American professor of chemistry; b. 31 Dec. 1921, Brussels, Belgium; s. of Jacques Stork and Simone Weil; m. Winifred Elizabeth Stewart 1944 (died 1992); one s. three d.; ed Univ. of Wisconsin; Instructor, Harvard Univ. 1946–48, Asst Prof. 1948–53; Assoc. Prof., Columbia Univ. 1953–55, Prof. 1955–67, Eugene Higgins Prof. of Chem. 1967–92, Prof. Emer. 1992–, Chair. of Dept 1973–76; mem. NAS, American Acad. of Arts and Sciences, American Philosophical Soc., Acad. des Sciences (France); Foreign mem. Royal Soc. 1999; Hon. Fellow, Royal Soc. of Chemistry; Hon. Fellow Pharmaceutical Soc. of Japan; Hon. DSc (Lawrence Coll.) 1961, (Paris) 1979, (Rochester) 1982, (Emory) 1988, (Columbia) 1993, (Wis.) 1997; Award in Pure Chemistry of ACS 1957, Baekeland Medal of N Jersey Section of ACS 1961, Harrison Howe Award 1962, Edward Curtis Franklin Memorial Award of Stanford Univ. 1966, ACS Award in Synthetic Organic Chemistry 1967, Nebraska Award 1973, Roussel Prize 1978, Nichols Medal 1980, Arthur C. Cope Award, ACS 1980, NAS Award in Chemical Sciences 1982, Willard Gibbs Medal 1982, Nat. Medal of Science 1983, Tetrahedron Prize 1985, Roger Adams Award 1991, George Kenner Award 1992, Robert Welch Award 1993, shared Wolf Prize 1995, first Barton Gold Medal, Royal Soc. of Chem. 2002; numerous other awards. *Publications:* The Enamine Alkylation 1963, Enolate Trapping 1965, Stereospecific Synthesis of Reserpine 1989, Stereospecific Synthesis of Quinine 2001. *Leisure interest:* tennis. *Address:* Department of Chemistry, Columbia University, Chandler Hall, New York, NY 10027 (Office); 188 Chestnut Street, Englewood Cliffs, NJ 07632, USA (Home). *Telephone:* (212) 854-2178 (Office); (201) 871-4032 (Home). *Fax:* (212) 932-1289 (Office). *E-mail:* gjs8@columbia.edu (Office).

STORM, Colin A.; British business executive; b. 26 June 1939, Jersey; s. of Archibald Storm and Dorothy Storm (née Lamy); m. Jennifer Pitcher 1965; one s. two d.; joined Guinness Group as Under-Brewer 1961, various posts in Personnel Dept 1966–76, Personnel Man. Guinness GB 1976–84, Personnel Dir 1984, later Personnel Dir Guinness Brewing Worldwide, Man. Dir Guinness Brewing Int. 1990–92, Man. Dir Guinness Ireland Group 1992–97, Deputy Man. Dir Guinness Brewing Worldwide and Man. Dir Guinness GB 1997–98, Chief Exec. Guinness 1998–; mem. Exec. Cttee, Dir and CEO Diageo PLC; Vice-Pres. Exec. Cttee Middx Young People's Clubs; mem. Inst. of Personnel Man. *Leisure interests:* sailing, fishing. *Address:* Diageo PLC, 8 Henrietta Place, London, W1G 0NB, England (Office). *Telephone:* (20) 7927-5200 (Office). *Fax:* (20) 7927-4600 (Office).

STORM, Kornelis (Kees), MA, CPA; Netherlands business executive; b. 6 June 1942, Amsterdam; m.; two d.; ed Univ. of Rotterdam; chartered accountant Moret & Limperg 1970–76; mem. Exec. Bd Kon. Scholten-Honig NV 1976–78, AGO 1978–83; mem. Exec. Bd AEGON NV 1983–93, Chair. 1993–2002; Chair. Supervisory Bd Koninklijke Wessanen NV; Chair. Laurus NV; mem. Supervisory Bds AEGON NV, KLM NV, PON Holding BV, Interbrew SA. *Publication:* Management With a Smile. *Address:* AEGON NV, Mariahoeveplein 50, PO Box 202, 2501 The Hague (Office); Vondellaan 24, 2111 CP Aerdenhout, Netherlands (Home). *Telephone:* (70) 3448287 (Office); (23) 5242619 (Home). *Fax:* (70) 3448271 (Office); (23) 5248076 (Home). *Website:* www.aegon.com (Office).

STÖRMER, Horst Ludwig, PhD; German physicist; b. 6 April 1949, Frankfurt am Main; s. of Karl-Ludwig Stormer and Marie Ihrig; m. Dominique A. Parchet 1982; ed Univ. of Stuttgart; with tech. staff AT&T Bell Labs. 1977–83, head of Dept 1983–91, Dir Physics Research Lab. 1992–; Prof. of Physics and Applied Physics, Columbia Univ. 1998–; Adjunct Physics Dir Lucent Technologies 1997–; Bell Labs. Fellow 1982; Fellow American Physics Soc., American Acad. of Arts and Sciences; Buckley Prize, American Physics Soc. 1984, Otto Klug Prize, Germany 1985; Officier, Légion d'honneur 1999, N.Y.C. Mayor's Award 2000. *Address:* Department of Physics, Columbia University, 538 West 120th Street, New York, NY 10027 (Office); Lucent Technologies, 700 Mountain Avenue, New Providence, NJ 07974, USA. *Website:* www.columbia.edu (Office).

STOTHARD, Sir Peter M., Kt, MA; British journalist and newspaper editor; b. 28 Feb. 1951, Chelmsford; s. of Wilfred Stothard and Patricia Savage; m. Sally Ceris Emerson 1980; one s. one d.; ed Brentwood School, Essex and Trinity Coll. Oxford; journalist, BBC 1974–77; Shell Petroleum 1977–79; business and political writer, Sunday Times 1979–80; Features Ed. and leader writer, The Times 1980–85; Deputy Ed. The Times 1985–92, US Ed. 1989–92, Ed. 1992–2002; Ed. The Times Literary Supplement 2002–; Hon. Fellow Trinity Coll. Oxford 2000. *Leisure interests:* ancient and modern literature. *Address:* The Times Literary Supplement, 1 Pennington Street, London, E98 1TT, England (Office). *Telephone:* (20) 7782-3380.

STOTT, Kathryn Linda, ARCM; British pianist; b. 10 Dec. 1958, Nelson, Lancs.; d. of Desmond Stott and Elsie Cheetham; m. 1st Michael Ardron 1979 (divorced 1983); m. 2nd John Elliot 1983 (divorced 1997); one d.; ed Yehudi Menuhin School (under Marcel Ciampi, Vlado Perlemuter, Louis Kentner) and Royal Coll. of Music, London (under Kendall Taylor); fifth prizewinner, Leeds Int. Piano 1978; has since performed extensively in recitals and concertos both in UK and in Europe, Far East, Australia, Canada and USA; ten appearances at Henry Wood Promenade concerts; 20 recordings including premieres of concertos by George Lloyd and Michael Nyman; Dir Fauré and the French Connection Festival, Manchester 1995, Piano 2000, Manchester 2000, Piano 2003, Manchester 2003; Chevalier Ordre des Arts et Lettres 1996. *Leisure interests:* horse-riding, travel, film noir. *Address:* c/o Jane Ward, 38 Townfield, Rickmansworth, Herts., WD3 7DD, England (Office). *Telephone:* (1923) 493903. *Fax:* (1923) 493903. *E-mail:* ward.music@ntlworld.com (Office). *Website:* www.kathrynstott.com (Office).

STOTT, Richard Keith; British journalist; b. 17 Aug. 1943, Oxford; s. of Fred B. Stott and Bertha Stott; m. Penny Scragg 1970; one s. two d.; ed Clifton Coll., Bristol; Bucks. Herald 1963–65; Ferrari Press Agency 1965–68; reporter Daily Mirror 1968–79, Features Ed. 1979–81, Asst Ed. 1981; Ed. The People 1984–85, 1990–91; Ed. Daily Mirror 1985–89, 1991–92, Today 1993–95; Political and Current Affairs Columnist, News of the World 1997–2000, Sunday Mirror 2001–; British Press Awards Reporter of the Year 1977; What the Papers Say Ed. of the Year 1993. *Publication:* Dogs and Lampposts 2002. *Leisure interests:* theatre, reading. *Address:* 20 Albany Park Road, Kingston-upon-Thames, Surrey, KT2 5SW, England.

STOWE, Madeleine; American actress; b. 18 Aug. 1958, Los Angeles, California; d. of the late Robert Stone and Mireya Mora; m. Brian Benben 1986; one d.; ed Univ. of Southern California; began acting career at Solari Theatre, Beverly Hills; appeared in TV series The Gangster Chronicles, mini-series Beulah Land and TV films The Nativity, The Deerslayer, Amazons, Blood and Orchids. *Films:* Stakeout 1987, Tropical Snow, Worth Winning 1989, Revenge 1990, The Two Jakes 1990, Closet Land 1991, China Moon, Unlawful Entry 1992, The Last of the Mohicans, Another Stakeout, Short Cuts 1993, Blink, Bad Girls, Twelve Monkeys 1995, The Proposition 1998, Dancing About Architecture 1999, Imposter 1999, The General's Daughter 1999, The Magnificent Ambersons 2002, We Were Soldiers 2002. *Address:* c/o David Schiff, UTA, 9560 Wilshire Boulevard, Suite 500, Beverly Hills, CA 90212, USA.

STOYANOV, Petar; Bulgarian politician and lawyer; b. 1952, Plovdiv; m. Antonina Stoyanova; one s. one d.; ed Sofia Univ.; fmr divorce lawyer; became politically active 1989; mem. Union of Democratic Forces (SDS); Deputy Minister of Justice 1992; mem. Parl. 1994–96; Pres. of Bulgaria 1997–2002. *Address:* 2 Dondukov blvd, Sofia 1123, Bulgaria (Office).

STRÅBERG, Hans, MSE; Swedish business executive; b. 1959, Västervik; ed Chalmers Univ. of Technology, Stockholm; Pres. and CEO AB Electrolux. *Leisure interests:* tennis, hunting, cars, family. *Address:* Office of the Chief Executive, AB Electrolux, St Göransgatan 143, Stockholm, Sweden (Office). *Telephone:* (8) 7386400 (Office). *Fax:* (8) 6564478 (Office). *Website:* www .electrolux.com (Office).

STRACHAN, Sir Ian Charles, Kt, MA, MPA; British business executive; b. 7 April 1943, Oldham; s. of Dr. Charles Strachan and Margaret Craig; m. 1st Diane Shafer 1967 (divorced 1987); one d.; m. 2nd Margaret Auchincloss 1987; one step-s. one step-d.; ed Fettes Coll. Edinburgh, Christ's Coll. Cambridge and Princeton and Harvard Univs; Assoc. Ford Foundation, Malaysia 1967–69; various positions, Exxon Corpn 1970–86; Sr Vice-Pres. and Chief Financial Officer, Johnson & Higgins, New York 1986–87; Finance Dir RTZ Corpn PLC 1987–91, Deputy Chief Exec. 1991–95; Man. Dir BTR PLC July–Dec. 1995, Chief. Exec. 1996–99; Deputy Chair. Invensys PLC 1999–2000; Dir (non-exec.) Commercial Union 1992–95, Transocean Sedco Forex 2000–, Reuters Group PLC 2000–. *Leisure interests:* tennis, golf, reading, oriental antiques. *Address:* c/o Reuters Group PLC, 85 Fleet Street, London EC4P 4AJ, England (Office). *Telephone:* (20) 7250-1122 (Office). *Fax:* (20) 7353-3002 (Office). *Website:* www.reuters.com (Office).

STRAKHOV, Vladimir Nikolayevich, D.PHYS.MATH.SC.; Russian physicist; b. 3 May 1932; ed Moscow Inst. of Geological Prospecting; sr engineer, researcher, Head of Lab. Prof. O. Schmidt Inst. of Earth Physics, USSR (now Russian) Acad. of Sciences 1959–89, Dir-Gen. 1989–; Corresp. mem. USSR (now Russian) Acad. of Sciences 1987, mem. 1992; main research in math., geophysics, gravitational and magnetic methods of prospecting mineral deposits, magnetic anomalies of oceans; went on hunger strike in protest at the state of scientific research and its financing 1996; mem. Russian Acad. of Natural Sciences. *Address:* Institute of Earth Physics, Bolshaya Gruzinskaya 10, 123 810 Moscow, Russia. *Telephone:* (095) 252-07-26 (Office).

STRANGE, Curtis Northrop; American golfer; b. 30 Jan. 1955, Norfolk, Va; s. of Thomas Wright Strange Jr and Nancy Neal; m. Sarah Jones; two s.; ed Wake Forest Univ.; turned professional 1976; won Pensacola Open 1979, Sammy Davis Jr Greater Hartford Open 1983, LaJel Classic 1984, Honda Classic, Panasonic-Las Vegas Int. 1985, Canadian Open 1985, Houston Open 1986, Canadian Open, Fed. Express-St Jude Classic, NEC Series of Golf 1987, Sandway Cove Classic, Australia 1988, Ind. Insurance Agent Open, Memorial Tournament, US Open, Nabisco Championships 1988, US Open, Palm Meadows Cup 1989, Holden Classic, Australia 1993; mem. PGA Tour Charity Team, Michelob Championship, Kingsmill 1996; Capt. US Ryder Cup Team 2002 after playing on five Ryder Cup Teams; golf analyst for

ABC Sports 1997–; Golfer of the Year 1986, 1987. *Leisure interests:* hunting, fishing, Harley Davidsons. *Address:* c/o IMG, 1 Erieview Plaza, Suite 1300, Cleveland, OH 44114; PGA America, P.O. Box 109601, 100 Avenue of the Champions, Palm Beach Gardens, FL 33410, USA.

STRÁNSKÝ, Jiří; Czech writer; b. 12 Aug. 1931, Prague; m. Jitka Balíková; one s., one d.; ed High School; manual worker until 1989; political prisoner 1950–58, 1970–72; after 'Velvet Revolution' 1989–, mem. of Confed. of Political Prisoners, Pres. of Czech Centre of Int. PEN 1992–; Chair. M. Havel Foundation; mem. Council for TV, Council for Grants and Devt of Czech Cinematography 2000–; Chevalier, Ordre des Arts et des Lettres 2002;Egon Hostovský Prize 1991, Medal for Merit 2001. *Publications include:* Happiness, Tales 1969, The Land that Became Wild (Zdivočelá země) 1991; prose Auction; script for film Boomerang 1996 (Czech Literary Fund Prize 1998), script for TV play The Uniform 2000. *Leisure interests:* scouting, riding. *Address:* Czech Centre of International PEN, 28 Oct. No. 9, 110 00 Prague 1, Czech Republic.

STRASSER, Valentine E. M.; Sierra Leonean politician and army officer; b. c. 1965, Allen Town, Freetown; m. Gloria Strasser; ed Sierra Leone Grammar School, Gbenguema Mil. School; rank of Capt., retd from army Sept. 1996; mem. mil. junta who overthrew Govt of Pres. Momoh April 1992; Chair. Nat. Provisional Ruling Council 1992–96, also fmr Minister of Defence; student, Warwick Univ., UK 1996.

STRATAS, Teresa, OC; Canadian opera singer; b. 26 May 1938, Toronto, Ont.; d. of Emmanuel Stratas and Argero Stratakis; ed Univ. of Toronto; began singing career in nightclubs in Toronto; début at Toronto Opera Festival 1958; noted opera performances at Metropolitan Opera, New York include Berg's Lulu and Jenny in Brecht and Weill's Mahagonny; appeared as Violetta in Zeffirelli's film of La Traviata 1983; appeared in Broadway musical Rags 1986; cr. role of Marie Antoinette in Ghosts of Versailles, premièred Metropolitan Opera, NY 1992; LLD hc (McMaster Univ.) 1986, (Toronto) 1994, (Rochester) 1998; Drama Desk Award for Leading Actress in a Musical on Broadway 1986–87, Gemini Award for Best Supporting Actress (for Under the Piano) 1997. *Address:* The Ansonia, 2109 Broadway, New York, NY 10023 (Office); c/o Vincent & Farrell Associates, 157 W 57th Street, Suite 502, New York, NY 10019; Metropolitan Opera Company, Lincoln Center Plaza, New York, NY 10023, USA.

STRATHCLYDE, 2nd Baron, cr. 1955; Thomas Galbraith, PC; British politician; b. 22 Feb. 1960; s. of the late Sir Thomas Galbraith and Simone Galbraith; m. Jane Skinner 1992; three d.; ed Sussex House, London, Wellington Coll., Univs. of E Anglia and Aix-en-Provence; insurance broker Bain Clarkson Ltd (fmrly Bain Dawes) 1982–88; Govt Whip House of Lords 1988–89; fmr spokesman for Dept of Trade and Industry, Under-Sec. of State 1993, Minister of State 1994; Parl. Under-Sec. of State Dept of Employment 1989–90, Dept of Environment July–Sept. 1990, 1992, Scottish Office 1990–92; Minister for Tourism 1989–90; Minister for Agric., Fisheries, Highlands and Islands 1990–92; Chief Govt Whip 1994–97; Opposition Chief Whip House of Lords 1997–98, Shadow Leader Dec. 1998–; Conservative cand. European Election, Merseyside E 1984. *Address:* House of Lords, Westminster, London, SW1A 0PW, England. *Telephone:* (20) 7219-5353.

STRAUME, Janis; Latvian politician; b. 1962, Sigulda, Latvia; m.; one s. two d.; ed Riga State Medical Inst.; physician, Riga City clinic, endoscopist, Latvian Diagnostics Centre 1986–90; political activities 1988–; mem. Latvian Human Rights Group Helsinki 86 (Riga Chapter), Latvian Nat. Independence Movt, Citizen's Congress of Latvian Repub., Union of 18th Nov.; mem. Saeima 1990–, Chair. 1999–; Chair., Union for Fatherland and Freedom Faction 1998–. *Address:* Saeima, Jecaba str. 11, 226811 Riga, Latvia. *Telephone:* (2) 708-7111 (Office).

STRAUS, Roger W., Jr; American publisher and editor; b. 3 Jan. 1917, New York; s. of Roger Williams and Gladys (Guggenheim) Straus; m. Dorothea Liebmann 1938; one s.; ed Hamilton Coll., Univ. of Missouri; reporter, Daily Reporter, White Plains, New York 1936, feature writer 1939–40; Editorial Writer, reporter Columbia Missourian 1937–49; Ed., Publr Asterisk 1939; Editorial Asst Current History 1940, Assoc. Ed. 1940–45; Assoc. Ed. Forum 1940–45; Pres. Book Ideas Inc. 1943–45; f. Farrar, Straus & Co. Inc. (now Farrar, Straus & Giroux Inc.) 1945, Pres. 1987–, also CEO; Pres. Hill & Wang 1971–87; Dir Univ. of Missouri Press; Chair. Publishing Bd American Judaism magazine 1955–65; Vice-Pres. Fred L. Lavanburg Foundation 1950–80, Daniel and Florence Guggenheim Foundation 1960–76; mem. Bd of Dirs. Harry Frank Guggenheim Foundation 1970–76, John Simon Guggenheim Foundation, Center for Inter-American Relations; mem. PEN, Emerson Literary Soc., Union of American Hebrew Congregations; Hon. D. Litt. (Missouri) 1976. *Publications:* (Co-Ed.) The Sixth Column 1941, War Letters from Britain 1941, The New Order 1941. *Address:* Farrar, Straus & Giroux Inc., 19 Union Square West, Fourth Floor, New York, NY 10003, USA (Office).

STRAUSS, Botho; German playwright and novelist; b. 2 Dec. 1944, Naumburg; moved with family to Remscheid, Ruhr region; on staff of Theater heute, West Berlin; Dramaturg at Schaubühne Theater, West Berlin 1970–75; Literaturpreis, Bayerische Akademie der Schönen Künste 1981, Mülheimer Drama Prize 1982. *Plays include:* Die Hypochonder (first play, 1971, winner Hannover Dramaturgie Award), Trilogie des Wiedersehens, Gross und Klein

Kalldeway and Der Park, Das Gleichgewicht 1994. *Novels include:* Die Widmung 1979, Rumor 1980, Paare, Passanten 1981, Der Junge Mann 1984, Niemand Anderes 1987.

STRAUSS, Robert Schwarz, LLB; American politician and trade negotiator; b. 19 Oct. 1918, South Central Texas; s. of Charles H. Strauss and Edith V. (née Schwarz) Strauss; m. Helen Jacobs 1941; two s. one d.; ed Univ. of Texas Law School; Special Agent for Fed. Bureau of Investigation (FBI) in Ia, Ohio and Dallas, Tex. 1941–45; admitted to Texas Bar 1941; co-founder of law firm Akin, Gump, Strauss, Hauer and Feld 1945; Pres. Strauss Broadcasting Co. 1965; Dir Archer Daniels Midland, Lone Star Industries, MCA, Memorex Telex; mem. Texas State Banking Bd 1963–68; mem. Advisory Cttee Forstmann Little & Co.; mem. Democratic Nat. Cttee 1968–70, Treas. 1970–72; Chair. 1972–77; U.S. Prin. Trade Negotiator (rank of Amb.) 1977–79; Special Envoy of Pres. to Middle East April–Nov. 1979; Chair. Pres. Carter's Campaign Cttee 1979–80; mem. Nat. Bipartisan Comm. of Cen. America 1983–84; Co-Chair. Nat. Econ. Comm. 1988–; Amb. to Russia 1991–93; partner Akin, Gump, Strauss, Hauer and Feld, Dallas 1945–77, 1981–; Presidential Medal of Freedom 1981. *Leisure interests:* golf, horse racing. *Address:* Akin, Gump, Strauss, Hauer & Feld, 4100 First City Center, Dallas, TX 75201; 1333 New Hampshire Ave, Suite 400, NW, Washington, DC 20036, USA.

STRAUSS-KAHN, Dominique Gaston André; French politician; b. 25 April 1949, Neuilly-sur-Seine; s. of Gilbert Strauss-Kahn and Jacqueline Fellus; m. 3rd Anne Sinclair 1991; one s. three d. from fmr marriages; lecturer Univ. of Nancy II 1977–80; Scientific Counsellor Nat. Inst. of Statistics and Econ. Studies (INSEE) 1978–80; Dir Cerepi (CNRS) 1980–; Prof. Univ. of Paris-X Nanterre 1981; Chief of Financial Services Commissariat Gen., Plan, Asst Commr Plan 1984–86; elected Socialist Deputy Val-d'Oise 1988–91; Pres. of Comm. on Finances, Assemblée Nationale 1988, Minister Del. of Industry and Foreign Trade to the Minister of State, Minister of the Economy, Finance and Budget 1991–92; Minister of Industry and Foreign Commerce 1992–93, of the Econ., Finance and Industry 1997–99; mem. Socialist Party Cttee of Dirs. 1983–, Nat. Sec. 1984–89; mem. Socialist Party Bureau 1995–; Mayor City of Sorcelles (Val d'Oise) 1995–97; apptd. First Deputy Mayor 1997; Chair. Scientific Cttee Jean-Jaurès Foundation 2000–; Special Councellor to Sec.-Gen. OECD 2000–; Dir of Research Nat. Foundation of Political Science 2000–; charged with forgery Oct. 2000; on trial for corruption Oct. 2001. *Publications:* La richesse des Français 1977, Economie de la famille et accumulation patrimoniale 1977, L'epargne et la retraite 1982. *Leisure interests:* piano, cinema, skiing, rugby. *Address:* Parti socialiste, 10 rue de Solférino, 75007 Paris (Office); Fondation Jean-Jaurès, 12 cité Malesherbes, 75009 Paris, France.

STRAW, Rt Hon. Jack (John Whitaker), PC, MP; British politician and lawyer; b. 3 Aug. 1946, Buckhurst Hill, Essex; s. of Walter A. W. Straw and Joan S. Straw; m. 1st Anthea L. Weston 1968 (divorced 1978); one d. (deceased); m. 2nd Alice E. Perkins 1978; one s. one d.; ed Brentwood School, Essex and Univ. of Leeds; Pres. Nat. Union of Students 1969–71; mem. Islington Borough Council 1971–78, Inner London Educ. Authority 1971–74 (Deputy Leader 1973–74); called to Bar, Inner Temple 1972, Bencher 1997, practised as barrister 1972–74; special adviser to Sec. of State for Social Services 1974–76, to Sec. of State for Environment 1976–77; on staff of Granada TV (World in Action) 1977–79; MP for Blackburn 1979–; Opposition Treasury Spokesman 1980–83, Environment 1983–87; mem. Parl. Cttee of Labour Party (Shadow Cabinet) 1987–97; Shadow Sec. of State for Educ. 1987–92, for the Environment (Local Govt) 1992–94; Shadow Home Sec. 1994–97; Home Sec. 1997–2001; Sec. of State for Foreign and Commonwealth Affairs 2001–; mem. Council, Inst. for Fiscal Studies 1983–2000, Lancaster Univ. 1984–92; Vice-Pres. Asscn of District Councils; Visiting Fellow, Nuffield Coll. Oxford 1990–98; Gov. Blackburn Coll. 1990–, Pimlico School 1994–2000 (Chair. 1995–98); Fellow Royal Statistical Soc. 1995–; Labour; Hon. LLD (Leeds) 1999. *Publications:* Policy and Ideology 1993; contribs to pamphlets, newspaper articles. *Leisure interests:* walking, cooking puddings, music. *Address:* Foreign and Commonwealth Office, King Charles Street, London, SW1A 2AH (Office); House of Commons, London, SW1A 0AA, England. *Telephone:* (20) 7219-3000 (Office). *Website:* www.fco.gov.uk (Office).

STRAWSON, Sir Peter Frederick, Kt, FBA, MA; British professor of metaphysical philosophy; b. 23 Nov. 1919, London; s. of Cyril Walter Strawson and Nellie Dora Strawson; m. Grace Hall Martin 1945; two s. two d.; ed Christ's Coll., Finchley, St John's Coll., Oxford; served in the army with rank of Capt. 1940–46; Asst Lecturer in Philosophy, Univ. Coll. of N Wales 1946–47; Lecturer in Philosophy, Univ. Coll., Oxford 1947–48, Fellow and Praelector 1948–68, Univ. Reader in Philosophy 1966–68, Waynflete Prof. of Metaphysical Philosophy and Fellow of Magdalen Coll., Oxford 1968–87; Woodbridge Lecturer, Columbia Univ., USA 1983; Visiting Prof., Collège de France, Paris 1985; Immanuel Kant Lecturer, Munich Univ. 1985; mem. Acad. Europaea 1990; Foreign Hon. mem. American Acad. of Arts and Sciences 1971; Hon. Fellow of St John's and Magdalen Colls; Dr. hc (Munich) 1998; John Locke Prize 1946, Int. Kant Prize, Berlin 2000. *Publications:* Introduction to Logical Theory 1952, Individuals 1959, The Bounds of Sense 1966, Logico-Linguistic Papers 1971, Freedom and Resentment 1974, Subject and Predicate in Logic and Grammar 1974, Naturalism and Skepticism 1985, Analyse et Metaphysique 1985, Analysis and Metaphysics: an Introduction to Philosophy 1992, Entity and Identity 1997. *Leisure interests:* reading, travel.

Address: Magdalen College, Oxford, OX1 4AU; University College, Oxford, OX1 4BH; 25 Farndon Road, Oxford, OX2 6RT, England (Home). *Telephone:* (1865) 276662 (Univ. Coll.); (1865) 515026 (Home).

STREEP, Meryl (Mary Louise), AB, MFA; American actress; b. 22 June 1949, Summit, NJ; d. of Harry Streep, Jr and Mary W. Streep; m. Donald Gummer 1978; one s. three d.; ed singing studies with Estelle Liebling; studied drama at Vassar, Yale School of Drama; stage début in New York in Trelawny of the Wells; 27 Wagons Full of Cotton, New York; New York Shakespeare Festival 1976 in Henry V, Measure for Measure; also acted in Happy End (musical), The Taming of the Shrew, Wonderland (musical), Taken in Marriage and numerous other plays; Hon. Dr (Dartmouth) 1981, (Yale) 1983, (Lafayette) 1985; Commdr, Ordre des Arts et des Lettres 2003; Acad. Award for Best Supporting Actress for Kramer vs. Kramer 1980; Best Supporting Actress awards from Nat. Soc. of Film Critics for The Deer Hunter, New York Film Critics Circle for Kramer vs. Kramer, The Seduction of Joe Tynan and Sophie's Choice; Emmy Award for Holocaust, British Acad. Award 1982, Acad. Award for Best Actress, for Sophie's Choice 1982, Bette Davis Lifetime Achievement Award 1998, Special Award Berlin Int. Film Festival 1999. *Films acted in include:* Julia 1976, The Deer Hunter 1978, Manhattan 1979, The Seduction of Joe Tynan 1979, The Senator 1979, Kramer vs. Kramer 1979, The French Lieutenant's Woman 1980, Sophie's Choice 1982, Still of the Night 1982, Silkwood 1983, Plenty 1984, Falling in Love 1984, Out of Africa 1985, Heartburn 1985, Ironweed 1987, A Cry in the Dark (Best Actress Award, New York Film Critics 1988, Cannes 1989) 1988, The Lives and Loves of a She Devil 1989, Hollywood and Me 1989, Postcards from the Edge 1991, Defending Your Life 1991, Death Becomes Her 1992, The House of the Spirits, The River Wild 1994, The Bridges of Madison County 1995, Before and After, Marvin's Room, One True Thing 1998, Dancing at Lughnasa 1999, Music of the Heart 1999, The Hours 2002, Adaptation (Golden Globe for Best Supporting Actress) 2003. *Plays include:* The Seagull 2001. *Television appearances include:* The Deadliest Season, Uncommon Women, Holocaust, Velveteen Rabbit, First Do No Harm 1997. *Leisure interests:* peace and anti-nuclear causes, gardening, skiing, raising family, visiting art galleries and museums. *Address:* c/o Creative Artists Agency, 9830 Wilshire Boulevard, Beverly Hills, CA 90212, USA.

STREET, Hon. Anthony Austin; Australian business executive and fmr politician; b. 8 Feb. 1926, Victoria; s. of Brig. the Hon. G. A. Street, MC; m. V. E. Rickard 1951; three s.; ed Melbourne Grammar; Royal Australian Navy; primary producer; mem. for Corangamite, House of Reps. 1966–84; Sec. Govt Mems. Defence and Wool Cttees. 1967–71; mem. Joint Parl. Cttee on Foreign Affairs 1969; Chair. Fed. Rural Cttee of Liberal Party 1970–74; mem. Fed. Exec. Council 1971–2; Asst Minister for Labour and Nat. Service 1971–72; mem. Liberal Party Shadow Cabinet for Social Security, Health and Welfare 1973, for Primary Industry, Shipping and Transport 1973, for Science and Tech. and ACT 1974, for Labour 1975; Minister for Labour and Immigration Nov.–Dec. 1975; Minister Assisting the Prime Minister in Public Service Matters 1975–77; Minister for Employment and Industrial Relations 1975–78, for Industrial Relations 1979–80, for Foreign Affairs 1980–83; resgnd from Parl. Jan. 1984; now Man. and Co. Dir. *Leisure interests:* flying, cricket, golf, tennis. *Address:* 153 The Terrace, Ocean Grove, Vic. 3226, Australia (Home).

STREET, Sir Laurence Whistler, AC, KCMG, LLB, QC; Australian lawyer and conciliator; b. 3 July 1926, Sydney, NSW; s. of the late Sir Kenneth Street and Jessie Street; m. 1st Susan Gai Watt 1952, two s. two d.; m. 2nd Penelope Patricia Ferguson 1989; one d.; ed Cranbrook School, Sydney, Univ. of Sydney; served in Royal Australian Navy 1943–47; barrister NSW 1951; lecturer Univ. Sydney Law School 1962–65; QC 1963; Commdr and Inaugural Sr Officer RANR Legal Br. 1964–65, Pres. Courts Martial Appeal Tribunal 1971–74; Judge Supreme Court NSW 1965–88; Judge Court of Appeal 1972–74; Chief Judge in Equity 1972–74; Chief Justice of NSW 1974–88; Lt-Gov. NSW 1974–89; Pres. Cranbrook School Council 1966–74, St John Ambulance Australia (NSW) 1974–; Chair. Inaugural Planning Cttee, Australian Commercial Disputes Centre 1985–86; Fellow UTS Sydney 1990; Hon. Col 1st/15th Royal NSW Lancers 1986–96; mem. London Court of Int. Arbitration 1988–; Pres. LCIA Asia-Pacific Council 1989–; Chair. Advisory Bd Dispute Resolution Centre, Bond Univ. 1989–99, UTS Centre for Dispute Resolution 1991–2001; Pres. Australian Br. Int. Law Asscn 1990–94, World Pres. 1990–92, Life Vice-Pres. 1992–; Pres. Sydney Univ. Law School Foundation 1990–; Chair. Australian Govt Int. Legal Services Advisory Council 1990–; Fellow Chartered Inst. of Arbitrators (UK) 1992; Dir John Fairfax Holdings Ltd 1991–94, Chair. 1994–97; mem. WIPO Arbitration Consultative Comm., Geneva 1994–; Chair. Judiciary Appeals Bd NSW Rugby League 1998–; Australian Govt Designated Conciliator to ICSID, Washington 1995–; ADR Consultant to Australian Defence Legal Office; Mediator Court of Arbitration for Sport, Lausanne; Hon. Fellow Inst. of Arbitrators Australia (Grade I) 1989; KStJ 1976; Grand Officer of Merit Order of Malta 1977; Hon. LLD (Sydney), (Macquarie), (Univ. of Tech.); Hon. DEcon (New England Univ.) 1996. *Publication:* Medication – A Practical Outline (5th edn) 2003. *Address:* 233 Macquarie Street, Sydney (Office); 1 Wolseley Crescent, Point Piper, NSW 2027, Australia. *Telephone:* (2) 9223-0888 (Office); (2) 9363-1480 (Home). *Fax:* (2) 9223-0588 (Office); (2) 9327-8871 (Home). *E-mail:* lstreet@laurencestreet.com.au (Office). *Website:* www.laurencestreet.com.au (Office).

STREET, Robert, AO, DSc, PhD, FAA; Australian physicist; b. 16 Dec. 1920, Wakefield, England; s. of Joe Street and Edith Elizabeth Street; m. Joan Marjorie Bere 1943; one s. one d.; ed Univ. of London; Scientific Officer, Dept of Supply, UK 1942–45; Lecturer Dept of Physics, Univ. of Nottingham 1945–54; Sr Lecturer, Dept of Physics, Univ. of Sheffield 1954–60; Foundation Prof. of Physics, Monash Univ., Melbourne, Victoria 1960–74; Dir Research School of Physical Sciences, Australian Nat. Univ. 1974–77; Vice-Chancellor Univ. of Western Australia 1978–86; Dir Magnetics Group, Research Centre for Advanced Materials and Minerals Processing 1991–; fmr Pres. Australian Inst. of Nuclear Science and Eng; mem. and Chair. Australian Research Grants Cttee 1970–76; Chair. Nat. Standards Comm. 1967–78; FAA 1973, Treas. 1976–77; Pres. Int. Inst. of Business and Tech., Perth, WA 1987–90; Chair. Child Health Research Foundation of Western Australia 1988–93; Consultant CRA Advanced Tech. Devt 1992–96. *Publications:* scientific papers on magnetism in learned journals. *Address:* The University of Western Australia, Department of Physics, 35 Stirling Highway, Crawley, WA 6009, Australia.

STREET-PORTER, Janet, FRTS, FRIBA; British journalist, television producer, presenter and newspaper editor; b. 27 Dec. 1946; m. 1st Tim Street-Porter 1967 (divorced 1975); m. 2nd A. M. M. Elliott 1976 (divorced 1978); m. 3rd Frank Cvitanovich (divorced 1988, died 1995); ed Lady Margaret Grammar School and Architectural Asscn; columnist and fashion writer, Petticoat Magazine 1968, Daily Mail 1969–71, Evening Standard 1971–73; own show, LBC Radio 1973; presenter, London Weekend Show, London Weekend Television (LWT) 1975; producer and presenter, Saturday Night People (with Clive James, q.v., and Russell Harty), The Six O'Clock Show (with Michael Aspel), Around Midnight 1975–85, co-cr. Network 7 (Channel 4) 1986–87; Head, Youth and Entertainment Features, BBC TV 1988–94; Head, Ind. Production for Entertainment 1994; with Mirror Group PLC 1994–95; TV presenter Design Awards, Travels with Pevsner, Coast to Coast, The Midnight Hour 1996–98, As The Crow Flies (series) 1999, Cathedral Calls 2000 (all BBC2), J'Accuse, Internet 1996 (Channel 4), Bloomberg TV 2001–; Ed. The Independent on Sunday 1999–2001, Ed.-at-Large 2001–; Pres. Ramblers' Asscn 1994–97 (now Vice-Pres.), Globetrotters Club 2003–; Prix Italia 1992, British Acad. Award for Originality 1988. *Publications:* Scandal 1980, The British Teapot 1981, Coast to Coast 1998, As the Crow Flies 1999. *Leisure interests:* walking, modern art. *Address:* c/o Bob Storer, Harbottle & Lewis, 14 Hanover Square, London, W1S 1HP, England. *Telephone:* (20) 7667-5000. *Fax:* (20) 7667-5100.

STREISAND, Barbra Joan; American actress and singer; b. 24 April 1942, Brooklyn, NY; d. of Emanuel Streisand and Diana (née Rosen) Streisand; m. 1st Elliot Gould 1963 (divorced 1971); one s.; m. 2nd James Brolin 1998; ed Erasmus Hall High School; nightclub debut at Bon Soir 1961; appeared in off-Broadway revue Another Evening with Harry Stoones 1961; appeared at Caucus Club, Detroit and Blue Angel New York 1961; played in musical comedy I Can Get It for You Wholesale 1962; began recording career with Columbia records 1963; appeared in musical play Funny Girl, New York 1964, London 1966; TV programme My Name is Barbra shown in England, Holland, Australia, Sweden, Bermuda and the Philippines, winning five Emmy awards; second programme Color Me Barbra also shown abroad; numerous concert and nightclub appearances; New York, Critics Best Supporting Actress Award 1962; Grammy awards for Best Female Pop Vocalist 1963, 1964, 1965, 1977, 1986; London Critics' Musical Award 1966; Acad. Award (Oscar) for film Funny Girl 1968; American Guild of Variety Artists' Entertainer of the Year Award 1970, Commdr des Arts et Lettres 1984; Nat. Medal of Arts; Emmy Award for Best Individual Performance in a Music or Variety Programme (for Barbra Streisand: Timeless) 2001. *Films include:* Funny Girl 1968, Hello Dolly 1969, On a Clear Day You Can See Forever 1969, The Owl and the Pussycat 1971, What's up Doc? 1972 Up the Sandbox 1973, The Way We Were 1973, For Pete's Sake 1974, Funny Lady 1975, A Star is Born 1977, Yentl 1983 (also Dir and produced), Nuts 1987, Sing 1989, Prince of Tides 1990 (also Dir, co-producer), The Mirror Has Two Faces 1996 (also Dir). *Address:* c/o Jeff Berg, ICM, 8942 Wilshire Boulevard, Beverly Hills, CA 90211, USA.

STREISSLER, Erich W., DrIur; Austrian professor of economics, econometrics and economic history; b. 8 April 1933, Vienna; s. of Albert Streissler and Erna Leithe; m. Monika Ruppe 1961; two s. (one deceased) three d.; ed Vienna Law School, Univ. of Vienna, Oxford Univ., UK, Hamilton Coll., New York, USA; studied also in France and Spain; Prof. of Statistics and Econometrics, Univ. of Freiburg Br., Germany 1962–68, twice Dean of Law and Social Science Faculty 1965–67; Prof., Univ. of Vienna 1968–, Dean of Law and Social Science Faculty 1973–74; Vice-Pres. Austrian Inst. of Econ. Research 1990–; Distinguished Austrian Visiting Prof., Stanford Univ., USA 1983; Pres. Austrian Economic Asscn 1988–94, Pres. Confed. of European Econ. Asscns. 1990–91; mem. Bd of Control, Vienna Stock Exchange 1990–98; Treas. Int. Econ. Asscn 1992–99; Foreign mem. Bavarian Acad. of Sciences; mem. Austrian Acad. of Sciences; Hon. mem. Hungarian Acad. of Sciences; various science prizes. *Publications:* numerous articles in scientific journals on econ. growth, distribution, monetary matters, analysis of econ. systems and especially on the history of thought in Econs. *Leisure interests:* hiking, history. *Address:* Faculty of Social Sciences and Economics, Vienna University, Hohenstaufeng 9, Vienna 1010 (Office); 18 Khevenhuellerstrasse 15, 1180 Vienna, Austria (Home). *Telephone:* 4277-374-25 (Office); 44-05-770 (Home). *Fax:* 4277-9374 (Office). *E-mail:* sylvie.hansbauer@univie.ac.at (Office).

STREITWIESER, Andrew, Jr., MA, PhD; American professor of chemistry; b. 23 June 1927, Buffalo, NY; s. of Andrew Streitwieser and Sophie Streitwieser; m. 1st Mary Ann Good 1950 (died 1965); m. 2nd Suzanne Cope 1967; one s. one d.; ed Stuyvesant High School and Columbia Univ.; Atomic Energy Comm. Postdoctoral Fellow, MIT 1951–52; Instructor in Chem. Univ. of Calif. at Berkeley 1952–54, Asst Prof. 1954–59, Assoc. Prof. 1959–63, Prof. of Chem. 1963, Prof. Emer. 1993–; Prof. Grad. School 1995–98; Consultant to Industry 1957–; Guggenheim Fellow 1969; mem. NAS, American Acad. of Arts and Sciences, Bavarian Acad. of Sciences; ACS awards: Calif. Section 1964, Award in Petroleum Chem. 1967; Humboldt Sr Scientist Award (Bonn) 1976, Humboldt Award (Bonn) 1979, Norris Award in Physical Organic Chem. 1982, Cope Scholar Award 1989. *Publications:* Molecular Orbital Theory for Organic Chemists 1961, Solvolytic Displacement Reactions 1962, Supplemental Tables of Molecular Orbital Calculations (with J. I. Brauman) Vols I and II 1965, Progress in Physical Organic Chemistry (co-ed.) Vols I-XI 1963–74, Dictionary of π-Electron Calculations (with C. A. Coulson) 1965, Orbital and Electron Density Diagrams (with P. H. Owens) 1973, Introduction to Organic Chemistry (with C. H. Heathcock) 1976, 1981, 1985, (also with E.L. Kosower) 1992, Solutions Manual and Study Guide for Introduction to Organic Chemistry (with C. H. Heathcock and P. A. Bartlett) 1985 (3rd Edn), A Lifetime of Synergy with Theory and Experiment 1996. *Leisure interests:* music (especially opera), wine, photography. *Address:* Department of Chemistry, University of California, Berkeley, CA 94720, USA. *Telephone:* (510) 642-2204. *Fax:* (510) 642-6072 (Home); (510) 643-6232. *E-mail:* astreit@socrates.berkeley.edu (Office).

STRENGER, Hermann-Josef; German business executive; b. 26 Sept. 1928, Cologne; m. Gisela Buchholtz 1956; two s. two d.; joined Bayer AG as commercial trainee 1949; Chemical Sales Dept –1954; assigned to subsidiary, Brazil 1954–57, to Bayer subsidiary, AB Anilin Kemi, Sweden 1958–61; Head, Sales Dept for raw materials for surface coatings, Leverkusen 1961–65; Head, Polyurethanes Dept 1965–69, Dir 1969–70; Commercial Head, Polyurethanes Div. 1970–72; mem. Bd of Man. 1972–; Deputy Chair. Man. Bd Bayer AG 1978–84, Chair. and Chief Exec. 1984–92, Chair. Supervisory Bd, CEO 1992–; Chair. Supervisory Bd VEBA AG; Chair. Carl Duisberg Gesellschaft 1987–; Chair. Supervisory Bd Linde AG 1996; mem. Supervisory Bd Hapag-Lloyd AG 1983, Karstadt AG 1983. *Address:* VEBA AG, Postfach 30 10 51, 40410 Düsseldorf; Bayer AG, 51368 Leverkusen, Germany.

STRETTON, James, BA, FFA; British business executive; b. 16 Dec. 1943; m. Isobel Christine Robertson 1968; two d.; ed Laxton Grammar School, Oundle, Worcester Coll., Oxford; Deputy Man. Dir Standard Life Assurance Co. 1988–94, Chief Exec. UK Operations 1994–2001; Dir Bank of England 1998–; Chair. The Wise Group 2002–; mem. Scottish Business Forum 1998–99, Court, Univ. of Edin. 1996–2002, Franchise Bd of Lloyds 2993; Dir Edin. Int. Festival Ltd 1997–; Trustee Lamp of Lothian Collegiate Trust 2003–. *Address:* Bank of England, Threadneedle Street, London, EC2R 8AH (Office); 15 Letham Mains, Haddington, EH41 4NW, Scotland (Home). *Telephone:* (20) 7601-4444 (Office). *Fax:* (20) 7601-4771 (Office). *Website:* www.bankofengland.co.uk.

STRETTON, Ross; Australian ballet dancer; b. Canberra, ACT; m. Valmai Strettan; three c.; ed Bryan Laurence School of Ballet, Canberra, Australian Ballet School; trained in Melbourne, graduating into corps de ballet, Australian Ballet 1972, soloist 1974, Prin. Artist 1976; scholarship to study in New York with Robert Helpmann 1974; joined Joffrey Ballet, New York 1979; guest dancer with American Ballet Theater 1980–81, then perm. mem. and Prin. Artist; performed as guest artist with many cos in USA and abroad; Dance Admin. with American Ballet Theater 1990, Asst Dir 1993; Artistic Dir Australian Ballet 1997–2001; Dir The Royal Ballet, London 2001–02. *Principal roles include:* Prince Siegfried (Swan Lake), Crassus (Spartacus), Paris and Romeo (John Cranko's Romeo and Juliet) 1974, Basilio (Don Quixote), Albrecht (Giselle), many other leading classical roles and cr. new roles in contemporary works. *Address:* c/o The Royal Ballet, Covent Garden, London, WC2E 9DD, England (Office).

STRICK, Joseph; American film director and company executive; b. 6 July 1923, Braddock, Pa; s. of Frank Strick and Rose Abramovitz; m. 1st Anne Laskin 1945 (divorced 1968); two s. one d.; m. 2nd Martine Rossignol 1970; one s. one d.; studied physics in LA; aerial photographer during World War II; formed Electrosolids Corpn, Physical Sciences Corpn; Venice Critics Award for The Savage Eye, Acad. Award for Interviews with My Lai Veterans. *Films directed:* Muscle Beach (also producer, documentary), The Savage Eye, The Balcony, Ulysses (also co-writer and producer), Interviews with My Lai Veterans (documentary), Portrait of the Artist, Tropic of Cancer, Underworld, Renaissance Farces.

STRICKLAND, John, MA, JP; British banker; b. 23 Oct. 1939; s. of William F. Strickland and Nora N. Strickland; m. Anthea Granville-Lewis 1963; three s.; ed Univ. of Cambridge; Asst Gen. Man. TSV, Hongkong and Shanghai Banking Corpn 1980–82, Gen. Man. TSV 1983–88, Exec. Dir Services 1989–96, Chair. 1996–99; Dir HSBC Holdings PLC 1988, Marine Midland Bank 1991–96, Midland Bank PLC 1993–96; Chair. Hongkong Bank Malaysia Berhad 1996–98; Vice-Chair. Hang Seng Bank Ltd 1996; mem. Council Outward Bound Trust of Hong Kong. *Leisure interests:* mountaineering, reading. *Address:* c/o The Hongkong and Shanghai Banking Corporation Ltd, Level 34, 1 Queen's Road Central, Hong Kong.

STRINGER, Sir Howard, Kt, MA; American/British broadcasting executive; b. 19 Feb. 1942, Cardiff, Wales; s. of Harry Stringer and Marjorie Mary Pook; m. Dr Jennifer A. K. Patterson 1978; ed Merton Coll., Oxford; served with US Army in Viet Nam 1965–67; researcher and producer, CBS News 1967–76; Exec. producer, CBS Reports 1976–81, CBS Evening News 1981–84; Exec. Vice-Pres. CBS News 1984–86, Pres. 1986–88; Pres. CBS Broadcast Group 1988–95; Chair., CEO Tele-TV 1995–97; Pres. Sony Corpn of America 1997, Chair. and CEO 1998; Vice-Chair. American Film Inst. –1999, Chair. Bd Trustees 1999–; mem. Bd Six Continents PLC; Gov. Motion Picture and TV Fund Foundation; Trustee Presbyterian Hosp., Museum of TV and Radio; Hon. Fellow Merton Coll., Oxford 1999. *Address:* Sony Corporation of America, 550 Madison Avenue, New York, NY 10022, USA. *Telephone:* (212) 833-6777 (Office). *Fax:* (212) 833-6932 (Office).

STRITCH, Elaine; American singer and actress; b. 2 Feb. 1926, Detroit; d. of George J. Stritch and Mildred (née Tobe) Stritch; m. John Bay 1973 (died 1982); ed Sacred Heart Convent, Detroit, Drama Workshop, New School for Social Research; Broadway début as Pamela Brewster in Loco 1946; other performances include, Three Indelicate Ladies 1947, Yes M'Lord 1949, Melba Snyder in revival of Pal Joey 1952, Bus Stop 1955, Mimi Paragon in Sail Away, New York 1961, London 1962, Martha in Who's Afraid of Virginia Woolf? 1962 and 1965, Joanne in Company, New York 1970, London 1971, Love Letters, London 1990, Elaine Stritch At Liberty (Old Vic, London) 2002. *Films include* The Scarlet Hour 1956, Three Violent People 1956, A Farewell to Arms 1957, The Perfect Furlough 1958, Who Killed Teddy Bear 1965, Pigeons 1971, September 1988, Cocoon: The Return, Cadillac Man 1990, Out to Sea 1997, Screwed 2000, Small Time Crooks 2000. *Television includes:* My Sister Eileen 1962, Two's Company (British Series) 1975–76 and 1979, Stranded 1986. *Publication:* Am I Blue?: Living With Diabetes and, Dammit, Having Fun 1984.

STROESSNER, Gen. Alfredo; Paraguayan politician and army officer; b. 3 Nov. 1912; ed Military Coll., Asunción; entered Paraguayan army; commissioned 1932, served through all ranks to Gen; C-in-C of Armed Forces 1951; Pres. of Paraguay 1954–89; overthrown in coup Feb. 1989; flown to exile in Brazil 1989; mem. Partido Colorado; Cruz del Chaco, Cruz del Defensor, decorations from Argentina and Brazil.

STRÖMHOLM, Stig Fredrik, LLD, DJur; Swedish fmr university vice-chancellor; b. 16 Sept. 1931, Boden; s. of Major Frederik Strömholm and Gerda Jansson; m. Gunilla M. Forslund 1958; one s. two d.; ed Univs of Uppsala, Cambridge and Munich; Clerk, Southern Dist Court of Uppsala 1958–60; Jr Judge, Stockholm Court of Appeal 1961; Asst Prof. of Comparative Law, Uppsala Univ. 1966, Prof. of Jurisprudence 1969, Dean, Faculty of Law 1973–79, Deputy Vice-Chancellor 1978–89, Vice-Chancellor 1989–97; Pres. Royal Swedish Acad. of Letters, History and Antiquities 1985–93, Academia Europaea, London 1997–2002; mem. several Swedish and foreign acads; Orden pour le Mérite (FRG) and other decorations; Dr hc at several Swedish and foreign univs; several prizes. *Publications:* 25 vols of legal science including Le droit moral de l'auteur, 3 vols 1967–73, A Short History of Legal Thinking in the West 1985; some 20 vols of criticism and fiction. *Leisure interests:* reading, travelling. *Address:* Norra Rudbecksgatan 5, 752 36 Uppsala, Sweden. *Telephone:* (18) 515-045; (18) 548-208. *Fax:* (18) 548-208 (Home).

STROMINGER, Jack L., MD; American professor of biochemistry; b. 7 Aug. 1925, New York; m.; four c.; ed Harvard and Yale Univs; Intern, Barnes Hosp., St Louis 1948–49; Research Fellow, American Coll. of Physicians, Dept of Pharmacology, Washington Univ. School of Medicine, St Louis 1949–50, Research Asst 1950–51; Sr Asst Surgeon, U.S. Public Health Service, Nat. Inst. of Arthritis and Metabolic Diseases, Bethesda 1951–54; leave of absence, Carlsberg Lab., Copenhagen, Denmark and Molteno Inst., Cambridge Univ., England, Commonwealth Fund Fellow 1955; Asst Prof. of Pharmacology, Dept of Pharmacology, Washington Univ. School of Medicine, Markel Scholar in Medical Science 1958–60, Prof., 1960–61, Forsyth Faculty Fellow 1960, Prof. of Pharmacology and Microbiology, Depts. of Pharmacology and Microbiology 1961–64; Prof. of Pharmacology and Chemical Microbiology, Univ. of Wis. Medical School, Madison, Chair. Dept of Pharmacology, mem. Univ. Cttee on Molecular Biology 1964–68; Prof. of Biochem., Dept of Biochem. and Molecular Biology, Harvard Univ., Cambridge, Mass. 1968–83, Chair. Dept of Biochem. and Molecular Biology 1970–73, Higgins Prof. of Biochem. 1983–, Dir of Basic Sciences, Sidney Farber Cancer Center 1974–77; Head Tumor Virology Div., Dana–Farber Cancer Inst., Boston 1977–; mem. Steering Cttee Biomedical Sciences Scientific Working Group, WHO; mem. NAS, American Acad. of Arts and Sciences, Nat. Inst. of Medicine, AAAS, American Soc. of Biological Chemists, of Microbiologists, of Pharmacology and Experimental Therapeutics, American Asscn of Immunologists, American Chemical Soc.; Hon. DSc (Trinity Coll., Dublin) 1975; Guggenheim Fellowship 1974–75; John J. Abel Award in Pharmacology 1960, Paul-Lewis Labs. Award in Enzyme Chem. 1962, NAS Award in Microbiology in Honour of Selman Waxman 1968, Rose Payne Award, American Soc. for Histocompatibility and Immunogenetics 1986, Pasteur Medal 1990, Albert Lasker Award for Basic Medical Research 1995, other awards. *Address:* Department of Molecular and Cell Biology, Harvard University, 7 Divinity Avenue, Cambridge, MA 02138 (Office); Department of Biochemistry, Dana Faber Cancer Institute, 44 Binney Street, Boston, MA 02115, USA. *Website:* www.harvard.edu (Office).

STRONG, David F., PhD, FRSC; Canadian geologist and university president; b. 26 Feb. 1944, Botwood, Newfoundland; m. Lynda Joan Marshall; two d.; ed Memorial Univ. of Newfoundland, Lehigh Univ., Pa, USA, Univ. of Edinburgh, Scotland; Asst Prof., Dept of Geology, Memorial Univ. of Newfoundland 1970–72, Assoc. Prof. 1972–74, Acting Head of Dept 1974–75, Prof., Dept of Earth Sciences 1974–90, Univ. Research Prof. 1985–90, Special Adviser to Pres. 1986–87, Vice-Pres. (Academic) 1987–90; Pres. and Vice-Chancellor Univ. of Vic. 1990–2000, Pres. Emer. 2000–; Chair. and CEO LearningWise Inc. 2002–; Visiting Prof., Université de Montpellier, France 1976–77; W. F. James Prof. of Pure and Applied Sciences, St Francis Xavier Univ., Nova Scotia 1981–82; mem. Bd of Dirs Seabright Corpn Ltd 1986–; Assoc. Ed. Canadian Journal of Earth Sciences 1977–83, Transactions of the Royal Soc. of Edinburgh 1980–; Chair. Natural Sciences and Eng Research Council of Canada 1983–86, mem. 1982–88; mem. Research Council, Canadian Inst. of Advanced Research 1986–, Newfoundland and Labrador Advisory Council on Science and Tech. 1988–, Governing Council, Nat. Research Council of Canada 1999– (mem. Exec. Cttee 2002–); Fellow Geological Asscn of Canada, Geological Soc. of America, Soc. of Econ. Geologists; mem. Canadian Inst. of Mining and Metallurgy, Mineralogical Asscn of Canada; Univ. of Edin. Swiney Lecturer 1981; Hon. Fellow Geological Asscn of Canada; Hon. DSc (Memorial Univ., Newfoundland) 1990; Hon. LLD (St Francis Xavier Univ.) 1992; APICS Young Scientist Award (now the Frazer Medal) 1973, Foreign Exchange Fellowships to Japan 1976, to France 1976–77, Canadian Inst. of Mining and Metallurgy Distinguished Service Award 1979, Geological Asscn of Canada Past Pres.'s Medal 1980. *Publications:* about 200 scientific and technical papers. *Leisure interests:* reading, music, gardening. *Address:* LearningWise Inc., Suite 135A, R-Hut, McKenzie Avenue, PO Box 3075 STN CSC, Victoria, BC V8W 3W2, Canada. *Telephone:* (250) 472-4331. *Fax:* (250) 721-6497. *E-mail:* dfstrong@learningwise.com.

STRONG, James Alexander; Australian business executive; b. 31 July 1944, Lismore, NSW; s. of R. J. Strong; m. Laile Strong 1968 (divorced 1993); two s.; ed Univ. of Queensland, Univ. of Sydney; industrial officer Sugar Producers Asscn, Brisbane 1964–70; industrial officer, Northern Territory, Nabalco Pty Ltd, 1970–74, Chief Industrial Officer 1974–78, Personnel and Legal Man. 1978–80, Admin. Man. Northern Territory and Sydney 1980–81, Site Man. 1981–83; admitted to Bar NSW 1976; Exec. Dir Australian Mining Council 1983–86; CEO Australian Airlines 1986–89; Chair. of Dirs. SEAS Sapfor Ltd 1990–92; Dir RGC Ltd 1990–98; Nat. Chair. of Partners Corrs Chambers Westgarth 1991–92 (fmr Man. Partner, CEO Corrs Australia Solicitors); Dir Clarks Shoes Australia Ltd 1991–92, Woolworths Ltd 2000–; Man. Dir, CEO, DB Group Ltd., Auckland, New Zealand 1992–93; Man. Dir Qantas Airways Ltd 1993– (Dir 1991–); Chair. Int. Air Transport Asscn 1999–; mem. Law School Advisory Bd, Flinders Univ. of S. Australia, Advisory Council Tasman Econ. Research; Trustee Vic. State Opera Foundation. *Leisure interests:* drama, music, opera, reading, tennis. *Address:* Qantas Airways Ltd., Qantas Centre, 203 Coward Street, Mascot, NSW 2020, Australia (Office). *Telephone:* (2) 9691-3636 (Office). *Fax:* (2) 9691-3277 (Office). *Website:* www.qantas.com.au (Office).

STRONG, Liam (Gerald Porter), BA; British business executive; b. 6 Jan. 1945, Enniskillen, Northern Ireland; s. of Gerald James Strong and Geraldine Crozier Strong; m. Jacqueline Gray 1970; one s. one d.; ed Trinity Coll. Dublin; joined Procter & Gamble, Newcastle-upon-Tyne 1967–71; Household Man., Reckitt & Colman 1971, moved to Corp. Planning Unit, London 1973, Marketing and Sales Dir, then Gen. Man. Reckitt & Colman 1975–80, Vice-Pres. Sunset Designs, Calif., USA 1980–82, Head Int. Pharmaceuticals Div., Reckitt & Colman 1982–86, Pres. Durkee French, USA 1986–89; Dir of Marketing British Airways 1989–90, Dir Marketing and Operations 1990–91; Chief Exec. Sears PLC 1991–97; CEO World Comm. Int. 1997–; Dir Skystream Inc., USA 2000–. *Leisure interests:* reading, shooting, opera. *Address:* c/o 40 Duke Street, London, W1A 2HP, England.

STRONG, Rt Hon. Maurice F., CC, PC, LLD, FRS, FRSA, FRSC; Canadian environmentalist, international official and business executive; b. 29 April 1929, Oak Lake, Manitoba; s. of Frederick Milton Strong and Mary Fyfe Strong (deceased); m. 1st Pauline Olivette Williams 1950 (divorced 1980); two s. two d. one foster d.; m. 2nd Hanne Marstrand 1981; ed Oak Lake High School, Manitoba; served in UN Secr. 1947; Pres. or Dir of various Canadian and int. corpns. 1954–66; also involved in leadership of various pvt. orgs. in field of Devt and int. affairs; Dir-Gen. External Aid Office of Canadian Govt 1966 (now Canadian Int. Devt Agency); Chair. Canadian Int. Devt Bd; Alt. Gov. IBRD, ADB, Caribbean Devt Bank; UN Under-Sec. Gen. with responsibility for environmental affairs 1970–72, Chief Exec. for 1972 Conf. on Human Environment, Stockholm, June 1972; Montague Burton Prof. of Int. Relations, Univ. of Edin. 1973; Exec. Dir UNEP 1973–75; Chair. Petro Canada 1976–78; Pres. Stronat Investments Ltd 1976–80; Chair. Bd of Govs Int. Devt Research Centre 1977–78; Chair. Strovest Holdings Inc., Procor Inc. 1978–79, AZL Resources Inc. 1978–83, Int. Energy Devt Corpn 1980–83, NS Round Table Soc. for Int. Devt, Canadian Devt Investment Corpn, 1982–84, Supercritical Combustion Corpn, Int. Advisory Group, CH2M Hill Cos Ltd; Chair. and Dir Tech. Devt Corpn; Dir or mem. numerous business and conservation groups in Canada and internationally including Foundation Bd World Econ. Forum, Leadership for Environment and Devt, Zenon Environmental, Inc., The Humane Soc. of the US; Under Sec.-Gen., UN 1985–87, 1989; Pres. World Fed. UNA 1987, The Baca Corpn; Dir Better World Soc. 1988; Chair., Pres. American Water Devt Inc., Denver 1986–89; Sec.-Gen. UN 1992 Conf. on Environment and Devt; Chair. Ontario Hydro 1992–95, World Resources Inst.; Sr Adviser to Pres. of World Bank 1995–; Under Sec.-Gen. and Exec. Co-ordinator for UN Reform 1997; Under Sec.-Gen. and Sr Adviser to Sec.-Gen. of UN 1998–; Pres. Council UN Univ. for Peace, San José, Costa Rica 2001–; Chair. Earth Council Foundation; mem. Bd Dirs UN Foundation, Int. Advisory Bd, Toyota Motor Corpn, Int. Advisory Bd, Center of Int. Devt at Harvard Univ., Int. Advisory Council, Liu Centre for the Study of Global Issues at Univ. of British Columbia, Lamont-Doherty Observatory Advisory Bd; Fellow Royal Agric. Soc. of Canada; hon. degrees from 49 univs; Royal Order of the Polar Star, Sweden 1996; Onassis Int. Award 1993, Jawaharlal Nehru Award for Int. Understanding 1994,Millennium Award, The Princes' Award Foundation, Denmark 2000, Global Steering Wheel Int. Prize, Russia 2001, Global Environment Leadership Award 2002 and numerous other awards, prizes and decorations. *Publications:* The Great Building Bee (with Jacques Hébert) 1980, A Life for the Planet 1999, Where On Earth Are We Going?; various articles in journals. *Address:* The Earth Council Institute, Suite #401, 255 Consumers Road, Toronto, Ont., M2J 5B6, Canada. *Telephone:* (416) 498-3150 (Office). *Fax:* (416) 498-7296 (Office).

STRONG, Sir Roy Colin, Kt, PhD, FSA, FRSL; British historian, writer on gardening and fmr museum director; b. 23 Aug. 1935, London; s. of George Edward Clement Strong and Mabel Ada Smart; m. Julia Trevelyan Oman (q.v.) 1971; ed Queen Mary Coll., Univ. of London and Warburg Inst.; Asst Keeper, Nat. Portrait Gallery, London 1959–67, Dir 1967–73; Dir Victoria and Albert Museum, London 1974–87; Vice-Chair. South Bank Bd (now South Bank Centre) 1985–90; Dir Oman Productions Ltd, Nordstern Fine Art Insurance 1988–2001; organizer of exhbns. including The Elizabethan Image (Tate Gallery) 1969, The Destruction of the Country House (Victoria and Albert Museum) 1974, Artists of the Tudor Court (Victoria and Albert Museum) 1983; mem. Arts Council of GB 1983–87 (Chair. Arts Panel 1983–87), Council, RCA 1979–87; Patron, Pallant House, Chichester 1986–; Fellow, Queen Mary Coll., Univ. of London, Royal Soc. of Literature 1999; High Bailiff and Searcher of the Sanctuary of Westminster Abbey 2000–; Pres. Garden History Soc. 2000–; Hon. DLitt (Leeds) 1983, (Keele) 1984; Shakespeare Prize 1980 (FVS Foundation, Hamburg). *Publications:* Portraits of Queen Elizabeth I 1963, Leicester's Triumph (with J. A. Van Dorsten) 1964, Holbein and Henry VIII 1967, Tudor and Jacobean Portraits 1969, The English Icon: Tudor and Jacobean Portraiture 1969, Van Dyck: Charles I on Horseback 1972, Inigo Jones: The Theatre of the Stuart Court 1972 (with S. Orgel), Elizabeth R (with Julia Trevelyan Oman) 1971, Mary Queen of Scots (with Julia Trevelyan Oman) 1972, Splendour at Court: Renaissance Spectacle and The Theatre of Power 1973, Nicholas Hilliard 1975, An Early Victorian Album (with Colin Ford) 1974, The Cult of Elizabeth: Elizabethan Portraiture and Pageantry 1977, And When Did You Last See Your Father? The Victorian Painter and British History 1978, The Renaissance Garden in England 1979, Britannia Triumphans, Inigo Jones, Rubens and Whitehall Palace 1980, Holbein 1980, The English Miniature (with J. Murdoch, J. Murrell and P. Noon) 1981, The English Year (with Julia Trevelyan Oman) 1982, The English Renaissance Miniature 1983, Artists of the Tudor Court (with J. Murrell) 1983, Glyndebourne, A Celebration (contrib.) 1984, Art and Power, Renaissance Festivals 1450–1650 1984, Strong Points 1985, Henry Prince of Wales and England's Lost Renaissance 1986, C. V. Wedgwood Festschrift (contrib.) 1986, Creating Small Gardens 1986, Gloriana, Portraits of Queen Elizabeth I 1987, The Small Garden Designers Handbook 1987, Cecil Beaton: the Royal Portraits 1988, Creating Small Formal Gardens 1989, Lost Treasures of Britain 1990, A Celebration of Gardens 1991, Small Period Gardens 1992, Royal Gardens 1992, Versace Theatre 1992, William Larkin 1994, A Country Life 1994, Successful Small Gardens 1994, The Tudor and Stuart Monarchy 1995, The Story of Britain 1996, The English Arcadia 1996, Country Life 1897–1997 1997, The Roy Strong Diaries 1967–1987 1997, On Happiness 1997, The Tudor and Stuart Monarchy 1998, The Spirit of Britain 1999, Garden Party 2000, The Artist and the Garden 2000, Ornament in the Small Garden 2001, Feast – A History of Grand Eating 2002, The Laskett – The Story of a Garden 2003; numerous articles in newspapers and periodicals. *Leisure interests:* gardening, cooking, country life. *Address:* The Laskett, Much Birch, Hereford, HR2 8HZ, England.

STROSSEN, Nadine, BA, JD; American human rights lawyer; b. 18 Aug. 1950, Jersey City; d. of Woodrow John Strossen and Sylvia Strossen; m. Eli Michael Noam 1980; ed Harvard Law School, Radcliffe Coll.; assoc. attorney Sullivan and Cromwell 1978–83; partner Harvis and Zeichner 1983–84; mem. Nat. Bd Dirs. American Civil Liberties Union 1983–, Pres. 1991–, mem. advisory Cttee on Reproductive Freedom Project 1983–, Nat. Exec. Cttee 1985–, Nat. Gen. Council 1986–91; Asst Prof. of Clinical Law Univ. of New York 1989–; Adjunct Prof. Grad. School of Business Univ. of Columbia 1990–; mem. Exec. Cttee Human Rights Watch 1989–91; mem. Bd Dirs. Coalition to Free Soviet Jewry 1984–; mem. Asia Watch 1987–, Vice-Chair. 1989–91; mem. Nat. Coalition Against Censorship 1988, Middle East Watch 1989–91, The Fund for Free Expression 1990–; mem. steering Cttee New York Legal Council for Soviet Jewry 1987–. *Publications include:* Regulating Campus Hate Speech; A Modest Proposal? 1990, Recent US and International Judicial Protection of Individuals Rights: A Comparative Legal Process Analysis and Proposed Synthesis 1990, In Defense of Pornography: Free Speech and the Fight for Women's Rights 1995, numerous articles in professional journals. *Leisure interests:* singing, skiing, travel. *Address:* New York Law School, 57 Worth Street, New York, NY 10013; 450 Riverside Drive, #51, New York, NY 10027, USA (Home).

STROYEV, Yegor Semyonovich, D.ECONS.; Russian politician; b. 25 Feb. 1937, Stroyevo, Khotynetsky, Orel Region; s. of Semyon Fedorovich Stroyev and Anna Ivanovna Stroyeva; m. Nina Semyvovna Stroyeva; one d.; ed I. V. Michurin Horticultural Inst., Acad. of Social Sciences, Moscow; mem CPSU 1958–91; worked at Progress collective farm, Khotynetsky Dist; Sec. Khotynetsky CPSU Dist Cttee, Chair. Exec. Cttee Pokrovsky Dist Soviet of People's Deputies, First Sec. Pokrovsky CPSU Dist Cttee, Sec., First Sec. Orel CPSU Regional Cttee 1985–89; Sec. CPSU Cen. Cttee 1989–91; mem. Politburo of CPSU Cen. Cttee 1990–91; resgnd after the Aug. coup d'état; fmr People's Deputy of USSR; mem. Council of Fed. Ass. of Russian Fed. 1995–2001, Chair. 1996–2001; Chair. Council of Interparl. Ass. of CIS Mem. States 1996–; Head of Admin. Orel Region 1993–; Dir All-Russia Scientific Research Inst. of Fruit Crop Breeding 1991–93; Academician Russian Acad. of Agricultural Sciences; Hon. mem. Russian Acad. of Literature; Order of the Oct. Revolution 1973; Order of the Red Banner of Labour 1987; Order of St Prince Vladimir 1997 and other awards. *Publications:* Methodology and Practices of Agrarian Restructuring 1994, To Give a Chance to the Peasant 1995, Land Issue 1999. *Leisure interest:* recreation in the countryside. *Address:* Governor's Office, Lenina pl. 1, 30200 Orel, Russia. *Telephone:* (862) 41-63-13. *Fax:* (862) 41-25-30 (Office). *Website:* www.adm.orel.ru (Office).

STRUBE, Jürgen, DJur; German business executive; b. 1939, Bochum; m.; one d.; joined BASF 1969, several posts, then with BASF Brasileira SA, São Paulo 1974–85, Head, Glasurit do Brasil Ltda 1980–, Head, Brazil Regional Div. 1982–, in charge of Information Systems and Fibres Operating Divs. and Regional Divs. in N America 1985–88, of Foams, Polyolefins and PVC and Information Systems Operating Divs. and Brazil and Latin American Regional Divs. 1988–90, mem. Bd Exec. Dirs. BASF AG, Ludwigshafen, Germany 1985–, Chair. 1990–; Pres. Asscn of Chemical Industry (VCI) 1996–97; Soc. of Chemical Industry's Centenary Medal 1999. *Address:* BASF Aktiengesellschaft, 67056 Ludwigshafen, Germany.

STRUCHKOVA, Raissa Stepanovna; Russian ballerina; b. 5 Oct. 1925, Moscow; ed Bolshoi Theatre Ballet School; Soloist, Bolshoi Theatre Ballet 1944–67; lecturer in classical dancing Lunacharsky State Inst. of Theatrical Art 1968, Prof. 1978–; mem. CPSU 1962–91; People's Artist of USSR 1958; Ed.-in.-Chief Sovetskiy Balet (now Balet) 1981–96; Coach, Bolshoi Theatre 1996–. *Principal roles include:* Cinderella (Cinderella, Prokofiev), Juliet (Romeo and Juliet, Prokofiev), Giselle (Giselle, Adan), Princess Aurora (Sleeping Beauty, Tchaikovsky), Odette-Odile (Swan Lake, Tchaikovsky), Kitri (Don Quixote), Parasha (Copper Rider, Glier), Tao Khoa (Red Poppy, Glier), Maria (Fountain of Bakhsisarai, Asafyev), Janne, also Diana de Mirrel (Flames of Paris, Asafyev), Gayane (Gayane, Khachaturyan), Vakchanka (Walpurgisnacht, Gounod); films: Crystal Slipper, Your Name. *Address:* Bolshoi Theatre, Teatralnaya pl. 1, 103009 Moscow, Russia. *Telephone:* (095) 915-40-57.

STRUCK, Peter, DJur; German lawyer and politician; b. 24 Jan. 1943, Göttingen; m.; three c.; ed Univs. of Göttingen and Hamburg; adviser to the govt, Hamburg 1971; personal adviser to Pres. of Univ. of Hamburg 1971–72; elected Town Councillor and Deputy Town Mayor of Uelzen 1973; admitted to Bar, 1983; worked in Dist Court of Uelzen and Regional Court of Lueneburg; mem. SDP 1964–, mem. Bundestag (representing Lower Saxony) 1980–, Chair. of Parl. Group 1998–; Minister of Defence 2002–; mem. ÖTV (Public Workers' Union); mem. Bd Hilden AHG Gen. Hosp., Rockwool Beteiligungs GmbH, Gladbeck. *Address:* Ministry of Defence, Stauffenbergstrasse 18, 10785 Berlin, Germany (Office). *Telephone:* (30) 200400 (Office). *Fax:* (30) 20048333 (Office). *E-mail:* peter.struck@bundestag.de (Office). *Website:* www .bundestag.de/~Peter.Struck (Office); www.bmvg.de.

STRUGATSKY, Boris Natanovich (S. Viticky); Russian science-fiction writer and astronomer; b. 15 April 1933, Leningrad; s. of Natan Strugatsky; m.; one s.; ed Leningrad State Univ.; astronomer's post in Pulkovo Observatory, Leningrad 1955–65; started publishing science-fiction (with his brother) 1957; Victor Hugo Prize (France). *Publications:* with A. N. Strugatsky over 25 novels including: The Land of Purple Clouds 1959, The Return 1962, Escape Attempt 1962, The Far-Away Rainbow 1964, Rapacious Things of the Century 1965, The Inhabited Island 1971, The Ugly Swans 1972, Stories 1975, The Forest 1982, The Lame Fortune 1986, One Billion Years Before the End of the World 1988, Collected Works 1991, Burdened by Evil 1988, The Search of Destination 1994, Collected Works 2001. *Address:* Pobeda Str. 4, Apt 186, 196070 St Petersburg, Russia. *Telephone:* (812) 291-37-55. *E-mail:* bns@tf.ru (Home).

STRUNK, Klaus Albert, DPhil; German professor of linguistics; b. 22 Aug. 1930, Düsseldorf; s. of Albert Strunk and Hedwig Schäfer; m. Marion Kriegeskotte 1957; two s. one d.; ed Univs. of Cologne and Bonn; Prof., Univ. of Saarland and Dir Inst. of Indo-European Linguistics and Indo-Iranian Philology 1967–77; Prof., Univ. of Munich and Dir Inst. of Gen. and Indo-European Linguistics 1977–, Dean Dept I (Linguistics and Literature) 1985–87; Ed. Kratylos review 1969–83; Co-Ed. Glotta review 1974–, series Studies in Indo-European Language and Culture (Berlin and New York) 1985–, Muenchener Studien zur Sprachwissenschaft review 1992–; Pres. Indogermanische Gesellschaft 1983–92; mem. Bayerische Akademie der Wissenschaften 1979–, Sec. Philosophy and History section 1989–; mem. Société de Linguistique de Paris 1978–, Philological Soc., London 1993–. *Publications:* Die sogenannten Aeolismen der homerischen Sprache 1957, Nasalpraesentien und Aoriste. Ein Beitrag zur Morphologie des Verbums im Indo-Iranischen und Griechischen 1967, Probleme der lateinischen Grammatik (Ed.) 1973, Lachmanns Regel für das Lateinische 1976, Generative Versuche zu einigen Problemen in der historischen Grammatik indogermanischer Sprachen 1976, Typische Merkmale von Fragesätzen und die altindische Pluti 1983, Zum Postulat 'vorhersagbaren' Sprachwandels bei unregelmässigen oder komplexen Flexionsparadigmen 1991, numerous articles and reviews on Greek, Latin, Indo-Iranian and Indo-European linguistics. *Leisure interests:* reading books on history, literature, classical music, sport. *Address:* Ringbergstrasse 11, 83707 Bad Wiessee, Germany. *Telephone:* (8022) 82198.

STRUZIK, Adam; Polish politician; b. 1 Jan. 1957, Kutno; m.; one s. one d.; ed Medical Acad., Łódź; Dir Voivodeships Joint Hosp. in Płock 1990–98; Councillor City and Commune of Gąbin 1990–98; Marshal (Speaker) of Nat. Regional Council of Territorial Self-Govt 1994–98; Councillor Regional Council of Mazovian Voivodeship 1998–; mem. Solidarity Trade Union 1980–; mem. Polish Peasant Party (PSL) 1989–, Exec. Council; Senator 1991–2001; Marshal of the Senate 1993–97; Marshal of Mazovian Vavodeship 2001–; mem. Programming Bd TVP SA; mem. Polish Hunting Asscn, Płock Scientific Soc., Polish Haematology Soc. *Leisure interests:* politics, literature, tourism. *Address:* Urząd Marsrałkowski Województwa Mazowieckiego, ul. Brechta 3, 03-472, Warsaw, Poland (Office). *Telephone:* (22) 5979100 (Office); (22) 5979104 (Office). *E-mail:* A.Struzik@mazovia.pl. *Website:* www.mazovia.pl.

STRZEMBOSZ, Adam Justyn, DrIur; Polish state official and lawyer; b. 11 Nov. 1930, Warsaw; s. of Adam Strzembosz and Zofia (née Gadomska) Strzembosz; m. Zofia Strzembosz 1957; two s. two d.; ed Jagiellonian Univ., Cracow, Warsaw Univ.; legal adviser, Ministry of Labour and Social Security 1953–56; judge, County Court 1956–68, Provincial Court 1968–81; researcher Research Inst. of Judicial Law 1974–81; Asst Prof. and Head Dept of Penal Law Catholic Univ. of Lublin 1982–89, Prof. 1986–; Vice-Minister of Justice 1989–90; judge, Supreme Court 1990–; First Pres. Supreme Court 1990–98; Head Tribunal of State 1990–98; Head Solidarity Group, Ministry of Justice 1980–81; mem. Bd Solidarity Mazowsze Region 1980; Del. to 1st Solidarity Conf., Jt Leader Appeal Comm., Gdańsk Oliwa 1981; Co-Founder Soc. for Promotion and Propagation of Sciences; mem. Catholic Univ. of Lublin Scientific Asscn, Penal Law Asscn. *Publications:* six books and more than over 200 treatises and articles. *Leisure interests:* cycling, literature. *Address:* ul. Stanisława Augusta 73 m. 20, 03-846 Warsaw, Poland (Home).

STUART, Sir Kenneth Lamonte, Kt, MD, FRCP, FACP, FFPM, FFPHM; Barbadian physician; b. 16 June 1920, Barbados; s. of Egbert Stuart and Louise Stuart; m. Barbara Cecille Ashby 1958; one s. two d.; ed Harrison Coll., Barbados, Queen's Univ., Belfast, Northern Ireland; Rockefeller Foundation Fellow in Cardiology, Mass. Gen. Hosp., Boston, USA 1956–57; Wellcome Research Fellow, Harvard Univ., USA 1960–61; Prof. of Medicine, Univ. of W Indies 1966–76, Dean Medical School 1969–73, Head Dept of Medicine 1972–76; Commonwealth Medical Adviser 1976–85; Consultant Adviser, Wellcome Tropical Inst. 1985–95; Gresham Prof. of Physic, Gresham Coll., London 1988–94; Dir Int. Medical Educ. Trust 2000 1998–; mem. Bd of Govs, Liverpool School of Tropical Medicine 1980–96, Int. Research Centre of Canada 1985–90; Chair. Court of Govs, London School of Hygiene and Tropical Medicine 1983–86; Chair. Commonwealth Caribbean Medical Research Council 1988; Chair. Errol Barrow Memorial Trust 1989–99; mem. of Council and Trustee The London Lighthouse 1994–2001; mem. of Council Royal Overseas League 1994–2000, United Medical and Dental Schools of Guy's and St Thomas's Hosps 1994–98, Guy's, King's and St Thomas's Hosp. Medical and Dental School 1998, King's Coll. London 1998–2002; Trustee Schools Partnership Worldwide 1990–; Hon. Medical and Scientific Adviser, Barbados High Comm., London 1991–; Freeman of City of London 1992; Hon. DSc (Queen's, Belfast) 1988. *Leisure interests:* tennis, music, literature. *Address:* 3 The Garth, Cobham, Surrey, KT11 2DZ, England (Home). *Telephone:* (1932) 863826 (Home). *Fax:* (1932) 860427. *E-mail:* kenstuart@lineone .net (Office).

STUART, Lyle; American publishing company executive; b. 11 Aug. 1922, New York; s. of Alfred Stuart and Theresa (Cohen) Stuart; m. 1st Mary Louise Strawn 1946; one s. one d.; m. 2nd Carole Livingston 1982; one d.; reporter, Int. News Service 1945, Variety 1945–46; script writer, Dept of State, Voice of America 1946; Ed. Music Business magazine 1946–48; f. Expose 1951; Publr The Independent 1951–75; Business Man. MAD magazine 1952–54; Pres. Lyle Stuart Inc. 1954–89, Citadel Press 1970–89, University Books Inc. 1983–, Hot News 1983, Barricade Books 1990–; f. N Bergen, NJ Public Library; Producer Chinese Festival of Music 1952–62; mem. American Booksellers' Asscn, Nat. Acad. of TV Arts and Sciences, New York Zoological Soc.; Hon. PhD (State of Calif.). *Publications:* God Wears a Bowtie 1949, The Secret Life of Water Winchell 1953, Mary Louise 1970, Casino Gambling for the Winner 1978, Lyle Stuart on Baccarat 1983, Map of Life 1993, Winning at Casino Gambling 1995, Map of Life 1996. *Address:* Barricade Books Inc., 185 Bridge Plaza North, Suite 308A, Fort Lee, NJ 07024 (Office); 1530 Palisade Avenue, Apartment 6-L, Fort Lee, NJ 07024, USA (Home).

STUBBS, Imogen Mary, MA; British actress; b. 20 Feb. 1961, Rothbury; d. of late Robin Stubbs and Heather McCracken; m. Trevor Nunn (q.v.) 1994; one s. one d.; ed St Paul's Girls School, London, Exeter Coll. Oxford and Royal Acad. of Dramatic Art; appeared with RSC in The Rover, Two Noble Kinsmen, Richard II 1987–88, Othello 1991, Heartbreak House 1992, St Joan 1994, Twelfth Night 1996, Blast from the Past 1998, Betrayal 1998, The Relapse

2001; Gold Medal, Chicago Film Festival. *Television appearances include:* The Rainbow, Anna Lee, After the Dance. *Films include:* Nanon, A Summer Story, Erik the Viking, True Colours, A Pin for the Butterfly, Fellow Traveller, Sandra c'est la vie, Jack and Sarah, Sense and Sensibility 1995, Twelfth Night 1996. *Leisure interests:* writing, skiing, collecting junk.

STUDER, Cheryl; American soprano opera singer; b. 24 Oct. 1955, Midland, Mich.; m. 2nd Ewald Schwarz; two d. (one by previous m.); ed Interlochen Arts Acad., Oberlin Coll. Cleveland, Ohio and Univ. of Tennessee; studied singing with Gwendolyn Pike, at Berks. Music Centre, at Tanglewood with Phyllis Curtin and at Hochschule für Musik, Vienna with Hans Hotter; engaged for concert series with Boston Symphony Orch. by Seiji Ozawa (q.v.) 1979; opera debut as the First Lady in The Magic Flute, Munich 1980–82; with Darmstadt State Theatre, Germany 1982–84; Deutsche Oper, Berlin 1984–86; U.S. debut as Micaela in Carmen, Lyric Opera of Chicago 1984; debut at Bayreuth 1985, Royal Opera House, Covent Garden 1987, Metropolitan Opera, New York 1988; sings wide variety of roles, especially Wagner, Verdi, Mozart and Strauss; Int. Music Award 1993, Vocalist of the Year (USA) 1994. *Address:* c/o Deutsche Oper Berlin, Richard Wagnerstrasse 10, 1000 Berlin, Germany (Office); c/o International Performing Artists Inc., 125 Crowfield Drive, Knoxville, TN 37922, USA.

STUHR, Jerzy; Polish actor and film director; b. 18 April 1947, Cracow; s. of Tadeusz Stuhr and Maria Stuhr; m. 1971; one s. one d.; ed Jagiellonian Univ. and Ludwik Solski State School of Drama, Kraków; main theatrical roles at Stary Theatre, Kraków with Andrzej Wajda (q.v.), notably Hamlet 1982, Dostoevsky's The Possessed and Crime and Punishment 1984, P. Süskind's Double Bass (actor and dir) 1985–, Le Bourgeois Gentilhomme 1993, Harold Pinter's Ashes to Ashes 1996, Merry Wives of Windsor (dir) 1998; film roles include: Blind Chance 1981, Decalogue X, Three Colours – White; dir, actor and teacher, Italy 1980–; film dir List of Adultresses 1994, Love Stories 1997, A Week of a Man's Life 1999, Big Animal 2000; Rector, Ludwik Solski State School of Drama, Kraków 1990–97, 2002–; lecturer 1998–; lecturer Faculty of Radio and TV, Silesia Univ. 1998–; mem. European Film Acad. 1998–; Best Actor, Chicago Festival 1978, Premio della Critica Teatrale 1982, Premio Fiprescii for Love Stories, Venice Film Festival 1997, Grand Prix for Love Stories, Polish Film Festival, Gdynia 1997, Nastro d'Argento 1997, Big Anima Special Jury Prize, Karlovy Vary 2000, Emerging Master, Int. Film Festival, Seattle 2001. *Publications:* Heart Illness, or My Life in Art (autobiog.) 1992, Big Animal 2000, True Pretender 2000. *Leisure interests:* literature, sport. *Address:* Ludwik Solski State School of Drama, ul. Straszewskiego 22, , 31-109 Kraków, Poland (Office). *Telephone:* (12) 4228196 (Office). *Fax:* (12) 4220209 (Office). *E-mail:* sekr@pwst.krakow.pl (Office). *Website:* www.stuhr.onet.pl (Office).

STUIVER, Minze, PhD; American professor of geological sciences; b. 25 Oct. 1929, Vlagtwedde, Netherlands; s. of Albert Stuiver and Griet Welles; m. Annie Hubbelmeyer 1956; two d.; ed Univ. of Groningen; Research Assoc. Yale Univ. 1959–62; Sr Research Assoc. and Dir Radiocarbon Lab. 1962–69; Prof. of Geological Sciences and Zoology, Univ. of Washington, Seattle 1969–82, Prof. of Geological Sciences and Quaternary Sciences 1982–, Dir Quaternary Isotope Lab. 1972–; Ed. Radiocarbon 1976–88; mem. Geological Soc. of America, American Quaternary Asscn; Alexander von Humboldt Sr Scientist, Fed. Repub. of Germany 1983. *Address:* University of Washington, Box 351360, Seattle, WA 98195, USA. *Telephone:* (206) 543-2100. *Website:* www .washington.edu (Office).

STUMP, Nicholas Withrington, M.APP.SC.; Australian mining executive; b. 16 Dec. 1941, Adelaide; s. of Stanley Withrington and Dorothy Ellen; m. Alison Goode 1966; one s. two d.; ed Scotch Coll. Adelaide, Unley High School, Univ. of Adelaide and S. Australian Inst. of Tech.; worked for CRA Group 1970–95; held several tech. and operating man. positions with Zinc Corpn Broken Hill 1970–77; transferred to Mary Kathleen Uranium Ltd (CRA subsidiary) 1977; Man. Planning and Evaluation, CRA Group, Melbourne 1980; Gen. Man. CRA's Sulphide Corpn zinc smelter, Cockle Creek, NSW 1983–85; Man. Dir Comalco Rolled Products, Sydney 1985–87; Pres. Commonwealth Aluminum Corpn Ltd USA 1988; Chief Exec. Comalco Ltd and Group Exec. CRA Ltd 1991–95; Chief Exec. M.I.M. Holdings Ltd 1995–; mem. Senate Univ. of Queensland 1996–; Pres. Minerals Council of Australia 1997–99 (mem. 1995–); Vice-Pres. Queensland Mining Council Ltd 1995–; Jt recipient of Arthur F. Taggart Award, American Inst. of Mining Engineers 1975. *Leisure interests:* cruising and offshore yacht racing. *Address:* M.I.M. Holdings Ltd, G.P.O. Box 1433, Brisbane, Queensland 4001, Australia (Office). *Telephone:* (7) 3833-8222. *Fax:* (7) 3832-6828.

STUMPF, Paul Karl, PhD; American professor of biochemistry; b. 23 Feb. 1919, New York; s. of Karl Stumpf and Annette Shreyer; m. Ruth Rodenbeck 1947; two s. three d.; ed Harvard and Columbia Univs.; Instructor, School of Public Health, Univ. of Mich. 1946–48; Asst Prof. of Plant Nutrition, Univ. of Calif., Berkeley 1948–52, Assoc. Prof. of Plant Biochem. 1952–57, Prof. 1957–58; Prof. of Biochem., Univ. of Calif., Davis 1958–84, Prof. Emer. 1984–; Consultant, Palm Oil Research Inst., Malaysia 1982–92; Chief Scientist Competitive Research Grants Office 1988–91, Nat. Research Initiative for Competitive Grants, USDA 1990–91; mem. scientific advisory Bd, Calgene Inc., Calif. 1990–93; Md Biotech. Inst. 1990–92; Guggenheim Fellow 1962, 1969, Alexander von Humboldt Fellow 1976; mem. Royal Danish Acad. of Sciences, NAS, American Soc. of Plant Physiologists (Chair., Bd of Trustees 1986–89, Pres. 1979–80); Fellow AAAS 1994; Stephens Hales Award 1974,

Lipid Chem. Award 1974, Charles Reid Barnes Life Membership Award 1992, Unit Award for Superior Service, USDA 1992, Award of Excellence, Calif. Aggie Alumni Foundation 1996. *Publications:* Outlines of Enzyme Chemistry (with J. B. Nielands), Outlines of Biochemistry (with E. E. Conn); Ed.-in-Chief Biochemistry of Plants (12 vols), Exec. Ed. Archives of Biochemistry 1965–88; over 250 scientific publs. *Leisure interests:* gardening, golf, travel. *Address:* Department of Molecular and Cellular Biology, University of California, Davis, CA 95616; 764 Elmwood Drive, Davis, CA 95616, USA (Home). *Telephone:* (916) 752-3523 (Office); (916) 753-5022 (Home). *Fax:* (916) 752-3085.

STURRIDGE, Charles; British television, film and theatre director; b. 24 June 1951, London; s. of Jerome Sturridge and Alyson Sturridge (née Burke); m. Phoebe Nichols; three c.; ed Univ. Coll., Oxford; fmr mem. Nat. Youth Theatre; fmr Pres. Oxford Univ. Dramatic Soc.; worked as actor and theatre Dir; debut as professional Dir, musical version of Hard Times, Belgrade Theatre, Coventry; joined Granada Television 1974; freelance 1981–; numerous awards for feature films and TV documentaries. *TV documentaries and drama include:* Brideshead Revisited; (17 awards including BAFTA award for Best Series, two American Golden Globe awards, Grand Award of New York Film and TV Festival), Soft Targets (BBC TV) 1982, The Storyteller 1988, Gulliver's Travels 1996 (12 int. awards, including Humanitas Prize and five US Primetime Emmys), A Foreign Field (BBC TV), Longitude (writer and Dir Channel 4) 2000 (5 BAFTA Awards including Best Series), Shackleton (writer/Dir, Channel 4), Ohio Impromptu (Beckett on Film — Channel 4) (LWT South Bank Award for Best TV Drama). *Feature films include:* Runners 1982, A Handful of Dust 1988, Where Angels Fear to Tread 1991, Fairytale—A True Story (co-writer) 1997 (BAFTA Best Children's Film 1998); Contrib. Dir to Aria (La Vergine degli angeli from La Forza del Destino). *Theatre includes:* Dir and Co-writer Hard Times, Belgrade Theatre, Coventry 1974; Dir own trans. of The Seagull, Queens Theatre, London 1985; trans. (with Tania Alexander) Uncle Vanya. *Address:* c/o Peters, Fraser & Dunlop Ltd, Drury House, 34–43 Russell Street, London, WC2B 5HA, England. *Telephone:* (20) 7344-1000 (Office).

STURUA, Robert Robertovich; Georgian theatrical director; b. 31 July 1938, Tbilisi; m. Dudana Kveselava 1968; two s.; trained at Georgian Theatre Inst. 1956–61; Dir Rustaveli Theatre, Tbilisi 1961–, Artistic Dir 1978–; has directed over 50 productions, including operas; first Guest Dir at Saarbrücken State Theatre; USSR State Prize 1979, Georgian State Prize 1981, USSR People's Artist 1982. *Opera productions include:* Music for Alive (G. Kancheli) 1984, Keto and Kote (V. Dolidze) 1986. *Plays include:* The Crucible (Miller), Italian Straw Hat (Labiche), The Good Woman of Szechuan (Brecht), Caucasian Chalk Circle, Medea (Anouilh), King Lear, Tartuffe (in Tel Aviv) 1989, Three Sisters (in London) 1990, Eugene Onegin (in Bologna) 1991, Comedy of Errors (in Helsinki) 1992, Hamlet (in London) 1992, Richard III (toured theatres around world), Antigone and many Russian and Georgian plays. *Address:* Rustaveli Theatre, Tbilisi, Georgia. *Telephone:* (32) 99-85-87.

STÜTZLE, Walther K. A., Dr rer. pol; German journalist; b. 29 Nov. 1941, Westerland-Sylt; s. of the late Moritz Stützle and of Annemarie Ruge; m. Dr. H. Kauper 1966; two s. two d.; ed Westerland High School and Univs. of Berlin, Bordeaux and Hamburg; researcher, Inst. for Strategic Studies, London 1967–68, Foreign Policy Inst. Bonn 1968–69; Desk Officer, Ministry of Defence, Planning Staff, Bonn 1969–72, Pvt. Sec. and Chef de Cabinet, 1973–76, Head, Planning Staff, Under-Sec. of Defence, Plans and Policy 1976–82; editorial staff, Stuttgarter Zeitung 1983–86; Dir Stockholm Int. Peace Research Inst. (SIPRI) 1986–91; Ed.-in-Chief Der Tagesspiegel 1994–98; Perm. Sec., Ministry of Defence 1998–. *Publications:* Adenauer und Kennedy in der Berlinkrise 1961–62 1972, Politik und Kräftverhältnis 1983; co-author: Europe's Future—Europe's Choices 1967, ABM Treaty—To Defend or Not to Defend 1987, SIPRI Yearbook (Ed.) 1986–90. *Leisure interests:* history, reading, sailing, mountain walking. *Address:* c/o Ministry of Defence, 10785 Berlin, Stauffenberg-str. 18 (Office); Traunsteiner Str. 2, 10781 Berlin, Germany. *Telephone:* (30) 20048120 (Office); (30) 2137742 (Home).

STYLES, Margretta, EdD; American professor of nursing; b. 19 March 1930, Mt. Union, Pa; d. of Russell B. and Agnes Wilson Madden; m. Douglas F. Styles 1954; two s. one d.; ed Juniata Coll., Yale Univ., Univ. of Florida; Prof. and Dean, School of Nursing, Univ. of Texas, San Antonio 1969–73, Wayne State Univ., Detroit 1973–77, Univ. of Calif., San Francisco 1977–87, Prof. and Livingston Chair. in Nursing 1987–; Pres. Int. Council of Nurses 1996–2001, American Nurses Credentialing Center 1996–; mem. Nat. Comm. on Nursing 1980–; First Distinguished Scholar, American Nurses' Foundation; mem. NAS, Inst. of Medicine; American Nurses' Asscn Hon. Recognition Award (Pres. 1986–88). *Publications:* On Nursing: Toward a New Endowment, Project on the Regulation of Nursing, Int. Council of Nurses 1985. *Leisure interest:* skydiving. *Address:* School of Nursing, N 531C-D, Box 0608, University of California (San Francisco), San Francisco, CA 94143 (Office); 12 Commons Lane, Foster City, CA 94404, USA (Home). *Telephone:* (415) 476-6701 (Office); (415) 754-3870 (Home).

STYLIANOU, Petros Savva, PhD; Cypriot politician, journalist and writer; b. 8 June 1933, Kythrea; s. of Savvas and Evanthia Stylianou; m. Voula Tzanetatou 1960; two d.; ed Pancyprian Gymnasium, Univs. of Athens and Salonika; served with Panhellenic Cttee of the Cyprus Struggle (PEKA) and Nat. Union of Cypriot Univ. Students (EFEK), Pres. EFEK 1953–54; co-founder Dauntless Leaders of the Cypriot Fighters Org. (KARI); joined liberation Movt of Cyprus 1955; imprisoned in Kyrenia Castle 1955, escaped; leader, Nat. Striking Group; sentenced to 15 years' imprisonment 1956, transferred to UK prison, released 1959; mem. Cen. Cttee United Democratic Reconstruction Front (EDMA) 1959; Deputy Sec.-Gen. Cyprus Labour Confed. (SEK) 1959, Sec.-Gen. 1960–62; f. Cyprus Democratic Labour Fed. (DEOK) 1962, Sec.-Gen. 1962–73, Hon. Pres. 1974–; mem. House of Reps. 1960–70, 1985–91, Sec. 1960–62; Deputy Minister of Interior 1980–82; Special Adviser to Pres. on Cultural Affairs 1982–85; Mayor of Engomi 1992–; Founder Pancyprian Orgs. for Rehabilitation of Spastics, Rehabilitation from Kidney Disease, from Haemophilia and from Myopathy; Pres. Cyprus Historical Museum and Archives; numerous awards and prizes from Cyprus, Greece and USA. *Publications:* numerous works on poetry, history, etc. *Address:* Erecthiou Street, P.O. Box 7504, Engomi (Office); Kimonos 10, Engomi, Nicosia, Cyprus (Home). *Telephone:* (2) 353240 (Office); (2) 445972 (Home).

STYRON, William, DLitt; American writer; b. 11 June 1925, Newport News, Va; s. of William Styron and Pauline Abraham; m. Rose Burgunder 1953; one s. three d.; ed Davidson Coll., Duke Univ.; Advisory Ed., Paris Review 1953–; Hon. Consultant, Library of Congress; Pres. Cannes Film Festival 1983; mem. Signet Soc. Harvard Univ.; Fellow, Silliman Coll., Yale Univ.; Fellow, American Acad. of Arts and Sciences; mem. American Acad. of Arts and Letters 1966–; Hon. mem. Acad. Goncourt; Duke Univ. Distinguished Alumni Award; Pulitzer Prize for best novel 1968, Howells Medal for Fiction 1970, Conn. Arts Award 1984, Prix Mondial Cino del Duca 1985, Edward MacDowell Medal 1988, Elmer Holmes Bobst Award 1989, Nat. Medal of Arts 1993, Nat. Arts Club Medal for Literature 1995, Common Wealth Award 1995, F. Scott Fitzgerald Award 1996; Commdr, Légion d'honneur, Ordre des Arts et des Lettres. *Publications:* Lie Down in Darkness 1951, The Long March 1955, Set this House on Fire 1960, The Confessions of Nat Turner 1967, In the Clap Shack (play) 1973, Sophie's Choice 1979 (American Book Award 1980), This Quiet Dust (Essays) 1982, Darkness Visible: A Memoir of Madness 1990, A Tidewater Morning 1993. *Leisure interests:* tennis, sailing. *Address:* 12 Rucum Road, Roxbury, CT 06783; Vineyard Haven, MA 02568, USA (Summer). *Telephone:* (508) 693-2535.

SU CHI, PhD; Taiwanese government official; b. 1 Oct. 1949, Taichung; s. of Chan-Wu Su and Kuo-Yin Ni; m. Grace Chen; one s. one d.; ed Nat. Chengchi Univ., Johns Hopkins Univ., Columbia Univ.; Assoc. Prof. Dept of Diplomacy Nat. Chengchi Univ. 1984–90, Prof. 1990–, Deputy Dir Inst. of Int. Relations 1990–93; Sec. Gen. Office of the Univ. Pres. 1989–90; mem. Exec. Yuan Research, Devt and Evaluation Comm. 1990–94; Sec.-Gen. China Political Science Asscn 1990–91; Deputy Dir Kuomintang Cen. Cttee Dept of Mainland Affairs 1992–93; Vice-Chair Exec. Yuan Mainland Affairs Council 1993–96; Dir-Gen. Govt Information Office 1996–97; Exec. Yuan Minister of State 1997; Nat. Policy Adviser to Pres. of Repub. 1997, Deputy Sec.-Gen. to Pres. 1997–99; Chair. Mainland Affairs Council 1999–. *Publications:* The Normalization of Sino-Soviet Relations, over 20 papers and articles. *Address:* Mainland Affairs Council, 5th–13th Floors, 2-2 Chi-nan Road, Section 1, Taipei, Taiwan (Office). *Telephone:* (2) 23975589 (Office). *Fax:* (2) 23975700 (Office). *E-mail:* macst@mac.gov.tw (Office).

SU RONG; Chinese politician; b. Oct. 1948, Taonan, Jilin Prov.; ed Jilin Univ.; joined CCP 1970; Sec. Najin Commune, Taoan Co., Jilin Prov.; Sec.-Gen. Jilin Prov. Cttee –1995, Vice-Sec. 1996–2001; Sec. Yanbian Korean Autonomous Prefecture Cttee 1995–97, Qinghai Prov. Cttee Oct. 2001–; alt. mem. 15th CCP Cen. Cttee 1997–2002. *Address:* Chinese Communist Party Qinghai Provincial Committee, Xining, Qinghai Province, People's Republic of China (Office).

SU SHAOZHI, MA; Chinese research professor; b. 25 Jan. 1923, Peking; s. of Su Xiyi and Jin Yunquan; m. Hu Jianmei; two d.; ed Chongqing Univ. and Nankai Inst. of Econs; Assoc. Prof. Fudan Univ. 1949–63; ed. Theoretical Dept Renmin Ribao (People's Daily) 1963–79; Deputy Dir Inst. of Marxism-Leninism-Mao Zedong Thought (MLMT) 1979–82, Dir 1982–87; Research Prof. Chinese Acad. of Social Sciences (CASS) 1982–87, mem. Acad. Cttee of CASS 1982–85, Prof. Graduate School of CASS 1982–; Ed. Studies of Marxism (quarterly) 1983–. *Publications:* Democracy and Socialism in China 1982, Marxism in China 1983, Democratization and Reform 1988; books and articles on politics and economics. *Leisure interests:* calligraphy and paintings, classical music. *Address:* Institute of Marxism-Leninism-Mao Zedong Thought, The Chinese Academy of Social Sciences, 5 Jianguomen Nei Dajie, Beijing 100732 (Office); 5–3 Building 28, Guang Hua Li, Jianguomen Wai, Beijing 100020, People's Republic of China (Home). *Telephone:* 5077443149 (Office); 594552 (Home).

SU SHUYANG (Su Yang, Yu Pingfu); Chinese writer; b. 1938, Baoding, Hebei Prov.; ed Renmin Univ.; fmrly teaching Asst Dept of CCP History, Renmin Univ.; lecturer Beijing Teachers' Coll.; worker Baoding Voltage Transformer Factory; lecturer Beijing Coll. of Chinese Medicine; currently playwright Beijing Film Studio; Vice-Chair. China Film Asscn. *Publications:* Wedding, Masquerade, The Death of Lao She, The Moon Goddess, I Am a Zero, Big Family Matter, Flying Moth, Taiping Lake, Sunset Boulevard: Selected Screenplays by Su Shuyang. *Address:* Beijing Film Studio, Beijing, People's Republic of China. (Office).

SU TONG; Chinese writer; b. 1963, Suzhou, Jiangsu Prov.; ed Beijing Normal Univ.; fmrly lecturer Nanjing Acad. of Arts; Ed. Zhongshan Magazine; mem. Jiangsu Provincial Writers Asscn. *Publications:* Collected Works of Su Tong

(7 vols.), The Eighth Is a Bronze Sculpture, The Escape of 1934, The Mournful Dance, A Crowd of Wives and Concubines. *Address:* Jiangsu Provincial Writers Association, Nanjing, Jiangsu Province, People's Republc of China. (Office).

SUÁREZ, The Duke of, Adolfo Suárez González; Spanish politician and lawyer; b. 25 Sept. 1932, Cebreros, Avila Province; m. Amparo Illana; five c.; ed Univs. of Salamanca and Madrid; Civil Gov. of Segovia 1969, then Dir-Gen. Radio and TV; Pres. Empresa Nacional de Turismo; Pres. Unión del Pueblo Español; Vice-Sec.-Gen. Falange until 1975, Sec.-Gen. 1975–76; Prime Minister and Pres. of Council of Ministers 1976–81; named Duke of Suárez 1981; Leader Unión Centro Democrático (UCD) 1977–81, Hon. Pres. Jan.–Dec. 1981, resigned July 1982; f. and Leader Centro Democrático y Social (CDS) 1982–91, Pres. 1982–91; MP for Madrid 1982–; Pres. Int. Liberals 1988–91; Pres. Inst. of European-Latin American Relations (IRELA).

SUÁREZ PERTIERRA, Gustavo, LLD; Spanish politician; b. 1949, Cudillero, Oviedo; m.; two c.; ed Univs. of Oviedo, Valladolid and Munich; Prof. in Canon Law, Complutense Univ., Madrid 1978, also sometime Vice-Dean of Law and mem. Academic Council of Human Rights Inst.; Dir-Gen. of Religious Matters, Ministry of Justice and Pres. of Advisory Comm. on Religious Freedom 1982; Deputy Sec. Ministry of Defence 1984; Sec. of State for Mil. Admin. 1990–93; Minister of Educ. and Science 1993–95, of Defence 1995–96; Pres. Parl. Comm. for Public Admin. 1996–. *Address:* Palacio de las Cortes, c/Carrera de San Jerónimo, Madrid 14, Spain.

SUBANDRIO; Indonesian politician, diplomatist and surgeon; b. 1914; ed Medical Univ., Jakarta; active in Nat. Movt as student and gen. practitioner; worked with underground anti-Japanese Forces during Second World War; forced to leave post at Jakarta Cen. Hosp. and then est. a pvt. practice at Semarang; following declaration of independence abandoned practice to become Sec.-Gen., Ministry of Information and was later sent by Indonesian Govt as special envoy to Europe; est. Information Office, London 1947; Chargé d'affaires, London 1949, Amb. to UK 1950–54, to USSR 1954–56; Foreign Minister 1957–66; Second Deputy First Minister 1960–66, concurrently Minister for Foreign Econ. Relations 1962–66; convicted of complicity in attempted communist coup and sentenced to death Oct. 1966; sentence commuted to life imprisonment 1970; pardoned by Pres. Suharto, released 15 Aug. 1995.

SUBBA ROW, Raman, CBE, MA; British cricketer (retd), company director and public relations consultant; b. 29 Jan. 1932, Streatham, London; s. of the late Panguluri Venkata Subba Row and of Doris Pinner; m. Anne Harrison 1960; two s. one d.; ed Whitgift School and Trinity Hall, Cambridge; Pilot Officer RAF 1956–58; left-hand opening batsman; played for Cambridge Univ. 1951–53, Surrey 1953–54, Northants. 1955–61 (Capt. 1958–61); 13 Tests for England 1958–61; toured Australia 1958–59; scored 14,182 first-class runs with 30 hundreds; Assoc. Dir W. S. Crawford Ltd 1963–69; Man. Dir Man. Public Relations Ltd 1969–92; Chair. Surrey Co. Cricket Club 1974–79, Test and County Cricket Bd 1985–90; Int. Cricket Council referee 1992–2001; apptd. to work with ICC on reform of int. umpiring and refereeing panels; mem. Inst. of Dirs; Wisden Cricketer of the Year 1961. *Leisure interests:* golf, sports generally. *Address:* Leeward, 13 Manor Way, South Croydon, Surrey, CR2 7BT, England. *Telephone:* (20) 8688-2991. *Fax:* (20) 8688-2991.

SUBBOTIN, Valery Ivanovich; Russian physicist; b. 12 Dec. 1919, Baku; s. of Ivan Subbotin and Tatiana Subbotin; m. Irina Subbotin 1945; two s. one d.; ed Baku Industrial Inst.; engineer, then chief of section Kavkazenergomash 1943–48; jr then sr researcher Energy Inst. Azerbaijan Acad. of Sciences 1952–53; Head of Lab., of Div., Deputy Dir Inst. of Physics and Energy Obninsk 1953–75; Dir Research Production enterprise Energiya 1975–77; Chair. Moscow Inst. of Physics and Eng 1977–88, also Prof.; Scientific Sec. Research group, Research Construction Inst. of Energy Tech. 1988–; Corresp. mem. USSR (now Russian) Acad. of Sciences 1967, mem. 1987, mem. Presidium 1991–, Chair. Scientific Council 'Physicotech. Analysis of Power Systems', Dept of Power, Mechanical Eng and Process Control, Chair. Comm. on Use of Energy-Accumulating Substances in Mechanics, Power Engineering and Ecology; main research on thermophysics of nuclear energy plants, methods of modelling of active zones of nuclear reactors, turbulence laws of liquid currents; Lenin Prize and other decorations. *Publications:* Liquid Metals 1967, Physical-Chemical Basis for Application of Liquid Metal Heat Carriers 1978, Structure of Turbulent Flow and Mechanism of Heat Exchange in Channels 1978, On Thermophysics of Focusing Mirrors of Laser Nuclear Reactors 1983, Interchannel Heat Exchange at Transversal Water Flow Around a Bunch of Pipes 1985, Reflections on Atomic Energetics 1995, 21st Century – Century of Nuclear Energy 1998; articles in scientific journals. *Leisure interest:* literature. *Address:* Leninsky prospect 14, Moscow, 117901; Institute of Mechanical Engineering (IMASH), Haribouevskij per. 4, 101990 Moscow, Russia (Office). *Telephone:* (095) 135-61-31 (Office); (095) 135-77–69 (Home). *E-mail:* subbotin@imash.ru (Office). *Website:* www.imash.ru (Office).

SUBBULAKSHMI, Madurai Shanmugavadivu; Indian classical Karnatic musician; b. 16 Sept. 1916, Madurai; m. Sri T. Sadasivam 1940; ed privately; recitals with her mother, Guru Veena Shanmugavadivu 1928–32; gave solo performances and became a leading musician before age 18; acted title role in Hindi film Meera; numerous benefit performances, donated royalties from many of her records to social and religious causes; rep. Karnatic music at Edin. Festival 1963; concerts in London, Frankfurt, Geneva, Cairo;

7-week tour of USA 1966; performed in Tokyo, Bangkok, Hong Kong, Manila, Singapore, Malaysia, New York, Pittsburgh, Moscow; Pres. Madras Music Acad. Conf. 1968; Nat. Prof. (Music) 1990–; Nat. Research Prof. 1995–; Producer Emer., All India Radio and Doordarshan 1979–; Life mem. Int. Music Council 1981; Trustee Indira Gandhi Nat. Centre for Arts; Hon. DLitt (Ravindra Bharati Univ.) 1967, (Shri Venkateswara Univ.) 1971, (Delhi Univ.) 1973, (Madhya Pradesh Univ.) 1979, (Banaras Hindu Univ.) 1980, (Madras Univ.) 1987, (Tirupati) 1989, (Madurai Kamaraj Univ.) 1994; numerous awards including: President's Award for Karnatic Music 1956, Ramon Magsaysay Award for Public Service (Philippines) 1974, Melvin Jones Fellowship Award for outstanding humanitarian services 1986, Indira Gandhi Award 1990, Woman of the Year Award (Int. Women's Assoc.) 1992, Swaralaya Puraskaram–Delhi Award 1997; Sangeet Natak Acad. Fellowship 1974; Padma Bhushan 1954; Padma Vibhushan 1975; hon. title Sangeetha Khalanidhi; hon. title Sapthagiri Sangeetha Vidwanmani 1975, Thanipperum Kalaignyar 1980, Gayaka Ratnam 1990. *Address:* 'Sivam-Subham', 11 First Main Road, Kotturpuram, Chennai 600085, India. *Telephone:* (44) 472288.

SUBOTNICK, Morton Leon, MA; American composer; b. 14 April 1933, Los Angeles; s. of Jack Jacob Subotnick and Rose Luckerman; m. 1st Linn Pottle 1953 (divorced 1971); one s. one d.; m. 2nd Doreen Nelson 1976 (divorced 1977); m. 3rd Joan La Barbara 1979; one s.; ed Univ. of Denver, Mills Coll.; Co-Founder, San Francisco Tape Music Center 1961–65; fmr Music Dir, Ann Halprin's Dance Co. and San Francisco Actors' Workshop, fmr Music Dir of Lincoln Center Repertory Theatre; Dir of electronic music at original Electric Circus, St Mark's Place, New York 1967–68; Artist-in-Residence at New York Univ. School of the Arts 1966–69; Co-Dir Center for Experiments in Art, Information and Tech., Calif. Inst. of Arts, Valencia 1969–, also Co-Chair. Composition Dept; Visiting Prof. in Composition, Univ. of Md 1968, Univ. of Pittsburgh 1969, Yale Univ. 1982, 1983; has toured extensively as a lecturer and composer/performer; Composer-in-Residence DAAD, West Berlin 1981, MIT 1986; Brandeis Award for Music 1983 and numerous other grants and awards. *Compositions include:* Silver Apples of the Moon, The Wild Bull, Trembling, The Double Life of Amphibians, The Key to Songs, Return: The Triumph of Reason (electronic composition in honour of the return of Halley's Comet) 1986, In Two Worlds 1987–88, And The Butterflies Begin to Sing 1988, A Desert Flowers 1989, All my Hummingbirds have Alibis, Jacob's Room (opera) 1993, Making Music 1996, Intimate Immensity 1997, Echoes from the Silent Call of Girona 1998. *Address:* 121 Coronado Lane, Santa Fe, NM 87507, USA.

SUBRAMANIAM, A.; Indian social worker and educationalist; b. 18 Oct. 1925, Kodungallur, Kerala State; s. of Ananthanarayanan Ammal and Lakshmi Ammal; jailed for six months in 1942 for participating in Quit India Movt; trade union worker; Tamil Nadu State Sec. of Socialist Party for several years; headed trade unions in textiles, Eng, road transport, ports and docks, papermaking, tea plantations, heavy electricals, etc.; Nat. Pres. Hind Mazdoor Sabha; mem. of Tamil Nadu Legis. Ass. 1971–76. *Address:* Thiagi N.G.R. Bhavan, 248 (Old 2112) Trichy Road, Singanallur, Coimbatore 641 005 (Office); Thamarai, 42 (Old 65) 2nd Street, Lal Bahadur Nagar, Coimbatore 641 004, India (Home). *Telephone:* (422) 573145 (Office); (422) 574460 (Home); (422) 574140. *Fax:* (422) 574140 (Office).

SUBRAMANYAN, Kalpathi Ganapathi; Indian artist and professor of art; b. 5 Feb. 1924, Kerala; s. of K. P. Ganapathi and Alamelu Ammal; m. Susheela Jasra 1951; one d.; ed Univ. of Madras, Kalabhavana, Visvabharati and Slade School of Art, London; Lecturer in Painting, Faculty of Fine Arts, M. G. Univ., Baroda 1951–59, Reader 1961–66, Prof. 1966–80, Dean, Faculty of Fine Arts 1968–74; Prof. of Painting, Kalabhavana, Visva Bharati, Santiniketan 1980–89, Prof. Emer. 1989–; Deputy Dir (Designs), All India Handloom Bd, Bombay 1959–61, Design Consultant 1961–65; Visiting Lecturer, Canada 1976; Visiting Fellow, Visvabharati, Santiniketan 1977–78; Christensen Fellow, St Catherine's Coll., Oxford 1987–88; JDR III Fund Fellowship, New York 1967–68; Fellow Lalit Kala Acad. 1984; numerous solo exhbns.; work has been displayed in many countries; Hon. DLitt (Rabindra Bharati Univ., Calcutta) 1992, (Banaras Hindu Univ., Varanasi) 1997; Hon. Mention (São Paulo Biennale) 1961, Nat. Award 1965, Gold Medal, 1st Indian Triennale 1968; Padma Shri (India) 1975; Kalidas Samman 1981. *Publications:* Moving Focus (essays on art) 1978, Living Tradition 1985, Creative Circuit (collection of lectures) 1991. *Leisure interests:* reading, handicraft. *Address:* Kalabhavana, Santiniketan, 731235, West Bengal (Office); Kailas, 13 Purvapalli, Santiniketan, 731235, West Bengal, India (Home).

SUBROTO, MA, PhD; Indonesian politician; b. 19 Sept. 1928, Surakarta; s. of Sindurejo Subroto and Ibu Subroto; m. Trisnowati Harsono 1958; three s.; ed Univ. of Indonesia, McGill, Stanford and Harvard Univs; fmr Dir-Gen. of Research and Devt, Ministry of Trade; Prof. in Int. Econs, Univ. of Indonesia; Minister of Resettlement and Co-operatives 1971–73, of Manpower, Transmigration and Co-operatives 1973–78, of Mines and Energy 1978–88; Chair. of Bd Pertamina 1978–88; Sec.-Gen. OPEC 1988–95. *Publications:* numerous books on econ. topics. *Leisure interests:* tennis, golf, reading. *Address:* c/o Ministry of Foreign Affairs, Jalan Taman Pejambon, 6 Jakarta Pusat, Indonesia.

SUCHARIPA, Ernst, LLB; Austrian diplomatist; b. 24 July 1947, Vienna; m.; ed Univ. of Vienna and Diplomatic Acad., Vienna; joined foreign service 1974, Dept of Int. Law, then with Perm. Mission to the UN 1975–80, Deputy Chief of Mission, Embassy GDR 1980–83, Asst Dir Dept of Int. Orgs., Ministry of Foreign Affairs, Deputy, then Chef de Cabinet Office of the Minister for Foreign Affairs 1984–85, Head Dept. for E Europe 1987–90, Dir.-Gen. for Political Affairs 1990–93, Perm. Rep. to the UN 1993–2000; Special Envoy for Restitution Issues 2001. *Address:* c/o Ministry of Foreign Affairs, Ballhauspl. 1014 Vienna, Austria (Office).

SUCHET, David, OBE; British actor; b. 2 May 1946, London; s. of the late Jack Suchet and Joan Suchet (née Jarché); m. Sheila Ferris 1976; one s. one d.; ed Wellington School, Somerset, LAMDA, London; fmr mem. Nat. Youth Theatre, Chester Repertory Co.; joined RSC 1973; Assoc. Artist Birmingham Rep., Connaught Theatre, Worthing, Northcott Theatre, Exeter, Liverpool Rep., Chichester Festival Theatre, Theatre Royal, Bath; Visiting Prof. of Theatre, Univ. of Neb., USA 1975; mem. Fight Directors' Asscn; Brown Belt in Aikido; a First Master of Japanese Samurai. *Roles for RSC include:* Tybalt in Romeo and Juliet 1973, Orlando in As You Like It 1973, Tranio in Taming of the Shrew 1973, Zamislov in Summerfolk 1974, 1975, Wilmer in Comrades 1974, The Fool in King Lear 1974, 1975, Pisanio in Cymbeline 1974, Hubert in King John, Ferdinand King of Navarre in Love's Labour's Lost 1975, Shylock in The Merchant of Venice 1978, Grumio in Taming of the Shrew 1978, Sir Nathaniel in Love's Labour's Lost 1978, Glougauer in Once in a Lifetime 1978, Caliban in The Tempest 1978, Sextus Pompey in Antony and Cleopatra 1978, Angelo in Measure for Measure 1979, Iago in Othello, Every Good Boy Deserves Favour, Bolingbroke in Richard II 1981, Achilles in Troilus and Cressida, Mercutio in Romeo and Juliet, Iago in Othello 1985. *Other stage roles include:* Lucio in Measure for Measure 1977, Thomas Gilthead in The Devil is an Ass 1977, The Kreutzer Sonata 1978, Tsaravitch and George Wochner in Laughter! 1978, Joe Green in Separation 1987, This Story of Yours, Litvanoy in The Wedding Feast, Estragon in Waiting for Godot, John Aubrey in Brief Lives, Mole in Toad of Toad Hall, Timon in Timon of Athens 1991, John in Oleanna (Variety Club Best Actor Award 1994) 1993, Sid Field in What a Performance 1994, George in Who's Afraid of Virginia Woolf? (Critic's Circle Best Actor Award 1997) 1996, Salieri in Amadeus (Variety Club Best Actor Award 1998, South Bank Award and Backstage Theatre Award 2000) 1998–2000. *Films:* Tale of Two Cities 1978, Schiele in Prison 1980, The Missionary 1982, Hunchback of Notre Dame 1982, Red Monarch (Best Actor, Marseilles Film Festival 1983) 1983, Trenchcoat 1983, Greystoke: The Legend of Tarzan, Lord of the Apes 1984, Little Drummer Girl 1984, Song for Europe (video title Cry for Justice) (Best Actor, Royal TV Soc. Performance Awards 1986) 1985, Thirteen to Dinner 1985, Falcon and the Snowman 1985, Gulag 1985, Iron Eagle 1986, Murrow 1986, Big Foot and The Hendersons 1986, Stress (Best Actor Award, British Industry/Scientific Film Asscn 1986) 1986, Crime of Honor 1987, The Last Innocent Man 1987, A World Apart 1988, To Kill a Priest (also known as Popielusko) 1988, The Lucona Affair, When the Whales Came 1990, Executive Decision 1995, Deadly Voyage 1995, Sunday 1996, A Perfect Murder 1997, RKO 1999, Sabotage 1999, Live From Baghdad 2002, The Wedding Party 2002, Foolproof 2002. *Work for radio includes:* The Kreutzer Sonata (one-man show) (Best Radio Actor of the Year 1979), Shylock in The Merchant of Venice, Bolingbroke in Richard II, First Night Impression, Rosenberg in the Trenches, Chimes at Midnight, The Isaac Babel Stories, Super Cannes (Book at Bedtime) and numerous other parts. *Television includes:* dramatization of Agatha Christie's Poirot novels (for LWT) Series I 1989, II 1990, III 1991, IV 1992, V 1993, VI 1994, VII 2000, 100th Anniversary Special: The Mysterious Affair at Styles 1990, Oppenheimer 1978, Being Normal, Saigon – the Last Days, Time to Die, The Life of Freud (Best Actor, Royal TV Soc. Performance Awards 1986), Blott on the Landscape (Best Actor, Royal TV Soc. Performance Awards 1986), Oxbridge Blues 1986, Playing Shakespeare 1983, Master of the Game 1984, Reilly – Ace of Spies 1984, Mussolini: The Untold Story 1985, James Joyce's Ulysses, Cause Célèbre 1988, The Life of Agatha Christie 1990, Once in a Lifetime, Bingo, Long Ago and Far Away 1989, Days of Majesty 1994, Fighting Fund (episode of The Protectors), Separation 1990, Secret Agent, Kings and Castles, Nobody Here but Us Chickens 1989, The Cruel Train, The Curious 1994, Moses 1995, Solomon 1997, See Saw 1997, The Way We Live Now 2001, National Crime Squad 2001–02, Maggie 2003. *Publications:* essays in Players of Shakespeare 1985. *Leisure interests:* photography, clarinet, ornithology, theology, narrow boating. *Address:* c/o Ken McReddie Ltd, 91 Regent Street, London, W1 7TB, England. *Telephone:* (20) 7439-1456. *Fax:* (20) 7734-6530.

SUCHOCKA, Hanna, DrIur; Polish politician and lawyer; b. 3 April 1946, Pleszew; ed Adam Mickiewicz Univ., Poznań; scientific worker, Dept of Constitutional Law of Adam Mickiewicz Univ., Poznań 1968–69, 1972–90, Catholic Univ. of Lublin 1988–92, Polish Acad. of Science 1990–; mem. Democratic Party (SD) 1969–84, Democratic Union 1991–94, Freedom Union 1994–; Deputy to Sejm (Parl.) 1980–85, 1989–2001; mem. Civic. Parl. Caucus 1989–91, mem. Democratic Union Parl. Caucus (now Freedom Union) 1991–, Deputy Chair. Parl. Legis. Cttee 1989–92; Chair. Council of Ministers (Prime Minister) 1992–93; Minister of Justice and Attorney-Gen. 1997–99; mem. Pontifical Acad. of Social Sciences, Rome 1994–; Amb. to the Holy See 2001–; Dr hc (Oklahoma Univ.); Max Schmidtheiny Prize 1994. *Publications:* author of reports and articles for professional pubs and int. confs. *Address:* Polish Embassy, via del Selfini, 300186 Rome, Italy.

SUCKLING, Charles W., CBE, DSc, PhD, FRSC, FRS; British chemist; b. 24 July 1920, Teddington; s. of Edward Ernest Suckling and Barbara Suckling (née Thomson); m. Eleanor Margaret Watterson 1946; two s. one d.; ed Oldershaw

Grammar School, Wallasey, Univ. of Liverpool; with Imperial Chemical Industries PLC 1942–82, Deputy Chair. Mond Div. 1969–72, Chair. Paints Div. 1972–77, Gen. Man. Research and Tech. 1977–82; Chair. Bradbury, Suckling and Partners Ltd 1981–92; Dir (non-exec.) Albright and Wilson 1982–89; Visiting Prof. Stirling Univ. 1969–92; mem. Science Consultative Group, BBC 1979–82; mem. Royal Comm. on Environmental Pollution 1981–92; Treas. Royal Coll. of Art, London 1984–90; mem. Nat. Curriculum Working Parties for English and Modern Foreign Languages 1988–91; numerous other appointments; Hon. DSc (Liverpool) 1980; Hon. DUniv (Stirling) 1985; John Scott Medal of City of Philadelphia for invention of anaesthetic halothane 1973, Leverhulme Prize Soc. Chem. Industry 1942, Gold Medal of Royal Coll. of Anaesthetists 1992. *Publications:* Research in the Chemical Industry 1969, Chemistry Through Models (with C. J. and K. E. Suckling) 1978. *Leisure interests:* music, writing, horticulture, languages. *Address:* 1 Desborough Drive, Tewin, Welwyn, Herts, AL6 0HQ, England. *Telephone:* (1438) 798250. *E-mail:* charlessuckling@compuserve.com (Home).

SUDHARMONO, Gen.; Indonesian politician; b. 12 March 1927, Gresik; ed Mil. Law Acad., Mil. Law Inst., Army Staff and Command Coll.; Commdr Reserve Troops, Ronggolawe Div., E and Cen. Java 1945–49; army officer, Bandung Educ. Centre 1950–52; Staff Officer, Cen. War Authority 1957–61; Alternate Mil. Attorney/Staff Officer, Supreme War Authority Office 1962–63; Asst to Special Affairs Div. of Consultative Team to Leadership of the Revolution 1963–66; Sec. Econ. Stabilization Council 1966; Cabinet Sec. 1966; Chair., Co-ordinator, Cttee for Int. Tech. Co-operation 1966; Sec. Audit Team 1971; became Maj.-Gen. 1971; State Sec. (and Cabinet Sec.) 1972; Minister, State Sec. 1973–88; Vice-Pres. of Indonesia 1988–93; Head Advisory Bd for Promotion of Pancasila (state ideology) 1994–. *Address:* Senopati Street 44B, Jakarta Selatan, Indonesia.

SUDJIC, Deyan, OBE; British architecture critic and arts administrator; b. 6 Sept. 1952, London; s. of the late Miša J. Sudjic and of Ceja Sudjic (née Pavlovic); m. Sarah Miller; one d.; ed Latymer Upper School, London and Univ. of Edin.; chose not to practise as an architect; Architecture Corresp. Sunday Times 1980–85; fmr Critic London Daily News; Critic Sunday Correspondent 1989–90; Architecture Critic The Guardian 1991–97; Visiting Prof. of Design Theory and History, Hochschule für Angewandte Kunst, Vienna 1993–97; Dir Glasgow 1999 UK City of Architecture and Design; Ed. Domus Magazine 2000–; Architecture Critic The Observer 2000–; Dir 8th Venice Architectural Biennale 2002; Founder Ed., later Editorial Dir Blue-print magazine, also f. Tate and Eye magazines. *Exhibitions curated include:* New British Architecture – Foster Rogers Stirling, Royal Acad., London (Co-Curator) 1986, The Public Realm, Heinz Gallery, London 1990, An Opera House for Wales, Nat. Museum of Wales/Oriel Gallery, Cardiff 1994, Design as Identity, Louisiana Museum, Humlebaek, Denmark 1996, Home, Glasgow Green 1999, The Architecture of Democracy, McLellan Galleries, Glasgow 1999, Norman Foster: Exploring the City, British Museum 2001. *Publications include:* Cult Objects 1985, New British Architecture: The Design of Richard Rogers, Norman Foster and James Stirling 1986, Rei Kawakubo: A Monograph of the Japanese Fashion Designer 1990, Cult Heroes: An Investigation of the Mechanics of Celebrity 1990, The Hundred Mile City: A Study of the Rapidly Evolving Modern City 1992, The Architecture of Richard Rogers 1995, The Architecture of Erick van Egeraat 1997, Ron Arad: A Monograph 1999, John Pawson Works 2000. *Address:* Editoriale Domus, Via Gianni Mazzocchi 1/3, 20089 Rozzano, Italy (Office). *Telephone:* (02) 82472265 (Office). *Fax:* (02) 82472386 (Office). *E-mail:* press@edidomus.it (Office). *Website:* www.edidomus.it/Domus (Office).

SUDOMO; Indonesian politician; b. 20 Sept. 1926, Malang, E Java; ed Navigation High School, Cilacap, Cen. Java, Artillerie School Koninklijke Marine Den Helder, Netherlands, Inst. for Nat. Defence (LEMHANAS), School for Marine Commdrs., Surabaya and Naval Staff and Command Coll., Jakarta; Battalion III Base IX 1945–50; Commdr Flores and First Officer Gajah Madah 1950–56; Head, Directorate of Operations and Training Credits, Naval H.Q., Commdr Special Fighting Unit, promoted Vice-Adm. 1956–62; Theatre Naval Commdr for liberation of W Irian 1962–64; Asst to Minister of Sea Communications 1964–66; Insp.-Gen. of Navy 1966–68; Commdr Cen. Maritime Territory 1968–69; Chief of Staff of Indonesian Navy, promoted Admiral 1969–73; Deputy Chief of Command for Restoration of Security and Order 1973–74; Chief of Staff 1974–78; Deputy Commdr in charge of Armed Forces 1978–83; Minister of Manpower 1983–88, Co-ordinating Minister of Political Affairs and Security 1988–93; Chair. Supreme Advisory Council 1993–98. *Address:* c/o Supreme Advisory Council, Jalan Merdeka Utara 15, Jakarta Pusat 10110, Indonesia.

SUGAÏ, Kumi; Japanese painter; b. 1919; ed Osaka School of Fine Arts; rep. at Pittsburgh Carnegie Int. Exhbn 1955, Salon des Réalités Nouvelles 1956, 1957, Salon de Mai 1957, 1958, Salon Biennale 1957 (all Paris) and Dunn Int. Exhbn, London 1963; Int. Painting Prize, São Paulo Biennale 1965. *Solo exhibitions include:* Galerie Cruen, Paris, Palais des Beaux Arts, Brussels 1954, St George's Gallery, London 1955, Galerie Legendre, Paris 1957. *Publication:* La quête sans fin.

SUGAR, Sir Alan Michael, Kt; British business executive; b. 24 March 1947, London; s. of Nathan Sugar and Fay Sugar; m. Ann Simons 1968; two s. one d.; ed Brooke House School, London; Chair. and Man. Dir Amstrad PLC 1968–97, CEO –1993, Chair. 1997–2001, Chair. and CEO 2001–; Chair., owner Tottenham Hotspur PLC 1991–2001; Chair. Viglen PLC 1997–; Hon.

Fellow City and Guilds of London Inst.; Hon. DSc (City Univ.) 1988. *Leisure interest:* tennis. *Address:* Amstrad PLC, 169 King's Road, Brentwood, Essex, CM14 4EF, England (Office). *Telephone:* (1277) 228888. *Fax:* (1277) 232818 (Office). *E-mail:* ams@amstrad.com (Office). *Website:* amstrad.com (Office).

SUGISAKI, Shigemitsu; Japanese international official and fmr civil servant; b. 1941, Tokyo; ed Univ. of Tokyo, Columbia Univ.; positions with Ministry of Finance 1964–76, 1979–94 including mem. Minister's Secr., Deputy Vice-Minister of Finance for Int. Affairs 1990–91, Deputy Dir-Gen. Int. Finance Bureau 1991–92, Commr Tokyo Regional Taxation Bureau 1992–93, Sec.-Gen. Exec. Bureau Securities and Exchange Surveillance Comm. 1993–94; Personal Asst to Pres. Asian Devt Bank 1976–79; Special Adviser to Man. Dir IMF 1994–97, Deputy Man. Dir 1997–. *Address:* IMF, 700 19th Street, NW, Washington, DC 20431, USA (Office); 4200 Massachusetts Avenue, NW, 802 Washington, DC 20016 (Home). *Telephone:* (202) 623-8257 (Office). *Fax:* (202) 623-4364 (Office). *E-mail:* ssugisaki@imf.org (Office). *Website:* www.imf.org (Office).

SUGITA, Katsuyuki, BEcons; Japanese banker; b. 13 Oct. 1942; ed Tokyo Univ.; joined Nippon Kangyo Bank 1966 (later merged with Dai-Ichi Bank Ltd to form Dai-Ichi Kangyo Bank); Man. Dir and Gen. Man. Planning and Co-ordination Div., Dai-Ichi Kangyo Bank 1995–96, Man. Dir of Div. V, Nat. Banking Admin. April–May 1996, Man. Dir 1996–2002; Pres. Mizuho Holdings (banking group formed with merger of Dai-Ichi Bank Ltd, Fuji Bank Ltd and Industrial Bank Ltd 2000) 2000–02. *Address:* c/o Mizuho Holdings, Marunouvhi Center Building, G1 Marunouchi, Chiyoda-ku, Tokyo, Japan (Office).

SUHARTO, Gen. Mohamed, T.N.I.; Indonesian politician and army officer; b. 8 June 1921, Kemusu, Yogjakarta; m. Siti Hartinah 1947 (died 1996); six c.; ed mil. schools and Indonesian Army Staff and Command Coll.; Officer in Japanese-sponsored Indonesian Army 1943; Battalion, later Regimental Commdr, Yogjakarta 1945–50; Regimental Commdr, Cen. Java 1953; Brig.-Gen. 1960, Maj.-Gen. 1962; Deputy Chief of Army Staff 1960–65; Chief of Army Staff 1965–68, Supreme Commdr 1968–73; Minister of Army 1965; assumed emergency exec. powers March 1966; Deputy Prime Minister for Defence and Security 1966; Chair. of Presidium of Cabinet, in charge of Defence and Security, also Minister of Army 1966–67; Full Gen. 1966; Acting Pres. of Indonesia 1967–68; Prime Minister 1967, concurrently Minister for Defence and Security 1967–73; Pres. of Indonesia March 1968–98; corruption charges against him dismissed when declared medically unfit to stand trial Sept. 2000; UN Population Award 1989. *Publication:* Suharto, My Thoughts, Words and Deeds 1989. *Address:* 8 Jalan Cendana, Jakarta, Indonesia (Home).

SUHL, Harry, PhD; American professor of physics; b. 18 Oct. 1922, Leipzig, Germany; s. of Bernhard Suhl and Klara Bergwerk; m. 1949 (deceased); ed Univ. Coll., Cardiff and Oriel Coll., Oxford; Temp. Experimental Officer, Admiralty, London 1943–46; Tech. Staff, Bell Labs., NJ 1948–60; Prof. of Physics, Univ. of Calif. (San Diego) 1961–; Consultant, Aerospace Corpn 1961–, Exxon Research and Eng, NJ 1977–; Fellow, American Physics Soc., NAS; Guggenheim Fellow 1968–69; Nat. Science Foundation Fellow 1971; Co-Ed. Magnetism 1961–74; Solid State Communications 1961–; Alexander V. Humboldt Sr Fellow 1991; Fellow American Acad. of Arts and Sciences. *Publication:* Magnetism—a Treatise on Modern Theory and Materials (with G.T. Rado) 1966. *Address:* Physics Department, University of California, 9500 Gilman Drive, La Jolla, CA 92093, USA. *Telephone:* (619) 534-4748. *Fax:* (619) 534-0173 (Office). *E-mail:* hsuhl@ucsd.edu (Office).

SUI, Anna; American fashion designer; b. 1955, Dearborn Heights, Mich.; d. of Paul Sui and Grace Sui; ed Parsons School of Design, New York; f. and designer Anna Sui Corpn 1988–; brought out first collection 1991; established reputation with 'baby-doll' collection 1993; designer Sui Anna Sui 1995–; launched new line of special-occasion gowns 1997; Perry Ellis Award. *Address:* Anna Sui Corporation, 275 West 39th Street, Floor 9, New York, NY 10018 (Office); 113 Green Street, New York, NY 10012, U.S.A. (Office). *Telephone:* (212) 768-1951 (Office).

SUI MINGTAI, Lt-Gen.; Chinese army officer; b. 1942, Zhaoyuan Co., Shandong Prov.; joined PLA 1960; joined CCP 1962; Vice-Dir then Dir Political Dept of PLA Second Artillery Force 1990–; mem. 15th CCP Cen. Cttee 1997–. *Address:* People's Liberation Army Second Artillery Force Headquarters, Beijing, People's Republic of China.

SUI YONGJU, Lt-Gen.; Chinese army officer; b. Nov. 1932, Dalian City; engaged in secret communist activities while still at school as mem. New Democratic Youth; joined CCP 1950; joined PLA; Clerk Luda Garrison Command responsible for Communist Youth League work; Sec. Political Office Public Security Militia Luda Border Defence Regt 1953; Co. Political Guidance Officer Eng Regt Second Artillery, Regt Org. Section Chief, Div. Chief Political Dept 1969, Political Commissar, Dir Base Political Dept, Asst Political Commissar, Base Political Commissar; elected. mil. rep. 7th NPC 1988; selected as activist to study Mao's works 1968; trained Second Artillery Eng Acad. 1985, Dir Political Office Second Artillery 1988, promoted to Maj. Gen. 1988; Second Asst Political Commissar Second Artillery 1990, Political Commissar 1992; mem. Cen. Comm. for Disciplinary Inspection; rank of Gen. 1996. *Address:* People's Liberation Army, c/o Ministry of National Defence, Jingshanqian Jie, Beijing, People's Republic of China.

SUISSA, Eliyahu; Israeli politician; b. 1956, Afula, Morocco; m.; four c.; mem. Shas (Sephardic Torah Guardians); joined Ministry of Interior, firstly in charge of Jerusalem Dist, then as Deputy Dir-Gen.; Minister of the Interior and of Religious Affairs 1996–99, of Nat. Infrastructure 1999–2000; Minister without Portfolio, responsible for Jerusalem Affairs 2001–02. *Address:* c/o Ministry of the Interior, P.O. Box 6158, 2 Rehov Kaplan, Kiryat Ben-Gurion, Jerusalem 9108, Israel (Office).

SUITNER, Otmar; Austrian conductor; b. 16 May 1922, Innsbruck; s. of Karl Suitner and Maria Rizzi; m. Marita Wilckens 1948; ed Pädagogium Innsbrück, Mozarteum Salzburg; Music Dir in Remscheid 1952–57; Gen. Dir of Pfalzorchester in Ludwigshafen 1957–60; Gen. Dir of State Opera Dresden 1960–64; Gen. Dir German State Opera Berlin 1964–89; Hon. Conductor Nippon Hoso Kyokai Orchestra, Tokyo 1973–88; Guest Conductor San Francisco, Tokyo, Vienna, Bayreuth Festival, etc.; many recordings; led course for conductors, Int. Summer Acad. Univ. Mozarteum, Salzburg 1975, 1976; Prof. 1968; Prof. in Conducting, Hochschule für Musik, Vienna 1977–; Commendatore, Gregorian Order 1973; Austrian Ehrenkreuz for Science and Art 1982. *Address:* Platanenstr. 13, 13156 Berlin, Germany; Widerhoferplatz 4/48, 1090 Vienna, Austria.

SUK, Josef; Czech violinist (retd); b. 8 Aug. 1929, Prague; s. of Josef Suk and Marie Suková; great-grandson of Antonín Dvořák; grandson of Josef Suk; m. Marie Poláková 1951; ed Prague Conservatory and studied with Jaroslav Kocian; First violinist, Prague String Quartet 1950; f. Suk Trio 1952; soloist with Czech Philharmonic Orchestra 1961–; Prof., Vienna Conservatoire 1979–86; has given concerts as a soloist or with trio throughout the world; announced retirement from professional career 2001; Pres. Prague Spring Foundation, Antonín Dvořák Foundation; numerous recordings; Hon. mem. Int. Antonín Dvořák Soc. 1999; Chevalier, Légion d'honneur 2002; Grand Prix du Disque 1960, 1966, 1968, 1974, 1978, Czechoslovak State Prize 1964, Edison Prize 1972, Wiener Flötenuhr 1974, Honoured Artist 1970, National Artist 1977, Golden Disc of Nippon Columbia 1978, Plaque of 100th Anniversary of Béla Bartók's Birth 1981, Czech State Prize 1999, Platinum Record Supraphon 1999, Medal of Merit 1999, Prize, Masaryk Acad. of Peforming Arts 2001. *Leisure interests:* music, literature. *Address:* Karlovo náměstí 5, 12000 Prague 2, Czech Republic. *Telephone:* (2) 24919765. *Fax:* (2) 24919765.

SUKARNOPUTRI, Megawati (see Megawati Sukarnoputri).

SUKSELAINEN, Vieno Johannes; Finnish politician and economist; b. 12 Oct. 1906, Paimio; m. Elma Bonden 1938; three s. one d.; Lecturer School of Social Sciences, Helsinki 1939; Sec. to Prime Minister 1941–45; teacher of political econs, Univ. of Turku 1945–47; Prof. School of Social Sciences, Univ. of Tampere 1947–54, Rector 1953–54, Chancellor 1969–78; Pres. of the Agrarian Union 1945–64; mem. Finnish Parl. 1948–70, 1972–79, Speaker 1956–57, 1958–59, 1968–70, 1972–75; Minister of Finance 1950–51, 1954; Minister of Interior 1951–53; Gen. Dir People's Pension Inst. 1954–71; Prime Minister May–Nov. 1957, 1959–61; fmr mem. Nordic Council, Pres. 1972, 1977. *Leisure interest:* agriculture.

SULAIM, Suliman Abd al aziz as-; Saudi Arabian politician; b. 1941; ed Cairo Univ., Univ. of Southern Calif., Johns Hopkins Univ.; Dir Dept of Foreign Relations and Confs., Ministry of Labour; Asst Dir-Gen. Gen. Org. of Social Insurance; Prof. Political Science, Riyadh Univ. 1972–74; Deputy Minister of Commerce and Industry for Trade and Provisions 1974–75; Minister of Commerce 1975–95; Chair. Bd Saudi Arabian Specifications and Standardization Org., Wheat Silos and Flour Mills Org. *Address:* c/o Ministry of Commerce, P.O. Box 1774, Airport Road, 11162 Riyadh, Saudi Arabia.

SULEIMENOV, Tuleutai Skakovich; Kazakhstan diplomatist; b. 1941, Semipalatinsk; ed Karaganda Polytech. Inst., Diplomatic Acad. of USSR Ministry of Foreign Affairs; foreman Karaganda Metallurgic factory –1969, Comsomol and CP functionary 1969–80; mem. USSR Ministry of Foreign Affairs 1980–; Counsellor USSR Embassy to Iran 1988–91; Kazakhstan Minister of Foreign Affairs 1991–94; Amb. to USA 1994–95; to Hungary 1995–2001, to Belgium 2001–. *Leisure interests:* chess, tennis. *Address:* 30 Avenue Van Bever, 1180 Brussels, Belgium (Office); Aiteke-bi 65, Alma-Ata, Kazakhstan. *Telephone:* (2) 374-9562 (Office). *Fax:* (2) 374-50-91 (Office). *E-mail:* kazakstan.embassy@linkline.be.

SULEYMANOGLU, Naim; Turkish weightlifter; b. 1967, Ptchar, Bulgaria; defected to Turkey in 1986; youngest world record breaker (16 years, 62 days) when he set records for clean and jerk (160 kg.) and combined total (285 kg.); triple Olympic gold medallist; seven-time World Championships (twice for Bulgaria); retd 1996; Vice-Pres. Int. Weightlifting Fed.; launched clothing and leather goods business; voted one of the 25 greatest athletes of the 20th century by Int. Sports Journalist Asscn. *Address:* c/o International Weightlifting Federation, Pf. 614, 1374 Budapest, Hungary (Office).

SULEYMENOV, Olzhas Omarovich; Kazakhstan politician and writer; b. 1936; ed Kazak State Univ., Maxim Gorky Inst. of Literature in Moscow; mem. CPSU 1989–90; debut as writer in 1960; Ed.-in-Chief Studio Kazakhfilm 1962–71; head of div. Prostor (magazine) 1971–; Sec. Bd Kazakh Writers' Union 1971–; Chair. Kazakh Cttee on relations with writers of Asia and Africa 1980–; actively participates in ecological movt, actions of protest against nuclear tests in Semipalatinsk since late 1980s; Deputy to USSR Supreme Soviet 1984–89; People's Deputy, mem. USSR Supreme Soviet 1989–91; Founder and Leader of People's Progress Party of Kazakhstan 1992–95; Amb. to Italy 1995–2001; USSR Komsomol Prize, State Abai Prize of Kazakh SSR.

Publications: collections of poetry including Argamaki 1961, Sunny Nights 1962, The Night of Paris 1963, The Kind Time of the Sunrise 1964, The Year of Monkey 1967, Above White Rivers 1970, Each Day – Morning 1973, Repeating in the Noon 1973, A Round Star 1975, Definition of a Bank 1976 and others. *Address:* Embassy of Kazakhstan, Piazza Farnese 101, 00186, Rome, Italy (Office); Karla Marksa str. 96, Apt. 6, 480100 Alma-Ata, Kazakhstan (Home). *Telephone:* (06) 68891360 (Office); (3272) 68-20-65 (Home). *E-mail:* Kazakhstan.emb@agora.stm.it (Office).

SULIOTIS, Elena; Greek soprano opera singer; b. 28 May 1943, Athens; d. of Constantino Souliotis and Gallia Cavalengo; m. Marcello Guerrini 1970; one d.; ed Buenos Aires and Milan; grew up in Argentina; went to Milan and was introduced to Gianandrea Gavazzeni 1962; studied singing with Mercedes Llopart; debut in Cavalleria Rusticana, Teatro San Carlo, Naples 1964; sang Amelia in Un Ballo in Maschera, Trieste 1965 and has since sung frequently throughout Italy; debut at La Scala as Abigail in Nabucco 1966; U.S. debut as Helen of Troy in Mefistofele, Chicago 1966; debut at Covent Garden as Lady Macbeth 1969; has also appeared at Teatro Colón, Buenos Aires and in Rio de Janeiro, São Paulo, Mexico City, New York, Dallas, Philadelphia, San Antonio, Montreal, Paris, Kiel, Lübeck, Höchst, Tokyo, Lisbon, Athens and Madrid. *Repertoire includes:* Manon Lescaut, La Gioconda, Macbeth, Norma, Otello, Aida, Luisa Miller, Il Trovatore, Tosca, Loreley, La Forza del Destino, etc.; has recorded Norma, Cavalleria Rusticana, Nabucco, Anna Bolena, Macbeth and arias for Decca; recipient of several prizes. *Leisure interests:* country life, looking after plants and animals. *Address:* Villa il Poderino, Via Incontri 38, Florence, Italy.

SULLIVAN, Andrew, PhD; British journalist; b. 20 Aug. 1963, Godstone, Surrey; ed Magdalen Coll., Oxford Univ., Dept of Govt, Harvard Univ., USA; joined New Republic magazine 1986, Ed. 1991–96; columnist The Sunday Times, London. *Publication:* Virtually Normal: An Argument About Homosexuality 1995. *Address:* c/o New Republic, Suite 600, 1220 19th Street, NW, Washington, DC 20036, USA.

SULLIVAN, Barry F., MBA; American politician and business executive; b. 21 Dec. 1930, Bronx, NY; m.; four s. one d.; ed Georgetown and Columbia Univs. and Univ. of Chicago; with Chase Manhattan Bank 1957–80, mem. Man. Cttee 1974–80; Chair. of Bd and CEO First Chicago Corpn, First Nat. Bank of Chicago 1980–91; apptd. Deputy Mayor, Finance and Econ. Devt, New York 1992; mem. Econ. Devt Comm. of Chicago, Asscn of Reserve City Bankers, Mayor's Airport Study Comm., Chicago Clearing House Cttee, World's Fair Finance Cttee; Vice-Pres. Exec. Cttee, Chicago Asscn of Commerce and Industry; Dir United Way; Crusade of Mercy Chicago, Campaign Dir 1985; Trustee and mem. Exec. Cttee, Univ. of Chicago, also Chair. of Council of Graduate School of Business; Trustee, Art Inst. of Chicago.

SULLIVAN, Dennis P., PhD; American mathematician; b. 12 Feb. 1941, Port Huron, Mich.; three s. two d.; ed Rice and Princeton Univs; NATO Fellow, Univ. of Warwick, UK 1966; Miller Fellow, Univ. of Berkeley 1967–69; Sloan Fellow of Math. MIT 1969–72, Prof. of Math. 1972–73; Prof. Perm., Institut des Hautes Etudes Scientifiques, Paris, France 1974–; Einstein Prof. of Sciences, Queens Coll. and CUNY Grad. School, CUNY, New York 1981; mem. NAS; Hon. Dr. (Warwick) 1984; Oswald Veblen Prize in Geometry 1971; Elie Cartan Prix en Géométrie, French Acad. of Sciences 1981. *Publications:* several papers in math. journals. *Leisure interest:* people.

SULLIVAN, Louis Wade, MD; American politician and physician; b. 3 Nov. 1933, Atlanta; s. of Walter Wade Sullivan and Lubirda Elizabeth (née Priester) Sullivan; m. Eve Williamson 1955; three c.; ed Morehouse Coll., Atlanta, Boston Univ.; Intern New York Hosp.-Cornell Medical Centre, New York 1958–59, resident in internal medicine 1959–60; Fellow in Pathology, Mass. Gen. Hosp., Boston 1960–61; Research Fellow Thorndike Memorial Lab., Harvard Medical School, Boston 1961–63, Instructor of Medicine 1963–64; Asst Prof. Medicine NJ Coll. Medicine 1964–66; Co-Dir Haematology, Boston Univ. Medical Centre 1966, Assoc. Prof. 1968–74, Prof. of Medicine and Physiology 1974–75; Dir Hematology, Boston City Hosp.; Dean School of Medicine, Morehouse Coll. 1975–89, Pres. –1989, 1993–; Sec. of State for Health and Human Services 1989–93; Dir (non-exec.) Gen. Motors 1993–; mem. sickle cell anaemia Advisory Cttee, Nat. Insts. of Health 1974–75, Medical Advisory Bd, Nat. Leukemia Asscn 1968–70, (Chair. 1970); mem. American Soc. of Hematology, American Soc. of Clinical Investigation, Inst. of Medicine. *Publications:* numerous papers on medical matters. *Address:* Office of the President, Morehouse School of Medicine, 720 Westview Drive, SW, Atlanta, GA 30310 (Office); 223 Chestnut Street, Atlanta, GA 30314, USA.

SULLIVAN, Michael J., BSc, JD; American politician, lawyer and diplomatist; b. 23 Sept. 1939, Omaha; s. of Joseph B. Sullivan and Margaret Hamilton; m. Jane Metzler 1961; one s. two d.; ed Univ. of Wyoming; Assoc. Brown, Drew, Apostolos, Barton & Massey, Casper, Wyoming 1964–67; partner, Brown, Drew, Apostolos, Massey & Sullivan, Casper 1967–; Gov. of Wyoming 1987–95; Amb. to Ireland 1998–2001; mem. ABA; Democrat. *Leisure interests:* jogging, tennis, golf, fly-fishing. *Address:* c/o Department of State, 2201 C Street, NW, Washington, DC 20520, USA (Office). *E-mail:* guvsuv@aol.com (Home).

SULLO, Fiorentino; Italian politician; b. 29 March 1921, Paternopoli, Avellino; s. of Clorindo Sullo and Giulia Emilia (née Calienno) Sullo; m. Elvira de Laurentiis 1961; one d.; mem. Constituent Ass. 1946–48, Chamber of

Deputies 1948–; fmr Under-Sec. for Defence, Under-Sec. for Industry and Commerce, Under-Sec. for State Participation; Minister of Transport 1960, of Labour and Social Insurance 1960–62, of Public Works 1962–63, of Educ. 1968–69; Minister without portfolio for scientific and tech. research 1972–73, for Regions 1973; Pres. Interior Comm., Chamber of Deputies 1966–68; Pres. Public Works Comm. 1979–81; now State Councillor; Ed. Le Discussione 1966–69; editorial contrib. Roma di Napoli; Contrib. to Il Punto, Politica and Mattino 1977–79, to Roma 1979–; Pres. Christian Democrat group in Parl. 1968; resigned from Christian Democrat Party 1974; mem. Social Democrat Party 1974–82; returned to Christian Democrat Party Aug. 1982, to Chamber of Deputies 1983–87; mem. Majority of Regulation, Constitutional Affairs Comm., Regional Questions Comm., Chamber of Deputies, Admin. Law Council in Sicilian Region 1988, Second Section of State Council 1989, Nat. Revenue Cttee 1989; Co-Pres. Italy-USSR Cultural Asscn; Grand Officier, Légion d'honneur, Kt Grand Cross of Italian Repub. *Publication:* Lo Scandalo Ubanistico 1964. *Leisure interest:* tennis. *Address:* Via Venanzio Fortunato 54, 00136 Rome, Italy. *Telephone:* (06) 3451031.

SULSTON, Sir John Edward, Kt, PhD, FRS; British scientist; b. 27 March 1942, Fulmer; s. of the late Rev. Canon Arthur Edward Aubrey Sulston and Josephine Muriel Frearson Blocksidge; m. Daphne Edith Bate 1966; one s. one d.; ed Merchant Taylor's School and Pembroke Coll., Cambridge; Postdoctoral Fellowship at the Salk Inst., Calif. 1966–69; Staff scientist, MRC Lab. of Molecular Biology, Cambridge 1969–; Dir The Sanger Centre 1992–2000; Hon. Fellow Pembroke Coll., Cambridge 2000; Hon. ScD (Trinity Coll., Dublin) 2000; Dr hc (Essex) 2002; W. Alden Spencer Award (jtly) 1986, Gairdner Foundation Award (jtly) 1991, Darwin Medal, Royal Soc. 1996, Rosenstiel Award jtly) 1998, Pfizer Prize for Innovative Science 2000, Sir Frederick Gowland Hopkins Medal, Biochemical Soc. 2000, Edinburgh Medal 2001, City of Medicine Award, Durham, NC 2001, Prince of Asturias Award (Spain) 2001, Daily Mirror Pride of Britain Award 2002, Fothergill Medal, Medical Soc. of London 2002, Dan David Prize, Tel-Aviv Univ. 2002, General Motors Sloan Prize 2002, Gairdner Award 2002, Nobel Prize in Physiology or Medicine (jtly) 2002. *Television:* Royal Inst. Christmas Lectures (Channel 4) 2001. *Publications:* The Common Thread – A Story of Science, Politics, Ethics and the Human Genome (jtly) 2002; papers in scientific journals. *Leisure interests:* gardening, walking, avoiding people. *Address:* 39 Mingle Lane, Stapleford, Cambridge, CB2 5SY, England (Home). *Telephone:* (1223) 842248 (Home). *E-mail:* jes@sanger.ac.uk (Office).

SULTAN, Altoon, BA, MFA; American artist; b. 29 Sept. 1948, Brooklyn, New York; s. of Raymond Sultan and Adele Chalom Sultan; ed Abraham Lincoln High School, Brooklyn and Brooklyn Coll.; work in public collections: Metropolitan Museum of Art, New York, Hunter Museum, Chattanooga, Tenn., Museum of Fine Arts, Boston, Yale Univ. Art Gallery and Walker Art Center, Minneapolis, Minn.; mem. Nat. Acad. of Design, New York; Nat. Endowment for the Arts Fellowship Grant 1983, 1989, Karolyi Foundation Fellowship 1984; Acad. Award in Art, American Acad. of Arts and Letters 1999, Prix Duc de Valverde d'Ayala Valva, Fondation Monaco 1999. *Solo exhbns. include:* Marlborough Gallery, New York 1977–98, Middendorf Gallery, Washington, DC 1987, Hokin-Kaufman Gallery, Chicago 1990, D.P. Fong & Spratt, San Jose, Calif. 1992, Pinnacle Gallery, Savannah, Ga 1997, Galleria Marieschi, Monza, Italy 1999, Tibor de Nagy Gallery, New York 2001. *Group exhbns. include:* Museum of Fine Arts, Boston 1982, San Francisco Museum of Modern Art 1985, Butler Inst. Youngstown 1987, Metropolitan Museum 1991, Flint Inst. of Arts, Mich., Nat. Museum of Women in the Arts, Washington, DC, Wichita Art Museum, Kan., Currier Gallery of Art, Manchester, NH. *Publication:* The Luminous Brush: Painting with Egg Tempera. *Leisure interests:* horseback riding, gardening. *Address:* P.O. Box 2, Groton, VT 05046, USA. *Telephone:* (802) 584-4052. *Fax:* (802) 584-4052 (Office). *E-mail:* asultan@together.net (Home).

SULTAN, Donald Keith, MFA; American painter, printmaker and sculptor; b. 5 May 1951, Asheville, NC; s. of Norman Sultan and Phyllis Sultan; m. Susan Reynolds 1978; one s. one d.; ed Univ. of N Carolina, Art Inst. of Chicago; represented by: Willard Gallery 1979–82, Blum Helman Gallery 1982–89, M. Knoedler Gallery New York 1989; work in collections: Art Inst. of Chicago, Hirsh Museum and Sculpture Garden, Washington DC, The Metropolitan Museum of Art, NY, The Museum of Fine Arts, Boston, The Museum of Modern Art, NY, The Solomon R. Guggenheim Museum, NY, Walker Art Center, Minneapolis, Bibliothèque Nationale, Paris 1992; Public Service Grant NY State 1978–79, Nat. Endowments for the Arts 1980–81. *Address:* 19 E 70th Street, New York, NY 10021, USA.

SULTAN, Fouad, BSc; Egyptian politician and business executive; b. 26 Jan. 1931; s. of Abdel Latif Sultan and Farida Torky; m. Ferial Fikry 1956, one s. one d.; ed Univ. of Cairo; worked for 21 years with Cen. Bank of Egypt; seconded to IMF, North Yemen 1971–74; CEO Misr-Iran Bank 1974–85; head of several cttees. in Fed. of Egyptian Banks; Minister of Tourism and Civil Aviation 1985–93; Chair. and CEO ADI 1995–. *Leisure interests:* rowing, tennis, swimming. *Address:* ADI, 38 Cornish El Nil, 4th Floor, MAADI, Cairo, Egypt (Office). *Telephone:* (2) 5780790 (Office). *Fax:* (2) 5780793 (Office). *E-mail:* adi@intouch.com (Office); adi@adi-alahly.com (Home).

SULTAN IBN ABDUL AZIZ AS-SA'UD, HRH Prince; Saudi Arabian government minister; b. 1928; s. of the late King Abdul Aziz ibn Saud and Hassa Bint Sudairi; brother of King Fahd and of the late King Khalid; Gov. of Riyadh 1947; Minister of Agric. 1954, of Transportation 1955; Vice-Pres.

Supreme Cttee of Educ. Policy; Minister of Defence and Aviation and Insp.-Gen. 1963–82; Chair. Bd Saudia Airlines 1963; Chair. Bd of Gen. Enterprise of Mil. Industries; Chair. Council of Manpower 1980; Second Deputy Prime Minister and Minister of Defence and Civil Aviation, Insp.-Gen. 1982–; Chair. Supreme Council for Islamic Affairs 1994; various orders and decorations. *Address:* Ministry of Defence and Civil Aviation, P.O. Box 26731, Airport Road, Riyadh 11165, Saudi Arabia. *Telephone:* (1) 476-9000. *Fax:* (1) 405-5500.

SULTANGAZIN, Umirzak Makhmutovich, D.PHYSICS AND MATHS.; Kazakhstan scientist; b. 10 April 1936, Kustanai Region; s. of Sultangazy Makhmutov and Nurila Makhmutova; m. Raikhan Meirmanova 1958, two c.; ed Kazakh State Univ. and USSR (now Russian) Acad. of Sciences, Novosibirsk; Asst Prof. Kazakh State Univ. 1958–60, Assoc. Prof. 1960–64, Prof. of Math. 1972–78; Dir Inst. of Math. and Mechanics, Acad. of Sciences of Kazakh SSR 1978–88, Vice-Pres. of Acad. 1986–88, Pres. 1988–94; Dir Space Research Inst. 1991–95; Visiting Prof. Karlov Univ. Czechoslovakia 1972, Kyoto Univ. Japan 1994–95; Chair. Fed. of Cosmonautics 1985, Peace Fund of Kazakh SSR 1987, Math Cttee of Rep. of Kazakhstan 1994; Corresp. mem. Acad. of Sciences of Kazakh SSR 1975, mem. 1983; CPSU 1968–91, Cen. Cttee 1989–91; mem. Parl. Kazakh SSR 1987–89, Parl. of USSR 1989–91; Korolev's Medal 1986, State Prize of USSR for Science and Tech. 1987, Red Banner Order 1987, Prize of Acad. of Sciences of USSR and Czechoslovakia for Nat. Sciences 1988. *Publications:* Concentrated Capacity in the Problems of Heat Physics and Microelectronics 1972, Method of Spherical Harmonics in Kinetic Transport Theory 1979, Mathematical Problems of Kinetic Transport Theory 1986, Discrete Nonlinear Models of Boltzmann Equation 1987, Ecological and Economical Model of Kazakhstan 1995; 150 articles on mathematical physics, numerical mathematics and ecology. *Leisure interests:* history, mountain tourism. *Address:* Institute of Space Research, 480034 Almaty, Akademgorodok (Office); Shevchenko 15, Almaty 480100, Kazakhstan. *Telephone:* (3272) 62-38-96 (Office); (3272) 61-68-53. *Fax:* (3272) 49-43-55.

SULTANOV, Otkir S.; Uzbekistan politician; b. 14 July 1939; m.; one d.; ed Tomsk State Polytech. Inst.; electrician Tomsk plant of cutting metals 1963; master, Head of lab., Head of production automatization, Deputy Chief Engineer, Deputy Dir-Gen. Tashkent Aviation Production Union 1964–85; Head Scientific Production Unit Vostok 1985–91; Chair. State Cttee for Foreign Trade and Int. Relations 1991–92; Minister of External Econ. Relations, Deputy Prime Minister 1992–95; Prime Minister of Uzbekistan Dec. 1995–; People's Deputy of Uzbekistan; awarded Mekhnat Shukhradi; Merited Engineer Repub. of Uzbekistan. *Address:* Government House, Mustarilik 5, 700008 Tashkent, Uzbekistan (Office). *Telephone:* (712) 139-86-19 (Office); (712) 139-82-95. *Fax:* (712) 139-86-01 (Office).

SULZBERGER, Arthur Ochs; American newspaper executive; b. 5 Feb. 1926, New York; s. of Arthur Hays and Iphigene (née Ochs) Sulzberger; m. 1st Barbara Grant 1948 (divorced 1956); one s. one d.; m. 2nd Carol Fox 1956 (died 1995); two d.; m. 3rd Allison Stacey Cowles 1996; ed Columbia Univ.; U.S. Marine Corps, Second World War and Korean War; joined The New York Times Co., New York 1951, Asst Treas. 1958–63, Pres. 1963–79, Publr 1963–92, Chair., CEO 1992–97, Chair. Emer. 1997–, mem. Bd Dirs. –2002 ; Co-Chair. Bd Int. Herald Tribune 1983; Chair. Newspaper Pres. Asscn 1988; Dir, Times Printing Co., Chattanooga, Gapesia Pulp and Paper Co. Ltd of Canada; Trustee Columbia Univ., mem. Coll. Council; Trustee Metropolitan Museum of Art, Chair. Bd of Trustees 1987–99; Hon. LHD (Montclair State Coll.), (Tufts Univ.) 1984; Columbia Journalism Award 1992; Alexander Hamilton Medal 1982, Vermeil Medal (City of Paris) 1992. *Address:* New York Times Co., 229 West 43rd Street, New York, NY 10036, USA. *Telephone:* (212) 556-1234.

SUMAYE, Frederick; Tanzanian politician; fmr Minister of Agric.; Prime Minister of Tanzania Oct. 1995–; mem. C.C.M. (Party for Democracy and Progress). *Address:* Office of the Prime Minister, P.O. Box 980, Dodoma, Tanzania. *Telephone:* (61) 20511.

SUMMER, Donna; American singer and actress; b. 31 Dec. 1948, Boston; d. of Andrew Gaines and Mary Gaines; m. 1st Helmut Sommer (divorced); one d.; m. 2nd Bruce Sudano; one s. one d.; singer 1967–; appeared in German stage production Hair; in Europe 1967–75, appearing in Vienna Folk productions of Porgy and Bess and German productions of The Me Nobody Knows; has sold over 20 million records; Best Rhythm and Blues Female Vocalist, Nat. Acad. of Recording Arts and Sciences 1978, Best Female Rock Vocalist 1979, Favourite Female Pop Vocalist, American Music Awards 1979, Favourite Female Vocalist of Soul Music 1979, Ampex Golden Reel Award for single and album On the Radio 1979, album Bad Girls, Soul Artist of Year, Rolling Stone Magazine 1979, Best Rock Performance, Best of Las Vegas Jimmy Award 1980, Grammy Award for Best Inspirational Performance 1984; several awards for best-selling records. *Albums:* The Wanderer, Star Collection, Love to Love You Baby, Love Trilogy, Four Seasons of Love, I Remember Yesterday, The Deep, Shut Out, Once upon a Time, Bad Girls, On the Radio, Walk Away, She Works Hard for the Money, Cats without Claws, All Systems Go 1988, Another Time and Place 1989, Mistaken Identity 1991, Endless Summer 1994, I'm a Rainbow 1996, Live & More Encore 1999. *Address:* 2401 Main Street, Santa Monica, CA 90405, USA.

SUMMERFIELD, Arthur, B.SC.TECH., BSc, C.PSYCHOL., F.B.PS.S., F.INST.D; British psychologist; b. 31 March 1923, Wilmslow; s. of the late Arthur Summerfield and Dora Gertrude (née Perman Smith) Summerfield; m. 1st

Aline Whalley 1946; one s. one d.; m. 2nd Angela Barbara Steer 1974; ed Manchester Grammar School, Victoria Univ. of Manchester, Univ. Coll. London; Electrical Officer, RDVR (Naval Air Stations 1943–46, Dept of Sr Psychologist to Admiralty 1946); lecturer in Psychology, Univ. Coll. London 1949–61, Hon. Research Assoc. 1961–70, Hon. Research Fellow 1970–; Prof. of Psychology, Univ. of London and Head, Dept of Psychology, Birkbeck Coll. 1961–88, Prof. Emer. 1988–, Gov. 1982–86; Chair. Cttee on 'Psychologists in Educ. Services' (Summerfield Report), Dept of Educ. and Science 1965–68; Chair. LearnIT Ltd 1991–2002; Pres. British Psychological Soc. 1963–64 (Hon. Life mem. 1993–), Int. Union of Psychological Science 1976–80, Section J (Psychology), British Asscn for the Advancement of Science 1976–77, Int. Social Science Council (UNESCO) 1977–81, mem. Exec. Cttee 1981–83; mem. Cttee on Int. Relations in Psychology, American Psychological Asscn 1977–79; mem. Bd of Dirs, European Co-ordination Centre for Research and Documentation in Social Sciences 1977–81, British Journal of Educ. Psychology Ltd 1976–93; mem. Social Science Research Council (GB) 1979–81; mem. Int. Council of Scientific Unions Study Group on the Biological, Medical and Physical Effects of the Large-scale Use of Nuclear Weapons 1983–87; Asst Ed. British Journal of Psychology (Statistical Section) 1950–54, Ed. British Journal of Psychology 1964–67; Scientific Ed. British Medical Bulletin (experimental psychology) 1964, (cognitive psychology) 1971, with D. M. Warburton (psychobiology) 1981. *Publications:* Animals and Men (translated and ed. jtly.) 1951, Meeting Points in Dyslexia (ed. jtly.) 1990. *Address:* Rose Bank, Sutton-under-Whitestonecliffe, Thirsk, North Yorks., YO7 2PR, England (Home). *Telephone:* (1845) 597395 (Home). *Fax:* (1845) 597005 (Home). *E-mail:* arthur.summerfield@btopenworld.com (Home).

SUMMERS, Lawrence, PhD; American economist; b. 30 November 1954, New Haven; s. of Dr Robert Summers and Anita Summers; one s. two d.; ed Mass. Inst. of Tech and Harvard Univ.; domestic policy economist, US Council of Econ. Advisers 1982–83; Prof. of Econs Harvard Univ. 1983–93, Nathaniel Ropes Prof. of Political Economy 1987; Chief Economist and Vice-Pres. of Devt Econs IBRD 1991–93; Econ. Adviser to Pres. Bill Clinton; Treasury Under-Sec. for Int. Affairs 1993–95; Deputy Treasury Sec. 1995–99; Sec. of Treasury 1999–2001; Arthur Okun Distinguished Fellow in Econs, Globalization and Governance, Brookings Inst. 2001–02; Pres. Harvard Univ. 2002–; Fellow, American Acad. of Arts and Sciences; Alan T. Waterman Award, Nat. Science Foundation 1987, John Bates Clark Medal 1993. *Publications:* Understanding Unemployment, Reform in Eastern Europe (co-author), more than 100 articles. *Leisure interests:* skiing, tennis. *Address:* Massachusetts Hall, Harvard University, Cambridge, MA 02138, USA (Office). *Telephone:* (617) 495-1502 (Office). *Fax:* (617) 495-8550 (Office). *E-mail:* lawrence_summers@harvard.edu (Office). *Website:* www.president.harvard.edu (Office).

SUMNER, Gordon Matthew (see Sting).

SUMPTION, Jonathan Philip Chadwick, QC, MA; British barrister and author; b. 9 Dec. 1948, London; s. of A. J. Sumption and Mrs. H. Sumption; m. Teresa Mary Whelan 1971; one s. two d.; ed Eton Coll., Magdalen Coll., Oxford; Fellow in History Magdalen Coll., Oxford 1971–75; called to Bar (Inner Temple) 1975; Recorder 1992–; Judge of Courts of Appeal of Guernsey and Jersey 1995–. *Publications:* Pilgrimage: An Image of Medieval Religion 1975, The Albigensian Crusade 1979, The Hundred Years War (Vol. 1) 1989, (Vol. 2) 1999. *Leisure interests:* music, history. *Address:* Brick Court Chambers, 7–8 Essex Street, London, WC2R 3LD, England. *Telephone:* (20) 7379-3550. *Fax:* (20) 7379-3558.

SUN CHEN; Chinese politician; fmrly Minister of Defence; mem. Kuomintang Cen. Standing Cttee 1994–. *Address:* c/o Ministry of National Defence, 2nd Floor, 164 PoAi Road, Taipei, Taiwan.

SUN DAO LIN; Chinese actor and film director; b. 18 Dec. 1921; s. of Sun Wen-Yao and Fan Nian-Hua; m. Wang Wenjuan 1962; one d.; ed Yanjing Univ.; Hon. mem. China Fed. of Literary and Art Circles 1996–; Best Film Actor (Lian-Ho Daily, Singapore) 1987, Outstanding Film Artist Prize (Wen-Hui Daily, Shanghai) 1989, One of Ten Most Popular Film Stars (China Film Weekly) 1990. *Films include:* Reconnaissance Over Yangtze River 1954, The Family 1956, Constant Beam 1958, Early Spring in February 1963, Go Master 1982 (Grand Prix, Montreal Film Festival 1984), Thunderstorm 1983, Special President 1986, Stepmother 1992. *Publication:* Anthology of Sun Daolin's Poems and Prose 1994. *Leisure interests:* literature, music (especially singing). *Address:* Shanghai Film Studio, 595 Tsao Hsi North Road, Shanghai 200030, People's Republic of China. *Telephone:* (21) 4387100. *Fax:* (21) 4391650.

SUN FULING; Chinese party official and business executive; b. 1921, Shaoxing City, Zhejiang Prov.; Vice-Mayor Beijing 1983–93; Vice-Chair. Beijing Mun. Cttee CPPCC 1988–92; mem. 5th Nat. Cttee CPPCC 1978–82; Perm. mem. 6th Nat. Cttee 1983–87, 7th Nat. Cttee 1988–92; Vice-Chair. 8th Nat. Cttee CPPCC 1993–98, 9th Nat. Cttee 1998–. *Address:* National Committee of Chinese People's Political Consultative Conference, 23 Taiping Qiao Street, Beijing, People's Republic of China.

SUN HONGLIE; Chinese agronomist; b. 2 Jan. 1932, Henan; m. Wu Huanning 1956; one s. one d.; ed Beijing Agric. Univ., Shenyang Inst. of Forestry and Soil Science, Chinese Acad. of Sciences; Research Fellow Comm. for Integrated Survey of Natural Resources (Chinese Acad. of Sciences) 1961–, Dir 1983; Head Multi-disciplinary Expedition of Qinghai-Tibet Plateau 1973; Visiting Scholar Inst. of Alpine and Arctic Research, Colorado Univ. 1981–82;

Vice-Pres. Chinese Acad. of Sciences 1984–; Chair. Academic Cttee of Antarctic Research of China 1986; Chair. Nat. Cttee of China for MAB, UNESCO; Vice-Chair. Int. Mountain Soc., State Antarctic Cttee; a Vice-Pres. Social Devt Science Soc. 1992–; Dir Cttee for Comprehensive Survey of Natural Resources; Fellow Third World Acad. of Sciences 1987; mem. Gen. Cttee of ICSU 1990; mem. Div. of Earth Sciences, Chinese Acad. of Sciences 1992–; mem. Standing Cttee of 8th Nat. People's Congress 1993–, mem. Credentials Cttee, Environmental and Resources Protection Cttee; mem. 4th Presidium of Depts., Chinese Acad. of Sciences 2000–; mem. 21st Century Cttee for China–Japan Friendship; Special Prize, Chinese Acad. of Sciences 1986; First Prize, State Natural Sciences Awards 1987; Chen Jiagen Prize 1989. *Publications:* The Soil of Heilongjiang River Valley 1960, The Land Resources Assessment of North-East China, Inner Mongolia and West China 1966, The Soils of Tibet 1970, Land Types of Qinghai-Tibet Plateau and the Principles of Agricultural Assessment 1980, Land Resources and Agricultural Utilization in Tibet Autonomous Region, Mountain Research and Development 1983, Integrated Scientific Survey on Tibetan Plateau (series) 1983–89. *Leisure interest:* photography. *Address:* Chinese Academy of Sciences, 52 Sanlihe Road, Beijing 100864, People's Republic of China. *Telephone:* 3297235.

SUN JIADONG; Chinese space scientist; b. 7 April 1948, Fuxian, Liaoning Prov.; ed Harbin Univ. of Tech.; USSR Ruchkovski Air Force Eng Inst.; Dir of Design Section, Vice-Dir Overall Design Dept, No. 5 Research Inst. of Ministry of Defence; Vice-Pres. No. 5 Research Inst. of Seventh Ministry of Machine Bldg Industry; Pres. Chinese Space Tech. Research Inst.; Dir Science and Tech. Cttee, Chief Engineer, fmr Vice-Minister of Ministry of Aerospace Industry; Fellow, Chinese Acad. of Sciences; instrumental in Devt of China's first atomic bomb and hydrogen bomb; presided over the overall design of China's first medium-range missile, first satellite and first telecommunications satellite; Meritorious Service Medal, CPP Cen. Cttee, State Council and Cen. Mil. Comm. 1999. *Address:* c/o State Commission of Science, Technology and Industry for National Defence, Aimin Daijie, Xicheng Qu, Beijing 100035, People's Republic of China. *Telephone:* (10) 66058958 (Office). *Fax:* (10) 66673811 (Office).

SUN JIAZHENG; Chinese politician; b. 1944, Siyang Co., Jiangsu Prov.; ed Nanjing Univ.; joined CCP 1966, mem. 14th CCP Cen. Cttee 1992–97, 15th CCP Cen. Cttee 1997–; Minister of Radio, Film and TV 1994–98; Minister of Culture 1998–; Hon. Chair. Bd of Dirs. Beijing Film Coll. *Address:* Ministry of Culture, 10 Chaoyangmen North Street, Beijing 199920, People's Republic of China. *Telephone:* (10) 65551114 (Office). *E-mail:* szw@ccnt.gov.cn (Office). *Website:* www.ccnt.gov.cn (Office).

SUN JOUN-YUNG; South Korean diplomatist and civil servant; b. 16 June 1939; m.; two c.; ed Seoul Nat. Univ. Coll. of Law, The American Univ. School of Int. Service, Washington, DC; with Ministry of Foreign Affairs, Dir-Gen. Int. Econ. Affairs Bureau 1987–88, Int. Trade Bureau 1988–90, Deputy Foreign Minister for Econ. Affairs 1993–96; Vice-Minister, Ministry of Foreign Affairs and Trade 1997–2000; Counsellor for Political Affairs, Embassy in London, UK 1978; Minister, Embassy in Brasilia, Brazil 1981, for Econ. Affairs in Washington, DC 1986; apptd Amb. to Czechoslovakia 1990; Minister at Perm. Mission to UN, Geneva 1984, Amb. and Perm. Rep. 1996–98 and to other int. orgs; Perm. Rep. to UN, New York March 2000–; Amb.-at-Large for Trade Negotiations 1993, Chief Negotiator on Repub. of Korea–EC Framework Agreement for Trade and Co-operation 1994–95; Govt Co-ordinator for Accession to OECD; Co-Chair. Korea's Econ. Jt Cttees with China, Canada, Viet Nam, UK, Germany, Australia and Asscn of SE Asian Nations (ASEAN) 1993–95; Chair. World Trade Org. Council for Trade Services 1997–98, Int. Textile and Clothing Bureau and also in Geneva Co-ordinator Western Group, Conf. on Disarmament 1997 and Head of Del. at Multi-Fiber Arrangement negotiations 1985–86; Order of Civil Service Merit (Red Stripes) Civil Service Merit Medal of Honour. *Address:* Permanent Mission of the Republic of Korea to the UN, 335 East 45th Street, New York, NY 10017, USA (Office). *Telephone:* (212) 439-4000 (Office). *Fax:* (212) 986-1083 (Office). *E-mail:* korea@un.int (Office). *Website:* www.un.int/korea (Office).

SUN SHU; Chinese geologist; b. 1933, Jintan, Jiangsu Prov.; ed Nanjing Univ.; Research Fellow Inst. of Geology, Chinese Acad. of Sciences, now Dir; Fellow Chinese Acad. of Sciences; Vice-Pres. Nat. Natural Science Foundation of China; mem. 4th Presidium, Chinese Acad. of Sciences 2000. *Publications:* ed. Geological Changes of Precambian Period in the South of North China Fault Block; The Geology of Xiaoxing'anling, Wandashan and Zhangguangchailing (jtly), over 50 research papers and research reports. *Address:* Institute of Geology, Chinese Academy of Sciences, Beijing, People's Republic of China (Office).

SUN WEIBEN; Chinese politician; b. 1928, Yingkou Co., Liaoning; joined CCP 1947; alt. mem. 12th CCP Cen. Cttee 1982, mem. 1985, mem. 13th Cen. Cttee 1987–92, 14th Cen. Cttee 1992–; Sec. CCP Cttee, Liaoning Prov. 1983–85; Chair. Heilongjiang 7th Provincial People's Congress Standing Cttee 1988, 8th Cttee 1993–; 1st Sec. Party Cttee, PLA Heilongjiang Provincial Command 1985–94; Ed.-in-Chief Dictionary of Party Affairs of the CCP June 1989–. *Address:* Heilongjiang Provincial 8th People's Congress, Heilongjiang, People's Republic of China.

SUN WEIYAN; Chinese economist; b. 1937, Cixi, Zhejiang Prov.; ed Beijing Foreign Trade Inst.; Pres. Univ. of Int. Business and Econs 1984–. *Publications:* A Handbook of International Commerce and Trade (Chief Ed.),

Multi-National Management Encyclopaedia for Chinese Enterprises (Chief Ed.). *Address:* University of International Business and Economics, Huixin Dong Jie, He Ping Jie N., Beijing 100029, People's Republic of China. *Telephone:* (10) 64965522. *Fax:* (10) 64968036. *E-mail:* uibe@chinaonline.com.cn.net (Office).

SUN WENSHENG; Chinese government official; b. Feb. 1942, Weihai City, Shandong Prov.; ed Shandong Metallurgical Inst.; joined CCP 1966; workshop Dir Zhuzhou Smeltery 1963–81, Deputy Dir 1981–83; Sec. CCP Zhuzhou City Cttee 1983; Vice-Dir Org. Dept CCP Hunan Prov. Cttee, CCP 1984, Dir 1985, Vice-Sec. 1989; alt. mem. 12th CCP Cen. Cttee 1985–, 13th CCP Cen. Cttee 1987, 14th CCP Cen. Cttee 1992; Vice-Sec. CCP Shanxi Prov. Cttee, Vice-Gov., Acting Gov. of Shanxi Prov. 1993, Gov. 1994–99; mem. 15th CCP Cen. Cttee 1997–. *Address:* c/o Office of the Governor, Shanxi Provincial Government, 101 Fudong Street, Taiyuan City, Shanxi Province, People's Republic of China.

SUN YING; Chinese politician; b. Nov. 1936, Baodi Co., Tianjin City; ed Shanxi Teachers College 1958; joined CCP 1956; Sec. CCP Taiyuan City Cttee; Vice-Sec. CCP Gansu Provincial Cttee 1992–98, Sec. 1998–2001; Dir Party History Research Centre of CPC Cen. Cttee 2001–; Gov. Gansu Prov. 1997–98; mem. 15th CCP Cen. Cttee 1997–. *Address:* Central Committee of Chinese Communist Party, Beijing, People's Republic of China.

SUN YUN-SUAN, BS; Chinese politician and engineer; b. 11 Nov. 1913, Penglai, Shantung; m. Yu Hui-hsuan 1947; two s. two d.; ed Harbin Polytechnic Inst.; engineer with Nat. Resource Comm. 1937–40; Supt Tienshui Electric Power Plant 1940–43; Training Engineer Tenn. Valley Authority, USA 1943–45; Head Engineer, Electrical and Mechanical Dept, Taiwan Power Co. 1946–50, Chief Engineer 1950–62, Vice-Pres. 1953–62, Pres. 1962–64; CEO and Gen. Man. Electricity Corpn of Nigeria 1964–67; Minister of Communications 1967–69, of Econ. Affairs 1969–78; Premier of Taiwan 1978–84; Sr Adviser to the Pres. 1984–; Fellow Int. Acad. of Man. 1983; Cravat of the Order of Brilliant Star 1952; Eng Award of the Chinese Inst. of Engineers 1954. *Leisure interests:* reading, Chinese opera, classical music, sports. *Address:* 7th Floor, 106 Ho Ping E Road, Section 2, Taipei, Taiwan 106. *Telephone:* (2) 27377338 (Office). *Fax:* (2) 27359049 (Office).

SUNDERLAND, Eric, OBE, LLD, PhD, FIBiol; British anthropologist and fmr university vice-chancellor; b. 18 March 1930, Ammanford, Carmarthenshire; s. of Leonard Sunderland and Mary Agnes Davies; m. Jean Patricia Watson 1957; two d.; ed Univ. of Wales, Univ. Coll. London; Prof. of Anthropology, Univ. of Durham 1971–84, Pro-Vice-Chancellor 1979–84; Prin. Univ. Coll. of N Wales, Bangor 1984–94, Vice-Chancellor 1994–95; Vice-Chancellor Univ. of Wales 1989–91, Prof. Emer. 1995–; Sec.-Gen. Int. Union of Anthropological and Ethnological Sciences (IUAES) 1978–98, Pres. 1998–2003; Pres. Royal Anthropological Inst., London 1989–91; Chair. of Dirs Gregynog Press 1991–; Chair. Local Govt Boundary Comm. for Wales 1994–2001, Chair. Wales Cttee; mem. Bd British Council 1996–2001, Chair. 1996; mem. BBC Broadcasting Council for Wales 1995–2000; Chair. Environment Agency Advisory Cttee for Wales 1996–2000; High Sheriff of Gwynedd 1998–99; DL; Pres. Univ. of Wales, Lampeter 1998–2002; Lord-Lt of Gwynedd 1999–; Chair. Wetlands for Wales Project 2001–, Comm. on Local Govt Electoral Arrangements in Wales 2001–02; Hon. mem. Gorsedd of Bards, Royal Nat. Eisteddfod of Wales; Hon. Fellow, Univ. of Wales, Lampeter, Univ. of Wales, Bangor; Gold Medal of IUAES, Zagreb XIIth Int. Congress 1988. *Publications:* Elements of Human and Social Geography – Some Anthropological Perspectives 1973, Genetic Variation in Britain (Co-Ed.) 1973, The Exercise of Intelligence: biological pre-conditions for the operation of intelligence (Co-Ed.) 1980, Genetic and Population Studies in Wales (Co-Ed.) 1986. *Leisure interests:* travelling, book collecting, gardening, paintings. *Address:* Y Bryn, Ffriddoedd Road, Bangor, Gwynedd, LL57 2EH, Wales (Home). *Telephone:* (1248) 353265. *Fax:* (1248) 355043.

SUNDERLAND, John Michael, MA; British business executive; b. 24 Aug. 1945, Oxford; m.; three d. one s.; ed King Edward VII School, Lytham, Lancs., Queen's Coll., Univ. of St Andrews, Scotland; joined Cadbury Ltd 1968, apptd. mem. Bd Cadbury Ireland 1978, Cadbury Schweppes SA 1981, Marketing Dir, then Man. Dir Schweppes Ltd UK 1983, Founding Dir Coca-Cola & Schweppes Beverages 1987, Man. Dir Trebor Bassett 1989, CS Confectionery and CS Main Bd Dir 1993, Group CEO Cadbury Schweppes 1996–2003, Chair. 2003–. *Address:* Cadbury Schweppes, 25 Berkeley Square, London, W1X 6HT, England (Office). *Telephone:* (20) 7830-5004 (Office). *Fax:* (20) 7830-5014 (Office). *Website:* www.cadburyschweppes.com.

SUNDLUN, Bruce George, LLB; American politician; b. 19 Jan. 1920, Providence, RI; s. of Walter I. Sundlun and Jane Z. Colitz; m. 2nd Marjorie G. Lee 1985; three s. three d. by previous m.; m. 3rd Susan Dittelman 2000; two step-c.; ed Williams Coll., Harvard Univ. and Air Command and Staff School; served to Capt. USAAF 1942–45; admitted Bars of RI and DC 1949; Asst US Attorney, Washington, DC 1949–51; special asst to US Attorney-Gen. 1951–54; partner, Amram, Hahn & Sundlun, Washington, DC 1954–72, Sundlun, Tirana & Scher 1972–76; Vice-Pres., Dir and Gen. Counsel, Outlet Co., Providence 1960–76, Pres. and CEO 1976–84, Chair. Bd and CEO 1984–91; Pres. Exec. Jet Aviation Inc., Columbus, 1970–76, Chair. of Bd 1976–84; Dir Questech Inc. 1972–91; Incorporator, Dir Communications Satellite Corpn 1962–91; Dir Hal Roach Studios Inc. 1986–91; numerous other public appointments; del. Democratic Nat. Convention 1964, 1968, 1980, 1990, RI Constitutional Convention 1985; Gov. of Rhode Island

1990–95; Gov-in-Residence Univ. of Rhode Island 1995–; Dir Nat. Security Bd 2000–2001; Hon. DSBA (Bryant Coll.) 1980; Hon. DBA (Roger Williams Coll.) 1980; DFC; Air medal with oak leaf cluster; Purple Heart; Chevalier, Légion d'honneur; Prime Minister's Medal (Israel). *Address:* University of Rhode Island, 216 University Library, Kingston, RI 02881 (Office); 257 Walmsley Lane, Saunderstown, RI 02874, USA (Home).

SUNDQUIST, Donald Kenneth (Don), BA; American politician and business executive; b. 15 March 1936, Moline, Ill.; s. of Kenneth Sundquist and Louise Rohren; m. Martha Swanson 1959; one s. two d.; ed Augustana Coll. Rock Island, Ill.; Div. Man. Josten's Inc. 1961–72; Exec. Vice-Pres. Graphic Sales of America, Memphis 1973, Pres. 1973–82; mem. 98th–103rd Congresses from 7th Tenn. Dist 1983–95; Gov. of Tennessee 1995–2003; Republican. *Leisure interests:* golf, reading. *Address:* c/o Office of the Governor, State Capitol Building, Nashville TN 37243, USA.

SUNDQVIST, Ulf Ludvig, M.POL.SC.; Finnish business consultant and fmr politician; b. 22 Feb. 1945, Sipoo; s. of Karl Eric Sundqvist and Helga Linnea Lönnkvist; m. Eine Kristiina Joki 1969; one s. one d.; ed Univ. of Helsinki; Asst Lecturer, Faculty of Political Science, Helsinki Univ. 1968–70; mem. Parl. 1970–83; Minister of Educ. 1972–75, of Trade and Industry 1979–81; Gen. Sec. Finnish Social Democratic Party 1975–81, Chair. 1991–93; mem. Supervisory Bd Neste Ltd 1970–, Chair. 1976–94; Deputy Chief Gen. Man. STS-Bank Ltd 1981, Chief Gen. Man. 1982–91, mem. Bd 1992–94; pvt. consultant 1993–; Hon. PhD (Kuopio). *Leisure interests:* music, literature.

SUNG CHUL-YANG, PhD; South Korean diplomatist and academic; b. 20 Nov. 1939; m.; one s. one d.; ed Seoul Nat. Univ., Univ. of Hawaii and Univ. of Kentucky, USA; mil. service 1960–62; taught at Eastern Kentucky Univ. and Univ. of Kentucky Fort Knox Center, USA 1970–75, Prof. of Political Science, Lexington 1978; Visiting Prof. at N Western Univ., Pembroke State Univ., Indiana Univ., USA and Seoul Nat. Univ.; taught at Grad. Inst. of Peace Studies (GIP), Kyung Hee Univ., Seoul 1986, Dean of Academic Affairs at GIP 1987–94; Sec.-Gen. Asscn of Korean Political Scientists in N America; Pres. Korean Asscn of Int. Studies; contrib. to journals and leading newspapers in Repub. of Korea; mem. Advisory Cttee, Ministry of Foreign Affairs, Ministry of Nat. Defence, Nat. Unification Bd; Amb. to USA Sept. 2000–. *Publications include:* numerous articles and essays. *Address:* Embassy of the Republic of Korea, 2450 Massachusetts Avenue, NW, Washington, DC 20008, USA (Office). *Telephone:* (202) 939-5600 (Office). *Fax:* (202) 797-0595 (Office). *E-mail:* information_usa@mofat.go.kr (Office). *Website:* www.koreaembassyusa.org (Office).

SUNGURLU, Mahmut Oltan; Turkish politician; b. 1936, Gümüşhane; m.; one c.; ed Bursa Lycée, Istanbul Univ.; practised law in Gümüşhane; f. Motherland Party prov. org. in Gümüşhane; Deputy for Gümüşhane 1983–; Minister of Justice 1986–87, 1987–88, 1989–92, 1997–98; Deputy Chair. Motherland Party June 1988. *Address:* c/o Ministry of Justice, Adalet Bakanlığı, Bakanlıklar, Ankara, Turkey.

SUNIA, Tauese, MA; American Samoa politician, teacher and administrator; b. Fagatogo; m. Fagaoalii Sunia; ten c.; ed Univ. of Nebraska, Univ. of Hawaii; many years in educ. as teacher, admin., coll. vice-pres., State Supt.; practised law; fmr. Pres. Bar Asscn.; fmrly Lieut.-Gov. American Samoa, Gov. of American Samoa 1996–; Democrat. *Address:* Office of the Governor, Pago Pago, AS 96799, American Samoa (Office). *Telephone:* 633-4116 (Office). *Fax:* 633-2269 (Office). *E-mail:* stanhist@samoatelco.com (Office).

SUNTRANGKOON, Gen. Prachuab; Thai army officer and politician; b. 4 April 1920, Sukhothai; m. Khunying Pimpa; one s. one d.; ed Mil. Acad. (now Chulachomklao Royal Mil. Acad.), Bangkok Metropolis and Cavalry School, Royal Thai Army, Ground Gen. School, Fort Riley and Armour School, Fort Knox, USA, Nat. Defence Coll.; rank of Col 1957; Dir Port Authority of Thailand 1959–72; Maj.-Gen., Chief Cavalry Div. 1962–69; Lt-Gen., Army Adviser 1969–72; Deputy Dir-Gen. Police Dept, with rank of Police Lt-Gen. 1972, Dir-Gen., then Police Gen.; Deputy Minister of Communications 1973–74; Deputy Minister of Interior 1974–75; attached to Office of Supreme Commdr of Armed Forces, with rank of Army Gen.; Deputy Prime Minister 1981–86; Minister of Interior 1986–88. *Address:* c/o Ministry of the Interior, Atasadang Road, Bangkok 10200, Thailand.

SUNUNU, John E., M.MECH.ENG., MBA; American politician; b. Salem, NH; m. Kitty Sununu; three c.; ed Salem High School, MIT and Harvard Grad. School of Business; worked for REMEC, Inc. 1987; man. and operations specialist with Pittiglio, Rabin Todd & McGrath 1990–92; Chief Financial Officer and Dir of Operations Teletrol Systems, Inc. 1992–96; Rep. (Republican) for First Congressional Dist, NH 1996–2002, Vice-Chair. Budget Cttee 2001; Senator from New Hampshire 2003–; mem. Appropriations Cttee (and subcttees. overseeing funding for Veteran Admin., NASA, Environmental Protection Agency, Treasury Dept and foreign aid programmes), Republican Policy Cttee (Chair. SubCttee on Retirement Security, Capital Markets and Tax Policy). *Address:* Office of the Senator from New Hampshire, U.S. Senate Buildings, Washington, DC 20510, USA (Office). *Website:* www.house.gov/sununu (Office).

SUNUNU, John H., PhD; American politician; b. 2 July 1939, Havana, Cuba; m. Nancy Hayes 1958; five s. three d.; ed Mass. Inst. of Tech.; founder, Chief Engineer Astro Dynamics 1960–65; Pres. JHS Eng Co. and Thermal Research Inc., Salem, NH 1965–82; Assoc. Prof. Mechanical Eng, Tufts Univ. 1966–82, Assoc. Dean Coll. of Eng 1968–73; mem. NH House of Reps. 1973–74, Govt

Energy Council; Chair. Govt Council on NH Future 1977–78; mem. Govt Advisory Cttee on Science and Tech. 1977–78; Gov. State of NH Concord 1983–89; Chair. coalition of NE Govs. 1985–86; White House Chief of Staff 1989–91, Counsellor to the Pres. 1991–92; Chair. Task Force on Tech.; Pres. JHS Assoc. Ltd 1992; Vice-Chair. Alliance for Acid Rain Control; Chair. Republican Gov.'s Asscn, New England Gov.'s Asscn; Vice-Chair. Advisory Comm. on Intergovt. Relations. *Address:* 24 Samoset Drive, Salem, NH 03079, USA (Office); JHS Associates Ltd, 815 Connecticut Avenue, NW, Suite 1200, Washington, DC 20006.

SUNYAYEV, Rashid Aliyevich; Russian astrophysicist; b. 1 March 1943; m.; three s. one d.; ed Moscow Inst. of Physics and Tech.; jr, sr researcher Inst. of Applied Math. USSR Acad. of Sciences; head of div., head of Dept Inst. of Space Studies USSR Acad. of Sciences; Scientific Head Int. Orbital Observatory ROENTGEN on complex space station Mir, Orbital Observatory GRANAT; Corresp. mem. USSR (now Russian) Acad. of Sciences 1984, mem. 1992; research in high energy astrophysics, cosmology, theoretical astrophysics, X-ray astronomy; Foreign mem. USA Nat. Acad. of Sciences, mem. European Acad. of Sciences, mem. Int. Acad. of Astronautics, Adjunct Prof. Columbia Univ. (USA); Bruno Rossi Prize. *Publications:* Black Holes in Double Systems 1973, Observation of Relict Irradiation as Method of Studying the Nature of X-ray Irradiation of Galaxy Clusters 1973, Comptonization of X-ray Irradiation in Plasma Clouds: characteristic spectra 1980; numerous articles. *Address:* Institute of Space Studies, Russian Academy of Sciences, Profsoyuznaya str. 84/32, 117910 Moscow, Russia. *Telephone:* (095) 333-33-73 (Office); (095) 331-38-05 (Home). *Fax:* (095) 233-53-77.

SUOMINEN, Ilkka Olavi, M.POL.SC.; Finnish business executive and fmr politician; b. 8 April 1939, Nakkila; s. of Leo Suominen and Anna Suominen; m. Riitta Suhonen 1977; one s. two d.; Dept Head, J. W. Suominen Oy 1960–72, Deputy Man. Dir 1972–74, Man. Dir 1975–79, mem. Man. Bd 1982–; mem. Parl. 1970–75, 1983–94; Leader Nat. Coalition Party 1979–91; Vice-Chair. European Democrat Union 1986–93; Speaker of Parl. 1987, 1991–96; Minister of Trade and Industry 1987–91; Pres. CSCE Parl. Ass. 1992–94; Chair. Admin. Bd Oy Alko AB 1980–88, 1991–94, Gen. Man. 1994; Chair. Bd of Dirs ICL Data (Finland) 1992–; Vice-Chair. Confed. of Finnish Industries 1978–79. *Leisure interests:* hunting, fishing.

SUONIO, Kaarina Elisabet, MA, LLM; Finnish politician, lawyer and psychologist; b. 7 Feb. 1941, Helsinki; d. of Prof. Karl Otto Brusiin and Ulla Helena Raassina; m. 1st Reino Kalevi 1961; m. 2nd Kÿosti Kullervo Suonio 1967; m. 3rd Ilkka Tanner 1993; one s. one d.; ed Helsinki Univ.; psychologist, Inst. of Occupational Health 1963–71; Researcher, Ministry of Justice 1971–75; mem. Helsinki City Council 1973–; MP 1975–86; Alt. mem. Exec. Finnish Social Democratic Party 1981–84; Second Minister of Educ. (Minister of Culture and Science) 1982–83, Minister of Educ. 1983–86; Deputy Mayor of Tampere 1986–94; Gov. Province of Häme 1994–97; Man. Dir Tampere Hall Conf. and Concert Centre 1997–; Commdr Ordre des Arts et des Lettres. *Address:* Tampere Hall, c/o Box 16, 33101 Tampere, Finland. *Telephone:* (3) 2434100 (Office); (50) 5509401 (Home). *Fax:* (3) 2434199 (Office); (3) 6372175 (Home); (3) 2434199. *E-mail:* kaarina.suonio@tampere-talo.fi (Office); kaarina.suonio@mail.htk.fi (Home). *Website:* www.tampere-talo.fi (Office).

SUPEK, Ivan, DSc; Croatian scientist and author; b. 8 April 1915, Zagreb; s. of Rudolf Supek and Marija Supek; m. Zdenka Supek; one s. two d.; ed Zagreb Univ., studied in Zurich and Leipzig with W. Heisenberg; arrested by Gestapo 1941; Prof. Zagreb Univ. 1946–; founder of R. Boskovic Inst. 1950; mem. Croatian Acad. of Sciences and Arts 1948; Pres. of Yagoslav Pagwash Movt 1963; Ed. Encyclopedia Moderna 1966; Rector Zagreb Univ. 1968–72; f. Interuniv. Cen. in Dubrovnik 1970; banned from public life because of his opposition to totalitarian rule; Pres. Croatian Acad. of Arts and Sciences 1991–97, Prof. Emer. 1997–; awarded int. prize for play 1976; several orders. *Plays include:* On Atomic Island, Heretic, The Lottery of the Emperor Augustus. *Publications:* Scientific Theoretical Physics and Structure of Matter, Superbomb and Crisis of Conscience 1962, Cognition 1971, Philosophy of Science and Humanism 1979, History of Physics 1980, Filosofija, znanost i humanizam 1995, Povijesne meditacije 1995, Mene, Takel, Fares 1998, At the Crossroads of the Millennia 2002; novels: Heretic 1969, Rebellion of Janus Pannonius 1990, Hrvatska tetralogiya 1995; plays: Mirakul 1965, Piramida, Poet and Ruler, Amalgami (10 plays) 1999. *Leisure interests:* music, tennis. *Address:* Hrvatska Akademija Znanosti i Umetnosti, Zringjski trg 11, 41000 Zagreb (Office); Rubeticéva 10, 41000 Zagreb, Croatia (Home). *Telephone:* (1) 4616314 (Home).

SUPLICY, Marta Teresa, MSc; Brazilian politician and psychologist; b. 1946, São Paulo; m. Eduardo Suplicy; ed Pontifícia Universidade Católica de São Paulo and Stanford and Michigan State Univs.; fmr psychotherapist War Veterans Hosp., Palo Alto, Calif.; TV presenter, Brazil 1980–86; fmr Fed. Rep.; Mayor of São Paulo Jan. 2001–; Assoc. mem. Sociedade Brasileira Psicanalítica de São Paulo 1990–. *Address:* Presidente da Câmara Municipal, São Paulo, SP, Brazil (Office).

SUPPES, Patrick, BS, PhD, FAAS; American philosopher and scientist; b. 17 March 1922, Tulsa, Okla; m. 1st Joan Farmer 1946 (divorced 1970); one s. two d.; m. 2nd Joan Elizabeth Sieber 1970 (divorced 1973); m. 3rd Christine Johnson 1979; one s. one d.; ed Univ. of Chicago and Columbia Univ.; mem. faculty Stanford Univ. 1950–, Prof. of Philosophy, Statistics Educ. and Psychology, Dir Inst. for Mathematical Studies in the Social Sciences 1959–92; Pres. Computer Curriculum Corpn 1967–90; Fellow American Psychological Asscn; mem. Nat. Acad. of Educ. (Pres. 1973–77), American Acad. of Arts and Sciences, Finnish Acad. of Science and Letters, NAS, European Acad. of Sciences and Arts; Corresp. mem. Yugoslav Acad. of Sciences and Arts 1990; Foreign mem. USSR (now Russian) Acad. of Pedagogical Sciences, Norwegian Acad. of Science and Letters; Hon. mem. Chilean Acad. of Sciences; Dr hc (Social Sciences) Nijmegen 1979, (Acad. de Paris, Univ. René Descartes) 1982, (Regensburg) 1999, (Bologna) 1999; Palmer O. Johnson Memorial Award, American Educational Research Asscn 1967, Distinguished Scientific Contribution Award, American Psychological Asscn 1972, Columbia Univ. Teachers College Medal for Distinguished Service 1978, E. L. Thorndike Award for Distinguished Psychological Contrib. to Educ., American Psychological Asscn 1979, Nat. Medal of Science 1990. *Publications:* Introduction to Logic 1957, Decision Making: An Experimental Approach (with D. Davidson and S. Siegel) 1957, Axiomatic Set Theory 1960, Markov Learning Models for Multiperson Interactions (with R. C. Atkinson) 1960, First Course in Mathematical Logic (with S. Hill) 1964, Experiments in Second-Language Acquisition (with E. Crothers) 1967, Computer Assisted Instruction: Stanford's 1965–66 Arithmetic Program (with M. Jerman and D. Brian) 1968, Studies in the Methodology and Foundations of Science 1970, A Probabilistic Theory of Causality 1970, Foundations of Measurement (with D. Krantz, R. D. Luce, A. Tversky) Vol. I 1971, Vol. II 1989, Vol. III 1990, Computer-assisted Instruction at Stanford, 1966–68 (with M. Morningstar); Probabilistic Metaphysics 1974, The Radio Mathematics Project: Nicaragua 1974–1975 (with B. Searle and J. Friend) 1976, Logique du Probable 1981, Estudios de Filosofía y Metodología de la Ciencia 1988, Language for Humans and Robots 1991, Models and Methods in the Philosophy of Science 1993, Language and Learning for Robots (with C. Crangle) 1994, Foundations of Probability with Applications (with M. Zanotti) 1996, Representation and Invariance of Scientific Structures 2002; and over 300 articles in professional journals. *Address:* 678 Mirada Avenue, Stanford, CA 94305, USA.

SUPPLE, Barry Emanuel, CBE, PhD, FRHistS, FBA; British professor of economic history; b. 27 Oct. 1930; s. of Solomon Supple and Rose Supple; m. Sonia Caller 1958; two s. one d.; ed Hackney Downs Grammar School, LSE and Christ's Coll. Cambridge; Asst Prof. of Business History, Grad. School of Business Admin., Harvard Univ., USA 1955–60; Assoc. Prof. of Econ. History, McGill Univ. 1960–62; Lecturer in Econ. and Social History, Univ. of Sussex, Reader, then Prof. 1962–78, Dean, School of Social Sciences 1965–68, Pro-Vice-Chancellor (Arts and Social Studies) 1968–72, Pro-Vice-Chancellor 1978; Reader in Recent Social and Econ. History, Univ. of Oxford 1978–81, Professorial Fellow, Nuffield Coll. 1978–81; Prof. of Econ. History Univ. of Cambridge 1981–93, Prof. Emer. 1993–, Professorial Fellow, Christ's Coll. 1981–83, Hon. Fellow 1984; Master of St Catharine's Coll., Cambridge 1984–93, Hon. Fellow 1993; Dir Leverhulme Trust 1993–2001; Pres. Econ. History Soc. 1992–95, Foreign Sec. British Acad. 1995–99; mem. Social Science Fellowship Cttee, Nuffield Foundation 1974–94; Co-Ed. Econ. History Review 1973–82; Hon. Fellow Worcester Coll., Oxford 1986; Hon. DLitt (Sussex) 1998, (Leicester) 1999, (Warwick) 2000, (Bristol) 2001; Hon. FRAM 2001. *Publications:* Commercial Crisis and Change in England, 1600–42, 1959, The Experience of Economic Growth (Ed.) 1963, Boston Capitalists and Western Railroads 1967, The Royal Exchange Assurance: a history of British insurance 1720–1970, 1970, Essays in Business History (Ed.) 1977, History of the British Coal Industry, Vol. IV (1914–46), The Political Economy of Decline 1987, The State and Economic Knowledge: the American and British Experience (ed.) 1990, The Rise of Big Business (ed.) 1992, articles and reviews in learned journals. *Leisure interests:* tennis, photography. *Address:* 41 Lensfield Road, Cambridge, CB2 1EN, England (Home). *Telephone:* (1223) 353726 (Home).

SUQUÍA GOICOECHEA, HE Cardinal Angel; Spanish ecclesiastic; b. 2 Oct. 1916, Zaldivia, San Sebastián; ordained 1940; consecrated Bishop of Almería 1966, of Málaga 1969; Archbishop of Santiago de Compostela 1973, of Madrid 1983, Archbishop Emer. 1994–; cr. Cardinal 1985; mem. Congregation for Catholic Educ., Congregation for the Bishops and several others. *Address:* c/o Javier de Barcaiztegui No. 7, 3°, 20010 San Sebastián, Spain.

SURÁNYI, György, PH.D, DEcon; Hungarian economist; b. 3 Jan. 1954, Budapest; m.; two c.; ed Univ. of Econ., Budapest, Hungarian Acad. of Sciences; Research Fellow, Head of Dept Financial Research Inst. Budapest 1977–86; Consultant World Bank, Washington, DC 1986–87; Counsellor to Deputy Prime Minister, Council of Ministers 1988–89; Sec. of State, Nat. Planning Office 1989–90; Pres. Nat. Bank of Hungary 1990–91; Man. Dir Cen. European Int. Bank Ltd 1992–95; Pres. Nat. Bank of Hungary 1995–2001; Head Multinat. Banking-IntesBci Group, Italy 2001–; Chair. Bd Cen. European Int. Bank Ltd 2001–, Pres. Supervisory Bd Privredna Banka, Zagreb 2001–; mem. Supervisory Bd VUB, Bratislava 2001–; Global Leader for Tomorrow, World Econ. Forum 1993, Leadership in Econ. Transition, East-West Inst. New York 2001. *Publications:* author of several articles and books on monetary and financial issues. *Address:* Central European International Bank Ltd., 1027 Budapest, Medve u. 4-14, Hungary. *Telephone:* (1) 489-6222. *Fax:* (1) 489-6226. *E-mail:* gsurauyi@cib.hu (Office).

SUREAU, Claude, MD; French obstetrician and gynaecologist; b. 27 Sept. 1927, Paris; s. of Maurice Sureau and Rita Jullian; m. Janine Murset 1956; one s. two d.; ed Paris Univ., Columbia Presbyterian Medical Center; Asst Prof., Paris Univ. 1956–61, Assoc. Prof. 1961–74; Prof. and Chair., Dept of Obstetrics and Gynaecology, St Vincent de Paul Hosp., Paris 1974–76, Univ. Clinique Baudelocque 1976–89; Pres., Int. Fed. of Obstetricians and Gynaecologists 1982–85, Pres., Standing Cttee on Ethical Aspects of Human Reproduction 1985–94; Pres. European Asscn of Gynaecology and Obstetrics 1988–91; Dir Unit 262, Physiology and Physiopathology of Reproduction, Nat. Inst. of Health and Medical Research 1983–90; Active Staff mem. American Hosp. of Paris 1989–93, Chief of Gynaecological Unit 1990–93, Medical Dir American Hosp. of Paris 1994–95; Pres. Theramex Inst. 1996–; mem. Nat. Acad. of Medicine of France 1978–, Pres. 2000–; Officier, Légion d'honneur 1989, Commdr Ordre nat. du Mérite 1996. *Publications:* Le danger de naître 1978, Ethical Dilemmas in Assisted Reproduction 1996, Alice au pays des clones 1999; Co-Ed.: Clinical Perinatology 1980, Immunologie de la réproduction humaine 1983, Aux débuts de la vie 1990, Ethical Aspects of Human Reproduction 1995, Ethical Problems in Obstetrics and Gynaecology 2000. *Address:* Institut Theramex, 38–40 avenue de New York, B.P. 398-16, 75768 Paris cedex 16 (Office); 16 rue d'Aubigny, 75017 Paris, France (Home). *Telephone:* 1-53-67-63-32 (Office); 1-42-67-44-08 (Home). *Fax:* 1-42-67-35-49 (Home); 1-53-67-63-03 (Office). *E-mail:* csureau@theramex.mc (Office).

SURJÁN, László, MD, PhD; Hungarian politician and physician; b. 7 Sept. 1941, Kolozsvár (now Cluj, Romania); s. of László Surján and Margit (née Göttinger) Surján; m. Zsófia Stverteczky 1966; one s. two d.; ed Roman Catholic Theologic Acad. Semmelweis Univ. Medical School, Budapest; specialist in pathology 1973; lecturer Semmelweis Medical Univ. 1969–70, Postgrad. Medical School 1970–90; mem. numerous socs.; joined Hungarian Christian Democratic Party (Pres. 1990–95); mem. Hungarian Parl. 1990–; Minister of Welfare 1990–94; Pres. Employment and Labour Affairs Cttee of Parl. 1994–98; Head Hungarian Del. to Parl. Ass. of Council of Europe and Vice-Chair. Foreign Affairs Cttee 1998–; Chair. WHO Regional Cttee for Europe 1992–93; Vice-Chair. European Union of Christian Democrats 1992–99. *Publications:* author of 48 scientific Publs. *Address:* Parlamenti Hivatal, Széchenyi rkp. 19, 1054 Budapest, Hungary. *Telephone:* (1) 441-5886. *Fax:* (1) 441-5464.

SURLYK, Finn C., PhD, DR.SCIENT.; Danish professor of geology; b. 17 March 1943, Copenhagen; s. of C. Surlyk and K. Surlyk; m. Nanna Noe-Nygaard; two s.; Adjunct Prof. Univ. of Copenhagen 1968–69, Assoc. Prof. 1969–80, Prof. 1984–; Head Dept of Oil Geology, Geological Survey of Greenland, Copenhagen 1981–84; Gen.-Sec. Int. Asscn of Sedimentologists 1986–94; Fellow Royal Danish Acad. of Arts and Letters; Hon. Fellow Geological Soc. of London; Ridder of Dannebrogordenen (Kt 2001); Gold Medal, Univ. of Copenhagen 1969, Recipient First Jubilee Prize, Danish Nat. Oil and Gas Co. *Publications:* over 100 papers, particularly on the geology of Greenland. *Leisure interests:* jazz, bass-playing, outdoor life. *Address:* Geological Institute, Øster Voldgade 10, 1350 Copenhagen K (Office); Islandsvej 11, 2800 Lyngby, Denmark (Home). *Telephone:* 35-32-24-53 (Office); 45-87-72-09 (Home). *Fax:* 33-14-83-22 (Office). *E-mail:* finns@geol.geol.ku.dk (Office).

SURTEES, John, MBE; British racing motorcyclist and driver; b. 11 Feb. 1934, Tatsfield, Surrey; s. of John Norman Surtees and Dorothy Cynthia Calla Surtees; m. Jane Sparrow 1987; one s. two d.; ed Ashburton Secondary School, London; only man to win both world motorcycling and world motor racing championships; began motorcycle road racing 1950, 350cc World Champion 1958, 1959 and 1960, 500cc World Champion 1956, 1958, 1959 and 1960; began car racing 1960, World Champion 1964, runner-up 1966, CanAm Champion 1966; Grand Prix wins (motorcycling): won 32 World Championship motor cycle Grand Prix and 6 Isle of Man TT races; (motor racing): 1963 German (Ferrari), 1964 German (Ferrari), 1964 Italian (Ferrari), 1966 Belgian (Ferrari), 1966 Mexican (Cooper-Maserati), 1967 Italian (Honda); racing car constructor and team owner (F5000, F2 and F1); closed down racing operation Team Surtees 1978; Founder-mem. Constructers' Asscn; drives for Mercedes Benz in historic demonstration events; motor sport consultant, journalist and property developer, Man. Dir John Surtees Ltd 1979–; Dir British Racing Drivers' Club; mem. Worshipful Co. of Carmen. *Publications:* Speed 1963, John Surtees – World Champion 1991. *Leisure interests:* restoration of period property, Grand Prix motor cycles and cars, antiques, food and wine. *Address:* John Surtees Ltd, Monza House, Fircroft Way, Edenbridge, Kent, TN8 6EJ, England. *Telephone:* (1732) 865496 (Office). *Fax:* (1732) 866945 (Office).

SURUR, Ahmad Fathi, M.L., PhD; Egyptian politician and professor of criminal law; b. 9 July 1932, Cairo; s. of Mostafa Kamel Sorour and Fatma Ali Hassan; m. Zeinab El-Housseiny; one s. two d.; ed Cairo Univ., Univ. of Michigan, USA; Prof. of Criminal Law, Cairo Univ. 1959–, Head of Criminal Law Dept 1978–83, Dean, Faculty of Law 1983–85, Vice-Rector Cairo Univ. 1985–86; Minister of Educ. 1986–90; Chair. Supreme Council of Univs. 1986–90; Speaker of the Egyptian People's Ass. 1990–; Pres. IPU Council 1994–; Science and Arts Medal (Class A), Highest Distinction Award 1993; Ordre au de la Pléiade, France. *Publications:* Theory of Nullity 1959, Offences against Public Interest 1963, Penal Law (Part I and II) 1980, Criminal Procedures Law 1993, Constitutional Legality and Human Rights 1995, Probation. *Address:* 11583 Majlis Al-Shaab, Cairo, Egypt. *Telephone:* (2) 3543130. *Fax:* (2) 3543116.

SUSCHITZKY, Wolfgang, BSc; British cameraman (retd) and photographer (retd); b. 29 Aug. 1912, Vienna, Austria; s. of Wilhelm Suschitzky and Mrs Suschitzky (née Bauer); m. three times; two s. one d.; ed Graphische Lehr- und Versuchsanstalt Vienna; started in documentary films with Paul Rotha 1937; first feature film No Resting Place 1950; freelance cameraman, exhbns.exhbns London 1982, 1988, 1989, 1995, 1997, 2000, 2001, Edin. 2002,

Amsterdam 1982, Vienna 1999; mem. British Soc. of Cinematographers; mem. BAFTA; Hon. mem. Asscn of Cinematograph, Television and Allied Technicians, Royal Photographic Soc. *Films as cameraman include:* The Small World of Sammy Lee 1962, Ulysses 1966, Entertaining Mr. Sloan 1969, Get Carter 1970, Staying On 1980; numerous documentaries and commercials. *Publications:* Photographing Animals 1941, Photographing Children 1942, Kingdom of the Beasts (with Julian Huxley) 1956, Charing Cross Road in the Thirties 1980. *Leisure interests:* photography, film, music, literature, travel. *Address:* Flat 11, Douglas House, 6 Maida Avenue, London, W2 1TG, England. *Telephone:* (20) 7723-6269.

SUSHCHENYA, Leonid Mikhailovich, D.BIOL.SC.; Belarus scientist; b. 11 Nov. 1929, Maly Luky, Brest Region; m. Nina Nikolayevna Khmeleva; three c.; ed Belarus Univ.; Asst Prof. Byelorussian State Univ., Minsk 1956–59; sr researcher, Inst. of Biology of Southern Seas, Ukrainian Acad. of Sciences 1959–67, Head of Div. of Marine Animal Physiology 1967–71; Head of Div., Dir Inst. of Zoology, Belarus Acad. of Sciences, 1971–95, Academician Sec., Div. of Biological Sciences 1979–92, Head of Div., Hon. Dir Inst. of Zoology 1995–; Pres. Belarus Acad. of Sciences 1992–97; Counsellor Nat. Belarus Acad. of Sciences 1997–; Vice-Pres. Int. Asscn of Acads. of Sciences of CIS and other cos. 1996–; Ed.-in-Chief Doklady Akademii nauk Belarusi; mem. Belarus and USSR (now Russian) Acads of Sciences; mem. Int. Soc. of Limnology, Hydrobiological Socs. of Belarus and Russia (Hon. Pres. –1989); mem. Peace Cttee (Chair. Environmental Protection section); mem. All European Acads. Ass.; Foreign mem. Polish and Lithuanian Acads of Sciences 1994; represents Belarus in ICSU; Hon. Scientist of Repub. of Belarus 1978; Order of People's Friendship 1986; Order of Red Banner of Labour USSR 1989; Order of Fatherland of Repub. of Belarus 1999; Order of Friendship of Russian Fed. 2000; Hon. Awards of Supreme Soviet of Repub. of Belarus 1979, 1994. *Publications:* more than 190 articles on hydrobiology, gen. ecology, ecology of animals and environment, including monographs Respiration of Crustacea 1972, Quantitative Regularities of Crustacea Feeding 1975, Growth of Water Animals at Changing Temperatures 1978, Fundamentals of Rational Use of Nature 1980, Biology and Products of Ice-age Relic Crayfish 1985, Ecology of Animals in the Radioactive Contaminated Zone 1993. *Leisure interests:* travelling, reading, music. *Address:* Presidium of the Academy of Sciences of Belarus, Prospekt F. Skoriny 66, 220072 Minsk (Office); 15 fl. 41 Kulman Street, 220100 Minsk, Belarus (Home). *Telephone:* (2) 84-04-77 (Office); (2) 34-44-05 (Home). *Fax:* (2) 39-31-63.

SÜSKIND, Patrick; German author; b. 1949; fmr writer for TV. *Publications:* Perfume: the Story of a Murderer (novel), The Double Bass, The Pigeon, Three Stories and a Reflection. *Address:* c/o Diogenes Verlag AG, Sprecherstr. 8, 8032 Zürich, Switzerland. *Telephone:* (1) 2548511. *Fax:* (1) 2528407.

SUŠNIK, Janez; Slovenian government official; b. 18 Sept. 1942; m.; two c.; ed Tech. Coll., Ljubljana; Pres. Admin. Bd Alpe Tour (forwarding agency) –2001; Asst Man. Viator–Vektor (forwarding agency) 2002; Pres. Nat. Council of Repub. of Slovenia Dec. 2002–. *Address:* Office of the President, Drzavni Svet, Subiceva 4, 1000 Ljubljana, Slovenia (Office). *Telephone:* (1) 4789799 (Office). *Fax:* (1) 4789851 (Office). *E-mail:* janez.susnik@ds-rs.si (Office). *Website:* www.ds-rs.si (Office).

SÜSSENGUTH, Hans, DIPL.ING.; German aviation executive; b. 8 Sept. 1913, Neustadt/Coburg; s. of Franz H. Süssenguth and Rosalie Süssenguth; m. Christa Reischel 1942; one s. one d.; ed Oberrealschule, Coburg and Tech. Hochschule, Darmstadt; Technician in Research and Devt and Maintenance and Operations Depts. Deutsche Lufthansa A.G., Berlin 1939–45; Engineer in father-in-law's business 1945–50; Engineer at Gummi-Werke Fulda 1950–52; rejoined Lufthansa in Eng Div., Hamburg 1952, Tech. Dir 1954, Head of Traffic Division 1958, Deputy mem. Exec. Bd 1959, mem. 1963–, responsible for sales, worldwide field org., in-flight services and marketing, retd June 1978, mem. Bd Deutsche Lufthansa AG June 1978–; Chair. Advisory Bd, Berlin Penta Hotelgesellschaft, DSG-Deutsche Schlafwagen- und Speisewagen GmbH Frankfurt, AMK-Ausstellungs-Messe-Kongress GmbH, Berlin; mem. Exec. Bd and Vice-Pres., German Tourist Bd; mem. Advisory Bd, Hansa Luftbild GmbH, Münster, Deutscher Aerokurier, Cologne; mem. Bd of Trustees, Hessian Inst. for Aviation; mem. Chartered Inst. of Air Transport, London; Dir START-Datentechnik für Reise und Touristik GmbH, Frankfurt; Hon. Consul Repub. of Togo; Hon. Prof. Technische Univ., Berlin; Grosses Bundesverdienstkreuz 1978. *Address:* 61476 Kronberg, Taunusstrasse 2, Germany (Home). *Telephone:* (6173) 79538 (Home).

SÜSSMUTH, Rita, D.PHIL; German politician; b. 17 Feb. 1937, Wuppertal; m. Prof. Dr. Hans Sussmüth; one d.; ed Univs. of Münster, Tübingen and Paris; Research Asst Univs. of Stuttgart and Osnabrück 1963–66; lecturer, Coll. of Educ. Pädagogische Hochschule Ruhr 1966; lecturer Ruhr Univ. Bochum 1969; Prof. of Educ. Univ. of Dortmund 1970; Dir Research Inst. Frau und Gesellschaft (Woman and Society), Hanover 1982–85; mem. Scientific Advisory Cttee on Family Affairs, Fed. Ministry for Youth, Family Affairs and Health 1985; Fed. Chair. Christian Democratic Union (CDU) Women's Asscn 1986–2001; Fed. Minister for Youth, Family Affairs and Health 1985–86, for Youth, Family Affairs, Women and Health 1986–88; mem. Bundestag 1987–; Pres. of Bundestag 1988–98; Chair. Comm. for Immigration 2000–01; Pres. German Asscn of Adult Educ. Centres 1998; mem. Advisory Council, Bertelsmann Stiftung 1997–; Dr. hc (Hildesheim) 1988, (Bochum) 1990, (Veliko

Tărnovo, Czech Repub.) 1994, (Timişoara, Romania) 1995, (Sorbonne Nouvelle) 1996, (Johns Hopkins) 1998, (Ben Gurion, Israel) 1998. *Publications:* Frauen: Der Resignation keine Chance 1985, Aids: Wege aus der Angst 1987, Kämpfen und Bewegen: Frauenreden 1989, Wenn der Zeit der Rhythmus ändert 1991, Die planlosen Eliten (jtly.) 1993, Wer nicht Kämpft, hat schon verloren 2000, Mut zur Macht in Fraunhand. *Leisure interest:* tennis. *Address:* Platz der Republik 1, 11011 Berlin, Germany (Office). *Telephone:* (30) 22777998 (Office). *Fax:* (30) 22776998 (Office).

SUTER, Albert Edward, B.M.E., MBA; American business executive; b. 18 Sept. 1935, New Jersey; s. of Joseph V. Suter and Catherine Clay; m. Michaela S. Suter 1966; two s. one d.; ed Cornell Univ.; Knight & Assocs., Chicago 1959–79, fmr Pres. and CEO; Vice-Chair. Emerson Electric Co., St Louis, Mo. 1979–87; Pres. and COO Firestone Tire & Rubber Co., Akron, Ohio 1987–88; Pres. and COO Whirlpool Co. 1988–89; Pres. COO Emerson Electric Co. 1990–92, Sr Vice-Chair., COO 1992–97, Sr Vice-Chair., CEO 1997–; mem. Bd Dirs. NationsBank Corpn. *Address:* Emerson Electric Co., P.O. Box 4100, St Louis, MO 63136, USA.

SUTHERLAND, Donald McNichol, OC; Canadian actor; b. 17 July 1935, St John, NB; s. of Frederick McLae and Dorothy Isabel (McNichol) Sutherland; m. 1st Lois May Hardwick 1959; m. 2nd Shirley Jean Douglas 1966 (divorced); one s. one d.; m. 3rd Francine Racette 1971; three s.; ed Bridgewater, NS, High School, Univ. of Toronto; TV Hallmark Hall of Fame; appeared on television (BBC and ITV) in Hamlet, Man in the Suitcase, The Saint, Gideon's Way, The Avengers, Flight into Danger, Rose Tattoo, March to the Sea, Lee Harvey Oswald, Court Martial, Death of Bessie Smith, Max Dugan Returns, Crackers, Louis Malle, The Disappearance; Pres. McNichol Pictures Inc.; Hon. PhD; Officier, Ordre des Arts et des Lettres. *Films include:* The World Ten Times Over 1963, Castle of the Living Dead 1964, Dr. Terror's House of Horrors 1965, Fanatic 1965, The Bedford Incident 1965, Promise Her Anything 1966, The Dirty Dozen 1967, Billion Dollar Brain 1967, Oedipus Rex 1968, Interlude 1968, Joanna 1968, The Split 1968, Start the Revolution Without Me 1969, Act of the Heart 1970, M*A*S*H* 1970, Kelly's Heroes 1970, Little Murders 1970, Alex in Wonderland 1971, Klute 1971, Johnny Got His Gun (as Christ) 1971, Steelyard Blues 1972, Lady Ice 1972, Alien Thunder 1973, Don't Look Now 1973, S*P*Y*S* 1974, The Day of the Locust 1975, 1900 1976, Casanova (Fellini) 1976, The Eagle Has Landed 1977, The Great Train Robbery 1978, Blood Relatives 1978, Bear Island 1979, Ordinary People 1980, Lolita 1981, Eye of the Needle 1981, Threshold 1982, Winter of Our Discontent, Ordeal by Innocence 1984, Revolution 1985, Gauguin 1986, The Wolf at the Door 1987, A Dry White Season 1988, Bethune: The Making of a Hero 1989, Lock Up 1989, Apprentice to Murder 1989, Lost Angels 1989, The Railway Station-man 1991, Scream from Stone 1991, Faithful 1991, JFK 1991, Backdraft, Agaguk, Buffy the Vampire Slayer, Shadow of the Wolf 1993, Benefit of the Doubt, Younger and Younger 1993, Six Degrees of Separation 1993, The Puppet Masters, Disclosure, Outbreak, Hollow Point, The Shadow Conspiracy, A Time to Kill, Virus 1999, Instinct 1999, Toscano 1999, The Art of War 2000, Panic 2000, Space Cowboys 2000, Uprising 2001, The Big Herst 2001, Final Fantasy: The Spirits Within 2001. *Television includes:* Path To War (Golden Globe for Best Supporting Actor in a TV series or TV movie 2003) 2002. *Plays:* Lolita (Broadway) 1981, Enigmatic Variations 2000. *Leisure interests:* sailing, baseball, Montreal. *Address:* 760 N La Cienega Boulevard, Los Angeles, CA 90069; c/o Katherine Olin, CAA, 9830 Wilshire Boulevard, Beverly Hills, CA 90212, USA. *Telephone:* (213) 306-1633.

SUTHERLAND, Grant Robert, AC, PhD, DSc, FRS, FAA; Australian geneticist; b. 2 June 1945, Bairnsdale, Victoria; s. of John Sutherland and Hazel Wilson Mason McClelland; m. Elizabeth Dougan 1979; one s. one d.; ed Numurkah High School, Univs. of Melbourne and Edinburgh; Dir Dept of Cytogenetics and Molecular Genetics, Women's and Children's Hosp., Adelaide 1975–2002, Foundation Research Fellow 2002–; Affiliate Prof. Dept of Paediatrics, Univ. of Adelaide 1991–, Dept of Genetics 1998–2001; Int. Research Scholar Howard Hughes Medical Inst., Bethesda, Md 1993–97; Pres. Human Genetics Soc. of Australasia 1989–91, Human Genome Org. 1996–97; Co-Founder and Co.-Chair., Scientific Advisory Bd of Bionomics Ltd; Hon. Fellow Royal Coll. of Pathologists of Australasia 1994; co-recipient Australia Prize in Molecular Genetics 1998, Nat. Australia Day Council Australian Achiever Award 2001, Ramaciotti Medal for Excellence in Biomedical Research 2001. *Publications include:* two books and over 400 papers in medical and scientific journals on human genetics. *Leisure interest:* beef cattle farming. *Address:* Department of Cytogenetics and Molecular Genetics, Women's and Children's Hospital, Adelaide, SA 5006; P.O. Box 300, Macclesfield, SA 5153, Australia. *Telephone:* (8) 8161-7284 (Adelaide); (8) 8388-9524 (Macclesfield). *Fax:* (8) 8161-7342 (Adelaide). *E-mail:* grant.sutherland@adelaide.edu.au (Office).

SUTHERLAND, Dame Joan, OM, AC, DBE, FRCM; Australian opera singer (retd); b. 7 Nov. 1926, Sydney; d. of William McDonald Sutherland and Muriel Beatrice Sutherland (née Alston); m. Richard Bonynge 1954; one s.; ed St Catherine's School, Waverley, Sydney; début as Dido in Purcell's Dido and Aeneas, Sydney 1947; Royal Opera Co., Covent Garden, London 1952–88; retd from performing 1991; Hon. life mem. Australia Opera Co. 1974; Commdr, Ordre des Arts et des Lettres 1989; Hon. DMus (Sydney) 1984. *Has sung leading soprano roles at:* the Vienna State Opera, La Scala, Milan, Teatro Fenice, Venice, the Paris Opera, Glyndebourne, San Francisco and Chicago Operas, The Metropolitan, New York, the Australian Opera, Hamburg, the Canadian Opera, etc.; leading roles in Lucia di Lammermoor, La Traviata,

Adriana Lecouvreur, Les Contes d'Hoffmann, Lucrezia Borgia, Semiramide, Don Giovanni, Faust, Die Zauberflöte, Dido and Aeneas, The Merry Widow, Les Huguenots, Norma and others. *Publications:* The Joan Sutherland Album (autobiog., with Richard Bonynge) 1986, A Prima Donna's Progress: the Autobiography of Joan Sutherland 1997. *Leisure interests:* reading, needlepoint. *Address:* c/o Ingpen & Williams, 26 Wadham Road, London, SW15 2LR, England. *Telephone:* (20) 8874-3222. *Fax:* (20) 8877-3113.

SUTHERLAND, John Andrew, PhD, FRSL; British professor of English Literature; b. 9 Oct. 1938; s. of Jack Sutherland and Elizabeth (née Salter) Sutherland; m. Guilland Watt 1967; one s.; ed Colchester Royal Grammar School, Leicester and Edinburgh Univs; nat. service, 2nd Lt Suffolk Regt 1958–60; lecturer in English Univ. of Edin. 1965–72; lecturer in English U.C.L. 1972–84, Lord Northcliffe Prof. of Modern English Literature 1992–; Hon. DLitt (Leicester) 1998. *Publications include:* Thackeray at Work 1974, Victorian Novelists and Publishers 1976, Fiction and the Fiction Industry 1978, Bestsellers 1980, Offensive Literature 1982, The Longman Companion to Victorian Fiction 1989, Mrs Humphry Ward 1992, The Life of Walter Scott: A Critical Biography 1995, Victorian Fiction: Writers, Publishers, Readers 1995, Is Heathcliffe a Murderer? 1996, Can Jane Eyre be Happy? 1997, Who Betrays Elizabeth Bennet? 1999. *Leisure interest:* walking. *Address:* Department of English, University College London, Gower Street, London, WC1E 6BT, England. *Telephone:* (20) 7387-7050.

SUTHERLAND, Kiefer; American actor; b. Dec. 1966, London, England; s. of Donald Sutherland (q.v.) and Shirley Douglas; m. 1st Camelia Kath 1987 (divorced 1990); two d.; m. 2nd Kelly Winn 1996 (separated 1999); two steps-.; debut with LA Odyssey Theatre in Throne of Straw aged 9. *Films:* Max Dugan Returns 1983, The Bay Boy 1984, At Close Range 1986, Crazy Moon 1986, Stand By Me 1986, The Lost Boys 1987, The Killing Time 1987, Promised Land 1987, Bright Lights, Big City 1988, Young Guns 1988, Renegades 1989, Chicago Joe and the Showgirl 1990, Flashback 1990, Flatliners 1990, The Nutcracker Prince (voice) 1990, Young Guns II 1990, Article 99 1991, Twin Peaks: Fire Walk With Me 1992, A Few Good Men 1992, The Vanishing 1993, The Three Musketeers, The Cowboy Way, Teresa's Tattoo, Eye for an Eye, A Time to Kill 1996, Truth or Consequences NM (also Dir) 1997, Dark City 1997, Ground Control 1998, The Breakup 1998, Woman Wanted 1999, The Red Dove 1999, Hearts and Bones 1999, Beat 2000, Picking up the Pieces 2000, Ring of Fire 2000. *Television appearances include:* Amazing Stories, Trapped in Silence, Brotherhood of Justice, Last Light (also Dir), 24 (Golden Globe for Best Actor in a TV Series 2002). *Address:* International Creative Management, 8942 Wilshire Boulevard, Beverly Hills, CA 90211, USA.

SUTHERLAND, Peter Denis, SC, BCL; Irish international civil servant, lawyer and politician; b. 25 April 1946; s. of W. G. Sutherland and Barbara Sutherland; m. Maria del Pilar Cabria Valcarcel 1971; two s. one d.; ed Gonzaga Coll., Univ. Coll., Dublin and King's Inns; called to Irish Bar (King's Inns), English Bar (Middle Temple) and New York Bar; admitted to Bar of the Supreme Court of the United States; practising mem. of Irish Bar 1968–81; Tutor in Law, Univ. Coll., Dublin 1968–71; apptd. Sr Counsel 1980; Attorney-Gen. 1981–82, 1982–85; mem. Strategy Cttee Fine Gael Party 1978–81, Dir Policy Programme, 1981 Gen. Election; mem. Comm. of the European Communities (responsible for Competition and Relations with the European Parl.) 1985–89; Dir-Gen. GATT (later World Trade Org.) 1993–95; Chair. Allied Irish Banks 1989–93; Dir Telefonaktiebolaget, L. M. Ericsson, Delta Airlines, ABB Asea Brown Boveri Ltd; Dir British Petroleum Co. PLC (Deputy Chair. 1995–97, Chair. 1997–; Chair Goldman Sachs Int. 1995–; Dir Investor AB 1995–, Royal Bank of Scotland Group PLC 2001–; Visiting Fellow Kennedy School of Govt, Harvard Univ. 1989; Visiting Prof. Univ. Coll. Dublin; Bencher of the Hon. Soc. of the King's Inns; mem. Bar Council of Ireland Action Cttee for Europe, Foundation Bd, World Econ. Forum; Hon. Fellow London Business School 1997;Grand Cross of Civil Merit (Spain) 1989; Grand Cross of King Leopold II (Belgium) 1989; Chevalier Légion d'honneur; Commdr du Wissam (Morocco) 1994; Order of Rio Branco (Brazil) 1996; Grand Cross of Order of Infante Dom Henrique (Portugal) 1998; Hon. LLD (St Louis, Nat. Univ. of Ireland, Bath, Suffolk Univ. (USA), Open Univ., Trinity Coll. (Dublin), Reading, Nottingham, Exeter); Hon. DPhil (Dublin City Univ.); Gold Medal of European Parl. 1988, First European Law Prize Paris 1988, NZ Centenary Medal 1990, David Rockefeller Int. Leadership Award 1998. *Publications:* 1er janvier 1993 – ce qui va changer en Europe 1989; and numerous articles in law journals. *Leisure interests:* reading, sport. *Address:* Goldman Sachs International, Peterborough Court, 133 Fleet Street, London, EC4A 2BB; BP PLC, 1 St James's Square, London, SW1Y 4PD, England; 68 Eglinton Road, Dublin 4, Ireland. *Telephone:* (20) 7774-4141 (Fleet Street).

SUTHERLAND, Dame Veronica Evelyn, DBE, MA; British diplomatist and college president; b. 25 April 1939; d. of the late Lt-Col Maurice G. Beckett and of Constance M. Cavenagh-Mainwaring; m. Alex J. Sutherland 1981; ed Royal School, Bath, Univs of London and Southampton; joined diplomatic service 1965, Second Sec., then First Sec. Copenhagen 1967–70, New Delhi 1975–78; with FCO 1970–75, 1978–80, Counsellor 1981, 1984–87, Asst Under-Sec. of State (Personnel) 1990–95; Perm Del. to UNESCO 1981–84; Amb. to Côte d'Ivoire 1987–90, to Ireland 1995–99; Deputy Sec. Gen. of the Commonwealth 1999–; Pres. Lucy Cavendish Coll., Cambridge 2001–; Hon. LL.D (Trinity Coll., Dublin) 1998. *Address:* Lucy Cavendish College, Cambridge, CB3 0BU, England. *Telephone:* (1223) 332192.

SUTHERLAND OF HOUNDWOOD, Baron (Life Peer), cr. 2001, of Houndwood in the Scottish Borders; **Stewart Ross Sutherland,** Kt, KT, MA, FBA, FRSE; British university vice-chancellor and company director (non-executive); b. 25 Feb. 1941, Scotland; s. of George Sutherland and Ethel Masson; m. Sheena Robertson 1964; one s. two d.; ed Woodside School, Robert Gordon's Coll., Univ. of Aberdeen and Corpus Christi Coll. Cambridge; Asst Lecturer in Philosophy, Univ. Coll. of N Wales 1965; Lecturer in Philosophy, Univ. of Stirling 1968, Sr Lecturer 1972, Reader 1976; Prof. of History and Philosophy of Religion, King's Coll. London 1977–85, Vice-Prin. 1981–85, Prin. 1985–90, Fellow 1983; Vice-Chancellor, Univ. of London 1990–94; HM Chief Insp. of Schools 1992–94; Vice-Chancellor and Prin. Univ. of Edin. 1994–2002; mem. Council of Science and Tech. 1993–2000; Chair. Royal Comm. on Long-term Care of the Elderly 1997–99; Univ. Grants Cttee (Hong Kong) 1999–; Liveryman, Goldsmiths Co. 1991, Courts Assistant 2002; Hon. Fellow, Corpus Christi Coll. Cambridge 1989, Univ. Coll. at Bangor 1991; Hon. LHD (Coll. of Wooster, Ohio) 1986, (Commonwealth Univ. of Va) 1992, (New York Univ.) 1996; Hon. LLD (Aberdeen) 1991, (Nat. Univ. of Ireland) 1992; Hon. DUniv (Stirling) 1993; Hon. DLitt (Richmond Coll.) 1995, (Univ. of Wales) 1996, (Glasgow) 1999, (Warwick) 2001, (St Andrews) 2002; Dr hc (Uppsala) 1995. *Publications:* Atheism and the Rejection of God 1977, The Philosophical Frontiers of Christian Theology (ed. with B. L. Hebblethwaite) 1983, God, Jesus and Belief 1984, Faith and Ambiguity 1984, The World's Religions (ed.) 1988, Religion, Reason and the Self (jtly) 1989; articles in books and learned journals. *Leisure interests:* Tassie medallions, theatre, jazz. *Address:* The Royal Society of Edinburgh, 22–26 George Street, Edinburgh, EH2 2PQ, Scotland (Office). *Telephone:* (131) 240-5030 (Office). *Fax:* (131) 240-5024 (Office). *E-mail:* president@royalsoced.org.uk (Office).

SÜTŐ, András; Hungarian writer; b. 17 June 1927, Pusztakamarás, Transylvania; s. of András Sütő and Berta Sütő; m. Éva Szabó 1949; two s.; ed Bethlen Gábor Coll., Nagyenyed and Reformed Coll., Kolozsvár (now Cluj, Romania); started as journalist with daily newspaper Világosság, Kolozsvár; contrib., later Ed.-in-Chief, Falvak Népe 1949–54; Deputy Chief Ed. literary monthly Igaz Szó, Marosvásárhely (Târgu Mureş) 1955–57; Chief Ed. pictorial Új Élet, Marosvásárhely 1957–89; Vice-Pres. Writers' Fed. of Socialist Repub. of Romania 1973–81; State Prize for Literature Romania 1953, 1954; Herder Prize, Vienna 1979, Kossuth Prize for Literature, Budapest 1992. *Publications include:* Emberek indulnak (short stories) 1953, Félrejáró Salamon (short novel) 1956, Anyám könnyü álmot igér (novel) 1970, Rigó és apostol (essays, travelogue) 1970, Engedjétek hozzám jönni a szavakat (novel) 1977, Az Idő markában (essays) 1984, A lőttlábú madár nyomában 1988, Mese és reménység (short stories) 1991, Vadpávamenyegző (tales) 1994; dramatic works: Tékozló szerelem (play) 1963, Pompás Gedeon (play) 1967, Egy lócsiszár virágvasárnapja 1978, Csillag a máglyán 1978, Káin és Ábel 1978, A szuzai menyegző 1979, Advent a Hargitán 1985, Fülesek és fejszéseh (diary notes) 2000, Erdélyi változatlanságok (essays) 2001, Kalandok Könyve (tales, play) 2001 Álomkommandó 1987, Szemet szóért (diary notes) 1993, Az ugató madár (play) 1993, Herodes napjai (diary notes) 1994; collected works: Színművek (plays) I, II, III, 1989, 1992, 1995, Omló egek alatt (essays) 1990, Sárkány alszik veled (interviews) 1991, Csipkerózsika ébresztése (essays) 1993, Engedjétek hozzám jönni a szavakat (essays, novel) 1994, Kék Álhalál (short stories) 1997, Napló (diary notes) 1998, Balkáni gerle (play, diary notes) 1999; books translated into Romanian, German, Russian, Bulgarian, Slovak and French; plays performed in Budapest, Bucharest, Cluj, Novi-Sad, Zagreb, Bratislava, New York and Aachen. *Address:* 4300 Târgu - Mureş (Marosvásárhely), Str. Mărăşti Nr. 36, Romania. *Telephone:* (65) 211179.

SUTRESNA, Nana S., MA; Indonesian diplomatist; b. 21 Oct. 1933, Ciamis; m. 1973; two s. one d.; ed Univ. of Wales, Aberystwyth, Acad. for the Foreign Service; foreign news for the Indonesian News Agency, ANTARA, 1955–57; joined Dept of Foreign Affairs 1957, Head of Public Relations and Spokesman 1972–76, Dir for European Affairs 1979–81, Dir-Gen. for Political Affairs 1984–88; served at Indonesian Embassy in Washington, DC and in Mexico City, as Minister Counsellor then Minister in Vienna 1976–79; Head of Indonesian Del. to Disarmament Conf., Geneva 1981–83; Deputy Perm. Rep. to the UN, Geneva 1981–84, Perm. Rep. to the UN (also Accred to Bahamas, Jamaica and Nicaragua) 1988–92; Amb.-at-large 1992–99; Amb. to UK 1999–. *Leisure interest:* golf. *Address:* Embassy of Indonesia, 38 Grosvenor Square, London, W1X 9AD, UK. *Telephone:* (20) 7499-7661. *Fax:* (20) 7491-4993. *E-mail:* kbri@indolondon.freeserve.co.uk. *Website:* www.indonesianembassy.org.uk.

SUTRISNO, Gen. Try; Indonesian army officer; mil. engineer; Aide-de-Camp to Pres. 1974–78; Army Chief of Staff 1986–88; Commdr of the Armed Forces 1988–93; Vice-Pres. of Indonesia 1993–97; left Golkan Party to found Justice and Unity Party (PKP) 1998–. *Address:* c/o Partai Keadilan dan Persatuan (PKP), c/o Dewan Perwakilan Rakyat, Jalan Gatot Subroto 16, Jakarta, Indonesia (Office).

SUTTON, Rt Rev Keith Norman, MA; British ecclesiastic; b. 23 June 1934, London; s. of Norman Sutton and Irene Sutton; m. Edith M. J. Geldard 1963 (died 2000); three s. one d.; ed Woking and Battersea Grammar Schools, Jesus Coll. Cambridge, Ridley Hall, Cambridge; Curate, St Andrew's, Plymouth 1959–62; Chaplain, St John's Coll. Cambridge 1962–67; Tutor and Chaplain, Bishop Tucker Coll. Mukono, Uganda 1968–72; Prin. Ridley Hall, Cambridge 1973–78; Bishop Suffragan of Kingston-upon-Thames 1978–84; Bishop of Lichfield 1984–2003; Hon. DUniv (Keele), Hon. DLitt (Wolverhampton) 1994. *Publication:* The People of God 1983. *Leisure interests:* Russian literature, Third World issues, music. *Address:* Bishop's House, 22 The Close, Lichfield, Staffs. WS13 7LG, England. *Telephone:* (1543) 306000 (Office); (1543) 306001 (Office); (1543) 306296 (Home). *Fax:* (1543) 306009 (Office). *E-mail:* bishop.lichfield@lichfield.anglican.org (Office).

SUTTON, Philip John, RA; British artist; b. 20 Oct. 1928, Poole, Dorset; s. of L. L. Sutton and Anne Sutton; m. Heather Cooke 1954; one s. three d.; ed Slade School of Fine Art and Univ. Coll., London; Lecturer, Slade School of Fine Art, Univ. Coll. 1954–; artist-in-residence, Fulham Pottery 1987–; one-man exhbns. bi-annually at Roland Browse & Delbanco and Browse & Darby 1956–84; Leeds City Art Gallery retrospective 1960; travelled in Australia and Fiji painting landscapes 1963–64; retrospective Exhbn Diploma Gallery, Royal Acad. 1977; toured Israel with ten British artists 1979; visited Australia 1980; exhbns. Royal Acad. of Arts, London 1992, 1997, Agnews, London 1992, 1997, Glyn Vivian Art Gallery, Graham Sutherland Gallery 1994, Tenby Museum 1995, Armoury Museum, Leeds 1997, Berkeley Square Gallery, London 1999; touring Exhbn, Wales 1993; Exhbn of 'Shell' tapestry at Royal Acad. 1985; ceramic wall, NMB Bank HQ, Amsterdam 1987; ceramic Exhbn Odette Gilbert Gallery, London 1987; painting Exhbn, Paris 1988; designed Post Office Greeting Stamps 1989. *Leisure interests:* swimming, running. *Address:* 3 Morfa Terrace, Manorbier, Tenby, Pembrokeshire, SA70 7TH, Wales. *Telephone:* (1834) 871474 (Home). *Website:* www.philip-sutton.co.uk (Home).

SUZMAN, Dame Helen, BCom; South African politician (retd); b. 7 Nov. 1917, Germiston, Transvaal; m. Dr. M. M. Suzman 1937 (died 1994); two d.; ed Parktown Convent, Univ. of Witwatersrand; Asst statistician, War Supplies Bd 1941–44; part-time lecturer, Dept of Econs and Econ. History, Univ. of Witwatersrand 1944–52; MP Houghton 1953–89; (United Party) 1953–61, Progressive Party (now Progressive Fed. Party) 1961–89 (merged with Democratic Party 1989); Hon. Vice-Pres. S. African Inst. of Race Relations 1991–93; part-time mem. S. African Human Rights Comm. 1996–98; Hon. Fellow St Hugh's Coll., Oxford 1973, LSE 1975, New Hall, Cambridge 1990; Hon. DBE 1989; Order of Merit (Gold) 1997; 28 hon. doctorates; UN Human Rights Award 1978; Medallion of Heroism (New York) 1980; American Liberties Medallion (American Jewish Cttee) 1984; recipient Moses Mendelssohn Award, Berlin Senate 1988, Liberal Int. Int. Prize for Freedom 2002. *Publication:* In No Uncertain Terms (memoirs) 1993. *Leisure interests:* bridge, fishing. *Address:* 52 Second Avenue, Illovo, Sandton 2196, South Africa (Home). *Telephone:* (11) 7882833. *Fax:* (11) 7882833.

SUZMAN, Janet, BA; British/South African actress and director; b. 9 Feb. 1939, Johannesburg; d. of Saul Suzman and Betty Sonnenberg; m. Trevor Nunn (q.v.) 1969 (divorced 1986); one s.; ed Kingsmead Coll., Univ. of the Witwatersrand, London Acad. of Music and Dramatic Art; moved to Britain 1960; The Spencer Memorial Lecture, Harvard Univ. 1987; The Tanner Lectures Brasenose Coll., Oxford 1995, The Drapers Lecture Queen Mary and Westfield Coll., Univ. of London 1996, The Morell Lecture Univ. of York 1999; Vice-Pres. Council of LAMDA; Hon. Assoc. Artist RSC; Hon. Patron the Market Theatre; Hon. MA (Open Univ.) 1984; Hon. DLit (Warwick) 1990, (Leicester) 1992, London (QMW) 1997, (Southampton) 2002, (Middlesex) 2003; Best Actress, Evening Standard Drama Award 1973, 1976, Plays and Players Award 1976, Barclays TMA Award for Best Director 1997. *Roles for RSC and West End include:* Lady Anne, La Pucelle, Lady Percy, Luciana, Lulu in The Birthday Party 1963–64, Portia, Rosalind 1965, Carmen in The Balcony, She Stoops to Conquer (Oxford Playhouse) 1966, (RSC) Katharina, Celia, Berinthia in The Relapse 1967, Beatrice, Rosalind 1968–69, Cleopatra and Lavinia 1972–73, Hester in Hello and Goodbye (Kings Head) 1973, Masha in Three Sisters (Cambridge Theatre) 1976, The Death of Bessie Smith (Market Theatre, Johannesburg 1976), Shen Te in The Good Woman of Setzuan (Tyneside Theatre Co.) 1976, at Royal Court Theatre 1977; Hedda Gabler (Duke of York's Theatre) 1977, Duchess of Malfi 1978, The Greeks (Aldwych) 1980, Boesman and Lena (Hampstead) 1984, Vassa (Greenwich Theatre) 1985, Andromache (Old Vic) 1987, Another Time (Wyndhams) 1989–90, Hippolytus (Almeida) 1991, The Sisters Rosensweig (Old Vic) 1994, The Retreat from Moscow (Chichester) 1999, The Free State (Birmingham Repertory and tour) 2000, The Hollow Crown (tour of Far East) 2003. *Directed:* (theatre) Othello, (Market Theatre, Johannesburg) 1987, A Dream of People (The Pit) 1990, The Cruel Grasp (Edinburgh Festival) 1991, No Flies on Mr. Hunter (Chelsea Centre) 1992, Death of a Salesman (Theatr Clwyd) 1993, The Deep Blue Sea (Theatr Clwyd) 1996, The Good Woman of Sharkville (Market Theatre, Johannesburg) 1996 and UK tour 1997, The Cherry Orchard (Birmingham Rep.) 1997, The Snow Palace (tour 1998) and Tricycle Theatre 1998, The Free State – A South African Response to The Cherry Orchard (Birmingham Rep.) and UK tour 2000; The Guardsman 2000; (television) Othello (Channel 4) 1988. *Film appearances:* A Day in the Death of Joe Egg 1970, Nicholas and Alexandra 1971, Nijinsky 1978, Priest of Love 1981, The Draughtsman's Contract 1981, E la Nave Va 1982, A Dry White Season 1988, Nuns on the Run 1990, Leon the Pig-Farmer 1992, Max 2001, Fairy Story 2002. *Television includes:* The Family Reunion 1967, Saint Joan 1968, The Three Sisters 1969, Macbeth 1970, Hedda Gabler 1972, Twelfth Night 1973, Shakespeare or Bust 1973, Antony and Cleopatra 1974, Miss Nightingale, Clayhanger (serial) 1975–76, Robin Hood (CBS TV) 1983, Mountbatten: The Last Viceroy 1985, The Singing Detective 1986, The Miser 1987, Revolutionary Witness 1989, Masterclass on Shakespearian Comedy 1990, Masterclass from Haymarket Theatre (Sky TV) 2001, White Clouds (BBC) 2002. *Publications:* Hedda Gabler: The Play in Performance 1980, Acting with

Shakespeare: Three Comedies 1996, The Free State 2000, A Commentary on Antony and Cleopatra 2001. *Address:* Steve Kenis and Co., Royalty House, 72–74 Dean Street, London, W1D 3SG, England. *Telephone:* (20) 7534-6001 (Office). *Fax:* (20) 7287-6328 (Office).

SUZUKI, Haruo, LLB; Japanese business executive; b. 31 March 1913, Hayama, Kanagawa Pref.; s. of Chuji and Masu Suzuki; m. Ito Hibiya 1941; two d.; ed Tokyo Imperial Univ.; with Nomura Securities Co. Ltd 1936–38; joined Showa Denko KK 1939, Exec. Vice-Pres. 1959–71, Pres. 1971–81, Chair. 1981–87, Hon. Chair. 1987–2000, Sr. Counsellor 2000–; Chair. Japan Chemical Industry Asscn 1976–78, New Materials Study Group 1983–, Japan Fine Ceramics Asscn 1986–91; Perm. Trustee Japan Cttee for Econ. Devt 1945–; Dir Int. Primary Aluminium Inst. 1974–76, 1980–82; Exec. Dir Fed. of Econ. Orgs. 1972–87; Chair. Japan-Southern US Asscn 1984–90; Dir and Sr Counsellor Japan Econ. Research Inst. 1997–; Chair. Asscn for Corp. Support for the Arts in Japan 1990–94, Hon. Chair. 1994–; Consultant Village Shonan Inc. 1996–; Industrial Structure Council of Ministry of Int. Trade and Industry (MITI) 1972–92, Legis. Council, Ministry of Justice 1982–92; mem. Industrial Property Council, Patent Office, MITI 1983–91, Comité de réflexion sur l'avenir des relations franco-japonaises, Ministry of Foreign Affairs 1982–84; First Class Order of the Sacred Treasure (Japan) 1989, Officier Légion d'honneur 1995; Hon. DEcon (Humboldt Univ., Berlin) 1975. *Publications:* Chemical Industry 1968, What the Classics Have Taught Me 1979 and others. *Leisure interests:* reading, art appreciation, painting, travelling. *Address:* Showa Denko KK, 13-9, Shiba Daimon 1-chome, Minato-ku, Tokyo, Japan (Office). *Telephone:* (3) 5470-3300 (Office). *Fax:* (3) 3455-5600 (Office).

SUZUKI, Ichiro; Japanese baseball player; b. 22 Oct. 1973, Kasugai; m. Yumiko Suzuki; ed Aikoudai Meiden, Aichi Pref.; right fielder player with Japanese Pacific League team Orix Blue Wave 1994–2000; set new Japanese records for continuous games and batting averages; signed with Seattle Mariners Nov. 2000 and by 4 Oct. 2001 had set an American League record for singles (190) in a season; seven Gold Glove awards. *Address:* c/o Seattle Mariners, P.O. Box 4100, Seattle, WA 98104, USA (Office). *Telephone:* (206) 346-4000 (Office).

SUZUKI, Osamu; Japanese business executive; b. 30 Jan. 1930, Gero, Gifu; s. of Shunzo Suzuki and Toshiko Suzuki; m. Shoko Suzuki 1958; two s. one d.; ed Chuo Univ.; joined Suzuki Motor Co. Ltd 1958, Dir 1963–66, Jr Man. Dir 1967–72, Sr Man. Dir 1973–77, Pres. 1978, now Chair. and CEO; Award 'Sitara-i-Pakistan' (Pakistan) 1985; Medal of Honour with Blue Ribbon 1987; Mil. Cross of Order of Repub. of Hungary 1993. *Leisure interest:* golf. *Address:* Suzuki Motor Corporation, 300 Takatsuka, Hamamatsu, Shizuoka 432-8611, Japan (Office). *Telephone:* (53) 440-2023 (Office). *Fax:* (53) 440-2776 (Office). *Website:* www.suzuki.co.jp (Office).

SUZUKI, Tadashi; Japanese theatre director and producer; b. 20 June 1939, Shimizu City; m. Hiroko Takeuchi 1969; one s.; ed Kitazono High School and Waseda Univ.; founded Waseda Sho-Gekijo 1966; changed name to Suzuki Co. of Toga (SCOT) 1984; apptd. Artistic Dir of Iwanami Hall 1974; built Toga Theatre, Toga Village, Toyama Pref. 1976; Guest Prof. at various schools including Juilliard School, Univ. of Wis. (Milwaukee), Univ. of Calif. (San Diego) and Univ. of Del.; founded Japan Performing Arts Center 1982–99; began annual Toga Int. Arts Festival 1982, Toga Int. Actor Training Programme 1983; apptd. Artistic Dir of Acting Co. Mito (ACM) Theatre 1989–94, Artistic Dir Shizuoka Performing Arts Center 1997; mem. Int. Cttee Theatre Olympics 1994; Kinokuniya Theatre Award 1976, Educ. Minister's Art Encouragement Prize of Theatre 1981. *Work includes:* own texts On the Dramatic Passions I 1969, II 1970, III 1970 and Night and Clock 1975, A Greek trilogy and plays by Chekhov and Shakespeare, many of these in theatres around the world. *Publications:* The Sum of the Internal Angles 1973, Dramatic Language 1977, On the Dramatic Passions 1977, Horizon of Deception 1980, Force that Crosses the Border 1984, The Way of Acting 1986, What Theatre Is 1988, The Way of Directing 1994, Dramatic Language II 1999. *Leisure interest:* collecting costumes (especially hats). *Address:* Shizuoka Performing Arts Center, 100-1, Hirasawa, Shizuoka-shi, Shizuoka, 422-8003, Japan (Home). *Telephone:* (54) 203-5730. *Fax:* (54) 203-5732 (Office).

SUZUMURA, Kotaro, PhD; Japanese economist; b. 7 Jan. 1944, Aichi; s. of Hidetaro Suzumura and Sumie Suzumura; three d.; ed Hitotsubashi Univ.; lecturer Dept of Econs, Hitotsubashi Univ. 1971–73, Prof. of Public Econs, Inst. of Econ. Research 1984–; Assoc. Prof. Inst. of Econ. Research, Kyoto Univ. 1973–82; lecturer LSE 1974–76; Visiting Assoc. Prof. of Econs, Stanford Univ. 1979–80; Visiting Fellow Dept of Econs, Univ. of Pennsylvania 1987, All Souls Coll., Oxford 1988; Dir-Gen. Tokyo Centre for Econ. Research 1990–92; Chair. Far Eastern Standing Cttee Econometric Soc. 1995–, Fellow 1990–, mem. Council 1995–; Ed.-in-Chief Japanese Econ. Review 1995–97; mem. Council Soc. for Social Choice and Welfare; Nikkei Prize 1984, 1988. *Publications:* Rational Choice, Collective Decisions and Social Welfare 1983, Competition, Commitment and Welfare 1995, Social Choice Re-examined (Jt Ed. 2 Vols) 1996, 1997, Development Strategy and Management of the Market Economy (jtly.) 1997. *Leisure interests:* reading novels. *Address:* Institute of Economic Research, Hitotsubashi University, Naka 2–1, Kunitachi, Tokyo (Office); 1–29–3 Asagaya Minami, Suginami-ku, Tokyo, Japan (Home). *Telephone:* (42) 850-8353 (Office); (3) 3311-5110 (Home). *Fax:* (42) 850-8353 (Office); (3) 3311-5110 (Home).

SVANHOLM, Poul Johan, LLB; Danish banker and business executive; b. 7 June 1933, Aalborg; s. of Poul Svanholm and Gerda Svanholm (née Stougaard); m. Lise Andersen 1957; one s. one d.; ed Univ. of Copenhagen; Pres. Vingaarden, Odense 1962–72; Pres. Carlsberg A/S, Copenhagen 1972–82, CEO Carlsberg Group 1982–96; Chair. Danske Bank 1983–; mem. Bd D/S Svendborg (A.P. Moeller Group) 1978–, European Advisory Cttee to NY Stock Exchange 1986–; Grand Cross of Order of Dannebrog 1977; Hon. CBE 1997. *Leisure interest:* his Ravnborg Estate. *Address:* Danske Bank, 2-12 Holmens Kanal, 1092 Copenhagen K (Office); 15 Helleruplund Allé, 2900 Hellerup, Denmark (Home). *Telephone:* 39-62-23-45 (Home). *Fax:* 39-62-75-46 (Home).

SVANIDZE, Nikolay Karlovich; Russian journalist; b. 2 April 1955, Moscow; m.; one s.; ed Moscow State Univ.; researcher Inst. of USA and Canada USSR Acad. of Sciences 1978–91; on staff Russian TV 1992–; commentator Information programme Vesti 1991–94; author and narrator Information programmes Contrasts, Mirror 1996–; Deputy Dir Information programmes, Head Studio Information and Analytical programmes 1996–97; Deputy Chair., Chair. All Russian State TV and Radio Co. 1996–98; political observer 1998–; Head news programme Zerkalo (Mirror); Teffi Prize of Russian Acad. of TV for the best information programme. *Address:* Russian TV and Radio Company, Leninsky prosp. 27/2, 125040 Moscow, Russia (Office). *Telephone:* (095) 234-85-22 (Office).

ŠVANKMAJER, Jan; Czech stage designer and film director; b. 4 Sept. 1934, Prague; m. Eva Dvořáková 1960; one s. one d.; ed Theatrical Acad. of Performing Arts, Prague 1954–58; freelance artist 1958–; numerous drawings, graphic sheets, collages, stage sets and (with his wife) art pottery; Prix Special ASIFA 1990, Award for Lifetime Work UK 1995, Freedom Prize, Berlin 2001, Czech Lion Prize 2002. *Exhibitions include:* Speaking Painting, Prague 1997, (with his wife) Netherlands 2001. *Films directed:* Dimensions of Dialogue 1990, The End of Stalinism in the Czechlands 1990, Food 1992, The Faust Lesson 1994, Conspirators of Pleasure 1996, Otesánek (Kristián Prize 2002) 2000, Chimaeras (co-dir) 2001, Little Otik 2001. *Publication:* Power of Imagination 2001. *Address:* Studio Athanor, Knovíz, 274 01 Slaný (Office); Čermínská 5, 118 00 Prague 1, Czech Republic (Home). *Telephone:* (2) 20514785 (Home).

SVARTVIK, Jan, PhD; Swedish professor of English; b. 18 Aug. 1931, Torsby; s. of Gustaf Svartvik and Sigrid Svartvik; m. Gunilla Berner 1958; two s. one d.; ed Uppsala Univ.; Research Asst and Asst Dir Survey of English Usage, Univ. Coll. London 1961–65; lecturer, Univ. of Gothenburg 1965–70; Visiting Prof. Brown Univ., RI, USA 1969; Prof. of English, Lund Univ. 1970–95; Pres. Asscn Int. de Linguistique Appliquée 1981–84; Chair. Org. Cttee, Nobel Symposium on Corpus Linguistics 1991; Chair. Steering Cttee for Evaluation of Linguistics in Sweden 1990–92; mem. Royal Acad. of Letters, History and Antiquities, Royal Swedish Acad. of Sciences, Academia Europaea, Societas Scientarum Fennica; Dr. hc (Bergen) 1996, (Masaryk Univ.) 1998, (Helsinki) 2000. *Publications:* On Voice in the English Verb 1966, The Evans Statements 1968, A Grammar of Contemporary English (jtly) 1972, A Comprehensive Grammar of the English Language (jtly) 1985, The London-Lund Corpus of Spoken English: Description and Research 1990, Directions in Corpus Linguistics: Proceedings of Nobel Symposium 82 1992 (Ed.), Words, Proceedings (Ed.) 1996, Engelska – öspråk världsspråk, trendspråk (August Prize for Swedish Non-fiction Book of the Year) 1999, Handbok i engelska (jtly) 2001, Politikens bog om engelsk 2001, A Communicative Grammar of English 2002. *Leisure interest:* sailing. *Address:* Tumlaregränden 7, SE-22651 Lund, Sweden. *Telephone:* (46) 248412. *E-mail:* jan.svartvik@telia.com (Home).

SVEDBERG, Bjoern, MSc; Swedish business executive; b. 4 July 1937, Stockholm; s. of Inge Svedberg and Anna-Lisa Svedberg; m. Gunnel Nilsson 1960; four c.; ed Royal Inst. of Tech., Stockholm and Man. Devt Inst. (IMEDE), Univ. of Lausanne; Man. Eng Telephone Exchange Div., L. M. Ericsson Telephone Co. 1972–76, Sr Vice-Pres. Research and Devt 1976–77, Pres. 1977–90, Chair. May 1990–; Mo och Domsjo AB, Chair. 1991–92; Dir AB Volvo 1994–; mem. Bd Fed. of Swedish Industry, L. M. Ericsson and several other cos.; mem. Royal Swedish Acad. of Eng Sciences. *Address:* Telefonaktiebolaget L. M. Ericsson, S 126 11 Stockholm 32, Sweden. *Telephone:* 719-00-00.

SVEJGAARD, Arne, MD, DSc; Danish scientist and professor of immunology; b. 13 March 1937, Odense; m. Else Lyngsoe 1960; two s. one d.; ed Univ. of Århus Medical School and Univ. Hosp. of Århus; Dir Tissue Typing Lab., Univ. Hosp. of Copenhagen 1970–87, Dept of Clinical Immunology 1987–; Prof. of Clinical Immunology, Univ. of Copenhagen 1991–; Councillor Int. Histocompatibility Workshops 1975–; Chair. Danish Cttee for Immunology 1985–; mem. Royal Danish Acad. of Sciences and Letters 1981–; Chair. Alfred Benzon Foundation 1996; Danish Medical Research Council 1997–2002; Kt of Dannebrog 1994; Tsuji Memorial Lecture 1981; Gaardon Prize 1980, Novo Prize 1981, Hess Thaysen Prize 1989, Europe and Medicine Senior Prize 2002. *Publications:* Iso-antigenic Systems of Human Blood Platelets 1969, The HLA System (with others) 1975, HLA and Disease (with J. Dausset) 1977, numerous scientific articles. *Address:* Department of Clinical Immunology, University Hospital, Blegdamsvej 9, 2100 Copenhagen (Office); Skovvang 67, 3450 Allerød, Denmark. *Telephone:* 35-45-76-30 (Office); 48-17-32-11 (Home).

SVĚRÁK, Jan; Czech film director; b. 6 Feb. 1965, Žatec; m.; one s. one d.; ed Film Acad. of Arts; partner of the film production co. Luxor 1996; Co. Biograf Jan Svěrák Pictures 1996–; numerous awards including Acad. Award for best foreign student film 1989, Czech Lion Awards for Direction 1996,

1997, 2001, Time for Peace Prize 1997. *Films directed include:* Ropáci 1988, Primary School 1991, Akumulátor I 1994, Ride 1994, Kolya (Golden Globe Award, Acad. Award and Czech Lion Award) 1996, Blue Dark World 2001. *Leisure interest:* painting. *Address:* P.O. Box 33, 155 00 Prague 515, Czech Republic.

SVERDLOV, Yevgeny Davidovich; Russian biochemist; b. 16 Nov. 1938; ed Moscow State Univ., Sr lab., Jr, Sr researcher Inst. of Bio-organic Chem. 1965–88; Dir Inst. of Molecular Genetics 1988–; corresp. mem. USSR (now Russian) Acad. of Sciences 1984, mem. 1994; research in molecular genetics, structure and functions of nucleic acids; mem. Russian Acad. of Agricultural Sciences 1994; mem. Scientific Council of Biotech. Russian Acad. of Sciences; Lenin Prize; USSR State Prize. *Publications include:* Organic Chemistry of Nucleic Acids 1970, over 200 scientific articles. *Address:* Institute of Molecular Genetics, Kurchatov pl. 46, 123182 Moscow, Russia. *Telephone:* (095) 196-00-00 (Office). *Fax:* (095) 196-02-21 (Office).

SVILANOVIČ, Goran, CandJur; Serbia and Montenegro (Serbian) politician and lawyer; b. 1963, Gnjilane, Kosovo; m.; two c.; ed Belgrade Univ., Inst. of Law, Strasbourg, Saarbrücken Univ., European Univ. of Peace, Austria; worked as asst researcher Belgrade Univ. 1986–89, discharged after protest 1989; collaborator with Yugoslavian Forum on Human Rights 1989–93; Head of telephone service for rescue of victims of nat., ethnic, religious and other discrimination, Centre for Anti-war Action 1993–97; Chair. Council on Human Rights 1996–98; Official Rep. Civic Alliance of Serbia 1997, Vice-Pres. 1998, Pres. 1999; Fed. Minister of Foreign Affairs 2000–03. *Publications:* Civil and Civil Process Law; books and numerous articles on the situation of refugees and problems of citizenship. *Address:* c/o Ministry of Foreign Affairs, Kneza Milosa 24, 11000 Belgrade, Serbia and Montenegro (Office). *Telephone:* (11) 3618073 (Office). *Fax:* (11) 3618052 (Office). *E-mail:* ksm@smip.sv.gov.yu (Office).

SVOBODA, Cyril; Czech politician and lawyer; b. 24 Nov. 1956, Prague; m.; four s.; ed Charles Univ.; legal officer, the notary Transgas 1980–93; Adviser to the Deputy Prime Minister for Human Rights, Restitution and Relations Between the State and the Church 1990; Dir Legis. Section, Office of the Govt –1992; Deputy Minister of Justice 1992–96; Deputy Minister of Foreign Affairs for issues related to accession to the EU 1996–98; Minister of the Interior Jan.–July 1998; Chair. Petition Cttee, Chamber of Deputies 1998–2002; Deputy Prime Minister and Minister of Foreign Affairs 2002–; joined Christian Democratic Union—Czecheslovak People's Party (KDU-CSL) 1995, First Deputy Chair. –2001, Chair. May 2001–; Leader of Coalition of Four Jan.–March 2001; mem. European Comm. for Democracy through Law 1994–, Deputy Chair. 1997–; Chair. Cttee for the Rules of Procedure and Immunity of the Parl. Ass., Council of Europe 2001–. *Publications include:* Annotations on the Constitution of the Czech Republic (co-author), The Act on Out-of-Court Rehabilitation in Questions and Answers; numerous articles and studies on legislation. *Address:* Ministry of Foreign Affairs, Loretánské nám 5, 118 00 Prague 1, Czech Republic (Office). *Telephone:* (2) 24181111 (Office). *Fax:* (2) 24310017 (Office). *Website:* www.mzv.cz (Office).

SVOBODA, Jiří; Czech film director; b. 5 May 1945, Kladno; s. of Jiří Svoboda and Božena Svobodová (née Procházková); m. 1973; two d.; ed Film Acad. of Performing Arts, Prague; studied drama at Acad. of Performing Arts, Prague, expelled for political reasons 1963; worked as warehouseman and driver 1963–66; Dir and script-writer, Film Studios Barrandov 1971–93; freelance film Dir and scriptwriter 1994–; mem. CP of Czechoslovakia 1975–90; Deputy Chair. Union of Czech Dramatic Artists 1987–89; Chair. Film Section of Union of Czech Dramatic Artists 1987–89; Chair. CP of the Czechlands and Moravia 1990–93; Deputy to House of Nations, Fed. Ass. of C.S.F.R. 1990–92; seriously wounded in attempt on his life Dec. 1992; Sr Lecturer, Acad. of Performing Arts; Prof. Film and TV and New Media 2000–; Merited Artist 1986; Grand Prize Karlovy Vary 1982, San Remo 1982, Jury Prize Cannes 1983. *Films include:* (as Dir or scriptwriter): Hostage 1975, A Mirror for Christine 1976, House on the Embankment 1976, The Break Time 1977, The Blue Planet 1979, Girl with a Shell 1980, The Chain 1981, A Meeting with Shadows 1982, The End of the Lonely Berhof Farmstead 1983, The Lancet, Please 1985, Papilio 1986, The World Knows Nothing 1987, A Curse on the Hajnůs' House 1988, Only About Family Orders (about political trials in 1950s) 1989; also directed many TV plays and part of a series on architecture 1999–2000. *Television films:* Blow Up 2001, The Act of Grace is Disproved 2002. *Leisure interests:* philosophy, political theory, literature. *Address:* Academy of Performing Arts, Famu Smetanovo Nab. 2, Prague 1 (Office); Na Balkáně 120, Prague 3, Czech Republic. *Telephone:* (2) 24221192 (Office); (2) 66317640 (Home). *E-mail:* ji.svoboda@email.cz (Home). *Website:* famu.cz (Office); www.mujweb.cz/kultura/svoboda_jiri (Home); www.volny .cz/ji.svoboda.

SWAELEN, Frank M. G., LLD; Belgian politician; b. 23 March 1930, Antwerp; m. M. J. Gobin 1958; one s. two d.; ed Coll. of St-Lievens, Antwerp, Catholic Univ. of Louvain, Harvard Int. Seminar; Sec.-Gen. Nat. Confed. of Parents' Assocns. 1956–66; Nat. Chair. Young Christelijke Volks Partij (CVP) 1964–66; Gen. Sec. Political CVP-PSC (Christian Democrats) 1966–76; mem. Nat. Bureau CVP 1966–71; mem. Chamber of Reps. 1968–85, Senator 1985–99, Nat. Bureau CVP 1971–; Vice-Chair. CVP group in Chamber of Reps. 1979–80; Chair. CVP group in Council of the Flemish Cultural Community 1979–80; Minister of Defence 1980–81; Nat. Pres. CVP 1981–88; Mayor of Herne Nov 1971–89; Pres. of Belgian Senate 1988–99; Pres. Parl. Ass. of

CSCE (now OSCE) 1994–96; Minister of State 1995–; Pres. Charlemagne Inst. 1995–; Grand Cross, Order of Leopold II, Grand Cross, Order of the Crown, Grand Cordon, Order of Leopold. *Leisure interests:* tennis, reading. *Address:* Leliestraat 82, 2540 Hove, Belgium (Home). *Telephone:* (3) 455-26-12 (Home). *Fax:* (3) 454-03-41 (Home). *E-mail:* frank.swaelen@belgacom.net (Home).

SWAN, Sir John William David, KBE, BA; Bermudan politician and business executive; b. 3 July 1935, Bermuda; s. of John Nicholas and Margaret Swan; m. Jacqueline Roberts 1965; one s. two d.; ed Cen. School and Howard Acad., Bermuda and W. Virginia Wesleyan Coll.; Real-Estate Salesman with Rego Ltd 1960–62; Founder, CEO and Chair. of John W Swan Ltd 1962–, Chair. Swan Group of Cos. 1996–; mem. Parl. 1972–95, Minister for Marine and Air Services, Labour and Immigration 1977–78, Home Affairs 1978–82, Premier of Bermuda 1982–95; fmr Parl. Sec. for Finance, Chair. Bermuda Hosp. Bd, Chair. Dept of Civil Aviation; mem. Chief. Execs. Org. and World Business Council; mem. and Fellow, Senate, Jr Chamber Int. 1992; United Bermuda Party; Hon. Freeman City of London 1985; Hon. LLD (Tampa Univ.) 1986, (W Va Wesleyan Coll.) 1987, (Atlantic Union Coll., Mass.) 1991; St Paul's Anniversary Citation 1969, Outstanding Young Man of the Year 1969, Int. Medal of Excellence (first recipient), Poor Richard Club of Phila 1987 and other awards. *Leisure interests:* tennis, sailing. *Address:* Swan Building, 26 Victoria Street, Hamilton, HM12; 11 Grape Bay Drive, Paget PG06, Bermuda (Home). *Telephone:* (441) 295-1785 (Office); (441) 236-1303 (Home). *Fax:* (441) 295-6270 (Office); (441) 236-7935 (Home). *E-mail:* sirjohn@challengerbanks .bm (Office).

SWANK, Hilary; American actress; b. 30 July 1974, Bellingham, Wash.; m. Chad Lowe 1997. *Films include:* Buffy the Vampire Slayer 1992, The Next Karate Kid 1994, Sometimes They Came Back . . . Again 1996, Heartwood 1997, Boys Don't Cry (Acad. Award for Best Actress) 1999, The Gift 2000, Affair of the Necklace 2000, Insomnia 2002, The Core 2003. *Television includes:* Terror in the Family 1996, Leaving LA 1997.

SWANSON, David Heath, MA; American business executive; b. 3 Nov. 1942, Illinois; s. of Neil H. Swanson and Helen M. Swanson; m. 1st Elizabeth Farwell 1963 (divorced); two s.; m. 2nd Cynthia Tripp 1990; m. 3rd Carolyn Breitinger; ed Harvard Coll. and Univ. of Chicago; Account Exec. First Nat. Bank of Chicago 1966–69; Deputy Man. Brown Bros. Harriman 1969–72; Treas. Borden Int. 1972–75; Chief Financial and Admin. Officer, Continental Grain, then Sr Vice-Pres. and Group Pres., Sr Vice-Pres. and Gen. Man. World Grain Div. 1975–86; Pres. and CEO Central Soya Co. Inc. 1986–94; Chair. Premier Agricultural Tech. Inst. 1994–; Chair., CEO Explorer Nutrition Group, New York 1994–96; Pres. CEO Countrymark Cooperative Inc., Indianapolis 1996–98; mem. Council on Foreign Relations; mem. Advisory Bd Export-Import Bank of U.S.; mem. Bd Int. Policy Council on Trade and Agric. *Publications:* articles on mountaineering and exploration. *Address:* Explorer Nutrition and Fiber Group, 46 East 70th Street, New York, NY 10021, USA (Office).

SWAR AL-DAHAB, Field Marshal (see Dahab, Field Marshal Abdul-Rahman Swar al-).

SWARAJ, Sushma, BA, LLB; Indian politician; b. 14 Feb. 1952, Ambala Cantonment; m. Swaraj Kaushal 1975; one d.; ed Punjab Univ., Chandigarh; Advocate, Supreme Court of India 1973–; Mem. (Janata Party) Haryana Legis. Ass. 1977–82, (Bharatiya Janata Party–BJP) 1987–90; All-India Sec. BJP 1985–87, 1990–92, All-India Gen. Sec. and Official Spokesperson 1992–96; Cabinet Minister 1977–78; Minister for Educ. 1987–89; Mem. Parl. (Rajya Sabha) 1990–96, 2000–; Chair. Cttee on Petitions 1994–96; Minister of Information and Broadcasting 1996–98, 2000–, with additional charge of Ministry of Communications 1998; Mem. Parl. (Lok Sabha) for S Delhi 1996–98, 1998–2000; Mem. Delhi Legis. Ass. 1998; Chief Minister of Delhi 1998. *Address:* Ministry of Information and Broadcasting, Room 561, A Wing, Shastri Bhawan, New Delhi 110 001, India (Office). *Telephone:* (11) 3384782 (Office); (11) 3384340 (Office). *Fax:* (11) 3782118 (Office). *Website:* www.mib .nic.in (Office).

SWART, Karel, B.CHEM.ENG.; Netherlands oil company executive; b. 26 May 1921, Singapore; m. Wilhelmina A. Bruinsma 1950; ed Delft Univ.; with Royal Dutch Shell-Laboratory, Amsterdam 1948; Refinery Start-up Team, Shell Berre 1953; Bombay 1954, Geelong 1955; Cen. Office, The Hague 1956; various tech. and managerial posts at Cardón Refinery, Compañía Shell de Venezuela Ltd 1958–65; Gen. Man. Curaçao 1965; Dir Mfg and Supply, Venezuela 1967; Special Assignment, Cen. Office, The Hague 1968; Man. Dir N.V. Koninklijke Nederlandsche Petroleum Maatschappij (Royal Dutch) 1979, The Shell Petroleum Co. Ltd 1979, Prin. Dir Shell Petroleum N.V. 1970–79; Chair. Supervisory Bd, Royal Boskalis Westminster NV (Papendrecht) 1980–; Kt Order of Netherlands Lion. *Address:* Brouwerlaan 6, Voorschoten, Netherlands (Home).

SWAYZE, Patrick; American actor and dancer; b. 18 Aug. 1954, Houston; s. of Patsy Swayze; m. Lisa Niemi 1976; ed Harkness and Joffrey Ballet Schools; began as dancer in Disney on Parade on tour as Prince Charming; appeared on Broadway as dancer in Goodtime Charley, Grease. *Television appearances include:* North and South: Books I and II, The New Season, Pigs vs. Freaks, The Comeback Kid, The Return of the Rebels, The Renegades. *Films:* Skatetown USA 1979, The Outsiders, Uncommon Valor, Red Dawn, Grandview USA (also choreographer), Dirty Dancing (co-wrote song and sings She's

Like the Wind), Steel Dawn, Tiger Warsaw, Road House, Next of Kin, Ghost, Point Break, City of Joy, Father Hood, Tall Tales, To Wong Foo–Thanks for Everything–Julie Newmar, Three Wishes, Letters from a Killer 1997, Vanished 1998, Black Dog 1998, Without a Word 1999, The Winddrinker 2000, Wakin' Up In Reno 2000, Forever Lulu 2000, Donnie Darko 2001. *Address:* c/o William Morris Agency, 151 South El Camino Drive, Beverly Hills, CA 90212, USA.

SWE, U Ba; Myanma politician; b. 19 April 1915, Tavoy; s. of U Tun Hlaing and Daw Pe Lay Swe; m. Daw Nu Nu Swe 1944; six s. four d.; ed Rangoon Univ.; Pres. Rangoon Univ. Students' Union 1940–41; one of the founders of People's Revolutionary Party 1939; Chief of Civil Defence in the "Kebotai" 1942–45; one of leaders of Anti-Japanese Resistance Movement, in charge of Rangoon, Hanthawaddy and Insein Dists. 1944–45, arrested and detained by Japanese; Pres. Socialist Party (originally People's Revolutionary Party) 1945, later Sec.-Gen.; Pres. Asia Socialist Conf. 1952–56, 1956–60; Sec.-Gen. Anti-Fascist People's Freedom League 1947–58; Leader of "Stable" Group 1958; fmr MP from Taikkyi; Minister of Defence 1952–58, concurrently Prime Minister 1956; Deputy Prime Minister 1957–59; Leader of Opposition 1958; under political arrest 1963–66; Yugoslav Banner, First Class, Noble Order of the White Elephant (Thailand), Star of Revolution, First Degree, Naing-Ngani Gon Yi, Title Class 1 1980. *Leisure interests:* gardening, billiards, writing. *Address:* 84 Innes Road, Yangon, Myanmar. *Telephone:* 21355.

SWEDEN, King of (see Carl Gustaf XVI, King Carl Gustaf Folke Hubertus).

SWEENEY, John Joseph, BSc; American trades union official; b. 5 May 1934, New York; s. of John Sweeney and Patricia Sweeney; m. Maureen Power; one s. one d.; ed Iona Coll.; with IBM (Int. Business Machines Corpn); researcher Int. Ladies Garment Workers Union; fmr Pres. Service Employees Int. Union; Pres. AFL-CIO (American Fed. of Labor and Congress of Industrial Orgs.) 1995–. *Publication:* America Needs a Raise 1996. *Address:* AFL-CIO, 815 16th Street, NW, Washington, DC 20006, USA. *Telephone:* (202) 637-5000. *Fax:* (202) 637-5058.

SWENSEN, Joseph Anton; American conductor and composer; b. 4 Aug. 1960, New York City; m. 2nd Kristina Algot-Sörensen; three s. (one from previous marriage); ed Juilliard School; Prin. Guest Conductor Stockholm Chamber Orchestra 1994–97, Lahti Symphony Orchestra 1995–2000; Prin. Conductor Scottish Chamber Orchestra (SCO) 1996–; Prin. Guest Conductor BBC Nat. Orchestra of Wales 2000–; toured Japan with SCO 1995, USA 1999; debut at Edinburgh Int. Festival with SCO 1998; cycle of Beethoven performances to mark 25th anniversary of SCO 1999; conducted new production of The Marriage of Figaro at the Royal Danish Opera 1999; regular appearances with Royal Stockholm Philharmonic and Swedish Radio Symphony Orchestras; guest conductor with Los Angeles Philharmonic, Toronto Symphony, Dallas Symphony, London Philharmonic, City of Birmingham Symphony, Oslo Philharmonic, Finnish Radio Symphony, Gothenburg Symphony and Ulster Orchestras, Lausanne Chamber Orchestra; own orchestral works have been performed by various orchestras. *Address:* c/o Victoria Rowsell, Van Walsum Management Ltd, 4 Addison Bridge Place, London, W14 8XP, England (Office). *Telephone:* (20) 7371-4343 (Office). *Fax:* (20) 7371-4344 (Office). *E-mail:* c/o edesmond@vanwalsum.co.uk (Office). *Website:* www.vanwalsum.co.uk (Office).

SWETT, Richard Nelson, BA, FAIA; American politician and architect; b. 1 May 1957, Lower Merion, Pennsylvania; s. of the late Philip Eugene Swett Sr and of Ann Parkhurst Swett; m.; three s. three d.; ed Yale Univ.; licensed architect in several states; has worked in real estate Devt, alternative energy Devt, energy conservation, industrial Devt and export promotion; mem. U.S. House of Reps. from 2nd Congressional Dist of NH 1990–98, mem. several Congressional Cttees., co-author Congressional Accountability Act, author Transportation for Livable Communities Act; Amb. to Denmark 1998–2001; Founding mem. Advisory Bd, European Center of Calif. 2001–; mem. Bd Sunrise Capital Partners 2001–; State Chair. U.S. Olympic Cttee 2001–; Hon. LLD (Franklin Pierce Coll.) and several other hon. degrees; Presidential Citation, AIA. *Publications:* A Nation Reconstructed, A Quest to Make Cities All That They Can Be (co-author). *Leisure interests:* tennis, reading, piano, sailing, skiing, running, basketball, golf, painting, travel, family. *Address:* 5 Coliseum Avenue, Nashua, NH 03063 (Office); 127 Main Street, Littleton, NH 03561, USA. *E-mail:* rswett@mediaone.net (Home).

ŚWIĘCICKI, Marcin, D.ECON.SC.; Polish politician and economist; b. 17 April 1947, Warsaw; s. of Andrzej Święcicki and Jadwiga Święcicka; m. Joanna Szyr 1969; three s., one d.; ed Warsaw Univ.; Asst. Econ. Sciences Inst., Warsaw Univ. 1971–72; Councillor, then Chief Specialist in Planning Comm. attached to the Council of Ministers 1972–82; Dir for study and analysis matters 1982–87, Gen. Sec. of Consultative Econ. Council 1987–89; mem. PZPR 1974–90, PZPR Cen. Cttee 1989–90, Sec. PZPR Cen. Cttee Aug.–Sept. 1989; participant Round Table debates, mem. group for economy and social policy Feb.–April 1989; Deputy to Sejm (Parl.) 1989–91, 1993–96; Minister for Foreign Econ. Co-operation 1989–91; Deputy Chair. Sejm Cttee on Foreign Econ. Relations 1993–95; Mayor of Warsaw 1994–99; Co-Chair. Govt and Territorial Self-Govt Jt Comm. 1994–99; Adviser to Lithuanian Govt 1993; Co-Founder Tax Reform Movt 1993–; Co-Founder Cen. European Forum 1995–; Pres. Union of Polish Metropolises 1994–99; mem. Polish Econ. Soc. 1978–; Co-Founder Consensus Dialogue Group 1986–90, mem. Secr. 1986–89; Co-Founder and Treas. Polish Asscn for the Club of Rome 1987–91; scientific worker, Inst. of Econ. Sciences, Polish Acad. of Sciences 1991–93;

independent adviser 1991–94; 2001–; Under-Sec. of State, Ministry of the Econ. 1999–; mem. Negotiating Team, Polish Accession to EU 1999–2000; Adviser to Pres. of Lithuania 1999–2000; mem. Democratic Union (now Freedom Union) 1991– (mem. Council, Warsaw br. 1991–93, mem. Nat. Council 1993–); Co-Founder and Vice-Pres. Polish Fulbright Alumni Asscn 1993–96; Pres. Polish Cttee of Support for Museum of the History of Polish Jews 1997–; Fellowship, George Washington Univ., Washington, DC 1975–76, Harvard Univ., Cambridge, Mass., USA 1984–85; Hon. mem. Union of Warsaw Uprising Veterans (Związek Powstańców Warszawskich); Labour and Wages Comm. Award 1971, Award of Chair. of Radio and TV Cttee 1988, Daily Trybuna Ludu Award 1989; Gold and Bronze Cross of Merit; Bronze Medal in long jump, European Junior Athletic Championship, Odessa 1966. *Publications include:* Perspektywiczne programowanie problemowe w Polsce 1978, Revolution in Social Sciences and Future Studies Movement 1978, Rozwój sytuacji i polityki gospodarczej (Ed.) 1985, Reforma własnościowa 1989, The Economy of Ukraine (with Stanisław Wellisz) 1993. *Leisure interests:* mountain hiking, jogging, volleyball, political books, memoirs, essays. *Address:* Ministerstwo Gospodarki, pl. Trzech Krzyzy 3/5, 00-507 Warsaw (Office); Węgrzyna 29, 00-769 Warsaw, Poland (Home). *Telephone:* (22) 64236 51; (22) 6422783 (Home). *Fax:* (22) 6423651; (22) 6422783 (Home). *E-mail:* m.swiecicki@melog.com.pl (Office).

ŚWIERZY, Waldemar; Polish graphic designer; b. 9 Sept. 1931, Katowice; ed Acad. of Fine Art, Cracow; lecturer Acad. of Fine Art, Poznań 1965–, Prof. 1987–; Prof. Acad. of Fine Art, Warsaw 1994–; Visiting Prof. Univ. of Mexico 1979–80, Hochschule der Kunste, Berlin 1985–86, Gesamthochschule Kassel 1989–90; has designed over 1,500 posters and 500 book covers; mem. Alliance Graphique Internationale; Hon. Prof. Acad. of Fine Art, Cracow 1997; Gold Cross of Merit 1955; Kt's Cross, Order of Polonia Restituta 1978, Officer's Cross 1989; Lautrec Grand Prix, Toulouse 1959, Minister of Culture and Arts Prize (1st Class) 1961, First Prize, Prix X Biennale di São Paulo 1970, Gold Medal, Int. Posters Biennale, Warsaw 1976, Gold and Bronze Medal, Int. Jazz Poster Exhbn., Bydgoszcz 1985, First Prize, Annual Film Posters Competition of Hollywood Reporter, Los Angeles 1985. *Exhibitions:* solo exhbns in Poland and abroad include: Galerie in der Biberstrasse, Vienna 1960, X Biennale di São Paulo 1969, Poster Museum Wilanow, Warsaw 1978, 1997, Poliforum Sigueros, Mexico City 1980, Galerie Oxe, Copenhagen 1982, Taidemuseo, Lahti 1989, GHK, Kassel 1990, Creation Gallery GB, Tokyo 1991, Festival d'Affiche, Chaumont 1993, Plakat Kunsthof, Essen 2000, Museum of Contemporary Art, Tehran 2001. *Address:* ul. Piwna 45/47 m. 14, 00-265 Warsaw, Poland (Home). *Telephone:* (22) 8312048 (Home). *Fax:* (22) 8312048 (Home).

ŚWIEŻAWSKI, Stefan; Polish professor of history of philosophy; b. 10 Feb. 1907, Hołubie; m.; two d.; ed Jan Kazimierz Univ., Lvov; Sr Asst Jan Kazimierz Univ., Lvov 1934; Head History of Philosophy Dept, Catholic Univ. of Lublin 1946–76, Prof. 1956–76, Prof. Emer. 1976–; researcher Research Centre of Medieval Philosophy, Poland Inst. of Philosophy and Sociology, Polish Acad. of Sciences, Warsaw 1957–63, Centre Nationale de la Recherche Scientifique, Paris 1960–61; mem. Polish Acad. of Arts and Sciences, Société Internationale pour l'Etude de la Philosophie Mediévale, Institut Internationale de Philosophie; Officier, Ordre des Palmes Académiques 1988, White Eagle Order 1997; Dr hc (Jagiellonian Univ., Kraków) 1989; Alfred Jurzykowski Foundation Award 1976. *Publications:* La philosophie à l'heure du Concile (co-author) 1965, Zagadnienia historii filozofii (Problems of History of Philosophy) 1966, Dzieje filozofii europejskiej w XV wieku (History of European Philosophy) Vols I–VIII 1974–90, Dzieje klasycznej filozofii europejskiej (History of Classical European Philosophy) 2000. *Address:* ul. Wiślna 2 m. 19, 00-317 Warsaw, Poland (Office).

SWIFT, Graham Colin, FRSL; British writer; b. 4 May 1949, London; s. of Lionel Allan Stanley Swift and Sheila Irene (née Bourne) Swift; ed Dulwich Coll., Queens' Coll., Cambridge, Univ. of York; Hon. LittD (East Anglia) 1998, Hon. DUniv (York) 1998; Geoffrey Faber Memorial Prize, Guardian Fiction Prize, Royal Society of Literature Winifred Holtby Award 1983, Premio Grinzane Cavour (Italy) 1987, Prix du meilleur livre étranger (France) 1994, Booker Prize, James Tait Black Memorial Prize 1996. *Publications:* (novels) The Sweet Shop Owner 1980, Shuttlecock 1981, Waterland 1983, Out of This World 1988, Ever After 1992, Last Orders 1996, The Light of Day 2003; (short stories) Learning to Swim and Other Stories 1982; The Magic Wheel (ed. with David Profumo) 1986. *Leisure interest:* fishing. *Address:* c/o A. P. Watt, 20 John Street, London, WC1N 2DR, England.

SWIFT, Jane, BA; American politician; b. 24 Feb. 1965, North Adams; d. of John Maynard and Jean Kent; m. Chuck Hunt 1994; three d.; ed Trinity Coll.; elected to Mass. State Senate 1991, becoming Asst Minority Leader, mem. Senate Ways and Means Cttee, Educ. Reform Conf. Cttee; Lieut.-Gov. of Mass. 1998–2001, Gov. 2001–03; Dir Regional Airport Devt, Mass. Port Authority –1997; Dir Mass. Office of Consumer Affairs and Business Regulation 1997–2001; mem. Fed. Trade. Comm. Advisory Cttee on Online Access and Security; mem. Bd W. Mass. Girl Scout Council, Mass. Coll. of Liberal Arts. *Address:* c/o Office of the Governor, State House, Room 360, Boston, MA 02133, USA (Office).

SWINBURNE, Richard Granville, MA, BPhil, F.B.A.; British professor of philosophy; b. 26 Dec. 1934, Smethwick; s. of William H. Swinburne and Gladys E. Swinburne; m. Monica Holmstrom 1960 (separated 1985); two d.; ed Univ. of Oxford; Fereday Fellow, St John's Coll., Oxford 1958–61; Leverhulme Research Fellow in History and Philosophy of Science, Univ. of Leeds

1961–63; lecturer in Philosophy, Univ. of Hull 1963–72; Prof. of Philosophy, Univ. of Keele 1972–84; Nolloth Prof. of the Philosophy of the Christian Religion, Univ. of Oxford 1985–2002; Visiting Assoc. Prof. Univ. of Md 1969–70. *Publications:* Space and Time 1968, The Concept of Miracle 1971, An Introduction to Confirmation Theory 1973, The Coherence of Theism 1977, The Existence of God 1979, Faith and Reason 1981, The Evolution of the Soul 1986, Responsibility and Atonement 1989, Revelation 1991, The Christian God 1994, Is There a God? 1996, Providence and the Problem of Evil 1998, Epistemic Justification 2001. *Address:* Oriel College, Oxford, OX1 4EW (Office); 50 Butler Close, Oxford, OX2 6JG, England (Home). *Telephone:* (1865) 276589 (Office); (1865) 514406 (Home). *Fax:* (1865) 791823. *E-mail:* richard.swinburne@oriel.ox.ac.uk (Office).

SWING, William Lacy, BA, BD; American diplomatist; b. 11 Sept. 1934, Lexington, North Carolina; s. of Baxter D. Swing and Mary F. (née Barbee) Swing; m. Yuen Cheong 1993; one s. one d. from previous marriage; ed Catawba Coll., Yale Univ., Tübingen Univ.; Vice-Consul, Port Elizabeth, S. Africa 1963–66; int. economist, Bureau of Econ. Affairs, Dept of State 1966–68; Consul, Hamburg 1968–72; Desk Officer for FRG, Dept of State 1972–74; Deputy Chief of Mission, U.S. Embassy, Bangui, Cen. African Repub. 1974–76; Sr Fellow, Center for Int. Affairs, Harvard Univ. 1976–77; Deputy Dir, Office of Cen. African Affairs, Dept of State 1977–79; Amb. to People's Repub. of Congo 1979–81, to Liberia 1981–85, to SA 1989–93, to Nigeria 1992–93, to Haiti 1993–98, to Democratic Repub. of Congo 1998–2001; Special Rep. of UN Sec.-Gen. for Western Sahara 2001–; Dir Office of Foreign Service Assignments and Career Devt 1985–87; Deputy Asst Sec. for Personnel 1987–89; Fellow, Harvard Univ.; Hon. LLD (Catawba Coll.) 1980; Hon. DHumLitt (Hofstra) 1994; Presidential Distinguished Service Award 1985; Distinguished Honor Award 1994, Award for Valor 1995, Presidential Meritorious Service Award 1987, 1990, 1994, 1998, Presidential Certificate of Commendation 1998. *Publications:* Education for Decision 1963, U.S. Policy Towards South Africa: Dilemmas and Priorities 1977, Liberia: The Road to Recovery 1982, Haiti: In Physical Contact with History 1994. *Leisure interests:* tennis, squash, golf. *Address:* Minurso-HQ, Laayoune, PO Box 5846, Grand Central Station, New York, NY 10163-5846 (Office); 6002 Paradise Point Drive, Miami, FL 33157, USA (Home). *Telephone:* (212) 963-1952 (ext. 5000); 61-38-68-20 (Morocco) (Home). *E-mail:* swing@un.org (Office); swingwl@yahoo.com (Home). *Website:* www.un.org.

SWINNERTON-DYER, Sir (Henry) Peter Francis, Bt, KBE, MA, FRS; British mathematician and university professor; b. 2 Aug. 1927, Ponteland; s. of the late Sir Leonard Dyer; m. Dr. Harriet Crawford 1983; ed Eton and Trinity Coll., Cambridge; Research Fellow, Trinity Coll. 1950–54; Commonwealth Fund Fellow, Univ. of Chicago 1954–55; Coll. Lecturer in Math., Trinity Coll. 1955–71, Dean 1963–70; Lecturer in Math., Cambridge Univ. 1960–71, Prof. of Math. 1971–88, Master of St Catharine's Coll. 1973–83; Vice-Chancellor, Cambridge Univ. 1979–81; Chair. Univ. Grants Cttee 1983–89, Chief Exec. Univs. Funding Council 1989–91, European Scientific and Tech. Ass. 1994–; Chair. Sec. of State for Nat. Heritage's Advisory Cttee, Library and Information Services Council 1992–95; mem. Advisory Bd for Research Councils 1977–90; Vice-Pres. Inst. of Manpower Studies 1983; Visiting Prof. Harvard Univ. 1970–71; Chair. Cttee on Acad. Org., Univ. of London 1980–81; mem. Advisory Council on Science and Tech. 1987–89; Hon. Fellow, Worcester Coll., Oxford 1980, St Catharine's Coll., Cambridge 1983, Trinity Coll., Cambridge 1983; Hon. DSc (Bath) 1981, (Wales) 1991; Hon. ScD (Ulster) 1991, (Birmingham) 1992, (Nottingham) 1992; Hon. LLD (Aberdeen) 1991. *Publications:* Analytic Theory of Abelian Varieties 1974 and papers in learned journals. *Leisure interest:* gardening. *Address:* The Dower House, Thriplow, Royston, Herts., SG8 7RJ, England. *Telephone:* (1763) 208220.

SWINNEY, John Ramsay, MA; British politician and management specialist; b. 13 April 1964; s. of Kenneth Swinney and Nancy Swinney (née Hunter); m. Lorna Ann King 1991 (divorced 1998); one s. one d.; ed Univ. of Edin.; Sr Man. Consultant, Devt Options Ltd 1988–92; Strategic Planning Prin., Scottish Amicable 1992–97; MP for North Tayside 1997–2001; mem. North Tayside, Scottish Parl. 1999–; Nat. Sec. SNP 1986–92, Vice-Convener for Publicity 1992–97, Treasury Spokesman 1995–2000, Deputy Leader 1998–2000, Leader 2000–; Leader of the Opposition, Scottish Parl. 2000–; Convener Enterprise and Lifelong Learning Cttee, Scottish Parl. 1999–2000. *Leisure interests:* hill walking, cycling. *Address:* Scottish Parliament, George IV Bridge, Edinburgh, EH99 1SP (Office); 35 Perth Street, Blairgowrie, PH10 6DL, Scotland (Home). *Telephone:* (131) 348-5717 (Office); (1250) 876576 (Home). *Fax:* (131) 348-5946 (Office); (1250) 876576 (Home).

SWINTON, Tilda; British actress; ed New Hall, Cambridge; performance art appearance sleeping in a glass case, Serpentine Gallery, London 1996. *Films include:* The Last of England, The Garden 1990, Edward II 1991, Orlando 1993, Wittgenstein 1993, Female Perversions 1996, Love is the Devil 1997, Conceiving Ada 1997, The War Zone 1998, The Beach 2000, The Deep End 2000, Vanilla Sky 2001; TV: Your Cheating Heart 1989.

SWIRE, Sir Adrian (Christopher), Kt, MA; British business executive; b. 15 Feb. 1932, London; s. of the late John Kidston Swire and Juliet Richenda Barclay; m. Lady Judith Compton 1970; two s. one d.; ed Eton, Univ. Coll., Oxford; served Coldstream Guards 1950–52; fmrly with RAFVR; joined Butterfield & Swire in Far East 1956; Dir John Swire & Sons Ltd 1961, Deputy Chair. 1966–87, Chair. 1987–97, 2002–, Hon. Pres., Exec. Dir 1998–2002; Pro-Chancellor Southampton Univ. 1995–; Chair. China Navi-

gation Co. Ltd 1968–88; Dir Brooke Bond Group 1972–82, Navy, Army and Air Force Insts. 1972–87; Pres. Gen. Council of British Shipping 1980–81; Chair. Int. Chamber of Shipping 1982–87; mem. Gen. Cttee Lloyds Register 1967–99, Int. Advisory Council, China Int. Trust and Investment Corpn 1995–; Chair. RAF Benevolent Fund 1996–2000; Pres. Spitfire Soc. 1996–; Trustee RAF Museum 1983–91; Hon. Air Commodore Royal Auxiliary Air Force 1987–2000; DL (Oxfordshire) 1989; Hon. DSc (Cranfield) 1995; Hon. DUniv (Southampton) 2002. *Address:* Swire House, 59 Buckingham Gate, London, SW1E 6AJ, England. *Telephone:* (20) 7834-7717 (Home). *Fax:* (20) 7630-0380 (Office).

SWITKOWSKI, Zygmunt Edward, PhD; Australian (b. German) business executive; b. 21 June 1948, Rheine, Germany; m. Jadzia Teresa 1970; one s. one d.; ed St Bernardo's Coll., Univ. of Melbourne; Sr Research Scientist Eastman Kodak Co., New York 1978–80, Man. Research and Devt 1980–82, Sales Man. 1982–83, Marketing Man. Consumer Products 1983–85, Dir Business Planning 1985–88; Deputy Man. Dir Kodak (Australasia) Ltd 1988–92, Chair., Man. Dir 1992–96; Dir Amcor Ltd 1995–99; Chair., Acting CEO Optus Vision Pty Ltd 1996–97, CEO Optus Communications Pty Ltd 1996–97; Group Man. Dir Business Int. Div. Telstra Corpn Ltd 1997–99, CEO 1999–; Chair. Australian Quality Council; mem. Business Council of Australia. *Address:* Telstra Corporation Ltd., Level 14, 231 Elizabeth Street, Sydney, NSW 2000, Australia (Office). *Telephone:* (2) 9287-4677 (Office). *Fax:* (2) 9287-5869 (Office). *Website:* www.telstra.com.au (Office).

SWOBODA, Peter, DBA; Austrian professor of finance; b. 13 April 1937, Bad-Deutsch Altenburg; s. of Gottfried Swoboda and Maria Magdalena Swoboda; m. 1st Eva Swoboda 1959; m. 2nd Birgit Swoboda 1978 (divorced 1988); one s. three d.; ed Hochschule für Welthandel, Vienna; Asst Prof. Hochschule für Welthandel, 1959–64; Visiting Assoc. Prof. in Accountancy, Univ. of Ill. (Urbana-Champaign) 1965–66; Full Prof. in Accountancy and Finance, Johann Wolfgang Goethe Univ., Frankfurt 1966–70; Prof. of Industrial Econs. Karl Franzens Univ., Graz 1970–; Pres. European Finance Asscn 1980–81; Assoc. mem. Austrian Acad. of Sciences 1980, Full mem. 1983. *Publications:* Investition und Finanzierung 1992, Betriebliche Finanzierung 1994. *Address:* c/o Faculty of Business Administration and Economics, Karl Franzens University Graz, Universitätsplatz 3, 8010 Graz, Austria.

SYAL, Meera, BA, MBE; British writer and actress; b. 27 June 1963, Wolverhampton; d. of Surendra Syal and Surrinder Syal; m. 1989; one d.; ed Queen Mary's High School for Girls, Walsall, Univ. of Manchester; actress in one-woman comedy One of Us after graduation (Nat. Student Drama Award); fmr actress Royal Court Theatre, London; writer of screenplays and novels; actress and comedienne in theatre, film and on TV; contrib. to The Guardian newspaper; Scottish Critics Award for Most Promising Performer 1984, Woman of the Year in the Performing Arts, Cosmopolitan Magazine 1994, Chair.'s Award, Asian Women of Achievement (AWA) Awards 2002. *Plays include:* Serious Money (London and Broadway, NY) 1987, Stitch, Peer Gynt 1990. *Radio includes:* Legal Affairs 1996, Goodness Gracious Me 1999, The World as We Know It 1999. *Film appearances include:* Sammie and Rosie Get Laid 1987, A Nice Arrangement, It's Not Unusual, Beautiful Thing 1996, Girls' Night 1997. *Television appearances include:* The Real McCoy (5 series) 1990–95, My Sister Wife (BBC TV series) 1992, Have I Got News For You 1992, 1993, 1999, Sean's Show 1993, The Brain Drain 1993, Absolutely Fabulous 1995, Soldier Soldier 1995, Degrees of Error 1995, Band of Gold 1995, Drop the Dead Donkey 1996, Ruby 1997, Keeping Mum (BBC sitcom) 1998, The Book Quiz 1998, Goodness Gracious Me (first UK Asian comedy sketch) 1998–99, Room 101 1999, The Kumars at No 42 2002–. *Publications include:* A Nice Arrangement (short TV film) 1991, My Sister Wife (TV film; Best TV Drama Award, Comm. for Racial Equality, Awards for Best Actress and Best Screenplay, Asian Film Acad. 1993) 1992, Bhaji on the Beach (film) 1994, Anita and Me (novel; Betty Trask Award 1996) 1996, Goodness Gracious Me (comedy sketch TV show; co-writer) 1999, Life is not all Ha Ha Hee Hee (novel) 2000, Bombay Dreams (musical) 2002. *Leisure interests:* singing in jazz quintet, netball. *Address:* c/o Rochelle Stevens, 2 Terretts Place, Islington, London, N1 1QZ, England (Office). *Telephone:* (1973) 417762 (Office).

SYBERBERG, Hans-Jürgen, DPhil; German film producer, theatre director and writer; b. 8 Dec. 1935, Nossendorf, Pomerania; m.; ed studies in literature and history of art at Munich; made over 80 short TV films 1963–65; later work includes documentaries, feature films and theatre; several Bundesfilmpreise and other awards including Bayerischer Filmpreis. *Films:* Fritz Kortner Rehearses Schiller's Intrigue and Love 1965, Shylock Monolog 1966, The Counts Pocci 1967, How Much Earth Does a Man Need 1968, Sexbusiness Made in Passing 1969, San Domingo 1970, After My Last Removal (Brecht) 1971, Ludwig—Requiem for a Virgin King 1972, Ludwig's Cook 1972, Karl May—In Search of Paradise Lost 1974, The Confessions of Winifred Wagner 1975, Hitler, A Film from Germany 1977, Parsifal (Kritiker Preis, Berlin 1983) 1982, Die Nacht 1984, Edith Clever liest Joyce-Molly 1985, Fräulein Else 1987, Penthesilea 1988, Marquise von O 1990, Ein Traum, was sonst? 1994. *Plays include:* (in collaboration with E. Clever) Die Nacht 1984, Penthesilea 1988, Die Marquise von O . . . 1989, Ein Traum, was sonst? 1990. *Publications:* The Film as the Music of the Future 1975, Syberbergs Filmbuch 1976, Die Kunst als Rettung aus der deutschen Misere (essay) 1978, Vom-Unglück und Glück der Kunst in Deutschland nach dem letzten Kriege 1990, Der verlorene Auftrag 1994. *Address:* Genter Strasse 15A, 80805 Munich, Germany. *Telephone:* (89) 3614882. *Fax:* (89) 3614905. *E-mail:* film@

syberberg.de (Office); hjs@syberberg.de (Home). *Website:* www.syberberg.de, www.syberberg2.de (Office); www.syberberg3.de, www.syberberg4.de (Home).

SYCHOV, Alyaksandr; Belarus diplomatist; b. 19 Sept. 1951, Homel, Belarus; m. Natalia Vedmedenko 1976; one s. one d.; ed Moscow State Inst. of Int. Relations; Third then Second Sec., Ministry of Foreign Affairs 1979–84; Del. Perm. Mission of the Repub. of Belarus to UN office and other int. orgs., Geneva 1984–90; Head Dept of Foreign Econ. Relations, Ministry of Foreign Affairs 1991–92, Deputy Minister for Foreign Affairs 1992–94; Perm. Rep. to UN 1994–2000; Deputy Minister of Foreign Affairs 2000–; Chair. First Cttee of the 51st session of the UN Gen. Ass., 19th Special Session 1996–97; Vice-Pres. ECOSOC 1998–99. *Publications:* numerous articles on Belarus foreign policy and int. affairs. *Leisure interests:* art, opera, tennis, soccer. *Address:* Ministry of Foreign Affairs, vul. Lenina 19, 220030 Minsk, Belarus. *Telephone:* (17) 227-29-22. *Fax:* (17) 227-45-21. *Website:* www.mfa.gov.by.

SYDOW, Max von; Swedish actor; b. 10 April 1929, Lund, Sweden; s. of Carl W von Sydow and Greta Rappe; m. 1st Kerstin Olin 1951 (divorced 1979); two s.; m. 2nd Catherine Brelet 1997; two s.; ed Royal Dramatic Theatre School, Stockholm; Norrköping-Linköping Theatre 1951–53, Hälsingborg Theatre 1953–55, Malmö Theatre 1955–60, Royal Dramatic Theatre, Stockholm 1960–74, 1988–94; Best Actor, European Film Award, Berlin 1988. *Plays acted in include:* Peer Gynt, Henry IV (Pirandello), The Tempest, Le misanthrope, Faust, Ett Drömspel, La valse des toréadors, Les sequestrés d'Altona, After the Fall, The Wild Duck, The Night of the Tribades 1977, Duet for One 1981, The Tempest 1988, Swedenhielms 1990, And Give Us the Shadows 1991, The Ghost Sonata 1994. *Films acted in include:* Bara en mor 1949, Miss Julie 1950, Det sjunde inseglet (The Seventh Seal) 1957, Ansiktet (The Face) 1958, The Virgin Spring 1960, Såsom i en spegel (Through a Glass Darkly) 1961, Nattvardsgästerna (Winter Light) 1963, The Greatest Story Ever Told 1963, 4×4 1965, Hawaii 1965, Quiller Memorandum 1966, The Hour of the Wolf 1966, The Shame 1967, A Passion 1968, The Emigrants 1969, The New Land 1969, The Exorcist 1973, Steppenwolf 1973, Heart of a Dog 1975, Three Days of the Condor 1975, The Voyage of the Damned 1976, The Desert of the Tartars 1976, Cadaveri Eccelenti 1976, Deathwatch 1979, Flash Gordon 1979, Victory 1980, The Flight of the Eagle 1981, Hannah and Her Sisters 1985, Duet for One 1986, Pelle the Conqueror 1986, Father 1989, Until the End of the World 1990, The Silent Touch 1991, Time is Money 1993, Needful Things 1994, Judge Dredd, Hamsun 1996, What Dreams May Come 1997, Snow Falling on Cedars 1999, Non ho sonno 2000, Intacto 2000, Minority Report 2001; Dir Katinka 1989. *Television:* The Last Civilian, Christopher Columbus, The Last Place on Earth 1984, The Belarus File 1984, Gosta Berling's Saga 1985, The Wisdom and the Dream 1989, Red King White Knight, Hiroshima Out of the Ashes 1990, Best Intentions 1991, Radetzky March 1994, Citizen X 1995, Confessions 1996, Solomon 1997. *Publication:* Loppcirkus (with Elisabeth Sörenson) 1989. *Leisure interests:* nautical history, environment preservation. *Address:* c/o London Management, 2-4 Noel Street, London W1V 3RB, England; c/o Agence Anne Alvares Correa, 18 rue Troyon, 75017 Paris, France.

SYKES, Alfred Geoffrey, PhD, DSc, CChem, FRSC, FRS; British professor of inorganic chemistry; b. 12 Jan. 1934, Huddersfield; s. of Alfred H. Sykes and Edith A. Wortley; m. Elizabeth Blakey; two s. one d.; ed Huddersfield Coll., Univ. of Manchester, Princeton and Adelaide Univs.; lecturer, Univ. of Leeds 1961–70, Reader 1970–80; Prof. of Inorganic Chem. Univ. of Newcastle upon Tyne 1980–99, Prof. Emer. of Chemistry; mem. SERC BBSRC/EPSRC Panels/Cttees.; Ed. Advances in Inorganic Chemistry, vols. 32–52; mem. editorial bds. various specialist journals; Visiting Prof. Argonne Nat. Labs. 1968, Heidelberg Univ. 1975, Northwestern Univ. 1978, Univ. of Sydney 1984, Univ. of Kuwait 1989, Univs. of Adelaide and Melbourne 1992, Newfoundland 1995, W Indies 1997, Lausanne 1998, S. Africa 1999, La Laguna, Spain 2000, City Univ., Hong Kong 2001; Fellow J.S.P.S. (Japan) 1986; Tilden Medal and Prize, Royal Soc. of Chem. 1984. *Publications:* Kinetics of Inorganic Reactions 1964; over 470 papers and reviews in chemistry journals. *Leisure interests:* travel, classical music, sport. *Address:* Department of Chemistry, University of Newcastle upon Tyne, NE1 7RU (Office); 73 Beech Court, Darras Hall, Newcastle upon Tyne, NE20 9NE, England (Home). *Telephone:* (191) 2226700 (Office); (1661) 825425 (Home).

SYKES, Eric, OBE; British actor, writer and director; b. 4 May 1923, Oldham; s. of Vernon Sykes and Harriet Sykes; m. Edith Eleanor Milbradt; one s. three d.; ed Ward Street School, Oldham; left school at 14; long-running TV comedy show Sykes (with Hattie Jacques); many other TV appearances; Freeman City of London 1988, Hon. Fellow Univ. of Lancashire 1999; Lifetime Achievement Award, Writers' Guild 1992. *Films include:* actor, Orders are Orders, Watch Your Stern, Very Important Person, Heavens Above, Shalako, Those Magnificent Men in Their Flying Machines, Monte Carlo or Bust!, The Boys in Blue, Absolute Beginners, The Others 2000. *Plays include:* Big Bad Mouse 1977–78, A Hatful of Sykes 1977–78, Run For Your Wife 1992, The 19th Hole 1992, Two of a Kind 1995, Fools Rush In 1996, The School For Wives 1997, Kafka's Dick 1998–99, Caught in the Wet 2001–02. *Radio includes:* (as writer) Educating Archie, The Frankie Howerd Show. *Television includes:* Sykes and A..., The 19th Hole, Curry and Chips, Gormenghast. *Publications:* The Great Crime of Grapplewick 1996, UFOs Are Coming Wednesday 1995, Smelling of Roses 1997, Sykes of Sebastopol Terrace 2000. *Leisure interest:* golf. *Address:* 9 Orme Court, London, W2 4RL, England. *Telephone:* (20) 7727-1544. *Fax:* (20) 7792-2110.

SYKES, Lynn R., PhD; American professor of geological sciences; b. 16 April 1937, Pittsburgh, Pa; s. of Lloyd A. Sykes and Margaret Woodburn Sykes; m. 1st Meredith Henschkel (divorced); m. 2nd Katherine Flanz 1986 (died 1996); m. 3rd Kathleen Mahoney 1998; ed Massachusetts Inst. of Tech. and Columbia Univ.; Research Asst, Lamont-Doherty Geological Observatory, Columbia Univ. 1961–64, Research Assoc. 1964–66, Adjunct Asst Prof. of Geology 1966–68, Head of Seismology Group 1973–83, Higgins Prof. of Earth and Environmental Sciences 1978–; main areas of interest are seismology, tectonics and arms control, earthquake prediction and the detection and identification of underground atomic tests; Chair. Nat. Earthquake Prediction Evaluation Council; Fellow American Geophysical Union, Geological Soc. of America, Royal Astronomical Soc., AAAS; mem. NAS, American Acad. of Arts and Sciences, Geological Soc. of London, Arms Control Asscn; Walter H. Bucher Medal of American Geophysical Union for original contribs. to basic knowledge of earth's crust 1975, Public Service Award, Fed. of American Scientists 1986, John Wesley Powell Award, US Geological Survey 1990, Vetleson Award for devt and testing of plate tectonics 2000. *Publications:* numerous articles in scientific journals. *Leisure interests:* hiking, canoeing, opera, travel. *Address:* Lamont-Doherty Earth Observatory, Columbia University, Palisades, New York, NY 10964; 100 Washington Spring Road, Palisades, NY 10964, USA. *Telephone:* (845) 365-8880. *Fax:* (845) 365-8150. *E-mail:* sykes@ldeo.columbia.edu (Office). *Website:* www.columbia.edu (Office).

SYKES, Peter, BSc, MSc, PhD, FRSC, CChem; British chemistry teacher; b. 19 Feb. 1923, Manchester; s. of Charles Hyde Sykes and Alice Booth; m. Joyce Tyler 1946; two s. one d.; ed Rydal School, Colwyn Bay, Univ. Manchester, Clare Coll., Cambridge; Research Fellow, St John's Coll., Cambridge 1947–50, Univ. Demonstrator in Organic Chem. 1947–55, Lecturer 1955–82, Fellow, Christ's Coll. 1956–, Vice-Master 1984–88; Visiting Research Prof., Coll. of William and Mary, Williamsburg, Va 1970–71, 1977–78; Visiting Prof., Univ. of Cape Town 1974, 1980, Univs of São Paulo and Campinas, Brazil 1976, Univ. of Melbourne 1983–84; Mellor Medal, Univ. of NSW 1984. *Publications:* The Search for Organic Reaction Pathways 1972, A Guidebook to Mechanism in Organic Chemistry 1986, A Primer to Mechanism in Organic Chemistry 1995 (all trans. into several languages); numerous papers on organic reaction mechanisms. *Leisure interests:* chamber music, church architecture, talking, wine. *Address:* N2, Christ's College, Cambridge, CB2 3BU, England. *Telephone:* (1223) 334917.

SYKES, Sir Richard (Brook), Kt., PhD, FRS, FMedSci; British research microbiologist, business executive and university rector; b. 7 Aug. 1942; s. of the late Eric Sykes and of Muriel Mary Sykes; m. Janet Mary Norman 1969; one s. one d.; ed Queen Elizabeth Coll., London, Bristol Univ., London Univ.; Head Antibiotic Research Unit, Glaxo Research Ltd 1972–77; Asst Dir, Dept of Microbiology, Squibb Inst. for Medical Research, Princeton 1977, Dir of Microbiology 1979, Vice-Pres., Infectious and Metabolic Diseases 1983–86; Deputy Chief Exec., Glaxo Group Research Ltd 1986; Group Research and Devt Dir, Glaxo PLC and Chair. and Chief Exec. Glaxo Group Research Ltd 1987; Deputy Chair. and Chief Exec. Glaxo PLC 1993; Chair. Glaxo Wellcome PLC 1997–2001, CEO 1997; Chair. (non-exec.) GlaxoSmithKline 2001–02; Rector, Imperial Coll. of Science, Tech. and Medicine 2001–; Visiting Prof., King's Coll., London and Bristol Univ.; Pres., British Asscn for the Advancement of Science 1998–99; Dir (non-exec.) Rio Tinto PLC 1997–; mem. Council for Science and Tech. 1993–2002; mem., Bd of Trustees, Nat. History Museum; Fellow Royal Soc., Acad. of Medical Sciences, Imperial Coll. School of Medicine; Fleming Fellow, Lincoln Coll., Oxford 1992; Hon. mem. Nat. Acad. of Medicine, Brazil; Hon. Fellow Royal Coll. of Physicians, Univ. of Wales, Cardiff, Royal Pharmaceutical Soc.; Hon. FRSC; Hon. D.Pharm. (Madrid) 1993; Hon. DSc (Brunel, Hull, Herts.) 1994, (Bristol, Newcastle) 1995, (Huddersfield, Westminster) 1996, (Leeds) 1997, (Edin., Strathclyde) 1998, (Cranfield, Leicester, Sheffield, Warwick) 1999; Hon. MD (Birmingham) 1995; Hon. LLD (Nottingham) 1997; Dr hc (Sheffield Hallam, Surrey); Hamao Umezawa Memorial Award (Int. Soc. of Chemotherapy) 1999, Singapore Nat. Day Public Service Star Award 1999. *Leisure interests:* tennis, swimming, opera, skiing. *Address:* Imperial College London, Exhibition Road, London, SW7 2AZ, England (Office). *Telephone:* (20) 7594-5002 (Office). *Fax:* (20) 7594-5004 (Office). *E-mail:* r.sykes@imperial.ac.uk (Office).

SYLLA, Jacques Hugues, LLB; Malagasy politician and lawyer; b. 1946, Holy Marie, Toamasina Prov.; m. Yvette Rakoto; four c.; Lawyer; Co-Founder Toamasina Br. of Nat. Cttee for Observation of the Elections (CNOE), First Foreign Minister of fmr Pres. Albert Zafy 1992–93; Minister of Foreign Affairs 1993–96; Prime Minister of Madagascar Feb. 2002–. *Address:* Office of the Prime Minister, BP 248, Lapan'ny Mahazoarivo, 101 Antananarivo, Madagascar (Office). *Telephone:* (20) 2225258 (Office). *Fax:* (20) 2235258 (Office). *Website:* www.madagascar.gov.mg.

SYMON, Lindsay, CBE, TD, MB, ChB, FRCS, FRCSE; British professor of neurological surgery; b. 4 Nov. 1929, Aberdeen; s. of William L. Symon and Isabel Symon; m. Pauline Barbara Rowland 1954; one s. two d.; ed Aberdeen Grammar School and Aberdeen Univ.; house physician/surgeon Aberdeen Royal Infirmary 1952–53; Clinical Officer/Jr. Specialist in Surgery, British troops in Austria 1953–55; Surgical Registrar Aberdeen Royal Infirmary 1956–58; Clinical Research Fellow MRC 1958–61; Major in charge No. 2 Mobile Neurosurgical Team, TA, RAMC 1960–68; Rockefeller Travelling Fellow Wayne Univ., USA 1961–62; Sr Registrar Neurosurgery Nat. Hosps 1962–65, Consultant Neurosurgeon 1965–78; mem. External Staff MRC

1965–78; Prof. of Neurological Surgery, Sr Surgeon, Nat. Hosps 1978–95; Hon. Consultant Neurosurgeon St Thomas' Hosp., London 1973–95, Hammersmith Hosp., London 1978–95, Royal Nat. Throat, Nose and Ear Hosp. 1979–95, The Italian Hosp. 1981–89; Adjunct Prof. Dept of Surgery, Southwestern Medical School, Dallas 1982–95; Civilian Adviser in Neurosurgery, RN 1979–95; Pres. World Fed. of Neurosurgical Socs. 1979–93, Hon. Pres. 1993–; Pres. Harveian Soc., London 1997–98, Trustee 1999–; Hon. FACS 1994; Jamieson Medal, Australasian Neurosurgical Soc. 1982, John Hunter Medal, Royal Coll. of Surgeons 1985, Joachim Zulch Prize, Max Planck Inst. 1993, Otfrid Förster Medal, German Soc. Neurosurgery 1998. *Publications:* texts on cerebrovascular surgery, physiology of the cerebral circulation, surgery of acoustic neuroma, general neurosurgical topics. *Leisure interests:* golf, prehistory. *Address:* Maple Lodge, Rivar Road, Shalbourne, nr Marlborough, Wilts., SN8 3QE, England. *Telephone:* (1672) 870501. *Fax:* (1672) 870501.

SYMONS OF VERNHAM DEAN, Baroness (Life Peer), cr. 1996, of Vernham Dean in the County of Hampshire; **Elizabeth Conway Symons,** MA, FRSA; British politician; b. 14 April 1951; d. of Ernest Vize Symons and Elizabeth Megan Symons (née Jenkins); partner Philip Alan Bassett; one s.; ed Putney High School for Girls, Girton Coll., Cambridge; Admin. Trainee Dept of the Environment 1974–77; Asst Sec. Inland Revenue Staff Fed. 1977–88, Deputy Gen. Sec. 1988–89; Gen. Sec. Asscn of First Div. Civil Servants 1989–96; Parl. Under-Sec. of State, FCO 1997–99; Minister of State, Ministry of Defence 1999–2001; Minister of State (Minister for Trade), Foreign and Commonwealth Office and Dept of Trade and Industry 2001–; Deputy Leader of House of Lords 2001–; mem. Gen. Council, TUC 1989–96, Council, RIPA 1989–97, Exec. Council, Campaign for Freedom of Information 1989–97, Hansard Soc. Council 1992–97, Advisory Council, Civil Service Coll. 1992–97, Council, Industrial Soc. 1994–97, Council, Open Univ. 1994–97; Employment Appeal Tribunal 1995, Equal Opportunities Comm. 1995–97; Exec. Mem. Involvement and Participation Asscn 1992; Gov. Polytechnic of N London 1989–94, London Business School 1993–97; Trustee Inst. for Public Policy Research 1993; Hon. Assoc. Nat. Council of Women 1989. *Leisure interests:* gardening, reading. *Address:* House of Lords, London, SW1A 0PW, England (Office).

SYMS, Sylvia; British actress and director; b. 6 Jan. 1934, London; m. Alan Edney 1957 (divorced 1989); one s. one d.; ed Royal Acad. of Dramatic Art; Founder-mem. and Artistic Dir Arbela Production Co.; numerous lectures, including Dodo White McLarty Memorial Lecture 1986; mem. The Actors' Centre 1986–91, Arts Council Drama Panel 1991–96, Council for R.A.D.A. 1992–; Variety Club Best Actress in Films Award 1958, Ondas Award for Most Popular Foreign Actress (Spain) 1966, Manchester Evening News Best Actress Award. *Films include:* Ice Cold in Alex 1953, The Birthday Present 1956, The World of Suzie Wong 1961, Run Wild Run Free 1969, The Tamarind Seed 1974, Chorus of Disapproval 1988, Shirley Valentine 1989, Shining Through 1991, Dirty Weekend 1992, Staggered 1994, Food for Love 1996, Mavis and the Mermaid 1999. *Television includes:* Love Story 1964, The Saint 1967, My Good Woman 1972–73, Nancy Astor 1982, Ruth Rendell Mysteries 1989, Dr. Who 1989–90, May to December 1989–90, The Last Days of Margaret Thatcher 1991, Natural Lies, Mulberry, Peak Practice, Ruth Randell Mysteries 1993, 1997–98, Ghost Hour 1995, Heartbeat 1998, At Home with the Braithwaites 2000, 2001. *Theatre includes:* Dance of Death, Much Ado About Nothing, An Ideal Husband, Ghosts, Entertaining Mr. Sloane 1985 (Best Actress Award, Manchester Evening News), Who's Afraid of Virgina Woolf? 1989, The Floating Lightbulb 1990, Antony and Cleopatra 1991, For Services Rendered 1993, Funny Money 1996, Ugly Rumours 1998. *Radio includes:* Little Dorrit, Danger in the Village, Post Mortems, Joe Orton, Love Story, The Change 2001. *Plays and television directed:* Better in My Dreams 1988, The Price 1991, Natural Lies 1991–92. *Leisure interests:* gardening, dogs. *Address:* c/o Barry Brown and Partners, 47 West Square, London, SE11 4SP, England. *Telephone:* (20) 7582-6622.

SYQUIA, Enrique, LLD; Philippine lawyer and professor of law; b. 22 May 1930, Manila; s. of the late Vicente A. Syquia and Consolacion P. Syquia; m. Leticia Corpus Syquia 1964; five s.; ed Univ. of Santo Tomas, Univ. of Madrid and Hague Acad. of Int. Law; Head Syquia Law Offices, Manila 1954–; Prof. of Law 1976–; Publr The Lawyers Review 1987–, The Diplomats Review 1989–91; Dir Philippine Bar Asscn 1971–92, Pres. 1981–84; mem. Exec. Council, Int. Bar Asscn 1974–92, Vice-Pres. 1982–84; Pres. Int. Law Asscn 1978–80, Vice-Chair. 1989–; Pres. Philippines Council for Foreign Relations 1987–94; Vice-Pres. Union Int. des Avocats 1989–; Pres. Int. Inst. of Humanitarian Law 1991–93; Special Adviser Philippine Del. to UN Gen. Ass. 1989–92; mem. and/or officer of numerous nat. and int. law orgs. including ABA, American Judicature Soc., American Soc. of Int. Law; mem. Inst. Hispano-Luso-Americano de Derecho Internacional 1980–, Dir 1991–, Pres. 1998–2000; Hon. Consul-Gen. of Kingdom of Jordan in the Philippines 1987–96; del. to numerous law confs. at home and abroad since 1953; Patron American Soc. of Int. Law 1989–; various hon. trusteeships etc.; Sovereign Mil. Order of Malta, Order de Isabel la Católica (Spain) 1999; Kt Pontifical Equestrian Order of Gregory the Great 1996, Kt Illustrious Spanish Order of Corpus Christi 1997 and numerous other awards and decorations. *Publications:* The Tokyo Trial 1955, A Manual on International Law 1957, Twenty Papers on World Affairs 1989; about 100 articles on law, especially int. law. *Leisure interests:* reading, heraldry, stamp-collecting. *Address:* 6th Floor, Cattleya Condominium, 235 Salcedo Street, Legaspi Village, Makati, Manila

(Office); 127 Cambridge Circle, North Forbes, Makati, Manila, Philippines (Home). *Telephone:* (2) 817-1095/1098 (Office); (2) 810-7975 (Home); (2) 817-1089; (2) 810-7975. *Fax:* (2) 817-1089 (Office); (2) 817-1724 (Home). *E-mail:* syquia@intlaw.com.ph (Office).

SYRADEGHYAN, Vano Sumbatovich; Armenian politician; b. 13 Nov. 1946, Koti, Noyemberyan Region; m.; five c.; ed Yerevan State Univ.; army service 1966–69; journalist in a number of pubs of the Repub. –1988; mem. Cttee Karabakh 1988; Chair. of Bd Armenian Nat. Movt; Deputy to Armenian Supreme Soviet 1990–92; Minister of Internal Affairs 1992–96; Mayor of Yerevan 1996–98; mem. of Parl. 1999–; investigated by police for criminal activity and corruption. *Publications include:* articles, essays in numerous publs of Armenia. *Address:* National Assembly, Marshal Bagramingan Prosp. 26, 375019, Yerevan, Armenia.

SYRON, Richard Francis, PhD; American bank executive and economist; b. 25 Oct. 1943, Boston; s. of Dominick Syron and Elizabeth (McGuire) Syron; m. Margaret Mary Garatoni 1972; one s. one d.; ed Boston Coll., Tufts Univ.; Deputy Dir Commonwealth of Mass. 1973–74; Vice-Pres., Economist Fed. Reserve Bank of Boston 1974–82, Sr Vice-Pres., Econ. Adviser 1982–85, Pres., CEO 1989–94; Chair. American Stock Exchange 1994–99; Chair. and CEO Thermo Electron, Mass. 1999–; Exec. Asst to Sec. U.S. Treasury, Washington 1979–80, Deputy Asst to Sec. for Econ. Policy 1980–81; Asst to Chair. Volcker Fed. Reserve, Washington 1981–82; Pres. Fed. Home Loan Bank of Boston 1986–88; mem. Bd of Dirs. John Hancock, Thermo Electron, The Dreyfus Corpn, U.S. Stock Exchange; Trustee Boston Coll. *Address:* Thermo Electron, 81 Wyman Street, Waltham, MA 02454, USA (Office).

SYRYJCZYK, Tadeusz Andrzej, DTech; Polish politician; b. 9 Feb. 1948, Kraków; m.; ed Acad. of Mining and Metallurgy, Kraków; lecturer Acad. of Mining and Metallurgy, Kraków 1971–89; with ABAKS, Kraków 1987–89; Minister of Industry 1989–90; Chief Prime Minister's team of advisers and Under-Sec. of State in Council of Ministers 1992–93; Minister of Transport and Maritime Economy 1998–2000; Deputy to Sejm (Parl.) 1991–2001; mem. Democratic Union Parl. Caucus 1991–94, Freedom Union Parl. Caucus 1994–2001, Chair. 1997–98; mem. Parl. Comm. for Privatization, Econ. System and Industry 1991–92, Parl. Comm. for Econ. Policy, Budget and Finances 1993–97, Parl. Comm. for Public Finances 1997–98, Parl. Comm. for Nat. Defence 1998; mem. Democratic Union 1991–94; mem. Solidarity Trade Union 1980–89; mem. Presidium Małopolska Region 1981; interned during state of martial law 1981–82; mem. regional authorities, Kraków 1982–84; mem. Freedom Union 1994–, Nat. Council and Regional Council, Kraków 1983–2001; Vice-Pres. Freedom Union 1995–2001; Co-Founder Industrial Soc. of Kraków 1987; mem. Polish Tourist Country-Lovers' Asscn, Polish Informatics Soc. *Publications:* papers on automatics and informatics, articles in nat. magazines. *Leisure interest:* tourism, mountaineering. *Address:* ul. Kazimierza Wielkiego 4 m. 9, 30-074 Kraków, Poland (Home). *Telephone:* (12) 6336427 (Home); (601) 471870. *Fax:* (601) 405999 (Home). *E-mail:* tadeusz@syryjczyk.krakow.pl (Home). *Website:* www.syryjczyk.krakow.pl (Home).

SYSUYEV, Oleg Nikolayevich; Russian politician; b. 23 March 1953, Kuybyshev (now Samara); m.; one s. one d.; ed Kuybyshev Moscow Aviation Inst.; master, head. of tech. div., engineer, Sec. CP Cttee Kuibyshev aviation team 1976–87; Sec. Krasnoglinsk Dist CP Cttee of Kuybyshev 1987–91; del. to 18th CP Congress; Head Samara Admin. 1991–94; Mayor of Samara 1994–97; active participant movt Russia Our Home; Co-Chair. Union of Mayors of Russian towns 1995–97; Deputy Head Russian Govt, Minister of Labour and Social Devt 1997–98; Co-ordinator Russian Comm. on Regulation of Trade-Social Relations 1997–98; First Deputy Head Admin. of Pres. Yeltsin 1998–99; first Deputy Chair. of Bd Alpha-Bank 1999–. *Leisure interests:* playing guitar, piano, violin. *Address:* Alpha-Bank, Mashi Poryvayevoy str. 9, 107078 Moscow, Russia. *Telephone:* (095) 974-25-15.

SZABAD, György, PhD; Hungarian politician and historian; b. 4 Aug. 1924, Arad, Romania; s. of Erzsébet Blantz; m. Andrea Suján; one d.; ed Loránd Eötvös Univ., Budapest; served in forced labour camp 1944; on staff of Nat. Archives 1949, univ. Asst lecturer 1954, lecturer 1956, Prof. 1970; Corresp. mem. Hungarian Acad. of Sciences 1982, mem. 1998–; mem. Revolutionary Cttee 1956; founding mem. and nat. Bd mem. Hungarian Democratic Forum 1987; founding mem. Hungarian Democratic People's Party; Speaker of Hungarian Parl. 1990–94, mem. Parl. 1994–98. *Publications include:* Kossuth on the Political System of the United States of America 1975, Hungarian Political Trends between the Revolution and the Compromise 1849–1867 1977, Conceptualization of a Danubian Federation 1998. *Address:* Kelenhegyi ut. 40/B.1118, Budapest, Hungary. *Telephone:* 385-3761.

SZABO, Denis, OC, DèsSc, FRSC; Canadian/Belgian professor of criminology; b. 4 June 1929, Budapest, Hungary; s. of Jenö Denes and Catherine Zsiga; m. Sylvie Grotard 1956; two d.; ed Univs of Budapest, Louvain and Paris; Asst Univ. of Louvain 1952–56; lecturer in Sociology, Catholic Univ. of Paris and Lyon 1956–58; Asst Prof. Univ. of Montreal 1958–59, Assoc. Prof. 1959–66, Prof. of Criminology 1966–95, Prof. Emer. 1995–; Founder and Dir School of Criminology, Univ. of Montreal 1960–70; Founder and Dir Int. Center for Comparative Criminology, Univ. of Montreal 1969–84, now Chair. of Bd; consultant to Canadian, US, French, Hungarian and UN comms and bodies on crime prevention; mem. Hungarian Acad. of Sciences 1993–; Hon. Pres. Int. Soc. of Criminology; Commdr Ordre Nat. du Mérite, Côte d'Ivoire 1986, Commdr Ordre du Mérite Répub., Hungary 1996, Chevalier des Arts et des Lettres, France 1996, Officier Ordre nat. du Québec 1998 and other decorations; Dr hc (Siena, Budapest, Aix-Marseille, Panteios-Athens); Sutherland Award, American Soc. of Criminology 1968, Golden Medal Beccaria, German Soc. of Criminology 1970 and other awards. *Publications:* Crimes et villes 1960, Criminologie et politique criminelle 1978, The Canadian Criminal Justice System (with A. Parizeau), Science et crimes 1986, Criminologie empirique au Québec (ed. with Marc Le Blanc), De l'anthropologie à la criminologie comparée 1993, Traité de criminologie empirique (ed. with Marc Le Blanc) 1994. *Leisure interest:* gardening, swimming. *Address:* International Centre for Comparative Criminology, University of Montreal, C.P. 6128, Montreal, H3C 3J7 (Office); 66, Square Copp, Georgeville, J0B 1T0, Canada (Home). *Telephone:* (514) 343-7065 (Office); (819) 843-4343 (Home). *Fax:* (514) 343-2269 (Office); (514) 343-2269. *E-mail:* dszabo@videotron.ca (Office). *Website:* www.cicc.umontreal.ca (Office).

SZABO, Gabriela; Romanian athlete; b. 14 Nov. 1975, Bistrita; m. Gyonyossy Zsolt 1999; Indoor European record-holder and Outdoor World record-holder 5000m; silver medal 1500m, Olympic Games, Atlanta 1996; world's fastest at 1500m, one mile, 2000m, 3000m and 5000m 1998; gold medal (5000m Olympic Games, Sydney 2000, bronze medal 1500m, Sydney 2000; set new world records indoor 5000m in Feb. 1999 (still stands as at end 2002), 3000m in Birmingham, England, Feb. 2001; gold medallist 1500m World Championships 2001; silver medallist European Championships 5000m 1998, 1500m 2002; first female track athlete to make a million dollars in prize money in one season; European Athlete of the Year 1999, IAAF Athlete of the Year 1999.

SZABÓ, István; Hungarian film director and writer; b. 18 Feb. 1938, Budapest; s. of Dr. István Szabó and Mária Vita; m. Vera Gyürey; ed Budapest Acad. of Theatre and Film Arts; started as mem. Balázs B. Studio, Budapest; leading mem. Hungarian Film Studios; Tutor, Coll. of Theatre and Film Arts, Budapest; mem. Acad. of Motion Picture Arts and Sciences, Akademie der Künste, Berlin; Béla Balázs Prize 1967, Kossuth Prize 1975. *Productions: short films:* Concert 1961, Variations upon a Theme 1961, Te (You) 1963 (Grand Prix de Tours), Budapest, amiért szeretem (Budapest, Why I Love It) 1971; *series:* Álom a házról (Dream about the House) 1971 (Main Prize of Oberhausen); *documentaries:* Kegyelet (Piety) 1967, Várostérkép (City Map) 1977 (Grand Prix of Oberhausen), Steadying the Boat 1996; *TV plays:* Osbemutató (Première) 1974, Katzenspiel (Cat Play) 1982, Bali 1983; *TV films:* Der grüne Vogel (The Green Bird) 1979, Offenbach 1995; *full-length films:* Álmodozások kora (The Age of Day-Dreaming) 1964, Apa (Father) 1966, Szerelmesfilm (A Film of Love) 1970, Tüzoltó utca 25 (No. 25 Fireman's Street) 1973 (Grand Prix of Locarno), Budapesti mesék (Budapest Tales) 1976, Bizalom (Confidence) 1979 (Silver Bear of Berlin, 1981), Mephisto 1981 (Acad. Award 1982, David di Donatello Prize (Italy), Italian Critics' Prize, Critics' Prize, UK), Colonel Redl 1985 (BAFTA Award 1986, Best W German Film—Golden Band), Hanussen 1988, Meeting Venus 1990, Sweet Emma, Dear Böbe 1991 (Silver Bear of Berlin, European Acad. Award for Best Screenplay), Steadying the Boat (for the BBC) 1996, Sunshine 1999 (European Acad. Award for Best Screenplay, Canadian Acad. Award for Best Film), Taking Sides 2001; *operas:* Tannhäuser, Paris 1987, Boris Godunov, Leipzig 1993, Il Trovatore, Vienna 1993, The Three Sisters, Budapest 2000. *Address:* I. S. L.-Film, 1149 Budapest, Róna utca 174; 1132 Budapest, Váci-6, Hungary. *Telephone:* (1) 251-9369; (1) 340-5559. *Fax:* (1) 340-5559.

SZABÓ, Iván, PhD; Hungarian politician, engineer and economist; b. 8 Jan. 1934, Budapest; s. of Ferenc Szabó and Mária Sallai; m. Ildikó Zemenszky; two d.; ed Budapest Tech. Univ. and Budapest Econ. Univ.; construction engineer with Road and Railway Bldg Co. 1957–59; tech. Dir Bldg Mechanization Trust 1959–69; Chief Engineer Civil Eng Co. 1969–78; export man. Water Construction Trust 1978–85; Pres. Eng and Constructing Co-operative 1985–90; arrested for activity in revolutionary students movt 1956; joined Hungarian Democratic Forum 1988; mem. of Parl. 1990–98; Chair. Econ. Comm. of Parl. 1990–91; Minister of Trade and Industry 1991–93, of Finance 1993–94, Man. Pres. and Leader of Parl. Group of Hungarian Democratic Forum 1994–96; Pres. and Leader of Parl. Group of Hungarian Democratic People's Party 1996–98, Hon. Pres. 1998–; Pres. Asscn for Consumer Protection; Bd mem. EU-2002 Fondation; mem. Pax Romana. *Publications include:* Acélhajbeton (1975), Töprengések pentatonben 1999, Üvegfalak (biog.) 2001. *Leisure interest:* gardening. *Address:* Hungarian Democratic People's Party, 1011 Budapest, Iskola u. 16 (Office); 1092 Budapest, Ra'day u. 4, Hungary (Home). *Telephone:* (1) 218-7475. *Fax:* (1) 218-7475.

SZABÓ, Magda; Hungarian author; b. 5 Oct. 1917, Debrecen; d. of Alex Szabó and Madeleine Jablonczay; m. Tibor Szobotka 1948; graduated as a teacher 1940; worked in secondary schools 1940–44, 1950–59; started literary career as poet and has since written novels, plays, radio dramas, essays and film scripts; works have been translated into 35 languages including English, French, German, Italian, Russian, Polish, Swedish; mem. Acad. of Sciences of Europe, Hungarian Széchenyi Acad. of Art and Literature; Fellow Univ. of Iowa; Hon. citizen Debrecen; Hon. DPhil; Baumgarten Prize 1949; József Attila Prize 1959 and 1972, Kossuth Prize 1978, Getz Corpn Prize (USA) 1992, Szén Ernő Prize for Dramatic Art. *Publications:* poems: Neszek (Noises); autobiog.: Ókut (Old Well); novels for children: Szigetkék (Island-Blue), Tündér Lala (Lala the Fairy), Abigél (Abigail); novels: Az őz (The Fawn), Fresko (Fresco), Disznótor (Night of Pig-Killing), Pilatus (Pilate), A Danaida (The Danaid), Mózes 1.22) (Genesis 1.22), Katalin utca (Kathleen Street), A szemlélők (The Onlookers), Régimódi történet (Old-Fashioned Story), Az ajtó (The Door), The Moment 1990; plays: Kiálts város (Cry Out, Town!), Az a szép fényes nap (That Bright Beautiful Day), A meráni fiu (The Boy of Meran), A csata (The Battle) 1982, Béla Király (King Béla), A Macskák Szerdája (The Wednesday of the Cats) 1985, Outside the Circle 1980, The Lethargy of the Semigods (essays) 1986, The Logic of the Butterfly (essays) 1997, Cakes for Cerberus (short stories), The Mondogue of Cseke (essays). *Leisure interest:* pets. *Address:* 1026 Budapest II, Julia-utca 3, Hungary. *Telephone:* (3) 565-013. *Fax:* (3) 565-013.

SZABÓ, Miklós, PhD, DSc; Hungarian archaeologist; b. 3 July 1940, Szombathely; s. of Dezső Szabó and Irén Süle; m. Ágnes Molnár; three s.; ed Eötvös Loránd Univ. of Arts and Sciences (ELTE); with Dept of Archaeology Hungarian Nat. Museum 1963–66; with Dept of Antiquities Museum of Fine Arts 1966–85, Deputy Dir Gen. 1985–87; Asst Prof. Dept of Classical Archaeology of ELTE 1983–89, Prof. and Head of Dept 1989, Gen. Vice-Rector 1991–93, Rector 1993–99; research into Ancient Greek and Celtic archaeology, involved in excavations in Greece by the French Inst. of Archaeology in Athens 1970–78; in France 1978, led the Hungarian excavation expedition in Bibracte, France 1988–; Visiting Prof. Sorbonne 1980–81, Ecole normale supérieure, Paris 1985, Coll. de France 1989, 2000–01; Pres. Archaeological Cttee Hungarian Acad. of Sciences 1994; Corresp. mem. Hungarian Acad. of Sciences 1995 (mem. 2001), German Archaeological Inst. 1977, Royal Acad. of Barcelona 1997, French Acad. 2002; Ed. Dissertationes Pannonicae; mem. Editorial Bd of Acta Archaeologica and Études Celtiques; Hon. mem. Greek Archaeological Soc. 1998; Chevalier de l'Ordre Nat. du Mérite 1995; Commdr Légion d'honneur 2001, Ordre des Arts et des Lettres 2001; Dr hc (Univs of Burgundy, Dijon) 1997, (Bologna) 1999; Kuzsinszky Medal 1984, College de France Medal 1989, Rómer Flóris Commemorative Medal 1990, City of Dijon Commemorative Medal 1991 . *Publications:* The Celtic Heritage in Hungary 1971, Hellász fénykora (The Golden Age of Greece) 1972, Világtörténelem képekben I, (World History in Pictures I, co-author) 1972, A keleti kelta művészet (Eastern Celtic Art, co-author) 1974, Les Celtes (co-author) 1978, Les Celtes en Pannonie. Contribution à l'histoire de la civilisation celtique dans la cuvette des Karpates 1988, I Celti (co-author) 1991, Les Celtes de l'Est: Le second âge du fer dans la cuvette des Karpates 1992, Decorated Weapons of the La Tène Iron Age in the Carpathian Basin (co-author) 1992, Archaic Terracottas of Boeotia 1994, Storia d'Europa II (co-author) 1994, A la frontière entre l'Est et l'Ouest (co-author) 1998, Prähistorische Goldschätze im Ungarischen Nationalmuseum (co-author) 1999, Trésors préhistoriques de Hongrie (co-author) 2001, Celtes de Hongrie (co-author) 2001, Celtas y Vettones (co-author) 2001. *Address:* ELTE, 1088 Budapest, Múzeum krt. 4/B, Hungary. *Telephone:* (1) 200-1743 (Home); (1) 266-0863. *Fax:* (1) 266-0861 (Office). *E-mail:* archinst@ludens.elte.hu (Office).

SZAJNA, Józef; Polish theatre director, author, scenographer and painter; b. 13 March 1922, Rzeszów; s. of Julian Szajna and Karolina Pieniążek; m. Bożena Sierosławska 1953; one s.; ed Acad. of Fine Arts, Kraków; mem. Anti-Nazi Resistance, in Auschwitz and Buchenwald 1939–45; Lecturer, Acad. of Arts, Kraków 1954–65; Co-founder and scenographer Teatr Ludowy, Nowa Huta 1955–63, Man. Dir 1963–66; Dir and Scenographer, Teatr Stary, Kraków 1966–70; Man. Dir Teatr Klasyczny, now Art Gallery and experimental theatre called Teatr Studio, Warsaw 1971–82; Prof. Acad. of Arts, Warsaw 1972– and Dir School for Stage Designers 1972–78; mem. jury World Council of Culture, Mexico; Dir Acropolis 1962, Inspector 1963, Puste Pole 1965, Zamek 1965; Dir and Scenario Faust 1971, Replika I, Göteborg 1971, Replika II, Edinburgh Festival 1972, Replika III, Nancy Festival 1973, Replika IV, Poland 1973, Replika V, France, Théâtre des Nations 1980, Replika VI, Istanbul Festival 1984, Replika VII, Tel Aviv 1986, Witkacy 1972, Gulgutiera 1973, Dante, Int. Theatre Festival, Florence 1974, Witkacy II 1975, Cervantes 1976, (Special Prize, XIII Kalisz Theatre Encounters 1977), Majakowski 1978, Śmierć na gruszy 1978, Dante żywy (Dante Alive), Dubrovnik 1981, Dante III, Essen 1985, Dante 1992, Ślady, Ślady II, Ankara 1993, Workshop, Ziemia, Cairo 1993, Vida y muerte del Poeta Cervantes, Alcalá de Henares 1993, Szczątki, Int. Theatre Festival, Portugal 1995, Déballage, Wanda Siemaszkowa Theatre, Rzeszów 1997; one-man exhbn Reminiscence, XXXV Venice Biennale 1970, Gegenwart einer Vergangenheit (Present of the Past), Frankfurt am Main 1978, Silhouettes, São Paulo 1979, Pictures of Man, West Berlin 1980, Essen 1984, Tel-Aviv, Jerusalem 1986, Cracow 1986, Warsaw 1987, Moscow 1987, Bienniale São Paulo 1989, Venice Biennale 1990, Paris 1990, Gdańsk 1991, Warsaw 1992, Poznań 1992, Centrum Scenografii, Katowice 1993, Museum, Ankara 1993, Círculo de Bellas Artes, Madrid 1993, Gallery of Contemporary Art Opole 1996, Museum of Kalisian District 1996, Deutsches Nationaltheater Weimar 1996, Gedenkstätte Buchanwald 1996, Museum of Contemporary Sculpture Orońsko 1997, Int. Exhbn, Graz 1998, Nat. Museums, Osaka 1998; contrib. to many int. exhbns. and theatre festivals, including Québec Festival 1986 (award winner); works of art in galleries and museums in Poland and abroad; mem. Polish Asscn of Art, Italian Acad. of Arts and Skills; Pres. Soc. Européenne de Culture, Poland 2001; Hon. mem. Int. Asscn of Art; Order of Banner of Labour (1st Class) 1982; Kt's and Commdr's Cross with Star of Order of Polonia Restituta; Great Cross of Polonia Restituta 1997; Hon. Citizen of Opole 1996, Rzeszów 1997, Tczew 2002; Dr hc (Oldenburg); numerous awards including Int. Quadrinnale Praha Award 1973, Gold Centaur Award 1982, Meritorious Award for Nat. Culture 1986, Gold Medal, 40th Anniversary of War Veterans, USSR 1987, Golden Lion Award, Int. Theatre Festival, Lvov 2000, Int. Hon. Citation from Experimental Theatre, Cairo 1992, Alfred Jurzykowski Foundation Award (USA) 1995, Prize of Minister of Culture (First, Second and Third Class) . *Films directed:* Art in Captivity: The World of Józef Szajna (video), Teatr według szajny (video). *Publications:* Teatr Organiczny (Organic Theatre), On the New Function of Scenography, The Open Theatre, The Matter of Spectacle, Visual Narrative, Bottum: Commemoration of Auschwitz. *Leisure interests:* sport, tourism. *Address:* ul. Smulikowskiego 14 m. 8, 00-389 Warsaw, Poland (Home). *Telephone:* (22) 8264752 (Home).

SZASZ, Thomas Stephen, MD; American psychiatrist, psychoanalyst, author and lecturer; b. 15 April 1920, Budapest, Hungary; s. of Julius Szasz and Lily Wellisch; m. Rosine Loshkajian 1951 (divorced 1971); two d.; ed Cincinnati Univ. and Medical Coll.; staff mem., Chicago Inst. for Psychoanalysis 1951–56; mil. service with US Naval Hosp., Bethesda (attained rank of Commdr) 1954–56; Prof. of Psychiatry, State Univ. of NY, Upstate Medical Center 1956–90, Prof. Emer. 1990–; Co-founder and Chair. Bd of Dirs, American Asscn for the Abolition of Involuntary Mental Hospitalization Inc.; mem. Bd of Dirs, Nat. Council on Crime and Delinquency; Consultant, Cttee on Mental Hygiene, NY State Bar Asscn and other advisory positions; mem. AAAS and other asscns, Int. Editorial Bd The Int. Journal of the Addictions, Contemporary Psychoanalysis, Editorial Bd Journal of Humanistic Psychology, The Humanist, also consulting positions with journals; Hon. Pres. Int. Comm. for Human Rights 1974; Hon. DSc (Allegheny Coll.) 1975, (Univ. Francisco Marroquín, Guatemala) 1979, (State Univ., New York) 2001; Hon. DHL (Towson Univ.) 1999. *Publications:* Pain and Pleasure 1957, The Myth of Mental Illness 1961, 1974, Law, Liberty and Psychiatry 1963, Psychiatric Justice 1965, The Ethics of Psychoanalysis 1965, Ideology and Insanity 1970, The Manufacture of Madness 1970, The Age of Madness 1973, The Second Sin 1973, Ceremonial Chemistry 1974, Heresies 1976, Schizophrenia: The Sacred Symbol of Psychiatry 1976, Karl Kraus and the Soul-Doctors 1976, Psychiatric Slavery 1977, The Theology of Medicine 1977, The Myth of Psychotherapy 1978, Sex By Prescription 1980, Sex: Facts, Frauds and Follies 1981, The Therapeutic State 1984, Insanity: The Idea and its Consequences 1987, The Untamed Tongue: A Dissenting Dictionary 1990, Our Right to Drugs 1992, A Lexicon of Lunacy 1993, Cruel Compassion 1994, The Meaning of Mind 1996, Fatal Freedom: The Ethics and Politics of Suicide 1999, Pharmacracy: Medicine and Politics in America 2001, Liberation by Oppression: A Comparative Study of Slavery and Psychiatry. *Leisure interests:* reading, hiking, swimming. *Address:* Department of Psychiatry, State University of New York, Upstate Medical Center, 750 East Adams Street, Syracuse, NY 13210 (Office); 4739 Limberlost Lane, Manlius, NY 13104, USA (Home). *Telephone:* (315) 464-3106 (Office); (315) 637-8918 (Home). *Fax:* (315) 464-3163 (Office).

SZCZEPAŃSKI, Jan, PhD; Polish sociologist; b. 14 Sept. 1913, Ustroń, Cieszyn Dist; s. of Paweł Szczepański and Ewa Szczepańska (née Cholewa); m. Eleonora Poczobut 1937; one s. one d.; ed Univ. of Poznań; Asst Poznań Univ. 1935–39; during Nazi occupation forced labour in Germany; Asst Łódź Univ. 1945–52, Extraordinary Prof. 1952–63, Prof. 1963–70, Rector 1952–56; Chief Sociological Dept Inst. of Philosophy and Sociology, Polish Acad. of Sciences 1957–58, Deputy Dir 1961–68, Dir 1968–75; Corresp. mem. Polish Acad. of Sciences 1964, ordinary mem. 1969, Vice-Pres. 1971–80; Pres. Int. Sociological Asscn 1966–70; Vice-Chair. All-Poland Cttee of Nat. Unity Front 1971–83; Deputy to Sejm (Parl.) 1957–60, 1972–85, Chair. Sejm Socio-Econ. Council 1982–84; Chair. Chief Council of Science, Higher Educ. and Tech., Ministry of Science, Higher Educ. and Tech. 1973–82; Chair. Scientific Council of Intercollegiate Inst. for Research on Higher Educ. 1973–91; mem. Council of State 1977–82; Chair., Sejm Extraordinary Comm. for Control of the Realization of Gdańsk, Szczecin and Jastrzębie Zdrój Agreements 1981; mem. Consultative Council attached to Chair. of State Council 1986–89; mem. Bd UNRISD, Asscn Int. de Sociologie (AIS); mem. Nat. Acad. of Educ., USA; Foreign mem. Finnish Acad. of Science and Literature; Hon. mem. American Acad. of Arts and Sciences 1972; Dr hc (Brno Univ.) 1969, (Łódź Univ., Silesian Univ., Katowice) 1973, (Warsaw Univ.) 1979, (Sorbonne) 1980; Hon. CBE 1978; Commdr's Cross with Star, Commdr.'s and Knight's Cross, Polonia Restituta Order, Order of the Builders of People's Poland 1974, State Prize (1st Class) 1974 and others. *Publications:* Structure of Intelligentsia in Poland (in Polish) 1960, History of Sociology (in Polish) 1961, Sociological Problems of Higher Education (in Polish, French, Hungarian) 1963, edited Studies in Polish Class Structure (28 Vols), Introduction to Sociology (in Polish, Czech, Russian, Hungarian and Finnish) 1963, Problems of Contemporary Sociology (in Polish) 1965, Industry and Society in Poland (in Polish) 1969, Sociology and Society (in Bulgarian) 1970, Changes of the Present Time (in Polish) 1970, Co-editor Social Problems of Work Production (in Polish, Russian) 1970, Considerations on the Republic (in Polish) 1971, Reflections on Education (in Polish) 1973, Changes of Polish Community in the Process of Industrialization 1973, Essays on Higher Education 1976, Sprawy ludzkie (Res Humanae) 1979, Konsumpcja a rozwój człowieka (Consumption and Development of Man) 1981, Zapytaj samego siebie 1983, Korzeniami wrosłem w ziemię 1985, O indywidualności 1985, Polska wobec wyzwań przyszłości 1989, Historia mistrzynią życia? 1990. *Address:* ul. Mokotowska 46a m. 23, 00-543 Warsaw, Poland. *Telephone:* (22) 6282193.

SZÉKELY, Gábor, MA; Hungarian theatre director and university professor of theatre direction; b. 26 May 1944, Jászberény; s. of late Árpád Székely and of Irma Csuka; m. Erika Székely 1967; one s. two d.; ed Könyves Kalmán Grammar School, Budapest, Budapest Acad. of Dramatic and Cinematic Art; Asst Dir, Szolnoki Szigligeti Theatre 1968–71, Prin. Dir 1971–72, Theatre Man. and Prin. Dir 1972–78; Prin. Dir Budapest Nat. Theatre 1978–82, apptd. Theatre Man. 1982; Theatre Man. Budapest Katona József Theatre 1982–89; teacher of dramatic art and theatre direction, Acad. of Dramatic and Cinematic Art 1972–, Head Theatre Dirs. Faculty 1990–; has directed in Novi Sad, Stuttgart, Prague Nat. Theatre; invited to direct at Deutsches Theater, Berlin, Comédie Française, Paris 1991, Helsinki City Theatre 1993; guest teacher Paris Acad. of Dramatic and Cinematic Art 1993; Jászai Mari Prize, Merited Artist, Outstanding Artist, Kossuth Prize, critics' prize for best theatre performance and best theatre direction, several times. *Plays directed include:* As You Like It, Troilus and Cressida, Timon of Athens (Shakespeare), Georges Dandin, L'impromptu de Versailles, Don Juan (Molière), The Death of Tarelkin (Kobilin), The Death of Danton, Woyzeck (Büchner); guest performances abroad with Budapest Nat. and Katona József theatres (among others): Cat's Play (Orkény), Family Toth (Orkény), Moscow, Bucharest, Prague, Helsinki; Catullus (Fust), Vienna, Paris (Odeon), Zürich; Le Misanthrope (Molière), Moscow; Coriolanus (Shakespeare), Berlin; The Escape (Bulgakov), Prague. *Leisure interests:* architecture, fine arts. *Address:* Jókai u. 36. II/12, 1066 Budapest, Hungary. *Telephone:* (1) 332-4284.

SZENTIVÁNYI, Gábor, GCVO; Hungarian diplomatist; b. 9 Oct. 1952, Vaskút; s. of József Szentiványi and Ilona Fejes; m. Gabriella Gönczi; one s. one d.; ed Univ. of Econ. Sciences, Budapest; joined Foreign Service 1975, positions in Baghdad 1976–81, Washington, DC 1986–91; mem. staff Protocol Dept, Ministry of Foreign Affairs 1982–85, Spokesman for Press and Int. Information Dept 1994–95, Spokesman and Dir-Gen. 1995–97, Deputy State Sec. 2002–; Amb. to UK 1997–2002; Man. Dir Burson-Marsteller's Budapest office 1991–94; mem. Hungarian Foreign Affairs Soc., Hungarian Atlantic Council, Hungarian Public Relations Asscn; Freeman of the City of London 2000; Officer Order of Prince Henry the Navigator 1982; Hon. Kt Grand Cross, Royal Victorian Order; Grand Cross of Merit (Chile) 2002. *Leisure interests:* boating, reading. *Address:* Ministry of Foreign Affairs, 1027 Budapest, Bem rkp. 47, Hungary (Office). *Telephone:* (1) 201-80-93 (Office). *Fax:* (1) 458-15-44 (Office). *E-mail:* GSzentivanyi@kum.hu (Office).

SZILÁGYI, János György, PhD; Hungarian art historian; b. 16 July 1918, Budapest; s. of Hugo Szilágyi and Adél Braun; m. Mária Rabinovszky; one d.; ed Pázmány Péter Univ. of Arts and Sciences; research fellow at the Classical Dept, Museum of Fine Arts of Budapest 1941, Head of Dept 1952–93, Prof. of Budapest Univ. of Arts and Sciences 1952–93; mem. Cttee History of Ancient Civilizations of the Hungarian Acad. of Sciences, Istituto Nazionale di Studi Etruschi, Florence, Deutsches Archäologisches Institut, Istituto per la Storia e l'Archeologia della Magna Grecia; Ábel Jenő Commemorative Medal, Móra Ferenc Commemorative Medal, Kossuth Award 1991, Eötvös Wreath 1996. *Publications include:* Ceramica etrusco-corinzia figurata I–II 1992–98, In Search of Pelasgian Ancestors 2002 and numerous works on Greek and Etruscan art and culture. *Address:* Museum of Fine Arts, Budapest 62, PF 463, 1396 (Office); Margit Körut 7, III, 1 Budapst, 1024 Hungary (Home). *Telephone:* (1) 469-7123 (Office); (1) 335-1298 (Home). *Fax:* (1) 469-7171 (Office).

SZINETÁR, Miklós; Hungarian theatre and film director; b. 8 Feb. 1932, Budapest; m. Ildikó Hámori, one s. one d.; ed High School of Dramatic Art; producer of Budapest Operetta Theatre, Chief Producer 1953–60; Chief Producer of Hungarian TV, artistic Dir Chief Artistic Dir 1962–, Deputy Chair. of Hungarian TV 1979–90; Man. Dir of Budapest Operetta Theatre 1993–96; Chief Man. Dir of Hungarian State Opera House 1996–2001, Intendant-Gen. Dir 2002–; also Univ. Prof.; Golden Nympha, Monte Carlo 1970, Best Director, Prague TV Festival 1976–79, Silver Asterix, Trieste 1980. *Films:* Forteresse, Csárdás Fürstine, Janos Háry, Bluebeard's Castle. *Television:* Così fan Tutte, Fidelio, The Barber of Seville, The Life of Franz Liszt. *Address:* (Hungarian State Opera House) Magyar Állami Operaház, 1061 Budapest, Andrássy út 22 (Office); 2011 Budakalász, Bethlen Gábor u. 16, Hungary (Home). *Telephone:* (36) 13124642 (Office); (36) 26343000 (Home). *Fax:* (36) 26540380 (Home). *E-mail:* szini1@accelero.hu (Home).

SZMAJDZIŃSKI, Jerzy Andrzej; Polish politician; b. 9 April 1952, Wrocław; m.; two s.; ed Acad. of Econs, Wrocław 1975; with Polish Socialist Youth Union 1975–89; Head of Dept, Cen. Cttee Polish United Workers' Party, (PZPR) 1989–90; mem. Social Democracy of Polish Repub. (SdRP) 1990–99, Sec. Gen. 1993–98, Deputy Chair. 1998–99; mem. Democratic Left Alliance Party 1999–; Deputy to Sejm (Parl.) 1985–89, 1991–; Chair. Cttee of Nat. Defence 1993–97, Deputy Chair. 1997–2001; Chair. Sejm Democratic Left Alliance (SLD) 1995–97, Deputy Chair. 1997–; Deputy Chair. Democratic Lef Alliance Dec. 1999–; Minister of Nat. Defence 2001–. *Leisure interests:* history, sport. *Address:* Ministry of National Defence, ul. Klonowa 1, 00-909 Warsaw, Poland. *Telephone:* (22) 6280031. *Fax:* (22) 8455378. *Website:* www.mon.gov.pl (Office).

SZOKA, HE Cardinal Edmund Casimir, BA; American ecclesiastic; b. 14 Sept. 1927, Grand Rapids; s. of Casimir Szoka and Mary Wolgat; ordained 1954, elected to Gaylord 1971, consecrated bishop of Detroit 1971, prefect 1981, Archbishop Emer. 1990; cr. Cardinal 1988; Pres. of Pref. of Econ. Affairs of Holy See 1990; Pres. Pontifical Comm. for Vatican City State, Governorate of Vatican City State; Second Sec. Council for Relations with States; mem. Congregations for the Causes of Saints, for the Bishops, for the Evangelization of Peoples, for the Clergy, for Insts. of Consecrated Life and for Socs. of Apostolic Life. *Address:* Prefecture Economic Affairs, 00120 Vatican City.

SZOKOLAY, Sándor; Hungarian composer; b. 30 March 1931, Kunágota; s. of Bálint Szokolay and Erzsébet Holecska; m. 1st Sári Szesztay 1952; m. 2nd

Maja Weltler 1970; four s. one d.; ed Békéstardos Music High School, Budapest Music Acad.; music teacher Budapest Conservatory 1952–55; Musical Adviser and Ed. Hungarian Radio 1955–59; composition teacher Budapest Music Acad. 1959–66; musical adviser Hungarian TV 1966–; Chair. Hungarian Kodály Soc.; has won prizes in Warsaw, Moscow, Vienna; Merited Artist Distinction 1976, Honoured Artist Distinction 1986, Bartók-Pásztory Prize 1987. *Works include:* Blood Wedding (opera) 1963, Hamlet (opera) 1968, Az iszonyat balladája (The Ballad of Horror), Tetemrehívás (Ordeal of the Bier), Samson (opera) 1973, Csalóka Péter (children's opera, text by Sándor Weöres) 1985, Ecce Homo (passion-opera) 1987; Oratorios: A tüz márciusa (March Fire), Istár pokoljárása (Ishtar's Descent to Hell), Hungarian Psalm; has also written cantatas, songs, chamber music and choral works. *Leisure interests:* driving, mountaineering. *Address:* c/o Martin Perdoux, 5014 Chaparral Way, San Diego, CA 92115, USA.

SZŐLLŐSY, András, D.PH.; Hungarian composer and music historian; b. 27 Feb. 1921, Szászváros, Transylvania; s. of János Szőllősy and Julia Tóth; m. Éva Keményfy 1944; ed Univ. of Budapest; studied composition, Music Acad., Budapest, under Zoltán Kodály, Accademia di Santa Cecilia, Rome, under Goffredo Petrassi; Prof. of History and Theory of Music, Liszt Ferenc Music Acad., Budapest 1950–; top qualifier, UNESCO Prize, Tribune Int. des Compositeurs, Paris 1970, Merited Artist title 1974, Outstanding Artist 1982, Kossuth Prize 1985, Bartok-Pásztory Prize 1986, 1998; Commdr, Ordre des Arts et Lettres 1987. *Compositions include:* Oly korban éltem (Improvisation of Fear) (ballet) 1963; orchestral works: five Concertos, Musica per Orchestra 1972, Trasfigurazioni 1972, Musica Concertante 1973, Preludio, Adagio e Fuga 1973, Sonorità 1974, Musiche per Ottoni 1975, Concerto for Harpsichord and Strings 1979, Pro Somno Igoris Stravinsky Quieto 1979, Fabula Phaedri for vocal ensemble 1982 (composed for the King's Singers), In Pharisaeos (for choir) 1982, Tristia (for strings) 1983, Planctus Mariae (for female choir) 1983, Suoni di tromba 1984, Miserere (composed for the King's Singers) 1985, Fragments 1985, Quartetto di Tromboni 1986, Canto d'autunno (for orchestra) 1986, Due Paesaggi (for piano) 1987, String Quartet 1988, Elegy (for dixtuor) 1992, Passacaglia Achatio Máthé in memoriam (for string quartet and cello) 1997, Addio (for 10 strings) 2002; songs; incidental music for plays and films. *Publications:* Kodály művészete 1943, Honegger 1960, 1980; Ed. writings of Kodály and Bartók. *Address:* 1118 Budapest, Somlói ut 12, Hungary. *Telephone:* (1) 466-0035.

SZŐNYI, Erzsébet; Hungarian musician; b. 25 April 1924; d. of Jenő Szőnyi and Erzsébet Piszanoff; m. Dr. Lajos Gémes 1948; two s.; ed Music Acad., Budapest and Paris Conservatoire; teacher of music at a Budapest grammar school 1945–48, Music Acad., Budapest 1948–; leading Prof. of Music Acad. 1960–81; Vice-Pres. Int. Soc. for Music Educ. 1970–74; Co-Chair. Hungarian Kodály Soc. 1978–, Bárdos Soc. 1988–, Forum of Hungarian Musicians 1995–; Hon. Pres. Hungarian Choir Asscn 1990–; Gen. adviser on methodology, Int. Kodály Soc. 1979–; mem. Chopin Soc. of Warsaw, Liszt Soc. of Hungary; mem. Bd Hungarian Composers' Soc. 1999–; Erkel Prize 1959, Hungarian Repub. Medal 1993 Apácai Csere János Prize 1994, Bartók-Pásztory Prize 1995, Prize for Artistic Excellence 2000, Zoltán Kodály Prize 2001. *Compositions include:* Concerto for Organ and Orchestra; symphonic works: Musica Festiva, Divertimento 1 and 2, Prelude and Fugue, Three Ideas in Four Movements; operas: Tragedy of Firenze, A Gay Lament, Break in Transmission, Elfrida (madrigal opera) 1987–, several children's operas; chamber music, oratorios, vocal compositions, etc. *Publications:* Methods of Musical Reading and Writing, Kodály's Principles in Practice, Travels in Five Continents, Twentieth-Century Musical Methods. *Leisure interests:* gardening, cooking. *Address:* Ormódi-utca 13, 1124 Budapest XII, Hungary. *Telephone:* (1) 356-7329.

SZÖRÉNYI, Levente; Hungarian musician, composer and songwriter; b. 26 April 1945, Gmunden, Austria; m. (divorced); ed Coll. of Music; guitar player; worked with János Bródy 1965–; pop musician with Mediterrán and Balassa 1963–64, with Illés 1965–73; dance participant Még fáj minden csók (song festival) 1966; founding mem. Fonográf 1974–81; retd from theatre 1984; First Prize Hungarian Radio Amateur Competition 1965, SZOT (Trade Union) Award 1981, Composer of the Year 1983, Erkel Ferenc Award 1983, KISZ (Youth Org.) Award. *Soundtracks include:* Ezek a fiatalok 1967, Extázis 5-7-ig 1969, Eltávozott a nap, Locsolókocsi, Pókfoci, A Koncert 1982, István a Király 1983, Attila Isten kardja (opera) 1993, Veled Uram! (opera) 2000, Ének a csodaszarvasról 2001. *Compositions include:* Human Rights (Oratory) 1968, Kömíves Kelemen (rock ballad) 1982, István a Király (rock opera) 1983, Fehér Anna (rock ballad) 1988, Fénylő Ölednek édes Örömében (Innin and Dumuzi—oratory) 1989. *Address:* Mátru u. 9, 1029 Budapest, Hungary.

SZOSTEK, Andrzej Ryszard, BPhil; Polish ecclesiastic and academic; b. 9 Nov. 1945, Grudziądz; ed Catholic Univ. of Lublin; ordained priest 1974; with Dept of Ethics, Catholic Univ. of Lublin 1970–, scientific worker 1971–, Extraordinary Prof. 1992–99, Ordinary Prof. 2000–, Head Dept of Ethics, mem. man. team Inst. of John Paul II 1983–98, Pro-Rector 1992–98, Rector 1998–; numerous visiting lectureships; lecturer, Superior Monastic House,

Lublin 1987–90; Provincial Councillor Marians 1987–93; mem. Cttee of Formation of Marians 1975–90, Scientific Soc., Catholic Univ. of Lublin 1980–, Polish Philosophical Soc., Lublin 1982, Int. Cttee of Theology, Vatican Congregation of Religious Studies 1992–98, Lublin Scientific Soc. 1998–2001 (Distinguished mem. 2001–), Pontificia Academia Pro Vita 2001–; Order of Merit 2001, Palmes Académiques (France) 2001; Hon. Fellow St. Mary's Coll., London 2000; Medal, Comm. of Nat. Educ. 2001. *Publications:* Rules and Exceptions – Philosophical Aspects of the Discussion about Absolute Norms in Contemporary Theology 1980, Nature–Reason–Freedom. Philosophical Analysis of the Concept of Creative Intellect in Contemporary Moral Theology 1989, Talks on Ethics 1993, On Dignity, Truth and Love 1995 and numerous other publs. *Leisure interests:* mountaineering, music, chess. *Address:* Katolicki Uniwersytet Lubelski, Al. Racławickie 14, 20-950 Lublin (Office); ul. Bazylianówka 54B, 20-160 Lublin, Poland (Home). *Telephone:* (81) 4454120 (Office); (81) 7433773 (Home). *Fax:* (81) 4454123 (Office). *E-mail:* rektorat@kul.lublin.pl (Office).

SZUMSKI, Henryk; Polish army officer; b. 6 April 1941, Potulice; m. Wiesława Jawor; three s. one d.; ed Officer's School, Poznan, Gen. Staff Acad. Polish Armed Forces, Warsaw, Gen. Staff Acad. Armoured Forces of USSR Armed Forces, Moscow; career soldier 1964–; Commdr section and co. of brigade 1964–68, Chief of Staff and Commdr 1971–76, Chief of Staff and Commdr of 16th Armoured Div. 1976–78, Commdr, 12th Mechanized Div., Szczecin 1980–84, Chief of Staff of Pomeranian Mil. Dist 1984–86, deputy chief Gen. Staff for Operational Matters, 1984–87, Commdr Silesian Mil. Dist 1987–89, First Deputy Chief Gen. Staff, 1989–90, Chief Main Bd of Combat Training, 1990–92; Brig.-Gen. 1983, Maj. Gen. 1988, Lt-Gen. 1997; Inspector of Leadership of Gen. Staff 1993–97, Chief of Gen. Staff 1997–; mem. Nat. Security Council 2000–05). *Leisure interests:* history, literature, sport. *Address:* Sztab Generalny WP, ul. Rakowiecka 4A, Warsaw, Poland.

SZŰRÖS, Mátyás, PhD; Hungarian politician and diplomatist; b. 11 Sept. 1933, Püspökladány; ed Moscow Univ. Inst. of Int. Relations, Budapest Univ. of Econ. Sciences; on staff of Foreign Ministry 1959–65; staff mem. HSWP 1965–74, Deputy Leader Foreign Dept HSWP Cen. Cttee 1974–75, Head 1982–83; Amb. to GDR 1975–78, to USSR 1978–82; mem. Cen. Cttee HSWP 1978, Secr. 1983–89; mem. Parl. 1985–, Chair. Foreign Relations Parl. Cttee 1985–89 (mem. 1998–), Pres. of Parl. March–Oct. 1989, Acting Pres. 1989, Deputy Speaker 1990–94; Chair. Hungarian Group of IPU 1989–90, 1994–, mem. Exec. Cttee IPU 1994–96; Chair. Ópusztaszer Historical Commemorative Cttee 1989–98, Bd Trustees Illyés Foundation 1994–99, Trustee 1999–; mem. Council of Hundreds (World Fed. of Hungarians) 1997–; Freeman of Püspökladány 1996, of Beregszász 1997; Bocskai Award 1996. *Publications:* Hazánk és a nagyvilág (Homeland and World) 1985, Hazánk és Európa (Homeland and Europe) 1987, Magyarságról-Külpolitikáról (On Being Hungarian and on Foreign Policy) 1989, Cselekvő politikával a magyarságért-Politikai portré (1988–96) (Active policy for Hungary, portrait of a politician) 1996, Köztársaság született haranszavú délben (1989. október 23) (The Republic Was Born and the Bells Rang at Noon, 23 October 1989) 1999, National Politics and Joining. Questions of Integration 2001. *Address:* Hungarian National Assembly, 1055 Budapest, Kossuth Lajos tér 1-3, Hungary. *Telephone:* (1) 441-5067; (1) 441-5068. *Fax:* (1) 441-5972. *E-mail:* secretariate@ipu.parlament.hu (Office).

SZYMANEK-DERESZ, Jolanta; Polish government official and lawyer; b. 12 July 1954, Przedbórz; d. of Tadeusz Szymanek and Zenajda Szymanek; m. Pawel Deresz; one d.; ed Warsaw Univ.; judge, Dist court 1982, attorney 1984; mem. Int. League of Right to Competition 1996–; Under-Sec. of State at the Chancellery 2000, Head of the Chancellery 2000–. *Publications include:* articles in Polish press on protection of personal rights, trade marks and patents. *Leisure interests:* tennis, skiing. *Address:* Chancellery of the President of the Republic of Poland, ul. Wiejska 10, 00-902 Warsaw, Poland (Office). *Telephone:* (22) 6952050 (Office). *Fax:* (22) 6952257 (Office).

SZYMBORSKA, Wisława; Polish poet, translator and literary critic; b. 2 July 1923, Kórnik, nr Poznań; ed Jagiellonian Univ., Kraków; first work published 1945; mem. Polish Writers' Asscn 1951–81, 1981–, mem. Gen. Bd 1978–83; mem. Editorial Staff Życie Literackie (weekly) 1953–81; Nobel Prize for Literature 1996; Gold Cross of Merit 1955, Goethe Award (Frankfurt) 1991, Herder Award 1995, Polish PEN Club Award 1996. *Publications:* poetry: Dlatego żyjemy (That's Why We're Alive) 1952, Pytania zadawane sobie (Questioning Oneself) 1954, Wołanie do Yeti (Calling Out to Yeti) 1957, Sól (Salt) 1962, Sto pociech (No End of Fun) 1967, Wybór wierszy (Selected Poems) 1967, 1973, Poezje 1970, Wszelki wypadek (Could Have) 1972, Wielka liczba (A Large Number) 1976, Poezje wybrane (Selected Poems II) 1983, Ludzie na moście (The People on the Bridge) 1986, Koniec i początek 1993, Widok z ziarnkiem piasku (View With a Grain of Sand) 1996, Poems New and Collected 1957–97 1998, Wiersze wybrane (Selected Poems III) 2000, Chwila (A Moment) 2002. *Address:* Polish Writers' Association, ul. Kanonicza 7, 31-002 Kraków, Poland.

T

TABACHNIK, Dmitro Volodimirovich; Ukrainian historian; b. 26 Nov. 1964, Kiev; s. of Volodomir Igorovich Tabachnik and Alla Viktorovna Tabachnik; m. Tetyana Ovgenyovna Nazarova; ed Kiev State Univ.; fmr copyist, then restorer Cen. State Archives of Cinematography, Documents of Ukraine; jr researcher Inst. of History of Ukraine, Ukrainian Acad. of Sciences, leading researcher Inst. of Politology 1997–; Deputy Kiev City Soviet 1990–94; Deputy Head Kiev City Exec. Comsomol Cttee 1991–92; Head of Press Service, Cabinet of Ministers 1992–93; First Deputy Head State Cttee on Publishing, Polygraphy and Book Trade 1993–94; Head of Admin., Presidency 1994–96, Counsellor 1997–98, Head Constitution Comm. 1994–96; Deputy Prime Minister of Ukraine 2002–; Prof. Ukrainian Acad. of State Man. 1995–; mem. Verkhovna Rada; corresp. mem. Acad. of Juridical Sciences. *Publications:* over 200 papers. *Leisure interests:* collecting cold steel, theatre. *Address:* Verkhovna Rada, M. Hrushevskogo str. 5, 252008 Kiev, Ukraine (Office). *Telephone:* (44) 226-24-72 (Office).

TABAI, Ieremia T., CMG; I-Kiribati politician and international organization official; b. 1950, Nonouti; m.; two c.; ed King George V School, Tarawa, St Andrew's Coll., Christchurch, NZ, Victoria Univ., Wellington, NZ; mem. Gilbert Islands (later Kiribati) House of Ass. 1974–91; fmr Leader of the Opposition; Chief Minister of the Gilbert Islands 1978–79, also Minister of Local Govt; Pres. of Kiribati and Minister of Foreign Affairs (fmrly Gilbert Islands) 1979–91; Sec.-Gen. South Pacific Forum 1991–98; Chair. Commonwealth Observer Group 2001; co-owner New Star newspaper; Hon. LLD (Vic. Univ. of Wellington). *Address:* c/o Ministry of Foreign Affairs, P.O. Box 68, Bairiki, Tarawa, Kiribati.

TABAKOV, Oleg Pavlovich; Russian film actor, stage actor and director; b. 17 Aug. 1935, Saratov; s. of Pavel K. Tabakov and Maria A. Beresovskaya; m. 1st Lyudmila Krilova 1959 (divorced); one s. one d.; m. 2nd Marina V. Zudina 1995; one s.; ed Moscow Arts Theatre Studio-School; Co-founder and actor with Sovremennik Theatre 1957–83; with Moscow Arts Theatre 1983–; stage debut 1956; film debut 1957; mem. CPSU 1965–91; master of theatre training 1976–; Assoc. Prof. State Inst. of Theatre Arts (GITIS) 1976–85; Prof. Moscow Arts Theatre Studio School 1985–, Chancellor 1986–; Founder and Producer, Moscow Theatre Studio (now Oleg Tabakov Theatre) 1974–; Artistic Dir Moscow A. Chekhov Arts Theatre; directed and taught in numerous countries; f. and teacher Stanislavsky Summer School, Cambridge, Mass. 1992–; Founder and Pres. Russian-American Performing Arts Center 1992–; State Prize for Acting 1967; People's Artist of the USSR 1987. *Film roles include:* Oleg Komelev in The Tight Knot 1956, Nikolay Rostov in War and Peace 1967, Oleg Savin in Noisy Day 1960, Iskremas in Light My Star, Light 1969, Clown in Kashtanka 1975, Shcherbuk in Unfinished Play for Mechanical Piano 1977, Oblomov in A Few Days of I. I. Oblomov's Life 1979 (Oxford Int. Festival Prize for best male actor 1980), Nikolay Pavlovich in Flights of Fancy 1983, Cudechkis in The Art of Living in Odessa 1989, Gen. Vlasik in The Inner Circle 1991, Klaverov in The Shadows 1991, Soukhodritchev in Shirly-Mirly 1995, etc. *Stage roles include:* Misha in Always Alive 1956, Aleksandr in The Same Old Story 1966, Brother Lymon in The Ballad of Sad Café 1966, Klava in Always on Sale 1965, Major in Tooth, Others and Major 1971, Balalaykin in Balalaykin and Co. 1974, Anchugin in Provincial Anecdotes 1975, 1996, Malvolio in Twelfth Night 1975, Peter Stockman in Dr. Stockman 1979, Salieri in Amadeus 1983, Hailmayer in Judgers 1985, Sorin in Seagull 1987, Buton in Cabal of Hippocrates 1989, Tacker in I Ought to be in Pictures 1990, Meyer Volf in My Big Land 1991, Famusov in Woe from Wisdom 1992, Uncle in The Same Old Story 1993, Tallyran in Le Souper 1994, Ivan Kolomiytsev in The Last Ones 1995; has directed Champions, Every Wise Man Has a Fool in his Sleeve, The Same Old Story, Goldoni's Revenge. *Publication:* My Real Life. *Leisure interest:* driving a car. *Address:* Moscow A. Chekhov Arts Theatre, Kamergurskiy per. 3, 103009 Moscow (Office); Chernysherskogo 39, Apt. 3, 103062 Moscow, Russia (Home). *Telephone:* (095) 229-33-12 (Office); (095) 924-76-90 (Home). *Fax:* (095) 975-21-96.

TABAKSBLAT, Morris; Netherlands business executive; b. Rotterdam; m.; two s. one d.; ed Leiden Univ.; joined Unilever 1964, mem. Bd 1984, mem. Unilever Special Cttee 1992–99, Chair. and CEO 1994–99; Chair. Reed Elsevier 1999–; Pres. Aegon NV 2000–; Chair. European Round Table of Industrialists, Bd of Govs., Leiden Univ. Medical Centre, Mauritshuis Museum, The Hague; Vice-Chair. USA Conf. Bd; Chair. Supervisory Bd, AEGON NV, TNT Post Group NV; mem. Int. Advisory Bds. Salomon Smith Barney, Renault Nissan; Hon. KBE. *Address:* Office of the Chairman, Reed Elsevier, Sara Burgerhartstraat 25, 1055 KV Amsterdam, The Netherlands (Office). *Telephone:* (20) 4852993 (Office). *Fax:* (20) 4852750 (Office). *E-mail:* morris.tabaksblat@reed-elsevier.nl (Office).

TABECARU, Nicolae; Moldovan politician and diplomatist; b. 20 Aug. 1955, Nadrechnoye, Odessa Region, Ukraine; m.; two c.; ed Moldovan State Univ., Moscow Diplomatic Acad., diplomatic service 1989–; Head, Protocol Dept, Moldovan Ministry of Foreign Affairs 1990; First Sec. Perm. Mission of Repub. of Moldova to UN 1991–92; Head, Dept for UN and Disarmament, Moldovan Ministry of Foreign Affairs 1992–93; Head, Protocol Diplomatic Dept 1993; Counsellor, Minister-Counsellor, Embassy, Belgium (also Accred to Luxembourg, UK, NATO and EC) 1993–96; Head, Dept of Europe and N America, Ministry of Foreign Affairs 1996–97; Adviser on Problems of Foreign Policy to Moldovan Pres. 1997–; Minister of Foreign Affairs 1997–99; Amb. to Germany 2001–. *Address:* Embassy of Modova, Gotlandstr. 16, 10439 Berlin,

Germany (Office); c/o Ministry of Foreign Affairs, Piaţa Marii Adunari Nationale 1, 2033 Chişinău, Moldova. *Telephone:* (30) 44652970 (Office). *Fax:* (30) 44652972 (Office). *E-mail:* botschaft_moldova_berlin@compuserve.com (Office).

TABIANI, Mahmoud, PhD; Iranian professor of electronics; b. 1950; ed Sharif Univ. of Tech., USA, Mass. Inst. of Tech.; Prof., Electrical Eng Dept, Sharif Univ. of Tech. 1979–, Dir Electronics Research Centre; Pres. Iranian Research Org. for Science and Tech. 1982–89; Fellow Islamic Acad. of Sciences. *Address:* Electronics Research Centre, Sharif University of Technology, P.O. Box 11365, Tehran, Iran (Office). *Telephone:* (21) 600-5419 (Office). *Fax:* (21) 601-2983 (Office). *E-mail:* scientia@sharif.ac.ir (Office).

TABONE, Anton; Maltese politician; b. 15 Nov. 1937; s. of Anton Tabone; m. Margerite Stivala; three s.; ed St Aloysius Coll.; employee, Nat. Bank of Malta 1955–66; mem. Parl. for Gozo (Nationalist Party) 1966–98; mem. Gozo Civic Council 1966–73; Party spokesman for Agric. and Fisheries, later for Gozo Affairs 1973–87; Minister for Gozo 1987–96; Shadow Minister for Gozo 1996–98; Speaker House of Reps. 1998–. *Address:* House of Representatives, The Palace, Valletta, Malta. *Telephone:* (356) 222294. *Fax:* (356) 242552.

TABONE, Vincent, GCB, MD, DO(Oxon), DOMS, DMJ, FRCS(E), FCS, KUOM; Maltese fmr politician and fmr ophthalmic specialist; b. Censu Tabone, 30 March 1913, Victoria, Gozo; s. of Dr. Nicholas Tabone and Elisa Calleja; m. Maria Wirth 1941; four s. (one deceased) five d.; ed St Aloysius Coll., Univ. of Malta, Univ. of Oxford and Royal Coll. of Surgeons of Edin.; served Royal Malta Artillery during World War II; has held sr ophthalmic posts in various hosps. in Malta; mem. Exec. Cttee Nationalist Party 1961, Sec.-Gen. 1962–72, First Deputy Leader 1972–77, Pres. 1978–85; mem. Parl. (Nationalist Party) 1966–89; Minister of Labour, Employment and Welfare 1966, of Foreign Affairs 1987–89; Pres. of Repub. of Malta 1989–94; Visiting Prof. Univ. of Malta; Corresp. mem. Accad. Pontificio Pro Vita; Hon. LLD (Univ. of Malta) 1989; UN Testimonial for Service to UN Programme on Aging 1989; Grand Cross, Order of Merit (Fed. Repub. of Germany) 1990, Pro Merito Medal (Council of Europe) 1991, Presidential Gold Medal (Royal Coll. of Surgeons of Edin.) 1991, Cavaliere di Gran Croce 1991, Hon. GCB. *Address:* 33 Carmel Street, St Julians, Malta (Home). *Telephone:* 330994 (Home). *E-mail:* ctabone@keyworld.net (Home).

TABOR, David, BSc, PhD, ScD, FRS, FInstP; British physicist; b. 23 Oct. 1913, London; s. of Charles Tabor and Rebecca Weinstein; brother of Harry Tabor (q.v.); m. Hannalene Stillschweig 1943; two s.; ed Royal Coll. of Science, London, Cambridge Univ.; Tribophysics, CSIRO, Melbourne, Australia 1940–46; Asst Dir of Research, Cambridge Univ. 1946–61, Lecturer in Physics 1961–64, Reader 1964–73, Prof. 1973–81, Emer. Prof. 1981–, Head of Physics and Chem. of Solids, Cavendish Lab. 1969–81; Visiting Prof. Imperial Coll. London 1981–88; Fellow of Gonville and Caius Coll. Cambridge 1957–; Int. Fellow, Stanford Research Inst. 1956; UNESCO Visiting Prof., Israel 1961; Russell Springer Visiting Prof. Univ. of Calif.at Berkeley 1970; Foreign Assoc. US Nat. Acad. of Eng 1995; Hon. DSc (Bath Univ.) 1985; Nat. Award, American Soc. for Lubrication Engineers 1955, Wilson Award, American Soc. of Metals 1969, Inaugural Gold Medal for Tribology, Inst. of Mechanical Engineers 1972, Mayo D. Hersey Award, American Soc. of Mechanical Engineers 1974, Guthrie Medal, Inst. of Physics 1974, Royal Medal, Royal Soc. 1992. *Publications:* Hardness of Metals 1951, Gases, Liquids and Solids 1969 (new edn Gases, Liquids and Solids and Other States of Matter 1991); (with F. P. Bowden) Friction and Lubrication of Solids, Part I 1950, 1986, Part II 1964, Friction – an Introduction to Tribology 1973; contributions to learned journals on friction and adhesion. *Leisure interest:* Judaica. *Address:* Cavendish Laboratory, Madingley Road, Cambridge, CB3 0HE (Office); 3 Westberry Court, Grange Road, Cambridge, CB3 9BG, England (Home). *Telephone:* (1223) 337200 (Office); (1223) 304585 (Home).

TABOR, Hans, Dr rer. pol; Danish diplomatist; b. 25 April 1922, Copenhagen; s. of Svend Tabor and Dagny Tabor Rasmussen; m. Inger Petersen 1945 (died 1998); two d.; ed Birkerød Statsskole and Univ. of Copenhagen; Sec., Gen. Secr. OEEC, Paris 1948–50; Sec. Ministry of Foreign Affairs, Copenhagen 1950–52; Asst Head Danish del. to OEEC 1952–56; Branch Head Ministry of Foreign Affairs 1956, 1957–59; Deputy Sec.-Gen. Suez Canal Users' Asscn. London 1957; Econ. Counsellor, Asst Head Danish Mission to the European Communities 1959–61, Minister and Head 1961–64, Amb. 1963–64; Perm. Rep. to the UN 1964–67; Minister of Foreign Affairs 1967–68; Rep. of Denmark on the UN Security Council 1967–68; Amb. to Italy (also accred to Malta) 1968–74; Perm. Rep. to UN 1974; Amb. to Canada 1975–79; Amb. and Perm. Rep. at OECD 1979–86, Chair. OECD Exec. Cttee 1983; Amb. to Norway 1986–92. *Publications:* Danmark og Marshallplanen (Denmark and the Marshall Plan) 1961, De Seks og det økonomiske samarbejde i Vesten (The Six and Economic Co-operation in the Western World), Krig og Krise – Trods FN (War and Crisis – in spite of the United Nations) 1977, Diplomat blandt politikere (Diplomat Among Politicians) 1995. *Leisure interests:* tennis, swimming, reading, writing. *Address:* Johannes V. Jensens Allé 48, 2000 Frederiksberg, Denmark. *Telephone:* 36-17-38-52.

TABOR, Harry Zvi, PhD, FInstP; British/Israeli research physicist; b. 7 March 1917, London; s. of Charles Tabor and Rebecca Tabor; brother of David Tabor (q.v); m. Vivienne Landau 1947; two d.; ed Quintin Hogg School, London, Univ. of London and Hebrew Univ. of Jerusalem; research physicist in UK instrument industry (including defence-related research and devt 1939–45) 1939–49; Research Council of Israel 1949–74; Dir Nat. Physical Lab. of Israel 1950–74; Chair. and Scientific Dir Scientific Research Foundation, Jerusalem 1969–; mem. research cttees Ministry of Science & Tech., Ministry of Energy and Infrastructure 1975–; Pres. Int. Solar Energy Soc. (ISES) 1981–83; guest lecturer NAS 1961 and at numerous univs; consultant to UNESCO and WEC; primarily responsible for widespread use of solar water heating in Israel; Hon. PhD (Weizmann Inst.) 1992; Royal Soc. Gold Medal Energy Award 1975 for pioneering work on exploitation of solar energy; Diesel Gold Medallist 1977; Farrington Daniels Award (ISES) 1981; Alfred Krupp Energy Prize 1981; Quality of Life Award (Knesset, Israel) 1995 and other honours. *Publications:* selected reprints of papers by Harry Zvi Tabor, Solar Energy Pioneer (ed. by Morton B. Prince) 1999, book chapters and some 90 papers in scientific journals. *Leisure interests:* music, theatre, study of social problems (non-party). *Address:* PO Box 3745, Jerusalem 91036, Israel. *Telephone:* 2-6435785. *Fax:* 2-6437470.

TACHI, Ryuichiro; Japanese professor of economics; b. 11 Sept. 1921, Yokohama; m. Yoko Shinmel 1951; two s.; ed Univ. of Tokyo; Assoc. Prof. of Econs, Univ. of Tokyo 1950–61, Prof. 1961–82, Prof. Emer. 1982–, Dean Faculty of Econs 1972, Vice-Pres. 1979–81; Prof. of Econs, Aoyama Gakuin Univ. 1984–; Chief Counsellor Inst. for Monetary and Econ. Studies, Bank of Japan 1982–; Dir Inst. of Public Finance 1982–84; Pres. Japan Soc. of Monetary Econs 1982–88, Inst. of Fiscal and Monetary Policy, Ministry of Finance 1985–; mem. Japan Acad. 1986–. *Address:* Bank of Japan, 2-1-1, Hongoku-cho, Nihonbashi, Chuo-ku, Tokyo, Japan. *Telephone:* (3) 3279-1111. *Fax:* (3) 5200-2256. *Website:* www.boj.or.jp.

TADDZHUDDIN, Talgat Safich; Russian (Tartar) ecclesiastic; b. 12 Oct. 1948, Kazan, Tatarstan, Russia; m.; five c.; ed El-Azkhar Theological Univ., Cairo; First Imam-Khatyb, mufti and Chair. of Sacred Bd Mosque El-Mardjani; Chair. Dept of Int. Relations of Muslim Orgs of the USSR 1990; Supreme Mufti of Russia and European cos. of CIS; awarded the sacred title Sheik-iul-Islam; Official Rep. of Muslims of Russia to maj. foreign and public Muslim orgs., Org. of Islam Confed., UNESCO, European League of Muslims. *Publications:* The Wild East 1999, Limit of Rationality 1998, and numerous scientific works on political and religious culture. *Leisure interest:* foreign languages. *Address:* Vypolzov per. 7, 129090 Moscow, Russia (Office). *Telephone:* (095) 281-49-04 (Office).

TADLAOUI, Mohammed, BSc; Moroccan engineer; b. 1939, Meknes; m.; two s. one d.; ed Imperial Coll. London and Inst. of Civil Engs., UK; research engineer UK 1963, project engineer 1966; consulting engineer Morocco 1973; Founder, Pres. and Gen. Dir SOCOPLAN (consulting engs.) 1975; Co-founder and mem. Moroccan Asscn of Consulting Engineers (AMCI) 1976; Gen. Sec. Regional Asscn Grande Ismailia, Rabat Section 1994, Ismailia Asscn. of Micro Credit. *Leisure interests:* swimming, tennis, history, Arabic literature. *Address:* Residence Al Mansour, Zankat Moulay Slimane, Rabat, Morocco. *Telephone:* (7) 721020 (Office). *Fax:* (7) 735663 (Office).

TADROS, Tharwat Fouad, MSc, PhD; British/Egyptian scientist and academic; b. 29 July 1937, Kena, Egypt; s. of Fouad Tadros Mikhail and Rosa Wasif El-Gouhary; m. Jantina Lodewijka Buter 1969; two s.; ed Secondary School, Luxor, Egypt, Alexandria Univ.; Lecturer in Physical Chem., Faculty of Science, Alexandria Univ. 1962–66; Agric. Univ. Wageningen, Netherlands 1966–68; research worker Lab. for Applied Research, Delft, Netherlands 1968–69; Tech. Officer ICI 1969–74, Sr Research Officer 1974–78, Research Assoc. 1978–89, Sr Research Assoc. 1989–; Visiting Prof. Bristol Univ. 1983–84, Imperial Coll. London 1988–; Industrial Lecturer; Royal Soc. of Chem. Colloid and Surface Chem. Award and Medal, Silver Medal 1990. *Publications:* over 160 scientific articles in learned journals. *Leisure interests:* chess, reading, debates. *Address:* 89 Nash Grove Lane, Wokingham, Berks., RG40 4HE, England (Home). *Telephone:* (118) 973-2621 (Home).

TAFROV, Stefan; Bulgarian diplomatist; b. 11 Feb. 1958, Sofia; ed Lycée de langue française, Sofia, Univ. of Sofia; staff writer, weekly newspaper ABV, Sofia 1983–87; First Deputy Minister of Foreign Affairs 1991–92, April–Dec. 1997; Amb. to Italy 1992–95, to UK 1995–97, to France 1998–2001; Perm. Rep. to UN, New York 2001–; Commdr Légion d'honneur. *Address:* Permanent Mission of Bulgaria to the UN, 11 East 84th Street, New York, NY 10028, USA (Office). *Telephone:* (212) 737-4790 (Office). *Fax:* (212) 472-9865 (Office). *E-mail:* bulgaria@un.int (Office). *Website:* www.un.int/bulgaria (Office).

TAFT, Bob, JD, MA; American politician; b. 8 Jan. 1942; m. Hope Taft; one d.; ed Yale, Princeton and Cincinnati Univs.; rep. Ohio House of Reps. 1976–80, Commr Hamilton Co., Ohio 1981–90, Sec. of State of Ohio 1990–99, Gov. of Ohio 1999–; Republican. *Address:* Office of the Governor, 30th Floor, 77 South High Street, Columbus, OH 43215, USA.

TAHER, Abdul Hadi, PhD; Saudi Arabian government official; b. 1930, Medina; ed Ain Shams Univ., Cairo and Univ. of Calif.; entered Saudi Arabian Govt service 1955; Dir-Gen. Ministry of Petroleum and Mineral Resources 1960; Gov., Gen. Petroleum and Mineral Org. (PETROMIN), Riyadh 1962–86; Man. Dir Saudi Arabian Fertilizers Co. (SAFCO) 1966–76, Jeddah Oil Refinery 1970–; Chair. Arab Maritime Petroleum Transport Co. –1981; Dir Arabian American Oil Co. (ARAMCO), Saudi Govt Railways Corpn; Trustee, Coll. of Petroleum and Minerals; mem. Industrial Research and Devt Center, Saudi Arabia; Hon. mem. American Soc. of Petroleum Engineers. *Publications:* Income Determination in the International Petroleum Industry 1966, Development and Petroleum Strategies in Saudi Arabia (Arabic) 1970, Energy—A Global Outlook 1981; lectures and papers on econ. and petroleum affairs. *Address:* c/o General Petroleum and Mineral Organization (PETROMIN), P.O. Box 757, Riyadh, Saudi Arabia.

TAILLANDIER, François Antoine Georges, MA; French writer; b. 20 June 1955, Chamalières; s. of Henri Taillandier and Denise Ducher; three c.; teacher 1980–83; full-time writer 1984–, also contrib. Le Figaro (newspaper), La Montagne (newspaper), L'Humanité (newspaper), L'Atelier du Roman (periodical) and Revue des Deux Mondes (periodical); Prix Roger Nimier 1992, Prix de la critique Acad. française 1997; Grand Prix du roman Acad. française 1999. *Publications:* (novels) Personnages de la rue du Couteau 1984, Tott 1985, Benoît ou les contemporains obscurs 1986, Les clandestins (Prix Jean-Freustié) 1990, Les nuits racine, Mémoires de Monte-Cristo 1994, Des hommes qui s'éloignent 1997, Anielka 1999, Le cas gentile 2001; (essays) Jorge Luis Borges 1993, Aragon 1997; Tous les secrets de l'avenir 1996, Journal de Marseille 1999, N6, la route de l'Italie 1999, Les parents lâcheurs 2001. *Address:* Editions Stock, 31 rue de Fleurus, 75006 Paris, France (Office).

TAILLIBERT, Roger René; French architect; b. 21 Jan. 1926, Châtres-sur-Cher; s. of Gaston Taillibert and Melina Benoit; m. Béatrice Pfister 1965; one d.; ed schools in Toulouse, Dreux, Argenton-sur-Creuse, Tours, Vaureal and Ecole Nat. des Beaux-Arts, Paris; own practice 1963–; Curator Grand Palais des Champs-Elysées 1977–82, of Palais de Chaillot 1983–86; Pres. Taillibert Gulf Int., USA; mem. Acad. d'architecture 1974–; mem. Acad. des Beaux-Arts, Inst. de France, Acad. des Sports, Royal Soc. of Arts; Commdr Légion d'honneur, Commdr, Ordre nat. du Mérite, Officier des Palmes Académiques, Commdr des Arts et des Lettres, Chevalier du Mérite industriel et commercial. *Main works:* Olympic Complex (Parc des Sports, indoor sports hall, swimming pool), Montréal, Canada; Olympic swimming pool, Luxembourg; Nat. Geographic Centre, Amman, Jordan; Officers' Club, Abu Dhabi, UAE; sports complex, Baghdad, Guests' Palace, Bahrain, univ. bldgs., Sousse, Gabès, Tunisia, sports facilities, Cameroon, sports and golf club houses, Yamoussoukro and Abidjan, Côte d'Ivoire; in France: School of Pharmacy, Toulouse, Coca Cola plant, Grigny, pharmaceutical lab. P. Fabre, Castres, DAF plant, Survilliers, skiing and mountaineering nat. school, Chamonix, Parc des Princes stadium, Paris, Nat. Inst. for Sports and Physical Educ., Paris, pre-Olympic centre, Font-Romeu, nuclear plants Penly and Civaux, swimming complex at Nogent-sur-Oise 1995; Lycée Raspail, Paris 1995, Commercial and residential complex, St-Quentin-en-Yvelines 1995; studies for projects in Iraq and Lebanon; feasibility studies for projects in Argentina and Uruguay (hotels, sports facilities, leisure parks, etc.). *Publications:* Montréal—Jeux Olympiques 1976, Construire l'avenir 1977, Roger Taillibert (autobiog.) 1978. *Leisure interests:* photography, music, painting. *Address:* Institut de France, 23 quai Conti, 75006 Paris; 163 rue de la Pompe, 75116 Paris, France. *Telephone:* 1-47-04-29-92. *Fax:* 1-42-27-37-71. *E-mail:* roger.taillibert@free.fr, roger.taillibert@online.fr (Office).

TAIPALE, Vappu Tuulikki, DM; Finnish politician and psychiatrist; b. 1 May 1940, Vaasa; m. 1965; two s. two d.; psychiatrist, Aurora Youth Polyclinic 1970–74; Paediatric Clinic 1975–79; Asst Prof. of Child Psychiatry, Kuopio Univ. 1980–83, Tampere Univ. 1983–; First Minister of Social Affairs and Health July 1982–May 1983, Second Minister 1983–84; Dir-Gen. Nat. Bd of Social Welfare 1984–90; Dir-Gen. Nat. Agency for Welfare and Health 1991–92, Nat. Research and Devt Centre for Welfare and Health 1992–; Chair. COST A5 Ageing and Tech. Inst. Soc. for Gerontech., EAG Key Action 6, EU 5th FP; mem. SDP; mem. UNU Council 2001–. *Address:* STAKES National Research and Development Centre for Welfare and Health, Lintulahaenkuja 4, P.O. Box 220, 00531 Helsinki, Finland. *Telephone:* (9) 39672011. *Fax:* (9) 39672417. *E-mail:* vappu.taipale@stakes.fi. (Office). *Website:* www.stakes.fi. (Office).

TAIT, Alan A., PhD; British international civil servant, academic and consultant; b. 1 July 1934, Edinburgh; s. of Stanley Tait and Margaret Anderson; m. Susan Somers 1963; one s.; ed Heriots School, Univs. of Edinburgh and Dublin; Lecturer Trinity Coll., Dublin Univ. 1959–70, Fellow 1967, Sen. Tutor 1968; Prof. of Money and Finance Univ. of Strathclyde 1970–76; Visiting Scholar IMF 1971; Consultant to Sec. of State for Scotland 1972–76; Adviser to Pakistan Taxation Comm. 1973, Chief Fiscal Analysis Div., IMF 1975–82, Dep. Dir Fiscal Affairs Dept 1982–94, Dir of Geneva Office 1994–98; Co-Chair. Working Group, WHO Cttee on Macroecons. and Health 2000–02; mem. Review Cttee GAVI 2003; Hon. Fellow Trinity Coll. Dublin 1996; Hon. Prof. Univ. of Kent at Canterbury 1999. *Publications:* Taxation of Personal Wealth 1967, Economic Policy in Ireland (ed. with J. Bristow) 1968, Value-Added Tax 1988; contribs to numerous academic journals on public finance and macroecons. *Leisure interest:* painting. *Address:* Cramond House, Harnet Street, Sandwich, Kent, CT13 9ES, England. *Telephone:* (1304) 621038 (Home). *E-mail:* alantait@lineone.net (Home).

TAIT, James Francis, PhD, FRS; British/American scientist; b. 1 Dec. 1925, Stockton-on-Tees; s. of H. Tait and C. L. Brotherton; m. Sylvia A. S. Wardropper 1956; ed Univ. of Leeds; Lecturer in Medical Physics, Middx Hospital Medical School 1947–57, Joel Prof. of Medical Physics 1970–82, Dir Biophysical Endocrinology Unit 1970–85; External Scientific Staff, MRC

1955–58; Sr Scientist, Worcester Foundation, USA 1958–70; Prof. Emer., Univ. of London 1982–; Hon. DSc (Hull) 1979; Reichstein Award, Int. Soc. of Endocrinology 1976, CIBA Award, American Heart Asscn for Hypertension Research 1977, Dale Medal, Soc. for Endocrinology 1979, R. Douglas Wright Lecturer, Melbourne 1989. *Publications:* numerous papers on medical physics and endocrinology. *Leisure interests:* gardening, walking, chess, photography. *Address:* Moorlands, Main Road, East Boldre, Nr. Brockenhurst, Hants., SO42 7WT, England. *Telephone:* (1590) 626312. *Fax:* (1590) 626312. *E-mail:* jftait@globalnet.co.uk (Home). *Website:* www.users.globalnet.co.uk/~jftait (Home).

TAIT, Marion, OBE; British ballet mistress and dancer; b. 7 Oct. 1950, London; d. of Charles Tait, OBE and Betty Hooper; m. David Morse 1971; ed Royal Acad. of Dancing and Royal Ballet School; joined Royal Ballet School aged 15, graduating to Royal Ballet's touring co. (later known as Sadler's Wells Royal Ballet, now Birmingham Royal Ballet); Prin. dancer 1974; danced all the classics and other prin. roles including Juliet, Elite Syncopations, Las Hermanas, The Invitation, Hobson's Choice, The Dream, The Burrow, Lizzie Borden in Fall River Legend and Hagar in Pillars of Fire; created many roles for Kenneth MacMillan and David Bintley; guest appearances worldwide; Ballet Mistress (to both company and students), and still performs character roles, Birmingham Royal Ballet 1995–; Dancer of Year 1994; Evening Standard Ballet Award 1994. *Leisure interest:* needlework. *Address:* Birmingham Royal Ballet, Thorp Street, Birmingham, B5 4AU, England. *Telephone:* (121) 245-3500.

TAITT, Branford Mayhew, LLB, MPA; Barbadian politician; b. 15 May 1938; m. Marjorie C. Taitt (deceased); one s. two d.; ed Univ. of West Indies, New York Univ. and Brooklyn Coll., New York; Cable and Wireless 1954–62; Conf. Officer, UN Secr. 1962–65; U.S. Rep. Barbados Industrial Devt Corpn 1965–67; mem. Barbados Del. to UN 1966–71; Consul-Gen. of Barbados, New York 1967–71; mem. Barbados Senate 1971–76; Minister of Trade, Industry and Commerce, of Tourism and Industry 1986–88, of Health 1988–93, of Foreign Affairs 1993–94; Pres. Democratic Labour Party 1978–84; fmr part-time Lecturer in Law, Univ. of W Indies, Cave Hill, Barbados and visiting or guest lecturer at univs. and colls. in USA. *Publications:* over 200 articles in newspapers and periodicals. *Address:* 10 Stanmore Crescent, Black Rock, St Michael, Barbados (Home). *Telephone:* 424-0363 (Office); 424-4113. *Fax:* 424-5436. *E-mail:* hontaitt@cariaccess.com (Home).

TAITTINGER, Anne-Claire; French business executive; d. of Jean Taittinger (q.v.) and Corinne Deville; m.; two s.; ed Inst. d'Etudes Politiques de Paris; fmr urban planner; fmrly held positions within several Soc. du Louvre cos, Head Soc. du Louvre 1997–; Dir Dexia. *Address:* Société du Louvre, 58 boulevard Gouvion Saint-Cyr, 75858 Paris cedex 17, France.

TAITTINGER, Jean; French politician and vintner; b. 25 Jan. 1923, Paris; s. of Pierre Taittinger and Gabrielle Guillet; m. Marie Corinne Deville 1948; three s. two d.; ed Coll. Stanislas, Paris; Dir Champagne Taittinger 1946, Vice-Chair. 1958–94, Chair. 1994–; Deputy for Marne, Nat. Ass. 1958–73; Mayor of Rheims 1959–77; Nat. Sec. UNR-UDT (Union Démocratique du Travail) 1967; mem. Exec. Office and Nat. Treas. UDR Feb.-Oct. 1968, Deputy Sec.-Gen. 1974–76; Vice-Pres. Finance Comm. of Nat. Ass. 1967–68, Pres. 1968–71; Sec. of State, Ministry of Finance and Econ. Affairs 1971–73; Minister of Justice 1973–74; Minister of State for Justice March–May 1974; Chair Imprimerie Union Républicaine 1960, Soc. du Louvre 1977, Soc. des Hôtels Concorde 1978–90, Cofidev 1979, Société Deville 1979, Société Hôtel-ière Martinez 1981, Banque Privée de Dépôt et de Crédit 1987; Vice-Chair. Société Taittinger 1947, Société Hôtelière Lutetia Concorde 1980–; Dir Banque de l'Union Occidentale 1976–85, Banque Worms 1978–82, Etablisse-ments VQ Petersen 1979–84; Pres., Dir-Gen. Banque du Louvre 1987–90 (Hon. Pres. 1990–), Cie Cristalleries de Baccarat 1992–94, Hon. Pres. 1994–; Dir Gen. Compagnie Financière Taittinger 1989–94, Chair. 1994–2000; Pres. Supervisory Council Euro Disneyand SA 1989–95; Vice-Chair. Deville SA 1993–95. *Leisure interest:* breeding basset hounds. *Address:* Compagnie Financière Taittinger, 58 boulevard Gourion Saint-Cyr, 75017 Paris (Office); Cristallerie de Baccarat, 30 bis rue de Paradis, 75010 Paris, France.

TAKABWEBWE, Michael, LLB; I-Kiribati lawyer; b. 11 Nov. 1945, Tabi-teuea North; s. of Teababa Taumeang and Nei Ana Neaua; m. Tebaniman Tito 1979; three d.; ed Univ. of Melbourne, Australia; State Advocate 1979–81, Sr State Advocate 1981–83; Attorney-Gen. of Kiribati 1983–2002; legal adviser to govt on contracts with foreign cos and orgs 1994–2002; mem. Parl. and Cabinet 1983–; apptd Puisne Judge 2002–(05); Judge High Court of Kitibati 2002–(05); Rep. to Commonwealth Law Ministers Meetings 1986, 1990, 1993, 1996; Rep. to Int. Bar Asscn Meeting, Fiji 2002. *Publications include:* Kiribati, Asia–Pacific Constitutional Yearbook 1995. *Address:* Justice's Chambers, High Court Kiribati, POB, Betio, Tarawa, Kiribati (Office). *Telephone:* (686) 26007 (Office); (686) 21849 (Home). *Fax:* (686) 26149 (Office). *E-mail:* michael.j@tskl.net.ki (Office).

TAKÁCS-NAGY, Gábor; Hungarian violinist; b. 17 April 1956, Budapest; s. of László Takács-Nagy and Matild Pataki; m. Lesley (née Townson) de Senger 1991; two d.; ed Béla Bartók Conservatory and Franz Liszt Music Acad. of Budapest; f. Takács String Quartet 1976, Takács Piano Trio 1996; concert tours from 1980 every year throughout Europe, every other year in Australia, USA, Japan, South America; Leader, Festival Orchestra of Budapest 1993–99; Prof. Conservatoire de Musique, Geneva 1997–; Acad. of Music, Sion 1998–; first prize Evian competition 1977, Menuhin competition (Ports-

mouth) 1981, Scholarship award, Banff School of Fine Arts, Liszt Prize 1983. *Leisure interests:* sport, theatre. *Address:* Case postale 186, 1245 Collonge-Bellerive, Switzerland. *Telephone:* (22) 752-55-68. *Fax:* (22) 752-55-68.

TAKAGAKI, Tasuku; Japanese banker; b. 1928, Tokyo; m.; two d.; ed Univ. of Tokyo; joined The Bank of Tokyo Ltd (merged with Mitsubishi Bank Ltd 1996, now Bank of Tokyo-Mitsubishi Ltd) 1953, Gen. Man. Int. Investment Div. 1975–76, mem. Bd 1979–, Dir and Gen. Man. Planning and Personnel Div. 1979–82, Resident Man. Dir for Europe 1982–84, Man. Dir Head Office 1984, Sr Man. Dir 1986, Deputy Pres. 1989, Pres. 1990–98, Chair. of Bd 1998–, Sr Adviser 2000–; Deputy Treas. Asian Devt Bank 1966–71; Gran Cruz, Orden Nacional al Mérito (Colombia), Medal of Honour with Blue Ribbon (Japan), Grã-Cruz, Ordem do Mérito Agrícola, Comercial e Industrial (Por-tugal), Commdr Orden del Libertador, Venezuela. *Address:* 7-1 Marunouchi 2-chome, Chiyoda-ku, Tokyo 100-8388, Japan (Office). *Telephone:* (3) 3240-1111 (Office). *Website:* www.btm.co.jp (Office).

TAKAHASHI, Naoko; Japanese athlete; b. 5 June 1972, Gifu; ed Osaka Univ.; began career with life insurance co., later becoming athlete sponsored by Sekisui Chemical Co.; won marathon, Asian Games, Bangkok 1998; Olympic Gold Medal winner, Sydney Sept. 2000; first woman to run marathon in under 2 hours 20 minutes (2 hours 19 minutes 46 seconds), Berlin Sept. 2001; top award in world road running, AIMS/ASICS World Athlete of Year, 2001. *Address:* c/o Sekisui Chemical Company, 4-4 Nishitenma 2-chome, Kita-ku, Osaka 530-8565, Japan (Office).

TAKAHASHI, Tomoko, BA; Japanese artist; b. 1966, Tokyo; ed Tama Art Univ., Tokyo, Goldsmiths Coll., Slade School of Fine Art; Assoc. Research Student, Goldsmiths Coll. 1996–; solo and group exhbns. in both Europe and USA; Seventh East Award 1997. *Solo exhibitions include:* Hales Gallery, London, The Drawing Center, New York, Entwistle, London 1999, Grant Selwyn, LA 1999. *Group exhibitions include:* EAST Int. Norwich 1997, Gonzo, London 1997, Generation Z, PS1, New York 1999, New Neurotic Realism, Saatchi Gallery, London 1999. *Address:* c/o Entwistle Gallery, 6 Cork Street, London, W.1 (Office). *Telephone:* (20) 7734-6440 (Office).

TAKAMATSU, Shin, PhD; Japanese architect; b. 5 Aug. 1948, Shimane Pref.; s. of Toshio Takamatsu and Yuriko Takamatsu; m. Toshiko Hariguchi 1970; two d.; ed Ohda High School, Kyoto Univ.; Prin. Architect, Shin Takamatsu Architects and Assocs., Kyoto 1980; mem. Nihon Kenchiku Gakai (Japan Architecture Inst.) 1989–, Japan Inst. of Architecture 1993–; work exhibited Venice Biennale 1985, Krin Plaza, Paris 1988, Killing Moon, London 1988, Nîmes 1989, Berlin 1991, San Francisco Museum of Modern Art 1992, Kyoto Municipal Museum of Art 1995; Hon. Fellow AIA 1995; several prizes and awards including Japan Architects Asscn Prize 1984, Venice Biennale Prize 1985, Second Int. Interior Design Award 1987, Architectural Inst. of Japan Prize 1989, Grand Prize, Journal of Japanese Soc. of Commercial Space Designers 1989, Architectural Inst. of Japan Prize 1990, Kyoto Pref. Merito-rious Cultural Service Award 1994, Art Encouragement Prize, Ministry of Educ. 1996, Public Architecture Prize 1998. *Publications:* Works-Shin Taka-matsu 1984, Architecture and Nothingness 1996, To the Poetic Space 1998. *Address:* Shin Takamatsu Architects and Associates, 195 Jobodaiin-cho Takeda, Fushimi-ku, Kyoto 612, Japan. *Website:* www.takamatsu.co.jp (Office).

TAKEI, Yasuo; Japanese financial services executive; m.; three c.; worked in family liquor store and later as vegetable vendor in Omiya, Saitama; using savings as capital, began offering loans to individuals 1966; f. Takefuji Corpn 1966, later Chair., CEO and Pres., Rep. Chair. and CEO 2002–; Hon. Founder Gregorian Univ. 1996; Ordine di San Silvestro. *Address:* Takefuji Corpo-ration, 15-1 Nishi-Shinjuku 8-chome, Shinjuku-ku, Tokyo 163-8654, Japan (Office). *E-mail:* info@takefuji.co.jp (Office). *Website:* www.takefuji.co.jp (Office).

TAKEMURA, Masayoshi; Japanese politician; b. 26 Aug. 1934, Youkaichi City, Shiga Pref.; ed Tokyo Univ.; joined Ministry of Home Affairs 1962, at Saitama Pref. offices 1967–70, Research Counsellor to Minister of Home Affairs 1970–71; Mayor of Youkaichi City, Shiga Pref. 1971–74, Gov. of Shiga Pref. 1974–86; Pres. New Party Sakigake (Harbinger) 1993–96; Minister of State, Chief Cabinet Sec. 1993–94; Minister of Finance 1994–96; mem. House of Reps., Shiga Pref. 1986–2000 (Chair. Environment Cttee).

TAKENAKA, Heizo, PhD; Japanese politician; b. 3 March 1951; ed Hitotsu-bashi Univ. and Osaka Univ.; joined Japan Devt Bank 1973, Research Inst. of Capital Formation 1977; Visiting Scholar Harvard Univ., USA 1981, Visiting Assoc. Prof. 1989; Visiting Scholar Univ. of Pennsylvania 1981; Assoc. Prof. Faculty of Econs. Osaka Univ. 1987; Visiting Fellow, Inst. of Int. Econs 1989; Assoc. Prof. Faculty of Policy Man., Keio Univ. 1990, Prof. 1996; Dir The Tokyo Foundation (fmrly Global Foundation for Research and Scholarship) 1997, Exec. Dir 1998, Pres. 1999; mem. Econ. Strategy Council 1998, IT Strategy Council 2000, IT Strategy Headquarters 2001; Minister of State (Econ. and Fiscal Policy, Information Tech. Policy), Cabinet Office 2001–, also Financial Services Agency 2002–. *Publications:* in Japanese: The Economics of Business Investment 1984, The Macroeconomic Analysis of External Imbalances 1987, The Economics of US–Japan Friction 1991, The Globalization of the Japanese Economy and Corporate Investment 1993, Wealth of People 1994, The Economy in Which Fast Movers Win 1998; in English: Contemporary Japanese Economy and Economic Policy 1991; pop-ular writing includes a cartoon book explaining economics. *Address:* Minister of State for Economic and Fiscal Policy, Cabinet Office, 1-6-1, Nagato-cho, Chiyoda-ku, Tokyo 100-8914, Japan (Office). *Telephone:* (3) 5253-2111. *Website:* www.cao.go.jp.

TAKRITI, Saddam Hussein (see Saddam Hussein).

TALAGI, Sisilia, BSc; Niuean diplomatist and civil servant; b. 27 Feb. 1952, Niue; one s. three d.; food technologist 1976–81, food industry trainer 1981–83; Agric. Projects Man. and Exports Promoter 1983–88; Dir Agric. and Fisheries 1988–94; Asst Head of External Affairs 1994–99; Sec. to the Govt 1999–. *Leisure interests:* research reading, golf, watching sports. *Address:* Secretary to the Government, P.O. Box 40, Alofi (Office); P.O. Box 175, Alofi, Niue (Home). *Telephone:* (683) 4200 (Office); (683) 4227 (Home). *Fax:* (683) 4232 (Office). *E-mail:* seegov.premier@mail.gov.nu (Office).

TALAKE, Koloa; Tuvaluan politician; b. 1934; Dir Tuvalu TV Corpn; fmr Minister for Finance; fmrly special ministerial adviser to Govt; Prime Minister of Tuvalu 2001–02. *Address:* c/o Office of the Prime Minister, Vaiaku, Funafuti, Tuvalu (Office).

TALAL, Walid ibn; Saudi Arabian prince and business executive; s. of Prince Talal ibn Abdul Aziz al-Saud and Princess Mona El-Solh; ed Menlo Coll., Syracuse Univ., New York; Chair. United Saudi Bank 1988–99; f. Kingdom Holding Co.; investments in Citigroup Inc., News Corpn, Euro Disney SCA, Planet Hollywood chain of restaurants, Apple Computers. *Address:* c/o United Saudi Bank, P.O. Box 25895, Riyadh 11476, Saudi Arabia (Office).

TALAL IBN ABDUL AZIZ AL-SAUD, HRH Prince; Saudi Arabian politician and international official; b. 1934; s. of the late King Abdul Aziz ibn Saud; ed Prince's School, Royal Palace, Riyadh; positions held in his early 20s include responsibility for the Royal Palaces, Minister of Communications; fmr Minister of Economy and Finance; fmr Amb. to France; f. Riyadh's first girls' school 1957, first pvt. hosp. 1957 and Mecca's first coll. for boys 1957; passport cancelled 1962; exile in Egypt (for activities promoting human rights and democracy); returned to Saudi Arabia 1964; fmr Special Envoy, UNICEF; Pres. Arab Gulf Programme for UN Devt Orgs. "AGFUND"; Pres. Arab Council for Childhood and Devt. *Leisure interests:* history, amateur radio, swimming. *Address:* 7 rue Beaujon, 75008 Paris, France. *Telephone:* 1-43-80-22-97.

TALBOTT, Strobe; American journalist and politician; b. 25 April 1946, Dayton, Ohio; s. of Nelson S. Talbott and Josephine Large; m. Brooke Lloyd Shearer 1971; two s.; ed Hotchkiss School, Connecticut, Yale and Oxford Univs.; joined Time magazine; Diplomatic Corresp., White House Corresp., Eastern Europe Corresp., Washington Bureau Chief 1984–89, Ed.-at-Large 1989–94; Amb.-at-Large State Dept Feb.–Dec. 1993; Deputy Sec. of State 1994–2001; Pres. The Brookings Inst. 2002–; Rhodes Scholar Oxford Univ. 1969; Dir Carnegie Endowment for Int. Peace; mem. Council on Foreign Relations. *Publications:* Khrushchev Remembers 1970, Khrushchev Remembers: The Last Testament (jtly.) 1974, Endgame: The Inside Story of Salt II 1979, Deadly Gambits: The Reagan Administration and the Stalemate in Nuclear Arms Control 1984, The Russians and Reagan 1984, Reagan and Gorbachev (jtly.) 1987, The Master of the Game: Paul Nitze and the Nuclear Peace 1988, At the Highest Levels: The Inside Story of the End of the Cold War (jtly.) 1993, The Age of Terror: America and The World After September 11 (co-ed.) 2001, The Russia Hand: A Memoir of Presidential Diplomacy 2002. *Address:* The Brookings Institution, 1775 Massachusetts Avenue, NW, Washington, DC 20036, USA. *Telephone:* (202) 797-6000. *Fax:* (202) 797-6004. *Website:* www.brookings.edu.

TALENT, Jim (James Matthes); American politician; b. 18 Oct. 1956, Des Peres, Mo.; s. of Milton Talent and Marie Talent (née Matthes); m. Brenda Talent 1984; one s. two d.; ed Kirkwood High School, Washington Univ., St Louis and Univ. of Chicago; clerk to Judge of U.S. Court of Appeals 1982–83; elected (Republican) to Mo. House of Reps. 1984–92, later Minority Leader –1992; elected to Congress (Second Dist, Mo.) 1992–2000, later Asst Minority Leader; mem. Armed Services Cttee 1992–2000, Small Business Cttee 1992–2000 (Chair. 1997), Educ. Cttee; Senator from Missouri 2003–; Arnold J. Lien Prize for Most Outstanding Undergrad. in Political Science, Nat. Asscn of Women Business Owners' Nat. Public Policy Award (first male recipient), named Legislator of the Year by Dept of Missouri Veterans of Foreign Wars, Int. Franchise Asscn and Ind. Electrical Contractors, Vietnam Veterans of America's Lifetime Achievement Award 2000. *Address:* Office of the Senator from Missouri, U.S. Senate Buildings, Washington, DC 20510 (Office); 9433 Olive Blvd., St. Louis, MO 63132, USA (Home). *Telephone:* (314) 453-0344 (Home). *Fax:* (314) 453-0805 (Home).

TALIB, Maj.-Gen. Naji; Iraqi politician and soldier; b. 1917; ed Iraqi Staff Coll. and Sandhurst, England; Mil. Attaché, London 1954–55; Commdr Basra Garrison 1957–58; Minister of Social Affairs 1958–59; lived abroad 1959–62; Minister of Industry 1963–64; mem. UAR-Iraq Jt Presidency Council 1964–65; Minister of Foreign Affairs 1964–65; Prime Minister and Minister of Petroleum Affairs 1966–67.

TALIBANI, Jalal; Iraqi (Kurdish) politician; b. 1933, Kelkan; ed high schools in Erbil and Kirkuk; f. secret student asscn at age of 13; mem. Kurdish Democratic Party 1947, elected to Cen. Cttee 1951; denied admission to medical school by govt due to political activities; allowed to enter law school 1953; forced to go into hiding to escape arrest for founding and becoming Sec.-Gen. of Kurdistan Student Union 1956; following overthrow of Hashemite

monarchy, returned to law school 1958; pursued career as journalist and ed. of Khabat and Kurdstan; mil. service 1959, later Commdr of tank unit; organized and led Kurdish revolt against Govt in Mawat, Rezan and Karadagh regions 1961; rep. Kurdish leadership on numerous diplomatic missions in Europe and Middle East 1960s; Founder and Sec.-Gen. Patriotic Union of Kurdistan 1975–. *Address:* c/o European Office, Patriotic Union of Kurdistan, POB 210213, 10502 Berlin, Germany (Office). *E-mail:* puk@puk.org (Office). *Website:* www.puk.org (Office).

TALLAWY, Mervat; Egyptian diplomatist and politician; b. 1 Dec. 1937, Menya; d. of Mehani Tallawy and Soraya Abdel-Hamid; m. Dr. Ali Abdel-Rahman Rahmy 1964; one d.; ed American Univ. Cairo, Inst. for Diplomatic Studies, Cairo and Grad. Inst. of Int. Studies, Geneva; joined Ministry of Foreign Affairs 1963; served Geneva, New York and Caribbean countries, Vienna and Tokyo; Deputy Dir UN Inst. for the Advancement of Women 1982–85; Minister Plenipotentiary, Deputy Dir Dept of Int. Orgs. Ministry of Foreign Affairs 1985–88; Amb. to Austria and Resident Rep. to IAEA, UNIDO and UN Centre for Social and Humanitarian Affairs 1988–91; Dir of Int. Econ. Dept, Ministry of Foreign Affairs 1991; Asst Minister for Int. Political and Econ. Affairs 1992–93; Amb. to Japan 1993–97; Minister of Insurance and Social Affairs 1997–99; Asst UN Sec. for UNDP, Arab countries 1997; Sec.-Gen. Nat. Council for Women 2000; Exec. Sec. UN Econ. and Social Comm. for Western Asia (ESCWA) Feb. 2001–; Rapporteur-Gen. UN Conf. on Adoption of Int. Convention on Prevention of Illicit Drug Trafficking, Vienna 1988; mem. UN Cttee on Elimination of Discrimination against Women (CEDAW) (Chair. 1990–92); Chair. UN Comm. on Status of Women 1991–93; Chair. workshop on Women and Violence leading to adoption of UN Declaration on Elimination of Violence Against Women, Vienna 1992; Chair. Working Group on Health, UN Int. Conf. for the Advancement of Women, Beijing 1995; Head Egyptian Del. to Multilateral Middle East Peace Talks Working Group on Econ. Regional Co-operation, Brussels 1992, Paris 1992, Rome 1993 and to Steering Cttee of Multilateral Middle East Talks, Tokyo 1994; Head Egyptian Del. to UN World Conf. on Natural Disasters, Yokohama 1994; Del. to UN Environment Conf., Rio de Janeiro 1992, to UN Int. Conf. on Population and Devt, Cairo 1994; initiator of proposal leading to adoption of UN Declaration for the Protection of Women and Children in Time of Armed Conflicts 1974; mem. Club of Rome; Amb. of the Year (Austria) 1991. *Leisure interests:* theatre, classical music, walking, reading, painting. *Address:* UN House (ESCWA), P.O. Box 118575, Beirut, Lebanon (Office); 18 el-Mansour Mohammed St, Apt. 15, Zamalek, 11211, Cairo, Egypt (Home). *Telephone:* (1) 198-1301 (Office); (2) 735-8102 (Home). *Fax:* (1) 198-1515 (Office); (2) 735-8102 (Home).

TALLCHIEF, Maria; American ballet dancer; b. 24 Jan. 1925, Fairfax, Okla; d. of Ruth Porter Tallchief and Alexander Tallchief; m. 1st George Balanchine 1946; m. 2nd Henry D. Paschen 1956, one d.; studied with Bronislava Nijinska; joined Ballet Russe de Monte Carlo 1942; Prima Ballerina, New York City Ballet 1948–66; toured worldwide with the co., cr. numerous roles including Four Temperaments, Stravinsky's Firebird; Guest Prima Ballerina, American Ballet Theatre, touring USSR, Romania, Bulgaria and Greece 1960; Guest Star, Paris Opéra Ballet 1947; Guest Artist, Royal Danish Ballet, Copenhagen 1961; fmr teacher, School of American Ballet, New York; gave up performing career 1966; Dir of Ballet, Lyric Opera of Chicago; guest speaker on dance and dance educ. at several univs.; mem. Nat. Soc. of Arts and Letters; numerous hon. degrees; received Woman of the Year Award from Pres. Eisenhower 1953, Hon. Princess, Osage Indian Tribe 1953, Achievement Award, Women's Nat. Press Club 1953, Dance Educators American Award 1956, Dance Magazine Award 1960, Capezio Award 1965, Distinguished Service Award, Univ. of Okla 1972, Kennedy Center Honor 1996; inducted into Nat. Women's Hall of Fame 1996, Int. Women's Forum Hall of Fame 1997; Nat. Medal of Arts 1999. *Address:* Lyric Opera Ballet, 20 North Wacker Drive, Suite 860, Chicago, IL 60606 (Office); 48 Prospect, Highland Park, IL 60035, USA. *Fax:* (847) 266-8782.

TALLCHIEF, Marjorie; American ballerina; b. 1927; d. of the Chief of the Osages Indians; m. George Skibine 1947 (died 1981); two s.; ed Beverly Hills High School, Calif.; studied with Bronislava Nijinska; joined American Ballet Theatre; created role of Medusa in Undertow; Prima Ballerina, Ballet de Monte Carlo 1948; American Ballet Theater 1960; created leading roles in Somnambula, Concerto Barrocco, Les Biches, Boléro, Idylle, Prisoner of the Caucasus and Annabel Lee; Première Danseuse Etoile, Paris Opera 1957–; leading roles in The Firebird, Les Noces Fantastiques, Giselle, Conte Cruel, Concerto and numerous other ballets; Prima Ballerina, Hamburg State Opera 1965–; Chevalier du Nicham-Iftikar.

TALLING, John Francis, PhD, FRS; British freshwater biologist; b. 23 March 1929, Grange Town; s. of Frank Talling and Miriam Talling; m. Ida Björnsson 1959; one s. one d.; ed Sir William Turner's School, Coatham, Yorks., Univ. of Leeds and Univ. of London; Lecturer in Botany, Univ. of Khartoum 1953–56; Postdoctoral Fellow, Univ. of Calif. 1957; Biologist, Freshwater Biological Asscn, England 1958–89, Sr Research Fellow 1991–; Visiting Prof. Univ. of Lancaster 1992–98. *Publications:* Ecological Dynamics of Tropical Inland Waters (with J. Lemoalle) 1998; and about 80 scientific papers. *Leisure interests:* walking, archaeology. *Address:* Freshwater Biological Association, Ambleside, Cumbria, England. *Telephone:* (15394) 42468.

TALMACI, Leonid; Moldovan banker; b. 26 April 1954; m. Nina Talmaci 1977; one d.; ed Financial Banking Coll., Chişinău, Financial-Econ. Inst.

Leningrad (now St Petersburg); Prin. Economist Stroibank USSR 1984–88; Deputy Head Dept, Promstroibank USSR 1988, Chair. Energomash Bank 1988–91; Gov. Nat. Bank of Moldova 1991–. *Address:* National Bank of Moldova, 7 Renaşterii Avenue, 2006 Chişinău, Moldova (Office). *Telephone:* (2) 22-16-79 (Office). *Fax:* (2) 22-05-91 (Office). *Website:* www.bnm.org (Office).

TALMI, Igal, DrScNat; Israeli professor of physics; b. 31 Jan. 1925, Kiev, Ukraine (USSR); s. of Moshe Talmi and Lea (née Weinstein) Talmi; m. Chana (née Kivelewitz) Talmi 1949; one s. one d.; ed Herzlia High School, Hebrew Univ. of Jerusalem and Swiss Fed. Inst. of Tech.; served in Israeli Defence Forces 1947–49; Research Fellow Princeton Univ. 1952–54, Visiting Assoc. Prof. 1956–57, Visiting Prof. 1961–62, 1966–67; Prof. of Physics, Weizmann Inst. of Science 1958–, Prof. Emer.1995–, Head Dept of Nuclear Physics 1967–76, Dean Faculty of Physics 1970–84; mem. Israel Acad. of Sciences and Humanities 1963–, Chair. Div. of Sciences 1974–80; Weizmann Prize of the Tel Aviv Municipality 1962, Israel Prize (with A. de Shalit) 1965, Rothschild Prize, 1971, Hans A. Bethe Prize, American Physical Soc. 2000. *Publications:* Nuclear Shell Theory (with A. de Shalit) 1963, Simple Models of Complex Nuclei 1993, numerous Publs on theoretical nuclear physics. *Leisure interest:* bird watching. *Address:* Department of Particle Physics, The Weizmann Institute of Science, Rehovot 76100, Israel (Office). *Telephone:* 8-9342060 (Office); 8-9468166 (Home).

TALU, Umur E., BA ECON.; Turkish journalist; b. 7 Aug. 1957, Istanbul; s. of M. Muvakkar and G. Güzin; m. Şule Talu 1987; two d.; ed Galatasaray High School and Bosphorus Univ.; Educ. specialist, Railway Workers' Union 1977–78; Int. Econ. Cooperation Sec. Union of Municipalities 1978–80; Econ. Corresp. Günaydin (newspaper) 1980–82; Chief, Econ. Dept Günes (newspaper) 1982–83; Ed. with Cumhuriyet (newspaper) 1983–85; Chief, Econ. Dept Milliyet (newspaper) 1985–86, News Ed. 1986–87, 1988–92, Ed.-in-Chief 1992–94, columnist 1994–; News Ed. Hürriyet (newspaper) 1987–88; Freedom of the Press Award (Turkish Journalists' Assn) 1996. *Publications:* Social Democracy in Europe (co-author) 1985, Keynes (trans.) 1986, Mr Uguran's Post Office 1996. *Leisure interests:* sport, music, films. *Address:* Milliyet, Dogan Medya Centre, Bagcilar 344554, İstanbul, Turkey. *Telephone:* (212) 5056111. *Fax:* (212) 5056233.

TALWAR, Rana Gurvirendra Singh, BA; Indian banker; b. 22 March 1948; s. of R. S. Talwar and Veera Talwar; m. 1st Roop Som Dutt 1970 (divorced); one s. one d.; m. 2nd Renuka Singh 1995; one s.; ed Lawrence School, Sanawar, St Stephen's Coll., Delhi; exec. trainee, Citibank 1969–70, numerous operational, corp. and institutional banking assignments, India 1970–76, Group Head for Treasury and Financial Inst. 1976, Regional Man. for Eastern India 1977, Group Head of Treasury and Financial Insts. Group, Saudi American Bank, Jeddah 1978–80, Regional Consumer Business Man., Singapore, Malaysia, Indonesia, Thailand and India 1982–88, Div. Exec., Asia Pacific 1988–91, Exec. Vice-Pres. and Group Exec., Consumer Bank, Asia Pacific, Middle East and Eastern Europe 1991–95, Exec. Vice-Pres. Citicorp and Citibank, responsible for USA and Europe 1996–97; Group Exec. Dir Standard Chartered PLC 1997–98, CEO 1998–2001; Dir (non-exec.) Pearson PLC 2000–. *Leisure interests:* bridge, golf, tennis, travel. *Address:* c/o Standard Chartered Bank, 1 Aldermanbury Square, London, EC2V 7SB, England (Office).

TAM YIU CHUNG; Chinese trade unionist and government official; b. 15 Dec. 1949, Hong Kong; m. Lai Xiang Ming; two c.; ed Australian Nat. Univ., LSE, UK; trade union officer; Vice-Chair. Hong Kong Fed. of Trade Unions; Chair. Employees' Retraining Bd, Elderly Comm.; fmr mem. Preparatory Cttee for Hong Kong Special Admin. Region; mem. Exec. Council Hong Kong Special Admin. Region, Legis. Council Hong Kong Special Admin. Region, Vocational Training Council, Standing Comm. on Civil Service Salaries and Conditions of Service, Ind. Comm. Against Corruption Complaints Cttee, Services Promotion Strategy Unit; Vice-Chair. Democratic Alliance for Betterment of Hong Kong; Justice of the Peace; Hon. Life Fellow Inst. of Commercial Man., UK; Gold Bauhinia Star. *Address:* 12F SUP Tower, 83 King's Road, North Point, Hong Kong Special Administrative Region (Office); Executive Council Secretariat, 1st Floor, Main Wing, Central Government Offices, Central, Hong Kong Special Administrative Region, People's Republic of China. *Telephone:* 25286888 (Office). *Fax:* 25282326 (Office). *E-mail:* yctam@dab.org.hk (Office). *Website:* www.yctam.org (Office).

TAMARÓN, Marqués de; Santiago de Mora-Figueroa, 9th Marqués de Tamarón; Spanish diplomatist; b. 18 Oct. 1941, Jerez de la Frontera; s. of José de Mora-Figueroa, 8th Marqués de Tamarón and Dagmar Williams; m. Isabelle de Yturbe 1966; one s. one d.; ed Univ. of Madrid and Escuela Diplomática; Lt Spanish Marine Corps 1967; Sec. Embassy, Nouakchott 1968–70, Paris 1970–73; Banco del Noroeste 1974; Counsellor, Copenhagen 1975–80; Minister-Counsellor, Ottawa 1980–81; Pvt. Sec. to Minister of Foreign Affairs 1981–82; Head of Studies and Deputy Dir Escuela Diplomática 1982–88; Dir Inst. de Cuestiones Internacionales y Política Exterior (INCIPE) 1988–96; Dir Instituto Cervantes 1996–99; Amb. to UK 1999–; mem. Trilateral Comm. 1989–96; Commdr Order of Carlos III, Officier, Ordre nat. du Mérite (France), Commdr Order of Dannebrog, Commdr Order of Merit (Germany), Gran Cruz Mérito Naval (Spain). *Publications:* Pólvora con Aguardiente 1983, El Guirigay Nacional 1988, Trampantojos 1990, El Siglo XX y otras Calamidades 1993, El Peso de la Lengua Española en el Mundo

(co-author) 1995. *Leisure interests:* philology, mountain walking, gardening. *Address:* Spanish Embassy, 39 Chesham Place, London, SW1X 8SB, England. *Telephone:* (20) 7235-5555. *Fax:* (20) 7235-9905.

TAMAZAWA, Tokuichiro; Japanese politician; mem. House of Reps.; Dir.-Gen. Defence Agency, fmr Parl. Vice-Minister for Agric., Forestry and Fisheries, Minister 1999–2001. *Address:* c/o Ministry of Agriculture, Forestry and Fisheries, 1-2-1, Kasumigaseki, Chiyoda-ku, Tokyo 100-0013, Japan (Office).

TAMEN, Pedro, LLB; Portuguese foundation executive and poet; b. 1 Dec. 1934, Lisbon; s. of Mário Tamen and Emília Tamen; m. Maria da Graça Seabra Gomes 1975; two s. two d.; ed Lisbon Univ.; Dir Moraes Publishing House 1958–75; Pres. Portuguese PEN Club 1987–90; Trustee Calouste Gulbenkian Foundation, Lisbon 1975–2000; mem. Bd Portuguese Asscn of Writers; D. Diniz Prize 1981; Grand Prix for Translation 1990; Critics Award 1993; INAPA Prize for Poetry 1993, Nicola Prize for Poetry 1998, Press Poetry Prize 2000, PEN Club Poetry Prize 2000. *Publications:* 12 books of poetry since 1958; Tábua das Matérias (Collected Works) 1991, Depois de Ver 1995, Guião de Caronte 1997, Memória Indescritível 2000, Retábulo das Matérias 2001. *Address:* Rua Luís Pastor de Macedo, lote 25, 5° esq., 1750-157 Lisbon, Portugal (Home). *E-mail:* ptamen@mail.tdepac.pt (Home).

TAMM, Ditlev, DJur, DPhilR; Danish professor of legal history; b. 7 March 1946, Copenhagen; s. of Henrik Tamm and Lizzie Knutzen; m. Maria Pilar Lorenzo 1973 (separated 1987); two d.; ed Univ. of Copenhagen and in Germany and France; Prof. of Legal History, Univ. of Copenhagen 1978–; mem. Royal Danish Acad., Accad. Europea and several other Danish and int. scientific bds and cttees; Dr hc (Helsinki) 2000; A.S. Orsted Award 1974. *Publications:* Fra lovkyndighed til retsvidenskab 1976, Retsopgøret efter besaettelsen 1984, Roman Law 1997; several books and articles on Danish and European legal history. *Address:* Studiestraede 6, 1455 Copenhagen, Denmark (Office); Attemovevej 80a, 2870 Holte (Home). *Telephone:* 35-32-31-67 (Office); 45-80-43-66 (Home). *Fax:* 35-32-32-05 (Office). *E-mail:* ditlev .tamm@jur.ku.dk (Office).

TAMM, Peter; German publisher; b. 12 May 1928, Hamburg; s. of Emil Tamm; m. Ursula Weisshun 1958; one s. four d.; ed Univ. of Hamburg; Shipping Ed., Hamburger Abendblatt 1948–58; Man. Dir Ullstein GmbH (Publr) 1960–62, 1984; Man. Dir Bild-Zeitung 1962–64; Dir, Verlagshaus Axel Springer, Berlin 1964–70, mem. Exec. Bd 1970–82, Chair. Man. Bd 1982–91; Vice-Pres. Bundesverband Deutscher Zeitungsverleger 1980–90; now Propr Koehler/Mittler-Verlagsgruppe and Schiffahrtsverlages Hansa, Propr and Dir Scientific Inst. for Maritime and Naval History; mem. Royal Swedish Soc. of Maritime Sciences, Stockholm 1999; Bayerischer Verdienstorden, Grosses Bundesverdienstkreuz, Vasco da Gama Naval Medal 1998, Gold Ehrenkreuz der Bundeswehr 2001. *Publication:* Maler der See 1980. *Leisure interests:* model ships, marine books, maritime and naval history. *Address:* Elbchaussee 277, 22605 Hamburg, Germany. *Telephone:* (40) 821341 (Office). *Fax:* (40) 8226300 (Office).

TAMUERA, Tekiree; I-Kiribati politician; b. 16 Feb. 1940, Maiana; s. of Tamuera Timau and Era Iobi; m. Raratu Rouatu; three s.; ed King George V School, Tarawa Teachers Coll., Geelong Teachers Coll., Australia, South Devon Tech. Coll., UK; teacher; admin. officer; Chair. Public Services Comm.; currently Speaker of Parl. *Leisure interests:* cutting toddy, fishing. *Address:* Maneaba Ni Maungatabu, Bairiki, Tarawa (Office); Betio, Tarawa, Kiribati (Home). *Telephone:* (686) 21880 (Office); (686) 21175 (Home). *Fax:* (686) 21278 (Office). *E-mail:* mnm@tski.net.ki (Office).

TAN, Amy Ruth, MA, LHD; American writer; b. 19 Feb. 1952, Oakland, Calif.; d. of John Yuehhan and Daisy Ching (née Tu) Tan; m. Louis M. DeMattei 1974; ed San José State Univ., Calif., Dominican Coll., San Rafael; specialist in language devt Alameda Co. Asscn for Mentally Retarded 1976–80; Project Dir MORE, San Francisco 1980–81; freelance writer 1981–88; Best Fiction Award for The Joy Luck Club 1990 (Commonwealth Club and Bay Area Book Reviewers), Best American Essays Award 1991. *Film:* The Joy Luck Club (screenwriter, producer) 1993. *Publications:* The Joy Luck Club 1989, The Kitchen God's Wife 1991, The Moon Lady 1992, The Chinese Siamese Cat 1994, The Hundred Secret Senses 1995, The Bonesetter's Daughter 2000, numerous short stories and essays. *Address:* c/o Ballantine Publications Publicity, 201 East 50th Street, New York, NY 10022, USA.

TAN, Lucio; Philippine business executive; Chair. Philippine Airlines Inc. (fmrly Pres., CEO); has investments in banking, brewing and tobacco sectors. *Address:* Philippine Airlines Inc., PAL Corporate Communications Department, PAL Center, Ground Floor, Legaspi Street, Legaspi Village, Makati City, Metro Manila, The Philippines (Office). *Telephone:* (2) 8171234 (Office). *Fax:* (2) 8136715 (Office). *E-mail:* rgeccd@pal.com.ph (Office). *Website:* www .philippineair.com (Office).

TAN, Melvyn; British concert pianist and early music specialist; b. 13 Oct. 1956, Singapore; s. of Tan Keng Hian and Wong Sou Yuen; ed Anglo-Chinese School, Yehudi Menuhin School, Royal Coll. of Music; performs on historical keyboard instruments, which he has introduced to audiences round the world; has now extended repertory to include modern piano; performs regularly in music festivals in USA, Japan, Far East, Australia and throughout Europe. *Leisure interests:* swimming, wine, travelling without having to perform.

Address: c/o Valerie Barber Management, Suite 305, Mappin House, 4 Winsley Street, London, W1N 7AR, England. *Telephone:* (20) 7436-1115. *Fax:* (20) 7436-5090.

TAN DUN, MA; Chinese composer; b. 18 Aug. 1957, Changsha, Hunan; s. of Tan Xiang Qiu and Fang Qun Ying; m. Jane Huang 1994; one s.; ed Cen. Conservatory of Music, Beijing, Columbia Univ., USA; fmr violinist, Beijing Opera; Vice-Pres. Cen. Conservatory of Music 1978–; Second place, Weber Int. Chamber Music Composition Competition, Dresden 1983; numerous awards; works performed by maj. orchestras in China and at Aspen Music Festival, USA 1982, Dresden Music Festival 1983, Contemporary Chinese Composers' Festival, Hong Kong 1986 and by Cen. Philharmonic of China during US tour 1987; four recordings of his maj. orchestral works, oriental instrumental music, chamber music and electronic music issued by China Nat. Recording Co.; works also include 14 film scores for US and Chinese films, six modern ballet scores, music for several stage plays; orchestral piece commissioned by Inst. for Devt of Intercultural Relations Through the Arts, USA for Beijing Int. Music Festival 1988; Artistic Dir Fire Crossing Water Festival Barbican Centre 2000; Suntory Prize 1992, Grawemeyer Award 1998, Grammy Award 2001, Acad. Award 2001, British Acad. Film Award 2001, Classical Brit Contemporary Music Award 2001, Musical America Composer of the Year 2003. *Films:* Film Score: Fallen 1997, Crouching Tiger, Hidden Dragon 2001, Hero 2002. *Works include:* (operas) Nine Songs 1989, Marco Polo 1993–94, Peony Pavilion 1998, Tea 2002; (orchestral works) Li Sao 1979, Feng Ya Song 1983, Death and Fire: Dialogue with Paul Klee 1992, Symphony 1997, Water Passion after St Matthew 2000, The Map: Concerto for Cello, Video and Orchestra 2003; (experimental performance work) Soundshape 1990, Silent Earth 1991, Jo-Ha-Kyu 1992, The Pink 1993. *Leisure interests:* painting in ink, calligraphy. *Address:* 367 West 19th Street, Suite A, New York, NY 10011, USA (Office). *Telephone:* (212) 627-0410 (Office). *Fax:* (917) 606-0247 (Office). *E-mail:* tan_dun@hotmail.com (Office). *Website:* www.tandun.com (Office).

TAN HAOSHENG, PhD; Chinese academic; b. 1 Dec. 1916, Wujin Co., Jiangsu Prov.; m. Deng Tuantz 1969; ed Jiaotong Univ., California Inst. of Tech., Cornell Univ., USA; Faculty mem. Cornell Univ. 1950–53, Notre Dame Univ. 1953–56; Dir Therm Advanced Research 1957–62; Prof. Ill. Inst. of Tech. 1962–65; returned to China from USA 1965; Prof. Mechanics Inst. 1966–; mem. Acad. Sinica 1980–; mem. Standing Cttee 6th CPPCC 1984–88, 7th CPPCC 1989–93, 8th CPPCC 1993–98. *Address:* Mechanics Institute, Academia Sinica, Zhong Guan Cun, Beijing 100080, People's Republic of China.

TAN JIAZHEN; Chinese biologist; b. 15 Sept. 1909, Ningbo; s. of C. Y. Tan and M. Y. Yang; m. 1st M. Y. Fu 1932 (deceased); m. 2nd Dr. Y. F. Qiu 1973; three s. one d.; ed Calif. Inst. of Tech., USA; Research Asst Calif. Inst. of Tech. 1936–37; Prof. Nat. Chekiang Univ. 1937–52, Dean, Science Coll. 1950–52; Visiting Prof. Colo Univ. 1945–46; Dir Genetics Inst., Fudan Univ. 1961–90, Vice-Pres. 1961–82, Provost, School of Life Sciences 1986–90; Sr Research Fellow, Eleanor Roosevelt Inst. for Cancer Research, Denver, Colo 1984–; Vice-Chair. Scientific Advisory Cttee, China Center of Biotech. Devt 1984–; Pres. Chinese Soc. of Biological Eng 1994–; Pres., 18th Int. Congress of Genetics 1998; Editorial Consultant, The Scientist 1986–96; mem. Bd Dirs. Int. Council for Devt of Underutilized Plants 1983–96; mem., NGO Steering Cttee, UN Centre for Science and Tech. for Devt 1984–96, Panel of Scientific Advisers, ICGEB, UNIDO 1984–96, Advisory Editorial Bd of Journal of Genetics 1985–, Int. Advisory Cttee for Global Science Journal 1987; Vice-Pres. Genetics Soc. of China 1978, Pres. 1983–91; a Vice-Chair. China Democratic League 1983–97, Hon. Chair. 1997–; Vice-Chair. Shanghai Municipal People's Congress 1983–98; mem. Chinese Acad. of Sciences 1980; Foreign mem. Italian Nat. Acad. of Sciences of 40 1987; Foreign Assoc. NAS 1985; Fellow Third World Acad. of Sciences 1985; Founding mem. World Inst. of Sciences 1991; Hon. Pres. Ningbo Univ. 1986–, Shanghai Agric. Coll. 1988–2000; mem. Standing Cttee 8th CPPCC 1993–97; Hon. life mem. NY Acad. of Sciences 1999; Hon. DSc (York Univ.) 1984, (Univ. of Md) 1985; Distinguished Alumni Award, Calif. Inst. of Tech. 1983; Medal of Merit, Konstanz Universität, Fed. Repub. of Germany 1989; Hon. Citizen of State of Calif. 1990; Distinguished Scientist Prize, Qiushi Science and Tech. Foundation 1995. *Achievements:* newly discovered planet No. 1542 named after him 1999. *Address:* Genetics Institute, Fudan University, 220 Handan Road, Shanghai 200433, People's Republic of China. *Telephone:* 65642426 (Office); 59173668 (Home). *Fax:* 65648376.

TAN KENG YAM, Tony, PhD; Singaporean politician and banker; b. 7 Feb. 1940, Singapore; s. of the late Tan Seng Hwee and of Lim Neo Swee; m. Mary Chee Bee Kiang 1964; four c.; ed St Patrick's School, St Joseph's Inst., Univ. of Singapore, Mass. Inst. of Tech., USA and Univ. of Adelaide, Australia; Lecturer in Mathematics, Univ. of Singapore 1967–69; Sub-Man. Overseas Chinese Banking Corpn 1969, Gen. Man. 1978; MP 1979–; Sr Minister of State (Educ.) 1979; Minister of Educ. 1980, concurrently Vice-Chancellor, Nat. Univ. of Singapore; Minister for Trade and Industry, concurrently Minister in charge of Nat. Univ. of Singapore and Nanyang Tech. Inst. 1981–83; Minister of Finance 1983–85, of Educ. and Health Jan.–April 1985, for Trade and Industry 1985–86, of Educ. 1985–91; Chair. People's Action Party Cen. Exec. Cttee 1993; Chair. and CEO Oversea-Chinese Banking Corpn Ltd 1992; Deputy Prime Minister of Singapore Aug. 1995–, concurrently Minister of Defence 1995–2003, of Defence and Homeland Security 2003–. *Leisure interests:* swimming, golf and walking. *Address:* Ministry of

Defence and Homeland Security, Gombak Drive, off Upper Bukit Timah Road, Mindef Building, Singapore 7646119, Singapore. *Telephone:* 7688828. *Fax:* 7646119. *E-mail:* mfu@starnet.gov.sg (Office). *Website:* www.mindef.gov.sg (Office).

TANABE, Makoto; Japanese politician; b. 25 Feb. 1922, Maebashi City, Gunma Pref.; Chair. All Japan Postal Workers Union, Gunma District 1949; Pres. Workers Unions Council, Gunma Dist 1951–60; mem. Gunma Pref. Ass. 1955–60; mem. House of Reps. 1960–; Vice-Chair. Cen. Exec. Cttee Socialist Party of Japan (SPJ) 1982–83, Gen. Sec. 1983–86, Vice-Chair. 1990–91; Chair. Cen. Exec. Cttee Social Democratic Party of Japan (SDPJ) 1991–. *Address:* Social Democratic Party of Japan, 1-8-1, Nagata-cho, Chiyoda-ku, Tokyo, Japan. *Telephone:* (813) 3592-7512.

TANAKA, Koichi, BEng; Japanese chemist; b. 3 Aug. 1959, Toyama City; ed Tohoku Univ.; joined Cen. Research Lab., Shimadzu Corpn 1983, seconded to subsidiary Kratos Group PLC, UK 1992, joined R&D Dept of Analytical Instruments Div., Japan 1992, seconded to Shimadzu Research Lab. (Europe) Ltd, UK 1997, seconded to Kratos Group PLC, UK 1999, Asst Man. Life Science Lab., Shimadzu Corpn, Japan May 2002–; Nobel Prize in Chemistry (co-recipient) 2002. *Address:* Shimadzu Corporation, 1 Nishinkyoko Kuwabaracho, Nakagyou-ku, Kyoto 604-8511, Japan (Office). *Website:* www.shimadzu.com (Office).

TANAKA, Makiko; Japanese politician; b. 14 Jan. 1944; m. Naoki Tanaka; ed Waseda Univ.; fmr Deputy Dir-Gen. LDP Int. Bureau; Minister of State, Dir-Gen. Science and Tech. Agency 1994–95; Ministry of Foreign Affairs 2001–02; mem. House of Reps. for Nigata –2002 (resgnd); mem. House Cttee on Health and Welfare. *Address:* c/o Ministry of Foreign Affairs, 2-2-1, Kasumig aseki, Chiyoda-ku, Tokyo 100-8919, Japan.

TANAKA, Shoji, PhD; Japanese research director; b. 19 Sept. 1927, Odawara, Kanagawa; m. Kimiko Tanaka 1956; one s.; ed Univ. of Tokyo; lecturer, Faculty of Eng Univ. of Tokyo 1955, Assoc. Prof. 1958, Prof. 1968, Prof. Emer. 1988; Prof. Tokai Univ. 1988–93; Vice-Pres. Int. Superconductivity Tech. Center (ISTEC) 1988–; Dir Superconductivity Research Lab. (SRL) 1988–; Hon. DSc (Purdue Univ., USA) 1999; Purple Ribbon Medal 1990 and other awards. *Publications:* Research of Semiconductor Physics 1950–75, Research of Superconductivity 1975, High-Temperature Superconductivity 1991, Industry Technology are the World of the Future 1994. *Leisure interests:* golf, reading. *Address:* Superconductivity Research Laboratory, 1-10-13, Shinonome, Koto-ku, Tokyo 135-0062 (Office); 2-5-26, Ichigaya kaga-cho, Shinjuku-ku, Tokyo 162, Japan (Home). *Telephone:* (3) 3536-5700 (Office); (3) 3260-5500 (Home). *Fax:* (3) 3536-5717 (Office); (3) 3260-9398 (Home). *E-mail:* tanaka@istec.or.jp (Office). *Website:* www.istec.or.jp (Office).

TANAKA, Shun-ichi, DEng; Japanese professor of optics; b. 28 May 1926, Tokyo; m. Yuriko Tanaka 1957; two d.; ed The First Higher School, Univ. of Tokyo; Assoc., Univ. of Tokyo 1954–58, Lecturer 1958–60, Assoc. Prof. 1960–71, Prof. 1971–87; Prof. Faculty of Physics, Scientific Univ. of Tokyo 1987–; Ed.-in-Chief Japanese Journal of Applied Physics 1976–78; Ed. Journal of Modern Optics (Taylor & Francis) 1984–97; Postdoctoral Fellow NRC Canada 1963–64; Fellow Optical Soc. of America 1986–; Optics Paper Award 1960 and Micro-optics Award 1991, Japanese Soc. of Applied Physics, Distinguished Service Award, Minister of Int. Trade and Industry 1990. *Publications:* Dictionary of Optical Terms 1981, Handbook of Optical Engineering 1986, Fundamentals and Applications of Lightwave Sensing 1990, Dictionary of Optoelectronic Terms 1996; more than 70 scientific papers on optics, mostly in English. *Address:* Faculty of Sciences, Department of Applied Physics, Science University of Tokyo, 1-3 Kagurazaka, Shinjuku-ku, Tokyo 162-8601 (Office); 3-7-7 Zoshigaya, Toshima-ku, Tokyo 171-0032, Japan (Home). *Telephone:* (3) 3260-4271 (Office); (3) 3982-0023 (Home). *Fax:* (3) 3260-4772 (Office); (3) 3982-0023 (Home). *E-mail:* ystanaka@t.toshima.ne.jp (Home).

TANAKA, Yasuo; Japanese writer and politician; b. 1956; ed Univ. of Hitotsubashi; community activist, Kobe, following 1995 earthquake; elected first ind. Gov. of Nagano Pref. 2000–02. *Publications:* Nantonaku Kurisutaru (Somehow Crystal, Bungei Prize) 1983. *Address:* c/o Nagano Prefectural Government, 692-2 Habashita Minaminagano, Nagano City, 380-8570, Japan (Office).

TANAYEV, Nikolai; Kyrgyzstan politician; b. 1945; fmr First Deputy Prime Minister; Head of Special Comm. into deaths of demonstrators shot by police March 2002; Acting Prime Minister of Kyrgyzstan May 2002, Prime Minister June 2002–. *Address:* Office of the Prime Minister, 720003 Bishkek, Government House, Kyrgyzstan (Office). *Telephone:* (312) 22-56-56 (Office). *Fax:* (312) 21-86-27 (Office). *Website:* www.gov.kg (Office).

TANDJA, Col Mamadou; Niger politician and army officer (retd); fmr army officer, rank of Col; mem. Nat. Movt for the Devt of Soc. (MNSD); Pres. of Niger 1999–. *Address:* Office of the President, Niamey, Republic of Niger (Office). *Telephone:* 722381 (Office).

TANDJUNG, Akbar; Indonesian politician; b. 14 Aug. 1945, Sibolga, N Sumatera; m. R. A. Krissnina Maharani; four d.; ed Univ. of Indonesia; mem. Functional Devt Faction, House of Reps. 1977–88, Deputy Chair. 1997–, Speaker House of Reps. 1999–; State Minister for Youth and Sports 1988–93, for People's Housing 1993–98, for People's Housing and Settlement 1998, Minister State Sec. 1998; mem. People's Consultative Ass. 1992–97; Chair.

Cen. Bd GOLKAR Parity 1998–; Mahaputra Adiprandana Star. *Leisure interest:* swimming. *Address:* House of Representatives, Jalan Gatot Subroto 16, Jakarta, Indonesia (Office). *Telephone:* 5734469 (Office). *Fax:* 5723635 (Office). *E-mail:* akbartandjung@pr.go.id (Office). *Website:* www.dpr.go.id (Office).

TANFORD, Charles, PhD; American professor of physiology; b. 29 Dec. 1921, Halle, Germany; s. of Max Tanford and Charlotte Tanford; m. 1st Lucia Brown 1948 (divorced 1969); two s. one d.; m. 2nd Jacqueline Reynolds 1971; ed New York and Princeton Univs.; Lalor Fellow, Harvard Univ. 1947–49; Asst Prof., Univ. of Iowa 1949–54, Assoc. Prof. 1954–59, Prof. 1959–60; Prof. Duke Univ. 1960–70, James B. Duke Prof. of Physical Biochem. 1970–80, James B. Duke Prof. of Physiology 1980–88; mem. Whitehead Medical Research Inst. 1977–83; George Eastman Visiting Prof., Oxford Univ. 1977–78; Pres. Biophysical Soc. 1979; Walker-Ames Prof. Univ. of Washington 1979, Reilly Lecturer, Univ. of Notre Dame 1979; Guggenheim Fellow 1956–57; mem. NAS, American Acad. of Arts and Sciences; Alexander von Humboldt Prize 1984, Merck Award (American Soc. for Biochem. and Molecular Biology) 1992. *Publications:* Physical Chemistry of Macromolecules 1961, The Hydrophobic Effect 1973, Ben Franklin Stilled the Waves 1989, The Scientific Traveller (with J. A. Reynolds) 1992, Travel Guide to Scientific Sites of the British Isles (with J. A. Reynolds) 1995, Nature's Robots: A History of Proteins (with J. A. Reynolds) 2001; 200 scientific articles in various journals. *Leisure interests:* photography, hiking, travel. *Address:* Tarlswood, Back Lane, Easingwold, York, YO61 3BG, England. *Telephone:* (1347) 821029. *E-mail:* candj@dial.pipex.com (Home).

TANG, Pan-Pan, MA; Taiwanese broadcasting executive; b. 3 April 1942, Hunan Prov.; m. Helen Chao; one s. one d.; ed Political Warfare Coll. Taipei and S. Illinois Univ., Carbondale, Ill.; Chief Ed. Free China Weekly 1968–72; Deputy Dir English Dept Central News Agency, Taipei 1973–79; City Ed. China News 1973–75; Chief Ed. Central Daily News (overseas edn, Chinese) Taipei 1976–77; Deputy Ed.-in-Chief, Cen. Daily News (Chinese-language daily), Taipei 1977–79, Ed.-in-Chief –1996; Dir Dept of Media Research, Govt Information Office 1979–80; News and Overseas Programmes Dir Broadcasting Corpn of China (BCC) 1980–83; Pres. BCC 1986–92; Pres. Chinese Taipei Baseball Assn 1986–; Commr Chinese Professional Baseball Org. 1990–. *Publications:* more than 500 features, commentaries and analytical articles.

TANG, Pascal Biloa, BA; Cameroonian diplomatist; b. 20 Nov. 1937, Ebolowa; m.; six c.; ed Univs. of Aix-en-Provence and Grenoble, France, Institut Universitaire des Hautes Etudes Internationales, Geneva, Switzerland; Dir Dept of Admin., Consular and Cultural Affairs, Ministry of Foreign Affairs 1965, Dept of African and Asian Affairs 1976–77, Dept of Legal Affairs and Treaties 1985–86; served in Embassy in Addis Ababa and London, then First Counsellor, Embassy in Bonn 1979–81, Chargé d'Affaires, Algiers 1982, First Counsellor, Brussels 1982–85; Chargé de Mission, Presidency of Repub. 1977–79, Diplomatic Adviser to Pres. and Tech. Adviser to Presidency 1986–90; Perm. Rep. of Cameroon to UN, New York 1990–95. *Address:* Embassy of Cameroon, 73 rue d'Auteuil, 75116 Paris, France. *Telephone:* 1-47-43-98-33. *Fax:* 1-46-51-24-52.

TANG, Raili Kaarina; Finnish painter; b. 19 Dec. 1950, Helsinki; d. of Leo Tang and Vilma Tang (née Urb); ed The Free Art School, Univ. of Industrial Arts, School of Finnish Acad. of Fine Arts; solo exhibitions in Helsinki, Malmö, Norrköping, Stockholm, Turku, Bonn 1980–; group exhibitions 1976–; Dukat Prize for Young Artist 1979. *Leisure interests:* jogging, dogs, art. *Address:* Lemuntie 6, 00510 Helsinki (Studio) (Office); Luotsikatu 11 A 3, 00160 Helsinki, Finland. *Telephone:* (9) 656450.

TANG AOQING, PhD; Chinese professor of chemistry; b. 18 Nov. 1915, Yixing Co., Jiangsu Prov.; s. of Tang Linking and Chu Yongmei; m. Shi Guangxia 1943; three s. three d.; ed Beijing and Colombia Univs.; taught at Nat. South-West Associated Univ., Kunming after graduation; Prof. Beijing Univ. 1950–52; Prof. Jilin Univ. 1952–, Vice-Pres. 1956–78, Pres. 1978–86, Hon. Pres. 1986–; Chair. Nat. Natural Science Foundation of China 1986–91, Hon. Chair. 1991–; Chair. Nat. Natural Science Reward Cttee of China 1991–; Vice-Pres. China Assn for Int. Tech. 1986–; Pres. Soc. of Chem. 1986–; Vice-Pres. China Assn for Int. Exchange of Personnel 1986–; a leading researcher in quantum chem. and in the physical chem. of macromolecules; announced irreducible tensorial method of Ligand field theory, Beijing symposium on physics symmetry conservation and the statistical theory of polymer reactions; mem. Presidium Chinese Acad. of Sciences 1981–, Acad. Degree Cttee, State Council of China 1981–, Int. Acad. of Quantum and Molecular Science 1982–, Advisory Editorial Bd 1982–88, Editorial Bd of Int. Journal of Quantum Chemistry 1989–, Standing Cttee 8th CPPCC 1993–98; Ed.-in-Chief, Chem. Journal of Chinese Univs. 1985–; Fellow Chinese Acad. of Sciences 1955–; Third Class Award, Chinese Acad. of Sciences 1956, Nat. Science Award (First Class) 1982, 1987, (Second Class) 1989, Chen Jiang Chem. Award 1994. *Publications:* Theoretical Method of Ligand and Field Theory 1979, Graph Theoretical Molecular Orbitals 1980, Quantum Chemistry 1982, Statistical Theory on Polymeric Reactions 1985, Applied Quantum Chemistry 1987, Introduction to Irreducible Density Matrix 1989, Dynamics of Molecular Reactions 1989, Supplement to Theoretical Method of Ligand and Field 1989; over 300 articles in various books and journals. *Leisure interests:* quantum chemistry, physical chemistry of macromolecules, liter-

ature. *Address:* Institute of Theoretical Chemistry, Jilin University, Changchun 130023 (Office); 35 Huayuan Beilu, Haidian District, Beijing 100083, People's Republic of China. *Telephone:* 89231893244 (Office); 2016655313.

TANG FEI; Taiwanese politician and army officer; fmr professional soldier; Minister of Defence 1999–2000; Premier of Taiwan April–Oct. 2000; mem. Kuomintang. *Address:* c/o Kuomintang, 11 Chang Shan South Road, Taipei 100, Taiwan (Office). *Telephone:* (2) 23121472 (Office). *Fax:* (2) 23434524 (Office).

TANG JIAXUAN; Chinese diplomatist; b. Jan. 1938, Zhenjiang City, Jiangsu Prov.; ed Peking Univ.; joined CCP 1973; First Sec., then Minister Embassy, Japan; Vice-Minister of Foreign Affairs 1993–98, Minister 1998–2003; mem. 15th CCP Cen. Cttee 1997–2002, 16th CCP Cen. Cttee 2002–. *Address:* Zhangguo Gongchan Dang (Chinese Communist Party), Beijing, People's Republic of China.

TANG SHUBEI; Chinese government official; b. Jan. 1931, Shanghai; m. Liang Wenfeng; one s. one d.; joined CCP 1953; fmrly official Shanghai Fed. of Trade Unions, Ed., Head of Reporters Centre Fujian Daily; Chief Editorial Dept New Vietnamese-Chinese News 1955–57; Sec., then Deputy Dir then Dir China News Service 1957–69; Deputy Div. Chief Dept of Consular Affairs 1971–78; First Sec. Tokyo Embassy 1978–82; Div. Chief Dept of Consular Affairs 1982–83; Consul-Gen. San Francisco 1983–86; Minister of Embassy, USA 1986–88; Dir Office for Taiwan Affairs of Foreign Ministry 1988–89, Deputy Dir for Taiwan Affairs of State Council 1989–2000; Deputy Dir CCP Cen. Cttee Taiwan Affairs Office 1991–; Exec. Vice-Chair. Assn for Relations Across the Taiwan Straits 1991–; Deputy Dir CPCC Cen. Cttee Coordinating Cttee for Reunification of the Motherland 1993–; mem. Standing Cttee 8th and 9th Nat. Cttees CPCC Cen. Cttee. *Address:* Office for Taiwanese Affairs, c/o State Council, Beijing, People's Republic of China. *Telephone:* 68328307; 68465315. *Fax:* 68328321; 68478780.

TANG TIANBIAO, Gen.; Chinese army officer; b. Oct. 1940, Shimen Co., Hunan Prov.; ed Harbin Inst. of Mil. Eng., Inst. of PLA Engineer Corps, Propaganda and Theoretical Cadre Training Course of CCP Cen. Cttee Party School and Univ. of Nat. Defence; mem. CCP 1961–; held various posts in Guangzhou Mil. Region; Deputy Dir Propaganda Dept Guangzhou Mil. Region 1983; Deputy Office Head and Deputy Dir Cadre Dept of PLA Gen. Political Dept; Deputy Dir PLA Navy's Political Dept; Dir Cadre Dept of Gen. Political Dept; Deputy Dir Leading Group for the Placement of Demobilized Army Officers 1993–; Asst Dir PLA Gen. Political Dept 1993–95, Deputy Dir 1995–; rank of Lt-Gen. 1994, Gen. 2000; Deputy to 8th NPC 1993; mem. 15th CCP Cen. Cttee 1997–. *Address:* c/o Ministry of National Defence, Jingshanqian Jie, Beijing, People's Republic of China. *Telephone:* (10) 6370000.

TANG XIAOWEI; Chinese physicist; b. Oct. 1931, Wuxi Co., Jiangsu Prov.; ed Qinghua Univ.; researcher Physics Inst. 1981–; mem. of Dept Math. and Physics, Academia Sinica 1985–; Nat. Scientific Prize of China. *Address:* High Energy Physics Institute, Yu Quan Lu, Beijing, People's Republic of China.

TANG YIAN-MIN, BSc; Taiwanese politician and fmr army officer; b. 29 Nov. 1938; m.; two s. one d.; ed Mil. Acad., Army Command and Gen. Staff Coll., Armed Forces Univ., Armed Forces War Coll., Armed Forces Univ.; Div. Commdr in army 1984–86, Corps Commdr 1988–90, Deputy Field Army Commdr 1990–93, Field Army Commdr 1993–95, Deputy C-in-C 1995–96, C-in-C 1996–99; Chief of Gen. Staff, Ministry of Nat. Defense 1999–2002; Minister of Nat. Defense 2002–. *Address:* Ministry of National Defense, 2nd Floor, 164 Po Ai Road, Taipei, Taiwan (Office). *Telephone:* (2) 231-16117 (Office). *Fax:* (2) 231-44221 (Office). *E-mail:* mnd@mnd.gov.tw (Office). *Website:* www.mnd.gov.tw (Office).

TANG YING YEN, Henry, JP, GBS; Hong Kong business executive and government official; b. 6 Sept. 1952, Hong Kong; m. Lisa Kuo; four c.; ed Univ. of Michigan; Man. Dir Peninsula Knitters Ltd; Chair. Fed. of Hong Kong Industries; Dir Meadville Ltd; Hong Kong Affairs Adviser to Chinese Govt; fmr mem. Legis. Council; mem. Exec. Council Hong Kong Special Admin. Region July 1997–; Sec. for Commerce, Industry and Technology July 2002–; mem. Selection Cttee for First Govt of the Hong Kong Special Admin. Region, CPPCC Shanghai Cttee, Hong Kong Trade Devt Council, Liberal Party. *Address:* 8th Floor, West Wing, Central Government Offices, 11 Ice House Street, Central, Hong Kong Special Administrative Region, People's Republic of China. *Telephone:* (852) 28102280 (Office). *Fax:* (852) 25373210 (Office).

TANG ZHISONG; Chinese computer scientist; b. 7 Aug. 1925, Changsha, Hunan; s. of Tang Shousong and Zhu Chunxuan; m. Tong Enjian 1959; two s.; researcher, Computer Tech. Inst., Acad. Sinica, 1956–, Software Inst. 1983–; visited Stanford Univ., USA 1979–81; mem. Acad. Sinica 1992; Hon. First Nat. Prize of Sciences 1989. *Publication:* Temporal Logic Programming and Software Engineering Vol. 1 (in Chinese) 1999. *Leisure interest:* Chinese classical poetry. *Address:* Institute of Software, Academia Sinica, P.O. Box 8718, 1000 80 Beijing, People's Republic of China. *Telephone:* (10) 62556910 (Office); (10) 62561363 (Home). *Fax:* (10) 62562533.

TANGAROA, Hon. Sir Tangaroa, Kt, MBE; Cook Islands administrator (retd); b. 6 May 1921; s. of Tangaroa and Mihiau; m. 1939; two s. seven d.; ed Avarua Primary School, Rarotonga; radio operator 1939–54; shipping clerk, Donald and Ingram Ltd 1955–63; MP for Penrhyn 1958–84; Minister of Educ., Works Survey Printing and Electric Power Supply, then Minister of Internal Affairs 1978–80; Minister of Educ. 1980–84; Queen's Rep. Cook Islands

1984–90; Pres. Cook Island Crippled Children's Soc. 1966–; Deacon Cook Islands Christian Church; fmr Pres. Cook Islands Boys Brigade; Del. Islands Sports Asscn; Silver Jubilee Medal 1952–1977, New Zealand Commemoration Medal 1990. *Address:* P.O. Box 870, Avarua, Rarotonga, Cook Islands. *Telephone:* 21690.

TANGE, Kenzo, DEng; Japanese architect; b. 4 Sept. 1913, Osaka; s. of Tokiyo Tange and Tei (née Komaki) Tange; m. 1st Toshiko Kato 1949; m. 2nd Takako Iwata 1973; one s. one d.; ed Tokyo Univ.; Prof. Univ. of Tokyo 1946–74, Emer. 1974–; Pres. Japanese Architects Asscn 1986–; Founding mem. Foundation Arquitectura y Urbanismo, Argentina 1978; Assoc. mem. Paris Acad. of Fine Arts 1984; Foreign corresp. l'Acad. d'Architecture pour Japon, France 1979; Academic corresp. in Japan of Nat. Acad. of Fine Arts, Argentina 1978; Hon. Prof. (Univ. Nacional Federico Villarreal, Peru) 1977, (Univ. Buenos Aires) 1978; Hon. mem. American Acad. of Arts and Letters, Akad. der Künste, West Berlin, Colegio de Arquitectos de Venezuela 1978; Hon. Fellow American Inst. of Architects; Hon. Dr. Arts (Harvard); Hon. doctorate (Sheffield Univ.); Hon. Dr. Fine Arts (Univ. of Buffalo); Hon. Dr.-Ing. (Technische Hochschule, Stuttgart); Hon. DrArch (Politecnico di Milano, Italy); Hon. DSc (Univ. of Hong Kong); Royal Gold Medal, RIBA 1965, AIA Gold Medal, American Inst. of Architects 1966; Medal of Honour, Danish Royal Acad. of Fine Arts, Grand Prix, Architectural Inst. of Japan 1986, Pritzker Architecture Prize 1987, Imperial Award (Japan) 1993 and several other awards; Grande Médaille d'Or, Acad. française 1973, Ordre pour le Mérite (Fed. Repub. of Germany) 1976, Commdr. Ordre nat. du Mérite 1977, Mexican Order of the Aguila Azteca (Grade Encomienda) 1978, Commendatore nell' Ordine al Merito della Repubblica Italiana 1979, Person of Cultural Merit, Japan 1979, Order of Culture, Japan 1980, Commdr, Ordre des Arts et des Lettres 1984, Grande Ufficiale nell'Ordine al Merito, Italy 1984, First Order of the Sacred Treasure 1994, Medal of Honour, Taiwan 1994, Légion d'honneur 1997. *Buildings include:* Peace Memorial Park and Buildings, Hiroshima, Tokyo City Hall, Kurashiki City Hall, Kagawa Prefectural Govt Office, Takamatsu, Roman Catholic Cathedral, Tokyo, Nat. Gymnasiums for 1964 Olympic Games, Tokyo, Kuwait Int. Air Terminal Bldg, Skopje City Centre Reconstruction Project, Yugoslavia, Yamanashi Press and Broadcasting Centre, Yamahashi, Master Plan for Expo 1970, Osaka, Int. Fairs' Fiera Dist Centre, Bologna, Italy, Univ. Hospital and Dormitory, Oran, Algeria, Baltimore Inner Harbour Project, residential redevt., Royal State Palace, Jeddah, Saudi Arabia 1977–82, Royal Palace for HM the King, Jeddah, Saudi Arabia 1977–82, new capital of Nigeria 'Abuja' Urban Design for Cen. Civic Axis 1979, Overseas Union Bank Centre Bldg, Singapore 1980, Naples Admin. Centre, Italy 1980, Int. Tech. Centre, Singapore 1982, Ekime Culture Centre, Japan 1982, Yokohama City Museum, Japan 1983, Singapore Indoor Stadium 1990, Ohutsu Prince Hotel, Japan 1994, The UN Univ., Tokyo 1990, New Tokyo City Hall Complex, 1991, BMW Italia Headquarters Bldg, Italy 1991, Sinjuku Park Tower, Tokyo 1994, FCG (Fuji-Sankei Communications Group) HQ Bldg, Tokyo 1996. *Publications:* Katsura, Tradition and Creation in Japanese Architecture 1960, A Plan for Tokyo, 1960 1961, Ise 1962, Japan in the Future 1966, Kenzo Tange, 1946–1958 1966, Kenzo Tange, 1958–1964 1966, Kenzo Tange 1964–1969 1970, Japan in the 21st Century 1971, Ippon no Enpitsu Kara 1985, Kenzo Tange 1987, Kenzo Tange 1946–1996 1996. *Address:* 7-2-21 Akasaka, Minato-ku, Tokyo (Office); 1702, 2-3-34 Mita, Minato-ku, Tokyo 108-0073, Japan (Home). *Telephone:* (3) 408-7121 (Office); (3) 455-2787 (Home).

TANGNEY, Lt-Gen. William Patrick; American military commander; b. 7 Oct. 1945, Worcester, Mass.; ed Syracuse Univ., US Naval Coll.; joined US Army 1968, advanced to rank of Lt.-Gen. 1998; Operational Staff Officer G-3 Training Div., US Army John F. Kennedy Center for Military Assistance, Fort Bragg 1972–74; Exec. Officer 2nd Special Forces Bn, 7th Special Forces Group 1974, 5th Special Forces Group 1981–83; Deputy Asst Chief of Staff G-3 1983–85; Commdr 3rd Bn 5th Special Forces Group 1985–87; Chief of Special Forces, US Total Army Personnel Command, Alexandria, VA 1987–88; Commdr 10th Special Forces Group, Fort Devens, Mass. 1990–92; Commanding Gen. Special Operations, MacDill Air Force Base, Fla 1993–94; Deputy Commanding Gen., Chief of Staff, US Army Special Operations Command, Fort Bragg 1994–95; Commanding Gen. US Army Special Forces Command (Airborne), Fort Bragg 1995–97, US Army John F. Kennedy Special Warfare Center, Fort Bragg 1996–98; Deputy Commdr in Chief, Special Operations Command, MacDill Air Force Base, Fla Oct. 2000–; Defense Superior Service Medal (with Oak Leaf Cluster), Legion of Merit (with Oak Leaf Cluster), Bronze Star, Meritorious Service Medal (with 2 Oak Leaf Clusters). *Address:* United States Special Operations Command, 7701 Tampa Point Boulevard, MacDill Air Force Base, FL 33621-5323, U.S.A. (Office).

TANIGUCHI, Makoto, MA; Japanese diplomatist and university professor; b. 1930, Osaka; s. of Yoshio Taniguchi and Tomiko Tamura; m. Hiroko Kanari 1972; one s.; ed Hitotsubashi Univ., St John's Coll. Cambridge, UK; joined Ministry of Foreign Affairs 1959; specialized in econ. affairs; Dir for UN Specialized Agencies 1972, Dir for UN Econ. Affairs 1973–74, Counsellor of Japanese Mission to Int. Orgs, Geneva, in charge of UNCTAD Affairs 1974–76, Minister and Consul-Gen., Manila 1976–79, Minister, Japanese Mission to UN, in charge of Econ. Matters 1979–83; Amb. to Papua New Guinea 1983–86, to UN, New York 1986–90; Deputy Sec.-Gen. OECD 1990–96; External Auditor Hitachi Metals 1995–; Special Adviser to Sec.-Gen. OECD 1997; Prof. Inst. of Asia-Pacific Studies, Waseda Univ., Tokyo 1998–2000, Toyo Eiwa Women's Univ., Tokyo 1997–; Dir Research Inst. of Current Chinese Affairs, Waseda Univ. 2000–; Chair. Preparatory Cttee for UN Conf. on New and Renewable Sources of Energy 1980–81, Chair. Cttee I 1981; Chair. Cttee I, UNCTAD VII; Vice-Pres., Pres. Exec. Bd UNICEF 1987–88; Visiting Prof. Univ. of Int. Trade and Econs Beijing 1995; Head Japanese Del. to UN Comm. on Human Rights 1987–89; Second Order of Merit 1999. *Publications:* North-South Issues – A Path to Global Solutions (in Japanese) 1993, North-South Issues in the 21st Century – A Challenge of Globalization (in Japanese) 2001, Japan and Asia in a New Global Age 2001; many articles. *Leisure interests:* music (opera), singing, walking. *Address:* Research Institute of Current Chinese Affairs, Waseda University, Bokusha Building 2F 1-101, Totsuka-machi, Shinjuku-ku, Tokyo 169-0071 (Office); Azabu House 901, 1-7-13 Roppongi, Minato-ku, Tokyo 106-0032, Japan (Home). *Telephone:* (3) 5286-3987 (Office); (3) 3585-2879 (Home). *Fax:* (3) 5286-3987 (Office); (3) 3585-2879 (Home). *E-mail:* xxchiang@mn.waseda.ac.jp (Office).

TANIGUCHI, Yoshio; Japanese architect; b. 1937, Tokyo; ed Keio Univ., Tokyo, Grad. School of Design, Harvard Univ., USA; won competition to design expansion of Museum of Modern Art, New York 1998. *Principal works include:* Higashiyama Kaii Gallery, Nagano City 1990, Marugame Genichiro Inokuma Museum 1991, Toyota Mun. Museum of Art 1995, Kanazawa Library, Kansai Rinkai Park.

TANKARD, Meryl; Australian choreographer; b. 8 Sept. 1955, Darwin; d. of (Mick) Clifford Tankard and Margot Tankard; ed Australian Ballet School; dancer with Australian Ballet Co. 1975–78; soloist, Pina Bausch Wuppertal Tanztheater, Germany 1978–84, Guest Performer and Choreographer 1984–89; Artistic Dir Meryl Tankard Co., Canberra 1989–92, Australian Dance Theatre, Adelaide 1993–99, Meryl Tankard Australian Dance Theatre 1993–; Sidney Myer Performing Arts Award for Individual Achievement 1993, Victoria Green Room Awards 1993, 1994, Betty Pounder Award for Original Choreography 1994, 'Age' Performing Arts Award for Best Collab. (Dance) 1995, Mobil Pegasus Award for Best Production 1997; Australian Dance Awards' Lifetime Achievement Award 2003. *Major works choreographed include:* Echo Point (Australia) 1984, 1990, Travelling Light (UK and Australia) 1986–87, Two Feet (Australia, NZ, Japan and Germany) 1988–94, VX 18504 (Australia) 1989–95, Court of Flora (Australia) 1990–93, Nuti & Kikimora (Italy, Indonesia, Australia, China and Germany) 1990–94, Chants of Marriage I and II (Australia) 1991–92, Furioso (Australia and overseas) 1993–99, O Let Me Weep (Australia) 1994, Aurora (Australia) 1994–96, Orphée et Eurydice (Australia) 1995–96, Possessed (Australia, France and Germany) 1995–99, The Deep End (Australia) 1996, Bolero (France, USA, Hong Kong) 1999, The Beautiful Game (UK) 2000, Merryland (Netherlands, Switzerland, Germany), The Wild Swans (Australia) 2003. *Address:* PO Box 3129, Bellevue Hill, NSW 2023, Australia (Office).

TANNER, Alain; Swiss film director; b. 1933, Geneva; ed in London; made numerous documentaries before directing feature films. *Films include:* Charles Dead or Alive 1969; The Salamander, The Middle of the World, Jonah Who Will be 25 in the Year 2000, Light Years Away (Special Jury Prize, Cannes Film Festival 1985) 1981, No Man's Land 1985, Une Flamme Dans Mon Coeur 1987, The Woman of Rose Hill 1989.

TANNER, Roger Ian, FAA, PhD, FRS; British professor of mechanical engineering; b. 25 July 1933, Wells, Somerset; s. of R. J. Tanner and E. Tanner; m. Elizabeth Bogen 1957; two s. three d.; ed Univs of Bristol, Calif. at Berkeley and Manchester; eng apprentice, Bristol Aero Engines 1950–53; Lecturer in Mechanical Eng Univ. of Manchester 1958–61; Sr Lecturer, Reader, Univ. of Sydney 1961–66, P.N. Russell Prof. of Mechanical Eng 1975–, Pro-Vice-Chancellor (Research) 1994–97; Prof. Brown Univ. Providence, RI 1966–75; Fellow Australian Acad. of Tech. Science and Eng 1977; Edgeworth David Medal 1966, Australian Soc. of Rheology Medallion 1993, A.G.M. Michell Medal 1999, British Soc. of Rheology Gold Medal 2000. *Publications:* Engineering Rheology 1985, 2000, Rheology: An Historical Perspective 1998. *Leisure interests:* tennis, opera. *Address:* Department of Mechanical and Mechatronic Engineering, University of Sydney, NSW 2006 (Office); Marlowe, Sixth Mile Lane, Roseville, NSW 2069, Australia (Home). *Telephone:* (2) 9351-7153 (Office). *Fax:* (2) 9351-7060. *E-mail:* rit@mech.eng.usyd.edu.au (Office).

TANZI, Vito, PhD; American/Italian economist; b. 29 Nov. 1935, Italy; s. of Luigi Tanzi and Maria Tanzi; m. Maria T. Bernabé 1997; three s.; ed George Washington and Harvard Univs.; Chair. of Econs Dept, American Univ. 1971–74, Prof. of Econs 1970–74; Head Tax Policy Div. IMF 1974–81, Dir Fiscal Affairs Dept 1981–2000; Under-Sec. of State, Ministry of Economy and Finance, Italy 2001–; Sr Assoc. Carnegie Endowment for Int. Peace 2001; Pres. Int. Inst. of Public Finance; Commendatore della Repubblica Italiana; Hon. degrees: (Córdoba, Argentina) 1998, (Liège) 1999, (Turin) 2001. *Publications:* ten books, over 200 articles in professional journals. *Leisure interests:* native art, African art, photography, music, travel. *Address:* Via XX Settembre 97, 00187 Rome (Office); Vicolo del Lupo 6, 00187 Rome, Italy (Home); 5912 Walhonding Road, Bethesda, MD 20816, USA. *Telephone:* (06) 4815665 (Rome) (Office); (06) 6786298 (Rome) (Home). *Fax:* (06) 47613505 (Office). *E-mail:* vito.tanzi@tesoro.it (Office); v2m1@aol.com (Home); vitotanzi@msn.com (Home).

TAO BOJUN, Gen.; Chinese army officer; Chief of Staff Guangzhou Mil. Region 1992; promoted to Lt-Gen. 1993; Deputy Commdr Guangzhou Mil.

Region 1993–96; Commdr Guangdong Mil. Region 1996–; rank of Gen. 1998; mem. 15th CCP Cen. Cttee 1997–2002. *Address:* People's Liberation Army, c/o Ministry of National Defence, Jingshanqian Jie, Beijing, People's Republic of China.

TAO DAYONG; Chinese economist; b. 12 March 1918, Shanghai; m. Niu Ping-Qing 1942; one s. one d.; ed Nat. Cen. Univ.; Lecturer Nat. Sun Yat-sen Univ. 1942–43; Assoc. Prof., Nat. Guangxi Univ. 1943–44, Nat. Jiaotong Univ. 1944–45; Prof. Nat. Szechwan Univ. 1945–46; Visiting Prof. (invited by British Council) 1946–48; Prof. Beijing Univ. 1949–51; Prof. Beijing Normal Univ. 1952–; Ed.-in-Chief, New Construction 1951–54, Qunyan 1985–; mem. Standing Cttee 6th CPPCC 1982–88; mem. Standing Cttee 6th, 7th, 8th NPC 1993–; Vice Chair. Cen. Cttee Chinese Democratic League 1985–97, Hon. Vice-Chair. 1997–; Vice-Pres. World Econs Soc. of China 1980–85, Chinese Soc. of Foreign Econ. Theories 1983–; Adviser, Centre for Hongkong and Macao Studies 1982; Int. Order of Merit 1990, Medal of The First Five Hundred 1991, Int. Register of Profiles 1993, 20th Century Award for Achievement 1993. *Publications:* Economic Reconstruction of Post-War Eastern Europe 1948, Post-war Capitalism 1950, History of Socialism 1949, Introduction to World Economy 1951, Studies in Contemporary Capitalistic Economy 1985, A Critique of Henry George's Economic Thought 1982, History of Social Development 1982, A New History of Foreign Economic Thoughts 1990, Selected Works of Tao Dayong (Vols I and II) 1992, (Vol. III) 1998, Outline of New Democratic Economics 2002. *Leisure interests:* reading, travel, music. *Address:* Economics Department, Beijing Normal University, Xinjiekouwai Street 19, Beijing 100875, People's Republic of China. *Telephone:* (10) 62200012.

TAO HO; Chinese artist and architect; b. 1936; ed Williams Coll. Massachusetts and Harvard Univ.; worked with architect Walter Gropius; in practice as architect in Hong Kong; art work includes acrylic paintings, lithographs, pen-and-ink sketches and sculptures in marble, wood and rusty scrap iron; works exhibited at Hong Kong Univ. Museum.

TAO SIJU; Chinese party official; b. 1935, Jingjiang Co., Jiangsu Prov.; joined CCP 1949; Vice-Minister of Public Security 1984–90, Minister 1990–98; Vice-Chair. Internal Affairs and Judicial Cttee 9th NPC 1998–; mem. 14th CCP Cen. Cttee 1992–97, 15th CCP Cen. Cttee 1997–; Chair. Nat. Narcotics Control Comm. 1993–; First Political Commissar Chinese People's Armed Police Force 1991–; mem. Cen. Comm. of Political Science and Law. *Address:* c/o Standing Committee of National People's Congress, Beijing, People's Republic of China. *Telephone:* (10) 65122831.

TAOFINU'U, HE Cardinal Pio; Samoan ecclesiastic; b. 8 Dec. 1923, Falealupo, Savaii; s. of Solomona Taofinu'u and Mau Solia; ordained priest 1954; Bishop of Samoa Apia 1968–73, Archbishop 1982–; cr. Cardinal by Pope Paul VI March 1973. *Publication:* The Kava Ceremony is a Prophecy 1973. *Leisure interests:* gardening, music, art. *Address:* Cardinal's Office, P.O. Box 532, Apia, Samoa. *Telephone:* 20400. *Fax:* 20402.

TAPE, Gerald Frederick, AB, MS, PhD; American physicist and scientific administrator; b. 29 May 1915, Ann Arbor, Mich.; s. of Henry A. Tape and Flora Simmons Tape; m. Josephine Waffen 1939; three s.; ed Eastern Michigan Univ. and Univ. of Michigan; Asst in Physics, Eastern Mich. Univ. 1933–35, Univ. of Mich. 1936–39; Instructor in Physics, Cornell Univ. 1939–42; staff mem. Radiation Lab. MIT 1942–46; Asst, later Assoc. Prof. of Physics Univ. of Ill. 1946–50; Asst to Dir 1950–51, Deputy Dir, Brookhaven Nat. Lab. 1951–62; Vice-Pres. Associated Univs Inc. 1962, Pres. 1962–63, 1969–80, Special Asst to Pres. 1980–82; US Atomic Energy Commr 1963–69; US Rep. to IAEA with rank of Amb. 1973–77; mem. Pres.'s Science Advisory Cttee 1969–73; mem. Defense Science Bd 1970–74, Chair. 1970–73; mem. AEC High Energy Physics Advisory Panel 1969–74, IAEA Scientific Advisory Panel 1972–74, Energy Research and Devt Admin. Gen. Advisory Cttee 1975–77, Nat. Science Foundation Advisory Group on Science Programs 1975–76, Dept of Energy Advisory Cttee on Nuclear Facility Safety 1988–91; Dir Atomic Industrial Forum Inc. 1970–73, Science Service Inc. 1971–; Electric Power Research Inst. Advisory Council 1978–85; Univ. Chicago, Bd of Govs for Argonne Nat. Lab. 1982–85; Consultant, Defense Nuclear Facilities Safety Bd 1990–2000; mem. Nat. Acad. of Eng, American Astronomical Soc.; Fellow, American Physical Soc., American Nuclear Soc., AAAS; Hon. DSc (E Mich. Univ. 1964); Army-Navy Certificate of Appreciation 1947; Dept of State Tribute of Appreciation 1969; Sec. of Defense Meritorious Civilian Service Medal 1969; Dept of Defense Distinguished Public Service Medal 1973; Henry DeWolf Smyth Nuclear Statesman Award, Atomic Industrial Forum, American Nuclear Soc. 1978; Commdr, Order of Leopold II (Belgium) 1978; Nat. Science Foundation Distinguished Public Service Award 1980; Distinguished Assoc. Award, Dept of Energy 1980, Enrico Fermi Award 1987. *Publications:* co-author (with L. J. Haworth) Relay Radar Chapter of MIT Radiation Laboratory Technical Series; co-author with Dr. F. K. Pittman and M. F. Searl Future Energy Needs and the Role of Nuclear Power 1964, Proceedings of Third International Conference on Peaceful Uses of Atomic Energy 1964, Proceedings of the Thermionic Electrical Power Generation Symposium, Stresa 1968, Why We Test 1968, National Policy on Peaceful Uses of Nuclear Explosives 1969, The Next Twenty Years—IAEA's Role 1977. *Address:* 9707 Old Georgetown Road 2518, Bethesda, MD 20814, USA. *Telephone:* (301) 530-6343.

TÁPIES PUIG, Antoni; Spanish painter; b. 13 Dec. 1923, Barcelona; m. Teresa Barba; three c.; ed Inst. Menéndez Pelayo and Univ. of Barcelona; first one-man exhbn, Barcelona 1948, later in Paris, New York, London, Zürich, Rome, Milan, Munich, Stockholm, Hanover, Washington, Pasadena, Buenos Aires, Caracas, Düsseldorf, Bilbao, Madrid and Barcelona; cr. Mural for Saint Gallen Theatre, Switzerland 1971; French Govt Scholarship 1950; Officier des Arts et des Lettres; UNESCO Prize, Venice Biennale and Pittsburgh Int. Prize 1958, Guggenheim Prize 1964, Rubens Prize 1972, City of Barcelona Prize 1979, Rembrandt Prize, Goethe Foundation, Basle 1984, French Nat. Grand Prize for Painting 1985, Prince of Asturias Prize 1990, Praemium Imperiale 1990, Golden Lion Venice Biennale 1993. *Publications:* La pràctica de l'art, L'art contra l'estètica, Memòria personal (autobiog.) 1978, La realitat com a art 1983, Valor de l'Art 1993, L'Art i els seus llocs 1999. *Address:* C. Zaragoza 57, 08006 Barcelona, Spain. *Telephone:* (93) 2173398.

TAPLIN, Guy Christie; British artist; b. 5 March 1939, London; s. of George Frederick Taplin and Gladys Lillian Taplin (née Peters); m. Robina Dunkery Jack 1989; one s. one d.; ed Norlington Secondary Modern School, Leyton; self-taught artist (sculptor) 1978–; fmrly worked as window cleaner; Post-Office messenger 1954–58, meat porter 1960, driver 1961, ladies' hairdresser 1961–62, lifeguard 1962–68, cook 1964, birdkeeper Regent's Park 1970–76; also had own fashion business during 1960s. *Exhibitions include:* Scottish Gallery, Edin., Portal and Kalmon Gallery, London, Portal Gallery, Bremen, The Gallery, Cork Street, London; bronzes at London Zoo, Charleston, USA and Hammer Gallery, Amsterdam. *Leisure interests:* life, art, folk art, travel, chance. *Address:* Anglesea Cottage, Anglesea Road, Wivenhoe, Colchester, Essex, CO7 9JR, England. *Telephone:* (1206) 822160.

TAPPER, Colin Frederick Herbert, MA, BCL; British professor of law; b. 13 Oct. 1934, W Drayton; s. of H. F. Tapper and F. G. Tapper (née Lambard); m. Margaret White 1961; one d.; ed Magdalen Coll. Oxford; teacher LSE 1959–65; barrister Grays Inn 1961; tutor Magdalen Coll. 1965–79, Fellow 1965–, Reader 1979–91, Prof. 1992–2002; Dir Butterworth Group 1979–84, Butterworth Telepublishing 1979–89; consultant to Masons (solicitors) 1990–. *Publications:* Computers and the Law 1973, Computer Law 1978, Cross on Evidence (ed.) 1990, Handbook of European Software Law (ed.) 1995, Cross and Tapper on Evidence (ed.) 1999. *Leisure interests:* computing, reading, writing. *Address:* Magdalen College, Oxford, OX1 4AU (Office); Corner Cottage, Woodstock Road, Stonesfield, Witney, Oxon., OX29 8QA, England (Home). *Telephone:* (1865) 276055 (Office); (1993) 891284 (Home). *Fax:* (1865) 276103 (Office); (1993) 891395 (Home).

TARAND, Andres; Estonian politician; b. 11 Jan. 1940, Tallinn; s. of Helmut Tarand and Leida Tarand; m. Mari (née Viiding) Tarand 1963; two s.; ed Tartu Univ.; hydrometeorologist 1963; research asst Tallinn Botanical Gardens 1965–68; researcher Antarctic Expedition 1968–70; engineer, Dir Tallinn Botanical Gardens 1970–89; Chair. Environment Cttee Supreme Soviet Estonian SSR 1990; mem. Council of Estonia 1990–92; mem. Constitutional Ass. 1991–92; mem. Riigikogu (Parl.) 1992, 1995–; Minister of Environment 1992–94; Prime Minister of Estonia 1994–95; Chair. People's Party Moderates (Moodukad) party 1995–2001, Cttee of Foreign Affairs 1999–2002; Order of Nat. Coat of Arms 2nd Class 2001, Légion d'honneur 2001. *Publications:* numerous articles on climatology, urban ecology, politics. *Leisure interests:* chess, ornithology, traditional style gardening. *Address:* Riigikogu, Lossi plats 1A, Tallinn 15165, Estonia (Office). *Telephone:* (372) 6316651 (Office). *Fax:* (372) 6316653 (Office).

TARANDA, Gediminas Leonovich; Russian/Lithuanian ballet dancer; b. 26 Feb. 1961, Kaliningrad; ed Moscow School of Choreography; soloist Bolshoi Theatre 1980–94, dismissed after conflict with admin.; Founder (with M. Plisetskaya) and Dir Imperial Russian Ballet of Vienna 1994. *Leading roles include:* classical and contemporary Russian repertoire including Espado (Don Quixote), Correchidor (Carmen), Forest Warden (Giselle), Kuman (Prince Igor), Severyan (Stone Flower), Yashka (Golden Age), Kurbsky (Ivan the Terrible), Abderakhman (Raimonda), Vizir (Legend of Love) and others. *Address:* Imperial Russian Ballet, Vienna, Austria; Imperial Ballet, Trekhprudny per. 11/13, building 2b, Office 45, 103001 Moscow, Russia. *Telephone:* (095) 299-13-98.

TARANTINO, Quentin; American film director; b. 27 March 1963, Knoxville, Tenn.; s. of Tony Tarantino and Connie McHugh; worked in Video Archives, Manhattan Beach; brief acting career; producer, Killing Zoe; wrote screenplay for True Romance, Natural Born Killers. *Films directed:* Reservoir Dogs, Pulp Fiction (Golden Palm, Cannes Film Festival) 1994, Jackie Brown 1997, 40 Lashes (also writer) 2000. *Film appearances include:* Sleep With Me 1994, Destiny Tunes on the Radio 1995, Desperado 1995, Girl 6 1996, From Dusk Till Dawn 1996. *Films produced:* Red Rain 1995, Four Rooms 1995, From Dusk Till Dawn 1996, Curdled 1996. *Publications:* screenplays: True Romance 1995, Natural Born Killers 1995, Jackie Brown 1998; novel: Kill Bill 2003. *Address:* WMA, 151 El Camino Drive, Beverly Hills, CA 90212; 6201 Sunset Boulevard, Suite 35, Los Angeles, CA 90028, USA.

ŢĂRANU, Cornel, DMus; Romanian composer and conductor; b. 20 June 1934, Cluj; s. of Francisc Ţăranu and Elisabeta Ţăranu; m. Daniela Mărgineanu 1960; one d.; ed Cluj Conservatory; Prof. of Composition, Cluj Conservatory; Conductor of Ars Nova, contemporary music ensemble; Vice-Pres. Romanian Composers' Union 1990–; Artistic Dir Modern Festival Cluj; mem. Romanian Acad. 1993–; Prize of the Romanian Composers' Union 1972, 1978, 1981, 1982, 2001, Prize of the Romanian Acad. 1973, The Koussevitsky Prize 1982, Chevalier des Arts et des Lettres. *Works include:* sonatas for flute, oboe, clarinet and percussion, sonata for double bass solo, viola sonata, one piano concerto, cantatas, four symphonies, Séquences, Incantations, Symmétries, Alternances, Raccords for orchestra, two Sinfoniettas for strings, Garlands (for chamber orchestra), Don Giovanni's Secret (chamber opera), Chansons nomades (oratorio), Chansons sans amour, lieder, Sempre Ostinato (saxophone and ensemble), Chansons sans réponse, Hommage à Paul Célan, Memento and Dedications (cantatas), Miroirs (for saxophone and orchestra), Prolégomènes (for chamber orchestra), Orpheus (cantata), Tombeau de Verlaine (mixed choir), Mosaïques (for saxophone and ensemble), Testament (for choir) 1988, Chansons interrompues (voice and ensemble) 1993, Cadenze Concertante (cello and chamber orchestra) 1993, Trajectoires (for ensemble) 1994, Crisalide (for saxophone, tape and ensemble), Five Tzara Songs (for voice and piano), Remembering Bartók (for oboe and ensemble), Enescu's 'Caprice Roumain' for violin and orchestra (new arrangement) 1995, Responsorial (for clarinet) 1996, Antiphona (for flute and orchestra) 1996, Flaine Quintette (for winds) 1997, Laudatio per Clusium (for voice and instruments) 1997, Saturnalii (baritone and ensemble) 1998, three Labiş Poems (bass and piano) 1998, Cadenze per Antiphona (flute and solo) 1998, Siciliana Blues (piano and chamber orchestra) 1998, Concerto (oboe and strings) 1998, Oreste-Oedipe (chamber opera) 1999–2001, Concerto Breve for flute orchestra 2001, Shakespeare Sonnets (voice and ensemble) 2002, Modra Rijeka (choir) 2002, Madrigals (verse by Blaga, Vinea, Attila, Ady); also film and theatre music. *Publication:* Enesco dans la conscience du présent 1981. *Leisure interest:* chess. *Address:* "Gh. Dima" Music Academy, str. I. I. C. Bratianu 25, 3400 Cluj (Office); Str. Nicolae Iorga 7, Cluj-Napoca 3400, Romania. *Telephone:* (64) 193879 (Office); (64) 443283 (Home). *Fax:* (64) 193879 (Office). *E-mail:* corneltaranu@yahoo.com (Office).

TARAR, Muhammad Rafiq; Pakistani politician and lawyer; b. 2 Nov. 1929, Pir Kot, Gujranwala Dist; ed Govt Islamia High School, Gujranwala, Guru Nanak Khalsa Coll., Gujranwala, Punjab Univ. Law Coll.; legal practice Gujranwala; Additional Sessions Judge, Gujranwala, Bahawalnagar, Sargodha; mem. Lahore High Court 1974, Chief Justice of Punjab 1989; mem. Electoral Comm. of Pakistan 1980–89; mem. Supreme Court 1991–94; Senator, Pakistan Muslim League March–Dec. 1997; Pres. of Pakistan 1998–2001. *Address:* House 457, G-3, Johar Town, Lahore, Pakistan.

TARASSOV, Gennadii Pavlovich; Russian diplomatist; b. 14 Sept. 1947; ed Moscow State Inst. of Int. Relations; on staff Ministry of Foreign Affairs 1970–; worked in Egypt, USSR Mission in UN and other posts –1986; Deputy Head of Dept Near E. and S. African Countries USSR Ministry of Foreign Affairs 1986–90; Amb. of USSR, then of Russia to Saudi Arabia 1990–96; Dir Dept of Information and Press, Ministry of Foreign Affairs 1996–98; Amb. to Portugal 1998–2001, to Israel 2002–. *Address:* Embassy of Russia, 120 Rehov Hayarkon, Tel-Aviv 63753 Israel. *Telephone:* 3-35226733 (Office). *Fax:* 3-35226713 (Office). *E-mail:* amb_ru@mail.netvision.net.il (Office).

TARASYUK, Boris Ivanovich; Ukrainian politician and diplomatist; b. 1 Jan. 1949, Dzerzhinsk, Zhitomir Region; m.; one s. two d.; ed Kiev State Univ.; attaché, Third, Second, First Sec. Ukrainian Ministry of Foreign Affairs 1975–81; Second, First Sec. Perm. Mission of Ukrainian SSR to UN 1981–86; First Sec. Div. of Int. Orgs, Ukrainian Ministry of Foreign Affairs 1986–87; instructor Div. of Foreign Relations, Ukrainian CP Cen. Cttee 1987–90; Head, Dept of Political Analysis and Planning, Ukrainian Ministry of Foreign Affairs 1991–92; Deputy, First Deputy Minister of Foreign Affairs, Head, Nat. Cttee on Disarmament Problems 1992–95; Amb. to Belgium (also Accred to Netherlands, Luxembourg) 1995–98; Head, Ukrainian Mission to NATO 1997–; Minister of Foreign Affairs 1998–2000; mem. Bd of Dirs East-West Inst.; Dir Inst. of Euro-Atlantic Co-operation 2001–. *Address:* c/o Ministry of Foreign Affairs, 1st Mikhaïlovska Square, 252018 Kiev, Ukraine. *Telephone:* (381) 293-24-72 (Office).

TARCHER, Jeremy Phillip, BA; American publisher; b. 2 Jan. 1932, New York; s. of Jack D. Tarcher and Mary Breger Tarcher; m. 1st Shari Lewis 1958 (died 1998); one d.; m. 2nd Judith Paige Mitchell 1999; ed St John's Coll., Annapolis, Md; Founder and Pres. Jeremy P. Tarcher Inc., LA 1964–; Vice-Pres. Houghton Mifflin, Boston 1980–83; Chair. Bd Audio Renaissance Tapes, L. A. 1985–; Pres. Tarcher/Putnam (a div. of Penguin/Putnam) 1991–; mem. Bd Trustees The Esalen Inst., Big Sur, Calif. 1986–; Producer Shari Lewis Show, NBC Network 1959–62; Exec. Producer A Picture of U.S. (Emmy Award for Children's Programming) 1976. *Leisure interests:* entheogenic research, travel, reading, primitive Oceanic art. *Address:* 144 South Beverly Drive, Beverly Hills, CA 90212 (Office); 1416 Stone Canyon, Bel Air, CA 90077, USA (Home). *Telephone:* (310) 274-7207 (Office). *Fax:* (310) 274-3611 (Office).

TARJANNE, Pekka, DTech; Finnish international telecommunications official; b. 19 Sept. 1937, Stockholm; s. of P.K. Tarjanne and Annu Ritavuori; m. Aino Kairamo 1962; two s. one d.; ed Helsinki Univ. of Tech.; research and teaching at univs. in Denmark and USA 1961–66; Prof. of Theoretical Physics, Univ. of Oulu 1965–66, Univ. of Helsinki 1967–77; mem. Parl. 1970–77; Minister for Transport and Communications 1972–75; Dir-Gen. of Posts and Telecommunications, Finland 1977–89; Sec.-Gen. Int. Telecommunication Union 1989–98; Vice-Chair. Project Oxygen 1999–2000; Exec. Co-ordinator, UN Information and Communication Technologies Task Force 2001–; Commdr Order of White Rose of Finland, Commdr Légion d'honneur, Grand Cross, Order of Finnish Lion 1998. *Publication:* A Group Theoretical Model

for Strong Interaction Dynamics 1962. *Address:* United Nations Information and Communication Technologies Task Force, United Nations Plaza, New York, NY 10017, U.S.A.

TARLEV, Vasile Pavlovich, DTechSci; Moldovan politician and business executive; b. 9 Oct. 1963, Başcalia, Basarabeasca; m.; three c.; ed Chişinău Polytech. Inst.; worked as tractor driver; served in army of USSR; Chief Mechanic Bucuria confectionery factory, Chief Engineer Bucuria SA 1991–93, First Deputy Dir-Gen. 1993–95, Chair. Bd of Admin., Dir-Gen. 1995–2001; fmr mem. Supreme Econ. Council of Pres., Econ. Council of Govt; mem. Repub. Comm. on Collective Negotiations between Businessmen and Trade Unions 1998–99; Prime Minister of Moldova 2001–; fmr Chair. Nat. Asscn of Mfrs 1995–2001; mem. Council Int. Union of Mfrs, Int. Acad. of Sciences and Computing Systems 1998–; Gen. Dir Bukuria Co. 2002–; mem. Int. Acad. of Sciences and Informational Systems 1998; 5 patents on tech. inventions; Businessman of the Year (six times) 1995–2000, Gold Medal for Efficient Man., Int. Acad. of Human Resources 2000, several medals for tech. inventions shown at int. exhbns 1997–; Order of Work Glory 1997. *Publications:* over 30 scientific publs. *Address:* Office of the Prime Minister, Great National Assembly Sq. 1, 277033 Chişinău, Moldova (Office). *Telephone:* (2) 23-35-72 (Office). *Fax:* (2) 23-77-95 (Office).

TARNOPOLSKY, Vladimir Grigor'yevich; Russian composer; b. 30 April 1955, Dniepropetrovsk, Ukraine; m. Yelena Ivanovna Snetko; one s.; ed Moscow State Conservatory; freelance composer 1988–; co-f. Moscow Asscn of Contemporary Music 1989; Prof. of Composition, Moscow Conservatory 1992–; Founder, Artistic Dir Cen. for Contemporary Music, Moscow Conservatory 1993–; f. Studio for New Music Ensemble 1993–; f. Moscow Forum – Int. Festival of Contemporary Music 1994–; works performed by Ensemble Modern, Schonberg Ensemble, Ensemble Recherche, Bayerische Rundfunk Symphony Orchestra in major European festivals; Dmitry Shostakovich Prize, Moscow 1991, Paul Hindemith Prize, Pion 1991. *Compositions include:* Cello Concerto 1988. *Address:* Centre for Contemporary Music, Bolshaya Nikitskaya str. 13, 109095 Moscow (Office); Arbat str., apt 41a, Moscow, Russia (Home). *Telephone:* (095) 290-51-81 (Office); (095) 241-56-66 (Office). *E-mail:* istar-priv@mtu-net.ru (Home).

TARSCHYS, Daniel, PhD; Swedish politician and political scientist; b. 21 July 1943, Stockholm; s. of Bernhard Tarschys and Karin Alexanderson; m. Regina Rehbinder 1970; two d.; ed Univs of Stockholm, Leningrad and Princeton; Research Assoc. Stockholm Univ. 1972–76, Prof. of Political Science and Public Admin. 1985–; adviser with Ministry of Finance 1976–78, 1979–83; Sec. of State, Prime Minister's Office 1978–79; Prof. of Soviet and E European Studies Uppsala Univ. 1983–85; contrib. to Dagens Nyheter 1983–94; mem. Parl. 1976–82, 1985–94; Chair. Parl. Social Affairs Cttee 1985–91, Foreign Affairs Cttee 1991–94; Vice-Pres. Liberal Int. 1992–94; mem. Council of Europe Parl. Ass. 1986–94, alt. mem. 1981–83; Sec.-Gen. Liberal, Democratic and Reformers Group (LDR) 1987–91, Chair. 1991–94; Sec.-Gen. Council of Europe 1994–99; Chair. of several insts and govt cttees. *Publications:* books and articles on political philosophy, budgetary policy, public admin. and comparative politics. *Address:* University of Stockholm, 10691 Stockholm, Sweden. *E-mail:* daniel.tarschys@statsvet.su.se (Office).

TARTAKOVSKY, Vladimir Aleksandrovich; Russian chemist; b. 10 Aug. 1932; m.; one d.; ed Moscow State Univ.; worked as researcher, teacher; Head of lab., Inst. of Organic Chem., USSR (now Russian) Acad. of Sciences 1955–86; Dir N D. Zelinsky Inst. of Organic Chem. 1987–; corresp. mem., USSR (now Russian) Acad. of Sciences 1987, mem. 1992–; main research in organic synthesis, chem. of nitrocompounds; Lenin Prize 1976, AM Butlerov Prize. *Address:* N D. Zelinsky Institute of Organic Chemistry, Leninsky prosp. 47, 117913 GSP-1 Moscow, Russia. *Telephone:* (095) 137-29-44 (Office).

TASCA, Catherine, LenD; French government official; b. 13 Dec. 1941, Lyons; d. of Angelo Tasca and Alice Naturel; one d.; ed Inst. d'Etudes Politiques, Paris and Ecole Nat. d'Admin; civil servant, Ministry of Culture 1967; Dir Maison de la Culture de Grenoble 1973; Gen. Man. Ensemble Intercontemporain 1978; Co-Dir Théâtre de Nanterre-Amandiers 1982; mem. Comm. Nat. de la Communication et des Libertés (CNCL) 1986; Minister Del. attached to the Minister of Culture and Communications 1988–91; Sec. of State for Francophone Countries and External Cultural Relations 1992–93; Minister of Culture and Communications March 2000–02; Pres. Admin. Bd Canal+Horizons 1993–97; Deputy to Nat. Ass. from Yvelines 1997–, mem. Socialist Party. *Publication:* Un Choix de vie 2002. *Address:* 21 rue Saint-Amand, 75015 Paris, France (Home).

TASMAGAMBETOV, Imangali Nurgaliyevich; Kazakhstan politician; b. 1956; served in various positions in govt, including Chair. State Cttee on Youth Affairs 1991–93; Asst to Pres. 1993–94; apptd Atyrau oblast akim (Gov.) 1998; Deputy Prime Minister for Cultural Affairs 1991–93, in charge of Social and Ethnic Policy 2000–02; Prime Minister of Kazakhstan Jan. 2002–. *Address:* Office of the Prime Minister, 473000 Astana, Beibitshilik 11, Kazakhstan (Office). *Telephone:* (3172) 32-31-04 (Office). *Fax:* (3172) 32-40-89 (Office).

TATA, Jamshed Rustom, DSc, FRS; British medical research scientist; b. 13 April 1930, Bombay, India; s. of Dr. Rustom J. Tata and Gool Tata (née Contractor); m. Renée S. Zanetto 1954; two s. one d.; ed Univ. of Bombay, Indian Inst. of Science, Bangalore, Coll. de France, Paris and Univ. de Paris, Sorbonne; Postdoctoral Fellow, Sloan-Kettering Inst., New York 1954–55;

Beit Memorial Fellow, Nat. Inst. for Medical Research, London 1956–60; Visiting Scientist, Wenner-Gren Inst., Univ. of Stockholm 1960–62; mem. Scientific Staff, MRC, Nat. Inst. for Medical Research, London 1962–96, Sr Scientist 1996–, Head, Lab. of Developmental Biochem. 1973–96; Visiting Prof., Univ. of Calif. at Berkeley 1969–70; Fogarty Int. Scholar, Nat. Insts. of Health, Bethesda, Md 1983–89, Visiting Scientist 1997; Chair. Cell and Molecular Panel, Wellcome Trust 1990–92, Int. Relations Group 1997; mem. Indian Nat. Acad. of Sciences; corresp. mem. Soc. de Biologie, France; Fellow Third World Acad. of Sciences; Chair. Trustee Oxford Int. Biomedical Centre 1996–; various awards. *Publications:* The Thyroid Hormones 1959, Chemistry of Thyroid Diseases 1960, Metamorphosis 1972, The Action of Growth and Developmental Hormones 1983, Metamorphosis 1986, Hormonal Signalling and Post-embryonic Development 1998. *Leisure interests:* gardening, reading, travel, tennis. *Address:* 15 Bittacy Park Avenue, Mill Hill, London, NW7 2HA, England (Home). *Telephone:* (20) 8959-3666 (Office); (20) 8346-6291 (Home). *Fax:* (20) 8913-8583 (Office). *E-mail:* jtata@nimr.mrc.ac.uk (Office); jtata@virgoans.co.uk (Home).

TATA, Ratan N.; Indian business executive; b. 28 Dec. 1937; nephew of J. R. D. Tata; Chair. Tata Sons Ltd (holding co. comprising 80 cos.) 1991–; also Chair. various cos. in Tata Group, including Tata Steel, Tata Eng and Tata Power. *Address:* Bombay House, 24 Homi Mody Street, Mumbai 400 001, India (Office). *Telephone:* (22) 2049131 (Office). *Fax:* (22) 2042333 (Office).

TATARINOV, Leonid Petrovich; Russian palaeontologist and zoologist; b. 12 Nov. 1926, Tula; s. of Petr Lukich Tatarinov and Anna Nikolayevna Tatatrinova; m. Bulat Susanna Gurgenovna 1959; two d.; ed Moscow Univ.; mem. CPSU 1964–91; served in Soviet Army 1943–44; Sr scientific of Foreign Language Publishing House 1953–54; mem. staff USSR Acad. of Sciences Inst. of Palaeontology (jr research fellow, then head of lab. and sr research fellow) 1955–73, Dir 1975–92, Vice-Sec. Dept of Gen. Biology of USSR (now Russian) Acad. of Sciences 1975–; Chair. Council for Study of Palaeobiology and Evolution 1981; mem. Council Russian Acad. of Sciences 1992–; Scientific Chief of Jt Soviet- (now Russian-) Mongolian Palaeontological Expedition 1975–96; Ed.-in-Chief Palaeontology Journal 1978–88, 1993–, Zoological Journal 1988–93; Corresp. mem. USSR (now Russian) Acad. of Sciences 1974, mem. 1981–; Foreign mem. Linnean Soc., London; USSR State Prize 1978, Order of Merit for the Fatherland 1999. *Publications:* Sketches on the Theory of Evolution 1987, Palaeontology and Evolutionary Doctrine 1989 and other works on origins and early evolution of tetrapods. *Leisure interests:* music, history. *Address:* Palaeontological Institute, Academy of Sciences, Profsoyuznaya str. 123, 117868 Moscow GSP-7, Russia. *Telephone:* (095) 339-07-00 (Office); 438-12-94 (Home). *Fax:* (095) 339-12-66. *E-mail:* postmaster@paleo.ru (Office).

TATE, Jeffrey Philip, CBE, MA, MB, BChir; British conductor; b. 28 April 1943, Salisbury, Wilts.; s. of Cyril H. Tate and Ivy Ellen Naylor (née Evans); ed Farnham Grammar School, Christ's Coll. Cambridge and St Thomas's Hosp. London; trained as medical dr. 1961–67; joined London Opera Centre 1969; joined staff of Royal Opera House, Covent Garden 1970; made recordings as harpsichordist 1973–77; Asst to Pierre Boulez for the Ring, Bayreuth 1976–81; Asst to Sir John Pritchard, Cologne Opera 1977; conducted Gothenburg Opera, Sweden 1978–80; Metropolitan Opera début 1979; Covent Garden début 1982; Chief Guest Conductor, Geneva Opera 1983–95; Prin. Conductor, English Chamber Orchestra 1985–, Royal Opera House, Covent Garden 1986–91; Prin. Guest Conductor, Royal Opera House, Covent Garden 1991–94, Orchestre Nat. de France 1989–98; Chief Conductor and Artistic Dir Rotterdam Philharmonic Orchestra 1991–94; Chief Conductor Minnesota Orchestra Summer Festival 1997–; Prin. Guest Conductor Teatro La Fenice 1999–; appears with maj. orchestras in Europe and America; numerous recordings with English Chamber orchestra; Pres. Asscn for Spina Bifida and Hydrocephalus 1989–, Music Space Trust 1991–; other charitable positions; Hon. Fellow Christ's Coll. Cambridge, St Thomas's and Guy's Hosp. Medical School; Hon. DMus (Leicester) 1993; Officier des Arts et des Lettres 1995, Chevalier, Légion d'honneur 1999; Grand Prix du Disque 1995 for complete recording of opera Lulu. *Leisure interests:* church-crawling, with gastronomic interludes. *Address:* c/o English Chamber Orchestra, 2 Coningsby Road, London, W5 4HR, England. *Telephone:* (20) 8840-6565. *Fax:* (20) 8567-7198.

TATE, Robert Brian, PhD, FBA, FRHistS; British professor of Hispanic studies; b. 27 Dec. 1921, Belfast, Northern Ireland; s. of Robert Tate and Jane Grantie Tate; m. Beth Ida Lewis 1951; one s. one d.; ed Royal Belfast Academical Inst., The Queen's Univ., Belfast; Asst Lecturer, Manchester Univ. 1949–52; Lecturer, The Queen's Univ., Belfast 1952–56; Reader in Hispanic Studies, Nottingham Univ. 1956–58, Prof. 1958–83, Emer. Prof. 1983–; Visiting Prof. Univ. of New York (Buffalo), Harvard and Cornell Univs., Univ. of Virginia and Univ. of Texas (Austin); Corresp. Fellow Institut d'Estudis Catalans, of Real Acad. de Buenas Letras, Barcelona, of Real Acad. de Historia, Madrid. *Publications:* numerous publications on Hispanic topics. *Leisure interests:* art, architecture, jazz. *Address:* 11 Hope Street, Beeston, Nottingham, England (Home). *Telephone:* (115) 925-1243 (Home). *E-mail:* brian@rbtate19.freeserve.co.uk (Home).

TATHAM, David Everard, CMG, BA; British diplomatist (retd) and consultant; b. 28 June 1939, York; s. of the late Lt-Col Francis Everard Tatham and of Eileen Mary Wilson; m. Valerie Ann Mylechreest 1963; three s.; ed St Lawrence Coll., Ramsgate, Wadham Coll. Oxford; entered HM Diplomatic Service 1960, Third Sec. UK Mission to UN, New York 1962–63; Vice-Consul

(Commercial), Milan 1963–67; Middle East Centre for Arabic Studies 1967–69; served Jeddah 1969–70, FCO 1971–74, Muscat 1974–77; Asst Head Middle East Dept FCO 1977–80; Counsellor, Dublin 1981–84; Amb. to Yemen Arab Repub. (also Accred to Djibouti) 1984–87; Head Falkland Islands Dept, FCO 1987–90; Amb. to Lebanon 1990–92; Gov. Falklands Islands 1992–96, concurrently Commr S. Georgia and S. Sandwich Islands; High Commr to Sri Lanka (also Accred to Maldives) 1996–99; Adviser on diplomatic training to Palestinian Authority 2000; Dist Man. UK Census 2000–01; Ed. Dictionary of Falklands Biography Project 2002. *Leisure interests:* walking uphill, historical research. *Address:* c/o Foreign and Commonwealth Office, Whitehall, London, SW1A 2AH, England (Office).

TATISHVILI, Tsisana Bezhanovna; Georgian opera singer (soprano); b. 30 Dec. 1939, Tbilisi, Georgia; m. Giorgi Totibadze; ed V. Sarandzhishvili Conservatoire, Tbilisi; soloist with Tbilisi (now Georgian) State Opera 1963–; has toured in Germany, Poland, fmr Czechoslovakia and other countries; Prof. V. Saradjishvili Conservatoire 1985–; vocal consultant at Georgian State Opera 1999–; mem. Artistic Council 2001–; People's Artist of Georgian SSR 1973, Paliashvili Prize 1979, 1987, People's Artist of USSR 1979; Order of Honour. *Roles include:* Tatiana in Eugene Onegin, Liza in Queen of Spades, Aida, Leonora in Il Trovatore, Donna Anna in Don Giovanni, Ortrud in Lohengrin, Salome, Desdemona in Otello, Santuzza in Cavalleria Rusticana, Eteri in Paliashvili's Absalom and Eteri. *Address:* 3 Ateni Street, Apt 12, Tbilisi (Home); c/o Georgian State Opera, Tbilisi, Georgia. *Telephone:* (32) 23-22-66 (Home). *E-mail:* Tatishvili@rambler.ru (Home).

TATTENBACH-YGLESIAS, Christian, LLB; Costa Rican diplomatist and politician; b. 1924; ed Univ. of Costa Rica; mem. Nat. Wage Bd 1949; Amb. to Guatemala 1951, to Nicaragua 1952; Deputy Legis. Ass. 1962–66, 1978–82, 1986–90, Pres. Legis. Ass. 1981–82; Minister of Interior, Police and Justice 1966–70; Alt. Sec.-Gen. Cen. American Inst. for Extension of Culture and Dir Escuela para Todos Publs programme 1970–77; Co-founder and Chair. Union Popular Party 1977; Head Parl. Group of Coalición Unidad 1980–81; Pres. Union Popular 1982–84, now Hon. Pres. Unidad Social Cristiana; Perm. Rep. to UN, New York 1990–94; mem. Bd Inter-American Inst. of Human Rights 1982. *Address:* c/o Ministry of Foreign Affairs, 1000 San José, Costa Rica.

TAUBE, Henry, BS, MS, PhD; American professor of chemistry; b. 30 Nov. 1915, Saskatchewan, Canada; s. of Samuel Taube and Albertina Tiledetzki Taube; m. Mary Alice (née Wesche) 1952; two s. two d.; ed Univs. of Sask. and Calif. at Berkeley; Instructor Univ. of Calif. at Berkeley 1940–41; Instructor-Asst Prof. Cornell Univ. 1941–46; Asst Prof., Prof. Univ. of Chicago 1946–61; Prof. of Chem., Stanford Univ., Calif. 1962–90, Prof. Emer. 1990–; Guggenheim Fellow 1949–55; mem. NAS, Royal Physiographical Soc. of Lund, American Philosophical Soc.; foreign mem. Royal Soc. 1988; Hon. mem. Hungarian Acad. of Science 1988; Hon. Fellow RSC 1989; Hon. Fellow Indian Chem. Soc. 1989; Hon. Fellow Royal Soc. of Canada 1997; Hon. LLD (Univ. of Sask.) 1973, PhD hc (Hebrew Univ. of Jerusalem) 1979, Hon. DrSc (Univ. of Chicago) 1983, (Lajos Kossuth Univ. of Debrecen) 1988, (Seton Hall Univ.) 1988; Baker Lecture, Cornell Univ. 1965, Priestley Lecture, Pa State 1976; American Chem. Soc. Awards 1955, 1960, Chandler Medal of Columbia Univ., Kirkwood Award, Harrison Howe Award, Rochester Section, ACS, 1960; Nichols Medal, New York Section, ACS 1971; Willard Gibbs Medal, Chicago Section, ACS 1971; F. P. Dwyer Medal, Univ. of NSW 1973; Nat. Medal of Science 1977; Allied Chemical Award for Excellence in Graduate Teaching and Innovative Science 1979; T. W. Richards Medal, Northeastern Sec. ACS 1980, ACS Award in Inorganic Chem. of the Monsanto Co. 1981, Linus Pauling Award, Puget Sound Section ACS 1981, NAS Award in Chemical Sciences 1983, Bailar Medal, Univ. of Ill. 1983, Robert A. Welch Foundation Award in Chem. 1983, Nobel Prize for Chem. 1983, Priestley Medal 1984, Distinguished Achievement Award, Precious Metals Inst. 1986, Oesper Award 1986, G. M. Kospaloff Award 1990, Brazilian Order of Science Merit Award 1994. *Publications:* approx. 330 scientific articles in chemical journals. *Leisure interests:* record-collecting, gardening. *Address:* Department of Chemistry, Stanford University, Stanford, CA 94305 (Office); 441 Gerona Road, Stanford, CA 94305, USA (Home). *Telephone:* (650) 725-9344 (Office); (650) 326-4662 (Home). *E-mail:* cdpiercy@stanford.edu (Office). *Website:* www.stanford.edu (Office).

TAUBMAN, A. Alfred; American entrepreneur; b. 31 Jan. 1925, Pontiac, Mich.; s. of Philip Taubman and Fannie Taubman; m. 1st Reva Kolodney 1949 (divorced 1977); two s. one d.; m. 2nd Judith Mazor 1982; ed Univ. of Michigan, Lawrence Inst. of Tech.; Chair. and CEO The Taubman Co., Bloomfield Hills, Michigan (specializing in shopping-centre design, planning and devt) 1950–; Chair. Sothebys Holdings 1983–2000; owner of Sotheby's (art auctioneers) 1983–2000; sentenced to one year and one day's imprisonment for price-fixing April 2002. *Address:* c/o The Taubman Co., 200 E Long Lake Road, Bloomfield Hills, MI 48304, USA.

TAUFA'AHAU Tupou IV, HM the King of Tonga, GCVO, GCMG, KBE, BA, LLB; b. 4 July 1918; s. (eldest) of the late Queen Salote Tupou III of Tonga and the late Hon. Uiliami Tungi Premier of Tonga; brother of Prince Fatafehi Tu'ipelahake; m. HRH Princess Halaevalu Mata'aho 1947; three s. one d., of whom the eldest, HRH Crown Prince Tupoutoa, is heir to the throne; ed Newington Coll. and Sydney Univ., NSW; Minister of Educ. 1943, of Health 1944–49, Premier of Tonga, also Minister of Foreign Affairs and Agric. 1949–65; King of Tonga 1965–; est. Teachers' Training Coll. and revised Tonga alphabet 1944; f. Tonga High School 1947, Broadcasting Station 1961,

Govt newspaper 1964; Chancellor Univ. of the S. Pacific 1970–73; Hon. LLD; Kt Commdr, Order of Merit (FRG) 1978; numerous citations and awards. *Address:* The Palace, P.O. Box 6, Nuku'alofa, Tonga. *Telephone:* Nuku'alofa 21-000.

TAUS, Josef, LLD; Austrian politician, banker and industrialist; b. 8 Feb. 1933, Vienna; s. of Josef Taus and G. Schinko; m. Martha Loibl 1960; ed Univ. of Vienna, Hochschule für Welthandel; Journalist; law practice; with Austrian Inst. of Econ. Research; Sec. and Head of Econ. Div., Girozentrale und Bank der Österreichischen Sparkassen AG 1958, mem. Man. Bd 1967–68, Chair. and Man. Dir 1968–75; fmr Man. Sparinvest-Kapitalanlage GmbH; mem. Parl. 1975–91; State Sec. Fed. Ministry of Communications and Nationalized Enterprises 1966–67; Fed. Chair. Austrian People's Party (ÖVP) 1975–79; Man. Partner Constantia Industrieverwaltungs GesmbH. 1979–86; mem. Bd Constantia Industrieholding AG 1986–89; mem. Bd ECO TRUST Holding AG 1989, Man. Trust Holding AG 1989–, Trust Invest AG 1990–; Man. Dir Fremdenverkehrsbetriebe GesmbH and Co. OHG. *Leisure interests:* skiing, music, reading, swimming. *Address:* Zahnradbahnstrasse 17, 1190 Vienna, Austria (Home).

TAVENER, Sir John, Kt; British composer; b. 28 Jan. 1944, London; s. of Kenneth Tavener and Muriel Tavener; m. 1st Victoria Marangopoulou 1974 (divorced 1980); m. 2nd Maryanna Schaefer 1991; two d.; ed Highgate School and RAM; Organist St John's Church, London 1960; Prof. of Composition, Trinity Coll. of Music, London 1968–; youngest composer ever performed at Promenade Concert, London 1969, at Royal Opera House, Covent Garden (Thérèse) 1979; works performed in UK, USA, fmr USSR, Greece, Poland, Australia, Germany, Scandinavia, S. America and elsewhere; converted to Russian Orthodox Church 1974; works recorded on numerous labels; Hon. FRAM, Hon. Fellow Royal School of Church Music, Hon. Fellow Trinity Coll. of Music, London; Hon. DMus (New Delhi) 1990, (City of London Univ.) 1996; Prince Rainier Int. Prize 1965, First Prize Sacred Music Int. Composition Contest 1972, Gramophone Award (for The Protecting Veil) 1992. *Compositions include:* The Whale, Celtic Requiem, Ultimos Ritos, Palintropos, Antigone, Thérèse, Akhmatova-Rekviem, Liturgy of St John Chrysostom, 16 Haiku of Seferis, Sappho—Lyrical Fragments, Great Canon of St Andrew of Crete, Prayer for the World, Kyklike Kinesis, Ikon of Light, A Gentle Spirit, All-Night Vigil Service of the Orthodox Church (commissioned by Orthodox and Anglican Churches, for Christ Church Cathedral, Oxford 1985), Two Hymns to the Mother of God, Trisāgion, Mandelion; Eis Thanaton (a ritual), Ikon of St Cuthbert, God is with Us, Acclamation for Patriarch Demetrios, Akathist of Thanksgiving, Meditation on the Light, Panikhida, Ikon of Saint Seraphim, The Protecting Veil, Resurrection, Magnificat and Nunc Dimittis, The Hidden Treasure, Eonia, Mary of Egypt, The Repentant Thief, We Shall See Him as He Is, The Last Sleep of the Virgin, The Annunciation, Hymns of Paradise, Akhmatova Songs, The Child Lived, The Apocalypse, Let's Begin Again, Wake Up and Die, The Toll Houses, Agraphon, Vlepondas, The Last Discourse, Diodia, Song for Athene (performed at funeral of Diana, Princess of Wales), Nipson Fall and Resurrection, Total Eclipse, A New Beginning, Eternity's Sunrise, The Bridegroom, Lamentations and Praises, Life Eternal, Song of the Cosmos. *Publication:* The Music of Silence—A Composer's Testament. *Leisure interests:* iconography, love of Greece. *Address:* c/o Chester Music, 8–9 Frith Street, London, W1D 3JB, England.

TAVERNE, Suzanna, BA; British business executive; b. 3 Feb. 1960; d. of Dick Taverne and Janice Taverne; m.; Marc Vlessing 1993; one s. one d.; ed Pimlico School, Westminster School, Balliol Coll. Oxford; with S. G. Warburg and Co. Ltd 1982–90; Head of Strategic Planning, Newspaper Publishing PLC 1990–92, Finance Dir 1992–94; consultant to Saatchi & Saatchi PLC 1994–95; Dir of Strategy and Devt, Pearson PLC then Man. Dir FT Finance, Financial Times Group 1995–98; Man. Dir British Museum, London 1999–2001. *Address:* 35 Camden Square, London, NW1 9XA, England (Home). *Telephone:* (20) 7284-2146 (Home). *Fax:* (20) 7284-2421 (Home). *E-mail:* taverne@vlessing.com (Home).

TAVERNER, Sonia; Canadian ballerina; b. 18 May 1936, Byfleet, Surrey; d. of H. F. Taverner and Evelyn N. Taverner; ed Elmhurst Ballet School, Royal Ballet School, London and Ballet Arts and American Ballet Theater, New York; joined Royal Ballet 1954, toured USA and Canada; joined Royal Winnipeg Ballet 1956, leading dancer 1957, ballerina 1962–66; appeared with Royal Winnipeg Ballet, Commonwealth Arts Festival, London 1964; joined "Les Grands Ballets Canadiens" as prin. dancer 1966–74; appeared as guest artist with the Boston Ballet Co., in Swan Lake 1967; Guest teacher Les Grands Ballets Canadiens Summer School 1970; prin. artist with The Pa Ballet 1971–72; Head of Ballet Div., Grant MacEwan Community Coll. 1975–80; Dir Professional Program Devt, Alberta Ballet School 1981–82; f. School of Classical Ballet, Spruce Grove, Alberta 1982–97; Producer own concert "Variations" 1977; guest artist with Vancouver Opera 1977, Les Grands Ballets Canadiens in Giselle and The Nutcracker 1977, 1978, Alberta Ballet Co. in The Nutcracker and Raymonda 1978, 1979; guest teacher with Alberta Ballet Summer School 1975, 1976, Pacific Ballet Theatre Summer School 1979; guest artist with Toronto, Winnipeg and Vancouver Symphony Orchestras; guest teaching in Penticton, BC 1984–85; guest teacher with Edmonton Dance Centre 1998–; has toured extensively over North America, Jamaica and UK; registered mem. Royal Acad. of Dancing, Actors Equity Asscn, American Guild of Musical Artists; Dame Adeline Genée Silver Medal 1954, Canada Council Exploration Grant 1977. *Principal classical roles*

include: Swan Lake, Sleeping Beauty, Giselle, Nutcracker, Raymonda and Les Sylphides. *Leisure interests:* cooking, books, gardening. *Address:* P.O. Box 2039, Stony Plain, Alberta T7Z 1X6, Canada.

TAVERNIER, Bertrand René Maurice; French film director; b. 25 April 1941, Lyon; s. of René Tavernier and Geneviève Dumond; m. Claudine O'Hagan 1965; one s. one d.; ed Ecole St-Martin de Pontoise, Lycées Henri-IV, Fénelon, Paris, Univ. de Paris (Sorbonne); press attaché and journalist, then film dir; mem. Société des réalisateurs de films, APR; Pres. Inst. Lumière 1982–. *Films include:* Le baiser de Judas, Une charge explosive, La chance et l'amour, L'horloger de Saint-Paul (Louis Delluc prize 1973), Que la fête commence (César Best Screenplay, Best Direction) 1975, Le juge et l'assassin (César Best Screenplay 1976) 1976, Des enfants gâtés 1977, La mort en direct (Foreign Press Award 1979) 1979, Une semaine de vacances 1980, Coup de torchon 1981, Mississippi Blues 1983, Un dimanche à la campagne (Best Dir Award, Cannes Film Festival, NY Critics Award) 1984, Autour de minuit 1986, La passion béatrice 1987, La vie et rien d'autre 1988 (European Film Festival Special Prize 1989), Daddy nostalgie 1990, La guerre sans nom 1991, L.627 1991, La fille d'Artagnan 1994, L'Appât 1995, De l'autre côté du periph (TV documentary) 1997; jt screenplay La trace 1983; (producer) Veillées d'Armes 1994, Capitaine Conan 1996 (Méliès Prize for Best French Film 1996, César for Best Dir 1997), Ça commence aujourd'hui 1999 (Prix de la Fipresci, Berlin, Prix du Public, San Sebastian and Tübingen, Prix Photogramas de Plata for Best Foreign Language Film, Spain), Histoires de vies brisées 2001, Laissez-passer 2002 (Best Film, Best Dir Fort Lauderdale 2002). *Publications:* 30 ans de cinéma américain (jtly) 1970, 50 ans de cinéma américain (jtly) 1991, Qu'est-ce qu'on attend? 1993, Amis américains 1994 and other books. *Leisure interests:* jazz, food, literature, movies. *Address:* Little Bear, 7–9 rue Arthur Groussier, 75010 Paris, France. *Telephone:* 1-42-38-06-55 (Office). *Fax:* 1-42-45-00-33 (Office).

TAVIANI, Paolo; Italian film director; b. 8 Nov. 1931, San Miniato; brother of Vittorio Taviani (q.v.); ed Univ. of Pisa. *Films:* co-dir (with Vittorio Taviani): Un uomo da bruciare 1963, I fuorilegge del metraimonio 1963, Sovversivi 1967, Sotto il segno dello scorpione 1969, San Michele aveva un gallo 1971, Allonsanfan 1974, Padre Padrone 1977, The Meadow 1979, La notte di San Lorenzo (The Night of the Shooting Stars) 1981, Xaos 1984, Good Morning, Babylon 1988, Il Sole anche di Notte 1990, Fiorile 1993, The Elective Affinities, You Laugh.

TAVIANI, Vittorio; Italian film director; b. 20 Sept. 1929, San Miniato; brother of Paolo Taviani (q.v.); ed Univ. of Pisa. *Films:* co-dir Un uomo da Bruciare 1963, I fuorilegge del metraimonio 1963, Sovversivi 1967, Sotto il segno dello scorpione 1969, San Michele aveva un gallo 1971, Allonsanfan 1974, Padre Padrone 1977, The Meadow (Italian-French) 1979, La notte di San Lorenzo (The Night of the Shooting Stars) 1981, Xaos 1984, Good Morning, Babylon 1988, Il Sole Anche di Notte 1990, Fiorile 1993, The Elective Affinities, You Laugh.

TAVOLA, Kaliopate, MAgrSc; Fijian politician and economist; b. 10 Oct. 1946, Dravuni; m. Helen Tavola; two d. one s.; ed Massey Univ., New Zealand, Australian Nat. Univ., Australia; Agric. Officer Ministry of Primary Industries 1973–77, Sr Agric. Officer 1977–79, Prin. Economist 1979, Prin. Agric. Officer Eastern Div./Projects 1980, Chief Economist 1980–81, 1982–84, Dir of Agric. (acting) 1981–82, later Minister of Primary Industries; London Rep. Fiji Sugar Marketing (FSM) Co. Ltd 1984–88, Deputy CEO 1998–2000; Commercial Counsellor Fiji High Comm. 1984–88; Head of Mission, EU, Brussels 1988–98; Amb. to Belgium, Luxembourg, Netherlands, France, Italy, Spain, Portugal, Greece 1988–98; Perm. Rep. to UNESCO, FAO, WTO, WCO, OPCW; responsible for IFAD, MFO, PCA 1988–98; Commr-Gen. S Pacific Pavilion, EXPO '92, Seville, Spain 1992; Minister of Foreign Affairs and External Trade 2000–. *Leisure interests:* reading, gardening, music, golf. *Address:* Ministry of Foreign Affairs and External Trade, Government Buildings, POB 2220, Suva, Fiji (Office). *Telephone:* 3211458 (Office). *Fax:* 3301741 (Office). *E-mail:* info@foreignaffairs.gov.fj (Office). *Website:* www .foreignaffairs.gov.fj.

TAXELL, (Lars Evald) Christoffer, LLM; Finnish business executive; b. 14 Feb. 1948, Turku; s. of Lars Erik Taxell and Elna Hillevi Brunberg; m. Rachel Margareta Nygård 1974; Chair. Youth Org., Swedish People's Party 1970–72, Party Chair. 1985–90; Political Sec. 1970–71; Asst, School of Econ., Åbo Akademi, Turku 1973–75; MP 1975–91; Minister of Justice 1979–87, of Educ. and Science 1987–90; Pres. and CEO Partek Corpn 1990–. *Address:* Partek Corporation, 21600 Pargas, Finland. *Telephone:* 21 74261. *Fax:* 21 742 6340. *Website:* www.partek.fi.

TAYA, Col Maawiya Ould Sid'Ahmed; Mauritanian politician and army officer; b. 1943; served in Saharan War 1976–78, Chief of Mil. Operations, then Commdr garrison at Bir Mogkrein; Minister of Defence 1978–79; Commdr nat. gendarmerie 1979–80; Minister in charge of Perm. Secr., Mil. Cttee for Nat. Recovery 1979–81; Army Chief of Staff 1980–81, March–Dec. 1984; Prime Minister and Minister of Defence 1981–84, Dec. 1984–92; Pres. of Mauritania and Chair. Mil. Cttee for Nat. Salvation 1984–92, elected Pres. of Mauritania 1992–. *Address:* Présidence de la République, B.P. 184, Nouackchott, Mauritania. *Telephone:* 525-23-17.

TAYLOR, Allan Richard, OC; Canadian banker; b. 14 Sept. 1932, Prince Albert, Saskatchewan; s. of Norman Taylor and Anna Lydia Norbeck Taylor; m. Shirley Irene Ruston 1957; one s. one d.; joined Royal Bank of Canada 1949,

Dir, Head Int. Div. 1977–83, Pres. and COO 1983–86, CEO 1986–94, Chair. 1986–95; Dir Fairmont Hotels and Resorts, Toronto, General Motors of Canada Ltd, Canadian Inst. for Advanced Research, Toronto, Neuroscience Network, Montréal, Max Bell Foundation, Calgary; Pres. Int. Monetary Conf. 1992–93; Chair. Canadian Bankers Asscn 1984–86; mem. Council of Patrons, Canadian Outward Bound; mem. Advisory Council Canadian Exec. Service Overseas; mem. Advisory Bd Canadian Journalism Foundation, Advisory Bd, Canadian Foundation for AIDS Research; Exec. Adviser, Public Policy Forum; Hon. DJur (Univ. of Regina) 1987, (Concordia Univ.) 1988, (Queen's Univ.) 1991; Hon. DBA (Laval) 1990; Dr hc (Ottawa) 1992. *Leisure interests:* golf, tennis, fishing. *Address:* Suite 1835, North Tower, Royal Bank Plaza, Toronto, Ont., M5J 2J5, Canada. *Fax:* (416) 974-8713.

TAYLOR, Ann (see Taylor, (Winifred) Ann).

TAYLOR, Arthur Robert, MA; American business executive; b. 6 July 1935, Elizabeth, NJ; s. of Arthur Earl Taylor and Marion Hilda Scott; m. Marion McFarland 1959 (divorced); three d.; m. 2nd Kathryn Pelgrift; ed Brown Univ.; Asst Dir of Admissions, Brown Univ. 1957–60; with The First Boston Corpn 1961–70, Vice-Pres. Underwriting Dept 1966–70, Dir 1970; Vice-Pres. (Finance), Int. Paper Co. 1970–71, Exec. Vice-Pres. 1971–72, Dir 1971–72; Pres. and Dir CBS Inc. 1972–76; Dir Arthur Taylor & Co., New York 1977– (Chair. 1977–), Travelers Corpn, Rockefeller Centre Inc., American Friends of Bilderberg, Pitney Bowes Inc., Louisiana Land and Exploration, Eastern Airlines, Nomura Pacific Basin Fund, etc.; Vice-Chair. Forum Corpn, Boston, Mass. 1988–; Dean, Faculty of Business, Fordham Univ. 1985–89; Pres. Muhlenberg Coll., Pa 1992–; mem. Council on Foreign Relations, Nat. Cttee on American Foreign Policy, Center for Inter-American Relations, Japan Soc.; Trustee, Brown Univ., Franklin Savings Bank, NY Hosp., William H. Donner Foundation; Commr Trilateral Comm. *Publications:* article in Harvard Review of Business History 1971, chapter in The Other Side of Profit 1975. *Address:* Office of the President, Muhlenberg College, 24th and Chew Streets, Allentown, PA 18104; Main Street, Salisbury, CT 06068, USA (Home). *Telephone:* (610) 821-3100. *Fax:* (610) 821-3234.

TAYLOR, Charles, DPhil, FBA; Canadian professor of philosophy; b. 5 Nov. 1931, Montréal; s. of Walter Margrave Taylor and Simone Beaubien; m. Alba Romer 1956 (deceased), five d.; m. 2nd Aube Billard; ed McGill and Oxford Univs.; Fellow of All Souls Coll., Oxford 1956–61; Asst Prof. of Political Science and Philosophy 1961, Prof. of Political Science and Prof. of Philosophy 1973–; Prof. of Philosophy, Univ. of Montréal 1962–71; Chichele Prof. of Social and Political Theory, Oxford Univ. and Fellow of All Souls Coll. 1976–81; Prof. of Political Science, then of Philosophy, McGill Univ. 1982–; mem. Royal Soc. of Canada, corresp. mem. American Acad. of Arts and Sciences; John Locke Prize, Oxford 1955. *Publications:* The Explanation of Behaviour 1964, Hegel 1975, Hegel and Modern Society 1979, Human Agency and Language 1985, Philosophy and the Human Sciences 1985, Sources of Self 1989, The Malaise of Modernity 1991, Philosophical Arguments 1995. *Leisure interests:* skiing, swimming, hiking. *Address:* Department of Philosophy, McGill University, Stephen Leacock Building, Room 908, 855 Sherbrooke Street W, Montréal, Québec, H3A 2T7; 6603 Jeanne Mance, Montréal, Québec, H2V 4L1, Canada (Home). *Website:* www.mcgill.ca.

TAYLOR, Charles Ghankay; Liberian Head of State; Leader Nat. Patriotic Front of Liberia (NPFL) which was part of combined rebel force which overthrew fmr Pres. Samuel Doe; engaged in civil insurrection 1991–96; mem. Transitional Exec. Council of State 1996–97; Pres. of Liberia 1997–. *Address:* Office of the President, Executive Mansion, P.O. Box 10-9001, Capitol Hill, 1000 Monrovia 10, Liberia. *E-mail:* emansion@liberia.net (Office).

TAYLOR, Derek H.; Turks and Caicos Islands politician; Leader People's Democratic Movement (PDM); Chief Minister and Minister of Finance, Devt and Commerce Jan. 1995–. *Address:* Office of the Chief Minister, Government Compound, Grand Turk, The Turks and Caicos Islands (Office). *Telephone:* 946-2801 (Office). *Fax:* 946-2777 (Office). *E-mail:* unfptc@tciway.tc (Office).

TAYLOR, Dame Elizabeth Rosemond, DBE; British film actress; b. 27 Feb. 1932, London; d. of Francis Taylor and Sara Sothern; m. 1st Conrad Nicholas Hilton, Jr 1950 (divorced); m. 2nd Michael Wilding 1952 (divorced); two s.; m. 3rd Mike Todd 1957 (died 1958); one d.; m. 4th Eddie Fisher 1959 (divorced); m. 5th Richard Burton 1964 (divorced 1974, remarried 1975, divorced 1976); one adopted d.; m. 7th Senator John Warner (q.v.) 1976 (divorced 1982); m. 8th Larry Fortensky 1991 (divorced 1996); ed Byron House, Hawthorne School and Metro-Goldwyn-Mayer School; active in philanthropic and relief charitable causes internationally including Israeli War Victims Fund for the Chaim Sheba Hosp. 1976, UNICEF, Variety Children's Hosps., medical clinics in Botswana; inititiated Ben Gurion Univ.-Elizabeth Taylor Fund for Children of the Negev 1982; supporter AIDS Project LA 1985; Founder, Nat. Chair. Council for AIDS Research (AmFAR) 1985–, int. fund 1985–; Founder Elizabeth Taylor AIDS Foundation 1991–; licensed fragrances: Elizabeth Taylor's Passion, Passion for Men, White Diamonds/Elizabeth Taylor, Elizabeth Taylor's Diamonds and Emeralds, Diamonds and Rubies, Diamonds and Sapphires; jewelry: The Elizabeth Taylor Fashion Jewelry Collection for Avon; Commdr des Arts et des Lettres 1985; Légion d'honneur (for work with AmFAR) 1987; Aristotle S. Onassis Foundation Award 1988, Jean Hersholt Humanitarian Acad. Award (for work as AIDS advocate), Life Achievement Award, American Film Inst. 1993, Lifetime Achievement Award, Screen Actors Guild 1998, BAFTA Fellowship 1999; honoured with dedication of Elizabeth Taylor Clinic, Washington 1993. *Films include:* Lassie Come Home

1942, There's One Born Every Minute 1943, The White Cliffs of Dover 1943, Jane Eyre 1943, National Velvet 1944, Courage of Lassie 1946, Life with Father 1946, Cynthia 1947, A Date With Judy 1948, Julia Misbehaves 1948, Little Women 1948, Conspirator 1949, The Big Hangover 1949, Father's Little Dividend 1950, Father of the Bride 1950, A Place in the Sun 1950, Love is Better Than Ever 1951, Ivanhoe 1951, Rhapsody 1954, Elephant Walk 1954, Beau Brummel 1954, The Last Time I Saw Paris 1955, Giant 1956, Raintree Country 1957, Cat on a Hot Tin Roof 1958, Suddenly Last Summer 1959, Butterfield 8 1960, Cleopatra 1962, The VIPs 1963, The Sandpiper 1965, Who's Afraid of Virginia Woolf? 1966, The Taming of the Shrew 1967, The Comedians 1967, Reflections in a Golden Eye 1967, Doctor Faustus 1968, Boom 1968, Secret Ceremony 1968, The Only Game in Town 1969, Under Milk Wood 1971, X, Y and Zee 1972, Hammersmith is Out 1972, Night Watch 1973, Ash Wednesday 1974, The Driver's Seat 1975, Blue Bird 1976, A Little Night Music 1977, The Mirror Crack'd 1980, Between Friends 1983, The Young Toscanini 1988, The Flintstones 1994. *Television appearances include:* Divorce His, Divorce Hers 1973, Victory at Entebbe 1977, Return Engagement 1979, Between Friends 1982, Hotel (series) 1984, Malice in Wonderland 1986, North and South (mini-series) 1986, There Must be a Pony 1986, Poker Alice 1987, Sweet Bird of Youth 1989. *Plays include:* The Little Foxes (New York) 1981, (Los Angeles) 1981, (London) 1982, Private Lives (New York) 1983. *Publications:* World Enough and Time (with Richard Burton) 1964, Elizabeth Taylor 1965, Elizabeth Taylor Takes Off – On Weight Gain, Weight Loss, Self-Esteem and Self Image 1988. *Address:* P.O. Box 55995, Sherman Oaks, CA 91413, USA (Office).

TAYLOR, Graham, OBE; British professional football manager; b. 15 Sept. 1944, Worksop; s. of Tommy Taylor; m. Rita Cowling 1965; two d.; ed Scunthorpe Grammar Sch.; player Grimsby Town 1962–68, Lincoln City 1968–72 (Man. 1972–77); Man. Watford FC 1977–87, 1996–2001, Aston Villa 1987–90, 2001–, England nat. team 1990–93, Wolverhampton Wanderers FC 1994–95; Dir (non-exec.) Aston Villa 2001–; patron Lincoln City FC. *Address:* c/o Aston Villa Football Club, Villa Park, Trinity Road, Birmingham, B6 6HE, England (Office).

TAYLOR, Gregory Frank, AO, BEcons; Australian civil servant and diplomatist; b. 1 July 1942, Adelaide; s. of Frank Taylor and Constance Rischbieth; m. Jill Beatrice Bodman 1967; one s. one d.; ed Univ. of Adelaide; Chair. Industries Assistance Comm., Canberra 1988; CEO Dept of Employment Educ. and Training 1989–94, Dept of Primary Industries and Energy 1993–95, Dept of Industry, Tech. and Commerce 1996; Exec. Dir IMF, Washington, DC 1997–2000. *Leisure interest:* skiing. *Address:* c/o International Monetary Fund, 700 19th Street, NW, Washington, DC 20431; 3915 Ivy Ice Court, NW, Washington, DC 20007, USA (Office).

TAYLOR, John B., BA, D. ECONS.; American economist; b. 1947, Yonkers, NY; m. Allyn Taylor; two c.; ed Princeton Univ., Stanford Univ.; Mary and Robert Raymond Prof. of Econs, Stanford Univ., also Sr Fellow Hoover Inst., Stanford Inst. for Econ. Policy Research, Vice-Chair. Faculty Senate, Stanford Univ., fmr Chair. Stanford Cttee on Undergrad. Studies, fmr Faculty Rep. Finance Cttee of Stanford Univ. Bd of Trustees; mem. Presidential Council of Econ. Advisers (CEA) under Presidents Gerald Ford and George Bush, Sr; Under-Sec. of Treasury for Int. Affairs June 2001–; Hoagland Prize 1992, Lilian and Thomas B. Rhodes Prize 1997. *Address:* US Treasury, 1500 Pennsylvania Ave, NW, Washington, DC 20220, U.S.A. (Office). *Telephone:* (202) 622-2000 (Office). *Fax:* (202) 622-6415 (Office).

TAYLOR, Rt Rev John Bernard, KCVO, MA; British ecclesiastic; b. 6 May 1929, Newcastle upon Tyne; s. of George Taylor and Gwendoline Taylor; m. Linda Courtenay Barnes 1956; one s. two d.; ed Watford Grammar School, Christ's and Jesus Colls. Cambridge, Hebrew Univ. of Jerusalem and Ridley Hall, Cambridge; RAF service 1952–54; ordained deacon 1956, priest 1957; Vicar of Henham and Elsenham, Essex 1959–64; Vice-Prin. Oak Hill Theological Coll. London 1964–72; Vicar of All Saints' Woodford Wells, Essex 1972–75; Archdeacon of West Ham 1975–80; Bishop of St Albans 1980–95; Chair. Council, Wycliffe Hall, Oxford 1985–99; Lord High Almoner to HM the Queen 1988–97; Pres. The Bible Soc. 1997–; Pres. and Chair. of Council, Haileybury 1980–95; Pres. Hildenborough Evangelistic Trust 1986–2000, Garden Tomb Asscn 1987–; Church's Ministry Among Jewish People 1996–; Chair. Council, Tyndale House, Cambridge 1996–; Hon. LLD. *Publications:* Tyndale Commentary on Ezekiel 1969, Preaching through the Prophets 1983, Preaching on God's Justice 1994. *Leisure interests:* bird-watching, walking. *Address:* 22 Conduit Head Road, Cambridge, CB3 0EY, England. *Telephone:* (1223) 313783.

TAYLOR, John Bryan, PhD, FRS; British physicist; b. 26 Dec. 1928, Birmingham; s. of Frank H. Taylor and Ada Taylor (née Stinton); m. Joan M. Hargest 1951; one s. one d.; ed Oldbury Co. High School and Birmingham Univ.; served RAF 1950–52; Physicist, Atomic Weapons Research Establishment, Aldermaston 1955–59, 1961–62; Harkness Fellow, Univ. of Calif. 1959–60; on staff of UKAEA, Culham Lab. 1962–89, Head of Theory Div. 1963–81, Chief Physicist Culham Lab. 1981–89, Consultant 1994–; Fondren Foundation Prof. of Plasma Theory, Univ. of Texas at Austin 1989–94; mem. Inst. for Advanced Study, Princeton, NJ 1969, 1980 and 1981; Fellow American Physical Soc.; Maxwell Medal (Inst. of Physics) 1971, Max Born Prize and Medal (German Physical Soc.) 1979, Award for Excellence in Plasma Research (American Physical Soc.) 1986, James Clerk Maxwell Prize (American Physical Soc.) 1999. *Publications:* contribs. to scientific learned journals. *Leisure interests:* gliding, model engineering. *Address:* Radwinter, Winterbrook Lane, Wallingford, OX10 9EJ, England. *Telephone:* (1491) 837269. *Fax:* (1235) 466435 (Office).

TAYLOR, (John) Maxwell (Percy); British insurance broker; b. 17 March 1948; s. of Harold Guy Percy Taylor and Anne Katherine Taylor (née Stafford); m. Dawn Susan Harling 1970; one s. one d.; joined Willis Faber & Dumas as Jr aviation broker 1970; Dir Willis Faber, then Willis Corroon Group PLC, Chair. and Chief Exec. Willis, Faber & Dumas, Group Exec. Dir 1997; elected to Council of Lloyd's 1997, Chair. of Lloyd's 1998–2000; fmr Chair. Lloyd' Insurance Brokers' Cttee, London Insurance Market Network; Vice-Pres. Insurance Inst. of London. *Leisure interests:* music, skiing, golf, travelling. *Address:* c/o Office of the Chairman, Lloyds, 1 Lime Street, London, EC3M 7HA, England (Office). *Telephone:* (20) 7327-1000 (Office). *Fax:* (20) 7327-5926 (Office).

TAYLOR, John Russell, MA; British writer and professor of cinema studies; b. 19 June 1935, Dover, Kent; s. of Arthur Russell Taylor and Kathleen Mary (née Picker) Taylor; ed Dover Grammar School, Jesus Coll. Cambridge, Courtauld Inst. of Art; Sub Ed., Times Educ. Supplement 1959–60; Editorial Asst, Times Literary Supplement 1960–62; Film Critic, The Times 1962–73; Prof., Div. of Cinema, Univ. of Southern Calif., USA 1972–78; Art Critic, The Times 1978–; Ed. Films and Filming 1983–90. *Publications:* Anger and After 1962, Anatomy of a Television Play 1962, Cinema Eye, Cinema Ear 1964, Penguin Dictionary of the Theatre 1966, The Art Nouveau Book in Britain 1966, The Rise and Fall of the Well-Made Play 1967, The Art Dealers 1969, The Hollywood Musical 1971, The Second Wave 1971, Directors and Directions 1975, Hitch 1978, Impressionism 1981, Strangers in Paradise 1983, Ingrid Bergman 1983, Alec Guinness 1984, Vivien Leigh 1984, Hollywood 1940s 1985, Portraits of the British Cinema 1986, Orson Welles 1986, Edward Wolfe 1986, Great Movie Moments 1987, Meninsky 1990, Impressionist Dreams 1990, Liz Taylor 1991, Muriel Pemberton 1993, Ricardo Cinalli 1993, Igor Mitoraj 1993, Claude Monet 1995, Bill Jacklin 1997, The World of Michael Parkes 1998, Antonio Smiola 1998, The Sun is God 1999, Geoffrey Dashwood 2001, Peter Coker 2001; edited: Look Back in Anger: A Casebook 1968, The Pleasure Dome (Graham Greene on Film) 1972, Masterworks of British Cinema 1974. *Leisure interest:* book collecting. *Address:* c/o The Times, 1 Pennington Street, London, E1 9XN, England. *Telephone:* (20) 7782-5000.

TAYLOR, Joseph Hooton, Jr., PhD; American radio astronomer and physicist; b. 29 March 1941, Philadelphia; s. of Joseph Taylor and Sylvia Evans; m. Marietta Bisson 1976; one s. two d.; ed Haverford Coll. and Harvard Univ.; Research Fellow and Lecturer, Harvard Univ. 1968–69; Asst Prof. of Astronomy, Univ. of Mass., Amherst 1969–72, Assoc. Prof. 1973–77, Prof. 1977–81; Prof. of Physics, Princeton Univ. 1980–, James McDonnell Distinguished Prof. of Physics 1986–, Dean of Faculty 1997–; Fellow, American Acad. of Arts and Sciences; mem. NAS, American Astronomy Soc., Int. Scientific Radio Union, Int. Astronomy Union; Wolf Prize in Physics 1992; shared Nobel Prize for Physics 1993; Hon. DSc (Chicago) 1985, (Mass.) 1994 and other awards and distinctions. *Publication:* Pulsars 1977. *Address:* Department of Physics, Princeton University, 215 Jadwin Hall, P.O. Box 708, Princeton, NJ 08544 (Office); 272 Hartley Avenue, Princeton, NJ 08540, USA (Home).

TAYLOR, Joyce, FRTS, BA; British television executive; b. 14 March 1948, Glasgow; d. of Lord and Lady Taylor of Gryfe; m. John Lloyd-Richards 1982; one s. one d.; ed Hutchesons' Girls' Grammar School, Glasgow and Univ. of Strathclyde; worked in production, BBC 1968–70; producer, audio-visual service, Univ. of Glasgow 1977–85; Head of Programming, Clyde Cablevision 1985–89; Chief Exec. Programming, United Artists 1989–95; Man. Dir Discovery Communications Europe 1995–2002; Lifetime Achievement Award (Royal TV Soc.) 1998. *Leisure interests:* theatre, reading, walking. *Address:* c/o Discovery Communications Europe, 160 Great Portland Street, London, W1, England.

TAYLOR, Ken; British screenwriter; b. 1922, Bolton, Lancs.; m. Gillian Dorothea Black 1953; two s. two d.; ed Greshams school; Writers' Guild Best Original Teleplay Award 1964, Guild of TV Producers and Dirs' Writer of the Year Award 1964, Royal Soc. Writer's Award 1984. *Plays for TV include:* One of Us, Special Occasion, The Tin Whistle Man, China Doll, Into the Dark, Parkin's Primitives, The Long Distance Blue, The Slaughtermen, The Devil and John Brown, The Seekers, The Magicians, The Edwardians: E. Nesbit, Death or Liberty (Churchill's People), The Pankhursts, Christabel Pankhurst, Sylvia Pankhurst (3 plays for BBC's Shoulder to Shoulder), The Poisoning of Charles Bravo, The Devil's Crown (5 plays on Henry II), Cause Célèbre 1988, The Camomile Lawn 1992, The Peacock Spring 1995; many adaptations for TV of works by Somerset Maugham, D. H. Lawrence, Jane Austen, Muriel Spark, Rebecca West, Mary Wesley etc., also The Jewel in the Crown from Paul Scott's The Raj Quartet. *Stage plays:* The Strange Affair of Charles Bravo 1979, Staying On 1997. *Publication:* Staying On 2001. *Leisure interests:* walking, music, theatre. *Address:* c/o Peters Fraser and Dunlop, Drury House, 34–43 Russell Street, London, WC2B 5HA, England. *Telephone:* (1736) 752287 (Home); (20) 7344-7000. *Fax:* (1736) 752536 (Home).

TAYLOR, Lance Jerome, BS, PhD; American university professor; b. 25 May 1940, Montpelier, Idaho; s. of W. Jerome Taylor and Ruth R. Taylor; m. Yvonne S. M. Taylor 1963; one s. one d.; ed Calif. Inst. of Tech., Harvard Univ. Asst and Assoc. Prof. Harvard Univ. 1968–74; Prof. MIT 1974–93; Arnhold Prof. of Int. Co-operation and Devt, New School Univ. 1993–; Visiting Prof. Univ. of Brasília 1973–74, Delhi School of Econs 1987–88, Stockholm School of Econs 1990; consultant for UN agencies and over 25 govts and agencies; Marshall Lecturer, Univ. of Cambridge 1987; V. K. Ramaswamy Lecturer, Delhi School of Econs 1988. *Publications:* Structuralist Macroeconomics 1983, Varieties of Stabilization Experience 1988, Income Distribution, Inflation and Growth 1991, The Market Meets its Match: Restructuring the Economies of Eastern Europe 1994, Global Finance at Risk 2000, Reconstructing Macroeconomics 2003. *Leisure interest:* raising cashmere goats. *Address:* Graduate Faculty, New School for Social Research, 65 Fifth Avenue, New York, NY 10003 (Office); 15 Old County Road, P.O. Box 378, Washington, ME 04574, USA (Home). *Telephone:* (207) 845-2722 (Home). *Fax:* (207) 845-2589 (Home). *E-mail:* lance@blacklocust.com (Home).

TAYLOR, Martin; British banker and retailing executive; b. 8 June 1952; m. Janet Davey 1976; two d.; ed Eton Coll. and Balliol Coll. Oxford; joined Reuters news agency, Paris; subsequently ed. Lex comment column, Financial Times; Personal Asst to Chair. of Courtaulds, later Dir Courtaulds Clothing Div.; CEO Courtaulds PLC 1990–93, Chair. 1993; Dir Barclays Bank PLC Nov. 1993–, Chief Exec. 1994–98; Leader New Whitehall Task Force 1997–; Dir (non-exec.) WH Smith Group PLC 1993–98, Chair. 1999–. *Address:* WH Smith Group PLC, Nations House, 103 Wigmore Street, London, W1H 0WH, England (Office).

TAYLOR, Martin; British jazz guitarist; b. Ayr; s. of Buck Taylor; self-taught; began playing at age four, playing in local bands at age 12, support act for Count Basie and his Orchestra, QE2; performed and recorded regularly with violinist Stéphane Grappelli late 1970s and 1980s alongside solo career; formed Martin Taylor's Spirit of Django 1994; played and recorded with Bill Wyman's Rhythm Kings 1998, 1999; featured on Prefab Sprout album Andromeda Heights; recent recordings (with Steve Howe) of guitars from the Chinery Collection; Dr. hc (Paisley); Freeman of London. *Albums:* Taylor Made (debut) 1978, numerous albums with Stéphane Grappelli and guest musicians, Sarabanda (with John Patitucci and Paulinho Da Costa) 1987, Don't Fret 1990, Artistry 1993, Reunion (with Stéphane Grappelli) 1993, Spirit of Django (Best Album 1995, Best Guitarist (for seventh time), British Jazz Awards), Portraits. *Video:* Martin Taylor in Concert. *Film soundtracks include:* (with Stéphane Grappelli) Milou en Mai, Dirty Rotten Scoundrels.

TAYLOR, Rev. Michael Hugh, OBE, MA, BD, DLitt, STM; British minister of religion, charity administrator and university teacher; b. 8 Sept. 1936, Northampton; s. of Albert Taylor and Gwendolen Taylor; m. Adele May Dixon 1960; two s. one d.; ed Northampton Grammar School, Manchester Univ., Union Theological Seminary, New York; Baptist Minister, North Shields, Northumberland and Hall Green, Birmingham 1960–69; Prin. Northern Baptist Coll., Manchester 1970–85; Lecturer in Theology and Ethics, Univ. of Manchester 1970–85; Examining Chaplain to Bishop of Manchester 1975–85; Dir Christian Aid 1985–97; Pres. Selly Oak Colls., Birmingham 1998–99; Prof. of Social Theology, Univ. of Birmingham 1999–, Dir World Faiths Devt Dialogue 2002–; Chair. Audenshaw Foundation Trustees 1979–93; mem. Comm. on Theological Educ., WCC 1972–91, Vice-Moderator 1985–91; mem. Council, Overseas Devt Inst. 1986–2000; mem. Comm. IV: Sharing and Service WCC; Chair. Asscn of Protestant Devt Agencies in Europe 1991–94; Pres. Jubilee 2000 UK Coalition 1997–; Trustee Mines Advisory Group 1998, Chair. 2000–; Chair. Burma Campaign –2000; Chair. Health Unlimited 2002; Hon. mem. of Foundation, Worcester Cathedral; Fulbright Travel Award 1969. *Publications:* Variations on a Theme 1971, Learning to Care 1983, Good for the Poor 1990, Christianity and the Persistence of Poverty 1991, Not Angels but Agencies 1995, Jesus and the International Financial Institutions 1996, Past their Sell-By Date? The Role of Northern NGOs in the Future of Development 1998, Poverty and Christianity 2000, Christianity, Poverty and Wealth in the 21st Century 2003. *Leisure interests:* walking, theatre, music, cinema, cooking. *Address:* University of Birmingham, Selly Oak, Birmingham, B29 6LQ, England. *Telephone:* (121) 415-2220. *E-mail:* m.h.taylor@bham.ac.uk (Office).

TAYLOR, Paul B.; American dancer and choreographer; b. 29 July 1930, Allegheny Co., Pa; s. of Paul B. Taylor and Elizabeth P. Rust; ed Virginia Episcopal School, Syracuse Univ., Juilliard School, Metropolitan School of Ballet and Martha Graham School of Contemporary Dance; fmr dancer with the cos. of Martha Graham, George Balanchine, Charles Weidman, Anna Sokolow, Merce Cunningham, Katherine Litz, James Waring and Pearl Lang; Dancer-Choreographer-Dir The Paul Taylor Dance Co. 1955–; co. has performed in 450 cities in more than 60 countries; choreographed 119 dances, many of them taken up by more than 50 other dance cos worldwide; Guggenheim Fellowship 1961, 1965, 1983; Hon. Mem. American Acad. and Inst. of Arts and Letters 1989; Hon. Dr Fine Arts (Connecticut Coll., Duke Univ.) 1983, (Syracuse Univ.) 1986; Centennial Achievement Award (Ohio State Univ.), 1970; Brandeis Univ. Creative Arts Award gold medal 1978, Dance Magazine Award 1980, Samuel H. Scripps/American Dance Festival Award 1983, MacArthur 'Genius' Award 1985, New York State Governor's Award 1987, New York City Mayor's Award of Honor for Art and Culture 1989, Kennedy Center Honour 1992, Nat. Medal of Arts 1993, Award from Chicago Int. Film Festival 1993, Algur H. Meadows Award for Excellence in the Arts 1995, Emmy Award for Speaking in Tongues 1991; Commdr des Arts et des Lettres 1990, Légion d'honneur 2000. *Choreography includes:* Three Epitaphs 1956, Rebus 1958, Tablet 1960, Junction 1961, Fibers 1961, Insects and Heroes 1961, Tracer 1962, Piece Period 1962, Aureole 1962, Party Mix 1963, Scudorama 1963, Duet 1964, From Sea to Shining Sea 1965, Post

Meridian 1965, Orbs 1966, Agathes' Tale 1967, Lento 1967, Public Domain 1968, Private Domain 1969, Churchyard 1969, Foreign Exchange 1970, Big Bertha 1970, Fêtes 1971, Book of Beasts 1971, Guests of May 1972, So Long Eden 1972, Noah's Minstrels 1973, American Genesis 1973, Untitled Quartet 1974, Sports and Follies 1974, Esplanade 1975, Runes 1975, Cloven Kingdom 1976, Polaris 1976, Images 1976, Dust 1977, Aphrodisiamania 1977, Airs 1978, Diggity 1978, Nightshade 1979, Profiles 1979, Le Sacre du Printemps (subtitled The Rehearsal) 1980, Arden Court 1981, Lost, Found and Lost 1982, Mercuric Tidings 1982, Sunset 1983, Snow White 1983, Musette 1983, Equinox 1983, Byzantium 1984, Roses 1985, Last Look 1985, A Musical Offering 1986, Ab Ovo Usted Mala 1986, Syzygy 1987, Kith and Kin 1987, Minikin Fair 1989, Speaking in Tongues 1989, The Sorcerer's Sofa 1989, Of Bright and Blue Birds and The Gala Sun 1990, Company B 1991, Fact and Fancy (3 Epitaphs and All) 1991, Oz 1992, A Field of Grass 1993, Spindrift 1993, Moonbine 1994, Funny Papers 1994, Offenbach Overtures 1995, Eventide 1996, Prime Numbers 1996, Piazzolla Caldera 1997, The World 1998, Oh, You Kid! 1999, Cascade 1999, Arabesque 1999, Fiends Angelical 2000, Dandelion Wine 2000, Black Tuesday 2001, Antique Valentine 2001, Promethean Fire 2002, Dream Girls 2002, In the Beginning 2003. *Television:* eight different programmes on Dance in America (PBS). *Publication:* Private Domain (autobiog.) 1987. *Leisure interests:* gardening, snorkelling. *Address:* Paul Taylor Dance Co., 552 Broadway, New York, NY 10012, USA.

TAYLOR, Richard Edward, PhD, FRSC, FRS; Canadian physicist; b. 2 Nov. 1929, Medicine Hat, Alberta; s. of Clarence Richard Taylor and Delia Alena (née Brunsdale) Taylor; m. Rita Jean Bonneau 1951; one s.; ed Univ. of Alberta, Edmonton, Stanford Univ., Calif., USA; Boursier, Laboratoire de l'Accélérateur Linéaire, Orsay, France 1958–61; physicist, Lawrence Berkeley Lab., Berkeley, Calif. 1961–62; staff mem. Stanford Linear Accelerator Center, Calif. 1962–68, Assoc. Prof. 1968–70, Prof. 1970–, Assoc. Dir 1982–86; Dr hc (Paris-Sud) 1980, (Blaise-Pascal) 1997; Hon. DSc (Alberta) 1991, (Lethbridge, Alberta) 1993, (Vic., BC) 1994; Hon LLD (Calgary, Alberta) 1993; Dr hc (Carleton Univ., Ont.) 1999; Hon. DSc (Liverpool) 1999, (Queen's, Ont.) 2000; Guggenheim Fellow 1971–72, A. von Humboldt Sr Scientist Award 1982, W.K.H. Panofsky Prize (with H.W. Kendall and J.I. Friedman) 1989, Nobel Prize in Physics (with H.W. Kendall and J.I. Friedman) 1990. *Publications:* numerous scientific papers. *Address:* Stanford Linear Accelerator Center (SLAC), Mail Stop 43 (Office); 2575 Sand Hill Road, Menlo Park, CA 94025 (Office); 757 Mayfield Avenue, Stanford, CA 94305, USA (Home). *Telephone:* (650) 926-2417 (Office); (650) 857-1345 (Home). *Fax:* (650) 926-2923 (Office). *E-mail:* retaylor@slac.stanford.edu (Office).

TAYLOR, Stuart Ross, MA, PhD, DSc, FAA; New Zealand geochemist; b. 26 Nov. 1925; s. of the late T. S. Taylor; m. Noel White 1958; three d.; ed Ashburton High School, NZ, Canterbury Univ. Coll., Univ. of NZ and Indiana Univ., USA; Lecturer in Mineralogy, Univ. of Oxford 1954–58; Sr Lecturer in Geochemistry, Univ. of Cape Town 1958–60; Professorial Fellow, Research School of Earth Science, Australian Nat. Univ. (ANU) 1961–90, Visiting Fellow, Research School of Physical Sciences 1991, 1993–99; mem. Council, ANU 1971–76; mem. Lunar Sample Preliminary Examination Team, Houston, Tex. 1969–70, Prin. Investigator, Lunar Sample Analysis Program 1970–90; Visiting Prof., Univ. of Vienna 1992, 1996; Foreign Assoc. NAS (USA); Fellow Geochemical Soc., American Geophysical Union; Hon. Fellow, UK and Indian Geological Socs, Royal Soc. of NZ; Goldschmidt Medal, Geochemical Soc. 1993, Gilbert Award, Geological Soc. of America 1994, Leonard Medal, Meteoritical Soc. 1998, Bucher Medal, American Geophysical Union 2002; Asteroid 5670 named Ross Taylor. *Publications include:* Spectrochemical Analysis (jtly) 1961, Moon Rocks and Minerals (jtly) 1971, Lunar Science: A Post-Apollo View 1975, Planetary Science: A Lunar Perspective 1982, The Continental Crust: Its Composition and Evolution (jtly) 1985, Solar System Evolution: A New Perspective 1992, Destiny or Chance: Our Solar System and Its Place in the Cosmos 1998 and some 220 papers in scientific journals. *Leisure interests:* reading history, gardening, classical music. *Address:* 18 Sheehan Street, Pearce, ACT 2607, Australia.

TAYLOR, Wendy Ann, CBE, LDAD, FZS, FRBS; British sculptor; b. 29 July 1945, Stamford, Lincs.; d. of Edward P. Taylor and Lilian M. Wright; m. Bruce Robertson 1982; one s.; ed St Martin's School of Art; mem. Fine Art Bd Council of Acad. Awards 1980–85, Specialist Adviser 1985–93; Specialist Adviser, Cttee for Art and Design 1988–93; mem. Cttee for Art and Design, Council of Nat. Acad. Awards; mem. Royal Fine Art Comm. 1981–99; mem. Council, Morley Coll. 1984–89; mem. Court RCA; design consultant, New Towns Comm. (Basildon) 1985–; design consultant, London Borough of Barking and Dagenham 1989–93, 1997–; Advisory Bd, London Docklands Devt Corpn 1989–98; mem. Advisory Group of the Polytechnics and Colls Funding Council 1989–90; mem. Council, Royal Soc. of British Sculptors 1999–; Fellow Queen Mary and Westfield Coll. (London Univ.); Trustee, Leicestershire's Appeal for Music and the Arts 1993–; Walter Neurath Award 1964, Pratt Award 1965, Sainsbury Award 1966, Arts Council Award 1977, Duais Na Riochta Gold Medal, Eire 1977. *Exhibitions include:* 12 one-woman exhbns; participated in more than 100 group exhbns 1964–82; work represented in collections in UK, Europe, USA etc.; over 60 major comms in towns and cities throughout UK. *Leisure interest:* gardening. *Address:* 73 Bow Road, London, E3 2AN, England. *Telephone:* (20) 8981-2037. *Fax:* (20) 8980-3153. *Website:* wendytaylorsculpture.com (Office).

TAYLOR, Sir William, Kt, CBE; British academic; b. 31 May 1930, Crayford, Kent; s. of Herbert Taylor and Maud Taylor; m. Rita Hague 1954; one s. two d.; ed London School of Econs; fmr school teacher and deputy head teacher, Kent; later worked in two colls. of educ. and Dept of Educ., Oxford Univ.; Prof. of Educ. Univ. of Bristol 1966; Dir London Inst. of Educ. 1973–83; Prin., Univ. of London 1983–85; Vice-Chancellor, Univ. of Hull 1985–91; Chair. Council for Accreditation of Teacher Educ. (CATE) 1984–93; Chair. Bd NFER/Nelson publishing co. 1988–99; Chair. of Convocation, Univ. of London 1994–97; Pres. Soc. for Research in Higher Educ. 1996–2001; Vice-Chancellor, Univ. of Huddersfield 1994–95, Thames Valley Univ. 1998–99; Chair. Northern Ireland Cttee for Teacher Educ. 1994–; Visiting Prof. Univ. of Oxford 1991–97, Univ. of Southampton 1998–; Gov. Univ. of Glamorgan 1992–2002, Christ Church Univ. Coll. Canterbury 1996–; mem. Council, Hong Kong Inst. of Educ. 1998–2003; Charter Fellow, Coll. of Preceptors; Hon. Fellow, Westminster Coll. Oxford, Thames Polytechnic, Commonwealth Council for Educ. Admin., Inst. of Educ.; Dr hc (Aston, Bristol, Leeds, London, Kent, Loughborough, Open Univ., Huddersfield, Hull, Kingston, Plymouth, Oxford Brookes, Univ. of West of England, Ulster, Queen's Univ. Belfast, Southampton). *Publications include:* The Secondary Modern School, Society and the Education of Teachers, Planning and Policy in Post-secondary Education, Heading for Change, Research and Reform in Teacher Education, The Metaphors of Education, Universities under Scrutiny. *Leisure interest:* books and music. *Address:* Yew Trees, 20 Hinton Fields, King's Worthy, Winchester, Hants., SO23 7QB, England. *Telephone:* (1962) 883485. *E-mail:* william.taylor@btinternet.com (Office).

TAYLOR, Rt Hon (Winifred) Ann, PC, MP; British politician; b. 2 July 1947, Motherwell; m. David Taylor 1966; one s. one d.; ed Bolton School and Univs. of Bradford and Sheffield; fmr teacher and part-time tutor, Open Univ.; MP for Bolton West 1974–83, for Dewsbury 1987–; Parl. Pvt. Sec. to Sec. of State for Educ. and Science 1975–76, to Sec. of State for Defence 1976–77; an Asst Govt Whip 1977–79; Opposition Spokesman on Educ. 1979–81, on Housing 1981–83, on Home Affairs 1987–90, on Environment 1990–92, on Educ. 1992–94; Shadow Leader of House of Commons 1994–97; Pres. of the Council and Leader of the House of Commons 1997–98; Chief Whip 1998–2001; Chair. Select Cttee on Modernization 1997–98; Spokesperson on Citizen's Charter 1994–95; mem. Select Cttee on Standards and Privileges 1995–97; Hon. Fellow, Birkbeck Coll. London; mem. Labour Party. *Address:* 12 Downing Street, London, SW1A 2AA (Office); House of Commons, London, SW1A 0AA, England. *Telephone:* (20) 7270-2020 (Office).

TAYLOR-WOOD, Sam; British artist, photographer and film maker; b. 1967; m. Jay Jopling; ed Hastings Coll. of Art and Tech., Goldsmiths Coll., London; uses highly choreographed photographic sequences; first solo exhbn, London 1994. *Group exhibitions include:* Information Dienst, Kunsthalle, Stuttgart 1993, Don't Look Now, Thread Waxing Space, New York 1994, Masculin/Féminin, Centre Georges Pompidou, Paris 1995 and Young British Artists (Project for General Release), 46th Venice Biennale 1995, Brilliant! New Art from London, Walker Art Center, Minneapolis and Contemporary Arts Museum, Houston 1995–96, Festival for Contemporary British Artists, Magazzini d'Arte Moderne, Rome, Prospect 96, Kunstverein, Frankfurt, Manifesta 1, Museum Boijmans Van Beuningen and Witte de With, Rotterdam, The Event Horizon, Irish Museum of Modern Art, Dublin, Contemporary British Art, Toyama Museum, Life/Live, Musée d'Art Moderne de la Ville de Paris and Centro de Exposições do Centro Cultural de Belém, Lisbon, Full House, Kunstmuseum Wolfsburg 1996, Creux de l'Enfer, Centre d'art contemporain, Thiers, 47th Venice Biennale, Home Sweet Home, Deichtorhallen Hamburg, Truce, SITE Santa Fe, NM, Sensation, Royal Acad. of Arts, London, Worldwide Video Festival, Stedelijk Museum, Amsterdam, Montreal Film Festival, Trade Routes: History and Geography, 2nd Johannesburg Biennale and 5th Int. Istanbul Biennale 1997. *Solo exhibitions include:* White Cube²/Jay Jopling, London 1995–96, Fundació 'la Caixa', Barcelona 1997, Hirshhorn Museum and Sculture Garden, Washington, DC 1999, Mute, White Cube², London 2001. *Works include:* Fuck, Suck, Spank, Wank 1993, Slut 1993, Five Revolutionary Seconds XI 1997, Five Revolutionary Seconds XIII 1998, Soliloquy I 1998, Soliloquy V 1998, Self Portrait in a Single Breasted Suit with Hare 2001, Hummmm 2001, Self Portrait as a Tree. *Films include:* Killing Time 1994, Method in Madness 1994, Mute 2001, Breach 2001, Still Life 2001. *Publications include:* Contact 2001. *Address:* c/o Booth-Clibborn Editors, 12 Percy Street, London, W1T 1DW, England (Office).

TCHAIKOVSKY, Aleksandr Vladimirovich; Russian composer and pianist; b. 19 Feb. 1946, Moscow; m. 1st; one s. one d.; m. 3rd; one d.; ed Moscow State Conservatory; performs as pianist and chamber musician 1967–; teacher Moscow State Conservatory 1976, Prof. 1994–; Artistic Consultant, Mariinski Theatre, St Petersburg; winner Hollybush Festival Prize (USA) 1987; People's Artist of Russia 1998. *Compositions include:* operas Grandfather Is Laughing 1976, Three Sisters (after A. Chekhov) 1988, ballets Inspector 1960, Battleship Potemkin 1988, symphonies 1985, 1991 (Aquarius), two piano concertos, two viola concertos, Distant Dreams of Childhood for violin and viola 1990, Concerto-Buff for violin and marimba 1990, Triple Concerto for piano, violin and cello 1994, folk operas Tsar Nikita and Motya and Savely for two soloists and folk instruments, Quartet (after A. Pushkin) 1997–99, chamber music, incidental music to theatre and film productions. *Leisure interests:* collecting models of cars, table hockey. *Address:* Leningradsky prosp. 14, Apt. 4, 125040 Moscow, Russia (Home). *Telephone:* (095) 151-54-18 (Home).

TCHERINA, Ludmila (Tchemerzine, Monika); French actress, dancer, painter, sculptor and writer; b. 10 Oct. 1924, Paris; d. of Prince Avenir Tchemerzine and Stéphane Finette; m. 1st Edmond Audran (deceased); m. 2nd Raymond Roi 1953; ed privately and studied under Yvan Clustine; first dancer and choreographer, Grands Ballets de Monte Carlo (youngest-ever prima ballerina) 1940–44, Ballets de Paris 1951–58; f. Compagnie de Ballet Ludmila Tcherina 1958; Prize for Best Feminine Performance, Vichy Film Festival for La nuit s'achève 1950, First Prize Dance Film Festival, Buenos Aires for A la mémoire d'un héros 1952, Acad. Award for Best Performance by a Foreign Actress in Tales of Hoffmann 1952, Paris Gold Medal 1959, Oscar Italien de la Popularité 1959, Prix Michel Ange 1973, Prix d'honneur Gemail 1973, Grande Médaille de Vermeil de la Ville de Paris 1978, Prix d'interpretation (Monte Carlo), Europa operanda 1995; Officier, Légion d'honneur 1980, Chevalier des Arts et des Lettres, des Palmes académiques. *Chief appearances include:* ballets: Romeo and Juliet (with Serge Lifar) Paris 1942, Giselle La Scala, Milan 1954, Bolshoi Theatre, Moscow 1959, Le martyre de Saint Sébastien Paris Opera 1957, Buenos Aires 1967, Les amants de Teruel Théâtre Sarah Bernhardt, Paris 1959, Gala (by Salvador Dali and Maurice Béjart) Venice 1961, Brussels and Paris 1962, La muette de Portici Florence 1968, Anna Karénine Versailles 1975, etc. *Films include:* The Red Shoes, The Tales of Hoffmann, Clara de Montargis, La légende de Parsifal, La nuit s'achève, Oh! Rosalinda, A la mémoire d'un héros, La fille de Mata-Hari, Honeymoon, Les amants de Téruel (Cannes Film Festival, French Entry 1962; New York Critics Award), Jeanne au bûcher, etc. *Television appearances include:* Le Mandarin marveilleux, Bonaparte (title role), Salomé, La possédée, La dame aux camélias, La passion d'Anna Karénine, La création de la Féminine (based on her career), La Reine de Saba, Portrait de Ludmila Tcherina. *Works:* exhibited Sully Museum and Centre Georges Pompidou, Paris, Universal Exhbn of Sevilla 1992, the European Parl., Strasbourg and in many capital cities worldwide. *Publications:* L'amour au miroir (novel) 1983, La Femme à l'envers (novel) 1986. *Address:* 42 cours Albert 1er, 75008 Paris, France. *Telephone:* 43-59-18-33.

TCHUKHONTSEV, Oleg Grigoryevich; Russian poet; b. 8 March 1938, Pavlov Posad, Moscow Region; m. Irina Igorevna Povolotskaya; ed Moscow Pedagogical Inst.; poetry section, mem. Editorial Bd Novy Mir; published in Druzhba Narodov, Yunost, Molodaya Gvardiya, Novy Mir; State Prize of Russia 1993. *Publications:* From Three Notebooks (cycles Road, Name, Sparrow's Night) 1976, The Dormer Window 1983, Poetry 1989, By Wind and Heat 1989, Passing Landscape 1997 and other books of poetry; translations of Goethe, Warren, Frost, Kits and numerous other poets. *Address:* Bolshoy Tishinsky per. 12, Apt. 10, 123557 Moscow, Russia (Home). *Telephone:* (095) 253-51-95 (Home).

TCHURUK, Serge; French engineer and business executive; b. 13 Nov. 1937, Marseille; s. of Georges Tchurukdichian and Mathilde Dondikian; m. Hélèna Kalfus 1960; one d.; ed Lycée Thiers à Marseille, Ecole nationale supérieure de l'armement, Ecole Polytechnique, Paris; various refining and research positions Mobil/Oil BV Rotterdam 1964–68, Dir French research centre 1968–70, Dir of Information, France 1971–73, attaché int. planning, New York and dir plans and programmes France 1973–77, Dir social and external relations 1977–79, Pres. and Dir-Gen. 1979–80; Dir-Gen. fertilizer div. Rhône-Poulenc Inc. 1981, Asst Dir-Gen. Rhône-Poulenc Group 1982, Dir-Gen. special chemicals 1983, Dir-Gen. Rhône-Poulenc Group 1983; Pres. Bd Dirs CdF Chimie 1986, Pres. Dir-Gen. 1987–90 (became Orkem 1988); mem. Bd Dirs Total 1989, 1995–, Pres. 1990–95; Chair., CEO Alcatel Alsthom (now Alcatel) 1995–; mem. Bd of Dirs Inst. Pasteur 2001–; Officier, Légion d'honneur, Officier, Ordre nat. du Mérite, Manager of the Year Award, Le Nouvel Economiste 2000. *Leisure interests:* music, skiing, tennis. *Address:* Alcatel, 54 rue La Boétie, 75008 Paris, France (Office).

TE KANAWA, Dame Kiri Jeanette Claire, DBE, ONZ, AO; New Zealand opera singer (soprano); b. 6 March 1944, Gisborne; m. Desmond Park 1967 (divorced 1997); one s. one d.; ed St Mary's Coll., Auckland, London Opera Centre; first appearance at Royal Opera, Covent Garden, London, 1970, Santa Fe Opera, USA 1971, Lyons Opera, France 1972, Metropolitan Opera, New York, USA 1974; appeared at Australian Opera, Royal Opera House Covent Garden, Paris Opera during 1976–77 season; appeared at Houston Opera, USA and Munich Opera 1977; début La Scala, Milan 1978, Salzburg Festival 1979; San Francisco Opera Co. 1980; Edinburgh Festival, Helsinki Festival 1980; song at Wedding of HRH the Prince of Wales 1981; appeared in "2000 Today" on 1 January 2000; Hon. Fellow Somerville Coll. Oxford 1983, Wolfson Coll. Cambridge 1997; Hon. LLD (Dundee) 1982, Hon. DMus (Durham) 1982, (Oxford) 1983, (Nottingham) 1992, (Waikato) 1995, (Cambridge) 1997; Hon. D.Litt. (Warwick) 1989. *Operas:* Boris Godunov 1970–71, Parsifal 1971, The Marriage of Figaro 1971, 1972, 1973, 1976, 1979, 1986, 1991, 1997, Otello 1972, 1973, 1974, 1987, 1988, 1991, 1992, Simon Boccanegra 1973, 1974, 1975, 1976, 1977, 1979, 1980, 1986, 1988, 1991, 1995, 1997, Carmen 1973, Don Giovanni 1974, 1975, 1976, 1979, 1981, 1983, 1988, 1996, Faust 1974, The Magic Flute 1975, 1980, La Bohème 1975, 1976, 1977, 1979, 1980, 1989, 1991, Eugene Onegin 1975, 1976, Così fan tutte 1976, 1981, 1986, 1987, 1988, Arabella 1977, 1980, 1981, 1983, 1984, 1990, 1993, 1994, 1995, Die Fledermaus 1978,1984, 1986, 1987, La Traviata 1978, 1980, 1983, 1984, Der Rosenkavalier 1981, 1984, 1985, Manon Lescaut 1983, Don Giovanni (film) 1979, Samson 1986, Don Carlos 1984, Capriccio 1990, 1991, 1993, 1998, Vanessa 2001. *Recordings include:* Don Giovanni (as Elvira), Così fan tutti (as Fiordiligi), Carmen (as Michela), Mozart Vespers, Mozart C Minor Mass, The Magic Flute (Pamina), The Marriage of Figaro, Hansel and Gretel, La Bohème, Capriccio, French and German arias and songs, Maori songs, Strauss songs with orchestra, recital records. *Publications:* Land of the Long White Cloud 1989, Opera for Lovers 1997. *Leisure interests:* golf, swimming, cooking. *Address:* c/o Jules Haefliger, Impresario AG, Postfach 3320, 6002 Lucerne, Switzerland. *Fax:* (41) 3201915 (Office).

TEANNAKI, Teatao; I-Kiribati politician; mem. Parl. for Abiang; fmr Vice-Pres. of Kiribati; Pres. of Kiribati 1991–94. *Address:* c/o Office of the President, Tarawa, Kiribati.

TEAR, Robert, CBE, MA, FRSA, RCM, RAM; British opera and concert singer; b. 8 March 1939, Barry, Wales; s. of Thomas Arthur Tear and Edith Tear; m. Hilary Thomas 1961; two d.; ed Barry Grammar School, King's Coll. Cambridge; embarked on solo career as tenor after singing as member of King's Coll. Choir 1957–60 and St Paul's Cathedral Choir; joined English Opera Group 1964; worked with leading conductors (including Karajan, Giulini, Bernstein, Solti) and appeared in numerous operas by Benjamin Britten 1964–68; Artistic Dir London Royal Schools Vocal Faculty; first Prof. of Int. Singing, Royal Acad. of Music 1985–; first appearance at Covent Garden in The Knot Garden, other appearances: Eugene Onegin 1970, Die Fledermaus 1977, Peter Grimes 1978, The Rake's Progess 1979, Thérèse 1979, Rheingold 1980, Alceste 1981, Die Meistersinger 1982, Billy Budd 1982, Turn of the Screw 1989, Death in Venice 1989; début with Scottish Opera in works including La Traviata, Alceste, Don Giovanni, Peter Grimes 1974; Paris Opera 1976, Lulu 1979; appearances in all major festivals; close asscn with Sir Michael Tippett 1970–97; numerous recordings including premier recording of Tippett's opera King Priam 1981; Hon. Fellow, King's Coll. Cambridge 1989, Welsh Coll. of Music and Drama 1994; Hon. DMus (Royal Scottish Acad. of Music and Drama). *Publications:* Victorian Songs and Duets, Tear Hear (autobiog.) 1990, Singer Beware 1995, 10 Christmas Carols. *Leisure interests:* sport, 18th- and 19th-century English watercolours. *Address:* c/o Askonas Holt Ltd, 27 Chancery Lane, London, WC2A 1PF, England. *Telephone:* (20) 7400-1700. *Fax:* (20) 7400-1799.

TEARE, Andrew, BA; British business executive; b. 8 Sept. 1942; s. of Arthur Hubert Teare and Rosalind Margaret Baker; m. Janet Skidmore; three s.; with Turner and Newall 1964–72, CRH 1972–83, Rugby Group 1983–90; Group Chief Exec. English China Clays 1990–96; Chief Exec. Rank Group. 1996–98; Dir (non-exec.) Heiton Holdings PLC 1984–90, Prudential Insurance Co. 1992–98, Nat. Freight Corpn 1989–96. *Leisure interests:* skiing, opera. *Address:* Flat 2, 34 Craven Street, London, WC2N 5PB, England.

TEBALDI, Renata; Italian soprano; b. 1 Feb. 1922, Pesaro; d. of Teobaldo Tebaldi and Guisseppina (née Barbieri) Tebaldi; ed Arrigo Boito Conservatory, Parma, Gioacchino Rossini Conservatory, Pesaro, then pupil of Carmen Melis and Guiseppe Pais; début as Elena in Mefistofele, Rovigo 1944; has sung the principal soprano operatic roles in America and Europe; has appeared at Metropolitan Opera in over 200 performances as Tosca, Mimi, La Gioconda, Desdemona, Adriana Lecouvreur, Manon Lescaut, Amelia Boccanegra, Violetta, Butterfly and Alice Ford 1955–; further appearances at Chicago Lyric Opera, Vienna Staatsoper, Paris Opéra, Deutsche Oper Berlin and in Japan; retd. from opera in 1974.

TEBBIT, Baron (Life Peer), cr 1992, of Chingford in the London Borough of Waltham Forest; **Norman Beresford Tebbit,** PC, CH; British politician; b. 29 March 1931, Enfield; s. of Leonard Tebbit and Edith Tebbit; m. Margaret Elizabeth Daines 1956; two s. one d.; ed state primary schools, Edmonton Co. Grammar School; RAF Officer 1949–51; commercial pilot and holder of various posts, British Air Line Pilots' Asscn 1953–70; MP for Epping 1970–74, for Chingford 1974–92; Parl. Pvt. Sec. Dept of Employment 1972–73; Under-Sec. of State, Dept of Trade 1979–81; Minister of State, Dept of Industry Jan.–Sept. 1981; Sec. of State for Employment 1981–83, for Trade and Industry 1983–85; Chancellor of the Duchy of Lancaster 1985–87; Chair. Conservative Party 1985–87; Dir B.E.T. PLC 1987–96, British Telecom PLC 1987–96, Sears PLC 1987–99, Spectator Ltd; Co-Presenter, Target, Sky TV 1989–97; columnist The Sun 1995–97, Mail on Sunday 1997–2001. *Publications:* Upwardly Mobile 1988, Unfinished Business 1991. *Leisure interests:* peace and quiet. *Address:* House of Lords, Westminster, London, SW1A 0PW, England. *Telephone:* (20) 7219-6929.

TÉCHINÉ, André Jean François; French author and film-maker; b. 13 March 1943, Valence, Tarn-et-Garonne. *Films:* Paulina s'en va 1969, Souvenirs d'en France 1975, Barocco 1976, Les Sœurs Bronté 1979, Hôtel des Amériques 1981, Rendez-vous 1985 (Prize for Best Director, Cannes Int. Film Festival 1985), Le Lieu du crime 1986, Les Innocents 1987, J'embrasse pas 1991, Ma Saison préférée 1993, Les Roseaux sauvages 1994 (Prix Louis-Delluc 1994, César for Best French Film, Best Dir and Best Original Screenplay or Adaptation 1995), Les Voleurs 1996, Alice et Martin 1998, Loin 2001; television: La Matiouette. *Address:* c/o Artmédia, 20 avenue Rapp, 75007 Paris, France.

TEER, Kees, DSc, FIEEE; Netherlands scientist; b. 6 June 1925, Haarlem; m. Jozina A. Kas 1951; four c.; ed Tech. Univ. Delft; joined Philips Research Labs, Eindhoven 1950, Sr Researcher, Deputy Head of Acoustics, 1958, Deputy Dir 1966, Man. Dir 1968, Chair. Man. Cttee 1982–85; Prof. Tech. Univ. Delft 1987–91; mem. Netherlands Scientific Council for Govt 1985–88; mem. Royal Netherlands Acad. of Sciences; mem. Bd of Dirs Royal Dutch PTT, Nedap Industries –1998; Officier, Order of Orange Nassau; C. J. de Groot plaquelle.

Publications: several publs on electro-acoustics, TV systems, electronic principles, information tech. and society, R&D man. etc. *Leisure interests:* philosophy, writing, society versus technology. *Address:* Hoge Duinlaan 3, 5582 KD Waalre, Netherlands. *Telephone:* (40) 2216861. *Fax:* (40) 2219222. *E-mail:* k.teer@wxs.nl.

TEICH, Malvin Carl, PhD, FIEEE; American professor of electrical and computer engineering, biomedical engineering and physics; b. 4 May 1939, New York; s. of Sidney R. Teich and Loretta K. Teich; ed Mass. Inst. of Tech. and Stanford and Cornell Univs; Research Scientist, MIT Lincoln Lab., Lexington, Mass. 1966–67; Prof. of Eng Science and Applied Physics, Columbia Univ. 1967–96, Prof. Emer. 1996–, Chair. Dept of Electrical Eng 1978–80, mem. Columbia Radiation Lab.; Prof. of Electrical and Computer Eng, Prof. of Biomedical Eng, Prof. of Physics, Boston Univ. 1995–, mem. Photonics Center, Hearing Research Center, Center for Adaptive Systems; Deputy Ed. Journal of European Optical Soc. B: Quantum Optics 1988–92; mem. Bd of Editors Optics Letters 1977–79, Journal of Visual Communication and Image Representation 1989–92, Jemná Mechanika a Optika 1994–; mem. Scientific Bd Czech Acad. of Sciences Inst. of Physics; Fellow AAAS, American Physical Soc., Optical Soc. of America, Acoustical Soc. of America; John Simon Guggenheim Memorial Foundation Fellow 1973; IEEE Browder Thompson Memorial Prize 1969, Citation Classic Award, Inst. for Scientific Information 1981, Memorial Gold Medal (Palacký Univ.) 1992, IEEE Morris E. Leeds Award 1997. *Publications:* Fundamentals of Photonics (with B. E. A. Saleh) 1991; 300 articles in tech. journals; two US patents. *Address:* Department of Electrical and Computer Engineering, Boston University, 8 Saint Mary's Street, Boston, MA 02215, USA. *Telephone:* (617) 353-1236. *Fax:* (617) 353-1459. *E-mail:* teich@bu.edu (Office). *Website:* www.people.bu.edu/teich (Office).

TEISSIER, Guy; French politician; b. 4 April 1945, Marseilles; ed Ecole de Notariat de Marseilles; mem. Parti Republicain; Conseiller Général for Bouches de Rhône 1982; elected Deputy to Nat. Ass. 1988– (invalidated by Conseil Constitutionel) re-elected 1993–; Deputy Mayor 9th and 10th arrondissements, Marseilles 1995, 2001, Sec. 1997–99; mem. Comm. of Cultural, Family and Social Affairs 1988; mem. Comm. of Nat. Defence 1993–2002, Sec. 1994–95, Pres. 2002–. *Address:* c/o Assemblée Nationale, 126 rue de l'Université, 75355 Paris (Office); Nouveau Parc Sevigne, 15 place Mignard, 13009 Marseilles, France (Home). *Telephone:* 1-40-63-73-83 (Office); 4-91-23-39-28 (Home). *Fax:* 1-40-63-79-63 (Office). *E-mail:* gteissier@assemblee-nat.fr (Office). *Website:* guy.teissier.free.fr (Office).

TEITELBAUM, Philip, PhD; American professor of psychology; b. 9 Oct. 1928, Brooklyn, New York; s. of Bernard Teitelbaum and Betty Schechter; m. 1st Anita Stawski 1955; m. 2nd Evelyn Satinoff 1963; m. 3rd Osnat Boné 1985; five s.; ed Johns Hopkins Univ.; Instructor and Asst Prof. in Psychology, Harvard Univ. 1954–59; Assoc., Full Prof., Univ. of Pa 1959–73; Prof., Univ. of Ill. 1973–85, Emer. Prof. 1985–; Fellow in Center for Advanced Studies, Univ. of Ill. 1979–85; Grad. Research Prof. in Psychology, Univ. of Fla 1984–; mem. NAS, AAAS; Guggenheim Fellow; Fulbright Fellow; American Psychology Asscn Scientific Contrib. Award. *Publications:* Fundamental Principles of Physiological Psychology 1967, Vol. on Motivation, Handbook of Behavioral Neurobiology (with Evelyn Satinoff) 1983. *Address:* 2239 NW 17th Avenue, Gainesville, FL 32605 (Home); Psychology Department, University of Florida, Gainesville, FL 32611, USA. *Telephone:* (352) 392-0615 (Office); (352) 372-5714 (Home). *E-mail:* teitelb@ufl.edu (Office).

TEKLE, Afewerk, OM; Ethiopian artist; b. 22 Oct. 1932, Ankober, Shoa Prov.; s. of Weizero Feleketch Yematawork and Ato Tekle Mamo; ed Cen. School of Arts and Crafts, London, Slade School of Art, Univ. of London, UK, and Academie di Michelangelo, Italy; sent to England to become a mining engineer 1947; artistic studies 1947–54; solo exhbns world-wide; has also produced drawings and designs for stamps, playing cards, posters, flags and nat. ceremonial dress; designed his own house, studio and gallery 'Villa Alpha'; exhibited and lectured in fmr USSR, USA, Senegal, Turkey, Zaïre, UAE, Bulgaria, Munich, Germany (XX Olympiad) Kenya and Algeria; mem. French Int. Acad. of Arts 1997; Hon. Citizen of USSR 1989, Order of Merit of Senegal; Haile Selassie I Prize for Fine Arts 1964, Grand Order of Cyril and Methodius, Bulgaria 1968, Int. Gold Mercury Award, Italy 1982, American Golden Acad. Award 1992, Cambridge Order of Excellence, UK 1992, Council of the ABI World Laureate, 27th Int. Millennium Congress on the Arts and Communication, Washington DC 2000; numerous other awards, medals and decorations by heads of state. *Works include:* King Solomon meets the Queen of Sheba, St George's Cathedral, Addis Ababa, Equestrian Statue of Ras Makonnen, Harar, The Struggles and Aspirations of the African People (stained glass), Africa Hall, UN Building 1960, Meskel Flower (considered his masterpiece) 1961, Mural of St Paul's Hosp. 1972, Last Judgment, Adigrat Cathedral, Tigrai, northern Ethiopia, Unity Triptych: (a) The Disunity of Man, (b) Towards the Unity of Man, (c) Symbol of Human Unity (Gold Medal, Algiers Int. Festival 1977), Self Portrait (first African painting to be included in perm. collection of Uffizi Gallery, Florence, Italy) 1981, The Victory of Ethiopia over Evil Forces 1992, The Chalice and the Cross in the Life of the African People (First Prize, Biennale of Aquitane 1997) 1997, The Sun of Senegal 1997, Mother Ethiopia, The Simien Mountains. *Solo exhibitions include:* Municipality Hall, Addis Ababa 1954, Second Retrospective Exhbn, Addis Ababa 1961, Moscow 1964, One-man show, Washington DC and New York, USA 1964, Pushkin Museum, Moscow 1980, Russian State Museum, Leningrad 1980, IFA Gallery, Bonn, W. Germany 1981, Biennale of Aqui-

taine, France (Laureate of the Biennale and Grand Cordon with the Easel of Gold) 1997. *Group exhibitions include:* Festival of Negro Arts, Dakar, Senegal 1965, Expo 67, Montréal, Canada. *Leisure interests:* fencing, walking, mountaineering. *Address:* Villa Alpha, off Jimma Road, Addis Ababa, Ethiopia (Office). *Telephone:* 71-59-41 (Office). *Fax:* 71-59-41 (Office). *E-mail:* hmal.afewerk.tekle@telecom.net.et (Office). *Website:* www.afewerktekle.org (Office).

TELEFONI RETZLAFF, Misa, LLB, CPA; Samoan politician and lawyer; b. 21 May 1952; ed King's Coll., Auckland and Auckland Univ., NZ; with Jackson Russell Tunks and West, Auckland, NZ 1974–76; admitted to Bar as Barrister and Solicitor of the Supreme Court, NZ 1975, Western Samoa 1976; pvt. legal practice as H. T. Retzlaff, Apia, Western Samoa 1976–92 (closed office on appointment as Minister of State); apptd Attorney-Gen. 1986–88, resgnd on running as MP; elected MP for Falelatai and Samatau Dist 1988–, served as Opposition MP 1988–91; Minister of State with portfolios of Agric., Forests, Fisheries and Meteorology and Minister of Shipping 1992–96, of Health 1996–2001; Deputy Prime Minister and Minister of Finance March 2001–; Vice-Pres. WHO 1999; Chair. FAO Asia/Pacific Regional Conf. and Inaugural Meeting FAO Minister 1995; admitted as CPA Samoa 1977, apptd Pres. of Samoa Chamber of Commerce 1977–79; Dir Retzlaff Group of Cos 1975–86, also of eight cos in Western Samoa, one in NZ and Suva, Fiji (resgnd from all 1992); Pro-Chancellor Nat. Univ. of Samoa 1986–98; elected to Komiti Tumau (Standing Cttee) of Methodist Church of Samoa 1996–; mem. Inaugural Council of Piula Theological Coll. 1998–; Signatory Latimer House Rules on Good Governance, The Commonwealth; spoke at numerous univs and int. confs including Econ. and Social Comm. for Asia and the Pacific (ESCAP) 1994, Commonwealth Law Conf., Kuala Lumpur 1999; Kelliher Econs Scholarship, NZ 1969, Sr Prize in Law, Auckland Univ. 1969. *Address:* Ministry of Finance, POB L 1861, Apia, Samoa (Office). *Telephone:* (685) 25210/24924 (Office); (685) 24363 (Home). *Fax:* (685) 25357 (Office); (685) 21721 (Home). *E-mail:* finmin@samoa.ws (Office).

TELIČKA, Pavel; Czech diplomatist, lawyer and university teacher; b. 24 Aug. 1965, Washington, USA; m. Eva Telička; one s. one d.; ed Charles Univ., Prague; with Ministry of Foreign Affairs 1986–, mem. of del. to negotiate Czech membership of EU 1991, with Czech Standing Mission to EU 1991–95, Deputy Amb. to Brussels 1993–95; Dir of Dept Ministry of Foreign Affairs 1995–98, Dir-Gen. Dept for EU and NATO 1998–; Deputy Chair. Comm. for Czech Integration to EU 1998–; Deputy Minister for Foreign Affairs 1998–; State Sec. for European Affairs 1999–. *Leisure interests:* sport, music, travel. *Address:* Mission of the Czech Republic to the European Community, 15 rue Caroly, 1050, Brussels. *Telephone:* (32) 22130110. *Fax:* (32) 22130185 (Office). *Website:* www.mfa.cz/missionEU (Office).

TELLEM, Nancy; American television executive; b. 1954; m. Arn Tellem; three c.; ed Univ. of California; began career as TV industry lawyer; fmr Exec. Lorimar Inc.; with Warner Bros. TV 1987–97, Exec. Vice-Pres. of Business and Financial Affairs; Exec. Vice-Pres. of Business Affairs, CBS Productions 1997–98, Pres. CBS Entertainment 1998–; Dir ThirdAge Media Inc. 2000–, Artful Style Inc. 2000–. *Address:* CBS Entertainment, 7800 Beverly Boulevard, Los Angeles, CA 90036, USA. *Telephone:* (323) 575-2345 (Office). *Website:* www.cbs.com (Office).

TELLEP, Daniel Michael, MS; American business executive (retd); b. 20 Nov. 1931, Forest City, Pa; m. Pat Tellep; six c.; ed Univ. of Calif. at Berkeley and Harvard Univ.; with Lockheed Missiles & Space Co. 1955–, Chief Eng Missile Systems Div. 1969–75, Vice-Pres., Asst Gen. Man. Advanced Systems Div. 1975–83, Exec. Vice-Pres. 1983–84, Pres. 1984–; Pres. Lockheed Missiles and Space Group 1986–; Chair. and CEO Lockheed Corpn 1989–95 (merged with Martin Marietta to form Lockheed Martin 1994), Chair., CEO Lockheed Martin 1996–97; now consultant; mem. Interstate Bancorp Bd 1991–, Bd Govs. Music Center LA Co. 1991–95, Calif. Business Round Table 1992–; Fellow, AIAA, American Astronautical Soc.; mem. Nat. Acad. of Eng; James V. Forrestal Award 1995, Calif. Mfrs Award 1996, Nat. Eng Award 1996, Karman Wings Award 1997 and numerous other awards. *Address:* c/o Lockheed Martin Corporation, 6801 Rockledge Drive, Bethesda, MD 20817, USA.

TELLER, Edward, PhD; American scientist; b. 15 Jan. 1908, Budapest, Hungary; s. of Ilona Teller and Max Teller; m. Augusta Maria Harkanyi 1934 (deceased); one s. one d.; ed Karlsruhe Technical Inst. and Univs. of Munich and Leipzig; Research Assoc., Leipzig 1929–31, Göttingen 1931–35; Rockefeller Fellow, Copenhagen 1934; Lecturer, Univ. of London 1934–35; Prof. of Physics, George Washington Univ. 1935–41, Columbia Univ. 1941–42; Physicist, Manhattan Engineer Dist 1942–46; Prof. of Physics, Univ. of Chicago 1946–52; Physicist and Asst Dir Los Alamos Scientific Lab. 1949–52; Consultant, Univ. of Calif. Radiation Lab. Livermore 1952–53, Assoc. Dir Lawrence Livermore Radiation Lab. 1953–75, Dir 1958–60, Dir Emer. 1975–; Prof. of Physics Univ. of Calif. 1953–60, Prof. of Physics-at-Large 1960–70, Univ. Prof. 1970–75, Prof. Emer. 1975–; Chair. Dept of Applied Science, Univ. of Calif. 1963–66; Sr Research Fellow, Hoover Inst. for War, Revolution and Peace 1975–; Visiting Prof., Arthur Spitzer Chair of Science, Pepperdine Univ. 1975–77; mem. NAS, American Acad. of Arts and Sciences, USAF Scientific Advisory Bd, etc.; mem. White House Science Council 1982–89; Fellow, American Nuclear Soc., American Acad. of Arts and Sciences etc.; Hon. DSc (Yale, Alaska, Fordham, George Washington, Southern Calif., St Louis, Clarkson Coll. Clemson Univ., Maryland); Hon. LLD (Mount Mary);

Joseph Priestley Memorial Award 1957, Albert Einstein Award 1958, Mid-West Research Inst. Award, Living History Award 1960, Enrico Fermi Award 1962, Robins Award of America 1963, Harvey Prize 1975, Nat. Medal of Science 1983, Sylvanus Thayer Award 1986, Presidential Citizen Medal 1989, Order of Banner with Rubies of Hungary 1990, Corvin Chain Award 2001, US Dept of Energy Sec.'s Gold Award 2002. *Publications:* The Structure of Matter (with F. O. Rice) 1949, Magneto-Hydrodynamic Shocks (with F. de Hoffmann) 1950, Theory of Origin of Cosmic Rays 1954, Our Nuclear Future (with A. Latter) 1958, The Legacy of Hiroshima (with Allen Brown) 1962, The Reluctant Revolutionary 1964, Constructive Uses of Nuclear Explosives (with Talley, Higgins & Johnson) 1968, Great Men of Physics (with others) 1969, General Remarks on Electronic Structure 1970, The Hydrogen Molecular Ion 1970, General Theory of Electron Structure 1970, Energy from Heaven and Earth 1979, The Pursuit of Simplicity 1980, Better a Shield than a Sword 1987, Conversations on the Dark Secrets of Physics 1991, Memoirs: A Twentieth-Century Journey in Science and Politics 2001. *Leisure interests:* chess, swimming, piano. *Address:* Hoover Institution, Stanford University, 434 Galvez Mall, Stanford, CA 94305 (Office); PO Box 808, Livermore, CA 94551, USA (Office). *Telephone:* (650) 723-0601. *Fax:* (650) 723-1687 (Office). *E-mail:* smith44@llnl.gov (Office).

TELLER, Juergen; German photographer; b. 28 Jan. 1964, Erlangen; partner Venetia Scott; one d.; ed Bayerische Staatslehranstalt für Photographie, Munich; living and working in London 1986–. *Solo exhibitions:* Photographers' Gallery, London 1998, Pitti Immagine Discovery, Florence 1999, Lehmann Maupin Gallery, New York 2000; "Märchenstüberl", Modern Art, London 2001; *Group exhibitions:* "New Universe", Biennale di Firenze 1996, "Living in the Real World", Museum Dhondt-Dhaenens, Belgium 2000, "90x60x90", Museo Jacobo Borges, Caracas, Venezuela 2000, "Remake Berlin", Fotomuseum, Winterthur, Zürich 2000, "Century City": Art and Culture in the Modern Metropolis, Tate Modern, London 2001, "Marchenstüberl", Modern Art, London 2001, FotoMuseum, Munich 2002, Museum Folwang Essen 2002, Galleria d'Arte Moderna, Bologna 2003, Frans Hals Museum, Haarlem 2003, "Werkstatt", Contemporary Fine Arts, Berlin 2003, "Citibank Photography Prize 2003", Photographers' Gallery, London 2003. *Address:* 1 Telford Road, London, W10 5SH, England (Office). *Telephone:* (20) 8964-0966 (Office). *Fax:* (20) 8964-0790 (Office). *E-mail:* juergenteller@ukf.net (Office).

TELLO, Manuel, BA; Mexican diplomatist (retd); b. 15 March 1935, Mexico City; s. of Manuel Tello and Guadalupe M. de Tello; m. Rhonda Mosesman 1983; three step-d.; ed Georgetown Univ., Washington, DC, USA, Escuela Libre de Derecho, Mexico City; Dir-Gen. for Int. Orgs., Ministry of Foreign Affairs 1970–72, Head of Div. of Int. Orgs. 1972–74, of Political Affairs 1975–76; Amb. to the UK 1977–79; Vice-Minister of Multilateral Affairs 1979–82; Perm. Rep. of Mexico to Geneva-based int. orgs. 1983–88, Rep. to GATT 1986–88; Amb. to France 1989–92; Perm. Rep. of Mexico to UN, New York 1993–94, 1995–2001; Minister of Foreign Affairs 1994–95; Alt. Rep. on Council of Agency for Prohibition of Nuclear Weapons in Latin America 1970–73; Rep. to Third UN Conf. on Law of the Sea 1971–82; several foreign decorations. *Publications:* various papers and articles on Mexico's foreign policy, the law of the sea etc. *Leisure interests:* reading, tennis. *Address:* c/o Secretary of State for Foreign Affairs, Avda Ricardo Flores Magón 2, 4°, Col Vonoalce Tlatelolco, 09600 México, DF, Mexico (Office).

TELMER, Frederick Harold, MA; Canadian business executive; b. 28 Dec. 1937, Edmonton, Alberta; s. of Ingar Telmer and Bernice Telmer; m. Margaret Goddard Hutchings; three s.; ed Garneau High School, Edmonton, Univ. of Alberta; joined Industrial Relations Dept, Stelco Inc. 1963, various man. positions in Marketing Div., subsequently Gen. Man. Field Sales, apptd. Gen. Man. Corp. Affairs and Strategic Planning 1984, Vice-Pres. 1985, Pres. Stelco Steel 1988, Dir Stelco Inc. 1989, Chair. and CEO 1991–97, Chair. 1997–; Founding Dir Japan Soc. *Leisure interests:* golf, tennis, skiing. *Address:* Stelco Inc., P.O. Box 2030 Hamilton, Ont., L8N 3T1 (Office); 4451 Lakeshore Road, Burlington, Ont., L7L 1B3, Canada (Home). *Telephone:* (905) 528-2511, ext. 4498 (Office). *Fax:* (905) 681-9088 (Office); (905) 681-9088 (Home).

TELTSCHIK, Horst; German fmr politician; b. 14 June 1940, Klantendorf; s. of Richard Teltschik and Anja Teltschik; m. Gerhild Ruff 1967; one s. one d.; ed Gymnasium Tegernsee and Freie Univ. Berlin; fmrly. held various positions in CDU offices and in State Govt of Rhineland-Palatinate; then Ministerial Dir Dept 2, Fed. Chancellery; CEO Bertelsmann Foundation, Herbert Quandt Foundation 1993; Chair. Teltschik Assocs. GmbH 2002; mem. Bd of Man. BMW AG 1993–2000, BMW Rep. Bd for Eastern Europe, Asia and Middle East; organizer Munich Conf. on Securities Policy; Hon. Gen. Consul of India for Bavaria and Thuringia; Diplompolitologe; Hon. DUniv (Budapest) 1991, (Sogang, Seoul) 1997; Bundesverdienstkreuz, First Class; Commdr, Légion d'honneur; Grande Ufficiale (Italy), Commdr (Luxembourg), Bavarian Verdienstorden. *Publication:* 329 Tage—Innenansichten der deutschen Einigung. *Leisure interests:* literature, tennis. *Address:* Herbert Quandt Foundation, Hanauer Strasse 46, 80788 Munich (Office); Karl-Theodor Strasse 38, 83700 Rottach-Egern, Germany (Home). *Telephone:* (89) 38211630 (Office); (8022) 26677 (Home). *Fax:* (89) 38211636 (Office); (8022) 662849 (Home). *E-mail:* horstmt@t-online.de (Home).

TEMERLIN, (Julius) Liener, BFA; American advertising executive; b. 27 Nov. 1928, Ardmore, Okla; s. of S. Pincus Temerlin and Julie Kahn Temerlin; m. Karla Samuelsohn 1950; two d.; ed Ardmore, Okla High School, Univ. of

Oklahoma; COO Glenn Advertising 1970–74; Pres. Glenn, Bozell & Jacobs 1974–79; Chair. of Bd Bozell & Jacobs 1979–85; Chair. Bozell, Jacobs, Kenyon & Eckhardt 1985–88, Bozell 1989–92, Temerlin McClain 1992–; Algur H. Meadows Distinguished Prof. of Advertising, Meadows School of the Arts, Southern Methodist Univ.; Chair. Dallas Museum of Art Devt Cttee 1993–96; Pres. Council Dallas Symphony Asscn 1989–; Chair. Lieberman Research Bldg, Baylor Medical Center, Fundraising Campaign 1997–; mem. Bd of Dirs., Madison Council, Library of Congress 1991–, East/West Inst. 1999–; mem. Steering Cttee for Capital Campaign, KERA (Public TV Council) 2000–01; Trustee American Film Inst. 1992–2000, Hon. Trustee 2000–; Bill D. Kerss Award, Dallas Advertising League 1983, Nat. Conf. of Christians and Jews Brotherhood Award 1984, Susan G. Komen Foundation for Breast Cancer Research 1989, Community Service Award, Jas. K. Wilson Silver Cup Award, Dallas 1990, Linz Award for civic service 1990, Volunteer Fundraiser of the Year 1991, Silver Medal Award, Dallas Advertising League 1991, Father of the Year 1991, Best Man in Advertising Award 1992, Servant Leader Award, Volunteer Center of Dallas 2001. *Address:* 6555 Sierra Drive, Irving, TX 75039, USA. *Telephone:* (972) 556-3100 (Office); (214) 363-6909 (Home). *Fax:* (972) 556-3120 (Office). *E-mail:* ltemerli@temmc.com (Office).

TEMIRKANOV, Yuriy Khatuyevich; Russian conductor; b. 10 Dec. 1938, Nalchik; s. of Khatu Sagidovich Temirkanov and Polina Petrovna Temirkanova; m. Irina Guseva (deceased); one s.; ed Leningrad Conservatoire; first violinist with Leningrad Philharmonic Orchestra 1961–66; Conductor for Maly Theatre and Opera Studio, Leningrad 1965–68; Chief Conductor, Leningrad Philharmonic Orchestra 1968–76, Kirov Opera and Ballet Co. 1976–88; Prof. Leningrad Conservatoire 1979–88; Artistic Dir State Philharmonia 1988–; Prin. Guest Conductor Royal Philharmonic Orchestra and Philadelphia Orchestra; Chief Conductor, London Philharmonic Orchestra 1992–97; Prin. Guest Conductor, Danish Radio Orchestra 1997–; Music Dir Baltimore Symphony Orchestra 1999–; guest conductor in a number of countries, including Scandinavia (Sweden 1968), USA and GB (Royal Philharmonic Orchestra 1981–); USSR People's Artist 1981, Glinka Prize, USSR State Prize 1976, 1985. *Opera productions include:* Porgy and Bess (at Maly), Peter the Great (at Kirov), Shchedrin's Dead Souls (at Bolshoi and Kirov), Tchaikovsky's Queen of Spades and Eugene Onegin (Kirov) 1979. *Address:* State Philharmonia, Mikhailovskaya 2, St Petersburg, Russia. *Telephone:* (812) 110-42-14.

TEMPLE, Shirley (see Black, Shirley Temple).

TEMPLEMAN, Baron (Life Peer), cr. 1982, of White Lackington in the County of Somerset; **Sydney William Templeman,** PC, QC, MBE, MA; British judge; b. 3 March 1920, London; s. of Herbert W. Templeman and Lilian (née Pheasant) Templeman; m. 1st Margaret Rowles 1946 (died 1988); two s.; m. 2nd Sheila Barton Edworthy 1996; ed Southall Grammar School and St John's Coll. Cambridge; served 4/1st Gurkha Rifles 1941–46; mem. Middle Temple 1946–, Treas. 1987–; mem. Bar Council 1961–65, 1970–72; QC 1964; Attorney-Gen., Duchy of Lancaster 1970; Judge, Chancery Div., 1972; Pres. Senate of Inns of Court and Bar 1974; mem. Royal Comm. on Legal Services 1976; Lord Justice of Appeal 1978–82; Lord of Appeal in Ordinary 1982–95; Visitor Essex Univ. 1990; Pres. Bar European Group 1987–95, Asscn of Law Teachers 1997–; Hon. Fellow, St John's Coll. Cambridge 1982; Hon. mem. Canadian Bar Asscn 1976, American Bar Asscn 1976, Newfoundland Law Soc. 1984; Hon. DLitt (Reading) 1980, Hon. LLD (Birmingham) 1986, (Exeter) 1991, Hon. LLD CNAA (Huddersfield Polytechnic) 1989, (West of England) 1993, Nat. Law School of India 1994. *Address:* Mellowstone, 1 Rosebank Crescent, Exeter, EX4 6EJ (Office); House of Lords, London, SW1A 0PW, England. *Telephone:* (1392) 275428 (Home).

TEMPLETON, Sir John M., Kt, MA; British investment counsellor; b. 29 Nov. 1912, Winchester, Tenn., USA; s. of Harvey Maxwell Templeton and Vella Handly Templeton; m. 1st Judith Dudley Folk 1937 (died 1951), two s. one d.; m. 2nd Irene Reynolds Butler 1958 (died 1993); one step-s. one step-d.; ed Yale Univ., Balliol Coll., Oxford Univ. (Rhodes Scholar); Sec.-Treas., Vice-Pres. and Dir Nat. Geophysical Co., Dallas and New York 1937–41; Pres. and Dir Templeton, Dobbrow and Vance, Inc., New York 1941–65, Templeton Growth Fund Canada Ltd, Toronto 1954–85, Templeton Funds, Inc. 1977–86, Templeton Global Funds, Inc. 1981–86; Chair. Templeton Damroth Corpn 1959–62; Vice-Pres. and Dir First Trust Bank Ltd 1963–; Dir Magic Chef, Inc., Cleveland, Tenn. 1965–86; Chase Manhattan Trust Co. 1972–82, British-American Insurance Co. 1973–82; Chair. Templeton, Galbraith and Hansberger Ltd 1986–92; Chair. Bd of Trustees Princeton Theological Seminary 1967–73, 1979–85; Chair. and Trustee Templeton Theological Seminary 1985–94; Pres. World Thanksgiving Alliance 1990–96; Trustee Templeton Foundation Inc. 1952–, Wilson Coll. 1951–73, Englewood Hosp. 1953–56, Center of Theological Inquiry, Princeton 1967–93, Buena Vista Coll. 1981–94, Soc. for Promoting Christian Knowledge (USA) 1984–88, Balliol Coll. Oxford Endowments Fund 1984–94, Templeton Project Trust (England) 1984–, America European Community Asscn; mem. Bd of Visitors Harvard Divinity School 1982–88, Advisory Bd Harvard Center for Study of World Religions 1975–85, Council on Theological Seminaries, United Presbyterian Church of the USA 1959–84, Bd Corporators Presbyterian Ministers' Fund Inc. 1960–93, Comm. on Ecumenical Mission 1961–70, Bd of Mans. American Bible Soc. 1973–93, Man. Council Templeton Coll. Oxford 1982–95, Bd of Trustees for Restoration of Westminster Abbey 1991–96; Chancellor Fla Southern Coll. 1992–94; mem. New York Soc. of Security Analysts 1942–; mem. Royal Inst. (UK) 1996; Hon. Rector Dubuque Univ. 1988–93; Hon.

Fellow Templeton Coll. 1991; Paul Harris Fellow (Rotary Int.) 1992; 20 Hon. degrees; Benjamin Franklin Medal of Royal Soc. of Arts 1995, R. E. Lee Distinguished Service Award 1996; Ind. Award, Brown Univ. 1998, KStJ. *Publications:* The Humble Approach 1981, The Templeton Touch (co-author) 1985, The Templeton Plan 1987, The God Who Would be Known 1989, Riches for the Mind and Spirit 1990, Looking Forward 1993, Is God the Only Reality? (co-author) 1994, Discovering the Laws of Life 1994, Evidence of Purpose (ed.) 1994, World Wide Laws of Life 1996, The Good News 1997, Pure Unlimited Love: An Eternal Creative Force and Blessing Taught by All Religions 2000, Wisdom from the World: Pathways toward Heaven on Earth 2002; articles in financial and religious journals. *Address:* P.O. Box N-7776, Lyford Cay, Nassau, Bahamas (Home). *Telephone:* 3624904. *Fax:* 3624880.

TEN HOLT, Friso; Netherlands painter and etcher; b. 6 April 1921, Argelès-Gazost, France; m. A. Taselaar 1946; two s. one d.; ed Rijksakademie van Beeldende Kunsten, Amsterdam; paintings mainly of swimmers, landscapes and nudes, portraits and figures; Prof. of Painting, Rijksakademie van Beeldende Kunsten, Amsterdam 1969–83; one-man exhbns in Netherlands since 1952, London 1959, 1962, 1963, 1965, 1969, 1973; group exhbns at Beaverbrook Art Gallery, Canada and Tate Gallery, London 1963, Biennale Salzburg 1964, Carnegie Inst., Pittsburgh 1964, Netherlands travelling exhbn 1957–58; works in collections in Netherlands, Sweden, UK, France and America. *Major works:* stained-glass windows for churches in Amsterdam and The Hague and for Haarlem Cathedral. *Leisure interest:* reading. *Address:* Keizersgracht 614, Amsterdam, Netherlands. *Telephone:* 022481727 (Studio); 6230736 (Home).

TENDULKAR, Sachin Ramesh; Indian cricketer; b. 24 April 1973, Mumbai; s. of the late Ramesh Tendulkar; m. Anjeli Mehtas; one s. one d.; right-hand batsman, right-arm off-break, leg-break bowler (over 100 One Day Ints. (ODI) wickets); teams: Mumbai, Yorkshire, India; in 104 Tests (25 as Capt.) scored 8,770 runs (average 58), to Dec. 2002; 300 matches in ODIs (73 as Capt.) for 11,544 runs (average 44.23), to Dec. 2001; first player to reach 10,000 runs in ODIs; 15,272 first-class runs (average 62.1), including 50 hundreds, to Jan. 2002; Arjuna Award 1994, Wisden Cricketer of the Year 1997, Rajiv Gandhi Khel Ratna Award 1998, Padma Shri Award 1999, Maharashtra Bhushan Award. *Address:* 7 Ushakkal, Sahitya Sahawas Colony, Bandra (East), Mumbai 400051, India (Office). *Website:* tendulkar@cricinfo.com (Office).

TENET, George J., MIA; American government official; b. New York; m. A. Stephanie Glakas; one s.; ed Georgetown Univ. School of Foreign Service, School of Int. Affairs, Columbia Univ.; Legis. Asst, Legis. Dir, staff of Senator John Heinz 1982–85; fmr head of supervision of arms control negotiations between USSR and USA, subsequently Staff Dir, Senate Select Cttee on Intelligence; fmr Special Asst to Pres. and Sr Dir for Intelligence Programs, Nat. Security Council; Deputy Dir of CIA 1995–96, Acting Dir 1996–97, Dir 1997–. *Publication:* The Ability of US Intelligence to Monitor the Intermediate Nuclear Force Treaty. *Address:* Central Intelligence Agency, Washington, DC 20505, USA.

TENG TENG; Chinese politician; b. 1930, Jiangyin Co., Jiangsu Prov.; ed Qinghua Univ. and in USSR; joined CCP 1948; Vice Minister in charge of State Educ. Comm. 1993; Vice-Pres. Chinese Acad. of Social Sciences 1993–98, Dir Sustainable Devt Research Centre; mem. 8th NPC, mem. Educ., Science, Culture and Public Health Cttee; mem. 9th NPC, Legislation Cttee 1993; Prof. Tsinghua Univ.; Pres. Chinese Ecological Econs Council; Govt Prize of Science and Tech. 1978. *Publication:* Future Outlook for the Environment and Sustainable Development 2002. *Address:* 5th Jianguomennei Dajie, Beijing 100732 (Office); Cuiweisili 1-2-401, Beijing 100036, People's Republic of China (Home). *Telephone:* (10) 65137697 (Office); (10) 68258097 (Home). *Fax:* (10) 65137815 (Office); (10) 68252720 (Home). *E-mail:* tengteng@cass.net.ch (Office); tengcass@yahoo.com (Home).

TENG WENSHENG; Chinese politician; b. 1940, Changning Co., Hunan Prov.; ed Chinese People's Univ., joined CCP 1965; research fellow Research Office, Secr. of CCP Cen. Cttee; Vice-Dir Policy Research Office of CCP Cen. Cttee; mem. 15th CCP Cen. Cttee 1997–. *Address:* Policy Research Office of Chinese Communist Party Central Committee, 1 Zhong Nan Hai, Beijing, People's Republic of China.

TENGBOM, Anders, D.ARCH.; Swedish architect; b. 10 Nov. 1911, Stockholm; s. of Ivar Tengbom and Hjördis Tengbom; m. Margareta Brambeck 1937; two s. two d.; ed Royal Inst. of Tech. and Royal Acad. of Fine Arts, Stockholm, Cranbrook Acad., Mich., USA; travelled in Europe, USA, Japan, China and the USSR 1935–36; architectural practice in Stockholm 1938–, designed bldgs. for many different functions in Sweden, Belgium, Venezuela and Saudi Arabia; Asst Prof. of Architecture, Royal Inst. of Tech., Stockholm 1947; Pres. Nat. Asscn of Swedish Architects (S.A.R.) 1963–65; mem. Bd Swedish Hospitals Fed. 1962–70; Pres. Swedish Asscn of Consulting Architects (S.P.A.) 1972–75; mem. Royal Acad. of Fine Arts, Stockholm 1973–, Pres. 1980–86; Hon. corresp. mem. RIBA 1963; Hon. Fellow AIA 1978. *Address:* Kornhamnstorg 6, 111 27 Stockholm (Office); Canton 2, 178 93 Drottningholm, Sweden (Home). *Telephone:* (8) 412-52-00 (Office); (8) 759-01-75 (Home).

TENNANT, Sir Anthony John, Kt, BA; British business executive; b. 5 Nov. 1930, London; s. of the late Maj. John Tennant and of Hon. Antonia (later Viscountess) Radcliffe; m. Rosemary Violet Stockdale 1954; two s.; ed Eton Coll., Trinity Coll. Cambridge; Mather and Crowther 1953–66, Dir 1960–66; Marketing Consultancy 1966–70; Marketing Dir then Deputy Man. Dir, Truman Ltd 1970–72; Sales and Marketing Dir then Deputy Chief Exec., Watney, Mann and Truman Brewers 1972–76; Deputy Man. Dir, later CEO, then Chair. Int. Distillers and Vintners Ltd 1976–87; Dir, later Group Man. Dir, then Deputy Chief Exec., Grand Metropolitan 1977–87; CEO Guinness PLC 1987–89, Chair. 1989–92; Dir (non-exec.) Christie's Int. PLC 1993–98, (non-exec. Chair. 1993–96); Chair. Priorities Bd 1992–93; Deputy Chair. (non-exec.) Wellcome PLC 1994–95; Deputy Chair. (non-exec.) Arjo Wiggins Appleton PLC 1996–2000; Dir (non-exec.) Guardian Royal Exchange 1989–99, Guardian Royal Exchange Assurance 1989–94, Banque Nat. de Paris 1990–91, BNP UK Holdings Ltd 1991–2002, London Stock Exchange 1991–94; Deputy Chair. Forte PLC 1992–96; Sr Adviser Morgan Stanley UK Group 1993–2000; Dir (non-exec.) Morgan Stanley Dean Witter Bank Ltd 1999–2000; Chair. Bd of Trustees, Royal Acad. Trust 1996–2002 (Trustee 1994–2002), Univ. of Southampton Devt Trust 1994–2002 (Trustee 1992–2002); mem. Supervisory Bd LVMH, Moët Hennessy Louis Vuitton, Paris 1988–92; Trustee Cambridge Foundation 1996–2001; Hon. DBA (Nottingham Trent Univ.) 1996; Hon. DUniv (Southampton) 2000; Médaille de la ville de Paris; Légion d'honneur. *Leisure interest:* gardening. *Address:* 18 Hamilton House, Vicarage Gate, London, W8 4HL, England. *Telephone:* (20) 7937-6203.

TENNANT, Emma Christina, FRSL; British author; b. 20 Oct. 1937; d. of 2nd Baron Glenconner and Elizabeth Lady Glenconner; one s. two d.; ed St Paul's Girls' School; fmr freelance journalist; Founder, Ed. Bananas 1975–78; Gen. Ed. In Verse 1982–, Lives of Modern Women 1985–; Hon. DLitt (Aberdeen) 1996. *Publications include:* The Colour of Rain (under pseudonym Catherine Aydy) 1963, The Time of the Crack 1973, The Last of the Country House Murders 1975, Hotel de Dream 1976, Bananas Anthology (ed.) 1977, Saturday Night Reader (ed.) 1978, The Bad Sister 1978, Wild Nights 1979, Alice Fell 1980, Queen of Stones 1982, Woman Beware Woman 1983, Black Marina 1985, Adventures of Robina by Herself (ed.) 1986, Cycle of the Sun: The House of Hospitalities 1987, A Wedding of Cousins 1988, The Magic Drum 1989, Two Women of London 1989, Faustine 1992, Tess 1993, Pemberley 1993, An Unequal Marriage 1994, Strangers: A Family Romance 1998; children's books: The Boggart (with M. Rayner), The Search for Treasure Island 1981, The Ghost Child 1984, Emma In Love 1996, Girlitude 1999, Burnt Diaries 1999, The Ballad of Sylvia and Ted (contrib.) 2001, Felony 2002. *Leisure interest:* planning trips that never happen. *Address:* c/o Jonathan Cape, Random House, 20 Vauxhall Bridge Road, London, SW1V 2SA, England (Office). *Fax:* (20) 7221-3917 (Office).

TENNANT, Stella, BA; British model; b. 1971; d. of The Hon. Tobias William Tennant and Lady Emma Tennant; granddaughter of Duke of Devonshire; m. David Lasnet 1999; one s. one d.; ed St Leonard's Girls' School, Kingston Polytechnic and Winchester School of Art; first assignment, cover shoot for Italian Vogue; now works in London, New York and Paris and with photographers including Mario Testino, Paolo Roversi and Bruce Weber; selected by Karl Lagerfeld as new face of Chanel 1996. *Address:* c/o Select Model Management, Thomas Archer House, 43 King Street, London, WC2E 8RJ, England. *Telephone:* (20) 7470-5220. *Fax:* (20) 7470-5233.

TENNEKES, Hendrik, DS(Eng); Netherlands meteorologist; b. 13 Dec. 1936, Kampen; s. of the late Cornelis Tennekes and of Harmpje Noordman; m. Olga Vanderpot 1964 (divorced 1998); one s. one d.; ed Delft Tech. Univ.; Asst Prof., Assoc. Prof., Prof. of Aerospace Eng, Pennsylvania State Univ. 1965–77; Dir of Research, Royal Netherlands Meteorological Inst. 1977–90, Dir of Strategic Planning 1990–95; Prof. of Meteorology, Free Univ., Amsterdam 1977–; Visiting Prof. Univ. of Washington, Seattle 1976–77; Visiting Sr Scientist, Nat. Center for Atmospheric Research, Boulder, Colo 1987; mem. Royal Netherlands Acad. of Sciences. *Publications:* A First Course in Turbulence (with J. L. Lumley) 1972, The Simple Science of Flight 1996; numerous publs on turbulence, predictability, chaos, boundary-layer meteorology and environmental philosophy. *Leisure interests:* poetry, landscape painting.

TENORIO, Pedro Pangelinan; American politician; b. 18 April 1934, Saipan, Northern Mariana Islands; s. of the late Blas Pangelinan Tenorio and of Guadalupe Sablan Pangelinan; m. Sophia Pangelinan 1959; four s. four d.; ed George Washington High School, Guam; mem. House of Reps., Congress of Micronesia; Senator Marianas Dist Legislature; Vice-Pres. The Senate, Northern Mariana Commonwealth Legislature 1978–80, Pres. 1980–82; Gov. Commonwealth of the Northern Mariana Islands 1982–91, 1998–2001; Hon. LLD (Univ. of Guam) 1998. *Leisure interest:* golf. *Address:* c/o Office of the Governor, Caller Box 10007, Capitol Hill, Saipan, MP 96950, Commonwealth of the Northern Mariana Islands.

TENYAKOV, Eduard Venyaminovich; Russian business executive; b. 25 Feb. 1952, Chelyabinsk; m.; one d.; ed Chelyabinsk Polytechnic Inst., Moscow Inst. of Finance; with production co. Polyot Chelyabinsk 1971–79; Deputy Dir Gen. on commercial problems 1979–82; Dir Chelyabinsk Factory 1982–85; Dir construction co-operative, Chelyabinsk 1985–87; Chair. Exec. Bd Chelyabinsk Rotorbank, Council of Exchange All-Union Asscn of Commercial Banks and Russian Banking Union 1987–89; one of founders Moscow Cen. Stock Exchange 1989, Pres. 1990–91; Pres. Jt Stock Finance Co. Fininvest, Chelyabinsk 1990–91; Founder and Pres. Chelyabinsk Universal Exchange and Moscow Cen. Stock Exchange 1991–; Co-Chair. Interregional Council of Exchanges and Congress of Exchanges. *Publications:* Optimally Possible

Variant 1991, People of the Future 1994. *Leisure interests:* reading, hunting, riding and breeding horses. *Address:* Chelyabinsk Universal Stock Exchange, Chelyabinsk, Russia (Office). *Telephone:* (095) 292-85-43 (Office).

TEO ENG CHENG, Michael, BBA, MA; Singaporean diplomatist and air force officer (retd); b. 19 Sept. 1947, Sarawak; s. of Teo Thian Lai and Lim Siew Kheng; m. Joyce Teo (née Ng Sinn Toh); one s. one d.; ed Auburn Univ., Fletcher School of Law and Diplomacy, Tufts Univ., USAF War Coll., USA; joined Repub. of Singapore Air Force (RSAF) 1968, Commdr RSAF 1985, Brig.-Gen. 1987, Chief of Air Force 1990, retd; joined Diplomatic Sevice 1993; High Commr to NZ 1994–96; Amb. to Repub. of Korea 1996–2001; High Commr to UK 2001–; The Most Noble Order of the Crown (Thailand) 1981, Legion of Merit, Degree of Commdr (USA) 1991, Order of Diplomatic Service Merit Gwanghwa Medal (Repub. of Korea) 2002; Public Admin. Medal (Singapore) 1989, Outstanding Achievement Award (Philippines) 1989, Bintang Swa Bhuana Paksa Utama (Indonesia) 1991. *Leisure interests:* golf, hiking, reading. *Address:* Singapore High Commission, 9 Wilton Crescent, London, SW1X 8SP, England (Office). *Telephone:* (20) 7201-5850 (Office). *Fax:* (20) 7245-6583 (Office). *E-mail:* info@singaporehc.org.uk (Office).

TER-MINASSIAN, Teresa, MS(Econs); Italian economist; ed Univ. of Rome, Harvard Univ., USA; began career in Research Dept Bank of Italy 1967–71; joined IMF as economist in Fiscal Affairs Dept 1971, Deputy Dir 1988–97, Dir Jan. 2001–, also experience in fmr European Dept, Deputy Dir Western Hemisphere Dept 1997–2001. *Publication:* Fiscal Federalism in Theory and Practice 1997. *Address:* IMF, 700 19th Street, NW, Washington, DC 20431, USA (Office). *Telephone:* (202) 623-8844 (Office). *Fax:* (202) 623-4259 (Office). *E-mail:* tterminassian@imf.org (Office).

TER-PETROSYAN, Levon Akopovich, DLit; Armenian politician and philologist; b. 9 Jan. 1945, Aleppo, Syria; m. Lyudmila Pletnitskaya; one s.; ed Yerevan State Univ., Leningrad Inst. of Orientology; family moved to Armenia in 1946; jr researcher Armenian Inst. of Literature 1972–78, sr researcher, then Scientific Sec. Matenadaran Archive 1978–90; took part in dissident movt, arrested 1966, 1988–89; mem. Chair. Karabakh Cttee in Matenadaran 1988; Deputy Supreme Soviet of Armenian SSR 1989, Chair. 1990–91; mem. Bd, Chair. Armenian Nat. Movt; Pres. of Armenia 1991–98. *Publications:* six books and over 70 papers on the history of Armenia. *Leisure interests:* reading, chess. *Address:* Marshal Baghramian Prospect 19, 375016 Yerevan, Armenia. *Telephone:* (2) 52-57-00; (2) 52-54-04.

TERASAWA, Yoshio, BA (Econs); Japanese international public servant; b. Tokyo; s. of Tsunesaburo Terasawa and Kura Terasawa; m. 1960; one s. three d.; ed Waseda Univ., Tokyo, Wharton Business School, Univ. of Pennsylvania, USA; Pres. Nomura Securities Int. 1970–80, Chair. 1980–85, Exec. Vice-Pres. Nomura Securities, Tokyo 1985–88; Dir-Gen. Econ. Planning Agency May–June 1994; Chair. Tokyo Star Bank; Exec. Vice-Pres. Multilateral Investment Guarantee Agency (MIGA) 1988–; Dir English-Speaking Union of Japan; fmr Fulbright Scholar; mem. New York Stock Exchange 1971–; Hon. Citizen New York City 1972. *Publications:* Night and Day on Wall Street, Windblown on Wall Street, Think Big!!, From the Window of Washington, DC.

TEREKHOVA, Margarita Borisovna; Russian actress and film maker; b. 25 Aug. 1942, Turinsk, the Urals; d. of Galina Stanislavovna Tomashevich and Boris Ivanovich Terekhov; one s. one d.; ed Tashkent Univ. and Mossoviet Studio School; with Mossoviet Theatre 1964–83; Founder and Dir of Theatre Studio (Balaganchik) 1987–; film début 1966; RSFSR Artist of Merit 1976, K. Stanislavsky Prize 1992. *Films include:* Hi! It's Me! 1966, Byelorussian Station 1971, My Life 1972, Monologue 1973, Mirror 1975, Day Train 1976, Who'll go to Truskovets? 1977, Dog in a Manger 1977, Kids, Kids, Kids 1978, D'Artagnan and the Three Musketeers 1978, Let's get Married 1983, Only for Crazy 1991 (San Remo Int. Film Festival Prize), Forbidden Fruit 1993, The Way 1995, The Seagull 2002 (also dir and scriptwriter)). *Theatre:* (dir and actress) When Five Years Elapse, The Tsar's Hunt, Mossoviet Theatre, Bel Ami. *Radio:* A Game for Two, adaptations from the Bible. *Television:* Players, Manon Lescaut, Childhood. *Leisure interest:* son's upbringing and educ. *Address:* Mossovet Theatre, B. Sadovaya str. 16, Moscow, Russia (Office); Bolshaya Gruzinskaya Str. 57, Apt. 92, 123056 Moscow, Russia. *Telephone:* (095) 254-96-95. *Fax:* (095) 254-96-95 (Home); (095) 299-44-37. *E-mail:* terekh.m@mail.ru.

TERENIUS, Lars Yngve, PhD; Swedish medical research scientist; b. 9 July 1940, Örebro; s. of Yngve Terenius and Margareta Hallenborg; m. 1st Malin Åkerblom 1962 (divorced 1986); m. 2nd Mona Hagman 1989; two s.; ed Faculties of Science and Medicine, Uppsala Univ.; Asst Prof. of Pharmacology, Medical Faculty, Uppsala Univ. 1969–79, Prof. of Pharmacology, Faculty of Pharmacy 1979–89; Prof. of Experimental Alcohol and Drug Dependence Research, Karolinska Inst. 1989–; Visiting Scientist Nat. Inst. for Medical Research, London 1972–73, Univ. of Aberdeen, Scotland 1975, Hebrew Univ., Jerusalem 1983, 1986; Fogarty Scholar, NIH, USA 1988–89; mem. Royal Swedish Soc. of Sciences, Royal Swedish Acad. of Sciences, Academia Europaea, American Acad. of Arts and Sciences, IPSEN Award 2000; Dr hc (Uppsala) 1981, (Trondheim) 1983; Olof Rudbeck Prize 1999; Pacesetter Award 1977, Gairdner Award 1978, Jahre Award 1980, Björkén Award of Uppsala Univ. 1984, IPSEN Award 2000. *Publications:* 400 papers on experimental endocrinology, cancer research, neurobiology. *Address:* Department of Experimental Drug Dependence Research, L8: 01, Karolinska Insti-

tute, 17176 Stockholm (Office); Kyrkogårdsgatan 29, 75312 Uppsala, Sweden (Home). *Telephone:* (8) 5177-48-60 (Office). *Fax:* (8) 34-19-39 (Office). *E-mail:* lars.terenius@cmm.ki.se (Office). *Website:* www.ki.se (Office).

TERENTYEVA, Nina Nikolayevna; Russian singer (mezzo-soprano); b. 9 Jan. 1946, Kusa, Chelyabinsk Region; d. of Nikolai Fedorovich and Tatyana Vladimirovna Terentyev; one d.; ed Leningrad State Conservatory (class of Olga Mshanskaya); soloist Kirov (now Mariinsky) Theatre 1971–77, Bolshoi 1979; leading solo mezzo-soprano; People's Artist of Russia. *Russian repertoire includes:* Marta (Khovanshchina), Lubasha (Tsar's Bride), Lubava (Sadko), Marina Mnishek (Boris Godunov), also Amneris (Aida), Azucena (Il Trovatore), Delila (Samson and Delila), Eboli (Don Carlos), Santuzza (Cavalleria Rusticana) and others; participated in productions of maj. theatres of the world including Covent Garden (Amneris, 1995), Metropolitan-Opera (Eboli, 1993), La Scala (oratorio Ivan Grozny with R. Muti, 1994), also in Deutsche Oper and Staatsoper Berlin, Munich, Hamburg, Bordeaux, Los Angeles opera houses; participated in int. festivals; concert repertoire comprises Russian classics. *Leisure interest:* driving. *Address:* Bolshoi Theatre, Teatralnaya pl. 1, 103009 Moscow, Russia. *Telephone:* (095) 971-67-61 (Home).

TERENZIO, Pio-Carlo, LLD; Italian international civil servant; b. 4 Sept. 1921, Lausanne, Switzerland; s. of Rodolfo Arnoldo Terenzio and Katherine Agopian; m. Luisa de Notaristefani 1950; two s.; ed Univs. of Rome and Geneva; joined Int. Labour Office (ILO) 1948; Officer in charge of Relations with Int. Orgs, UNESCO 1948–60, Dir in charge of Congo Operations 1960–63, Dir Bureau of Relations with Member States 1963–69, Dir Bureau of Personnel 1969–70; Sec.-Gen. Inter-Parl. Union (IPU) 1970–86; mem. cttees. on human rights and disarmament, of Italian Nat. Acad. of Sciences 1986–. *Publications:* La rivalité anglo-russe en Perse et en Afghanistan 1947. *Address:* Via della Minerva, 12, 00186 Rome, Italy. *Telephone:* (06) 69920922.

TERESHCHENKO, Sergei, BSc; Kazakhstan politician; b. 30 March 1951, Lesozavodsk, Primorskiy Region; s. of Aleksandr Ivanovich Tereshchenko and Tamara Ivanovna Tereshchenko; m. Yevgenya Tsykunov; two d.; ed Alma-Ata Inst. of Agric., Moscow Univ. of Commerce; held offices in state power organs of Chimkent Region 1986–89, Chair. of the Exec. Cttee of Chimkent Region 1990–91; First Deputy-Chair. Council of Ministers of Kazakh Soviet Repub. 1989–90; Vice-Pres. of Kazakhstan April–May 1991; Prime Minister of Kazakhstan 1991–94; Minister of Foreign Affairs 1994–95; Chair. Bd of Dirs Integrazia Fund 1994–; Vice-Chair. Republican (Otan) Party 1999–2002, Deputy Chair. Ass. of the Peoples of Kazakhstan Oct. 2002–; Order of Dostyk (First Class) 1999; State Prize for Peace and Spiritual Content 1999. *Publications include:* Kazakh Land is My Cradle 1999, Kazakhstan, Reforms, Market 2000. *Leisure interests:* hunting, swimming, fashion, travelling. *Address:* 92 Maoulenov str., 480012 Almaty (Office); 121-18 Kounaev str., 480100 Almaty, Kazakhstan (Home). *Telephone:* (3272) 62-40-57 (Office); (3272) 63-36-18 (Home). *Fax:* (3272) 62-14-96 (Office). *E-mail:* tyelena@nursat.kz (Home).

TERESHKOVA, Maj.-Gen. Valentina Vladimirovna, CandTechSc; Russian politician and fmr cosmonaut; b. 6 March 1937, Maslennikovo, Yaroslavl Region; d. of the late Vladimir Aksyonovich Tereshkov and Elena Fyodorovna Tereshkova; m. 1963 (divorced); one d.; ed Yaroslavl Textile Coll. and Zhukovsky Air Force Engineering Acad.; fmr textile worker, Krasny Perekop textile mill, Yaroslavl; Textile Mill Sec., Young Communist League 1960; joined Yaroslavl Air Sports Club 1959 and started parachute jumping; mem. CPSU 1962–91, Cen. Cttee CPSU 1971–90; began cosmonaut training March 1962; made 48 orbits of the Earth in spaceship Vostok VI 16th–19th June 1963; first woman in world to enter space; Deputy to USSR Supreme Soviet 1966–90; USSR People's Deputy 1989–91; Chair. Soviet Women's Cttee 1968–87; mem. Supreme Soviet Presidium 1970–90; Head Union of Soviet Socs. for Friendship and Cultural Relations with Foreign Countries 1987–92; Chair. then Dir of Presidium, Russian Asscn of Int. Co-operation (now Russian Centre of Int. Scientific and Cultural Co-operation) 1992–; Pres. Moscow House of Europe 1992–; Head Russian Centre for Int. Scientific and Cultural Co-operation 1994–; Visit to UK 1977; Pilot-Cosmonaut of USSR, Hero of Soviet Union, Joliot-Curie Gold Medal, World Peace Council 1966, Order of the Nile (Egypt) 1971 and other decorations. *Address:* Russian Centre of International Co-operation, Vozdvizhenka Str. 14–18, 103885 Moscow, Russia. *Telephone:* (095) 290-12-45.

TERFEL JONES, Bryn, CBE; British bass baritone singer; b. 9 Nov. 1965, Pantglas, Snowdonia; s. of Hefin Jones and Nesta Jones; m. Lesley Halliday 1987; three s.; ed Ysgol Duffryn Nantlle, Pengroes, Gwynedd and Guildhall School of Music and Drama; has appeared at world's leading opera houses including Welsh Nat. Opera 1990–, English Nat. Opera 1991–, Salzburg 1992–, Royal Nat. Opera, Covent Garden 1992–, Vienna State Opera 1993–, NY Metropolitan Opera 1994–; Sydney Opera House 1999–; roles at Royal Opera House include Mozart's Figaro, Masetto, Balstrode, Jochanaan, Wotan and Falstaff; many concert appearances in Europe, USA, Canada, Japan and Australia; frequent guest soloist with Berlin Philharmonic Orchestra; Pres. Nat. Youth Choir of Wales, Festival of Wales; Vice-Pres. Llangollen Int. Eisteddfod; Founder, Faenol Festival 2000; Hon. Fellow, Univ. of Wales, Aberystwyth, Welsh Coll. of Music and Drama, Univ. of Wales, Bangor; Hon. DMus (Glamorgan) 1997; White Robe, Gorsedd; recipient, Kathleen Ferrier Scholarship 1988; Gold Medal Award 1989; Lieder Prize, Cardiff Singer of World Competition 1989; Young Singer of the Year, Gramophone magazine

1992; British Critics' Circle Award 1992; Newcomer of Year, Int. Classic Music Awards 1993; Caecillia Prize for recording of Vagabond 1995; Grammy Award for best classical vocal performance for recording of opera arias 1996; People's Award, Gramophone awards for recording of Vagabond 1996; Britannia Record Club Members' Award for recording of Something Wonderful 1997. *Recordings include:* The Marriage of Figaro, Britten's Gloriana, Beethoven's Ninth Symphony, Brahms' Requiem. *Leisure interests:* golf, collecting fob watches, supporting Manchester United. *Address:* c/o Harlequin Agency, 203 Fidlas Road, Cardiff, CF4 5NA, Wales. *Telephone:* (29) 2075-0821. *Fax:* (29) 2075-5971.

TERKEL, Studs Louis, PhB, JD; American author, actor and interviewer; b. 16 May 1912, New York; s. of Samuel Terkel and Anna (née Finkel) Terkel; m. Ida Goldberg 1939; one s.; ed Chicago Univ.; star TV programme Studs Place 1950–53, radio programme Wax Museum 1945–, Studs Terkel Almanac 1952–, Studs Terkel Show (station WFMT-FM Chicago 1952–97); master of ceremonies, Newport Folk Festival 1959, 1960, Ravinia Musical Festival 1959, Chicago Univ. Folk Festival 1961 and others; Distinguished Scholar in Residence, Chicago History Soc. 1998–; lecturer and film narrator; Prix Italia, UNESCO Award for best Radio Programme (East-West Values) 1962; Communicator of the Year Award (Chicago Univ. Alumni Asscn) 1969; Nat. Humanities Medal 1997. *Stage appearances include:* Detective Story 1950, A View from the Bridge 1958, Light up the Sky 1959, The Cave Dwellers 1960. *Publications:* Giants of Jazz 1956, Division Street America 1966, Amazing Grace (play) 1959, Hard Times 1970, Working 1974, Talking to Myself 1977, American Dreams: Lost and Found 1980, The Good War: An Oral History of World War Two 1985, Talking to Myself: A Memoir of My Times 1986, Chicago 1986, The Great Divide: Second Thoughts on the American Dream 1988, Race: How Blacks and Whites Think and Feel About the American Obsession 1992, Coming of Age 1995, My American Century 1997, The Spectator: Talk About Movies and Plays with Those Who Made Them 1999 and short stories. *Address:* c/o Chicago History Society, Clark Street at North Avenue, Chicago, IL 60614, USA (Office).

TERRAGNO, Rodolfo H., DJur; Argentine politician; b. 16 Nov. 1945, Buenos Aires; m. Sonía Pascual Sánchez; two s.; ed Univ. de Buenos Aires; Asst Prof. Univ. de Buenos Aries 1973–80; researcher Inst. of Latin American Studies, London 1980–82, LSE 1980–82; Pres. Terragno SA de Industrias Químicas 1970–76; Exec. Vice-Pres. El Diario de Caracas SA 1976–80; Vice-Pres. Alas Enterprises Inc., NY 1982–86; Dir Letters S.A.R., Luxembourg 1982–86; Latin American Newsletters Ltd, London and Paris 1982–86; also columnist on several newspapers; rep. at int. conferences, including dispute with UK over Falkland Islands 1983–85; Sec. to Cabinet 1987, Minister of Works and Public Services 1987–89; Pres. Fundación Argentina Siglo 21 1986–87. *Publications:* Los dueños del poder 1972, Los 400 días de Perón 1974–75, Contratapas 1976, Muerte y resurrección de los políticos 1981, La Argentina del Siglo 21 1985–87, also numerous research papers.

TERRAINE, John Alfred, FRHistS; British writer; b. 15 Jan. 1921, London; s. of Charles William Terraine and Evelyn Holmes; m. Joyce Elizabeth Waite 1945; one d.; ed Stamford School, Keble Coll. Oxford; Recorded Programmes Section, BBC 1943, Radio Newsreel 1945, Russian Section 1947, Pacific and S. African Programme Organizer 1953; freelance writer 1963–; Founder and Pres. Western Front Asscn 1980–97, Patron 1997–; Screenwriters' Guild Documentary Award 1964, Soc. of Film and TV Arts Script Award 1969, Chesney Gold Medal, Royal United Service Inst. 1982, Yorkshire Post Book of the Year 1985, C. P. Robertson Memorial Trophy, Air Public Relations Asscn 1985. *Publications:* Mons 1960, Douglas Haig: The Educated Soldier 1963, The Great War (TV series) 1964, The Western Front 1964, General Jack's Diary (Ed.) 1964, The Life and Times of Lord Mountbatten 1968 (TV series), Impacts of War, 1914 and 1918 1970, The Mighty Continent 1974 (TV series), Trafalgar 1976, The Road to Passchendaele 1977, To Win a War: 1918 The Year of Victory 1978, The Smoke and the Fire 1980, White Heat: the New Warfare 1914–18 1982, The First World War 1914–18 1983, The Right of the Line: The Royal Air Force in the European War 1939–45 1985, Business in Great Waters: The U-Boat Wars 1916–1945 1989, White Heat: The New Warfare 1914–18 1992, The Smoke and the Fire: Myths and Anti-Myths of War 1992. *Leisure interest:* convivial and congenial conversation. *Address:* 77 Sirdar Road, London, W11 4EQ, England. *Telephone:* (20) 7229-8152.

TERRAZAS SANDOVAL, HE Cardinal Julio; Bolivian ecclesiastic; b. 7 March 1936, Vallegrande; ordained priest 1962; consecrated Titular Bishop 1978; Bishop of Oruro 1982–91; Archbishop of Santa Cruz 1991–; cr. Cardinal 2001. *Address:* Arzobispado, Casilla 25, Calle Ingavi 49, Santa Cruz, Bolivia (Office). *Telephone:* (3) 32-4286 (Office). *Fax:* (3) 33-0181 (Office). *E-mail:* asc@scbbs-bo.com (Office).

TERRY, John Quinlan, AADip, FRIBA; British architect; b. 24 July 1937, London; s. of the late Philip Terry and Phyllis Terry; m. Christina de Ruttié 1961; one s. four d.; ed Bryanston School, Architectural Asscn; joined late Raymond Erith RA 1962–73; work includes Kingswalden Bury, the New Common Room Bldg at Gray's Inn, the restoration of St Mary's Church on Paddington Green; Partner Erith and Terry 1967–; in pvt. practice 1973–, work includes large classical pvt. houses in stone erected in England, USA and Germany including six pvt. villas in Regent's Park for Crown Estate Commrs, offices, shops and flats at Richmond Riverside, new Lecture Theatre, Jr Common Room, Library and residential bldgs for Downing Coll. Cambridge, Brentwood Cathedral, restoration of the three State Rooms at No. 10 Downing Street, restoration of St Helen's Church, Bishopsgate, new commercial bldg 20–32 Baker Street; mem. Royal Fine Art Comm. 1994–97; Rome Scholar 1969, Prix International de la Reconstruction 1983. *Publications:* Architectural Monographs 1991, Architects Anonymous 1993. *Leisure interest:* the Pauline Epistles. *Address:* Old Exchange, Dedham, Colchester, Essex, CO7 6HA, England. *Telephone:* (1206) 323186.

TERZIEFF, Laurent Didier Alex; French actor and theatre director; b. 27 June 1935, Toulouse; s. of Jean Terzieff and Marie (née Lapasset) Terzieff; ed Lycée Buffon, Paris; actor 1953–; Officier Ordre nat. du Mérite, Commdr des Arts et des Lettres; numerous prizes and awards including Prix du disque français 1975, Grand prix nat. du théâtre (Ministry of Culture) 1984, Molière Prizes for best dir and for best play of the year for Ce que voit Fox 1988, Pirandello Prize (Italy) 1989, Molière Prizes for best dir and for best play at a pvt. theatre, for Temps contre temps 1993. *Theatre includes:* (as dir and actor): Zoo Story 1964, Tango 1968, Fragments 1978, Le Pic du bossu 1979, Le Philanthrope 1979, Les Amis 1981, L'Ambassade 1982, Guérison americaine 1984–85, Témoignage sur Ballybeg 1986, A pied 1987, Ce que voit Fox 1988, 1990, Henri IV 1989, Richard II 1991, Temps contre temps 1993; (as actor): Meurtre dans la cathédrale 1994, Le Bonnet de fou 1997, Brulés par la glace 1999, Brecht, poète 2000, Le Regard 2002. *Cinema includes:* Les tricheurs 1958, Kajo 1966, La prisonnière 1967, Vanina Vanini 1967, La voie lactée 1968, Medea 1973, Noces de sang 1980, La flambeuse 1981, Détective 1984, Diésel 1984, Rouge baiser 1985, Hiver 54 1989, Germinal 1993, Fiesta 1994, Pianiste 1997, Le manuscrit du prince 1999, Sur la plage 1999, Territori d'omba 2000. *Television includes:* Bérénice, Le Beau françois, Moïse, Hedda Gabler, Rimbaud, Le Martyre de Saint Sébastien, La Flèche dans le coeur 1985, La Fille aux lilas 1985. *Address:* 8 rue du Dragon, 75006 Paris, France.

TESAURO, Giuseppe; Italian professor of international law; b. 15 Nov. 1942, Naples; m. Paola Borrelli 1967; three c.; ed Liceo Umberto, Naples, Univ. of Naples, Max Planck Inst. Volkerrecht-Heidelberg; Asst Prof. of Int. Law, Univ. of Naples 1965–71; Prof. of Int. Law and Int. Org., Univs. of Catania, Messina, Naples, Rome 1971–88; Dir EEC Law School, Univ. of Rome 1982–88; mem. Council Legal Affairs, Ministry of Foreign Affairs 1986–; Judge, First Advocate Gen. European Court of Justice 1988–98; Pres. Italian Competition Authority 1998–. *Publications:* Financing International Institutions 1968, Pollution of the Sea and International Law 1971, Nationalizations and International Law 1976, Movements of Capital in the EEC 1984, Course of EEC Law 1988. *Leisure interests:* tennis, football, sailing.

TESCH, Emmanuel Camille Georges Victor; Luxembourg iron and steel company executive and engineer; b. 9 Dec. 1920, Hespérange; s. of Georges Tesch and Marie-Laure Weckbecker; m. Thérèse Laval 1949; one s.; ed Technische Hochschule, Aachen and Eidgenössische Technische Hochschule, Zürich; Engineer, Manufacture de Tabacs Heintz van Landewyck 1948–51; fmr Man. Dir Soc. Générale pour le Commerce de Produits Industriels (SOGECO); joined ARBED as auditor 1958, Dir 1968, Chair. Bd of Dirs. 1972–91; Chair. Bd of Dirs. ARBED Finance SA –1992, Electro Holding Co., SA Luxembourgeoise d'Exploitations Minières; Dir SIDMAR SA, Compagnie Maritime Belge, SOGECO SA, LE FOYER SA, Banque Générale du Luxembourg SA; Adviser Société Générale de Belgique, Companhia Siderurgica Belgo-Mineira; mem. Internationaler Beraterkreis der Allianz-Versicherungs-Gesellschaft, Conseil Economique et Social (Luxembourg); Pres. Chambre de Commerce du Grand-Duché de Luxembourg; Médaille de la Résistance (France); Grand Officer Ordre de la Couronne de Chêne (Luxembourg); Commdr avec Couronne dans l'Ordre de mérite civil et militaire d'Adolphe de Nassau (Luxembourg); Ordre de la Couronne (Belgium); Commdr Order of Orange-Nassau (Netherlands); Cavaliere di Gran Croce (Italy); Order of Tudor Vladimirescu (Romania); Hon. KBE; Grosses Goldenes Ehrenzeichen mit Stern des Verdienstordens der Republik Österreich; Grosses Verdienstkreuz mit Stern des Verdienstordens der Bundesrepublik Deutschland; Encomienda de numero, Mérito Civil, Spain. *Leisure interests:* fishing, literature. *Address:* La Cléchère, 45 Route de Bettembourg, 1899 Kockelscheuer, Luxembourg (Home). *Telephone:* 47-921 (Office); 36-81-68 (Home).

TESHABAEV, Fatikh, PhD; Uzbekistan diplomatist; b. 18 Oct. 1939, Tashkent; s. of Gulam Ahmad Teshabaev and Hajiniso Teshabaev; m. Mauluda Teshabaev 1966; two s. one d.; ed Univs. of Tashkent and Delhi; First Deputy Minister for Foreign Affairs 1991–93; Amb. to USA and Perm. Rep. to UN 1993–96; Amb.-at-Large 1996–97; Amb. to UK 1997–99; Special Adviser UNDP in Uzbekistan 2000–; Nehru Award. *Publications:* articles on political thought in oriental countries. *Leisure interest:* tennis. *Address:* Birinchitor Kucha Topqairagoch 12, Tashkent 700081, Uzbekistan (Home). *Telephone:* (71) 2791786 (Home); (71) 1055860. *Fax:* (Home). *E-mail:* fatih.teshabaev@undp.org (Office); teshabaev2002@yahoo.com.

TESSON, Philippe, DèsSc; French journalist; b. 1 March 1928, Wassigny (Aisne); s. of Albert Tesson and Jeanne Ancely; m. Dr. Marie-Claude Millet 1969; one s. two d.; ed Coll. Stanislas, Inst. of Political Studies, Paris; Sec. of Parl. Debates 1957–60; Ed.-in-Chief, Combat 1960–74; candidate in legis. elections 1968; Diarist and Drama Critic, Canard Enchaîné 1970–83; Co-Man. and Dir Société d'Editions Scientifiques et Culturelles 1971, Pres. 1980; Dir and Ed.-in-Chief, Quotidien de Paris 1974; Dir Nouvelles Littéraires 1975–83; Drama Critic, L'Express Paris 1986; Dir and Co.-Man. Quotidien du Maire 1988; Animator (TV programme with France 3) A Quel Titre 1994–; Ed. Valeurs actuelles 1994–; Drama Critic Revue des deux Mondes 1990–, Figaro

Magazine 1995–; Dir Avant-scène Théâtre 2001–; Chevalier, Légion d'honneur. *Publication:* De Gaulle 1er 1965, Où est passée l'autorité? 2000. *Address:* 205 boulevard Saint-Germain, 75007 Paris, France (Office).

TESTINO, Mario; Peruvian fashion photographer; b. 1954, Lima; portfolio includes Madonna for Versace, Princess of Wales for Vanity Fair 1997, advertising campaign for Gucci, Sir Hardy Amies, John Galliano, Jade Jagger, Naomi Campbell, Devon Aoki and Alexander McQueen for Vogue's Millennium souvenir issue 2000; work exhibited in Nat. Portrait Gallery, London 2001–02. *Address:* c/o National Portrait Gallery, St Martin's Place, London, WC2H 0HE, England (Office). *Telephone:* (20) 7306-0055 (Office). *Fax:* (20) 7306-0056. *Website:* www.npg.org.uk (Office).

TETLEY, Glen, BS; American ballet director and choreographer; b. 3 Feb. 1926, Cleveland, Ohio; s. of Glenford Andrew Tetley and Mary Eleanor Byrne; ed Franklin and Marshall Coll., Lancaster, Pa and New York Univ.; performed with Hanya Holm, José Limon, Pearl Lang, John Butler modern dance cos.; choreographer Major Ballet Co. 1948–; prin. dancer, New York City Opera 1951–54; leading soloist, Robert Joffrey Ballet 1955–56, Martha Graham Dance Co. 1957–59, American Ballet Theater 1959–61, Jerome Robbins' Ballet USA 1961–62; f. own co. 1962–69; dancer and choreographer, Nederlands Dans Theater, Co-Artistic Dir 1969; guest choreographer Royal Danish, Swedish, Norwegian Ballets, Hamburg State Opera; choreographer Royal Ballet, Covent Garden, American Ballet Theatre, Ballet Rambert; Dir Stuttgart Ballet 1974–76; Artistic Assoc. Nat. Ballet of Canada 1987–; German Critics Award (for Die Feder) 1969, Queen Elizabeth II Coronation Award 1981, Prix Italia 1982, RAI Prize 1982, Tennant Caledonian Award 1983, Ohioana Career Medal for 1986, NY Univ. Achievement Award 1988; Kt, Order of Merit, Norway 1997–; Hon. Dr of Fine Arts, Franklin and Marshall Co. 2001. *Performances:* Kiss me Kate, Out of this World, Amahl and the Night Visitors, Juno; choreography: Pierrot Lunaire, Sargasso, The Anatomy Lesson, Circles, Imaginary Film, Arena, Small Parades, Mutations, Embrace Tiger and Return to Mountain, Ziggurat, Rag Dances, Ricercare, Field Figures, Laborintus, Mythical Hunters, Gemini, Chronocromie, Threshold, Moveable Garden, Voluntaries, Le sacre du printemps, Greening, Nocturne, Sphinx, Praeludium, Contredances, The Tempest, Summer's End, Dances of Albion, Dark Night: Glad Day, Fire Bird, Murderer Hope of Women, Revelation and Fall, Pulcinella, Dream Walk of the Shaman, Alice, Orpheus, La Ronde, Tagore, Dialogues, Oracle, Amores, Lux in Tenebris. *Major roles:* (American Ballet Theatre) Pillar of Fire, Lilac Garden, Miss Julie, Lady from the Sea, Billy the Kid; (Joffrey Ballet) Pas de Déesses; (Martha Graham Co.) Embattled Garden, Diversion of Angels; (Limon Co.) Moor's Pavane, Passacaglia; (Jerome Robbins Ballet, USA) Afternoon of a Faun, Cage, The Concert Moves, Events; (John Butler Co.) Masque of the Wild Man, Sebastian, The Sybil, Glory Folk, Carmina Burana. *Leisure interests:* farming, reading, archaeology. *Address:* 860 United Nations Plaza, Apt. 10/6, New York, NY 10017, USA.

TETTAMANZI, HE Cardinal Dionigi; Italian ecclesiastic; b. 14 March 1934, Renate; ordained priest 1957; Bishop 1989; Archbishop of Genoa 1995–; cr. Cardinal Feb. 1998. *Address:* Arcivescovado, Piazza Matteotti 4, 16123 Genoa, Italy. *Telephone:* (10) 27001. *Fax:* (10) 292554.

TEUFEL, Erwin; German politician; b. 4 Sept. 1939, Rottweil; m.; four c.; Dist Admin. Rottweil and Trossingen municipality 1961–64; Mayor of Spaichingen 1964–72; mem. State Parl. of Baden-Württemberg 1972–; Leader CDU Parl. Group 1978–91; Minister-Pres. of Baden-Württemberg Jan. 1991–; Chair. CDU-Baden-Württemberg 1991–; mem. Fed. Cttee of CDU. *Address:* Landtag von Baden-Württemberg, Haus des Landtags, Konrad-Adenauer-strasse 3, 70173 Stuttgart (Office); Dreifaltigkeitsbergstrasse 44, 78549 Spaichingen, Germany (Home). *Telephone:* (711) 20630 (Office). *Fax:* (711) 2063299 (Office). *E-mail:* post@lantag-bw.de. *Website:* www.landtag-bw.de (Office).

TÉVOÉDJRÈ, Albert, LèsL; Benin politician and international civil servant; b. 10 Nov. 1929, Porto Novo; s. of Joseph Tévoédjrè and Jeanne Singbo Tévoédjrè; m. Isabelle Ekué 1953; three s.; ed Toulouse Univ., France, Fribourg Univ., Switzerland, Institut Universitaire de Hautes Etudes Internationales, Geneva, Sloan School of Management and MIT, USA (Advanced Programme for Sr Executives); teaching assignments include: Lycée Delafosse, Dakar, Senegal 1952–54, Ecole Normale d'Institutrices, Cahors, France 1957–58, Lycée Victor Ballot, Porto Novo 1959–61, Geneva Africa Inst. 1963–64, Georgetown Univ., Washington DC 1964; Sec. of State for Information 1961–62; Sec.-Gen. Union Africaine et Malgache (UAM) 1962–63; Research Assoc. Harvard Univ., Centre for Int. Affairs 1964–65; Int. Labour Office 1965–, Regional Dir for Africa March 1966, Asst Dir-Gen. 1969–75, Deputy Dir-Gen. 1975; Dir Int. Inst. for Labour Studies 1975–84; Sec.-Gen. World Social Prospects Asscn (AMPS) 1980–; fmr Chief Ed. L'Etudiant d'Afrique Noire; Minister of Planning and Employment Promotion 1997–99; founding-mem. Promotion Africaine (soc. to combat poverty in Africa); founding-mem. Nat. Liberation Movt and mem. Cttee 1958–60; Deputy Sec.-Gen. of Nat. Syndicate of Teachers, Dahomey 1959–60; Visiting Prof. Sorbonne, Paris 1979–, Univ. des Mutants, Dakar 1979–, Nat. Univ. of Côte d'Ivoire 1979–, Northwestern Univ., Ill. 1980; Int. Humanitarian Medal 1987. *Publications:* L'Afrique revoltée 1958, La formation des cadres africains en vue de la croissance économique 1965, Pan-Africanism in Action 1965,

L'Afrique face aux problèmes du socialisme et de l'aide étrangère 1966, Une stratégie du progrès social en Afrique et la contribution de l'OIT 1969, Pour un contrat de solidarité 1976, La pauvreté—richesse des peuples 1978, etc.

THAHANE, Timothy T., BComm, MA; Lesotho government official and diplomatist; b. 2 Nov. 1940, Leribe; s. of Nicodemus Thahane and Beatrice Thahane; m. Dr. Edith Mohapi 1972; one s. one d.; ed Lesotho High School, Univs. of Newfoundland and Toronto, Canada; Asst Sec., Prin. Asst Sec., Cen. Planning Office 1968–70, Dir of Planning 1968–73; Amb. to EEC for Negotiations of Lomé Convention 1973–74; Alt. Exec. Dir (Africa Group 1) World Bank 1974–76, Exec. Dir 1976–78, representing 15 African countries and Trinidad and Tobago; Vice-Chair. and Chair., Jt Audit Cttee of World Bank Group 1976–78; Amb. to the USA 1978–80; Vice-Pres. UN Affairs, IBRD 1990–96; Deputy Gov. SA Reserve Bank 1996–; Vice-Pres. and Sec., IBRD 1980–96; Dir Bd of Global Coalition for Africa, Washington 1992–; mem. Bd of Lesotho Bank (Vice-Chair. 1972–73), Third World Foundation, Centre for Econ. Devt and Population Activities, Washington. *Publications:* articles on econ. planning and investment in Lesotho, Southern Africa and Africa in general. *Leisure interests:* reading, music. *Address:* South African Reserve Bank, 370 Church Street, P.O. Box 427, Pretoria 0001, South Africa. *Telephone:* (12) 3133911. *Fax:* (12) 8133197. *E-mail:* info@gwise.resbank.co.za (Office). *Website:* www.resbank.co.za (Office).

THAILAND, King of (see Bhumibol Adulyadej).

THAKSIN SHINAWATRA, PhD; Thai politician and police officer; b. 26 July 1949, Chiangmai; ed Police Cadet Acad., Eastern Kentucky Univ., Sam Houston State Univ., USA; joined Royal Thai Police Dept 1973, Lt-Col 1987, resgnd 1987; Chair. Shinawatra Computer and Communications Group 1987–94; Minister of Foreign Affairs 1994–95; Leader Palang Dharma Party 1995–96; Deputy Prime Minister in charge of Traffic and Transportation in Bangkok 1995–96, Deputy Prime Minister 1997; Prime Minister of Thailand 2001–; Founder and Leader Thai Rak Thai Party 1998–; Founder and Vice-Chair. THAICOM Foundation for Secondary Educ. 1993–; Hon. (External) mem. Police Cadet Acad. Council 1996–; Hon. mem. Asscn Ex-Mil. Officers 1998–; Pres. Northerners' Asscn of Thailand 1998–; 1992 ASEAN Businessman of the Year Award, Lee Kuan Yew Exchange Fellowship 1994 and other awards. *Address:* Office of the Prime Minister, Government House, Thanon Nakhon Patnom, Bangkok, 10300, Thailand (Office). *Telephone:* (2) 280-3526 (Office). *Fax:* (2) 282-8792 (Office). *Website:* www.pmoffice.go.th (Office).

THALÉN, Ingela; Swedish politician; b. 1 Oct. 1943, Gothenburg; m. Lars Thalén; one s. two d.; fmr shop asst, later clerk at Social Democratic Youth League, Gothenburg, Social Democratic Party, Stockholm County Council and at ARE-Bolagen 1959–74; District Sec. Gothenburg br., Social Democratic Party 1975–78, Stockholm City br. 1979; engaged in local politics, Järfälla 1979–87, Municipal Commr and Chair. Municipal Exec. Bd 1983–87; Minister of Labour 1987–90; mem. of Parl. 1988–; Minister of Health and Social Affairs 1990–91, 1994–96; Sec. Gen. Social Democratic Party 1996–99; Minister for Social Security 1999–. *Address:* Ministry of Health and Social Affairs, Fredsgt. 8, 10333 Stockholm, Sweden (Office). *Telephone:* (8) 405-10-00 (Office). *Fax:* (8) 723-11-11 (Office). *E-mail:* registrator@social.ministry.se (Office). *Website:* www.regeringen.se (Office).

THALER, Zoran; Slovenian politician; b. 21 Jan. 1962, Kranj; m.; one c.; ed Univ. of Ljubljana; with Yugoslavian Foreign Ministry 1987; took part in various int. confs; Deputy Minister of Foreign Affairs Slovenian Repub. 1990–93; mem. of Parl. 1990; mem. Liberal Democracy of Slovenia 1992; Chair. Parl. Cttee for Foreign Affairs 1993–95; Pres. Slovenian Interparl. Group; Minister of Foreign Affairs 1995–96; in pvt. business 1996–. *Leisure interests:* sailing, skiing, gardening, travelling. *Address:* c/o Ministry of Foreign Affairs, Gregorciceva 25, 61000 Ljubljana, Slovenia.

THAN SHWE, Sr Gen.; Myanmar politician and army officer; Prime Minister and Minister of Defence April 1992–; Chair. State Law and Order Restoration Council (SLORC) 1992–97, Chair. State Peace and Devt Council (SDP) 1997–. *Address:* Office of the Prime Minister, Theinbyu Road, Botahtaung Township, Yangon, Myanmar. *Telephone:* (1) 283742.

THANHAWLA, Lal, BA; Indian politician; b. 19 May 1942, Durtlang, Aizawl, Mizoram; s. of H. P. Sailo and Lalsawmliani Thanhawla; m. Lal Riliani 1970; one s. two d.; ed Gauhati Univ.; joined Indian Nat. Congress 1968, mem. All India Congress Cttee 1973, Pres. Mizoram Pradesh Congress Cttee 1973–98; mem. Mizoram Legis. Ass. 1978–, Chief Minister 1984–87, 1989–98, Leader of Opposition 1978–84, 1987–89; mem. Congress Working Cttee; mem. 9th Finance Comm. of India; Chair. Sports Comm. NE Region of India; Founder-Ed. Remna Arsi & Mizo Aw (daily newspaper); Chair. Literary Cttee of Nat. Devt Council; Pres. Mizoram Olympic Asscn; Life mem. YMCA, Evangelical Fellowship of India, Bible Soc. of India; 10 nat. and int. awards for contribs. to peace etc. *Leisure interests:* gardening, reading. *Address:* Zarkawt, Aizawl (Mizoram), India. *Telephone:* 22150; 22274.

THANI, Sheikh Abdul Aziz ibn Khalifa ath-, BS; Qatari politician; b. 12 Dec. 1948, Doha; one s. three d.; ed Northern Indiana Univ., USA; Deputy Minister of Finance and Petroleum June–Dec. 1972, Minister of Finance and Petroleum, State of Qatar 1972; Chair. State of Qatar Investment Bd 1972–, Qatar Nat. Bank 1972, Qatar Gen. Petroleum Corpn 1973–; Gov. IMF and IBRD (World Bank) 1972; rep. at numerous int. confs. including OPEC,

OAPEC and Arab, Islamic and Non-Aligned summit confs. *Leisure interest:* scuba diving. *Address:* c/o Qatar General Petroleum Corporation, P.O. Box 3212, Doha, Qatar.

THANI, Sheikh Abdullah bin Khalifa ath-; Qatari politician; fmrly Deputy Prime Minister, Minister of the Interior; Prime Minister of Qatar 1996–. *Address:* Office of the Prime Minister, P.O. Box 923, Doha, Qatar. *Telephone:* 4323377 (Office). *Fax:* 4435249 (Office). *Website:* www.diwan.gov .qa (Office).

THANI, Sheikh Hamad bin Khalifa ath-, Amir of Qatar; b. 1950, Doha; ed Royal Mil. Coll., Sandhurst, UK; apptd. Heir-Apparent May 1977; Commdr First Mobile Bn (now Hamad Mobile Bn); Maj., then Maj.-Gen., Commdr-in-Chief Armed Forces of Qatar; Minister of Defence May 1977–; Amir of Qatar June 1995–; Prime Minister 1995–96; Supreme Pres. Higher Planning Council; Pres. Higher Youth Council 1979–91; f. Mil. Sports Fed.; mem. Int. Mil. Sports Fed.; Orders of Merit from Egypt, France, Indonesia, Lebanon, Morocco, Oman, Saudi Arabia, UK, Venezuela. *Address:* The Royal Palace, P.O. Box 923, Doha, Qatar.

THANI, Sheikh Khalifa bin Hamad ath-, fmr Amir of Qatar; b. 1932, Doha; s. of the late Heir Apparent Sheikh Hamad bin Abdullah bin Jassim al-Thani; ed Royal Mil. Coll., Sandhurst, UK; appointed Heir-Apparent 1948; served successively as Chief of Security Forces, Chief of Civil Courts, Minister of Educ., Finance and Petroleum; Deputy Ruler 1960–72, also Minister of Educ. 1960–70; Prime Minister 1970–72, Minister of Finance 1970–72; Chair. Investment Bd for State Reserves 1972; deposed his cousin Sheikh Ahmad and took office as Amir of Qatar 1972, deposed by his son June 1995.

THANIN KRAIVICHIEN (see Kraivichien, Thanin).

THAPA, Surya Bahadur; Nepalese politician; b. 20 March 1928, Muga, East Nepal; s. of Bahadur Thapa; m. 1953; one s. two d.; ed Allahabad Univ., India; House Speaker, Advisory Ass. to King of Nepal 1958; mem. Upper House of Parl. 1959; Minister of Forests, Agric., Commerce and Industry 1960; Minister of Finance and Econ. Affairs 1962; Vice-Chair. Council of Ministers, Minister of Finance, Econ. Planning, Law and Justice 1963; Vice-Chair. Council of Ministers, Minister of Finance, Law and Gen. Admin. 1964–65; Chair. Council of Ministers, Minister of Palace Affairs, 1965–69; Prime Minister of Nepal and Minister of Palace Affairs 1979–83; Minister of Finance 1979–80, of Defence 1980–81, 1982–83, of Foreign Affairs 1982; Prime Minister of Nepal 1997–98; Pres. Nat. Democratic Party (NDP); mem. Royal Advisory Cttee 1969–72; arrested and released 1972, 1975; Tri-Sahkti-Patta 1963, Gorkha Dakshinbahu I 1965, Om Rama Patta 1980; several Nepalese and foreign awards. *Address:* National Democratic Party (NDP) (Chand), Maitighar, Kathmandu, Nepal. *Telephone:* 223044. *Fax:* 223628.

THAQI, Hashim; Serbia and Montenegro (Serbian/Kosovan) politician and guerrilla leader; b. 1970; fmr Commdr Kosovo Liberation Army (KLA); Pres. Democratic Party of Kosovo (fmrly Party for the Democratic Progress of Kosovo) May 2000–; mem. Interim Admin. Council (IAC), Kosovo 1999–2001. *Address:* Democratic Party of Kosovo, Pristina, Kosovo, Serbia and Montenegro (Office).

THAROOR, Shashi, PhD; Indian international organization executive and author; b. 1956, London, UK; two s.; ed Tuft's Univ. Fletcher School of Law and Diplomacy, USA; professional author; joined UN 1978; with UNHCR, served at Geneva HQ, Head of Office in Singapore; Special Asst for UN Peacekeeping operations; Exec. Asst to UN Sec.-Gen. 1997–98, Dir Communications and Special Projects, Office of the Sec.-Gen. 1998–2000; Interim Head of Dept of Public Information 2001–02, Head and Under-Sec.-Gen. for Communication and Public Information May 2002–; Commonwealth Writers' Prize, several journalism and literary awards; named Global Leader of Tomorrow by World Econ. Forum, Davos, Switzerland 1998. *Publications include:* India: From Midnight to the Millennium 1997, The Great Indian Novel 1989; six other books. *Address:* Department of Public Information, United Nations, New York, NY 10017, USA (Office). *E-mail:* dpingo@un.org (Office). *Website:* www.un.org (Office).

THARP, Twyla, BA; American dancer and choreographer; b. 1 July 1941, Portland, Ind.; m. 1st Peter Young (divorced); m. 2nd Robert Huot (divorced); one s.; ed Pomona Coll., American Ballet Theatre School, Barnard Coll.; studied with Richard Thomas, Merce Cunningham, Igor Schwezoff, Louis Mattox, Paul Taylor, Margaret Craske, Erick Hawkins; with Paul Taylor Dance Co. 1963–65; freelance choreographer with own modern dance troupe and various other cos., including Joffrey Ballet and American Ballet Theatre 1965–87; Artistic Assoc. Choreographer American Ballet Theatre, New York 1988–91; Hon. mem. American Acad. of Arts and Letters 1997; has received 15 Hon. degrees, two Emmy Awards and numerous other awards including Dance Magazine Annual Award 1981, Laurence Olivier Award 1991, Doris Duke Awards for New York 1999. *Major works choreographed include:* Tank Dive 1965, Re-Moves 1966, Forevermore 1967, Generation 1968, Medley 1969, Fugue 1970, Eight Jelly Rolls 1971, The Raggedy Dances 1972, As Time Goes By 1974, Sue's Leg 1975, Push Comes to Shove 1976, Once More Frank 1976, Mud 1977, Baker's Dozen 1979, When We Were Very Young 1980, Amadeus 1984, White Nights 1985, Rules of the Game 1989; choreographed Cutting Up 1993 for US tour, Demeter and Persephone 1993, 1994, Waterbaby Bagatelles 1994, Red White and Blues 1995, How Near Heaven 1995, Mr. Worldly Wise 1996; films Hair 1979, I'll do Anything 1992; videotape Making Television Dance 1977, CBS Cable Confessions of a Corner Maker

1980. *Publication:* Push Comes to Shove (autobiog.) 1992. *Address:* Tharp Productions, 336 Central Park West, Flat 17B, New York, NY 10025, USA. *Website:* twylatharp.org (Office).

THATCHER, Baroness; (Life Peer), cr. 1992, of Kesteven in the County of Lincolnshire; **Rt Hon Margaret Hilda Thatcher,** LG, OM, PC, BSc, MA, FRS; British stateswoman and barrister; b. 13 Oct. 1925; d. of the late Alfred Roberts and of Beatrice Ethel Stephenson; m. Denis Thatcher (now Sir Denis Thatcher, Bt) 1951; one s. one d. (twins); ed Grantham High School and Somerville Coll. Oxford; research chemist 1947–51; called to the Bar, Lincoln's Inn 1953; MP for Finchley 1959–92; Parl. Sec. Ministry of Pensions and Nat. Insurance 1961–64; Chief Opposition Spokesman on Educ. 1969–70; Sec. of State for Educ. and Science 1970–74; Leader of Conservative Party 1975–90; Leader of HM Opposition 1975–79; Prime Minister 1979–90; First Lord of the Treasury and Minister for the Civil Service 1979–90; retd from public life 2002; Pres. No Turning Back Group 1990–; Dir Tiger Man. 1998–; Vice-Pres. Royal Soc. of St George 1999–; Hon. Pres. Bruges Group 1991–; Chair. Advisory Bd Univ. of London's Inst. of US Studies 1994–; Hon. Bencher, Lincoln's Inn 1975; Hon. Master of the Bench of Gray's Inn 1983; Freedom of Royal Borough of Kensington and Chelsea 1979, of London Borough of Barnet 1980, of Falkland Is. 1983, of City of London 1989, of the City of Westminster 1990; Chancellor Univ. of Buckingham 1992–98, William and Mary Coll., Va 1994–2000; mem. Worshipful Co. of Glovers 1983–, Int. Advisory Bd British-American Chamber of Commerce 1993–; Conservative Companion of Guild of Cambridge Benefactors 1999–; Hon. Fellow Royal Inst. of Chem. 1979; Hon. LLD (Univ. of Buckingham) 1986, Dr. hc (Rand Afrikaans Univ. SA) 1991, (Weizmann Inst. of Science) 1992, (Mendeleyev Univ.) 1993, (Brunel) 1996; MacArthur Foundation Fellowship 1992; Presidential Medal of Freedom (USA) 1991, Order of Good Hope (SA) 1991; Hilal-i-Imitaz 1996; Hon. Citizen of Gorasde 1993. *Publications:* In Defence of Freedom 1986, The Downing Street Years 1979–1990 1993, The Path to Power 1995, The Collected Speeches of Margaret Thatcher 1997, Statecraft 2002. *Address:* House of Lords, Westminster, London, SW1A 0PW; POB 1466, London, SW1X 9HY, England.

THAWLEY, Michael; Australian diplomatist; joined Foreign Affairs Dept 1972, served in Rome, Moscow, Tokyo; Foreign Policy Adviser to the Prime Minister 1996–99; fmr staff mem. Office of Nat. Assessments, Dept of Prime Minister and Cabinet; Amb. to USA 1999–. *Address:* Australian Embassy, 1601 Massachusetts Avenue, NW, Washington, DC 20036, USA (Office). *Telephone:* (202) 797-3000 (Office). *Fax:* (202) 797-3168 (Office). *E-mail:* library.washington@dfat.gov.au (Office).

THÉ, Guy Blaudin de (see de Thé, Guy Blaudin).

THEOCHARIS, Reghinos D., PhD; Cypriot economist; b. 10 Feb. 1929, Larnaca; s. of Demetrios Theocharis and Florentia Theocharis; m. Madeleine Loumbou 1954; one s. one d.; ed Athens School of Economics, Univ. of Aberdeen and London School of Econs; Insp. of Commercial Educ., Cyprus 1953–56; at LSE 1956–58; Bank of Greece, Athens 1958–59; Minister of Finance in Cyprus Provisional Govt 1959–60; Minister of Finance 1960–62; Gov. of Bank of Cyprus 1962–75; Prof. Athens Univ. of Econs and Business 1975–96, Prof. Emer. 1996–; Dir-Gen. Centre of Planning and Econ. Research (KEPE), Athens 1978–81; Hon. Fellow, LSE 1971. *Publications:* On the Stability of the Cournot Solution on the Oligopoly Problem 1960, Early Developments in Mathematical Economics 1983, The Development of Mathematical Economics: from Cournot to Jevons 1993. *Leisure interests:* chess, gardening. *Address:* 2 Raidestou Street, Kessariani, Athens, 16122, Greece. *Telephone:* 7214531.

THEODORAKIS, Mikis; Greek composer; b. 29 July 1925, island of Chios; s. of Georges Michel Theodorakis and Aspasia Poulaki; m. Myrto Altinoglou 1953; one s. one d.; ed Athens Conservatoire and Paris Conservatoire; joined resistance against German occupation of Greece 1942; arrested and deported during civil war 1947–52; moved to Paris 1953 and studied under Olivier Messiaen; first public concert Sonatina (for pianoforte), Paris 1954; set to bouzouki music the poem Epitaphios by Iannis Ritsos 1958–59 and subsequently wrote numerous other successful songs; Ballet music for Antigone (first performed in London by Dame Margot Fonteyn), Stuttgart Ballet, etc.; returned to Greece 1962; leader Lambrakis youth movt; MP 1963; imprisoned for political activities 1967, released April 1970; lived in Paris 1970–74; resgnd from CP March 1972; MP 1981–1986 (resgnd), 1989–93 (resgnd), Minister of State 1990–92 (resgnd); f. Cttee for Greek-Turkish Friendship 1986; Gold Medal, Moscow Shostakovich Festival 1957, Copley Prize, USA 1957, First Prize Athens Popular Song Festival 1961, Sibelius Award, London 1963, Gold Medal for Film Music, London 1970, Socrates Prize, Stockholm 1974, First Literary Prize, Athens 1987; Lenin Int. Peace Prize 1982. *Works include:* Sinfonia (oratorio) 1944, Love and Death (voice, strings) 1945–48, Assi-Gonia (orchestra) 1945–50, Sextet for Flute 1946, Oedipus Tyrannus (strings) 1946, Greek Carnival (ballet suite) 1947, First Symphony (orchestra) 1948–50, Five Cretan Songs (chorus, orchestra) 1950, Orpheus and Eurydice (ballet) 1952, Barefoot Battalion (film) 1953, Suite No. 1 (four movements, piano and orchestra) 1954, Poèmes d'Eluard (Cycle 1 and Cycle 2) 1955, Suite No. 2 (chorus, orchestra) 1956, Suite No. 3 (five movements, soprano, chorus, orchestra) 1956, Ill Met by Moonlight (film) 1957, Sonatina No. 1 (violin, piano) 1957, Les amants de Teruel (ballet) 1958, Piano Concerto 1958, Sonatina No. 2 (violin, piano) 1958, Antigone (ballet) 1958, Epitaphios (song cycle) 1959, Deserters (song cycle) 1958, Epiphania (song cycle) 1959, Honeymoon (film) 1960, Phoenician Women—Euripides (theatre music) 1960, Axion Esti (pop oratorio) 1960, Electra-Euripides (film), Phaedra (film) 1962, The Hostage (song cycle) 1962, The Ballad of the Dead Brother (musical tragedy) 1962, Zorba the Greek (film), The Ballad of Muthausen (song cycle) 1965, Romiossini (song cycle) 1965, Lisistrata—Aristophanes (theatre music) 1966, Romancero Gitano (Lorca) (song cycle) 1967, Sun and Time (song cycle) 1967, Arcadias Nos. 1–10 (song cycles) 1968–69, Canto General (Pablo Neruda) (pop oratorio) 1972, Z (film), Etat de Siège (film) 1973, Ballads (song cycle) 1975, Symphony No. 2 (orchestra and piano) 1981, Messe Byzantine (Liturgie) 1982, Symphony No. 3 (orchestra, chorus, soprano) 1982, Sadoukeon Passion (cantata for orchestra, chorus, soloists) 1983, Liturgie No. 2 1983, Symphony No. 7 (orchestra, chorus, soloists) 1983, Requiem 1985, Kostas Kariotakis (opera in two acts) 1985, Beatrice (song cycle) 1987, Faces of the Sun (song cycle) 1987, Symphony No. 4 1987, Memory of Stone (song cycle) 1987, Like an Ancient Wind (song cycle) 1987, Canto Olympico (symphony) 1991, Medea (opera) 1990, Electra (opera) 1993. *Publications include:* La Dette, Journals of Resistance 1972, Ballad of the Dead Brother, Culture et dimensions politiques 1973, Star System, Antimanifeste, Les chemins de l'Archange (autobiog.), 4 Vols 1986–92. *Address:* Epifanous 1, Akropolis, 117 42 Athens, Greece. *Telephone:* (1) 9214863. *Fax:* (1) 9236325.

THÉODORE, Jean-François; French public servant; b. 5 Dec. 1946, Paris; s. of Charles Théodore and Aimée Chevallier; m. Claudine Lefèbvre 1976; one s. two d.; ed Lycées Montaigne and Louis-le-Grand, Faculty of Law, Paris, Institut d'études politiques de Paris; Ecole nat. d'admin. 1971–74; civil servant, Ministry of Econ. and Finance 1974–78, Crédit nat. 1978–80, Head, Bureau des états africains et de la zone franc 1980–82, Head, Bureau des investissements étrangers en France et français à l'étranger 1982–84, Asst Dir Etablissements de crédit 1984–86, Deputy Dir, Head of Funding and Investment Dept, Treasury 1986–90; Gen. Man. Société des bourses françaises 1990–91, Chair. and CEO 1991–; Pres. Int. Fed. of Stock Exchanges 1993–94, Fed. of European Stock Exchanges 1998–; Vice-Pres. Société inter-professionnelle de compensation des valeurs mobilières (Sicovam) 1992, Chair. 1993–; Pres. Matif SA 1998–; Chair. Euronext 2000–; Chevalier, Ordre nat. du Mérite, Légion d'honneur, Prix Andese du financier 2000. *Leisure interests:* opera, American cinema, theatre. *Address:* Matif, 115 rue Réaumur, Paris; Société des bourses françaises, 39 rue Cambon, 75001 Paris, France.

THERON, Charlize; South African actress; b. 7 Aug. 1975, Benoni, SA; trained as ballet dancer; went to Milan aged 16 to become a model; moved to New York to dance with Joffrey Ballet; knee injury ended dancing career; moved to Los Angeles to take up acting. *Films include:* Children of the Corn III 1994, Two Days in the Valley 1996, That Thing You Do! 1996, Trial and Error 1997, Hollywood Confidential 1997, Devil's Advocate 1997, Cop Land/ The Yards 1997, Mighty Joe Young 1998, Celebrity 1998, The Cider House Rules 1999, The Astronaut's Wife 1999, The Yards 2000, Reindeer Games 2000, Men of Honor 2000, The Legend of Bagger Vance 2000, Navy Diver 2000, Sweet November 2001, The Curse of the Jade Scorpion 2001, 15 Minutes 2001, The Yards/Nightwatch 2002, Waking Up in Reno 2002, Trapped 2002, 24 Hours 2002, Sweet Home Alabama (exec. producer) 2002. *Address:* c/o Spanky Taylor, 3727 West Magnolia, Burbank, CA 91505, USA (Office).

THEROUX, Paul Edward, BA, FRSL, FRGS; writer; b. 10 April 1941, Medford, Mass.; s. of Albert Eugene Theroux and Anne Dittami Theroux; m. 1st Anne Castle 1967 (divorced 1993), two s.; m. 2nd Sheila Donnelly 1995; ed Univ. of Massachusetts, USA; lecturer, Univ. of Urbino, Italy 1963, Soche Hill Coll., Malawi 1963–65, Makerere Univ., Kampala, Uganda 1965–68, Univ. of Singapore 1968–71; Writer-in-Residence, Univ. of Va 1972; Hon. DLitt (Tufts Univ., Trinity Univ.) 1983, (Univ. of Mass.) 1988. *Publications:* (*novels*) Waldo 1967, Fong and the Indians 1968, Girls at Play 1969, Murder in Mount Holly 1969, Jungle Lovers 1971, Sinning with Annie 1972, Saint Jack 1973 (filmed 1979), The Black House 1974, The Family Arsenal 1976, The Consul's File 1977, Picture Palace 1978 (Whitbread Award 1978), A Christmas Card 1978, London Snow 1980, World's End 1980, The Mosquito Coast 1981 (James Tait Black Award), The London Embassy 1982, Doctor Slaughter 1984 (filmed as Half Moon Street 1987), O-Zone 1986, My Secret History 1989, Chicago Loop 1990, Dr. DeMarr 1990, Millroy the Magician 1993, My Other Life 1996, Collected Short Novels 1998; (*play*) The White Man's Burden 1987; (*criticism*) V. S. Naipaul 1972; (*travel*) The Great Railway Bazaar 1975, The Old Patagonian Express 1979, The Kingdom by the Sea 1983, Sailing through China 1983, Riding the Iron Rooster: By Train Through China (Thomas Cook Prize for Best Literary Travel Book 1989) 1988, Travelling the World 1990, The Happy Isles of Oceania: Paddling the Pacific 1992, The Pillars of Hercules 1995, Collected Stories 1997, Kowloon Tong 1997, Sir Vidia's Shadow 1998, Fresh-Air Fiend 1999, Hotel Honolulu 2000, Dark Star Safari: Overland from Cairo to Cape Town 2002; (*screenplay*) Saint Jack 1979; reviews in New York Times, etc. *Leisure interest:* rowing. *Address:* The Wylie Agency, 250 West 57th Street, New York NY 10107, USA.

THESIGER, Sir Wilfred Patrick, KBE, DSO, MA, FRSL; British traveller; b. 3 June 1910, Addis Ababa, Ethiopia; s. of the Hon. Wilfred Thesiger, DSO, and Kathleen Mary Vigors, CBE; ed Eton Coll. and Magdalen Coll., Oxford; explored Danakil country of Abyssinia 1933–34; Sudan Political Service, Darfur and Upper Nile Provinces 1935–39; served in Ethiopia, Syria and Western Desert with Sudan Defence Force and Special Air Service, Second World War; explored the Empty Quarter of Arabia 1945–50; lived with the Madan in the Marshes of Southern Iraq 1950–58; Hon. Fellow, British Acad. 1982, Magdalen Coll., Oxford 1982; Hon. DLitt (Leicester) 1967, (Bath) 1992;

awarded Back Grant, Royal Geographical Soc. 1936, Founder's Medal 1948, Lawrence of Arabia Medal, Royal Central Asian Soc. 1955, David Livingstone Medal, Royal Scottish Geographical Soc. 1961, W. H. Heinemann Bequest, Royal Soc. of Literature 1964, Burton Medal, Royal Asiatic Soc. 1966. *Publications:* Arabian Sands 1959, The Marsh Arabs 1964, Desert, Marsh and Mountain: The World of a Nomad 1979, The Life of My Choice (autobiog.) 1987, Visions of a Nomad (photographs) 1987, My Kenya Days 1994, The Danakil Diary 1996, Travels in Asia 1998, Among the Mountains 1998, Crossing the Sands 1999, A Vanished World 2001, My Life and Travels 2002. *Leisure interests:* photography, travel in remote places. *Address:* Woodcote Grove House, Meadow Hill, Coulsdon, Surrey, CR5 2XL, England. *Telephone:* (20) 8668-5309.

THEWLIS, David; British actor; b. 20 March 1963; s. of Alec Raymond Wheeler and Maureen Wheeler (née Thewlis); m. Sara Jocelyn Sugarman 1992; ed Highfield High School, Blackpool, St Anne's Coll. of Further Educ., Guildhall School of Music and Drama, London. *Theatre includes:* Buddy Holly at the Regal, Ice Cream, Lady and the Clarinet (winner Edin. Fringe First), The Sea. *Television includes:* Dandelion Dead, Valentine Park, Road, The Singing Detective, Bit of a Do, Skulduggery, Journey to Knock (Best Actor, Rheims Film Festival 1992), Filipina Dreamgirls, Frank Stubbs Promotes, Prime Suspect 3. *Films include:* Short and Curlies, Vroom, Resurrected, Afraid of the Dark, Life is Sweet, Damage, The Trial, Naked (Best Actor, Cannes Film Festival 1993), Black Beauty, Divorcing Jack, The Big Lebowski. *Leisure interest:* painting.

THEWS, Gerhard, Dr rer. nat, DR. MED.; German professor of physiology; b. 22 July 1926, Königsberg; m. Dr. Gisela Bahling 1958; three s. one d.; ed Univ. of Kiel; Research Fellow Univ. of Kiel 1957–61, Asst Prof. 1961–62, Assoc. Prof. 1962–63, Prof. 1964–, Dir Physiological Inst. 1964–, Dean Faculty Medicine 1968–69; Vice-Pres. Acad. Science and Literature 1977–85, Pres. 1985–93; Pres. German Physiological Soc. 1968–69; mem. German Scientific Council 1970–72; Pres. Int. Soc. for Oxygen Transport 1973–75; Wolfgang Heubner Prize (Berlin) 1961, Feldberg Prize (London) 1964, Carl Diem Prize 1964, Adolf Fick Prize (Würzburg) 1969, Ernst von Bergmann Medal (Germany) 1986. *Publications:* Human Anatomy, Physiology and Pathophysiology 1985, Autonomic Functions in Human Physiology 1985, Human Physiology 1989. *Address:* Weidmannstrasse 29, 55131 Mainz, Germany.

THIAM, Habib, LenD; Senegalese politician; b. 21 Jan. 1933, Dakar; ed Ecole Nat. de la France d'Outre-mer; Sec. of State for the Devt Plan 1963; Minister for the Plan and Devt 1964–67, of Rural Econ. 1968–73; mem. Nat. Ass. 1973–, Pres. 1983–84; Prime Minister 1981–83, 1991–96; Press Sec. Union pro-gressiste sénégalaise (now Parti socialiste sénégalais—PS); Pres. Parl. Group PS 1978; Chair. Bd Banque Int. pour le Commerce et l'Industrie du Sénégal; Dir Ethiopique 1976–, L'Unité Africaine 1976–.

THIANDOUM, HE Cardinal Hyacinthe; Senegalese ecclesiastic; b. 2 Feb. 1921, Poponguine; s. of François Fari Thiandoum and Anne Ndiémé Sène; ed Univ. de la Propagande and Gregorian Univ., Rome; ordained Priest at Dakar Cathedral April 1949; Dir of Works at Dakar 1955–60; Vicar-Gen. at Dakar 1960–62; Archbishop of Dakar 1962–2000; cr. Cardinal 1976; fmrly mem. Congregation for the Doctrine of the Faith; fmr Pres. Episcopal Conf. of Senegal and Mauritania; fmrly mem. Perm. Cttee Episcopal Conf. of Franco-phone West Africa (CERAO); fmrly Pres. Symposium of Episcopal Confs of Africa and Madagascar (SECAM); mem. Pontifical Comm. for Social Communications, Congregation for Consecrated Life Inst. and Apostolic Life Socs, Sacred Congregation for the Clergy, Congregation for People Evangelization; fmr mem. Pontifical Council for Culture, Council of Secr. Gen. of the Rome Synod of Bishops (Deputy Pres. 1977); Gen. Reporter to the Synod 1987, to the African Synod 1994; mem. Post-Synodal Council of African Synod; mem. Episcopal Comm. for Mass Media, CERAO; Hon. Chaplain with Grand Cross, Order of Malta 1972; Grand Cross, Order of Lion 1976; Commdr Légion d'honneur 1980. *Address:* B.P. 5082, Villa 'Les Bodamiers', Dakar-Fann, Senegal. *Telephone:* 823-69-18.

THIBAUDET, Jean-Yves; French pianist; b. 7 Sept. 1961, Lyon; ed Paris Conservatoire, Lyon Conservatory of Music; now based in LA and Paris; appears with maj. orchestras in USA and Europe including Royal Concertgebouw, London Philharmonic, Royal Philharmonic, Orchestre Nat. de France etc.; regular visitor to maj. US and European music festivals; in recital has collaborated with mezzo-sopranos Brigitte Fassbaender and Cecilia Bartoli, Renee Fleming and cellist Truls Mørk; debut, BBC Promenade Concerts 1992, continuing to 2001; records exclusively for Decca (over 20 recordings); Prix du Conservatoire, Paris Conservatory 1976, Echo Award for Conversations with Bill Evans, Germany 1998, Choc de la Musique for Reflections on Duke 1999, Diapason d'Or for his recordings of works by Debussy 2000; Chevalier Ordre des Arts et des Lettres 2001. *Leisure interests:* tennis, swimming, riding, water-skiing, museums, movies, racing cars. *Address:* Mastroinni Associates, 161 West 61st Street, Suite 17E, New York, NY 10023 (Office); c/o M. L. Falcone Public Relations, 55 West 68th Street, Suite 1114, New York, NY 10023, USA. *Telephone:* (212) 580-4302. *Fax:* (212) 787-9638.

THICH QUANG DO; Vietnamese Buddhist leader; in exile in India and Sri Lanka; taught Buddhist philosophy in Saigon in the 1960s and 1970s; fmr leader Unified Buddhist Church of Vietnam; imprisoned by Communist authorities; released 1998. *Address:* Thanh Zinh Zen Monastery, Ho Chi Minh City, Vietnam (Office).

THIEBAUD, Wayne, MA; American artist; b. 15 Nov. 1920, Mesa, Ariz.; m. 1st Patricia Patterson 1945 (divorced 1959); two d.; m. 2nd Betty Jean Carr 1959; one s. one step s.; ed Frank Wiggins Trade School, Long Beach Jr Coll., San. José State Coll. (now San José State Univ.), California State Coll. (now California State Univ.); worked as commercial artist and freelance cartoonist from 1938; served USAAF 1942–45; started career as painter 1947; Asst Prof., Dept of Art, Univ. of Calif. at Davis 1960, Assoc. Prof. 1963–67, Prof. 1967–, Faculty Research Lecturer 1973–; co-founder Artists Co-operative Gallery (now Artists Contemporary Gallery), Sacramento 1958; numerous one-man exhbns in USA since 1950; one-man exhbn Galleria Schwarz, Milan, Italy 1963; represented USA at São Paulo Bienal, Brazil 1968; commissioned to do paintings of Wimbledon tennis tournament, England 1968; selected as Nat. Juror for Nat. Endowment for the Arts, Washington, DC 1972; commissioned by US Dept of Interior to paint Yosemite Ridge Line for Bicentennial Exhbn, America 1976; mem. American Acad., Inst. of Arts and Letters, New York City 1985, Nat. Acad. of Design, New York City; Award of Distinction, Nat. Art Schools Asscn and Special Citation Award, Nat. Asscn of Schools of Art and Design 1984, Nat. Medal of the Arts 1994. *Publication:* Wayne Thiebaud: Private Drawings—The Artist's Sketchbook 1987. *Address:* Department of Art, University of California (Davis), 1 Shields Avenue, Davis, CA 95616, USA. *Telephone:* (530) 752-1011. *Fax:* (530) 752-6363. *Website:* www.ucdavis .edu (Office).

THIELEN, Gunter, DEng; German business executive; b. 4 Aug. 1942, Quierschied, Saarland; ed Tech. Univ. of Aachen; various man. positions with BASF, Ludwigshafen 1970; Tech. Dir Wintershall Refinery, Kassel 1976; joined Bertelsmann AG as CEO Maul Belser printing co., Nuremberg 1980, mem. Exec. Bd Bertelsmann AG 1985, Head Print and Industrial Operations Div. (renamed Bertelsmann Arvato AG) 1985–2002, Chair. and CEO 2002–; Chair. Bertelsmann Foundation 2001; Chair. Bertelsmann Verwaltungsge-sellschaft mbH (BVG) 2001; mem. Bertelsmann AG Supervisory Bd 2002–. *Address:* Bertelsmann AG, Carl-Bertelsmann-Strasse 270, 33311 Gütersloh, Germany (Office). *Telephone:* 5241800 (Office). *Fax:* 5241809662 (Office). *E-mail:* info@bertelsmann.de (Office). *Website:* www.bertelsmann.de (Office).

THIER, Samuel Osiah, MD; American physician; b. 23 June 1937, Brooklyn, New York; s. of Sidney Thier and May H. Kanner Thier; m. Paula Dell Finkelstein 1958; three d.; ed Cornell Univ., State Univ. of New York, Syracuse; Intern, Mass. Gen. Hosp. 1960–61, Asst Resident 1961–62, 1964–65, Postdoctoral Fellow 1965; Clinical Assoc. Nat. Inst. of Arthritis and Metabolic Diseases 1962–64; Chief Resident in Medicine, Mass. Gen. Hosp. 1966; Instr. to Asst Prof. Harvard Medical School 1967–69; Assoc. Prof. then Prof. of Medicine, Univ. of Pa Medical School 1969–74; Prof. and Chair. Dept of Medicine, Yale Univ. School of Medicine and Chief of Medicine, Yale-New Haven Hosp. 1975–85; Pres. Inst. of Medicine, NAS 1985–91; Pres. and Prof. Brandeis Univ. 1991–94; Pres. Mass. Gen. Hosp. 1994–97; Pres., Partners Healthcare System Inc. 1994–, CEO 1996–; Prof. of Medicine and Health Care Policy Harvard Medical School 1994–. *Publications:* numerous articles and chapters in medical journals and textbooks. *Address:* Partners HealthCare System Inc., 800 Boylston Street, Suite 1150, Boston, MA 02199 (Office); 99–20 Florence Street, Apartment 4B, Chestnut Hill, MA 02467, USA (Home). *Telephone:* (617) 278-1004 (Office). *Fax:* (617) 278-1047 (Office).

THIERSE, Wolfgang; German politician; b. 22 Oct. 1943, Breslau; ed Humboldt Univ., Berlin; fmr typesetter; teaching asst, Dept of Cultural Theory and Aesthetics, Humboldt Univ. Berlin 1964; mem. staff Ministry of Culture, GDR 1975–76, Cen. Inst. for History of Literature, Acad. of Sciences, GDR 1977–90; Chair. Social Democratic Party, GDR (which later factioned) 1990; mem. Bundestag (Parl.) 1990–, Pres. Oct. 1998–. *Publications:* The Right Life in a False System, The Future of the East. *Address:* Bundestag, Platz der Republik 1, 11011 Berlin, Germany. *Telephone:* (30) 22735500/1 (Office). *Fax:* (30) 22736500 (Office). *Website:* www.bundestag.de (Office).

THIESSEN, Gordon, PhD; Canadian banker; b. 14 Aug. 1938, South Porcu-pine, Ont.; m. Annette Hillyar 1964; two c.; ed Univ. of Saskatchewan and London School of Econs and Political Science; joined Bank of Canada 1963; Visiting Economist, Reserve Bank of Australia 1973–75; Adviser to Gov. Bank of Canada 1979, Deputy Gov. responsible for econ. research and financial analysis 1984, Sr Deputy Gov. 1987, Chair. Bd Dirs.; mem. Exec. Cttee 1987–, Gov. 1994–2001. *Leisure interests:* skiing, sailing. *Address:* c/o Bank of Canada, 234 Wellington Street, Ottawa, ON, K1A OG9, Canada.

THINLEY, Lyonpo Jigmi Yozer; Bhutanese politician; fmr Chair. Council of Ministers; Minister of Foreign Affairs 1998–. *Address:* Ministry of Foreign Affairs, Convention Centre, P.O. Box 103, Thimphu, Bhutan. *Telephone:* 323297. *Fax:* 323240.

THINOT, Dominique Pierre; French painter, teacher and diplomatist; b. 3 Oct. 1948, Paris; s. of Y. Hervé and Pierre Thinot; m. Claire Moreau 1977; two s.; Prof. École Nationale Supérieure des Arts Décoratifs, Paris 1972–; has taught at various univs in Asia 1980–; leader several cultural missions to Japan, Singapore, Korea and China 1985–; Pres. Asscn of Artists of the Bateau-Lavoir, Paris; mem. Gruppe Sieben, Germany 1975–; Prix de la Création Artistique, Ministry of Cultural Affairs 1971, 1974, Prix de l'Acad. des Beaux-Arts 1983, Distinction du Govt de la Répub. Arabe d'Egypte 1996. *Exhibitions include:* Saarland Museum, Saarbrucken, N.B. Museum, Canada, Galerie Il Navile, Bologna, Museum Alma-Ata, Kazakhstan, Munici-pal Museum, Kyoto, Museum of Modern Art, Taipei, Nat. Arts Centre, Cairo, Inoue Galleries, Tokyo, Musée de Xi'an and Qingao, China. *Television:*

numerous reports for TV networks in France, Japan, Korea and China. *Leisure interests:* music, oenology. *Address:* Bateau-Lavoir, 13 place Emile Goudeau, 75018 Paris, France; 13 route des Vieilles-Vignes, 17880 Les Portes, Ile-de-Ré, France. *Telephone:* 1-42-54-30-08 (Home). *Fax:* 1-42-57-33-58.

THIRSK, (Irene) Joan, CBE, PhD, FBA, FRHistS; British historian and aca-demic (retd); b. Irene Joan Watkins, 19 June 1922, London; d. of William Henry Watkins and Daisy Watkins (née Frayer); m. James Wood Thirsk 1945; one s. one d.; ed Camden School for Girls, London and Westfield Coll., Univ. of London; war service in Auxiliary Territorial Service (ATS) 1942–45; Asst Lecturer in Sociology, LSE 1950–51; Sr Research Fellow in Agrarian History, Dept of English Local History, Leicester Univ. 1951–65; Reader in Econ. History, Oxford Univ. 1965–83, Professorial Fellow of St Hilda's Coll. 1965–83, Hon. Fellow 1983–; mem. Royal Comm. on Historical Monuments of England 1977–86, Historical Manuscripts 1989–96; Pres. British Agricul-tural Hist. Soc. 1983–86, 1995–98, British Asscn for Local History 1986–92, Kent History Fed. 1990–99; Gen. Ed. Agrarian History of England and Wales 1975–2000; Mellon Sr Fellow, Nat. Humanities Center, NC, USA 1986–87; Foreign mem. American Philosophical Soc.; Corresp. mem. Colonial Soc. of Massachusetts; Hon. Fellow Queen Mary and Westfield Coll. London 1997; Hon. DLitt (Leicester) 1985, (East Anglia) 1990, (Kent) 1993, (Sussex) 1994, (Southampton) 1999, (Greenwich) 2001; Hon. DUniv (Open Univ.) 1991; Hon. Dr of Agricultural and Environmental Sciences (Wageningen, Netherlands) 1993. *Publications:* ed. and contrib. The Agrarian History of England and Wales, IV 1500–1640 1967, V 1640–1750 1985; Seventeenth-Century Eco-nomic Documents (with J. P. Cooper) 1972, The Restoration 1976, Economic Policy and Projects: The Development of a Consumer Society in Early Modern England 1978, The Rural Economy of England: Collected Essays 1984, England's Agricultural Regions and Agrarian History 1500–1750 1987, Alternative Agriculture: a History from the Black Death to the Present Day 1997, The English Rural Landscape 2000. *Leisure interests:* gardening, sewing and machine knitting. *Address:* 1 Hadlow Castle, Hadlow, Tonbridge, Kent, TN11 0EG, England. *Telephone:* (1732) 850708 (Home). *Fax:* (1732) 850708 (Home).

THOM, Gertel; Antigua and Barbuda lawyer; b. Guyana; ed Univ. of the West Indies and Sir Hugh Wooding Law School; fmr State Counsel, Office of Dir of Public Prosecutions, Guyana; fmr Prin. Crown Counsel and Chief Legal Adviser to Gov. of Montserrat; fmr Attorney-Gen. of Montserrat; Deputy Solicitor-Gen. of Antigua and Barbuda –2001, Attorney-Gen. (first female to hold position) 2001–. *Address:* Office of the Attorney General, Hadeeg Building, Redcliffe Street, St John's, Antigua and Barbuda (Office).

THOMAS, Betty; American director and actress; b. 27 July 1949, St Louis, Mo.; ed Ohio Univ., Chicago Art Inst., Roosevelt Univ.; fmr mem. Second City improvisation group, Chicago; performed at the Comedy Store, LA. *Films:* (dir) Only You, The Brady Bunch Movie 1995, Private Parts, Dr Dolittle 1998, 28 Days 1999; (actress) Tunnelvision, Chesty Anderson—US Navy, Loose Shoes, Used Cars, Homework, Troop Beverly Hills 1989, Jackson County Jail. *Television:* (dir) (series) Doogie Howser MD, Dream On (Emmy Award 1993), Hooperman, Mancusco FBI, Arresting Behavior, Couples; (film) My Breast; (documentary drama) The Late Shift (Dirs' Guild of America Award 1997); (actress) (series) Hill Street Blues (Emmy Award 1985); (films) Outside Chance, Nashville Grab, When Your Lover Leaves, Prison for Children. *Address:* c/o Directors' Guild of America, 7920 Sunset Boulevard, Los Angeles, CA 90046, USA (Office).

THOMAS, Clarence, BA, JD; American judge; b. 23 June 1948, Pinpoint, Savannah, Ga; ed Immaculate Conception Seminary, Conception Junction, Mo., Holy Cross Coll. Worcester and Yale Law School; worked for Mo. Attorney-Gen. for 2½ years; pvt. legal practice 1977–79; Legislative Asst US Senate 1979; Asst Sec. for Civil Rights, Dept of Educ. Washington, DC 1981; Chair. Equal Employment Comm. 1982–90; Judge US Court of Appeals, DC 1990–91; Assoc. Justice US Supreme Court 1991–. *Address:* United States Supreme Court, 1 First Street, NE, Washington, DC 20543, USA.

THOMAS, Craig, BS; American politician; b. 17 Feb. 1933, Cody, Wyo.; s. of Craig E. Thomas and Marge Lynn; m. Susan Roberts; four s.; ed Univ. of Wyoming; Exec. Vice-Pres. Wyo. Farm Bureau, Laramie 1960–69; Asst Legis. Dir American Farm Bureau, Washington, DC 1969–71; Dir Nat. Resource, American Farm Bureau, Chicago 1971–75; Gen. Man. Wyo. Rural Electrical Asscn 1975–89; mem. Wyo. House of Reps. 1985–89; mem. 101st–103rd US Congresses from Wyo. 1989–94; Senator from Wyoming 1995–; Republican. *Address:* US Senate, 109 Hart Senate Office Building, Washington, DC 20510, USA.

THOMAS, David; British singer; b. 26 Feb. 1943, Orpington; m. Veronica Joan Dean 1982; three d.; ed St Paul's Cathedral Choir School, London, King's School, Canterbury, King's Coll., Cambridge; has performed all over the world in most of the maj. concert halls with leading conductors, particularly works of the Baroque and Classical period; Chair. Artistic Advisory Cttee; mem. Bd Blackheath Concert Halls. *Works include:* more than 100 records, including Handel's Messiah, Athalia, La Resurrectione, Suzanna, Orlando, Bach's B Minor Mass, Cantata "Ich habe genug", St John Passion, St Matthew Passion, Haydn's Creation, Mozart's Requiem; solo record Aria for Montagnana. *Leisure interests:* woodwork, the island of Dominica. *Address:* Allied Artists, 42 Montpelier Square, London, SE10 8HP (Office); 74 Hyde Vale, Greenwich, London, SE10 8HP, England.

THOMAS, (David) Craig Owen, MA; British author; b. 24 Nov. 1942; s. of late John Brinley George Thomas and Gwendoline Megan Thomas (née Owen); m. Jill Lesley White 1967 (died 1987); ed Cardiff High School, Univ. Coll. Cardiff; schoolteacher 1966–77; full-time novelist 1977–; mem. Bd Lichfield Int. Arts Festival; mem. Soc. of Authors. *Publications:* Rat Trap 1976, Firefox 1977, Wolfsbane 1978, Snow Falcon 1979, Sea Leopard 1981, Jade Tiger 1982, Firefox Down 1983, The Bear's Tears 1985, Winter Hawk 1987, All the Grey Cats 1988, The Last Raven 1990, There to Here—Ideas of Political Society 1991, A Hooded Crow 1992, Playing with Cobras 1993, A Wild Justice 1995, A Different War 1997, Slipping into the Shadow 1998; (as David Grant) Moscow 5000 1979, Emerald Decision 1980. *Leisure interests:* history, philosophy, jazz, classical music, gardening, cricket.

THOMAS, Sir Derek Morison David, KCMG, MA; British fmr diplomatist and business consultant; b. 31 Oct. 1929, London; s. of K. P. D. Thomas and Mali Thomas; m. Lineke Van der Mast 1956; one s. one d.; ed Radley Coll. and Trinity Hall, Cambridge; articled apprentice, Dolphin Industrial Devts. Ltd 1947; entered HM Foreign Service 1953; RDVR 1953–55; appointments overseas included Moscow, Manila, Sofia, Ottawa, Paris, Washington; Deputy Under-Sec. of State for Europe and Political Dir FCO 1984–87; Amb. to Italy 1987–89; European Adviser to NM Rothschild and Sons Ltd 1990–, Dir 1991–99, now Sr Adviser; Dir Rothschild Italia 1990–97, Christow Consultants Ltd 1990–99, Rothschild Europe 1991–97; Dir, Assoc. CDP Nexus 1990–92; Dir New Court Int. Ltd, Moscow, Consilium Spa, Prague 1994–2001; mem. Export Guarantees Advisory Council 1991–97; Chair. British Invisibles Lotis Cttee 1992–96, Council S.O.S. Sahel 1991–2000, Council Royal Inst. of Int. Affairs 1994–97, Council Reading Univ. 1990–99; Chair. British Inst. of Florence 1996–2002; Hon. Fellow Trinity Hall, Cambridge 1998. *Leisure interests:* exploring the past and present, music, theatre, wines, reading when there is time, grandchildren. *Address:* Flat 1, 12 Lower Sloane Street, London, SW1W 8BJ, England. *Telephone:* (20) 7730-1473. *Fax:* (20) 7730-4674. *E-mail:* derek.thomas@rothschild.co.uk (Office).

THOMAS, Deroy C., BA, LLB; American business executive and lawyer; b. 16 Feb. 1926, Utica, NY; ed Iona Coll. and Fordham Univ.; admitted NY Bar 1952; Asst Prof. of Law, Fordham Univ. 1953–58; Asst counsel, Asscn of Casualty and Surety Cos. New York 1959–64; with firm Watters & Donovan 1964; with Hartford Fire Insurance Co. and subsidiaries, Conn. 1964–, gen. counsel 1966–69, Vice-Pres. 1968–69, Sr Vice-Pres. 1969–73, Exec. Vice-Pres. 1973–76, Pres. and CEO 1976–83, Chair. and CEO 1979–; Exec. Vice-Pres. ITT Corpn New York 1983–85, Vice-Chair. 1985–88, Pres. and COO 1988–; Pres. and CEO ITT Diversified Services Corpn 1983–. *Address:* Hartford Life Insurance Co., Hartford Place, Hartford, CT 06115, USA.

THOMAS, Donald Michael, MA; British novelist and poet; b. 27 Jan. 1935, Redruth, Cornwall; s. of Harold Redvers Thomas and Amy Thomas (née Moyle); two s. one d.; ed Redruth Grammar School, Univ. High School, Melbourne, New Coll., Oxford; English teacher, Teignmouth, Devon 1959–63; lecturer, Hereford Coll. of Educ. 1963–78; full-time author 1978–; Gollancz/Pan Fantasy Prize, PEN Fiction Prize, Cheltenham Prize, Los Angeles Times Fiction Prize. *Publications:* Two Voices 1968, Logan Stone 1971, Love and Other Deaths 1975, Honeymoon Voyage 1978, The Flute-Player 1978, Birthstone 1980, The White Hotel 1981, Dreaming in Bronze 1981, Ararat 1983, Selected Poems 1983, Swallow 1984, Sphinx 1986, Summit 1987, Memories and Hallucinations 1988, Lying Together 1989, Flying in to Love 1992, The Puberty Tree (new and selected poems) 1992, Pictures at an Exhibition 1993, Eating Pavlova 1994, Lady with a Laptop 1996, Alexander Solzhenitsyn 1998 (biog.), Charlotte 2000. *Leisure interests:* travel, Russia, Cornwall, the life of the imagination. *Address:* The Coach House, Rashleigh Vale, Truro, Cornwall, TR1 1TJ, England. *Telephone:* (1872) 261724. *E-mail:* dmthomas@btconnect.com (Home).

THOMAS, Edward Donnall, MD; American physician; b. 15 March 1920, Mart, Tex.; s. of Edward E. Thomas and Angie Hill Donnall Thomas; m. Dorothy Martin 1942; two s. one d.; ed Univ. of Tex., Harvard Univ.; US Army 1948–50; Chief Medical Resident, Sr Asst Resident Peter Bent Brigham Hosp. 1951–53; Research Assoc. Cancer Research Foundation Children's Medical Centre, Boston 1953–55; Instructor in Medicine, Harvard Medical School 1953–55; Physician-in-Chief Mary Imogene Bassett Hosp., Cooperstown, NY 1955–63; Assoc. Clinical Prof. of Medicine Coll. of Physicians and Surgeons, Columbia Univ. 1955–63; Prof. of Medicine Univ. of Wash. Medical School, Seattle (Head Div. of Oncology 1963–85), Attending Physician, Univ. of Wash. Hosp., Seattle 1963–90, Prof. Emer. 1990–; mem. Fred Hutchinson Cancer Research Centre, Seattle 1974–, Dir Medical Oncology 1974–89, Assoc. Dir Clinical Research Programs 1982–89; mem. Haematology Study Section Nat. Insts. of Health 1965–69; mem. Bd of Trustees and Medical Science Advisory Cttee Leukaemia Soc. America, Inc. 1969–73; mem. Clinical Cancer Investigation Review Cttee, Nat. Cancer Inst. 1970–74; mem. numerous editorial bds.; numerous guest lectures; Hon. MD (Cagliari) 1981, (Verona) 1991, (Parma) 1992, (Barcelona) 1994; hon. mem. numerous socs.; received McIntyre Award 1975, Levine Award 1979, Kettering Prize 1981, de Villiers Award 1983, Landsteiner Award 1987, Fox Award 1990, Gairdner Foundation Award 1990, Nat. Medal of Science 1990, shared Nobel Prize for Medicine and Physiology 1990 for pioneering bone marrow transplants in leukaemia patients, Kober Medal 1992. *Publications:* numerous articles. *Address:* Fred Hutchinson Cancer Center, 1100 Fairview Avenue North, D5-100, P.O. Box 19024, Seattle, WA 98109, USA.

THOMAS, Eric Jackson, MD, FRCOG, FMedSci; British doctor and academic; b. 24 March 1953, Hartlepool; s. of Eric Jackson Thomas and Margaret Mary Murray; m. Narell Marie Ronnard 1976; one s. one d.; ed Ampleforth Coll., Univ. of Newcastle upon Tyne; lecturer in Obstetrics and Gynaecology, Univ. of Sheffield 1985–87; Sr Lecturer in Obstetrics and Gynaecology, Univ. of Newcastle upon Tyne 1987–90; Prof. of Obstetrics and Gynaecology, Univ. of Southampton 1991–2001, Head School of Medicine 1995–98, Dean Faculty of Medicine, Health and Biological Sciences 1998–2000; Vice-Chancellor Univ. of Bristol 2001–; consultant obstetrician and gynaecologist Newcastle Gen. Hosp. 1987–2000, Southampton Univ. Hosps Trust 1991–2001; Dir (non-exec.) Southampton Univ. Hosps Trust 1997–2000, Southampton and SW Hants. Health Authority 2000–01; Exec. Sec. Council of Heads of Medical Schools 1998–2000; mem. Council Royal Coll. of Obstetricians and Gynaecologists 1995–2001; mem. Bd South West Regional Devt Agency 2003–; William Blair Bell Memorial Lecturer, Royal Coll. of Obstetricians and Gynaecologists 1987. *Publications:* Modern Approaches to Endometriosis (jtly) 1991; publs on endometriosis and reproductive medicine. *Leisure interests:* keeping fit, golf, Newcastle United. *Address:* Office of the Vice-Chancellor, University of Bristol, Senate House, Tyndall Avenue, Bristol, BS8 1TU, England (Office). *Telephone:* (117) 928-7499 (Office). *Fax:* (117) 930-4263 (Office). *Website:* www.bris.ac.uk (Office).

THOMAS, Gareth, PhD; American professor of science; b. 9 Aug. 1932, Maesteg, Wales; s. of David Basset Thomas and Edith May Gregory; m.; one s.; ed Univ. of Wales, Cambridge Univ.; with Univ. of Calif., Berkeley 1960–, Prof. 1967–; Assoc. Dean, Graduate Div. 1968–69, Asst to Chancellor 1969–72, Acting Vice-Chancellor, Acad. Affairs 1971–72, Chair. Faculty of Coll. of Eng 1977–78, Sr Faculty Scientist, Materials and Molecular Research Div., Scientific Dir., Nat. Center for Electron Microscopy, Prof. Dept of Materials and Mineral Eng 1982–93; mem. NAS, Nat. Acad. of Eng and numerous cttees.; Hon. ScD (Cambridge) 1969, (Lehigh Univ.) 1978, (Crakow Univ., Poland) 1999 and numerous other awards. *Publications:* several books and 600 research papers. *Leisure interests:* squash, skiing, cricket. *Address:* Department of Materials Science and Mineral Engineering, University of California, 561 Evans Hall, Berkeley, CA 94720, USA. *Telephone:* (510) 486-5696. *Fax:* (510) 643-0965.

THOMAS, Harvey, CBE, FRSA; British international public relations consultant; b. 10 April 1939, London; s. of the late John Humphrey Kenneth Thomas and Olga Rosina Thomas; m. Marlies Kram 1978; two d.; ed Westminster School, London, Northwestern Coll., Minn., USA, Univ. of Minnesota, Univ. of Hawaii, Honolulu; articled in law 1957–60; Billy Graham Evangelistic Assen 1960–75, N of England Crusade 1960–61, Direct Mail, Minneapolis 1961–63, Press Relations, Southern Calif. Crusade 1963, KAIM Radio, Honolulu 1963–64, London Crusades 1965–67, World Congress on Evangelism, Berlin 1966, Australasian Crusades 1967–69, Dir Euro 70 Crusades 1969–70, Dir European Congress on Evangelism, Amsterdam 1970–71, research in 80 countries for 1974 Int. Congress on World Evangelization Lausanne 1971–72, SPRE-E 73, London 1973, Dir Billy Graham LAUSTADE Rally, Lausanne 1974, Gen. Sec. EUROFEST Brussels 1975; int. public relations and presentation consultant 1976–; Co-ordinator Int. Exposition for Tech. Transfer 1984; Public Relations, Luis Palau Mission to London 1984; Dir of Presentation, Conservative Party 1978; Field Dir Prime Minister's Election Tour 1987; Chair. Fellowship of European Broadcasters; mem. Bd London Cremation Co. PLC; Chair. 5th World Productions Ltd, Trans World Radio UK; mem. Inst. of Dirs; Fellow Inst. of Public Relations; Fellow Chartered Inst. of Journalists; int. political consultant; conf. speaker and moderator; broadcaster and commentator on politics, religion and media; exec. coach; Individual Achievement Int. Broadcasting Award 2000. *Publications:* In the Face of Fear 1985, Making an Impact 1989, If They Haven't Heard It – You Haven't Said It 1995. *Leisure interests:* family, travel, broadcasting, public speaking, trains. *Address:* 23 The Service Road, Potters Bar, Herts., EN6 1QA, England. *Telephone:* (1707) 649910. *Fax:* (1707) 662653. *E-mail:* harvey@hthomas.net (Office). *Website:* www.hthomas.net (Office).

THOMAS, Iwan, MBE, BSc; British athlete; b. 5 Jan. 1974, Farnborough, Hants.; ed Stamford School, Brunel Univ.; fourth-ranked BMX rider, Europe 1988; fifth Olympic Games 400m 1996, silver medal 4x400m relay; gold medal Amateur Athletics Asscn Championships 400m 1997 (British record, 44.36 seconds), 1998; silver medal World Championships 4x400m relay 1997; gold medal European Championships 400m 1998; gold medal World Cup 400m 1998; gold medal Commonwealth Games 400m 1998; Patron Norwich Union Startrack Scheme; after-dinner speaker; British Athletics Writers Male Athlete of the Year 1998. *Leisure interests:* music, Playstation, socializing with friends. *Address:* c/o UK Athletics, Athletics House, 10 Harborne Road, Edgbaston, Birmingham, BI5 3AA, England (Office). *Website:* www.iwanthomas.com.

THOMAS, Jean Olwen, CBE, SCD., FRS, CChem; British professor of macromolecular biochemistry; b. 1 Oct. 1942; d. of John Robert Thomas and Lorna Prunella (née Harris) Thomas; ed Llwyn-y-Bryn High School for Girls, Swansea, Univ. Coll., Swansea, Univ. of Wales; demonstrator in Biochem., Univ. of Cambridge 1969–73, lecturer 1973–87, reader in the Biochem. of Macromolecules 1987–91, Prof. of Macromolecular Biochem., Univ. of Cambridge 1991–, Chair. Cambridge Centre for Molecular Recognition 1993–; coll. lecturer 1969–91; tutor, New Hall, Cambridge 1970–76, Vice-Pres. 1983–87; mem. European Molecular Biology Org.; Royal Soc. Council, SERC, Academia

Europaea, Council and Scientific Advisory Cttee Imperial Cancer Research Fund 1994–, Scientific Advisory Cttee Lister Inst. 1994–2000; Trustee British Museum 1994–; Fellow, New Hall, Cambridge 1969–; mem. Royal Soc. of Chem.; Beit Memorial Fellow; Gov. Wellcome Trust 2000–; Hon. Fellow, UCW, Swansea 1987, Cardiff Univ. 1998; Hon. DSc (Wales) 1992; Ayling Prize 1964, Hinkel Research Prize 1967, K. M. Stott Research Prize, Newnham Coll., Cambridge 1976. *Publications:* Companion to Biochemistry: Selected Topics for Further Study Vol. 1 1974, Vol. 2 1979 (jt and contrib.); numerous papers in scientific journals. *Leisure interests:* reading, music, walking. *Address:* Department of Biochemistry, 80 Tennis Court Road, Cambridge, CB2 1QW (Office); 26 Eachard Road, Cambridge, CB3 0HY, England (Home). *Telephone:* (1223) 333670 (Office); (1223) 362620 (Home).

THOMAS, Jeremy; British film producer; b. 26 July 1949, London; s. of Ralph and Joy Thomas; m. 1st Claudia Frolich 1977 (divorced 1981); one d.; m. 2nd Vivien Coughman 1982; two s.; began work in film-processing lab., later worked as asst and in cutting room; worked with Dir Philippe Mora, editing Brother Can You Spare a Dime; went to Australia where he produced first film Mad Dog Morgan 1974; f. Recorded Picture Co. Ltd 1975; returned to UK 1976; Chair. BFI 1993–97; set up own film distribution co. Recorded Releasing 1985; f. Hanway Films 1998; Grand Prix de Jury, Cannes Film Festival for The Shout, Crash; Vittorio de Sica Prize 1986, Special Award, Evening Standard Film Awards 1991, Michael Balcon BAFTA Award 1991, BFI Fellowship. *Films:* Mad Dog Morgan 1976, The Shout 1978, The Great Rock'n'Roll Swindle 1979, The Kids are Alright (Special Consultant) 1979, Bad Timing 1980, Eureka 1982, Merry Christmas Mr Lawrence 1982, The Hit 1983, Insignificance 1984, The Last Emperor 1987 (winner of 9 Acad. Awards), Everybody Wins 1990, The Sheltering Sky 1990, The Naked Lunch 1991, Let Him Have It (Exec. Producer) 1991, Little Buddha 1993, Rough Magic (Exec. Producer) 1994, Victory (Exec. Producer) 1994, Stealing Beauty 1995, The Ogre (Exec. Producer) 1996, The Brave (Exec. Producer) 1996, Crash (Exec. Producer) 1996, Blood and Wine 1996, All The Little Animals (Dir) 1998, The Cup (Exec. Producer) 1999, Gohatto 2000, Brother 2000, Sexy Beast 2001, Rabbit Proof Fence (Exec. Producer) 2000, Triumph of Love (Exec. Producer) 2002, Young Adam (Producer) 2003, The Dreamers (Producer) 2003. *Address:* Recorded Picture Company Ltd, 24 Hanway Street, London, W1T 1UH, England. *Telephone:* (20) 7636-2251 (Office). *Fax:* (20) 7636-2261 (Office). *E-mail:* jj@recordedpicture.com (Office).

THOMAS, (John David) Ronald (J. D. R. Thomas), DSc, FRSC; British professor of chemistry; b. 2 Jan. 1926, Gwynfe, Wales; s. of John Thomas and Betty (née Watkins); m. Gwyneth Thomas 1950; three d.; ed Llandovery Grammar School, Univ. of Wales (Cardiff); served RAMC (India) 1944–47; analytical chemist Spillers Ltd, Cardiff 1950–51, Glamorgan County Council 1951–53; Asst Lecturer, Cardiff Coll. of Tech. 1953–56; Lecturer, S. East Essex Tech. Coll. 1956–58; Sr Lecturer, Newport and Monmouthshire Coll. of Tech. 1958–61; Sr Lecturer and Reader, UWIST and Univ. of Wales, Cardiff 1961–90; Counsellor, Open Univ. 1970–71; Prof., Univ. of Wales, Cardiff 1990–93, Prof. Emer. 1994–; Hon. Ed. Newsletter, Analytical Div., Royal Soc. of Chem. 1995–; Hon. Prof. Univ. 'Politehnica', Bucharest, Romania 1996–; Hon. Course Adviser Hong Kong Baptist Univ. 1991–; mem. Court Univ. of Wales 1989–2001, 2002–, Council 1997–2001; mem. Council UWIST, Cardiff 1976–79, Univ. of Wales Coll. of Medicine 1993–99; mem. Court Univ. of Wales, Aberystwyth 1995–; Foreign Expert Academia Sinica (Nanjing), Hunan (Changsha), North West (Xian) and Shanghai Teachers Univs. 1983, 1985; Visiting Prof. Japan Soc. for the Promotion of Science 1985, NEWI, Wrexham 1995–96; Assessor Univ. Pertanian Malaysia 1992–94, 1997–99, Univ. Sains Malaysia 1996–98, Univ. Nova de Lisboa and Univ. of Porto 1998–99; RSC Schools Lecturer in Analytical Chem. 1986; Distinguished Visiting Fellow La Trobe Univ., Australia 1989; mem. Govt High-Level Mission on Analytical Instrumentation to Japan 1991; Adviser to RSC on privatization of UK Lab. of Govt Chemist 1995–97; Vice-Pres. Analytical Div. Chem. Soc. 1974–76, mem. Council Chem. Soc. 1977–80; Hon. Sec. Analytical Div. RSC 1987–90, Pres. 1990–92, mem. Council RSC 1990–2002; Chair. Analytical Ed. Bd RSC 1985–90; Hon. mem. Romanian Soc. of Analytical Chem. 1994–; Sec. Baptist Union of Wales Superannuation Appeal 1976–78; mem. Council, Baptist Union of Wales 1994–97; L. S. Theobald Lectureship, Royal Soc. of Chem. 2001; Enrico Casassas Memorial Lecturer Univ. of Barcelona 2002–; Hon. mem. Romanian Chem. Soc. 1999; Electroanalytical Chem. Medal and Award, RSC 1981, J. Heyrovsky Centenary Medal, Czechoslovak Acad. of Sciences 1990, White Robe, Gorsed of Bards 2000; Royal Soc. of Chem. symposium in his honour, Cardiff 1994. *Publications:* Ed.: Selective Electrode Reviews, Vols 1–14 1979–92; Trans. Ed.: Membrane Electrodes in Drug Substances Analysis (Cosofret) 1982; Author: History of the Analytical Division, Royal Society of Chemistry 1999; Co-author: Calculations in Advanced Physical Chemistry 1962, Noble Gases and Their Compounds 1964, Selective Ion-Sensitive Electrodes 1971, Dipole Moments in Inorganic Chemistry 1971, Practical Electrophoresis 1976, Chromatographic Separations and Extraction with Foamed Plastics and Rubbers 1982; over 300 articles in scientific journals on chemical and bio-sensors, reaction kinetics and separation chemistry. *Leisure interests:* travel, reading (current affairs and history), browsing and things of Wales. *Address:* 4 Orchard Court, Gresford, Wrexham, LL12 8EB, Wales. *Telephone:* (1978) 856771. *Fax:* (1978) 856771. *E-mail:* jdrthomas@aol.com (Home).

THOMAS, Sir John Meurig, Kt, MA, DSc, LLD, FRS; British scientist; b. 15 Dec. 1932, Llanelli, Wales; s. of David J. Thomas and Edyth Thomas; m. Margaret Edwards 1959; two d.; ed Gwendraeth Grammar School, Univ. Coll., Swansea, Queen Mary Coll., London; Scientific Officer, UKAEA 1957–58; Asst Lecturer, Lecturer, Sr Lecturer then Reader, Dept of Chem., Univ. Coll. of N Wales, Bangor 1958–69; Prof. and Head Dept of Chem., Univ. Coll. of Wales, Aberystwyth 1969–78; Head of Dept of Physical Chem., Cambridge Univ., Professorial Fellow of King's Coll. 1978–86, Master of Peterhouse 1993–2002; Distinguished Hon. Research Fellow, Dept of Materials Science, Univ. of Cambridge 1993–2002, Hon. Prof. in Solid State Chemistry, Univ. of Cambridge 2002–; Dir Royal Inst. of GB 1986–91, Resident Prof. 1986–88, Fullerian Prof. of Chem. 1988–94, Prof. of Chem. 1994–; Deputy Pro-Chancellor, Univ. of Wales 1991–94; Dir Davy Faraday Labs. 1986–91; Chair. Chem. Research Applied to World Needs, IUPAC 1987–95; Pres. Chem. Section, BAAS 1988–89; Hon. Visiting Prof. of Physical Chem., Queen Mary Coll., London 1986–, of Chem., Imperial Coll., London 1986–91, Miller Prof., Univ. of Calif., Berkeley 1998; Linus Pauling Lectureship, Calif. Inst. of Tech. 1999; Baker Lecturer, Cornell Univ. 1983; John C. Polanyi Nobel Laureate Lecturer, Univ. of Toronto 2000; Trustee British Museum (Natural History) 1986–91, Science Museum 1989–95; Commr, 1851 Royal Exhbn 1995– (Chair. Scientific Research Cttee 1996–); Tetelman Fellow, Yale Univ. 1997; Hon. Professorial Fellow Academia Sinica (Shanghai), Imperial Coll. London, Queen Mary Coll. London; Hon. F.R.Eng.; Hon. FRSE; Hon. Fellow Indian Acad. (Bangalore), Indian Acad. (Delhi), UMIST, Univ. Coll. Swansea, American Acad. of Arts and Science, American Philosophical Soc., Venezuelan Acad. of Sciences, Russian Acad. of Sciences, Inst. of Physics; Hon. Foreign Fellow Eng Acad. Japan 1991, Hungarian and Polish Acad. of Sciences 1998, Royal Spanish Acad. of Sciences 1999, Göttingen Acad. of Sciences 2003–; mem. Academia Europaea 1989; Rutherford Memorial Lecturer of Royal Soc. in New Zealand 1997; Hon. Bencher, Gray's Inn 1986; Hon. DSc (Heriot-Watt Univ.) 1989, (Birmingham) 1991, (Claude Bernard Univ., Lyon) 1994, (Complutense Univ., Madrid) 1994, (Western Univ., Ont.) 1995, (Eindhoven Univ., Netherlands, Hull Univ.) 1996, (Aberdeen, Surrey) 1997, (American Univ. Cairo) 2002; Hon. DUniv (Open Univ.) 1992; numerous awards including Faraday and Longstaff Medals, Royal Soc. of Chem. 1990, Bakerian Prize Lectureship, Royal Soc. 1990, Messel Gold Medal, Soc. of Chemical Industry 1992, Davy Medal, Royal Soc. 1994, Willard Gibbs Gold Medal (ACS) 1995, Hon. Medal Polish Acad. of Sciences, Warsaw 1996, Semonov Centenary Medal, Russian Acad. of Sciences 1996, Award for Creative Research in Catalysis, American Chemical Soc. 1999, Linus Pauling Gold Medal for advances in science (Stanford) 2003; new mineral meurigite named in his honour 1995; symposium in his honour organized by Microscopy and Microanalysis Soc. of America, Philadelphia 2000 and by RSC London 2002. *Publications:* Principles of Heterogeneous Catalysis 1967, Characterization of Catalysts 1980, Heterogeneous Catalysis: Principles and Practice 1997, Michael Faraday and the Royal Institution: the genius of man and place 1991, Perspectives in Catalysis (with K. I. Zamaraev) 1992; Pan Edrychwyf ar y Nefoedd (Welsh Radio Lecture) 1978; Founding Co-Ed.-in-Chief Catalysis Letters 1988–, Topics in Catalysis 1992–; over 950 articles on catalysis solid-state and surface science. *Leisure interests:* walking, Welsh literature, ancient civilizations, birdwatching, popularization of science. *Address:* Dept of Materials Science, Cambridge, CB2 3QZ; The Royal Institution, 21 Albemarle Street, London, W1X 4BS, England. *Telephone:* (1223) 334300 (Cambridge); (20) 7409-2992 (London). *Fax:* (1223) 334567 (Cambridge); (20) 7670-2958 (London).

THOMAS, Sir Keith Vivian, Kt, MA, FBA; British historian; b. 2 Jan. 1933, Wick, Glamorgan, Wales; s. of Vivian Thomas and Hilda Thomas; m. Valerie June Little 1961; one s. one d.; ed Barry County Grammar School and Balliol Coll. Oxford (Brackenbury Scholar); nat. service in Royal Welch Fusiliers 1950–52; Fellow of All Souls Coll. Oxford 1955–57; Fellow of St John's Coll. Oxford 1957–86, Tutor 1957–85; Reader in Modern History, Univ. of Oxford 1978–85, Prof. 1986, Pres. Corpus Christi Coll. 1986–2000, Pro-Vice-Chancellor, Univ. of Oxford 1988–2000, Fellow All Souls Coll. 2001–; Del., Oxford Univ. Press 1980–2000; G. M. Trevelyan Lecturer, Univ. of Cambridge 1979; Ford's Lecturer, Univ. of Oxford 2000; mem. Econ. and Social Research Council 1985–90, Reviewing Cttee on Export of Works of Art 1990–92, Royal Comm. on Historical Manuscripts 1992–2002; Trustee, Nat. Gallery 1991–98, British Museum 1999–; Pres. British Acad. 1993–97; Chair. British Library Advisory Cttee for Arts, Humanities and Social Sciences 1997–2002, Advisory Cttee, Warburg Inst., Univ. of London 2000–; Hon. Fellow Balliol Coll., Oxford 1984, St John's Coll., Oxford 1986, Corpus Christi Coll., Oxford 2000; Hon. Vice-Pres. Royal Historical Soc. 2001–; Foreign hon. mem. American Acad. of Arts and Sciences 1983; mem. Academia Europaea 1993; Hon. DLitt (Kent) 1983, (Wales) 1987, (Hull) 1995, (Leicester) 1996, (Sussex) 1996, (Warwick) 1998; Hon. LittD (Sheffield) 1992, (Cambridge) 1995; Hon. LLD (Williams) 1988, (Oglethorpe, Atlanta, Ga) 1996; Wolfson Literary Award for History 1971; Cavaliere Ufficiale, Ordine al Merito della Repubblica Italiana 1991. *Publications:* Religion and the Decline of Magic 1971, Puritans and Revolutionaries (Ed., with Donald Pennington) 1978, Man and the Natural World 1983, The Oxford Book of Work (Ed.) 1999. *Leisure interest:* visiting second-hand bookshops. *Address:* All Souls College, Oxford, OX1 4AL (Office); The Broad Gate, Broad Street, Ludlow, Shropshire, SY8 1NJ (Home); 15 Duke Street, Oxford, OX2 0HX, England (Home). *Telephone:* (1865) 279379 (Office); (1584) 877797 (Ludlow) (Home); (1865) 427508 (Oxford) (Home). *Fax:* (1865) 279299 (Office). *E-mail:* keith.thomas@all-souls.oxford.ac.uk (Home).

THOMAS, Robert Kemeys, MA, DPhil, FRS; British chemist; b. 25 Sept. 1941, Harpenden; s. of Rev. Herbert Thomas and Agnes Thomas (née McLaren); m.

Pamela H. Woods 1968; one s. two d.; ed St John's Coll., Oxford; researcher Univ. of Oxford 1968–78, Fellow Merton Coll. 1975–78, lecturer in Physical Chemistry 1978–, Fellow and tutor Univ. Coll. 1978–; Tilden Lecturer, Royal Soc. of Chemistry; Hon. Prof. Inst. of Chemistry, Chinese Acad. of Sciences, Beijing 1999–. *Publications:* papers in scientific journals. *Leisure interests:* music, flora, fungi, Chinese language. *Address:* Physical and Theoretical Chemistry Laboratory, South Parks Road, Oxford, OX1 3QZ, England; University College, High Street, Oxford, OX1 4BH. *Telephone:* (1865) 275422, (1865) 276602. *Fax:* (1865) 275410.

THOMAS ELLIS, Alice (see Haycraft, Anna Margaret).

THOMAS OF SWYNNERTON, Baron (Life Peer), cr. 1981, of Notting Hill in Greater London; **Hugh Swynnerton Thomas,** MA; British historian; b. 21 Oct. 1931, Windsor; s. of Hugh Whitelegge and Margery (née Swynnerton) Thomas; m. Vanessa Jebb 1962; two s. one d.; ed Sherborne School, Queens' Coll., Cambridge and Sorbonne, Paris; Foreign Office 1954–57; Sec. UK Del. to UN Disarmament Sub-Cttee 1955–56; lecturer Royal Mil. Acad., Sandhurst 1957; worked for UNA 1959–61; Prof. of History, Univ. of Reading 1966–76; Chair. Graduate School of European Studies 1973–76, Centre for Policy Studies 1979–91; King Juan Carlos I Prof. New York Univ. 1995; Visiting Prof. of History Univ. of Boston 1996, Univ. Prof. 1997–; Corresp. mem. Real Academia de la Historia, Madrid; Fellow, Royal Historical Soc.; Somerset Maugham Prize 1962, Arts Council Nat. Book Award for History 1980, Order of the Aztec Eagle 1995, Grand Cross, Order of Isabel la Católica, Spain 2001. *Publications include:* The Spanish Civil War 1961, The Suez Affair 1966, Cuba or the Pursuit of Freedom 1971, Goya and the Third of May 1808 1973, John Strachey 1973, An Unfinished History of the World 1979, A Case for the Round Reading Room 1983, Havannah! (novel) 1984, Armed Truce: The Beginnings of the Cold War 1945–46 1986, Klara (novel) 1988, Madrid: A Traveller's Companion (ed.) 1988, Ever Closer Union: Britain's Destiny in Europe 1991, The Conquest of Mexico 1993, The Slave Trade 1997, The Future of Europe 1998, Who's Who of the Conquistadors 2000. *Address:* 29 Ladbroke Grove, London, W11 3BB.

THOMPSON, Alan Eric, MA, PhD, FRSA, FSA (Scot); British professor of economics; b. 16 Sept. 1924; s. of Eric Thompson and Florence Thompson; m. Mary Heather Long 1960; three s. one d.; ed Univ. of Edin.; Lecturer in Econs, Univ. of Edin. 1953–59, 1964–71; Labour MP for Dunfermline 1959–64; Econ. Consultant, Scotch Whisky Asscn 1965–70; Visiting Prof., Graduate School of Business, Stanford Univ., Calif. 1966, 1968; A. J. Balfour Prof. of Econs of Govt, Heriot-Watt Univ., Edin. 1972–87, Prof. of Econs, School of Business and Financial Studies 1987–88, Prof. Emer. 1988–; mem. Scottish Council for Adult Educ. in HM Forces 1973–; mem. Local Govt Boundaries Comm. for Scotland 1975–82; mem. Joint Mil. Educ. Cttee, Edin. and Heriot-Watt Univs 1975–; mem. Court, Heriot-Watt Univ. 1980; Chair. Northern Offshore Maritime Resources Study 1974–84; BBC Nat. Gov. for Scotland 1976–79; mem. Royal Fine Art Comm. for Scotland 1975–80, Scottish-Russian Co-ordinating Cttee for Trade and Industry 1985–90; Parl. Adviser to Scottish TV 1966–76, to Pharmaceutical Gen. Council (Scotland) 1985–99; Adviser, Robert Burns Memorial Trust 1995–97; Chair. Bd of Govs, Newbattle Abbey Coll. 1980–82; Hon. Vice-Pres. Asscn of Nazi War Camp Survivors 1960–; Dir Scottish AIDS Research Foundation 1991–. *Publications:* The Development of Economic Doctrine (with Alexander Gray) 1980; contributions to learned journals. *Leisure interests:* writing children's stories and plays, croquet, bridge. *Address:* 11 Upper Gray Street, Edinburgh, EH9 1SN (Home); Ardtrostan Cottage, St Fillian's, Perthshire, PH6 2NL, Scotland. *Telephone:* (131) 667-2140 (Edinburgh); (1764) 685275 (Perthshire).

THOMPSON, Caroline Warner, BA; American screenwriter, film producer and director; b. 23 April 1956, Washington, DC; d. of Thomas Carlton Jr and Bettie Marshall Thompson (née Warner); m. Alfred Henry Bromell 1982 (divorced 1985); ed Amherst Coll., Harvard Univ.; fmr freelance journalist. *Screenplays include:* Edward Scissorhands (also assoc. producer) 1990, The Addams Family 1991, Homeward Bound: The Incredible Journey 1993, The Secret Garden (also assoc. producer) 1993, Tim Burton's The Nightmare Before Christmas (also dir) 1994, Black Beauty (also dir) 1994, Buddy (also dir) 1997. *Publication:* First Born 1993. *Leisure interest:* horseback riding. *Address:* c/o William Morris Agency Inc., 151 El Camino Drive, Beverly Hills, CA 90212, USA.

THOMPSON, Sir Clive Malcolm, Kt, BSc; British business executive; b. 4 April 1943, Bristol; s. of H. L. Thompson and P. D. Thompson (née Stansbury); m. Judith Howard 1968; two s.; ed Clifton Coll., Bristol and Birmingham Univ.; Marketing Exec. Royal Dutch Shell Group 1964–67; Marketing Exec. and Gen. Man. Boots Co. PLC 1967–70; Gen. Man. Jeyes Group Ltd 1970–78; Man. Dir Health and Hygiene Div., Cadbury Schweppes 1978–82; Chief Exec. Rentokil Initial PLC 1983–2003, Chair. (non-exec.) 2003–; Pres. CBI 1998–2000; Deputy Chair. Financial Reporting Council; fmr Dir (non-exec.) Wellcome PLC, Sainsbury PLC, Seeboard PLC, Caradon PLC, BAT Industries PLC; now Chair. Kleeneze PLC; mem. Hampel Cttee on Corp. Governance; Hon. DSc (Birmingham) 1999. *Leisure interests:* the stock market, current affairs, walking, golf. *Address:* Rentokil Initial PLC, Felcourt, East Grinstead, West Sussex, RH19 2JY, England.

THOMPSON, Daley (Francis Morgan), CBE; British athlete; b. 30 July 1958, Notting Hill, London; m. Tisha Quinlan 1987; one c.; Sussex Schools 200m title 1974; first competitive decathlon, Welsh Open Championship June 1975; European Junior Decathlon Champion 1977; European Decathlon

silver medallist 1978, gold medallist 1982 and 1986; Commonwealth Decathlon gold medallist 1978, 1982 and 1986; Olympic Decathlon gold medallist 1980 (Moscow) and 1984 (LA); World Decathlon Champion 1983; est. new world record for decathlon (at Olympic Games, LA); set four world records in all and was undefeated between 1978 and 1987; retd July 1992; invited to run leg of the Olympic Torch relay at the opening of the Sydney Olympic Games 2000. *Publications:* Going for Gold 1987, The Greatest 1996. *Address:* Church Row, Wandsworth Plain, London SW18, UK.

THOMPSON, David; Barbadian politician and attorney-at-law; ed Combermere School, Hugh Wooding Law School, Trinidad and Tobago, Univ. of the W Indies; in pvt. law practice 1986–91; pnr. Thompson & Patterson 1994–; mem. House of Ass.; Minister of Community Devt and Culture 1991; Minister of Finance 1992–93; Leader of Democratic Labour Party, currently Leader of the Opposition; mem. Barbados Bar Asscn, Barbados Museum and Historical Soc. *Address:* Democratic Labour Party, George Street, Belleville, St. Michael, Barbados (Office). *Telephone:* 429-3104 (Office). *Fax:* 427-0548 (Office). *E-mail:* dlp@sunbeach.net (Office).

THOMPSON, Emma; British actress and screenwriter; b. 15 April 1959; d. of Eric Thompson and Phyllida Law; m. Kenneth Branagh 1989 (divorced); partner Greg Wise; one d.; ed Camden Girls' School and Newnham Coll. Cambridge; appeared with Cambridge Footlights. *Films:* The Tall Guy 1988, Henry V 1989, Impromptu 1989, Howards End 1991 (eight awards for Best Actress, including New York Film Critics, LA Critics, Golden Globe, Acad. Award, BAFTA, Nat. Bd of Review; David di Donatella Award for Best Foreign Actress (Italy)), Dead Again 1991, Cheers 1992, Peter's Friends 1992, Much Ado About Nothing 1993, Remains of the Day 1993 (David di Donatella Award for Best Foreign Actress (Italy)), In the Name of the Father 1993, Junior 1994, Carrington 1995, Sense and Sensibility (nine awards for Best Screenplay, including Acad. Award, Golden Globe, LA Film Critics, New York Film Critics, Writers Guild of America, Evening Standard British Film Award; awards for Best Actress from BAFTA and Nat. Bd of Review), The Winter Guest 1996 (Panisetti Award for Best Actress, Venice Film Festival), Primary Colors 1997, Judas Kiss 1997, Imagining Argentina 2002, Love Actually 2002. *Stage appearances include:* The Cellar Tapes, Edin. Festival 1981–82 (Perrier Pick of the Fringe Award 1981), A Sense of Nonsense (revue tour) 1983, Short Vehicle, Edin. Festival 1984, Me and My Girl, Adelphi 1984–85, Look Back in Anger, Lyric 1989, A Midsummer Night's Dream (world tour) 1990, King Lear (world tour) 1990. *Television appearances include:* Emma Thompson Special, Channel 4 1983, Alfresco (two series), Granada 1983–84, The Crystal Cube, BBC 1984, Tutti Frutti, BBC 1986 (BAFTA Award for Best Actress), Fortunes of War, BBC 1986–87 (BAFTA Award for Best Actress), Thompson 1988, Knuckle, BBC 1988, The Winslow Boy, BBC 1988, Look Back in Anger, Thames 1989, Blue Boy, BBC Scotland 1994, Ellen, Touchstone TV/ABC 1998 (Emmy Award for Outstanding Guest Actress in a Comedy Series), Wit (Best Actress Award, Semana Internacional de Cine de Valladolid) 2000, Angels in America 2002. *Address:* c/o Hamilton Hodell Ltd, 1st Floor, 24 Hanway Street, London, W1T 1UH, England. *Telephone:* (20) 7636-1221. *Fax:* (20) 7636-1226 (Office). *E-mail:* lorraine@hamiltonhodell.co.uk (Office).

THOMPSON, Francis Michael Longstreth, CBE, DPhil, FBA; British professor of history; b. 13 Aug. 1925, Purley, Surrey; s. of Francis Longstreth-Thompson; m. Anne Challoner 1951; two s. one d.; ed Bootham School, York and The Queen's Coll., Oxford; Lecturer in History, Univ. Coll. London 1951–63, Reader in Econ. History 1963–68; Prof. of Modern History, Univ. of London and Head of Dept of History, Bedford Coll. London 1968–77, Prof. of History and Dir of Inst. of Historical Research 1977–90, Prof. Emer. 1990–; Ford's Lecturer, Univ. of Oxford 1993–94; Pres. Econ. History Soc. 1983–86, Hon. Vice-Pres. 1986–; British mem. Standing Cttee for Humanities, European Science Foundation 1983–93; Pres. Royal Historical Soc. 1988–92; Pres. British Agric. History Soc. 1989–92. *Publications:* English Landed Society in the 19th century 1963, Chartered Surveyors: the growth of a profession 1968, Victorian England: the horse-drawn society 1970, Hampstead: building a borough, 1650–1964 1974, Countrysides (in The Nineteenth Century; ed. Asa Briggs) 1970, Britain (in European Landed Elites in the Nineteenth Century; ed. David Spring) 1977, Landowners and Farmers (in The Faces of Europe; ed. Alan Bullock) 1980, The Rise of Suburbia (Ed.) 1982, Horses in European Economic History (Ed.) 1983, The Rise of Respectable Society: A Social History of Victorian Britain 1988, The Cambridge Social History of Britain 1750–1950, 3 Vols (Ed.) 1990, The University of London and the World of Learning 1836–1986 (Ed.) 1990, Landowners, Capitalists and Entrepreneurs (Ed.) 1994, Gentrification and the Enterprise Culture: Britain, 1780–1980 2001. *Leisure interests:* gardening, walking, carpentry. *Address:* Holly Cottage, Sheepcote Lane, Wheathampstead, Herts., AL4 8NJ, England. *Telephone:* (158) 283-3129 (Home).

THOMPSON, Fred Dalton, JD; American politician, actor and lawyer; b. 19 Aug. 1942, Sheffield, Ala; m. (divorced); three c.; ed Vanderbilt Univ., Memphis State Univ.; Minority Staff Counsel to Watergate Cttee; Senator from Tennessee 1994–2003; Chair. Senate Cttee to Investigate Fund Raising during 1996 Presidential Election 1997; Chair. Senate Governmental Affairs Cttee 1997–2001; Republican. *Films include:* In the Line of Fire, The Hunt for Red October, No Way Out and 15 others. *Address:* c/o United States Senate, 511 Dirksen Senate Building, Washington, DC 20510, USA.

THOMPSON, Harold Lindsay, MB, BS, FRACGP, AM; Australian medical practitioner; b. 23 April 1929, Aberdeen, Scotland; s. of Harold Thompson and

Johan D. Thompson; m. 1st Audrey J. Harpur 1957 (died 1996); three s. two d.; m. 2nd Jennifer Manton 1997; ed Aberdeen, Melbourne and Sydney Grammar Schools and postgrad. training in UK; Surgeon-Lt Royal Australian Navy 1956–60; now in gen. practice in Lakemba, NSW; Exec. Dir Canterbury Div. of Gen. Practice 1996–; Assoc. Prof., Faculty of Medicine, Univ. of Sydney 1996–; Fellow Australian Medical Assen 1973, Pres. 1982–85; Pres. Confed. of Medical Assens. of Asia and Oceania 1985–87, Immediate Past Pres. 1987–89; Chair. Australian Urban Divs of Gen. Practice 1995–; Vice-Chair. Australian Council on Healthcare Standards 1985–89; Vice-Pres. Australian Council of Professions 1985–87, Pres. 1989–91; mem. Council, World Medical Assen 1984–90, Pres. 1988–89; mem. Econ. Planning Advisory Cttee 1989–91, Bd Southern Sydney Area Health Service 1991–95; Chair. Australian Confed. of Medical Assens of Asia and Oceania 1989–95, GP Advisory Cttee NSW Health 1997–; Gold Medal, Australian Medical Assen 1986; Medal, Australian Council on Healthcare Standards 1990, Award of Merit, Confed. of Medical Assens of Asia and Oceania 1996. *Leisure interests:* golf, fishing, bridge. *Address:* 601/2 Roseby Street, Drummoyne, NSW 2047 (Office); 4/100 Milsom Road, Cremorne, NSW 2090, Australia (Home). *Telephone:* (2) 9719-8391 (Office); (2) 9908-2980 (Home). *E-mail:* hlthompson@iprimus.com.au.

THOMPSON, James R., LLD; American politician and lawyer; b. 8 May 1936, Chicago, Ill.; s. of Dr J. Robert Thompson and Agnes Thompson; m. Jayne Carr 1976; one d.; ed Univ. of Illinois, Washington Univ., St Louis, Missouri, Northwestern Univ. Law School; admitted to Illinois Bar 1959; Prosecutor, State Attorney's Office, Cook County, Ill. 1959–64; Assoc. Prof. North Western Univ. Law School, Ill. 1964–69; Chief, Dept of Law Enforcement and Public Protection, Office of Ill. Attorney-Gen. 1969–70, First Asst US Attorney 1970–71, US Attorney for Northern Dist of Ill. 1971–75; Counsel, Winston and Strawn law firm, Chicago 1975–77, partner, Chair. Exec. Cttee 1991–; Gov. of Ill. 1977–91; mem. Exec. Cttee Nat. Govs' Assen (NGA) 1980–82, Chair. 1983–84; Co-Chair. Attorney-Gen.'s Task Force on Violent Crime 1981; Chair./President's Intelligence Oversight Bd 1989–93; mem. Presidential Advisory Cttee on Federalism 1981, Advisory Bd of Fed. Emergency Man. Agency 1991–93; Chair. Republican Govs' Assen, Midwestern Govs' Conf., NGA Task Force on Job Creation and Infrastructure 1982; Chair. Council of Great Lakes Govs 1985; Vice-Chair. Martin Luther King Jr Nat. Holiday Cttee 1985; Chair. Ill. Math. and Science Foundation; Republican; Hon. LLD (Lincoln Coll.) 1975, Hon. DHumLitt (Roosevelt Univ.) 1979, Hon. DJur (Northwestern Univ. and Illinois Coll.) 1979, Hon. LLD (Monmouth Coll.) 1981, (Marshall Law School) 1984, (Elmhurst Coll.) 1985, Dr hc (Pratt Inst.) 1984; Justice in Legislation Award, American Jewish Congress 1984; Distinguished Public Service Award, Anti-Defamation League 1984, Swedish-American of the Year, Vasa Order of America 1985. *Publications:* co-author of four textbooks incl. Cases and Comments on Criminal Procedure; numerous articles in professional journals. *Address:* Winston & Strawn, 35 W Wacker Drive, Suite 4200, Chicago, IL 60601, USA.

THOMPSON, John M.; Canadian business executive; ed Univ. of Western Ont., Richard Ivey Business School at Univ. of Western Ont. and Kellogg Grad. School at Northwestern Univ.; joined IBM Canada Ltd 1966, systems engineer, marketing man., Pres. and CEO 1986; Corp. Vice-Pres. marketing and services IBM Corpn 1991, head AS/400 server business, Sr Vice-Pres. and Group Exec. IBM Software Group 1995, Vice-Chair. Bd Dirs. 2000; Dir Toronto-Dominion Bank (Chair. Man. Resources Cttee). *Address:* IBM Corporation, New Orchard Road, Armonk, NY 10504, USA (Office). *Telephone:* (914) 499-1900 (Office).

THOMPSON, Mark John, BA, FRTS, FRSA; British broadcasting executive; b. 31 July 1957; s. of Duncan John Thompson and Sydney Columba Corduff Thompson; m. Jane Emilie Blumberg 1987; two s. one d.; ed Stonyhurst Coll., Merton Coll. Oxford; Research Asst Trainee, BBC TV 1979–1980, Asst Producer Nationwide 1980–1982, Producer Breakfast Time 1982–84, Output Ed. London Plus 1984–85, Newsnight 1985–87, Ed. Nine O'Clock News 1988–90, Panorama 1990–92, Head of Features 1992–94, Head of Factual Programmes 1994–96, Controller BBC2 1996–98; Dir of Nat. and Regional Broadcasting 1998–2000; Dir of TV, BBC 2000–02; CEO Channel 4 March 2002–. *Leisure interests:* walking, cooking. *Address:* Channel 4 Television, 124 Horseferry Road, London, SW1P 2TX, England (Office). *Telephone:* (20) 7396-4444 (Office).

THOMPSON, Sir Michael Warwick, Kt, DSc, FInstP; British physicist and university vice-chancellor; b. 1 June 1931; s. of Kelvin W. Thompson and Madeleine Walford; m. 1st Sybil N. Spooner 1956 (died 1999); two s.; m. 2nd Jenny Mitchell 2000; ed Rydal School and Univ. of Liverpool; research scientist, AERE, Harwell, Reactor Physics and Metallurgy 1953–65; Prof. of Experimental Physics, Univ. of Sussex 1965–80, Pro-Vice-Chancellor 1972–78; Vice-Chancellor, Univ. of E Anglia 1980–86; Vice-Chancellor and Prin. Univ. of Birmingham 1987–96, Emer. Prof. 1996–; Chair. Council John Innes Research Inst. 1980–86, British Council Cttee for Academic Research Collaboration with Germany 1988–; mem. SRC Physics Cttee (also Chair.) 1972–79, E Sussex Educ. Cttee 1973–78, E Sussex Area Health Authority 1973–80, W Midlands Regional Health Authority 1987–90 (non-exec. Dir 1990–96), Council for Nat. Academic Awards 1988–91, Council of Assen of Commonwealth Univs 1990–95, Council for Industry and Higher Educ. 1991–96; Dir (non-exec.) Alliance Bldg Soc. 1979–85 (Alliance and Leicester Bldg Soc., now Alliance & Leicester PLC) 1985–2000, Deputy Chair. 1995–2000; COBUILD Ltd 1987–96, TPIC Ltd 1987–, Council of the Cttee of Vice-Chancellors and Prins 1989–96 (Chair. Medical Cttee 1994–); Trustee

Barber Inst. of Fine Art 1987–, St Bartholomew's Medical Coll. 1998–; Hon. LLD (Birmingham) 1997; Hon. DSc (Sussex) 1998; CV Boys Prize, Inst. of Physics; Grosses Bundesverdienstkreuz 1997. *Publications:* Defects and Radiation Damage in Metals 1968; over 100 papers in scientific journals on the interaction of radiation with solids. *Leisure interests:* sailing, the arts. *Address:* The University of Birmingham, Edgbaston, Birmingham, B15 2TT (Office); Stoneacre, The Warren, Polperro, Cornwall, PL13 2RD, England (Home). *Telephone:* (121) 414-4536 (Office).

THOMPSON, (Rupert) Julian (de la Mare), MA; British business executive; b. 23 July 1941; s. of Rupert Spens Thompson and Florence Elizabeth (de la Mare) Thompson; m. Jacqueline Julie Ivimy 1965; three d.; ed Eton Coll. and King's Coll., Cambridge; joined Sotheby's 1963, Dir 1969–, Chair. 1982–86, Deputy Chair. 1987–92, Chair. Sotheby's Asia 1992–. *Address:* 47 Warrington Crescent, London, W9 1EJ, England. *Telephone:* (20) 7289-3145.

THOMPSON, Tommy George, JD; American state governor; b. 19 Nov. 1941, Elroy, Wis.; s. of Allan Thompson and Julie Dutton; m. Sue Ann Mashak 1969; one s. two d.; ed Univ. of Wisconsin; political intern, US Rep. Thomson 1963; legis. messenger, Wis. State Senate 1964–66; sole practice, Elroy and Mauston, Wis. 1966–87; self-employed real estate broker, Mauston 1970–; mem. Dist 87 Wis. State Ass. 1966–87, Asst Minority Leader 1972–81, Floor Leader 1981–87; Gov. of Wisconsin 1987–2001; Sec. of State of Health and Human Services 2001–; Chair. Republican Govs' Assen 1991–92; Chair. Bd Dirs Amtrak 1998–99; mem. Exec. Cttee Nat. Govs' Assen; mem. American Bar Assen; Republican; Nature Conservancy Award 1988, Thomas Jefferson Freedom Award (American Legis. Exchange Council) 1991; Leadership in Natural Energy Conservation Award, US Energy Assen 1994, Horatio Alger Award, and numerous other awards. *Leisure interests:* hunting, fishing, sports. *Address:* Department of Health and Human Services, 200 Independence Avenue, SW, Washington, DC 20201, USA (Office). *Telephone:* (202) 690-6343 (Office). *Website:* www.os.dhhs.gov (Office).

THOMSEN, Niels Jørgen, DPhil; Danish university professor; b. 21 April 1930, Copenhagen; s. of late Sigurd Thomsen and Gudrun Kirkegaard; m. Birgit Nüchel Petersen 1953; two s.; ed Univ. of Copenhagen; Dir Danish Press Museum, Aarhus 1958–65; lecturer, School of Journalism, Aarhus 1962–65; Asst Prof. of Econ. History, Univ. of Copenhagen 1965–71, Asst Prof. of Political Science 1971–73, Prof. of Modern History 1973–2000; Danish Ed. Pressens Årbog 1968–82; Chair. Soc. for History and Econs, Copenhagen 1980–83; Chair. Soc. for Contemporary History 1982–; mem. Royal Danish Acad. of Science and Letters. *Publications:* Partipressen 1965, Dagbladskonkurrencen 1870–1970 I–II 1972, Københavns Universitet 1936–66 1986, De danske aviser 1634–1989 (with Jette Søllinge) I–III 1987–91, Industri, stat og samfund 1870–1939 1991, Hovedstrømninger 1870–1914 1998; about 80 articles on political and media history in professional journals. *Address:* Institute of History, University of Copenhagen, Njalsgade 102, 2300 Copenhagen S (Office); Vitus Berings Allé 15, 2930 Klampenborg, Denmark (Home). *Telephone:* 35-32-82-43 (Office); 39-64-33-16 (Home). *Fax:* 35-32-82-41. *E-mail:* n.thomsen@mail.tele.dk (Home). *Website:* www.hum.ku.dk.

THOMSON, Brian Edward; Australian film, theatre and opera designer; b. 5 Jan. 1946, Sydney; s. of Austin Thomas Thomson and Adoree Gertrude Thomson; ed Applecross Sr High School, Perth Tech. Coll., Univ. of New South Wales; Supervising Designer, closing ceremony of Olympic Games, Sydney 2000; Production Designer, Centennial of Fed. Ceremony 2001; Australian Film Inst. Award for production design, Rebel 1985, Ground Zero 1987, Sydney Theatre Critics' Award for Best Designer 1989, 1992, 1993, 1994, Mo Award 1994, 1995, Tony Award for The King and I 1996. *Musicals:* Hair, Jesus Christ Superstar (London and Australia), The Rocky Horror Show (original London production and worldwide), Chicago, The Stripper, Company, Chess, The King and I (Broadway production 1996, London Palladium), How to Succeed in Business Without Really Trying, South Pacific, Hello, Dolly!, Merrily We Roll Along, Grease, Happy Days. *Theatre:* Housewife Superstar!!! (London and New York); The Threepenny Opera (opening season, Drama Theatre, Sydney Opera House); Big Toys (the Old Tote); A Cheery Soul, Chinchilla, Macbeth, The Doll Trilogy, The Ham Funeral, A Midsummer Night's Dream, The Crucible, The Homecoming, Uncle Vanya, Death and the Maiden, Coriolanus, Falsettos, King Lear, Arcadia, Medea, Mongrels, Third World Blues, After the Ball, White Devil (also at Brooklyn Acad. of Music); Up for Grabs (all for Sydney Theatre Co.); Arturo Ui, Rock-Ola (Nimrod); Lulu, Shepherd on the Rocks Crow (State Theatre Co. of S. Australia); Ghosts, The Tempest, The Master Builder, Buzz, Frogs, Aftershocks, Radiance, Up the Road, Burnt Piano, The Laramie Project (Company B Belvoir); Angels in America (Melbourne Theatre Co.); Soulmates, One Day of the Year (Sydney Theatre Co.), My Zinc Bed, Buried Child (Company B Belvoir). *Film and television:* Barlow and Chambers, Shadow of the Cobra (both mini-series); Shirly Thompson vs. the Aliens, The Rocky Horror Picture Show, Starstruck, Rebel, Night of Shadows (also Dir), Ground Zero, Turtle Beach, Frauds. *Dance:* Synergy, Fornicon (Sydney Dance Co.), Tivol (Sydney Dance Co. and Australian Ballet). *Opera:* Death in Venice, The Makropulos Affair (Adelaide Festival); Turandot, Aida, Summer of the Seventeenth Doll (Vic. State Opera); Voss, Death in Venice, Tristan und Isolde, Katya Kabanova, The Eighth Wonder (The Australian Opera); Billy Budd (Welsh Nat. Opera, Opera Australia, Canadian Nat. Opera), Sweeney Todd (Lyric Opera of Chicago). *Leisure interests:* movies, sport (Aussie rules, cricket, tennis). *Address:* 5

Little Dowling Street, Paddington, NSW 2021, Australia. *Telephone:* (2) 9331-1584. *Fax:* (2) 9360-4314. *E-mail:* bt@brianthomson.biz (Office). *Website:* www.brianthomson.biz (Office).

THOMSON, James Alan, MS, PhD; American business executive; b. 21 Jan. 1945, Boston, Mass.; ed Univ. of New Hampshire and Purdue Univ.; Research Fellow, Univ. of Wis. Madison 1972–74; Systems Analyst, Office of Sec. of Defense, US Dept of Defense, Washington, DC 1974–77; staff mem. Nat. Security Council, Washington, DC 1977–81; Vice-Pres. RAND, Santa Monica, Calif. 1981–88, Pres. and CEO 1989–; Dir LA World Affairs Council; Dir AK Steel Holdings Corpn, Texas Biotech. Corpn; mem. Int. Inst. for Strategic Studies, Council on Foreign Relations 1985–, Bd Los Angeles World Affairs Council; Hon. DSc (Purdue) 1992; Hon. LLD (Pepperdine) 1996. *Publications:* Conventional Arms Control and the Security of Europe 1988; articles on defence issues. *Address:* RAND, 1700 Main Street, Santa Monica, CA 90401, USA. *Telephone:* (310) 451-6936. *Fax:* (310) 451-6972 (Office).

THOMSON, Sir John Adam, GCMG, MA; British diplomatist (retd); b. 27 April 1927, Aberdeenshire; s. of the late Sir George Thomson, Kt, FRS and Kathleen Smith; m. 1st Elizabeth Anne McClure 1953 (died 1988); three s. one d.; m. 2nd Judith Ogden Bullitt 1992; ed Philips Exeter Acad., NH, USA, Aberdeen Univ., Trinity Coll., Cambridge; Third Secretary, Embassy in Jeddah 1951, in Damascus 1954; Foreign Office 1955; Private Sec. to Perm. Under-Sec. 1958; First Sec., Embassy in Washington, DC 1960; Foreign Office 1964; Acting Head of Planning Staff 1966; Counsellor, Head of Planning Staff 1967; seconded to Cabinet Office as Chief of Assessment Staff 1968; Minister, Deputy Perm. Rep. to NATO 1972; Asst Under-Sec. of State, Foreign and Commonwealth Office 1973; High Commr in India 1977–82; Perm. Rep. to UN 1982–87; Leader CSCE Humanitarian Mission to Bosnia-Herzegovina 1992; Prin. Dir, 21st Century Trust 1987–90; Chair. Minority Rights Group Int. 1991–, Flemings Emerging Markets Investment Trust 1991–98; int. adviser ANZ Grindlays Bank 1996–97 (Dir 1987–96); mem. Council Int. Inst. of Strategic Studies, Governing Body Inst. of Devt Studies, Sussex, Council Overseas Devt Inst., London, Howie Cttee for Secondary Educ. in Scotland 1990–92; Trustee Nat. Museums of Scotland 1991–99 (Dir 1987–96); Assoc. mem. Nuffield Coll., Oxford 1988–91; Hon. LLD (Ursinus Coll., Penn.) 1984, (Aberdeen) 1986. *Publication:* Crusader Castles (with Robin Fedden) 1956. *Leisure interests:* castles, oriental carpets, walking. *Address:* Fleming Emerging Markets Investment Trust PLC, 25 Copthall Avenue, London, EC2R 7DR, England.

THOMSON, Peter William, AO, CBE; Australian golfer; b. 23 Aug. 1929, Melbourne; m. Stella Mary 1960; one s. three d.; turned professional 1949; British Open Champion 1954, 1955, 1956, 1958, 1965 (only player to win three successively since Open became 72-hole event 1892); won British PGA Match-Play Championship four times and 16 major tournaments in Britain; Australian Open Champion 1951, 1967, 1972, NZ Open Champion nine times; won open titles of Italy, Spain, Hong Kong, Philippines, India and Germany; played 11 times for Australia in World Cup (won twice); won World Seniors Championship 1984, PGA Seniors Championship of America 1984; Capt. Pres.'s Cup Int. Team 1996, 1998, 2000; fmr Pres. Professional Golfers' Assocn of Australia; Dir Thomson, Wolveridge, Perrett; mem. James McGrath Foundation, Vic.; Hon. DBA (Queen Margaret Univ. Coll. Edin.) 2002. *Leisure interests:* classical music, literature, discussing politics. *Address:* Carmel House, 44 Mathoura Road, Toorak, Vic. 3142, Australia.

THOMSON, Richard Murray, OC, BASs(Eng), MBA; Canadian banker; b. 14 Aug. 1933, Winnipeg, Man.; s. of H. W. Thomson and Mary Thomson; m. Heather Lorimer 1959; ed Univ. of Toronto, Harvard Business School, Queen's Univ., Kingston, Ont.; joined Toronto-Dominion Bank, Head Office 1957, Senior Asst Man., St James & McGill, Montreal 1961, Asst to Pres., Head Office 1963, Asst Gen. Man. 1965, Chief Gen. Man. 1968, Vice-Pres., Chief Gen. Man., Dir 1971, Pres. 1972–79, Pres. and CEO 1977–79, CEO 1978–97, Chair. 1978–98; Dir Canada Pension Plan Investment Bd., Nexen Inc., Ontario Power Generation Inc., INCO Ltd, S. C. Johnson & Son Inc., Prudential Financial Inc., The Thomson Corpn, The Toronto-Dominion Bank, Trizec Hahn Corpn, Stuart Energy Systems Inc. *Leisure interests:* golf, tennis, skiing. *Address:* c/o Toronto-Dominion Bank, P.O. Box 1, Toronto-Dominion Centre, 55 King Street, P.O. Box 1, Toronto, Ont., M5K 1A2, Canada. *Telephone:* (416) 982-8354 (Office). *Fax:* (416) 983-9607 (Office).

THOMSON, Robert; Australian journalist and newspaper editor; b. 11 March 1961, Torrumbarry; m. Ping Wang; two s.; financial and gen. affairs reporter, then Sydney Corresp. The Herald, Melbourne 1979–83; sr feature writer Sydney Morning Herald 1983–85; corresp. for the Financial Times, Beijing 1985–89, Tokyo 1989–94, Foreign News Ed., London 1994–96, Asst Ed. Financial Times and Ed. Weekend FT 1996–98, US Man. Ed. Financial Times 1998–2002; Ed. The Times March 2002–; mem. Knight-Bagehot Fellowship Bd, Columbia Univ.; Chair., Arts International 2001–02; Business Journalist of the Year, The Journalist and Financial Reporting Group (TJFR) 2001. *Television:* regular appearances on ABC News, CNN, Fox News Channel. *Publications:* The Judges – A Portrait of the Australian Judiciary, The Chinese Army, True Fiction (ed.). *Leisure interests:* cinema, tennis, reading. *Address:* The Times, 1 Pennington Street, Wapping, London, E98 1TT, England (Office). *Telephone:* (20) 7782-5000 (Office). *Fax:* (20) 7782-5988 (Office). *Website:* www.the-times.co.uk (Office).

THOMSON, Sir Thomas James, Kt, CBE, MB, CH.B., FRCP (GLASGOW), FRCP (UK), F.R.C.P.(E.), FRCPI; British gastroenterologist (retd) and consultant physi-

cian; b. 8 April 1923, Airdrie; s. of Thomas Thomson and Annie Jane Grant; m. Jessie Smith Shotbolt 1948; two s. one d.; ed Airdrie Acad. and Univ. of Glasgow; posts in clinical medicine continuously 1945–87, teacher 1948–87; posts as Lecturer in Dept Materia Medica, Univ. of Glasgow 1953–87, Hon. Lecturer 1961–87; Consultant Physician and Gastroenterologist Stobhill Gen. Hosp., Glasgow 1961–87; Postgraduate Clinical Tutor to Glasgow Northern Hosps. 1961–80; Chair., Greater Glasgow Health Bd 1987–93; mem. Court, Univ. of Strathclyde 1992–97, Chair. Staff Cttee 1993–97; Sec. Specialist Advisory Cttee for Gen. Internal Medicine for UK 1970–74; Chair., Medico-Pharmaceutical Forum 1978–80; ed. Advisory Bd 1979–84, Conf. of Royal Colls. and Faculties in Scotland 1982–84, Nat. Medical Consultative Cttee for Scotland 1982–87; Hon. Sec. Royal Coll. of Physicians and Surgeons, Glasgow 1965–73, Pres. 1982–84; Hon. Fellow American Coll. of Physicians; Hon. LLD (Glasgow) 1988; Hon. DUniv (Strathclyde) 1997. *Publications:* Dilling's Pharmacology (Jt) 1969, Gastroenterology—an integrated course 1972. *Leisure interests:* swimming and golfing. *Address:* 1 Varna Road, Glasgow, G14 9NE, Scotland. *Telephone:* (141) 959-5930.

THOMSON, William Cran, CA, CBIM; British business executive; b. 11 Feb. 1926, Glasgow; s. of William Thomson and Helen Cran; m. Jessie Wallace 1951; four s.; ed Hutchesons (Boys) Grammar School; joined Royal Dutch/Shell Group 1951, Shell Co. of Egypt 1951–54, of Sudan 1954–56, of Aden 1956–58, Finance Dir P.T. Shell Indonesia 1961–64, Finance Co-ordinator Shell Int. Chemical Co. 1966–70, Chemical Co-ordinator Shell Int. Chemical Co. 1970–79, Chair. Shell Chemicals UK 1974–79, Finance Dir Shell Petroleum Co. 1979–86, Man. Dir Royal Dutch/Shell Group 1979–86, Man. Dir Shell Transport and Trading 1979–86 (Dir 1986–), Chair. Shell Holdings (UK) 1981–86; Chair. Shell Pensions Trust Ltd 1986–, (Dir 1976–); Chair. The Nickerson Group 1990– (Dir 1986–); Dir Coats Viyella PLC 1986–, Romaga AG 1986–. *Leisure interests:* golf, shooting. *Address:* Royal Dutch/Shell Group, Shell Centre, London, SE1 7NA, England.

THOMSON, William Reid, M.PHIL., MSc; American/British international financial adviser and writer; b. 10 Aug. 1939, London, England; s. of the late Wing-Commdr W. Thomson and of Nellie Hendry Thomson; m. 1st Mary Cormack 1967 (divorced 1986); m. 2nd Jeannette Vinta 1987; two s. one d.; ed George Washington Univ., Univ. of Washington and Univ. of Manchester (UK); operations analyst and economist various cos. 1961–72; investment analyst Legg Mason & Co. 1973–74; mem. staff US Treasury Dept, in posts including financial economist, Office of Debt Analysis and later as sr economist, Office of Int. Devt Banks 1974–85; Exec. Dir African Devt Bank 1982–83; Alt. Exec. Dir Asian Devt Bank (ADB) 1985–90, Vice-Pres. (Operations) ADB 1990–94, Sr Counsellor to Pres. of ADB 1994–95; Sr Adviser Fiduciary Trust Int. Asia 1995–; Man. Dir Economic and Financial Consultants 1995–; Chair. Yamamoto Int. Co (Japan) 1996–, Siam Recovery Fund 1997–, Momentum Asia Ltd 1997–, PEDCA LLC 1997–; writer on Asian political/econ. affairs. *Publication:* Confidential Inside Asia Report 1996–. *Leisure interests:* jogging, cricket, reading, writing. *Address:* Rumah, Martyr Road, Guildford, GU1 4LF, England (Home). *Telephone:* (2) 814-0131 (Manila) (Office); 2869-1995 (Hong Kong) (Office); (1483) 440825 (Home). *Fax:* (2) 814-0130 (Manila) (Office); 2869-4111 (Hong Kong) (Office); (1483) 440825 (Home). *E-mail:* wt@momentum-asia.com.hk (Office); wt@momentum-asia.com.hk (Home).

THOMSON OF FLEET, 2nd Baron (cr. 1964), of Northbridge in the City of Edinburgh; **Kenneth Roy Thomson,** MA; Canadian newspaper proprietor; b. 1 Sept. 1923, Toronto; s. of the late Roy Thomson, the 1st Lord Thomson of Fleet and Edna Anna Irvine; m. Nora Marilyn Lavis 1956; two s. one d.; ed Upper Canada Coll. and Cambridge Univ.; served with Canadian Air Force during Second World War; in Editorial Dept, Timmins Daily Press, Timmins, Ont. 1947; Advertising Dept Galt Reporter 1948–50, Gen. Man. 1950–53; directed US and Canadian Operations of Thomson Newspapers in Toronto 1953–68; Deputy Chair. Times Newspapers Ltd 1966–67, Chair. 1968–70, Co-Pres. 1971–81; Dir The Thomson Corpn, Chair. The Woodbridge Co. Ltd; Pres. Thomson Works of Art Ltd. *Leisure interests:* collecting paintings and works of art, golf and walking. *Address:* The Thomson Corporation, 65 Queen Street West, Suite 2500, Toronto, Ont., M5H 2M8 (Office); The Thomson Corporation, The Quadrangle, P.O. Box 4YG, 180 Wardour Street, London WIA 4YG, England (Office); 8 Castle Frank Road, Toronto, Ont., M4W 2Z4, Canada (Home); 8 Kensington Palace Gardens, London, W.8, England (Home). *Telephone:* 364-8700 (Canada) (Office); (20) 7437-9787 (England) (Office). *Website:* www.thomson.com (Office).

THOMSON OF MONIFIETH, Baron (Life Peer), cr. 1977, of Monifieth in the District of the City of Dundee; **George Morgan Thomson,** KT, PC, FRTS, FRSE; British politician and journalist; b. 16 Jan. 1921, Stirling, Scotland; s. of late James Thomson; m. Grace Jenkins 1948; two d.; ed Grove Acad., Dundee; Royal Air Force 1940–45; Ed. Forward 1946–53; MP 1952–72; Chair. Commonwealth Educ. Council 1959–64; Chair. Parl. Group for World Govt 1962–64; Minister of State, Foreign Office 1964–66, Jan.–Aug. 1967; Chancellor of Duchy of Lancaster 1966–67; Sec. of State for Commonwealth Affairs 1967–68; Minister without Portfolio 1968–69; Chancellor of Duchy of Lancaster and Deputy Foreign Sec. (with special responsibility for European Affairs and Common Market negotiations) 1969–70; Opposition Spokesman on Defence 1970–72; Chair. Standing Conf. of British Refugee Orgs. 1971–72, David Davies Memorial Inst. 1971–77, Labour Cttee for Europe 1972–73, European Movement 1977–79; mem. Comm. of European Communities, with special responsibility for Regional Policy 1973–76; First Crown Estate Commr

1977–80; Chair. Advertising Standards Authority 1977–80; Deputy Chair. Ind. Broadcasting Authority 1980–81, Chair. 1981–88; mem. SLD 1989–; Vice-Pres. Royal TV Soc. 1982–89; Chair. Franco-British Council 1979–81, Anglo-Romanian Round Table 1979–81; Chancellor, Heriot-Watt Univ. 1977–92; Chair. Value & Income Investment Trust; Dir ICI 1977–89, Royal Bank of Scotland 1977–90, Woolwich Equitable Bldg Soc. (Sr Vice-Chair. 1988–90); Pres. History of Advertising Trust 1985–2001, Prix Italia 1989–91; Dir English Nat. Opera 1987–92; Chair. Suzy Lamplugh Trust 1990–92; Trustee Thomson Foundation; mem. Standing Cttee Standards in Public Life 1994–97; Chair. Leeds Castle Foundation 1994–2001; Scottish Peers Asscn 1996–98; Hon. LLD (Dundee) 1967, DLitt (Heriot-Watt) 1973, (New Univ. of Ulster) 1984; Hon. DSc (Aston) 1976, (Loughborough) 1980; Hon. DCL (Kent) 1989. *Leisure interests:* swimming, hill walking. *Address:* House of Lords, London, SW1A 0PW, England.

THONEMANN, Peter Clive, MSc, DPhil; British physicist and emeritus professor; b. 3 June 1917, Melbourne, Australia; s. of Frederick Emil Thonemann and Mabel Jessie Thonemann; one s. one d.; ed Univs. of Melbourne and Sydney and Trinity Coll., Oxford; Commonwealth Research Scholar Sydney Univ. 1944–46; ICI Fellow, Clarendon Lab., Oxford; proposed principles and initiated research for a fusion reactor, 1946–49; Head of Research on Controlled Thermonuclear Reactions, AERE, Harwell 1949–60, designed and built prototype fusion reactor Zeta, Deputy Dir, Culham Lab. of the Atomic Energy Authority 1965–66; Prof. of Physics and Head of Dept, Univ. Coll. of Swansea (now Univ. of Wales Swansea) 1968–84. *Leisure interests:* physics, musical composition. *Address:* 130 Bishopston Road, Swansea, SA3 3EU, Wales. *Telephone:* (1792) 232669.

THORBURN, Cliff(ord) Charles Devlin, CM; Canadian snooker player; b. 16 Jan. 1948, Victoria, BC; s. of James Thorburn and Adel Hanna Thorburn; m. 1981; two s.; World Professional Champion 1980; 27 tournament wins (worldwide); winner 13 Canadian Championships; first player in World Professional Championship to make a 147 break (Crucible Theatre, Sheffield) 1983; Canadian Snooker Hall of Fame 1990, mem. Canada's Sports Hall of Fame. *Publications:* Cliff Thorburn's Snooker Skills, Playing for Keeps (autobiog.). *Leisure interests:* golf, chess, reading. *Address:* 31 West Side Drive, Markham, Ontario, Canada. *Website:* www.thorburn-wych-.on.ca (Office).

THORENS, Justin Pierre, DenD; Swiss professor of law and attorney-at-law; b. 15 Sept. 1931, Collonge-Bellerive; s. of Paul L. Thorens and Germaine Falquet; m. Colette F. Vecchio 1963; one s. one d.; ed Univ. of Geneva, Freie Univ. Berlin and Univ. Coll. London; attorney-at-law, Geneva Bar 1956–; Alt. Pres. Jurisdictional Court, Geneva 1971–78; Lecturer, Faculty of Law, Univ. of Geneva 1967, Assoc. Prof. 1970, Prof. 1973–96, Dean 1974–77, Hon. Prof. 1996–; Rector, Univ. of Geneva 1977–83; Visiting Scholar, Stanford and Calif. (Berkeley) Univs. 1983–84; Guest Prof. Univ. of Munich 1984; mem. Cttee European Centre for Higher Educ. (CEPES), Bucharest 1981–95, Pres. 1986–88; mem. Admin. Council Asscn des Universités Partiellement ou Entièrement de Langue Française (AUPELF), Montreal 1978–87, Vice-Pres. 1981–87, Hon. Vice-Pres. 1987–, mem. Gov. Council 1987–; Pres. Bd Int. Asscn of Univs (AIU), Paris 1985–90, Hon. Pres. 1990–; mem. Council UN Univ. Tokyo 1986–92, Pres. 1988–89; mem. UNESCO Swiss Nat. Comm. 1989–2001, Int. Acad. of Estate and Trust Law; Pres. Latsis Int. Foundation 1989–; various prizes, awards and distinctions. *Publications:* publs on pvt. law, civil procedure, arbitration, Anglo-American property law, univ. politics, cultural questions. *Leisure interests:* history and all its aspects, both European and the rest of the world; interaction of cultures of various times and regions. *Address:* 18 chemin du Nant d'Aisy, 1246 Corsier (Geneva), Switzerland. *Telephone:* (22) 7518081 (Office); (22) 7511262 (Home). *Fax:* (22) 7518082 (Office and Home). *E-mail:* etude.jthorens@bluewin.ch (Office); justin.thorens@bluewin.ch (Home).

THORN, Gaston, DenD; Luxembourg politician; b. 3 Sept. 1928, Luxembourg; s. of Edouard Thorn and Suzanne Weber; m. Liliane Petit 1957; one s.; ed Univs. of Montpellier, Lausanne and Paris; admitted to Luxembourg Bar 1955; Pres. Nat. Union of Students, Luxembourg; mem. Legis. 1957–; mem. European Parl. 1959–69, Vice-Pres. Liberal Group; Pres. Democratic Party, Luxembourg 1961–80; Minister of Foreign Affairs and Minister of Foreign Trade 1968–80, also Minister of Physical Educ. and Sport 1968–77, Prime Minister and Minister of State 1974–79, Minister of Econ. Affairs, Small Firms and Traders 1977–80, of Justice 1979–80; Deputy Prime Minister 1979–80; Pres. Comm. of the European Communities 1981–85, also responsible for Secr. Gen., Legal Service, Spokesman's Group, Security and Cultural Affairs; Pres. Int. Liberal Party 1970–82; Pres. of 30th Session of the UN Gen. Ass. 1975–76; Pres. Fed. of Liberal and Democratic Parties of European Community 1976–80; Chair. Banque Int., Luxembourg 1985–; Pres. Mouvement Européen Int. 1985; Pres., Dir-Gen. RTL Luxembourg 1985–, Pres. 1987–; Chair., CEO CLT Multi-Media 1987–93, Chair. CLT-UFA SA Group 1997–; Pres. Centre of European Studies, Strasbourg 1994; numerous decorations. *Leisure interests:* lecturing, tennis, golf. *Address:* 1 rue de la Forge, Luxembourg (Home). *Telephone:* 420-77 (Home).

THORN, George Widmer, MD; American physician; b. 15 Jan. 1906, Buffalo, NY; s. of George W. Thorn and Fanny R. (Widmer) Thorn; m. 1st Doris Weston 1931 (died 1984); one s.; m. 2nd Claire Steinert 1985 (died 1990); ed Coll. of Wooster, Ohio; House Officer, Millard Fillmore Hosp., Buffalo (NY) 1929–30; Asst Univ. of Buffalo 1931–34; Rockefeller Fellow in Medicine,

Harvard Medical School and Mass. Gen. Hosp. 1934–35; Asst Prof. Dept of Physiology, Ohio State Univ. 1935–36; Assoc. Prof. of Medicine, Johns Hopkins Medical School, Assoc. Physician Johns Hopkins Hosp. 1936–42; Physician-in-Chief, Peter Bent Brigham Hosp., Hersey Prof. of Theory and Practice of Physic, Harvard Univ. 1942–72, Emer. 1972–; Samuel A. Levine Prof. of Medicine, Harvard Medical School 1967–72, Emer. 1972–; Dir of Research, Howard Hughes Medical Inst. 1956–78, mem. Exec. Cttee 1978–, Chair. Medical Advisory Bd 1978–, Pres. 1981–84, Chair. Bd Dirs and Trustee 1984–; mem. Corpn and of Exec. Cttee of Corpn of MIT 1965–; First Wingate Johnson Visiting Prof., Bowman Gray School of Medicine, Wake Forest Univ. 1972; Consultant US Public Health Service etc.; Fellow, Royal College of Physicians, London; mem. Nat. Advisory Cttee on Radiation; Trustee, Diabetic Fund; Chair. Scientific Review Bd, Whitaker Foundation Biomed. Eng, Bd, Hippocrates Int. Medical Foundation; mem. Royal Acad. of Medicine (Belgium), Norwegian Medical Soc., Swedish Medical Soc.; First Lilly Lecturer, Royal Coll. of Physicians, London 1966; Hon. mem. Soc. Colombiana de Endocrinología (Bogotá), Royal Soc. of Medicine (Great Britain); numerous awards including John Philips Memorial Award (American Coll. of Physicians) 1955, Modern Medicine Award 1961, George Minot Award (American Medical Asscn) 1963, Robert H. Williams Award (Asscn of Profs. of Medicine) 1972; Commdr Order of Hipólito Unanue (Peru), Public Welfare Medal, NAS 1997. *Leisure interests:* tennis, arboretum. *Address:* Howard Hughes Medical Institute, 320 Longwood Avenue, Enders 661, Boston, MA 02115; 16 Gurney Street, Cambridge, MA 02138, USA. *Telephone:* (617) 876-1230.

THORNBURGH, Dick, BEng, LLB; American lawyer; b. 16 July 1932, Pittsburgh; s. of Charles G. Thornburgh and Alice Sanborn; m. Virginia W Judson 1963; four s.; ed Yale Univ. and Univ. of Pittsburgh; admitted to Pa Bar 1958, US Supreme Court Bar 1965; attorney, Kirkpatrick & Lockhart LLP, Pittsburgh 1959–79, 1977–79, 1987–88, 1994–; US attorney for Western Pa, Pittsburgh 1969–75; Asst Attorney-Gen. Criminal Div. US Justice Dept 1975–77; Gov. of Pennsylvania 1979–87; Dir Inst. of Politics, J.F. Kennedy School of Govt, Harvard Univ. 1987–88; Attorney-Gen. of USA 1988–91; Under Sec. Gen. for Admin. and Man. UN 1992–93; Chair. State Science and Tech. Inst., Legal Policy Advisory Bd, Washington Legal Foundation; Vice-Chair. World Cttee on Disability; Fellow, American Bar Foundation; mem. American Judicature Soc., Council on Foreign Relations; Trustee Urban Inst., Nat. Acad. of Public Admin.; Republican; 30 hon. degrees; Special Medallion Award, Fed. Drug Enforcement Admin. 1973, Distinguished Service Medal, American Legion 1992. *Publications:* articles in professional journals. *Address:* Kirkpatrick and Lockhart LLP, 1800 Massachusetts Avenue, NW, Washington, DC 20036-1800, USA.

THORNE, Kip Stephen, PhD; American research physicist, university professor and writer; b. 1 June 1940, Logan, Utah; s. of David Wynne Thorne and Alison Comish; m. 1st Linda Jeanne Peterson 1960 (divorced 1977); one s. one d.; m. 2nd Carolee Joyce Winstein 1984; ed Calif. Inst. of Tech. and Princeton Univ.; Postdoctoral Fellow, Princeton Univ. 1965–66; Research Fellow in Physics, Calif. Inst. of Tech. 1966–67, Assoc. Prof. of Theoretical Physics 1967–70, Prof. 1970–, William R. Kenan Jr Prof. 1981–91; Feynman Prof. of Theoretical Physics 1991–; Adjunct Prof. of Physics, Univ. of Utah 1971–98; Fulbright Lecturer, France 1966; Visiting Prof., Moscow Univ. 1969, 1975, 1978, 1981, 1982, 1986, 1988, 1990, 1998; Andrew D. White Prof.-at-Large, Cornell Univ. 1986–92; Chair. Topical Group on Gravity of American Physical Soc. 1997–98; Alfred P. Sloan Research Fellow 1966–68; Guggenheim Fellow 1967; mem. Int. Cttee on Gen. Relativity and Gravitation 1971–80, 1992–, Cttee on US-USSR Co-operation in Physics 1978–79, Space Science Bd, NASA 1980–83; Fellow American Acad. of Arts and Sciences, American Physical Soc., AAAS; Foreign mem. Russian Acad. of Sciences 1999; mem. American Philosophical Soc. 1999; mem. NAS 1973; Hon. DSc (Ill. Coll.) 1979, (Glasgow) 2001; Dr. hc (Moscow State Univ.) 1981; American Inst. of Physics Science Writing Award in Physics and Astronomy 1967 and 1994, Julius Edgar Lilienfeld Prize; American Physical Soc. 1996, Karl Schwarzschild Medal, German Astronomical Soc. 1996, Robinson Prize in Cosmology, Univ. of Newcastle 2002. *Publications:* (co-author) Gravitation Theory and Gravitational Collapse 1965, High Energy Astrophysics, Vol. 3 1967, Gravitation 1973, Black Holes: The Membrane Paradigm 1986; (sole author) Black Holes and Time Warps: Einstein's Outrageous Legacy 1994. *Address:* California Institute of Technology, 130-33 Theoretical Astrophysics, 1200 East California Boulevard, Pasadena, CA 91125, USA. *Telephone:* (626) 395-4598. *Fax:* (626) 796 5675. *Website:* www.cco.caltech.edu/~kip (Office).

THORNTON, Billy Bob; American actor, director and writer; b. 4 Aug. 1955, Hot Springs, Ariz; m. Angelina Jolie (q.v.) 2000; one adopted s. *Films include:* Sling Blade (also dir, screenplay; Acad. Award for Best Adapted Screenplay 1996, Chicago Film Critics Award for Best Actor, Independent Spirit Awards), U-Turn 1997, A Thousand Miles 1997, The Apostle 1997, A Gun A Car A Blonde, Primary Colors 1997, Homegrown 1998, Armageddon 1998, A Simple Plan 1998, Pushing Tin 1998, The Man Who Wasn't There 2001, Bandits 2001. *Television:* The 1,000 Chains, Don't Look Back (actor, writer), The Outsiders (series), Hearts Afire. *Address:* c/o William Morris Agency, 151 S. El Camino Drive, Beverly Hills, CA 90212 (Office); c/o Miramax, 7966 Beverly Boulevard, Los Angeles, CA 90048, USA.

THORNTON, Clive Edward Ian, CBE, LLB, BA, FCIB; British lawyer and business executive; b. 12 Dec. 1929, Newcastle upon Tyne; s. of Albert Thornton and Margaret Thornton; m. Maureen Crane 1956; one s. one d.; ed St Anthony's School and Coll. of Commerce, Newcastle upon Tyne and Coll.

of Law, London; articled, Kenneth Hudson, Solicitor, London 1959; Solicitor to Cassel Arenz (merchant bankers), London 1964; Chief Solicitor, Abbey Nat. Bldg Soc. 1967, Deputy Chief Gen. Man. 1978, Chief Gen. Man. 1979–83, Dir 1980–83; Chair. Commerce and Industry Group, The Law Soc. 1974–75; mem. Council, Bldg Socs. Asscn 1979–83, Housing Corpn 1980–86; Chair. Shelter Housing Aid Centre 1983–86, Mirror Group of Newspapers Jan.–July 1984, Thorndale Farm 1984–, Financial Weekly Ltd 1984–87, Thamesmead Town Ltd 1986–90, Gabriel Communications Ltd 1986–96, Universe Publs 1986–96, Armstrong Capital Holdings Ltd 1988–; Dir Investment Data Services 1986–90, Melton Mowbray Building Soc. 1988–, (Chair. 1991–), LHW Futures 1988–96, Burgon Hall Ltd 1988–96; Council mem., St Mary's Hosp. Medical School 1986–96; Partner, Stoneham Langton and Passmore (int. lawyers) 1984–88; Solicitor of Supreme Court. *Publications:* Building Society Law: Cases and Materials 1975, 1989, History of Devon Cattle 1999. *Leisure interests:* antique collecting, music, reading, breeding Devon cattle. *Address:* Lansbury House, 3 St Mary's Place, Stamford, Lincs., PE9 2DN; Keythorpe Grange, East Norton, Leics., LE7 9XL; Belford Hall, Belford, Northumberland, England. *Telephone:* (1162) 598201 (East Norton); (1668) 213667 (Belford).

THORNTON, Janet Maureen, CBE, PhD, FRS; British professor of molecular biology; b. 23 May 1949; d. of Stanley James McLoughlin and Kathleen Barlow; m. Alan Thornton 1970; one s. one d.; ed Nottingham Univ., King's Coll. London, Nat. Inst. of Medical Research; tutor Open Univ. 1976–83; molecular pharmacologist Nat. Inst. of Medical Research 1978; Science and Eng Research Council Advanced Fello79–83, lecturer 1983–89, Sr lecturer 1989–90, Bernal Chair. of Crystallography 1996–; Dir Biomolecular Structure and Modelling Unit, Univ. Coll. London 1990–, Prof. of Biomolecular Structure 1990–; consultant European Molecular Biology Lab., European Bioinformatics Inst. (EMBL–EBI) 1994–2000, Dir EMBL-EBI 2000–; Head Jt Research School in Molecular Sciences, Univ. Coll. London and Birkbeck Coll. 1996–2000; Hon. Prof. Dept of Chem., Fellow of Churchill Coll., Univ. of Cambridge; Hans Neurath Award, Protein Soc. (USA) 2000. *Publications:* numerous articles in scientific journals. *Leisure interests:* reading, music, gardening, walking. *Address:* EMBL-EBI, Wellcome Trust Genome Campus, Hinxton, Cambridge CB10 1SD, UK (Office). *Telephone:* (1223) 494444 (Office). *Fax:* (1223) 494468 (Office). *E-mail:* thornton@ebi.ac.uk (Office).

THORNTON, John L.; American business executive; b. 2 Jan. 1954, New York; ed Hotchkiss School, Harvard Coll., Oxford Univ., Yale School of Org. and Man.; joined Goldman Sachs 1980, f. and built merger and acquisition business for co. in Europe 1983–91, partner 1988 with exec. responsibility for operations in Europe, Middle East and Africa, mem. Bd of Dirs. 1996, Pres., Co-COO 1999–2003; Prof. Tsinghua Univ., China 2003–; mem. Audit Cttee, Org. Review and Nominating Cttee. *Address:* Tsinghua University, 1 Qinghuayuan, Beijing 100084, People's Republic of China (Office). *Telephone:* (10) 62782015 (Office). *Fax:* (10) 62770349 (Office). *E-mail:* info@tsinghua.edu.cn (Office). *Website:* www.tsinghua.edu.cn (Office).

THORPE, Ian; Australian swimmer; b. 13 Oct. 1982, Sydney; s. of Kenneth William Thorpe and Margaret Grace Thorpe; ed East Hills Boys Technical High School; world freestyle long-course record holder for 200m, 400m, 800m; winner 3 Olympic gold medals, 2 silver medals 2000; set new world record in 400m freestyle and 4x200m relay; winner 8 World Championship gold medals 1998–2001; won six gold medals and broke own 400m freestyle world record Commonwealth Games, Manchester 2002; won five gold medals Pan-Pacific Games, Yokohama, Japan 2002; world-record holder for 200, 400, 800m long course and as mem. of 4x100m and 4x200m relay teams; numerous awards including NSW Athlete of the Year 1998, three times Australian Swimmer of the Year, four times World Swimmer of the Year, Swimming World Magazine 1998, 1999, Male Athlete of the Year, Australian Sports Awards 2000, Young Australian of the Year 2000, The Sport Australia Hall of Fame's "Don Award" 2000, Jesse Owens American Int. Athlete Trophy Award 2001, China Sports Daily's Most Popular World Athlete 2002. *Achievements:* Ian Thorpe's Fountain for Youth Trust launched by Australian Prime Minister John Howard. *Publications:* The Journey, Live Your Dreams. *Leisure interests:* surfing, cooking, movies, dinner, water skiing, computer games, music, TV. *Address:* c/o Grand Slam International Pty Ltd, P.O. Box 402, Manly, NSW 1655, Australia (Office). *Telephone:* (2) 9976-0844 (Office). *Fax:* (2) 9976-0767 (Office). *E-mail:* gsi@grandslamint.com (Office).

THORPE, James, MA, PhD, LittD, LHD, LLD, HHD; American literary scholar; b. 17 Aug. 1915, Aiken, SC; s. of J. Ernest Thorpe and Ruby H. Holloway; m. Elizabeth M. Daniells 1941; one s. one d.; ed The Citadel, Charleston, SC, Univ. of N Carolina and Harvard Univ.; Col, USAF 1941–46; Prof. of English, Princeton Univ. 1946–66; Dir Huntington Library, Art Gallery and Botanical Gardens 1966–83, Sr Research Assoc. 1966–99, Dir Emer. 1983–; Pres. Soc. for Textual Scholarship; Guggenheim Fellow 1949–50, 1965–66; Fellow, American Philosophical Soc., AAAS, American Antiquarian Soc.; Bronze Star Medal. *Publications:* Rochester's Poems 1950, Etherege's Poems 1963, Literary Scholarship 1964, Principles of Textual Criticism 1972, Use of Manuscripts in Literary Research 1974, Gifts of Genius 1980, A Word to the Wise 1982, John Milton: The Inner Life 1983, The Sense of Style: Reading English Prose 1987, Henry Edwards Huntington: A Biography 1994, Henry Edwards Huntington: A Brief Biography 1996, A Pleasure of Proverbs 1996, Proverbs for Friends 1997, Proverbs for Thinkers 1998, Poems Written at the Hun-

tington Library 2000. *Leisure interest:* walking. *Address:* Duncaster T-320, 20 Loeffler Road, Bloomfield, CT 06002, USA (Home). *Telephone:* (860) 726-2174 (Home).

THORPE, Rt Hon (John) Jeremy, PC; British politician; b. 29 April 1929; m. 1st Caroline Allpass 1968 (died 1970); one s.; m. 2nd Maria (Marion) Stein, fmr Countess of Harewood, 1973; ed Rectory School, Conn., Eton Coll. and Trinity Coll., Oxford; Barrister, Inner Temple 1954; MP for N Devon 1959–79; Treas. UN Parl. Group 1962–67; Hon. Treas. Liberal Party 1965–67, Leader 1967–76; Pres. N Devon Liberal Asscn 1987–; Consultant, Stramit; Chair. Jeremy Thorpe Assocs Ltd 1984–; Hon. Fellow, Trinity Coll. Oxford Univ.; Hon. DCL, Exeter Univ. *Publications:* To All Who Are Interested in Democracy 1951, Europe: The Case for Going In 1971, In My Own Time (autobiog.) 1999. *Leisure interests:* collecting Chinese ceramics. *Address:* 2 Orme Square, Bayswater, London, W2 4RS, England.

THORPE, Nigel James, CVO, BA; British diplomatist; b. 3 Oct. 1945; three d.; ed East Grinstead Co. Grammar School, Cardiff Univ.; joined Diplomatic Service 1969, with Embassy, Warsaw 1970–72, High Comm., Dhaka 1973–74; at FCO, London 1975–79, High Comm., Ottawa 1979–81; seconded to Dept of Energy, London 1981–82; Deputy Head Southern Africa Dept, FCO 1982–85; Deputy Head of Mission, Warsaw 1985–88; Deputy High Commr, Harare 1989–92; Head Cen. European Dept, FCO 1992–96; Sr Directing Staff, Royal Coll. of Defence Studies, London 1996–98; Amb. to Hungary 1998–2003. *Publication:* Harmincad Utca 6: A Twentieth Century History of Budapest. *Leisure interests:* family, his dog, music. *Address:* c/o Foreign and Commonwealth Office, King Charles Street, London, SW1A 2AH, England.

THOULESS, David James, PhD, FRS; American (b. British) physicist; b. 21 Sept. 1934, Bearsden, Scotland; s. of Robert Thouless and Priscilla (née Gorton) Thouless; m. Margaret Scrase 1958; two s. one d.; ed Winchester Coll., Trinity Hall, Cambridge, Cornell Univ.; Physicist, Lawrence Radiation Lab., Berkeley 1958–59; ICI Research Fellow, Birmingham Univ. 1959–61, Prof. of Mathematical Physics 1965–79; Lecturer at Cambridge and Fellow of Churchill Coll. 1961–65, Royal Soc. Research Prof. and Fellow of Clare Hall, Cambridge 1983–86; Prof. of Applied Science, Yale Univ. 1979–80; Prof. of Physics, Univ. of Washington 1980–; mem. NAS 1995; Fellow American Acad. of Arts and Sciences 1980, American Physical Soc. 1987; Maxwell Prize 1973, Holweck Medal 1980, Fritz London Award 1984, Wolf Prize for Physics 1990, Dirac Prize 1993, Onsager Prize 2000. *Publications:* Quantum Mechanics of Many-Body Systems 1961, Topological Quantum Numbers in Nonrelativistic Physics 1998. *Address:* Department of Physics, Box 351560, University of Washington, Seattle, WA 98195, USA. *Telephone:* (206) 685-2393.

THRANE, Hans Erik, MEcon; Danish diplomatist; b. 14 April 1918, Copenhagen; s. of Julius Peter Thrane and Frieda Jensen; m. Gerda Boye 1941; two s.; ed Copenhagen Univ.; Danish Foreign Service 1945–88; Econ. Attaché, Paris 1948–52; Ministry of Foreign Affairs, Copenhagen 1952–56; Econ. Counsellor, Washington 1956–59; Alt. Exec. Dir, IBRD (World Bank) 1958–59; Ministry of Foreign Affairs, Copenhagen 1959–66, Minister 1962, Asst Under-Sec. of State for Econ. Affairs 1964; Amb. and Perm. Rep. EFTA and Perm. Rep. to UN Office and other int. orgs in Geneva 1966–74; Chair. Council, GATT 1968–71; Amb. to Norway 1974–79, to Switzerland 1980–86, to the Holy See 1982–86; Ministry of Foreign Affairs 1986–88; mem. Bd of Dirs, Nordic Investment Bank 1986–92, (Chair. 1988–90), Nordic Devt Fund for the Western North 1987–92. *Leisure interests:* sailing, skiing, mountaineering, modern art. *Address:* Rude Vang 53, 2840 Holte, Denmark.

THRUSH, Brian Arthur, MA, ScD, FRS; British professor emeritus of physical chemistry; b. 23 July 1928, London; s. of late Arthur Thrush and Dorothy Thrush; m. Rosemary C. Terry 1958; one s. one d.; ed Haberdashers' Aske's Hampstead School and Emmanuel Coll., Cambridge; Univ. Demonstrator, Asst Dir of Research, Lecturer, Reader in Physical Chem. Univ. of Cambridge 1953–78, Prof. of Physical Chem. 1978–95; Head Dept of Chem., Univ. of Cambridge 1988–93; Fellow, Emmanuel Coll., Cambridge 1960–, Vice-Master 1986–90; mem. Natural Environment Research Council 1985–90; Visiting Prof. Chinese Acad. of Sciences 1980–; mem. Council, Royal Soc. 1989–91, Academia Europaea 1992–98; Tilden Lecturer (Royal Soc. of Chem.) 1965; M. Polanyi Medal (Royal Soc. of Chem.) 1980, Rank Prize for Opto-Electronics 1992. *Publications:* papers on spectroscopy, gas reactions and atmospheric chem. in learned journals. *Leisure interests:* wine, gardens. *Address:* Department of Chemistry, University of Cambridge, Lensfield Road, Cambridge, CB2 1EW (Office); Brook Cottage, Pemberton Terrace, Cambridge, CB2 1JA, England (Home). *Telephone:* (1223) 336458 (Office); (1223) 357637 (Home). *Fax:* (1223) 336362.

THUBRON, Colin Gerald Dryden, FRSL; British author; b. 14 June 1939, London; s. of Brig. Gerald Ernest Thubron and Evelyn Kate Dryden; ed Eton Coll.; mem. Editorial Staff, Hutchinson & Co. Publishers Ltd 1959–62; freelance documentary film maker 1963–64; Production Ed., The Macmillan Co., USA 1964–65; freelance author 1965–; Hon. DLitt (Warwick) 2002; Silver Pen Award of PEN 1985, Thomas Cook Award 1988, Hawthornden Prize 1988, Mungo Park Medal, Royal Scottish Geographical Soc. 2000, Lawrence of Arabia Medal, Royal Soc. of Asian Affairs 2001. *Scenario:* The Prince of the Pagodas (ballet at The Royal Opera House, Covent Garden). *Publications:* Mirror to Damascus, The Hills of Adonis, Jerusalem, Journey into Cyprus, The God in the Mountain (novel), Emperor (novel), Among the Russians, A Cruel Madness (novel), Behind the Wall, Falling (novel), Turning Back the

Sun (novel), The Lost Heart of Asia, Distance (novel), In Siberia, To the Last City. *Address:* Garden Cottage, 27 St Ann's Villas, London, W11, England. *Telephone:* (20) 7602-2522.

THULIN, Ingrid; Swedish actress and director; b. 27 Jan. 1929, Sollefteå; d. of Adam Thulin and Nanna Larsson; m. 1st Claes Sylwander 1951; m. 2nd Harry Schein 1956; ed Royal Dramatic Theatre School, Stockholm; has appeared in many modern and classical plays for Royal Dramatic Theatre, Stockholm and for municipal theatres of Malmö and Stockholm until 1962; has also appeared on Broadway, the Italian stage and US TV; many nat. and int. awards. *Films include:* When Love Comes to the Village 1950, Wild Strawberries 1957, So Close to Life 1958, The Face 1958, The Judge 1960, The Four Horsemen of the Apocalypse 1961, Winter Light 1962, The Silence 1963, La guerre est finie 1968, The Damned 1970, Cries and Whispers 1973, A Handful of Love 1974, La cage 1975, Cassandra Crossing 1976, Agnes Will Die 1977, One and One 1978, The Rehearsal, Il Corsario 1983, La Casa Sorire 1991, Rabbit Face; wrote and directed feature film Broken Skies 1983. *Publication:* Någon jag kände (Somebody I Knew) 1993. *Address:* Kevingestrand 7B, 18257 Danderyd, Sweden; 00060 Sacrofano di Roma, Italy. *Telephone:* (8) 755-68-98 (Sweden); (06) 9084171 (Italy).

THUN, Matteo; Italian designer; b. 1952, Bozen; ed Univ. of Florence; co.-f. and fmr partner Sottsass Associati, Milan; co.-f. Memphis Group; f. own studio 1984; Applied Art Chair., Vienna; recipient of six awards for design 1987–96.

THUNBORG, Anders; Swedish diplomatist; b. 9 June 1934, Stockholm; m. Ingalill Thunborg; three s. two d.; Organizing Sec. of Stockholm branch, Social Democratic Party 1958, transferred to party Exec. 1960, later Information Sec. and then Int. Sec.; Asst Party Sec. 1967–69; Under-Sec. of State, Ministry of Defence 1969–74, Ministry of Foreign Affairs 1974–76; Perm. Rep. to UN 1977–83; Chair. UN Trust Fund SA 1977–82; Vice-Chair. UN Comm. on Decolonization 1978–79; Chair. UN Study Group on Nuclear Weapons 1979–82; Minister of Defence 1983–85; Amb. to USSR and Mongolia 1986–89, to USA 1989–93, to Greece 1993; Consultant, Ministry of Foreign Affairs 1994–95; Amb. to the Holy See 1996–99; mem. Int. Steering Bd, The Southeast European Legal Devt. Initiative. *Publications:* a number of books, handbooks and essays mainly on int. affairs and defence policy. *Address:* c/o Ministry of Foreign Affairs, Gustav Adolfstorg 1, P.O. Box 16121, 103 39 Stockholm, Sweden (Office).

THURAU, Klaus Walther Christian, MD; German physiologist; b. 14 June 1928, Bautzen; s. of Walther Thurau and Helene Engel; m. Antje Wiese 1957; two s.; ed High School, Berlin and Univs. of Erlangen and Kiel; Lecturer in Physiology, Univ. of Göttingen 1955–65; Chair. Dept of Physiology, Univ. of Munich 1968–; Visiting Prof. American Heart Asscn 1964; Gilman Prof., Dartmouth Medical School 1968; Visiting Prof., American Kidney Foundation 1980; Pres. Int. Soc. of Nephrology; Treas. and Councillor Int. Union of Physiological Science; mem. Exec. Bd Int. Council of Scientific Unions; Chair. Verum-Foundation, German UNESCO Comm. on Natural Sciences; mem. German Physiological Soc., Soc. for Clinical Investigation, American Soc. of Physiology, Int. Soc. for Hypertension, Int. Soc. of Nephrology; Emer. Ed. European Journal of Physiology (Pflügers Archiv.); Hon. mem. Australian Soc. of Nephrology, S. African Soc. of Nephrology, Int. Soc. of Nephrology, Heidelberg Acad. of Sciences, Acad. Europaea, London; Dr hc; Civil Service Cross 1st Class, Germany, Homer Smith Award. *Publications:* various papers on renal function (in medical journals). *Leisure interest:* music. *Address:* Department of Physiology, 12 Pettenkaferstr., 80336 Munich (Office); Josef-Vötterstrasse 6, 81545 Munich, Germany (Home). *Telephone:* (89) 5996558 (Office); (89) 6422618 (Home). *Fax:* (89) 5996532 (Office); (89) 64254517 (Home). *E-mail:* thurau@physiol.med.uni-muenchen.de (Office).

THURLEY, Simon John, MA, PhD; British foundation executive and museum administrator; b. 29 Aug. 1962; s. of the late Thomas Manley Thurley and Rachel Thurley (née House); ed Kimbolton School, Bedford Coll., London and Courtauld Inst.; Insp. of Ancient Monuments, Crown Buildings and Monuments Group, English Heritage 1988–90; Curator Royal Historic Palaces 1990–97; Dir Museum of London 1997–2002; Chief Exec. English Heritage March 2002–; mem. Cttee, Soc. for Court Studies 1996–; Adviser, Council of Royal Collection Studies 1996–, Cttee Lambeth Palace Chapel 1999–; Pres. City of London Archaeological Soc. 1997–2002; mem. Metropolitan History Advisory Cttee; Editorial Adviser, The London Journal 1997–, Journal of British Art, BBC History Magazine; Trustee Dickens House Museum 1998–2002. *Publications:* Henry VIII: Images of a Tudor King (jt author) 1989, The Royal Palaces of Tudor England 1993, Whitehall Palace 2000; frequent contribs to historical publs. *Leisure interest:* ancient buildings. *Address:* English Heritage, 23 Savile Row, London, W1X 1AB, England (Office).

THURLOW, 8th Baron, cr. 1792; **Francis Edward Hovell-Thurlow-Cumming-Bruce,** KCMG; British diplomatist; b. 9 March 1912, London; s. of 6th Baron Thurlow and Grace Catherine Trotter; m. Yvonne Diana Aubyn Wilson 1949 (died 1990); two s. (one deceased) two d.; ed Shrewsbury School and Trinity Coll., Cambridge; Asst Prin., Dept of Agric. for Scotland 1935–37, Dominions Office 1937; Asst Sec. Office of UK High Commr in New Zealand 1939–44, in Canada 1944–46; Prin. Pvt. Sec. to Sec. of State 1946–48; Asst Sec. Commonwealth Relations Office (CRO) 1948; Head of Political Div., UK High Commr in India 1949–52; Establishment Officer, CRO 1952–54, Head of Commodities Dept 1954–55; Adviser on External Affairs to Gov. of Gold

Coast 1955–57, Deputy High Commr for UK in Ghana 1957–58; Asst Under-Sec. of State, CRO 1958; Deputy High Commr for UK in Canada 1958–59, High Commr in New Zealand 1959–63, in Nigeria 1964–66; Gov. and C-in-C Bahamas 1968–72; KStJ 1969. *Address:* 102 Leith Mansions, Grantully Road, London, W9 1LJ; Philham Water, Hartland, Bideford, N Devon, EX39 6EZ, England. *Telephone:* (20) 7289-9664 (London); (1237) 441433 (Bideford). *Fax:* (20) 7289-9664. *E-mail:* francisthurlow@compuserve.com (Home).

THURMAN, Uma; American actress; b. 29 April 1970, Boston; d. of Robert Thurman and Nena Schlebrugge; m. 1st Gary Oldman (q.v.) 1991 (divorced 1992); m. 2nd Ethan Hawke (q.v.) 1997; one d.; worked as model. *Films:* The Adventures of Baron Munchhausen 1988, Dangerous Liaisons 1988, Even Cowgirls Get the Blues, Final Analysis, Where the Heart Is, Henry and June, Mad Dog and Glory 1993, Pulp Fiction 1994, Robin Hood, Dylan, A Month by the Lake 1995, The Truth About Cats and Dogs 1996, Batman and Robin 1997, Gattaca 1997, The Avengers 1998, Les Miserables 1998, Vatel 2000, The Golden Bowl 2001, Chelsea Walls 2002. *Television includes:* Hysterical Blindness (Golden Globe for Best Actress in a mini-series or TV movie 2003) 2002. *Address:* c/o Brian Lourd, CAA, 9830 Wilshire Boulevard, Beverly Hills, CA 90212, USA.

THURMOND, Strom; American politician, farmer and lawyer; b. 5 Dec. 1902, Edgefield, SC; s. of J. William Thurmond and Eleanor Gertrude (née Strom) Thurmond; m. 1st Jean Crouch 1947 (died 1960); m. 2nd Nancy Moore 1968 (separated 1991); two s. two d. (one deceased); ed Clemson Coll.; Teacher, S Carolina Schools 1923–29, Supt 1929–33; admitted to the Bar 1930, served as City and County Attorney; State Senator 1933–38; Circuit Judge 1938–46; active service in Europe and Pacific 1942–46; Maj.-Gen. in US Army Reserve (retd); Gov. of S Carolina 1947–51; US Senator from S Carolina 1954–2003; Chair. Senate Judiciary Cttee 1981–87, Ranking Minority mem. 1987–92; Chair. Senate Armed Services Cttee 1995–99; Pres. US Senate Pro Tempore 1981–87, 1995–2003; Trustee, Bob Jones Univ.; Chair. SC Democratic del. and mem. Nat. Exec. Cttee 1948; mem. American Bar Asscn, Clemson Alumni Asscn; Republican; numerous hon. degrees; decorations include Legion of Merit with Oak Leaf Cluster, Bronze Star with "V", Purple Heart, Croix de guerre, Croix de la Couronne, Army Commendation Ribbon, Congressional Medal, Honor Soc. Nat. Patriot's Award 1974, American Legion Distinguished Public Service Award 1975, American Judges Distinguished Service Award 1981, Presidential Citizens Medal 1989, Presidential Medal of Freedom 1993 and numerous other awards. *Address:* c/o US Senate, 217 Russell Senate Office Building, Washington, DC 20510; Aiken, SC 29801, USA (Home).

THWAITE, Anthony (Simon), OBE, MA, FRSL, FSA, DLitt; British writer; b. 23 June 1930, Chester; s. of Hartley Thwaite and Alice Thwaite (née Mallinson); m. Ann Harrop 1955; four d.; ed Kingswood School, Bath, Christ Church, Oxford; Visiting lecturer in English Literature Univ. of Tokyo 1955–57; radio producer BBC 1957–62; Literary Ed. The Listener 1962–65; Asst Prof. of English, Univ. of Libya, Benghazi 1965–67; Literary Ed. New Statesman 1968–72; Co-Ed. Encounter 1973–85; Editorial Dir, Editorial Consultant André Deutsch 1986–95; Hon. DLitt (Hull) 1989; Richard Hillary Memorial Prize 1968; Cholmondeley Award 1983. *Publications:* Philip Larkin: Collected Poems (ed.) 1988, Poems 1953–88 1989, Selected Letters of Philip Larkin (ed.) 1992, Selected Poems 1956–1996 1997, A Different Country: New Poems 2000, Philip Larkin: Further Requirements (ed.) 2001, A Move in the Weather 2003. *Leisure interests:* archaeology, travel. *Address:* The Mill House, Low Tharston, Norfolk, NR15 2YN, England. *Telephone:* (1508) 489569. *Fax:* (1508) 489221.

THYS, Willy Lucien Ghislain; Belgian trade unionist and international organization official; b. 18 July 1943, Le Roeulx; m. Micheline Berteau; three c.; ed FOPES/UCL Inst. for Adult Educ.; shop steward ACV-CSC at Belgian Rail 1963, mem. Exec. Cttee railway workers' fed. in ACV-CSC 1970; Sec.-Gen. Belgian Christian Fed. of Communication and Cultural Workers 1976–87; Nat. Sec. ACV-CSC 1987; Sec.-Gen. World Confed. of Labour (WCL) 1996–. *Address:* World Confederation of Labour, 33 rue de Trèves, 1040 Brussels, Belgium (Office). *Telephone:* (2) 285-47-00 (Office); (67) 63-70-66 (Home). *Fax:* (2) 230-87-22 (Office); (67) 63-80-82 (Home). *E-mail:* willy.thys@cmt-wcl.org (Office); willy.t@skynet.be (Home). *Website:* www.cmt-wcl.org (Office).

TIAN CHENGPING; Chinese administrator; b. 1940; alt. mem. 13th Cen. Cttee CCP 1987–91; a Deputy Sec. CPC 8th Qinghai Prov. Cttee 1988–; mem. 14th CCP Cen. Cttee 1992–97, 15th CCP Cen. Cttee 1997–2002; Gov. of Qinghai Prov. 1993; Sec. CCP Qinghai Prov. Cttee 1997–99, Sec. CCP Shanxi Prov. 1999–. *Address:* c/o Chinese Communist Party Shanxi Provincial Committee, Taiy Yan, Shanxi Province, People's Republic of China (Office).

TIAN CONGMING; Chinese politician; b. May 1943, Fugu, Shaanxi Prov.; ed Beijing Normal Univ.; joined CCP 1965; corresp. Xinhua News Agency Nei Monggol Br., Chief Sec. then Vice-Sec. CCP Nei Monggol Autonomous Region Cttee, Vice-Sec. CCP Tibetan Autonomous Region Cttee 1970–90; Vice-Minister of Radio, Motion Picture and TV 1990–98; Dir State Gen. Admin. of Radio, Motion Picture and TV 1998–2000; Dir Xinhua News Agency 2000–; mem. CCP Cen. Cttee for Discipline Inspection 1992–. *Address:* Xinhua News Agency, 57 Xuanwumen Xidajie, Beijing 100803, People's Republic of China. *Telephone:* (10) 63071114. *Fax:* (10) 63071210. *Website:* www.xinhuanet.com (Office).

TIAN FENGSHAN; Chinese administrator; b. Oct. 1940; joined CCP 1970; mem. CCP Suihua Prefectural Cttee Heilongjiang Prov. 1985–88; Deputy Commr, Prov. Admin. Office 1985–88; alt. mem. 13th CCP Cen. Cttee 1987–91; Sec. CCP Mudanjiang Municipal Cttee 1988–89; Vice-Gov. Heilongjiang Prov. 1989–94, Acting Gov. 1994–95, Gov. 1995–2000; Minister of Land and Natural Resources 2000–; Sec. CCP Harbin Municipal Cttee 1992; alt. mem. 14th CCP Cen. Cttee 1992–97; mem. 15th CCP Cen. Cttee 1997–2002, 16th CCP Cen. Cttee 2002–; Deputy to 8th NPC from Heilongjiang Prov. 1996; Deputy Sec. CCP Heilongjiang Prov. Cttee. *Address:* Ministry of Land and Natural Resources, 37 Guanyingyuanxiqu, Xicheng Qu, Beijing 100035, People's Republic of China (Office). *Telephone:* (10) 66127001 (Office). *Fax:* (10) 66175348 (Office). *Website:* www.mlr.gov.cn (Office).

TIAN JIYUN; Chinese politician; b. June 1929, Feicheng Co., Shandong; joined CCP 1945; Deputy Sec.-Gen. State Council 1981–83, Sec.-Gen. 1983–88; mem. 12th CCP Cen. Cttee 1982–87, 13th CCP Cen. Cttee 1987–92, 14th CCP Cen. Cttee 1992–97, 15th CCP Cen. Cttee 1997–2002; mem. Politburo 1985–; Vice-Premier 1983–93; Head, Commodity Prices Group, State Council 1984–93; mem. Secr. CCP Cen. Cttee 1985–87; Head State Flood Control HQ 1988–93, Cen. Forest Fire Prevention HQ 1987–93; Vice-Chair. Standing Cttee, 8th NPC 1993–98, 9th NPC 1998. *Address:* Standing Committee of National People's Congress, Beijing, People's Republic of China.

TIAN ZENGPEI; Chinese politician; b. 1930, Raoyang Co., Hebei Prov.; Nankai Univ.; Vice-Minister of Foreign Affairs 1988–96; mem. 14th CCP Cen. Cttee 1992–97; Chair. Foreign Affairs Cttee, 9th Nat. Cttee of CPPCC 1998. *Address:* National Committee of Chinese People's Political Consultative Conference, Taipingqiao Street, Beijing, People's Republic of China. *Telephone:* (10) 553831.

TIAN ZHAOWU; Chinese scientist and university administrator; b. 1927, Fuzhou City, Fujian Prov.; ed Xiamen Univ.; mem. Dept of Chem. Academia Sinica 1985–; Pres. of Xiamen Univ. 1986; mem. Standing Cttee 8th CCP Nat. Cttee 1993–; Hon. Nat. Prize of Sciences 1987. *Address:* c/o Xiamen University, Xiamen, Fujian Province, People's Republic of China.

TIBAIJUKA, Anna Kajumulo; Tanzanian agricultural economist; m. (deceased); four c.; ed Swedish Univ. of Agricultural Sciences, Uppsala; Assoc. Prof. Dar-es-Salaam Univ. 1993–98; Founding Chair. Tanzanian Nat. Women's Council; UNCTAD Special Co-ordinator for Least Developed Countries, Landlocked and Small Island Developing Countries 1998–2000; Exec. Dir UN Centre for Human Settlements (Habitat) 2000–, Under-Sec.-Gen. 2002–; Exec. Sec. for Third UN Conf. on Least Developed Countries, Brussels, Belgium 2001. *Address:* P.O. Box 30030, Nairobi, Kenya (Office). *Telephone:* (2) 621234 (Office). *Fax:* (2) 624266 (Office). *E-mail:* habitat@unchs.org (Office). *Website:* www.unchs.org (Office).

TIBERI, Jean, LenD; French politician; b. 30 Jan. 1935, Paris; s. of Charles Tiberi and Hélène Pallavicini; m. Xavière Casanova; two d.; ed Coll. Sainte-Barbe, Lycées Montaigne and Louis-le-Grand and Faculté de Droit, Paris; Acting Judge, Colmar 1958; Deputy Public Prosecutor, Metz 1959, Meaux 1959; Judge, Beauvais 1959, Nantes 1960; Chancellery 1960–63; Dir of Studies, Faculté de Droit, Paris 1961–; Conseiller de Paris 1965–; First Vice-Pres. Conseil de Paris 1983–95; Deputy to Mayor of Paris 1977–83, First Deputy 1983–95; Deputy to Nat. Ass. 1968–; fmr Sec. of State at Ministries of Agric., Industry and Research; Mayor of 5th arrondissement of Paris 1983–95; Sec. Paris RPR 1985–2000; Mayor of Paris 1995–2000. *Publications:* Le quartier latin, Paris capitale des siècles 1988, La nouvelle Athènes, Paris capitale de l'espirit 1992. *Address:* Assemblée Nationale, 75355 Paris (Office); 1 place du Panthéon, 75005 Paris, France (Home).

TICKELL, Sir Crispin (Charles Cervantes), GCMG, KCVO, FRGS, FZS, FGS; British university chancellor and fmr diplomatist; b. 25 Aug. 1930, London; s. of the late Jerrard Tickell and Renée Haynes; m. 1st Chloë Gunn 1954 (divorced 1976); two s. one d.; m. 2nd Penelope Thorne-Thorne 1977; ed Westminster School and Christ Church, Oxford; entered HM Diplomatic Service 1954; served at The Hague 1955–58, Mexico 1958–61, Paris 1964–70; Pvt. Sec. to Chancellor of Duchy of Lancaster 1970–72; Head, Western Orgs. Dept FCO 1972–75; Fellow, Center for Int. Affairs Harvard Univ. 1975–76; Chef de Cabinet to Pres. of Comm. of EC 1977–81; Visiting Fellow, All Souls Coll. Oxford 1981; Amb. to Mexico 1981–83; Deputy Under-Sec. of State FCO 1983–84; Perm. Sec. Overseas Devt Admin. 1984–87; Perm. Rep. to UN 1987–90; Warden Green Coll. Oxford 1990–97; Dir Green Coll. Centre for Environmental Policy and Understanding 1992–; Chancellor Univ. of Kent at Canterbury 1996–; Dir (non-exec.) IBM UK 1990–95 (mem. IBM Advisory Bd 1995–2000), Govett Mexican Horizons Investment 1991–96, Govett American Smaller Companies Trust 1996–98, Govett Enhanced Investment Trust 1999–; mem. Friends Provident Stewardship Cttee. of Reference 1999–; Dir BOC Foundation 1990–; Pres. Royal Geographical Soc. 1990–93, Earth Centre 1996–, Nat. Soc. for Clean Air 1997–99, Gaia Soc. 1998–2001; Chair. Int. Inst. for Environment and Devt 1990–94, Earthwatch Europe 1990–97, Climate Inst. of Washington, DC 1990–2002, Marine Biological Asscn 1990–2001, Advisory Cttee on Darwin Initiative 1992–99; Trustee Nat. History Museum 1991–2001, World Wildlife Fund (UK) 1993–99, Reuters Foundation 2000–; Convenor Govt Panel on Sustainable Devt 1994–2000; mem. Govt Task Force on Urban Regeneration 1998–99, on Potential Risks from Near Earth Objects 2000; Hon. Fellow Westminster School 1993, St Edmund's Coll., Cambridge 1995, Green Coll., Oxford 1997; Dr hc (Univs. of Stirling, E Anglia, Mass., Bristol, Birmingham, Sussex, Westminster, Cran-

field, Loughborough, Sheffield Hallam, East London, Kent, Exeter, Hull, Plymouth, St Andrews, Southampton, Oxford Brookes, Univ. du Littoral Côte d'Opale); Officer, Order of Orange-Nassau (Netherlands), Order of Aztec Eagle with Sash (Mexico). *Publication:* Climatic Change and World Affairs 1977, Mary Anning of Lyme Regis 1996; contribs to many other works. *Leisure interests:* climatology, palaeohistory, art, mountains. *Address:* Ablington Old Barn, Ablington, Cirencester, Glos., GL7 5NU, England. *Telephone:* (1285) 740569. *Fax:* (1285) 740671.

TICKNER, Robert, LLM, BEcons; Australian politician; b. 24 Dec. 1951, Sydney; m. Jody Tickner; one c.; ed Univ. of Sydney; lecturer, Faculty of Business Studies, NSW Inst. of Tech. 1974–78, Faculty of Law 1978–79; Prin. Solicitor, Aboriginal Legal Service, Redfern, Sydney 1979–83; Alderman Sydney City Council 1977–84; MP for Hughes, NSW 1984–96; Minister for Aboriginal and Torres Strait Islander Affairs 1990–96; Office holder Fed. Electorate Council and other Australian Labor Party bodies; Pres. NSW Soc. of Labor Lawyers; Cttee mem. NSW Council for Civil Liberties; Founding Cttee mem. Citizens for Democracy; Convenor Labor Parliamentarians for Nuclear Free Australia; Chair. Parl. Group of Amnesty Int. *Leisure interests:* golf, tennis.

TIDBURY, Sir Charles Henderson, Kt; British company director; b. 26 Jan. 1926, Camberley; s. of the late Brig. O. H. Tidbury, MC and Beryl (née Pearce) Tidbury; m. Anne Russell 1950; two s. three d.; ed Eton Coll.; King's Royal Rifle Corps 1944–52; joined Whitbread & Co. Ltd 1952, a Man. Dir 1959, Chief Exec. 1974, Deputy Chair. 1977, Chair. 1978–84; Chair. Brickwoods Brewery Ltd 1966–71; Dir Whitbread & Co. PLC 1984–88, Whitbread Investment Co. PLC, Barclays PLC 1978–91, Barclays Bank PLC 1985–91, Barclays Bank UK Ltd, Mercantile Group PLC 1988–91, Nabisco Group Ltd 1985–88, Vaux Group PLC 1985–91, ICL (Europe) 1985–94, Pearl Assurance PLC 1985–94, Gales Brewery 1990–96; Deputy Chair. Int. Speciality Chemicals (Inspec) PLC 1994–98; Pres. Inst. of Brewing 1976–78, Vice-Pres. 1978; Chair. Brewers' Soc. 1982–84, Vice-Pres. 1985–; Pres. Shire Horse Soc. 1986–88, British Inst. of Innkeeping 1985–92 (Vice-Pres. 1992–); Chair. Mary Rose Devt Trust 1980–86, William and Mary Tercentenary Trust Ltd 1986–93, Brewing Research Foundation (now Brewing Research Foundation Int.) 1985–93 (Pres. 1993–); mem. Portsmouth and SE Hants. Health Comm. 1992–96, Hants. Enterprise Partnership 1992–; Trustee, Nat. Maritime Museum 1984–96; Gov. Nat. Heart and Chest Hosps. 1988–90, Portsmouth Polytechnic (now Univ.) 1988–96; mem. Centre for Policy Studies 1988–93; Hon. LLD (Portsmouth) 1997. *Leisure interests:* family, sailing, shooting, countryside. *Address:* Crocker Hill Farm, Forest Lane, Wickham, Hants., PO17 5DW, England (Home). *Telephone:* (1329) 833229. *Fax:* (1329) 833229.

TIE NING; Chinese writer; b. 1957, Beijing; d. of Tie Yang and Xu Zhi-ying; Council mem. of Chinese Writers' Asscn 1985–, Vice-Chair. 2001–. *Publications:* Path in the Night 1980, Xiangxue (won Nat. Short Story Prize) 1982, Red Shirt With No Buttons (won Nat. Fiction Prize) 1984, Rose Gate 1988, Cotton Stack 1988, Hay Stack (short stories) 1991, Women's White Night (non-fiction) 1991, Straw Ring (non-fiction) 1992, For Ever and Ever 1999, The Great Bather 2000. *Leisure interests:* music, gourmet cooking. *Address:* 40-2-201 Luo Si-zhuang, Baoding City, Hebei Prov., People's Republic of China. *Telephone:* (312) 34341.

TIEMANN, Susanne, D. JUR.; German lawyer; b. 20 April 1947, Schwandorf; d. of Hermann Bamberg and Anna-Maria Bamberg; m. Burkhard Tiemann 1969; one s. two d.; ed Ludwig-Maximilian Univ. Munich; called to the Bar and est. as lawyer in Munich 1975; lawyer, Cologne 1980; Prof. for Social and Admin. Law Univ. of Bonn, Catholic Univ. of Cologne; mem. Bundestag 1994–; mem. Econ. and Social Cttee of EC 1987–, Chair. 1992–; mem. Bd German Fed. of Liberal Professions 1988–; mem. Exec. Bd and Vice-Pres. European Secr. of the Liberal, Intellectual and Social Professions (SEPLIS) 1988, Pres. 1989–95; Chair. German Taxpayers' Asscn 1992–94; Frauen für Europa Prize 1993. *Address:* OberLänder Ufer 174, 50968 Cologne, Germany. *Telephone:* (221) 9347540. *Fax:* (221) 93475420.

TIEN, Chang-Lin, PhD; Chinese/American academic; b. 24 July 1935, Wuhan, China; s. of Yun Chien and Yun Di (Lee) Tien; m. Di-Hwa Liu 1959; one s. two d.; ed Nat. Univ. of Taiwan, Univ. of Louisville, USA, Univ. of Princeton, USA; acting Asst Prof. Dept of Mechanical Eng Univ. of Calif., Berkeley 1959–60, Asst Prof. 1960–64, Assoc. Prof. 1964–88, Prof. 1968–88, 1990–, A. Martin Berlin Prof. 1987–88, 1990–97, NEC Distinguished Prof. of Eng 1997–, Univ. Prof. 1999–, Dept Chair. 1974–81, Vice-Chancellor for Research 1983–85, Chancellor 1990–97; Exec. Vice-Chancellor Univ. of Calif. at Irvine 1988–90; Chair. Int. Advisory Panel, Univ. of Tokyo Inst. of Ind. Science 1995; Gov. Bd of Dirs, Cttee of 100 1991–; mem. Bd of Dirs Wells Fargo Bank 1991–, AAAS 1992–96, Berkeley Community Foundation 1993–97, Raychem Corpn 1996–; mem. Bd of Trustees, Chiang Industrial Charity Foundation Ltd, Hong Kong 1991–, Princeton Univ. 1991–95, Asia Foundation 1993– (Chair. 1998–), Carnegie Foundation for the Advancement of Teaching 1994–97, US Cttee on Econ. Devt 1994–, Council on Foreign Relations 1996; mem. Aspen Inst. Domestic Strategy Group 1992–97; mem. Nat. Advisory Council, American Soc. for Eng Educ. 1993, Int. Advisory Panel, Nat. Univ. of Singapore 1993; Ed. Int. Journal of Heat and Mass Transfer 1981–, Int. Communications in Heat and Mass Transfer 1981–; Ed.-in-Chief Experimental Heat Transfer 1987–, Microscale Thermophysical Eng 1997–; consultant for numerous industrial, governmental and educational orgs; Guggenheim Fellow 1965; Hon. mem. or fellow of numerous socs including mem. Nat. Acad. of Eng 1976, Fellow Academia Sinica (Taiwan) 1988, Fellow AAAS 1989, Fellow American Acad. of Arts and Sciences 1991; Hon. Prof. at 12 leading univs in China since 1981; 12 hon. doctor's degrees; Heat Transfer Memorial Award 1974, Gustus L. Larson Memorial Award 1975, Thermophysics Award 1977, Max Jakob Memorial Award 1981; asteroid Tien Chang-Lin Star named in his hon. by Int. Astronomy Union 1999; mega oil tanker named in his hon. 2000. *Publications:* Statistical Thermodynamics (jtly) 1971; ed. of 16 titles, author of 312 research papers. *Address:* Department of Mechanical Engineering, University of California, 6101 Etcheverry Hall # 1740, Berkeley, CA 94720, USA. *Telephone:* (510) 643-3886 (Office). *Fax:* (510) 643-3887 (Office). *E-mail:* nancie@newton.berkeley.edu (Office). *Website:* www.me.berkeley.edu/faculty/tien/index.html (Office).

TIEN, Ping-King, MS, PhD; Chinese research engineer; b. 2 Aug. 1919, Checkang Prov., China; s. of N. S. Tien and C. S. (Yun) Tien; m. Nancy Chen 1952; two d.; ed Nat. Cen. Univ., China and Stanford Univ.; Vice-Pres. Tien-Sun Industrial Co. 1942–47; Research Assoc. Stanford Univ. 1948–52; mem. Tech. Staff, AT & T Bell Labs. (now Bell Labs) 1952–61, Head, Electronics Physics Research 1961–80, Head, Microelectronics Research 1980–84, Ed.-in-Chief High Speed Electronics and Systems; Fellow, Bell Labs. 1984 (Fellow Emer. 1990–), IEEE, Optical Soc. of America; mem. Nat. Acad. of Eng, NAS, Third World Acad. of Sciences, NAS (Taiwan); Chinese Inst. of Eng Achievement Award 1966, Morris N. Liebmann Award, IEEE 1979. *Publications:* numerous technical publs. *Address:* Bell Laboratories, Lucent Technologies, Room 4B-433, 101 Crawfords Corner Road, Holmdel, NJ 07733 (Office); 9 Carolyn Court, Holmdel, NJ 07733, USA (Home). *Telephone:* (201) 949-6925 (Office). *E-mail:* pkt@bell-labs.com (Office).

TIEN HUNG-MAO, MA, PhD; Taiwanese professor of political science and diplomatist; b. 7 Nov. 1938, Tainan; m. Amy Tien; one s. one d.; ed Tunghai Univ. and Univ. of Wisconsin; fmr Prof. of Political Science, Univ. of Wisconsin; Pres. Inst. for Nat. Policy Research 1991–; mem. Nat. Unification Research Council, Office of Pres. of Taiwan 1994–; Nat. Policy Adviser to Pres. of Taiwan 1996–; Dir Foundation for Int. Co-operation and Devt 1996–, Minister of Foreign Affairs 2000–02; Rep. to UK 2002–. *Publications include:* Government and Politics in Kuomintang China 1927–37, The Great Transition, Social and Political Change in the Republic of China, Taiwan's Electoral Politics and Democratic Transition: Riding the Third Wave 1995. *Leisure interests:* golf, tennis, table-tennis. *Address:* Ministry of Foreign Affairs, 2 Chiehshou Road, Taipei 10016 (Office); #225, Tung-shih Street, Hsichih, Taipei County, Taiwan (Home). *Telephone:* (2) 23119292 (Office); (2) 660-0145 (Home). *Fax:* (2) 23144972 (Office). *Website:* www.mofa.gov.tw.

TIETMEYER, Hans, Dr rer. pol; German banker, economist and civil servant; b. 18 Aug. 1931, Metelen; s. of Bernhard Tietmeyer and Helene Tietmeyer; m. 1st Marie-Luise Tietmeyer (died 1978); m. 2nd Maria-Therese Tietmeyer 1980; one s. one d.; ed Univs. of Münster, Bonn and Cologne; Sec. Bischöfliche Studienforderung Cusanuswerk 1959–62; Fed. Ministry of Econs 1962–82, Head of Div. of Gen. Econ. Policy 1973–82; mem. Econ. Policy Cttee of EC and OECD 1972–82; Sec. of State, Ministry of Finance 1982–89; mem. Bd of Dirs., Bundesbank 1990, Vice-Pres. 1991–93, Pres. 1993–99; Hon. Prof. of Public Econ. of Halle-Wittenberg 1996–; Monetary Policy Adviser to IMF 2002–; Dr. hc (Münster) 1994, (Maryland) 1997; Grosses Bundesverdienstkreuz. *Publications:* The Social Market Economy and Monetary Stability 1999; more than 100 articles on economics. *Leisure interests:* sport, rambling. *Address:* International Monetary Fund, 700 19th Street, NW, Washington, DC 20431, USA. *Telephone:* (202) 623-7300. *Fax:* (202) 623-6220. *E-mail:* publicaffairs@imf.org. *Website:* www.imf.org.

TIGERMAN, Stanley, MArch, FAIA; American architect; b. 20 Sept. 1930, Chicago, Ill.; s. of Samuel B. Tigerman and Emma L. Stern; m. Margaret I. McCurry 1979; one s. one d.; ed Mass. Inst. of Tech. and Yale Univ.; architectural draughtsman, George Fred Keck, Chicago 1949–50; Skidmore Owings & Merrill, Chicago 1957–59; Paul Rudolph, New Haven 1959–61; Harry Weese 1961–62; partner, Tigerman & Koglin, Chicago 1962–64; Prin. Stanley Tigerman & Assoc. Chicago 1964–82; partner, Tigerman Fugman McCurry, Chicago 1982–88, Tigerman McCurry, Chicago 1988–; co-founder, Archeworks Design Lab. Chicago 1993; Prof. of Architecture, Univ. of Ill. Chicago 1967–71, 1980–93, Dir School of Architecture 1985–93; Davenport Prof. of Arch. Yale Univ. 1979, Bishop Prof. 1984; Architect-in-residence, American Acad. Rome 1980; Visiting Prof. Harvard 1982; mem. Advisory Cttee Princeton Univ. 1997; ACSA Citation 1989 and numerous other awards. *Publications:* Chicago's Architectural Heritage: A Romantic Classical Image . . . & Work of the Current Generation of Chicago Architects 1979, VERSUS: An American Architect's Alternatives 1982, Stanley Tigerman Architoons 1988, The Architecture of Exile 1988, Stanley Tigerman, Buildings & Projects 1966–89 1989. *Leisure interests:* tennis, skiing, reading. *Address:* Tigerman McCurry Ltd, 444 North Wells Street, Suite 206, Chicago, IL 60610, USA (Office). *Telephone:* (312) 644-5880.

TIGRID, Pavel; Czech journalist, publisher, radio presenter and politician; b. 27 Oct. 1917, Prague; m. Ivana Myšková 1947; one s. two d.; radio presenter BBC, London 1939–45; returned to Czechoslovakia 1945; fled Czechoslovakia 1948; set up and worked for Czech Section of Radio Free Europe, Munich 1952–89; returned to Czechoslovakia 1990–; adviser to Pres. Havel 1991–92; Minister of Culture Govt of Czech Repub. 1994–95; Adviser to Pres.'s Office for Czech-German Relations 1997–; a Co-ordinator, Co-ordination Council of Czech-German Discussion Forum 1998–2000; Officier, Légion d'honneur

1992, Order of T. G. Masaryk 1995; European Cultural Prize 1998, Annual Prize of Pangea Foundation (Czech. Repub.) 1999. *Radio:* Radio Prague 1995–2000 (Sunday morning commentaries). *Publications:* The Prague Spring 1968, An Intelligent Woman's Guidebook through Her Own Life 1988, On Czech Politics 2000, Marx at Hradčany 2001; articles and radio plays. *Leisure interests:* skiing, tourism. *Address:* U starého hřbitova 248/3, 110 00 Prague 1, Czech Republic (Home).

TIGYI, József; Hungarian biophysicist; b. 19 March 1926, Kaposvár; s. of András Tigyi and Julianna Mátrai; m. Anna Sebes; two s.; ed Medical Univ. of Pécs; Prof. and Dir of Biophysical Inst. Medical Univ. Pécs 1971–91, Vice-Rector 1967–73, Rector 1973–79; corresp. mem. Hungarian Acad. of Sciences 1967–76, mem. 1976–, Vice-Pres. 1988, Pres. Regional Cttee, Pécs 1996–; Pres. Acad. Section No. 8 (Biological Sciences) 1980–88; Pres. Hungarian Biophysical Soc. 1972–91, Hon. Pres. 1991–; Pres. UNESCO European Collaboration in Biophysics 1976–86; Chief Ed. Acta Biochimica et Biophysica 1981–91; mem. Royal Soc. of Medicine, New York Acad. of Sciences 1980–, European Acad. of Arts, Sciences and Humanities, Paris 1990–; WHO Exec. Bd 1972–75; Int. Council of Scientific Unions (ICSU) Gen. Cttee; Cttee on the Teaching of Science 1986–93; Gesellschaft für mathematische u. physikalische Biologie (GDR), Biophysical Soc. of Romania, of India; Gen. Sec. Int. Union of Pure and Applied Biophysics (IUPAB) 1984–93, Co-Chair. Special Cttee on Radiation and Environmental Biophysics 1993–; Labour Order of Merit (Silver) 1966, (Gold) 1970, 1979. *Publications:* Application of Radioactive Isotope in Experimental Medicine 1965; Biophysics – Theory of Bioelectric Phenomena, Biological Semi-conductors; Energetics of Cross-Striated Muscle 1977, Physical Aspects of the Living Cell 1991. *Address:* Biophysical Institute of the Medical University, 7643 Pécs, Szigeti ut 12, Hungary. *Telephone:* (72) 536-264. *Fax:* (72) 536-261.

TIINGA, Beniamina; I-Kiribati politician; Vice-Pres. of Kiribati 2000–; also Minister of Finance and Economic Planning. *Address:* Ministry of Finance and Economic Planning, P.O. Box 67, Bairiki, Tarawa, Kiribati (Office). *Telephone:* 21820 (Office). *Fax:* 21307 (Office).

TIJDEMAN, Robert; Netherlands professor of mathematics; b. 30 July 1943, Oostzaan; ed Univ. of Amsterdam; scientific worker, Univ. of Amsterdam 1967–70; Reader, Univ. of Leiden 1970–75, Prof. of Math. 1975–; mem. Royal Netherlands Acad. of Sciences 1987; Dr hc (Debrecen, Hungary) 1999. *Publication:* Exponential diophantine equations (with T. N. Shorey) 1986. *Address:* Mathematical Institute, POB 9512, 2300 RA Leiden, Netherlands. *Telephone:* (71) 5277138. *Fax:* (71) 527 7101. *E-mail:* tijdeman@math.leidenuniv.nl (Office).

TIKHVINSKY, Sergej Leonidovich; Russian historian; b. 1 Sept. 1918, Petrograd; s. of Leonid Tikhvinsky and Kira Tikhvinsky; m. Vera Nikitichna Tikhvinskaya 1940; one s. one d.; ed Oriental Inst., Moscow; mem. CPSU 1941–91; diplomatic service in China, UK and Japan 1939–57; Head of Asian Dept of USSR State Cttee with Council of Ministers for Foreign Cultural Relations 1957–60; Prof. Moscow Univ. 1959; Dir USSR Acad. of Sciences Inst. of Sinology 1960–61; Deputy Dir of Acad. of Sciences Inst. of the Peoples of Asia 1961–63; Deputy Dir of Acad. of Sciences Inst. of World Socialist Economies 1963–65; Corresp. mem. of Acad. of Sciences 1968–81, mem. 1981–; Chief of History of Diplomacy Dept, Head of Asia Section in Foreign Policy Planning Dept USSR Ministry of Foreign Affairs 1965–80; Rector of Diplomatic Acad. of USSR Ministry of Foreign Affairs 1980–86; Academician-Sec. of Historical Section of USSR Acad. of Sciences 1982–88; Pres. Nat. Cttee of Soviet (now Russian) Historians 1980–; Chair. Scientific Council for The History of Russia's Foreign Policy and Int. Relations 1987–; Hon. Chair. All-Russia Asscn of Sinologues 1988; Adviser to the Presidium of Acad. of Sciences 1988–; Hon. mem. Accademia Fiorentina delle Arti 1984. *Publications include:* The Reform Movement in China and K'ang Youwei 1959, Sun Yatsen Foreign Affairs Theories and Practice 1964, Manchu Rule in China 1966, History of China and Present Time 1976, The Reform Movements in China at the end of the 19th Century 1980, China and her Neighbours 1980, China and World History 1988, China: History through Personalities and Events 1991, China in my Life 1992, China's Road to Unity and Independence 1996, Eternal Sleep in China's Earth: Memorial Album 1996, Russia–Japan, Doomed to Good Neighbourhood 1996; numerous articles on Soviet and Russian foreign policy and int. affairs. *Leisure interest:* angling. *Address:* National Committee of Historians, Leninsky prosp. 32A, 117334 Moscow, Russia. *Telephone:* (095) 938-00-08, 123-90-73 (Office); (095) 915-45-20 (Home).

TILEY, John, CBE, LLD, MA, BCL; British professor of law of taxation; b. 25 Feb. 1941, Leamington Spa; s. of the late William Tiley and Audrey Tiley; m. Jillinda Draper 1964; two s. one d.; ed Winchester Coll. and Lincoln Coll. Oxford; called to the Bar, Inner Temple 1964, Hon. Bencher 1993; Recorder 1989–97; Lecturer, Lincoln Coll. Oxford 1963–64, Univ. of Birmingham 1964–67; Fellow, Queens' Coll. Cambridge 1967–; Asst Lecturer, Univ. of Cambridge 1967–72, Lecturer 1972–87, Reader 1987–90, Prof. of Law of Taxation 1990–, Chair. Faculty Bd of Law 1992–95; Pres. Soc. of Public Teachers of Law 1995–96; Visiting Prof. Dalhousie Univ., Canada 1972–73, Univ. of Auckland 1973, Univ. of Western Ont. 1978–79, Univ. of Melbourne 1979, Case Western Reserve Univ. 1985–86, 1996, 2002. *Publications:* Revenue Law 1976; ed. of various works on taxation and contribs to legal journals. *Leisure interests:* walking, visits to art galleries, listening to music. *Address:* Queens' College, Cambridge, CB3 9ET, England. *Telephone:* (1223) 335511.

TILGHMAN, Shirley Marie, PhD; Canadian university president and professor of biology; ed Queen's Univ., Kingston, Ont., Canada, Temple Univ., Philadelphia; mem. Inst. for Cancer Research 1979–86; Howard A. Prior Prof. of the Life Sciences, Princeton Univ. 1986–; Head, Inst. for Integrative Genomics 1998–, Pres. Princeton Univ. 2001–; Pres.'s Award for Distinguished Teaching 1996. *Address:* Department of Molecular Biology, Princeton University, Princeton, NJ 08544, USA (Office). *Telephone:* (609) 258-2900 (Office). *Fax:* (609) 258-3345 (Office). *E-mail:* stilghman@molbio.princeton .edu (Office). *Website:* www.princeton.edu (Office).

TILL, Jeremy, MA, RIBA; British architect and university professor; pnr Peter Currie Architects 1985–92; Dir Sarah Washington Architects 1992–; Sr Lecturer Kingston Univ. 1986–92; Sr Lecturer and Sub-Dean of Faculty, The Bartlett School of Architecture, Univ. Coll. London 1992–98; Prof. of Architecture and Head School of Architecture Univ. of Sheffield 1999–; Fulbright Arts Fellowship 1990, Civic Trust Award 2002. *Radio includes:* Shaping Our Spaces (two part series), BBC Radio 4. *Publications include:* The Everyday and Architecture 1997, 9 Stock Orchard Street: A Guidebook 2002. *Leisure interests:* cooking, eating, drinking. *Address:* School of Architecture, University of Sheffield, Western Bank, Sheffield, S10 2TN (Office); 9 Stock Orchard Street, London, N7 9RW, England (Home). *Telephone:* (142) 220347 (Office); (20) 7700-1081 (Home). *Fax:* (142) 228276 (Office). *E-mail:* j.till@ sheffield.ac.uk (Office). *Website:* www.swarch.co.uk (Office).

TILLMANS, Wolfgang; German artist; b. 1968, Remscheid; ed Bournemouth and Poole Coll. of Art and Design; Turner Prize 2000. *Art exhibitions include:* solo exhbns: Royal Acad.'s Apocalypse 2000, Andrea Rosen Gallery, New York 2001–02, Wako Works of Art, Tokyo 2001–02, Super Collider at Galerie Daniel Bucholz, Cologne 2001–02, Aufsicht at Deichtorhallen Hamburg 2001–02, Castello di Rivoli-Museo d'Arte Contemporanea, Rivoli, Turin 2001–02, Palais de Tokyo, Paris 2001–02, Louisiana Museum of Modern Art, Humlebæ, Denmark 2001–02, Regen Projects, Los Angeles 2002, Maureen Paley Interim Art, London 2002; group exhbns: Open City: Street Photography 1950–2000, Museum of Modern Art, Oxford 2001, Neue Welt at Frankfurter Kunstveren 2001, Zero Gravity at Kunsthalle Düsseldorf 2001, Contemporary Utopia at Latvian Centre for Contemporary Art, Riga 2001, Century City: Art and Culture in the Modern Metropolis, Tate Modern, London 2001, Uniforms, Order and Disorder at Pitti Imagine, Florence and Contemporary Art Center, New York 2001. *Address:* c/o Maureen Paley Interim Art, 21 Herald Street, London, E 6JT, England (Office). *Telephone:* (20) 7729-4112 (Office). *Fax:* (20) 7729-4113 (Office).

TILSON, Joseph (Joe), ARCA, RA; British artist; b. 24 Aug. 1928, London; s. of Frederick Albert Edward Tilson and Ethel Stapley Louise Saunders; m. Joslyn Morton 1956; one s. two d.; ed St Martin's School of Art, Royal Coll. of Art, British School, Rome; Visiting Lecturer Slade School, Univ. of London, 1962–63, King's Coll., Univ. of Durham 1962–63, exhibited at Venice Biennale 1964; Lecturer School of Visual Arts, New York 1966, Staatliche Hochschule, Hamburg 1971–72; Rome Prize 1955, Grand Prix Fifth Biennale, Cracow 1974, Henry Moore Prize, Bradford 1984, Grand Prix, 15th Biennale, Ljubljana 1985 and 21st Biennale 1995. *Art exhibitions:* retrospective exhbn Boymans van Beuningen Museum, Rotterdam 1973, Sackler Galleries, Royal Acad., London 2002. *Address:* 93 Bourne Street, London, SW1W 8HF, England. *Telephone:* (20) 7259-0024.

TILSON THOMAS, Michael; American conductor, pianist and composer; b. 21 Dec. 1944, Los Angeles; s. of Theodor Thomas and Roberta Thomas; ed Univ. of S. Calif.; conductor, Young Musicians' Foundation Debut Orchestra, Los Angeles 1963–67; conductor and pianist, Monday Evening Concerts 1963–68; musical Asst Bayreuth 1966–67; Asst Conductor, Boston Symphony Orchestra 1969, Assoc. Conductor 1970–71, Prin. Guest Conductor 1972–74; New York début 1969; London début with London Symphony Orchestra (LSO) 1970; Music Dir Buffalo Philharmonic 1971–79; Prin. Guest Conductor, Los Angeles Philharmonic 1981–85; Music Dir Great Woods Inst. 1985, Music Dir Great Woods Festival 1987–88; Prin. Conductor, LSO 1988–95, Prin. Guest Conductor 1995–; Founder and Artistic Dir, New World Symphony 1988–; Music Dir San Francisco Symphony 1995–; Artistic Dir Pacific Music Festival; guest conductor with orchestras and opera houses in USA and Europe; Koussevitzky Prize, Tanglewood 1968; Ditson Award for contribs to American music 1994, Musical America's Conductor of the Year 1994, American Music Center Award 2001, two Gramophone Awards and three Grammy Awards. *Recordings include:* Bach, Beethoven, Mahler, Stravinsky and Prokofiev as well as pioneering work with the music of Ives, Ruggles, Reich, Cage and Gershwin. *Address:* Van Walsum Management Ltd., 4 Addison Bridge Place, London, W14 8XP, England (Office). *Telephone:* (20) 7371-4343 (Office). *Fax:* (20) 7371-4344 (Office). *E-mail:* c/o nmcghee@vanwalsum.co.uk (Office). *Website:* www.vanwalsum.co.uk (Office).

TIMAKATA, Fred; Ni-Vanuatu politician; b. 1936, Shepard Islands; Speaker of Parl. 1985–88; Minister of Health 1988–89; Pres. of Vanuatu 1989–94. *Address:* c/o Office of the President, Port Vila, Vanuatu.

TIMBERLAKE, Justin Randall; American singer, songwriter and actor; b. 31 Jan. 1981, Memphis, TN; started vocal training aged 8; guest appearance at Grand Ole Opry 1991; early TV appearances: Star Search 1992, The Mickey Mouse Club 1993–94; mem. *NSYNC vocal quintet 1995–, first headline US tour 1998; also solo artist 2002–; presented with keys to City of Orlando 2000; American Music Award, Favourite Pop/Rock Band, Duo or Group 2002. *Recordings:* Albums with *NSYNC: *NSYNC 1998, Home For Christmas

1998, No Strings Attached 2000, Celebrity 2001; Solo Album: Justified 2002; Singles with *NSYNC: I Want You Back 1997, Tearin' Up My Heart 1997, Let The Music Heal Your Soul (various artists charity single credited to Bravo All Stars) 1999, Music Of My Heart (with Gloria Estefan) 1999, Bye, Bye, Bye 2000, I'll Never Stop 2000, It's Gonna Be Me 2000, This I Promise You 2000, Pop 2001, Gone 2001; Solo Singles: Like I Love You 2002, Cry Me A River 2003. *Address:* c/o Wright Entertainment Group, PO Box 590009, Orlando, FL 32859-0009, USA (Office). *Website:* www.nsync.com (Office).

TIMON, Clay S.; American business executive; m. Barbara Timon; two c.; ed Univ. of Colorado; fmr Bd Dir, Man. Supervisor (Paris) McCann-Erickson, Man. Services Dir (Tokyo), Sr Vice-Pres./Man. Supervisor; fmr Sr Vice-Pres. Int. Doyle Dane Bernbach; fmr Vice-Pres./Dir. Worldwide Advertising Colgate-Palmolive; fmr Regional Vice-Pres. Saatchi & Saatchi, Paris; Chair., Pres., CEO Landor Assocs. 1994–; World Pres. Int. Advertising Asscn 1988–90; fmr Chair. Int. Cttee of American Asscn of Advertising Agencies; mem. Business Advisory Council School of Business, Univ. of Colorado. *Leisure interests:* travel, reading, tennis, vintage automobiles. *Address:* Landor Associates, 1001 Front Street, San Francisco, CA 94111, USA. *Telephone:* (415) 955-1400.

TINDEMANS, Leo; Belgian politician; b. 16 April 1922, Zwyndrecht; s. of Frans Tindemans and Margaret Vercruyssen; m. Rosa Naesens 1960; two s. two d.; ed State Univ. of Ghent, Catholic Univ. of Louvain, Univ. of Antwerp; mem. Chamber of Deputies 1961–89; Mayor of Edegem 1965–76; Minister of Community Affairs 1968–71; Minister of Agric. and Middle Class Affairs 1972–73; Deputy Prime Minister and Minister for the Budget and Institutional Problems 1973–74; Prime Minister 1974–78; Minister of Foreign Affairs 1981–89, Minister of State 1992; Vice-Pres. European Union of Christian Democrats, Leader 1992–94; Pres. European People's Party 1976–85; mem. European Parl. 1979–81, 1989–99; Pres. Group of European People's Party, European Parl. 1992–94; Pres. Belgian Christian People's Party (CVP) 1979–81; Pres. Antwerp Business School; Hon. Prof., Faculty of Social Sciences, Catholic Univ., Louvain; Christian Democrat; Hon. DLitt (City Univ., London) 1976; Dr hc (Heriot-Watt Univ., Edin.) 1978, (Georgetown Univ.) 1984, (Deusto Univ., Bilbao) 1991; Charlemagne Prize 1976; St-Liborius-Medaille für Einheit und Frieden 1977; Stresemann Medal 1979; Robert Schuman Prize 1980. *Publications:* Ontwikkeling van de Benelux 1958, L'autonomie culturelle 1971, Regionalized Belgium, Transition from the Nation State to the Multinational State 1972, Een handvest voor woelig België 1972, Dagboek van de werkgroep Eyskens 1973, European Union 1975, Europe, Ideal of Our Generation 1976, Open Brief aan Gaston Eyskens 1978, Atlantisch Europa 1980, Europa zonder Kompas 1987, L'Europe de l'Est vue de Bruxelles 1989, Duel met de Minister 1991, De toekomst van een idee 1993, Cain in the Balkans 1996. *Leisure interests:* reading, writing, walking. *Address:* Jan Verbertlei 24, 2650 Edegem, Belgium (Home). *Fax:* (3) 455-66-58.

TINDLE, David, RA; British artist; b. 29 April 1932, Huddersfield, Yorks.; m. 1st Jillian Evans 1953 (divorced) 1957); one s. one d.; m. 2nd Sheila Pratt 1957 (divorced 1969); three s. one d.; m. 3rd Janet Trollope 1969 (divorced 1992); one s. two d.; ed Coventry School of Art; worked as scenic artist for theatre until moving to London in 1951; numerous exhbns in London and provinces since 1952; works in many public and private collections including the Tate Gallery, Nat. Portrait Gallery; designed and painted set for Iolanta (Tchaikovsky), Aldeburgh Festival 1988; Visiting Tutor, Royal Coll. of Art 1973–83; Fellow 1981, Hon. Fellow 1984; Ruskin Master of Drawing, St Edmund Hall, Oxford 1985–87, lives and works in Italy; Hon. Fellow St Edmund Hall, Oxford 1988–; Hon. mem. Royal Birmingham Soc. of Artists; Hon. MA (St Edmund Hall, Oxford) 1985; RA Johnson Wax Award 1983. *Art exhibitions include:* first one-man exhbn London 1953, regular one-man shows, Piccadilly Gallery 1954–83, Hamburg Gallerie XX 1974–85, Los Angeles and San Francisco 1964, Bologna and Milan 1968; one-man show, Fischer Fine Art 1985, 1989, 1992, Redfern Gallery, London 1994, 1996, 1998–99, 2000, 2001, 2003, St Edmund Hall, Oxford 1994, The Shire Hall Gallery, Stafford 1994; has participated in numerous group exhbns and int. biennales in Europe. *Leisure interests:* music, films, cats and dogs, visiting the towns and museums of Italy. *Address:* Via C. Barsotti 194, S. Maria del Giudice, 55058 Lucca (Office); Via Giovanni Pacchini 118B, S. Maria del Giudice, 55058 Lucca, Italy (Home); c/o The Redfern Gallery, 20 Cork Street, London, W1, England.

TING, Samuel Chao Chung, BSE, PhD; American physicist; b. 27 Jan. 1936, Ann Arbor, Mich.; s. of Prof. Kuan Hai Ting and Prof. Tsun-Ying Wang; m. 1st Kay Louise Kuhne; two d.; m. 2nd Susan Carol Marks 1985; one s. two d.; ed primary and secondary schools in China, Univ. of Michigan; Ford Foundation Fellow, European Org. for Nuclear Research (CERN), Geneva 1963; Instructor, Columbia Univ., NY 1964, Asst Prof. 1965–67; Group Leader, Deutsches Elektronen Synchrotron (DESY), Hamburg, Fed. Repub. of Germany 1966; Assoc. Prof. of Physics, MIT, Cambridge 1967–68, Prof. 1969–, Thomas Dudley Cabot Inst. Prof. 1977–; Programme Consultant, Div. of Particles and Fields, American Physical Soc. 1970; Hon. Prof. Beijing Normal Coll., China 1984, Jiatong Univ., Shanghai, China 1987; Assoc. Ed. Nuclear Physics B 1970; mem. Editorial Bd Nuclear Instruments and Methods 1977, Mathematical Modelling, Chinese Physics; worked chiefly on physics of electron or muon pairs, investigating quantum electro-dynamics, production and decay of photon-like particles, searching for new particles which decay to electron or muon pairs, studying physics and astrophysics phenomena in space; Fellow, American Acad. of Arts and Sciences 1975; mem. American, Italian and European Physical Socs.; Foreign mem. Academia Sinica, Taiwan 1975, Pakistani Acad. of Science 1984, USSR (now Russian) Acad. of Science 1989, Hungarian Acad. of Science 1993; mem. NAS 1977–, Deutsche Akademie der Naturforscher Leopoldina 1996; Hon. ScD (Michigan) 1978, (Chinese Univ. of Hong Kong) 1987, (Bologna) 1988, (Columbia) 1990, (Univ. of Science and Tech., China) 1990, (Moscow State Univ.) 1991, (Bucharest) 1993; Ernest Orlando Lawrence Award 1976, Nobel Prize for Physics (jtly with Burton Richter, q.v.) for discovery of the heavy, long-lived 'J' (or 'psi') particle 1976, Eringen Medal, Soc. of Eng Scientists 1977, De Gasperi Gold Medal for Science, Italy 1988, Gold Medal for Science, City of Brescia, Italy 1988, Forum Engelberg Prize 1996. *Address:* Department of Physics, Massachusetts Institute of Technology, 51 Vassar Street, Cambridge, MA 02139, USA. *Telephone:* (617) 253-1000. *Fax:* (617) 253-8000. *Website:* web.mit.edu (Office).

TINKHAM, Michael, MS, PhD; American professor of physics; b. 23 Feb. 1928, nr Ripon, Wisconsin; s. of Clayton H. Tinkham and Laverna Krause Tinkham; m. Mary S. Merin 1961; two s.; ed Ripon Coll., Ripon, Wis., MIT and Univ. of Oxford; Research Asst, Univ. of Calif. (Berkeley) 1955–57, Asst Prof. of Physics 1957–59, Assoc. Prof. of Physics 1959–61, Prof. of Physics 1961–66; Gordon McKay Prof. of Applied Physics and Prof. of Physics, Harvard Univ. 1966–80, Rumford Prof. of Physics and Gordon McKay Prof. of Applied Physics 1980–, Chair. Dept of Physics 1975–78; Richtmyer Lecturer (of American Physical Soc. and American Asscn of Physics Teachers) 1977; Visiting Miller Research Prof., Univ. of Calif. (Berkeley) 1987; Visiting Prof., Delft Univ. of Tech. 1993; mem. NAS; Fellow, American Acad. of Arts and Sciences; Guggenheim Fellow 1963–64; Hon. DrScNat (ETH Zürich) 1997; Buckley Prize 1974, Alexander von Humboldt Foundation Award 1978–79. *Publications:* Group Theory and Quantum Mechanics 1964, Superconductivity 1965, Introduction to Superconductivity 1996 (2nd Edn); numerous articles in journals. *Address:* Department of Physics, Harvard University, Cambridge, MA 02138 (Office); 98 Rutledge Road, Belmont, MA 02478, USA (Home). *Telephone:* (617) 495-3735 (Office).

TIRIMO, Martino, FRAM, Dip RAM; British concert pianist and conductor; b. 19 Dec. 1942, Larnaca, Cyprus; s. of Dimitri Tirimo and Marina Tirimo; m. Mione J. Teakle 1973; one s. one d.; ed Bedales School, England (Cyprus Govt Scholarship), Royal Acad. of Music, London, Vienna State Acad.; first public recital, Cyprus 1949; conducted 7 performances of La Traviata with singers and musicians from La Scala, Milan, at Cyprus Opera Festival 1955; prizewinner Int. Beethoven Competition, Vienna 1965; London début Wigmore Hall 1965; jt winner Munich Int. Piano Competition 1971; winner Geneva Int. Piano Competition 1972; gave first public performance of complete Schubert sonatas (including unfinished ones with own completions), London 1975; first public performance of Beethoven piano concertos cycle directed from keyboard in two consecutive evenings, Dresden 1985, London 1986; first performance Tippett piano concerto in several European countries 1986–87; concerto performances with major orchestras worldwide as well as recitals, radio and TV appearances Europe, USA, Canada, SA and Far East 1965–; four series of performances of complete Beethoven piano sonatas 2000, two series devoted to the maj. piano works of Robert and Clara Schumann 2001; six-concert series devoted to the major piano works of Chopin 2002; began Mozart piano concertos series, directing from keyboard 2001–; composed film score "The Odyssey" 1998; Liszt Scholarship, Boise Foundation Scholarship, Gulbenkian Foundation Fellowship 1967–69; mem. jury in various int. piano competitions 1995–; Gold Medal, Associated Bd of Royal Schools of Music 1959, Macfarren Medal, Royal Acad. of Music 1964, Silver Disc 1988 and Gold Disc 1994 for recording of Rachmaninov 2nd Concerto and Paganini Rhapsody and other prizes and awards. *Recordings include:* Brahms piano concertos, Chopin concertos, Tippett piano concerto, Rachmaninov concertos, complete Debussy piano works, complete Schubert piano sonatas, complete Mendelssohn works for piano and cello, several other recordings with mixed repertoire. *Television:* live performance of Tippett piano concerto from Coventry Cathedral for BBC TV in celebration of composer's 90th birthday and the 50th birthday of the UN. *Publications include:* urtext edn of complete Schubert piano sonatas in 3 vols 1997–99. *Leisure interests:* chess, reading, self-knowledge, theatre, badminton. *Address:* 1 Romeyn Road, London, SW16 2NU, England. *Telephone:* (20) 8677-4847. *Fax:* (20) 8677-6070. *E-mail:* martino@tirimo.fslife.co.uk.

TISHCHENKO, Boris Ivanovich; Russian composer; b. 23 March 1939, Leningrad; s. of Ivan I. Tishchenko and Zinaida A. Tishchenko; m. Irina A. Donskaya 1977; three s.; ed Leningrad Conservatory, with post-grad. course under Shostakovich; Prof. at St Petersburg Conservatory; 1st Prize, Int. Contest of Young Composers, Prague 1966, RSFSR State Prize (Glinka) 1978, People's Artist of RSFSR 1987, Prize of Mayor of St Petersburg 1995, Pushkin Gold Medal 2000, Russian Order of Merit for the Homeland, IVth class 2002. *Compositions include:* The Stolen Sun (opera) 1968, The Twelve (ballet) 1963, Fly-bee (ballet) 1968, Yaroslavna (The Eclipse, ballet) 1974, Beatriche (ballet) 2003, Lenin Lives (cantata) 1959, Requiem (words by A. Akhmatova) 1966, A Cockroach (operetta) 1968. *Symphonies:* French Symphony 1958, Sinfonia Robusta 1970, Violin Symphony (2nd Violin Concerto) 1981, The Siege Chronicle 1984, Pushkin's Symphony 1998, 7 symphonies 1961–94. *Other works:* 10 piano sonatas 1957–97; violin and cello solo sonatas; Sonata for family of flutes and organ 1999; Rondo, Capriccio and Fantasy for violin and piano; also concertos for violin, piano, cello, flute and harp 1962–77, Concerto alla marcia for 16 soloists 1989, The Dog's Heart—Novels for chamber

ensemble based on M. Bulgakov 1988, Concerto for clarinet and piano trio 1990, Piano Quintet 1985, String quartets 1957–84, Twelve Inventions and Twelve Portraits for Organ 1964, 1994, orchestral and instrumental suites and pieces, vocal cycles and ensembles, choral works, music for drama productions and films; edns. and instrumentations of some works by Monteverdi, Grieg, Mahler, Prokofiev and Shostakovich. *Leisure interest:* reading. *Address:* Rimsky-Korsakoff Avenue 79, Apt. 10, St Petersburg 190121, Russia. *Telephone:* (812) 114-75-16.

TISHKOV, Valery Aleksandrovich, DHist; Russian historian and anthropologist; b. 1941; m.; one s.; ed Moscow State Univ.; teacher, Magadan State Pedagogical Inst. 1964–66; aspirant, Moscow State Pedagogical Inst. 1966–69; docent, Dean, Magadan State Pedagogical Inst. 1969–72; researcher, Inst. of Gen. History USSR (now Russian) Acad. of Sciences, Scientific Sec., Div. of History, USSR Acad. of Sciences, also Head of Dept, Inst. of Ethnography; Deputy Dir, Inst. of Ethnology and Anthropology Russian Acad. of Sciences 1972–89, Dir 1989–; Fed. Minister for Nationalities, Russian Govt 1992; Vice-Pres. Int. Union of Ethnological and Anthropological Sciences 1993 (re-elected 1998); Distinguished Scholar of the Russian Fed. 1998. *Publications:* Ethnicity, Nationalism and Conflict in and after the Soviet Union. The Mind Aflame 1997, Peoples and Religions of the World (Russian Encyclopaedia) 1998. *Leisure interests:* fishing, collection of Arctic ivory art. *Address:* Institute of Ethnology and Anthropology, Russian Academy of Sciences, Leninsky prosp. 32A, 117334 Moscow, Russia. *Telephone:* (095) 938-17-47 (Office). *Fax:* (095) 938-06-00 (Office). *E-mail:* tishkov@orc.ru (Home). *Website:* www.tower.iea.ras.ru (Office).

TITARENKO, Mikhail Leontyevich, PhD; Russian specialist on international relations with the Far East and Chinese philosophy; b. 27 April 1934, Bryansk region; s. of the late Leonty Titarenko and Maria Titarenko; m. Galina Titarenko 1957 (died 1997); two s.; ed Moscow State Univ., Beijing Univ., Fudan Univ., Shanghai; diplomatic service 1961–65; researcher and consultant in Govt bodies 1965–85; Dir Inst. of Far East Studies, Russian Acad. of Sciences 1985–; mem. Editorial Bd of Far Eastern Affairs 1986–; Chair. of Academic Council on Problems of Modern China, Russian Acad. of Sciences 1987–; Pres. All-Russian Asscn of Sinologists 1988–; Corresp. mem. Russian Acad. of Sciences 1997–; mem. Russia Acad. of Natural Sciences, Int. Acad. of Informatization; Honour of the Russian Federation 1994, Merited Scholar of Russia 1995, 200 Years of Russian Foreign Service Medal 2002. *Publications:* Anthology of Ancient Chinese Philosophy (two Vols), Ancient Chinese Philosopher Mo Di 1985, Development of Productive Forces in China 1989, History of Chinese Philosophy 1989, Economic Reform in China: Theory and Practice 1990, Russia and East Asia: Issues of International and Cross-Civilization Relations 1994, Russia Towards Asia 1998, China: Civilization and Reforms 1999, Russia's Co-operative Security: East Asian Vector 2003; and numerous articles. *Leisure interests:* collecting stamps, matchboxes, skiing, mushroom hunting. *Address:* Institute of Far East Studies, Russian Academy of Sciences, 32 Nakhimovsky pr., 117218 Moscow, Russia (Office). *Telephone:* (095) 124-01-17 (Office); (095) 198-55-38 (Home). *Fax:* (095) 718-96-56 (Office). *E-mail:* ifes@cemi.rssi.ru (Office). *Website:* www.ifes-ras.ru (Office).

TITHERIDGE, John Edward, PhD, FRSNZ, FInstP; New Zealand research scientist; b. 12 June 1932, Auckland; s. of Leslie Edward Titheridge and Clarice Muriel Barnes; m. Patricia Joy Brooker 1970; one s. one d.; ed Avondale Coll., Univ. of Auckland and Univ. of Cambridge; Research Fellow Univ. of Auckland 1960–, Sr Research Fellow 1961, Assoc. Prof. 1967–; Fellow NZ Inst. of Physics; Cheeseman-Pond Memorial Prize 1962, Michaelis Memorial Prize 1972, NZ Geophysics Prize, Wellington Br. Royal Soc. of NZ 1977. *Publications:* more than 120 refereed scientific papers 1959–. *Leisure interests:* music, photography, reading, woodwork, electronics. *Address:* Physics Department, University of Auckland, Auckland (Office); 1500 Dominion Road, Auckland 4, New Zealand (Home). *Telephone:* (9) 373-7599 Ext. 88866 (Office); (9) 620-6231 (Home). *Fax:* (9) 373-7445. *E-mail:* j.titheridge@auckland.ac.nz (Office).

TITO, Teburoro, BSc; I-Kiribati politician; b. 25 Aug. 1953, Tabiteuea North; m. Nei Keina; one c.; ed King George V Secondary School, Univ. of South Pacific, Suva, Papua New Guinea Admin. Coll.; student co-ordinator, Univ. of S. Pacific Students' Asscn 1977–79; scholarship officer, Ministry of Educ. 1980–82, Sr Educ. Officer 1983–87; mem. Maneaba ni Maungatabu (Parl.) and Leader of Opposition 1987–94; mem. Parl. Public Accounts Cttee 1987–90; Pres. of Kiribati 1994–, also Minister of Foreign Affairs; and Int. Trade mem. CPA Exec. Cttee for Pacific Region 1989–90; Chair. Kiribati Football Asscn 1980–94; Dr of World Peace (Maharishi Univ. of World Peace) 2001. *Leisure interests:* sports, especially soccer, tennis and table tennis. *Address:* Office of the President, P.O. Box 68, Bairiki, Tarawa (Office); Tabuarorae, Eita Village, South Tarawa, Kiribati (Home). *Telephone:* 21650 (Office); 21183. *Fax:* 21466 (Office); 21145. *E-mail:* mfa@tskl.net.ki (Office).

TITOV, Konstantin Alekseyevich, CandEconSc; Russian politician; b. 30 Oct. 1944, Moscow; m. Natalia Borisovna Titova; one s.; ed Kuybyshev (now Samara) Aviation Inst., Kuybyshev Inst. of Planning; milling-machine operator, Kuybyshev aviation factory 1962–63, flight engineer 1968–69, Deputy Sec. Komsomol Cttee 1969–70; Deputy Head Students Div., Kuybyshev City Komsomol Cttee 1970–73; Sec. Komsomol Cttee, Jr, Sr Researcher, Head of Group, Head Research Lab. Kuybyshev Inst. of Planning 1973–88; Deputy Dir Research Cen. Informatika (Samara br.) 1988–90; Chair. Samara City

Council 1990–91; Head of Admin. Samara Region 1991–96; Gov. Samara Region 1996–; mem. Council of Fed. of Russia 1993–2001, Chair. Cttee on Budget, Taxation Policy, Finance and Customs Regulation 1996–2001; Pres. Interregional Asscn of Econ. Interaction 'Bolshaya Volga' 1994; Deputy Chair. 'Our Home Is Russia' political movt 1995; Chair. of Council, Union of Right Forces 1998–; Cand. for Pres. of Russian Fed. 2000; Chair. Russian Party of Social Democracy 2000, Co-Founder Union of Social Democratic Parties 2001; mem. Russian Acad. of Natural Sciences; Golden Mask Prize, Russian Theatre Artists Union; Order of St Faithful Prince Daniil Moskovsky (3rd Degree), Order of St Grand Duke Vladimir (2nd Degree); Order of Friendship, Green Man of the Year, Russian Ecological Union 1996, Honoured Economist of the Russian Fed., Gov. of the Year 1998. *Leisure interests:* football, photography, music, painting, reading. *Address:* Molodogvardeyskaya str. 210, 443006 Samara, Russia (Office). *Telephone:* (8462) 32-22-68 (Office). *Fax:* (8462) 32-13-40 (Office). *E-mail:* governor@samara.ru (Office). *Website:* www .titov.samara.ru (Office).

TITOV, Col. Vladimir Georgievich; Russian cosmonaut; b. 1 Jan. 1947, Sretensk, Chita Region; m. Vera Evdokimovna Titova; one s. one d.; ed Chernigov Higher Mil. Aviation School, Yuriy Gagarin Air Force Acad.; pilot instructor, Commdr of aviation unit 1970–76; mem. Cosmonauts' team since 1976; Commdr of space flights on spacecraft Soyuz T-8 1983 and record-breaking flight on Soyuz TM-4 and space station MiR; Deputy Head Dept of Man. Centre of Cosmonauts' Training 1988–99; Dir for Foreign Econ. Relations, Kosmos i Svyaz (Cosmos and Communications) br., Boeing Corpn 1999–; Hero of Soviet Union; Officier Légion d'honneur and other decorations. *Address:* Yuriy Gagarin Centre for Cosmonauts' Training, Zvezdny Gorodok, Moscow Region, Russia.

TITOV, Yuriy Evlampievich; Russian gymnast; b. 27 Nov. 1935, Omsk; s. of Evlampiy Titov and Marina Titova; m. Valerie Kouzmenko 1960; one s. one d.; ed Kiev Inst. of Physical Culture; all-round champion of USSR 1958, 1961, of Europe 1959 and the world 1962; Honoured Master of Sports 1956; Olympic gymnastics champion 1956; won 13 gold medals at European, world championships and Olympic Games; int. class judge 1968; mem. CPSU 1969–91; Vice-Pres. Int. Gymnastic Fed. 1972–76, Pres. 1976–96, Hon. Life Pres. 1996–; Head Dept of Gymnastics, USSR State Sports Cttee 1968–87; lecturer Moscow Acad. of Physical Culture 1980–, Leningrad (now St Petersburg) Acad. of Physical Culture 1988–, Prof. 1993–; Sec. Nat. Olympic Cttee 1987–88, mem. Int. Olympic Cttee (IOC) Working Group on Women and Sport 1995–, ex officio mem. IOC 1995–96; Olympic Order 1992, inducted into Int. Gymnastics Hall of Fame 1999. *Publications:* The Sum of Points 1971, The Ascent 1982, The Notes of the President 1984, Rhythmic Gymnastics (jtly.) 1998, works on methodology of gymnastics. *Leisure interests:* history, carpentry, doing nothing with pleasure. *Address:* Kolokolnikov per. 6, Apt. 19, 103045 Moscow, Russia. *Telephone:* (095) 208-46-57. *Fax:* (095) 208-46-57.

TITS, Jacques Léon, DrSc; French professor of mathematics; b. 12 Aug. 1930, Uccle, Belgium; s. of Léon Tits and Louisa (née André) Tits; m. Marie-Jeanne Dieuaide 1956; ed Univ. of Brussels; Asst Univ. of Brussels 1956–57, Assoc. Prof. 1957–62, Prof. 1962–64; Prof. Univ. of Bonn 1964–74; Assoc. Prof. Coll. de France, Paris 1973–74, Prof. of Group Theory 1975–2000; Visiting Teacher and Prof. Eidgenössische Technische Hochschule, Zürich 1950, 1951, 1953, Inst. for Advanced Study, Princeton 1951–52, 1963, 1969, 1971–72, Univ. of Rome 1955, 1956, Univ. of Chicago 1963, Univ. of Calif., Berkeley 1963, Univs. of Tokyo and Kyoto 1971, Yale Univ. 1966–67, 1976, 1980, 1984, 1990; mem. editorial bds. of periodicals and scientific collections; Ed.-in-Chief Math. Publs of IHES 1980–99; guest speaker at Int. Congresses of Mathematicians, Stockholm 1962, Nice 1970, Vancouver 1974; lecture tours in USA, UK, Israel, etc.; mem. Deutsche Akad. der Naturforscher Leopoldina 1977; Corresp. mem. Acad. des Sciences, Paris 1977, mem. 1979; Foreign mem. Royal Netherlands Acad. of Arts and Sciences 1988; Foreign Assoc. Royal Belgian Acad. 1991; mem. American Acad. of Arts and Sciences 1992, NAS 1992; Foundation mem. Academia Europaea; Hon. mem. London Math. Soc. 1993; Dr. hc (Utrecht) 1970, (Ghent) 1979, (Bonn) 1987, (Louvain) 1992; Prix scientifique Interfacultataire L. Empain 1955, Prix Wettrems, Acad. de Belgique 1958, Grand Prix des Sciences mathématiques et physiques, Acad. des Sciences 1976, Wolf Prize 1993; Chevalier, Légion d'honneur, Commdr des Palmes académiques. *Publications:* over 150 scientific papers. *Leisure interests:* languages, literature, arts. *Address:* Institut de France, 23 quai Conti, 75006 Paris (Office).

TIWARI, Narayan Datt, MA LLB; Indian politician; b. 18 Oct. 1925, Balyuti, Nainital Dist, UP; s. of Poorna Nand Tiwari; m. Sushila Tiwari 1954; ed Allahabad Univ.; joined Indian Freedom Movt aged 13; joined "Quit India Movt." 1942; imprisoned for 15 months; Pres. Allahabad Univ. Students' Union 1947; Sec. Political Sufferers' Distress Relief Soc.; Ed. Hindi monthly Prabhat; mem. UP Ass. 1952–62; Leader of Opposition and Chair. Public Accounts Cttee 1957; mem. UP Vidhan Sabha 1969; Minister for Planning, Labour and Panchayats, also Deputy Chair. State Planning Comm., Govt of UP 1969, Minister for Finance and Parl. Affairs 1970–76, for Heavy Industries and Cane Devt 1973–76; Chief Minister of UP 1976–77, 1984–85, 1988–89; Leader of Opposition (UP Congress (I) Legis. Party) 1977–80; mem. Lok Sabha 1980–; Minister of Planning, Govt of India 1980–81, of Labour 1980–82, of Industry 1981–84, 1985–86, of External Affairs 1986–87, of Finance and Commerce 1987–88, of Steel and Mines 1982–83. *Publication:* European Miscellany. *Leisure interests:* cricket, hockey. *Address:* C-1/9 Tilak Lane, New Delhi, 110 001, India. *Telephone:* (11) 338 2218.

TIZARD, Dame Catherine (Anne), GCMG, GCVO, DBE, QSO; New Zealand public official; b. 4 April 1931, Auckland; d. of Neil Maclean and Helen Montgomery Maclean; m. Hon. Robert James Tizard 1951 (divorced 1983); one s. three d.; ed Matamata Coll. and Auckland Univ.; Tutor in Zoology, Univ. of Auckland 1967–84; Mayor of Auckland 1983–90; Gov.-Gen. of New Zealand 1990–96; Chair. NZ Worldwide Fund for Nature 1996–2000, NZ Historic Places Trust 1996–; mem. Auckland City Council 1971–83, Auckland Regional Authority 1980–83; Hon. Fellow Lucy Cavendish Coll. Cambridge, UK and Winston Churchill Fellow 1981; Hon. LLD (Auckland) 1992. *Leisure interests:* music, reading, drama, scuba diving. *Address:* 12A Wallace Street, Herne Bay, Auckland 1, New Zealand. *Telephone:* (9) 376-2555. *Fax:* (9) 360-0656. *E-mail:* cath.tizard@xtra.co.nz (Home).

TJEKNAVORIAN, Loris-Zare; American/Armenian composer and conductor; b. 13 Oct. 1937; s. of Haikaz and Adriné Tjeknavorian; m. 1st Linda Pierce 1964 (divorced 1979); one s.; m. 2nd Julia Cory Harley-Green 1986; ed Vienna Acad. of Music, Salzburg Mozarteum; studied with the late Carl Orff 1963–64; worked in USA until 1970; fmr Teaching Fellow, Univ. of Michigan; fmr Composer-in-Residence, Concordia Coll., Minnesota; Composer-in-Residence, Ministry of Culture and Fine Arts; Prin. Conductor, Tehran Opera 1972–79; artist with RCA 1976–; Composer-in-Residence American-Armenian Int. Coll., La Verne Univ., Calif. 1979–; Prin. Conductor and Artistic Dir Armenian Philharmonic Orchestra, Yerevan, Armenia 1989–; principally associated with London Symphony Orchestra with whom he has recorded; Chair. Bd of Trustees, Inst. of Armenian Music, London 1976–80; Order of Homayoun; several int. tours as a conductor. *Works include:* Requiem for the Massacred 1975, Simorgh (ballet music), Lake Van Suite, Erebouni for 12 strings 1978, a piano concerto, several operas, several chamber works, Credo Symphony Life of Christ (after medieval Armenian chants) 1976, Liturgical Mass, Violin Concerto, oratorios Lucifer's Fall and Book of Revelation, Mass in Memoriam 1985, Othello (ballet), ballet suites for orchestra, five symphonies. *Address:* c/o Thea Dispeker Artist Representative, 59 East 54th Street, New York, NY 10022 (Agent); 347 West 57th Street, Apt. 37C, New York, NY 10019, USA (Home); c/o State Philharmonia, Mashtotsi Prospekt 46, Yerevan, Armenia. *Telephone:* (212) 421-7676 (Agent).

TKACHENKO, Oleksander Mikolayevich, CandTechSc; Ukrainian politician; b. 7 March 1939, Shpola, Cherkassy Region; m. Larissa Mitrofanivna Tkachenko; one d.; ed Belotsekivski Agric. Inst., Higher Party School, CPSU Cen. Cttee; worked as First Sec., Tarashansk Comsomol Cttee 1966–70, then Ukrainian CP functionary in agric. sector 1970–82; State Minister, Head Cttee on Agric. Policy and Food Ukrainian SSR 1985–91; Head, Agric. Asscn Zemlya i Lyudi 1992–94; leader Ukrainian Farmers' Party; mem. Verkhovna Rada (Parl.) 1994–; First Vice-Chair. Verkhovna Rada 1994–98, Chair. (Speaker) 1998–99, Pres. Cand. 1991. *Address:* Verkhovna Rada, M. Hrushevskoga str. 5, 252008 Kiev, Ukraine. *Telephone:* (381) 226-28-25 (Office).

TLASS, Lt-Gen. Mustafa el; Syrian politician and army officer; b. 11 May 1932, Rastan City, Mouhafazat Homs; m. Lamyaa al-Jabri 1958; two s. two d.; ed Mil. and Law Colls. and Voroshilov Acad., Moscow; active mem. Baath Arab Socialist Party 1947–, Sec. of Rastan Section 1951; Sports teacher, Al-Kraya School, Mouhafazat al-Soueda 1950–52; attended Mil. Coll. 1952–54; seconded to Egyptian army 1959–61; Insp. Ministry of Supply 1962; mem. Free Officers' Movement 1962–63, detained 1962–63; Commdr Tank Bn and Chief of Cen. Region of Nat. Security Court 1963; Chief of Staff, 5th Armoured Brigade 1964–66; mem. Regional Command, Regional Congress of Baath Arab Socialist Party 1965, 1968, 1969, 1975, of Politbureau 1969–, of Nat. Council of Revolution 1965–71; participated in movement of 23 Feb., promoted to Commdr of Cen. Region and of 5th Armoured Brigade; rank of Maj.-Gen. 1968, Chief of Staff of Armed Forces 1968–70, First Deputy Minister of Defence 1968–72; participated in coup installing Pres. Hafez Al-Assad Nov. 1970; First Deputy C-in-C Armed Forces 1970–72, Deputy C-in-C 1972–; mem. People's Council 1971–; Minister of Defence 1972–, now also Deputy Prime Minister; Deputy Chief of Jt Supreme Mil. Council of Syrian and Egyptian Armed Forces 1973; rank of Lt-Gen. 1978; 33 orders and medals. *Publications include:* Guerilla War, Military Studies, An Introduction to Zionist Strategy, The Arab Prophet and Technique of War, The Armoured Brigade as an Advanced Guard, Bitter Memories in the Military Prison of Mezzah, The Fourth War between Arabs and Israel, The Second Chapter of the October Liberation War, Selections of Arab Poetry, The Steadfastness Front in Confrontation with Camp David, The Algerian Revolution, Art of Soviet War, American Policy under the Carter Regime, The Technological Revolution and Development of the Armed Forces. *Leisure interests:* reading and writing books, military and historical studies, photography. *Address:* Ministry of Defence, Place Omayad, Damascus, Syria. *Telephone:* (11) 7770700.

TLOU, Thomas, MA, PhD; Botswana professor of history and diplomatist; b. 1 June 1932, Gwanda, S. Rhodesia (now Zimbabwe); s. of Malapela Tlou and Moloko Nare; m. Sheila Dinotshe 1977; two s. one d.; ed schools in Rhodesia, Luther Coll., Decorah, Iowa, Johns Hopkins Univ., Baltimore and Univ. of Wisconsin; primary school teacher, Rhodesia 1957–62; Lecturer in History, Luther Coll. 1969, Univ. of Wis. 1970–71; Lecturer in History, Univ. of Botswana, Lesotho and Swaziland 1971, later Prof., Dean of Faculty of Humanities and Head of History; mem. Bd Nat. Museum and Art Gallery of Botswana 1974–76, 1981–, mem. Univ. Senate and Council of UBLS 1974–76; Acting Dir Nat. Research Inst. 1976; Perm. Rep. to UN 1977–80; Deputy Vice-Chancellor Univ. of Botswana 1980, Vice-Chancellor 1984–98, mem. Senate and Council of Univ. of Botswana and Swaziland (now Univ. of Botswana) 1980–, mem. Nat. Archives Advisory Council, mem. Univ. of Botswana Review Comm.; mem. Pres.'s Comm. on Incomes Policy 1989–90; mem. Namibian Pres. Comm. on Higher Educ. 1991, Univ. of Botswana Review Comm. 1990, UNESCO Bd 1992–95; Chair. SADCC Consultancy on Human Resources Devt 1991, Asscn of Eastern and Southern African Univs. 1992–93; Vice-Chair. Asscn of Commonwealth Univs 1993, Chair. 1994; mem. Bd Botswana Tech. Centre; mem. Nat. Employment, Manpower and Incomes Council; Chair. Asscn of Eastern and Southern Africa Univs; mem. Exec. Bd Asscn of African Univs 1993–96, Botswana Inst. of Devt Policy Analysis (Chair. 1999–), Botswana Nat. Council on Educ. (Chair. 1999–); mem. Council, Univ. of Swaziland 1993–95; mem. American-African Studies Asscn, Life mem. Botswana Soc.; mem. Bd Lutheran World Fed. (LWF) 1998–, mem. LWF Study Group on African Religion 1998–; Hon. DLitt (Luther Coll.) 1978; Hon. LLD (Ohio) 1986; Chevalier des Palmes académiques 1982, Presidential Order of Honour 1994. *Publications:* History of Botswana (co-author), A History of Ngamiland 1750–1906: The Formation of an African State, Biography of Seretse Khama 1995; and several articles and book chapters on history of Botswana and Ngamiland. *Leisure interest:* swimming, reading, walking. *Address:* P.O. Box 1004, Gaborone, Botswana. *Telephone:* 3552661 (Office); 3927645 (Home). *Fax:* 585098. *E-mail:* tlout@mopipi-ub.bw (Office).

TOBIA, Maguid, BSc; Egyptian author; b. 25 March 1938, Minia; teacher of math. 1960–68; mem. Higher Council of Arts and Literature 1969–78; mem. staff Ministry of Culture 1978–; mem. Writers' Union, Chamber of Cinema Industry, Soc. of Egyptian Film Critics, Fiction Cttee of Supreme Council of Culture; Medal of Science and Arts (First Class); several literary prizes. *Film scripts include:* Story from Our Country, Sons of Silence, Stars' Maker, Harem Cage. *Play:* International Laugh Bank. *Television:* Friendly Visit (series). *Publications:* (collections of short stories): Vostock Reaches the Moon, Five Unread Papers, The Coming Days, The Companion; (novels): Circles of Impossibility, Sons of Silence, The They, The Room of Floor Chances, The Music Kiosk, Hanan, The Strange Deeds of Kings and the Intrigues of Banks, The Emigration to the North Country of Hathoot's Tribe (3 vols), The Story of Beautiful Reem; contribs to Al Ahram and several Arabic magazines. *Leisure interests:* reading, travel. *Address:* 15 El-Lewaa Abd El Aziz Aly, Heliopolis 11361, Cairo, Egypt. *Telephone:* 2917801. *Fax:* 2917801.

TOBIAS, Phillip Vallentine, PhD, DSc, MBBCh, FRS, FRCP; South African professor emeritus of anatomy and anthropologist; b. 14 Oct. 1925, Durban; s. of late Joseph Newman Tobias and Fanny Rosendorff; ed St Andrew's School, Bloemfontein, Durban High School, Univ. of the Witwatersrand and Emmanuel Coll., Cambridge; Lecturer in Anatomy, Univ. of Witwatersrand 1951–52, Sr Lecturer 1953–58, Dir Palaeo-anthropology Research Unit 1966–96, Prof. and Head of Anatomy Dept 1959–90, Dean of Faculty of Medicine 1980–82, Hon. Professorial Research Fellow 1994–, Prof. Emer. 1994–; Dir Sterkfontein Research Unit 1999–; fmr Visiting or Hon. Prof. Univs of Cambridge, Pennsylvania, Cornell, Vienna, Palma de Mallorca, Florence, Namjing Normal, IVPP, Accad. Sinica, Beijing; Founder-Pres. Inst. for the Study of Mankind in Africa, Anatomical Soc. of Southern Africa, S. African Soc. for Quaternary Research; Hon. mem. and mem. numerous int. asscns.; Foreign Assoc. NAS; Fellow Linnean Soc. of London; sometime Vice-Pres. and acting Exec. Pres. S. African Asscn for the Advancement of Science; Pres. Royal Soc. of S. Africa 1970–72. Int. Asscn of Human Biologists 1994–98; Perm. Council mem. Int. Union of Prehistoric and Protohistoric Sciences, Pan-African Congress of Prehistory and Quaternary Studies, Int. Asscn of Human Biologists; Trustee, Leakey Foundation, Pasadena, Calif.; Vice-Pres. World Cultural Council 2001–; Hon. Prof. of Palaeo-anthropology, Bernard Price Inst. for Palaeontological Research; Hon. Prof. of Zoology; Hon. Corresp. mem., Austrian Acad. of Sciences 1978; Hon. Fellow, Royal Anthropological Inst. of Great Britain and Ireland, Royal Soc. of S. Africa, Coll. of Medicine of S. Africa, American Philosophical Soc.; Foreign Hon. mem. American Acad. of Arts and Sciences 1986–; Hon. DSc (Natal) 1980, (Cambridge) 1988, (Univ. of Western Ont.) 1986, (Alberta) 1987, (Cape Town) 1988, (Guelph) 1990, (S. Africa) 1990, (Durban-Westville) 1993, (Pennsylvania) 1994, (Witwatersrand) 1994, (Musée Nat. d'Histoire Naturelle, Paris) 1996, (Barcelona) 1997, (Turin) 1998, (Charles Univ. Prague) 1999, (Stellenbosch) 1999; British Asscn Medal 1952, Simon Biesheuvel Medal 1966, South Africa Medal 1967, Sr Captain Scott Medal 1973, Rivers Memorial Medal 1978, Anisfield-Wolf Award for Race Relations 1978, Rotary Int. Paul Harris Award 1981, 1991, Percy Fox Foundation Award 1983, Phillip Tobias Medal 1983, Certificate of Honour, Univ. of Calif. 1983, Balzan Prize 1987, John F.W. Herschel Medal 1990, Silver Medal-Medical Asscn of S. Africa 1990, 1st John Grant Distinguished Lecturer Award, Univ. of Toronto 1991, 1st L.S.B. Leakey Prize 1991, Carmel Merit Award (Haifa) 1992, Huxley Memorial Medal of Royal Anthropological Inst. 1996; Order for Meritorious Service (Gold Class) of S. Africa 1992, Commdr Ordre National du Mérite (France) 1998, Order of Southern Cross, Silver Class (S. Africa) 1999, Wood Jones Medal of the Royal Coll. of Surgeons 1997, Charles R. Darwin Lifetime Achievement Award, American Asscn of Physical Anthropologists 1997, Gold Medal, Charles Univ. 1999, Hrdlicka Memorial Medal 1999, Gold Medal of Simon van der Stel Foundation (S. Africa) 1999, Commdr Order of Merit (Italy) 2000, Plaque of Honour, Univ. of S. Amaro, São Paulo 2001, UNESCO Medal 2001, Medal of Honour, Univ. of Cagliari 2001, Hon. Cross for Science and Arts (First Class) (Austria) 2002, Siriraj Foundation Sangvichien Medal, Thailand 2002. *Achievements:* only person at Witwatersrand Univ. to hold three chairs simultaneously (anatomy, palaeoanthropology, zoology). *Publications:* Chromosomes, Sex-cells and Evolution 1956, Olduvai Gorge Vol. II 1967, Man's Anatomy (with M. Arnold) 1968, The Brain in Hominid Evolution 1971, The Meaning of Race 1972, The Bushmen 1978, Dart, Taung and the Missing Link 1984, Hominid Evolution: Past, Present and Future 1985, Olduvai Gorge Vol. IV*A* and *B* 1991, Images of Humanity 1991, Paleo-antropologia 1992, Il Bipede Barcollante 1992 The Origins and Past of Modern Humans 1998, Humanity from African Naissance to Coming Millennia 2001; over 1,100 scientific and other publs. *Leisure interests:* people, books, music, philately, art, writing. *Address:* School of Anatomical Sciences, University of the Witwatersrand Medical School, 7 York Road, Parktown, Johannesburg, 2193 (Office); 409 Summerhill, Sally's Alley, Kentview, Johannesburg 2196, South Africa (Home). *Telephone:* (11) 7172516 (Office); (11) 8852748 (Home). *Fax:* (11) 7172773 (Office). *E-mail:* tobiaspv@anatomy.wits.ac.za (Office).

TOBIAS, Randall L., BS; American business executive; b. 20 March 1942, Lafayette, Ind.; m. 1st Marilyn Jane Salyer 1966 (died 1994); one s. one d.; m. 2nd Marianne Williams 1995; one step-s. one step-d.; ed Indiana Univ.; served U.S. Army 1964–66; numerous positions Ind. Bell 1964–81, Ill. Bell 1977–81; Vice-Pres. (residence marketing, sales and service) AT & T 1981–82; Pres. American Bell Consumer Products 1983–84, Sr Vice-Pres. 1984–85, Chair. and CEO AT & T Communications, New York 1985–91, AT & T Int., Basking Ridge, NJ 1991–93, Vice-Chair. Bd AT & T, New York and Chair. Bd Dirs. 1986–93; Chair., Pres. and CEO Eli Lilly & Co., Indianapolis 1993–98, Chair. Emer. 1999; mem. Bd Dirs. Eli Lilly & Co., Kimberly-Clark, Knight-Ridder, Phillips Petroleum; Chair. Bd of Trustees Duke Univ.; Vice-Chair. Colonial Williamsburg Foundation; mem. Council on Foreign Relations, numerous other appointments. *Leisure interests:* skiing, shooting. *Address:* c/o Eli Lilly & Co., 500 East 96th Street, Suite 110, Indianapolis, IN 46240, USA.

TOBIN, Brian; Canadian politician; b. 21 Oct. 1954, Stephenville, Newfoundland; s. of Patrick Tobin and Mary Frye; m. Jodean Smith 1977; two s. one d.; ed Memorial Univ., St. John's, Newfoundland; worked as a journalist; MP for Humber-St Barbe-Baie Verte 1980–96; MP for Bonavista-Trinity-Conception 2000–; Parl. Sec. to Minister of Fisheries and Oceans 1980; Minister of Fisheries and Oceans 1993, of Industry and Minister responsible for the Atlantic Canada Opportunities Agency and for Western Econ. Diversification and Francophonie and for the Econ. Devt Agency of Canada for the Regions of Québec 2000–01; Premier of Newfoundland 1996–2000; Chair. Nat. Liberal Caucus 1989; mem. numerous House of Commons Cttees. *Address:* c/o Ministry of Industry, CD Howe Building, 235 Queen Street, Ottawa, Ont., K1A 0H5, Canada (Office).

TODD, Damian Roderic, BA; British diplomatist; b. 29 Aug. 1959, Crawley, Surrey; s. of George Todd and Annette Todd; ed Worcester Coll. Oxford; joined diplomatic service 1980; Third, later Second Sec., Cape Town and Pretoria 1981–84; at FCO, London 1984–87, 1989–91, 1997–98; Consul and First Sec., Prague 1987–89; First Sec. (Econ.), Bonn 1991–95; seconded to Treasury, London 1995–97, Head Agric. Team 1996–97, Head EU Co-ordination and Strategy Team 1998–2001; Amb. to Slovakia 2001–. *Leisure interests:* history, family life, looking at buildings. *Address:* Embassy of UK, Panska 16, 811 01 Bratislava, Slovakia (Office).

TODD, Sir David, Kt, CBE, MD, FAM, FRCP, FRCPE, FRCPGLAS, FRACP, FRCPATH; British professor of medicine; b. 17 Nov. 1928, China; s. of Paul J. Todd and Margaret S. Todd; ed Univ. of Hong Kong; Prof. Dept of Medicine, Univ. of Hong Kong 1972–96, Head, Dept of Medicine 1974–89, Sub-Dean, Faculty of Medicine 1976–78, Pro-Vice-Chancellor 1978–80; consultant (medicine) to Govt of Hong Kong 1974–89; Pres. Hong Kong Acad. of Medicine 1992–96, Council for AIDS Trust Fund, Hong Kong 1993–96; Hon. DSc (Chinese Univ. of Hong Kong) 1990, (Hong Kong Univ.) 1992. *Publications:* numerous articles in professional journals. *Leisure interests:* classical music, stamp collecting, swimming. *Address:* D12 Breezy Court, 2A Park Road, Mid-levels, Hong Kong Special Administrative Region, People's Republic of China.

TODD, Olivier, MA; French writer; b. 19 June 1929, Neuilly; s. of Julius Oblatt and Helen Todd; m. 1st Anne-Marie Nizan 1948; m. 2nd France Huser 1982; two s. two d.; ed Sorbonne, Corpus Christi Coll., Cambridge; teacher Lycée Int. du Shape 1956–62; Univ. Asst St-Cloud 1962–64; reporter Nouvel Observateur 1964–69; Ed. TV Programme Panorama 1969–70; Asst Ed. Nouvel Observateur 1970–77; columnist and Man. Ed. L'Express 1977–81; worked for BBC (Europa, 24 Hours) 1964–69; Hon. PhD (Stirling, Bristol); Prix Cazes 1981, Prix France Télévision 1997, Prix du Mémorial 1997, Chevalier Légion d'honneur, Commdr des Arts et Lettres. *Publications:* Une demi-campagne 1957, La traversée de la Manche 1960, Des trous dans le jardin 1969, L'année du Crabe 1972, Les Canards de Ca Mao 1975, La marelle de Giscard 1977, Portraits 1979, Un fils rebelle 1981, Un cannibale très convenable 1982, Une légère gueule de bois 1983, La balade du chômeur 1986, Cruel Avril 1987, La Négociation 1989, La Sanglière 1992, Albert Camus, une vie 1996, André Malraux, une vie 2001. *Leisure interests:* walking, Luxembourg Gardens. *Address:* 21 rue de l'Odéon, 75006 Paris; 8 rue du Pin, 83310 La Garde Freinet, France. *Telephone:* 1-43-29-55-26.

TODD, Richard Andrew Palethorpe, OBE; British actor and producer; b. 11 June 1919, Dublin, Ireland; s. of Major A. W. Palethorpe Todd and Marvilla Palethorpe Todd (née Agar-Daly); m. 1st Catherine Stewart Crawford Grant-Bogle 1949 (divorced 1970); one s. one d.; m. 2nd Virginia Anne Rollo Mailer 1970 (divorced 1992); two s. (one deceased); ed Shrewsbury, privately; began theatrical career, London 1937; founder-mem. Dundee Repertory Co. 1938–39, rejoined 1947; served in King's Own Yorkshire Light Infantry and

Parachute Regt 1940–46; entered film industry in For Them That Trespass 1948; Past Grand Steward, Grand Lodge of England, Past Master Lodge of Emulation No.21; Pres. Birmingham Age Concern 1990–; nominated for Best Actor Award, Acad. Awards 1950, won British Nat. Film Award, PictureGoer Award, Hollywood Golden Globe. *Other films include:* The Hasty Heart 1949, Stage Fright 1950, Lightning Strikes Twice (USA) 1951, Robin Hood 1952, Twenty-Four Hours of a Woman's Life, The Venetian Bird 1953, Rob Roy 1954, The Sword and the Rose 1954, The Dam Busters 1955, A Man Called Peter 1955, The Virgin Queen (USA) 1955, The Sixth of June, Yangtse Incident 1956, Saint Joan, Chase a Crooked Shadow 1957, The Naked Earth, Danger Within 1958, The Long, the Short and the Tall 1959, Don't Bother to Knock (for own film co. Haileywood Films Ltd) 1960, The Hellions 1960, Never Let Go 1961, The Longest Day 1962, The Boys 1962, Sanders 1963, Operation Crossbow 1965, Coast of Skeletons 1965, The Last of the Long-Haired Boys 1968, Dorian Gray 1970, Asylum 1972, Secret Agent 008 1976, The House of the Long Shadows 1982, The Olympus Force 1988; returned to London stage as Lord Goring (An Ideal Husband) 1965, Nicholas Randolph (Dear Octopus), Haymarket 1967; formed Triumph Theatre Production 1970, appeared in numerous productions in Britain, as the Comte (The Marquise), USA 1972, as Andrew Wyke (Sleuth), Australia and New Zealand 1972–73, English tour 1976, RSC productions of The Hollow Crown and Pleasure and Repentance, Canada and USA 1974, as Martin Dysart (Equus) for Australian Nat. Theatre Co., Perth Festival 1975, toured as John (Miss Adams Will Be Waiting) 1975, toured SA in On Approval 1976, in Quadrille 1977, The Heat of the Moment 1977, appeared in Double Edge in UK and Canada 1978, in Nightfall, South Africa 1979, in This Happy Breed, UK 1980; The Business of Murder (Duchess Theatre 1981, Mayfair Theatre 1981–88), The Woman in Black (Sydney Opera House) 1991; as Lord Caversham (An Ideal Husband), Old Vic 1996, Albery Theatre, Theatre Royal Haymarket 1998, Lyric Theatre 1999. *TV appearances include:* Wuthering Heights, Dr. Who, Virtual Murder, as H.G. Wells in Beautiful Lies, Carrington V.C., Silent Witness. *Publications:* Caught in the Act (Vol. I of autobiog.) 1986, In Camera (Vol. II of autobiog.) 1989. *Leisure interests:* game shooting, fishing, gardening. *Address:* Chinham Farm, Faringdon, Oxon., SN7 8EZ; c/o Richard Stone Partnership, 2 Henrietta Street, London, WC2E 8PS (Office); Little Ponton House, nr Grantham, Lincs. NG33 5BS, England. *Telephone:* (20) 7497-0849 (Office); (1367) 710294. *Fax:* (1367) 710294; (20) 7497-0869 (Office).

TODD, Ronald (Ron); British trade union official (retd); b. 11 March 1927, Walthamstow; s. of George Todd and Emily Todd; m. Josephine Tarrant 1945; one s. two d.; ed St Patrick's School, Walthamstow; served Royal Marine Commandos; joined Transport and Gen. Workers' Union (T&GWU) while employee of Ford Motor Co., Deputy Convenor 1954–62, full-time Union Officer, Metal, Eng and Chemical Sections 1962–69, Regional Officer 1969–75, Regional Secretary, Region No. 1 1976–78, Nat. Organizer 1978–84, Gen. Sec. 1985–92; mem. TUC Gen. Council, TUC Econ. Cttee, Equal Rights, Health Service Cttees., TUC Gen. Council mem. of NEDC 1985–92, TUC/Labour Party Liaison Cttee; Chair. TUC Int. Cttee; Commr on Manpower Services Comm.; mem. Employment Appeal Tribunal; Pres. Unity Trust 1986–89; Hon. Vice-Pres. Campaign for Nuclear Disarmament, Nat. Cttee World Disarmament Campaign; mem. Nat. Council Royal Marines Asscn; Trades Union rep. Anti-Apartheid Cttee, T&GWU rep. on Nat. Union of Mineworkers Dispute Co-ordinating Cttee, Past Commr, Manpower Services Comm.; Past Pres. Unity Trust; Vice-Pres. British Deaf Asscn. *Publications:* On His Todd (collection of poems, sold in aid of Royal London Hosp. Leukaemia Appeal Fund), Still on His Todd (collection of poems, sold in aid of David Jenkinson Memorial Fund), Odd Thoughts in Retirement (collection of poems, sold in aid of One World Action), Odd Thoughts Collection of poems, sold in aid of Jimmy Knapp Cancer Fund). *Leisure interests:* palaeontology and collecting Victorian music covers and political autographs. *Address:* 65 Surrey Road, Dagenham, RM10 8ET, England. *Telephone:* (20) 8593-8683.

TODOROVSKY, Piotr Yefimovich; Russian film director, cameraman and scriptwriter; b. 26 Aug. 1925; m. Myra Grigoryevna Todorovskaya; one s.; ed All-Union Inst. of Cinematography; started as cameraman film studios of Kishinev (Moldovafilm) and Odessa in films Moldavian Tunes 1955, Spring in the Zarechnaya Street 1956, Two Fyodors 1958, Thirst 1960; debut as film Dir Never 1962; numerous prizes All-Union and Int. Festivals in Tokyo, Venice, Berlin, San-Remo and others; Nica Prize 1992, State Prize 1995; People's Artist of Russia 1985. *Film productions include:* Faithfulness 1965 (Prize of Int. Festival in Venice), Juggler 1968, City Romance 1971, Our Own Land 1973, The Last Victim 1976, On Holiday 1979, The Beloved Woman of Mechanic Gavrilov 1982, Wartime Romance 1984, Intergirl 1988, Encore, Encore 1993, What a Wonderful Game 1995, Retro for Three Together 1998; frequently author of scripts and music for his own films. *Leisure interests:* composition and performance of guitar music. *Address:* Vernadskogo prospect 70A, Apt. 23, 117454 Moscow, Russia (Home). *Telephone:* (095) 193-52-06 (Home).

TODOROVSKY, Valery Petrovich; Russian film director; b. 8 May 1962, Odessa; s. of Piotr Yefimovich Todorovsky and Maiya Grigoriyevna Todorovskaya; ed All-Union Inst. of Cinematography; began career as scriptwriter. *Films include:* (scriptwriter) Sea Wolf, A Man of the Retinue, Cynics, Above Dark Water, (Dir) Hearse (Mannheim Film Festival Prize 1991), Live (UNICEF Prize, Chicago Film Festival), Moscow Nights (Green Apple Prize,

Golden Leaf), Land of Deaf, Love, Kamenskaya (for TV). *Address:* Ramenki str. 11, korp. 2, Apt. 272, 117607 Moscow, Russia. *Telephone:* (095) 931-56-63.

TOENNIES, Jan Peter, PhD; American physicist; b. 3 May 1930, Philadelphia, Pa; s. of Dr. Gerrit Toennies and Dita Jebens; m. Monika Zelesnick 1966; two d.; ed Amherst Coll., Brown Univ.; Asst, Bonn Univ., Fed. Repub. of Germany 1962–65, Privat Dozent 1965–67, Dozent 1967–69; Scientific mem. and Dir Max-Planck-Inst. für Strömungsforschung (Fluid Dynamics) 1969–98, Dir Emer. 1998–2004, Admin. Dir 2001–02; Assoc. Prof. Göttingen Univ. 1971–; Corresp. mem. Acad. of Sciences, Göttingen; mem. German Acad. of Natural Sciences 'Leopoldina'; Hon. Prof. Bonn Univ. 1971– Hon. DPhil (Gothenburg) 2000; Physics Prize, Göttingen Acad. of Sciences 1964, Gold Heyrovsky Medal of the Czechoslovak Acad. of Sciences 1991, 1991 Hewlett-Packard Europhysics Prize (for outstanding achievement in condensed matter research), Max Planck Prize, Alexander von Humboldt Foundation 1992, Stern-Gerlach Medal, German Physical Soc. 2002. *Publications:* Chemical Reactions in Shock Waves (with E.F. Greene) 1964, A Study of Intermolecular Potentials with Molecular Beams at Thermal Energies (with H. Pauly) in Advances in Atomic and Molecular Physics 1965, Molecular Beam Scattering Experiments, contribution in Physical Chemistry, an Advanced Treatise 1974, Rotationally and Vibrationally Inelastic Scattering of Molecules (Chem. Soc. Review) 1974, Scattering Studies of Rotational and Vibrational Excitation of Molecules (with M. Faubel) 1977, Advances in Atomic and Molecular Physics 1977, The Study of the Forces between Atoms of Single Crystal Surfaces 1988; over 560 publs in scientific journals. *Leisure interest:* sailing. *Address:* Max-Planck-Institut für Strömungsforschung, Bunsenstrasse 10, 37073 Göttingen (Office); Ewaldstrasse 7, 37085 Göttingen, Germany (Home). *Telephone:* (551) 5176600 (Office); (551) 57172 (Home). *Fax:* (551) 5176607 (Office). *E-mail:* jtoenni@gwdg.de (Office).

TOH CHIN CHYE, PhD; Singaporean politician and physiologist; b. 10 Dec. 1921, Malaya; s. of Toh Kim Poh and Tan Chuan Bee; m. Yeapp Sui Phek; one d.; ed Raffles Coll., Singapore, Univ. Coll., London Univ. and National Inst. for Medical Research, London; Founder, People's Action Party, Chair. 1954–; Reader in Physiology, Univ. of Singapore 1958–64; Research Assoc., Univ. of Singapore 1964; Deputy Prime Minister of Singapore 1959–68; Minister for Science and Tech. 1968–75, for Health 1975–81; MP Singapore 1959–88; Chair. Bd of Govs, Singapore Polytechnic 1959–75; Vice-Chancellor, Univ. of Singapore 1968–75; Chair. of Bd of Govs Regional Inst. for Higher Educ. and Devt 1970–75; Chair. Applied Research Corpn 1973–75; Hon. DLitt (Univ. of Singapore) 1976; Nila Utama, First Class 1990. *Leisure interests:* orchids, reading. *Address:* 23 Greenview Crescent, Singapore 289332, Singapore.

TOIBIN, Colm; Irish journalist and writer; b. 1955; journalist, columnist Dublin Sunday Independent 1985–; E. M. Forster Award, American Acad. of Arts and Letters 1995. *Publications:* Seeing is Believing: Moving Statues in Ireland 1985, Walking Along the Border 1987, Homage to Barcelona 1990, Dubliners 1990, The South (novel) 1990, The Trial of the Generals: Selected Journalism 1980–90, The Heather Blazing 1993, Soho Square 6: New Writing from Ireland 1993; articles. *Address:* 23 Carnew Street, Dublin 7, Ireland.

TOIVO, Andimba Toivo ya; Namibian politician; b. 22 Aug. 1924, Omangundu, Ovamboland; s. of Andimba Toivo ya Toivo and Nashikoto Elizabeth; m. 2nd Vicki Lynn Erenstein 1990; three s. two d.; ed St Mary's Mission School, Odimbo; taught at St Mary's Mission School, Odimbo; served in SA Army 1942–43; worked in SA gold mines and on railways; mem. African National Congress and Modern Youth Soc.; deported to Ovamboland 1958; f. (with Sam Nujoma) SW African People's Org. (SWAPO); arrested 1966; sentenced to 20 years' imprisonment, Robben Island 1968; released in Windhoek, Namibia 1984; mem. Politburo and Sec.-Gen. SWAPO 1984–91; Minister of Mines and Energy 1990–98, of Labour 1999–; leader SWAPO del. to UN 1984. *Leisure interests:* volleyball, tennis, jogging, swimming and reading. *Address:* Private Bag 19005, 32 Mercedes Street, Khomasdal, Windhoek (Office); 9 Bruce Street, Klein, Windhoek; P.O. Box 2038, Windhoek, Namibia. *Telephone:* (61) 2066321 (Home). *Fax:* (61) 210047.

TOKAREVA, Victoria Samoilovna; Russian writer and script writer; b. 20 Nov. 1937, Leningrad; ed All-Union Inst. of Cinematography; literary debut 1969; freelance writer; mem. Russian Writers' Union 1971. *Film scripts include:* Gentlemen of Luck, Mimino, A Dog Was Walking on the Piano. *Publications:* A Day Without Lies 1967, About What That Has Never Been 1969 (collected stories), Flying Swing (collected stories) 1978, Nothing Particular 1983; numerous works of prose 1994–97. *Address:* Dovzhenko str. 12, korp. 1, apt. 148, 119590 Moscow, Russia (Home). *Telephone:* (095) 147-99-71 (Home).

TOKAEV, Kasymzhomart Kemelevich; Kazakhstan diplomatist and politician; b. 17 May 1953, Almaty, Kazakhstan; s. of the late Kemel Tokaev and of Turash Shabyrbayeva; m. Nadeyda Tokaeva (née Poznanskaya) 1983; one s.; ed Moscow Inst. of Int. Relations, Diplomatic Acad., USSR Ministry of Foreign Affairs, Inst. of the Chinese Language, Beijing; with USSR Ministry of Foreign Affairs 1975; Embassy, Singapore 1975–79; Attaché, Third Sec. Ministry of Foreign Affairs 1979–83; Second Sec. of Dept 1984–85; Second, First Sec. Embassy, People's Repub. of China 1985–91; rank of Amb. of Kazakhstan 1994; Deputy, First Deputy Minister of Foreign Affairs Repub. of Kazakhstan 1992–94, State Sec. and Minister 1994–99; Deputy Prime Minister March–Oct. 1999, Prime Minister of Kazakhstan 1999–2002, Sec. of State, Minister of Foreign Affairs Jan. 2002–; Parasat (Nat. Award) 1996,

Astana Medal. *Publications:* How it was...Disturbance in Beijing 1993, United Nations: Half a Century of Serving for Peace 1995, Under the Banner of Independence 1997, Kazakhstan Foreign Policy in the context of Globalisation 2000, Diplomacy of the Republic of Kazakhstan 2001. *Leisure interests:* reading, playing tennis. *Address:* Ministry of Foreign Affairs, Beybitshikik str. 10, 473000 Astana, Kazakhstan (Office). *Telephone:* (3172) 15-30-03 (Office). *Fax:* (3172) 32-76-67. *E-mail:* ministr@mid.kz (Office). *Website:* www .mfa.kz.

TŐKEI, Ferenc, MA, D.LITT.SC.; Hungarian philosopher and sinologue; b. 3 Oct. 1930, Budapest; s. of Ferenc Tőkei and Irma Kiss; m. Margit Egry; two s. one d.; ed Eötvös Loránd Univ. Budapest; on staff Hopp Ferenc Museum of East-Asian Arts, Budapest 1956–57; Ed. Europa Publishing House, Budapest 1957–67; acad. researcher 1967–69; Dir Inst. of Philosophy, Hungarian Acad. of Sciences 1969–72; corresp. mem. of Acad. 1973–, mem. 1985–; Head of Orientalistic Research Group 1972–; Chair. Hungarian Philosophical Asscn 1987–90; mem. Bd Kőrösi Csoma Soc.; ed. Acta Orient. Hung. 1977–90; Pres. Cttee for Orientalistic Studies, Hungarian Acad. of Sciences 1976–86; Prof. of Philosophy Eötvös L. Univ. Budapest 1970–90, Prof. of Chinese 1990–2000; State Prize Award 1970. *Publications:* A kínai elégia születése 1959, Naissance de l'élégie chinoise 1967, Az ázsiai termelési mód kérdéséhez 1965, Zur Frage der asiatischen Produktionsweise 1969, Műfajelmélet Kínában a III-VI. században 1967, Genre Theory in China in 3rd–6th Centuries 1971, Kínai filozófia, Ókor I-III 1962–67, 1980, 1986, A szépség szíve 1973, Sinológiai műhely 1974, A társadalmi formák marxista elméletének néhány kérdése 1977, 1988, Zur marxistischen Geschichtstheorie I–II 1977, Essays on the Asiatic Mode of Production 1979, Primitive Society and the Asiatic Mode of Production 1989, Kortársunk-e Marx? 1984, Karl Marx—unser Zeitgenosse? 1990, Kínai buddhista filozófia 1993, 1996, Kínai szofisztika és logika 1997, A kínai festészet elmélete 1997, A kínai költészet elméleteiből 1998, Kínai-magyar irodalmi gyűjtemény I-II 1997–99, A kínai zene elméletéből 2000. *Leisure interests:* travelling, tourism. *Address:* 1022 Budapest, Felvinci út 22, Hungary. *Telephone:* (1) 316-6244. *Fax:* (1) 316-6244. *E-mail:* ferenc.tokei@ ella.hu.

TŐKÉS, Rev. László; Romanian ecclesiastic; b. 1 April 1952, Cluj/Kolozsvár; s. of István Tőkés and Erzsébet Vass; m. Edit Joó 1985; two s. one d.; ed Protestant Theological Inst. Cluj; Asst minister at Brașov/Brassó, then at Dej/Dés 1975–84; discharged for political reasons and suspended from church service 1984–86; reinstalled as chaplain then pastor, Timișoara/Temesvár 1986–89; banished to small parish of Mineu/Menyő, threatened with eviction; demonstration by supporters was beginning of revolution that overthrew Communist Govt 1989; Oradea Bishop of (Királyhágómellék Diocese, Nagyvárad) 1990–; mem. Temporary Nat. Salvation Council; Co-Chair. Hungarian Reformed Synod of Romania; Hon. Pres. Hungarian Democratic Alliance of Hungarians in Romania; Hon. Pres. Hungarian World Fed.; Pres. Reformed Hungarian World Fed.; Dr. hc (Theological Acad. of Debrecen) 1990, (Regent Univ., Va Beach, USA) 1990, (Hope Coll., Holland, Mich.) 1991; Berzsenyi Prize, Hungary 1989, Roosevelt Prize of The Netherlands 1990, Bethlen Gábor Prize, Hungary 1990, Geuzenpenning Prize, Netherlands 1991, Pro Fide Prize, Finland 1993, Bocskay Prize, Hungary 1995, Hungarian Heritage Prize 1996, Minority Prize of Catalan CIEMEN Centre, Spain 1996, Leopold Kunschak Prize, Austria 1998; Freeman Cities of Sárospatak amd Székelyudvarhely and of 5th and 11th dists. of Budapest; mem. Johannit Order of Knighthood. *Publications:* Where the Lord's Soul, there Freedom (selections of sermons) 1990, The Siege of Timișoara '89 1990, With God for the People 1990, There is a Time to Speak (with David Porter) 1993, A Phrase—and what is Behind 1993, In the Spirit of Timișoara. Ecumenism and Reconciliation 1996, Hope and Reality—selected writings 1999, Timișoara Memento—Self Confessions 1999, Timișoara Siege 1999; sermons, articles in ecclesiastical and secular Publs. *Address:* 3700 Oradea, Str. Craiovei 1, Romania (Office). *Telephone:* (991) 131708 (Office).

TOKODY, Ilona; Hungarian soprano; b. Szeged; d. of András Tokody and Ilona Nagy; ed Liszt Ferenc Music Acad., Budapest; won Kodály singing competition 1972, Erkel competition of Inter-konzert Agency 1973, Ostend competition operatic category 1976; joined State Opera, Budapest 1976; regular guest performer Staatsoper Wien and Deutsche Oper West-Berlin; appearances in opera houses and concert halls worldwide, including Metropolitan Opera House, Royal Opera House Covent Garden, Vienna State Opera, San Francisco Opera, Teatro Colón, Buenos Aires, Liceo, Barcelona, Bavarian State Opera, San Carlo, Naples, Rome Opera, Bolshoi, Carnegie Hall, New York, Musikverein, Vienna, Royal Opera, Copenhagen. *Operatic roles include:* leading roles in La Forza del Destino, Don Carlos, Suor Angelica, Madama Butterfly, Il Trovatore, Aida, La Juive, La Bohème, Manon Lescaut; Nedda (I Pagliacci), Micaela (Carmen), Alice (Falstaff), Giselda (I Lombardi), Desdemona (Otello). *Recordings:* Suor Angelica, Nerone, La Fiamma, Brahms Requiem, Il Tabarro, Guntram, Iris. *Leisure interests:* cooking, badminton, gymnastics, table tennis, reading. *Address:* c/o Hungarian State Opera, 1062 Budapest, Andrássy ut 22, Hungary. *Telephone:* (1) 312-550.

TOKOMBAYEVA, Aysulu Asanbekovna; Kyrgyzstan ballerina; b. 22 Sept. 1947, Frunze (now Bishkek); d. of Asanbek Tokombayev and Munjiya Sultanova; m. Kuvan Aliyev; ed Vaganova Dancing School, Leningrad (now Ballet Acad., St Petersburg, Russia); ballet soloist Opera and Ballet Theatre of Kyrgyzstan 1966–95; Prof. of Ballet Conservatoire, Ankara, Turkey 1995–; Youth Prize 1968, USSR State Prize 1976, Aitmatov Int. Prize 1994; People's

Artist of Kirghizia 1976; USSR People's Artist 1981. *Major roles include:* Odette-Odile (Swan Lake), Aurore (Sleeping Beauty), Giselle, La Bayadère, Frigia (Spartacus), Lady Macbeth (by K. Molchanov), Cholpon (by Rauhverger), Carmen, Tomiris (by Musaev), Mariya (Bakhchiserai Fountain), Chopiniana, Tolgonay (Mother's Field), Pakhita, Spanish Pictures. *Leisure interests:* classical music, poetry, nature. *Address:* Kyrgyz State Opera and Ballet Theatre, Bishkek (Office); Usenbaev Str. 37, Apt. 33, 720021 Bishkek, Kyrgyzstan (Home). *Telephone:* (312) 28-29-57 (Home).

TOLEDO, Francisco; Mexican artist; b. 1940, Juchitan, Tehuantepec; worked in Paris until 1965; returned to Mexico 1965; worked at Casa de la Cultura, Juchitan and Inst. de Artes Gráficas, Oaxaca; associated with Museo de Arte Contemporaneo de Oaxaca, Jorge Luis Borges Library for the Blind, Cine El Pochote, Centro Cultural de Santo Domingo. *Art Exhibitions include:* Planos de Juchitan, Titulos Primordiales, Venado con zapatos 1970, Tamazul (Sapo) 1977, Canonazo 1998, Self Portrait 1999, Retrospective, Whitechapel Art Gallery, London 2000.

TOLEDO MANRIQUE, Alejandro ('Cholo'), PhD; Peruvian politician and economist; b. 28 March 1946, Cabana, Ancash Prov.; m. Eliane Karp; ed Univs. of Stanford and San Francisco, USA; fmr mem. staff World Bank; adviser to UN, World Bank, IDB, ILO and OECD; Research Fellow, Inst. for Int. Devt, Harvard Univ., 1991–94; Perm. Prof. of ESAN Univ. Lima; Visiting Prof. Univ. of Waseda & Japan Foundation, Tokyo; Founder-mem. and Leader Perú Posible party (opposition alliance); Presidential cand. 2000, subsequently boycotted election; Pres. of Peru July 2001–. *Publications:* Las Cartas sobre la Mesa, Social Inversion for Growth, Economic Structural Reforms, Peru's Challenge: The Transition to Sustained Economic Growth; and several books on econs and devt. *Address:* Ministry of the Presidency, Avda Paseo de la República 4297, Lima 1, Peru (Office); Perú Posible, Bajada Balta 131, Miraflores, Lima. *Telephone:* (1) 4465886 (Office); (1) 2419307 (pp). *Fax:* (1) 4470379 (Office); (21) 2419307. *E-mail:* Preisa@perupossible.org.pe (Office). *Website:* www.perupossible.org (Office).

TOLNAY, Lajos, PhD; Hungarian business executive; b. 27 Sept. 1948, Sajószentpéter; m.; four c.; ed Heavy Industries Tech. Univ. Miskolc and Budapest Univ. of Econs; various positions DIMAG Co. Ltd 1971–92, Gen. Dir 1989–92; Man. Dir Dunaferr Trading House Ltd 1992–93; Pres.-Man. Dir PTW Investment Co. Ltd 1993–95; Pres.-Man. Dir Rákóczi Bank 1994, Pres. Aug. 1994–; Chair. Hungarian Chamber of Commerce 1990–93, Hungarian Chamber of Commerce and Industry 1994–; Man. Dir Inota Aluminium Co. Ltd 1996–; Chair. Bd Magyar Aluminium Inc. 1997–; Chair. Controlling Cttee Életút First Nat. Pension Fund; Chair. NAT Hungarian Accreditation Bd; mem. Exec. Bd ICC, Hon. Chair. ICC Hungary; mem. Supervisory Bd Hungexpo Co. Ltd, Bankár Investment Co. Ltd; various awards and decorations. *Address:* Magyar Kereskedelmi és Iparkamara, 1372 Budapest, V, P.O. Box 452, Hungary (Office). *Telephone:* (1) 368-6890 (Office). *Fax:* (1) 250-5138 (Office). *E-mail:* mkik@mail.mkik.hu.

TOLSTAYA, Tatyana Nikitichna; Russian writer; b. 3 May 1951, Leningrad (now St Petersburg); d. of Mikhail Lozinsky; m. Andrey V. Lebedev; two s.; ed Univ. of Leningrad; Ed. of Eastern Literature Nauka Publishing, Moscow 1987–89; lecturer, Skidmore Coll., NJ, USA. *Publications:* On the Golden Porch (short story) 1983, Sleepwalkers In A Fog 1992, Night 1995, Day 1997, Kys 1998. *Address:* c/o Penguin Books Ltd, Bath Road, Harmondsworth, Middx UB7 0DA, England. *Telephone:* (095) 238-22-15 (Moscow); (908) 821-3007 (USA); (1856) 770474 (UK).

TOMALIN, Claire, MA, FRSL; British writer; b. 20 June 1933, London; d. of Emile Delavenay and Muriel Emily Herbert; m. 1st Nicholas Osborne Tomalin 1955 (died 1973); two s. three d. (one d. and one s. deceased); m. 2nd Michael Frayn (q.v.) 1993; ed Hitchin Girls' Grammar School, Dartington Hall School, Newnham Coll., Cambridge; publr.'s reader and Ed. 1955–67; Asst Literary Ed. New Statesman 1968–70, Literary Ed. 1974–77; Literary Ed. Sunday Times 1979–86; Vice-Pres. English PEN 1997, Royal Literary Fund 2000; mem. London Library Cttee 1997–2000, Advisory Cttee for the Arts, Humanities and Social Sciences, British Library 1997–, Council Royal Soc. of Literature 1997–2000; Trustee Nat. Portrait Gallery 1992–; Whitbread Prize 1974, James Tait Black Prize 1990, NCR Book Award 1991, Hawthornden Prize 1991. *Exhibitions:* Mrs. Jordan, English Heritage Kenwood 1995, Hyenas in Petticoats: Mary Wollstonecraft and Mary Shelley, Wordsworth Trust and Nat. Portrait Gallery 1997–98. *Play:* The Winter Wife 1991. *Publications:* The Life and Death of Mary Wollstonecraft 1974, Shelley and his World 1980, Katherine Mansfield: A Secret Life 1987, The Invisible Woman 1990, The Winter Wife 1991, Mrs Jordan's Profession 1994, Jane Austen: A Life 1997, Maurice by Mary Shelley (ed.) 1998, Several Strangers: Writing from Three Decades 1999, Samuel Pepys: The Unequalled Self (Whitbread Awards for Book of the Year and Best Biog.) 2002. *Address:* c/o David Godwin, 55 Monmouth Street, London, WC2H 9DG; 57 Gloucester Crescent, London, NW1 7EG, England. *E-mail:* clairetomalin@dial.pipex.com (Office).

TÓMASSON, Tómas Ármann, MA; Icelandic diplomatist; b. 1 Jan. 1929, Reykjavik; s. of Tómas Tómasson and Gudrun Thorgrimsdóttir; m. Heba Jónsdóttir 1957 (divorced); three s. one d.; ed Reykjavik Grammar School, Univ. of Illinois, Fletcher School of Law and Diplomacy and Columbia Univ.; entered Icelandic foreign service 1954; Sec. Moscow 1954–58; Ministry for Foreign Affairs 1958–60; Deputy Perm. Rep. to NATO and OECD 1960–66; Chief of Div., Ministry for Foreign Affairs 1966–69, Deputy Sec.-Gen. of

Ministry 1970–71; Amb. to Belgium and EEC and Perm. Rep. on N Atlantic Council 1971–77, 1984–86, also accred to Luxembourg 1976–77, 1984–86; Perm. Rep. to UN 1977–82, 1993–94; Amb. to France (also accred to Portugal, Spain, Cape Verde) 1982–84, to USSR (also accred to Bulgaria, GDR, Hungary, Mongolia and Romania) 1987–90; Amb., Head of Del. to CSBMs and CFE negotiation, Vienna 1990; Amb. to USA (also accred to Canada) 1990–93; Amb., Head of Del. to CSCE Review Conf. and Summit, Budapest Oct.–Dec. 1994; mem. staff, Ministry for Foreign Affairs, Reykjavik 1994–; Order of the Falcon (Iceland) and decorations from France, Belgium, Luxembourg, Portugal and Sweden. *Address:* Ministry for Foreign Affairs, 150 Reykjavik; Espigerdi 4/9H, 108 Reykjavik, Iceland (Home). *Telephone:* 5609900. *Fax:* 5622386; 5623152 (Office). *E-mail:* tomas.a.tomasson@utn.stjr.is (Office); tat@islandia.is (Home).

TOMASZEWSKI, Henryk; Polish graphic artist; b. 10 June 1914, Warsaw; m. Teresa Pągowska one s.; ed Acad. of Fine Arts, Warsaw; Ordinary Prof., Lecturer Acad. of Fine Arts 1952–85 Warsaw; mem. Union of Polish Artists and Designers 1944–83, Alliance Graphique Int. 1958–; works in numerous pvt. collections and museums including Nat. Museum, Warsaw and Poznań, Museum of Modern Art, New York and Kanagawa, Japan, Museo de Arte Contemporánea, São Paulo, Kunstgewerbe Museum, Zurich, Stedelijk Museum, Amsterdam Nat. Museum, Warsaw and Poznań, Museum of Modern Art, New York, Museo de Arte Contemporánea, São Paulo, Kunstgewerbe Museum, Zurich, Stedelijk Museum, Amsterdam, Kamakura Museum of Modern Art, Japan; Hon. Royal Designer for Industry, London 1976; Polish Prime Minister's Award 1958, Przegląd Kultury Prize 1960, Alfred Jurzykowski Foundation Award, New York 1984, Icograda Excellence Award 1986, Special Warsaw City Award 1989 and numerous other prizes and awards; Commdr's Cross with Star, Order of Polonia Restituta 1994. *Exhibitions include:* Seventh Biennale d'Arte Moderna, São Paulo (First Prize) 1963, Int. Poster Biennale, Warsaw (Silver Medal) 1966, (Gold and Silver Medal) 1991, Poster Biennale, Lahti (Finland) (Gold Medal) 1981, Third Int. Poster Triennale, Toyama Int. Poster Triennale, Japan (Bronze Medal) 1991; one-man exbns. include Société des Beaux Arts, Bienne-Biel (Switzerland) 1969, Homage à Henryk Tomaszewski – Communauté de Belgique, La Lauviée 1989, Stedelijk Museum, Amsterdam 1991, Ginza Graphic Gallery, Tokyo 1992, Henryk Tomaszewski Poster, Visual Arts Museum, School of Arts, New York 1996, Poster Museum, Wilanów, Warsaw – Nat. Museum – Retrospective 1999. *Address:* ul. Jazgarzewska 13, 00-730 Warsaw, Poland (Home). *Telephone:* (22) 840-11-51 (Home).

TOMBS, Baron (Life Peer), cr. 1990, of Brailes in the County of Warwickshire; **Francis Leonard Tombs,** BSc, LLD, DSc, FEng; British business executive; b. 17 May 1924, Walsall; s. of Joseph Tombs and Jane Tombs; m. Marjorie Evans 1949; three d.; ed Elmore Green School, Walsall and Birmingham Coll. of Tech.; with British Electricity Authority 1948–57; Gen. Man., Gen. Electric Co. Ltd 1958–67; Dir and Gen. Man. James Howden and Co. 1967–68; Dir of Eng, South of Scotland Electricity Bd 1969–73, Deputy Chair. 1973–74, Chair. 1974–77; Chair. Electricity Council for England and Wales 1977–80; Dir N. M. Rothschild and Sons Ltd 1981–94; Chair. The Weir Group Ltd 1981–83; Dir Rolls-Royce Ltd 1982–92, Chair. 1985–92; Chair. Old Mutual SA Fund 1994–99; Dir Shell (UK) Ltd 1983–94; Chancellor Univ. of Strathclyde 1991–97; Chair. Eng Council 1985–88; Hon. FICE; Hon. FIMechE; Hon. FIChemE; Hon. FIEE (and fmr Pres.); Hon. FRSE 1996; Hon. DSc (Aston) 1979, (Lodz, Poland) 1980, (Cranfield Inst. of Tech.) 1985, (The City Univ., London) 1986, (Bradford) 1986, (Queen's Univ., Belfast) 1988, (Surrey) 1988, (Nottingham) 1989, (Cambridge) 1990, (Warwick) 1990; Hon. DUniv. (Strathclyde) 1991; Hon. DTech. (Loughborough) 1979; Dr hc (Council for Nat. Acad. Awards) 1988; Papal Knighthood of the Order of St Gregory 2002. *Publications:* Nuclear Energy Past, Present and Future—Electronics and Power 1981, Reversing the Decline in Manufacturing Industry (Mountbatten Lecture 1993). *Leisure interests:* music and golf. *Address:* Honington Lodge, Honington, Shipston on Stour, Warwicks., CV36 5AA, England.

TOMCIĆ, Zlatco, B.SC.(ENG.); Croatian politician; b. 10 July 1945, Zagreb; ed Belgrade Univ.; f. underground Croatian Peasant Party (HSS), Zagreb 1984, mem. re-est. HSS 1990–, Pres. 1994–; mem. Sabor (Ass.), Pres. 2000–, also Pres. Chamber of Reps. 2000–. *Address:* Sabor, trg sv. Marka 617, 10000 Zagreb, Croatia (Office). *Telephone:* (1) 4569444 (Office). *Fax:* (1) 6303010 (Office). *E-mail:* predsjednik@sabor.hr (Office).

TOMIĆ, Dragan; Serbia and Montenegro (Serbian) politician and engineer; b. 9 Dec. 1935, G. Bukovica; s. of Boško Tomić and Mitra Tomić; m. Milica Tomić 1964; two d.; ed Belgrade Univ.; various positions Rekord Rubber Works, Rakovica 1962–86, Gen. Dir 1986; Pres. Eng Soc. of Yugoslavia; Gen. Dir NIS – Jugopetrol Co.; Chair. Man. Bd RTV Politika Co. 1993–; mem. Nat. Parl. (Skupština) of Serbia 1994–, Chair. 1994–97; Chair. Union of Yugoslav Engineers and Technicians 1993–. *Leisure interests:* chess, walking with his dog. *Address:* Skupština Srbije, Srpskih Vladara 14, 11000 Belgrade, Serbia and Montenegro. *Telephone:* (11) 324-8604. *Fax:* (11) 685-092.

TOMKA, Peter, LLM, PhD; Slovak diplomatist, lawyer and judge; b. 1 June 1956, Banska Bystrica; s. of Jan Tomka and Kornélia Tomková; m. Zuzana Halgasová 1990; one s. one d.; ed Charles Univ., Prague; Asst. Faculty of Law, Charles Univ., Prague 1980–84, Lecturer 1985–86, Adjunct Lecturer 1986–91, Asst Legal Adviser, Ministry of Foreign Affairs, Czechoslovakia 1986–90, Head of Public Int. Law Div. 1990–91; Counsellor and Legal Adviser, Czechoslovak Mission to the UN 1991–92; Deputy Perm. Rep. of

Slovakia to the UN 1993–97, Perm. Rep. 1999–2003; Agent of Slovakia before the Int. Court of Justice 1993–2003, Judge, Int. Court of Justice 2003–; Legal Adviser to Slovak Ministry of Foreign Affairs 1997–99; Chair. UN Legal Cttee 1997, Cttee of Advisers on Public Int. Law, Council of Europe 2001–02; mem. Perm. Court of Arbitration, The Hague 1994–, UN Int. Law Comm. 1999–2003. *Address:* International Court of Justice, Peace Palace 2517 KJ, The Hague, Netherlands (Office). *Telephone:* (70) 3022323 (Office). *Fax:* (70) 3649928 (Office). *E-mail:* mail@icj-cij.org (Office). *Website:* www.icj-cij.org (Office).

TOMKO, HE Cardinal Jozef, DTheol, DrIur; Slovak ecclesiastic; b. 11 March 1924, Udavské, Humenné; s. of Andrej Tomko and Anna Tomko; ordained priest 1949; consecrated Bishop (Titular See of Doclea) 1979; cr. HE Cardinal 1985; Sec.-Gen. of Synod of Bishops; mem. Comm. for Admin. of State of Vatican 1985–; Prefect of the Congregation for the Evangelization of Peoples 1985–; Adviser, Sec. of Vatican State 1996–; numerous missions worldwide; Prize of Grand Duchy of Luxembourg 1988. *Publications include:* Light of Nations 1972, Christianity and the World 1974, Christ Yesterday and Today 1976, Ecumenism 1977. *Address:* Via Urbano VIII 16, 00165 Rome, Italy. *Telephone:* (06) 6870331.

TOMKYS, Sir (W.) Roger, KCMG, DL, MA; British diplomatist and academic; b. 15 March 1937, Bradford; s. of Arthur Tomkys and Edith Tomkys; m. Margaret Abbey 1963; one s. one d.; ed Bradford Grammar School and Balliol Coll. Oxford; entered HM Diplomatic Service 1960; served Amman, Benghazi, Athens, Rome; Amb. to Bahrain 1981–84, to Syria 1984–86; Asst Under-Sec., later Deputy Under-Sec. of State, FCO 1986–90; High Commr in Kenya 1990–92; Master of Pembroke Coll., Cambridge 1992–; Commendatore dell'Ordine al Merito, Order of Bahrain. *Leisure interests:* travel, books, golf. *Address:* The Master's Lodge, Pembroke College, Cambridge, CB2 1RF, England. *Telephone:* (1223) 338129. *Fax:* (1223) 338163.

TOMLINSON, John, CBE; British (bass) opera singer; b. 22 Sept. 1946, Accrington, Lancs.; s. of Rowland Tomlinson and Ellen Greenwood; m. Moya Joel 1969; one s. two d.; ed Accrington Grammar School, Manchester Univ. and Royal Manchester Coll. of Music; debut at Glyndebourne Festival 1972, English Nat. Opera 1974, Royal Opera House, Covent Garden 1976; since then has appeared in many operas throughout Europe and N America, including Parsifal, Tristan und Isolde and Lohengrin; has sung role of Wotan/Wanderer in The Ring Cycle, Bayreuth Festival 1988–98; other significant roles include Boris in Boris Godunov, ENO (Manchester) 1982, Don Basilio in Il Barbiere di Siviglia, Covent Garden 1985, Moses, ENO 1980, Fiesco in Simon Boccanegra, ENO 1988, Mephistopheles in Damnation of Faust, Santiago, Chile 1990, Attila, Opera North 1990, Filippo II in Don Carlos, Opera North 1992, König Marke in Tristan and Isolde, Bayreuth Festival 1993, Mephistopheles in Damnation of Faust, La Fenice, Venice 1993, Claggart in Billy Budd, Covent Garden 1994, Hans Sachs in Die Meistersinger, Berlin Staatsoper 1995, Kingfisher in Midsummer Marriage, Covent Garden 1996, Bluebeard in Bluebeard's Castle, Berlin Philharmonic 1996, Four Villains in Tales of Hoffmann, ENO 1998, Moses in Moses and Aaron New York Met. 1999, Golaud in Pelléas et Mélisande, Glyndebourne 1999, Mephistopheles in Damnation of Faust, Munich Staatsoper 2000, Hagen in Götterdämmerung, Bayreuth 2000, Baron Ochs in Rosenkavalier, Staatsoper Dresden 2000, Borromeo in Palestrina, Covent Garden 2001, Gurnemanz in Parsifal, New York Metropolitan 2001; numerous broadcasts, recordings, opera videos and concert performances; Hon. FRNCM; Hon. DMus (Sussex) 1997, (Manchester) 1998; Singer of the Year, Royal Philharmonic Soc. 1991, 1998, Evening Standard Opera Award 1998. *Address:* c/o Music International, 13 Ardilaun Road, Highbury, London, N5 2QR, England. *Telephone:* (20) 7359-5183.

TOMLINSON, Lindsay Peter, MA, FIA; British financial executive; b. 7 Oct. 1951, Derby; s. of P. Tomlinson and J. M. Tomlinson; m. Sarah Caroline Anne Martin 1973; four s. one d.; ed Clifton Coll., St John's Coll., Cambridge; actuarial student Commercial Union Assurance Co. 1973–77; sr pensions consultant Metropolitan Pensions Asscn 1977–81; Sr Investment Man. Provident Mutual Managed Pension Funds 1981–87; Chief Exec. (Europe) Barclays Global Investors (fmrly BZW Investment Man.) 1987–. *Address:* Barclays Global Investors Limited, Murray House, 1 Royal Mint Court, London, EC3N 4HH, England. *Telephone:* (20) 7668-8866. *Fax:* (20) 7668-6866.

TOMLINSON, Mel Alexander, BFA; American dancer; b. 3 Jan. 1954, Raleigh, NC; s. of Tommy W. A. Tomlinson and Marjorieline Henry Tomlinson; ed F. J. Carnage Jr High School, J. W. Ligon High School, NC Gov.'s School and NC School of the Arts; Prin., Agnes DeMille's Heritage Dance Theater 1973, Dance Theatre of Harlem Inc. 1974–77, Alvin Ailey American Dance Theatre 1977–78, Dance Theatre of Harlem Inc. 1978–81; mem. corps de ballet, New York City Ballet 1981, soloist 1982–; guest appearance, DeMille Tribute, Joffrey Ballet. *Leisure interests:* knitting, swimming, gymnastics, reading, sewing, games. *Address:* New York City Ballet, Lincoln State Theater, New York, NY 10023; 790 Riverside Drive, Apt. 6B, New York, NY 10032; 1216 Bunche Drive, Raleigh, NC 27610, USA. *Telephone:* (212) 234-3320; (919) 834-7010.

TOMOS; Chinese artist; b. 26 Nov. 1932, Tumed Banner, Inner Mongolia (Nei Monggol); s. of Yun Yao and Xing Yu; m. Xiahe-xiou 1967; two s.; ed Cen. Inst. of Fine Arts, Beijing; Assoc. Prof. of Fine Arts, Inner Mongolia Normal Coll.; Dean of Fine Arts, Inner Mongolia Teachers' Training Coll. 1984–; Adviser on Fine Arts to Children's Palace, Huhehot, Inner Mongolia; Vice-Chair. Inner

Mongolian Branch of Chinese Artists' Asscn 1980–; Dir Standing Cttee, Chinese Artists' Asscn May 1985–, mem. Oil Art Cttee 1985–; mem. Selection Cttee for Sixth Nat. Art Exhbn of oil paintings; mem. Art Educ. Cttee of Nat. Educ. 1986–; Dir Inner Mongolia branch of China External Culture Exchange Asscn; Dir Cheng's Style Tai-Chi Chuan Asscn 1993–; Chair. Judges' Cttee for 8th Annual Chinese Art Exhbn, Inner Mongolia 1994, 8th Annual Best Chinese Artwork Exhbn 1994; Consultant, The Watercolour Asscn, Inner Mongolia 1994; Dir China Oil Painting Asscn 1995–; Chair. Inner Mongolian Artists' Asscn 1996–; Head of del. of Inner Mongolian painters to Hong Kong 1993; First Prize for Art, Inner Mongolia, Merit of Art Educ. Award, Wu Zuo Ren Int. Art Foundation 1990, Expert and Scholar award of Govt 1991 and medals awarded for individual paintings. *Exhibitions include:* oil paintings and sketches, Huhehot 1979, oil paintings Exhbn Hall of Cen. Inst. of Fine Arts, Cultural Palace of minority nationalities, Beijing 1981, oil paintings and sketches, Changsha, Hunan Prov. 1984, Modern Oil Painting Exhbn, China Art Gallery, China Modern Oil Painting Exhbn, USA 1987, Far East Art Museum of USSR 1991, Modern Gallery, Tai Zhong, Taiwan 1993. *Works include:* Mine, Wind on the Grasslands, Having a Break, Dawn, Milkmaid, A Woman Hay-making, At Dusk, Polo, Spring Wind, White Horse and Wind, At Dark and many others. *Publications:* Selection of oil-paintings, Tomos's Album of Paintings (sketches and oil paintings) 1993, The Techniques of Oil Painting 1999. *Leisure interests:* Chinese Gongfu, Peking opera, Chinese medicine. *Address:* Art Department, Normal College, Nei Monggol Autonomous Region, People's Republic of China.

TOMOWA-SINTOW, Anna; Austrian opera singer; b. 22 Sept. 1943, Stara Zagora, Bulgaria; m. Albert Sintow 1963; one d.; ed Nat. Conservatory of Sofia; début Leipzig Opera 1967; joined Deutsche Staatsoper, Berlin 1969; guest engagements at most leading European and U.S. opera houses, including La Scala, Milan, Vienna, Covent Garden, London, Paris, Bavarian State Opera and Bolshoi, Moscow; début N America at Metropolitan Opera, New York 1978; has toured Japan with La Scala di Milano and Berlin Philharmonic under von Karajan; regular guest at Salzburg Festival since 1973; has sung in several TV productions; recording and film of Verdi Requiem with von Karajan; winner Kammersängerin Prize. *Recordings include:* Lohengrin, Le Nozze di Figaro, Don Giovanni, Die Zauberflöte, Mozart Coronation Mass, Mozart Requiem, Brahms German Requiem, Strauss Four Last Songs and Capriccio monologue, Beethoven Missa Solemnis, Ariadne auf Naxos (in preparation), Madame Butterfly, La Traviata, Tosca, Eugen Onegin, recitals of Verdi arias and of Italian and German arias. *Major roles include:* Arabella, Ariadne, Madelaine (in Capriccio), Countess Almaviva, Elsa (in Lohengrin), Elisabeth (in Tannhäuser), Aida, Tosca, Madame Butterfly, Traviata, Manon Lescaut, Maddalena (in Andrea Chenier), Leonora (in La Forza del Destino), Marschallin (Rosenkavalier), Yaroslavna, etc. *Leisure interests:* nature, reading books, singing.

TOMUR DAWAMAT; Chinese party official; b. 1927, Toksun, Xinjiang; s. of Ziweidihan Dawamat; m. Gulzirahan 1944; five s. two d.; ed Cen. Nationalities Coll., Beijing; village chief 1950; joined CCP 1952; Sec. CCP Cttee, Toksun Cttee, Tunpan Basin 1956, First Sec. 1960; Vice-Chair. Xinjiang Autonomous Region 1964; Deputy for Xinjiang, 3rd NPC; mem. Standing Cttee, Autonomous Regional Revolutionary Cttee, Xinjiang 1968; disappeared until 1976; Deputy for Xinjiang, 5th NPC 1978; mem. Standing Cttee, 5th NPC 1978; Deputy Sec. CCP Cttee Xinjiang 1978–; Vice-Minister of State Nationalities Affairs Comm., State Council 1979; Chair. Autonomous Regional People's Congress, Xinjiang 1979–85; mem. 12th Cen. Cttee, CCP 1982; Gov. Xinjiang Autonomous Region 1986–93; Vice-Sec. Xinjiang Autonomous Region CCP Cttee 1985; mem. 13th Cen. Cttee, CCP 1987–92; mem. 14th Cen. Cttee CCP 1992–; a Vice-Chair. Standing Cttee 8th NPC 1993–98, 9th NPC 1998–. *Leisure interests:* writing poetry, playing Chinese Checkers. *Address:* Standing Committee of National People's Congress, Beijing, People's Republic of China.

TONČIĆ-SORINJ, Lujo, LLD; Austrian politician and landowner; b. 12 April 1915, Vienna; s. of Dušan Tončić-Sorinj and Mabel Plason de la Woesthyne; m. Renate Trenker 1956; one s. four d.; ed Grammar School, Salzburg and Univs. of Vienna and Zagreb; Asst to Chair. SE Europe Dept, Berlin Univ. 1940–44; Mil. Service 1941–44; Head of Political Dept, Austrian Research Inst. for Econs and Politics 1946–49, Ed. Berichte und Informationen 1946–49; MP for Land Salzburg 1949–66; Chair. Legal Cttee of Austrian Parl. 1953–56, Foreign Affairs Cttee 1956–59; in charge of Foreign Affairs questions, Austrian People's Party 1959–66; Austrian mem. Consultative Ass. of Council of Europe 1953–66, Vice-Chair. Political Cttee; Vice-Pres. Council of Europe 1961–62; Minister of Foreign Affairs 1966–68; Sec.-Gen. Council of Europe 1969–74; Pres. Austrian Asscn of UN 1977–92; Perm. Rep. Austrian People's Party to Christian-Democratic Group in European Parl. 1980–92; Perm. Rep. Croatian Democratic Union to EU of Christian Democratic Parties 1991–; Pres. Union Int. de la Propriété Immobilière 1987–99; Grosses Goldenes Ehrenzeichen am Bande (Austria), Hon. GCMG, and other decorations. *Publications:* Erfüllte Träume (autobiog.) 1982, Am Abgrund vorbei 1991, Usamljena borba Hrvatske 1998, Die welt der Kroaten am Beginn des dritten Jahrtausends 2002; and about 400 articles and essays on history and int. politics. *Leisure interests:* history, geography, swimming, diving. *Address:* 5020 Salzburg, Schloss Fürberg, Pausingerstrasse 11, Austria. *Telephone:* (662) 64-28-86.

TONEGAWA, Susumu, PhD; Japanese immunologist and neuroscientist; b. 5 Sept. 1939, Nagoya; s. of Tsutomu Tonegawa and Miyuko Tonegawa; m. Mayumi Yoshinari 1985; three c.; ed Kyoto Univ. and Univ. of Calif. San Diego; postgraduate work at Dept of Biology, Univ. of Calif. San Diego 1968–69, The Salk Inst. San Diego 1969–70; mem. Basle Inst. for Immunology, Basle, Switzerland 1971–81; Prof. of Biology, Center for Cancer Research and Dept of Biology, MIT 1981–; investigator Howard Hughes Medical Inst. 1988–; Dir Center for Learning and Memory, MIT 1994–; mem. American Acad. of Arts and Sciences; Foreign Assoc. mem. NAS; Hon. mem. American Asscn of Immunologists, Scandinavian Soc. for Immunology; numerous awards and prizes including Avery Landsteiner Prize 1981, Gairdner Foundation Int. Award 1983, Robert Koch Prize 1986, Lasker Prize 1987, Nobel Prize for Medicine 1987; Bunkakunsho Order of Culture 1984. *Address:* Center for Learning and Memory, Room E17-353, Massachusetts Institute of Technology, 77 Massachusetts Avenue, Cambridge, MA 02139, USA. *Telephone:* (617) 253-1000. *Fax:* (617) 253-8000. *Website:* web.mit.edu (Office).

TONG YIN CHU; Chinese politician; b. 1915, Hefei City, Anhui Prov.; ed Shanghai Jiaotong Univ.; living in Indonesia 1938–47; joined China Democratic Construction Asscn 1948; Chair. Cen. Cttee of China Zhi Gong Dang 1988–97, Hon. Chair. 1997–; Vice-Chair. 8th Nat. Cttee CPPCC 1993–98; Adviser, China Council for Promotion of Peaceful Nat. Reunification, All China Fed. of Returned Overseas Chinese. *Address:* National Committee of Chinese People's Political Consultative Congress, 23 Taiping Qiao Street, Beijing, People's Republic of China.

TONG ZENGYIN; Chinese banker; b. 1934, Yinxian, Zhejiang Prov.; joined CCP 1954; fmrly Vice-Gov. Chinese People's Bank; Vice-Chair. China Securities Supervisory Cttee; Founding Pres. Minsheng Bank (China's first privately owned nat. bank) 1996. *Address:* China Minsheng Banking Corporation, 4 Zhengyi Lu, Dongcheng Qu, Beijing 100006, People's Republic of China. *Telephone:* (10) 65269610. *Fax:* (10) 68588570. *E-mail:* msbgs@cmbc.com.cn (Office). *Website:* www.cmbc.com.cn (Office).

TONG ZHIGUANG; Chinese international official and professor of economics; ed Univ. of Int. Business and Econs, Bombay Univ.; mem. Standing Cttee 8th NPC, mem. NPC Foreign Affairs Cttee, del. of Hebei Prov. to 8th NPC; Deputy Head State Council Leading Group for Right to Intellectual Property 1991–; Vice-Minister of Foreign Trade and Econ. Co-operation 1991–93; Chair. Bd of Dirs, The Export-Import Bank of China 1994–99; Chair. WTO Research Soc. of China 2001–; Vice-Chair. China–UK Friendship Group; mem. China–US Inter-parliamentarian Exchange Group of the NPC; fmr Chief Negotiator and Del. Leader for China's accession to GATT/WTO and Sino–US Trade Negotiations; fmr sr diplomat to India, Myanmar, USA and UN; fmr Adviser to Chinese Del. of UN Gen. Ass.; fmr Chair. China Exim Bank; fmr Pres. and CEO of China Resources (Holdings) Co. Ltd, Hong Kong. *Publications:* several articles on foreign trade, int. econs and the WTO. *Leisure interests:* golf, classical music, Chinese calligraphy. *Address:* 2212, 28 Dong Holi Xiang, Anwai Beijing 100710 (Office); 7202 Yin Zha Hu Tong, Xicheng Qu, Beijing (Home); c/o The Export-Import Bank of China, 75 Chongnei St, Beijing 100005, People's Republic of China. *Telephone:* (10) 84255121 (Office); (10) 64259703 (Home). *Fax:* (10) 84255122 (Office). *E-mail:* wtori@sina.com.cn (Office).

TONGA, King of (see Taufa'ahau Tupou IV).

TONKIN, Peter Frederick, BSc(ARCH.), BArch; Australian architect; b. 10 Jan. 1953, Blayney, NSW; s. of John Ebenezer Tonkin and Veronica Mariea Tonkin (née Perry); m. Ellen Claire Woolley; ed Univ. of Sydney; in practice with Lawrence Nield and Partners 1979–81; independent practice 1981–, co-founder of Tonkin Zulaikha 1987, Tonkin Zulaikha Greer 1988–; Visiting Design Tutor, Sydney Univ., Univ. of NSW, Univ. of Tech., Sydney; mem. Royal Australian Inst. of Architects (fmr Vice-Pres. and Chair. of Practice Bd), Historic Houses Trust Exhbns. Cttee, Sydney City Council Urban Design Task Force; numerous awards and prizes including Royal Australian Inst. of Architects Merit Awards 1988, 1991, 1993, 1996, 2000, winner, Vietnam Memorial Competition 1990, Tomb of the Unknown Soldier Competition 1993, Master Builders Asscn Merit Award 1993, ACEA Engineering Excellence Award 1999, Property Council of NSW Devt of the Year 1999, Int. RICS Award for Conservation 2000; winner, Nat. Gallery of Australia Competition 2000. *Achievements:* design projects include refurbishment of Sydney Customs House; Fed. Museum and Library, Tenterfield, Royal Blind Soc. Library, Nat. Memorial to Australian Vietnam Forces; Tomb of the Unknown Australian Soldier, Canberra, Australian War Memorial, London. *Leisure interests:* mountain sports, motorcycling. *Address:* Tonkin Zulaikha Greer Architects, 117 Reservoir Street, Surry Hills, NSW 2010, Australia (Office). *Telephone:* (2) 9215-4900 (Office). *Fax:* (2) 9215-4901 (Office). *E-mail:* peter@tzg.com.au (Office). *Website:* www.tzg.com.au (Office).

TONOMURA, Hitoshi; Japanese banker; fmr Pres. and Chair. Nomura Int., Head of Overseas Operations 1995–, now Sr Adviser. *Address:* 2-1-14, Nihombashi, Chuo-ku, Tokyo, 103-8260, Japan (Office). *Telephone:* (3) 3241-9500 (Office). *Fax:* (3) 3241-9599 (Office).

TOOLEY, Sir John, Kt, MA; British administrator and arts consultant; b. 1 June 1924, Rochester, Kent; s. of late H. R. Tooley; m. 1st Judith Craig Morris 1951 (dissolved 1965); three d.; m. 2nd Patricia J. N. Bagshawe 1968 (divorced 1990); one s.; m. 3rd Jennifer Anne Shannon 1995; ed Repton School and Magdalene Coll., Cambridge; Sec. Guildhall School of Music and Drama 1952–55; Asst to Gen. Admin., Royal Opera House, Covent Garden 1955–60,

Asst Gen. Admin. 1960–70, Gen. Admin. 1970–80, Gen. Dir 1980–88; Chair. Almeida Theatre 1990–97, Fabric Advisory Cttee Salisbury Cathedral 1992–, Nureyev Foundation 1995–; Chair. Monument Insurance Brokers Ltd 1997–2002; Pres. Salisbury Festival 1988–; Consultant Int. Man. Group 1988–97, Ballet Opera House, Toronto 1989–90, Istanbul Foundation for Culture and Arts 1992–, Antelope Films 1993–; Dir London Philharmonic Orchestra 1998–, Britten Estate 1989–96, South Bank Bd 1991–97, Compton Verney Opera Project 1991–97, Welsh Nat. Opera 1992–2000, David Gyngell Holdings Ltd 1996–97; Trustee Britten Pears Foundation 1988–99, Walton Trust 1988–2000, Wigmore Hall 1989–2001, Almeida Theatre 1990–2002, Performing Arts Labs 1992–97, Cardiff Bay Opera House 1995–96, Sidney Nolan Trust 1995–, Mozartfest, Bath 2001–; Gov. Royal Ballet 1994–97; Hon. FRAM, Hon. GSM; Hon. mem. Royal Northern Coll. of Music, ISM; Hon. DUniv (Univ. of Central England) 1996; Commendatore of Italian Repub. *Publication:* In House 1999. *Leisure interests:* walking, theatre. *Address:* 5 Royal Crescent, Bath, BA1 2LR, England. *Telephone:* (1225) 335079. *Fax:* (1225) 335108. *E-mail:* tooley@btinternet.com (Home).

TOON, Malcolm, MA, LLD; American diplomatist (retd); b. 4 July 1916, Troy, NY; s. of George Toon and Margaret Broadfoot; m. Elizabeth J. Taylor 1943; one s. two d.; ed Tufts Univ., Fletcher School of Law and Diplomacy and Harvard Univ.; Research Technician, Nat. Resources Planning Bd 1939–41; Ensign, Lt.-Commdr, US Naval Reserve 1942–46; in US Foreign Service 1946–79; Amb. to Czechoslovakia 1969–71, to Yugoslavia 1971–75, to Israel 1975–76, to USSR 1976–79; Dir McKesson Corpn, San Francisco; mem. Bd of Trustees Tufts Univ., Bd of Visitors, Fletcher School of Law and Diplomacy 1992; Co-Chair. US–Russian Jt Comm. on POWs and MIAs 1992–98; Hon. LLD (Tufts Univ.) 1977, (Middlebury Coll.) 1978, (Drexel Univ.) 1980, (American Coll. of Switzerland) 1985, (Grove City Coll.); degree of Prof. Acad. of Natural Sciences of the Russian Fed. 1996; Superior Honor Award, Dept of State 1965; Distinguished Honor Award, Dept of State 1979; Freedom Leadership Award Hillsdale Coll., Mich. 1980, Freedom Award 1981, Wallace Award 1984, Gold Medal, Nat. Inst. of Social Sciences 1987. *Leisure interests:* golf, tennis, hunting, fishing. *Address:* 375 Pee Dee Road, Southern Pines, NC 28387, USA (Home). *Telephone:* (910) 692-5992 (Home).

TOPCHEYEV, Yuriy Ivanovich, DTechSc; Russian cyberneticist; b. 26 Sept. 1920, Yaroslavl; s. of Ivan Yakovlevich Topcheyev and Vera Aleksandrovna Topcheyeva; m. Inna Ivanovna Smirnova 1965; one s.; ed Moscow Aviation Inst.; mem. CPSU 1948–91; Chief Dept of Scientific Research Inst. of Automatic Systems 1943–72; mem. staff and Prof., Inst. of Physical Eng, Moscow 1968–89, Chief of Faculty 1972–88; Prof. Int. G. Soros Science Educ. Programme 1996–97, Emer. Prof. 1997–; mem. Comm. of Co-ordination Cttee on Computers of USSR (now Russian) Acad. of Sciences 1978–85, Co-ordination Cttee on Robotics 1980–87; Chair. Council on Systems of Automated Design, Ministry of Higher Educ. 1977–87; mem. Council Specialized Scientific and Technological Activities of USSR (now Russian) Acad. of Sciences 1989–, Russian Cosmonautics 1992–, World Innovation Foundation 2001–; Order of Labour Banner 1950, State Prize 1972, Korolev Medal 1977, Gagarin Medal 1981. *Publications include:* Encyclopaedia for Automatic Regulation Systems Design 1989; (co-author) Basics of Automatic Regulation 1954, Modern Methods of Automatic Control System Design (ed. and co-author) 1967, Technical Cybernetics (4 Vols) 1967–89, Philosophy of Nonlinear Control Systems 1990, Nonlinear Systems of Automatic Control (Vols 1–9) 1970–92, People and Robotics (Vol. 1) 1995, (Vol. 2) 1998, Development of Robotics 2000, Robotics: A Historical Overview 2001, Robotics – History and Perspectives 2002, Biography of Mstislavh Vsevolodovich Keldysh 2002; over 290 articles, including 12 on great contemporary Russian scientists in A History of Science Engineering 2002, and 2 pieces on contemporary biosphere ecology. *Leisure interests:* nonlinear systems design, the history of the development of automatic systems and robotics. *Address:* Leningradskoye sch. 31, Apt. 147, 125212 Moscow, Russia. *Telephone:* (095) 156-63-06.

TÖPFER, Klaus, PhD; German politician and international organization official; b. 29 July 1938, Waldenburg, Silesia; m.; three c.; ed Univs. of Mainz, Frankfurt am Main and Munster; family expelled from Silesia, settled in Höxter/Weser 1945; Head, Political Economy Dept, Inst. of Devt Planning, Munster 1970–71; Head, Planning and Information Section, Saarland State Chancellery, Saarbrücken; lecturer, Coll. of Admin., Speyer 1971–78; Prof. Ordinarius, Hanover Univ., Dir Inst. of Environmental Research and Regional Planning 1978–79; Hon. Prof. Mainz Univ. 1985–; joined Christian Democratic Union (CDU) 1972, CDU Dist Chair., Saarbrücken, mem. CDU State Exec., Saar 1977–79; State Sec., Rhineland Palatinate Ministry of Social Affairs, Health and Environment, Mainz 1978–85; Deputy Chair. CDU Fed. Cttee of Experts on the Environment 1983; Minister of Environment and Health, Rhineland Palatinate 1985–87; CDU Dist Chair., Rhein-Hunsrück 1987–; Fed. Minister for the Environment, Nature Conservation and Nuclear Safety 1987–94, of Regional Planning, Housing and Urban Devt 1994–98; Exec. Dir UN Environment Programme (UNEP), Nairobi 1998–; Acting Dir UN Centre for Human Settlements (Habitat) 1998–2000; TÜV Environment Prize 2000, German Environment Prize 2002. *Address:* UNEP, P.O. Box 30552, Nairobi, Kenya (Office). *Telephone:* (2) 624001/2 (Office). *Fax:* (2) 624275/624006 (Office). *E-mail:* cpiinfo@unep.org (Office). *Website:* www.unep.org (Office).

TOPOL, Chaim; Israeli actor, producer and director; b. 9 Sept. 1935, Tel Aviv; s. of Yaakov Topol and Rela Goldman; m. Galia Finkelstein 1956; one s. two d.; joined entertainment unit during army service 1953; f. The Green Onion satirical theatre 1956, Municipal Theatre of Haifa 1959; starred in stage productions of Fiddler on the Roof in London 1967, 1983, 1994, on Broadway NY, 1990 and in Melbourne 1998, in Ziegfield 1988, in The Caucasian Chalk Circle, Romanov and Juliet, Othello, View From The Bridge, Chichester Festival Theatre; Actor, Producer, Director for the Genesis Project, filming the Bible, New York; Golden Globe Award, San Francisco Film Festival Winner. *Films include:* Cast A Giant Shadow 1965, Sallah 1966, Before Winter Comes 1969, A Time for Loving, Fiddler on the Roof 1971, The Public Eye, Galileo 1974, Flash Gordon, For Your Eyes Only 1980, The Winds of War 1981, A Dime Novel, Ervinka, Left Luggage 1997; several TV films. *Albums include:* Fiddler on the Roof (cast album), It's Topol, War Songs, Topol 68, Fiddler on the Roof (film album), Topol's Israel. *Publication:* Topol by Topol (autobiog.) 1981, To Life! (A Treasury of Jewish Wisdom, Wit and Humour) 1995. *Address:* 22 Vale Court, 28 Maida Vale, London, W9 1RT, England. *Telephone:* (20) 7286-5361. *Fax:* (20) 7266-2155.

TOPORNIN, Boris Nikolayevich; Russian legal specialist; b. 29 Dec. 1929; m.; two s.; ed Moscow Inst. of Int. Relations; Jr, Sr researcher, Scientific Sec. Inst. of Law USSR (now Russian) Acad. of Sciences 1955–62; Deputy Chief Scientific Sec. Presidium of USSR Acad. of Sciences 1962–67; head of div., First Deputy Dir Inst. of Law and State USSR Acad. of Sciences 1967–89; Dir 1989–; corresp. mem. USSR (now Russian) Acad. of Sciences 1987, mem. 1991, Acad. Sec. Dept of Phil. and Law; research in constitutional law and state law 1991–; Deputy Pres. Int. Asscn of Constitutional Law; Mem. Int. Acad. of Law; Humboldt Inst. Prize 1999, Femida Prize 2000. *Publications include:* Political Foundation of Socialism 1972, New Constitution of USSR 1980, Development of Socialist Democracy 1985, Foreign Policy and Science 1990. *Publications:* Federalismus zwischen Integration und Sezession. Chancen und Risiken bundesstaatlicher Ordnung 1993, Legal Foundation of Russian Economy 2000. *Address:* Institute of State and Law, Russian Academy of Sciences, Znamenka str. 10, 119841 Moscow, Russia. *Telephone:* (095) 291-87-56; (095) 203-92-12.

TOPOROV, Col-Gen. Vladimir Mikhailovich; Russian army officer; b. 7 Feb. 1946, Baranovichi; ed Odessa Artillery School, Frunze Mil. Acad., Gen. Staff Acad.; Commdr of platoon, battery 1968–75, Deputy Commdr of Regt, Commdr 1976–79, Deputy Commdr of Div., Commdr 1979–84, First Deputy Commdr, Commdr of army 1987–89; Head of Staff, First Deputy Commdr of troops of Far East Mil. Dist 1989–92; Commdr of troops of Moscow Mil. Dist 1991–92; Deputy Minister of Defence 1992–; C-in-C of airborne (expeditionary) forces 1995–98. *Address:* Ministry of Defence, Znamenka 19, Moscow, Russia. *Telephone:* (095) 295-12-84 (Office).

TOPOROV, Vladimir Nikolayevich; Russian linguist, semiotician and literary historian; b. 5 July 1928, Moscow; m.; two d.; ed Moscow Univ.; first articles published 1958; Sr Research Fellow at Inst. of Slavic and Balkan Studies, USSR (now Russian) Acad. of Sciences 1954–86, Chief Scientific Researcher 1986–; specialist in Indo-European languages and semiotics; mem. USSR (now Russian) Acad. of Sciences 1990–; Hon. Prof. Vilnius Univ., Russian Univ. of Humanities, Moscow; Hon. mem. Latvian Acad. of Sciences; USSR State Prize 1990, Order of the Grand Duke of Lithuania Godiminas 1999. *Publications:* Studies in the Field of Slavic Antiquities 1974; Dictionary of the Prussian Language (5 Vols) 1975–90, Akhmatova and Blok 1981, Gospodin Prokharchin 1982, Pushkin and Goldsmith 1992, Aeneas—the Man of Fate 1993, Sanctity and the Saints in Russian Spiritual Culture, Vols I–II 1995–98; articles in Soviet and int. professional journals, some in collaboration with Vyacheslav Ivanov (q.v.), many works published abroad. *Address:* Institute of Slavic and Balkan Studies, Leninski prosp. 32A, 117334 Moscow (Office); 5–49 ul. Sameda Vurguna, 125315 Moscow, Russia (Home). *Telephone:* (095) 938-19-43 (Office); (095) 155-32-71 (Home).

TORKUNOV, Anatoly Vassilyevich, CandHist, DrPolSci; Russian academic and fmr diplomatist; b. 26 Aug. 1950, Moscow; m.; one d.; ed Moscow State Inst. of Int. Relations; teacher Moscow State Inst. of Int. Relations 1974–, Pro-Rector 1977–, Dean Chair. of Int. Relations, then First Pro-Rector 1986–; diplomatic service in People's Democratic Repub. of Korea 1971–72, in USA 1983–86; Rector Moscow State Inst. of Int. Relations 1992–; Pres. Russian UN Asscn; mem. Expert Analytical Council, Attestation Bd Ministry of Russian Asscn of Int. Studies, Scientific Council of Security Council of Russian Fed., Russian Acad. of Nat. Sciences, Acad. of Sciences of Higher Schooling, Nat. Russian Cttee on problems of UNESCO; mem. Editorial Bd journals Global Gov. (USA), Mezhdunarodnaya Zhizn, Moscovsky Zhurnal Mezhdunarodnogo Prava, Bisnes i Politika; Medals for Labour Merit, 850th Anniversary of Moscow, 300 Years of Russian Navy, Order of Friendship between Peoples, Order of Merit Before the Fatherland. *Publications:* 5 monographs and over 150 scientific publs on int. relations, problems of Russian foreign policy, Asian-Pacific Region, Korea. *Leisure interests:* theatre, music. *Address:* Moscow State Institute of International Relations, Vernadskogo prosp. 76, 117454 Moscow, Russia (Office). *Telephone:* (095) 434-00-89 (Office). *Fax:* (095) 434-90-61 (Office). *E-mail:* tork@mgimo.ru (Office). *Website:* www.mgimo.ru (Office).

TÖRMÄLÄ, Pertti, DPhil; Finnish professor of biomaterials technology; b. 26 Nov. 1945, Tampere; s. of Matti Törmälä and Elma Virtanen; m. 1st Kirsti Miettinen 1967 (dissolved); two d.; m. 2nd Mirja Talasoja 1995; Assoc. Prof. of Non-Metallic Materials, Tampere Univ. of Tech. 1975, Prof. of Fibre Raw Materials, Prof. of Plastics Tech. and Head Inst. of Plastics Tech. 1985–; fmr Research Prof. Acad. of Finland, Acad. Prof. 1995–; Hon. DMed; Nat. Inventor

Prize 1986, Nordic Tech. Prize 1988. *Publications:* eight textbooks, 150 patents, over 800 scientific papers. *Leisure interests:* exercise, music. *Address:* Tampere University of Technology, Institute of Biomaterials, P.O. Box 589, 33101 Tampere, Finland. *Telephone:* (3) 311511; (40) 5146944.

TORNATORE, Giuseppe; Italian film director; b. 1956, Bagheria, Palermo, Sicily; debut as Dir at age 16, with short film Il Carretto. *Television films include:* Ritratto di un Rapinatore, Incontro con Francesco Rosi, Scrittori Siciliani e Cinema: Verga, Pirandello, Brancati and Sciascia and Il Diario di Guttuso. *Feature films include:* Il Camorrista 1987, Cinema Paradiso 1988 (Special Jury Prize, Cannes Festival 1989), Stanno Tutti Bene 1991, A Pure Formality 1994, Uomo delle Stelle 1995. *Documentaries include:* Ethnic Minorities in Sicily (Best Documentary, Salerno Film Festival 1982).

TÖRNUDD, Klaus, PhD; Finnish diplomatist and professor; b. 26 Dec. 1931, Helsinki; s. of Allan Törnudd and Margit Niininen; m. Mirja Siirala 1960; one s. one d.; ed Univ. of Helsinki, Univ. of Paris and School of Advanced Int. Studies, Johns Hopkins Univ., Washington DC; entered Finnish Foreign Service 1958, served at Finnish Mission to UN 1961–64, Cairo Embassy 1964–66, Moscow Embassy 1971–73, CSCE 1973–74; Prof. of Int. Politics, Univ. of Tampere, Finland 1967–74; Deputy Dir of Political Affairs in the Ministry for Foreign Affairs 1974–77, Dir 1977–81, Under-Sec. of State for Political Affairs 1983–88; Perm. Rep. to the UN 1988–91; Fellow Harvard Univ., USA 1991–92; Sr Adviser, Ministry for Foreign Affairs 1992–93; Amb. to France and to UNESCO 1993–96; mem. Sr Faculty, Geneva Centre for Security Policy 1997–98; Visting Prof. Nat. Defence Coll. of Finland 1998–; Ed. Co-operation and Conflict (Nordic Journal of Int. Politics) 1968–70, mem. Editorial Bd 1976–79; mem. Editorial Bd of Ulkopolitiikka-Utrikespolitik 1983–87; Chair. of Bd Tampere Peace Research Inst. 1978–82; Chair. UN Study Group on Nuclear Weapon-Free Zones 1983–85; mem. Bd of Trustees UNITAR 1984–88; mem. of Bd of Govs. IAEA 1985–87; mem. UN Sec.-Gen.'s Advisory Bd on Disarmament Matters 1991–96; Dr hc (Åbu Akademi Univ., Finland) 2002. *Publications:* several books on Finnish politics and int. affairs. *Address:* National Defence College, Department of Strategic and Defence Studies, P.O. Box 266, 00171 Helsinki (Office); Tempelgatan 8A, 00100 Helsinki, Finland (Home). *Telephone:* (9) 18126340 (Office); (9) 490159 (Home). *Fax:* (9) 18126324 (Office); (9) 448849 (Home). *E-mail:* klaus .toernudd@kolumbus.fi (Home).

ToROBERT, Sir Henry Thomas, KBE, BEcons; Papua New Guinea banker; b. 1942, Kokopo; ed Univ. of Sydney; Asst Research Officer, Reserve Bank of Australia, Port Moresby 1965, Deputy Man. 1971, Man. 1972; Gov. and Chair. of Bd Bank of Papua New Guinea 1973–93; Chair. Papua New Guinea Inst. of Applied Social and Econ. Research 1975–82; Chair. Man. Bd Bankers' Coll. 1973–; partner Deloitte Touche Tohmatsu 1993–; Chair. Credit Corpn (PNG) Ltd 1993–, Govt Super Task Force on Project Implementation 1994–; Pres. Amateur Sports Fed. and PNG Olympic and Commonwealth Games Cttee 1980–. *Address:* P.O. Box 898, Port Moresby, Papua New Guinea.

TÖRÖK, László; Hungarian archaeologist; b. 13 May 1941, Budapest; s. of László Török and Mária Giesz; m. Erzsébet Sződy 1984; ed Budapest Univ. of Tech. Sciences, Eötvös Loránd Univ.; research fellow Archaeological Inst. Hungarian Acad. of Sciences 1964, Sr research fellow 1985, adviser 1991; Lecturer, Eötvös Loránd Univ. of Arts and Sciences, Dept of Egyptology 1972, Hon. Prof. 1992–; Visiting Prof. Dept of Classics, Univ. of Bergen, Norway 1980, 1989–92, 1994–99; Overseas Visiting Scholar, St John's Coll. Cambridge 1998; Vice-Pres. of the Int. Soc. for Nubian Studies 1990–; Gen. Ed. of Antaeus (periodical) 1984–99; mem. Norwegian Acad. of Science 1994; Albert Reckitt Archaeological Lecture, British Acad. 1995; research into ancient history and archaeology of Middle Nile Region and Hellenistic and late antique art of Egypt; Dr. hc (Univ. of Bergen, Norway) 2000. *Publications:* Economic Offices and Officials in Meroitic Nubia 1978, Der meroitische Staat 1986, The Royal Crowns of Kush 1987, Late Antique Nubia 1988, Coptic Antiquities I–II 1993, Fontes Historiae Nubiorum I 1994, II 1996, III 1998, IV 2000 (with co-authors), Hellenistic and Roman Terracottas from Egypt 1995, The Birth of an Ancient African State 1995, Meroe City: An Ancient African Capital 1997, The Kingdom of Kush: Handbook of the Napatan-Meroitic Civilization 1997, The Hunting Centaur 1998, The Image of the Ordered World in Ancient Nubian Art 2002; over 100 articles. *Leisure interest:* reading (belles-lettres). *Address:* MTA Régészeti Intézete, 1014 Budapest, Úri utca 49, Hungary. *Telephone:* (1) 375-9011. *Fax:* (1) 224-6719 (Office).

TORP, Niels A., DipArch; Norwegian architect; b. 8 March 1940, Oslo; s. of Ernst Torp and Nini Torp (née Butenschøn); m. Bente Poulsson; one s. three d.; ed Norges Tekniske Høgskole, Trondheim, The Norwegian Inst. Rome; joined Torp & Torp Arkitekter MNAL 1965, partner 1970, Man. 1974, Man. Niels Torp Arkitekter MNAL 1984; visiting lecturer at architectural schools in Norway and other European countries; awards include: A. C. Houens Legacy, Sundts Prize for Architectural Merits, Awards from the Stone Asscn, Fine Art Award (Oslo City Council), Carl M. Egers Legacy, Europa Nostra Awards, Prize for Built Environment (Norwegian Dept of Environment), Kasper Salin Prize (Sweden), European Award for Steel Structures, Swedish Stone Asscn Award, Concrete Award (Norway), British Construction Industry Award 1998, Brunel Award 1998, Aesthetic Counsel Diploma, Bærum, Norway 1998, Parelius Scholarship 1998, Glulam Award 1999 (with Aviaplan), RIBA Award for Architecture 1999, Jacob Award for Design 1999. *Major works:* Giskehagen residential homes 1986, Scandinavian Airlines System (SAS) HQ, Stockholm 1987, Aker Brygge (dockland devt Oslo) 1988,

HQ Den Norske Bank 1988, Hamar Olympiahall 1991, Alna Shopping Centre, Oslo 1996, railway station/bus terminal, Gothenburg 1996, Christiania Qvartalet 1996, BA HQ, London 1997, Colosseum Park, Oslo 1997, Oslo Airport Gardermoen (with Aviaplan) 1998, airport control tower and airport hotel, Oslo 1998, Papendrop – Utrecht, The Netherlands, five office bldgs 1999, NSB (Norwegian Railway) HQ, Oslo 1999, devt plans for towns Larvik, Sandefjord, Drammen, Ås, Elverum, Hamar and Bodø. *Leisure interests:* music, playing piano, sailing. *Address:* Industrigaten 59, PO Box 5387, 0304 Oslo, Norway (Office). *Telephone:* 23-36-68-00 (Office). *Fax:* 23-36-68-01.

TORRANCE, Sam, OBE; British golfer; b. 24 Aug. 1953, Largs; s. of Bob Torrance and June Torrance; m. Suzanne Torrance 1995; one s. two d.; professional golfer 1970–; has played in eight Ryder Cups and represented Scotland on numerous occasions; winner Scottish PGA Championship 1978, 1980, 1985, 1991, 1993; mem. Dunhill Cup team (eight times), World Cup team (11 times), Hennessy Cognac Cup team (five times), Double Diamond team (three times); Capt. winning European team in Asahi Glass Four Tours Championship, Adelaide 1991; Capt. British Ryder Cup Team 2002–; winner of 28 tournaments worldwide since 1972 including Italian Open 1987, Germany Masters 1990, Jersey Open 1991, Kronenbourg Open 1993, Catalan Open 1993, Honda Open 1993, Hamburg Open 1993, British Masters 1995, French Open 1998. *Leisure interests:* snooker, tennis. *Address:* c/o Parallel Murray Management, 56 Ennismore Gardens, Knightsbridge, London, SW7 1AJ, England (Office). *Telephone:* (20) 7225-4600 (Office). *Website:* www .samtorrance.com.

TORRANCE, Very Rev. Thomas Forsyth, MBE, MA, DTheol, DD, DLitt, DSc, FBA, FRSE; British minister of religion and university professor; b. 30 Aug. 1913, Chengtu, China; s. of Rev. Thomas and Annie Elizabeth (Sharp) Torrance; m. Margaret Edith Spear 1946; two s. one d.; ed Bellshill Acad., Univs of Edin., Basel and Oxford; war service with Church of Scotland Huts and Canteens, Middle East and Italy 1943–45; Prof. of Systematic Theol., Auburn Theol. Seminary, USA 1938–39; Minister, Alyth Barony Parish, Church of Scotland 1940–47, Beechgrove Parish Aberdeen 1947–50; Prof. of Church History, Univ. of Edin. 1950–52, of Christian Dogmatics, also Head of Dept 1952–79; Cross of St Mark, Cross of Aksum, Protopresbyter of Greek Orthodox Church; Hon. DD (Montreal, St Andrews, Edin. 1996); Hon. DTheol (Geneva, Faculté Libre Paris, Oslo, Debrecen 1988); Hon. DSc (Heriot-Watt Univ.) 1983; Collins Prize 1969, Templeton Prize 1978. *Publications:* The Doctrine of Grace in the Apostolic Fathers 1948, Calvin's Doctrine of Man 1949, Royal Priesthood 1955, Kingdom and Church 1956, Conflict and Agreement in the Church (two vols) 1959, 1960, Karl Barth: Introduction to his Early Theology 1962, Theology in Reconstruction 1965, Theological Science 1969, Space, Time and Incarnation 1969, God and Rationality 1971, Theology in Reconciliation 1975, Space, Time and Resurrection 1976, The Ground and Grammar of Theology 1980, The Incarnation (ed.) 1980, Belief in Science and in Christian Life (ed.) 1980, Christian Theology and Scientific Culture 1980, Divine and Contingent Order 1981, Reality and Evangelical Theology 1981, Juridical Law and Physical Law 1982, Transformation and Convergence in the Frame of Knowledge 1984, James Clerk Maxwell. A Dynamical Theory of the Electromagnetic Field (ed.) 1982, Reality and Scientific Theology 1985, The Mediation of Christ 1983, The Christian Frame of Mind 1985, The Trinitarian Faith 1988, The Hermeneutics of John Calvin 1988, Karl Barth, Biblical and Evangelical Theologian 1990, Trinitarian Perspectives 1994, Preaching Christ Today, The Gospel and Scientific Thinking 1994, Divine Meaning, Studies in Patristic Hermeneutics 1995, The Christian Doctrine of God, One Being, Three Persons 1996, Scottish Theology from John Knox to John McLeod Campbell 1996, A Passion for Christ (with J.B. and D.W. Torrance) 1999, The Soul and the Person of the Unborn Child 1999, The Person of Jesus Christ 1999, H.R. Mackintosh, Theologian of the Cross 2000. *Leisure interests:* walking, travel. *Address:* 37 Braid Farm Road, Edinburgh, EH10 6LE, Scotland (Home). *Telephone:* (131) 447-3224 (Home). *Fax:* (131) 447-3224. *E-mail:* ttorr@globalnet.co.uk (Home).

TORRES Y TORRES LARA, Carlos; Peruvian politician; fmr Minister of Labour; Prime Minister and Minister of Foreign Affairs 1991–92. *Address:* c/o Office of the Prime Minister, Ucayali 363, Lima, Peru.

TORRICELLI, Robert G., JD, MPA; American politician; b. 26 Aug. 1951, Paterson, NJ; ed Rutgers and Harvard Univs.; called to bar, NJ 1978; Deputy legis. counsel, Office of Gov. of NJ 1975–77; counsel to Vice-Pres. Mondale, Washington, DC 1978–81; pvt. practice, Washington, DC 1981–82; mem. 98th-104th Congresses 1983–97; Senator from New Jersey 1996–2002; Democrat. *Address:* c/o United States Senate, 113 Dirksen Senate Office Building, Washington, DC 20510, USA.

TORSHIN, Aleksander Porfiryevich; Russian politician; b. 27 Nov. 1953, Mitoga, Kamchatsk region; m. Nina Valer'yevna Torshina; two d.; ed All Union Inst. of Law, Moscow State Univ.; teacher, docent Acad. of Public Sciences, then functionary, Cen. CPSU Cttee; Deputy Head Div. on Public Relations with Chambers, Factions and Public Orgs, Fed. Ass. of Russian Fed. 1993–95; Statistics Sec., Deputy Chair. Cen. Bank 1995–98; Deputy Chair. Admin of Russian Fed. Govt, Rep. of Russian Fed. Gov. to State Duma (Parl.) 1998–99; Deputy Dir-Gen. Statistics-Sec., State Corp. Agency on Restructuring of Credit Orgs (ARKO) 1999–2001; mem. Council of Feds representing Mari-El Repub. 2001–, Deputy Chair 2002–; mem. Cttee on Agrarian-Food Policy, Comm. on Reglementation and Org. of Parl. Activities, Comm. on Controlling Council of Fed. Activities; Rep. of Govt of Mary-El Repub. to Parl.

Ass. *Address:* Leninsky prosp. 29, office 114, Yoshkar-Ola, 424001 Republic of Mari-El (Office); Council of Federations, Bolshaya Dmitrovka str. 26, 103426 Moscow, Russia (Office). *Telephone:* (88326) 12-68-04 (Office); (095) 292-59-21 (Office). *Fax:* (095) 292-76-03 (Office).

TORSTENDAHL, Rolf, PhD; Swedish professor of history; b. 9 Jan. 1936, Jönköping; s. of Torsten Torstendahl and Ragnhild (née Abrahamsson) Torstendahl; m. 1st Anna-Maria Ljung 1960 (died 1987); two s.; m. 2nd Tamara A. Salycheva 1996; ed Uppsala Univ.; Lecturer, Dept of History, Uppsala Univ. 1964–67, Assoc. Prof. 1968–78, Sven Warburg Prof. of History 1978–80, Stockholm Univ.; Prof. Uppsala Univ. 1981–2000, Prof. Emer. 2001–; Prof. Mälardalen Univ. 2002–03; Dir Swedish Collegium for Advanced Study in the Social Sciences 1985–90, Dean of Faculty 1994–99; mem. Royal Swedish Acad. of Letters, History and Antiquities 1982, Norwegian Acad. of Science and Letters 1989, Acad. Europaea 1989, Russia Acad. of Sciences, Urals Div. 1995; Björnstiernas pris (Royal Swedish Acad. of Letters, History and Antiquities) 1976. *Publications include:* Teknologins nytta 1975, Dispersion of Engineers in a Transitional Society 1975, Professions in Theory and History (Ed.) 1990, The Formation of Professions (Ed.) 1990, Bureaucratization in Northwestern Europe 1880–1985 1991, State Theory and State History (Ed.) 1992, History-making (Ed.) 1996, State Policy and Gender System (Ed.) 1999, An Assessment of Twentieth-Century Historiography (Ed.) 2000. *Address:* Uppsala University, St Larsgatan 2, 75310 Uppsala (Office); Mälardalen University, Department of Humanities, POB 883, SE—72123 Västerås (Office); St Olofsgatan 4, 75312 Uppsala, Sweden (Home). *Telephone:* (18) 471-15-34 (Office); (21) 10-70-58 (Office); (18) 12-52-98 (Home). *E-mail:* rolf.torstendahl@hist.uu.se (Office); rolf.torstendahl@mdh.se (Office).

TORTELIER, Yan Pascal; French conductor and violinist; b. 19 April 1947, Paris; s. of the late Paul Tortelier and of Maud Tortelier; m. Sylvie Brunet-Moret 1970; two s.; ed Paris Conservatoire and Berks. Music Centre; début as concert violinist, Royal Albert Hall 1962; has since toured extensively all over the world; Konzertmeister, Assoc. Conductor of Orchestre du Capitole de Toulouse 1974–82; Prin. Conductor and Artistic Dir, Ulster Orchestra 1989–92; Prin. Conductor BBC Philharmonic 1992–2002; Hon. DLitt (Ulster) 1992, Dr. hc (Lancaster) 1999. *Publication:* première orchestration of Ravel's Piano Trio (world première concert 1992). *Leisure interests:* skiing, windsurfing, scuba diving, nature. *Address:* c/o IMG Artists Europe, 616 Chiswick High Road, London, W4 2RX, England.

TORVALDS, Linus; Finnish computer software executive; b. 1969; m. Tove Torvalds; two d.; ed Univ. of Helsinki; fmr teacher and research asst; creator of Linux operating system; with Transmeta 1997–. *Publication:* Just for Fun (with David Diamond) 2001. *Address:* c/o Transmeta, 3940 Freedom Circle, Santa Clara, CA 95054, USA (Office). *Telephone:* (408) 919-6836 (Office). *Fax:* torvalds@transmeta.com. *Website:* www.transmeta.com (Office).

TORVILL, Jayne, OBE; British ice skater; b. 7 Oct. 1957; d. of George Torvill and Betty (née Smart) Torvill; m. Philip Christensen 1990; ed Clifton Hall Grammar School for Girls; insurance clerk 1974–80; British Pair Skating Champion (with Michael Hutchinson) 1971; British Ice Dance Champion (with Christopher Dean, q.v.) 1978–83, 1994; European Ice Dance Champion (with Christopher Dean) 1981–82, 1984, 1994; World Ice Dance Champion (with Christopher Dean) 1981–84; World Professional Ice Dance Champion (with Christopher Dean) 1984, 1985, 1990, 1995, 1996; Olympic Ice Dance Champion (with Christopher Dean) 1984; Olympic Ice Dance Bronze Medal (with Cristopher Dean) 1994; Tours include: Australia and NZ 1984, Royal Variety Performance London 1984, world tour with own co. of int. skaters 1985, guest artists with IceCapades 1987, world tour with co. of skaters from Soviet Union 1988, Australia as guests of S. Australian Govt 1991, GB with co. of skaters from Ukraine 1992, "Torvill & Dean, Face the Music, World Tour", UK, Australia and N America 1994, Stars on Ice tour in USA and Canada 1997, "Torvill & Dean Ice Adventures" in UK 1997–98, Stars on Ice Tour in USA and Canada 1997–98; choreography includes "Stars on Ice" in USA 1998–99, 1999–2000, O'Connor and O'Dougherty 1999–2000, GB Nat. Champion Synchronized Skating Team 1999–2000; Hon. MA (Nottingham Trent) 1994; BBC Sportsview Personality of the Year (with Christopher Dean) 1983–84; Figure Skating Hall of Fame (with Christopher Dean) 1989. *Television:* Path of Perfection (Thames Television video) 1984, Fire & Ice (also video) 1986, World Tour (video) 1988, Bladerunners (BBC documentary) 1991, Great Britain Tour (TV special and video) 1992, The Artistry of Torvill and Dean (ABC) 1994, Face the Music (video) 1995, Torvill & Dean: The Story So Far (video) 1996, Bach Cello Suite (with Yo-Yo Ma) 1996. *Publications:* (with Christopher Dean) Torvill and Dean: An Autobiography 1984, Torvill and Dean: Fire on Ice (with Christopher Dean) 1984, Torvill and Dean: Face the Music and Dance 1995, Facing the Music (with Christopher Dean) 1995. *Leisure interests:* theatre, ballet, dogs. *Address:* c/o Mrs Sue Young, POB 32, Heathfield, East Sussex, TN21 0BW, England. *Telephone:* (1435) 867825.

TOŠOVSKÝ, Josef, BCom; Czech banker; b. 28 Sept. 1950, Náchod; m. Bohdana Světlíková; two d.; ed Univ. of Econs Prague; Assoc. Prof. Univ. of Econs, Prague; banker with Czechoslovak State Bank 1973–, Deputy Dir 1978–, consultant to Bank Chair. 1982; Chief Economist, Živnostenská banka, London 1984–85, Deputy Dir June–Dec. 1989; Consultant to Bank Chair., Prague 1986–89; Chair. Czechoslovak State Bank 1989–92, Gov. 1992, for Czech Nat. Bank 1993–97, 1998–2000; Prime Minister of Czech Repub. 1997–98; Chair. Inst. for Financial Stability, Basel, Switzerland 2000–; Cen. Banker of the Year, IMF 1993, European Man. of the Year, European Business Press Fed. 1994, Karel Engliš Prize 1994, European Banker of the Year, Group 20+1 1996, East-West Inst. Award for Leadership in Transition (USA) 2001. *Publications:* numerous articles in professional press. *Leisure interest:* tennis. *Address:* Financial Stability Institute, Bank for International Settlements, Centralbahnplatz 2, 4002 Basel, Switzerland. *Telephone:* (61) 2806074 (Office). *Fax:* (61) 2809100 (Office). *E-mail:* josef.tosovsky@bis.org. *Website:* www.bis.org (Office).

TÓTH, Július, CSc; Slovak politician and engineer; b. 6 May 1935, Zvolen; m. Mária Tóthová; held numerous positions in various iron-processing plants, participated in the privatization of these plants 1990; Minister of Finance 1992–94; Chair. Econ. Council of Slovak Repub. 1992–98, Council for Regional Devt 1992–; Vice-Premier, Govt of Slovakia –March 1994; Alt. Gov. IMF 1992–98; mem. Party for Democratic Slovakia 2000–; Chair. Bd of Supervisors, E Slovak Iron Works, Košice 1994–99; Deputy Chair. Bd of Dirs Industrial Bank, Košice 1994–. *Address:* Party for Democratic Slovakia, Tomášikova 32/A, Bratislava, Slovakia. *Telephone:* (2) 43330144.

TÓTHOVÁ, Katarína, JuDr, DrSc; Slovak politician and lawyer; b. 6 Feb. 1940, Bratislava; m. Lůdovít Tóthová; one d.; ed Univ. Komenského; legal counsellor; Minister of Justice 1992–94; Chair. Legis. Council of Slovak Repub. 1992–97, 1997–98; Vice-Premier of Slovakia 1994–98; Chair. Govt Council for Mass Media 1995–96; mem. Parl. 1998–2002; mem. Party for Democratic Slovakia 2000–; mem. Republican Party Bd; A. Hlinka Order of the first degree, Gold Medal Univ. Komenského, Medal of Nat. Centre of Human Rights. *Publications include:* Selected Issues of Administrative Law in the Management of Universities 1986, Decision-making in State Administration 1989. *Leisure interests:* culture, literature, classic and modern art. *Address:* nr Sr, nām. Alexandra Dubčeka č.1, 81280 Bratislava (Office); Údolná č.1, 81280 Bratislava (Home); Party for Democratic Slovakia, Tomášikova 32/A, Bratislava, Slovakia. *Telephone:* (903) 707000.

TOTSKY, Col-Gen. Konstantin Vasilyevich; Russian army officer; b. 23 Feb. 1950, Kagan, Uzbekistan; m.; two d.; ed Higher Frontier Mil. School, Frunze Mil. Acad., Gen. Staff Mil. Acad.; army service in Pacific, Cen. Asian, Transcaucasian, NW Border Dist 1977–89; participated in mil. operations in Afghanistan; Head, Acad. of Fed. Border Service of Russian Fed. 1996–; Dir Fed. Border Service 1998–; Chair. Council of Border Forces of CIS Countries 1998–. *Address:* Federal Border Service, Myasnitskaya str. 1, 101000 Moscow, Russia. *Telephone:* (095) 224-19-73 (Office).

TÖTTERMAN, Richard Evert Björnson, JurLic, DPhil; Finnish diplomatist; b. 10 Oct 1926, Helsinki; s. of B. Björn Tötterman and Katharine Clare Wimpenny; m. Camilla S. Veronica Huber 1953; one s. one d.; ed Univ. of Helsinki and Brasenose Coll., Oxford; entered Ministry for Foreign Affairs 1952; diplomatic posts in Stockholm 1954–56, Moscow 1956–58, at Ministry of Foreign Affairs 1958–62, Berne 1962–63, Paris 1963–66; Deputy Dir Ministry of Foreign Affairs 1966; Sec.-Gen. Office of Pres. of Finland 1966–70; Sec. of State Ministry of Foreign Affairs 1970–75; Amb. to UK 1975–83, to Switzerland 1983–90, concurrently to the Holy See 1988–90; Chair. Multilateral Consultations preparing Conf. on Security and Co-operation in Europe 1972–73; Hon. Fellow, Brasenose Coll. Oxford 1982; Hon. GCVO, Hon. OBE; Kt Commdr Order of the White Rose (Finland); Grand Cross, Order of Dannebrog (Denmark), Order of Merit (Austria), Order of Orange-Nassau (Netherlands), Order of the Pole Star (Sweden), Order of the Falcon (Iceland); Grand Officier Ordre de la Couronne (Belgium), Order of St Olav (Norway), Order of Merit (Poland), Order of Lion (Senegal), Order of the Banner (Hungary), Commdr, Ordre Nat. du Mérite (France). *Address:* Parkgatan 9A, 00140 Helsinki, Finland. *Telephone:* (9) 627721.

TOTTIE, Thomas, FilLic; Swedish librarian; b. 3 July 1930, Waxholm; s. of the late John Tottie and Gerda (née Willers) Tottie; m. 1st; two d.; m. 2nd Marianne Sandels 1972; two s.; ed Stockholm Univ.; Asst Librarian, Royal Library, Stockholm 1961; Sec. Swedish Council of Research Libraries 1966–73; Deputy Dir Stockholm Univ. Library 1975–76; Dir Library of Royal Carolingian Medico-Chirurgical Inst., Stockholm 1977; Chief Librarian, Uppsala Univ. 1978–96; mem. and official of various professional orgs.; Dr. hc (Uppsala) 1994. *Publications:* 2 books and numerous articles and reports on librarianship. *Leisure interests:* biography, sailing. *Address:* University Publications from Uppsala, Uppsala University Library, P.O. Box 510, 751 20 Uppsala (Office); Kyrkogardsgatan 5A, 753 10 Uppsala, Sweden. *Telephone:* (18) 51-46-83 (Office); (18) 12-32-00 (Home). *E-mail:* thomas.tottie@ub.uu.se (Home). *Website:* www.ub.uu.se/upu (Office).

TOUBERT, Pierre Marcel Paul, PhD; French professor of medieval history; b. 29 Nov. 1932, Algiers; s. of André Toubert and Paola Garcia y Planes; m. Hélène Poggioli 1954; one s.; ed Ecole Normale Supérieure, Paris, Ecole des Hautes-Etudes, Paris, Univ. of Paris and Ecole Française d'Archéologie, Rome; mem. Ecole Française, Rome 1958–61; Dir of Studies, Ecole des Hautes-Etudes 1964–92; Prof. Dept of History, Univ. of Paris (Sorbonne) 1969–92; Prof. Coll. de France 1991–; mem. Nat. Council for Scientific Research, CNRS 1992–; mem. Acad. des Inscriptions et Belles-Lettres, Inst. de France, Acad. Europaea 1989–, Nat. Cttee of Evaluation of Univs 1996–, High Council of Technological Research 1999–; Dr hc (Siena) 1999, (Liège) 2002; Chevalier, Légion d'honneur, Officier Ordre nat. du Mérite, Ordre des Arts et des Lettres, Commdr des Palmes académiques. *Publications include:* Les structures du Latium médiéval, 2 Vols 1973, Etudes sur l'Italie médiévale 1976, Histoire du haut Moyen Age et de l'Italie médiévale 1987, Dalla terra aì castelli nell'Italia medioevale 1994; many other books and publs on medieval Italy, econ. and social history of the Middle Ages. *Address:* Collège de France, 11 place Marcelin Berthelot, 75231 Paris Cedex 05; 34 rue Guynemer, 75006 Paris, France. *Telephone:* 1-44-27-10-32. *Fax:* 1-44-27-11-09. *E-mail:* pierre.toubert@college-de-france.fr (Office).

TOUBON, Jacques, LenD; French politician; b. 29 June 1941, Nice; s. of Pierre-Constant Toubon and Yolande (Molinas) Toubon; m. 1st Béatrice Bernascon; m. 2nd Lise Weiler 1982; ed Lycée Masséna, Nice, Lycée Jean Perrin, Lyon, Faculté de Droit, Lyon, Inst. d'Etudes Politiques, Lyon and Ecole Nat. d'Admin; civil servant 1965–76, Chef de Cabinet, to Minister of Agric. 1972–74, to Minister of Interior 1974, Tech. Adviser, Office of Prime Minister 1974–76; Asst Sec.-Gen. Rassemblement pour la République (RPR) 1977–81, Sec.-Gen. 1984–88; Deputy to Nat. Ass. 1981–93; Mayor 13th Arrondissement, Paris 1983–2001, Deputy Mayor of Paris 1983–2001; Pres. Club 89 1993–; Minister of Culture and the French Language 1993–95, of Justice 1995–97; adviser to Pres. Jacques Chirac 1997–98; Dir Fondation Claude Pompidou 1970–77; Chevalier du Mérite Agricole. *Publication:* Pour en finir avec la peur 1984. *Leisure interests:* collecting modern art, volleyball, tennis. *Address:* Présidence de la République, 55–57 rue du Faubourg-Saint-Honoré, 75008 Paris (Office); Hôtel de Ville, 9 place de l'Hôtel de Ville, 750046 Paris, France (Home).

TOULOUSE, Gérard, DSc; French research scientist; b. 4 Sept. 1939, Vattetot-sur-mer; s. of Robert Toulouse and Thérèse Toulouse (née Tiret); m. Nicole Schnitzer 1970; one s. one d.; ed Ecole Normale Supérieure, Ulm, Orsay; research scientist CNRS 1965–, Laboratoire de Physique de l'Ecole Normale Supérieure 1976–; post-doctoral Fellow UCSD, La Jolla, CA 1969–71; Vice-Pres. Cttee of Exact and Natural Sciences (French nat. comm. for UNESCO) 1997 (Pres. 1999); Sec.-Gen. Foundation La Ferthé 1996; Vice-Pres. Pugwash France 1998; Visitor Ecole Supérieure de Physique et Chimie, Paris 1985–86; Fellow Inst. for Advanced Studies, Jerusalem 1987–88; Corresp. Acad. of Sciences, Paris 1990; Founding mem. Nat. Acad. of Technologies of France, Paris 2000; Foreign hon. mem. American Acad. of Arts and Sciences 1996; Chevalier Ordre nat. du Mérite; Langevin Prize 1976, Triossi Prize 1979, Holweck Prize 1983, CEA Prize 1989; Cecil Powell Medal 1999. *Publications:* Introduction au groupe de renormalisation 1975, Biology and Computation: a Physicist's Choice 1994, Regards sur l'éthique des sciences 1998. *Address:* Laboratoire de physique de l'ENS, 24 rue Lhomond, 75231 Paris, France. *Telephone:* 1-44-32-34-87. *Fax:* 1-43-36-76-66. *E-mail:* toulouse@physique.ens.fr (Office).

TOURAINE, Alain Louis Jules François, DèsSc; French sociologist; b. 3 Aug. 1925, Hermanville; s. of Albert Touraine and Odette Cleret; m. Adriana Arenas 1957 (deceased); one s. one d.; ed Lycées Montaigne and Louis-le-Grand, Paris and Ecole Normale Supérieure; Dir of Studies, Ecole Pratique des Hautes Etudes (now Ecole des Hautes Etudes en Sciences Sociales) 1960–; Prof. Faculté des Lettres de Paris-Nanterre 1966–69; f. Lab. de Sociologie Industrielle (now Centre d'Etude des Mouvements Sociaux) 1958–80; founder and Dir Centre d'Analyse et d'Intervention Sociologiques 1980; mem. Haut Conseil à l'Intégration 1994–96; mem. Acad. Europaea, American Acad. of Arts and Sciences, Polish Acad. of Sciences 1991, Mexican Acad. of Sciences 1998, Brazilian Acad. of Letters 1998; Officier Légion d'honneur, Officier des Arts et Lettres. *Publications:* Sociologie de l'Action 1965, La Société post-industrielle 1969, Production de la société 1973, Pour la sociologie 1974, La voix et le regard 1978, Mort d'une gauche 1979, L'après-socialisme 1980, Solidarité 1982, Le mouvement ouvrier (with Dubet and Wieviorka) 1984, Le retour de l'acteur 1984, La parole et le sang. Politique et société en Amérique Latine 1988, Critique de la modernité 1992, Qu'est-ce que la démocratie? 1994, Lettre à Lionel, Michel, Jacques, Martine, Bernard, Dominique . . . et vous 1995, Le Grand refus, réflexion sur la grève de décembre 1995 (with Dubet, Khosrokhavar, Lapeyronnie and Wieviorka), Pourrons-nous vivre ensemble? Egaux et différents 1997, Comment sortir du libéralisme? 1999, La recherche de soi. Dialogue sur le sujet (with F. Khosrokhavar) 2000. *Leisure interest:* Latin America. *Address:* CADIS, 54 blvd Raspail, 75006 Paris (Office); 32 blvd de Vaugirard, 75015 Paris, France (Home). *Telephone:* 1-49-54-24-57 (Office); 1-43-20-04-11 (Home). *Fax:* 1-42-84-05-91 (Office); 1-45-38-54-05 (Home). *E-mail:* touraine@ehess.fr (Office). *Website:* www.ehess.fr/centres/cadis (Office).

TOURÉ, Lt-Col Amadou Toumani; Malian army officer and head of state; b. 1948; with Armed Forces of Mali, Lt 1972–78, Capt. 33rd Parachute Bn 1978–84, Commdr 1985–90, rank of Lt-Col 1986; Commdr Presidential Guard 1978–86; led coup which overthrew Gen. Moussa Traoré (q.v.) March 1991; Leader Nat. Reconciliation Council 1991–92; Chair. Transition Cttee for the Salvation of the People (acting Head of State) 1991–92; participated in diplomatic initiatives in Rwanda, Burundi 1996, Cen. African Repub. 1997; Head Inter-African Mission to Monitor the Implementation of the Bangui Agreements 1997–; Pres. of Mali 2002–. *Address:* Office of the President, B.P. 1463, Koulouba, Bamako, Mali.

TOURÉ, Sidia; Guinean politician; fmr Dir Office of the Prime Minister of Côte d'Ivoire; Prime Minister of Guinea 1996–99, Minister of Economy, Finance and Planning 1996–97; Pres. Union des forces républicaines. *Address:* c/o Union des forces républicaines, Conakry, Guinea.

TOURÉ, Younoussi; Malian politician; b. 27 Dec. 1941, Niodougou, Timbuktu Region; s. of Singoro Touré and Santadji Tamoura; m. Alimata Traore 1970; two s. three d.; studied in Dakar, Senegal and Abidjan, Côte d'Ivoire;

joined Cen. Bank of Mali 1969, Dir Gen. 1983; rep. at Banque Centrale des états de l'Afrique de l'ouest (BCEAO); Prime Minister 1992–93; Special Adviser to Gov. of BCEAO 1993–94; Commissaire, Union Economique et Monétaire Ouest Africaine (UEMOA) 1994–. *Leisure interests:* reading, sport. *Address:* c/o Union Economique et Monétaire Ouest Africaine (UEMOA), 01 BP 543, Ouagadougou 01, Burkina Fasso. *Telephone:* (226) 306015.

TOURET, Jacques Léon Robert; French geologist; b. 2 Jan. 1936, Fumay; s. of late Martial Touret and Suzanne Gouilly; m. 1st Christiane Poinsignon 1960 (divorced 1972); one s. two d.; m. 2nd Lydie Mohammed 1974; one d.; ed Lycée Chanzy, Charleville, Ecole Nat. Supérieure de Géologie Appliquée, Nancy and Univ. of Nancy; Asst, Ecole Nat. Supérieure de Géologie, Nancy 1958–64, Asst Lecturer in Geology 1964–69; Lecturer in Geology, Univ. of Nancy 1969–74; Prof. Univ. of Paris 7 1974–80; Prof. Earth Science Inst., Free Univ., Amsterdam, Netherlands 1980–2001, Prof. Emer. 2001–; Invited Prof., Ecole Normale Supérieure, Paris 1994–97; chargé de mission, CNRS, Paris 1978–80; mem. Royal Netherlands Acad. of Sciences, Norwegian Acad. of Science and Letters, Academia Europaea; Hon. Fellow European Union of Geologists; Dr. hc (Liège Univ., Belgium) 2001; Prix Carrière, Acad. des Sciences, Paris 1970; Dumont Medal (Belgian Geological Soc.) 1992, Van Waterschoot van der Gracht Medal (Netherlands) 1996; Chevalier, Ordre nat. du mérite. *Publications include:* Le Socle précambrien de Norvège méridionale 1969, The deep Proterozoic Crust in the North Atlantic province (with A. C. Tobi) 1985, Fluid Inclusions: Phase Relationships-Methods-Applications 2001. *Leisure interests:* classical music, French literature. *Address:* Musée de Minéralogie (ABC Mines), 60 blvd Saint Michel, 75006 Paris (Office); 121 rue de la Réunion, 75005 Paris, France (Home). *Telephone:* 1-40-51-91-43 (Office); 1-43-48-32-76 (Home). *Fax:* 1-46-34-25-96 (Office). *E-mail:* jtouret@musee.ensmp.fr (Office).

TOURNIER, Michel, LèsL, LenD, DPhil; French author; b. 19 Dec. 1924, Paris; s. of Alphonse Tournier and Marie-Madeleine (née Fournier) Tournier; ed Saint-Germain-en-Laye and Univs. of Paris (Sorbonne) and Tübingen (Germany); radio and TV production 1949–54; press attaché, Europe No. 1 1955–58; head of literary services, Editions Plon 1958–68; contrib. to Le Monde, Le Figaro; mem. Acad. Goncourt 1972–; Dr hc (Univ. Coll. London) 1997; Officier, Légion d'honneur; Commdr, Ordre nat. du Mérite; Grand Prix du Roman, Acad. Française 1967, Prix Goncourt 1970; Goethe Medal 1993. *Publications:* Vendredi ou les limbes du Pacifique 1967, Le Roi des Aulnes 1970, Les météores 1975, Le vent paraclet 1977, Le coq de bruyère 1978, Des clefs et des serrures 1979, Gaspard, Melchior et Balthazar 1980, Le vol du Vampire 1981, Gilles et Jeanne 1983, La Goutte d'Or 1986, Le Tabor et le Sinaï 1989, Le Médianoche amoureux 1989, Le Crépuscule des masques 1992, Le Miroir des Idées 1994, Le Pied de la lettre 1994, La Couleuvrine 1994, Célébrations 1999. *Leisure interest:* photography. *Address:* Le Presbytère, Choisel, 78460 Chevreuse, France. *Telephone:* 1-30-52-05-29.

TOUSIGNANT, Claude, OC; Canadian artist; b. 23 Dec. 1932, Montreal; s. of Alberic Tousignant and Gilberte Hardy-Lacasse; m. Judith Terry 1968; two d.; ed School of Art and Design, The Montreal Museum of Fine Arts; many solo and group nat. and int. exhbns. 1956–; works included in major N American public and pvt. collections; 1st Prize, Salon de la jeune peinture 1962, 1st Prize, Painting, Art Gallery of Ont. 1967, Canadian Inst. in Rome Award 1973, Prix Paul-Emile Borduas 1989. *Address:* 181 Bourget Street, Montreal, Québec, H4C 2M1 (Studio); 460 Avenue Bloomfield, Outremont, Québec, H2V 3R8, Canada (Home). *Telephone:* (514) 934-3012 (Studio); (514) 948-1463 (Home).

TOWNE, Robert; American scriptwriter; b. 1936; m. Luisa Towne; two c.; ed Pomona Coll. *Screenplays include:* The Tomb of Ligeia 1964, Villa Rides 1967, The Last Detail 1967, Chinatown 1974, Shampoo (with Warren Beatty) 1974, The Yazuka (jtly) 1975, Personal Best (also producer-dir 1984), Greystoke 1984, Tequila Sunrise 1988, Days of Thunder, The Two Jakes, The Firm (co-screenwriter) 1993, Love Affair (co-screenwriter), Mission Impossible (co-screenwriter), Without Limits (also dir) 1998, Mission Impossible 2 1999. *Address:* c/o CAA, 9830 Wilshire Boulevard, Beverly Hills, CA 90212, USA.

TOWNES, Charles Hard, PhD; American physicist; b. 28 July 1915, Greenville, S. Carolina; s. of Henry Keith Townes and Ellen Sumter Hard; m. Frances H. Brown 1941; four d.; ed Furman and Duke Univs, California Inst. of Technology; Asst Calif. Inst. of Tech. 1937–39; mem. Tech. staff, Bell Telephone Labs. 1939–47; Assoc. Prof. of Physics, Columbia Univ. 1948–50, Prof. 1950–61; Exec. Dir Radiation Lab. 1950–52; Chair. Dept of Physics 1952–55; Vice-Pres. and Dir of Research, Inst. for Defense Analyses 1959–61; Provost and Prof. of Physics, MIT 1961–66, Inst. Prof. 1966–67; Univ. Prof., Univ. of Calif. 1967–86, Prof. Emer. 1986–94, Prof. in the Grad. School 1994–; Trustee Carnegie Inst. of Washington 1965–, Bd of Dirs. Perkin-Elmer Corpn 1966–85, Gen. Motors 1973–86, Bulletin of the Atomic Scientists 1964–69; Chair. Science and Tech. Advisory Comm. for Manned Space Flight, Nat. Aeronautics and Space Admin. 1964–69; Chair. Space Science Bd, NAS 1970–73; Guggenheim Fellow 1955–56; Fulbright Lecturer, Paris 1955–56, Tokyo 1956; Richtmeyer Lecturer, American Physical Soc. 1959; Scott Lecturer, Cambridge 1963; Centennial Lecturer, Univ. of Toronto 1967; Jansky Lecturer, Nat. Radio Astronomy Observatory 1971; Lincoln Lecturer 1972–73; Halley Lecturer, Oxford 1976; Schiff Memorial Lecturer, Stanford 1982, Michelson Memorial Lecturer, US Naval Acad. 1982; Faculty Research Lecturer, Univ. of Calif. at Berkeley 1986; Beckman Lecturer, Univ. of Ill. 1986; Schultz Lecturer, Yale Univ. 1987; Fulbright Fellow Lecturer, Collège de France 1987; Darwin Lecturer, Cambridge Univ. 1988; Houston Memorial Lecturer, Rice Univ., Houston 1990; VanVleck Lecturer, Univ. of Minn. 1990; Henry Norris Russell Lectureship, American Astronomical Soc. 1998; Sackler Lecturer, Univ. of Leiden 1999; Loeb Lecturer, Harvard Univ. 2000; Hamilton Lecturer, Princeton Univ. 2000; Bunyan Lecturer, Stanford Univ. 2000, Ford/Nobel Lecture, MIT 2001, Karl Schwarzschild Lecture, Astronomische Gesellschaft 2002, Schroedinger Lecture, Centre for Philosophy and Foundations of Science, New Delhi 2003, Birla Lecture, Birla Science Centre, Hyderabad 2003; mem. Bd of Trustees Rand Corpn 1965–70; Trustee, Calif. Inst. of Tech. 1979–; mem. Pres.'s Science Advisory Cttee 1966–70, Vice-Chair. 1967–69; Trustee Pacific School of Religions 1983–93; mem. Bd of Dirs Grad. Theological Union 1993–96, Center for Theology and the Natural Sciences 1989–; mem. Bd of Advisers, Templeton Foundation Humility Theology Center 1993–; mem. Astronomical Soc. of the Pacific 1989–; mem. Editorial Bd Review of Scientific Instruments 1950–52, Physical Review 1951–53, Journal of Molecular Spectroscopy 1957–60, etc.; Fellow, American Physical Soc. (Council mem. 1959–62, 1965–71, Pres. 1967), Inst. of Electrical and Electronics Engineers; mem. American Acad. of Arts and Sciences, American Philosophical Soc., American Astronomical Soc., Space Program Advisory Council, NASA, NAS (council mem. 1967–72, 1978–81); Foreign mem. Royal Soc. 1976, Nat. Acad. of Sciences, India, Indian Nat. Science Acad.; mem. Pontifical Acad. of Science 1983, Russian Acad. of Sciences 1993, Nat. Acad. of Eng; Fellow of Calif. Acad. of Sciences; holder of patents in electronics, including fundamental patents on masers and lasers, etc.; Hon. mem. Optical Soc. of America; Hon. Fellow Rozhdestvensky Optical Soc. of Russia 1995; hon. degrees include DLitt, ScD, DottIng, LLD, LHD, DMedSc; awards include Comstock Award (NAS) 1959, Stuart Ballantine Medal (Franklin Inst.) 1959, 1962, Rumford Premium (American Acad. of Arts and Sciences) 1961, David Sarnoff Award in Electronics (American Inst. of Electrical Engineers) 1961, John A. Carty Medal (NAS) 1962, Thomas Young Medal and Prize (Inst. of Physics and Physical Soc., England) 1963, Nobel Prize for Physics 1964, Distinguished Public Service Medal (NASA) 1969, Medal of Honor, Inst. of Electrical and Electronics Engineers 1967, Wilmer Exner Award 1970, Plyler Prize American Physical Soc. 1977, Niels Bohr Int. Gold Medal 1979, LeConte Medal 1980, Nat. Medal of Science 1982, L. W. Frolich Award 1986, Berkeley Citation 1986, Nat. Inventors' Hall of Fame 1976, Eng and Science Hall of Fame 1983, Commonwealth Award 1993, ADION Medal, Observatory of Nice 1995, Frederick Ives Medal, Optical Soc. of America 1996, Frank Annunzio Award 1999, Rabindranath Tagore Centenary Plaque 1999, Founder's Award, Nat. Acad. of Eng 2000, Author of Best Science Book of the Year, American Physical Soc. 2000, Lomonosov Gold Medal, Russian Acad. of Sciences 2001, Karl Schwarzschild Medal, Astronomische Gesellschaft 2002; Officier, Légion d'honneur. *Publications:* Microwave Spectroscopy 1955, Quantum Electronics 1960, Quantum Electronics and Coherent Light 1964, Making Waves 1995, How the Laser Happened; Adventures of a Scientist 1999; other scientific papers on microwave spectroscopy, molecular and nuclear structures, radio and infra-red astronomy, masers and lasers, etc. *Leisure interest:* natural history. *Address:* University of California, Department of Physics, 366 LeConte, # 7200, Berkeley, CA 94720, USA. *Telephone:* (510) 642-1128. *Fax:* (510) 643-8497.

TOWNSEND, Sue; British author; b. 2 April 1946, Leicester; m. (divorced); three c.; started writing professionally early 1980s; stage plays include Ten Tiny Fingers, Nine Tiny Toes, Groping for Words 1984, Womberang 1984, The Great Celestial Cow 1985; wrote, narrated and presented Think of England (TV) 1991; Hon. MA (Leicester) 1991. *Publications:* The Secret Diary of Adrian Mole Aged 13¾ (trans. in 20 languages), The Growing Pains of Adrian Mole, True Confessions of Adrian Albert Mole, Margaret Hilda Roberts and Susan Lilian Townsend, Rebuilding Coventry, Ten Tiny Fingers, Nine Tiny Toes 1990, Adrian Mole: From Minor to Major 1991, The Queen and I (adapted for stage 1994) 1992, Adrian Mole: The Wilderness Years 1993, Plays 1996, Ghost Children 1997, Adrian Mole: The Cappuccino Years 1999, Number Ten 2002. *Leisure interests:* canoeing, reading. *Address:* Reed Books, Michelin House, 81 Fulham Road, London, SW3 6RB (Office); c/o The Sale Agency, 11 Jubilee Place, London, SW3 3TD; c/o Curtis Brown Group Ltd, 28–29 Haymarket, London, SW1Y 4SP, England (Office). *Telephone:* (116) 283-1176 (Office).

TOWNSHEND, Peter Dennis Blandford; British composer, performer of rock music, publisher and author; b. 19 May 1945, Isleworth, London; s. of Clifford Townshend and Betty Townshend; m. Karen Astley 1968; one s. two d.; ed Acton County Grammar School and Ealing Art Coll.; contracted as mem. of The Who to Fontana Records 1964, M.C.A. Records 1965, W.E.A. Records 1979; retd from The Who 1984; contracted as solo artist to Atco Records (USA) 1979–, to Virgin Records 1986–; owner, Eel Pie Recording Ltd 1972–83; est. Eel Pie (bookshops and publishing co.) 1976–83; est. Meher Baba Oceanic (UK archival library) 1976–81; Ed., Faber & Faber (publrs.) 1983–; final tour with The Who 1989; Ivor Novello Award 1981, British Phonographic Industry Award 1983; Rock and Roll Hall of Fame 1990, Olivier Award 1997, Q Magazine Lifetime Achievement Award 1997, Ivor Novello Lifetime Achievement Award 2001. *Recordings include:* with The Who: I Can't Explain 1965, My Generation, Tommy (rock opera), Quadrophenia (rock opera), The Iron Man 1989; solo: Empty Glass 1980, Chinese Eyes 1982, White City 1985, Iron Man 1989. *Publications:* The Story of Tommy (with Richard Barnes), Horse's Neck: 1985, Tommy: The Musical 1995, London 1996. *Leisure interest:* sailing. *Address:* c/o Trinifold Management, 12 Oval Road, London, NW1 7DH; Box 305, Twickenham, TW1 1TT, England. *Telephone:* (20) 7419-4300. *Fax:* (20) 7419-4325 (London).

TOYE, Wendy, CBE; British theatrical director, film director, choreographer, actress and dancer; b. 1 May 1917, London; d. of Ernest W. Toye and Jessie Crichton (Ramsay) Toye; ed privately, trained with Euphen MacLaren, Tamara Karsavina, Anton Dolin, Morosoff, Legat, Marie Rambert, Ninette de Valois; first performance aged 3 years, Albert Hall; first professional appearance as Cobweb (Midsummer Night's Dream), Old Vic 1929; prin. dancer Hiawatha, Albert Hall 1931; played Marigold and Phoebe and produced dances, Toad of Toad Hall, Royalty 1931–32; masked dancer Ballerina, Gaiety 1933; danced and choreographed for Carmargo Soc. of Ballet; mem. Ninette de Valois' original Vic Wells Ballet, danced in C. B. Cochran's The Miracle, Lyceum 1932, prin. dancer The Golden Toy, Coliseum 1934; toured with Anton Dolin's Ballet (choreographer for divertissements and short ballets) 1934–35; Tulip Time, Alhambra, then prin. dancer and choreographer, Markova-Dolin Ballet 1935; arranged dances and ballets for many shows and films 1935–42, including most of George Black's productions notably Black Velvet (also prin. dancer) 1939; Shakespearean season, Open Air Theatre 1939; musicals, variety, cabaret; Guest Artist with Sadler's Wells Ballet and Mme Rambert's Ballet Club; prin. dancer with British Ballet organized by Adeline Genée, Denmark 1932; lectured in Australia 1977; Adviser, Arts Council Training Scheme 1978–; mem. Grand Council, Royal Acad. of Dancing, Council LAMDA, Wavendon All Music scheme, Richard Stilgoe Award scheme, original Accreditation Bd, Nat. Council of Drama Training for Acting Courses; Dir Royal Theatrical Fund; Vice-Pres. TACT; Pres. Vic Wells Asscn; Patron Millennium 2000 Dance; Hon. DLitt (City) 1997; The Queen's Silver Jubilee Medal. *Theatre productions:* Big Ben, Bless the Bride, Tough at the Top (for C. B. Cochran), Adelphi, The Shepherd Show, Prince's, Peter Pan (co-dir and choreographer), New York, And So To Bed, New Theatre, Feu d'Artifice (co-dir and choreographer), Paris, Night of Masquerade, Queen, Second Threshold, Vaudeville, Three's Company (choreographer) in Joyce Grenfell Requests the Pleasure, Fortune, Wild Thyme, Duke of York's, Lady at the Wheel and Robert and Elizabeth, Lyric, Hammersmith, Majority of One, Phoenix, Magic Lantern and On the Level, Saville, As You Like It, Old Vic, Virtue in Danger, Mermaid and Strand, A Midsummer Night's Dream, Shakespeare quatercentenary, Latin American tour 1964, Soldier's Tale, Edin. Festival 1967, Boots and Strawberry Jam, Nottingham Playhouse 1968, The Great Waltz, Drury Lane 1970, Showboat, Adelphi 1971, She Stoops to Conquer, Young Vic 1972, Cowardy Custard, Mermaid 1972, Stand and Deliver, Roundhouse 1972; at Chichester R. Loves J 1973, The Confederacy 1974, Follow The Star 1974, Made in Heaven 1975, Make Me a World 1976, Once More with Music 1976, Oh Mr. Porter, Mermaid 1977, Gingerbread Man, Watermill Theatre 1981, This Thing Called Love, Watermill Theatre 1982, Ambassadors Theatre 1983, Singing in the Rain (Assoc. Producer), Palladium 1983, Noel and Gertie, Monte Carlo 1983, Birds of A Feather 1984, Barnum (Assoc. Producer) 1985, Madwoman of Chaillot, Torville and Dean World Tour (Assoc. Producer) 1985, Once Upon A Mattress, Watermill Theatre 1985, Kiss Me Kate, Copenhagen 1986, Laburnham Grove, Palace Theatre, Watford 1987, Miranda, Chichester Festival Theatre 1987, Get the Message, Molecule 1987, Songbook, Watermill 1988, Mrs Dot, Watford 1981, When that I was, Manitoba 1988–89, Cinderella, Watford 1989, Penny Black, Wavendon 1990, Moll Flanders, Watermill 1990, Heaven's Up, Playhouse 1990, Bernard Shaw and Mrs Patrick Campbell (musical), Wavendon 1990, Mrs Pat's Profession, Wavendon 1991, The Drummer, Watermill 1991, Sound of Music 1992, See How They Run, Watermill 1992, Vienna 1992, The Kingfisher, Vienna 1993, Under Their Hats, King's Head 1994, Vienna 1995, The Anastasia File, Watermill 1994, Der Apotheker, Menton, France 1995, Warts and All, Watermill 1996, Sadler's Wells Finale Gala 1996, Rogues to Riches, Watermill 1996. *Opera productions:* Bluebeard's Castle (Bartók), Sadler's Wells and Brussels, The Telephone (Menotti), Rusalka (Dvořák) and La Vie Parisienne, Sadler's Wells, Die Fledermaus, Coliseum and Sadler's Wells, Orpheus in the Underworld, Sadler's Wells and Australia, The Abduction from the Seraglio, Bath Festival 1967, The Impresario, Don Pasquale (for Phoenix Opera Group) 1968, The Italian Girl in Algiers, Coliseum 1968, Orpheus 1978, Merry Widow 1979–80, Orpheus 1981, Mikado (Turkey) 1982, The Italian Girl in Algiers 1982, Serva Padrona and the Apothecary Operas for Aix-en-Provence Festival 1991. *Films directed:* The Stranger Left No Card 1952, The Teckman Mystery, Raising a Riot, The Twelfth Day of Christmas, Three Cases of Murder 1954, All for Mary 1955, True as a Turtle 1956, We Joined the Navy 1962, The King's Breakfast, Cliff in Scotland, A Goodly Manor for a Song, Girls Wanted – Istanbul; retrospective of films, Paris Film Festival 1990, Nat. Film Theatre 1995. *Television productions include:* Chelsea at 8 and Chelsea at 9 and Orpheus in the Underworld (dir) for Granda TV; directed Esmi Divided 1957, Follow the Star 1979, Tales of the Unexpected 1981, Trial by Jury 1982 for the BBC; choreographed many revues for the BBC. *Leisure interests:* embroidery, gardening. *Address:* 5 Wedderburn House, 95 Lower Sloane Street, London, SW1W 8BZ (Home); c/o Jean Diamond, London Management, 2 Noel Street, London W1, England. *Telephone:* (20) 7823-4530.

TOYODA, Shoichiro, DEng; Japanese business executive; b. 27 Feb. 1925, Nagoya; s. of Kiichiro Toyoda and Hatako Toyoda; m. Hiroko Mitsui 1952; one s. one d.; ed Nagoya and Tohoku Univs.; joined Toyota Motor Corpn 1952, Man. Dir 1961, Sr Man. Dir 1967, Exec. Vice-Pres 1972, Pres. Marketing Org. 1981, Pres. Toyota Motor Corpn 1982, Chair. 1992–99, Hon. Chair. 1999–, Sr

Adviser, mem. Bd June 1996–; fmr Chair. Japanese Automobile Mfrs Asscn; Vice-Chair. Keidanren (Fed. of Industrial Orgs.) 1990–94, Chair. 1994–98; Deming Prize 1980; Medal with Blue Ribbon for Outstanding Public Service (Japan) 1984, FISITA Medal (France) 2000, Order of Merit (Turkey) 1998, Commdr Légion d'honneur and numerous other honours. *Leisure interests:* gardening, golf. *Address:* Toyota Motor Corporation, 1 Toyota-cho, Toyota, Aichi 471-8571, Japan (Office).

TOYODA, Tatsuro, BMechEng, MBA; Japanese motor manufacturing executive; b. 1 June 1929, Nagoya; s. of Kiichiro Toyoda and Hatako Iida; m. Shimizu Ayako; one s. one d.; ed Univ. of Tokyo, New York Univ.; joined Toyota Motor Corpn 1953, apptd Dir 1974, supervised creation of New United Motor Mfg Inc. (NUMMI), jt venture with General Motors in Calif., USA 1984, Pres. NUMMI 1984–86; Sr Man. Dir Toyota 1986–88, Exec. Vice-Pres. 1988–92, Pres. 1992–95, Vice-Chair 1995–96, Sr Adviser to the Bd 1996–; fmr Chair. Japan Automobile Mfrs' Asscn; Vice-Chair. Japan Asscn of Corp. Execs (Keizai Doyukai); Grand Cordon of the Orders of the Sacred Treasure 1999. *Leisure interest:* listening to music. *Address:* c/o Toyota Motor Corporation, 1 Toyota-cho, Toyota, Aichi 471-8571, Japan.

TRACHTENBERG, Stephen Joel, JD, MPA; American university president; b. 14 Dec. 1937, Brooklyn; s. of Oscar Trachtenberg and Shoshana Weinstock; m. Francine Zorn 1971; two s.; ed Columbia, Yale and Harvard Univs.; admitted New York Bar 1964, U.S. Supreme Court Bar 1967; attorney, Atomic Energy Comm. 1962–65; Special Asst to U.S. Educ. Comm., Health, Educ. and Welfare, Washington, DC 1966–68; Assoc. Prof. of Political Science, Boston Univ. 1969–77, Assoc. Dean 1969–70, Dean 1970–74, Assoc. Vice-Pres., co-Counsel 1974–76, Vice-Pres. Academic Services 1976–77; Pres., Prof. of Law, Univ. of Hartford, Conn. 1977–88; Pres., Prof. of Man. George Washington Univ., Washington 1988–; Dir NationsBank, Greater Washington Bd of Trade, Nat. Educ. Telecommunications Org., Washington Research Library Consortium, DC Tax Revision Comm., Newcomen Soc.; Adviser to Presidency; numerous awards and several hon. degrees. *Address:* Office of the President, George Washington University, Washington, DC 20052; 843 Bruce Avenue, Flossmoor, IL 60422, USA. *Telephone:* (202) 994-1000. *Fax:* (202) 994-9025. *Website:* www.gwn.edu.

TRAHAR, Anthony (Tony) John, BComm, CA (SA); South African business executive; b. 1 June 1949, Johannesburg; m. Patricia Trahar; one s. one d.; ed St. John's Coll., Univ. of the Witwatersrand; qualified CA 1973, served articles Whiteley Bros. (now Deloitte & Touche); Man. Trainee Anglo American Corpn 1974–76, Personal Asst to Chair. of Exec. Cttee and of Corpn 1976–77, Asst Div. Man. 1977–79, Div. Industrial Financial Man. 1979–82, Exec. Dir 1991–2000, CEO 2000–, Chair. Anglo Forest Products, Anglo Industrial Minerals Div.; Financial Dir Anglo American Industrial Corpn 1982–92, Deputy Chair. 1992–; Man. Dir Mondi 1986–89, Exec. Chair. 1989, Chair. Mondi Europe 1993–; Deputy Chair. Neusiedler AG (Austria) 1990, Frantschach AG 1992; Chair. Anglo American Corpn of SA, Paleo Anthropological Scientific Trust; Dir Anglo Platinum, Anglo Gold, DB Investments, Highveld Steel; mem. Exec. Cttee World Wildlife Fund. *Leisure interests:* shooting, fishing, gym, classic cars and music. *Address:* Anglo American PLC, 20 Carlton House Terrace, St. James's, London, SW1Y 5AN, England (Office); POB 650876, Benmore 2010 South Africa. *Telephone:* (20) 7698-8888 (Office). *Fax:* (20) 7698-8500 (Office). *E-mail:* ajtrahar@angloamerican.co.za (Office). *Website:* www.angloamerican.co.uk (Office).

TRAILL, Sir Alan, GBE, QSO, MA, DMus; British insurance broker; b. 7 May 1935, London; s. of George Traill and Margaret (Matthews) Traill; m. Sarah Jane Hutt 1964; one s.; ed Charterhouse and Jesus Coll., Cambridge; Dir Morice Tozer Beck (insurance brokers) 1960; Underwriting mem. Lloyd's 1963–89; Founder Dir Traill Attenborough (Lloyd's brokers) 1973, Chair. 1980; Man. Dir Colburn Traill Ltd 1989–96; Div. Dir First City Insurance Brokers Ltd 1996–2000; Dir City Arts Trust Ltd, Grandactual Ltd 1993–97; Hon. Sec. and Treas. ARIAS (Insurance Arbitration Soc.) 1997–2002; mem. Pathfinder Team Consulting 1992–; mem. Advisory Council and Educ. Cttee, London Symphony Orchestra 1997–; Chair. UK/NZ 1990 Cttee 1989–90; Chair. Trustees, Waitangi Foundation 1991–99; Trustee, St Paul's Cathedral Choir School Foundation 1985–; Gov./Almoner Christ's Hosp. 1980–2003; Gov. Lord Mayor Treloar Coll. 1985–2002; Trustee Morden Coll. 1995–; mem. Court of Common Council (of City of London) 1970, Alderman 1975, Sheriff 1982–83, Lord Mayor of London 1984–85; Master Worshipful Co. of Musicians 2000; Gov. Menuhin School 2000–; Vice-Pres. Bridewell Royal Hosp. 2003–; Patron Lord Mayor Treloar Trust 2002–; K.StJ. 1985. *Leisure interests:* DIY, travel, opera, music, assisting education. *Address:* Wheelers Farm, Thursley, Godalming, Surrey, GU8 6QE, England. *Telephone:* (1252) 702939 (Office); (1252) 703271 (Home). *Fax:* (1252) 703271 (Home). *E-mail:* atraill.granary@btinternet.com (Office).

TRAJKOVSKI, Boris, GCMG; Macedonian politician; b. 25 June 1956, Strumica; m. Vilma Trajkovska; one s.; ed Univ. St Cyril and Methodius, Skopje; fmr head of legal Dept; adviser Sloboda (construction co.) –1997; Chair. Comm. on Foreign Relations, Internal Macedonian Revolutionary Org.-Democratic Party for Macedonian Nat. Unity (IMRO-DPMNU); Pres. Pan-European Movt for Repub. of Macedonia; Head Cabinet of Mayor, Kisola Voda municipality, Skopje 1997–98; Deputy Minister of Foreign Affairs 1999; Pres. of Macedonia 1999–; Insignia of the Collar of the Order of Merit "Pro Merito Melitense", Malta 2000, Knight Grand Cross of the Order of St Michael

and St George 2000, World Methodist Peace Award 2002. *Address:* Office of the President, 1000 Skopje, 11 Oktomvri bb, Macedonia. *Telephone:* (2) 113318. *Fax:* (2) 112147. *Website:* www.president.gov.mk (Office).

TRÂN DUC LUONG; Vietnamese politician and fmr mining engineer; b. 1937; apptd. a Vice-Prime Minister 1992; mem. Dang Cong san Viet Nam (Communist Party of Viet Nam) Politburo 1996–97. *Address:* c/o Dang Cong san Viet Nam, 1 Hoang Van Thu, Hanoi, Viet Nam.

TRAN TAM TINH, Rev., PhD, FRSC; Vietnamese/Canadian professor of classical archaeology; b. 16 April 1929, Nam Dinh; ed Séminaire Pontifical, Università Laterano, Université de Fribourg, Ecole Pratique des Hautes Etudes, Paris, CNRS; ordained Priest 1956; excavations at Soli, Cyprus 1965–74, Pompeii and Herculaneum 1969–76; Co-f. Fraternité Vietnam 1976; Prof. of Classical Archaeology, Laval Univ. 1964–, Sr Prof. 1971–94; Tatiana Warscher Award for Archaeology (American Acad. at Rome) 1973, Prix G. Mendel (Académie des Inscriptions et Belles-Lettres, France) 1978. *Publications:* Le culte d'Isis à Pompéi 1964, Le culte des divinités orientales à Herculanum 1971, Le culte des divinités orientales en Campanie 1972, Isis lactans 1973, Catalogue des peintures romaines au musée du Louvre 1974, I cattolici nella storia del Vietnam 1975, Dieu et César 1978, Sérapis debout 1983, Soloi I, La Basilique 1985, La casa dei Cervi à Herculanum 1988, Tôi vê Hanoi 1974, Tro vê nguôn 1974, Corpus des lampes antiques conservées au Québec I 1991, Corpus des lampes à sujets asiatiques du musée gréco-romain d'Alexandrie 1993; and numerous articles on classical iconography and religion. *Address:* Université Laval, Cité Universitaire, Québec, G1K 7PQ (Office); 2995 Maricourt, Suite 300, Ste.-Foy, Québec, G2W 4T8, Canada. *Telephone:* (418) 653-3513. *Website:* www.ulaval.ca (Office).

TRÂN THIEN KHIEM, Gen.; Vietnamese politician and army officer; b. 15 Dec. 1925; Army service 1947–75; held off attempted coup against Pres. Diem 1960, took part in coup against him 1963; with Gen. Nguyen Khan led coup removing Gen. Duong Van Minh 1964; Defence Minister and C-in-C 1964; Amb. to USA 1964–65, to Repub. of China 1965–68; Minister of the Interior 1968–73, Deputy Prime Minister March–Aug. 1969, Prime Minister of Viet Nam 1969–75, Minister of Defence 1972–75; fled to Taiwan April 1975.

TRAN VAN HUONG; Vietnamese politician; b. 1 Dec. 1903; fmr schoolteacher; participated in Viet-Minh resistance against French; Prefect of Saigon 1954 and 1964; Prime Minister Repub. of Viet Nam 1964–65, 1968–69; Vice-Pres. of Repub. of Viet Nam 1971–75, Pres. 21–28 April 1975.

TRAORÉ, Col Diara; Guinean politician and army officer; Prime Minister of Guinea April–Dec. 1984, Minister of Nat. Educ. 1984–85; mem. Comité militaire de redressement nat. (CMRN) 1984–85; staged abortive coup d'état July 1985; arrested and sentenced to death; sentence commuted to life imprisonment; released Dec. 1988.

TRAORÉ, Gen. Moussa; Malian politician and army officer; b. 25 Sept. 1936, Kayes; ed Training Coll., Fréjus, Cadets Coll., Kati; became NCO in French Army; returned to Mali 1960; promoted Lt 1964, Col 1971, Brig.-Gen. 1978; at Armed Forces Coll., Kati until 1968; led coup to depose Pres. Modibo Keita Nov. 1968; Pres. Mil. Cttee for Nat. Liberation (Head of State) and C-in-C of the Armed Forces 1968–91, also Prime Minister 1969–80; Pres. of Mali 1979–91; Minister of Defence and Security 1978–86, of the Interior 1978–79, of Nat. Defence 1988–90 (overthrown in coup, under arrest); Chair. OAU 1988–89; Sec.-Gen. Nat. Council Union Démocratique du Peuple Malien 1979–80; fmr mem. Cen. Exec. Bureau; Pres. Conf. of Heads of State, Union Douanière des Etats de l'Afrique de l'Ouest 1970; overthrown March 1991; stood trial Nov. 1992; sentenced to death for mass murder Feb. 1993; sentence commuted to life imprisonment 1997; charged with embezzlement Oct. 1998; sentenced to death Jan. 1999; sentence commuted to life imprisonment Sept. 1999.

TRAPATTONI, Giovanni; Italian professional football manager; b. 17 March 1939, Milan; player AC Milan; 17 caps for Italy; coach Italy nat. team 2000–; fmr Man. Juventus (won six Serie A titles), Inter (won one Serie A title), Bayern Munich (won one Bundesliga title); winner of numerous other trophies including the World Club Cup, European Cup, Cup Winner's Cup, European Supercup, UEFA Cup (three times). *Publication:* Fischia il Trap (biog.).

TRAPP, Joseph Burney, CBE, MA, FBA, FSA; British/New Zealand administrator and scholar; b. 16 July 1925, Carterton, NZ; s. of H.M.B. Trapp and Frances M. Trapp (née Wolters); m. Elayne Margaret Falla 1953; two s.; ed Dannevirke High School and Victoria Univ. Coll., Wellington, NZ; Asst Librarian, Alexander Turnbull Library, Wellington 1946–50; Jr Lecturer, Victoria Univ. Coll. 1950–51; Asst Lecturer, Univ. of Reading, England 1951–53; Asst Librarian, then Librarian, Warburg Inst., London 1953–76, Dir and Prof. of the History of the Classical Tradition 1976–90, Hon. Fellow 1990–; Vice-Pres. British Acad. 1983–85, Foreign Sec. 1988–95; Chair. Advisory Cttee and Trustee, Lambeth Palace Library 1987–98; Chair. Panizzi Lectures Selection Cttee 1996–2000; Gray Lecturer (Cambridge) 1990, Panizzi Lecturer (British Library) 1990, Lyell Reader (Oxford) 1994; Foreign mem. Royal Swedish Acad. of Letters, History and Archaeology 1995–. *Publications:* Ed. Apology of Sir Thomas More 1979, Essays in the Renaissance and the Classical Tradition 1990, Erasmus, Colet and More: The Early Tudor Humanists and their Books 1991, Cambridge History of The Book in Britain, III: 1400–1557 (co-ed.) 1999; articles in learned journals. *Address:*

Warburg Institute, Woburn Square, London, WC1H 0AB, England. *Telephone:* (20) 7862-8905. *Fax:* (20) 7862-8955. *E-mail:* joseph.trapp@sas.ac.uk (Office); joseph.trapp@sas.ac.uk (Home).

TRAUNER, Sergio; Italian business executive and lawyer; b. 9 March 1934, Athens, Greece; s. of Livio Trauner and Nada Mandich; m. (divorced); ed Univ. of Trieste; lawyer in pvt. practice; counsellor to Trieste Municipality 1962–75, 1982–, to Friuli Venezia Giulia Region 1964–78; Dir Finmare Co. (IRI Group) 1981–84, EFIM 1984–87; mem. Presidential Cttee and Bd of Dirs. IRI 1986–91; Pres. ILVA SpA 1991–; Commendatore of Italian Repub., Officer, Order of Merit of Italian Repub. *Publications:* books on art and history. *Leisure interests:* reading, travel.

TRAUTMAN, Andrzej; Polish theoretical physicist and professor of physics; b. 4 Jan. 1933, Warsaw; s. of Mieczysław Trautman and Eliza Trautman (née André); m. Róża Michalska 1962; two s.; ed Warsaw Univ. of Tech., Warsaw Univ.; asst, Inst. of Radiolocation, Warsaw Univ. of Tech. 1952–53, Inst. of Applied Math. 1953–55; postgraduate studies, Inst. of Physics, Polish Acad. of Sciences (PAN) 1955–58, doctorate 1959; lecturer 1959; scientific training, Imperial Coll., King's Coll., London, Univ. of Syracuse, USA 1959–61; scientist, Inst. of Theoretical Physics, Warsaw Univ. 1961–, Asst Prof. and Head of Dept Electrodynamics and Theory of Relativity 1962–68, Extraordinary Prof. 1964–71, Ordinary Prof. 1971–; Deputy Dir Inst. of Theoretical Physics 1968–74, Dir 1975–85; Corresp. mem. Polish Acad. of Sciences 1969–76, mem. 1977–, mem. Presidium 1972–83, Vice-Pres. 1978–80, Chair. Cttee of Physics; Corresp. mem. Polish Acad. of Arts and Science, Krakow; Deputy Chair. Gen. Bd of Polish Physics Asscn 1970–73, Foreign mem. Czechoslovak Acad. of Sciences 1980–90; mem. Int. Cttee of Theory of Relativity and Gravitation 1965–80, Int. Journal of Theoretical Physics, Journal of Geometry and Physics; Visiting Prof., American Math. Soc., Santa Barbara 1962, Coll. de France, Paris 1963 and 1981, Brandeis Univ., USA 1964, Univ. of Chicago 1971, Univ. of Pisa, Italy 1972, The Schrödinger Professorship, Univ. of Vienna 1972, State Univ. of NY at Stony Brook 1976–77, Univ. of Montreal 1982, 1990, Univ. of Tex. at Dallas 1985, 1986; Dr hc (Silesian Univ., Czech Repub.) 2001; State Prize 1st Class 1976, Alfred Jurzykowski Foundation Award in Physics 1984, Gold Cross of Merit, Cross of Order of Polonia Restituta. *Publications:* Differential Geometry for Physicists 1984, The Spinorial Chessboard (with P. Budinich) 1988, Space Time and Gravitation (with W. Kopczyński) 1992; and numerous works on theory of gravitational waves, energy of gravitation field, modern methods of differential geometry and their application in physics, Einstein-Cartan's Theory, Dirac operator and spin structures on manifolds. *Leisure interest:* chess. *Address:* Instytut Fizyki Teoretycznej UW, ul. Hoża 69, 00-681 Warsaw, Poland (Office). *Telephone:* (22) 5532295 (Office). *Fax:* (22) 6219475 (Office). *E-mail:* Andrzej.Trautman@fuw.edu.pl (Office). *Website:* www.fuw .edu.pl/~amt/amt.html (Office).

TRAVKIN, Nikolai Ilyich; Russian politician; b. 19 March 1946, Novo-Nikolskoe, Moscow region; m.; two s.; ed Kolomna Pedagogical Inst., Higher Party School; mem. CPSU 1970–90; worker, brigade-leader, Head of the Dept of "Glavmosstroi"; initiator self-financing and self-man. into construction industry 1969–; Deputy Head of construction union 1967–89; mem. of the movt "Democratic Russia" 1988–; People's Deputy of the USSR 1989–91; People's Deputy of Russia 1990–93; a founder and Chair. Democratic Party of Russia 1990–94; Chair. of the Subcttee, Supreme Soviet of the USSR (supervising local soviets and devt of self-man.) 1989–90; Chair. Cttee Supreme Soviet of Russia; supervising local soviets and devt of self-man. May–Dec. 1990; head of local admin. Shakhovskoy Dist 1991–96; co-leader Civic Union coalition 1992–93; mem. State Duma (Parl.) Yabloko group (now Union of Right Forces faction) 1993–; Minister without Portfolio 1994–96; mem. Cttee on Problems of Fed. and Regional Politics 1996–; Pres. Fund in Support of Farmers; Hero of Socialist Labour 1986. *Leisure interests:* theatre, literature. *Address:* State Duma, Okhotny Ryad 1, 103265 Moscow, Russia. *Telephone:* (095) 292-33-47 (Duma).

TRAVOLTA, John; American actor; b. 18 Feb. 1954, Englewood, NJ; s. of Salvatore Travolta and late Helen (née Burke) Travolta; m. Kelly Preston 1991; one s. one d.; TV series Welcome Back Kotter 1975–77; l.p. records 1976, 1977; Billboard Magazine Best New Male Vocalist Award 1976; Best Actor Award, Nat. Bd of Review 1978; Male Star of the Year, Nat. Asscn of Theatre Owners 1983, Alan J. Pakula Prize 1998, Lifetime Achievement Award, Palm Springs Int. Film Festival 1999. *Films:* Carrie 1976, The Boy in the Plastic Bubble (for TV) 1976, Saturday Night Fever 1977, Grease 1978, Moment by Moment 1978, Urban Cowboy 1980, Blow-Out 1981, Staying Alive 1983, Two of a Kind 1983, Perfect 1985, The Experts 1988, Chains of Gold 1989, Look Who's Talking 1989, Look Who's Talking Now 1990, The Tender 1991, All Shook Up 1991, Look Who's Talking 3 1994, Pulp Fiction 1994, White Man's Burden 1995, Get Shorty 1995, Broken Arrow 1996, Phenomenon 1996, Michael 1997, Face Off 1997, She's So Lovely 1997, Primary Colors 1998, A Civil Action 1998, The General's Daughter 1999, Battlefield Earth 2000, Lucky Numbers 2000, Swordfish 2001, Domestic Disturbance 2001. *Publication:* Staying Fit 1984. *Leisure interest:* flying.

TREACY, Philip, MA, RCA; Irish milliner; b. 26 May 1967, Ballinsoe, Co. Galway; s. of the late James Vincent Treacy and Katie Agnes Treacy; ed Nat. Coll. of Art and Design, Dublin, Royal Coll. of Art, London; while still a student, worked for designers including Rifat Ozbek, John Galliano and Victor Edelstein; f. Philip Treacy Millinery, London 1991; house milliner for

Marc Bohan at Hartnell and for Victor Edelstein; has collaborated with Karl Lagerfeld, Chanel's couture and ready-to-wear shows 1991–; his own ready-to-wear range sold in New York and London 1991–; designed head dresses for Pola John's production of My Fair Lady 1992; presented own show, London 1993; launched accessory range 1997; first show in New York 1997; British Accessory Designer of the Year award 1991, 1992, 1993, 1996, 1997, Irish Fashion Oscar 1992, Haute Couture Paris 2000. *Address:* Philip Treacy Ltd, 69 Elizabeth Street, London, SW1W 9PJ, England. *Telephone:* (20) 7824-8787. *Fax:* (20) 7824-8559.

TRECHSEL, Stefan, DIur; Swiss lawyer; b. 25 June 1937, Berne; s. of Manfred F. Trechsel and Steffi Friedlaender; m. Franca Julia Kinsbergen 1967; two d.; ed Univ. of Berne and Georgetown Univ., Washington; Asst and Main Asst for Criminal Law, Univ. of Berne 1964–71; Swiss Fed. Dept for Tech. Cooperation 1966–67; Public Prosecutor, Dist of Bern-Mittelland 1971–75; Guest Prof. of Criminal Law and Procedure, Univ. of Fribourg 1975–77; Prof., Hochschule St Gallen 1979–99; Prof. of Criminal Law and Legal Instruction, Univ. of Zurich 1999–; mem. European Comm. of Human Rights 1975–99, 2nd Vice-Pres. 1987, Chamber Pres. 1993–94, Pres. 1995–99; Dr. hc New York Law School 1975. *Publications:* Der Strafgrund der Teilnahme 1967, Die Europäische Menschenrechtskonvention, ihr Schutz der persönlichen Freiheit und die Schweizerischen Strafprozessrechte 1974, Strafrecht Allgemeiner Teil I (4th Edn of textbook by Peter Noll) 1994, Schweizerisches Strafgesetzbuch, Kurzkommentar 1997. *Leisure interests:* skiing, music, literature, psychology, chamber music ('cello). *Address:* Rechtswissenschaftl. Seminar der Universität Zürich, Wilfriedstr. 6, 8032, Zürich, Switzerland. *Telephone:* (1) 6343052 (Office). *Fax:* (1) 6344393 (Office). *E-mail:* trechsel@rws.unizh.ch (Office). *Website:* www.rws.unizh.ch (Office).

TREDE, Michael, MB, BChir, MD; German surgeon; b. 10 Oct. 1928, Hamburg; s. of Hilmar Trede and Gertrud (Daus) Trede; m. Ursula Boettcher 1956; one s. four d.; ed The Leys School, Cambridge and Univ. of Cambridge; Surgeon-in-training, Freie Universität Berlin 1957–62, Heidelberg Univ. 1962–72; Prof. and Chair. Dept of Surgery, Klinikum Mannheim, Univ. of Heidelberg, now Prof. Emer. and Chair.; Pres. Deutsche Gesellschaft für Chirurgie, Int. Surgical Soc. 1993–95; Hon. mem. Austrian, American, Swiss, Italian and Portuguese Surgical Asscns.; Hon. FRCS (England, Ireland, Glasgow, Edin.); Hon. FACS, Dr. hc (Edin.) 1995. *Publications:* Surgery of the Pancreas (with D. C. Carter), The Art of Surgery 1999, Der Rückbehrer. Skizzenbuch eines Chirurgen 2001; 500 articles on surgery in scientific journals. *Leisure interests:* painting, violin-playing, mountaineering, skiing. *Address:* Nadlerstrasse 1A, 68259 Mannheim, Germany. *Telephone:* (621) 383-2728 (Office); (621) 796301.

TREFILOVA, Tatyana Ivanovna; Russian lawyer and financier; b. 13 Feb. 1957, Moscow; ed All-Union Inst. of Law; Insp. Chief Dept of Foreign Tourism, USSR Council of Ministers 1975–77; Sec., Head of Secr. Procurator's Office, Leninsky Dist, Moscow 1977–80; legal adviser 2nd Moscow Device Construction plant 1980–81; Procurator, Deputy Head of Div. Procurator's Office of Moscow region 1981–87; Sr Asst to Procurator of Magadan region 1987–93, 1994–95, advocate Magadan Coll. of Advocates 1993–94; Asst to Chief Procurator of Krasnogorsk, Moscow region 1995–96; Deputy Head, then Head of Dept CB Kredfitprombank 1996–97; Head of Rosuglesbyt legal service 1997; Head of Div., Deputy Head Legal Dept Vneskeconombank 1997–2000; Deputy Head Dept of Budget, Credits and Guarantees, Ministry of Finance 2000–01; Head Fed. Service of Financial Rehabilitation and Banking 2001–. *Address:* FSFO, Shchepkina str. 42, 129857 Moscow, Russia (Office). *Telephone:* (095) 971-90-90 (Office). *Fax:* (095) 945-47-15 (Office).

TREGLOWN, Jeremy Dickinson, BLitt, MA, PhD, FRSL; British university professor, writer and journalist; b. 24 May 1946, Anglesey, N Wales; s. of late Rev. G. L. Treglown and of Beryl Treglown; m. 1st Rona Bower 1970 (divorced 1982); one s. two d.; m. 2nd Holly Eley (née Urquhart) 1984; ed Bristol Grammar School, St Peter's Coll., Oxford; Lecturer in English Literature, Lincoln Coll., Oxford 1973–76, Univ. Coll., London 1976–79; Asst Ed. The Times Literary Supplement 1979–81, Ed. 1982–90; Prof. of English, Univ. of Warwick 1993– (Chair. Dept. of English and Comparative Literary Studies 1995–98); Chair. of Judges, Booker Prize 1991, Whitbread Book of the Year Award 1998; Co-ed. Liber, a European Review of Books 1989; Contributing Ed., Grand Street magazine, New York 1991–98; Visiting Fellow, All Souls Coll., Oxford 1986; Fellow Huntington Library 1988; Mellon Visiting Assoc., Calif. Inst. of Tech. 1988; Ferris Visiting Prof., Princeton Univ. 1992; Jackson Brothers Fellow, Beinecke Library, Yale Univ. 1999; Leverhulme Research Fellow 2001–03; Margaret and Herman Sokol Fellow, Cullnan Center for Scholars and Writers, New York Public Library 2002–03; Hon. Research Fellow, Univ. Coll. London 1991–; Fellow, Royal Soc. of Literature 1989–. *Publications:* The Letters of John Wilmot, Earl of Rochester 1980, Spirit of Wit 1982, The Lantern-Bearers and Other Essays by R. L. Stevenson 1988, Roald Dahl: A biography 1994, Grub Street and the Ivory Tower: Literary Journalism and Literary Scholarship from Fielding to the Internet (co-ed.) 1998, Romancing: The Life and Work of Henry Green 2000; various articles and introductions on poetry, drama and literary history. *Address:* Gardens Cottage, Ditchley Park, Enstone, Oxfordshire, OX7 4EP, England.

TREICHL, Heinrich; Austrian banker; b. 31 July 1913, Vienna; s. of Dr. Alfred Treichl and Dorothea (née Baroness Ferstel) Treichl; m. Helga Ross 1946; two s.; ed Univs. of Frankfurt, Germany and Vienna; Dir Banque des

Pays de l'Europe Centrale, Paris, Mercur Bank AG and Länderbank Wien AG, Vienna 1936–39; Partner, Ullstein and Co., Vienna 1946–55; Dir Österreichische Industrie- und Bergbauverwaltungs GmbH, Vienna 1956–58; Dir Creditanstalt-Bankverein, Vienna 1958, Chair. of Man. Bd 1970–81 (merged with Bank Austria 1998); Hon. Chair. Supervisory Bd Bank für Kärnten und Steiermark AG, Bank für Oberösterreich und Salzburg, Bank für Tirol und Vorarlberg AG; mem. Int. Advisory Bd Verwaltungs-und Privatbank AG, Vaduz; Pres. Austrian Red Cross Soc.; Grande Ufficiale Ordine del Merito (Italy); Commdr, Order Homayoun; Commdr, Légion d'honneur; Kt Commdr, Order of St Gregory, Grand Decoration of Honour in Gold for Services to Repub. of Austria, Grand Decoration in Silver with Star for Services to Repub. of Austria. *Leisure interests:* literature, hunting, skiing. *Address:* 1030 Vienna, Salmgasse 2, Austria. *Telephone:* 713-31-50.

TREIKI, Ali A., PhD; Libyan diplomatist and politician; b. 10 Oct. 1938, Misurata; s. of Abdussalem Treiki and Amna Treiki; m. Aisha Dihoum 1969; one s. three d.; ed Univ. of Benghazi, Libya and Toulouse Univ., France; joined Foreign Ministry 1970; Minister Plenipotentiary 1970, Dir of Political Admin. 1970–73, Dir of African Admin. 1973–74, Asst Deputy for Political Affairs 1974–76; Sec. of State for Foreign Affairs 1971–77, Foreign Sec. 1977–81, Sec. of Liaison for Foreign Affairs 1981–86; Foreign Minister 1984–86; Head of Libyan del. to UN Gen. Ass. 1977–80; Perm. Rep. of Libya to the UN 1982–84, 1986–91, to League of Arab States, Cairo 1991–93; Amb. to France 1995–2001; Sec. Libyan Popular Cttee for African Unity 2000–. *Address:* c/o Libyan People's Bureau, 2 rue Charles Lamoureux, 75116 Paris, France.

TREITEL, Sir Guenter Heinz, Kt, QC, MA, DCL, FBA; British professor of law; b. 26 Oct. 1928, Berlin, Germany; s. of Dr Theodor Treitel and Hanna (née Levy) Treitel; m. Phyllis M. Cook 1957; two s.; ed Kilburn Grammar School and Magdalen Coll., Oxford; came to UK 1939; Fellow of Magdalen Coll., Oxford 1954–79, Emer. Fellow 1979–; All Souls Reader in English Law 1964–79; Vinerian Prof. of English Law, Univ. of Oxford and Fellow of All Souls Coll. 1979–96, Prof. Emer. and Fellow Emer. 1996–; Visiting Lecturer, Univ. of Chicago 1963–64, Visiting Prof. 1968–69, 1971–72; Visiting Prof., Univ. of W Australia 1976, Univ. of Houston 1977, Southern Methodist Univ. 1978, 1988–89, 1994, Distinguished Visiting Prof. 2000, Univ. of Va 1978–79, 1983–84, Univ. of Santa Clara 1981; Visiting Scholar, Ernst von Caemmerer Gedächtnisstiftung 1990; Clarendon Lecturer in Law, Univ. of Oxford 2001; Consultant to Law Comm. on law of contract 1972–84; Trustee, British Museum 1983–98; mem. Council Nat. Trust 1984–93; Hon. Bencher, Gray's Inn. *Publications:* The Law of Contract 1962, An Outline of the Law of Contract 1975, Remedies for Breach of Contract: a comparative account 1988, Unmöglichkeit, "Impracticability" und "Frustration" im anglo-amerikanischen Recht 1991, Frustration and Force Majeure 1994, Benjamin's Sale of Goods (co-author) 1974, English Private Law (co-author) 2000, Carver on Bills of Lading (co-author) 2001, Some Landmarks of Twentieth Century Contract Law 2002; ed. of other law books. *Leisure interests:* reading, music. *Address:* All Souls College, Oxford, OX1 4AL, England. *Telephone:* (1865) 279379. *Fax:* (1865) 279299.

TREJOS FERNÁNDEZ, José Joaquín; Costa Rican politician and university professor; b. 18 April 1916, San José; s. of Juan Trejos and Emilia F. de Trejos; m. Clara F. de Trejos 1936; five s.; ed Univ. of Chicago; Prof. of Statistical Theory and Dean, Faculty of Econ., Univ. de Costa Rica 1952–56, Dean, Faculty of Sciences and Letters 1957–62, Prof. Emer. School of Statistics 1979–; Pres. of Costa Rica 1966–70; Partido Unidad Social Cristiana. *Publications:* Reflexiones sobre la Educación, 2nd Edn 1968, Ocho Años en la Política Nacional—Ideales Políticos y Realidad Nacional, Vol. I 1973, Vol. III 1973, Vol. IV 1973, Vol. II 1974, Ideas Políticas Elementales 1985, Reflexiones Políticas 1995, Por Esfuerzo Propio 1999. *Leisure interests:* music, history. *Address:* Apartado 10.096, San José, Costa Rica. *Telephone:* 224-2411.

TRELFORD, Donald Gilchrist, MA, FRSA; British journalist; b. 9 Nov. 1937, Coventry; s. of the late T.S. Trelford and the late Doris Gilchrist; m. 1st Janice Ingram 1963 (divorced 1978); two s. one d.; m. 2nd Katherine Louise Mark 1978 (divorced 1998); one d.; m. 3rd Claire Elizabeth Bishop 2001; ed Bablake School, Coventry, Selwyn Coll., Cambridge; Pilot Officer, RAF 1956–58; worked on newspapers in Coventry and Sheffield 1961–63; Ed. Times of Malawi and Corresp. in Africa, The Times, Observer, BBC 1963–66; joined Observer as Deputy News Ed. 1966, Asst Man. Ed. 1968, Deputy Ed. 1969–75, Dir and Ed. 1975–93, CEO 1992–93; Dir Optomen Television 1988–97; Observer Films 1989–93, Cen. Observer TV 1990–93; Dir, Prof. Dept of Journalism Studies, Sheffield Univ. 1994–2000, Visiting Prof. 2001–; Chair. Soc. of Gentlemen, Lovers of Musick 1996–, London Press Club 2002–; mem. British Exec. Cttee, Int. Press Inst. 1976–, Asscn of British Eds. 1984–, Guild of British Newspaper Eds. 1985– (mem. Parl. and Legal Cttee 1987–91); Vice Pres. British Sports Trust 1988–2002; Ind. Assessor BBC TV Regional News 1997; mem. Council, Media Soc. 1981– (Pres. 1999–2002), Judging Panel, British Press Awards 1981– (Chair. 2003), Scottish Press Awards 1985, Olivier Awards Cttee, SWET 1984–93, Defence, Press and Broadcasting Cttee 1986–93, Cttee, MCC 1988–, Competition Comm.'s Newspaper Panel 1999–, Council Advertising Standards Authority 2002–; Vice-Pres. Newspaper Press Fund 1992– (Chair. Appeals Cttee 1991), Acting Ed. The Oldie 1994; Judge, Whitbread Literary Awards 1992, George Orwell Prize 1998; Sports columnist Daily Telegraph 1993–; Dir St Cecilia Int. Festival of Music 1995–; Freeman City of London 1988; Hon. DLitt (Sheffield), Granada Newspaper of the Year Award 1983, 1993; commended, Int. Ed. of the Year (World Press

Review) 1984. *Radio:* presenter LBC Breakfast News 1994; regular panellist BBC Radio Five Live. *Television:* presenter sports and current affairs series, Channel 4 and BBC2. *Publications:* Siege 1980, Snookered 1986, Child of Change (with Garri Kasparov) 1987, Saturday's Boys 1990, Fine Glances 1990; (contrib.) County Champions 1982, The Queen Observed 1986, Len Hutton Remembered 1992, World Chess Championships (with Daniel King) 1993, W. G. Grace 1998; (Ed.) Sunday Best 1981, 1982, 1983, The Observer at 200 1992; contrib. Animal Passions 1994. *Leisure interests:* golf, snooker. *Address:* 15 Fowler Road, London, N1 2EP, England. *Telephone:* (20) 7226-9356. *E-mail:* donald@donaldgtrelford.demon.co.uk (Home).

TREMAIN, Edwin Garrick; New Zealand landscape artist and cartoonist; b. 4 Feb. 1941, Wellington; s. of Edwin Rex Tremain and Linda Joyce Tremain; m. Jillian Mary Butland; two d.; ed Palmerston North Boys' High School; fmrly worked as shepherd; fmr artist and art dir for advertising cos in NZ, UK and elsewhere; full-time artist 1973–; syndicated cartoonist 1988–; NZ Commemoration Medal 1990; Cartoonist of the Year 1996, 1999. *Leisure interests:* golf, piano, jazz music. *Address:* Stonebridge, 188 Domain Road, RDI, Queenstown, Otago, New Zealand. *Telephone:* (3) 409-8244. *Fax:* (3) 409-8245 (Home); (3) 409-8245. *E-mail:* tremain@queenstown.co.nz (Office); tremain@queenstown.co.nz (Home).

TREMAIN, Rose, BA, FRSL; British writer; b. 2 Aug. 1943, London; d. of Keith Thomson and Viola Mabel Thomson; m. 1st Jon Tremain 1971; one d.; m. 2nd Jonathan Dudley 1982 (dissolved 1990); ed Sorbonne, Paris and Univ. of East Anglia; full-time novelist/playwright 1971–; part-time lecturer Univ. of East Anglia 1988–95; Hon. DLitt (Univ. of East Anglia) 2001; Dylan Thomas Short Story Prize 1984, Giles Cooper Award 1985, Angel Literary Award 1986, Sunday Express Book of the Year Award 1989, James Tait Black Memorial Prize 1993, Prix Fémina Etranger 1994, Sony Award 1996, Whitbread Novel of the Year 1999. *Plays for radio include:* Who Was Emily Davison? 1996, The End of Love 1999, One Night in Winter 2001. *Television:* A Room for the Winter 1979, Daylight Robbery 1982. *Publications:* (novels) Sadler's Birthday 1976, Letter to Sister Benedicta 1978, The Cupboard 1981, The Swimming Pool Season 1984, Restoration 1989, Sacred Country 1992, The Way I Found Her 1997, Music and Silence 1999, The Colour 2003; (short stories) The Colonel's Daughter 1982, The Garden of the Villa Mollini 1988, Evangelista's Fan 1994. *Leisure interests:* yoga, gardening. *Address:* 2 High House, South Avenue, Thorpe St Andrew, Norwich, NR7 0EZ, England. *Telephone:* (1603) 439682. *Fax:* (1603) 434234.

TREMAINE, Scott Duncan, PhD, FRS, FRSC; Canadian astrophysicist; b. 25 May 1950, Toronto; s. of Vincent Tremaine and Beatrice (Sharp) Tremaine; ed McMaster Univ., Princeton Univ.; mem. Inst. for Advanced Study 1978–81; Assoc. Prof. MIT 1981–85; Prof. Univ. of Toronto 1985–97; Dir Canadian Inst. for Theoretical Astrophysics 1985–96; Prof. and Chair. Dept of Astrophysical Sciences, Princeton Univ. 1998–; Foreign Hon. mem. American Acad. of Arts and Sciences 1992; mem. NAS 2002. *Publication:* Galactic Dynamics (with J. Binney) 1987. *Address:* Princeton University Observatory, Peyton Hall, Princeton, NJ 08544, USA (Office). *Telephone:* (609) 258-3800 (Office). *Fax:* (609) 258-1020 (Office). *E-mail:* tremaine@astro.princeton.edu (Office).

TREMBLAY, Marc-Adélard, OC, MA, LSA, PhD, FRSC, GOQ; Canadian fmr professor of social anthropology; b. Joseph Adélard, 24 April 1922, Les Eboulements; s. of Wellie Tremblay and Lauretta Tremblay; m. Jacqueline Cyr 1949; one s. five d.; ed Montreal, Laval and Cornell Univs; research assoc., Cornell Univ. 1953–56; Asst Prof., Dept of Sociology and Anthropology, Laval Univ. 1956, Prof. of Social Anthropology 1963–93, Prof. Emer. 1994–; Founding Pres., Canadian Sociology and Anthropology Asscn 1965–67; Pres. Canadian Ethnology Soc. 1976–77, Royal Soc. of Canada 1981–84, Asscn of Canadian Univs for Northern Studies 1985–87, Québec Council for Social Research 1987–91; Dir Groupe d'études Inuit et Circumpolaires 1990–94; mem. many other professional and scientific orgs; Dr hc (Ottawa) 1982, (Guelph) 1984, (Univ. of N British Columbia) 1994, (Carleton) 1995, (Ste-Anne) 1997, (McGill) 1998; Prix de la Province de Québec 1964, Innis-Gérin Medal, Royal Soc. of Canada 1979; Molson Prize, The Canada Council 1987, Marcel Vincent Prize, French Canadian Asscn for the Advancement of Science 1988; Grand Officier Ordre Nat. du Québec 1995. *Publications:* People of Cove and Woodlot: communities from the viewpoint of social psychiatry 1960, Les comportements économiques de la famille salariée 1964, Initiation à la recherche dans les sciences humaines 1968, Famille et Parenté en Acadie 1971, Communities and culture in French Canada 1973, Patterns of Amerindian Identity 1976, L'identité québécoise en péril 1983, Conscience et Enquête 1983, L'Anthropologie à l'Université Laval: Fondements historiques, pratiques, académiques, dynamismes d'évolution 1989, Les Fondements historiques et pratiques de l'anthropologie appliquée 1990; 25 books and monographs and 200 articles. *Leisure interests:* gardening, cross-country skiing, classical music, skating. *Address:* Département d'Anthropologie, Université Laval, Cité Universitaire, Ste-Foy, Québec (Office); 835 rue Nouvelle-Orléans, Ste-Foy, Québec, G1X 3J4, Canada (Home). *Telephone:* (418) 653-5411 (Home). *Fax:* (418) 653-9865. *E-mail:* matremgt@globetrotter.net (Home). *Website:* pages.globetrotter.net/matrem (Home).

TREMBLAY, Michel; Canadian writer; b. 25 June 1942, Montreal; ed Graphic Arts Inst. of Québec; worked as linotypist 1963–66; won first prize for young writers sponsored by CBC for play Le Train (written 1959) 1964; Dr hc (Concordia, McGill, Stirling, Windsor); several hon. degrees, numerous prizes and awards, including Gov.-Gen.'s Performing Arts Award 1999;

Officier des Arts et des Lettres (France). *Film scripts include:* Françoise Durocher, Waitress 1972, Il était une fois dans l'Est 1973, Parlez-nous d'amour 1976, Le Soleil se lève en retard 1977. *Plays include:* Les Belles Sœurs 1968, En pièces detachées 1969, La Duchesse de Langeais 1969, Les Paons 1971, Hosanna 1973, Bonjour Là, Bonjour 1974, Ste Carmen de la Main 1976, Damnée Manon, Sacrée Sandra 1977, L'Impromptu d'Outremont 1980, Les grandes vacances 1981, Les Anciennes Odeurs 1981, Albertine en cinq temps 1984, Le vrai monde? 1987, La Maison suspendue 1990, Marcel poursuivi par les chiens 1992; opera libretto: Nelligan, Opéra de Montréal 1990, Messe solennelle pour une pleine lune d'été 1996, Encore une fois, si vous permettez 1998, L'État des lieux 2002, Le Passé antérieur 2003. *Radio plays include:* Le Cœur découvert 1986, Le Grand Jour 1988, Six Heures au plus tard 1988. *Television:* Le Cœur découvert 2000. *Publications:* Contes pour buveurs attardés 1966 (English trans. 1977), La Cité dans l'oeuf 1969, C't'à ton tour, Laura Cadieux 1973, La Grosse Femme d'à côté est enceinte 1973 (English trans. 1981), Thérèse et Pierrette à l'école des Saints-Anges 1980 (English trans. 1984), La Duchesse et le roturier 1982, Des Nouvelles d'Edouard 1984, Le Coeur découvert 1986 (English trans. 1988), Le Premier Quartier de la lune 1989, Les vues animées 1991, Douze coups de théâtre 1992 (English trans. 2002), Le Cœur éclaté 1995, Un Ange cornu avec des ailes de tôle 1996, L'Homme qui entendait siffler une bouilloire 2001, Bonbons assortis 2002. *Leisure interests:* painting water colours. *Address:* c/o Agence Goodwin, 839 Sherbrooke est, Suite 2, Montréal, Québec, H2L 1K6, Canada. *Telephone:* (514) 598-5252. *Fax:* (514) 598-1878.

TREMLETT, David Rex; British artist; b. 13 Feb. 1945, Cornwall; s. of Rex Tremlett and Dinah Tremlett; m. Laure Florence 1987; one s. two d.; ed St Austell Grammar School, Falmouth Art Coll. and Royal Coll. of Art; exhibited widely in UK, USA, Europe, Africa, Australia, Mexico, Japan etc.; recent projects include: walls of Law Courts, Amsterdam, Benesse Guesthouse, Naoshima Island, Japan, façade of St Denis Univ., Paris, main hall of BBL Bank Kortrijk, Belgium, walls at Eaton Hall, Chester, UK, walls of castle of Marchese di Barolo, Barolo, Italy, lobby of Central Landesbank, Dresden, Germany, ceiling at Eaton Hall, Chester, Chapel of Barolo, Italy, interior wall at ABN AMRO HQ, Amsterdam, walls of British Embassy Berlin, walls at Obayashi HQ, Tokyo, walls and floor of Palazzo Fantuzzi, Bologna, wall for the Grosvenor Estates, London, walls and floor of the Re Enzo Chapel, Bologna, walls of Rione Alto metro station, Naples. *Art exhibitions include:* Tate Gallery, London 1972, Museum of Modern Art, New York 1973, Inst. of Contemporary Arts, London 1976, Stedelijk Museum, Amsterdam 1979, Pompidou Centre, Paris 1985, Serpentine Gallery, London 1989, Palais des Beaux Arts, Brussels 1990, Joán Miró Foundation, Barcelona 1996, Southampton Art Gallery 1997, Museum of Contemporary Art, Trento, Italy 2001. *Music:* Hand Up/Too Bad (CD). *Publications:* Some Places to Visit 1974, On the Waterfront 1978, Scrub 1978, On the Border 1979, Restless 1983, Rough Ride 1985, Ruin 1987, Dates/Differents 1987, Sometimes We All Do 1988, Tremlett-West Bengal 1990, Written Form 1990, Internal 1991, From Wall to Wall 1991, Mjimwema Drawings 1991, A Quiet Madness 1992, PAC Catalogue 1993, Abandoned Drawings 1993, Casa de Dibujos 1993, Nouveaux Plans 1994, Rooms in Vienne 1994, Walls at the Palais Jacques Coeur, Bourges 1994, Wall Drawings 1969–1995, Columns 1995, How Far in that Direction 1996, Walls and their Drawings 1997, Pages (Eritrea) 1998, Clear and Fuzzy 1999, Passa Dentro 2000, If Walls Could Talk 2001, If Things Could Talk 2002. *Leisure interests:* pole vaulting, African music, Saharan architecture, cross-country running. *Address:* Broadlawns, Chipperfield Road, Bovingdon, Herts., England. *Telephone:* (1442) 832214. *Fax:* (1442) 832533. *E-mail:* d.tremlett@ntlworld.com (Home). *Website:* www.laudanum.net/tremlett.

TREMONTI, Giulio; Italian politician and lawyer; b. 18 Aug. 1947, Sondrio, Lombardy; ed Univ. of Pavia; teacher of tax law, Univ. of Pavia; fmr Sr Teaching Fellow Inst. of European and Comparative Law, Oxford Univ., UK; mem. Chamber of Deputies 1994–; Minister of Finance 1994–95, of Economy and Finance 2001–; Pres. Comm. for Monetary Reform 1994–95; mem. Parl. Special Cttee for Reform of Italian Constitution 1994–95; mem. Forza Italia Party; fmr Vice-Pres. Aspen Inst. Italia; mem. Italy/Vatican Cttee for Treaty on Financing of Ecclesiastical Insts., Comm. on Deregulation; Ed. Rivista di Diritto Finanziario e Scienza delle Finanze; regular contrib. to Corriere della Sera. *Publications:* several books on tax and public policy. *Address:* Ministry of Economy and Finance, Viale Europa 242, 00144 Rome, Italy. *Telephone:* (06) 59971 (Office). *Fax:* (06) 5910993 (Office). *Website:* www.finanze.it (Office).

TRENGGANU, HRH The Sultan of; Mizan Zainal Abidin; Malaysian ruler of Trengganu State; b. 22 Jan. 1962, Kuala Trengganu; s. of the late Sultan Mahmud Al Muktafi Billah Shah and Bariah binti Hishamuddin Alam Shah; m. Permaisuri Nur Zahirah Cik Puan Seri Rozita Adil Bakeri 1996; one s. one d.; apptd Heir Apparent Yang di-Pertuan Muda of Trengganu 1979; 16th Sultan of Trengganu 1998–; Timbalan Yang di-Pertuan Agong (Deputy Supreme Head of State) 1999–; Col-in-Chief Royal Armoured Corps. *Address:* Istana Badariah, 20500 Kuala Trengganu, Malaysia (Office).

TRENTHAM, David R., FRS, PhD; British medical research scientist; b. 22 Sept. 1938, Solihull; s. of John A. Trentham and Julia A. M. Trentham; m. Kamalini Bhargava 1966; two s.; ed Uppingham School and Cambridge Univ.; Faculty mem., Biochem. Dept, Bristol Univ. 1972–77; Chair. and Edwin M. Chance Prof., Dept of Biochem. and Biophysics, School of Medicine, Univ. of Pa, Philadelphia, USA 1977–83; Head, Physical Biochem. Div., Nat. Inst. for Medical Research, London 1984–; Colworth Medal, Biochem. Soc. 1974, Wilhelm Feldberg Prize 1990. *Publications:* numerous articles in biochemical and academic journals. *Address:* Physical Biochemistry Division, National Institute for Medical Research, The Ridgeway, Mill Hill, London, NW7 1AA, England (Office). *Telephone:* (20) 8959-3666.

TRETYAKOV, Viktor Viktorovich; Russian violinist; b. 17 Oct. 1946, Krasnoyarsk; m. Natalia Likhopoi; one d.; ed Moscow Conservatory (pupil of Yury Yankelevich); First Prizes, All-Union Competition of Violinists 1965, Int. Tchaikovsky Competition 1966; concert career since mid-1960s, soloist of Moscow Philharmonic 1969; tours Europe, America, Japan; participant in numerous European music festivals; Artistic Dir and Conductor Moscow (now Russian) Chamber Orchestra 1983–90; Prof., Head of Chair of Violin, Moscow Conservatory 1983–90; Prof., Hochschule für Musik, Cologne 1996–; State Prize of Russia 1981, USSR People's Artist 1987, "Triumph" Prize (Russia) 2003. *Address:* Berliner Konzertagentur Monika Ott, Dramburger, Str. 46, 12683 Berlin (Office); Burgblick 9b, 53177 Bonn, Germany (Home). *Fax:* (228) 9329641 (Home).

TRETYAKOV, Vitaly Toviyevich; Russian journalist; b. 2 Jan. 1953, Moscow; m.; one s.; ed Moscow State Univ.; jr ed to Ed. Press Agency Novosti (APN) 1976–88; reviewer, political reviewer, Deputy Ed.-in-Chief Moskovskiye Novosti (weekly) 1988–90; f. Nesavisimaya Gazeta (newspaper) 1990, Ed.-in-Chief 1990–2000; Dir-Gen. Indpendent Publishing Group 2001–; mem. Exec. Bd Council on Foreign and Defence Policy. *Publications include:* Philanthropy in Soviet Society 1989, Gorbachev, Ligachev, Yeltsin: Political Portraits on the Perestroika Background 1990, Titus of Sovietologists: Their Struggle for Power: Essays on Idiotism of Russian Policy 1996; numerous articles on political problems. *Leisure interests:* theatre, collecting of art albums. *Address:* Independent Publishing Group, Moscow, Russia (Office). *E-mail:* wt1t@narod.ru (Office).

TREVES, Vanni E., MA, LLM; British/Italian business executive; b. 3 Nov. 1940, Italy; s. of the late Giuliano Treves and of Marianna Treves; m. Angela Treves; two s. one d.; ed St Paul's, London, Univ. Coll. Oxford, Univ. of Illinois; joined City law firm Macfarlanes as articled clerk 1963, qualified 1965, Asst Solicitor 1965–68, Visiting Attorney White & Case, NY 1968–69, Partner Macfarlanes 1970–, Sr. Partner 1987–99; Chair. Equitable Life Assurance Soc. 2001–; Chair. Channel Four Television Corpn 1998–, BBA Group PLC 1989–2000, McKechnie PLC 1991–; Dir Intertek Testing Services PLC, Amplifin; Chair. NSPCC Justice for Children Appeal 1997–2000; Gov. Coll. of Law 1999–, Sadlers Wells Foundation 1999–; Trustee J. Paul Getty Charitable Trust and many other private cos. and pension schemes; mem. Devt Bd, Nat. Art Collections Fund; mem. Law Soc. *Leisure interests:* art, walking, food. *Address:* Macfarlanes, 10 Norwich Street, London, EC4A 1BD, England (Office). *Telephone:* (20) 7831-9222 (Office). *E-mail:* vet@macfarlanes.com (Office). *Website:* www.macfarlanes.com (Office).

TREVINO, Lee Buck; American golfer; b. 1 Dec. 1939, Dallas, Tex.; s. of Joe Trevino and Juanita Barrett; m. Claudia Bove 1983; three s. three d.; professional 1960–; US Open Champion 1968, 1971; British Open Champion 1971, 1972; Canadian Open Champion 1971 and numerous other championships 1965–80; US PGA Champion 1974, 1984; Champion US Sr Open 1990, PGA Sr Championship 1994; won Australian PGA Sr Championship 1996; Chair. Bd Lee Trevino Enterprises, Inc. 1967–; US PGA Player of the Year 1971, Sr Tour Player of the Year 1990, 1992, 1994. *Publication:* Super Mex (autobiog.) 1983. *Leisure interest:* fishing. *Address:* Senior PGA Tour, 112 Tpc Boulevard, Ponte Vedra Beach, FL 32082, USA (Office).

TREVOR, William, CLit; Irish author; b. 24 May 1928, Co. Cork; s. of James William Cox and Gertrude Cox; m. Jane Ryan 1952; two s.; ed St Columba's, Dublin, Trinity Coll., Dublin; Hawthornden Prize 1965, Royal Soc. of Literature Prize 1978, Whitbread Prize for Fiction 1978, Allied Irish Banks Award for Services to Literature 1978, Whitbread Prize for Fiction 1983, Whitbread Book of the Year 1994; Sunday Express Book of the Year Award 1994, David Cohen British Literature Prize 1999, PEN Prize for Short Stories 2001, Irish Times Prize for Irish Fiction 2001; Hon. DLitt (Exeter) 1984, (Dublin) 1986, (Queen's Univ., Belfast) 1989, (Nat. Univ. Cork) 1990; Hon. KBE 2002. *Publications:* The Old Boys 1964, The Boarding House 1965, The Love Department 1966, The Day We Got Drunk on Cake 1967, Mrs Eckdorf in O'Neill's Hotel 1968, Miss Gomez and the Brethren 1969, The Ballroom of Romance 1970, Elizabeth Alone 1972, Angels at the Ritz 1973, The Children of Dynmouth 1977, Lovers of Their Time 1979, Other People's Worlds 1980, Beyond the Pale 1981, Fools of Fortune 1983, A Writer's Ireland: Landscape in Literature 1984, The News from Ireland 1986, Nights at the Alexandra 1987, The Silence in the Garden 1988, Family Sins and Other Stories 1989, The Oxford Book of Irish Short Stories (ed.) 1989, Two Lives 1991, William Trevor: The Collected Stories 1992, Juliet's Story 1992, Excursions in the Real World (essays) 1993, Felicia's Journey 1994, Ireland: Selected Stories 1995, After Rain 1996, Cocktails at Doney's and Other Stories 1996, Death in Summer 1998, The Hill Bachelors 2000, The Story of Lucy Gault 2002. *Address:* c/o A. D. Peters, 34–43 Russell Street, London, WC2B 5HA, England.

TRIANTAFYLLIDES, Michalakis Antoniou; Cypriot judge; b. 12 May 1927, Nicosia; m.; two c.; ed Gray's Inn, London; practised as a lawyer in Cyprus 1948–60, serving for three years as Sec. of Human Rights Cttee of Bar; mem. Greek Cypriot del. to Joint Constitutional Comm. which drafted Cyprus Constitution 1959–60; Greek Cypriot Judge, Supreme Constitutional Court

1960–64, Judge 1964–71, Pres. Supreme Court 1971–88; Attorney Gen. 1988–94. *Address:* c/o Office of the Attorney General, Supreme Court, Char. Mouskos Street, Nicosia, Cyprus.

TRIBOULET, Raymond, LenDr, LèsL; French politician; b. 3 Oct. 1906, Paris; s. of Maurice Triboulet and Josèphe Wagner; m. Luce Chauveau 1928 (died 1995); three s. (one deceased) three d.; ed Univ. of Paris; active in French Resistance 1941–44; Sous-Préfet for Bayeux region 1944–46; Regional Insp. for Rhine-Palatinate 1946; MP 1946–; founder of European Federalist group in French Parl.; Pres. of Gaullist Parl. Group (Social Republicans) 1954–58; Minister of War Veterans Jan.–Oct. 1955; mem. ECSC Common Ass. 1957; Pres. Union of New Republic (UNR) Parl. Group 1958; Minister of War Veterans 1959–63, of Co-operation 1963–66; re-elected Deputy 1958, 1962, 1967 and 1968; mem. European Parl. 1967–73; Pres. UDE group 1968–73; Pres. and founder D-Day Commemoration Cttee, Hon. Pres. 1999; mem. Inst. (Acad. des Sciences morales et politiques) 1979; Grand Officier Légion d'honneur, Croix de guerre; Médaille de la Résistance; Hon. KBE 2000, and other decorations. *Publications:* Les Billets du Négus 1939, Sens dessus dessous 1951, Des Vessies pour des Lanternes 1958, Halte au Massacre 1966, Correspondance de Gaston de Renty (1611–1649) 1978, A tous ceux qui sont mal dans leur peau 1980, Un gaulliste de la IVe 1985, Un Ministre du général 1986, Vie de Gaston de Renty, homme de ce monde et homme de Dieu 1992, Tous comptes faits 1998. *Address:* 119 rue Brancas, 92310 Sèvres, France. *Fax:* 1-45-07-11-39.

TRICART, Jean Léon François; French university professor; b. 16 Sept. 1920, Montmorency; s. of François Tricart and Lea Cordonnier; m. Denise Casimir 1944; four s.; ed Lycée Rollin, Paris and Univ. de Paris à la Sorbonne; Asst Lecturer, Univ. de Paris 1945–48; Lecturer Univ. of Strasbourg 1948–49, Asst Prof. 1949–55, Prof. 1955–88, Emer. Prof. 1988–93; Vice-Dean, mem. of Univ. Senate 1967–70; Prin. Asst, Geological Map of France 1960; Founder-Dir Centre of Applied Geography, Strasbourg 1956–; Pres. Applied Geomorphology Comm. of Int. Geographical Union 1960–68; head of numerous tech. co-operation missions in Senegal, Mauritania, Ivory Coast, Guinea, Togo, Mali, Argentina, Brazil, Chile, Venezuela, Peru, Panama, El Salvador, Colombia, Uruguay, Mexico; Sr Consultant FAO, UNDP, WMO and UNESCO 1968; scientific assessor of Inst. de Recherche Agronomique Tropicale; Expert, Int. Hydrological Programme, UNESCO; Chair. French Nat. Cttee of INQUA 1976–79; Chair. Comm. of Arid and Subarid Regions, CNFG 1989–94; Corresp. mem. Colombian Acad. of Science 1986–, GAEA 1991–; mem. titulaire Acad. Européenne; Dr hc (Łódź, Poland, Bahia, Brazil, Los Andes, Venezuela); Prix Bastian French Acad. of Sciences 1943; Busk Medal (Royal Geographical Soc.) 1985; medals and prizes in Argentina, Belgium, France, Germany, Hungary, Italy, Netherlands; Chevalier, Légion d'honneur 1992; Officier des Palmes académiques. *Publications include:* numerous scientific articles and Principes et méthodes de la Géomorphologie 1965, Traité de Géomorphologie (with A. Cailleux), 5 Vols, La terre, Planète vivante, Ecogeography and Rural Management (with Kiewiet de Jonge), Ecogéographie des espaces ruraux. *Leisure interest:* philately. *Address:* 85 route de la Meinau, 67100 Strasbourg Meinau, France. *Telephone:* 3-88-39-09-86 (Home).

TRICHET, Jean-Claude, LèsL ECON.; French banker; b. 20 Dec. 1942, Lyon; s. of Jean Trichet and Georgette Vincent-Carrefour; m. Aline Rybalka 1965; two s.; ed Ecole des Mines, Nancy, Inst. d'Etudes Politiques, Paris, Faculté Sciences Economiques, Paris and Ecole Nat. d'Admin; Insp. of Finances 1971–76; Sec.-Gen. Business Restructuring Interministerial Cttee 1976–78; Adviser, Minister of Economy 1978; Counsellor to Pres. of Repub. 1978–81; Deputy Asst Sec. and Asst Sec. of Treasury 1981–86; Chief of Staff to Minister of Finance 1986–87; Under-Sec. of Treas. and Censor Bank of France 1987–93; Gov. Bank of France 1993–; Pres. Paris Club 1985–93; mem. Bd of Dirs BIS 1993–, EMI 1994–98; a Gov. IBRD 1993–95; Vice-Gov. IMF 1995; Chair. Monetary Cttee of EC 1992–93; Dir Cen. European Bank 1998–; on trial for financial scandal involving state-owned Credit Lyonnais Bank in early 1990s Jan.(–June) 2003; Officier, Légion d'honneur, Ordre Nat. du Mérite; decorations (Commdr) from Austria, Argentina, Brazil, Ecuador, Germany, Ivory Coast, Yugoslavia; Policy Maker of the Year, Int. Econ.; Prize Zebilli Marimo, Acad. des Sciences Morales et Politiques, Int. Prize Pico della Mirandola. *Publications:* various articles on finance and economy. *Leisure interest:* poetry. *Address:* Banque de France, 39 rue Croix des Petits Champs, 75001 Paris (Office); 5 rue de Beaujolais, 75001 Paris, France. *Telephone:* 1-42-92-20-01 (Office). *Fax:* 1-42-92-20-10 (Office). *Website:* www .banque-france.fr.

TRIER, Peter Eugene, CBE, MA, MSc, FREng, FIEE, FInstP, FIMA; British research director and consultant; b. 12 Sept. 1919, Darmstadt, Germany; s. of Ernst J. Trier and Nellie M. (née Bender) Trier; m. 1st Margaret N. Holloway 1946 (died 1998); three s.; m. 2nd Teresa (née Keogh) Watson 2000; ed Mill Hill School, London and Trinity Hall, Cambridge; Royal Naval Scientific Service 1941–50; Mullard Research Labs (now Philips Research Labs), Redhill 1950–69, Dir 1953–69; Dir of Research and Devt Philips Electronics 1969–81, mem. Bd 1969–85; Chair. of Council, Brunel Univ. 1973–79, Pro-Chancellor 1980–99; Chair. Electronics Research Council 1976–80, Defence Scientific Advisory Council 1981–85; Faraday Lecturer Inst. of Electrical Engineers 1968–69; Pres. Inst. of Math. and its Applications (IMA) 1982, 1983; mem. Man. Cttee The Wine Soc. 1977–92; Hon. DTech (Brunel) 1975; Glazebrook Prize and Medal, Inst. of Physics 1984. *Publications:* Mathematics & Information 1983; papers in scientific and technical

journals. *Leisure interests:* travel, mathematics, railway history, Trier family history. *Address:* 14 Mill View Gardens, Shirley, CR0 5HW, England. *Telephone:* (20) 8655-0835.

TRIESMAN, David Maxim, MA, FRSA; British politician and trade unionist; b. 30 Oct. 1943, Hertfordshire; s. of Michael Triesman and Rita Triesman (née Lubran); ed Stationers' Co. School, London, Univ. of Essex and King's Coll., Cambridge; Resident Officer in Addiction, Inst.of Psychiatry 1970–74; secondment to Asscn of Scientific, Tech. and Managerial Staff(ASTMS) 1974–75; Sr Lecturer and Co-ordinator Postgrad. Research, Polytech. of South Bank 1975–84; Deputy Sec.-Gen. (Nat. Negotiating Sec.) Nat. Asscn of Teachers in Further and Higher Educ. (NATFHE) 1984–93; Gen. Sec. Asscn of Univ. Teachers (AUT) 1993–2001; Gen. Sec. Labour Party 2001–; Visiting Prof. in Social Econs, St Lawrence Univ. 1977; Visiting Fellow in Econs, Wolfson Coll., Cambridge 2000–; mem. Greater London Manpower Bd 1981–86, Home Office Consultative Cttee on Prison Educ. 1980–83, Burnham Further and Higher Educ. Cttee 1980–84, Univ. Entrance and Schools Exams Bd for Social Science 1980–84, Standing Cttee on Business and the Community, Higher Educ. Funding Council for England (HEFCE) 1999–; mem. Kensington, Chelsea and Westminster Area Health Authority 1976–82; mem. Industrial Relations Public Appointments Panel, Dept of Trade and Industry 1996–2001, Ind. Review of Higher Educ. Pay and Conditions 1998–99, Cabinet Office Better Regulation Task Force 2000–01, Treasury Public Services Productivity Panel 2000–, British N American Cttee 1999–; Chair. (non-exec.) Mortgage Credit Corpn 1978–2001, Vic. Man. Ltd 2000–01; Chair. Usecolor Foundation 2001; mem. Fabian Soc. 1974–, Charles Rennie Mackintosh Soc., Glasgow 1986–, Highgate Literary and Scientific Inst. 1990–; mem. Council Ruskin Coll., Oxford 2000–; Hon. Fellow Nene Coll. of Higher Educ. 1995. *Publications include:* The Medical and Non-Medical Use of Drugs 1969, Football Mania (with G. Viani) 1972, Football in London 1985, College Administration (jtly) 1988, Managing Change 1991, Can Unions Survive (Staniewski Memorial Lecture) 1999, Higher Education for the New Century 2000. *Leisure interests:* football, art, reading, blues guitar, hill walking. *Address:* Labour Party, 16 Old Queen Street, London, SW1H 9HP, England (Office). *Telephone:* (20) 7802-1199 (Office). *E-mail:* info@new.labour.org.uk (Office). *Website:* www.labour.org.uk (Office).

TRILLO-FIGUEROA MARTÍNEZ CONDE, Federico, PhD; Spanish politician and jurist; b. 23 May 1952, Cartagena; ed Univ. of Salamanca, Univ. Complutense of Madrid; Counsel to State Council 1979–; lawyer for Coll. of Madrid 1980–; mem. Cuerpo Jurídico de la Armada –1989; Gen. Coordinator of the reformation of the Partido Popular and Asst Sec. Gen. 1989–90, Nat. Deputy for Alicante 1989–, Spokesperson for Justice and Constitution 1991–96; Vice-Speaker of Congress 1988–96; Cttee mem. Constitutional Court 1991–96; Speaker of Congress and Nat. Ass. 1996–2000; Minister of Defence 2000–. *Publication:* El poder político en los dramas de Shakespeare. *Leisure interests:* opera, Shakespeare. *Address:* Ministry of Defence, Paseo de la Castellana 109, 28071 Madrid, Spain (Office). *Telephone:* (91) 5555000 (Office). *Fax:* (91) 5563958 (Office). *Website:* www.mde.es (Office).

TRIMBLE, Rt Hon David, PC, LLB, MLA; British politician, barrister and university lecturer; b. 15 Oct. 1944, Belfast; s. of the late William Trimble and of Ivy Jack; m. 1st Heather McComb (divorced); m. 2nd Daphne Orr 1978; two s. two d.; ed Bangor Grammar School and Queen's Univ. Belfast; Lecturer in Law, Queen's Univ. Belfast 1968–77, Sr Lecturer 1977–90; mem. N Ireland Constitutional Convention 1975–76; mem. Parl. for Upper Bann 1990–; Leader Ulster Unionist Party 1995–; First Minister, Northern Ireland Ass. 1998–2000, 2001–02 (Ass. suspended Oct. 2002); mem. N Ireland Ass. for Upper Bann 1998–; Chair. Lagan Valley Unionist Asscn 1985–90, Ulster Soc. 1985–90; Hon. LLD (Queen's) 1999, (New Brunswick) 2000, (Wales) 2002; shared Nobel Peace Prize 1998. *Leisure interests:* music, reading. *Address:* Ulster Unionist Party, 429 Holywood Road, Belfast, BT4; 2 Queen Street, Lurgan, Co. Armagh, BT66 8BQ, Northern Ireland. *Telephone:* (28) 9076-5500 (Office); (28) 3832-8088 (Home). *Fax:* (28) 9052-1772 (Office); (28) 3832-2343. *E-mail:* uup@uup.org (Office).

TRINH, Xuan Lang, BA; Vietnamese diplomatist; b. 4 Sept. 1927, Hanoi; m.; three c.; took part in Viet Nam's independence movt 1945–54; joined Ministry of Foreign Affairs 1955, Consul-Gen., Rangoon 1960–64, Counsellor of Embassy in New Delhi 1969–73; Amb. to Indonesia 1981–84; Dir Press and Information Dept and spokesman for Ministry of Foreign Affairs 1984–88; Perm. Rep. to the UN 1988–93. *Address:* c/o Ministry of Foreign Affairs, Hanoi, Viet Nam.

TRINTIGNANT, Jean-Louis (Xavier); French actor; b. 11 Dec. 1930, Piolenc (Vaucluse); s. of Raoul Trintignant and Claire Tourtin; m. 1st Colette Dacheville (the actress Stéphane Audran) 1954 (divorced); m. 2nd Nadine Marquand 1961; one s. two d. (one deceased); ed Faculté de Droit, Aix-en-Provence; theatre début 1951; film roles 1955–; Prix d'interprétation de l'Acad. du Cinéma (for Mata Hari, Agent H21) 1965; Prize, Cannes Festival (for Z) 1969; Prix David de Donatello, Taormina Festival 1972; Officier des Arts et des Lettres. *Plays include:* Macbeth, Jacques ou la Soumission (Ionesco), Hamlet, Bonheur, impaire et passe (Sagan), Deux sur la balançoire, Art 1998, Poèmes à Lou 1999, Comédie sur un quai de gare 2001. *Films include:* Et Dieu créa la femme 1956, Club de femmes 1956, Les liaisons dangereuses 1959, L'été violent 1959, Austerlitz 1959, La millième fenêtre 1959, Pleins feux sur l'assassin 1960, Coeur battant 1960, Le jeu de la vérité 1961, Horace 62 1961, Les sept péchés capitaux 1961, Il sorpasso 1962, Il successo 1962, Chateau en Suède 1963, La bonne occase 1964, Mata Hari, Agent H21 1964, Angélique marquise des anges 1964, Meurtre à l'italienne 1965, La longue marche 1965, Le 17e ciel 1965, Paris brûle-t-il? 1965, Un homme et une femme 1966, Safari diamants 1966, Trans-Europ-Express 1966, Mon amour, mon amour 1967, L'homme qui ment 1967, Les biches 1968, Le voleur de crimes 1968, Z 1969, Ma nuit chez Maud 1969, Disons un soir à diner 1969, L'Américain 1969, La mort a pondu un oeuf 1969, Le conformiste 1970, Si douces, si perverses 1970, Le grand silence 1971, Une journée bien remplie (author and dir) 1973, Le train 1973, Les violins du bal 1973, Le mouton enragé 1974, Le secret 1974, Le jeu avec le feu 1975, Shattering 1977, Le désert des Tartares 1977, The French Way 1978, L'argent des autres 1978, Le maitre nageur 1979 (also dir), La terrasse 1980, Je vous aime 1980, La femme d'à côté 1981, Un assassin qui passe 1981, Malevil 1981, Passion d'amour 1981, Une affaire d'hommes 1981, Eaux profondes 1981, Le grand-pardon 1982, Boulevard des assassins 1982, Le bon plaisir 1983, Vivement dimanche! 1983, La crime 1983, Le bon plaisir, Femmes de personne 1984, Under Fire, Viva la vie 1984, L'été prochain, Partir, revenir 1985, Rendez-vous, David, Thomas et les autres 1985, L'homme aux yeux d'argent 1985, Un homme et une femme: vingt ans déja 1986, La femme de ma vie 1986, La vallée fantôme 1987, Le Moustachu 1987, Bunker Palace Hotel 1989, Merci la vie 1991, L'Instinct de l'ange 1993, Rouge 1994, Regarde les hommes tomber 1994, Fiesta 1995, C'est jamais loin 1996, Ceux qui m'aiment prendront le train 1998. *Address:* c/o Artmédia, 20 avenue Rapp, 75007 Paris; 30 rue des Francs-Bourgeois, 75003 Paris, France (Home).

TRITTIN, Jürgen; German politician; b. 25 July 1954, Bremen; one d.; worked as journalist 1973; business man. Alternative-Greens-Initiative List (AGIL) group Göttingen City Council 1982–84; press spokesman for Green Party group Lower Saxony Landtag 1984–85, Chair. 1985–86, 1988–90, Deputy Chair. Alliance '90/Greens group 1994–95, spokesman Fed. Exec. 1994–98; mem. Lower Saxony Landtag 1985–90, 1994–95, Lower Saxony Minister for Fed. and European Affairs 1990–94, also head state mission to fed. insts. in Bonn; mem. Bundestag 1998–; Fed. Minister for the Environment, Nature Conservation and Nuclear Safety 1998–. *Address:* Ministry of the Environment, Nature Conservation and Nuclear Safety, 10178 Berlin, Alexanderplatz 6, Germany (Office). *Telephone:* (1888) 3052000 (Office). *Fax:* (1888) 3052046 (Office). *E-mail:* service@bmu.de (Office). *Website:* www.bmu .de (Office).

TRIVEDI, Ram Krishna, MA; Indian state governor (retd); b. 1 Jan. 1921, Myingyan, Burma (now Myanmar); s. of Pandit Mahavir Trivedi and Rama Trivedi; m. Krishna Trivedi 1944 (deceased); four s. one d.; joined civil service 1943; Dist Magistrate, Tehri Garhwal, Faizabad, Allahabad and Kanpur; Vice-Prin., IAS Training School, Delhi 1957–58, Acting Prin. 1958–59, Deputy Dir Nat. Acad. of Admin. 1959–62; Sec. Medical and Health Dept Govt of Uttar Pradesh 1968–70; Commr and Sec. Dept of Finance 1968–71; Commr Allahabad 1970–71; Chair. UP State Electricity Bd 1972–73; Sec. Dept of Civil Supplies and Cooperation 1974–75; Dept of Personnel & Admin. Reforms, Govt of India 1975–77; Chair. and Man. Dir STC 1978; Vice-Chancellor, Bundelkhand Univ. 1979; Adviser to Gov. of Madhya Pradesh; Chair. British India Corpn Kanpur 1980; Central Vigilance Commr Govt of India 1980–82; Chief Election Commr of India 1982–85; Gov. of Gujarat 1986–90; fmr Vice-Pres. Exec. Council, Indian Inst. of Public Admin.; mem. Gov. Body, Asian Centre for Devt Admin. Kuala Lumpur; Pres. Ramkrishna Mission, Lucknow; Hon. DLitt (Lucknow); Hon. LLD (Bundelkhand); Padma Bhushan Award 1986. *Publication:* The Greening of Gujarat. *Leisure interests:* yoga, serious reading, philately, photography. *Address:* Anand Niwas, B-7, Niralanagar, Lucknow, UP, 226020, India. *Telephone:* (522) 2787180.

TROISGROS, Pierre Emile René; French hotelier and restaurateur; b. 3 Sept. 1928, Châlon-sur-Saône; s. of Jean-Baptiste Troisgros and Marie Badaut; m. Olympe Forte 1955; two s. one d.; ed Lycée Bourgneuf, Roanne; worked Roanne-Etretat 1944–45, Armenonville, Paris 1946, St Jean de Luz 1947; mil. service, Tunisia 1948; at Lucas Carton, Paris 1950–52, Point, Vienne 1954, then Maxim's and Retour à Roanne; now Pres. Supervising Cttee Restaurant Troisgros SA, Roanne; Ordre Nat. du Mérite 1969, Officier des Arts et des Lettres 1985, Chevalier, Légion d'honneur 1987. *Publications:* Cuisiniers à Roanne (with Jean Troisgros) 1977, Toc et Toque 1983, Les Petits Plats des Troisgros (with Michel Troisgros) 1985, Cuisine de famille chez les Troisgros (jtly) 1998. *Leisure interests:* tennis, basketball. *Address:* Place Jean Troisgros, 42300 Roanne; 20 route de Commelle, 42120 Le Coteau, France. *Telephone:* 4-77-71-66-97.

TRØJBORG, Jan; Danish politician; b. 14 Dec. 1955, Horsens; ed Ealing Coll., London, Horsens Tech. Coll.; bricklayer 1976; engineer A/S Samfund-steknik 1986, Dept Head Horsens br. 1987; Chair. Social Democratic Youth Org. 1973–78; mem. Horsens Town Council 1978–86; Deputy Chair. Social Democratic Party, Horsens 1981–82; mem. Parl. for Horsens 1987–; Chair. Trade and Industry Cttee 1991–93; Minister of Industry 1993–94, of Transport 1994–96, of Business and Industry 1996–98, of Research and Information Tech. 1998–99, of Devt Co-operation 1999–2000, of Defence 2000–01; Personal Rep. of OSCE Chair. for Preventing and Combating Terrorism 2002–. *Address:* Organization for Security and Co-operation in Europe, Kärtner Ring 5–7, 1010 Vienna, Austria (Office). *Telephone:* (1) 514-36-0 (Office). *Fax:* (1) 514-36-105 (Office). *E-mail:* info@osce.org (Office). *Website:* www.osce.org (Office).

TROLLOPE, Joanna, OBE, MA, DL; British author; b. 9 Dec. 1943; d. of Arthur Trollope and Rosemary Hodson; m. 1st David Potter 1966; two d.; m. 2nd Ian Curteis 1985 (divorced 2001); two step-s.; ed Reigate Co. School and St Hugh's Coll. Oxford; Information and Research Dept Foreign Office 1965–67; various teaching posts 1967–79; Chair. Advisory Cttee on Nat. Reading Initiative, Dept of Nat. Heritage 1996; mem. Advisory Cttee on Nat. Year of Reading, Dept of Educ. 1998, Council, Soc. of Authors 1997–, Campaign Bd, St Hugh's Coll., Oxford; Vice-Pres. Trollope Soc., West Country Writers' Asscn; Trustee Joanna Trollope Charitable Trust 1995–; Patron County of Glos. Community Foundation 1994–; apptd Deputy Lieutenant for County of Gloucestershire 2002; Romantic Historical Novel of the Year 1980. *Publications:* Britannia's Daughters: A Study of Women in the British Empire 1983, The Choir 1988, A Village Affair 1989, A Passionate Man 1990, The Rector's Wife 1991, The Men and the Girls 1992, A Spanish Lover 1993, The Country Habit (ed.) 1993, The Best of Friends 1995, Next of Kin 1996, Faith 1996, Other People's Children 1998, Marrying the Mistress 2000, Girl From the South 2002; as Caroline Harvey: Eliza Stanhope 1978, Parson Harding's Daughter 1979, Leaves from the Valley 1980, The City of Gems 1981, The Steps of the Sun 1983, The Taverners' Place 1986, Legacy of Love 1992, A Second Legacy 1993, A Castle in Italy 1993, The Brass Dolphin 1997; contribs. to newspapers and magazines. *Leisure interests:* reading, conversation, very long baths. *Address:* c/o Peters Fraser and Dunlop, Drury House, 34–43 Russell Street, London WC2B 5HA, England.

TRONCHETTI PROVERA, Marco; Italian business executive; b. 1948, Milan; three c.; ed Bocconi Univ., Milan; worked in family maritime transport business 1973–86; joined Pirelli Group as Partner, Pirelli & C. 1986, Man. Dir and Gen. Man. Soc. Int. Pirelli SA, Basle 1988–92, Man. Dir and Gen. Man. (Finance and Admin. and Gen. Affairs) Pirelli SpA 1991–92, Exec. Deputy Chair. and Man. Dir Pirelli SpA 1992–96, Deputy Chair. Pirelli & C. 1995–99, Chair. and CEO Pirelli SpA 1996–, Chair. Pirelli & C. 1999–; Chair. Olivetti 2001–, Chair. Bd and Exec. Cttee CAMFIN SpA, Milan; Chair. Bd Il Sole 24 Ore; Deputy Chair. Confindustria (nat. employers' org.), Chair. 2000–; mem. Bd Mediobanca, Banca Commerciale Italiana, Banca Intesa, GIM, RAS, Università Commerciale Luigi Bocconi; mem. European Round Table of Industrialists, Int. Advisory Bd of Allianz, Int. Council of J. P. Morgan, New York Stock Exchange Advisory Cttee, Italian Group of Trilateral Comm. *Address:* Office of the Chairman, Pirelli SpA, Viale Sarca 202, 20126, Milan, Italy (Office); CONFINDUSTRIA, Viale dell'Astronamia 30, EVR, 00144 Rome. *Telephone:* (02) 6442.2650 (Office); (06) 59031. *Fax:* (02) 64423733 (Office); (06) 5919615. *E-mail:* confindustria@confindustria.it (Office). *Website:* www.confindustria.it.

TROSHEV, Col.-Gen. Gennady Nikolayevich; Russian army officer; b. 15 March 1947, Russia; ed Kazan Higher Mil. Tank School, Mil. Acad. of Armoured Forces, Mil. Acad. of Gen. Staff; with tank troops; Commdr 10th Ural-Lvov volunteer tank div.; Commdr 42nd tank corps; Commdr United Group of Troops of Moscow Mil. Command in Chechnya; Commdr 58th Army 1995–97; Deputy C-in-C N Caucasus Mil. Command 1997–; Commdr Group of United Fed. Armed Forces Vostok in N Caucasus 1999–2000, N Caucasus Mil. Dist 2000–; Hero of Russia for operations in Dagestan and Chechnya 1999. *Publication:* My War 2001. *Address:* c/o Ministry of Defence, 103160 Moscow, Russia (Office).

TROŠKA, Zdeněk, MA; Czech film and theatre director and scriptwriter; b. 18 May 1953, Strakonice; s. of Václav Troška and Růžena Troška; ed Lycée Carnot, Dijon, France, Acad. of Film and Musical Arts; Prin./Head Prize for Luck From Hell II, St Petersburg, Russia 2002. *Films:* Boot 1982, The Sun, Hay and Strawberries 1983, The Treasure of Count Chamaré 1984, About Princess Jasněnka 1987, Flying Shoemaker 1987, The Sun, Hay and Some Slaps 1989, The Time of Examinations 1990, The Sun, Hay and Erotics 1991, The Princess from Mill 1999. *Plays:* Don Carlos (Nat. Theatre, Prague) 1989, Rusalka, Hamlet (musical version) 2000, Luck From Hell 2000, Luck From Hell II 2001. *Leisure interests:* literature, music: piano and organ, cooking, mushrooming, hiking. *Address:* Hoštice u Volyně 77, Volyně 387 01, Czech Republic (Office).

TROST, Barry Martin, PhD; American professor of chemistry; b. 13 June 1941, Philadelphia, Pa; s. of Joseph and Esther Trost; m. Susan Paula Shapiro 1967; two s.; ed Univ. of Pennsylvania and MIT; Asst Prof. of Chem., Dept of Chem., Univ. of Wis. 1965–68, Assoc. Prof. 1968–69, Prof. 1969–76, Helfaer Prof. 1976–82, Vilas Prof. 1982–87; Prof. of Chemistry, Stanford Univ. 1987–, Tamaki Prof. of Humanities and Sciences 1990–; Consultant E.I. du Pont de Nemours and Merck, Sharp & Dohme; mem. ARCO Science Bd; mem. Cttee on Chemical Sciences, NAS 1980–83; mem. and Chair. NIH Medicinal Chem. Study Section 1982–; Commr, Nat. Research Council Comm. on Eng and Tech. Systems; Ed.-in-Chief Comprehensive Organic Synthesis (Vols 1–9) 1991, Chair. 1996–; Ed. Chemical Tracts/Organic Chem.; mem. NAS, American Chemical Soc., AAAS; Dr hc (Univ. Claude Bernard, Lyon), (Technion, Israel); ACS Award in Pure Chem. 1977, for Creative Work in Synthetic Organic Chem. 1981, Backland Award 1981, Chemical Pioneer Award of AIC 1983, Alexander von Humboldt Award (Fed. Repub. of Germany) 1984, Cope Scholar Award of ACS 1989, Guenther Award of ACS 1990, Dr. Paul Janssen Prize for Creativity in Organic Synthesis 1990, Merit Award (NIH) 1988, Roger Adams Award 1995, Herbert C. Brown Award 1999, Nichols Medal 2000, Elsevier Boss Award 2000, Yamada Prize 2001, ACS Nobel Laureate, Signature Award for Grad. Educ. in Chem. 2002. *Publications:* Problems in Spectroscopy 1967, Sulfur Ylides 1974, Organic Synthesis Today and

Tomorrow (Ed.) 1981, Selectivity: a Goal for Synthetic Efficiency (Ed.) 1984; more than 700 scientific articles in leading chemical journals. *Address:* Department of Chemistry, Stanford University, Stanford, CA 94305, USA. *Telephone:* (650) 723-3385. *Fax:* (650) 725-0002.

TROTMAN, Baron (Life Peer), cr. 1999, of Osmotherley in the County of North Yorkshire; **Alexander Trotman,** Kt, MBA; British business executive; b. 22 July 1933, Middx; m.; ed Mich. State Univ.; joined Ford Motor Co. 1955, car planner, Chief Product Analyst 1960s, Dir Sales and Marketing Planning 1971–72, Exec. Dir Product Planning Research 1972–75, Corp. Vice-Pres. 1979, Pres. Ford Asia-Pacific 1983–84, Pres. Chair. Ford Europe 1984, Head World-Wide Auto Operations 1992–93, Pres., Chair., CEO 1993–99; Dir Imperial Chemical Industries (ICI) PLC 1997–, Chair. (Non-exec.) 2002–; mem. Bd IBM Corpn, New York Stock Exchange; Dr. hc (Edin.) 1998. *Address:* House of Lords, London, SW1A 0PW, England (Office).

TROTMAN-DICKENSON, Sir Aubrey Fiennes, Kt, DSc; British university vice-chancellor and principal (retd); b. 12 Feb. 1926, Wilmslow, Cheshire; s. of late Edward Trotman-Dickenson and Violet Murray (née Nicoll); m. Danusia Hewell 1953; two s. one d.; ed Winchester Coll., Balliol Coll. Oxford and Univs of Manchester and Edin.; Fellow, Nat. Research Council, Ottawa, Ont. 1948–50; Asst lecturer, ICI Fellow, Univ. of Manchester 1950–53; E.I. Du Pont de Nemours, Wilmington, USA 1953–54; Lecturer, Univ. of Edin. 1954–60; Prof. of Chem. Univ. Coll. of Wales, Aberystwyth 1960–68; Prin. Univ. of Wales Inst. of Science and Tech. 1968–88, Univ. Coll. Cardiff 1987–88, Univ. of Cardiff 1988–93; Vice-Chancellor Univ. of Wales 1975–77, 1983–85, 1991–93; Tilden Lecturer 1963; Hon. LLD (Wales). *Publications:* Gas Kinetics 1955, Free Radicals 1959, Tables of Biomolecular Gas Reactions 1967, Comprehensive Inorganic Chemistry (ed. 1973); 150 contribs to learned journals. *Address:* Siston Court, Bristol, BS16 9LU, England. *Telephone:* (117) 937-2109.

TROVOADA, Miguel dos Anjos da Cunha Lisboa; São Tomé e Príncipe politician; fmrly in charge of foreign relations for the São Tomé e Príncipe Liberation Movt (MLSTP), fmr mem. Political Bureau; Prime Minister of São Tomé e Príncipe 1975–78, also Minister of Defence and Foreign Affairs July–Dec. 1975, of Econ. Co-ordination, Co-operation and Tourism 1975–78, of Trade, Industry and Fisheries 1978–79; arrested and imprisoned 1979, released 1981, then in exile in Lisbon; Pres. and C-in-C of the Armed Forces of São Tomé e Príncipe 1991–95 (deposed in coup 15 Aug. 1995), reinstalled 1995–2001. *Address:* c/o Office of the President, São Tomé, São Tomé e Príncipe.

TROWBRIDGE, Alexander Buel, Jr.; American business executive; b. 12 Dec. 1929, Englewood, NJ; s. of Alexander Buel Trowbridge and Julie Chamberlain; m. 1st Nancey Horst 1955; two s. one d.; m. 2nd Eleanor Hutzler 1981; ed Phillips Acad., Andover, Mass. and Princeton Univ.; U.S. Marine Corps during Korean War; with overseas operations of several petroleum cos. in Cuba, El Salvador, Panama and Philippines; Pres. and Div. Man. Esso Standard Oil Co. of Puerto Rico 1963–65; Asst Sec. of Commerce for Domestic and Int. Business 1965–67; Acting Sec. of Commerce Feb.–May 1967, Sec. of Commerce 1967–68; Pres. American Man. Asscn 1968–70, Conf. Bd Inc. 1970–76; Dir Allied Chemical Corpn, then Vice-Chair. of Bd 1976–79; mem. Bd Dirs. Nat. Asscn of Mfrs 1978–, Pres. 1980–89; Dir New England Life Insurance Co., The Rouse Co., Waste Management Inc., The Sun Co., The Gillette Co., Harris Corpn, ICOS Corpn, Warburg Pincus Counsellors Funds, Sun Resorts Int., SA; I.R.I. Int. Corpn; Charter Trustee Phillips Acad., Andover, Mass.; mem. Competitiveness Policy Council, Washington, DC, Council on Foreign Relations. *Leisure interests:* tennis, skiing. *Address:* 1317 F Street, NW, Suite 500, Washington DC 20004 (Office); 1823 23rd Street, NW, Washington, DC 20008, USA (Home).

TROYAT, Henri (pseudonym of Tarassoff); French writer; b. 1 Nov. 1911, Moscow, Russia; s. of Aslan Tarassoff and Lydie Abessolomoff; m. Marguerite Saintagne 1948 (deceased); one s. one step-d.; ed Lycée Pasteur and Law Faculty, Univ. of Paris; mem. Acad. Française 1959–; Grand Officier Légion d'honneur, Commdr Ordre nat. du Mérite, Ordre des Arts et des Lettres. *Publications:* Faux-jour (Prix Populiste) 1935, L'araignée (Prix Goncourt) 1938, La neige en deuil (Grand prix littéraire de Monaco) 1952, Tant que la terre durera (three Vols) 1947–50, Les semailles et les moissons (five Vols) 1953–58, La lumière des justes (five Vols) 1960–, Les Eygletière (three Vols) 1965–67, Les héritiers de l'avenir 1968, Anne Predaille 1973, Le Moscovite 1974, La dérision 1983, Le bruit solitaire du coeur 1985, Aliocha, A Demain Sylvie 1986, Le Troisième bonheur 1987, Toute ma vie sera mensonge 1988, Le Défi d'Olga 1995; biographies: Dostoïevsky, Pouchkine, Tolstoï, Gogol, Catherine la Grande, Pierre le Grand, Alexandre Ier, Ivan le Terrible, Tchekhov, Turgenev, Gorki, Flaubert, Maupassant, Alexandre II, Nicolas II, Zola, Verlaine, Baudelaire, Raspoutine, L'Affaire Crémonnière 1997, Le fils du satrape 1998, Terribles tsarines 1998, Namouna ou la chaleur animale 1999. *Address:* Académie Française, 23 quai de Conti, 75006 Paris, France.

TRPEVSKI, Ljube, MSc, PhD; Macedonian banker and politician; b. 3 Aug. 1947, Velmej, Ohrid; m.; one s. one d.; ed Univ. of St Cyril and St Methodius, Skopje, Univ. of Tallahassee, Fla; teaching Asst, Faculty of Econs, Univ. of St Cyril and St Methodius, Skopje 1970–77, lecturer 1977–80, Docent 1980–85, Assoc. Prof. 1985–91, Prof. 1991; Deputy Gov. Nat. Bank of Macedonia 1987–91, Gov. 1997–; Minister, Pres. Securities and Exchange Comm. 1992–95; Vice-Pres. of Macedonia 1996. *Publications:* Lexicon of Contemporary Market Economy (co-author, ed.) 1993, Money and Banking 1995, The

Republic of Macedonia (co-author) 1996 and numerous articles. *Address:* Office of the Governor, National Bank of the Republic of Macedonia, Kompleks banki bb, P.O. Box 401, *1000 Skopje (Office); Mile Pop Jordanov 52, 91000 Skopje, Republic of Macedonia (Home). *Telephone:* (2) 112177 (Office). *Fax:* (2) 113481 (Office). *E-mail:* governorsoffice@nbrm.gov.mk (Office). *Website:* www.nbrm.gov.mk (Office).

TRUBETSKOI, Kliment Nikolayevich; Russian geochemist; b. 3 July 1933; m.; two c.; ed Moscow Inst. of Nonferrous Metals and Gold; Jr, Sr researcher Moscow Inst. for Problems of Complex Utilization of Mineral Resources 1961–81; Head of Lab. 1981–87, Deputy Dir 1987–92, Dir 1992–; Corresp. mem. USSR (now Russian) Acad. of Sciences 1987, mem. 1991; Vice-Pres. Acad. of Mining Sciences; took part in Devt of tech. to save resources in quarries, developed theoretical fundamentals of projecting, prognosis and tech. of complex utilization of mineral deposits; USSR State Prize 1990, N Melnikov Gold Medal and Prize. *Publications:* author of books and scientific articles in periodicals. *Leisure interests:* chess, swimming, photography, travelling. *Address:* Institute of Problems of Complex Utilization of Mineral Resources, Krukovsky tupik 4, 111020 Moscow, Russia. *Telephone:* (095) 360-89-60 (Office); 331-52-55 (Home).

TRUBETSKOV, Dmitry Ivanovich, DPhys-MathSc; Russian physicist; b. 14 June 1938, Saratov; s. of Ivan Trubetskov and Varvara Trubetskova; m. Sofya Vasilyeva 1962; one s.; ed Saratov State Univ.; aspirant 1960–64; teacher 1961–68; docent 1968; Prof. Saratov State Univ. 1981–, Head Chair of Electronics and Wave Processes 1981–, Rector 1994–; mem. IEEE Electron Devices Soc. 1995; corresp. mem. USSR (now Russian) Acad. of Sciences 1991; research in theoretical radiophysics and electronics, microwave electronics, applied nonlinear dynamics; Educ. Award of the Pres. of Russian Fed. *Publications include:* Analytical Methods of Calculation in Microwave Electronics (with V. N. Shevchik) 1970, Electronics of Backward-Wave Tubes 1975, Introduction into the Theory of Oscillations and Waves 1984, Nonlinear Dynamics in Action (with A. A. Koronovsky) 1995, Lectures on Microwave Vacuum Microelectronics (with A. G. Rozjenev and D. V. Sokolov) 1996, Nonlinear Waves (with N. M. Ryskyn) 2000, Linear Oscillators and Waves (with A. G. Rozjenev) 2001, Linear Oscillations and Waves, Problems (with A. P. Kuznetsov and A.G. Rozjenev) 2001. *Leisure interest:* reading. *Address:* Saratov State University, Astrakhanskaya str. 83, 410071 Saratov, Russia. *Telephone:* (8452) 241-696 (Office); (8452) 261-993 (Home). *Fax:* (8452) 240-446; (8452) 511-438. *E-mail:* true@cds.ssu.runnet.ru (Office).

TRUBNIKOV, Gen. Vyacheslav Ivanovich; Russian security officer and politician; b. 25 April 1944, Irkutsk; m.; one d.; ed Moscow State Inst. of Int. Relations; served in USSR KGB (First Main Directorate, intelligence) 1967–91; staff mem. HQ of First Main Dept (intelligence) 1977–84; KGB station officer in India (as corresp. Press Agency Novosti) 1971–77; mem. Union of Journalists 1973; resident in Bangladesh and India 1984–90; Head Div. of S. Asia KGB 1990–92; First Deputy Dir Russian Intelligence Service 1992–96, Dir 1996–98; mem. Security Council, Defence Council and Foreign Policy Council of Russia 1996; First Deputy Minister of Foreign Affairs 2000–. *Address:* Ministry of Foreign Affairs, Smolenskaya-Sennaya pl. 32/34, 121200 Moscow, Russia. *Telephone:* (095) 244-29-00. *Fax:* (095) 244-29-27.

TRUDEAU, Garry B., MFA; American cartoonist; b. 1948, New York; m. Jane Pauley 1980; one s. one d.; ed Yale Univ. School of Art and Architecture; cr. comic strip Doonesbury syndicated nationwide, Pinhead; selected cartoons from You Ask for Many; conceived (with Robert Altman) Tanner '88 (TV) 1988; Pulitzer Prize for Editorial cartooning 1975. *Plays include:* Doonesbury 1983, Rapmaster Ronnie, A Partisan Review (with Elizabeth Swados) 1984. *Publications include:* Any Grooming Hints for Your Fans, Rollie, But the Pension Fund was Just Sitting There, The Doonesbury Chronicles, Guilty, Guilty, Guilty, We Who are about to Fry, Salute You: selected cartoons in In Search of Reagan's Brain, Vol. 2, Is This Your First Purge, Miss ?, Vol. 2, It's Supposed to be Yellow, Pinhead; selected cartoons from You Ask for Many, Seetle for June, Vol. 1, The Wreck of the Rusty Nail, Dressed for Failure 1983, Confirmed Bachelors are Just So Fascinating 1984, Sir I'm Worried About Your Mood Swings 1984, Doonesbury Dossier: The Reagan Years 1984, Check Your Egos at the Door 1986, Talking 'Bout My G-G-Generation 1988, We're Eating More Beets 1988, Read My Lips, Make My Day, Eat Quiche and Die 1989, Recycled Doonesbury 1990, You're Smoking Now Mr Butt! 1990, In Search of a Cigarette Holder Man: A Doonesbury Book 1994, Doonesbury Nation 1995, Flashbacks 1995; The Portable Doonesbury 1993; contribs. to The People's Doonesbury and many others.

TRUJILLO, Solomon, MBA; American telecommunications executive; b. 1951; ed Univ. of Wyoming; began career with Mountain Bar Telephone 1974; Pres. and CEO USWest 1995–99; Chair. 1999–2000; Chair. and CEO Graviton Inc. 2001–; mem. Exec. Bd Orange SA 2001–, CEO 2003–; mem. Chair.'s Council Alcatel 2000–; mem. Bd Dirs Pepsi Co., Target Stores, Gannet. *Address:* Orange Media Centre, 50 George Street, London, W1U 7DZ, England (Office). *Telephone:* (20) 7984-2000 (Office). *Fax:* (20) 7984-2001 (Office). *E-mail:* media.centre@orange.co.uk (Office). *Website:* www.orange.co.uk (Office).

TRUJILLO MOLINA, Gen. Héctor Bienvenido; Dominican Republic army officer and politician; b. 1908; ed Univ. Autónoma de Santo Domingo; entered Army 1926; Chief of Staff of Army 1936; Supervisor-Gen. of Nat. Police 1938–43; Secretary of War, C-in-C of Army and Navy 1944; succeeded his brother as Pres. of the Dominican Republic 1952–60; Prof. American Int.

Acad., Washington; corresp. mem. Nat. Athenaeum Arts and Sciences, Mexico; living abroad; holds numerous military and other decorations of his own and foreign countries.

TRUMAN, Edwin M.; American economist; m.; one s. one d.; trained as economist; fmr lecturer Yale Univ.; joined Div. of Int. Finance, Bd of Govs. of Fed. Reserve System 1972, Dir (later Staff Dir) 1977–98 ; Asst Sec.., US Treasury for Int. Affairs 1998–2001; Asst Sec. (Int. Affairs) Senate Finance Cttee 1999–; Sr Fellow, Inst. for Int. Econs, Washington, DC; mem. G-7 Working Group on Exchange Market Intervention 1982–83, G-10 Working Group on the Resolution of Sovereign Liquidity Crises 1995–96, G-10-sponsored Working Party on Financial Stability in Emerging Market Econs 1996–97, G-22 Working Party on Transparency and Accountability 1998, Financial Stability Forum's Working Group on Highly Leveraged Insts 1999–2000. *Publications:* numerous articles on int. monetary econs, int. debt problems, econ. devt and European econ. integration. *Address:* Institute for International Economics, 1750 Massachusetts Avenue, NW, Washington, DC 20036-1903, USA (Office). *Telephone:* (202) 328-9000. *Fax:* (202) 659-3225. *E-mail:* ttruman@iie.com (Office); tnttruman2@aol.com (Home). *Website:* www.iie.com (Office).

TRUMKA, Richard Louis, JD; American lawyer and industrialist; b. 24 July 1949, Waynesburg, Pa; s. of Frank Richard Trumka and Eola Elizabeth Bertugli; m. Barbara Vidovich 1982; one s.; ed Philadelphia State Univ., Villanova Univ.; served at bar US Dist Court 1974, US Court of Appeals 1975, US Supreme Court 1979; Attorney United Mine Workers of America, Washington 1974–77, 1978–79, mem. Int. Exec. Bd Dist 4, Masontown, Pa 1981–83, Int. Pres., Washington 1982–95; Sec. Treas. AFL-CIO, Washington 1995–; Miner-Operator Jone and Loughlin Steel, Nemacolin, Pa 1977–78, 1979–81; Pres. Emer. United Mine Workers Asscn 1995–; Dir Nat. Bank, Washington 1983–85, Dinamo Corpn 1983–; mem. Bd Dirs American Coal Fund 1983–; Trustee Philadelphia State Univ.; Labor Responsibility Award, Martin Luther King Center for Non-Violent Social Change 1990. *Address:* AFL-CIO, 815 16th Street, NW, Washington, DC 20006, USA.

TRUMP, Donald John, BA; American property developer; b. 14 June 1946, New York; s. of Fred C. Trump and Mary Trump; m. 1st Ivana Zelnicek 1977 (divorced 1991); two s. one d.; m. 2nd Marla Maples 1993 (divorced 1999); one d.; ed Fordham Univ., Univ. of Pennsylvania; Pres. Trump Org.; holdings include: (New York) Trump Tower on Fifth Avenue; (Fla) Mar-A-Lago at Palm Beach, Trump Plaza; (Atlantic City) Trump Plaza Hotel Casino, Trump Castle Casino, Trump Taj Mahal Casino Resort; acquired 50 per cent stake in Empire State Bldg 1994; mem. Bd of Dirs Police Athletic League; Advisory Bd mem., Lenox Hill Hosp. and United Cerebral Palsy; Dir Fred C. Trump Foundation; Founder-mem. cttee to complete construction of Cathedral of St John the Divine and Wharton Real Estate Center; fmr Co-Chair. New York Vietnam Veterans Memorial Fund. *Publications:* Trump: The Art of the Deal 1987, Trump: Surviving at the Top 1990, The Art of the Comeback 1997. *Address:* Trump Organization, 725 Fifth Avenue, New York, NY 10022, USA. *Telephone:* (212) 832-2000. *Fax:* (212) 755-3230.

TRUONG NHU TANG; Vietnamese lawyer and politician; b. 1923, Cholon; ed Univ. of Paris; Controller-Gen., Viet Nam Bank for Industry and Commerce; Dir-Gen. Viet Nam Sugar Co., Saigon; Sec.-Gen. People's Movt for Self-Determination 1964–65; mem. Saigon Cttee for Restoration of Peace; Pres. Viet Nam Youth Union 1966–67; imprisoned 1967–68; joined Nat. Liberation Front 1968; Minister of Justice, Provisional Revolutionary Govt of S. Viet Nam 1969–76 (in Saigon 1975–76). *Address:* c/o Council of Ministers, Hanoi, Viet Nam.

TRUSZCZYNSKI, Jan; Polish politician and diplomatist; b. 30 July 1949, Warsaw; m.; two c.; ed Main School of Planning and Statistics, Warsaw ; with Ministry of Foreign Affairs 1972–93, Dept of Human Resources and Training 1972–74, 1975–78, European Integration Desk Officer, Western Europe Dept 1982; Second Sec., Polish Embassy, The Hague 1978–82, Adviser, Brussels 1988–89, Adviser, Mission to EC, Brussels 1989–93; Adviser to the Chair., Dept Dir Inicjatyw Gospodarczych Bank (BIG) SA 1993–94; Dir Poland Office, Kreditbank NV 1995–96; Amb. to the EU 1996–2001; Under-Sec. of State, Chancellery 2001; Under-Sec. of State, Ministry of Foreign Affairs, Govt Plenipotentiary for Poland's Accession Negotiations to the EU 2001–. *Address:* Ministry of Foreign Affairs, al. J.Ch. Szucha 23, 00-580 Warsaw, Poland (Office). *Telephone:* (22) 5239610 (Office). *Fax:* (22) 6219614 (Office). *E-mail:* jantruszczynski@mszgov.pl (Office). *Website:* www.negocjacje.gov.pl (Office).

TRZECIAKOWSKI, Witold Mieczysław, DEconSc; Polish economist and politician; b. 6 Feb. 1926, Warsaw; s. of Witold Trzeciakowski and Zofia Trzeciakowska; m. Anna Przedpełska 1951; three s.; ed Cen. School of Planning and Statistics, Warsaw, Harvard Univ., Cambridge, Mass. and Columbia Univ., New York, NY; mem. underground Home Army 1942–44, took part in Warsaw uprising 1944; Asst Prof. 1966, Extraordinary Prof. 1972, Ordinary Prof. 1979; Dir Podkowiak Metal Wares Factory, Szydłowiec 1946–49; Vice-Pres. Asscn of Pvt. Producers of Metal Wares 1946–49; designer, Transport Design Office, Warsaw 1949–57; consultant, Inst. of Foreign Trade Conjuncture and Prices, Warsaw 1959–60, Deputy Dir 1960–76, Dir 1976–78, Prof. 1972–81; Prof., Econ. Sciences Inst., Polish Acad. of Sciences (PAN), Warsaw 1981–91; mem. Solidarity Trade Union 1980–, Civic Cttee attached to Chair. of Solidarity Trade Union, Lech Wałęsa (q.v.) 1988–; participant Round Table plenary debates, co-Chair. group for econ.

and social policy Feb.–April 1989; Senator 1989–91, Chair. Senate Comm. of Nat. Econ. 1989–91; Minister, mem. Council of Ministers 1989–90, Chair. Econ. Council 1989–91; Hon. Pres. Inst. of Econs, Polish Acad. of Sciences; mem. Primatial Social Council 1983–85; Chair. Church Agric. Cttee 1987–89, mem. 1987–; Commdr's Cross with Star, Officer's Cross and Kt's Cross, Order of Polonia Restituta, Gold Cross of Merit, Cross of Valour, Prime Minister's Prize for achievements in economics of transformation 1995. *Publications include:* Modele pośredniego kierowania gospodarką planową w sterowaniu handlem zagranicznym 1975, Structural Adjustments in Trade-Dependent Small Centrally Planned Economies 1984, Reforma–restrukturyzacja–zadłużenie 1987, Transition in Poland 1993, Dynamika Transformacji Polskiej Gospodarki 1996. *Leisure interests:* skiing, horse-riding. *Address:* ul. Langiewicza 2 m. 2, 02-071 Warsaw, Poland. *Telephone:* (22) 8256615. *Fax:* (22) 6295897. *E-mail:* wtrzecia@staszic.inepan.waw.pl (Home).

TSABAN, Yair; Israeli journalist and politician; b. 1930, Tel Aviv; Chair. political bureau of Maki (Israeli CP) 1972–73; co-founder of Sheli Coalition 1977; Political Sec. Mapam (United Workers' Party), Chair. Mapam's faction in the Histadrut; Minister of Immigrant Absorption 1992–96; mem. Knesset 1981– (Meretz), served on numerous cttees. 1981–92. *Publications:* various articles on political, social and econ. topics. *Address:* c/o Ministry of Immigrant Absorption, P.O. Box 883, 2 Rehov Kaplan, Kiryat Ben-Gurion, Jerusalem 91006, Israel.

TSAGOLOV, Maj.-Gen. Kim Makedonovich, PhD; Russian/Ossetian; b. 1930, N Ossetia, Russia; ed School of Fine Arts, Yeysk Mil. School of Marine Aviation; Sr mil. adviser Limited Contingent of Soviet armed forces in Afghanistan 1981–84; expelled from army for public criticism of Afghanistan war 1989; headed defence of the N Ossetian Capital during attack of Georgian troops of Pres. Gamsakhurdia 1989–91; Deputy Minister on Problems of Nationalities Russian Fed. 1993–98; Deputy Minister on Nat. Policy of Russian Fed. 1999–2000; Dir Inst. of Peoples of Russia 2000–. *Art exhibition:* Exhbn in Moscow 1998. *Leisure interest:* painting. *Address:* Institute of Peoples of Russia, Smolenskaya str. 14, 125493 Moscow, Russia (Office). *Telephone:* (095) 456-72-13 (Home).

TSAI ING-WEN, LLM, PhD; Taiwanese politician and professor of law; b. 31 Aug. 1956; ed Nat. Taiwan Univ., Cornell Univ., USA and LSE, UK; Assoc. Prof., Law Dept, Nat. Chengchi Univ. 1984–90, Prof., Grad. School of Law 1990–91, Prof. of Law, Grad. Inst. of Int. Trade 1993–2000 (mem. Int. Trade Comm.); Prof., Grad. School of Law, Soochow Univ. 1991–93; Adviser on Int. Econ. Orgs., Ministry of Econ. Affairs 1992–2000; Convener, Drafting/Research Group on 'Statute Governing Relations with Hong Kong and Macao' 1994–95; mem. Advisory Cttee Mainland Affairs Council, Exec. Yuan 1994–98, Chair. 2000– ; mem. Fair Trade Comm., Exec. Yuan 1995–98, Advisory Cttee of Copyright Comm., Ministry of Interior 1997–99; Sr Adviser Nat. Security Council 1999–2000. *Address:* Mainland Affairs Council, 5th–13th Floors, 2-2 Chi Nan Road, Sec. 1, Taipei, Taiwan (Office). *Telephone:* (2) 239-75589 (Office). *Fax:* (2) 239-75700 (Office); (2) 239-75300 (Office). *E-mail:* macso@mac.gov.tw (Office). *Website:* www.mac.gov.tw (Office).

TSANG, Sir Donald Yam-kuen, KBE; Chinese government official; b. Tsang Yam-kuen, 7 Oct. 1944, Hong Kong; m.; two s.; ed in Hong Kong and USA; joined Govt of Hong Kong 1967; served in various Govt depts. and brs. of Govt Secr.; Dist Officer, Shatin; Deputy Dir of Trade responsible for trade relations with N America; Deputy Sec. of Gen. Duties Br. responsible for Sino-British Jt Declaration 1985; Dir of Admin. Office of Chief Sec. 1989; Dir-Gen. of Trade 1991–93; Sec. for Treasury 1993–95; Financial Sec. 1995–2001; Chief Sec. for Admin. 2001–; Hon. LLD 1999; Hon. DBA 1999. *Leisure interests:* bird-watching, music. *Address:* Central Government Offices, West Wing, 12/F, Lower Albert Road, Hong Kong Special Administrative Region, People's Republic of China (Office). *Telephone:* (852) 28102323 (Office). *Fax:* (852) 28820099 (Office).

TSANG YOK-SING; Hong Kong politician; Chair. Democratic Alliance for the Betterment of Hong Kong (DAB); currently Legis. Councillor, Special Admin. Region of Hong Kong, People's Repub. of China, apptd. mem. Exec. Council (Cabinet) June 2002; mem. political section, Preparatory Cttee for Hong Kong Special Admin. Region (SAR). *Address:* Democratic Alliance for the Betterment of Hong Kong, SUP Tower, 12/F, 83 King's Road, North Point, Hong Kong Special Administrative Region, People's Republic of China. *Telephone:* 25280136. *Fax:* 25284339. *E-mail:* info@dab.org.hk (Office). *Website:* www.dab.org.hk (Office).

TSAO, Robert H.C., MS; Taiwanese electronics industry executive; b. 24 Feb. 1947, Shantung; ed Nat. Univ. of Taiwan, Nat. Chiao Tung Univ.; Deputy Dir Electrical Research Service Org. 1979–81; Vice-Pres. United Microelectronics Corpn (UMC) 1980, Pres. 1981–91, Chair. 1991–; Chair. Unipac Microelectronics Corpn 1989–, World Wiser Electrical Inc. 1989–; Vice-Chair. TECO Information System Co. Ltd 1995–; mem. Standing Bd Chinese Nat. Fed. of Industry (CNFI), Chair. Intellectual Property Protection Cttee 1991–94; Chair. Asscn of Allied Industries in Science-Based Industry Park 1987–93. *Address:* United Microelectronics Corporation Ltd., 13 Chuang Hsin 1st Road, Science-Based Industry Park, Hsinchu, Taiwan. *Telephone:* (35) 782258. *Fax:* (35) 774767.

TSAPOGAS, Makis Joakim, MD, DSc, MCh, MRCS, LRCP, FACS; professor of vascular diseases; b. Greece; m. Lily Philossopoulou; lecturer in Surgery, King's Coll. Hosp. Medical School, London 1961–63, Sr lecturer 1963–67;

Assoc. Prof. of Surgery, Albany Medical Coll. Union Univ. New York 1967–70; Prof. 1970–75; Adjunct Prof. Rensselear Polytechnic Inst. New York 1970–75; Prof. of Surgery, Rutgers Medical School, NJ 1976; Prof. of Vascular Diseases, State Univ. of New York 1977–; Prof. Univ. of London 1993–; adviser, WHO 1986–; consultant, UN, New York 1993–; Visiting Prof. in many univs. in Europe and N America; Hunterian Prof. Royal Coll. of Surgeons; corresp. mem. Acad. of Athens; hon. mem. many scientific socs.; Red Cross Gold Medal; Hon. PhD; Hon. DM. *Publications include:* Atherosclerosis in the Lower Limb 1959, Treatment of Thrombosis 1965, Management of Vascular Diseases 1985, Medical Education 1992; numerous articles in scientific medical journals. *Leisure interests:* classical music, reading, travelling. *Address:* P.O. Box 457, Northport, NY 11768, USA. *Telephone:* (516) 261-4114. *Fax:* (516) 261-4114.

TSCHIRA, Klaus; German computer executive; with IBM –1972; co.-f. of SAP. *Address:* SAP AG, P.O. Box 1461, 69185, Walldorf, Germany (Office). *Telephone:* (6227) 747474 (Office).

TSCHUDI-MADSEN, Stephan, PhD; Norwegian art historian; b. 25 Aug. 1923, Bergen; s. of Dr. Stephan Tschudi Madsen and Aagot (née Stoltz) Tschudi Madsen; m. Elizabeth Kverndal 1954; two s. one d.; ed Univ. of Oslo; Keeper, Nat. Gallery, Oslo 1950–51, Vigelands Museum, Oslo 1951–52; Asst Prof. Univ. of Oslo 1953–58; Chief Antiquarian, Cen. Office of Historic Monuments, Oslo 1959–78, Dir-Gen. 1978–91, Special Counsellor 1991–93; Keeper, Akershus Castle 1961–79; Prof. Univ. of Calif. 1966–67, 1973; Sec. Gen. The Architectural Heritage Year 1974–76; Pres. Advisory Cttee of Int. Council on Monuments and Sites 1981–88, Vice-Pres. 1988–90; Pres. Norwegian Nat. Comm. 1978–92; Chair. Akershus Slotts Venner 1992–; Vice-Pres. World Heritage Comm. 1984–87; Chair. State Council of Cultural Heritage 1992–96, Council of Norsk Folkemuseum 1992–2001; mem. Norwegian Nat. Comm. of UNESCO 1988–92; mem. Norwegian Acad.; Hon. mem. Norwegian Soc. of Preservation, Icomos (int. and nat.), Friends of Norsk Folkemuseum, Friends of Akershus Castle; Cultural Prize of Science and Letters of Oslo City; Commdr of the Order of St Olav, Commdr of Order of Oranje-Nassau, Kt of Order of King Leopold; Hon. Medal of Norwegian Soc. of Preservation, Norsk Folkemuseum. *Television:* several programmes on antiquities and Art Nouveau, Norwegian Broadcasting. *Publications:* To kongeslott 1952, Vigelands Fontenerelieffer 1953, Sources of Art Nouveau 1957, Rosendal 1965, Art Nouveau 1967, Chateauneuf's Works in London and Oslo 1968, Restoration and Anti-Restoration 1976, Henrik Bull 1983, (Ed.) Norges Kulturhistorie, 8 Vols 1979–81, (Ed.) Norges Kunsthistorie, 7 Vols 1981–83, (Ed.) Norsk Kunstnerleksikon, 4 Vols 1981–86, (Ed.) Norway: A Cultural Heritage 1987, Vakrest i Norge 1991, På Nordmanns vis 1993, Norske antikviteter 1994, Quantum Satis (Ed.) 1995, Our Nordic Heritage (Ed.), The Norwegian Supreme Court (Ed.) 1998, Akershus Castle 1999, 50 år for Akershus (Ed.) 2001, The British Ambassador's Residence in Oslo 2001. *Leisure interest:* mountain walking, grandchildren. *Address:* Bjørn Farmannsgt. 8, Oslo 0271, Norway (Home). *Telephone:* 22430373.

TSELKOV, Oleg; Russian artist; b. 1934, Moscow; ed Moscow secondary school, Minsk Inst. of Theatre Art and Leningrad Acad. of Art; expelled from both for 'formalism'; later graduated from Leningrad Theatre Inst. as stage-designer 1958; designed numerous productions; mem. of Artists' Union; left USSR 1977; now lives in Paris. *Exhibitions:* Moscow 1965, 1970, 1975, Austria 1975, Fed. Germany, France 1976, in Russia after 1991.

TSENG CHENG KUI, DSc; Chinese scientist; b. 18 June 1909, Xiamen (Amoy), Fujian Prov., China; s. of Tseng Pi-chang and Lin Sui-qing; m. 1st Ye Nu-ying 1931; m. 2nd Zhang Yi-fan 1954; two s. two d.; ed Amoy, Lingnan and Mich. Univs; asst. Botany Dept Amoy Univ. 1930–32; instructor, Biology Dept 1934–35; lecturer in Biology Nat. Shandong Univ. 1935–37, Assoc. Prof. 1937–38; Assoc. Prof. in Biology, Lingnan Univ. 1938–40; Rackham Postdoctoral Fellow, Univ. of Mich. 1942–43; Research Assoc. in charge of Seaweed Research, Scripps Inst. of Oceanography, UCLA, La Jolla, Calif., USA 1943–46; Prof. and Chair. Dept of Botany and Deputy Dir, Inst. of Oceanography Nat. Shandong Univ., Qingdao 1946–52, Chair., Dept of Fisheries, 1946–47; Research Prof., Deputy Dir, Marine Biological Lab. 1950–56, with Inst. of Marine Biology 1957–58; Deputy Dir, Inst. of Oceanography 1959–77, Dir 1978–84, Dir Emer. 1984–; Dir, Experimental Marine Biology (Open) Lab., CAS 1987–91, Dir Emer. 1991–; mem. Chinese Acad. of Sciences 1980; Fellow, Third World Acad. of Sciences 1985; mem. Chinese Society of Oceanology and Limnology 1951–63 (Pres., 1979–88, Pres. Emer. 1988–), Chinese Fisheries Soc. 1964–77 (Vice-Pres. 1981–90, Hon. mem. 1991–), Chinese Phycological Soc. (Pres. 1979–84, Pres. Emer. 1985–), Pres., Chinese Scientific Cttee of Oceanic Research 1985–89, Pres. Emer., Chinese Oceanographic Soc. 1989–; Hon. Life mem. World Aquaculture Soc. 1991; Dr hc (Ohio State Univ.) 1987; Nat. Natural Science Award, 1956, 1987, Nat. Science Congress Award 1978, Nat. Educational Comm. Textbook Award 1987; CAS Natural Science Award 1990, Shintoshi Hatai Medal, Pacific Science Asscn 1995, Quishi Natural Science Prize, Quishi Science and Tech. Foundation 1996, Science and Tech. Progress Prize, HLHL Science and Tech. Foundation 1997, PSA Award of Excellence in Phycology, Phycological Soc. of America. *Publications:* 12 books and more than 360 scientific articles. *Leisure interest:* music. *Address:* Institute of Oceanology, Chinese Academy of Sciences, 7 Nanhai Road, Qingdao 266071 (Office); 5 Qihe Road, Qingdao 266003, People's Republic of China. *Telephone:* (532) 2870220 (Office); (532) 2869117 (Home). *Fax:* (532) 2964965; (532) 2879235. *E-mail:* cktseng@qd-public.sd .cninfo.net (Office).

TSEPOV, Boris Anatolyevich, CJur; Russian diplomatist; b. 13 June 1948; ed Moscow Inst. of Int. Relations, Diplomatic Acad.; diplomatic service 1971–; different posts in USSR Embassy, Kuwait 1971–76; in Third African Div., USSR Ministry of Foreign Affairs 1976–78; Secr. of Deputy Minister 1978–86, with Dept for Int. Humanitarian Cooperation and Human Rights 1986–90; Counsellor Perm. USSR (now Russian) Mission to UN (New York) 1991–94; Dir of Dept, concurrently Exec. Sec. Russian Ministry of Foreign Affairs 1994–98; Amb. to Kenya (also accred Perm. Rep. to int. orgs, Nairobi) 1998–2001; Dir Dept of Compatriots Affairs and Human Rights 2001–. *Address:* Ministry of Foreign Affairs, Smolenskaya-Sennaya 32/34, 121200 Moscow, Russia. *Telephone:* (095) 244-30-25. *Fax:* (095) 244-30-45. *E-mail:* dgpch@mid.ru (Office).

TSERETELI, Zurab Konstantinovich; Georgian sculptor and artist; b. 4 Jan. 1934, Tbilisi; m. Inessa Andronikashvili; one d.; ed Tbilisi Acad. of Arts; mem. Russian Acad. of Fine Arts, Pres. 1997–, Head Dept of Design; Pres. Int. UNESCO Foundation in Moscow; Vice-Pres. Russian Acad. of Creativity; author of numerous sculptures, mosaics, monumental murals, stained-glass windows, revived old technique of traditional Georgian enamel; author of numerous monuments including Friendship in Moscow (with poet A. Voznesensky), Kindness Wins over Evil (New York, UN Bldg), Happiness for Children of the World (Univ. of Fine Arts, Brockport), Columbus (Miami), Birth of a New Man (London), Moment of Victory (Moscow), Peter the Great (Moscow) and others in Tbilisi, Tokyo, Seville, Osaka, Brasília; USSR People's Deputy 1989–90; Hero of Labour 1990, USSR People's Artist 1980, People's Artist of Russia; Lenin and State Prizes. *Address:* Bolshaya Gruzinskaya str. 17, Moscow, Russia. *Telephone:* (095) 254-77-67.

TSHERING, Lyonpo Dago; Bhutanese diplomatist and politician; b. 17 July 1941, Paro; ed Univ. of Bombay, Indian Admin. Service Training, Mussoorie and Indian Audit and Accounts Service Training, Simla, India, Univ. of Manchester, England; Asst. Ministry of Devt 1961–62; Asst, Office of the Chief Sec., Royal Secretariat 1962–63; returned to Ministry of Devt 1963, Sec. 1965–70; mem. Nat. Ass.; mem. Royal Advisory Council 1968–70; First Sec. Bhutan Embassy in India 1971–73; Deputy Perm. Rep. to UN 1973–74, Perm. Rep. 1974–80, 1984–85; Amb. to Bangladesh 1980–84; Minister of Home Affairs 1985–98; Amb. to India 1998–; Orange Scarf. *Address:* Embassy of Bhutan, Chandragupta Marg, Chanakyapuri, New Delhi 110 021, India. *Telephone:* (11) 6889807. *Fax:* (11) 6876710.

TSHERING, Ugyen, BA; Bhutanese public servant; b. 8 Aug. 1954, Thimphu; m.; ed Univ. of California, Berkeley, USA; joined Govt Planning Comm. 1978, Co-ordinator bilateral and multilateral assistance to Govt 1983–, Project Co-ordinator, Computer Support Centre 1984, Sec. Computerization Cttee 1983–, Dir Planning Comm. 1986–89, now Vice-Chair.; Perm Rep. of Bhutan to UN 1989–98; Editorial Adviser to Nat. Ass. 1980–; fmr Chair. Asian Devt Bank; Chair. World Bank Projects Implementation Cttee 1984–; Chair. Tech. Cttee on Rural Devt, S-E Asian Asscn of Regional Co-operation 1988–89; Sec., Ministry of Foreign Affairs 2001–. *Address:* Ministry of Foreign Affairs, Convention Centre, P.O. Box 103, Thimphu, Bhutan. *Telephone:* 323297. *Fax:* 323240.

TSHISEKEDI, Etienne; Democratic Republic of the Congo politician; Leader, Union pour la démocratie et le progrès social (UDPS)); Prime Minister of Zaire (now Democratic Repub. of the Congo) and C-in-C of Armed Forces Sept.–Oct. 1991, Prime Minister 1992–93 (dismissed by Pres. Mobutu March 1993), April 1997. *Address:* Union pour la démocratie et le progrès social (UDPS), Twelfth Street, Limete Zone, Kinshasa, Democratic Republic of Congo. *E-mail:* udps@globalserve.net. *Website:* www.udps.org/udps.html.

TSISKARIDZE, Nikolai; Georgian ballet dancer; b. 31 Dec. 1973, Tbilisi; s. of Maxim Tsiskaridze and Lamara Tsiskaridze; ed Tbilisi Ballet School, Bolshoi Ballet Acad., Moscow Choreographic Inst.; joined the Bolshoi Ballet 1992, now prin. dancer; numerous prizes including Silver Medal, 7th Japan World Ballet Competition, Osaka 1995, Soul of Dance Rising Star Nat. Prize 1995, First Prize and Gold Medal, 8th Moscow Int. Ballet Competition 1997, Merited Artist of Russia 1997, La Sylphide Russian Nat. Dance Org. Diploma Dancer of the Year 1997, Gold Mask, Russian Nat. Award for Best Male Role 1999, 2000, Benois de la Danse Int. Award, Dancer of the Year 1999, Mayor of Moscow Prize in Literature and Art 2000. *Dance:* roles in numerous ballets including Sleeping Beauty, Gisèle, Raymonda, La Sylphide, La Bayadére, The Nutcracker, Swan Lake, Romeo and Juliet, Legend of Love, Narcissus, Pharaoh's Daughter, etc. *Leisure interest:* reading. *Address:* Bolshoi Theatre, Teatralnaya Pl.2, Moscow 103009 (Office); Komsomolsky Prospekt 35, Apt. 106, Moscow 119146, Russian Federation (Home). *Telephone:* (095) 292-06-55 (Office); (095) 242-29-79 (Home). *Fax:* (095) 242-47-53 (Office).

TSOHATZOPOULOS, Apostolos Athanasios; Greek politician; b. 1939, Athens; m. Gudrun Moldenhauer; one s. one d.; ed Tech. Univ. of Munich, FRG; deprived of citizenship by mil. dictatorship 1969; active in Panhellenic Liberation Movt, mem. Nat. Council during dictatorship; returned to Greece 1974; mem. Cen. Cttee and Exec. Office PASOK 1974–90, Gen. Sec. 1990–95, mem. Exec. Office 1995–; mem. Parl. 1981–; Minister of Public Works 1981–84, to the Prime Minister 1986–87, of the Interior 1987–89, of Transport and Communications 1989, of Interior 1993–94, 1995–96, of Nat. Defence 1996–2001, of Devt 2002–. *Address:* Ministry of Development, Odos Mihalakopoulou 80, 115 28 Athens (Office); Komna Traka 3, 11257 Athens; Omirou 8, 10564 Athens, Greece. *Telephone:* (1) 07708615 (Office). *Fax:* (1) 07788279 (Office). *Website:* www.ypan.gr (Office).

TSOVOLAS, Dimitris; Greek politician; b. 1942, Melissourgi, Arta; m. Ekaterini Yoti; one s. one d.; ed Salonika Univ.; practised law at Arta until 1977; mem. Parl. 1977–92, mem. Parl. Working Cttees. on Labour, Public Order and Premiership 1977–81; elected Sec. of Presidium of Parl.; Minister of Finance 1985–89; Founder and Leader Democratic Social Movt (DHKKI) 1995–; Parl. Deputy (DHKKI) for Athens II 1996–. *Address:* Democratic Social Movement, Odos Halkokondili 9, 106 77 Athens (Office); 48 Serifou Street, 112 54, Athens, Greece. *Telephone:* (1) 3801712 (Office); (1) 2020469. *Fax:* (1) 3839047 (Office). *E-mail:* dikki@otenet.gr (Office).

TSUI, Daniel C., PhD; American (b. Chinese) professor of physics; b. 1939, Henan, China; ed Univ. of Chicago; Prof. Dept of Electrical Eng, Princeton Univ. 1982–; mem. NAS, Acad. Sinica, American Acad. of Arts and Sciences, Chinese Acad. of Sciences; Fellow American Physics Soc.; Nobel Prize in Physics for discovery of fractional quantum Hall effect (jtly with Robert B. Laughlin and Horst L. Störmer) 1998, Benjamin Franklin Medal 1998. *Publications:* numerous articles in scientific journals. *Address:* Department of Electrical Engineering, Princeton University, POB 5263, Princeton, NJ 08544, USA. *Telephone:* (609) 258-4621. *Fax:* (609) 258-6279. *E-mail:* tsui@ee .princeton.edu (Office).

TSUI, Lap-Chee, OC, OOnt, PhD, FRSC, FRS; Canadian geneticist; b. 21 Dec. 1950, Shanghai, China; s. of Jing Lue Hsue and Hui Ching Wang; m. (Ellen) Lan Fong 1977; two s.; ed The Chinese Univ. of Hong Kong, Univ. of Pittsburgh, USA; staff geneticist, Dept of Genetics and scientist, The Research Inst., Hosp. for Sick Children, Toronto, Canada 1983–, Sr Research Scientist 1988–, Sellers Chair in Cystic Fibrosis Research 1989–, Geneticist-in-Chief 1996–; Asst Prof. Depts of Medical Genetics and Medical Biophysics, Univ. of Toronto 1983–88, Assoc. Prof. 1988–90, Prof., Dept of Molecular and Medical Genetics 1990–, Univ. Prof. 1994–, H. E. Sellers Chair in Cystic Fibrosis 1998–; Howard Hughes Int. Scholar 1991–96; Assoc. Ed. Clinical Genetics 1991–; Ed. Int. Journal of Genome Research 1990, Assoc. Ed. Genomics 1994–; mem. Editorial Bd several scientific journals; Adviser, European Journal of Human Genetics 1992–; Dir American Soc. of Human Genetics, Mon Sheong Foundation, Educ. Foundation, Fed. of Chinese Canadian Professionals; mem. or fmr mem. numerous scientific cttees; Pres. The Human Genome Org.; mem. other professional bodies; Lee Kuan Yew Distinguished Visitor, Singapore 2000; Hon. DSc (Univ. New Brunswick) 1991, (Chinese Univ. of Hong Kong) 1992, Hon. DCL (Univ. King's Coll.) 1991; numerous prizes and awards including Scientist Award, Medical Research Council (Canada) 1989–93, Gold Medal of Honor, Pharmaceutical Mftrs Asscn of Canada 1989, Royal Soc. of Canada Centennial Award 1989, Award of Excellence, Genetic Soc. of Canada 1990, Gairdner Int. Award 1990, Canadian Achiever Award 1991, Sarstedt Research Prize 1993, XII San Remo Int. Award for Genetic Research 1993, J. P. Lecocq Prize 1994, Henry Friesen Award, Canadian Soc. of Clinical Investigation and Royal Coll. of Physicians and Surgeons of Canada 1995, Medal of Honour, Canadian Medical Asscn 1996, Distinguished Scientist Award, MRC 2000. *Publications:* numerous scientific papers and reviews. *Leisure interests:* travel, good food. *Address:* Department of Genetics, The Hospital for Sick Children, 555 University Avenue, Toronto, Ont., M5G 1X8, Canada. *Telephone:* (416) 813-6015. *Fax:* (416) 813-4931.

TSUJI, Yoshifumi; Japanese business executive; b. 6 Feb. 1928, Kagawa Pref.; ed Univ. of Tokyo; joined Nissan Motor Co., Ltd 1954, Gen. Man. Tochigi Plant 1984, Dir, mem. Bd and Gen. Man. Tochigi Plant 1985, Man. Dir in charge of Product Planning 1987, Exec. Man. Dir in charge of Plant Operations, Eng Depts. 1989, Exec. Vice-Pres. in charge of Product Operation Group, Purchasing Group, Non-Automotive Operations Group, etc. 1990, Exec. Vice-Pres. in charge of Production Operation Group, Non-automotive Operations Group 1991, Pres. 1992–96, Chair. 1996–2000, Consultant 2000–. *Leisure interests:* golf, reading. *Address:* Nissan Motor Co., 17-1 Ginza 6-chome, Chuo-ku, Tokyo 104-23, Japan. *Telephone:* (3) 3543-5523.

TSUKA, Kohei (Bong Woong Kim); South Korean author and theatre director; b. 24 April 1948, Iizuka City, Fukuoka Pref., Japan; m. Naoko Ikoma; one d.; ed Keio Univ. Tokyo; wrote first play, Red Beret for You 1969; writer and dir for Waseda Univ. Theatre Club 1972; published first play The Murder of Atami 1975; est. Thukakoahei office for plays 1975–82; est. Kitaku Thukakoahei Gekidan 1994, Ōita City Thukakoahei Gekidan 1996; Dir Ginchan Ga Yuku, New Nat. Theatre 1997; Japan Acad. Award for film Kamata March Song 1983; 42nd Yomiuri Literature Prize for play of The Tale of Hiryu '90 1990, and other awards. *Publications:* novels: The Murder of Atami 1975, For the Father Who Couldn't Die in the War 1976, Introduction to Revolution, The Tale of Hiryu 1977, Sun is in Your Mind 1978, Kamata March Song 1981, Town with Well 1985, The Day that they Bombed Hiroshima 1986, A Stripper's Story 1984, Birth of a Star 1986, My Country, Tell it to my Daughter 1990, The Story of Ryoma 1992–2000; many other plays and essays. *Address:* Room 401, Villa Kamimura, Tabata, 6-3-18 Tabata, Kita-ku, Tokyo 114-0014, Japan. *Telephone:* (3) 5814-5177. *Fax:* (3) 5814-5178.

TSUMBA, Leonard Ladislas, PhD; Zimbabwean banker; b. 27 June 1943, Harare; s. of Ladislus Million Tsumba and Regina Tsumba; m. Nola Arne Yasinski 1969; two d.; Instructor in Econs Hampton Inst. USA 1970–72; Asst Prof. of Econs Trinity Coll. USA 1975–77; consultant, Money and Finance Div. UNCTAD 1979; CitiBank NA, USA 1977–81; Exec. Asst to Gov. Reserve Bank of Zimbabwe 1981–82, Gen. Man. 1982–86, Deputy Gov. 1986–87, Group

Chief Exec. 1987–83, Gov. 1993–; Man. Dir Finhold/Zimbabwe Banking Corpn 1987–93. *Leisure interest:* golf. *Address:* Reserve Bank of Zimbabwe, P.O. Box 1283, 80 Samora Machel Avenue, Harare, Zimbabwe (Office). *Telephone:* (4) 703000 (Office). *Fax:* (4) 705890 (Office). *E-mail:* ltsumba@rbz .co.zw (Office).

TSUNG, Christine Tsai-yi, MBA; Taiwanese business executive; b. 1949; m. Jerome Chen; ed Nat. Taiwan Univ. and Univ. of Missouri, USA; fmr exec. farm machinery co. in Texas, USA; fmr Budget Man., Columbia Pictures; Consultant Kaohsiung Mass Rapid Transit System 1999; Pres. and CEO China Airlines 2000–02; Minister of Econ. Affairs Feb.–March 2002 (first woman in position); Chair. The Grand Hotel, Taipei 2002–. *Address:* The Grand Hotel, Sec. 4 Chung Shan North Road, Taipei, Taiwan (Office).

TSURUMI, Kazuko, PhD; Japanese professor of sociology; b. 10 June 1919, Tokyo; s. of Yusuke Tsurumi and Aiko Tsurumi; ed Peeresses' School, Tsuda Coll., Vassar Coll. and Princeton Univ.; Asst Prof. Univ. of British Columbia 1964–65, Seikei Univ. 1966–69; Prof. of Sociology and mem. Inst. of Int. Relations, Sophia Univ. 1969–89, Prof. Emer. 1989–; Visiting Prof. Univ. of Toronto 1973–74, Princeton Univ. 1976–77; Mainichi Publication-Culture Prize 1979, Tohata Prize (Nat. Inst. for Research and Achievement) 1990, Minakata Kumagusu Prize 1995, Asahi Prize 1999; Bobbs-Merrill Award 1964. *Publications:* Social Change and the Individual: Japan Before and After Defeat in World War II 1970, Itinerants and the Settled: Yanagita Kunio's Theory of Social Change 1977, Minakata Kumagusu: A Globe-oriented Comparativist 1979, A Theory of Endogenous Development (co-ed.) 1989, Collected Works (9 Vols) 1997–99. *Leisure interests:* Japanese Tanka poetry, Japanese theatrical dancing. *Address:* 14-1-7711, Nabekurayama Shira-kawa, Uji-shi, Kyoto-fu 611-0022, Japan. *Telephone:* (774) 28-1001 (Office); (774) 28-1744 (Home). *Fax:* (774) 21-1260 (Office).

TSURUMI, Shunsuke, BS; Japanese author; b. 25 June 1922, Tokyo; s. of Yusuke Tsurumi and Aiko Tsurumi; m. Sadako Yokoyama 1960; one s.; ed Harvard Coll.; f. The Science of Thought (philosophical journal) 1946; Asst Prof. Univ. of Kyoto 1949, Tokyo Inst. of Tech. 1954; Prof. Doshisha Univ. 1960; freelance author 1970–; Visiting Prof. El Colegio de México 1972–73, McGill Univ. 1979–80; Takano Chóei Prize 1976; Osaragi Jiro Prize 1982; Mystery Writers' Soc. Prize 1989, Asahi Prize 1994. *Publications:* Collected Works (5 Vols) 1974, An Intellectual History of Wartime Japan 1986, A History of Mass Culture in Postwar Japan 1987, Collected Works (12 Vols) 1992, Conversation (10 Vols) 1996, Further Collected Works (5 Vols) 2000. *Leisure interest:* reading. *Address:* 230-99 Nagatanicho, Iwakura, Sakyōku, Kyoto, Japan (Home).

TSUZUKI, Kunihiro; Japanese politician; mem. House of Councillors; Chair. House of Councillor's Cttee on Judicial Affairs and Cttee on Oversight of Admin.; Dir.-Gen. Man. and Co-ordination Agency 1999–2000. *Address:* c/o Management and Co-ordination Agency, 3-1-1, Kasumigaseki, Chiyoda-ku, Tokyo 100-0013, Japan (Office).

TSVANGIRAI, Morgan; Zimbabwean trade unionist and politician; b. 1952, Gutu, Masvingo; m. Susan Tsvangirai 1978; six c.; ed Silveria and Gokomere High Schools, Harvard Univ., USA; with Mutare Clothing Co. 1972–74; mem. local textile union; rose from plant operator to foreman Trojan Nickel Mine, Bindura 1974–84; mem. Associated Mine Workers' Union, apptd Br. Chair. 1984; fmr exec. mem. Nat. Mine Workers' Union; elected Sec.-Gen. Zimbabwe Congress of Trade Unions (ZCTU) 1988; charged with being a spy for SA, imprisoned for six weeks 1989; Founder and Chair. Nat. Constitutional Ass.; organized series of anti-Govt strikes against tax rises 1997; Founder and Pres. Movement for Democratic Change (MDC) 1999–; Parl. Opposition Leader 2000–; Presidential Cand. 2002; charged with treason Feb. 2002 for allegedly plotting the assassination of Pres. Robert Mugabe (q.v.), on trial Feb. 2003. *Leisure interests:* reading, spending time with the family. *Address:* Movement for Democratic Change, 127B Fife Avenue, Harare, Zimbabwe (Office). *E-mail:* mdc@africaonline.co.zw (Office). *Website:* www.in2zw.com/mdc (Office).

TSVETKOV, Aleksey, PhD; Russian poet and critic; b. 2 Feb. 1947, Stanislaw (now Ivano-Frankivsk), Ukraine; s. of Petr Tsvetkov and Bella Tsvetkov (née Tsyganov); m. Olga Samilenko 1978; ed Odessa and Moscow Univs, Univ. of Mich., USA; journalist in Siberia and Kazakhstan; poetry recitals and participant in Volgin's Moscow Univ. literary soc. Luch 1970–75; emigrated to USA 1974; co-of Russkaya zhizn', San Francisco 1976–77; Prof. of Russian Language and Literature, Dickinson Coll., Pa 1981–85; broadcaster, Voice of America; poetry has appeared in Kontinent, Ekho, Vremya i my, Apollon, Glagol and elsewhere; Dr hc (Univ. of Mich.) 1977. *Publications include:* A Collection of Pieces for Life Solo 1978, Three Poets: Kuzminsky, Tsvetkov, Limonov, 1981, Dream State 1981, Eden 1985, Simply Voice 1991. *Leisure interest:* collecting baroque opera records.

TU GUANGCHI, PhD; Chinese scientist; b. 14 Feb. 1920; ed Univ. of Minnesota; Deputy, 5th NPC 1978–83, 6th NPC 1983–87, 7th NPC 1988–; Pres. Soc. of Mineral-Rocks Geochem. 1980–; Dir Dept of Earth Sciences, Acad. Sinica 1981–; Dir Guiyang Inst. of Geochem. 1985–; Vice-Chair. People's Congress of Guizhou Prov. 1987–; mem. Nat. Acad. Degrees Cttee 1988. *Address:* Institute of Geochemistry, Guiyang City, Guizhou Province, People's Republic of China.

TUCCI, H.E. Cardinal Roberto; Italian ecclesiastic and broadcasting official; ordained priest; Gen. Man. and Pres. Vatican Radio Coordinating

Cttee; cr. Cardinal 2001. *Address:* Radio Vaticana, Palazzo Pio, Piazza Pia 3, 00193 Rome, Italy (Office). *Telephone:* (06) 69883551 (Office). *Fax:* (06) 69883237 (Office). *E-mail:* dirgen@vatiradio.va (Office). *Website:* www .radiovaticana.org (Office).

TUCKWELL, Barry Emmanuel, AC, OBE, FRCM, FRSA; Australian musician; b. 5 March 1931, Melbourne, Australia; s. of Charles Tuckwell and Elizabeth Hill; m. 1st Sally E. Newton 1958; one s. one d.; m. 2nd Hilary J. Warburton 1971; one s.; m. 3rd Susan T. Levitan 1992; ed Sydney Conservatorium; French horn player with Melbourne Symphony Orchestra 1947, Sydney Symphony Orchestra 1947–50, Hallé Orchestra 1951–53, Scottish Nat. Orchestra 1954–55, Bournemouth Symphony Orchestra, London Symphony Orchestra 1955–68; Horn Prof., RAM 1963–74; f. Tuckwell Wind Quintet 1968; int. soloist and recording artist; Conductor of Tasmanian Symphony Orchestra 1980–83; Music Dir and Conductor Md Symphony Orchestra 1982–98; Pres. Int. Horn Soc. 1969–76, 1993–95; Guest Conductor Northern Sinfonia 1993–; mem. Bd of Dirs., London Symphony Orchestra 1957–68, Chair. 1961–68; mem. Chamber Music Soc. of Lincoln Center 1974–81; Fellow Royal Coll. of Music, Royal Soc. of Arts; hon. degrees from RAM, Guildhall School of Music and Drama, Sydney Univ.; Harriet Cohen Int. Award for Solo Instruments 1968, George Peabody Medal for outstanding contribs to music in America. *Publications:* Playing the Horn, 50 1st Exercises 1978, The Horn (Yehudi Menuhin Music Guides) 1981, entire horn repertoire of G. Schirmer Inc. (Ed). *Address:* Gallo & Giordano, 76 West 86th Street, New York, NY 10024 (Office); 13140 Fountain Head Road, Hagerstown, MD 21742, USA.

TUENI, Ghassan, MA; Lebanese publishing executive; b. 5 Jan. 1926, Beirut; s. of Gebran Tueni and Adèle (née Salem) Tueni; m. 2nd Chadia El-Khazen; one s.; ed American Univ. of Beirut and Harvard Univ.; lecturer in Political Science, American Univ. of Beirut 1947–48; Ed.-in-Chief, An-Nahar (daily newspaper) 1948, Pres.; Man.-Dir An-Nahar Publishing Co. (now Dar an-Nahar SAL) 1963–; Co-founder Lebanese Acad. of Law and Political Science 1951, lecturer 1951–54; MP for Beirut 1953–57; mem. Lebanese del. to UN Gen. Ass. 1957; founded Middle East Business Services and Research Corpn 1958, Chair. 1958–70; founder, Chair. and Man.-Dir of Press Co-operative, SAL 1960–; Deputy Prime Minister and Minister of Information and Nat. Educ. 1970–71; arrested Dec. 1973, appeared before mil. tribunal and then released in accordance with press laws; Minister for Social Affairs and Labour, Tourism, Industry and Oil 1975–76; Perm. Rep. to UN 1977–82; Pres. Annahar Daily –2000; Pres. Dar Annahar Publishing 'Les Editions Dar an-Nahar' SAL 2000–; mem. Nat. Dialogue Cttee 1975. *Publications:* Peace-Keeping Lebanon 1979, Laissez vivre mon peuple 1984, Une guerre pour les autres 1985, El Bourj (Place de la liberté et porte du Levant) 2000; books and pamphlets in Arabic. *Address:* Dar an-Nahar SAL, PO Box 11-226, 36 Andraos str., Achrafieh, Beirut (Office); Ras Kafra, Beit Mery, Lebanon (Home). *Telephone:* (1) 444642 (Office). *Fax:* (1) 561877 (Office). *E-mail:* ghs@annahar .com.lb (Office).

TUGENDHAT, Baron (Life Peer), cr. 1993, of Widdington in the County of Essex; **Christopher Samuel Tugendhat,** Kt, MA; British company chairman, fmr international official and politician; b. 23 Feb. 1937, London; s. of late Dr. Georg Tugendhat; m. Julia Lissant Dobson 1967; two s.; ed Ampleforth Coll., Gonville and Caius Coll., Cambridge; Pres. Cambridge Union; Mil. Service, Commissioned in The Essex Regt 1955–57; Leader and Feature Writer, The Financial Times 1960–70; Consultant to Wood Mackenzie & Co. Ltd, stockbrokers 1968–77; Conservative MP for Cities of London and Westminster 1970–74, for City of London and Westminster South 1974–76; Dir Sunningdale Oils 1971–77, Phillips Petroleum Int. (UK) Ltd 1972–77, Nat. Westminster Bank PLC 1985–91 (Deputy Chair. 1990–91), BOC Group PLC 1985–96, Commercial Union PLC 1988–91, LWT (Holdings) PLC 1991–94; Dir (non-exec.), Eurotunnel PLC 1991–, Rio Tinto PLC; Chair. Civil Aviation Authority 1986–91, Abbey Nat. PLC 1991–2002, Blue Circle Industries PLC 1996–2001; Chair. (non-exec.) Lehman Brothers Europe 2002–; mem. Comm. of EEC with responsibility for Budget and Financial Control, Financial Institutions, Personnel and Admin. 1977–81, Vice-Pres. with responsibility for Budget and Financial Control, Financial Institutions and Taxation 1981–85; Chancellor Univ. of Bath 1998–; Chair. Royal Inst. of Int. Affairs (Chatham House) 1986–95; Gov. and mem. Council of Man., Ditchley Foundation; Patron and Vice-Pres. British Lung Foundation; Chair. Gonville & Gaius Devt Campaign Cttee, Cambridge Univ.; Hon. Fellow Gonville and Caius Coll., Cambridge; Hon. LLD (Bath Univ.) 1998, Hon. DLitt (UMIST) 2002; McKinsey Foundation Book Award 1971; Freeman City of London. *Publications:* Oil: the Biggest Business 1968, The Multinationals 1971, Making Sense of Europe 1986, Options for British Foreign Policy in the 1990s (with William Wallace) 1988; numerous articles. *Leisure interests:* reading, family, conversation. *Address:* 35 Westbourne Park Road, London, W2 5QD, England.

TUGWELL, Very Rev. Simon Charles ffoster, OP, STM, DD, STD; British ecclesiastic; b. 4 May 1943, Brighton; s. of Major Herbert Tugwell and Mary Brigit Tugwell (née Hutchinson); ed Lancing Coll. and Corpus Christi Coll. Oxford; received into Roman Catholic Church 1964; joined Dominican Order 1965; ordained priest 1971; lecturer and tutor, Blackfriars, Oxford 1972–92, Regent of Studies 1976–90; mem. Faculty of Theology, Oxford Univ. 1982–92; Fellow Istituto Storico Domenicano 1987– (Pres. 1992–97); Ed. Monumenta Ordinis Praedicatorum Historica 1992–; Visiting Lecturer, Pontifical Univ. of St Thomas, Rome 1977–93; Flannery Prof. of Theology, Gonzaga Univ.

Spokane 1982–83; Read-Tuckwell Lecturer on Human Immortality, Bristol Univ. 1988; Consultor to Congregation for Causes of Saints 1994–97; has lectured in many countries around the world. *Publications:* The Way of the Preacher 1979, Early Dominicans 1982, Ways of Imperfection 1984, Albert and Thomas 1988, The Apostolic Fathers 1989, Letters of Bede Jarrett (ed.) 1989, Human Immortality and the Redemption of Death 1990, Saint Dominic 1995, Miracula S. Dominici . . . Petri Calo legendae S. Dominici (ed.) 1997, Bernardi Guidonis: Scripta de Sancto Dominico (ed.) 1998; articles on aspects of theology and Dominican history, especially sources for the life of St Dominic. *Leisure interests:* music, science fiction, teddy bears, avoiding sightseeing. *Address:* Istituto Storico Domenicano, Largo Angelicum 1, 00184 Rome, Italy.

TUITA, Baron Siosaia Aleamotu'a Laufilitonga Tuita, CBE; Tongan government official and civil servant; b. 29 Aug. 1920, Lapaha, Tongatapu; s. of 'Isileli Tupou Tuita and Luseane Halaevalu Fotofili; m. Fatafehi Lapaha Tupou 1949; two s. two d.; ed Tupou Coll., Wesley Coll., Auckland, New Zealand, Oxford Univ.; Lt Officer, Tonga Defence Service 1942–43; Court Interpreter and Registrar, Supreme Court 1945; Asst Sec. Prime Minister's Office 1954; Acting Gov. of Vava'u 1956, Gov. 1957; Acting Minister of Lands 1962, of Police 1964–65; Chair. Niuafo'ou evacuation 1965; Minister of Lands and Survey and Minister of Health 1965; assumed title of Tuita 1972, conferred with title of Baron Tuita of 'Utungake 1980; Deputy Prime Minister and Minister of Lands, Survey and Natural Resources 1972–89; mem. Privy Council; Chair. Town Planning Cttee, Energy Standing Cttee, Royal Land Comm., Tonga Broadcasting Comm.; mem. numerous socs. *Leisure interests:* rugby, cricket, driving, fishing. *Address:* Mahinafekite, Nuku'alofa, Tonga (Home). *Telephone:* 22451 (Home).

TUIVAGA, Hon. Sir Timoci (Uluiburotu), Kt, BA; Fijian judge; b. 21 Oct. 1931; s. of Isimeili Siga Tuivaga and Jessie Hill; m. Vilimaina Leba Parrott Tuivaga 1958; three s. one d.; ed Univ. of Auckland, New Zealand; native magistrate 1958–61, called to the Bar, Gray's Inn 1964, NSW 1968; Crown Counsel 1965–68, Prin. Legal Officer 1968–70, Puisne Judge 1972, Acting Chief Justice 1974, Chief Justice of Fiji 1980–87, 1988–; Acting Gov.-Gen. 1983–87. *Leisure interests:* golf, gardening. *Address:* 228 Ratu Sukuna Road, Suva, Fiji. *Telephone:* 301-782.

TULEYEV, Aman Gumirovich (Amangeldy Moldagazyevich), DPolSc; Russian politician; b. 13 May 1944, Krasnovodsk, Turkmenistan; m.; two s.; ed Tikhoretsk Railway Tech. School, Novosibirsk Inst. of Railway Eng, Acad. of Social Sciences at Cen. Cttee CPSU; worked on railway station Kemerovo Region, head Mezhdurechensk Railway Station, Head Novokuznetsk Dept Kemerovo Railway 1978–88; Head Div. of Transport and Communications Regional Cttee CPSU 1988–90; Chair, Kemerovo Regional Soviet 1991; Peoples' Deputy of Russian Fed. 1990–93; Cand. for Presidency 1991, 1996, 2000; supported coup d'état attempt 1991; mem. CP of Russian Fed. 1993; Chair. Legis. Ass. Kemerovo Region 1994–96; Minister of Co-operation with CIS 1996–97; Gov. Kemerovo Region 1997–; mem. Council of Fed. 1993–95, 1997–2001. *Address:* Office of the Governor, Sovetsky prosp. 62, 650099 Kemerovo, Russia (Office). *Telephone:* (3842) 36-34-09 (Office). *Fax:* (3842) 36-48-33. *Website:* www.kemerovo.su.

TULIN, Dmitri Vladislavovich, MBA, PhD; Russian economist; b. 26 March 1956; s. of the late Vladislav Tulin and of Emma S. Tulin; m. Vera Nerod 1977; two s.; ed Moscow Financial Inst. and USSR Inst. of Econs and Finance; economist, Int. Monetary and Econ. Dept USSR State Bank (Gosbank) 1978, Sr Economist 1980, Chief Economist 1985, Man. 1989, Man. Dir, mem. Bd Securities Dept 1990; Deputy Chair. Russian Fed. Bank 1991–94; Exec. Dir for Russian Fed. IMF 1994–96; Chair. Bd Vneshtorgbank (Bank for Foreign Trade) 1996–98; Sr Adviser EBRD 1999–. *Publications:* articles on monetary econs and banking in Russian professional journals. *Leisure interests:* gardening, chess. *Address:* European Bank for Reconstruction and Development, 1 Exchange Square, 175 Bishopsgate, London, EC2A 2EH, England (Office). *Telephone:* (20) 7338-6000 (Office).

TULLY, Daniel Patrick; American finance executive; b. 2 Jan. 1932, New York; m. Grace Tully; four c.; ed St John's Univ. New York and Harvard Business School; army service 1953–55; joined Merrill Lynch & Co. Inc. 1955; Account Exec. Stamford Office 1959, Man. 1970, Vice-Pres. 1971; Individual Sales Dir New York HQ 1976; mem. Bd Dirs. Merrill Lynch, Pierce, Fenner & Smith 1977, Chair. and CEO 1985; Exec. Vice-Pres. Marketing 1979; Pres. Individual Services Group 1982 and Exec. Vice-Pres. Merrill Lynch & Co. Inc. 1982, Pres. and COO 1985–92, Chair. Bd and CEO 1992–96, Chair., CEO, Pres. 1993–97, now Chair. Emer.; Vice-Chair. American Stock Exchange 1984–86, Securities Industry Asscn 1985–86; Dir New York Stock Exchange. *Address:* Merrill Lynch & Co. Inc., 301 Tresser Boulevard, 12th Floor, Stamford, CT 06901, USA (Office).

TULLY, Sir (William) Mark, KBE, MA; British journalist; b. 24 Oct. 1935, Calcutta, India; s. of William S. C. Tully and Patience T. Tully; m. Frances M. Butler 1960; two s. two d.; ed Marlborough Coll., Trinity Hall, Cambridge; Regional Dir Abbeyfield Soc. 1960–64; Personnel Officer BBC 1964–65, Asst Rep. then Rep. (a.i.), BBC, Delhi 1965–69, Hindi Programme Organizer BBC External Services, London 1969–70, Chief Talks Writer 1970–71, Chief of Bureau BBC, Delhi 1971–93, BBC South Asia Corresp. 1993–94; now freelance writer, broadcaster, journalist 1994–; Hon. Fellow Trinity Hall, Cambridge 1994; Hon. DLitt (Strathclyde) 1997; Dimbleby Award (BAFTA) 1984, Padma Shri (India) 1992 etc. *Publications:* Amritsar Mrs Gandhi's Last Battle (jtly) 1985, Raj to Rajiv (jtly) 1988, No Full Stops in India 1991, The Heart of India 1995, The Lives of Jesus 1996, India in Slow Motion (with Gillian Wright) 2002. *Leisure interests:* bird watching, reading, railways, theology. *Address:* 1 Nizamuddin East, Delhi 110013, India (Office). *Telephone:* (11) 4352878. *Fax:* (11) 4359687. *E-mail:* tulwri@ndf.vsnl.net.in (Office).

TŮMA, Zdeněk, CSc, MCom; Czech banker; b. 19 Oct 1960, České Budějovice; m.; two s. one d.; ed School of Econs, Prague; researcher Inst. for Forecasting, Prague 1986–90; teacher School of Econs, Prague, Faculty of Social Sciences Charles Univ., Prague 1990–98; Adviser to Minister of Trade and Industry 1993–95; Chief Economist Patria Finance 1995–98; Exec. Dir EBRD 1998–99; Vice-Gov. Czech Nat. Bank 1999–2000, Gov. 2000–; Pres. Czech Econ. Soc. 1999–2001. *Publications:* articles and chapters on econ. transition. *Leisure interests:* skiing, squash, tennis, cycling. *Address:* Czech National Bank, Na Příkopě 28, Prague 1, 11503, Czech Republic (Office). *Telephone:* (2) 24412001 (Office). *Fax:* (2) 24412150 (Office). *E-mail:* governor@cnb.cz (Office). *Website:* www.cnb.cz (Office).

TUMANOV, Vladimir Aleksandrovich, DJur; Russian lawyer; b. 20 Oct. 1926, Kropotkin, Krasnodar Dist; s. of Aleksandr Tumanov and Serafima Tumanov; m. 1948; one s.; ed Inst. of Foreign Trade, USSR Ministry of Foreign Trade, All-Union Inst. of Law; Scientific Researcher All-Union Inst. of Law 1952–59; Chief Scientific Researcher, Head of Comparative Law Dept, Inst. of State and Law USSR (now Russian) Acad. of Sciences; Pres. Int. Asscn of Legal Science at UNESCO (resgnd); mem. State Duma (Russian Parl.) 1993–94; mem. Constitutional Court of Russian Fed. 1994–, Chair. 1995–97, Adviser 1997–; mem. European Court of Human Rights 1997–, Acad. of Comparative Rights; Pres. Int. Asscn of Legal Sciences; Chair. Council on Problems of Improving Legal System, Admin. of Russian Pres. 2000–. *Publications include:* Force-majeure in Civil Law 1958, Constitutional Law of Foreign Countries (Vols 1, 2) 1987–88, Legal Nihilism and Prospects of the Rule of Law 1991, Constitution of the Russian Federation of 1993 (an encyclopaedic guide) 1994. *Leisure interests:* canoeing, travel. *Address:* 13th Parkovaya str. 25, Korp. 1, Apt. 40, 105215 Moscow, Russia (Home). *Telephone:* (095) 206-18-39 (Home).

TUMI, HE Cardinal Christian Wiyghan; Cameroonian ecclesiastic; b. 15 Oct. 1930, Kikaikelaki; ordained 1966, elected to Yagoua 1979, consecrated Bishop 1980, Coadjutor Bishop 1982, Diocesan Bishop 1984; now Archbishop of Douala; cr. Cardinal 1988. *Address:* Archevêché, B.P. 179, Douala, Cameroon. *Telephone:* 423714. *Fax:* 421837. *E-mail:* christiantumi@camnet.com (Office).

TUMIM, Sir Stephen, Kt, MA; British judge; b. 15 Aug. 1930, London; s. of Joseph Tumim and Renee Tumim; m. Winifred Borthwick 1962; three d.; ed St Edward's School, Oxford, Worcester Coll., Oxford; called to the Bar 1955; Co. Court Judge 1978; HM Chief Insp. of Prisons in England and Wales 1987–95; Prin. St Edmund's Hall, Oxford 1996–98; Bencher Middle Temple 1990; Pres. Royal Literary Fund 1990–; Chair. Arthur Koestler Trust 1993–; Chair. Bryan Shaw Art School, London 2000–02; Dr hc (N London) 2001. *Publications:* Great Legal Disasters 1983, Great Legal Fiascos 1985, Crime and Punishment 1997. *Leisure interests:* books and pictures. *Address:* 8 Stafford Place, London, SW1E 6NP, England (Home). *Telephone:* (20) 7931-0047 (Home). *Fax:* (20) 7233-8635.

TUNE, Tommy (Thomas James), BFA; American theatrical performer, director and choreographer; b. 28 Feb. 1939, Witchita Falls, Tex.; s. of Jim Tune and Eva Tune; ed Lamar High School, Houston, Lon Morris Junior Coll., Univ. of Tex. at Austin and Univ. of Houston; began professional career as chorus dancer on Broadway 1963; appeared in films Hello, Dolly! and The Boyfriend; appeared on Broadway in Seesaw (Tony Award, Best Supporting Actor); Off-Broadway Dir The Club, Cloud 9 (Obie and Drama Desk Awards), Stepping Out 1987; Choreographer, A Day in Hollywood/A Night in the Ukraine (Tony Award); Dir The Best Little Whorehouse in Texas, Nine (Tony Award 1982); actor and choreographer, My One and Only (Tony Award 1983), Grand Hotel 1989 (London 1992), The Will Rogers Follies, Bye, Bye Birdie 1991–92; recipient of many other awards. *Leisure interests:* cooking, yoga, reading, drawing. *Address:* c/o International Creative Management, 40 W 57th Street, New York, NY 10019; Tommy Tune Inc., 50 East 89th Street, New York, NY 10128, USA (Office). *Telephone:* (212) 719-2166.

TUNG CHEE-HWA, BSc; Hong Kong business executive and politician; b. 29 May 1937, Shanghai; m. Betty Chiu Hung Ping 1961; two s. one d.; ed Univ. of Liverpool; with Gen. Electric, USA; Chair. Island Navigation Corpn Ltd, fmr Chair. Orient Overseas (Holdings) Ltd; Dir Sing Tao Newspapers Ltd, Sun Hung Kai Bank Ltd, Hsin Chong Properties Ltd, Mass Transit Railway Corpn; Vice-Chair. Preparatory Cttee for Hong Kong Special Admin. Region; mem. Exec. Council, Hong Kong Govt 1992–96; Chief Exec. of Hong Kong Special Admin. Region 1997–; mem. 8th NPC 1993–; numerous civic appointments etc.; Hon. Consul of Monaco in Hong Kong 1982–96. *Leisure interests:* reading, hiking, watching sport, Tai Chi, swimming. *Address:* Office of the Chief Executive, 5/F Main Wing, Central Government Offices, Lower Albert Road, Hong Kong Special Administrative Region, People's Republic of China. *Telephone:* 28783300. *Fax:* 25090577.

TUNLEY, David Evatt, AM, DLitt, MMus, FAHA; Australian professor of music; b. 3 May 1930, Sydney; s. of Dr. Leslie Tunley and Dr. Marjorie Tunley; m. Paula Patricia Laurantus 1959; one s. two d.; ed The Scots Coll., Sydney, State Conservatorium of Music, Sydney; music master, Fort Street Boys' High School, Sydney 1952–57; joined staff of Dept of Music, Univ. of Western Australia 1958, Personal Chair. of Music 1980–, now Emer., Head Dept of Music 1985–90, Hon. Sr Research Fellow in Music 1994–; studied under Nadia Boulanger with French Govt Scholarship 1964–65; Scholar-in-residence, Rockefeller Foundation, Bellagio, Italy 1987; Fowler Hamilton Visiting Research Fellow, Christ Church, Oxford 1993; Visiting Scholar, Wolfson Coll. Oxford 1996; Founder/Conductor Univ. Collegium Musicum, 1976–83; Founder/Chair. York Winter Music Festival, 1982–; Founder/Dir The Terrace Proms, Perth; Nat. Pres. Musicological Soc. of Australia 1980–81; Chair. Music Bd, Australia Council 1984–85; Hon. DMus (Western Australia); Chevalier Ordre des Palmes Académiques. *Compositions include:* Concerto for Clarinet and Strings 1966 (revised 2000), A Wedding Masque 1970, Immortal Fire 1999. *Publications:* The 18th-Century French Cantata 1974, Couperin 1982, Harmony in Action 1984, The French Cantata in Facsimile, 17 Vols 1990, Romantic French Song in Facsimile (6 Vols) 1994, The Bel Canto Violin: the life and times of Alfredo Campoli 1906–1991 1999, Salons, Singers and Songs: A Background to Romantic French Song 1830–70 2002; contribs to the New Grove Dictionary of Music and Musicians, The New Oxford History of Music. *Leisure interests:* reading, travel, theatre. *Address:* Department of Music, University of Western Australia, Nedlands 6009, Western Australia (Office); 100 Dalkeith Road, Nedlands 6009, Western Australia, Australia (Home). *Telephone:* (8) 9386-1934 (Home). *E-mail:* dtunley@cyllene.uwa.edu .au (Home).

TUNNEY, John V., BA, LLB; American politician; b. 26 June 1934, New York City; s. of Gene Tunney and Mary Lauder Tunney; m. 2nd Kathinka Osborne 1977; two s. two d.; ed Westminster School, Simsbury, Conn., Yale Univ., Univ. of Virginia School of Law and Acad. of Int. Law, The Hague; practised law, New York City 1959–60, Riverside 1963–; Judge Advocate, US Air Force 1960–63; taught Business Law at Univ. of Calif., Riverside; mem. US House of Reps 1964–70; Senator from California 1971–77; mem. Manatt, Phelps, Rothenberg and Tunney, LA 1977–86; Chair., Bd of Dirs Cloverleaf Group Inc., LA 1986–; Enterprise Plan Inc., Trusted Brands Inc.; Gen. Partner Sun Valley Ventures 1994–; Democrat. *Leisure interests:* tennis, sailing, skiing, handball. *Address:* 1819 Ocean Ave, Santa Monica, CA 90401, USA.

TUOMIOJA, Erkki, MBA, Dr rer. pol; Finnish politician; b. 1 July 1946, Helsinki; s. of Sakari Tuomioja and Vappu Wuolijoki; m. Marja-Helena Rajala 1979; MP 1970–79, 1991–; Deputy Mayor of Helsinki 1979–91; Minister of Trade and Industry 1999–2000, for Foreign Affairs 2000–. *Publications:* 18 books on history, politics and int. affairs. *Leisure interests:* history, literature, running. *Address:* Ministry of Foreign Affairs, Merikasarmi, P.O. Box 176, 00161 Helsinki, Finland (Office). *Website:* www.tuomioja.org (Office).

TURABI, Hassan Al-; Sudanese politician; Leader Nat. Islamic Front (NIF) 1986–; established Popular Arab Islamic Conference (PAIC) in Khartoum 1990–; Pres. Nat. Ass. 1996–2000; Sec.-Gen. Nat. Congress; arrested and imprisoned 2001. *Address:* National Islamic Front, Khartoum, Sudan.

TURAJONZODA, Haji Akbar; Tajikistan ecclesiastic and politician; b. 16 Feb. 1954, Kafarnikhon; s. of Ishan-e Tourajon; two s., four d.; ed Tashkent Islam Inst., Amman Univ., Jordan, Mir-e Arab School, Bukhara; teacher Tashkent Islam Inst. 1987–88; Head of Office of Kasiat of Tajikistan 1988–; elected mem. Supreme Soviet Tajik SSR, active participant in democratic movt against Islamic fundamentalists; forced to emigrate, in hiding 1993; First Deputy Chair. Islamic Renaissance Movt of Tajikistan 1993–; headed United Tajik Opposition in negotiations with the Govt leading to peace settlement 1995–97; First Deputy Prime Minister of Tajikistan 1998–; Ismael Somoni Medal of Honour, World Islamic Centre Prize for Peace 1999. *Publication:* Between Water and Fire: The Peace Plan. *Leisure interests:* reading, sports. *Address:* House of Government, Rudaki prospect 42, 734051 Dushanbe, Tajikistan (Office). *Telephone:* (2) 216524 (Office); (2) 211506 (Home); (2) 215956; (2) 212557. *Fax:* (2) 212547 (Office); (2) 212547 (Home). *E-mail:* pakhta@tojikiston.com (Home).

TURBAY AYALA, Julio César; Colombian diplomatist and politician; b. 18 June 1916, Bogotá; m.; one s. three d.; mem. House of Reps. 1943–53; Minister of Mines and Energy 1957–58, of Foreign Affairs 1958–61; Senator 1962–70; twice elected Vice-Pres. of Colombia; Pres. of Colombia 1978–82; Perm. Rep. to UN 1967; Amb. to UK 1970, to USA 1974–76, fmr Amb. to Holy See; Hon. LLD (Univ. Cauca) 1957. *Address:* c/o Ministry of Foreign Affairs, Palacio de San Carlos, Calle 10A, No 5-51, Santa Fe de Bogotá DC, Colombia (Office).

TURECK, Rosalyn; American concert artist, conductor and professor; b. 14 Dec. 1914, Chicago; d. of Samuel Tureck and Monya Lipson; m. George Wallingford Downs 1964; ed Juilliard School of Music, New York; debut in Chicago 1924; first New York appearance 1932; concert tours in USA and Canada 1937–, Europe 1947–, S. Africa 1959, S. America 1963, Israel 1963, World Tour (Far East and India) 1971, Europe, Israel, S. America, N American Bach Festivals 1985/86; repeated appearances at maj. int. festivals; specializes in the keyboard works of J. S. Bach, played on the piano, harpsichord, clavichord, organ, antique and electronic instruments; conductor 1956–; conductor-soloist, London Philharmonic 1958, New York Philharmonic 1958, Israel Philharmonic 1963, Kol Israel Orchestra 1963, Int. Bach Soc. Orchestra 1967, 1968, 1970, Madrid Chamber Orchestra 1972, Washington Nat. Symphony 1972, Tureck Bach Players (Carnegie Hall) 1981, Bach Triennial Celebration Series (solo recitals and orchestral concerts conducting Tureck Bach Players), Carnegie Hall 1984/85, soloist, Casals Festival 1991; Visiting Prof. of Music, Washington Univ., St Louis 1963–64;

Prof. of Music, Univ. of Calif., San Diego 1966–72, Regents Lecturer 1966; Visiting Prof., Univ. of Md 1982–84, Yale Univ. 1992; Regents Prof. UCLA 1995–; lecturer numerous univs and colls of music, including Univ. of Winnipeg, Canada, Southern Methodist Univ., Dallas, Tex. 1989, Brandeis and Yale Univs, Menéndez Pelayo Inst., Univ. of Santander, Spain 1990; Visiting Fellow, St Hilda's Coll., Oxford 1974, Hon. Life Fellow 1974–; Visiting Fellow, Wolfson Coll., Oxford 1975–; Founder-Dir of Composers of Today 1951–55, Tureck Bach Players 1957, Int. Bach Soc. 1966 (now Tureck Bach Inst.), Int. Bach Soc. Orchestra 1967, Inst. for Bach Studies 1968, Tureck Bach Research Foundation 1994; mem. many musical socs; Hon. DMus, (Colby Coll. 1964, Roosevelt Univ. 1968, Wilson Coll. 1968, Oxford Univ. 1977, etc.); First Prize, Greater Chicago Piano Playing Tournament 1928, Winner Schubert Memorial Contest, Nat. Fed. of Music Clubs 1935; Officer's Cross of Order of Merit, Fed. Repub. of Germany 1979. *Recordings:* The Well-tempered Clavier (Books I and II), Goldberg Variations, Six Partitas, Italian Concerto, French Overture, Introduction to Bach, A Bach Recital, A Harpsichord Recital, Goldberg Variations and Aria and Ten Variations in the Italian Style (harpsichord), Italian Concerto, Chromatic Fantasia and Fugue, Four Duets (piano), Rosalyn Tureck Plays Bach (Live at the Teatro Colón, Buenos Aires) 1992, Live in St Petersburg (5 Vols) 1995. *Films:* Fantasy and Fugue: Rosalyn Tureck plays Bach 1972, Rosalyn Tureck plays Bach on Harpsichord and Organ 1977, Joy of Bach (Rosalyn Tureck Soloist and Consultant) 1979, Bach on the Frontier of The Future 1980, Rosalyn Tureck Plays Bach in Ephesus, Turkey 1985, Rosalyn Tureck plays Bach, Live at the Teatro Colón, Buenos Aires 1992, Live in St Petersburg 1995. *Publications:* An Introduction to the Performance of Bach (3 Vols) 1959–60 (trans. into Japanese 1966, Spanish 1972), A Critical and Performance Edition of J. S. Bach's Chromatic Fantasia and Fugue; numerous articles in various periodicals; Editor: Paganini, Niccolo—Perpetuum Mobile 1950, J. S. Bach—Sarabande, C Minor 1960, Scarlatti, Alessandro—Sarabande and Gavotte; Ed. Tureck Bach Urtext Series, Publr Italian Concerto 1983, Lute Suite, E Minor 1984, Lute Suite C Minor 1985, Authenticity 1994. *Address:* c/o Askonas Holt Ltd, Lonsdale Chambers, 27 Chancery Lane, London WC2A 1PF, England (Office); Hotel El Paradiso, Ctra Cádiz, Km. 167, Apdo 134, 29680 Marbella, Spain. *Telephone:* (952) 883000.

TÜRK, Danilo, PhD; Slovenian diplomatist and lawyer; b. 19 Feb. 1952, Maribor; m.; one d.; ed Ljubljana and Belgrade Univs; Lecturer in Public Int. Law, Univ. of Ljubljana 1978–88, Prof. of Int. Law 1988–, Head Inst. of Int. Law and Int. Relations 1983–95; mem. UN Subcomm. on Prevention of Discrimination and Protection of Minorities 1984–92; Special Rapporteur 1989–92, Chair. 1990; Perm. Rep. of Slovenia to the UN 1992–2000; mem. UN Security Council 1998–99, Pres. Aug. 1998, Nov. 1999; mem. Security Council Mission to Jakarta and E. Timor, Indonesia Sept. 1999, Asst Sec.-Gen. of UN for Political Affairs 2000–; active in the field of human rights with several NGOs; Chair. Int. Law Asscn, Slovenia 1990–. *Publications:* book on the principle of non-intervention in int. relations and int. law and over 100 articles in legal journals and other pubs. *Address:* United Nations, Room 3327A, New York, NY 10017, USA (Office). *Telephone:* (212) 963-9606 (Office). *Fax:* (212) 963-9297 (Office). *E-mail:* turk@un.org (Office).

TURKI, Abdul Aziz Al-Abdullah Al-, BA; Saudi Arabian oil official; b. 12 Aug. 1936, Jeddah; m.; two d.; ed Univ. of Cairo; U.S. Embassy, Jeddah 1953–54; ARAMCO 1954–66; Dir Office of Minister of Petroleum and Mineral Resources 1966–68; Dir of Gen. Affairs, Directorate of Mineral Resources 1968–70; Asst Sec.-Gen. OAPEC 1970–75, Sec.-Gen. 1990–; Sec.-Gen. Supreme Advisory Council for Petroleum and Mineral Affairs, Saudi Arabia 1975–90; Saudi Gov. for OPEC 1975–90; Deputy Minister, Ministry of Petroleum and Mineral Resources 1975–; Chair. Arab Maritime Petroleum Transport Co., Kuwait 1981–87, Pemref 1982–89; mem. Bd of Dirs. Petromin 1975–89, ARAMCO 1980–89. *Leisure interests:* tennis, swimming. *Address:* Organization of Arab Petroleum Exporting Countries, P.O. Box 20501, Safat 13066, Kuwait. *Telephone:* 4844500. *Fax:* 4815747. *E-mail:* oapec@qualitynet.net (Office). *Website:* www.oapecorg.org (Office).

TÜRKMEN, Ilter; Turkish politician and diplomatist; b. 1927, Istanbul; s. of Behçet Türkmen and Nuriye Türkmen; m. Mina Türkmen 1953; one s. one d.; ed Galatasaray Lycée, Istanbul, Faculty of Political Sciences, Ankara; Dir-Gen. of Policy Planning Dept, Ministry of Foreign Affairs 1964, Asst Sec.-Gen. for Political Affairs 1967; Amb. to Greece 1968, to USSR 1972, to France 1988–90; Perm. Rep. to UN in New York 1975–78, 1985–88, in Geneva 1983–85; Special Rep. to UN Sec.-Gen. for Human Affairs in South East Asia 1979–80; Minister of Foreign Affairs 1980–83; fmr Commr-Gen. UNRWA. *Address:* c/o Ministry of Foreign Affairs, Dişişleri Bakanligi, Yeni Hizmet Binasi, 06520 Balgat, Ankara, Turkey.

TURLINGTON, Christy; American fashion model; b. 2 Jan. 1969, Walnut Creek, Calif.; d. of Dwain Turlington and Elizabeth Turlington; discovered at age 14; with Ford Models Inc. 1985; model for Calvin Klein 1986; model for Revlon, Maybelline 1993; face of Calvin Klein's Eternity Fragrance 1988–; promotes advertisement campaigns for Michael Kors, Camay Soap, Special K Cereal. *Film:* Catwalk 1996; appeared in George Michael's video Freedom. *Address:* United Talent Agency, 9560 Wilshire Boulevard, Suite 500, Beverly Hills, CA 90212 (Office); 344 East 59th Street, New York, NY 10022, U.S.A. (Office).

TURNAGE, Mark-Anthony; British composer; b. 10 June 1960, Corringham, Essex; s. of Roy Turnage and Patricia Knowles; m. 1st Susan Shaw

1989 (divorced 1990); m. 2nd Helen Reed 1992; two s.; ed Hassenbrook Comprehensive School, Palmers Sixth Form, Grays and Royal Coll. of Music (RCM); studied composition at RCM with Oliver Knussen and John Lambert; Mendelssohn scholarship to study with Gunther Schuller and Hans Werner Henze in Tanglewood, USA 1983; first opera, Greek, premiered at first Munich Biennale 1988; Composer in Asscn with City of Birmingham Symphony Orchestra (CBSO), composing three maj. works 1989–93; Composer in Asscn with ENO 1995–99; Assoc. Composer in asscn. with BBC Symphony Orchestra 2000–. *Works include:* Night Dances 1980–81, On All Fours 1985, Greek 1986–88, Three Screaming Popes 1988–89, Some Days 1989, Drowned Out 1992–93, Your Rockaby 1992–93, Blood on the Floor 1994–95, Dispelling the Fears 1995, Twice Through the Heart 1997, Country of the Blind 1997, Four-Horned Fandango 1997, The Silver Tassie 1997–99, Silent Cities 1998, About Time 1999, Fractured Lines 2000, Another Set To 2000, Bass Inventions 2001, Dark Crossing 2001, A Quick Blast 2001. *Leisure interests:* football, films, theatre. *Address:* c/o Van Walsum Management Ltd., 4 Addison Bridge Place, London, W14 8XP, England. *Telephone:* (20) 7371-4343. *Fax:* (20) 7371-4344. *E-mail:* vwm@vanwalsum.co.uk (Office). *Website:* www.vanwalsum.co.uk (Office).

TURNBERG, Baron (Life Peer), cr. 2000, of Cheadle in the County of Cheshire; **Leslie Arnold Turnberg,** Kt, MB, ChB, MD, FRCP, FMedSci; British professor of medicine; b. 22 March 1934, Manchester; s. of Hyman Turnberg and Dora Bloomfield; m. Edna Barme 1968; one s. one d.; ed Stand Grammar School, Whitefield and Univ. of Manchester; Lecturer, then Sr Lecturer in Gastroenterology, Univ. of Manchester, Manchester Royal Infirmary 1968–73; Prof. of Medicine Univ. of Manchester 1973–97, Dean Faculty of Medicine 1986–89; Hon. Consultant Physician, Hope Hosp. 1973–97; Pres. Royal Coll. of Physicians 1992–97, Asscn of Physicians of GB and Ireland 1996–97; Chair. Conf. of Medical Royal Colls. 1993–95, Strategic Review of London's Health Services 1997; Pres. Medical Protection Soc. 1997–, Medical Council on Alcoholism 1997–2002; Chair. Bd of Public Health Lab. Service 1997–2002; Scientific Adviser Asscn of Medical Research Charities 1997–; Pres. British Soc. of Gastroenterology 1999–2000; Chair. Bd of Health Quality Service 2000–; Chair. UK Forum on Genetics and Insurance 2000–02; Vice-Pres. Acad. of Medical Sciences 1998–; Hon. FRCP (Edin.), FRCP (Glasgow), FRCPI, FRCOG; Hon. Fellow Royal Colls. of Ophthalmologists, Psychiatrists, Surgeons of England; Hon. Fellow Royal Australian Coll. of Physicians, S. African Coll. of Medicine, Pakistan Coll. of Physicians, Acad. of Medicine of Hong Kong and of Singapore and several others; Hon. DSc (Salford) 1996, (Manchester) 1998, (Imperial Coll. London) 2000. *Publications:* Intestinal Secretion 1982, Mechanisms of Mucosal Protection in the Upper Gastro-Intestinal Tract 1983, Clinical Gastroenterology 1989. *Leisure interests:* reading, antiquarian books, walking, talking, Chinese ceramics. *Address:* House of Lords, Westminster, London, SW1A 0PW, England. *Telephone:* (20) 7435-8223. *Fax:* (20) 7435-9262 (Office).

TURNBULL, Sir Andrew, KCB, CVO; British civil servant; b. 21 Jan. 1945, Enfield; s. of Anthony Turnbull and Mary Turnbull; m. Diane Clarke 1967; two s.; ed Enfield Grammar School, Christ's Coll., Cambridge; Overseas Devt Inst. Fellow working as economist to Govt of Zambia 1968–70; Asst Principal HM Treasury 1970, Prin. 1972, seconded to IMF 1976–78, Asst Sec. 1978, Head of Gen. Expenditure Policy Group 1985–88, Deputy Sec. (Public Finance) 1992, Second Perm. Sec. 1993–94; Pvt. Sec. to Prime Minister 1983–85, Under Sec. 1985, Prin. Pvt. Sec. to Prime Minister 1988–92; Perm. Sec. Dept of Environment 1994–97, Dept of Environment, Transport and the Regions 1997–98, HM Treasury 1998–2002, Cabinet Sec. Sept. 2002–. *Leisure interests:* walking, opera, golf, sailing. *Address:* Cabinet Office, 70 Whitehall, London, SW1A 2AS, England (Office).

TURNBULL, Charles Wesley, PhD; American governor and educationalist; b. 1935, St. Thomas, US Virgin Islands; s. of John W. Turnbull and Ruth Ann Turnbull; ed Charlotte Amalie High School, Hampton Univ. and Univ. of Minn.; elementary school teacher, secondary teacher, Asst Prin., High School Prin.; Prof. of History and Trustee Univ. of the VI; Asst Commr of Educ., Commr Dept of Educ., est. Cultural Educational Div., Chair. VI Bd Educ.; Gov. of US VI 1998–; mem. Territorial Cttee VI Democratic Party; served on all four Constitutional conventions of VI; mem. Bd Roy Lester Schneider Hosp. *Address:* Office of the Governor, Government House, 21–22 Kongens Gade, Charlotte Amalie, United States Virgin Islands 00802 (Office). *Telephone:* (340) 774-0001 (Office). *Fax:* (340) 774-1361 (Office). *E-mail:* rcanton@govhouse.gov.vi (Office).

TURNBULL, Malcolm Bligh, BA, LLB, BCL; Australian banker and lawyer; b. 24 Oct. 1954, Sydney; s. of Bruce B. Turnbull and Coral Lansbury; m. Lucinda M. F. Hughes 1980; one s. one d.; ed Sydney Grammar School, Univ. of Sydney and Univ. of Oxford (Rhodes Scholar); State Parl. Corresp. for Nation Review 1976; journalist, The Bulletin 1977–78; Exec. Asst to Chair. Consolidated Press Holdings Ltd 1978; journalist, The Sunday Times, London 1978–79; barrister, Sydney 1980–82; Gen. Counsel and Sec. Consolidated Press Holdings Ltd 1983–85; solicitor in pvt. practice, Turnbull McWilliam, Sydney 1986–87; Prin. Turnbull and Co. (Solicitors) 1987; Man. Dir Turnbull & Partners Pty Ltd (Investment Bankers), Sydney 1987–97, 2002–; Chair. Axiom Forest Resources Ltd (HK) 1991–92; Dir Perseverance Corpn Ltd 1993–94, Star Mining Corpn NL 1993–95, FTR Holdings Ltd; Chair. Oz Email Ltd 1995–99; Dir Australian Republican Movt 1991–, Chair. 1993–; Chair. Cttee to advise on changing Australia to Repub.; Chair., Man. Dir Goldman Sachs Australia 1997–; Partner Goldman Sachs (US) 1998–2001; Chair.

Menzies Research Centre 2002–; Fed. Hon. Treas. Liberal Party 2001–; Henry Lawson Prize for Poetry 1975. *Publications:* The Spycatcher Trial 1988, The Reluctant Republic 1993, Fighting for the Republic 1999. *Leisure interests:* reading, walking, riding, gardening. *Address:* Turnbull & Partners Pty Ltd, GPO Box 4298, Sydney, NSW 2001, Australia (Office).

TURNBULL, Rt Rev Michael, MA, DIP.THEOL.; British ecclesiastic; b. 27 Dec. 1935, Yorks.; s. of George Turnbull and Adeline Awty; m. Brenda Merchant 1963; one s. two d.; ed Ilkley Grammar School, Keble Coll. Oxford and St John's Coll. Durham; ordained deacon 1960, priest 1961; curate, Middleton 1960–61, Luton 1961–65; Domestic Chaplain to Archbishop of York 1965–69; Rector of Heslington and Chaplain, York Univ. 1969–76; Chief Sec. Church Army 1976–84; Archdeacon of Rochester 1984–88; Bishop of Rochester 1988–94, of Durham 1994–2003; Hon. Asst Bishop, Diocese of Canterbury 2003–; mem. Gen. Synod of Church of England 1970–75, 1987–2003; mem. Archbishops' Council 1999–2001, Chair. Ministry Div. 1999–2001; Chair. Archbishops' Comm. on Org. of Church of England; Hon. DLitt 1994, Hon. DD 2003. *Publications:* Unity: the Next Step? (contrib.) 1972, God's Front Line 1979, Parish Evangelism 1980, Learning to Pray 1981; numerous articles in journals. *Leisure interests:* cricket, family life. *Address:* 67 Strand Street, Sandwich, Kent, CT13 9HN, England. *Telephone:* (1304) 611389.

TURNBULL, William; British sculptor, painter and print-maker; b. 11 Jan. 1922, Dundee, Scotland; m. Cheng Kim Lim 1960; two s.; ed Slade School of Fine Art, London; has participated in numerous group exhbns. around the world since 1950; works in public collections in UK, USA, Australia and Germany. *One-man exhibitions:* London, New York, San Francisco, Berlin, Stuttgart, Latin America, Toronto, Luxembourg, Singapore etc. since 1950 including IX Bienal, São Paulo and tour of S. American countries (sculpture and painting) 1967, Hayward Gallery, London (painting) 1968, Tate Gallery Retrospective (sculpture and painting) 1973 and exhbns at Waddington Galleries, London 1967, 1969, 1970, 1976, 1978, 1981, 1985, 1987, 1991, 1998, 2001, Serpentine Gallery 1995. *Leisure interests:* reading, music. *Address:* c/o Waddington Galleries, 11 Cork Street, London, W1S 3LT, England.

TURNER, George William, MA, FAHA; Australian reader in English (retd); b. 26 Oct. 1921, Dannevirke, NZ; s. of Albert George Turner and Elinor Jessie Turner; m. Beryl Constance Barbara Horrobin 1949; two s.; ed Univ. of NZ, Univ. Coll. London and NZ Library School; secondary school teacher, NZ 1944–46; Dip. NZ Library School; librarian, Christchurch 1949–54; English Dept, Univ. of Canterbury 1955–64; Reader in English, Univ. of Adelaide, Australia 1965–86. *Publications:* The English Language in Australia and New Zealand 1966, Stylistics 1973, The Australian Pocket Oxford Dictionary (Ed.) 1984, The Australian Concise Oxford Dictionary (Ed.) 1987, The Australian Oxford Paperback Dictionary (Ed. with Beryl C. B. Turner) 1989, The Annotated Such Is Life (with others) 1991. *Leisure interests:* lexicography, reading, walking. *Address:* 3 Marola Avenue, Rostrevor, South Australia 5073, Australia. *Telephone:* (8) 8337-2257.

TURNER, Grenville, DPhil, FRS; British professor of isotope geochemistry; b. 1 Nov. 1936, Todmorden; s. of Arnold Turner and Florence Turner; m. Kathleen Morris 1961; one s. one d.; ed St John's Coll., Cambridge and Balliol Coll., Oxford; Asst Prof., Univ. of Calif., Berkeley 1962–64; Lecturer, Sheffield Univ. 1964–74, Sr Lecturer 1974–79, Reader 1979–80, Prof. of Physics 1980–88; Prof. of Isotope Geochem., Manchester Univ. 1988–2002, Research Prof. 2002–; Visiting Assoc. in Nuclear Geophysics, Calif. Inst. of Tech. 1970–71; Council mem. Royal Soc. 1990–92; Fellow Meteoritical Soc. 1980, Geochemical Soc. and European Asscn of Geochem. 1996, American Geophysical Union 1998; Rumford Medal, Royal Soc. 1996, Leonard Medal, Meteoritical Soc. 1999, Urey Medal European Asscn of Geochemists 2002. *Achievements:* developed Ar-Ar method for rock dating, used it to determine first ages of Apollo lunar samples. *Publications:* scientific papers on the application of naturally occurring isotopes to earth science and the evolution of the solar system. *Leisure interests:* photography, walking, theatre. *Address:* Department of Earth Sciences, University of Manchester, Manchester, M13 9PL (Office); 42 Edgehill Road, Sheffield, S7 1SP, England (Home). *Telephone:* (161) 275-3800 (Office). *Fax:* (161) 275-3947 (Office); (161) 275-3947. *E-mail:* grenville.turner@man.ac.uk (Office).

TURNER, Rt Hon John Napier, PC, CC, QC, MA, BCL; Canadian politician and lawyer; b. 7 June 1929, Richmond, Surrey, England; s. of Leonard Turner and Phyllis Turner (née Gregory); m. Geills McCrae Kilgour 1963; three s. one d.; ed schools in Ottawa and Univs. of British Columbia, Oxford and Paris; MP 1962–76, 1984–93; Minister without Portfolio 1965; Registrar-Gen. 1967–68; Minister of Consumer and Corp. Affairs Jan.–July 1968; Solicitor-Gen. April–July 1968; Minister of Justice and Attorney-Gen. 1968–72; Minister of Finance 1972–75; Leader Liberal Party of Canada 1984–90; Prime Minister of Canada June–Sept. 1984, Leader of Opposition 1984–90; Partner, McMillan, Binch (law firm), Toronto 1976–84; Partner, Miller Thomson (law firm), Toronto 1990–; mem. Bd Dirs Purolator Courier Ltd. *Publications:* The Senate of Canada 1961, Politics of Purpose 1968. *Leisure interests:* tennis, canoeing, skiing. *Address:* Miller Thomson, 20 Queen Street West, Box 27, Suite 2500, Toronto, Ont., M5H 3S1 (Office); 59 Oriole Road, Toronto, Ont., M4V 2E9, Canada (Home). *Telephone:* (416) 595-8500 (Office). *Fax:* (416) 595-8695 (Office). *E-mail:* jturner@millerthomson.ca (Office).

TURNER, (Jonathan) Adair, MA; British business executive and political adviser; b. 5 Oct. 1955; s. of Geoffrey Vincent Turner and Kathleen Margaret Turner; m. Orna Ni Chionna 1985; two d.; ed Hutcheson's Grammar School, Glasgow, Glenalmond School and Gonville & Caius Coll. Cambridge; Pres. Cambridge Union; began career with BP (British Petroleum) PLC 1979; with Chase Manhattan Bank 1979–82; McKinsey & Co. 1982–95, Dir 1994–95; Dir-Gen. CBI 1995–99; Vice-Chair. Merrill Lynch Europe 2000–; Dir (non-exec.) United News and Media 2000–, Netscalibur Ltd 2000–01; Chair. (non-exec.) Group.Trade.com 2000; mem. British Overseas Trade Bd 1995–99; Visiting Prof. LSE 1999–; Chair. Policy Cttee, Centre for Econ. Performance 1999–; Chair. Low Pay Comm. 2002–; Chair. Ind. Pension Comm. 2003–; Strategic Adviser to British Prime Minister 2001–02; mem. Council of Man. of Nat. Inst.of Econ. and Social Renewal 2002–; Trustee Worldwide Fund for Nature 2002–. *Publication:* Just Capital: The Liberal Economy 2001. *Leisure interests:* skiing, opera, theatre, gardening. *Address:* Merrill Lynch Europe, 2 King Edward Street, London, EC1A 1HQ, England (Office).

TURNER, Kathleen, BFA; American actress; b. 19 June 1954, Springfield, Mo.; m. Jay Weiss 1984; one d.; ed Cen. School of Speech and Drama, London, SW Missouri State Univ., Univ. of Maryland; various theatre roles including Broadway debut, Gemini 1978, The Graduate, London 2000. *Television series include:* The Doctors 1977, Style and Substance 1996. *Films include:* Body Heat 1981, The Man With Two Brains 1983, Crimes of Passion 1984, Romancing the Stone 1984, Prizzi's Honour 1985, The Jewel of the Nile 1985, Peggy Sue Got Married 1986, Julia and Julia 1988, Switching Channels 1988, The Accidental Tourist 1989, The War of the Roses 1990, V.I. Warzhawski 1991, House of Cards, Undercover Blues 1993, Serial Mom 1994, Naked in New York 1994, Moonlight and Valentino, A Simple Wish, The Real Blonde, The Virgin Suicides 1999, Prince of Central Park 1999, Love and Action in Chicago 1999, Baby Geniuses 1999, Beautiful 2000, The Man Who Cried 2001; producer Hard Boiled 1990. *Address:* c/o Chris Andrews, ICM, 8942 Wilshire Boulevard, Beverly Hills, CA 90211, USA.

TURNER, Michael, CBE, BA, ACIS, FRAeS; British aerospace industry executive; b. 1948; m.; four c.; ed Didsbury Technical High School, Manchester and Manchester Polytechnic; joined Hawker Siddeley Aviation as undergrad. commercial apprentice 1966, later Contracts Officer; Contracts Man. (Mil.) British Aerospace (BAe) Aircraft Group, Manchester Div. 1978, Admin. Man. 1980, Exec. Dir of Admin. 1981, Divisional Admin. Dir 1982 (led Advanced Turboprop Project Team 1982–84), Divisional Dir and Gen. Man., Kingston 1984, Dir Divisional Man. Cttee and Gen. Man. Mil. Aircraft Div. 1986, Dir Marketing and Product Support, Mil. Aircraft Div. 1987, Exec. Vice-Pres. Defence Marketing British Aerospace PLC 1988; Chair. and Man. Dir British Aerospace Regional Aircraft Ltd and Chair. Jetstream Aircraft 1992; Chair. Commercial Aerospace 1994 (mem. Main Bd British Aerospace PLC), assumed responsibility for all BAe's defence export business 1996, mem. Airbus Supervisory Bd (renamed AIC) 1998, mem. Shareholders' Cttee AIC, COO BAe Systems (following merger of British Aerospace PLC and Marconi Electronic Systems) 1999, CEO March 2002–; Vice-Pres. Soc. of British Aerospace Cos. 1995, Pres. 1996–97; Dir (non-exec.) Babcock Int. Group PLC 1996–. *Leisure interests:* Manchester United Football Club, golf, cricket, rugby. *Address:* BAe Systems, 6 Carlton Gardens, London, SW1Y 5AD (Office); BAe Systems, Farnborough, Hampshire, GU14 6YU, England (Office). *Telephone:* (1252) 373232 (Office). *Fax:* (1252) 383991 (Office); (1252) 383000 (Office). *Website:* www.baesystems.com (Office).

TURNER, Adm. Stansfield, MA; American naval officer (retd), lecturer and author; b. 1 Dec. 1923, Chicago, Ill.; s. of Oliver Stansfield Turner and Wilhelmina Josephine (née Wagner) Turner; m. Eli Karin Gilbert 1985 (died 2000); m. Marion Weiss Sept. 2002; ed Amherst Coll., US Naval Acad., Annapolis, Oxford Univ., UK; Rhodes Scholar, Oxford Univ. 1947; active duty, US Navy, serving minesweeper, destroyers, USS Horne (guided missile cruiser in action in Vietnamese conflict); served in Office of Chief of Naval Operations, then in Office of Asst Sec. of Defence for Systems Analysis; Advanced Man. Program, Harvard Business School; Exec. Asst and Naval Aide to Sec. of the Navy 1968–70; Rear Admiral 1970; CO Carrier Task Group in USS Independence, US Sixth Fleet 1970; Dir Systems Analysis Div. of Office of Chief of Naval Operations, Dept of the Navy 1971–72; Vice-Adm. 1972; Pres. US Naval War Coll., Newport, RI 1972–74; Commdr US Second Fleet and NATO Striking Fleet Atlantic 1974–75; Admiral 1975; C-in-C Allied Forces Southern Europe, NATO 1975–77; Dir Cen. Intelligence (CIA) 1977–81; Sr Research Scholar, Center for Int. and Security Studies, Univ. of Maryland 1991–; Hon. Fellow, Exeter Coll., Oxford 1981–; Nat. Security Medal, Legion of Merit, Bronze Star. *Publications:* Secrecy and Democracy: The CIA in Transition 1985, Terrorism and Democracy 1991, Caging the Nuclear Genie: An American Challenge for Global Security 1997, Caging the Genies: A Workable Plan for Nuclear, Chemical and Biological Weapons 1998. *Leisure interests:* tennis, reading. *Address:* 600 New Hampshire Avenue, N.W., 8th Floor, Washington, DC 20037, USA (Office). *Telephone:* (202) 266-5441 (Office). *Fax:* (202) 266-5429 (Office). *E-mail:* admturner@aol.com (Office).

TURNER, Ted (Robert Edward, III); American broadcasting executive and yachtsman; b. 19 Nov. 1938; s. of Robert Turner and Frances Rooney; m. 1st Judy Nye (divorced); one s. one d.; m. 2nd Jane S. Smith 1965 (divorced 1988); one s. two d.; m. 3rd Jane Fonda (q.v.) 1991 (separated 1999); ed Brown Univ.; Gen. Man. Turner Advertising, Macon, Ga 1960–63; Pres. and CEO various Turner cos., Atlanta 1963–70; Chair. Bd and Pres. Turner Broadcasting System, Inc. (merged with Time Warner to form Time Warner Inc.) 1970–96; Vice-Chair. Time Warner Inc. 1996–2003; Pres. Atlanta Braves

1976– and now owner; Chair. Bd Atlanta Hawks 1977–, Better World Soc., Wash. 1985–90; f. and Chair. UN Foundation; Dir Martin Luther King Center, Atlanta; acquired New Line Cinema Corpn 1993; sponsor, creator, The Goodwill Games, Moscow 1986; winner 1977 America's Cup in yacht Courageous; named Yachtsman of Year four times; U Thant Peace Award 1999, numerous other awards. *Publication:* The Racing Edge 1979. *Leisure interests:* fishing, sailing. *Address:* Turner Broadcasting System Inc., One CNN Center, Box 105366, Atlanta, GA 30348, USA.

TURNER, Tina (Annie Mae Bullock); American singer; b. 26 Nov. 1939, Brownsville, Tenn.; m. Ike Turner 1956 (divorced 1978); four s.; singer with Ike Turner Kings of Rhythm, Ike and Tina Turner Revue; concert tours of Europe 1966, 1983–84, Japan and Africa 1971; Grammy Award 1972, 1985 (three), 1986; Chevalier des Arts et des Lettres. *Films:* Gimme Shelter 1970, Soul to Soul 1971, Tommy 1975, Mad Max Beyond Thunderdome 1985, What's Love Got to Do with It (vocals) 1993, Last Action Hero 1993. *Recordings include:* River Deep, Mountain High 1966, Proud Mary 1970, Blues Roots 1972, Nutbush City Limits 1973, The Gospel According to Ike and Tina 1974; solo albums: Let Me Touch Your Mind 1972, Tina Turns the Country On 1974, Acid Queen 1975, Rough 1978, Private Dancer 1984, Break Every Rule 1986, Foreign Affair 1989, Simply the Best 1991, The Collected Recordings: Sixties to Nineties (with others) 1994, Wildest Dreams 1996. *Publication:* I, Tina (autobiog.) 1985 (filmed as What's Love Got to Do with It? 1993). *Address:* c/o CAA, 9830 Wilshire Boulevard, Beverly Hills, CA 90212, USA.

TURNER, William Cochrane, BS; American diplomatist and business executive; b. 27 May 1929, Red Oak, Iowa; s. of James Lyman Turner and Josephine Cochrane Turner; m. Cynthia Dunbar 1955; two s.; ed Northwestern Univ.; Vice-Pres. and Dir, Western Man. Consultants Inc. 1955–60, Pres., CEO and Dir 1960–74, Chair. and Dir Western Man. Consultants Europe SA 1969–74; Dir Ryan-Evans Drug Stores Inc. 1964–68, First Nat. Bank of Arizona 1970–74; Trustee Thunderbird American Graduate School of Int. Man. 1972–, Vice-Chair. 1972–86, Chair. 1986–88; mem. Advisory Cttee for Trade Negotiations 1982–84; Amb. and US Rep. to OECD 1974–77; mem. US Advisory Comm. on Int. Educ. and Cultural Affairs 1969–74, Nat. Review Bd, Center for Cultural and Tech. Interchange between East and West 1970–74, Western Int. Trade Group, US Dept of Commerce 1972–74; Pres. and Dir Phoenix Symphony Asscn 1957–72; Gov. Atlantic Inst. for Int. Affairs, Paris 1977–88, Joseph H. Lauder Inst. of Man. and Int. Studies, Univ. of Pa 1983–2001; Chair. and CEO Argyle Atlantic Corpn 1977–, Avon Int. Advisory Council, Avon Products Inc. 1985–98, Int. Advisory Council, Plasma Tech. Inc. 1992–97; Chair Bd GO Wireless Int. Ltd 1995–97; Chair. European Advisory Council, Asia Pacific Advisory Council, AT&T Int. 1981–88; Dir Pullman Inc. 1977–80, Nabisco Brands Inc. 1977–85, Goodyear Tire and Rubber Co. 1978–2001, Salomon Inc. 1980–93, Energy Transition Corpn (also Vice-Chair.) 1979–86, The Atlantic Council of the US 1977–92, AT&T Int. 1980–84, Swensen's Inc. 1981–84, Atlantic Inst. Foundation Inc. 1984–90, Rural/Metro Corpn 1993–, Microtest Inc. 1995–2001; mem. IBM European Advisory Council 1977–80, Gen. Electric of Brazil Advisory Council 1979–81, Caterpillar of Brazil Advisory Council 1979–84, American Asia Pacific Advisory Council 1981–85, Caterpillar Tractor Co. Asia Pacific Advisory Council 1984–90, Spencer Stuart Advisory Council 1984–90; mem. European Community-US Business Council, Washington, DC 1978–79, Advisory Bd Center for Strategic and Int. Studies, Georgetown Univ. 1978–81, Nat. Councils, The Salk Inst. 1978–82, Council of American Ambs. 1984–, Council on Foreign Relations 1980–2002, US-Japan Business Council 1987–93, Nat. Advisory Council on Business Educ., Council on Int. Educ. Exchange, New York City 1987–2000, Trade and Environment Cttee Nat. Advisory Council for Environmental Policy and Tech., US Environmental Protection Agency, Washington, DC 1991–95, Gov.'s Strategic Partnership for Econ. Devt, Phoenix 1992–95; Chair. and mem. ASM Int. Advisory Council, Advanced Semi-conductor Materials Int. NV, Bilthoven 1985-88; Trustee and mem. Exec. Cttee, US Council for Int. Business 1977–, Heard Museum, Phoenix 1983–85 (mem. Nat. Advisory Bd 1985–93); Nat. Trustee, Nat. Symphony Orchestra Asscn 1973–84; mem. Bd of Govs. American Hosp. of Paris 1974–77, Bd of Trustees, American School of Paris, St-Cloud 1975–77, Vestry, American Cathedral, Paris 1976–77, Greater Phoenix Leadership 1979–97; Co-Chair. Int. Advisory Bd, Univ. of Nations 1985–; Dir and fmr Founding Chair. Bd of Dirs Mercy Ships Int., A Ministry of Youth with a Mission, Lindale, Tex. 1986–2000; Dir Ariz. Econ. Council, Phoenix 1989–93, mem. Nat. Council, World Wildlife Fund and The Conservation Foundation, Washington, DC 1989–95; f. mem. Pacific Council on Int. Policy 1995–; Chair. and Dir WorldWideTalk Inc. 1999–; Chair. Advisory Bd Arris Ventures 2001–, One Touch 2002–, Significant Ventures Inc. 2002–; Hon. LLD (Thunderbird American Grad. School of Int. Man.) 1993, East-West Center Distinguished Service Award 1977. *Leisure interests:* tennis, fly fishing, opera, symphonic and chamber music, international political and economic relations. *Address:* 5434 East Lincoln Drive, No. 74, Paradise Valley, AZ 85253, USA. *Telephone:* (480) 998-1890. *Fax:* (480) 948-4674. *E-mail:* wct-aac@mindspring.com (Office).

TURNER-WARWICK, Dame Margaret, DBE, BCh, MA, DM, PhD, FRCP, FMedSci, FRCPE, FRACP, FFPHM, FACP, FRSM; British consultant physician; b. 19 Nov. 1924, London; d. of William Harvey Moore, QC and Maude Baden-Powell; m. Richard Turner-Warwick 1950; two d.; ed Maynard School, Exeter, St Paul's School for Girls, Univ. of Oxford and Univ. Coll. Hosp.; consultant physician, Royal Brompton Hosp., London Chest Hosp. 1965–72; Prof. of Medicine, Cardiothoracic Inst. 1972–87, Dean 1984–87; Pres. Royal Coll. of Physicians 1989–92; Emer. Prof. of Medicine, London Univ.; Chair. Royal Devon & Exeter Health Care NHS Trust; Fellow Univ. Coll. London 1991; Hon. Bencher, Middle Temple; Fellow Royal Coll. of General Practitioners, Faculty of Occupational Medicine, Royal Coll. of Physicians Canada, Royal Coll. of Pathologists, Royal Coll. of Physicians Ireland, Royal Coll. of Physicians and Surgeons (Canada) and others; Founder mem. Nuffield Bioethics Council, Round Table on Sustainable Devt; Hon. Fellow Lady Margaret Hall, Oxford, Green Coll., Oxford, Girton Coll., Cambridge, Imperial Coll., London, Univ. Coll., London; Hon. DSc (New York, Sussex, Hull, Exeter, London, Oxford, Cambridge, Leicester) and numerous other honours, including Osler Medal (Oxford Univ.) and President's Medal (British Thoracic Soc. & European Respiratory Soc.). *Publications:* Immunology of the Lung 1978, Occupational Lung Disease (jtly) 1981; chapters in textbooks and articles in medical journals on asthma, fibrosing connective tissue disorders and occupational lung diseases. *Leisure interests:* gardening, water-colour painting, violin playing, country life and family. *Address:* Pynes House, Thorverton, Exeter, EX5 5LT, Devon, England. *Telephone:* (1392) 861173. *Fax:* (1392) 860940.

TURNQUEST, Sir Orville (Alton), GCMG, QC, LLB, JP; Bahamian politician, lawyer and judge; b. 19 July 1929, Grants Town, New Providence; s. of the late Robert Turnquest and Gwendolyn Turnquest; m. Edith Louise Thompson 1955; one s. two d.; ed Govt High School, Univ. of London, Lincoln's Inn, London; articled in chambers of Hon. AF Adderley 1947–53; called to The Bahamas Bar 1953, to English Bar (Lincoln's Inn) 1960; Counsel and Attorney of Supreme Court of Bahamas; Notary Public; in pvt. practice 1953–92; stipendiary and circuit magistrate and coroner 1959; law tutor and mem. Examining Bd, The Bahamas Bar 1965–92; Pres-Bahamas Bar Asscn; Chair. Bahamas Bar Council 1970–72; Sec.-Gen. Progressive Liberal Party 1960–62; MP for S. Cen. Nassau 1962–67, for Montagu 1982–94; Opposition Leader in Senate 1972–79; Deputy Leader Free Nat. Movt 1987–94; Attorney-Gen. 1992–94, Minister of Justice 1992–93, of Foreign Affairs 1992–94, Deputy Prime Minister 1993–94; Gov.-Gen. The Bahamas 1995–2001; mem. Del. to first Bahamas Constitutional Conf., London 1963, Bahamas Independence Conf., London 1972; Pres. Commonwealth Parl. Asscn 1992–93; Patron The Bahamas Games; Chancellor of Diocese of Nassau and The Bahamas 1965–2002; mem. Anglican Cen. Educational Authority, Nat. Cttee of United World Colls , Bd of Govs St John's Coll., St Anne's High School; fmr mem. Prov. Synod, Anglican Church of West Indies; Life mem. Rotary Int., Salvation Army Advisory Bd; Hon. LLD (Elmira Coll. NY, USA) 1998, (Univ. of West Indies) 2000; Hon. LHD (Sojourner-Douglass Coll., USA) 2002; Hon. Bencher, Lincoln's Inn; President's Assocs (Nova Southeastern Univ. Fla USA). *Leisure interests:* tennis, swimming, music, reading. *Address:* Librery House, Dowdeswell Street, POB N-8181, Nassau, Bahamas (Office); Kalamalka, Skyline Drive, POB N-682, Nassau, Bahamas (Home). *Telephone:* (242) 3232942 (Office); (242) 3277951 (Home). *Fax:* (242) 3282222 (Office); (242) 3274994 (Home). *E-mail:* oatchambers@batelnet.bs (Office).

TUROW, Scott F., JD; American author and lawyer; b. 12 April 1949; s. of David Turow and Rita Pastron; m. Annette Weisberg 1971; three c.; ed Amherst Coll. and Stanford and Harvard Univs.; mem. Bar, Ill. 1978, US Dist Court. Ill. 1978, US Court of Appeals (7th Circuit) 1979; Assoc. Suffolk Co. Dist Attorney, Boston 1977–78; Asst US Attorney, US Dist Court, Ill., Chicago 1978–86; partner Sonnenschein, Nath & Rosenthal, Chicago 1986–; mem. Chicago Council of Lawyers. *Publications:* One L.: An Inside Account of Life in the First Year at Harvard Law School 1977, Presumed Innocent 1987, The Burden of Proof 1990, Pleading Guilty 1993, The Laws of our Fathers 1996, Personal Injuries 1999, Reversible Errors 2002; contribs to professional journals. *Address:* Sonnenschein, Nath & Rosenthal, Sears Tower, Suite 8000, 233 S. Wacker Drive, Chicago, IL 60606, USA.

TURRO, Nicholas John, PhD; American professor of chemistry; b. 18 May 1938, Middletown, Conn.; s. of Nicholas J. Turro and Philomena Russo; m. Sandra J. Misenti 1960; two d.; ed Wesleyan Univ. and California Inst. of Tech.; Instr. Columbia Univ. 1964–65, Asst Prof. 1965–67, Assoc. Prof. 1967–69, Prof. of Chem. 1969–82, William P. Schweitzer Prof. of Chem. 1982–, Chair. Dept of Chem. 1981–84, Co-Chair. Dept of Chemical Eng and Applied Chem. 1997–; Prof. of Earth and Environment Eng 1998–; Sloan Fellowship 1966–70; Guggenheim Fellowship, Univ. of Oxford 1984; mem. NAS, American Acad. of Arts and Sciences; Fellow, New York Acad. of Science; several awards and distinctions including Gibbs Medal Award 2000; Hon. DSc (Wesleyan Univ.) 1984. *Publications:* Molecular Photochemistry 1965, Modern Molecular Photochemistry 1978. *Leisure interests:* racquet ball, music, reading. *Address:* Department of Chemistry, Columbia University, 3000 Broadway, New York, NY 10027 (Office); 125 Downey Drive, Tenafly, NJ 07670, USA (Home).

TURTURRO, John; American actor; b. 28 Feb. 1957, Brooklyn; s. of Nicholas Turturro and Katherine Turturro; m. Katherine Borowitz; one s.; ed State Univ. of New York at New Paltz and Yale Drama School; fmr labourer; Best Actor Award, Cannes Film Festival, for role in Barton Fink 1991; Obie Award for stage appearance in Danny and the Deep Blue Sea. *Films include:* Raging Bull, Desperately Seeking Susan, Exterminator III, The Flamingo Kid, To Live and Die in LA, Hannah and Her Sisters, Gung Ho, Offbeat, The Color of Money, The Italian Five Corners, Do the Right Thing, Miller's Crossing, Men of Respect, Mo' Better Blues, Jungle Fever, Barton Fink, Brain Doctors, Mac (co-author, dir and actor), Being Human, Quiz Show, Fearless, Clockers, Search and Destroy, Unstrung Heroes, Sugartime (dir), Grace of My Heart (dir), Box of Moonlight (dir), The Truce (dir), The Big Lebowski 1997, Animals

1997, Lesser Prophets 1998, Rounders 1998, Illuminata (dir) 1998, The Source 1999, The Cradle Will Rock 1999, Company Man 1999, Two Thousand and None 1999, Oh Brother, Where Art Thou? 1999, The Man Who Cried 1999, The Luzhin Defense 1999, Thirteen Conversations About One Thing (dir) 2000, Collateral Damage (dir) 2001, Mr Deeds 2002, Secret Passage 2002, Fear X 2003, Anger Management 2003. *Address:* c/o ICM, 40 West 57th Street, New York, NY 10019; 16 North Oak Street, 2A Ventura, CA 93001, USA.

TUSA, John, MA; British broadcaster and administrator; b. 2 March 1936, Zlín, Czechoslovakia (now Czech Repub.); s. of Jan Tusa and Lydie Sklenarova; m. Ann Hilary Dowson 1960; two s.; ed Gresham's School, Holt, Trinity Coll., Cambridge; joined BBC as general trainee 1960; Producer, Talks and Features, BBC World Service 1964–66; Ed., Forum World Features 1966–67; Presenter, The World Tonight, Radio 4 1970–78, 24 Hours, BBC World Service 1972–76, Newsweek, BBC2 1978–79, Newsnight, BBC2 1979–86, Timewatch, BBC2 1982–84, One O'Clock News BBC 1993–95; Chair. London News Radio 1993–94; Pres. Wolfson Coll., Cambridge Feb.–Oct. 1993; Man. Dir BBC World Service 1986–92; Man. Dir Barbican Centre 1995–; Chair. Advisory Cttee, Govt Art Collection 1993, BBC Marshall Plan of the Mind Trust 1992–99; mem. Bd English Nat. Opera 1994–; Freeman City of London 1997; Trustee Nat. Portrait Gallery 1988–2000, Design Museum 1998–2000, British Museum 2000–; Chair. Wigmore Hall Trust, 1999–; Visiting Prof., Dept of Arts Policy and Man., City Univ.; Hon. mem. Royal Acad. of Music 1999, Guildhall School of Music and Drama 1999; Dr. hc (Heriot Watt) 1993; Hon. LLD (London) 1993; Hon. DLitt (City Univ.) 1997; Royal TV Soc. TV Journalist of the Year 1984, BAFTA Richard Dimbleby Award 1984, Broadcasting Press Guild Award 1991, RTS Presenter of the Year 1995, Broadcasting Press Guild Radio Programme of the Year (for "20/20—A View of the Century") 1995, Order of the White Rose (Finland) 1998. *Publications:* The Nuremberg Trial 1983 (with Ann Tusa), The Berlin Blockade (with Ann Tusa) 1988, Conversations with the World 1990, A World in Your Ear 1992, Art Matters 1999, On Creativity 2003. *Leisure interests:* tennis, string quartets, listening. *Address:* Barbican Centre, Silk Street, London, EC2Y 8DS (Office); 16 Canonbury Place, London, N1 2NN, England. *Telephone:* (20) 7382-7001 (Office). *Fax:* (20) 7382-7245 (Office); (20) 7704-2451.

TUSK, Donald Franciszek; Polish politician; b. 22 April 1957, Gdańsk; m.; one s. one d.; ed Gdańsk Univ.; journalist Maritime Publishing House, with magazines Pomerania and Samorządność; with Gdańsk Height Services Work Co-operative; ed. Gazeta Gdańska 1990; mem. Liquidation Cttee RSW Press-Books-Ruch; assoc. Free Trade Unions by the Coast; co.-f. Independent Students Union (NZS); mem. Solidarity Trade Union 1980–; Founder and Ed. underground Publ Przegląd Polityczny; Leader Programme Council for Liberals Foundation; Leader Congress of Liberals 1989, later the Liberal-Democratic Congress (KLD), Chair. 1991–94; Vice-Chair. Freedom Union (UW) 1994 following the merger with Democratic Union (UD); Deputy to Sejm (Parl.) 1991–93, 2001–, Deputy Marshal of Sejm 2001–, mem. Civic Platform Parl. Caucus 2001–; Chair. Parl. Liberal-Democratic Caucus and Special Cttee for Consideration of Constitutional Acts 1991–93; Senator and Vice-Marshal of Senate 1997–2001; Co-Founder Civic Platform 2001–. *Publications:* Kashubian Lake District 1985, Once There Was Gdańsk 1996, Gdańsk 1945, 1998, Old Sopot 1998, Ideas of Gdańsk's Liberalism 1998. *Leisure interests:* football, old photography. *Address:* Sejm RP, ul. Wiejska 4/6/8, 00-902 Warsaw, Poland. *Telephone:* (22) 6942500. *Fax:* (22) 6942252.

TUSQUETS BLANCA, Oscar; Spanish architect and designer; b. 14 June 1941, Barcelona; m. Victoria Roqué; one с.; ed Arts & Crafts School, Barcelona, School of Architecture, Barcelona; with Luis Clotet, Studio Per 1964–84; co-founder BD Ediciones de Diseño 1972; Prof., School of Architecture, Barcelona 1975–76, 1979–80; f. Tusquets, Diaz & Assoc. Architects' Office, with Carlos Diaz 1987; FAD Architecture Prize (five times); FAD Design prize (six times), Sant Jordi Cross 1987, Ciutat de Barcelona Prize 1988, 1989, Nat. Prize for Design 1988, Fukuoka Beautification Award 1994, Medalla de Oro 1998; Chevalier des Arts et des Lettres. *Work includes:* Casa Fullá, Barcelona, Belvedere Regas, Girona, Casa Vittoria, Sala Mae West, Dali Museum, Figueras, re-modelling of Music Palace, Barcelona, Pavilion, Parc de la Villette, Paris, Chandon Vinery, Barcelona, dwellings in Kashii, Fukuoka and in Olympic Village, Barcelona, La Coupole, Montpellier, music auditorium, Canary Islands, public square, shopping mall and dwellings, Den Bosch, Netherlands; design of furniture and objects for various producers, bus stop for Hanover, Germany. *Leisure interest:* painting. *Address:* Tusquets, Diaz & Assoc., Cavallers 50, 08034 Barcelona, Spain (Office). *Telephone:* (93) 2065580 (Office). *Fax:* (93) 2804071 (Office). *E-mail:* tusquets@tda.es (Office).

TUTT, Leo Edward, FCA, FAIM, FCPA; Australian business executive; b. 6 April 1938, Sydney; s. of Leo Edward Tutt and Dorothy Tutt; m. Heather Coombe 1961; two s. one d.; ed Knox Grammar School, Univ. of Sydney and Inst. of Chartered Accountants, Australia; CA 1966–71; Man. Dir Tutt Bryant Ltd 1971–74; CEO Bowater Industries Australia Ltd 1974–96; Chair. Royal and Sun Alliance Insurance Australia Ltd 1994–, MIM Holdings Ltd (Australia) 1998– (Dir 1991–), Pirelli Cables Australia Ltd 1999–, ITG Ltd 2001–; Dir Rexam PLC (fmrly Bowater PLC) 1978–96, Friends Provident 1984–94, Grad. School of Man., Univ. of Sydney 1989–, Australian Grad. School of Man. 1999–, State Rail Authority of NSW (Australia) 1989–94, Metway Bank Ltd (Australia) 1992–96, Crane Group Ltd 2001–; Hon. Fellow Univ. of Sydney 1996. *Leisure interests:* sailing, golf, reading. *Address:* 58 Prince Alfred Parade, Newport, NSW 2106, Australia 2106. *Telephone:* (2) 9221-1966 (Office); (2) 9979-5744 (Home). *Fax:* (2) 9235-2585 (Office); (2) 9997-3119 (Home). *E-mail:* letutt@mim.com.au (Office).

TUTU, Most Rev. Desmond Mpilo, MTh; South African ecclesiastic (retd); b. 7 Oct. 1931, Klerksdorp; s. of Zachariah Tutu and Aletta Tutu; m. Leah Nomalizo Tutu 1955; one s. three d.; ed Bantu High School, Bantu Normal Coll., Univ. of South Africa, St Peter's Theological Coll., Rosettenville, King's Coll., Univ. of London; schoolmaster 1954–57; parish priest 1960–; Theological Seminary Lecturer 1967–69; Univ. Lecturer 1970–71; Assoc. Dir Theological Educ. Fund, World Council of Churches 1972–75; Dean of Johannesburg 1975–76; Bishop of Lesotho 1977–78, of Johannesburg 1984–86; Archbishop of Cape Town, Metropolitan of the Church of the Prov. of Southern Africa 1986–95, Archbishop Emer. 1995–; Chancellor Univ. of Western Cape 1988–; Chair. Truth and Reconciliation Comm. 1995–99; Pres. All Africa Conf. of Churches 1987–97; Sec.-Gen. South African Council of Churches 1979–84; Visiting Prof. of Anglican Studies New York Gen. Theological Seminary 1984; elected to Harvard Univ. Bd of Overseers 1989; Dir Coca-Cola 1986–; Visiting Prof. Emory Univ., Atlanta 1998–2000; mem. Third Order of the Soc. of St Francis; Hon. DD, DCL, LLD, ThD (Gen. Theol. Sem. New York, Kent Univ., Harvard Univ., Ruhr Bochum Univ.); Hon. DDiv (Aberdeen) 1981; Hon. STD (Columbia) 1982; Dr hc (Mount Allison Univ., Sackville, NB, Strasbourg) 1988, (Oxford) 1990; Hon. LLD (South Bank Univ.) 1994; Hon. DD (Exeter) 1997; FKC (Fellow of King's Coll. London); numerous awards including Onassis Award, Family of Man Gold Medal 1983, Nobel Peace Prize 1984, Carter-Menil Human Rights Prize 1986, Martin Luther King Jr Humanitarian Award 1986, Third World Prize (jt recipient) 1989, Grand Cross of Merit, Germany 1996, Bill of Rights Award, American Civil Liberation Union Fund 1997, Henry W. Edgerton Civil Liberties Award, American Civil Liberties Union 1997, One Hundred Black Men Award, USA 1997, Peace Prize, Int. Community of UNESCO, Athens 1997; Order of Jamaica; Freedom of Borough of Merthyr Tydfil (Wales), Durham, Hull, Borough of Lewisham (UK), Florence, Lecco (Italy), Kinshasa (Democratic Repub. of Congo), Krugersdorp, Cape Town (SA). *Publications:* Crying in the Wilderness 1982, Hope and Suffering 1983 (both collections of sermons and addresses), The Rainbow People of God 1994, An African Prayer Book 1996, No Future Without Forgiveness 1999. *Leisure interests* reading, music, jogging. *Address:* c/o Truth and Reconciliation Commission, POB 3162, Cape Town 8000, South Africa. *Telephone:* (21) 4245161. *Fax:* (21) 4245227.

TUWAIJRI, Abdulrahman Al-, PhD; Saudi Arabian economist; b. 23 Feb. 1955, Almajmaah; s. of Abdulaziz Al-Tuwaijri and Hussah Al-Tuwaijri; m. Norah Alabdulatif 1982; three s. two d.; ed King Saud Univ. and Iowa State Univ., USA; grad. asst Dept of Econs, King Saud Univ. 1978–84, Asst Prof. 1985–88; Econ. Adviser Gen. Secr. Cooperation Council for the Arab States of the Gulf 1988–90; Alt. Exec. Dir IMF 1991–95, Exec. Dir 1995–2001; Sec.-Gen., Supreme Econ. Council 2002–. *Leisure interests:* reading, swimming. *Address:* c/o Ministry of Finance and National Economy, Airport Road, Riyadh 11177, Saudi Arabia. *Telephone:* (1) 405-0000. *Fax:* (1) 401-0583.

TUYAA, Nyam-Osoryn, MA; Mongolian politician; b. 1958, Ulan Bator; m.; two s. one d.; ed Moscow State Inst. of Int. Relations, Univ. of Sorbonne, Univ. of Leeds; later Ed.-in-Chief Foreign Service Broadcasting Dept State Cttee for Radio, TV and Information 1980–90; researcher Strategic Studies Centre 1990–95; Sec. Elections Cttee Mongolian Nat. Democratic Party 1995–96; Head Policy Planning Dept, Ministry of External Relations 1996–98; Minister for External Relations 1998–2000. *Address:* c/o Ministry of External Relations, Government Building 6, Ulan Bator, Mongolia.

TUYAKBAYEV, Col-Gen. Zharmakhan Aitbaiuly, CandJur; Kazakhstan politician and jurist; b. 22 Nov. 1947; m. Bagilya Aptayeva; two s. one d.; ed Kirov Kazakh State Univ.; worked in prosecutor's bureaus in S. Kazakhstan until 1978; Deputy Prosecutor-Gen. Kazakh SSR 1981; prosecutor Mangyshlak region, then Guryev region 1987–90; mem. Supreme Soviet Repub. of Kazakhstan 1990; Prosecutor-Gen. Repub. of Kazakhstan 1990–95, Deputy Prosecutor-Gen., Chief Mil. Prosecutor 1997–99; Chair. State Investigation Comm. 1995–97; elected mem. Majlis (Parl.) Oct. 1999, Chair. Dec. 1999–; Order of Barys 2001, Sodruzhestvo 2002. *Publications:* Development Prosecution in Kazakhstan in the period of reforms 1997; numerous articles. *Leisure Interests:* golf, reading. *Address:* House of Parliament, Astana, Kazakhstan (Office). *Telephone:* (3172) 15-30-19 (Office). *Fax:* (3172) 32-77-81 (Office). *E-mail:* protocol@parlam.kz (Office). *Website:* www.parlam.kz (Office).

TUYMANS, Luc; Belgian artist; b. 14 July 1958, Mortsel. *Art exhibitions:* numerous solo exhbns including: Repulsion, Cologne 1992, Superstition, Toronto 1994, London and Chicago 1995, The Agony, Warsaw 1995, The Heritage, NY 1996, Premonition, Berkeley, Calif. 1997, Der Architekt, Berlin 1998, The Passion, Antwerp 1999, Sincerely, Tokyo Opera Art Gallery 2000, Mwana Kitok (Beautiful White Man), Venice Biennale 2001, The Rumour, White Cube², London 2001; numerous group exhbns including Imperfectum, Norway 2000, Apocalypse, Royal Acad., London. *Address:* c/o White Cube², 48 Hoxton Square, London, N1, England (Office).

TVRDÍK, Lt-Col Jaroslav, MSc (Econ.); Czech politician and military officer; b. 11 Sept. 1968, Prague; m. Blanka Tvrdíková; one d.; ed Military School., Vyškov; Head Financial Services, Schooling and Training Centre, Ministry of Defence 1990–91; Commanding Sr Officer, Foreign Relations Section 1991–92; Head of Dept 1993–95; Dir Interior Admin. 1996, Deputy Minister of Defence 2000–01, Minister of Defence 2001–; Dir Military Spa and recreations facilities 1996–2000; Chief, Financial Services, Czechoslovak contingent, UNPROFOR 1993–95; UN Medal for Activity in UNPROFOR 1992–93, Anniversary Medal of Honour, NATO 2002. *Publication:* Transformation of the Army 2001. *Leisure interests:* squash, swimming, historical literature. *Address:* Ministerstvo obrany, Ministry of Defence, Tychonova 1, 160 01 Prague 6, Czech Republic (Office). *Telephone:* (2) 20201111 (Office). *Fax:* (2) 220210125 (Office). *E-mail:* sekretariat.mo@army.cz (Office). *Website:* www.army.cz (Office).

TWAIN, Shania; Canadian country music singer; b. Eileen Regina Edwards, 28 Aug. 1965, Windsor, Toronto; d. of Gerry Twain and Sharon Twain; m. Robert John Lange 1993, one s.; fmr cabaret singer; Favorite New Country Artist, American Music Award 1995, Female Vocalist Award, Canadian Country Music Awards 1995, Female Artist of the Year, Country Music TV/Europe 1996, Juno Songwriter of the Year 2000, Juno Best Country Female Artist 2000 and numerous other awards. *Singles include:* From This Moment On, That Don't Impress Me Much, Man! I Feel Like a Woman, Don't Be Stupid (You Know I Love You), I'm Gonna Get You Good 2002, Up! 2003, Ka-Ching! 2003. *Albums include:* Shania Twain 1993, The Woman in Me 1995 (Grammy Award for Best Country Album 1996, numerous other awards), Come on Over 1998, Up! 2002. *Address:* c/o Georgette Pascale, Shore Fire Media, 32 Court Street, Floor 16, Brooklyn, NY 11201, USA (Office); Mercury Nashville, 54 Music Square E, Nashville, TN 37203, USA. *Website:* www.shaniatwain.com.

TWEEDIE, Sir David Philip, Kt, PhD, CA; British chartered accountant; b. 7 July 1944; s. of Aidrian Ian Tweedie and Marie Patricia Tweedie (née Phillips); m. Janice Christine Brown 1970; two s.; ed Grangemouth High School, Edin. Univ.; accountancy training Mann, Judd, Gordon (Glasgow) 1969–72; Lecturer in Accounting, Edin. Univ. 1973–78; Tech. Dir Inst. of Chartered Accountants, Scotland 1978–81; partner KMG Thomson McLintock 1982–87, KPMG Peat Marwick McLintock 1987–90; Chair. Accounting Standards Bd 1990–2000, Int. Accounting Standards Bd 2001–; Hon. FIA 1999; several hon. degrees; Founding Socs. Award, Inst. of Chartered Accountants in England and Wales 1997, Chartered Inst. of Man. Accounting Award 1998. *Publications:* Financial Reporting, Inflation & The Capital Maintenance Concept 1979; co-author of three other books and contribs. to professional and academic journals. *Leisure interests:* athletics, watching rugby, walking, gardening. *Address:* International Accounting Standards Board, 1st Floor, 30 Cannon Street, London, EC4M 6XH, England (Office). *Telephone:* (20) 7246-6480 (Office). *Fax:* (20) 7246-6411 (Office). *E-mail:* dtweedie@iasb.org.uk (Office). *Website:* www.iasb.org.uk (Office).

TWIGGY (see Lawson, Lesley).

TWIN, Peter John, OBE, PhD, FRS; British professor emeritus of experimental physics; b. 26 July 1939, London; s. of Arthur James Twin and Hilda Ethel Twin; m. Jean Leatherland 1963; one s. one d.; ed Sir George Monoux Grammar School, Walthamstow, London and Univ. of Liverpool; Lecturer, Univ. of Liverpool 1964, Sr Lecturer 1973, Prof. of Experimental Physics 1987–2001, Sr Fellow and Prof. Emer. 2001–; Head, Nuclear Structure Facility, Daresbury Lab. Cheshire 1983–87; Weatherill Medal, Franklin Inst. USA 1991; Bonner Prize, Americal Physical Soc. 1991. *Publications:* articles in professional journals. *Address:* Oliver Lodge Laboratory, University of Liverpool, Liverpool, L69 3BX, England. *Telephone:* (151) 794-3378 (Office). *Fax:* (151) 794-3348 (Office).

TWITCHETT, Denis Crispin, FBA; British professor of Chinese studies (retd); b. 23 Sept. 1925, London; m. Umeko Ichikawa 1956 (divorced 1993); two s.; ed St Catharine's Coll., Cambridge and Inst. of Far Eastern Culture, Tokyo Univ.; Lecturer in Far Eastern History, SOAS, London Univ. 1954–56; Lecturer in Classical Chinese, Cambridge Univ. 1956–60; Prof. of Chinese and Head of Dept of Far East, SOAS 1960–68; Prof. of Chinese, Cambridge Univ. 1968–80, Professorial Fellow of St Catharine's Coll. 1968–80; Visiting Fellow, Inst. for Advanced Study, Princeton, USA 1973–74; Visiting Prof., Princeton Univ. 1978–79, Gordon Wu Prof. of Chinese Studies 1980–94. *Publications:* Financial Administration of the T'ang Dynasty 1963, Confucian Personalities (with A. F. Wright) 1963, Perspectives on the T'ang (with A. F. Wright) 1973, Times Atlas of China 1974, Printing and Publishing in Medieval China 1984, Reader T'ang History 1986, The Writing of Official History under the T'ang 1992, The Historian, His Readers and the Passage of Time 1997; Gen. Ed. of Cambridge History of China 1977–. *Leisure interests:* music, fine arts. *Address:* 24 Arbury Road, Cambridge, CB4 2JE, England.

TWOMBLY, Cy; American artist; b. 25 April 1929, Lexington, Va; ed Boston Museum School of Fine Arts, Washington & Lee Univ., Art Students League and Black Mountain Coll. with Frank Kline and Robert Motherwell; Head, Art Dept Southern Seminary and Jr Coll. Buena Vista, Va 1955–56; retrospective exhbn Whitney Museum of Art, New York 1979; works in numerous public and pvt. collections in USA and Europe; Fellow American Acad. of Arts and Letters; Imperial Praemium Prize 1996. *Solo exhibitions:* Milwaukee 1968, Nicholas Wilder Gallery 1969, Heron Inst. of Art, Indianopolis 1969, Guggenheim Museum, New York 1976, Museum of Modern Art, New York 1976, Vancouver Art Gallery 1982, Museum Hans Lange, Krefeld, Germany 1982, Santa Barbara Contemporary Arts Forum 1984. *Group exhibitions include:* New York Univ. 1967, Whitney Museum American Art Annual 1967,

Royal Acad. London 1981, Larry Gagosian Gallery, LA 1982, Young Hoffman Gallery, Chicago 1982, Blum Gallery, New York 1982. *Address:* c/o Gagosian Gallery, 980 Madison Avenue, New York, NY 10021, USA.

TYAGACHEV, Leonid Vassilyevich; Russian sports administrator, politician and skier; b. 1946, Dedenevo, Moscow region; ed Moscow Pedagogical Inst., Mountain Ski School Kirschberg, Austria; participated in All-Union and int. ski competitions until 1971; fmr USSR Ski Champion; Sr Ski Coach, Moscow region 1971–76; Chief Coach USSR Ski team, has coached numerous skiers including Zhirov, Zelenskaya, Tsyganov, Makeyev, Gladyshev 1976–81; took part in organizing World Cup competitions in Saalbach, Schladming, Saint Anton 1981–95; Minister of Sport and Tourism 1995–99; First Vice-Pres. Russian Olympic Cttee 1991–2001, Pres. July 2001–; numerous medals. *Address:* Olympic Committee of Russian Federation, Luzhnetskaya nab. 8, 119871 Moscow, Russia (Office). *Telephone:* (095) 725-45-01 (Office).

TYAZHLOV, Anatoly Stepanovich; Russian politician; b. 11 Oct. 1942, Kopeisk, Chelyabinsk Region; m.; two c.; ed Chelyabinsk Polytech. Inst.; metalworker, master, head of workshop, head of div., chief engineer Orenburg factory of prefabricated ferro-concrete structures 1959–69; chief engineer Orekhovo-Zuyevo house construction factory, Egoryevsk agric. construction factory 1969–73; chief engineer, man. of div., Head Moscow Region Dept of Construction, Chair. State Production Asscn Mosoblstroimateliay 1973–82; Head Elektrostal Construction Trust 1982–90; Chair. Exec. Cttee Moscow Region Soviet 1990–91; Head Moscow Region Admin. 1991–; Gov. of Moscow Region 1995–99; mem. Russian Council of Fed. 1993–99; Pres. Int. Asscn of Fraternized Towns; Pres. Asscn of Admin. Heads of Regions and Territories, Chair. Union of Govs of Russia 1992–99; elected to State Duma 1999–; mem. Otechestvo faction; mem. Co-ordination Council on Introduction of Privatization Cheques by Russian Govt 1992–; mem. Fed. State Comm. on Problems of Reforms 1993–; mem. Int. Acad. of Ecological Sciences. *Address:* State Duma, Okhotny Ryad 1, 103265 Moscow, Russia (Office). *Telephone:* (095) 292-80-00.

TYCZKA, Mieczysław; Polish lawyer; b. 13 April 1925, Witków; s. of Szczepan Tyczka and Maria Tyczka; m. 1956; two d.; ed Adam Mickiewicz Univ., Poznan; with Investment Bank 1950–53, Dist Arbitration Comm., Poznan 1953–61, Adam Mickiewicz Univ., Poznań 1961–; Prof. and Head of Dept of Civil Proceedings Adam Mickiewicz Univ.; Prof. Higher School of Man. and Banking, Dept of Econ., Civil and Labour Law, Poznań 1996; Inst. for Environmental Foundations of Tourism and Recreation of Physical Educ. Acad., Poznan; Pres. of Constitutional Tribunal 1989–93; mem. Cttee for Legal Sciences of Polish Acad. of Sciences; mem. Poznan Friends of Learning Soc. (Chair. Comm. for Legal Sciences), Democratic Party (SD) 1963–. *Publications:* Organization of the Polish Judicature, Law-making Procedure in the Polish National Economy Governmental Agencies, Arbitration Proceedings, Proceedings in Law on Inventions and Industrial Designs. *Leisure interest:* tourism. *Address:* Katedra Postępowania Cywilnego Univ. im. Adama, Mickiewicza, ul. Sw. Marcin 90, 61-809 Poznań, Poland. *Telephone:* (61) 8536251.

TYLER, Anne, BA; American author; b. 25 Oct. 1941, Minneapolis; d. of Lloyd Parry Tyler and Phyllis (Mahon) Tyler; m. Taghi M. Modarressi 1963 (died 1997); two c.; ed Duke Univ., Columbia Univ.; Pulitzer Prize for Fiction for Breathing Lessons 1989. *Publications:* If Morning Ever Comes 1964, The Tin Can Tree 1965, A Slipping-Down Life 1970, The Clock Winder 1972, Celestial Navigation 1974, Searching for Caleb 1976, Earthly Possessions 1977, Morgan's Passing 1980, Dinner at the Homesick Restaurant 1982, The Accidental Tourist 1985, Breathing Lessons 1988, Saint Maybe 1991, Tumble Tower (for children) 1993, Ladder of Years 1995, A Patchwork Planet 1998, Back When We Were Grown-ups 2001; short stories in magazines. *Address:* 222 Tunbridge Road, Baltimore, MD 21212, USA. *E-mail:* atmBaltimore@aol.com (Home).

TYLER, Liv; American actress; b. 1 Jul. 1977, Portland, Maine; d. of Steve Tyler and Bebe Buell; m. Royston Langdon 2003; fmrly model Eileen Ford Agency. *Film appearances include:* Silent Fall, Empire Records, Heavy, Stealing Beauty, That Thing You Do!, Inventing the Abbotts, Plunkett and Macleane 1999, Armageddon 1998, Cookie's Fortune 1999, Onegin 1999, The Little Black Book 1999, Dr. T. and the Women 2000, The Lord of the Rings: The Fellowship of the Ring 2001, One Night at McCool's 2001, The Lord of the Rings: The Two Towers 2002. *Address:* c/o CAA, 9830 Wilshire Boulevard, Beverly Hills, CA 90212, USA (Office).

TYNDALE-BISCOE, Cecil Hugh, PhD; Australian research scientist and university teacher; b. 16 Oct. 1929, Kashmir, India; s. of Eric Dallas Tyndale-Biscoe and Phyllis Mary (née Long) Tyndale-Biscoe; m. Marina Szokoloczi 1960; two s. one d.; ed Wycliffe Coll., England, Canterbury Univ., NZ, Univ. of Western Australia and Washington Univ., St Louis, USA; Animal Ecology, Dept of Scientific and Industrial Research, NZ 1951–55; lecturer Edwardes Coll., Peshawar, Pakistan 1955–58, Univ. of WA, Perth 1961; Deputy Leader, Biologist, NZ Alpine Club Antarctic Expedition 1959–60; Lecturer, Sr Lecturer, Reader in Zoology, Australian Nat. Univ., Canberra 1962–75, Adjunct Prof. 1996–2002; Sr Prin. Research Scientist Div. of Wildlife Research, CSIRO, Canberra 1976–78, Chief Research Scientist Div. of Wildlife and Ecology 1978–91; Dir Co-operative Research Centre for Biological Control of Vertebrate Pest Populations 1992–95; Hayward Fellow, Manaaki Whenua Landcare Research, NZ 1996–97; mountaineering in NZ, including first north-south traverse of Mt. Cook, first ascent of Torres from the Balfour; in the Karakorum, including first ascents of Falak Sar, Barteen and Buni Zom; Fellow Australian Acad. of Science, Australian Inst. of Biologists; Life mem. Australian Mammal Soc.; Hon. mem. RSNZ; Clarke Medal, Royal Soc. of NSW, Troughton Medal, Aitken Medal, CSIRO Medal. *Publications:* Life of Marsupials 1973, Reproduction and Evolution (Ed.) 1977, Reproductive Physiology of Marsupials (with M. B. Renfree) 1987, Developing Marsupials (Ed. with P. A. Janssens) 1988; about 120 papers in scientific journals of reproduction, ecology and endocrinology. *Leisure interests:* mountaineering, agroforestry, earth houses, woodwork, history of N India. *Address:* 114 Grayson Street, Hackett, ACT 2602, Australia (Home). *Telephone:* (2) 6249-8612 (Home). *Fax:* (2) 6242-1511. *E-mail:* hugh.tyndale-biscoe@csiro.au (Office).

TYRA; American model; b. (Tyra Banks), 4 Dec. 1973; d. of Carolyn London; ed Immaculate Heart High School; has modelled since 1991 for Karl Lagerfeld (q.v.), Yves St Laurent, Oscar De La Renta (q.v.), Chanel, etc.; featured on covers of Elle, GQ, Sports Illustrated, German Cosmopolitan, Spanish Vogue, Scene, Arena. *Video appearances include:* Too Funky by George Michael (q.v.), Black or White by Michael Jackson (q.v.), Love Thing by Tina Turner (q.v.). *Film appearances include:* Higher Learning, Love Changes. *Television appearances include:* Fresh Prince of Bel Aire, NY Undercover. *Address:* c/o IMG Models, 13–16 Jacob's Well Mews, George Street, London, W1H 5PD, England. *Telephone:* (20) 7486-8011. *Fax:* (20) 7487-3116.

TYSON, Harvey Wood; South African journalist; b. 27 Sept. 1928, Johannesburg; two s. one d.; ed Kingswood Coll., Rhodes Univ., Grahamstown; Ed.-in-Chief The Star and the Sunday Star, Johannesburg 1974–90; Dir Argus Holdings 1991–94, Argus Newspapers 1991–94, Sussens Mann Tyson Ogilvie & Mather, Omni Media Holdings 1994–. *Publication:* Editors Under Fire 1993. *Leisure interests:* writing, golf. *Address:* c/o The Star, 47 Sauer Street, P.O. Box 1014, Johannesburg 2000, South Africa. *Telephone:* (11) 8867153. *Fax:* (11) 8867676.

TYSON, Keith, MA; British artist; b. Ulverston, Cumbria; s. of David Tyson and Audrey Rigby; ed Dowdales School, Dalton-in-Furness, Carlisle Coll. of Art and Univ. of Brighton; studied mechanical eng craft before taking up art studies; worked as metal turner and draftsman at Vickers shipyard; has exhibited across Europe and N America; Turner Prize 2002. *Group exhibitions include:* Pandemonium Show, Inst. of Contemporary Arts 1996, Venice Biennale 2001, São Paulo Bienal 2002. *Solo exhibitions include:* From The Artmachine, Anthony Reynolds Gallery 1995. *Address:* c/o Tate Britain, Millbank, London, SW1, England.

TYSON, Laura D'Andrea, PhD; American professor of economics; b. 28 June 1947, New Jersey; m. Erik Tarloff; one s.; ed Smith Coll., Northampton, Mass and MIT; Asst Prof. Princeton Univ. 1974–77; Nat. Fellows Program Fellowship, Hoover Inst. 1978–79; consultant, IBRD 1980–86, Pres.'s Comm. on Industrial Competitiveness 1983–84, Hambrecht & Quist 1984–86, Plan-

Econ 1984–86, Western Govs. Asscn 1986, Council on Competitiveness 1986–89, Electronics Industry Asscn 1989, Motorola 1989–90; Visiting Prof. Harvard Business School 1989–90; Prof. Dept of Econs and Business Admin. and Dir Inst. of Int. Studies, Univ. of Calif. Berkeley 1978–98; Dean Haas School of Business 1998–2001, London Business School 2001–; Chair. Council of Econ. Advisers to Pres. Clinton 1993–95, Nat. Econ. Adviser to Pres. US Nat. Econ. Council 1995–97; Visiting Scholar, Inst. of Int. Econs; mem. Bd of Economists, Los Angeles Times; mem. Council on Foreign Relations, numerous other professional and public appointments. *Publications:* The Yugoslav Economic System and its Performance in the 1970s 1980, Economic Adjustment in Eastern Europe 1984, Who's Bashing Whom?, Trade Conflict in High Technology Industries 1992; articles in professional journals. *Address:* London Business School, Sussex Place, Regents Park, London, NW1 4SA, England.

TYSON, Mike G.; American boxer; b. 30 June 1966, New York City; s. of the late John Kilpatrick Tyson and Lorna Tyson; m. Robin Givens 1988 (divorced 1989); defeated Trevor Berbick to win WBC heavyweight title 1986; winner WBA heavyweight title March 1987, IBF heavyweight title Aug. 1987; fmr undefeated world champion, winner all 32 bouts, lost to James Buster Douglas 1990, defeated Donovan Ruddock 1991; Hon. Chair. Cystic Fibrosis Asscn 1987–, Young Adult Inst. 1987–; sentenced to six years' imprisonment for rape and two counts of deviant sexual practice March 1992; appealed against March sentence; appeal rejected by US Supreme Court March 1994; released March 1995; regained title of heavyweight world champion after defeating Frank Bruno March 1996; lost to Evander Holyfield Dec. 1996; licence revoked by Nevada State Athletics Comm. after disqualification from rematch against Holyfield 1996, reinstated on appeal Oct. 1998; sentenced to a year's imprisonment for assault Feb. 1999; released on probation May 1999; fought Lennox Lewis (q.v.) June 2002 for the WBC and IBF titles, knocked out in eighth round. *Address:* Don King Productions, 501 Fairway Drive, Deerfield Beach, FL 33441, USA (Office).

TZANNETAKIS, Tzannis; Greek politician; b. 13 Sept. 1927, Gytheion; s. of Petros Tzannetakis and Maria Tzannetakis; m. Maria Ragoussi 1954; one s. one d.; ed Naval Acad., War Acad.; served Greek Navy 1945–67; business exec. 1967–74; Sec.-Gen. Nat. Tourist Org. 1975; mem. Parl. 1977, 1981, 1985, 1993–; Minister of Public Works 1980–81; Prime Minister 1989; Minister of Defence 1990; Vice-Premier 1990–91; Deputy Prime Minister 1992–93; Minister of Culture 1990–93; founder of project to restore traditional villages in Greece; has promoted diverse cultural activities including exhbns.; Grand Cross (Greece, Luxembourg), First Prize, Fed. of Indian Publrs., for India: Another Way of Life. *Publications:* The Greek Agora: Public Political Space 1994, India: Another Way of Life 1994; translations into Greek. *Leisure interests:* reading, sailing, travelling. *Address:* Omirou 54, Athens 10672 (Office); Odos Pefkon 25, Kifissia, Athens, Greece (Home). *Telephone:* (10) 3608573 (Office); (10) 8087520 (Home). *Fax:* (10) 3645028.

U

UBAYDULLAYEV, Makhmadsaid; Tajikistan politician and political scientist; b. 1 Feb. 1952, Khatlon region; s. of Ubaidullo Mahmudov and Sababul Nazarova (died 1986); m. R. Karimova; two s., one d.; ed Tajik Polytech. Inst., Kharkov Polytech. Inst., Tashkent Higher CPSU School; engineer, sr engineer, then Dir Kulyab Regional Dept of Statistics, Dir Computation Centre 1974–79; instructor, Head of Div. Kulyab Regional CP Cttee 1979–83, 1986–88; Deputy Dir Cen. Dept of Statistics 1985–86; Chair. Regional Statistical Cttee, Khatlon region 1988–90; Head Kurgan-Tube Regional Dept of Statistics 1988–90; Deputy Chair. Kulyab Regional Soviet of People's Deputies 1990–92; Deputy Chair. Council of Ministers 1992–94; First Deputy Prime Minister 1994–96; Mayor of Dushanbe 1996–2000; mem. People's Democratic Party; Chair. Majlisi Milliy (Nat. Ass., Parl.) 2000–; Order of the DUSTI (Friendship), Tajikistan 1998, Order of the Ismoili Somoni, Tajikistan 1999, 21st Century Achievement Award 2001, and other awards. *Address:* Majlisi Milliy, Majlisi Oli, Rudaki prosp. 42, 734001 Dushanbe, Tajikistan (Office). *Telephone:* (372) 21-27-04 (Office). *Fax:* (372) 21-94-38 (Office). *E-mail:* abris@tajnet.com (Office).

UCHIDA, Mitsuko; Japanese pianist; b. 20 Dec. 1948, Tokyo; d. of Fujio Uchida and Yasuko Uchida; ed Vienna Acad. of Music; First Prize Beethoven Competition Vienna 1969, Second Prize Chopin Competition Warsaw 1970, Second Prize Leeds Competition 1975; Co. Dir Marlboro Music Festival; Artist-in-Residence, Cleveland Orchestra; Gramophone Award (Mozart Piano Sonatas) 1989, Hon. CBE 2001, Gramophone Award (Schoenberg Piano Concerto) 2001. *Performances:* recitals and concerto performances with all maj. London orchestras, Chicago Symphony, Boston Symphony, Cleveland Orchestra, Berlin Philharmonic, Vienna Philharmonic, New York Philharmonic, LA Philharmonic and others; played and directed the cycle of 21 Mozart piano concertos with the English Chamber Orchestra in London 1985–86; gave US premiere of piano concerto Antiphonies by Harrison Birtwistle 1996. *Recordings include:* Mozart Complete Piano Sonatas and 21 Piano Concertos (English Chamber Orchestra and Jeffrey Tate), Chopin Piano Sonatas, Schubert Piano Sonatas, Beethoven Piano Concertos, Schoenberg Piano Concerto. *Leisure interest:* bicycling (preferably on the flat). *Address:* c/o Van Walsum Management Ltd, 4 Addison Bridge Place, London, W14 8XP, England (Office). *Telephone:* (20) 7371-4343 (Office). *Fax:* (20) 7371-4344 (Office). *E-mail:* c/o nmcghee@vanwalsum.co.uk (Office).

UCHITEL, Aleksei Yefimovich; Russian film director; b. 31 Aug. 1931, Leningrad; s. of Yefim Uchitel; ed All Union State Inst of Cinematography; Meritied Worker of Arts; with documentary film studio, St Petersburg 1975–90; Founder and Artistic Dir ROR studio 1990–; Int. Film Festival Prizes, Leipzig, Krakow, Berlin, Mexico, Montreal, Palm Springs. *Documentaries:* Its Name is Novgorod 1974, Leningrad: Years of Achievement 1975, Leningrad – Hero City 1975, Hundreds of Thousands of I, Irina Kolpakova, Snow Fantasy 1977, October and Youth 1977, Portrait of One Event 1978. *Fiction includes:* Mania of Giselle 1995, Elite 1997, Diary of His Wife 2001. *Address:* 4th Krasnokararmennaya str. 6–5, apt 4, 198052 St Petersburg, Russia (Home). *Telephone:* (812) 292-59-45 (Home).

UCISIK, Ahmet Hikmet, PhD; Turkish professor of engineering; ed Istanbul Univ.; Assoc. Prof. Istanbul Tech. Univ.; Dir Marmara Scientific and Industrial Research Inst., Turkish Scientific and Tech. Research Council; instructor Metallurgical Eng Dept, Istanbul Tech. Univ.; Prof. of Materials Science, Bogazici Univ.; mem. American and Japanese Socs. for Dental Materials and Devices; Fellow Islamic Acad. of Sciences. *Address:* Boğaziçi University, 80815 Bebek, Istanbul, Turkey (Office). *Telephone:* (212) 263-15-00 (Office). *Fax:* (212) 265-63-57 (Office). *E-mail:* halkilis@boun.edu.tr (Office). *Website:* www.boun.edu.tr (Office).

UDAY HUSSEIN; Iraqi militia leader and media executive; b. 1964; s. of Saddam Hussein (fmr Pres. of Iraq) and Sajida Saddam; ed Baghdad Univ.; Ed. Babil (pro-Govt newspaper); Ed. and owner Al-Baath ar-Riyadhi; owner, TV and radio station; Head, Fedaycen of Saddam (militia) –2003, Iraqi army and militia defeated in invasion of Iraq by US-led coalition forces March–April 2003, whereabouts of Uday Hussein not known as at April 2003.

UDOVENKO, Hennadiy Yosipovich, PhD; Ukrainian diplomatist and politician; b. 22 June 1931, Kryvy Rih; s. of Yosyp Petrovich Udovenko and Maria Maksimivna Kharenko; m. Dina Grigorivna Boutenko 1953; one d.; ed Kiev State Univ.; joined Diplomatic Service 1959, First Sec., Counsellor 1959–64; Sr Recruitment Officer, UN Tech. Assistance Recruitment Service, Geneva 1965–71; Chief of Depts., Ministry of Foreign Affairs 1972–76; Dir Interpretation and Meetings Div., Dept of Conf. Services, UN Secr., New York 1977–80; Deputy Minister for Foreign Affairs of Ukrainian SSR 1980–85; Rep. of Ukrainian SSR on Governing Body of ILO 1981–85; Rep. to UN Security Council 1985; Perm. Rep. of Ukrainian SSR to UN 1985–91; Deputy Minister of Foreign Affairs 1991–92, Minister of Foreign Affairs 1994–98; Ukrainian Amb. to UN 1992; Amb. to Poland 1992–94; Pres. UN Gen. Ass. 1997–98; mem. Verkhovna Rada (Parl.), Head Standing Cttee on Human Rights, leader RUKH Faction 1999–; Head Narodnyy Rukh Ukrainy political party 1999–; Hon. DHumLitt (Bridgeport Univ., USA) 1997; Dr. hc (Ukrainian Free Univ., Munich) 1996, (Int. Human Rights Acad., Kiev, Int. Solomon Univ., Kiev) 1998; Diplomatist of the Year 1996, 1998. *Leisure interest:* jogging. *Address:* Narodnyy Rukh Ukrainy, O Honchara Str. 33, 01034 Kiev (Office); Desyatynna Str. 10, Apt. 2, 01025 Kiev, Ukraine (Home). *Telephone:*

(44) 246-47-67 (Office); (44) 229-65-08 (Home). *Fax:* (44) 246-47-67 (Office); (44) 226-28-79 (Home). *E-mail:* nru@bigmir.net (Office); udovenko@rada.gov .ua (Office). *Website:* www.nru.org.ua (Office).

UDUGOV, Brig.-Gen. Movladi; Russian/Chechen politician; b. 9 Feb. 1962, Grozny; m. 1st; m. 2nd; four c.; ed Chechen-Ingush State Univ.; trained as economist; political activities 1986–; one of founders Soc. Kavkaz, political group Bart and newspaper Bart 1987; Founder and Ed. Orientir (newspaper) banned by Soviet regime 1988; organizer Mil. Patriotic Union Mansur 1990; participant Congress of Chechen People 1990; Sec. all sessions of Chechen Nat. Congress, Leader Formation Cttee Nat. Congress of Chechen People, one of orgs. of anti-Russian resistance Nov. 1991; participant overthrowing of Communist leadership of Chechen-Ingushetia 1991; Minister of Information and Press, Dudayev Govt 1991; Head propaganda service of separatists 1994–; took part in negotiations on peaceful resolution of conflict; First Vice-Minister Coalition Govt Chechen Repub. Ichkeria 1996–97; First Deputy Prime Minister 1997–98; Foreign Minister 1998–99; currently Pres. Kavkaz-Center News Agency.

UEBERROTH, Peter; American sports administrator; b. 2 Sept. 1937, Evanston, Ill.; s. of Victor Ueberroth and Laura Larson; m. Ginny Nicolaus 1959; one s. three d.; ed San Jose Univ.; Operations Man., Trans Int. Airlines 1959, later part owner; f. Transportation Consultants (later First Travel); Head, LA Olympic Games Organizing Cttee 1984; Maj. League Baseball Commr 1984–89; named Head "Rebuild L.A." 1992–93; Co-Chair. Doubletree Hotels Corpn 1999–; mem. Young Pres.'s Org.; Chair. Contrarian Group; owner and Co-Chair. Pebble Beach Co.; mem. Bd Coca-Cola Co., Hilton Hotel Corpn; Chair. Bd Ambassadors International (AMIE) 1995–; 12 honorary degrees; Time magazine's Man of the Year 1984, Scopus Award 1985. *Publication:* Made in America (autobiog.) 1986. *Leisure interests:* reading (especially historical non-fiction), golf. *Address:* Doubletree Hotels Corporation, 755 Crossover Lane, Mailroom Department, Memphis, TN 38117, USA.

UEMATSU, Kunihiko, DEng; Japanese engineer; b. 1931, Kochi; m.; three c.; ed Kyoto Univ. and MIT; Head, Fuel and Materials Devt for Fast Breeder Reactor Project, Japanese Power Reactor and Nuclear Fuel Devt Corpn (PNC) 1968, Dir Fuel Devt Div. 1982, Exec. Dir 1983–88, Exec. Vice-Pres. 1995–98, Special Tech. Adviser 1998–; Dir-Gen. OECD Nuclear Energy Agency (NEA) 1988–95; currently Sr Adviser, Japan Atomic Industrial Forum and Research Adviser, Cen. Research Inst. of Electric Power Industry. *Publications:* numerous papers on tech. and policy issues in field of nuclear energy. *Address:* NKK Building, 1-1-2, Marunouchi, Chiyoda-ku, Tokyo (Office); 1-27-3-611, Nishigahara, Kita-ku, Tokyo, Japan (Home). *Telephone:* (3) 5220-3311 (Office); (3) 5394-8259 (Home). *Fax:* (3) 3212-2020 (Office); (3) 5394-8259 (Home). *E-mail:* uematsu@jnc.go.jp (Office). *Website:* www.jnc.go.jp (Office).

UFFEN, Robert James, OC, PhD, DSc, PEng, FRSC, FGSA, FCAE; Canadian geophysicist; b. 21 Sept. 1923, Toronto, Ont.; s. of James Frederick Uffen and Elsie May (Harris) Uffen; m. Mary Ruth Paterson 1949; one s. one d.; ed Univ. of Toronto, Western Ontario; war service 1942–45; Lecturer, Univ. of Western Ont. 1951–53, Asst Prof. of Physics and Geology 1953–57, Assoc. Prof. of Geophysics 1957–58, Prof. and Head of Dept of Geophysics 1958–61, Acting Head Dept Physics 1960–61; Prin. Univ. Coll. of Arts and Science, London, Ont. 1961–65; Dean, Coll. of Science, Univ. of Western Ont. 1965–66; Vice-Chair. Defence Research Bd, Ottawa 1966–67, Chair. 1967–69; Chief Science Adviser to the Cabinet 1969–71; Dean, Faculty of Applied Science, Queen's Univ., Kingston, Ont. 1971–80, Prof. of Geophysics 1971–89, Prof. Emer. 1989–; Commr Ont. Royal Comm. on Asbestos 1980–84, on Truck Safety 1981–83; Research Fellowship, Inst. of Geophysics, Univ. of Calif., LA 1953; mem. Council of Regents Colls. of Applied Arts and Tech. 1966–69, 1973–76, Nat. Research Council of Canada 1963–66, Science Council of Canada 1967–71; Dir Canadian Patents and Devt Ltd 1965–70; mem. Club of Rome 1969–83; Chair. Canadian Eng Manpower Council 1973–74; Dir Centre for Resource Studies 1973–76, 1980–83, Ont. Hydro 1974–79, Vice-Chair. 1975–79); Councillor, Asscn of Professional Engineers of Ont. 1975–78; Chair. Ont. Exploration Tech. Devt Fund 1981–84; Consultant to EEC on energy research 1987–88; Tech. Adviser to AECL on nuclear waste 1988–91; mem. Fisheries Research Bd of Canada 1974–78; Visiting Fellow, Univ. of Sussex 1976–77; Fellow American Asscn for the Advancement of Science 1986, Canadian Acad. of Eng 1988–; Hon. DSc (Queen's Univ.) 1967, (Univ. of Western Ont.) 1970, (Royal Mil. Coll. of Canada) 1978, Hon. DSc (McMaster Univ.) 1983; Centennial Medal, Canada 1967, APEO Public Service Award 1985, Distinguished Service Award, Queen's Univ. 1990, Eng Hall of Distinction, Univ. of Toronto 1990, 1867–1992 Commemorative Medal 1992, John Orr Award (Queen's Univ.) 1993. *Publications:* papers on geophysics, operations research, evolution, science policy and radioactive waste management. *Leisure interests:* painting, boating, old bottles. *Address:* 185 Ontario Street, No. 1504, Kingston, Ont., K7L 2Y7, Canada. *Telephone:* (613) 546-4981.

UGEUX, Georges; Belgian financier; b. 20 April 1945, Brussels; m. Francine Godet 1970; two s. two d.; ed Catholic Univ. of Louvain; lecturer in Economics,

Faculty of Law, Univ. of Louvain 1970–72; fmr Gen. Man. Investment Banking & Trust Div., Générale Bank; Man. Dir Morgan Stanley 1985–88; Group Finance Dir Société Générale de Belgique 1988–92; Pres. Kidder Peabody-Europe 1992–95; Chair. Belgian Privatization Comm. 1995–96; Pres. European Investment Fund 1995–96; Group Exec. Vice-Pres., Int., New York Stock Exchange 1996–. *Publication:* Floating Rate Notes 1985. *Leisure interests:* music, arts, philosophy. *Address:* New York Stock Exchange, 11 Wall Street, New York, NY 10005, USA (Office). *Telephone:* (212) 656-2077 (Office). *Fax:* (212) 656-2016 (Office). *E-mail:* gugeux@nyse.com (Office).

UGGLAS, Baroness Margaretha af, BA; Swedish politician; b. 5 Jan. 1939; ed Harvard-Radcliffe Program in Business Admin., Stockholm School of Econs; leader-writer Svenska Dagbladet 1968–74; Chair. Save the Children Fed., Stockholm 1970–76; mem. Stockholm Co. Council 1971–73; mem. Parl. 1974–; fmr Moderate Party Spokesman on Foreign Affairs; Chair. Swedish Section European Union of Women 1981–; mem. Parl. Standing Cttee on Foreign Affairs 1982–, Advisory Council on Foreign Affairs, Swedish Del. to Council of Europe; observer European Parl.; Minister for Foreign Affairs 1991–94; Vice-Pres. European People's Party (EPP) 1996; Robert Schuman Medal 1995. *Leisure interests:* art, walking, sailing, mountains and country-side. *Address:* c/o Moderata Samlingspartiet, P.O. Box 1243, 111 82 Stockholm, Sweden.

UGOLINI, S. E. Giovanni Francesco; San Marino politician; b. 28 Feb. 1953, Borgo Maggiore; m. Loredana Mularoni; one d.; industrial chemical expert, technician in state hosp. 1974–81; with family hotel business 1981–; Pres. of San Marino Union of Tourist Hospitality (USOT); joined Partito Democratico Cristiano Sammarinese (PDCS) 1973–, mem. Cen. Council 1993–, Sec. Borgo Maggiore Br. 1989–93; elected Mem. of Govt 2001–; Head of State (Capt. Regent) 2002–; mem. Foreign Policy Advisory Comm., Council of the XXII. *Address:* Partito Democratico Cristiano Sammarinese (PDCS), Via delle Scalette 6, 47890 San Marino (Office). *Telephone:* (549) 991193 (Office). *Fax:* (549) 992694 (Office). *E-mail:* pdcs@omniway.sm (Office). *Website:* www.pdcs.sm (Office).

UHDE, Milan, PhD; Czech politician, journalist and playwright; b. 28 July 1936, Brno; m.; two c.; ed Masaryk Univ., Brno; Ed. of literary monthly A Guest Is Coming 1958–70; signed Charter 77; published essays in unofficial periodicals and abroad; Reader, Faculty of Philosophy, Masaryk Univ., Brno Dec. 1989–; Ed.-in-chief, Atlantis Publishing House, Brno March–June 1990; Minister of Culture, Czech Repub. 1990–92; Pres. of Foundation for Preservation of Cultural Monuments 1991–; mem. Civic Democratic Party (ODS) 1991–98, Unie Svobody 1998; Deputy to Czech Nat. Council June 1992–; mem. Presidium; Pres. of Parl., Czech Repub. 1992–96; Chair. Civic Democratic Party in Parl. 1996–97; mem. State Radio Council 1999–; Czechoslovak Radio Prize 1966, Medal for Merit 2000. *Plays include:* King Vávra 1964, The Tax-Collector 1965, Witnesses 1966, The Tart from the Town of Thebes 1967, The Gang 1969, A Dentist's Temptation 1976, Lord of the Flames 1977, The Hour of Defence 1978, The Blue Angel 1979. *Publications:* novels: Like Water off a Duck's Back 1961, A Mysterious Tower in B. 1967. *Address:* Barvičova 59, 602 00 Brno, Czech Republic. *Telephone:* (5) 43240201. *Fax:* (5) 43240201.

UHL, Petr; Czech/Slovak human rights activist; b. 8 Oct. 1941, Prague; s. of Bedřich Uhl and Marie Kohoutová; m. Anna Šabatová 1974; three s. one d.; ed Czech. Univ. of Tech., Prague; designer and patent clerk 1964–66; teacher, Coll. of Tech. Prague 1966–69; imprisoned for political activities 1969–73; designer 1974–78; Co-Founder of Charter 77; Co-Founder of Cttee for Protection of the Unjustly Prosecuted 1978; imprisoned for political activities 1979–84; stoker 1984–89; ed. of East European Information Agency 1988–90; leading rep. of Civic Forum, Prague 1989–90; Dir-Gen., Czechoslovak News Agency 1990–92, Ed. 1992–94; Ed.-in-Chief Listy (magazine) 1994–96; Ed. Právo (daily) 1996–98, 2001–; Commr of Govt of Czech Repub. for Human Rights 1998–2001; Deputy to House of the Nations, Fed. Ass. 1990–92; Chair., Control and Auditing Comm. of Prison Staff Corps, Czech Repub. 1990; mem. Working Group on Arbitrary Detention of UN Comm. on Human Rights 1991–2001; State Honours of Czech Repub. 1998, of Poland 2000, of Germany 2001, of Austria 2002, Order of Merit, France 2002; Press Freedom Award, Reporter without Borders, Austria 2002. *Publications:* The Programme of Social Self-government 1982, On Czechoslovak Prison System (co-author) 1998, Justice and Injustice in the Eyes of Petr Uhl 1999, and numerous articles in Czech and foreign press. *Address:* Právo, Slezská 13, 121 50 Prague (Office); Anglická No 8, 120 00 Prague 2, Czech Republic (Home). *Telephone:* (2) 24228865 (Home); 724027545. *Fax:* (2) 21001276 (Office). *E-mail:* uhl@seznam.cz (Home).

UHLIG, Harald Friedrich Hans Volker Sigmar, PhD; German economist; b. 26 April 1961, Bonn; s. of Jan Peter Uhlig and Anjuli Sarah Uhlig; ed Technische Univ., Berlin, Univ. of Minnesota; Research Asst, Fed. Reserve Bank of Minneapolis and Inst. for Empirical Macroeconomics 1986–89; teaching asst, Univ. of Minn. 1987; Asst Prof., Dept of Econs, Princeton Univ. 1990–94; Research Prof. for Macroeconomics, Center for Econ. Research, Tilburg Univ., Netherlands 1994–2000; Prof. of Macroecon. and Econ. Policy, Humboldt Univ. 2000–; main field of work macroecons, secondary fields Bayesian time series econometrics and financial econs; assoc. ed., Journal of Econ. Dynamics and Control 1995–98, Macroecon. Dynamics 1997–, Computational Econs 1998–, Econometric Theory 2000–; Asst, Review of Econ. Studies 1998–; co-ed. European Econ. Review 1997–; mem. Econometric Soc., American Econ. Asscn, European Econ. Asscn; Alfred P. Sloan Doctoral Dissertation Fellowship 1989–90. *Publications:* numerous articles in econ. journals. *Address:* Department of Business Administration and Economics, Spandauer Str. 1, 10178 Berlin (Office); Neidenburger Allee 22, 14055 Berlin, Germany (Home). *Telephone:* (30) 20935926 (Office). *Fax:* (30) 20935934 (Office). *E-mail:* uhlig@wiwi.hu-berlin.de. *Website:* www.wiwi.hu-berlin.de/wpol.

UHRIG, John Allan, AC; Australian business executive; b. 24 Oct. 1928, Newcastle, NSW; s. of L. J. Uhrig; m. Shirley Attwood 1956; two s. two d.; ed Newcastle Tech. High School, Univ. of New South Wales; Man. Dir Simpson Ltd 1975–85; Dir CRA Ltd (now Rio Tinto Ltd) 1983–, Chair. (non-exec.) 1987–; Chair. Codan Pty Ltd 1986–, Australian Mineral Devt Laboratories Ltd (Amdel) 1989–, Australian Minerals and Energy Environment Foundation 1991–; fmr Chair. Australian Mfg Council; Dir Westpac Banking Corpn 1989–, Chair. Oct. 1992–; Deputy Chair. Santos Ltd 1992–94, Chair. 1994– (Dir 1991–); Deputy Chair. RTZ 1995–; mem. Remuneration Tribunal of South Australia 1985–89. *Address:* c/o Rio Tinto Ltd, G.P.O. Box 384D, Melbourne, Vic. 3001, Australia.

ULLENDORFF, Edward, MA, DPhil, DLitt, FBA; British university professor; b. 25 Jan. 1920; s. of Frederic Ullendorff and Cilli Ullendorff; m. Dina Noack 1943; ed Univs. of Jerusalem and Oxford; war service in Eritrea and Ethiopia 1941–46; Asst Sec., Govt of Palestine 1946–47; Research Officer, Oxford Univ. Inst. of Colonial Studies 1948–49; Lecturer, later Reader, in Semitic Languages, St Andrews Univ. 1950–59; Prof. of Semitic Languages, Manchester Univ. 1959–64; Prof. of Ethiopian Studies, London Univ. 1964–79, of Semitic Languages 1979–82, Prof. Emer. 1982–; Head of Africa Dept, School of Oriental and African Studies (SOAS) 1972–77; Chair. Asscn of British Orientalists 1963–64, Anglo-Ethiopian Soc. 1965–68, Editorial Bd of Bulletin of SOAS 1968–78; Schweich Lecturer, British Acad. 1967; Pres. Soc. for Old Testament Study 1971; Vice-Pres. Royal Asiatic Soc. 1975–79, 1981–85; Fellow, British Acad. 1965–, Vice-Pres. 1980–82; Foreign Fellow, Accad. Nazionale dei Lincei, Rome 1998; Hon. Fellow Oxford Centre of Hebrew Studies 1998; Hon. DLitt (St Andrews Univ.) 1972; Hon. DPhil (Hamburg Univ.) 1990; Haile Selassie Prize for Ethiopian Studies 1972. *Publications:* Exploration and Study of Abyssinia 1945, Catalogues of Ethiopic MSS in the Bodleian Library 1951, The Royal Library, Windsor Castle 1953, Cambridge Univ. Library 1961; The Semitic Languages of Ethiopia 1955, The Ethiopians 1960, 3rd Edn 1973, Comparative Grammar of the Semitic Languages 1964, An Amharic Chrestomathy 1965, Ethiopia and the Bible 1968, Solomon and Sheba 1974, translated and annotated Emperor Haile Selassie's autobiography 1976, Studies in Semitic Languages and Civilizations 1977, The Ethiopic Enoch (with M. A. Knibb, 2 Vols) 1978, The Amharic Letters of Emperor Theodore to Queen Victoria (jtly) 1979, The Bawdy Bible, The Hebrew Letters of Prester John (jtly) 1982, A Tigrinya Chrestomathy 1985, Studia Aethiopica et Semitica 1987, The Two Zions 1988, From the Bible to Enrico Cerulli 1990, H.J. Polotsky's Selected Letters 1992, From Emperor Haile Selassie to H. J. Polotsky 1995 and others; articles and reviews in journals of learned socs. *Leisure interests:* music, motoring in Scotland. *Address:* 4 Bladon Close, Oxford, OX2 8AD, England.

ULLMAN, Tracey; British actress and singer; b. 30 Dec. 1959, Slough; d. of the late Anthony John Ullman and of Dorin Cleaver; m. Allan McKeown 1984; one s. one d.; ed Italia Conti Stage School, London; record album: You Broke My Heart in Seventeen Places; British Acad. Award 1983, Rudolph Valentino Cinema Lifetime Achievement Award 1992. *Films include:* The Rocky Horror Picture Show, Give My Regards to Broad Street, Plenty 1985, Jumpin' Jack Flash 1986, I Love You To Death 1990, Robin Hood: Men in Tights 1993, Household Saints, Bullets over Broadway 1995, Pret-a-Porter 1995, Everybody Says I Love You 1996, Small Town Crooks 2000. *Stage appearances include:* Gigi, Elvis, Grease, Four in a Million (London Theatre Critics' Award 1981). *Television appearances include:* The Tracey Ullman Show 1987–90, The Best of the Tracey Ullman Show 1990, Tracey Takes On 1996–. *Leisure interests:* hiking, riding. *Address:* c/o ICM, Oxford House, 76 Oxford Street, London, W1N 0AX, England; IFA Talent Agency, 8730 W. Sunset Boulevard, Suite 490, Los Angeles, CA 90069, USA. *Telephone:* (20) 7636-6565 (London). *Fax:* (20) 7323-0101 (London).

ULLMANN, Liv Johanne; Norwegian actress; b. 16 Dec. 1938, Tokyo, Japan; d. of late Viggo Ullmann and of Janna (née Lund) Ullmann; m. 1st Dr Gappe Stang 1960 (divorced 1965); one d.; m. 2nd Donald Saunders 1985; worked in repertory co., Stavanger 1956–59; has appeared in Nat. Theatre and Norwegian State Theatre, Oslo; work for UNICEF as Goodwill Amb. 1980–; Vice-Chair. Int. Rescue Cttee; 12 hon. doctorates; Best Actress of the Year, Nat. Soc. of Critics in America 1969, 1970, 1974; NY Film Critics Award 1973, 1974; Hollywood Foreign Press Asscn.'s Golden Globe 1973; Best Actress of the Year, Swedish T.V. 1973, 1974; Donatello Award (Italy) 1975; Bambi Award (Fed. Repub. of Germany) 1975; nominated for Tony Award as Best Stage Actress, debut on Broadway in A Doll's House 1975; LA Film Critics' Award (Face to Face) 1976; New York Film Critics' Award (Face to Face) 1977; Nat. Bd of Review of Motion Pictures Award (Face to Face) 1977; Peer Gynt Award (Norway), Eleanor Roosevelt Award 1982, Roosevelt Freedom Medal 1984, Dag Hammarskjöld Award 1986; Commdr of Olav 1994. *Films include:* Pan 1965, Persona 1966, The Hour of the Wolf 1968, Shame 1968, The Passion of Anna 1969, The Night Visitor 1971, The Emigrants 1972, Cries and Whispers 1972, Pope Joan 1972, Lost Horizon 1973, 40 Carats 1973, The New Land 1973, Zandy's Bride 1973, Scenes from a Marriage 1974, The Abdication 1974, Face to Face 1975, The Serpent's Egg 1978, Sonate d'automne 1978, Richard's Things 1980, The Wild Duck 1983, Love Streams 1983, Let's Hope It's a Girl 1985, Baby Boy 1984, Dangerous Moves 1985, Gaby Brimmer 1986, Moscow Adieu 1986, Time of Indifference 1987, La Amiga 1987, Mindwalk, The Ox, The Long Shadow; Dir: Sophie 1993, Kristin Lavrandsdatter (wrote screenplay also), Faithless 2000. *Plays include:* Brand 1973, A Doll's House 1975, Anna Christie 1977, I Remember Mama 1979, Ghosts 1982, Old Times 1985, The Six Faces of Women (TV), Mother Courage. *Publication:* Changing (autobiog.) 1976, Choices (autobiog.) 1984. *Leisure interest:* reading. *Address:* c/o London Management, 235 Regent Street, London, W1, England.

ULLRICH, Jan; German cyclist; b. 2 Dec. 1973, Rostock; s. of Werner Ullrich and Marianne Kaatz; ed S.C. Dynamo sports school, Berlin; wins as an amateur include: World Championships (Road) 1993, South Africa Tour (three stage wins) 1994, Lower Saxony Tour (two stage wins); turned professional 1995; wins as a professional include: German Time Trial Champion (50km) 1995, Regio Tour (one stage win) 1996, Tour de France 1997 (two stage wins), 2001, German Road Championships 1997, silver and gold Olympic medals, Sydney 2000; in 2002 tested positive in dope test and given 6-month suspension by German Cycling Fed.; now lives in Switzerland; German Sportsman of the Year 1997, World Cyclist of the Year 1997. *Leisure interests:* cars, cinema, music. *Address:* Burgunderweg 10, 79291 Merdingen, Germany.

ULLSTEN, Ola; Swedish politician and diplomatist; b. 23 June 1931, Umeå; s. of C. A. Ullsten and Ṣtina Ullsten; graduated in social sciences 1956; Sec. Parl. Group Liberal Party 1957–61; journalist Dagens Nyheter 1962–64; mem. Riksdag (Parl.) 1965–84; Chair. Liberal Party Stockholm County 1972–76; Minister of Int. Devt Co-operation 1976–78; Deputy Prime Minister March–Oct. 1978, Prime Minister 1978–79; Minister for Foreign Affairs 1979–82, Deputy Prime Minister 1980–82; Chair. Liberal Party 1978–83; Amb. to Canada 1983–89, to Italy 1989; mem. Interaction Council of Former Heads of Govt.

ULMANIS, Guntis, BEcon; Latvian politician; b. 13 Sept. 1939, Riga; m. Aina Ulmane (née Stelce); one s. one d.; ed Univ. of Latvia; as a child was exiled to Russia together with his parents, returned to Latvia in 1946; mil. service 1963–65; economist bldg industry and Riga Public Transport Bd; Man. Riga Mun. Community Services 1965–92; fmr lecturer in construction econs Riga Polytechnic Inst. and econ. planning Latvian State Univ.; mem. CPSU 1965–89; mem. Bd of Cen. Bank of Latvia 1992–93, Deputy to Parl. (Saeima) June–July 1993; Pres. of Latvia 1993–99; Hon. Chair. Union of Farmers party 1993–; Dr hc (Charleston Univ., USA) 1996; Award of US Inst. for East West Studies 1996, Cen. and E European Law Initiative Award, American Bar Asscn 1997, Distinguished Statesman Award, Anti-Defamation League 1998; numerous decorations including Order of St Michael and St George 1996, Légion d'honneur 1997, Order of Merit (Germany) 1999. *Publications:* Autobiography 1995, My Time as President 1999. *Leisure interests:* hunting, reading, playing with grandchildren. *Address:* Brīvības iela 38, Apt. 5, 1050 Riga, Latvia (Home). *Telephone:* 709 2112 (Office); 927 8758. *Fax:* 732 5800. *E-mail:* eva@president.lv (Office).

ULUFA'ALU, Bartholomew; Solomon Islands politician; Leader Solomon Islands Liberal Party (SILP); Prime Minister of Solomon Islands 1997–2000; Acting Minister of Finance 1998–99. *Address:* Solomon Islands Liberal Party, Honiara, Solomon Islands.

'ULUKALALA-LAVAKA-ATA, HRH Prince; Tongan politician and army officer; b. Nuku'alofa; s. of HM King Taufa'ahau Tupou IV (q.v.); m.; three c.; ed in New Zealand, Britannia Royal Naval Coll., Dartmouth, Univ. of New South Wales, Australian Jt Services Staff Coll., US Naval War Coll.; joined Tonga Defence Services 1981, Second-in-Command 1995; Commanding Officer, Navy 1993; Minister of Foreign Affairs and Defence 1998–; Prime Minister of Tonga 2000–, also Minister of Agric., Forestry and Fisheries, Civil Aviation and Telecommunications. *Address:* Office of the Prime Minister, POB 62, Taufa'ahau Road, Kolofo'ou, Nuku'alofa, Tonga (Office). *Telephone:* 24644 (Office). *Fax:* 23888 (Office).

ULUSU, Adm. Bülent; Turkish politician and naval officer; b. 7 May 1923, Istanbul; s. of M. Salih Ulusu and Seniye Ulusu; m. Mizat Erensoy 1951; one d.; ed Naval Acad.; various command posts in navy; rank of Rear-Adm. 1967, Vice-Adm. 1970, Adm. 1974; fmr Commdr of War Fleet; Commdr of Turkish Naval Forces until 1980; fmr Under-Sec., Ministry of Defence; Prime Minister of Turkey 1980–83; MP 1983–87. *Address:* Ciftehavuzlar Yesilbahar 50K. 8/27, Kadikoy Istanbul, Turkey.

ULYANOV, Mikhail Aleksandrovich; Russian actor and director; b. 20 Nov. 1927, Tara, Omsk Dist; s. of Aleksandr Andreevich Ulyanov and Elizaveta Mikhailovna Ulyanova; m. Alla Petrovna Parfanyi 1958; one d.; ed Shchukin Theatre School; worked with Vakhtangov Theatre 1950–, Chief Theatre Dir 1987–; mem. CPSU 1951–91; with Soviet TV; début as dir 1973; Chair. Russian Union of Theatre Workers 1986–96; USSR People's Deputy 1989–91; USSR People's Artist 1969, RSFSR State Prize 1975 for work in theatre; Hero of Socialist Labour 1986; Pres. of Russia's Prize 1998. *Roles in films include:* They Were The First 1956, The Volunteers 1958, A Simple Story 1960, The Battle on the Way 1961, The Chairman 1964 (Lenin Prize 1966), Brothers Karamazov 1969, Escape 1971, Egor Bulychev and Co. 1973, Liberation 1970–72, The Blockade 1975–78, Soldiers of Freedom 1977, Call me to the Bright Distant Horizon 1978, The Last Escape 1981, Private Life

1982 (USSR State Prize 1988), Unless the Enemy Surrenders 1983, No Witnesses 1983, Choice 1987, Our Armoured Train 1989, The Home under Starry Skies 1991, The Co-operative Store called 'Political Bureau' 1992, Me I'm the Native of Viatka 1992, The Master and Margarita 1992, Composition by the Day of Victory 1997, Voroshilovi's Shooter 1999. *Films directed include:* The Very Last Day 1973, Brothers Karamazov (part 3). *Radio appearances:* The Calm Don, The Dead Souls, poems. *Television:* (films) Islands in the Stream 1972, Tevie the Milkman 1985, Imposters (series) 2001. *Publications:* I Work as an Actor, My Profession, The Philtre. *Leisure interest:* reading. *Address:* Theatre Vakhtangov, 26 Arbat, 121002 Moscow, Russia (Office). *Telephone:* (095) 241-10-77 (Office); (095) 241-07-44 (Office); (095) 299-96-76 (Home). *Fax:* (095) 241-26-25.

ULYUKAYEV, Alexei Valentinovich, DrEcon; Russian politician and economist; b. 23 March 1956, Russia; m.; ed Moscow State Univ.; Asst, then Docent Moscow Inst. of Construction Eng 1982–88; Adviser, Head of Div. Communist (journal); political reviewer Moskovskiye Novosti (weekly) 1991; Deputy Dir Int. Cen. of Studies of Econ. Reforms 1997; Deputy Dir Inst. of Econs in Transition 1998–2000; Head Group of Advisers to Chair. of Govt Russian Fed. 1992–93; Deputy Minister of Finance 2000–, First Deputy 2001–. *Leisure interests:* tourism, swimming, literature. *Address:* Ministry of Finance, Ilyinka str. 9, 103097 Moscow, Russia (Office). *Telephone:* (095) 928-56-40 (Office). *Fax:* (095) 913-43-17 (Office). *Website:* www.miufiu.ku (Office).

UMBA DI LUTETE, LenD; Democratic Republic of the Congo diplomatist and former government official; b. 30 June 1939, Kangu; s. of late Umba Julien and Mdbuilu Matsumba; m. Diomi Kiese 1967; three s. three d.; ed Univ. of Lovanium, Univ. Libre de Bruxelles, Belgium; training with US Agency for Int. Devt and with Belgian Parl. and Foreign Ministry; taught at Univ. of Lovanium, at Nat. Univ. of Zaire; Minister at the Presidency 1969–70, of Energy 1970–71, of Mining 1971–74, for Foreign Affairs 1974–75, for Politics 1975–76, for State Affairs, Foreign Affairs and Int. Co-operation 1977–79, for Nat. Guidance, Culture and the Arts 1979–80; mem. Political Bureau of Mouvement populaire de la révolution (MPR), also MPR Perm. Cttee; Perm. Rep. to UN 1976–77, 1982–84; State Commr for Foreign and Int. Affairs 1984–85; fmr leader of dels to UN Gen. Ass. and Security Council, to OAU, OCAM, UNCTAD. *Address:* c/o Ministry of Foreign Affairs, Kinshasa, Democratic Republic of the Congo.

UMRI, Gen. Hassan; Yemeni politician; took part in revolution against Imamate 1962; Minister of Transport Sept.–Oct. 1962, of Communications 1962–63; mem. Council of Revolutionary Command 1962–63; Vice-Pres. of Yemen 1963–66; mem. Political Bureau 1963–66; Prime Minister Jan.–April 1965, 1965–66, 1967–68; Mil. Gov.-Gen. of Yemen 1968–69; also C-in-C of Army; Prime Minister Aug.–Sept. 1971; in exile in Lebanon until Jan. 1975; returned to Yemen Arab Repub. Jan. 1975.

UNAKITAN, Kemal; Turkish politician; b. 1946, Edirne; ed Ankara Econ. and Commerical Sciences Acad.; fmr Financial Comptroller Ministry of Finance, Minister of Finance 2002–; fmr mem. Exec. Bd SEKA Directorate Gen., Albaraka Türk and Family Finance. *Address:* Ministry of Finance, Maliye Bakanlıği, Dikmen Cad., Ankara, Turkey (Office). *Telephone:* (312) 4250018 (Office). *Fax:* (312) 4250058 (Office). *E-mail:* bshalk@maliye.gov.tr (Office). *Website:* www.maliye.gov.tr (Office).

UNCKEL, Per; Swedish politician; b. 24 Feb. 1948, Finspång, Östergötland; m. Christina Lagenquist 1977; two s.; ed Uppsala Univ.; Chair. Swedish Young Moderates 1971–76, MP (Östergötland) 1976–86, 1994–, Moderate Party Spokesman on Energy Questions 1978–82, Nat. Campaign Leader 1980 Referendum on Nuclear Power, Party Spokesman on Educ. and Science 1982–86, Sec.-Gen. Moderate Party 1986–91; Minister of Educ. and Science 1991–94; Spokesman on Employment 1994–98, Chair. Parl. Standing Cttee. on the Constitution 1998–, Parl. Group Leader Moderate Party 1999–; Sec.-Gen. Nordic Council of Ministers 2003–. *Publications:* Knowledge as a Personal Investment 1998, No One Behind. *Leisure interests:* music, carpentry. *Address:* Nordic Council of Ministers, Store Strandstrasse 18, 1255 Copenhagen, Denmark. *Website:* www.norden.org (Office).

UNDERWOOD, Cecil H., LLD; American politician and businessman; b. 5 Nov. 1922, Joseph's Mills, West Va; s. of Silas H. Underwood and Della N. Underwood; m. Hovah Hall 1948; one s. two d.; ed Salem Coll., West Virginia Univ.; US Army Reserve Corps 1942–43; high-school teacher 1943–46; mem. staff Marietta Coll. 1946–50; Vice-Pres. Salem Coll. 1950–56; mem. West Virginia House of Dels 1944–56 and Minority Floor Leader 1949–54; Gov. of West Virginia 1957–61, 1997–2000; Temporary Chair. Republican Nat. Convention 1960; Vice-Pres. Island Creek Coal Co. 1961–64; Dir Civic Affairs, Northeastern Region, Monsanto Co. 1965–66; Vice-Pres. Govt and Civic Affairs, Monsanto Co., Washington, DC 1967; Pres. Franswood Inc., Huntington 1968–75; Pres. Cecil H. Underwood Asscns 1965–80; field underwriter New York Life Insurance Co. 1976–78; Pres. Bethany Coll. 1972–75, Princess Coals Inc. 1978–81, Chair. Bd 1981–83; Pres. Morgantown Industrial Park Inc. 1983–86, Chair. Bd 1986–96; Pres. Software Valley Corpn 1989–92, Mon View Heights of West Va 1993–96; Bd of Dirs. Huntington Fed. Savings and Loan Asscn 1961–96, American Cancer Soc. 1973–; mem. Bd of Trustees Salem-Teikyo Univ. 1990–; Chair. W Va State Council on Vocational Educ. 1982–96; Pres. Nat. Asscn of State Councils on Vocational Educ. (NASCOVE) 1994–96; mem. Bd West Va State Coll. System (Chair. 1991–93); Vice-Chair.

Huntington Foundation 1986–94, Chair. 1994–; 12 hon. degrees. *Address:* c/o Governor's Mansion, 1578 Kanawha Boulevard East, 1-C Charleston, WV 25311, USA (Home).

UNGARO, Emanuel Mattéotti; French fashion designer; b. 13 Feb. 1933, Aix-en-Provence; s. of Cosimo Ungaro and Concetta Casalino; m. Laura Bernabei; one d.; ed Lycée d'Aix-en-Provence; worked as tailor at Aix-en-Provence then with Camps, Paris, Balenciaga Paris and Madrid 1958–64, Courrèges, Paris 1964; Couturier, Paris 1965–. *Leisure interests:* music, reading, skiing. *Address:* 2 avenue Montaigne, 75008 Paris, France.

UNGER, Felix, DrMed; Austrian surgeon; b. 2 March 1946, Klagenfurt; s. of Carl Unger and Maria Unger; m. Monika von Fioreschy 1971; two s.; lecturer Univ. of Vienna 1978–83, Prof. Univ. of Innsbruck 1983–; Head of Heart Surgery Salzburg State Hosp.; Founder and Pres. European Acad. of Sciences and Arts; Hon. DrMed (Temeschwar, Budapest, Tokyo, Maribor and Riga) 1990–2003; Bundesverdienstkreuz 1992; Dr. Karl Renner Prize 1975, Sandoz Prize 1980, Plannsee Prize 1982. *Publications:* 15 books and more than 500 articles in specialist journals. *Leisure interest:* arts. *Address:* European Academy of Sciences and Arts, Waagplatz 3, A-5020 Salzburg (Office); Schwimmschulstrasse 31, 5020 Salzburg, Austria. *Telephone:* (66) 2841345 (Office); (66) 2824741 (Home). *Fax:* (66) 2841343 (Office); (66) 2433840 (Home). *E-mail:* felix.unger@european-academy.at (Office); f.unger@lks.at (Office). *Website:* www.european-academy.at (Office); www.ehi.at; www.eomed.at.

UNGER, Michael Ronald; British newspaper editor and executive; b. 8 Dec. 1943, Surrey; s. of Ronald Unger and Joan Stanbridge; m. 1st Eunice Dickens 1966 (divorced 1992); one s. one d. (deceased); m. 2nd Noorah Ahmed 1993; ed Wirral Grammar School, Liverpool Polytechnic; trainee journalist, Stockport 1963–65; Production Ed., Reading Evening Post 1965–67; News Ed., Perth, Australia 1967–71; Deputy Ed. Daily Post, Liverpool 1971–79, Ed. 1979–82; Ed. Liverpool Echo 1982–83; Ed. Manchester Evening News 1983–97; Dir Guardian Media Group 1983–97, Manchester Evening News PLC 1983–97; Gen. Man. Jazz FM; Chair. The Lowry Centre 1996–, Youth Charter for Sport 1996–2000; mem. Broadcasting Standards Comm. 1999–2000; Trustee Scott Trust 1986–97; various newspaper awards including Newspaper Design 1980, 1981, 1982, 1994; Ed. of the Year 1988. *Publication:* The Memoirs of Bridget Hitler 1979. *Leisure interests:* books, theatre.

UNGERER, Werner, Dr rer. pol; German diplomatist; b. 22 April 1927, Stuttgart; s. of Max Ungerer and Elisabeth (Mezger) Ungerer; m. Irmgard Drenckhahn 1959; one s. two d.; ed Dillman Gymnasium, Stuttgart, Technical Univ. Stuttgart, Univ. of Tübingen and Coll. of Europe, Bruges; Attaché, diplomatic service 1952–54; Vice-Consul, Boston 1954–56; Consul, Bombay 1956–58; Head of Div. Euratom Comm. Brussels 1958–64; Ministry of Foreign Affairs 1964–70; Resident Lecturer on Diplomacy and European Integration, Univ. of Bonn 1965–66; rep. to int. orgs in Vienna 1970–75; Consul-Gen. New York 1975–79; Ministry of Foreign Affairs 1979–85; Dir-Gen. Dept of Econ. Affairs 1984–85; Perm. Rep. to EEC Brussels 1985–89; Rector Coll. of Europe 1990–93; lecturer, Univ. of Bonn 1994–98; Pres. European Co-operation Fund 1994–98; mem. Bd of Trustees, Trier Acad. of European Law 1993–2003; Bundesverdienstkreuz, Order Leopold II of Belgium, Medal of Merit, Europa-Union Germany. *Music:* piano recitals in Carnegie Hall, NY 1979, Brussels Opera 1989. *Publications:* numerous articles on European integration, energy problems and int. orgs in reviews and anthologies. *Leisure interests:* history, religions, playing piano and composing. *Address:* Nachtigallenweg 19, 53343 Wachtberg, Germany. *Telephone:* (228) 325572.

UNGERS, Oswald Mathias, DipEng; German architect and university professor; b. 12 July 1926, Kaisersesch; s. of Anton Ungers and Maria (née Mitchels) Ungers; m. Liselotte Gabler 1956; one s. two d.; ed Technical Univ., Karlsruhe; architectural practice, Cologne 1950–62, Berlin 1962–69, Ithaca, NY 1969–; Prof. of Architecture, Technische Universität, Berlin 1963–73, Dean, Faculty of Architecture 1965–67; Prof. of Architecture, Cornell Univ. 1968–, Chair. of Dept 1968–74; Visiting Prof., Harvard Univ. 1972, 1977, Univ. of Calif. (LA) 1973; mem. Accademia Nazionale di San Luca, Rome, Akademie der Wissenschaft, Berlin. *Publications:* Optimization Models for Housing, New York State Pattern Development, Settlements of the 20th Century, The Urban Block, The Urban Villa, The Urban Garden, O.M. Ungers 1951–84: Bauten und Projekte, O. M. Ungers-Architektur 1951–90, O. M. Ungers Architektur 1991–98. *Address:* Belvederestrasse 60, 50933 Cologne, Germany. *Telephone:* (221) 492343.

UNO, Osamu, BL; Japanese business executive; b. 29 May 1917, Kyoto; s. of Kenichiro Uno and Tami Uno; m. Yoshie Uno 1945; one s. two d.; ed Tokyo Univ.; Dir Toyobo Co. Ltd 1971, Man. Dir 1974–76, Sr Man. Dir 1976–77, Deputy Pres. 1977–78, Pres. 1978–83, Chair. 1983–92, Hon. Chair. and Dir 1992–94, Sr Adviser 1994–97, Hon. Sr Adviser 1997–; Vice-Pres. Japan Chemical Fibres Assn 1980–81, Pres. 1981–82; Vice-Pres. Japanese Spinners' Assn 1982–83, Pres. 1983–84; Vice-Chair. Kansai Econs Fed. 1983–87, Chair. 1987–94, Exec. Adviser 1994–; Blue Ribbon Medal Japan 1982, Kt Commdr's Cross (Badge and Star) of Order of Merit of Fed. Repub. of Germany 1990, Officier, Légion d'honneur 1990, Grand Cordon, Order of the Sacred Treasure 1991, Order of Diplomatic Service Merit, Heung-In Medal 1992. *Leisure interest:* golf. *Address:* 2-8 Dojima Hama, 2-chome Kita-ku, Osaka 530-8230 (Office); 1-46 Showa-cho, Hamadera Sakai, Osaka 592-8345, Japan (Home). *Telephone:* (6) 348-3252 (Office).

UNSWORTH, Barry; British writer; b. 10 Aug. 1930, Wingate, Co. Durham; s. of the late Michael Unsworth and Elsie Unsworth; m. 1st Valerie Irene Moore 1959 (divorced 1991); three d.; m. 2nd Aira Pohjanvaara-Buffa 1992; ed Manchester Univ.; nat. service; taught English in France and at Univs of Athens and Istanbul; Writer-in-Residence Ambleside, Cumbria 1979, Univ. of Liverpool 1985; Visiting Literary Fellow Univs of Durham and Newcastle 1982; moved to Helsinki 1987; now lives in Italy; Hon. Litt. D. (Manchester) 1998. *Publications:* The Partnership 1966, The Greeks Have A Word For It 1967, The Hide 1970, Mooncranker's Gift (winner Heinemann Fiction Prize) 1973, The Big Day 1976, Pascali's Island 1980, The Rage of the Vulture 1982, Stone Virgin 1985, Sugar and Rum 1988, Sacred Hunger 1992 (jt winner, Booker Prize 1992), Morality Play 1995, After Hannibal 1996, Losing Nelson 1999, The Songs of the Kings 2002. *Leisure interests:* gardening, bird-watching. *Address:* c/o Giles Gordon, Curtis Brown, Haymarket House, 28–29 Haymarket, London, SW1Y 4SP, England; Casella Postale 24, 06060 Agello (PG), Italy (Home). *Telephone:* (20) 7396-6600 (London). *Fax:* (20) 7396-0110 (London).

UNTERMANN, Jürgen, DPhil; German professor of linguistics; b. 24 Oct. 1928, Rheinfelden; ed Univs of Frankfurt and Tübingen; Asst Prof. Univ. of Tübingen 1953–58, Pvt. Tutor 1962–65; project on Pre-Roman inscriptions in the Iberian Peninsula 1958–62; Full Prof. Comparative Linguistics, Univ. of Cologne 1965–94, Dean, Faculty of Letters 1971–72, Emer. Prof. 1994–; Dr hc (Salamanca, Santiago de Compostela). *Publications:* Die Venetischen Personennamen 1961, Monumenta Linguarum Hispanicarum, Vol. I 1975, Vol. II 1980, Vol. III 1990, Vol. IV 1997, Einführung in die Sprache Homers 1987, Oskisch-Umbrisches Wörterbuch 2000. *Address:* Pfalzgrafenstrasse 11, 50259 Pulheim, Germany (Home). *Telephone:* (2234) 82274 (Home). *E-mail:* juergen.untermann@epost.de (Home).

UNWIN, Geoff (Eric Geoffrey), BSc; British business executive; b. 9 Aug. 1942, Radcliffe-on-Trent, Notts.; s. of Maurice Doughty Unwin and Olive Milburn (née Watson); m. Margaret Bronia Element 1967; one s. one d.; ed Heaton Grammar School, Newcastle upon Tyne, King's Coll., Durham Univ.; with Cadbury Bros 1963–68; joined John Hoskyns & Co. 1968, Man. Dir Hoskyns Systems Devt 1978, Dir Hoskyns Group 1982, Man. Dir 1984; COO Cap Gemini 1993–2000, COO and Vice-Chair. Exec. Bd 1996–2000, Chair. Cap Programmator AB 1993–2000, CEO, mem. Bd Cap Gemini Ernst & Young (fmrly Cap Gemini) 2000–02; Dir (non-exec.) Volmac Software Group NV 1990, Gemini Consulting Holding SA 1994–2000, United News & Media PLC 1995– (Chair. 2001–); Pres. Computing Services Asscn 1987–88; mem. Information Tech. Advisory Bd 1988–91; Deputy Chair. (Chair. Elect) Halna PLC 2002–; Chair. 3G Lab, United Business Media PLC 2002–; Dir (non-voting) CGEY; Freeman City of London 1987. *Leisure interests:* golf, riding, skiing, gardening. *Address:* United Business Media plc, Ludgate House, 245 Blackfriars Road, London, SE1 9UY (Office); 17 Park Village West, London, NW1 4AE, England (Home). *Telephone:* (20) 921-5980 (Office). *Fax:* (20) 921-5982 (Office). *E-mail:* geoff.unwin@gunwin.co.uk (Office).

UNWIN, Sir (James) Brian, KCB, MA; British banker and fmr government official; b. 21 Sept. 1935, Chesterfield; s. of Reginald Unwin and Winifred Walthall; m. Diana Scott 1964; three s.; ed Chesterfield School, New Coll. Oxford and Yale Univ.; Asst Prin. Commonwealth Relations Office 1960; Pvt. Sec. to British High Commr Salisbury, Rhodesia 1961–64; First Sec. British High Comm. Accra 1964–65; FCO 1965–68; transferred to HM Treasury 1968; Pvt. Sec. to Chief Sec. Treasury 1970–72, Asst Sec. 1972, Under-Sec. 1976, Deputy Sec. 1983–85; seconded to Cabinet Office 1981–83; Dir European Investment Bank (EIB) 1983–85, Pres. 1993–2000, Hon. Pres. 2000–; Deputy Sec. Cabinet Office 1985–87; Chair. Bd HM Customs & Excise 1987–93; Gov. EBRD 1993–2000; Chair. Supervisory Bd European Investment Fund 1994–2000; Hon. Pres. Euronem (Athens) 2000–; mem. Advisory Bd IMPACT 1990–93; mem. Bd of Dirs ENO 1993–94, 2000–, Fondation Pierre Werner; mem. Bd Centre d'Etudes Prospectives (CEPROS) 1996–2000; mem. Bd of Dirs Dexia Bank 2000– (Pres. 2001–), European Centre for Nature Conservation 2000– (Pres. 2001–), "Britain in Europe" Council 2002–; Hon. Fellow New Coll. Oxford 1997, Inst. of Indirect Taxation 2002; Gold Medal, Fondation du Mérite Européen, Officier du Wissam Al Alloui (Morocco) 1999, Grand Officier Ordre de la Couronne (Belgium) 2000, Grand Croix Ordre Grand Ducal de la Couronne de Chêne (Luxembourg) 2001. *Publication:* Corporate Social Responsibility and Socially Responsible Investing (co-author) 2002. *Leisure interests:* opera, bird-watching, Wellingtoniana, cricket. *Address:* c/o Reform Club, Pall Mall, London, SW1Y 5EW, England. *Telephone:* (1306) 877481 (Home). *Fax:* (1372) 877528 (Home).

UOSUKAINEN, Riitta, MA, LicPhil; Finnish politician and teacher; b. 18 June 1942, Jääski; d. of Reino Vainikka and Aune Vainikka; m. Toivo Uosukainen; one s.; ed Univ. of Helsinki; teacher Imatrankoski Upper Second School 1969–; Prov. Instructor in Finnish Language, Kymi Prov. 1976–83; mem. Imatra Town Council 1977–92, Vice-Chair. 1980–86; mem. Eduskunta (Parl.) 1983–2003, Minister of Educ. 1991–94, Speaker of Parl. 1994–2003; Dr. hc (Finlandia Univ., USA) 1997, (Lappeenranta Inst. of Tech.) 1999; Commdr Order of White Rose 1992, Commdr Italian Repub. 1993, Order of First Class of White Star (Estonia) 1995, Grand Cross First Class, Order of Merit (Germany) 1996, Grand Cross, Order of the Crown (Belgium) 1996, Commdr Grand Cross, Royal Order of Polar Star (Sweden) 1996, Grand Cross, Order of Honour (Greece) 1996, Commdr Cross, Order of Falcon (Finland) 1997; Speaker of the Year Award 1985. *Publications:* (as co-author): Clues for Mother Tongue Teaching 1979, Link Exercises in Mother Tongue 1981,

Mother Tongue Fountain 1984, Liehuva Liekinvarsi (speeches and letters) 1996. *Leisure interest:* literature. *Address:* Olkinuorankatu 11, 55910 Imatra, Finland (Home). *Telephone:* (5) 4337766 (Home). *Fax:* (5) 4337700 (Home).

UPDIKE, John Hoyer, AB; American writer; b. 18 March 1932, Shillington, Penn.; s. of Wesley R. Updike and Linda Grace Hoyer Updike; m. 1st Mary Pennington 1953; two s. two d.; m. 2nd Martha Bernhard 1977; ed Shillington High School, Pennsylvania and Harvard Univ.; reporter on the magazine New Yorker 1955–57; mem. Nat. Inst. of Arts and Letters, American Acad. of Arts and Sciences; Dr hc (Harvard) 1992; Rosenthal Award, Nat. Inst. of Arts and Letters 1960; O'Henry Story Award 1967, 1991, US Nat. Book Critics Circle Award 1982, Pulitzer Prize 1982, 1991, Nat. Medal of Arts 1989, Scanno Prize 1991, Harvard Arts Medal 1998, Nat. Book Foundation Award for Lifetime Achievement 1999. *Publications:* The Carpentered Hen (poems) 1958, The Poorhouse Fair (novel) 1959, The Same Door (short stories) 1959, Rabbit, Run (novel) 1960, Pigeon Feathers and Other Stories 1962, The Centaur (novel) 1963, Telephone Poles and Other Poems 1963, Assorted Prose 1965, Of the Farm (novel) 1965, The Music School (short stories) 1966, Couples (novel), Midpoint and other poems 1969, Bech: A Book 1970, Rabbit Redux (novel) 1972, Museums and Women and Other Stories 1972, Buchanan Dying (play) 1974, A Month of Sundays (novel) 1975, Picked-up Pieces 1976, Marry Me (novel) 1976, The Coup (novel) 1978, Tossing and Turning (poems) 1978, Problems (short stories) 1979, Your Lover Just Called 1980, Rabbit is Rich (novel) 1981, Bech is Back 1982, Hugging the Shore (essays and criticism) 1984, The Witches of Eastwick (novel) 1984, Facing Nature 1984, The Year's Best American Short Stories (ed.) 1985, Roger's Version (novel) 1986, Trust Me (short stories) 1987, S (novel) 1988, Self-Consciousness (autobiog.) 1989, Just Looking (essays) 1989, Rabbit at Rest 1990, Odd Jobs (essays and criticism) 1991, Memories of the Ford Administration (novel) 1992, Collected Poems 1953–1993 1993, Brazil (novel) 1993, The Afterlife and Other Stories 1994, In the Beauty of the Lilies 1996, Golf Dreams (writings on golf) 1996, Toward the End of Time 1997, Bech at Bay: A quasi-novel 1999, More Matter (essays and criticism) 1999, Gertrude and Claudius (novel) 2000, The Best American Short Stories of the Century (ed.) 2000, Licks of Love 2001. *Leisure interest:* golf. *Address:* Beverly Farms, MA 01915, USA.

URANO, Yasuoki; Japanese politician; fmr Parl. Vice-Minister of Foreign Affairs, of Int. Trade and Industry; mem. House of Reps., Chair. Cttee on Commerce and Industry; Minister of State, Dir-Gen. Science and Tech. Agency 1995–96. *Address:* c/o Science and Technology Agency, 2-2-1, Kasumigaseki, Chiyoda-ku, Tokyo 100, Japan. *Telephone:* (3) 3581-5271.

URBAIN, Robert; Belgian politician; b. 24 Nov. 1930, Hornu; three s.; ed Ecole Normale, Mons; math. teacher 1950–58; Deputy for Mons 1971–95; Sec. of State for Planning and Housing 1973, for Econ. Affairs (French region) 1977–78; Minister of Posts and Telephones 1979, of Foreign Trade 1980–81, of Health and Educ. (French sector) 1981–85, of Social Affairs and Health Feb.–May 1988, of Foreign Trade 1988–92, of Foreign Trade and European Affairs 1992–95; mem. Senate 1995–99; Minister of State 1998–; Prés. du Conseil d'Admin. de la Faculté Polytechnique de Mons; Grand-Croix Ordre de Léopold II, Croix civique (1st Class); Officier Ordre de la Pléiade, Grand-Croix Ordre de la Couronne, and numerous foreign awards. *Leisure interests:* cycling, swimming. *Address:* Hôtel de Ville, 7300 Boussu (Office); Rue de Bavay 42, 7301 Hornu, Belgium (Home). *Telephone:* (65) 76-21-11 (Office). *Fax:* (65) 79-36-14 (Office); (65) 65-02-65 (Home).

URBAN, Jerzy; Polish journalist; b. 3 Aug. 1933, Łódź; s. of Jan Urban and Maria Urban; m. 1st 1957; one d.; m. 3rd Małgorzata Daniszewska 1986; ed Warsaw Univ.; staff writer, weekly Po Prostu, Warsaw 1955–57; head of home section, weekly Polityka, Warsaw 1960–63, 1968–81; columnist of satirical weekly Szpilki, articles written under pen-names including Jan Rem and Jerzy Kibic; Govt Press Spokesman 1981–89; Minister without portfolio, Head Cttee for Radio and Television April–Sept. 1989; Dir and Ed.-in-Chief, Nat. Workers' Agency Nov. 1989–90; Dir and Ed.-in-Chief Unia-Press Feb.–May 1990; Pres. Kier Co. Ltd 1990–; Pres. URMA Co. Ltd, Warsaw 1991–; Ed.-in-Chief, political weekly Nie Oct. 1990–; participant Round Table debates, mem. group for mass media Feb.–April 1990; mem. Journalists' Asscn of Polish People's Repub. 1982–; mem. Polish Writers' Union; Victor Prize (TV) 1987, Złoty KrzyżZastTugi, KrzyżKomandorski Polonia Restituta. *Screenplays include:* Sekret, Otello. *Publications:* Kolekcja Jerzego Kibica 1972, Impertynencje: Felietony z lat 1969–72 1974, Wszystkie nasze ciemne sprawy 1974, Grzechy chodzą po ludziach 1975, Gorączka 1981, Romanse 1981, Robak w jabłku 1982, Na odlew 1983, Samosądy 1 1984, Felietony dla cudzych zon 1984, Samosądy 2 1984, Z pieprzem i solą 1986, Jakim prawem 1988, Rozkosze podglądania 1988, Cały Urban 1989, Alfabet Urbana 1990, Jajakobyły 1991, Prima aprilis towarzysze 1992, Klątwa Urbana 1995, Druga Klątwa Urbana 2000. *Leisure interest:* social life. *Address:* URMA Co. Ltd, ul. Słoneczna 25, 00 789 Warsaw, Poland (Office). *Telephone:* (22) 8485290 (Office). *Fax:* (22) 8497258 (Office). *E-mail:* nie@atcom.net.pl (Office); nie@redakya.nie.aom.pl (Office).

URBANOVÁ, Eva; Czech opera and concert singer (soprano); b. 20 April 1961, Slaný; ed Acad. of Musical Arts; opera début Plzeň Josef Kajetan Tyl Theatre 1987; soloist Plzeň Opera 1988–90; Chief of opera singer section Conservatory Plzeň 1989; soloist Nat. Theatre Prague 1990–, Metropolitan Opera New York 1996–; charity concert tours with Karel Gott, Czech Repub. 1998; concert tours and opera performances in Canada, France, Italy, USA (Dvořák operas), Hong Kong (Janáček operas) and Germany (Verdi opera);

charity concerts after floods in Czech Repub. 2002–; Classic Prize for propagation of Czech music in the world 1999. *Recordings:* Duets (with Karel Gott) 1998, Czech Opera Airs 1998, Czech Christmas Carols 2000. *Leisure interests:* cooking, piano. *Address:* Národní divadlo, National Theatre, Prague 1 Ostrovní, 1 110 00, Czech Republic. *Telephone:* (2) 24910312. *Fax:* (2) 24911524.

URE, Sir John Burns, KCMG, LVO, MA; British diplomatist, author and company director; b. 5 July 1931, London; s. of the late Tam Ure; m. Caroline Allan 1972; one s. one d.; ed Uppingham School, Magdalene Coll., Cambridge, Harvard Business School, USA; served in Scottish Rifles, Malaya 1950–51; appointments in British Embassies Moscow, Léopoldville, Santiago and Lisbon and at Foreign Office, London 1956–79, Asst Under-Sec. of State (Americas) in FCO 1981–83; Amb. to Cuba 1979–81, to Brazil 1984–87, to Sweden 1987–91; UK Commr-Gen. for Expo '92, Seville; Dir Thomas Cook Group 1991–99, Sotheby's Scandinavia Advisory Bd, CSE Aviation Ltd 1992–94; consultant, Robert Fleming (merchant bankers) 1995–98, Ecosse Films 1996–99; Chair. Anglo-Swedish Soc. 1992–96, Brazilian Chamber of Commerce 1994–96, Panel of judges for Travel Book of the Year Award 1991–99; Trustee Leeds Castle Foundation. *Publications:* Cucumber Sandwiches in the Andes 1973, Prince Henry the Navigator 1977, The Trail of Tamerlane 1980, The Quest for Captain Morgan 1983, Trespassers on the Amazon 1986, Royal Geographical Soc. History of World Exploration (section on Cen. and S. America) 1991, A Bird on the Wing 1992, Diplomatic Bag 1994, The Cossacks 1999; regular book reviews in Times Literary Supplement; travel articles for Daily Telegraph and Sunday Telegraph. *Leisure interests:* travel, writing. *Address:* Netters Hall, Hawkhurst, Kent, TN18 5AS, England. *Telephone:* (1580) 752191. *Fax:* (1580) 754532.

UREN, Thomas, AO; Australian politician (retd); b. 28 May 1921, Balmain, NSW; s. of Thomas Uren and Agnes Uren; m. 1st Patricia Uren 1947 (died 1981); one s. one d.; m. 2nd Christine Anne Logan 1992; one d.; served with Royal Australian Artillery 1939, 2nd Australian Imperial Force 1941, in Japanese prisoner-of-war camp 1942–45 (Burma–Siam Railway); Labor MP for Reid 1958–90; mem. Opposition cabinet 1969–72; mem. Fed. Parl. Labor Party Exec. 1969–72, Deputy Leader 1976–77; First Minister of Urban and Regional Devt 1972–75; Fed. Labor Spokesman, Urban and Regional Devt 1976–77, on Urban and Regional Affairs, Decentralization, Local Govt, Housing and Construction 1977–80, on Urban and Regional Affairs 1980–83; Minister for the Territories and Local Govt and Minister assisting Prime Minister for Community Devt and Regional Affairs 1983–84, Minister for Local Govt and Admin Services 1984–87; del. to Australasian Area Conf. of Commonwealth Parl. Asscn, Darwin 1968, to Australian Parl. Mission to Europe 1968, to Commonwealth Parl. Asscn Conf., Canberra 1970; Leader Australian del. to IPU 1987–90, Chair. Asian-Pacific Group 1989–90; brought back Australian hostages from Baghdad 1990; Chair. Australia-Vietnam Soc., Parramatta Park Trust; Pres. H. V. Evatt Foundation; Patron Defenders of Sydney Harbour Foreshores; Life Mem. Australian Labor Party 1993; Hon. DUniv (Charles Sturt Univ.) 1997, Hon. DSciArch (Sydney) 2002. *Publication:* Tom Uren Stright Left 1994. *Leisure interests:* gardening, theatre, opera, music, art, environmental issues, photography. *Address:* 8 Gilchrist Place, Balmain, NSW 2041, Australia.

URIBE VÉLEZ, Alvaro, LLB; Colombian politician; b. 4 July 1952, Medellín; m. Lina Moreno; two s.; ed Univ. of Antioquia, Harvard Univ., Mass., USA, Univ. of Oxford, UK; Sec.-Gen. Ministry of Labour 1977–78; Dir of Civil Aviation 1980–82; Mayor of Medellín 1982, Councillor 1984–86, Senator of Antioquia Prov. 1986–90, 1990–94; Gov. of Antioquia 1995–97; Presidential Cand. for Movimiento Primero Colombia 2002; Pres. of Colombia May 2002–. *Address:* Office of the President, Palacio de Nariño, Carrera 8A, No. 7–26, Santafé de Bogotá, Colombia. *Telephone:* (1) 562-9300. *Fax:* (1) 286-8063. *E-mail:* primerocolombia@md.impsat.net.co (Office). *Website:* www.alvarouribevelez.com.co (Office).

URINSON, Yakov Moiseyevich, DEcon; Russian fmr politician and economist; b. 12 Sept. 1944; m.; one s. one d.; ed Moscow Plekhanov Inst. of Nat. Econs; researcher Centre Inst. of Econ. and Math. USSR Acad. of Sciences 1968–72; Deputy Head of Div., Deputy Dir Computation Centre USSR State Planning Cttee 1972–91; Dir Centre of Econ. Conjuncture and Prognosis, Russian Govt 1992–94; First Deputy Minister of Econs 1993–97; Deputy Chair. Russian Govt, Minister of Econs 1997–98; mem. Defence Council 1997–98; Chief Expert on econ. and financial problems United Power Grids of Russia Jan.–Sept. 1999, Deputy Chair. Sept. 1999–; Chair. Bd of Pvt. Pensions Fund of Energy Industry 2001–. *Publications:* over 50 papers and articles in specialized periodicals. *Leisure interest:* football. *Address:* United Power Grids, Kitaigorodsky Proyezd 7, 103074 Moscow, Russia (Office). *Telephone:* (095) 220-40-87 (Office). *Fax:* (095) 220-40-87 (Office). *E-mail:* uym@rao.elektra.ru (Office).

URIS, Leon Marcus; American writer; b. 3 Aug. 1924, Baltimore; s. of Wolf William Uris and Anna (Blumberg) Uris; m. 1st Betty Beck 1945 (divorced 1968); two s. one d.; m. 2nd Margery Edwards 1968 (died 1969); m. 3rd Jill Peabody 1971; one d.; ed High School, Baltimore City Coll; served with the US Marine Corps 1942–45. *Publications:* Battle Cry 1953 (novel and screenplay), The Angry Hills 1955, Exodus 1957, Mila 18 1960, Gunfight at the OK Corral (screenplay), Armageddon 1964, Topaz 1967, QB VII 1970, Trinity 1976, Ireland: A Terrible Beauty (with Jill Uris) 1976, The Haj 1984, Mitla Pass

1988, Redemption 1995, A God in Ruins 2000; (with others) Exodus Revisited (photo essay) 1959. *Address:* c/o Doubleday & Co. Inc., 1540 Broadway, New York, NY 10036, USA.

URNOV, Mark Yuryevich, CandEcon; Russian politician; b. 12 May 1947, Moscow; m.; one d.; ed Moscow State Inst. of Int. Relations; on staff Inst. of Conjuncture USSR Ministry of Foreign Trade 1970–76; researcher Inst. of World Econs and Int. Relations USSR Acad. of Sciences 1976–79; sr researcher Inst. of Culture Ministry of Culture RSFSR 1979–82; sr researcher Leningrad Inst. of Information and Automatization 1982–86; sr researcher Inst. of Int. Workers' Movt USSR Acad. of Sciences 1986–89; leading researcher USSR Acad. of Nat. Econ. 1989–90; Dir of political programmes and studies Research Cen. Ekspertiza, concurrently worked in All-Union Cen. on study of public opinion Int. Foundation of Social Econ. and Political Studies Gorbachev Foundation 1990–94; Head of div. Politika Analytical Centre, Russian Presidency April 1994–; Deputy Head, Dir Analytical Centre, Russian Presidency 1994–98; mem. Political Council, Russian Presidency 1994–98, Dir 1995–98; First Deputy Head, Centre for Econ. Reforms 1998–2000. *Address:* c/o Centre for Economic Reforms, Ilyinka str. 23 entr. 10, 103132 Moscow, Russia (Office). *Telephone:* (095) 206-46-86 (Office).

URQUHART, Sir Brian, KCMG, MBE; British international official (retd); b. 28 Feb. 1919, Bridport, Dorset; s. of Murray Urquhart and Bertha Urquhart (née Rendall); m. 1st Alfreda Huntington 1944 (dissolved 1963); two s. one d.; m. 2nd Sidney Howard 1963; one s. one d.; ed Westminster School and Christ Church, Oxford; Army service 1939–45; Personal Asst to Exec. Sec. of Preparatory Comm. of UN London 1945–46; Personal Asst to Trygve Lie, First Sec.-Gen. of UN 1946–49; served in various capacities relating to peace-keeping operations in Office of UN Under-Sec.-Gen for Special Political Affairs 1954–71; Exec. Sec. 1st and 2nd UN Int. Confs on Peaceful Uses of Atomic Energy 1955, 1958; Deputy Exec. Sec. Preparatory Comm. of IAEA 1957; Asst to Sec.-Gen.'s Special Rep. in the Congo July–Oct. 1960; UN Rep. in Katanga, Congo, 1961–62; Asst Sec.-Gen. UN 1972–74; Under-Sec.-Gen. for Special Political Affairs UN 1974–86; Scholar-in-residence, Ford Foundation 1986–95; Hon. LLD (Yale Univ.) 1981, (Tufts Univ.) 1985; Dr hc (Essex Univ.) 1981, (Westminster) 1993; Hon. DCL (Oxford Univ.) 1986, hon. degrees (City Univ. of New York, Grinnell Coll., State Univ. of New York—Binghamton) 1986, (Univ. of Colorado, Keele) 1987, (Hobart Coll., William Smith Coll.) 1988, (Warwick Univ.) 1989, (Williams Coll.) 1992, (Lafayette Coll.) 1993, (Ohio State Univ.) 2000, (Hamilton Coll.) 2000, (Brown Univ.) 2003; Roosevelt Freedom Medal 1984, Int. Peace Acad. Prize 1985. *Publications:* Hammarskjöld 1973, A Life in Peace and War 1987, Decolonization and World Peace 1989, A World in Need of Leadership: Tomorrow's United Nations (with Erskine Childers) 1990, Ralph Bunche: An American Life 1993, Renewing the United Nations System (with Erskine Childers) 1994, A World in Need of Leadership: A Fresh Appraisal (with Erskine Childers) 1996. *Address:* 50 West 29th Street, New York, NY 10001; Jerusalem Road, Tyringham, MA 01264, USA.

URQUHART, Lawrence McAllister, LLB, CA; British business executive; b. 24 Sept. 1935, Liverpool; s. of the late Robert Urquhart and Josephine McEwan Urquhart (née Bissell); m. Elizabeth Catherine Burns 1961; three s. one d.; ed Strathallan School, Perthshire, King's Coll., London Univ., Inst. of Chartered Accountants of Scotland; Price Waterhouse 1957–62; Shell Int. Petroleum 1962–64; PA Man. Consultants 1964–68; Sr Group Exec. Charterhouse Group Ltd 1968–74; Group Finance Dir Tozer Kemsley & Millbourn Holdings 1974–77, Burmah Oil Co. Ltd 1977–82; Chief Exec. Castrol Ltd 1982–85; Group Man. Dir The Burmah Oil PLC 1985–88, Group Chief Exec. 1988–90; CEO Burmah Castrol PLC 1988–93, Chair. 1990–98; Dir (non-exec.) Premier Consolidated Oilfields PLC 1986, English China Clays PLC 1991–99 (Chair. 1995–99), BAA PLC 1993–2002 (Deputy Chair. 1997–98, Chair. 1998–2002), Scottish Widows' Fund and Life Assurance Soc. 1992– (Deputy Chair. 1993–95, Chair. 1995–), Kleinwort Benson PLC 1994–98. *Leisure interests:* golf, music. *Address:* c/o BAA, 130 Wilton Road, London, SW1V 1LQ, England (Office).

URRUTIA MONTOYA, Miguel, PhD; Colombian banker; b. 20 April 1939, Bogotá; s. of Francisco Urrutia and Genoveva Montoya; m. Elsa Pombo 1963; three c.; ed Univ. de los Andes, Bogotá, Univs. of Harvard and Calif., Berkeley; Gen. Sec. Ministry of Finance 1967–68, Adviser to Monetary Bd 1969; Deputy Tech. Man. Banco de la República 1970–74; Dir Nat. Planning Dept 1974–76; Minister of Mines and Energy 1977; Vice-Rector Univ. of the UN, Tokyo 1981–85; Man. Econ. and Social Devt Dept, Interamerican Devt Bank 1985–89; Exec. Dir Fedesarrollo 1978–81, 1989–91; mem. Bd of Dirs. Banco de la República 1991–93; Gov. Cen. Bank of Colombia (Banco de la República) 1993–; has taught various courses at Univ. de los Andes at various times; fmr weekly columnist for El Tiempo newspaper. *Publications:* Empleo y Desempleo en Colombia 1968, The Development of the Colombia Labor Movement 1969, Income Distribution in Colombia 1975, Winners and Losers in Colombia's Economic Growth of the 1970s 1985, Development Planning in Mixed Economies (with Setsuko Yukawa) 1988, Financial Liberalization and the Internal Structure of Capital Markets in Asia and Latin America 1988, Economic Development Policies in Resource Rich Countries (with Setsuko Yukawa) 1988, The Political Economy of Fiscal Policy (with Shinichi Ichimura and Setsuko Yukawa) 1989. *Leisure interests:* golf, reading. *Address:* Banco de la República, Carrera 7A No. 14–78, piso 5°, Apdo Aéreo 3531, Santa Fé de Bogotá, DC, Colombia. *Telephone:* (1) 343-0190. *Fax:* (1) 286-1731. *Website:* www.banrep.gov.co (Office).

URSI, HE Cardinal Corrado; Italian ecclesiastic; b. 26 July 1908, Andria, Bari; s. of Riccardo Ursi and Apollonia Sterlicchio; ordained Priest 1931; Bishop of Nardo 1951, Archbishop of Acorensa 1961, Archbishop of Naples 1966–87, Archbishop Emer. 1987–; created Cardinal by Pope Paul VI 1967; mem. Congregation for Catholic Educ. *Address:* c/o Palazzo delle Congregazioni, Piazza Pio XII 3, 00193 Rome; Via Capodimonte 13, 80136 Naples, Italy. *Telephone:* (081) 7413985, (06) 69884167. *Fax:* (06) 69884172.

URSU, Ioan, PhD; Romanian physicist; b. 5 April 1928, Mânăstireni Commune, Cluj Co.; s. of Ioan Ursu and Ana Abrudan; m. Lucia Flămându 1930; two s. one d.; ed Univ. of Cluj and Univ. of Princeton, USA; Asst Prof., Univ. of Cluj 1949, Prof. and Head of Dept 1960–68; Prof. and Head of Dept, Univ. of Bucharest 1968–89, Sr Scientist 1990–; Visiting Prof., ICTP (Italy) 1991; Dir-Gen., Inst. for Atomic Physics 1968–76; Pres. State Cttee for Nuclear Energy 1969–76; Pres. Nat. Council for Science and Tech. 1976–79, Vice-Chair. 1979–86, First Vice-Chair. Nat. Cttee for Science and Tech. 1986–89; Corresp. mem. Romanian Acad. 1963, mem. 1974, Pres. Physics Section 1988–; mem. Scientific Council of the Jt Inst. for Nuclear Research, Dubna 1969; mem. Bd of Govs. IAEA 1971, Vice-Pres. 1972; mem. Scientific Advisory Cttee, IAEA 1979–90; mem. Exec. Council, European Physical Soc. 1968, Vice-Pres. 1975, Pres. 1976–79; Pres. Balkan Physical Union 1987; Ed. two Romanian journals of physics and int. journals of magnetic resonance, lasers, materials and energy; mem. Romanian Soc. of Physics and Chem., Physical Socs. of USA, Belgium, France; mem. Bd of Int. Soc. of Magnetic Resonance; mem. Cttee Atomes et Molécules par Etudes Radioélectriques (AMPERE); mem. American Nuclear Assocn 1976, Canadian Nuclear Assocn 1976; Corresp. mem. Ecuadorian Inst. of Natural Sciences 1976, Centre for Scientific Culture "Ettore Majorana" (Erice, Italy) 1977; mem. European Acad. of Sciences, Arts and Humanities 1980. *Publications:* Rezonanța Electronică de Spin 1965, La résonance paramagnétique électronique 1968, Magnetic Resonance and Related Phenomena (Ed.) 1971, Energia atomică 1973, Magnetic Resonance in Uranium Compounds 1979, Magnitny Rezonans v Soedynenyah Urana 1982, Fizica și Tehnologia Materialelor Nucleare 1982, Physics and Technology of Nuclear Materials 1985, Interactiunea Radiației Laser cu Metalele (with others) 1986, Fizika i technologyia iadernyh materialov, Vzaimodeistwie lazernovo ižluchenyia s metallami 1988, Laser Heating of Metals 1990; and about 300 papers on atomic and nuclear physics, nuclear materials, nuclear technologies, solid state physics, interaction of radiation with matter. *Address:* Str. Iuliu Tetrat 26, Bucharest 1, Romania (Home).

URWICK, Sir Alan (Bedford), KCVO, CMG, MA; British fmr parliamentary official and retd diplomatist; b. 2 May 1930, London; s. of the late Lyndall Fownes Urwick and Joan Saunders; m. Marta Yolanda (née Montagne) 1960; three s.; ed Dragon School, Rugby, New Coll. Oxford; joined Foreign Service 1952; served in embassies in Belgium 1954–56, USSR 1958–59, Iraq 1960–61, Jordan 1965–67, USA 1967–70, Egypt 1971–73; seconded to Cabinet Office as Asst Sec., Cen. Policy Review Staff 1973–75; Head of Near East and North Africa Dept, Foreign and Commonwealth Office 1975–76; Minister, British Embassy in Madrid 1977–79; Amb. to Jordan 1979–84, to Egypt 1984–87; High Commr in Canada 1987–89; Serjeant at Arms, House of Commons 1989–95; Chair. Anglo-Jordanian Soc. 1997–2001. *Leisure interests:* reading, gardening. *Address:* The Moat House, Slaugham Place, Nr Haywards Heath, W Sussex, RH17 6AL, England. *Telephone:* (1444) 400458.

USHAKOV, Yurii Viktorovich, PhD; Russian diplomatist; b. 13 March 1947, Moscow; m.; one d.; ed Moscow State Inst. of Int. Relations, Diplomatic Acad.; joined diplomatic service 1970; trans., expert, attaché USSR Embassy, Denmark 1970–75, Second then First Sec. 1978–82, Minister-Counsellor 1986–92; adviser Gen. Secr. USSR Ministry of Foreign Affairs 1982–86; Head Dept of All-Europe Co-operation, Ministry of Foreign Affairs 1992–96; Perm. Rep. of Russia to Org. for Security and Co-operation in Europe (OSCE) 1996–98; Deputy Minister of Foreign Affairs 1998; Amb. to USA 1999–. *Leisure interests:* tennis, alpine skiing. *Address:* Embassy of the Russian Federation, 2650 Wisconsin Ave, NW Washington, DC 20007 (Office); 1125 16th Street, NW, Washington, DC 20036, USA. *Telephone:* (202) 298-5700 (Office). *Fax:* (202) 298-5749 (Office). *E-mail:* rusembus@erols.com (Office). *Website:* www.russianembassy.org (Office).

USHER ARSÉNE, Assouan, MA; Côte d'Ivoirian politician and lawyer; b. 24 Oct. 1930; ed Dakar, Bordeaux and Poitiers Univ.; Lawyer, Court of Appeals, Poitiers 1955–56; Cabinet attaché de M. Houphouët-Boigny 1956; Asst Dir Caisse des Allocations Familiales 1957–59; Conseiller Général 1957–59; Deputy Vice-Pres. Nat. Ass. 1959–60; Lawyer, Court of Appeals, Abidjan 1959; Head, Ivory Coast (now Côte d'Ivoire) Perm. Mission to UN 1961–67; Minister of Foreign Affairs 1967–77; mem. UN Security Council 1964–67, Political Bureau Parti Démocratique de Côte d'Ivoire responsible for Mass Educ. 1970; Pres. Société des Ananas de la Côte d'Ivoire 1987; Nat. Order of Côte d'Ivoire.

USHERWOOD, Nicholas John, BA; British curator and art critic; b. 4 June 1943, Bucks.; s. of Stephen Usherwood and Hazel Usherwood (née Weston); m. 1st Henrietta Mahaffy (dissolved 1990); one s. one d.; m. 2nd Jilly Szaybo 1991; ed Westminster School, Courtauld Inst. of Art, Univ. of London; lecturer in art history, Portsmouth and Wimbledon Colls. of Art 1965–68; researcher, Pelican History of Art 1966–68; Admin., Press Officer RA 1969–74, Exhbns Sec. 1974–77; Deputy Keeper in charge of exhbns and public relations, British Museum 1977–78; freelance exhbn curator and organizer, art-critic, lecturer, writer 1978–; Features Ed. Galleries Magazine 1998–; Curator Topolski C

Sections 2001–02; Pres. UK Chapter, Int. Asscn of Art Critics (AICA) 2000–03; Chevalier Order of Léopold II of Belgium. *Publications include:* Exhbn catalogues for Algernon Newton 1980, Tristram Hillier 1983, Alfred Munnings 1986, Richard Eurich 1991, 1994, Nolan's Nolans 1997, Julian Trevelyan 1998. *Leisure interests:* new maps, reading poetry, talking to artists, contemporary music. *Address:* 82 High Street, Hampton Wick, Surrey, KT1 4DQ, England (Office). *Telephone:* (20) 8973-0921 (Office). *Fax:* (20) 8255-6892 (Office).

USPENSKY, Boris Andreyevich, PhD, DLitt; Russian/Italian linguist, philologist, critic, semiotician and historian; b. 1 March 1937, Moscow; s. of Andrej Uspensky and Gustava Mekler; m. 1st Galina Korshunova 1963 (died 1978); m. 2nd Tatiana Vladyshevskaya 1985; two s.; ed Moscow Univ.; dissertation on structural typology of languages published 1965 and partly translated into English 1968; dissertation on history of Russian church pronunciation partly published 1968; studied under Hjelmslev at Univ. of Copenhagen 1961; expedition to Siberia to study Ket language 1962; research at USSR Acad. of Sciences Inst. of African Languages 1963–65; research mem. of Lab. of Computational Linguistics, Moscow Univ. 1965–77, Prof., Moscow Univ. 1977–92; Fellow Inst. for Advanced Studies, Russian State Univ. for the Humanities 1992–93; Visiting Prof. Vienna Univ. 1988, Harvard Univ. 1990–91, Graz Univ. 1992, Cornell Univ. 1994, Univ. of Italian Switzerland 1997–2002; Fellow Wissenschaftskolleg (Berlin) 1992–93; Prof., Oriental Univ. of Naples 1993–; major structuralist publs 1962–; Foreign Corresp. mem. Austrian Acad. of Science 1987, Foreign mem. Norwegian Acad. of Science and Letters 1999; mem. Int. Asscn for Semiotic Studies 1976, Academia Europaea 1990, Russian Acad. of Natural Science 1992, Russian PEN Centre 1994, Soc. Royale des Lettres de Lund 1996; Hon. mem. Slavonic and E European Medieval Studies Group 1987, Asscn Int. de sémiologie de l'image 1990, Hon. Cttee, American Friends of the Warburg Inst. 1993; Dr hc (Russian State Univ. for the Humanities) 2001. *Publications include:* Principles of Structural Typology 1962, Structural Typology of Languages 1965, The Archaic System of Church Slavonic Pronunciation 1968, The History of Church-Slavonic Proper Names in Russia, A Poetics of Composition 1970 The First Russian Grammar in the Native Language 1975, The Semiotics of the Russian Icon 1976, Tipologia della cultura (with Yu. M. Lotman) 1975, Philological Investigations in the Field of Slavic Antiquities 1982, The Semiotics of Russian Culture (with Yu. M. Lotman) 1984, The Semiotics of Russian Cultural History (with Yu. M. Lotman and L. Ja. Ginsburg) 1985, The History of the Russian Literary Language of XVIII to early XIX centuries 1985, The History of the Russian Literary Language XI–XVII centuries 1987, Storia e Semiotica 1988, Sémiotique de la culture russe (with Yu. M. Lotman) 1990, Semiotik der Geschichte 1991, Storia della lingua letteraria russa: Dall'antica Rus' a Puškin 1993, Semiotics of Art 1995, Linguistica, semiotica, storia della cultura 1996, Selected Works (3 Vols) 1996–97, Tsar and Patriarch 1998, Boris and Gleb: The Perception of History in the Old Rus' 2000, "In regem unxit..." 2001; numerous articles. *Leisure interest:* travelling. *Address:* Istituto Universitario Orientale di Napoli, Dipartimento di Studi dell'Europa Orientale, Via Duomo 219, Naples 80138 (Office); Via Principe Eugenio 15, Rome 00185, Italy (Home); Chasovaya ul. 19/8 Apt. 20, Moscow 125315, Russia (Home). *Telephone:* (Office); (06) 4468157 (Italy); (095) 152-52-39 (Russia). *Fax:* (081) 5630220 (Office). *E-mail:* buspenskij@iuo.it (Office); borisusp@tiscalinet.it (Home).

USPENSKY, Vladislav Aleksandrovich; Russian composer and professor of composition; b. 7 Sept. 1937, Omsk; s. of Alexander Grigoryevich Kolodkin and Vera Pavlovna Uspenskaya; m. Irina Yevgenyevna Taimanova 1963; ed Leningrad State Conservatory; postgrad. studies under Dmitri Shostakovich; teacher of music theory Leningrad State Conservatory 1965–67, Dean of Musicology 1967–72, Prof. of Composition 1982–; Guest Composer-in-Residence Seoul Univ., Korea 1995, Lima Univ., Peru 1997, Boston Univ. USA; Chair. Music Council of Cultural Cttee, St Petersburg Govt 1996–; Vice-Pres. Union of Composers of St Petersburg 1972–; Gen. Dir Int. Musical Children's Festival 1995–; People's Artist of Russia, D. Shostakovich Prize 1997, Order of Merit of Homeland 1998, Order of Catherine the Great 2002; music festival in his honour, St Petersburg autumn 2002. *Compositions:* operas: The War Against Salamanders 1967, Intervention 1970; 8 ballets including A Road to the Day 1974, For You to the Sea 1978, Cranes Flying 1984, The Mushroom's Alarm 1990; four musicals including Anna Karenina; works for orchestra, choir, instrumental ensembles, songs (over 100), music for films, theatre and TV productions. *Publication:* D. Shostakovich in My Life. *Leisure interest:* love. *Address:* Composers' Union, B. Morskaia 45, St Petersburg (Office); Admiralteysky canal 5 Apt. 26, St Petersburg, Russia (Home). *Telephone:* (812) 311-35-48 (Office); (812) 311-74-35 (Home). *Fax:* (812) 311-35-48 (Office).

USTINOV, Sir Peter Alexander, Kt, CBE, FRSA; British actor and dramatist; b. 16 April 1921; s. of late Iona Ustinov and Nadia Benois; m. 1st Isolde Denham 1940 (divorced 1950); one d.; m. 2nd Suzanne Cloutier 1954 (divorced 1971); one s. two d.; m. 3rd Hélène du Lau d'Allemans 1972; ed Westminster School and London Theatre Studio; entered theatre as actor 1939; first appearance in revue writing own material Ambassador's Theatre, London 1940; served in army 1942–46; UNICEF Amb. of Goodwill; Pres. World Federalist Movt 1992–96; has appeared in numerous TV productions; dir operas The Magic Flute, Hamburg 1968, Don Quichotte, Paris 1973 (also designed and produced), Don Giovanni, Edin. 1973 (also designed), Les Brigands, Berlin 1978, Mavra, Milan 1982, Katia Kabanova, Hamburg 1985,

The Marriage of Figaro (Salzburg and Hamburg) 1987, The Love of the Three Oranges (Moscow) 1997; recorded Peter and the Wolf (Grammy Award); Rector Univ. of Dundee 1968, 1971–73; Chancellor Durham Univ. 1992–; Pres. World Federalist Movt 1992; Foreign mem. Acad. of Fine Arts, Paris 1988; Hon. DMus (Cleveland Inst. of Music) 1967, Hon. LLD (Univ. of Dundee) 1969, (La Salle Coll., Philadelphia) 1971, (Ottawa Univ.) 1991; Hon. DLitt (Univ. of Lancaster) 1972; Hon. Dr (Univ. of Toronto) 1984, (Pontifical Inst. of Medieval Studies, Univ. of Toronto) 1995; Hon. DHL (Georgetown Univ.) 1988, Dr hc (Free Univ. of Brussels) 1995; UNICEF Award 1978, 1995, Variety Club Award 1979; Benjamin Franklin Medal, RSA; Gold Medal (City of Athens) 1990; Greek Red Cross Medal 1990; Medal of Honour (Prague Univ.) 1991; Britannia Award (BAFTA) 1992; Critics' Circle Award 1993; Commdr Ordre des Arts et des Lettres 1985; Ordem Nacional do Cruzeiro de Sul (Brazil) 1994; German Cultural Award 1994, German Bambi Award 1994; Int. Child Survival Award, UNICEF 1995; German Video Prize (for lifetime achievement) 1997; Order of Istiqlal (Jordan); Order of the Yugoslav Flag; Bundesverdienstkreuz 1998; Bayerischer Fernsehpreis 1998. *Films include:* The Way Ahead (collaborated on screenplay) 1944, Odette 1950, Hotel Sahara 1951, Quo Vadis 1951, Beau Brummel 1954, The Egyptian 1954, We're no Angels 1955, Lola Montes 1955, Spartacus 1961 (Acad. Award for Best Supporting Actor, Golden Globe Award), Billy Budd 1962, Topkapi 1963 (Acad. Award for Best Supporting Actor), John Goldfarb 1964, Lady L 1965, Blackbeard's Ghost 1966, The Comedians 1967, Viva Max! 1970, Hot Millions (part-author and star) 1968, Hammersmith is Out (also dir) 1971, One of Our Dinosaurs is Missing 1975, Treasure of Matcumbe 1977, The Last Remake of Beau Geste 1977, The Thief of Baghdad 1978, Death on the Nile 1978, Ashanti 1978, Charlie Chan and the Curse of the Dragon Queen 1981, Evil Under the Sun 1981, Memed My Hawk (writer and dir) 1984, Appointment with Death 1988, The French Revolution 1989, The Man Who Loved Hitchcock 1989, Lorenzo's Oil 1992, The Old Curiosity Shop 1994, The Phoenix and the Magic Carpet 1994, Stiff Upper Lips 1998, Alice in Wonderland 1998, My Khmer Heart 2000. *Plays include:* Crime and Punishment 1946, Frenzy 1948, Love in Albania 1949, The Love of Four Colonels 1951, Romanoff and Juliet 1956 (British Critics' Best Play Award), Photo Finish 1962, The Unknown Soldier and his Wife 1973, King Lear 1979–80, Beethoven's Tenth 1983, (in Berlin) 1987–88, An Evening with Peter Ustinov 1990–94, 1995–97, Love of the Three Oranges (opera) 1997. *Publications:* plays: House of Regrets 1942, Blow Your Own Trumpet 1943, The Banbury Nose 1944, The Tragedy of Good Intentions 1945, The Indifferent Shepherd 1948, The Man in the Raincoat 1949, The Love of Four Colonels 1951, The Moment of Truth 1951, No Sign of the Dove 1953, Romanoff and Juliet 1956, Photo Finish 1962, The Life in My Hands 1963, Half Way up the Tree 1967, The Unknown Soldier and his Wife 1967, Who's Who in Hell 1974, Overheard 1981, Beethoven's Tenth 1983; short stories: Add a Dash of Pity 1959, The Frontiers of the Sea 1966; novels: The Loser 1960, Krumnagel 1971, The Old Man and Mr Smith 1990; autobiogs: Dear Me 1977, My Russia 1983; Ustinov at Large 1991, Ustinov Still at Large 1993, Quotable Ustinov 1995, Monsieur René 1998; The Disinformer (novellas) 1989; articles, etc. *Leisure interests:* sailing, travel. *Address:* The Ustinov Foundation Office, Höhenberg Strasse 20, 82340 Feldafing, Germany (Office); c/o William Morris Agency (UK) Ltd, 1 Stratton Street, London, W1X 6HB, England; 11 rue de Silly, 92100 Boulogne, France. *Telephone:* (20) 7355-8500 (London). *Fax:* (20) 7355-8600.

USTINOV, Vladimir Vassilyevich; Russian lawyer; b. 25 Feb. 1953, Nikolayevsk-on-Amur, Khabarovsk Territory, Russia; m.; one s. one d.; ed Kharkov Inst. of Law; prosecutor of Krasnodar Territory 1978–92; prosecutor of Sochi 1992–97; concurrently First Deputy Prosecutor Krasnodar Territory, Deputy Procurator-Gen. Russian Fed. 1997; also Head of Dept Office of Procurator-Gen., N Caucasus 1998–99; Acting Procurator-Gen. Russian Fed. 1999–2000, Procurator-Gen. 2000–; Merited Jurist of Russian Fed. *Address:* Office of the Procurator-General, Bolshaya Dmitrovka str. 15a, 103793 Moscow, Russia (Office). *Telephone:* (095) 292-88-69 (Office).

USTVOLSKAYA, Galina Ivanovna; Russian composer; b. 17 June 1919, Petrograd (now St Petersburg); ed Leningrad Conservatory (pupil of Shostakovich); teacher, then Prof. of Composition N Rimsky-Korsakov School of Music in St Petersburg 1947–. *Compositions:* author of maj. orchestral compositions rarely performed in USSR up to late 1980s due to ban on contemporary sacred music including 5 symphonies: 1 1955, 2 (Genuine Eternal Beauty) 1979, 3 (Jesus, Messiah, Rescue Us) 1983, 4 (Pray) 1987, 5 (Amen) 1989/90; also numerous compositions for different instruments and piano pieces, including Dona nobis pacem, for piccolo, tuba and piano 1970/71, Dies irae, for 8 double basses, percussion and piano 1972/73, Benedictus qui Venit, for 4 flutes, 4 bassoons and piano 1974/75. *Address:* Prospect Gagarina 27, Apt. 72, 196135 St Petersburg, Russia (Home). *Telephone:* (812) 373-15-12 (Home).

UTEEM, Cassam, GCSK, LèsL; Mauritian politician; b. 22 March 1941, Plaine Verte; m. 1967; two s. one d.; ed Univs. of Mauritius and Paris VII; fmr supervisor, Cable & Wireless Ltd; Personnel Man. Currimjee Jeewanjee & Co., Ltd; Sec.-Gen. Mauritius Nat. Youth Council 1971–72; Treas. Mauritius Council of Social Service 1971–73; Rep. of World Ass. of Youth (WAY) to UNESCO 1974–76; municipal councillor, Port Louis 1969, 1977–79, 1986–88; Lord Mayor of City of Port Louis 1986; mem. Legis. Ass. 1976–92; Minister of Employment, Social Security and Nat. Solidarity 1982–83; Opposition Whip 1983–87; Chair. Public Accounts Cttee 1988–90; Deputy Leader, Mouvement Militant Mauricien (MMM) 1988; Deputy Prime Minister and

Minister of Industry and Industrial Tech. 1990–92; Pres. Repub. of Mauritius 1992–2002; mem. hc Acad. Nationale Malgache 1995; Hon. DCL (Univ. of Mauritius) 1994; Dr hc (Univ. of Marseille III) 1994. *Address:* c/o State House, Le Réduit, Port Louis, Mauritius.

UTSUMI, Yoshio, LLB, MA.; Japanese international civil servant; b. 14 Aug. 1942; m. Masako Utsumi 1970; one s. one d.; ed Tokyo and Chicago Univs.; joined Ministry of Posts and Telecommunications 1966, Head of Investment Postal Life Insurance Bureau 1986–88, Head Gen. Affairs Div., Broadcasting Bureau 1988, with Communications Policy Bureau, Deputy Minister, Asst Vice-Minister, Dir.-Gen. MPT 1988–98; First Sec. Perm. Mission of Japan, Int. Telecommunications Union (ITU), Geneva 1978–81, Chair. ITU Plenipotentiary Conf. 1994, Sec.-Gen. ITU 1998–; Prof. of Public Admin. MPT Postal Coll. 1972; del. to numerous int. negotiations. *Address:* Office of the Secretary-General, International Telecommunications Union, Place des Nations, 1211 Geneva 20, Switzerland (Office). *Telephone:* (22) 7305111 (Office). *Fax:* (22) 7337256 (Office). *E-mail:* itumail@itu.int (Office). *Website:* www.itu.int (Office).

UTTLEY-MOORE, William James, CBE, BSc, FREng, FRAeS; British electronic engineer; b. 19 July 1944, Crayford, Kent; s. of late William Uttley-Moore and of Louisa Clara Dixon; m. Jennifer Bencer 1966; one s.; ed Erith Tech. School, London Univ.; student apprentice and devt engineer, Cintel Ltd 1960–68; project leader, Molins Machine Co. Ltd 1968–69; Chief Engineer, Computing Devices Co. Ltd 1969–75, Tech. Dir 1979–85, Chair. and Man. Dir 1985–; Founder Dir Southern FM 1989–92, Conqueror Broadcasting Ltd 1996–; Chair. E Sussex Econ. Partnership 1998–; mem. Bd, Defence Scientific Advisory Council 1994–. *Publications:* numerous tech. papers on reconnaissance, avionics and digital battlefield. *Leisure interests:* practical eng, farming, running, classical music. *Address:* Computing Devices Co. Ltd, St Leonards-on-Sea, E Sussex, TN38 9JN (Office); Tilekiln Farm, Fairlight Road, Ore, Hastings, E Sussex, TN35 5EL, England. *Telephone:* (1429) 426322 (Office). *Fax:* (1424) 447306 (Office). *E-mail:* WUM@mhs.compd.com (Office).

UTZERATH, Hansjörg; German theatre director; b. 20 March 1926, Tübingen; m. Renate Ziegfeld 1957; one s. two d.; ed Kepler Oberschule, Tübingen; began as actor, later in theatre man. in Düsseldorf and then in production; Chief Stage Man., Düsseldorfer Kammerspiele 1955–59; Dir 1959–66; Intendant, Freie Volksbühne, Berlin 1967–73; Dir Städtische Bühnen, Nuremberg 1977–92; freelance dir 1993–; guest producer at Staatstheater Stuttgart, Municher Kammerspiele and Schiller-Theater, Berlin 1959–; Visiting Prof. Univ. Mozarteum, Sazburg. *Productions include:* Tango 1971, Der Vater 1972, Viele heissen Kain (TV), Waiting for Godot 1980, Mother Courage 1981, King Lear 1982, Der Hauptmann von Köpenick 1986, Liebeskonzil 1988, Richard III 1990, Lila 1990, Beiliegend 1999. *Address:* Knesebeckstr. 98A, 10623 Berlin, Germany.

UTZON, Jørn, OA, FRIBA; Danish architect; b. 9 April 1918, Copenhagen; ed Royal Acad. of Fine Arts, Copenhagen; joined Helsinki Office of Alvar Aalto after Second World War; won travelling scholarships to Morocco and USA; designer of furniture and glassware; won competition for design of Sydney Opera House 1957, worked on project in Denmark 1957–63, in Sydney 1963–66 (resgnd as architect); won competition for design of Zürich Schauspielhaus 1966; other projects include housing scheme near Fredensborg, his own house, Bank Melli Iran, Tehran; Fellow, Royal Australian Inst. of Architects 1965; Ehrenpreis, Bund Deutscher Architekten 1966, Gold Medal, Royal Australian Inst. of Architects 1973, Wolf Prize (jtly) 1992, Pritzker Architecture Prize (for Sydney Opera House) 2003, and other awards. *Address:* 3150 Hellebaek, Denmark.

UVAROV, Andrei Ivanovich; Russian ballet dancer; b. 28 Sept. 1971, Moscow; m. Filippova Svetlana; one d.; ed Moscow School of Choreography; soloist Bolshoi Theatre 1989–; Merited Artist of Russian Fed., Benoit de la Danse Int. Prize 1993, 1st Prize Int. Ballet Competition, Japan 1995. *Ballets:* has danced leading roles with Bolshoi Theatre including Swan Lake, Cho-

piniana, Ivan the Terrible, Romeo and Juliet, Giselle, La Bayadère, Sleeping Beauty. *Address:* State Academic Bolshoi Theatre, Teatralnaya pl. 1, 103009 Moscow, Russia. *Telephone:* (095) 292-99-86 (Office).

UYEDA, Seiya, DSc; Japanese geophysicist; b. 28 Nov. 1929, Tokyo; s. of the late Seiichi Uyeda and Hatsuo Uyeda; m. Mutsuko Kosaka 1952; one s. two d.; ed Univ. of Tokyo; Research Fellow Earthquake Research Inst., Univ. of Tokyo 1955–63, Assoc. Prof. Geophysical Inst. 1963–69, Prof. Earthquake Research Inst. 1969–89; Prof., School of Marine Science and Tech., Tokai Univ. 1990–95; Harris Prof. of Geophysics, Texas A & M Univ. 1990–95; RIKEN Int. Frontier Program on Earthquake Research 1996–; Tanakadate Prize, Soc. of Terrestrial Electricity and Magnetism 1955; Okada Prize, Oceanographical Soc. of Japan 1968; Alexander Agassiz Medal, Nat. Acad. of Sciences 1972, Japan Acad. Prize 1987, George P. Woollard Award, Geological Soc. of America 1989, Walter H. Bucher Medal, American Geophysical Union 1991. *Publications:* Debate about the Earth 1967, Island Arcs 1973, The New View of the Earth 1977; 300 scientific papers. *Leisure interest:* skiing. *Address:* Earthquake Prediction Research Centre, Tokai University, 3-20-1 Orido, Shimizu City 424-8610 (Office); 2-39-6 Daizawa, Setagaya-ku, Tokyo 155-0032, Japan (Home). *Telephone:* 543-36-2862 (Office); (3) 3412-0237 (Home). *Fax:* 543-36-0920 (Office). *E-mail:* kikakn@tsc.u-tokai.ac.jp. *Website:* www.u-tokai.ac.jp.

UYS, Pieter-Dirk, BA; South African playwright, performer and producer; b. 28 Sept. 1945, Cape Town; s. of Helga Bassel and Hannes Uys; ed Univ. of Cape Town, London Film School, UK; joined Space Theatre, Cape Town 1973; f. Syrkel Theatre Co.; Dir P. D. Uys Productions, Bapetikosweti Marketing Enterprises; produced and performed 30 plays in revues throughout SA and in UK, USA, Australia, Canada, Netherlands; several videos and TV films and documentaries; Hon. DLitt (Rhodes Univ.) 1997. *Theatre:* cr. Mrs Evita Bezuidenhout – the most famous white woman in South Africa. *Television:* Evita Live and Dangerous, weekly talk/satire show 1999. *Publications:* Die van Aardes van Grootoor 1979, Paradise is Closing Down 1980, God's Forgotten 1981, Karnaval 1982, Selle ou storie 1983, Farce about Uys 1984, Appassionata 1985, Skote! 1986, Paradise is Closing Down and Other Plays 1989, No one's Died Laughing 1986, P.W. Botha: In His Own Words 1987, A Part Hate, A Part Love 1990, Funigalore 1995. *Leisure interests:* films, music, people, South African politics. *Address:* Evita SE Perron Theatre/Cafe/Bar Darling Station, Darling 7345 (Office); 17 Station Road, Darling 7345, South Africa. *Telephone:* (22) 4922831 (Office); (22) 4923208 (Home). *Fax:* (22) 4923208 (Home). *E-mail:* evita@africa.com (Office); evitadarling@hotmail.com (Home). *Website:* millennia.co.za/evita (Office).

UZAN, Cem; Turkish media executive and politician; ed Pepperdine Univ.; owner of eight radio channels, four TV channels, two newspapers and Telsim mobile telephone network; f. Youth Party, cand. in parl. elections Nov. 2002. *Address:* Telsim, Ikitelli, Istanbul 38600, Turkey (Office).

UZAWA, Hirofumi, PhD; Japanese professor of economics; b. 21 July 1928, Tottori Province; s. of Tokio Uzawa and Toshiko Uzawa; m. Hiroko Aoyoshi 1957; two s. one d.; ed Univ. of Tokyo; Research Assoc., Lecturer, Asst Prof., Dept of Econs, Stanford Univ., Calif. 1956–60, Assoc. Prof. of Econs and Statistics 1961–64; Asst Prof. of Econs and Math., Univ. of Calif., Berkeley 1960–61; Prof. of Econs Univ. of Chicago 1964–68, Univ. of Tokyo 1969–89, Prof. Emer. 1989–; Prof. of Econs, Niigata Univ. 1989–94; mem. The Japan Acad. 1989–; Matsunaga Memorial Prize 1969, Yoshino Prize 1971, Mainichi Prize 1974, desig. as Person of Cultural Merits 1983, Order of Culture 1997. *Publications:* in English: Studies in Linear and Nonlinear Programming (co-author) 1958; in Japanese: Economic Development and Fluctuations (co-author) 1972, Social Costs of the Automobile 1974, A Re-examination of Modern Economic Theory 1977, Transformation of Modern Economics 1986, A Critique of Japanese Economy 1987, Towards a Theory of Public Economics 1987, Preference, Production and Capital 1988, Optimality, Equilibrium and Growth 1988, A History of Economic Thought (in Japanese) 1989, Poverty Amid Economic Prosperity (in Japanese) 1989, Economic Analysis (in Japanese) 1990, Collected Papers of Hirofumi Uzawa (12 Vols) 1994–95, Introduction to Mathematics (6 Vols) 1997–2000. *Leisure interest:* walking. *Address:* Kamiyama-cho 20-23, Shibuya-ku, Tokyo, Japan (Home).

V

VĂCĂROIU, Nicolae; Romanian politician and economist; b. 5 Dec. 1943, Bolgrad, Bessarabia; m. Marilena Văcăroiu; one s.; ed Bucharest Acad. of Econ. Studies; Economist, Ilfov Co. Inst. of Design and Systemization; then with State Planning Cttee, promoted to Dir Econ.-Financial Synthesis Dept; apptd. Deputy Minister of Nat. Economy 1990; subsequently Head of Price Dept, Ministry of Finance, Sec. of State and Head of Tax Dept, Chair. Interministerial Cttee of Foreign Trade Guarantees and Credits; Prime Minister 1992–96; Senator 1996–, Vice-Pres. of Senate 1999–2000, Chair. 2000–; Pres. Privatisation Cttee 1997–; Chair. Romania-Brazil Friendship Asscn 1997–. *Publications:* numerous articles on econ. and financial matters. *Address:* Romanian Senate, Piața Revoluției, 71243 Bucharest, Romania.

VACEK, Miroslav; Czech politician and army officer (retd); b. 29 Aug. 1935, Kolín; m. Helena Vacek 1958; one s.; ed A. Zápotocký Mil. Acad. Brno and Mil. Acad. of USSR; Commdr Western Mil. Dist 1985; Chief of Gen. Staff of Czechoslovak Army and First Deputy of Minister of Nat. Defence 1987; Minister of Nat. Defence 1989–90; Adviser to Ministry of Defence 1990–91; Pres. Victoria (business) 1992–; mem. Parl. of Czech Repub. 1996–98; mem. Comm. for Defence and Security in Parl. 1996–98; Communist Party of Bohemia and Moravia (KSČM). *Publications:* Why Should I Keep Silent? 1991, In Fairness 1994, Úsměvy v barvě (Smiles in Khaki) 2002; articles on mil. problems published in mil. press. *Address:* Communist Party of Bohemia and Moravia, Politických vězňů 9, 110 00 Prague 1, Czech Republic. *Telephone:* 222-897-111.

VACHON, HE Cardinal Louis-Albert, CC, D.PH., D.TH., FRSC; Canadian ecclesiastic; b. 4 Feb. 1912, St Frédéric, Beauce Co., Québec; s. of Napoléon Vachon and Alexandrine Gilbert; ed Laval Univ. and St Thomas Aquinas Univ., Rome; ordained priest 1938; Prof. of Philosophy, Laval Univ. 1941–47, of Theology 1949–55; Superior, Grand Seminaire de Québec 1955–59, Gen. Superior 1960–77; Domestic Prelate 1958; Vice-Rector Laval Univ. 1960–72; Vicar-Gen., Diocese of Québec 1960–81; Protonotary Apostolic 1963–77; Auxiliary Bishop of Québec 1977–81; Archbishop of Québec and Primate of Canada 1981–90, Archbishop Emer. 1990; cr. Cardinal 1985; mem. Sacred Congregation for the Clergy 1986–, Canadian Soc. of Theology, Canadian Soc. of Authors, Admin. Bd of English Speaking Union of Commonwealth in Canada, Royal Soc. of Canada, Admin. Bd of Canadian Conf. Catholic Bishops and many other bodies; Hon. degrees from several univs.; Kt Great Cross, Equestre du Saint-Sépulchre de Jérusalem 1985, Officier, Légion d'honneur (France) 1988. *Publications:* Espérance et présomption 1958, Vérité et liberté 1962, Unité de l'université 1962, Apostolat de l'universitaire catholique 1963, Mémorial 1963, Communauté universitaire 1963, Progrès de l'université et consentement populaire 1964, Responsabilité collective des universitaires 1964, Les humanités d'aujourd'hui 1966, Excellence et loyauté des universitaires 1969. *Leisure interests:* reading, fine art. *Address:* Séminaire de Québec, 1 rue des Remparts, Québec City, Qué., G1R 5L7, Canada. *Telephone:* (418) 692-3981. *Fax:* (418) 692-4345.

VĂDUVA, Leontina; French soprano; b. 1962, Romania; d. of Maria Ciobanu; m. Gheorghe Codre; ed Bucharest Conservatoire; came to West in 1988, subsequently gaining political asylum in France; début in Massenet's Manon, Toulouse 1987; Covent Garden début as Manon 1988; appeared at Covent Garden as Gilda in Rigoletto 1989 and as Juliet in Romeo and Juliet 1995; performed Ismene in Mozart's Mitridate at the Châtelet, Micaela in Carmen at Covent Garden 1996, Mimi and Adina at Barcelona 1998; has also sung in Munich, Hamburg, Zürich, Brussels, Florence, Buenos Aires, San Francisco and Tokyo; Olivier Award for Outstanding Achievement in Opera 1988, Chevalier Ordre des Arts et des Lettres 1998. *Recordings include:* Mitridate, Le nozze di Figaro (conducted by J.E. Gardiner) 1993. *Address:* Stafford Law Associates, 6 Barnham Close, Weybridge, KT13 9PR, England (Office); c/o Theateragentur Luisa Petrov, Glauburgstr. 95, 60318 Frankfurt, Germany.

VAEA, (Baron Vaea of Houma); Tongan politician; b. 15 May 1921, Nuku'alofa; s. of Vilai Tupou and Tupou Seini Vaea; m. Hon. Tuputupu-'o-Pulotu Ma'afu 1952; three s. three d.; ed Tupou Coll., Wesley Coll., NZ, St Edmund's Hall, Oxford Univ., Kidlington Air Training School; inherited title 'Vaea' 1942; military service with RN Z.A.F. 1942–44; joined Tonga Civil Service 1948; Aide-de-Camp to HM Queen Salote Tupou III 1954–59; Gov. of Ha'apai 1960–68; Commr and Consul for Tonga in London 1969–70, High Commr and Consul 1970–72; given title of Baron by HM King Taufa'ahau Tupou IV 1970; Minister for Labour, Commerce and Industries 1973–91; Acting Deputy Prime Minister 1989; Prime Minister, Minister for Agric. and Forestry, for Fisheries 1991–2000, for Telecommunications 1991, for Women's Affairs 1991, of Marines and Ports 1994–2000; mem. Tonga Defence Bd 1973; Chair. Shipping Corpn of Polynesia 1978, Nat. Reserve Bank 1989, Tonga Telecommunications Comm. 1991–2000, Tonga Broadcasting Comm. 1991–2000, Tonga Investments Ltd 1991–; FAO Agricola Medal 2001. *Leisure interests:* tennis, rugby, farming. *Address:* P.O. Box 262, Nuku'alofa, Tonga. *Telephone:* 24-644. *Fax:* 23-888.

VAGELOS, Pindaros Roy, MD; American pharmaceutical industry executive; b. 8 Oct. 1929, Westfield, NJ; s. of Roy John Vagelos and Marianthi Lambrinides; m. Diana Touliatos 1955; two s. two d.; ed Univ. of Pennsylvania and Columbia Univ. Coll. of Physicians and Surgeons; Intern in Medicine, Mass. Gen. Hosp. 1954–55, Asst Resident in Medicine 1955–56; Surgeon, Lab.

of Cellular Physiology, Nat. Insts. of Health 1956–59, Surgeon, Lab. of Biochem. 1959–64, Head, Section on Comparative Biochem. 1964–66; Prof. of Biochem., Chair. Dept of Biological Chem., Washington Univ. School of Medicine, St Louis, Mo. 1966–75, Dir Div. of Biology and Biomedical Sciences 1973–75; Sr Vice-Pres. Research, Merck Sharp & Dohme Research Labs., Rahway, NJ 1975–76, Pres. 1976–84, Corporate Sr Vice-Pres. Merck & Co., Inc. 1982–84, Exec. Vice-Pres. 1984–85, CEO 1985–86, Chair. and CEO 1986–95; Chair Regeneron Pharmaceuticals Inc. (now called Merck Pharmaceuticals Inc.) 1995–; Trustee Rockefeller Univ. 1976–94, Univ. of Pa 1988– (Chair. Bd 1994–), Danforth Foundation 1978–; Dir TRW Inc. 1987–, Prudential Insurance Co. of America 1989–, PepsiCo Inc. 1992–, numerous other appointments; mem. NAS, American Acad. of Arts and Sciences; discoverer of acyl-carrier protein; Enzyme Chem. Award, American Chemical Soc. 1967, NJ Science/Tech. Medal 1983, Pupin Medal 1995. *Leisure interests:* jogging, tennis. *Address:* Merck Pharmaceuticals Inc., 1 Crossroads Drive, Building A, Bedminster, NJ 07921 (Office); 82 Mosle Road, Far Hills, NJ 07931, USA (Home).

VAGNORIUS, Gediminas, D.ECON.SC.; Lithuanian politician; b. 10 June 1957, Plunge Dist; m. Nijole Vagnorenė; one s. one d.; ed Inst. of Eng and Construction, Vilnius; engineer-economist, Jr researcher, then researcher, Inst. of Econs, Lithuanian Acad. of Sciences 1980–90; Deputy to Lithuanian Supreme Soviet, mem. Presidium 1990–91; Chair. Council of Ministers of Lithuania 1991–92, 1996–99; mem. Seimas (Parl.) 1992–; Chair. Bd Homeland Union/Lithuanian Conservative Party 1993–2000; Chair. Moderate Conservative Union July 2000–. *Leisure interest:* jogging. *Address:* Parliament of Lithuania, Gedimino Prospekt 53, 2002 Vilnius, Lithuania (Office). *Telephone:* (2) 396-725 (Office). *Fax:* (2) 396-288 (Office). *E-mail:* gevagn@lrs .lt (Office). *Website:* www.lrs.lt (Home).

VAGO, Constant, PhD, DSc; French pathologist and university professor; b. 2 May 1921, Debrecen, Hungary; s. of Vincent Vago and Françoise Schibl; m. Catherine Sary 1944; one s. one d.; ed Lycée of Debrecen, Univ. of Marseilles; Dir Lab. of Cytopathology, Nat. Inst. for Agron. Research, St-Christol 1958–; Prof. of Pathology and Microbiology, Univ. of Science, Montpellier 1964–; Dir Centre of Comparative Pathology, Univ. of Montpellier and WHO Research Centre 1970–; mem. Acad. of Sciences of France 1971–, Acad. of Agric. of France, New York Acad. of Sciences, Hungarian Acad. of Sciences, Nat. Acad. of Sciences of India, European Acad. of Sciences, Int. Acad. of Sciences; Past Pres. Int. Soc. for Invertebrate Pathology; Pres. Nat. Cttee of Biological Sciences of France; mem. numerous scientific socs.; Dr. hc (Medical Univ., Debrecen, Hungary); Prof. hc (Univ. of Cen. China); Int. Ishida Prize of Cytology, Int. El Fasi Great Prize for Science, Institut Pasteur Prize; Légion d'honneur, Ordre nat. du Mérite and other decorations. *Publications:* Invertebrate Tissue Culture 1972 and about 400 publications on comparative pathology, tissue culture, molecular virology, chlamydial diseases, comparative oncology. *Leisure interests:* sculpture, swimming. *Address:* Centre of Comparative Pathology, University of Sciences, Place Eugène Bataillon, 34000 Montpellier; Institut de France, 23 quai Conti, 75006 Paris; Chemin Serre de Laurian, 30100 Alès, France (Home). *Telephone:* (4) 67-14-32-20. *Fax:* (4) 66-52-46-99.

VÄHI, Tiit; Estonian politician; b. 10 Jan. 1947, Valgamaa; m.; two c.; ed Tallinn Polytechnic Inst.; fmr Production Man. Valga Motor Depot, later Deputy Dir, Chief Engineer, Dir, Chair. Transport Cttee; fmr Minister of Transport and Communications; Prime Minister of Estonia Jan.–Oct. 1992, 1995–97; mem. of Bd, Coalition Party, Chair. 1995–99; attended refresher courses in Germany 1993; Chair. Tallinn City Council 1993–95. *Address:* Coalition Party Eesti Koonderakond, Raekoja plats 16, Tallinn 10146, Estonia (Office). *Telephone:* (2) 631-41-61 (Office). *Fax:* (2) 631-40-41 (Office).

VAILE, Hon. Mark Anthony James; Australian politician; b. 18 April 1956, Sydney; s. of George Strafford Vaile and Suzanne Elizabeth Vaile; m. Wendy Jean Vaile 1976; three d.; jackaroo 1973–76; farm machinery retailer 1976–79; Real Estate and Stock and Station Agent 1979–92; Chair, Wingham Chamber of Commerce 1980–85; fmr Deputy Speaker, then Chair. House of Reps. Standing Cttee on Communications, Transport and Micro-Econ. Reform; mem. House of Reps. for Lyne (Nat. Party), NSW 1993–; Nat. Party Whip, House of Reps. 1994; Minister for Transport and Regional Devt 1997–98, for Agric., Fisheries and Forestry 1998–99, for Trade 1999–; Deputy Leader Nat. Party of Australia 1999–. *Leisure interests:* squash, tennis, water skiing, golf. *Address:* Suite MG-46, Parliament House, Canberra, A.C.T. 2600 (Office); 219 Victoria Street, Taree, NSW 2430, Australia. *Telephone:* (2) 6277-7420 (Office). *Fax:* (2) 6273-4128 (Office). *Website:* www.dfat.gov.au (Office).

VAILLANT, Daniel; French politician; b. 19 July 1949, Lormes (Nièvre); s. of Raymond Vaillant and Germaine Andre; three c.; ed Ecole supérieure de biologie et biochimie; joined Convention des Institutions Républicaines 1966; Parti Socialiste (PS) official, 18th arrondissement Paris 1971–95; Special Asst to François Mitterrand, presidential election campaign 1981; Asst Nat. Sec. for PS Feds. 1986, Nat. Sec. for PS Feds. 1988–94, Nat. Sec. without specific assignment 1994–95; Campaign Dir, Lionel Jospin's parl. and regional election campaigns 1986, Organizer and Co-ordinator of Lionel Jospin's gen.

election campaign 1997; City Councillor 18th arrondissement Paris 1977–95, Mayor of 18th arrondissement 1995–2001, 2003– (First Deputy Mayor 2001–03); Ile-de-France Regional Councillor 1986–89; Nat. Ass. Deputy for 19th Paris constituency 1988–93, 1994–97, 2002–; Minister for Relations with Parl. 1997–2000, of the Interior 2000–02. *Publications:* C'est ça ma gauche 2000, Sécurité, priorité à gauche 2003. *Address:* Mairie, 1 place Jules Joffrin, 75877 Paris cedex 18, France.

VAILLAUD, Pierre; French oil executive; b. 15 Feb. 1935, Paris; s. of Marcel Vaillaud and Rose Larrat; m. Geneviève Dreyfus 1960; two s.; ed Lycée Janson-de-Sailly, Paris, Ecole Polytechnique, Ecole des Mines, Ecole Nat. Supérieure du Pétrole et des Moteurs; engineer, Ministry of Industry 1959–63; project man. Technip 1964–68, Dir, Vice-Pres. Eng and Construction Atochem (affiliate of Total) 1968–72; Vice-Pres. Natural Gas Div., Total 1972–74, Vice-Pres. Devt and Construction Div., Vice-Pres. Exploration and Production Operations then Pres., Total Exploration Production 1974–89, Exec. Vice-Pres. Total, Pres. and CEO Total Chimie 1989–92, Chair. and CEO Technip 1992–99, Elf Aquitaine SA 1999–2000; Pres. Asscn des techniciens du pétrole 1985–87; Commdr, Ordre nat. du Mérite, Officier, Légion d'honneur. *Leisure interests:* tennis, sailing, golf. *Address:* 5 villa Madrid, 92200 Neuilly-sur-Seine, France (Home).

VAINIO, Vesa Veikko; Finnish business executive; b. 2 Dec. 1942, Helsinki; s. of Veikko Vainio and Aune Vainio; m. Marja-Liisa Harjunen 1968; two s.; Circuit Court Notary, Rovaniemi Circuit Court 1966–67; Counsellor, Union of Finnish Lawyers 1968; Sec. Finnish Employers' Confed. 1969, Counsellor and Asst Head of Dept 1969–72; Admin. Dir Aaltonen Footwear Factory 1972, Deputy Man. Dir 1974–76; Man. Dir Aaltonen Factories Oy 1976–77; Dir Confed. of Finnish Industries 1977–83, Deputy Man. Dir 1983–85; Exec. Vice-Pres. Kymmene Corpn 1985–91, Pres. 1991–92; Pres. and CEO Unitas Ltd 1992–94; Chair. and CEO Union Bank of Finland 1992–94 (after merger with Kansallis-Osake-Pankki into Merita Bank Ltd) Merita Bank Ltd 1994–97, Pres. and CEO of Merita Ltd 1994–97, Pres. Merita PLC 1998–2000, Chair. Bd MeritaNordbanken PLC 1998, Vice-Chair. Nordbanken Holding PLC 1998–2000, Vice-Chair. Bd MeritaNordbanken PLC 1999, Chair. Nordea AB (publrs) 2000–02; Kt, Order of Finnish Lion, Commdr of Finnish Lion. *Leisure interests:* hunting, fishing. *Address:* UPM-Kymmene Corporation, PO Box 380, FIN-00101, Helsinki, Finland (Office). *Telephone:* 20415111 (Office). *Fax:* 204150304 (Office).

VAINSHTEIN, Aleksander Lvovich; Russian media executive; b. 1 Sept. 1953, Moscow; m. Lia Vainchteine; one s. one d.; ed Moscow Inst. of Radio Tech., Electronics and Automation; worked in light bulb factory, Moscow 1976–86, Dir Club of Moscow factory 1986–89; Commercial Dir Moscow News newspaper 1989–90, Pres. Information-Publishing co. Moscow News 1995–; Dir-Gen. Acad. of Free Press; Exec. Dir Cup of Kremlin tennis tournament 1990–95; mem. Union of Journalists, Exec. Cttee Russian Football Union until 1998; USSR Council of Ministers Prize in the field of science and tech.; TEFFI Prize for Best Sports TV Show 1998. *Television:* writer and producer: Century of Football, Football in Dialogues. *Publication:* N. Starostin: Football Through the Years. *Address:* Moscow News Publishing House, Tverskaya str. 16/2, 125009 Moscow, Russia (Office). *Telephone:* (095) 200-63-90 (Office). *Fax:* (095) 937-45-29 (Office). *Website:* www.mn.ru (Office).

VAINSHTOK, Semen Mikhailovich; Russian business executive; b. 5 Oct. 1947, Klimatsy, Moldova; m.; one d.; ed Kiev Inst. of Construction and Engineering, Acad. of KGB; engineer in Chernovtsy, Ukraine 1969–74; Head Chernovtsy regional Dept of Provision and Trade 1974–82; Deputy Head Povkhneft 1982–86; Deputy Dir-Gen. Bashneft, W. Siberia 1986–88; Deputy Head Kolymneftgas 1988–93; Dir-Gen. LukOil–Kolymneftgas 1993–95, LukOil, W. Siberia 1995–, Vice-Pres., mem. Bd Dirs. LukOil co. 1995; Pres. Transneft 1999–; initiated direct oil transport from Russia to Europe; mem. Acad. of Mining Sciences; Order for Service to Motherland. *Address:* Transneft Co., B. Polyanka str. 57, 109180, Moscow, Russia (Office). *Telephone:* (095) 953-86-94 (Office).

VAISEY, David George, CBE, MA, FSA, FRHistS; British librarian and archivist; b. 15 March 1935; s. of William Thomas Vaisey and Minnie Vaisey (née Payne); m. Maureen Anne Mansell 1965; two d.; ed Rendcomb Coll., Glos., Exeter Coll. Oxford; archivist, Staffordshire Co. Council 1960–63; Asst, then Sr Librarian, Bodleian Library 1963–75, Keeper of Western Manuscripts 1975–86, Bodley's Librarian 1986–96, Bodley's Librarian Emer. 1997–; Deputy Keeper, Oxford Univ. Archives 1966–75, Keeper 1995–2000; Professorial Fellow, Exeter Coll. Oxford 1975–96, Fellow by Special Election 1997–2000, Emer. Fellow 2000–; Visiting Prof. Library Studies, Univ. of Calif. at LA 1985; Chair. Nat. Council on Archives 1988–91; mem. Royal Comm. on Historical Manuscripts 1986–98, Advisory Council on Public Records 1989–94; Vice-Pres. British Records Asscn 1999–; Pres. Soc. of Archivists 1999–2002; Hon. Fellow, Kellogg Coll. Oxford 1996–; Hon. Research Fellow, Dept of Library, Archive and Information Studies, Univ. Coll. London 1987–. *Publications:* Staffordshire and the Great Rebellion (jtly) 1964, Probate Inventories of Lichfield and District 1568–1680 1969, Victorian and Edwardian Oxford from Old Photographs (jtly) 1971, Oxford Shops and Shopping 1972, Art for Commerce (jtly) 1973, Oxfordshire: A Handbook for Students of Local History 1973, The Diary of Thomas Turner 1754–65 1984. *Address:* 12 Hernes Road, Oxford, OX2 7PU, England.

VAJDA, György; Hungarian engineer; b. 18 June 1927, Budapest; s. of László Vajda and Mária Daróczi; m. 1st Magdolna Krasznai 1969 (died 1987); one s. one d.; m. 2nd Dr Klára Berei 1988; ed Tech. Univ., Budapest; Asst Lecturer 1949–50; on staff of Hungarian Acad. of Sciences 1950–52; Deputy Dir Inst. of Measurements 1952–57, Research Inst. of Electric Energetics 1957–63; Deputy Section Leader, Ministry of Heavy Industry 1963–70; Dir Inst. for Electrical Power Research 1970–93, Prof. 1993–97; Dir Gen. Nat. Atomic Energy Authority 1997–99 (Vice-Pres. 1979–97); Pres. European Atomic Energy Soc.; Hon. Pres. Hungarian Electrotech. Soc.; mem. Hungarian Nat. Comm. for Tech. Devt, Hungarian Acad. of Eng; Corresp. mem. Hungarian Acad. of Sciences 1976–81, mem. 1982, Section Pres. 1985–92; mem. Admin. Comm. Conf. Int. des Grands Reseaux Électriques, Paris; Chair. ECE Electric Power Comm. 1972–76; mem. New York Acad. of Sciences; State Prize 1975, Szilárd Prize 1999, Széchenyi Award 2000, Renovanda Kult. Hung Grand Award 2002. *Publications:* A szigetelések romlása (Deterioration of Insulations) 1964, Szigetelések villamos erőterei (Electric Power Fields of Insulation) 1970, Energia és Társadalom (Energy and Society) 1975, Energetika (Energetics), Vols I–II 1984, Risk and Safety 1998, Energy Policy 2001; 150 papers in int. journals. *Leisure interest:* gardening. *Address:* National Atomic Energy Authority, Fényes A.4, 1036 Budapest (Office); Bem rkp. 32, 1027, Budapest, Hungary (Home). *Telephone:* (1) 436-4809 (Office). *Fax:* (1) 436-4804 (Office). *E-mail:* vajda@haea.gov.hu (Office).

VAJPAYEE, Atal Bihari, MA; Indian politician; b. 25 Dec. 1924, Gwalior, Madhya Pradesh; s. of Krishna Bihari Vajpayee; ed Victoria (now Laxmibai) Coll., Gwalior, D.A.V. Coll., Kanpur; mem. Rashtriya Swayamsewak Sangh 1941, Indian Nat. Congress 1942–46; mem. Lok Sabha 1957–62, 1967–84 (for New Delhi 1977–84), 1991–, Rajya Sabha 1962–67, 1986; Founder mem. Bharatiya Jana Sangh 1951, Parl. Leader 1957–77; Chair. Cttee on Govt Assurance 1966–67, Public Accounts Cttee Lok Sabha 1967–70, 1991–93; detained during Emergency 1975–77; Founder mem. Janata Party 1977, Pres. Bharatiya Janata Party 1980–86, Parl. Leader 1980–84, 1986; Minister of External Affairs 1977–79; Leader of Opposition, Lok Sabha 1993–98, Chair. Standing Cttee on External Affairs 1993–96; Minister of External Affairs 1998; Prime Minister of India 15–28 May 1996, March 1998–, also Minister of Health and Family Welfare, Atomic Energy and Agric. March 1998–; Chair. Nat. Security Council 1998–; mem. Nat. Integration Council 1961–; fmr Ed. Rastradharma (monthly), Panchjanya (weekly), Swadesh and Veer Arjun (dailies); Hon. PhD (Kanpur Univ.) 1993; Bharat Ratna Pt. Govind Ballabh Pant Award 1994; Padma Vibhushan 1992; Lokmanya Tilak Puruskar. *Publications:* New Dimensions of India's Foreign Policy, Jan Sangh Aur Musalmans, Three Decades in Parliament; collections of poems and numerous articles. *Leisure interests:* reading, writing, travelling, cooking. *Address:* Office of the Prime Minister, S Block, New Delhi 110001 (Office); 7 Race Course Road, New Delhi 110011, India (Home). *Telephone:* (11) 3013040 (Office); (11) 3018939 (Home). *Fax:* (11) 3016857 (Office); (11) 3019545 (Home). *Website:* www.pmindia.nic.in (Office).

VAKHROMEYEV, Geliy Sergeyevich, D.GEOLOGY; Russian scientist; b. 21 June 1934, Sverdlovsk; ed Sverdlovsk Ore Inst.; participated in geological expeditions with Irkutsk Geology Dept 1957–68; teacher, Head of Chair of Geophysics Irkutsk State Tech. Univ. 1960–77; Dir Inst. of Ecological Geophysics, Russian Acad. of Natural Sciences 1992–; Ed. Geophysical Searches for Ore and Non-Ore Sources (yearbook) 1976–91; mem. Russian Acad. of Natural Sciences 1996, Scientific Council on Geology and Identification; Hon. Prof. Mongolian Tech. Univ. *Publications:* numerous scientific publications. *Address:* Institute of Ecological Geophysics, Irkutsk, Russia (Office). *Telephone:* (3952) 43-08-54 (Office).

VAKHROMEYEV, Kyril Varfolomeyevich (see Philaret).

VAKSBERG, Arkady Iosifovich, DJur; Russian writer, journalist and lawyer; b. 11 Nov. 1933, Novosibirsk; m.; one d.; ed Moscow State Univ.; barrister Moscow City Bd of Bar –1973; political corresp. in Paris, Literaturnaya Gazeta; Vice-Pres. Russian PEN Centre; mem. Russian Writer's Union, Journalist's Union, Union of Cinematography Workers, Int. Cttee of Writers in Prison. *Screenplays for films:* The Storm Warning, The Provincial Romance. *Plays:* A Shot in the Dark, The Supreme Court, The Alarm. *TV work includes:* The Special Reporter (serial), A Dangerous Zone (actor and scriptwriter). *Publications:* three books and numerous articles on copyright law; over 35 works of fiction, collections of essays, biogs. *Leisure interests:* collecting reference books and encyclopaedias. *Address:* Krasnoarmeiskaya str. 23, Apt. 65, 125319 Moscow, Russia (Home); 17 blvd Garibaldi, 75015 Paris, France. *Telephone:* (095) 151-33-69 (Home); 1-45-66-45-31. *Fax:* 1-45-66-45-31. *E-mail:* vaksberg@noos.fr (Home).

VALDÉS, Juan Gabriel, PhD; Chilean politician and diplomatist; b. June 1947; m. Antonia Echenique Celis; four c.; ed Catholic Univ. of Chile, Santiago, Univ. of Essex, UK, Princeton Univ., NJ, USA; Researcher, Political Science Inst. of Catholic Univ. of Chile, Inst. for Policy Studies, Washington DC, USA 1972–76; Officer Latin American Inst. for Transnational Studies, Prof. of Int. Relations, Econ. Research and Devt Centre, Mexico City, Mexico 1976–1984; Research Fellow Kellogg Inst. of Int. Studies, Notre Dame Univ., IN, USA, Center for Latin American Studies, Princeton Univ., NJ, USA 1984, 1987; Consultant Econ. Comm. for Latin America 1985; Amb. to Spain 1990–94; Dir Int. Div. and Co-ordinator NAFTA Negotiating Team, Ministry of Finance 1994–96, Lead Negotiator Chile–Canada Free

Trade Agreement 1996; Consultant UN Programme for Devt, Santiago 1994; mem. Nat. TV Council 1995; Vice-Minister Int. Econ. Affairs, Ministry of Foreign Affairs 1996–99, Minister 1999–2000; Perm. Rep. to UN, New York 2000–; concurrently Amb. to Iran 2001–. *Publications include:* numerous articles on int. relations. *Address:* Permanent Mission of Chile to the UN, 305 East 47th Street, 10th/11th Floor, New York, NY 10017, USA (Office). *Telephone:* (212) 832-3323 (Office). *Fax:* (212) 832-0236 (Office). *E-mail:* chile@un.int (Office). *Website:* www.un.int/chile.

VÁLDEZ ALBIZÚ, Héctor, B.ECONS.SC.; Dominican Republic central bank governor; b. 10 Nov. 1947, Dominican Repub.; s. of Hector Manuel Valdez Albizu and Ana Rita Valdez Albizu; m. Fior d'Aliza Martinez 1971; one s.; Tech. Asst (Publs), Cen. Bank of Dominican Repub. 1970–75, Head of Banking and Monetary Div., Tech. Co-ordinator of Econ. Studies 1975–82, Econ. Asst to Gov. 1982–84, Dir Econ. Studies Dept 1984–86, Asst Man., Monetary and Exchange Policy 1986–90, Adviser to Monetary Bd 1987–89, Rep. of Cen. Bank at Banco de Reservas (State commercial bank) 1991–92, Asst Gen. Man. and Gen. Admin. Banco de Reservas 1992–94, Gov. Cen. Bank and Pres. Monetary Bd 1994–2000; mem. Bd of Dirs. Consejo Estatal del Azucar (State Sugar Council) 1993–94; Prof., Universidad Cen. del Este and Instituto de Estudios Superiores 1975–89. *Publications:* Financial Programs for the Dominican Republic 1976–1990, Dimensions of the National Banking System and its Enhancement 1976, Exchange Emergency Regime 1985. *Address:* c/o Banco Central de la Republica Dominicana, Calle Pedro Henriquez Ureña, Esq. Leopoldo Navarro, Apdo. 1347, Santo Domingo, DN, Dominican Republic.

VALDIVIESO SARMIENTO, Alfonso, LLD; Colombian diplomatist and politician; b. Oct. 1949, Bucaramanga; m.; two s.; ed Javerian Univ., Bogotá, Boston, Toronto and Stanford Univs.; Admin. Vice-Rector and Dir of Planning, Autonomous Univ. of Bucaramanga 1978–86; mem. House of Reps. 1982–86; mem. Council, Bucaramanga 1988–89, Pres. 1989; Senator 1986–90, 1990–94; Minister for Nat. Educ. 1990–91; Amb. to Israel 1992–93; Attorney-Gen. in charge of criminal investigations 1994–97; Presidential Cand. 1998; Perm. Rep. to UN 1998–. *Address:* Permanent Mission of Colombia to the United Nations, 140 East 57th Street, 5th Floor, New York, NY 10022, USA (Office). *Telephone:* (212) 355-7776 (Office). *Fax:* (212) 371-2813 (Office). *E-mail:* columbia@un.int (Office). *Website:* www.un.int/columbia (Office).

VALE CÉSAR, Carlos Manuel Martins do; Portuguese politician; b. 30 Oct. 1956, Ponta Delgada; s. of Aurélio Augusto César and Maria Natália Martins do Vale César; m.; one s.; ed Antero de Quental High School, Faculty of Law, Lisbon; f. Socialist Youth and Socialist Party 1974, mem. Nat. Exec. Socialist Party 1975–; Asst to State Sec. for Public Admin. 1977–78; Deputy, Regional Ass. 1980–96, Vice-Pres. –1996; Pres. Regional Govt of the Azores 1996–; mem. State Council, Higher Nat. Defence Council, Higher Internal Security Council, Cttee of the Regions, Ass. of European Regions, Conf. of Presidents of Ultra-peripheral Regions, Conf. of Peripheral Maritime Regions of Europe, Congress of Local Regional Authorities of Europe. *Address:* Residência do Presidente, Goberno Regional, Ponta Delgada, The Azores (Office). *Telephone:* (296) 301000 (Office). *Fax:* (296) 283697 (Office). *E-mail:* GRPresidencia@pg.raa.pt (Office). *Website:* www.pg.raa.pt (Office).

VÁLEK, Vladimír; Czech conductor; b. 2 Sept. 1935, Nový Jičín; m. 1st Jana Adamová; m. 2nd Hana Patočková 1986; two s. one d.; ed Acad. of Musical Arts, Bratislava, Acad. of Performing Arts, Prague; conductor with several Czech orchestras 1962–75; Conductor FOK Prague Symphony Orchestra 1975–87; Chief Conductor Prague Radio Symphony Orchestra 1985–; Conductor Czech Philharmonic 1996–; Prin. Guest Conductor Orchestra Osaka Symphoniker 2003–; Guest Conductor with many orchestras world-wide including The Big Radio Orchestra Leipzig, Tonkuenstler and ORF (Vienna), Israeli and Japan Philharmonics; Music Critics' Award, MIDEM Classic Cannes (for recording of piano concertos by Ervin Schulhoff) 1996. *Performances:* concert tours include Japan, France, Spain, USA. and Singapore; has appeared as guest conductor with numerous symphony orchestras in many countries. *Recordings:* more than 100 classical music recordings and more than 1,000 recordings for radio. *Leisure interest:* aviation. *Address:* Český rozhlas, Vinohradská 12, 120 00 Prague 2 (Office); Nad údolím 24, 140 00 Prague 4, Czech Republic (Home). *Telephone:* (2) 2155-1400 (Office); (2) 4177-1463 (Home). *Fax:* (2) 2155-1413 (Office). *E-mail:* socr@cro.cz (Office). *Website:* www.cro.cz/socr (Office).

VALENCIA-RODRÍGUEZ, Luis, LLD; Ecuadorean diplomatist and professor of law; b. 5 March 1926, Quito; s. of Pedro Valencia and María Rodríguez; m. Cleopatra Moreno 1952; two s. three d.; ed Cen. Univ., Quito; entered Ecuadorean Foreign Service 1944; Counsellor, Buenos Aires 1957–59; Minister-Counsellor, UN, New York 1959–64; Minister of Foreign Affairs 1965-66, 1981–84; legal adviser on foreign affairs 1964–65, 1966–69, 1980–81, 1990–94, 2001–; Amb. to Bolivia 1969–71, to Brazil 1971–74, to Peru 1974–78, to Venezuela 1978–79, to Argentina 1988–91; Perm. Rep. to UN 1994–99; Prof. Cen. Univ., Quito 1994–; mem. UN Cttee on the Elimination of Racial Discrimination 1974–86, 1992–; special citation of Ecuadorean Nat. Ass. 1966 and decorations from Ecuador, Italy, Nicaragua, Bolivia, Brazil, Peru, Venezuela, Colombia, Argentina, El Salvador, Dominican Republic and

Korea. *Publications:* books on legal matters, foreign affairs etc. *Leisure interests:* swimming, reading. *Address:* c/o Ministry of Foreign Affairs, Avenida 10 de Agosto y Carrión, Quito, Ecuador.

VALENTI, Jack; American film executive and fmr government official; b. 5 Sept. 1921, Houston, Tex.; s. of the late Mr. and Mrs. Joseph Valenti; m. Mary Margaret Wiley 1962; one s. two d.; ed High School, Houston, Univ. of Houston and Harvard Business School; fmr office boy, oil company; USAF, Second World War; co-f. Weekly & Valenti Advertising 1951; Special Asst to Pres. Johnson 1963–66; Pres. and CEO Motion Picture Asscn of America 1966–; Chair. Alliance of Motion Picture and TV Producers Inc. 1966–; Chair., CEO Motion Picture Export Asscn of America; Dir American Film Inst. 1967–; mem. Bd Riggs Nat. Corpn; mem. Bd of Trustees, J.F.K. Center for the Performing Arts, American Film Inst.; Chevalier, Légion d'honneur. *Publications:* The Bitter Taste of Glory 1971, A Very Human President 1976, Speak Up with Confidence 1982, Protect and Defend 1992. *Address:* Motion Picture Association, 1600 Eye Street, NW, Washington, DC 20006; MPAA, 15503 Ventura Boulevard, Encino CA 91436, USA.

VALENTIČ, Nikica; Croatian politician and business executive; b. 24 Nov. 1950, Gospić; m. Antoneta Valentič; one s. one d.; ed Zagreb Univ.; journalist for Radio Zagreb 1969–71; Ed. Pravnik (magazine) 1972–74; legal adviser in Zeljko Jurkovič office; f. and Gen. Man. S2 Stanograd and Stanogradinvest consultancy co. 1978–83; own legal firm 1984–90; Gen. Man. INA Industria Nafte 1990–93; Prime Minister of Croatia 1993–95; Pres. Niva co. 1995–. *Leisure interests:* painting, music. *Address:* c/o Office of the Prime Minister, 41000 Zagreb, Jordanovac 71, Croatia.

VALENTINO, (Valentino Garavani); Italian fashion designer; b. 11 May 1932, Voghera, nr Milan; ed Ecole des Beaux-Arts, Paris, Ecole de la Chambre Syndicale de la Couture, Paris; Asst designer at Paris fashion houses of Jean Dessès 1950–55, Guy Laroche 1956–58; est. Valentino fashion house with Giancarlo Giammetti in Rome 1959; owner boutiques Rome, Milan and other cities; other Valentino boutiques opened and licensing agreements signed Europe, USA and Far East since 1970s; f. Valentino Acad. for AIDS research and assistance to victims of the disease; f. L.I.F.E. 1990; retrospective Exhbn of creations at Columbus Festivities, New York 1991; numerous int. awards; Ufficiale di Gran Croce. *Address:* Palazzo Mignanelli, Piazza Mignanelli 22, 00187 Rome, Italy (Office); 823–825 Madison Avenue, New York, NY 10021, USA (Office).

VALENZUELA, Luisa; Argentine writer and journalist; b. 26 Nov. 1938, Buenos Aires; d. of Luisa Mercedes Levinson and Pablo F. Valenzuela; m. Théodore Marjak 1958 (divorced); one d.; ed Belgrano Girls' School, Colegio Nacional Vicente Lopez, Buenos Aires; lived in Paris, writing for Argentinian newspapers and for the RTF 1958–61; Asst Ed. La Nación Sunday Supplement, Buenos Aires 1964–69; writer, lecturer, freelance journalist in USA, Mexico, France, Spain 1970–73, Buenos Aires 1973–79; taught in Writing Div., Columbia Univ., New York 1980–83; conducted writers' workshops, English Dept, New York Univ. and seminars, Writing Div. 1984–89; returned to Buenos Aires 1989; Fulbright Grant 1969–70; Guggenheim Fellow 1983; Fellow New York Inst. for the Humanities; mem. Acad. of Arts and Sciences, Puerto Rico; Dr. hc (Knox Coll., Ill., USA) 1991; Machado de Assis Medal, Brazilian Acad. of Letters 1997. *Publications:* novels: Hay que sonreír 1966, El Gato Eficaz 1972, Como en la guerra 1977, Cambio de armas 1982, Cola de largartija 1983, Novela negra con argentinos 1990, Realidad Nacional desde la cama 1990, Antología personal 1998; short stories: Los heréticos 1967, Aquí pasan cosas raras 1976, Libro que no muerde 1980, Donde viven las águilas 1983, Simetrías (Cuentos de Hades) 1993, Antología Personal 1998, Cuentos Completos y Uno Más 1999, La travesía 2001, Peligrosas palabras 2001; most books in English trans. *Leisure interests:* masks, anthropology, ceremonies. *Address:* Artilleros 2130, 1428 Buenos Aires, Argentina. *Telephone:* (11) 4781-3593.

VALIONIS, Antanas, PhD; Lithuanian politician, engineer and diplomatist; b. 21 Sept. 1950, Kedainiai Dist; m. Romualda Valionis; two s.; ed Kaunas Polytechnic Inst., Warsaw Univ.; foreman, Kaunas Meat Processing Plant, 1974–76, Man., Taurage Meat Processing Plant 1976–80; Chief Instructor, Taurage Regional Cttee, Industry and Transport Dept 1980–85, Instructor, Agric. and Food Industry Dept 1985–89; Head of Div. of Perspective Planning and Foreign Relations, Food Industry Dept, Ministry of Agric. 1990–94; Amb. to Poland 1994–2000, to Romania (also Accred to Bulgaria) 1996–2000; Minister of Foreign Affairs Oct. 2000–; Commdr Cross with Star (Poland). *Publications:* numerous press articles. *Leisure interest:* music. *Address:* Ministry of Foreign Affairs, J. Tumo-Vaizganto Str. 2, Vilnius 2600, Lithuania (Office). *Telephone:* (2) 362-401 (Office). *Fax:* (2) 313-090 (Office). *E-mail:* urm@urm.lt (Office). *Website:* www.urm.lt (Office).

VALIYEV, Kamil Akhmedovich; Russian/Tatar physicist; b. 15 Jan. 1931, Verkhny Shendar, Tatarstan; m.; two c.; ed Kazan State Univ.; Sr teacher, then Head of Lab. Kazan State Pedagogical Inst.; Dir Research Inst. of Molecular Physics; Head of Sector Ledebev Inst. of Physics; Deputy Dir, then Dir Inst. of Gen. Physics (FTIAN), USSR Acad. of Sciences; mem. Russian Acad. of Sciences 1984, Presidium Tatarstan Acad. of Sciences; Lenin Prize, State Prize of Azerbaijan; Order of October Revolution, Order of Labour Red Banner. *Publications include:* Microelectronics: Achievements and Ways of

Development 1986, Physics of Submicronic Lithography 1990. *Leisure interests:* chess, photography. *Address:* FTIAN, Nakhimovsky prosp. 34, 117218 Moscow, Russia (Office). *Telephone:* (095) 125-77-09 (Office).

VALLANCE, Sir Iain David Thomas, Kt, BA, MSc; British business executive; b. 20 May 1943, London; s. of Edmund Thomas Vallance and Janet Wright Bell Ross Davidson; m. Elizabeth Mary McGonnigill 1967; one s. one d.; ed Edinburgh Acad., Dulwich Coll., Glasgow Acad., Brasenose Coll. Oxford, London Grad. School of Business Studies; Asst Postal Controller, Post Office 1966, Personal Asst to Chair. 1973–75, Head of Finance Planning Div. 1975–76, Dir Cen. Finance 1976–78, Telecommunications Finance 1978–79, Materials Dept 1979–81; mem. Bd for Org. and Business Systems, British Telecommunications 1981–83, Man. Dir, Local Communications Services Div. 1983–85, Chief of Operations 1985–86, Chief Exec. 1986–95, Chair. 1987–2001, Pres. Emer. 2001–02; Vice-Chair. Royal Bank of Scotland 1994–; founding mem. Pres.'s Cttee of European Foundation for Quality Man. 1988–; mem. CBI Pres.'s Cttee, Pres. CBI 2000–; mem. Advisory Council of Business in the Community, Allianz Int. Advisory Bd, Advisory Council of Prince's Youth Business Trust 1988–, Advisory Bd British-American Chamber of Commerce 1991–; Vice-Chair. European Advisory Cttee to New York Stock Exchange, Chair. 2000–, Financial Reporting Council; fmr mem. Bd Scottish Enterprise, Mobil Corpn; Trustee Monteverdi Trust; Fellow London Business School 1989; Hon. Fellow Brasenose Coll.; Hon. Gov. Glasgow Acad. 1993–; Hon. DSc (Ulster) 1992, (Napier) 1994, Hon. DTech (Loughborough) 1992, (Robert Gordon) 1994, Hon. DBA (Kingston) 1993, Hon. DEng (Heriot-Watt) 1995, Hon. DSc (City Univ.) 1996; Liveryman of Worshipful Co. of Wheelwrights; Freeman of the City of London. *Leisure interests:* walking, playing the piano, listening to music. *Address:* c/o 81 Newgate Street, London, EC1A 7AJ, England (Office).

VALLANCE-OWEN, John, MA, MD, FRCP, FRCPI, FRCPath; British professor of medicine and physician; b. 31 Oct. 1920, London; s. of Edwin Augustine Vallance-Owen and Julia May; m. Renee Thornton 1950; two s. two d.; ed Epsom Coll., Surrey, Cambridge Univ., The London Hosp.; various appts including Pathology Asst and Medical First Asst, London Hosp. 1946–51; Medical Tutor, Royal Postgrad. Medical School, Hammersmith Hosp., London 1952–55, 1956–58; Consultant Physician and Lecturer in Medicine, Univ. of Durham 1958–64; Consultant Physician and Reader in Medicine, Univ. of Newcastle-upon-Tyne 1964–66; Prof. and Chair., Dept of Medicine, Queen's Univ., Belfast and Consultant Physician to Royal Victoria Hosp., Belfast City Hosp. and Forster Green Hosp., Belfast 1966–82; Dir of Medical Services, The Maltese Islands 1981–82; Foundation Prof. and Chair. Dept of Medicine, The Chinese Univ. of Hong Kong 1983–88, Assoc. Dean 1984–88; Consultant in Medicine to Hong Kong Govt 1984–88, to British Army in Hong Kong 1985–88; Medical Adviser on Clinical Complaints, NE Thames Regional Health Authority 1989–96; Visiting Prof. Imperial Coll. of Science, Tech. and Medicine, Hammersmith Hosp. 1989–; Consultant Physician London Ind. Hosp. 1989–99, Wellington Hosp. 1999–2003; Rockefeller Travelling Fellowship, held at Univ. of Pa, USA 1955–56; Fellow Royal Hong Kong Coll. of Physicians; Oliver-Sharpey Prize, Royal Coll. of Physicians 1976. *Publications:* Essentials of Cardiology 1961, Diabetes: Its Physiological and Biochemical Basis 1974; numerous papers in scientific journals on carbohydrates and fat metabolism and the aetiology of diabetes mellitus, with special reference to insulin antagonism. *Leisure interests:* music, tennis, golf. *Address:* 17 St Matthews Lodge, Oakley Square, London, NW1 1NB; 10 Spinney Drive, Great Shelford, Cambridge, England; Cuildochart, Killin, Perthshire, Scotland. *Telephone:* (20) 7388-3644; (1223) 842767; (1567) 820337. *E-mail:* renee@vallance-owen.freeserve.co.uk (Office).

VALLARINO BARTUANO, Arturo Ulises, BSc, D.JUR.SC.; Panamanian politician and lawyer; b. 15 Dec. 1943, Capiro Dist, Panamá; s. of Ismael Vallarino and María Concepción Bartuano; m. Elka Aparicio de Vallarino; five c.; ed Univ. of Panama, Universidad Nacional Autónoma de México, Univ. of Costa Rica; Legal Adviser Ministry of Foreign Affairs 1966; elected Councillor for Panamá Dist 1968; lawyer pvt. firm Carillo, Villalaz & Muñoz; Sr Partner Bufete, Vallarino y Asociados until 1999; Prof. of Political Science and Commercial Law Univ. of Panama 1979–; fmr Chargé d'affaires for Business, Argentina; fmr Legal Adviser Ministry of Planning and Econ. Politics, Nat. Banking Comm.; fmr Pres. Legis. Ass.; currently Sec.-Gen. Partido Movimiento Liberal Republicano Nacionalista (MOLIRENA); First Vice-Pres. of Panama 1999–. *Address:* Oficina del Primer Vice-Presidente, Palacio Presidencial, Valija 50, Panamá 1, Panama (Office).

VALLEE, Bert Lester, MD; American biochemist, physician and university professor; b. 1 June 1919, Hemer, Westphalia, Germany; s. of Joseph Vallee and Rosa (née Kronenberger) Vallee; m. Natalie Kugris 1947; ed Univ. of Berne, Switzerland and New York Univ. Coll. of Medicine; went to USA 1938, naturalized 1948; Research Fellow, Harvard Medical School, Boston 1946–49, Research Assoc. 1949–51, Assoc. 1951–56, Asst Prof. of Medicine 1956–60, Assoc. Prof. 1960–64, Prof. of Biological Chem. 1964–65, Paul C. Cabot Prof. of Biological Chem. 1965–80, Paul C. Cabot Prof. of Biochemical Sciences 1980–89, Prof. Emer. 1989–, Distinguished Sr Prof. Biochemical Sciences 1989–90, Edgar M. Bronfman Distinguished Sr Prof. 1990–; Research Assoc., Dept of Biology, MIT 1948–; Physician Peter Bent Brigham Hosp., Boston 1961–80; Biochemist-in-Chief, Brigham and Women's Hosp., Boston 1980–89, Emer. 1989–; Scientific Dir Biophysics Research Lab., Harvard Medical School, Peter Bent Brigham Hosp. 1954–80; Head, Center for

Biochemical and Biophysical Sciences and Medicine, Harvard Medical School 1980–; Founder and Trustee Boston Biophysics Foundation 1957–; Founder, Pres. Endowment for Research in Human Biology, Inc. 1980–; Fellow AAAS, NAS, American Acad. of Arts and Sciences, NY Acad. of Sciences; mem. American Chemical Soc.; Hon. mem. Swiss Biochem. Soc. 1976; Hon. Foreign mem. Royal Danish Acad. of Sciences and Letters; Hon. Prof., Tsinghua Univ. 1987, Stellenbosch Univ. 1995, Shanghai Inst. of Biochem. 1997; Messenger Lecturer, Cornell Univ. 1988; Hon. mem. Japan Soc. for Analytical Chem.; Hon. AM (Harvard) 1960, Hon. MD (Karolinska Inst.) 1987, Hon. DSc (Naples Univ.) 1991, Hon. PhD (Ludwig Maximillian Univ., Munich) 1995; LinderstrømLang Award and Gold Medal 1980, Willard Gibbs' Gold Medal 1981, William C. Rose Award in Biochem. 1982; Order Andres Bello (1st Class) (Venezuela), Raulin Award (ISTERH) 2002. *Publications:* over 500 Publs on zinc and other metalloenzymes; their structure, function and mechanism of action; emission, absorption, CD and MCD spectroscopy; organic chemical modification of proteins; organogenesis. *Leisure interest:* riding. *Address:* Harvard Medical School, 25 Shattuck Street, Boston, MA 02115 (Office); 300 Boylston Street, Apartment 712, Boston, MA 02116, USA (Home). *Telephone:* (617) 695-1701 (Home). *Fax:* (617) 621-6111 (Office); (617) 695-1702 (Home). *E-mail:* bert_vallee@hms.harvard.edu (Office).

VALTICOS, Nicholas, DenD; Greek judge; b. 8 April 1918, Cairo, Egypt; s. of Michael Valticos and Helen Valticos; m. Nelly Valticos 1951; one s. one d.; ed Univ. of Paris; barrister at law in Athens 1941–42; Chief of section Comm. administering Relief in Greece 1942–45; joined ILO 1949, Chief of Application of Conf. Decisions Div. 1955–64, Chief Int. Labour Standards Dept 1964–76, Asst Dir-Gen. and Adviser for Int. Labour Standards 1976–81; Assoc. Prof. at Faculty of Law, Univ. of Geneva 1972–81; Sec.-Gen. Inst. de droit int. 1981–91; ad hoc Judge at Int. Court of Justice 1984–94 (case concerning Continental Shelf, Libya/Malta), (case-frontier dispute, El Salvador/ Honduras), (Qatar-Bahrain); Judge at the European Court of Human Rights 1986–98, First Vice-Pres. Inst. of Int. Law 1991–93; Henri Rolin Professor of Int. Law, Belgium 1979–80; Pres. Curatorium, Acad. of Int. Law, The Hague 1996–; mem. Perm. Court of Arbitration; mem. and Chair. of various int. arbitral tribunals and comms. of inquiry; mem. Société française de droit int., Int. Law Asscn, Greek Soc. of Int. Law, Acad. of Athens; Assoc. Acad. des Sciences Morales et Politiques, Paris; Hon. mem. American Soc. of Int. Law, Hellenic Inst. of Int. and Foreign Law; Dr. hc (Univs. of Athens, Leuven, Utrecht, Neuchâtel); Prix de la Faculté and Prix Dupin Aîné, Paris; Grand Cross of San Raimundo de Peñafort, Spain 1989; Officier, Légion d'honneur 1981, Commdr Order of Isabella la Catolica (Spain) 1986, Order of Merit (Poland) 1992, Great Commdr Order of Honour (Greece) 1998, Commdr Order of Merit (Italy) 2001. *Publications:* Droit International du Travail 1970; about 200 studies on int. law. *Leisure interest:* writing.

VALTINOS, Thanassis; Greek author; b. 16 Dec. 1932, Karatoula Kynourias; m.; one d.; ed Athens Univ.; Visiting Prof. War Research Inst., Frankfurt 1993–; Pres. Greek Soc. of Authors; mem. European Acad. of Sciences and Arts, Int. Inst. of Theatre, Greek Society of Playwriters; Scenario Award Cannes Festival 1984; Nat. Literary Award 1990. *Address:* 66 Astidamantos Street, 116 34 Athens, Greece. *Telephone:* 7218793.

VÁMOS, Éva, PhD; Hungarian museologist; b. 22 May 1950, Budapest; d. of Endre Vamos and Lilly (née Vigyázó) Vámos; ed Eötvös Loránd Univ. of Budapest, Tech. Univ. of Budapest; affiliated to Hungarian Museum for Science and Tech. (Országos Műszaki Múzeum) 1973–, Curator 1973–78; scientific co-worker 1978–86; Head of Ind. Group of History of Science, scientific sec. in charge of public relations 1986–87, Sr scientific co-worker 1987–89, Head of Dept 1989–91, Scientific Deputy Dir Gen. 1991–93, Dir Gen. 1994–; Memorial Medal 1997, Justus von Liebig Memorial Medal 2000. *Achievements:* Chapters from the History of Communication 1979, History of Writing and Writing Utensils 1980–82, Creative Hungarians 1988, László József Bíró 1996. *Publications:* German-Hungarian Relations in the Fields of Science with Special Regard to Chemistry, Chemical Industry and Food Industry 1876–1914 1995. *Leisure interests:* university women's movement, gardening, classical music. *Address:* Hungarian Museums for Science and Technology, 1117 Budapest, Kaposvár u. 13 (Office); 1015 Budapest, Batthyány u. 3. VI. 32, Hungary (Home). *Telephone:* (1) 204-4095 (Office); (1) 204-4090 (Office); (1) 201-7317 (Home). *Fax:* (1) 204-4088 (Office). *E-mail:* vam13378@helka.iif.hu (Office); evamos@freemail.hu (Home). *Website:* www .omm.hu.

VÁMOS, Tibor, DSc, PhD; Hungarian research professor; b. 1 June 1926, Budapest; s. of Miklós Vámos and Ilona Rausnitz; m. Mária Fekete; one s.; ed Tech. Univ. Budapest; started in process control automation of power plants and systems, worked later in computer control of processes, robot vision, artificial intelligence; Chief Eng Research Inst. of Power System Eng Co. 1950–54, Automation Dept Head 1954–64; Dir Computer and Automation Inst. of the Hungarian Acad. of Sciences 1964–85, Chair. 1986–; Prof. Budapest Tech. Univ. 1969–; Distinguished Visiting Prof., George Mason Univ. 1992–93, Distinguished Affiliate Prof. 1993–94; Corresp. mem. Hungarian Acad. of Sciences 1973, mem. 1979, mem. Governing Bd 1980–; Pres. Int. Fed. of Automatic Control 1981–84, IFAC Lifetime Adviser 1987–; mem. editorial Bd 6 int. scientific journals; Fellow IEEE Inc. 1986–, Life mem. 2001–; mem. Austrian Computer Soc. 1992, Austrian Soc. for Cybernetic Studies 1994; Hon. Pres. John v. Neumann Soc. of Computer Science 1986–; Dr. hc (Tallinn Univ.); State Prize 1983; Chorafas Prize (Swiss Acads.) 1994;

Order of Hungarian Repub. 1996. *Publications:* Nagy ipari folyamatok irányitása (Control of Large-Scale Processes) 1970, Computer Epistemology 1991; Co-author: Applications of Syntactic Pattern Recognition 1977, Progress in Pattern Recognition 1981; Co-ed.: The Neumann Compendium 1995; 130 contribs to scientific journals and 170 to other publications. *Leisure interests:* fine arts, mountaineering. *Address:* Lágymányosi u. 11, 1111 Budapest, Hungary. *Telephone:* (1) 209-5274. *Fax:* (1) 209-5275.

VAN AGT, Andries A. M. (see Agt, Andries A. M. van).

VAN ALLAN, Richard, CBE; British opera singer; b. 28 May 1935, Clipstone, Notts.; s. of Joseph Arthur Jones and Irene Hannah Jones; m. 1st Elizabeth Mary Peabody 1963 (divorced 1974); m. 2nd Rosemary Pickering 1976 (divorced 1987); two s. one d.; ed Brunt's Grammar School, Mansfield, Worcester Teaching Training Coll., Birmingham School of Music; studied singing under David Franklin and Jani Strasser; with Sadler's Wells Opera (now English Nat. Opera) 1968, as prin. bass, Royal Opera House, Covent Garden 1971–, with Paris Opera 1975, with Boston Opera, Mass. and San Diego Opera, Calif. 1976; Dir Nat. Opera Studio, London 1986–2001; mem. Bd of Dirs. English Nat. Opera 1995–98; Fellow Birmingham Schools of Music 1991; John Christie Award, Glyndebourne 1967, Grammy Award (The Nat. Acad. of Performing Arts and Sciences) for Don Alfonso (Così fan tutte), Sir Charles Santley Memorial Prize, Worshipful Co. of Musicians 1995; Hon. mem. RAM 1987; Hon. Fellow Birmingham Conservatoire. *Performances:* first appearance with Glyndebourne Festival Opera 1964; with Welsh Nat. Opera 1967, debut Colón Theatre, Buenos Aires 1978, Le Monnaie, Brussels 1982, Miami 1985, Seattle 1987, Metropolitan, New York 1987, Madrid 1991, Barcelona 1992, Vic. State Opera, Melbourne 1995, Saito Kinen and Florence Festivals 2002, Die Zauberflöte (Royal Opera House) 2003. *Television:* world premiere of Flight. *Leisure interests:* cricket, tennis, shooting. *Address:* 18 Octavia Street, London, SW11 3DN, England. *Telephone:* (20) 7228-8462. *Fax:* (20) 7228-4367. *E-mail:* rvanallan@aol.com (Home).

VAN ALLEN, James Alfred, PhDFIEEEFAAS; American physicist; b. 7 Sept. 1914, Mount Pleasant, Iowa; s. of Alfred Morris Van Allen and Alma (née Olney) Van Allen; m. Abigail Fithian Halsey 1945; two s. three d.; ed Iowa Wesleyan Coll. and State Univ. of Iowa; Research Fellow, Carnegie Inst., Washington 1939–41, Physicist (Dept of Terrestrial Magnetism) 1941–42; Applied Physics Lab., Johns Hopkins Univ. 1942, 1946–50; Lt-Commdr in US Navy 1942–46; Prof. of Physics, Univ. of Iowa, Head of Dept 1951–85, Carver Prof. of Physics 1985–92, Regent Distinguished Prof. 1992–, now Prof. Emer.; Prin. Investigator, Pioneers 10 and 11 and Interdisciplinary Scientist, Galileo project; Guggenheim Research Fellow at Brookhaven Nat. Lab. 1951; Research Assoc. Princeton Univ. Project Matterhorn 1953–54; Dir expeditions to study cosmic radiation, Cen. Pacific 1949, Alaska 1950, Arctic 1952, 1957, Antarctic 1957; mem. Rocket and Satellite Research Panel 1946, Chair. 1947–58, Exec. Cttee 1958; mem. Advisory Cttee on Nuclear Physics, Office of Naval Research 1957–60; mem. Space Science Bd, NAS 1958–70, Foreign mem. The Royal Swedish Acad. of Sciences 1981; Consultant, Pres.'s Science Advisory Cttee; mem. Cosmic Radiation, Rocket Research and Earth Satellite Panel, Int. Geophysical Year; Fellow American Physical Soc., American Geophysical Union, American Rocket Soc., Inst. of Electrical and Electronics Engineers, American Astronautical Soc., American Acad. of Arts and Sciences, Regents' Fellow, Smithsonian Inst. 1981; Pres.-elect American Geophysical Union 1980–82, Pres. 1982–84; mem. NAS, Royal Astronomical Soc. (UK) (Gold Medal 1978); Founder mem. Int. Acad. of Astronautics; Assoc. Ed. Physics of Fluids 1958–62, Journal of Geophysical Research 1959–67; mem. Editorial Bd Space Science Reviews 1962–; discoverer of the 'Van Allen Belt' of radiation around the Earth and a pioneer of high-altitude rocket research; Hon. DSc (numerous univs); Distinguished Civilian Service Medal (US Army) 1959, NASA Medal for Exceptional Scientific Achievement 1974, Distinguished Public Service Award (USN) 1976, Award of Merit, American Consulting Engineers Council 1978, Space Science Award, American Inst. of Aeronautics and Astronautics 1982, Crawford Prize, Swedish Royal Acad. of Sciences 1989. *Publications:* Physics and Medicine of the Upper Atmosphere, Rocket Exploration of the Upper Atmosphere, Origins of Magnetospheric Physics 1983 and 225 scientific papers; Ed.: Scientific Use of Earth Satellites. *Address:* Department of Physics and Astronomy, 701 Van Allen Hall, University of Iowa, Iowa City, IA 52242 (Office); 5 Woodland Mounds Road, R.F.D. 6, Iowa City, IA 52240, USA (Home). *E-mail:* james-vanallen@uiowa.edu (Office).

VAN BASTEN, Marco; Netherlands footballer; b. 31 Oct. 1964, Utrecht; m. Elizabeth Van Basten 1992; one s. two d.; player Ajax 1981–97 (won Golden Boot Award for top-scoring with 37 goals in 1986, 3 Dutch Championships, 3 Dutch Cups, Cup Winner's Cup) scoring 128 goals in 143 appearances; player AC Milan 1987–95 (won 2 European Cups, 2 World Club Cups) scoring 90 goals in 147 games; player nat. team, 58 caps, 24 goals; European Footballer of the Year 1988, 1989, 1992, World Footballer of the Year 1988, 1992. *Leisure interest:* golf.

VAN BENTHEM, Johannes F. A. K., MA, PhD; Netherlands professor of mathematical logic; b. 12 June 1949, Rijswijk; s. of A. K. van Benthem and J. M. G. Eggermont; m. Lida Blom 1977; two s.; ed 's Gravenhaags Christelijk Gymnasium and Univ. of Amsterdam; Asst Prof. of Philosophical Logic, Univ. of Amsterdam 1972–77, Chair. Dept of Philosophy 1974–75; Assoc. Prof. of Philosophical Logic, Univ. of Groningen 1977–86, Chair. Dept of Philosophy

1979–81; Prof. of Mathematical Logic, Univ. of Amsterdam 1986–, Chair. Dept of Math. and Computer Science 1987–89; Scientific Dir Research Inst. for Logic, Language and Computation 1991–98; Sr Researcher, Center for Study of Language and Information, Stanford Univ., USA 1992–; Bonsall Visiting Chair. in the Humanities, Stanford Univ. 1994–; Vice-Pres. Int. Fed. of Computational Logic 1999–; Chair. Nat. Cognitive Science Programme 2001–; mem. Academia Europaea, Royal Dutch Acad. of Sciences, Institute Int. de Philosophie; Dr hc (Liège Univ.) 1998; Spinoza Prize, Netherlands Org. for Scientific Research 1996. *Publications:* The Logic of Time 1983, Modal Logic and Classical Logic 1985, Essays in Logical Semantics 1986, A Manual of Intensional Logic 1988, Language in Action, Categories, Lambdas and Dynamic Logic 1991, Exploring Logical Dynamics 1996; co-author of various textbooks in logic; (ed.) Handbook of Logic and Language 1997, Logic and Games 2001; articles in scientific journals. *Address:* Institute for Logic, Language and Computation, University of Amsterdam, Plantage Muidergracht 24, 1018 TV Amsterdam, Netherlands (Office). *Telephone:* (20) 5256051 (Office). *Fax:* (20) 5255206 (Office). *E-mail:* johan@science.uva.nl (Office). *Website:* turing.science.uva.nl/~johan (Office).

VAN BERKEL, Ben (Bernard Franciscus); Dutch architect; b. 25 Jan. 1957, Utrecht; s. of Magchiel van Berkel and Maria Therese Mattaar; ed Rietved Acad., Amsterdam, Architectural Asscn, London; graphic designer 1977–82; Co-Founder, Dir Van Berkel & Box 1988–99; Co-Founder, Dir UN Studio 1999. Projects include: switching substation, Amersfoort 1989–93, Erasmus Bridge, Rotterdam 1990–96, Villa Wilbrink, Amersfoort 1992–94, Möbius House, 't Gooi 1993–98, Museum Het Valkhof, Nijmegen 1995–99, Masterplan station area, Arnhem 1996—, City hall and theatre, Ijsselstein 1996–2000, switching station, Innsbruck 1998–2001, Music Faculty, Graz 1998–; Eileen Gray Award 1983, British Council Fellowship 1986, Charlotte Köhler Prize 1991, winning entry for Police HQ, Berlin 1995, Museum Het Valkhof 1995, music theatre, Graz, Austria 1998. *Art exhibitions:* work included in numerous architectual exhbns. including Architecture et Utopie, Paris and Berlin 1989–90, Architectural Biennale of Venice 1991–93, 1996, 2000, Das Schloss, Berlin, Vienna and Stuttgart 1993–94, Mobile Forces, LA, New York 1997, The Un-Private House, Museum of Modern Art, New York 1999, LA 2000–01. *Address:* UN Studio Van Berkel & Box, Stadhouderskade 113, 1073 AX Amsterdam, The Netherlands (Office). *Telephone:* (20) 5702040 (Office). *Fax:* (20) 5702041 (Office). *E-mail:* info@unstudio.com (Office). *Website:* www.unstudio.com (Office).

VAN CAENEGEM, Baron Raoul C.; Belgian academic; b. 14 July 1927, Ghent; s. of Jozef Van Caenegem and Irma Barbaix; m. Patricia Carson 1954; two s. one d.; ed Univs. of Ghent, Paris and London; Ordinary Prof. 1964, Prof. Emer. Univ. of Ghent 1992–; Visiting Fellow, Univ. Coll. Cambridge 1968; Goodhart Prof. of Legal Science, Cambridge 1984–85; Visiting Fellow, Peterhouse, Cambridge 1984–85; Sir Henry Savile Fellow, Merton Coll. Oxford 1989; Fiftieth Anniversary Fellow, Univ. of Queensland, Australia 1990; Erasmus Lecturer on History and Civilization of the Netherlands, Harvard Univ. 1991; Francqui Prize 1974; Solvay Prize, Nat. Fund for Scientific Research, Brussels 1990; Dr. hc (Tübingen) 1977, (Louvain) 1984, (Paris) 1988. *Publications:* Royal Writs in England from the Conquest to Glanvill. Studies in the Early History of the Common Law 1959, The Birth of the English Common Law 1973, Guide to the Sources of Medieval History 1978, English Lawsuits from William I to Richard I (two Vols) 1990–91, An Historical Introduction to Private Law 1992, Judges, Legislators and Professors: Chapters in European Legal History 1993, An Historical Introduction to Western Constitutional Law 1995, Introduction aux sources de l'histoire médiévale 1997, European Law in the Past and the Future: Unity and Diversity over Two Millennia 2002. *Leisure interests:* bridge, swimming, wine. *Address:* Veurestraat 47, 9051 Afsnee, Belgium. *Telephone:* (9) 222-62.11. *Fax:* (9) 222-62-11. *E-mail:* annie.dolieslagers@rug.ac.be.

VAN CITTERS, Robert L., MD; American professor of medicine, physiology and biophysics; b. 20 Jan. 1926, Alton, Ia; s. of Charles J. Van Citters and Wilhelmina T. Van Citters; m. Mary E. Barker 1949; two s. two d.; ed Univ. of Kansas; Intern, Univ. of Kansas Medical Center 1953–54; Medical Officer, Air Research and Devt Command, Kirtland AFB, NM 1954–55; Resident, Internal Medicine, Univ. of Kansas Medical Center 1957–58; Research Fellow Cardiovascular Physiology, Univ. of Washington 1958–62; Research Assoc. Cardiopulmonary Inst., Scripps Clinic and Research Foundation, La Jolla, Calif. 1962; Exchange Scientist, Jt US–USSR Scientific Exchange Agreement 1962; Robert L. King Chair. of Cardiovascular Research 1963–; Asst Prof. of Physiology and Biophysics School of Medicine, Univ. of Washington 1963–65, Assoc. Prof. 1965–68, Assoc. Dean for Research and Grad. Programs 1968–70, Chair. Bd of Health Sciences 1970, Dean, School of Medicine 1970–81, Dean Emer. 1981–, Prof. of Medicine (Cardiology), Prof. of Physiology and Biophysics 1981–; mem. Inst. of Medicine, NAS; Hon. DSc (Northwestern Coll.) 1978. *Publications:* 150 publs in scientific journals. *Leisure interests:* fishing, gardening. *Address:* Division of Cardiology, Box 356422, School of Medicine, University of Washington, Seattle, WA 98195, USA (Office). *Telephone:* (206) 543-9952 (Office). *Fax:* (206) 543-3639 (Office).

VAN CREVELD, Martin L.; Israeli academic; b. 5 March 1946, Rotterdam; s. of L. van Creveld and M. van Creveld (née Wyler); two step c.; ed Hebrew Univ., LSE; Lecturer, later Prof. in History, Hebrew Univ. 1971–; Fellow War Studies Dept King's Coll. Univ., London 1975–76; Fellow von Humboldt Inst., Freiburg 1980–81; Faculty mem. Nat. Defense Univ., Washington DC

1986–87; Prof. Marine Corps. Univ., Quantico, Va 1991–92; Best Book Award, Mil. History Inst. USA 1990. *Publications:* Supplying War 1977, Fighting Power 1987, Command in War 1985, Technology and War 1988, The Transformation of War 1991. *Leisure interests:* reading, walking. *Address:* Hebrew University of Jerusalem, Mount Scopus, 91 905 Jerusalem, Israel (Office). *Telephone:* 2-588211 (Office); 2-5344923 (Home). *Fax:* 2-5322545 (Office).

VAN-CULIN, Rev. Canon Samuel, OBE, AB, BD; American ecclesiastic; b. 20 Sept. 1930, Honolulu; s. of Samuel Van-Culin and Susie Mossman; ed Princeton Univ. and Virginia Theological Seminary; Curate St Andrew's Cathedral, Honolulu 1955–56; Canon Precentor and Rector Hawaiian Congregation, Honolulu 1956–58; Asst Rector St John's, Washington DC 1958–60; Gen. Sec. Lyman Int., Washington DC 1960–61; Asst Sec. Overseas Dept, Exec. Council of the Episcopal Church USA 1962–68, Sec. for Africa and Middle E 1968–76, Exec. for World Mission 1976–83; Sec. Gen. Anglican Consultative Council 1983–94; Asst Priest All Hallows Church, London 1995–; Sec. to Lambeth Conf. 1988; Hon. DD (Virginia Theological Seminary); Hon. Canon Canterbury, Jerusalem, Honolulu, Ibadan and Cape Town. *Leisure interests:* music and travel. *Address:* 16A Burgate, Canterbury, Kent, CT1 2HG, England. *Telephone:* (1227) 458018.

VAN DAM, José; Luxembourg opera singer; b. 25 Aug. 1940, Brussels, Belgium; m.; ed Académie de Musique, Brussels, Conservatoire Royal, Brussels; début in Paris in Carmen (Escamillo) 1961, with Grand Théâtre, Geneva 1965–67, Deutsche Oper, Berlin 1967–, Salzburg Festival, opera and concerts 1966–, Festival d'Aix en Provence 1966–, title role in St-François d'Assise (Messiaen) Paris 1983–84, Wozzeck at Royal Opera House, Covent Garden 1983–84, début in Meistersinger (Hans Sachs), Brussels 1985; awards include Grand Prix de l'Académie Française du Disque 1979, Orphée d'Or, Académie Lyrique Française 1980, Prix Européen des Critiques 1985. *Address:* c/o Artist's Management Zürich, Frau Rita Schütz, Rütistrasse 52, CH-8044 Zürich Gockhausen, Switzerland.

VAN DAMME, Jean-Claude; Belgian actor; b. 18 Oct. 1961, Brussels; m. 1st Gladys Portugues; m. 2nd Darcy LaPier 1994; one s. one d.; fmr European Professional Karate Asscn Middleweight Champion. *Films include:* Predator, Bloodsport, Death Warrant, Kickboxer, Cyborg, AWOL, Universal Soldier, No Retreat, No Surrender, Nowhere to Run, Monaco Forever, Hard Target, Streetfighter, Time Cop, Sudden Death, The Quest (also Dir), Maximum Risk, Double Team, Universal Soldier: The Return 1999, Coyote Moon 1999, Desert Heat 1999, The Order 2001, Replicant 2001. *Address:* United Talent Agency, Suite 500, 9560 Wilshire Boulevard, Beverly Hills, CA 90212, USA.

VAN DE KAA, Dirk Jan, PhD; Netherlands professor of demography; b. 5 Jan. 1933, Scherpenzeel; m. Anna Jacomina van Teunenbroek 1961; one s. one d.; ed Univ. of Utrecht, ANU; Dept Dir, Demographic Research Project, Western New Guinea 1961–66; Research Fellow, Dept of Demography, Research School of Social Sciences, Inst. for Advanced Studies, ANU, Canberra 1966–71; Dir Netherlands Interuniversity Demographic Inst. (NIDI), The Hague 1971–87; Project Dir World Fertility Survey, London 1981–82; Dir Int. Statistical Research Centre, The Hague 1982–84; Prof. of Demography, Univ. of Amsterdam 1977–; Dir Netherlands Inst. for Advanced Study (NIAS), Wassenaar 1987–95; Vice-Chair. Nat. Science Foundation, The Hague 1988–; mem. Royal Netherlands Acad. of Arts and Sciences (Vice-Pres. 1984–87); Pres. European Asscn for Population Studies 1983–87, Hon. Pres. 1987–. *Publications:* (author, co-author or ed.) Results of the Demographic Research Project Western New Guinea 1964–67, The Demography of Papua and New Guinea's Indigenous Population 1971, Science for Better and for Worse 1984, Population: Growth and Decline 1986, Europe's Second Demographic Transition 1987. *Address:* Van Hogenhoucklaan 63, 2596 TB The Hague, Netherlands.

VAN DE WALLE, Leslie; French business executive; b. 27 March 1956, Paris; s. of Philippe Van de Walle and Marie Van de Walle; m. Domitille Noel 1982; two d.; ed Hautes Etudes Commerciales, Paris; Man. Dir Schweppes Benelux 1990–92, France and Benelux 1992–93, Spain and Portugal 1993–94; Snacks Div., United Biscuits Continental Europe 1994–95 (CEO 1996–97), CEO McVities Group 1998, United Biscuits Group 1999–2000; Pres. Shell Latin America and Africa 2000–03, Shell Oil Products Europe 2003–. *Leisure interests:* golf, travel. *Address:* Shell Centre, London, SE1 7NA (Office); 34 Rose Square, Fulham Road, London, SW3 6RS, England (Home). *Telephone:* (20) 7934-5655 (Office); (20) 7584-1218 (Home). *Fax:* (20) 7934-7663 (Office); (20) 7584-9339 (Home). *E-mail:* Leslie.VandeWalle@shell.com (Office).

van den BERGH, Maarten Albert; Dutch business executive; b. 19 April 1942, New York, USA; s. of Sidney James van den Bergh and Maria Mijers; m. Marjan Désirée; two d.; ed Univ. of Groningen; joined the Shell Group 1968, East and Australasia Area Co-ordinator 1981, Deputy Group Treas. Shell Int. 1983, Chair. Shell Cos. in Thailand 1987, Western Hemisphere and Africa Regional Coordinator Shell Int. 1989, Group Man. Dir Royal Dutch/Shell Group 1992, Vice-Chair. Cttee of Man. Dirs. and Pres. Royal Dutch Petroleum Co. 1998–2000; Dir Shell Petroleum Co. 1992–; Dir Royal Dutch Petroleum Co. and Shell Petroleum NV; Dir British Telecommunications PLC 2000–01, BT Group PLC 2001–; Deputy Chair. Lloyds TSB Group PLC 2000–01, Chair. 2001–; Vice-Pres. and Fellow Inst. of Financial Services 2001–; mem. Pres. of the Philippines' Special Bd of Advisers 2001–; mem. Advisory Council, Amsterdam Inst. of Finance 2001–; mem. Guild of Int. Bankers 2001–; Adviser to Chief Exec. of Hong Kong Special Admin. Region 1998–2002;

Companion Chartered Man. Inst. 2001. *Leisure interests:* European history, collector of Asian art. *Address:* Lloyds TSB Group PLC, 25 Gresham Street, London, EC2V 7HN, England (Office). *Telephone:* (20) 7356-2074 (Office). *Fax:* (20) 7356-2050 (Office).

VAN DEN BERGH, Sidney, OC, MSc, Dr rer. nat, FRS; Canadian astronomer; b. 20 May 1929, Wassenaar, Netherlands; s. of Sidney J. van den Bergh and S. M. van den Berg; m. 2nd (wife deceased); one s. two d.; m. 3rd Paulette Brown; ed Leiden Univ., Princeton Univ. and Ohio State Univ., USA, Univ. of Göttingen, Fed. Repub. of Germany; Asst Prof., Ohio State Univ. 1956–58; Prof., Univ. of Toronto, Canada 1958–77; Dir Dominion Astrophysical Observatory, Victoria 1977–86, Astronomer 1986–98, Researcher Emer. 1998–; Adjunct Prof., Univ. of Vic. 1978–; Pres. Canadian Astronomy Soc. 1990–92; Assoc. Royal Astronomical Soc.; Hon. DSc 1998, 2001; Killam Laureate 1990; NRC Pres.'s Medal. *Publications:* about 600 scientific Publs including Galaxy Morphology and Classification 1998, The Galaxies of the Local Group 2000. *Leisure interests:* archaeology, photography. *Address:* Dominion Astrophysical Observatory, 5071 West Saanich Road, Victoria, BC, V9E 2E7; 418 Lands End Road, Sidney, BC, V8L 5L9, Canada (Home). *Telephone:* (250) 363-0006 (Office); (250) 656-6020 (Home). *Fax:* (250) 363-0045 (Office); (250) 363-0045. *E-mail:* sidney.vandenbergh@nrc.ca (Office). *Website:* www.nrc.ca (Office).

VAN DEN BOOGAARD, Hans Albert Dirk; Netherlands business executive; b. 5 Nov. 1939, Hengelo; m. Ina Mulder 1967; one s. one d.; ed Rotterdam School of Econs; joined Stork N.V. 1968, mem. Man. Bd 1986–, Chief Financial Officer and Exec. Vice-Pres., Bd of Man. 1991–; Chair. Supervisory Bd NethCorp V, Van der Hoop Effektenbank; mem. Supervisory Bd ICT Automatisering, Royal IBC; Chair. Foundation Certifying Friesland Coberco Dairy Foods, Stork Pension Fund Foundation; retd. 2001; mem. Advisory Bd Netherlands Energy Research Foundation (ECN) 1996–; Treas. Exec. Cttee FME-CWM (Employers' Asscn); mem. Bd Coöperatie Achmea, Stichting Continuiteit Polynorm. *Leisure interests:* hockey, skiing, reading.

VAN DEN BROEK, Hans; Netherlands politician; b. 11 Dec. 1936, Paris, France; m.; two c.; ed Alberdingk Thym Grammar School, Hilversum, Univ. of Utrecht; attended Sr Man. training, De Baak, Noordwijk; solicitor in Rotterdam 1965–68; Sec. Man. Bd ENKA B.V., Arnhem 1969–73, Commercial Man., 1973–76; City Councillor, Rheden 1970–74; mem. Second Chamber, States-Gen. (Parl.) 1976–81; served on Standing Cttees. on Foreign Affairs, Devt Co-operation and Justice; Sec. of State for Foreign Affairs 1981–82, Minister 1982–93; Commr for External Relations, Foreign and Security Policy Enlargement Negotiations, Comm. of EC (now European Comm.) 1993–95, for External Relations with Cen. and Eastern Europe, fmr Soviet Union and others for Common Foreign and Security Policy and External Service 1995–99.

VAN DEN HOUT, Tjaco T., LLB; Netherlands lawyer, politician and international organization executive; ed Leiden Univ., Harvard Univ., USA; Deputy Sec.-Gen. Ministry of Foreign Affairs –1999; Sec.-Gen. Perm. Court of Arbitration (PCA), The Hague 1999–. *Address:* Permanent Court of Arbitration, Peace Palace, Carnegieplein 2, 2517 KJ The Hague, Netherlands (Office). *Telephone:* (70) 3024165 (Office). *Fax:* (70) 3024167 (Office). *E-mail:* secgen@pca-cpa.org (Office). *Website:* www.pca-cpa.org (Office).

VAN DER AVOIRD, Ad, PhD; Netherlands professor of theoretical chemistry; b. 19 April 1943, Eindhoven; s. of H. J. van der Avoird and M. A. van der Avoird (née Kerkhofs); m. T. G. M. Lange 1964; two s.; ed Tech. Univ., Eindhoven; Research Fellow, Inst. Battelle, Geneva, Switzerland 1965–67; Section Man. Unilever Research Lab., Vlaardingen 1967–71; Assoc. Prof., Univ. of Nijmegen, Nijmegen 1968–71, Prof. 1971–; mem. Netherlands Acad. of Sciences 1979–, Int. Acad. of Quantum Molecular Sciences 1997–. *Publications:* Interacties tussen moleculen 1989; articles in scientific journals. *Address:* Institute of Theoretical Chemistry, University of Nijmegen, Toernooiveld, 6525 ED Nijmegen, Netherlands (Office). *Telephone:* (24) 3653037 (Office). *Fax:* (24) 3653041 (Office). *E-mail:* avda@theochem.kun.nl (Office).

VAN DER EB, Alex Jan, PhD; Netherlands professor of molecular carcinogenesis; b. 16 Jan. 1936, Bandung, Java; s. of Wijnand Jan van der Eb and Gertrude Leonie van der Eb-Blekkink; m. Titia Brongersma 1961; two s. one d.; ed Univ. of Leiden; mil. service 1962–63; Assoc. Prof. of Tumor Virology, Univ. of Leiden 1974–80, Prof. of Molecular Carcinogenesis 1980–; mem. Royal Acad. of Sciences and Letters 1987–, European Molecular Biology Org. 1981–, Acad. Europaea, Human Genome Org., Holland Science Asscn of 1752 1987–; Postdoctoral Fellow, Calif. Inst. Tech., Pasadena, USA 1968–69; AKZO Prize 1975, Korteweg Overwater Fund Award 1977, Beijerinck Virology Medal 1978, Robert Koch Prize 1989. *Publications:* numerous Publs on virology. *Address:* Sylvius Laboratory, Wassenaarseweg 72, 2333 AL Leiden (Office); Prinses Beatrixlaan 53, 2341 TW Oegstgeest, Netherlands (Home). *Telephone:* (71) 5276115 (Office); (71) 5172178 (Home). *Fax:* (71) 5276284.

VAN DER KLAAUW, Christoph Albert; Netherlands politician and diplomatist; b. 13 Aug. 1924, Leyden; m. 1st Henriette van Everdingen (deceased); five c.; m. 2nd Leontine van Noort 1989; ed Leyden Municipal Gymnasium, State Univ. of Leyden; entered Ministry of Foreign Affairs as trainee 1952; Legation Attaché, Budapest 1952–53; Staff mem., Western Co-operation Dept (NATO and European Defence Affairs Section), Ministry of Foreign Affairs; Second Sec., Oslo 1956–59; First Sec., Combined Perm.

Netherlands Del. to N Atlantic Council and OEEC, Paris 1959–63; Head of NATO and WEU Political Affairs Section, Ministry of Foreign Affairs and Sec. of dels. to ministerial NATO and WEU Council sessions 1963–66; Counsellor, Rio de Janeiro 1966–70; Deputy Perm. Rep. to UN, New York 1970–74; Amb. serving as Perm. Rep. at UN and other int. orgs., Geneva 1975–77; Dir-Gen. for European Co-operation 1977; Minister for Foreign Affairs 1977–81; Amb. to Belgium 1981–86, to Portugal 1986–89; mem. People's Party for Freedom and Democracy (VVD), Advisory Cttee on Foreign Policy 1964–66; mem. Telders Foundation 1964–66; fmr Corresp. mem. Univ. Alumni Fund and advisory mem. Student Asscn, State Univ. of Leyden; Vice-Chair. Dutch Protestant League, Paris 1961–63; Chair. Asscn of Liberal Reformed Protestants of The Hague and Scheveningen 1964–66; Chair. Supervisory Bd Netherlands Inst. for Int. Relations 1989–98; Commdr of Order of Orange-Nassau, Kt of the Order of the Netherlands Lion, Grand Cross of the Order of Leopold (Belgium), Grand Cross of the Order of the Crown (Belgium) and other foreign decorations. *Publications:* Political Relations between the Netherlands and Belgium 1919–1939 1953, Integration at the Ministry of Foreign Affairs (article in Internationale Spectator) March 1977, Een Diplomatenleven (memoirs) 1995. *Leisure interests:* family, water sports, reading, contemporary and 19th century history. *Address:* Ary Schefferstraat 151, 2597 VS The Hague, Netherlands. *Telephone:* (70) 3282427.

VAN DER MEER, Jan, MD; Netherlands physician; b. 30 Aug. 1935, Leeuwarden; s. of L. van der Meer and G. Bakker; m. Joan Alkema 1962; one d.; ed Univ. of Amsterdam; intern 1968; Sr Registrar in Internal Medicine, Binnengasthuis, Amsterdam 1970–76; Head of Coagulation Lab., Cen. Lab. of Bloodtransfusion Service of Dutch Red Cross 1969–76; Prof. of Internal Medicine, Chair. of Dept, Acad. Hosp. of Free Univ. Amsterdam 1976–2000; Chair. Govs., Cen. Lab. of Blood Transfusion Service, Netherlands Red Cross 1994–98; Chair. Landsteiner Foundation for Blood Transfusion Research 1998–, Dutch Diabetes Research Foundation. *Publication:* Meting van de plasma renine-activiteit met behulp van een radioimmunologische bepaling van angiotensine I 1969. *Address:* De Wijde Blik 19, 1189 WJ Amsterdam, Netherlands (Home). *Telephone:* (297) 582553 (Home).

VAN DER MEULEN, Robert Paul, LLM, MCL; Netherlands diplomatist; b. 25 May 1950, Eindhoven; m. Christine Bayle 1982; two d.; ed Univ. of Leyden; Asst, European Inst., Univ. of Leyden 1974–76; Dir European Integration, Foreign Econ. Relations Dept, Ministry of Econ. Affairs 1976, Head of Bureau, Accession of Greece, Spain and Portugal, Co-operation with Mediterranean cos and EFTA cos 1979; with Perm. Representation of Netherlands to EC, Brussels 1981–82; First Sec. Embassy in Washington, DC 1982–84, Counsellor 1984–85; Deputy Head Office of Vice-Pres. of EC 1985–88; Amb., Head of Del. of European Comm. to Brunei, Indonesia and Singapore 1989–94, to Tunisia 1994–98, to Jordan 2002–; Head Maghreb Div. (DG RELEX-F3), European Comm. 1998–2001, Acting Dir S Mediterranean and Middle East 2001–02; Grand Officier, Ordre de la Répub. Tunisienne. *Leisure interests:* collecting Chinese porcelain, nineteenth-century paintings. *Address:* c/o European Commission, Delegation Amman, PO Box 926794, Amman 11110, Jordan (Office); 1 rue du Genève (valise diplomatique), 1049 Brussels, Belgium (Home). *Telephone:* (6) 5668191 (Office); (6) 5931042 (Home). *E-mail:* robert.van-der-meulen@cec.eu.int (Office); vdmeulen@go.com.jo (Home). *Website:* www.deljor.cec.eu.int (Office).

VAN DER STOEL, Max, LLM, MA; Netherlands politician; b. 3 Aug. 1924, Voorschoten; one s. four d.; ed Univ. of Leiden; Int. Sec. Labour Party (Partij van de Arbeid) 1958–65; mem. Exec. Bd Socialist Int. 1958–65; mem. First Chamber of States-Gen. (Parl.) 1960–63, Second Chamber 1963–65, 1967–73, 1978–; State Sec. of Foreign Affairs 1965–66; mem. Ass. Council of Europe 1967–72; N Atlantic Ass., European Parl. 1972–73; Minister of Foreign Affairs 1973–77, 1981–82; Perm. Rep. to the UN 1983–86; mem. Council of State 1986–92; OSCE High Commr on Nat. Minorities 1993–2001; Minister of State of the Netherlands 1991; apptd. a Special Rapporteur of UN Comm. on Human Rights on the situation of human rights in Iraq 1991–99; Special Rep. of Chair. of OSCE on Macedonia 2001–; Dr. h.c. (Athens) 1997, (Charles Univ. Prague) 1993, (Utrecht) 1994, (Péter Pázmány Catholic Univ., Budapest) 1999, (Univ. Coll. London) 2001; Gold Medal, Comenius Univ., Bratislava, Slovakia 1998. *Address:* Lubeckstr. 138, 2517 SV The Hague, Netherlands.

VAN DER WEE, Baron Herman Frans Anna, LLD, PhD; Belgian historian (retd); b. 10 July 1928, Lier; s. of Jos Van der Wee and Martha Planckaert; m. Monique Verbreyt 1954; one s. one d.; ed Leuven Univ., Sorbonne, Paris, London School of Econs, UK; Fellow Nat. Foundation for Scientific Research of Belgium 1953–55; lecturer, Leuven Univ. 1955, Assoc. Prof. 1966, Prof. of Econ. History 1969–93, Prof. Emer. 1993–, Sec. Dept of Econs 1970–72, Chair. 1972–74, Chair. Bd of Trustees Leuven Univ. Press 1971–93; Visiting Prof. St Aloysius Univ., Brussels 1972–76, Dean Faculty of Econ., Political and Social Sciences 1972–75; Visiting Prof. Université Catholique de Louvain, Louvain-la-Neuve 1972–80, 1991–92; Research Fellow, Woodrow Wilson Int. Center for Scholars, Washington, DC 1975–76; Visiting Fellow, Inst. for Advanced Study, School of Historical Studies, Princeton, NJ, USA 1981–82, 1991, All Souls Coll. Oxford 1985; Ellen MacArthur Chair., Cambridge Univ. 1989; P.P. Rubens Chair., Univ. of Calif. at Berkeley 1994; Visiting Fellow Inst. for Advanced Study (RSSC), Canberra, Australia 1994; Erasmus Chair, Harvard Univ. (1997); Chair. of Banking History Univ. of St.-Gallen 1999; Guest of the Rector Netherlands Inst. for Advanced Study; Visiting Prof. or

Fellow at various univs. in USA, UK, Australia, Netherlands, France and Switzerland 1968–94; Pres. Belgian-Luxembourg American Studies Asscn. 1985–92, Int. Econ. History Asscn 1986–90 (Hon. Pres. 1990–); Chair. Leuven Univ. Press 1972–85, Royal Acad. of Belgium (Class of Letters) 1987, Leuven Inst. of Cen. and E European Studies 1990–93, Advisory Council of W European Program at Wilson Int. Center for Scholars, Washington, DC 1986–91, Academic Advisory Council of European Asscn for Banking History 1991–99; mem. Research Council European Univ. Inst., Florence 1985–94, 1999–, Bd of Trustees Cité Int. Universitaire, Paris 1993–; mem. Royal Acad. of Belgium 1977–; Corresp. Foreign mem. Royal Acad. of Netherlands 1983–; Corresp. Fellow British Acad. 1987; Foundation mem. Acad. Europaea 1997–; Foreign Hon. mem. American Acad. of Arts and Sciences 1993–; Dr. hc (Brussels) 1994, (Leicester) 1995; De Stassart Prize for Nat. History 1961–67 (Royal Acad. of Belgium) 1968, Fulbright-Hayes Award 1975, 1981, Quinquennial Solvay Prize for the Social Sciences 1976–80 (Nat. Foundation of Scientific Research of Belgium) 1981, Amsterdam Prize for Historical Sciences 1992, Golden Medal for Special Merits, Flemish Parl. 1995. *Publications:* Prix et salaires: Manuel Méthodologique 1956, The Growth of the Antwerp Market and the European Economy (14th–16th centuries), 3 Vols 1963, The Great Depression Revisited 1972, The Rise of Managerial Capitalism 1974, La Banque Nationale de Belgique et la politique monétaire entre les deux guerres 1975, Monetary, Credit and Banking Systems in Western Europe, 1400–1750, in The Cambridge Economic History of Europe (part V) 1977, Productivity of Land of Agricultural Innovation in the Low Countries 1250–1800 1978, Mint Statistics of Flanders and Brabant 1300–1506 (two Vols) 1980, 1985, Prosperity and Upheaval, the World Economy, 1945–1980 1983 (trans. in several languages), The Rise and Decline of Urban Industries in Italy and in the Low Countries (Late Middle Ages—Early Modern Times) 1988, Histoire économique mondiale 1945–1990 1990, History of European Banking 1991, Winkler Prins. History of the Low Countries, 1500–1800 (Ed.) 1992, The Economic Development of Europe, 950–1950 1992, Constructing the World Economy 1750–1990 1992, The Low Countries in the Early Modern World 1993, The General Bank 1822–1997: A Continuing Challenge 1997, Economic Development in Belgium Since 1870 (Ed.) 1997, Urban Achievement in Early modern Europe: Golden Ages in Antwerp, Amsterdam and London (Ed.) 2001, A Century of Banking Consolidation in Europe: The History and Archives of Mergers and Acquisitions (Ed.) 2001, Cera 1892–1997: The Power of Cooperative Solidarity (Ed.) 2002. *Leisure interests:* literature, music, tennis, skiing. *Address:* Katholieke Universiteit Leuven, Centrum voor Economische Studiën, Naamsestraat 69, 3000 Leuven (Office); Ettingestraat 10, 9170 Sint-Pauwels, Belgium (Home). *Telephone:* (16) 32-67-25 (Office); (3) 776-03-33 (Home). *Fax:* (16) 32-67-96 (Office); (3) 765-90-28 (Home). *E-mail:* ces@econ.kuleuven.ac.be (Office); Herman.VanDerWee@econ.kuleuven.ac.be (Home).

Van DEURSEN, Arie Theodorus; Netherlands professor of modern history (retd); b. 23 June 1931, Groningen; s. of Arie van Deursen and Trijntje Smilde; m. Else Ruth Junkers 1962; two s. two d.; ed Groningen Grammar School and Groningen State Univ.; Research Asst Univ. of Groningen 1957; staff mem. Bureau, Royal Comm. of Dutch History 1958–67; Prof. of Modern History, Free Univ. Amsterdam 1967–96; mem. Royal Acad. of Science 1978; Wijnaends Francken Award 1983. *Publications:* Professions et métiers interdits 1960, Honni soit qui mal y pense 1965, Jacobus de Rhoer 1970, Bavianen en slijkgeuzen 1974, Het kopergeld van de gouden eeuw (4 vols) 1978–80, Willem van Oranje (with H. C. de Schepper) 1984, Plain Lives in a Golden Age 1991, Een Dorp in de Polder 1994, Graft: Ein Dorf im 17. Jahrhundert 1997, Maurits van Nassau 2000. *Address:* Bispinck Park 35, 2061 SH Bloemendaal, Netherlands. *Telephone:* (23) 5265592. *E-mail:* athvandeursen@cs.com (Home).

VAN DIJK, Petrus, LLM, SJD; Netherlands state official and fmr professor of international law; b. 21 Feb. 1943, De Lier; s. of A. A. M. van Dijk and J. H. van Straelen; m. Francisca G. M. Lammerts 1969; one s. one d.; ed Utrecht and Leyden Univs.; Lecturer in Int. Law, Utrecht Univ. 1967–76, Prof. 1976–90; State Councillor 1990–, Pres. Admin. Jurisdiction Div., Council of State 2000–; Judge European Court of Human Rights 1996–98, Deputy Pres. Admin. Tribunal of Council of Europe; Fullbright-Hays Scholar, Univ. of Mich. Law School 1970–71; Visiting Prof. Wayne State Univ. Law School 1978; Chair. Netherlands Inst. of Human Rights 1982–97, Netherlands Inst. of Social and Econ. Law 1986–90; mem. Court of Appeal of The Hague 1986, Court of Appeal for Business and Industry 1992; mem. Bd of Trustees Inst. of Social Sciences 1992–98, Anne Frank Foundation 1994–; mem. various advisory cttees.; mem. Royal Netherlands Acad. of Arts and Sciences; mem. Netherlands Del. to UN Gen. Ass. 1981, 1983, 1986. *Publications include:* Theory and Practice of the European Convention on Human Rights (with G. J. H. van Hoof) 1979, The Final Act of Helsinki: Basis for a Pan-European System? 1980, Contents and Function of the Principle of Equity in International Economic Law 1987, Normative Force and Effectiveness of International Economic Law 1988, Access to Court 1993, Universality of Human Rights 1994; book chapters and ed. of numerous legal Publs. *Address:* Council of State, P.O. Box 20019, 2500 EA The Hague, Netherlands. *Telephone:* (70) 4264645 (Office). *Fax:* (70) 3465145 (Office). *E-mail:* pvandijk@raadvanstate.nl (Office).

VAN DÚNEM, Fernando José França; Angolan politician; fmr Minister of External Affairs; Prime Minister of Angola 1991–98; mem. Marxist-Leninist Popular Movt for the Liberation of Angola-Worker's Party (MPLA).

VAN DUYN, Mona, MA; American poet; b. 9 May 1921, Waterloo, Iowa; d. of Earl Van Duyn and Lora Kramer; m. Jarvis Thurston 1943; ed Univ. of Iowa; instructor in English, Univ. of Iowa 1943–46, Univ. of Louisville, Ky 1946–50; Lecturer in English, Washington Univ., St Louis 1950–67; Ed. Perspective: A Quarterly of Literature, St Louis 1947–67; Chancellor Acad. of Poets 1985–99; named U.S. Poet Laureate 1992–93; mem. Nat. Acad. of Arts and Letters, N.A.A.S.; Fellow Acad. of American Poets; numerous awards and hon. degrees; Pulitzer Prize for Poetry 1991. *Publications:* Valentines to the Wide World 1959, A Time of Bees 1964, To See, To Take 1970, Bedtime Stories 1972, Merciful Disguises 1973, Letters from a Father and Other Poems 1982, Near Changes 1990, Firefall 1993, If It Be Not I 1993. *Leisure interests:* gardening, reading. *Address:* 7505 Teasdale Avenue, St Louis, MO 63130, USA.

VAN EEKELEN, Willem Frederik, D.LL.; Netherlands politician and diplomatist; b. 5 Feb. 1931, Utrecht; s. of Dr. Marie van Eekelen and Anna Maria van Eekelen; m. Johanna Wentink; two c.; ed Utrecht and Princeton Univs.; diplomatic service 1957–77; mem. Consultative Ass. Council of Europe and WEU 1981–82; Sec. Gen. WEU 1989–94; Sec. of State for Defence 1978–81, for Foreign Affairs 1982–86; Minister of Defence 1986–88; Senator 1995–; Chair. European Movt in the Netherlands 1995–; Grand Officer Légion d'honneur, Grand Cross of Germany, Belgium, Luxembourg. *Publications:* The Security Agenda for 1996, Debating European Security 1948–1998. *Leisure interests:* old maps, trekking, sailing. *Address:* Else Manhslaan 187, 2595 HE The Hague, Netherlands. *Telephone:* (70) 3241103. *Fax:* (70) 3241103.

VAN FRAASSEN, Bastiaan Cornelis, PhD; American/Canadian professor of philosophy; b. 5 April 1941, Goes, The Netherlands; s. of Jan Bastiaan van Fraassen and Dina Landman; m. Judith Ann Brown 1962; two s.; Univ. of Alberta, Canada, Univ. of Pittsburgh, USA; Asst Prof., Yale Univ. 1966–68, Assoc. Prof. 1969, Assoc. Prof., Univ. of Toronto 1969–73, Prof. 1973–82; Prof., Univ. of Southern Calif. 1976–81; Prof. of Philosophy, Princeton Univ. 1982–; John Simon Guggenheim Fellowship 1970–71; co-winner Franklin Matchette Award 1982, co-winner Imre Lakatos Award 1986. *Publications:* Introduction to the Philosophy of Time and Space 1970, Formal Semantics and Logic 1971, The Scientific Image 1980, Laws and Symmetry 1989, Quantum Mechanics: An Empiricist View 1991, The Empirical Stance 2002. *Leisure interest:* rock climbing. *Address:* 308 Western Way, Princeton, NJ 08544, USA. *Telephone:* (609) 258-4304. *Fax:* (609) 258-1502.

VAN GERVEN, Walter M., DJur; Belgian lawyer; b. 11 May 1935, St Niklaas; s. of Willy van Gerven and Germaine van Bel; m. Frieda Sintobin 1959; four s.; ed Catholic Univ. of Louvain; Teaching Fellow, Univ. of Chicago Law School 1959–60; Assoc. Prof. of Law, Catholic Univ. of Louvain 1962–67, Prof. of Law 1967–82, Extraordinary Prof. 1982–, Vice-Rector 1970–76; Extraordinary Prof., Univ. of Amsterdam 1981–86; mem. Brussels Bar. 1970–80; Pres. Banking Comm. of Belgium 1982–88; mem. Bd of Dirs. of several commercial cos.; Advocate-Gen. Court of Justice of European Communities 1988–95; Visiting Prof. Univ. of Chicago 1968–69; mem. Royal Belgian Acad., Royal Netherlands Acad., Acad. Europaea. *Publications:* Principles of Belgian Private Law 1968, Commercial and Economic Law (3 Vols) 1973–86, The Policy of the Judge 1973, In Law and Equity 1987. *Leisure interests:* modern art, music, golf. *Address:* Demarsinstraat 42, 3010 Wilsele, Belgium (Home). *Telephone:* (16) 22-91-54 (Home).

VAN GINKEL, Hans J. A., MSc, PhD; Netherlands university administrator and academic; b. 22 June 1940, Kota-Radjah, Indonesia; m. Bep Teepen; one s. one d.; ed Utrecht Univ.; Teacher of Geography and History, Thomas à Kempis Coll., Arnhem 1965–68; joined Faculty of Geographical Sciences, Utrecht Univ. 1968, apptd Prof. of Human Geography and Planning 1980, Dean of Faculty 1981–85, mem. Exec. Bd 1985, Rector Magnificus 1986; Treas. Netherlands Foundation for Int. Co-operation in Educ. 1986–97; mem., then Chair. Bd Netherlands Interdisciplinary Demographic Inst. 1986–2000; Ind. Chair. Regional Council of Utrecht 1988–93; Pres. Governing Bd Int. Training Centre for Aerial Survey and Earth Sciences, Enschedé 1990–98; mem. Governing Bd UN Univ. 1992–97, Rector 1997–; Vice-Pres. Bd European Asscn of Univs 1994–98; mem. European Science and Tech. Ass., Brussels, Belgium 1994–98; Vice-Pres. Bd Int. Asscn of Univs 1995–2000, Pres. 2000–; mem. Nat. Council, Chair. Organizing Cttee. 28th Int. Geographical Congress, The Hague 1996; Vice-Chair. Bd of Trustees, Asian Inst. of Tech., Bangkok, Thailand 1997–; mem. Steering Cttee, UNESCO World Conf. on Higher Educ. 1998; mem. Academia Europaea; fmr mem. UNESCO Advisory Group for Higher Educ.; fmr Chair. Co-ordinating Cttee of Advisory Councils on Science Policy; fmr Bd mem. Utrecht Network for Innovation and Economy; fmr mem. Nat. Foresight Cttee on Science Policy; Hon. Mem. Comm. on the History of Geographical Thought, Int. Geographical Union; Kt Netherlands Order of the Lion 1994. *Address:* United Nations University, 53–70 Jingumae 5-chrome, Shibuya-ku, Tokyo 150-8925, Japan (Office). *Telephone:* (813) 3499-2811 (Office). *Fax:* (813) 3499-2828 (Office). *E-mail:* mbox@hq.unu.edu (Office). *Website:* www.unu.edu (Office).

VAN HAMEL, Martine; American ballerina; b. 16 Nov. 1945, Brussels, Belgium; d. of D. A. van Hamel and Manette van Hamel-Cramer; ed Nat. Ballet School of Canada; started ballet training at age four; début aged 11 with Nat. Ballet of Venezuela; joined Nat. Ballet of Canada as soloist 1963; moved to New York and danced with Joffrey Ballet 1969–70; joined American Ballet Theatre 1970, as Prin. Ballerina (1973–91) danced classic roles including Swan Lake, Sleeping Beauty, Raimonda as well as contemporary works choreographed by Petipa, Balanchine, Glen Tetley, Anthony Tudor, Kenneth MacMillan, Mark Morris, Twyla Tharp, Alvin Ailey; danced with Nederlands Dans Theater III 1993–98; Artistic Dir New Amsterdam Ballet (f. 1986); mem. Founding Bd Kaatsbaan Int. Dance Center, New York Choral Soc.; Gold Medal, Varna Competition 1966, Prix de Varna 1966, Dance Magazine Award, Cue Magazine Award, Award for Excellence, Washington Coll., Dance Educators of America Award. *Choreography:* Amnon V'Tamar for American Ballet Theatre 1984 and creator of works for Milwaukee Ballet, Washington Ballet, Royal Winnipeg Ballet and New Amsterdam Ballet. *Leisure interest:* singing. *Address:* 290 Riverside Drive, New York, NY 10025, USA. *Telephone:* (212) 749-1942. *Fax:* (212) 678-0320.

VAN HEERDEN, Neil Peter, BA; South African diplomatist; b. 30 July 1939, East London; s. of J. van Heerden and C. Nel; m. Evelin Nowack 1961; one s. one d.; ed Wonderbom High School, Pretoria and Univ. of S. Africa, Pretoria; joined Dept of Foreign Affairs 1959; Vice-Consul, Tokyo 1963; opened S Africa's first mission in Taipei 1967–68; opened first S African mission in Tehran 1970–71; First Sec. Washington, DC 1971–75; Amb. to FRG 1980; Deputy Dir Gen., Dept of Foreign Affairs, Pretoria 1985–87, Dir-Gen. of Foreign Affairs 1987–92, Amb. to EC (now EU) 1992–96; Exec. Dir S Africa Foundation 1996–; Hon. D.Litt. et Phil. (Rand Afrikaans Univ.) 2000. *Publications:* articles in journals dealing with foreign affairs. *Leisure interests:* music, hiking, sailing, golf. *Address:* South Africa Foundation, St Margaret's, 3 Rockridge Road, Parktown 2193 (Office); PO Box 7006, Johannesburg 2000, South Africa. *Telephone:* (11) 356-4650 (Office). *Fax:* (11) 726-4705 (Office). *E-mail:* safouond@safoundation.org.za (Office).

VAN HOOFF, Jan A. R. A. M.; Netherlands professor of comparative physiology and ethology; b. 15 May 1936, Arnhem; s. of R. A. Th. van Hooff and L. E. Burgers; m. Anna C. M. Bluemink 1964; two s. one d.; ed Canisius Coll., Nijmegen; scientific collaborator, Faculty of Biology, Utrecht Univ. 1963–73, Lecturer in Comparative Physiology 1973–80, Prof. of Comparative Physiology 1980–2001, Dean Faculty of Biology 1993–96; Dir Science Bd, Burgers Zoo, Arnhem 1969–; Pres. Research Council of Ethology, Netherlands Foundation for Biological Research 1972–78, Dir 1978–83; Pres. Soc. pour l'Etude et la Protection des Mammifères 1985–89, Royal Netherlands Zoological Soc. 1997; Sec. Gen. Int. Primatological Soc. 2000–; mem. numerous scientific foundations and socs; Fellow, Royal Netherlands Acad. of Arts and Sciences; Officer Royal Order of Orange-Nassau 2000. *Publications include:* Facial Expressions in Higher Primates 1962, The Comparison of Facial Expressions in Man and Higher Primates 1976, Categories and Sequences of Behavior: Methods of Description and Analysis 1982, Oorlog 1990, Relationships Among Nonhuman Primate Males 2000, Economics in Nature 2001. *Address:* Faculty of Biology, Utrecht University, PO Box 80.086, Sorbonnelaan 16, 3584 CB Utrecht (Office); Vermeerlaan 24, 3723 EN Bilthoven, Netherlands (Home). *Telephone:* (30) 2535404 (Office); (30) 2287639 (Home). *Fax:* (30) 2521105. *E-mail:* j.a.r.a.m.vanhooff@bio.uu.nl (Office).

VAN HOOVEN, Eckart, DJur; German company executive; b. 11 Dec. 1925; Chair. Supervisory Bd Giesecke & Devrient GmbH, Munich, Mobil Oil AG, Hamburg; Deputy Chair. Supervisory Bd Hapag-Lloyd AG, Hamburg; mem. Supervisory Bd Kaufhof AG, Cologne, Reemtsma Cigarettenfabriken GmbH, Hamburg; fmr mem. Bd Deutsche Bank AG. *Address:* Deutsche Bank AG, Taunusanlage 12, 60325 Frankfurt am Main, Germany. *Telephone:* (69) 71503075.

van INWAGEN, Peter Jan, PhD; American professor of philosophy and scholar; b. 21 Sept. 1942, Rochester, New York; s. of George Butler van Inwagen and Mildred Gloria Knudsen; m. 1st Margery Naylor 1967 (divorced 1988); one d.; m. 2nd Elisabeth Bolduc 1989; ed Rensselaer Polytechnic Inst., Univ. of Rochester; served U.S. Army 1969–70; Visiting Asst Prof. of Philosophy, Univ. of Rochester 1970–71; Asst Prof., Assoc. Prof., then Prof. of Philosophy, Syracuse Univ. 1971–95; John Cardinal O'Hara Prof. of Philosophy, Univ. of Notre Dame, S. Bend, Ind. 1995–; Visiting Prof., Univ. of Ariz. 1981, Rutgers Univ. 1987; Research grants, Nat. Endowment for the Humanities 1983–84, 1990–91. *Publications:* An Essay on Free Will 1983, Material Beings 1990, Metaphysics 1993, God, Knowledge and Mystery (essays) 1995, The Possibility of Resurrection and Other Essays in Christian Apologetics 1997, Ontology, Identity and Modality: Essays in Metaphysics 2001. *Address:* Department of Philosophy, University of Notre Dame, IN 46556, USA (Office). *Telephone:* (219) 631-5910 (Office). *Fax:* (219) 631-0588 (Office). *E-mail:* peter.vaninwagen.1@nd.edu (Office).

VAN ITTERSUM, Baron Boudewijn F.; Netherlands financial official; b. 7 June 1939; s. of Paul A. L. A. Van Ittersum and Henriette F. Van Lennep; m. Karin R. W. Van der Ven 1967; three c.; ed Univ. of Amsterdam; joined Ministry of Finance; seconded to IMF, IBRD, Washington, DC 1970–72; subsequently Dir of Int. Affairs, Ministry of Finance; Chair. Amsterdam Stock Exchange 1981–96, Dir 1996–2000 (merged with Paris Bourse and Brussels Exchanges to form Euronext Amsterdam 2000). *Address:* c/o Euronext Amsterdam, Beursplein 5, 1012 JW Amsterdam, Netherlands. *Telephone:* (20) 5504444. *Fax:* (20) 5504897.

VAN LINT, Jacobus Hendricus, PhD; Netherlands professor of mathematics; b. 1 Sept. 1932, Bandung, Indonesia; s. of J. H. van Lint and P. C. E. Minkman; m. Elisabeth Barbara Janna Teunissen 1961; one s. one d.; ed

Univs. of Utrecht, Göttingen and Munster; Prof. of Math., Eindhoven Univ. of Tech. 1959–, Rector Magnificus 1991–96; Dir Stan Ackermans Inst. 1997–99; mem. Tech. Staff, Bell Labs. 1966, 1971, 1977; Visiting Prof. Calif. Inst. of Tech. 1970–71, 1988–89; Pres. Wiskundig Genootschap 1968–70; mem. Royal Netherlands Acad. of Arts and Sciences; Dr. hc (Politehnica Bucarest, Univ. of Bergen) 1996, (Univ. of Ghent) 2000; Kt Order of the Lion (Netherlands). *Publications:* Coding Theory 1971, Algebra en Analyse (with S. T. M. Ackermans) 1974, Combinatorial Theory Seminar 1973, Graphs, Codes and Designs (with P. J. Cameron) 1980, Introduction to Coding Theory 1983, A Course in Combinatorics (with R. M. Wilson) 1991. *Leisure interests:* philately, swimming, bridge. *Address:* Department of Mathematics and Computing Science, Eindhoven University of Technology, Den Dolech, P.O. Box 513, 5600 MB Eindhoven (Office); Beukenlaan 15, Nuenen 5671 AH, Netherlands (Home). *Telephone:* (40) 2831466 (Home); (40) 2474763 (Office). *Fax:* (40) 2435810 (Office). *E-mail:* j.h.v.lint@tue.nl (Office).

VAN MIERLO, Henricus Antonius Franciscus Maria Oliva (Hans), DJur; Netherlands politician; b. 18 Aug. 1931, Breda; ed Canisius Coll. Nijmegen and Univ. of Nijmegen; journalist, Het Algemeen Handelsblad, Amsterdam 1960–67; first Chair. newly formed political party Democrats '66 (D66) 1966; mem. Lower House of States Gen. 1967–77, 1986–94; Leader D66 Parl. Party 1967–74, 1986–94; mem. Upper House of States Gen. 1983–86; Deputy Prime Minister and Minister of Foreign Affairs 1994–98; fmr mem. Netherlands-Suriname Devt Comm., Advisory Council on Defence; co-producer of TV programmes; various positions in literary and other cultural orgs. *Address:* c/o Ministry of Foreign Affairs, Bezuidenhoutseweg 67, P.O. Box 20061, 2500 EB The Hague, Netherlands.

VAN MIERT, Karel; Belgian international official and politician; b. 17 Jan. 1942, Oud-Turnhout; m.; one c.; ed State University of Ghent; Researcher, Fonds National de la Recherche Scientifique 1968–70; Asst in Int. Law, Free Univ. of Brussels 1971–73; Head. Admin. attached to Pvt. Office of Vice-Pres. of EC 1973–75; part-time lecturer, Free Univ. of Brussels 1978–; Int. Sec. Belgian Socialist Party 1976, Co-Chair. 1977; subsequently Chair. Flemish Socialists; Vice-Chair. Confed. of Socialist Parties of European Community 1978–80; MEP 1979–85; mem. House of Reps 1985–88; Vice-Chair. Socialist Int. 1986–92; EEC (now EU) Commr for Transport, Credit, Investment and Consumer Affairs 1989–94, for Environment (acting) 1992–93, for Competition Policy, Personnel and Admin. 1993–95, for Competition 1992–99, a Vice-Pres. 1993–95; Pres. Nijenrode Univ., Netherlands Business School 2000–; Dir (non-exec.) Anglo-American 2002–. *Address:* Office of the President, Nijenrode University, Netherlands Business School, Straatweg 25, 3621 BG Breukelen, Netherlands (Office). *Telephone:* (346) 291211 (Office). *Fax:* (346) 264204 (Office). *E-mail:* info@nijenrode.nl (Office). *Website:* www.nijenrode .nl (Office).

VAN MONTAGU, Baron Marc Charles Ernest, PhD; Belgian plant geneticist; b. 10 Nov. 1933, Ghent; s. of Jean Van Montagu and Irene Van Beveren; m. Nora Podgaetchi 1957; ed State Univ. Ghent; Asst, State Univ. Ghent 1962–64, Lab. Dir and Lector, Dept of Histology 1964–78, Assoc. Prof. and Co-Dir Lab. of Genetics 1979–87, Full Prof. and Dir Lab. of Genetics 1987–99; Chair. Steering Cttee IPBO 1999–; Scientific Dir Plant Genetic Systems N.V. 1983–95; mem. Royal Belgium Acad. of Sciences; Foreign Assoc. NAS (USA); Foreign mem. Russian Agric. Acad., Royal Swedish Acad. of Eng Sciences, Acad. d'Agric. de France; Assoc. Fellow Third World Acad. of Sciences 2001; title of Baron granted by King Baudoin I; Hon. DPhil (Helsinki) 1990; Rank Prize for Nutrition, UK 1987, IBM-Europe Prize 1988, Prize of the Flemish Community 1989, Dr. A. De Leeuw-Damry-Bourlart Prize 1990, Charles Leopold Mayer Prize, Acad. of Sciences, Paris 1990, Japan Prize 1998, Theodor Bücher Medal 1999. *Publications:* about 800 articles in specialized journals and books. *Leisure interest:* travel. *Address:* IPBO, Institute of Plant Biotechnology for Developing Countries, Department of Molecular Genetics, University of Ghent, Ledeganckstraat 35, 9000 Ghent (Office); De Stassartstraat 120, 1050 Brussels, Belgium (Home). *Telephone:* (9) 264-87-27 (Office); (2) 511-25-57 (Home). *Fax:* (9) 264-87-95 (Office); (9) 264-87-95. *E-mail:* mamon@gengenp.rug.ac.be (Office). *Website:* www.ipbo.rug.ac.be (Office).

van MUNSTER, Hans, DPhil; Netherlands ecclesiastic; b. 17 Nov. 1925, Gouda; s. of J. M. van Munster and A. C. B. Faay; ed Univ. of Louvain; entered Order of St Francis of Assisi 1944; ordained priest 1951; Lecturer in Logic and Methodology, Philosophical Inst., Venray 1955–67; Regent, RC Lycee, Venray 1963–67; Prof. of Philosophy, Catholic Theological Faculty of Utrecht 1967–71, Rector 1968–71; Vicar-Gen. of Archdiocese of Utrecht 1970–81; Sec.-Gen. Dutch Bishops' Conf. 1981–91; Pres. Cttee on Justice and Peace 1991–99; Pres. European Conf. of Justice and Peace Comms. 1996–99; Pres. Catholic Bible Soc. 1992–98, Franciscan Asscn 1992–98; Officer Order of Oranje-Nassau, Kt of Netherlands Lion. *Publications include:* Kierkegaard een keuze uit zijn dagboeken 1957, De filosofische gedachten van de jonge Kierkegaard 1958, Kierkegaards redevoeringen 1959, Over de vertwijfeling 1963, Sören Aabye Kierkegaard 1963, Naar woorden moet je luisteren 1981, Vanwaar? Waarheen? 1982, Drie prioriteiten voor de kerk van Europa 1983, Kantelt de Koets wel? 1989, Een steen in de vijver, vrede en gerechtigheid na de dood van Marx 1993, Te Doen gerechtigheid 1993, De ware vrede 1993, 't is een vreemdeling zeker 1994, Een ryke heeft het murilyk 1997, De mystick van Franciscus 2002. *Leisure interests:* cycling, literature. *Address:* Jan van Scorelstraat 75, 3583 CL Utrecht, Netherlands. *Telephone:* (30) 2510153. *Fax:* (30) 2523326.

VAN NIEKERK, André Isak (Kraai), PhD; South African politician and agricultural scientist; b. 7 Oct. 1938, Eshowe, Natal; m. Theresa Claassens 1964; three s.; ed Univ. of Stellenbosch; taught Science and Agric. Eshowe Bantu Training Coll. 1962; specialist officer, Dept of Agric. Tech. Services, Univ. of Stellenbosch 1964–67; Research at Rowett Inst., Aberdeen, Scotland 1968, Wageningen Agricultural Univ., The Netherlands 1969; farmer, Kenhardt Dist 1971–81; elected MP for Prieska 1981; Deputy Minister of Agric. 1986, of Agric. and Water Supply in Ministers' Council 1989, of Agricultural Devt 1989; Minister of Agric. in Cabinet, of Agricultural Devt in Ministers' Council 1991–94, of Agric., Govt of Nat. Unity 1994–96; Leader Nat. Party for the Northern Cape 1994–; mem. Senate (for Northern Cape) 1994–, Deputy Leader 1994–. *Address:* Private Bag X5066, Kimberley 8300, South Africa.

VAN PEEBLES, Mario, BEcons; American actor and film director; b. 15 Jan. 1957, Mexico; s. of Melvin Van Peebles and Maria Marx; ed Columbia Univ.; film début aged 11, A Thousand Clowns, then appeared in Dirty Harry, Sweet Sweetback's Badass Song; worked as budget analyst in New York Mayor's office; studied acting and script interpretation with Stella Adler. *Theatre:* Champion, Jungle Fever, Midnight, Friday The 13th, Deadwood Dick, Bodybags (also co-Dir). *Television:* The American Masters Series, Children of the Night, LA Law, One Life to Live, Gang in Blue, Riot. *Films include:* Cotton Club, Exterminator II, Rappin (also as singer), Hot Shots, The Last Resort, Heartbreak Ridge, New Jack City (also Dir), Posse (also Dir), Gunmen (also Dir), Panther (also Dir, producer), Jaws IV: The Revenge, Solo, Los Locos (also Dir, wrote screenplay), Stag 1997, Love Kills (also Dir, producer) 1998, Crazy Six, Raw Nerve, Standing Knockdown 1999.

Van ROIJEN, Jan Herman Robert Dudley, LLM; Netherlands diplomatist; b. 17 Dec. 1936, Tokyo, Japan; s. of the late Dr. Jan Herman van Roijen and Anne van Roijen (née Jonkvrouwe Snouck Hurgronje); m. Jonkvrouw Caroline H.W. Reuchlin 1963; one s. two d.; ed Groton School, Mass., USA and Univ. of Utrecht; entered foreign service 1963; Third Sec. Jakarta 1965–67; Second Sec. Perm. Mission at NATO, Paris and Brussels 1967–70; Head, Recruitment and Training Section, Foreign Office 1970–73; Chargé d'Affaires, Saigon 1973–75; Counsellor, Athens 1975–78, Ottawa 1978–81; Minister Plenipotentiary, Jakarta 1981–83; Deputy Dir-Gen. Int. Cooperation, Ministry of Foreign Affairs 1983–86; Amb. to Israel 1986–89; Prin. Dir Personnel, Diplomatic Budget and Bldgs., Ministry of Foreign Affairs 1989–91; Amb. to Indonesia 1992–94, to UK 1995–99 (also Accred to Iceland); Chair. Netherlands Helsinki Cttee; Kt Order of Netherlands Lion, Officer Order of Orange Nassau. *Leisure interests:* tennis, skiing. *Address:* Jagerslaan 9, 2243 EH Wassenaar, Netherlands (Home). *Telephone:* (70) 5144470 (Home). *Fax:* (70) 5142751 (Home). *E-mail:* vanroijen-reuchlin@hetnet.nl (Home).

VAN SANT, Gus Jr, BA; American film director and screenwriter; b. 1952, Louisville, Ky; ed Rhode Island School of Design; fmr production asst to Ken Shapiro; Nat. Soc. of Film Critics Awards for Best Dir and Screenplay 1990, New York Film Critics and LA Film Critics Award for Best Screenplay 1989, PEN Literary Award for Best Screenplay Adaptation (jtly) 1989. *Films include:* Mala Noche (dir, writer), Drugstore Cowboy 1989 (dir, writer, with Daniel Yost), My Own Private Idaho (dir, writer) 1991, Even Cowgirls Get the Blues (dir, writer) 1993, To Die For (dir)1995, Kids (producer) 1995, Ballad of the Skeletons (dir) 1996, Good Will Hunting (dir) 1997, Psycho (dir) 1998, Finding Forrester 2000. *Publications:* 108 Portraits 1995, Pink 1997. *Address:* c/o William Morris Agency Inc., 151 El Camino Drive, Beverly Hills, CA 90212, USA.

Van SCHAIK, Ben; Netherlands business executive; b. 1945; worked in sales for Mercedes Benz in UK, Netherlands, Germany; Chair. Fokker (aircraft maker) 1994–. *Address:* Fokker, P.O. Box 1222, 1100 AE Amsterdam Juidoost, Netherlands.

VAN SCHAIK, Gerard, FCIS; Netherlands business executive (retd); b. 29 March 1930, Haarlem; s. of the late Gerard Van Schaik and Maria Mulder; m. Moyra Colijn 1963; two s. one d.; ed Free Univ. of Amsterdam, IMEDE, Switzerland; officer Royal Netherlands Air Force 1956–58; joined Heineken's Bierbrouwerij Maatschappij N.V. 1959, mem. Exec. Bd Heineken N.V. 1974, Deputy Chair. 1983, Chair. 1989–93; Pres. Supervisory Bd Aegon NV 1993–2000; Pres. European Foundation of Man. Devt, Brussels; Dr. hc (State Acad. for Man., Moscow) 1997; Hon. Fellow London Business School; Kt Order of Dutch Lion. *Leisure interests:* golf, music. *Address:* Duinvoetlaan 7, 2243 GK Wassenaar, Netherlands. *Telephone:* (70) 5179008. *Fax:* (70) 5179008. *E-mail:* g.vanschaike@wanadoo.nl (Home).

VAN SCHALKWYK, Marthinus Christopher Johannes, MA; South African politician; b. 10 Nov. 1959, Pietersburg; m.; one s. one d.; ed Pietersburg High School, Rand Afrikaans Univ.; fmr Nat. Pres. Afrikaanse Studentebond, Chair. Youth for SA, Fed. Youth Leader, Nat. Party; mil. service 1978–79; Lecturer in Political Science, Rand Afrikaans Univ., Univ. of Stellenbosch; MP for Randburg 1990–94; mem. Nat. Ass. 1994–, mem. Parl. Portfolio Cttee on Communications, Nat. Party Rep. at Int. Democratic Union and African Dialogue Group; apptd. Exec. Dir Nat. Party 1997, Leader New Nat. Party (NNP) 1997–; Deputy Leader Democratic Alliance (f. 2000 by Democratic Party, NNP and others to contest municipal elections) 2000–; Abe Bailey Bursary to GB and Europe, Award for Academic Achievement, Transvaal Lawyers' Asscn. *Address:* New National Party, P.O. Box 1698, Cape

Town 8000, South Africa (Office). *Telephone:* (21) 4618180 (Office). *Fax:* (21) 4623008 (Office). *E-mail:* mcjvs@natweb.co.za (Office). *Website:* www.natweb.co.za (Office).

VAN SWAAIJ, Willibrordus Petrus Maria, PhD; Netherlands professor of chemical engineering; b. 18 Jan. 1942, Nijmegen; s. of Christian van Swaaij and C. Bosman; m. J. J. T. van den Berk 1966; one s. four d.; ed Tech. Univ. of Eindhoven, Univ. of Nancy, France; joined Shell Research 1965, worked in lab. Shell Research B.V. (KSLA), Amsterdam 1966–72, Section Chief, Gasification 1971–72; Prof. of Chemical Eng Science, Twente Univ.; Consultant to DSM, AKZO, Unilever, Netherlands Govt, EEC; mem. Royal Netherlands Acad. of Sciences 1986; Australian European Fellowship Award 1984; Dr. hc (Inst. Nat. Polytechnique de Lorraine, France) 1996; Dow Energy Prize 1985, Grand Prix du Génie des Procédés, Inst. de France 1996; Golden Hoogewerff Medal for Lifetime Achievement 2000; Australian European Fellowship Award 1984; Kt Order of the Lion (Netherlands) 1997. *Publications:* Chemical Reactor Design and Operation (with Westerterp and Beenackers); about 340 scientific papers, contribs. to books etc. *Leisure interests:* sailing, surfing, photography, gardening, history. *Address:* University of Twente, Department of Chemical Technology, P.O. Box 217, 7500 AE Enschede (Office); Sportlaan 60, 7581 BZ Losser, Netherlands (Home). *Telephone:* (53) 4892880 (Office); (53) 5382677 (Home). *Fax:* (53) 4894774 (Office); (53) 5384368 (Home).

VAN VUUREN, Jacobus Lukas Jansen, BCom; South African banker; b. 6 June 1931, De Aar; s. of Stephanus van Vuuren; m. Anna van der Merwe 1953; three d.; ed De Aar High School and UNISA; Chief Accountant, Volkskas Bank Ltd 1978, Asst Gen. Man. 1980, Gen. Man. 1981, Sr Gen. Man. 1984, now Man. Dir and CEO; Exec. Dir Volkskas Group Ltd; Chair. MLS Bank Ltd, Volkskas Motor Bank Ltd; Exec. Dir Amalgamated Banks of SA Ltd; Dir Bank of Transkei Ltd, United Bank Ltd, Priceforbes Federale Volkskas Holdings (Pty) Ltd. *Leisure interests:* gardening, golf.

VAN WACHEM, Lodewijk Christiaan; Netherlands business executive and mechanical engineer; b. 31 July 1931, Pangkalan Brandan, now Indonesia; m. Elisabeth G. Cristofoli 1958; two s. one d.; ed Technological Univ., Delft; joined Bataafsche Petroleum Maatschappij, The Hague 1953; Mech. Engineer, Cía Shell de Venezuela 1954–63; Chief Engineer, Shell-BP Petroleum Devt Co. of Nigeria 1963–66, Eng Man. 1966–67, Chair. and Man. Dir 1972–76; Head Tech. Admin. Brunei Shell Petroleum Co. Ltd 1967–69, Tech. Dir 1969–71; Head of Production Div. Shell Int. Petroleum Maatschappij, The Hague 1971–72, Co-ordinator Exploration and Production 1976–79; Man. Dir Royal Dutch Petroleum Co. until 1982, Pres. 1982–92; mem. Presidium of Bd of Dirs., Shell Petroleum N.V.; Man. Dir Shell Petroleum Co. Ltd 1977–92, Chair. Shell Oil Co. USA 1982–92, Dir Shell Canada Ltd 1982–92; Chair. Jt Cttee of Man. Dirs. of the Royal Dutch/Shell Group 1985–92, Chair. Supervisory Bd Royal Dutch Petroleum Co. 1992–2002; mem. Bd of Dirs. Crédit Suisse Holding 1992–96, Zürich Insurance Group (now Zürich Financial Services) 1993– (Vice-Chair. 2001–02, Chair. 2002–) Supervisory Bd Akzo-Nobel NV 1992–2002, Philips Electronics NV 1993– (Chair. Supervisory Bd 1999–), BMW (Munich) 1994–2002, Bayer AG 1997–2002; Dir (non-exec.) IBM Corpn 1992–, ATCO Ltd 1993–, AAB Brown Boveri Ltd 1996–99; Hon. KBE 1989, Kt Order of Netherlands Lion 1981, Commdr, Order of Oranje Nassau 1990, Public Service Star, Singapore 1998. *Address:* Zurich Financial Services, PO Box 16999, 2500 BZ The Hague, Netherlands (Office). *Telephone:* (70) 4184799 (Office). *E-mail:* loes.van.der.heijden@zurich.com (Office).

VAN WALSUM, Arnold Peter, LLB; Netherlands diplomatist; b. 1934, Rotterdam; m.; two c.; ed Univ. of Utrecht; First Sec. Perm. Mission to UN 1970–74, First Sec. New Delhi 1974–79, Counsellor, London 1975–79, Counsellor Perm. Mission to EC 1979–81, Head Western Hemisphere Dept, Ministry of Foreign Affairs 1981–85; Amb. to Thailand 1985–89, to Germany 1993–98; Dir.-Gen. Political Affairs, Ministry of Foreign Affairs 1989–93; Perm. Rep. to UN 1998–2001. *Address:* c/o Ministry of Foreign Affairs, Bezuidenhoutseweg 67, P.O. Box 20061, 2500 EB The Hague, Netherlands (Office).

VAN WIJNGAARDEN, Leendert, PhD; Netherlands professor of fluid mechanics; b. 16 March 1932, Delft; s. of Cornelis M. van Wijngaarden and Jeanne Severijn; m. Willy F. de Goede 1962; two s.; ed Gymnasium B, Delft and Technological Univ. of Delft; Netherlands Ship Model Basin, Wageningen 1962–66, latterly Head of Hydrodynamics Dept; Prof. of Fluid Mechanics, Twente Univ. 1966–97, Prof. Emer. 1997–; mem. of Bureau and Treasurer Int. Union of Theoretical and Applied Mechanics 1984–88, Pres. 1992–96, Vice-Pres. 1996–; mem. Royal Netherlands Acad. of Science. *Publications:* about 60 Publs in professional journals. *Leisure interests:* tennis, chess, literature, music. *Address:* University Twente, P.O. Box 217, 7500 AE Enschede (Office); Von Weberlaan 7, 7522 KB Enschede, Netherlands (Home). *Telephone:* (53) 893086 (Office); (53) 352078 (Home).

VAN WINDEN, Jacobus Cornelis Maria; Netherlands ecclesiastic and professor of Greek; b. 10 Oct. 1922, Schipluiden; ed in Franciscan convents and Leiden Univ.; mem. Franciscan Order (OFM) 1941; ordained priest 1948; Asst to J. H. Waszink, Prof. of Latin, Leiden 1954–56; teacher of Greek and Latin, Rotterdam 1956–66; Reader, Leiden Univ. 1966–80, Prof. of Greek of Late Antiquity 1980–87, Prof. Emer. 1987–; Ed.-in-Chief Vigiliae Christianae (review of Early Christian Life and Language) 1977–; mem. Royal Netherlands Acad. *Publications:* Calcidius on Matter: His Doctrine and Sources 1959, An Early Christian Philosopher: Justin Martyr's Dialogue with Trypho

(ch. 1-9) 1971, Tertullianus, De idolatria (critical text, trans. and commentary with J. H. Waszink) 1987, De ware wijsheid: Wegen van vroeg-christelijk denken 1992, Bonaventura, Itinerarium. De Weg die de geest naar God voert 1996, Arche. A Collection of Patristic Studies 1997, Bonaventura, Breviloquium, De theologie in kort bestek 2000. *Address:* Haarlemmerstraat 106, 2312 GD Leiden, Netherlands. *Telephone:* (71) 5120401.

VAN WYK, Andreas Herculas, BA, LLD; South African professor of law and university rector; b. 17 Sept. 1941, Pretoria; s. of Andries Hercules du Preez van Wyk and Hendrina Louise van Wyk (née Kruger); m. Magdalena Krüger 1967; two d.; ed Helpmekaar Boys' High School, Johannesburg, Univs. of Stellenbosch and Leiden; Lecturer, then Prof., then Dean, Faculty of Law, Univ. of Stellenbosch 1966–84, Dir Gen. Dept of Constitutional Devt 1984–87, Prof. Faculty of Law 1987–91, Vice-Rector Operations 1991–93, Rector and Vice-Chancellor 1993–2001; Chair. South African Univs. Vice-Chancellors Asscn (SAUVCA) 2001; mem. Bd Comm. of Old Mutual 1992–; guest USA/SA Leadership Exchange Programme 1978; Alexander von Humboldt Foundation Fellowship 1981; mem. SA Akad. vir wetenskap en kuns; Hon. LLD (Leuven); William of Orange Medal (Leiden) 1995. *Publications:* The Power to Dispose of the Assets of the Universal Matrimonial Community of Property 1976, Die Suid-Afrikaanse Kraktereg en Handelsreg (jtly.) 1992, Family, Property and Succession 1983 and numerous articles in academic journals; has drafted various pieces of legislation. *Address:* c/o Rector's Office, University of Stellenbosch, Private Bag XI, Matieland 7602, Cape Province, South Africa (Office). *Telephone:* (21) 8084654 (Office). *Fax:* (21) 8083714 (Office).

VAN ZYL SLABBERT, Dr. F. (see Slabbert, F. Van Zyl).

VANDENBROUCKE, Frank, DPhil; Belgian politician; b. 21 Oct. 1955, Louvain; ed Catholic Univ. of Louvain, Univs of Cambridge and Oxford, UK; Research Asst, Centrum voor Economische Studiën, Catholic Univ. of Louvain 1978–80; staff mem. SEVI (Research Dept of Socialist Party of Flemish Region) 1982–85; MP 1985–96; Leader Socialist Party 1989–94; Leader Parl. Group of Socialist Party 1995–96; Deputy Prime Minister and Minister of Foreign Affairs 1994–95; Minister of Social Affairs and Pensions July 1999–. *Address:* Ministry of Social Affairs and Pensions, rue de la Loi 62, 1040 Brussels, Belgium (Office). *Telephone:* (2) 238-28-11 (Office). *Fax:* (2) 230-38-95 (Office). *E-mail:* cabinetas@minsoc.fed.be (Office). *Website:* www .vandenbroucke.fgov.be (Office).

VANDEPUTTE, Robert M. A. C., DenD, D. EN SC., POL. ET SOC.; Belgian banker and university professor; b. 26 Feb. 1908, Antwerp; m. Marie-Louise Cauwe 1938; three c.; ed Univs. of Louvain, Nijmegen, Paris, Berlin and Berne; called to Antwerp Bar 1930–40; Prof. Univ. of Louvain 1936–78; Chef de Cabinet, Ministry of Econ. Affairs 1939–40; Sec.-Gen. Assoc. Belge des Banques 1940–42; Dir Banque Nat. de Belgique 1943–44, Regent 1954–71, Gov. 1971–75; Man. Dir Soc. Nat. de Crédit à l'Industrie 1944–48, Pres. 1948–71; mem. Caisse Gén. d'Epargne et de Retraite 1958–75; Dir and mem. Directing Cttee Société Nat. d'Investissement 1962–71; Pres. Inst. de Réescompte et de Garantie 1973–78; Minister of Finance April–Dec. 1981; Administrateur, Palais des Beaux-Arts de Belgique 1966–84; mem. Conseil Supérieur des Finances 1969–71; Pres. Administratieve en Economische Hogeschool 1959–91; Pres. Faculty Univ. Saint-Louis 1982–93; Commdr, Order of the Crown and Kt, Order of Léopold (Belgium); Officer, Order of Merit (Italian Repub.); Commdr, Order of St Gregory the Great (Holy See); Grand Officer, Order of Léopold II (Belgium) and other awards. *Publications:* Beginselen van Nijverheidsrecht, Handboek voor Verzekeringen en Verzekeringsrecht, Wat ik rondom mij zag, De Overeenkomst, Een Machteloos Minister, De harde strijd—Beknopte geschiedenis van het A.C.V., Economische geschiedenis van Belgie 1944–84, Het Aquilaans foutbegrip, Verbintenissen en Overeenkomsten in Kort bestek, Sociale geschiedenis van België 1944–85, Economie in België in Kort Bestek, De Schoolkwestie en de Guimardstraat; in French: Quelques aspects de l'activité de la Société Nationale de Crédit à l'industrie, Le statut de l'entreprise, Ministre sans pouvoir, Les institutions financières belges. *Address:* Rue au Bois 376, Bte. 21, 1150 Brussels, Belgium (Home).

VANDER ESPT, Georges J. H.; Belgian diplomatist; b. 16 Jan. 1931, Ostend; m. Marie-Jeanne Schaeverbeke; two s. two d.; ed Univ. of Ghent; public prosecutor 1957; joined diplomatic service 1961; served in the Netherlands 1963, UK 1969, Portugal 1975, Italy 1979; Dir Cabinet of Minister of Foreign Affairs 1980–88; Amb. to Germany 1988–96; many Belgian and foreign distinctions. *Leisure interests:* reading, swimming, modern painting.

VANDER ZALM, William N.; Canadian politician and business executive; b. 29 May 1934, Noordwykerhout, Netherlands; s. of Wilhelmus Nicholaas van der Zalm and Agatha C. Warmerdam; m. Lillian B. Mihalick 1956; two s. two d.; ed Phillip Sheffield High School, Abbotsford, BC, Canada; emigrated to Canada 1947, became Canadian citizen; purchased Art Knapp Nurseries Ltd, became Co. Pres. 1956; elected to Surrey Municipal Council as Alderman 1965, as Mayor 1969–; elected to Prov. Legis. for Social Credit Party, Minister of Human Resources 1975; Minister of Municipal Affairs and Minister responsible for Urban Transit Authority (now BC Transit) 1978; Minister of Educ. and Minister responsible for BC Transit 1982; est. Fantasy Garden World, major tourist attraction in Richmond 1983; Leader BC Social Credit Party July 1986–; Premier of BC 1986–91; Pres. Van's Int. Projects Inc. 1991–, Mitsch Nursery Inc., Oregon, USA 1994–; Leader Reform B.C. Party 1996–2001; Chair. Water on Net Corpn Inc. 1998–. *Publication:* Northwest's Gardener's Almanac. *Leisure interests:* fishing, swimming. *Address:* 3553

Arthur Drive, Ladner BC, V4K 3N2, Canada. *Telephone:* (604) 946-1774. *Fax:* (604) 946-1981. *E-mail:* vans@lilac-king.com (Office); billvanderzalm@dccnet .com (Home). *Website:* www.lilac-king.com (Office).

VANDERHAEGHE, Guy; Canadian writer and playwright; b. 5 April 1951; s. of Clarence Earl Vanderhaeghe and Alma Beth Allen. *Publications:* (novels) Man Descending (Gov. Gen.'s Literary Award for Fiction 1982, Geoffrey Faber Memorial Prize 1987) 1982, The Trouble With Heroes 1983, My Present Age 1984, Homesick (City of Toronto Book Award 1990) 1989, Things As They Are? 1992, The Englishman's Boy (Gov. Gen.'s Literary Award for Fiction 1996) 1996; (plays): I Had a Job I Liked, Once (Canadian Authors' Asscn Award for Drama 1993) 1991, Dancock's Dance 1995. *Address:* c/o McClelland and Stewart, 481 University Avenue, Toronto, Ont., M5G 2E9, Canada (Office).

VANDERPOORTEN, Herman, LLD; Belgian politician; b. 25 Aug. 1922; ed Atheneum Berchem-Antwerp and Rijksuniversiteit te Gent; Attorney 1945; Co. Councillor, Antwerp 1949–58; Town Councillor and Deputy Justice of the Peace, Lier 1959; mem. Chamber of Reps. 1961–65; Senator 1965; Minister of Interior 1966–68, of Justice 1973–77; Deputy Prime Minister and Minister of Justice and Institutional Reforms May–Oct. 1980; Pres. Liberal Flemish Asscn 1957–66; MEP 1979–80; Govt Councillor to the King 1981–. *Address:* Antwerpsesteenweg 2, Lier, Belgium.

VANDEVELDE, Luc; Belgian business executive; b. 1951; joined Kraft Gen. Foods Ltd 1971, later apptd. CEO Kraft Jacobs Suchard France and Italy –1995, Pres., COO 1995–99, Chair., CEO 1999–2000; participated in merger of Promodès and Carrefour Aug. 1999 (apptd. Exec. Vice-Chair. new group); Exec. Chair. Marks & Spencer PLC Feb. 2000–, CEO 2000–02; Exec. Chair. Change Capital Partners 2003–. *Address:* Marks and Spencer PLC, Michael House, Baker Street, London, W1U 8EP, England (Office). *Telephone:* (20) 7935-4422 (Office). *Fax:* (20) 7487-2679 (Office). *Website:* www .marksandspencer.com (Office).

VANDROSS, Luther; American singer, songwriter and producer; b. New York; s. of Mary Ida Vandross; started career by singing advertising jingles and with backing groups; featured on David Bowie's record Young Americans 1975; signed contract with Epic Records 1981; has produced albums by Aretha Franklin and Cheryl Lynn. *Albums include:* Never Too Much, Forever, for Always, for Love, Busy Body, Give Me The Reason, The Night I Fell In Love, Any Love, Never Let Me Go, The Best of Luther Vandross, The Power of Love, One Night With You, The Best of Love, Always & Forever – The Classics 1998, Greatest Hits 1999. *Address:* Epic Records, 550 Madison Avenue, Floor 27, New York, NY 10022, USA.

VANE, Sir John Robert, DSc, DPhil, FRS; British pharmacologist; b. 29 March 1927, Tardebigg, Worcs.; s. of Maurice Vane and Frances Florence Vane; m. Elizabeth Daphne Page 1948; two d.; ed King Edward VI High School, Birmingham and Univs. of Birmingham and Oxford; Therapeutic Research Council Fellow, Oxford 1946–48; research worker, Sheffield and Nuffield Inst. for Medical Research, Oxford 1948–51; Stothert Research Fellow, Royal Soc. 1951–53; Instructor in Pharmacology, Yale Univ. 1953–54, Asst Prof. 1954–55; Sr Lecturer in Pharmacology, Inst. of Basic Medical Sciences of Univ. of London at Royal Coll. of Surgeons of England 1955–61, Reader 1961–65, Prof. of Experimental Pharmacology 1966–73; Group Research and Devt Dir, The Wellcome Foundation Ltd 1973–85; Dir The William Harvey Research Inst., St Bartholomew's Hosp. Medical Coll. 1986–90, Dir-Gen. 1990–97, Hon. Pres. 1997–; Prof. of Pharmacology and Medicine New York Medical Coll. 1986–; mem. British Pharmacological Soc. (Foreign Sec. 1979–85), Physiological Soc., Soc. for Drug Research, Royal Acad. of Medicine of Belgium; Fellow, Inst. of Biology; Foreign mem. NAS, Polish Acad. of Sciences, AAAS, Royal Netherlands Acad. of Arts and Sciences, Nat. Acad. of Medicine, Buenos Aires; numerous memorial lectures in UK and abroad, especially USA; Hon. Fellow, Royal Coll. of Physicians, American Coll. of Physicians, Swedish Soc. of Medical Sciences, St Catherine's Coll., Oxford, American Physiological Soc., Council on Clinical Cardiology, American Heart Asscn, British Pharmacological Soc., Physiological Soc., Royal Coll. of Surgeons, Royal Nat. Acad. of Medicine, Spain; Hon. Fellow Inst. of Biology; Hon. doctorates from Copernicus Acad. of Medicine, Cracow, René Descartes Univ., Paris, Aberdeen Univ., London Univ., Mount Sinai Medical School, New York, New York Medical Coll. and Birmingham, Surrey, Camerino, Louvain and Buenos Aires Univs.; shared Nobel Prize for Physiology or Medicine for discoveries concerning prostaglandins and related substances 1982, Royal Medal, Royal Soc. 1989; numerous other awards, prizes and distinctions. *Publications:* numerous review articles and over 700 papers on pharmacology and related topics; Jt of five books. *Leisure interests:* photography, travel, underwater swimming. *Address:* The William Harvey Research Foundation, St Bartholomew's and The Royal London School of Medicine and Dentistry, Charterhouse Square, London, EC1M 6BQ, England. *Telephone:* (20) 7982-6119. *Fax:* (20) 7251-1685.

VANGELIS (pseudonym of Vangelis Papathanassiou); Greek composer and conductor; began performing own compositions at age of six; moved to Paris in late 1960s; composed and recorded symphonic poem Faire que ton rêve soit plus long que la nuit and album, Terra; composed La Cantique des Créatures for film-maker Frederic Rossif; returned to Greece, after period in London, 1989; formed band Formynx in Greece. *Film scores:* Chariots of Fire (Acad.

Award), Antarctica, Missing, Blade Runner, The Bounty, Wonders of Life, Wild and Beautiful, Francesco, 1492: Conquest of Paradise, Bitter Moon, Cavafy.

VANIN, Mikhail Valentinovich; Russian civil servant; b. 1960, Moscow Region; ed Moscow State Univ., Acad. of State Service; Insp., then Head of Div. against Contraband, Deputy Head Customs, Sheremetyevo Airport 1982–91; Chief Counsellor Div. of Contracts and Legal Problems, Ministry of Foreign Affairs 1991–92; Head Div. for Fight Against Contraband and Violation of Customs Law, State Customs Cttee 1992–98, Vice-Chair. 1998–, Chair. Customs Inspection April 1999–, Chair. State Customs Cttee May 1999–; Rep. Russian Customs Service, Kyrgyzstan 1998–99. *Address:* State Customs Committee, Nóvozavodskaya stz. 1 1/5, 121087 Moscow, Russia (Office). *Telephone:* (095) 449-70-50, 975-32-89 (Office). *Fax:* (095) 244-45-08 (Office).

VANNI, Carla, LLD; Italian journalist; b. 18 Feb. 1936, Leghorn; m. Vincenzo Nisivoccia; two c.; ed Univ. of Milan; joined Mondadori publrs., working on fashion desk of Grazia magazine 1959, Head fashion desk 1964, Jt Ed.-in-Chief 1974, Ed.-in-Chief 1978–, responsible for launch of Marie Claire magazine in Italy 1987, Publishing Dir Marie Claire and Cento Cose-Energy 1987–99, Donna Moderna 1995–; has created several new supplements of Grazia: Grazia Bricolage, Grazia Blu and Grazia Int., Grazia Accessori and Grazia Uomo and introduced coverage of social problems; also Ed.-in-Chief Grazia Casa; mem. juries of several nat. and int. literary awards and many beauty competitions; Montenapoleone d'Oro (Best Journalist) 1970, The Oner (Journalist of the Year) 1987, Gullace (for coverage of women's interest issues) 1995, Premio Letterario Castigloncello 2001. *Address:* c/o Grazia, Via Arnoldo Mondadori, 20090 Segrate, Milan, Italy (Office). *Telephone:* (02) 754212390 (Office). *Fax:* (02) 75422515 (Office). *E-mail:* vanni@mondadori.it (Office).

VANNI D'ARCHIRAFI, Raniero; Italian diplomatist; entered diplomatic service 1956; attached to office of Italy's Perm. Rep. to EC, Brussels 1961–66; with Ministry of Foreign Affairs 1966–73; First Counsellor, Madrid 1973; Minister Plenipotentiary 1980; Prin. Pvt. Sec. to Minister of Foreign Affairs 1980; Amb. to Spain 1984–87, 1995–99, to Germany 1987–90; Dir-Gen. for Econ. Affairs 1990, for Political Affairs 1991; mem. Comm. for Institutional Questions, The Internal Market, Financial Services, Enterprise Policy, Small and Medium-sized Enterprises, Trade Services, Crafts and Tourism, EC 1993–95. *Address:* c/o Ministry of Foreign Affairs, Piazzale della Farnesina 1, 00194 Rome, Italy (Office).

VANRIET, Jan; Belgian artist; b. 21 Feb. 1948, Antwerp; m. Simone Lenaerts 1971; two s. one d.; ed Royal Acad. of Fine Arts, Antwerp; Dir Antwerp Acad. of Fine Arts, Hoboken 1980–2000; works in several museums in Europe, USA and Asia; Special Prize, Art Festival, Seoul 1990, Prize, Van Acker Foundation 2001. *Exhibitions:* participated in São Paulo Biennale 1979, Venice Biennale 1984, Art at Olympics, Seoul 1988; Café Aurora, Cultureel Centrum, Knokke 2000, Hallen, Bruges 2001. *Achievements:* monumental works for KCB-Bank, Brussels, Metro, Brussels, Roularta, Bourla-Theatre Antwerp, UFSIA Univ. *Publications:* poetry: Staat van Beleg 1982, Geen Hond die Brood Lust 1984, Café Aurora 2000, De Reiziger is Blind 2001, Transport 2002. *Address:* Louizastraat 22, 2000 Antwerp 1, Belgium. *Telephone:* (3) 232-47-76; (3) 248-07-03. *Fax:* (3) 226-13-50.

VANSITTART, Peter, FRSL; British novelist and historian; b. 27 Aug. 1920, Bedford; s. of Edwin Vansittart and Mignon Vansittart; ed Haileybury Coll. and Worcester Coll. Oxford; school teacher 1940–60; writer 1942–; Hon. Fellow Worcester Coll. Oxford. *Publications:* The Overseer 1948, The Game and the Ground 1955, The Friends of God 1963, The Story Teller 1968, Dictators 1973, The Death of Robin Hood 1983, Paths from a White Horse 1985, London 1994, A Safe Conduct 1995, In the Fifties 1995, In Memory of England 1998, Survival Tactics 1998, Hermes in Paris 2000, John Paul Jones 2003. *Leisure interests:* walking and gardening. *Address:* Little Manor, Church Hill, Kersey, Ipswich, Suffolk, IP7 6DZ, England. *Telephone:* (1473) 823163.

VARADHAN, Srinivasa, MA, PhD, FRS, FAAS; American mathematician; b. 2 Jan. 1940; s. of S. V. Rangaiyengar and S. R. Janaki; m. Vasundara Narayanan; two s.; ed Madras Univ., Indian Statistical Inst., Courant Inst., New York Univ.; Visiting Member, Courant Inst., New York Univ. 1963–66, Asst Prof. 1966–68, Assoc. Prof. 1968–72, Dir 1980–84, 1992–94, Prof. of Math. 1972–; Assoc. Fellow, Third World Acad. of Sciences 1988; mem. NAS. *Publications:* Multi-dimensional Diffusion Processes 1979, On Diffusion Problems and Partial Differentiation Equations 1980; Large Deviations and Applications 1984. *Leisure interests:* squash, bridge, travel. *Address:* Courant Institute, New York University, 251 Mencer Street, New York, NY 10012, USA (Office). *Telephone:* (212) 998-3334 (Office). *Website:* (Office).

VARDA, Agnès; French film writer and director; b. 30 May 1928, Ixelles, Belgium; d. of Eugène Jean Varda and Christiane Pasquet; m. Jacques Demy 1962 (died 1990); one s. one d.; ed Sète, Hérault and Univ. de Paris à la Sorbonne and Ecole du Louvre; Official Photographer, Théâtre Nat. Populaire 1951–61; reporter and photographer, film-maker 1954–; Prix Méliès 1962 (Cleo de 5 à 7), Prix Louis Delluc 1965 (Le Bonheur), David Selznick Award 1965 (Le Bonheur), Bronze Lion, Venice Festival 1964 (Salut les Cubains), Silver Bear, Berlin Festival 1965 (Le Bonheur); 1st Prize, Oberhausen (Black Panthers), Popular Univs. jury (Lions Love) 1970, Grand Prix, Taormina,

Sicily 1977 (L'une chante, l'autre pas), Firenze 1981 (Mur Murs); César Award 1984 (Ulysse); Golden Lion, Best Film Venice Film Festival (Sans toit ni loi) 1985; Prix Méliès (Sans toit ni loi) 1985; LA Critics Best Foreign Film (Sans toit ni loi) 1985; César d'honneur 2001; Commdr des Arts et des Lettres, Chevalier Légion d'honneur. *Full-length films:* La pointe-courte 1954, Cleo de 5 à 7 1961, Le bonheur 1964, Les créatures 1965, Loin du Vietnam 1967, Lions Love 1969, Nausicaa 1970, Daguerreotypes 1975, L'une chante, l'autre pas 1976, Mur Murs 1980, Documenteur (An Emotion Picture) 1981, Sans toit ni loi (Vagabond) 1985, Jane B par Agnés V 1987, Kung Fu Master 1987, Jacquot de Nantes 1990, Les demoiselles ont eu 25 ans 1992, L'univers de Jacques Demy 1993, Les Cent et Une nuits 1994, Les Glaneurs et La Glaneuse 2000 (Acad. of European Cinema Award, Prix du Meilleur Film Française). *Short-length films:* O saisons, O châteaux 1957, L'opéra-Mouffe 1958, Du côté de la côte 1958, Salut les cubains 1963, Uncle Yanco 1967, Black Panthers 1968, Réponse de femmes 1975, Plaisir d'amour en Iran 1975, Ulysse 1982, Les dites Cariatides 1984, T'as de beaux escaliers . . . tu sais 1986. *Publication:* Varda par Agnès 1994. *Address:* c/o Ciné-Tamaris, 86–88 rue Daguerre, 75014 Paris, France. *Telephone:* 1-43-22-66-00. *Fax:* 1-43-21-75-00.

VARENNIKOV, Gen. Valentin Ivanovich; Russian army officer (retd) and politician; b. 15 Dec. 1923, Krasnodar; m.; two s.; ed Frunze Mil. Acad., Higher Mil. Acad. of Gen. Staff; mem. CPSU 1944–91; joined army 1941; active service 1941–45; Commdr of a corps 1967–69, of a unit 1969–71; First Deputy Supreme Commdr Soviet Forces in Germany 1971–73; Commdr Carpathian Mil. Dist 1973–82; First Deputy Chief of Gen. Staff 1982–91; First Deputy Head of HQ of USSR Armed Forces 1984–91; People's Deputy of the USSR 1989; Army Gen. 1978; arrested Aug. 1991 as an alleged accomplice in attempted coup d'état; charged with conspiracy; released 1992; on trial 1993–94, released 1994; cleared of high treason by Supreme Court after rejecting amnesty Aug. 1994; active in Communist Movt; mem. State Duma (Parl.) 1995–, Chair. Cttee on War Veterans 1996–; mem. CP of Russian Fed. 1994–. *Address:* State Duma, Okhotny Ryad 1, Moscow, Russia (Office). *Telephone:* (095) 292-93-60, 292-92-10 (Office).

VARFIS, Grigorios; Greek politician; b. 1927, Athens; ed Univs. of Athens and Paris; journalist in Paris, 1952–58; on staff of OECD 1953–62; Econ. Adviser to Perm. Greek Del. to the EEC, Brussels 1963–74; apptd. Gen. Dir, Co-ordination Ministry, with jurisdiction over Directorate of Relations with the European Communities 1974, resgnd Jan. 1977; contributed to econ. programme of Panhellenic Socialist Movt (PASOK) 1979–; Co-ordination Under-Sec. and Under-Sec. at Foreign Affairs Ministry, responsible for EEC Affairs 1981–83; mem. European Parl. 1984; mem. Comm. of the European Communities (responsible for Regional Policy and Relations with European Parl.) 1985–86, for Structural Funds and Consumer Protection 1986–89. *Address:* Spefsipou 35, 10676 Athens, Greece.

VARGA, Imre; Hungarian sculptor; b. 1 Nov. 1923, Budapest; s. of Mátyás Varga and Margit Csepeli; m. Ildikó Szabó 1944; two s.; ed Budapest Coll. of Visual Arts; Pres. FÉSZEK Artists Club; mem. American Acad. of Arts and Sciences, Académie Européenne des Arts et des Sciences, Paris; Munkácsy Prize 1969, Kossuth Prize 1973, Merited Artist 1975, Eminent Artist 1980, Herder Prize 1981; Order of the Flag 1983, Commdr, Ordre des Arts et des Lettres (France), Cavaliere dell'Ordine al Merito (Italy). *Works:* Prometheus 1965 and The Professor 1969 in Middelheim, Belgium, Madách Memorial 1968, Radnóti Memorial 1970, Partisans Memorial 1971, Lenin Memorial, Heroes Monument, Oslo 1974, plurifigural St Stephen composition, St Peter's Basilica, Vatican 1980, Bartók Memorial, Paris 1983, Béla Kun Memorial, Budapest 1986, Raoul Wallenberg Memorial 1987; perm. collection of work in Budapest; smaller sculptures: Erőlltetett menet (Forced March), A la Recherche, Baudelaire kedvese (Baudelaire's Sweetheart), Páholy (Theatre box), statue of St Stephen in Aachen Cathedral, Germany 1993, Bartók Memorial, Carrefour de l'Europe Square, Brussels 1995, Ferenc Rákóczi II, commemorative statue, Bad Kissingen, Germany 1992. *Address:* 1126 Budapest XII, Bartha-utca 1, Hungary. *Telephone:* (1) 560-278.

VARGA, Mihály; Hungarian economist and politician; b. 1965, Karcag; m.; three c.; ed Budapest Univ. of Econ. Sciences; econ. adviser Water Man. Inst. of E. Hungary, Szolnok 1989–90; mem. FIDESZ (Alliance of Young Democrats) 1988, Vice-Pres. 1994, Deputy Head of Parl. Faction 1995–98; elected MP 1990; mem. Parl. Cttee of State Budget and Finances 1990–98, of State Audit; Political State Sec. Ministry of Finance 1998–2001, Minister of Finance 2001–02; mem. Inter-Parl. Union (IUP) 1995, Chair. Parl. Advisory Cttee for Debtors and Banking Consolidation 1995–97; Visiting Prof. Szolnok Business School 1995–97; elder presbyter Reformed Church Community of Karcag and Kt of St John. *Address:* c/o Pénzügyminisztérium, József nádor tér 2/4, 1051 Budapest, Hungary (Office).

VARGAS LLOSA, Mario, PhD; Spanish/Peruvian writer; b. 28 March 1936, Arequipa, Peru; s. of Ernesto Vargas Maldonado and Dora Llosa de Vargas; m. 1st Julia Urquidi 1955 (divorced 1964); m. 2nd Patricia Llosa Urquidi 1965; two s. one d.; ed Colegio Nacional San Miguel, Piura, Peru, Leoncio Prado Military Acad., Lima, Universidad Nacional Mayor de San Marcos, Lima and Universidad Complutense de Madrid, Spain; journalist on local newspapers, Piura, Peru 1951, for magazines Turismo and Cultura Peruana and for Sunday supplement of El Comercio 1955; news ed. Radio Panamericana, Lima 1955; journalist Agence-France Presse 1959; broadcaster Latin American services of Radiodiffusion Télévision Française 1959; Lecturer in Latin American Literature, Queen Mary Coll., London Univ. 1967, Prof. King's Coll. 1969; trans. UNESCO 1967; Visiting Prof. Washington State Univ., USA 1968, Univ. de Puerto Rico 1969, Columbia Univ., USA 1975; Prof. Univ. of Cambridge 1977; writer-in-residence Woodrow Wilson Int. Center for Scholars, Smithsonian Inst., USA 1980; f. Movimiento Libertad political party and co-f. Frente Democrático (FREDEMO) coalition 1988; cand. for Pres. of Peru 1990; Prof. of Ibero-American Literature and Culture, Georgetown Univ., Washington, DC 2001–; Visiting Prof. Harvard Univ., USA 1992, Princeton Univ., USA 1993, Georgetown Univ., USA 1994, 1999; Pres. PEN Club Int. 1976–79; mem. Acad. Peruana de la Lengua 1977, Real Acad. Española 1994, Int. Acad. of Humanism 1996; Neil Gunn Int. Fellow, Scottish Arts Council 1986; Fellow Wissenschaftskolleg, Berlin 1991–92, Deutscher Akademischer Austauschdienst, Berlin 1997–98; Hon. Fellow Hebrew Univ., Israel 1976, Modern Language Asscn of America 1986, American Acad. and Inst. of Arts and Letters 1986; Hon. D.Hum.Litt (Conn. Coll., USA) 1991; Dr. hc of 16 univs.; numerous prizes including Revue Française Prize for El desafío 1957, Leopoldo Alas Prize for Los Jefes 1959, Biblioteca Breve Prize for La Ciudad y los Perros 1963, Crítica Española Prize 1966, Premio Nacional de Novela (Peru) 1967 for La Casa Verde 1967, Premio de la Crítica, Argentina 1981, ILLA Prize (Italy) for La tía Julia y el escribidor 1982, Ritz Paris Hemingway Prize 1985, Pablo Iglesias Literature Prize 1982 for La Guerra del findel mundo, etc., Príncipe de Asturias Prize, Spain 1986, Castiglione de Sicilia Prize, Italy 1990, Miguel de Cervantes Prize, Spain 1994, Jerusalem Prize, Israel 1995; Congressional Medal of Honour, Peru 1982, Golden Palm Award, INTAR Hispanic American Arts Center, New York 1992, Pluma de Oro Award, Spain 1997, Medal and Diploma of Honour, Univ. Católica de Santa María, Arequipa, Peru 1997, Nat. Book Critics Circle Award, New York 1998, Medal of the Univ. of Calif. 1999, PEN Nabakov Award 2002; Légion d'honneur, Commdr Ordre des Arts et Lettres. *Films:* (co-dir.) of film version of his novel Pantaleón y las visitadoras. *Publications include:* (plays) La huída del Inca 1952, La señorita de Tacna (The Lady of Tacna) 1981, Kathie y el hipopótamo (Kathie and the Hippopotamus) 1983, La Chunga 1986, El loco de los balcones (The Madman of the Balconies) 1993, Ojos bonitos, cuadros feos 1994; (short stories) El desafío (The Challenge) 1957, Los jefes 1959, Los cachorros (The Cubs) 1967; (novels) La cuidad y los perros (The Time of the Hero) 1963, La casa verde (The Green House) 1966, Conversación en La Catedral (Conversation in the Cathedral) 1969, Pantaleón y las visitadoras (Captain Pantoja and the Special Service) 1973, La tía Julia y el escribidor (Aunt Julia and the Scriptwriter) 1977, La guerra del fin del mundo (The War of The End of the World) 1981, Historia de Mayta (The Real Life of Alejandro Mayta) 1984, ¿Quién mató a Palomino Molero? (Who Killed Palomino Molero?) 1986, El hablador (The Storyteller) 1987, Elogio de la madrastra (In Praise of the Stepmother) 1988, Lituma en los Andes (Death in the Andes) 1993, Los cuadernos de Don Rigoberto (The Notebooks of Don Rigoberto) 1997, La Fiesta del Chivo (The Feast of the Goat) 2000; (anthologies) Contra viento y marea, vol. I (1962–72) 1986, vol. II (1972–83) 1986, vol. III (1983–90) 1990, Desafíos a la libertad 1994, Making Waves 1996, Cartas a un joven novelista (literary essay) 1997; (autobiog.) El pez en el agua (A Fish in the Water) 1993; (criticism) The Perpetual Orgy 1975. *Address:* Las Magnolias 295, 6° Piso, Barranco, Lima 4, Peru. *Telephone:* (1) 477-3868. *Fax:* (1) 477-3518.

VÁRKONYI, Ágnes R., PhD; Hungarian historian; b. 9 Feb. 1928, Salgótarján, Nógrád Co.; d. of József Várkonyi and Mária Bérczy; m. Kálmán Ruttkay; two d.; ed Eötvös Lóránd Univ. of Budapest; Asst Prof. Inst. for Historical Research of Hungarian Acad. of Sciences 1951–83; Prof., Head of Dept of Medieval and Early Modern Hungarian History in Eötvös Lóránd Univ. of Budapest 1983–98, Prof. Emer. 1998–; Corresp. Fellow of Royal Historical Soc.; several awards including Széchenyi Prize. *Publications:* 31 books including Selected Studies 2000; numerous articles. *Leisure interests:* gardening, travelling. *Address:* Eötvös Lóránd University of Budapest, Faculty of Arts, 1088 Budapest, Múzeum krt 6-8 (Office); 1021 Budapest, Széher út 24, Hungary (Home). *Telephone:* (1) 267-0966 (Office); (1) 200-9093 (Home). *Fax:* (1) 266-5699 (Office). *E-mail:* h7621var@ella.hu (Office).

VARKULEVICIUS, Rimas; Lithuanian administrator and engineer; b. 10 March 1956, Vilnius; m. Vitalija Zukelyte 1980; one s.; ed Kaunas Tech. Univ., Moscow Food Industry Tech. Univ., Georgetown Univ. (USA); Chief Engineer, Tauras State Brewery 1979–83; Adviser and Chief Engineer, Food Processing Co., Erdenet, Mongolia 1983–85; Exec. Officer, Food Industry Bd of Lithuania 1986; Head of Food Industry Devt Div., Ministry of Agric. 1989–91, Dir Dept of Int. Relations 1991–95, Dir Dept of Int. Integration 1995–97; Chief Consultant, Inst. for Nat. and Int. Meat and Food Industry IFW Heidelberg GmbH 1997–98; Dir.-Gen. Asscn of Lithuanian Chambers of Commerce, Industry and Crafts Sept. 1998–; has represented the Lithuanian Ministry of Agric. at numerous int. orgs. and confs., adviser to the Econ. Cttee of Seimas (Parl.). *Leisure interest:* yachting. *Address:* J. Tumo Vaižganto 9/1 Apt. 63a, 2001 Vilnius (Office); Mindaugo 16-10, 2029 Vilnius, Lithuania (Home). *Telephone:* (2) 335670 (Office); (2) 332849 (Home). *Fax:* (2) 235338 (Office). *E-mail:* lppra@post.omnitel.net (Office); varkl@post.5ci.lt (Home). *Website:* www.lithuaniachambers.lt (Office); www.5ci.lt/varkl/ (Home).

VARLEY, Baron (Life Peer), cr. 1990, of Chesterfield in the County of Derbyshire; **Eric Graham Varley;** British politician; b. 11 Aug. 1932, Poolsbrook, Derbyshire; s. of Frank Varley and Eva Varley; m. Marjorie Turner 1955; one s.; ed Secondary Modern and Tech. Schools and Ruskin Coll. Oxford; apprentice engineer's turner 1947–52; engineer's turner 1952–55; mining industry craftsman 1955–64; Nat. Union of Miners' Br. Sec. 1955–64;

mem. Area Exec. Cttee, Derbyshire 1956–64; MP for Chesterfield 1964–84; Asst Govt Whip 1967–68; Parl. Pvt. Sec. to Prime Minister 1968–69; Minister of State, Ministry of Tech. 1969–70; Chair. Trade Union Group of Labour MP's 1971–74; Sec. of State for Energy 1974–75, for Industry 1975–79; Opposition Spokesman for Employment 1979–83; Treas. Labour Party 1981–83; mem. Nat. Exec. Cttee Labour Party 1981–83; Exec. Deputy Chair. Coalite Group Jan.–Nov. 1984, Chair. and CEO 1984–89; N and E Midlands Regional Dir Lloyds Bank Group 1987–89, Midlands and N Wales Regional Dir 1989–91; mem. House of Lords European Communities Select Cttee 1992–96; Dir Ashgate Hospice Ltd 1987–96, Cathelco Ltd 1989–, Laxgate Ltd 1991–92. *Leisure interests:* gardening, reading, music, sport. *Address:* c/o House of Lords, London, SW1A 0PW, England.

VARLOOT, Denis; French engineer; b. 25 Oct. 1937, Lille; s. of Jean Varloot and Madeleine (née Boutron) Varloot; m. Marie J. Kennel 1963; two s.; ed Lycées in Paris, Ecole Polytechnique and Ecole Nat. Supérieure des Télécommunications; Centre Nat. d'Etudes des Télécommunications 1962–68; with Direction Gén. des Télécommunications, Service des Programmes et des Etudes Economiques 1968–73, deputized for head of service 1973–75; Dir of Telecommunications, Orléans 1975–76; Head of Telecommunications Personnel 1976–81; Dir of Scientific and Tech. Information, Ministry of Educ. 1981–82; Dir Libraries, Museums and Scientific and Tech. Information, Ministry of Educ. 1982–87; Special Adviser to Pres. of France-Télécom 1987, Adviser 1992–98; Chair. and CEO Télésystemes 1988–92; Chair. Admin. Bd Palais de la découverte 1996–; Chair. Musée des télécom de Pleumeur Bodou 1994; Chevalier des Arts et Lettres, Ordre des Palmes Académiques, Officier, Légion d'honneur, Ordre nat. du Mérite. *Leisure interest:* sailing. *Address:* Palais de la découverter, avenue Franklin D. Roosevelt, 75008 Paris (Office); 14 rue Campagne Première, 75014 Paris, France (Home). *Telephone:* 1-43-22-31-31 (Home).

VARMUS, Harold Eliot, MA, MD; American microbiologist and university professor; b. 18 Dec. 1939, Oceanside, NY; s. of Frank Varmus and Beatrice (née Barasch) Varmus; m. Constance Louise Casey 1969; two s.; ed Amherst Coll., Harvard Univ., Columbia Univ.; physician, Presbyterian Hosp., New York 1966–68; Clinical Assoc., NIH, Bethesda, Md 1968–70; lecturer, Dept of Microbiology, Univ. of Calif. at San Francisco 1970–72, Asst Prof. 1972–74, Assoc. Prof. 1974–79, Prof. 1979–83, American Cancer Soc. Research Prof. 1984–93; Dir Nat. Insts. of Health 1993–99; Pres. and CEO Memorial Sloan-Kettering Cancer Centre 2000–; Consultant, Chiron Corp., Emoryville, Calif.; Assoc. Ed. Cell Journal; mem. Editorial Bd Cancer Surveys; mem. American Soc. of Virology, American Soc. of Microbiology, AAAS; Calif. Acad. of Sciences Scientist of the Year 1982, Lasker Foundation Award 1982 (Co-recipient), Passano Foundation Award 1983, Armand Hammer Cancer Prize 1984, Gen. Motors Alfred Sloan Award, Shubitz Cancer Prize (NAS) 1984, Nobel Prize 1989. *Publications:* (Ed.) Molecular Biology of Tumor Viruses 1982, 1985, Readings in Tumor Virology 1983. *Address:* Memorial Sloan-Kettering Cancer Centre, 1275 York Avenue, New York, NY 10021, USA (Office).

VARNEY, David Robert, BSc, MBA; British telecommunications executive; b. 11 May 1946, London; s. of Robert Varney and Winifred Varney; m. Patricia Varney; one d. one s.; ed Univs of Surrey and Manchester; fmrly with Shell, Man. Dir AB Svenska Shell, Sweden, Dir Shell Int.; CEO BG Group (fmrly British Gas) 1996–2000; Chair. mmO2 2001–; Chair. Business in the Community 2001–. *Address:* mmO2, Wellington Street, Slough SL1 1YP (Office); Riverthatch, The Abbotsbrook, Bourne End, Bucks., SL8 5QU, England (Home). *Telephone:* (1753) 628339 (Office); (1628) 521077 (Home). *Fax:* (1753) 628340 (Office). *E-mail:* david.varney@o2.com (Office); david@varney.uk.com (Home). *Website:* www.o2.com (Office); www.varney.uk.com (Home).

VARSHAVSKY, Alexander J., PhD; American research scientist and professor of biology; b. 8 Nov. 1946, Moscow, USSR; s. of Jacob Varshavsky and Mary Zeitlin; m. Vera Bingham; one s. two d.; ed Dept of Chem., Moscow Univ., Inst. of Molecular Biology, Moscow; Research Fellow Inst. of Molecular Biology, Moscow 1973–76; Asst Prof. of Biology, Dept of Biology, MIT, Cambridge, Mass., 1977–80, Assoc. Prof. 1980–86, Prof. 1986–92; Howard and Gwen Laurie Smits Prof. of Cell Biology, Div. of Biology, Calif. Inst. of Tech., Pasadena, 1992–; Fellow American Acad. of Arts and Sciences, American Acad. of Microbiology; mem. NAS, American Philosophical Soc.; Merit Award, NIH 1998, Novartis-Drew Award 1998, Gairdner Int. Award, Canada 1999, Shubitz Prize in Cancer Research, Univ. of Chicago 2000, Hoppe-Seyler Award, Soc. for Biochem. and Molecular Biology, Germany 2000, Sloan Prize 2000, Merck Award, American Soc. for Biochem. and Molecular Biology 2001, Wolf Prize in Medicine, Israel 2001, Pasarow Award in Cancer Research 2001, Massry Prize 2001, Horwitz Prize 2001, Max Planck Research Prize, Germany 2001, Wilson Medal, American Soc. for Cell Biology 2002. *Achievements:* discoveries in fields of DNA replication, chronome structure, ubiquitin system and regulated protein degradation. *Publications:* more than 150 articles in professional journals in the fields of genetics and biochem.; 14 patents in these fields. *Address:* Division of Biology, 145-75, California Institute of Technology, 1200 East California Boulevard, Pasadena, CA 91125, USA (Office). *Telephone:* (626) 395-3785 (Office). *Fax:* (626) 440-9821 (Office). *E-mail:* avarsh@caltech.edu (Office). *Website:* www.caltech.edu/~biology/brochure/faculty/varshavs.html (Office).

VÁSÁRY, Tamás; Hungarian concert pianist and conductor; b. 11 Aug. 1933, Budapest; s. of Jozsef Vasary and Elizabeth (née Baltazàr) Vasary; m. Henriette Tunyogi 2000; ed Ferenc Liszt Acad. of Music, Budapest under Lajos Hernádi, József Gát and Zoltán Kodály; first solo performance at age eight; studied at Ferenc Liszt Acad. of Music until 1954; remained at Ferenc Liszt Acad. to teach theory; recitals in Leningrad (now St Petersburg), Moscow and Warsaw; settled in Switzerland 1958; London début 1961, New York 1962; début as conductor in Menton Festival of Music 1971; has since appeared in Europe, S. Africa, S. America, USA, Canada, India, Thailand, Hong Kong, Australia, Japan and Mexico; Jt Music Dir Northern Sinfonia, Newcastle 1979–; Musical Dir Bournemouth Sinfonietta 1988–96, Hungarian Radio Orchestra 1993–; performances at Salzburg, Edin. and Merano Music Festivals; records for Deutsche Grammophon; Liszt Prizes: Queen Elizabeth (Belgium), Marguerite Longue (Paris); Chopin Prizes: Int. Competition, Warsaw, Int. Competition, Brazil; Bach and Paderewski Medals (London), Kossuth Prize, Presidential Gold Medal 1998, Hungarian Heritage Prize. *Principal recordings:* three records of works of Liszt; eight of works of Chopin and various recordings of works of Rachmaninoff, Dohnányi, Debussy and Mozart; all symphonies and overtures of Beethoven, Schubert and Schumann 1997–98; further records for Hungaroton. *Leisure interest:* writing fiction. *Address:* Magyar Rádió Zenekari Iroda, 1800 Budapest, Bródy Sándor u. 5–7, Hungary (Office). *Telephone:* (1) 328-8326. *Fax:* (1) 328-8910.

VÁŠÁRYOVÁ, Magdaléna; Slovak diplomatist, actress and writer; b. 26 Aug. 1948, Banská Štiavnica; d. of Jozef Vášáry and Hermína Vášáry (née Schmidt); m. Milan Lasica; two d.; ed Comenius Univ., Bratislava; actress with Nová Scéna, Bratislava 1971–83, Slovak Nat. Theatre 1984–90; Amb. to Austria, to Poland 1990–; Silver Medal 2000; Artist of Merit 1988, Prize for Dramatic Performance in ... a pozdravuji vlaštovky, Italy 1972, Gold Crocodile for Za frountou 1974, Andrea 1993. *Films include:* Senzi mama 1964, Markéta Lazarová 1967, Sladký cas Kalimagdory 1968, Zbehovia a pútnici 1968, Královská polovacka 1969, Na komete 1970, Radúz a Mahulena 1970, Princ Bajaja 1971, ...a pozdravuji vlaštovky 1972, Rusalka 1977, Postřižiny 1980. *Plays include:* Ubohý moj Marat 1970, Woyzeck 1971, Three Sisters 1972, Hamlet 1074, Clavio 1976, Výnosné miesto 1984, Sleena Júlia 1986, Samovrah 1989. *Publications include:* Short Sheets to One City 1988, Diskrétní pruvodce - co možná nevíte o spolecesnkém chování. *Leisure interests:* literature, charity fundraising. *Address:* Embassy of Slovakia, ul. Litewska 6, 00-581 Warsaw, Poland (Office). *Telephone:* (22) 5258110 (Office). *Fax:* (22) 5258122 (Office). *E-mail:* slovakia@waw.pdi.net (Office). *Website:* www .ambasada-slovacji.pdi.pl (Office).

VASELLA, Daniel, PhD; Swiss pharmaceutical executive; b. 1953; ed Univ. of Berne; began career as hosp. physician; Head of Corp. Marketing, Sandoz Group 1993, Sr Vice-Pres. and Head of Worldwide Devt, Sandoz Pharma Ltd, COO, mem. Exec. Cttee, then CEO 1995–96; Chair. Bd of Dirs., CEO and Head of Exec. Cttee Novartis AG April 1999– (following merger of Sandoz and Ciba-Geigy 1996); Dir Crédit Suisse 2000–; mem. Supervisory Bd, Siemens AG, Munich, Int. Bd of Govs., Perez Center for Peace, Tel Aviv, Israel; mem. several industry asscns., including Int. Business Leaders Advisory Council for the Mayor of Shanghai; mem. Bd INSEAD (Inst. Européen d'Admin. des Affaires), IMD (Int. Inst. of Man. Devt); mem. Global Leaders for Tomorrow Group, World Econ. Forum, Davos, Switzerland. *Leisure interests:* skiing, motorcycles, collecting rare books. *Address:* Novartis AG, Lichtstrasse 35, 4056 Basel, Switzerland (Office). *Website:* www.novartis.com (Office).

VASILE, Radu, PhD; Romanian politician and academic; b. 10 Oct. 1942, Sibiu; m. Mariuca Vasile; two s. one d; ed Univ. of Bucharest; historian The Village Museum, Bucharest 1967–69; scientific researcher History Inst. Nicolae Iorga, Romanian Acad. 1969–72; Asst lecturer Acad. of Econ. Studies, Bucharest 1972; Asst Prof., Vice-Dean, Faculty of Trade, Acad. of Econ. Studies, Bucharest 1990, Prof. 1993; Vice-Pres. Romanian Senate 1996–98, Head Romanian Del. to Parl. Ass. of Council of Europe 1996–98; Vice-Pres. Parl. Ass. of Council of Europe 1997–98; Dir Dreptatea (daily newspaper) 1992–94; mem. Christian Democratic Nat. Peasant Party CDNPP 1990–99, Sec. Gen. 1996–98, Pres. Senate Parl. Group 1996–98; Prime Minister of Romania 1998–99; Senator 2000–. *Publications:* World Economy: Avenues and Stages of Modernization 1987, Currency and Economy 1994, Currency and Fiscal Policy 1995, From the Iron Century to the Second World War 1998. *Leisure interests:* poetry, satirical literature, chess, football.

VASILIU, Emanuel Kant, PhD; Romanian professor of linguistics; b. 7 Sept. 1929, Chişinău; s. of Nicolae Vasiliu and Gabriela Vasiliu; m. Maria-Laura Vasiliu 1952; ed Univ. of Bucharest; Assoc. Prof. Univ. of Bucharest 1968, Prof. 1970; Visiting Prof. Univ. of Chicago 1964–65, 1970–71, Univ. of Boston 1971; Dean Faculty of Letters, Univ. of Bucharest 1990–92; Dir "Al. Rosetti" Inst. of Phonetics and Dialectology 1990–; mem. Romanian Acad. 1992; mem. Soc. Linguistica Europaea, Soc. Européenne de Culture, Romanian Linguistic Soc. (SRL), Romanian Soc. of Romance Linguistics (SRLR), Int. Cttee of Linguists 1977–87; mem. editorial Bd Studii şi cercetări lingvistice (Linguistic Studies and Researches), Revue roumaine de linguistique, Fonetică şi dialectologie (Phonetics and Dialectology), Cahiers de linguistique théorique et appliquée; State Prize (Second Class) 1953, B. P. Hasden Prize, Romanian Acad. 1960. *Publications:* Fonologia limbii române (Romanian Phonology) 1965, Fonologia istorică a dialectelor dacoromâne (Historical Phonology of Daco-Romanian Dialects) 1968, Elemente de teorie semantică a limbilor naturale (Some Principles of a Semantic Theory of Natural Languages) 1970, Outline of a Semantic Theory of Kernel Sentences 1972, Preliminarii logice la semantica frazei (Logic Preliminaries to Compound Sentence Semantics)

1978, Scrierea limbii române în raport cu fonetica şi fonologia (Romanian Writing in relation to Phonetics and Phonology) 1979, Sens, adevăr analitic, cunoaştere (Meaning, Analytic Truth and Knowledge) 1984, Introducere în teoria textului (Introduction to Textual Theory) 1990, Introducere în teoria limbii (Introduction to the Theory of Language) 1992, Elemente de filosofie a limbajului (Elements of Language Philosophy) 1995, The Transformational Syntax of Romanian (with Sanda Golopentia-Eretescu) 1972, Limba Română în Secolele al XII-lea–al XV-lea. Fonetică—Fonologie—Gramatică (Romanian in the XII–XV Centuries: Phonetics—Phonology—Grammar) (with Liliana Ionescu-Ruxăndoiu) 1986; contrib. to several works on Romanian language. *Leisure interest:* music. *Address:* Institutul de Fonetică şi Dialectologie "Al. Rosetti", Str. 13 Septembrie 13, Sector 5, 76117 Bucharest (Office); Intrarea Lucaci 3, 74111 Bucharest, Romania (Home). *Telephone:* (1) 3206337, 6412757 (Home).

VASILYEV, Anatoli Aleksandrovich; Russian theatre director; b. 4 May 1942, Danilovka, Penza Region; m. Nadezhda Kalinina; one d.; ed Rostov State Univ., State Inst. of Dramatic Art, Moscow; Founder and Dir Theatre Co. School of Dramatic Art, Moscow 1987; staged all works by Pirandello; numerous tours in Europe 1985–2002; Nuova Realtà Europea Prize, Taormina, Italy 1990, Pirandello Prize, Agrigento, Italy 1992, Stanislavsky Fund Prize 1995, Stanislavsky Prize of Russian Fed. 1998; Chevalier Ordre des Arts et des Lettres 1989, Honoured Art Worker of Russia 1993; Golden Mask Prize of Russian Fed. for The Lamentation of Jeremiah (Martynov) 1997, Nat. State Prize of Russian Fed. for creation of School of Dramatic Art 1999, Triumph Prize 2001. *Productions include:* Vassa Zheleznova 1978, Grown-up Daughter of a Young Man (V. Slavkin) 1979, Cerceau (V. Slavkin) 1985, Six Characters in Search of an Author (Pirandello) 1987, Masquerade (Lermontov) at Comédie Française 1992, Uncle's Dream (Dostoyevsky), Budapest 1994, The Lamentation of Jeremiah (Martynov) 1996, The Queen of Spades (Tchaikovsky), German Nat. Theatre, Weimar 1996, Don Juan (Pushkin) 1998, Mozart and Salieri (Pushkin) 2000, Requiem (Martynov) 2000, Medee Materiaux (Heiner Muller) 2001. *Publications:* A propos de bal masqué de Mikhail Lermontov 1997, Szinházi Fuga 1998, Sept ou huit leçons de théâtre 1999, Ione e Menone di Platone 1999, A un unico lettore 2000. *Address:* School of Dramatic Art, Povarskaya 20, Moscow, Russia (Office). *Telephone:* (095) 291-50-39 (Office); (095) 951-37-71 (Home). *Fax:* (095) 291-86-42 (Office). *E-mail:* rezy@orc.ru (Office).

VASILYEV, Boris Lvovich; Russian writer, dramatist and essayist; b. 21 May 1924, Smolensk; m. Zorya Albertovna Vasilyeva; two adopted s.; ed Mil. Acad. of Armoured Troops; served in Red Army in World War II, seriously wounded; engineer with Acad. of Armoured Troops 1943–54; USSR People's Deputy 1989–91; mem. USSR Supreme Soviet 1991; USSR State Prize 1975; Konstantin Simonov Prize; Dovzhenko Gold Medal. *Publications include:* Dawns are Quiet Here 1969, Do Not Shoot the White Swans 1975, My Horses are Flying 1983, And Tomorrow was War (novel) 1984, The Burning Bush 1987, Regards from Baba Vera 1988, Absent from the Casualty List (novel) 1988, There was Evening, There was Morning 1989, The Short Castling 1989, The Carnival (novel) 1990, The House Built by the Old Man 1991, Kahunk and Prince Prophetic Oleg (novel) 1996, Two Bananas in one Peel (novel) 1996, A Gambler and Rabid Duellist 1998; many screenplays. *Leisure interests:* gardening, history, English literature. *Address:* Chasovaya Str. 58, Apt. 40, 125319 Moscow, Russia. *Telephone:* (095) 152-99-01.

VASILYEV, Sergey Aleksandrovich, DEcon; Russian politician; b. 8 June 1957, Leningrad; m.; two d.; ed Leningrad State Univ.; Head Research Lab. Leningrad Inst. of Finance and Econs 1985–90; took part in activities of Moscow-Leningrad group of young economists 1983–; mem. Leningrad Political Club Perestroika 1986; deputy Leningrad City Soviet 1990; Head Working Cttee for Econ. Reforms, Russian Govt 1991–94; Deputy Minister of Econs Russian Fed. 1994–97; First Deputy Head Office of Russian Govt 1997–98, Deputy Head 1998–2001; Chair. Bd Int. Investment Bank Moscow 1998–99; Chair. Cttee on Financial Markets; Pres. Int. Centre for Social and Econ. Research St Petersburg 1999–2001; Rep. of St. Petersburg Regional Govt to Council of Fed. 2001–; mem. Cttee on Budget and Taxes 2001–. *Publications:* Economics and Power 1998, Ten Years of Russian Econ. Reform 1999. *Leisure interest:* travel. *Address:* Council of Federation, Bolshaya Dmitrovka 26, 103426 Moscow (Office); Govt of Leningrad Region, Suvorovsky prosp. 67, 191311 St Petersburg, Russia (Office). *Telephone:* (095) 292-67-12 (Office); (812) 274-47-23 (Office). *Fax:* (095) 926-66-36 (Office); (812) 274-47-23 (Office). *E-mail:* SAVasilev@couoncil.gov.ru (Office); savasiliev@lenreg.ru (Office).

VASILYEV, Vladimir Viktorovich; Russian ballet dancer, ballet director and choreographer; b. 18 April 1940, Moscow; s. of Viktor Vasilyev and Tatiana Vasilyeva; m. Yekaterina Maksimova (q.v.); ed Bolshoi Theatre Ballet School, State Inst. of Theatrical Arts; with Bolshoi Theatre Ballet 1958–88; toured widely 1988–94; guest appearances with Ballet of Maurice Béjart 1977, 1978, Ballet de Marseille 1987, Teatro di S. Carlo di Napoli 1988–89, Arena di Verona 1988, Opera di Roma, Kirov Ballet, Paris 1988; Kremlin Ballet 1990; Man. and Artistic Dir Bolshoi Theatre 1995–2000; Choreographer and Pres. Galina Ulanova Foundation 2000–; Nijinsky Prize Paris Dance Acad. 1964, Grand Prix at Varna Int. Competition 1964, Maruis Petipa Prize Paris Dance Acad. 1972, People's Artist of USSR 1973, Order of Lenin 1976, USSR State Prize 1977, Order of People's Friendship 1981, UNESCO Pablo Picasso Medal 1990, 2000, Diagilev Prize 1990, State Prize of Russian Fed. 1991, Order of Merit (France) 1999, State Order of Merit of Russian Fed. 2000. *Principal roles:* The Prince (Nutcracker), Pan (Valpurgis Night), The Poet (Chopiniana), Danila (Stone Flower), Prince Charming (Cinderella), Batyr (Shurale), Andrei (A Page of Life), Basil (Don Quixote), Albert (Giselle), Frondoso (Laurencia), Nutcracker/Prince (Nutcracker), Medjnun (Leili and Medjnun), Ivanushka (The Little Humpbacked Horse), Spartacus (Spartacus), Petrushka (Petrushka) and Icarus (Icarus), Macbeth (Macbeth), Narcissus (Narcissus), Lukash (Song of the Woods), Paganini (Paganini), Romeo (Romeo and Juliet), Prince Desire (Sleeping Beauty), Ivan (Ivan the Terrible), Sergey (Angara), Baron (Gaite Parisienne), Zorba (Greek Zorba) Nijinsky (Nijinsky), Balda (Balda), Pyotr Leontyevich (Anyuta), Professor Unrat (The Blue Angel), Maestro (Lungo Viaggio Nella Notte de Natale) *Ballets choreographed:* Anyuta, Macbeth, Icarus, These Charming Sounds, Romeo and Juliet, Swan Lake, Cinderella, Paganini, Balda, new version of Giselle, Bolshoi Theatre and Don Quixote *Operas staged:* La Traviata, Bolshoi Theatre 1996, Mozart, Mozart..., Novaya Opera of Moscow 1999. *Films:* principal roles in Trapezium, House at the Road, Adam and Eva, Gospel for the Sly, Gigolo and Gigolette, Fouette, Katya and Volodya, Duet; appeared in Traviata (Zeffirelli). *Art exhibition:* Paintings of V. Vasilyev (Museum of Svyatoslav Richter Moscow). *Publication:* poems: The Chain of Days 2000. *Leisure interests:* painting, writing poetry. *Address:* Smolenskaya naberezhnaya 5/13 62, 121099 Moscow, Russia (Home). *Telephone:* (095) 244-02-27 (Home). *Fax:* (095) 244-02-27 (Home). *Website:* www.vasiliev.com (Home).

VASILYEVA, Larisa Nikolayevna; Russian poet and writer; b. 23 Nov. 1935, Kharkov, Ukraine; d. of Nikolai Alekseyevich Kucherenko and Yekaterina Vasilievna Kucherenko; m. Oleg Vasiliyev 1957; one s.; ed Moscow Univ.; started publishing 1957; first collection of verse 1966; Sec. of Moscow Br. of Russian Union of Writers; Pres. Fed. of Russian Women Writers 1989–, Int. Publishing League Atlantida 1992–; Moscow Komsomol Prize 1971. *Publications include:* (Stories, prose works) Albion and the Secret of Time 1978, Novel About My Father 1983, Cloud of Fire 1988, Selected Works (2 Vols) 1989, The Kremlin Wives 1992, The Kremlin Children 1996, The Wives of the Russian Crown; (Poetry) Fire-fly 1969, The Swan 1970, Blue Twilight 1970, Encounter 1974, A Rainbow of Snow 1974, Meadows 1975, Fire in the Window 1978, Russian Names 1980, Foliage 1980, Fireflower 1981, Selected Poetry 1981, Grove 1984, Mirror 1985, Moskovorechie 1985, Lantern 1985, Waiting For You In The Sky 1986, A Strange Virtue 1991. *Address:* Usiyevicha str. 8, Apt. 86, 125319 Moscow, Russia. *Telephone:* (095) 155-74-86.

VASILYEVA, Tatyana Grigoryevna; Russian actress; b. 28 Feb. 1947, Leningrad; two s. one d.; ed Studio-School of Moscow Art Theatre; with Moscow Satire Theatre –1984; actress Moscow Mayakovsky Theatre 1984–93; later freelance; People's Artist of Russia, Nika Prize 1992. *Theatre roles include:* Princess in Ordinary Miracle, Clown in Pippi Long Stocking, Luska in Run, Maria Antonovna in Inspector, Jenny in The Threepenny Opera. *Films include:* Hello, I'm Your Auntie, To See Paris and Die. *Address:* Goncharny proyezd 8/40, Apt. 62, 121248 Moscow, Russia.

VASNETSOV, Andrei Vladimirovich; Russian painter; b. 24 Feb. 1924, Moscow; ed Moscow Inst. of Applied Arts; Sec. USSR Union of Artists 1983–88, Chair. 1988–92; First Sec. of Bd RSFSR Union of Artists 1987–88; USSR People's Deputy 1989–91; mem. Presidium, Russian Acad. of Arts; Hon. Pres. Vasnetsovs' Foundation; People's Artist of Russia, USSR State Prize 1979, Pres.'s Prize, Russian Fed. 1998. *Exhibitions:* author of monumental panels for Soviet pavilions at exhbns. in Leipzig 1953, New York 1957, Brussels 1958, participated in decorating maj. architectural edifices in Moscow; one-man exhbns. 1962–; solo Exhbn Moscow 1987, Sofia 1988; Exhbn of the Vasnetsov's Generation, Moscow 1998. *Publications:* From Creative Experience, Conquerors of Space, Elkonin's Creative Method. *Address:* Russian Academy of Fine Arts, Prechistenka str. 21, 119034 Moscow (Office); Maly Patriarshiy per. 5, Apt. 43, 103001 Moscow, Russia (Home). *Telephone:* (095) 201-39-71. *Fax:* (095) 201-39-71 (Office).

VASSANJI, Moyez G., PhD; Canadian fiction writer; b. 30 May 1950, Nairobi, Kenya; s. of Gulamhussein V. Nanji and Daulatkhanu V. Nanji; m. Nurjehan Vassanji (née Aziz); two s.; ed Mass. Inst. of Tech. and Univ. of Pennsylvania; grew up in Dar es Salaam, Tanzania; Post-doctoral Fellow Atomic Energy of Canada Ltd 1978–80; Research Assoc. Univ. of Toronto 1980–89; first novel published 1989, full-time writer 1989–; Writer-in-Residence Int. Writing Program, Univ. of Ia 1989; Commonwealth (Regional) Prize 1990, Giller Prize for Best Novel (Canada) 1994, Harbour Front Literary Award 1994, Bressani Award 1994. *Publications:* The Gunny Sack (novel), No New Land (novel) 1991, Uhuru Street (short stories) 1992, The Book of Secrets (novel) 1994, Amriika (novel) 1999. *Address:* P.O. Box 6996, Station A, Toronto, Ont., M5W 1X7 (Office); 39 Woburn Avenue, Toronto, Ont., M5M 1K5, Canada.

VASSILIKOS, Vassilis; Greek author; b. 18 Nov. 1934, Kavala; m. Vasso Papantoniou 1985; one d.; ed Univ. of Salonika Law School and School of Radio and Television, New York; Dir-Gen. of Greek TV (public) 1981–85; presenter of weekly TV show on books; Amb. to UNESCO 1996–; Commdr, Ordre des Arts et des Lettres. *Publications:* (in English trans.): The Plant, The Well, The Angel 1963, Z– 1968, The Harpoon Gun 1972, Outside the Walls 1973, The Photographs 1974, The Monarch 1976, The Coroner's Assistant 1986, ... And

Dreams Are Dreams 1996; some 80 titles in Greek; translations into many languages (15 French titles). *Address:* 27 rue Galilée, 75116 Paris, France. *Telephone:* 1-45-68-30-64.

VASSILIOU, Georghios Vassos, DEcon; Cypriot politician and consulting company executive; b. 20 May 1931, Famagusta; s. of Vasos Vassiliou and Sophia Othonos (née Yiavopoulou) Vassiliou; m. Androulla Georgiadou 1966; one s. two d.; ed Univ. of Budapest; Market Researcher Reed Paper Group, London 1960–62; Founder, Chair Middle E Marketing Research Bureau (now MEMRB Int.) and Ledra Advertising 1962–; mem. Exec. Cttee Cyprus Chamber of Commerce 1970–86; mem. Bd Exec. Cttee Bank of Cyprus 1981–88; Pres. of Cyprus 1988–93; Leader, United Democrats Movt 1993–; mem. Parl. 1996–99; Chief Negotiator for the Accession of Cyprus to the EU 1998–2003; Visiting Prof., Cranfield School of Man.; Chair. World Inst. for Devt Econ. Research, UN Univ. 1995–2000; mem. InterAction Council 1998–, Trilateral Comm. 2000–; Fellow Royal Econ. Soc., Royal Statistical Soc.; mem. European Soc. of Opinion and Marketing Research, Market Research Soc., Industrial Market Research, Market Research Asscn; Grand Cross, Order of Merit, Cyprus, Grand Cross, Légion d'honneur, Grand Cross of the Saviour, Greece, Grand Cross of the Order of the Repub. of Italy, Grand Star, Austria, Grand Collar, Order of Infante D. Henrique, Portugal, Grand Collar of the Nile, Egypt, Standard (Flag) Order, Hungary and other distinctions, awards and decorations. *Publications:* Marketing in the Middle East 1980, The Middle East Markets 1977, Towards the Solution of the Cyprus Problem 1992, Overcoming Indifference 1994, Tourism and Sustainable Development 1995, Towards a Larger, Yet More Effective European Union 1999; numerous articles in various int. publs. *Leisure interests:* listening to music, reading, swimming, body-exercise. *Address:* PO Box 22098, 1583 Nicosia (Office); 9A Orpheos Street, 1070, Cyprus (Home). *Telephone:* (2) 2336142 (Office); (2) 2374888 (Home). *Fax:* (2) 2336301 (Office). *E-mail:* gvassiliou@memrb.com.cy (Office).

VASSILYEV, Alexey Mikhailovich, DR.HIST.; Russian scientist; b. 26 April 1939, Leningrad; m.; two d.; ed Moscow State Inst. of Int. Relations; with Pravda, political columnist, corresp. in Vietnam, Turkey, Egypt 1962–83; Deputy Dir Inst. of Africa (now of African and Arab Studies), USSR (now Russian) Acad. of Sciences 1983–92, Dir 1992–; Ed.-in-Chief Asia and Africa Today (magazine) 1998–; Pres. Asscn of Cultural and Business Co-operation with African Cos.; Pres. Centre of Regional and Civilisation Studies; mem. Council on Foreign Policy, Ministry of Foreign Affairs, Russian Fed.; Visiting Prof. univs. in USA, UK, France, Egypt, Saudi Arabia etc.; Medals for Labour Merit, for Labour Heroism. *Publications:* more than 20 monographs, numerous scientific works and over 100 articles published in Russia and abroad on Middle East, Central Asia, Africa, Arab-Israeli conflict, Islam including History of Saudi Arabia, Russian Policy in the Middle East, Egypt and the Egyptians, Post-Soviet Central Asia. *Leisure interest:* Russian literature, skiing. *Address:* Institute of Africa, Russian Academy of Sciences, Spiridonovka str. 30/1, 103001 Moscow (Office); 11/13-103 Pravda str., 125040 Moscow, Russia (Home). *Telephone:* (095) 290-63-85 (Office); (095) 214-47-28 (Home). *Fax:* (095) 202-07-86 (Office). *E-mail:* dir@inafr.ru (Office). *Website:* www.inafr.ru (Office).

VASTAGH, Pál, PhD; Hungarian politician and jurist; b. 23 Sept. 1946; m. Erzsébet Fenyvesi; one s. two d.; ed József Attila Univ. of Arts and Sciences, Szeged; Asst Lecturer, later Lecturer, then Sr Lecturer Dept of Theory of State and Law, József Attila Univ. of Arts and Sciences 1988–89, Dean 1989; mem. of Presidium of Hungarian Socialist Party (HSP) 1989; mem. Parl. 1990–; mem. Parl.'s Cttee on Constitutional Affairs, Chair 2002–; mem. Codification and Justice Cttee on European Integration Affairs; Minister of Justice 1994–98; Prof. Budapest School of Man. 1999–; Deputy Leader of Socialist faction 1998–2002; mem. Convention on the Future of Europe 2002–. *Publications:* articles in nat. newspapers and professional periodicals. *Leisure interests:* reading, hiking, travelling, soccer. *Address:* Képviselői Irodaház, 1358 Budapest, Széchenyi Rkp. 19, Hungary (Office). *Telephone:* (1) 441-4484 (Office). *Fax:* (1) 441-4823 (Office). *E-mail:* pal.vastagh@parlament.hu (Office). *Website:* www.parlament.hu (Office).

VATOLIN, Nikolay Anatolyevich; Russian metallurgist; b. 13 Nov. 1926, Yekaterinburg; m.; one s.; ed Urals Polytech. Inst.; scientific researcher, scientific sec., Head of Lab., Dir USSR (now Russian) Acad. of Sciences Inst. of Metallurgy (Urals Branch) 1950–98, Adviser Russian Acad. of Sciences 1998–; mem. CPSU 1952–91; Prof. at Urals Mining-Geological Acad. 1973–; Corresp. mem. of USSR (now Russian) Acad. of Sciences 1970–81, mem. 1981; USSR State Prize 1982, 1991, Kurnakow Gold Medal, Russian Acad. of Sciences 1995, Govt Prize, Russian Fed. 1997, Demidov's Prize 1997, Russian Fed. State Prize 2000. *Publications:* (co-author): Physico-chemical Foundations of Steel Hot Leading 1977, Oxidation of Vanadium Slags 1978, Interparticle Interaction in Molten Metals 1979, Diffraction Studies of High Temperature Melts 1980, Computerization of Thermodynamic Calculations of Metallurgical Processes 1982, Electrical Properties of Oxide Melts 1984, Hydrometallurgy of Ferropowders 1984, Computer Simulation of Amorphous Metals 1985, Vanadium Slags 1988, Thermodynamic Modelling in High Temperature Inorganic Systems 1994, Temperature Dependences of Gibbs Reduced Energy of Some Inorganic Substances 1997, Fire Processing of Integrated Ores 1997, Some Regularities of Changes of Thermochemical Properties of Inorganic Compounds and Computational Methods for these Properties 2001. *Address:* Institute of Metallurgy of Ural Div. of Russian

Academy of Sciences, 101 Amundsen Street, 620016 Yekaterinburg (Office); 17 Polyanka Street, 620016 Yekaterinburg, Russia (Home). *Telephone:* (3432) 67-94-21 (Office); (3432) 67-89-01 (Home). *Fax:* (3432) 67-91-86 (Office). *E-mail:* vatolin@imet.mplik.ru (Home).

VAUGHAN, David Arthur John, CBE, QC, FRSA; British lawyer; b. 24 Aug. 1938; s. of the late Capt. F.H.M. Vaughan and J.M. Vaughan; m. 1st 1967 (divorced); m. 2nd Leslie A. F. Irwin 1985; one s. one d.; ed Eton Coll. and Trinity Coll. Cambridge; called to Bar, Inner Temple 1962, Bencher 1988; mem. Bar Council 1968–72, 1984–86, Bar Cttee 1987–88; mem. Int. Relations Cttee of Bar Council 1968–86, Bar/Law Soc. Working Party on EEC (now EU) Competition Law 1977– (Chair. 1978–88), UK Del. to Consultative Cttee of Bars and Law Socs of the EC 1978–81 and other cttees etc.; Chair. EC Section, Union Int. des Advocats 1987–91; a Recorder 1994–2001; Chair. Editorial Bd European Law Reports 1997–; a Deputy High Court Judge 1997–; Judge of the Courts of Appeal of Jersey and Guernsey 2000–; Visiting Prof. of Law Durham Univ. 1989–; mem. Advisory Bd, Centre for European Legal Studies, Cambridge Univ. 1991–; mem. Council of Man., British Inst. of Int. and Comparative Law 1992–; mem. Editorial Advisory Bd European Business Law Review 1998–; Fellow Soc. for Advanced Legal Studies 1998; Bronze Medal, Bar of Bordeaux 1985. *Publications:* co-ordinating ed. vols on EC Law, Halsbury's Laws of England 1986; Vaughan on the Law of the European Communities (ed.) 1986–97; consultant ed. European Court Practice 1993, Current EC Legal Development series. *Leisure interests:* fishing, tennis. *Address:* Brick Court Chambers, 7–8 Essex Street, London, WC2R 3LD, England (Office). *Telephone:* (20) 7379-3550. *Fax:* (20) 7379-3558.

VAUTRIN, Jean (Jean Herman); French novelist and film director; b. 17 May 1933, Pagny sur-Moselle, Meurthe-et-Moselle; s. of Raymond Herman and Maria Schneider; m. 2nd Anne Doat; two s. one d. (and one s. from first m.); ed Lycée Jacques-Amyot, Auxerre, Institut des hautes études cinématographiques; Lecturer in French Literature, Univ. of Bombay 1955; Asst to Roberto Rossellini 1955–57, to Jacques Rivette 1958, to Vincente Minelli 1958; Asst at ORTF, Dir, Armed Forces film div. 1959–61; Asst to Jean Cayrol, then made advertising films and shorts 1958–63, full-length films 1963–; Dir Julliard 1990–; began writing career 1973; films (made under name Jean Herman) include: Voyage en Boscavie 1958 (Prix Emile Cohl), Actua-Tilt 1960 (Grand Prix, Festival Int. de Tours, Critics' Prize, Oberhausen), La Quille 1961 (Jury's Special Prize, Venice Festival), Le Dimanche de la Vie 1965 (Marilyn Monroe Prize), Garde à vue 1981 (Prix de l'Académie française); several films for TV; Ed. Atelier Julliard series; Conseiller Régional d'Aquitaine; Chevalier Légion d'honneur, Officier du Mérite, Commdr des Arts et des Lettres; Prix Goncourt 1989. *Films:* Le Dimanche de la vie d'après queneau 1965, Adieu l'abri (with Alain Delon and Charles Bronson) 1968; Garde à vous (scriptwriter) 1981. *Publications:* (under name of Jean Vautrin) include: A bulletins rouges 1973, Billy-Ze-Kick 1974, Bloody Mary 1979 (Prix Mystère de la Critique), Canicule 1982, Patchwork 1984 (Prix des Deux-Magots), Baby Boom 1985 (Prix Goncourt de la Nouvelle), La Vie Ripolin 1986 (Grand Prix du Roman de la Société des gens de lettres), Un grand pas vers le Bon Dieu 1989 (Prix Goncourt), 18 Tentatives pour devenir un saint 1989; (with Dan Franck): La Dame de Berlin 1988, Le Temps des cerises 1991, Romans Noirs 1991, Courage, chacun 1992, Les Noces de Guernica (jtly.) 1994, Symphonie-Grabuge 1994 (Prix Populiste); Mademoiselle Chat (jtly.) 1996, Jamais comme avant (co-author) 1996, Le Roi des ordures 1997, Un Monsieur bien mis 1997, Histoires déglinguées 1998, Le cri du peuple 1999, Boro s'en va-t-en guerre (jtly.) 2000, L'Homme qui assassinait sa vie 2001, Le Journal de Louise B. 2002. *Leisure interest:* drawing cartoons, painting. *Address:* 170 Rte de Toulouse, 33130 Bègles, France. *Telephone:* (5) 56-85-33-87. *Fax:* (5) 56-85-15-23.

VAUZELLE, Michel Marie; French politician and lawyer; b. 15 Aug. 1944, Montelimar, Drome; s. of Fernand Vauzelle and Marine Faure; m. Sylvie Fauvet 1980; two s. one d.; ed Collège St-Joseph, Lyon, Faculty of Law, Paris, Inst. of Political Studies, Paris; barrister 1968; Chargé de mission Prime Minister's Office 1969–72; mem. Finance Section Econ. and Social Council 1972–73; town councillor, Arles 1983–95; Nat. Del. of Socialist Party Council of Civil Liberties 1978–81; Spokesman for the President of the Republic 1981–86; Préfet hors cadre 1985; Socialist Deputy for Bouches-du-Rhône 1986–92, 1997–; Pres. Comm. for Foreign Affairs Nat. Assembly 1989–92; Minister of Justice and Keeper of the Seals 1992–93; Pres. Nat. School of Photography 1982–86; Vice-Pres. Gen. Bouches du Rhône 1992–97; Mayor of Arles 1995–98; Pres. Regional Council Provence-Alpes-Côte d'Azur 1998–. *Publication:* Éloge de Daniel Manin, avocat venitien 1978. *Leisure interest:* riding. *Address:* Hôtel de la Région, 27 place Jules Guesde, 13481 Marseille cedex 20, France (Office).

VAVAKIN, Leonid Vassilyevich; Russian architect; b. 6 April 1932, Moscow; ed Moscow State Inst. of Architecture; Chief Architect, Chair. Moscow Cttee on Architecture and City Construction; Prof. Moscow Inst. of Architecture; corresp. mem. Russian Acad. of Fine Arts; mem. Int. Acad. of Architecture; Academician-Sec. Russian Acad. of Architecture; USSR Council of Ministers Prize; RSFSR Merited Architect. *Address:* Russian Academy of Architecture, Dmitrova str. 24, 103874 Moscow, Russia (Office). *Telephone:* (095) 229-65-26 (Office).

VAVILOV, Andrei Petrovich; Russian business executive and politician; b. 10 Jan. 1961, Perm; m.; ed Moscow Inst. of Man.; Eng programmer Computation Centre USSR Ministry of Public Health 1982–85; Jr researcher Cen. Inst. of Econs and Math., USSR Acad. of Sciences 1985–88, Head of Lab. Inst. of Marketing Problems 1991–92; Sr researcher Inst. of Econ. Prognosis of Tech. Progress 1988–91; Head Dept of Macroecon. Policy, Ministry of Econs and Finance 1992; First Deputy Minister of Finance 1992–97; Pres. Int. Financial Initiative Bank 1997–; mem. Bd of Dirs. RAO Gazprom (Counsellor to Chair. 1998–), Norilsk Nikel; Dir., Inst. of Financial Studies 1998–; mem. Observation Council Savings Bank 1997; Chair. Bd. of Dirs. N. Oil Co. 2000–. *Publications:* over 20 papers. *Leisure interests:* hunting, skiing, tennis. *Address:* International Financial Initiative, B. Gruzinskaya str. 12, korp. 2, 123242 Moscow, Russia (Office). *Telephone:* (095) 725-58-33 (Office).

VÁVRA, Otakar; Czech scriptwriter and film director (retd); b. 28 Feb. 1911, Hradec Králové; s. of Alois Vávra and Marie Vávrová; m. 1st Helena Vávrová 1946 (deceased); m. 2nd Jitka Němcová 1997; one s.; ed Czech Tech. Coll.; scriptwriter, Dir Moldavia-film, Elektafilm, Lucernafilm cos 1931–45; scriptwriter, Dir Barrandov Film Studios, Prague 1945–89; art team man. Barrandov Film Studios, Prague 1947–51; teacher, Film Faculty, Acad. of Music and Dramatic Arts, Prague 1949–51, Head, Film and Television Direction Dept 1956–70, Prof. 1963–; mem. collective man. Bd, Barrandov Film Studios, Prague 1951–54; art team man. Barrandov Film Studios, Prague 1954–56; Chair. feature film section, Union of Czechoslovak Film and Television Artists 1965, mem. Cen. Cttee 1966–70; Pro-Rector Acad. of Music and Dramatic Arts, Prague 1967–70; awards from San Sebastián, Acapulco, Moscow, Phnom-Penh, Mar del Plata (Argentina) Film Festivals; Finale Award, Plzen (Special Award for work over previous ten years) 1990, Karlovy Vary Int. Film Festival Prize for contrib. to world film 2001; Czechoslovak Film Prize 1937, 1938, Luce Award for The Guild of Maids of Kutná Hora 1938, Nat. Prize 1941, Czech Land Prize 1948, State Prize 1949, Artist of Merit Award (Edin.) 1955, Order of Labour 1961, State Prize of Klement Gottwald 1968, Nat. Artist 1968, Prize of Antonín Zápotocký 1973, State Prize of Klement Gottwald 1977, Order of Repub. 1981 and various other awards. *Author and co-author of films:* 89 screenplays including The Eleventh Commandment, Maryša 1935, The Lane in Paradise, A Camel through a Needle's Eye 1936, Guard No. 47, Morality Above All 1937, The Case of Jan Masaryk 1998, Dammed Beauty 1998. *Films directed:* 46 films including Gaudeamus igitur, Virginity 1937, scriptwriter and dir of short films Light Penetrates Darkness 1931, We Live in Prague 1934, November 1935 Guild of the Maids of Kutná Hora 1938, Humoresque 1939, The House of Magic 1939, The Enchanted Masqued Lover, The Girl in Blue, The Mistress in Disguise, Dr Hegl's Patient, The May Tale 1940, The Turbine 1941, Come Right Back 1942, Happy Journey 1942, Rozina the Bastard 1945, The Mischievous Bachelor 1946, Presentiment 1947, Krakatit 1948, The Silent Barricade 1949, Deployment 1952, Jan Hus 1955, A Hussite Warrior 1956, Against All 1957, Citizen Brych 1958, The First Rescue Party 1959, The Curfew 1960, August Sunday 1960, The Night Guest 1961, The Burning Heart 1962, The Golden Queening 1965, Romance for a Bugle 1966, 13 Chamber 1968, Witch-Hunt 1969, The Days of Betrayal 1973, Sokolovo 1974, The Liberation of Prague 1977, A Story of Love and Honour 1977, The Dark Sun 1980, Jan Amos Commenius 1982, Comedian 1983, Oldřich a Božena 1984, Veronika 1985, Temptation Catherine, Chief Witness 1985–87, Till 1987, Europe was Waltzing 1989, Genus 1996. *Publications:* Contemplations of the Film Director 1982, Three Times in Front of the Camera (with M. V. Kratochvil) 1986, Strange Life of the Film Director 1996. *Leisure interests:* literature, cinema, theatre, golf. *Address:* Academy of Music and Dramatic Arts, Faculty of Film and TV, Smetanovo nábřeží 2, 11000 Prague 1, Czech Republic (Office). *Telephone:* (2) 24229468 (Office). *Fax:* (2) 24230285 (Office).

VÄYRYNEN, Paavo Matti, D.POL.SC.; Finnish politician; b. 2 Sept. 1946, Keminmaa; s. of Juho Eemeli Väyrynen and Anna Liisa (née Kaijankoski) Väyrynen; m. Vuokko Kaarina Tervonen 1968; one s. two d.; MP 1970–; Political Sec. to Prime Minister 1970–71; Vice-Chair. Centre Party 1972–80, Chair. 1980; mem. Nordic Council 1972–75; Minister of Educ. 1975–76, of Labour 1976–77; Minister for Foreign Affairs 1977–82, 1991–93; Chair. Supervisory Bd Rautaruukki Oy 1994–. *Publications:* Köyhän asialla (Speaking for the Poor) 1971, On muutoksen aika (This is a Time of Change) 1974, Kansallisia kysymyksiä 1981. *Address:* Keskustapuolue (KP), Pursimiehenkatu 15, 00150 Helsinki, Finland.

VAZQUEZ ROSAS, Tabaré Ramón, PhD; Uruguayan politician and doctor; b. Jan. 1940; m. Maria Auxiliadora Delgado; four c.; ed Universidad de la Republica; Prof. Faculty of Medicine, Universidad de la Republica 1987–; Pres. of Encuentro Progresista—Frente Amplio (EP—FA); Pres. Cand. March 2000. *Address:* Encuentro Progresista—Frente Amplio, Colonia 1367, 2° Montevideo, Uruguay (Office). *Telephone:* (2) 9022176 (Office).

VEASEY, Josephine, CBE; British (mezzo-soprano) opera singer (retd) and vocal consultant; b. 10 July 1930, London; m. Ande Anderson 1951 (divorced 1969); one s. one d.; mem. chorus Covent Garden Opera Company 1948–50, returned as soloist 1955; prin. mezzo-soprano, Royal Opera House, Covent Garden; has sung every major mezzo-soprano role in repertory; many foreign engagements have included Salzburg Festival, La Scala, Milan, Metropolitan Opera House, New York and Paris Opera; Prof. Royal Acad. of Music 1982–83; Vocal consultant, English Nat. Opera 1985–94; Hon. RAM. *Recordings:* has made recordings with Karajan, Solti, Bernstein and Colin Davis. *Address:* 5 Meadow View, Whitchurch, Hants., RG28 7BL, England. *Telephone:* (1256) 896813.

VEBER, Francis Paul; French film screenplay writer and director; b. 28 July 1937, Neuilly; s. of Pierre Gilles Veber and Catherine Veber (née Agadjaniantz); m. Françoise Marie Ehrenpreis 1964; two s.; ed Paris Univ. of Science, Paris Medical School; began career as journalist, also wrote short stories, stand-up comedy material and theatre plays; Pres. EFVE Films 1976, Escape Film Production Co. 1988; fmr mem. Bd Dirs EuroDisney; Chevalier, Légion d'honneur, Commdr des Arts et des Lettres, Officier de l'Ordre Nat. du Mérite. *Screenplays:* wrote first film screenplay 1969. *Films directed:* first film, Le Jouet, 1976; first American film, Three Fugitives 1989 Le Dîner de Cons 1997 (based on his stage play), Le Placard 2001. *Plays directed include:* Le Dîner de Cons 1993. *Publications:* Le Grand Blond avec une Chaussure Noire 1972, L'Emmerdeur 1973, Le Magnifique 1973, Le Jouet 1976, La Cage aux Folles (adaptation) 1978, La Chèvre 1981, Les Compères 1983, Les Fugitifs 1986, Le Jaguar 1996, Le Dîner de Cons 1998, Le Placard 2001. *Leisure interests:* tennis, swimming. *Address:* c/o Artmédia, 20 avenue Rapp, 75007 Paris, France (Office); Creative Artists Agency, 9830 Wilshire Boulevard, Beverly Hills, CA 90210, USA. *Telephone:* (310) 288-4545.

VECSEI, Eva Hollo, BArch, FRAIC; Canadian/Hungarian architect; b. 21 Aug. 1930, Vienna, Austria; m. André Vecsei 1952; one s. one d.; ed School of Architecture, Univ. of Tech. Sciences, Budapest; Assoc. Prof., School of Architecture, Univ. of Budapest, designer of various public bldgs. and winner of housing competition, Budapest 1952–56; Assoc., ARCOP Architects, Montréal, Canada 1958–71; Assoc. of D. Dimakopoulos, architect, Montréal 1971–73; in pvt. practice, Eva Vecsei, architect 1973–84, in partnership with husband, Vecsei Architectes 1984– (now Prin.); mem. Nat. Capital Comm. Advisory Cttee on Design 1982–87; juror for several architectural competitions; lecture tour in China 1984; adviser to Master of Architecture programme, McGill Univ. 2000; Hon. Fellow AIA, O.A.Q.; Award of Excellence, The Canadian Architect, for office Bldg McGill Coll. Ave., Montréal 1983, Prix Orange for renovation of Passage du Musée, Montréal. *Exhibitions include:* Int. Union of Women Architects, Paris 1978, La Cité and Centre Karachi Centre Georges Pompidou, Paris, Travelling Canadian Exhbn, Europe, "La Cité Linéaire", Boston. *Major projects include:* planning, design devt. and design control of Life Science Bldg., Halifax, McGill Univ. Student Centre, Montréal and other projects 1958–71; design and execution La Cité 7-acre redevelopment project, Montréal 1973–76, commercial and financial centre, Karachi, Pakistan, drama faculty and experimental theatre, Sainte-Thérèse, Canada, Inter-Municipal Library and Recreational Centre, Dollard-des-Ormeaux, Canada, Residence Montefiore, Montréal. *Publications:* History of American Literature 1980, Encyclopedia of Contemporary Architects 1980, 1997–98, La Bâtisseuse de la Cité 1993, Designing Women 2000; articles in architectural journals. *Address:* Vecsei Architectes, 1425 rue du Fort, Montréal, Québec, H3H 2C2 (Office); 4417 Circle Road, Montréal, Québec, H3W 1Y6, Canada. *Telephone:* (514) 932-7100 (Office). *Fax:* (514) 932-7987 (Office). *E-mail:* vecsei@total.net (Office).

VEDERNIKOV, Alexander Aleksandrovich; Russian conductor; b. 11 Jan. 1964, Moscow; s. of Aleksander F. Vedernikov and Natalya Guryeva; m. Olga Aleksandrovna Vedernikova; ed Moscow P. I. Tchaikovsky State Conservatory; Asst, then Conductor Prin. Symphony Orchestra of Russian TV and Radio 1989–95; Founder and Chief Conductor Russian Philharmonic Orchestra 1995–98, 2000–; Musical Dir and Chief Conductor Bolshoi Theatre of Russia 2001–; conducted opera and ballet productions in European theatres including Covent Garden, London, La Scala, Milan and symphony orchestras in Russia. *Address:* Bolshoi Theatre, Teatralnaya pl. 1, Moscow (Office); Pyryeva str. 4, korp. 1, apt. 24, 119285 Moscow, Russia (Home). *Telephone:* (095) 292-18-48 (Office); (095) 147-52-17 (Home).

VÉDRINE, Hubert; French politician, lawyer and civil servant; b. 31 July 1947, Saint-Silvain-Bellegarde; s. of Jean Védrine and Suzanne Védrine; m. Michèle Froment; two s.; ed Lycée Albert–Camus, Univ. of Nanterre, Institut d'Etudes Politiques, Paris, Ecole Nat. d'Admin.; Sr Civil Servant, Ministry of Culture 1974–78, Ministry for Capital Works 1978–79; Co-ordinator for Cultural Relations, nr and Middle East, Ministry of Foreign Affairs 1979–81; Technical Adviser External Affairs, Office of the Sec.-Gen. of the Pres. 1981–86, Legal Adviser, Conseil d'Etat 1986, 1995–96; Spokesman for Presidency of Repub. 1988–91, Sec.-Gen. 1991–95; Minister of Foreign Affairs 1997–2002; partner in pvt. law firm Jeantet et Associés 1996–97. *Publications:* Mieux aménager sa ville 1979, Les Mondes de François Mitterrand, A l'Elysée 1981–95 1996, Dialogue avec Dominique Moïsi: Les Cartes de la France à l'heure de la mondialisation 2000. *Address:* c/o Ministry of Foreign Affairs, 37 quai d'Orsay, 75700 Paris Cédex 07, France.

VEGA DE SEOANE AZPILICUETA, Javier; Spanish mining engineer; b. 13 Sept. 1947, San Sebastián; s. of Joaquín Vega de Seoane and Rosa Azpilicueta; m. Mercedes Pérez de Villaamil Lapiedra 1970; two s. one d.; ed Escuela Técnica Superior de Ingenieros de Minas, Madrid and Glasgow Business School, Scotland; Asst Production Dir, Fundiciones del Estanda SA 1972–75; Asst to CEO, Leyland Ibérica SA 1975–77; Gen. Man. SKF Española SA 1977–83, Pres. and CEO 1983–84; Gen. Man. Instituto Nacional de Industria 1984–. *Leisure interests:* golf, squash, scuba diving.

VEIGA, Carlos Alberto Wahnon de Carvalho, PhD; Cape Verde politician and lawyer; b. 21 Oct. 1949, Mindelo; Prime Minister of Interim Govt Jan. 1991, Prime Minister of Cape Verde 1991–2000, also with responsibility for Defence; Presidential Cand. 2001; fmr Chair. Movimento para a Democracia

(MPD). *Address:* NV Consultones Lda, CP43K, Praia, Santiago, Cape Verde (Office). *Telephone:* 60-36-70 (Office); 62-12-10 (Home). *Fax:* 61-85-93 (Office); 62-12-20 (Home). *E-mail:* wrjtv@cvtelecom.cv (Office); carlos.veiga@cvtelecom.cv (Home).

VEIGA, Maria de Fátima Lima; Cape Verde politician and diplomatist; b. 22 June 1957, São Vicente; Amb. to Cuba 1999–2001; fmr adviser, Ministry of Foreign Affairs, Sec. of State for Foreign Affairs 2001–02; mem. Nat Comm. CILSS. *Address:* c/o Ministry of Foreign Affairs, Co-operation and Communities, Praça Dr Lorenza, CP 60, Praia, Santiago, Cape Verde (Office).

VEIL, Simone, LenD; French politician and fmr lawyer; b. 13 July 1927, Nice; d. of André Jacob and Yvonne Steinmetz; m. Antoine Veil 1946; three s.; ed Inst. d'Etudes Politiques de Paris; Attaché Ministry of Justice 1957–59; Tech. Adviser to Office of René Pleven, Keeper of the Seals 1969; Sec.-Gen. Conseil Supérieur de la Magistrature 1970–74; mem. ORTF Admin. Council 1971–74; Minister of Health 1974–76, of Health and Social Security 1976–79, of Social Affairs, Health and Urban Devt 1993–95; mem. European Parl. 1979–93, (Pres. 1979–82, Chair. of Legal Affairs Cttee 1982–84), Chair. Liberal and Democratic Group 1984–89; mem. Conseil Constitutionnel 1998–; Leader Centre-Right List for European elections 1989; Pres. Fondation pour la Mémoire de la Shoah 2001–; Dr hc (Princeton) 1975, (Weizmann Inst.) 1976, (Bar Ilan) 1980, (Yale) 1980, (Cambridge) 1980, (Edin.) 1980, (Georgetown) 1981, (Urbino) 1981, (Sussex) 1984, (Yeshiva) 1982, (Free Univ., Brussels) 1984, (Brandeis) 1989, (Pennsylvania) 1997; Hon. LLD (Glasgow) 1995; Onassis Foundation Prize 1980, Charlemagne Prize 1981, Louise Weiss Foundation Prize 1981, Louise Michel Prize 1983, European Merit Prize 1983, Jabotinsky Prize (USA) 1983, Prize for Everyday Courage 1984, Special Freedom Prize 1984, Fiera di Messina 1984, Thomas Dehler Prize 1988, Klein Foundation Prize, Phila 1991, Truman Prize for Peace, Jerusalem 1991, Giulietta Prize, Verona 1991, Atlantide Prize, Barcelona 1991 and other prizes; Chevalier Ordre nat. du Mérite, Médaille pénitentiaire, Médaille de l'Education surveillée; numerous foreign decorations including Grand Officer, Nat. Order of the Lion (Senegal), Order of Merit of the Repub. (Ivory Coast), Isabel la Católica (Spain), Grand Cross Order of Merit (FRG), Order of Rio Branco (Brazil), Order of Merit (Luxembourg), Order of the Phoenix (Greece); Hon. DBE (UK) 1997. *Publication:* Les données psycho-sociologiques de l'adoption (with Prof. Launay and Dr. Soule) 1969. *Address:* 10 rue de Rome, 75008 Paris (Office); Conseil constitutionnel, 2 rue Montpensier, 75001 Paris; 11 Place Vauban, 75007 Paris, France (Home). *Telephone:* 1-42-93-00-60 (Office). *Fax:* 1-40-08-03-62 (Office).

VEINBERG, Lev Iosifovich, PhD; Russian business executive; b. 6 May 1944, Samara; m. Sofia D. Landau; one d.; ed Moscow Aviation Inst., Moscow State Univ.; scientific research and teaching (automation of tests, metrology), Moscow Aviation Inst. –1987; Founder and Gen. Dir Interquadro (French/Italian/Soviet computer co.—first jt computer venture in USSR) 1987–90; owner and Pres., SOLEV holding group 1990–; IBM consultant in Russia 1990–92; Vice-Pres., Int. Foundation for Promotion of Privatization and Foreign Investments 1991–93; Chair. Bd of Dirs, AO Centrinvest (reconstruction of Moscow city centre) 1992–, AO Rosvtordragmet 1993–, Russian Bank for Reconstruction and Devt 1993–96; Pres. Asscn of Jt Ventures, Int. Unions and Orgs 1988–, Chair. Supervisory Bd 1998–; Vice-Pres. Scientific-Industrial Union of USSR 1990–91; Vice-Pres. Russian Union of Industrialists and Entrepreneurs 1991–; mem. Presidium, Council on Foreign and Defence Policy of Russia 1992–; Chair. of Bd BAM Credit Bank 1996, AKB Technobank 1997; Order of Friendship 1998; Council of Ministers of the USSR Prize 1988. *Publications:* more than 50 articles in specialized journals. *Leisure interest:* reading history books. *Address:* International Consortium SOLEV, Svetly Proyezd 4, corp. 4, 125080 Moscow (Office); Apt. 139, 3 Facultetsky Per., 125080 Moscow, Russia (Home). *Telephone:* (095) 158-53-39 (Office). *Fax:* (095) 943-00-15 (Office). *E-mail:* solev@solev.ru (Office).

VELASCO GARCÍA, HE Cardinal Ignacio Antonio; Venezuelan ecclesiastic; b. 17 Jan. 1929, Acarigua; ordained priest 1955; Bishop 1990; Archbishop of Caracas 1995–; cr. Cardinal 2001. *Address:* Arzobispado, Apartado 954, Plaza Bolívar, Caracas 1010-A, Venezuela (Office). *Telephone:* (2) 545-0212 (Office). *Fax:* (2) 545-0297 (Office).

VELASQUEZ-GÁZTELU RUIZ, Cándido; Spanish business executive; b. 1937, Jerez de la Frontera; ed Univ. of Granada; Dir Coca-Cola and other cos.; Head of sales and Commercial Dir Tabalcera SA 1973, Gen. Dir 1981, Chair. 1982–89; Pres. Compañía Telefónica Nacional de España 1989–. *Address:* c/o Telefónica SA, Beatriz de Bobadilla 3, 9°, 28040 Madrid, Spain.

VELAYATI, Ali Akbar; Iranian politician; b. 1945, Tehran; s. of Ali Asghar and Zobeideh Asgah; m. Skina Khosshnevissan; three c.; ed Tehran Univ.; joined Nat. Front (of Mossadegh) 1961; a founder of the Islamic Asscn of Faculty of Medicine, Tehran Univ. 1963; underground political activities in support of Ayatollah Khomeini 1979; Vice-Minister, Ministry of Health 1979–80; proposed for Prime Minister by Ayatollah Khomeini Oct. 1981 (candidature rejected by the Majlis); Minister of Foreign Affairs 1981–97. *Publications:* Infectious Diseases (3 Vols) 1979, numerous articles. *Address:* c/o Ministry of Foreign Affairs, Tehran, Iran.

VELDHUIS, Johannes (Jan) G. F.; Netherlands university president; b. 4 Oct. 1938, Hengelo; m. Monica M. H. Thier 1969; three s.; ed Univs. of Utrecht and Minnesota; Ministry of Foreign Affairs 1968–70; Sec. Univ. Bd Univ. of Leiden 1970–74; Deputy Sec.-Gen. Ministry of Educ. and Science 1974–79, Dir-Gen. and Insp.-Gen. of Educ. and Science 1979–86; Pres. Utrecht Univ. 1986–; Chair. Netherlands del. OECD Educ. Cttee 1984–86; Chair. Bd Netherlands-America Comm. for Educational Exchange (Fulbright Comm.) 1984–2001, Netherlands Inst. for Art History, Florence, Fondation Descartes Amsterdam, Museum Catharÿneconvent Utrecht, Stichting Carmelcollege Hengelo; mem. Bd Netherlands History Inst., Rome, Netherlands Archaeological Inst., Cairo, Japan-Netherlands Inst., Tokyo; mem. bds. of several hosps. in The Hague area; Chevalier, Légion d'Honneur 1997, Officer Order Orange Nassau 1998, Commdr Order Isabel la Católica (Spain) 2001; Hon. doctorate (Florida Gainesville). *Publications:* various publs in the field of educ. and public admin. *Leisure interests:* comparative educ., literature, botany, tennis, skiing, bridge. *Address:* Heidelberglaan 8, PO Box 80125, 3508 TC Utrecht (Office); Roucooppark 12, 2251 AV Voorschoten, Netherlands (Home). *Telephone:* (30) 2535150 (Office); (71) 5617696 (Home). *Fax:* (30) 2537745 (Office); (71) 5620029 (Home). *E-mail:* voorzitter@cvb.uu.nl (Office); monica.jan.veldhuis@planet.nl (Home).

VELICHKO, Vladimir Makarovich; Russian fmr politician and business executive; b. 23 April 1937, Mozhaisk, Voronezh Region; s. of Makar Petrovich Velichko and Maria Ivanovna Velichko; m. Eleanora Dmitrievna Bestouzheva 1961, one d.; ed Leningrad Inst. of Mechanics, Leningrad Inst. of Eng and Econs; joined CPSU 1962; started career as foreman, later Dir of machine Bldg plant; First Deputy Minister, Ministry of Power Eng of USSR 1975–83, Minister 1983–87; Minister of Heavy Power and Transport Eng 1987–89; Minister of Heavy Machine-Building Industry 1989–91; USSR First Deputy Prime Minister Jan.–Dec. 1991; Deputy to USSR Supreme Soviet 1984–89; Deputy of the USSR 1989; mem. Political Consultative Council, Sept.–Dec. 1991; Chair. Bd Tyazhenergomash (now Jt stock co. TENMA) 1992; Pres. Financial and Industrial Group Heavy Eng Industry 1996; Academician, mem. Presidium Russian Acad. of Eng; USSR State Prize 1974. *Leisure interests:* literature, art. *Address:* TENMA, Nizhni Kislovsky per. 5, GSP, 103906 Moscow K-9, Russia. *Telephone:* (095) 203-15-00. *Fax:* (095) 291-68-26.

VELIKHOV, Yevgeniy Pavlovich; Russian physicist; b. 2 Feb. 1935, Moscow; s. of Pavel Pavlovich Velikhov and Natalia Vsevolodoma Velikhova; m. Natalia Alekseevna Arseniyeva 1959; two s. one d.; mem. of staff, Kurchatov Inst. of Atomic Energy 1958–, Head of Lab. 1962–70, Deputy Dir, then Dir of branch of Inst. 1971–89; Dir Russian Scientific Centre, Kurchatov Inst. 1989–; f. and Dir Inst. for Security Problems of Nuclear Energy Devt 1988–91; Prof., Moscow Univ. 1973–; mem. CPSU Cen. Cttee 1989–90; mem. USSR (now Russian) Acad. of Sciences 1974, Presidium, Vice-Pres. 1978–96, 2002–, Academician-Sec. Dept of Information Technology, Cybernetics and Automatic Systems 1985–92; mem. Supreme Soviet of USSR; People's Deputy of the USSR 1989–91; mem. Pres. Council 1992–93; Chair. Cttee of Soviet Scientists for Peace against Nuclear Threat; Co-founder Int. Foundation for Survival and Devt of Humanity; del. to numerous scientific and peace confs.; Chair. Soviet Nuclear Soc. 1989–; Co-Chair. Jr Achievement of Russia 1991–; Chair. Council, Int. Thermonuclear Experimental Reactor 1992–; mem. Presidential Council of Science and Tech. 1995–; Pres. Shelf-Developing Co. Rosshelf 1992–; mem. American Geophysical Soc. 1981; Foreign mem. Swedish Royal Acad. of Eng Sciences 1989; Dr. hc (Notre Dame, Susquachana, Tafts, London); USSR State Prize 1977, Lenin Prize 1984, Hero of Socialist Labour 1985, Science for Peace Prize, Italy, Szillard Award, American Physical Soc.; Order of Lenin (three times). *Publications:* numerous, related both to science and the problems of prevention of nuclear war. *Leisure interests:* mountain skiing, underwater swimming, windsurfing. *Address:* RNTs Kurchatovskiy Institute, Kurchatova pl. 1, 123182 Moscow, Russia. *Telephone:* (095) 196-92-41.

VELLIDIS, Katerina; Greek publisher; b. 1947, Thessaloniki; d. of Ioannis Vellidis and Anna Vellidis; m. (divorced); one d.; ed Univ. of Geneva and Sorbonne, Paris; Pres. Bd and Man. Dir I. K. Vellidis Press Org. of Northern Greece (publrs of newspapers and magazines) 1980–; Pres. Ioannis and Anna Vellidis Foundation; numerous awards including Silver Medal of Acad. of Athens.

VELTMAN, Martinus J. G., PhD; Netherlands physicist; b. 1931; ed Univ. of Utrecht; Prof. of Physics Univ. of Utrecht 1966–81, Univ. of Mich. 1981–, now Prof. Emer.; mem. Dutch Acad. of Sciences; High Energy and Particle Physics Prize (European Physical Soc.) 1993, Jt winner Nobel Prize in Physics 1999. *Publications:* Facts and Mysteries in Particle Physics.

VELYAMINOV, Petr Sergeyevich; Russian actor; b. 7 Dec. 1926, Moscow; m.; four c.; arrested and imprisoned on charge of membership of anti-Soviet org. 1943, acquitted 1952; worked in theatres in Abakan, Perm, Tumen, Cheboksary, Sverdlovsk, Moscow (Sovremennik), St Petersburg (N. Akimov Comedy Theatre 1995–); People's Artist of Russia, USSR State Prize. *Theatre roles include:* Leander Nodan in Men in Her Life, Rodion Nikolayevich in Old-Fashioned Comedy. *Films include:* Commander of the Lucky Pike, Sweet Woman, Yaroslav the Wise, Glass Labyrinth, Here is our Home, A Tale about the Human Heart, Dust Under the Sun, Version of Colonel Zorin, Poem of Wings, Dangerous Friends. *Address:* N. Akimov Comedy Theatre, Nevski prosp. 56 St. Petersburg, Russia. *Telephone:* (812) 314-26-10.

VENABLES, Terry Frederick; British football manager and commentator; b. 6 Jan. 1943; m. Yvette Venables; two d.; ed Dagenham High School;

professional footballer, Chelsea 1958–66 (Capt. 1962), Tottenham Hotspur 1966–68 (FA Cup winners 1967), Queens Park Rangers 1968–73; coach, Crystal Palace 1973–76, Man. 1976–80; Man. Queens Park Rangers 1980–84; Man. Barcelona 1984–87 (winners Spanish Championship 1984, European Cup finalists 1985); Man. Tottenham Hotspur 1987–91 (FA Cup winners 1991); Chief Exec. Tottenham Hotspur PLC 1991–93; coach, England Nat. Team 1994–96; Dir of Football, Portsmouth Football Club 1996–98; coach, Australian Nat. Team 1996–98; head coach Crystal Palace 1998; coach Middlesbrough 2001; Man. Leeds Utd 2002–03; only player to have rep. England at all levels; co-author, Hazell (TV detective series); Hon. Fellow Univ. of Wolverhampton. *Publications:* They Used to Play on Grass 1971, Terry Venables: The Autobiography 1994, The Best Game in the World 1996, Venables' England—The Making of the Team 1996. *Address:* Terry Venables Holdings Ltd, 213 Putney Bridge Road, London, SW15 2NY, England. *Telephone:* (20) 8874-5001. *Fax:* (20) 8874-0064.

VENDLER, Helen Hennessy, AB, PhD; American professor and literary critic; b. 30 April 1933, Boston, Mass.; d. of George Hennessy and Helen Conway; one s.; ed Emmanuel Coll. and Harvard Univ.; Instructor Cornell Univ. 1960–63; Lecturer, Swarthmore Coll., Pa and Haverford Coll., Pa 1963–64; Asst Prof. Smith Coll. Northampton, Mass. 1964–66; Assoc. Prof. Boston Univ. 1966–68, Prof. 1968–85; Visiting Prof. Harvard Univ. 1981–85, Kenan Prof. 1985–, Assoc. Acad. Dean 1987–92, A. Kingsley Porter Univ. Prof. 1990–; Sr Fellow, Harvard Soc. of Fellows 1981–92; poetry critic, New Yorker 1978–; mem. American Acad. of Arts and Sciences, Norwegian Acad., American Philosophical Soc., Educ. Advisory Bd Guggenheim Foundation, Pulitzer Prize Bd 1990–99; Fulbright Fellow 1954; A.A.U.W. Fellow 1959; Guggenheim Fellow 1971–72; American Council of Learned Socs. Fellow 1971–72; N.E.H. Fellow 1980, 1985, 1994; Wilson Fellow 1994; Fulbright Lecturer, Univ. of Bordeaux 1968–69; Overseas Fellow, Churchill Coll. Cambridge 1980; Parnell Fellow, Magdalene Coll. Cambridge 1996, Hon. Fellow 1996–; 17 hon. degrees; Lowell Prize 1969, Explicator Prize 1969, Nat. Inst. of Arts and Letters Award 1975, Nat. Book Critics Award 1980, Newton Arvin Award, Jefferson Medal. *Publications include:* Yeats's Vision and the Later Plays 1963, On Extended Wings: Wallace Stevens' Longer Poems 1969, The Poetry of George Herbert 1975, Part of Nature, Part of Us 1980, The Odes of John Keats 1983, Wallace Stevens: Words Chosen Out of Desire 1985, Harvard Book of Contemporary American Poetry 1985, The Music of What Happens 1988, The Given and the Made 1995, The Breaking of Style 1995, Soul Says 1995, Poems, Poets, Poetry 1996, The Art of Shakespeare's Sonnets 1997, Seamus Heaney 1998. *Leisure interests:* travel, music. *Address:* Harvard University, Department of English, Barker Center, Cambridge, MA 02138; 54 Trowbridge Street, Apt. B, Cambridge, MA 02138, USA. *Telephone:* (617) 496-6028 (Office); (617) 547-9197 (Home). *Fax:* (617) 496-8737; (617) 496-8737 (Office).

VENEMAN, Ann M.; American politician and lawyer; Assoc. Admin. Foreign Agric. Service, U.S. Dept of Agric. 1986–89, Deputy Under-Sec. of Agric. for Int. Affairs and Commodity Programmes 1989–91, Deputy Sec. of Dept 1991–93; Sec. Calif. Dept of Food and Agric. 1995–99; partner Nossaman, Guthner, Knox and Elliott 1999–2001; Sec. of Agric. Jan. 2001–. *Address:* Department of Agriculture, 14th & Independence Avenue, SW, Washington, DC 20250, U.S.A. (Office). *Telephone:* (202) 720-2791 (Office). *Website:* www.usda.gov (Office).

VENETIAAN, Runaldo Ronald; Suriname politician; b. 1936; leader Suriname Nat. Party; Pres. of Suriname 1991–96, 2000–. *Address:* Office of the President, Paramaribo, Suriname.

VENGEROV, Maxim; Israeli violinist; b. 20 Aug. 1974, Novosibirsk, Western Siberia, USSR; s. of Alexander Vengerov and Larissa Vengerov; studied with Galina Tourchaninova and Zakhar Bron; first recital aged five; 1st Prize Jr Wieniawski Competition Poland 1984; winner Carl Flesch Int. Violin Competition 1990; Prof. of Violin, Musikhochschule des Saarlandes; performs with all maj. int. orchestras, recitals world-wide; apptd. UNICEF Envoy for Music 1997; many recordings, exclusive EMI artist May 2000–; Gramophone Young Artist of the Year 1994, Ritmo Artist of the Year 1994, Gramophone Record of the Year 1996, Edison Award 1997, Gramophone Artist of the Year 2002. *Address:* c/o Askonas Holt Ltd., Lonsdale Chambers, 27 Chancery Lane, London, WC2A 1PF, England. *Telephone:* (20) 7400-1780. *Fax:* (20) 7400-1799. *E-mail:* nicola-fee.bahl@askonasholt.co.uk (Office).

VENIAMIN, Christodoulos; Cypriot government official; b. Sept. 1922; ed in Nicosia and Middle Temple, London; junior officer in Govt service 1942, admin. officer 1949; served as Asst Sec. in Depts. of Local Govt and Admin., Personnel, Finance, Commerce and Industry, Social Services, Communications and Works, Agric. and Natural Resources; Asst Dist Commr, Larnaca; Asst Sec. Ministry of Interior during transitional period; Dist Officer, Limassol Dist 1960–68; Dir-Gen. Ministry of Foreign Affairs 1968; Minister of Interior and Defence 1975–84, of Interior 1988–93; mem. House of Reps. 1997–2001; Grosse Verdienstkreuz mit Stern und Schulterband (Germany), Onorifiecenza di Grande Ufficiale (Italy), Order of the Cedar (Lebanon). *Leisure interests:* reading and walking. *Address:* Kleanthi Ierodiaconou No. 5, 2411 Engomi, Nicosia, Cyprus. *Telephone:* (22) 680339 (Office); (22) 352400 (Home). *Fax:* (22) 671821.

VENIZELOS, Evangelos, PhD; Greek politician; b. 1957, Thessaloniki; m. Vasiliki Bakatselou; one d.; ed Aristotle Univ. of Thessaloniki, Univ. of Paris II (Paris-Sorbonne); Asst Prof., then Prof. of Constitutional Law Aristotle Univ. of Thessaloniki 1984–87; Attorney at Law for Council of State and Supreme Court 1984–87; apptd mem. Bd Nat. Centre of Public Admin 1987; apptd mem. Bd Nat. Bank of Greece 1988; mem. Local Radio Cttee; elected to Cen. Cttee of the Panhellenic Socialist Movement (PASOK) 1990; mem. Parl. 1993–; Deputy Minister to the Prime Minister's Office, responsible for Press Affairs 1993–94; Minister for Press and Media Affairs 1994–95; Minister of Transportation and Communications 1995–96; Minister of Justice Jan.–Sept. 1996; Minister of Culture 1996–98, 2000–; Minister of Devt 1999–2000. *Address:* Ministry of Culture, 20–22 Bouboulinas Sreet, 10682 Athens, Greece (Office). *Telephone:* (1) 08201648 (Office). *E-mail:* minister@culture.gr (Office). *Website:* www.culture.gr (Office).

VENKATARAMAN, Ramaswamy, MA, BL; Indian politician; b. 4 Dec. 1910; s. of Ramaswami Iyer; m. Janaki Venkataraman; three d.; ed Madras Univ.; Advocate, Madras High Court and Supreme Court; detained during Quit India Movt 1942–44; Man. Ed. Labour Law Journal 1949; mem. Provisional Parl. 1950–52; mem. Lok Sabha 1952–57, 1977–84; Sec. Congress Party 1952–54; mem. Standing Finance Cttee, Estimates Cttee, Public Accounts Cttee, Privileges Cttee; Minister for Industry and Labour and Leader of the House, Govt of Madras 1957–67, mem. Planning Comm. 1967–71; Chair. Nat. Research and Devt Corpn; Minister of Finance and Industry 1980–82, of Defence 1982–84; Vice-Pres. of India 1984–87, Pres. of India 1987–92; Chair. Governing Body, Kalakshetra Foundation 1993–; mem. UN Admin. Tribunal 1956–79, Pres. 1968–79; Del. to ILO 1958, UN Gen. Ass. 1953–61; Dr. hc from several univs.; Soviet Land Prize for book on travel in the Soviet Union and Eastern Europe. *Publications:* Travelogue in Socialist Countries 1966, My Presidential Years (in English) 1994. *Leisure interests:* arts, music, tennis, photography. *Address:* No. 5 Safdar Jung Road, New Delhi 110011, India. *Telephone:* (11) 3794366 (Office); (11) 3014925 (Home). *Fax:* (11) 3014925 (Home).

VENNER, Sir K. Dwight, Kt; central banker; ed Univ. of the W. Indies; Research Asst Univ. of the W. Indies, Jr Research Fellow, Inst. of Social and Econ. Reseach, Lecturer, Dept of Econs; Dir Finance and Planning, Govt of St Lucia; Gov. Eastern Caribbean Cen. Bank 1989–; numerous articles on econs; Chair. Air and Seaports Authority, St Lucia 1981–89, Nat. Insurance Investment Cttee 1981–89, Caricom Cen. Bank Govs, Eastern Caribbean Home Mortgage Bank; Chair. Technical Restructuring Cttee, Org. of Eastern Caribbean States (OECS); Dir St Lucia Devt Bank, Nat. Commercial Bank, St Lucia; mem. Chancellor's Governance Cttee, Univ. of the W. Indies; mem. Univ. Strategy Cttee. *Address:* East Caribbean Central Bank, Fairplay Commercial Complex, The Valley, Anguilla (Office). *Telephone:* 497-5050 (Office). *Fax:* 497-5150 (Office). *E-mail:* eccbaxa@aguillanet.com (Office). *Website:* www.eccb-centralbank.org (Office).

VENTER, J. Craig, PhD; American scientist; m. Claire Fraser; ed Univ. of California at San Diego; USN, served in Vietnam 1967; teacher, SUNY, Buffalo; Section and Lab. Chief, NIH, Bethesda, MD 1984–92; Founder, Chair. and Chief Scientist, The Inst. for Genomic Research (TIGR) 1992–; Pres. and Chief Scientific Officer, Celera Genomics Corpn, Rockville, MD 1998–2002, Chair. Scientific Advisory Bd 2002–; Beckman Award 1999, Chiron Corpn Biotech. Research Award 1999. *Publications:* more than 160 articles in scientific journals. *Leisure interest:* sailing. *Address:* Institute of Genomic Research, 9712 Medical Center Drive, Rockville, MD 20850, USA (Office).

VENTURA, Jesse; American politician, wrestler, radio presenter and actor; b. James George Janos, 15 July 1951, Minneapolis; s. of George Janos and Bernice Janos; m. Terry Ventura; two c.; ed N Hennepin Community Coll.; served in US Navy 1969–73, USNR 1973–75; fmr bodyguard for The Rolling Stones; professional wrestler 1973–84; fmr TV commentator; actor 1984–97; Brooklyn Park Mayor 1991–95; radio talk show host 1995–98; Gov. of Minn. 1998–2002; fmr mem. Reform Party. *Films include:* Predator 1987, Running Man 1987, Abraxas, Guardian of the Universe 1991, Demolition Man 1993, Batman & Robin 1997. *Publication:* I 'Aint Got Time to Bleed 2000. *Address:* c/o 130 State Capitol Building, 75 Constitution Avenue, St. Paul, MN 55155, USA (Office).

VENTURI, Robert, AB, MFA, FAIA; American architect; b. 25 June 1925, Philadelphia, Pa; s. of Robert C. Venturi and Vanna Lanzetta; m. Denise (Lakofski) Scott Brown 1967; one s.; ed Princeton Univ.; Designer, Oskar Stonorov 1950, Eero Saarinen & Assoc. 1950–53; Rome Prize Fellow, American Acad. in Rome 1954–56; Designer, Louis I. Kahn 1957; Assoc. Prof., School of Fine Arts, Univ. of Pennsylvania 1957–65; Charlotte Shepherd Davenport Prof., Yale Univ. 1966–70; Prin., Venturi, Cope & Lippincott 1958–61, Venturi and Short 1961–64, Venturi and Rauch 1964–80, Venturi, Rauch and Scott Brown (architects and planners) 1980–89; Venturi, Scott Brown and Assocs June 1989–; Fellow American Acad. in Rome, Accademia Nazionale di San Luca, American Acad. of Arts and Sciences; Hon. FRIBA; Hon. Fellow Royal Incorporation of Architects in Scotland, American Acad. and Inst. of Arts and Letters; Hon. DFA (Oberlin, Yale, Penn., Princeton, Phila Coll of Art); Hon. LHD (NJ Inst. of Tech.); Laurea hc (Univ. of Rome La Sapienza) 1994; Nat. Medal of Arts 1992 and numerous other awards. *Works include:* Vanna Venturi House, Phila, Pa 1961, Guild House, Phila 1961, Franklin Court, Phila 1972, Allen Memorial Art Museum Addition, Oberlin, Ohio 1973, Inst. for Scientific Information Corpn HQ, Phila 1978, Gordon Wu

Hall, Princeton Univ., NJ 1980, Seattle Art Museum, Seattle, Wash. 1984, Clinical Research Bldg, Univ. of Pa 1985 (with Payette Assocs.), Nat. Gallery, Sainsbury Wing, London, UK 1986, Fisher-Bendheim Hall, Princeton Univ. 1986, Charles P. Stevenson Library, Bard Coll. 1989, Regional Govt Bldg, Toulouse, France 1992, Kirifuri Resort facilities, Nikko, Japan 1992, Univ. of Del. Student Center, Newark, Del. 1992, Memorial Hall Restoration and Addition, Harvard Univ. 1992, The Barnes Foundation Restoration and Renovation, Merion, Pa 1993, Disney Celebration Bank, Celebration, Fla 1993, Irvine Auditorium, Perelman Quadrangle, Univ. of Pa 1995, Princeton Campus Center, Princeton Univ. 1996, Congress Avenue Building, Yale Univ. School of Medicine 1998, Master Plan and Bldgs for Univ. of Michigan 1997–. *Publications:* Complexity and Contradiction in Architecture 1966, Learning from Las Vegas (with Denise Scott Brown and Steven Izenour) 1972, A View from the Campidoglio: Selected Essays, 1953–1984 (with Denise Scott Brown) 1984, Iconography and Electronics upon a Generic Architecture 1996; numerous articles in professional journals. *Leisure interest:* travel. *Address:* Venturi, Scott Brown and Associates, 4236 Main Street, Philadelphia, PA 19127, USA (Office). *Telephone:* (215) 487-0400 (Office). *Fax:* (215) 487-2520 (Office). *E-mail:* venturi@vsba.com (Office). *Website:* www.vsba.com (Office).

VENTURONI, Adm. Guido; Italian naval officer and international organization official; b. 10 April 1934, Teramo; m. Giuliana Marinozzi; two s. one d.; ed Naval Acad. 1952–56; Navigator, Communications Officer, maritime patrol pilot and tactical instructor; Head of Naval Helicopter Studies and Projects Office; Exec. Asst to Chief of Navy Staff, to Chief of Defence at Naval Personnel Directorate; Head of Plans and Operation Dept at Navy Gen. Staff, at Defence Gen. Staff 1982–86; Commdr, First Naval Div. 1986–87; Head Financial Planning Bureau, Naval Gen. Staff 1987–89; Deputy Chief of Staff of Navy 1989–90; Vice-Adm. 1990–91; C-in-C of Fleet and NATO Commdr of Cen. Mediterranean 1991–92; Chief of Staff of Navy 1992–93, Chief of Defence Gen. Staff 1994–; Over Commdr, Int. Security Mission to Albania 1997–; Chair. Mil. Cttee, NATO 1999–; Kt of Grand Cross of Order of Merit, Silver Medal for sea-duty service, Gold Medal for air service; Medal for Merit (Mauritius); Officer Légion d'honneur; Grand Cross of Orden de Mayo al Mérito Naval (Argentina); First Class Cross of Order of Mérito Naval (Spain); Second Class Decoration of Order of Mérito Naval (Venezuela). *Address:* NATO, blvd Léopold III, 1110 Brussels, Belgium (Office). *Telephone:* (2) 707-41-11 (Office). *Fax:* (2) 707-45-79 (Office).

VERA BEJARANO, Candido; Paraguayan politician; b. 16 July 1957, San Pedro de Yeuamandyzú; s. of Candido Vera and Florencia Bezarano; m.; two s. two d.; ed Escuela Agricola Carlos Pfnnl, Universidad del Horte, Asunción; elected mem. Nat. Congress (Liberal Party) 1993, re-elected 1998; Pres. Nat. Congress 2000–; elected Senator 2003–. *Publications include:* Proyecto de Modificacion del Estatuto Agraiio 2002, Proyecto de ley que creo el Instituto de Desarollo Rural y de la Tierra 2003. *Address:* Officina del Presidente, Congreso Nacional, Asunción (Office); Pedro Ciancio 1075, Concordia, Asunción, Paraguay (Home). *Telephone:* 21452013 (Office); 21214612 (Home). *Fax:* 21452013 (Office); 21214612 (Home).

VERBA, Sidney, PhD; American academic; b. 26 May 1932, Brooklyn, New York; s. of Morris Verba and Recci Salman; m. E. Cynthia Winston 1955; three d.; ed Harvard Coll. and Princeton Univ.; Asst, then Assoc. Prof. of Politics Princeton Univ. 1960–64; Prof. of Political Science, Stanford Univ. 1964–68; Sr Study Dir Nat. Opinion Research Center 1968–72; Prof. of Political Science, Univ. of Chicago 1968–72; Prof. of Govt, Harvard Univ. 1972–, Clarence Dillon Prof. of Int. Affairs 1983–84, Carl H. Pforzheimer Prof. 1984–, Assoc. Dean for Undergraduate Educ., Faculty of Arts and Sciences 1981–84, Dir Harvard Univ. Library 1984–; Chair. Bd of Dirs Harvard Univ. Press 1991–; Pres. American Political Science Asscn 1994–95; mem. NAS, American Acad. of Arts and Sciences; Guggenheim Fellow; Woodrow Wilson and Kammerer Book Awards, James Madison Award (American Political Science Asscn). *Publications:* Small Groups and Political Behavior 1961, The Civic Culture 1963, Participation in America 1972, Participation and Political Equality 1978, The Changing American Voter 1979, Injury to Insult 1979, Equality in America 1985, Elites and the Idea of Equality 1987, Designing Social Inquiry 1994, Voice and Equality 1995. *Address:* Wadsworth House, Harvard University, Cambridge, MA 02138 (Office); 142 Summit Avenue, Brookline, MA 02146, USA (Home). *Telephone:* (617) 495-3650 (Office); (617) 232-4987 (Home).

VERBITSKAYA, Ludmila Alekseyevna, D. LINGUISTICS; Russian philologist; b. 17 June 1936; m.; two d.; ed Leningrad State Univ.; lab. Asst, then Jr researcher, docent Chair. of Philology, Leningrad (now St Petersburg) State Univ. –1979, Prof. Chair. of Phonetics 1979–85, Head Chair. of Gen. Linguistics 1985–, Pro-Rector on scientific work, First Pro-Rector 1989, Acting Rector 1994, Rector 1995–; Vice-Pres. UNESCO Comm. on Problems of Women's Educ.; Rep. to Exec. Council of Int. Asscn of Univs.; mem. Russian Acad. of Humanitarian Sciences, Acad. of Sciences of Higher School, Presidium Int. Asscn of Russian Language and Literature Teachers, Presidium Conf. of Rectors of European Univs.; mem. of Council Our Home Russia Movt 1996–99; hon. degrees from numerous foreign univs. *Publications:* over 150 Publs. *Address:* St Petersburg State University, Universitetskaya nab. 7/9, 199034 St. Petersburg, Russia (Office). *Telephone:* (812) 218-51-52 (Office).

VERDAN, Claude Edouard; Swiss hand surgeon (retd); b. 21 Sept. 1909, Yverdon; s. of Edouard Verdan and Adeline Verdan (née Henrioud); m. 1st

Sylva Malan 1934 (died 1999); one s. (deceased) one d.; m. 2nd Suzanne Léon-Forestier 2000; ed Faculty of Medicine, Univ. of Lausanne, Univ. of Zürich; specialist in surgery, Foederatio Medicorum Helveticorum (FMH); Chief surgeon and founder of Clinique chirurgicale et Permanence de Longeraie, Lausanne; Prof. Univ. of Lausanne; Sr Dean Faculty of Medicine 1972–74; Pres. Soc. suisse de médecine des accidents et des maladies professionnelles 1961–66; Pres. Soc. française de chirurgie plastique et reconstructive 1964; Sec.-Gen. and Founder, Groupe suisse d'étude de chirurgie de la main 1966–72; Pres. Comm. for war surgery, Fed. Mil. (Defence) Dept (médecin-Col) 1965–69; Pres. Soc. française de chirurgie de la main 1975–76; retd from medical practice 1980; f. Museum of the Human Hand (Foundation Claude Verdan), Lausanne 1981, first Exhbn "Man's Hand" 1983, several other exhbns. in Switzerland and France; Corresp. mem. Belgian Soc. for Forensic Traumatology 1963, Italian Soc. for Hand Surgery 1970; Assoc. mem. Acad. of Surgery, Paris 1974; Specialist FMH in plastic and reconstructive surgery 1977; Ed. Annales de chirurgie de la main 1982–, Ed.-in-Chief Emer. 1985; Hon. Pres. Claude Verdan Foundation 1990; Hon. mem. British Soc. for Surgery of the Hand 1959; Hon. mem. American Soc. for Surgery of the Hand 1960, Swiss Soc. for Medicine in Casualty 1966, Swiss Soc. for Orthopedics 1967, German-speaking Asscn for Hand Surgery 1971, Soc. vaudoise de médecine 1975, Spanish Soc. for Hand Surgery, French Soc. for Orthopedics and Traumatology 1979, French Soc. of Hand Surgery 1979; Hon. mem. de l'Association française de chirurgie 1981; Hon. Prof. Univ. of Lausanne 1979; Gold Medal and Prix César Roux (Faculty of Medicine, Lausanne) 1933; nominated Pioneer of Hand Surgery, 3rd Congress JFSSH, Tokyo 1986; Officier Légion d'honneur. *Publications:* The Hand—A Whole Universe, with catalogue of Museum of the Human Hand 1994 and numerous other books and articles on the hand. *Leisure interests:* sculpting, painting, collecting articles concerning the hand, objets d'art, writing memoirs. *Address:* The Museum of the Human Hand (Foundation Claude Verdan), 21 rue du Bugnon, 1005 Lausanne; 63 route de Lausanne, 1096 Cully, Switzerland. *Telephone:* (21) 3144955; (21) 7991330. *Fax:* (21) 3144963. *E-mail:* mmain@hospvd.ch (Office). *Website:* verdan.hospvd.ch.

VERE-JONES, David, MSc, DPhil, FRSNZ; British professor of mathematics; b. 17 April 1936, London; s. of Noel W. Vere-Jones and Isabel M. I. Wyllie; m. Mary To Kei Chung 1965; two s. one d.; ed Cheadle Hulme School, Cheshire, Hutt Valley High School, NZ, Vic. Univ. of Wellington and Univ. of Oxford; emigrated to New Zealand 1949; Rhodes Scholar 1958–61; Sr Scientist, Applied Math. Div. Dept of Scientific and Industrial Research, NZ 1961–65; Fellow, Sr Fellow, Dept of Statistics, ANU 1965–69; Prof. of Statistics Vic. Univ. of Wellington 1970–; Founding Pres. NZ Math Soc. 1975; Chair. Int. Statistical Inst. (ISI) Educ. Comm. 1987–91; Pres. Interim Exec., Int. Asscn for Statistical Educ. 1991–93; other professional affiliations; Hon. mem. ISI Henri Willem Methorst Medal 1995, Science and Tech. Medal in gold NZ Math. Soc. 2000. *Publications:* An Introduction to the Theory of Point Processes (with D. J. Daley) 1988; about 100 papers on probability theory, seismology, mathematical educ. *Leisure interests:* tennis, walking, languages. *Address:* School of Mathematics and Computing Science, Victoria University of Wellington, P.O. Box 600, Wellington (Office); 15 Farm Road, Northland, Wellington 5, New Zealand (Home). *Telephone:* (4) 499-4601 (Office); (4) 475-7249 (Home). *Fax:* (4) 495-5239 (Office). *E-mail:* postmaster@vuw.ac.nz (Office). *Website:* www.vuw.ac.nz (Office).

VEREKER, Sir John (Michael Medlicott), KCB, KStJ, BA, CIMgt, FRSA; British civil servant; b. 9 Aug. 1944; s. of the late Commdr Charles W.M. Vereker and Marjorie Vereker (née Whatley); m. Judith Diane Rowen 1971; one s. one d.; ed Marlborough Coll., Keele Univ.; Asst Prin. Overseas Devt Ministry 1967–69, Prin. 1972, Pvt. Sec. to Minister of Overseas Devt 1977–78, Asst Sec. 1978; Asst Sec. Prime Minister's Office 1980–83, Under-Sec. 1983–88; Prin. Finance Officer Overseas Devt Admin., FCO 1986–88; Deputy Sec. Dept of Educ. and Science, then Dept for Educ. 1988–93; Perm. Sec. Dept for Int. Devt 1994–2002; Gov. of Bermuda Feb. 2002–; Asst Prin. World Bank, Washington 1970–72; Chair. Students Loans Co. Ltd 1989–91; Vice-Pres. Raleigh Int. 2002–; mem. Council, Inst. of Manpower Studies 1989–92, Bd British Council 1994–2002, IDS 1994–2001, VSO 1994–2002, Advisory Bd for British Consultants Bureau 1998–; Hon. DLitt (Keele) 1997. *Address:* Government House, 11 Langton Hill, Pembroke, HM 13, Bermuda (Office).

VERESHCHETIN, Vladlen Stepanovich, DJur; Russian jurist; b. 8 Jan. 1932, Briansk; m.; one d.; ed Moscow Inst. of Int. Relations; mem. staff, Presidium of USSR Acad. of Sciences 1958–67; First Vice-Chair. and Legal Counsel, Intercosmos, USSR Acad. of Sciences 1967–81; Prof. of Int. Law, Univ. of Friendship of Peoples 1979–82; Deputy Dir and Head, Dept of Int. Law, Inst. of State and Law, Russian Acad. of Sciences 1981–95; mem. Perm. Court of Arbitration, The Hague 1984–85; mem. Int. Court of Justice, The Hague 1995–(2006); Vice-Pres. Russian (fmrly Soviet) UN Asscn 1984–97; Vice-Pres. Russian (fmrly Soviet) Asscn of Int. Law 1985–97; mem. UN Int. Law Comm. 1992–95; Hon. Awards from German Acad. of Sciences 1978, Bulgarian Acad. of Sciences 1979, Int. Acad. of Astronautics 1987, 1994; Prof. of Int. Law Badge of Honour 1967, Friendship of Peoples Award 1975, October Revolution Award 1981, Hugo Grotius Award 2001. *Publications:* books and over 150 articles on int. law, law of the sea, space law, state responsibility, int. criminal law. *Address:* International Court of Justice, Peace Palace, Carnegieplein 2, 2517 KJ The Hague, Netherlands. *Telephone:* (70) 302-2323 (Office). *Fax:* (70) 302-2409 (Office). *E-mail:* v.s.vereshchetin@icj-cij.org (Office). *Website:* www.icj-cij.org (Office).

VERGE, Pierre, MA, LLL, LLM, LLD, FRSC; Canadian professor of law; b. 9 Jan. 1936, Québec City; m. Colette Habel 1963; two s. one d.; ed Univ. Laval, McGill Univ. and Univ. of Toronto; mem. Québec Bar 1961; QC 1976; Prof. of Law, Univ. Laval 1967–, Dean, Faculty of Law 1973–77; Commonwealth Fellowship, St John's Coll. Cambridge 1977; mem. Canadian Asscn of Law Teachers (Pres. 1972–73), Royal Soc. of Canada. *Publications:* Le droit de grève, fondement et limites, Le droit et les syndicats (co-author) 1991, Un droit du travail? (co-author) 1997, La représentation syndicale: vision juridique actuelle et future (co-author) 1999. *Address:* Faculté de droit, Université Laval, Québec, G1K 7P4 (Office); 2542 de la Falaise, Sillery, Québec, G1T 1W3, Canada (Home). *Telephone:* (418) 656-5009 (Office); (418) 651-4829 (Home). *Fax:* (418) 656-7230 (Office). *E-mail:* pierre.verge@fd.ulaval.ca (Office).

VERGÈS, Jacques; French lawyer; b. 5 March 1925, Thailand; m. Djamila Bouhired; two c.; ed legal studies in Paris; served with Free French in World War II in N Africa, Italy, France and Germany; mem. French CP 1945–57; Sec. Int. Union of Students, Prague 1951–55; joined Paris Bar 1955; defended many Algerian FLN militants; pvt. legal practice in Algeria 1965–70; activities unknown 1970–78; returned to Paris Bar 1978; appeared for defence, at trial in Lyons of Nazi war criminal Klaus Barbie who was jailed for atrocities committed during World War II, 1987; adviser to several African heads of state. *Publications:* De la stratégie judiciare 1968, Beauté du Crime 1988, La justice est un jeu 1992, Dictionnaire amoureux de la justice 2002, Que sais-je: les erreurs judiciaires 2002. *Address:* 20 rue de Vintimille, 75009 Paris, France (Office). *Telephone:* 1-42-81-51-61 (Office). *Fax:* 1-42-82-90-30 (Office).

VERGHESE, Rev. Thadikkal Paul (see Gregorios, Bishop Paul).

VERHAEGEN, Georges, PhD; Belgian university professor; b. 26 March 1937, Brussels; s. of Col J. Verhaegen and L. Nefcoeur; m. M. van de Keere 1965; two s.; ed Ashbury Coll., Ottawa, Canada, Univ. Libre, Brussels, CNRS, France; Pres. Dept of Chem., Univ. Libre de Bruxelles 1973–75, Dean Faculty of Sciences 1978–81, Prof. 1979–, mem. Governing Body 1975–84, 1986–, Rector 1986–90, Pro-Rector 1990; Pres. Belgian Conf. of Rectors (French speaking) 1986–90, Belgian Nat. Science Foundation 1990, Network of Univs. of Capital Cities of Europe (UNICA) 1989–97; Expert for Univ. Man. (European Univ. Asscn, IBRD, European Comm.) 1993–; winner of three Belgian scientific prizes. *Publications:* around sixty scientific Publs. *Leisure interests:* reading, tennis, handicrafts, travelling. *Address:* C.P. 160/09, Université Libre de Bruxelles, 50 ave. F.D. Roosevelt, B 1050 Brussels (Office); 2 rue du Bois des Aulnes, B 7090 Braine le Comte, Belgium (Home). *Telephone:* (2) 650-24-24 (Office); (6) 763-82-86 (Home). *Fax:* (2) 650-42-32 (Office); (6) 763-82-86 (Home). *E-mail:* gverhaeg@ulb.ac.be (Office).

VERHEUGEN, Günter; German politician; b. 28 April 1944, Bad Kreuznach; s. of Leo Verheugen and Leni Verheugen (née Holzhaüser); m. Gabriele Verheugen (née Schäfer); ed in Cologne and Bonn; trainee, Neue Rhein-Neue Ruhr-Zeitung 1963–65; Head of Public Relations Div., Fed. Ministry of the Interior 1969–74; Head of Analysis and Information Task Force, Fed. Foreign Office 1974–76; Fed. Party Man., Free Democratic Party (FDP) 1977–78; Gen. Sec. FDP 1978–82; joined Sozialdemokratische Partei Deutschlands (SPD) 1982; mem. Bundestag 1983–99, Chair. EU Special Cttee 1992–, mem. Foreign Affairs Cttee 1983–98; Spokesman, SPD Nat. Exec. 1986–87; Ed.-in-Chief Vorwärts (SPD newspaper) 1987–89; Chair. Radio Broadcasting Council, Deutsche Welle 1990–99; Fed. Party Man. SPD 1993–95; Deputy Chair. SPD Parl. Group for Foreign, Security and Devt Policy 1994–97; Chair. Socialist Int. Peace, Security and Disarmament Council 1997–; mem. SPD Nat. Exec.; Minister of State, Fed. Foreign Office 1998–99; EU Commr for Enlargement 1999–; Commdr Distinguished Service Cross (Italy). *Publications:* Eine Zukunft für Deutschland 1980, Das Programm der Liberalen Baden-Baden 1980, Der Ausverkauf-Macht und Verfall der FDP 1984, Apartheid-Südafrika und der Deutschen Interessen am Kap 1986. *Address:* European Commission, 200 rue de la Loi, 1049 Brussels, Belgium (Office). *Telephone:* (2) 298-11-00 (Office). *Fax:* (2) 298-11-99 (Office).

VERHOEVEN, Michael; German screenplay writer, director and producer; b. 13 July 1938, Berlin; s. of the late Paul Verhoeven and Doris Kiesow; m. Senta Berger 1966; two s.; actor stage, TV and cinema 1953–; Head Sentana Filmproduktion GmbH, Munich 1965–; medical studies Munich, Berlin and Worcester, Mass., LA, Calif., USA; worked as doctor Munich –1973; taught at Film Acad. Baden-Württemberg; Jerusalem Film Festival Award, New York Critics Circle Award, BAFTA Award; several other awards for writing, directing and producing; Joseph Neuberger-Medaille 1996; Cross of Merit. *Films:* Dance of Death 1967, "O.K." 1970, Great Escape 1973, Sunday Children 1979, The White Rose 1981, Killing Cars 1985, The Nasty Girl 1989, My Mother's Courage 1995. *Plays (Dir and producer):* The Guns of Mrs Carrar, Believe Love Hope, The Tribades Night, Volpone. *Television (Dir and producer):* The Challenge 1974, The Reason 1978, Dear Melanie 1983, Gunda's Father 1986, Semmelweis MD 1987, The Fast Gerdi 1989, Land of Milk and Honey 1991, Unholy Love 1993, Tabori – Theatre is Life (documentary) 1998, Room to Let 1999, Metamorphosis 2000. *Publications:* Liebe Melanie 1974, Sonntagskinder 1979, Die Weisse Rose 1980. *Address:* Sentana Filmproduktion GmbH, Gebsattelstr. 30, 81541 Munich (Office); Robert-Koch-Str. 10, 82031 Grünwald, Germany (Home). *Telephone:* (89) 4485266 (Office). *Fax:* (89) 4801968 (Office). *E-mail:* sentana@sentana.de (Office).

VERHOEVEN, Paul, PhD; Netherlands film director; b. 18 July 1938, Amsterdam; ed Leiden Univ.; worked as a documentary film-maker for the Dutch navy and then for TV; directed: (shorts) A Lizard too Much 1960, Let's have a Party 1963, The Wrestler 1971; (feature length) Wat zien ik (Business is Business/Any Special Way) 1971, Turks fruit (Turkish Delight) 1973, Keetje Tippel 1975, Soldaat van Oranje 1940–45 (Soldier of Orange/Survival Run) 1978, Spetters 1980, De vierde man (The Fourth Man) 1984, Flesh and Blood 1985, RoboCop 1987, Total Recall 1989, Basic Instinct, Showgirls, Starship Troopers, Hollow Man. *Address:* c/o Beth Swofford, 9830 Wilshire Boulevard, Beverly Hills, CA 90212, USA (Office).

VERHOFSTADT, Guy, LLB; Belgian politician; b. 11 April 1953, Dendermonde; s. of Marcel Verhofstadt and Gaby Stockmans; m. Dominique Verkinderen 1981; one s. one d.; ed Koninklijk Atheneum, Ghent and Univ. of Ghent; Began career as attorney-at-law Ghent Bar; Pres. Flemish Liberal Students' Union, Ghent 1972–73 and 1974–75; Councillor Ghent 1976–82; Political Sec. to Willy De Clerq, Nat. Pres. Party for Freedom and Progress (PVV) 1977–81; mem. House of Reps Ghent-Eeklo Dist 1978–84; Vice-Pres. PVV Ghent-Eeklo Dist Fed. 1979; Nat. Pres. PVV Youth Div. 1979–81, Nat. Pres. PVV 1982–85; Deputy Prime Minister and Minister for the Budget, Scientific Research and the Nat. Plan 1985–88; Pres. of Shadow Cabinet 1988–91; Nat. Pres. of PVV 1989–92, of Flemish Liberals and Democrats (VLD) 1992–95, 1997–99; Minister of State 1995–99; Senator VLD 1995–99, Vice-Pres. of Senate 1995–99; Prime Minister of Belgium July 1999–. *Publications:* Het Radicaal Manifest: Handvest voor een nieuwe liberaale omwenteling 1979, Burgermanifest 1991, De Weg naar politieke vernieuwing: Het tweede burgermanifest 1992, Angst, afgunst en het algemeen belang 1994, De Belgische Ziekte: Diagnose en remedies 1997, In goede banen: VLD-plan voor meer tewerks telling 1999; De vierde golf – een liberaal project voor de nieuwe eeuw 2002; contribs to books and articles in periodicals. *Leisure interests:* cycling, literature, Italy. *Address:* Office of the Prime Minister, 16 rue de la Loi, 1000 Brussels, Belgium (Office). *Telephone:* (2) 501-02-11 (Office). *Fax:* (2) 511-69-53 (Office). *Website:* www.premier.fgov.be (Office).

VERNIER, Jacques; French politician and environmentalist; b. 3 July 1944, Paris; s. of Charles Vernier and Georgette Mangin; m. Bertille Janssen 1968; two s. two d.; ed Ecole Polytechnique and Ecole des Mines, Paris; engineer Service des Mines, Strasbourg 1968–72; Sec.-Gen. Agence de l'eau Seine-Normandie 1972–74; Dir Agence de Bassin Artois-Picardie 1974–83; Mayor of Douai 1983–; Conseiller Régional 1983–90, 1998–; mem. European Parl. 1984–93; Deputy (RPR) to Nat. Ass. 1993–97; Pres. Agence de l'Environnement 1994–97, Ineris 2003–; Chevalier, Légion d'honneur, Officier Ordre nat. du Mérite, Officier Ordre du Palmes académiques. *Publications:* several Publs on environmental matters. *Leisure interests:* tennis, flying aircraft. *Address:* Mairie de Douai, 59500 Douai; 162 quai du Petit Bail, 59500 Douai, France (Home). *Telephone:* (3) 27-93-58-00. *Fax:* (3) 27-96-58-22. *E-mail:* cabinet@ville-douai.fr (Office).

VERNON, Sir (William) Michael, Kt, MA, CCMI; British business executive (retd); b. 17 April 1926, Cheshire; s. of the late Sir Wilfred Vernon; m. 1st Rosheen O'Meara 1952 (divorced 1977); one s.; m. 2nd Jane Kilham-Roberts 1977 (died 1998); m. 3rd Penelope Cuddeford 2001; ed Marlborough Coll. and Trinity Coll. Cambridge; joined Spillers (millers and animal food mfrs) as trainee 1948, Dir 1960–80, Joint Man. Dir 1962–67, Deputy Chair. 1967–68, Chair. 1968–80; Chair. Famous Names Ltd 1981–85, Granville Meat Co. Ltd 1981–94; Dir Electrical and Musical Industries (later EMI) Ltd 1973–80, Strong and Fisher (Holdings) PLC 1980–91; Pres. British Food Export Council 1977–79; Vice-Pres. Royal Nat. Lifeboat Inst. 1975–2001, Deputy Chair. 1980–89, Chair. 1989–96, Life Vice-Pres. 2001. *Leisure interests:* boating, shooting. *Address:* Fyfield Manor, Andover, Hants., SP11 8EN, England (Home).

VEROSTA, Stephan Eduard, LLD; Austrian lawyer and diplomatist; b. 16 Oct. 1909, Vienna; s. of Rudolf Verosta and Elisabeth Verosta (née Szalay); m. Maria Stuehler, MD 1942; two s. one d.; ed Gymnasium, Vienna, Univ. of Vienna and studied in Paris, Geneva and Acad. of Int. Law, The Hague; legal practice 1932–35, Judge 1936; Legal Dept, Austrian Foreign Office 1935–38, Deputy Legal Adviser 1945–48, 1949–51; Counsellor, Austrian Legation, Rome, Minister, Budapest 1951–52; Head of Legal Dept, Foreign Office 1953–56; Amb. to Poland 1956–61; Austrian del. to various int. confs and UN; mem. Perm. Court of Arbitration, The Hague 1957–; Consultant to Foreign Office 1962; Dozent in Int. Law, Univ. of Vienna 1946, Prof. of Int. Law, Jurisprudence and Int. Relations 1962–80; Chair. U.S-Finnish Comm. of Conciliation 1964; mem. Dutch-Fed. German Comm. of Conciliation, Inst. de Droit Int. 1961; mem. Founding Cttee UN Univ. 1972; mem. Appeals Bd, Council of Europe 1974; mem. Int. Law Comm. of UN 1977–82, Council, UN Univ. 1977–83; mem. Austrian Acad. of Science 1964; numerous decorations. *Publications:* Les avis consultatifs de la Cour Permanente de Justice Internationale, etc. 1932, Jean Dumont und seine Bedeutung für das Völkerrecht 1934, Liberale und planwirtschaftliche Handelspolitik (with Gottfried Haberler) 1934, Richterliches Gewohnheitsrecht in Österreich 1942, Die Satzung der Vereinten Nationen 1946, Die internationale Stellung Österreichs von 1938–1947 1947, Die geschichtliche Kontinuität des österreichischen Staates und seine europäische Funktion 1954, Johannes Chrysostomus, Staatsphilosoph 1960, Geschichte des Völkerrechts 1964, International Law in Europe and Western Asia between 100–650 AD 1966, Dauernde Neutralität 1967, Theorie und Realität von Bündnissen Heinrich Lammasch, Karl Renner und der Zweibund 1897-1914 1971, L'histoire de l'Académie de Droit International de la Haye 1973, History of the Law of Nations 1648 to 1815 1984, Kollektivaktionen der Mächte des Europäischen Konzerts bis 1914 1988, Die völkerrechtliche Praxis der Donaumonarchie von 1859 bis 1918, 2 vols (co-author with Ignaz Seidl-Hohenveldern) 1996. *Leisure interest:* collecting old books. *Address:* 1180 Vienna, Hockegasse 15, Austria. *Telephone:* 479-13-48.

VERPLAETSE, Viscount Alfons Remi Emiel; Belgian central banker; b. 19 Feb. 1930, Zulte; m. Odette Vanhee 1954; three s. two d.; ed Katholieke Universiteit Leuven; Nat. Bank of Belgium 1953–81; Office of the Prime Minister 1981–88; Dir Nat. Bank of Belgium 1988–, Deputy Gov. 1988–89, Gov. 1989–99, Hon. Gov. 1999–; Hon. Gov. and Vice-Pres. Higher Finance Council, Admin. BIS, Basle; Gov. IMF 1989–99; Deputy Gov. IBRD 1989–99, IFC 1989–99; Grand Officier, Ordre de la Couronne (Belgium) 1991, Grande Ufficiale, Ordine al Merito (Italy) 1986, Officier, Légion d'Honneur 1994. *Address:* c/o National Bank of Belgium, Boulevard de Berlaimont 14, 1000 Brussels (Office); Schaveyslaan 25, 1650 Beersel, Belgium (Home).

VERRETT, Shirley; American soprano singer; b. 31 May 1931, New Orleans; d. of Leon Verrett and Elvira Verrett; m. Louis Lomonaco 1963; one d.; ed Juilliard School of Music, New York; Prof. of Voice, School of Music, Univ. of Mich. 1996–; operatic début as mezzo-soprano taking title role of Carmen, Spoleto Festival 1962; same role for début at Bolshoi Opera, Moscow 1963, New York City Opera 1966, Florence 1968, Metropolitan Opera, New York 1968; sang at Covent Garden, London in roles of Ulrica (Un Ballo in Maschera) 1966, Amneris (Aida) 1967, Eboli (Don Carlos) 1968, Azucena (Il Trovatore) 1970; début at San Carlo, Naples as Elisabetta (Maria Stuarda) 1969, at La Scala, Milan as Delilah (Samson et Dalila) 1970, at Vienna Staatsoper as Eboli 1970, at Teatro Liceo, Barcelona as Eboli 1971, at Paris Opera as Azucena 1972; other mezzo-soprano roles in Orfeo (Gluck), as Dido (Les Troyens), Judith (Bluebeard's Castle), Neocle (Siege of Corinth), Adalgisa (Norma, first performance at Metropolitan, New York 1976); made début as soprano in title role of La Favorita, Dallas Civic Opera 1971; début at San Francisco Opera in title role of L'Africaine 1972; first artist to sing roles of both Dido and Cassandra in one single full-length production of Les Troyens, Metropolitan 1973; other soprano roles: Lady Macbeth, La Scala 1975 and with La Scala at Kennedy Center, Washington, DC 1976, also with Opera Co. of Boston 1976; title role of Norma, Metropolitan Opera 1976 (in the same season took mezzo-soprano role of Adalgisa, being the first singer since Grisi to sing both roles); New Prioress in Dialogues of the Carmelites, Metropolitan 1977; now sings only soprano roles; Amellia, La Scala 1978, title role in Favorita, Metropolitan 1978; in Tosca at Metropolitan, New York 1978; début appearance at Opera Bastille, Paris 1990; appeared in film Maggio Musicale 1990, as Nettie Fowler in Broadway production of Carousel 1994–95; frequent appearances with U.S. and European opera houses, with U.S. symphony orchestras; has appeared as soloist on Milan's RAI; was subject of BBC TV feature Profiles in Music 1971, of documentary Black Diva 1985; Dr. hc (Holy Cross Coll., Worcester, Mass., Northeastern Univ.); Commdr des Arts et des Lettres 1984. *Address:* Herbert Breslin Inc., 6124 Liebig Avenue, Bronx, NY 10471 (Office); School of Music, University of Michigan, 1100 Baits Drive, Ann Arbor, MI 48109, USA.

VERSACE, Donatella; Italian designer; b. 1955, Reggio Calabria; d. of Antonio Versace and Francesca Versace; sister of the late Gianni Versace; m. Paul Beck; one s. one d.; joined Versace 1978, fmrly overseer of advertising and public relations, accessories designer, children's collection designer, sole designer Versus and Isante lines; Creative Dir Gianni Versace Group 1997–. *Address:* c/o Keeble Cavaco and Duka Inc., 450 West 15th Street, Suite 604, New York, NY 10011, USA.

VERSHBOW, Alexander R., MA; American diplomatist; b. 3 July 1952, Boston; s. of Arthur E. Vershbow and Charlotte Z. Vershbow; m. Lisa K. Vershbow 1976; two s.; ed Yale Coll. and Russian Inst., Columbia Univ.; joined Foreign Service 1977, Bureau of Politico-Military Affairs 1977–79, US Embassy, Moscow 1979–81, Office of Soviet Union Affairs 1981–85, US Embassy, London 1985–88; adviser US Del. to SALT II and START negotiations; Dir State Dept's Office of Soviet Union Affairs 1988–91; US Deputy Perm Rep. to NATO and Chargé d'affaires US Mission 1991–93; Prin. Deputy Asst Sec. of State for European and Canadian Affairs (responsibilities covered the Balkan conflict) 1993–94; Special Asst to the Pres. and Sr Dir for European Affairs at Nat. Security Council 1995–97 (worked on US policy which laid foundations of the Dayton Peace Agreement, adaptation and enlargement of NATO and its new relationship with Russia); Perm. Rep. to NATO Jan. 1998–2001; Amb. to Russian Fed. July 2001–; Anatoly Sharansky Freedom Award, Union of Councils of Soviet Jews 1990, first Joseph J. Kruzel Award for contribs to the cause of peace, US Dept of Defense 1997, Distinguished Award for Work at NATO, US State Dept 2001. *Publications:* articles on arms control, speeches on NATO issues. *Leisure interests:* music, theatre. *Address:* American Embassy, B. Devyatinskii per. 8, Moscow 121099, Russia (Office). *Telephone:* (095) 728-51-80 (Office). *Fax:* (095) 728-51-59 (Office). *E-mail:* pamoscow@pd.state.gov. *Website:* www.usembassy.ru (Office).

VERSTRAETE, Baron Marc, MD, PhD, FRCP, FACP; Belgian professor of medicine; b. 1 April 1925, Bruges; s. of Louis Verstraete and Jeanne Coppin; m. Bernadette Moyersoen 1955; one s. four d.; ed Leuven and Oxford Univs. and Cornell Univ. Medical Coll., New York; Lecturer, Univ. of Leuven 1957,

Asst Prof. 1961, Assoc. Prof. 1963, Prof. 1968–, Dir Centre for Molecular and Vascular Biology; Visiting Prof., Harvard Medical School, Boston, USA; Past-Pres. Royal Acad. of Medicine of Belgium; mem. Acad. of Medicine of South Africa and of Argentina; Dr hc (Edinburgh, Córdoba (Argentina), Bologna, Bordeaux, London). *Publications:* Arterial Hypertension 1966, 1972, Haemostatic Drugs 1977, Methods in Angiology 1980, Haemostasis 1980, Thrombosis 1982, Thrombolysis 1985, Thrombosis and Haemostasis 1987, Thrombosis in Cardiovascular Disorders 1992; numerous articles in scientific journals. *Leisure interests:* reading, skiing, swimming, tennis. *Address:* Centre for Molecular and Vascular Biology, Campus Gasthuisberg, University of Leuven, Herestraat 29, 3000 Leuven (Office); Minderbroedersstraat 29, 3000 Leuven, Belgium (Home). *Telephone:* (16) 34-57-75 (Office); (16) 22-66-74 (Home). *Fax:* (16) 34-59-90 (Office); (16) 22-66-74 (Home). *E-mail:* marc.verstraete@med.kuleuven.ac.be (Office).

VERTINSKAYA, Anastasiya Aleksandrovna; Russian actress; b. 19 Dec. 1944, Moscow; d. of Aleksander Vertinsky and Lidiya Vertinskaya; one s.; ed Schukin Theatre School; actress Theatre Sovremennik 1969–80, Moscow Art Theatre 1980–90; works as theatre teacher in Oxford, Switzerland (European Film School), France (Comédie Française); f. Russian Drama troupe in Paris; Dir production Mirage or The Route of The Russian Pierrot, Chekhov, Act III (with A. Kalyagin); cinema début 1961; Dir Benefit Fund for Actors 1996; Honoured Artist of Russia 1980, People's Artist of Russia 1988. *Films include:* Red Sails 1961, A Man-Amphibia 1962, Hamlet 1964, War and Peace 1967, Anna Karenina 1968, Do Not Grieve! 1969, A Man Before His Time 1973, Master and Margarita 1994, Gad-Fly, Occurence with Polynin, Bremen Musicians 1999 and others. *Theatre:* You Can Only Dream about Rest 1962, Princess Turaudot 1964, Naked King 1967, Craftsmen 1967, Seagull 1968, 1980, Norodovoltsy 1968, Decembrists 1969, Bolmsheviks 1970, Twelfth Night 1969, Provincial Jokes 1970, The Cherry Orchard 1973, Echelon 1975, Do Not Part with Beloved Once 1976, Valentin and Valentina 1972, Tartuffe 1981, The Living Corpse 1982, In Private with All 1983, The Ball at the Candles 1984, Uncle Vanya 1986, Pearl Zinaida 1988, The Mirage 1989. *Television:* (films) Unnamed Star 1989, Theft and others. *Address:* Benefit Fund for Actors, Office 540, Arbat str., 121002 Moscow (Office); Malaya Dmitrovka str. 31/22, Apt. 38, 103006 Moscow, Russia (Home). *Telephone:* (095) 248-30-22 (Office). *Fax:* (095) 248-30-22 (Office).

VERWAAYEN, Ben, LLM; Netherlands telecommunications executive; b. Feb. 1952, Utrecht; m.; two c.; ed State Univ. of Utrecht; various man. posts with ITT Nederland BV 1975–88, rising to Gen. Man.; joined Koninklijke PTT Nederland (KPN) 1996, Chair. Unisource European Venture 1996–97, Pres. and Man. Dir PTT Telecom 1997–98; Exec. Vice-Pres. of Int. Div., Lucent Technologies Inc. Sept.–Oct. 1997, Exec. Vice-Pres. and COO 1997–99, Vice-Chair. Man. Bd 1999–2002; CEO British Telecommunications (BT) PLC Jan. 2002–; mem. Advisory Council, ING; mem. Bd Astro All Asia Networks (ASTRO), Health Center Internet Services Inc. *Leisure interest:* Arsenal football club. *Address:* British Telecommunications PLC, Centre, 81 Newgate Street, London, EC1A 7AJ, England (Office). *Telephone:* (20) 7356-5000 (Office). *Fax:* (20) 7356-5520 (Office). *Website:* www.bt.com (Office).

VERWILGHEN, Marc, BL; Belgian politician and lawyer; b. 21 Sept. 1952, Dendermonde; ed Free Univ. of Brussels; practising lawyer 1975–; Deputy 1991–99; Senator 1999–; Chair. Comms. of Inquiry on Dutroux-Nihoul and on Missing and Murdered Children 1996–98; Chair. Chamber Comm. on Justice; mem. Vlaamse Liberalen en Demokraten-Partij van de Burger (PVV-VLD); Minister of Justice July 1999–; Dr hc (Univ. of Ghent) 1999. *Publications:* Het V-Plan 1999, Over bruggen bouwen 1999. *Address:* Ministry of Justice, 115, boulevard de Waterloo, 1000 Brussels, Belgium (Office). *Telephone:* (2) 542-79-11 (Office). *Fax:* (2) 538-07-67 (Office). *Website:* www.just.fgov.be (Office).

VESHNYAKOV, Aleksander Albertovich, CAND.JUR.SC.; Russian government official and lawyer; b. 24 Nov. 1952, Baikalovo, Arkhangelsk Region; m.; two c.; ed Arkhangelsk Navigational School, Leningrad Higher School of Marine Eng, Leningrad Higher Communist Party School, Diplomatic Acad., Russian Ministry of Foreign Affairs; worked for Northern Sea steamship line, Arkhangelsk 1973–87; Sec. Arkhangelsk City CP Cttee 1987–90; Deputy Chair. Council of Repub. Supreme Soviet Russian Fed. 1990–91; Chair. sub-comm., Comm. for Transportation, Communications, Information Science and Space, Council of Repub. 1991–93; Econs Adviser Marine Transport Dept, Ministry of Transportation 1993–94; Consultant Information and Analysis Dept, Cen. Election Comm. 1994, Sec. 1995–99, Chair. March 1999–; Medal in Commemoration of 850th Anniversary of Moscow 2000, Rank IV Order for Service to the Fatherland 2000. *Address:* Central Election Commission, Bolshoi Cherkassky per. 9, 103012 Moscow, Russia (Office). *Telephone:* (095) 206-99-66 (Office). *Fax:* (095) 956-39-30 (Office). *E-mail:* intdiv@A5.kiam.ru (Office). *Website:* www.fci.ru (Office).

VESSEY, Gen. John W., Jr, DSC, DSM; American army officer; b. 22 June 1922, Minneapolis, Minn.; s. of John William and Emily (née Roche) Vessey; m. Avis C. Funk; two s. one d.; enlisted in Minn. Nat. Guard 1939; commissioned 2nd Lt, Field Artillery, Anzio May 1944; served successively with 34th Infantry Div., N Africa and Italy, 4th Infantry and 3rd Armoured Div., Germany, 25th Infantry Div., S Viet Nam; promoted Gen. 1976; Commdr US Forces, S Korea 1976–79; Army Vice-Chief of Staff 1979–82; Chair. Joint Chiefs of Staff 1982–85; Presidential Emissary to Hanoi 1987–93; Chair. Bd Center for Preventive Action (Council on Foreign Relations) 1995–; mem.

Defense Science Bd 1987–90, 1992–2000, Defense Policy Bd 1990–93, Bd of Dirs Martin Marietta, Illinois Tool Works, Nat. Computer Syst., United Services Life Insurance, Nat. Flag Day Foundation, Youth Services USA, Advisory Bd Gen. Atomics; Trustee AAL Mutual Funds; Legion of Merit, Bronze Star, Air Medal, Jt Services Commendation Medal, Purple Heart, Presidential Medal of Freedom 1992 and other decorations. *Address:* 27650 Little Whitefish Road, Garrison, MN 56450, USA. *Telephone:* (320) 692-4488. *Fax:* (320) 692-4939.

VEST, Charles Marstiller, MSE, PhD, FAAS; American university president; b. 9 Sept. 1941, Morgantown, W Va; s. of Marvin Vest and Winifred Buzzard; m. Rebecca McCue 1963; one s. one d.; ed W Va Univ. and Univ. of Mich.; Asst Prof., Assoc. Prof. Univ. of Mich. Ann Arbor 1968–77, Prof. of Mechanical Eng 1977–90, Assoc. Dean of Academic Affairs, Coll. of Eng 1981–86, Dean, Coll. of Eng 1986–89, Provost, Vice-Pres. for Academic Affairs 1989–90; Pres. MIT, Mass. 1990–; Visiting Assoc. Prof. Stanford Univ., Calif. 1974–75; Fellow, Optical Soc. of America, American Acad. of Arts and Sciences. *Publications:* Holographic Interferometry 1979; articles in professional journals. *Address:* Office of the President, Massachusetts Institute of Technology, 77 Massachusetts Avenue, Cambridge, MA 02139, USA.

VESTERDORF, Bo; Danish judge and international official; b. 1945; fmr Jurist-Linguist Court of Justice; fmr Admin. Ministry of Justice, later Head Constitutional and Admin. Law Dept, then apptd. Dir Ministry of Justice; fmr Legal Attaché with Perm. Representation of Denmark to European Communities; fmr temporary judge Eastern Regional Court; fmr mem. Human Rights Steering Cttee, then Bureau, Council of Europe; Judge Court of First Instance of the European Communities 1989–, Pres. 1998–. *Address:* Court of the First Instance of the European Communities, blvd Konrad Adenauer, 2925 Luxembourg, Luxembourg (Office). *Telephone:* 4303-1 (Office). *Fax:* 4303-2100 (Office). *Website:* www.curia.eu.int (Office).

VESTEY, Edmund Hoyle, DL, FRSA, F.C.I.T.; British business executive (retd); b. 19 June 1932; s. of Ronald Arthur Vestey; m. Anne Moubray Scoones 1960; four s.; ed Eton Coll.; 2nd Lt Queens Bays 1951; Lt City of London Yeomanry; Dir Vestey Group Ltd –2000; Chair. Albion Insurance Co. 1970–91, Blue Star Line 1971–95, Union Int. PLC and assoc. cos. 1988–91; Pres. Essex Co. Scout Council 1979–87, Gen. Council of British Shipping 1981–82; Pres. Chamber of Shipping 1992–94; Chair., Masters of Foxhounds Asscn 1992–96; High Sheriff, Essex 1977; DL Essex 1978–91, Suffolk 1991–. *Leisure interest:* fox-hunting. *Address:* Little Thurlow Hall, Haverhill, Suffolk, England.

VETCHÝ, Vladimír, Dr rer. nat, CSc; Czech politician; b. 8 May 1949, Třebíč; m. Alena Vetchá; one s. one d.; ed Masaryk Univ., Brno, Pedagogue Mil. Acad., Brno; mem. Czech Social Democratic Party 1991–; various functions 1989–98 including mem. Council, Brno, mem. Czecho-Moravian Chamber of Labour Unions; Minister of Defence 1998–2000; Lecturer Mil. Acad. Brno. *Leisure interests:* sport, especially basketball, volleyball. *Address:* Ministry of Defence, Tychonova 1, 160 00 Prague 6, Czech Republic (Office). *Telephone:* (2) 20201111. *Website:* www.army.cz (Office).

VEYRAT, Marc; French chef and restaurant owner; b. 1950; worked as shepherd before opening first restaurant aged 29; Owner and Chef restaurants L'Auberge de l'Eridan, Annecy 1987–, La Ferme de Mon Père Megève 1999– (both received three stars from Michelin and GaultMillau magazine 2003). *Address:* c/o Christina Egal, Press Relations, 17 rue des Erables, 78150 Rocquencourt, France (Office). *Website:* www.marcveyrat.com (Office).

VÉZINA, Monique; Canadian politician; b. July 1935, Rimouski; m.; four c.; Dir and Chair. Fédération des caisses populaires Desjardins du Bas Saint-Laurent; Chair. Gérardin-Vaillancourt Foundation; Sec. and Dir Confédération des caisses populaires Desjardins du Québec; Minister for External Relations 1984–86, of Supply and Services 1986–87, of State (Transport) 1987–88, of State for Employment and Immigration 1988–93, for Sr Citizens 1988–93, for External Affairs Jan.–Nov. 1993; mem. Bd of Dirs., Rimouski Chamber of Commerce, Soc. immobilière du Québec; fmr Chair. Comm. on Secondary Educ.; fmr Vice-Pres. Régie de l'assurance automobile du Québec; fmr mem. Superior Council of Educ.; mem. Progressive Conservative Party. *Address:* c/o Progressive Conservative Party of Canada, 275 Slater Street, Suite 501, Ottawa, Ont., K1P 5H9; 408 Notre Dame East, Apartment 203, Montréal, Québec, H2Y 1C9, Canada (Home).

VIAL, Martin Marie-Charles François; French civil servant and economist; b. 8 Feb. 1954, Lyon; s. of René Vial and Thérèse Giuliani; m. Nelly Waldmann 1978; two s. two d.; ed Lycée Ampère, Inst. of Political Studies Paris; Prof. of Econ. and Reform Inst. of Tech. of Commerce Algiers 1977–78, Prof. of Finance Higher School of Applied Commercial Sciences 1978–82; with Office of Gen. Compatibility and Budget for External Services 1982–84, also Head; Head of Office of the Treasury and Financial Man. 1984–86; with Office of Banks and Nat. Financial Cos. 1986–88, tech. adviser Postal sector 1988–89, charged with reform of Post, Telecommunications and Broadcasting (PTT) 1989–91, Jt Dir office of Minister for Post, Telecommunications and Space 1991, Dir Ministry of Post and Telecommunications 1992–93, Jt Dir for Space Equipment, Accommodation and Transport 1991, Dir 1991–92; Pres. Aéropostale 1993–97; Dir La Poste 1997–2000, Pres. 2000–02; mem. Cen. Cttee Union of Air Transport and Nat. Fed. of Aviation Trade 1994–96, Pres.

1996–. *Publication:* La Lettre et la toile 2000. *Leisure interests:* tennis, skiing. *Address:* La Poste, 4 quai du Point du Jour, 92777 Boulogne Billancourt cedex (Office); 2 rue Alençon, 75015 Paris, France (Home).

VIARDO, Vladimir Vladimirovich, DJur; Russian pianist; b. 14 Nov. 1949; m. Natalia Viardo; two s.; ed Moscow State Conservatory; Asst Prof., Prof., Moscow State Conservatory 1975–; Grand Prix Marguerite Long Int. Competition; Gold Medal and 1st Prize, Van Clibern Int. Competition, USA 1973; resident in USA 1988–; Prof. Univ. of N Texas 1988–; Visiting Prof. Moscow State Conservatory 1998–2000. *Performances:* played with conductors Mehta, Kitayenko, Maazel, Spivakov, Comissiona, Penderecki; toured in major European, N American and Canadian cities, Asia and S Africa, Israel, Cen. and S America. *Address:* 457 Piermont Road, Cresskill, NJ 07626, USA. *Telephone:* (201) 8161339 (Home). *Fax:* (201) 8945352 (Home).

VIBE, Kjeld, LLD; Norwegian diplomatist; b. 5 Oct 1927, Stavanger; s. of Christopher Andreas Vibe and Thordis Amundsen; m. Beate Meyer 1953; one s. three d.; ed Univ. of Oslo; entered foreign service 1954; Sec., Del. to NATO and OEEC, Paris 1956–59; First Sec. Ministry of Foreign Affairs 1959–62; Temp. Head, Norwegian Mil. Mission, Berlin 1961; Personal Sec. to Minister of Foreign Affairs 1962–65; Counsellor, Norwegian Embassy, Wash. 1965–69; Deputy Dir-Gen. for Political Affairs, Ministry of Foreign Affairs 1969–72, Dir-Gen. 1972–77; Amb., Perm. Rep. to NATO 1977–84; Sec.-Gen. Ministry of Foreign Affairs 1984–89; Amb. to USA 1989–97; mem. Norwegian Govt.'s Comm. on Freedom of Speech 1996–2002; Commdr with Star of the Royal Norwegian Order of Sanct Olav; several foreign decorations. *Publications:* regular contribs. on foreign affairs to newspaper Aften Posten 1996–2002. *Leisure interests:* skiing, history, music. *Address:* Holmenkollv 35, Oslo 0376, Norway (Home). *Telephone:* 22-14-98-36 (Home).

VICARI, Andrew; British artist; b. 20 April 1938, Port Talbot, Wales; s. of Vittorio Vicari and Italia Bertani; ed Slade School of Art and Univ. Coll. London; works held in many perm. and pvt. collections including Dallas Museum of Fine Arts, Nat. Library of Wales, Museum of Tel-Aviv, Contemporary Arts Soc. of GB, Columbus Museum of Fine Arts, USA, Pezzo Pozzoli Museum, Milan, Petit Palais Museum of Modern Art, Geneva; official painter of King and Govt of Saudi Arabia; Fellow London Zoological Soc.; Freedom of the City of London 2002, Liveryman of Wales 2002, Liveryman of the Guilds of London 2002; European Beaux Arts Prize 1995, Chevalier, Order of Merit (Monaco), Brig. d'honneur, Compagnie Républicaine de Sécurité (France). *Exhibitions include:* New Burlington Galleries, London 1955, Grand Palais des Champs Elysées, Paris 1957, 1959, The Last Supper, Foyle's Art Gallery, London 1960, Columbus Museum of Art, Ohio 1963, Harrison Library, NY 1963, Circola della Stampa, Rome 1965, The Triumph of the Bedouin, Riyadh 1974–78, Vicari Retrospective, Geneva 1984, Monaco 1991, Beijing 1995, Triptych of Gen. de Gaulle, Versailles 1994, Vicari Exhbn, St Petersburg 1995, Retrospective, Palais des Arts, Beijing. *Publication:* Triumph of the Bedouin 1984. *Address:* c/o The East India Club, 16 St James's Square, London, SW1Y 4LH, England. *Telephone:* (7976) 310352 (Office). *Fax:* (709) 200-6234 (Office). *E-mail:* executive@andrewvicariworld .com (Office). *Website:* www.andrewvicariworld.com (Office).

VICKERS, John Stuart, FBA, MA, DPhil; British economist; b. 7 July 1958, Eastbourne; s. of Aubrey Vickers and Kay Vickers; m. Maureen Freed 1991; one s. two d.; ed Eastbourne Grammar School and Oriel Coll. Oxford; Fellow, All Souls Coll. Oxford 1979–84, 1991–; Shell UK Oil 1979–81; Roy Harrod Fellow, Nuffield Coll. Oxford 1984–90; Drummond Prof. of Political Econ. Univ. of Oxford 1991–98; Chief Economist, Bank of England 1998–2000; Dir Gen. of Fair Trading 2000–; Fellow Econometric Soc. 1998–; Visiting Lecturer, Princeton Univ. 1988, Harvard Univ. 1989, 1990; Visiting Prof. London Business School 1996. *Publications:* Privatization: An Economic Analysis (jtly.) 1988, Regulatory Reform (jtly.) 1994; articles on innovation, competition, regulation, industrial org. etc. *Address:* Office of Fair Trading, Fleetbank House, 2–6 Salisbury Square, London, EC4Y 8JX, England (Office). *Telephone:* (20) 7211-8920 (Office). *Fax:* (20) 7211-8966 (Office). *Website:* www.oft .gov.uk (Office).

VICKERS, Jon, CC; Canadian tenor; b. 29 Oct. 1926, Prince Albert, Saskatchewan; s. of William Vickers and Myrle Mossip; m. 1st Henrietta Outerbridge 1953 (died 1991); three s. two d.; m. 2nd Judith Stewart 1993; began career as concert and opera singer in Canada; joined Royal Opera House, Covent Garden (London) 1957; sang at Bayreuth Festival, Vienna State Opera, San Francisco, Chicago Lyric Opera, Metropolitan Opera, La Scala, Milan, Paris Opera, Boston, Buenos Aires, Athens, Ottawa, Houston, Dallas, Hamburg, Berlin, Munich, Athens Festival, Salzburg Festival, Festival of Orange, Tanglewood Festival, Rio de Janeiro; mem. Royal Acad. Music, London; Hon. LLD (Sask.); Hon. CLD (Bishop's Univ.); Mus.D. (Brandon Univ., Univ. of Western Ont.), LLD (Univ. of Guelph), Civ. L.D. (Univ. of Laval), DMus (Univ. of Ill.); Critics Award, London 1978, Grammy Award 1979. *Films include:* Carmen, Pagliacci, Norma, Otello. *Recordings:* Messiah, Otello, Aida, Die Walküre, Samson and Delilah, Fidelio, Italian Arias, Verdi Requiem, Peter Grimes, Das Lied von der Erde, Les Troyens, Tristan und Isolde; Enock Arden (poem by Alfred Lord Tennyson, piano played by Mark Ammelain). *Address:* Collingtree, 18 Riddells Bay Road, Warwick, WK 04, Bermuda.

VICTOR, Ed(ward), MLitt; British literary agent; b. 9 Sept. 1939, New York, USA; s. of Jack Victor and the late Lydia Victor; m. 1st Mecheline Dinah

Samuels 1963 (divorced); two s.; m. 2nd Carol Lois Ryan; one s.; ed Dartmouth Coll. USA, Pembroke Coll., Univ. of Cambridge; Arts Book Ed., then Editorial Dir Weidenfeld & Nicholson 1964–67; Editorial Dir Jonathan Cape Ltd 1967–71; Sr Ed. Alfred A. Knopf Inc., NY 1972–73, literary agent and Dir John Farquharson Ltd 1974–76; f. Ed Victor Agency 1977; mem. Council Aids Crisis Trust 1986–98; Vice-Chair. Almeida Theatre 1994– (Dir 1993–); Trustee, The Arts Foundation 1991–. *Publications include:* The Obvious Diet (with Nigella Lawson) 2001. *Leisure interests:* golf, tennis, travel, opera. *Address:* Ed Victor Ltd., 6 Bayley Street, Bedford Square, London WC1B 3HB (Office); 10 Cambridge Gate, Regents Park, London NW1 4JX, England (Home). *Telephone:* (20) 7304-4100 (Office); (20) 7224-3030 (Home). *Fax:* (20) 7304-4111 (Office); (20) 7935-3096 (Home). *E-mail:* ed@edvictor.com.

VID, Leonard Bernhardovich, CAND. ECON.; Russian banker; b. 9 Nov. 1931, Zaporozhye, Ukraine; m.; two d.; ed Moscow Inst. of Non-ferrous Metals and Gold; with Norilsk Ore Mining and Processing enterprise, master then Deputy Dir 1955–77; First Deputy Chair. USSR State Planning Cttee 1977–91; Deputy Minister of Econs of USSR 1991–92; Dir Cen. of Econ. State of Affairs at Russian Govt 1992–95, Chair. Bd Alfa-Bank 1996–; Exec. Dir Our Home Russia Movt 1995–96; mem. Comm. on Co-ordinating State Programme of Transition to the Int. System of Statistics and Accountancy. *Address:* Alfa-Bank, Mashi Poryvayevoy str. 11, Moscow, Russia (Office). *Telephone:* (095) 208-8-42 (Office). *Fax:* (095) 913-7142 (Office). *Website:* www .alfabank.com (Office).

VIDAL, Gore; American writer; b. 3 Oct. 1925, West Point, NY; s. of Eugene L. Vidal and Nina (née Gore) Vidal; ed Phillips Acad., Exeter, NH; served in U.S. Army 1943–46; Drama Critic Reporter (magazine) 1959, Democratic-Liberal Cand. for U.S. Congress from New York 1960; Pres. Kennedy's Advisory Council on the Arts 1961–63; Co-Chair. People's Party 1970–72; Edgar Allen Poe Award for Television 1955; Hon. Citizen, Ravello, Italy 1983; Chevalier Ordre nat. des Arts et des Lettres. *Short stories:* A Thirsty Evil 1956. *Plays:* Visit to a Small Planet 1956, The Best Man 1960, Romulus 1962, Weekend 1968, An Evening with Richard Nixon 1972, Gore Vidal's Lincoln 1988. *TV Includes:* Dress Gray, NBC 1988, Gore Vidal's Lincoln, NBC 1989, Billy the Kid, TNT 1990. *Film scripts and adaptations:* Wedding Breakfast, I Accuse 1958, Suddenly Last Summer 1959, The Best Man (Cannes Critics' Prize 1964), Is Paris Burning? 1966, The Last of the Mobile Hotshots 1970. *Essays:* Rocking the Boat 1963, Reflections upon a Sinking Ship 1969, Homage to Daniel Shays 1972, Matters of Fact and Fiction: Essays 1973–76, 1977, The Second American Revolution 1982, Armageddon? 1987, At Home: Essays 1982–88 1988, A View from the Diners Club: Essays 1987–1991 1991, United States: Essays 1952–1992 1993 (Nat. Book Award), Virgin Islands: A Dependency of United States Essays 1992–97 1997, The Last Empire 2001; acted in film Bob Roberts 1992; writes thrillers under pseudonym Edgar Box. *Memoirs:* Screening History 1992, Palimpsest 1995; criticism in Partisan Review, The Nation, New York Review of Books, Times Literary Supplement. *Novels:* Williwaw 1946, In a Yellow Wood 1947, The City and the Pillar 1948, The Season of Comfort 1949, A Search for the King 1950, Dark Green, Bright Red 1950, The Judgment of Paris 1952, Messiah 1954, Julian 1964, Washington, DC 1967, Myra Breckinridge 1968, Two Sisters 1970, Burr 1972, Myron 1974, 1876 1976, Kalki 1978, Creation 1980 (Prix Deauville), Duluth 1983, Lincoln 1984, Empire 1987, Hollywood 1990, Live from Golgotha 1992, With Honors 1994, Dark Green, Dark Red 1995, The Season of Conflict 1996, The Essential Vidal 1998, The Smithsonian Institution: a novel 1998, The Golden Age 2000.

VIDAL, HE Cardinal Ricardo; Philippine ecclesiastic; b. 6 Feb. 1931, Mogpog, Marinduque; s. of Fructuoso Vidal and Natividad Jamin; ordained 1956; consecrated Bishop (Titular Church of Claterna) 1971; Archbishop of Lipa 1973–82, of Cebu 1982–; cr. Cardinal 1985; Chair. Episcopal Comm. on Clergy; mem. Congregation for the Evangelization of Peoples, Congregation for Catholic Educ., Pontifical Council for Pastoral Assistance to Health Care Workers. *Leisure interests:* walking, classical music, gardening. *Address:* 234 D. Jakosalem Str., P.O. Box 52, Cebu City 6000, Philippines. *Telephone:* (32) 2533382. *Fax:* (32) 2544458. *E-mail:* rcv@cebu.pworld.net.ph (Office).

VIDAL-NAQUET, Pierre Emmanuel; French historian (retd); b. 23 July 1930, Paris; s. of Lucien Vidal-Naquet and Marguerite Valabrègue; m. Geneviève Railhac 1952; three s.; ed Lycées Périer, Carnot, Henri-IV and Thiers, Faculté des lettres, Paris; teacher Lycée d'Orléans 1955–56; Asst Faculté des lettres Univ. de Caen 1955–60, Univ. de Lille 1961–62; research Asst CNRS 1962–64; lecturer Faculté des lettres Univ. of Lyon 1964–66; Deputy Dir of Studies School of Higher Studies in Social Sciences 1966–69, Dir of Studies 1969–97; Corresp. FBA; Dr hc (Free Univ. of Brussels) 1987, (Dublin) 1989, (Bristol) 1999; Officier Légion d'honneur, Commdr Order of Phoenix, Greece; Eschilo Oro, Syracuse 1986; Grand Prix des sciences humaines de la Ville de Paris 1996. *Publications include:* L'Affaire Audin 1958, La Raison d'Etat 1962, Torture–Cancer of Democracy 1963, Flavius Josèphe ou du bon usage de la trahison 1977, Le Chasseur noir 1981, Les Assassins de la mémoire 1987, Atlas historique 1987, Face à la raison de l'Etat: Un historien dans la guerre d'Algérie 1989, La Démocratie grecque vue d'ailleurs 1990, Les Juifs, la mémoire et le présent (2 Vols) 1981, 1991, Le Trait empoisonné, Réflexions sur l'affaire de Jean Moulin 1993, Réflexions sur le génocide 1995, Mémoires: la Brisure et l'attente (Vol. 1) 1995, Le Trouble et la lumière (Vol. 2) 1998, Le monde d'Homère 2000, Los grecs, les historiers la démocratie 2000, Le miroir brisé, Tragédie grecque et politique 2001,

Fragments sur l'art antique 2002. *Address:* Centre Louis Gernet, 10 rue Monsieur le Prince, 75006 Paris (Office); 72 blvd de la Villette, 75019 Paris, France (Home). *Telephone:* 1-44-41-46-50 (Office). *Fax:* 1-44-41-46-61 (Office).

VIDELA, Lt-Gen. Jorge Rafael; Argentine fmr Head of State and army officer; b. 2 Aug. 1925, Mercedes, Prov. of Buenos Aires; m. Alicia Hartridge; six c.; ed Nat. Mil. Coll. and War School; commissioned in Infantry 1944; Lt in Vigilance Co., Ministry of War 1946; with Motorized Army Regt 1947–48; Nat. Mil. Coll. 1948; Student, War School, with rank of Army Capt. 1951–54; Staff Officer, Nat. Mil. Coll. 1954–56; Adviser to Office of Mil. Attaché, Washington, DC 1956–58; Staff Officer, Army Gen. Command 1962–65, 1966–68; Col 1965; engaged on course in Strategy, Army Centre of Higher Studies 1965–66; Lt-Col, Chief of Cadet Corps 1968; Second in Command and Chief of Staff, Fifth Infantry Brigade 1968–70; Chief of Operations, Third Army Corps 1970–71; Brig., Head of Nat. Mil. Coll. 1971–73; Chief of Army Gen. Staff 1973–75, of Joint High Command 1975; C-in-C of Army 1975–78; led coup to depose Pres. María Perón (q.v.) March 1976; Pres. of Argentina 1976–81; fmr mem. Inter-American Defence Bd, Washington, DC; arrested Aug. 1984, on trial for human rights offences 1985, sentenced to life imprisonment Dec. 1985, granted pardon Dec. 1990.

VIDENOV, Jan Vassilev; Bulgarian politician; b. 22 March 1959, Plovdiv; m.; one c.; ed Moscow State Inst. for Int. Relations; specialist with Biotech Corpn and Autoelectronics; mem. Supreme Council of Presidency, Bulgarian Socialist Party (BSP) 1990, Chair. 1994; mem. Parl.; Prime Minister of Bulgaria 1995–97.

VIEGAS FILHO, José; Brazilian politician and diplomatist; m. 1st Rosa Maria Amorim (died 1999); three c.; m. 2nd Erika Stockholm; joined Instituto Rio Branco 1964; apptd consul-aid in New York 1969; responsible for Brazilian businesses in Cuba 1987–90; apptd Chief Dept of Int. Bodies within Foreign Office 1992; Amb. to Denmark 1995–98, to Peru 1998–2001, to Russia 2001–02; Minister of Defence Jan. 2003–. *Leisure interests:* literature, translation. *Address:* Ministry of Defence, Esplanada dos Ministérios, Bloco Q, 70049-900 Brasília, Brazil (Office). *Telephone:* (61) 223-5356 (Office). *Fax:* (61) 321-2477 (Office). *Website:* www.defesa.gov.br (Office).

VIEIRA, Brig.-Gen. João Bernardo; Guinea-Bissau politician; b. 1939, Bissau; joined Partido Africano da Independência da Guiné e Cabo Verde (PAIGC) 1960; Political and Mil. Chief of Catió 1961–64; Mil. Chief of the Southern Front and mem. Political Bureau 1964–65; Vice-Pres. Council of War 1965–67; Rep. of the Political Bureau for the Southern Front 1967–70; mem. Council of War, responsible for mil. operations 1970–71; mem. Exec. Cttee and Council of War 1971–73; mem. Perm. Secr. of PAIGC 1973–; Pres. of People's Nat. Ass. 1973–78; State Commr for the Armed Forces Sept. 1973–78; Chief State Commr 1978–84; Pres. of Guinea–Bissau 1980–99; C-in-C of Armed Forces 1982, Minister of Defence and Interior 1982–92; led coup to depose Pres. Luiz Cabral; Sec. Gen. Revolutionary Council 1980–99; in exile in The Gambia.

VIEIRA DE MELLO, Sergio, PhD; Brazilian United Nations official and international civil servant; b. 15 March 1948; two s.; ed Univ. of Panthéon-Sorbonne, Paris; numerous HQ and field posts in UN humanitarian and peacekeeping operations, fmr. Special Envoy for UNHCR for Cambodia, Dir of Repatriation for UN Transitional Authority in Cambodia (UNTAC), Head of Civil Affairs of UN Protection Force (UNPROFOR), UN Regional Humanitarian Co-ordinator for the Great Lakes; UN Asst High Commr for Refugees 1996–98; Under-Sec.-Gen., Emergency Relief Co-ordinator, UNOCHA 1998–99; apptd. Acting Special Rep. of the Sec.-Gen. for Kosovo June 1999; Special Rep. of Sec.-Gen. for Timor-Leste 1999–2000; Special Envoy of Sec.-Gen. for Fiji 2000; Head of UN Transitional Admin. in Timor-Leste (UNTAET) 2000–02; UN High Commr for Human Rights July 2002–. *Address:* Office of the United Nations High Commissioner for Human Rights (OHCHR), Palais Wilson, 52 rue de Paquis, 1201 Geneva, Switzerland (Office). *Telephone:* (22) 9179290 (Office). *Fax:* (22) 9179022 (Office). *E-mail:* scrt.hchr@unog.ch. *Website:* www.unhchr.ch (Office).

VIENOT, Marc, LèsL; French banker; b. 1 Nov. 1928, Paris; s. of the late Jacques Vienot and Henriette Brunet; m. Christiane Regnault 1953; two s. two d.; ed Nat. Inst. of Political Studies and Ecole Nat. d'Admin.; Inspector of Finance 1955; special envoy to Cabinet of Minister of Econ. and Finance April–June 1957, to Cabinet of Minister of Finance, Econ. and Planning June–Nov. 1957; special envoy to cabinet of Pres. of French Parl. 1957–58; special envoy to Treasury Div. July 1958; Chair. Study Cttee OECD 1961–65; Sec. to Bd of Econ. and Social Devt Fund 1963–65; Under-Sec. Treasury Div. 1965; Head, Financial Activities Service, Treasury Div. 1967; Minister (Financial Counsellor), French Embassies in USA and Canada and Dir IBRD and IMF 1970–73; Deputy Gen. Man. Société Générale 1973, Gen. Man. 1977–86, Chair. and CEO 1986–97, now Hon. Chair and Dir; Interim Pres. Alcatel Alsthom April–July 1995; Pres. Paris Europlace 1998–; Chair. Bd of Avensis, Dir Alcatel Vivendi Universal, Cimets Français; mem. Supervisory Bd Compagnie bancaire, Carnaud Metalbox; mem., fmr Vice-Pres. French Banks Asscn; Officier, Légion d'honneur; Commdr, Ordre nat. du Mérite. *Address:* 4 avenue Raymond Poincaré, 75016 Paris, France.

VIERECK, Peter, BS, MA, PhD; American poet, historian and dramatist; b. 5 Aug. 1916, New York; s. of George S. Viereck and Margaret (née Hein) Viereck; m. 1st Anya de Markov 1945 (divorced 1970); one s. one d.; m. 2nd

Betty Martin Falkenberg 1972; ed Harvard Univ. and Christ Church, Oxford; Teaching Asst, Harvard Univ. 1941–42, Instructor in German Literature and tutor 1946–47; History Instructor, US Army, Univ. of Florence, Italy 1945; Asst Prof. History, Smith Coll. 1947–48; Assoc. Prof. Mount Holyoke Coll. 1948–55, Prof. of European and Russian History 1955–, Distinguished William R. Kenan Prof. 1979–; US State Dept mission of cultural exchange to USSR 1961; Guggenheim Fellow, Rome 1949–50; Visiting Lecturer Univ. of Paris, American Univ., Beirut and American Univ. Cairo 1966; LHD (Olivet Coll.) 1959; awarded Tietjens Prize for Poetry 1948, Pulitzer Prize for Poetry 1949, Sadin Poetry Prize New York Quarterly 1977, Varoujan Prize 1983. *Publications:* Metapolitics – From the Romantics to Hitler 1941, Terror and Decorum (poems) 1948, Who Killed the Universe? 1948, Conservation Revisited – The Revolt Against Revolt 1815–1849 1949, Strike Through the Mask: New Lyrical Poems 1950, The First Morning: New Poems 1952, Shame and Glory of the Intellectuals 1953, Dream and Responsibility: The Tension Between Poetry and Society 1953, The Unadjusted Man: a New Hero for Americans 1956, Conservatism: From John Adams to Churchill 1956, The Persimmon Tree (poems) 1956, The Tree Witch: A Poem and Play 1961, Metapolitics: The Roots of the Nazi Mind 1961, Conservatism Revisited and the New Conservatism: What Went Wrong? 1962, New and Selected Poems 1967, Soviet Policy Making 1967, Outside Looking In 1972, A Question of Quality 1976, Archer in the Marrow (poems) 1987, Tide and Continuities: Last and First Poems 1995, Metapolitics from Wagner to Hitler 2002; numerous articles and poems. *Address:* 12 Silver Street, South Hadley, MA 01075, USA (Office). *Telephone:* (413) 534-5504 (Home).

VIGNAL, Renaud; French diplomatist; b. 18 April 1943, Valence; s. of Jean Vignal and Reine Roulet; m. 1st Monique Tuffelli 1966 (divorced); two d.; m. 2nd Anne de Villiers de la Noue 1983 (deceased); one s.; ed Lycées Montaigne and Louis-le-Grand, Paris, Facultés de Droit et des Lettres, Paris, Inst. d'Etudes Politiques and Ecole Nat. d'Admin.; Second Sec. Embassy Cairo 1971–74; mem. policy planning staff, Ministry of Foreign Affairs 1974–75; Press Officer, Washington 1975–77; Deputy Spokesman, Ministry of Foreign Affairs 1980–81; Prin. Sec. to Minister for Co-operation and Devt 1981–82; Consul-Gen. Québec 1983–87; Amb. to Seychelles 1987–89, to Romania 1990–93, to Argentina 1993–97; Del. Gen. for Int. Relations for the Mayor of Paris 1997–98; Insp. of Foreign Affairs 1998–2001; Amb. to Côte d'Ivoire 2001–; Conseiller Gen. de la Drôme 1988–94; Chevalier Légion d'honneur, Ordre nat. du Mérite, Grande croix du Mérite (Argentina); Commdr du Mérite (Egypt). *Leisure interest:* horses. *Address:* French Embassy, rue Lecoeur, 01 B.P. 175, Abidjan, Côte d'Ivoire (Office); Ministère des Affaires étrangères, 37 quai d'Orsay, 75007 Paris; 15 rue Moncey, 75009 Paris; La Guerimande, 26270 Loriol, France (Home). *Telephone:* 20-20-04-04 (Office). *Fax:* 20-22-42-54 (Office). *E-mail:* presse@ambafrance-abidjan.org (Office). *Website:* www.ambafrance-abidjan.org (Office).

VIKE-FREIBERGA, Vaira, MA, PhD; Latvian head of state and psychologist; b. 1 Dec. 1937, Riga; m. Imants Freibergs 1960; one s. one d.; ed Univ. of Toronto, McGill Univ.; Prof. of Psychology Univ. of Montréal 1965–99; Prof. Emer. Victoria Univ., Toronto 2000–; Vice-Chair. Science Council of Canada 1988–97; Dir Latvian Inst. in Riga 1998–99; Pres. of Latvia 1999–; fmr Pres. Canadian Psychological Asscn; Pres. Social Science Fed. of Canada; Chair. Assen for Advancement of Baltic Studies, USA; Pres. Acad. des Lettres et des Sciences Humaines of Royal Soc. of Canada; mem. Latvian Acad. of Sciences; lectures and seminars on Latvian culture in USA, Canada, Latvia and numerous cos.; Hon. Prof. Victoria Univ. (Canada) 2000, (Latvia Univ.); Hon. LLD (Latvia) 1991; Anna Abele Prize 1979, Marcel-Vincent Prize and Medal 1992, Pierre Chauveau Medal 1995; Three Star Order of Latvia 1995; and awards from Latvian Acad. of Science 1992, McGill Univ. Canada 2002, Kaunas Vytautas Magnus Univ. Lithuania 2002. *Publications include:* La Frequence Lexicalle des Mots au Québec 1974, Latvian Sun-Songs (jtly.) 1988, Linguistic and Poetics of Latvian Folk Songs 1989, On the Amber Mountain 1993, 1999 Against the Current 1993, The Cosmological Sun 1997, The Chronological Sun 1999, The Warm Sun 2002; and over 400 articles and papers. *Address:* Chancery of the President, Pils Laukums 3, Riga, Latvia (Office). *Telephone:* 709-2101; 709-2131 (Office); 781-1032 (Home). *Fax:* 709-2157 (Office); 781-1035 (Home). *E-mail:* prezidents@president.lv (Office). *Website:* www.president.lv (Office).

VIKHAREV, Anatoly Anatolyevich; Russian politician; b. 16 Oct. 1962; ed Ural Polytechnic Inst.; metal worker, mechanic, foreman then head of workshop, Uralenergostroi factory, Sverdlovsk 1982–94; Dir-Gen. Ural Inst. of Heavy Machine Construction 1994–98; Chair. Bd of Dirs Joint-Stock co. Uralgidrotyazhmash 1998–2000; mem. Tutorial Council, Inst. of Human Rights; mem. Council of Feds representing Kurgan Regional Duma 2001, Deputy Chair. 2001, mem. Comm. on Reglementation and Org. of Parl. Activities, Comm. on Problems of Youth and Sports. *Address:* Gogol str. 56, Office 63, 640024 Kurgan (Office); Council of Federations, Bolshaya Dmitrovka str. 26, 103426 Moscow, Russia (Office). *Telephone:* (83522) 4183-94 (Office); (095) 292-57-88 (Office); (095) 926-63-81 (Office).

VIKTYUK, Roman Grigoryevich; Russian/Ukrainian theatre director; b. 28 Oct. 1936, Lvov; ed A. Lunacharcky State Inst. of Theatre Art; Chief Dir Kalinin Theatre of Lenin Komsomol 1968–71; Dir Russian Drama Theatre in Vilnius 1971–77; Artistic Dir Students' Theatre of Moscow Univ. 1977–91; concurrently theatre productions in maj. theatres of Moscow and Leningrad (now St Petersburg); Founder and Artistic Dir Viktyuk Theatre 1991–;

directed productions in Swedish Theatre Helsinki, theatres of Brescia, Rome, San Diego; USA tour 1998; several TV productions. *Address:* Roman Victyuk Theatre, Stromynka str. 6, 107014 Moscow (Office); Tverskaya 4, Apt. 87, 103009 Moscow, Russia (Office); (095) 268-06-69 (Office). *Telephone:* (095) 292-6895 (Home).

VILADECANS, Joan-Pere; Spanish artist; b. 1948, Barcelona; s. of Joan-Pere Viladecans and Carme Viladecans; Chevalier, Ordre des Arts et des Lettres. *Solo exhhibitions include:* Sala Gaspar, Barcelona 1967, Galerie Dresdnere, Toronto 1967, Galerie Dreiseitel, Cologne 1971, 1990, Galeria Pecanins, Mexico 1974, Galleri Uddenberg, Gothenburg 1975, M.L. Museum Gallery, New York 1977, Aaron Gallery, Washington, DC 1978, Guild Gallery, New York 1981, Museo Español Arte Contemporáneo, Madrid 1983, Duszka Patÿn-Karolczak Galerie d'Art, Brussels 1983, Galeria Art-Inter, Luxembourg 1985, Brompton Gallery, London 1985, Baukunst Galerie, Cologne 1988, Galerie Dreiseitel, Cologne 1990, Museo Rufino Tamayo, Mexico 1991, Casa de Goya, Bordeaux 1991, Espace Sphonisbe, Tunis 1991, Expo '92, Seville 1992, Sala Gaspar, Barcelona 1992, Galeria Quadrado Azul, Oporto 1993, Galerie Joan Gaspar, Barcelona 1994, Galeria Benedet, Oviedo 1995. *Address:* Córcega 589, 08025 Barcelona, Spain. *Telephone:* (3) 455-93-85.

VILARDELL, Francisco, MD, D.SC.(MED.); Spanish physician; b. 1 April 1926, Barcelona; s. of Jacinto Vilardell and Mercedes Viñas; m. Leonor Vilardell 1958; one s. two d.; ed Univs. of Barcelona and Pennsylvania; Dir Gastroenterology Service, Hosp. Santa Cruz y San Pablo, Barcelona 1963–; Dir Postgrad. School of Gastroenterology, Autonomous Univ. of Barcelona 1969–; Pres. European Soc. for Digestive Endoscopy 1970–74, European Asscn for Study of the Liver 1975–76, World Org. of Gastroenterology 1982–90 (Sec.-Gen. 1974–82), Council of Int. Orgs. in Medical Science 1987–93, Perm. Adviser 1994–; Dir-Gen. Health Planning, Ministry of Health 1981–82, mem. Advisory Council 1997–; Gold Medal, Barcelona Acad. of Medicine; Gold Medal, Spanish Soc. of Gastroenterology; Chevalier, Légion d'honneur. *Publications:* ed. of six books; 170 papers in medical journals. *Leisure interests:* music, philology. *Address:* Escuela de Patología Digestiva, Hospital de la Santa Cruz y San Pablo, 08025 Barcelona (Office); CIOMS, c/o World Health Organization, 1211 Geneva 27, Switzerland; Juan Sebastian Bach 11, 08021 Barcelona, Spain (Home). *Telephone:* (93) 2197343 (Office); (22) 913406 (CIOMS); (93) 2014511 (Home). *Fax:* (93) 2010191 (Home).

VILARIÑO PINTOS, Daría; Spanish librarian (retd); b. 26 Jan. 1928, Santiago de Compostela; d. of José Vilariño de Andrés and Daría Pintos Castro; mem. staff, state library, museum and archives depts. 1957–70; Deputy Dir Library of Univ. of Santiago 1970–73, Dir 1973–93; Insignia de Oro de la Universidad de Santiago 1993; Medalla de Bronce de Galicia 1993. *Publications:* O Libro Galego onte e hoxe (with Virtudes Pardo) 1981, Hechos de D. Berenguel de Landoria (co-author) 1983, Vasco de Aponte: Recuento de las Casas Antiguas del Reino de Galicìa. Edición crítica (co-author) 1986, Ordoño de Celanova: Vida y Milagros de San Rosendo. Edición crítica (co-author) 1990, Guía do Fondo Antigo de Monografías da Biblioteca Xeral da USC: Literaturas Hispánicas Séculos XV–XVIII (co-author) 2000; articles in professional journals, bibliographical catalogues. *Leisure interest:* reading. *Address:* Calle San Miguel No. 5, 2°, 15704 Santiago de Compostela, La Coruña, Spain. *Telephone:* (981) 583658.

VILHJALMSSON, Thor; Icelandic lawyer; b. 9 June 1930, Reykjavik; s. of Vilhjalmur Th. Gislason and Inga Arnadóttir Gislason; m. Ragnhildur Helgadóttir Vilhjalmsson 1950; one s. three d.; ed Reykjavik Grammar School, St Andrews Univ., Scotland, Univ. of Iceland, New York Univ. and Univ. of Copenhagen; Asst Lecturer, Univ. of Iceland 1959–62, part-time Lecturer 1962–67, Prof. 1967–76 and Dean, Faculty of Law 1968–70, Dir Inst. of Law 1974–76; Deputy Judge Reykjavik Civil Court 1960–62, Judge 1962–67; Judge European Court of Human Rights 1971–98, Vice-Pres. 1998; Assoc. Justice of the Supreme Court of Iceland 1976–93, Pres. 1983–84, 1993; Judge, EFTA Court, Geneva 1994–96, Luxembourg 1996– (Pres. 2000–); mem. Icelandic Del. to UN Gen. Ass. 1963, UN Sea-Bed Cttee 1972, 1973 to Law of the Sea Conf. 1974, 1975 and other int. confs.; Pres. Asscn of Icelandic Lawyers 1971–74; Ed. Icelandic Law Review 1973–83. *Publications:* Civil Procedure I–IV and studies on constitutional law, human rights and legal history. *Address:* EFTA Court, 1 rue du Fort Thüngen, 1499 Luxembourg, Luxembourg. *Telephone:* 42-108-1. *Fax:* 43-43-89.

VILINBAKHOV, Georgy Vadimovich, D.HIST.SC.; Russian historian; b. 13 April 1949; ed Leningrad (now St Petersburg) State Univ.; researcher, later Prof. State Hermitage Museum 1969–, treasurer collection of banners and mil. graphic works 1970–92, Deputy, then First Deputy Dir 1991–; Head State Heraldic Council 1992–; Head of State Heraldry 1994, then Chair. Herald Council, State Heraldmeister 1999–; mem. Exec. Cttee Int. Asscn of Mil. Museums and Museum of Arms; Pres. St Petersburg Foundation of Culture; Order Sign of Honour 1997, Order for Service to Motherland 1999. *Publications:* over 50 articles and Publs on Russian history and heraldry. *Leisure interests:* collecting tin soldiers, opera music. *Address:* State Hermitage Museum, Dvortsovaya nab. 34, St Petersburg, Russia (Office). *Telephone:* (812) 110-96-25 (Office).

VILJOEN, Gerrit van Niekerk, DLitt ET PHIL., MA; South African fmr politician and academic; b. 11 Sept. 1926, Cape Town; s. of the late Hendrik Geldenhuys Viljoen; m. Magdalena Maria van der Merwe 1951; two s. five d.; ed Afrikaanse Hoër Seunskool, Pretoria, Univ. of Pretoria, King's Coll.

Cambridge, Ryksuniversiteit, Leiden, Sorbonne, Paris; Sr Lecturer in Classics, Univ. of SA 1955–57, Prof. 1957–67; Admin.-Gen. Namibia (SW Africa) 1979–80; Minister of Nat. Educ. 1980–84, of Co-operation and Devt and (Black) Educ. (renamed Devt Aid and Educ.) 1984–86, of Devt Aid and Educ. 1986–89, of Nat. Educ. 1989–90, of Constitutional Devt, Planning 1989–92, of State Affairs May–Nov. 1992; Rector, Rand Afrikaans Univ. 1967–79; Chancellor Rand Afrikaans Univ. 1985–2000; Corresp. mem. Royal Netherlands Acad. of Sciences; mem. Suid-Afrikaanse Akad.; Hon. Pres. Classical Asscn of SA; Hon. LLD (Rand Afrikaans) 1980, Hon. D.Ed. (Orange Free State Univ.). *Address:* c/o Rand Afrikaans University, P.O. Box 524, Auckland Park, Johannesburg 2006 (Office); P.O. Box 95173, Waterkloof 0145, Pretoria, South Africa.

VILJOEN, Hendrik Christo, PhD; South African academic and electronics engineer; b. 31 Aug. 1937, Graaff-Reinet; s. of Hendrik Christoffel Viljoen and Anna Pienaar; m. Hana Stehlik 1965; one s. two d.; ed Univ. of Stellenbosch; engineer, Dept of Posts and Telecommunications, Pretoria 1961–65; Sr Lecturer, Univ. of Stellenbosch 1966–70, Prof. 1970–, Dean of Eng 1979–93, Vice-Rector of Operations 1993–98; Chair. SABC 1989–93; Visiting Prof. Ga Inst. of Tech., Atlanta, USA 1975–76, Nat. Chiao Tung Univ., Hsinchu, Taiwan 1981; Dir Office for Intellectual Property; Chair. Task Group on Broadcasting in SA 1987–91; Sr mem. Inst. of Electrical and Electronic Engineers, USA 1978–; Fellow SA Akademie vir Wetenskap en Kuns; Sir Ernest Oppenheimer Memorial Trust Award; Engineer of the Year, SA Asscn for Professional Engineers 1991; Order for Meritorious Service; Merit Medal, SA Acad. for Arts and Science 2000. *Leisure interests:* philately, genealogy, website design. *Address:* 6 Hof Avenue, Stellenbosch 7600, South Africa. *Telephone:* (2231) 8833754. *Fax:* (2231) 8083743. *E-mail:* viljoen@mail.com (Home).

VILKAS, Eduardas, D.PHYS.-MATH.SC.; Lithuanian mathematician and economist; b. 3 Oct. 1935, Gargždai; m. Stefa Vilkienė; two s. one d.; ed Vilnius Univ.; researcher Inst. of Physics and Math., Lithuanian Acad. of Sciences 1958–77; researcher Inst. of Math. and Cybernetics 1977–79, Deputy Dir 1979–85; Dir Inst. of Econs 1985–; teacher Vilnius Univ. 1958–, Prof. 1976; Chair. Parl. Comm. for Privatization (later State Privatization Cttee) 1996; mem. Lithuanian Acad. of Sciences, Vice-Pres. 1991–99; main research on probability theory, game theory, math. economics and its application in nat. econ. *Publications:* What is the Theory of Games? 1976, Mathematical Methods in the Economy 1980, Solutions: Theory, Information, Modelling (together with E. Maiminas) 1981, Optimality in Games and Decisions 1991, Decision-Making Theory 2003; articles in scientific periodicals. *Leisure interest:* tennis. *Address:* Ekonomikos Institutas, A. Goštanto 12, 2600 Vilnius (Office); Žirgo 20, 2040 Vilnius, Lithuania. *Telephone:* (5) 2623502 (Office); (5) 2700404 (Home). *Fax:* (5) 2227506 (Office). *E-mail:* ei@ktl.mii.lt (Office); evilkas@takas.lt (Home).

VILLA, José García, AB; Philippine poet and critic; b. 5 Aug. 1914, Manila; s. of Dr. Simeon Villa and Maria García; two s.; ed Univs of the Philippines, of New Mexico and Columbia Univ.; Assoc. Ed. New Directions Books 1949; Cultural Attaché Philippine Mission to UN 1953–63; Dir NY City Coll. Poetry Workshop 1952–63, Prof. of Poetry, New School for Social Research 1964–73; Philippines Presidential Adviser on Cultural Affairs 1968–; Guggenheim Fellowship 1943, Bollingen Fellowship 1951, Rockefeller Grant 1964; Hon. DLitt (Far Eastern Univ.) 1959, Hon. LHD (Philippines) 1973; American Acad. of Arts and Letters Award 1942, Shelley Memorial Award 1959, Pro Patria Award 1961, Philippines Cultural Heritage Award 1962, Nat. Artist in Literature 1973. *Publications:* Footnote to Youth (stories) 1933, Many Voices 1939, Poems by Doveglion 1941, Have Come, Am Here 1942, Volume Two 1949, Selected Poems and New 1958, Poems Fifty-five 1962, Poems in Praise of Love 1962, Selected Stories 1962, The Portable Villa 1963, The Essential Villa 1965, Appassionata 1979; Ed.: A Celebration for Edith Sitwell 1948, Doveglion Book of Philippine Poetry 1975, Bravo: the Poet's Magazine 1981, New Doveglion Book of Philippine Poetry 1993. *Leisure interests:* dogs, plants, cooking.

VILLA-VICENCIO, Rev. Charles, STM, PhD; South African professor of religion and society; b. 7 Nov. 1942, Johannesburg; s. of Charles Villa-Vicencio and Paula Villa-Vicencio; m. Eileen van Sittert 1968; two d.; ed Rhodes Univ. Grahamstown and Natal, Yale and Drew Univs; with Standard Bank of SA 1961–64; Probationer Minister, Methodist Church of Southern Africa 1965–70; ordained Minister 1970; Minister of various congregations in S Africa and USA; Teaching Fellow, Drew Univ. 1974–75; part-time lecturer, Univ. of Cape Town 1976–77; Sr Lecturer, Univ. of S Africa 1978–81, Assoc. Prof. 1981–82; Sr Lecturer, Univ. of Cape Town 1982, Assoc Prof. 1984–88, Head, Dept of Religious Studies 1986–97, Prof. of Religion and Society 1988–97; mem. S African Theological Soc.; del. to numerous confs etc. *Publications include:* Between Christ and Caesar: Classical and Contemporary Texts 1986, Trapped in Apartheid 1988, Civil Disobedience and Beyond 1990, A Theology of Reconstruction 1992, A Spirit of Hope: Conversations on Politics, Religion and Values 1993; ed. or co-ed. of and contrib. to several vols of essays; numerous articles including many on the church and politics in S Africa. *Address:* 14 Annerley Road, Rosebank, Cape Town 7700, South Africa (Home). *Telephone:* (21) 6868643 (Home). *Fax:* (21) 6503761.

VILLAGRAN DE LEON, Francisco, MA; Guatemalan diplomatist; b. 29 March 1954, Guatemala City; m.; one c.; ed Georgetown Univ., Washington,

DC and Universidad Rafael Landivar, Guatemala; Deputy Dir Guatemalan Foreign Service 1979; Political Counsellor, Washington, DC 1983; Alt. Rep. Guatemalan Mission to OAS 1984; Deputy Chief of Washington Embassy 1985; Deputy Minister of Foreign Affairs 1986; Amb. to OAS 1987, to Canada 1995–98; Perm. Rep. to UN 1988–92. *Address:* c/o Ministry of Foreign Affairs, Palacio Nacional, Guatemala City, Guatemala.

VILLAIN, Claude Edouard Louis Etienne, LenD; French civil servant; b. 4 Jan. 1935, Paris; s. of Etienne Villain and Marie Louise (née Caudron) Villain; m. Bernadette Olivier 1962; two s.; ed Lycée Voltaire, Lycée Louis-le-Grand, Univ. of Paris, Ecole Nat. de la F.O.M.; Trainee in French Overseas Admin. 1956–59, Officer in Dept of Algerian Affairs 1959–61; Officer for Econ. Studies in Agricultural Devt Bureau 1962–64; Officer in Ministry of Econ. and Finance 1964, Head of Dept 1969, Deputy Dir of Ministry 1973; Tech. Adviser in Office of Valéry Giscard d'Estaing (then Minister of Econ. and Finance) 1973–74; Dir-Gen. of Competition and Prices in Ministry of Econ. and Finance 1974–78; Administrateur Soc. Nat. des Chemins de fer Français (SNCF) 1974–78; Administrateur Soc. Nat. Elf Aquitaine 1974–79; Dir-Gen. of Agric., Comm. of EEC 1979–85; Dir-Gen. Socopa Int., Vice-Pres. Socopa France 1985; Special Adviser to Minister of Econ. and Finance 1986–88; Inspector-Gen. of Finances 1987–; Del. Interministerial Mission for Cen. and Eastern Europe (MICECO) 1992–93, for Euro-Disneyland 1993; Chair. Admin. Bd Comilog S.A. 1996–; mem. Intergovernmental Comm. of the Channel Tunnel 1990, of the Lyon-Turin rail project 1996–2001; Admin. Soc. Nat. RATP 1998; Officier, Légion d'honneur; Officier, Ordre nat. du Mérite; Croix de Valeur Mil.; Commdr du Mérite Agricole. *Leisure interests:* tennis, skiing. *Address:* Inspection générale des finances, 139 rue de Bercy, 75572 Paris, cedex 12 (Office); 103 avenue Félix Faure, 75015 Paris, France (Home). *Telephone:* 1-53-18-38-31 (Office). *Fax:* 1-53-18-69-34 (Office). *E-mail:* claude_edouard.villain@igf .finances.gouv.fr (Office).

VILLANUEVA SARAVIA, Eladio; Spanish trade union official; b. Valladolio; fmr railroad man.; currently Pres. Gen. Confed. of Workers (CGT). *Address:* Confederacion General de Trabajo, Sagunto 15, 28010 Madrid, Spain (Office). *Telephone:* (91) 4475769 (Office). *Fax:* (91) 4453132 (Office). *E-mail:* spcc.cgt@cgt.es (Office). *Website:* www.cgt.es (Office).

VILLAPALOS-SALAS, Gustavo; Spanish university rector; b. 15 Oct. 1949, Madrid; s. of Gustavo Villapalos-Salas and Juana Villapalos-Salas; Prof., Faculty of Law, Universidad Complutense de Madrid 1970–75, Prof. of Law 1976, Dir Dept of History of Law 1980–84, Dean Faculty of Law 1984–87, Rector of Univ. 1987–2000; Research Fellow Instituto de Estudios Jurídicos 1972–74, Centro de Investigaciones Juridícas, Económicas y Sociales 1975; Visiting Prof., Univ. of Calif. at Berkeley, USA 1976, Univ. of Freiburg 1976–77; Dr. hc (Paris-Sud, St Louis, USA, Guanajuato, Mexico, La Plata, Argentina); Gran Cruz de la Orden de Alfonso X el Sabio, Gran Cruz del Mérito Civil, Hon. CBE. *Publications:* Colección Diplomática del Archivo Municipal de Santander: Documentos Reales II (1525–1599) 1982, Los Regímenes Económicos Matrimoniales en la Historia del Derecho Español: Prelección 1983, El Fuero de León: Comentarios 1984, Cortes de Castilla en el siglo XV 1986, La Baja Edad Media, Vol. IV, Historia General de Cantabria 1986, La Alta Edad Media, Vol. III 1987. *Leisure interests:* astronomy, cinema, classical music, reading. *Address:* Calle Alberto Aguilera 11, 28015 Madrid, Spain (Home). *Telephone:* (91) 4452929 (Home).

VILLARROEL LANDER, Mario Enrique; Venezuelan Red Cross official, lawyer and professor; b. 20 Sept. 1947, Caracas; m. Norka Sierraalta 1969; three s. one d.; ed Cen. Univ. of Venezuela, Santa María Univ., Caracas; joined Red Cross as a volunteer 1967, Nat. Pres. 1978–, Pres. Int. Fed. of Red Cross and Red Crescent Socs. 1987–98; Pres. Mirandino Historical Studies Inst., Henry Dunant Inst. 1992–93; Prof. of Penal Law, Chair. of Criminal Law Santa María Univ.; lawyer pvt. legal practice; fmr Dir La Voz del Derecho (legal review); numerous memberships of int. orgs.; numerous distinctions from Red Cross orgs. *Publications:* El Cuerpo Técnico de Policía Judicial en el Proceso Penal Venezolano, Habeas Corpus y antejuicio de Mérito; legal articles in Venezuelan and foreign periodicals. *Leisure interest:* journalism. *Address:* c/o International Federation of Red Cross and Red Crescent Societies, 17 Chemin des Crêts, Petit-Saconnex, Case Postale 372, 1211 Geneva 19, Switzerland.

VILLAS-BOAS, José Manuel P. de; Portuguese diplomatist; b. 23 Feb. 1931, Oporto; s. of João de Villas-Boas and Maria Margarida de Villas-Boas; m. Maria do Patrocinio de Almeida Braga 1956; ed Lisbon Univ.; Attaché, Ministry of Foreign Affairs 1954; Embassies, Pretoria 1959, London 1963; Counsellor 1969; Head of African Dept, Ministry of Foreign Affairs 1970–72; Consul-Gen., Milan 1972–74; Minister Plenipotentiary, Asst Dir-Gen. of Political Affairs, Ministry of Foreign Affairs 1974–77, Dir-Gen. of Political Affairs 1977–79; Amb. and Perm. Rep. to NATO 1979–84, Amb. to South Africa 1984–89, to People's Repub. of China 1989–93, to Russia 1993–97; Prof. Univ. of Minho, Braga 1997–; Grand Cross Order of Merit (Portugal), Hon. KCMG (UK), Grand Cross of St Olav (Norway), of Merit (Spain), Cruzeiro do Sul (Brazil), of Rio Branco (Brazil), of Good Hope (S. Africa), Grand Officer of the Order of Merit (F.R.G.), of the Lion (Senegal), Commdr, Légion d'honneur (France), Order of Merit (Italy), etc. *Publication:* Orthodoxy and Political Power in Russia 1999. *Leisure interests:* music, travelling. *Address:* Department of Political Science and International Relations, Universidade do

Minho, Largo do Paço, 4704-553 Braga (Office); Casa de Esteiro, Vilarelho 4910 Caminha, Portugal (Home). *Telephone:* (253) 605513 (Office); (258) 721333 (Home). *Fax:* (258) 921356 (Home). *Website:* www.eeg.uminho.pt.

VILLELLA, Edward, BS; American ballet dancer; b. 1 Oct. 1936, New York; s. of Joseph Villella and Mildred (née De Giovanni) Villella; m. 1st Janet Greschler 1962 (divorced 1980); one s.; m. 2nd Linda Carbonetta 1981; two d.; ed NY State Maritime Coll.; joined NY City Ballet 1957, becoming soloist within a year, now Premier Dancer; originated leading roles in George Balanchine's Bugaku, Tarantella, Stars and Stripes, Harlequinade, Jewels, Glinkaiana, A Midsummer Night's Dream; first danced his famous role of Prodigal Son 1960; has also danced leading roles in Allegro Brillante, Jeux, Pas de Deux, Raymonda Variations, Scotch Symphony, Swan Lake; choreographed Narkissos; has appeared at Bolshoi Theatre, with Royal Danish Ballet and in London and made numerous guest appearances; choreographed and starred in revivals of Brigadoon, Carousel; Chair. NY City Comm. of Cultural Affairs 1978; Artistic Co-ordinator Eglersky Ballet Co. (now André Eglersky State Ballet of New York) 1979–84, Choreographer 1980–84; Choreographer NJ Ballet 1980; Artistic Dir Ballet Okla 1983–86, Miami City Ballet 1985–; Heritage Chair in Arts and Cultural Criticism George Mason Univ. 1992–93, 1993–94; mem. Nat. Council on the Arts 1968–74; Artist-in-Residence Dorothy F. Schmidt Coll. of Arts and Letters 2000–01; Robert Kiphuth Fellow Yale Univ. 2001; Dance magazine award 1965; Hon. DFA (S.U.N.Y. Maritime Coll.) 1998; Golden Plate Award (American Acad. of Achievement) 1971, Emmy Award 1975, Gold Medal Award Nat. Soc. of Arts and Letters 1990, Nat. Medal of Arts Award 1997, other awards. *Publication:* Prodigal Son (jtly.) 1992.

VILLEMÉJANE, Bernard de; French business executive; b. 10 March 1930, Marseille; s. of Pierre Villeméjane and Marie-Thérèse (née Getten) de Villeméjane; m. Françoise Boucheronde 1965; two s.; ed Ecole Polytechnique and Ecole des Mines, Paris; with Direction des Mines et de la Géologie, French W Africa 1955–60; Ministry of Industry 1960–61; Eng Adviser, Banque Rothschild 1961–62; Deputy Man. Dir Société Penarroya 1963, Man Dir 1967, Chair. of Bd and Man. Dir 1971–86, Dir 1986–88, Vice-Pres. Supervisory Bd 1988–91; Man Dir Société Le Nickel 1971–74; Chair. of Bd and Man. Dir SM le Nickel S.L.N. 1974–83, Dir 1984; Dir Imetal 1974, Man. Dir 1974, Chair. 1979–93, Hon. Pres. 1993–; Vice-Chair. Supervisory Bd Metaleurop 1986–91; Dir Copperweld Corpn, USA 1976, Cookson PLC (UK) 1977–86; Dir Financière d'Angers 1989–, Chair. 1989–91; Chair., Man. Dir Gravograph 1994–95; Vice-Pres. Moulinex; Dir of various other European and American cos., including Origny-Desvroise, C-E Minerals Inc., DBK Minerals Inc., Minemet SA; Officier, Légion d'honneur, Officier, Ordre nat. du Mérite, Grand Cross, Orden del Mérito (Spain), Commdr Ordre de l'Etoile Equatoriale (Gabon). *Address:* Imetal, Tour Maine-Montparnasse, 33 avenue du Maine, 75755 Paris Cedex 15 (Office); 102 rue d'Assas, 75006 Paris, France (Home). *Telephone:* 45-38-48-48 (Office).

VILLENEUVE, Jacques; Canadian racing car driver; b. 9 April 1971, St Jean sur Richelieu, QC; s. of the late Gilles Villeneuve and of Joanne Barthe; started racing in Italian touring car championship Italian Formula 3 1989, 1990, with Reynaud and Alfa Romeo 1992, Japanese Formula 3 1993, Formula Atlantic 1993, IndyCar driver 1994–95; IndyCar racing champion 1995 (youngest ever winner); fmrly. drove Formula 1 cars with Williams Renault team, now with British American Racing (BAR) team; Grand Prix winner: Britain 1996, 1997, Brazil 1997, Argentina 1997, Spain 1997, Hungary 1997, Austria 1997, Luxembourg 1997; Formula 1 Champion 1997; owns restaurant/bar Newtown in Montreal; lives in Monaco. *Leisure interests:* reading, music, skiing, computers. *Address:* British American Racing, Brackley, Northants, NN13 7BD, England.

VILLENEUVE, Jeanne Madeleine; French journalist; b. 29 Jan. 1949, Paris; d. of Henry Villeneuve and Jacqueline Picq; ed Inst. d'Etudes Politiques; Financial Analyst, Banque Nat. de. Paris 1974–78; Chef de Service, Soc. Générale de Presse 1978–82, daily newspaper Libération 1982–86, weekly l'Express Feb.–Sept. 1986; Chief Reporter, l'Evènement du Jeudi 1986–91; Asst Ed. Parisien 1991–95; Ed. Libération 1996–97. *Publication:* Le mythe Tapie 1988. *Address:* c/o Journal Libération, 11 rue Béranger, 75003 Paris, France.

VILLEPIN, Dominique Marie François René Galouzeau de, LenD; French politician, diplomatist and civil servant; b. 14 Nov. 1953, Rabat, Morocco; s. of Xavier Galouzeau de Villepin and Yvonne Hétier; m. Marie-Laure Le Guay 1985; one s. two d.; ed Collège Français, Caracas, Ecole de Caousou, Toulouse, Lycée Français, New York, Paris Univ.; responsible for Horn of Africa, Office of African Affairs 1980–81, Head of Mission attached to Dir.'s Office 1981–84, Asst Dir 1992–93; with Centre d'Analyse et de Prévision 1981–84; Adviser, Middle East 1984–87; Embassy Press and Information Dir, New York 1987–89, Ministerial Councillor, India 1989–92; Dir de Cabinet to Alain Juppé (q.v.), Minister of Foreign Affairs 1993–95; Sec. Gen. to Presidency 1995–2002; Minister of Foreign Affairs 2002–; Chair. Admin. Council Nat. Forests Office (ONF) 1996–99; Rep. Convention on the Future of Europe 2002–. *Publications:* Parole d'Exil 1986 (poetry), Le Droit d'Aînesse 1988 (poetry), Elégies barbares 1996, Secession 1996, Les Cent-Jours ou l'esprit de sacrifice (Amb.'s Prize) 2001. *Leisure interest:* marathon

running. *Address:* Ministry of Foreign Affairs, 37 quai d'Orsay, 75007 Paris, France. *Telephone:* 1-43-17-53-53. *Fax:* 1-43-17-52-03. *Website:* www.diplomatie.gouv.fr.

VILLIERS de SAINTIGNON, Philippe le Jolis de; French politician; b. 25 March 1949, Boulogne; s. of Jacques le Jolis de Villiers de Saintignon and Hedwige d'Arexy; m. Dominique de Buor de Villeneuve 1973; four s. three d.; ed Saint-Joseph Inst., Ecole Nat. d'Admin.; civil servant Ministry of Interior 1978; Prin. Pvt. Sec. to Prefect of La Rochelle 1978; Deputy Prefect Vendôme 1979; f. Alouette FM (regional radio station) 1981, Fondation pour les Arts et les Sciences de la Communication, Nantes 1984; Jr Minister of Culture and Communications 1986–87; mem. Conseil Gen. de la Vendée 1987–, Pres. 1988–; Deputy to Nat. Ass. from Vendée 1988–94 (U.D.F.), 1997– (Ind.); MEP 1994–97, majorité pour l'autre Europe; Nat. Del. UDF (in charge of youth and liaising with cultural groups) 1988; f. and Pres. Mouvement pour la France 1994; Co-Founder Rassemblement pour la France 1999, Vice-Pres. 1999–2000. *Publications:* Lettre Ouverte aux Coupeurs de Têtes et aux Menteurs du Bicentenaire 1989, La Chienne qui Miaule 1990, Notre Europe sans Maastricht 1992, Avant qu'il ne soit trop tard 1993, La Société de connivence 1994, Dictionnaire du politiquement correct à la française 1996, La machination d'Amsterdam 1998. *Address:* Assemblée nationale, 75355 Paris; Conseil Général de la Vendée, 40 rue Foch, 85923 La Roche-sur-Yon cedex 9, France. *Telephone:* 1-40-63-82-05 (Paris). *Fax:* 1-40-63-82-80 (Paris).

VILLIGER, Kaspar; Swiss politician; b. 5 Feb. 1941, Pfeffikon, Lucerne; m.; two d.; ed Swiss Fed. Inst. of Tech., Zürich; man. of cigar factory Villiger Söhne AG, Pfeffikon 1966; subsequently bought bicycle factory in Buttisholz; fmr Vice-Pres. Chamber of Commerce of Cen. Switzerland and mem. Cttee Swiss Employers' Cen. Asscn; mem. Lucerne Cantonal Parl. 1972–82; mem. Nat. Council, Liberal Party of Switzerland (FDP) 1982; mem. Council of States 1987; Swiss Fed. Councillor 1989–; Head, Fed. Mil. (Defence) Dept 1989–95, Dept of Finance 1996–2001; Vice-Pres. of Swiss Confed. 1994, 2001; Pres. Swiss Confed. Jan.–Dec. 1995, Jan. 2002–. *Address:* Federal Department of Finance, Bernerhof, Bundesgasse 3, 3003, Berne, Switzerland (Office). *Telephone:* (31) 3226033 (Office). *Fax:* (31) 3233852 (Office). *E-mail:* info@gs-efd.admin.ch (Office). *Website:* www.efd.admin.ch (Office).

VILSACK, Thomas, JD; American state official and lawyer; b. 13 Dec. 1950, Pittsburg, Pa; s. of Bud Vilsack and Dolly Vilsack; m. Christine Bell 1973; twos.; ed Hamilton Coll., NY, Union Univ.; pvt. law practice, Mt.Pleasant, Iowa 1975–98; Mayor of Mt. Pleasant 1987–92; Senator from Iowa 1993–98; Gov. of Iowa 1998–; mem. Bd Dirs. United Way, Mt. Pleasant. *Address:* Office of the Governor, State Capitol Building, Des Moines, IA 50319-0001, USA (Office). *Website:* www.state.ia.us (Office).

VIMOND, Paul Marcel; French architect; b. 20 June 1922, La Meurdraquière; s. of Ernest Vimond and Marie Lehuby; m. Jacqueline Lefèvre 1945; two s. two d.; ed Lycée de Coutances, Ecole préparatoire des beaux-arts de Rennes and Ecole nat. supérieure des beaux-arts, Paris; Acad. de France at Rome 1950–52; Chief architect, public bldgs. and nat. monuments 1954; mem. Jury of Nat. School of Fine Arts; mem. Diocesan Comm. on Sacred Art, Paris; Nat. Expert for Cour de Cassation, Cours d'Appel, Tribunaux Administratifs and all French courts; Pres. Architecture section, Salon des Artistes Français; Officier Ordre nat. du mérite; Chevalier, Légion d'honneur, des Palmes académiques, des Arts et des Lettres and of Pontifical Order of Merit; Premier Grand Prix de Rome 1949. *Major architectural works:* architect in charge of Int. Exhbn of Sacred Art, Rome 1953; responsible for films and architectural reconstructions of tomb of Saint Peter, Rome; Buildings in Paris for: Assemblée de l'Union française, Conseil économique et social, Union de l'Europe occidentale, Org. de co-opération et de développement économiques; planner and architect for Palais d'Iéna, Paris; town planner for Cherbourg; Atomic Power Station, The Hague; two theatres, three churches in Paris, hotels, restaurants, hospitals and numerous lycées in France; 800 pvt. houses; 15,000 flats in six new towns; technical insts. at Besançon, Montpellier, Paris, Orsay, Nice, Toulon, Troyes; Faculty of medicine, Nice; a hosp. and a coll. in Lebanon; French Lycée, Brussels; numerous telephone exchanges and 14 large postal sorting offices in Paris region and provinces; sorting offices in Riyadh, Jeddah and Dammam and project for TV centre in Saudi Arabia, project for town in Zaire. *Leisure interests:* painting, golf.

VINCENT, Jean-Pierre, LèsL; French theatre director; b. 26 Aug. 1942, Juvisy-sur-Orge, Essonne; s. of André Vincent and Paulette Loyot; one s.; ed Lycées Montaigne, Louis-le-Grand, Paris, Univ. de Paris (Sorbonne); amateur actor Univ. theatre Lycée Louis-le-Grand 1958–64; mem. Patrice Chéreau theatre co. 1965–68, Dir 1968–72; Dir. Admin. Dir Espérance Theatre 1972–74; Dir at Théâtre Nat. and École Supérieure d'art dramatique, Strasbourg 1975–83; Gen. Admin. Comédie-Française 1983–86; Dir Théâtre de Nanterre-Amandiers 1990–2001; Lecturer Inst. d'études théâtrales de Paris 1969–70; Studio Dir Conservatoire Nat. Supérieur d'art dramatique 1969–70, Prof. 1986–89; Pres. Syndicat Nat. de Dirs. d'entreprises artistiques et culturelles (Syndeac) 1978–82, Vice-Pres. 1992; numerous critics' prizes, including Molière Prize for Best Dir 1987, Prix de la Critique 1988. *Plays include:* Le suicide 1984, Six personnages en quête de l'auteur 1986, Fantasio, Les caprices de Mariane 1991, Woyzeck 1993, Violences à Vichy 1995, Pièces de guerre 1999, Homme pour homme, Lorenzaccio 2000, Drame de la vie 2001.

Opera includes: Les Noces de Figaro 1994, Mitridate 2000, Le drame et la vie 2001. *Address:* Nanterre-Amandiers, 6 avenue Pablo Picasso, 92000 Nanterre, France.

VINCENT, Rev. John James, DTheol; British minister of religion; b. 29 Dec. 1929, Sunderland; s. of David Vincent and Beatrice Ethel Vincent (née Gadd); m. Grace Johnston Stafford 1958; two s. one d.; ed Manchester Grammar School, Richmond Coll., London Univ., Drew Univ., Madison, NJ, USA, Basel Univ., Switzerland; ordained in Methodist Church 1956; Minister, Manchester and Salford Mission 1956–62; Supt Minister, Rochdale Mission 1962–69, Sheffield Inner City Ecumenical Mission 1970–77; Dir Urban Theology Unit, Sheffield 1969–97, Dir Emer. and Doctoral Supervisor 1997–; Pres. Methodist Conf. 1989–90; Visiting Prof. of Theology, Boston School of Theology, USA 1969, New York Theological Seminary 1970, Theological School, Drew Univ. 1977; elected mem. Studiorum Novi Testamenti Societas 1961; Sec. Regional Working Party, WCC Faith and Order 1958–63; mem. British Council of Churches Comm. on Defence and Disarmament 1963–65, 1969–72; NW Vice-Pres. Campaign for Nuclear Disarmament 1957–69; Founding mem. Methodist Renewal Group 1961–70; Founding mem. and Leader Ashram Community 1967–; Chair. Alliance of Radical Methodists 1971–74, Urban Mission Training Asscn of GB 1976–77, 1985–90; Co-ordinator, British Liberation Theology Project 1990–; mem. Bd Int. Urban Ministry Network 1991–; presented Petition of Distress from the Cities to HM the Queen 1993; mem. Independent Human Rights Del. to Colombia 1994; Chair. Methodist Report on The Cities 1997; Hon. Lecturer Biblical Studies Dept, Sheffield Univ. 1990–. *Publications:* Christ in a Nuclear World 1962, Christ and Methodism 1965, Secular Christ 1968, The Race Race 1970, The Jesus Thing 1973, Stirrings 1975, Starting All Over Again 1981, Into the City 1982, O.K. Let's Be Methodists 1984, Radical Jesus 1986, Mark at Work 1986, Britain in the 90s 1989, Discipleship in the 90s 1991, Liberation Theology UK (ed.) 1995, Gospel from the City (ed.) 1997, Hope from the City 2000, Journey: Explorations into Discipleship 2001, Faithfulness in the City (ed.) 2003. *Leisure interests:* jogging, writing. *Address:* 178 Abbeyfield Road, Sheffield, S4 7AY, England. *Telephone:* (114) 243-6688. *Fax:* (114) 243-5342.

VINCENT, John Russell, PhD, FRHistS; British historian; b. 20 Dec. 1937, Cheshire; s. of J. J. Vincent; m. Nicolette Kenworthy 1972; two s. (one deceased); ed Bedales School, Christ's Coll. Cambridge; Fellow of Peterhouse, Cambridge 1962–70, Lecturer in History Univ. of Cambridge 1967–70; Prof. of Modern History, Univ. of Bristol 1970–84, Prof. of History 1984–2002; Visiting Prof. Univ. of E Anglia Norwich 2003–. *Publications:* The Formation of the Liberal Party 1966, The Governing Passion 1974, The Crawford Papers 1984, Disraeli 1990, An Intelligent Person's Guide to History 1995, Derby Diaries, 1869–1878 1995, Derby Diaries 1878–93 2003; various works on political history. *Leisure interest:* journalism. *Address:* Senate House, Univ. of Bristol, Bristol, BS8 1TH, England. *Telephone:* (117) 929-2700 (Home).

VINCENT, Olatunde Olabode, CFR; Nigerian banker; b. 16 May 1925, Lagos; s. of Josiah O. Vincent and Comfort A. Vincent; m. Edith Adenike Gooding 1958; three s. one d.; ed CMS. Grammar School, Lagos, Chartered Inst. of Secs, London, Univ. of Manchester and Admin. Staff Coll., Henley, England; Nigerian Army 1942–46; Financial Sec.'s Office 1947–56; Fed. Ministry of Finance 1956–61; Asst Gen. Man. Cen. Bank of Nigeria 1961–62, Deputy Gen. Man. 1962, Gen. Man. 1963–66, Adviser 1973–75, Deputy Gov. 1975–77, Gov. 1977–82; co-f., then Vice-Pres. African Devt Bank, Abidjan, Ivory Coast 1966–73; part-time Lecturer in Econs, Extra-Mural Dept, Univ. Coll. of Ibadan 1957–60; mem. Lagos Exec. Devt Bd 1960–61; Dir Nigerian Industrial Devt Bank 1964–66, Nigerian Security Printing and Minting Co. Ltd, Lagos, 1975–77; Chair. Sona Dairies Ltd 1985–90, City Business Computers Ltd 1985–, Equity and Trust Ltd 1986–; Chair. Capital Issues Comm., Lagos 1975–77, Southern Africa Relief Fund 1977–82, Cttee on Motor Vehicle Advances and Basic Allowance 1978; Chair. Visitation Panel, Lagos State Univ. (LASU) 1993–, Governing Bd, Centre for Environment and Science Educ., LASU 1996–; Chair. Bd of Trustees, Nigerian Lions Charity Foundation 1993–; Life mem. Soc. for Int. Devt; Fellow Nigerian Inst. of Bankers, Inst. of Dirs, Nigerian Inst. of Man.; mem. Nat. Econ. Council 1979–82, Nigerian Econ. Soc., Nigerian Stock Exchange, Nigeria-Britain Asscn, Nigerian Conservation Foundation Trustee, African Church Cathedral (Bethel), Cancer Aid Foundation; Patron Lagos State Chapter, Spinal Cord Injuries Asscn of Nigeria; Hon. DSc (Lagos State Univ.) 2000; African Church Primatial Honours Award 1981, Distinguished Nigerian Community Leader Award 1983; Commdr Order of Fed. Repub. 1982. *Leisure interests:* reading, listening to African and light classical music, gardening. *Address:* 8 Balarabe Musa Crescent, Victoria Island, P.O. Box 8780, Lagos, Nigeria. *Telephone:* 615687; 619291.

VINCENT OF COLESHILL, Baron (Life Peer), cr. 1996, of Coleshill in the County of Oxfordshire; **Field Marshal The Lord Richard (Frederick) Vincent,** GBE, KCB, DSO, FIMechE, FRAeS, F.I.C.; British army officer; b. 23 Aug. 1931, London; s. of the late Frederick Vincent and Frances Elizabeth (née Coleshill) Vincent; m. Jean Paterson (née Stewart) 1955; two s. (one deceased) one d.; ed Aldenham School, Royal Mil. Coll. of Science; nat. service 1950; Germany 1951–55, Gunnery Staff 1959, Radar Research Establishment, Malvern 1960–61, BAOR 1962, Tech. Staff Training, Royal Mil. Coll. of Science 1963–64; Staff Coll. 1965, Commonwealth Brigade, Malaysia 1966–68, Ministry of Defence 1968–70; Commdr 12th Light Air Defence Regt, Germany, England and N.I. 1970–72; Instructor Staff Coll. 1972–73; Mil. Dir

of Studies, RMCS 1974–75; Commdr 19 Airportable Brigade 1975–77; RCDS 1978; Deputy Mil. Sec. 1979–80; Commandant Royal Mil. Coll. of Science 1980–83; Master Gen. of Ordnance, Ministry of Defence 1983–87; Vice-Chief Defence Staff 1987–91, Chief 1991–92; Chair. Mil. Cttee of NATO 1993–96; Chair. MoDeM Consortium 1997–99; Chancellor Cranfield Univ. 1998–; Col Commandant, REME 1981–87, RA 1983–2000; Hon. Col 100 (Yeomanry) Field Regt RA, TA 1982–91, 12th Air Defence Regt 1987–91; Chair (non-exec.) Hunting Defence Ltd 1996–; Dir (non-exec.) Hunting Eng Ltd 1996–2001 (Chair. 1998–2001), Vickers Defence Systems 1996–2002, R. A. Museums Ltd 1996–2000, INSYS Ltd 2001–; Pres. Cranfield Trust 1999–, Old Aldenhamian Soc. 1999–; Vice-Pres. The Defence Mfrs Asscn 1996–2000 (Pres. 2000–), Officers' Pension Soc. 1997–; Dir Hunting-BRAE 1997– (Chair. 1998–); Kermit Roosevelt Lecturer 1988; mem. Court, Cranfield Inst. of Tech. 1981–83, Greenwich Univ. 1997–2000; mem. Guild of Freemen of the City of London 1992–, Comm. on Britain and Europe (Royal Inst. for Internal Affairs) 1996–97, Advisory Council, RMCS 1983–91; Freeman City of London 1992, Freeman of Worshipful Co. of Wheelwrights 1997; Fellow Imperial Coll. London 1996; Gov. Aldenham School 1987–, Ditchley Foundation 1992–, Imperial Coll. London 1995– (Chair. Bd of Govs. 1996–); Master Gunner St James's Park 1996–2000; Patron Inspire Foundation 1999–; Hon. DSc (Cranfield) 1985; Jordanian Order of Merit (First Class), USA Legion of Merit (Degree of Cdre). *Publications:* contrib. to journals and Publs. *Leisure interests:* seven grandchildren, pursuing a second career. *Address:* House of Lords, London, SW1A 0PW, England.

VINE, Barbara (see Rendell, Ruth).

VINE, Jeremy, BA; British broadcaster; b. 17 May 1965; s. of Guy Vine and Diana Vine; ed Epsom Coll. and Univ. of Durham; journalist, Coventry Evening Telegraph 1986–87; joined BBC 1987, News Trainee 1987–89, Programme Reporter, Today 1989–93, Political Corresp. 1993–97, Africa Corresp. 1997–99, Presenter, Newsnight 1996–2002 (full-time 1999–2002); Presenter, The Jeremy Vine Show, BBC Radio Two 2003–. *Leisure interest:* Chelsea Football Club. *Address:* c/o Room G680, BBC Television Centre, Wood Lane, London, W12 7RJ, England (Office). *Telephone:* (20) 8624-9800 (Office). *Website:* www.bbc.co.uk (Office).

VINES, David Anthony, PhD; British/Australian economist; b. 8 May 1949, Oxford; s. of Robert Vines and Vera Vines; m. 1st Susannah Lucy Robinson 1979 (divorced 1992); three s.; m. 2nd Jane E. Bingham 1995; two step-s.; ed Scotch Coll. Melbourne and Univs of Melbourne and Cambridge; Fellow, Pembroke Coll. Cambridge 1976–85; Research Officer, Sr Research Officer, Dept of Applied Econs, Univ. of Cambridge 1979–85; Adam Smith Prof. of Political Econ. Univ. of Glasgow 1985–92; Fellow and Tutor in Econs Balliol Coll. Oxford 1992–, Prof. of Econs, Univ. of Oxford 2000–; Adjunct Prof. of Econs, Inst. of Advanced Studies, ANU 1991–; Dir ESRC Research Programme on Global Econ. Insts 1993–2000; mem. Bd Channel 4 TV 1986–92, Glasgow Devt Agency 1990–92, Analysys, Scottish Early Music Asscn 1988–95; econ. consultant to Sec. of State for Scotland 1988–92; consultant to IMF 1988, 1989; mem. Acad. Panel, HM Treasury 1986–; mem. Research Programmes Bd, ESRC 1990–92; mem. Int. Policy Forum, HM Treasury 1999–; Houblon Norman Fellow, Bank of England 2001–02. *Publications:* Stagflation, Vol. II: Demand Management (with J. E. Meade and J. M. Maciejowski) 1983, Macroeconomic Interactions Between North and South (with D. A. Currie) 1988, Macroeconomic Policy: inflation, wealth and the exchange rate (jtly) 1989, Deregulation and the Future of Commercial Television (with G. Hughes) 1989, Information, Strategy and Public Policy (with A. Stevenson) 1991, North South Macroeconomic Interactions and Global Macroeconomic Policy (ed. with D. A. Currie) 1995, Europe, East Asia and APEC: a Shared Global Agenda (with P. Drysdale) 1998, The Asian Financial Crisis: Causes Contagion and Consequences (ed., with P. Agenor, M. Miller and A. Weber) 1999, Integrity in the Public and Private Domains (ed. with A. Montefiore) 1999, The World Bank: Structure and Policies (ed. with C. L. Gilbert) 2000, papers in professional journals. *Leisure interests:* hillwalking, music. *Address:* Balliol College, Oxford, OX1 3BJ; Department of Economics, Manor Road, Oxford, OX1 3UQ, England. *Telephone:* (1865) 277719 (Coll.); (1865) 271067 (Dept). *Fax:* (1865) 277803 (Coll.); (1865) 271094 (Dept). *E-mail:* david.vines@economics.ox.ac.uk (Office and Home).

VINES, Sir William Joshua, Kt, AC, CMG; Australian business executive and farmer (retd); b. 27 May 1916, Terang; s. of Percy V. Vines and Isabella Vines; m. 1st Thelma J. Ogden 1939 (died 1988); one s. two d.; m. 2nd Judith Anne Ploeg 1990; ed Haileybury Coll., Victoria; army service, Middle East, New Guinea and Borneo 1939–45; Sec. Alexander Fergusson Pty Ltd 1938–40, 1945–47; Dir Goodlass Wall and Co. Pty Ltd 1947–49, Lewis Berger and Sons (Australia) Pty Ltd and Sherwin Williams Co. (Aust.) Pty Ltd 1952–55; Man. Dir Lewis Berger and Sons (Victoria) Pty Ltd 1949–55, Lewis Berger & Sons Ltd 1955–60, Berger, Jensen & Nicholson Ltd 1960–61, Int. Wool Secr. 1961–69, mem. Bd 1969–79; Chair. Dalgety Australia Ltd 1969–80, Carbonless Papers (Wiggins Teape) Pty Ltd 1970–78, Assoc. Pulp & Paper Mills Ltd 1978–82; Deputy Chair. and Dir Tubemakers of Australia Ltd 1970–86; Dir Commercial Union Assurance Co. of Australia Ltd 1969–78, Port Phillip Mills Pty Ltd, Conzinc Riotinto of Australia Ltd 1976–89, Dalgety Australia Holdings Ltd 1980–92, A.N.Z. Banking Group Ltd (Deputy Chair. 1980–82, Chair. 1982–89), Grindlays Holdings (now A.N.Z. UK Holdings PLC) 1985–89, Grindlays Bank 1987–89; Chair. Sir Robert Menzies Memorial Trust 1978–92; Chair. Council, Hawkesbury Agricultural Coll. 1975–85; Hon.

D.Sc.(Econs) (Sydney Univ.). *Leisure interests:* golf, writing, reading biographies. *Address:* 1/10 West Street, Balgowlah, NSW 2093, Australia (Home). *Telephone:* (2) 9948-1147.

VINKEN, Pierre; Netherlands publishing executive (retd); b. 25 Nov. 1927, Heerlen; ed Univs. of Utrecht and Amsterdam; consultant neurosurgeon, Univ. of Amsterdam 1964–71; Man. Dir Excerpta Medica Publishing Co. Amsterdam 1963–71, Elsevier Science Publrs., Amsterdam 1971–73; Exec. Dir Elsevier NV, Amsterdam (now Reed/Elsevier PLC London) 1972–79, Chair. 1993–95; hon. mem. various scientific asscns.; Kt. Order of Netherlands Lion 1984, Commdr Order of Hipólito Unanul (Peru) 1984, Commdr. Order of Orange Nassau 1995; Dr hc (Paris). *Publications:* Handbook of Clinical Neurology (77 Vols), The Shape of the Heart 2000; articles on medicine and art history in journals. *Address:* 142 Bentveldsweg, 2111 EE Aerdenhout, Netherlands (Home). *Telephone:* (23) 5246342 (Home). *Fax:* (23) 5246032 (Home). *E-mail:* vinken@euronet.nl (Home).

VINOGRADOV, Oleg Mikhailovich; Russian ballet master; b. 1 Aug. 1937; ed Vaganov Choreographic School, Leningrad; danced with Novosibirsk Acad. Theatre and Dir Cinderella 1964, Romeo and Juliet 1965; ballet master at Kirov Ballet, Leningrad 1968–72; RSFSR State Prize 1970 for Kazhlaev's Goryanka; Chief Ballet Master of Maly Theatre Dance Co. 1973–77; Chief Ballet Master of Kirov (now Mariinsky) Theatre 1977–99; works in USA and S. Korea; People's Artist of USSR 1983; Marius Petipa Prize, Paris 1978. *Productions include:* Useless Precaution (Hérold) 1971, Coppélia 1973, Yaroslavna (B. Tishchenko) 1974, The Hussar's Ballad (Khrennikov), The Government Inspector, The Battleship Potemkin (A. Chaikovsky), Behests of the Past 1983 and numerous others.

VINOGRADOV, Vasily Valentinovich; Russian diplomatist; b. 19 Sept. 1948, Port Arthur; m.; one s.; ed Moscow Inst. of Int. Relations; with USSR (now Russian) Ministry of Foreign Affairs 1971–; Consulate Dept 1971–79; Third Sec. USSR Gen. Consulate in New York 1979–88; Third, Second Sec. USSR Embassy, USA 1980–84; First Sec., Head of Div., Deputy Head, Head Consulate Dept Ministry of Foreign Affairs 1984–92; Dir Dept of Consulate Service Russian Ministry of Foreign Affairs 1992–96; Amb. to Australia 1997–98; on staff Ministry of Foreign Affairs 1998–. *Address:* Ministry of Foreign Affairs, Smolenskaya-Sennaya 32/34, Moscow, Russia.

VINOGRADOV, Vladimir Alekseyevich; Russian information specialist and economist; b. 2 July 1921, Kazan; s. of Aleksei Alexandrovich and Maria Alexandrovna; m. Marianna B. Antsuta 1943; one s.; ed Inst. of Int. Relations, Moscow; served in Soviet Army 1939–41; mem. staff Presidium of USSR (now Russian) Acad. of Sciences 1948–60, Deputy Chief Scientific Sec. 1961–71, Dir Inst. of Scientific Information on Social Sciences 1972–98, mem. Acad. 1984–, Counsellor 1998–; Lecturer, Dept of Political Economy, Moscow Univ. 1954–60; mem. Soviet Cttee of UNESCO 1965–91; Vice-Pres. Int. Asscn for Econ. History 1968–78, Int. Social Sciences Council 1978–81; Hon. Vice-Pres. Vienna Centre 1981–93; mem. New York Acad. of Sciences; USSR State Prize 1982, Chernishevski Prize (Presidium of Acad. of Sciences) and other awards and prizes. *Publications:* numerous books and articles on the genesis of property in Russian and West European countries and on problems of information in the social sciences and the humanities, including Social Sciences and Information 1978, Workers' Control over Production: Theory, History and Contemporaneity 1983, What Type of Privatization do we Need? 1991, State Property and Privatization in France 1998, Privatization in the Global Context 1998. *Leisure interest:* poetry. *Address:* Institute of Scientific Information in Social Sciences, Nakhimovski prosp. 51/21, 117418 Moscow, Russia. *Telephone:* (095) 128-89-30 (Office); (095) 331-32-16 (Home). *Fax:* (095) 420-22-61.

VIOT, Jacques Edmond, CVO, CBE, LèsL; French diplomatist; b. 25 Aug. 1921, Bordeaux; m. Jeanne de Martimprey de Romecourt 1950; ed Bordeaux and Paris lycées, Ecole Normale Supérieure and Ecole Nat. d'Admin.; Lecturer in French, Univ. of Dublin 1945–47, Ecole Nat. d'Admin. 1948–50; Foreign Office 1951–53, Second Sec., London 1953–57; First Sec., Rabat 1957–61; held various posts in cen. admin. 1961–72; Amb. to Canada 1972–77; Gen. Insp. for Foreign Affairs 1977–78; Dir de Cabinet, Ministry of Foreign Affairs 1978–81; Gen. Insp. for Foreign Affairs 1981–84; Amb. to UK 1984–86; Chair. Review Cttee on Foreign Affairs, Paris 1986–87; Chair. France-Grande Bretagne 1987–2000; mem. Admin. Council Alliance-Française 1987–94, Ecole Normale supérieure 1988–94, Conseil supérieur Agence France-Presse 1988–94; Chair. Franco-British Council (French Section) 1992, Alliance Française 1994–; Ambassadeur de France; Commdr, Légion d'honneur, Commdr, Ordre nat. du Mérite. *Address:* 19 rue de Civry, 75016 Paris, France. *Telephone:* 1-42-75-79-83 (Office); 1-42-84-90-36 (Office). *Fax:* 1-42-84-90-30 (Office); 1-42-75-79-87 (Office).

VIOT, Pierre, LèsL, L. END.; French barrister; b. 9 April 1925, Bordeaux; s. of Edmund Viot and Irma Viot; m. Monique Fruchier 1952 (deceased); two s. two d.; ed Faculté de droit de Bordeaux, Inst. d'études politiques de Paris, Ecole Nat. d'Admin.; Jr Official Cour des Comptes 1953, Chief Counsel; Asst Bureau des Commrs. aux Comptes, NATO 1957–61; Regional and Urban Dept Head, Gen. Planning Office 1961; Spokesman Nat. and Regional Devt Cttee 1961; Sec.-Gen. Conseil des Impôts 1971; Dir-Gen. Centre nat. de la Cinématographie 1973–84; Pres. Cannes Film Festival 1984–2000, Cinefondation Cannes Film Festival 2000–; Pres. Bd of Dirs., Establissement public de l'Opéra de la Bastille 1985–89; Commdr, Légion d'honneur, Croix de guerre,

Grand Officier, Ordre nat. du Mérite, Commdr Arts et Lettres. *Leisure interests:* tennis, gardening. *Address:* 38 avenue Emile Zola, 75015 Paris, France (Home).

VIRATA, Cesar Enrique, B.S.BUS.ADM., B.S.MECH.ENG., MBA; Philippine politician and banker; b. 12 Dec. 1930, Manila; s. of Enrique Virata and Leonor Aguinaldo; m. Joy Gamboa 1956; two s. one d.; ed Univ. of Pennsylvania, USA and Univ. of the Philippines; Dean, Coll. of Business Admin., Univ. of the Philippines 1961–69; Chair. and Dir Philippine Nat. Bank 1967–69; Deputy Dir-Gen. Presidential Econ. Staff 1967–68; Under-Sec. of Industry 1967–69; Chair. Bd of Investments 1968–70; Minister of Finance 1970–86; Prime Minister of the Philippines 1981–86; Chair. Land Bank of the Philippines 1973–86; mem. Nat. Ass. 1978–86, Monetary Bd, Nat. Econ. and Devt Authority 1972–86, Comm. on the Future of the Bretton Woods Insts. 1992–; Adviser to the Co-ordinating Council for the Philippines Aid Plan 1989–90; Chair. IMF and IBRD Devt Cttee 1976–80; Prin. C. Virata & Assocs. (Man. Consultants) 1986–; Chair. Bd of Govs., Asian Devt Bank 1979–80; Dir Philippine Stock Exchange, Inc. 1992; Chair. and CEO Rizal Commercial Banking Corpn 1996–; LHD hc, D.P.A. hc, Dr. hc (Philippines). *Leisure interests:* tennis, reading. *Address:* Rizal Commercial Banking Corporation, 333 Sen. Gil. J. Puyat Avenue, Ext., Makati City, P.O. Box 1005, Metro Manila (Office); 63 East Maya Drive, Quezon City, Philippines (Home). *Telephone:* (2) 8949000 (Office). *Fax:* (2) 8910988.

VIREN, Lasse; Finnish athlete and politician; b. 22 July 1949, Myrskylä; m. Päivi Kajander 1976; three s.; competed Olympic Games, Munich 1972, won gold medal at 5,000m and 10,000m; Montréal 1976, won gold medal at 5,000m and 10,000m, 5th in marathon; Moscow 1980, 5th in 10,000m; only athlete to retain 5,000m and 10,000m titles at successive Olympics; has held world records at 2 miles, 5,000m and 10,000m; sports promoter in schools at the Union Bank of Finland; elected Pres. of his local town council while running own transport business; MP (Conservative Party) 1999–. *Publication:* The Golden Seconds. *Address:* Suomen Urheilulitto ry, Box 25202, 00250, Helsinki 25, Finland.

VIRILIO, Paul; French writer and artist; b. 1932, Paris; ed Ecole des Metiers d'Art, Paris, Univ. of the Sorbonne, Paris; worked as artist in stained glass alongside Matisse in various churches in Paris; untrained architect; Chair. and Dir Ecole Spéciale d'Architecture, Paris 1968–98, Prof. Emer. 1998–; Ed. Espace Critique, Editions Galilee, Paris 1973–; Co-Founder and Program Dir Collège Int. de Philosophie 1990–; mem. French Comm. concerned with housing for the poor (HCLD) 1992–; fmr mem. Editorial Bds Esprit, Cause Commune, Critiques, Traverses; has worked with Fondation Cartier pour l'art contemporain on several exhbns including Bunker Archeology, Pompidou Centre 1975, Speed, Jouy-en-Josas 1991, Unknown Quantity, Paris 2002; Grand Prix Nat. de la Critique 1987. *Publications include:* Bunker Archeologie 1975, L'Insecurité du territoire 1976, Speed and Politics 1977, Popular Defense and Ecological Struggles 1978, L'Esthetique de la disparition 1980, Pure War (with Sylvère Lotringer) 1983, War and Cinema: The Logistics of Perception 1984, L'Espace critique 1984, Polar Inertia 1990, The Art of the Motor 1995, Politics of the Very Worst 1996, Open Sky 1997, The Information Bomb 1998, The Strategy of Deception 1999, A Landscape of Events 2000, Ground Zero 2002; numerous technical works. *Address:* Editions Galilee, 9 rue de Linné, 75005 Paris, France (Office). *Telephone:* 1-43-31-23-84 (Office). *Fax:* 1-45-35-53-68 (Office). *E-mail:* editions.galilee@free.fr (Office).

VIRSALADZE, Eliso Konstantinovna; Georgian pianist; b. 14 Sept. 1942, Tbilisi; studied under grandmother, Prof. Anastasia Virsaladze; then at Tbilisi Conservatory; won first prize at All-Union Competition of Performing Musicians, Moscow 1961; Bronze Medal at Tchaikovsky Competition 1962, Prize at Schumann Competition; teacher Moscow Conservatory 1962, Prof.; played as a soloist all over the world and on tour in Europe and USA with Leningrad Philharmonic; soloist with USSR Symphony Orchestra in UK 1983–84, Germany 1984–85; f. Tkvarcheli Music Festival and Summer School; many other tours as soloist in Europe and Japan; master classes in Munich 1996; USSR People's Artist 1989, Georgian State Prize 1983. *Address:* Moscow Conservatory, Bolshaya Nikitskaya str. 13, Moscow, Russia. *Telephone:* (095) 268-69-12 (Home).

VISHNEVSKAYA, Galina Pavlovna; Russian soprano; b. 25 Oct. 1926, Leningrad (now St Petersburg); m. Mstislav Rostropovich (q.v.); two d.; studied with Vera Garina 1942–52; Leningrad Musical Theatres 1944–52; leading soloist, Bolshoi Theatre 1952–74; left Soviet Union 1974; stripped of citizenship 1978 (citizenship restored 1990); retd from operatic stage as Tatiana (Eugene Onegin) Paris 1982; numerous parts in operas, notably Leonora in Fidelio and Tatiana in Eugene Onegin (also in the film), Aida (Aida), Kupava (Snow Maiden), Liza (Queen of Spades), Cio-Cio-San (Madame Butterfly), Margaret (Faust), Natasha (War and Peace), Cherubino (Marriage of Figaro), Marfa (Tsar's Bridge), Violetta (Traviata), Liu (Turandot), Katerina (Lady Macbeth of Mtsensk); acted in A. Chekhov Moscow Arts Theatre 1993–94; f. opera School in Moscow 1999. *Publication:* Galina (autobiog.) 1985. *Address:* Gazetny per. 13, Apt. 79, 103009 Moscow, Russia. *Telephone:* (095) 229-04-96 (Moscow); 1-42-27-85-06 (Paris).

VISHNEVSKY, Yuri Georgyevich; Russian geophysicist and civil servant; b. 13 May 1943, Orlovorozka, Kemerovo region; m.; one s.; ed Tomsk Polytech. Inst.; engineer, Sr engineer Tomsk-7 (chemical co.), Siberia for Ministry of

Machine Construction 1966–85; Head of Volzhsk br., then Cen. Br. State Inspection of Atomic and Energy Safety (Balakovo Nuclear Station) 1985–91; Chair. State Cttee for Inspection of Radiation Safety 1991, Chair. RSFSR State Cttee for Inspection of Nuclear and Radiation Safety at Russian Presidency 1991–92; Dir Fed. Inspection of Nuclear and Radiation Safety 1992–. *Address:* Federal Inspection of Nuclear and Radiation Safety of Russian Federation, Taganskaya str. 34, 109147 Moscow, Russia (Office). *Telephone:* (095) 911-15-68 (Office). *Fax:* (095) 912-40-41 (Office).

VISHNYOVA, Diana Viktorovna; Russian ballerina; b. 13 July 1976, Leningrad; ed Vaganova Acad. of Russian Ballet; soloist Mariinsky Theatre 1995–; first Russian ballerina to have won Prix de Lausanne 1994; Prizes Divine Isadora, Benoit de la Dance. *Main roles include:* Masha (Nutcracker), Kitri (Don Quixote), Aurore (Sleeping Beauty), Henriette (Raymonda), Gulnary (Corsaire). *Address:* Mariinsky Theatre, Teatralnaya pl. 1., St Petersburg, Russia. *Telephone:* (812) 315-57-24.

VITA, Giuseppe, DR. MED.; Italian business executive; b. 28 April 1935, Sicily; ed in Catania and Rome; qualified as specialist in radiology; Asst Röntgeninstitut, Univ. of Mainz 1962; joined Schering AG as Asst in clinical research 1964; Gen. Dir Schering SpA Milan 1965; Deputy mem. Man. Bd Schering AG 1987, mem. 1988, Chair. 1989–2001, Chair. Supervisory Bd 2001–; Cavaliere del Lavoro; Verdienstorden des Landes Berlin, Verdienstkreuz am Bande des Verdienstordens der Bundesrepublik Deutschland. *Address:* Schering AG, 13342 Berlin, Germany.

VITALE, Alberto; American publishing executive; b. 22 Dec. 1933, Vercelli, Piedmont, Italy; s. of Sergio Vitale and Elena Segre; m. Gemma G. Calori 1961; two s.; ed Turin Univ., IPSOA Business School and Wharton School, Univ. of Pa (Fulbright Scholar); joined Olivetti 1958; moved to USA to assist in Olivetti's acquisition of Underwood 1959; Exec. IFI (Agnelli family holding co.) 1971; Exec. Vice-Pres. for Admin. Bantam Books, New York 1975, Co-CEO 1985, Sole CEO 1986; Pres. and CEO Bantam-Doubleday-Dell 1987; Chair., Pres. and CEO Random House 1990–96, Chair., CEO 1996–98; Chair. Supervisory Bd Random House Inc., New York 1998–; mem. Bd Dirs. Transworld Publrs. *Address:* 745 Fifth Avenue, Suite 1512, New York, NY 10151 (Office); Random House Inc., 299 Park Avenue, New York, NY 10171; 505 Alda Road, Mamaroneck, NY 10543, USA.

VITHAYATHIL, HE Cardinal Varkey; Indian ecclesiastic; b. 29 May 1927, Parur, Ernakulam; s. of Justice Joseph Vithayathil; ordained priest 1954; Archbishop 1997; Archbishop Maj. of Syro-Malabar Church, Ernakulam-Angamaly 1999–; cr. Cardinal 2001. *Address:* Archdiocesan Curia, P.O. Box 2580, Kochi 68 2031, Kerala (Office); Major Archbishop's House, Ernakulam, P.O. Box 2580, Kochi 682031, Kerala, India (Home). *Telephone:* (484) 352629 (Office). *Fax:* (484) 366028 (Office). (484) 355010 (Home). *E-mail:* abperang@vsnl.com (Office). *Website:* www.ernakulamarchdiocese.org (Office).

VITIER, Cintio; Cuban poet and writer; b. 25 Sept. 1921, Key West, USA; s. of Medardo Vitier; m. Fina García Marruz; ed Univ. of Havana; worked on Orígenes magazine 1944–56; lecturer, Escuele normal para Maestros, Havana, Universidad Cen. de las Villas; researcher, José martí Nat. Library 1962–77; Pres. Centre of Martianos Studies; Ofícier des Arts et des Lettres; Dr hc (Univ. of Havana), (Universidad Central de las Villas), (Soka Univ., Japan); Nat. Literature Prize 1988, 30th Anniversary Medal, Acad. of Sciences, Order of Jose Marti 2002, Juan Rulfo Prize for Literature 2002. *Publications include:* poetry: Vísperas 1953, Testimonios 1968, La fecha al pie 1981, Nupcias 1993; fiction: De Peña Pobre 1980, Los Papeles de Jacinto Finalé 1984, Rajando la leña está 1986; essays: Lo cubano en la poesía 1958, Temas Martianos (with Fina García Marruz) 1969, 1982; Crítica Sucesiva 1971, Ese sol del mundo moral 1975, Rescate de Zenea 1987, Crítica cubana 1988. *Address:* c/o Editorial Letras Cubanas, Ediciones Unión, No. 4, esq. Tacón, Hababa Vieja, Havana, Cuba (Office). *Website:* www.cubaliteraria.cu (Office).

VITORGAN, Emmanuil; Russian film and theatre director; b. 27 Dec. 1939, Baku, Azerbaijan; m.; one s. one d; ed Leningrad State Inst. of Theatre Arts; with Leningrad Theatre of Drama and Comedy 1961–63, Leningrad Theatre of Leninsky Komsomol 1964–71, Moscow Stanislavsky Drama Theatre 1971–82, Moscow Taganka Theatre 1982–84, Moscow Academic Mayakovsky Theatre 1984–; Merited Artist of Russia 1990, People's Artist of Russia 1998. *Films include:* King Lear 1972, And This is All about Him 1974, Fortress 1978, Two People in a New House 1979, Profession - Investigator 1982, Devout Marta 1983, The Grown-up Daughter of a Young Man 1990, When Saints are Marching 1990, Lady in Spectacles with a Gun in a Car 2002. *Plays include:* Westside Story, Humiliated and Insulted, Rain Seller, Shadows, Grown-Up Daughter of a Young Man, Sirano de Berjerac, Circle, Nora or Doll's House. *Address:* Moscow Academic Mayakovsky Theatre, Bolshaya Nikitskaya str. 19, 103009 Moscow (Office); Maly Kislovsky per.7, apt 26, 103009 Moscow, Russia (Home). *Telephone:* (095) 290-30-31 (Office); (095) 291-89-89 (Office).

VITORINO, António; Portuguese politician and lawyer; b. 1958; mem. Parl. 1981; Sec. of State for Parl. Affairs 1985; has served in Govt of Macao; Judge, Constitutional Court; Minister for Defence and the Presidency 1995; EU Commr for Freedom, Security and Justice July 1999–. *Address:* Commission of the European Communities, 200 rue la Loi, 1049 Brussels, Belgium (Office).

VITRENKO, Natalia Mikhailovna, DEcon; Ukrainian politician; b. 28 Dec. 1958, Kiev; m.; one s. one d.; ed Kiev State Inst. of Nat. Econs; Sr Economist Cen. Dept of Statistics 1973–76; Sr researcher Research Inst. of Information, State Planning Comm. 1979–89; Docent Kiev Inst. of Nat. Econs 1979–89; Sr Researcher Council on Production Forces, Ukrainian Acad. of Sciences 1989–94; ed. Vybor (journal) 1993–; People's Deputy 1994–; Counsellor on Socio-econ. Problems, Verkhovna Rada; mem. Socialist Party of Ukraine 1991, Progressive Socialist Party 1998–, Presidium of Political Council 1993–, Acad. of Construction, Acad. of Econ. Cybernetics 1997. *Address:* Verkhovna Rada, M. Hrushevskogo str. 5, Kiev, Ukraine (Office).

VITRUK, Nikolai Vasilievich, LLD; Russian lawyer; b. 4 Nov. 1937, Zharovka, Tomsk Region; m. (divorced 1988); one d.; ed Tomsk State Univ.; Man. Legal Advice Bureau, Tomsk Regional Lawyers' Bd 1959; Asst Chair. of Theory and History of State and Law, Tomsk Univ. 1960–63; Asst, Sr Teacher, Asst Prof. Chair. of Theory of State and Law, T. G. Shevchenko Kiev State Univ. 1966–71; Sr Scientific Researcher, Inst. of State and Law, USSR Acad. of Sciences 1971–81; Prof. Chair. of Theory of State and Law and Constitutional Law, Acad. of Ministry of Internal Affairs of USSR 1981–84; Chief, Chair of State and Law Discipline, High Correspondence Law Coll. Ministry of Internal Affairs of USSR 1984–91; Justice, Constitutional Court of Russian Fed. 1991–, Deputy Chair. 1991–96, Acting Chair. 1993–95; mem. Venice Comm., Strasbourg, France 1992; Rep. of Russian Fed., European Comm. for Democracy Through Law; Labour Veteran Medal, Medal for Irreproachable Service, Honoured Scientist of Russian Fed. *Publications:* about 300 legal works. *Leisure interests:* theatre, modern realistic painting, poetry, art, culture of Russia during the 'Silver Age'. *Address:* Constitutional Court, 21 Ilyinka Street, 103132 Moscow, Russia (Office). *Telephone:* (095) 206-06-29 (Office). *Fax:* (095) 206-17-49 (Office).

VITRYANSKY, Vassily Vladimirovich, DJur; Russian lawyer; b. 8 May 1956, Gomel, Belarus; m.; one s. two d.; ed Moscow State Univ.; mem. staff RSFSR State Court of Arbitration 1978–86; Sr Asst Admin. RSFSR Council of Ministers 1986–89, consultant Dept of Law 1989–90; Deputy Chief State Arbiter of RSFSR 1990–92; Deputy Chair. Higher Court of Arbitration of Russian Fed. 1992–; teacher Moscow State Univ., participated in Devt of civil law in Russian Fed. *Monographs:* Protection of Property Rights of Businessmen, Protection of Property Rights of Stock Companies and Shareholders, Law and Bankruptcy; numerous publications on protection of civil rights, civil and legal responsibility, bankruptcy, etc. *Address:* Higher Court of Arbitration, M. Kharitonyevsky per. 12, 111001 Moscow, Russia (Office). *Telephone:* (095) 208-12-81 (Office).

VITTI, Monica (Monica Luisa Ceciarelli); Italian actress; b. 3 Nov. 1931, Rome; ed Nat. Acad., Rome. *Films include:* L'Avventura 1959, La Notte 1960, L'Eclisse 1962, Dragées au Poivre 1963, The Red Desert 1964, Modesty Blaise 1966, The Chastity Belt 1967, Girl With a Pistol 1969, Le Coppie 1971, La Pacifiste 1971, La Tosca 1971, Teresa la larda 1973, A mezzanotte va la ronda di piacere 1975, Duck in Orange Sauce 1975, An Almost Perfect Affair 1979, Teresa the Thief 1979, The Oberwald Mystery 1981, Tigers in Lipstick, The Flirt, When Veronica Call's, Broadway Danny Rose 1984, Secret Scandal (also wrote and Dir) 1990. *Publication:* A Bed is Like a Rose 1997.

VITUKHNOVSKAYA, Alina Aleksandrovna; Russian poet; b. 27 March 1973, Moscow; first verses published late 1980s in periodicals; arrested on charge of drugs trafficking, freed Oct. 1995, arrested Nov. 1997; mem. Russian PEN Centre, Writers' Union; Pushkin Scholarship, Hamburg, Germany 1998. *Publications include:* Anomaly 1993, Children's Book of the Dead 1994, Pavlov's Dog (with K. Kedrov) 1996, The Last Old Woman Money-lender of Russian Literature (stories) 1996, Land of Zero 1996, Romance with Phenamine (novel). *Address:* Leningradskoye shosse 80, Apt. 89, 125565 Moscow, Russia. *Telephone:* (095) 452-15-31.

VIVARELLI, Roberto; Italian professor of history; b. 8 Dec. 1929, Siena; s. of Lavinio Vivarelli and Margherita Cosci; m. Ann Sheldon West 1960 (died 1999); two s. one d.; ed Univs of Siena, Florence and Pennsylvania, USA and Istituto Italiano di Studi Storici; Research Fellow, St Antony's Coll. Oxford, UK 1961–62; Asst Prof., Univ. of Siena 1962–70, Full Prof. 1972–75; Assoc. Prof., Univ. of Florence 1970–72, Full Prof. 1975–86; Prof. of History, Scuola Normale Superiore, Pisa 1986–; Visiting Prof., Inst. for Advanced Study, Princeton, USA 1969–70, 1980–81, Harvard Univ. 1976; Visiting Fellow, All Souls Coll. Oxford 1993–94; mem. Editorial Bd Rivista Storica Italiana; mem. Academia Europaea. *Publications:* Gaetano Salvemini's Scritti sul Fascismo (Ed.) 1961, 1974, Georges Sorel's Scritti politici (Ed.) 1963, Il dopoguerra in Italia e l'avvento del fascismo 1967, Il fallimento del liberalismo 1981, Storia delle origini del fascismo (2 Vols) 1991, Profilo di storia (3 Vols) 1996, La fine di una stagione: Memoria 1943–1945 2000. *Address:* Scuola Normale Superiore, Piazza dei Cavalieri, 56100 Pisa (Office); Via Dante da Castiglione 1, 50125 Florence, Italy (Home). *Telephone:* (050) 509221 (Office); (055) 223190 (Home). *Fax:* (050) 563513 (Office).

VIVES, Xavier, MA, PhD; Spanish economist; b. 23 Jan. 1955, Barcelona; m. Aurora Bastide; two s.; ed Autonomous Univ. of Barcelona, Univ. of Calif. at Berkeley, USA; Sr Researcher, Fundación de Estudios de Economía Aplicada (FEDEA); Programme Dir Applied Microecons. and Industrial Org. Programmes, Centre for Econ. Policy Research, London; Dir Institut d'Analisi Económica, Barcelona 1991–2001; Prof. of Econs and Finance, Institut Européen d'Administration des Affaires (INSEAD) 2001–; Visiting Prof. Harvard Univ., Univs of Pa, Calif. at Berkeley and New York; Fellow Econometric Soc. 1992; Premio Extraordinario de Licenciatura, Autonomous

Univ. of Barcelona 1978, King Juan Carlos I Prize for Research in Social Science 1988, Societat Catalana d'Economía Prize 1996. *Publications:* Monitoring European Integration: The Future of European Banking (co-author) 1999, Oligopoly Pricing: Old Ideas and New Tools 2000, Corporate Governance: Theoretical and Empirical Perspectives (ed.) 2000. *Address:* INSEAD, boulevard de Constance, 77305 Fantainebleu Cedex (Office); 24 rue Casimir Périer, 77300 Fontainebleu, France (Home). *Telephone:* 1-60-72-42-79 (Office); 1-60-72-83-01 (Home). *Fax:* 1-60-74-67-19 (Office). *E-mail:* xavier.vives@insead.edu (Office). *Website:* faculty.insead.edu/vives.

VIVIAN, Young; Niue politician; b. 1935; Leader Niue People's Party; Premier Dec. 1992–March 1993, May 2002–, also Minister for External Affairs, Int. Relations and Aid Co-ordination, Niue Public Service Comm., the Crown Law Office, Community Affairs, Arts, Culture and Village Councils, Religious Affairs, Population Devt and Niueans Abroad, Women's Affairs, Youth and Sport and Pvt. Sector Devt May 2002–. *Address:* Niue People's Party, Alofi, Niue (Office).

VIZZINI, Carlo; Italian politician and university teacher; b. 28 April 1947, Palermo; elected Social Democrat MP for Palermo-Trapani-Agrigento-Caltanisetta 1976, now Senator; Nat. Deputy Sec. Italian Social Democrat Party and Head of Dept 1980–88; Under-Sec. of State in Ministry of Budget and Econ. Planning; Minister for Regional Affairs 1986–87, of Cultural Heritage 1987–88, of the Merchant Navy 1989–91, of Posts and Telecommunications 1991–92; Sec. Partido Socialista Democratica Italiano (PSDI); Pres. Bicameral Comm. for Regional Questions; mem. Parliamentary Comm. of Inquiry into Organized Crime and the Mafia; Prof. of History of Econs, Univ. of Palermo. *Address:* Segretaria Politica, Centro Studi – Laboratorio Politico, Via di Stefano 19, Palermo, Italy. *Telephone:* (91) 332697 (Office). *Fax:* (91) 321038 (Office). *E-mail:* carlovizzini@carlovizzini.it (Office).

VLAAR, Nicolaas Jacob; Netherlands professor emeritus of geophysics; b. 17 March 1933, Mijnsheerenland; m. 1st Joanna Lambermont 1956 (died 1976); m. 2nd Everdina den Hartog 1980; three s. (one s. deceased) one d.; ed Bisschoppelijk Coll., Tech. Univ., Delft and Utrecht Univ.; Asst Calif. Inst. of Tech. 1965–66, St Louis Univ. 1966–67, Utrecht Univ. 1963–, Prof. of Theoretical Geophysics 1973; Prof. of Theoretical Geophysics, Free Univ. 1983–, now Emer., Dean of Faculty 1989–92; mem. Royal Netherlands Acad. of Science 1984–; mem. Hollandsche Maatschappij der Wetenschappen 1983–, Bd Netherlands Science Org. (Biology, Oceanography and Earth Science) 1988–; Hon. mem. European Geophysical Soc. 1995; Royal Dutch/Shell Prize 1982, Kt Royal Order of the Lion of the Netherlands 1994. *Publications:* numerous works on seismology and geodynamics. *Leisure interests:* nature, esoterics. *Address:* Mauritslaan 5, 3818 GJ Amersfoort, Netherlands. *Telephone:* (33) 4613516. *E-mail:* (Home).

VLADIMIR, Metropolitan (Victor Markianovich Sabodan), B.THEOL.; Ukrainian ecclesiastic; b. 23 Nov. 1935, Khmelnitsky Region; ed Leningrad and Moscow Theological Acads.; ordained as deacon, then priest 1962–66; Bishop, Archbishop 1966–82; Metropolitan 1982; taught in Odessa Seminary, then Rector; Deputy Chief Russian Orthodox Mission in Jerusalem 1966–68; Bishop of Pereslavl-Zalessky; Archbishop of Dmitrov, Rector Moscow Theological Acad., Prof. 1973–82; Metropolitan of Rostov and Novocherkassk 1982–86; Patriarch Rep. in West Europe 1986–87; man. Moscow Patriarchy, perm. mem. Holy Synod 1987–; Metropolitan of Kiev and All Ukraine 1992–. *Address:* Ukrainian Orthodox Church, Perchevsk Monastery, Sichnevoho Povstannia 25, Kiev, Ukraine. *Telephone:* (44) 290-15-08.

VLADIMIROV, Vasiliy Sergeyevich, DSc; Russian mathematician; b. 9 Jan. 1923, Djaglevo, Petrograd Region; s. of Sergey Ivanovich Vladimirov and Maria Semyonovna Vladimirova; m. Nina Yakovlevna Vladimirov (née Ovsyannikova) 1948; two s.; ed Leningrad State Univ.; served in Soviet Army 1941–45; Jr Research Worker, Leningrad Dept, V. A. Steklov Inst. of Math., USSR Acad. of Sciences 1948–50; Head Dept Computer Math., All Russian Research Inst. of Experimental Physics, Arsamas-16, 1950–56; Sr Research Worker, Steklov Inst. of Maths, Moscow 1956–69, Head, Dept of Math. Physics 1969–; Prof. Physico-tech. Inst. 1964–87; Vice-Dir Steklov Inst. 1986–88, Dir 1988–93, Counsellor 1993–; mem. CPSU 1944–91; Corresp. mem. USSR (now Russian) Acad. of Sciences 1968–70, mem. 1970–, Counsellor 1993–; mem. Saxony Akad. der Wissenschaften zu Leipzig 1985, Int. Asscn of Math. Physics 1980, Acad. of Sciences and Arts Voivodina (Yugoslavia) 1987, Serbian Acad. of Science and Arts (Belgrade) 1991; Hon. mem. Soc. Math. and Physics of the Czech Repub.; State Prize 1953, 1987 (twice), Order of Lenin 1975, 1983 (twice), Order of the Great Patriotic War 1985, Bogolyubov Prize, Nat. Acad. of Sciences of Ukraine 1997; Gold Medal of A. N. Liapounov 1971, Gold Medal Bernarda Bolzana CSR Acad. of Science 1982, Gold Star of Hero of Socialist Labour 1983, Gold Medal of N.N. Bogolyubov Award 1999 and numerous other awards. *Publications:* Mathematical Problems of the One-Velocity Particles Transfer 1961, Methods of the Theory of Functions of Several Complex Variables 1964, Equations of Mathematical Physics 1967, Distributions in Mathematical Physics 1976, Many Dimensional Tauberian Theorems for Distributions (with others) 1986, p-Adic Analysis and Mathematical Physics (with others) 1994, Equations and Mathematical Physics (jtly, in Russian) 2001, Methods of the Theory of Generalized Functions 2002, and works in the field of number theory and numerical methods, analysis of transfer equation, theory of holomorphic

functions of several complex variables and distribution theory and their applications in mathematical physics; about 300 papers and articles. *Leisure interests:* skiing, fishing. *Address:* Steklov Institute of Mathematics, Gubkin Street 8, 117966 GSP-1 Moscow (Office); Fersmen Str. 9, fl. 37, 117312 Moscow, Russia (Home). *Telephone:* (095) 135-14-49 (Office); (095) 124-78-64 (Home). *Fax:* (095) 135-05-55 (Office). *E-mail:* vsv@vsv.mian.su (Office); vsv@vsv.mian.su (Home).

VLADIMOV, Georgij Nikolayevich; Russian writer and literary critic; b. 19 Feb. 1931, Kharkov; ed Leningrad State Univ.; started literary activity as critic 1954 and as prose-writer 1960; expelled from USSR Writers' Union 1977 and refused visa to emigrate; subsequently emigrated and worked for some time as ed. of Grani 1983–86; Russian Booker Prize 1995, Andrey Sakharov Prize 2000. *Publications include:* Bolshaya Ruda (novel) 1961, Letter to the Presidium of USSR Writers' Union (samizdat) 1967, Faithful Ruslan 1975, Three Minutes of Silence 1969, The Sixth Soldier (play) 1981, Do Not Pay Attention, Maestro (short story) 1982, The General and his Army (novel) 1994, (Russian Booker Prize 1995), Collected Works (4 Vols) 1998. *Address:* Lenzhahner Weg 38, Niedernhausen TS, Germany. *Telephone:* (6127) 5896. *E-mail:* GVladimov@aol.com.

VLADISLAVLEV, Alexander Pavlovich, D.TECH.SC.; Russian politician; b. 21 May 1936, Moscow; m. Karina Lisitsian; one s.; ed Gubkin Petroleum Inst., Moscow, Oil and Gas Inst., Bucharest; mem. CPSU 1959–91; researcher, Sr teacher, docent, Pro-Rector Gubkin Moscow Inst. 1959–74; Vice-Pres. All-Union Soc. Znanie 1974–86; First Vice-Chair. USSR Council of Scientific and Eng Socs. 1988–90; Chair. Exec. Cttee, First Vice-Pres. USSR (now Russian) Scientific-Industrial Union 1990–92; Chair. Council of Business of USSR, Pres. 1991; First Deputy Minister of Foreign Econ. Relations of USSR Nov.–Dec. 1991; First Vice-Pres. Russian Union of Industrialists and Entrepreneurs 1990–; USSR People's Deputy 1989–91; f. and Co-Chair. Democratic Reform Movt 1991–92; a leader of Civic Union 1992–93; mem. State Duma (Parl.) 2000– Chair. Sub-Cttee on Investment Policy; Chair. Bd, ZIL motor co. 1994–95; Pres. Ind. Fund for Realism in Politics 1994–; mem. Presidium of Eng Acad., founder and mem. of admin. of non-Govt foundations and socs.; mem. Advisory Council of UNO on Science and Tech.; mem. faction Otechestvo. *Publications:* 6 books; over 200 articles and papers; 15 patents. *Address:* Novy Arbat prosp. 15, Suite 2424, Moscow, Russia (Office). *Telephone:* (095) 202-26-25 (Office); (095) 203-55-15 (Home).

VLK, HE Cardinal Miloslav, BSc; Czech ecclesiastic; b. 17 May 1932, Sepekov-Líšnice; ed Faculty of Philosophy, Charles Univ. Prague, Faculty of Theology, Litoměřice; archivist Třeboň and Jindřichův Hradec 1960–61, České Budějovice 1961–64; ordained priest 1968; sec. to Roman Catholic Bishop of České Budějovice 1968–71; parish priest Lažiště and Rožmitál pod Třemšínem 1971–78; denied permission to work as priest 1978; window cleaner, Prague 1978–1986; archivist, Czechoslovak State Bank, Prague 1986–88; parish priest, parishes in Šumava Mountains 1989–90; cr. Bishop of České Budějovice 1990, Archbishop of Prague 1991–, cr. Cardinal 1994; mem. Consilium Conferentiarum Episcopalium Europae 1990–2001 (Pres. 1993–2001), Pontificium Consilium de Cultura 1991–93, Pontificum Consilium de Communicationibus Socialibus 1994–, Congregatio pro Ecclesiis Orientalibus 1994–; Hon. LHD (Ill. Benedictine Coll., USA, Univ. of St Thomas, Minn., USA) 1992; Hon. DTheol (Univ. Passau, Germany) 1993, (Pontificia Academia Theologica Cracoviensys, Poland) 2001, (Univ. Opole, Poland) 2002; Hon. Citizen, Rožmitál pod Třemšínem 1992, Cedar Rapids, USA 1992, Baltimore, USA 1992, Kłodzko, Poland 1996, Třeboň 1996, Roudnice nad Labem 1997, Mníšek pod Brdy 1998; Grosses Verdienstkreuz, Germany 1999, TGM Order 2002. *Publications:* numerous ecclesiastical articles. *Leisure interests:* classical and oriental languages, classical music, mountain tourism, skiing, cycling. *Address:* Arcibiskupství pražské, Hradčanské nám. 16/56, 119 02 Prague 1, Czech Republic. *Telephone:* (2) 20392111; (2) 20392201. *Fax:* (2) 20514647; (2) 20515396. *E-mail:* sekretar.vlk@apha.cz (Office). *Website:* www.apha.cz (Office).

VLOK, Adriaan; South African politician; b. 11 Dec. 1937, Sutherland; m. Cornelia Burger; two s. one d.; joined Dept of Justice 1957; became prosecutor and Sr magistrate, Asst Pvt. Sec. to Prime Minister John Vorster 1967; subsequently entered pvt. business; later Deputy Sheriff, E Pretoria; MP 1974–94; fmr Deputy Speaker of House of Ass.; Deputy Minister of Defence and Deputy Minister of Law and Order 1985–86; Minister of Law and Order 1986–91, of Correctional Services and the Budget 1991–92, of Correctional Services and of Housing and Works 1992, of Correctional Services 1992–94; Leader House of Ass. 1992–94; mem. Truth and Reconciliation Comm. for amnesty for criminal acts 1998. *Leisure interests:* rugby (referee in Northern Transvaal), military history, chewing biltong.

VO CHI CONG; Vietnamese politician; b. 1913, Central Viet Nam; fmr mem. Vietcong force; fmr Sec. Southern People's Party, a main element in Nat. Liberation Front (NLF); mem. Cen. Cttee of Lao Dong party for many years; Minister for Fisheries, Socialist Repub. of Viet Nam 1976–77; Vice-Premier, Council of Ministers 1976–82, now mem.; Minister for Agric. 1977–78; mem. Politburo of CP of Viet Nam 1976; Pres. of Viet Nam 1987–92. *Address:* c/o Council of Ministers, Bac Thao, Hanoi, Viet Nam.

VO NGUYEN GIAP, Gen.; Vietnamese army officer; b. 1912, Quangbinh Prov.; ed French Lycée in Hué and law studies at Univ. of Hanoi; History teacher, Thang Long School, Hanoi; joined Viet Nam CP in early 1930s; fled to China 1939, helped organize Vietminh Front, Viet Nam 1941; Minister of Interior 1945, became C-in-C of Vietminh Army 1946; defeated French at Dien Bien Phu 1954; Vice-Chair. Council of Ministers 1976–91, Minister of Defence, C-in-C, Democratic Repub. of Viet Nam to 1976, Socialist Repub. of Viet Nam 1976–80; mem. Politburo Lao-Dong Party until 1976, CP of Viet Nam 1976–82. *Publications:* People's War, People's Army, Big Victory, Great Task 1968. *Address:* Dang Cong san Viet Nam, 1c boulevard Hoang Van Thu, Hanoi, Viet Nam.

VO VAN KIET; Vietnamese politician; b. 1922, S. Viet Nam; joined CP of Indo-China in 1930s; mem. Lao Dong Party (renamed Communist Party of Viet Nam Dec. 1976), mem. Cen. Cttee CP 1958–; mem. Cen. Office for S. Viet Nam during war; alt. mem. Politburo, CP of Viet Nam 1976, now mem.; Vice-Chair. Council of Ministers 1982–91, Chair. 1991; Chair. State Planning Cttee 1982–88; Chair. CP Cttee in Ho Chi Minh City; Prime Minister of Viet Nam 1992–97. *Address:* c/o Council of Ministers, Hanoi, Viet Nam.

VODIČKA, Jindřich; Czech politician; b. 22 July 1952, Prague; m.; two s.; ed Univ. of Maritime Studies, Odessa; sailed as deck engineer, later First Officer in merchant navy 1977–90; First Deputy Dir, Office for Protection of Constitutional Officials –1990; Dir Job Centre, Prague-West Dist 1990–92; mem. Civic Democratic Party (CDP) 1991–97, 1998–, Unie Svobody Jan.–March 1998; Deputy to House of Nations (Fed. Ass. of Č.S.F.R.) June–Dec. 1992; Minister of Labour and Social Affairs of Czech Repub. 1992–97; Minister of Interior 1997–98; Dir-Gen. České přístavy (Czech Ports Ltd). *Address:* Civic Democratic Party, Sněmovní 3, 110 00 Prague 1, Czech Republic. *Telephone:* (2) 33334800. *E-mail:* info@ods.cz (Office). *Website:* www.ods.cz (Office).

VOGEL, Bernhard, DPhil; German politician; b. 19 Dec. 1932, Göttingen; s. of Prof. Dr Hermann Vogel and Caroline Vogel (née Brinz); ed Univs of Heidelberg and Munich; Lecturer, Inst. für Politische Wissenschaft, Heidelberg 1961–67; mem. Bundestag 1965–67; Minister of Educ. and Culture, Rhineland-Palatinate 1967–76; mem. Rhineland-Palatinate State Parl. 1971–88; Chair. CDU Rhineland-Palatinate 1974–88 (Chair Exec. Cttee CDU of Palatinate 1967–69, later Rheinhessen/Palatinate 1969–75); Minister-Pres., Rhineland-Palatinate 1976–88, Thuringia 1992–; Pres. Bundesrat 1976–77, 1987–88; Chair. Advisory Bd, Zweites Deutsches Fernsehen 1979–92; Pres. Bundesverband "Schutzgemeinschaft Deutscher Wald" 1980–84, Stiftung Wald in Not 1984–; Pres. Maximilian-Kolbe Works 1984–; Senator Max-Planck Asscn 1984–96; Konrad Adenauer Foundation 1989–95, Chair. 2001–; mem. Fed. Exec. Cttee of CDU 1975–, Chair. CDU Thuringia 1993–2000; Vice-Pres. European Democratic Union (EDU) 1985–; mem. Christian Democrats; Grosses Bundesverdienstkreuz mit Stern und Schulterband; decorations from France, Luxembourg, UK, Senegal and Vatican; Grosskreuz St Gregorius; Gold Medal of Strasbourg. *Publications:* Wahlen und Wahlsysteme 1961, Kontrolliert der Bundestag die Regierung? 1964, Wahlkampf und Wählertradition 1965, Wahlen in Deutschland 1848–1970 (with D. Nohlen and R-O Schultze), Schule am Scheideweg 1974; numerous essays and speeches. *Leisure interests:* mountaineering, literature, swimming. *Address:* Thüringer Staatskanzlei, Postfach 102151, 99021 Erfurt, Germany. *Telephone:* (361) 3792802. *Fax:* (361) 3792805. *E-mail:* tsk@thueringen.de. *Website:* www.thueringen.de.

VOGEL, Dieter H., DrIng; German industrialist; b. 14 Nov. 1941; m. Ursula Gross 1970; two c.; ed Tech. Univ. of Darmstadt, Tech. Univ. of Munich; Asst Prof., Thermic Turbo Engines, Tech. Univ. of Munich 1967–69; Vice-Pres., Printing Div., Bertelsmann AG 1970–74, Pegulan AG 1975–85 (Chair. 1978); Vice-Chair. Man. Bd Batig (BAT Industries) 1978–85; joined Thyssen Group 1986, Chair. Thyssen Handelsunion AG 1986–96, mem. Exec. Bd 1986–91, Deputy Chair. Thyssen AG 1991–96, Chair. 1996–98; Chair. Supervisory Bd Deutsche Bahn AG 1999–2001. *Leisure interest:* skiing. *Address:* c/o Deutsche Bahn AG, 60326 Frankfurt am Main, Stephensonstr. 1, Germany.

VOGEL, Hans-Jochen, DJur; German politician; b. 3 Feb. 1926, Göttingen; m. 1st Ilse Leisnering 1951 (divorced 1972); one s. two d.; m. 2nd Liselotte Sonnenholzer (née Biersack) 1972; ed Univs of Munich and Marburg; Asst, Bavarian Justice Ministry 1952–54; lawyer, Traunstein Dist Court 1954–55; Bavarian State Chancellery 1955–58; mem. Munich City Council 1958–60; Chief Burgomaster of Munich 1960–72; mem. Bundestag 1972–81, 1983–94; Minister for Regional Planning, Building and Urban Devt 1972–81, of Justice 1974; Mayor, West Berlin Jan.–June 1981; Chair. SPD Parl. Party 1984–91; Deputy Chair. SPD 1984–87, Chair. 1987–90; Vice-Pres. Org. Cttee for Munich Olympic Games 1972; Chair. Gegen Vergessen (Against Forgetting) Project 1993–; numerous decorations including Grosses Bundesverdienstkreuz, Bayerischer Verdienstorden, Hon. CBE and honours from France, Italy, etc. *Publications:* four books. *Leisure interests:* mountain walking, history. *Address:* Gegen Vergessen – Für Demokratie eV, Max Planck Strasse 3, 53177 Bonn, Germany (Office).

VOGT, Marthe Louise, DrMed, DPhil, PhD, FRS; British scientist; b. 1903; d. of Oskar Vogt and Cécile Mugnier; ed Univ. of Berlin; Research Asst, Dept of Pharmacology, Univ. of Berlin 1930; Research Asst and Head, Chemical Div., Kaiser Wilhelm Inst. für Hirnforschung, Berlin 1931–35; Rockefeller Travelling Fellow 1935–36; Research Worker, Dept of Pharmacology, Univ. of Cambridge 1935–40; Alfred Yarrow Research Fellow, Girton Coll. Cambridge 1937–40; mem. Staff, Coll. of Pharmaceutical Soc., London 1941–46; Lecturer, later Reader in Pharmacology, Univ. of Edin. 1947–60; Head, Pharmacology

Unit, Agricultural Research Council, Inst. of Animal Physiology 1960–68; Visiting Assoc. Prof. in Pharmacology, Columbia Univ., New York 1949; Visiting Prof., Sydney Univ. 1965, Montréal 1968; Life Fellow, Girton Coll. Cambridge 1970; Hon. mem. Physiological Soc. 1974, British Pharmacological Soc. 1974, Hungarian Acad. of Sciences 1981, British Asscn for Psychopharmacology 1983; Foreign Hon. mem. American Acad. of Arts and Sciences 1977; Hon. FRSM; Hon. DSc (Edin.) 1974, (Cambridge) 1983; Schmiedeberg Plakette 1974; Royal Medal, Royal Soc. 1981. *Publications:* papers in neurological, physiological and pharmacological journals. *Leisure interests:* gardening, travel. *Address:* Chateau La Jolla Terrace, 7544 La Jolla Boulevard, La Jolla, CA 92037, USA.

VOGT, Peter K., PhD; American professor of molecular and experimental medicine; b. 10 March 1932; s. of Josef Vogt and Else (née Thiemann) Vogt; m. Hiroko Ishino 1993; ed Univ. of Tubingen; Asst Prof. of Pathology, Univ. of Colorado 1962–66, Assoc. Prof. 1966–67; Assoc. Prof. of Microbiology, Univ. of Washington 1967–69, Prof. 1969–71; Hastings Prof. of Microbiology, Univ. of Southern Calif. 1971–78, Hastings Distinguished Prof. of Microbiology 1978–80, Chair. Dept of Microbiology 1980–; Chair. Div. of Oncovirology, Prof. Dept of Molecular and Experimental Medicine, The Scripps Research Inst. 1993–; Calif. Scientist of the Year 1975, Award of Nat. Acad. of Sciences 1980, Alexander von Humboldt Prize 1983, Ernst Jung Prize for Medicine 1985, Howard Taylor Ricketts Award 1991, Charles S. Mott Prize 1991. *Publications:* Genetics of RNA Tumor Viruses 1977, The Genetic Structure of RNA Tumor Viruses 1977 and numerous articles in scientific journals. *Leisure interest:* painting. *Address:* Department of Molecular and Experimental Medicine, Division of Oncovirology, The Scripps Research Institute, 10550 North Torrey Pines Road, BCC–239, La Jolla, CA 92037, USA (Office). *Telephone:* (858) 784-9728 (Office). *Fax:* (858) 784-2070 (Office). *E-mail:* pkvogt@scripps.edu (Office).

VOHOR, Serge; Ni-Vanuatu politician; fmr Minister of Econ. Affairs; Pres. Union of Moderate Parties (UMP); Prime Minister of Vanuatu 1995–98; Minister of Foreign Affairs 2000–, Deputy Prime Minister 2001–. *Address:* Office of the Deputy Prime Minister, PMB 057, Port Vila, Vanuatu (Office). *Telephone:* 22750. *Fax:* 27714.

VOIGHT, Jon; American actor; b. 29 Dec. 1938, Yonkers, New York; s. of Elmer Voight and Barbara (née Kamp) Voight; m. 1st Lauri Peters 1962 (divorced 1967); m. 2nd Marcheline Bertrand 1971 (divorced); one s. one d.; ed Catholic Univ.; Acad. Award (Best Actor) for Coming Home 1979, Best Actor Awards for Midnight Cowboy 1969, Coming Home 1979, Cannes Int. Film Festival, Golden Globe Award for Best Actor for Coming Home. *Theatre includes:* A View From the Bridge (New York); That Summer That Fall (New York) 1966; played Romeo at the San Diego Shakespeare Festival; Stanley Kowalski in A Streetcar Named Desire, Los Angeles 1973, Hamlet 1975. *Films include:* Hour of the Gun 1967, Fearless Frank 1968, Out of It 1969, Midnight Cowboy 1969, The Revolutionary 1970, The All-American Boy 1970, Catch 22 1970, Deliverance 1972, Conrack 1974, The Odessa File 1974, Coming Home 1978, The Champ 1979, Lookin' to Get Out (also wrote screenplay) 1982, Table for Five 1983, Runaway Train 1985, Desert Bloom 1986, Eternity, Heat, Rosewood, Mission Impossible 1996, U-Turn 1997, The Rainmaker 1997, Varsity Blues 1998, The General 1998, Enemy of the State 1998, Dog of Flanders 1999, Lara Croft: Tomb Raider 2001, Pearl Harbor 2001, Ali 2001, Zoolander 2002, Holes 2003, Superbabies 2003, Karate Dog 2003. *Television includes:* End of the Game 1976, Gunsmoke and Cimarron Strip, Chernobyl: The Final Warning 1991, The Last of His Tribe 1992, The Tin Soldier (also Dir), Convict Cowboy 1995, The Fixer 1998, Noah's Ark 1999, Second String 2000, Jasper Texas 2003. *Address:* c/o Martin Baum and Patrick Whitesell, CAA, 9830 Wilshire Boulevard, Beverly Hills, CA 90212, USA. *Telephone:* (310) 288-4545.

VOINEA, Radu, PhD; Romanian civil engineer and scientist; b. 24 May 1923, Craiova; s. of Policarp Voinea and Gabriela Voinea; m. 1st Maria Marta Gorgos 1951 (divorced 1957); one s. one d.; m. 2nd Aurica Daghie 1959 (died 2000); ed Polytech. School, Bucharest; Asst Prof. 1947; Sr Lecturer, Inst. of Civil Eng, Bucharest 1951; Prof., Polytech. Inst., Bucharest 1962, Pro-Rector 1964–67, Rector 1972–81; Corresp. mem. Romanian Acad. 1963, mem. 1974–, Gen. Sec. 1967–74, Pres. 1984–90; mem. European Acad. of Arts, Sciences and Humanities 1985, Elemente de Mecanica Medülor Continue (Elements of Mechanics of Continuous Media) (jtly.) 2000. *Publications:* Curs de rezistența materialelor (Lectures on the Strength of Materials), with A. Beles 1958, Mecanica teoretică (Theoretical Mechanics), with V. Vâlcovici and Ș. Bălan 1959, Metode analitice în teoria mecanismelor (Analytical Methods in the Theory of Mechanisms), with M. C. Atanasiu 1964, Mecanica (Mechanics), with D. Voiculescu and V. Ceausu 1975, 1983, Elasticitate și Plasticitate (Elasticity and Plasticity), with D. Voiculescu and V. Ceausu 1976, Vibratii mecanice (Mechanical Vibrations) with D. Voiculescu 1979, Introducere în Mecanica Solidului pentru ingineri (Introduction to mechanics of solids for engineers) with D. Voiculescu and F. Simion 1989, Technical Mechanics (co-author) 1996, Introduction to Mechanics of Elastic Continuous Bodies (co-author) 1997, Mechanics and Mechanical Vibrations 1998, Introducere în Teoria Sistemelor Dinamice (Introduction to the Theory of Mechanical Systems, with Ion Stroe) 1999. *Address:* Academia Română, Calea Victoriei 125, 70102 Bucharest 1 (Office); Bd Dacia 88, Ap. 4, 70 256, Bucharest 2, Romania (Home). *Telephone:* (1) 6594815 (Office); (1) 6105496 (Home). *E-mail:* bratosin@acad.ro (Office).

VOINOVICH, George, V., BA, JD; American lawyer and politician; b. 15 July 1936, Cleveland; m. Janet Voinovich; two s. one d.; ed Ohio State Univ.; called to the Bar, Ohio 1961; Asst Attorney Gen., Ohio 1963–64; mem. Ohio House of Reps. 1967–71; auditor Cuyahoga Co., Ohio 1971–76, Commr 1977–78; Lt. Gov. of Ohio 1979; Mayor of Cleveland 1979–89; Gov. of Ohio 1991–98; Senator from Ohio 1999–; mem. Nat. Govs. Asscn (Chair. Educ. Action Team on School Readiness 1991, Child Support Enforcement Work Group 1991–92, Co-Chair. Task Force on Educ. 1992–93, mem. Exec. Cttee 1993–; Co-Lead Gov. on Fed. Mandates 1993–; Chair. Nat. Governors' Asscn 1997–98); Certificate of Merit Award, Dist Urban Mayor Award Nat., Urban Coalition, 1987 Ohio Univ., Humanitarian Award N.C.C.J. 1986 and many others. *Address:* 317 Hart Senate Office Building, Washington, DC, 20510-0001, USA. *Telephone:* (202) 224-3353 (Office). *Fax:* (202) 228-1382 (Office). *Website:* www.senate.gov/~voinovich.

VOINOVICH, Vladimir Nikolayevich; Russian writer; b. 26 Sept. 1956, Dushanbe, Tajikistan; m.; one d.; ed Moscow Regional Pedagogical Inst.; active in dissident movt. 1960s; freelance writer; mem. USSR Writers' Union, expelled 1974, expulsion revoked 1990; deprived of Soviet citizenship 1981, emigrated and lived in Germany 1980–92; Prof. Princeton Univ., USA; mem. Bavarian Acad. of Fine Arts; Triumph Prize. *Publications:* I want to Be Honest (short story), We Live Here 1963, The Degree of Confidence 1972, Life and Extraordinary Adventures of the Soldier Ivan Chonkin, Hat, Ivankyada, By Mutual Correspondence, Moscow-2042. *Address:* Russian Pen-Centre, Neglinnaya str. 18/1, Bldg 2, Moscow, Russia (Office). *Telephone:* (095) 209-45-89 (Office). *Fax:* (095) 200-02-93 (Office).

VOITOVICH, Aliaksander Pavlavich, DR.PHYS-MATH.SCI.; Belarus physicist and politician; b. 5 Jan. 1938, Radkevichi, Minsk region; s. of Pavel Voitovich and Nadezhda Voitovich; m.; one s.; ed Belarus State Univ.; mem. research staff Inst. of Physics Belarus Acad. of Sciences (BAS) 1962–84 (Deputy Research Dir 1984–92); Deputy Research Dir, then Dir Inst. of Molecular and Atomic Physics, BAS 1992–97; mem. 1996, then Pres. Nat. Acad. of Sciences of Belarus 1997–2000; Chair. Nat. Ass. of Repub. of Belarus Council of Repub. 2000–; author of 24 scientific inventions; State Prize 1966; Badge of Hon. 1981; Order of Francisk Skaryna 1998. *Publications:* Magneto-Optics of Gas Lasers 1984, Lasers with Anisotropic Resonators (with V. Severikov) 1990; some 200 research papers. *Leisure interests:* fishing, carpentry. *Address:* Houses of Government, Council of Republic, 220010 Minsk, Belarus (Office). *Telephone:* (17) 226-66-94 (Office). *Fax:* (17) 226-67-65 (Office).

VOLACHIT, Boungnang; Laotian politician and army officer; b. 1936; m. Keosaychay Sayasone; fmr army officer; fmr Gov. Savannaket, then Mayor Vientiane Municipality; apptd. mem. Politburo 1996; Minister of Finance and Deputy Prime Minister 1999–2001; Prime Minister of Laos 2001–. *Address:* Office of the Prime Minister, Vientiane, Laos (Office). *Telephone:* (21) 213650 (Office). *Fax:* (21) 213650 (Office).

VOLCHEK, Galina Borisovna; Russian stage director and actress; b. 19 Dec. 1933, Moscow; d. of Boris Volchek and Vera Maimyna; m. 1st Yevgeniy Yevstigneyev 1957 (divorced 1964); m. 2nd Mark Abelev 1966 (divorced 1976); one s.; ed Studio-School of Moscow Art Theatre; one of founders, actress and Stage Dir Theatre Sovremennik 1956–72, Artistic Dir 1972–; Deputy to State Duma (Parl.) 1995–99; over 40 productions including Common Story by Goncharov, On the Bottom by Gorky, Cherry Orchard, Three Sisters by Chekhov, Ascent over Fujiyama by Aitmatov, Echelone by Roshchin, Anfissa by Andreyev, Steep Route by Ginzburg, Pygmalion by G. B. Shaw, We Go On... by Kalida, Three Comrades by E. M. Remorque; roles include Martha (Who's Afraid of Virginia Woolf?), Miss Amelia (The Ballad of the Sad Café by Albee), Wife of Governor (Inspector by Gogol), roles in films by dirs Kozintsev (King Lear), Yutkevich, Danelia and others; stage productions in many countries including USA (first Soviet stage dir to work in USA, Alley Theatre, Houston (Echelone by M. Roshchin)), Ireland (Abbey Theatre), Hungary, Finland, Bulgaria, Germany, Czechoslovakia; master classes in Tisch School NY Univ.; USSR People's Artist, State Prize, State Orders of USSR, Hungary, Bulgaria and Russia. *Leisure interest:* designing clothes. *Address:* Chistoprudny blvd 19A, 101000 Moscow (Theatre); Povarskaya str. 26, Apt. 43, Moscow, Russia (Home). *Telephone:* (095) 921-25-43 (Theatre). *Fax:* (095) 921-66-29 (Office). *E-mail:* teatr@sovremennik.ru (Office). *Website:* sovremennik.ru (Office).

VOLCKER, Paul A., MA; American government official and banker; b. 5 Sept. 1927, Cape May, NJ; s. of Paul A. Volcker and Alma Klippel Volcker; m. Barbara Marie Bahnson 1954 (died 1998); one s. one d.; ed Princeton Univ., Harvard Univ. Graduate School of Public Admin. and LSE, UK; Special Asst Securities Dept, Fed. Reserve Bank of NY 1953–57; Financial Economist, Chase Manhattan Bank, NY 1957–62, Dir of Forward Planning 1965–69; Dir Office of Financial Analysis, U.S. Treasury Dept 1962–63, Deputy Under-Sec. for Monetary Affairs 1963–65, Under-Sec. Monetary Affairs 1969–74; Sr Fellow, Woodrow Wilson School of Public and Int. Affairs, Princeton Univ. 1974–75; Pres. NY Fed. Reserve Bank 1975–79; Chair. Bd of Govs., Fed. Reserve System 1979–87; Chair. James D. Wolfensohn Inc. 1988–; CEO 1995–; Frederick H. Schultz Prof. of Inst. Econ. Policy, Princeton Univ. 1988; Henry Kaufman Visiting Prof., Stern School of Business, NY Univ. 1998; Consultant IBRD on Debts; Dir (non-exec.) ICI 1988–93, Exec. Dir 1993–; Hon. LLD (Adelphi Univ., Notre Dame Univ.) 1980, (Farleigh Dickinson Univ.) 1981, (Princeton Univ., Univ. of NH) 1982, (New York Univ., Lamar

Univ., Dartmouth Coll.) 1983; Admin. Fellowship (Harvard), Rotary Foundation Fellow (LSE), Arthur S. Fleming Award (Fed. Govt), U.S. Treasury Dept Exceptional Service Award, Alexander Hamilton Award, Fred Hirsch Memorial Lecture 1978, Public Service Award (Tax Foundation) 1981, Courage Award 1989.

VOLENÍK, Lubomír, JU.DR.; Czech politician and civil servant; b. 1 March 1950, Prague; m.; two s.; ed Charles Univ. Prague (corresp. student); electromechanic, EZ Bystřany 1970–75, tech. controller 1975–78; disability pension from 1978; co. lawyer, SČVK Teplice 1983–90; mem. People's Chamber of Fed. Ass. (Civic Forum) 1990–92; mem. Civic Democratic Party 1991–; mem. Cttee of Conciliation 1991–92; mem. People's Chamber of Fed. Ass. (Civic Democratic Party) 1992; mem. Constitution-Legal Cttee 1992; Pres. N Bohemia Regional Asscn until June 1992; mem. Czech Broadcast Liquidation Group 1993; Pres. Supreme Audit Office 1993–2002, 2002–(11); Vice-Pres. EUROSAI Governing Bd 1993–96, Pres. 1996–99. *Publications:* Luxembourg Conception of the Czech State (legal-historical study); numerous articles. *Address:* Nejvyšší kontrolní úřad, Jankovcova 63, 170 04, Prague 7, Czech Republic (Office). *Telephone:* (2) 33045500 (Office). *Fax:* (2) 33045536 (Office). *E-mail:* lubomir.volenik@nku.cz (Office). *Website:* www.nku.cz (Office).

VOLK, Igor Petrovich; Russian cosmonaut; b. 12 April 1937; m.; two d.; ed Kirovograd Mil. Pilot School, School of Pilot Testers, Moscow Aviation Inst.; army service 1956–63; joined Cosmonauts' Team 1978, first space flight 1984; leading test pilot for Buran aircraft 1984–95; Dir V. Chkalov Test Flights Centre, M. Gromov Research Flight Inst. (GNC RFLII) 1995–. *Leisure interests:* flying, football, skiing, tennis. *Address:* GNC RFLII, 140160 Zhukovskiy-2, Moscow, Russia (Office). *Telephone:* (095) 556-56-07 (Office).

VOLK, Patricia, BFA; American writer; b. 16 July 1943, New York; d. of Cecil Sussman Volk and Audrey Elayne Morgen Volk; m. Andrew Blitzer 1969; one s. one d.; ed Syracuse Univ., Acad. de la Grande Chaumière, Paris, School of Visual Arts, The New School, Columbia Univ.; Art Dir Appelbaum and Curtis 1964–65, Seventeen Magazine 1967–68; copy-writer, Assoc. Creative Dir, Sr Vice-Pres. Doyle Dane Bernbach Inc. (DDB Needham Worldwide Inc.) 1969–88; Adjunct Instructor of fiction Yeshiva Coll. 1991; columnist Newsday, NY 1995–96; mem. PEN Authors Guild; Yaddo Fellow; MacDowell Fellow; Word Beat Fiction Book Award 1984 and numerous other awards. *Publications include:* The Yellow Banana 1985, White Light 1987, All It Takes 1990, Stuffed 2001; contribs. to The New York Times Magazine, The Atlantic, Quarterly, Cosmopolitan, Family Circle, Mirabella, Playboy, 7 Days, Manhattan Inc., The New Yorker, New York Magazine, Red Book, Good Housekeeping, Allure; Anthologies: Stories About How Things Fall Apart and What's Left When They Do 1985, A Reader for Developing Writers 1990, Exploring Language 1992, Magazine and Feature Writing 1992, Hers 1993, Her Face in the Mirror 1994. *Leisure interests:* fly-fishing, gardening, travel. *Address:* c/o Gloria Loomis, 133 East 35th Street, New York, NY 10016, USA.

VOLKOV, Vladimir Konstantinovich, DHist; Russian historian; b. 15 Dec. 1930, Voronezh; m.; two d.; ed Moscow State Univ.; started career as journalist; broadcasting for Bulgaria and Albania 1954–56; researcher, Prof. and Head of Div., Deputy Dir Inst. of Slavonic Studies USSR (now Russian) Acad. of Sciences 1956–87, Dir 1987–; mem. Council Pres. Boris Yeltsin 1993–98; Vice Pres. Nat. Cttee of Historians, mem. several scientific socs. *Publications:* over 160 works on problems of culture and history of Slavic peoples. *Address:* Institute of Slavonic Studies, Leningradsky pr. 7, 125040 Moscow, Russia. *Telephone:* (095) 250-77-08 (Office).

VOLLEBAEK, Knut, MSc; Norwegian politician; b. 11 Feb. 1946; m. Ellen Sofie Aadland Vollebaek; one s.; ed Inst. Catholique de Paris, Univs. of Oslo, Madrid and Calif., Norwegian School of Econs and Business Admin., Bergen; joined Foreign Service 1973; Second Sec. Embassy of Norway, Delhi 1975–78, First Sec. Embassy of Norway, Madrid 1978–81, Exec. Officer, then Sr Exec. Officer, Ministry of Foreign Affairs 1981–84, Counsellor Embassy of Norway, Harare 1984–86; Head First Political Affairs Div., Ministry of Foreign Affairs 1986–89, State Sec. and Deputy Minister of Foreign Affairs 1989–90; Amb. to Costa Rica 1991–93; Dir Gen. Dept of Bilateral Devt Cooperation, Ministry of Foreign Affairs 1993; Deputy Co-Chair. Int. Conf. on the fmr Yugoslavia, Geneva 1993; Asst Sec. Gen. for Devt Cooperation 1994–97; Minister of Foreign Affairs 1997–2000; Chair. Barents Euro-Arctic Council 1997–98; Chair.-in-Office Org. for Security and Co-operation in Europe (OSCE) 1999; Amb. to USA March 2001–. *Address:* Embassy of Norway, 2720 34th Street, NW, Washington, DC 20008-2714, USA. *Telephone:* (202) 333-6000. *Fax:* (202) 337-0870. *E-mail:* norcons@interport.net. *Website:* www.norway.org.

VOLOCHKOVA, Anastasiya; Russian ballet dancer; b. 20 Jan. 1976, St Petersburg; ed Russian Vaganova Acad. of Ballet; soloist, Maryinsky Theatre, St Petersburg 1994–98; with Bolshoi Theatre 1998–; Gold Medal, 2nd Ballet Contest, Kiev. *Roles include:* Odyllia and Swan Princess in Swan Lake, Giselle in Gisele, Raimonda in Raimonda, Niknya in Bayder, Aurora and Lilac Fairy in Sleeping Beauty, Zarema in Fountain of Bakhchisarai, Girl in Spirit of Rose, Medora in Corsair, Carmen in Carmen-Suite. *Leisure interests:* walking, reading, classical and modern music. *Address:* Bolshoi Theatre, Teatralnaya pl. 1, Moscow, Russia (Office). *Telephone:* (095) 126-17-53 (Home).

VOLODARSKY, Eduard Yakovlevich; Russian scriptwriter and writer; b. 3 Feb. 1941, Kharkov, Ukraine; s. of Yakov Isaakovich Volodarsky and Maria

Yakovlevna Brigova; m. Tagirova Farida Abdurakhmanovna; ed All-Union Inst. of Cinematography; mem. Union of Cinematographers, Sec. 1990–95; mem. Union of Writers; mem. Exec. Bd Studio Slovo 1997; Ed.-in-Chief Cen. Scenario Studio 1998–; Pres. Guild of Scriptwriters 1997–; Hon. Dr. Acad. of Arts, St Marino; USSR State Prize, State Prize of Russian Fed., Merited Worker of Arts; Dovzhenko Golden Medal. *Film scripts include:* White Explosion 1968, A Road Home 1969, Sixth Summer 1969, Anthracite 1970, Check-up on Roads 1971, Risk 1973, Killed in Performance 1974, Hatred 1975, My Friend Ivan Lapshin 1975, Second Attempt of Victor Krokhin 1976, Eight Days of Hope 1977, Forget the Word Death 1979, Smoke of Motherland 1980, Emelyan Pugachev 1981, People in the Ocean 1981, Look Back 1982, Guilt of Lieutenant Nekrasov 1982, War 1983, Partings 1983, Blackmailer 1984, Appellation 1986, Vagabond 1987, Moonzund 1987, Behind the Deadline 1987, Abyss or Seventh Circle 1992, Lonely Gambler 1993, Ordinary Bolshevism 1999. *Plays include:* The Happiest, Moscow Vakhtangov Drama Theatre, Our Debts, Leaving, Look Back, Moscow Art Theatre, Trap, Moscow Ostrovsky Maly Theatre, Stars for the Lieutenant, Moscow Ermolova Drama Theatre, Run, Run, Evening Star, Tzwilling Theatre. *Publications:* Russian or Crime Without Punishment, Each Has a War of His Own. *Telephone:* (095) 330-96-64 (Home).

VOLODIN, Vyacheslav Viktorovich, DJur; Russian politician; b. 4 Feb. 1964, Alekseyevka, Saratov region; m.; one d.; ed Saratov Inst. of Agric. Mechanisation, Acad. of Civil Service; teacher, Docent, Saratov Inst. of Agric. Mechanisation 1987–92; Deputy Head Admin. of Saratov 1992–93; Prof., Head of Chair., Pro-Rector Povolzhye Personnel Centre 1993–94; mem., Deputy Chair. Saratov Regional Duma 1994–, Vice-Gov., First Deputy Chair. Saratov Regional Govt 1996–99; Prof. Povolzhye Acad. of Civil Service until 1999; mem. State Duma (Parl.) 1999–; mem. Homeland–All Russia faction, Deputy Sec. Political Council 1999–; mem. United Party Yedinstvo and Otechestvo 2001–. *Leisure interests:* painting, sports. *Address:* State Duma, Okhotny Ryad 4, 103009 Moscow, Russia (Office). *Telephone:* (095) 292-47-70 (Office). *Fax:* (095) 292-73-55 (Office).

VOLONTIR, Mikhai; Moldovan actor; b. 9 March 1934; s. of Ermolae Volontir and Feodosia Volontir; m. Eufrosinia Volontir 1961; one d.; ed Actors' Training School; actor and producer with Alecsandri Moldavian Music and Drama Theatre in Beltsy 1957–; work in TV and films 1968–; mem. Pres. Council 1997–2001; USSR People's Artist 1984. *Theatre includes:* Misfortune (producer), The Twilight (actor, producer), Alecsandri's Agaki Flutur, Bayescu's Preshul (actor, producer), Drutsa's Beautiful and Saint (producer), Tanev's The Last Night of Socrates (actor, producer). *Films:* leading and title roles in numerous films including: A Movement of Answer, The Only Man, The Hunting of Deer, Am I Guilty?, Traces of a Wolf, We Shall Remain Faithful, One-Sided Love. *Leisure interest:* protection of animals. *Address:* Str. Independentsei 34, Apt. 4, 3100 Beltsy, Moldova. *Telephone:* (31) 2-80-52.

VOLOSHIN, Alexander Stalyevich; Russian government official; b. 3 March 1956, Moscow; m.; three s.; ed Moscow Inst. of Transport Eng, All-Union Acad. of Foreign Trade; Head Lab. of Scientific Org. of Labour; Sec. Comsomol Org.; Moskva-Sortirovochnaya railway station 1973–83; Researcher, then Sr Researcher, Head of Sector, Deputy Head of Section All-Union Research Inst. of Conjuncture 1986–92; Exec. Dir Analysis, Consultations and Marketing 1992–; Pres. ESTA Corpn 1993–96; Pres. Fed. Funds Corpn 1996–97; Asst to Head of Admin. of Presidency (for Econ. Problems) 1997–, Deputy Head 1998–99, Head 1999–; Chair. Bd of Dirs. RAO EES 1999–; Chair. Collegium of Reps., State Bd of Public Radio and TV. *Address:* President of Russia Administration, Kremlin, Staraya p.4, 103132 Moscow, Russia (Office). *Telephone:* (095) 206-62-55 (Office).

VOLPINARI III, Antonio Lazzaro; San Marino politician; b. 2 Oct. 1943, Domagnano; m. Claudia Berti; one d.; joined Partito Socialista Sammarinese (PSS) 1959, elected to Cen. Cttee 1963–, with Secr. Youth Movt, Vice-Sec. PSS 1980–82, Gen.-Sec. before and after Conf. Socialist Unification 1991, mem. Secr., Pres. of Group of Advisers; elected mem. of Govt 1969–, Mayor of Govt 1974–76, Deputy to Agric., Communications and Transport 1976–78, to Agric. and Commerce 1978–83, to the Territory and Atmosphere 1983–86, Sec. of State for Internal Affairs 1992–2000; Supreme Magistracy of Captain Regent 1973–74, April–Sept. 1977; Head of State (Capt. Regent) 2002–; mem. Advisory Comm. on Internal Affairs; Del. to the Council of Europe. *Address:* Partito Socialista Sammarinese (PSS), Via G. Ordelaffi 46, 47890 San Marino (Office). *Telephone:* (549) 902016 (Office). *Fax:* (549) 906438 (Office). *E-mail:* pss@omniway.sm (Office). *Website:* www.pss.sm (Office).

VOLSKY, Arkadiy Ivanovich; Russian politician; b. 15 May 1932, Dobrush, Byelorussian SSR; s. of Ivan Pavlovich Volsky and Anna Semyonovna Volsky; m. Ludmila Aleksandrovna Semyonova 1953; one s. one d.; ed Moscow Steel Inst.; foreman, shop Supt, Sec. of Party Cttee of Likhachev Automobile Plant, Moscow 1955–69; Deputy Head, First Deputy Head of Dept of Machine Bldg, Cen. Cttee CPSU 1969–83; Aide to Gen. Sec. Cen. Cttee 1983–84; Head of Dept of Machine Bldg, Cen. Cttee CPSU 1984–91; Rep. of Cen. Cttee CPSU and Presidium of USSR Supreme Soviet in Nagorny-Karabakh autonomous region (Azerbaijan SSR) 1988–89; Chair. Emergency Powers Cttee in Nagorny-Karabakh 1989–90; Deputy Head Russian Govt's del. to negotiations on crisis in Chechen Repub. June 1995; Pres. USSR League of Industrial and Industrial Assocns. 1990–92, Russian Industrialists and Entrepreneurs' Union 1992–; Deputy to RSFSR Supreme Soviet 1984–86; Deputy to USSR

Supreme Soviet 1986–89; USSR People's Deputy 1989–91; mem. Cen. Cttee CPSU 1986–91; Deputy Head Governing Cttee on Nat. Econ. of USSR Aug.–Dec. 1991; mem. Constitutional Comm. of Russian Fed. 1993–; Chair., Pres.'s Comm. on Political Stability of Public Chamber 1994–99; USSR State Prize 1971. *Leisure interest:* football. *Address:* RSSP, Staraya Pl. 10/4, 103070 Moscow, Russia. *Telephone:* 206-54-92. *Fax:* (095) 973-20-13.

VON BÜLOW, Andreas, DJur; German politician and lawyer; b. 17 July 1937, Dresden; s. of Georg-Ulrich Bülow and Susanne (née Haym) von Bülow; m. Anna Barbara Duden 1961; two s. two d.; law studies in Heidelberg, Berlin and Munich, studied in France and USA; entered higher admin. service of State of Baden-Württemberg 1966, on staff of Rural Dist Offices of Heidelberg and Balingen, Pres. Admin. Dist of Süd-Württemberg Hohenzollern at Tübingen; mem. Bundestag (Parl.) 1969–94; Parl. State Sec. Fed. Ministry of Defence 1976–80; Fed. Minister for Research and Tech. 1980–82; mem. Social Democratic Party 1960–, Public Services and Transport Workers' Union. *Publications:* Die Überwachung der Erdgasindustrie durch die Federal Power Commission als Beispiel der Funktionen der unabhängigen Wirtschaftsüberwachungskommissionen der amerikanischen Bundesverwaltung 1967 (dissertation), Gedanken zur Weiterentwicklung der Verteidigungsstrategien in West und Ost 1984, Alpträume West gegen Alpträume Ost—ein Beitrag zur Bedrohungsanalyse 1984, Skizzen einer Bundeswehrstruktur der 90er Jahre 1985, Die eingebildete Unterlegenheit—das Kräfteverhältnis West-Ost, wie es wirklich ist 1985, The Conventional Defense of Europe, New Technologies and New Strategies 1986, Im Namen des Staates, CIA, BND und die Kriminellen Machenschaften der Geheimdienste 1998. *Leisure interests:* music, geology, history, swimming, hiking, skiing.

VON DER DUNK, Hermann Walther; Netherlands professor of history; b. 9 Oct. 1928, Bonn, Germany; s. of Heinrich M. von der Dunk and Ilse Löb; m. Goverdina Schuurmans Stekhoven 1958; two s. one d.; ed Univ. of Utrecht and Inst. für Europäische Geschichte, Mainz; school teacher, Bilthoven 1961–63; Asst Prof. Dept of History, Univ. of Utrecht 1963–67, Prof. of Contemporary History and Head of Dept 1967–88, Prof. and Head, Dept of Cultural History 1988–90, now Prof. Emer.; mem. Royal Netherlands Acad., Acad. Europaea, Dutch Soc. of Science; Grosses Bundesverdienstkreuz 1989, Ridder Nederlandse Leeuw 1991, Vondel Prize 1994, Goethe-Medaille 1995. *Publications:* Der deutsche Vormärz u. Belgien (thesis) 1966, Kleio heeft 1000 ogen (essays) 1974, Conservatisme 1976, De organisatie van het verleden 1982, Voorbij de verboden drempel: de Shoah 1990, Cultuur & Geschiedenis (articles) 1990, Sprekend over identiteit en geschiedenis 1992, Twee buren, twee culturen 1994, Elke tijd is overgangstijd 1996, De verdwijnende hemel. Over de Cultuur van Europa in de twintigste eeuw (2 Vols) 2000, Mensen, Machten, Moyelÿ Kheden (essays) 2002; articles and contribs. to textbooks, journals and newspapers. *Leisure interests:* music (playing piano), drawing and painting, literature. *Address:* Nicolailaan 20, 3723 HS Bilthoven, Netherlands (Home). *Telephone:* 302285401 (Home).

VON DOHNÁNYI, Christoph; German conductor; b. 8 Sept. 1929, Berlin; s. of Hans von Dohnányi and Christine (née Bonhoeffer) von Dohnányi; brother of Klaus von Dohnányi; m. 1st Renate Zillessen; one s. one d.; m. 2nd Anja Silja (q.v.) 1979; one s. two d.; abandoned legal training to study music 1948; studied in USA under grandfather, Ernst von Dohnányi 1951; répétiteur and conductor under Georg Solti, Frankfurt Oper 1952; Gen. Music Dir Lübeck 1957–63, Kassel 1963–66; Chief Conductor of Cologne Radio Symphony Orchestra 1964–69; Gen. Music Dir and Opera Dir, Frankfurt 1968–77; Chief Conductor and Intendant, Hamburg State Opera 1977–84; Music Dir (desig.) Cleveland Orchestra 1982–84, Music Dir 1984–; Prin. Guest Conductor Philharmonia Orchestra 1994, Prin. Conductor 1997–; numerous guest appearances; numerous recordings of symphonies with Cleveland Orchestra and opera recordings; Dr. hc (Kent State Univ., Case Western Univ., Oberlin Coll., Eastman School of Music, Cleveland Inst. of Music); Commdr Ordre des Arts et des Lettres; Commdr.'s Cross, Order of Merit (Germany); Commdr.'s Cross (Austria); recipient Richard Strauss Prize, Bartok Prize, Goethe Medal, Frankfurt, Arts and Science Prize, City of Hamburg. *Address:* The Cleveland Orchestra, Severance Hall, Cleveland, OH 44106, USA. *Telephone:* (216) 231-7300.

VON DOHNÁNYI, Klaus, DJur, LLB; German politician; b. 23 June 1928, Hamburg; s. of Johann-Georg von Dohnányi and Christine (née Bonhoeffer) von Dohnányi; brother of Christoph von Dohnányi; m. Ulla Hahn 1997; two s. one d.; ed Munich, Columbia, Stanford and Yale Univs.; frmly. with Ford Motor Co., Detroit, Mich. and Cologne; Dir Planning Div. Ford-Werke, Cologne 1956–60; Dir Inst. für Marktforschung und Unternehmensberatung, Munich 1960–68; Sec. of State, Fed. Ministry of Economy 1968–69; mem. Bundestag 1969–81; Parl. Sec. of State, Ministry of Educ. and Science 1969–72; Minister of Educ. and Science 1972–74; Minister of State and Parl. Sec. of State, Fed. Foreign Office 1976–81, First Burgomaster and Pres. Senate, Hamburg 1981–88; Chair. Bd TAKRAF AG, Leipzig 1990–94; mem. Club of Rome 1996–; mem. SPD; Heuss Medal Theodor Heuss Foundation 1988; Gold Medal for Distinguished Leadership and Service to Humanity, B'nai B'rith 1988. *Publications:* Japanese Strategies 1969, Brief an den Deutschen Demokratischen Revolutionäre 1990, Das Deutsche Wagnis 1990, Im Joch des Profits? (The German Model) 1999. *Leisure interests:* writing, reading. *Address:* Heilwig Str. 5, 20249 Hamburg, Germany.

VON KLITZING, Klaus; German physicist; b. 28 June 1943, Schroda; s. of Bogislav von Klitzing and Anny (née Ulbrich) von Klitzing; m. Renate Falkenberg 1971; two s. one d.; ed Tech. Univ. Brunswick, Univ. Würzburg; Prof., Tech. Univ., Munich 1980–84; Dir Max-Planck Inst. for Solid State Research, Stuttgart 1985–; Schottky Prize, Hewlett-Packard Prize, Nobel Prize for Physics 1985. *Address:* Max-Planck Institut für Festkörperforschung, Heisenbergstr. 1, Postfach 800665, 70506 Stuttgart, Germany. *Telephone:* (711) 6891571.

VON MEHREN, Arthur Taylor, SB, LLB, PhD; American professor of law; b. 10 Aug. 1922, Minn.; s. of Sigurd Anders von Mehren and Eulalia M. Anderson; m. Joan E. Moore 1947; three s.; ed Harvard Univ., Univ. of Zürich and Faculté de Droit, Paris; law clerk, US Court of Appeals 1945–46; Asst Prof. Harvard Univ. 1946–53, Prof. of Law 1953–76, Story Prof. of Law 1976–93, Prof. Emer. 1993–; Fulbright Research Prof. Univ. of Tokyo 1956–57, Rome 1968–69; Guggenheim Fellow 1968–69; Goodhart Prof. of Legal Science Univ. of Cambridge 1983–84, Fellow, Downing Coll. 1983–84, Hon. Fellow, Downing Coll. 1984–; gave Gen. Course on pvt. int. law, Hague Acad. of Int. Law 1996; other visiting professorships etc.; mem. US del. Hague Conf. on Pvt. Int. Law 1966, 1968, 1978, 1980, 1985, 1993, 1996, 2001; mem. American Bar Asscn, American Acad. of Arts and Sciences, Int. Acad. of Comparative Law, Inst. de Droit Int., American Soc. of Comparative Law; Hon. DrIur (Katholieke Univ. Leuven) 1985, (Univ. Panthéon-Assas, Paris) 2000; Order of the Rising Sun; Theberge Award, American Bar Asscn 1997; Grand Prize of Int. Acad. of Comparative Law (Canada Prize) 2002. *Publications include:* The Civil Law System 1957, 2nd Edn 1977, The Law of Multistate Problems 1965, Law in the United States: A General and Comparative View 1988, Conflict of Laws: American, Comparative International (co-ed.) 1998, International Commercial Arbitration (co-ed.) 1999. *Leisure interests:* travel, gardening. *Address:* Harvard Law School, AR-231, 1545 Massachusetts Avenue, Cambridge, MA 02138 (Office); 68 Sparks Street, Cambridge, MA 02138, USA (Home). *Telephone:* (617) 495-3193 (Office); (617) 547-8977 (Home). *Fax:* (617) 496-4866 (Office). *E-mail:* vonmehre@law.harvard.edu (Office).

VON OTTER, Anne Sofie; Swedish singer; b. 9 May 1955, Stockholm; ed Conservatorium, Stockholm, studied interpretation with Erik Werba (Vienna) and Geoffrey Parsons (London) and vocal studies since 1981 with Vera Rozsa; mem. Basel Opera, Switzerland 1982–85; début France at Opéra de Marseille (Nozze di Figaro—Cherubino) and Aix-en-Provence Festival (La Finta Giardiniera) 1984, Rome, Accad. di Santa Cecilia 1984, Geneva (Così fan tutte—Dorabella) 1985, Berlin (Così fan tutte) 1985, USA in Chicago (Mozart's C minor Mass) and Philadelphia (Bach's B minor Mass) 1985, London at Royal Opera, Covent Garden (Le Nozze di Figaro) 1985, Lyon (La Finta Giardiniera) 1986, La Scala, Milan (Alceste) 1987, Munich (Le Nozze di Figaro) 1987, Stockholm (Der Rosenkavalier) 1988, The Metropolitan Opera, New York (Le Nozze di Figaro) 1988, The Royal Albert Hall, London (Faust) 1989, numerous recordings for Philips, EMI, Deutsche Grammophon and Decca; has given recitals in New York, Paris, Brussels, Geneva, Stockholm, Vienna and London; Hon. DSc (Bath) 1992. *Address:* c/o IMG, Lovell House, 616 Chiswick High Road, London, W4 2TH, England. *Telephone:* (20) 8233-5800 (Office). *Fax:* (20) 8233-5801 (Office).

VON PLOETZ, Hans-Friedrich; German diplomatist; b. 12 July 1940, Nimptsch; m. Päivi Leinonen; two s.; ed Univs. of Marburg, Berlin and Vienna; lawyer in Bad Arolsen, Hesse 1960; Asst Lecturer Univ. of Marburg 1965–66; Fed. Foreign Office, Bonn 1966–68, 1973–78; Trade Mission, German Embassy, Helsinki 1968–73; German Embassy, Washington, DC 1978–80; Fed. Foreign Office, Bonn (Private Office of the Foreign Minister 1980–85, Deputy Political Dir 1985–88); Perm. Rep. NATO Council 1989–93; Dir-Gen. for European Affairs, Bonn 1993–94; State Sec., Ministry for Foreign Affairs, Bonn 1994–99; Amb. to UK 1999–2002, to Russian Fed. 2002–. *Leisure interests:* music, golf, gardening. *Address:* German Embassy, ul. Mosfilmowskaya 56, 119285 , Moscow, Russia (Office). *Telephone:* (095) 937-9500 (Office). *Fax:* (095) 939-9887 (Office). *E-mail:* L@mosk.auswaertiges-amt.de (Office). *Website:* www.deutschebotschaft-moskau.ru (Office).

VON RINGELHEIM, Paul Helmut, BS, MA; American sculptor; b. Vienna, Austria; s. of Henry von Ringelheim and Rosita von Ringelheim (née Altschuler); ed Brooklyn Coll., Fairleigh Dickinson Univ., Art Students League, New York, Acad. of Fine Arts, Munich; teacher of printmaking Brooklyn 1957–58; Prof. of Sculpture School of Visual Arts, New York 1967–71; one-man shows include Niveau Art Gallery, New York 1958, Am Haus, Berlin, Munich and Hamburg 1960–61, Rose Fried Gallery, New York 1964, 1967, Fairleigh Dickinson Univ. 1964, New Vision Galleries, London 1964, New York Cultural Center 1975, O.K. Harris Gallery, New York 1971–73, 1976, 1978, 1980, 1982, Mitzi Landau Gallery, LA 1974, Amarillo Museum of Art 1987, Amarillo Art Center 1987, Robert Berman Gallery, LA 1988, Obelisk Gallery 1992, 1994; has participated in numerous group exhbns. internationally; Fulbright scholar 1974–75; mem. Architectural League, New York; Outstanding Young Man of the Year Award, New York World's Fair 1964. *Address:* 9 Great Jones Street, New York, NY 10012-1128, USA. *Telephone:* (212) 777-8757.

VON ROHR, Hans Christoph (see Rohr, Hans Christoph von).

VON SCHENCK, Michael U. R., DrIur; Swiss diplomatist; b. 21 April 1931, Basel; s. of Dr. Ernst von Schenck and Selma Oettinger; ed Humanistisches

Gymnasium and Univ., Basel and in Lausanne; Swiss Trade Fair 1950–55; Die Woche 1950–55; Swiss Foreign Ministry 1957–67, 1973–93, Del. to OECD 1958, Del. to UN 1959–61, UN Narcotics Conf. 1961, Swiss Tech. Assistance Authority 1961–67; Founder and Dir Swiss Volunteers for Devt 1962–67; Sec.-Gen. Int. Sec. for Volunteer Service (ISVS) 1967–71; Harvard Univ. 1972–73; Rep. to IAEA and UNIDO, Swiss Embassy, Vienna 1973–77; Head Econ. Dept, Swiss Embassy, Bonn 1977–79; Amb. to Ghana (also Accred to Liberia, Sierra Leone and Togo) 1979–83, to Finland 1983–86, to Bulgaria 1987–89, to NZ, (also Accred Samoa, Tonga and Fiji) 1989–93. *Publications:* Der Statutenwechsel im internationalen Obligationenrecht 1955, Volunteer Manpower for Development 1967, Conferencia Regional sobre Servicio Voluntario 1968, An International Peace Corps 1968, Youth Today 1968, Youth's Role in Development 1968, International Volunteer Service 1969. *Leisure interests:* skiing, hiking. *Address:* P.O. Box 641, 4010 Basel 10, Switzerland.

VON SCHLABRENDORFF, Fabian Gotthard Herbert, MA, DrIur; German lawyer; b. 23 Dec. 1944, Berlin; s. of Fabian von Schlabrendorff and Luitgarde von Schlabrendorff (née von Bismarck); m. Maria de la Cruz Caballero Palomero 1977; one s. one d.; ed Univs. of Tübingen, Berlin, Geneva, Frankfurt and Chicago; service in Bundeswehr 1964–68; Research co-ordinator, Inst. of Int. and Foreign Trade and Business Law, Frankfurt 1975–82; lawyer with Pünder, Volhard, Weber & Axster, Frankfurt 1982, partner 1984; CEPES Award 1987. *Publications:* (co-author) Mining Ventures in Developing Countries (parts 1 and 2) 1979/81, The Legal Structure of Transnational Forest-Based Investments in Developing Countries 1987; various articles on business law. *Leisure interest:* classical music. *Address:* Clifford Chance Pünder, Mainzer Landstrasse 46, 60325 Frankfurt am Main, Germany. *Telephone:* (69) 719901. *Fax:* (69) 71994000.

VON STADE, Frederica; American mezzo-soprano; b. 1 June 1945, Somerville, NJ; m. 1st Peter Elkus 1973 (divorced); two d.; m. 2nd Michael G. Gorman 1991; ed Mannes Coll. of Music, New York; opera début with Metropolitan Opera, New York (in Le Nozze di Figaro) 1970; has also sung Paris Opera, San Francisco Opera, Lyric Opera of Chicago, LA Music Center Opera, Salzburg Festival, Covent Garden, London, Spoleto Festival, Boston Opera Co., Santa Fe Opera, Houston Grand Opera, La Scala, Milan; recital and concert artist; Hon. Dr. (Yale Univ.), (Boston Univ.), (Georgetown Univ. School of Medicine), (Mannes School of Music); two Grand Prix du Disc awards, Deutsche Schallplattenpreis, Premio della Critica Discografica and many other awards and prizes; Officier Ordre des Arts et des Lettres. *Music:* over 60 recordings include Frederica von Stade Sings Mozart and Rossini Opera Arias, French Opera Arias, Songs of the Cat with Garrison Keillor. *Address:* c/o Columbia Artists Management Inc., Jeffrey D. Vanderveen, 165 W 57th Street, New York, NY 10019, USA.

VON SYDOW, Björn, MS, PhD; Swedish politician; b. 26 Nov. 1945, Stockholm; s. of Bengt Sköldenberg and Tullia von Sydow; m. Madeleine von Sydow; three s. one d.; ed Stockholm and Linköping Univs.; worked as librarian 1970–74; Lecturer in Political Science Linköping Univ. 1974–78; Assoc. Prof. of Political Science Stockholm Univ. 1978–83, 1992–96; Prin. School of Social Work and Public Admin. 1983–88; work on study of gen. election of Bd of Dirs. of Nat. Pension Insurance Fund 1984–86; Visiting Research Scientist Case Western Reserve Univ., Ohio 1986, Pomona and Scripps Colls. Clairmont, Calif. 1992; active in municipal politics in Solna 1979–96, Chair. Swedish Social Democratic Party (SAP), Solna 1983–; mem. Editorial Cttee Tiden (political journal) 1983–89; mem. SAP programme comm. 1987–; MP 1994–; mem. Parl. Cttee on Constitutional Affairs 1994–96, mem. SI Cttee on Econ. Policy, Devt And Environment 1995–96, Chair. SAP Cttee on EU Affairs, mem. IGC and EU Enlargement Cttee of Party of European Socialists, Chair. EU Cttee of Nordic Labour Movt (SAMAK) 1996–98; Head of Political Planning responsible for Research and Devt, Econ. Growth and Environment, Office of Prime Minister 1988–91; mem. Cttee on Civil Rights, Ministry of Justice 1993–94; Chair. Cttee on Environmental Protection, Ministry of Environment 1994–96, Parl. Cttee preparing EU Treaty revision, Ministry for Foreign Affairs 1995–96; Minister of Trade at Ministry for Industry and Commerce 1996–97; Minister of Defence 1997–2002; Chair. Univ. Centre for Physics and Astronomy, Stockholm 1992–95. *Publications:* Parliamentarism in Sweden: Development and Forms up to 1945 1997, The Swedish Defence Decision and the Swedish View of the European Security Structures 1997, Defence up to Date: National and International Hand in Hand 1998, Sweden's Security in the 21st Century 1999. *Leisure interest:* horse riding. *Address:* c/o Ministry of Defence, Jakobsgatan 9, 103 33 Stockholm, Sweden.

VON TRIER, Lars; Danish film director; b. 30 April 1956; ed Danish Film Institute; co-founder Dogmei school of film. *Films include:* The Element of Crime, Zentropa, Epidemic, The Kingdom, Breaking the Waves, Idiots, Dancer in the Dark (Palme d'Or, Cannes), Dogville.

VON TROTTA, Margarethe; German film director and actress; b. 21 Feb. 1942, Berlin; has written scripts for The Sudden Wealth of the Poor People of Kombach 1971, Summer Lightning 1972, Fangschuss 1974, Unerreichbare Nahe 1984. *Films include:* Die Verlorene Ehre der Katharina Blum (The Lost Honour of Katharina Blum) 1975, Das zweite Erwachen der Christa Klages (The Second Awakening of Christa Klages) 1978, Schwestern, oder die Balance des Glücks (Sisters, or the Balance of Happiness) 1979, Die Bleierne Zeit (The German Sisters) 1981, Heller Wahn (Friends and Husbands) 1983, Rosa Luxemburg 1985, Felix 1987, Paura e amore (Love and Fear) 1988,

L'Africana 1990, Il lungo silenzio 1992, Das Versprechen (The Promise) 1994, Winterkind (TV film) 1996, Dunkle Tage (TV film) 1998. *Address:* Bioskop-Film, Turkenstrasse 91, 80799 Munich, Germany.

VON WILPERT, Gero, PhD, FAHA; Australian professor of German; b. 13 March 1933, Dorpat, Estonia; s. of Arno von Wilpert and Gerda Baumann; m. Margrit Laskowski 1953; three s.; ed Univs. of Heidelberg and NSW; publrs. reader and literary Dir Stuttgart 1957–72; Sr Lecturer in German, Univ. of NSW 1973–78, Assoc. Prof. 1978–81; McCaughey Prof. of German, Univ. of Sydney 1982–94, now Emer. *Publications include:* Sachwörterbuch der Literatur 1955, Deutsche Literatur in Bildern 1957, Schiller-Chronik 1958, Deutsches Dichterlexikon 1963, Der verlorene Schatten 1978, Die deutsche Gespenstergeschichte 1994, Goethe-Lexikon 1998. *Leisure interests:* 18th century French art and antiques. *Address:* Werrington House, Werrington, NSW 2747, Australia. *Telephone:* (2) 9623-1026 (Home).

VONDRAN, Ruprecht, DrIur; German business executive and politician (retd); b. 31 Dec. 1935, Göttingen; s. of Rudolf Vondran and Anneliese Unterberg; m. Jutta Paul 1970; two s. two d.; ed Univs. of Göttingen, Bonn and Würzburg; Pres. Wirtschaftsvereinigung Stahl 1988–2000; Chair. German-Japanese Industrial Co-operation Cttee; mem. Bundestag 1987–94; Hon. DEng. *Leisure interests:* modern graphics, Japanese porcelain. *Address:* Urdenbacher Allee 63, 40593 Düsseldorf, Germany (Home). *Telephone:* (211) 7182231 (Office). *Fax:* (211) 7118734 (Office).

VONNEGUT, Kurt, Jr, MA; American author; b. 11 Nov. 1922, Indianapolis; s. of Kurt Vonnegut and Edith Lieber; m. 1st Jane Marie Cox 1945 (divorced 1979); one s. two d. and three adopted s.; m. 2nd Jill Krementz 1979; one d.; ed Cornell Univ., Univ. of Chicago; served with US Army as Infantry Combat Scout, World War II; POW, Dresden 1945; police reporter, Chicago City News Bureau 1946; in public relations, Gen. Electric Co., Schenectady, NY 1947–50; freelance writer, New York 1950–65, 1974–; lecturer, Writers' Workshop, Univ. of Iowa 1965–67; Lecturer in English, Harvard Univ. 1970; Distinguished Prof., City Coll. of NY 1973–74; Hon. Pres. American Humanist Asscn 1992–; Guggenheim Fellow 1967–68; mem. Nat. Inst. Arts and Letters (Literary Award 1970). *Publications:* novels: Player Piano 1951, The Sirens of Titan 1959, Mother Night 1961, Cat's Cradle 1963, God Bless you, Mr. Rosewater 1965, Slaughterhouse-Five 1969, Breakfast of Champions 1973, Slapstick 1976, Jailbird 1979, Deadeye Dick 1982, Galápagos 1985, Bluebeard 1987, Hocus Pocus 1990, Timequake 1997, Bagombo Snuff Box 1999, God Bless You, Dr Kevorkian 2000; play: Happy Birthday, Wanda June 1971; short stories: Welcome to the Monkey House 1968; essays: Wampeters, Foma and Granfalloons 1974, Sun Moon Star 1980, Palm Sunday (autobiographical collage) 1981; TV script: Between Time and Timbuktu or Prometheus-5 1972, Fates Worse Than Death: An Autobiographical Collage of the 1980s. *Address:* c/o Donald C. Farber, Jacob, Medingeka Finnegan, LLP, 1270 Avenue of the Americas, New York, NY 10020, USA. *Telephone:* (212) 332-7735 (Office). *Fax:* (212) 332-7235 (Office).

VORA, Motilal; Indian politician; b. 29 Dec. 1928, Nagor, Rajasthan; s. of Mohanlal Vora; m. Shanti Vora; two s. four d.; fmr journalist; elected Councillor, Durg Municipality 1968, Congress Party mem. Madhya Pradesh Vidhan Sabha 1972; Minister of State for Educ. and Minister for Local Govt 1981–82; Minister of Transport, Science and Tech. 1982–83, of Higher Educ. 1983–84, of Health and Family Welfare and Civil Aviation 1988–89; Pres. Madhya Pradesh Congress (I) Cttee 1984–85; elected Leader Congress (I) Legis. Party 1985; Chief Minister, Madhya Pradesh 1985–88, Jan.–Dec. 1989; Gov. of UP 1995–96. *Address:* c/o Raj Bhavan, Lucknow, Uttar Pradesh, India.

VOROBYEV, Andrei Ivanovich, DR. MED.; Russian haematologist; b. 1 Oct. 1928; m.; two s.; ed First Inst. of Medicine; worked as house-painter 1941–44; practitioner, Head of Polyclinics Volokolamsk Moscow Region 1953–54; Prof. Cen. Inst. of Advanced Medical Studies 1956–66; Head of div. Inst. of Biophysics 1966–84; mem. Acad. of Medical Sciences 1986; Dir All-Union (now All-Russian) Scientific Cen. of Haematology 1987–91; Minister of Health of Russia 1991–92; Dir Haematological Scientific Centre, Russian Acad. of Medical Sciences 1993–; USSR State Prize. *Leisure interest:* history of Russian Acad. of Science. *Address:* Haematological Scientific Centre, Novy Zhukovsky pr. 4a, 125167 Moscow, Russia (Office). *Telephone:* (095) 212-21-23 (Office).

VOROBYEV, Yuri Leonidovich; Russian politician and engineer; b. 2 Feb. 1948, Krasnoyarsk; m.: two s.; ed Krasnoyarsk Inst. of Non-Ferrous Metals; mem. staff Krasnoyarsk plant; Sec. Sosnovoborsk dist. CPSU Cttee, Krasnoyarsk 1971–88, instructor Krasnoyarsk regional CPSU Cttee 1989–90; Dir-Gen. Foundation for Protection of Small Business and Devt of Econ. Reforms 1990–91; Deputy Chair. Russian Rescue Corps 1991–92; First Deputy Chair. Russian Fed. State Cttee on Problems of Civil Defence and Emergency Situations 1992–94; First Deputy Minister of Civil Defence and Emergency Situations 1994–; mem. Tech. Comm. at Russian Presidency 1993–; Order for Personal Courage. *Leisure interests:* sports, tourism. *Address:* Ministry of Civil Defence and Emergency Situations, Teatralny pr. 3, 103012 Moscow, Russia (Office). *Telephone:* (095) 924-43-75 (Office).

VORONENKOVA, Galina, D.PHIL, DR.HABIL; Russian professor of journalism; b. 30 Jan. 1947, Kostroma Region; d. of late Fyodor Smirnov and Alexandra Smirnova; m. Mikhail Voronenkov; one d.; ed Moscow State Univ., Leipzig Univ., GDR; literary contrib. to local newspaper, Kostroma Region

1965–67; mem. staff Journalism Dept, Moscow State Univ. 1974–87; teacher of Russian language, House of Soviet Science and Culture, Berlin, GDR and Business Man. Journalists' Club, Berlin 1987–90; reporter for Soviet Women, Germany 1990–92; Prof. Faculty of Journalism, Moscow State Univ. 1992–; Dir Free Russian-German Inst. for Publishing 1994–; Corresp. mem. Acad. of Information and Communication; award from Fed. Council of Russian Fed. 1996. *Publications include:* Bürger in der Demokratie (Russian ed.) 1997, Sredstva massovoy Informatii Germanii v 90-e gody 1998, Neue Technologien und die Entwicklung der Medien in Russland und Deutschland (Russian ed.) 1998, Russland vor den Wahlen. Die Rolle der Medien bei den Wahlen–ein deutsch-russischer Vergleich (Russian ed.) 2000. *Leisure interests:* classical music, world history, science fiction. *Address:* Mochovaya ul. 9, Apt. 235, 103009 Moscow (Office); Fadeyva ul. 6, Apt. 60, 125047 Moscow, Russia (Home). *Telephone:* (095) 203-26-43 (Office); (095) 251-97-76 (Home). *Fax:* (095) 251-97-76 (Home); (095) 203-26-43 (Office). *E-mail:* frdip@journ.msu.ru (Office); galine-w@dataforce,net (Home). *Website:* www.frdip.ru (Office).

VORONIN, Vladimir Nikolayevich; Moldovan politician; b. 25 May 1941, Corjova, Chişinău region; m.; three c.; ed Tech. Coll., Chişinău, All-Union Inst. of Food Industry, Acad. of Social Sciences, Cen. CPSU Cttee, Acad. of Ministry of Internal Affairs; man. bakery, Criuleni 1961–66, Dubasari 1966–71; fmr Deputy Supreme Council Soviet Socialist Repub. of Moldova (SSRM), First Sec. Party Cttee, Bender 1985–89, Minister of Internal Affairs SSRM 1989–90; mem. Police Reserve, Russian Fed. 1989–93; Co-Pres. Organizational Cttee for Consolidation of Communist Party 1993; Deputy, Parl. Repub. of Moldova 1998–; Pres. of Moldova April 2001–. *Address:* Office of the President, Great National Assembly sq. 1, 277033 Chişinău, Moldova (Office). *Telephone:* (2) 23-72-17 (Office).

VORONKOV, Mikhail Grigorievich, DrChemSc; Russian chemist; b. 6 Dec 1921, Orel; s. of Grigorii Vasilievich and Raisa Mikhailovna Voronkov; m. Lilia Iliinichna Makhnina 1943; one s. one d.; ed Leningrad Univ.; Sr Scientist, Chemical Dept, Leningrad Univ. 1944–54; Head of Lab., Inst. of Chem. of Silicates, USSR Acad. of Sciences 1954–61; Head of Lab. Inst. of Organic Synthesis, Latvian Acad. of Sciences 1961–70; Dir Inst. of Organic Chem., Siberian br. of USSR (now Russian) Acad. of Sciences, Irkutsk 1970–94; Scientific Adviser 1994–; Corresp. mem. USSR (now Russian) Acad. of Sciences 1970, mem. 1990; Corresp. mem. Latvian Acad. of Sciences 1966–91, Foreign mem. 1991–; mem. Braunschweig Scientific Soc., FRG 1976, Chem. Soc. of Japan 1991–, Asia-Pacific Acad. of Advanced Materials 1992; Emer. mem. Fla Center of Heterocyclic Chem., USA 1998; Dr hc (Gdansk Tech. Univ., Poland); Laureate, State Prize of Ukrainian SSR 1981, Hon. Chemist of the USSR 1983, Prize of the USSR Council of Ministers 1991, Laureate, State Prize of Russia 1997; orders and medals for services to the motherland. *Publications:* more than 2,000 scientific papers including 45 monographs. *Leisure interests:* numismatics, humour in chem. *Address:* Institute of Chemistry, 1 Favorsky Street, 664033 Irkutsk; Lermontova Street, 297B-196, 664033, Irkutsk, Russia (Home). *Telephone:* (3952) 42-64-00 (Office); (3952) 42-85-81 (Home). *Fax:* (3952) 39-60-46 (Office). *E-mail:* voronkov@irioch.irk.ru (Office).

VORONTSOV, Nikolai Nikolayevich, D.BIOL.SC.; Russian geneticist, zoologist and politician; b. 1 Jan. 1934, Moscow; m. Elena Lyapunova 1955; two d.; ed Moscow Univ.; worked as jr researcher Leningrad Inst. of Zoology, Docent, Pirogov Second Medical Inst., Moscow; Scientific Sec. Presidium of the Siberian br. of USSR Acad. of Sciences on problems of biology, Head of Lab. Inst. of Cytology and Genetics; mem. Presidium of the Far East Scientific Centre of Acad. of Sciences, Dir Inst. of Biology and Soil 1972–77; Sr Researcher, Koltsov Inst. of Biology of Devt, Moscow 1977–88, Leading Researcher 1988–; Chair. USSR State Cttee on Nature Preservation, then Minister of Use of Nature (the first minister not mem. of CPSU) 1989–91; USSR People's Deputy 1989–91; People's Deputy of Russia 1990–93; Visiting Scholar, Prof. Harvard Univ. 1992–93; mem., Vice-Pres. Russian Acad. of Natural Sciences 1991–; active participant in democratic reforms movt; mem. State Duma (Parl.) 1993–96; participant in more than 40 scientific expeditions; mem. Swedish Royal Acad. of Sciences, American Acad. of Art and Science; mem. Lithuanian Acad. of Sciences 1997–; A. N. Severtsov Prize 1982, First Prize, Moscow Soc. for Nature 1984, USSR State Prize 1990, Bruno Schubert Prize (Germany) 1990, Znamya Literature Prize 1996. *Publications:* more than 500 works on evolutionary biology, mammalian taxonomy, genetics, biodiversity, politology, ecology and preservation of environment. *Address:* N. K. Koltsov Institute of Biology of Development, Vavilova Str. 26, 117334 Moscow, Russia. *Telephone:* (095) 135-75-83.

VORONTSOV, Yuliy Mikhailovich; Russian diplomatist (retd); b. 7 Oct. 1929, Leningrad; m.; one d.; ed Moscow Inst. of Int. Relations; various posts in Ministry of Foreign Affairs 1952–54; mem. CPSU 1956–91; USSR Rep. at UN 1954–58, 1963–65; Counsellor, USSR Embassy to USA 1966–70, Counsellor-Envoy 1970–77; Amb. to India 1977–83, to France 1983–86, to Afghanistan 1988–90; First Deputy Minister of Foreign Affairs 1988–89; USSR (then Russian) Amb. to UN 1990–92; Adviser to Pres. Yeltsin 1992–94; Amb. to USA 1994–98; Under-Sec. Gen. with responsibility for conflict resolution Feb.–Aug. 1999; Chair. Russian-American Investment Bank Feb. 1999–; Special Rep. of UN Sec.-Gen. on CIS 1999–. *Address:* United Nations, United Nations Plaza, New York, NY 10017, USA; Ministry of Foreign Affairs, Smolenskaya-Sennaya 32/34, Moscow, Russia.

VOROSHILO, Aleksander Stepanovich; Russian singer (baritone), theatre manager and business executive; b. 15 Dec. 1944, Dniepropetrovsk region, Ukraine; m. Svetlana Voroshilo; one d.; ed Odessa State Conservatory; served in the army; began vocal studies 1969; soloist Odessa Opera Theatre 1972–75, Bolshoi Theatre, Moscow 1975–91; ended singing career 1991; employee sausage production cos. 1992–; owner of two meat processing, sausage production plants 1997–; Exec. Dir Bolshoi Theatre 2000–02; Gen. Dir Moscow Int. House of Music 2002–; USSR State Prize, USSR Peoples' Artist. *Opera:* leading roles in Bolshoi Theatre include Onegin in Eugene Onegin, Chichikov in Dead Souls, Iago in Othello and Rigoletto in Rigoletto. *Address:* Moscow Int. House of Music, Kosmodamianskaya Naberezhnaya 52, Bldg 8, 115054, Moscow, Russia (Office). *Telephone:* (095) 730-43-50 (Office). *Fax:* (095) 730-43-55 (Office). *E-mail:* international@col.ru (Office). *Website:* www.mmdm.ru (Office).

VORRES, Ian, MA; Canadian/Greek art museum president; b. 19 Sept. 1924, Athens; s. of Andrew Vorres and Stephanie Vorres; one adopted c.; ed Queen's Univ. and Toronto Univ.; Founder and Pres. Bd Vorres Museum 1983–; Mayor of Paiania 1991–98; decorations from the govts. of Portugal, Austria and Finland. *Publication:* The Last Grand Duchess (biog. of Duchess Olga of Russia) 1964. *Leisure interests:* collection of antiques, collection of contemporary Greek art, writing, architecture, gardening. *Address:* Vorres Museum of Contemporary Greek Art, Paiania, Attica; 190 02 Paiania, Attica, Greece. *Telephone:* 6642520; 6644771. *Fax:* 6645775. *E-mail:* vorres@otenet.gr.

VOSCHERAU, Henning, LLD; German politician; b. 13 Aug. 1941, Hamburg; m.; three c.; qualified as notary public; joined SPD 1966; mem. Borough of Wandsbek Dist Ass. 1970–74, Chief Whip SPD Parl. Group 1971–74; mem. Hamburg City Parl., mem. SPD Parl. Exec. Cttee 1974–, Deputy Chair. 1976–82, Chair. 1982–87, Chair. City Parl. Cttee on Home Affairs 1974–82, Deputy Party Chair. SPD, Hamburg 1981–89; First Mayor and Pres. of Senate, City of Hamburg 1988–97; Pres. Bundesrat 1990–91; Chair. Jt Comm. for Reform of the Fed. Constitution 1992–93; SPD Speaker on Financial Policy 1995–97; Chair. Mediation Cttee 1996–97. *Address:* Alstertor 14, 20095 Hamburg, Germany.

VOUTILAINEN, Pertti Juhani, MSc; Finnish banker; b. 22 June 1940, Kuusjärvi; s. of Otto Voutilainen and Martta Voutilainen; m. Raili Juvonen 1963; two s.; ed Helsinki Univ. of Tech., Helsinki School of Econs, Pennsylvania State Univ., USA; joined Outokumpu Oy 1964, Man. Corp. Planning 1973–76, Dir Corp. Planning 1976–78, mem. Bd 1978–91, Pres. 1980–91, Chair. Exec. Bd 1983–91; Chair. and CEO Kansallis-Osake-Pankki (to merge with Unitas Ltd) 1992–; currently Pres. Merita Nordbanken; Commdr Order of Lion of Finland. *Leisure interests:* hunting, fishing. *Address:* Merita Bank PLC, Aleksanterinkatu 36 B, FIN-00020 MERITA, Finland. *Telephone:* (9) 1651. *Fax:* (9) 16542838. *Website:* www.merita.fi/s (Office).

VOYNET, Dominique; French politician and doctor; b. 4 Nov. 1958, Montbéliard; d. of Jean Voynet and Monique Richard; two d.; ed Faculty of Medicine, Besançon; anaesthetist and intensive care specialist, Dole (Jura) public hosp. 1985–89; activist in several ecological and other orgs., Belfort and Besançon 1976–; Co-founder Les Verts ('Green' Movt) 1984, Gen. Sec. Green Group in European Parl. 1989–91, Nat. Spokesperson 1991–, Nat. Sec. 2001–; Municipal Councillor, Dole 1989–; Co. Councillor 1998–; mem. Franche-Comté regional council 1992–94 (resgnd); cand. presidential election 1995; elected Nat. Ass. Deputy (for Les Verts and Parti Socialiste) in Dole-Arbois 1997; Minister for Town and Country Planning and the Environment 1997–2001; Councillor-Gen., Jura 1998–. *Address:* Les Verts, 107 avenue Parmentier, 75011 Paris, France. *Telephone:* 1-43-55-10-01 (Office). *Fax:* 1-43-55-16-15 (Office). *E-mail:* secretar@les-verts.org (Office). *Website:* www.les-verts.org (Office).

VOYNOVICH, Vladimir Nikolayevich; author, playwright and film scriptwriter; b. 26 Sept. 1932, Stalinabad (now Dushanbe), Tajikistan; s. of Nikolai Pavlovich Voinovich and Rosa (née Goikhman) Voinovich; m. 1st Valentina Voinovich; one s. one d.; m. 2nd Irina Braude 1970; one d.; served in Soviet Army 1951–55; worked as carpenter 1956–57; studied Moscow Pedagogical Inst. 1958–59; started literary activity (and song-writing for Moscow Radio) 1960; various dissident activities 1966–80; expelled from USSR Writers' Union 1974; elected mem. French PEN Centre 1974; emigrated from USSR 1980; USSR citizenship restored 1990; mem. Bavarian Acad. of Fine Arts. *Publications include:* The Life and Unusual Adventures of Private Ivan Chonkin (samizdat 1967) 1975 (English trans. 1977), Ivankiada 1976, By Way of Mutual Correspondence 1979, Pretender to the Throne 1981, Moscow–2042 1987, The Fur Hat 1989, The Zero Decision 1990, Case N3484 1992, The Conception 1994, Tales for Adults 1996.

VOZNESENSKY, Andrey Andreyevich; Russian poet; b. 12 May 1933, Moscow; s. of Andrey N. Voznesensky and Antonina S. Voznesensky; m. Zoya Boguslavskaya 1965; one s.; ed Moscow Architectural Inst.; mem. Union of Soviet Writers, mem. Bd 1967–; Vice-Pres. Soviet (now Russian) PEN Centre 1989–; Hon. mem. American Acad. of Arts and Letters 1972, Bayerischen Kunst Akad., French Acad. Merimé; Int. Award for Distinguished Achievement in Poetry 1978, State Prize 1978. *In English:* Selected Poems 1964, Anti-worlds 1966, Anti-worlds and the Fifth Ace 1967, Dogalypse 1972, Story under Full Sail 1974, Nostalgia for the Present 1978. *Publications:* poems: The Masters 1959, Forty Lyrical Digressions from a Triangular Pear 1962,

Longjumeau 1963, Oza 1964, Story Under Full Sail 1970, Ice-69 1970, Queen of Clubs 1974, The Eternal Flesh 1978, Andrey Polisadov 1980, Unaccountable 1981, The Ditch 1981; collections: Parabola 1960, Mosaic 1960, Anti-Worlds 1964, Heart of Achilles 1966, Verses 1967, The Shadow of a Sound 1970, The Glance 1972, Let The Bird Free 1974, Violoncello Oak Leaf 1975, The Master of Stained Glass 1976, Temptation 1978, Metropol (poetry and prose, co-author with 22 others) 1979, Selected Poems 1979, Collected Works (Vols 1–3) 1984, Aksioma Samoiska 1990, Videomes 1992, Rossia-Casino 1997, On the Virtual Wind 2000. *Address:* Kotelnicheskaya nab. 1/15, korp. B., Apt. 62, Moscow 109240, Russia. *Telephone:* (095) 915-49-90.

VRAALSEN, Tom Eric, M.ECON.; Norwegian diplomatist; b. 26 Jan. 1936, Oslo; m.; five c.; ed Århus School of Econs and Business Admin., Denmark; joined Norwegian Foreign Service 1960; various diplomatic positions, Beijing 1962–64, 1969–70, Cairo 1964–67, Manila 1970–71, Jakarta 1971; in charge of Norwegian relations with Africa, Asia and Latin America, Political Dept, Ministry of Foreign Affairs 1971–73, in charge of UN and int. org. affairs 1973–75; Deputy Perm. Rep. to UN 1975–79, Perm. Rep. 1982–89; Dir-Gen. Political Dept, Ministry of Foreign Affairs 1981–82; Minister for Devt Co-operation, for Nordic Co-operation 1989–90; Sr Vice-Pres. Saga Petroleum 1991–92; Asst Sec.-Gen. Ministry of Foreign Affairs 1992–94; Amb. to UK 1994–96, to USA 1996–2001; UN Special Envoy for Humanitarian Affairs for the Sudan 1998–. *Address:* Department of Peace-Keeping Operations, Room S-3727-B, United Nations, New York, NY 10017, USA (Office). *Telephone:* (212) 963-8079 (Office). *Fax:* (212) 963-9222 (Office). *Website:* www.un.org/Depts/dpko (Office).

VRACAR, Milenko; Bosnia and Herzegovina politician and banker; b. 15 May 1956, Omarska-Prijedor; m.; two d.; ed Belgrade Univ.; Sector Man., rising to Gen. Dir for Finance, AIPK 1979–90; Gen. Man. Agroprom Bank, Banja Luka 1991–92, 1993–2000; Gov. Nat. Bank of Republika Srpska 1992–93; Gen. Man. Zepter Commerc Bank 2000–01; Minister of Finance 2001–. *Leisure interests:* football, numismatics. *Address:* Ministry of Finance, Vuka Karadzica 4, 78000 Banja Luka (Office); N. Pasica 70, Banja Luka, Bosnia and Herzegovina (Home). *Telephone:* (51) 331350 (Office); (51) 300550 (Home). *Fax:* (51) 331351 (Office). *E-mail:* mf@vladars.net (Office). *Website:* www.vladars.net (Office).

VRANITZKY, Franz, DComm; Austrian politician and banker; b. 4 Oct. 1937, Vienna; s. of Franz Vranitsky and Rosa Vernitsky; m. Christine Kristen; one s. one d.; ed Vienna XVII High School, Coll. (now Univ.) of Commerce, Vienna; joined Siemens-Schuckert GmbH, Vienna 1961; Dept of Nat. Econs, Austrian Nat. Bank 1961–69, seconded to the Office of the First Vice-Pres. 1969–70; Adviser on Econ. and Financial Policy to Minister of Finance 1970–76; Deputy-Chair. Bd of Dirs. Creditanstalt-Bankverein 1976–81, Österreichische Länderbank 1981, Chair. Bd of Dirs. 1981–84; Fed. Minister of Finance 1984–86; Fed. Chancellor 1986–96; fmr Chair. Austrian Socialist Party (now Social Democratic Party of Austria); Pres. Vienna Inst. for Devt and Co-operation 1990–; Hon. KCMG 1995. *Address:* c/o Office of the Federal Chancellor, Ballhausplatz 2, 1014 Vienna, Austria.

VUJANOVIĆ, Filip; Serbia and Montenegro (Montenegrin) politician and lawyer; b. 1 Sept. 1954, Belgrade; m.; one s. two d.; ed Univ. of Belgrade; began career with First Municipal Court; Official Assoc., Dist Attorney's Office, Belgrade; Sec. to Dist Court, Podgorica 1981, mem. Attorney's Chamber, Chair. Chamber 1989; Minister of Justice, Repub. of Montenegro–1996, of the Interior 1996; Prime Minister of the Repub. of Montenegro, with responsibility for Religious Affairs 2001–02; Speaker of Parl. 2002–03; Pres. of Repub. of Montenegro 2003–; mem. Democratic Party of Montenegrin Socialists (DPMS). *Address:* Office of the President, Podgorica, Serbia and Montenegro (Office). *Fax:* (81) 42329 (Office).

VULF, Vitaly Yakovlevich, DHist; Russian broadcaster and writer; b. 23 May 1930, Baku, Azerbaijan; s. of Yakov Vulf; ed Moscow State Univ.; barrister, Baku and Moscow 1961–67; Sr, then leading researcher Inst. of Int. Workers' Movt (now Inst. of Comparative Politology), USSR (now Russian) Acad. of Sciences 1967–97; Broadcaster VID TV Co. 1997–; creator of Silver Ball TV programme; mem. editorial Bd Ballet (magazine); mem. Union of Theatre Workers. *Publications:* Theatre of the USA of the Seventies and Political Reality, A Little Aside from Broadway, A. Stepanova—Actress of Moscow Art Theatre, Idols, Stars, People, Stars of Difficult Destiny, Theatre Rain and numerous other works on Russian and foreign theatre. *Address:* Panfilovskiy per. 5, Apt. 35, 121099 Moscow, Russia. *Telephone:* (095) 241-97-44.

VUNIBOBO, Berenado, CBE, BAgrSc; Fijian government official and agronomist; b. 24 Sept. 1932, Nukutubu, Rewa; s. of Mateo Vunibobo and Maria Kelekeletabua; m. Luisa Marama Tabumoce 1953; two s. three d.; ed St Joseph's Catholic Mission School, Rewa, Marist Brothers High School, Suva, Queensland State Agric. Coll., Queensland Univ. Imperial Coll. of Tropical Agric., Trinidad; Govt Service 1951–, Dist Agric. Officer 1962–67, Sr Agric. Officer and later Chief Agric. Officer 1968–69; Deputy Dir of Agric. 1969–70, Dir of Agric. 1970–71; Perm. Sec. for Agric., Fisheries and Forests 1971–72, for Works 1973–76; Perm. Rep. to UN, Amb. to USA, High Commr in Canada 1976–80; Perm. Sec. for Tourism, Transport and Civil Aviation 1980–81; Resident Rep. UNDP, Repub. of Korea 1981–86; Resident Rep. UNDP, Pakistan 1986–87; Minister of Trade and Commerce 1987–92, for Home Affairs, Immigration, Employment, Youth and Sports 1994, of Finance and

Econ. Devt 1994–97, for Foreign Affairs and External Trade 1997–99; Chair. UN Visiting Mission to Cayman Islands and U.S. Virgin Islands 1978; Vice-Pres. UN Gen. Ass.; Pres. UN Pledging Conf., Governing Council, UNDP; Chair. UN Observer Mission to New Hebrides (now Vanuatu); Chair. Coconut Pests and Diseases Bd, Banana Marketing Bd, Nat. Marketing Authority 1970–72; Chair. Civil Aviation Authority, Fiji, Air Terminal Services, Fiji; mem. Bd, Fiji Devt Bank 1970–72; mem. Native Lands Trust Bd 1968–75, Fijian Affairs Bd 1968–76, Great Council of Chiefs 1968–76, Cen. Whitley Council 1970–76, Jt Industrial Council 1970–76, Fiji Electricity Authority 1975–76; Gold Medal (Queensland Agric. Coll.) 1986. *Leisure interests:* reading, debating, walking, gardening, swimming, golf. *Address:* c/o Ministry of Foreign Affairs, Government Buildings, P.O. Box 2220, Suva, Fiji.

VURAL, Volkan, MA; Turkish diplomatist; b. 29 Dec. 1941, Istanbul; m.; ed Ankara Coll. and Univ.; joined Foreign Ministry 1964, Third Sec. Econ. Affairs Dept 1964–65; mil. service 1965–67; Third Sec. Dept of Bilateral and Regional Econ. Affairs 1967–68, Second then First Sec. Embassy, Seoul 1968–71, Consul then Deputy Consul Gen. Consulate, Munich 1971–73, Acting Head Dept of Int. Econ. Insts., Foreign Ministry 1973–76, Int. Officer Political Dept NATO Headquarters 1976–82, Deputy Dir Gen. for Bilateral Econ. Affairs, Foreign Ministry 1982–87; Amb. to Iran 1987–88, to USSR 1988–93, to Germany 1995–98; Spokesman Foreign Ministry 1993, Chief Adviser to the Prime Minister 1993–95; Perm. Rep. to the UN 1998–2000. *Address:* c/o Ministry of Foreign Affairs, Dişişleri Bakanlığı, Yeni Mizmet Binası, 06520 Balgat, Ankara, Turkey (Office).

VUURSTEEN, Karel; Netherlands business executive; b. 25 July 1941, Arnhem; s. of Cornelis Vuursteen and Hendrika Weddepohl; m. Juliette Pronk 1964; one s. two d.; ed Agricultural Univ. Wageningen; several marketing functions, Philips, Netherlands 1968; Man. Dir Consumer Goods, Philips Sweden 1979; CEO Philips Norway 1982; Man. Dir Consumer Goods, Philips Germany 1984; CEO Philips Austria 1987, Philips Lighting Co. USA 1990; mem. Exec. Bd Heineken N.V. 1991, Deputy Chair. Exec. Bd 1992, Chair. and CEO 1993–2002; Dir of numerous co.s. *Leisure interest:* golf. *Address:* c/o Corporate Communications Department, Heineken N.V., Tweede Weteringplantsoen 21, Postbus 28, 1000 AA Amsterdam, Netherlands (Office).

VYACHIREV, Rem Ivanovich; Russian business executive; b. 23 Aug. 1934, Bolshaya Chernigovka, Kuibyshev Dist; m.; two c.; ed Kuibyshev Inst. of Oil and Gas; worked in Oil Producers' Union, Ozenburg (Ordobycha)

1976–78; Chief Engineer Orenburggazprom 1978–82; Deputy Minister of Gas Industry of USSR 1983–85, 1986–89; Gen. Man. Tyumengazprom 1985–86; Deputy Chair. Bd, State (later Jt Stock) Gazprom Co. 1989–92, CEO 1992–2001, Chair. Bd. of Dirs. 2001–; Chair Bd of Dirs. Siberian Oil Co. 1996–; mem. Int. Eng Acad.; Chair. of Bd, Promstroybank 1998–. *Address:* RAO Gazprom, Nametkina str. 16, 117884 Moscow, Russia. *Telephone:* (095) 719-30-01; (095) 719-21-09. *Fax:* (095) 719-83-33.

VYACHORKA, Vintsuk; Belarus politician and linguist; b. 7 July 1961, Bieraście; s. of Ryhor Viačorka and Alaucina Viačorka; m. 1980; two s. one d.; ed Belarus State Univ., Acad. of Sciences; Lecturer, Minsk Pedagogical Univ. 1986–; f. Belarusian Popular Front (BPF) 1988, Chair. BPF – 'Revival' ('BPF – Adradzhennye') 1999–; Deputy Ed.-in-Chief bi-monthly Spadčyna. *Publication:* Orthography: An Attempt at Comprehensive Standardization 1994. *Leisure interest:* ethno-music. *Address:* BPF – "Adradzhennye", vul. Varvasheni 8, 220005 Minsk, Belarus (Office). *Telephone:* (17) 213-30-09 (Office). *Fax:* (17) 284-50-12 (Office). *E-mail:* cscsc@user.unibel.by (Office). *Website:* www.pbnf.org (Office).

VÝBORNÝ, Miloslav, DIur; Czech politician and lawyer; b. 19 Feb. 1952, Chrudim; m. Václava Výborná; three s.; ed Charles Univ., Prague; mem. Parl. 1990–, Chair. Parl. Constitutional Juridical Cttee 1992–96; Vice-Chair. Christian Democratic Union–Czech People's Party (CDU–CPP) 1993–; Chair. CDU–CPP Parl. Club 1995–96, Vice-Chair. 2001–; Minister of Defence 1996–97, of Legislative Affairs Jan.–July 1998; Vice-Pres. Govt Cttee for Integration of Czech Repub. into NATO 1997–98; Chair. Mandate and Immunities Cttee 1998–. *Address:* Parliament of the Czech Republic, Sněmovní 4, 118 26 Prague 1, Czech Republic. *Telephone:* (2) 57171111 (Office). *Fax:* (2) 57532223 (Office). *E-mail:* c/o havlickova@psp.cz (Office). *Website:* www.psp.cz (Office).

VYUGIN, Oleg Vyacheslavovich, CAND. PHYS.-MATH.SC.; Russian economist; b. 29 July 1952, Ufa, Bashkortostan; m.; one d.; ed Moscow State Univ.; researcher, then Sr researcher, Head of Lab. Inst. of Prognosis of Nat. Econ., Russian Acad. of Sciences 1989–92; Head Dept of Macroecons. Policy, Ministry of Finance 1993–96, Deputy Minister of Finance 1996–99, First Deputy 1999–2000; mem. Bd, Exec. Vice-Pres., Chief Economist Troyka-Dialog investment Co. 2000–. *Address:* Troyka-Dialog Investment Company, Romanov per. 4, 103009 Moscow, Russia (Office). *Telephone:* (095) 258-05-00 (Office).

WAAGSTEIN, Finn, MD, PhD; Swedish professor of cardiology; Prof. of Cardiology, Inst. of Heart and Lung Diseases, Gothenberg Univ.; pioneered treatment of heart failure with beta-blockers 1973; King Faisal Int. Prize for Medicine 2002 (Jt recipient). *Address:* Wallenberg Laboratory, Bruna stråket 16, SU/Sahlgrenska, 413 45 Gothenberg, Sweden (Office). *Telephone:* (31) 342-30-14 (Office). *Fax:* (31) 82-37-62 (Office). *E-mail:* Finn.Waagstein@wlab.wall.gu.se (Office).

WACHTMEISTER, Count Wilhelm Hans Frederik; Swedish fmr diplomatist; b. 29 April 1923, Wanås; s. of Count Gustaf Wachtmeister and Countess Margaretha Wachtmeister (née Trolle); m. Countess Ulla Wachtmeister (née Leuhusen) 1947; one s. one d.; ed Stockholm Univ.; Attaché, Foreign Office 1946–47, Embassy in Vienna 1947–49, in Madrid Feb.–May 1949, in Lisbon 1949–50, Foreign Office 1950–52; Second Sec. Foreign Office 1952–55; Second Sec. Embassy in Moscow 1955–56, First Sec. 1956–58; Special Asst to Sec.-Gen. of UN 1958–62; Head of Div. for UN Affairs, Foreign Office 1962–63, Head of Div. 1963–65, Head of Dept July–Oct. 1965, Asst Under-Sec. of State 1965–66; Amb. to Algeria 1966–68; Deputy Under-Sec. of State and Head of Political Div. 1968–74; Amb. to USA 1974–89; Dean of the Diplomatic Corps 1986–89; Sr Adviser to Chair. of AB Volvo 1989–93; Int. Adviser Coudert Bros (law firm) 1989–93; Chair. Swedish-American Chamber of Commerce (US) 1993–96; Hon. LLD. *Publications:* Som Jag Sås Det (As I Saw It) 1996. *Leisure interest:* tennis. *Address:* Karlavagen 59, SE 11449, Stockholm, Sweden. *Telephone:* (8) 660-3823 (Home).

WADA, Akiyoshi, PhD; Japanese research director; b. 28 June 1929, Tokyo; s. of Koroku Wada and Haruko Kikkawa; m. Sachiko Naito 1958; two s.; ed Gakushūin High School and Univ. of Tokyo; Prof. of Physics, Univ. of Tokyo 1971–90, Prof. Emer. 1990–, Dean Faculty of Science 1989–90; Dir Sagami Chemical Research Center 1991–2001; Vice-Pres. Advanced Tech. Inst. 1988–; Dir Kazusa DNA Research Inst. 1991–; mem. Science Council of Japan 1991–2000; Pres. Nestlé Science Foundation (Japan) 1992–; Dir Genomic Sciences Centre (RIKEN) 1998–; Matsunaga Prize 1971, Shimadu Prize 1983, Polymer Soc. Prize 1995, Purple Ribbon Medal 1995, 10th Anniversary Award, Human Frontier Science Program 1998, Second Order of the Sacred Treasure 2002. *Publications:* Macrodipole of α-helix 1976, Molten Globule State of Proteins 1980, Automated DNA Sequencing 1987, Stability Distribution of DNA Double Helix 1987. *Leisure interests:* orchid cultivation, stamp collection. *Address:* 11-1-311, Akasaka 8, Minato-ku, Tokyo 107, Japan. *Telephone:* (3) 3408-2932.

WADA, Emi; Japanese costume designer; b. 18 March 1937, Kyoto; d. of Nobu Wada and Sumiko Noguchi; m. Ben Wada 1957; one s.; ed Kyoto City Coll. of Arts (now Kyoto Univ. of Arts); mem. Acad. of Motion Picture Art and Sciences, USA, Costume Designers' Guild, USA; Acad. Award, Best Costume Design for Ran 1986, Gold Medal, Cannes Film Festival 1987, Grand Prix, Montreux Int. HDTV Festival for Silk Art by Emi Wada 1991. *Costumes designed:* (theatre) Aoi Hi (Blue Fire) 1957, Image Mandala 1987, King Lear 1993; (films) Marco 1972, Ran 1985, Rokumeikan 1986, Princess from the Moon 1987, Momotaro Forever 1988, Rikyu 1989, Dreams 1990, Prospero's Books 1991; (dance) Carmen 1991; (TV) Silk Art by Emi Wada 1991; (opera) Oedipus Rex 1992; (Exhbn) Emi Wada Recreates the Momoyama Period, Kyoto 1989. *Publication:* My Costume—Emi Wada 1989. *Leisure interest:* reading. *Address:* 3-31-3-105 Kinuta, Setagaya-ku, Tokyo 157, Japan. *Telephone:* (3) 3417-0425. *Fax:* (3) 3417-1773.

WADDELL, (John) Rankin; British photographer; b. 1966, Glasgow; m. Kate Hardie (divorced); one s.; ed Brighton Polytechnic, London Coll. of Printing; co-f. Dazed and Confused magazine; co-f. Vision On Publishing; photographed Queen's Jubilee 2002. *Publications include:* Nudes, Male Nudes 2000. *Address:* Vision On Publishing, 112–116 Old Street, London EC1V 9BG, England (Office). *Telephone:* (20) 7549-6808 (Office). *Fax:* (20) 7336-0966 (Office). *E-mail:* web@visiononpublishing.com (Office).

WADDINGTON, Baron (Life Peer), cr. 1990, of Read in the County of Lancashire; **David Waddington,** GCVO, PC, QC, DL; British politician; b. 2 Aug 1929, Burnley; s. of Charles Waddington and Minnie Hughan Waddington; m. Gillian Rosemary Green 1958; three s. two d.; ed Sedbergh and Hertford Coll. Oxford; Pres. Oxford Union Conservative Assen 1950; called to the Bar, Gray's Inn 1951, Recorder of the Crown Court 1972; MP for Nelson and Colne 1968–74, for Clitheroe (Ribble Valley constituency from 1983) March 1979–91; Parl. Pvt. Sec. to Attorney-Gen. 1970–72; Lord Commr of the Treasury 1979–81, Parl. Under-Sec. of State for Employment 1981–83; Minister of State at the Home Office 1983–87, Parl. Sec. to HM Treasury and Govt Chief Whip 1987–89, Home Sec. 1989–90, Lord Privy Seal and Leader of the House of Lords 1990–92; Gov. and C-in-C of Bermuda 1992–97. *Leisure interests:* golf, sailing. *Address:* House of Lords, Westminster, London, SW1A 0PW (Office); Flat 4, 39 Chester Way, London, SE11 4UR; Stable House, Sabden, nr Clitheroe, Lancs., BB7 9HP, England (Home). *Telephone:* (20) 7219-6448 (Office); (1282) 771070 (Home); (20) 7820-9338. *Fax:* (20) 7820-9338 (Office); (1282) 774407 (Home). *E-mail:* wadding@parliament.uk (Office).

WADDINGTON, Leslie; British art dealer; b. 9 Feb. 1934, Dublin; s. of Victor Waddington and Zelda Waddington; m. 2nd Clodagh F. Waddington 1985; two d. by first marriage; ed Portora Royal School, Enniskillen and Ecole du Louvre, Paris; Dir Waddington Galleries 1957, Man. Dir 1966–; Chair.

Modern Painting Section Maastricht Art Fair 1994–, Pictura Section 1996–2000; Sr Fellow RCA 1993; Dr hc (Royal Coll. of Art) 1993. *Leisure interests:* chess, reading. *Address:* Waddington Galleries, 11 Cork Street, London, W1S 3LT, England. *Telephone:* (20) 7851-2200.

WADE, Abdoulaye; Senegalese politician and lawyer; b. 1927; m.; two c.; ed Univ. of Besançon, France; univ. teacher in Senegal and abroad; barrister, Court of Appeal, Senegal; Founder and Pres., Senegalese Democratic Party 1974–; Pres. of Senegal 2000–. *Address:* Office of the President, Avenue Léopold Sédar Senghor, B.P. 168, Dakar, Senegal. *Telephone:* 823-10-88. *Website:* www.gouv.sn/prosid.html (Office).

WADE, Sir (Henry) William (Rawson), Kt, QC, LLD, DCL, FBA, LittD; British professor of law (retd); b. 16 Jan. 1918, London; s. of Col H. O. Wade and E. L. Wade; m. 1st Marie Osland-Hill 1943 (died 1980); m. 2nd Marjorie Grace Hope Browne 1982 (died 2001); two s.; ed Shrewsbury School, Gonville and Caius Coll. Cambridge and Harvard Law School, USA; Temporary Officer, HM Treasury 1940–45; Barrister, Lincoln's Inn 1946; Fellow, Trinity Coll. Cambridge and Univ. Lecturer/Reader 1946–61; Prof. of English Law, Oxford Univ. and Fellow of St John's Coll. 1961–76; Master of Gonville and Caius Coll. Cambridge 1976–88; Prof. of English Law, Cambridge Univ. 1978–82; Guest Lecturer in many countries; mem. Council on Tribunals 1958–71, Relationships Comm., Uganda 1961, Royal Comm. on Tribunals of Inquiry 1966; Vice-Pres. British Acad. 1981–83; Hon. Bencher, Lincoln's Inn 1964; Hon. Fellow, St John's Coll. Oxford 1976, Trinity Coll. Cambridge 1991. *Publications:* The Law of Real Property (with Sir Robert Megarry), 6th Edn 2000, Administrative Law (with C. F. Forsyth), 8th Edn 2000, Towards Administrative Justice 1963, Legal Control of Government (with B. Schwartz) 1972, Constitutional Fundamentals (Hamlyn Lectures) 1980; articles in legal journals. *Leisure interests:* climbing, gardening and music. *Address:* Gonville and Caius College, Cambridge, CB2 1TA (Office); The Green, 1A Ludlow Lane, Fulbourn, Cambridge, CB1 5BL, England (Home). *Telephone:* (1223) 332400 (Office); (1223) 881745 (Home).

WADE, Kenneth, DSc, FRS; British university professor; b. 13 Oct. 1932, Sleaford, Lincs.; s. of the late Harry K. Wade and Anna E. Wade (née Cartwright); m. Gertrud Rosmarie Hetzel 1962 (separated); one s. two d.; ed Carre's Grammar School, Sleaford, Lincs., Nottingham Univ.; postdoctoral research Asst Cambridge Univ. 1957–59, Cornell Univ., Ithaca, NY 1959–60; Lecturer in Chem. Derby Coll. of Tech. 1960–61; Lecturer in Chem. Durham Univ. 1961–71, Sr Lecturer 1971–77, Reader 1977–83, Head of Inorganic Chem. 1980–98, Prof. 1983–2001, Prof. Emer. 2001–; Chair. Dept of Chem. 1986–89; Visiting Prof. Warsaw 1974, Amsterdam 1977, USCLA 1979, Notre Dame 1983, McMaster 1984, London, Ont. 1990; Pres. Royal Soc. of Chem. Dalton Div. 1995–97; Main Group Award Royal Soc. of Chem. 1982, Tilden Lecturer 1987, Mond Lecturer 1998, E. Merck Lecturer, Darmstadt 1994. *Publications:* Organometallic Compounds: The Main Group Elements (jtly.) 1967, Principles of Organometallic Chemistry (jtly.) 1968, Electron Deficient Compounds 1971, Hypercarbon Chemistry (jtly.) 1987, Electron Deficient Boron and Carbon Clusters (jtly.) 1990. *Leisure interest:* walking. *Address:* Chemistry Department, Durham University Science Laboratories, South Road, Durham, DH1 3LE (Office); 7 Hill Meadows, High Shincliffe, Durham, DH1 2PE, England (Home). *Telephone:* (191) 374-3122 (Office); (191) 386-5139 (Home). *Fax:* (191) 384-4737. *E-mail:* kenneth.wade@durham.ac.uk (Office).

WADE, Rebekah; British newspaper editor; b. 27 May 1968; d. of the late Robert Wade and of Deborah Wade; ed Appleton Hall, Cheshire and Univ. of the Sorbonne, Paris; began career as Features Ed., later Assoc. Ed. and Deputy Ed. News of the World –1998, Ed. 2000–03; Deputy Ed. The Sun 1998–2000, Ed. 2003–; Founder-mem. and Pres. Women in Journalism. *Address:* The Sun, 1 Virginia Street, Wapping, London, E1 9XR, England (Office). *Telephone:* (20) 7782-4108 (Office). *E-mail:* news@the-sun.co.uk (Office). *Website:* www.thesun.co.uk (Office).

WADE, (Sarah) Virginia, OBE, BSc; British tennis player and broadcaster; b. 10 July 1945, Bournemouth, Hants. (now Dorset); d. of the late Canon Eustace Wade (fmr Archdeacon of Durban, SA) and of Joan Barbara Wade; ed Univ. of Sussex; amateur player 1962–68, professional 1968–87; British Hard Court Champion 1967, 1968, 1973, 1974; USA Champion 1968 (singles), 1973, 1975 (doubles); Italian Champion 1971; Australian Champion 1972; Wimbledon Ladies Champion 1977; played Wightman Cup for GB 1965–85, Capt. 1973–80; played Fed. Cup for GB 1967–83 (a record), Capt. 1973–81; won 55 singles titles; commentator BBC 1980–; mem. Cttee All England Lawn Tennis Club 1983–91 (first woman to be elected) 1982–; Hon. LLD (Sussex) 1985; Int. Tennis Hall of Fame 1989; Fed. Cup Award of Excellence 2002. *Publications:* Courting Triumph (with Mary Lou Mellace) 1978, Ladies of the Court 1984. *Leisure interest:* reading. *Address:* c/o International Management Group, Pier House, Strand on the Green, London, W4 3NN, England.

WADE-GERY, Sir Robert (Lucian), KCMG, KCVO, MA; British fmr diplomatist and banker; b. 22 April 1929, Oxford; s. of Prof. H. T. Wade-Gery and V. Wade-Gery; m. Sarah Marris 1962; one s. one d.; ed Winchester Coll. and

New Coll., Oxford; Fellow, All Souls Coll. Oxford 1951–73, 1987–89, 1997–; joined Foreign (now Diplomatic) Service 1951; in Foreign Office (FO) Econ. Relations Dept 1951–54; at Embassy in Bonn 1954–57, Tel-Aviv 1961–64, Saigon (now Ho Chi Minh City) 1967–68; FO 1957–60, 1964–67; Cabinet Office 1968–69; Counsellor 1969; on loan to Bank of England 1969; Head of Financial Policy and Aid Dept, FCO 1970; Under-Sec., Cen. Policy Review Staff, Cabinet Office 1971–73; Minister at Embassy, Madrid 1973–77, Moscow 1977–79; Deputy Sec. of Cabinet 1979–82; High Commr in India 1982–87; Vice-Chair. Barclays de Zoete Wedd 1994–98 (Exec. Dir 1987–93), Vice-Chair. Barclays Capital 1998–99; Sr Consultant to Int. Financial Services London 1991–2001 and to Barclays Private Bank 1999–2002; Chair. SOAS 1990–98; Chair. Anglo-Spanish Soc. 1995–98. *Leisure interests:* walking, sailing, travel, history. *Address:* 14 Hill View, 2 Primrose Hill Road, London, NW3 3AX (Home); The Old Vicarage, Cold Aston, Cheltenham, Glos., GL54 3BW, England (Home). *Telephone:* (20) 7722-4754 (Home); (1451) 821115 (Home). *Fax:* (20) 7586-5966, (1451) 822496 (Home).

WADHWANI, Sushil Baldev, CBE, MSc, PhD; British economist; b. 7 Dec. 1959, Kenya; s. of Baldev Wadhwani and Meena Wadhwani; m. Renu Wadhwani; one s. one d.; ed London School of Econs; Reader in Econs LSE 1984–91; Dir of Equity Strategy, Goldman Sachs Int. 1991–95; Dir of Research, Tudor Proprietary Trading LLC 1995–99; mem. Bank of England Monetary Policy Cttee 1999–2002; Allyn Young Prize, C. S. McTaggart Scholarship, Clothworkers' Co. Exhbn, Gonner Prize, Raynes Undergrad. Prize, Sir Edward Stern Scholarship, Ely Devons Prize, Sayers Prize. *Publications:* numerous articles in academic journals. *Leisure interest:* cricket. *Address:* Wadhwani Asset Management LLP, 51 Gresham Street, London, EC2V 7EL, England (Office). *Telephone:* (20) 7663-3420 (Office). *Fax:* (20) 7663-3410 (Office). *E-mail:* sushilw@waniasset.com (Office). *Website:* www.waniasset.com (Office).

WADIA, Jim, FCA, FRSA; British chartered accountant; b. 12 April 1948; m. Joelle Garnier 1972; one s. one d.; ed Le Rosey, Rolle, Switzerland, Inns of Court School of Law; called to Bar, Inner Temple 1969; Partner, Arthur Andersen 1982–2000, Managing Partner, UK 1993–97, Worldwide Managing Partner 1997–2000; COO Linklaters 2001–. *Leisure interests:* tennis, theatre. *Address:* Linklaters, 1 Silk Street, London, EC2Y 8MQ (Office); 28 Eldon Road, London, W8 5PT, England (Home). *Telephone:* (20) 7456-4982 (Office); (20) 7937-7045. *E-mail:* jim.wadia@linklaters.com (Office).

WAELSCH, Salome G., PhD; American geneticist; b. 6 Oct. 1907, Danzig, Germany (now Gdańsk, Poland); d. of Ilyia Gluecksohn and Nadia Gluecksohn; m. Heinrich B. Waelsch 1943; one s. one d.; ed Univs. of Königsberg, Berlin, Freiburg; Research Assoc. in Genetics, Columbia Univ., New York 1936–55; Assoc. Prof. of Anatomy (Genetics), Albert Einstein Coll. of Medicine, Bronx, NY 1955–58, Prof. of Anatomy (Genetics) 1958–63, Chair. of Dept of Genetics 1963–76, Prof. of Genetics 1963–; mem. NAS; Fellow, American Acad. of Arts and Sciences. *Publications:* more than 100 articles in the field of developmental genetics in various scientific journals. *Address:* Department of Molecular Genetics, Albert Einstein College of Medicine, 1300 Morris Park Avenue, Bronx, NY 10461 (Office); 90 Morningside Drive, New York, NY 10027, USA (Home). *Telephone:* (718) 430-3185 (Office). *Fax:* (718) 822-0845 (Office). *E-mail:* gradus@aecom.yu.edu (Office).

WAGGONER, Paul Edward, PhD, FAAS; American scientist; b. 29 March 1923, Appanoose County, Ia; s. of Walter Loyal Waggoner and Kathryn Maring Waggoner; m. Barbara Ann Lockerbie 1945; two s.; ed Univ. of Chicago and Iowa State Coll., Ames; Asst, then Assoc., then Chief Scientist, Connecticut Agricultural Experiment Station, New Haven 1951–71, Vice-Dir 1969–71, Dir 1972–87, Distinguished Scientist 1987–; lecturer, Yale Forestry School, New Haven 1962–; Guggenheim Fellow 1963; mem. NAS; Fellow American Soc. of Agronomy, American Phytopathological Soc.; Anton-de Bary Medal 1996. *Publications:* Agricultural Meteorology (ed.) 1965, Climate Change and US Water Resources 1990, How Much Land Can 10 Billion People Spare for Nature? 1994 and articles on phytopathology. *Leisure interests:* gardening, bicycling. *Address:* The Connecticut Agricultural Experiment Station, Box 1106, New Haven, CT 06504 (Office); 314 Vineyard Point Road, Guilford, CT 06437, USA (Home). *Telephone:* (203) 974-8494 (Office); (203) 453-2816 (Home). *E-mail:* paul.waggoner@po.state.ct.us.

WAGNER, Falk (Oskar Paul Alfred), DTheol; German professor of theology; b. 25 Feb. 1939, Vienna, Austria; s. of Robert Wagner and Friedel Wagner; m. Inamaria Winnefeld 1968; two d.; ed Gymnasium Wiesbaden and Univs. of Frankfurt and Mainz; Research Fellow for Economic Ethics and Adult Educ., Karlsruhe 1968–69; Research Fellow, Deutsches Inst. für Int. Pädagogische Forschung, Frankfurt am Main 1969–72; Asst Univ. of Munich 1970–72, Lecturer in Systematic Theology 1972, Prof. 1978–; now Prof. Vienna Univ. *Publications include:* Über die Legitimität der Mission 1968, Der Gedanke der Persönlichkeit Gottes bei Fichte und Hegel 1971, Schleiermachers Dialektik 1974, Geld oder Gott? 1985, Was ist Religion? 1986, Die vergessene spekulative Theologie 1987, Was ist Theologie? 1989, Zur gegenwärtigen Lage des Protestantismus 1995, Ende der Religion—Religion ohne Ende? (with M. Murrmann-Kahl) 1996, Religion und Gottesgedanke 1996, Zeitenwechsel und Beständigkeit (co-Ed.) 1997; numerous articles on theological, philosophical and ethical questions. *Address:* Universität Wien, Evangelisch-Theologische Fakultät, Institut für Systematische Theologie, Rooseveltplatz 10, 1090 Vienna (Office); Kaiserstrasse 32, 1070 Vienna, Austria (Home). *E-mail:* public@univie.ac.at (Office). *Website:* www.univie.ac.at (Office).

WAGNER, Heinz Georg, Dr rer. nat; German professor of physical chemistry; b. 20 Sept. 1928, Hof, Bavaria; s. of Georg Wagner and Frida Spiess; m. Renate C. Heuer 1974; ed Tech. Hochschule, Darmstadt and Univ. of Göttingen; lecturer, Univ. of Göttingen 1960–65, Prof. of Physical Chem. 1971–97; Prof. Ruhr Univ. Bochum 1965–70, now Prof. Emer.; Dir Max-Planck-Inst. für Strömungsforschung, Göttingen 1971–97; Vice-Pres. Deutsche Forschungsgemeinschaft 1983–89; mem. Exec. Council ESF; scientific mem. Max-Planck-Gesellschaft; mem. Göttingen Acad., Acad. Leopoldina, Int. Acad. of Astronautics, Heidelberg Acad., Acad. of Natural Sciences of Russia, Academia Europaea, American Physical Soc., Royal Soc. of Chem. etc.; Drs. hc; Grosses Bundesverdienstkreuz; Fritz-Haber Prize, Bernard Lewis Gold Medal, Achema Medal, Numa Manson Medal, Dionizy Smoleński Medal, Walther-Nernst-Denkmünze, Dechema Medal; Hon. mem. Bunsen-Gesellschaft. *Publications:* articles on combustion, reaction kinetics, thermodynamics of liquid mixtures. *Address:* Institut für Physikalische Chemie, Universität Göttingen, Tammannstr. 6, 37077 Göttingen, Germany. *Telephone:* (551) 393112. *Fax:* (551) 393117. *E-mail:* jkupfer@gwdg.de (Office).

WAGNER, Robert; American actor; b. 10 Feb. 1930, Detroit; m. 1st Natalie Wood 1957 (divorced 1962, re-married 1972, died 1981); one d. one step-d.; m. 2nd Marion Marshall Donen; one d. *Films include:* Halls of Montezuma, The Frogmen, Let's Make It Legal, With a Song in My Heart, What Price Glory?, Stars and Stripes Forever, The Silver Whip, Titanic, Star of Tomorrow, Beneath the 12-Mile Reef, Prince Valiant, Broken Lance, White Feather, A Kiss Before Dying, The Mountain, The True Story of Jesse James, Stopover Tokyo, In Love and War, Say One For Me, Between Heaven and Hell, The Hunters, All the Fine Young Cannibals, Sail a Crooked Ship, The Longest Day, The War Lover, The Condemned of Altona, Harper, Banning, The Biggest Bundle of Them All, The Pink Panther, The Curse of the Pink Panther, Winning, The Affair, The Towering Inferno, Critical List, Pearl, Dragon, Austin Powers: International Man of Mystery, Crazy in Alabama, Wild Things, No Vacancy, Love and Fear, Austin Powers: The Spy Who Shagged Me 1999, The Mercury Project 2000, Becoming Dick 2000, Rocket's Red Glare 2000, The Retrievers 2001. *Television series include:* Hart to Hart 1979–84, It Takes a Thief 1967–70, Madame Sin (producer and actor); numerous other TV appearances. *Address:* c/o William Morris Agency, 151 El Camino Drive, Beverly Hills, CA 90212, USA. *Website:* www.robert-wagner.com (Office).

WAGNER, Wolfgang; German opera director; b. 30 Aug. 1919, Bayreuth; s. of Siegfried Wagner and Winifred (née Williams) Wagner; m. 1st Ellen Drexel 1943; one s. one d.; m. 2nd Gudrun Mack (née Armann) 1976; one d.; mil. service 1938–40; stage man. at Bayreuth Festival 1940; Asst with Preussische Staatsoper, Berlin 1940–44; returned to Bayreuth after war, worked with brother (the late Wieland Wagner) as Dir annual Wagner operatic festival 1951–66, on his own 1967–; Dir more than 400 performances 1953–; numerous guest appearances and int. tours; mem. Bayerische Akademie der Schönen Künste 1986; Dr hc (Univ. of Bagreuth) 1994; Bayerischer Maximiliansorden 1984; Ehrensenator Graz 1987, Munich 1988, Tübingen 1988. *Productions include:* Andreasnacht (Berlin 1944), The Rhinegold (Naples 1952), The Valkyrie (Naples 1952, 1953, Barcelona 1955, Venice 1957, Palermo 1962, Osaka 1967), Lohengrin (Bayreuth 1953, 1967, Taormina 1991, Tokyo 1997), Siegfried (Naples 1953, Brussels 1954, Venice 1957, Bologna 1957), The Flying Dutchman (Bayreuth 1955, Dresden 1988), Tristan and Isolde (Barcelona 1955, Bayreuth 1957, Venice 1958, Palermo 1960, Osaka 1967, Milan 1978), Parsifal (Barcelona 1955, Bayreuth 1975, 1989), Don Giovanni (Brunswick 1955), The Mastersingers of Nuremberg (Rome 1956, Bayreuth 1968, 1981, 1996, Dresden 1985), The Nibelung's Ring (Venice 1957, Bayreuth 1960, 1970), Götterdämmerung (Venice 1957), Tannhäuser (Bayreuth 1985). *Publication:* Acts (autobiog.). *Address:* c/o Bayreuther Festspiele, PO Box 100262, 95402 Bayreuth, Germany. *Telephone:* 92178780.

WAGNER TIZON, Allan; Peruvian politician and diplomatist; b. 7 Feb. 1942, Lima; ed Universidad Católica and Universidad de San Marcos; joined Ministry of Foreign Affairs 1963; joined Diplomatic Service 1968; fmr. Amb. to Venezuela; Minister of Foreign Affairs 1985–88; Amb. to Spain 1988–1991; Prof. Diplomatic Acad. 1991; Founder-mem. Peruvian Centre of Int. Studies (CEPEI), Pres. 1999–; Founder-mem. Inst. of European–Latin American Relations (IRELA); Amb. to USA 2002; Adviser to Sec.-Gen. of ANDEAN Community of Nations –2002; Orden Bernardo O'Higgins (Chile) 2001, Orden en el Grado de Gran Cruz (Chile) 2001. *Address:* Peruvian Centre of International Studies, Lima, Peru.

WAGONER, Dan; American dancer, choreographer and dance company director; b. 1932, West Va; studied pharmacy; joined Martha Graham co. 1957; danced with Merce Cunningham's and Paul Taylor's cos; f. own dance co. 1969; has choreographed about 40 works; Artistic Dir London Contemporary Dance Theatre (LCDT), 1989–90. *Address:* c/o Contemporary Dance Theatre, The Place, 17 Duke's Road, London, WC1H 9AB, England.

WAGONER, David Russell, MA; American writer and university professor; b. 5 June 1926, Massillon, Ohio; m. 1st Patricia Parrott 1961 (divorced 1982); m. 2nd Robin H. Seyfried 1982; two d.; ed Pennsylvania State Univ., Indiana Univ.; served USN 1944–46; Instructor DePauw Univ., Greencastle, Ind. 1949–50, Pennsylvania State Univ. 1950–54; Assoc. Prof. Univ. of Washington, Seattle 1954–66, Prof. of English 1966–2000, Prof. Emer. 2000–; Elliston Lecturer Univ. of Cincinnati 1968; Ed. Poetry Northwest, Seattle 1966–, Ed. Princeton Univ. Press Contemporary Poetry Series 1977–81;

Poetry Ed. Mo. Press 1983–; Guggenheim Fellowship 1956, Ford Fellowship 1964, American Acad. Grant 1967, Nat. Endowment for the Arts Grant 1969; Morton Dauwen Zabel Prize (Poetry, Chicago) 1967, Ruth Lilly Prize 1991, Levinson Prize (Poetry, Chicago) 1994, Union League Prize (Poetry, Chicago) 1997; Pacific NW Booksellers Award 2000. *Short Stories:* Afternoon on the Ground 1978, Wild Goose Chase 1978, Mr. Wallender's Romance 1979, Cornet Solo 1979, The Water Strider 1979, Fly Boy 1980, The Bird Watcher 1980, Snake Hunt 1980. *Play:* An Eye for an Eye for an Eye 1973. *Verse:* Dry Sun, Dry Wind 1953, A Place to Stand 1958, Poems 1959, The Nesting Ground 1963, Five Poets of the Pacific Northwest (with others) 1964, Staying Alive 1966, New and Selected Poems 1969, Working Against Time 1970, Riverbed 1972, Sleeping in the Woods 1974, A Guide to Dungeness Spit 1975, Travelling Light 1976, Who Shall Be the Sun? Poems Based on the Lore, Legends and Myths of Northwest Coast and Plateau Indians 1978, In Broken Country 1979, Landfall 1981, First Light 1983, Through the Forest 1987, Walt Whitman Bathing 1996, Traveling Light: Collected and New Poems 1999. *Novels:* The Man in the Middle 1955, Money, Money, Money 1955, Rock 1958, The Escape Artist 1965, Baby, Come On Inside 1968, Where is My Wandering Boy Tonight? 1970, The Road to Many a Wonder 1974, Tracker 1975, Whole Hog 1976, The Hanging Garden 1980. *Address:* University of Washington, P.O. Box 354330, Seattle, WA 98105; 5416 154th Place, SW, Edmonds, WA 98026, USA (Home). *Telephone:* (425) 745-6964. *E-mail:* renogawd@aol.com (Home).

WAGONER, G. Richard, Jr, BEcons, MBA; American automobile industry executive; b. 9 Feb. 1953, Richmond, VA; ed Duke Univ., Harvard Univ.; joined General Motors (GM) 1977, analyst Office of the Treas., NY 1977, Treas. of GM do Brasil (GMB), São Paulo 1981–84, Exec. Dir of Finance, GMB 1984–87, Vice-Pres. and Finance Man. GM Canada Ltd 1987–88, Group Dir (Strategic Business Planning) Chevrolet-Pontiac-GM, Canada 1988–89, Vice-Pres. Finance GM Europe, Zürich, Switzerland 1989–90, Pres. and Man. GMB 1991–92, Exec. Vice-Pres. and Chief Financial Officer 1992–94, Head of Worldwide Purchasing 1993–94, Exec. Vice-Pres. and Pres. N. American Operations 1994–98, Pres. and COO 1998–2000, Chair. Automotive Strategy Bd, Pres. and CEO 2000–03, Chair. and CEO May 2003–; Chair. A World in Motion Exec. Cttee, Soc. of Automotive Engineers; mem. Business Council, Business Roundtable; mem. Bd Trustees Duke Univ., Detroit Country Day School; mem. Bd Dean's Advisers, Harvard Business School. *Address:* General Motors, 300 Renaissance Center, Detroit, MI 48264-3000, USA (Office). *Telephone:* (313) 556-5000 (Office). *Fax:* (248) 696-7300 (Office). *Website:* www.gm.com (Office).

WAHID, Abdurrahman (Gus Dur); Indonesian politician and religious leader; b. 4 Aug. 1940, Jombang, East Java; s. of K. H. Wahid Hasyim (founder of Nahdlatul Ulama—NU); m. Sinta Nuriyah; four d.; ed Al-Azhar Univ., Cairo, Baghdad Univ.; lecturer, Hasyim As'yari Univ.; Leader Nahdlatul Ulama 1984–; Jt founder Nat. Awakening Party (PKB); Pres. of Indonesia 1999–2001; impeached July 2001. *Address:* c/o Office of the President, Istana Merdeka, Jakarta, Indonesia (Office).

WAHL, Jacques Henri; French administrator; b. 18 Jan. 1932, Lille; s. of Abraham Wahl and Simone Kornbluth; m. Inna Cytrin 1969; two s. one d.; ed Inst. d'Etudes Politiques, Paris, Univs. of Lille and Paris, Ecole Nat. d'Admin.; Insp. des Finances 1961–; Treasury Dept 1965–68; Special Asst to Ministers of Econ. and Finance, François Ortoli 1968–69, Valéry Giscard d'Estaing 1969–71; Asst Dir of the Treasury for Int. Affairs 1971–73; Chair. Invisible Transactions Cttee, OECD 1971–73; lecturer, Inst. d'Etudes Politiques and Ecole Nat. d'Admin., Paris 1969–73; Financial Minister, French Embassies, USA and Canada 1973–78; Exec. Dir IMF, IBRD 1973–78; Sec.-Gen. to the Presidency of the French Repub. 1978–81; Insp.-Gen. des Finances 1981; Dir-Gen. Banque Nat. de Paris 1982 (Vice-Chair. 1993–97, Adviser to Chair. 1994); Chair. Banque Nat. de Paris Intercontinentale 1993–97, mem. Bd 1994–; Officier, Légion d'honneur, Officier Ordre nat. du Mérite, Commdr Ordre Nat. de Côte d'Ivoire, Officier Ordre du Mérite de la République Centrafricaine, Chevalier Ordre du Mérite de Haute Volta. *Address:* BNP Paribas, 19 boulevard des Italiens, 75009 Paris (Office); 15 avenue de la Bourdonnais, 75007 Paris, France (Home).

WAHLBERG, Mark Robert; American actor; b. 5 June 1971, Dorchester, Mass.; s. of Donal E. Wahlberg and Alma Wahlberg. *Films:* Renaissance Man 1994, The Basketball Diaries 1995, Fear 1996, Traveller 1997, Boogie Nights 1997, The Big Hit 1998, The Corruptor 1999, Three Kings 1999, The Yards 2000, The Perfect Storm 2000, Metal God 2000, Planet of the Apes 2001, Rock Star 2001, The Truth About Charlie 2003. *Television:* Teen Vid II (Video) 1991, The Substitute 1993. *Website:* www.markwahlberg.com (Office).

WAIGEL, Theodor, DJur; German politician; b. 22 April 1939, Oberrohr; s. of August Waigel and Genoveva Konrad; m. 1st Karin Hönig 1966 (divorced 1994); m. 2nd Irene Epple 1994; two s. one d.; ed Univs. of Munich and Würzburg; Bavarian Ministries of Finance and of Econ. and Transport 1969–72; mem. Bundestag 1972–; Chair. CSU Land (Bavarian) Group in Bundestag 1982–89; Chair. of CSU 1988–98; Minister of Finance 1989–98; Bayerischer Verdienstorden, Dr. hc (Univ. of S. Carolina) 1997. *Leisure interests:* climbing, theatre. *Address:* c/o Bundestag, 11011 Berlin, Germany.

WAIHEE, John David, III, BA, JD; American state governor; b. 19 May 1946, Honokaa, Hawaii; m. Lynne Kobashigawa; one s. one d.; ed Andrews Univ., Central Mich. Univ. and Univ. of Hawaii; admitted to Hawaii Bar 1976; Community Educ. Co-ordinator, Benton Harbor (Mich.) area schools 1968–70;

Asst Dir Community Educ. 1970–71; Program Evaluator, Admin. Asst to Dirs., Planner, Honolulu Model Cities Program 1971–73; Sr Planner, Office of Human Resources, City and Co. of Honolulu 1973–74, Program Man. 1974–75; Assoc. Shim, Sigal, Tam & Naito, Honolulu 1975–79; partner, Waihee, Manuia, Yap, Pablo & Hoe, Honolulu 1979–82; mem. Hawaiian House of Reps. 1980–82; Lt Gov. of Hawaii 1982–86, Gov. 1986–95; Democrat. *Address:* 745 Fort Street Mall, # 600, Honolulu, HI 96813, USA.

WAINWRIGHT, Rev. Geoffrey, MA, DD, DrThéol; British ecclesiastic and university professor; b. 16 July 1939, Yorkshire; s. of Willie Wainwright and Martha Burgess; m. Margaret H. Wiles 1965; one s. two d.; ed Gonville & Caius Coll. Cambridge and Univ. of Geneva; Prof. of Dogmatics, Protestant Faculty of Theology, Yaoundé, Cameroon 1967–73; Lecturer in Bible and Systematic Theology, Queen's Coll. Birmingham 1973–79; Roosevelt Prof. of Systematic Theology, Union Theological Seminary, New York 1979–83; Cushman Prof. of Christian Theology, Duke Univ. 1983–; mem. Faith and Order Comm. WCC 1977–91; Pres. Soc. Liturgica 1985–87; Co-Chair. Jt Comm. between World Methodist Council and Roman Catholic Church 1986–; Sec. American Theological Soc. 1988–95, Pres. 1996–97; Leverhulme European Fellow 1966–67; Pew Evangelical Fellow 1996–97; Hon. DD (North Park Univ.) 2001; Berakah Award, N American Acad. of Liturgy 1999; Festschrift: 'Ecumenical Theology in Worship, Doctrine and Life: Essays Presented to Geoffrey Wainwright on his Sixtieth Birthday' (ed. David Cunningham and others), Oxford Univ. Press, 1999; Outstanding Ecumenist Award, Washington Theological Consortium 2003. *Publications include:* Christian Initiation 1969, Eucharist and Eschatology 1971, Doxology 1980, The Ecumenical Moment 1983, On Wesley and Calvin 1987, Methodists in Dialogue 1995, Worship With One Accord 1997, For Our Salvation: Two Approaches to the Work of Christ 1997, Is the Reformation Over? Protestants and Catholics at the Turn of the Millennia 2000, Lesslie Newbigin: A Theological Life 2000. *Leisure interests:* music, art, cricket, tennis, travel. *Address:* The Divinity School, Duke University, Durham, NC 27708 (Office); 4011 W Cornwallis Road, Durham, NC 27705, USA (Home). *Telephone:* (919) 660-3460 (Office); (919) 489-2795 (Home). *Fax:* (919) 660-3473 (Office). *E-mail:* gwainwright@div.duke.edu (Office).

WAISMAN RJAVINSTHI, David; Peruvian politician and business executive; b. 4 May 1937, Chiclayo (Lambayeque); fmr Chair. Cttee for Small Industries and mem. Bd of Dirs. Nat. Soc. of Industries in Peru; nat. spokesman Bd of Co-ordination, Corpn of Small and Micro Enterprises; Man. Dir Industrial Gameda; Founder-mem. and Chair. COPEI 1997–2000; mem. and Congressman Perú Posible (PP) party; elected mem. Congreso (Parl.) 2000; Second Vice-Pres. of Peru and Minister of Defence 2000–02. *Address:* c/o Ministry of Defence, Avda Arequipa 291, Lima 14, Peru (Office).

WAITE, Terence Hardy, CBE; British fmr religious adviser, author and broadcaster; b. 31 May 1939, Bollington; s. of Thomas William Waite and Lena Waite (née Hardy); m. Helen Frances Watters 1964; one s. three d.; ed Wilmslow School, Stockton Heath, Cheshire, Church Army Coll., London; Lay Training Adviser to Bishop and Diocese of Bristol 1964–68; Adviser to Archbishop of Uganda, Rwanda and Burundi 1968–71; int. consultant working with Roman Catholic Church 1972–79; Adviser to Archbishop of Canterbury on Anglican Communion Affairs 1980–92, Iranian hostages mission 1981, Libyan hostages mission 1985; kidnapped in Beirut Jan. 1987, released Nov. 1991; mem. Church of England Nat. Asscn 1966–68; Co-ordinator Southern Sudan Relief Project 1969–71; mem. Royal Inst. of Int. Affairs 1980–; Trustee Butler Trust (Prison Officers Award Project); Pres. Y-Care Int. (YMCA Int. Devt Cttee) 1998; Pres. Emmaus UK 1998; Dir Educ. Interactive 2000; Founder Chair. Friends of Victim Support 1992–; Patron Strode Park Foundation for the Disabled, Hearne, Kent, Rainbow Trust, Warrington Male Voice Choir, One to One Children's Fund and many other orgs.; Trustee FreePlay Foundation; Fellow Commoner Trinity Hall, Cambridge 1992–; Hon. DCL (Kent) 1986, (City of London), (Sussex) 1992; Hon. LLD (Durham), (Liverpool) 1992; Hon. LHD (Wittenberg) 1992; Dr hc (Yale Univ. Divinity School) 1992; Hon. DHumLitt (Florida Southern) 1992, (Virginia Commonwealth) 1996; Hon. DPhil (Anglia Polytechnic) 2001; Hon. DLitt (Nottingham Trent) 2001; Templeton UK Award 1986, Roosevelt Four Freedoms Medal 1992, Freeman City of Canterbury 1992, Borough of Lewisham 1992. *Publications:* Taken on Trust 1993, Footfalls in Memory 1995, Travels with a Primate 2000; numerous contribs to journals and periodicals. *Leisure interests:* music, walking, travel, Jungian studies, int. affairs and politics. *Address:* Trinity Hall, Cambridge, CB2 1TJ, England.

WAITT, Theodore (Ted) W.; American computer executive; f. Gateway (with Mike Hammond) 1985, CEO Gateway 2000 Inc. 1992–, also Chair., Pres.; Hon. DSc (Univ. of S Dakota); US Small Business Asscn Young Entrepreneur of the Year, US Jr Chamber of Commerce Ten Outstanding Young Americans Award, Nat. Alliance of Business Henry Ford II Award. *Address:* Gateway 2000, Inc., 4545 Towne Centre Court, San Diego, CA 92121, USA.

WAJDA, Andrzej; Polish film and theatrical director; b. 6 March 1926, Suwałki; s. of Jakub Wajda and Aniela Wajda; m. 1st Beata Tyszkiewicz 1967 (divorced); one d.; m. 2nd Krystyna Zachwatowicz 1975; ed Acad. of Fine Arts, Kraków and Higher Film School, Łódź; Film Dir 1954–; Theatre Dir Teatr Stary, Kraków 1962–98; Man. Dir Teatr Powszechny, Warsaw 1989–90; Senator of Repub. of Poland 1989–91; Pres. Polish Film Asscn 1978–83, Solidarity Lech Wałęsa Council 1981–89, Presidential Council for Culture

1992–94; Founder Centre for Japanese and Technology Manggha, Kraków 1987; mem. Inst. de France 1997–, Acad. des Beaux Arts, France 1997–; Hon. mem. Union of Polish Artists and Designers (ZPAP) 1977; Dr hc (American Univ. Washington) 1981, (Bologna) 1988, (Jagiellonian Univ., Kraków) 1989, (Lyon Univ.) 1995, (Univ. Libre, Brussels) 1995 (Acad. of Fine Arts, Warsaw) 2000, (Polish. Nat. Films, TV and Theatre School, Łódź) 2000; numerous prizes including State First Class Prize 1974, Konrad Swinarski Prize 1976, Premio David di Donatello 'Luchino Visconti' 1978, Prize of Cttee for Polish Radio and TV 1980, Onassis Prize, Greece 1982, Kyoto Prize, Japan 1987, Praemium Imperiale, Japan 1997, BAFTA Fellowship 1982, César Award, France 1983, Pirandello Artistic Award, Italy 1986, 'Felix' European Film Awards—Lifetime Achievement Award 1990, Golden Lion, Venice 1998; Order of the Banner of Labour (Second Class) 1975, Officer's Cross of Polonia Restituta Order, Order of Kirill and Methodius (First Class), Bulgaria 1978, Order of Rising Sun, Japan 1995, Acad. Award (Oscar) 2000, Commdr Légion d'honneur 2001, Grosses Verdienstkreuz des Verdienstordens der Bundesrepublik Deutschland 2001. *Films:* Pokolenie (A Generation) 1954 (Polish State Prize), Idę do słońca (I'm Going to the Sun) 1955, Kanal 1957 (Jury Special Silver Palm Award, Cannes 1957), Popiół i diament (Ashes and Diamonds) 1957 (Fipresci Prize, Venice 1959, David O. Selznick's 'Silver Laurel' Award 1962), Lotna 1959, Niewinni czarodzieje (Innocent Sorcerers) 1960, Samson 1961, Sibirska Ledi Makbet (Siberian Lady Macbeth) 1962, L'Amour à Vingt Ans (Love at Twenty) 1962, Popioły (Ashes) 1965, Gates to Paradise 1968, Wszystko na sprzedaż (Everything for Sale) 1969, Polowanie na muchy (Hunting Flies) 1969, Krajobraz po bitwie (Landscape After Battle) 1970 (Golden Globe, Milan 1971), Brzezina (The Birch Wood) 1970 (Fipresci Prize, Milan 1970, Golden Medal, Moscow 1971), Wesele (The Wedding) 1973 (Silver Shell, San Sebastián 1973), Ziemia obiecana (The Promised Land) 1975 (Gdańsk Golden Lions 1975, Golden Medal, Moscow 1975), Człowiek z marmuru (Man of Marble) 1977 (Fipresci Prize, Cannes 1978, Jury Special Prize, Cartagena 1980), Bez znieczulenia (Without Anaesthetic) 1978 (OCIC Prize, Cannes 1979), Panny z Wilka (The Maids of Wilko) 1979, Dyrygent (The Orchestral Conductor) 1980, Człowiek z żelaza (Man of Iron) 1981 (Palme d'Or, Cannes 1981), Danton 1982 (Prix Luis Delluc 1982), Eine Liebe in Deutschland (A Love in Germany) 1983, Kronika wypadków miłosnych (Chronicle of Love Affairs) 1986, Les Possédés (The Possessed) 1987, Korczak 1990, Pierścionek z orłem w koronie (The Crowned-Eagle Ring) 1992, Nastasya 1994, Wielki Tydzień (The Holy Week) 1995 (Silver Bear, Berlin 1996), Panna Nikt (Miss Nobody) 1996, Pan Tadeusz (The Last Foray in Lithuania) 1999, Zemsta (Revenge) 2002, Zekcja polskiego kina (Lesson of Polish Cinema, document) 2002. *TV:* Przekładaniec (Roly-Poly) 1968, Macbeth 1969, Pilatus und Andere (for German TV ZDF) 1971 (Bambi Award 1972), Noc listopadowa (November Night) 1975, The Shadow Line (for Thames TV, London) 1976, Z biegiem lat z beiegiem dni (Gone with the Years, Gone with the Days) 1978–79, Zbrodnia i kara (Schuld und Suhne) 1985, Wieczernik (The Last Supper) 1985, Hamlet IV 1989, Silniejsza (The Stronger One) 1990, Mishima 1995, Bigda idzie (Bigda Comes) 1999, Wyrok na Franciszka Kłosa (Judgment on Franciszek Kłos) 2000, Noc czerwcowa (June Night) 2002. *Plays:* Kapelusz pełen deszczu (Hatful of Rain) 1959, Hamlet 1960, 1980, 1989, Dwoje na huśtawce (Two on the Seesaw) 1960, 1990, Demons 1963, Wesele (The Wedding) 1962, 1991, Play Strindberg 1970, Sticks and Bones (Moscow) 1972, Noc listopadowa (November Night) 1974, Sprawa Dantona (The Danton Case) 1975, 1980, Kiedy rozum śpi (When Reason is Asleep) 1976, Emigranci (Emigrés) 1976, Nastasya Filipowna (improvisation based on Dostoyevsky's The Idiot) 1977, Rozmowy z Katem (Conversation with the Executioner) 1977, White Marriage (Yale Repertory) 1977, Z biegiem lat z biegiem dni (Gone with the Years, Gone with the Days) 1978, Antygona 1984, Zbrodnia i kara (Crime and Punishment) 1984, Wieczernik (The Last Supper) 1985, Zemsta (Revenge) 1986, Panna Julia (Miss Julia) 1988, Dybuk 1988, Lekcja polskiego (Lesson of Polish Language) 1988, Romeo and Juliet 1990, The Ghost Sonata (Stockholm) 1994, Mishima 1994, Klątwa (The Curse) 1997, Słomkowy kapelusz (The Straw Hat) 1998. *Publications:* Powtórka z caìosci) 1986, My Life in Film 1989, Wajada mówi o sobie (Wajda Talks about Himself) 1991, Wajda o polityce, o srtuce, o sobie (Wajda about Politics, Arts and Himself) 2000, Podwojne spojnenie (Double Take), Kino i reszta świata (Cinema and the Rest of the World) 2000. *Address:* Centre for Japanese and Technology, ul. Konopnickiej 26, 30-302 Kraków, Poland.

WAKEFIELD, Sir Peter George Arthur, KBE, CMG; British diplomatist; b. 13 May 1922; s. of John Bunting Wakefield and Dorothy Ina Wakefield (née Stace); m. Felicity Maurice-Jones 1951; four s. one d.; ed Cranleigh School and Corpus Christi Coll. Oxford; served in Army 1942–47; Mil. Govt, Eritrea 1946–47; Hulton Press 1947–49; entered Diplomatic Service 1949; Middle East Centre for Arab Studies 1950; Second Sec., British Embassy, Jordan 1950–52; Foreign Office 1953–55, 1964–66; First Sec., British Middle East Office, Nicosia, Cyprus 1955–56; First Sec. (Commercial), Egypt 1956, Austria 1957–60, Japan 1960–63; Admin. Staff Coll., Henley 1957; Consul-Gen. and Counsellor, Benghazi 1966–69; Econ. and Commercial Counsellor, Tokyo 1970–72, Econ. and Commercial Minister 1973; seconded as Special Adviser on the Japanese Market, British Overseas Trade Bd 1973–75; Amb. to Lebanon 1975–78, to Belgium 1979–81; Dir Nat. Art Collections Fund London 1982–92; UK Dir, Trust for Museum Exhbns.; Gov. European Cultural Foundation 1988–92; Chair. Heritage Co-ordination Group 1993–97, Asia House, London, Richmond Theatre 1993–2001; Chair. of Judges, Jerwood Painting Prize 1994/95; Hon. LLD (St Andrews) 1991. *Leisure interests:* modern British painting, ceramics, restoring ruins. *Address:* Asia House, 105 Piccadilly, London, W1J 7NJ (Office); Lincoln House, Montpelier Row, Twickenham, Middx, England; La Molineta, Frigiliana, nr Málaga, Spain. *Telephone:* (20) 8892-6390 (England), 952533175 (Spain). *Fax:* (20) 8744-0961.

WAKEHAM, Baron (Life Peer), cr. 1992, of Maldon in the County of Essex; **John Wakeham,** JP, FCA; British politician; b. 22 June 1932, Godalming, Surrey; s. of the late Maj. W. J. Wakeham and Mrs E. R. Wakeham; m. 1st Anne Roberta Bailey 1965 (died 1984); two s.; m. 2nd Alison Bridget Ward 1985; one s.; ed Charterhouse; JP Inner London 1972–; MP for Maldon 1974–83, for Colchester S and Maldon 1983–92; Asst Govt Whip 1979–81, Govt Chief Whip 1983–87; Lord Commr of HM Treasury 1981, Minister of State 1982–83; Parl. Under-Sec. of State, Dept of Industry 1981–82; Lord Privy Seal 1987–88; Leader of House of Commons 1987–89, Sec. of State for Energy 1989–92; Lord Privy Seal and Leader of the House of Lords 1992–94; Lord Pres. of Council 1988–89; Chair. Carlton Club 1992–98, Press Complaints Comm. 1995–2002, British Horseracing Bd 1996–98 (mem. 1995–98); Chair. Vosper Thornycroft PLC 1995–2002, Genner Holdings Ltd 1994–, Alexandra Rose Day 1998–, Michael Page Int. PLC 2001–02; Chair. Royal Comm. on Lords Reform 1999–2000; Dir (non-exec.) Bristol & West PLC 1995–2002, NM Rothschild & Sons Ltd 1995–2002, Enron Corpn 1994–2002; Chancellor Brunel Univ. 1998–; Trustee, mem. Cttee of Man. Royal Nat. Lifeboat Inst. 1995–; Trustee HMS Warrior 1860 1997–. *Leisure interests:* farming, sailing, racing and reading. *Address:* House of Lords, London, SW1A 0PW, England.

WAKELEY, Amanda; British fashion designer; b. 15 Sept. 1962, Chester; d. of Sir John Wakeley; ed Cheltenham Ladies' Coll.; worked in fashion industry, NY 1983–85; began designing for pvt. clients in UK 1986; launched own label 1990; operation includes retail, wholesale worldwide, bridal and corporatewear consultancy and diffusion range; Co-Chair. Fashion Targets Breast Cancer Campaign 1996, 1988, 2000, 2002; Glamour Award, British Fashion Awards 1992, 1993, 1996. *Achievements:* raised over £4 million for 'Breakthrough' in 1996, 1998, 2000 and 2002 as Co-Chair. of Fashion Targets Breast Cancer Campaign. *Leisure interests:* travel, driving, waterskiing, snowskiing, rollerblading. *Address:* Amanda Wakeley Ltd, 26–28 Conway Street, London, W1T 6BQ, England. *Telephone:* (20) 7692-6744 (Office). *Fax:* (20) 7692-6770. *Website:* www.amandawakeley.com (Office).

WAKIL, Abdul; Afghanistan politician; b. 1945, Kabul province; ed Kabul Univ.; fmr Sec. Gen. of Afghan Foreign Ministry, Minister of Finance, Amb. to UK and to Viet Nam; mem. People's Democratic Party of Afghanistan (PDPA) 1964, mem. Cen. Cttee 1977; mem. of Revolutionary Council of Afghanistan; Minister of Foreign Affairs 1986–89. *Address:* c/o Ministry of Foreign Affairs, Kabul, Afghanistan.

WAKOSKI, Diane, BA; American poet; b. 3 Aug. 1937, Whittier, Calif.; ed Univ. of Calif. at Berkeley; began writing poetry, New York 1960–73; worked as a book shop clerk, a junior high school teacher and by giving poetry readings on coll. campuses; Poet-in-Residence Michigan State Univ. 1975–; Prof. of English, Michigan State Univ. 1975–; Guggenheim Grant 1972, Mich. Arts Foundation Award 1989, William Carlos Williams Prize (PSA) 1989. *Publications:* Coins and Coffins 1962, Discrepancies and Apparitions 1966, The George Washington Poems 1967, Inside the Blood Factory 1968, The Magellanic Clouds 1970, The Motorcycle Betrayal Poems 1971, Smudging 1972, Dancing on the Grave of a Son of a Bitch 1973, Trilogy (reprint of first three collections) 1974, Virtuoso Literature for Two and Four Hands 1975, Waiting for the King of Spain 1976, The Man Who Shook Hands 1978, Cap of Darkness 1980, The Magician's Feastletters 1982, Norii Magellanici (collection of poems from various Vols trans. into Romanian) 1982, The Collected Greed 1984, The Rings of Saturn 1986, Emerald Ice (selected poems 1962–87) 1988 (William Carlos Williams Prize 1989), The Archaeology of Movies and Books: Vol. I Medea The Sorceress 1991, Vol. II Jason The Sailor 1993, Vol. III The Emerald City of Las Vegas 1995, Vol. IV Argonaut Rose 1998, The Butcher's Apron: New Selected Poems 2000; (criticism) Towards A New Poetry 1980. *Leisure interests:* cooking, films, letters, gambling. *Address:* 607 Division Street, East Lansing, MI 48823, USA (Home). *Telephone:* (517) 355-0308 (University); (517) 332-3385 (Home).

WALA, Adolf; Austrian banker; b. 18 May 1937, Dürnholz; m.; three c.; ed Commercial School of Vienna Merchants' Asscn; Deputy Supervisor, later Supervisor, Foreign Exchange Dept, Creditanstalt-Bankverein 1957–65; joined Credit and Loans Dept, Austrian Nat. Bank (OeNB) 1965, Head of Office of First Deputy Gov. 1973–80, Deputy Exec. Dir Credit and Loans Dept 1980–88, Pres. of OeNB 1998–; mem. Supervisory Bd Casinos Austria AG 1999, Burgtheater GmbH 1999; Order of Merit, Order of Kts of Malta 1998, Grand Decoration of Hon. in Gold with Star for Services to Repub. of Austria 1999; Gold Medal for Outstanding Services to State of Vienna 1994, Arthur von Rosthon Medal 2000. *Address:* Oesterreichische Nationalbank, Otto-Wagner-Platz 3, Postfach 61, 1090 Vienna, Austria (Office). *Website:* www.oenb.at (Office).

WALCOTT, Sir Clyde Leopold, G.C.M., OBE; Barbadian cricketer and business executive; b. 17 Jan. 1926, St Michael; s. of the late Frank Eyre Walcott and Ruth Walcott (née Morris); m. Muriel Edith Ashby 1951; two s.; ed Harrison Coll.; right-hand batsman, right-arm fast-medium bowler, wicket-keeper; teams: Barbados, West Indies; in 44 Tests scored 3,789 runs (average 56.68) including 15 hundreds; in first-class cricket scored 11,820 runs (average 56.55) including 40 hundreds and making 174 catches and 33 stumpings 1941–64; fmr Pres. Guyana Cricket Bd of Control 1968–70; Pres.

W Indies Cricket Bd of Control 1988–93; Umpire Int. Cricket Council (ICC) 1992 (3 Tests), fmr Chair. ICC; Dir Barbados Shipping and Trading Co. 1980–91; Hon. Life Vice-Pres. Barbados Cricket Asscn; Wisden Cricketer of the Year 1958. *Publications:* Island Cricketers 1958, Sixty Years on the Back Foot. *Leisure interest:* football. *Address:* Wildey Heights, St. Michael, Barbados, West Indies (Home). *Telephone:* 429-4938 (Home).

WALCOTT, Derek; Saint Lucia poet and playwright; b. 23 Jan. 1930, Castries; s. of Warwick Walcott and Alix Walcott; m. 1st Fay Moston 1954 (divorced 1959); one s.; m. 2nd Margaret R. Maillard 1962 (divorced); two d.; m. 3rd Norline Metivier (divorced 1993); ed Univ. of Wisconsin, Univ. of the West Indies; Prof. of Creative Writing, Univ. of Boston, USA; Queen's Gold Medal for Poetry 1988, W. H. Smith Literary Award 1991 for epic poem Omeros; awarded Nobel Prize for Literature 1992. *Publications:* numerous vols of poetry, Collected Poems 1948–1984; plays include Odyssey, The Last Carnival, Dream on Monkey Mountain, The Joker of Seville, O Babylon!, Steel, The Bounty 1997, The Capeman 1997 (musical, jtly), What the Twilight Says 1998, Homage to Robert Frost (jtly) 1998, Tiepolo's Hound 2000. *Address:* c/o Faber & Faber, 3 Queen Square, London, WC1N 3AU, England; PO Box GM 926, Castries, St. Lucia, West Indies (Home). *Telephone:* 450-0559 (Home). *Fax:* 450-0935 (Home).

WALD, Nicholas John, MBBS, DMedSc, FRCP, FFPHM, FRCOG, FMedSci, CBiol, FIBiol; British professor of environmental and preventive medicine; b. 31 May 1944; s. of Adolf Max Wald and Frieda Shatsow; m. Nancy Evelyn Miller 1966; three s. one d.; ed Univ. Coll. London, Univ. Coll. Hosp. Medical School; mem. science staff MRC 1971–; mem. science staff Imperial Cancer Research Fund (ICRF) Cancer Epidemiology and Clinical Trials Unit, Oxford 1972–82, Deputy Dir 1982–83, Prof. and Head Dept of Environmental and Preventive Medicine, St Bartholemew's Hosp. 1983–, Hon. Consultant 1983–, Chair. Wolfson Inst. of Preventive Medicine 1991–95, 1997–; Ed.-in-Chief Journal of Medical Screening 1994–; Hon. Dir Cancer Research Campaign Screening Group 1986–2000; Chair. Study Monitoring Cttee of MRC Randomised Clinical Trial of Colo-Rectal Cancer Screening 1986–, Steering Cttee for Multicentre Aneurysm Screening Study 1997–; mem. Scientific Cttee on Tobacco and Health, Dept of Health 1993–2002, Medicines Control Agency Expert Advisory Panel 1996–; mem. Cttee on Ethical Issues in Medicine, Royal Coll. of Physicians 1988–, HPV/LBC Pilots Screening Group 2000–; mem. Information Sub-Cttee, Faculty of Public Health 2001–; mem. Wellcome Trust Physiology and Pharmacological Panel 1995–2000; Kennedy Foundation Int. Award in Scientific Research 2000, Foundation for Blood Research Award 2000, Obstetrical Soc. of Philadelphia Int. Speakers' Award 2001, BMA Medical Book Competition Award 2001, US Public Health Service and Centers for Disease Control Award 2002. *Publications:* Alpha-Fetoprotein Screening – The Current Issues (co-ed.) 1981, Antenatal and Neonatal Screening 1984 (2nd edn co-ed. 2000), Nicotine Smoking and the Low Tar Programme (co-ed.) 1989, Passive Smoking: A Health Hazard (co-ed.) 1991, International Smoking Statistics (co-author) 1993. *Leisure interests:* economics, boating, skiing. *Address:* Barts and The London, Queen Mary's School of Medicine and Dentistry, Charterhouse Square, London, EC1M 6BQ (Office); Department of Environmental and Preventive Medicine, Wolfson Institute of Preventive Medicine, Barts and The London, Queen Mary's School of Medicine and Dentistry, Charterhouse Square, London, EC1M 6BQ; 9 Park Crescent Mews East, London, WIN 5HB, England (Home). *Telephone:* (20) 7882-6269 (Office); (20) 7636-2721 (Home). *Fax:* (20) 7882-6270 (Office). *E-mail:* n.j.wald@qmul.ac.uk (Office). *Website:* www.smd.Qmul.ac.uk/wolfson (Office).

WALD, Patricia McGowan, LLB; American judge; b. 16 Sept. 1928, Torrington, Conn.; d. of Joseph McGowan and Margaret (née O'Keefe) McGowan; m. Robert L. Wald 1952; two s. three d.; ed Connecticut Coll. for Women, Yale Law School; Law Clerk, US Court of Appeals for the Second Circuit 1951–52; Assoc. Arnold, Fortas and Porter, Washington, DC 1952–53; mem. Nat. Conf. on Bail and Criminal Justice 1963–64; Consultant, Nat. Conf. on Law and Poverty 1965; mem. President's Comm. on Crime in the Dist of Columbia 1965–66, on Law Enforcement and Admin. of Criminal Justice 1966–67; Attorney, Office of Criminal Justice, Dept of Justice 1967–68; Neighborhood Legal Services Program 1968–70; Co-Dir, Ford Foundation Drug Abuse Research Project 1970; Attorney, Center for Law and Social Policy 1971–72, Mental Health Law Project 1972–77; Asst Attorney for Legis. Affairs, Dept of Justice 1977–79; Circuit Judge, US Court of Appeals for the Dist of Columbia Circuit 1979–99, Chief Judge 1986–91; First Vice-Pres. American Law Inst.1993–98; mem. Exec. Bd CEELI (ABA) 1994–97; Judge Int. Criminal Tribunal for fmr Yugoslavia, The Hague, Netherlands 1999–2001; Chair Open Soc. Inst. Justice Initiative 2002–; numerous hon. degrees including Hon. L.L.D. (Yale) 2001; August Voelmer Award, American Soc. of Criminology 1976, Woman Lawyer of the Year, Women's Bar Asscn 1984; Sandra Day O'Connor Medal of Honor (Seton Hall Law School) 1993; Margaret Brent Award for Distinguished Women in the Legal Profession 1994. *Publications:* Bail in the United States (with Daniel J. Freed) 1964, Bail Reform: A Decade of Promise Without Fulfillment, Vol. 1 1972, Juvenile Detention in 'Pursuing Justice for the Child' 1977, The Rights of Children and the Rites of Passage in 'Child Psychiatry and the Law' 1980, Dealing with Drug Abuse: A Report to the Ford Foundation (with Peter Barton Hutt) 1972, Law and Poverty: Report to the Nat. Conf. on Law and Poverty 1965; and numerous learned articles. *Address:* 2101 Connecticut Avenue, NW, Apartment 38, Washington, DC 20008, USA (Home). *Telephone:* (202) 232-1158 (Home).

WALD, Richard C., MA; American journalist and academic; b. New York; s. of Joseph S. Wald and Lily (née Forstate) Wald; m. Edith May Leslie; two s. one d.; ed Columbia Univ. and Clare Coll. Cambridge; reporter, later Man. Ed. NY Herald Tribune 1955–66; Asst Man. Ed. Washington Post 1967; Exec. Vice-Pres. Whitney Communications Corpn New York 1968; Pres. NBC News, 1968–77; Sr Vice-Pres. ABC News 1978–2000; Prof. of Media and Society Columbia Univ. 2000–; Chair. of Bd Columbia Spectator; Chair. Worldwide TV News. *Leisure interests:* reading, running. *Address:* ABC News, 47 West 66th Street, New York, NY 10023, USA (Office).

WÄLDE, Thomas, DrIur, LLM; German lawyer; b. 9 Jan. 1949, Pluderhausen; s. of Dr. Ernst Wälde; m. Gabriele Wälde-Sinigoj 1981; one s.; ed Univs of Heidelberg, Lausanne, Berlin and Frankfurt and Harvard Law School, USA; Research Fellow, Inst. for Foreign and Int. Econ. Law, Frankfurt 1973–77; Legal Officer, UN Centre on Transnational Corpns. New York 1976–77; Resident Investment Adviser, UNIDO, Vienna 1978–79; Interregional Adviser on Mineral Devt Legislation, Dept of Tech. Co-operation for Devt, UN, New York 1980–85, Interregional Adviser on Petroleum and Mineral Legislation 1986–; Maier Leibnitz Award 1978; American Inst. of Mining Engineers Award 1985. *Publications:* Decision Analysis and Economic Legislation 1976, Transnational Investment Agreements 1978, Renegotiation of Transnational Agreements 1978, Methods and Mechanisms of International Industrial Enterprise Cooperation 1979, International Economic Development Law 1982, Permanent Sovereignty over Natural Resources 1985, Petroleum Investment in Developing Countries 1988. *Leisure interests:* history, anthropology. *Address:* DC1-846, NRED/DTCD, United Nations, One UN Plaza, New York, NY 10017, USA. *Telephone:* (212) 963-8783.

WALDEGRAVE OF NORTH HILL, Baron (Life Peer), cr. 1999, of Chewton Mendip in the County of Somerset; **William Waldegrave,** PC, JP; British banker and fmr politician; b. 15 Aug. 1946; s. of the late Earl Waldegrave, KG, GCVO and Mary Hermione Waldegrave (née Grenfell); m. Caroline Burrows 1977; one s. three d.; ed Eton Coll., Corpus Christi Coll. Oxford, Harvard Univ., USA; fmr Pres. Oxford Union; Fellow All Souls Coll. Oxford 1971–86, 1999–; attached to Cabinet Office as mem. Cen. Policy Review Staff 1971–73; mem. staff political office of Rt Hon Sir Edward Heath (q.v.) 1973–76; MP for Bristol W 1979–97; Parl. Under-Sec. of State, Dept of Educ. and Science 1981–83, Dept of Environment and Spokesman for the Arts 1983–85; Minister of State, Dept of the Environment (Minister for the Environment, Countryside and Local Govt, subsequently Minister for Housing and Planning) 1985–88; Minister of State, FCO 1988–90; Sec. of State for Health 1990–92, Chancellor of the Duchy of Lancaster 1992–94; Sec. of State for Agric., Fisheries and Food 1994–95; Chief Sec. to Treasury 1995–97; Dir Bank of Ireland Financial Services (UK) PLC 1997–, Corp. Finance, Dresdner Kleinwort Benson 1998–; Man. Dir Dresdner Kleinwort Wasserstein 1998–; Chair. Rhodes Trust 2002–, Nat. Museum of Science and Industry 2002–; several other directorships; worked for GEC PLC 1975–81; Hon. Fellow, Corpus Christi Coll., Oxford 1991. *Publication:* The Binding of Leviathan—Conservatism and the Future 1977. *Address:* PO Box 560, 20 Fenchurch Street, London, EC3P 3DB (Office); 66 Palace Gardens Terrace, London, W8 4RR, England. *Telephone:* (20) 7475-5845 (Office).

WALDEN, (Alastair) Brian; British broadcaster and journalist; b. 8 July 1932; s. of W. F. Walden; m. Hazel Downes; one s. (and three s. from fmr marriages); ed West Bromwich Grammar School, Queen's Coll. and Nuffield Coll., Oxford; univ. lecturer; MP (Labour) for Birmingham All Saints 1964–74, Birmingham Ladywood 1974–77; TV presenter, Weekend World (London Weekend TV) 1977–86; mem. W Midland Bd, Cen. Ind. TV 1982–84; columnist London Standard 1983–86, Thomson Regional Newspapers 1983–86, The Sunday Times; presenter, The Walden Interview (London Weekend TV for ITV network) 1988, 1989, 1990–94, Walden on Labour Leaders (BBC) 1997, Walden on Heroes (BBC) 1998, Walden on Villains 1999; Chair. Paragon 1997–, Ten Alps 2001–; Shell Int. Award 1982, BAFTA Richard Dimbleby Award 1985; Aims of Industry Special Free Enterprise Award 1990; ITV Personality of the Year 1991. *Publication:* The Walden Interviews 1990. *Leisure interests:* chess, reading. *Address:* Landfall, Fort Road, St Peter Port, GY1 1ZU, Guernsey.

WALDENSTRÖM, Jan Gosta, MD; Swedish professor of medicine; b. 17 April 1906, Stockholm; s. of Prof. Henning Waldenström and Elsa Laurin; m. 1st Elisabet Waldenström 1932; m. 2nd Karin Nordsjö 1957; five s. two d.; ed Univs. of Uppsala and Cambridge, Tech. Hochschule, Munich; various positions at Academic Hosp., Uppsala; Prof. of Theoretical Medicine, Uppsala 1947; Prof. of Practical Medicine, Univ. of Lund 1950–72; Physician-in-Chief, Dept of Gen. Medicine, Gen. Hospital, Malmö 1950–72; Foreign mem. NAS, USA, French Acad. of Sciences; mem. Academia Europaea; Hon. mem. Royal Soc. of Medicine, London and other foreign acads.; Jahre Scandinavian Prize in Medicine 1962, Gairdner Award 1966, Paul Ehrlich Prize 1972; Hon. degrees from Univs. of Oslo, Dublin, Mainz, Oxford, Paris, London, Innsbruck and Poitiers, Freiburg im Breisgau. *Publications:* Studien über Porphyrie, 1937, Monoclonal and polyclonal hypergammaglobulinemia 1968, Diagnosis and Treatment of Multiple Myeloma 1970, Paraneoplasia 1978, Reflections and Recollections from a Long Life with Medicine 1994; numerous Publs on metabolic, hematologic and other subjects of internal medicine; chapters in many textbooks. *Leisure interests:* history, botany, travelling, art. *Address:* Roskildevägen 11A, 217 46 Malmö, Sweden. *Telephone:* 40-91-62-02.

WALDHEIM, Kurt, LLD; Austrian fmr Head of State, fmr United Nations official and diplomatist; b. 21 Dec. 1918; m. Elisabeth Ritschel Waldheim 1944; one s. two d.; ed Consular Acad. of Vienna, Univ. of Vienna; entered foreign service 1945; served Ministry of Foreign Affairs; mem. Austrian Del. to Paris, London and Moscow for negotiation on Austrian State Treaty; First Sec. 1945–47; served Paris 1948–51; Counsellor and Head of Personnel Div., Ministry of Foreign Affairs 1951–55; Perm. Austrian Observer to UN 1955–56; Envoy to Canada 1956–58, Amb. to Canada 1958–60; Dir-Gen. for Political Affairs, Ministry for Foreign Affairs 1960–64; Perm. Rep. to UN 1964–68; Chair. Outer Space Cttee of UN 1965–68, 1970–71; Fed. Minister for Foreign Affairs 1968–70; Perm. Rep. to UN 1970–71; Cand. for Pres. of Austria 1971, Pres. of Austria 1986–92; Sec.-Gen. of UN 1972–82; Pres. UNA Austria; Guest Prof. of Diplomacy, Georgetown Univ., Washington, DC 1982–84; Chair. InterAction Council of Fmr. Heads of State and Govt 1982–85; numerous hon. degrees; several decorations include Order of Pius IX (Vatican) 1994. *Publications:* Der österreichische Weg (The Austrian Example), Un métier unique au monde, Der schwierigste Job der Welt, The Challenge of Peace 1980, Building The Future Order 1980, In the Eye of the Storm 1985, Die Antwort 1996. *Leisure interests:* horseback riding, swimming, sailing, skiing. *Address:* Lobkowitz-Platz 1, 1010 Vienna, Austria. *Telephone:* (1) 513-08-38 (Office). *Fax:* (1) 513-08-37-15 (Office). *E-mail:* una .austria@afa.at (Office). *Website:* www.una.austria.at (Office).

WALES, HRH Prince Charles Philip Arthur George, The Prince of and Earl of Chester (cr. 1958); Duke of Cornwall, Duke of Rothesay, Earl of Carrick, Baron Renfrew, Lord of the Isles and Great Steward of Scotland (cr. 1952), KG, KT, GCB, OM, PC, MA; b. 14 Nov. 1948, London; s. (eldest) of Princess Elizabeth (now HM Queen Elizabeth II, q.v.) and Prince Philip, Duke of Edinburgh (q.v.); m. Lady Diana Spencer (subsequently Diana, Princess of Wales) 29 July 1981 (divorced 28 Aug. 1996, died 31 Aug. 1997); two s., HRH Prince William Arthur Philip Louis, b. 21 June 1982, HRH Prince Henry Charles Albert David, b. 15 Sept. 1984; ed Cheam School, Gordonstoun School, Geelong Grammar School, Trinity Coll. Cambridge and Univ. Coll. of Wales, Aberystwyth; mem. Gray's Inn 1974, Hon. Bencher 1975; Personal ADC to HM the Queen 1973–; Capt. RN 1988, Rear Adm. 1998–; Maj.-Gen. Army 1998–; Group Capt. RAF 1988–, Air Vice-Marshal 1998–; Col-in-Chief The Royal Regt of Wales (24th/41st Foot) 1969–; Col Welsh Guards 1974–; Col-in-Chief The Cheshire Regt 1977–, Lord Strathcona's Horse (Royal Canadian) Regt 1977–, The Parachute Regt 1977–, The Royal Australian Armoured Corps 1977–, The Royal Regt of Canada 1977–, The Royal Winnipeg Rifles 1977–, Royal Pacific Islands Regt, Papua New Guinea 1984–, Royal Canadian Dragoons 1985–, Army Air Corps 1992–, Royal Dragoon Guards 1992–, Royal Gurkha Rifles 1994–; Deputy Col-in-Chief The Highlanders (Seaforth, Gordons, Camerons) 1994–; Air Cdre-in-Chief RNZAF 1977–; Col-in-Chief Air Reserves Group of Air Command in Canada 1977–; Pres. Soc. of St George's and Descendants of Knights of the Garter 1975–; Adm. Royal Thames Yacht Club 1974–; High Steward, Royal Borough of Windsor and Maidenhead 1974–; Chair. The Mountbatten Memorial Trust 1979–, King Edward VII Fund for London Hosps 1987, The Prince of Wales's Cttee 1971–; Pres. The Prince's Trusts 1977–, Royal Forestry Soc. 1982–, RAM 1985–, Prince's Youth Business Trust 1986–, The Prince's Scottish Youth Business Trust, Business in the Community 1985, Prince of Wales's Foundation for Architecture and the Urban Enviroment 1992–, Prince of Wales's Business Leaders Forum 1990–; Chancellor, Univ. of Wales 1976–; mem. Bd Commonwealth Devt Corpn 1979–89; Hon. Pres. Royal Acad. Trust 1993–; Trustee, Royal Opera House, Gurkha Welfare Fund 1989; Patron Oxford Centre for Islamic Studies 1993–, British Orthopaedic Asscn 1993–, Royal Coll. of Music 1993–, Prague Heritage Fund 1993–, Nat. Gallery 1993–, Nat. Trust Centenary Appeal 1994–, ActionAid 1995–, Help the Aged 1997–, Welsh Nat. Opera 1997–, Guinness Trust 1997–; represented HM the Queen at Independence Celebrations in Fiji 1970, at Requiem Mass for Gen. Charles de Gaulle 1970, at Bahamas Independence Celebrations 1973, at Papua New Guinea Independence Celebrations 1975, at Coronation of King of Nepal 1975, at funeral of Sir Robert Menzies 1978, at funeral of Jomo Kenyatta 1978, at funeral of Rajiv Gandhi 1990, at funeral of King Olav of Norway 1991; Pres. Royal Ballet, Birmingham Royal Ballet 2003–; Hon. Air Cdre RAF Valley 1994–; Dr hc (Royal Coll. of Music) 1981; Spoleto Prize 1989; Author of the Year 1989; Premio Fregene 1990; Coronation Medal 1953, The Queen's Silver Jubilee Medal 1977, Grand Cross of The Southern Cross of Brazil 1978, Grand Cross of The White Rose of Finland 1969, Grand Cordon of the Supreme Order of the Chrysanthemum of Japan 1971, Grand Cross of The House of Orange of the Netherlands 1972, Grand Cross Order of Oak Crown of Luxembourg 1972, Kt of The Order of Elephant of Denmark 1974, Grand Cross of The Order of Ojasvi Rajanya of Nepal 1975, Order of the Repub. of Egypt (First Class) 1981; Grande Croix, Légion d'honneur 1984; Order of Mubarak the Great of Kuwait 1993; cr. Prince of Wales and Earl of Chester (invested July 1969); KG 1958 (invested and installed 1968), KT 1977, PC 1977, GCB and Great Master of Order of the Bath 1975; Royal Fellowship of the Australian Acad. of Science 1979; Hon. Fellowship of Royal Coll. of Surgeons 1978, Royal Aeronautical Soc. 1978, Inst. of Mechanical Engineers 1979, Inst. of Architecture 1992; received Freedom of City of Cardiff 1969, of Royal Borough of New Windsor 1970, of City of London 1971, of Chester 1973, of City of Canterbury 1978, of City of Portsmouth 1979, of City of Lancaster 1993, of City of Swansea 1994; Hon. Fellow, Trinity Coll. Cambridge 1988; Liveryman of Fishmongers' Co. 1971; Freeman of Drapers' Co. 1971; Freeman of Shipwrights' Co. 1978; Hon. Freeman and Liveryman of Goldsmiths Co. 1979, Liveryman of Farmers' Co.

1980, of Pewterers' Co. 1982, of Fruiterers' Co. 1989; Hon. Liveryman of Worshipful Co. of Carpenters 1992; Hon. mem. of Hon. Co. of Master Mariners 1977 (Master 1988), of Merchants of City of Edinburgh 1979; Hon. Life mem. Incorporation of Gardeners of Glasgow 1989; Hon. DCL (Durham) 1998. *Publications:* The Old Man of Lochnagar 1980, A Vision of Britain 1989, HRH The Prince of Wales Watercolours 1990, Urban Villages 1992, Highgrove: Portrait of an Estate 1993, Prince's Choice: A Selection from Shakespeare by the Prince of Wales 1995, Travels with the Prince 1998. *Address:* St James's Palace, London, SW1A 1BS; Highgrove House, Doughton, Nr Tetbury, Gloucestershire, GL8 8TN, England. *Website:* www.princeofwales.gov.uk (Office).

WALES, HRH Prince William Arthur Philip Louis, Prince William of; b. 21 June 1982; elder s. of HRH The Prince of Wales and of the late Diana, Princess of Wales; ed Mrs Mynors' Nursery School, Wetherby School, Ludgrove School, Eton Coll., St Andrews Univ. *Address:* St James's Palace, London, SW1A 1BS, England.

WAŁĘSA, Lech; Polish fmr politician and trade union activist; b. 29 Sept. 1943, Popowo; s. of Bolesław Wałęsa and Feliksa Wałęsa; m. Danuta Wałęsa 1969; four s. four d.; ed primary and tech. schools; electrician, Lenin Shipyard, Gdańsk 1966–76, 1983–; Chair. Strike Cttee in Lenin Shipyard 1970; employed Zremb and Elektromontaż 1976–80; Chair. Inter-institutional Strike Cttee, Gdańsk Aug.–Sept. 1980; Co-Founder and Chair. Solidarity Independent Trade Union 1980–90, Chair. Nat. Exec. Comm. of Solidarity 1987–90; interned 1981–82; Founder of Civic Cttee attached to Chair. of Solidarity 1988–90; participant and co-Chair. Round Table debates 1989; Pres. of Polish Republic 1990–95,Chair. Country Defence Cttee 1990–95, Supreme Commdr of Armed Forces of Polish Republic for Wartime 1990–95; Founder of Lech Wałęsa Inst. Foundation 1995, Christian Democratic Party of the Third Republic (ChDTRP) 1997, Pres. 1998–; retd from politics; 100 hon. doctorates; Man of the Year, Financial Times 1980, The Observer 1980, Die Welt 1980, Die Zeit 1981, L'Express 1981, Le Soir 1981, Time 1981, Le Point 1981; awarded Let us Live peace prize of Swedish journal Arbetet 1981, Love International Award (Athens) 1981, Freedom Medal (Philadelphia) 1981, Medal of Merit (Polish American Congress) 1981, Free World Prize (Norway) 1982, Int. Democracy Award 1982, Social Justice Award 1983, Nobel Peace Prize 1983, Humanitarian Pub. Service Medal 1984, Int. Integrity Award 1986, Phila Liberty Medal 1989, Human Rights Prize, Council of Europe 1989, White Eagle Order (Poland) 1989, US Medal of Freedom 1989, Meeting-90 Award (Rimini) 1990, Path for Peace Award, Apostolic Nuncio to the UN 1996, Freedom Medal of Nat. Endowment for Democracy (Washington USA) 1999, Int. Freedom Award (Memphis USA); Order of the Bath 1991, Grand Cross of Légion d'honneur 1991, Grand Order of Merit (Italy) 1991, Order of Merit (FRG) 1991, Great Order of the White Lion 1999, Orden Heraldica do Cristobal Colon 2001; and other awards, orders and prizes. *Publications:* autobiogs.: Droga nadziei (The Road to Hope) 1987, Droga douwolności (The Road to Freedom) 1991, Wszystko co robię, robię dla Polski (Everything I Do, I Do for Poland) 1995. *Leisure interests:* crossword puzzles, fishing. *Address:* Christian Democratic Party of the Third Republic (ChDTRP), Al. Jerozolimskie 11/19, Warsaw, Poland.

WALEWSKA, Malgorzata; Polish mezzo-soprano opera singer; b. 5 July 1965, Warsaw; one d.; ed Acad. of Music, Warsaw, Nat. Opera, Warsaw; has sung at Bremer Theater 1994, Staatsoper, Vienna 1996–98, Semperoper, Dresden 1999 and Rome (Teatro della Opera), Berlin (Deutsche Open), Düsseldorf (Deutsche Open am Rhein), Florida (Palm Bech Opera) and others; has participated in numerous festivals in Brussels, Seville, London, Bregenz, Nantes and Athens; numerous honours or prizes including 1st Prize Alfredo Kraus Int. Competition 1992, Prize for Best Mezzo-Soprano, Stanislaw Moniuszko Int. Competition, Warsaw 1992, Laureate Luciano Pavarotti Vocal Competition, Phila 1992, Best Graduate, Chopin Acad. of Music, Warsaw, 1994. *Roles include:* Carmen (Carmen), Delilah (Samson and Delilah) Charlotte (Werther), Emilia (Otello), Olga (Eugene Onegin), Jocaste (Oedipus Rex). *CD Recordings include:* Voce di Donna (a compilation of famous mezzo-soprano arias) 2000, Mezzo (songs and arias in contemporary arrangements) 2000.

WALI, Yousuf Amin, PhD; Egyptian politician; b. 1930; ed Faculty of Agric., Cairo Univ. and in USA; Reader, later Prof. Faculty of Agric., Cairo Univ.; consultant, Ministry of Scientific Research and Ministry of Agric. and Land Reform; fmr Agric. Planning Consultant in Libya; mem. Nat. Democratic Party, Sec.-Gen. –2002, Deputy Chair. in charge of Internal Affairs 2002–; Deputy Prime Minister Sept. 1985–; Minister of State for Agric. and Food Security 1982–87, Minister of Agric. and Land Reclamation 1987–. *Address:* Ministry of Agriculture and Land Reclamation, Sharia Nadi es-Sayed, Dokki, Egypt. *Telephone:* (2) 3772566. *Fax:* (2) 3498128. *E-mail:* sea@idsc.gov.eg (Office). *Website:* www.agri.gov.eg (Office).

WALKEN, Christopher; American actor; b. 31 March 1943, Astoria, NY; s. of Paul Walken and Rosalie Walken; ed Hofstra Univ. *Films include:* The Anderson Tapes, Next Stop Greenwich Village, Roseland, Annie Hall, The Deer Hunter (New York Film Critics and Acad. Awards for Best Supporting Actor), Dogs of War, Heaven's Gate, Pennies from Heaven, The Dead Zone 1983, Brainstorm 1983, A View to a Kill 1984, At Close Range 1986, The Milagro Beanfield War 1988, Biloxi Blues 1988, Communion 1989, The Comfort of Strangers 1989, King of New York 1990, True Romance 1993, A Business Affair 1994, Scam 1994, Wayne's World II 1994, Pulp Fiction 1994, Things To Do In Denver When You're Dead, Nick of Time, The Funeral, Last

Man Standing, Touch, Excess Baggage, Suicide Kings, Blast from the Past 1999, Sleepy Hollow, Kiss Toledo Goodbye, The Opportunists, The Affairs of the Necklace 2001, America's Sweethearts 2001, Joe Dint 2001, Scotland PA 2002, Catch Me If You Can (BAFTA Award for Best Supporting Actor) 2003. *Stage appearances include:* West Side Story, Macbeth, The Lion in Winter (Clarence Derwent Award 1966), The Night Thoreau Spent in Jail (Joseph Jefferson Award 1970–71), Cinders 1984, A Bill of Divorcement 1985, The Seagull 2001. *Address:* William Morris Agency, 151 El Camino Drive, Beverly Hills, CA 90212, USA.

WALKER, Alan Cyril, BA, PhD; British medical scientist; b. 23 Aug. 1938; s. of Cyril Walker and Edith Walker (née Tidd); m. 1st Patricia Dale Larwood 1963 (marriage dissolved); one s.; m. 2nd Patty Lee Shipman 1976; ed St John's Coll. Cambridge, Royal Free Hosp., London; Asst Lecturer in Anatomy, Royal Free Hosp. School of Medicine 1965; Lecturer in Anatomy, Makerere Univ. Coll., Kampala, Uganda 1965–69; Hon. Keeper of Paleontology, Uganda Museum 1967–69; Sr Lecturer in Anatomy, Univ. of Nairobi, Kenya 1969–73; Visiting Lecturer, Dept of Anatomy, Harvard Univ. 1973–74, Assoc. Prof. of Anatomy 1974–78, Assoc. Prof. of Anthropology 1974–78; Research Assoc. Peabody Museum 1974–78; Prof. of Cellular Biology and Anatomy, Johns Hopkins Univ. School of Medicine 1978–95 (part-time 1995–97); Prof. of Anthropology and Biology, Pa State Univ. 1995–96, Distinguished Prof. 1996–; Assoc. Ed. American Journal of Physical Anthropology 1974–79, Journal of Human Evolution 1994–98; John Guggenheim Memorial Foundation Fellow 1986, MacArthur Foundation Fellow 1988–93; mem. American Acad. of Arts and Sciences 1996; Hon. DSc (Univ. of Chicago) 2000; Rhône-Poulenc Prize 1997, Int. Foundation Fyssen Prize 1998. *Publications:* Prosimian Biology (Jt Ed.) 1974, Structure and Function of the Human Skeleton (Jt author) 1985, Nariokotome Homo Erectus Skeleton (Jt Ed.) 1993, The Wisdom of the Bones (Jt author) 1996, numerous papers published in scientific journals. *Address:* Department of Anthropology, 409 Carpenter Building, Pennsylvania State University, University Park, Pittsburgh, PA 168802, U.S.A. (Office). *Telephone:* (814) 865-3122 (Office). *Website:* www.psu .edu (Office).

WALKER, Alice Malsenior, BA; American author; b. 9 Feb. 1944, Eatonton, Ga; d. of Willie L. Walker and Minnie (née Grant) Walker; m. Melvyn R. Leventhal 1967 (divorced 1977); one d.; ed Sarah Lawrence Coll.; Hon. PhD (Russell Sage Univ.) 1972; Hon. DHL (Univ. of Mass.) 1983; Lillian Smith Award 1974, Rosenthal Award, Nat. Inst. of Arts and Letters 1973, Guggenheim Foundation Award 1979, American Book Award 1983, Pulitzer Prize 1983. *Publications:* Once 1968, The Third Life of George Copeland 1970, In Love and Trouble 1973, Langston Hughes, American Poet 1973, Revolutionary Petunias 1974, Meridian 1976, I Love Myself When I am Laughing 1979, You Can't Keep a Good Woman Down 1981, Good Night Willi Lee, I'll See You in the Morning 1979, The Colour Purple 1982, In Search of Our Mothers' Gardens 1983, Horses Make a Landscape Look More Beautiful 1984, To Hell with Dying 1988, Living By the Word 1988, The Temple of My Familiar 1989, Her Blue Body Everything We Know: Earthling Poems (1965–90) 1991, Possessing the Secret of Joy 1992, Warrior Marks (with Pratibha Parmar) 1993, Double Stitch; Black Women Write About Mothers and Daughters (jtly) 1993, Everyday Use 1994, Alice Walker Banned 1996, Everything We Love Can Be Saved 1997, The Same River Twice 1997, The Way Forward is Hitha Broken Heart (ed.) 2000. *Address:* c/o Random House, 299 Park Avenue, New York, NY 10171, USA.

WALKER, Catherine, M. ÈS L., FRSA; French couturier; b. 27 June 1945, Pas de Calais; d. of Remy Baheux and Agnes Lefèbvre; m. John Walker (deceased); two d.; ed Univs. of Lille and Aix-en-Provence; Dir Film Dept, French Inst., London 1970, Lecture Dept, French Embassy, London 1971, The Chelsea Design Co. Ltd 1978–; Founder sponsor Haven Trust; Fellow RSA 2000; Designer of the Year for British Couture 1990–91, Designer of the Year for Glamour Award 1991–92. *Publications:* Catherine Walker, an Autobiography by the Private Couturier to Diana, Princess of Wales 1998, Catherine Walker Twenty Five Years 1977–2002 British Couture. *Address:* 65 Sydney Street, Chelsea, London, SW3 6PX, England. *Telephone:* (20) 7352-4626.

WALKER, Charls Edward, MBA, PhD; American economist; b. 24 Dec. 1923, Graham, Tex.; s. of Pinkney Clay Walker and Sammye McCombs Walker; m. Harmolyn Hart 1949; one s. one d.; ed Univs. of Texas and Pennsylvania; Pilot instructor, USAF World War II; Instructor in Finance and later Asst and Assoc. Prof., Univ. of Tex. 1947–54; Instructor in Finance, Wharton School 1948–50; Assoc. Economist, Fed. Reserve Bank of Philadelphia 1953–54; Economist and Special Asst to Pres. of the Repub. Nat. Bank of Dallas 1955–56; Vice-Pres. and Financial Economist, Fed. Reserve Bank of Dallas 1958–61; Asst to the Sec. of the Treasury 1959–61; Exec. Vice-Pres., American Bankers' Asscn 1961–69; Under-Sec. of the Treasury 1969–72; Deputy Sec. of the Treasury 1972–73; Adjunct Prof. for Finance and Public Affairs Univ. of Texas at Austin 1986–; Distinguished Visiting Prof., Emory Univ.; Adjunct Prof. Texas A & M Univ. 2001; Chair. Walker and Walker L.L.C.; Chair. American Council for Capital Formation; Co-Chair. Presidential Debates 1976; Chair., Pres. Reagan's Task Force on Tax Policy 1980; Co-founder Cttee on the Present Danger; Founder Chair. Bretton Woods Cttee, Advisory Cttee on Nat. Issues Convention; Chair. Pres. Nixon's Advisory Cttee on Minority Enterprise; Hon. LLD (Ashland Coll.) 1970; Alexander Hamilton Award, US Treasury, Distinguished Alumnus Award, Univ. of Texas, Baber Award for Exemplary Service to Econ. Educ., Distinguished Service Award, Urban League Award for Contributions to Minority Enterprise and Educ. *Publications:* The Banker's Handbook 1978 (co-Ed.), New Directions in Federal Tax Policy 1983 (co-Ed.), The Consumption Tax: A Better Alternative (co-Ed.) 1987, Intellectual Property Rights and Capital Formation in the Next Decade 1988, Saving: The Challenge for the US Economy 1990; numerous articles in newspapers, magazines and economic and other journals. *Leisure interests:* golf, music. *Address:* 10120 Chapel Road, Potomac, MD 20854, USA. *Telephone:* (301) 299-5414 (Home). *Fax:* (301) 299-5024 (Home).

WALKER, David Alan, PhD, DSc, FRS; British professor of photosynthesis; b. 18 Aug. 1928, Hull; s. of Cyril Walker and Dorothy Walker; m. Shirley Wynne Mason 1956; one s. one d.; ed Univ. of Newcastle; Royal Naval Air Service 1946–48; at Univ. of Newcastle 1948–58, Purdue Univ., Indiana 1953–54; Reader in Botany, Queen Mary Coll., Univ. of London 1963; Reader in Enzymology, Imperial Coll., Univ. of London 1964–70; Prof. of Biology, Univ. of Sheffield 1970–84, Dir Research Inst. for Photosynthesis 1984–88, Prof. of Photosynthesis 1988–93, Prof. Emer. 1993–; Visiting Fellow, Connecticut Agricultural Experimental Station 1965; Corresp. mem. American Soc. of Plant Physiology 1979, Academia Europaea 1994; von Humboldt Prize 1991. *Publications:* Energy, Plants and Man 1979, 1992, C_3C_4 (with Gerry Edwards) 1983, A Leaf in Time 1999, Like Clockwork 2000; over 200 Publs on photosynthetic carbon assimilation. *Leisure interests:* singing the Sheffield carols and changing the Biddlestone landscape. *Address:* 6 Biddlestone Village, Morpeth, Northumberland, NE65 7DT, England. *Telephone:* (114) 230-5904. *E-mail:* david@algeba.demon.co.uk (Home). *Website:* www .oxygraphics.co.uk (Office); www.algeba.demon.co.uk/index.html (Home).

WALKER, Sir David Alan, Kt, MA; British financial executive; b. 31 Dec. 1939; m. Isobel Cooper 1963; one s. two d.; ed Chesterfield School and Queens' Coll. Cambridge; joined HM Treasury 1961, Pvt. Sec. to Jt Perm. Sec. 1964–66, Asst Sec. 1973–77; seconded to staff IMF, Washington, DC 1970–73; joined Bank of England as Chief Adviser, then Chief Econ. Intelligence Dept 1977, Asst Dir 1980, Dir 1982–88 (non-exec. 1988–93); Chair. Johnson Matthey Bankers Ltd (later Minories Finance Ltd) 1985–88, Financial Markets Group, LSE 1987–95, Securities and Investments Bd 1988–92, Agric. Mortgage Corpn PLC 1993–94, Morgan Stanley (Europe) (now Morgan Stanley Dean Witter (Europe) Ltd) 1994–2000, Morgan Stanley Int. 1995–2000 (Sr Adviser 2001–), Reuters Venture Capital; Deputy Chair. Lloyds Bank Ltd 1992–94; Dir (non-exec.) British Invisibles 1993–, Nat. Power 1990–93; part-time Bd mem. Cen. Electricity Generating Bd 1987–89; mem. Council, Lloyd's of London 1988–92; Gov. Henley Man. Coll. 1993–99, LSE 1993–; Chair. Exec. Cttee of Int. Org. of Securities Comms 1990–92, Cttee of Inquiry into Lloyd's Syndicate Participations and the LMX Spiral; mem. Group of Thirty 1993–; Trustee Cambridge Univ. Devt Foundation; Amb. for Community Links; Hon. Fellow Queens' Coll. Cambridge 1989; Hon. LLD (Exeter) 2002. *Leisure interests:* music, architecture, long-distance walking. *Address:* Morgan Stanley International Ltd, 25 Cabot Square, Canary Wharf, London, E14 4QA, England. *Telephone:* (20) 7425-5400. *Fax:* (20) 7425-8975.

WALKER, David Maxwell, CBE, QC, PhD, LLD, FBA, FRSE, F.S.A.SCOT., FRSA; British university professor and barrister; b. 9 April 1920, Glasgow; s. of James Mitchell Walker and Mary Paton Colquhoun Irvine; m. Margaret Knox, OBE 1954; ed High School of Glasgow, Univs of Glasgow, Edinburgh and London; army service in India, N Africa and Italy, Capt., Indian Army 1939–46; practised at Scottish Bar 1948–53; Prof. of Jurisprudence, Glasgow Univ. 1954–58, Regius Prof. of Law 1958–90, Dean of Faculty of Law 1956–59, Convener of School of Law 1984–88, Sr Research Fellow 1990–; retd 1990; Chair. Hamlyn Trust 1988–93; Hon. LLD (Edin.) 1974. *Publications:* Law of Damages in Scotland 1955, Law of Civil Remedies in Scotland 1974, The Oxford Companion to Law 1980, Law of Delict in Scotland (2nd edn) 1981, Stair's Institutions (ed.; 6th edn) 1981, The Scottish Jurists 1985, Principles of Scottish Private Law (4th edn, four vols) 1988–90, Legal History of Scotland, Vol. I 1988, Vol. II 1990, Vol. III 1995, Vol. IV 1996, Vol. V 1997, Vol. VI 2001, Law of Contracts in Scotland (3rd edn) 1994, The Scottish Legal System (8th edn) 2001, Law of Prescription in Scotland (6th edn) 2002. *Leisure interest:* book collecting. *Address:* School of Law, University of Glasgow, Glasgow, G12 8QQ (Office); 1 Beaumont Gate, Glasgow, G12 9EE, Scotland (Home). *Telephone:* (141) 339-8855 (Office); (141) 339-2802 (Home).

WALKER, Derek, MArch, RIBA, FRCA, FRSA; British architect, town planner, university professor and designer; b. 15 June 1931, Ribchester, Lancs.; s. of the late William Walker and Ann Nicholson; m. 1st Honora Jill Messenger 1957; two s.; m. 2nd Jan Larrance 1983; one d.; f. Derek Walker Assocs., Architects & Urban Planners 1960, Walker, Wright, Schofield, Interior Design/Furniture Design 1966; Chief Architect and Planner, New City of Milton Keynes 1969–76; re-formed practices, Sr Partner Derek Walker Assocs., Walker Wright 1976–; Prof. of Architecture & Design, RCA 1984–90, Chair. Design Faculty; Architectural Design Awards, pvt. houses, urban devts., village plans 1965 (two), 1966 (two), 1967, 1968, Civic Trust Awards 1965, 1967, 1968, Financial Times Architectural Awards 1969, first prize numerous nat. and int. competitions for theatres, new towns, shopping bldgs., waterside devts. and parks, RIBA Awards 1979, 1980. *Principal projects:* New City of Milton Keynes 1969–82, Sculpture Park, Milton Keynes 1972, Master Planning New City of Jubail, Saudi Arabia 1979–82, WonderWorld Themepark 1982–, StarSite Birmingham Urban Plan 1984, Commodores Point, Jacksonville, Fla Urban Plan, USA 1985, Ski Resort, Telluride, Colo, USA 1986–88, Lijnbaan Shopping Centre, Rotterdam 1987–89, Gyosei Japanese School 1985–87, Kowloon Park, Hong Kong 1985–87, Energy World, Corby

1986, Olympic Pool and Sports Hall, Kowloon 1986–88, Happy Valley Racecourse Redevt., Hong Kong 1990–96, Ushiku New Town Plan, Japan 1991–95, Clarence Dock Master Plan, Leeds 1991, Royal Armouries Museum, Leeds 1992–96, Museum of British History, London 1996–, Newmarket Racing Museum and Stables 1996–. *Publications:* British Architects 1981, Los Angeles 1982, Architecture and Planning of Milton Keynes 1982, Animated Architecture 1995, The Royal Armouries: The Making of a Museum (with Guy Wilson) 1996; numerous articles. *Leisure interests:* fine art, classical music, jazz, literature and most sports. *Address:* 80 Warwick Gardens, London, W14 8PR, England; 12 North Drive, Marion, MA 02738, USA. *Telephone:* (20) 7371-1749 (England); (508) 748-0203 (USA). *Fax:* (508) 748-0203 (USA).

WALKER, George Alfred; British business executive; b. 14 April 1929, London; s. of William James Walker and Ellen Walker (née Page); m. Jean Maureen Hatton 1957; one s. two d.; ed Jubilee School, Bedford, Essex; fmr boxer and boxing man.; Chief Exec. Walkers Int. 1992; declared bankrupt April 1993; Chair. Premier Telesports Ltd 1995–; Freeman City of London 1978. *Leisure interests:* skiing, ocean racing, climbing. *Address:* Pell House, High Road, Fobbing, Essex, SS17 9JJ, England. *Telephone:* (1375) 672082. *Fax:* (1375) 643315.

WALKER, George P. L., PhD, FRS; British geologist and volcanologist; b. 2 March 1926, London; s. of L. R. T. Walker and E. F. Walker (née McConkey); m. Hazel R. Smith 1958; one s. one d.; ed Wallace High School, Lisburn, Northern Ireland, Queen's Univ. Belfast and Univ. of Leeds; Asst Lecturer, Imperial Coll. of Science and Tech., Univ. of London 1951–54, Lecturer 1954–64, Reader in Geology 1964–80; Capt. James Cook Research Fellow of Royal Soc. of NZ, based at Univ. of Auckland 1978–80; Gordon A. Macdonald Prof. of Volcanology, Univ. of Hawaii, Manoa 1981–96, Prof. Emer. 1999–; Visiting Prof. Univ. of Bristol; Fellow Geological Soc. of America 1987; Fellow American Geophysical Union 1988; Hon. mem. Visindafelag Islendinga (Iceland), Royal Soc. of NZ; Hon. DSc (Univ. of Iceland) 1988; Moiety of Lyell Fund, Lyell Medal and Wollaston Medal, Geological Soc. of London 1963, 1982, 1995, McKay Hammer Award, Geological Soc. of NZ 1982, Excellence in Research Award, Univ. of Hawaii 1985, Thorarinsson Medal, Int. Asscn of Volcanology and Geochem. of Earth's Interior 1989; Icelandic Order of the Falcon, Kt's Class 1980. *Publications:* scientific papers on the geology and mineralogy of Iceland and processes in volcanology. *Leisure interest:* visiting volcanoes. *Address:* Department of Earth Sciences, University of Bristol, Queens Road, Bristol, BS8 1RJ (Office); Department of Geology, University of Bristol, Bristol BS8 1RJ; Geology Department, Cheltenham and Gloucester College of Higher Education, Gloucester, GL50 4AZ, England; Department of Geology and Geophysics, University of Hawaii, Honolulu, HI 96822, USA. *Telephone:* (117) 928 9000. *Fax:* (117) 925 3385 (Office).

WALKER, Sir John Ernest, Kt, MA, DPhil, ScD, FRS; British scientist; b. 7 Jan. 1941, Halifax; s. of Thomas Ernest Walker and Elsie Walker (née Lawton); m. Christina Jane Westcott 1963; two d.; ed Rastrick Grammar School, W Yorks., St Catherine's Coll. Oxford; Visiting Research Fellow Univ. of Wis., USA 1969–71; NATO Research Fellow, CNRS, Gif-sur-Yvette, France 1971–72; EMBO Research Fellow, Pasteur Inst., Paris 1972–74; Staff Scientist, MRC Lab. of Molecular Biology, Cambridge 1974–; Dir MRC Dunn Human Nutrition Unit, Cambridge 1998–; mem. EMBO 1983; Fellow Sidney Sussex Coll. Cambridge 1997–; mem. Netherlands Acad. of Arts and Science 1998; Hon. Prof. (Pekin Union Medical Coll., Beijing) 2001, (Cambridge) 2002; Hon. Fellow St Catherine's Coll. Oxford; Hon. DSc (London) 2002; Dr hc (Univs of Bradford, Leeds, Oxford, Gröningen, Manchester, Huddersfield, Buenos Aires); Johnson Foundation Prize, Univ. of Pa 1994, CIBA Medal and Prize, Biochemical Soc. 1996, Nobel Prize for Chem. (jtly, with Paul Boyer) 1997, Soc. of Chemical Industry Messel Medal 2000. *Publications:* research papers and reviews in scientific journals. *Leisure interests:* cricket, opera music, walking. *Address:* Medical Research Council Dunn Human Nutrition Unit, Hills Road, Cambridge, CB2 2XY, England. *Telephone:* (1223) 252701. *Fax:* (1223) 252705 (Office). *E-mail:* walker@mrc-dunn.cam.ac.uk (Office).

WALKER, Gen. Sir Michael John Dawson, GCB, CMG, CBE; British army officer; b. 7 July 1944, Salisbury, Rhodesia (now Zimbabwe); s. of William Hampden Dawson Walker and Dorothy Helena (née Shiach) Walker; m. Victoria Margaret Holme 1973; two s. one d.; ed Royal Mil. Acad. Sandhurst; joined Royal Anglian Regt 1966, Regimental and Staff Duties 1966–82, with Staff Coll. 1976–77, Mil. Asst to Chief of Gen. Staff 1982–85, CO 1985–87, Col 1996–; Commdr 20th Armoured Brig. 1987–89; Chief of Staff 1 (Br.) Corps 1989–91; GOC NE Dist and Commdr 2nd Infantry Div. 1991–92; Col Commdt Queen's Div. 1991–2000, Army Air Corps 1994–; GOC Eastern Dist 1992; Asst Chief of the Gen. Staff Ministry of Defence 1992–94; Commdr Ace Rapid Reaction Corps 1994–97; Head NATO Ground Forces, Bosnia 1995–96; C-in-C Land Command 1997–2000; Aide de Camp Gen. to the Queen 1997–; Chief of the Gen. Staff 2000–03; Chief of the Defence Staff 2003–. *Leisure interests:* skiing, sailing, golf, shooting. *Address:* Ministry of Defence, Whitehall, London, SW1A 2EU, England.

WALKER, Sir Miles Rawstron, Kt, CBE; British politician (retd); b. 13 Nov. 1940, Isle of Man; s. of George D. Walker and Alice Rawstron; m. Mary L. Cowell 1966; one s. one d.; ed Castle Rushen High School and Shropshire Agricultural Coll.; co. Dir farming and retail trade; mem. and fmr Chair. Arbory Parish Commrs. 1970–76; mem. House of Keys (Ind.) 1976–; mem. Bd of Agric., Local Govt Bd, Manx Museum 1976–81; Chair. Broadcasting Comm. 1979, Local Govt Bd 1981–86; mem. Exec. Council 1981–; mem. Assessment Bd 1983–86; Vice-Chair. Post Office Authority 1984–86; Chief Minister, Isle of Man Govt 1986–96; mem. Isle of Man Treasury 1996–2000; Chair. Isle of Man Swimming Asscn; Pres. Rotary Club 2000–01, Southern Amateur Swimming Club, Port St Mary Rifle Club; LLD hc (Liverpool) 1994. *Publications:* Isle of Man Govt Policy Documents 1987–1996. *Leisure interest:* Rotary club. *Address:* Magher Feailley, Main Road, Colby, IM9 4AD, Isle of Man (Home). *Telephone:* (1624) 833728 (Home). *Fax:* (1624) 833728 (Office). *E-mail:* miles.walker@talk 21.com (Home).

WALKER, Robert Mowbray, PhD; American physicist; b. 6 Feb. 1929, Philadelphia; s. of Robert Walker and Margaret Seivwright; m. 1st Alice J. Agedal 1951 (divorced 1973); two s.; m. 2nd Ghislaine Crozaz 1973; ed Union Coll., Schenectady, New York, Yale Univ.; Research Physicist, Gen. Electric Lab., Schenectady, NY 1954–66; Adjunct Prof. Metallurgy Dept Rensselaer Polytechnic Inst., Troy, NY 1958, Physics Dept 1965–66; Nat. Science Foundation Sr post-doctoral Fellow and Visiting Prof. Univ. of Paris 1962–63; McDonnell Prof. of Physics, Washington Univ. 1966–; Visiting Prof. of Physics and Geology, Calif. Inst. of Tech. Jan.–June 1972; Visiting Scientist, Laboratoire René Bernas, Univ. of Paris, France May–Aug. 1975; Dir McDonnell Center for the Space Sciences, Washington Univ. 1975–99; Chair. Antarctic Meteorite Working Group 1990–92; mem. NAS Polar Research Bd 1995–, Cosmic Dust Allocation Cttee, NASA 1998; Visiting Scientist Physical Research Lab., Ahmedabad, India 1981; Visiting Scientist, Inst. d'Astrophysique, Paris and Laboratoire René Bernas, France March–Aug. 1981; Visiting Prof. Univ. Libre de Bruxelles 2001; Founder Vols in Tech. Assistance (VITA) 1960, Pres. 1960–62, 1965–66; Fellow American Physical Soc., AAAS; Officier Ordre des Palmes Académiques and other honours and awards. *Publications:* more than 200 scientific papers and book: Nuclear Tracks in Solids. *Address:* Physics Department, Box 1105, Washington University, 1 Brookings Drive, St Louis, MO 63130 (Office); 3 Romany Park Lane, St Louis, MO 63132, USA (Home). *Telephone:* (314) 935-6257.

WALKER, Roger Neville, BArch, FNZIA; New Zealand architect; b. 21 Dec. 1942, Hamilton; s. of Andrew Frank Walker and Margaret Clothier; m. 1985; three s. one d.; ed Hamilton Boys' High School, Univ. of Auckland School of Architecture; with corp. architectural practice, Wellington 1968–70; own practice 1970–; designs include Rainbow Springs, Rotorua, Waitomo Visitor Centre, Whakatane Airport, Gardens Park Royal Hotel, Queenstown, City Centre Shopping Devt, New Plymouth, Marist Provincial Bldg, Ropata Medical Centre, Thorndon New World Shopping Devt, Willis Street Village, Wellington, over 120 houses and apartment devts. in New Zealand, Australia and UK; lecturer Auckland School of Architecture, Wellington School of Architecture; received New Zealand Steel Award 1984; 16 NZ Inst. of Architecture Awards; 5 NZ Tourism Awards; New Zealand Order of Merit for services to architecture 1999. *Leisure interests:* photography, travel, motor sport, basketball. *Address:* 8 Brougham Street, Mount Victoria, Wellington, New Zealand. *Telephone:* (4) 385-9307. *Fax:* (4) 385-9348.

WALKER, Sarah Elizabeth Royle, CBE, FRCM, FGSM, LRAM; British mezzo-soprano; b. Cheltenham; d. of Elizabeth Brownrigg and Alan Royle Walker; m. Graham Allum 1972; ed Pate's Grammar School for Girls, Cheltenham and Royal Coll. of Music (RCM); studied violin and cello and then voice (with Ruth Packer and Cuthbert Smith) at RCM; Martin Musical Trust Scholarship to begin vocal studies with Vera Rozsa 1967; operatic débuts: Kent Opera, Ottavia in Coronation of Poppea 1969, Glyndebourne Festival, Diana/Giove in La Calisto 1970, Scottish Opera, Didon in Les Troyens 1971, ENO, Wellgunde in The Ring 1971; prin. singer with ENO 1972–76; début Royal Opera House, Covent Garden as Charlotte in Werther 1979; début Metropolitan Opera, New York, as Micha in Handel's Samson 1986; has sung opera in Chicago, San Francisco, Göttingen, Geneva, Vienna and Brussels; concert repertoire includes, in addition to standard works, contemporary and avant-garde works by Berio, Boulez, Cage, Ligeti, Xenakis and others; sang Rule Britannia at last night of 1985 and 1989 BBC Promenade Concerts, London; recital début, Wigmore Hall, London 1979; recital tours Australia, N America, Europe; numerous recordings including Handel's Hercules and Julius Caesar and Stravinsky's Rake's Progress; video recordings of Gloriana (title role), Julius Caesar (Cornelia) and King Priam (Andromache); Prince Consort Prof. of Singing RCM 1993–; vocal performance consultant Guildhall School of Music and Drama 1999–; Pres. Cheltenham Bach Choir 1986–; Liveryman Worshipful Co. of Musicians. *Leisure interests:* interior design, gardening, battling against incipient laziness. *Address:* c/o Askonas Holt Ltd, Lonsdale Chambers, 27 Chancery Lane, London, WC2A 1PF; 152 Inchmery Road, London, SE6 1DF, England. *Fax:* (20) 8461-5659. *E-mail:* megamezzo@sarahwalker.com (Home). *Website:* www.sarahwalker.com (Home).

WALKER OF WORCESTER, Baron (Life Peer), cr. 1992, of Abbots Morton in the County of Hereford and Worcester; **Peter Edward Walker,** PC, MBE; British politician and businessman; b. 25 March 1932; s. of Sydney Walker and Rose Walker; m. Tessa Joan Pout 1969; three s. two d.; ed Latymer Upper School; Chair. Rose, Thomson, Young and Co. Ltd (Lloyd's Brokers) 1956–70; Deputy Chair. Slater Walker Securities Ltd 1964–70; Dir Adwest Ltd 1963–70; mem. Lloyd's 1969–75; Parl. cand. for Dartford 1955 and 1959, MP for Worcester 1961–92; mem. Nat. Exec. of Conservative Party 1956–; Nat. Chair. Young Conservatives 1958–60; mem. Conservative Commonwealth Council Gen. Cttee 1960–61; Parl. Pvt. Sec. to Leader of House of Commons 1963–64; Opposition Spokesman Finance and Econs 1964–66, Transport 1966–68, Housing and Local Govt 1968–70; Minister of Housing and Local Govt 1970; Sec. of State for the Environment 1970–72, for Trade and Industry

1972–74; Opposition Spokesman on Trade and Industry 1974, Defence 1974–75; Sec. of State for Agric., Fisheries and Food 1979–83, for Energy 1983–87, for Wales 1987–90; Dir NM Rothschild (Wales) 1990–93, DC Gardner 1990–93, Tate and Lyle 1990–2001, British Gas 1990–96, Worcester Group 1990–96, Dalgety 1990–96, Smith New Court 1990–95, Liffe 1995–; Chair. (non-exec.) Kleinwort Benson 1997–99; Dept Co-ordinator on Coal Industry 1992–98; Chair. Thornton and Co. 1991–97, Cornhill Insurance 1992–, English Partnerships' (urban regeneration agency) 1992–98; Dir (non-exec.) London Int. Financial Futures and Options Exchange 1995–, Kleinwort Benson Group 1996–98; Vice-Chair. Dresdner Kleinwort Benson 1999–2000, Dresdner Kleinwort Wasserstein 2001–; Pres. British German Chamber of Commerce 1999–; Chair. Viet Nam Fund; mem. Conservative Party; Hon. LLD (Wales) 1991; Commdr.'s Cross of Order of Merit (Germany) 1994. *Publications:* The Ascent of Britain 1977, Trust the People 1987, Staying Power (autobiog.) 1991. *Address:* Abbots Morton Manor, Gooms Hill, Abbots Morton, Worcester, WR7 4LT, England (Home).

WALL, Brian; American sculptor; b. 5 Sept. 1931, London, England; s. of Arthur F. Wall and Dorothy Seymour; m. Sylvia Brown 1973; two s.; ed Luton Coll. of Art, England; numerous one-man exhbns since 1957 including: Lowinsky Gallery, New York City 1987, 1998, Francis-Graham-Dixon Gallery, London 1992, Sheldon Memorial Art Gallery, Univ. of Nebraska 1995, Jernigan Wicker Fine Arts, San Francisco 1995, 1999, Flowers East, London 1999, Flowers West, LA 2002; has participated in numerous group exhbns in UK, Europe, N America, Australia and NZ; retrospective exhbns in Seattle Art Museum 1982, San Francisco Museum of Modern Art 1983; works in many public collections including Tate Gallery, London, Art Gallery of NSW, Sydney, Museum of Art, Dublin, Seattle Art Museum, Univ. Art Museum, Berkeley, Oakland Museum, Calif., Sheldon Memorial Art Gallery, Univ. of Neb.; Asst Prof. of Art, Univ. of Calif. at Berkeley 1975–77, Assoc. Prof. 1977–81, Prof. 1981–94, Emer. Prof. 1994–. *Address:* 306 Lombard Street, San Francisco, CA 94133, USA. *Telephone:* (510) 652-6042.

WALL, Charles Terence Clegg, PhD, FRS; British professor of mathematics; b. 14 Dec. 1936, Bristol; s. of Charles Wall and Ruth Wall (née Clegg); m. Alexandra Joy Hearnshaw 1959; two s. two d.; ed Marlborough Coll. and Trinity Coll. Cambridge; Fellow of Trinity Coll. 1959–64; Harkness Fellow, Inst. for Advanced Study, Princeton, USA 1960–61; lecturer, Univ. of Cambridge 1961–64; Reader in Math. and Fellow of St Catherine's Coll. Oxford 1964–65; Prof. of Pure Math. Univ. of Liverpool 1965–99, now Prof. Emer.; Royal Soc. Leverhulme Visiting Prof., CIEA, Mexico 1967; Science and Eng Research Council (SERC) Sr Research Fellow 1983–88; mem. Council of Royal Soc. 1974–76, Council of London Math. Soc. 1972–80, 1992–96, Pres. 1978–80; Foreign mem. Royal Danish Acad.; Hon. mem. Irish Math Soc. 2001; Treas. Wirral Area SDP 1985–88, Wirral West Liberal Democrat Party 1988–; Jr Berwick Prize 1965, Sr Whitehead Prize 1976, Polya Prize (London Math. Soc. 1988), Sylvester Medal (Royal Soc. 1988). *Publications:* Surgery on Compact Manifolds 1971, A Geometric Introduction to Topology 1971, The Geometry of Topological Stability 1995; over 140 research Publs in math. journals. *Leisure interests:* reading, walking, gardening, home winemaking. *Address:* Department of Mathematical Sciences, The University of Liverpool, Liverpool, L69 3BX (Office); 5 Kirby Park, West Kirby, Wirral, Merseyside, CH48 2HA, England (Home). *Telephone:* (151) 794-4060 (Office); (151) 625-5063 (Home). *E-mail:* ctcw@liv.ac.uk (Office); *Website:* www.liv.ac.uk/~ctcw/homepage.html (Office).

WALL, Frank A., BCL, LLB, LLM.; Irish public official and solicitor; b. 10 Oct. 1949, Limerick; s. of Frank M. Wall and Eileen Pierse; m. Margot Hourigan 1977; three s. one d.; ed Mungret Coll., Limerick, Univ. Coll., Cork, Inc. Law Soc., Dublin and Free Univ. of Brussels; Adviser Group of European Progressive Democrats, European Parl. 1974–79; Adviser to Minister for Agric., Dublin 1980; Nat. Dir of Elections 1982; Senator 1982–83; mem. Exec. Cttee, Irish Council of the European Movt 1980–91; Gen. Sec. Fianna Fáil 1981–91; mem. Bd, Friends of Fianna Fáil Inc., USA 1986–91; Chair. Irish Council of European Movt 1987–91; Co-founder Inst. of European Affairs 1990, Chair. Brussels Br. 1998–2001; Dir Inter-Institutional Affairs, Council of the European Union 1991, currently Dir Directorate-General Legal Service, Gen. Secr. *Publications:* European Regional Policy (with Sean Brosnan) 1978, Changing Balance between European Institutions 1999. *Leisure interests:* politics, gaelic football, golf, rugby, gardening. *Address:* Council of the European Union, rue de la Loi 175, 1048 Brussels, Belgium. *Telephone:* (2) 285-80-55. *Fax:* (2) 285-73-93. *E-mail:* frank.wall@consilium.eu.int (Office).

WALL, Frederick Theodore, B.CHEM., PhD; American physical chemist; b. 14 Dec. 1912, Chisholm, Minn.; s. of Peter Wall and Fanny Rauhala Wall; m. Clara Vivian 1940; two d.; ed Univ. of Minnesota; Instructor to Prof. of Chem., Univ. of Ill. 1937–64, Dean of Grad. Coll. 1955–63; Prof. of Chem., Univ. of Calif. at Santa Barbara 1964–66, Vice-Chancellor Research 1965–66; Vice-Chancellor Grad. Studies and Research and Prof. of Chem., Univ. of Calif. at San Diego 1966–69; Ed. Journal of Physical Chemistry 1965–69; Exec. Dir of American Chem. Soc. 1969–72; Prof. of Chem., Rice Univ. 1972–78, San Diego State Univ. 1979–81; Adjunct Prof. Univ. of Calif., San Diego 1982–90; Fellow American Acad. of Arts and Sciences; mem. NAS; Corresp. mem. Finnish Chemical Soc.; American Chemical Soc. Award in Pure Chem. 1945, Univ. of Minn. Outstanding Achievement Award 1959. *Publications:* Chemical Thermodynamics 1958; numerous scientific articles on polymers, statistics of

macromolecular configurations and theory of reaction probabilities. *Address:* 8515 Costa Verde blvd, Apt. 606, San Diego, CA 92122, USA. *Telephone:* (858) 558-3730. *E-mail:* ftwall@worldnet.att.net (Home).

WALL, Jeff D., MA; Canadian artist and academic; b. 1946, Vancouver; ed Univ. of BC, Courtauld Inst., Univ. of London, UK; Asst Prof. Nova Scotia Coll. of Art and Design 1974–75; Assoc. Prof. Simon Fraser Univ., Vancouver 1976–87; Prof. of Fine Arts, Univ. of BC; works include Destroyed Room 1978, The Children's Pavilion (with Dan Graham), Woman and Her Doctor 1980, Mimic 1982, The Storyteller 1986, Dead Troops Talk 1992, A Sudden Gust of Wind (After Hokusai) 1993; Int. Photography Prize, Hasselblad Foundation 2002. *Exhibitions include:* solo: Nova Gallery, Vancouver 1978, Inst. of Contemporary Arts, UK 1984, Ydessa Gallery, Toronto 1986, 1990, Galerie Johnen & Schottle, Cologne, Germany 1986, 1987, 1989, 1991, 1998, 1999, 2001, Centro d'Arte Reina Sofia, Madrid, Spain 1994, Chicago–Paris Tour 1995–96, Museum of Contemporary Art, LA, USA 1997, Mies van der Rohe Foundation, Barcelona, Spain 1999, Marion Goodman Gallery, New York, USA; group: Vancouver Art Gallery 1969, Information, Museum of Modern Art, New York, USA 1970, Documenta 7, Museum Fridericianum, Kassel, Germany 1982, Nightfire, De Appel, Amsterdam, Netherlands 1987, Galleri Contur, Stockholm, Sweden 1988. *Publications include:* Jeff Wall: Transparencies 1987, De Duve, Thierry and Boris Groys 1996. *Address:* University of British Colombia, Department of Fine Arts, Vancouver, BC V6T 121, USA (Office).

WALL, Sir (John) Stephen, KCMG, LVO; British diplomatist; b. 10 Jan. 1947, Croydon; s. of John Wall and Maria Whitmarsh; m. Catharine Reddaway 1975; one s.; ed Douai School and Selwyn Coll. Cambridge; entered FCO 1968; served Addis Ababa 1969-72, Paris 1972–74; First Sec. FCO 1974–76; Press Officer, No. 10 Downing St 1976–77; Asst Pvt. Sec. to Sec. of State for Foreign and Commonwealth Affairs 1977–79; First Sec. Washington, DC 1979–83; Asst Head, later Head, European Community Dept FCO 1983–88; Pvt. Sec. to Sec. of State for Foreign and Commonwealth Affairs 1988–90, to Prime Minister 1991–93; Amb. to Portugal 1993–95; Perm. Rep. of UK to the European Union 1995–2000; Head European Secr., Cabinet Office 2000–; Hon. Fellow Selwyn Coll. Cambridge 2000. *Leisure interests:* walking, photography, running. *Address:* c/o Cabinet Office, 70 Whitehall, London SW1A 2AS, England (Office).

WALLACE, Bruce, PhD; American professor of genetics; b. 18 May 1920, McKean, Pa; s. of George E. Wallace and Rose Paterson Wallace; m. Miriam Covalla 1945; one s. one d.; ed Columbia Coll. and Columbia Univ.; Research Assoc., Dept of Genetics, Carnegie Inst. of Washington 1947–49; Geneticist, later Asst Dir, Biological Lab., Cold Spring Harbour, NY 1949–58; Assoc. Prof., Cornell Univ. 1958–61, Prof. of Genetics 1961–81; Univ. Distinguished Prof. of Biology, Virginia Polytech. Inst. and State Univ. 1981–94, Prof. Emer. 1994–; mem. NAS, American Acad. of Arts and Sciences; Alexander von Humbolt Sr US Scientist Award 1986. *Publications:* Radiation, Genes and Man (with Th. Dobzhansky) 1959, Adaptation (with A. M. Srb) 1961, Chromosomes, Giant Molecules and Evolution 1966, Topics in Population Genetics 1968, Genetic Load 1970, Essays in Social Biology (3 vols) 1972, Basic Population Genetics 1981, Dobzhansky's Genetics of Natural Populations I–XLIII (with others) 1982, Human Culture: A Moment in Evolution (with others) 1983, Biology for Living (with G. M. Simmons, Jr) 1987, Fifty Years of Genetic Load: An Odyssey 1991, The Search for the Gene 1992, The Study of Gene Action (with J. O. Falkinham) 1997, The Environment: As I See It, Science Is Not Enough 1998, The Environment 2: As I See It, The Mold Must Be Broken 2000. *Leisure interest:* promotion of environmental literacy. *Address:* 940 McBryde Drive, Blacksburg, VA 24060, USA. *Telephone:* (540) 951-2464. *Fax:* (540) 951-2464. *E-mail:* kojima@swva.net (Home).

WALLACE, David James, CBE, DL, PhD, FRS, FREng, FRSE, FInstP, FRSA, CEng; British university vice-chancellor; b. 7 Oct. 1945, Hawick, Scotland; s. of Robert Elder Wallace and Jane McConnell Wallace (née Elliot); m. Elizabeth Anne Yeats 1970; one d.; ed Hawick High School and Edinburgh Univ.; Harkness Fellow, Princeton Univ., USA 1970–72; Lecturer in Physics, Univ. of Southampton 1972–78, Reader 1978–79; Tait Prof. of Math. Physics, Univ. of Edinburgh 1979–93, Head of Physics 1984–87; Vice-Chancellor Loughborough Univ. 1994–; Assoc. Dir Research Initiative on Pattern Recognition, RSRE, Malvern 1986–90; Dir Edin. Concurrent Supercomputer 1987–89, Edin. Parallel Computing Centre 1990–93; mem. Science and Eng Research Council 1990–94 and Chair. Science and Materials Bd; mem. Scottish Higher Educ. Funding Council 1993–97; mem. Eng and Physical Sciences Research Council and Chair. Tech. Opportunities Panel 1994–98; served on various cttees for Tech. Transfer, including LINK/TCS Bd.; currently Chair. Quinquennial Review of TCS; Chair. UK e-Science Steering Cttee.; mem. Bd. UK e-Universities Worldwide Ltd; Dir (non-exec.) Taylor & Francis Group PLC; mem. Council Royal Soc. 2001–; Pres.-elect Inst. of Physics; Maxwell Medal, Inst. of Physics 1980. *Leisure interests:* eating at la Potinière, running. *Address:* Loughborough University, Loughborough, Leics., LE11 3TU, England. *Telephone:* (1509) 222001. *Fax:* (1509) 223900.

WALLACE, Helen, CMG, PhD, FBA; British professor of European studies; b. 25 June 1946, Manchester; d. of the late Edward Rushworth and of Joyce Rushworth (née Robinson); m. William Wallace (now Lord Wallace of Saltaire) 1968; one s. one d.; ed Univs. of Oxford, Bruges, Belgium and Manchester; Lecturer in European Studies, UMIST 1974–78, Visiting Prof. Coll. of Europe, Bruges 1976–2001; in Public Admin., Civil Service Coll. 1978–85;

mem. Planning Staff, FCO 1979–80; Head W European Programme, Royal Inst. of Int. Affairs 1985–92; Prof. of Contemporary European Studies and Dir Sussex European Inst., Univ. of Sussex 1992–2001; Dir Robert Schuman Centre, European Univ. Inst. 2001–; mem. Acad. for Learned Socs. for the Social Sciences 2000; Ordre nat. du Mérite (France) 1996. *Publications:* Policy-Making in the European Community (jtly.) 1983, French and British Foreign Policies in Transition (jtly.) 1990, The Wider Western Europe (Ed.) 1991, The European Community: the Challenge of Enlargement (jtly.) 1992, The Council of Ministers (jtly.) 1997, Participation and Policy-Making (jtly.) 1997, Policy Making in the European Union (Ed.) 2000, Interlocking Dimensions of European Integration (Ed.) 2001. *Leisure interests:* gardening, walking. *Address:* Robert Schuman Centre for Advanced Studies, European University Institute, Via dei Roccettini 9, 50016 San Domenico di Fiesole, Italy (Office). *Telephone:* (55) 4685-792 (Office); (55) 4685-796. *Fax:* (55) 4685-730. *E-mail:* helen.wallace@iue.it (Office).

WALLACE, Ian Bryce, OBE, MA; British singer, actor and broadcaster; b. 10 July 1919, London; s. of the late Sir John Wallace and Mary Temple; m. Patricia G. Black 1948; one s. one d.; ed Charterhouse and Trinity Hall, Cambridge; appeared in buffo roles at Glyndebourne 1948–60 and continued to appear in opera in Britain and briefly in Italy until 1970s; later appeared on concert platforms and also in straight plays, reviews, musicals and pantomimes as well as in many television and radio shows notably My Music; Pres. Inc. Soc. of Musicians 1979–80, Council for Music in Hosps 1987–99; Hon. mem. RAM, Royal Coll. of Music; Hon. MusD (St Andrews Univ.) 1991. *Film appearances include* Plenty, Tom Thumb. *Radio:* panellist, 'My Music', BBC. *Television appearances include:* The Mikado, Singing for Your Supper (opera series, Scottish TV), Porterhouse Blue. *Publications:* autobiog.: Vol. I Promise Me You'll Sing Mud 1975, Vol. II Nothing Quite Like It 1982, Reflections on Scotland 1988. *Leisure interests:* music, theatre, watching sport, reading. *Address:* c/o Peters, Fraser & Dunlop Ltd, Drury House, 34–43 Russell Street, London, WC2B 5HA, England. *Telephone:* (20) 7344-1010.

WALLACE, Rt Hon James Robert (Jim), QC, MA, LLB; Scottish politician; b. 25 Aug. 1954, Annan; s. of John F. T. Wallace and Grace Hannah Maxwell; m. Rosemary Janet Fraser 1983; two d.; ed Annan Acad., Downing Coll. Cambridge, Edinburgh Univ.; Chair. Edin. Univ. Liberal Club 1976–77; called to Scots Bar 1979; advocate 1979–83; mem. Scottish Liberal Exec. 1976–85; Vice-Chair. (Policy) Scottish Liberal Party 1982–85; MP for Orkney and Shetland 1983–2001 (Liberal 1983–88, Liberal Democrat 1988–2001); Hon. Pres. Scottish Young Liberals 1984–85; Liberal Spokesman on Defence 1985–87; Deputy Whip 1985–87; Chief Whip 1987–88; first Liberal Democrat Chief Whip 1988–92; Alliance Spokesman on Transport 1987; Liberal Democrat Spokesman on Employment and Training 1988–92, on Fisheries 1988–97, on Scottish Affairs 1992–, on Maritime Affairs 1994–97; Leader Scottish Liberal Democrats 1992–; Deputy First Minister of the Scottish Exec. and Minister for Justice 1999–. *Leisure interests:* golf, music, travel. *Address:* Scottish Parliament, Edinburgh, EH99 1SP (Office); Northwood House, Tankerness, Orkney, KW17 2QS, Scotland (Home). *Telephone:* (131) 348-5815 (Office); (1856) 861-383 (Home). *Fax:* (131) 348-5807 (Office); (1856) 861-383 (Home). *E-mail:* jim.wallace.msp@scottish.parliament.uk (Office); jimwallace@cix.compulink.co.uk.

WALLACE-CRABBE, Christopher Keith, MA, FAHA; Australian poet and critic; b. 6 May 1934, Melbourne; s. of Kenneth Eyre Inverell Wallace-Crabbe and Phyllis Vera May Wallace-Crabbe (née Cock); m. 1st Helen Margaret Wiltshire 1957; one s. one d.; m. 2nd Marianne Sophie Feil 1979; two s.; ed Melbourne Univ., Yale Univ., USA; cadet metallurgist 1951–52; then journalist, clerk, schoolteacher; Lockie Fellow in Australian Literature, Univ. of Melbourne 1962; Harkness Fellow, Yale Univ. 1965–67; Sr Lecturer in English, Univ. of Melbourne 1967, Reader 1976, Prof. 1987–, Personal Chair. 1987–97; Prof. Emer. Australian Centre 1997–; Visiting Chair. in Australian Studies, Harvard Univ., USA 1987–88; Masefield Prize for Poetry 1957, Farmer's Poetry Prize 1964, Grace Leven Prize 1986, Dublin Prize 1987, Christopher Brennan Award 1990, Age Book of the Year Prize 1995, Philip Hodgins Memorial Medal 2002, Centenary Medal 2003. *Publications:* The Music of Division 1959, Selected Poems 1974, Melbourne or the Bush 1974, The Emotions are not Skilled Workers 1980, Toil and Spin: Two Directions in Modern Poetry 1980, Splinters (novel) 1981, The Amorous Cannibal 1985, I'm Deadly Serious 1988, Sangue è l'Acqua 1989, For Crying out Loud 1990, Falling into Language 1990, Poetry and Belief 1990, From the Republic of Conscience 1992, Rungs of Time 1993, Selected Poems 1956–94 1995, Whirling 1998, By and Large 2001. *Leisure interests:* drawing, tennis, surfing, making artist's books. *Address:* Department of English, University of Melbourne, Parkville, Vic. 3052; Ca d'Oro, 12 Burchett Street, Brunswick, Vic. 3056, Australia. *Telephone:* (3) 9387-3662 (Home); (3) 8344-6864. *E-mail:* ckwc@unimelb.edu.au (Office). *Website:* www.hlc.unimelb.edu.au/cwc/ (Office).

WALLACH, Eli, MS(Educ.); American actor; b. 7 Dec. 1915, Brooklyn, NY; s. of Abraham Wallach and Bertha Schorr; m. Anne Jackson 1948; one s. two d.; ed Univ. of Texas, City Coll. of New York, Neighborhood Playhouse School of Theatre; started theatre career 1946, film career 1955; Donaldson Award, Tony Award, British Film Acad. Award 1956. *Films include:* Baby Doll 1956, The Line-Up 1958, Seven Thieves 1959, The Magnificent Seven 1960, The Misfits 1961, How the West Was Won 1962, The Victors 1963, The Moonspinners 1964, Lord Jim 1965, Genghis Khan 1965, How to Steal a Million 1966, The Good, the Bad and the Ugly 1967, The Tiger Makes Out 1967, Mackenna's Gold 1968, Cinderella Liberty 1973, Domino Principle 1975, The Sentinel 1975, The Deep 1975, Winter Kills 1975, The Silent Flute 1978, Movie Movie 1978, The Hunter 1979, The Wall 1980, The Executioner's Song 1982, Sam's Son 1985, Tough Guys 1986, Rocket to the Moon 1986, Nuts 1987, The Rose Garden 1989, The Godfather III 1990, The Two Jakes 1990, Article 99, Mistress 1991, Night and the City 1991, Honey Sweet Love 1993, Two Much Film 1995, The Associate 1996, Keeping the Faith 1999. *Plays include:* The Rose Tattoo, The Teahouse of the August Moon 1954–55, Camino Real, Luv, Typists and Tiger 1964, Promenade All 1973, Waltz of the Toreadors 1974, The Diary of Anne Frank 1978, Opera Comique 1987, The Flowering Peach in Florida 1987, Visiting Mr. Green 1997, Down the Garden Paths 1998–99, Remembered 1999. *Leisure interest:* photography.

WALLENBERG, Peter, LLM; Swedish business executive; b. 29 May 1926, Stockholm; s. of Dr. Marcus Wallenberg and Dorothy Mackay; m. (divorced); two s. one d.; ed Univ. of Stockholm; various positions with Atlas Copco Group; fmr Chair. Atlas Copco AB, STORA, ASEA; fmr Co-Chair. ASEA Brown Boveri (AAB); First Vice-Chair. Skandinaviska Enskilda Banken 1984–96; Chair. Investor AB 1982–97, Wallenberg Foundation 1982–; Dr. hc (Stockholm School of Econs, Augustana Coll. and Uppsala Coll., USA, Uppsala Univ., Royal Inst. of Tech., Stockholm); Hon. Kt 1989. *Leisure interests:* hunting, tennis, sailing. *Address:* Investor AB, 10332 Stockholm, Sweden. *Telephone:* 86-14-20-00. *Fax:* 86-14-28-15.

WALLER, Rev. Ralph, PhD; British minister of religion and academic; b. 11 Dec. 1945; m. Carol Roberts 1968; one d.; ed John Leggott Grammar School, Scunthorpe, Richmond Coll. Divinity School, Univ. of London, Univ. of Nottingham, King's Coll. London; Service in India, teaching math. and physical educ., House Master Shri Shivah Mil. School, Poona 1967–68; Math. Teacher Riddings Comprehensive School, Scunthorpe 1968–69; Methodist Minister, Melton Mowbray 1972–75; ordained 1975; Minister Elvet Methodist Church, Durham City, Methodist Chaplain, Durham Univ. 1975–81, Chaplain St Mary's Coll. and St Aidan's Coll. 1979–81; Chaplain, Tutor in Theology and Resident Tutor Westminster Coll. Oxford 1981–88; Prin. and Tutor in Theology, Harris Manchester (fmrly Manchester) Coll., Oxford Univ. 1988–, Chair. Faculty of Theology, Oxford Univ. 1995–97, mem. Hebdomadal Council 1997–2000; Chair. Environmental Cttee 1997–2000; Dir Farmington Inst. 2001–; Hon. DLitt (Menlo Coll., Calif.) 1994; Hon. DHum (Ball State Univ., Ind.) 1998; Hon. DHL (St Olaf Coll., Minn.) 2001; Hon. DTheol (Uppsala) 1999; Templeton Prize UK 1993. *Publications:* Christian Spirituality (co-ed.) 1999, John Wesley 2003, Basic Texts in Christian Spirituality (co-ed.) 2003. *Leisure interests:* swimming, walking, browsing round second-hand bookshops. *Address:* Principal's Lodgings, Harris Manchester College, Mansfield Road, Oxford, OX1 3TD, England (Home). *Telephone:* (1865) 271006 (Office). *Fax:* (1865) 281474 (Office). *Website:* www.hmc.ox.ac.uk (Office).

WALLER, Robert James; American writer and musician; b. 1 Aug. 1939; s. of Robert Waller Sr and Ruth Waller; m. Georgia A. Wiedemeier; one d.; ed Northern Iowa and Indiana Univs.; Prof. of Man. Univ. of N Iowa 1968–91, Dean Business School 1979–85; singer; guitarist; flautist. *Album:* The Ballads of Madison County 1993. *Publications:* Just Beyond the Firelight 1988, One Good Road is Enough 1990, Iowa: Perspectives on Today and Tomorrow 1991, The Bridges of Madison County 1992, Slow Waltz at Cedar Bend 1994, Old Songs in a New Café 1994, Selected Essays 1994, Border Music 1995, Puerto-Vallarta Squeeze 1995. *Leisure interests:* photography, basketball. *Address:* c/o Aaron Priest Literary Agency, 708 3rd Avenue, 23rd Floor, New York, NY 10017, USA.

WALLERSTEIN, Ralph O., MD; American professor of medicine; b. 7 March 1922, Düsseldorf, Germany; s. of O. R. Wallerstein and Ilse Hollander; m. Betty A. Christensen 1952; two s. one d.; ed Univ. of California Medical School, San Francisco; Chief of Clinical Hematology, San Francisco Gen. Hosp. 1953–81, Clinical Dir of Blood Bank 1955–80; Chief of Staff, Children's Hosp. 1968–72; Clinical Prof., Univ. of Calif. 1969–; mem. Exec. Cttee American Soc. of Hematology 1971–78, Pres. 1978; Chair. Bd of Govs. American Bd of Internal Medicine 1982–83, Chair. Cttee on Hematology 1974–77; Gov., N Calif., American Coll. of Physicians 1977–81, Chair. Bd of Govs. 1980–81, Regent 1981–87, Pres. 1987–88; mem. Residency Review Cttee for Internal Medicine 1985–; Fellow AAAS, ACP; mem. American Medical Assn, American Fed. for Clinical Research, American Assn of Blood Banks, American Soc. of Hematology, Inst. of Medicine, American Soc. of Clinical Oncology. *Publications:* Iron in Clinical Medicine (with S. R. Mettier) 1958, 27 articles in specialized journals. *Leisure interest:* photography. *Address:* 3447 Clay Street, San Francisco, CA 94118, USA (Home). *Telephone:* (415) 518-5586. *Fax:* (415) 922-6555. *E-mail:* rowmdsf@aol.com (Home).

WALLIS, Stanley David Martin, BCom, FAIM, FCIS, FCIM; Australian financial services executive; b. 23 July 1939, Melbourne; s. of S. E. Wallis; m. Judith Logan 1962; three s. two d.; ed Wesley Coll., Melbourne, Univ. of Melbourne, Stanford Univ., USA; joined APM/Amcor 1960, Chief Accountant 1986, Financial Man. 1972, Deputy Man. Dir 1975, Man. Dir 1977–96; Chair. Amcor Ltd 1997–2000; Dir AMP Ltd 1990–2003, Chair. 2000–03; Chair. Pineapplehead Ltd 2000–; Dir Coles Myer Ltd 1996–, Chair. 1997–; Dir Walter & Eliza Hall Inst. of Medical Research; Chair. and Dir Santos Ltd 1989–94; Dir Australian Foundation Investment Co. 1987–; fmr Dir Nicholas-Kiwi Australasia Ltd, NZ Forest Products Ltd, Mayne Nickless Ltd, Spicers Paper Ltd; Chair. Inquiry into Australian Financial System 1996–97; Pres. Business Council of Australia 1996–98; fmr Vice-Pres. Melbourne Business School,

Univ. of Melbourne; Hon. LLD (Monash); Award for Outstanding Achievement in Business, Melbourne Univ. Grad. School of Man. 1990, Bulletin Deloitte Business Leader Award 1995. *Leisure interests:* tennis, skiing, sailing. *Address:* c/o AMP, AMP Sydney Core Building, 33 Alfred Street, Sydney, NSW 2000, Australia (Office).

WALLOT, Jean-Pierre, OC, LesL, PhD, FRSC; Canadian historian and archivist; b. 22 May 1935, Valleyfield, Québec; s. of the late Albert Wallot and of Adrienne Thibodeau; m. 1st Rita Girard 1957; m. 2nd Denyse Caron 1990; two s. one d.; ed Univ. de Montréal; Prof. and Dir History Dept Univ. de Montreal 1961–66, 1973–85, Vice-Pres. (Academic) 1982–85; Historian Museum of Man of Canada 1966–69; Prof. Univ. of Toronto 1969–71, Concordia Univ. 1971–73; Nat. Archivist of Canada 1985–97; Dir d'études associé, Ecole des Hautes Etudes en Sciences Sociales, Paris 1975, 1979, 1981, 1983, 1984, 1985, 1987, 1989, 1994; Guest Lecturer Univ. of Ottawa 1986–97, Visiting Prof. Dept of History 1997–2000, Dir Centre for Research on French Canadian Culture 2000–; mem. Bd of Govs Univ. of Ottawa 1988–90; Pres. Int. Council of Archives 1992–96; Pres. RSC 1997–99; Pres. Int. Advisory Cttee on Memory of the World, UNESCO 1993–99; mem. European Acad. of Sciences, Arts and Letters 1997–; Dr hc (Rennes) 1987, (Ottawa) 1996; Jacques Ducharme Prize, Asscn Archiv. du Québec 1997; Marie Tremaine Medal (Canadian Bibliographic Soc.) 1973, RSC Tyrrell Medal 1983, Centenary Medal of RSC 1994; Officier Ordre des Arts et Lettres (France) 1987. *Publications:* Intrigues françaises et américaines au Canada 1965, Les Imprimés dans le Bas-Canada (with John Hare) 1967, Un Québec qui bougeait 1973, Patronage et Pouvoir dans le Bas-Canada (with G. Paquet) 1973, Evolution et Eclatement du Monde Rural, France-Québec, XVIᵉ–XXᵉ Siècles (with Joseph Goy) 1986, Constructions identitaires et pratiques sociales (ed.) 2002, La Commission Cepin-Robart quelque vingtans après (ed.). *Leisure interests:* reading, hiking, drums. *Address:* 26-635 Richmond Road, Ottawa, Ont., K2A 0G6, Canada. *Telephone:* (613) 761-7472; (613) 562-5710 (Office). *Fax:* (613) 761-9405; (613) 562-5143 (Office). *E-mail:* jpwallot@ uottowa.ca (Office).

WALLS, Gen. (George) Peter, MBE; Zimbabwean fmr army officer; b. 28 July 1926, Salisbury; ed Plumtree School, Royal Mil. Acad., Sandhurst and Camberley Staff Coll., UK; enlisted in Southern Rhodesian Army 1944; commissioned into the Black Watch (Royal Highland Regt), British Army 1946; attested back to Southern Rhodesian Perm. Staff Corps 1948, commissioned 1949; Commdr C. Squadron, 22nd Special Air Service in Malaya 1951–53; Officer Commdg Tactical Wing, later Chief Instructor, School of Infantry 1954–56; Co. Commdr Northern Rhodesian Regt 1956–59; Brigade Maj. Copperbelt Area and later N Rhodesia District 1961–62; Adjutant-Gen. Rhodesian Army 1962–64; CO 1st Bn Rhodesian Light Infantry 1964–67; Commdr 2nd Brigade 1967–68; Chief of Staff, Rhodesian Army 1968–72, Commdr 1972–77; Commdr Combined Operations 1977–80, of Jt Operations 1980; Grand Officer of the Legion of Merit, Defence Cross for Distinguished Service.

WALLSTRÖM, Margot; Swedish politician; b. 28 Sept. 1954, Kåge, Västerbotten Co.; m. Håkan Wallström; two s.; Organizing Sec. Värmland br., Social Democratic Youth League; bank clerk, Sparbanken Alfa, Värmland 1977–79; Chief Accountant 1986–88; MP 1979–85; fmr mem. Värmland Co. Council, Directorate of Bd of Civil Aviation, Directorate of Nat. Environment Protection Bd etc.; Minister with responsibility for Ecclesiastical, Consumers, Equality and Youth Affairs, Ministry of Public Admin. 1988–92; Minister of Cultural Affairs 1994–96, of Health and Social Affairs 1996–98; EU Commr for the Environment July 1999–. *Address:* Commission of the European Communities, 200 rue de la Loi, 1049 Brussels, Belgium (Office).

WALMSLEY, David George, PhD, DSc, MRIA; British professor of physics; b. 3 Feb. 1938, Newtownstewart, N Ireland; s. of Robert Gwynne Walmsley and Elizabeth Johnston; m. Margaret Heather Edmonstone 1965; two s.; ed Royal School, Armagh, Queen's Univ. Belfast and McMaster Univ., Hamilton, Ont.; NRC Canada Post-doctoral Fellow, MacMaster Univ. 1965; Scientific Officer, Sr Scientific Officer, AERE Harwell 1966–70; Lecturer, Sr Lecturer, Reader in Physics, New Univ. of Ulster 1970–84; Prof. of Physics, Univ. of Ulster 1984–88; Prof. of Physics, Queen's Univ. Belfast 1988–, Dir School of Math. and Physics 1993–98, Dean Faculty of Science and Agric. 1998–2002; Fellow Inst. of Physics 1980, American Physical Soc. 2001. *Publications:* articles in learned journals. *Address:* Department of Pure and Applied Physics, Queen's University, Belfast, BT7 1NN (Office); 5 Newforge Grange, Belfast, BT9 5QB (Home); 25 Swilly Road, Portstewart, BT55 7DJ, Northern Ireland. *Telephone:* (2890) 273531 (Office); (2890) 664141 (Home); (2870) 833257. *E-mail:* dg.walmsley@qub.ac.uk (Office).

WALPORT, Mark Jeremy, MA, MB, BChir, PhD, FRCP, FRCPath, FMedSci; British professor of medicine; b. 25 Jan. 1953; s. of Samuel Walport and Doreen Walport (née Music); m. Julia Elizabeth Neild 1986; one s. three d.; ed St Paul's School, London, Clare Coll. Cambridge, Middx Hosp. Medical School; house officer, Middx. Hosp. and Queen Elizabeth II Hosp., Welwyn 1977–78, House Officer 1978–80; Hon. Registrar, Brompton Hosp. 1980; Registrar, Hammersmith Hosp. 1980–82, Hon. Consultant Physician 1985–, Dir Research and Devt 1994–98; MRC Training Fellow, MRC Mechanisms in Tumour Immunity Unit, Cambridge 1982–85; Harrison–Watson Student, Clare Coll. Cambridge 1982–85; Sr Lecturer in Rheumatology, Imperial Coll. School of Medicine 1985–90, Reader Rheumatological Medicine 1990–91, Prof. of Medicine 1991–, Head of Div. of Medicine 1997–; Gov. Wellcome Trust

2000–03, Dir 2003–; mem. Scientific Advisory Bd, Cantab Pharmaceuticals, Cambridge 1989–2000, Research and Devt Advisory Bd, Smithkline Beecham 1998–2000; mem. Council, British Soc. for Rheumatology 1989–95, British Soc. for Immunology 1998–; Asst Ed. British Journal of Rheumatology 1990–97; Ed. Clinical and Experimental Immunology 1990–97; Series Ed. British Medical Bulletin 1998–; Roche Prize for Rheumatology 1991, Graham Bull Prize in Clinical Science 1996. *Publications:* Immunobilogy (Jt author); Clinical Aspects of Immunology (Jt Ed.); numerous papers published in scientific journals on immunology and rheumatology. *Leisure interest:* natural history. *Address:* Division of Medicine, Imperial College School of Medicine, Hammersmith Hospital, Du Cane Road, London, W12 0NN, England (Office). *Telephone:* (20) 8383-3299 (Office).

WALSER, Martin, DPhil; German writer; b. 24 March 1927, Wasserburg/ Bodensee; s. of Martin Walser and Augusta Schmid; m. Käthe Jehle 1950; four d.; ed Theologisch-Philosophische Hochschule, Regensburg and Univ. of Tübingen; writer 1951–; Group 47 Prize 1955, Hermann-Hesse Prize 1957, Gerhart-Hauptmann Prize 1962, Schiller Prize 1980, Büchner Prize 1981, Orden pour le mérite 1994, Friedenspreis des Deutschen Buchhandels 1998; Grosses Bundesverdienstkreuz mit Stern 1997. *Publications:* short stories: Ein Flugzeug über dem Haus 1955, Lügengeschichten 1964; novels: Ehen in Philippsburg 1957, Halbzeit 1960, Das Einhorn 1966, Fiction 1970, Die Gallistlische Krankheit 1972, Der Sturz 1973, Jenseits der Liebe 1976, Ein fliehendes Pferd 1978, Seelenarbeit 1979, Das Schwanenhaus 1980, Brief an Lord Liszt 1982, Brandung 1985, Dorle und Wolf 1987, Jagd 1988, Die Verteidigung der Kindheit 1991, Ohne einander 1993, Finks Krieg 1996, Ein springender Brunnen 1998, Der Lebenslauf der Liebe 2001, Death of a Critic 2002; plays: Der Abstecher 1961, Eiche und Angora 1962, Überlebensgross Herr Krott 1963, Der schwarze Schwan 1964, Die Zimmerschlacht 1967, Ein Kinderspiel 1970, Das Sauspiel 1975, In Goethe's Hand 1982, Die Ohrfeige 1986, Das Sofa 1992, Kaschmir in Parching 1995; essays: Beschreibung einer Form, Versuch über Franz Kafka 1961, Erfahrungen und Leseerfahrungen 1965, Heimatkunde 1968, Wie und wovon handelt Literatur 1973, Wer ist ein Schriftsteller 1978, Selbstbewusstsein und Ironie 1981, Messmers Gedanken 1985, Über Deutschland reden 1988, Vormittag eines Schriftstellers 1994, Messmers Reisen 2003; poems: Der Grund zur Freude 1978. *Address:* 88662 Überlingen-Nussdorf, Zum Hecht 36, Germany. *Telephone:* (7551) 4131. *Fax:* (7551) 68494.

WALSH, Arthur Stephen, CBE, MA, FEng, FIEE; British business executive; b. 16 Aug. 1926, Wigan; s. of Wilfrid Walsh and Doris Walsh; m. 1st. Gwendoline Mary Walsh (divorced 1983); m. 2nd Judith Martha Westenborg 1985; one s. one d.; ed Selwyn Coll. Cambridge; joined GEC 1952, various sr appointments, including Tech. Dir of GEC/AEL 1952–79; Man. Dir Marconi Space and Defence Systems 1979–82; Man. Dir The Marconi Co. 1982–85; Chief Exec. STC PLC (now Northern Telecom Europe Ltd) 1985–91; Chair. Telemetrix PLC 1991–97, Simoco Int. Ltd 1997–; Dir FKI PLC 1991–99, Deputy Chair. 1993; Hon. DSc (Ulster) 1988, (Southampton) 1993. *Leisure interests:* sailing, skiing, golf. *Address:* Aiglemont, Trout Rise, Loudwater, Rickmansworth, Herts., WD3 4JS, England.

WALSH, Courtney Andrew, OJ; Jamaican cricketer; b. 30 Oct. 1962, Kingston; s. of Joan Woollaston; right-hand batsman, right-arm fast bowler; player with maj. teams West Indies, Gloucs. and Jamaica; played in 132 Tests; Test debut with West Indies against Australia at Perth 1984–85; world record 519 Test wickets (average 24.44) at time of his retirement in April 2001 and 1,807 first-class wickets (average 21.71); Wisden Cricketer of the Year 1987. *Leisure interests:* cooking, dancing, music, cars.

WALSH, Don, MA, MS, PhD; American business executive, fmr university administrator and fmr naval officer; b. 1931, Berkeley, Calif.; s. of J. Don Walsh and Marta G. Walsh; m. Joan A. Betzmer 1962; one s. one d.; ed San Diego State Coll., Texas A & M Univ. and US Naval Acad.; entered navy 1950, submarine service 1956; became Officer-in-Charge Submersible Test Group and Bathyscaph Trieste 1959, made record dive to 35,780 ft., Jan. 1960; Submarine Service 1962–64; at Dept of Oceanography, Texas A & M Univ. 1965–68; commanded submarine Bashaw 1968–69; Scientific Liaison Officer Submarine Devt Group One 1969–70; Special Asst to Asst Sec. of the Navy for Research and Devt, Washington, DC 1970–73; Resident Fellow, Woodrow Wilson Int. Center for Scholars 1973–74; Deputy Dir Naval Labs. 1974–75; retd from navy with rank of Capt. 1975; Dir Inst. for Marine and Coastal Studies and Prof. of Ocean Eng. Univ. of Southern Calif. 1975–83; Pres., CEO Int. Maritime Inc. 1976–; Vice-Pres. Parker Diving Service 1985–94; mem. Marine Bd, Nat. Research Council 1990–93; Exec. Dir Deep Ocean Eng 1990–2000; mem. Bd of Dirs Explorers Club 1994–2000; mem. AAAS, US Naval Inst., Nat. Advisory Cttee on Oceans and Atmosphere 1979–86, Law of the Sea Advisory Cttee (US State Dept) 1979–83, Soc. of Naval Architects and Marine Engineers, American Soc. for Naval Engineers, Bd of Govs, Calif. Maritime Acad. 1985–94; Ed. Marine Tech. Soc. Journal 1976–80; mem. Nat. Acad. of Eng 2001–; Hon. Life mem. Explorers Club, Adventurers Club, Marine Tech. Soc. 1980, American Geographical Soc. 2000; Legion of Merit (two awards); Gold Medals from City of Trieste and Chicago Geographic Socs, US Coast Guard Meritorious Public Service Medal 1980, Meritorious Service Medal (two awards), Lowell Thomas Award, Explorers' Club 1987, Compass Distinguished Achievement Award, Marine Tech. Soc. 1996, Explorers' Medal, Explorers' Club 2001, L'Etoile Polaire, Jales Verne Adventures 2001. *Publications:* author of more than 200 papers, articles, etc. on marine subjects; ed. and contrib. Law of the Sea: Issues in Ocean Resources Management; Energy and Resource Development of the Continental Margins (co-ed.) 1980, Energy from the Sea: Challenge for the Decade (ed.) 1982, Waste Disposal in the Oceans: Minimum Impact, Maximize Benefits (co-ed.) 1983, Twenty Thousand Jobs Under the Sea: A History of Diving. *Leisure interests:* writing, travel, sailing, flying. *Address:* International Maritime Inc., 14578 Sitkum Lane, Myrtle Point, OR 97458, USA (Office). *Telephone:* (541) 572-2313. *Fax:* (541) 572-4041.

WALSH, Edward M., B.ENG, MSc, PhD, FIEE, FRSA; Irish university president; b. 3 Dec. 1939, Cork; s. of Michael Walsh and Margaret Walsh (née Leonard); m. Stephanie Barrett 1965; three s. one d.; ed Nat. Univ. of Ireland, Iowa State Univ., USA; Assoc., U.S. Atomic Energy Comm. Lab., Ames, Ia 1963–65; Assoc. Prof. Va Polytechic Inst. and State Univ. 1965–69; Dir Energy Research Group Programme, Va 1966–69; Founding Pres. Univ. of Limerick 1970–98, now Pres. Emer.; Founding Chair. Nat. Self-Portrait Collection of Ireland 1979–, Nat. Technological Park 1983–88, Nat. Council for Curriculum and Assessment 1984–90; mem. Bd Nat. Microelectronics Applications Centre 1981–84, Shannon Devt 1976– (Chair. 1987); Vice-Pres. Int. Asscn of Univ. Pres.'s 1987–99; Chair. Cttee of Heads of Irish Univs. 1991–92, Irish Council for Science, Tech. and Innovation 1997–, Citywest Growcorp 1998–; mem. Royal Irish Acad., NY Acad. of Science 1988; Hon. mem. Royal Hibernian Acad. of Arts 1994, Nat. Coll. of Art and Design 1997; Fellow Inst. of Engineers of Ireland, Irish Acad. of Eng 1998; Freeman of the City of Limerick 1995; Hon. LLD (Dublin) 1992, (Queen's, Belfast) 1995, (Nat. Univ.) 1998; Hon. DSc (Ulster) 1997. *Publications:* Energy Conversion: electro-mechanical-direct-nuclear 1967, Fluid Dynamic Energy Conversion 1967; and over 50 Publs in various journals and proceedings. *Leisure interests:* sailing, skiing, gardening, silversmithing, painting, violin. *Address:* University of Limerick, Limerick (Office); Oakhampton House, Newport, Co. Tipperary, Ireland (Home). *Telephone:* (61) 213198 (Office). *Fax:* (61) 213197.

WALSH, Joe; Irish politician; b. May 1943, Ballineen, Co. Cork; m. Marie Donegan; three s. two d.; ed Univ. Coll. Cork; fmr dairy man.; mem. Irish Creamery Mans. Asscn, Soc. of Dairy Tech., mem. Cork Co. Council 1974–91; mem. Dáil 1977–81, 1982–; Senator 1981–82; Minister of State, Dept of Agric. and Food 1987, 1989–93; Minister for Agric., Food and Forestry 1993–94, Agric., Food and Rural Devt 1997–; mem. Fianna Fáil. *Address:* Department of Agriculture, Food and Rural Development, Agriculture House, Kildare Street, Dublin 2 (Office); Dáil Eireann, Dublin 2; 5 Emmet Square, Clonakilty, Co. Cork, Ireland. *Telephone:* (1) 6072000 (Office); (23) 33575 (Home). *Fax:* (1) 6616263 (Office). *E-mail:* information@daff.irlgov.ie/ (Office). *Website:* www.gov.ie/daff (Office).

WALSH, Lawrence Edward, LLD; American lawyer; b. 8 Jan. 1912, Port Maitland, NS, Canada; s. of Dr Cornelius E. Walsh and Lila M. Sanders; m. Mary A. Porter; one s. four d.; ed Columbia Univ.; mem. Bar, New York State 1936, Dist of Columbia 1981, Oklahoma 1981, US Supreme Court 1951; Special Asst Attorney-Gen. Drukman Investigation 1936–38; Deputy Asst Dist Attorney, NY Co. 1938–41; Assoc. Davis Polk, Wardwell, Sunderland and Kiendl 1941–43; Asst Counsel to Gov. of New York 1943–49, Counsel to Gov. 1950–51; Counsel, Public Service Comm. 1951–53; Gen. Counsel, Exec. Dir Waterfront Comm. of NY Harbor 1953–54; US Judge, S Dist NY 1954–57; US Deputy Attorney-Gen. 1957–60; Partner, Davis, Polk & Wardwell 1961–81; Counsel, Crowe & Dunlevy, Oklahoma City 1981–; Independent Counsel, 'Iran-Contra' investigation 1986–93; Pres. American Bar Asscn 1975–76; Trustee Emer., Columbia Univ.; many other public appointments and mem. numerous bar and lawyers' asscns. *Address:* 1800 Mid-America Towers, Oklahoma City, OK 73102 (Office); 1902 Bedford Drive, Oklahoma City, OK 73116, USA (Home).

WALSH, Paul S.; British business executive; joined GrandMet's brewing div. Watney Mann and Truman Brewers 1982, Finance Dir 1986, Chief Financial Officer Inter-Continental Hotels 1987, GrandMet's Food Div. 1989, CEO Pillsbury 1990, mem. Bd 1995; mem. Bd Diageo PLC (f. after merger of GrandMet and Guinness) 1997–, COO 2000–01, CEO 2001–; CEO Guinness/UDV. *Address:* Diageo PLC, 8 Henrietta Place, London, W1M 9AG, England (Office). *Telephone:* (20) 7927-5200 (Office). *Fax:* (20) 7927-4641 (Office). *Website:* www.diageo.com (Office).

WALTER, Bernhard; German banker; joined Dresdner Bank on leaving school; fmr responsibilities include operations in the fmr GDR, corp. finance, Eastern European operations; mem. Bd 1987–2000, Chair. 1998–2000. *Leisure interests:* golf, jogging, music. *Address:* c/o Dresdner Bank AG, Jurgen-Ponto-Platz 1, 60301 Frankfurt am Main, Germany.

WALTER, Norbert, Dr rer. pol; German economist; b. 23 Sept. 1944, Weckbach/Unterfranken; s. of Heinrich Walter and Erna Walter; m. Christa Bayer 1967; two d.; ed Johann Wolfgang Goethe Univ., Frankfurt; affiliated Inst. for Capital Market Research, Frankfurt 1968–71; mem. staff Kiel Inst. of World Econs, Kiel 1971–86, Asst to Pres. and head various research groups 1971–77, Head Dept on Business Cycle in the World Economy, subsequently Resource Econs Dept 1977–85; fmr Professorial Lecturer, Christian Albrechts Univ., Kiel; John McCloy Distinguished Research Fellow and Resident Scholar, Johns Hopkins Univ., Washington, DC 1986–87; Sr Economist Deutsche Bank, Frankfurt 1987–90, Chief Economist Deutsche Bank Group 1990–, Man. Dir Deutsche Bank Research 1992–; mem. EU Inter-institutional Monitoring Group for Securities Markets 2002–. *Publications include:* Was würde Erhard heute tun?, Wohin treibt die Wirtschaft?—Die Wende zu mehr Markt (co-author) 1984, Strengths, Weaknesses and Prospects of the German

Economy, in The Future of Germany (Ed. Gary Geipel) 1990, Weniger Staat—Mehr Markt 1993, Der neue Wohlstand der Nation 1993, Ein Plädoyer für die Marktwirtschaft (with Astrid Rosenschon) 1996, Der Euro—Kurs auf die Zukunft 1997. *Leisure interests:* jogging, rock/glacier climbing. *Address:* Deutsche Bank Research, Postfach, 60272 Frankfurt am Main (Office); Bismarckstr. 28, 65812 Bad Soden, Germany (Home). *Telephone:* (69) 91031810 (Office). *Fax:* (69) 91031826. *E-mail:* norbert.walter@db.com (Office). *Website:* www.norbert-walter.com (Office).

WALTERS, Sir Alan Arthur, Kt, BSc; British economist; b. 17 June 1926, Leicester; s. of James Arthur Walters and Clarabel Walters; m. 2nd Margaret Patricia Wilson 1975; one d. by previous m.; ed Alderman Newton's Secondary School, Leicester, Univ. Coll., Leicester and Nuffield Coll. Oxford; Prof. of Econometrics and Social Statistics, Univ. of Birmingham 1961–68; Sir Ernest Cassel Prof. of Econs, LSE 1968–75; Prof. of Econs, Johns Hopkins Univ., Baltimore, Md 1976–91; Visiting Fellow, Nuffield Coll. Oxford 1982–83; Econ. Adviser to World Bank, Washington, DC 1976–80; Econ. Adviser to Margaret Thatcher (now Baroness Thatcher, q.v., 1981–89 (part-time 1983–89); Deputy Chair. and Dir AIG Trading Co. 1991–; mem. Referendum Party 1995–; Hon. DLitt (Leicester) 1981; Hon. D.Soc.Sci. (Birmingham) 1984; Hon. PhD (Francisco Marroquin Univ.) 1994. *Publications:* Growth without Development 1966, Economics of Road User Charges 1968, Money in Boom and Slump 1968, An Introduction to Economics 1969, The Economics of Ocean Freight Rates 1969, Noise and Prices 1975, Port Pricing and Investment for Developing Countries 1979, Microeconomic Theory (with Richard Layard) 1978, Britain's Economic Renaissance: Margaret Thatcher's Reforms 1979–1984 1986, Sterling in Danger 1990, The Economics and Politics of Money 1998. *Leisure interests:* theatre, opera, music. *Address:* AIG Trading Group, 9 Thomas More Square, Thomas More Street, London, E1W 1WZ (Office); 3 Chesterfield Hill, London, W1J 5BJ, England. *Telephone:* (20) 7491-7345; (20) 7709-2504 (Office). *Fax:* (20) 7499-3982 (Home); (20) 7709-2998 (Office). *E-mail:* sir_alan@aigtc.com, siralan@aigi.rom (Office); paddie.walters@ukgateway.net (Home).

WALTERS, Barbara, BA; American television broadcaster; b. 25 Sept. 1931, Brookline, Mass.; d. of Lou Walters and Dena (née Selett) Walters; m. 1st Lee Guber 1963 (divorced 1976); one adopted d.; m. 2nd Merv Adelson 1986 (divorced 1993); ed Sarah Lawrence Coll., Bronxville, NY; fmr writer and producer with WNBC TV, then with Station WPIX and CBS TV morning broadcasts; Producer, NBC TV; joined Today programme, NBC TV 1961 as a writer, then gen. reporter, regular panel mem. 1963–74, Co-Host 1974–76; Moderator, Not for Women Only (syndicated TV programme) for five years; Corresp., ABC News, Co-Anchor of evening news programme 1976–78, Co-Host 20/20 1979–; Host Barbara Walters Specials 1976–, Ten Most Fascinating People 1994–; Co.-Exec. producer The View (ABC), NY 1997–; contrib. Issues and Answers; retrospective of career at Museum of Broadcasting, NY 1988; Hon. LHD (Ohio State Univ., Marymount Coll., New York Temple Univ., Wheaton Coll., Hofstra Univ.); Broadcaster of the Year, Int. Radio and TV Soc. 1975, Emmy Award of Nat. Acad. of TV Arts and Sciences 1975, 1983, Silver Satellite Award, American Women in Radio and TV 1985, named one of the 100 Most Important Women of the Century, Good Housekeeping 1985, Pres.'s Award, Overseas Press Club 1988, Lowell Thomas Award for Journalism 1990, 1994, Lifetime Achievement Award, Int. Women's Media Foundation 1992, Lifetime Achievement Award, Daytime Emmy Awards 2000 and several other awards. *Publications include:* How to Talk with Practically Anybody about Practically Anything 1970; contribs. to Good Housekeeping, Family Weekly, Reader's Digest. *Address:* 20/20, 147 Columbus Avenue, 10th Floor, New York, NY 10023; Barwall Productions, The Barbara Walters Specials, 825 7th Avenue, Third Floor, New York, NY 10019, USA.

WALTERS, John P., MA; American government administrator; ed Mich. State Univ., Univ. of Toronto; Lecturer Mich. State Univ., Boston Coll.; acting Asst Dir and Programme Officer Educ. Programmes Div., Nat. Endowment for the Humanities 1982–85; Asst to Sec. of Educ., US Dept of Educ. 1985–88; Chief of Staff White House Office of National Drug Control Policy (ONDCP) 1989–91, Deputy Dir Supply Reduction 1991–93, Dir ONDCP 2001–; Visiting Fellow Hudson Inst. 1993; Pres. New Citizenship Project –1996; Pres. Philanthropy Round Table 1996–2001. *Publications include:* Body Count: Moral Poverty and How to Win America's War Against Crime and Drugs (with William J. Bennett and John J. Di Iulio Jr). *Address:* Office of National Drug Control Policy, 750 17th Street, NW, Washington, DC 20006, USA (Office). *Telephone:* (202) 395-6700 (Office). *Fax:* (202) 395-6708 (Office). *Website:* www.whitehousedrugpolicy.gov (Office).

WALTERS, Julie, OBE; British actress; b. 22 Feb. 1950, Birmingham; d. of the late Thomas Walters and Mary Bridget O'Brien; m. Grant Roffey 1998; one d.; ed St Pauls Prep. School, Edgbaston, Holly Lodge Grammar School for Girls, Smethwick, Manchester Polytechnic; School Gov., Open Univ. 1990; Variety Club Best Newcomer Award 1980, Best Actress Award 1984, British Acad. Award for Best Actress 1984, Golden Globe Award 1984, Show Business Personality of the Year Variety Club Award 2001. *Stage appearances include:* Educating Rita 1980, Fool for Love 1984/85, When I was a Girl I used to Scream and Shout 1986/87, Frankie and Johnny in the Clair de Lune 1989, The Rose Tattoo 1991, All My Sons (Olivier Award 2001) 2000. *Films include:* Educating Rita 1983, She'll be Wearing Pink Pyjamas 1984, Personal Services 1986, Pick Up Your Ears 1986, Buster 1987, Mack the Knife 1988, Killing Dad 1989, Stepping Out (Variety Club Award for Best Actress 1991) 1991, Just Like a Woman 1992, Sister My Sister 1994, Intimate Relations 1996,

Titanic Town 1997, Girls Night 1997, All Forgotten 1999, Dancer 1999, Billy Elliot (Evening Standard Award, BAFTA Award) 2000, Harry Potter 2001. *TV includes:* Talent 1980, Wood and Walters 1981, Boys from the Blackstuff 1982, Say Something Happened 1982, Victoria Wood as seen on TV 1984, 1986, 1987, The Birthday Party 1986, Her Big Chance 1987, GBH 1991, Stepping Out 1991, Julie Walters and Friends 1991, Clothes in the Wardrobe 1992, Wide Eyed and Legless 1993, Bambino Mio 1993, Pat and Margaret 1994, Jake's Progress 1995, Little Red Riding Hood 1995, Intimate Relations 1996, Julie Walters is an Alien 1997, Dinner Ladies 1998, Jack and the Beanstalk 1998, Dinner Ladies 1999, Oliver Twist 1999, My Beautiful Son (BAFTA Award) 2001, Murder (BAFTA and Royal TV Soc. Awards for Best Actress 2003) 2002. *Publication:* Baby Talk 1990. *Leisure interests:* reading, travel. *Address:* c/o ICM, 76 Oxford Street, London, W1N 0AX, England.

WALTERS, Sir Peter Ingram, Kt, BCom; British oil executive; b. 11 March 1931, Birmingham; s. of the late Stephen Walters and of Edna F. Walters (née Redgate); m. 1st Patricia Anne Tulloch 1960 (divorced 1991); two s. one. d.; m. 2nd Meryl Marshall 1992; ed King Edward's School, Birmingham and Univ. of Birmingham; served Royal Army Service Corps 1952–54; joined BP 1954, Vice-Pres. BP N America 1965–67, Gen. Man. Supply and Devt 1969–70, Regional Dir Western Hemisphere 1971–72; Dir BP Trading Ltd 1971–73, BP Chemicals Int. 1972, Chair. 1978–90; Deputy Chair. The British Petroleum Co. Ltd 1980–81, Chair. 1981–90; Vice-Pres. Gen. Council of British Shipping 1974–76, Pres. 1977–78; Pres. Soc. of Chemical Industry 1978–79, Inst. of Manpower Studies 1980–86; Dir Post Office 1978–79, Nat. Westminster Bank 1981– (Deputy Chair. 1988–89); Dir Thorn EMI (now EMI) 1989–, Deputy Chair. 1990–99; Dir SmithKline Beecham PLC 1989–, Deputy Chair. 1990–94, Chair. 1994–2000; Chair. Blue Circle Industries Ltd 1990–96, Midland Bank PLC 1992; Deputy Chair. HSBC Holdings 1992–2001; Adviser Union Bank of Switzerland 1990–92; Dir (non-exec.) Saatchi and Saatchi 1993–2000; Deputy Chair. GlaxoSmithKline PLC 2000–; mem. of Council, Industrial Soc.; Gov. London Business School 1981–91; Pres. Inst. of Dirs 1986–92; Trustee, mem. Foundation Bd, Nat. Maritime Museum 1982–89; Chair. Int. Man. Inst., Geneva 1984–86; Hon. D.Univ. (Birmingham) 1986, (Stirling) 1987; Commdr Order of Léopold (Belgium). *Leisure interests:* golf, gardening, sailing. *Address:* GlaxoSmithKline PLC, New Horizons Court, Brentford, TW8 9EP; 22 Hill Street, London, W1X 7FU, England. *Telephone:* (20) 8975-2000. *Fax:* (20) 8975-2040.

WALTERS, Sir Roger Talbot, MSc, KBE, RIBA, F.I.STRUCT.E.; British architect; b. 31 March 1917, Chorley Wood, Herts.; s. of Alfred Bernard Walters; m. 1st Gladys Millie Evans 1946 (divorced); m. 2nd Claire Myfanwy Chappell 1976; ed Oundle School, Architectural Asscn School of Architecture, Liverpool Univ. and Birkbeck Coll.; entered office of Sir E. Owen Williams 1936; Directorate of Constructional Design, Ministry of Works 1941–43; served in Royal Engineers 1943–46; Architect, Timber Devt Assn 1946–49; Prin. Asst Architect, E Region, British Railways 1949–59; Chief Architect (Devt), Directorate of Works, War Office 1959–62; Deputy Dir-Gen. Research and Devt, Ministry of Public Bldgs. and Works 1962–67, Dir-Gen. for Production 1967–69, Controller Gen. 1969–71; Architect and Controller of Construction Services, Greater London Council 1971–78; Prin. The Self-Employed Agency 1981–83; pvt. practice 1984–87; Hon. FAIA. *Address:* 46 Princess Road, London, NW1 8JL, England (Home). *Telephone:* (20) 7722-3740.

WALTHER, Herbert, Dr rer. nat; German professor of physics; b. 19 Jan. 1935, Ludwigshafen; s. of Philipp Walther and Anna Lorenz; m. Margot Gröschel 1962; one s. one d.; ed Univ. of Heidelberg and Tech. Univ. of Hanover; Asst Univ. of Hanover 1963–68, Lecturer in Physics 1968–69; Prof. of Physics, Univ. of Bonn 1971, Univ. of Cologne 1971–75, Univ. of Munich 1975–; Dir Max-Planck-Inst. für Quantenoptik 1981–; Vice-Pres. Max-Planck Soc. 1991–96; mem. Bavarian Acad. of Sciences, Acad. Leopoldina, Academia Europaea; Corresp. mem. Acad. of Sciences, Heidelberg, Nordrhein-Westfälische Akademie der Wissenschaften; mem. Convent for Tech. Sciences of the German Acads; Hon. mem. Loránd Eötvös Physical Soc., Hungary, Hungarian Acad. of Science, Romanian Acad.; Foreign mem. Russian Acad. of Sciences 1999–; Foreign Hon. mem. American Acad. of Arts and Sciences; Hon. Prof. Academia Sinica, China; Dr. hc (Hanover Univ., Lomonosov Univ., Moscow); Max Born Prize, Inst. of Physics and the German Physics Soc. 1978, Einstein Prize 1988, Carl-Friedrich-Gauss Medal 1989, Townes Medal (American Optical Soc.) 1990, Michelson Medal (Franklin Inst.) 1993, King Faisal Prize for Physics 1993, Humboldt Medal, Alexander von Humboldt-Stiftung 1997, Stern Gerlach Medal, German Physical Soc. 1998, Ernst Hellmut-Vits Prize 1998; Willis E. Lamb Medal for Laser Physics, Physics of Quantum Electronics Winter Colloquium, Snowbird, Salt Lake City 1999, EPS Quantum Electronics Prize 2000, Alfried Krupp Prize for Science 2002. *Publications:* 10 books on laser spectroscopy and high power lasers and applications, including Was ist Licht? Von der Klassischen Optik zur Quantenoptik 1999; 550 articles in professional journals. *Address:* Max-Planck-Institut für Quantenoptik und Sektion Physik der Universität München, 85748 Garching (Office); Egenhoferstrasse 7a, 81243 Munich, Germany (Home). *Telephone:* (89) 28914142; (89) 32905704 (Office); (89) 8349859 (Home). *Fax:* (89) 32905200; (89) 32905710 (Office); (89) 8349859 (Home). *E-mail:* Herbert.Walther@mpq.mpg.de (Office). *Website:* mste.laser.physik .uni-muenchen.de (Office).

WALTON, Henry John, MD, PhD, FRCP, F.R.C.PSYCH., DPM; British psychiatrist, physician and medical educator; b. 15 Feb. 1924, Kuruman, South Africa; m. Dr Sula Wolff 1959; ed Univs of Cape Town, London and Edinburgh and Columbia Univ., New York; Registrar in Neurology and Psychiatry, Univ. of Cape Town 1946–54, Head, Dept of Psychiatry 1957–60; Sr Registrar, Maudsley Hosp. London 1955–57; Sr Lecturer in Psychiatry, Univ. of Edin. 1962–70, Prof. of Psychiatry 1970–85, Prof. Emer. 1990–, Prof. of Int. Medical Educ. 1986–; Ed. Medical Educ. 1976–98, Ed. Emer. 1998–; Pres. Asscn for Medical Educ. in Europe 1972–86, Hon. Life Pres. 1986–; Pres. World Fed. for Medical Educ. 1983–97, mem. Exec. Bd 1997–; frequent consultant to WHO and mem. Advisory Panel on Health Manpower; led worldwide inquiry into training of doctors since 1983; presided at World Summit on Medical Educ., Edin. 1988, 1993, organized six Regional Confs 1986–88, 1994–95; Deputy Dir Edin. Printmakers; mem. Soc. of Medical Studies of Greece; Academician, Acad. of Medical Sciences of Buenos Aires, Polish Acad. of Medicine, Royal Acad. of Medicine of Belgium; Foundation mem. Nat. Asscn for Medical Educ. of Czechoslovakia; Hon. MD (Uppsala, New Univ. of Lisbon, Tucuman); Hermann Salhi Medal, Univ. of Berne 1976, Thureus Prize, Swedish Acad. of Medical Sciences 1982, De Lancey Prize, Royal Soc. of Medicine 1984, Jofre Medal, Spanish Soc. for Advancement of Psychiatry 1985, WHO Medal 1988, Medicus Magnus Medal, Polish Acad. of Medicine, Grand Medal, Albert Schweitzer World Acad. of Medicine 2003. *Publications:* Alcoholism (with N. Kessel) 1966, 1988, Small Group Psychotherapy (ed.) 1974, Dictionary of Psychiatry (ed.) 1985, Newer Developments in Assessing Clinical Competence (ed. with others), Problem-based Learning (with M. B. Matthews) 1988, Proc. of World Summit on Medical Educ. (ed.) 1994, Psychiatric Education and Training in Contemporary Psychiatry 2001, "Education in Psychiatry", International Encyclopedia of the Social and Behavioral Sciences 2001. *Leisure interests:* literature, visual arts, particularly Western painting, Chinese and Japanese art. *Address:* 38 Blacket Place, Edinburgh, EH9 1RL, Scotland. *Telephone:* (131) 667-7811. *Fax:* (131) 662-0337. *E-mail:* h.walton@ed.ac.uk (Home).

WALTON, Jim; American media executive; b. 1958; m.; two s.; joined CNN 1980, various positions including journalist in sports news div., launched CNN Sports Illustrated (all-sports TV channel), Deputy Pres., Pres. CNN Domestic Networks –2001, Pres. and COO 2001–03, Pres. CNN News Group Jan. 2003–; Emmy Award for Journalism. *Leisure interests:* Nebraska football, Allman brothers. *Address:* CNN Center, 1 CNN Center, Marietta Street NW, Atlanta, GA 30303, USA (Office). *Telephone:* (404) 827-2201 (Office). *Website:* www.cnn.com (Office).

WALTON, S. Robson; American retailing executive; b. 1945; s. of Sam Moore Walton; m.; ed Columbia Univ.; fmrly with Conner, Winters, Ballaine, Barry & McGowen; with Wal-Mart Stores Inc., Bentonville, Ark. 1969–, Sr Vice-Pres. 1978–82, Dir, Vice-Chair. Bd 1982–92, Chair. 1992–. *Address:* Wal-Mart Stores Inc., 702 8th Street SW, Bentonville, AR 72716, USA (Office).

WALTON OF DETCHANT, Baron (Life Peer), cr. 1989, of Detchant in the County of Northumberland; **John Nicholas Walton,** Kt, TD, MA, MD, DSc, FRCP, FMedSci; British neurologist; b. 16 Sept. 1922, Rowlands Gill, Co. Durham; s. of Herbert Walton and Eleanor Watson Walton (née Ward); m. Mary Elizabeth Harrison 1946; one s. two d.; ed Alderman Wraith Grammar School, Spennymoor, Co. Durham, King's Coll., Medical School, Univ. of Durham; served RAMC 1947–49, Col L/RAMC OC 1(N) Gen. Hosp. (TA) 1963–66 (Hon. Col 1968–73); Medical Registrar, Royal Victoria Infirmary, Newcastle-upon-Tyne 1949–51; Nuffield Foundation Travelling Fellow, Mass. Gen. Hosp., Harvard Medical School, Boston, USA, King's Coll. Travelling Fellow, MRC Neurology Unit, Nat. Hosp., Queen Sq., London 1954–55; First Asst in Neurology, Univ. of Durham (Newcastle-upon-Tyne) 1955–58; Consultant Neurologist, Newcastle Hosps. 1958–83; Prof. of Neurology, Univ. of Newcastle-upon-Tyne 1968–83, Dean of Medicine 1971–81; Warden, Green Coll. Oxford 1983–89; mem. MRC 1974–78, Gen. Medical Council (Chair. Educ. Cttee) 1971–89, Pres. 1982–89; Chair. Muscular Dystrophy Group of GB 1971–95, Hamlyn Foundation Nat. Comm. on Educ. 1990–96, House of Lords Select Cttee on Medical Ethics 1992–93; Pres. British Medical Asscn 1980–82; Pres. Royal Soc. of Medicine 1984–86; First Vice-Pres. World Fed. of Neurology 1981–89, Pres. 1989–97; Hon. FACP; Hon. FRCP (Edin.); Hon. FRCP (Canada); Hon. F.R.C. Path.; Hon. F.R.C. Psych.; Hon. F.R.C.P.C.H., Hon. Fellow Inst. Educ. (London) 1995, Hon. mem. Norwegian Acad. of Arts and Sciences 1992; Hon. Dr. de l'Univ. (Aix-Marseille) 1975; Hon. DSc (Leeds) 1979, (Leicester) 1980, (Hull) 1988, (Oxford Brookes) 1994, (Durham) 2002; Hon. MD (Sheffield) 1987, (Mahidol Univ., Thailand) 1998; Hon. DCL (Newcastle) 1988; Dr. hc (Genoa) 1992. *Publications:* Subarachnoid Haemorrhage 1956, Polymyositis (with R. D. Adams) 1958, Oxford Companion to Medicine (Ed.) 1986, Essentials of Neurology (6th Edn) 1989, Skeletal Muscle Pathology (with F. L. Mastaglia, 2nd Edn) 1992, Brain's Diseases of the Nervous System (Ed., 10th Edn) 1993, The Spice of Life (autobiog.) 1993, Disorders of Voluntary Muscle (Ed., 6th Edn) 1994, Oxford Medical Companion (Ed.) 1994 and numerous articles in scientific journals. *Leisure interests:* music, golf, reading, cricket. *Address:* The Old Piggery, Detchant, Belford, Northumberland, NE70 7PF, England. *Telephone:* (1668) 213374. *Fax:* (1668) 213012. *E-mail:* waldetch@aol.com (Office).

WAMALWA, Michael Kijana; Kenyan politician; b. 1944, Kitale, Trans-Nzoia Dist, Rift Valley Prov.; s. of William Wamalwa; ed Chewoyet Secondary School, Strathmore Coll., Kings Coll. Cambridge, LSE, UK; called to Bar, Lincoln's Inn, London, UK; Lecturer in Law Univ. of Nairobi 1970–76; mam. family farming business, Kitale; Gen. Man. Kenya Stone Mining Co.; Dir Kenya-Japan Asscn; MP for Saboti 1979–97; mem. KANU party, Parl. Sec. 1983–88; Co-Founder and Second Vice-Chair. Forum for the Restoration of

Democracy (FORD–Kenya) 1992–94, Chair. 1994–; Leader of the Opposition 1994–97, Chair. Public Accounts Cttee 1994–97; Vice-Pres. of Kenya 2003–. *Address:* Office of the Vice President, Jogoo House 'A', Taifa Road, POB 30520, Nairobi Kenya (Office). *Telephone:* (20) 228411 (Office).

WAMBAUGH, Joseph, MA; American author; b. 22 Jan. 1937, East Pittsburgh, Pa; s. of Joseph A. Wambaugh and Anne Malloy; m. Dee Allsup 1955; two s. (one deceased) one d.; ed Calif. State Coll., Los Angeles; served U.S. Marine Corps 1954–57; police officer, LA 1960–74; creator, TV series, Police Story 1973. *Publications:* The New Centurions 1971, The Blue Knight 1972, The Onion Field 1973, The Choirboys 1975, The Black Marble 1978, The Glitter Dome 1981, The Delta Star 1983, Lines and Shadows 1984, The Secrets of Harry Bright 1985, Echoes in the Darkness 1987, The Blooding 1989, The Golden Orange 1990, Fugitive Nights 1992, Finnegan's Week 1993, Floaters 1996.

WAMYTAN, Roch, MA; New Caledonian politician; b. 13 Dec. 1950, Nouméa; s. of the late Benjamin Wamytan and Philomène Pidjot; three s. one d.; ed Grand Séminaire St Paul, Nouméa, Univ. of Lyon II and Centre d'Etudes Financières Economiques et Bancaires, Paris; fmr Head, Office for the Devt of the Interior and Islands; Attaché to Econ. Devt Sec. 1988; mem. Union Calédonienne (UC), now Pres.; Chief, St Louis tribal village; mem. Mt. Dore town council; mem. Southern Provincial Govt; Deputy Speaker, Congress of New Caledonia, responsible for external relations 1989–; Vice-Pres. Kanak Socialist National Liberation Front (FLNKS) 1990, Pres. 1995; Pres. New Caledonian Diocese Pastoral Council 1996. *Address:* B.P. 288, Mont-Dore, 98810 New Caledonia. *Telephone:* 26-58-83; 27-31-29. *Fax:* 26-58-88; 27-32-04.

WAN GUOQUAN; Chinese politician; b. March 1919, Taoan Co., Jilin Prov.; ed Zhonghua Univ.; Man. Lizhong Acid Factory, Tianjin 1947–56, Chair. Hedong Dist Fed. of Industry and Commerce 1957–63; Perm. mem. Exec. Cttee, All-China Fed. of Industry and Commerce 1978–83; Vice-Pres. China Democratic Nat. Construction Asscn 1983–97, Hon. Vice-Pres. 1997–; mem. 5th Nat. Cttee CPPCC 1978–82, Perm. mem. 6th Nat. Cttee 1983–87, 7th Nat. Cttee 1988–92, 8th Nat. Cttee 1993–98 (Vice-Chair. 1994–98), Vice-Chair. 9th Nat. Cttee 1998–; Jt Pres. China Council for Promoting Peaceful Reunification 1993–99, Pres. 1999–; Vice-Pres. Asscn for Int. Understanding of China 1993–. *Address:* National Committee of Chinese People's Political Consultative Conference, 23 Taipingqiao Street, Beijing, People's Republic of China.

WAN LI; Chinese government official (retd); b. Dec. 1916, Dongping Co., Shandong Prov.; m. Bian Tao; four s. one d.; joined CCP 1936; trained as teacher; various posts in Dongping Co. CCP Cttee; served on Hebei-Shangdong CCP Cttee, Deputy Dir Financial and Econ. Cttee, Nanjing Mil. Control Comm.; Head Econ. Dept and Dir Construction Bureau 1947–49; Deputy Head, then Head Industrial Dept, Southwest China Mil. and Admin. Cttee; Vice-Minister of Bldg, Minister of Urban Construction 1949–58; subsequently Sec. Beijing Municipal CCP Cttee, Deputy Mayor of Beijing, Asst to Premier Zhou Enlai in planning and organizing work of Ten Maj. Projects of the Capital (including Great Hall of the People) and other important construction projects; persecuted during Cultural Revolution 1966–73; Vice-Chair. Municipal Revolutionary Cttee; fmr Minister of Railways, Head Provisional Leading Party mems.' group in Ministry; closely allied with Deng Xiaoping's policies; dismissed as Minister when latter fell from favour 1976; First Vice-Minister of Light Industry 1977; First Sec. Anhui Prov. CCP Cttee, Chair. Anhui Prov. Revolutionary Cttee, First Political Commissar, Anhui Mil. Area 1977–80; Vice-Premier, State Council and Chair. State Agricultural Comm., Sec. Leading Party Group, Chair. Cen. Afforestation Comm. 1982–89, State People's Air Defence Comm. 1980; Deputy to 2nd, 3rd, 4th, 5th and 7th NPC, Chair. Standing Cttee 7th NPC 1988–93; elected mem. CCP 11th Cen. Cttee, mem. Secr. CCP 11th Cen. Cttee; elected mem. Politburo CCP Cen. Cttee and mem. Secr. 1982, 1987; mem. Presidium 14th Nat. Congress CCP 1992; Hon. Chair. Chinese Tennis Asscn 1982–; Hon. Pres. Bridge Asscn 1980–, Literature Foundation 1986–, Hon. Pres. Chinese Youth Devt Foundation 1993–, Greening Foundation 1989–, China Environmental Protection Foundation 1993–; visited Canada and USA 1989. *Leisure interests:* tennis, bridge. *Address:* Standing Committee, National People's Congress, Tian An Men Square, Beijing, People's Republic of China.

WAN SHAOFEN; Chinese party official, economist and lawyer; b. 1930, Nanchang; ed Zhongzheng Univ.; joined CCP 1952; Leading Sec. CCP Cttee, Jiangxi 1985–87; mem. 13th CCP Cen. Cttee 1985–92; Chair. Prov. Women's Fed., Jiangxi 1983–85; Deputy Head United Front Work Dept of CCP Cen. Cttee 1988–; Vice-Chair. Overseas Chinese Affairs Cttee; mem. CCP Cen. Discipline Inspection Comm. 1992–97, 8th NPC Standing Cttee 1993–98, Preliminary Working Cttee of the Preparatory Cttee of the Hong Kong Special Admin. Region 1993–96; Vice-Chair. Internal Affairs and Judicial Cttee of the 9th NPC 1998. *Address:* c/o Standing Committee of National People's Congress, Beijing, People's Republic of China.

WAN XUEYUAN; Chinese administrator; b. 1941; joined CCP 1964; alt. mem. 13th CCP Cen. Cttee 1987–91; mem. 14th CCP Cen. Cttee 1992; Gov. of Zhejiang Prov. 1994–97; Deputy Sec. CCP 9th Zhejiang Prov. Cttee 1994–97; Vice-Minister of Personnel 1997, Head of Bureau of Foreign Experts 1997. *Address:* c/o Ministry of Personnel, 12 Hepinglizhong Jie, Dongcheng Qu, Beijing 100716, People's Republic of China.

WAN ZHEXIAN; Chinese mathematician; b. Nov. 1927; s. of Wan Cheggui and Zhou Weijin; m. Wang Shixiau; two d.; ed Qinghua Univ.; Prof. of Mathematics, Inst. of Systems Science (now Chinese Acad. of Math. and System Sciences) 1978–; mem. Chinese Acad. of Sciences 1992; Hua Lookeng Award for Mathematics 1995. *Publications:* Classical Groups 1963, Geometry of Classical Groups over Finite Fields 1993, Geometry of Matrices 1996. *Address:* Acad. of Math. and System Science, 1A Nansi Street, Zhongguancun, Beijing 100080, People's Republic of China (Office). *Telephone:* (10) 62553005 (Office); (10) 62559148 (Home). *Fax:* (10) 62568364 (Office). *E-mail:* issb@bamboo.iss.ac.cn.

WANAMAKER, Zoë, CBE; British/American actress; b. New York; d. of the late Sam Wanamaker and Charlotte Wanamaker; m. Gawn Grainger 1994; one step-s. one step-d.; ed Cen. School of Speech and Drama; professional debut as Hermia in A Midsummer Night's Dream, Manchester 1970; repertory at Royal Lyceum 1971–72, Oxford Playhouse 1974–75, Nottingham 1975–76; work with RSC and Nat. Theatre includes Toine in Piaf, London and New York 1980, Viola in Twelfth Night 1983, Adriana in A Comedy of Errors 1983, Kitty Duval in Time of Your Life 1983, Kattrin in Mother Courage 1984, Othello 1989, The Crucible 1990, The Last Yankee 1993; other performances include Fay in Loot, Broadway 1986, Ellie in Terry Johnson's new play Dead Funny, London 1994, Amanda in The Glass Menagerie, London 1995/96, Sylvia 1996, Electra, Chichester and London 1997, Princeton and Broadway 1998, The Old Neighbourhood, Royal Court 1998, Battle Royal, Nat. Theatre 1999, Boston Marriage, Donmar Warehouse, London 2001, New Ambassadors, London 2001–02; Hon. Vice-Pres. Voluntary Euthanasia Soc.; Hon. DLitt (South Bank Univ.) 1993; Dr hc (Richmond American Int. Univ. of London); Soc. of West End Theatres Award (Once in a Lifetime) 1979, Drama Award (Mother Courage) 1985, Olivier Award for Best Actress (Electra) 1998, Variety Club Award for Best Actress (Electra) 1998, BAFTA Award for Best Actress (Love Hurts and Wilde), Calaway Award (New York) for Best Actress (Electra) 1998, Gold Hugo for Narration 1998. *Films include:* The Last Ten Days of Hitler, Inside the Third Reich, The Hunger 1982, The Raggedy Rawney 1987, Wilde, Swept by the Sea 1997, Harry Potter: The Philosopher's Stone 2001. *Television appearances include:* Enemies of the State, Edge of Darkness (BBC), Paradise Postponed, Poor Little Rich Girl (NBC miniseries), Love Hurts, Prime Suspect, The Widowing of Mrs Holroyd, BBC 1995, David Copperfield, Leprechauns, Gormenghast, My Family (BBC series) 2000–03, Adrian Mole: The Cappuccino Years (BBC series) 2001. *Radio:* The Golden Bowl, Plenty Bay at Nice, A February Morning, Carol, Such Rotten Luck. *Address:* c/o Conway van Gelder Ltd, 18–21 Jermyn Street, London, SW1Y 6HP, England. *Telephone:* (20) 7287-0077. *Fax:* (20) 7287-1940.

WANCER, Józef, MA; Polish banker and economist; b. 26 May 1942, Komi, Russia; s. of Jakub Wancer and Edwarda Wancer; m. Krystyna Antoniak; one s. one d.; ed Univ. of New York City, Webster Univ., Saint Louis Missouri, USA; Vice-Pres. Citibank of New York, managerial posts at Citibank units, including Japan, Austria, UK, France; Vice-Pres., then Pres. Raiffeisen Centrobank 1995–2000; Pres. Przemyslowo-Handlowy Bank SA 2000–. *Leisure interests:* cycling, logotherapy, history. *Address:* Bank Przemyslowo-Handlowy PBK S.A., al. Pokoju 1, 31-548 Cracow, Poland (Office). *Telephone:* (22) 5319230 (Office). *Fax:* (22) 5319286 (Office). *E-mail:* joseph.wancer@bphpbk.pl (Office). *Website:* www.bphpbk.pl (Office).

WANG, Charles B., BS; Chinese computer executive; b. 19 Aug. 1944, Shanghai; ed Queen's Coll.; programming trainee Reverside Research Inst., Columbia Univ., USA 1976–; Founder, Chair., CEO Computer Assocs 1976–2002, Chair. Emer. 2002–; owner, CEO NY Islanders 1999–. *Publications:* Techno Vision 1994, Techno Vision II: Every Executive's Guide to Understanding and Mastering Technology and the Internet 1997. *Leisure interests:* basketball, cooking. *Address:* NY Islanders Nassau Veterans Memorial Coliseum, Uniondale, NY 11553, USA.

WANG, Wayne; Chinese/American film director; b. 1949, Hong Kong; m. Cora Miao; ed Coll. of Arts and Crafts, Oakland, Calif. *Films directed:* Chan is Mission, Dim Sum, Slamdance, Eat a Bowl of Tea, Life is Cheap . . . But Toilet Paper is Expensive, The Joy Luck Club, Smoke, Blue in the Face, Chinese Box, Anywhere But Here, The Centre of the World. *Address:* 916 Kearny Street, Sun Francisco, CA 94133 (Office); c/o Bob Walker, ICM, 40 West 57th Street, Floor 16, New York, NY 10019, USA.

WANG ANYI; Chinese writer; b. 1954, Tong'an, Fujian Prov.; ed Xiangming Middle School; fmrly musician Xuzhou Pref. Song and Dance Ensemble; Ed. Children's Time; Vice-Chair. Shanghai Writers Asscn; Mao Dun Prize for Literature for Song of Eternal Hatred. *Publications:* Song of Eternal Hatred, Xiaobao Village, The Love of a Small Town, The Story of a School Principal, Self-selected Works of Wang Anyi (6 Vols). *Address:* Shanghai Writers Association, Shanghai, People's Republic of China (Office).

WANG BINGQIAN; Chinese politician; b. 1925, Li Co., Hebei Prov.; Deputy Section Chief, Auditing Div., Dept of Finance 1948–49; Section Chief, later Dir, Vice-Minister, Minister of Finance, Cen. Govt; Dir Budget Dept 1963; Deputy Minister of Finance 1973–80, Minister of Finance 1980–92; mem. 12th Cen. Cttee CCP 1982, 13th Cen. Cttee 1987; Pres. Accounting Soc. 1980–; Chinese Gov., World Bank 1986; Hon. Chair. Bd of Dirs., China Investment Bank 1981–; State Councillor 1983–93; Chair. Cen. Treasury Bond Sales Promotion Cttee 1984–; Vice-Chair. Standing Cttee of 8th NPC 1993–98; mem. State Planning Comm. 1988–92; Hon. Pres. Auditing Soc. 1984–, China

Scientific Research Soc. for Policy Study; NPC Deputy Hebei Prov. *Address:* c/o Standing Committee of National People's Congress, Beijing, People's Republic of China.

WANG BINGZHANG; Chinese political activist; b. 1947; one d.; actively participated in Cultural Revolution, jailed twice by Chinese authorities; moved to USA 1979; f. China Spring magazine 1980s; Founder and Leader Chinese Alliance for Democracy, NY 1980s; attempted to return to China, but expelled 1998; entered Viet Nam to hold meetings with activists 2002; allegedly abducted by Chinese security forces and held at secret location July 2002; arrested in Fanchenggang City, S. China Dec. 2002; convicted of espionage and leading terrorist group (sentenced to life imprisonment), Guangdong Prov. Court, S. China Jan. 2003.

WANG CHANG-CHING, MSc; Taiwanese politician; b. 22 Sept. 1920, Chingshan Co., Hupeh; s. of C. S. Wang and late Si Teng; m. Hsueh Chen L. Wang; one s. one d.; ed Nat. Chiaotung Univ. and Johns Hopkins Univ., USA; Sr Eng and concurrently Div. Chief, Dept of Communications, Taiwan Provincial Govt 1949–58; Dir Public Works Bureau, Taiwan Provincial Govt 1958–69; Dir Dept of Public Works, Taipei City Govt 1967–69; Vice-Minister, Ministry of Communications 1969–77; Vice-Chair. Council for Econ. Planning and Devt 1977–84; Sec.-Gen. Exec. Yuan 1984–88; Chair. China External Trade Devt Council 1988–; Vice-Chair. Straits Exchange Foundation 1993–. *Leisure interest:* golf. *Address:* 7th Floor, 333 Keelung Road, Sec. 1, Taipei 10548, Taiwan. *Telephone:* (2) 7576293. *Fax:* (2) 7576653.

WANG CHAOWEN; Chinese politician; b. 1930, Huangping, Guizhou; joined CCP 1951; Sec. Guizhou Communist Youth League 1973; Vice-Chair. Prov. Revolutionary Cttee, Guizhou 1977–79; Sec. CCP Cttee, Guizhou 1980–81, Deputy Sec. 1981–; Vice-Gov. of Guizhou 1980–83, Gov. 1983–93; Chair. Guizhou Prov. 8th People's Congress 1994–98; Chair. Nationalities Cttee of 9th NPC 1998–; mem. 12th Cen. Cttee CCP 1982–87, 13th Cen. Cttee 1987–92, 14th Cen. Cttee 1992–97; Deputy Sec. CPC 6th Guizhou Prov. Cttee 1980–93. *Address:* The Standing Committee of the National People's Congress, 19 Xi-Jiaoming Xiang Road, Xicheng District, Beijing 100805, People's Republic of China.

WANG CHEN; Chinese journalist and editor; b. Wen'an Co., Hebei Prov.; ed School of Postgrad. Studies, Chinese Acad. of Social Sciences, Beijing; fmr reporter CCP Yijun Co. Cttee, CCP Yan'an Municipal Cttee, Shaanxi Prov.; reporter Guangming Daily, then successively Ed., Dir Chief Ed.'s Office, Assoc. Chief Ed., Chief Ed. 1982–2000; Deputy Dir Dept of Propaganda, CCP Cen. Cttee 2000; Ed.-in-Chief Renmin Ribao (People's Daily) Aug. 2001–. *Address:* Renmin Ribao (People's Daily), 2 Jin Tai Xi Lu, Chao Yang Men Wai, Beijing 100733, People's Republic of China (Office). *Telephone:* (10) 65092121 (Office). *Fax:* (10) 65091982 (Office). *E-mail:* rmrb@peopledaily.com.cn (Office). *Website:* www.people.com.cn (Office).

WANG CHIEN-SHIEN; Taiwanese politician; b. 7 Aug. 1938, Anhwei; m. Fa-jau Su; ed Harvard Univ., USA; Sr Specialist Taxation & Tariff. Comm. Ministry of Finance 1971–73; Dir 1st Div. Dept of Taxation 1973–76, 4th Dept Exec. Yuan 1976–80; Dir.–Gen. Dept of Customs Admin. Ministry of Finance 1980–82, Public Finance Training Inst. 1982–84; Admin. Vice-Minister of Econ. Affairs 1984–89, Political Vice-Minister 1989–90, Minister of Finance 1990–92; mem. Legis. Yuan 1993–, Sec.-Gen. New Party 1994; Asian Finance Minister of the Year 1992. *Publications:* several works on income tax and business. *Address:* c/o New Party, 4th Floor, 65 Guang Fuh S. Road, Taipei, Taiwan. *Telephone:* (2) 7562222.

WANG DAN; Chinese dissident; imprisoned for four years for role in Tiananmen Square pro-democracy demonstrations 1989; sentenced to eleven years' imprisonment for conspiring to subvert govt 1996.

WANG DAOHAN; Chinese politician; b. 1915, Jiashan, Anhui Prov.; ed Jiaotong Univ.; joined CCP 1938; Minister of Industry, East China Mil. and Political Comm.; Vice-Minister of First Machine Bldg Industry; Vice-Minister of Foreign Econ. Relations; Vice-Dir State Admin. for Imports and Exports; Vice-Dir Foreign Investment Admin. Comm.; Sec. CCP Shanghai Municipal Cttee; Vice-Mayor, then Mayor of Shanghai 1949–91; Chair. Cross-Strait Relations Cttee 1991–. *Address:* c/o General Office of the State Council, 2 Fuyou Jie, Beijing 100017, People's Republic of China (Office).

WANG DAZHONG, DSc; Chinese scientist; b. 1935, Changli, Hebei Prov.; ed Tsinghua Univ.; Assoc. Prof., Prof., Research Fellow, Dir of Nuclear Energy Research Inst., Qinghua Univ. 1958–99, Pres. Qinghua Univ. 1999–; mem. 4th Presidium of Depts. Chinese Acad. of Sciences 2000–. *Address:* Qinghua University, 1 Qinghuayuan, Beijing 100084, People's Republic of China (Office). *Telephone:* (10) 62561144 (Office). *Fax:* (10) 62562768.

WANG DEMIN; Chinese petroleum engineer; b. 1937, Tangshan, Hebei Prov.; ed Beijing Petroleum Inst.; technician, engineer, Chief Engineer, Daqing Petroleum Admin. 1960–; Fellow Chinese Acad. of Eng. 1994. *Address:* Daqing Petroleum Administration, Daqing, Heilongjiang Province, People's Republic of China (Office).

WANG DESHUN; Chinese mime artist; b. 1938; m. Zhao Aijun; one s. one d.; fmr street performer; with army drama co. 1960–70; joined state-run Changchun Theatre Troupe, NE China 1970; since 1984 has been appearing in 'modelling pantomime' show in which he adopts series of sculpture-like poses to develop a theme; has taken his show to France, Germany and Macao and China's first int. mime festival, Shanghai 1994.

WANG DEYAN; Chinese banker; b. 1931; ed Qinhua Univ., Cen. Inst. of Finance and Econ., Beijing Foreign Languages Inst.; joined Bank of China 1953, served as Sec., Asst Man., Deputy Gen. Man. 1953–84, Vice-Pres. 1984–85, Pres. 1985–93, Chair., Bd Dirs. 1986–93; Dir, Council's Office of People's Bank of China, Welfare Fund for Chinese Disabled Persons; Guest Adviser, China Council for Promotion of Int. Trade; Adviser to Coordination Group for Sino-Japanese Econ. and Trade Affairs; Vice-Chair. China Int. Finance Soc.; Hon. Dir Research Fund for Prevention of AIDS in China; mem. Leading Group for Introduction of Foreign Capital under State Council; mem. Nat. Geographic Soc., USA; Asian Banker of 1987, Asian Finance. *Address:* Bank of China, 410 Fuchengmennei Dajie, Beijing, People's Republic of China.

WANG DIANZUO; Chinese metallurgist; b. 23 March 1934, Jinxian, Liaoning Prov.; ed Zhongnan Univ. of Eng; Foreign Assoc. Mem. Nat. Acad. of Eng, USA 1990–; Fellow Chinese Acad. of Sciences; Fellow Chinese Acad. of Eng, now Vice-Pres.; made pioneering contribs. in flotation theory for mineral processing; won many nat., provincial and ministerial awards including He Liang and He Li Prizes 1994. *Publications:* 8 monographs and over 300 research papers. *Address:* Beijing Nonferrous Metallurgy Research General Institute, 2 Xinjiekou Wai Street, Beijing 100088, People's Republic of China (Office). *Telephone:* (10) 62055356 (Office). *Fax:* (10) 62055345 (Office). *E-mail:* wangdz@mail.grinm.edu.cn (Office).

WANG FOSONG; Chinese administrator and chemist; b. 1933, Xingning Co., Guangdong Prov.; ed Wuhan Univ.; Vice-Pres. Chinese Sciences Acad. 1988; mem. 8th Nat. People's Congress 1993–, 4th Presidium of Depts. Chinese Acad. of Sciences 2000–. *Address:* Chinese Academy of Sciences, 52 San Li He Road, Beijing 100864, People's Republic of China.

WANG FULI; Chinese actress; b. Nov. 1949, Xuzhou, Jiangsu Prov.; ed Jiangsu Prov. Drama Acad.; actress Jiangsu Prov. Peking Opera Troupe, then Jiangsu Prov. Drama Troupe 1968–90; with China Broadcasting Art Co. 1990–; won TV Gold Eagle Award for Best Actress, Hundred-Flower Award for Best Supporting Actress, Gold Rooster Award for Best Supporting Actress, New Decade Movie Award for Best Actress. *Films:* The Legend of Tianyun Mountain 1980, Xu Mao and His Daughters 1981, Our Niu Baisui, Sunrise 1985, God of Mountains 1992, The Romance of Blacksmith Zhang, The Wooden Man's Bride 1993. *Address:* China Broadcasting Art Company, Beijing, People's Republic of China (Office).

WANG FUZHOU; Chinese mountaineer and sports administrator; b. 1931, Xihua, Henan Province; s. of Wang Daikuang and Shen Xiozhen; m. Lia Aihua; one d.; mem. of Chinese mountaineering team which conquered Mt. Everest for first time from North 1960; Sec.-Gen. Chinese Mountaineering Asscn 1980–93, Pres. 1993–; Gen. Man. of China Int. Sports Travel Co. 1983–. *Address:* State Physical Culture and Sports Commission, 9 Tiyuguang Road, Beijing; Chinese Mountaineering Association, 10 Zuoanmen Nei Street, Beijing, People's Republic of China. *Telephone:* 7017810. *Fax:* 5114859.

WANG GANG; Chinese archivist; b. Oct. 1942, Fuyu, Jilin Prov.; ed Jilin Univ.; joined CCP 1971; Sec. Gen. Office of CCP Xinjiang Autonomous Region Cttee 1977–81; Sec. Taiwan Affairs Office of CCP Cen. Cttee 1981–85; Vice-Dir Petition Letters Bureau, Gen. Office of CCP Cen. Cttee and Gen. Office of the State Council 1985–90; Vice-Dir Cen. Archives 1990–93; Dir Cen. Archives, Dir Nat. Archives Bureau 1994–99; Chair. Int. Archives Council 1996–; alt. mem. 15th CCP Cen. Cttee 1997–2002; Dir Gen. Office of CCP Cen. Cttee and Sec. Working Cttee of Dept CCP Cen. Cttee 1999. *Address:* 21 Fengsheng Hutong, Beijing 100032, People's Republic of China. *Telephone:* (10) 63096115.

WANG GUANGYING; Chinese business executive; b. 1919, Beijing; m. 1943; ed Catholic Fudan Univ.; set up own business in Tianjin 1943; Vice-Chair. China Democratic Nat. Construction Asscn 1954; jailed for eight years during cultural revolution 1967–75; Vice-Chair. All China Fed. of Industry and Commerce 1982, Hon. Chair. 1993–; Founder, Chair. and Pres. China Everbright Co. (China's first trans-nat. corpn), Hong Kong 1983–90; Exec. Chair. Presidium CPPCC 1983–; Vice-Chair. 6th CPPCC 1983–87, 7th CPPCC 1988–, Standing Cttee of 8th NPC 1993–98, 9th NPC 1998–; NPC Deputy Tianjin Municipality; a Pres. China Council for Promoting Peaceful Reunification 1990–98; Hon. Vice-Chair. Red Cross Soc. of China 1994–. *Address:* All China Federation of Industry and Commerce, 93 Beiheyan Dajie, Beijing, People's Republic of China.

WANG GUNGWU, CBE, PhD, FAHA; Malaysian historian and university vice-chancellor; b. 9 Oct. 1930, Indonesia; s. of Wang Fo Wen and Ting Yien; m. Margaret Lim Ping-Ting 1955; one s. two d.; ed Nat. Cen. Univ., Nanjing, Univ. of Malaya and Univ. of London; Asst Lecturer Univ. of Malaya, Singapore 1957–59, lecturer 1959; lecturer, Univ. of Malaya, Kuala Lumpur 1959–61, Sr Lecturer 1961–63, Dean of Arts 1962–63, Prof. of History 1963–68; Rockefeller Fellow, Univ. of London 1961–62, Sr Visiting Fellow 1972; Prof. of Far Eastern History, ANU 1968–86, Prof. Emer. 1986–, Dir Research School of Pacific Studies 1975–80; Visiting Fellow, All Souls Coll. Oxford 1974–75; John A. Burns Distinguished Visiting Prof. of History, Univ. of Hawaii 1979; Rose Morgan Visiting Prof. of History, Univ. of Kansas 1983; Vice-Chancellor, Univ. of Hong Kong 1985–93; Chair. Inst. of E Asian Political Economy, Nat. Univ. of Singapore 1996–97; Dir East Asian Inst. 1997–; Distinguished Sr Fellow Inst. of Southeast Asian Studies, Singapore 1996–99; Distinguished Professorial Fellow 1999–; Fellow and Hon. Corresp. mem. for

Hong Kong of Royal Soc. of Arts 1987–95; Pres. Australian Acad. of the Humanities 1980–83, Asian Studies Asscn of Australia 1978–80; Chair. Australia-China Council 1984–86, Environmental Pollution Advisory Cttee 1988–95, Council for the Performing Arts 1989–94, Asia-Pacific Council, Griffith Univ. 1997–2001; mem. Exec. Council, Hong Kong 1990–92; Adviser Chinese Heritage Centre, Nanyang Tech. Univ. 1995–2000 (Vice-Chair.) 2000–, Southeast Asian Studies, Academia Sinica, Taipei 1994–; mem. Council Int. Inst. for Strategic Studies, London 1992–2001; mem. Nat. Arts Council, Singapore 1996–2000, Nat. Heritage Bd 1997–99 (Adviser 2000–), Nat. Library Bd 1997–; mem. Academia Sinica, Taipei, DD Social Science Research Council, NY 1999–; Foreign Hon. mem. American Acad. of Arts and Science; Hon. Fellow SOAS, London; Hon. Sr Fellow Chinese Acad. of Social Sciences, Beijing; Hon. Prof. Beijing Univ., Fudan Univ., Hong Kong; Hon. DLitt (Sydney, Hull, Hong Kong, Nanjing); Hon. LLD (Monash, ANU, Melbourne); Hon. DUniv (Griffith, Soka). *Publications:* 21 books, including The Chineseness of China 1991, China and the Chinese Overseas 1991, Community and Nation: China, South-East Asia and Australia 1992, Zhongguo yu Haiwai Huaren 1994, The Chinese Way: China's Position in International Relations 1995; Hong Kong's Transition: A Decade after the Deal (ed.) 1995, Global History and Migrations (ed.) 1997, The Nanhai Trade 1998, The Chinese Overseas: From Earthbound China to the Quest for Autonomy 2000, Joining the Modern World: Inside and Outside China 2000, Only Connect: Sino-Malay Encounters 2001, Don't Leave Home: Migration and the Chinese 2001, To Act is to Know: Chinese Dilemmas 2002, Bind Us in Time: Nation and Civilisation in Asia 2002; also numerous articles on Chinese and South-East Asian history; Gen. Ed. East Asian Historical Monographs series. *Leisure interests:* music, reading, walking. *Address:* East Asian Institute, Block AS5, 7 Arts Link, National University of Singapore, Kent Ridge, Singapore 117571. *Telephone:* 7752033. *Fax:* 7793409. *E-mail:* eaiwgw@nus.edu.sg (Office). *Website:* nus.edu.sg/nusinfo/eai (Office).

WANG HAI, Gen.; Chinese army officer; b. 1925, Weihai City, Shandong Prov.; ed China's North-East Aviation Acad.; joined PLA 1945; Group Commdr, air force brigade and sent to Korean battlefield 1950; promoted Col PLA 1964; Commdr, Air Force of Guangzhou Mil. Region 1975–83; Deputy Commdr, PLA Air Force 1983–85; Commdr, PLA Air Force 1985; mem., CCP 12th Cen. Cttee 1985–87, 13th Cen. Cttee 1987–92, 14th Cen. Cttee 1992–; promoted Gen. PLA 1988. *Address:* Ministry of Defence, Beijing, People's Republic of China.

WANG HANBIN; Chinese state and party official; b. 28 Aug. 1925, Fujian Prov.; m. Peng Peiyun; two s. two d.; joined CCP in Burma 1941; Deputy Sec.-Gen. NPC Legal Comm. 1979–80; Vice-Chair. and Sec.-Gen. NPC Legal Comm. 1980–83; Deputy Sec.-Gen., Political and Legal Comm. of CCP Cen. Cttee 1980–82, Constitution Revision Cttee of P.R.C. 1980–82; Vice-Pres. Chinese Law Soc. 1982–91, Hon. Pres. 1991–; mem. 12th CCP Cen. Cttee 1982–86, 13th Cen. Cttee 1987–92, 14th Cen. Cttee 1992–97; Sec.-Gen. NPC Standing Cttee 1983–87, Vice-Chair. NPC 7th Standing Cttee 1988–93; Chair. Legis. Affairs Comm. 1983–87; Vice-Chair. Cttee for Drafting Basic Law of Hong Kong Special Admin. Zone of People's Repub. of China 1985–90, for Drafting Basic Law of Macau Special Admin. Region of People's Republic of China 1988–, Preparatory Cttee, Hong Kong Special Admin. Region 1995–97; alt. mem. Politburo CCP 1992–97; Vice-Chair. Standing Cttee 8th NPC 1993–98. *Leisure interest:* bridge. *Address:* c/o National People's Congress Standing Committee, Beijing, People's Republic of China.

WANG JIDA; Chinese sculptor; b. 27 Oct. 1935, Beijing; s. of Wang Sho Yi and Chiu Chen Shin; m. Jin Gao 1971; one s. one d.; ed Cen. Inst. of Fine Arts, Beijing; worked in Nei Monggol 1966, 1976–84; moved to USA 1984; Exhbn in Grand Cen. Art Gallery 1986, 1987; Asst Dir Standing Council, Nei Monggol Sculptors' Asscn; mem., Chinese Artist's Asscn, American Nat. Sculpture Soc. 1988–; Honour Prize, China 1977. *Works include:* The Struggle 1987, (commissioned by Exec. Council on Foreign Diplomats), Natural Beauty 1987 (a collection of 18 pieces portraying women and animals), Statue of Liberty (commissioned by Statue of Liberty/Ellis Island Foundation), several monumental sculptures in Chairman Mao's image, in China. *Leisure interests:* athletics, music, literature. *Address:* Inner Mongolia Artist's Association, 33 W Street, Hohhot, Inner Mongolia, People's Republic of China; 76-12 35th Avenue, Apartment 3E, Jackson Heights, NY 11372, USA. *Telephone:* 25775 (China); (718) 651-3944 (USA).

WANG JIN-PYNG, BS; Taiwanese politician; b. 17 March 1941, Kaohsiung Co.; m. Chen Tsai-Lien; one s. two d.; ed Nat. Taiwan Normal Univ.; Vice-Chair. Cen. Policy Cttee of Kuomintang (KMT) 1990, Chair. Finance Cttee 1990–92; Vice-Chair. KMT 2000–; mem. Legis. Yuan 1975–, various positions including Sec.-Gen. of KMT Caucus, Dir and Dir-Gen. Dept. of Party–Govt Co-ordination, Convenor Finance Cttee 1981–88, Vice-Pres. 1993–99, Pres. Li-Fa Yuan (Legis. Yuan) 1999–; mem. CSC 1993–; Pres. Sino–Japanese Inter-Parl. Friendship Asscn 1992–, Taiwan Maj. League of Professional Baseball 1997–, Volunteer Fire-Fighter Asscn of the ROC 1997–. *Address:* Legislative Yuan, 1 Chuanshan S. Road, Taipei, Taiwan (Office). *Telephone:* (2) 3211531 (Office). *Fax:* (2) 3222558 (Office). *Website:* www.ly.gov.tw.

WANG JUN; Chinese business executive; b. 11 April 1941, Munan, Human; s. of the late Wang Zhen; joined China Int. Trust and Investment Corpn (CITIC) 1979, served as Deputy Gen. Man. then Gen. Man. Business Dept, Vice-Pres., Vice-Chair. and Pres. CITIC Hong Kong (Holdings), Vice-Pres. CITIC 1986–93, then Pres. 1993–95, Chair. of Bd 1994–; Chair. Bd of Dirs. Poly

Group 1991–, Planning Comm. Gansu Prov. People's Govt; Chief Procurator Guangdong Prov. People's Procuratorate; Chair. China Professional Golfers' Asscn. *Leisure interests:* golf, go. *Address:* China International Trust and Investment Corporation (CITIC), Capital Mansion, 6 Xianyuan Nan Ju, Chaoyang Qu, Beijing 100004, People's Republic of China. *Telephone:* (10) 4660088; (10) 64665509 (Office). *Fax:* (10) 4661186; (10) 64665526 (Office). *E-mail:* sugx@citic.com.cn (Office).

WANG JUNXIA; Chinese athlete; b. Jan. 1973, Dalian, Liaoning Prov.; under tutelage of coach Ma Junren set new world record for women's 10,000m race and 3,000m race in 1993 (both still standing at end of 2002), won gold medal in women's 5,000m race (under different coach) in the 26th Olympics in Atlanta; Female Int. Athlete of the Year 1993, Jesse Owens Int. Trophy Award 1994. *Address:* c/o State General Bureau for Physical Culture and Sports, 9 Tiyuguan Road, Chongwen District, Beijing, People's Republic of China.

WANG KE, Gen.; Chinese army officer; b. Aug. 1931, Xiaoxian Co., Jiangsu Prov.; joined CCP-led armed work team 1944; joined CCP 1947; ed PLA Military Acad.; took part in the Korean War 1953; Div. Commdr, Army Group Commdr 1980–86; Vice-Commdr Xinjiang Mil. Area Command 1986–90; Vice-Commdr Lanzhou Mil. Area Command, Commdr Xinjiang Mil. Area Command 1990–92; rank of Lt-Gen. 1988, Gen. 1994; mem. 14th CCP Cen. Cttee 1992–97, mem. 15th CCP Cen. Cttee 1997–2002; Commdr Shenyang Mil. Area Command 1992–95; mem. Cen. Mil. Comm. 1995–; Dir PLA Gen. Logistics Dept 1995–. *Address:* People's Liberation Army General Logistics Department, Beijing, People's Republic of China.

WANG KEFEN; Chinese dance historian; b. 1 April 1927, Yunyang, Sichuan; d. of Wang Baifan and Liao Huiqing; m. Zhang Wengang 1949; one s. one d.; choreographer and dancer Cen. Nat. Song and Dance Co. 1952–58; Research Fellow Chinese Nat. Dance Asscn 1956–66, Inst. of Dance, China Nat. Arts Acad. (CNAA) 1977–; Academic Prize, Arts Acad. of China 1989, Award for Special Contrib., Award for Outstanding Contribs. of Culture and Educ. Exchange. *Publications:* The History of Chinese Dance 1980, The Stories of Ancient Chinese Dancers 1983, The History of Chinese Dance: Ming Dynasty, Qing Dynasty 1984, Sui Dynasty and Tang Dynasty 1987 (CNAA Research Excellence Award 1989), The History of Chinese Dance Development (CNAA Research Excellence Award 1994, Chinese Ministry of Culture Art Research Award 1999); Dictionary of Chinese Dance (Chief Ed.) (Nat. Award for Best Dictionary 1995); Chief Ed. on subject of dance in 10 vol. History of Chinese Civilization (Nat. Award for Best Book 1994); Sui and Tang Culture (Co-Ed. and contrib.) 1990 (Social Science Book Award 1992), Chinese Dance of the 20th Century 1991 (Nat. Best Book Award 1993), Buddhism and Chinese Dance 1991, Chinese Ancient Dance History (Co-author), The Past and Future of Chinese Dance, The Chinese Contemporary History of Dance 1840–1996 (Ed. in chief), The Music and Dance of the Tang Dynasty recorded in Japanese History 1999, The Culture of the Wei Dynasty, Jin Dynasty, Northern Dynasty and Southern Dynasty (jtly.) 2000, Chinese Dance: An Illustrated History 2002, The Complete Works of Dnnhuang Caves – Dance Vol. 2001, and other works on Chinese Dance. *Leisure interests:* choreography, writing and dance. *Address:* 1601-4 Building, Changyungong, Xi Sahuan Bei Lu, Beijing 100044, People's Republic of China. *Telephone:* (10) 68411250.

WANG KUI; Chinese chemist; b. 7 May 1928, Tianjin; ed Yanjing Univ.; teaching Asst Beijing Medical Univ., Instructor, Assoc. Prof., Prof., Chair. of Dept, Dean Pharmaceutics School, Dean Coll. of Pharmaceutics, now Dir Nat. Laboratory of Natural Medicine and Bionic Medicine 1950–; Chair. Chem. Dept of Nat. Natural Science Foundation; Fellow Chinese Acad. of Science 1991–; mem. 4th Presidium, Chinese Acad. of Sciences 2000–; Chinese Acad. of Sciences Award for Advancement in Science and Tech. (2nd Class), State Educ. Comm. Award for Advancement in Science and Tech. (2nd Class). *Publications:* over 100 research papers. *Address:* Beijing Medical University, 38 Xue Yuan Ju, Beijing 100083, People's Republic of China (Office). *Telephone:* (10) 62091334 (Office). *Fax:* (10) 62015681 (Office). *E-mail:* dxb@mail.bjmu.edu.cn (Office). *Website:* www.bjmu.edu.cn (Office).

WANG LEQUAN; Chinese politician; b. Dec. 1944, Shouguang Co., Shandong Prov.; joined CCP 1966; Vice-Sec. Communist Youth League Shandong Provincial Cttee; Vice-Sec. then Sec. CCP Liaocheng Prefectural Cttee; Vice-Gov. Shandong Prov.; alt. mem. 14th CCP Cen. Cttee 1992; Vice-Sec. CCP Xinjiang Uygur Autonomous Regional Cttee, Vice-Chair. Xinjiang Uygur Autonomous Region 1993, then Sec. CCP Xinjiang Uygur Autonomous Regional Cttee; mem. 15th CCP Cen. Cttee 1997–. *Address:* Chinese Communist Party Xinjiang Uygur Autonomous Regional Committee, Urumqi City, Xinjiang Uygur Autonomous Region, People's Republic of China.

WANG LIANZHENG; Chinese agronomist and administrator; b. 15 Oct. 1930, Haicheng, Liaoning Prov.; s. of Wang Dianche and Wang Youzhen; m. Li Shuzhen 1959; two d.; ed Northeast Agricultural Coll., Harbin and Moscow Timiryazeev Agricultural Acad.; Asst Prof. Heilonjiang Acad. of Agricultural Sciences (HAAS) 1964–78, Assoc. Prof. 1979–82, Prof. 1983–; Dir Soybean and Crop Breeding Inst. HAAS 1970–78; Vice-Pres. HAAS 1978–82, Pres. 1983–86, Vice-Gov. Heilonjiang Prov. (in charge of Agricultural Production, Science and Tech.) 1983–87; Vice-Minister of Agric. 1988–91; mem. Agricultural Devt Group at State Council 1988–93; mem. and Convenor Plant Genetics, Breeding, Cultivation Academic Degree Cttee at State Council 1991–96; Pres. Chinese Acad. of Agricultural Sciences (CAAS) 1987–94, Chair. and Prof. Grad. School CAAS 1988–95; Hon. Chair. Acad. Cttee of CAAS

1995–; Vice-Chair. Chinese Crop Science Soc. 1988–94, Chair. 1994–2002; Vice-Chair. Scientific Tech. Cttee (Ministry of Agric.) 1988–96, Chinese Cttee for Release of New Crop Varieties 1989–96, Vice-Pres. China Asscn for Science and Tech. 1991–2001, Heilonjiang Asscn of Science and Tech., Chinese Asscn of Agricultural Science Socs.; Chair. China Int. Exchange Asscn of Agricultural Science and Tech. 1992–96; mem. Bd IFAD 1988–91, CABI 1994–97; Co-Chair. Advisory Cttee China-EC Centre for Agricultural Tech. 1992–97; Pres. China Seed Asscn 1998–, China Agricultural Tech. Soc. 2000–; mem. Chinese dels. to numerous int. confs.; Deputy to People's Congress of China and mem. Agricultural and Rural Affairs Cttee of Congress 1998–; has developed 19 soya bean cultivars; during 1991–2003 developed seven soya bean cultivars: Zhonghuan No. 12, Zhonghuan No. 13 with high yielding and broad adaptation, Zhonghuan No. 17, Zhongzuo No. 983 with high oil content, Zhongzuo 011 with high protein content, Zhongzuo RN02 with high resistance to cyst nematode, and Zhongzuo 962 with early maturity; Foreign mem. Russian Acad. of Agricultural Sciences; Foreign Fellow Indian Nat. Acad. of Agricultural Sciences; Second Class Chinese State Prize for Invention, for new soyabean cultivar "Heinong 26", Second Class Chinese State Prize for Invention, for new potato cultivar "Kexin No. 1", First Class Prize for Scientific Progress, Ministry of Agric.; Second Class Heilongjiang Prov. Prize for Tech. Progress, for high-yielding high-protein soyabean cultivar "Heinong 35" 1994. *Publications:* Feeding a Billion (co-author) 1987, Soyabean Breeding and Genetics (Ed.-in-chief) 1992, Agriculture in Modern China (Co-ed.) 1992, Soyabean Cultivation for High Yielding (Ed.-in-chief) 1994 and more than 162 papers. *Leisure interest:* classical music. *Address:* Chinese Academy of Agricultural Sciences, 12 Zhongguan chun Nan (Southern) Street, Haidian District, Beijing 100081; Cui wei xili 14-12-2, Haidian District, Beijing, 100081, People's Republic of China. *Telephone:* (10) 68975138 (Office); (10) 68258061 (Home); (10) 68919388. *Fax:* (10) 68975184 (Office); (10) 68975138. *E-mail:* wanglz@mail.caas.net.cn (Office).

WANG LINXIANG; Chinese business executive; b. 1951, Baotou, Nei Monggol Autonomous Region; joined CCP 1974; Dir Erdos Cashmere Sweater Mill 1983–89; Pres. Erdos Group 1989–. *Address:* Erdos Group, Baotou, Nei Monggol, People's Republic of China.

WANG LIQIN; Chinese table tennis player; b. 1 June 1978; singles finalist Int. Table Tennis Fed. (ITTF) Pro Tour Grand Finals 1997, Yugoslav Open 1997, Japan Open 1997, Hong Kong 1997, winner ITTF Pro Tour Grand Finals 1998, 2000, Lebanon Open 1998, Asian Championships 1998, Kenshoen Grand Finals 2000; men's doubles semi-finalist ITTF Pro Tour Grand Finals 1997, finalist China Grand Prix 1998, Australian Open 1998, Malaysian Open 1998, Qatar Open 1998, World Table Tennis Championships 1999, winner ITTF Pro Tour Grand Finals 2000, British Open 2001; doubles gold medallist Sydney Olympic Games; ranked number 1 in the World 2000–. *Address:* International Table Tennis Federation, Avenue Mon Repos 30, 1005 Lausanne, Switzerland (Office). *Telephone:* (21) 3407090 (Office). *Fax:* (21) 3407099 (Office). *Website:* www.ittf.com (Office).

WANG LUOLIN; Chinese economist; b. June 1938, Wuchang City., Hunan Prov.; ed Beijing Univ.; joined CCP 1978; Asst Lecturer, Lecturer, Assoc. Prof. Amoy Univ. 1961–84; Vice-Pres. Amoy Univ. 1984; currently Vice-Pres. Chinese Acad. of Social Sciences; alt. mem. 13th CCP Cen. Cttee 1987, mem. 14th CCP Cen. Cttee 1992, 15th CCP Cen. Cttee 1997–2002. *Publications:* Blue Book of China's Economoy (co-ed. annually). *Address:* Chinese Academy of Social Sciences, Jianguomennei Dajie 5 Hao, Beijing 100732, People's Republic of China. *Telephone:* (10) 65137744 (Office). *Fax:* (10) 65138154 (Office). *E-mail:* wangll@cass.net.cn (Office). *Website:* www.cass.net.cn (Office).

WANG MAOLIN; Chinese party and government official; b. 1935, Qidong, Jiangsu; ed Shanghai Financial and Econ. Coll.; Vice-Chair. Shanxi Prov. Revolutionary Cttee 1977–78; Vice-Gov. Shanxi Prov. 1979–88; Vice-Chair. Shanxi Prov. People's Congress 1981–88; Deputy Sec. Shanxi Prov. Cttee 1988–91, Sec. 1991; Chair. CPPCC 7th Shanxi Prov. Cttee 1993; Sec. CPC 7th Hunan Prov. Cttee 1993–98; mem. CCP 13th Cen. Cttee 1987–92, 14th Cen. Cttee 1992–97; mem. 15th CCP Cen. Cttee 1997–2002. *Address:* c/o Central Committee of the Chinese Communist Party, Zhongnanhai, Beijing, People's Republic of China.

WANG MAORUN, Gen.; Chinese army officer; b. May 1936, Rongcheng, Shandong Prov.; ed PLA Mil. Acad.; joined PLA 1951; mem. CCP 1956–; staff officer, Qingdao Garrison 1962; various posts in a corps political dept 1969–73; Deputy Sec.-Gen. Political dept Jinan Mil. Region 1973–76; Dir of a corps political dept 1976–83; corps deputy political commissar 1983–85; Dir Political Dept PLA Lanzhou Mil. Region 1985–90; Deputy Political Commissar and Sec. CCP Comm. for Inspecting Discipline, Lanzhou Mil. Region 1990; Political Commissar, Nat. Defence Univ. 1995–; rank of Gen. 1998; mem. 15th CCP Cen. Cttee 1997–2002. *Address:* National Defence University, Beijing, People's Republic of China.

WANG MENG; Chinese politician and writer; b. 15 Oct. 1934, Beijing; s. of Wang Jindi and Tong Min; m. Cui Ruifang 1957; two s. one d.; criticized 1957–76; rehabilitated 1979; alt. mem. 12th Cen. Cttee CCP 1982, mem. 12th Cen. Cttee CCP 1985, mem. 13th Cen. Cttee 1987–92; Minister of Culture 1986–89; mem. Secr. Chinese Writers' Asscn 1981–86, Vice-Chair. 1985–; Vice-Pres. China PEN Centre 1982–; Vice-Pres. Asscn for Int. Understanding 1985–; Chief Ed. People's Literature 1983–86; mem CPPCC 8th Nat. Cttee March 1994–; Vice-Chair. Chinese Writers' Asscn 2001. *Publications include:*

The Young Newcomer in the Organization Department 1956, Long Live the Youth 1957, Bolshevik State: A Modernist Chinese Novel 1979, The Barber's Tale 1979, A Night in the City 1979, A Spate of Visitors 1980, The Butterfly 1980, The Metamorphosis of Human Nature 1986, Selected Works (Vols I–IV) 1986, Adventures of a Soccer Star 1990, You Can Come into My Dream Again 1991, Revelation from The Dream of Red Mansion 1991, Notes on Styles (collection of literary criticisms) 1991, The Seasons for Love 1992, Hard Gruel (short stories) 1992, The Season for Losing Self-Control 1995, The Season for Hesitation 1997, The Season for Carnivals 2000. *Leisure interests:* swimming, drinking. *Address:* China PEN, Shatan Beijie 2, Beijing, People's Republic of China.

WANG MENGKUI; Chinese academic; b. April 1938, Wenxian Co., Henan Prov.; ed Beijing Univ.; joined CCP 1956; Assoc. Research Fellow then Research Fellow, Research Office of Secr. CCP Cen. Cttee 1981–87; Exec. Vice-Dir Econs Research Centre of State Planning Comm. 1987; Vice-Dir Research Office of State Council 1990, Dir 1995–; alt. mem. 14th CCP Cen. Cttee 1992, mem. 15th CCP Cen. Cttee 1997–. *Address:* Research Office of the State Council, Beijing, People's Republic of China.

WANG NAN; Chinese table tennis player; singles finalist Int. Table Tennis Fed. (ITTF) Pro Tour Grand Final 1997, 2000, 2001, China Open 1997, winner Lebanon Open 1997, US Open 1997, ITTF Pro Tour Grand Final 1998, China Open 1998, World Cup 1997, 1998, World Table Tennis Championships 1999, 2001; doubles winner ITTF Pro Tour Grand Final 1997, Lebanon Open 1997; Olympic gold medallist 2000 singles and doubles (with Li Ju). *Address:* International Table Tennis Federation, Avenue Mon Repos 30, 1005 Lausanne, Switzerland (Office). *Telephone:* (21) 3407090 (Office). *Fax:* (21) 3407099 (Office). *Website:* www.ittf.com (Office).

WANG QIMIN; Chinese business executive; b. 1937; ed Beijing Petroleum Inst.; joined CCP 1978; technician, Vice-Chief Geologist, Sr Engineer and then Vice-Pres. Oilfield Devt Research Inst. of Daqing Oilfield 1961–96, Pres. 1996–. *Address:* Oilfield Development Research Institute, Daqing, Heilongjiang Province, People's Republic of China.

WANG QISHAN; Chinese politician; b. July 1948, Tianzhen, Shanxi Prov.; ed Northwest Univ.; joined CCP 1983; div. head, Rural Devt Research Centre of State Council, acting Dir then Dir Rural Devt Inst. 1982–87; Gen. Man. China Rural Trust and Investment Corp. 1988–89; Vice-Pres. Construction Bank of China 1989–93, Pres. 1994–97; Vice-Gov. People's Bank of China 1993–94; Chair. of China Investment Bank 1994–97; Chair. China Int. Capital Corpn Ltd 1995–97; Exec. Vice-Gov. Guangdong Prov. 1998–2000; Dir Econ. Restructuring Office of the State Council 2000–; apptd Mayor of Beijing (acting) April 2003. *Address:* Economic Restructuring Office of the State Council, Beijing, People's Republic of China (Office).

WANG RUILIN, Gen.; Chinese army officer and party official; b. Dec. 1929, Zhaoyuan Co., Shandong Prov.; joined PLA 1946, CCP 1947; decoder and staff officer, Confidential Div., PLA Northeast Mil. Dist 1947–49; Deputy Section Chief, Confidential Div., Govt Admin. Council 1949–52; Sec. Office of Vice-Premier Deng Xiaoping 1973–76; Dir Vice-Chair.'s Office of CCP Cen. Cttee Mil. Comm., then Chair.'s Office; Deputy Dir of Gen. Office, CCP Cen. Cttee 1983–97, Vice-Dir PLA Gen. Political Dept 1992– (concurrently Dir Office of Deng Xiaoping –1997); rank of Lt-Gen. 1988; mem. 13th CCP Cen. Cttee 1987–92; Sec. Comm. for Discipline Inspection CCP Cen. Cttee Mil. Comm. 1990–93; mem. 14th CCP Cen. Cttee 1992–97, mem. Cen. Mil. Comm. 1995–; mem. 15th CCP Cen. Cttee 1997–2002. *Address:* Central Office, Chinese Communist Party Central Committee, Beijing, People's Republic of China.

WANG SENHAO; Chinese government official; b. 1932, Cixi, Zhejiang; two s.; Deputy Sec. CCP Cttee, Shaanxi 1983–93; Gov. of Shaanxi Prov. 1983–93; Minister of Coal Industry 1993–98; mem. CCP 12th Cen. Cttee 1985–87, 13th Cen. Cttee 1987–92, 14th Cen. Cttee 1992–97; Chair. Soc. and the Rule of Law Cttee, 9th Nat. Cttee of CPPCC 1998–. *Address:* National Committee of Chinese People's Political Consultative Conference, 23 Taipingqiao Street, Beijing, People's Republic of China.

WANG SHI; Chinese business executive; b. Jan. 1951, Liuzhou, Guanxi Prov.; ed Lanzhou Railway Inst.; f. Modern Scientific and Educational Instrument Exhbn Centre, Gen. Man. 1984; initiated China Urban Real Estate Developers' Collaborative Network 1999; initiated and organized "New Residence Forum" Shanghai Conf. and promoted New Residence Campaign 2000; Chair. and CEO Shenzhen Wanke Enterprise Ltd 1988; elected one of the Top Ten Econ. Figures in China 2000. *Address:* Shenzhen Wanke Enterprise Ltd., Shenzhen, People's Republic of China (Office).

WANG SHOUGUAN; Chinese astronomer and university professor; b. 15 Jan. 1923, Fuzhou; s. of B. L. Wang and S. Y. Gao; m. Lin Zhihuan 1955; one s. one d.; Deputy Head, Div. of Math. and Physics, Chinese Acad. of Sciences 1981–; Prof. Beijing Normal Univ. 1987–, Univ. of Science and Tech. of China 1991–; Hon. Dir Beijing Astronomical Observatory 1987–; Hon. Pres. Chinese Astronomical Soc. 1988–; Chief Ed. Vol. Astronomy, Chinese Encyclopaedia 1980; Chief Ed. Astrophysics Sinica; mem. Chinese Acad. of Sciences 1981; Nat. Science Congress Award 1978, Nat. Science and Tech. Progress Award 1985. *Leisure interest:* poetry. *Address:* Beijing Normal University, Xinyiekouwai Street 19, Beijing 100875 (Office); No. 404, Block 808, Zhong-Guan-Cun, Beijing 100080, People's Republic of China. *Telephone:* (10) 62207960 (Office). *Fax:* (10) 62200074 (Office). *E-mail:* ipo@bnu.edu.cn (Office). *Website:* www.bnu.edu.cn (Office).

WANG SHUWEN; Chinese constitutional lawyer; b. 3 April 1927, Qingshen, Sichuan Prov.; ed Sichuan Univ., Univ. of Moscow; joined CCP 1957; Asst Researcher, Law Research Inst. of Chinese Acad. of Sciences 1957–79; Research Fellow and Dir Nat. Law Research Section of Law Research Inst. of Chinese Acad. of Social Sciences, then Dir of the Inst.; Vice-Chair. Chinese Law Soc. 1979–; took part in drafting the Basic Laws for Hong Kong and Macao and in revising the Chinese Constitution; mem. Standing Cttee 8th NPC and Vice-Chair. Law Cttee of NPC. *Publications:* Xianfa Jiben Zhishi Jianghua (The ABC of the Constitution), Faxue Jiben Zhishi Jianghua (The ABC of the Science of Law), Wo Guo Renmin Daibiao Dahui Zhidu (The System of China's People's Congress), Xianggang Tebie Xingzheng Qu Jiben Fa Daolun (Introduction to the Basic Law of Hong Kong Special Admin. Region) and Aomen Tebie Xingzheng Qu Jiben Fa Daolun (Introduction to the Basic Law of Macao Special Admin. Region). *Address:* 15 Shatan Bei Jie, Beijing 100720, People's Republic of China. *Telephone:* (10) 64043942.

WANG TAIHUA; Chinese politician; b. Oct. 1945, Xingguo, Jiangxi Prov.; ed Jiangxi Teachers Coll.; joined CCP 1973; Vice-Sec. CCP Anhui Prov. Cttee and Sec. CCP Hefei City Cttee 1992–98; Deputy Gov. Anhui Prov. 1998–99, Gov. 1999–2000; Sec. CCP Anhui Prov. Cttee 2000–; alt. mem. CCP 14th and 15th Cen. Cttees 1992–2002. *Address:* c/o Anhui Provincial People's Government, 1 Changjiang Road, Hefei, Anhui Province, People's Republic of China.

WANG TAO; Chinese politician and geologist; b. 1931, Leting, Hebei; Chief Geologist, Dagang Oil Field; Chief Geologist, Liaohe Petroleum Prospecting Bureau; Gen. Man., South China Sea Eastern Br. of China Nat. Offshore Oil Corpn; Minister of Petroleum Industry 1985–88; Pres. China Nat. Petroleum Corpn 1988–97; mem. CCP 12th Cen. Cttee 1985–87, 13th Cen. Cttee 1987–92, 14th Cen. Cttee 1992–97, Vice-Chair. Environment and Resources Protection Cttee, 9th NPC 1998–. *Address:* c/o Standing Committee of the National People's Congress, Beijing, People's Republic of China.

WANG TIAN-REN; Chinese sculptor, artist and calligrapher; b. 26 July 1939, Henan; s. of Zheng-gang Wang and Shu-zheng Ren; m. Zhang Pei 1969; one s.; ed Xian Acad. of Fine Arts; worked as art designer and sculptor at Shaanxi Exhbn Hall 1963–79, worked on construction 1964–65; cr. sculptures for Yanan Revolution Memorial Hall 1968–71; Dir group sculptures for Shaanxi Exhbn Hall 1972–75; participated in group sculptures for Chairman Mao Memorial Hall 1976–78; calligraphy works exhibited in Chinese and Japanese cities; Pres. Shaanxi Sculpture Inst. 1995–; Vice-Dir of Sculpture Art Cttee, Shaanxi Br. Nat. Asscn of Artists; Art Dir, Dir of Creation Office, Shaanxi Sculpture Inst.; mem. Nat. Calligraphers Asscn, Shaanxi Folk Art Inst., Shaanxi Industrial Artists Asscn. *Works include:* Hou Ji 1980–81, Flower, The Morning Rooster, Qin Ox, Zebra, Tang Dynasty Musicians in Nishang and Yuyi (Copper Medal, Nat. City Sculptures Designing Exhbn 1983), Letter Carrier Goose (Copper Medal, Nat. City Sculptures Designing Exhbn 1983), Biaoqi General of Han Dynasty Huo Qu-bing' (Excellent Prize, 6th Nat. Art Works Exhbn 1984, First Prize, Shaanxi Art Works Exhbn 1984), Rising to the Sky (for Urumuqi, Xinjing; Prize for Excellence, Nat. Ministry of Urban Construction, Nat. Asscn of Artists 1987) 1985, Qin Unification 1992, Unification of Qin Dynasty (selected for 2nd Nat. City Sculpture, Nat. Prize from Nat. Construction Ministry, Ministry of Culture and Asscn of Nat Artists) 1994, Yu Youren (selected for 8th Nat. Arts Exhbn) 1994, sign sculpture for Xijiang Chemical Fertilizer Factory 1995, civic scenery sculpture for Hejin, Shaanxi Prov. 1995, Soar Aloft (sign sculpture for Xian Yanliang city) 1996, Zhao Hongzhang (granite-sculpture) 1996, Hou Ji (stone sculpture for Shaanxi) 1996, large city sign sculpture for Shanxi 1996. *Leisure interests:* Chinese classical literature, poetry, music. *Address:* Shaanxi Sculpture Institute, Longshoucun, Xian, Shaanxi 710016, People's Republic of China. *Telephone:* (29) 6261002 (Office); (29) 6253551 (Home). *Fax:* (29) 3237768.

WANG TIEYA, PhD; Chinese lawyer; b. 1913, Fuzhou, Fujian Prov.; ed Fudan Univ., Tsinghua Univ., London School of Econs, UK; Prof. of Int. Law, Wuhan Univ. 1940–47; Prof. Peking Univ. 1947–97; Chair. Chinese Soc. of Int. Law 1988–; Judge, Second Int. Tribunal on Former Yugoslavia 1997–2000.

WANG WEICHENG; Chinese party official; b. 1929, Tonglu Co., Zhejiang Prov.; joined CCP 1948; Deputy head of Propaganda Dept, CCP Cen. Cttee 1987; Dir Cen. Policy Research Center 1989–; mem. 14th CCP Cen. Cttee 1992–97; Vice-Pres. China Asscn for Int. Exchange of Personnel, Soc. for study of Workers' Political and Ideological Work; Chair. Legal Affairs Cttee of 9th NPC 1998–. *Address:* c/o Standing Committee of National People's Congress, Beijing, People's Republic of China.

WANG WENSHI; Chinese writer; b. 21 Nov. 1921, Shaanxi Prov.; s. of Wang Zhitong and Cui Jinxiu; m. Gao Bin 1949; two s. one d. *Publications:* Comrade-in-Arms (opera libretto), The Night of Wind and Snow, Hei Feng (novel), The Dunes, New Acquaintance, Yiyun Ji (Echo the Views of Others: essay), Wang Wenshi's Prose, Selected Short Stories. *Leisure interests:* playing marjang pieces, calligraphy. *Address:* Union of Chinese Writers, Shaanxi Branch Xian, Shaanxi Province, People's Republic of China.

WANG WENYUAN; Chinese politician and economist; b. Feb. 1931, Huangpi, Hubei Prov.; ed Northeast China Finance and Econs Inst.; teaching Asst, lecturer, Assoc. Prof., Prof. and Head, Econs Dept of Liaoning Univ. 1958–88; Vice-Gov. of Liaoning Prov. 1988–92; Vice-Chair. Cen. Cttee of Jiu San Soc. 1988–; Vice-Chair. Supreme People's Procuratorate 1992–98; Vice-Chair. 9th Nat. Cttee of CPPCC 1998–; Pres. 6th Council of China Council for the Promotion of Peaceful Reunification 1999–. *Address:* National Committee of Chinese People's Political Consultative Conference, 23 Taipingqiao Street, Beijing, People's Republic of China.

WANG XIANJIN; Chinese politician; b. 1930, Haiyang, Shandong; fmr Vice-Sec. Jilin, concurrently Dir State Bureau of Land Admin.; Pres. Asscn of Land Valuers of China 1994–. *Address:* Association of Land Valuers of China, Beijing, People's Republic of China.

WANG XIAOFENG; Chinese politician; b. Oct. 1944, Cili Co., Hunan Prov.; ed Beijing Mining Inst.; joined CCP 1973; Vice-Sec. CCP Changde Prefectural Cttee, Commdr Changde Prefectural Admin. Comm. 1983; Dir Hunan Provincial Planning Comm. 1986; Vice-Gov. Hunan 1990; Vice-Sec. CCP Hunan Prov. Cttee 1992; alt. mem. 14th CCP Cen. Cttee 1992–97; Vice-Sec. CCP Hainan Provincial Cttee; Vice-Gov. Hainan Prov. 1993–98, Gov. 1998–; mem. 15th CCP Cen. Cttee 1997–2002. *Address:* Office of the Governor, Haikou City, Hainan Province, People's Republic of China.

WANG XIAOGUANG; Chinese jurist; b. 1924, Anguo, Hebei; Deputy Procurator-Gen. 1983; mem. CCP Discipline Inspection Comm. 1982; Sec. Party Cttee Beijing Univ. 1985; Deputy Procurator Gen., Supreme People's Procuratorate, Pres. Soc. of Procuratorial Work; NPC Deputy Hebei Prov.; mem. 8th NPC 1993–98, Internal and Judicial Affairs Cttee. *Address:* Supreme People's Procuratorate, Beijing, People's Republic of China.

WANG XIJI, BEng, MS; Chinese engineer; b. 1921, Dali, Yun'nan Prov.; ed Nat. Southwest Assoc. Univ., Virginia Polytechnic Inst., USA; returned to China 1950; fmrly Assoc. Prof. Dalian Polytechnic; Prof. Shanghai Jiaotong Univ. and Shanghai Univ. of Science and Tech.; Chief Engineer Shanghai Mechanical and Electrical Designing Inst., Chinese Acad. of Sciences; Chief Engineer Ministry of Aerospace Industry; Vice-Pres. Research Inst. No. 5, Ministry of Aerospace Industry; Fellow Chinese Acad. of Sciences 1993–; was in charge of the research and Devt of 12 types of sounding rockets and the technical design of China's first launch vehicle Long March I in the 1960s; was first chief designer of Chinese recoverable satellites (CRSAT) and successfully conducted China's micro-gravity space experiments on CRSAT; Special Prize of Nat. Science and Tech. Advancement Award 1985, Meritorious Service Medal for the Devt of China's Atomic and Hydrogen Bombs and Satellites by the CCP Cen. Cttee, the State Council and the Cen. Mil. Comm. 1999. *Address:* c/o Chinese Academy of Sciences, 52 Sanlihe Road, Beijing 100864, People's Republic of China (Office).

WANG XUAN; Chinese computer scientist; b. 5 Feb. 1937, Shanghai; s. of Wang Shou-Qi and Zhou Miao-Qin; m. Chen Kun-Qiu 1967; ed Beijing Univ.; Prof. and Dir Research Inst. of Computer Tech., Peking Univ.; mem. Chinese Acad. of Sciences 1992–, Third World Acad. of Sciences 1993–, Chinese Acad. of Eng 1994–; Vice-Chair. Cttee of Educ., Science and Public Health of 9th NPC 1998–; Science and Tech. Progress Award, UNESCO Science Prize 1995, State Pre-eminent Science and Tech. Award 2001. *Leisure interests:* Peking Opera, sightseeing. *Address:* Peking University Computer Science & Technology Research Institute, Beijing 100871, People's Republic of China. *Telephone:* (10) 62981435. *Fax:* (10) 62981501. *E-mail:* xwang@founder.com.cn (Office).

WANG XUDONG; Chinese politician; b. Jan. 1946, Yancheng, Jiangsu Prov.; ed Tianjin Science and Tech. Refresher Coll.; joined CCP 1972; fmrly Sec. of Chinese Communist Youth League Cttee; Vice-Sec. CCP Cttee PLA 1418 Research Inst.; Dir Research Inst. No. 18, Ministry of Electronics Industry; Dir Dept of Org., CCP Tianjin Mun. Cttee, also Vice-Sec.; Vice-Dir Dept of Org., CCP Cen. Cttee 1993–2000; Sec. CCP Hebei Prov. Cttee 2000–; Minister of Information Industry 2003–. *Address:* Ministry of Information Industry, 13 Xichangan Jie, Beijing 100804, People's Republic of China (Office). *Telephone:* (10) 66014249 (Office). *Fax:* (10) 66034248 (Office). *E-mail:* webmaster@mii .gov.cn (Office). *Website:* www.mii.gov.cn (Office).

WANG XUEBING; Chinese banker; ed Univ. of Int. Business and Econs, Beijing; Adviser Steering Group, Gold and Exchange Rate Man. of State Council; Gen. Man. U.S. Operations, Bank of China 1988–93; Chair. and Pres. Bank of China 1993–2000; Pres. and CEO China Construction Bank 2000–02; dismissed following alleged financial irregularities at Bank of China; alt. mem. Cen. Cttee CCP 1997; Chair. China Int. Capital. Corpn; Dir Inst. of Int. Finance, Hong Kong Inst. for Monetary Research. *Address:* c/o Bank of China, 410 Fu Cheng Men Nei Dajie, Beijing 100818, People's Republic of China.

WANG YING-FAN, BA; Chinese diplomatist; m.; one d.; ed Beijing Univ.; on staff, Office of Chargé d'Affaires of People's Repub. of China, London 1964; joined Dept of Translation and Interpreting, Ministry of Foreign Affairs 1967; attaché, Embassy, Ghana then Embassy, Philippines; Deputy Div. Dir, Dept of Asian Affairs, Foreign Ministry 1978, Deputy Dir-Gen. 1988; Amb. to the Philippines 1988–90; Dir-Gen. Dept of Asian Affairs, Foreign Ministry 1990–94, Asst Foreign Minister 1994–95, Vice-Minister for Foreign Affairs 1995–2000; Perm. Rep. to UN 2000–. *Address:* Permanent Mission of the People's Republic of China to the United Nations, 350 East 35th Street, New York, NY 10016, U.S.A. (Office). *Telephone:* (212) 655-6100 (Office). *Fax:* (212) 634-7626 (Office). *E-mail:* china@un.int (Office). *Website:* www.un.fmprc.gov .cn/eng/index.html (Office).

WANG YONGYAN; Chinese doctor; b. Sept. 1938, Tianjin; ed Beijing Chinese Medical Coll.; Assoc. Prof., Prof., Chief Doctor, Pres. Beijing Chinese

Medical Univ. 1962; Fellow, Chinese Acad. of Sciences; Vice-Chair. Chinese Medical Soc. of China. *Address:* c/o 11 Beisanhuan Dong Lu, Beijing 100029, People's Republic of China (Office).

WANG YONGZHI; Chinese aerospace scientist; b. Nov. 1932, Changtu, Liaoning Prov.; ed Moscow Aeronautics Inst.; Dir Research Section, Dir Design Dept, Pres. No. 1 Research Inst. of Ministry of Aerospace Industry; Gen. Designer of Rockets 1961–91; Vice-Dir Science and Tech. Cttee of Ministry of Aerospace Industry 1991–98; gen. designer of rocket launcher series 1991–. *Address:* The People's Liberation Army General Equipment Department, 4 Beisanhuan Middle Road, Beijing 100720, People's Republic of China (Office). *Telephone:* (10) 66350660 (Office). *Fax:* (10) 66061566 (Office). *E-mail:* engach@mail.cae.ac.cn (Office).

WANG YOU-TSAO, MSc, PhD; Taiwanese politician; b. 2 July 1925, Chinchiang Co., Fukien; s. of Wang Hsiao-kwei and Wang-Huang Pei-feng; m. Jean Eng-ling 1954; two s. one d.; ed Nat. Taiwan Univ., Iowa State Univ., USA; Asst. Instructor, Assoc. Prof., Dept of Agric. Econs. Nat. Taiwan Univ. 1954–60, Prof. 1960–73; Specialist, Rural Econs Div., Jt Comm. on Rural Reconstruction (JCRR) 1960–63, Sr Specialist 1965–66, Chief, Rural Econs Div. 1966–71, Chief, Office of Planning and Programming 1971–72, Deputy Sec.-Gen. JCRR 1972–73, Sec.-Gen. 1973–79; Sec.-Gen. Council for Agric. Planning and Devt, Exec. Yuan 1979, Vice-Chair. 1979–84, Chair. 1984, Chair. and Chief Operating Admin. 1984–88, Adviser 1990–; Minister without Portfolio, Exec. Yuan 1988–90; Nat. Policy Adviser to Pres. 1990–96; Dir Asian Agric. Tech. Service Center 1993–95; Pres. Rural Devt Foundation 1995–98 (Chair. 1998–); Chair. Bd of Dirs. Harvest (farm magazine) 1995–2002; mem. Agric. Asscn of China, Rural Econs Asscn of China. *Publications:* Statistical Analysis of Resources Productivity in Shihmen Reservoir Area of Taiwan 1963, Technological Changes and Agricultural Development of Taiwan 1946–65 1966. *Address:* Council of Agriculture, Executive Yuan, 37 Nanhai Road, Taipei 100 (Office); 14-6 Alley 1, Lane 194, Sect. 4, Chung Hsiao East Road, Taipei, Taiwan (Home).

WANG YUAN; Chinese mathematician; b. 30 April 1930; Dir Inst. of Math., Acad. Sinica March–Oct. 1985; mem. Dept of Math. and Physics, Acad. Sinica 1985–; mem. Nat. Cttee 6th CPPCC 1986; Pres. Mathematics Soc. 1989–; Deputy Dir State Pharmaceutical Admin. 1991–; mem. Presidium Chinese Acad. of Sciences 1996–. *Address:* Institute of Mathematics, Academia Sinica, Zhong Guan Cun, Beijing 100080, People's Republic of China.

WANG YUNG-CHING; Taiwanese business executive; b. 18 Jan. 1917; m. Yueh-Lan Wang; two s. eight d.; founder/owner Formosa Plastics Group, a multinational petrochemical conglomerate consisting of over 20 cos. including Nan Ya Plastics Corpn, Formosa Plastics Corpn, Formosa Chemicals & Fibre Corpn, Cyma Plywood & Lumber Co. and three cos. in USA; Chair. Ming-chi Inst. of Tech. *Address:* Formosa Chemicals and Fibre Corporation., 201 Tun Hua North Road, Taipei, Taiwan.

WANG YUNKUN; Chinese politician; b. Dec. 1942, Liyang Co., Jiangsu Prov.; ed Tianjin Univ.; joined CCP 1966; Mayor of Jilin City and Vice-Sec. CCP Jilin City Cttee; Vice-Gov. Jilin Prov.; Sec. CCP Changchun City Cttee; Acting Gov. Jilin Prov. 1995, Gov. 1996–98; Sec. Jilin Prov. Cttee 1998–; Chair. Jilin Provincial People's Congress Standing Cttee 1999–; mem. 15th CCP Cen. Cttee 1997–2002. *Address:* c/o Jilin Provincial Government, Changchun City, Jilin Province, People's Republic of China.

WANG ZHAOGUO; Chinese party official; b. 1941, Fengrun, Hebei; ed Harbin Technological Univ.; First Sec. China Youth League 1982–84; mem. 12th Cen. Cttee CCP 1982–87, 13th Cen. Cttee 1987–92, 14th Cen. Cttee 1992–97, 15th Cen. Cttee 1997–2002; Deputy for Hubei to 6th NPC 1983; Dir-Gen. Office Cen. Cttee CCP 1984–86; Chief Rep. 21st Century Cttee for Chinese-Japanese Friendship 1984–89; Vice-Gov. and Acting Gov. of Fujian 1987–88, Gov. 1988–90; Dir Taiwan Affairs Office, State Council 1990–96; mem. Secr., CCP Cen. Cttee 1985–87; mem. Presidium 6th NPC 1986–88, Standing Cttee 6th NPC 1986–88; Head United Front Work Dept 1992–; Vice-Chair. 8th Nat. Cttee CPPCC 1993–98, 9th Nat. Cttee 1998–; Pres. China Overseas Friendship Asscn 1997–. *Address:* National Committee of the Chinese People's Political Consultative Conference, 23 Taipingqiao Street, Beijing, People's Republic of China.

WANG ZHENYI, DMed; Chinese haematologist; b. 3 Nov. 1924, Shanghai; ed Fudan Univ. Medical Coll.; fmrly doctor in charge, Shanghai Ruijin Hosp.; Pres. Shanghai Second Medical Univ.; Fellow, Chinese Acad. of Eng 1994–; Dir Shanghai Haematology Research Inst.; numerous prizes. *Address:* Shanghai Haematology Research Institute, Shanghai, People's Republic of China (Office).

WANG ZHIBAO; Chinese administrator; b. July 1938, Zhaoyuan, Shandong Prov.; ed Northeast Electric Power Inst.; joined CCP 1965; Vice-Minister of Forestry 1992–98; Dir State Forestry Bureau 1998–2000. *Address:* c/o State Forestry Bureau, Beijing, People's Republic of China.

WANG ZHIXIN; Chinese biophysicist; b. 10 Aug. 1953, Beijing; ed Tsinghua Univ.; Research Fellow, Vice-Dir Biophysics Research Inst. of Chinese Acad. of Sciences 1993–; Dir Nat. Biomolecular Lab.; Fellow, Chinese Acad. of Sciences; Hon. DSc (Biophysics Research Inst. of Chinese Acad. of Sciences) 1988. *Address:* Biophysics Research Institute of Chinese Academy of Sciences, 15 Datun Lu, Beijing 100012, People's Republic of China (Office). *Telephone:* (10) 64889910 (Office). *Fax:* (10) 62027837 (Office).

WANG ZHONGCHENG; Chinese neurosurgeon; b. 20 Dec. 1925, Yantai, Shandong Prov.; ed Peking Univ. Medical School; chief surgeon, Beijing Tongren Hosp.; Dir Beijing Neurosurgery Research Inst.; Pres. Beijing Tiantan Hosp.; Pres. and Hon. Dir; Beijing Neurosurgical Inst. Prof. Beijing Second Medical Coll.; Fellow, Chinese Acad. of Eng; neuroscience consultant to WHO; Heliangheli Science and Tech. Achievement Award 1997; numerous other scientific awards. *Publications:* Cerebral Aneurysms by Angiography, Neurosurgery, Practical Tumourology, Cerebral Vascular Diseases and Surgical Treatment; 278 papers and 24 monographs. *Leisure interests:* table tennis, swimming, calligraphy. *Address:* c/o Chinese Academy of Engineering, 3 Fuxing Lu, Beijing 100008 (Office); 6 Tiantan Xili, Beijing Chongwen Qu, Beijing, People's Republic of China (Home). *Telephone:* (10) 67014212 (Office); (10) 67027880 (Home). *Fax:* (10) 67018349 (Office). *E-mail:* wang.zhch@mail.cae.ac.cn (Office).

WANG ZHONGSHU; Chinese archaeologist; b. 15 Oct. 1925, Ningbo; s. of Wang Xuanbing and Ling Sujuan; m. Chen Kai 1960; one s.; ed Univ. of Beijing; Sr Fellow Inst. of Archaeology, Chinese Acad. of Social Sciences 1979–, Dir 1982–88; Prof. and Tutor for Doctoral Studies, Grad. School Chinese Acad. of Social Sciences 1982–; mem. Nat. Council of Cultural Relics 1983–; corresp. Fellow German Archaeological Inst. 1988–; Hon. Prof., Nat. Univ. of San Antonio Abad (Cuzco, Peru) 1973; 7th Fukuoka Grand Asian Cultural Prize, Fukuoka, Japan 1996. *Publications:* Han Civilization 1982, An Outline of Archaeology of the Han Period 1984, Triangular-rimmed Bronze Mirrors with Mythical Figure and Animal Designs unearthed from Japan 1992, Ancient Japan seen from China 1992. *Leisure interests:* Chinese and Japanese classical literature. *Address:* Institute of Archaeology, Chinese Academy of Social Sciences, 27 Wangfujing Dajie, Beijing 100710 (Office); 1-2-602 Chang Yun Gong, Zi Zhu Yuan, Beijing 100044, People's Republic of China (Home). *Telephone:* (10) 65234003 (Office); (10) 68411820 (Home). *Fax:* (10) 65135532 (Office). *E-mail:* liu.jg@history.cass.net.cn (Office); yidan@pku.edu.cn (Home). *Website:* www.archaeology.cass.net.cn (Office).

WANG ZHONGYU; Chinese politician; b. 1933, Changchun, Jilin; two s. one d.; joined CCP 1956; Sec. Gen. Jilin Prov. CCP Cttee 1984, Deputy Sec. 1985–89; Gov. 1989–93; alt. mem. 13th Cen. Cttee CCP 1987–92, 14th Cen. Cttee 1992; Deputy, Jilin Prov., 7th NPC 1988–93; Vice-Gov. Jilin Prov. 1988–89, Gov. 1989–93; Minister in charge of State Econ. and Trade Comm. 1993–98; State Councillor and Sec. Gen. State Council 1998–2003; mem. 15th Cen. Cttee CCP 1997–2002, 16th Cen. Cttee CCP 2002–. *Address:* c/o State Council, Xi Chang'an Jie, Beijing, People's Republic of China.

WANG ZIKUN, DSc; Chinese professor and university administrator; b. 30 April 1929, Jiangxi Prov.; s. of Wang Zhao-ji and Guo Xiang-e; m. Tian Der-Lin 1958; two s.; ed Wuhan Univ. and Moscow Univ.; Asst Prof., then Prof. Nankai Univ. 1952–84; Pres. and Prof. Beijing Normal Univ. 1984; Prof. Shantou Univ. 1993–; Dir of China Math. Soc.; mem. of Standing Bd China Probilistical-Statistics Soc., China Higher Educational Soc.; mem. of editorial Bd Society, Scientia Sinica, Science Bulletin of China; mem. Chinese Acad. of Sciences 1991–; DSc hc (Macquarie Univ., Australia) 1988; China Science Conf. Award 1978, China Natural Science Prize 1982, China Excellent Popular Science Works Award 1981 and numerous other awards. *Publications:* Foundations of Probability Theory and Their Applications 1976, Theory of Stochastic Processes 1965, Brownian Motion and Potentials 1982, Probability Theory and Statistical Prediction 1978, Talks on Scientific Discovery 1978, Birth-Death Processes and Markov Chains 1992 and many other math. articles and popular scientific Publs. *Leisure interest:* literature.

WANG ZUXUN, Gen.; Chinese army officer; b. May 1936, Qujing, Yunnan Prov.; joined PLA 1951; Vice-Commdr, then Commdr Yunnan Mil. Command 1984–89; Commdr Army Group 1989–93; Vice-Pres. PLA Acad. of Mil. Science 1993–99, Pres. 1999–; rank of Gen. 2000. *Address:* Xianghongqi, Beijing 100091, People's Republic of China (Office).

WANGCHUCK, Jigme Singye, King (Druk Gyalpo) of Bhutan; b. 11 Nov. 1955; s. of the late Druk Gyalpo Jigme Dorji Wangchuk and of Queen Ashi Kesang; m.; eight c.; ed North Point, Darjeeling, Ugyuen Wangchuk Acad., Paro, also in England; Crown Prince March 1972; succeeded to throne 24 July 1972, crowned 2 June 1974; Chair. Planning Comm. of Bhutan March 1972–; C-in-C of Armed Forces; Chair. Council of Ministers 1972–98. *Address:* Royal Palace, Thimphu, Bhutan.

WANIEK, Danuta, DJur; Polish politician and political scientist; b. 26 Oct. 1946, Włocławek; d. of Jerzy Waniek and Juzefina Waniek; m. (husband died); two s.; ed Warsaw Univ., Institut für Höhere Studien und Wissenschaft, Vienna; Inst. of Political Studies, Polish Acad. of Sciences (PAN) 1989–; mem. Polish United Workers' Party (PZPR) 1967–90; mem. Social Democracy of Polish Repub. (SDRP) 1990–; Deputy to Sejm (Parl.) 1991–, mem. Parl. Cttee of Nat. Defence; Chair. Women's Democratic Union 1990–; Deputy Minister of Nat. Defence 1994–95; Minister of State and Head of Chancellery of Pres. of Poland 1995–97; Krzyz Kastugi (Cross of Merit). *Publications:* Compromise within the Political System of Germany: Partnership or Struggle? 1988, Constitution and Political Reality 1989, Debate over 'Little Constitution' (ed.) 1992, Creating New Constitutional Order in Poland (ed.) 1993. *Leisure interests:* opera, reading newspapers, embroidering, painting, music (listening and playing). *Address:* Sejm, ul. Wiejska 4/6, 00-902 Warsaw, Poland.

WANKE, Maj. Daouda Mallam; Niger army officer; Head Nat. Reconciliation Council April 1999; fmr Head Presidential Guard. *Address:* National Reconciliation Council, Niamey, Niger.

WANLESS, Derek, MA, M.I.S., FCIB; British banker; b. 29 Sept. 1947, Newcastle; s. of the late Norman Hall Wanless and of Edna Charlton; m. Vera West 1971; one s. four d.; ed Royal Grammar School, Newcastle-upon-Tyne, King's Coll. Cambridge and Harvard Univ.; joined Nat. Westminster Bank PLC 1970, Marketing Man. Domestic Banking Div. 1980–82, Area Dir North-East Area 1982–85, W Yorks Area 1985–86, Dir of Personal Banking Services 1986–88, Gen. Man. UK Br. Business 1989–90, Chief Exec. UK Financial Services 1990–92, Deputy Group Chief Exec. and Group Head of NatWest Markets (now Hawkpoint Partners Ltd) 1992, Dir 1991–99, Group Chief Exec. 1992–99; Chair. Advisory Cttee on Business and the Environment 1993–95, Nat. Forum for Man. Educ. and Devt (NFMED) 1996–; consultant to Dept of Health 2001–; mem. Investors in People UK Bd, Statistics Comm. 2000–; Hon. DSc (City) 1995. *Leisure interests:* all sports, chess, music, walking, gardening.

WAPAKHABULO, James Francis Wambogo, LLB; Ugandan politician; b. 23 March 1945; ed Univ. of E Africa, Dar es Salaam, Tanzania, Kenya Inst. of Admin., Legis. Drafting Inst., Canberra, Australia, Legal Training Inst., Papua New Guinea; Asst Sec., Office of the Sec.-Gen., East African Community 1970–72; Clerk, East African Legis. Ass. 1973–77; Legal Officer, Office of the Attorney-Gen., Govt of Australia 1977–79; Sr Legis. Draftsman, Legis. Counsel, Papua New Guinea 1979–83; Prin. Legal Officer, later Asst Sec. of Justice, Ministry of Justice 1983–86; MP for Mbale municipality 1989–; Minister of Housing and Urban Devt 1986–88, of Co-operatives and Marketing 1988–91, of Industry and Tech. 1991–92, of Tourism, Wildlife and Antiquities 1992–94, without Portfolio, Office of the Pres. 1994–96; Chair. Constituency Ass. 1995–95; Speaker of Parl. 1996–98; Nat. Political Commissar 1998–2001; Sec.-Gen. Nat. Movt 1998–2001; Third Deputy Prime Minister and Minister of Foreign Affairs July 2001–; mem. Nat. Resistance Council 1986–89. *Leisure interests:* watching cricket and football. *Address:* Ministry of Foreign Affairs, Parliament Building, POB 7048, Kampala, Uganda (Office). *Telephone:* (41) 258251 (Office). *Fax:* (41) 258733 (Office). *E-mail:* info@mofa.go.ug (Office). *Website:* www.mofa.go.ug (Office).

WAPNEWSKI, Peter, DPhil; German professor of medieval literature; b. 7 Sept. 1922, Kiel; s. of Harald Wapnewski and Gertrud (née Hennings) Wapnewski; m. 1st Caroline Gräfin Finckenstein 1950 (divorced 1959); m. 2nd Monica Plange 1971; ed Univs. of Berlin, Freiburg, Jena and Hamburg; Prof. of Medieval German Literature, Heidelberg 1959, Free Univ. of Berlin 1966, Univ. of Karlsruhe 1969, Tech. Univ. of Berlin 1982–; Rector, Wissenschaftskolleg, Berlin 1980–86, Perm. mem. 1986–; Vice-Pres. Goethe Inst. 1977–2002; mem. Deutsche Akademie für Sprache und Dichtung, PEN Club, American Medieval Acad.; Dr hc (Heidelberg) 2002; Grosses Bundesverdienstkreuz 1986, (with star) 1992, Rahel Varnhagen von Ense Medal 1999, Ehrensenator, Tech. Univ. Berlin. *Publications:* Wolframs Parzival 1955, Deutsche Literatur des Mittelalters 1960, Walther von der Vogelweide (ed.), Hartmann von Aue 1962, Die Lyrik Wolframs von Eschenbach 1972, Richard Wagner—Die Szene und ihr Meister 1978, Der Traurige Gott 1978, Zumutungen 1979, Tristan der Held Richard Wagners 1981, Minnesang des Codex Manesse 1982, Eduard Hanslick, Aus meinem Leben (Ed.) 1987, Götternot und Göttertrauer 1988, Die unerhörten Künste (Ed.) 1989, Eduard Hanslick: Aus dem Tagebuch eines Rezensenten (Ed.) 1989, Peter Huchel, Gedichte (Ed.) 1989, Betrifft Literatur: Über Marcel Reich-Ranicki (Ed.) 1990, Richard Wagner Handbuch 1992, Zuschreibungen: Gesammelte Aufsätze von P.W. Hildesheim 1994, Weisst Du Wie das Wird? Richard Wagner: Der Ring des Nibelungen 1995, 2000; about 200 articles on medieval and modern German literature. *Address:* Wallotstrasse 19, 14193 Berlin, Germany. *Telephone:* (30) 890010.

WAQAR YOUNIS; Pakistani cricketer; b. 16 Nov. 1971, Vehari; ed Pakistani Coll. Sharjah and Govt Coll. Vehari; right-hand lower-order batsman, right-arm fast bowler; played for Multan 1987–88 to 1990–91, United Bank 1988–89 to date, Surrey 1990–91 and 1993, Glamorgan 1997–98 (took career-best 8 for 17 against Sussex); played in 87 Tests for Pakistan 1989–90 to 2 Jan. 2003, 17 as Capt. taking 373 wickets (average 23.56); has taken 912 wickets in first-class cricket to 15 Jan. 2003; toured England 1992, 1996 and 2001; 256 limited-overs internationals to 18 Dec. 2002 (56 as Capt.); Wisden Cricketer of the Year 1992. *Leisure interests:* football, badminton, squash. *Address:* c/o Pakistan Cricket Board, Gaddafi Stadium, Ferozepur Road, Lahore 54600, Pakistan. *Telephone:* (42) 571-7231.

WARBURTON, Dame Anne Marion, DCVO, CMG, MA; British diplomatist; b. 8 June 1927, London; d. of Capt. Eliot Warburton and Mary Louise Warburton (née Thompson); ed Barnard Coll., Columbia Univ. USA, Somerville Coll. Oxford; with Econ. Co-operation Admin., London 1949–52; NATO Secr., Paris 1952–54; Lazard Bros., London 1955–57; entered Diplomatic Service 1957; Second Sec., Foreign Office 1957–59; Second, then First Sec., UK Mission to UN, New York 1959–62; First Sec., Bonn 1962–65; Diplomatic Service Admin. Office, London 1965–67; Foreign Office, then FCO 1967–70; Counsellor, UK Mission to UN, Geneva 1970–75; Head of Guidance and Information Policy Dept, FCO 1975–76; Amb. to Denmark 1976–83, to UN at Geneva 1983–85; Pres. Lucy Cavendish Coll. Cambridge 1985–94, Hon. Fellow 1994–; Equal Opportunities Commr 1986–87; Leader EU Investigative Mission on the Abuse of Bosnian Muslim Women 1992–93; mem.

British Library Bd 1989–95, Council of Univ. of E Anglia 1991–97, Cttee on Standards in Public Life (Nolan Cttee) 1994–97; Hon. Fellow Somerville Coll. Oxford 1977–; Dr. hc (Arkansas) 1994; Verdienstkreuz (First Class), Fed. Repub. of Germany 1995; Grand Cross, Order of Dannebrog, Denmark 1979; Order of Isabel la Católica, Spain 1988. *Leisure interests:* the arts, walking, travel. *Address:* Ansted, Thornham Magna, Eye, Suffolk, IP23 8HB, England.

WARCHUS, Matthew, BA; British theatre director; b. 24 Oct. 1966, Rochester; ed Univ. of Bristol; Dir Nat. Youth Theatre 1989, 1990, Bristol Old Vic 1991; Asst Dir RSC 1991–92; Assoc. Dir W Yorks. Playhouse 1993; freelance Dir; Shakespeare's Globe Award 1994, Sydney Edwards Award 1995, Evening Standard Award 1995. *Films directed include:* Simpático (feature film) 1999. *Plays directed include:* (for R.S.C.) Henry V 1995, The Devil is an Ass 1995, Hamlet 1997; (for W Yorkshire Playhouse) Life is a Dream, Who's Afraid of Virginia Woolf?, The Plough and the Stars, Death of a Salesman, Betrayal, True West; other productions The Stuff of Life (Donmar Warehouse) 1994, Volpone (Royal Nat. Theatre) 1995, Art (Wyndhams) 1996, The Unexpected Man (Duchess) 1998, Life x 3 (West End) 2001, Art, True West, Follies (all Broadway). *Opera:* Troilus and Cressida (Opera North), The Rake's Progress, Falstaff, Così fan tutte (ENO). *Address:* c/o Hamilton Asper Management, 24 Hanway Street, London, W1T 1OH, England (Office). *Telephone:* (20) 7636-1221.

WARD, Ian Macmillan, MA, DPhil, FRS; British professor of physics; b. 9 April 1928, Stockton-on-Tees; s. of Harry Ward and Joan Moodie (née Burt); m. Margaret Linley 1960; two s. one d.; ed Royal Grammar School, Newcastle-upon-Tyne and Magdalen Coll. Oxford; Tech. Officer, ICI Fibres 1954–61; seconded to Div. of Applied Math. Brown Univ., USA 1961–62; Head, Basic Physics Section, ICI Fibres 1962–65; Sr Lecturer in Physics of Materials, Univ. of Bristol 1965–69; Prof. of Physics, Univ. of Leeds 1970–93, Cavendish Prof. 1977–94 (Chair. of dept 1975–78, 1987–89, Research Prof. Emer. 1994; Dir, IRC in Polymer Science and Tech. 1989–94); Pres. British Soc. of Rheology 1984–86; Hon. DSc (Bradford) 1993; A. A. Griffith Medal 1982, S. G. Smith Memorial Medal 1984, Swinburne Award 1988, Charles Vernon Boys Medal 1993. *Publications:* Mechanical Properties of Solid Polymers 1971, Structure and Properties of Oriented Polymers (Ed.) 1975, Ultra High Modulus Polymers (Ed.) 1979, An Introduction to Mechanical Properties of Solid Polymers (with D. W. Hadley) 1993, Solid Phase Processing of Polymers (Ed.) 2000. *Leisure interests:* music, walking. *Address:* Kirskill, 2 Creskeld Drive, Bramhope, Leeds, West Yorks., LS16 9EL, England. *Telephone:* (113) 267-3637 (Home).

WARD, Most Rev. John Aloysius; British ecclesiastic; b. 24 Jan. 1929, Leeds; s. of Eugene Ward and Hannah Cheetham; ed Prior Park Coll., Bath and Theological Seminaries of Franciscan Order, Olton, Crawley; entered Capuchin Franciscan Order 1945, Profession 1950, Priest 1953–; Travelling Missioner of Diocese of Menevia, Wales 1954–60; Superior (Guardian) and Parish Priest of Franciscan Friary, Peckham, London 1960–66; Provincial Definitor (Councillor) of British Prov. of Order 1963–69, Minister Provincial 1969–70; Gen. Definitor (Councillor) of Order in Rome 1970–80; Coadjutor Bishop of Menevia July 1980, Bishop Oct. 1980, succeeded to See 1981; Archbishop of Cardiff and Metropolitan of Welsh Prov. 1983–2001; Order of Friars Minor Capuchin. *Address:* c/o Archbishop's House, 41–43 Cathedral Road, Cardiff, CF11 9HD, Wales.

WARD, John Stanton, CBE, RP; British artist; b. 10 Oct. 1917; s. of the late Russell S. Ward and Jessie E. Ward; m. Alison C. M. Williams 1950; four s. twin d.; ed St Owen's School, Hereford and Royal Coll. of Art; served Royal Engineers 1939–46; with Vogue Magazine 1948–52; exhbns at Thomas Agnew Gallery and Maas Gallery; fmr Vice-Pres. Royal Soc. of Portrait Painters; mem. Exec. Nat. Art-Collections Fund 1976–87; Trustee, Royal Acad. (R.A.) 1976–87; resgnd from RA 1997; Hon. DLitt (Kent) 1982. *Art Exhibitions:* Hazlitt, Goaden & Fox, Fine Art Soc.; pictures in the Tate Gallery, Victoria and Albert Museum, Nat. Portrait Gallery, HM Royal Collection, Ashmolean and Fitzwilliam, Canterbury Royal Museum. *Publication:* The Paintings of John Ward. *Leisure interest:* book illustration. *Address:* Bilting Court, Bilting, Ashford, Kent, TN25 4HF, England. *Telephone:* (1233) 812478.

WARD, Michael Phelps, CBE, MD, FRCS; British consultant surgeon; b. 26 March 1925, London; s. of the late Wilfrid Arthur Ward and Norah Anne Phelps; m. Felicity Jane Ewbank 1957; one s.; ed Marlborough Coll., Peterhouse, Cambridge, London Hosp.; House Surgeon, Registrar, Sr Registrar, London Hosp. 1950–64; Lecturer in Clinical Surgery, London Hosp. Medical Coll. 1975–93; Consultant Surgeon, City and East London Area Hosp. Authority (Teaching) 1964–93, St Andrew's Hosp., Bow 1964–93, Newham Hosp. 1983–93; took part in Everest Reconnaissance 1951, First Ascent 1953, Himalayan Scientific Expedition 1960–61; Leader scientific expeditions N Bhutan 1964, 1965, Southern Xinjiang (First Ascent Mt. Kongur) 1980, 1981; Royal Soc./Chinese Acad. of Sciences Tibet Geotraverse 1985–86; Chair. Mt. Everest Foundation 1978–80; mem. Court of Assistants, Soc. of Apothecaries 1985; Hunterian Prof., Royal Coll. of Surgeons 1954; Cuthbert Peek Award, Royal Geographical Soc. 1973, Founders (Royal) Medal, Royal Geographical Soc. 1982, Cullum Medal, American Geographical Soc. 1954. *Publications:* Mountaineer's Companion 1966, In This Short Span 1972, Mountain Medicine 1975, High Altitude Medicine and Physiology (Co-Author) 1989; articles and medical papers on the effects of great altitude, exposure to cold and on exercise; also on exploratory journeys in Nepal, Bhutan, Chinese Cen. Asia and Tibet. *Leisure interests:* mountaineering, skiing. *Address:* c/o St Andrew's Hospital, Bow, London, E3 3NT, England.

WARD, Simon; British actor; b. 19 Oct. 1941, Beckenham; s. of Leonard Fox Ward and Winifred Ward; m. Alexandra Malcolm; three d.; ed Alleyn's School, Dulwich and Royal Acad. of Dramatic Art; mem. Nat. Youth Theatre from its foundation (as Youth Theatre) 1956; first professional stage appearance in Hobson's Choice, Northampton Repertory Theatre 1963; London début in The Fourth of June, St Martin's Theatre 1964; film début in Frankenstein Must Be Destroyed 1969. *Stage roles include:* Konstantin in The Seagull, Birmingham Repertory 1964; Abel Drugger in The Alchemist and Hippolytus in Phèdre, Playhouse, Oxford 1965–66; Dennis in Loot, Jeannetta Cochrane and Criterion 1966; the Unknown Soldier in The Unknown Soldier and His Wife, Ferdinand in The Tempest and Henry in The Skin of Our Teeth, Chichester Festival 1968; Donald in Spoiled, Haymarket 1971; Romeo in Romeo and Juliet, Shaw 1972; Troilus in Troilus and Cressida, Young Vic 1976. *Other stage performances include:* House Guest 1982, Whose Life is it Anyway?, Birmingham 1982, Heartbreak House 1983, Dial M for Murder 1983, Ross 1986, Paris Match 1988, Henceforward 1990, Rumours 1990, Don't Dress for Dinner 1992, Cell Mates 1995, An Ideal Husband 1997, Mindgame 2000. *Films include:* I Start Counting 1970, Young Winston 1971, Hitler—The Last Ten Days 1972, The Three Musketeers 1973, The Four Musketeers, Deadly Strangers, All Creatures Great and Small 1974–75, Aces High 1975, Battle Flag 1976, The Four Feathers 1978, Zulu Dawn 1979, Supergirl, Around The World in 80 Days, Double X 1992, Wuthering Heights, Ghost Writers. *Television includes:* The Black Tulip, The Roads to Freedom, Holocaust (serials). *Leisure interests:* music, gardening, reading, badminton. *Address:* c/o Shepherd & Ford Associates Ltd, 13 Radner Walk, London, SW3 4BP, England. *Telephone:* (20) 7352-2200. *Fax:* (20) 7352-2277.

WARD, Vincent; New Zealand film director; b. 1956, Greytown; ed Elam School of Fine Art, Christchurch. *Films include:* A State of Siege 1977, In Spring one Plants Alone 1979 (Grand Prix co-winner in 1982 Cinéma du Réel, Silver Hugo at Chicago Film Festival), Vigil 1984 (Grand Prix at Madrid and Prades Film Festivals), The Navigator 1988, Map of the Human Heart, Leaving Las Vegas (actor), What Dreams May Come. *Publication:* Edge of the Earth 1990. *Address:* P.O. Box 423, King's Cross, Sydney, NSW 2011, Australia. *Telephone:* (2) 360-2769.

WARDHANA, Ali, MA, PhD; Indonesian politician and economist; b. 6 May 1928, Surakarta, Central Java; m. Renny Wardhana 1953; one s. three d.; ed Univ. of Indonesia, Jakarta and Univ. of California at Berkeley, USA; Dir, Research Inst. of Econ. and Social Studies 1962–67; Prof. of Econs, Univ. of Indonesia 1967–, Dean Faculty of Econs 1967–78; Adviser to Gov. of Cen. Bank 1964–68; mem. team of experts of Presidential Staff 1966–68; Minister of Finance 1968–83; Co-ordinating Minister for Econ., Finance, Industry and Devt Control 1983–88; Chair. Cttee of Bd of Governors of the IMF on Reform of the Int. Monetary System and Related Issues 1972–74; Grand Cross Order of Léopold II (Belgium) 1970, Grand Cross Order of Orange Nassau (Netherlands) 1971, Mahaputra Adipradhna II Award (Indonesia) 1973. *Leisure interests:* reading, tennis, bowling, swimming. *Address:* 5, Jalan Brawijaya III, Kebayoran Baru, Jakarta, Indonesia.

WARLOW, Charles Picton, MD, FRCP; British professor of medical neurology; b. 29 Sept. 1943, Nottingham; s. of Charles Warlow and Nancy Hine; m. Ilona McDowell 1976; three c.; ed Univ. of Cambridge and St George's Hosp. Medical School, London; Lecturer in Medicine, Aberdeen 1971–74; specialist training in neurology, London and Oxford 1974–77; Clinical Reader in Neurology and Hon. Consultant Neurologist, Oxford 1977–87; Prof. of Medical Neurology, Univ. of Edin. 1987–; Pres. Asscn of British Neurologists 2001–03; Tenovus-Scotland Margaret MacLellan Award 1989–90, Soc. of Authors and Royal Soc. of Medicine Medical Book Award, Advanced Author Book Category 1997, Osler Oration, Royal Coll. of Physicians 1998. *Publications include:* Handbook of Clinical Neurology 1991, Transient Ischaemic Attacks of the Brain and Eye (with G. J. Hankey) 1994, Stroke: A Practical Guide to Management (co-author) 1996. *Leisure interests:* sailing, photography, mountains. *Address:* Department of Clinical Neurosciences, Western General Hospitals, Crewe Road, Edinburgh, EH4 2XU, Scotland. *Telephone:* (131) 537-2082. *Fax:* (131) 332-7886. *E-mail:* cpw@skull.dcn.ed.ac.uk (Office).

WARNE, Shane Keith; Australian cricketer; b. 13 Sept. 1969, Ferntree Gully, Melbourne; m. Simone Warne; one s. two d.; ed Hampton High School, Mentone Grammar School; leg-break and googly bowler; right-hand lower-order batsman; in 183 first-class matches for Hampshire took 70 wickets (average 23.1) to 2000; Australia's highest-ever wicket taker in Tests; 107 Tests for Australia 1991–92 to 29 Nov. 2002, taking 491 wickets (average 25.71) and scoring 2,238 runs; took hat-trick vs England, Melbourne, 1994; took 850 wickets and scored 4,103 runs in first-class cricket to 15 Jan. 2003; toured England 1993, 1997, 2001; 191 limited-overs ints (11 as Capt.) to 15 Jan. 2003; Capt. Vic. Sheffield Shield Team (Bushrangers) 1996–99; received 12-month ban in Feb. 2003 for testing positive for a banned substance; Wisden Cricketer of the Year 1994; selected as one of five Wisden Cricketers of the Century 2000. *Publication:* Shane Warne: The Autobiography 2001. *Address:* c/o Victorian Cricket Association, 86 Jolimont Street, Vic. 3002, Australia.

WARNER, Bishop Bennie D., MSc, ThM, DD; Liberian ecclesiastic; b. 30 April 1935, Caresburg District; ed Monrovia Gbargna United Methodist Mission School, Booker Washington Inst., Kakata, Cuttington Univ. Coll., Suakoto, Syracuse Univ. and Boston Univ. School of Theology (USA); ordained Deacon 1961; Acting Dir Pastors' Inst. of the United Methodist Church 1961; educ. counsellor and maths. and social studies teacher, W.V.S. Tubman Elementary School 1962–68; fmr Chair. Nat. Student Christian Council of Liberia; later ordained Elder; fmr Pastor, St John's United Methodist Church, Gbarnga and Reeves Memorial United Methodist Church, Crozierville; fmr Chair. Interim Cttee for the Admin. of the Coll. of W Africa, Bd of Ministry, Liberia Annual Conf. of United Methodist Church; ordained Bishop 1973; later Chair. Bd of Trustees of the Coll. of W Africa; Vice-Pres. of Liberia 1977–80; mem. Bd of Trustees, Cuttington Coll. and Divinity School, Bd of the Booker Washington Inst., Nat. Disaster Comm., Council of Bishops, World Methodist Council; in exile in USA; Grand Band, Order of the Star of Africa.

WARNER, Brian, MA, PhD, DSc; British astronomer; b. 25 May 1939, Crawley Down, Sussex; s. of Leslie Warner and Edith M. Warner (née Bashford); m. 1st Carole Christian 1965 (divorced 1973); one s. one d.; m. 2nd Nancy Russell 1976 (divorced 1987); ed Univs of London and Oxford; Research Asst, Univ. of London Observatory 1964–65; Radcliffe-Henry Skynner Sr Research Fellow, Balliol Coll. Oxford 1965–67; Asst Prof., Univ. of Texas at Austin 1967–69, Assoc. Prof. 1969–72; Prof. and Head, Dept of Astronomy, Univ. of Cape Town 1972–99 Distinguished Prof. of Natural Philosophy 1999–, Fellow 1978–; Alfred P. Sloan Fellow 1969–71; Visiting Fellow, Univ. of Colo 1977; Visiting Sr Fellow, Dept of Astrophysics Univ. of Oxford 1985; Visiting Prof. Dartmouth Coll. and Univ. of Texas 1986–87, Univ. of Sussex 1997; Visiting Fellow, Univ. of Calif. at Santa Cruz 1990, ANU 1989, 1993, 1996, 1998; Visiting Scientist, European Southern Observatory 1996; Pres. Royal Soc. of South Africa 1981–83, Foreign Sec. 1996–2001, Fellow; Founder mem. Acad. of Sciences of S Africa 1994–; Pres. Comm. 42 of Int. Astronomical Union 1978–82; Pres. Astronomical Soc. of Southern Africa 1977–78, The Owl Club 1985–86; mem. Bd of Trustees, South African Museum 1981–99, Deputy Chair. 1988–91, Chair. 1991–99; mem. Council S Africa Library 1991–99; Ernest Oppenheimer Travelling Fellowship 1990; Assoc. Royal Astronomical Soc. 1994; Hon. mem. Royal Astronomical Soc. of NZ 1995; Boyden Premium, Franklin Inst. 1980; McIntyre Award, Astronomical Soc. of Southern Africa 1983, John F. W. Herschel Medal, Royal Soc. of S Africa 1988, South African Medal, S African Asscn for the Advancement of Science 1989, Gill Medal, Astronomical Soc. of Southern Africa 1992, Univ. of Cape Town Book Award 1997. *Publications:* Astronomers at the Royal Observatory, Cape of Good Hope 1979, Charles Piazzi Smyth 1983, Maclear and Herschel 1984, The Journal of Lady Jane Franklin 1985, High Speed Astronomical Photometry 1988, William Mann 1989, Lady Herschel 1991, Cataclysmic Variable Stars 1995, Dinosaurs' End 1996, Flora Herscheliana 1998; over 300 scientific research papers. *Leisure interests:* 19th-century science and exploration, baroque music. *Address:* Department of Astronomy, University of Cape Town, Rondebosch, 7700 Cape (Office); 401 Blenheim, Marlborough Park, Claremont, 7700 Cape, South Africa (Home). *Telephone:* (2721) 6502391 (Office); (2721) 6711850 (Home). *Fax:* (2721) 6503342 (Office). *E-mail:* warner@physci.uct.ac.za (Office). *Website:* mensa.ast.uct.ac.za (Office).

WARNER, David; British actor; b. 29 July 1941, Manchester; s. of Herbert Simon Warner; ed Feldon School, Leamington Spa and Royal Acad. of Dramatic Art; worked as bookseller; stage début as Snout in A Midsummer Night's Dream, Royal Court 1962; film début in Tom Jones 1963; joined RSC 1963 and appeared as Trinculo in The Tempest, title role in Henry VI, Edward IV in adaptation of Henry VI (Parts I, II and III) comprising first two parts of trilogy The Wars of the Roses (Stratford). *Other roles include:* Henry VI in The Wars of the Roses, Aldwych 1964; Richard II, Mouldy in Henry IV (Part II) and Henry VI in The Wars of the Roses, RSC, Stratford 1964; Valentine Brose in Eh?, Aldwych 1964, Hamlet, Stratford and Aldwych 1965; the Postmaster in The Government Inspector, Aldwych 1965; Hamlet, Sir Andrew Aguecheek in Twelfth Night, Stratford 1966; Claudius in I, Claudius, Hampstead 1972. *Films include:* Morgan – A Suitable Case for Treatment 1966, Work is a Four Letter Word 1967, The Bofors Gun, The Fixer, The Seagull 1968–69, The Ballad of Cable Hogue 1970, Straw Dogs 1971, A Doll's House 1972, The Omen 1975, Cross of Iron, Providence, Silver Bears 1976, The Disappearance 1977, The Thirty Nine Steps 1978, Nightwing, Time After Time 1979, The Island 1980, Hanna's War 1988, The Secret Life of Ian Fleming 1990, Dark at Noon, Mortal Passions, In the Mouth of Madness, Titanic 1997, Scream 2 1997, Money Talks 1997, Shergar 2000, In the Beginning 2000, Horatio Horn Blower 2001. *Television includes:* Clouds of Glory 1977, Holocaust 1977, Charlie 1984, The Choir 1995.

WARNER, Deborah; British theatre and opera director; b. 12 May 1959, Oxford; d. of Ruth Warner and Roger Warner; ed Sidcot School, Avon, St Clare's, Oxford, Cen. School of Speech and Drama, London; Artistic Dir Kick Theatre Co. 1980–86; Resident Dir RSC 1987–89; Assoc. Dir Royal Nat. Theatre 1989–98; Assoc. Dir Abbey Theatre, Dublin 2000; has also staged productions at English Nat. Opera, Glyndebourne Festival Opera, Royal Opera House and Opera North and productions for Fitzroy Productions, Odeon Theatre and Bobigny Theatre, Paris, Salzburg Festival, L.I.F.T. and Perth Int. Arts Festival; Dir Fitzroy Productions; Evening Standard Award 1988, 1998, 2002, Laurence Olivier Award 1989, 1992, New York Drama Desk Award 1997, S. Bank Arts Award 1998; Officier, Ordre des Arts et des Lettres. *Productions include:* The Turn of the Screw, Royal Opera House 2002. *Films:* The Waste Land 1996, The Last September 1999. *Television includes:* Richard II (BBC), Hedda Gabler (BBC), Don Giovanni (Channel 4). *Leisure interest:*

travelling. *Address:* c/o Conway van Gelder Ltd, 18–21 Jermyn Street, London, SW1Y 6HP, England. *Telephone:* (20) 7287-0077. *Fax:* (20) 7287-1940.

WARNER, Douglas Alexander III, BA; American banker; b. 9 June 1946, Cincinnati; s. of Douglas Alexander Warner Jr and Eleanor (née Wright) Warner; m. Patricia Grant 1977; two s. one d.; ed Yale Univ.; Officer's Asst Morgan Guaranty Trust Co., New York 1968–70, Asst Treas. 1970–72, Asst Vice-Pres. 1972–75, Vice-Pres. 1975–85, Sr Vice-Pres. Morgan Guaranty Trust Co., London 1983–87, Exec. Vice-Pres. Morgan Guaranty Trust Co., New York 1987–89, Man. Dir 1989–90, Pres. 1990–95, Chair. and CEO 1995–2000; Chair. J.P. Morgan Chase & Co. 2000–01; mem. Bd Dirs. General Electric Co., Anheuser-Busch Cos. Inc.; Chair. Bd of Man. Overseers Memorial Sloan-Kettering Cancer Center, New York; Trustee Pierpoint Morgan Library, Cold Spring Harbor Lab. *Leisure interests:* golf, tennis, shooting. *Address:* JP Morgan Chase & Co. Inc., 270 Park Avenue, New York, NY 10017 (Office); P.O. Box 914, New York, NY 10268, USA (Home).

WARNER, Sir Frederick Edward, Kt, F.R.ENG., FRS; British engineer and university professor; b. 31 March 1910, London; s. of Frederick Warner; m. 1st Margaret Anderson McCrea; two s. two d.; m. 2nd Barbara Ivy Reynolds; ed Bancrofts School, Univ. Coll. London; chemical engineer with various cos. 1934–56; partner in firm of consulting chemical engineers working in UK, Ireland, USSR, India, Iran, Jordan, Africa 1956–80; Sr Partner, Cremer and Warner 1963–80; Visiting Prof. Bartlett School of Arch., Univ. Coll. London 1970; Visiting Prof. Imperial Coll. London 1970–78, 1993–2001; Visiting Prof. Univ. of Essex 1983–; Pro-Chancellor, Open Univ. 1974–79; mem. Advisory Council on Energy Conservation, Dept of Energy 1974–80; Pres. British Standards Inst. 1980–83, Vice-Pres. 1976–80, 1983–89; Pres. British Asscn for Commercial and Industrial Educ. 1977–90, Inst. of Quality Assurance 1987–90; Chair. British Nat. Cttee on Problems of Environment, Royal Soc. 1973–80, Council of Science and Tech. Insts. 1987–90; Treas. SCOPE 1982; Pres. Fédération Européenne d'Associations Nationales d'Ingénieurs 1968–71; Fellow, Univ. Coll. London 1967; Académico Correspondiente la Academia de Ingeniería, Mexico; Hon. mem. Royal Inst. of Engineers, Netherlands 1972; Hon. Fellow, School of Pharmacy, London 1979, UMIST 1986; Hon. DTech (Bradford) 1969; Hon. DSc (Aston) 1970, (Cranfield) 1978, (Heriot-Watt) 1978, (Newcastle) 1979; Hon. DUniv (Open) 1980, (Essex) 1992; Gold Medal, Czechoslovak Soc. for Int. Relations 1969; Medal, Insinöö riliitto, Finland 1969, Bronze Medal, Associazione Nazionale Ingegneri e Architetti d'Italia 1971, Leverhulme Medal (Royal Soc.) 1978, Buchanan Medal 1982, Gold Medal World Fed. of Eng Orgs., Tuev Rheinland Prize 1984, Gerard Piel Scientific American Award. *Publications:* Problem in Chemical Engineering Design (with J. M. Coulson) 1949, Risk (ed.) 1983, Quality 2000 1992 (ed.), Radioecology after Chernobyl (with J. M. Harrison) 1993, Nuclear Test Explosions (ed. with R. J. Kirchmann) 1999; papers on nitric acid, heat transfer, underground gasification of coal, air and water pollution, contracts, planning, safety, risk, technology transfer, professional and continuous educ., nuclear winter, Chernobyl, nuclear weapons tests. *Leisure interests:* monumental brasses, ceramics, gardens. *Address:* 1 Ropewalk, Southwell, Notts., NG25 0AL, England. *Telephone:* (1636) 816483. *Fax:* (1636) 814219.

WARNER, John W., BS, LLB; American politician; b. 18 Feb. 1927, Washington, DC; s. of the late Dr John W. Warner and of Martha (née Budd) Warner; m. 1st Catherine Conover Mellon (divorced 1973); one s. two d.; m. 2nd Elizabeth Taylor (q.v.) 1976 (divorced 1982); ed public schools in Washington, DC, school of Naval Research Laboratory, Washington, DC, Washington and Lee Univ. and Univ. of Virginia Law School; in USN, attained rank of Electronic Technician 3rd Class 1944–46; subsequently enlisted in US Marine Corps Reserve, active duty as Communications Officer 1950–52, Capt. in Marine Corps Reserve 1952–61; admitted to the Bar 1954; pvt. practice 1954–56; in US Attorney's office as Special Asst 1956, Asst 1957, fmr trial lawyer; joined campaign staff of then Vice-Pres. Richard Nixon 1960; associated with law firm Hogan & Hartson 1960, gen. partner 1964; Dir of Ocean Affairs as rep. of Dept of Defense 1971; Under-Sec. of US Navy 1969–72, Sec. 1972–74; Dir American Revolution Bicentennial Admin. 1974–76; Senator from Virginia 1979–; Head of US Del. to Moscow on Naval Affairs; Republican. *Address:* 225 Russell Senate Office Building, The Senate, Washington, DC 20510, USA (Office).

WARNER, Marina Sarah, MA; British author; b. 9 Nov. 1946, London; d. of Esmond Warner and Emilia Terzulli; m. 1st William Shawcross 1971; one s.; m. 2nd John Dewe Mathews 1981; ed St Mary's Convent, Ascot and Lady Margaret Hall, Univ. of Oxford; Getty Scholar, Getty Centre for the History of Art and the Humanities 1987–88; Tinbergen Prof. Erasmus Univ. Rotterdam 1990–91; Visiting Prof., Queen Mary and Westfield Coll., Univ. of London 1994, Univ. of Ulster 1994, Univ. of York 1996–; Tanner Lecturer, Yale Univ. 1999; Clarendon Lecturer, Oxford 2001; Fellow Commonership, Trinity Coll. Cambridge 1998; Visiting Fellow, All Souls Coll. Oxford 2001, Univ. Paris XIII 2003; mem. Exec. Cttee Charter 88 –1997, Literature Panel Arts Council of England –1997, Advisory Council British Library –1997, Man. Cttee Nat. Council for One-Parent Families, Bd Artangel, Cttee London Library, Cttee PEN; Hon. DLitt (Exeter) 1998, (Univ. of E London) 1999; Dr. hc (Sheffield Hallam, York, N London, St Andrews) 1998; Fawcett Prize 1986; Harvey Darton Award 1996, Mythopoeic Fantasy Award 1996, Katherine M. Briggs Award 1999, Rosemary Crawshay Prize, British Acad. 2000, Chevalier des Arts et des Lettres 2000. *Publications:* Alone of All Her Sex: The Myth and the Cult of the Virgin Mary 1976, Joan of Arc 1982, Monuments and Maidens:

The Allegory of the Female Form 1985, The Lost Father 1988, Indigo 1992, Mermaids in the Basement (short stories) 1993, Six Myths of Our Time—The 1994 Reith Lectures, From the Beast to the Blonde: On Fairy Tales and Their Tellers 1994, The Inner Eye: Art Beyond the Visible 1996, No Go the Bogeyman: On Scaring, Lulling and Making Mock 1998, The Leto Bundle 2001, Fantastic Metamorphoses, Other Worlds: The Clarendon Lectures 2002, Wonder Tales (ed.) 1994, Murderers I Have Known (short stories) 2002. *Leisure interests:* travel, friendship. *Address:* c/o Rogers, Coleridge & White, 20 Powis Mews, London, W11 1JN, England. *Telephone:* (20) 7221-3717. *Fax:* (20) 7229-9084.

WARNER, Mark R., BA, BLL; American politician; b. 15 Dec. 1954; m. Lisa Collis; three d.; ed George Washington Univ., Harvard Law School; founding pnr Columbia Capital Corpn; f. Virginia Health Care Foundation; developed SeniorNavigator.com, TechRiders; launched Virginia High-Tech Partnership 1997; developed Tek.Xam technology skills test; Gov. of Va Jan. 2002–. *Address:* Office of the Governor, State Capitol Building, Richmond, VA 23219, USA (Office). *Telephone:* (804) 786-2211 (Office). *Fax:* (804) 371-6351 (Office). *Website:* www.governor.state.va.us (Office).

WARNER, Ty; American business executive; s. of Harold Warner and Georgia Warner; Pres., CEO Ty Inc., creator of Beanie Babies. *Address:* Ty Inc., P.O. Box 5377, Oakbrook, IL 60522, USA (Office). *Telephone:* (630) 920-1515 (Office).

WARNKE, Jürgen, LLD; German politician; b. 20 March 1932, Berlin; s. of Dr Franz Warnke and Marianne (née Gensel) Warnke; m.; six c.; registered for legal practice 1961; Sec. Chemical Industry Asscn in Bavaria 1962–64; Gen. Sec. Ceramics Industry Assn., Selb, Bavaria; joined Christian Social Union (CSU) 1958, Academic Asst to CSU Group in Deutscher Bundestag 1959–62; mem. Bavarian State Parl. 1962–70; mem. Deutscher Bundestag 1969–; apptd. Chair. Bundestag Cttee on Trade Policy 1971, Vice-Pres. Cttee for European and Int. Co-operation 1978; Fed. Minister of Econ. Co-operation 1982–87, 1989–91, of Transport 1987–89; Chair. Supervisory Bd Königliche Porzellan Manufaktur GmbH, Berlin 1995–; mem. Synod, Protestant Church of Germany (EKD) 1985–; Grosses Bundesverdienstkreuz (with star) 1994. *Address:* Bundestag, Reichstagegebäude, Scheidemannstrasse 2, Berlin 10557, Germany.

WARNOCK, Baroness (Life Peer), cr. 1985, of Weeke in the City of Winchester; **(Helen) Mary Warnock,** DBE, F.C.P., FRSM; British philosopher and university administrator; b. 14 April 1924, Winchester; d. of the late Archibald Edward Wilson; m. Geoffrey J. Warnock 1949 (died 1995); two s. three d.; ed St Swithun's, Winchester and Lady Margaret Hall, Oxford; Tutor in Philosophy, St Hugh's Coll. Oxford 1949–66; Headmistress, Oxford High School 1966–72; Talbot Research Fellow, Lady Margaret Hall 1972–76; Sr Research Fellow, St Hugh's Coll. 1976–84; Mistress of Girton Coll. Cambridge 1985–91; Chair. Cttee of Inquiry into Special Educ. 1974–78, Advisory Cttee on Animal Experiments 1979–86, Cttee of Inquiry into Human Fertilization 1982–84, Educ. Cttee Girls' Day School Trust 1994–2001; mem. Ind. Broadcasting Authority1973–81, Royal Comm. on Environmental Pollution 1979–84, Social Science Research Council 1981–85, UK Nat. Comm. for UNESCO 1981–85, Archbishop of Canterbury's Advisory Group on Medical Ethics 1992–; Hon. Master of the Bench, Gray's Inn 1986; Chair. Planning Aid Trust 2002–; Hon. F.I.C. 1986; Hon. Fellow, Hertford Coll. Oxford 1997; Hon. FBA 2000; Hon. DUniv (Open Univ.) 1980, (St Andrews) 1992; Hon. LLD (Manchester) 1987, (Liverpool) 1991, (London) 1991; Hon. DLitt (Glasgow) 1988; Dr hc (Univ. of York) 1989; RSA Albert Medal 1998. *Publications:* Ethics since 1900 1960, J.-P. Sartre 1963, Existentialist Ethics 1966, Existentialism 1970, Imagination 1976, Schools of Thought 1977, What Must We Teach? (with T. Devlin) 1977, Education: A Way Forward 1979, A Question of Life 1985, Teacher Teach Thyself (Dimbleby Lecture) 1985, Memory 1987, A Common Policy for Education 1989, Universities: Knowing Our Minds 1989, The Uses of Philosophy 1992, Imagination and Time 1994; Women Philosophers (ed.) 1996, An Intelligent Person's Guide to Ethics 1998, A Memoir: People and Places 2000, Making Babies 2002, Nature and Mortality 2003, Utilitarinasim (ed.) 2003. *Leisure interests:* music, gardening. *Address:* 60 Church Street, Great Bedwyn, Wilts., SN8 3PF, England. *Telephone:* (20) 7219-8619 (Office); (1672) 870214.

WARNOCK, John E., MS, PhD; American computer executive; ed Univ. of Utah; fmrly with Evans & Sutherland Computer Corpn, Computer Sciences Corpn, IBM and Univ. of Utah; Principal Scientist Xerox Palo Alto Research Centre (PARC) until 1982; co-Founder and Jt Chair. Adobe Systems Inc. 1982–; mem. Bd of Dirs. Octavo Corpn, mem. Bd, fmr Chair. Tech. Museum of Innovation; mem. Entrepreneurial Bd Advisory Cttee, American Film Inst.; mem. Nat. Acad. of Engineering, Utah Information Tech. Asscn 2000; numerous awards including Distinguished Service to Art and Design Int. Award and Corp. Outstanding Achievement Award, Rhode Island School of Design 1998; Award for Technical Excellence, Nat. Graphics Asscn; Lifetime Achievement Award for Technical Excellence, PC Magazine; Cary Award, Rochester Inst. of Tech.; ACM Software Systems Award. *Publications:* numerous articles in technical journals and industry magazines. *Address:* Adobe Systems Inc., 375 Park Avenue, San José, CA 95110-2704, USA (Office). *Website:* www.adobe.com (Office).

WARRELL, David Alan, MA, DM, DSc, FRCP, F.R.C.P.(E.), FMedSci; British specialist in tropical medicine and venoms; b. 6 Oct. 1939, Singapore; s. of Mr and Mrs A. T. Warrell; m. Dr. Mary J. Prentice 1975; two d.; ed Portsmouth

Grammar School, Christ Church, Oxford and St Thomas's Hosp. Medical School, London; Oxford Univ. Radcliffe Travelling Fellow, Univ. of Calif. at San Diego 1969; Sr Lecturer, Ahmadu Bello Univ., Nigeria and Lecturer and Consultant Physician, Royal Postgrad. Medical School, London and Hammersmith Hosp. 1970–75; Founding Dir Wellcome-Mahidol Univ., Oxford Tropical Medicine Research Programme, Bangkok and Wellcome Reader in Tropical Medicine, Univ. of Oxford 1979–86; Prof. of Tropical Medicine and Infectious Diseases and Dir Emer. (fmrly Dir) Centre for Tropical Medicine, Univ. of Oxford 1987–2001, Head Nuffield Dept Clinical Medicine 2002–; Sr Adviser to M.R.C. on Research relevant to Developing Socs. 2001–; Hon. Consultant in Malariology to British Army 1989–; Hon. Medical Adviser, Royal Geographical Soc. 1993–; WHO Consultant 1979–; mem. WHO Expert Advisory Panel on Malaria 1989–; Fellow St Cross Coll. 1975–; Chair. AIDS Therapeutic Trials Cttee, MRC; Trustee, Tropical Health and Education Trust; Patron, Cambodia Trust; Pres. British Venom Gp. 1992–, Int. Fed. for Tropical Medicine 1996–2000, Royal Soc. of Tropical Medicine and Hygiene 1997–99; Del. Oxford Univ. Press 1999–; Marc Daniels, Bradshaw, Croonian and Coll. Lecturer and Harveian Orator 2001, Royal Coll. of Physicians; Runme Shaw Lecturer, Acad. of Medicine, Singapore 1997; Hon. mem. Asscn of Physicians GB and NI 2003; Ambuj Nath Bose Prize, Royal Coll. of Physicians 1994; Chalmer's Medal, Royal Soc. of Tropical Medicine and Hygiene 1981; Queen's Award for Higher and Further Educ. 2000. *Publications:* scientific papers and book chapters; Ed. Oxford Textbook of Medicine, Essential Malariology, Expedition Medicine. *Leisure interests:* book-collecting, music, bird-watching, mountain-walking. *Address:* Millfield Dept Clinical Medicine, University of Oxford, John Radcliffe Hospital, Headington, Oxford, OX3 9DU, England. *Telephone:* (1865) 220968. *Fax:* (1865) 220984. *E-mail:* david.warrell@ndm.ox.ac.uk (Office).

WARREN, Sir Frederick Miles, KBE, FNZIA, ARIBA, DIP.ARCH.; New Zealand architect; b. 10 May 1929, Christchurch; s. of M. B. Warren and J. Warren (née Hay); ed Christ's Coll., Auckland Univ. School of Architecture; worked for the late C. W. Wood, 1946–47, for the late R. C. Munroe, ANZIA 1948; joined partnership with the late G. T. Lucas 1956; started firm Warren and Mahoney 1958, Sr Partner 1958–; Fellow, New Zealand Inst. of Architects (NZIA) 1965; Pres. Canterbury Soc. of Arts 1972–76; Warren and Mahoney awarded NZIA Gold Medal for Dental Nurses' Training School 1960, for Christchurch Memorial Garden Crematorium 1964, for Christchurch Coll. Halls of Residence 1969, for Christchurch Town Hall and Civic Centre 1973; won Architectural Competition for design of Condominium Offices, New Hebrides 1966; Gold Medal NZIA 1980, 1981, 1983, 1984, 1985, 1986, 1988–91. *Publication:* Warren & Mahoney Architects 1990. *Leisure interests:* yachting, water-colouring, sketching. *Address:* 65 Cambridge Terrace, Christchurch 1, New Zealand. *Telephone:* 799-640.

WARREN, Jack Hamilton, OC; Canadian diplomatist and business executive (retd); b. 10 April 1921; m. Hilary J. Titterington; four c.; ed Queen's Univ., Kingston, Ont.; Royal Canadian Navy 1941–45; joined Dept of External Affairs 1945; served in London 1948–51; transferred to Dept of Finance and served as Financial Counsellor, Washington, DC and as Alt. Dir for Canada, IMF and IBRD 1954–57; Canadian Del. to OECD and NATO 1957–58; Asst Deputy Minister of Trade and Commerce 1958–64; Chair. GATT Contracting Parties 1962–65; Deputy Minister of Trade and Commerce 1964–68, of Industry, Trade and Commerce 1968–71; High Commr in UK 1971–74; Amb. to USA 1975–77; Canadian Coordinator for the Multilateral Trade Negotiations 1977–79; Vice-Chair. Bank of Montréal 1979–86; Prin. Adviser on trade policy, Govt of Québec 1986–94; Deputy N American Chair. Trilateral Comm. 1986–90; Hon. LLD (Queen's Univ.) 1974; Outstanding Achievement Award, Public Service of Canada 1975. *Leisure interests:* travel, salmon fishing, food and wine. *Address:* 37 Larrimac Road, Chelsea, Québec, J9B 2C4, Canada (Home). *Telephone:* (819) 827-3715 (Home). *Fax:* (819) 827-3715 (Home).

WARRINGTON, Elizabeth Kerr, PhD, DSc, FRS; British professor of clinical neuropsychology; d. of the late Prof. John A. V. Butler, FRS and Margaret L. Butler; m.; one d.; ed Univ. Coll. London; Research Fellow, Inst. of Neurology 1956; Sr Clinical Psychologist, Nat. Hosp. 1960, Prin. Psychologist 1962, Top Grade Clinical Psychologist 1972–82, Prof. of Clinical Neuropsychology 1982–96, Consultant Neuropsychologist to Dementia Research Group 1996–; Emer. Prof. of Clinical Neuropsychology, London Univ. 1996–; Fellow Univ. Coll. London; Dr. hc (Bologna) 1998, (York) 1999. *Publications:* Cognitive Neuropsychology (co-author) 1990; numerous papers in professional journals. *Leisure interests:* gardening, entertaining granddaughters. *Address:* Dementia Research Group, National Hospital for Neurology and Neurosurgery, Queen Square, London, WC1N 3BG, England. *Telephone:* (20) 7837-3611.

WARWICK, Dionne; American singer; b. 12 Dec. 1941, East Orange, NJ; m. Bill Elliott (divorced 1975); two s.; ed Hartt Coll. of Music, Hartford, Conn.; as teenager formed Gospelaires; later sang background for recording studio 1966; début, Philharmonic Hall, Lincoln Center, New York 1966; appearances at London Palladium, Olympia, Paris, Lincoln Center; co-host, Solid Gold (TV show); host, A Gift of Music (TV show) 1981; star, Dionne Warwick Special (TV show); appeared in Sisters in the Name of Love on TV 1986; Grammy Awards 1969, 1970, 1980. *Films:* The Slaves 1969, No Night, So Long, Hot! Live and Otherwise. *Singles include:* I'll Never Love this Way Again, That's What Friends are For. *Albums include:* Valley of the Dolls and Others 1968, Promises, Promises 1975, Dionne 1979, Then Came You, Friends 1986, Reservations for Two 1987, Greatest Hits 1990, Dionne Warwick Sings Cole

Porter 1990, Hidden Gems: The Best of Dionne Warwick (Vol. 2) 1992, Friends Can Be Lovers (with Whitney Houston) 1993, Dionne Warwick and Placido Domingo 1994, Aquarela do Brasil 1994, From the Vaults 1995, Dionne Sings Dionne 1998, I Say a Little Prayer For You 2000. *Address:* c/o Arista Records Inc., 6 West 57th Street, New York, NY 10019, USA.

WARWICK OF UNDERCLIFFE, Baroness (Life Peer), cr. 1999, of Undercliffe in the County of West Yorkshire; **Diana Warwick,** BA; British academic; b. 16 July 1945, Bradford; d. of Jack Warwick and Olive Warwick; m. Sean Young 1969; ed Bedford Coll., Univ. of London; Gen. Sec. Asscn of Univ. Teachers 1983–92; mem. Employment Appeals Tribunal 1984–99; mem. Bd British Council 1985–95; Chief Exec. Westminster Foundation for Democracy 1992–95; Chair. VSO 1994–; mem. Standing Cttee on Standards in Public Life (Nolan/Neill Cttee) 1994–99; Chief Exec. Universities UK (fmrly Cttee of Vice-Chancellors and Prins) 1995–; Trustee St Catharine's Foundation, Windsor 1996–; mem. Tech. Foresight Steering Group; Hon. DLitt (Bradford) 1993, (Open Univ.) 1998. *Address:* Universities UK, Woburn House, 20 Tavistock Square, London, WC1H 9HQ, England. *Telephone:* (20) 7419-5402 (Office). *Fax:* (20) 7380-0137 (Office). *E-mail:* diana.warwick@universitiesuk .ac.uk (Office). *Website:* www.universitiesuk.ac.uk (Office).

WARWICK-THOMPSON, Paul, PhD; British museum director; b. 9 Aug. 1959, Oxford; s. of Sir Michael Thompson; m. Adline Finlay 1984; one s. one d.; ed Bryanston School, Univ. of Bristol, Univ. of East Anglia; Curator Design Museum, London 1989–92, Dir 1992–2000; Dir Cooper-Hewitt Nat. Design Museum, New York 2001–; Hon. Fellow RCA 2000. *Leisure interests:* theatre, cinema, gardening. *Address:* Cooper-Hewitt National Design Museum, c/o Smithsonian Institution, 2 East 91st Street, New York, NY 10128, USA (Office). *Telephone:* (212) 849-8370 (Office). *Fax:* (212) 849-8367 (Office).

WĄSACZ, Emil; Polish economist; b. 1 Aug. 1945, Zabratówka, Rzeszów Prov.; m.; three c.; ed Łódź Tech. Univ., Main School of Commerce (SGH), Warsaw; employee Katowice Steelworks 1976–94, Supreme Dir then Chair. Katowice Steelworks SA 1991–94; adviser Chair. Bank Śląski SA, Bank PeKaO SA and enterprise Stalexport SA; Chair. Szczecin Steelworks SA 1995–97; Vice-Leader Supervisory Bd, later Chair. Progress Nat. Investment Fund 1995–97; Minister of the Treasury 1997–2001; mem. Solidarity Trade Union, leader Plant Cttee in the Katowice Steelworks 1989–90; voluntary worker Catholic Family Clinic, Sosnowiec 1983–90. *Leisure interests:* tourism, history, astronomy, literature and romantic poetry. *Address:* c/o Ministerstwo Skarbu Państwa, ul. Krucza 36, 00-522 Warsaw, Poland.

WASER, Peter Gaudenz, MD, DPhil; Swiss professor of pharmacology; b. 21 July 1918, Zürich; s. of Ernst Waser and Margrit Ruttiman; m. Marion Edmée Bodmer 1946; one s. two d.; ed Univ. of Zürich, Basle Univ. Hosp., Calif. Inst. of Tech., USA; Prof. of Medicine, Univ. of Zürich 1959, Dir Inst. of Pharmacology 1963–87, Prof. of Pharmacy 1965–87, Dean of Faculty of Medicine 1970–72, Rector 1978–80; research in psychopharmacology, Univ. Clinic, Zürich 1987–95; Pres. Engadine Collegium in Philosophy 1967–, Int. Union of Pharmacology 1978–81, Int. Council of Scientific Unions 1981–84. *Publications:* Mechanisms of Synaptic Transmission 1969 (with Akert), Cholinergic Mechanisms 1975, Praktische Pharmakotherapie 1987 (with C. Steinbach), The Cholinergic Receptor 1987, Psychiatrie, Psychopharmaka und Drogen in Zürich 1990. *Leisure interests:* mountaineering, skiing, gardening, painting. *Address:* Research Department of Psychiatry, University Clinic, Lenggstrasse 31, 8029 Zürich; Ob. Heuelsteig 12, 8032 Zürich, Switzerland (Home). *Telephone:* (1) 3842111 (Psychiatry); (1) 2512814 (Home).

WASHINGTON, Denzel, BA; American film actor; b. 28 Dec. 1954, Mt. Vernon, NY; m. Pauletta Pearson 1983; two s. two d.; ed Fordham Univ. and American Conservatory Theater, San Francisco; worked at New York Shakespeare Festival and American Place Theater; off-Broadway appearances include: Ceremonies in Dark Old Men, When the Chickens Come Home to Roost and A Soldier's Play (Negro Ensemble Co.); played young doctor in TV series St Elsewhere; Harvard Foundation Award 1996. *Films include:* A Soldier's Story 1984, The Mighty Quinn, Cry Freedom 1987, Heart Condition 1989, Glory (Acad. Award for Best Supporting Actor) 1990, Love Supreme 1990, Mo' Better Blues 1990, Ricochet 1991, Mississippi Masala 1991, Much Ado About Nothing, Malcolm X 1992, The Pelican Brief 1993, Philadelphia 1993, Devil in a Blue Dress 1995, Courage Under Fire 1996, The Preacher's Wife 1996, Fallen 1997, He Got Game 1998, The Siege 1998, The Bone Collector 1999, The Hurricane 1999, Remember the Titans 2001, Training Day (Acad. Award for Best Actor 2002) 2001, John Q (Award for Best Actor, Nat. Asscn for the Advancement of Colored People (NAACP) Awards 2003) 2002, Antwone Fisher (also producer and dir—Awards for Best Supporting Actor and Best Dir, NAACP Awards 2003) 2002. *Leisure interests:* cooking, reading, basketball. *Address:* c/o ICM, 8942 Wilshire Boulevard, Beverly Hills, CA 90211, USA.

WASIM AKRAM; Pakistani cricketer; b. 3 June 1966, Lahore; ed Islamia Coll.; left-hand middle-order batsman, left-arm fast bowler; played for Pakistan Automobile Corpn 1984–85, Lahore 1985–86, Lancashire 1988–98 (Capt. 1998); only bowler to have captured more than 400 wickets both in Test and one-day cricket; played in 104 Tests for Pakistan 1984–85 as at 16 Jan. 2003, 25 as Capt., scoring 2,898 runs (average 22.64) including 3 hundreds and taking 414 wickets (average 23.6); has scored 7,106 runs (7 hundreds) and taken 1,022 wickets in first-class cricket to 24 Dec. 2001; toured England 1987, 1992 and 1996 (Capt.); 350 limited-overs internationals (109 as Capt.)

taking record 490 wickets to 15 Jan. 2003; Wisden Cricketer of the Year 1993. *Publication:* Wasim (autobiog.). *Address:* c/o Pakistan Cricket Board, Gaddafi Stadium, Ferozepur Road, Lahore 54600, Pakistan. *Telephone:* (42) 571-7231.

WASMOSY, Juan Carlos, DCE; Paraguayan politician and civil engineer; b. 15 Dec. 1938, Asunción; s. of Dr. Juan Bautista Wasmosy and María Clotilde Monti Paoli; m. Maria Teresa Carrasco Dos Santos; five s. (one deceased) one d.; ed San José School, Asunción and Nat. Univ. of Asunción; fmr Asst Prof. Univ. of Asunción; sometime Pres. ECOMIPA, CONEMPA, COCEP, GOYA (pvt. construction and industrial cos.); other business affiliations; mem. construction holding which built Itaipú Hydroelectric Power Station; currently engaged in construction of Yacyretá power station; Pres. Int. Fed. of Zebu Cattle Breeders; mem. Colorado Party 1973–; Minister of Integration 1993; Pres. of Paraguay 1993–98, Senator for Life 1998–; Orden de Solidaridad de Brasil; other medals and awards. *Address:* The Senate, Asunción, Paraguay.

WASS, Sir Douglas William Gretton, GCB, MA; British fmr civil servant and business executive; b. 15 April 1923, Wallasey, Cheshire; s. of the late Arthur W. Wass and Elsie W. Wass; m. Dr Milica Pavičić 1954; one s. one d.; ed Nottingham High School, St John's Coll. Cambridge; Scientific Research with Admiralty 1943–46; Asst Prin., Treasury 1946, Prin. 1951; Commonwealth Fund Fellow, USA 1958–59; Fellow, Brookings Inst., Washington 1959; Pvt. Sec. to Chancellor 1959–61; Pvt. Sec. to Chief Sec. 1961–62; Alt. Exec. Dir to IMF and Financial Counsellor, British Embassy, Washington, DC 1965–67; Under-Sec. of Treasury 1968, Deputy Sec. 1970, Second Perm. Sec. 1973, Perm. Sec. 1974–83; Jt Head, Home Civil Service 1981–83; Chair. Econ. Policy Cttee, OECD 1982; Reith Lecturer, BBC 1983; Chair. British Selection Cttee, Harkness Fellowships 1981–84, Governing Body of the Ditchley Foundation, Council of the Policy Studies Inst.; Chair. Nomura Int. PLC 1986–98 (Sr Adviser 1998–2002), Axa Equity and Law Life Assurance Soc. PLC 1986–95, N.C.M. (Credit Insurance) Ltd 1991–95; Gov. Centre for Econ. Policy Research 1983–90; Adviser to Campaign for Freedom of Information; Dir De La Rue Co. PLC 1983–93, Coopers and Lybrand 1984–86, Barclays Bank PLC 1984–87, African Capacity Bldg Foundation, Harare 1991–98, Equitable Cos Inc. New York 1992–95; Administrateur, Cie du Midi SA (now Axa SA) 1987–95; Vice-Pres. Constitutional Reform Centre 1984–92; mem. Council of Univ. of Bath 1985–91; Pres. Market Research Soc. 1987–91; mem. Overseas Devt Council 1990–96; mem. Council British Heart Foundation 1990–96; Dir Soho Theatre Co. 1996–2000; Hon. Fellow, St John's Coll. Cambridge; Hon. DLitt (Bath). *Publications:* The Changing Problems of Economic Management 1978, The Public Service in Modern Society 1982, Government and the Governed 1984, The Civil Service at the Crossroads 1985, What Sort of Industrial Policy? 1986, Checks and Balances in Public Policy Making 1987. *Leisure interest:* swimming. *Address:* 6 Dora Road, Wimbledon, London, SW19 7HH, England. *Telephone:* (20) 8946-5556. *Fax:* (20) 8241-4626 (Home). *E-mail:* douglas.wass@blueyonder.co.uk (Home).

WASSENER, Albert; German cultural institute director; b. 25 April 1936, Essen; s. of Albert Wassener and Gertrud Wassener (née Forstbauer); m. Renate Wassener 1962; one s. one d.; ed Univ. of Bonn, Univ. of Munich; Dir Goethe Inst., Tripoli, Libya 1965–66; Officer, Cultural Programmes, Goethe Inst., Rome 1966–74; Head, Teachers' Training Dept., Goethe Inst. Head Office, Munich 1974–78; Dir Goethe Inst., Tel-Aviv 1978–84, Copenhagen 1984–89, Istanbul 1989–90; Head, Talks Dept, Goethe Inst. Head Office, Munich 1990–95; Dir Goethe Inst., London and Regional Dir, Great Britain and Northern Ireland 1995–2000. *Address:* c/o Goethe Institute, 50 Prince's Gate, Exhibition Road, London, SW7 2PH, England.

WASSERBURG, Gerald Joseph, MSc, PhD; American professor of geology and geophysics; b. 25 March 1927, New Brunswick, NJ; s. of Charles Wasserburg and Sarah Levine Wasserburg; m. Naomi Z. Orlick 1951; two s.; ed Univ. of Chicago; Rifleman, US Army Second Infantry Div. 1943–46; with Resurrection Mining Co. 1947; Juneau Ice Field Research Project, Alaska 1950; Consultant Argonne Nat. Laboratory, Lamont, Ill. 1952–55; Research Assoc., Inst. for Nuclear Studies, Chicago 1954–55; Asst Prof. of Geology, Calif. Inst. of Tech. 1955–59, Assoc. Prof. of Geology 1959–62, Prof. of Geology and Geophysics 1962–82; Adviser to NASA 1968–88; Vice-Chair. Lunar Sample Analysis Planning Team, MSC, NASA 1970; mem. Lunar Sample Review Bd 1970–72, Science Working Panel 1971–73, Physical Sciences Cttee 1971–75; Ed. Earth and Planetary Science Letters 1967–74; Chair. Comm. for Planetary and Lunar Exploration, NAS, Space Science Bd 1975–78; Vinton Hayes Sr Fellow, Harvard 1980; Jaeger-Hales Lecture, ANU 1980; Harold Jeffreys Lecture, Royal Astronomical Soc. 1981; John D. MacArthur Prof. of Geology and Geophysics, Calif. Inst. of Tech. 1982– (Prof. Emer. 2002–), Chair. Div. of Geological and Planetary Sciences 1987–89; Pres. Meteoritical Soc. 1987–88; mem. NAS; Fellow, American Acad. of Arts and Sciences, American Geophysical Union, Geological Soc. of America; Regents Fellow, Smithsonian Inst. 1982; Geochemistry Fellow Geochemical Soc. and European Asscn for Geochemistry 1996; mem. American Philosophical Soc.; Foreign mem. Norwegian Acad. of Science and Letters 1988; Hon. Fellow Geological Soc. London; Hon. Foreign Fellow European Union of Geosciences (EUG) 1983; Distinguished Visiting Scholar, Harvard Univ. 2001; Dr hc (Brussels) 1985, (Paris) 1986, (Chicago) 1992, (Rennes) 1998, (Torino) 2000; Hon. DSc (Ariz.) 1987; Combat Infantryman's Badge; Exceptional Scientific Achievement Medal, NASA 1970; Arthur L. Day Medal, Geological Soc. of America 1970; Distinguished Public Service Medal, NASA 1972 and with cluster 1978; James Furman Kemp Medal, Columbia Univ. 1973, Leonard Medal, Meteoritical Soc. 1975; V. M. Goldschmidt Medal, Geochemical Soc. 1978, Univ. of Chicago Alumni Asscn Professional Achievement Award 1978; Arthur L. Day Prize, NAS 1981, J. Lawrence Smith Medal, NAS 1985, Wollaston Medal, Geological Soc. of London 1985, Sr US Scientist Award, Alexander von Humboldt-Stiftung 1985, Harry H. Hess Medal, American Geophysical Union, Crafoord Prize, Swedish Royal Acad. 1986, Holmes Medal, EUG 1987, Gold Medal (Royal Astronomical Soc.) 1991. *Publications:* research papers in several scientific journals, in the fields of geochemistry, geophysics and astrophysics, cosmology and the application of the methods of chemical physics to problems in the earth and planetary sciences; major researches: determination of the time scale of the solar system, chronology of the moon, establishment of dating methods using long-lived natural radioactivities, study of geological processes using nuclear and isotopic effects as a tracer in nature and the application of thermodynamic methods to geological systems. *Leisure interests:* hiking, music, art. *Address:* California Institute of Technology, Division of Geological and Planetary Sciences, Pasadena, CA 91125 (Office); PO Box 2959, Florence, OR 97439, USA (Home). *Telephone:* (626) 395-6139 (Office); (541) 992-9224 (Home). *Fax:* (626) 796-9823 (Office). *E-mail:* isotopes@gps.caltech.edu (Office).

WASSERMAN, Robert Harold, PhD; American professor of biological sciences; b. 11 Feb. 1926, Schenectady, New York; s. of Joseph Wasserman and Sylvia Rosenburg; m. Marilyn Mintz 1950; three d.; ed Mount Pleasant High School, NY, Cornell Univ., Michigan State Univ.; Research Assoc. and Assoc. Prof. of Biochem. Univ. of Tenn. Atomic Energy Comm. Agricultural Research Program, Oak Ridge 1953–55; Sr Scientist Medical Div., Oak Ridge Inst. of Nuclear Studies 1955–57; Research Assoc. in Radiation Biology NY State Veterinary Coll., Cornell Univ. 1957–59; Assoc. Prof. of Radiation Biology, Dept of Physical Biology 1959–63, Prof. of Radiation Biology 1963–80, Prof. of Physiology, Coll. of Veterinary Medicine 1980–89, Prof. and Chair. of Dept and Section 1983–87, James Law Prof. of Physiology 1989–97, Prof. Emer. 1998–; Chair. Cttee Meat and Poultry Inspection, Nat. Research Council 1983–85, mem. Food and Nutrition Bd 1984–87; Visiting Scientist Inst. of Biological Chem., Copenhagen, Denmark 1964–65; Guggenheim Fellowship 1964, 1972; mem. NAS 1980–; Fellow American Inst. of Nutrition 1992; Wise and Helen Burroughs Lectureship 1974, 1987; Mead-Johnson Award in Nutrition 1969; A. Lichtwitz Prize (INSERM) 1982, Merit Status, NIH 1989, Newman Award (American Soc. Bone and Mineral Research) 1990, Career Recognition Award, Vitamin D Workshop 1994. *Publications:* numerous articles in specialist journals. *Leisure interests:* reading, sports, computers, cards, writing. *Address:* Department of Biomedical Sciences—T8-020B VRT, College of Veterinary Medicine, Cornell University, Ithaca, NY 14853; 207 Texas Lane, Ithaca, NY 14850, USA (Home). *Telephone:* (607) 253-3437. *E-mail:* RHWZ@cornell.edu (Office).

WASSERSTEIN, Bruce, MBA; American investment banker; b. 25 Dec. 1947, New York; s. of Morris Wasserstein and Lola Wasserstein; m. Christine Parrott; two s. one d.; ed Univ. of Mich., Harvard Univ. and Univ. of Cambridge, UK; Assoc. Cravath, Swaine & Moore, New York 1972–77; Man. Dir First Boston Corpn 1977–88; Pres. Wasserstein, Perella & Co. 1988–2000; Chair. Dresdner Kleinwort Wasserstein (formed after acquisition of Wasserstein, Perella & Co. by Dresdner 2000) 2001–02; CEO Lazard Jan. 2002–; mem. Council on Foreign Relations. *Publications:* Big Deal: The Battle for Control of America's Leading Corporations 2000. *Address:* Lazard LLC, 30 Rockefeller Plaza, New York, NY 10020, USA (Office). *Telephone:* (212) 632-6000 (Office). *Website:* www.lazard.com (Office).

WASSERSTEIN, Wendy, MFA; American playwright and author; b. 18 Oct. 1950, Brooklyn; d. of Morris Wasserstein and Lola Wasserstein; ed Mount Holyoake Coll. and Yale School of Drama; mem. Council, Dramatists' Guild; mem. Bd British American Arts Asscn; mem. Artistic Bd Playwrights Horizons; taught fmrly at Columbia and New York Univs.; contrib. New York Woman; other plays include: Isn't It Romantic, Any Woman Can't, Montpelier, Pa-Zazz, Miami, Uncommon Women and Others, The Sisters Rosenzweig, Old Money; Dir Channel Thirteen, MacDowell Colony, British American Arts Asscn; Dr. hc (Mt. Holyoake Coll.); recipient of Pulitzer Prize, NW Drama Critics Circle Prize, Drama Desk Award, Outer Critics Circle Award, Susan Smith Blackburn Prize and Tony Award, all for play The Heidi Chronicles. *Publications:* Bachelor Girls, The Heidi Chronicles and Other Plays; collection of essays, Pamela's First Musical (for children) 1995. *Address:* c/o Royce Carlton Inc., 866 United Nations Plaza, Suite 4030, New York, NY 10017, USA. *Telephone:* (212) 355-7700.

WÄSTBERG, Olof, BA; Swedish politician, writer and banker; b. 6 May 1945, Stockholm; s. of Erik Wastberg and Greta Hirsch; m. Inger Claesson 1968; two s.; ed Univ. of Stockholm; Vice-Pres. Liberal Youth Sweden 1968–71; mem. Bd Liberal Party 1972–93, 1997–, Pres. Exec. Cttee 1982–83, teacher of political science, Univ. of Stockholm 1967–68; journalist, political Dept Expressen 1968–71, Ed. 1994–95; Research Fellow, Business and Social Research Centre 1971–76; Pres. Akieframjandet 1976–82; mem. Parl. 1976–82; Pres. Swedish Newspaper Promotion Asscn 1983–91; Under-Sec. of State, Ministry of Finance 1991–93; Consul Gen. of Sweden in NY 1999–; Dir Stockholm Stock Exchange 1977–82, 1988–94; Pres. Nordic Investment Bank 1992–94; Chair. Bd Swedish Broadcasting Corpn 1996–, Stockholm City Theatre 1998–; mem. Govt comms. on S. African consumer politics, stock market and media; Gold Medal, Swedish Marketing Group 1982. *Publications:* books on African problems, immigration policies and economic topics; articles in professional journals. *Address:* Consulate General of Sweden, 1 Dag Hammarskjöld Plaza,

885 Second Avenue, 45th Floor, New York, NY 10017 (Office); 600 Park Avenue, New York, NY 10021, USA (Home); Bellmangatan 6, 11820 Stockholm, Sweden. *Telephone:* (212) 583-2550 (Office); (8) 643-68-79. *Fax:* (212) 517-6515 (Home). *E-mail:* olle@wastberg.nu. *Website:* www.webcom.com/sis (Office); www.wastberg.nu (Office).

WATANABE, Youji; Japanese architect; b. 14 June 1923, Naoetsu City; ed Waseda Univ.; Asst to Prof. Takamasa Yosizaka, Architectural Inst., Waseda Univ. 1955–58; Lecturer in Architecture, Waseda Univ. 1959, Special Postgraduate Student of City Planning 1968–73; Visiting Lecturer, Montana State Univ. 1983; Oceanic Architectural Students' Congress, Auckland Univ. 1983; prizes in architectural competitions. *Exhibitions include:* VIII Salone Internazionale della Industrializzazione Edilizia, Bologna 1972, Georges Pompidou Centre, Paris 1977, Centro Edile, Milan 1977, Museum of Modern Art, New York 1978, The Peak Competition, Hong Kong 1982, Paris Opera Bastille Competition 1982. *Publication:* Approach to Architecture 1974.

WATERHOUSE, (Gai) Gabriel Marie, BA; Australian racehorse trainer; b. 3 Sept. 1954, Sydney; d. of the late Thomas John Smith and Valerie Lillian Smith; m. Robert Waterhouse; one s. one d.; ed Univ. of New South Wales; actress 1974–78; journalist, stable foreman 1978–92; racehorse trainer 1992–; Dir Gayval Investments Pty Ltd, Gail Waterhouse Racing Pty Ltd; Australian Racing Personality of the Year 1994–95, fmr NSW Sports Star of the Year, Sarah Kennedy Award for Contrib. to Racing, Silver Horseshoe Award for Best Trainer 1995, NSW Businesswoman of the Year 2000, Nat. Trust Living Treasure 2001. *Publication:* Against All Odds (biog.). *Leisure interests:* skiing, movies, theatre. *Address:* Gai Waterhouse Racing Pty Ltd, P.O. Box 834, Kensington, NSW 1465, Australia (Office). *Telephone:* (2) 9662-1488 (Office). *Fax:* (2) 9662-6328 (Office). *E-mail:* Gai.Waterhouse@bigpond.com (Office). *Website:* www.gaiwaterhouse.com.au (Office).

WATERHOUSE, Keith Spencer, CBE, FRSL; British writer; b. 6 Feb. 1929, Leeds; s. of Ernest Waterhouse and Elsie Edith Waterhouse; m. 2nd Stella Bingham 1984 (divorced 1989); one s. two d. by previous marriage; journalist 1950–, columnist, Daily Mirror 1970–86, Daily Mail 1986–, contrib. to various periodicals; mem. Kingman Cttee on Teaching of the English Language 1987–88; Granada Columnist of the Year Award 1970; IPC Descriptive Writer of the Year Award 1970; IPC Columnist of the Year Award 1973; British Press Awards Columnist of the Year 1978, 1989; Granada Special Quarter Century Award 1982; Evening Standard Comedy of the Year 1990 (Jeffrey Bernard is Unwell); Press Club Edgar Wallace Award 1996; Gerald Barry Lifetime Achievement Award 2000. *Films (with Willis Hall) include:* Billy Liar, Whistle Down the Wind, A Kind of Loving, Lock Up Your Daughters. *Plays:* Mr. and Mrs. Nobody 1986, Jeffrey Bernard is Unwell 1989, Bookends 1990, Our Song 1992, Good Grief 1998, Bing-Bong 1999. *Plays (with Willis Hall) include:* Billy Liar 1960, Celebration 1961, All Things Bright and Beautiful 1963, Say Who You Are 1965, Whoops-a-Daisy 1968, Children's Day 1969, Who's Who 1972, The Card (musical) 1973, Saturday, Sunday, Monday (adapted from play by de Filippo) 1973, Filumena (adapted from de Filippo) 1977, Worzel Gummidge 1981, Budgie (musical) 1988. *TV series:* Budgie, Queenie's Castle, The Upper Crusts, Billy Liar, The Upchat Line, The Upchat Connection, Worzel Gummidge, West End Tales, The Happy Apple, Charters and Caldicott. *TV films:* Charlie Muffin 1983, This Office Life 1985, The Great Paperchase 1984. *Others:* Café Royal (with Guy Deghy) 1956, Writers' Theatre (Ed.) 1967, The Passing of the Third-floor Buck 1974, Mondays, Thursdays 1976, Rhubarb, Rhubarb 1979, Fanny Peculiar 1983, Mrs Pooter's Diary 1983, Waterhouse At Large 1985, Collected Letters of a Nobody 1986, The Theory and Practice of Lunch 1986, The Theory and Practice of Travel 1988, Waterhouse on Newspaper Style 1989, English Our English 1991, Jeffrey Bernard is Unwell and Other Plays 1992, Sharon & Tracy and the Rest 1992, City Lights 1994, Streets Ahead 1995. *Publications:* (novels) There is a Happy Land 1957, Billy Liar 1959, Jubb 1963, The Bucket Shop 1968, Billy Liar on the Moon 1975, Office Life 1978, Maggie Muggins 1981, In the Mood 1983, Thinks 1984, Our Song 1984, Bimbo 1990, Unsweet Charity 1992, Good Grief 1997, Soho 2001, Palace Pier 2003. *Address:* c/o Alexandra Cann Representation, 12 Abingdon Road, London, W8 6AF; 84 Coleherne Court, London, SW5 0EE, England.

WATERLOW, John Conrad, CMG, MD, ScD, FRS; British professor of human nutrition (retd); b. 13 June 1916, London; s. of Sir Sydney Waterlow and Margery H. Eckhard; m. Angela P. Gray 1939; two s. one d.; ed Eton Coll., Trinity Coll. Cambridge and London Hosp. Medical Coll.; Persia/Iraq force 1943; mem. scientific staff, MRC 1942–70; Dir Tropical Metabolism Research Unit, Univ. of the West Indies 1954–70; Prof. of Human Nutrition, London School of Hygiene and Tropical Medicine 1970–82, Prof. Emer. 1982–; Foreign Assoc. mem. NAS (USA); Murgatroyd Prize for Tropical Medicine, Bristol-Myers Prize for Nutrition, Rank Prize Fund Prize for contribs. to nutrition 2000. *Publications:* Protein Turnover in the Whole Body and in Mammalian Tissues 1978, Protein Energy Malnutrition 1992; many papers and reviews on malnutrition and protein metabolism. *Leisure interest:* mountain walking. *Address:* 15 Hillgate Street, London, W8 7SP; Parsonage House, Oare, Marlborough, Wilts., SN8 4JA, England. *Telephone:* (20) 7727-7456 (London).

WATERMAN, Ewen Leith, BEcons; Australian civil servant; b. 2 Dec. 1943, Adelaide, S Australia; s. of Gordon Waterman and Elsie Waterman (née Batty); m. Barbara Prideaux 1966; two s. one d.; ed Pulteney Grammar School, Adelaide, Univ. of Adelaide; Gen. Financial and Econ. Policy Div., Australian Treasury 1967–72; Overseas Econ. Relations Div., 1973–75, Asst

Sec. State and Local Govt Finances Br. 1982–84, Prin. Adviser, Gen. Financial and Econ. Policy Div., 1984–85, First Asst Sec., Revenue Loans and Investment Div. 1985–87, Capital Markets Div. 1987–89, Deputy Sec. (Financial) 1989–93; Prime Minister's Dept 1972; Counsellor (Financial), Australian Embassy, Washington, DC 1976–79; Sec. Australian Loan Council 1986–87, Australian Nat. Debt Comm. 1986–87; Exec. Dir IMF, Washington, DC 1993–97; Exec. Dir Access Economics 1997–2001; Man. Dir Export Finance and Insurance Corpn (EFIC) 2001–. *Leisure interests:* tennis, golf. *Address:* Export Finance and Insurance Corporation, 22 Pitt Street, Sydney, NSW 2000, Australia. *Telephone:* (2) 9201-2111. *Fax:* (2) 9201-5222. *E-mail:* info@efic.gov.au. *Website:* www.efic.gov.au.

WATERSTONE, Timothy John Stuart, MA; British business executive; b. 30 May 1939; s. of Malcolm Waterstone and Sylvia Sawday; m. 1st Patricia Harcourt-Poole (divorced); two s. one d.; m. 2nd Clare Perkins (divorced); one s. two d.; m. 3rd Mary Rose (Rosie) Alison; two d.; ed Tonbridge School and St Catharine's Coll. Cambridge; Carritt Moran, Calcutta 1962–64; Allied Breweries 1964–73; W. H. Smith 1973–81; Founder, Chair. and Chief Exec. Waterstone's Booksellers Ltd 1982–93; Chair. Priory Investments Ltd 1990–95, Golden Rose Radio (London Jazz FM) 1992–93; Founder and Chair. Chelsea Stores Ltd children's stores 1996–; Chair. HMV Media Group PLC 1998–2001; Deputy Chair. Sinclair-Stevenson Ltd 1989–92; mem. Bd Yale Univ. Press 1992–, Futurestart 1992–, Virago Press 1995–96, Hill Samuel UK Emerging Cos Investment Trust PLC 1996–2000, Downing Classic VCT 1998–; Chair. Dept of Trade and Industry Working Group on Smaller Quoted Cos and Pvt. Investors 1999, Shelter 25th Anniversary Appeal Cttee 1991–92; mem. Bd London Philharmonic Orchestra 1990–97 (Trustee 1995–98), Portman House Trust 1994–96; Chair. Acad. of Ancient Music 1990–95, London Int. Festival of Theatre 1991–92, Elgar Foundation 1992–98, King's Coll. Library Bd 2000–; Co-Founder BOOKAID 1992–93; Advisory mem. Booker Prize Man. Cttee 1986–93; Chair. of Judges Prince's Youth Business Trust Awards 1990. *Publications:* Lilley and Chase 1994, An Imperfect Marriage 1995, A Passage of Lives 1996. *Leisure interest:* being with Rosie Alison. *Address:* c/o Ed Victor Ltd, 6 Bayley Street, London, WC1B 3HB, England.

WATKINS, Alan Keith, PhD; British business executive; b. 9 Oct. 1938, Birmingham; s. of the late Wilfred Watkins and of Dorothy Watkins; m. Diana E. Wynne 1963; two s.; ed Moseley Grammar School and Univ. of Birmingham; Mfg Process Research, Lucas Group Research 1962–69; Mfg and Production Eng Lucas Batteries Ltd 1969–75; Div. Dir Electrical Div. Lucas Aerospace Ltd 1975–82; Man. Dir Lucas Aerospace Ltd 1982–87; Man. Dir Aerospace, Lucas Industries PLC 1987–89; Man. Dir and Chief Exec. Hawker Siddeley Group PLC 1989–91; CEO London Transport 1992–94, Vice-Chair. 1992–93, Deputy Chair. 1993–94; Dir Senior Eng Group (now Senior PLC) 1994–2001, Deputy Chair. 1995–96, Chair. 1996–2001; Dir (non-exec.) Dobson Park Industries PLC 1992–95, Hepworth PLC 1995–98; Chair. High Duty Alloys Ltd 1997–2000; mem. Review Bd for Govt Contracts 1993–. *Leisure interests:* tennis, photography, golf, hot-air ballooning, vintage cars. *Address:* Senior PLC, 59/61 High Street, Rickmansworth, Herts., WD3 1RH, England. *Telephone:* (1923) 714703 (Office).

WATKINS, Winifred May, DSc, FRCPath, FMedSci, FRS; British scientist; b. 6 Aug. 1924, London; d. of Albert E. Watkins and Annie B. Watkins; ed Godolphin and Latymer School, London, Univ. of London; Research Student, St Bartholomew's Hosp. Medical School, London 1948–50; MRC Grantee, Lister Inst. Preventive Medicine, London 1950–52, Beit Memorial Research Fellow 1952–55, mem. scientific staff 1955–75, Prof. of Biochem. and Head, Dept of Biochem. 1968–75; Wellcome Travelling Fellow, Univ. of Calif. at Berkeley 1960–61; Reader in Biochem., Univ. of London 1965–68; Head of Div. of Immunochemical Genetics, MRC Clinical Research Centre 1976–89; Visiting Prof. and Sr Research Fellow, Royal Postgrad. Medical School 1990–; Foreign mem. Polish Acad. of Sciences 1988, Royal Swedish Acad. of Sciences 1998; Fellow Acad. of Medical Sciences 1998; Hon. mem. Int. Soc. of Blood Transfusion 1984, British Blood Transfusion Soc. 1996; Hon. mem. Japanese Biochemical Soc. 1990, British Biochemical Soc. 2000; Hon. FRCP 1990; Hon. DSc Chem. (Utrecht) 1990; Award of Oliver Memorial Fund for outstanding contribs in blood transfusion 1965, Karl Landsteiner Award, American Asscn of Blood Banks (jtly) 1967, Paul Erhlich-Ludwig Darmstädter Medal and Prize (jtly) 1969, William Julius Mickle Fellowship Award, Univ. of London 1970, Kenneth Goldsmith Award of British Blood Transfusion Soc. 1986, Royal Medal of Royal Soc. 1988, Franz-Oehleckler Medal of the German Soc. of Transfusion Medicine and Immunohaematology 1989, Philip Levine Award (jtly) (American Soc. of Chemical Pathologists 1990). *Publications:* numerous papers in scientific journals. *Leisure interest:* reading. *Address:* Department of Haematology, Imperial College School of Medicine, Hammersmith Hospital, Du Cane Road, London, W12 0NN, England (Office). *Telephone:* (20) 8383-2171. *Fax:* (20) 8742-9335. *E-mail:* w.watkins@ic.ac.uk (Office).

WATSON, Emily; British actress; b. 14 Jan. 1967, London; ed London Drama Studio, Bristol Univ. *Films:* Breaking the Waves (New York Soc. of Film Critics Award, Nat. Soc. of Film Critics Award), Mill on the Floss, Metroland, The Boxer, Hilary and Jackie, Angela's Ashes 1999, The Cradle Will Rock, Trixie, The Luzhin Defense, Equilibrium, Gosford Park 2001, Red Dragon 2002, Punch-Drunk Love 2002, Equilibrium 2003. *Theatre includes:* Uncle Vanya, Twelfth Night (both at Donmar Warehouse, London 2002, at Brooklyn Acad. of Music, NY 2003). *Address:* c/o ICM Ltd, Oxford House, 76 Oxford Street, London, W1N 0AX, England.

WATSON, James Dewey, BS, PhD; American biologist; b. 6 April 1928, Chicago, Ill.; s. of James D. Watson and Jean Mitchell Watson; m. Elizabeth Lewis 1968; two s.; ed Univ. of Chicago and Univ. of Indiana; Research Fellow, US Nat. Research Council, Univ. of Copenhagen 1950–51; Fellow US Nat. Foundation, Cavendish Lab., Univ. of Cambridge, England 1951–53, 1955–56; Sr Research Fellow in Biology, Calif. Inst. of Tech. 1953–55; Asst Prof. of Biology, Harvard Univ. 1956–58, Assoc. Prof. 1958–61, Prof. 1961–76; Dir Cold Spring Harbor Lab. 1968–93, Pres. 1994–; Assoc. Dir NIH (USA) 1988–89, Dir Nat. Center for Human Genome Research, NIH 1989–92; Newton-Abraham Visiting Prof., Oxford Univ., UK 1994; discovered structure of DNA (with F. W. Crick) 1953; mem. NAS, Danish Acad. of Arts and Sciences, American Acad. of Arts and Sciences, American Soc. of Biological Chemists; Sr Fellow, Soc. of Fellows, Harvard Univ. 1964–70; mem. American Philosophical Soc. 1978; Foreign mem. Royal Soc. 1981, USSR (now Russian) Acad. of Sciences 1989; Hon. Fellow of Clare Coll., Univ. of Cambridge 1967; Hon. DSc (Chicago, Indiana, Long Island, Adelphi, Brandeis, Hofstra, Harvard, Rockefeller, State Univ. of New York, Albert Einstein Coll. of Medicine, Clarkson Coll., Stellenbosch, Fairfield, Cambridge, Oxford, Charleston Medical Coll., Washington Coll., Univ. of Judaism, UCL, Wesleyan, Widener, Dartmouth, Trinity Coll. Dublin); Hon. LLD (Notre Dame) 1965; Hon. MD (Buenos Aires) 1986, (Charles Univ., Prague) 1998; Hon. DSc (Rutgers Univ.) 1988, (Bard Coll.) 1991, (Melbourne) 1997; Eli Lilly Award in Biochem. 1959, Lasker Prize (American Public Health Asscn) 1960, Nobel Prize for Medicine (with F. H. C. Crick and M. F. H. Wilkins) 1962, John J. Carty Gold Medal (Nat. Acad. of Sciences) 1971, Medal of Freedom 1977, Gold Medal Award, Nat. Inst. of Social Sciences 1984, Kaul Foundation Award for Excellence 1992, Copley Medal of Royal Soc. 1993, Nat. Biotech. Venture Award 1993; Lomosonov Medal 1994, Nat. Medal of Science 1997, Liberty Medal Award 2000, Benjamin Franklin Medal 2001; Hon. KBE 2002. *Publications:* Molecular Biology of the Gene 1965, The Double Helix 1968, The DNA Story 1981 (with John Tooze), Recombinant DNA: A Short Course 1983 (jtly), The Molecular Biology of the Cell (jtly) 1986, Recombinant DNA, 2nd Edn 1992 (jtly), A Passion for DNA 2000, Genes, Girls and Gamow 2001; papers on structure of deoxyribonucleic acid (DNA), on protein synthesis and on the induction of cancer by viruses. *Address:* Cold Spring Harbor Laboratory, PO Box 100, Cold Spring Harbor, Long Island, New York, NY 11724 (Office); Bungtown Road, Cold Spring Harbor, New York, NY 11724, USA (Home). *Telephone:* (516) 367-8310.

WATSON, James Kay Graham, PhD, FRS, FRSC; British research scientist; b. 20 April 1936, Denny, Scotland; s. of Thomas Watson and Mary C. Miller; m. Carolyn M. L. Kerr 1981; ed Denny High School, High School of Stirling and Univ. of Glasgow; Carnegie Sr Scholar, Dept of Chem., Univ. Coll. London 1961–63; Postdoctoral Fellow, Nat. Research Council, Ottawa, Canada 1963–65; ICI Research Fellow, Univ. of Reading 1965–66, Lecturer in Chemical Physics 1966–71; Visiting Assoc. Prof. in Physics, Ohio State Univ. 1971–75; SRC Sr Research Fellow in Chem. Univ. of Southampton 1975–79, 1980–82; Visiting Scientist, Nat. Research Council, Ottawa, Canada 1979–80, Sr Research Officer 1982–87, Prin. 1987–; Fellow American Physical Soc. 1990; Chem. Soc. Award 1974; Plyler Prize, American Physical Soc. 1986; Henry Marshall Tory Medal, Royal Soc. of Canada 1999. *Publications:* 150 articles on molecular physics in learned journals. *Leisure interests:* music, golf, tree-watching. *Address:* Steacie Institute for Molecular Sciences, National Research Council of Canada, Ottawa, Ont., K1A 0R6 (Office); 183 Stanley Avenue, Ottawa, Ont., K1M 1P2, Canada (Home). *Telephone:* (613) 990-0739 (Office); (613) 745-7928 (Home). *Fax:* (613) 991-2648 (Office). *E-mail:* james.watson@nrc-cnrc.gc.ca (Office).

WATSON, (Malcolm) Lyall, PhD, FZS, FLS; British author and biologist; b. 12 April 1939, South Africa; m. Vivienne Mawson 1961 (divorced 1966); ed Rondebosch Boys High School, Witwatersrand Univ. and Univs of Natal and London; Dir Johannesburg Zoo 1964–65; Producer and Reporter, BBC TV 1966–67; Founder and Dir Biologic of London (Consultancy) 1968–; organizer and leader of numerous expeditions 1970–; Commr for Seychelles on Int. Whaling Comm. 1978–82; lives on ocean-going trawler "Amazon" and in a cottage in West Cork, Ireland; Kt Order of Golden Ark, Netherlands 1983. *Television:* Documentary series for ITV and Discovery Channel. *Miscellaneous:* sailed single-handed across the Atlantic Ocean. *Publications:* Omnivore 1970, Supernature 1972, The Romeo Error 1974, Gifts of Unknown Things 1976, Lifetide 1978, Lightning Bird 1980, Whales of the World 1982, Heavens Breath 1984, Earthworks 1986, Beyond Supernature 1986, Supernature II 1986, The Water Planet 1987, Sumo 1988, Neophilia 1988, The Nature of Things 1990, Turtle Islands 1995, Dark Nature 1996, Monsoon 1996, Warriors, Warthogs and Wisdom 1997, Perfect Speed 1998, Jacobson's Organ 1999, Natural Mystery 2000, Elephantoms 2002, The Whole Hog 2003. *Leisure interests:* bird-watching, ethnobotany, archaeology, tribal art, conchology. *Address:* c/o BCM-Biologic, London, WC1N 3XX, England; Castle Melligan, Goleen, Co. Cork, Ireland (Home).

WATSON, Thomas Sturges (Tom), BS; American golfer; b. 4 Sept. 1949, Kansas City, Mo.; s. of Raymond Etheridge Watson and Sarah Elizabeth Ridge; m. 1st Linda Tova Rubin 1973; one s. one d.; m. 2nd Hilary Watson; three step-c.; ed Stanford Univ.; professional 1971–; British Open Champion 1975, 1977, 1980, 1982, 1983; record low aggregate for British Open of 268, record two single round scores of 65, lowest final 36-hole score of 130, Turnberry 1977; won US Masters title 1977, 1981; won US Open 1982; won World Series 1975, 1977, 1980; winner numerous other open championships;

top money winner on US Professional Golf Asscn (PGA) circuit 1977, 1978, 1979, 1980; first player ever to win in excess of $500,000 in prize money in one season 1980; Ryder Cup Player 1977, 1981, 1983, 1989 (Capt. 1993); Sr Tour victories: 1999 Bank One Championship, 2000 IR Sr Tour Championship, 2001 Sr PGA Championship, 2002 Sr Tour Championship; Hon. mem. Royal and Ancient Golf Club of St Andrews 1999; US PGA Player of the Year 1977, 1978, 1979, 1980, 1982; PGA World Golf Hall of Fame 1988. *Publication:* Getting Back into Basics (jtly) 1992. *Leisure interests:* current affairs, outdoor life, baseball (Kansas City Royals fan). *Address:* PGA America, PO Box 109801, 100 Avenue of the Champions, Palm Beach Gardens, FL 33410; 1901 West 47th Place, Suite 200, Shawnee Mission, KS 66205, USA.

WATSON, William, CBE, FBA; British professor of Chinese and Japanese Art History; b. 9 Dec. 1917, Darley Abbey; s. of Robert Scoular Watson and Lily Waterfield; m. Katherine Sylvia Mary Armfield 1940; four s.; ed Glasgow High School, Herbert Strutt School and Gonville and Caius Coll. Cambridge; Asst Keeper, British Museum, first in Dept of British and Medieval Antiquities, then in Dept of Oriental Antiquities 1947–66; Slade Prof. of Fine Art, Cambridge Univ. 1975–76; Prof. of Chinese Art and Archaeology, Univ. of London (SOAS) 1966–83, Prof. Emer. 1983–; Pres. of Oriental Ceramic Soc. 1981–84; Trustee British Museum 1980–90; Hon. D.Litt. (Chinese Univ. of Hong Kong) 1973. *Publications:* The Sculpture of Japan 1959, Archaeology in China 1960, China before the Han Dynasty 1961, Ancient Chinese Bronzes 1961, Jade Books in the Chester Beatty Library 1963, Cultural Frontiers in Ancient East Asia 1971, The Genius of China 1973, Style in the Arts of China 1974, L'Art de l'Ancienne Chine 1980; Ed. Catalogue of the Great Japan Exhibition 1981–82, Tang and Liao Ceramics 1984, Pre-Tang Ceramics of China 1991, The Arts of China to AD 900 1995, The Arts of China 900–1620, Collected Papers 1997, 1998. *Leisure interests:* Iberia, claret, Welsh literature. *Address:* Cefn y Maes, Parc, Bala, Gwynedd, LL23 7YS, Wales. *Telephone:* (1678) 540302.

WATT, James Gaius, BS, JD; American politician and lawyer; b. 31 Jan. 1938, Lusk, Wyo.; s. of William G. Watt and Lois M. (née Williams) Watt; m. Leilani Bomgardner 1957; one s. one d.; ed Univ. of Wyoming; Instructor, Coll. of Commerce and Industry, Univ. of Wyo. 1960–62; admitted to Wyo. Bar 1962; US Supreme Court Bar 1966; Legis. Asst, Counsel to Senator Simpson of Wyo. 1962–66; Sec. Natural Resources Comm. and Environmental Pollution Advisory Panel, US Chamber of Commerce 1966–69; Deputy Asst Sec. for Water and Power, Dept of the Interior 1969–72; Dir Bureau of Outdoor Recreation, US Dept of the Interior 1972–75; Vice-Chair. Fed. Power Comm. 1975–77; Pres., Chief Legal Officer, Mountain States Legal Foundation, Denver 1977–80; US Sec. of the Interior 1981–83; practising law, Washington 1983–86, Jackson Hole, Wyo. 1986–; Chair. of Bd Environmental Diagnostics Inc. 1984–87, Disease Detection Int. 1987–90. *Publication:* The Courage of a Conservative (with Doug Wead) 1985. *Address:* P.O. Box 3705, 755 East Paintbrush Drive, Box 3705, Jackson, WY 83001, USA.

WATT, James Park (Jim), MBE; Scottish boxer; b. 18 July 1948, Glasgow; s. of James Watt and Ina Watt; m. Margaret Black; two s. one d.; ed Glasgow Grammar School; rep. Scotland, amateur boxing; Amateur Boxing Asscn (ABA) lightweight champion 1968; declined invitation to join British Olympic team 1968; turned professional Oct. 1968; beaten in British lightweight championship fight v. Willie Reilly Feb. 1972; won title, beating Tony Riley after Willie Reilly relinquished it May 1972; lost title to Ken Buchanan Jan. 1973; won vacant title vs Johnny Cheshire Jan. 1975; won Lonsdale Belt outright by retaining British title vs Johnny Claydon Feb. 1977; beaten by Jonathan Dele for vacant Commonwealth lightweight title May 1975; won vacant European title, beating André Holyk in first round Aug. 1977; relinquished British title July 1977; retained European title twice in 1978; won vacant World Boxing Council (WBC) version of world lightweight championship April 1979, beating Alfredo Pitalua; defended it vs Roberto Vasquez Nov. 1979, Charlie Nash March 1980, Howard Davis June 1980 and Sean O'Grady Nov. 1980; 45 fights, 38 wins; now works as TV commentator; Freeman of the City of Glasgow 1981. *Leisure interests:* football and music. *Address:* c/o Gordon Poole Agency Ltd, The Limes, Brockley, Bristol, BS48 3BB, England. *Telephone:* (1275) 463222.

WATTS, Sir Arthur Desmond, KCMG, QC, LLM; British international lawyer; b. 14 Nov. 1931, Wimbledon; s. of the late Col A. E. Watts and Eileen May Watts (née Challons); m. Iris Ann Collier 1957; one s. one d.; ed Haileybury, Royal Mil. Acad. and Downing Coll. Cambridge; called to Bar, Gray's Inn 1957, Bencher 1996; Legal Asst Foreign Office 1957–59, Asst Legal Adviser 1962–67; Legal Adviser British Property Comm. (later British Embassy), Cairo 1959–62; Legal Adviser (First Sec.), British Embassy, Bonn 1967–69; Asst Solicitor Law Officer's Dept 1969–70; Legal Counsellor FCO 1970–73, 1977–82; Legal Counsellor, Perm. Rep. to EEC, Brussels 1973–77; Deputy Legal Adviser 1982–87, Legal Adviser 1987–91; practising barrister 1991–; Special Negotiator for Succession Issues (Fmr Yugoslavia) 1996–2001. *Publications:* Legal Effects of War (with Lord McNair) 1966, Encyclopaedic Dictionary of International Law (with Parry, Grant) 1986, Oppenheim's International Law, Vol. I (with Sir Robert Jennings) 1992, International Law and the Antarctic Treaty System 1992, Self-Determination and Self-Administration (with Danspeckgruber) 1997, International Law Commission 1949–1998 (3 vols) 1999. *Leisure interest:* cricket. *Address:* 20 Essex Street, London, WC2R 3AL, England. *Telephone:* (20) 7583-9294 (Office). *Fax:* (20) 7583-1341 (Office).

WATTS, Charlie (Charles Robert); British musician; b. 2 June 1941; m. Shirley Anne Shepherd 1964; one d.; drummer with Rolling Stones 1963–; toured with Charlie Watts Orchestra 1985–86. *Albums include:* (with the Rolling Stones) The Rolling Stones 1964, The Rolling Stones No. 2 1965, Out of Our Heads 1965, Aftermath 1966, Big Hits 1966, got LIVE if you want it! 1967, Between the Buttons 1967, Their Satanic Majesties Request 1967, Beggars Banquet 1968, Let it Bleed 1969, Get Yer Ya-Ya's Out! 1970, Stone Age 1971, Sticky Fingers 1971, Goats Head Soup 1973, It's Only Rock 'N' Roll 1974, Black and Blue 1976, Love You Live 1977, Some Girls 1978, Emotional Rescue 1980, Tattoo You 1981, Still Life 1981, Dirty Work 1986, Steel Wheels 1989, Flashpoint 1991, Voodoo Lounge 1994; solo albums include: Charlie Watts Orchestra – Live at Fulham Town Hall 1986, From One Charlie 1992, Warm and Tender 1993, From One Charlie 1995, Long Ago and Far Away 1996. *Films include:* Sympathy For The Devil 1969, Gimme Shelter 1970, Ladies and Gentlemen, The Rolling Stones 1977, Let's Spend the Night Together 1983, Flashpoint 1991. *Publication:* Ode to a High Flying Bird 1965. *Leisure interest:* jazz music. *Address:* c/o Munro Sounds, 5 Church Row, Wandsworth Plain, London, SW18 1ES, England.

WATTS, Donald Walter, AM, PhD, F.T.S.E., F.R.A.C.I., FACE, FAIM; Australian business executive; b. 1 April 1934, Western Australia; s. of Horace Frederick Watts and Esme Anne White; m. Michelle Rose Yeomans 1960; two s.; ed Hale School, Perth, Univ. of Western Australia, University Coll. London, UK; Personal Chair. in Physical and Inorganic Chem., Univ. of Western Australia 1977–79; Dir Western Australian Inst. of Tech. 1980–86; Vice-Chancellor Curtin Univ. of Tech. 1987; Pres. and Vice-Chancellor Bond Univ. 1987–90, Emer. Prof. 1990; CEO Trade Devt Zone Authority, Darwin 1990–91; Chair. NT Employment & Training Authority 1991–93; Dean Coll. of Arts and Sciences, Univ. of Notre Dame, Western Australia 1995–97, Dean of Research 1998–; Prof. of Science and Educ. 1995–; Dir Advanced Energy Systems 1995–96 (Chair. 1997–); Chair. and Dir Tech. Training Inst. Pty Ltd 2001–03; Councillor Australian Acad. of Technological Sciences and Eng 2001–; Fellow Royal Australian Chemical Inst., Australian Acad. of Tech. Sciences and Eng; mem. American Chemical Soc., Chemical Educ. Sub.-Cttee, Australian Acad. of Science; Hackett Scholar 1953, Gledden Fellow 1957, CSIRO Postdoctoral Fellow 1959, DSIR Postdoctoral Fellow 1961, Fulbright Scholar 1967; Japan Foundation Visiting Fellow 1984; Hon. Fellow Marketing Inst. of Singapore; Hon. DTech (Curtin Univ. of Tech.) 1987, Hon. D.Ed. (Univ. of WA) 2001; Rennie Medal 1967, Leighton Medal Royal Australian Chemical Inst. 1987, ANZAAS Medal 1998. *Publications:* The School Chemistry Project—A Secondary School Chemistry Syllabus for Comment (with N. S. Bayliss) 1978, Chemical Properties and Reactions (with A. R. H. Cole and R. B. Bucat) 1978, Chemistry for Australian Secondary School Students (with N. S. Bayliss) 1979, Elements of Chemistry: Earth, Air, Fire and Water 1984, Higher Education in Australia: A Way Forward, Policy Paper No. 8 1986, The Private Potential of Australian Higher Education 1987, A Private Approach to Higher Education 1987; numerous articles. *Leisure interests:* golf, tennis, reading. *Address:* University of Notre Dame Australia, Mouat Street, Freemantle, PO Box 1225, WA 6959; 87 Evans Street, Shenton Park, WA 6008, Australia. *Telephone:* (8) 9239-5533 (Office); (8) 9381-1667 (Home). *E-mail:* dwatts@nd .edu.au (Office).

WATTS, Helen Josephine, CBE; British contralto (retd); b. 7 Dec. 1927, Milford Haven, Wales; d. of Thomas Watts and Winifred Morgan; m. Michael Mitchell 1980; ed St Mary and St Anne's School, Abbot Bromley; singer in Glyndebourne and BBC choruses; toured Russia with English Opera Group 1964; concert tours in USA 1967–85 (retd); has appeared with all major European and American orchestras; numerous recordings; has sung at the Salzburg Festival, Covent Garden and the Hong Kong Festival; major appearances include: The Ring at Covent Garden; Mozart Opera at Salzburg Festival; four Promenade concerts 1974; Hon. FRAM. *Recordings include:* Handel Arias, Orfeo, Bach's B Minor Mass, Beethoven's Mass in C Minor, The Dream of Gerontius, The Apostles, Götterdämmerung. *Leisure interest:* gardening. *Address:* c/o Askonas Holt Ltd, Lonsdale Chambers, 27 Chancery Lane, London, WC2A 1PF, England (Office).

WATTS, Philip Beverley, KCMG, MSc; British oil company executive; b. 25 June 1945, Leicester; s. of Samuel Watts and Philippa Watts (née Wale); m. Janet Edna Watts (née Lockwood) 1966; one s. one d.; ed Wyggeston Grammar School, Leicester and Leeds Univ.; science teacher, Methodist Boys High School, Freetown, Sierra Leone 1966–68; joined Shell Int. 1969; held various posts: seismologist, Indonesia 1970–74, geophysicist UK/Europe 1974–77, Exploration Man., Norway 1978–81, Div. Head, Malaysia, Brunei, Singapore, London 1981–83, Exploration Dir, UK 1983–85; Head EP Liaison—Europe, The Hague 1986–88, Head EP Econs and Planning, The Hague 1989–91, Man. Dir, Nigeria 1991–94, Regional Co-ordinator, Europe, The Hague 1994–95; Dir Planning, Environment and External Affairs, London 1996–97; Chair. Royal Dutch/Shell Group 2001 (Group Man. Dir 1997–); Chair. Shell Transport and Trading 2001 (Man. Dir 1997–); Chair. World Business Council for Sustainable Devt 2001 (mem. Exec. Cttee 1998–); Chair. ICC-UK 1998– (mem. Governing Body 1997–), Worldwide ICC, Exec. Bd 1997–2000; Trustee Said Business School Foundation, Univ. of Oxford. *Leisure interests:* travel, gardening, reading. *Address:* Shell Centre, London, SE1 7NA, England (Office). *Telephone:* (20) 7934-5554 (Office). *Fax:* (20) 7934-5557 (Office).

WAUGH, John Stewart, PhD; American professor of chemistry; b. 25 April 1929, Willimantic, Conn.; s. of Albert E. Waugh and Edith S. Waugh; m. Susan M. Walsh 1983; one s. one d.; ed Windham High School, Dartmouth Coll. and Calif. Inst. of Tech.; mem. Faculty, MIT 1953–, A. A. Noyes Prof. of Chem. 1973–88, Inst. Prof. 1989–96, Inst. Prof. Emer. 1996–; Visiting Scientist, USSR Acad. of Sciences 1962, Univ. of Calif. 1963, Harvard Univ. 1975; Visiting Prof. Max Planck Inst. for Medical Research 1971, East China Normal Univ., Shanghai 1984, Texas A & M Univ. 1986; Joliot-Curie Prof. Ecole Supérieure de Physique et Chimie, Paris 1985, 1997; Fairchild Scholar, Calif. Inst. of Tech. 1989; Chair. Div. of Chem. Physics, American Physical Soc. 1984–85; Vice-Pres. Int. Soc. of Magnetic Resonance 1996–98, Pres. 1998–2001; mem. NAS, American Acad. of Arts and Sciences 1962–96, Slovenian Acad. of Sciences and Arts; Hon. ScD (Darmouth Coll.) 1989; von Humboldt Award 1971, Langmuir Award 1974, Pittsburgh Spectroscopy Award 1978, Wolf Laureate 1984, Pauling Medal 1985, Richards Medal 1992. *Publications:* many scientific research papers. *Leisure interests:* sailing, harpsichord. *Address:* Department of Chemistry, Massachusetts Institute of Technology, 77 Massachusetts Avenue, Cambridge, MA 02139 (Office); 60 Conant Road, Lincoln, MA 01773, USA (Home). *Telephone:* (617) 253-1901. *Fax:* (617) 253-7030. *E-mail:* jswaugh@mit.edu (Office).

WAUGH, Stephen (Steve) Rodger; Australian cricketer; b. 2 June 1965, Canterbury, Sydney; s. of Rodger Waugh and Beverley Waugh; elder twin of Mark Edward; m. Lynette Waugh; one s. two d.; ed East Hills High School; right-hand batsman and right-arm medium-fast bowler; teams—New South Wales 1984–85, Somerset 1987–88; 156 Tests for Australia 1985–86 to 2 Jan. 2003, scoring over 10,000 runs (average 49.45) including 29 hundreds and taking 91 wickets (average 35.6); has scored 21,989 first-class runs (average 51.61) with 71 hundreds to 15 Jan. 2003; shared world record 5th wicket stand of 464 (unbroken) with brother M. E. Waugh for NSW v.s Western Australia, Perth, 1990–91; toured England 1989, 1993, 1997, 2001; 325 limited-overs internationals to end Dec. 2002 (106 as Capt.); Capt. Australian Test Cricket Team 1999–; Patron Camp Quality, Cerebral Palsy Asscn, Udayan Home for Girls, India; Wisden Cricketer of the Year 1989, Australian Cricketer of the Year 2000–01; Allan Border Medal 2001, Laureus Sports Award (World's Best Team) 2001. *Publications:* South African Tour Diary 1995, Steve Waugh's West Indies Tour Diary 1996, Steve Waugh's World Cup Diary 1997, Images of Waugh, Never Satisfied, Ashes Summer (co-author), Ashes Diary 1997, 2001, Captain's Diary 2002. *Leisure interests:* golf, photography, reading, writing. *Address:* c/o Team-Duet, 3 Winnie Street, Cremorne, NSW 2090, Australia. *Telephone:* (2) 9909-2188 (Office). *Fax:* (2) 9909-2157 (Office).

WAX, Ruby; American comedienne, actress and writer; b. 19 April 1953, Ill.; d. of Edward Wax and Berta Wax (née Goldmann); m. Edward Richard Morison Bye 1988; one s. two d.; ed Evanston High School, Berkeley Univ., Royal Scottish Acad. of Music and Drama; with Crucible Theatre 1976; with RSC 1978–82; Performer of the Year, British Comedy Awards 1993. *Television includes:* Not the Nine O'Clock News 1982–83, Girls on Top 1983–85, Don't Miss Wax 1985–87, Hit and Run 1988, Full Wax 1987–92, Ruby Wax Meets... 1996, 1997, 1998, Ruby 1997, 1998, 1999, Ruby's American Pie 1999, 2000, Hot Wax 2001, The Waiting Game 2001, 2002, Ruby 2002. *Films include:* Miami Memoirs 1987, East Meets Wax 1988, Class of 69, Ruby Takes a Trip 1992. *Plays include:* Wax Acts (one woman show) 1992, Stressed (one woman show) 2000. *Publication:* How Do You Want Me? (autobiog.) 2002. *Address:* c/o ICM, Oxford House, 76 Oxford Street, London, W1N 0AY, England. *Telephone:* (20) 7636-6565; (20) 7323-0101.

WEAH, George; Liberian footballer; b. 1 Oct. 1966, Monrovia; m.; four c.; played for Liberian and Cameroonian clubs; player AC Monaco, Cameroon national team 1988–92 (47 goals, 93 games), Paris St Germain 1992–95 (32 goals, 96 games), AC Milan 1995–99 (34 goals, 78 games); played with Chelsea, Manchester City and Marseille; player Liberia nat. team, also Technical Dir until retired after the African Nations Cup Jan. 2002; signed for Al Jazira, UAE 2001; special rep. for sport UNICEF; Amb. for SOS Children's Villages; African Player of the Year 1989, 1994, 1995, World Player of the Year 1995, European Player of the Year 1995, FIFA Fair Player 1996, African Footballer of the Century.

WEAIRE, Denis Lawrence, PhD, FRS, MRIA, MAE; British/Irish physicist; b. 17 Oct. 1942; s. of Allen M. Weaire and Janet E. Rea; m. Colette O'Regan 1969; one s.; ed Belfast Royal Acad. and Cambridge Univ.; Harkness Fellowship 1964–66; Fellow, Clare Coll. Cambridge 1967–69; Instructor, Assoc. Prof. Yale Univ. 1970–74; Sr Lecturer, Prof. Heriot-Watt Univ. 1974–79; Chair. of Experimental Physics, Univ. Coll. Dublin 1980–84; Erasmus Smith's Prof. of Natural and Experimental Philosophy, Trinity Coll. Dublin 1984–, Dean of Science 1989; mem. Acad. Europaea; Hon. Sec. European Asscn of Deans of Science 1991–93; Vice-Pres. European Physical Soc. 1995–96, 1999–2000, Pres. 1997–99; Dr hc (Tech. Univ., Lisbon) 2001; Cecil Powell Medal 2002. *Publications:* Introduction to Physical Mathematics (co-author) 1985, The Physics of Foams (co-author) 2000, The Pursuit of Perfect Packing (co-author) 2000; co-ed. of several other vols. *Leisure interests:* sport, sea-fishing, theatre, humorous writing. *Address:* University of Dublin, Trinity College, Faculty of Science, Dublin 2; 26 Greenmount Road, Terenure, Dublin, Ireland (Home). *Telephone:* (1) 4902063 (Home).

WEALE, Martin Robert, BA, CBE; British economist; b. 4 Dec. 1955, Barnet, Herts.; s. of R. A. Weale and M. E. Weale; ed Clare Coll. Cambridge; Overseas Devt Inst. Fellow, Nat. Statistical Office, Malawi 1977–79; researcher and lecturer, Faculty of Econs and Politics, Cambridge Univ. 1979–95, Econs Fellow Clare Coll. 1981–95; Dir Nat. Inst. of Econ. and Social Research 1995–, Statistics Commr 2000–; Hon. Fellow Inst. of Actuaries 2001. *Publications* *include:* Macroeconomic Policy: Inflation, Wealth and the Exchange Rate (co-author) 1989, Reconciliation of National Income and Expenditure (co-author) 1995, Econometric Modelling: Techniques and Applications (co-ed.) 2000. *Leisure interests:* bridge, walking, art exhbns., music. *Address:* National Institute of Economic and Social Research, 2 Dean Trench Street, London, SW1P 3HE (Office); 63 Noel Road, London, N1 8HE, England (Home). *Telephone:* (20) 7654-1945 (Office). *E-mail:* mweale@niesr.ac.uk (Office). *Website:* www.niesr.ac.uk (Office).

WEARING, Gillian, BA; British artist; b. 1963, Birmingham; ed Chelsea School of Art, Goldsmith's Coll. London; first solo exhbn City Racing, London 1993, numerous exhbns around the world; concentrates on video and photography; Turner Prize 1997; New Contemporaries Award 1993. *Solo exhibitions include:* Kunsthaus Zurich, Chisenhale Gallery, London 1997, Centre d'Art contemporain, Geneva 1998, Serpentine Gallery, London 2000, Fundación "la Caixa", Madrid 2001, ARC, Paris 2001, Cento Gallego de Arte Contemporánea, Santiago 2001, Museo do Chiado, Lisbon 2001, Kunsthens, Glarus 2002, Trilogy, Vancouver Art Gallery 2002, Mass Observation MCA Chicago and touring. *Group exhibitions include:* Museum of Contemporary Art, Sydney 2000, Tate Britain, London 2000, Ikon Gallery, Birmingham 2001, Kunstmuseum, Lichtenstein 2001, Tate Modern, London 2001, I Promise it's Political, Museum Ludwig, Cologne 2002, Remix: Contemporary Art and Pop, Tate Liverpool 2002, Bienal de São Paolo, Brazil 2002, ABBILD recent portraiture and depiction, Landesmuseum Joanneum, Graz 2001, Ikon Gallery, Birmingham 2001. *Publications:* Signs that say what you want them to say and not signs that say what someone else wants you to say 1997, Gillian Wearing 1999, 2000, 2001, Gillian Wearing Sous Influence 2001, Mass Observation 2002. *Address:* c/o Maureen Paley Interim Art, 21 Herald Street, London, E2 6JT, England. *Telephone:* (20) 7729-4112. *Fax:* (20) 7729-4113.

WEATHERALL, Sir David John, Kt, MD, FRCP, FRS; British professor of medicine (retd); b. 9 March 1933, Liverpool; s. of the late Harry Weatherall and Gwendoline Weatherall; m. Stella Nestler 1962; one s.; ed Calday Grammar School and Univ. of Liverpool; various resident posts in medicine 1956–58; Jr medical specialist, Royal Army Medical Corps, Singapore 1959–60; Research Fellow, Johns Hopkins Hosp. 1961–65; Reader in Haematology, Univ. of Liverpool 1969–71, Prof. 1971–74; consultant to WHO 1967–82; Nuffield Prof. of Clinical Medicine, Univ. of Oxford 1974–92, Regius Prof. of Medicine 1992–2000, Regius Prof. Emer. 2000–; Fellow, Magdalen Coll. 1974–92, Emer. Fellow 1992, Student, Christ Church 1992–2000; Hon. Dir MRC Molecular Haematology Unit 1979–2000, Inst. of Molecular Medicine 1988–2000; Trustee Wellcome Trust 1990–2000; Pres. British Asscn for the Advancement of Science 1993, Int. Soc. of Haematology 1993; Pres. Kennedy Foundation 2000–02; Trustee Wolfson Trust 2000–, Imperial Cancer Research Fund 2000–02; mem. American Acad. of Arts and Sciences; Watson-Smith Lecture 1974, Croonian Lecture 1984, Foundation Lecture (FRCPath) 1979, Darwin Lecture (Eugenics Soc.) 1979; Sims Visiting Prof. 1982; Fellow Imperial Coll. 1984; Foreign Assoc. NAS 1990, Inst. of Medicine 1991, Founder Fellow Acad. Med. Sci.; Hon. FRCOG; Hon. FACP; Hon. FRCPCH; Hon. MD (Leeds) 1988, (Sheffield) 1989, (Nottingham) 1993; Hon. DSc (Manchester) 1989, (Edin.) 1989, (Aberdeen) 1991, (Leicester) 1991, (London) 1992, (Keele) 1993, (Mahidol Univ., Thailand) 1997, (Exeter) 1999, (McGill Univ., Canada) 1999; Hon. DHumLitt (Johns Hopkins Univ.) 1990; Hon. DSc (Oxford Brookes) 1995, (South Bank) 1995, (Exeter) 1998; Hon. LLD (Liverpool) 1992, (Bristol) 1994; Stratton Award and Medal (Int. Soc. of Haematology) 1982, Ballantyne Prize (R.C.P. Edin.) 1983, Feldberg Foundation Award 1984, Royal Medal (Royal Soc.) 1989, Conway Evans Prize (Royal Soc. and Royal Coll. Physicians) 1991, Gold Medal, Royal Soc. of Medicine 1992, Buchanan Medal (Royal Soc.) 1994, Helmut Horten Int. Prize in Biomedical Science 1995, Manson Medal, Royal Soc. of Tropical Medicine 1998, Prince Mahidol Award, Thailand 2001. *Publications:* The New Genetics and Clinical Practice 1982, The Thalassaemia Syndromes (with J. B. Clegg) 1982, 2001, Oxford Textbook of Medicine (with others) 1983, Science and the Quiet Art 1995. *Leisure interest:* music. *Address:* Weatherall Institute of Molecular Medicine, John Radcliffe Hospital, Headington, Oxford, OX3 9DU (Office); 8 Cumnor Rise Road, Cumnor Hill, Oxford, OX2 9HD, England (Home). *Telephone:* (1865) 222360 (Office). *Fax:* (1865) 222501.

WEATHERALL, Vice-Adm. Sir James (Lamb), KCVO, KBE; British naval officer and Marshal of the Diplomatic Corps; b. 28 Feb. 1936, Newton Mearns, Renfrewshire; s. of the late Lt Commdr Alwyne Weatherall and Joan Cuthbert; m. Hon. Jean Stewart Macpherson 1962; two s. three d.; ed Glasgow Acad., Gordonstoun School; commanded HM Ships Soberton 1966–67, Ulster 1970–72, Tartar 1975–76, Andromeda 1982–84 (in Falklands Conflict), Ark Royal 1985–87; on staff of Supreme Allied Commander Europe (NATO) as Rear-Adm. 1987–89; Deputy Supreme Allied Commdr Atlantic 1989–91; HM Marshal of the Diplomatic Corps 1992–2001; Extra Equerry to HM The Queen 2001; one of HM The Queen's Commrs. of the Lieutenancy for the City of London 2002; Liveryman Worshipful Co. of Shipwrights 1985, Asst to Court 1989, Prime Warden 2001–02; Younger Brother Trinity House 1986; Trustee Marwell Zoological Preservation Trust 1992 (Chair. 1999–); Gov. Box Hill School 1992– (Chair. 1994–2003), Gordonstoun School 1994– (Chair. 1996–2003); Pres. Int. Social Service 1996–2001; Chair. Lord Mayor of London's Appeal 1997–98; Chair. Sea Cadet Asscn 1992–98; Trustee World Wildlife Fund UK 2001. *Leisure interests:* fishing, stamp collecting. *Address:* Craig House, Ashton Lane, Bishop's Waltham, Hants., SO32 1FS, England (Home). *Telephone:* (1489) 892483 (Home). *Fax:* (1489) 892483 (Home).

WEATHERILL, Baron (Life Peer), cr. 1992, of North East Croydon in the London Borough of Croydon; **(Bruce) Bernard Weatherill,** KStJ, PC; British politician and master tailor; b. 25 Nov. 1920, Sunningdale, Surrey; s. of the late Bernard Weatherill and of Gertrude Creak; m. Lyn Eatwell 1949; two s. one d; ed Malvern Coll.; served Royal Dragoon Guards, Indian Army, 19th King George V's Own Lancers 1939–45; Man. Dir Bernard Weatherill Ltd 1957–70, Pres. 1992–; MP for Croydon North East 1964–92; Opposition Whip 1967–70; Lord Commr of HM Treasury 1970–71; Vice-Chamberlain of the Royal Household 1971–72, Comptroller 1972–73; Treasurer of the Household and Deputy Chief Whip 1974–79; Chair. Ways and Means and Deputy Speaker 1979–83; Speaker of the House of Commons 1983–92; Convenor of Cross-bench Peers, House of Lords 1995–99; Chair. Commonwealth Speakers and Presiding Officers 1986–88; High Bailiff of Westminster Abbey 1989–99; Chair. Industry and Parl. Trust; Vice-Chancellor The Order of St John of Jerusalem 1992–99; K.St.J.; Hon. Bencher Lincoln's Inn; Hon. DCL (Kent) 1990, (Univ. of William and Mary, Williamsburg), (Denver, Colo); Hon. DUniv (Open Univ.); Hilal.i. Pakistan. *Publication:* Acorns to Oaks. *Leisure interests:* golf, tennis. *Address:* House of Lords, Westminster, London, SW1A 0PW (Office); Emmetts House, Ide Hill, Kent, TN14 6BA, England (Home). *Telephone:* (20) 7219-2224 (Office). *Fax:* (20) 7219-5979 (Office).

WEATHERSTONE, Sir Dennis, KBE, FIB; British banker; b. 29 Nov. 1930, London; s. of Henry Philip Weatherstone and Gladys Hart; m. Marion Blunsum 1959; one s. three d.; ed Acland High School, North London Univ.; Vice-Pres. Morgan Guaranty Trust Co. 1965–72, Sr Vice-Pres. 1972–77, Exec. Vice-Pres. and Treas. 1977–79; Vice-Chair. Morgan Guaranty Trust Co. (now J. P. Morgan Chase & Co. Inc.) 1979–80, Chair. Exec. Cttee 1980–86, Pres. 1987–89, Chair. 1989–94, CEO 1990–94; mem. Bd of Banking Supervision of Bank of England 1994–; Dir General Motors, Merck & Co. Inc., Air Liquide. *Leisure interest:* tennis. *Address:* JP Morgan Chase & Co., 270 Park Avenue, New York, NY 10017, USA. *Telephone:* (212) 622-9162 (Office).

WEAVER, A. Vernon; American diplomatist; b. 16 April 1922, Miami, Fla; s. of A. Vernon Weaver, Sr and Genevieve Weaver; m. Joyce McCoy 1947; three d.; ed U.S. Naval Acad.; with U.S. Navy 1946–49, 1951–53; with Southern Venetian Blind Co., Miami 1949–51 (Vice-Pres.), 1953–59; Pres. Lanotan Inc., Miami 1952–62; Man. Hollis & Co., Little Rock 1962–64; Pres. Union Life Insurance, Little Rock 1954–77; Admin. U.S. Small Business Admin., Washington DC 1977–81; Asst to Chair., Stephens Inc., Washington, DC 1981–96; Amb. to EU 1996–99. *Leisure interests:* reading, tennis.

WEAVER, Sigourney, BA, MFA; American actress; b. 8 Oct. 1949, New York; d. of Pat Weaver and Elizabeth Inglis; m. James Simpson 1984; one d.; ed Stanford Univ., Yale Univ. *Films include:* Annie Hall 1977, Tribute to a Madman 1977, Camp 708 1978, Alien 1979, Eyewitness 1981, The Year of Living Dangerously 1982, Deal of the Century 1983, Ghostbusters 1984, Une Femme ou Deux 1985, Half Moon Street 1986, Aliens 1986, Gorillas in the Mist (Golden Globe Best Actress Award) 1988, Working Girl (Best Supporting Actress Award Golden Globe) 1988, Ghostbusters II 1989, Aliens 3 1992, 1492: Conquest of Paradise 1993, Dave 1993, Death and the Maiden 1994, Jeffrey 1995, Copycat 1996, Snow White in the Black Forest 1996, Ice Storm 1996, Alien Resurrection 1997, A Map of the World 1999, Galaxy Quest 1999, Get Bruce 1999, Company Man 1999, Airframe 1999, Heartbreakers 2001. *Address:* c/o ICM, 8942 Wilshire Boulevard, Beverly Hills, CA 90211, USA.

WEBB, Sir Adrian Leonard, Kt, B.SOC.SCI., MSc, DLitt, FRSA; British academic and university administrator; b. 19 July 1943; s. of Leonard Webb and Rosina Webb; m. 1st Caroline Williams 1966 (divorced 1995); two s.; m. 2nd Monjulee Dass 1996; ed Birmingham Univ., London School of Econs; Lecturer, LSE 1966–74; Research Dir Personal Social Services Council 1974–76; Prof. of Social Policy, Loughborough Univ. 1976–93; Dir Centre for Research in Social Policy 1983–90, Dean, later Pro-Vice-Chancellor, 1986–93; Vice-Chancellor, Univ. of Glamorgan 1993–; mem. Nat. Cttee of Inquiry into Higher Educ. (Dearing Cttee) 1996–97; BBC Broadcasting Council for Wales 1998–; Dir (non-exec.) E Glamorgan NHS Trust 1997–. *Publications:* Change, Choice and Conflict in Social Policy 1975; Planning Need and Scarcity 1986; The Economic Approach to Social Policy 1986; Social Work, Social Care and Social Planning 1987; Joint Approaches to Social Policy 1988. *Leisure interests:* birdwatching, walking. *Address:* University of Glamorgan, Pontypridd, Mid Glamorgan, CF37 1DL, Wales (Office). *Telephone:* (1443) 482001 (Office). *Fax:* (1443) 482390 (Office). *E-mail:* alwebb@glam.ac.uk (Office).

WEBB, Leslie Roy, BCom, PhD; Australian university vice-chancellor (retd); b. 18 July 1935, Melbourne; s. of Leslie Hugh Charles Webb and Alice Myra Webb; m. Heather Brown 1966; one s. one d.; ed Wesley Coll., Melbourne, Univ. of Melbourne, London School of Econs; Sr Lecturer in Econs, Univ. of Melbourne 1964–68, Truby Williams Prof. of Econs 1973–84, Prof. Emer. 1985–, Pro-Vice-Chancellor 1982–84, Chair. Academic Bd 1983–84; Reader in Econs, La Trobe Univ. 1969–72; Vice-Chancellor Griffith Univ. 1985–2002; Chair. Queensland Non-State Schools Accreditation Bd 2001; Visiting Prof. Cornell Univ., USA 1967–68; Consultant, UNCTAD 1974–75; Jt Ed. The Economic Record 1973–77; Chair. Cttee of Inquiry into S Australian Dairy Industry 1977, Library Bd of Queensland; Assoc. mem. Prices Justification Tribunal 1978–79, 1980–81; mem. Council of Advice, Bureau of Industry Econs 1982–84; Chair. Bd of Dirs. Australian-American Educational Foundation (Fulbright Program) 1986–90; mem. Bd of Govs., Foundation for Devt Co-operation 1990–; Dir and mem. Australian Vice-Chancellors' Cttee Bd of Dirs. 1991–94; Pres. Victorian Br., Econ. Soc. of Australia and NZ 1976; Award for

Outstanding Achievement, U.S. Information Agency 1987; Cavaliere, Ordine al Merito (Italy) 1995. *Publications:* Industrial Economics: Australian Studies (Jt Ed.) 1982; articles in learned journals. *Leisure interests:* music, art. *Address:* 3 Davrod Street, Robertson, Queensland 4109, Australia (Home). *Telephone:* (7) 3345-7141 (Home). *Fax:* (7) 3344-6797 (Home). *E-mail:* roywebb@bigpond.com (Home).

WEBBER, Tristan, MA; British fashion designer; ed SE Essex Coll. of Arts and Tech., Cordwainers Coll., London and St Martin's School of Art and Design; work exhibited at Colette, Paris and Powerhouse Exhbn, London 1998; third collection shown at London Fashion Week (Sept. 1998) and MTV Fashionably Loud event, Miami (Dec. 1998). *Address:* c/o Brower Lewis PR, 74 Gloucester Place, London, W1H 3HN, England. *Telephone:* (20) 7935-2735. *Fax:* (20) 7935-2739.

WEBER, Bruce; American photographer, film director and producer; b. 29 March 1946, Greensburg, Pa; ed Hun School at Princeton, Denison Univ., Ohio, New York Univ. Art and Film Schools, New School for Social Research, New York; numerous exhbns. New York, Los Angeles, Chicago, Dallas, San Francisco, Atlanta, New Orleans, St Louis, Paris, London, Dortmund, Basel, Lausanne, Tokyo, Frankfurt etc. 1973–; photographs in perm. collections of Victoria and Albert Museum, London and Photography Div., City of Paris; numerous commercials 1988–; numerous awards including: Council of Fashion Designers of America for Achievement in Photography 1984, 1985, American Soc. of Magazine Photographers Fashion Photographer of the Year 1984, Int. Film and TV Festival of New York Silver Medal 1985, Cannes Int. Advertising Film Festival Silver Lion for Beauty Brothers (commercial) 1988, Int. Center of Photography Award for use of Photography in Advertising 1994, Best Advertising in Print and TV, Fragrance Foundation 1997, First Alfred Eisenstaedt Award for Portrait Photography, Life magazine 1998. *Films as Producer and Director include:* Broken Noses 1987 (Int. Documentary Asscn. Award 1988), Let's Get Lost 1988 (Critics' Award, Venice Film Festival 1988, Int. Documentary Asscn. Award 1989), Backyard Movie 1991, Gentle Giants 1994, The Teddy Boys of the Edwardian Drape Society 1996, Chop Suey 1999. *Music Videos:* Being Boring, The Pet Shop Boys 1990 (Video of the Year Award, Music Week 1990), Blue Spanish Sky, Chris Isaak 1991, Se A Vida E, The Pet Shop Boys 1996. *Publications:* Sam Shepard 1990, Bear Pond 1990, Hotel Room with a View (photographs) 1992, Gentle Giants: A Book of Newfoundland 1994, A House is Not a Home 1996, Branded Youth and other stories 1997, The Chop Suey Club 1999. *Address:* c/o Little Bear Inc., 135th Watts Street, 5th Floor, New York, NY 10013, USA. *Telephone:* (212) 226-0814 (Office). *Fax:* (212) 334-5180 (Office).

WEBER, George Brian, MA; Canadian Red Cross official; b. 18 April 1946, Montréal; s. of Harry Weber and Johanna Alexopoulos; m. Mary Morris 1976; ed McGill Univ., Harvard Univ., USA; voluntary instructor/examiner Canadian Red Cross 1963–73; Field Del. Vietnam, Int. Red Cross 1973–74; Disaster Relief Officer, Chief Del. League of Red Cross Socs. 1974–76; Nat. Dir Int. Affairs, Canadian Red Cross 1976–81, Nat. Dir of Programmes 1981–83, Sec. Gen. Canadian Red Cross 1983–93, Hon. Vice Pres. 1993–, Sec. Gen. and CEO Int. Fed. of Red Cross and Red Crescent Socs. 1993–2000, Emer. 2000–; mem., Dir numerous bodies, including Canadian Inst. of Int. Affairs, Amundsen Foundation, Earth Foundation, American Coll. of Sports Medicine, Canadian Soc. Assoc. Execs.; awards include Vanier Award 1984. *Leisure interests:* diving, tennis, squash, skiing.

WEBER, John William, BA; American art dealer; b. 10 Dec. 1932, Los Angeles, Calif.; s. of John William Weber and Helen M. Curran; m. Joyce Nereaux 1981 (divorced); four c.; ed Admiral Farragut Acad., Fla, Antioch Coll. Yellow Springs, Ohio and Inst. of Fine Arts, New York Univ.; Assoc. Curator, Dayton Art Inst. Dayton, Ohio 1958; Dir Martha Jackson Gallery, New York 1960–62, Dwan Gallery, LA and New York 1962–71; Founder and Pres. John Weber Gallery, New York 1971–; Chevalier, Ordre des Arts et des Lettres. *Publications:* de Europa 1972, Papunya Tula 1989, Political Arm 1991. *Leisure interests:* amateur radio, boating, mountaineering. *Address:* John Weber Gallery, 529 W 20th Street, New York, NY 10011, USA. *Telephone:* (212) 691-5711. *Fax:* (212) 691-5848.

WEBER, Jürgen, DR. ING.; German business executive; b. 17 Oct. 1941; m. Sabine Rossberg 1965; one s. one d.; ed Stuttgart Tech. Univ., MIT; with Lufthansa Eng Div. 1967–74, Dir Line Maintenance Dept 1974–78, with Aircraft Eng Sub-div. 1978–87, COO (Tech.) 1987–89, Deputy mem. Exec. Bd 1989–90, CEO (Tech.) 1990–91, Chair. Exec. Bd Lufthansa German Airlines 1991–2003, CEO 1998–2003; Champion of Liberty Award, Asscn of European Airlines 1999. *Leisure interests:* jogging, skiing. *Address:* c/o Deutsche Lufthansa AG, Lufthansa Basis, 60546 Frankfurt, Germany. *Telephone:* (69) 6962200.

WEBER, Manfred, Dr rer. pol; German banking official; b. 18 Dec. 1950, Altenkofen, Landshut; ed Johann Wolfgang Goethe Univ. Frankfurt am Main; Research Asst, Research Dept, Deutsche Bundesbank 1980, Head, Office of Deputy Gov. 1986–91; Monetary and Econ. Dept B.I.S., Basle 1991–92; Gen. Exec. Man.and mem. Bd of Dirs. Bundesverband deutscher Banken, Berlin 1992–. *Address:* Burgstrasse 28, 10178 Berlin, Germany. *Telephone:* (30) 16631000.

WEBSTER, Paul; British film executive; b. 19 Sept. 1952; co-Dir Osiris Film, London 1979–81; founder Palace Pictures 1982–88; launched Working Title Film LA 1990–92; Head of Production Miramax Films 1995–97; CEO Film Four Ltd 1998–; mem. BAFTA Council, BAFTA Film Council. *Films include:* The Tall Guy 1988, Drop Dead Fred 1990, Bob Roberts (exec. producer) 1992, Romeo is Bleeding 1993, Little Oddessa (Silver Lion Venice Film Festival 1994), The Pallbearer 1995, Gridlock'd 1996, The English Patient, Welcome to Sarajevo, Wings of the Dove, The Yards 1998. *Address:* FilmFour Ltd, 76-78 Charlotte Street, London, S1P 1LX, England (Office). *Telephone:* (20) 7306-8621 (Office). *Fax:* (20) 7306-6457.

WEBSTER, Peter; Irish business executive; joined Jefferson Smurfit Group 1978, fmr Regional Operations Dir, Chair. and Chief Exec. 1996–. *Address:* Jefferson Smurfit Group PLC, Beech Hill, Clonskeagh, Dublin 14, Ireland. *Telephone:* (1) 2696622. *Fax:* (1) 2694481.

WEBSTER, William Hedgcock, LLB; American government official and judge; b. 6 March 1924, St Louis, Mo.; s. of Thomas M. Webster and Katherine (née Hedgcock) Webster; m. 1st Drusilla Lane 1950 (died 1984); one s. two d.; m. 2nd Lynda Clugston 1990; ed Amherst Coll., Washington Univ. Law School; admitted to Mo. Bar 1949; attorney with Armstrong, Teasdale, Kramer and Vaughan and predecessors, St Louis 1949–50, 1952–59, partner 1956–59, 1961–70; U.S. Attorney, Eastern Dist, Mo. 1960–61; Judge U.S. Dist Court, Eastern Mo. 1971–73, U.S. Court of Appeals 1973–78; Dir FBI 1978–87; Dir Cen. Intelligence Agency (CIA) 1987–91; Sr Partner Millbank, Tweed, Hadley & McCloy 1991–; Trustee, Washington Univ. 1974–; Head investigation into police response to LA Riots 1992; served as Lt USNR 1943–46, 1951–52; mem. American, Fed., Mo. and St Louis Bar Asscns., American Law Inst., Council 1978–, Inst. of Judicial Admin. Inc.; Fellow, American Bar Foundation; Hon. LLD (Amherst Coll. 1975, DePauw Univ. 1978, Washington Univ. 1978, William Woods Coll. 1979 and numerous others); Washington Univ. Distinguished Alumnus Award 1977; American Legion Distinguished Service Award 1979; Order of the Coif; St Louis Globe-Democrat Man of the Year 1980; Washington Univ. William Greenleaf Elliot Award 1981; Riot Relief Fund of NY Award 1981, Young Lawyers of the American Bar Asscn Award 1982, Fordham-Stein Award 1982, William Moss Inst.-American Univ. Award 1983, Freedoms Foundation Medal 1985. *Leisure interest:* tennis. *Address:* Milbank, Tweed, Hadley and McClay, 1825 I Street, NW, Suite 1100, Washington, DC 20006, USA.

WECHMAR, Rüdiger Baron von; German diplomatist and journalist; b. 15 Nov. 1923, Berlin; s. of Irnfried Baron von Wechmar and Ilse Baroness von Wechmar (née von Binzer); m. 1st Rosemarie Warlimont 1947 (divorced); one s. one d.; m. 2nd Susanne Woldenga 1961; one d.; with German News Service (DPD); joined United Press 1948, Head of Bonn Bureau 1954–58; Press Attaché, German Consulate-Gen., NY 1958; Head of E European Bureau, Zweites Deutsches Fernsehen, Vienna 1963; Dir German Information Center, New York 1968; Deputy Head of Govt Press and Information Office 1969, State Sec., Head of Govt Press and Information Office, Chief Govt Spokesman 1972–74; Perm. Rep. to UN 1974–81, Pres. UN Gen. Ass. 1980–81; Amb. to Italy 1981–83, to UK 1984–88; mem. European Parl. 1989–94; mem. Deutsche Gesellschaft für Auswärtige Politik; Paul Klinger Prize 1973, Dag Hammarskjöld Gold Medal 1981, UN Gold Medal 1981 and other decorations. *Publications:* numerous works and articles on foreign and UN affairs. *Address:* Hiltensperger Strasse 15, 80798 Munich, Germany. *Telephone:* (89) 2711224. *Fax:* (89) 2711224.

WECKMANN-MUÑOZ, Luis, PhD, LLD, MA; Mexican diplomatist and historian; b. 7 April 1923, Ciudad Lerdo, Durango; s. of José Bernardo Weckmann and Ana Muñoz; ed Univ. Nacional Autónoma de México, Univs. of Paris and Calif., Inst. des Hautes Etudes Int. and Ecole des Chartes, Paris; successively Sec. of Legation and Chargé d'affaires, Czechoslovakia, Sec. of Embassy and Chargé d'affaires, France 1952–59; Dir-Gen. for Int. Educ. Affairs and Exec. Sec.-Gen. Mexican Nat. Council for UNESCO 1959–64; Minister Plenipotentiary and Chargé d'affaires, France 1965–66; Amb. to Israel 1967–69, to Austria 1969–72, to Fed. Repub. of Germany 1973–74; Special Rep. of UN Sec.-Gen. to Iran and Iraq 1974; Special Rep. of UN Sec.-Gen. in Cyprus 1974–75; Amb. to Iran 1976–79, to UN 1979–80, to Italy 1981–86, to Belgium and the EEC 1986–88; Consul-Gen. in Rio de Janeiro 1988–90; Vice-Pres. 1st Inter-american Meeting on Science and Tech., Washington; UNESCO's expert for Latin America on Cultural Exchanges. *Publications:* La Sociedad Feudal 1944, Las Bulas Alejandrinas de 1943 y la Teoría Política del Papado Medieval 1949, El Pensamiento Político Medieval y una nueva base para el Derecho Internacional 1950, Les origines des Missions Diplomatiques Permanentes 1953, Panorama de la Cultura Medieval 1962, Las Relaciones Franco-Mexicanas (1823-1885) vol. I 1961, vol. II 1963, vol. III 1972, La Herencia Medieval de México, Vols I and II 1984, new edn in one vol. 1994, Carlota de Bélgica: Correspondencia y Escritos sobre México en los archivos Europeos, 1861–1868 1989, Constantino el Grande y Cristóbal Colón 1992, The Medieval Heritage of Brazil 1993. *Leisure interest:* reading. *Address:* Villa del Cardo, Calzado del Cardo 4, 37700 San Miguel Allende, Gto., Mexico.

WEDDERBURN OF CHARLTON, Baron (Life Peer), cr. 1977, of Highgate; **Kenneth William Wedderburn,** QC, MA, LLB, FBA; British professor of law; b. 13 April 1927, London; s. of Herbert John Wedderburn and Mabel Ethel Wedderburn; m. 1st Nina Salaman 1951 (divorced 1961); one s. two d.; m. 2nd Dorothy Cole 1962 (divorced 1969); m. 3rd Frances Ann Knight 1969; one s.; ed Aske's (Hatcham) Grammar School, Whitgift School, Queens' Coll. Cambridge; Lecturer in Law, Cambridge Univ. 1952–64; Fellow, Clare Coll. Cambridge; Cassel Prof. of Commercial Law, LSE 1964–92, Prof. Emer.

1992–; Visiting Prof., Harvard Law School 1969–70, Univ. of Calif. at LA 1969; Barrister at Law (Middle Temple) 1953–, QC 1990; Gen. Ed. Modern Law Review 1970–88; mem. Civil Service Arbitration Tribunal 1973–; Chair. Trades Union Congress Ind. Review Cttee 1975–; Hon. Pres. Industrial Law Soc. 1996–; Fellow, British Acad. 1981; Hon. Fellow Clare Coll. Cambridge 1996, LSE 1997; Hon. D.Giur. (Pavia); Hon. D.Econ. (Siena); Hon. LLD (Stockholm); George Long Prize for Jurisprudence (Cambridge) 1948, Chancellor's Medal for English Law (Cambridge) 1949. *Publications:* Employment Grievances and Disputes Procedures in Britain (with P. L. Davies) 1969, Cases and Materials on Labour Law 1967, The Worker and the Law 1971, 1986, Industrial Conflict—A Comparative Legal Survey (co-ed. with B. Aaron) 1972, Democrazia Politica e Democrazia Industriale 1978, Discrimination in Employment (co-ed.) 1978, Labour Law and the Community (with W. T. Murphy) 1983, Labour Law and Industrial Relations (with R. Lewis and J. Clark) 1983, Diritto del Lavoro in Europa (with B. Veneziani and S. Ghimpu) 1987, The Social Charter, European Company and Employment Rights 1990, Employment Rights in Britain and Europe 1991, Labour Law and Freedom 1995, I Diritti del Lavoro 1998; numerous articles on legal subjects. *Leisure interest:* Charlton Athletic Football Club. *Address:* London School of Economics, Houghton Street, London, WC2A 2AE (Office); 29 Woodside Avenue, Highgate, London, N6 4SP, England (Home). *Telephone:* (20) 8444-8472 (Home). *Fax:* (20) 8444-8472 (Home).

WEDGEWORTH, Robert, AB, MS, LHD; American university librarian and academic; m. Chung-Kyun Wedgeworth; one d.; ed Wabash Coll., Univ. of Illinois; Exec. Dir American Library Asscn (ALA) 1972–85; Dean School of Library Service, Columbia Univ. 1985–92; Librarian, Prof. of Library Admin. Univ. of Ill. at Urbana-Champaign 1993–99; Pres. Int. Fed. of Library Asscns. and Insts. (IFLA) 1991–97, Hon. Pres. 1997–; Chair. Advisory Cttee ALA Office of Information Tech. Policy 1995–97; mem. Cttee to Visit Harvard Coll. Library 1994–97; Trustee Newberry Library, Chicago; ALA Joseph Lippincott Award 1989, Medal of Honor, Int. Co-operation Admin. 1996, Melvil Dewey Award 1997. *Publications:* World Encyclopaedia of Library and Information Services (Ed.) 1993, Issues Affecting the Development of Digital Libraries in Science and Technology (UNESCO) 1996, Courtship, Marriage and Librarianship: a Vision of a 21st Century Profession (IFLA) 1996, Beyond Unification 1997, Reaffirming Professional Values 1997. *Address:* University of Illinois at Urbana-Champaign Library, Urbana, IL 61801, USA (Office). *Telephone:* (217) 333-1000 (Office). *E-mail:* rwedge@uiuc.edu (Office). *Website:* www.uiuc.edu (Office).

WEE CHONG JIN, MA; Singaporean judge; b. 28 Sept. 1917, Penang, Malaya; s. of the late Wee Gim Puay and Lim Paik Yew; m. Cecilia Mary Henderson 1955; three s. one d.; ed Penang Free School, St John's Coll. Cambridge; called to Bar, Middle Temple, London 1938, admitted Advocate and Solicitor of Straits Settlements 1940; practised in Penang and Singapore 1940–57; Puisne Judge, Singapore 1957; Chief Justice 1963–90; Acting Pres. of Singapore March–Aug. 1985; Head Presidential Council for Religious Harmony 1992–; Hon. DCL (Oxford) 1987. *Leisure interest:* golf.

WEE KIM WEE; Singaporean journalist and diplomatist; b. 4 Nov. 1915; s. of Wee Choong Lay and Chua Hay Luan; m. Koh Sok Hiong 1936; one s. six d.; ed Raffles Inst.; clerk Circulation Dept Straits Times, then Advertising Dept then reporter, rejoined as Deputy Ed. (Singapore) 1959, covered civil war in Belgian Congo (now Democratic Repub. of Congo) and was first Singapore journalist to enter Jakarta during Confrontation 1966; joined United Press Asscn 1941, rejoined 1945–59; served in Air Raid Precautions during attack on Malaya and Singapore; worked as clerk in Japanese mil. establishments during occupation; High Commr to Malaysia 1973–80; Dean Diplomatic Corps, Kuala Lumpur 1978–80; mem. Singapore Del. to UN Gen. Ass. 1977; Amb. to Japan 1980–84, to Repub. of Korea 1981–84; Chair. Singapore Broadcasting Corpn 1984–85; Pres. Repub. of Singapore 1985–93; fmr Pres. Singapore Badminton Asscn, Chair. Singapore Anti-Tuberculosis Asscn; fmr mem. Rent Control Bd, Film Appeal Cttee, Land Acquisition Bd, Bd of Visiting Justices, Nat. Theatre Trust; JP 1966; Hon. DLitt (Nat. Univ. of Singapore) 1994; Public Service Star 1963, Meritorious Service Medal 1979; Hon. GCB 1989, Laila Utama (Brunei) 1990; Order of Temasek (First Class) 1993; Jr Singles Badminton Champion of Singapore 1937. *Leisure interests:* golf, walking and writing. *Address:* 25 Siglap Plain, Singapore 456014, Singapore.

WEEDON, Basil Charles Leicester, CBE, FRS, DSc, FRSC; British chemist and university administrator; b. 18 July 1923, London; s. of the late Charles William Weedon and Florence May Weedon; m. Barbara Mary Dawe 1959; one s. one d.; ed Wandsworth School, Imperial Coll. of Science and Tech., Univ. of London; Research Chemist, ICI Ltd (Dyestuffs Div.) 1945–47; Lecturer in Organic Chem., Imperial Coll. 1947–55, Reader 1955–60; Prof. of Organic Chem., Queen Mary Coll., Univ. of London 1960–75; Vice-Chancellor, Univ. of Nottingham 1976–88; Chair. Food Additives and Contaminants Cttee 1968–83, Nat. Stone Centre 1985–91, East Midlands Electricity Consumers' Cttee 1990–95; Hon. Prof. (Nottingham) 1988–; Scientific Ed., Pure and Applied Chemistry 1960–75; mem. EEC Scientific Cttee for Food 1974–81; Fellow Queen Mary Coll. 1984; Tilden Lecturer of Chem. Soc.; Hon. DTech (Brunel) 1975; Hon. LLD (Nottingham) 1988; Meldola Medal, Royal Inst. of Chem. *Publications:* numerous papers in scientific journals, mainly in Journal of the Chemical Society. *Leisure interests:* music, gardening. *Address:* Sheepwash Grange, Heighington Road, Canwick, Lincoln, LN4 2RJ, England. *Telephone:* (1522) 522488.

WEEKES, Sir Everton de Courcy, KCMG, GCM, OBE; Barbadian cricketer; b. 26 Feb. 1925, St Michael; ed St Leonard's School, Bridgetown; right-hand batsman; teams: Barbados, West Indies; in 48 Tests scored 4,445 runs (average 58.6) including 15 hundreds; scored 12,010 first-class runs (average 55.3) including 36 hundreds 1944–64; Umpire ICC (4 Tests, 3 One Day Ints); Wisden Cricketer of the Year 1951. *Leisure interest:* int. bridge player. *Address:* c/o West Indies Cricket Board of Control, Letchworth Complex, The Garrison, St Michael, Barbados, West Indies.

WEERAMANTRY, Christopher Gregory, BA, LLD; Sri Lankan judge; b. 17 Nov. 1926, Colombo; ed Univ. of London; advocate Supreme Court of Sri Lanka 1948–65, Commr of Assize 1965–67, Justice of Supreme Court 1967–72; Sir Hayden Starke Prof. of Law, Monash Univ., Melbourne, Australia 1972–91, Prof. Emer. of Law 1991–; Judge Int. Court of Justice 1991–2000 (ad-hoc 1999–2000), Vice-Pres. 1997–99; lecturer and Examiner, Council of Legal Educ. 1951–56; mem. Council of Legal Educ. 1967–72; Visiting Prof. Univs. of Tokyo 1978, Stellenbosch 1979, Papua New Guinea 1981, Fla 1984, Lafayette Coll., Pa 1985, Hong Kong 1989; Hon. Visiting Prof. Univ. of Colombo 1984; Chair Comm. of Inquiry into Int. Responsibility for Phosphate Mining on Nauru 1987–88; mem. Editorial Bd Sri Lankan Journal of Int. Law, Human Rights Quarterly (Johns Hopkins Univ.), Interdisciplinary Peace Research (La Trobe Univ.), Journal of Ceylon Law; mem. Advisory Bd China Law Reports; Vice Chair. UN Centre against Apartheid/Govt. of Nigeria Conf. on Legal Status of Apartheid Regime, Lagos 1984; Co-ordinator UN Univ./Netherlands Inst. of Human Rights Workshop on Science, Tech. and Human Rights, Utrecht 1989; Assoc. Academician, Int. Acad. of Comparative Law, Paris; Vice-Pres. Int. Comm. of Jurists, Vic.; Past Pres. World Fed. of Overseas Sri Lankan Orgs.; Vice-Patron UN Asscn of Sri Lanka; Chair. Cttee of Chief Justices of Asia and Africa; mem. Europa Mundi (UNESCO project), Club of Rome (Australia), Commonwealth Lawyers' Asscn and other professional bodies; Hon. Life mem. Bar Asscn of Sri Lanka; Hon. LLD (Colombo), Dr. hc (Monash Univ.) 2000; Mohamed Sahabdeen Award for Int. Understanding in the SAARC Region 1993; Order of Deshamanya. *Publications:* numerous books on law, human rights and other topics; numerous articles in law journals worldwide and published lectures. *Address:* 5/1 Roland Towers, Dharmaraja Mawatha, off Alfred House Avenue, Colombo 3, Sri Lanka. *Telephone:* (1) 555028. *Fax:* (74) 720480. *E-mail:* cgw@lanka.ccom .lk.

WĘGLEŃSKI, Piotr; Polish molecular geneticist; b. 29 June 1939, Swidniki; m. Teresa Juszczyk; two d.; ed Warsaw Univ.; Academic Warsaw Univ. 1961–, Pro-Rector 1985–88, 1990–96, Ordinary Prof. 1989–, Rector 1999–2002, 2002–; Visiting Prof. MIT 1987–88, Univ. Paris-Sud 1991; mem. Polish Genetic Soc., Warsaw Scientific Soc., corresp. mem. Polish Acad. of Sciences 1994; Officier des Palmes académiques 2002; Dr hc (Prikarpatsky State Univ.) 2002. *Publications:* Genetic Engineering (jtly.) 1980, Molecular Genetics (jtly. and Ed.) 1996; and numerous scientific articles. *Leisure interests:* tennis, travel, volleyball. *Address:* Uniwersytet Warszawski, ul. Krakowskie Przedmieście 26/28, 00-927, Warsaw, Poland (Office). *Telephone:* (22) 5520355 (Office). *Fax:* (22) 5524000 (Office). *E-mail:* rektor@mercury.ci .uw.edu.pl (Office). *Website:* www.uw.edu.pl (Office).

WEI CHUNSU; Chinese administrator; b. 1929; joined CCP 1941; del. 12th Nat. Conf. CCP 1982–85, 13th 1986–91, 14th 1992–97; del. 6th NPC 1983–87, 7th NPC 1988–92, 8th NPC 1993; Admin. Head, Self-Govt of Guangxi Zhuang Autonomous Region 1992–. *Address:* Office of the Governor, Guangxi Dangwei, 1 Minlelu Road, Nanning City, People's Republic of China.

WEI JIANXING; Chinese state official; b. Jan. 1931, Xinchang Co., Zhejiang Prov.; ed Dalian Eng Inst. and in USSR; joined CCP 1949; section chief, Northeast China Light Alloy Processing Factory 1961–64, Dir 1977–81; Deputy Sec. Harbin Municipality CCP Cttee 1981–83; Mayor of Harbin City 1981–83; Sec. and mem. Exec. Cttee All-China Fed. of Trade Unions 1983, Vice-Pres. 1983–84, Pres. 1993–; Deputy Dir CCP Cen. Cttee Org. Dept 1984–85, Dir 1985–87; Minister of Supervision 1987–93; Sec. Beijing Municipal CCP Cttee 1995–97; mem. CCP Cen. Cttee Politburo, Cttee and Secr. for Inspecting Discipline 1992–2002; Head Cen. Leading Group for Party Bldg Work; Sec. Secr. CCP Cen. Cttee; mem. 15th Cen. Cttee CCP 1997–2002; mem. CCP Politburo Standing Cttee 1997–2002. *Address:* All-China Federation of Trade Unions, 10 Fu Xing Men Wai Jie, Beijing 100865, People's Republic of China. *Telephone:* (10) 8012200. *Fax:* (10) 8012922.

WEI JINGSHENG; Chinese dissident; fmr mem. Red Guards and PLA; active in pro-democracy movt, contrib. to underground magazine Exploration 1978; sentenced to 15 years' imprisonment for allegedly leaking mil. secrets to a foreign journalist and for counter-revolutionary activities Spring 1979, released Sept. 1993; held incommunicado and without charge April 1994; sentenced to 14 years' imprisonment for alleged subversive activities 1995; deported March 1998; Sakharov Prize 1996. *Publication:* The Courage to Stand Alone.

WEI WEI; Chinese singer; m. Michael Smith; one s.; singer at 11th Asian Games, Beijing 1990, performed a duet with Julio Iglesias at East Asian Games, Shanghai 1993; tour of China 1995. *Albums include:* Twilight.

WEI YUNG, PhD; Taiwanese university professor, politician and consultant; b. 5 May 1937, Wuhan City, China; s. of Shao-cheng Wei and Pei-chih Shing; m. Serena Ning Sun Wei 1964; two d.; ed Nat. Chengchi Univ., Taipei, Univ. of Oregon, USA; Instructor to Asst Prof., Dept of Political Science, Univ. of

Nevada 1966–68; Asst Prof., Dept of Political Science, Memphis State Univ. 1968–69, Assoc. Prof. of Political Science 1969–74, Prof. and Chair. of Grad. Program in Political Science 1974; Visiting Scholar, Survey Research Centre, Univ. of Mich. 1969; Visiting Assoc. Prof., Nat. Chengchi Univ. 1970–71; Nat. Fellow, Hoover Inst., Stanford Univ. 1974–75, Distinguished Visiting Fellow 1999–2000; Deputy Dir Inst. of Int. Relations 1975–76; Eisenhower Exchange Fellow 1977; Chair. Research, Devt and Evaluation Comm., Exec. Yuan (Cabinet), Taiwan 1976–88; Chancellor, Sun Yat-sen Inst. on Policy Research and Devt 1988–90; Prof. of Political Science, Nat. Chiao-tung Univ. 1990–2002, Shih Hsin Univ. 2002–; mem. Legis. Yuan (Parl.) and Chair. Foreign Relations Cttee 1992–96; Adjunct Prof., Depts of Political Science, Nat. Taiwan Univ. and Nat. Chengchi Univ.; Pres. Chinese Asscn of Political Science 1988–92; Chair. Bd Vanguard Foundation, Dir Vanguard Inst. for Policy Studies 1991–; Pres. Sino-American Cultural and Econ. Asscn 1997–; mem. Cen. Cttee, Kuomintang 1979–; Medal for Outstanding Service, Exec. Yuan 1987, First Class Medal for Policy Planning and Evaluation, Exec. Yuan 2000. *Art exhibitions include:* exhibitions of calligraphy and paintings, 1991 and 1995. *Publications:* The Nature and Methods of the Social Sciences, Taiwan: A Modernizing Chinese Society, Political Development in the Republic of China on Taiwan: Analysis and Projections, A Methodological Critique of Current Studies on Chinese Political Culture, Policy Planning of the Republic of China in the 1980s, Science, Elite and Modernization, From Multi-System Nations to Linkage Communities, Therapeutic Politics, Advocacy Politics and the Eclipse of Democracy, Recognition of Divided States. *Leisure interests:* Chinese calligraphy, painting, boating, golf. *Address:* Vanguard Foundation, 2nd Floor, 15 Chi-Nan Road, Sec. 1, Taipei (Office); 5 Floor, No 1-1, Lane 21, Li-shui Street, Taipei 106, Taiwan (Home). *Telephone:* (2) 23952045 (Office). *Fax:* (2) 23952052 (Office).

WEICKER, Lowell Palmer, Jr., LLB; American senator; b. 16 May 1931, Paris, France; s. of Lowell Palmer Weicker and Mary (née Bickford) Paulsen; m. 1st Camille Di Lorenzo Butler; eight c.; m. 2nd Claudia Testa Ingram 1984; ed Lawrenceville School, Yale Univ. and Univ. of Virginia; State Rep. in Conn. Gen. Ass. 1963–69; U.S. Rep., Fourth Congressional District, Conn. 1969–71; Senator from Conn. 1971–89; Gov. of Connecticut 1991–95; 1st Selectman of Greenwich 1964–68; mem. Select Cttee for Investigation of the Watergate Case 1973; fmr mem. Senate Appropriations Cttee, Senate Labor and Human Resources Cttee, fmr Chair. Senate Small Business Cttee, Sub-Cttee on State, Justice, Commerce, the Judiciary and related agencies, Senate Energy and Natural Resources Cttee; fmr Republican, then Independent. *Publication:* Maverick: My Life in Politics 1995. *Leisure interests:* tennis, scuba, history. *Address:* c/o Office of the Governor, 210 Capitol Avenue, Room 202, Hartford, CT 06106, USA.

WEIDENBAUM, Murray Lew, BBA, MA, PhD, LLD; American government official and economist; b. 10 Feb. 1927, Bronx, New York; s. of David Weidenbaum and Rose (née Warshaw) Weidenbaum; m. Phyllis Green 1954; one s. two d.; ed City Coll. New York, Columbia Univ., New York and Princeton Univ.; Fiscal Economist, Budget Bureau, Washington 1949–57; Corpn Economist, Boeing Co., Seattle 1958–62; Sr Economist, Stanford Research Inst., Palo Alto, Calif. 1962–63; mem. Faculty, Washington Univ., St Louis, Mo. 1964–, Dir of Center for Study of American Business at Washington Univ. 1975–81, 1982–95, Chair. 1995–2000, Prof. and Chair. Dept of Econs 1966–69, Mallinckrodt Distinguished Univ. Prof. 1971–; Asst Sec. for Econ. Policy, Treasury Dept, Washington 1969–71; Head, Council of Econ. Advisers, US Govt 1981–82; Chair. Research Advisory Cttee, St Louis Regional Industrial Devt Corpn 1965–69; Pres. Midwest Econ. Asscn 1985; Chair. US Trade Deficit Review Comm 1999–2000; Exec. Sec. Pres.'s Cttee on Econ. Impact of Defense and Disarmament 1964; mem. US Financial Investment Advisory Panel 1970–72; mem. Pres.'s Econ. Policy Advisory Bd 1982–89, Bd of Dirs Harbour Group Ltd 1982–, May Dept Stores Co. 1982–99, Tesoro Petroleum Corpn 1992–2002, Macroeconomic Advisers 1996–; consultant to various firms and insts; Fellow, Nat. Asscn of Business Economists; mem. Acad. of Missouri Squires; Hon. Chair. Weidenbaum Center on the Econ., Govt and Public Policy 2001; Hon. Fellow Soc. for Tech. Communication; Townsend Harris Medal for Distinguished Achievement, City Coll. of NY 1970, Treasury Dept Alexander Hamilton Medal 1971, Distinguished Writer Award, Georgetown Univ. 1975, Free Market Hall of Fame 1983, Officier, Ordre nat. du Mérite 1985, Founder's Day Medal, Washington Univ. 1998. *Publications:* Federal Budgeting 1964, Economic Impact of the Vietnam War 1967, Modern Public Sector 1969, Economics of Peacetime Defense 1974, Government-Mandated Price Increases 1975, The Future of Business Regulation 1979, Business, Government and the Public 1990, Rendezvous with Reality: The American Economy After Reagan 1990, Small Wars, Big Defense 1992, Bamboo Network 1996, Business and Government in the Global Marketplace 1999; articles in econ. journals. *Leisure interest:* writing. *Address:* Weidenbaum Center on the Economy, Government and Public Policy, Washington University, Box 1027, One Brookings Drive, St Louis, MO 63130 (Office); 303 N Meramec No. 103, St Louis, MO 63105, USA (Home). *Telephone:* (314) 727-8950 (Home); (314) 935-5662 (Office). *Fax:* (314) 935-5688 (Office).

WEIDENFELD, Baron (Life Peer), cr. 1976, of Chelsea in Greater London; **Arthur George Weidenfeld,** Kt; British publisher; b. 13 Sept. 1919, Vienna, Austria; s. of the late Max Weidenfeld and Rosa Weidenfeld; m. 1st Jane Sieff 1952; one d.; m. 2nd Barbara Skelton Connolly 1956 (divorced 1961); m. 3rd Sandra Payson Meyer 1966 (divorced 1976); m. 4th Annabelle Whitestone 1992; ed Piaristen Gymnasium, Vienna, Univ. of Vienna and Konsular Akademie; came to England 1938; BBC Monitoring Service 1939–42; BBC News Commentator on European Affairs on BBC Empire and N American service 1942–46; Foreign Affairs columnist, News Chronicle 1943–44; Political Adviser and Chief of Cabinet of Pres. Weizmann of Israel 1949–50; Founder of Contact Magazine 1945, George Weidenfeld & Nicolson Ltd 1948–; Chair. George Weidenfeld & Nicolson Ltd 1948–, Wheatland Corpn, NY 1985–90, Grove Press, NY 1985–90, Wheatland Foundation, San Francisco and New York 1985–92; Dir (non-exec.) Orion 1991–; Consultant Bertelsmann Foundation 1991–, Axel Springer AG Germany; Chair. Bd of Govs., Ben Gurion Univ. of the Negev 1996–; Gov. of Tel Aviv Univ. 1980–, Weizmann Inst. of Science 1964–; Columnist Die Welt, Die Welt am Sonntag; mem., South Bank Bd 1986–99; mem. Bd English Nat. Opera 1988–98, Herbert-Quandt-Foundation 1999–; Trustee Royal Opera House 1974–87, Nat. Portrait Gallery 1988–95, Potsdam Einstein Forum, Jerusalem Foundation; Chair. Cheyne Capital 2000–, Trialogue Educational Trust 1996–; mem. Governing Council, Inst. of Human Science, Vienna; Vice-Chair. Oxford Univ. Devt Programme 1994–99; Freeman City of London; Hon. Senator Bonn Univ. 1996; Hon. Fellow St Peter's Coll. Oxford 1992, St Anne's Coll. Oxford 1993; Hon. MA (Oxon.) 1992; Hon. PhD (Ben Gurion Univ.); Hon. DLitt (Exeter) 2001; Golden Kt.'s Cross of Order of Merit (Austria) 1989, Chevalier, Légion d'honneur 1990, Kt Commdr.'s Cross (Badge and Star) of Order of Merit (Germany) 1991, Austrian Cross of Honour First Class for Arts and Science, Vienna 2003, Honour of City of Vienna 2003; Charlemagne Medal 2000. *Publications:* The Goebbels Experiment 1943, Remembering My Good Friends 1994. *Leisure interests:* opera, travel. *Address:* 9 Chelsea Embankment, London, SW3 4LE, England. *Telephone:* (20) 7351-0042.

WEIDENFELD, Werner, DPhil; German professor of political science; b. 2 July 1947, Cochem; s. of Dr. Josef Weidenfeld and Maria Weidenfeld (née Walther); m. Gabriele Kokott-Weidenfeld 1976; ed Univ. of Bonn; Prof. of Political Science, Univ. of Mainz 1976–95; Assoc. Prof., Sorbonne, Paris 1986–88; Co-ordinator for German-American Co-operation 1987–99; Prof. of Political Science, Univ. of Munich 1995–, Dir Centre for Applied Policy Research; Dr hc; Bundesverdienstkreuz (First Class) 1998. *Publications:* Die Englandpolitik Gustav Stresemanns 1972, Konrad Adenauer und Europa 1976, Europa 2000 1980, Die Frage nach der Einheit der deutschen Nation 1981, Die Identität der Deutschen 1983, Die Bilanz der Europäischen Integration 1984, Nachdenken über Deutschland 1985, 30 Jahre EG 1987, Geschichtsbewusstsein der Deutschen 1987, Der deutsche Weg 1990, Jahrbuch der Europäischen Integration (ed.), Die Deutschen—Profil einer Nation 1991, Handwörterbuch zur deutschen Einheit 1992, Osteuropa: Herausforderungen-Probleme-Strategien 1992, Technopoly, Europa im globalen Wettbewerb 1993, Maastricht in der Analyse, Materialien zur Europäischen Union (ed.) 1994, Europa '96: Reformprogramm für die Europäische Union (ed.) 1994, Reform der Europäischen Union 1995, Kulturbruch mit Amerika? 1996, Handbuch zur deutschen Einheit 1996, Demokratie am Wendepunkt? (ed.) 1996, Europa öffnen—Anforderungen an die Erweiterung (ed.) 1997, Aussenpolitik für die deutsche Einheit: Die Entscheidigungsjahre 1989/90 1998, Amsterdam in der Analyse: Strategien für Europa (ed.) 1998, Handbuch zur deutschen Einheit 1949–1989–1999 (ed.) 1999, Deutschland-Trendbuch (ed.) 2001, Europa—Handbuch 2002. *Address:* Oettingenstr. 67, 80538 Munich, Germany. *Telephone:* (89) 21809040. *Fax:* (89) 21809042.

WEIDINGER, Christine, BA; American soprano; b. 31 March 1946, Springville, NY; m. Kenneth Smith 1976; ed Grand Canyon Coll., Phoenix; fmrly with Stuttgart Opera; joined Bielefeld Opera 1979; appearances at Bielefeld include Malvina in Heinrich Marschner's Der Vampyr, title role in Thea Musgrave's Mary, Queen of Scots, Donizetti's Lucia di Lammermoor, Anina in Bellini's La Sonnambula, Berthe in Meyerbeer's Le Prophète, Elizabeth I in Donizetti's Roberto Devereux and title role in Bellini's Norma 1989; appearances abroad include: Inez in L'Africaine (Barcelona), Lucia and Juliet in I Capuleti e i Montecchi, Pamira in Rossini's Siege of Corinth (Marseilles), title role in Bellini's Beatrice di Tenda (Catania), Eupaforice in Heinrich Graun's Spanish Conquest (Spoleto/Charleston Festival of Two Worlds) and in Tancredi (Los Angeles Music Center Opera) 1989, Lucia di Lammermoor (Cincinnati) 1990, Violetta (San Diego) 1991. *Leisure interests:* yoga, jogging, electric trains. *Address:* c/o Robert Lombardo, 1 Harkness Plaza, 61 West 62nd Street, Suite 6F, New York, 10023, USA.

WEIDLINGER, Paul, MS; American engineer; b. 22 Dec. 1914, Budapest, Hungary; s. of Andrew Weidlinger and Juliette Weidlinger; m. Solveig Højberg 1964; two s. one d.; ed Tech. Inst., Brno, Czechoslovakia, Swiss Polytechnic Inst., Zürich; Chief Engineer, Bureau of Reclamation, La Paz, Bolivia 1939–42; Prof. of Eng, San Andrés Univ. La Paz 1939–42; went to USA 1944, naturalized 1949; Chief Engineer, Atlas Aircraft, New York 1944–46; Dir of Div., Nat. Housing Agency, Washington, DC 1946–47; engineer, pvt. practice 1947–; Sr partner Weidlinger Assocs., New York 1948–; Visiting Lecturer, Harvard Univ., MIT; mem. Scientific Advisory Bd, USAF; Consultant to Rand Corpn; Fellow of Hudson Inst., American Soc. of Civil Engineers (ASCE), American Concrete Inst., Int. Asscn of Bridge and Structural Engineers, New York Acad. of Sciences, AIAA, Nat. Acad. of Eng; J. R. Croes Medal 1963, Moisseiff Award 1975, Ernest E. Howard Award (all ASCE) 1985. *Publications:* articles in journals. *Address:* Weidlinger Associates, 375 Hudson Street, New York, NY 10014, USA.

WEIKL, Bernd; Austrian baritone; b. 29 July 1942, Vienna; ed Mainz Conservatoire and Hochschule für Musik, Hanover; mem. Hamburg State

Opera 1973–, Deutsche Oper Berlin 1974–; guest artist, Bayreuth Festivals 1973–75; Covent Garden debut in 1975 as Rossini's Figaro; Metropolitan Opera debut in 1977 as Wolfram; guest engagements at La Scala Milan, Bavarian State Opera, Salzburg Festival; performed Iago at Stuttgart 1990, Bovccanegra at Hamburg 1991, Dutchman at Bayreuth 1990, Sachs at the Metropolitan 1993, Jochanaan at San Francisco 1997, Kurwenal in Tristan und Isolde at Munich 1998. *Address:* c/o Askonas Holt Ltd., Lonsdale Chambers, 27 Chancery Lane, London, WC2A 1PF, England (Office).

WEILL, Sanford I., BA; American banker; b. 16 March 1933, New York; s. of Max Weill and Etta (née Kalika) Weill; m. Joan Mosher 1955; one s., one d.; ed Peekskill Mil. Acad., Cornell Univ., School Business and Public Admin.; CEO Carter, Berlind and Weill (now Shearson/American Express Inc.) New York 1960–, Pres. and CEO 1978–85; Chair., Pres., CEO Commercial Credit Co., Baltimore 1986–; Chair., CEO Primerica Corpn 1989–, Pres. 1989–92; Chair., CEO Travelers Group 1996–98; Co-Chair. Citigroup (merger between Citicorp and Travelers Group) 1999–, now Chair. and CEO; f. Acad. of Finance; Dir Terra Nova Insurance Co. 1984–; Chair. Carnegie Hall 1991–; mem. Midwest Stock Exchange Bd; Assoc. mem. New York Stock Exchange, Bd of Overseers Cornell Medical Coll., Business Cttee Museum of Modern Art, NY. *Address:* Citigroup, 153 East 53rd Street, New York, NY 10043 (Office); Travelers Group, 399 Park Avenue, New York, NY 10013, USA.

WEINBACH, Lawrence, BS; American business executive; b. 1 Jan. 1940, Brooklyn, New York; s. of Max Weinbach and Winnefred Weinbach; m. Patricia Lieter 1961; two s. one d.; ed Univ. of Pennsylvania, Wharton; joined Arthur Andersen 1961, Man. Partner and Chief Exec. 1989–97; as Chair., Pres. and CEO Unisys Corpn 1997–. *Leisure interests:* reading, golf. *Address:* Unisys Corporation, Unisys Way, Blue Bell, PA 19424, USA. *Telephone:* (215) 986-4011. *Fax:* (215) 986-2886.

WEINBERG, Alvin M., SM, PhD; American physicist and scientific administrator; b. 20 April 1915, Chicago, Ill.; s. of Jacob Weinberg and Emma Levinson Weinberg; m. 1st Margaret Despres 1940 (died 1969); two s.; m. 2nd Gene K. de Persio 1974; ed Univ. of Chicago; Biophysics research Univ. of Chicago 1939–42; Hanford reactor design Univ. of Chicago Metallurgical Laboratory 1942–45; Section Chief Physics Div., Oak Ridge Nat. Laboratory 1945–47, Dir Physics Div. 1947–48, Research Dir 1948–55; Dir Oak Ridge Nat. Lab. 1955–73; Dir Office of Energy Research and Devt, Fed. Energy Office 1974, Inst. for Energy Analysis 1975–85 (Distinguished Fellow 1985–); mem. Scientific Advisory Bd to the Air Force 1955–59; mem. President's Science Advisory Cttee 1960–63; Chair. Advisory Cttee on Carbon Dioxide, Dept of Energy 1978–80; Fellow, American Nuclear Soc., American Physical Soc.; mem. American Acad. of Arts and Sciences, Nat. Acad. of Eng, NAS, Cttee on Science and Public Policy of Nat. Acad. of Sciences 1963–66, Council of NAS 1967–70, American Philosophical Soc.; Foreign mem. Royal Netherlands Acad. of Sciences; mem. Pres. Nixon's Task Force on Science Policy 1969, Nat. Cancer Plan Evaluation Cttee 1972; Regents' Lecturer Univ. of Calif. at San Diego 1980; contributions to nuclear tech. in reactor theory, reactor design, breeder reactor systems, implications of nuclear energy; formulation of science policy; energy supply and demand; co-recipient Atoms for Peace Award 1960, Ernest O. Lawrence Memorial Award of Atomic Energy Comm. 1960, Univ. of Chicago Alumni Medal 1966, Heinrich Hertz Energy Prize 1975, New York Acad. of Sciences Award 1976, Enrico Fermi Award 1980, Harvey Prize 1982, Alvin M. Weinberg Medal of American Nuclear Soc. 1997, Eugene P. Wigner Medal, American Nuclear Soc. *Publications:* The Physical Theory of Neutron Chain Reactors (with Eugene P. Wigner) 1958, Reflections on Big Science 1967, Continuing the Nuclear Dialogue 1985, The Nuclear Connection (Co-Ed.) 1985, Strategic Defenses and Arms Control (Co-Ed.) 1987, Stability and Strategic Defenses (Co-Ed.) 1991, Nuclear Reactions: Science and Trans-Science 1992, The First Nuclear Era: The Life and Times of a Technological Fixer 1994. *Leisure interests:* piano, tennis, swimming. *Address:* Oak Ridge Associated Universities, P.O. Box 117, Oak Ridge, TN 37831 (Office); 111 Moylan Lane, Oak Ridge, TN 37830, USA (Home). *Telephone:* (865) 576-3249 (Office); (865) 483-6045 (Home). *Fax:* (865) 576-3816 (Office).

WEINBERG, Felix Jiri, DSc, PhD, FRS, MRI, CEng, FInstP, FCGI; British physicist; b. 2 April 1928, Ústí, Czechzlovakia (now in Czech Repub.); s. of Victor Weinberg and Nelly Marie Weinberg (née Altschul); m. Jill Nesta Piggott 1954; three s.; ed Univ. of London; Lecturer, Dept of Chemical Eng and Chemical Tech., Imperial Coll. London 1956–60, Sr Lecturer 1960–64, Reader in Combustion 1964–67, Prof. of Combustion Physics 1967–93, Emer. Prof. and Sr Research Fellow 1993–, Leverhulme Emer. Research Fellow 1993–95; Dir Combustion Inst. 1978–88, Chair. British Section 1975–80; Founder and First Chair. Combustion Physics Group, Inst. of Physics 1974–77, Rep. on Watt Cttee on Energy 1979–84; mem. Council, Inst. of Energy 1976–79; Foreign Assoc. U.S. Nat. Acad. of Eng 2001; Hon. DSc (Technion) 1989; Combustion Inst. Silver Combustion Medal 1972, Bernard Lewis Gold Medal 1980, Royal Soc. Rumford Medal 1988, Italgas Prize in Energy Sciences (Turin Acad.) 1991, Smolenski Medal (Polish Acad. of Science) 1999. *Publications:* Optics of Flames 1963, Electrical Aspects of Combustion 1969, Combustion Inst. European Symposium (ed.) 1973, Advanced Combustion Methods 1986; over 200 scientific papers. *Leisure interests:* Eastern philosophies, travel, archery. *Address:* Imperial College, London, SW7 2BY (Office); 59 Vicarage Road, London, SW14 8RY, England (Home). *Telephone:* (20) 7594-5580 (Office); (20) 8876-1540 (Home). *Fax:* (20) 7594-5604. *E-mail:* f.weinberg@imperial.ac.uk (Office).

WEINBERG, Robert A., PhD; American biochemist; b. 11 Nov. 1942, Pittsburgh, Pa; s. of Dr. Fritz E. Weinberg and Lore W. (née Reichhardt) Weinberg; m. Amy Shulman 1976; one s. one d.; ed M.I.T; Instructor in Biology, Stillman Coll., Ala 1965–66; Fellow Weizmann Inst., Israel 1969–70; Fellow Salk Inst., Calif. 1970–72; Research Assoc. Fellow MIT 1972–73, Asst Prof., Dept of Biology and Center for Cancer Research 1973–76, Assoc. Prof. 1976–82, Prof. Whitehead Inst. for Biomedical Research 1982–, mem. 1984–; mem. NAS; numerous awards including Hon. ScD (Northwestern Univ., Ill.) 1984. *Leisure interests:* house building, gardening, genealogy. *Address:* Whitehead Institute, 9 Cambridge Center, Cambridge, MA 02142; Department of Biology, Massachusetts Institute of Technology, Cambridge, MA 02139, USA.

WEINBERG, Steven, PhD; American physicist; b. 3 May 1933, New York; s. of Fred Weinberg and Eva Weinberg; m. Louise Goldwasser 1954; one d.; ed Cornell Univ., Univ. of Copenhagen and Princeton Univ.; Columbia Univ. 1957–59; Lawrence Radiation Lab. 1959–60; Univ. of Calif. at Berkeley 1960–69; Prof. of Physics, MIT 1969–73; Higgins Prof. of Physics, Harvard Univ. 1973–83; Sr Scientist, Smithsonian Astrophysical Observatory 1973–83, Sr Consultant 1983–; Josey Regental Prof. of Science, Univ. of Texas, Austin 1982–; Co-Ed. Cambridge Univ. Press Monographs on Mathematical Physics 1978; Dir Jerusalem Winter School of Theoretical Physics 1983–, Headliners Foundation 1993–; mem. A.P. Sloan Foundation Science Book Cttee 1985–90, Einstein Archives Int. Advisory Bd 1988–, Scientific Policy Cttee, Supercollider Lab. 1989–93, American Acad. of Arts and Sciences 1968–, NAS 1972–, Council for Foreign Relations, President's Cttee on the Nat. Medal of Science 1979–80, Royal Soc. 1982–, American Philosophical Soc. 1983–; fmr mem. Council, American Physical Soc., Int. Astronomical Union, Philosophical Soc. of Tex. (Pres. 1994); Loeb Lecturer, Harvard Univ. and Visiting Prof. MIT 1966–69, Richtmeyer Lecturer of American Asscn of Physics Teachers 1974, Scott Lecturer, Cavendish Lab. 1975, Silliman Lecturer, Yale Univ. 1977, Lauritsen Lecturer, Calif. Inst. of Tech. 1979, Bethe Lecturer, Cornell Univ. 1979, Harris Lecturer, Northwestern Univ. 1982, Cherwell-Simon Lecturer, Oxford Univ. 1983, Bampton Lecturer, Columbia Univ. 1983, Hilldale Lecturer, Univ. of Wisconsin 1985, Brickweede Lecturer, Johns Hopkins Univ. 1986, Dirac Lecturer, Univ. of Cambridge 1986, Klein Lecturer, Univ. of Stockholm 1989, Sackler Lecturer, Univ. of Copenhagen 1994, Brittin Lecturer, Univ. of Colorado 1994, Gibbs Lecturer, American Math. Soc. 1996, Bochner Lecturer, Rice Univ. 1997, Sanchez Lecturer, Witherspoon Lecturer, Washington Univ. 2001.; Tex. A & M Int. Univ. 1998; Hon. DSc (Knox Coll.) 1978, (Chicago, Yale, Rochester) 1979, (City Univ., New York) 1980, (Clark Univ.) 1982, (Dartmouth) 1984, (Weizmann Inst.) 1985, (Columbia) 1990, (Salamanca) 1992, (Padua) 1992, (Barcelona) 1996, (Bates Coll.) 2002; Hon. DLitt (Washington Coll.) 1985; J. R. Oppenheimer Prize 1973, Dannie Heinemann Mathematical Physics Prize 1977, American Inst. of Physics-U.S. Steel Foundation Science Writing Award 1977, Elliott Cresson Medal, Franklin Inst. 1979, Joint Winner, Nobel Prize for Physics 1979, James Madison Medal (Princeton) 1991, Nat. Medal of Science 1991, Andrew Gemant Award 1997, Piazzi Prize 1998, Lewis Thomas Prize Honoring the Scientist as Poet 1999. *Publications:* Gravitation and Cosmology 1972, The First Three Minutes 1977, The Discovery of Subatomic Particles 1982, Elementary Particles and the Laws of Physics (with R. P. Feynman) 1987, Dreams of a Final Theory 1993, The Quantum Theory of Fields (Vol. I) 1995, (Vol. II) 1996, (Vol. III) 2000, Facing Up 2001; and over 250 articles. *Leisure interest:* medieval history. *Address:* Department of Physics, University of Texas, Austin, TX 78712, USA. *Telephone:* (512) 471-4394.

WEINBERGER, Caspar Willard, AB, MCL; American government official and publishing executive; b. 18 Aug. 1917, San Francisco; s. of Herman Weinberger and Cerise Carpenter (née Hampson) Weinberger; m. Jane Dalton 1942; one s. one d.; ed Harvard Coll. and Law School; served with AUS 1941–45; with Heller, Ehrman, White and McAuliffe 1947–69, partner 1959–69; mem. Calif. State Legislature 1952–58; Vice-Chair. Calif. Repub. Cen. Cttee 1960–62, Chair. 1962–64; Chair. Calif. Govt Cttee on Org. and Econ. 1967–68; Dir of Finance, Calif. 1968–69; Chair. Fed. Trade Comm. 1970; Deputy Dir Office of Man. and Budget 1970–72, Dir 1972–73; Counsellor to Pres. 1973; Sec. of Health, Educ. and Welfare 1973–75; Sec. of Defense 1981–87; specialist in int. law and finance, Rogers & Wells, Washington 1988–94; Publr Forbes Magazine 1988–92, Chair. 1989–; Distinguished Visiting Prof. Inst. for Advanced Studies in the Humanities, Edin. Univ., UK 1988; Gen. Counsel for the Bechtel Group of Cos. including Bechtel Power Corpn and Bechtel Inc. 1975–80; Chair. Pres.'s Cttee on Mental Retardation 1973–75; mem. Pres.'s Foreign Intelligence Advisory Bd 1987–88; Chair. Bd USA-ROC Econ. Council 1990–94; Earl Mountbatten Memorial Lecture 1991; fmr Dir Pepsico Corpn, Quaker Oats Corpn, American Ditchley Foundation, Yosemite Inst.; fmr Treas. Episcopal Diocese of Calif.; fmr Pres. Nat. Trustees of the Nat. Symphony, Washington, DC; fmr mem. American Ass. Bd of Trustees, Trilateral Comm.; American Bar Asscn, State Bar Calif.; admitted to Dist of Columbia Bar 1990; Dr. hc (Leeds) 1989; Hon. DLitt (Buckingham) 1995; Harvard Univ. John F. Kennedy School of Govt Medal 1982, 1986; Hon. GBE (UK) 1988; Grand Cordon of the Order of the Rising Sun (Japan) 1988; Presidential Medal of Freedom (with Distinction) 1987. *Publications:* Fighting for Peace 1990, The Next War (with Peter Schweizer) 1996, In the Arena 2000. *Address:* Forbes Inc., 1101 17th Street, NW, Suite 406, Washington, DC 20036, USA.

WEINGARTEN, David Michael, BA, MArch; American architect; b. 22 Jan. 1952, Fort Ord, Calif.; s. of Saul M. Weingarten and Miriam E. Moore; one s.; ed Monterey High School, Yale Univ. and Univ. of Calif. at Berkeley; partner, Ace Architects 1979–, now Prin.; Lecturer, Univ. of Calif. at Berkeley 1980–81; Graham Foundation for Advances Studies Award 1987, Interiors Magazine '40 under 40' Award 1990, Architectural Digest 'AD 100' Award 1994, 1996. *Exhibitions:* Oakland Museum 1985, San Francisco Fine Arts Comm. 1987, St Louis Design Center 1988, Avery Library, Columbia Univ. 1991, Smithsonian Inst. 1992, Limn Gallery 1993, San Francisco Museum of Modern Art 1996, Art Inst. of Chicago 1997, Octagon Museum, Washington DC 1997, Smith Coll. Museum of Art, Northampton Mass. 1998–99, Museum of the City of New York 1998–99. *Publications:* Souvenir Buildings/Miniature Monuments 1996, Monumental Miniatures 1997, Ten Houses: Ace Architects 2000. *Address:* Ace Architects, 330 2nd Street, Oakland, CA 94607, USA. *Telephone:* (510) 452-0775. *Fax:* (510) 452-1175. *E-mail:* ace@dnai.com (Office). *Website:* www.aceland.com (Office).

WEINGARTNER, Paul Andreas, DPhil; Austrian professor of philosophy; b. 8 June 1931, Innsbruck; s. of Karl Weingartner and Maria Weingartner; five s. one d.; ed Univ. of Innsbruck; Research Fellow, Univ. of London 1961–62; Research Asst Inst. für Wissenschaftstheorie, Int. Research Centre, Salzburg 1962–67, Chair. Dept I (Philosophy of Natural Science) 1967–72; Assoc. Prof. of Philosophy, Univ. of Salzburg 1970, Prof. of Philosophy 1971–, Chair. Inst. für Philosophie 1971–79, 1988–90, 1994–98, Chair. Inst. für Wissenschaftstheorie 1972–; mem. New York Acad. of Sciences 1997–; Dr. hc (M. Curie Univ., Poland) 1995. *Publications:* Wissenschaftstheorie (2 Vols) 1976, 1978, Logisch-philosophische Untersuchungen zu Werten und Normen 1996, Zu philosophie-historischen Themen 1996, Basic Questions on Truth 2000; Edn of 30 Vols; about 130 research articles. *Leisure interests:* sport (climbing, skiing), photography. *Address:* Institut für Philosophie, Universität Salzburg, Franziskanergasse 1, 5020 Salzburg, Austria. *Telephone:* (662) 8044-4071. *Fax:* (662) 8044-629.

WEINSTEIN, Harvey; American film company executive; b. 1952; s. of Mira Weinstein and Max Weinstein; brother of Robert Weinstein (q.v.); Co-Chair. Miramax Films Corpn, New York with brother Robert 1979–. *Films produced include:* Playing for Keeps 1986, Scandal 1989, Strike it Rich 1990, Hardware 1990, A Rage in Harlem 1991, The Crying Game 1992, The Night We Never Met 1993, Benefit of the Doubt 1993, True Romance 1993, Mother's Boys 1994, Like Water for Chocolate 1994, Pulp Fiction 1994, Pret-A-Porter 1994, Smoke 1995, A Month by the Lake 1995, The Crossing Guard 1995, The Journey of August King 1995, Things To Do In Denver When You're Dead 1995, The Englishman Who Went Up A Hill But Came Down A Mountain 1995, Blue in the Face 1995, Restoration 1995, Scream 1996, The Pallbearer 1996, The Last of the High Kings 1996, Jane Eyre 1996, Flirting with Disaster 1996, The English Patient 1996, Emma 1996, The Crow: City of Angels 1996, Beautiful Girls 1996, Addicted to Love 1997, Shakespeare in Love 1998, Allied Forces, She's All That 1999, My Life So Far 1999, The Yards 1999, Bounce 2000, Scary Movie 2000, Boys and Girls 2000, Love's Labour's Lost 2000, Scream 3 2000, About Adam 2000. *Address:* Miramax Films Corporation, 375 Greenwich Street, Floor 4, New York, NY 10013, USA. *Website:* www.miramax.com (Office).

WEINSTEIN, Robert; American film producer and executive; b. 1954; s. of Mira Weinstein and Max Weinstein; brother of Harvey Weinstein (q.v.); Co-Chair. Miramax Films Corpn with brother Harvey 1979–. *Films produced include:* (all with Harvey Weinstein, q.v.) Playing for Keeps (with Alan Brewer) 1986, Scandal (with Joe Boyd and Nik Powell) 1989, Strike it Rich 1990, Hardware (with Nik Powell, Stephen Woolley and Trix Worrell) 1990, A Rage in Harlem (with Terry Glinwood, William Horberg and Nik Powell) 1991, The Night We Never Met (with Sidney Kimmel) 1993, Benefit of the Doubt 1993, True Romance (with Gary Barber, Stanley Margolis and James G. Robinson) 1993, Mother's Boys (with Randall Poster) 1994, Pulp Fiction (with Richard N Gladstein) 1994, Pret-A-Porter (with Ian Jessel) 1994, Smoke (with Satoru Iseki) 1995, A Month By the Lake (with Donna Gigliotti) 1995, The Crossing Guard (with Richard N Gladstein) 1995, The Journey of August King 1995, Things To Do In Denver When You're Dead (with Marie Cantin) 1995, The Englishman Who Went Up a Hill But Came Down a Mountain (with Sally Hibbin and Robert Jones) 1995, Blue in the Face (with Harvey Keitel) 1995, Restoration (with Donna Gigliotti) 1995, Velvet Goldmine 1998, Shakespeare in Love 1998, Allied Forces 1999, My Life So Far 1999, The Yards 1999, Music of the Heart 1999, The Cider House Rules 1999, Down To You 2000, Boys and Girls 2000, Scream 3 2000, Love's Labour's Lost 2000, Scary Movie 2000, About Adam 2000. *Address:* Miramax Films Corporation, 375 Greenwich Street, Floor 4, New York, NY 10013, USA. *Website:* www.miramax.com (Office).

WEIR, Dame Gillian Constance, DBE; British/New Zealand concert organist and harpsichordist; b. 17 Jan. 1941, Martinborough, New Zealand; d. of Cecil Alexander Weir and Clarice Mildred Foy Weir (née Bignell); m. 1st Clive Rowland Webster 1967 (divorced 1971); m. 2nd Lawrence Irving Phelps 1972 (died 1999); ed Wanganui Girls' Coll., NZ and Royal Coll. of Music, London, pvt. studies with Marie-Claire Alain, Anton Heiller, Nadia Boulanger; winner St Albans Int. Organ Festival Competition 1964; débuts Royal Festival Hall and Royal Albert Hall, London 1965; worldwide career since 1965 as organist and latterly as harpsichordist; has appeared with all leading British orchestras and with many abroad, under leading conductors; many radio and TV appearances; adjudicator in int. competitions and artist-in-

residence at major univs.; gives lectures and master classes in many countries; organ consultant, Birmingham Symphony Hall; Visiting Prof. of Organ, Royal Acad. of Music, London 1996–98; Prince Consort Prof. of Organ, Royal Coll. of Music, London 1999–; many premières including first British performance of Messiaen's Méditations of 1972; many works written for her including concertos by William Mathias and Peter Racine Fricker; many recordings including 7-CD set complete organ works of Olivier Messiaen 1995 and complete works of César Franck 1997; presenter and performer 6-part BBC TV series 1989; Pres. Inc. Asscn of Organists (first woman Pres.) 1981–83, Inc. Soc. of Musicians 1992–93; mem. Exec. Council, Royal Coll. of Organists (first woman mem.) 1981–85, Council (first woman mem.) 1977–, Pres. (first woman Pres.) 1994–96; mem. Council Royal Philharmonic Soc. 1996–2002; subject of South Bank Show, ITV 2000; Hon. mem. Royal Acad. of Music; Hon. FRCO; Hon. FRCM; Hon. DMus (Victoria Univ. of Wellington, NZ) 1983, (Hull Univ.) 1999, (Univ. of Exeter) 2001; Hon. DLitt (Univ. of Huddersfield) 1997; Hon. DUniv (Univ. of Cen. England) 2001; Int. Performer of Year Award, American Guild of Organists 1983; Turnovsky Prize for Outstanding Achievement in the Arts 1985; Silver Medal, Albert Schweitzer Asscn (Sweden) 1998, Evening Standard Award for Outstanding Solo Performance in 1998. *Publications:* contrib. to The Messiaen Companion 1995; articles in professional journals. *Leisure interests:* theatre, reading. *Address:* c/o Denny Lyster Artists' Management, PO Box 155, Stanmore, Middx, HA7 3WF, England. *Telephone:* (20) 8954-5521 (Office). *Fax:* (20) 8954-9168 (Office). *Website:* www.dennylyster.free-online.co.uk (Office).

WEIR, Judith, CBE, MA; British composer; b. 11 May 1954, Cambridge; ed North London Collegiate School, King's Coll. Cambridge; composer-in-residence, Southern Arts Asscn 1976–79; Fellow in Composition Univ. of Glasgow 1979–82, Creative Arts Fellowship, Trinity Coll. Cambridge 1983–85, composer-in-residence Royal Scottish Acad. of Music and Drama 1988–91; Fairbairn Composer in Asscn with City of Birmingham Symphony Orchestra 1995–98; Artistic Dir Spitalfields Festival 1995–2000; Visiting Prof. in Opera Studies, Univ. of Oxford 1999–2000; Visiting Prof., Princeton Univ., USA 2001; mem. Bd of Govs Royal Opera House 2003–; Hon. Dr. (Aberdeen) 1995; Critics' Circle Award for most outstanding contrib. to British Musical Life 1994. *Works include:* King Harald's Saga 1979, Consolations of Scholarship 1985, A Night At The Chinese Opera 1987, Missa Del Cid 1988, Heaven Ablaze In His Breast 1989, The Vanishing Bridegroom 1990, Music Untangled 1991–92, Heroic strokes of the Bow 1992, Blond Eckbert 1993, Musicians Wrestle Everywhere 1994, Moon and Star 1995, Forest 1995, Storm 1997, We Are Shadows (South Bank Show Award 2001) 2000. *Address:* c/o Chester Music, 8/9 Frith Street, London, W1D 3JB, England. *Telephone:* (20) 7434-0066. *Fax:* (20) 7287-6329.

WEIR, Peter Lindsay; Australian film director; b. 21 Aug. 1944, Sydney; s. of Lindsay Weir and Peggy Barnsley; m. Wendy Stites 1966; one s. one d.; ed Scots Coll., Sydney, Vaucluse Boys' High School, Sydney Univ.; worked in real estate until 1965; worked as stagehand in television, Sydney 1967; dir film sequences in variety show 1968; Dir amateur univ. reviews 1967–69; dir for Film Australia 1969–73; made own short films 1969–73, independent feature-film dir and writer 1973–; various film awards. *Films:* Cars that Ate Paris 1973, Picnic at Hanging Rock 1975, The Last Wave 1977, The Plumber (television) 1978, Gallipoli 1980, The Year of Living Dangerously 1982, Witness 1985, The Mosquito Coast 1986, Dead Poets Society 1989, Green Card 1991, Fearless 1994, The Truman Show (BAFTA Award for Best Dir) 1997. *Address:* c/o Australian Film Commission, 8 West Street, North Sydney, NSW 2060 (Office); Salt Pan Films Pty Ltd, c/o P.O. Box 29, Palm Beach, NSW 2108, Australia.

WEIR, Stuart Peter, BA; British journalist and academic; b. 13 Oct. 1938, Frimley, Surrey; s. of Robert H. Weir and Edna F. Lewis; m. 1st Doffy Burnham 1963; two s.; m. 2nd Elizabeth E. Bisset 1987; one s. two d.; ed Peter Symonds School, Winchester and Brasenose Coll. Oxford; Feature Writer, Oxford Mail 1964–67; Diarist, The Times 1967–71; Dir Citizens Rights Office 1971–75; Founding Ed. Roof Magazine (Shelter) 1975–77; Deputy Ed. New Society 1977–84; Ed. New Socialist 1984–87; Political Columnist, London Daily News 1987; Ed. New Statesman 1987–88, New Statesman and Society 1988–90; Founder Charter 88 1988; Dir Democratic Audit and Prof. and Sr Research Fellow Human Rights Centre, Univ. of Essex 1991–; Visiting Prof. Essex Univ. 1999–; Series Consultant The People's Parl. (Channel 4 TV) 1994–97; Consultant State of Democracy Project, Int. IDEA, Stockholm 1997–2003; Assoc. Consultant (Governance) British Council 1997–; Consultant on Governance Dept for Int. Devt 1999–2002; Sr Int. Facilitator Namibian Govt and Democracy Project 1994–95; UK Facilitator Zimbabwe Parl. Democracy Project; Chair. Parl. Assessment Team, Zimbabwe 2002–03; Lecturer on Politics and the Media, LSE 1994. *Publications:* Manifesto 1981; contributor to: The Other Britain 1982, Consuming Secrets 1982, Defining and Measuring Democracy 1995; Ego Trip (ed.) 1995, Behind Closed Doors 1995, The Three Pillars of Liberty 1996, Making Votes Count 1997, Political Power and Democratic Control in Britain 1998, Voices of the People (jtly.) 2001, The IDEA Handbook on Democracy Assessments (jtly.) 2001, The State of Democracy (jtly) 2002, Democracy Under Blair 2003. *Leisure interests:* children, cooking, walking, football. *Address:* Butts Orchard, Butts Batch, Wrington, Bristol, BS40 5LN, England. *Telephone:* (1934) 863668. *E-mail:* stuart@democraticaudit.demon.co.uk (Office). *Website:* www.essex.ac.uk (Office).

WEIR, Viscount; William Kenneth James Weir, FRSA, BA; British business executive; b. 9 Nov. 1933, Glasgow, Scotland; s. of Lord Weir and Lady Weir (née Crowdy); m. 1st Diana Lucy MacDougall 1964 (divorced 1972); one s. one d.; m. 2nd Jacqueline Mary Marr 1976 (divorced); m. 3rd Marina Sevastopoulo 1988; one s.; ed Eton Coll., Trinity Coll. Cambridge; served Royal Navy 1955–56; Chair. Weir Group PLC 1972–99, Balfour Beatty PLC (fmly. BICC PLC) 1996–, CP Ships Ltd 2001–; Dir Bank of England 1972–84, British Steel Corpn 1972–76, British Bank of Middle East 1977–79, Canadian Pacific Ltd 1989–2001, St James Place Capital 1990–, Canadian Pacific Railway Co. 2001–; Pres. British Electrotechnical Mfrs Asscn 1988-89, 1993–95; mem. London Advisory Cttee, Hong Kong Shanghai Bank 1980–92, Export Credit Advisory Cttee 1991–98; Chair. British Waters 1999–2000; Hon. Fellow, Hon. DEng (Glasgow). *Leisure interests:* shooting, golf. *Address:* Balfour Beatty PLC, 130 Wilton Road, London, SW1V 1LQ, England (Office); Rodinghead, Mauchline, Ayrshire, KA5 5TR, Scotland (Home). *Telephone:* (20) 7216-6800 (Office); (1563) 884233 (Home).

WEISKRANTZ, Lawrence, PhD, FRS; American professor of psychology; b. 28 March 1926, Philadelphia; s. of Benjamin Weiskrantz and Rose Weiskrantz (née Rifkin); m. Barbara Collins 1954; one s. one d.; ed Girard Coll. of Philadelphia, Swarthmore and Univs. of Oxford and Harvard; part-time Lecturer, Tufts Univ. 1952; Research Assoc., Inst. of Living 1952–55; Sr Postdoctoral Fellow, NAS 1955–56; Research Assoc., Cambridge Univ., England 1956–61, Asst Dir of Research 1961–66, Fellow, Churchill Coll. 1964–67, Reader in Physiological Psychology 1966–67; Prof. of Psychology and Head of Dept of Experimental Psychology, Oxford Univ. 1967–93; Fellow of Magdalen Coll. Oxford; Kenneth Craik Research Award, St John's Coll. Cambridge 1975–76; Sir Frederick Bartlett Memorial Lecturer 1980; Ferrier Lecturer, Royal Soc. 1989; Hughlings Jackson Lecturer/Medallist (Royal Soc. of Medicine) 1990; Harry Camp Memorial Lecturer, Stamford Univ. 1997; Werner Heisenburg Lecturer, Bavarian Acad. of Science 1998; John P. McGovern Award Lecture, AAAS 2002; Deputy Ed. Brain 1981–91; mem. NAS. *Publications:* Analysis of Behavioral Change (Ed.) 1967, Animal Intelligence (Ed.) 1985, Neuropsychology of Cognitive Function (Ed.) 1986, Blindsight 1986, Thought Without Language (Ed.) 1988, Consciousness Lost and Found 1997 and articles in Science, Nature, Quarterly Journal of Experimental Psychology, Journal of Comparative Physiological Psychology, Animal Behaviour and Brain. *Leisure interests:* music, walking. *Address:* Department of Experimental Psychology, University of Oxford, South Parks Road, Oxford, OX1 3UD, England. *Telephone:* (1865) 271444.

WEISS, Ulrich; German banker; b. 3 June 1936; fmr mem. Bd of Man. Dirs., Deutsche Bank AG, Frankfurt; Chair. Supervisory Bd Continental AG, Hanover; Chair. Admin. Council, Deutsche Bank SAE, Barcelona/Madrid, Deutsche Bank de Investimento SA, Lisbon, Deutsche Bank Luxembourg SA; Chair. Admin. Council, Deutsche Bank SpA, Milan; mem. Supervisory Bd Asea Brown Boveri AG, Mannheim, BASF AG, Ludwigshafen, Heidelberger Zement AG, Klein, Schanzlin & Becker AG, Frankenthal, Rheinelektra AG, Mannheim, Südzucker AG, Mannheim; mem. Admin. Council Fiat SpA, Turin. *Address:* c/o Deutsche Bank AG, 60325 Frankfurt am Main, Germany.

WEISSENBERG, Alexis; Bulgarian pianist; b. 26 July 1929, Sofia; studied piano and composition with Pancho Vladigerov at age 3, also with Olga Samaroff at Juilliard School, New York 1946; début at age 14; numerous appearances in Europe, South America, USA, Japan; American début with New York Philharmonic; soloist with Berlin, Vienna, Japan, Czechoslovak Philharmonics, Philadelphia, Cleveland, Minnesota, Royal Danish and Salzburg Festival orchestras, Boston, Chicago, Pittsburgh Symphony orchestras, Orchestre de Paris and others; recording artist with RCA, Angel; first prize Int. Leventritt competition and Philadelphia Youth competition 1946. *Address:* c/o Michal Schmidt, Thea Dispeker Inc., 59 East 54th Street, New York, NY 10022, USA (Office).

WEISSMAN, Myrna, PhD; American professor of psychiatry; b. Boston, Mass.; one s. three d.; ed Yale Univ.; Prof. of Psychiatry and Epidemiology, Yale Univ. School of Medicine, Dir Depression Research Unit –1987; Prof. of Epidemiology in Psychiatry, Coll. of Physicians and Surgeons and School of Public Health, Columbia Univ., Chief of Dept, Clinical-Genetic Epidemiology, NY State Psychiatric Inst. 1987–; Visiting Sr Scholar, Inst. of Medicine, NAS, Washington, DC 1979–80 (mem. 1996–); mem. editorial bd of several journals including Archives of General Psychiatry; mem. Nat. Advisory Mental Health Council, Inst. of Medicine, NAS 1998–, Nat. Inst. of Mental Health 1999–2000, Council, American Coll. of Neuropsychopharmacology 1999–2002; Pres. American Psychopathological Asscn, New York 1998–99; Fellow Royal Soc. of Psychiatrists (UK) 1998–, NY Acad. of Science; American Psychiatric Asscn Foundation's Fund Prize 1978, Rema Lapouse Mental Health Epidemiology Award, American Public Health Asscn 1985, Research Award, American Suicide Foundation 1990, Joseph Zubin Award, American Psychopathological Asscn 1996 and other prizes and awards. *Publications:* author or co-author of over 400 scientific articles and book chapters and 7 books including The Depressed Woman: A Study of Social Relationships 1974, Interpersonal Psychotherapy of Depression 1984, A Comprehensive Guide to Interpersonal Psychotherapy 2000. *Address:* College of Physicians and Surgeons, Columbia University, 1051 Riverside Drive, Unit 24, New York, NY 10032 (Office); 39 East 79th Street, New York, NY 10021, U.S.A. (Home). *Telephone:* (212) 543-5880 (Office); (212) 737-2562 (Home). *Fax:* (212) 568-3534 (Office); (212) 396-3437 (Home). *E-mail:* MMW3@columbia.edu (Office).

WEISZ, Rachel; British actress; b. 1972. *Film roles:* Seventeen, Chain Reaction, Stealing Beauty, Going All the Way, Amy Foster, Bent, I Want You 1998, Land Girls 1998, The Mummy 1999, Sunshine 2000, Beautiful Creatures 2001, Enemy at the Gates 2001, The Mummy Returns 2001, About a Boy 2002. *Plays:* Design for Living 1995, Suddenly Last Summer 1999. *Address:* c/o ICM Ltd., Oxford House, 76 Oxford Street, London, W1N 0AX, England (Office). *Telephone:* (20) 7636-6565 (Office). *Fax:* (20) 7323-0101 (Office).

WEIZMAN, Maj.-Gen. Ezer; Israeli politician and air force officer; b. 15 June 1924, Tel-Aviv; nephew of Chaim Weizmann (1st Pres. of Israel); m.; two c.; ed RAF Staff Coll.; Officer, Israel Air Force 1948–66 and fmr CO, I.A.F.; Chief General Staff Branch 1966–69; Minister of Transport 1969–70, of Defence 1977–80, of Communications 1984–88, of Science 1988–92; Chair. Exec. Cttee Herut Party 1971–73; mem. Likud front 1973–80; in pvt. business 1980–84; Minister without Portfolio in Cabinet, Head of Yahad Party in Nat. Unity Govt 1984–89; Pres. of Israel 1993–2001. *Publications:* On Eagles Wings 1978, The Battle for Peace 1981. *Address:* Beit Amot Mishpat, 8 Shaul Hamelech blvd., Tel-Aviv 64733 (Office); 2 Hadekel Street, Caesarea 38900, Israel. *Telephone:* 3-6919888 (Office). *Fax:* 3-6917999 (Office).

WEIZSÄCKER, Carl Friedrich, Freiher von, PhD; German professor of philosophy and director of research; b. 28 June 1912, Kiel; s. of Ernst von Weizsäcker and Marianne Graevenitz; m. Gundalena Wille 1937; four c.; ed Univs. of Berlin, Göttingen and Leipzig; lecturer Kaiser-Wilhelm-Institut, Berlin 1936–42; Assoc. Prof. Univ. of Strasbourg 1942–44; Head Dept Max-Planck-Inst. for Physics, Göttingen 1946–57; Hon. Prof. Univ. of Göttingen 1946–57; Prof. of Philosophy Univ. of Hamburg 1957–69; Dir Max-Planck-Inst. for Research on Preconditions of Human Life in the Modern World, Starnberg 1970–80; Emer. Scientific mem. Max-Planck-Gesellschaft, Munich 1980–; Hon. Prof. Univ. of Munich; mem. Deutsche Akademie der Naturforscher, Leopoldina, Göttinger Akademie der Wissenschaften, Sächsische Akademie der Wissenschaften, Leipzig, Österreichische Akademie der Wissenschaften, Bayerische Akademie der Wissenschaften, Bayerische Akademie der Schönen Künste, Deutsche Physikalische Gesellschaft, American Physical Soc., Ordre Pour le Mérite, Académie des Sciences Morales et Politiques, Institut de France; Hon. DrIur (Vrije Universiteit, Amsterdam) 1975, (Alberta) 1981; Hon. DTheol (Catholic Theol. Faculty, Tubingen) 1977; Hon. Dr. rer. nat. (Karl-Marx-Universität, Leipzig) 1987; Hon. DPhil (Freie Universität, Berlin) 1987; numerous prizes and medals including John M. Templeton Prize for Progress in Religion (jtly.) 1989; Bundesverdienstkreuz. *Publications:* Die Atomkerne 1937, Zum Weltbild der Physik 1943, Die Geschichte der Natur 1948, Bedingungen des Friedens 1963, Die Tragweite der Wissenschaft 1964, Gedanken über unsere Zukunft 1966, Der ungesicherte Friede 1969, Die Einheit der Natur 1971, Fragen zur Weltpolitik 1975, Wege in die Gefahr 1977, Der Garten des Menschlichen 1978, Deutlichkeit 1978, Der bedrohte Friede 1981, Wahrnehmung der Neuzeit 1983, Aufbau der Physik 1985, Die Zeit drängt 1986, Bewusstseinswandel 1988, Bedingungen der Freiheit 1990, Der Mensch in seiner Geschichte 1991, Zeit und Wissen 1992, Der bedrohte Friede-heute 1994, Wohin gehen wir? 1997. *Address:* Alpenstrasse 15, 82319 Starnberg, Germany. *Telephone:* (8151) 7091.

WEIZSÄCKER, Richard von, DJur; German politician and lawyer; b. 15 April 1920, Stuttgart; s. of the late Baron Ernst von Weizsäcker; m. Marianne von Kretschmann 1953; three s. one d.; ed Berlin, law studies at Oxford, Grenoble, Göttingen; army service 1938–45; prof. lawyer 1955–; fmr mem. bd Allianz Lebensversicherung-AG, Stuttgart, Robeco-Gruppe, Amsterdam; mem. Robert Bosch Foundation, Stuttgart; mem. Synod and Council of German Protestant Church 1969–84, Pres. Protestant Church Congress 1964–70; mem. Fed. Bd CDU, Deputy Chair. CDU/CSU Party 1972–79; mem. Bundestag 1969–81, Vice-Pres. 1979–81; Governing Mayor of West Berlin 1981–84; Pres. Fed. Repub. of Germany 1984–94; Hon. Pres. Int. Council of Christians and Jews 1994–; Co-Chair. Ind. Working Group on the Future of the UN 1994–95; Chair. Comm. Common Security and the Future of the German Fed. Army 1999–2000; mem. Nomination Cttee Praemium Imperiale 1998–, "Three Wise Men" Comm. on Institutional Reforms of the EU 1999; mem. Eminent Persons Group requested by UN Sec.-Gen. Kofi Annan to write report Crossing the Divide – Dialogue Among Civilizations 2001; Hon. Senator Max Planck Soc.; Hon. DCL (Oxford) 1988; Dr hc (Cambridge) 1994; Theodor Heuss Prize 1983, Leopold Lucas Prize 2000. *Publications:* Die deutsche Geschichte geht weiter 1983, Von Deutschland aus 1985, Die politische Kraft der Kultur 1987, Von Deutschland nach Europa 1991, Vier Zeiten 1997, Drei Mal Stunde Null? 2001. *Address:* Am Kupfergraben 7, 10117 Berlin, Germany (Office).

WELCH, John Francis, Jr, PhD; American business executive; b. 19 Nov. 1935, Peabody, Mass.; s. of John Francis Welch and Grace (née Andrews) Welch; m. 1st Carolyn B. Osburn 1959 (divorced 1987); two s. two d.; m. 2nd Jane Beasely 1989 (divorced 2002); ed Univs. of Massachusetts and Illinois; joined Gen. Electric Co., Fairfield, Conn. 1960–, Vice-Pres. 1972, Vice-Pres. Exec. Components and Materials Group 1973–77, Sr Vice-Pres. Sector Exec., Consumer Products and Services Sector 1977–79, Vice-Chair. CEO 1979–81, Chair., CEO 1981–2001; Pres. and CEO Nat. Broadcasting Co. 1986–2000; Dir. Fiat, Idealab; Pvt. Leadership Consultant 2001–; with Clayton, Dubilier & Rice 2001–. *Publication:* Jack: Straight from the Gut 2001. *Address:* c/o General Electric Co., 3135 Easton Turnpike, Fairfield, CT 06431, USA.

WELCH, Raquel; American actress; b. 5 Sept. 1940, Chicago, Ill.; d. of Armand Tejada and Josepha (née Hall) Tejada; m. 1st James Westley Welch 1959 (divorced); one s. one d.; m. 2nd Patrick Curtis (divorced); m. 3rd Andre Weinfeld 1980 (divorced); fmr model for Neiman-Marcus stores. *Films include:* Fantastic Voyage 1966, One Million Years BC 1967, Fathom 1967, The Biggest Bundle of Them All 1968, Magic Christian 1970, Myra Breckinridge 1970, Fuzz 1972, Bluebeard 1972, Hannie Caulder 1972, Kansas City Bomber 1972, The Last of Sheila 1973, The Three Musketeers 1974, The Wild Party 1975, The Four Musketeers 1975, Mother, Jugs and Speed 1976, Crossed Swords 1978, L'Animal 1979, Chair. of the Board 1998; Right to Die 1987, Scandal in a Small Town 1988, Trouble in Paradise 1989, Naked Gun 33¹/₃ 1993, Folle d'Elle 1998. *Plays include:* Woman of the Year (Broadway) 1982, Torch Song 1993. *Videos:* Raquel: Total Beauty and Fitness 1984, A Week with Raquel 1987, Raquel: Lose 10lbs in 3 Weeks 1989. *Publication:* The Raquel Welch Total Beauty and Fitness Program 1984. *Address:* Innovative Artists, 1999 Avenue of the Stars, Suite 2850, Los Angeles, CA 90067, USA.

WELD, Tuesday Ker (Susan Ker Weld); American actress; b. 27 Aug. 1943, New York; d. of Lathrop M. Weld and Aileen Ker; m. 1st Claude Harz 1965 (divorced 1971); one d.; m. 2nd Dudley Moore 1975 (divorced); one s.; m. 3rd Pinchas Zukerman (q.v.) 1985; ed Hollywood Professional School; fashion and catalogue model aged three; regular appearances as magazine cover-girl and in child roles on TV by age twelve; appears in numerous TV programmes and TV films including Cimarron Strip, Playhouse 90, Climax, Ozzie and Harriet, 77 Sunset Strip, The Millionaire, Tab Hunter Show, Dick Powell Theatre, Adventures in Paradise, Naked City, The Greatest Show on Earth, Mr Broadway, Fugitive. *Films include:* Rock Rock (debut) 1956, Serial, Rally Round the Flag Boys, The Five Pennies, The Private Lives of Adam and Eve, Return to Peyton Place, Wild in the Country, Bachelor Flat, Lord Love a Duck, Pretty Poison, I Walk the Line, A Safe Place, Play it as it Lays, Because They're Young, High Time, Sex Kittens Go to College, The Cincinnati Kid, Soldier in the Rain, Looking for Mr Goodbar, Thief, Author!, Once Upon a Time In America, Heartbreak Hotel, Falling Down, Feeling Minnesota 1996.

WELD, William Floyd, JD; American politician; b. 31 July 1945, New York; s. of David Weld and Mary Nichols; m. Susan Roosevelt 1975; two s. three d.; ed Harvard and Oxford Univs; admitted Mass. Bar 1970; law clerk, Supreme Judicial Court, Mass. 1970–71; partner, Hill & Barlow, Boston 1971–81; Assoc. Minority Counsel, U.S. House of Reps. Judiciary Comm. Impeachment Inquiry 1973–74; U.S. Attorney for Dist of Mass. 1981–86; Asst Attorney-Gen. Criminal Div. U.S. Justice Dept, Washington, DC 1986–88; Gov. of Massachusetts 1990–97; mem. American Law Inst., Boston Bar Asscn, American Bar Asscn; Republican. *Address:* c/o Office of the Governor, State House, Boston, MA 02133, USA.

WELDON, Fay, CBE, MA; British author; b. 22 Sept. 1931, Alvechurch, Worcs.; d. of Frank T. Birkinshaw and Margaret J. Birkinshaw; m.1st Ronald Weldon 1960 (divorced 1994); four s.; m. 2nd Nicholas Fox 1995; ed Girls' High School, Christchurch, New Zealand, South Hampstead School for Girls and Univ. of St Andrews; Chair. of Judges, Booker McConnell Prize 1983; fmr mem. Arts Council Literary Panel; mem. Video Censorship Appeals Cttee; Fellow City of Bath Coll. 1999; Hon. DLitt (Bath) 1989, (St Andrews) 1992; Women in Publishing Pandora Award 1997. *Theatre plays:* Words of Advice 1974, Friends 1975, Moving House 1976, Mr Director 1977, Action Replay 1979, I Love My Love 1981, Woodworm 1981, Jane Eyre 1986, The Hole in the Top of the World 1987, Jane Eyre (adaptation), Playhouse Theatre, London 1995, The Four Alice Bakers, Birmingham Repertory 1999; more than 30 television plays, dramatizations and radio plays. *Television:* Big Women (series), Channel 4 1999. *Publications:* novels: The Fat Woman's Joke 1967 (published in USA as And the Wife Ran Away 1968), Down Among the Women 1972, Female Friends 1975, Remember Me 1976, Little Sisters 1977 (USA Words of Advice), Praxis 1978, Puffball 1980, The President's Child 1982, The Life and Loves of a She-Devil 1984, The Shrapnel Academy 1986, The Heart of the Country 1987, The Hearts and Lives of Men 1987, The Rules of Life (novella) 1987, Leader of the Band 1988, The Cloning of Joanna May 1989, Darcy's Utopia 1990, Growing Rich 1992, Life Force 1992, Affliction 1994 (USA Trouble), Splitting 1995, Worst Fears 1996, Big Women 1997, Rhode Island Blues 2000, Bulgari Connection 2001, Godless in Eden (essays) 2000; children's books: Wolf the Mechanical Dog 1988, Party Puddle 1989, Nobody Likes Me! 1997; short story collections: Watching Me Watching You 1981, Polaris 1985, Moon Over Minneapolis 1991, Wicked Women 1995, Angel All Innocence and Other Stories 1995, A Hard Time to be a Father 1998, Nothing to Wear, Nowhere to Hide 2002, Auto-da-Fay (autobiog.) 2002. *Address:* Casarotto Co. Ltd, National House, 62/66 Wardour Street, London W1V 3HP, England.

WELDON, Virginia Verral, AB, MD; American university administrator and physician; b. 8 Sept. 1935, Toronto, Canada; d. of John Edward Verral and Carolyn Edith Swift; m. (divorced); two d.; ed Smith Coll., State Univ. of New York at Buffalo, Johns Hopkins Univ. School of Medicine, USA; Instructor in Paediatrics, Johns Hopkins Hosp. 1967–68; Washington Univ. School of Medicine 1968–69, Asst Prof. of Paediatrics 1973–79, Prof. 1979–89, Asst Vice-Chancellor for Medical Affairs 1975–81, Assoc. Vice-Chancellor 1981–83, Deputy Vice-Chancellor 1983–89, Vice-Pres. Washington Univ. Medical Center 1980–89; Vice-Pres. Scientific Affairs, Monsanto Co. 1989, Vice-Pres. Public Policy 1989–93, Sr Vice-Pres. Public Policy 1993–98; Dir Center for Study of American Business, Washington Univ., St Louis 1998–99; Adviser, Dir Monsanto Co. 1989–98; Trustee Calif. Inst. of Tech. 1996–,

Whitaker Foundation 1997–, Whitfield School 1997–; mem. Environmental Protection Agency Risk Assessment Man. Comm. 1992–97, Pres's Cttee of Advisors on Science and Tech. 1994–; Fellow AAAS; Smith Coll. Medal 1984. *Publications:* numerous articles in scientific journals. *Leisure interest:* civic affairs. *Address:* 242 Carlyle Lake Drive, St Louis, MO 63141, USA (Home).

WELLAND, Colin; British playwright and actor; b. Colin Williams, 4 July 1934, Liverpool; s. of John Arthur Williams and Norah Williams; m. Patricia Sweeney 1962; one s. three d.; ed Newton-le-Willows Grammar School, Bretton Hall, Goldsmiths' Coll., London; art teacher 1958–62; entered theatre 1962, Library Theatre, Manchester 1962–64; Fellow Goldsmiths Coll., Univ. of London 2001. *Film roles:* Kes (BAFTA Award for Best Supporting Actor), Villain, Straw Dogs, Sweeney, The Secret Life of Ian Fleming, Dancing through the Dark. *Wrote screenplay for:* Yanks 1978, Chariots of Fire 1980 (Acad. Award), Twice in a Lifetime 1986, A Dry White Season, War of the Buttons 1994. *Stage roles:* Waiting for Godot 1987, The Churchill Play, Man of Magic, Say Goodnight to Grandma, Ubu Roi. *Wrote plays:* Say Goodnight to Grandma 1973, Roll on Four O'Clock 1981. *TV plays include:* Kisses at 50, Leeds United, Your Man from Six Counties, Bambino Mio, Slattery's Mounted Foot, Jack Point, The Hallelujah Handshake, Roll on Four O'Clock (BAFTA Award for Best TV Screenplay). *TV appearances in:* Blue Remembered Hills, The Fix, United Kingdom. *Publications:* plays: Roomful of Holes 1972, Say Goodnight to Grandma 1973. *Leisure interests:* sport (particularly Rugby League), films, dining out, politics, travel. *Address:* c/o Peters, Fraser & Dunlop, Drury House, 34–43 Russell Street, London, WC2B 5HA, England.

WELLER, Malcolm Philip Isadore, MA, MB, BS; British medical practitioner; b. 29 May 1935, Manchester; s. of Solomon George Weller and Esther Weller; m. Davina Reisler 1966; two s.; ed Perse School, Cambridge, Cambridge and Newcastle Univs; Consultant Emer., Barnet Enfield & Haringey Mental Health NHS Trust; Hon. Sr Lecturer, London Univ., Royal Free Hosp. School of Medicine –1997; Hon. Research Prof. Middx Univ. 1997–; Chair. N Thames Region Psychiatric Cttee 1997, London Region Psychiatric Cttee 1995–; Vice-Chair. NE Thames Regional Cttee for Hosp. Medical Services 1984–96; Hon. Medical Adviser, Nat. Alliance of Relatives of the Mentally Ill, Jewish Asscn of the Mentally Ill, Nat. Schizophrenia Fellowship and Founder-mem. Parl. Cttee; Chair. CONCERN 1992–99; co-opted mem. Bd of Studies in Psychology, London Univ. and Higher Degrees Sub-Cttee 1976–; Founder, Ed.-in-Chief Baillière's Clinical Psychiatry series (11 Vols); External Examiner for Master in Medicine (Psychiatry) Degree, Nat. Univ. of Singapore 1988, 1989; External Examiner Manchester Univ. MSc 1990; mem. Standing Cttee Bd of Studies in Medicine, London Univ. 1981–84; mem. Gen. Psychiatry Exec. Cttee Royal Coll. of Psychiatry, also of Pharmacology and Social, Community and Rehabilitation Cttees.; Concert organizer, Newcastle Festival 1970–71; co-opted mem. Laing Art Gallery Cttee 1972–73; Chair. Govs. Gosforth Middle School 1971–74; Fellow British Psychological Soc., Royal Coll. of Psychiatrists, Collegium Internationale Neuro-Psycho-Pharmacologicum (CINP); Mental Health Foundation Undergraduate Scholarship, British Council Travel Award; Invited Fellow, RSA Ver Heyden de Lancey Prize, Cambridge Univ., Wilfred Kingdom Prize, Newcastle Univ. *Publications:* Scientific Basis of Psychology (Ed.) 1983, International Perspectives in Schizophrenia (Ed.) 1989, Dimensions of Community Care 1993, Progress in Clinical Psychiatry 1997, about 150 editorials and papers in learned journals, mainly on schizophrenia, depression, psychological medicine and medico-legal matters; about 100 publs on music in various music journals. *Leisure interests:* fine art, music. *Address:* 30 Arkwright Road, Hampstead, London, NW3 6BH, England (Home). *Telephone:* (20) 7794-5804 (Home). *Fax:* (20) 7431-1589.

WELLER, Paul; British musician; b. 1958; m.; two c.; founded The Jam 1972, The Style Council 1982; solo 1989–. *Songs include:* Eton Rifles 1979, Going Underground/Dreams of Children 1980, Start 1980, Town Called Malice/Precious 1982, Bitterest Pill (I ever had to swallow) 1982, Beat Surrender 1982, Long Hot Summer 1982. *Albums:* In the City 1977, This is the Modern World 1977, All Mod Cons 1978, Setting Sons 1979, Sound Affects 1980, The Gift 1982, Dig the New Breed 1982, In the City (re-issue), Snap 1983, Greatest Hits 1991, Extras 1992, Live Jam 1993, (The Jam) Cafe Bleu 1984, Our Favourite Shop 1985, Home and Abroad 1986, The Cost of Loving 1987, Confessions of a Pop Group 1988, Singular Adventures of the Style Council 1989, (The Style Council) Paul Weller 1992, Here's Some That Got Away 1993, Wild Wood 1993, Live Wood 1994, Stanley Road 1995, Heavy Soul 1997, Modern Classics 1998, Heliocentric 2000, Illumination 2002. *Address:* c/o Go Discs Ltd, 72 Black Lion Lane, Hammersmith, London, W6 9BE, England. *Telephone:* (20) 8910-4600. *Fax:* (20) 8741-2184. *Website:* www.paulweller .com.

WELLER, Thomas Huckle, AB, MS, MD; American scientist and university professor; b. 1915, Ann Arbor, Mich.; s. of Carl V. Weller and Elsie H. Weller; m. Kathleen R. Fahey 1945; two s. two d.; ed Harvard Univ. and Univ. of Michigan; Teaching Fellow, Harvard Medical School 1940–42; served Medical Corps, US Army 1942–45; Asst Resident, Children's Hospital, Boston 1946–47; Research Fellow, Harvard Medical School 1947–48, Instructor 1948–49; Asst Prof. Tropical Public Health, Harvard School of Public Health 1949, Assoc. Prof. 1950–54, Richard Pearson Strong Prof. 1954–85, Emer. 1985 and Head of Dept 1954–81; Asst Dir Research Div. of Infectious Diseases, Children's Medical Center, Boston 1949–55; Dir Comm. on Parasitic Diseases, Armed Forces Epidemiological Bd 1953–59; Consultant on Tropical Diseases, US Public Health Service; Dir Center for Prevention of

Infectious Diseases, Harvard School of Public Health 1966–81; Consultant practice: viral and parasitic diseases, int. health 1985–; mem. NAS; Hon. Fellow Royal Soc. of Tropical Medicine and Hygiene 1987, Faculty of Public Health Medicine of Royal Coll. of Physicians 1990; Hon. LLD (Mich.); Hon. ScD (Gustavus Adolphus), LHD (Lowell); winner (jtly.) of E. Mead Johnson Award 1953, Kimble Methodology Award 1954, Nobel Prize in Medicine and Physiology 1954, Weinstein Cerebral Palsy Award 1973, Ledlie Prize 1963, Bristol Award, Infectious Diseases Soc. of America 1980, Gold Medal and Diploma of Honor, Univ. Costa Rica, 1984, VZV Foundation Award for Scientific Achievement 1993, Walter Reed Medal, American Soc. of Tropical Medicine and Hygiene 1996. *Publications:* papers on infectious diseases, tropical medicine, virus cultivation (especially poliomyelitis and mumps), the etiology of varicella, cytomegalic inclusion disease and rubella, herpes zoster, laboratory diagnosis of schistosomiasis. *Leisure interests:* gardening, ornithology, photography. *Address:* 56 Winding River Road, Needham, MA 02492, USA (Home). *Telephone:* (781) 235-3905. *Fax:* (781) 235-9059.

WELLER, Walter; Austrian conductor; b. 30 Nov. 1939; s. of Walter and Anna Weller; m. Elisabeth Samohyl, 1966; one s.; ed Realgymnasium, Vienna, Akademie für Musik, Vienna; f. Weller Quartet 1958–69; mem. Vienna Philharmonic 1958–60, First Leader 1960–69; Conductor, Vienna State Opera 1969–75; Guest Conductor with all main Austrian, American and Japan Broadcasting Corpn orchestras 1973–; Chief Conductor, Tonkünstler Orchestra, Vienna 1974–77; Principal Conductor and Artistic Adviser, Royal Liverpool Philharmonic Orchestra 1977–80, Guest Conductor Laureate 1980; Prin. Conductor, Royal Philharmonic Orchestra 1980–85, Chief Guest Conductor 1985–; Chief Guest Conductor, Nat. Orchestra of Spain 1987–; Prin. Conductor, Music Dir Royal Scottish Nat. Orchestra 1992–97, now Conductor Emer.; Chief Conductor and Artistic Adviser, Opera Basel and Allgemeine Musikgesellschaft Basel 1994–95; Medal of Arts and Sciences (Austria) 1968, Grand Prix du Disque, Charles Cross for Duke's Symphony in C, Great Silver Cross of Honour (Austria) 1998. *Leisure interests:* magic, model railways, sailing, swimming, stamp-collecting, skiing. *Address:* c/o Harrison-Parrott Ltd, 12 Penzance Place, London, W11 4PA, England. *Telephone:* (20) 7229-9166 (Office). *E-mail:* info@harrisonparrott.co.uk (Office). *Website:* www .harrisonparrott.co.uk (Office); www.music.at/walter-weller (Home).

WELLERSHOFF, Dieter, DPhil; German writer; b. 3 Nov. 1925, Neuss/ Rhein; s. of Walter Wellershoff and Kläre Weber; m. Dr Maria von Thadden 1952; one s. two d.; ed Gymnasium in Grevenbroich and Univ. Bonn; Ed. 1952–55; freelance writer 1956–59, 1981–; Reader Kiepenheuer and Witsch Publishing House, Cologne 1959–81; author of 11 radio plays and 10 TV plays; Hörspielpreis der Kriegsblinden 1961; Literaturpreis Verband der deutschen Kritiker 1970, Heinrich Böll Prize, Cologne 1988, Hölderlin Prize 2001, Breitbach Prize 2001. *Publications:* Gottfried Benn, Phänotyp dieser Stunde 1958, Der Gleichgültige 1963, Ein schöner Tag 1966, Literatur und Veränderung 1969, Einladung an alle 1972, Die Schönheit des Schimpansen 1977, Die Sirene 1980, Der Sieger nimmt alles 1983, Die Arbeit des Lebens 1985, Die Körper und die Träume 1986, Der Roman und die Erfahrbarkeit der Welt 1988, Pan und die Engel. Ansichten von Cologne 1990, Blick auf einen fernen Berg 1991, Das geordnete Chaos 1992, Angesichts der Gegenwart 1993, Der Ernstfall. Innenansichten des Krieges 1995, Zikadengeschrei 1995, Werke in 6 Bänden 1996–97, Der Liebeswunsch 2000, Der verstörter Eros 2001; (ed.) Gottfried Benn, Gesammelte Werke 1958; works translated into 15 languages. *Address:* Mainzer Strasse 45, 50678 Cologne, Germany. *Telephone:* (221) 388565.

WELLINK, Arnout H. E. M., PhD; Netherlands international banking executive; b. 1943; m. M.V. Volmer; five c.; ed Leyden Univ., Univ. of Rotterdam; teacher Leyden Univ. 1965–70; staff mem. Ministry of Finance 1970–75, Head of Directorate-Gen. Financial and Econ. Policy 1975–77, Treas.-Gen. 1977–81; Exec. Dir The Netherlands Bank 1982–, Pres. 1997–; Chair. of Bd and Pres. Bank for Int. Settlements (BIS) March 2002–; mem. Council, European Cen. Bank; mem. Bd of Trustees Museum Meermanno-Westreenianum; Kt of Order of the Netherlands. *Address:* Bank for International Settlements, Centralbahnplatz 2, 4002 Basel, Switzerland (Office). *Telephone:* (61) 2808080 (Office). *Fax:* (61) 2809100 (Office). *E-mail:* email@ bis.org (Office). *Website:* www.bis.org (Office).

WELLS, Rufus Michael Grant, PhD, DSc, FRSNZ; New Zealand professor of zoology; b. 3 July 1947, Cardiff, Wales; s. of Peter F. Wells and Jean Chiles; m. Jane Nelson 1969; one s. one d.; ed Hamilton Boys' High School, Univ. of Auckland, Bedford Coll., Univ. of London, UK; researcher in molecular physiology of haemoglobin and respiration (medical, animal and fisheries science), Antarctic biology; Asst Lecturer in Statistics, Univ. of Auckland 1970–71; Research Asst and PhD student Bedford Coll., London 1971–74; Biochemist and MRC Fellow, Univ. Coll. Hosp., London 1974–75; lecturer, then Sr Lecturer in Zoology, then Prof., Univ. of Auckland 1975–; biological and editorial consultant, specializing in Antarctic Science and Science Educ.; fmr mem. Nat. Comm. for Antarctic Research; Physiological Soc. of NZ Medal 1983, Royal Soc. of NZ Hutton Medal 1989. *Publications:* 220 scientific papers. *Address:* School of Biological Sciences, University of Auckland, Private Bag 92019, Auckland 1, New Zealand. *Telephone:* (9) 373-7999. *Fax:* (9) 373-7400. *Website:* www.auckland.ac.nz (Office).

WELSER-MÖST, Franz; Austrian conductor; b. 16 Aug. 1960, Linz; ed Musikgymnasium, Linz and Staatliche Musikhochschule, Munich; Chief Conductor, Jeunesse Orchestra, Linz 1982–85, Norrköping Symphony

Orchestra 1985, Musikkollegium Winterthur, Switzerland 1986; Music Dir London Philharmonic Orchestra (LPO) 1990–96, Zürich Opera 1995–, (desig.) Cleveland Orchestra 2002–; Outstanding Achievement Award from Western Law Centre, LA, for work for people with disabilities. *Recordings include:* Mendelssohn Symphonies 3 and 4, Schumann Symphonies 2 and 3, Bruckner Symphony 7, Strauss Waltzes, Carl Orff's Carmina Burana, Stravinsky's Oedipus Rex, Bartok's Miraculous Mandarin, Kodaly's Peacock Variations, Kancheli's Symphony 3, Pärt's Symphony 3, Fratres, Schmidt's Symphony 4 (Gramophone Award 1996) (all with LPO). *Leisure interests:* literature, mountain hiking, marathons. *Address:* c/o Van Walsum Management Ltd., 4 Addison Bridge Place, London, W14 8XP, England (Office). *Telephone:* (20) 7371-4343 (Office).

WELSH, Moray Meston, BA, LRAM, ARCM; British cellist; b. 1 March 1947, Haddington; s. of D. A. Welsh and C. Welsh (née Meston); ed York Univ. and Moscow Conservatoire; 'cello solo appearances in UK, USA, USSR, Europe and Scandinavia; appeared in concertos and chamber music with major UK orchestras, radio, TV; also festivals at Bath, Edinburgh, Aldeburgh, Bergen and Helsinki; Prin. cellist, London Symphony Orchestra 1992–; regular concert appearances with London Symphony Orchestra; British Council Scholarship 1969, Gulbenkian Fellowship 1970. *Records include:* concertos by Boccherini, Vivaldi, Goehr, Hoddinott, Hugh Wood (record of the year); recorded with James Galway, Kyung-Wha Chung, Allegri Quartet, Alberni Quartet; cello and orchestra music by Herbert Howells with L.S.O.; Rachmaninov Complete Works for Cello and Piano. *Radio:* frequent broadcasts on BBC Radio 3. *Leisure interests:* art, gardening, skiing, writing. *Address:* 28 Summerfield Avenue, Queens Park, London, NW6 6JY, England. *Telephone:* (20) 8960-9122. *Fax:* (20) 8960-9122.

WELTEKE, Ernst; German economist; b. 21 Aug. 1942, Korbach; ed Univ. Marburg, Univ. Frankfurt am Main; Chair. Parl. Group of Social Democratic Party in Hessen Land Parl. 1984–87, 1988–91; Minister for the Economy, Transport and Tech. in Hessen 1991–94, for Finance 1994–95; Pres. Land Cen. Bank, Hessen 1995–99; Pres. Deutsche Bundesbank Sept. 1999–; mem. Governing Council European Central Bank 1999–. *Address:* Deutsche Bundesbank, Wilhelm-Epstein-Str. 14, 60006 Frankfurt am Main, Postfach 100602, Germany. *Telephone:* (69) 95661 (Bundesbank). *Fax:* (69) 5601071 (Bundesbank). *E-mail:* presse-information@bundesbank.de (Office). *Website:* www.bundesbank.de (Office).

WELTY, John D., MA, EdD; American university president; b. 24 Aug. 1944, Amboy, Ill.; s. of John D. Welty and Doris E. Donnelly; m. Sharon Brown 1996; three d. two s.; ed Western Illinois, Michigan State and Indiana Univs; Admissions Counsellor, Mich. State Univ. 1966–67; Asst Vice-Pres. for Student Affairs, Southwest Minn. State Univ. 1967–74; Dir of Residences and Asst Prof. SUNY, Albany 1974–77, Assoc. Dean of Students and Dir of Residences 1977–80; Vice-Pres. for Student and Univ. Affairs, Ind. Univ. of Pa 1980–84, Pres. 1984–91; Pres. Calif. State Univ., Fresno 1991–; several distinguished service awards. *Publication:* Alcohol and Other Drugs: A Guide for College Presidents and Governing Boards. *Leisure interests:* golf, jogging, reading, racquetball. *Address:* Office of the President, California State University, 5241 N Maple Ave, Thomas Administration Building, Fresno, CA 93740 (Office); 4411 N Van Ness Boulevard, Fresno, CA 93704, USA (Home). *Telephone:* (559) 222-2920; (559) 278-2324 (Office). *Fax:* (559) 278-4715 (Office). *E-mail:* john-welty@csufresno.edu (Office). *Website:* www.csufresno .edu (Office).

WEN, Carson, MA, JP (Hong Kong); Hong Kong lawyer; b. 16 April 1953, Hong Kong; s. of Sir Yung Wen and Tsi Fung Chu; m. Julia Fung Yuet Shan 1983; one c.; ed Diocesan Boys' School, Hong Kong, Nat. Jr Coll. Singapore, Columbia Univ. New York and Univ. of Oxford; Singapore Govt Scholar 1971–72; partner, Siao, Wen and Leung (Solicitors and Notaries), Hong Kong 1982–; Dir and Sec.-Gen. Hong Kong Kwun Tong Industries and Commerce Asscn 1982–, Pres. Emer. 1989–; Hon. Life Pres. Hong Kong Sze Yap Industry and Commerce Asscn 1983–; mem. Kwun Tong Dist Bd 1983–85; Dir Banco Delta Asia SARL, Macau 1992–; Hon. Pres. Hong Kong Industrial Dists., Industry and Commerce Asscn Ltd 1993–; Attesting Officer apptd. by Ministry of Justice of China 1992–; Special Adviser to China Sr Prosecutors Educ. Foundation under the auspices of the Supreme People's Procurate of People's Repub. of China 1993–; Hong Kong Affairs Adviser to Govt of China 1993–; mem. Selection Cttee for First Govt of Hong Kong Special Admin. Region 1996; Vice-Chair. The Hong Kong Progressive Alliance 1994–; Deputy, Nat. People's Congress, People's Repub. of China 1998–. *Publications:* contribs. to 13 lectures on Hong Kong Law; articles in journals, magazines and newspapers. *Leisure interests:* reading, golf. *Address:* 15th Floor, Hang Seng Building, 77 Des Voeux Road, Central, Hong Kong Special Administrative Region (Office); 6B, Wealthy Heights, 35 Macdonnell Road, Hong Kong Special Administrative Region, People's Republic of China (Home). *Telephone:* (852) 28104113 (Office); (852) 28401118 (Home). *Fax:* (852) 28697060 (Office); (852) 28684179 (Home). *E-mail:* swlcw@siaowenleung.com (Office); wens@ netvigator.com (Home). *Website:* www.-siaowenleung.com (Office).

WEN JIABAO; Chinese party and state official; b. Sept. 1942, Tianjin; m.; one s. one d.; ed Beijing Geological Coll.; joined CCP 1965; geological research worker in Gansu Prov. 1968–1982; Dir Reform Research Office of the Geological and Mining Bureau of the State Council 1982–83; Deputy Minister of Geology and Mining 1983–85; Dir Gen. Office of CCP Cen. Cttee 1986–97; Alt. mem. Secr. of Cen. Cttee 1987; Sec. CCP Cen. Organs Working

Cttee 1988; mem. 14th CCP Cen. Cttee 1992–97, alt. mem. CCP Politburo 1992–97, mem. 1997–; Sec. Secr. of Cen. Cttee 1992; mem. 15th CCP Cen. Cttee 1997–2002, 16th CCP Cen. Cttee 2002–; Head Financial Work Cttee of Cen. Cttee 1998–; mem. Standing Cttee CCP Politburo 2002–; Vice-Premier State Council 1998–2003, Premier State Council (Prime Minister), People's Repub. of China 2003–. *Address:* State Council, Beijing, People's Republic of China. *Website:* www.gov.cn.

WEN SHIZHEN; Chinese administrator; b. 1940, Haicheng Co., Liaoning Prov.; ed Faculty of Mechanical Eng, Dalian Inst. of Tech.; joined CCP 1979; with Dalian Oil Pump Nozzle Plant 1980–82; Deputy Dir Dalian City Machinery Bureau 1983–85; alt. mem. 13th Cen. Cttee CCP 1987–91, mem. 14th Cen. Cttee CCP 1992; del. 8th NPC; Vice-Gov. Liaoning Prov. 1986–94, Acting Gov. 1994–95, Gov. 1995, Deputy Sec. CCP 7th Liaoning Prov. Cttee 1995, Sec. 1997–; mem. 15th Cen. Cttee CCP 1997–. *Address:* c/o Office of the Governor, Liaoning Provincial Government, Shengyang City, People's Republic of China.

WEN ZONGREN; Chinese army officer; b. Nov. 1940, Chaoxian Co., Anhui Prov.; ed PLA Tank School, PLA Political Acad., PLA Mil. Acad.; joined PLA 1959; joined CCP 1961; Regimental Political Commissar 1976; Dir Divisional Political Dept 1980; Divisional Political Commissar 1982; Dir Group Army Political Dept 1983; Group Army Political Commissar; Dir Political Dept of Nanjing Mil. Area Command, Political Commissar Lanzhou Mil. Area Command 1985–; alt. mem. 14th CCP Cen. Cttee 1992; mem. 15th CCP Cen. Cttee 1997–. *Address:* People's Liberation Army Lanzhou Military Area Command, Lanzhou City, Gansu Province, People's Republic of China.

WENDERS, Wim; German film director; b. 14 Aug. 1945, Düsseldorf; m. Donata Schmidt 1993; ed Filmhochschule, Munich; film critic Die Suddeutsche Zeitung, Filmkritik 1968–70; Chair. European Film Acad. 1991–96, Pres. 1996–; mem. Akademie der Künste; Dr. hc (Sorbonne, Paris). *Films include:* Summer in the City 1970, The Goalie's Anxiety at the Penalty Kick 1972, The Scarlet Letter 1973, Alice in the Cities 1974, The Wrong Move 1975, Kings of the Road 1976, The American Friend 1977, Lightning Over Water 1980, The State of Things 1982, Hammett 1982, Paris, Texas 1984, Wings of Desire 1987 (Cannes Film Festival Award), Aufzeichnungen zu Kleidern und Städten 1989, Until the End of the World 1991, Faraway, So Close! 1993, Lisbon Story, The Million Dollar Hotel 1999, Buena Vista Social Club 1999, Vill Passiert. *Publications:* Emotion Pictures 1986, Written in the West 1987, Die Logik der Bilder 1988, The Act of Seeing 1992.

WENDT, Albert; Samoan/New Zealand author; b. 1939, Apia; three c.; Prof. Head of English Dept, Auckland Univ.; Hon. PhD (Univ. de Bourgogne, France) 1993; Order of Merit (Western Samoa). *Publications include:* Pouliuli (novel), Leaves of the Banyan Tree (novel), Flying Fox in a Freedom Tree (short stories), Sons for the Return Home (novel), Ola (novel), Black Rainbow (novel), The Best of Albert Wendt's Short Stories, Photographs (poems). *Address:* Department of English, University of Auckland, Private Bag 92019, Auckland 1, New Zealand. *Telephone:* (9) 373-7999. *Fax:* (9) 373-7400. *Website:* www.auckland.ac.nz (Office).

WENDT, Henry, III, AB; American business executive; b. 19 July 1933, Neptune City, NJ; s. of Henry Wendt and Rachel Lindsey Wendt; m. Holly Ann Peterson 1956; one s. one d.; ed Hackley School, Tarrytown, NY and Princeton Univ., NJ; joined SmithKline and French Labs. 1955; Pres. SmithKline Corpn 1976–89, CEO 1982–89; Chair. SmithKline Beckman Corpn Feb.–July 1989; Chair. SmithKline Beecham PLC 1989–94, Global Health Care Partners –2001, DLJ Merchant Banking 1997–; Dir West Marine Inc. 1997–2001; Chair. Computerized Medical Systems Inc ., Arrail Dental (China) Ltd; Dir Cambridge Labs. PLC, Bio Partners SA, Wilson Greatbatch Techs. Ltd., Focus Techs. Inc., Prometheus Labs. Inc.; Propr Quivira Estate Vineyards and Winery 1983–; Order of the Rising Sun with Gold and Silver Star, Japan 1994; Hon. CBE 1995. *Publications:* Global Embrace 1993; various articles. *Leisure interests:* viticulture, oenology, 16th and 17th century cartography, fly fishing, sailing. *Address:* 4900 West Dry Creek Road, Healdsburg, CA 95448, USA.

WENG, Yueh-Sheng, LLB, DrJur; Taiwanese judge; b. 1 July 1932, Chia-yi, three d.; ed Heidelberg Univ., Germany, Nat. Taiwan Univ.; Assoc. Prof. Nat. Taiwan Univ. 1966–70, Prof. 1970–72; Grand Justice, Judicial Yuan 1972–99; Commr of Legal Comm. Exec. Yuan 1971–72; Commr of Research, Devt and Evaluation Comm. 1972; Commr and Convenor of Admin. Procedure Act Research Comm., Judicial Yuan 1981–92; Presiding Justice, Constitutional Court 1992–99; currently Pres. of Judicial Yuan and Chair. Grand Justices Council; mem. Council of Academic Review Evaluation, Ministry of Educ. 1998–99; Visiting Prof. School of Law, Univ. of Wasg. 1991; Commr. Academic Consultation Comm., Sun Yat-Sen Inst. of Social Sciences and Philosophy, Academia Sinica 1991–2001, Convenor 1998–2001. *Publications include:* Die Stellung der Justiz im Verfassungsrecht der Republik China 1970, Administrative Law & Rule of Law 1976, Administrative Law & Judiciary in a State Under the Principle of the Rule of Law 1994, Administrative Law I & II 1998. *Leisure interests:* reading, hiking. *Address:* Judicial Yuan, 124 Chungking South Road, Section 1, Taipei (Office); 19, Alley 9, Lane 143, Jiung Gong Road, Taipei 116, Taiwan (Home). *Telephone:* (2) 23141936 (Office); (2) 22306339 (Home). *Fax:* (2) 23898923 (Office); (2) 22306339 (Home). *E-mail:* president@judicial.gov.tw (Office). *Website:* www.judicial.gov.tw (Office).

WENGER, Antoine, Rév. Père; French ecclesiastic, theologian and historian; b. 2 Sept. 1919, Rohrwiller (Bas-Rhin); s. of Charles Wenger and Philomène Gambel; ed Sorbonne, Strasbourg Univ.; ordained Priest 1943; Dir of Oriental Theology, Univ. Catholique de Lyon 1948–56, Prof. 1956; Chief Ed. La Croix 1957–69; Pres. Fédération Internationale des Directeurs de Journaux Catholiques 1957–65; mem. Pontifical Marian Acad., Rome 1959; Prof. of Ancient Christian Literature, Strasbourg Univ. 1969–73; Ecclesiastical Counsellor to the French Amb. to the Holy See 1973–83; Adviser to Council for Church (Vatican) and Public Affairs 1983–92, to Pontifical Council for non-believers 1987–92, Counsellor for Religious Affairs, French Embassy in Russia 1992–96; Croix d'Or du Patriarcat de Constantinople 1964; Officier, Légion d'honneur; Commdr Ordre nat. du Mérite. *Publications:* L'Assomption dans la tradition orientale 1955, Homélies baptismales inédites de St Jean Chrysostome 1957, La Russie de Khrouchtchev 1959, Vatican II, première session 1963, Vatican II, deuxième session 1964, Vatican II, troisième session 1965, Vatican II quatrième session 1966, Upsal, le défi du siècle aux eglises 1968, Rome et Moscou, 1900–1950 1987, Le cardinal Jean Villot, Secrétaire d'Etat de trois Papes 1989, Les trois Romes 1991, Martyrs et confesseurs de l'Eglise catholique en Russie communiste 1917–1980 d'après les archives du KGB 1998. *Leisure interests:* old books, stamps. *Address:* Le Relars, B.P. 113, 83510 Lorgues, France. *Telephone:* (4) 98-10-10-40.

WENNING, Werner; German business executive; b. 21 Oct. 1946, Leverkusen-Opladen; m.; two d.; joined Bayer AG, Leverkusen 1966, Commercial Trainee, mem. staff Corp. Auditing Dept, Man. Finance and Accounting Dept Bayer Industrial SA, Lima, Peru 1970–75, Man. Dir and Admin. Head 1978–83, Head Staff Dept Health Care Sector, Leverkusen 1983–86, Head Marketing Thermoplastics, Plastics Business Group 1986, Head Worldwide Marketing Operations 1987–91, seconded to Treuhandanstalt privatization agency, Berlin 1991–92, Man. Dir Bayer Hispania Industrial SA, Sr Bayer Rep. Spain 1992–96, Head Corp. Planning and Controlling, Leverkusen 1996–97, mem. Bd of Man. Bayer AG 1997–2002, Chair. Bd Cttee for Finance, mem. Bd Cttees. for Corp. Co-ordination and for Human Resources, Rep. Cen. and S. America, Africa and Middle East regions 1997–2002, Chair. Bd of Man. 2002–; mem. Supervisory Bd Dresdner Bank Latinamerika AG, Gerling-Konzern Versicherungs-Beteiligungs AG, Rheinhyp Rheinische Hypothekenbank AG; Vice-Pres. Asscn of the German Chemical Industry. *Address:* Bayer AG, 51368 Leverkusen, Germany (Office). *Telephone:* (214) 301 (Office). *Fax:* (214) 3058923 (Office). *Website:* www.bayer.com (Office).

WENSLEY, Penelope Anne, AO, BA; Australian diplomatist; b. 18 Oct. 1946, Toowoomba; m. Dr Stuart McCosker 1974; two d.; ed Univ. of Queensland; diplomatic service 1968–, Paris 1969–72, Mexico City 1975–77, Wellington, NZ 1982–85, Consul Gen. Hong Kong 1986–88; Head Int. Orgs. Div., Dept of Foreign Affairs and Trade 1991–92, Perm. Rep. to UN, Geneva 1993–95, also Amb. for Environment, UN 1992–95, Head N Asia Div. 1996–97; Perm. Rep. to UN, New York 1997–2002; Sr Adviser Australian del. to UN Conf. on Environment and Devt 1992; Vice-Pres. World Conf. on Human Rights, Vienna 1993–; Vice-Chair. UN Climate Change Convention Negotiations 1993–96; Coordinator Western Group Negotiations on UN Conventions on Biodiversity and Desertification 1994–96; Chair. Preparatory Process UN Conf. for the Sustainable Devt of Small Island Developing States 1993–94; Chair. Int. Coral Reef Initiative Conf. 1995; Vice-Chair. UN Inst. for Training and Research; mem. WHO High Level Advisory Council on Health and the Environment; Chair. UN Gen. Ass. Fifth Cttee (Admin. and Budgetary) 1999; Co-Chair. Preparatory Process for UN Gen. Ass. Special Session on HIV/AIDS 2001; High Commr to India 2002–; Amb. to Bhutan 2002–; Patron UN Youth Asscn of Australia; Fellow Women's Coll., Univ. of Queensland; Adjunct. Prof. Univ. of Queensland 2000; Hon. PhD, Alumnus of the Year (Univ. of Queensland) 1994. *Leisure interests:* music, theatre, reading, tennis, bush-walking. *Address:* Australian High Commission, 1/50-G Shanti Path, Chanakyapuri, New Delhi 110 021, India (Office). *Telephone:* (11) 26888223 (Office). *Fax:* (11) 26885199 (Office). *E-mail:* penny.wensley@dfat.gov.au (Office). *Website:* www.ausgovindia.com (Office).

WENT, David, BA, LLB, BL; Irish business executive; b. 25 March 1947, Dublin; s. of Arthur Went and Phyllis Went (née Howell); m. Mary Christine Milligan 1972; one s. one d.; ed Trinity Coll. Dublin; Barrister-at-Law, King's Inns, Dublin; grad. trainee, Citibank, Dublin 1970, Gen. Man. 1975, Gen. Man., Jeddah 1975–76; Dir Ulster Investment Bank 1976, Chief Exec. 1982, Deputy Chief Exec. Ulster Bank Belfast 1987, Chief Exec. 1988–94; CEO Coutts & Co. Group 1994–97; CEO Irish Life Assurance PLC 1998–; Group CEO Irish Life and Permanent PLC 1999–; Brook Scholar, King's Inns 1970; Paul Prize, Trinity Coll. 1969. *Leisure interests:* tennis, reading. *Address:* Irish Life & Permanent PLC, Lower Abbey Street, Dublin, Ireland. *Telephone:* (1) 7042717.

WERGER, Marinus Johannes Antonius, PhD; Netherlands professor of plant ecology and vegetation science; b. 3 May 1944, Enschede; s. of Johannes G. Werger and Gezina M. Zwerink; m. Karin E. Klein 1968; one d.; ed Jacobus Coll. Enschede and Utrecht, Groningen and Nijmegen Univs; professional research officer, Botanical Research Inst. Pretoria, S Africa 1968–73; Asst Prof., Assoc. Prof. Nijmegen Univ. 1974–79; Prof. of Plant Ecology and Vegetation Science, Utrecht Univ. 1979–, Dean, Faculty of Biology 1990–93; Consultant Prof. SW China Univ. Beibei 1984–; Visiting Prof. Univ. of Tokyo 1985; mem. Royal Netherlands Acad.; Mid-America State Univs. Asscn Award 1986. *Publications:* Biogeography and Ecology of Southern Africa (2 Vols) 1978, The Study of Vegetation 1979, Man's Impact on Vegetation 1983,

Plant Form and Vegetation Structure 1988, Tropical Rain Forest Ecosystems 1989. *Leisure interests:* history, travel, cooking. *Address:* Faculty of Biology, Universiteit Utrecht, POB 80084, 3508 TB Utrecht (Office); Nieuwe Gracht 145, 3512 LL Utrecht, Netherlands (Home). *Telephone:* (30) 2536700 (Office); (30) 311969 (Home).

WERLEIGH, Claudette; Haitian politician and social worker; b. 26 Sept. 1946, Cap-Haitien; m. Georges Werleigh; two d.; worked for Caritas (Catholic aid org.) 1976–87; Minister of Social Affairs March–Aug. 1990, of Foreign Affairs 1993–95; Prime Minister of Haiti 1995–96; Rep. to OAS summit 1998; Dir of Conflict Transformation Programmes, Life and Peace Inst., Uppsala, Sweden; fmr Vice-Pres. Pax Christi Int.; fmr bd mem. Forum on Early Warning and Early Response (FEWER), London, UK. *Address:* The Life & Peace Institute, POB 1520, SE-751, Uppsala, Sweden. *Telephone:* (18) 169775 (Office). *Fax:* (18) 693059 (Office). *E-mail:* claudette.werleigh@life-peace.org (Office). *Website:* www.life-peace.org (Office); www.fewer.org.

WERNER, Helmut; German business executive; b. 2 Sept. 1936, Cologne; m. Erika Werner; one s. one d.; ed business studies in Cologne; various man. posts with Englebert & Co. GmbH, Aachen 1961–78, Man. Dir for marketing, mfg and devt, Europe 1978; mem. Exec. Bd Continental Gummi-Werke AG 1979, Chair. 1983–87; mem. Exec. Bd Daimler-Benz AG 1987–; Chair. Bd of Man. Mercedes-Benz AG 1993–97; Chair Supervisory Bd EXPO 2000 Hannover GmbH 1994–, Metallgesellschaft AG 1998–. *Address:* Metallgesellschaft AG, Bockenheimer Landstrasse 73–74, 60325 Frankfurt am Main, Germany (Office).

WERNER, Karl Ferdinand, DPhil; German historian (retd.); b. 21 Feb. 1924, Neunkirchen; s. of Karl Werner and Johanna Kloepfer; m. Brigitte Hermann 1950; one d.; ed schools in Saarbrücken and Dresden and Univs. of Heidelberg and Paris; Asst Prof. of Medieval History, Univ. of Heidelberg 1961–65; Prof. of Medieval History, Univ. of Mannheim 1965–68, Hon. Prof. 1968–; Dir Inst. Historique Allemand, Paris 1968–89; mem. Inst. de France 1992–; Corresp. mem. Munich and Dijon acads., Soc. des Antiquaires, France; Dr. hc (Sorbonne, Orléans); Prix Courcel, Acad. des Sciences morales et Politiques (France) 1985, Prix Maurice Baumont, Acad. des Sciences et Politiques 1998; Médaille d'Argent, CNRS (France) 1989; Commdr Ordre des Arts et des Lettres; Grosses Bundesverdienstkreuz. *Publications:* Untersuchungen zur Frühzeit des französischen Fürstentums 9–10 Jh. 1960, NS-Geschichtsbild 1967, Kingdom and Principality in Twelfth Century France 1978, Structures politiques du Monde Franc 1979, L'histoire médiévale et les ordinateurs 1981, Vom Frankenreich zur Entfaltung Deutschlands und Frankreichs 1984, Les origines 1984, (German version Ursprünge Frankreichs 1989), Hof, Kultur und Politik im 19. Jahrhundert 1985, Volk, Nation (in Gesch. Grundbegriffe Vol. 7) 1992, Karl d. Gr. oder Charlemagne? 1995, Marc Bloch 1995, Naissance de la noblesse en Europe 1998, Einheit der Geschichte. Studien zur Historiographie 1999. *Leisure interests:* music, chess. *Address:* Karl Theodor Strasse 30, 83700 Rottach-Egern, Germany. *Telephone:* (8022) 65840. *Fax:* (8022) 670181.

WERTENBAKER, Timberlake, FRSL; British playwright; m. John Man; one d.; Resident Playwright, Royal Court Theatre 1984–85; Dr hc (Open Univ.); Plays and Players Most Promising Playwright (for The Grace of Mary Traverse) 1985, Evening Standard Most Promising Playwright, Olivier Play of the Year (for Our Country's Good) 1988, Eileen Anderson Cen. Drama Award (for The Love of the Nightingale) 1989, Critics' Circle Best West End Play 1991, Writers' Guild Best West End Play, Susan Smith Blackburn Award (for Three Birds Alighting on a Field) 1992, Mrs Giles Whiting Award (for gen. body of work) 1989. *Plays include:* (for the Soho-Poly): Case to Answer 1980; (for the Women's Theatre Group): New Anatomies 1982; (for the Royal Court): Abel's Sister 1984, The Grace of Mary Traverse 1985, Our Country's Good 1988, Three Birds Alighting on a Field 1991, Credible Witness 2001; (for Out of Joint): The Break of Day 1995; (for RSC): The Love of the Nightingale 1988; (for Hampstead Theatre): After Darwin 1998; (for Birmingham Rep.): The Ash Girl 2000; (for RSC): trans. Arianne Mnouchkine's Mephisto, trans. Sophocles' Thebans; (for San Francisco ACT): trans. Euripides' Hecuba; (for Peter Hall Co): trans. Eduardo de Filippo's Filumena 1998, Anouilh's Wild Orchids (Chichester) 2002; other trans. include Successful Strategies, False Admissions, La Dispute (Marivaux), Come tu mi vuoi (Pirandello), Pelleas and Mélisande (Maeterlinck). *Radio includes:* Credible Witness, Dianeira (trans. and adaptation Euripides' Hecuba). *Television:* Belle and the Beast (BBC). *Films:* The Children (Channel 4), Do Not Disturb (BBC TV). *Publications:* Timberlake Wertenbaker: Plays 1996, The Break of Day 1996, After Darwin 1999, Filumena 1999, The Ash Girl 2000, Credible Witness 2001, Timberlake Wertenbaker: Plays 2 2002. *Leisure interest:* mountains. *Address:* c/o Casarotto Ramsay, National House, 60–66 Wardour Street, London, W1V 4ND, England.

WERTMULLER, Lina; Italian film director; b. (Arcangela Felice Assunta Wertmuller von Elgg), 14 Aug. 1928, Rome; m. Enrico Job; ed Rome Theatre Acad.; toured Europe with a puppet show after graduating; worked in theatre for ten years as actress, director and playwright. *Films as director and screenwriter:* I Basilischi (The Lizards) 1963, Questa Volta parliamo di Uomini (Let's Talk About Men) 1965, Rita la zanzara (Rita the Mosquito) 1966, Non stuzzicate la zanzara (Don't Sting the Mosquito) 1967, Mimi Metallurgio Ferito nell'Onore (The Seduction of Mimi) 1972, Film d'amore e d'anarchia (Love and Anarchy) 1973, Tutto a Posto e Niente in Ordine (All Screwed Up), Travolti da un Insolito Destino nell'Azzurro Mare d'Agosto (Swept Away) 1974, Pasqualino Settebellezze (Seven Beauties) 1976, The End of the World in our Usual Bed in a Night Full of Rain, Shimmy Lagano Tarantelle e Vino 1978, Revenge 1979, Summer Night, On a Moonlit Night, Saturday, Sunday, Monday, Ciao, Professore! *Address:* Piazza Clotilde 5, 00196 Rome, Italy.

WESKER, Arnold, FRSL; British playwright and director; b. 24 May 1932, Stepney, London; s. of Joseph Wesker and Leah Wesker (née Perlmutter); m. Doreen (Dusty) Cecile Bicker 1958; two s. one d.; ed mixed elementary schools and Upton House Central School, Hackney, London; left school 1948, worked as furniture maker's apprentice, carpenter's mate, bookseller's asst; RAF 1950–52 (ran drama group); plumber's mate, road labourer, farm labourer, seed sorter, kitchen porter and pastry-cook; studied 9 months, London School of Film Technique; Dir Centre 42, 1961–70; Chair. British Cen. of Int. Theatre Inst. 1978–82; Pres. Int. Cttee of Playwrights 1979–83; Arts Council Bursary 1959; Hon. Fellow Queen Mary Coll. London 1995; Hon. DLitt (Univ. of E Anglia) 1989; Hon. DHumLitt (Denison Univ., Ohio) 1997; Evening Standard Award for Most Promising Playwright (for Roots) 1959, Encyclopaedia Britannica Competition, 3rd Prize 1961 (for The Kitchen), Premio Marzotto Drama Prize (for Their Very Own and Golden City) 1964, Gold Medal, Premios el Espectador y la Critica (for The Kitchen) 1973, (for Chicken Soup with Barley) 1979, The Goldie Award (for Roots) 1986. *Film scripts:* The Wesker Trilogy 1979, Lady Othello 1980, Homage to Catalonia (from George Orwell's autobiog.) 1991, Maudie (from Doris Lessing's novel Diary of a Good Neighbour) 1995. *Opera libretto:* Caritas 1988 (music by Robert Saxton). *Plays:* The Kitchen, Royal Court Theatre 1959, 1961, 1994, Chicken Soup with Barley, Roots, I'm Talking about Jerusalem (Trilogy), Belgrade Theatre, Coventry 1958–60, Royal Court Theatre 1960, Chips with Everything, Royal Court 1962, Vaudeville 1962, Broadway 1963, The Four Seasons, Belgrade Theatre and Saville 1965, Their Very Own and Golden City, Brussels and Royal Court 1966, The Friends (Stockholm and London) 1970, The Old Ones, Royal Court 1972, The Wedding Feast, Stockholm 1974, Leeds 1977, The Journalists, Coventry 1977, Germany 1981, The Merchant (later entitled Shylock), Stockholm and Aarthus 1976, Broadway 1977, Birmingham 1978, Love Letters on Blue Paper, Nat. Theatre 1978, Fatlips 1978, Caritas, Nat. Theatre 1981, Sullied Hand 1981, Edin. Festival and Finnish TV 1984, Four Portraits, Tokyo 1982, Edin. Festival 1984, Annie Wobbler, Birmingham 1983, Fortune Theatre 1984, New York 1986, One More Ride on the Merry-Go-Round, Leicester 1985, Yardsale, Edin. Festival and Stratford-on-Avon 1985, When God Wanted a Son 1986, Whatever Happened to Betty Lemon, Yardsale, London 1987, Little Old Lady, Sweden 1988, The Mistress 1988, Beorhtel's Hill, Towngate, Basildon 1989, Three Women Talking (now Men Die Women Survive) 1990, Chicago 1992, Letters to a Daughter 1990, Blood Libel 1991, Wild Spring 1992, Tokyo 1994, Denial, Bristol Old Vic 2000, Groupie 2001 (based on radio play), Longitude 2002 (adaptation of book by Dava Sobel). *Own plays directed:* The Four Seasons, Cuba 1968, world première of The Friends at Stadsteatern, Stockholm 1970, London 1970, The Old Ones, Munich, Their Very Own and Golden City, Aarhus 1974, Love Letters on Blue Paper, Nat. Theatre 1978, Oslo 1980, Annie Wobbler, Birmingham 1983, London 1984, Yardsale and Whatever Happened to Betty Lemon, London 1987, Shylock (workshop production), London 1989, The Kitchen, Univ. of Wis. 1990, The Mistress, Rome 1991, The Wedding Feast, Denison Univ., Ohio 1995, Letter to a Daughter, Edin. Festival 1998; also Dir Osborne's The Entertainer, Theatre Clwyd 1983, The Merry Wives of Windsor, Oslo 1989. *Radio includes:* Bluey (Cologne Radio) 1985, (BBC) 1985, Groupie (commissioned by BBC) 2001. *Adaptations for TV:* Menace 1961, Thieves in the Night (Arthur Koestler) 1984–85, Diary of a Good Neighbour (Doris Lessing) 1989, Phoenix Phoenix Burning Bright (from own story, The Visit) 1992, Barabbas 2000. *Publications:* plays: The Kitchen 1957, Chicken Soup with Barley 1958, Roots 1959, I'm Talking About Jerusalem 1960, Chips with Everything 1962, The Four Seasons 1965, Their Very Own and Golden City 1966, The Old Ones 1970, The Friends 1970, The Journalists 1972, The Wedding Feast 1974, Shylock (previously The Merchant) 1976, Love Letters on Blue Paper (TV play) 1976, (stage play) 1977, One More Ride on the Merry-Go-Round 1978, Fatlips 1980, Caritas 1980, Annie Wobbler 1982, Four Portraits—of Mothers 1982, Yardsale 1983, Cinders 1983, Bluey 1984, Whatever Happened to Betty Lemon 1986, When God Wanted a Son 1986, Badenheim 1939 1987, Shoeshine & Little Old Lady 1987, Lady Othello 1987, Beorhtel's Hill 1988, The Mistress 1988, Three Women Talking 1990, Letter to a Daughter 1990, Blood Libel 1991, Wild Spring 1992, Break My Heart 1997; essays, stories, etc.: Fears of Fragmentation 1971, Six Sundays in January 1971, Love Letters on Blue Paper 1974, Journey into Journalism 1977, Said the Old Man to the Young Man 1978, Distinctions 1985, As Much As I Dare (autobiog.) 1994, The Birth of Shylock and the Death of Zero Mostel (non-fiction) 1997, The King's Daughters 1998, The Wesker Trilogy 2001, One Woman Plays 2001. *Leisure interest:* listening to music. *Address:* Hay on Wye, Hereford, HR3 5RJ, England. *Telephone:* (1497) 820473 (Home). *Fax:* (1497) 821005 (Home). *E-mail:* wesker@compuserve.com (Home). *Website:* www.arnoldwesker.com (Home).

WESSELMANN, Tom (Slim Stealingworth), BA; American artist; b. 23 Feb. 1931, Cincinnati, Ohio; s. of Edwin W. Wesselmann and Grace D. Wesselmann; m. 2nd Claire Selley 1963; one s. two d.; ed Hiram Coll., Ohio, Univ. of Cincinnati, Art Acad. of Cincinnati and Cooper Union, NY; taught art New York City Jr and Sr High Schools 1959–62. *Exhibitions:* more than 60 one-man exhbns. 1961–, including Sidney Janis Gallery, New York (19 exhbns.) and many other galleries in the USA, Düsseldorf, Paris, Montreal, Bogotá,

London, Tokyo, etc.; touring graphics and multiples retrospective in US galleries and Tokyo 1989–91; retrospective exhbn painting and sculpture touring Japan, Germany, Belgium, Netherlands, France and Spain 1993–96. *Publications:* Wesselmann (by Slim Stealingworth) 1980. *Leisure interest:* writing country music. *Address:* 7A 115 East 9th Street, New York, NY 10003, USA. *Telephone:* (212) 228-3930.

WESSELS, Wolfgang, Dr rer. pol; German academic; b. 19 Jan. 1948, Cologne; s. of Theodor Wessels and Emma Wessels; m. Aysin Wessels 1973; two d.; Dir Institut für Europäische Politik, Bonn 1973–94; Dir Admin. Studies and Prof., Coll. of Europe, Bruges, Belgium 1980–96; Jean Monnet Prof., Univ. of Cologne 1994–. *Publications include:* The European Council, Decision-Making in European Politics (with Simon Bulmer) 1987; (Co-Ed.) Die Europäische Politische Zusammenarbeit in den achtziger Jahren—Eine gemeinsame Aussenpolitik für Westeuropa? 1989, Jahrbuch der Europäischen Integration 1980–, Europa vom A–Z. Taschenbuch der Europäischen Integration 1994, 1995, Foreign Policy of the European Union. From EPC to CFSP and Beyond (jtly.) 1997, Die Öffnung des Staates. Modelle und Wirklichkeit grenzüberschreitender Verwaltungspraxis 2000; papers and articles on European integration. *Address:* Forschungsinstitut für Politische Wissenschaft und Europäische Fragen, Universität zu Cologne, Gottfried-Keller-Strasse 6, 50931 Cologne, Germany. *Telephone:* (221) 4704131. *Fax:* (221) 9402542. *E-mail:* wessels@uni-koeln.de (Office). *Website:* www.uni-koeln.de./wiso-fak/powi/wessels/index.html (Office).

WESSEX, HRH The Earl of Wessex; Viscount Severn, Prince Edward Antony Richard Louis, CVO, MA; b. 10 March 1964; s. of Queen Elizabeth II (q.v.) and Prince Philip, The Duke of Edinburgh; m. Sophie Rhys-Jones (now HRH The Countess of Wessex) 1999; ed Heatherdown Prep. School, Gordonstoun School, Jesus Coll. Cambridge; fmrly Second Lt Royal Marines; worked in theatre production with Really Useful Group, Theatre Div.; f. Ardent Productions Ltd 1993; opened Commonwealth Games, Auckland 1990 and Malaysia 1998, Pres. Commonwealth Games Fed.; UK and Int. Trustee, The Duke of Edinburgh's Award; Chair. Int. Council, The Duke of Edinburgh's Award Int. Asscn; Patron Nat. Youth Music Theatre, Nat. Youth Theatre, Royal Exchange Theatre Co., Manchester, Haddo Arts Trust, Nat. Youth Orchestras of Scotland, City of Birmingham Symphony Orchestra and Chorus, London Mozart Players, Scottish Badminton, Globe Theatre, Saskatchewan, Canada, Friends of Wanganui Opera House, New Zealand, British Ski and Snowboard Fed. *Publication:* Crown and Country 1999. *Leisure interests:* the arts, horse-riding, sailing, skiing, badminton, Real Tennis. *Address:* Buckingham Palace, London, SW1A 1AA; Bagshot Park, Bagshot, Surrey, GU19 5PJ, England.

WEST, Francis James, PhD, FRHistS, FAHA; British/Australian professor of history; b. 26 June 1927, E Yorks.; s. of George H. West and Florence C. Selby; m. 1st Katharine White 1963 (divorced 1976); one d.; m. 2nd Margaret Rose 1982; ed Hymers Coll. E Yorks, Univ. of Leeds and Trinity Coll. Cambridge; Fellow, ANU 1952–55; Sr Lecturer, Victoria Univ. of Wellington 1955–59; Professorial Fellow, Inst. of Advanced Studies, ANU 1960–73; Dean of Arts and Social Studies, Univ. of Buckingham 1973–75; Prof. of History and Govt and Dean of Social Sciences, Deakin Univ. Geelong 1976–90, Pro Vice-Chancellor (Research) 1986–90, Prof. Emer. 1990–; Overseas Fellow, Churchill Coll. Cambridge 1981–82, 1984–85; mem. Australian Humanities Research Council 1966; Visiting Lecturer Australian Jt Services Staff Coll. 1967–78, Command and Staff Coll. 1978–94, Ed. Advisory Cttee, Dept of Foreign Affairs 1984–94; Carnegie Commonwealth Award 1965, "Thank Offering to Britain" Fellow, British Acad. 1971. *Publications:* Political Advancement in the South Pacific 1961, The Justiciarship in England 1966, Hubert Murray: Australian Pro Consul 1968, Biography as History 1973, University House 1979, Gilbert Murray: A Life 1984, From Alamein to Scarlet Beach 1989. *Leisure interests:* music, occasional journalism and broadcasting. *Address:* Churchill College, Cambridge, CB3 0DS, England. *Telephone:* (1223) 354162 (Home).

WEST, John C., BA, LLB; American fmr state governor, lawyer and diplomatist; b. 27 Aug. 1922, Camden, SC; s. of the late Shelton J. West and of Mattie (Ratterree) West; m. Lois Rhame 1942; two s. one d.; ed The Citadel, SC, Univ. of SC; US Army, rank of Maj. 1942–46; elected to SC Senate 1954, re-elected 1958, 1962; Lt-Gov. of SC 1966–70; Gov. of SC 1971–75; Amb. to Saudi Arabia 1977–81; with law firm John C. West, P.A. and Sr Partner West & West, P.A., Hilton Head Is. and Camden 1981–88; Distinguished Prof. of Middle East Studies, Univ. of South Carolina 1981–; of Counsel McNair Law Firm 1988–92, Bethea, Jordan & Griffin 1993–; seven hon. degrees; Army Commendation Medal, Freedom Award, SC Chamber of Commerce; Kt Commdr Order of Merit, Fed. Repub. of Germany. *Address:* PO Drawer 13, Hilton Head Island, SC 29938, USA. *Telephone:* (843) 785-4300. *Fax:* (843) 785-5545.

WEST, Martin Litchfield, D.PHIL, DLitt, FBA; British scholar; b. 23 Sept. 1937, London; s. of the late Maurice Charles West and Catherine Baker West (née Stainthorpe); m. Stephanie Roberta Pickard 1960; one s. one d.; ed St Paul's School, London and Balliol Coll., Oxford; Woodhouse Jr Research Fellow, St John's Coll., Oxford 1960–63; Fellow and Praelector in Classics, Univ. Coll., Oxford 1963–74; Prof. of Greek, Univ. of London (Bedford Coll., now Royal Holloway and Bedford New Coll.) 1974–91; Sr Research Fellow, All Souls Coll., Oxford; corresp. mem. Akad. der Wissenschaften, Göttingen; mem. Acad. Europaea, London; Hon. Fellow, Univ. Coll. Oxford 2001; Balzan

Prize for Classical Antiquity 2000, British Acad. Kenyon Medal for Classical Studies 2002. *Publications:* Hesiod, Theogony (ed.) 1966, Fragmenta Hesiodea (ed. with R. Merkelbach) 1967, Early Greek Philosophy and the Orient 1971, Sing Me, Goddess 1971, Iambi et Elegi Graeci (ed.) 1971–72 (revised Edn 1989–92), Textual Criticism and Editorial Technique 1973, Studies in Greek Elegy and Iambus 1974, Hesiod, Works and Days (ed.) 1978, Theognidis et Phocylidis fragmenta 1978, Delectus ex Iambis et Elegis Graecis 1980, Greek Metre 1982, The Orphic Poems 1983, Carmina Anacreontea 1984, The Hesiodic Catalogue of Women 1985, Introduction to Greek Metre 1987, Euripides Orestes (ed.) 1987, Hesiod (trans.) 1988, Aeschyli Tragoediae 1990, Studies in Aeschylus 1990, Ancient Greek Music 1992, Greek Lyric Poetry (trans.) 1993, The East Face of Helicon 1997 (Runciman Prize 1998), Homeri Ilias (ed.) Vol. I 1998, Vol. II 2000, Studies in the Text and Transmission of the Iliad 2001, Documents of Ancient Greek Music (with E. Pöhlmann) 2001, Homeric Hymns, Homeric Apocrypha, Lives of Homer 2003, Greek Epic Fragments 2003. *Leisure interest:* music. *Address:* All Souls College, Oxford, OX1 4AL; 42 Portland Road, Oxford, OX2 7EY, England (Home). *Telephone:* (1865) 279289 (College).

WEST, Paul, MA; American author; b. 23 Feb. 1930, Eckington, Derbyshire, England; s. of Alfred West and Mildred Noden; ed Oxford and Columbia Univs; arrived USA 1961, became naturalized 1971; served with RAF 1954–57; Asst Prof. of English Memorial Univ., Newfoundland 1957–58, Assoc. Prof. 1958–60; contrib. Washington Post, New York Times 1962–95, also contributes to Harper's and GQ magazines, Paris Review; mem. of staff Pa State Univ. 1962–, Prof. of English and Comparative Literature 1968–1995, Prof. Emer. 1995–; Crawshaw Prof. Colgate Univ. 1972; Melvin Hill Distinguished Visiting Prof. Hobart and William Smith Colls. 1973; Distinguished Writer-in-Residence Wichita State Univ. 1982; Writer-in-Residence Univ. of Arizona 1984; Visiting Prof. of English Cornell Univ. 1986, Brown Univ. 1992; Guggenheim Fellow 1962–63; Nat. Endowment for Arts Creative Writing Fellow 1979, 1984; mem. Author's Guild; Aga Khan Fiction Prize 1973, Hazlett Memorial Award for Excellence in Arts (Literature) 1981, Literature Award, American Acad. and Inst. of Arts and Letters 1985, Pushcart Prize 1987, 1991, Best American Essays Award 1990, Grand Prix Halpérine Kaminsky Award 1992, Lannan Fiction Award 1993, Teaching Award NE Asscn of Grad. Schools 1994, Art of Fact Prize, State Univ. of NY 2000; Outstanding Achievement Medal, Pa State Univ. 1991, Chevalier Ordre Arts et Lettres. *Publications include:* Byron and the Spoiler's Art 1960, I, Said the Sparrow 1963, The Snow Leopard 1965, Tenement of Clay 1965, The Wine of Absurdity 1966, I'm Expecting to Live Quite Soon 1970, Words for a Deaf Daughter 1970, Caliban's Filibuster 1971, Bela Lugosi's White Christmas 1972, Colonel Mint 1973, Gala 1976, The Very Rich Hours of Count von Stauffenberg 1980, Out of My Depths: A Swimmer in the Universe and Other Fictions 1988, The Place in Flowers Where Pollen Rests 1988, Lord Byron's Doctor 1989, Portable People, The Women of Whitechapel and Jack the Ripper 1991, James Ensor 1991, Love's Mansion 1992, A Stroke of Genius 1995, Sporting with Amaryllis 1996, Terrestrials 1997, Life with Swan 1999, O.K.: The Corral 2000, The Earps 2000, Doc Holliday 2000, The Dry Danube: A Hitler Forgery 2000, The Secret Lives of Words 2000, A Fifth of November 2001, Master Class 2001, New Portable People 2001. *Leisure interests:* swimming, astronomy, classical music, cricket, films. *Address:* c/o Elaine Markson Agency, 44 Greenwich Avenue, Floor 3, New York, NY 10011, USA. *Telephone:* (212) 243-8480. *Fax:* (607) 257-0631.

WEST, Richard G., MA, ScD, FRS; British professor of botany; b. 31 May 1926, Hendon, Middx; m. 1st Janet Abram 1958; one s.; m. 2nd Hazel Gristwood 1973 (died 1997); two d.; ed King's School, Canterbury and Univ. of Cambridge; Fellow, Clare Coll., Cambridge 1954–; lecturer in Botany, Univ. of Cambridge 1960–68, Reader in Quaternary Research 1968–74, Prof. of Palaeoecology 1974–77, Prof. of Botany and Head, Dept of Botany 1977–91, Dir Sub-Dept of Quaternary Research 1966–87; Hon. mem. Royal Belgian Acad.; Foreign mem. Finnish Acad. of Sciences and Letters 1999; Hon. MRIA; Bigsby Medal, Geological Soc. 1968, Lyell Medal, Geological Soc. 1988. *Publications:* Pleistocene Geology and Biology 1968, The Ice Age in Britain (jtly.) 1972, The Pre-glacial Pleistocene of the Norfolk and Suffolk Coasts 1980, Pleistocene Palaeoecology of Central Norfolk 1991, Plant Life in the Quaternary Cold Stages 2000. *Leisure interest:* sailing. *Address:* Clare College, Cambridge; 3A Woollards Lane, Great Shelford, Cambridge, CB2 5LZ, England (Home). *Telephone:* (1223) 842578 (Home).

WEST, Stephen Craig, PhD, FRS, FMedSci; British scientist; b. 11 April 1952, Hull; s. of Joseph West and Louisa West; m. Phyllis Fraenza 1985; ed Univs of Newcastle and Yale; research scientist Yale Univ. 1983–85; Sr Scientist Imperial Cancer Research Fund 1985–89, Prin. Scientist 1989–; Hon. Prof. Univ. Coll. London 1997–; mem. European Molecular Biology Org. 1995–. *Publications:* over 180 research articles. *Leisure interests:* sport, music. *Address:* Cancer Research UK, London Research Institute, Clare Hall Laboratories, South Mimms, Herts., EN6 3LD (Office); Meadowbank, Riverside Avenue, Broxbourne, Herts., EN10 6RA, England (Home). *Telephone:* (20) 7269-3868 (Office); (1992) 470147 (Home). *Fax:* (20) 7269-3811 (Office). *E-mail:* stephen.west@cancer.org.uk (Office).

WEST, Timothy Lancaster, CBE, FRSA; British actor and director; b. 20 Oct. 1934, Bradford, Yorks.; s. of the late H. Lockwood West and Olive Carleton-Crowe; m. 1st Jacqueline Boyer 1956 (dissolved); one d.; m. 2nd Prunella Scales (q.v.) 1963; two s.; ed John Lyon School, Harrow and Regent Street Polytechnic; repertory seasons, Wimbledon, Hull, Salisbury, Northampton

1956–60; mem. Royal Shakespeare and Prospect Theatre Cos. 1962–79; Artistic Dir, Old Vic 1980–81; Dir-in-Residence Univ. of WA 1982; Assoc. Dir Bristol Old Vic. –1991; Pres. London Acad. of Music and Dramatic Art, Soc. for Theatre Research; Hon. DLitt (E Anglia, W of England); Hon. DUniv (Bradford); Hon. LLD (Westminster). *Stage appearances:* (in London) Caught Napping 1959, Galileo 1960, Gentle Jack 1963, The Trigon 1963, The Italian Girl 1968, Abelard and Heloise 1970, Exiles 1970, The Critic as Artist 1971, The Houseboy 1973, A Month in the Country 1974, A Room with a View 1975, Laughter 1978, The Homecoming 1978, Beecham 1980, Master Class 1984, The War at Home 1984, When We are Married 1986, The Sneeze 1988, Long Day's Journey into Night 1991, It's Ralph 1991, Twelve Angry Men 1996, Henry IV Parts 1 and 2 1996, King Lear 1997, The Birthday Party 1999, Luther 2001; numerous appearances with Prospect Theatre Co., Royal Shakespeare Co. and regional theatres. *Radio:* has appeared in more than 500 programmes since 1960. *TV appearances include:* The Monocled Mutineer, The Good Doctor Bodkin Adams, Harry's Kingdom, When We Are Married, Breakthrough at Reykjavik, Strife, A Shadow on the Sun, The Contractor, Blore MP, Survival of the Fittest, Why Lockerbie?, Framed, Smokescreen, Reith to the Nation, Eleven Men Against Eleven, Cuts, Place of the Dead, Midsomer Murders, Murder in Mind, Bedtime. *Film appearances include:* The Looking Glass War, Nicholas and Alexandra, The Day of the Jackal, The Devil's Advocate, The Thirty-Nine Steps, Oliver Twist, Cry Freedom, Ever After, Joan of Arc, 102 Dalmatians, The Fourth Angel, Villa des Roses, Iris, Beyond Borders. *Concerts:* with London Philharmonic Orchestra, Royal Philharmonic Orchestra, Britten Ensemble, Sinfonia 21 etc. *Publications:* I'm Here I Think, Where Are You? 1997, A Moment Towards the End of the Play 2001. *Leisure interests:* music, travel, inland waterways, old railways. *Address:* c/o Gavin Barker Associates, 2D Wimpole Street, London, W1M 7AA, England.

WESTBROOK, Roger, CMG, MA; British diplomatist (retd); b. 26 May 1941, Surrey; s. of Edward George Westbrook and Beatrice Minnie Marshall; ed Dulwich Coll. and Hertford Coll., Oxford; Foreign Office 1964; Asst Pvt. Sec. to the Chancellor of the Duchy of Lancaster 1965; held posts in Yaoundé 1967, Rio de Janeiro 1971, Brasília 1972; Private Sec. to Minister of State, FCO 1975; Head of Chancery, Lisbon 1977; Deputy Head, News Dept, FCO 1980, Deputy Head, Falkland Islands Dept 1982, Overseas Inspectorate 1984; High Commr, Brunei Darussalam 1986–91; Amb. to Zaire 1991–92; High Commr in Tanzania 1992–95; Amb. to Portugal 1995–99; British Commr-Gen. EXPO 98; Chair. Spencer House 2000–, Anglo-Portuguese Soc. 2000–. *Leisure interests:* doodling, sightseeing, theatre. *Address:* Spencer House, 27 St. James's Place, London, SW1A 1NR (Office); 33 Marsham Court, Marsham Street, London, SW1P 4JY, England (Home). *Telephone:* (20) 7514-1948 (Office).

WESTERBERG, Bengt, MED.KAND., FIL.KAND.; Swedish politician; b. 23 Aug. 1943; s. of the late Carl-Eric and of Barbro Westerberg; m. 2nd Marie Ehrling; one s., two d. from a previous marriage; ed Karolinska Inst., Univ. of Stockholm; joined Liberal Youth League 1965, held elected office at all levels, Chair. Exec. Cttee 1970–71; joined Liberal Party 1965, held municipal office in Södertälje, elected to Nat. Bd 1983, mem. Party Exec. 1983, Chair. 1984–95; Pres. Liberal Party 1993–95; Deputy Sec. to Commr for Greater Stockholm 1969, Sec. to Commr for Municipal Services 1970, Sec. to Stockholm County Council Traffic Commr 1971, Research Dir Traffic Cttee 1972, Adviser Govt Comm. on Traffic Policy 1975, Adviser Ministry of Labour 1976, Liberal Party's Coordination Office 1978; Under-Sec. Ministry of Industry 1978, Ministry of the Budget 1979–82; f. Foundation for a Market-Economy Alternative for Sweden (MAS) 1983; MP 1984–94; Minister of Social Affairs and Deputy Prime Minister 1991–94; Research and Devt Leader, Centre of Gender Studies, Univ. of Karlstad 1995–; Chair. Bd Telia AB 1995–, BTJ 1995–, Media Technology MT AB 1996–; Vice-Chair. Bd Riksbank (Cen. Bank of Sweden) 1994–; mem. Bd Morgondagen AB 1995–; Pres. Swedish Athletics Asscn 1995–, Swedish Foundation of Dyslexia 1995–.

WESTERFIELD, Putney, BA; American business executive; b. 9 Feb. 1930, New Haven, Conn.; s. of Ray Bert Westerfield and Beatrice Putney; m. Anne Montgomery 1954; two s. one d.; ed Choate School and Yale Univ.; Vice-Pres. and Co-f., Careers Inc. 1950–52; Man. SE Asia Operations, Swen Publs; service with Dept of State in Korea, Washington, Saigon 1953–59; Asst to Publr of Time 1957–59, Asst to Circulation Dir 1959–61, Circulation Dir 1961–66, Asst Publr 1966–68; Asst Publr of Life 1968–69; Publr of Fortune 1969–73; Pres. Chase World Information Corpn 1973–75; Vice-Pres. Boyden Assocs. Int. 1976–80, Sr Vice-Pres., Western Man. 1980–84, Pres. and CEO 1984–90, Man. Dir 1990–; Dir East Meets West Foundation 1991–; Chair. Bd Dirs. Upside Media Inc. *Leisure interests:* reading, music, tennis, swimming. *Address:* Boyden International, 275 Battery Street, Suite 420, San Francisco, CA 94111 (Office); 10 Green View Lane, Hillsborough, CA 94010, USA (Home). *Telephone:* (415) 981-7900. *Fax:* (415) 981-0644. *E-mail:* putneyw@ pacbel.net.

WESTHEIMER, Frank Henry, MA, PhD; American professor of chemistry; b. 15 Jan. 1912, Baltimore, Md; s. of Henry F. Westheimer and Carrie (Burgunder) Westheimer; m. Jeanne Friedman 1937; two d.; ed Dartmouth Coll. and Harvard Univ.; Nat. Research Fellow, Columbia Univ. 1935–36; Research Assoc., Instr., Asst Prof. of Chem., Univ. of Chicago 1936–44; Research Supervisor, NDRC Explosives Research Lab. 1944–45; Assoc. Prof. Dept of Chem., Univ. of Chicago 1946–48, Prof. 1948–54; Visiting Prof. of Chem. Harvard Univ. 1953–54, Prof. 1954–83, Morris Loeb Prof. of Chem.

Emer. 1983–; Visiting Prof., Univ. of Calif. (Berkeley) 1958, Boston Univ. 1984, Ohio State Univ. 1985, Univ. of Calif. (San Diego) 1986, 1988; mem. Pres.'s Science Advisory Cttee 1967–70; mem. American Acad. of Arts and Sciences, (Sec. 1985–90), NAS, American Philosophical Soc.; Foreign mem. Royal Soc.; seven hon. degrees; numerous awards and prizes including Willard Gibbs Medal, Ingold Medal, NAS Award in the Chemical Sciences, Nichols Medal, James Flack Norris Award, Richards Medal, Welch Award, Nat. Medal of Science, Paracelsus Medal (Swiss Chemical Soc.), Priestley Award (American Chemical Soc.), Repligen Award 1992, Nakanishi Prize 1997. *Publications:* Chemistry, Opportunities and Needs 1965; about 200 articles in scientific journals. *Address:* Department of Chemistry, Harvard University, 12 Oxford Street, Cambridge, MA 02138 (Office); 3 Berkeley Street, Cambridge, MA 02138, USA (Home). *E-mail:* westheimer@chemistry .harvard.edu (Office).

WESTMINSTER, 6th Duke, cr. 1874; **Gerald Cavendish Grosvenor,** OBE, TD, DL, FRSA; British landowner and company director; b. 22 Dec. 1951, Northern Ireland; s. of the late 5th Duke of Westminster and Hon. Viola Lyttelton; m. Natalia Phillips 1978; one s. three d.; ed Harrow School; succeeded to title 1979; served Queen's Own Yeomanry 1970–85, Col 1995–97, Deputy Commdr 143 W Midlands Brigade 1997–99; rank of Brig., TA HQ AG 2000–02; Dir Reserves Forces and Cadets 2002–; fmr Dir Grosvenor Estate Holdings (now Grosvenor Group Holdings), currently Chair.; Dir Claridges Hotel Ltd 1980–92, Marcher Sound Ltd 1982–97, Royal & Sun Alliance Group 1995–97, NW Business Leadership Team Ltd 1990–97; Pres. Arthritis Care 1987–, Chester Zoo, Game Conservancy Trust, Scope (fmrly The Spastics Soc.), British Limbless Ex-Servicemen's Asscn, Drug and Alcohol Foundation 1987–97, Hill Farmers' Initiative, Youth Sports Trust, Holstein Friesian Soc. and many other orgs.; Vice-Pres. Country Landowners Asscn, NSPCC; Chancellor Manchester Metropolitan Univ. (fmrly Manchester Polytechnic) 1993–2003; Patron Emeka Anyaoku Chair in Commonwealth Studies, The Prince's Trust (NW), Parents Against Drug Abuse, British Holstein Soc., Royal Fine Art Comm., Worcs. Co. Cricket Club; Gov. and Pres. Royal Agricultural Soc. of England; mem. cttee N American Advisory Group of British Overseas Trade Bd, Nat. Army Museum, Prince's Youth Business Trust, RICS Foundation 2000–; Trustee The Grosvenor Estate, TSB Foundation for England and Wales, Westminster Abbey Trust, Westminster Foundation, Westminster Housing Trust; Cubitt Memorial Trust, Falcon Trust, Habitat Research Trust, Royal Agricultural Soc. of the Commonwealth; Freeman of Chester, of London, of England; Fellow The Royal Agricultural Socs., Chartered Inst. of Marketing, Chartered Inst. of Bldg, Liverpool John Moores Univ.; mem. Royal Inst. of Chartered Surveyors; DL Co. of Cheshire; Hon. Col 7 Regt AAC 1993, Northumbrian Universities OTC, RMLY 2001, Col in Chief Royal Westminster Regt Vancouver; Hon. Fellow (Lancashire) 2001; Hon. LLD (Keele, Westminster Coll., Foulton, Mo., Liverpool); Hon. DLitt (Manchester Metropolitan Univ.), (Westminster) 1999, (Salford) 2000, Dr hc (Salford) 2000; KStJ. *Leisure interests:* shooting, fishing, scuba diving. *Address:* Eaton Hall, Eaton, Chester, Cheshire CH4 9EJ, England. *Telephone:* (1244) 680333.

WESTMINSTER, Archbishop of (see HE Cardinal Cormac Murphy-O'Connor).

WESTMORELAND, Gen. William Childs; American retd army officer; b. 26 March 1914, Spartanburg County, S. Carolina; s. of James R. Westmoreland and Eugenia Childs Westmoreland; m. Katherine S. Van Deusen 1947; one s. two d.; ed U.S. Mil. Acad.; U.S. Army 1936–72; Maj. Gen. 1956, Lt-Gen. 1963, Gen. 1964; Battery Officer, Oklahoma and Hawaii 1936–41; Commdg Officer, 34th Field Artillery Battalion 1942–44; Exec. Officer 9th Infantry Div. Artillery 1944, Chief of Staff 1944–45, Commdr 60th Infantry Regt, Germany 1945, 504th Parachute Infantry Regt, Fort Bragg 1946–47; Chief of Staff, 82nd Airborne Div. 1947–50; Instructor, Command and Gen. Staff Coll. and Army War Coll. 1950–52; Commdr 187th Airborne Regimental Combat Team, Korea and Japan 1952–53; Deputy Asst Chief of Staff G1, for Manpower Control, Dept of Army 1953–54, Sec. Gen. Staff 1955–58; Commdg Gen. 101st Airborne Div. and Fort Campbell, Kentucky 1958–60; Supt U.S. Mil. Acad., West Point 1960–63; Commdr 18th Airborne Corps, Fort Bragg 1963–64; Deputy Commdr U.S. Mil. Assistance Command Viet Nam 1964, Commdr 1964–68; Chief of Staff, U.S. Army, The Pentagon 1968–72; retd from army 1972; Man of the Year, Time Magazine 1966, S. Carolina Hall of Fame 1986; numerous awards from veteran and patriotic orgs.; numerous mil. decorations from foreign govts. *Publications:* Report on the War in Vietnam, A Soldier Reports and numerous articles in mil. publs and the press. *Address:* 1 Gadsden Way, CTG, Charleston, SC 29412, USA.

WESTON, Sir John (see Weston, Sir (Philip) John).

WESTON, John Pix, CBE, MA; British aerospace industry executive; b. 16 Aug. 1951, Kendal; s. of John Pix Weston and Ivy Weston (née Glover); m. Susan West 1974; one s. one d.; ed Kings School, Worcester and Trinity Hall, Cambridge; under-grad. apprentice British Aircraft Corpn 1970–74, various positions in Dynamics and Maths Services Div., later Marketing and Gen. Man. 1974–82, seconded to Ministry of Defence 1982–84, Man. Dir British Aerospace Military Aircraft Div. 1990–92, mem. Bd 1993–2002, CEO BAe (later BAE Systems following merger with Marconi Electric Systems) 1998–2002; mem. Dept of Trade and Industry (DTI) Council for Science and Tech.; mem. CBI Pres.'s Cttee, Chair. CBI Europe Cttee 2001–; Vice-Pres. Royal United Services Inst.; mem. Royal Coll. of Defence Studies Advisory Bd;

Council mem., European Assen of Aerospace Industries (AECMA), Soc. of British Aerospace Cos. (SBAC); Fellow, Royal Acad. of Eng, Royal Aeronautical Soc., Royal Soc. for the Encouragement of Arts, Mfg and Commerce; Freeman, City of London. *Leisure interests:* skiing, photography, mountain walking. *Address:* c/o BAE Systems PLC, Warwick House, Farnborough Aerospace Centre, Farnborough, Hants., GU14 6YU, England (Office).

WESTON, Sir Michael Charles Swift, KCMG, CVO, MA; British diplomatist (retd.); b. 4 Aug. 1937, Crowborough, Sussex; s. of the late Edward C. S. Weston and Kathleen M. Mockett; m. 1st Veronica A. Tickner 1959 (divorced 1990); two s. one d.; m. 2nd Christine J. Ferguson 1990; one s. one d.; ed Dover Coll. and St Catharine's Coll. Cambridge; joined HM Diplomatic Service 1961; Third Sec. Kuwait 1962; First Sec. Tehran 1968; UK mission, New York 1970; Counsellor, Jeddah 1977; Royal Coll. of Defence Studies 1980; Counsellor, Paris 1981, Cairo 1984; Head, S. European Dept FCO 1987–90; Amb. to Kuwait 1990–92; Leader UK del. to Conf. on Disarmament, Geneva 1992–97; mem. Special Immigration Appeals Comm. 1999–. *Leisure interests:* squash, tennis, walking. *Address:* c/o Foreign and Commonwealth Office, King Charles Street, London, SW1A 2AH; Beech Farm House, Beech Lane, Matfield, Kent, TN12 7HG, England (Home). *Telephone:* (1892) 824921 (Home). *Fax:* (1892) 824921 (Home).

WESTON, Sir (Philip) John, KCMG; British diplomatist and company director; b. 13 April 1938; s. of the late Philip G. Weston and Edith Ansell; m. Sally Ehlers 1967; two s. one d.; ed Sherborne School and Worcester Coll. Oxford; served Royal Marines 1956–58; entered HM Diplomatic Service 1962; Treasury Centre for Admin. Studies 1964; Chinese language student, Hong Kong 1964–66; Beijing 1967–68; Office of UK Perm. Rep. to EEC 1972–74; Asst Pvt. Sec. to Sec. of State for Foreign and Commonwealth Affairs 1974–76; Counsellor, Head of EEC Presidency Secr., FCO 1976–77; Visiting Fellow, All Souls Coll. Oxford 1977–78; Counsellor, Washington, DC 1978–81; Head, Defence Dept FCO 1981–84, Asst Under-Sec. of State 1984–85; Minister, Paris 1985–88; Deputy Sec. to Cabinet, Cabinet Office 1988–89; Deputy Under-Sec. of State, FCO 1989–90, Political Dir 1990–91; Amb. and Perm. Rep. to N Atlantic Council (NATO) 1992–95; Perm. Rep. to UN 1995–98; Dir (non-exec.) British Telecommunications 1998–2002, Rolls Royce 1998–; Hakluyt & Co. 2001–; Hon. Pres. Community Foundation Network (UK) 1998–; mem. Council Int. Inst. of Strategic Studies 2001–; Chair. Govs. Sherborne School 2002–; Gov. Ditchley Foundation 2000–; Trustee, Nat. Portrait Gallery; Hon. Fellow Worcester Coll. Oxford 2003; Order of Merit (with Star), Fed. Repub. of Germany. *Leisure interests:* poetry, fly-fishing, running, birds. *Address:* 13 Denbigh Gardens, Richmond, Surrey, TW10 6EN, England. *E-mail:* John.Weston@PJWeston.btinternet.com (Home).

WESTWOOD, Lee; British golfer; b. 24 April 1973, Worksop, Nottinghamshire; s. of John Westwood and Trish Westwood; m. Laurae Coltart 1999; one s.; England Boys, Youths and Srs. amateur teams 1989–93; won Peter McEvoy Trophy 1990, British Youth Championships 1993; turned professional 1993, won Volvo Scandinavian Masters 1996, 2000, Sumitomo Taiheiyo Masters 1996, 1997, 1998, Benson and Hedges Malaysian Open 1997, Volvo Masters 1997, Holden Australian Open 1997, McDermott-Freeport Classic 1998, Deutsche Bank SAP Open 1998, 2000, English Open 1998, Loch Lomond Invitation 1998, Belgacom Open 1998, 2000, Dunlop Phoenix Tournament 1998, Macau Open 1999, TNT Dutch Open 1999, Smurfit European Open 1999, 2000, Canon European Masters 1999, Dimension Data Pro Am 2000, Compaq European Grand Prix 2000, Cisco World Match Play Championship 2000; mem. Ryder Cup Team 1997, 1999, 2002; Volvo Order of Merit 2000. *Leisure interests:* snooker, horse racing (racehorse owner), sports cars, Nottingham Forest football team, cinema, shows. *Address:* c/o International Sports Management Ltd, Colshaw Hall, Cheshire, England (Office). *Website:* www.westyuk.com.

WESTWOOD, Vivienne, OBE; British fashion designer; b. 8 April 1941, Tintwistle, Derbys.; d. of Gordon Swire and Dora Swire; m. 1st Derek Westwood; one s.; m. 2nd Andreas Kronthaler 1993; one s. with Malcolm McLaren; during 1970s worked with Malcolm McLaren, developing 'punk' look; designed for the Sex Pistols, Boy George and Bananarama; created Pirate collection (adopted by Adam Ant and Bow Wow Wow) 1980; ended partnership with Malcolm McLaren 1983; moved to Italy for deal with Sergio Galeotti (partner of Giorgio Armani), 1984; launched 'Mini Crini' 1985; produced collection featuring Harris tweed suits and princess coats; Pagan 5 (latest of England Goes Pagan Collections) 1989; regular fashion shows, Paris, NY, London; launch of signature fragrance Boudoir 1998; Prof. of Fashion Acad. of Applied Arts 1989–91, Hochschule der Künste, Berlin 1993–; Dr. hc (Royal Coll. of Art) 1992, (Heriot-Watt) 1995; Designer of the Year 1990, 1991; Queen's Award for Export 1998. *Address:* Westwood Studios, 9–15 Elcho Street, London, SW11 4AU, England. *Telephone:* (20) 7924-4747.

WETHERILL, George West, PhD; American geophysicist; b. 12 Aug. 1925, Philadelphia, Pa; s. of George W. Wetherill and Leah Hardwick Wetherill; m. Phyllis May Steiss 1950 (died 1995); one s. two d.; m. 2nd Mary Bailey 1998; ed Univ. of Chicago; served U.S. Navy 1943–46; mem. Science Staff, Dept of Terrestrial Magnetism, Carnegie Inst. of Washington 1953–60, Dir Dept 1975–91, mem. Science Staff 1991–, Dir Emer. 2001–; Prof. of Geophysics and Geology, Univ. of Calif., Los Angeles 1960–75, Chair. Dept of Planetary and Space Science 1968–72; Ed. Annual Review of Earth and Planetary Science 1981–96; Pres. Geochemical Soc. 1975–76, Int. Assen of Geochemistry and Cosmochemistry 1977–80, Meteoritical Soc. 1983–85; Consultant to NASA,

NSF, Nat. Acad. of Sciences; Fellow American Acad. of Arts and Sciences; mem. NAS, American Philosophical Soc.; Leonard Medal (Meteoritical Soc.) 1981, G. K. Gilbert Award (Geological Soc. of America), 1984, G. P. Kuiper Prize (American Astronomical Soc.) 1986, Hess Medal (American Geophysical Union) 1991, Nat. Medal of Science 1997, J. Lawrence Smith Medal (Nat. Acad. of Sciences) 2000, Russell Lectureship, American Astronomical Soc. 2003. *Publications:* about 200 papers in scientific journals. *Address:* Dept of Terrestrial Magnetism, Carnegie Institution of Washington, 5241 Broad Branch Road, NW, Washington, DC 20015 (Office); 3003 Van Ness Street NW, W201 Washington, DC 20008, USA (Home). *Telephone:* (202) 478-8855 (Office); (202) 244-3435 (Home). *Fax:* (202) 478-8821 (Office). *E-mail:* wetherill@dtm.ciw.edu (Office).

WETHINGTON, Charles T., Jr, PhD; American university president; b. 2 Jan. 1936, Merrimac, Ky; m. Judy Woodrow 1962; two c.; Instr. Univ. of Ky 1965–66; Dir Maysville Community Coll. 1967–71; Asst Vice-Pres. for the Community Coll. System, Univ. of Ky 1971–81, Vice-Pres. 1981–82, Chancellor 1982–88, Chancellor for the Community Coll. System and Univ. Relations 1988–89, Interim Pres. Univ. of Ky 1989–90, Pres. 1990–2001; Dir Nat. Coll. Athletic Assen Foundation 1999–2002. *Address:* University of Kentucky, 5-52 Wm. T. Young Library, Lexington, KY 40506 (Office); 2926 Four Pines Drive, Lexington, KY 40502, USA (Home). *Telephone:* (606) 257-5646 (Office). *Fax:* (859) 323-3777 (Office).

WETTER, HE Cardinal Friedrich; German ecclesiastic; b. 20 Feb. 1928, Landau, Speyer; s. of Peter Wetter and Hedwig Böttinger; ed Univ. Gregoriana Rom; ordained 1953; consecrated Bishop of Speyer 1968–82; Archbishop of Munich and Freising 1982–; cr. Cardinal 1985; Hon. Prof. Univ. of Mainz 1967–; Grosses Bundesverdienstkreuz mit Stern, Bayerischer Verdienstorden. *Publications:* Zeit-Worte 1993, Er allein trägt 1996, Mit Euch auf dem Weg 1998. *Address:* Postfach 10 05 51, 80079 Munich, Germany. *Telephone:* (89) 296955. *Fax:* (89) 229871.

WETTSTEIN, Diter von, Dr rer. nat, FIL.DR.; Danish geneticist; b. 20 Sept. 1929, Göttingen, Germany; s. of Fritz von Wettstein and Elsa Jesser; m. Penny von Wettstein-Knowles 1967; two d.; ed school in Innsbruck, Austria, Univ. of Tübingen, Germany, Univ. of Stockholm, Sweden; Research Asst, Genetics Dept, Forest Research Inst., Stockholm 1951–54; Asst and Assoc. Prof. in Genetics, Univ. of Stockholm 1954–62; Prof. of Genetics and Head, Inst. of Genetics, Univ. of Copenhagen, Denmark 1962–75; Acting Head, Dept of Physiology, Carlsberg Lab., Copenhagen 1972–75, Prof. of Physiology and Head of Dept 1975–96; Distinguished Prof. Washington State Univ., Pullman, Wash., USA 1994–; Rockefeller Fellow 1958; Visiting Prof., Univ. of Calif., Davis 1966, 1972, 1973, 1974, Washington State Univ. 1969; Dr. Agr. hc *Publications:* 300 scientific papers on mutation research, developmental physiology and cell research. *Address:* Department of Crop and Soil Sciences, Washington State University, Pullman, WA 99164, USA (Office); Aasevej 13, 3500 Vaerløse, Denmark (Home). *Telephone:* (509) 335-3635 (Office); 44-48-19-98 (Home). *Fax:* (509) 335-8674.

WEYLAND, Joseph, DIur; Luxembourg diplomatist; b. 24 April 1943; m.; two s.; ed Institut d'Etudes Politiques, Paris, France; Attaché Ministry of Foreign Affairs (MFA) 1967; First Sec. Embassy in Bonn 1969–72; Deputy Dir of Protocol and Legal Matters, MFA 1972–76; Deputy Perm. Rep. to EEC, Brussels 1976–79; Dir Econ. Relations and Co-operation, MFA 1979–83; Amb., Perm. Rep. to UN, New York 1983–84; Amb., Perm. Rep. to EEC, Brussels 1984–91; Rep. to Inter-Governmental Conf. on Single European Act 1985; Chair. Cttee on Political Union at Inter-Governmental Conf. on Maastricht Treaty 1991; Sec.-Gen. MFA 1991–92; Amb. to UK, Ireland and Iceland 1993–2003; Perm. Rep. to NATO, Brussels 2003–; mem. Bd Luxair 1979–83, 1991–92; mem. Bd SNCI and CFL 1979–83; Grand Officer, Order of Merit (Luxembourg), Commdr, Order of the Crown of Oak (Luxembourg), Commdr, Légion d'honneur (France), Grand Cross of the Order of Merit (Spain), Grand Cross (Belgium, Italy, Netherlands, Portugal). *Leisure interests:* modern art, sculpture, music, travel. *Address:* Permanent Mission of Luxembourg to NATO, Boulevard Léopold III, 1110 Brussels, Belgium (Office). *Telephone:* (2) 707-50-93 (Office). *Fax:* (2) 726-89-00 (Office). *E-mail:* luxdel@hq.nato.int (Office). *Website:* www.nato.int (Office).

WEYMANN, Gert; German theatre director and playwright; b. 31 March 1919, Berlin; s. of Hans Weymann and Gertrud Israel; ed Grammar School, Berlin and Berlin Univ.; Asst Dir, later Dir Berlin theatre 1947–; worked as Dir in several W German cities and New York; lecturer in Drama Dept, American univs. 1963, 1966; lecturer at Goethe Inst., Berlin 1970–; perm. ind. mem. SFB (radio and TV plays); Gerhart Hauptmann Prize for Generationen 1954. *Plays:* Generationen, Eh' die Brücken verbrennen, Der Ehrentag; TV Plays: Das Liebesmahl eines Wucherers, Familie; Radio Plays: Der Anhalter, Die Übergabe. *Address:* Karlsruher Strasse 7, 10711 Berlin, Germany. *Telephone:* (89) 11861.

WHALLEY, Joanne; British actress; b. 25 Aug. 1964, Salford; m. Val Kilmer 1988 (divorced 1996); stage career began during teens and has included season of Edward Bond plays at Royal Court Theatre, London and appearances in The Three Sisters, What the Butler Saw (NW Manhattan Theatre Club), Lulu (Almeida, London); television appearances include: The Singing Detective, A Kind of Loving, A Quiet Life, The Gentle Touch, Bergerac, Reilly, Edge of Darkness, A Christmas Carol, Save Your Kisses, Will You Love Me Tomorrow?, Scarlett, 40 (Channel 4) 2003. *Films:* Pink Floyd—The Wall, Dance With a Stranger, No Surrender, The Good Father, To Kill a Priest,

Willow, Scandal, Kill Me Again, The Big Man, Navy Seals, Miss Helen, Shattered, Crossing the Line, Storyville, Mother's Boys, A Good Man in Africa, Trial By Jury, The Man Who Knew Too Little, Run the Wild Fields, The Guilty, Jacqueline Kennedy Onassis: A Life 2000. *Address:* Creative Artists Agency, 9830 Wilshire Boulevard, Beverly Hills, CA 90212, USA.

WHARTON, Clifton R., Jr., PhD; American educator, financial services executive and government official; b. 13 Sept. 1926, Boston, Mass.; s. of Hon. Clifton R. Wharton Sr and Harriette B. Wharton; m. Dolores Duncan 1950; two s.; ed Boston Latin School, Harvard Univ., Johns Hopkins Univ. School of Advanced Int. Studies and Univ. of Chicago; Head of Reports and Analysis Dept, American Int. Assn for Econ. and Social Devt 1948–53; Research Assoc., Univ. of Chicago 1953–57; Assoc., Agricultural Devt Council 1957–58, stationed in SE Asia 1958–64, Dir of the Council's American Univs. Research Program 1964–66, Vice-Pres. 1967–69, mem. Bd of Dirs 1973–80; Pres. Mich. State Univ. and Prof. of Econs 1970–78; Chancellor, State Univ. of NY System 1978–87; Chair. and CEO TIAA-CREF 1987–93; Deputy Sec. of State, US Dept of State 1993; Visiting Prof., Univ. of Malaya 1958–64, Stanford Univ. 1964–65; fmr Chair. Bd for Int. Food and Agric. Devt (AID), US Dept of State; mem. Presidential Comm. on World Hunger, Presidential Mission to Latin America, Presidential Mission to S Viet Nam; Chair. Bd Rockefeller Foundation 1982–87; Dir of numerous cos and orgs including Ford Motor Co. 1973–93, 1994–97, Tenneco Inc. 1994–99, NY Stock Exchange 1991–93, 1994–2000, Harcourt Gen. 1994–2001, Equitable Life 1969–82, Overseas Devt Council 1969–79, 1994–2000, Aspen Inst. 1980–93, Time Inc. 1982–89, Federated Dept Stores 1985–88, Rockefeller Foundation 1970–87; Comm. for Econ. Devt 1980–93, 1994–; Deputy Chair. Fed. Reserve Bank, New York 1985–86; mem. Knight Foundation Comm. on Inter-collegiate Athletics 1990–93, Council on Foreign Relations 1983–93, Advisory Comm. on Trade Policy and Negotiations 1990–93; 61 hon. degrees. *Publications:* Subsistence Agriculture and Economic Development (ed.) 1969, Patterns for Lifelong Learning (co-author) 1973. *Address:* TIAA-CREF, 730 Third Avenue, New York, NY 10017, USA.

WHEATLEY, Glenn Dawson; Australian media executive; b. 23 Jan. 1948, Nambour, Queensland; s. of William Dawson Wheatley and Freda Aileen Evans; m. Gaynor Cherie Martin 1982; one s. two d.; guitarist Purple Hearts 1966, Bay City Union 1966–67, The Master's Apprentices 1967–72; Founder, Man. Dir The Wheatley Org. (TWO Australia Ltd) 1975–92, Hoyts Media (fmrly Wheatley Communications Pty Ltd) 1987–89, Emerald City Records 1991–, TalentWORKS Pty Ltd 1996–; a founding Dir 92.3 EON FM radio station 1980; Man. Dir Radio 2BE Bega NSW 1987–89, Radio 3CV Vic. 1987–89; Co-owner and Dir Sydney Swans Football Club 1988–90; Dir Advantage Int. (fmrly Wheatley Sport Pty Ltd) 1985–88, Sydney Hard Rock Cafe 1988–89; Bd mem. Ausmusic 1993; mem. Tourism Task Force 1990–92; Cttee mem. Austrade (Music) 1986; Trustee AIDS Trust Australia 1990–93; Outstanding Contrib. in Entertainment Industry award, Advance Australia 1987, Marketing Award, Business Review Weekly 1988, Queensland Apprentice of the Year 1965, Aria Hall of Fame 1999. *Leisure interest:* golf. *Address:* TalentWORKS Pty Ltd, Suite 1A, 663 Victoria Street, Abbotsford, Vic. 3067, Australia. *Telephone:* (3) 9429-6933. *Fax:* (3) 9428-7433.

WHEELER, Sir (Harry) Anthony, Kt, OBE, BArch, P.P.R.S.A., P.P.R.I.A.S., FRSA, FRIBA; British architect and town planner (retd); b. 7 Nov. 1919, Stranraer; s. of Herbert G. Wheeler and Laura E. Groom; m. Dorothy J. Campbell 1944; one d.; ed Stranraer High School, Royal Tech. Coll. Glasgow, Glasgow School of Art and Glasgow School of Architecture, Univ. of Strathclyde; Asst City Architect, Oxford 1949; Asst Sir Herbert Baker & Scott, London 1949; Sr Architect, Glenrothes New Town 1949–51; Sr lecturer, Dundee School of Architecture 1952–58; commenced pvt. practice, Fife 1952; Sr partner, Wheeler & Sproson, Edinburgh and Kirkcaldy 1954–86, consultant 1986–89; various public appts.; Pres. Royal Scottish Acad. 1983–90; prin. works include St Columba's Parish Church, Glenrothes, reconstruction The Giles, Pittenweem, redevt. Dysart and Old Buckhaven, Students' Union, Univ. of St Andrews, Leonard Horner Hall and Students' Union, Heriot-Watt Univ., Hunter Bldg Edinburgh Coll. of Art, St Peter's Episcopal Church, Kirkcaldy, Museum of Childhood, Edinburgh, town centre renewal, Grangemouth and Community and Outdoor Educ. Centre, Linlithgow; Hon. Pres. Saltire Soc. 1995; Hon. RA; Hon. Royal Glasgow Inst.; Hon. mem. Royal Hibernian Acad., Royal Soc. of British Sculptors; Hon. D. Design (Rebort Gordon's Univ. Aberdeen 1991; 22 Saltire Soc. Housing Awards; 12 Civic Trust Awards and commendations. *Leisure interests:* sketching and watercolour painting, fishing, gardens, music, drama. *Address:* South Inverleith Manor, 31/6 Kinnear Road, Edinburgh, EH3 5PG, Scotland. *Telephone:* (131) 552-3854.

WHEELER, John Archibald, DSc, PhD; American physicist; b. 9 July 1911, Jacksonville, Fla; s. of Dr Joseph Lewis Wheeler and Mabel Archibald; m. Janette Latourette Zabriskie Hegner 1935; one s. two d.; ed Johns Hopkins Univ.; Nat. Research Council Fellow, New York and Copenhagen 1933–35; Asst Prof. of Physics, Univ. of NC 1935–38; Asst Prof. of Physics, Princeton Univ. 1938–42, Assoc. Prof. 1945–47, Prof. 1947–66, Joseph Henry Prof. of Physics 1966–76, Emer. 1976–; Prof. of Physics, Univ. of Texas at Austin 1976–86; Ashbel Smith Prof. of Physics 1979–86; Blumberg Prof. of Physics 1981–86, Prof. Emer. 1986–; Physicist, Manhattan project of US Govt, Chicago, Wilmington, Hanford 1942–45; Dir Project Matterhorn, Princeton 1951–53; Lorentz Prof., Univ. of Leiden 1956; Fulbright Prof., Univ. of Kyoto 1962; Guggenheim Fellow, Paris and Copenhagen 1949–50; Visiting Fellow, Clare Coll., Cambridge 1964; Chair. Jt Cttee of American Physical Soc. and American Philosophical Soc. on History of Theoretical Physics; mem. US Gen. Advisory Cttee on Arms Control and Disarmament 1969–76; Fellow, American Physical Soc. (Pres. 1966, mem. Council), American Philosophical Soc., Tex. Philosophical Soc., AAAS (mem. Bd of Dirs 1963–68); mem. American Acad. of Arts and Sciences, NAS, Accad. Naz. dei Lincei, Royal Acad. of Science Uppsala, Sweden, Royal Acad. of Sciences of Denmark, The Royal Soc., London; Trustee Battelle Memorial Inst. 1959–89, Southwest Research Inst. 1977–93; Hon. ScD (Western Reserve, Yeshiva, Rutgers and Yale Univs., Univs. of NC and Pa, Middlebury Coll., Catholic Univ. of America, Univ. of Conn., Gustavus Adolphus Univ. and Princeton Univ.); Hon. DSc (Newcastle Univ., England) 1983; Hon. DHumLitt (Johns Hopkins) 1976; Hon. PhD (Uppsala, Maryland) 1976; Hon. D. Litt. (Drexel) 1987; A. Cressy Morrison Prize, NY Acad. of Sciences 1947, Albert Einstein Prize, Strauss Foundation 1965, Enrico Fermi Award, US Atomic Energy Comm. 1968, Franklin Medal of Franklin Inst. 1969, Nat. Medal of Science 1971, Herzfeld Award 1975, Outstanding Graduate Teaching Award (Univ. of Texas at Austin) 1981, Niels Bohr Int. Gold Medal 1982, Oersted Medal 1983, J. Robert Oppenheimer Memorial Prize 1984, Franklin Medal, American Philosophical Soc. 1989, Wolf Foundation Prize in Physics 1997, Einstein Prize of American Physical Soc. 2003. *Publications:* Geometrodynamics 1962, Gravitation Theory and Gravitational Collapse 1965, Einstein's Vision 1968, Black Holes, Gravitational Waves and Cosmology (with M. Rees and R.Ruffini) 1974, Gravitation (with Thorne and Misner) 1973, Frontiers of Time 1979, Quantum Theory and Measurement (with Zurek) 1983, Journey into Gravity and Spacetime 1990, At Home in the Universe 1993, Spacetime Physics (with E. Taylor) 1994, Gravitation and Inertia (with Ciufolini) 1995, Geons, Black Holes and Quantum Foam: A Life in Physics (with K. Ford) 1998. *Leisure interests:* swimming, sculpture in nature. *Address:* Department of Physics, Princeton University, Princeton, NJ 08544; 1904 Meadow Lakes, Hightstown, NJ 08520, USA (Home). *Telephone:* (609) 258-5824 (Princeton Univ.); (609) 426-6239 (Home). *E-mail:* jawheeler@pupgg.princeton.edu (Office).

WHEELER, Gen. Sir Roger Neil, GCB, CBE, MA, FRGS; British army officer; b. 16 Dec. 1941, Fulmer, Bucks.; s. of Maj.-Gen. T.N.S. Wheeler, C.B., CBE; m. Felicity Hares 1980; three s. one d. from a previous marriage; ed All Hallows School, Devon and Hertford Coll. Oxford; commissioned Royal Ulster Rifles 1964; early service in Borneo, the Middle East and Cyprus; Chief of Staff, Falkland Islands June–Dec. 1982; Command, 11th Armoured Brig. 1985–87; Dir Army Plans 1987–89; Command, 1st Armoured Div. 1989–90; Asst Chief of Gen. Staff, Ministry of Defence 1990–92; G.O.C. Northern Ireland 1993–96; C-in-C Land Command 1996–97; Chief of Gen. Staff. 1997–2000; ADC Gen. to Queen 1996–2000; Constable HM Tower of London 2001–; Pres. Army Rugby Football Union 1995–99, Army Rifle Assoc. 1995–2000; Col The Royal Irish Regt 1996–2001; Col Commdt Intelligence Corps 1996–2001; Pres. Combat Stress 2001–; Dir Thales 2001–, Affinitas 2001–; Patron Police Foundation 2001–; Hon. Fellow, Hertford Coll. Oxford. *Leisure interests:* fly fishing, ornithology, cricket, shooting. *Address:* Constable, HM Tower of London, London, EC3N 4AB, England.

WHELAN, Michael John, PhD, FRS, FInstP; British university professor; b. 2 Nov. 1931, Leeds; s. of William Whelan and Ellen Whelan (née Pound); ed Gonville and Caius Coll., Cambridge; Royal Soc. Mr and Mrs John Jaffé Donation Research Fellow 1959–61; Demonstrator in Physics, Univ. of Cambridge 1961–65, Asst Dir of Research 1965–66, Fellow of Gonville and Caius Coll. 1958–66; Reader, Dept of Materials, Univ. of Oxford 1966–92, Prof. 1992–97, Emer. Prof. 1997–; Fellow, Linacre Coll., Univ. of Oxford 1968–; Hon. Prof. of Univ. of Science and Tech., Beijing 1995; Hon. Fellow Royal Microscopical Soc. 2001; C. V. Boys Prize, Inst. of Physics 1965; Hughes Medal, Royal Soc. 1988, Distinguished Scientist Award, Microscope Soc. of America 1998. *Publications:* Electron Microscopy of Thin Crystals (co-author) 1965, Worked Examples in Dislocations, numerous papers and articles in scientific journals. *Leisure interests:* gardening, tinkering, Japanese language. *Address:* Department of Materials, Parks Road, Oxford, OX1 3PH; 18 Salford Road, Old Marston, Oxford, OX3 0RX, England (Home). *Telephone:* (1865) 273779 (Office); (1865) 244556 (Home). *Fax:* (1865) 244556 (Home); (1865) 283333. *E-mail:* michael.whelan@materials.ox.ac.uk (Office).

WHELAN, Noel, BComm, M.ECON.SC., PhD, D.P.A., F.I.MGT.I.; Irish civil servant, international public servant, academic and banker; b. Noel Whelan, 28 Dec. 1940, Cork; s. of Richard Whelan and Ann Whelan (née Crowley); m. Joan Gaughan 1970; two s. two d.; ed Nat. School, Buttevant, Co. Cork, Sacred Heart Coll., Buttevant, Univ. Coll., Dublin; Nat. Univ. of Ireland; Exec. Officer, Irish Civil Service 1960–62; Sr Admin. Officer and Head of Research Evaluation, an Foras Taluntais (Agricultural Research Inst. of Ireland) 1962–69; Asst Gen. Man. Córas Iompair Éireann (Irish Transport Authority) 1969–74; Deputy Sec. Dept of Public Service and Dept of Finance 1974–77; Special Consultant, OECD (part-time) 1975–80; Sec. Dept of Econ. Planning and Devt 1977–80; Sec. Dept of the Taoiseach (Prime Minister) 1979–82, 1988–; Chair. Sectoral Devt Cttee, Irish Govt 1980–82; Vice-Pres. and Vice-Chair., Bd of Dirs. European Investment Bank, Luxembourg 1982–88, Hon. Vice-Pres. 1988–; Vice-Pres. Univ. of Limerick, Dean Coll. of Business 1989–; Chair. Sectoral Devt Cttee 1989–97; Special Consultant UN and World Bank 1989–; Chair./Dir corp. Bds. 1989–; Chair. Nat. Econ. and Social Council of Ireland 1978–84; Adviser to Irish Ministry of Foreign Affairs on Ireland's Foreign Aid Programme 1999–; Chair. Telephone Users' Advisory Council 1993–98; Chair. Caritas Consultative Forum (Health Sector) 1998–, Nat. Adult Learning Council of Ireland 2000–, St Vincent's Healthcare Group

2002–, Chair. State Claims Agency 2002–; Dir (non-exec.) on various pvt. sector corp. bds.; Pres. and Chair. Inst. of Public Admin. (part-time); Council mem. and mem. Exec. Cttee, Econ. and Social Research Inst.; Council mem. Statistical and Social Enquiry Soc.; Council mem. and Fellow Irish Man. Inst. 1984–; mem. NY Acad. of Sciences 1999. *Publications:* miscellaneous papers and reports in various academic and research journals. *Leisure interests:* reading, photography, music. *Address:* Office of the Vice-President External, University of Limerick, Limerick (Office); 74 Northbrook Avenue, Ranelagh, Dublin 6, Ireland (Home). *Telephone:* (61) 202115 (Office); (1) 4960646. *Fax:* (61) 234250 (Office); (1) 4977562. *E-mail:* noel.whelan@ul.ie (Office); nwhelan@iol.ie (Home).

WHICKER, Alan Donald, FRSA; British television broadcaster, journalist and author; b. 2 Aug. 1925; s. of the late Charles Henry Whicker and Anne Jane Cross; ed Haberdashers' Aske's School; Dir Army Film and Photo Unit, with 8th Army and US 5th Army; war corresp., Korea; Foreign Corresp. Exchange Telegraph 1947–57, BBC TV 1957–68; Founder mem. Yorkshire TV 1968; various awards, including Guild of TV Producers and Dirs., Personality of the Year 1964, Silver Medal, Royal TV Soc., Dimbleby Award, BAFTA 1978, TV Times Special Award 1978, first to be named in Royal Television Soc.'s new Hall of Fame for outstanding creative contrib. to British TV 1993, Travel Writers' Special Award, for truly outstanding achievement in travel journalism 1998, BAFTA Grierson Documentary Tribute Award 2001, Nat. Film Theatre tribute, sixth Television Festival 2002. *Radio includes:* Whicker's Wireless World (BBC Radio series) 1983; Around Whicker's World (six programmes for Radio 2) 1998, Whicker's New World (7 programmes for Radio 2) 1999, Whicker's World Down Under (6 programmes for Radio 2) 2000, Fabulous Fifties (4 programmes for Radio 2) 2000, It'll Never Last—The History of Television (6 programmes for Radio 2) 2001, Fifty Royal Years (6 programmes celebrating Queen's Golden Jubilee, Radio 2), Around Whicker's World (series of Radio 4 essays) 2002. *Television:* joined BBC TV 1957; regular appearances on "Tonight" programme, then series Whicker's World 1959–60, Whicker Down Under 1961, Whicker in Sweden 1963, Whicker's World 1965–67; made 122 documentaries for Yorkshire TV including Whicker's New World Series, Whicker in Europe, World of Whicker; returned to BBC TV 1982; programmes include: Whicker's World—The First Million Miles! (4 programmes) 1982, Whicker's World, A Fast Boat to China (4 programmes) 1983, Whicker! (series talk shows) 1984, Whicker's World—Living with Uncle Sam (10 programmes) 1985, Whicker's World—Living with Waltzing Matilda (10 programmes) 1988, Whicker's World—Hong Kong (eight programmes) 1990, Whicker's World—A Taste of Spain (eight programmes) 1992, Around Whicker's World (four programmes, for ITV) 1992, Whicker's World—The Sultan of Brunei 1992, South Africa: Whicker's Miss World and Whicker's World—The Sun King 1993, South-East Asia: Whicker's World Aboard the Real Orient Express, Whicker's World — Pavarotti in Paradise 1994, Travel Channel (26 programmes) 1996, Whicker's Week, BBC Choice 1999; Travel Amb. on the Internet for AOL 2000; One on One 2002. *Publications:* Some Rise by Sin 1949, Away—With Alan Whicker 1963, Best of Everything 1980, Within Whicker's World (autobiog.) 1982, Whicker's Business Travellers Guide 1983, Whicker's New World 1985, Whicker's World Down Under 1988, Whicker's World–Take 2! 2000. *Address:* Le Gallais Chambers, St Helier, Jersey, Channel Islands.

WHINNERY, John Roy, PhD; American professor of electrical engineering; b. 26 July 1916; s. of Ralph Vincent Whinnery and Edith Bent Whinnery; m. Patricia Barry 1944; three d.; ed Modesto Junior Coll. California, Univ. of California, Berkeley; Student Engineer to Research Engineer, Gen. Electric Co. 1937–46; Lecturer, Union Coll., Schenectady, NY, 1945–46; Lecturer, Univ. of Calif., Berkeley, Assoc. Prof., Prof., Chair. of Dept, Dean of Coll. 1959–63, Univ. Prof. 1980–; Guggenheim Fellow E.T.H., Zurich, Switzerland 1959; Head of Microwave Tube Research at Hughes Aircraft Co., Culver City, Calif. 1952–53; visiting mem. of Tech. Staff, Bell Telephone Labs. 1963–64; Visiting Prof. Stanford Univ. 1969–70; Research Professorship in Miller Inst. for Basic Research in Science 1973–74; mem. Visiting Review Bd, Dept of Electrical Eng, MIT 1968, Div. of Applied Science, Harvard Univ. 1974, 1979, 1980, 1981, 1982, 1983, Dept of Eng and Applied Science, Calif. Inst. of Tech. 1977, 1979, 1980; Hon. Prof. of Chengdu Inst. of Tech., Sichuan, Chengdu, People's Repub. of China 1986; Fellow, Univ. of Calif., Berkeley 1990; IEEE Microwave Theory and Techniques Soc. Distinguished Lecturer for U.S. 1990; mem. Nat. Acad. of Eng 1965, Pres.'s Cttee Nat. Medal of Science 1970–72, 1979–81, NAS 1973, Optical Soc. of America, American Acad. of Arts and Sciences; life mem. Inst. of Electronics and Electrical Eng, American Soc. for Eng Educ.; Fellow AAAS; Okawa Prize in Information and Telecommunications 1997; Educ. Medal Inst. Electronics and Electrical Engineers, Outstanding Educators of America Award (Univ. of Calif., Berkeley) 1974, Lamme Award of American Soc. on Eng Educ. 1975, Microwave Career Award of Inst. Electronics and Electrical Eng 1976, Distinguished Eng Alumnus Award, Univ. of Calif., Berkeley 1980, Inst. of Electronics and Electrical Eng Centennial Medallist 1984, Medal of Honor Award from Inst. Electronics and Electrical Eng 1985, Founder's Award, Nat. Acad. of Eng 1986, Berkeley Citation, Univ. of Calif., Berkeley 1987, Nat. Medal of Science 1992, American Soc. for Eng Educ. Hall of Fame and Centennial Medal awards 1993, John R. Whinnery Chair in Electrical Eng est. at Univ. of Calif., Berkeley 1994. *Publications:* Fields and Waves in Modern Radio (with Simon Ramo) 1944, 1952, World of Engineering 1965, Fields and Waves in Communication Electronics (with Simon Ramo and T. Van Duzer) 1965, Introduction to Electronic Systems Circuits and Devices (with D. O Pederson and J. J. Studer)

1966, 140 tech. articles and patents on microwaves and lasers. *Leisure interests:* hiking, skiing, golf, writing poetry and children's stories. *Address:* Department of Electrical Engineering and Computer Sciences, Univ. of California., Berkeley, CA 94720 (Office); 1804 Wales Drive, Walnut Creek, CA 94595, USA (Home). *Telephone:* (510) 642-1030 (Office); (925) 256-9136 (Home). *Fax:* (510) 642-6330.

WHIPPLE, Fred Lawrence, PhD; American astronomer; b. 5 Nov. 1906, Red Oak, Iowa; s. of Harry Lawrence Whipple and Celestia (MacFarland) Whipple; m. 1st Dorothy Woods 1928 (divorced 1935); one s.; m. 2nd Babette Samelson 1946; two d.; ed Univ. of California; mem. Staff Harvard Coll. Observatory 1931–77; in charge of Oak Ridge Station 1932–37; Instructor Harvard Univ. 1932–38, Lecturer 1938–45, Assoc. Prof. 1945–50, Prof. of Astronomy 1950–77, Chair. Dept of Astronomy 1949–56, Phillips Prof. of Astronomy 1968–77; Chair. Cttee on Concentration in the Physical Sciences 1947–49; Research Associate Radio Research Lab. 1942–45, in charge of Confusion Reflectors "Window" (radar countermeasure); Dir Smithsonian Inst. Astrophysical Observatory 1955–73, Sr Scientist 1973–; mem. Rocket and Satellite Research Panel 1946–58, U.S. Nat. Advisory Cttee on Aeronautics Sub-Cttee 1946–52, U.S. Research and Devt Bd Panel 1947–52, U.S. Nat. Cttee I.G.Y. 1955–59, Advisory Panel on Astronomy to the Nat. Science Foundation 1952–55 and Chair. 1954–55, mem. Div. Cttee for Mathematical and Physical Sciences 1964–70, many other scientific cttees., etc.; Project Leader, Harvard Radio Meteor Project 1958–65; mem. NASA Optical Astronomy Panel, Astronomy Missions Bd 1968; mem. NASA Science and Tech. Advisory Cttee 1969; mem. NASA Comet and Asteroid Working Group 1971–72, Chair. 1972; Voting Rep. of USA in Int. Astronomical Union 1952 and 1955; Assoc. Ed. Astrophysical Journal 1952–54, Astronomical Journal 1954–56, 1964–71; Ed. Planetary and Space Science 1958–83, Hon. Ed. 1983–, Harvard's Announcement Cards 1952–60, Smithsonian Contributions to Astrophysics 1956–73; Lowell Lecturer, Lowell Inst. Boston 1947; Vice-Pres. American Astronomical Soc. 1948–50, 1960–67, Cttee on Space Research (COSPAR) 1960; Editorial Bd Space Science Reviews 1961–70; Editorial Cttee Annual Review of Astronomy and Astrophysics 1965–69; mem. RSA, Benjamin Franklin Fellow 1968–; Assoc. Royal Astronomical Soc. 1970; depicted on postage stamp of Mauritania 1986, of St Vincent and the Grenadines 1994; numerous hon. degrees; Donohue Medals, Pres. Certificate of Merit, J. Lawrence Smith Medal of Nat. Acad. of Sciences, Exceptional Service Award (USAF), Liège Univ. Medal, Space Flight Award, Commr of Order of Merit for Research and Invention; Distinguished Federal Civilian Service Award from President Kennedy, Alumnus of the Year Achievement Award (Univ. of Calif.), Leonard Medal, Meteoritical Soc. 1970, Nat. Civil Service League's Career Service Award for Sustained Excellence 1972, Kepler Medal, AAAS, Gold Medal, Royal Astronomical Soc., London and Astronomical Soc. of the Pacific, Kuiper Award, American Astronomical Soc., Univ. of Calif. at Los Angeles Medal 1997, Living Legend Medallion, U.S. Congregational Library 2000. *Publications:* Earth, Moon and Planets 1942, Orbiting the Sun 1981, The Mystery of Comets 1985; and many scientific papers. *Leisure interests:* scuba diving, stochastic painting, cycling. *Address:* Smithsonian Astrophysical Observatory, 60 Garden Street, Cambridge, MA 02138; 35 Elizabeth Road, Belmont, MA 02178, USA (Home). *Telephone:* (617) 864-7383 (Office); (617) 484-0988 (Home). *Fax:* (617) 495-7356.

WHISHAW, Anthony, RA, RWA, ARCA; British artist; b. 22 May 1930, London; s. of Robert Whishaw and Joyce Wheeler; m. Jean Gibson 1957; two d.; ed Chelsea School of Art, Royal Coll. of Art; work for BBC Monitor, work in collections including Arts Council of GB, Bolton Art Gallery, Chantrey Bequest, City Art Galleries, Sheffield, Coventry Art Gallery, Dept of the Environment, European Parl., Strasbourg, Huddersfield Museum and Art Gallery, Leicester City Art Gallery, Museu de Arte da Bahia, Brazil, Museo de Murcia, Spain, Nat. Gallery of Victoria, Melbourne, Australia, Museum of Contemporary Art, Helsinki, Nat. Gallery of Wales, RCA, London, Royal Acad., London, Seattle Museum of Art, USA, Tate Gallery, London, Western Australia Gallery and several pvt. and corp. collections; Royal Coll. of Art Travelling Scholarship 1952, Royal Coll. of Art Drawing Prize 1953, Abbey Minor Scholarship 1954, Spanish Govt Scholarship 1954, Spanish Govt Scholarship 1955, Perth Int. Drawing Biennale Prize 1973, Byer Int. Painting Prize 1973, South East Arts Asscn Painting Prize 1975, Greater London Arts Council Award 1978, Greater London Council Painting Prize 1981, Abbey Premier Scholarship 1982, Lorne Scholarship 1982, Jt Wmuer Hunting Group Nat. Art Competition 1986, Korn Ferry Carre Oban Int. Picture of the year 1996. *Exhibitions:* numerous one-man exhbns UK, including ICA, London 1971, 1992, 1993, Royal Acad. of Arts, London 1986, 1987, Hamburg 1989, Shanghai 1989, Barbican Centre (London); touring exhbn, UK and Dublin 1994–95; numerous group exhbns 1957–2003. *Address:* 7A Albert Place, Victoria Road, London, W8 5PD, England. *Telephone:* (20) 8981-2139 (Studio); (20) 7937-5197 (Home). *Fax:* (20) 7937-5197.

WHITACRE, Edward E., Jr., BEng; American business executive; b. 4 Nov. 1941, Ennis, Tex.; ed Texas Tech. Univ.; joined Southwestern Bell Telephone Co., Dallas, Tex. 1963, subsequently facility engineer, Lubbock and various posts in operational depts., Texas, Arkansas and Kansas; Pres. Kansas Div. 1982–85; Group Pres., subsequently Vice-Pres. (Revenues and Public Affairs), Vice-Chair. and Chief Financial Officer, Southwestern Bell Corpn 1986–88, Pres. and COO 1988–90, Chair. of Bd and CEO (now SBC Communications Inc.) 1990–; Dir Anheuser-Busch Cos. Inc., May Department Stores Co., Emerson Electric Co., Burlington Northern Inc.; mem. Bd of Regents, Texas

Tech. Univ. and Texas Tech. Univ. Health Sciences Center, Bd of Govs., Southwest Foundation for Biomedical Research; Trustee Southwest Research Inst.; Int. Citizen of the Year Award, World Affairs Council, San Antonio 1997, Spirit of Achievement Award, Nat. Jewish Medical and Research Center 1998, Freeman Award, San Antonio Chamber of Commerce 1998. *Address:* SBC Communications Inc., Room 40, 175 E Houston Street, San Antonio, TX 78205, USA.

WHITBREAD, Fatima, MBE; British fmr athlete; b. 3 March 1961, Stoke Newington; adopted d. of Margaret Whitbread; m. Andrew Norman 1997; one s.; UK int. debut as javelin thrower 1977; European jr champion 1979; European Cup champion 1983; European Cup silver medallist 1985; European champion 1986; Commonwealth Games bronze medallist 1982, silver medallist 1986; Olympic Games bronze medallist 1984, silver medallist 1988; World Championships silver medallist 1983; world record-holder 1986; world champion 1987; retd 1990; founder-mem. and Pres. Chafford Hundred AC; marketing consultant; mem. Bd Eastern Region Sports Council 1992–96; Dir (non-exec.) Thameside Community Health Care NHS Trust 1993–; Voluntary Service Overseas Amb. 1992–93; Pres. Thurrock Harriers Athletic Club 1993–; Gov. King Edward Grammer School, Chelmsford 2000–02; BBC Sports Personality of the Year 1987; British Sports Writers Sportswoman of the Year 1986, 1987; British Athletic Writers Woman Athlete of the Year, 1986, 1987. *Leisure interests:* interior design, theatre. *Address:* Javel-Inn, Mill Hill, Shenfield, Brentwood, Essex, CM15 8EU (Home); Chafford Hundred Information Centre, Elizabeth Road, Chafford Hundred, Grays, Essex, RM16 6QZ, England. *Telephone:* (1375) 391099. *Fax:* (1277) 211979 (Home); (1375) 391374. *E-mail:* champinternational@tinyworld.co.uk (Home).

WHITBREAD, Samuel Charles, JP; British business executive; b. 22 Feb. 1937, London; s. of Major Simon Whitbread and H. B. M. Trefusis; m. Jane M. Hayter 1961; three s. one d.; ed Eton Coll.; served Beds. and Herts. Regt 1955–57; Dir Whitbread & Co. 1972, Deputy Chair. 1984, Chair. Whitbread & Co. (Whitbread PLC from 1991) 1984–92, Dir 1972–2001; Chair. Herts. Timber Supplies 2000–; Vice-Pres. East Anglia TA and VRA 1991–2000; Lord-Lt of Bedfordshire 1991–. *Leisure interests:* shooting, travel, painting, music. *Address:* Southill Park, Biggleswade, Beds., SG18 9LL, England (Home). *Telephone:* (1462) 813272 (Home).

WHITE, Sir Christopher John, Kt, CVO, PhD, FBA; British arts administrator (retd); b. 19 Sept. 1930; s. of Gabriel Ernest E. F. White; m. Rosemary Katharine Desages 1957; one s. two d.; ed Downside School, Courtauld Inst. of Art, London Univ.; army service 1949–50; Asst Keeper, Dept of Prints and Drawings, British Museum 1954–65; Dir P. and D. Colnaghi 1965–71; Curator of Graphic Arts, Nat. Gallery of Art, Washington 1971–73; Dir of Studies, Paul Mellon Centre for Studies in British Art 1973–85; Assoc. Dir Yale Centre for British Art, New Haven 1976–85; Adjunct Prof. of History of Art, Yale Univ. 1977–85; Dir Ashmolean Museum, Oxford 1985–97; Fellow, Worcester Coll., Oxford 1985–97; Prof. of the Art of the Netherlands, Oxford 1992–97; Hermione Lecturer, Alexandra Coll., Dublin 1959; Adjunct Prof., Inst. of Fine Arts, New York Univ. 1973, 1976; Visiting Prof., Yale Univ. 1976; Conf. Dir, European-American Ass. on Art Museums 1975; Reviews Ed., Master Drawings 1967–80; Gov. British Inst. of Florence 1994–2002; Trustee Victoria and Albert Museum 1997; mem. Exec. Cttee N.A.C.F. 1998, Raad van Toezicht, Mauritshuis, The Hague 1999; Dir Burlington Magazine 1981– (Chair. 1995–2001). *Publications:* Rembrandt and His World 1964, The Flower Drawings of Jan van Huysum 1965, Rubens and His World 1968, Rembrandt as an Etcher 1969, Rembrandt's Etchings: a catalogue raisonné (jtly) 1970, Dürer: the Artist and His Drawings 1972, English Landscape 1630–1850 1977, The Dutch Paintings in the Collection of HM The Queen 1982, Rembrandt in Eighteenth Century England (Ed.) 1983, Peter Paul Rubens: Man and Artist 1987, Drawing in England from Hilliard to Hogarth (jtly) 1987, Rubens in Oxford (jtly) 1988, One Hundred Old Master Drawings from the Ashmolean Museum (jtly) 1991, Dutch and Flemish Drawings at Windsor Castle (jtly) 1994, Anthony van Dyck: Thomas Howard, the Earl of Arundel 1995, Rembrandt by Himself (jtly) 1999, Ashmolean Museum Catalogue of the Dutch, Flemish and German Paintings 1999. *Address:* 34 Kelly Street, London, NW1 8PH, England. *Telephone:* (20) 7485-9148 (Home). *Fax:* (20) 7428-9786 (Home). *E-mail:* cjwhite@ukonline.co.uk (Home).

WHITE, Sir David Harry, Kt; British business executive; b. 12 Oct. 1929, Nottingham; s. of Harry White and Kathleen White; m. Valerie White 1971; one s. four d.; ed Nottingham High School; Master Mariner's Certificate, HMS Conway; apprentice, Shell Co. 1946–56; Terminal Man., Texaco (UK) Ltd 1956–64; Operations Man., Gulf Oil (GB) 1964–68; Asst Man. Dir Samuel Williams, Dagenham 1968–70; Man. Dir Eastern British Road Services 1970–76; Group Man. Dir British Road Services 1976–82, Pickfords 1982–84; Deputy Chair. Nat. Freight Corpn 1984–89; Group Man. Dir Nat. Freight Consortium Property Group 1984–87; Chair. Pension fund, Nat. Freight Co. 1985–99; Chair. Nottingham Devt Enterprise 1987–93; Dir (non-exec.) British Coal 1993–94; Chair. Nottingham Health Authority 1986–98, Bd of Govs. Nottingham Trent Univ. 1988–99, Mansfield Brewery PLC 1993–99, The Coal Authority 1994–99, EPS Ltd 1997–2000; Dir Hilda Hanson 1997–, James Bell 1998–, Nottingham Forest 1999–; Coutts & Co. 1999–; DL 1989; Alkane Ltd 2000–; Hon. DBA (Nottingham Trent) 1999. *Leisure interests:* football, walking. *Address:* Whitehaven, 6 Croft Road, Edwalton, Notts., NG12 4BW, England. *Telephone:* (115) 923-4199 (Home). *Fax:* (115) 945-2407 (Home). *E-mail:* dvwhite@btinternet.com (Home).

WHITE, Edmund; American author; b. 13 Jan. 1940; s. of E.V. White and Delilah Teddlie; ed Univ. of Michigan; Prof. of English, Brown Univ., Providence, RI; 1990–92; Prof. of Humanities, Princeton Univ. 1999–; Guggenheim Fellowship; mem. Acad. of Arts and Letters 1998; Officier Ordre des Arts et des Lettres 1999. *Publications include:* novels: Forgetting Elena 1973, Nocturnes for the King of Naples 1978, A Boy's Own Story 1982, Caracole 1985, The Darker Proof 1987, The Beautiful Room is Empty 1988, Skinned Alive 1995, The Farewell Symphony 1997, The Married Man 2000, Funny: A Fiction 2003; non-fiction: States of Desire: Travels in Gay America 1980, Proust 1999, The Burning Library 1994, Sketches from Memory 1994, The Flâneur 2001; biog.: Jean Genet 1992. *Address:* c/o Amanda Urban, ICM, 40 West 57th Street, New York, NY 10019, USA. *Telephone:* (212) 556-5764 (Office).

WHITE, Gilbert F(owler), PhD; American geographer (retd); b. 26 Nov. 1911, Chicago; s. of Arthur E. White and Mary (Guthrie) White; m. Anne E. Underwood 1944 (deceased); one s. two d.; ed Univ. of Chicago; Geographer, Miss. Valley Comm. of P.W.A. 1934, Nat. Resources Bd 1934–35; Sec. Land and Water Comm., Nat. Resources Comm. and Nat. Resources Planning Bd 1935–40; Bureau of Budget, Exec. Office of Pres. 1941–42; Relief Admin. in France 1942–43; interned Baden-Baden 1943–44; Sec. American Relief for India 1945–46; Pres. Haverford Coll. 1946–55; Prof. of Geography Univ. of Chicago 1956–69; Prof. of Geography and Dir Inst. of Behavioral Sciences, Univ. of Colorado 1970–78, Gustavson Distinguished Prof. Emer. 1979–; Dir Natural Hazards Research Information Center 1976–84, 1992–94, American Soc. of Flood Plain Man.'s Foundation 1996–; mem. numerous nat. and int. advisory comms. etc.; Exec. Ed. Environment 1983–93; Visiting Prof. Univ. of Oxford 1962–63; mem. NAS, Asscn of American Geographers; Hon. mem. Royal Geographical Soc., Russian Geographical Soc.; Foreign mem. Russian Acad. of Sciences; numerous hon. degrees; Sasakawa UN Prize 1985, Tyler Prize 1987, Volvo Prize 1995, NAS Public Service Medal 2000, Nat. Medal of Science 2001. *Publications:* author, co-author and ed. of books on flood management and other environmental issues including Human Adjustment to Floods 1945, Science and the Future of Arid Lands 1960, Strategies of American Water Management 1969, Selected Writings 1986. *Address:* Campus Box 482, University of Colorado, Boulder, CO 80309 (Office); 624 Pearl Street, Boulder, CO 80302, USA (Home). *Fax:* (303) 492-2151. *E-mail:* gilbert.white@colorado.edu (Office).

WHITE, Guy Kendall, AM, MSc, DPhil, FAA; Australian physicist; b. 31 May 1925, Sydney; s. of Perceval George White and Eugenie White (née Kendall); m. Judith Kelly McAuliffe 1955 (separated); one s. two d.; ed The Scots Coll., Sydney, Univ. of Sydney, Magdalen Coll., Oxford, UK; Research Officer CSIRO Div. of Physics 1950–54; Assoc. Research Officer, Nat. Research Council of Canada 1955–58; Prin. Research Scientist, CSIRO 1958–62, Sr Prin. Research Scientist 1962–69, Chief Research Scientist 1969–90, Hon. Fellow 1990–; Visiting Fellow A.N.U. 2000–01; Hon. DSc (Wollongong) 1994; Syme Medal (Melbourne Univ.) 1966, Armco Iron Award, USA 1983, Touloukian Award, USA 1994. *Publication:* Experimental Techniques in Low Temperature Physics 1958, (2nd edn jtly 2002) Heat Capacity and Thermal Expansion (jtly) 1999. *Leisure interests:* golf, tennis, swimming. *Address:* 6 Abbott Street, Bellerive, Tasmania 7018, Australia (Home). *Telephone:* (3) 6244-8256 (Home). *E-mail:* guy.white@csiro.au (Office).

WHITE, Adm. Sir Hugo (Moresby), GCB, CBE, DL; British naval officer (retd); b. 22 Oct. 1939, Torquay; s. of the late Hugh F.M. White, C.M.G. and Betty White; m. Josephine Pedler 1966; two s.; ed Dragon School, Nautical Coll. Pangbourne and Britannia Royal Naval Coll. (BRNC) Dartmouth; HMS Blackpool 1960; submarine training 1961; HMS Submarines Tabard, Tiptoe, Odin 1961–65; navigation course 1966; Navigator, HMS Warspite 1967; First Lt HMS Osiris 1968–69; CO HMS Oracle 1969–70; staff, BRNC Dartmouth 1971–72; submarine sea training 1973–74; CO HMS Salisbury (cod war) 1975–76; Naval Sec.'s Dept 1976–78; Asst Dir Naval Plans 1978–80; CO HMS Avenger (Falklands) and 4th Frigate Squadron 1980–82; Prin. Staff Officer to Chief of Defence Staff 1982–85; CO HMS Bristol and Flag Capt. 1985–87; Flag Officer, Third Flotilla and Commdr Anti-Submarine Warfare Striking Force Atlantic 1987–88; Asst Chief of Naval Staff 1988–89; Flag Officer, Scotland and N Ireland 1991–92; C-in-C Fleet, Allied C-in-C Channel and E Atlantic 1992–94; C-in-C Fleet, Allied C-in-C Atlantic and Naval Commdr NW Europe 1994–95; Gov. and C-in-C Gibraltar 1995–97; DL Devon 1999. *Leisure interests:* sailing, travelling, gardening, reading, biography. *Address:* c/o Naval Secretary, Victory Building, HM Naval Base, Portsmouth, PO1 3AS, England (Office).

WHITE, James Boyd, AM, LLB; American university professor; b. 28 July 1938, Boston, Mass.; s. of Benjamin White and Charlotte Green White; m. 1st Constance Southworth 1959; m. 2nd Mary Fitch 1978; two s. two d.; ed Groton School, Amherst Coll. and Harvard Univ.; pvt. practice of law, Foley Hoag & Eliot 1964–67; Prof. of Law, Univ. of Colorado 1967–75, Univ. of Chicago 1975–82; Hart Wright Prof. of Law, Prof. of English Language and Literature and Adjunct Prof. of Classics, Univ. of Mich. 1982–. *Publications:* The Legal Imagination 1973, When Words Lose Their Meaning 1984, Heracles' Bow: Essays on the Rhetoric and Poetics of the Law 1986, Justice as Translation: An Essay in Cultural and Legal Criticism 1990, This Book of Starres: Learning to Read George Herbert 1994, Acts of Hope: Creating Authority in Literature, Law and Politics 1994, From Expectation to Experience: Essays in Law and Legal Education 1999, The Edge of Meaning 2001. *Leisure interests:* reading, walking, swimming. *Address:* The University of Michigan

Law School, Ann Arbor, MI 48109 (Office); 1606 Morton, Ann Arbor, MI 48104, USA (Home). *Telephone:* (734) 936-2989 (Office); (734) 662-6464 (Home). *Fax:* (734) 763-9375.

WHITE, Marco Pierre; British chef and restaurateur; b. 11 Dec. 1961, Leeds; s. of the late Frank White and Maria Rosa Gallina; m. 1st Alexandra McArthur 1988 (divorced 1990); one d.; m. 2nd Lisa Butcher 1992 (divorced 1994); m. 3rd Matilda Conejero-Caldera 2000; two s. one d.; ed Allerton High School, Leeds; Commis Chef Hotel St George, Harrogate 1978, Box Tree, Ilkley 1979; Chef de Partie Le Gavroche 1981, Tante Claire 1983; Sous Chef Manoir aux Quat' Saisons 1984–85; Propr and Chef Harveys 1986–93, The Canteen Restaurant, Chelsea Harbour (co-owner Michael Caine) 1992–96, Restaurant Marco Pierre White 1993–, Criterion Marco Pierre White (co-owner Sir Rocco Forte, q.v.) 1995–, Quo Vadis 1996–, Oak Room, Le Meridien 1997–99, MPW Canary Wharf 1997–, Café Royal Grill Room 1997–, Mirabelle Restaurant, Curzon Street 1998–, L'Escargot, Belvedere 1999, Wheelers of St James 2002; Catey Award for Newcomer of the Year 1987, Chef of the Year, Egon Ronay 1992, youngest and first British chef to win 3 Michelin stars 1995, Restaurant of the Year, Egon Ronay (for The Restaurant) 1997. *Publications:* White Heat 1990, White Heat II 1994, Wild Food from Land and Sea 1994, Canteen Cuisine 1995, Glorious Puddings 1998, The Mirabelle Cookbook 1999. *Leisure interests:* fishing, shooting, bird-watching. *Address:* c/o Mirabelle Restaurant, 56 Curzon Street, London, W1Y 7PF, England.

WHITE, Michael Simon; British theatrical and film producer and impresario; b. 16 Jan. 1936; s. of Victor White and Doris White; m. 1st Sarah Hillsdon 1965 (divorced 1973); two s. one d.; m. 2nd Louise Moores 1985; one s.; ed Lyceum Alpinum, Zuoz, Switzerland, Pisa Univ. and Sorbonne, Paris; began career by bringing Cambridge Footlights to London's West End; Asst to Sir Peter Daubeny 1956–61. *Stage productions include:* Rocky Horror Show, Jabberwocky, Sleuth, America Hurrah, Oh, Calcutta!, The Connection, Joseph and the Amazing Technicolour Dreamcoat, Loot, The Blood Knot, A Chorus Line, Deathtrap, Annie, Pirates of Penzance, On Your Toes, The Mystery of Edwin Drood, Metropolis, Bus Stop, Crazy for You, Looking Through a Glass Onion, Me and Mamie O'Rourke, She Loves Me, Fame, Voyeurz 1996, Notre Dame de Paris 2000–01, Contact 2002. *Films include:* Monty Python and the Holy Grail, Rocky Horror Picture Show, My Dinner with André, Ploughman's Lunch, Moonlighting, Strangers' Kiss, The Comic Strip Presents, The Supergrass, High Season, Eat the Rich, White Mischief, The Deceivers, Nuns on the Run 1989, Robert's Movie, The Pope Must Die, Widow's Peak, Enigma 2000. *Publication:* Empty Seats 1984. *Leisure interests:* art, skiing, racing. *Address:* 48 Dean Street, London, W1V 5HL, England. *Telephone:* (20) 7734-7707.

WHITE, Miles D., MA; American pharmaceutical industry executive; b. 1955, Minneapolis, Minn.; ed Stanford Univ.; began career as Man. Consultant with McKinsey & Co.; Man. Nat. Account Sales and later other Sr Man. posts, Diagnostics Div., Abbott Laboratories 1984–93, Vice-Pres. Diagnostics Systems and Operations 1993–94, Sr Vice-Pres. 1994–98, Exec. Vice-Pres. 1998–99, mem. Bd of Dirs. 1998–, CEO Jan. 1999–, Chair. April 1999–; mem. Bd of Trustees Exec. Cttee, Pharmaceutical Research and Mfrs of America; mem. Bd of Dirs. Evanston Northwestern Healthcare, Culver Educ. Foundation; mem. Bd of Trustees Field Museum, Chicago, Art Inst. of Chicago, Joffrey Ballet of Chicago. *Address:* Abbott Laboratories, Abbott Park, IL 60064, USA (Office). *Website:* www.abbott.com (Office).

WHITE, Norman A., PhD, FIMechE, FRSA; British business executive, academic and international consultant; b. 11 April 1922, Hetton-le-Hole, Durham; s. of Charles Brewster White and Lilian Sarah White (née Finch); m. 1st Joyce Marjorie Rogers 1944 (died 1982); one s. one d.; m. 2nd Marjorie Iris Rushton 1983; ed Manchester Inst. of Science and Technology, Univ. of London, Univ. of Philippines, London Polytechnic (now Univ. of Westminster), Harvard Business School, London School of Econs; apprenticeship with George Kent Ltd and D. Napier and Sons Ltd 1936–43; Flight Test Engineer, Mil. Aircraft Devt 1943–45; with Royal Dutch Shell Group 1945–72, numerous posts, including Chair. and Dir of Royal Dutch/Shell Oil and int. mining cos. 1963–72; f. Norman White Assocs. 1972, Prin. Exec. 1972–92, Chair. 1992–95; tech. consultant to numerous cos. 1972–96; Chair. and Dir numerous eng and oil cos. 1972–97; Chair. Millennium Satellite Centre 1995–2000, Spacelink Learning Foundation 2000–; mem. Council and Chair. Eng-Man. Div., Inst. Mechanical Engineers 1980–85, 1987–91; mem. Council and Vice-Pres. Inst. of Petroleum 1975–81; Founder, Chair. Jt Bd for Engineering Man., IMechE, ICE, IEE, IChem.E 1990–94, Chair. Academic Bd 1994–97; Visiting Prof. Univ. of Manchester, Henley Man. Coll., City Univ. 1971–96; mem. numerous academic and educational cttees. including Senate and Advisory Bd in Eng, Univ. of London; Chair. Transnational Satellite Educ. Centre, Univ. of Surrey 1991–94; mem. House of Commons Parl. and Scientific Cttee 1977–83, 1987–92; Chair. British Nat. Cttee of World Petroleum Congresses (WPC) 1987–95 (Deputy Chair. 1977–87), UK Rep. WPC Int. Exec. Bd and Perm. Council 1979–97, Treas. 1983–91, 1994–97, Vice-Pres. 1991–94; mem. Conservation Comm. for World Energy 1979–87; Chair. Int. Task Force on Oil Substitution 1979–84; mem. int. energy/petroleum dels. to U.S.S.R, People's Repub. of China, Romania, GDR, Japan, Korea, India, Mexico, Argentina, Brazil, Venezuela, Nepal, Indonesia, Southern Africa, Iran 1979–97; mem. numerous professional Eng insts.; f. mem. British Inst. of Energy Econs; Fellow, Inst. of Man.; mem. American Soc. of Petroleum Engineers, Canadian Inst. of Mining and Metallurgy; Liveryman, Worshipful Co. of Engineers, Worshipful Co. of Spectacle Makers, Worshipful Co. of World Traders; Freeman of the City of London; Hon. Calgarian, Alberta, Canada; Hon. Dip.E.M. 1998; numerous honours. *Publications:* Financing the International Petroleum Industry 1978, The International Outlook for Oil Substitution to 2020 1983, Handbook of Engineering Management 1989, articles in professional journals in UK, USA and Canada. *Leisure interests:* family, walking, international affairs, comparative religions, odd-jobbing. *Address:* Spacelink Learning Foundation, POB 415, Guildford, Surrey, GU5 7WZ (Office); Green Ridges, Downside Road, Guildford, Surrey, GU4 8PH, England (Home). *Telephone:* (1483) 855329 (Office); (1483) 567523 (Home). *Fax:* (1483) 504314. *E-mail:* n.white@spacelink.org (Office); normanwhite@norsco-demon.co.uk (Home). *Website:* www.spacelink.org (Office).

WHITE, Raymond P., DDS, PhD; American oral and maxillofacial surgeon; b. 13 Feb. 1937, New York; s. of Raymond P. White and Mabel S. White; m. Betty P. White 1961; one s. one d.; ed Medical Coll. of Virginia and Washington & Lee Univ.; Asst Prof. of Oral Surgery, Univ. of Kentucky 1967–70, Assoc. Prof. 1970–71, Chair. Oral Surgery Dept 1969–71; Prof. of Oral Surgery, Virginia Commonwealth Univ. 1971–74; Dalton L. McMichael Prof. of Oral and Maxillofacial Surgery, Univ. of NC School of Dentistry 1974–, Dean 1974–81; Assoc. Dean. Univ. of NC School of Medicine 1981–93; Research Assoc. Univ. of NC Health Services Research Center 1982–98; mem. Inst. of Medicine, NAS; William Gies Award, American Asscn of Oral and Maxillofacial Surgeons 2000. *Publications:* co-author, Fundamentals of Oral Surgery 1971, Surgical Correction of Dentofacial Deformities 1980, Surgical Orthodontic Treatment 1990, Rigid Fixation for Maxillofacial Surgery 1991, Contemporary Treatment of Dentofacial Deformity 2002. *Leisure interests:* tennis, sailing. *Address:* Department of Oral and Maxillofacial Surgery, CB 7450, University of North Carolina, Chapel Hill, NC 27599-7450 (Office); 1506 Velma Road, Chapel Hill, NC 27514, USA (Home). *Telephone:* (919) 966-1126 (Office); (919) 967-4064 (Home). *Fax:* (919) 966-6019 (Office). *E-mail:* ray_white@dentistry.unc.edu (Office).

WHITE, Robert James, AO, F.A.I.B.; Australian banker; b. 18 Oct. 1923, Deniliquin, NSW; s. of the late A. W White and S. J. White; m. 1st Molly McKinnon 1950 (died 1994); m. 2nd Janice Anne White 1996; ed War Memorial High School, Hay, NSW; joined Bank of NSW 1940, Asst Chief Man., New Zealand 1965–66, Deputy Chief Accountant 1967–69, Man., Sydney 1970–71, Chief Man., UK and Europe 1972–74, Gen. Man. 1974–77, Dir and CEO Bank of NSW 1977–82, Man. Dir Westpac Banking Corpn (merger of Bank of NSW with Commercial Bank of Australia) 1982–87, Dir 1977–90; Dir ICI Australia Ltd 1987–93, IBM Australia Ltd 1988–95, Atlas Copco Australia Pty Ltd 1989–94; Commr Electricity Comm. of NSW 1989–95; Pres. Australian Inst. of Bankers 1980–86; Chair. Australian Bankers' Asscn 1978–79, 1983–84, 1987; Dir Int. Monetary Conf. 1982–85; Pres. Asian Pacific Bankers' Club 1983–84, Business Council of Australia 1984–86, Australian Coalition of Service Industries 1988–94, Australian Inst. for Int. Affairs 1988–91, German-Australian Chamber of Industry and Commerce 1988–91, Council for Int. Business Affairs 1992–95; mem. Trade Devt Council 1981–84, Australian Pacific Econ. Co-operation Cttee 1984–91; mem. Exec. Bd ICC 1987–90; Fellow Australian Inst. of Co. Dirs.; Storey Medal, Australian Inst. of Man. 1987; Commdr.'s Cross, Order of Merit (Germany). *Publication:* Cheques and Balances (memoir) 1995. *Address:* G.P.O. Box 4046, Sydney, NSW 2001, Australia. *Telephone:* (2) 9417-4989.

WHITE, Robert M., II, AB; American journalist; b. 6 April 1915, Mexico, Mo.; s. of L. Mitchell White and Maude White (née See); m. 1st Barbara Spurgeon 1948 (died 1983); one s. three d.; m. 3rd Linda Hess Grimsley 1992; ed Missouri Military Acad. and Washington and Lee Univ.; with United Press 1939; Army service 1940–45; Pres., Ed. and Publr Mexico (Missouri) Ledger 1945–87, Ed. Emer. 1987–; Ed. and Pres. New York Herald Tribune 1959–61: Dir American Newspaper Publishers' Asscn 1955–63, Treas. 1962–63; Dir New York World's Fair 1964–65; fmr Chair. Associated Press Nominating Cttee; fmr Chair. and Pres., Inland Daily Press Asscn; Pres. See TV Co. 1965–81; Vice-Chair. American Cttee Int. Pres. Inst. 1968–71, 1981–91, Chair. 1982–86; Dir American Soc. of Newspaper Eds. 1968–70; Pres. Soc. of Professional Journalists 1967; Dir Stephen's Coll., Missouri Mil. Acad.; Visiting Prof., Univ. of Missouri 1968–69; mem. Pulitzer Prize Jury for Journalism 1964–66; Chair. American Soc. of Newspaper Eds. Freedom of Information Cttee 1970-72; Chair. Missouri Free Press-Fair Trial Cttee 1970–74; Pres. Missouri Press Asscn; Vice-Pres. Mo. Inst. for Justice 1978–82, Bd of Dirs. 1982–87; Vice-Pres. Gen. Douglas MacArthur Foundation 1979–81, Pres. 1981–; mem. Bd of Dirs. Associated Press 1971–80, Bd of Dirs. Washington Journalism Center 1972–84, State Historical Soc. of Missouri, Missouri Public Expenditure Survey 1980–85 (Pres. 1981–83), Bd of Dirs. Washington and Lee Univ. Alumni Inc. 1976–80, World Press Freedom Comm. 1984–; Dir Commerce Bank of Mexico 1971–85, Commerce Bancshares Inc. 1971–85; Dir Thomson Newspapers (Toronto) 1986–92; mem. Bd of Dirs. Int. Eye Foundation 1987–89; Distinguished Service to Journalism Award, Univ. of Missouri 1967, Nat. Newspapers Asscn Pres. Award of Merit 1967. *Publications:* A Study of the Printing and Publishing Business in the Soviet Union (co-author), China Journey 1972, Second Journey To China 1977. *Leisure interests:* hunting, fishing. *Address:* Apartment 1037, 4000 Massachusetts Avenue, NW, Washington, DC 20016 (Office); 4871 Glenbrook Road, NW, Washington DC 20016, USA.

WHITE, Robert Mayer, ScD; American meteorologist; b. 13 Feb. 1923, Boston, Mass.; s. of David and Mary (Winkeller) White; m. Mavis Seagle 1948; one s. one d.; ed Harvard Univ. and MIT; war service with USAF, exec. at

Atmospheric Analysis Lab., Geophysics Research Directorate, Air Force Cambridge Research Center 1952–58, Chief of Meteorological Devt Lab. 1958; Research Assoc. MIT 1959; Travelers Insurance Cos. 1959–60, Pres. Travelers Research Center, Hartford 1960–63; Chief of Weather Bureau, US Dept of Commerce 1963–65; Admin. Environmental Science Services Admin., US Dept of Commerce 1965–70; Perm. Rep. and mem. Exec. Cttee of World Meteorological Org. 1963–77; Administrator Nat. Oceanic and Atmospheric Admin. 1971–77; Chair. Joint Oceanographic Inst., Inc., 1977–79; Chair. Climate Research Bd of NAS 1977–79; Admin. Nat. Research Council, Exec. Officer 1979–80; Pres. Univ. Corpn for Atmospheric Research 1979–83, Sr Fellow 1995–; Karl T. Compton Lecturer, MIT, Cambridge 1995–96; Pres. Washington Advisory Group 1996–98; mem. Exec. Cttee American Geophysical Union, Council Nat. Acad. of Eng, (Pres. 1983–), Marine Tech. Soc., Royal Meteorological Soc., Nat. Advisory Cttee on Oceans and Atmosphere 1979–84, Nat. Advisory Cttee on Govt and Public Affairs, Univ. of Ill. 1987–; Bd of Overseers Harvard Univ. 1977–79; mem. of numerous weather research cttees.; Commr Int. Whaling Comm. 1973–77; Cleveland Abbe Award, American Meteorological Soc. 1969, Rockefeller Public Service award 1974, David B. Stone Award, New England Aquarium 1975, Matthew Fontaine Maury Award Smithsonian Inst., Int. Conservation Award Nat. Wildlife Fed. 1976, Neptune Award American Oceanic Org. 1977, Charles Franklin Brooks Award 1978, Int. Meteorological Asscn Prize 1980, Tyler Prize, Univ. of Calif 1992, Vannevar Bush Award 1998. *Leisure interests:* gardening, reading. *Address:* 1275 K Street, NW, Suite 1025, Washington, DC 20005 (Office); Somerset House II, 5610 Wisconsin Avenue, Apt. 1506, Bethesda, MD 20815, USA (Home). *Telephone:* (202) 682-0164 (Office); (301) 652-2901 (Home). *Fax:* (202) 682-9335 (Office). *E-mail:* rwhite@theadvisorygroup.com (Office).

WHITE, Terrence Harold, PhD; Canadian university president; b. 31 March 1943, Ottawa; s. of William H. White and Shirley M. Ballantine; m. Susan E. Hornaday 1968; two d.; ed Univ. of Toronto; Head, Dept of Sociology and Anthropology, Univ. of Windsor 1973–75; Chair. Dept of Sociology, Univ. of Alberta 1975–80, Dean, Faculty of Arts 1980–88; Pres. and Vice-Chancellor Brock Univ. 1988–96, Univ. of Calgary 1996–2001, Prof. of Man. and Pres. Emer. 2001–; Rotary Int. Paul Harris Fellow; Canada 125 Commemorative Medal 1999. *Publications:* Power or Pawns: Boards of Directors in Canadian Corporations 1978, Quality of Working Life 1984. *Leisure interests:* hockey, skiing, squash, tennis, painting. *Address:* Haskayne School of Business, 452 Scurfield Hall, The University of Calgary, 2500 University Drive NW, Calgary, Alberta, T2N 1N4, Canada (Office). *Telephone:* (403) 220-4382 (Office). *Fax:* (403) 282-8343 (Office). *E-mail:* twhite@ucalgary.ca (Office).

WHITE, Tony; American business executive; b. 1947; ed Western Carolina Univ.; Exec. Vice-Pres. Baxter Int. Inc., Group Vice-Pres. 1986–92; Dir and Chair., Pres. and Chief Exec. PE Corpn (Applera Corpn. 2000–) Sept. 1995–; co-f. Celera Genomics Group 1998, Pres. (acting) 2002; Dir C.R. Bard Inc., Ingersoll-Rand Co., Tecan AG, NewCoGen Group; mem. Advisory Bd Kellogg Center for Biotech., Northwestern Univ.; Trustee N Carolina Univ., Centenary Coll. *Address:* PE Corporation, 761 Main Avenue, Norwalk, CT 06859, USA (Office).

WHITE, Willard Wentworth, CBE, BA; Jamaican/British opera singer; b. 10 Oct. 1946, Ewarton, St Catherine, Jamaica; s. of Egbert White and Gertrude White; m. Gillian Jackson 1972; three s. one d.; ed Excelsior School, Kingston and Juilliard School of Music, NY; with New York City Opera 1974–75; European début as Osmin with Welsh Nat. Opera 1976; has performed in most int. opera houses, including Royal Opera House, Covent Garden, England, La Scala, Italy, Glyndebourne, England, Scotland; roles include: Porgy, Orestes, Banquo, King Henry (Lohengrin), Pizarro, Wotan, Golau, Leporello, Prince Kovansky, Napoleon; extensive concert appearances; appeared as Othello, RSC, Stratford-upon-Avon; Prime Minister of Jamaica's Medal of Appreciation 1987. *Recordings include:* Porgy and Bess, Mozart Requiem and Orfeo. *Address:* c/o I.M.G. Artists Europe, 616 Chiswick High Road, London, W4 5RX, England.

WHITE, William James, BS, MBA; American business executive; b. 30 May 1938, Kenosha, Wis.; s. of William H. White and Dorothy Caroline White; m. Jane Schulte 1960; two s. two d.; ed Northwestern and Harvard Univs; Mechanical Planning Engineer, Procter & Gamble Corpn 1961–62; Corp. Vice-Pres. Hartmarx Corpn, Chicago 1963–74; Group Vice-Pres. Mead Corpn, Dayton, Ohio 1974–81; Pres., COO and Dir Masonite Corpn, Chicago 1981–85; Exec. Vice-Pres. and Dir USG Corpn 1985–88; Pres., CEO Whitestar Enterprises Inc. 1989–90; Chair., Pres., CEO Bell & Howell Co. 1990–95; Chair. CEO Bell and Howell Holdings Co. 1995–; Dir Midwest Stock Exchange, Chicago, Evanston Hosp., Evanston, Ill., Ill. Math. and Science Foundation, Business Advisory Council, Univ. of Ill.; mem. The Chicago Cttee, Advisory Council Tech. Inst., Northwestern Univ.; Trustee Northwestern Univ., Evanston. *Publication:* Creative Collective Bargaining (Co-author) 1965. *Address:* Bell & Howell Co., 5215 Old Orchard Road, Skokie, IL 60077, USA.

WHITEHEAD, George William, PhD; American mathematician; b. 2 Aug. 1918, Bloomington, Ill.; s. of George William Whitehead and Mary Gutschlag Whitehead; m. Kathleen Ethelwyn Butcher 1947; ed Univ. of Chicago; Instructor in Math. Purdue Univ. 1941–45, Princeton Univ. 1945–47; Asst Prof. of Math. Brown Univ. 1947–48, Assoc. Prof. 1948–49; Asst Prof. of Math. MIT 1949–51, Assoc. Prof. 1951–57, Prof. 1957–85, Prof. Emer. 1985–; Fellow, American Acad. of Arts and Sciences 1954; mem. NAS 1972–; Guggenheim

Fellow and Fulbright Research Scholar 1955–56; Nat. Science Foundation Sr Postdoctoral Fellow 1965–66. *Publications:* Homotopy Theory 1966, Recent Advances in Homotopy Theory 1970, Elements of Homotopy Theory 1978 and articles in scientific journals. *Leisure interests:* bridge, archaeology, genealogy. *Address:* 53 Hill Road, Apt. 706, Belmont, MA 02478-4307, USA (Home). *Telephone:* (617) 489-0817 (Home). *E-mail:* whthd@math.mit.edu (Home).

WHITEHEAD, Sir John Stainton, GCMG, CVO, MA; British diplomatist (retd) and consultant; b. 20 Sept. 1932; s. of John William Whitehead and Kathleen Whitehead; m. Mary Carolyn Hilton 1964; two s. two d.; ed Christ's Hosp. and Hertford Coll., Oxford; served HM Forces 1950–52; Foreign Office 1955–56, Third Sec., later Second Sec., Tokyo 1956–61, Foreign Office 1961–64, First Sec. Washington 1964–67, First Sec. Econ., Tokyo 1968–71, FCO 1971–73, Head of Personnel Services Dept 1973–76, Counsellor and Head of Chancery, Bonn 1976–80, Minister, Tokyo 1980–84, FCO, Deputy Under-Sec. of State (Chief Clerk) 1984–86; Amb. to Japan 1986–92; adviser to Pres. of Bd of Trade 1992–96; Sr adviser, Morgan Grenfell Group PLC 1992–99, Deutsche Asset Man. 1999–2000; Chair. Deutsche Morgan Grenfell Trust Bank, Tokyo 1996–2000; Dir (non-exec.) Cadbury Schweppes 1993–2001, Serco PLC 1994–96, BPB Industries PLC 1995–2002; adviser to Cable & Wireless PLC 1992–2001, Guiness PLC 1992–97, Inchcape 1926–96, Sanwa Bank 1993–2000, Tokyo Electric Power Co. 1993–2002; mem. Advisory Bd Powergen Int. 1996–2001, All Nippon Airways 2001–; Hon. Fellow Hertford Coll. Oxford 1992. *Leisure interests:* new challenges, music, travel, tree-felling, walking, golf. *Address:* Bracken Edge, High Pitfold, Hindhead, Surrey, England (Home). *Telephone:* (1428) 604162. *Fax:* (1428) 607950.

WHITELAW, Billie, CBE; British actress; b. 6 June 1932, Coventry; d. of Perceval Whitelaw and Frances Whitelaw; m. 1st Peter Vaughan (divorced); m. 2nd Robert Muller; one s.; ed Thornton Grammar School, Bradford; Annenberg-Beckett Fellow, Univ. of Reading 1993; Hon. DLitt (Bradford) 1981, (Birmingham, St Andrew's) 1997; Variety Club Silver Heart Award 1961, TV Actress of Year 1961, 1972, British Acad. Award 1968, U.S. Film Critics' Award 1977, Evening News Film Award as Best Actress 1977, Sony Best Radio Actress Award 1987, Evening Standard Best Film Actress Award 1988. *Plays include:* Hotel Paradiso, Winter Garden 1954 and Oxford Playhouse 1956, Progress to the Park, Theatre Workshop and Saville 1961, England our England, Prince's 1962, Touch of the Poet, Venice and Dublin 1962; with Nat. Theatre 1963–65, Othello, London and Moscow, Hobson's Choice, Play (Beckett), Trelawny of the Wells, The Dutch Courtesan, After Haggerty, Criterion 1971, Not I, Royal Court 1973 and 1975, Alphabetical Order, Mayfair 1975, Footfalls, Royal Court 1976, Molly, Comedy 1978, Happy Days, Royal Court 1979, The Greeks, Aldwych 1980, Passion Play, Aldwych 1981, Rockaby, Nat. Theatre 1982, New York 1982, 1984, Riverside Studios 1986, world tour 1985/86, Tales from Hollywood, Nat. Theatre 1983, Who's Afraid of Virginia Woolf?, Young Vic 1987. *Films include:* No Love For Johnnie 1961, Charlie Bubbles 1968, Twisted Nerve 1968, The Adding Machine 1968, Start the Revolution Without Me, Leo the Last, Eagle in a Cage 1969, Gumshoe 1971, Frenzy 1972, Night Watch 1973, The Omen 1976, Leopard in the Snow, The Water Babies 1977, An Unsuitable Job for a Woman 1981, Slayground 1983, The Chain 1984, Shadey 1985, Maurice 1986, The Dressmaker 1988, Joyriders 1989, The Krays 1990, Deadly Advice 1993, Jane Eyre 1994, Canterbury Tales (animated film), Quills 2000. *Television includes:* No Trams to Lime Street, Lena Oh My Lena, Resurrection, The Skin Game, Beyond the Horizon, Anna Christie, Lady of the Camelias, The Pity of It All, Love on the Dole, A World of Time, You and I, Poet Game, Sextet (8 plays), Napoleon and Love (9 plays, as Josephine), The Fifty Pound Note (Ten From the Twenties), The Withered Arm (Wessex Tales), The Werewolf Reunion (2 plays), Shades by Samuel Beckett, Not I, Eustace and Hilda (2 plays), The Serpent Son, Happy Days (Dir by Beckett), A Tale of Two Cities, Jamaica Inn, Private Schultz, Camille, Old Girlfriends, The Picnic, The Secret Garden, Imaginary Friends, The Entertainer, The 15 Streets, Footfalls, Rockaby, Eh Joe, Duel of Love, Lorna Doone, Murder of Quality, The Cloning of Joanna May, Firm Friends, Born to Run, Shooting the Past. *Plays for radio:* The Master Builder, Hindle Wakes, Jane Eyre, The Female Messiah, Alpha Beta, Marching Song, The Cherry Orchard, Vassa, Beckett's All that Fall, Embers, Beckett Evening (one-woman) 1997. *Publication:* Billie Whitelaw—Who he? (memoirs) 1995. *Leisure interest:* pottering about the house. *Address:* c/o Michael Foster, I.C.M., Oxford House, 76 Oxford Street, London, W1N 0AX, England. *Telephone:* (20) 7636-6565. *Fax:* (20) 7323-0101.

WHITELAW, James Hunter, PhD, DSc(Eng), FCGI, FIMechE, F.R.ENG., FRS; British professor; b. 28 Jan. 1936, Newry, Scotland; s. of James Whitelaw and Jean Ross Whitelaw (née Scott); m. Elizabeth Shields 1959; three s.; ed High School, Glasgow, Univ. of Glasgow; Research Asst. Univ. of Glasgow 1957–63; lecturer, Imperial Coll., London 1963–69, Reader 1969–74, Prof. of Convective Heat Transfer 1974–; Chair. Prof. of Pollution and Combustion, Hong Kong Polytechnic Univ. 2000–; Hon. DSc (Lisbon) 1980, (Valencia) 1996, (Dublin) 1999, (Athens) 2000; Nusselt-Reynolds Prize 1979. *Publications:* three books (co-author) and more than 360 scientific papers. *Leisure interests:* music, tennis, walking. *Address:* Department of Mechanical Engineering, Imperial College, London, SW7 2BX (Office); 149A Coombe Lane W., Kingston-upon-Thames, Surrey, KT2 7DH, England (Home). *Telephone:* (20) 7594-7028 (Office); (20) 8842-1836 (Home). *Fax:* (20) 7589-3905 (Office). *E-mail:* j .whitelaw@ic.ac.uk; JHWhitelaw<100773.2135@CompuServe.com (Home).

WHITEREAD, Rachel; British sculptor; b. 20 April 1963, London; d. of Thomas Whiteread and Patricia Whiteread; ed Brighton Polytechnic and Slade School of Art, Univ. Coll. London; some works use casts of sinks, baths, beds, mattresses, floors and mortuary slabs; work includes 'Ghost', a white plaster cast of an entire room shown at Chisenhale Gallery, London 1990 and 'House', a cast of an entire London terraced house on show in Bow, East London 1993–94; Hon. DLitt (Brighton Polytechnic) 1998, (Univ. of E London) 1998; Turner Prize 1993; Venice Biennale Award for Best Young Artist 1997. *Exhibitions:* one-woman exhbns. London 1988, 1990, 1991, 1994, 1996, 1998, 2001, Bristol 1991, New York 1992, 1994, 1996, 1999, Barcelona 1992, Eindhoven 1992, Paris, Chicago, Berlin 1993, Basle, Cologne, Philadelphia, Boston 1994, Madrid 1997, The British Pavilion Venice Biennale 1997, 'Water Tower Project', New York 1998, Fourth Plinth Project, Trafalgar Square 2000, Holocaust Memorial, Judenplatz, Vienna 2000; participant in numerous group exhbns. in UK and abroad 1987–. *Address:* c/o Anthony d'Offay, 29 Dering Street, London, W1R 9AA, England. *Telephone:* (20) 7499-4100. *Fax:* (20) 7493-4443.

WHITHAM, Gerald Beresford, PhD, F.A.A.A.S., FRS; American professor of applied mathematics; b. 13 Dec. 1927, Halifax; s. of Harry Whitham and Elizabeth E. Whitham; m. Nancy Lord 1951; one s. two d.; ed Elland Grammar School and Univ. of Manchester; Research Assoc. New York Univ. 1951–53; Lecturer in Applied Math. Manchester Univ. 1953–56; Assoc. Prof. of Applied Math., Inst. of Mathematical Sciences, New York 1956–59; Prof. of Math. MIT 1959–62; Prof. of Aeronautics and Math. Calif. Inst. of Tech. 1962–67, of Applied Math. 1967–83, Charles Lee Powell Prof. of Applied Math. 1983–98, Prof. Emer. 1998–; Wiener Prize 1980. *Publications:* Linear and Nonlinear Waves 1974, Lectures on Wave Propagation 1980. *Address:* Applied Mathematics 217-50, California Institute of Technology, Pasadena, CA 91125, USA. *Telephone:* (626) 395-4561.

WHITLAM, (Edward) Gough, AC, QC, BA, LLB; Australian politician and diplomatist; b. 11 July 1916, Melbourne; s. of the late H. F. E. Whitlam and Martha (née Maddocks) Whitlam; m. Margaret Dovey 1942; three s. one d.; ed Knox Grammar School, Sydney, Canberra High School, Canberra Grammar School and Univ. of Sydney; RAAF 1941–45; admitted to NSW Bar 1947; mem. House of Reps. 1952–78; mem. Parl. Cttee on Constitutional Review 1956–59; mem. Federal Parl. Exec. of Australian Labor Party 1959–77; Deputy Leader of Australian Labor Party in Fed. Parl. 1960–67, Leader 1967–77; Leader of the Opposition 1967–72, 1975–77; Prime Minister 1972–75, concurrently Minister of Foreign Affairs 1972–73; Rep. to UNESCO, Paris 1983–86, mem. Exec. Bd 1985–89; mem. Australian Constitutional Convention 1973–76, Independent Comm. on Int. Humanitarian Issues 1983–86, Constitutional Comm. 1986–88; Chair. Australia-China Council 1986–91, Australian Nat. Gallery 1987–90; Vice-Pres. Socialist Int. 1976–77, Hon. Pres. 1983–; Visiting Fellow (lecturing in Political Science and Int. Relations) Australian Nat. Univ. 1978–80, Nat. Fellow 1980–81; Fellow Univ. of Sydney Senate 1981–83, 1986–89; Pres. Int. Comm. of Jurists (Australian Section) 1982–83; Visiting Prof. Harvard Univ. 1979; Hon. Pres. Australian Nat. Council for the Celebration of the Bicentenary of the French Revolution 1989; f. Hanoi Architectural Heritage Foundation 1993; mem. Sydney Olympics 2000 del. to Africa 1993; Corresp. mem. Acad. of Athens 1992; Fellow Australian Acad. of the Humanities; Hon. LLD (The Philippines) 1974; Hon. DLitt (Sydney) 1981, (Wollongong) 1989, (La Trobe, Wodonga) 1992, (Univ. of Tech., Sydney) 1995, (Univ. of Western Sydney) 2002; Socialist Int. Silver Plate of Honour 1976, Mem. of Honour Int. Union for Nature Conservation (now World Conservation Union) 1988; Grand Cross, Order of Makarios III (Cyprus) 1983, Australian Library and Information Asscn Redmond Barry Award 1994, Grand Commdr Order of Honour (Greece) 1996, Grand Cross of the Order of the Phoenix (Greece) 1998, Grande Ufficiale nell' Ordine Al Merito (Italy) 1999, Grand Cross of the Apostle Andrew (Greek Orthodox Archdiocese of Australia) 2002. *Publications:* On Australia's Constitution (articles and lectures 1957–77) 1977, The Truth of the Matter 1979, A Pacific Community (Harvard lectures) 1981, The Whitlam Government 1985, Living with the United States: British Dominions and New Pacific States 1990, Hellenism in the Antipodes 1993, Abiding Interests 1997, Approaching Australia 1999, My Italian Notebook 2002. *Address:* 100 William Street, Sydney, NSW 2011, Australia. *Telephone:* (2) 9358-2022. *Fax:* (2) 9358-2753.

WHITMAN, Christine Todd; American politician; b. 26 Sept. 1946; d. of Webster Bray Todd and Eleanor Schley Todd; m. John Whitman 1974; two c.; ed Wheaton Coll.; fmr freeholder, Somerset Co., NJ; fmr Pres. State Bd of Public Utilities; fmr host, radio talk show, Station WKXW, Trenton, NJ; fmr newspaper columnist; Chair. Comm. for an Affordable NJ; Gov. of New Jersey 1994–2001; Head Environmental Protection Agency 2001–03; Republican. *Address:* c/o Environmental Protection Agency, Ariel Rios Building, 1200 Pennsylvania Avenue, NW, Washington, DC 20460, USA (Office).

WHITMAN, Margaret, BA, MBA; American business executive; ed Princeton Univ., Harvard Univ.; Brand Asst Procter & Gamble, Brand Man., responsible for global marketing of Playskool and Mr. Potato Head brands; Gen. Man. Hasbro Inc.'s Pre-school Div.; Pres. and CEO Florists Transworld Delivery, led launch of its Internet Strategy; Pres. Stride Rite Div., Exec. Vice-Pres. Keds Div. Stride Rite Corpn; Sr Vice-Pres. Marketing in Consumer Products Div. Walt Disney Co.; Vice-Pres. Bain & Co.; Pres. and CEO eBay Inc. *Address:* eBay Inc., 2125 Hamilton Avenue, San Jose, CA 95125, USA (Office). *Website:* www.ebay.com (Office).

WHITMAN, Marina von Neumann, PhD; American economist; b. 6 March 1935, New York; d. of John von Neumann and Mariette Kovesi (Mrs. J. B. H. Kuper); m. Robert F. Whitman 1956; one s. one d.; ed Radcliffe Coll. and Columbia Univ.; Lecturer in Econs, Univ. of Pittsburgh 1962–64, Asst Prof. 1964–66, Assoc. Prof. 1966–71, Prof. of Econs 1971–73, Distinguished Public Service Prof. 1973–79; Sr Staff Economist, Council of Econ. Advisers 1970–71; mem. President's Price Comm. 1971–72; mem. President's Council of Econ. Advisers (with special responsibility for int. monetary and trade problems) 1972–73; Vice-Pres., Chief Econ. Gen. Motors Corpn, New York 1979–85, Group Exec. Vice-Pres. for Public Affairs 1985–92; Distinguished Visiting Prof. of Business Admin. and Public Policy Univ. of Mich. 1992–94, Prof. 1994–; mem. Trilateral Comm. 1973, Bd of Dirs. Council on Foreign Relations 1977–87; mem. Bd of Dirs. J. P. Morgan Chase Corpn 1973–2002, Procter and Gamble Co. 1976–, Alcoa 1993–2002, Unocal 1993; mem. Bd of Overseers Harvard Univ. 1972–78, Bd of Trustees, Princeton Univ. 1980–90; mem. Consultative Group on Int. Econ. and Monetary Affairs 1979–; more than 20 hon. degrees. *Publications:* New World, New Rules: The Changing Role of the American Corporation 1999; many books and articles on economic topics. *Address:* Gerald R. Ford School of Public Policy, University of Michigan, 411 Lorch Hall, Ann Arbor, MI 48109, USA. *Telephone:* (734) 763-4173 (Office). *Fax:* (734) 763-9181 (Office). *E-mail:* marinaw@umich.edu (Office).

WHITNEY, John Norton Braithwaite, FRSA; British broadcasting official; b. 20 Dec. 1930, Burnham, Bucks.; s. of Willis Bevan Whitney and Dorothy Anne Whitney; m. Roma Elizabeth Hodgson 1956; one s. one d.; ed Leighton Park Friends' School, Reading; radio producer 1951–64; set up Ross Radio Productions Ltd 1951, Autocue Ltd 1955; f. Radio Antilles 1963; Man. Dir Capital Radio 1973–82; Dir-Gen. Ind. Broadcasting Authority 1982–89; Man. Dir The Really Useful Group 1989–90, Chair. 1990–95, Dir 1990–97; Dir VCI PLC 1995–98; Chair. The Radio Partnership Ltd 1996–99; Chair. Caspian Publishing Ltd 1996–2002; Dir Galaxy Media Corp PLC 1997–2000, Bird and Co. Int. 1999–2001, Friends Provident PLC 2001–02; wrote, edited and devised numerous TV series 1956–82; mem. Bd Royal Nat. Theatre 1992–94, City of London Sinfonia 1994–2001; Founder-Dir Sagitta Productions 1968–82; Dir Duke of York's Theatre 1979–82, Consolidated Productions (UK) Ltd 1980–82, Friends' Provident Life Office 1982–2001 (Chair. Friends' Provident Stewardship Cttee of Reference 1985–2000); Chair. Theatre Investment Fund 1990–2001, Trans-World Communications PLC 1992–94, Sony Music Pace Partnership (Nat. Bowl) 1992–95, Rajar Ltd 1992–2002, Friends' Provident Ethical Investment Trust PLC 1992–2001; Trustee Pension and Life Assurance Plan RNT 1994–; Chair. and co-f. Local Radio Asscn 1964; Chair. Asscn of Ind. Local Radio Contractors 1973–75, 1980; f. Recidivists Anonymous Fellowship Trust 1962; mem. Films, TV & Video Advisory Cttee, British Council 1983–89, Royal Coll. of Music Centenary Devt Fund 1982– (Chair. Media & Events Cttee 1982–94), Royal Jubilee Trusts Industry & Commerce Liaison Cttee 1986– (mem. Admin. Council of Trusts 1981–85); mem. Council Royal London Aid Soc. 1966–90, Fairbridge Drake Soc. 1981–96, Intermediate Tech. Group 1982–85; mem. Council for Charitable Support 1989–92; Pres. TV & Radio Industries Club 1985–86, London Marriage Guidance Council 1983–90; Vice-Pres. Commonwealth Youth Exchange Council 1982–85, RNID 1988–; Chair. Trustees, Soundaround 1981–2000, Artsline 1983–2000; Chair. Festival Media Cttee 1991–92; Trustee Japan Festival Educ. Trust 1992–; Trustee Venture Trust 1982–86; mem. Bd Open Coll. 1987–89; Gov. English Nat. Ballet 1989–91, Performing Arts and Tech. School; Patron Music Space Trust 1990–; Chair. British American Arts Asscn 1992–95, Sony Radio Awards 1996–99, Friends Provident Charitable Foundation 2002–; Fellow, Vice-Pres. RTS 1986–89; Hon. FRCM; Hon. mem. BAFTA. *Leisure interests:* chess, photography, sculpture. *Address:* 39 Hill Street, London, W1J 5NA, England. *Telephone:* (20) 7409-7332 (Office). *Fax:* (20) 7491-0046 (Office). *E-mail:* john@johnwhitney.co.uk (Office).

WHITTAM SMITH, Andreas, CBE; British journalist; b. 13 June 1937; s. of Canon J. E. Smith; m. Valerie Catherine Sherry 1964; two s.; ed Keble Coll., Oxford; with N. M. Rothschild 1960–62, Stock Exchange Gazette 1962–63, Financial Times 1963–64, The Times 1964–66; Deputy City Ed. The Telegraph 1966–69; City Ed. The Guardian 1969–70; Ed. Investors Chronicle, Stock Exchange Gazette and Dir Throgmorton Publs 1970–77; City Ed. Daily Telegraph 1977–85; Ed. The Independent 1986–94, Ed.-in-Chief Independent on Sunday 1991–94, Dir Newspaper Publishing PLC 1986–, CEO 1987–93, Chair. 1994–95; Chair., Publr Notting Hill 1995–, Sir Winston Churchill Archive Trust 1995–2000, Financial Ombudsman Service Ltd. 1999–2003; Pres. British Bd of Film Classification 1998–2002; First Church Estates Commr; Vice-Pres. Nat. Council for One Parent Families 1982–86, 1991–; Hon. Fellow Keble Coll., Oxford, UMIST 1989, Liverpool John Moores 2001; Hon. DLitt (St Andrew's, Salford) 1989; Wincott Award 1975; Journalist of the Year 1987. *Leisure interests:* music, history, walking. *Address:* 154 Campden Hill Road, London, W8 7AS, England.

WHITTLE, Peter, PhD, FRS; New Zealand mathematician; b. 27 Feb. 1927, Wellington; s. of Percy Whittle and Elsie (née Tregurtha) Whittle; m. Kathe Hildegard Blomquist 1951; three s. three d.; ed Wellington Boys' Coll., Victoria Univ. Coll., NZ, Uppsala Univ., Sweden; NZ Sr Prin. Scientific Officer 1953–59; Lecturer in Math. Univ. of Cambridge 1959–61, Churchill Prof. of the Math. of Operational Research 1967–94, Prof. Emer. 1994–; Prof. of Math. Statistics, Univ. of Manchester 1961–67; Sr Fellow Eng and Science Research Council 1988–91; mem. Royal Soc. of NZ 1981; Hon. DSc (Victoria Univ. of

Wellington) 1987; Lanchester Prize, Operational Research Soc. of America 1987; Sylvester Medal (Royal Soc.) 1994, Guy Medal in Gold, Royal Statistical Soc. 1996, J. von Neumann Theory Medal, Inst. of Operational Research Man. Science 1997. *Publications:* Hypothesis Testing in Time Series Analysis 1951, Prediction and Regulation 1963, Probability 1970, Optimisation under Constraints 1971, Optimisation over Time 1982, Systems in Stochastic Equilibrium 1986, Risk-sensitive Optimal Control 1990, Probability via Expectation 1992, Optimal Control; Basics and Beyond 1995, Neural Nets and Chaotic Carriers 1998. *Address:* Statistical Laboratory, Pavilion D, Centre for Mathematical Studies, Wilberforce Road, Cambridge, CB3 0WB (Office); 268 Queen Edith's Way, Cambridge, CB1 8NL, England (Home). *Telephone:* (1223) 245422 (Home). *Fax:* (1223) 337956.

WHITTLE, Stephen Charles, LLB; British broadcasting executive; b. 26 July 1945; s. of Charles William Whittle and Vera Lillian Whittle (née Moss); m. Claire Walmsley 1988 (divorced 1999); ed St Ignatius Coll., Stamford Hill, Univ. Coll. London; Asst Ed. New Christian 1968–70; Communications Officer World Council of Churches, Geneva 1970–73; Ed. One World 1973–77, Asst Head Communications Dept 1975–77; Sr Producer BBC Religious Programmes, Manchester 1977–82, Producer Newsnight 1982, Ed. Songs of Praise and Worship 1983–89, Head of Religious Programmes 1989–93, Chief Adviser Editorial Policy 1993–96; Dir Broadcasting Standards Council 1996–97, Broadcasting Standards Comm. 1997–2001; Controller of Editorial Policy BBC 2001–; Gov. European Inst. for the Media, Düsseldorf 1997; Freeman, City of London 1990; Personal Award Sandford St Martin Trust 1993. *Publications:* Tickling Mrs. Smith 1970. *Leisure interests:* cinema, theatre, music, reading, exercise. *Address:* Room 330, Henry Wood House, 3–6 Langham Place, London, W1A 1AA, England (Office).

WHITWORTH-JONES, Anthony, CA; British arts administrator; b. 1 Sept. 1945, Bucks; s. of Henry Whitworth-Jones and Patience Martin; m. Camilla Barlow 1974; one d.; ed Wellington Coll.; Admin. Dir London Sinfonietta 1972–81; Admin. Glyndebourne Touring Opera 1981–89, Opera Man. Glyndebourne Festival Opera 1981–89, Gen. Dir Glyndebourne 1989–98; Chair. Michael Tippett Musical Foundation 1998–; Gen. Dir The Dallas Opera 2000–02; mem. Bd Spitalfields Festival 2003–. *Leisure interests:* contemporary art, jazz, golf, Greece. *Address:* 81 St Augustine's Road, London, NW1 9RR, England. *Fax:* (20) 7482-7017.

WIATR, Jerzy Józef, M.PH; Polish politician and sociologist; b. 17 Sept 1931, Warsaw; s. of Wilhelm Wiatr and Zofia Wiatr; m. Ewa Żurowska-Wiatr; one s.; ed Warsaw Univ.; scientific worker Warsaw Univ. 1951–59; Mil. Political Acad. 1959–65; Polish Acad. of Sciences (PAN) 1965–69; Prof. Warsaw Univ. 1969–2001, Dean of Social Sciences 1977–80; participant Round Table debates 1989; Deputy to Sejm (Parl.) 1991–2001; mem. Cttee for Nat. Defence and Cttee for Constitutional Responsibility 1991–97; Minister of Educ. 1996–97; Dir Inst. for Social and Int. Studies, Keller-Krauz Foundation 1998–; Pres. Cen. European Political Science Asscn 2000–; Vice Pres. Int. Political Science Asscn 1979–82; Vice-Pres. Int. Studies Asscn 1980–81; mem. Polish United Workers Party (PZPR) 1949–90; mem. Social Democracy of Polish Repub. (SdRP) 1990–99; mem. Democratic Left Alliance 1999–; Dr. hc; Commdr.'s Cross with Star of Polonia Restituta Order 1996. *Publications:* over 30 books and numerous articles on sociology and political science. *Leisure interests:* tourism, books, chess. *Address:* ul. Komisji Edukacji Narodowej 98/49, 02-777 Warsaw, Poland (Home). *Telephone:* (22) 6435441 (Home). *Fax:* (22) 6435441 (Home).

WIBERG, Kenneth Berle, PhD; American professor of chemistry; b. 22 Sept. 1927, New York; s. of Halfdan Wiberg and Solveig Berle; m. Marguerite Louise Koch 1951; two s. one d.; ed Mass. Inst. of Technology and Columbia Univ.; Instructor, Univ. of Washington 1950–52, Asst Prof. 1952–55, Assoc. Prof. 1955–57, Prof. 1958–62; Prof., Yale Univ. 1962–68, Chair. Dept of Chem. 1968–71, Whitehead Prof. of Chem. 1968–90, Eugene Higgins Prof. 1990–97, Prof. Emer. 1997–; Visiting Prof., Harvard Univ. 1957–58; A. P. Sloan Foundation Fellow 1958–62, J. S. Guggenheim Fellow 1961–62; mem. NAS, AAAS; California Section Award of American Chemical Soc. 1962, J. F. Norris Award of American Chemical Soc. 1973, Arthur C. Cope Award of American Chemical Soc. 1988, Linus Pauling Award 1992. *Publications:* Laboratory Technique in Organic Chemistry 1960, Interpretation of NMR Spectra 1964, Physical Organic Chemistry 1964, Oxidation in Organic Chemistry (Ed.) 1965, Computer Programming for Chemists 1966, Sigma Molecular Orbital Theory (with Sinanoglu) 1970; approx. 400 articles in scientific journals. *Address:* Department of Chemistry, Yale University, 225 Prospect Street, New Haven, CT 06520 (Office); 160 Carmalt Road, Hamden, CT 06517, USA (Home). *Telephone:* (203) 432-5160 (Office); (203) 288-3408 (Home). *Fax:* (203) 432-5161 (Office). *E-mail:* kenneth.wiberg@yale.edu (Office).

WICKER, Thomas Grey, AB; American journalist (retd) and author; b. 18 June 1926, Hamlet, NC; s. of Delancey D. Wicker and Esta Cameron; m. 1st Neva J. McLean 1949 (divorced 1973); one s. one d.; m. 2nd Pamela A. Hill 1974; ed Univ. of North Carolina; Exec. Dir Southern Pines (NC) Chamber of Commerce 1948–49; Ed. Sandhill Citizen, Aberdeen, NC 1949; Man. Ed. The Robesonian, Lumberton, NC 1949–50; public information dir NC Bd of Public Welfare 1950–51; copy-ed. Winston-Salem (NC) Journal 1951–52, sports ed. 1954–55, Sunday feature ed. 1955–56, Washington corresp. 1957, editorial writer 1958–59; Nieman Fellow, Harvard Univ. 1957–58; assoc. Nashville Tennessean 1959–60; mem. staff, Washington Bureau, New York Times 1960–71, chief of bureau 1964–68; Assoc. Ed. New York Times 1968–85;

columnist 1966–91; Visiting Scholar, First Amendment Center, Nashville 1998; Visiting Prof. of Journalism, Middle Tenn. State Univ. 1999, Univ. of S. Calif. 1999. *Publications:* novels (under pseudonym Paul Connolly): Get Out of Town 1951, Tears Are for Angels 1952, So Fair, So Evil 1955; novels (under own name): The Kingpin 1953, The Devil Must 1957, The Judgment 1961, Facing the Lions 1963, Unto This Hour 1984, Donovan's Wife 1992, Easter Lilly 1998; non-fiction: Kennedy without Tears 1964, JFK and LBJ: The Influence of Personality Upon Politics 1968, A Time To Die 1975, On Press 1978, One of Us: Richard Nixon and the American Dream 1991, Tragic Failure: Racial Integration in America 1996; book chapters, contribs. to nat. magazines.

WICKER-MIURIN, Fields; American stock exchange official; Dir of Global Finance and Strategy, London Stock Exchange 1994–; Vice-Pres. A. T. Kearney (strategy consultancy), London; named Global Leader for Tomorrow (World Econ. Forum); contrib. Earth Times. *Address:* The London Stock Exchange, Old Broad Street, London, EC2N 1HP, England (Office). *Telephone:* (20) 7797-1000 (Office). *Fax:* (20) 7334-8916 (Office).

WICKI-FINK, Agnes; Swiss actress; b. 14 Dec. 1919, Frankfurt am Main, Germany; d. of Ludwig Fink and Anna Agnes Klotz; m. Bernhard Wicki 1945 (died 2000); ed Dr. Hoch's Konservatorium für Schauspielstudium, Frankfurt am Main; has appeared in Heidelberg, Leipzig, Munich, Zürich, Stuttgart, Hamburg, Vienna and Berlin; Maria Theater, Hamburg 1989–90; TV Kritikerpreis 1957; Goldene Bildschirm (twice), Grosses Bundesverdienstkreuz. *Address:* c/o Weisgerberstrasse 2, 8000 Munich 40, Germany (Office).

WICKRAMANAYAKE, Ratnasiri; Sri Lankan politician; elected mem. Mahajana Eksath Peramuna for Horana 1960; apptd. Deputy Minister of Justice 1970; Gen. Sec. Sri Lankan Freedom Party 1977; won Kalutara Dist seat 1994; appt. Minister of Public Admin. Home Affairs and Plantation and Leader of the House 1994; Prime Minister of Sri Lanka 2000–01; Minister of Buddha Sasana and Religious Affairs 2000–02; ex-officio Chair. Bd Govs. Cen. Cultural Fund. *Address:* c/o Prime Minister's Office, Sir Ernest de Silva Mawatha, Colombo 7, Sri Lanka (Office).

WICKRAMASINGHE, Nalin Chandra, MA, PhD, ScD; British astronomer and mathematician; b. 20 Jan. 1939, Colombo, Sri Lanka; s. of Percival H. Wickramasinghe and Theresa E. Wickramasinghe; m. Nelum Priyadarshini Pereira 1966; one s. two d.; ed Royal Coll., Colombo and Univs. of Colombo and Cambridge; Research Fellow, Jesus Coll., Cambridge 1963–66, Fellow 1967–73, Tutor 1970–73; Staff mem. Inst. of Theoretical Astronomy, Univ. of Cambridge 1968–73; Prof. and Head of Dept of Applied Math. and Astronomy, Univ. Coll., Cardiff 1973–88; Prof. of Applied Math. and Astronomy, Univ. of Wales Coll. of Cardiff 1988–; Dir Cardiff Centre for Astrobiology 2000–; Dir Inst. of Fundamental Studies, Sri Lanka 1982–83; UNDP Consultant and Scientific Adviser to Pres. of Sri Lanka 1970–81; Visiting Prof., Univs. of Ceylon, Maryland, Arizona and Kyoto 1966–70, Univ. of W Ontario 1974–76, Inst. of Space and Astronomical Science, Japan 1993, Univ. of W Indies, Mona, Kingston, Jamaica 1994; Dr. hc (Soka Univ., Tokyo) 1996; Dag Hammarskjöld laureate in science 1986, Scholarly Achievement Award of Inst. of Oriental Philosophy, Japan 1989, Sahabdeen Award for Science 1996; Vidya Jyothi (Sri Lanka Nat. Honour) 1992. *Publications:* Interstellar Grains 1967, Light Scattering Functions for Small Particles with Applications in Astronomy 1973, The Cosmic Laboratory 1975; with Sir Fred Hoyle: Life Cloud: The Origin of Life in the Universe 1978, Diseases from Space 1979, The Origin of Life 1980, Evolution from Space 1981, Space Travellers, The Bringers of Life, Is Life an Astronomical Phenomenon? 1982, Why Neo-Darwinism Doesn't Work 1982, Proofs That Life Is Cosmic 1982, Fundamental Studies and the Future of Science 1984, From Grains to Bacteria 1984, Living Comets 1985, Archaeopteryx, the Primordial Bird: a case of fossil forgery 1986, Cosmic Life Force 1987, The Theory of Cosmic Grains 1991, Our Place in the Cosmos: the Unfinished Revolution 1993, Life on Mars? The Case for a Cosmic Heritage 1996; with F. D. Kahn and P. G. Mezger: Interstellar Matter 1972; with D. J. Morgan: Solid State Astrophysics 1976; with Daisaku Ikeda: 2000 A.D.—Emergent Perspectives 1992, Glimpses of Life, Time and Space 1994, Space and Eternal Life 1997; Cosmic Dragons 2001. *Leisure interests:* photography, poetry. *Address:* Univ. of Cardiff, Cardiff CF1 1XL (Office); 24 Llwynypia Road, Lisvane, Cardiff, CF14 0SY, Wales (Home). *Telephone:* (29) 2087-4201 (Office); (29) 2075-2146. *Fax:* (29) 2075-3173. *E-mail:* wickramasinghe@cf.ac.uk (Office); xdw20@dial.pipex.com (Home).

WICKREMASINGHE, Ranil, LLB; Sri Lankan politician and lawyer; b. 24 March 1949, Colombo; s. of Esmond Wickremasinghe; m. Maithree Wickremasinghe 1995; ed Royal Coll. Colombo, Univ. of Colombo and Sri Lanka Law Coll.; attorney-at-law, Supreme Court; elected mem. Parl. 1977, 1989; Leader of House 1989–93; Deputy Minister of Foreign Affairs 1977–79; Minister of Youth Affairs and Employment 1978–89, of Educ. 1980–89, of Industries 1989–90, of Industries, Science and Tech. 1990–94; Prime Minister of Sri Lanka 1992, Dec. 2001– (also Minister of Policy Devt and Implementation 2001–); Leader United Nat. Party 1994–, Leader of the Opposition 1994–2001; cand. presidential elections 1999. *Address:* Prime Minister's Office, Sir Ernest do Silva Mawatha, Colombo 7 (Office); Parliament Building, Sri Jayewardanapura, Kotte, Sri Lanka. *Telephone:* (1) 575317 (Office). *Fax:* (1) 575454 (Office).

WICKS, Sir Nigel Leonard, GCB, CVO, CBE; British civil servant (retd); b. 16 June 1940; s. of the late Leonard Charles Wicks and Beatrice Irene Wicks; m. Jennifer Mary Coveney 1969; three s.; ed Beckenham and Penge Grammar

School, Portsmouth Coll. of Tech., Univ. of Cambridge, Univ. of London; British Petroleum 1958–68; served HM Treasury 1968–75, 1978–83, Second Perm Sec. (Finance) 1989–2000; Pvt. Sec. to Prime Minister 1975–78; mem. BNOC Bd 1980–82; Econ. Minister Embassy, Washington and UK; Exec. Dir IMF and IBRD 1983–85; Prin. Pvt. Sec. to Prime Minister 1985–88; Pres. Monetary Cttee of EC 1993–98; Chair. Cttee on Standards in Public Life 2001–, CRESTCO 2001–; Gov. King's Coll. School Wimbledon; Hon. LLD (Bath) 1999; Grand Officier de l'Order grand-ducal de la Couronne de Chêne (Luxembourg). *Address:* Steeple Ashton, Lime Grove, West Clandon, Guildford, GU4 7UT, England. *E-mail:* nigel.wicks@bigfoot.com (Home).

WIDDECOMBE, Rt Hon Ann (Noreen), PC, MA; British politician; b. 4 Oct. 1947, Bath, Somerset; d. of the late James Murray Widdecombe and of Rita Noreen Plummer; ed La Sainte Union Convent, Bath, Univ. of Birmingham, Lady Margaret Hall Oxford; with Marketing Dept Unilever 1973–75; Sr Admin. Univ. of London 1975–87; contested Burnley 1979, Plymouth Devonport 1983; MP for Maidstone 1987–97, Maidstone and The Weald 1997–; Parl. Pvt. Sec. to Tristan Garel-Jones, MP 1990; Parl. Under-Sec. State Dept of Social Security 1990–93, Dept of Employment 1993–94; Minister for Employment 1994–95, Home Office 1995–97; Shadow Health Minister 1998–99, Shadow Home Sec. 1999–2001; Conservative; Spectator/Highland Park Minister of the year 1996, Despatch Box Best Front Bencher 1998, Talk Radio Straight Talker of the Year 1998. *Publications:* Layman's Guide to Defence 1984, Inspired and Outspoken 1999, The Clematis Tree (novel) 2000, An Act of Treachery 2001. *Leisure interests:* reading, researching Charles II's escape. *Address:* 39 Searles Road, London, SE1 4YX (Home); House of Commons, Westminister, London, SW1A 0AA (Office); Kloof Cottage, Sutton Valence, Maidstone, Kent, England. *Telephone:* (20) 7219-5091 (Office); (20) 7701-6684 (Home); (1622) 843868. *Fax:* (20) 7219-2413 (Office); (20) 7708-3632 (Home). *E-mail:* nichollg@parliament.uk (Office). *Website:* www.annwiddecombemp.com (Home).

WIDMARK, Richard, BA; American actor; b. 26 Dec. 1914, Sunrise, Minn.; s. of Carl H. Widmark and Ethel Barr; m. Ora Jean Hazlewood 1942; one d.; ed Lake Forest Coll.; Drama instructor at Lake Forest Coll. 1936–38; radio actor for New York networks 1938–47; Pres. Heath Productions 1955–; Vice-Pres. Widmark Cattle Enterprises 1957–; Commdr des Arts des Lettres. *Broadway appearances include:* Kiss and Tell 1943, Get Away Old Man 1943, Trio 1944, Kiss Them For Me 1944, Dunnigan's Daughter 1945, Dream Girl 1946. *Films include:* Kiss of Death 1947, Road House 1948, Yellow Sky 1949, Slattery's Hurricane 1949, Night and the City 1950, No Way Out 1950, Halls of Montezuma 1950, Red Skies of Montana 1950, Full House 1952, Destination Gobi 1953, Hell and High Water 1954, Garden of Evil 1954, Broken Lance 1954, Backlash 1956, St Joan 1957, Tunnel of Love 1958, The Alamo 1960, Secret Ways 1961, Judgement at Nuremberg 1961, How the West Was Won 1963, Madigan 1969, The Moonshine War 1970, When Legends Die 1972, Murder on the Orient Express 1974, To the Devil a Daughter 1975, The Sellout 1976, The Domino Principle 1976, Roller Coaster 1976, The Swarm 1977, Coma 1978, Bear Island 1979, All God's Children 1980, Who Dares Wins 1982, The Final Option 1983, Against All Odds 1984, True Colours 1990. *Television includes:* Vanished 1970 and the series Madigan 1972.

WIDNALL, Sheila Evans, PhD; American professor of aeronautics and astronautics; b. 13 July 1938; d. of Rolland Evans and Genevieve Krause; m. William Widnall 1960; one s. one d.; ed Mass. Inst. of Tech.; Research Staff Engineer, MIT 1961–62, Research Asst 1962–64, Asst Prof. 1964–70, Assoc. Prof. 1970–74, Prof. 1974–86, Abby Rockefeller Mauze Prof. of Aeronautics and Astronautics 1986–93, Assoc. Provost 1992–93, Inst. Prof. 1998–; Dir Univ. Research, U.S. Dept of Transportation, Washington, DC 1974–75; Sec. of U.S. Air Force 1993–98; Vice-Pres. Nat. Acad. of Eng; Pres. American Inst. of Aeronautics and Astronautics 2000–01; Trustee Sloan Foundation 1998; Hon. DSc (Princeton) 1994; numerous awards including Outstanding Achievement Award, Soc. of Women Engineers 1975, Distinguished Service Award, Nat. Acad. of Eng 1993, Women in Aviation Pioneer Hall of Fame 1996, Goddard Award, Nat. Space Club 1998. *Publications:* articles in professional journals. *Address:* Massachusetts Institute of Technology, 77 Massachusetts Avenue, Building 33–411, Cambridge, MA 02139, USA.

WIDOM, Benjamin, PhD; American professor of chemistry; b. 13 Oct. 1927, Newark, NJ; s. of Morris Widom and Rebecca Hertz Widom; m. Joanne McCurdy 1953; two s. one d.; ed Stuyvesant High School, New York and Columbia and Cornell Univs.; Research Assoc., Univ. of NC 1952–54; Instructor in Chem., Cornell Univ. 1954–55, Asst Prof. 1955–59, Assoc. Prof. 1959–63, Prof. 1963–, Goldwin Smith Prof. 1983–; van der Waals Prof., Univ. of Amsterdam 1972; Visiting Prof. of Chem., Harvard Univ. 1975; IBM Visiting Prof. of Theoretical Chem., Oxford Univ. 1978; Lorentz Prof., Leiden Univ. 1985; Visiting Prof., Katholieke Univ., Leuven 1988, Université d'Aix Marseille III 1995; Kramers/Debye Prof., Univ. of Utrecht 1999; Fellow American Acad. of Arts and Sciences, New York Acad. of Sciences; mem. NAS, American Philosophical Soc.; Hon. DSc, (Chicago); Dr. hc (Utrecht); Boris Pregel Award (New York Acad. of Sciences), Langmuir Award (American Chemical Soc.), Dickson Prize for Science (Carnegie-Mellon Univ.), Hildebrand Award (American Chemical Soc.), Hirschfelder Prize in Theoretical Chem. (Univ. of Wis.), Bakhuis Roozeboom Medal (Royal Netherlands Acad. of Arts and Sciences), Onsager Medal (Univ. of Trondheim), Boltzmann Medal (IUPAP Comm. on Statistical Physics), Award in Theoretical Chem. (American Chemical Soc.). *Publications:* Molecular Theory of Capillarity (with J. S. Rowlinson) 1982, Statistical Mechanics: A Concise Introduction for Chemists

2002. *Address:* Department of Chemistry, Baker Laboratory, Cornell University, Ithaca, NY 14853, USA. *Telephone:* (607) 255-3363. *Fax:* (607) 255-4137. *E-mail:* bw24@cornell.edu (Office).

WIECZOREK-ZEUL, Heidemarie; German politician; b. 21 Dec. 1942, Frankfurt-am-Main; ed Frankfurt Univ.; teacher Friedrich Ebert School, Rüsselsheim 1965–74; joined SPD 1965, mem. Nat. Exec. 1984, mem. Presidium 1986, SPD Dist Chair. for S. Hesse 1988, Deputy Chair. SPD 1993; City Councillor, Rüsselsheim 1968; mem. Gross-Gerau Dist Council 1972; Fed. Chair. Young Socialists 1974–77; Chair. European Co-ordination Bureau for Int. Youth Asscns 1977–79; MEP 1979–87; mem. German Bundestag and SPD Parl. Spokesperson on European Policy 1987; Fed. Minister for Econ. Co-operation and Devt 1998–. *Address:* Federal Ministry for Economic Co-operation and Development (BMZ), Europahaus, Stresemannstrasse 92, 10963 Berlin, Germany (Office). *Telephone:* (30) 25030 (Office). *Fax:* (30) 25034827 (Office). *E-mail:* poststelle@bmz.bund.de (Office). *Website:* www.bmz.de (Office).

WIEDEKING, Wendelin; German business executive; b. 28 Aug. 1952, Ahlen; m.; fmrly engineer Porsche; left Porsche 1988; mem. Bd Porsche 1991–; Chair. 1994–. *Publication:* Das Davidprinzip. *Address:* Porsche AG, Porschestrasse 42, 70435 Stuttgart Zuffenhausen, Germany. *Telephone:* (711) 9110. *Fax:* (711) 9115777.

WIEDEMANN, Kent, MA; American diplomatist; m.; one s.; ed San Jose State Univ., Univ. of Oregon; with Peace Corps in Micronesia; joined State Dept 1974; served in Poznań, Shanghai and Beijing; Deputy Chief of Mission, Singapore and Tel Aviv; on staff Nat. Security Council, White House; on assignment, Bureau of Int. Security Affairs, Dept of Defense; Dir Office of Chinese and Mongolian Affairs, Bureau of East Asian and Pacific Affairs; Deputy Asst Sec., Bureau of East Asian and Pacific Affairs; Chargé d'affaires and Chief of Mission, Rangoon; Amb. to Cambodia 1999–. *Address:* American Embassy, 16 rue 228, Phnom-Penh, Cambodia (Office). *Telephone:* (23) 216436 (Office). *Fax:* (23) 216437 (Office). *Website:* usembassy.state.gov/cambodia (Office).

WIEHAHN, Nicholas E., LLD; South African university professor and consultant; b. 29 April 1929, Mafeking (now Mafikeng); s. of Johannes Wiehahn and Anna C. Wiehahn; m. Huiberdina J. Verhage 1956; two s.; ed Univ. of OFS, Univ. of S. Africa; research work in Univs. of Hamburg, Cologne, Heidelberg, Munich and London; research visits to labour insts. and univs. in Europe, Israel, Canada, USA and Japan; Advocate, Supreme Court of SA and High Court of Lesotho; Prof. in Labour and Industrial Law at various univs.; Chair. Transkei Nat. Manpower Comm.; Prof. Extra-Ordinarius, Univ. of SA 1980–, Dir Inst. of Labour Relations 1976–77; Prof. Siemens Chair of Industrial Relations, School of Business Leadership, Univ. of SA, Pretoria, Dir Oct. 1984–; mem. Council, Univ. of Port Elizabeth 1973–75, Free State Univ. 1980–; Chair. Council, Univ. of Zululand 1981–90; Dir Bureau for Int. Labour Affairs, Dept of Manpower 1977–78, Ed.-in-Chief EMPACT 1977–78, Labour Adviser to Minister of Manpower 1977–79; mem. Prime Minister's Econ. Advisory Council 1977; Pres. Industrial Court of SA 1979–80, Industrial Court of KwaNdebele; Chair. Comm. of Inquiry into Labour Legis. (Wiehahn Comm.) 1977–80, into Labour Matters (Namibia) 1987–88; Chair. Labour Council, SA Transport Services 1988; Chair. Wiehahn Comm., Transkei 1989, KwaNdebele 1990, Royal Comm. of Inquiry, Swaziland; Chair. Lotteries and Gambling Bd; mem. various Govt comms., advisory cttees., etc.; other public and educational appointments; Chair. and Dir of several public and pvt. cos. 1981–; three hon. doctorates; recipient of several awards and bursaries; Order for Meritorious Service (Gold Class) 1993. *Publications:* articles on labour law and industrial relations in periodicals, commentaries and other publs; Change in South Africa 1983. *Leisure interests:* reading, gardening. *Address:* P.O. Box 5862, Pretoria 0001, South Africa. *Telephone:* (12) 34246014 (Office); 474438 (Home). *Fax:* (12) 3424609 (Office).

WIELAND, Joyce, OC; Canadian artist and film maker; b. 30 June 1931, Toronto; ed Cen. Tech. School; solo exhbns. at Isaacs Gallery Toronto 1960, 1963, 1967, 1972, 1974, 1981, 1983, 1987, Vancouver Art Gallery 1968, Museum of Modern Art, New York 1971, Cannes Film Festival 1976, Canadian Film Arts Centre, Hong Kong 1981, Nat. Gallery of Canada 1978, Yajima Gallery, Montreal 1982; has participated in several group exhbns. including Canadian Pavilion at Expo 67, Montreal 1967; maj. travelling retrospective, Art Gallery of Ont., Toronto 1981–82, 1987–88, Canada House, London 1988–89; film The Far Shore received three Canadian awards 1977; Retrospective Films of Joyce Wieland, Whitney Museum, New York 1973, San Francisco Art Inst. 1985, Art Gallery of Ontario (touring) 1987–88, Nat. Film Theatre, London 1988, Georges Pompidou Centre 1989; selection of films screened at Ciné-Club de Saint-Charles, Univ. of Paris, Sorbonne 1986; Artists on Fire film documentary 1987; Artist in Residence, Univ. of Toronto 1988–89; YWCA Woman of Distinction Award 1987. *Films include:* Rat Life (Third Ind. Filmmakers Festival Award, NY 1969), Diet in North America (Third Ind. Filmmakers Festival Award, NY 1969), The Far Shore (three Canadian awards 1977), A and B in Ontario (Ann Arbor Film Festival Award 1986), Artists on Fire (documentary) 1987. *Publications:* True Patriot Love 1971, Joyce Wieland 1987, Joyce Wieland: Quilts, Paintings and Works on Paper 1988. *Address:* 497 Queen Street East, Toronto, Ont. M5A 1V1; 179 John Street, Toronto, Ont. M5T 1X4, Canada. *Telephone:* (416) 366-2986.

WIELGUS, Bishop Stanisław; Polish ecclesiastic and professor of history of philosophy; b. 23 April 1939, Wierzchowiska; ed Catholic Univ. of Lublin,

Univ. of Munich; ordained Priest 1962; curate and parish catechist 1962–69; professor, Catholic Univ. of Lublin 1969–, Pro-rector 1988–92, Rector 1989–98; Ordinary Bishop of Płock 1999–; Head Dept of the History of Philosophy in Poland, head Interdisciplinary Centre of the History of Medieval Culture; Head Catholic Univ. of Lublin (KUL) Catholic Encyclopaedia Editing Offices; Vice-Pres. Conf. of Polish Univ. of Rectors 1990–93; del. Extraordinary Synod of European Bishops, Rome 1991; canon Lublin Cathedral Chapter; leader Coll. of Rectors, Lublin Region 1992–93; mem. Ethical Team of Scientific Research attached to Minister of Educ. 1998–; Chair. Educ. Council of the Nat. Conf. of Bishops in Poland 2001–; Chair. Council of the Polish Rectors Foundation 2001; mem. KUL Science Soc. (Gen. Sec. 1985–88), Acad. Council of the John Paul Second Inst., mem. numerous socs.; Award of the Minister of Nat. Educ., Officer's Cross, Order of Polonia Restituta 1993, Catholic Soc. Civitas Christiana Award 1998, Honour of the Societas Scientiarum Lublinensis Resolutio Pro Laude 1999. *Publications:* Quaestiones Nicolai Peripatetici 1973, Benedykta Hessego Quaestiones super octo libros Physicorum Aristotelis 1983, Bible Research in Ancient Times and in the Middle Ages 1990, Foreign Biblical Literature in Medieval Poland 1990, Mediaeval Biblical Literature in the Polish Language 1991, Mediaeval Polish Bible Studies in the Latin Language 1992, From Research into the Middle Ages 1995, The Medieval Polish Doctrine of the Law of Nations: Jus Gentium 1998, Deo et Patriae, vol. 1 1996, vol. II 1999, Dobra jest więcej 2001, Na Skale budujmy nasz świat 2002, Z obszaròw średniowiecznej mysli islamshiej, żydowskiej i chrzescijańskiej 2002, Filozofie ur Rzeczypospolitej 2002. *Leisure interests:* factual literature, memoirs, film. *Address:* pl. Narutowicza 10, 09-402 Płock, Poland.

WIELICKI, Krzysztof; Polish mountaineer and businessman; b. 5 Jan. 1950, Szklarka Przygodzka; m.; one s. two d.; ed Tech. Univ. of Wrocław; owner of four commercial cos. (distribution of alpine and outdoor equipment and garments) and mountain agencies; began climbing 1970; joined 27 high mountain expeditions including Dolomites, Alps, Caucasus, Pamir, Hindukush, Karakoram and Himalayas; leader of 12 expeditions; the fifth man in the world to climb all 8,000m peaks; first person to climb in winter: Mount Everest (with partner Leszek Cichy) 1980, Kanchenjunga 1986, Lhotse (solo) 1988; leader climbing expedition on K-2 (Karakoram); mem. The Explorers' Club 1997, Group de Haute Montagne (France) 2001–. *Publications:* Talks about Everest (co-author) 1980, The Crown of the Himalayas 1997. *Leisure interest:* travelling. *Address:* ul. A. Frycza Modrzewskiego 21, 43-100 Tychy, Poland (Home). *Telephone:* (32) 227-15-00 (Home).

WIELOWIEYSKI, Andrzej Jan, LLM; Polish politician, economist and publicist; b. 16 Dec. 1927, Warsaw; m.; one s. six d.; ed Jagiellonian Univ., Kraków; trainee, Radomsko Forest Inspectorate 1942–44; Head Foreign Dept Bratnia Pomoc students' org. Jagiellonian Univ., Kraków 1945–48; mem. Wici Rural Youth Union (ZMW Wici) 1945–48; subsequently councillor and inspector in Ministry of Finance 1948–52; Ed., Słowo Powszechne, Warsaw 1948; inspector, Head Office of Workers' Housing Estates Enterprise Warsaw-South, subsequently Warsaw-Śródmieście 1952–55; inspector, Head Urban Devt Dept, Municipal Comm. of Econ. Planning, Warsaw 1956–62; Head of Section Więź, Warsaw 1961–80; lecturer, Doświadczenie i Przyszłość (Experience and the Future) Conversatorium, Warsaw 1978–82; Ed. Królowa Apostołów, Warsaw 1982–84, Gość Niedzielny, Katowice 1982–90; mem. Solidarity Ind. Self-governing Trade Union 1980–, adviser to Nat. Comm. of Solidarity 1980–81; Head of Social and Labour Study Centre attached to Nat. Comm. of Solidarity, Warsaw 1981; adviser to Nat. Executive Comm. of Solidarity 1987–89; mem. Civic Cttee attached to Lech Wałęsa (q.v.), Chair. of Solidarity 1988–90; participant Round Table plenary debates, Co-Chair. group for economy and social policy Feb.–April 1989; Senator 1989–91, 2001–, Vice-Marshal of the Senate 1989–91; Chair. Civic Parl. Caucus of Senate 1989–90; Deputy to Sejm (Parl.) 1991–, mem. Parl. Comm. Foreign Affairs 1991–, 2001–; Polish del. and Vice-Pres. Council of Europe Parl. Ass. 1992–; mem. Democratic Action of Civic Movement (ROAD) 1990, Democratic Union 1991–94, Freedom Union 1994–; mem. Pax Romana Catholic Intelligentsia Int. Fed., mem. of Council 1979–83; mem. of European Council 1987–89; co-f. Int. Fed. of Family Life Promotion 1979–; Silver Cross of Merit with Swords, Cross of Valour, Partisan Cross, Cross of Home Army (AK), Victory and Freedom Medal. *Publications:* Przed trzecim przyśpieszeniem 1969, Przed nami małżeństwo 1972, over 300 articles on politics, religion, educ. and history. *Leisure interests:* gardening, skiing, yachting, historical and detective stories. *Address:* Sejm RP, ul. Wiejska 4/6/8, 00-902 Warsaw (Office); Biuro Senatora UW, Andrzeja Wielowiejskiego, ul. Marsza łkowska 77/79, 00-683 Warsaw, Poland (Home). *Telephone:* (22) 8275047 (Office). *Fax:* (22) 8277851 (Office).

WIEMAN, Carl E., BS, PhD; American physicist; b. 26 March 1951, Corvallis, Oregon; ed MIT, Stanford Univ.; Asst Research Scientist Dept of Physics, Univ. of Mich. 1977–79, Asst Prof. 1979–84; Assoc. Prof. of Physics Univ. of Colo 1984–87, Prof. 1987–, Distinguished Prof. 1997–, Fellow Jt Inst. for Lab. Astrophysics (JILA) 1985–, Chair. 1993–95; Fellow American Physical Soc. 1990, Nat. Acad. of Sciences 1995, American Acad. of Arts and Sciences 1998; mem. Optical Soc. of America, American Assn of Physics Teachers; Hon. DS (Univ. of Chicago) 1997; numerous awards including Sloan Research Fellowship 1984, Guggenheim Fellowship 1990–91, E.O. Lawrence Award in Physics 1993, Fritz London Award 1996, King Faisal Int. Prize for Science 1997, Schawlow Prize for Laser Science 1999, Benjamin Franklin Medal in Physics 2000, Nobel Prize in Physics (Jt recipient) 2001. *Address:* Joint Institute for Laboratory Astrophysics (JILA), University of Colorado at Boulder, Boulder, CO 80309-0440, USA (Office). *Telephone:* (303) 492-6963 (Office). *Fax:* (303) 492-8994 (Office). *Website:* www.colorado.edu (Office).

WIESCHAUS, Eric F., PhD; American molecular biologist; b. 8 June 1947, South Bend, Ind.; s. of Leroy Joseph Wieschaus and Marcella Carner Wieschaus; m. Trudi Schupbach 1982; three d.; ed Univ. of Notre Dame, Yale Univ.; Research Fellow Zoological Inst., Univ. of Zurich 1975–78; Group Leader European Molecular Biology Lab., Germany 1978–81; Asst Prof. then Assoc. Prof., Princeton Univ. 1981–87, Prof. of Biology 1987–; Visiting Researcher Center for Pathobiology, Univ. of Calif., Irvine 1977; Fellow Laboratoire de Génétique Moléculaire, France, AAAS; mem. Damon Runyon-Walter Winchell Cancer Fund 1987–92, NAS; shared Nobel Prize for Medicine and Physiology 1995. *Publications:* numerous articles. *Address:* Department of Molecular Biology, Princeton University, Princeton, NJ 08544, USA. *Website:* www.princeton.edu (Office).

WIESEL, Elie; American author; b. 30 Sept. 1928, Sighet, Romania; s. of Shlomo Wiesel and Sarah (née Feig) Wiesel; m. Marion E. Wiesel 1969; one s.; ed Sorbonne, Paris; naturalized US citizen 1963; Distinguished Prof. Coll. of City of New York 1972–76; Andrew Mellon Prof. in Humanities, Boston Univ. 1976–, Prof. of Philosophy 1988–; Founder The Elie Wiesel Foundation for Humanity 1986; mem. bd Fund for the Holocaust 1997–; Founding Pres. Universal Acad. of Cultures, Paris 1993; mem. numerous bds. of dirs., trustees, govs. and advisers including Int. Rescue Cttee, American Jewish World Service, Yad Vashem, Mutual of America, AmeriCares, US Cttee for Refugees; mem. PEN, The Authors' Guild, Foreign Press Assn, Writers and Artists for Peace in the Middle East, Council of Foreign Relations, American Acad. of Arts and Sciences, American Acad. of Arts and Letters (Dept of Literature), Jewish Acad. of Arts and Sciences, European Acad. of Arts, Sciences and Humanities, Royal Norwegian Soc. of Sciences and Letters; recipient of numerous hon. degrees; Prix Rivarol 1964, Jewish Heritage Award 1965, Remembrance Award 1965, Prix Médicis 1968, Prix Bordin (Acad. Française) 1972, Eleanor Roosevelt Memorial Award 1972, American Liberties Medallion, American Jewish Comm. 1972, Martin Luther King Jr Award (Coll. of City of New York) 1973, Faculty Distinguished Scholar Award, Hofstra Univ. 1973–74, Congressional Gold Medal of Achievement 1985, Nobel Peace Prize 1986, Medal of Liberty Award 1986, Ellis Island Medal of Honor 1992, Presidential Medal of Freedom 1993 and numerous other awards; Grand Officer, Légion d'honneur. *Publications:* Night 1960, Dawn 1961, The Accident 1962, The Town Beyond the Wall 1964, The Gates of the Forest 1966, The Jews of Silence 1966, Legends of Our Time 1968, A Beggar in Jerusalem 1970, One Generation After 1971, Souls on Fire 1972, The Oath 1973, Ani Maamin, Cantata 1973, Zalmen or the Madness of God (play) 1975, Messengers of God 1966, A Jew Today 1978, Four Hasidic Masters 1978, The Trial of God 1979, Le testament d'un poète juif assassiné 1980 (Prix Livre-Inter 1980, Prix des Bibliothéquaires 1981), The Testament 1980, Images from the Bible 1980, Five Biblical Portraits 1981, Somewhere a Master: Further Tales of the Hasidic Master 1982, Paroles d'étranger 1982, The Golem 1983, The Fifth Son (Grand Prix de la Littérature, Paris) 1985, Signes d'exode 1985, Against Silence 1985, A Song for Hope 1987, Job ou Dieu dans la tempête (with Josy Eisenberg) 1987, The Nobel Address 1987, Twilight (novel) 1988, The Six Days of Destruction (with Albert Friedlander) 1988, L'oublie 1989, Silences et mémoire d'hommes 1989, From the Kingdom of Memory, Reminiscences (essays) 1990, Evil and Exile 1990, A Journey of Faith 1990, Sages and Dreamers 1991, Célébration Talmudique 1991, The Forgotten 1992, A Passover Haggadah 1993, All Rivers Run to the Sea (Memoirs, Vol.I) 1995, Et la mer n'est pas remplie (Memoirs, Vol.II) 1996, Célébration prophétique 1998, King Solomon and His Magic Ring 2000, And the Sea Is Never Full: Memoirs 1969–. *Address:* Boston University, 745 Commonwealth Avenue, Boston, MA 02215, USA. *Telephone:* (617) 353-4566.

WIESEL, Torsten Nils, MD; Swedish professor of neurobiology; b. 3 June 1924, Uppsala, Sweden; ed Karolinska Inst. Stockholm; Instr. Karolinska Inst. 1954–55; Asst Karolinska Hosp. 1954–55; Fellow in Ophthalmology, Johns Hopkins Univ. Medical School, Baltimore, Md 1955–58, Asst Prof. of Ophthalmic Physiology 1958–59; Assoc. in Neurophysiology/Neuropharmacology, Harvard Medical School, Boston 1959–60, Asst Prof. 1960–64, Asst Prof. Dept of Psychiatry 1964–67, Prof. of Physiology 1967–68, Prof. of Neurobiology 1968–74, Chair. Dept of Neurobiology 1973–82, Robert Winthrop Prof. of Neurobiology 1974–83; Vincent & Brooke Astor Prof. and Head, Lab. of Neurobiology, The Rockefeller Univ. New York 1983–2001, Gen. Sec. Human Frontier Science Program 2000–; Pres. The Rockefeller Univ. 1992–98, Pres. Emer. 1998–; Pres. Int. Brain Research Org. 1998–; Dir Shelby White & Leon Levy Center for Mind, Brain and Behavior 1999–; Chair. Borderline Personality Disorder Research Foundation 2001–02; Chair. New York Acad. of Sciences 2001–; mem. American Physiology Soc., American Acad. of Arts and Sciences, AAAS, NAS, etc.; Foreign mem. Royal Soc.; Nobel Prize for Medicine 1981; numerous honours and awards. *Publications:* over 80 articles in medical journals. *Address:* The Rockefeller University, 1230 York Avenue, New York, NY 10021, USA. *Telephone:* (212) 327-7093 (Office). *Fax:* (212) 327-8988 (Office). *E-mail:* wiesel@mail.rockefeller.edu (Office).

WIESENTHAL, Simon; Austrian fmr investigator of Nazi crimes and fmr architect; b. 31 Dec. 1908, Buczacz, Austro-Hungarian Empire (now Buchach, Ukraine); s. of Asher Wiesenthal and Rosa Wiesenthal (née Rapp); m. Cyla Müller 1936; one d.; ed Buczacz High School, architectural studies in Prague and Lvov (Lemberg); practised architecture until World War II; prisoner in

Nazi concentration camps 1941–43, 1944–45; liberated from Mauthausen May 1945; active since the war in searching for Nazi criminals, assisting Jewish victims of Nazi regime and in Jewish civic affairs; Head of Jewish Documentation Centre, Linz, Austria 1947–54; Dir Jewish Documentation Centre, Vienna 1961–2003; announced retirement April 2003; Chair. Soc. of Jewish Victims of the Nazi regime in Austria; First Vice-Pres. Union Int. des Résistants et Déportés, Paris; mem. Int. Council of Yad Vashem, Jerusalem; Simon Wiesenthal Center for Holocaust Studies f. at Yeshiva Univ., Los Angeles 1977; Hon. Pres. Australian League for Human Rights 1991; numerous hon mems including Dutch Resistance, Danish Asscn of Freedom Fighters; 19 hon. degrees; many awards and honours, including Diploma of Honour, Internationale de Résistance (Brussels), Org. of Jewish War Veterans (USA), Congressional Gold Medal (USA) 1980, Dutch Medal for Freedom, Medal for Freedom of Luxembourg, Jean-Moulin-Médaille of the French Resistance, Kaj-Munk-Medal, Denmark, Justice Louis Brandeis Award of Zionist Org. in USA 1980, Jerusalem Medal, Medal of Honour, Yad Vashem Foundation (Jerusalem), F.D. Roosevelt Four Freedoms Award (Netherlands) 1990, UNESCO Medal of Honour 1992, Erasmus Prize 1992; Great Medal of Merit, Fed. Repub. of Germany 1985, Chevalier, Légion d'honneur, Commdr of Oranje-Nassau (Netherlands), Commendatore della Repubblica Italiana, Austrian Cross of Honour of the Sciences and Arts, Vienna 1993, Commdr.'s Cross, Order of Polonia Restituta (Poland) 1994, Order of the White Lion, (Czech Repub.) 1999, World Tolerance Award 2000. *Publications:* KZ Mauthausen 1946, Head Mufti, Head Agent of the Axis 1947, I Hunted Eichmann 1961, Limitation 1964, The Murderers Among Us 1967, The Sunflowers 1969, Sails of Hope 1973, The Case of Krystyna Jaworska 1975, Max and Helen 1982, Every Day Remembrance Day—A Chronicle of Jewish Martyrdom 1986, Flight from Destiny 1988, Justice not Vengeance 1988, For They Knew What They Were Doing 1995. *Leisure interest:* philately. *Address:* c/o Jewish Documentation Centre, Salztorgasse 6, 1010 Vienna, Austria.

WIGGINS, David, MA, FBA; British university teacher; b. 8 March 1933, London; s. of Norman Wiggins and Diana Wiggins (née Priestley); m. Jennifer Hornsby 1980 (separated 1987); one s.; ed St Paul's School and Brasenose Coll., Oxford; Asst Prin. Colonial Office 1957–58; Jane Eliza Procter Visiting Fellow, Princeton Univ. 1958–59; Lecturer, New Coll., Oxford 1959, Fellow and Lecturer 1960–67; Prof. of Philosophy, Bedford Coll., London 1967–78; Fellow and Praelector in Philosophy, Univ. Coll., Oxford 1981–89; Prof. of Philosophy, Birkbeck Coll., London 1989–94; Wykeham Prof. of Logic, New Coll., Oxford Univ. 1994–; visiting appts. Stanford Univ. 1964, 1965, Harvard Univ. 1968, 1972, All Souls Coll., Oxford 1973, Princeton Univ. 1980, Univ. Coll., Oxford 1989–; Fellow, Center for Advanced Study in Behavioral Sciences, Stanford 1985–86; mem. Independent Comm. on Transport 1973–74, Cen. Transport Consultative Cttee; Chair. Transport Users' Consultative Cttee for South-East 1977–79; Foreign Hon. mem. American Acad. of Arts and Sciences 1992. *Publications:* Identity and Spatio Temporal Continuity 1967, Truth, Invention and the Meaning of Life 1978, Sameness and Substance 1980, Needs, Values, Truth 1987, Sameness and Substance Renewed 2001; articles in learned journals. *Address:* New College, Oxford, OX1 3BN, England.

WIGHTMAN, Arthur Strong, PhD; American professor of mathematics and physics; b. 30 March 1922, Rochester, NY; s. of Eugene Pinckney Wightman and Edith Stephenson Wightman; m. 1st Anna-Greta Larsson 1945 (died 1976); one d. (died 2001); m. 2nd Ludmila Popova 1977; ed Yale Coll. and Princeton Univ.; Instructor in Physics, Yale Univ. 1943–44; US Navy 1944–46; Instructor in Physics, Princeton Univ. 1949, Asst Prof., Assoc. Prof., Prof. of Math. Physics, 1960–, Thomas D. Jones Prof. of Math. Physics 1971–92, Prof. Emer. 1992–; Visiting Prof. Sorbonne, Paris 1957, École Polytechnique, Palaiseau 1977–78; Fellow American Acad. of Arts and Sciences, Royal Society of Arts, American Physical Soc.; mem. NAS, American Math. Soc.; Hon. DSc (ETH, Zürich) 1969, (Göttingen) 1987; Dannie Heinemann Prize in Mathematical Physics 1969, Poincaré Prize, Int. Asscn for Math. Physics 1997. *Publication:* PCT, Spin and Statistics and All That (with R. F. Streater) 1964, 1978, 2000. *Leisure interests:* art, music, tennis. *Address:* Physics Department, Princeton University, PO Box 708, Princeton, NJ 08544 (Office); 16 Balsam Lane, Princeton, NJ 08540, USA (Home). *Telephone:* (609) 921-7779 (Home); (609) 258-5835 (Office). *E-mail:* wightman@princeton.edu (Home).

WIGLEY, Dafydd, PC, BSc; Welsh politician; b. 1 April 1943, Derby; s. of Elfyn Edward Wigley and Myfanwy (née Batterbee) Wigley; m. Elinor Bennett Owen 1967; three s. (two deceased) one d.; ed Sir Hugh Owen School, Caernarfon, Rydal School, Colwyn Bay, Victoria Univ. of Manchester; Econ. Analyst, Ford Motor Co. 1964–67; Chief Cost Accountant, Mars Ltd 1967–71; Financial Controller, Hoover Ltd 1971–74; Pres. S Caernarfon Creamery 1987–; Co. Borough Councillor, Merthyr Tydfil 1972–74; Vice-Chair. Plaid Cymru 1972–74, Pres. 1981–84, 1991–2000; MP for Caernarfon 1974–2001; Chair. All Party House of Commons Reform Group 1983, Vice-Chair. All-Party Disablement Group 1992–2001; Vice-Chair. Parl. Social Services Group 1985–88; mem. Nat. Ass. for Wales 1999–, Leader of the Opposition 1999–2000, Chair Audit Cttee of Nat. Ass. 2002–; Chair Ymddiriedolaeth Hybu Gwydoniaeth 2002–; Pres. Spastic Soc. of Wales 1985–90, Mencap Wales 1991–; Vice-Pres. Welsh Asscn of Community Councils 1978–, Nat. Fed. of Industrial Devt Authorities 1981–2001; Sponsor, Disabled Persons Act 1981; Chair. Alpha Dyffryn Cyf/Ltd 1980–91; Dir (non-exec.) Gwernafalau

Cyf/Ltd2001–; Hon. mem. Gorsedd of Welsh Bards; Hon. Fellow Univ. of N Wales Bangor 1995; Hon. LLD (Univ. of Wales) 2002; Grimshaw Memorial Award, Nat. Fed. of the Blind 1982; Freedom of the Borough of Arfon 1994, Royal Town of Caernafon 2001. *Publications:* An Economic Plan for Wales 1970, O Ddifri 1992, Dal Ati 1993, A Democratic Wales in a United Europe 1995, A Real Choice for Wales 1996, Maen i'r Wal 2001. *Leisure interests:* football, tennis, chess, hill walking, writing. *Address:* Hen Efail, Bontnwydd, Caernarfon (Home); National Assembly for Wales, Cardiff Bay, Cardiff, CF99 1NA; 8 Stryd y Castell, Caernarfon, Gwynedd, LL55 1SE, Wales (Constituency Office) (Office). *Telephone:* (1286) 672076 (Office); (1286) 830010 (Home); (29) 2089-8711 (Cardiff); (1286) 672076 (Caernarfon). *Fax:* (1286) 672003 (Office); (1286) 830010 (Home); (29) 2089-8266. *E-mail:* dafydd.wigley@wales.gov.uk (Office).

WIGZELL, Hans, MD, PhD; Swedish professor of immunology; b. 28 Oct. 1938; m. Kerstin Largell 1964; one s. three d.; ed Karolinska Inst., Stockholm; Prof. of Immunology, Uppsala Univ. 1972–82; Prof. of Immunology, Karolinska Inst. 1982–, Pres. 1995–; Dir Nat. Bacteriological Lab., Stockholm 1988–; Chair. Nobel Cttee, Karolinska Inst. 1990; Hon. mem. American Asscn of Immunologists; Anders Jahres Prize, Oslo 1975, Erik Fernstrom Prize, Uppsala 1981. *Play:* The Gene Scene 1989. *Publications:* about 500 scientific articles, textbooks and popular science books. *Leisure interests:* music, nature, tropical plants. *Address:* Karolinska Institute, Microbiology and Tumour Biology Centre, 171 77 Stockholm, Sweden. *Telephone:* (8) 728-66-80 (Office). *Fax:* (8) 31-11-01 (Office). *Website:* www.ki.se (Office).

WIIG, Ole, BArch, MArch; Norwegian architect; b. 22 Oct. 1946, Trondheim; s. of Thorvald Wiig and Esther-Marie Wiig; m. 1st Alison Wiig 1972; two d.; m. 2nd Cathrine Lerche 2002; ed Manchester Univ., Dundee Univ., Harvard Univ.; joined Kallmann, McKinnel & Wood, Boston 1973; Community Design Services, Boston 1974; City Architects Dept, Edin. 1974–80; lecturer and studio critic, Edin. Univ. Dept of Architecture 1979–80, Visiting Lecturer and studio critic 1999–2000; External Examiner Dublin Inst. of Tech. Dept of Architecture 2000–; founding partner Narud-Stokke-Wiig AS 1979–, now Sr Pnr; Pres. Nat. Asscn of Norwegian Architects 1990–94; British Tourist Authority Cert. of Distinction, Museum of the Year Award, Edin. Civic Trust Award 1981, RIBA Award, Civic Trust Award, Disabled Design Award 1983, Homansbyen Environmental Award 1991, Nordic Copper Award 1994, First Prize Int. Competition for Scottish Architecture and Design Centre 1995; several first prizes in Norwegian architecture competitions. *Art Exhibitions:* architectural exhbns. in Norway and Scotland and worldwide as part of travelling exhbn of Norwegian architecture. *Publications:* numerous articles on architecture and planning topics in books, newspapers and magazines. *Leisure interest:* introducing modern architecture and design into medieval Italian villages. *Address:* c/o Narud-Stokke-Wiig AS, Rådhusgaten 27, 0158, Oslo (Office); Bryggegaten 16, 0250 Oslo, Norway (Home). *Telephone:* 22-40-37-40 (Office); 22-83-41-01 (Home). *Fax:* 22-40-37-41 (Office); 22-83-21-86 (Home). *E-mail:* ole.wiig@nsw.no (Office). *Website:* www.nsw.no (Office); www.olewiig.no (Home).

WIIN-NIELSEN, Aksel Christopher, DrSc; Danish professor of physics; b. 17 Dec. 1929, Klakring; s. of Aage Nielsen and Marie Petre (née Kristoffersen) Nielsen; m. Bente Havsteen Zimsen 1953; three d.; ed Univs. of Copenhagen and Stockholm; staff mem. Danish Meteorological Inst. 1952–55, Int. Meteorological Inst. 1955–58, Jt Numerical Weather Prediction 1959–61, Nat. Centre for Atmospheric Research 1961–63; Prof. (Chair.), Univ. of Mich., USA 1963–73; Dir European Centre for Medium-Range Weather Forecasts 1974–80; Sec.-Gen. WMO 1980–84; Dir Danish Meteorological Inst. 1984–87; Prof. of Physics, Univ. of Copenhagen 1988–94; mem. Danish Acad. of Tech. Sciences 1980 (Vice-Pres. 1989–92), Finnish Acad. of Sciences and Letters 1980, Royal Swedish Acad. of Sciences 1981, Royal Danish Acad. of Sciences 1982; Hon. DSc (Reading, Copenhagen); Ohridsky Medal, Univ. of Sofia, Bulgaria, Buys-Ballot Medal, Royal Netherlands Acad. of Science, Wihuri Int. Science Prize, Wihuri Foundation, Helsinki, Finland, Rossby Prize, Swedish Geophysical Soc., Silver Medal, Univ. of Helsinki, Palmen Medal, Finnish Geophysical Soc. *Publications:* Problems in Dynamic Meteorology 1970, Dynamic Meteorology 1973, Predictability 1987, Chaos and Causality 1992, Fundamentals of Atmospheric Energetics (with C.-T. Chen) 1993 and about 100 articles on dynamic meteorology, numerical weather prediction and atmospheric energetics.

WIJDENBOSCH, Jules Albert, CERT.ED., PhD; Suriname politician; b. 2 May 1941, Paramaribo; one d.; customs officer 1962–66; civil servant Municipality of Amsterdam 1966–81; mem. State Cttee on Remigration of Surinamese est. by Dutch Govt 1978–81; Sr civil servant Ministry of Dist Admin. and Decentralization 1981, Under-Dir in charge of Bureau for Decentralization of Admin. 1983, Dir of Dist Admin., Ministry of Dist Admin. and Decentralization and Nat. Mobilization 1985; Minister of Home Affairs, Dist Admin. and Nat. Mobilization and Minister of Justice and Police 1986–87; Prime Minister, Minister of Gen. Affairs and Minister of Foreign Affairs 1987–88; Sr civil servant Ministry of Regional Devt 1988–91; Vice-Pres. Repub. of Suriname and Minister of Finance Jan.–Sept. 1991, Pres. 1996–2000; Sr civil servant Ministry of Regional Devt 1991–; co-ordinator Jongerengroep (Youth Section) of Suriname Nat. Party 1962–63; co-ordinator Vereinigung van Bestuurskundigen 1982–; mem. and Acting Chair. Political Advisory Group 25th Feb. Movt 1983; mem. Higher Political Council on the political and admin. future of Suriname 1985–87; first Chair. Nationale Democratische Partij (NDP) 1987–91, Deputy Chair. 1992–96; mem. Nat.

Ass. and floor leader NDP 1991–; Deputy Chair. Foundation for the promotion of remigration of Surinamese; Chair. Amsterdam Welfare Foundation; Chair. Union of Customs Officers 1962–66; co-f. Algemene Jongeren Organisatie (Youth Org.) 1962, Dir 1963; Chair. Surinamese Basketball Fed., Deputy Chair. Surinamese Football Fed.; mem. editorial Bd Lanti; Grand Master, Order of the Yellow Star, Order of the Palm. *Publications:* Schets voor de Republiek Suriname eigen stijl (A Personal View of the Repub. of Suriname) 1974, Bestuurlijke organisatie in een leefgemeenschap (Administrative Organisation in Surinamese Society) 1980, Politieke orde en legitimiteit (Political Order and Legitimacy) 1981, Statuut van het Koninkrijk der Nederlanden (Charter for the Kingdom of the Netherlands) 1979, Participatie in een waarachtige democratie (Participating in a Modern Democracy) 1983. *Address:* c/o Office of the President, Kleine Combeweg 1, Paramaribo, Suriname.

WIJESEKERA, Nandadeva, MA, DLitt, PhD; Sri Lankan anthropologist, archaeologist and government official (retd); b. 11 Dec. 1908, Moonamalwatta, Sri Lanka; s. of Muhandiram N. G. de S. Wijesekera and Dona Emaliya de Alwis Gunatilaka; m. Leila Jayatilaka 1941; one d.; ed Ananda Coll., Colombo, Univ. Coll. Colombo, Trinity Coll. Cambridge, England, Univ. Coll. London, Vienna Univ. and Calcutta Univ.; Asst in Ethnology, Colombo Museum 1937–44; war service in civilian duties 1940–44; Deputy Supt of Census 1945–50; Dir Census and Statistics 1950–55; mem. UNESCO Nat. Comm. 1950; Asst Sec., Ministry of Finance 1951; Sec. Royal Comm. on Languages 1951; Sec. Gal-Oya Devt Bd 1952; Liaison Officer, World Bank Comm. 1952–53; Dir Official Language Dept 1956; Deputy Commr Official Language Affairs 1959–60, Commr 1960–67; Amb. 1967–70; Leader Science Del. to China 1964, Ceylon Del. to Colombo Plan Conf. 1967; Adviser to Dept of Archaeology 1983–; mem. Bd of Man. Inst. of Indigenous Medicine 1983–; has been mem. of numerous Govt dels. and has held many official appointments; Ed.-in-Chief Mahavamsa (in Pali and Sinhala); represented All-Ceylon cricket team 1932; Pres. Nondescripts Cricket Club 1982; Pundit, Oriental Studies Soc. 1959; Fellow Acad. of Arts, Nat. Acad. of Sciences; mem. Sri Lanka Asscn for the Advancement of Science 1964; Pres. All-Ceylon Football Asscn 1963, Royal Asiatic Soc. 1966–67, 1971, 1973–75; Founder Pres. Archaeological Soc. 1966; Hon. D. Litt. (Sri Jayawardene-pura; Gold Medal, Royal Asiatic Soc. 1973, Purā vidyā Chakravarti 1986, Desamanya Sri Lanka 1990. *Publications:* many books, including (Sinhala) Lanka Janatawa 1955, Perani Bitusituvam 1964, Perani Murti Kalawa 1970, Proper Names in Sinhala Literature 1988; (English) People of Ceylon 1949, Early Sinhalese Painting 1959, Veddas in Transition 1964, Biography of Sir D. B. Jayatilaka 1973, Selected Writings 1983, Heritage of Sri Lanka 1984, Anthropological Gleanings from Sinhala Literature 1985, Contacts and Conflicts with Sri Lanka 1986, The Sinhalese 1990, Sri Lankave Urumaya 1991, Archaeology Department's Centenary 1890–1990, 5 Vols (Ed.-in-chief); also (autobiog.) 1995, 25 children's books and 200 articles. *Leisure interests:* reading and writing. *Address:* No. 34 Dudley Senanayake Mawata, Borella, Colombo 8, Sri Lanka. *Telephone:* (1) 694089.

WIJETUNGA, Dingiri Banda; Sri Lankan politician; b. 15 Feb. 1922, Polgahanga, Kandy; m.; one d.; official in Co-operative Dept 1942–47; joined United Nat. Party 1946; MP for Udunuwara 1965; apptd. Minister of Information and Broadcasting 1977, of Power and Highways 1978, of Power and Energy 1979, of Agricultural Devt and Research and Minister of Food 1987, Gov. Northwestern Prov. 1988; Prime Minister of Sri Lanka and Minister of Finance 1989–93; elected Exec. Pres. of Sri Lanka 1993–94. *Address:* c/o Office of the President, Republic Square, Colombo 1, Sri Lanka.

WIJNHOLDS, Johannes de Beaufort, PhD; Netherlands international civil servant and economist; b. 24 Oct. 1943, Amsterdam; m. Jolanthe de Graaf 1968; one s. one d.; ed Univ. of Amsterdam; economist, De Nederlandsche Bank, Amsterdam 1968, various positions in bank 1974–84, Deputy Exec. Dir 1987–94; Asst to Exec. Dir IBRD and IMF, Washington, DC 1972–74, Alt. Exec. Dir IMF 1985–87, Exec. Dir 1994–2003; Perm. Rep. of European Central Bank Washington, DC and its Observer at the IMF; Alt. mem. Social Econ. Council of the Netherlands 1987–94; Prof. of Money and Banking, Univ. of Groningen 1992–95; Order of the Duke of Branimir (Croatia) 2003. *Publications:* The Need for International Reserves and Credit Facilities 1977, The International Banking System (in Dutch) 1985, A Framework for Monetary Stability (ed. and co-author) 1994; numerous articles on int. financial subjects. *Address:* International Monetary Fund, 700 19th Street, NW, Washington, DC 20431, USA. *Telephone:* (202) 623-8350. *Fax:* (202) 623-8377. *E-mail:* publicaffairsd@imf.org (Office). *Website:* www.imf.org (Office).

WIJNSCHENK, Harry; Netherlands politician; b. 1964; fmr motorcycle and watch magazine publisher; fmr mem. Liberal party; fmr State Gen. Lijst Pim Fortuyn, Leader 2002–. *Address:* Lijst Pim fortuyn, Vlaardingweg 62, 3044 CK Rotterdam, Netherlands (Office). *Telephone:* (10) 7507050 (Office). *Fax:* (10) 7507051 (Office). *E-mail:* info@lijst-pimfortuyn.nl (Office). *Website:* www.lijst-pimfortuyn.nl (Office).

WIKTORIN, Gen. Owe Erik Axel; Swedish army officer; b. 7 May 1940, Motala; s. of Erik Wiktorin and Ester Wiktorin (née Johnsson); m. Cajs Gårding 1965; two s.; ed AF Flying Training School, AF Acad., Armed Forces Staff and War Coll., USAF Air Command and Staff Coll.; fighter pilot Skaraborg Wing 1964–69, CO squadron 1969–71; staff officer Swedish Defence Staff 1973–79, Head of Planning Section 1980–83, Dir of Plans and Policy and Deputy Chief 1986–91, Chief 1991–92; Deputy CO Jämtland

(Sector) Wing 1983–84; Head of Planning Section AF Staff 1984–86; CO Southern Jt Command Swedish Armed Forces 1992–94, apptd. Supreme Commdr 1994; Kt Commdr of White Rose of Finland, Chevalier, Légion d'honneur; Gold Medal for Merit, Southern Skåne Regt, Swedish Home Guard; Gold Medal for Merit, Nat. Fed. of AF Asscns. *Leisure interests:* sailing, skiing, cooking, sky-diving, hunting.

WILANDER, Mats; Swedish tennis player; b. 22 Aug. 1964, Vaxjo; m. Sonja Mulholland 1987; turned professional 1981; Australian Open Champion 1983, 1984, 1988, French Open Champion 1982, 1985, 1988 (finalist 1983, 1987), US Open Champion 1988; winner Wimbledon Men's Doubles Championship (with Joakim Nystrom) 1986; mem. victorious Swedish Davis Cup Team 1984, 1987, 1988; ranked world No. 1 1988; voted official World Champion 1988; won 33 singles and 6 doubles titles (including 7 Grand Slam titles); coach of Russian player Marat Safin 2001–. *Leisure interests:* art, music. *Address:* c/o Tennis HOF, 194 Bellevue Avenue, Newport, RI, 02840-3515, USA.

WILBUR, Richard (Purdy), MA; American poet and fmr university professor; b. 1 March 1921, New York City; s. of Lawrence L. Wilbur and Helen Purdy Wilbur; m. Charlotte Ward; three s. one d.; ed Amherst Coll. and Harvard Univ.; Asst Prof. of English, Harvard Univ. 1950–54; Assoc. Prof. Wellesley Coll. 1954–57; Prof. Wesleyan Univ. 1957–77; Writer in Residence, Smith Coll., Northampton, Mass. 1977–86; mem. American Acad. of Arts and Sciences, Soc. of Fellows of Harvard Univ. 1947–50; Guggenheim Fellow 1952–53, 1963, Ford Fellow 1961; Chancellor, Acad. of American Poets 1961; Poet Laureate of USA 1987–88; mem. PEN; Pres. American Acad. of Arts and Letters 1974–76, Chancellor 1977–78; mem. Dramatists Guild; Hon. Fellow, Modern Language Asscn 1986; Chevalier, Ordre des Palmes Académiques 1984; Harriet Monroe Prize 1948, Oscar Blumenthal Prize 1950, Prix de Rome from American Acad. of Arts and Letters 1954–55, Edna St Vincent Millay Memorial Award 1956, Nat. Book Award, Pulitzer Prize 1957, co-recipient Bollingen Translation Prize 1963, co-recipient Bollingen Prize in Poetry 1971, Prix Henri Desfeuilles 1971, Brandeis Creative Arts Award 1971, Shelley Memorial Prize 1973, Harriet Monroe Poetry Award 1978, Drama Desk Award 1983, PEN Translation Prize 1983, St Botolph's Foundation Award 1983, Aiken Taylor Award 1988, L.A. Times Book Award 1988, Pulitzer Prize 1989, Gold Medal for Poetry, American Acad. of Arts and Letters 1991, MacDowell Medal 1992, Nat. Arts Club Medal of Honour for Literature 1994, PEN/Manheim Medal for Translation 1994, Nat. Medal of Arts 1994, Milton Center Prize 1995, Robert Frost Medal, Poetry Soc. of America 1996, T. S. Eliot Award 1996. *Publications:* The Beautiful Changes and Other Poems 1947, Ceremony and Other Poems 1950, A Bestiary (anthology, with Alexander Calder) 1955, The Misanthrope (trans. from Molière) 1955, Things of This World (poems) 1956, Poems 1943–1956 1957, Candide (comic opera, with Lillian Hellman and others) 1957, Poe (edition of his poems with introduction and notes) 1959, Advice to a Prophet (poems) 1961, Tartuffe (trans. from Molière) 1963, The Poems of Richard Wilbur 1963, Loudmouse (for children) 1963, Poems of Shakespeare (with Alfred Harbage) 1966, Walking to Sleep (new poems and translations) 1969, School for Wives (trans. from Molière) 1971, Opposites (children's verse, illustrated by the author) 1973, The Mind-Reader 1976, Responses: Prose Pieces 1953–1976 1976, The Learned Ladies (trans. from Molière) 1978, Selected Poems of Witter Bynner (editor) 1978, Seven Poems 1981, Andromache (trans. from Racine) 1982, The Whale (translations) 1982, Molière: Four Comedies (contains 4 plays translated previously listed) 1982, Phaedra (trans. from Racine) 1986, Lying and Other Poems 1987, New and Collected Poems 1988, More Opposites 1991, School for Husbands (trans. from Molière) 1992, The Imaginary Cuckold (trans. from Molière) 1993, A Game of Catch 1994, Amphitryon (trans. from Molière) 1995, The Catbird's Song (prose pieces) 1997, The Disappearing Alphabet (for children and others) 1998, Bone Key and Other Poems 1998, Mayflies (poems) 2000, Don Juan (trans. from Molière) 2000, The Bungler (trans. from Molière) 2000, Opposites, More Opposites and Some Differences (for children) 2000, The Pig in the Spigot (for children) 2000. *Leisure interests:* tennis, walking, herb gardening. *Address:* 87 Dodwells Road, Cummington, MA 01026; 715R Windsor Lane, Key West, FL 33040, USA (Winter). *Telephone:* (413) 634-2275; (305) 296-7499.

WILBUR, Richard Sloan, MD, JD; American association executive and physician; b. 8 April 1924, Boston; s. of Blake Colburn Wilbur and Mary Caldwell Sloan; m. Betty Lou Fannin 1951; three s.; ed John Marshall Law School, Stanford Univ.; Intern, San Francisco County Hosp. 1946–47; Resident, Stanford Hosp. 1949–51, Univ. of Pa Hosp. 1951–52; mem. staff, Palo Alto Medical Clinic, Calif. 1952–69; Deputy Exec. Vice-Pres., American Medical Asscn, Chicago 1969–71, 1973–74; Asst Sec., Health and Environment Dept 1971–73; Sr Vice-Pres., Baxter Labs Inc., Deerfield, Ill. 1974–76; Exec. Vice-Pres. Council Medical Speciality Socs. 1976–91, Emer. 1992–; Sec., Accreditation Council for Continuing Medical Educ. 1979–91; Assoc. Prof. of Medicine, Stanford Medical School 1952–69, Georgetown Univ. Medical School 1971–77; Vice-Pres. Nat. Resident Matching Plan 1980–91, Chair. 1991–92; Chair. Bd Calif. Medical Asscn 1968–69; Chair. Calif. Blue Shield 1966–68; Chair. American Medico-Legal Foundation 1987–, Professional Advisory Bd, Royal Soc. of Medicine Foundation 1995–; Pres. American Coll. of Physician Executives 1988–89; Pres. American Bd Medical Man. 1992–93; Pres. MedicAlert Foundation Int. 1992–94, MedicAlert Foundation, USA 1992–94, Dir MedicAlert Germany 1992–94, Iberica 1992–94, Europe (UK) 1992–95; Chair. Bd and CEO Inst. for Clinical Information 1994–; Sr Vice-

Pres. Healthcare, Buckeye Corpn Pte. Ltd 1997–; Chair. Medical Advisory Bd, Medical City, Bangalore 1997–2000; Pres. Royal Soc. of Medicine Foundation 1998–; mem. numerous other medical asscns; Distinguished Service Medal, Dept of Defense 1973. *Publications:* contribs to medical journals. *Address:* APT Management Inc., 207 Westminster Road, Suite 201, Lake Forest, IL 60045 (Office); 985 North Hawthorne Place, Lake Forest, IL 60045, USA (Home). *Telephone:* (847) 234-6337 (Office). *Fax:* (847) 234-6511. *E-mail:* aptmgmnt@aol.com (Office).

WILBY, James; British actor; b. 20 Feb. 1958, Rangoon, Burma; s. of Geoffrey Wilby and Shirley Wilby; m. Shana Louise Magraw 1988; three s. one d.; ed Sedbergh School, Durham Univ., Royal Acad. of Dramatic Art, London; Best Actor, Venice Film Festival 1988. *Stage appearances:* Another Country (West End début), Who's Afraid of Virginia Woolf (Belgrade Theatre, Coventry), Chips With Everything (Leeds Playhouse), As You Like It (Royal Exchange Theatre, Manchester and tour), Jane Eyre (Chichester), A Patriot for Me (Barbican), Helping Harry (Jermyn Street). *Films:* Dreamchild, Maurice, A Handful of Dust, A Summer Story, Howards End 1991, Immaculate Conception 1992, Une partie d'echec, Regeneration, An Ideal Husband, Tom's Midnight Garden, Cotton Mary, Jump Tomorrow, Gosford Park. *Television:* Sherlock Holmes, The Crooked Man, Dutch Girls, A Tale of Two Cities, Mother Love, Tell Me That You Love Me, Adam Bede, You, Me And It, Lady Chatterley, Crocodile Shoes, Woman in White 1997, The Dark Room, Trial and Retribution IV, Bertie and Elizabeth. *Leisure interests:* playing piano, tennis, sailing. *Address:* c/o Sue Latimer, A.R.G., 4 Great Portland Street, London, W1W 8PA, England. *Telephone:* (20) 7436-6400. *Fax:* (20) 7436-6700.

WILD, Earl; American pianist and composer; b. 26 Nov. 1915, Pittsburgh, Pa; s. of Royland Wild and Lillian G. Wild; ed Carnegie Technical Coll., Pittsburgh; studied with Selmar Jansen, Egon Petri, Helene Barrere, Volya Cossack and Paul Doguereau; first American soloist to perform with NBC Orchestra conducted by Toscanini 1942, has performed with symphony orchestras and given recitals in many cos.; staff pianist, composer, conductor ABC TV, New York 1945–68; has appeared with Sir Malcolm Sargent, Jascha Horenstein, Sir Georg Solti, Arthur Fiedler; played first TV piano recital 1939; has played for 7 Presidents of U.S., including inauguration of Pres. J. F. Kennedy; teacher Juilliard School of Music 1977–, Manhattan School of Music 1981–83; numerous recordings for RCA, EMI, Columbia, Nonesuch, Readers Digest and Vanguard Records. *Compositions include:* Piano Concerto, The Turquoise Horse (choral work) and ballet music, oratorios, solo piano music, choral work and popular songs. *Leisure interests:* writing poetry, playing piano.

WILD, John Paul, AC, CBE, MA, ScD, FRS, FAA, FTSE; Australian radio astronomer; b. 17 May 1923, Sheffield, England; s. of the late Alwyn H. Wild and Bessie Wild (née Arnold); m. 1st Elaine Poole Hull 1948 (died 1991); two s. one d.; m. 2nd Margaret Lyndon 1991; ed Whitgift School, Croydon, England and Peterhouse, Cambridge; Radar Officer, Royal Navy 1943–47; Research Scientist, Div. of Radiophysics, Commonwealth Scientific and Industrial Research Org. (CSIRO), Australia 1947–71, Chief of Div. 1971–77, Assoc. mem. 1977–78, full-time mem. of CSIRO Exec. 1978–85, Chair. and Chief Exec. 1978–85; Chair. Very Fast Train (VFT) Jt Venture 1986–91; Pres. Radio Astronomy Comm. of Int. Astronomical Union 1967–70; mem. Anglo-Australian Telescope Bd 1973–82, Chair. 1975–80; Foreign mem. American Philosophical Soc.; Corresp. mem. Royal Soc. of Sciences, Liège; Foreign Hon. mem. American Acad. of Arts and Sciences; Hon. Fellow Peterhouse, Cambridge, Royal Soc. of NSW, Royal Soc. of Arts, Inst. of Engineers, Australia; Hon. DSc (Aust. Nat. Univ.) 1979, (Newcastle Univ.) 1982; Hale Prize for Solar Astronomy, American Astronomical Soc. 1980; Edgeworth David Medal, Hendryk Arctowski Gold Medal of NAS, Balthasar van der Pol Gold Medal of Int. Union of Radio Science, Herschel Medal of Royal Astronomical Soc., Thomas Rankin Lyle Medal of Australian Acad. of Science, Royal Medal, Royal Soc. of London 1980, ANZAAS Medal 1984, Hartnett Medal, Royal Soc. of Arts 1988. *Publications:* various papers on radio astronomy in scientific journals. *Address:* Unit 4, 1 Grant Crescent, Griffith, ACT 2603, Australia; 800 Avon Road, Ann Arbor, MI 48104, USA. *Telephone:* (2) 6295-3473 (Australia); (734) 663-8333 (USA). *Fax:* (734) 761-1586.

WILDER, Gene (pseudonym of Jerry Silberman), BA; American film actor, director and producer; b. 11 June 1935, Milwaukee, Wis.; s. of William J. Silberman and Jeanne Silberman (née Baer); m. 1st Mary Joan Schutz 1967 (divorced 1974); one d.; m. 2nd Gilda Radner 1984 (deceased); m. 3rd Karen Boyer 1991; ed Univ. of Iowa, Bristol Old Vic. Theatre School; served with U.S. Army 1956–58; Broadway play: The Complaisant Lover 1962, West End play Laughter on the 23rd Floor 1996. *Films include:* Bonnie and Clyde 1966, The Producers 1967, Start the Revolution Without Me 1968, Quackser Fortune Has a Cousin in the Bronx 1969, Willy Wonka and the Chocolate Factory 1970, The Scarecrow 1972, Everything You Always Wanted to Know About Sex, But Were Afraid to Ask 1971, Young Frankenstein 1974, The Little Prince 1974, Rhinoceros 1972, Blazing Saddles 1973, Thursday's Game 1974, The Adventure of Sherlock Holmes's Smarter Brother 1975, Silver Streak 1976, The World's Greatest Lover 1977, The Frisco Kid 1979, Stir Crazy 1980, Sunday Lovers 1980, Hanky Panky 1982, The Woman in Red 1984, Haunted Honeymoon 1986, See No Evil, Hear No Evil 1989, Funny About Love 1990, Another You 1991, Stuart Little (voice) 1999, Murder in a Small Town 1999. *Television appearances include:* The Scarecrow 1972, The Trouble With People 1973, Marlo Thomas Special 1973, Thursday's Games 1973, Something Wilder

1994–, Alice in Wonderland (film) 1999, The Lady in Question (film) 1999. *Address:* c/o Ames Cushing, William Morris Agency, 151 El Camino Drive, Beverly Hills, CA 90212, USA.

WILDHABER, Luzius, DrIur, LLM, JSD; Swiss judge and professor of law; b. 18 Jan. 1937, Basle; m. 1st Simone Wildhaber-Creux 1963 (died 1994); two d.; m. 2nd Gill Reilly 1998; ed Basle, Paris, Heidelberg, London and Yale Univs; Int. Law Div. Fed. Dept of External Affairs 1968–71; Prof. of Int. Constitutional and Admin. Law, Univ. of Fribourg 1971–77; Prof. of Int. and Constitutional Law, Univ. of Basle 1977–98, Rector (desig.) 1990–92, Rector 1992–94, Pro-Rector 1994–96; Judge, Supreme Court of Liechtenstein 1975–88, Admin. Tribunal, IDB 1989–94, European Court of Human Rights 1991–; Pres. European Court of Human Rights 1998–; Star of Romania 2000; Dr hc (Charles Univ., Prague) 1999, (Sofia Univ.) 1999, (American Univ. in Bulgaria) 1999, (Bratislava) 2000, (State Univ. of Moldova) 2000, (Bucharest) 2000, (Russian Acad. of Sciences) 2000, (Law Univ. of Lithuania) 2000, (Tbilisi) 2001, (Nat. Law Acad. of Ukraine) 2001; Hon. LLD (McGill Univ., Montreal) 2001; Marcel Benoist Prize 1999. *Publications:* Advisory Opinions—Rechtsgutachten höchster Gerichte 1962, Treaty-making Power and Constitution 1971, Praxis des Völkerrechts (with J. P. Müller) 1977, Erfahrungen mit der Europäischen Menschenrechtskonvention 1979, Wechselspiel zwischen Innen und Aussen 1996; more than 200 articles. *Leisure interests:* travel, skiing, hiking, mountaineering. *Address:* European Court of Human Rights, Council of Europe, 67075 Strasbourg, France. *Telephone:* (3) 88-41-31-53. *Fax:* (3) 88-41-27-92.

WILES, Sir Andrew John, KBE, PhD, FRS; British mathematician; b. 11 April 1953; s. of Rev. M. F. Wiles; m.; two d.; ed Merton Coll. Oxford, Clare Coll. Cambridge; fmr Fellow Clare Coll.; Prof. of Math., Princeton Univ., USA 1982–88, 1990–; Royal Soc. Research Prof. in Math. and Professorial Fellow Merton Coll. Oxford 1988–90; Hon. DSc (Oxon) 1999; Jr Whitehead Prize (jtly.), London Math. Soc. 1988, Wolfskehl Prize (for proving Fermat's Last Theorem), Göttingen 1997, Special Award, Berlin Int. Congress of Mathematicians 1998. *Address:* Department of Mathematics, Princeton University, Fine Hall, Washington Hall, Princeton, NJ 08544, USA. *Website:* www.princeton.edu (Office).

WILES, Rev. Maurice Frank, MA, DD, FBA; British ecclesiastic and fmr university professor; b. 17 Oct. 1923, London; s. of Sir Harold Wiles and Lady Wiles; m. Patricia M. Mowll 1950; two s. one d.; ed Tonbridge School, Christ's Coll. Cambridge and Ridley Hall, Cambridge; curate, St George's Church, Stockport 1950–52; chaplain, Ridley Hall, Cambridge 1952–55; lecturer, Univ. Coll. Ibadan, Nigeria 1955–59; Dean, Clare Coll. Cambridge and Univ. lecturer, Faculty of Divinity 1959–67; Prof. of Christian Doctrine, King's Coll. London 1967–70; Regius Prof. of Divinity, Univ. of Oxford and Canon of Christ Church Cathedral 1970–91. *Publications:* The Spiritual Gospel 1960, The Christian Fathers 1966, The Divine Apostle 1967, The Making of Christian Doctrine 1967, The Remaking of Christian Doctrine 1974, What Is Theology? 1976, Working Papers in Doctrine 1976, Explorations in Theology 4 1979, Faith and the Mystery of God 1982, God's Action in the World 1986, Christian Theology and Interreligious Dialogue 1992, A Shared Search 1994, Archetypal Heresy 1996, Reason to Believe 1999. *Address:* Christ Church, Oxford, OX1 1DP, England.

WILHELM, Ivan, CSc; Czech scientist; b. 1 May 1942, Trnava, Slovakia; m.; one d.; ed Czech Tech. Univ. (CVUT), Prague; Asst, Dept of Nuclear Physics, CVUT 1964–67; study attachment to Neutron Physics Lab., United Inst. for Nuclear Research, Dubna, USSR 1967–71; Sr Research Officer Faculty of Math. and Physics, Charles Univ. 1971–89, Chief Research Officer 1989–91, Dir Nuclear Centre 1990–94, Vice-Rector for Devt 1994–2000, Rector of Charles Univ. 2000–; Pres. Czech Rectors' Conf.; mem. Exec. Council European Univ. Asscn (EUA). *Publications include:* more than 80 research papers on nuclear and neutron physics. *Leisure interests:* cycling, walking. *Address:* Charles University, Ovocný trh 5, 11636 Prague 1, Czech Republic (Office). *Telephone:* (2) 24210663 (Office). *Fax:* (2) 24491312 (Office). *E-mail:* ivan.wilhelm@ruk.cuni.cz (Office). *Website:* www.ruk.cuni.cz (Office).

WILHELMSSON, Hans K. B., DTech; Swedish professor of physics; b. 4 Oct. 1929, Göteborg; s. of Wilhelm Petterson and Clara M. Johansson; m. 1st Birgitta Fredrikson 1960 (divorced 1995); one s. one d.; m. 2nd Julie Baudin 1995; ed Chalmers Univ. of Tech.; Prof. and Dir Inst. for Electromagnetic Field Theory, Chalmers Univ. of Tech. Göteborg 1971; Prof. of Plasma Physics, Fondation de France, Ecole Polytechnique, Palaiseau 1987–93, Prof. Emer. 1994–; mem. Royal Swedish Acad., Royal Swedish Acad. of Eng Science, Acad. Nationale des Sciences, Belles-Lettres et Arts de Bordeaux; John Ericson Medal (Chalmers Univ.) 1952. *Publications:* Fusion: A Voyage Through the Plasma Universe 2000; more than 200 scientific articles in theoretical and plasma physics. *Leisure interests:* art, travel. *Address:* 2 rue Marcellin Berthelot, 33200 Bordeaux, France. *Telephone:* (5) 56-02-19-80 (Home). *Fax:* (5) 56-02-19-80 (Home). *E-mail:* lotus15@infonie.fr (Home).

WILKES, Joanne; university lecturer and writer; Lecturer in English, Univ. of Auckland; Rose Mary Crawshay Prize 2000. *Publications:* Lord Byron and Mme de Staël: Born for Opposition 2000, ed. Geraldine Jewsbury's The Half Sisters, numerous articles. *Address:* Department of English, University of Auckland, Private Bag 92019, Auckland 1, New Zealand (Office). *Telephone:* (9) 373-7999 (Office). *Fax:* (9) 373-7400 (Office). *E-mail:* j.wilkes@auckland.ac.nz (Office). *Website:* www2.arts.auckland.ac.nz (Office).

WILKES, Sir Maurice Vincent, Kt, PhD, FRS, FREng, FIEE, FBCS; British computer engineer (retd); b. 26 June 1913, Dudley; s. of the late Vincent J. Wilkes, OBE; m. Nina Twyman 1947; one s. two d.; ed King Edward VI School, Stourbridge and St John's Coll., Cambridge; Univ. Demonstrator 1937; Radar and Operational Research, Second World War; Univ. Lecturer and Acting Dir of Mathematical Lab., Cambridge 1945, Dir 1946–70; Head of Computer Lab. 1970; Prof. of Computer Tech., Univ. of Cambridge 1965–80; Staff Consultant, Digital Equipment Corpn 1980–86; Adjunct Prof. MIT 1981–85; mem. for Research Strategy, Olivetti Research Bd 1986–96; Adviser on Research Strategy, Olivetti and Oracle Research Lab. 1996–99; Staff Consultant AT&T Laboratories Cambridge 1999–2002; mem. Measurement and Control Section Cttee, Inst. of Electrical Engineers 1956–59; First Pres. British Computer Soc. 1957–60; mem. Council, Int. Fed. for Information Processing 1960–63, Council, Inst. of Electrical Engineers 1973–76, Council, Asscn for Computing Machinery 1991–94; Turing Lecturer Asscn for Computing Machinery 1967; Distinguished Fellow, British Computer Soc. 1973; Foreign Assoc. US Nat. Acad. of Engineering 1977, NAS 1980; Foreign Hon. mem. American Acad. Arts and Sciences 1974; Hon. ScD (Cambridge) 1993; Dr hc (Amsterdam) 1978, (Newcastle-on-Tyne, Hull, Kent, City Univ. London, Linköping, Munich, Bath); Harry Goode Memorial Award, American Fed. of Information Processing Socs. 1968, Eckert-Mauchly Award, American Fed. of Information Processing Socs. 1980, McDowell Award, IEEE 1981, Faraday Medal, IEE 1981, Pender Award, Univ. of Pa 1982, C and C Prize, Tokyo 1988, Italgas Prize, Turin 1991, Kyoto Prize 1992, John von Neumann Medal, IEEE 1997, Mountbatten Medal, Nat. Electronics Council 1997. *Publications:* Oscillations of the Earth's Atmosphere 1949, Preparation of Programs for an Electronic Digital Computer 1951, 1957, Automatic Digital Computers 1956, A Short Introduction to Numerical Analysis 1966, Time-Sharing Computer Systems 1968, The Cambridge CAP Computer and its Operating System 1979, Memoirs of a Computer Pioneer 1985, Computing Perspectives 1995. *Address:* Computer Lab, University of Cambridge, William Gates Building, J. J. Thomson Road, Cambridge, CB3 0FD, England (Office). *Telephone:* (1223) 763699 (Office).

WILKES, Gen. Sir Michael (John), KCB, CBE; British army officer; b. 11 June 1940, Steep, Hants.; s. of the late Lt-Col Jack Wilkes and of Phyllis Wilkes; m. Anne Jacqueline Huelin 1966; two s.; ed Royal Mil. Acad., Sandhurst; commissioned RA 1960; joined 7 Para Regt, Royal Horse Artillery 1961; served Middle East Troop, Commdr Special Forces, Radfan, Saudi Arabia, Borneo 1964–67; Staff Coll. 1971–72; Brig. Maj. RA, HQ 3 Armoured Div. 1973–74; Battery Commdr Chestnut Troop, 1 Royal Horse Artillery (BAOR) 1975–76; CO 1977–79; Mil. Asst to Chief of Gen. Staff 1980–81; Chief of Staff, 3 Armoured Div. 1982–83; Commdr 22 Armoured Brigade 1984–85; Arms Dir, Ministry of Defence 1986–88; Gen. Officer Commdg 3 Armoured Div. 1988–90; Commdr UK Field Army and Insp.-Gen., TA 1990–93; Middle East Adviser to Ministry of Defence 1992–95; Adjutant-Gen. 1993–95; Lt-Gov. and C-in-C, Jersey 1995–2000; Col Commdt and Pres., Hon. Artillery Co. 1992–98; Pres. Army Cadet Force Asscn 1999–; Kermit Roosevelt Lecturer 1995; Order of Mil. Merit 1st Class (Jordan) 1994, Freeman City of London 1993; KStJ. *Leisure interests:* mil. history, sailing, skiing. *Address:* c/o Le Riche House, P.O.Box 4, 1-3 l'avenue le Bas, Longveville, St Saviour, Jersey, JE4 8NB (Office).

WILKINS, Maurice Hugh Frederick, CBE, PhD, FRS; British molecular biologist; b. 15 Dec. 1916, Pongaroa, New Zealand; s. of the late E. H. Wilkins and of Eveline Whittaker; m. Patricia Chidgey 1959; two s. two d.; ed St John's Coll., Cambridge; Research on luminescence of solids, Physics Dept Birmingham Univ.; Ministry of Home Security and Aircraft Production 1938; Manhattan Project (Ministry of Supply), Univ. of Calif. 1944; Lecturer in Physics, St Andrews Univ. 1945; Medical Research Council, Biophysics Unit, King's Coll., London 1946, Deputy Dir 1955–70, Dir 1970–72, Dir Neurobiology Unit (Cell Biophysics Unit 1974–80), MRC 1972; Prof. of Biophysics and Head of Dept, King's Coll. 1970–82, Prof. Emer. 1981–, Fellow 1973–; mem. Russell Cttee against Chemical Weapons 1981; Pres. British Soc. for Social Responsibility in Science 1969–91, Food and Disarmament Int. 1984–; Hon. mem. American Soc. of Biological Chemists 1964; Foreign Hon. mem. American Acad. of Arts and Sciences 1970; Hon. LLD (Glasgow) 1972, Hon. ScD (Birmingham) 1992, Hon. DSc (London) 1998; Albert Lasker Award, American Public Health Asscn 1960; Nobel Prize for Physiology or Medicine (Jt recipient) 1962. *Publications:* Papers on luminescence and topics in biophysics, e.g. molecular structure of nucleic acids and structure of nerve membranes. *Address:* 30 St John's Park, London, SE3 7JH, England. *Telephone:* (20) 7836-5454; (20) 8858-1817.

WILKINSON, Sir Denys Haigh, Kt, DSc, PhD, ScD, FRS; British physicist and university professor; b. 5 Sept. 1922, Leeds; s. of Charles Wilkinson and Hilda Wilkinson; m. 1st Christiane Clavier 1947; three d.; m. 2nd Helen Sellschop 1967; ed Jesus Coll., Cambridge; worked on British Atomic Energy Project 1943–46, on Canadian Atomic Energy Project 1945–46; Demonstrator Cavendish Lab., Univ. of Cambridge 1947–51, Lecturer 1951–56 and Reader 1950–57, Fellow, Jesus Coll., Cambridge 1944–59, Hon. Fellow 1961–; Student of Christ Church, Oxford 1957–76, Emer. 1976–79, Hon. 1979–; Prof. of Nuclear Physics Clarendon Laboratory of Univ. of Oxford 1957–59, Prof. of Experimental Physics 1959–76, Head of Dept of Nuclear Physics 1962–76; Vice-Chancellor Sussex Univ. 1976–87, Prof. Emer. 1987–; Pres. Inst. of Physics 1980–82, Hon. Fellow 2002–; Rutherford Memorial Lecturer of British Physical Soc. 1962; mem. Governing Bd Nat. Inst. for Research in

Nuclear Science 1958–64; Queen's Lecturer, Berlin 1966, Cherwell-Simon Memorial Lecturer, Oxford 1970, Tizard Memorial Lecturer 1975, Lauritsen Memorial Lecturer, Calif. Inst. of Tech. 1976, Schiff Memorial Lecturer, Stanford Univ. 1977, Racah Memorial Lecturer, Univ. of Jerusalem 1977, Solly Cohen Memorial Lecturer, Hebrew Univ. of Jerusalem 1985, Axel Memorial Lecturer, Univ. of Ill. 1985, Breit Memorial Lecturer, Yale Univ. 1987, W. B. Lewis Memorial Lecturer, Chalk River 1989, Humphry Davy Lecturer, Acad. of Science (Paris) 1990, Rutherford Memorial Lecturer, NZ 1991, W. V. Houston Memorial Lecturer, Rice Univ., Houston, Tex. 1994, Hudspeth Lecturer, Univ. of Tex. Austin 1994, McPherson Memorial Lecturer, McGill Univ., Montreal 1995, Pickavance Memorial Lecturer, Rutherford Lab., Oxford 1997, Sargent Memorial Lecturer, Queen's Univ., Kingston, Ont. 1998, Saha Memorial Lecturer, Kolkata 2001; mem. Science Research Council 1967–70; Chair. SRC Nuclear Physics Bd 1968–70, Physics III Cttee CERN, Geneva 1971–75, Radioactive Waste Man. Advisory Cttee 1978–83; Vice-Pres. IUPAP 1985–93; mem. Council of the Asscn of Commonwealth Univs 1981–87; mem. Academia Europaea; Foreign mem. Royal Swedish Acad. of Sciences; Battelle Distinguished Prof., Univ. of Washington 1970; Hon. DSc (Univ. of Saskatchewan, Utah State Univ., Univ. of Guelph, Queen's Univ., Ont.); Hon. FilDr (Univ. of Uppsala); Hon. LLD (Sussex); Hon. DSc (Coll. of William and Mary, Williamsburg); Holweck Medallist of French and British Physical Socs 1957, Hughes Medal of the Royal Soc. 1965, Bruce-Preller Prize of Royal Soc. of Edinburgh 1969, Tom W. Bonner Prize of American Physical Soc. 1974, Royal Medal, Royal Soc. 1980, Guthrie Medal of Inst. of Physics 1986, CCSEM Gold Medal 1988. *Publications:* Ionization Chambers and Counters 1950, Our Universes 1991; Ed.: Isospin in Nuclear Physics 1969, Progress in Particle and Nuclear Physics 1977–84; Mesons in Nuclei (jt ed.) 1979; many articles in learned journals. *Leisure interests:* early music and art, ornithology. *Address:* Gayles Orchard, Friston, Eastbourne, BN20 0BA, England. *Telephone:* (1323) 423333. *Fax:* (1323) 423956.

WILKINSON, Paul, MA, FRSA; British professor of international relations; b. 9 May 1937, Harrow, Middx; s. of Walter Ross Wilkinson and Joan Rosemary Paul; m. Susan Wilkinson 1960; two s. one d.; ed Lower School of John Lyon, Harrow, Univ. Coll., Swansea and Univ. of Wales; regular officer RAF 1959–65; Asst Lecturer in Politics, Univ. Coll., Cardiff 1966–68, Lecturer 1968–75, Sr Lecturer 1975–78; Reader in Politics, Univ. of Wales 1978–79; Chair. in Int. Relations, Aberdeen Univ. 1979–89; Head Dept of Int. Relations, Univ. of St Andrews 1990–94, Prof. of Int. Relations 1990–, Head School of History and Int. Relations 1994–96, Dir Centre for the Study of Terrorism and Political Violence 1998–2002, Chair. 2002–; Dir Research Inst. for the Study of Conflict and Terrorism 1989–94; Visiting Fellow, Trinity Hall, Cambridge 1997–98; Hon. Fellow Univ. Coll., Swansea 1986. *Publications:* Social Movement 1971, Political Terrorism 1974, Terrorism versus Liberal Democracy 1976, Terrorism and the Liberal State (revised edn) 1986, British Perspectives on Terrorism 1981, Terrorism: Theory and Practice (jtly) 1978, The New Fascists (revised edn) 1983, Contemporary Research on Terrorism 1987, Lessons of Lockerbie 1989, Terrorism and Political Violence (ed., with David Rapoport) 1990, Technology and Terrorism (ed.) 1993, Terrorism: British Perspectives (ed.) 1993, Research Report (Vol. Two) Lord Lloyd's Inquiry into Legislation Against Terrorism 1996, Aviation Terrorism and Security Versus (ed., with Brian Jenkins) 1998, Terrorism Versus Democracy: The Liberal State Response 2000 and numerous articles in specialist journals. *Leisure interests:* modern art, poetry, walking. *Address:* Department of International Relations, University of St Andrews, North Street, St Andrews, Fife, KY16 9AL, Scotland. *Telephone:* (1334) 462938. *Fax:* (1334) 463005. *E-mail:* gm39@st-andrews.ac.uk (Office).

WILKINSON, Sir Philip William, Kt, FCIB; British business executive; b. 8 May 1927; m. Eileen Patricia Malkin 1951 (died 1991); one s. two d.; ed Leyton County High School; joined Westminster Bank (later Nat. Westminster Bank) 1943, Dir 1979–90, Deputy Chair. 1987–90; Chief Exec. Lombard North Cen. Ltd 1975; Gen. Man. Related Banking Services Div. 1978, Deputy Group Chief Exec. 1980, Group Chief Exec. 1983–87; Dir HandelsBank 1983–90 (Deputy Chair. 1987–90); Dir British Aerospace 1987–91, English Nat. Opera 1988–93, National Power 1990–92; Chair Wishbone Trust 1994–; Vice-Pres. Chartered Inst. of Bankers 1989–; Trustee Baptist Bldg Fund 1987–; Council mem. Imperial Cancer Research Fund 1990–2000; mem. Finance Cttee, Union Internationale contre le Cancer (UICC) 1993–2002; Hon. Fellow British Orthopaedic Asscn 2001. *Leisure interests:* opera, theatre, golf, watching sport. *Address:* Pine Court, Whichert Close, Knotty Green, Beaconsfield, Bucks., HP9 2TP, England.

WILKINSON, Tom; British actor. *Films:* Sylvia 1985, Wetherby 1985, Sharma and Beyond 1986, Paper Mask 1990, In the Name of the Father 1993, All Things Bright and Beautiful 1994, Priest 1994, A Business Affair 1994, Sense and Sensibility 1995, The Ghost and the Darkness 1996, Oscar and Lucinda 1997, Smilla's Sense of Snow 1997, Wilde 1997, The Full Monty 1997, Jilting Joe 1997, The Governess 1998, Shakespeare in Love 1998, Rush Hour 1998, Father Damien 1999, Ride with the Devil 2000, Chain of Fools 2000, In the Bedroom 2001, Black Knight 2001, The Importance of Being Earnest 2002, The Gathering Storm 2002. *Plays:* Plays with Royal National Theatre, RSC and Oxford Playhouse include Peer Gynt, Brand, Henry V, Three Sisters, Uncle Vanya, Julius Caesar, Hamlet, The Merchant of Venice, The Crucible, As You Like It. *Television includes:* Prime Suspect, Martin Chuzzlewit.

WIŁKOMIRSKA, Wanda; Polish violinist; b. 11 Jan. 1929, Warsaw; d. of Alfred Wiłkomirski and Dorota Temkin; divorced since 1976; two s.; ed Higher

State of Music, Łódź, Franz Liszt Acad. of Music, Budapest and pvt. studies with Henryk Szeryng, Paris; public debut at age of 7 years; first appearance with orchestra aged 15, in Cracow; numerous recordings; concerts in 50 countries with most of the maj. orchestras throughout the world; defected whilst on tour of FRG March 1982; Prof. Hochschule für Musik, Heidelberg-Mannheim 1983–98; Visiting Prof. Conservatory of Music, Sydney 1999—; Officer's Cross of Polonia Restituta Order 1953, Commdr's Cross with Star 2001; Order of Banner of Labour 2nd Class 1959, (1st Class) 1964; Polish State Prize 1952, 1964; several foreign prizes, including Bach Competition Award of Democratic German Radio, Culture and Arts Prize (1st Class) 1975, Orpheus Prize, Polish Musicians' Asscn 1979. *Leisure interests:* films, literature, sports.

WILLATS, Stephan; British artist; b. 17 Aug. 1943, London; m. Stephanie Craven 1983; three s.; ed Drayton School and Ealing School of Art; Ed. and Publr Control magazine 1965–; Lecturer, Ipswich School of Art 1965–67; Lecturer, Nottingham Coll. of Art 1968–72; Organiser, Centre for Behavioural Art, Gallery House, London 1972–73; numerous group exhbns. in the UK, Netherlands, Italy, Fed. Repub. of Germany, Switzerland, Belgium, Australia; numerous project works, including Inside an Ocean, Mile End, London 1979, Two Worlds Apart, Hayes 1981 and Blocks, Avondale Estate, London 1982, Brentford Towers, W London 1985, White Towers, Helsinki 1989, Private Network, Oxford 1990; D.A.A.D. Fellowship, Berlin 1979–81. *Solo exhibitions include:* Concerning Our Present Way of Living, Whitechapel Art Gallery, London 1979, Four Islands in Berlin, National Gallery, Berlin 1980, Meta Filter and Related Works, Tate Gallery, London 1982, Another City, Riverside Studios, London 1984, Doppelgänger, Lisson Gallery, Double Crossing, Ralph Wernicke Gallery, Stuttgart 1985, City of Concrete, Ikon Gallery, Birmingham, Fragments of Modern Living, in Regensburg and Cologne, Fed. Repub. of Germany and Utrecht, Netherlands, Concepts and Models, ICA Gallery, London, Vier Huizen in Den Haag, Netherlands, Striking Back, Mappin Art Gallery, Sheffield 1986, Between Objects and People, Leeds City Art Gallery 1987, Transformers, People's Lives in the Modern World, Laing Art Gallery, Newcastle 1988, Gallery Torch, Amsterdam 1988, Secret Language, Cornerhouse Gallery, Manchester 1989, Mosaics, Kaj Fovsblom Gallery, Helsinki, Barbara Farber Gallery, Amsterdam 1990, Multiple Clothing Inst. of Contemporary Art (ICA) 1993, Tate Gallery, London 1994, Victoria Miro Gallery London 1994, Tramway Glasgow 1995, Galerie Kaj Forsblom, Helsinki 1995. *Publications:* several books, including The Artist as an Instigator of Changes in Social Cognition and Behaviour 1973, Art and Social Function 1976, The Lurky Place 1978, Doppelgänger 1985, Intervention and Audience 1986, Concepts and Projects, Bookworks by Stephen Willats; numerous articles in art magazines. *Address:* c/o Lisson Gallery, 67 Bell Street, London, NW1 5DA, England.

WILLCOCKS, Sir David (Valentine), Kt, CBE, MC, MusB, MA, FRCO, FRCM; British musician; b. 30 Dec. 1919, Newquay, Cornwall; s. of T. H. Willcocks; m. Rachel Blyth 1947; two s. (one deceased) two d.; ed Clifton Coll. and King's Coll., Cambridge; Fellow, King's Coll., Cambridge 1947–51, Fellow and Dir of Music 1957–73, Lecturer in Music, Cambridge Univ. and Cambridge Univ. Organist 1957–74; Conductor Cambridge Univ. Music Soc. 1958–73; Organist Salisbury Cathedral 1947–50, Worcester Cathedral 1950–57; Conductor, Worcester Three Choirs Festival and City of Birmingham Choir 1950–57; Musical Dir Bach Choir, London 1960–98; Pres. Royal Coll. of Organists 1966–68, Incorporated Soc. of Musicians 1978–79, Nat. Fed. of Music Socs 1980–89, Asscn of British Choral Dirs 1993–; Dir Royal Coll. of Music, London 1974–84; conductor in many recordings with the Choir of King's Coll. Cambridge, the Bach Choir and the Royal Coll. of Music Chamber Choir; Hon. RAM, GSM, FRNCM, FRSAMD, FRSCM, FTCL; Freeman, City of London 1981; Hon. Fellow, Royal Canadian Coll. of Organists, King's Coll., Cambridge; Hon. mem. Royal Philharmonic Soc. 1999; Hon. DMus (Exeter, Bristol and Leicester Univs., Westminster Choir Coll., Princeton, St Olaf Coll., Luther Coll., Ia, Royal Coll. of Music, Univ. of Victoria, BC); Hon. DLitt (Sussex Univ.); Hon. DSL (Trinity Coll., Toronto); Hon. LLD (Toronto) 2001; Hon. MA (Bradford Univ.); Harvard Glee Club Medal 1992, Distinguished Musician Silver Medal, Inc. Soc. of Musicians 1998, Distinguished Visitor Silver Medal, Univ. of Toronto 1999, Silver Medal Worshipful Co. of Musicians 1999. *Address:* 13 Grange Road, Cambridge, CB3 9AS, England. *Telephone:* (1223) 359559. *Fax:* (1223) 355947. *E-mail:* david_willcocks@dvwcambs.freeserve.co.uk.

WILLEBRANDS, HE Cardinal Johannes Gerardus Maria, DPhil; Netherlands ecclesiastic; b. 4 Sept. 1909, Bovenkarspel; s. of Herman Willebrands and Afra Kok; ed Warmond Seminary, Holland, Angelicum, Rome; ordained 1934; Chaplain, Begijnhof Church, Amsterdam 1937–40; Prof. of Philosophy, Warmond 1940, Dir 1945; Pres. St Willibrord Asscn 1946; organized Catholic Conf. on Ecumenical Questions 1951; Sec. Vatican Secretariat for Promoting Christian Unity 1960, Pres. 1969–89; Pres. Emer. Pontifical Council for Promoting Christian Unity 1989–; cr. Bishop 1964; cr. Cardinal 1969; now Chamberlain of the Coll. of Cardinals; apptd. Archbishop of Utrecht 1975 (retd 1983); Hon. DD (Oxford) 1987 and numerous other hon. degrees. *Publications:* La liberté religieuse et l'oecuménisme; Ecumenismo e problemi attuali, Oecuménisme et problèmes actuels; Bibel, ekumenik och sekularisering; Christus, Zeichen und Ursprung der Einheit in einer geteilten Welt, Mandatum Unitatis: Beiträge zur Oekumene 1989, Church and Jewish People: New Considerations 1992, Una sfida ecumenica, La nuova Europa 1995. *Address:* Pontificio Collegio Olandese, Via Ercole Rosa 1, 00153 Rome,

Italy (Office); Nicolaasstichting, Zrs. Franciscanessen van Denekamp, Gravenallee 30, 7591 PE Denekamp, Netherlands (Home). *Telephone:* (06) 5717011 (Office); (541) 358358 (Home). *Fax:* (06) 5744350 (Office); (541) 354178 (Home).

WILLES, Mark Hinckley, PhD; American media executive and economist; b. 16 July 1941, Salt Lake City; s. of Joseph Simmons Willes and Ruth (née Hinckley) Willes; m. Laura Fayone 1961; three s. two d.; ed Columbia Univ.; with Banking and Currency Cttee House of Reps. 1966–67; Asst Prof. of Finance Univ. of Pennsylvania 1967–69; economist Fed. Reserve Bank 1967, Sr economist 1969–70, Dir Research 1970–71, Vice-Pres. 1971, First Vice-Pres. 1971–77; Pres. Fed. Reserve Bank of Minneapolis 1977–80; Exec. Vice-Pres., Chief Finance Officer Gen. Mills Inc. 1980–85, Pres., COO 1985–92, Vice-Chair. 1992–95; Chair., Pres., CEO Times Mirror Co. 1995–2000; Publr LA Times 1997–99; Pres. Hawaii Honolulu Mission, Church of the Latter Day Saints 2001. *Address:* Hawaii Honolulu Mission, Church of the Latter Day Saints, 1500 South Beretania Street, # 410, Honolulu, HI 96826, USA (Office). *E-mail:* mark_willes@byu.edu (Office).

WILLIAM, David, BA; British/Canadian director, actor and lecturer; b. 24 June 1926, London, England; s. of Eric Hugh Williams and Olwen Roose; ed Bryanston School, Blandford, Dorset, Univ. Coll. Oxford; nat. service in British Army 1945–48; Artistic Dir New Shakespeare Co., London, England 1962–66, Nat. Theatre of Israel 1968–70; Assoc. Dir Mermaid Theatre, London 1964–66; founder and first Artistic Dir Ludlow Festival; Artistic Dir Stratford Festival, Stratford, Ont., Canada 1989–93; Visiting Prof. Theatre Dept, De Paul Univ., Chicago 1985–88. *Productions include:* (at Stratford, Ont.): Bacchae, The Importance of Being Earnest, The Winter's Tale, Murder in the Cathedral, Troilus and Cressida, Twelfth Night, Volpone, Albert Herring; (elsewhere): Richard II (Nat. Theatre of GB), Dear Daddy (Ambassadors Theatre, London), world premieres of Thérèse (Royal Opera House, Covent Garden), The Lighthouse (Edinburgh Festival), world première of opera Red Emma (Canadian Opera Co.) 1995, Così fan Tutte, Opera St Louis, Tosca (Canadian Opera Co.) 1998, Mrs Mozart, Hartford, Conn. 1999 and many others in London, New York, San Francisco, Washington, DC, Gulbenkian Festival, Lisbon; recent roles performed on stage include Jacques (As You Like It), Serebryakov (Uncle Vanya), Malvolio (Twelfra Night) at Startford, Ontario, A.E.H. (The Inventory of Love), Guthrie Theater, Minneapolis and Studio Theater, Washington DC. *Operas directed include:* Albert Herring, The Fairy Queen, Iphigénie en Tauride, Fennimore and Gerda, Il Re Pastore, Xerxes, The Rake's Progress, A Midsummer Night's Dream, The Knot Garden, La Traviata. *TV roles include:* Richard II in Age of Kings, BBC and Octavius Caesar in Spread of the Eagle, BBC 2. *Publications:* The Tempest on the Stage 1960, Hamlet in the Theatre 1963. *Leisure interests:* walking, dogs. *Address:* 194 Langarth Street, London, Ont., N6C 1Z5, Canada. *Fax:* (519) 673-3755. *E-mail:* may.king@rogers.com (Home).

WILLIAMS, Sir Alwyn, Kt, PhD, FRS, FRSE, MRIA; British geologist and academic; b. 8 June 1921, Aberdare; s. of D. Daniel Williams and E. May Williams (née Rogers); m. Edith Joan Bevan 1949; one s. one d.; ed Aberdare Boys' Grammar School and Univ. Coll. of Wales, Aberystwyth; Fellow of Univ. of Wales, Sedgwick Museum, Cambridge 1947–48; Commonwealth Fund (Harkness) Fellow, U.S. Nat. Museum 1948–50; Lecturer in Geology, Univ. of Glasgow 1950–54; Prof. of Geology, Queen's Univ., Belfast 1954–74; Lapworth Prof. of Geology, Univ. of Birmingham 1974–76; Prin. and Vice-Chancellor, Univ. of Glasgow 1976–88; Hon. Sr Research Fellow, Univ. of Glasgow 1988–; Pres. Royal Soc., Edin. 1985–88; Foreign mem. Polish Acad. of Sciences; Hon. FRCPS, FDS, RCPS; Hon. Fellow, Geological Soc. of America; Hon. DSc (Wales) 1973, (Queen's Univ. Belfast) 1975, (Edinburgh) 1979, (Strathclyde) 1982; Hon. DCL (Oxford) 1988; Hon. LLD (Glasgow) 1988; Hon. DUniv (Paisley) 1993. *Publications:* Treatise on Invertebrate Paleontology (Brachiopoda); monographs in professional journals. *Leisure interests:* music, art. *Address:* Palaeobiology Unit, University of Glasgow, Glasgow, G12 8QQ (Office); 25 Sutherland Avenue, Pollokshields, Glasgow, G14 4HG, Scotland (Home). *E-mail:* alwyn@dcs.gla.ac.uk (Office).

WILLIAMS, Anthony A., JD; American government official; m. Diana Lynn Simmons; one c.; ed Yale and Harvard Univs.; law clerk U.S. Dist Court Boston 1987–88; Asst Dir Boston Redevt. Authority 1988–89; Exec. Dir Community Devt Agency St Louis 1989–91; Deputy Comptroller State of Conn. 1991–93; Chief Finance Officer Dept of Agric. 1993–98; Mayor of Washington, DC 1999–; Adjunct Prof. of Public Affairs Columbia Univ. 1992–93; Nat. Fellow Kellogg Foundation 1991; Democrat. *Address:* Office of the Mayor, 441 Fourth Street, NW, Washington, DC 20001, USA (Office).

WILLIAMS, Arthur Ronald, OBE; British business executive; b. 29 Oct. 1942, Rawalpindi, India (now Pakistan); s. of Alfred Arthur Williams and Marjory Williams (née Heenan); m. 1st Lynne Diana Merrin 1967; m. 2nd Antoinette Catherine Naldrett 1993; two d.; ed Rossall School, Fleetwood, Lancs. and Selwyn Coll., Cambridge; joined diplomatic service 1964, served in Jakarta 1966–67, Singapore 1967–69, Budapest 1971–74, Nairobi 1976–78; Chief Exec. Timber Growers UK 1980–87; Exec. Dir Forestry Industry Council of GB 1987–97; Chief Exec. The Publrs Asscn 1998–. *Publications:* Montrose, Cavalier in Mourning 1975, The Lords of the Isles 1985, The Heather and the Gale 1997, Sons of the Wolf 1998. *Leisure interests:* fly fishing, Scottish history, walking, real tennis. *Address:* The Publishers Association, 29B Montague Street, London, WC1B 5BH (Office); Starlings, Wildhern, nr. Andover, Hampshire, SP11 0JE, England. *Telephone:* (20)

7691-9191 (Office); (1264) 735389 (Home). *Fax:* (20) 7691-9191 (Office); (1264) 735435 (Home). *E-mail:* mail@publishers.org.uk (Office). *Website:* www .publishers.org.uk (Office).

WILLIAMS, Sir Bernard Arthur Owen, Kt, MA, FBA; British philosopher; b. 21 Sept. 1929, Westcliff; s. of Owen Williams and Hilda Williams; m. 1st Shirley Catlin (now Baroness Williams of Crosby, q.v., 1955 (divorced 1974); one d.; m. 2nd Patricia Skinner 1974; two s.; ed Chigwell School, Essex, Balliol Coll., Oxford; Fellow, All Souls Coll., Oxford 1951–54, 1997–, New Coll., Oxford 1954–59; Lecturer, Univ. Coll., London 1959–64; Prof. Bedford Coll., London 1964–67; Knightbridge Prof. of Philosophy, Cambridge 1967–79; Provost, King's Coll., Cambridge 1979–87; Monroe Deutsch Prof. of Philosophy, Univ. of Calif., Berkeley 1988–; White's Prof. of Moral Philosophy and Fellow Corpus Christi Coll., Univ. of Oxford 1990–96; visiting appointments, Univ. Coll. of Ghana 1958–59, Princeton 1963, 1978, ANU 1969, Harvard 1973, Univ. of California, Berkeley 1986; Dir ENO 1968–86; Hon. Fellow Balliol Coll., Oxford 1984, Corpus Christi Coll., Oxford 1996; Hon. LittD (Dublin) 1981; Hon. DLitt (Aberdeen) 1987, (Keele) 1995, (Yale) 2001, (Cambridge) 2002; Hon. DHL (Chicago) 1999; Hon. LLD (Harvard) 2002. *Television:* author and presenter What Is Truth? series (Channel 4) 1988. *Publications:* Morality 1972, Problems of The Self 1973, A Critique of Utilitarianism 1973, Descartes: The Project of Pure Enquiry 1978, Moral Luck 1981, Ethics and the Limits of Philosophy 1985, Shame and Necessity 1993, Making Sense of Humanity 1995, Plato 1998, Der Wert der Wahrheit 1998, Truth and Truthfulness 2002. *Leisure interest:* music. *Address:* All Souls College, Oxford, OX1 4AL, England.

WILLIAMS, Betty; British peace campaigner; b. 22 May 1943, Belfast; m. 1st Ralph Williams 1961 (divorced); one s. one d.; m. 2nd James T. Perkins 1982; ed St Teresa's Primary School, Belfast; worked as office receptionist; Jt winner of Nobel Peace Prize for launching the Northern Ireland Peace Movt (later renamed Community of the Peace People) 1976, Jt Leader 1976–78; Hon. DHumLitt (Coll. of Siena Heights, Mich.) 1977; Carl von Ossietzky Medal for Courage (Berlin Section, Int. League of Human Rights); Hon. LLD (Yale Univ.). *Leisure interest:* gardening. *Address:* P.O. Box 725, Valparaiso, FL 32580, USA.

WILLIAMS, Brian; American television journalist; b. 1959; m. Jane Stoddart Williams; two c.; ed Catholic and George Washington Univs; fmrly intern The White House, TV reporter KOAM-TV, with WTTG-TV, WCAU-TV; joined WCBS-TV 1993; Chief White House Corresp. 1994–96; anchor, Man. Ed. The News With Brian Williams MSNBC 1996–; Emmy Awards for reporting 1987, 1989, 1993. *Address:* c/o MSNBC NBC/Microsoft Corporation, 1 Msnbc Boulevard, Secaucus, NJ 07094, USA (Office).

WILLIAMS, Sir Bruce (Rodda), KBE, MA; economist; b. 10 Jan. 1919, Warragul, Vic.; s. of the late Rev. W J. Williams and of Helen Baud; m. Roma Olive Hotten 1942; five d.; ed Wesley Coll., Melbourne, Queen's Coll., Univ. of Melbourne; Prof. of Econs, Univ. Coll., North Staffordshire 1950–59; Robert Otley Prof., Stanley Jevons Prof., Univ. of Manchester 1959–67; Sec. and Jt Dir of Research, Science and Industry Cttee 1952–59; mem. UK Nat. Bd for Prices and Incomes 1966–67; Econ. Adviser to UK Ministry of Tech. 1966–67; mem. UK Cen. Advisory Council on Science and Tech. 1967; Vice-Chancellor and Principal, Univ. of Sydney 1967–81, Prof. 1967–; Dir Tech. Change Centre 1981–86; Chair. Australian Inquiry into the Eng Disciplines 1987–88; Chair. NSW State Cancer Council 1967–81; mem. Bd of Reserve Bank of Australia 1969–81; Chair. Australian Vice-Chancellors' Cttee 1972–74, Nat. Cttee of Inquiry into Educ. and Training 1976–79; Dir Parramatta Hospitals Bd 1978–81; mem. Commonwealth Working Group on the Man. of Technological Change 1984–85, on Distance Teaching and Open Learning 1986–87; Visiting Fellow ANU 1989–90, 1993–94, Univ. of London Inst. of Educ. 1991–92; Fellow Univ. of Sydney Senate 1994–98; Pres. Sydney Conservatorium of Music Foundation 1994–98, Sydney Spring Festival of New Music 1999–2002; Chair. Exec. Sydney Int. Piano Competition 1986–; Hon. FIE Australia 1989; Hon. DLitt (Univ. of Keele) 1973, (Univ. of Sydney) 1982; Hon. DEcon (Univ. of Queensland) 1980; Hon. LLD (Univ. of Melbourne) 1981, (Univ. of Manchester) 1982; Hon. DSc (Univ. of Aston) 1982. *Publications:* The Socialist Order and Freedom 1942, Industry and Technical Progress (with C. F. Carter) 1957, Investment in Innovation (with C. F. Carter) 1958, Science in Industry (with C. F. Carter) 1959, Technology, Investment and Growth 1967, Science and Technology in Economic Growth 1973, Systems of Higher Education, Australia 1978, Education, Training and Employment 1979, Disappointed Expectations 1981, Living with Technology 1982, Knowns and Unknowns in Technical Change 1985, The Influence of Attitudes to New Technology on National Growth Rates 1986, Review of the Discipline of Engineering 1988, Academic Status and Leadership (with D. Wood) 1990, University Responses to Research Selectivity 1991, Higher Education and Employment 1994, Liberal Education and Useful Knowledge 2001. *Leisure interests:* music, theatre. *Address:* 61 Hill Rise, Rickmansworth, Herts., WD3 7NY, England; 24 Mansfield Street, Glebe, NSW 2037, Australia.

WILLIAMS, C(harles) K(enneth), BA; American poet; b. 4 Nov. 1936, Newark, NJ; s. of Paul Bernard and Dossie (née Kasdin) Williams; m. 1st Sarah Dean Jones 1966 (divorced 1975); one d.; m. 2nd Catherine Justine Mauger 1975; one s.; ed Univ. of Pennsylvania; Visiting Prof. of Literature, Beaver Coll., Jenkintown, Pa 1975, Drexel Univ., Philadelphia 1976, Franklin and Marshall Coll., Pa 1977, Univ. of Calif. 1978, Boston Univ. 1979–80, Brooklyn Coll. 1982–83; Prof. of Writing, Columbia Univ. NY

1981–85, of Literature George Mason Univ., Fairfax Va 1982–95; Halloway Lecturer Univ. of Calif. 1986, Princeton Univ. 1995–; contributing Ed. American Poetry Review 1972–; Fellow Guggenheim Foundation 1975–, Nat. Endowment for Arts 1985, 1993; Nat. Book Critics Circle Award for Poetry 1987, Morton Dauwen Zabel Prize, American Acad. of Arts and Letters 1989, Harriet Monroe Prize 1993, Berlin Prize, American Acad. in Berlin 1998, Voelcker Career Achievement Award, PEN 1998, Pulitzer Prize 2000, LA Times Book Award 2000, Weathertop Prize 2000. *Publications:* A Day for Anne Frank 1968, Lies 1969, I am the Bitter Name 1972, With Ignorance 1977, The Lark, The Thrush, The Starling 1983, Tar 1983, Flesh and Blood 1987, Poems 1963–1983, 1988, The Bacchae of Euripides 1990, Helen 1991, A Dream of Mind 1992, The Vigil 1997, Poetry and Consciousness 1998, Repair 1999, Misgivings – A Memoir 2000. *Leisure interests:* drawing, piano, guitar. *Address:* 82 Rue d'Hauteville, 75010 Paris, France (Home).

WILLIAMS, Sir Daniel Charles, GCMG, QC, LLB; Grenadian governor-general and fmr lawyer; b. 4 Nov. 1935; s. of Adolphus D. Williams and Clare Stanislaus; m. Cecilia Patricia Gloria Modeste 1969; one s. three d.; ed London Univ.; called to Bar, Lincoln's Inn, London 1968; barrister 1969–70, 1974–84, 1990–96; magistrate, St Lucia 1970–74; MP (New Nat. Party) 1984–89; Minister of Health, Housing and Environment 1984–89, of Legal Affairs and Attorney-Gen. 1988–89; Acting Prime Minister July 1988; Gov.-Gen. of Grenada 1996–; fmrly several lay positions in RC Church; Chief Scout. *Publications:* Index of Laws of Grenada 1959–79, The Office and Duties of the Governor-General of Grenada 1998, A Synoptic View of the Public Service of Grenada 1999, Prescription of a Model Grenada 2000, God Speaks 2001, The Layman's Lawbook 2002; (contrib.) Modern Legal Systems Cyclopedia: Central America and the Caribbean, Vol. 7 1985. *Leisure interests:* lawn tennis, gardening. *Address:* Government House, St. George's, Grenada (Office). *Telephone:* 4402401 (Office). *Fax:* 4406688 (Office).

WILLIAMS, David; British international finance official; b. 1934; ed London School of Econs; mem. Basle Centre for Econ. and Financial Research; Asst lecturer, Univ. of Leeds; lecturer, Univ. of Hull; economist, European Dept IMF 1963; economist and Sr economist, IMF Research Dept; joined Treasurer's Dept 1969; Deputy Treas. IMF 1978, Treas. 1991–99. *Address:* c/o International Monetary Fund, 700 19th Street, NW, Washington, DC 20431, USA.

WILLIAMS, Sir David Glyndwr Tudor, Kt, MA, LLM; British university president and professor of law (retd); b. 22 Oct. 1930, Carmarthen; s. of Tudor Williams and Anne Williams; m. Sally G. M. Cole 1959; one s. two d.; ed Queen Elizabeth Grammar School, Carmarthen, Emmanuel Coll. Cambridge, Univ. of California, Berkeley and Harvard Law School; called to Bar, Lincoln's Inn 1956; Commonwealth Fund (Harkness) Fellow, Univ. of Calif., Berkeley and Harvard Univ. 1956–58; lecturer in Law, Univ. of Nottingham 1958–63; Fellow, Keble Coll., Oxford 1963–67; Fellow, Emmanuel Coll., Cambridge 1967–80, Sr Tutor 1970–76; Pres. Wolfson Coll., Cambridge 1980–92; Rouse Ball Prof. of English Law, Univ. of Cambridge 1983–92, Emer. Prof. 1992–; Vice-Chancellor, Univ. of Cambridge 1989–96, Vice-Chancellor Emer. 1996–; Prof. of Law, Professorial Fellow Emmanuel Coll. 1996–98; Pres. Univ. of Wales, Swansea Dec. 2001–; mem. Royal Comm. on Environmental Pollution 1976–83, Council on Tribunals 1972–83, Sr Salaries Review Body 1998–; Chair. Animal Procedures Cttee 1987–89; mem. Int. Jury for the Indira Gandhi Prize for Peace, Disarmament and Devt 1992–2002; Trustee Rajiv Gandhi (UK) Foundation; mem. American Law Inst.; Hon. Bencher, Lincoln's Inn 1985; Hon. QC 1994; Foreign Hon. mem. American Acad. of Arts and Sciences; Hon. Fellow, Emmanuel Coll., Cambridge 1984, Keble Coll., Oxford 1991, Pembroke Coll., Cambridge 1993, Wolfson Coll., Cambridge 1993; Hon. DLitt (Loughborough, William Jewell Coll., Mo.); Hon. LLD (Hull, Nottingham, Sydney, Davidson Coll., NC, Liverpool, McGill, De Montfort, Duke, Cambridge, Anglia Polytechnic). *Publications:* Not in the Public Interest 1965, Keeping the Peace 1967; articles in legal periodicals and chapters in books. *Address:* Emmanuel College, Cambridge, CB2 3AP (Office); Grange House, Selwyn Gardens, Cambridge, CB3 9AX, England (Home). *Telephone:* (1223) 334217 (Office); (1223) 350726 (Home). *Fax:* (1223) 350726 (Home). *Website:* www.swarv.ac.uk (Office).

WILLIAMS, Sir Denys Ambrose, KCMG, G.C.M., MA, BCL; Barbadian attorney-at-law; b. 12 Oct. 1929; s. of George Cuthbert Williams and Violet Irene Gilkes; m. Carmel Mary Coleman 1954; two s. four d.; ed Combermere School, Harrison Coll., Worcester Coll., Oxford and Middle Temple, London; Asst Legal Draftsman, Asst to Attorney Gen., Barbados; Asst Legal Draftsman, Fed. of West Indies; Sr Parl. Counsel, Barbados 1963–67; Supreme Court Judge 1967–86, Chief Justice 1987–2001; Gold Crown of Merit. *Leisure interests:* horse-racing, tennis, gardening, walking. *Address:* 9 Garrison, St Michael, Barbados. *Telephone:* 4271164.

WILLIAMS, Dudley Howard, PhD, ScD, FRS; British professor of biological chemistry; b. 25 May 1937, Leeds; s. of Lawrence Williams and Evelyn Williams; m. Lorna Patricia Phyllis Bedford 1963; two s.; ed Univ. of Leeds, Stanford Univ., Calif.; Asst Dir Research, Univ. Chem. Lab., Univ. of Cambridge 1966–74, Fellow Churchill Coll. 1964–, Reader in Organic Chem. 1974–96, Prof. of Biological Chem. 1996–; Visiting Prof. and Lecturer, Univs. of Calif. 1967, 1986, 1989, 1997, Cape Town 1972, Sydney 1972, Fla 1973, Wis. 1975, Copenhagen 1976, ANU, Canberra 1980, Queensland 1994; co-discoverer of metabolism of vitamin D 1971 and of mechanism of action of glycopeptide antibiotics which inhibit resistant bacteria; mem. Academia

Europaea; Tilden Lecturer, Royal Soc. of Chem. (RSC) 1983, Arun Guthi-konda Memorial Award Lectureship (Columbia Univ.) 1985, Distinguished Visiting Lecturer, Texas A & M Univ. 1986, Rorer Lecturer, Ohio State Univ. 1989, Univ. of Auckland Foundation Lecturer 1991, Pacific Coast Lecturer 1991, Steel Lecturer, Univ. of Queensland 1994, Lee Kuan Yew Distinguished Visitor, Singapore 2000, Marvin Carmack Distinguished Lecture, Indiana Univ. 2001, Merck Distinguished Lecturer 2001, James Sprague Lecturer, Univ. of Wisconsin 2002; Meldola Medal, Royal Inst. of Chem. 1966, Corday-Morgan Medal, Chemical Soc. 1968, RSC Award for Structural Chem. 1984, RSC Bader Award in Organic Chem. 1990, ACS Leo Friend Award 1996, Paul Ehrlich Award for Medicinal Chemistry (France) 2001, RSC Merck Research Prize 2002. *Publications:* 10 books, including Spectroscopic Methods in Organic Chemistry (with I. Fleming), more than 400 scientific publications dealing with the devt of mass spectrometry and nuclear magnetic resonance, the structure elucidation of complex molecules, the modes of action of antibiotics and molecular recognition phenomena. *Leisure interests:* music, gardening, hill-walking. *Address:* University Chemical Laboratory, Lensfield Road, Cambridge, CB2 1EW (Office); 7 Balsham Road, Fulbourn, Cambridge, CB1 5BZ, England (Home). *Telephone:* (1223) 336368 (Office); (1223) 740971 (Home). *Fax:* (1223) 336913 (Office). *E-mail:* dhw1@cam.ac.uk (Office).

WILLIAMS, Elizabeth (see Williams, Betty).

WILLIAMS, George Christopher, PhD; American biologist; b. 12 May 1926, Charlotte, NC; s. of George Felix Williams and Margaret Steuart; m. Doris Lee Calhoun 1951; one s. three d.; ed Univ. of California, Berkeley, Univ. of California at LA; army service 1944–46; instructor and Asst Prof. Mich. State Univ., E Lansing 1955–60; Assoc. Prof. Dept of Ecology and Evolution, State Univ. of NY, Stony Brook 1960–66, Prof. 1966–90; Adjunct Prof. Queen's Univ., Kingston, Ont., Canada 1980–; Prof. Emer. 1991–95; Ed. Quarterly Review of Biology; Fellow AAAS, NAS 1993–; Hon. ScD (Queens Univ., Kingston) 1995; Eminent Ecologist Award (Ecological Soc. of America 1989), NAS Daniel Giraud Elliot Medal 1992, Crafoord Prize (jtly) 1999. *Publications:* Adaptation and Natural Selection 1966, Sex and Evolution 1975, Natural Selection: Domains, Levels and Challenges 1992, Why We Get Sick: The New Science of Darwinian Medicine 1995, Plan and Purpose in Nature 1996 (also published under the title The Pony's Fish Glow) 1997. *Leisure interests:* music, swimming, fiction. *Address:* State University of New York, Quarterly Review of Biology, Stony Brook, NY 11794 (Office); 1 Jefferson's Ferry Drive, Apt. 3322, Sout Setauket, NY 11720, USA (Home). *Telephone:* (631) 632-6977 (Office); (631) 650-3122 (Home). *E-mail:* dcwilliams@ms.ca.sunysb.edu (Home).

WILLIAMS, Sir Glanmor, Kt, CBE, MA, DLitt, LLD, FBA, FSA, FRHistS; British professor of history (retd); b. 5 May 1920, Dowlais, Glam.; s. of Daniel Williams and Ceinwen Williams; m. Margaret F. Davies 1946; one s. one d.; ed Cyfarthfa Secondary School, Merthyr Tydfil and Univ. Coll. of Wales, Aberystwyth; Lecturer and Sr Lecturer in History, Univ. Coll. of Swansea 1945–57, Prof. of History 1957–82, Vice-Prin. 1975–78; Vice-Pres. Univ. of Wales, Aberystwyth 1986–96; mem. Bd of Govs. BBC 1965–71, British Library Bd 1973–80; Chair. Ancient Monuments Bd (Wales) 1983–95, Royal Comm. on Ancient and Historical Monuments (Wales) 1986–90; Chair. British Library, Advisory Council 1981–86; Freeman, Merthyr Tydfil 2001. *Publications:* The Welsh Church 1962, Welsh Reformation Essays 1966, Religion, Language and Nationality in Wales 1979, Henry Tudor 1985, Recovery, Reorientation and Reformation: Wales, 1415–1642 1987; Glamorgan County History, Vols I–VI 1971–88 (Ed.), The Welsh and their Religion 1991, Owain Glyndŵr 1993, Wales and the Reformation 1997, Cymru A'r Gorffennol 2000, A Life (autobiog.) 2002. *Leisure interests:* music, cine-photography. *Address:* 11 Grosvenor Road, Sketty, Swansea, SA2 0SP, Wales. *Telephone:* (1792) 204113.

WILLIAMS, Jody, MA; American international organization official and campaigner; b. 9 Oct. 1950; m. Stephen D. Goose 2001; ed Univ. of Vermont, Johns Hopkins School of Advanced Int. Studies; English teacher, Mexico, UK and Washington DC 1978–81; campaigned to spread awareness of U.S. policy in Cen. America 1981–92; co-ordinator Nicaragua-Honduras Educ. Project 1984–86; Deputy Dir Medical Aid for El Salvador, Los Angeles 1986–92; Founding Co-ordinator Int. Campaign to Ban Landmines (ICBL) 1992–, currently ICBL Campaign Amb.; Tech. Adviser UN Study on the Impact of Armed Conflict on Children; Nobel Peace Prize 1997 (Jt recipient with ICBL), Distinguished Peace Leadership Award, Nuclear Age Peace Foundation 1998, Peacemaker of the Year 1999; numerous hon. degrees. *Publications:* The International Campaign to Ban Landmines (with Stephen Goose) 1998, various articles and reports in journals. *Address:* International Campaign to Ban Landmines, 663 Lancaster Street, Fredericksburg, VA 22405, USA (Office). *E-mail:* williams@icbl.org (Office). *Website:* www.icbl.org (Office).

WILLIAMS, John, AO, OBE; guitarist; b. 24 April 1941, Melbourne, Australia; s. of Len Williams and Melaan Ket; m. 1st Linda Susan Kendall 1964 (divorced); one d.; m. 2nd Sue Cook 1981 (divorced); one s.; m. 3rd Kathleen Panama 2000; ed Friern Barnet Grammar School and Royal Coll. of Music, London; studied guitar with father, Segovia and at Accad. Chigiana, Siena; has toured widely and appears frequently on TV and radio; numerous transcriptions and gramophone recordings as solo guitarist and with leading orchestras; f. The Height Below (ensemble) with Brian Gascoigne 1974, John Williams and Friends (ensemble) and founder mem. groups Sky 1979–84 and John Williams' Attacca 1991–; Artistic Dir South Bank Summer Music

Festival 1984–85, Melbourne Arts Festival 1987; Hon. FRCM, FRAM, Hon. Fellow Royal Northern Coll. of Music; Dr. hc (Melbourne). *Films:* composed and played music for film Emma's War. *Leisure interests:* people, living, chess, table tennis, music. *Address:* c/o Askonas Holt Ltd, 27 Chancery Lane, London, WC2A 1PF, England. *Telephone:* (20) 7400-1700. *Fax:* (20) 7400-1799.

WILLIAMS, (John) Gwynn, CBE, MA; British historian; b. 19 June 1924; s. of the late John Ellis Williams and Annie Maude Rowlands; m. Beryl Stafford Thomas 1954; three s.; ed Holywell Grammar School, Univ. Coll. of North Wales; with RN 1943–46; staff tutor Dept of Extra Mural Studies Univ. of Liverpool 1951–54; Asst lecturer Univ. of North Wales 1955, Prof. of Welsh History 1963–83, Dean Faculty of Arts 1972–74, Vice-Prin. 1974–79, Vice-Pres. 1993–98; Chair. Press Bd Univ. of Wales 1979–91; Dir Gregynog Press 1979–2002; Vice-Pres. Nat. Library of Wales 1984–86, Pres. 1986–96; Pres. Cambrian Archaeological Asscn 1987–88; Vice-Pres. Hon. Soc. of Cymmrodorion 1988–; mem. Royal Comm. on Ancient and Historical Monuments in Wales 1967–91; Hon. mem. Gorsedd of Bards; Hon. DLitt (Univ. of Wales) 1999. *Publications include:* The Founding of the University College of North Wales, Bangor 1985, The University College of North Wales: Foundations 1985, University and Nation 1893–1939 (The Thomas Jones Pierce Memorial Lecture) 1992, The Report on the Proposed University of Wales (ed.) 1993, The University Movement in Wales 1993, The University of Wales 1893–1939 1997; numerous articles on 17th-century Wales for learned journals. *Leisure interests:* travelling, walking. *Address:* Llywenan, Siliwen, Bangor, Gwynedd, LL57 2BS, Wales. *Telephone:* (1248) 353065.

WILLIAMS, Sir (John) Kyffin, Kt, OBE, RA; Welsh artist; b. 9 May 1918, Llangefni; s. of Henry Inglis Wynne Williams and Essyllt Mary Williams (née Williams); ed Shrewsbury School, Slade School of Art; Sr Art Master, Highgate School 1944–73; one-man shows Leicester Galleries 1951, 1953, 1956, 1960, 1966, 1970; Colnaghi Galleries 1948, 1949, 1965, 1970; Thackeray Galleries 1975, 1977, 1979, 1981, 1983, 1985, 1987, 1989, 1991; retrospective Nat. Museum of Wales 1987; Pres. Royal Cambrian Acad. 1969–76, 1992–; Winston Churchill Fellow 1968; DL Gwynedd 1985; Hon. Fellow, Univ. Coll., Swansea 1989, Univ. Coll. N Wales, Bangor 1991, Univ. Coll. Wales, Aberystwyth 1992; Hon. MA (Wales) 1973; Hon. DLitt (Wales) 1993; Medal of Hon. Soc. of Cymmrodorion. *Publications:* Across The Straits (autobiog.) 1973, A Wider Sky (autobiog. Vol. II) 1991, Boyo Ballads 1995, Portraits 1996, Land and Sea 1998, Drawings 2000. *Leisure interests:* the countryside, sport.

WILLIAMS, John Peter Rhys, MBE, MRCS, LRCP, MB, BS, FRCSE; Welsh rugby player and orthopaedic surgeon; b. 2 March 1949, Cardiff; s. of Peter Williams and Margaret Williams; m. Priscilla Parkin 1973; one s. three d.; ed Bridgend Grammar School, Millfield, St Mary's Hosp. Medical School; British Junior Tennis Champion, Wimbledon 1966; Welsh int. rugby player 1969–79, 1980–81; 55 caps for Wales; on tour with British Lions to New Zealand 1971, South Africa 1974; 8 test matches for British Lions, winning both series; qualified as medical doctor 1973; surgical Registrar, Cardiff Hosp. 1977–80, Orthopaedic Registrar 1980–82; Orthopaedic Sr Registrar, St Mary's Hosp., London 1982–85; Consultant Orthopaedic Surgeon, Princess of Wales Hosp., Bridgend Jan. 1986–; Captain of Welsh rugby team 1978–79; Primary FRCS 1976; inducted into Int. Rugby Hall of Fame 1997. *Publications:* Irish Conference on Sporting Injuries, Dublin (ed.) 1975, JPR (autobiog.) 1979, Cervical Neck Injuries in Rugby Football, British Medical Journal 1978, Trans-Oral Fusion of the Cervical Spine, Journal of Bone and Joint Surgery 1985. *Leisure interests:* sport, music. *Address:* Llansannor Lodge, Llansannor, Nr. Cowbridge, Vale of Glamorgan, CF71 7RX, Wales.

WILLIAMS, John T.; American composer of film music; b. 8 Feb. 1932, Flushing, NY; ed Juilliard School; Conductor Boston Pops Orchestra 1980–98; numerous hon. degrees; Acad. Awards for Fiddler on the Roof, Jaws, Star Wars, E.T., Schindler's List. 14 Grammys; two Emmys; Golden Globe Award 1978. *Filmscores:* The Secret Ways 1961, Diamond Head 1962, None But the Brave 1965, How to Steal a Million 1966, Valley of the Dolls 1967, The Cowboys 1972, The Poseidon Adventure 1972, Tom Sawyer 1973, Earthquake 1974, The Towering Inferno 1974, Jaws 1975, The Eiger Sanction 1975, Family Plot 1976, Midway 1976, The Missouri Breaks 1976, Raggedy Ann and Andy 1977, Black Sunday 1977, Star Wars 1977, Close Encounters of the Third Kind 1977, The Fury 1978, Jaws II 1976, Superman 1978, Dracula 1979, The Empire Strikes Back 1980, Raiders of the Lost Ark 1981, E.T.: The Extra Terrestrial 1982, Return of the Jedi 1983, Indiana Jones and the Temple of Doom 1984, The River 1985, Space Camp 1986, The Witches of Eastwick 1987, Empire of the Sun (BAFTA Best Score Award) 1988, Always 1989, Born on the Fourth of July 1989, Stanley and Iris 1990, Presumed Innocent 1990, Home Alone 1990, Hook 1991, JFK, Far and Away, Home Alone 2: Lost in New York, Jurassic Park 1993, Schindler's List 1993, Sabrina 1995, Nixon 1995, Sleepers 1996, Rosewood 1996, Seven Years in Tibet 1997, The Lost World, Amistad 1997, Saving Private Ryan 1998, The Phantom Menace 1999, Angela's Ashes 1999, Attack of the Clones 2001, Catch Me If You Can 2002. *Address:* c/o Michael Gorfaine, Gorfaine & Schwartz, 13245 Riverside Drive, Suite 450, Sherman Oaks, CA 91423, USA.

WILLIAMS, Joseph Dalton, BSc; American business executive; b. 15 Aug. 1926, Washington, Pa; s. of Joseph Dalton Williams and Jane Day; m. Millie E. Bellaire 1973; one s. one d.; ed Univ. of Nebraska; Sales Rep., Parke-Davis, Kan. City 1950, Field Man. 1956, Asst Man. Market Research 1958, Asst to Dir Sales Research and Devt 1962, Dir Medical-Surgical Market Devt 1967,

Dir U.S. Marketing 1968, Group Vice-Pres., Marketing and Sales 1970; following merger of cos., Vice-Pres., Warner-Lambert, mem. Bd, Parke-Davis; Exec. Vice-Pres. and COO, Parke-Davis 1971, Pres. and CEO 1973; mem. Bd of Dirs. Warner-Lambert 1973–97, Sr Vice-Pres. 1973, Exec. Vice-Pres. and Pres. Pharmaceutical Group 1976, Sr Exec. Vice-Pres., mem. Office of Chair. and Pres. Int. Group 1977, Pres., Dir Warner-Lambert Corpn 1979–80, Pres. and COO 1980–84, Chair., CEO 1985–91, Chair. Exec. Cttee 1991–97; Bd Dirs. AT&T, Exxon Corpn, Rockefeller Financial Services Inc.; numerous hon. degrees; Remington Honor Medal, American Pharmaceutical Asscn, Rutgers Univ. Award 1982. *Leisure interests:* golf, antique cars. *Address:* Warner-Lambert Co., 55 Madison Avenue, Norristown, NJ 07960 (Home); P.O. Box 836, Bernardsville, NJ 07924, USA (Home).

WILLIAMS, Mack Geoffrey Denis, BA; Australian diplomatist; b. 16 July 1939, Sydney; s. of Bernard George Williams and Thelma A. McMillan; m. Carla Lothringer 1966; one s. three d.; ed Fort Street Boys High School, Sydney and Univ. of Sydney; joined Dept of Foreign Affairs 1961; Third Sec. Brussels 1962–65; Second Sec. Saigon 1965–67; First Sec. Phnom Penh 1969–71; Counsellor, Washington, DC 1971–74; Office of Minister of Foreign Affairs, Canberra 1975–76; Deputy High Commr in Papua New Guinea 1977–78; Royal Coll. of Defence Studies, London 1979; High Commr in Bangladesh 1980–82; Dept of Prime Minister, Canberra 1986–87; First Asst Sec. Dept of Foreign Affairs and Trade 1987–89; Amb. to the Philippines 1989–94, to Repub. of Korea 1994–98; Bd mem. Australia-Korea Foundation 1998–; Exec. Australia-Korea Business Council 1998–, Vice-Pres. 2000–; Hon. Investment and Trade Rep., Republic of Philippines 1999–; Korean Pres. Order of Merit 1998, Hon. Fellow Senate Univ. of Sydney 1996. *Leisure interests:* golf, travel. *Address:* 87 Ferry Road, Glebe, NSW 2037, Australia.

WILLIAMS, Marion V., PhD, FCIB; Barbadian banking official; ed Univ. of Surrey, UK, Univ. of the W. Indies; fmr Deputy Man. Research Dept, E. Caribbean Currency Authority, Man.; joined Cen. Bank of Barbados 1973–, Adviser, Sr Adviser, Deputy Gov. 1993–99, Gov. 1999–; numerous articles for professional journals; consultant, USAID, Commonwealth Secr., ILO; Pres. Barbados Inst. of Banking and Finance; mem. Barbados Econs Soc., Asscn of Caribbean Econs. *Address:* Central Bank of Barbados, Tom Adams Financial Centre, P.O.B. 1016, Spry Street, Bridgetown, Barbados (Office). *Telephone:* 436-6870 (Office). *Fax:* 427-9559 (Office). *E-mail:* cbb.libr@caribsurf.com (Office). *Website:* www.centralbank.org.bb (Office).

WILLIAMS, Martin John, CVO, OBE, BA; British consultant and diplomatist (retd); b. 3 Nov. 1941; s. of John Henry Stroud Williams and Barbara Williams (née Benington); m. Susan Dent 1964; two s.; ed Manchester Grammar School, Corpus Christi Coll. Oxford; joined Commonwealth Relations Office 1963; various posts including Embassy, Manila 1966–69, Consulate-Gen., Milan 1970–72, Embassy, Tehran 1977–80, High Comm., New Delhi 1982–86, Embassy, Rome 1986–90; Head S. Asian Dept, FCO 1990–92; seconded to NI Office, Belfast as Asst Under-Sec. (Political Affairs) 1993–95; High Commr in Zimbabwe 1995–98, in NZ (also accred to Samoa and Gov. Pitcairn Island) 1998–2001. *Leisure interests:* music, gardening, woodwork. *Address:* Russet House, Lughorse Lane, Yalding, Kent, ME18 6EG, England (Home). *Telephone:* (1622) 815403 (Home).

WILLIAMS, Nigel, MA; British writer and television producer; b. 20 Jan. 1948, Cheshire; s. of the late David Ffrancon Williams; m. Suzani Harrison 1973; three s.; ed Highgate School, Oriel Coll. Oxford; trainee BBC 1969–73, Producer/Dir Arts Dept 1973–85, Ed. Bookmark 1985–92, Omnibus 1992–96, writer and presenter 1997–2000. *Television includes:* Double Talk, Talking Blues, Real Live Audience 1977, Baby Love 1981, Breaking Up 1986, The Last Romantics 1992, Skallagrig (BAFTA Award) 1994. *Stage plays include:* Class Enemy 1978 (Plays and Players Award for most promising playwright 1978), Trial Run 1980, Line 'Em 1980, Sugar & Spice 1980, My Brother's Keeper 1985, Country Dancing 1986, Nativity 1989, Harry & Me 1995, The Last Romantics 1997. *Publications:* (novels) My Life Closed Twice 1977 (Jt winner Somerset Maugham Award), Jack Be Nimble 1980, Star Turn 1985, Witch-craft 1987, The Wimbledon Poisoner 1990, They Came from SW19 1992, East of Wimbledon 1994, Scenes from a Poisoner's Life 1994, Stalking Fiona 1997, Fortysomething 1999; (travel) Wimbledon to Waco 1995. *Leisure interests:* dogs, drinking, talking, family, swiming, walking. *Address:* c/o Judy Daish Associates, 2 St Charles Place, London, W10 6EG; 18 Holmbush Road, Putney, London, SW15 3LE, England (Home). *Telephone:* (20) 8964-8811. *Fax:* (20) 8964-8966.

WILLIAMS, Peter Orchard, CBE, FRCP; British medical director and doctor; b. 23 Sept. 1925, Trinidad; s. of Robert O. Williams and Agnes A. Birkinshaw; m. Billie I. Brown 1949; two d.; ed Caterham School, Queen's Royal Coll., Trinidad, St John's Coll., Cambridge and St Mary's Hosp. Medical School; House Physician, St Mary's Hosp., London 1950–51; Registrar, Royal Free Hosp. 1951–52; Medical Specialist, RAMC 1954; Medical Officer, Medical Research Council HQ 1955–60; Asst and Deputy Scientific Sec. Wellcome Trust 1960–64, Scientific Sec. 1964–65, Dir 1965–91; Pres. Royal Soc. of Tropical Medicine and Hygiene 1991–93; Visiting Fellow, Green Coll. Oxford; Hon. Fellow, London School of Hygiene and Tropical Medicine; Hon. DSc (Birmingham) 1989, (Univ. of the West Indies) 1991, (Glasgow) 1992; Hon. DM (Nottingham) 1990, (Oxford) 1990. *Publication:* Careers in Medicine 1952. *Leisure interest:* gardening. *Address:* Courtyard House, Bletchingdon, Kidlington, Oxon., OX5 3DL, England.

WILLIAMS, Richard Edmund; Canadian animated film producer, director and writer; b. 19 March 1933, Toronto, Ont.; s. of Kenneth D. C. Williams and Kathleen (née Bell) Williams; m. 2nd Margaret French 1976; four c. (including two from a previous m.); ed Royal Ontario Coll. of Art; f. Richard Williams Animation Ltd 1962; produced and directed: The Little Island 1955 (British Acad. Award, 1st Prize Venice Film Festival), Love Me, Love Me, Love Me 1962, A Christmas Carol 1973 (Oscar for Best Animated Short Subject); designed film sequences and titles for: What's New Pussycat 1965, A Funny Thing Happened on the Way to the Forum 1966, Casino Royale 1975, The Charge of the Light Brigade 1967, The Return of the Pink Panther 1975, The Pink Panther Strikes Again 1976; animation for Who Framed Roger Rabbit 1988 (Special Achievement Oscar), Arabian Knight (Dir, produced); mem. Acad. of Motion Picture Arts and Sciences; mem. Asscn of Cinematographers and TV Technicians.

WILLIAMS, Robbie (Robert Peter); British popular singer; b. 13 Feb. 1974, Stoke-on-Trent; s. of Pete Williams and Theresa Janette Williams; played the Artful Dodger in Oliver 1982; mem. group Take That 1991–95 (eight 'No. 1' singles); solo artist 1995–; 14 Brit Awards (10 solo); Levi's Nordoff-Robbins Music Therapy Original Talent Award 1998, MTV Award for Best Male 1998. *Film:* Nobody Someday 2002. *Albums:* with Take That: Take That And Party 1992, Everything Changes 1993, Greatest Hits 1996; Solo: Life Thru' a Lens 1997, I've Been Expecting You 1998, The Ego Has Landed (USA) 1999, Sing When You're Winning 2000, Swing When You're Winning 2001, Escapology 2002. *Singles:* with Take That: It Only Takes A Minute 1992, I Found Heaven 1992, A Million Love Songs 1992, Could It Be Magic 1993, Pray 1993, Relight My Fire (with Lulu) 1993, Babe 1993, Why Can't I Wake Up With You 1993, Love Ain't Here Anymore 1994, Everything Changes 1994, Sure 1994, Back For Good 1995, Never Forget 1995; Solo: Freedom 1996, Old Before I Die 1997, Lazy Days 1997, South Of The Border 1997, Angels 1997, Let Me Entertain You 1998, Millennium 1998, No Regrets 1998, Strong 1999, She's The One/It's Only Us 1999, Rock DJ 2000, Kids (with Kylie Minogue) 2000, Supreme 2000, Let Love Be Your Energy 2001, Eternity/ Road To Mandalay 2001, Better Man 2001, Somethin' Stupid (with Nicole Kidman) 2001, Feel 2002, My Culture 2002, Come Undone 2003. *Publications:* F for English 2000, Robbie Williams: Performance (with Mark McCrun) 2001, Robbie Williams: Somebody Someday 2001. *Leisure interests:* golf, roll-erblading. *Address:* IE Music Ltd, 59A Chesson Rd, London, W14 9QS; c/o EMI Group PLC, 4 Tenterden St, Hanover Square, London, W1A 2AY, England. *Website:* www.robbiewilliams.com.

WILLIAMS, Robert Joseph Paton, DPhil, FRS, FRCS; British professor of chemistry; b. 25 Feb. 1926, Wallasey; s. of Ernest Ivor Williams and Alice Roberts; m. Jelly Klara Buchli 1952; two s.; ed Oxford Univ.; Rotary Int. Fellow 1951–52; Research Fellow, Merton Coll. Oxford Univ. 1952–55; Tutor and Lecturer (Fellow), Wadham Coll., Oxford 1955–74, Professorial Fellow 1974–93, Prof. Emer. 1991–, Fellow Emer. 1993–, Lecturer, Oxford Univ. 1955–70, Reader 1970–72, Royal Soc. Napier Research Prof. 1974–91; Pres. Dalton Div. Royal Soc. of Chemistry 1991–93; Foreign mem. Royal Swedish Acad. of Science, Lisbon Acad. of Science, Czechoslovak Acad. of Science, Royal Soc. of Science, Liège; Lord Goodman Lecturer 1992; J. D. Bernal Lecturer 1993; Canada Lecturer, Royal Soc. 1996; J. D. Birchall Lecturer 1999, Huxley Lecturer 2000; Hon. Fellow, Merton Coll., Oxford 1991; Hon. DSc (Louvain, Leicester, East Anglia, Keele, Lisbon); Tilden Medal (Chem. Soc. of England), Liversidge Medal (Chem. Soc. of England), Keilen Medal (Biochem. Soc.), Hughes Medal (Royal Soc.), Sir Hans Krebs Medal (European Biochem. Soc.), Linderstrøm-Lang Medal (Denmark), Sigillum Magna (Univ. of Bologna), Heyrovsky Medal (Int. Union of Biochem.), Sir Frederick Gow-land Hopkins Medal (Biochem. Soc.), Royal Medal (Royal Soc.), Longstaff Medal (Chem. Soc. of England). *Publications:* Inorganic Chemistry (with C. S. G. Phillips), NMR in Biology, Recent Trends in Bioinorganic Chemistry, The Biological Chemistry of the Elements (with J. J. R. Frausto da Silva) 1991, The Natural Selection of the Chemical Elements (with J.J.R. Frausto da Silva) 1996, Bringing Chemistry to Life (with J. J. R. Frausto da Silva) 1999. *Leisure interests:* walking in the country, local planning. *Address:* Wadham College, Oxford, OX1 3QR (Office); Corner House, 1A Water Eaton Road, Oxford, OX2 7QQ, England (Home). *Telephone:* (1865) 272600 (Office); (1865) 558926 (Home). *Fax:* (1865) 272690 (Office); (1865) 558926 (Home). *E-mail:* bob.williams@chem.ox.ac.uk (Office).

WILLIAMS, Robin; American actor and comedian; b. 21 July 1951, Chicago; s. of Robert Williams and Laurie Williams; m. 1st Valerie Velardi 1978 (divorced); one s.; 2nd Marsha Garces 1989; one s. one d.; ed Claremont Men's Coll., Marin Coll., Kentfield, Calif., Juillard School, New York; started as stand-up comedian. *Television appearances include:* Laugh-In, The Richard Pryor Show, America 2-Night, Happy Days, Mork and Mindy 1978–82, Carol and Carl and Whoopi and Robin (Emmy Award), Royal Gala: Prince's Trust (Emmy Award). *Stage appearances include:* Waiting for Godot. *Films include:* Popeye 1980, The World According to Garp 1982, The Survivors 1983, Moscow on the Hudson 1984, Club Paradise 1986, Good Morning Vietnam 1987 (Golden Globe Award 1988), Dead Poets' Society 1989, Awakenings 1990 (Best Actor, Nat. Bd of Review), The Fisher King 1991 (Golden Globe Award), Hook 1991, Dead Again 1991, Toys 1992, Being Human 1993, Aladdin (voice) 1993, Mrs Doubtfire 1993, Jumanji 1996, The Birdcage 1996, Jack, Hamlet, Joseph Conrad's The Secret Agent 1996, Good Will Hunting 1997 (Acad. Award), Flubber 1997, What Dreams May Come 1998, Patch Adams 1998, Jakob the Liar 1999, Bicentennial Man 1999, Get Bruce 1999, One Hour

Photo 2001, Insomnia 2002, Death to Smoochy 2002. *Recordings:* Reality, What a Concept 1979 (Grammy Award), Throbbing Python of Love, A Night at the Met. *Address:* CAA Creative Artists Agency, 9830 Wilshire Boulevard, Beverly Hills, CA 90212; P.O. Box 480909, Los Angeles, CA 90048, USA.

WILLIAMS, Robin Murphy, Jr., PhD, DSc; American professor of social sciences; b. 11 Oct. 1914, Hillsborough, NC; s. of Robin Murphy Williams, Sr and Mabel Strayhorn Williams; m. Marguerite York 1939; one s. (deceased) two d.; ed North Carolina State Coll. and Harvard Univ.; Instructor and Research Asst, Univ. of Ky 1939–42; Statistical Analyst, US War Dept 1942–46; Assoc. Prof., Cornell Univ. 1946–48, Prof. 1948–67, Dir Social Science Research Center 1949–54, Chair. Dept of Sociology and Anthropology 1956–61, Henry Scarborough Prof. of Social Science 1967–85, Prof. Emer. 1985–; Visiting Prof. Univ. of Calif., Irvine 1990–2003; Ed. Sociological Forum 1984–91; Chair. Cttee on Status of Black Americans, Nat. Research Council; mem. American Philosophical Soc., American Acad. of Arts and Sciences, NAS. *Publications:* Strangers Next Door 1964, American Society 1970, Mutual Accommodation 1977 (ed. with Gerald David Jaynes), A Common Destiny: Blacks and American Society 1989, The Wars Within: Peoples and States in Conflict 2003. *Leisure interest:* work. *Address:* 342 Uris Hall, Cornell University, Ithaca, NY 14853; 414 Oak Avenue, Ithaca, NY 14850, USA (Home). *Telephone:* (607) 255-1416 (Univ.); (607) 273-9119 (Home).

WILLIAMS, Roger Stanley, CBE, MD, FRCP, FRCS, FRCPE, FRACP, FRCPI, FMedSci; British consultant physician; b. 28 Aug. 1931; s. of Stanley George Williams and Doris Dagmar Clatworthy; m. 1st Lindsay Mary Elliott 1954 (divorced 1977); two s. three d.; m. 2nd Stephanie Gay de Laszlo 1978; one s. two d.; ed St Mary's Coll., Southampton, London Hosp. Medical School, Univ. of London; House Doctor London Hosp. 1953–56; Jr Medical Specialist, Queen Alexandra Hosp. 1956–58; Medical Registrar and Tutor, Royal Postgraduate Medical School 1958–59; Lecturer in Medicine Royal Free Hosp. 1959–65; Consultant Physician Royal S. Hants. and Southampton Gen. Hosp. 1965–66; Consultant Physician and Dir, Inst. of Liver Studies, King's Coll. Hosp. (now King's Coll. School of Medicine and Dentistry), London 1966–96, Prof. of Hepatology; Dir Inst. of Hepatology and Hon. Consultant Physician, Univ. Coll. London Hosps and Medical School 1996–; mem. WHO Scientific Group on Viral Hepatitis, Geneva 1972, Transplant Advisory Panel DHSS 1974–83, Advisory Group on Hepatitis DHSS 1980–, European Asscn for the Study of the Liver (Pres. 1983) 1966–, Harveian Soc. of London (Pres. 1974–75), British Asscn for the Study of the Liver (Pres. 1984), Royal Soc. of Medicine, British Soc. of Gastroenterology (Pres. 1989); Vice-Pres. Royal Coll. of Physicians 1991; Hon. Consultant in Medicine to the Army 1988–98; Rep. to Select Cttee of Experts on Organizational Aspects of Co-operation in Organ Transplantation, Congress of Europe; Sir Ernest Finch Visiting Prof. Univ. of Sheffield 1974; Hon. FACP; Hon. FRCPI. *Publications:* Fifth Symposium on Advanced Medicine (Ed.) 1969, Immunology of the Liver 1971, Artificial Liver Support 1975, Immune Reactions in Liver Disease 1978, Drug Reactions and the Liver 1981, Clinics in Critical Care Medicine – Liver Failure 1986, Liver Tumours (Baillière's Clinical Gastroenterology) 1987, The Practice of Liver Transplantation 1995, International Developments in Health Care. A review of Health Systems in the 1990s 1995, Acute Liver Failure 1997; author of over 2,500 papers, reviews and book chapters. *Leisure interests:* tennis, sailing, opera. *Address:* Institute of Hepatology, University College London, 69–75 Chenies Mews, London, WC1E 6HX (Office); 8 Eldon Road, London, W8 5PU, England (Home). *Telephone:* (20) 7679-6510/6511 (Office); (20) 7937-5301 (Home). *Fax:* (20) 7380-0405 (Office). *E-mail:* roger.williams@ucl.ac.uk (Office).

WILLIAMS, Most Rev. Rowan Douglas, MA, DPhil, DD; British ecclesiastic and academic; b. 14 June 1950, Swansea; m. Jane Paul 1981; one s. one d.; ed Christ's Coll. Cambridge, Wadham Coll. Oxford; Tutor Westcott House, Cambridge Univ. 1977–80, Lecturer in Divinity 1980–1986, Dean and Chaplain, Clare Coll. 1984–1986; Deacon 1977; Priest 1978; Canon Theologian Leicester Cathedral 1981–82; Canon Residentiary, Christ Church, Oxford 1986–92; Lady Margaret Prof. of Theology, Oxford Univ. 1986–92; Bishop of Monmouth 1991–2000; Archbishop of Wales 2000–03; Archbishop of Canterbury Feb. 2003–; fmr mem. Dearing Working Party on Church Schools; Hon. Curate Chesterton St George, Ely 1980–1983, Fellow British Acad. 1990. *Publications include:* The Wound of Knowledge, A Ray of Darkness 1996, Resurrection, Teresa of Avila, Writing in the Dust: Reflections on September 11 2002; contribs to Our Selves, Our Souls and Bodies, Sexuality and the Household of God. *Address:* Lambeth Palace, London, SE1 7JU, England. *Telephone:* (20) 7898-1200. *Fax:* (20) 7261-1765. *Website:* www .archbishopofcanterbury.org.

WILLIAMS, Serena; American tennis player; b. 26 Sept. 1981, Saginaw, Michigan; d. of Richard Williams and Oracene Williams; sister of Venus Williams (q.v.); turned professional in 1994; coached by her father Richard Williams; won mixed doubles (with Mirryi) at Wimbledon and US Open 1998; doubles winner (with Venus Williams) Oklahoma City 1998, French Open 1999, Hanover 1999, Wimbledon 2000, 2002, Australian Open 2001, 2003; singles semi-finalist Sydney Open 1997, Chicago 1998; singles finalist Wimbledon 2000; winner US Open 1999, Paris Indoors 1999, Indian Wells 1999, 2001, LA 1999, 2000, Grand Slam Cup 1999, Hanover 2000, Tokyo 2000, Canadian Open 2001, French Open 2002, Wimbledon 2002, Australian Open 2003; US Fed. Cup Team 1999; US Olympic Team (won doubles gold medal with sister, Venus) 2000; ranked world number 1 2002; 19 WTA Tour singles titles (including 4 Grand Slam titles) and over 10 million dollars in prize

money at end 2002; Sanex WTA Tour Most Impressive Newcomer Award 1998, Most Improved Player 1999, Teen Awards Achievement Award (shared with sister, Venus) 2000, Associated Press Female Athlete of the Year 2002. *Leisure interests:* watching movies, playing football and basketball, reading, acting, music, designing clothing. *Address:* c/o USTA, 70 W Red Oak Lane, White Plains, NY 10604, USA (Office).

WILLIAMS, Stephen, PhD; American professor of anthropology, archaeologist and museum curator; b. 28 Aug. 1926, Minneapolis, Minn.; s. of Clyde G. Williams and Lois M. (Simmons) Williams; m. Eunice Ford 1962; two s.; ed Yale Univ. and Univ. of Michigan; Historical and Archaeological Research on Caddo Indians for U.S. Dept of Justice 1954–55; Research Fellow in N American Archaeology, Peabody Museum of Archaeology and Ethnology, Harvard Univ. 1955–58; Lecturer in Anthropology, Harvard Univ. 1956–58, Asst Prof. of Anthropology 1958–62, Assoc. Prof. 1962–67, Prof. of Anthropology 1967–72, Peabody Prof. 1972–93, Chair. Dept of Anthropology 1967–69, mem. of Bd of Freshmen Advisers, Harvard Univ. 1959–60, 1961–65; Asst Curator of N American Archaeology, Peabody Museum 1957–58, Curator of N American Archaeology 1962–93; Dir Peabody Museum, Harvard Univ. 1967–77, Dir Lower Mississippi Survey 1958–93, Peabody Prof. Emer. and Hon. Curator N American Archaeology, 1993–; mem. Bd of Dirs Archaeological Conservancy 1984–88; Distinguished Fellow School of American Research, Santa Fe 1977–78; Hon. MA (Harvard Univ.); Distinguished Service Award, Southeast Archaeological Conf. 1992, Dean's Distinguished Service Award, Harvard Extension Program 1993. *Publications:* six books and monographs including Excavations at the Lake George Site, Yazoo County, Miss. 1958–60 (with Jeffrey P. Brain), Fantastic Archaeology: The Wild Side of North American Prehistory 1990; numerous articles in journals and magazines. *Address:* P.O. Box 22354, Santa Fe, NM 87502 (Office); 1017 Foothills Trail, Santa Fe, NM 87505, USA (Home). *Telephone:* (505) 983-8836 (Office). *Fax:* (505) 983-1589. *E-mail:* williamsstephen@msn .com (Home).

WILLIAMS, HE Cardinal Thomas Stafford, ONZ, STL, B.SOC.SC.; New Zealand ecclesiastic; b. 20 March 1930, Wellington; s. of Thomas S. Williams and Lillian M. Williams (née Kelly); ed St Patrick's Coll., Wellington, Victoria Univ., Wellington, St Kevin's Coll., Oamaru, Holy Cross Coll., Mosgiel, Pontifical Urban Coll. de Propaganda Fide, Rome and Univ. Coll., Dublin; ordained priest, Rome 1959; Asst St Patrick's Parish, Palmerston North 1963; Dir of Studies, Catholic Enquiry Centre, Wellington 1965; parish priest, St Anne's, Leulumoega, Western Samoa 1971, Holy Family Parish, Porirua East, Wellington 1976; Archbishop of Wellington and Metropolitan of NZ 1979–; cr. Cardinal 1983. *Address:* P.O. Box 1937, Wellington 6015; Viard, 21 Eccleston Hill, Wellington 1, New Zealand. *Telephone:* (4) 496-1795. *Fax:* (4) 496-1728. *E-mail:* archbishop@wn.catholic.org.nz (Office).

WILLIAMS, Venus Ebone Starr; American tennis player; b. 17 June 1980, Lynwood, Calif.; d. of Richard Williams and Oracene Williams; sister of Serena Williams (q.v.); made professional debut Bank of West Classic, Oakland, Calif. 1994; Bausch & Lomb Championships 1996; winner numerous singles titles (WTA Tour) including Oklahoma City 1998, Lipton 1998, 1999, Hamburg 1999, Italian Open 1999, Grand Slam Cup 1998, Wimbledon 2000; five Grand Slam doubles titles (with Serena Williams): French Open 1999, Wimbledon 2000, 2002, Australian Open 2001, 2003; singles finalist Wimbledon 2002, Australian Open 2003; with Serena Williams, first sisters in tennis history to have each won a Grand Slam singles title; first sisters to win Olympic Gold Medal in doubles 2000; only sisters in 20th century to win a Grand Slam doubles title together; US Fed. Cup Team 1995, 1999; finished 2002 season ranked world number 2; awarded largest-ever endorsement contract for a female athlete by Reebok 2002; Sports Image Foundation Award 1995, Tennis Magazine Most Impressive Newcomer 1997, Most Improved Player 1998, Sanex WTA Tour Player of the Year and Doubles Team of the Year (with sister, Serena) 2000, Women's Sports Foundation Athlete of the year 2000, ESPY Awards for Best Female Athlete and Best Female Tennis Player of 2001 2002. *Leisure interests:* sumo wrestling, surfing, reading, languages, antique furniture, writing poetry. *Address:* US Tennis Association, 70 West Red Oak Lane, White Plains, NY 10604, USA (Office).

WILLIAMS-JONES, Michael Robert; British/South African film executive; b. 3 June 1947, Sussex; s. of Hugh E. Williams-Jones and Valerie Lyons; m. 1st. Lynne Williams-Jones 1969 (deceased); m. 2nd Eve Foreman 1994; two s. one step-.s. one step-d.; ed Selborne Coll. East London, S. Africa; trainee, United Artists, Southern Africa region 1967, Man. Dir 1969, Brazil 1971, UK 1975; Sr Vice-Pres. United Artists Int. 1978; Pres. United Int. Pictures Film Group 1981; Pres. and CEO United Int. Pictures Corpn 1994–96; owner/co-founder, Merlin Anglesey UK, Ltd 1996–; City of Rio de Janeiro Honour 1974, Golden Horse Lifetime Achievement Award, Taiwan 1986, Lifetime Achievement Award, Locarno 1989, Int. Distributor of the Year 1995. *Leisure interests:* movies, theatre, reading, opera, walking, snorkelling. *Address:* Merlin Anglesey (UK), Ltd, 49C Princes Gate, London, SW7 2PG (Office); 11 Kingston House South, Ennismore Gardens, London, SW7 1NF, England (Home). *Telephone:* (20) 7584-6065 (Office). *Fax:* (20) 7584-7057 (Office). *E-mail:* merlina@dial.pipex.com (Office).

WILLIAMS OF CROSBY, Baroness (Life Peer), cr. 1993, of Stevenage in the County of Hertfordshire; **Rt Hon Shirley Williams,** PC, MA; British politician; b. 27 July 1930, London; d. of the late Sir George Catlin and Vera Brittain; m. 1st Bernard Williams (q.v.) 1955 (divorced 1974); one d.; m. 2nd

Prof. Richard Neustadt (q.v.) 1987; ed Summit School, Minn., USA, St Paul's Girls' School, Somerville Coll., Oxford and Columbia Univ.; Gen. Sec. Fabian Soc. 1960–64; Labour MP for Hitchin 1964–74, for Hertford and Stevenage 1974–79; SDP MP for Crosby 1981–83; Parl. Pvt. Sec., Minister of Health 1964–66; Parl. Sec. Minister of Labour 1966–67; Minister of State, Dept of Educ. and Science 1967–69; Minister of State, Home Office 1969–70; Opposition Spokesman on Health and Social Security 1970–71, on Home Affairs 1971–73, on Prices and Consumer Affairs 1973–74; Sec. of State for Prices and Consumer Protection 1974–76, for Educ. and Science 1976–79; Paymaster-Gen. 1976–79; Sr Research Fellow (part-time) Policy Research Inst. 1979–85; mem. Labour Party Nat. Exec. Cttee 1970–81; mem. Council for Social Democracy Jan.–March 1981; left Labour Party March 1981; Co-Founder SDP March 1981, Pres. 1982–88; Public Service Prof. of Elective Politics, John F. Kennedy School of Govt, Harvard Univ. 1988–2000, Prof. Emer. 2000–, Dir Inst. of Politics 1988–89; mem. Social and Liberal Democratic Party 1988–; Deputy Leader Liberal Democrat Party, House of Lords 1999–2001, Leader Nov. 2001–; Visiting Fellow, Nuffield Coll., Oxford 1967–75; Fellow Inst. of Politics, Harvard 1979–80 (mem. Sr Advisory Council 1986–); Regents Lecturer and Fellow Inst. of Politics, Univ. of Calif., Berkeley; Dir Turing Inst., Glasgow 1985–90, Learning by Experience Trust 1986–94, Project Liberty 1990–98; Janeway Lecturer, Princeton Univ., NJ; Pick Lecturer, Chicago Univ.; Godkin Lecturer, Harvard Univ.; Montgomery Lecturer, Dartmouth Coll.; Heath Fellow, Grinell Coll.; Rede Lecturer and Darwin Lecturer, Univ. of Cambridge; Hoover Lecturer, Strathclyde Univ.; Dainton Lecturer, British Library; Gresham Lecturer, Mansion House; mem. EC Comité des Sages 1996–97, Council Int. Crisis Group 1998–, Int. Advisory Council, Council on Foreign Relations (US); Chair. EC Job Creation Competition 1997–98; Trustee The Century Foundation, New York, Inst. for Public Policy Research, London, RAND Europe UK; Gov. The Ditchley Foundation; mem. Bd Moscow School of Political Studies; Hon. Fellow Somerville Coll., Oxford, Newnham Coll., Cambridge; Grand Cross (FRG); Hon. DEd, CNAA; Hon. DrPolEcon (Univ. of Leuven, Belgium, Radcliffe Coll., Harvard, USA); Hon. LLD (Leeds) 1979, (Southampton) 1981, (Ulster) 1997; Dr hc (Aston, Bath, Essex, Heriot-Watt, Napier, Sheffield, Washington Coll. (USA)); RSA Silver Medal. *Radio:* Snakes and Ladders – A Political Diary (BBC Radio 4) 1996, Women in the House (BBC Radio 4) 1998. *Television:* Shirley Williams in Conversation (BBC series) 1979. *Publications:* Youth Without Work (OECD Study) 1981, Politics is for People 1981, A Job to Live 1985, 'Human Rights in Europe' for Human Rights: What Work? (ed. Power and Alison) 2000; pamphlets on EC and economics of Central Africa; articles for The Times, Guardian, Independent, Int. Herald Tribune, Political Quarterly, Prospect etc. *Leisure interests:* riding, rough walking, music. *Address:* House of Lords, Westminster, London, SW1A 0PW, England.

WILLIAMS OF ELVEL, Baron (Life Peer), cr. 1985, of Llansantffraed in Elvel in the County of Powys; **Charles Cuthbert Powell Williams**, CBE, MA; British business executive and politician; b. 9 Feb. 1933; s. of the late Dr. Norman P. Williams and Muriel Cazenove; m. Jane G. Portal 1975; one step-s.; ed Westminster School, Christ Church, Oxford and London School of Econs; British Petroleum Co. Ltd 1958–64; Bank of London and Montreal 1964–66; Eurofinance SA, Paris 1966–70; Baring Brothers & Co. Ltd 1970–77, Man. Dir 1971–77; Chair. Price Comm. 1977–79; Man. Dir Henry Ansbacher & Co. Ltd 1980–82, Chair. 1982–85; Chief Exec. Henry Ansbacher Holdings PLC 1982–85; Chair. Acoustiguide UK Ltd 1989–95; Pres. Campaign for the Protection of Rural Wales 1989–95, Vice-Pres. and Pres. Radnor Br. 1995–; Pres. Fed. of Econ. Devt Authorities 1990–96, Vice-Pres. 1996–; parl. cand. (Labour) 1964; Opposition Spokesman for Trade and Industry, House of Lords 1986–92, for Defence 1990–, for Environment 1992–; Deputy Leader of Opposition in House of Lords 1989–92. *Publications:* The Last Great Frenchman: A Life of General de Gaulle 1993, Bradman: An Australian Hero 1996, Adenauer: The Father of the New Germany 2000. *Leisure interests:* cricket, music, real tennis. *Address:* 48 Thurloe Square, London, SW7 2SX, England; Pant-y-Rhiw, Llansantffraed in Elvel, Powys, LD1 5RH, Wales. *Telephone:* (20) 7581-1783 (London).

WILLIAMS OF MOSTYN, Baron (Life Peer), cr. 1992, of Great Tew in the County of Oxfordshire; **Gareth Wyn Williams**, PC, LLB, MA; British lawyer; b. 5 Feb. 1941; s. of Albert Thomas Williams and Selina Williams; m. 1st Pauline Clarke (divorced); one s. two d.; m. 2nd Veena Maya Russell 1994; one d.; ed Rhyll Grammar School, Queens' Coll., Cambridge; called to the Bar, Gray's Inn 1965, Bencher 1991, Recorder 1978–97, Deputy High Court Judge 1986–97, Leader Wales and Chester Circuit 1987–89; Parl. Under-Sec. of State, Home Office 1997–98, Minister of State, Home Office 1998–99; Attorney Gen. July 1999–; Deputy Leader House of Lords 1998–2001, Leader June 2001–; mem. Bar Council 1986–92 (Chair. 1992–93); Pro-Chancellor, Univ. of Wales 1994–; Fellow Univ. Coll. of Wales, Aberystwyth 1993; Pres. Welsh Coll. of Music and Drama; Hon. Prof. School of Sociology and Social Policy, Univ. Coll. of N Wales 1994. *Address:* House of Lords, London, SW1A 0PW, England (Office).

WILLIAMSON, David Keith, AO, BE; Australian playwright and screenwriter; b. 24 Feb. 1942, Melbourne; s. of Edwin Keith David Williamson and Elvie May (née Armstrong) Williamson; m. Kristin Ingrid Lofven 1974; two s. one d.; ed Monash Univ., Melbourne Univ.; Design Engineer Gen. Motors-Holden's Ltd 1966–72; lecturer Swinbourne Tech. Coll. 1966–72; freelance writer 1972–; numerous writing, TV and cinema awards. *Plays:* The Removalists 1972, Don's Party 1973, Three Plays 1974, The Department 1975, A Handful of Friends 1976, The Club 1977, Travelling North 1979, The Perfectionist 1981, Sons of Cain 1985, Emerald City 1987, Top Silk 1989, Siren 1990, Money and Friends 1992, Brilliant Lies 1993, Sanctuary 1994, Dead White Males 1995, Corporate Vibes 1999, Face to Face 1999, The Great Man 2000. *Screenplays:* Gallipoli 1981, Phar Lap 1983, The Year of Living Dangerously 1983, Travelling North 1986, Emerald City 1988, The Four Minute Mile (2-part TV series) 1988, A Dangerous Life (6-hour TV series) 1988, Top Silk 1989, Siren 1990, Money and Friends 1992, Dead White Males 1995, Heretic 1996, Third World Blues 1997, After the Ball 1997, Brilliant Lies 1996, On the Beach 2000. *Address:* c/o Anthony Williams Management Pty Ltd, P.O. Box 1379, Darlinghurst, NSW 2010, Australia, NSW 2010, Australia.

WILLIAMSON, G. Malcolm, FIB, FBIM; British banker; b. 27 Feb. 1939, Oldham; m. Hang Thi Ngo; one s. one d.; one s. one d. by previous marriage; local dir Barclays Bank PLC, N London 1980–81; Asst Gen. Man. Barclays Bank PLC 1981–83, Regional Man. 1983–85; Dir Barclays Unit Trust & Insurance Ltd 1983–85; Man. Dir Girobank PLC and mem. bd The Post Office 1985–89; Group Exec. Dir Banking (Eastern Hemisphere), Standard Chartered Bank 1989–90, Group Exec. Dir Banking 1990–91, Group Man. Dir 1991–93, Group Chief Exec. 1993–98; Dir Nat. Grid Group 1995–99; UK Chair. Thai-British Group 1997–; Pres. and Chief Exec. Visa Int. 1998–; Deputy Chair. Britannic Group 2002–; Fellow, Inst. of Dirs. *Leisure interests:* mountaineering, walking, chess, bridge. *Address:* Visa International, P.O. Box 8999, San Francisco, CA 94128, USA (Office).

WILLIAMSON, John, PhD; British economist; b. 7 June 1937, Hereford; s. of A. H. Williamson and Eileen Williamson; m. Denise R. de Souza 1974; two s. one d.; ed London School of Econs and Princeton Univ.; Lecturer, Reader, Univ. of York 1963–68; HM Treasury 1968–70; Prof. Univ. of Warwick 1970–77; adviser, IMF 1972–74; Prof. Catholic Univ. of Rio de Janeiro 1978–81; Sr Fellow, Inst. for Int. Econs 1981–; Chief Economist South Asia, World Bank 1996–99; Project Dir UN High-Level Panel on Financing for Devt 2001. *Publications:* The Crawling Peg 1965, The Failure of World Monetary Reform 1977, The Exchange Rate System 1983, Targets and Indicators (with M. H. Miller) 1987, Latin American Adjustment: How Much Has Happened? 1990, The Political Economy of Policy Reform 1993, The Crawling Band as an Exchange Rate Regime 1996, A Survey of Financial Liberalization (co-author) 1998, Exchange Rate Regimes for Emerging Markets 2000. *Leisure interest:* birding. *Address:* Institute for International Economics, 1750 Massachusetts Avenue, NW, Washington, DC 20036-1903 (Office); 3919 Oliver Street, Chevy Chase, MD 20815, USA. *Telephone:* (202) 454-1340 (Office); (301) 654-5312 (Home). *Fax:* (202) 328-5432 (Office). *E-mail:* jwilliamson@iie.com (Office). *Website:* www.iie.com/jwilliamson.htm (Office).

WILLIAMSON, Kevin; American screenwriter and producer; b. New Bern, NC; ed E. Carolina Univ., UCLA; fmr actor, asst dir, music videos; f. Outerbanks Entertainment 1995; Entertainer of the Year, Entertainment Weekly 1997, mem. Power 100 List, Premiere Magazine 1998. *Films include:* Scream 1996, Scream 2 1997, I Know What You Did Last Summer, Halloween: H20 (producer), The Faculty, Teaching Mrs. Tingle (dir) 1999, Her Leading Man (dir), Cursed (producer). *TV series include:* Dawson's Creek, Wasteland (producer) 1998. *Address:* c/o WMA, 151 El Camino Drive, Beverly Hills, CA 90212, USA (Office).

WILLIAMSON, Matthew, BA; British fashion designer; ed St Martin's School of Art and Design; worked as freelance designer for two years; travelled frequently to India for Marni, Georgina von Ertzdorf and Monsoon fashion retailers; f. Matthew Williamson (with Joseph Velosa) 1996; collections shown in British Fashion Week 1997, 1998, 1999; trademark details are embroidery, beading and sequins. *Address:* c/o Beverly Cable PR, 11 St Christopher's Place, London, W1M 5HB, England. *Telephone:* (20) 7935-1314. *Fax:* (20) 7935-8314.

WILLIAMSON, Nicol; British actor; b. 14 Sept. 1938, Hamilton, Scotland; m. Jill Townsend 1971 (divorced 1977); one s.; began career with Dundee Repertory Theatre 1960–61; London début at Royal Court, That's Us 1961; joined RSC 1962; New York Drama Critics Award for Inadmissible Evidence 1965–66; Evening Standard Award for Best Actor, for Inadmissible Evidence 1964, for Hamlet 1969. *Theatre appearances include:* Satin in The Lower Depths 1962, Leantio in Women Beware Women 1962, Kelly's Eye 1963, The Ginger Man 1963, Vladimir in Waiting for Godot 1964, Bill Maitland in Inadmissible Evidence 1964, 1965, 1978, Diary of A Madman 1968, Hamlet 1969, Uncle Vanya 1973, Coriolanus 1973, Malvolio in Twelfth Night 1974, Macbeth 1974, Rex 1975, Inadmissible Evidence 1981, Macbeth 1982, The Entertainer 1983, The Lark 1983, The Real Thing 1985, Jack—A Night on the Town with John Barrymore 1994, King Lear 2001. *Films include:* Inadmissible Evidence 1967, Laughter in the Dark 1968, Bofors Gun 1968, The Reckoning 1969, Hamlet 1969, The Jerusalem File 1972, The Wilby Conspiracy 1974, Robin and Marian 1976, The Seven Per Cent Solution 1976, The Human Factor 1980, Knights 1980, Excalibur 1980, Venom 1980, I'm Dancing as Fast as I Can 1981, Return to Oz 1984, Black Widow 1986, The Hour of the Pig 1994. *Television includes:* Terrible Jim Fitch, Arturo Ui, I Know What I Meant, The Word 1977, Macbeth 1982, Mountbatten—the Last Viceroy 1985, Passion Flower 1985. *Publication:* Ming's Kingdom (novel) 1996. *Address:* c/o Jonathan Altaras Associates, 13 Shorts Gardens, London, WC2H 9AT, England.

WILLIAMSON, Sir (Robert) Brian, Kt, CBE, MA, FRSA; British business executive; b. 16 Feb. 1945; m. Diane Marie Christine de Jacquier de Rosée

1986; ed Trinity Coll., Dublin; Personal Asst to Maurice Macmillan (later Viscount Macmillan) 1967–71; Ed. Int. Currency Review 1971; Man. Dir Gerrard & Nat. Holdings (later Gerrard Group PLC) 1978–89, Chair. 1989–98; Dir London Int. Financial Futures and Options Exchange (LIFFE) 1982–89, Chair. 1985–88, 1998–2003; Chair. GNI Ltd 1985–89; Dir Fleming Int. High Income Investment Trust PLC 1990–96, Deputy Chair. Fleming Worldwide Investment Trust PLC 1996; Dir Bank of Ireland 1990–98 (mem. Bd Bank of Ireland Britain Holdings 1986–90); Dir Electra Investment Trust PLC 1994– (Chair. 2000–), Barlows PLC 1998–; mem. British Invisible Exports Council, Financial Services Authority 1986–98; Gov. at Large Nat. Asscn of Securities Dealers, USA 1995–98; mem. Int. Markets Advisory Bd, NASDAQ Stock Market (Chair. 1997–99); mem. Supervisory Bd Euronext. *Leisure interests:* tobogganing, hot air ballooning. *Address:* 23 Paultons Square, London, SW3 5AP, England (Office).

WILLIAMSON OF HORTON, Baron (Life Peer), cr. 1999, of Horton in the County of Somerset; **David Francis Williamson,** GCMG, CB, MA, DCL, D.ECON.SC.; British government official (retd); b. 8 May 1934; m. Patricia M. Smith 1961; two s.; ed Tonbridge School and Exeter Coll. Oxford; Army service 1956–58; entered Ministry of Agric., Fisheries and Food 1958; seconded to HM Diplomatic Service as First Sec. (Agric. and Food), Geneva, for Kennedy Round Trade Negotiation 1965–67; Prin. Pvt. Sec. to successive Ministers, Ministry of Agric., Fisheries and Food 1967–70; Head of Milk and Milk Products Div. 1970–74; Under-Sec. 1974; Deputy Dir-Gen. (Agric.), Comm. of European Communities 1977–83; Deputy Sec. and Head of European Secr. Cabinet Office 1983–87; Sec.-Gen. Comm. of European Communities (now European Comm.) 1987–97; mem. EU Cttee, House of Lords; Pres. Univ. Asscn for Contemporary European Studies; Visiting Prof., Univ. of Bath 1997–2001; Dir (non-exec.) Whitbread PLC; Trustee Thomson Foundation; Knight Commdr's Cross of the Order of Merit (Germany); Commdr, Légion d'honneur; Commdr, Grand Cross of the Royal Order of the Polar Star (Sweden). *Address:* Thatchcroft, Broadway, Ilminster, Somerset, TA19 9QZ, England.

WILLIS, Bruce Walter; American actor and singer; b. 19 March 1955, Fed. Repub. of Germany; s. of David Willis and Marlene Willis; m. Demi Moore (q.v.) (divorced 2000); three d.; ed Montclair State Coll.; moved to USA 1957; studied with Stella Adler; mem. First Amendment Comedy Theatre. *Stage appearances:* (off-Broadway): Heaven and Earth 1977, Fool for Love 1984, The Bullpen, The Bayside Boys, The Ballad of Railroad William. *Films:* Prince of the City 1981, The Verdict 1982, Blind Date 1987, Sunset 1988, Die Hard 1988, In Country 1989, Die Hard 2, Die Harder 1990, Bonfire of the Vanities 1990, Hudson Hawk 1991, The Last Boy Scout 1991, Death Becomes Her, Striking Distance, Color of Night 1994, North 1994, Nobody's Fool 1994, Pulp Fiction 1994, Die Hard with a Vengeance 1995, 12 Monkeys 1995, Four Rooms, Last Man Standing 1996, The Jackal 1997, The Fifth Element 1997, Mercury Rising 1998, Armageddon 1998, Breakfast of Champions 1998, The Story of US 1999, The Sixth Sense 1999, Unbreakable 2000, Disney's the Kid 2000, Bandits 2001, Hart's War 2002. *Television:* Trackdown (film), Miami Vice (series), The Twilight Zone (series), Moonlighting 1985–89 (series; People's Choice award 1986, Emmy award 1987, Golden Globe award 1987), Friends (guest) 2000. *Recordings:* The Return of Bruno 1987, If It Don't Kill You, It Just Makes You Stronger 1989.

WILLIS, Norman David; British trade union official; b. 21 Jan. 1933; s. of Victor J. M. Willis and Kate E. Willis; m. Maureen Kenning 1963; one s. one d.; ed Ashford County Grammar School, Ruskin and Oriel Colls, Oxford; Personal Research Asst to Gen. Sec. Transport & General Workers' Union (TGWU) 1959–70; Nat. Sec. Research and Educ. TGWU 1970–74; Asst Gen. Sec. Trades Union Congress 1974–77, Deputy Gen. Sec. 1977–84, Gen. Sec. 1984–93; Councillor (Labour), Staines Urban Dist Council 1971–74; Chair. Nat. Pensioners Convention Steering Cttee 1979–93; Vice-Pres. European TUC 1984–91 (Pres. 1991–93), ICFTU 1984–93, Inst. of Manpower Studies 1985–93; Trustee Anglo-German Foundation for Study of Industrial Soc. 1986–95, Duke of Edinburgh's Commonwealth Study Conf. 1986–93; Patron West Indian Welfare (UK) Trust 1986; mem. NEDC 1984, Council, Overseas Devt Inst. 1985–93, Council, Motability 1985–93, Exec. Bd UNICEF 1986–90, Trade Union Advisory Cttee to OECD 1986–93, Council of Prince of Wales Youth Business Trust 1986–93, Employment Appeal Tribunal 1995–2003; Pres. The Arthur Ransome Soc.; Vice-Pres. Poetry Soc., West Indian Welfare Trust (UK) 1986–93; Patron Docklands Sinfonietta 1986–; monthly column 'Cross Stitcher'; Hon. Fellow Oriel Coll., Oxford. *Leisure interests:* embroidery, poetry, natural history, architecture, canals. *Address:* c/o Trades Union Congress, Congress House, Great Russell Street, London, WC1B 3LS, England.

WILLIS, Ralph; Australian politician; b. 14 April 1938, Melbourne; s. of Stanley Willis and Doris Willis; m. Carol Joyce Dawson 1970; one s. two d.; ed Univ. High School and Melbourne Univ.; research officer, Australian Council of Trade Unions (ACTU) 1960, industrial advocate 1970; mem. House of Reps. 1972; Minister for Employment and Industrial Relations and Minister assisting Prime Minister in Public Service Industrial Matters 1983–87, Minister for Industrial Relations and Minister assisting Prime Minister in Public Service Matters 1987–88, for Transport and Communications 1988–90, for Finance 1990–91, Treas. 1991, Minister for Finance 1991–93, Treas. 1993–96; Vice-Pres. Exec. Council 1992; mem. Australian Labor Party. *Leisure interests:* tennis, reading, watching football. *Address:* 24 Gellibrand Street, Williamstown, Vic. 3016, Australia.

WILLOCH, Kåre Isaachsen, CAND.OECON.; Norwegian politician (retd); b. 3 Oct. 1928, Oslo; s. of Haakon Willoch and Agnes Saure; m. Anne Marie Jørgensen 1954; one s. two d.; ed Ullern Gymnasium and Univ. of Oslo; Sec. Fed. of Norwegian Shipowners 1951–53, Counsellor Fed. of Norwegian Industries 1954–63; mem. Storting 1958–89; mem. Nat. Cttee Conservative Party 1961–89, Sec.-Gen. Conservative Party 1963–65, Chair. 1970–74, Chair. Conservative Party Parl. Group 1970–81; Minister of Trade and Shipping 1963, 1965–70; World Bank Group 1967; mem. Nordic Council 1970–86, Pres. 1973; Prime Minister 1981–86; Chair. Int. Democratic Union 1987–89; Chair. Foreign Affairs Cttee of Parl. 1986–89; Co-Gov. of Oslo and Akershus 1989–98; Chair. Norwegian Defence Comm. 1990–92; Chair. Supervisory Bd, Norwegian Bank 1990–96; Chair. Bd of Norwegian Broadcasting Corpn 1998–2000; Chair. Norwegian Comm. on the Vulnerability of Soc. 1999–2000; Dir Fridtjof Nansen Inst. 1999–2001; Commdr with Star, Royal Norwegian Order of St Olav; Dr hc (St Olav's Coll. Minn., USA); Fritt Ords Pris, Norwegian Inst. for Free Speech 1997, Opinion Maker of the Year, Asscn of Norwegian Eds 1996, C. J. Hambro's Prize 2000. *Publications:* Personal Savings 1955, Price Policy in Norway (with L. B. Bachke) 1958, Memoirs (Vol. I) 1988, (Vol. II) 1990, Krisetid 1992, A New Policy for the Environment 1996, Ideas (Tanker i Tiden) 1999, Myths and Realities (Mytirog virkelighet) (memoirs) 2002. *Leisure interests:* skiing, touring. *Address:* Blokaveien 6B, 0282 Oslo, Norway (Home). *Telephone:* 22-50-72-89 (Home). *E-mail:* fmoa@frisurf.no (Home).

WILLOTT, (William) Brian, C.B., PhD; British public official; b. 14 May 1940, Swansea; s. of William Harford and Beryl P. M. Willott; m. Alison Leyland Pyke-Lees 1970; two s. two d.; ed Trinity Coll., Cambridge; Research Assoc., Univ. of Md 1965–67; Asst Prin. Bd of Trade 1967–69, Prin. 1969–73; HM Treasury 1973–75; Asst Sec. Dept of Industry 1975–78, Sec. Ind. Devt Unit 1978–80; Sec. Nat. Enterprise Bd 1980–81; CEO British Tech. Group (Nat. Enterprise Bd and Nat. Research and Devt Corpn) 1981–84; Head, Information Tech. Div., Dept of Trade and Industry 1984–87, Head, Financial Services Div. 1987–91; Chief Exec. Export Credit Guarantee Dept 1992–97; CEO Welsh Devt Agency 1997–2000; Dir Dragon Int. Studios Ltd, Gwent NHS Trust; mem. Council Nat. Museums and Galleries of Wales 2001–; Visiting Prof. Univ. of Glamorgan 2000. *Leisure interests:* music, reading, ancient history, gardening. *Address:* Coed Cefn, Tregare, Monmouth, NP25 4DT, Wales (Home).

WILLOUGHBY, Christopher R., MA; British economist; b. 24 Feb. 1938, Guildford; s. of Ronald James Edward Willoughby and Constance Louisa (née Sherbrooke) Willoughby; m. Marie-Anne Isabelle Normand 1972; ed Lambroke School, Marlborough Coll., Univ. of Grenoble, Jt Services School for Linguists, Balliol Coll., Oxford, Univ. of California, Berkeley; RN 1956–58, Lt, RN Reserve 1958; New York Times Wash. Bureau 1962–63; economist World Bank 1963–, Dir Operations Evaluation Dept 1973–76, Transport, Water and Telecommunications Dept 1976–83, Econ. Devt Inst. 1983–90, Chief, World Bank Mission in Bangladesh 1990–94, in Belarus 1994–97, Infrastructure Lead Adviser Europe and Cen. Asia Region 1997–, Lead Specialist Infrastructure Dept 1999–. *Leisure interests:* running, swimming, house re-modelling. *Address:* World Bank, 1818 H Street, NW, Washington, DC 20433 (Office); 5340 Falmouth Road, Bethesda, MD 20816, USA (Home). *Telephone:* (202) 473-3407 (Office); (301) 263-9116 (Home). *Fax:* (202) 522-3223.

WILLS, Dean Robert, AO; Australian business executive; b. 10 July 1933, Australia; s. of the late Walter W. Wills and Violet J. Dryburgh; m. Margaret F. Williams 1955; one s. two d.; ed Sacred Heart Coll., S. Australia and S. Australian Inst. of Tech.; Dir W. D. & H. O. Wills (Australia) 1974–, Man. 1977–83, Chair. 1983–86; Dir AMATIL Ltd 1975–, Deputy Chair. 1983–84, Man. Dir Coca-Cola AMATIL Ltd 1984–94, Chair. 1984–99; mem. Business Council of Australia 1984–94, Vice-Pres. 1987–88, Pres. 1988–90; mem. Bd Australian Grad. School of Man. (Univ. of NSW) 1985–92; Gov. Medical Foundation (Univ. of Sydney) 1990–94; mem. Corps. and Securities Panel 1991–94; Vice-Chair. Nat. Mutual Life 1992–97, Chair. 1997–2000; Deputy Chair. Nat. Mutual Holdings 1995–97, Chair. 1997–2000; Chair. Transfield Services Ltd 2001, Coca-Cola Australia Foundation Ltd 2002–; Dir Microsurgery Foundation, Melbourne 1992–, John Fairfax Holdings Ltd 1994– (Chair. 2002–), Westfield Holdings Ltd 1994–; Trustee Museum of Applied Arts and Sciences 1986–90; Gov. Australian Naval Aviation Museum; Deputy Chair. Australian Grand Prix Corpn 1994–2002. *Leisure interests:* tennis, performance cars. *Address:* 71 Circular Quay East, Sydney, NSW 2000, Australia. *Telephone:* (2) 9259-6401 (Office). *Fax:* (2) 9259-6700 (Office).

WILLSON, Francis Michael Glenn, MA, DPhil; British university administrator and professor; b. 29 Sept. 1924, Carlisle; s. of the late Christopher Glenn Willson and Elsie Katrine Mattick; m. Jean Carlyle 1945; two d.; ed Carlisle Grammar School, Univ. of Manchester, Balliol and Nuffield Colls., Oxford; war service in Merchant Navy 1941–42 and RAF 1943–47; seconded to BOAC 1946–47; Research Officer, Royal Inst. of Public Admin. 1953–60; Research Fellow, Nuffield Coll., Oxford 1955–60; Lecturer in Politics, St Edmund Hall, Oxford 1958–60; Prof. of Govt, Univ. Coll. of Rhodesia and Nyasaland 1961–64, Dean of Social Studies 1962–64; Prof. of Govt and Politics, Univ. of Calif., Santa Cruz 1965–74, Provost of Stevenson Coll. 1967–74, Vice-Chancellor Coll. and Student Affairs 1973–74, Visiting Prof. 1985–92; Warden of Goldsmiths Coll., London 1974–75; Prin. of London Univ. 1975–78; Vice-Chancellor Murdoch Univ., Western Australia 1978–84, Prof. Emer. 1985–. *Publications:* Organization of British Central Government 1914–1956 (with D. N. Chester) 1957, 2nd edn 1914–1964 1968, Administrators in Action 1961, A Strong Supporting Cast – The Shaw Lefevres 1789–1936 1993, Our Minerva – The Men and Politics of the University of London 1836–1858 1995, In Just Order Move – The Progress of the Laban Centre for Movement and Dance 1946–96 1997. *Leisure interests:* listening to music, reading. *Address:* 32 Digby Mansions, Hammersmith Bridge Road, London, W6 9DF, England. *Telephone:* (20) 8741-1247.

WILMOTT, Peter Graham, CMG, MA; British consultant and fmr civil servant; b. 6 Jan. 1947, Cuckfield; s. of John Wilmott and Violet Wilmott; m. Jennifer Plummer 1969; two d.; ed Hove Grammar School and Trinity Coll. Cambridge; Asst Prin., HM Customs & Excise 1968, Prin. 1973, Asst Sec. 1983, Commr 1988; seconded to UK Perm. Rep. to EC 1971–73, 1977–79, to EC Court of Auditors 1980–82; Dir-Gen. Customs and Indirect Taxation, EC Comm. 1990–96; partner with Prisma Consulting Group 1996–2000; Chair. Int. Value Added Tax Asscn 1998–2000; Pres. Office du Développement pour l'Automatisation et la Simplification du Commerce Extérieur, Paris 2000–; Dir (non-exec) SITPRO 2001–. *Address:* Ad Valorem International Ltd, 31 Wilbury Avenue, Hove, East Sussex, BN3 6HS, England.

WILMUT, Ian, OBE, PhD; British geneticist; b. 7 July 1944; s. of Leonard (Jack) Wilmut and Mary Wilmut; m. Vivienne Mary Craven 1967; two d. one adopted s.; ed Nottingham Univ., Darwin Coll., Cambridge; Post-doctoral Fellow, Unit of Reproductive Physiology and Biochem., Cambridge 1971–73; various research posts Animal Breeding Research Org. (ARC, now BBSRC Roslin Inst.) 1973–, now Head of Div. Gene Expression and Devt, jtly. responsible (with Keith Campbell) for cloning of Dolly (a sheep, first animal produced from an adult cell) 1996; Hon. Prof. Edin. Univ. 1998–; Hon. DSc (Nottingham) 1998, (North Eastern Univ., Boston) 1999, (Edin.) 2002. *Publications:* The Second Creation (jtly.) 2000; and contribs. to numerous papers on cloning of Dolly the sheep. *Leisure interests:* curling, photography, walking in the countryside. *Address:* Roslin Institute, Roslin, Midlothian, EH25 9PS, Scotland (Office). *Telephone:* (131) 527-4219 (Office).

WILSEY, Gen. Sir John, GCB, CBE, DL; British former army officer and business executive; b. 18 Feb. 1939, Frimley, Hants.; s. of the late Maj.-Gen. J.H.O. Wilsey and B.S.F. Wilsey; m. Elizabeth P. Nottingham 1975; one s. one d.; ed Sherborne School and Royal Mil. Acad. Sandhurst; served Cyprus, North Africa, Guyana, USA, Malta, Germany, UK (mem. Blue Nile Expedition 1968), Staff Coll. 1973; Commdg 1st Bn, The Devonshire & Dorset Regt 1979–82, Col 1990–97 (commissioned 1959); Chief of Staff, H.Q. N Ireland 1982–84; Commdg 1st Infantry Brigade and UK Mobile Force 1985–86; Royal Coll. of Defence Studies 1987; Chief of Staff, H.Q. UK Land Forces 1988–90; G.O.C. and Dir Mil. Operations, Northern Ireland 1990–93; C-in-C Land Command 1993–96; ADC Gen. to the Queen 1994–96; Chair. Western Provident Asscn 1996–; Hon. Col Royal Jersey Militia, Royal Engineers 1993–; Vice-Chair. Sherborne School 1996–; mem. Council Royal Bath & West 1996–, Commonwealth War Graves Comm. 1998– (Vice-Chair. 2001–); Commr Royal Hosp., Chelsea 1996–; Gov. Suttons Hosp. in Charterhouse 1996–2001, Sherborne School for Girls 1996–2001. *Publications:* Service for the Nation 1987, Biography of Lt.-Gen C. H. Jones, VC OBE 2002. *Leisure interests:* skiing, fishing, sailing, breeding alpacas. *Address:* Western Provident Association, Rivergate House, Blackbrook Park, Taunton, Somerset, TA1 2PE, England. *Telephone:* (1823) 623502.

WILSON, Sir Alan Geoffrey, Kt, MA, DSc, FBA, FCGI; British professor of geography, mathematician and university vice-chancellor; b. 8 Jan. 1939, Bradford, Yorks.; s. of Harry Wilson and Gladys Naylor; m. Sarah Fildes 1987; ed Queen Elizabeth Grammar School, Darlington, Corpus Christi Coll., Cambridge; Chartered Geographer; Scientific Officer, Rutherford High Energy Lab. 1961–64; Research Officer, Inst. of Econs and Statistics, Univ. of Oxford 1964–66; Math. Adviser to Ministry of Transport 1966–68; Asst Dir Centre for Environmental Studies, London 1968–70; Prof. of Urban and Regional Geography, Univ. of Leeds 1970–, Pro-Vice-Chancellor 1989–91, Vice-Chancellor 1991–; Ed. Environment and Planning 1969–91; Dir GMAP 1991–2001; mem. Academia Europaea 1991–, Acad. of Learned Socs for the Social Sciences; Gill Memorial Award, Royal Geographical Soc. 1978, Hons Award, Asscn of American Geographers 1987, Founder's Medal, Royal Geographical Soc. 1992. *Publications:* Entropy in Urban and Regional Modelling 1970, Urban and Regional Models in Geography and Planning 1974, Spatial Population Analysis (with P. H. Rees) 1977, Mathematics for Geographers and Planners (with M. J. Kirkby) 1980, Models of Cities and Regions (jt ed.) 1977, Catastrophe Theory and Bifurcation: applications to urban and regional systems 1981, Geography and the Environment: Systems Analytical Methods 1981, Mathematical Methods in Geography and Planning (with R. J. Bennett) 1985, Urban Systems (jt ed.) 1987, Urban Dynamics (jt ed.) 1990, Modelling the City: Performance, Policy and Planning (with Bertuglia, Clarke and others) 1994, Intelligent Geographical Information Systems (with Birkin, Clarke and Clarke) 1996, Complex Spatial Systems 2000. *Leisure interests:* writing, miscellaneous fads. *Address:* University of Leeds, Leeds, LS2 9JT, England. *Telephone:* (113) 343-3000. *Fax:* (113) 343-4122. *E-mail:* a.g.wilson@ adm.leeds.ac.uk.

WILSON, Alexander (Sandy) Galbraith; British writer and composer; b. 19 May 1924, Sale, Cheshire; s. of George Wilson and Caroline Humphrey; ed Harrow School, Oxford Univ. and Old Vic Theatre School; contributed to revues Slings and Arrows, Oranges and Lemons 1948; wrote revues for Watergate Theatre, London, See You Later, See You Again 1951–52; wrote musical The Boy Friend for Players Club Theatre 1953, transferred to

Wyndhams Theatre and on Broadway 1954 (London revival 1984), The Buccaneer 1955, Valmouth London 1958, USA 1960, Chichester 1982, Divorce me Darling! 1965 (revival Chichester 1997); Dir London revival of The Boy Friend 1967; Composed music for As Dorothy Parker Once Said, London 1969; songs for BBC TV's Charley's Aunt 1969; wrote and performed Sandy Wilson Thanks the Ladies (one man show) London 1971; wrote His Monkey Wife London 1971, The Clapham Wonder 1978, Aladdin (London) 1979. *Publications:* This is Sylvia 1954, The Poodle from Rome 1962, I Could be Happy (autobiog.) 1975, Ivor 1975, The Roaring Twenties 1977. *Leisure interests:* cinema, cookery, travel. *Address:* Flat 4, 2 Southwell Gardens, London, SW7 4SB, England. *Telephone:* (20) 7373-6172.

WILSON, Andrew N., MA, FRSL; British author; b. 27 Oct. 1950; s. of the late N. Wilson and of Jean Dorothy Wilson (née Crowder); m. 1st Katherine Dorothea Duncan-Jones 1971 (divorced 1989); two d.; m. 2nd Ruth Guilding 1991; one d.; ed Rugby School and New Coll., Oxford; Asst Master Merchant Taylors' School 1975–76; Lecturer St Hugh's Coll. and New Coll., Oxford 1976–81; Literary Ed. Spectator 1981–83, Evening Standard 1990–97; Hon. mem. American Acad. of Arts and Letters 1984; Chancellor's Essay Prize 1975, Ellerton Theological Prize 1975. *Publications:* fiction: The Sweets of Pimlico 1977, Unguarded Hours 1978, Kindly Light 1979, The Healing Art (Somerset Maugham Award) 1980, Who Was Oswald Fish? 1981, Wise Virgin (W. H. Smith Award) 1982, Scandal 1983, Gentleman in England 1985, Love Unknown 1986, Stray 1987, Incline Our Hearts 1988, A Bottle in the Smoke 1990, Daughters of Albion 1991, The Vicar of Sorrows 1993, A Watch in the Night 1996, Hazel the Guinea-pig (for children) 1997, Dream Children 1998; non-fiction: The Laird of Abbotsford 1980, A Life of John Milton 1983, Hilaire Belloc 1984, How Can We Know? An Essay on the Christian Religion 1985, The Church in Crisis (jtly.) 1986, The Lion and the Honeycomb 1987, Penfriends from Porlock 1988, Tolstoy (Whitbread Award for Biography and Autobiography) 1988, Eminent Victorians 1989, John Henry Newman: prayers, poems, meditations (ed.) 1989, C. S. Lewis: A Biography 1989, Jesus 1992, The Faber Book of Church and Clergy (ed.) 1992, The Rise and Fall of the House of Windsor 1993, The Faber Book of London (ed.) 1993, Hearing Voices 1995, A Life of Walter Scott: The Laird of Abbotsford 1996, A Life of John Milton 1996, Paul: The Mind of the Apostle 1997, God's Funeral 1999, The Victorians 2002. *Address:* 5 Regent's Park Terrace, London, NW1 7EE, England.

WILSON, August; American playwright; b. 1945, Pittsburgh, Pa; s. of David Bedford Wilson and Daisy Wilson; one d.; f. Black Horizons Theatre Co.; worked in Science Museum of Minn., St Paul, writing short plays to accompany exhbns. *Plays:* The Homecoming 1976, The Coldest Day of the Year 1977, Black Bart and the Sacred Hills 1977, Jitney 1979, Ma Rainey's Black Bottom 1982 (NY Drama Critics' Circle Award for Best Play), Fences (NY Drama Critics' Circle Award for Best Play, Tony Award, Pulitzer Prize for Drama), 1983 Joe Turner's Come and Gone 1984 (NY Drama Critics' Circle Award for Best Play), The Piano Lesson 1986 (Pulitzer Prize for Drama, New York Drama Critics' Circle Award, Drama Desk Award), Two Trains Running 1990, Seven Guitars 1995 (NY Drama Critics' Circle Award for Best Play). *Address:* c/o John Breglio, Paul, Weiss, Rifkind, Wharton & Garrison, 1285 Avenue of the Americas, New York, NY 10019, USA.

WILSON, Brian G., AO, PhD, FTS; Australian academic (retd); b. 9 April 1930, Belfast, N Ireland; s. of Charles W. Wilson and Isobel C. Wilson (née Ferguson); m. 1st Barbara Wilkie 1959 (divorced 1975); two s. one d.; m. 2nd Jeanne Henry 1978 (divorced 1988); m. 3rd Joan Opdebeeck 1988; three s.; ed Methodist Coll., Belfast, Queens Univ. Belfast and Nat. Univ. of Ireland; Postdoctoral Fellow, Nat. Research Council of Canada 1955–57; Officer-in-charge, Sulphur Mount Lab., Banff, Alberta 1957–60; Assoc. Prof. of Physics, Univ. of Calgary 1960–65, Prof. 1965–70, Dean of Arts and Science 1967–70; Vice-Pres. Simon Fraser Univ., Burnaby, BC 1970–78; Vice-Chancellor Univ. of Queensland 1979–95; Deputy Chair. Australian Univ. Vice-Chancellors' Cttee 1987–88, Chair. 1989–90; mem. Council, Northern Territory Univ. 1988–93, Univ. of the South Pacific 1991–95; Pres. Int. Devt Program of Australian Univs. and Colls. 1991–92; Chair. Australian Cttee for Quality Assurance in Higher Educ. 1993–95; Hon. LLD (Calgary) 1984; Hon. DUniv (Queensland Univ. of Tech.) 1995; Hon. DSc (Queensland) 1995. *Publications:* one book and over 50 scientific articles in int. journals. *Leisure interests:* golf, viniculture. *Address:* Domaine des Tisseyres, 11270 Fanjeaux, France. *Telephone:* (4) 68-24-61-75. *Fax:* (4) 68-24-61-75. *E-mail:* opdebeeck.wilsonz@tiscali.fr (Home).

WILSON, Charles; British journalist; b. 18 Aug. 1935, Glasgow, Scotland; s. of Adam Wilson and Ruth Wilson; m. 1st Anne Robinson 1968 (divorced 1973); one d.; m. 2nd Sally O'Sullivan 1980 (divorced 2001); one s. one d.; m. 3rd Rachel Pitkeathley 2001; ed Eastbank Acad., Glasgow; copy boy, The People 1951; later reporter with Bristol Evening World, News Chronicle and Daily Mail; Deputy Ed. Daily Mail (Manchester) 1971–74; Asst Ed. London Evening News 1974–76; Ed., Evening Times, Glasgow 1976; later Ed., Glasgow Herald; Ed. Sunday Standard, Glasgow 1981–82; Exec. Ed., The Times 1982, Jt Deputy Ed. 1984–85, Ed. 1985–90; Int. Devt Dir News Int. 1990–91; Ed.-in-Chief, Man. Dir The Sporting Life 1990–98; Editorial Dir Mirror Group Newspapers 1991–92, Group Man. Dir Mirror Group 1992–98; Acting Ed. The Independent 1995–96; Dir (non-exec.) Chelsea and Westminster Hosp.; mem. Competition Comm. 1999–; mem. Jockey Club 1993–, Youth Justice Bd 1998–; Trustee World Wildlife Fund-UK 1997–, Royal Naval Museum 1999–. *Leisure interests:* current affairs, National Hunt racing, hunting, reading. *Address:* c/o Competition Commission, New Court, 48 Carey Street, London, WC2A 2JT, England (Office); 23 Campden Hill Square, London, W8 7JY. *Telephone:* (20) 7727-3366 (Home).

WILSON, Sir Colin Alexander St. John, Kt, RA, FRIBA; British architect; b. 14 March 1922; s. of the late Rt Rev Henry A. Wilson; m. 1st Muriel Lavender 1955 (divorced 1971); m. 2nd Mary J. Long 1972; one s. one d.; ed Felsted School, Corpus Christi Coll. Cambridge and London Univ. School of Architecture; served RDVR 1942–46; Asst Housing Div. Architects Dept London County Council 1950–55; lecturer, School of Architecture, Univ. of Cambridge 1955–69, Prof. of Architecture 1975–89, now Prof. Emer.; Fellow, Churchill Coll. Cambridge 1962–71, Pembroke Coll. 1977–; Visiting Critic, Yale School of Architecture 1960, 1964, 1983; Bemis Prof. of Architecture, MIT 1970–72; practised in association with Sir Leslie Martin 1955–64; works included bldgs at Univs of Oxford, Cambridge, London and Leicester; in own pvt. practice; works include extension to British Museum, The British Library, St Pancras, Library for Queen Mary Coll., London, School of Architecture, Cambridge; Hon. Fellow Corpus Christi Coll. Cambridge, Churchill Coll. Cambridge 1999; Commdr, Order of the Lion (Finland) 1992; Dr Univ. (Essex) 1998; Hon. LittD (Cambridge) 1999, Hon. LLD (Sheffield) 1999; Sconul Award for Design Excellence 1984–89, A J Bovis RA Grand Award 2000. *Art Exhibitions:* Architectural Biennale, Venice 1996, Colin St. John Wilson – Touring Retrospective, London, Bristol, Glasgow 1997–98, Touring Exhbn. of British Library – Harvard, Chicago, New York, Yale School of Architecture 2000. *Publications:* Architectural Reflections 1992, The Other Tradition of Modern Architecture 1995, The Design and Construction of the British Library 1998, The Artist at Work 1999; articles in The Observer, in professional journals in numerous cos. *Address:* Colin St John Wilson & Associates, Clarendon Buildings, 27 Horsell Road, London, N5 1XL, England. *Telephone:* (20) 7607-3084. *Fax:* (20) 7607-5621.

WILSON, Colin Henry; British writer; b. 26 June 1931, Leicester; s. of Arthur Wilson and Annetta Jones; m. 1st Dorothy Troop 1951; one s.; m. 2nd Joy Stewart 1960; two s. one d.; ed Gateway Secondary Technical School, Leicester; laboratory asst 1948–49, civil servant (taxes) 1949–50; RAF 1950, discharged on medical grounds 1950; then navvy, boot and shoe operative, dish washer, plastic moulder; lived Strasbourg 1950, Paris 1953; later factory hand and dish washer; writer 1956–; Writer in Residence, Hollins Coll., Virginia, USA 1966–67; Visiting Prof., Univ. of Washington 1967–68, Dowling Coll., Majorca 1969, Rutgers Univ., NJ 1974. *Publications include: philosophy:* The Outsider 1956, Religion and the Rebel 1957, The Age of Defeat 1958, The Strength to Dream 1961, Origins of the Sexual Impulse 1963, Beyond the Outsider 1965, Introduction to the New Existentialism 1966; *other non-fiction:* Encyclopaedia of Murder 1960, Rasputin and the Fall of the Romanovs 1964, Brandy of the Damned (music essays) 1965, Eagle and Earwig (literary essays) 1965, Sex and the Intelligent Teenager 1966, Voyage to a Beginning (autobiog.) 1968, Shaw: A Reassessment 1969, A Casebook of Murder 1969, Poetry and Mysticism 1970, The Strange Genius of David Lindsay (with E. H. Visiak) 1970, The Occult 1971, New Pathways in Psychology 1972, Strange Powers 1973, A Book of Booze 1974, The Craft of the Novel 1975, The Geller Phenomenon 1977, Mysteries 1978, Beyond The Occult 1988; *novels:* Ritual in the Dark 1960, Adrift in Soho 1961, The World of Violence 1963, Man Without a Shadow 1963, Necessary Doubt 1964, The Glass Cage 1966, The Mind Parasites 1967, The Philosopher's Stone 1969, The Killer 1970, The God of the Labyrinth 1970, The Black Room 1970, The Schoolgirl Murder Case 1974, The Space Vampires 1976, Men of Strange Powers 1976, Enigmas and Mysteries 1977; *other works include:* The Quest for Wilhelm Reich 1979, The War Against Sleep: the Philosophy of Gurdjieff 1980, Starseekers 1980, Frankenstein's Castle 1980, The Directory of Possibilities (ed. with John Grant) 1981, Poltergeist! 1981, Access to Inner Worlds 1983, Encyclopaedia of Modern Murder (with Donald Seaman) 1983, The Psychic Detectives 1984, The Janus Murder Case 1984, The Personality Surgeon 1984, A Criminal History of Mankind 1984, Encyclopaedia of Scandal (with Donald Seaman) 1985, Afterlife 1985, Rudolf Steiner 1985, Strindberg (play) 1970, Spiderworld—The Tower 1987, Encyclopaedia of Unsolved Mysteries (with Damon Wilson) 1987, Aleister Crowley: the nature of the beast 1987, The Misfits 1988, Spiderworld—The Delta 1988, Written in Blood 1989, The Serial Killers 1990, Mozart's Journey to Prague (play) 1991, Spider World: the Magician 1992, The Strange Life of P. D. Ouspensky 1993, From Atlantis to the Sphinx 1996, Atlas of Sacred Sites and Holy Places 1996, Alien Dawn 1998, The Books in My Life 1998, The Devil's Party 2000, Atlantis Blueprint (with Rand Fle'math) 2000, Spiderworld—Shadowland. *Leisure interests:* music, mathematics, wine. *Address:* Tetherdown, Trewallock Lane, Gorran Haven, Cornwall, PL26 6NT, England.

WILSON, Sir David Mackenzie, Kt, LittD, FBA, FSA; British fmr museum director; b. 30 Oct. 1931, Dacre Banks; s. of Rev. J. Wilson; m. Eva Sjögren 1955; one s. one d.; ed Kingswood School, St John's Coll., Cambridge, Lund Univ., Sweden; Asst Keeper, The British Museum 1955–64; Reader in Archaeology, Univ. of London 1964–71, Prof. of Medieval Archaeology 1971–76; Dir British Museum 1977–92; Commr English Heritage 1990–97; mem. Royal Swedish Acad. of Science, Norwegian Acad. of Science and Letters; Hon. Fellow Univ. Coll., London; numerous other honours and awards. *Publications:* The Anglo-Saxons 1960, Catalogue of Anglo-Saxon Metalwork 700–1100 in the British Museum 1964, Anglo-Saxon Art 1964, The Bayeux Tapestry 1965, Viking Art (with O. Klindt-Jensen) 1966, Three Viking Graves in the Isle of Man (with G. Bersu) 1966, The Vikings and their Origins 1970, The Viking Achievement (with P. Foote) 1970, St Ninian's Isle and its Treasure (with A. Small and A. C. Thomas) 1973, The Viking Age in the Isle of Man 1974; Editor: The Archaeology of the Anglo-Saxons 1976, The Northern World 1980, The Art of the Anglo-Saxons 1984, The Bayeux Tapestry 1985, The British Museum: Purpose and Politics 1989, Awful Ends 1992, Showing the Flag 1992, Vikingetidens Konst 1995, Vikings and Gods in European Art 1997; The British Museum – A History 2002; many articles and pamphlets. *Address:* The Lifeboat House, Castletown, IM9 1LD, Isle of Man. *Telephone:* (1624) 822800.

WILSON, Donald M.; American journalist and publishing executive; b. 27 June 1925; m. Susan M. Neuberger 1957; one s. two d.; ed Yale Univ.; Air Corps Navigator, Second World War; magazine assignments in 35 countries 1951–61; fmr Far Eastern Corresp., Life magazine, Chief Washington Correspondent 1957–61; Deputy Dir US Information Agency 1961–65; Gen. Man. Time-Life Int. 1965–68; Assoc. Publisher Life magazine 1968–69; Vice-Pres. Corp. and Public Affairs, Time Inc. 1969–81, Corp. Vice-Pres. Public Affairs Time Inc. 1981–89; Publr NJBIZ 1989–. *Address:* NJBIZ, 104 Church Street, New Brunswick, NJ 08901 (Office); 4574 Province Line Road, Princeton, NJ 08540, USA (Home).

WILSON, Edward Osborne, PhD; American university professor and author; b. 10 June 1929, Birmingham, Ala; s. of the late Edward Osborne Wilson Sr and Inez Freeman Huddleston; m. Irene Kelley 1955; one d.; ed Univ. of Alabama and Harvard Univ.; Jr Fellow, Soc. of Fellows, Harvard Univ. 1953–56, Prof. of Zoology 1964–76, F. B. Baird Prof. of Science 1976–94, Pellegrino Univ. Prof. 1994–97, Research Prof. 1997–, Curator of Entomology, Museum of Comparative Zoology, 1974–97 (Hon. Curator 1997–); Fellow, Guggenheim Foundation 1977–78, Advisory Bd 1979–90, mem. Selection Cttee 1982–90; mem. Bd of Dirs., World Wildlife Fund 1983–94, Org. for Tropical Studies 1984–91, American Museum of Natural History 1992–, American Acad. of Liberal Educ. 1993–, Nature Conservancy 1994–, Conservation Int. 1997–; Foreign mem. Royal Soc. 1990; Nat. Medal of Science 1976, Pulitzer Prize for Gen. Non-Fiction 1978, 1981, Tyler Prize for Environmental Achievement 1983, Crafoord Prize, Royal Swedish Acad. of Sciences 1990, Int. Prize for Biology, Govt of Japan 1993, Schubert Prize (Germany) 1996, Franklin Prize for Science, American Philosophical Soc. 1999; Nonino Prize (Italy) 2000, King Faisal Prize 2000 and some 60 other awards and prizes. *Publications:* The Theory of Island Biogeography (with R. H. MacArthur) 1967, The Insect Societies 1971, Sociobiology: The New Synthesis 1975, On Human Nature 1978, Caste and Ecology in the Social Insects (with G. F. Oster) 1978, Genes, Mind and Culture (with C. J. Lumsden) 1981, Promethean Fire (with C. J. Lumsden) 1983, Biophilia 1984, Biodiversity (ed.) 1988, The Ants (with B. Hölldobler) 1990, Success and Dominance in Ecosystems 1990, The Diversity of Life 1992, Naturalist 1994, Journey to the Ants (with Bert Hölldobler) 1994, Consilience: The Unity of Knowledge 1998, Biological Diversity: The Oldest Human Heritage 1999; The Future of Life 2002; Pheidole in the New World: A Dominant, Hyperdiverse Ant Genus 2002; numerous articles on evolutionary biology, entomology and conservation. *Address:* Museum of Comparative Zoology, Harvard University, Cambridge, MA 02138 (Office); 1010 Waltham Street, Lexington, MA 02421, USA (Home). *E-mail:* ewilson@oeb.harvard.edu (Office).

WILSON, Hon. Geoffrey Hazlitt, CVO, BA, FCA, FCMA; British accountant and business executive; b. 28 Dec. 1929, London; s. of Lord Moran and Dorothy Dufton; m. Barbara Jane Hebblethwaite 1955; two s. two d.; ed Eton Coll. and King's Coll., Cambridge; with English Electric Co. Ltd 1956–68, Deputy Comptroller 1967–68; Financial Controller (Overseas), General Electric Co. Ltd 1968–69; Financial Dir, Cables Div., Delta PLC 1969, Group Financial Dir 1972, Jt Man. Dir 1977, Dir 1977, Deputy Chief Exec. 1980, Chief Exec. 1981–88, Chair. 1982–94; Dir Blue Circle Industries PLC 1981–87, Drayton English & Int. Trust PLC 1978–95, Nat. Westminster Bank PLC (W Midlands and Wales Regional Bd) 1985–92 (Chair. 1990–92), Southern Electric PLC 1989–96 (Chair. 1993–96), Johnson Matthey PLC 1990–97 (Deputy Chair. 1994–97); Hon. Treas., mem. Admin. Council The Prince's and the Royal Jubilee Trusts 1979–89; Vice-Pres. Eng Employers' Fed. 1983–86, 1990–94, Deputy Pres. 1986–90; Vice-Chair. King's Coll., Cambridge Campaign Appeal 1994–97; Pres. British Fed. of Electrotechnical and Allied Mfrs'. Asscns. 1987–88; mem. Court, Worshipful Co. of Chartered Accountants in England and Wales 1982–95, Master 1988–89, Financial Repertoire Council 1990–93; mem. O St J. 1997; Hon. mem. The Hundred Group of Chartered Accountants (Chair. 1979–81). *Leisure interests:* family, reading, vintage cars, skiing.

WILSON, Georges; French theatre and film director; b. 16 Oct. 1921, Champigny-sur-Marne; m. Nicole Mulon 1956; two s.; ed Centre dramatique de la rue Blanche, Paris; acted in two plays in Grenier-Hussenot Company 1947; entered Comédie de l'Ouest 1950; entered Théâtre Nat. Populaire (T.N.P.) 1952, played important roles in almost all the plays; Dir T.N.P. 1963–72; Chair. Interim Action Cttee British Film Authority 1979; several TV appearances; Chevalier, Légion d'honneur, Officier, Ordre nat. du Mérite, Commdr, Ordre des Arts et Lettres. *Films directed include:* Une aussi longue absence, La jument verte, Le Caïd, Terrain vague, Lucky Joe, Dragées au poivre, Chair de poule, Max et les ferrailleurs 1970, Blanche 1971, Nous sommes tous en liberté provisoire 1973, Asphalte 1981, L'honneur d'un capitaine 1982, Itinéraires bis 1983, Tango, l'exil de Gardel 1985, La Vouivre 1989, Le Château de ma mère 1990, La Tribu 1991, Marquise 1997. *Plays directed include:* L'école des femmes, Le client du matin (Théâtre de l'Oeuvre), Un otage (Théâtre de France), La vie de Galilée, Lumières de Bohème, La folle de Chaillot, Le diable et le bon Dieu, Chêne et lapins angora, Les prodiges 1971, Turandot 1971, Long voyage vers la nuit 1973, Othello 1975, Un habit pour l'hiver 1979, Huis clos, K2 1983, L'Escalier 1985, Je ne suis Rappaport 1987, Météore (Dir, Actor) 1991, Les Dimanches de Monsieur Riley 1992, Show Bis 1994, Henry IV 1994, Le cerisaie 1999. *Address:* Moulin de Vilgris, 78120 Rambouillet, France (Home).

WILSON, Gordon (see Wilson, (Robert) Gordon).

WILSON, Jean Donald, MD; American professor of internal medicine; b. 26 Aug. 1932, Wellington, Tex.; s. of J. D. Wilson and Maggie E. Wilson (née Hill); ed Hillsboro Coll., Univ. of Texas at Austin and Univ. of Texas Southwestern Medical Center, Dallas; Medical Intern and Asst Resident in Internal Medicine, Parkland Memorial Hosp. Dallas 1955–58; Clinical Assoc. Nat. Heart Inst. Bethesda, Md 1958–60; Instr. Univ. of Texas Health Science Center 1960–, Prof. of Internal Medicine 1968–; Established Investigator, American Heart Asscn 1960–65; Travelling Fellow, Royal Soc. of Medicine, Strangeways Research Lab. Cambridge 1970; mem. NAS, American Acad. of Arts and Sciences etc.; several honours and awards. *Publications:* more than 300 scientific articles in various medical journals. *Leisure interests:* birding, opera. *Address:* Division of Endocrinology and Metabolism, Department of Internal Medicine, University of Texas Southwestern Medical Center at Dallas, 5323 Harry Hines Boulevard, Dallas, TX 75390–8857, USA. *Telephone:* (214) 648-3685. *Fax:* (214) 648-8917. *E-mail:* jwils1@mednet.swmed .edu (Office).

WILSON, John P., MA, LLD, TD; Irish politician and university lecturer (retd); b. 8 July 1923, Co. Cavan; s. of John Wilson and Brigid Wilson; m. Ita M. Ward 1953; one s. four d.; ed St Mel's Coll., Longford, Nat. Univ. of Ireland, Univ. of London and Zaragoza Univ.; taught in England and Ireland 1947–73; mem. of the Dáil 1973–; Opposition Spokesman on Educ. and the Arts 1973–77, Jan.–Dec. 1982; Minister for Educ. 1977–81, for Transport and for Posts and Telegraphs 1982; Opposition Spokesman on Transport 1983–87; Minister for Tourism and Transport 1987–89, for the Marine 1989–93, for Defence 1992–93; Minister for the Gaeltacht, Tánaiste (Deputy Prime Minister) 1990–93; Chair. Irish Govt del., Northern Ireland talks 1992; apptd Victims' Commr by Irish Govt 1998; apptd by Irish Govt to Comm. for Recovery of Bodies/Remains 1999; Pres. European Council of Fisheries Ministers; Pres. Perm. Comm., Eurocontrol 1989–; mem. Arts Council, Nat. Archives Advisory Council; fmr Dir Tyrone Guthrie Centre, Annaghmakerrig; Order of Honour of Hellenic Repub.; Hon. LLD 2001. *Television:* Laochra Gael (TG4), I Clár. *Publications:* numerous articles on local history. *Leisure interests:* politics, Irish language and literature, theatre, reading, fishing, Gaelic football and hurling, cruising, arts. *Address:* Kilgolagh, Co. Cavan, via Finea, Mullingar; 13 Braemor Avenue, Churchtown, Dublin 14, Ireland. *Telephone:* (43) 81130 (Mullingar); (1) 2981861 (Dublin). *Fax:* (1) 2981861 (Dublin).

WILSON, Kenneth Geddes, PhD; American physicist and educationalist; b. 8 June 1936, Waltham, Mass.; s. of Edgar Bright Wilson, Jr and Emily Fisher Buckingham Wilson; m. Alison Brown 1982; ed Harvard Univ., Calif. Inst. of Tech.; Fellow Harvard Univ. 1959–62, Ford Foundation Fellow 1962–63; joined Cornell Univ. NY 1963, Prof. 1970–88, James A. Weeks Chair. in Physical Sciences 1974–88, Dir Center for Theory and Stimulation in Science and Eng (Cornell Theory Center) 1985–88; Hazel C. Youngberg Distinguished Prof. Ohio State Univ. 1988–; Co-Prin. Investigator Ohio's Project Discovery 1991–96; mem. NAS, American Acad. of Arts and Sciences, American Physical Soc.; Heinemann Prize 1973, Boltzmann Medal 1975, Wolf Prize 1980, Nobel Physics Prize 1982. *Publications:* Redesigning Education 1994; articles in journals. *Address:* Department of Physics, The Ohio State University, 174 W 18th Avenue, Columbus, OH 43210, USA. *Telephone:* (614) 292-8686. *Fax:* (614) 292-3221.

WILSON, Linda S., PhD, FAAS; American university administrator and chemist; b. Linda Lee Smith, 10 Nov. 1936, Washington DC; d. of Fred M. Smith and Virginia T. Smith; m. 1st Malcolm C. Whatley 1957 (divorced); one d.; m. 2nd Paul A. Wilson 1970; one step-d.; ed Tulane Univ. and Univ. of Wisconsin (Madison); Asst Vice-Chancellor for Research, Washington, Univ., St Louis, Mo. 1968–74, Assoc. Vice-Chancellor 1974–75; Assoc. Vice-Chancellor for Research, Univ. of Ill., Urbana, Ill. 1975–85, Assoc. Dean, Graduate Coll. 1978–85; Vice-Pres. for Research, Univ. of Mich., Ann Arbor, Mich. 1985–89; Pres. Radcliffe Coll., Cambridge, Mass. 1989–99, Pres. Emerita 1999; Chair. Advisory Cttee Office of Science and Eng Personnel, Nat. Research Council 1990–96; mem., Council on Govt Relations 1971–77, Nat. Inst. of Health Advisory Council on Research Resources 1978–82, Nat. Comm. on Research 1978–80, NSF Dirs. Advisory Council 1980–89, Govt-Univ.-Industry Research Roundtable (NAS) 1984–88, Inst. of Medicine Council 1986–89, Inst. of Medicine Cttee on Govt-Industry Collaboration in Research and Educ. 1988–89, Inst. of Medicine Cttee on NIH Priority-Setting 1998–99; mem. Bd of Dirs. AAAS 1984–88, Mich. Materials Processing Inst. 1986–89, Mich. Biotech. Inst 1986–89, Inst. of Medicine, American Chemical Soc., American Asscn for Advancement of Science; Overseer Museum of Science, Boston 1992–2001; Trustee Mass. Gen. Hosp. 1992–99 (Hon. Trustee 1999–2002), Cttee on Econ. Devt 1995–; Dir Citizens Financial Group 1996–99–, Inacom Corpn 1997–, ValueLine Inc. 1998–2000, Myriad Genetics Inc. 1999–, Internet Corpn. for Assigned Names and Numbers (ICANN) 1998–; Dr hc (Tulane Univ., Univ. of Md); Distinguished Contribution to Research Admin. Award, Soc. of Research Admins., Distinguished Service

Award, Univ. of Ill., Centennial Award for Outstanding Accomplishments, Newcomb Coll, Distinguished Alumni Award, Coll. of Medicine, Univ. of Wis. 1997, Endowed Chair. for Dir of Radcliffe Public Policy Center 1999, Radcliffe Medal 1999. *Publications:* 7 book chapters, 10 journal articles, 6 maj. reports, 4 commissioned studies, 12 papers on chem., science policy and research policy. *Leisure interests:* cello, reading, music, woodland man. and preservation. *Address:* 47 Keene Neck Road, Bremen, ME 04551, USA (Office). *Telephone:* (207) 529-2979 (Office). *Fax:* (207) 529-2981 (Office).

WILSON, The Very Rev. The Hon. Lois Miriam, OC, BA, BD, MDiv; Canadian ecclesiastic; b. 8 April 1927, Winnipeg, Man.; d. of Rev. Dr. E. G. D. Freeman and Ada M. Davis; m. Rev. Dr. Roy F. Wilson 1950; two s. two d.; ed Univ. of Winnipeg; ordained United Church of Canada 1965; Minister, First Church United, Thunder Bay, Ont. 1965–69, Hamilton, Ont. 1969–78, Chalmers United Church, Kingston, Ont. 1978–80; Pres. Canadian Council of Churches 1976–79; Moderator, United Church of Canada 1980–82; Dir Ecumenical Forum of Canada 1983–89; Pres. World Council of Churches 1983–91, World Federalists (Canada) 1996–; The United Church of Canada McGeachy Sr Scholar 1989–91; mem. Bd Amnesty Int. 1978–90, Canadian Inst. for Int. Peace and Security 1984–89, Refugee Status Advisory Bd 1985–89, Canadian Asscn of Adult Educ. 1987–90, Civil Liberties Asscn of Canada 1987–, Co-op Program in Int. Devt, Univ. of Toronto 1987–93, Public Review Bd, Canada 1989–, Bd of Regents, Victoria Univ. 1990–; Govt appointee to Environmental Assessment Panel reviewing nuclear waste disposal 1989–97; Chair. Urban Rural Mission (Canada) 1990–95; Senator (ind.) 1998–; Canada's Special Envoy to Sudan 1999–; Chancellor Lakehead Univ. 1990–2000; Nat. Pres. UNIFEM 1993–95, Int. Centre for Human Rights and Democratic Devt 1997–; mem. Advisory Bd, Canadian Women's Studies Journal, York Univ., Toronto 1993–, Centre for Studies in Religion and Society, Victoria, BC 1992–; Monitor, El Salvador elections 1994; Keynote speaker Christian/Jewish Conf., Jerusalem 1994; 11 hon. degrees in law and divinity; Pearson Peace Prize 1985, World Federalist Peace Prize 1985, Queen's Jubilee Medal, Order of Ont. 1991, commemorative medal for 125th anniversary of Canadian Confed. 1992. *Publications:* Like a Mighty River 1981, Turning the World Upside Down (memoir) 1989, Telling Her Story 1992, Miriam, Mary and Me 1992, Stories Seldom Told 1997, Nuclear Waste—Exploring the Ethical Options 2000. *Leisure interests:* skiing, sailing, canoeing, reading. *Address:* The Senate, VB #807, Ottawa, Ont., K1A 0A4 (Office); 40 Glen Road, Apt. 310, Toronto, Ont., M4W 2V1, Canada (Home). *Telephone:* (613) 992-7396 (Office); (416) 975-0395 (Home). *Fax:* (613) 9432-2269 (Office); (613) 975-0848 (Home). *E-mail:* wilsonl@sen.parl.gc.ca (Office). *Website:* sen.parl.gc.ca/lwilson (Office).

WILSON, Gen. Louis Hugh, BA; American marine corps officer; b. 11 Feb. 1920, Brandon, Miss.; s. of Louis Wilson and Bertha (née Buchann) Wilson; m. Jane Clark 1944; one d.; ed Millsaps Coll.; enlisted in Marine Corps Reserve 1941, Second Lt 1941, 9th Marine Regt, San Diego, Guadalcanal, Efate, Bougainville; Capt. 1943; participated in assault on Guam 1944; Company CO, Camp Pendleton 1944; Detachment Commdr, Washington, DC 1944–46; Dean, later Asst Dir Marine Corps Inst., later ADC to Commdg Gen. of Fleet Marine Force, Pacific; Recruiting Officer, NY; Lt-Col 1951; exec. posts at Basic School, Quantico, Va; CO, Camp Barrett 1951–54; with 1st Marine Div. as Asst G-3 in Korea 1954–55; Head of Operations, HQ Marine Corps 1956–68; CO, Test and Training Regt, then of Basic School, Quantico 1958–61; Deputy Chief of Staff, HQ Marine Corps 1962–65; Asst Chief of Staff, G-3 1st Marine Div., Repub. of Viet Nam 1965; Command, 6th Marine Corps District, Atlanta, Ga 1966; Brig.-Gen. 1966; Legis. Asst to Commdt of Marine Corps 1967–68; Chief of Staff, HQ Fleet Marine Force, Pacific 1968–70; Maj.-Gen. 1970; Command, 1st Marine Amphibious Force, 3rd Marine Div., Okinawa 1970; Dir of Educ., Quantico 1971–72; Lt-Gen. 1972; Command, Fleet Marine Force, Pacific 1972–75; 26th Commdt Marine Corps 1975–79; designated mem. Jt Chiefs of Staff Oct. 1978–; mem. Bd Dirs. Merrill Lynch and Co., Fluor Corpn, La. Lands Exploration Co.; Hon. LLD 1976; Hon. DHumLitt 1978; Medal of Honor 1944, Legion of Merit with Combat V and 2 Gold Stars, Purple Heart with 2 Stars, Cross of Gallantry with Gold Star (Repub. of Viet Nam) 1965, Order of Nat. Security Merit (Repub. of Korea), GUK-SEON Medal, Commdr, Legion of Honour (Philippines), Outstanding American Award 1975, Int. Order of Merit 1976, Spanish Grand Cross of Naval Merit 1977, Order of Nat. Security Merit, Tong-Il Medal (Korea) 1977, Distinguished American Award 1977, DSM. *Leisure interests:* hunting, golf.

WILSON, Lynton Ronald, OC, MA; Canadian business executive (retd); b. 3 April 1940, Port Colborne, Ont.; s. of Ronald Alfred Wilson and Blanche Evelyn Matthews; m. Brenda Jean Black; one s. two d.; ed Port Colborne High School, McMaster Univ., Cornell Univ., USA; Deputy Minister, Ministry of Industry and Tourism, Govt of Ont. 1978–81; Pres. and CEO Redpath Industries Ltd, Toronto 1981–88, Chair. Bd 1988–89; Man. Dir N America, Tate & Lyle PLC 1986–89; Vice-Chair. Bank of Nova Scotia, Toronto 1989–90; Pres. and COO BCE Inc., Montreal 1990–96, COO 1990–92, CEO 1992–98, Chair. 1993–98; Chair. Bd Dirs. 1998–2000; Chair. Bell Canada; Nortel Newtworks Corpn; Dir BCE Mobile Communications Inc., Bell Canada Int. Inc., Northern Telecom Ltd, Bell-Northern Research Ltd, Teleglobe Inc., Chrysler Canada Ltd, Chrysler Corpn, Tate & Lyle PLC, UK, Stelco Inc., CD Howe Inst., Canadian Inst. for Advanced Research; mem. Business Council on Nat. Issues (Policy Cttee), Trilateral Comm., Int. Council JP Morgan & Co., New York, Bd of Trustees Montreal Museum of Fine Arts Foundation; Gov. Olympic Trust of Canada, McGill Univ.; Dr. hc (Montreal) 1995; Hon. LLD

(McMaster) 1995; (Cape Breton) 1998; (Mount Allison) 2000. *Address:* North Tower, A83 Bay Suite, 7th Floor, Toronto, Ont., M5G 2E1 (Office); 2038 Lakeshore Road East, (Oakville), Ont. L6J 1M3, Canada (Home). *Telephone:* (416) 364-4612. *Fax:* (416) 364-7610.

WILSON, Nigel Guy, MA, FBA; British academic; b. 23 July 1935, London; s. of Noel Wilson and Joan L. Wilson; m. Hanneke Marion Wirtjes 1996; ed Univ. Coll. School and Corpus Christi Coll., Oxford; Lecturer, Merton Coll., Oxford 1957–62; Fellow and Tutor in Classics, Lincoln Coll., Oxford 1962–2002; James P. R. Lyell Reader in Bibliography 2003; Hon. LittD (Uppsala) 2001; Gordon Duff Prize 1968, Premio Anassilaos 1999. *Publications:* Scribes and Scholars (with L. D. Reynolds) (3rd edn) 1991, An Anthology of Byzantine Prose 1971, Medieval Greek Bookhands 1973, St Basil on the Value of Greek Literature 1975, Scholia in Aristophanis Acharnenses 1975, Menander Rhetor (with D. A. Russell) 1981, Scholars of Byzantium 1983, Oxford Classical Text of Sophocles (with Sir Hugh Lloyd-Jones) 1990, From Byzantium to Italy 1992, Photius: the Bibliotheca 1994, Aelian: Historical Miscellany 1997, Pietro Bembo: Oratio pro litteris graecis 2003. *Leisure interests:* bridge, real tennis. *Address:* Lincoln College, Oxford, OX1 3DR, England. *Telephone:* (1865) 558066 (Home). *Fax:* (1865) 279802. *E-mail:* nigel.wilson@lincola.ox.ac.uk.

WILSON, Pete, LLB; American politician and lawyer; b. 23 Aug. 1933, Lake Forest, Ill.; s. of James Boone Wilson and Margaret (Callahan) Wilson; m. 1st Betty Robertson (divorced); m. 2nd Gayle Edlund Graham 1983; admitted to Calif. Bar; Asst Exec. Dir Republican Asscn, San Diego Co. 1963–64; Exec. Dir San Diego Co. Republican Cen. Comm. 1964–65; legal service officer, Calif. State Republican Cen. Comm. 1965; mem. Calif. Ass. 1967–71; Mayor of San Diego 1971–83; Senator from Calif. 1983–91; Gov. of Calif. 1991–99; Man. Dir Pacific Capital Group, Calif. 1999–; mem. Presidential Advisory Cttee on Environmental Quality, Task Force Land Use and Urban Growth Policy.

WILSON, Peter L.; Australian architect; b. 27 Sept. 1950, Melbourne; s. of the late Jack Wilson and of Betty Wilson; m. Julia B. Bolles; one s. one d.; ed Univ. of Melbourne, Architectural Asscn School of Architecture, London; Unit Master Architectural Asscn 1978–88; f. Wilson Partnership, London (with Julia Bolles-Wilson) 1980, Architekturbüro Bolles + Wilson, Münster 1988; Guest Prof. Kunsthochschule Weisensee, Berlin 1996–98; winner of more than 20 int. architectural competitions. *Buildings include:* Suzuki House, Tokyo 1993, New City Library, Münster 1993, WLV Office Bldg, Münster 1993, Quay Landscape, Rotterdam 1998, New Luxor Theatre, Rotterdam 2001, BEIC Library and Media Centre, Milan 2001–06, Nord LB Bank, Cathedral Square, Magdeburg, Germany 2002. *Address:* Architekturbüro Bolles + Wilson, Alter Steinweg 17, 48143 Münster, Germany (Office). *Telephone:* (251) 482720 (Office); (251) 43888 (Home). *Fax:* (251) 4827224 (Office). *E-mail:* info@bolles-wilson.com (Office).

WILSON, (Robert) Gordon, BL, LLD; Scottish politician and solicitor; b. 16 April 1938, Glasgow, Scotland; s. of Robert George Wilson and Robina Wilson; m. Edith Hassall 1965; two d.; ed Douglas High School and Edin. Univ.; Asst Nat. Sec. Scottish Nat. Party 1963–64, Nat. Sec. 1964–71, Exec. Vice-Chair. 1972–73, Sr Vice-Chair. 1973–74, Chair. 1979–90, Vice-Pres. 1992–; MP for Dundee E 1974–87; Party Spokesman on Oil and Energy 1974–87, on Energy 1992–93, on Treasury 1993–94; Jt Spokesman on Devolution 1976–79; Rector, Univ. of Dundee 1983–86; Chair. Marriage Counselling (Tayside) 1989–92; Gov. Dundee Inst. of Tech.; Court mem. Univ. of Abertay Dundee 1991–96; mem. Church and Nation Cttee of Church of Scotland, Bd Dundee Age Concern. *Leisure interests:* photography, reading, sailing. *Address:* 48 Monifieth Road, Dundee, DD5 2RX, Scotland (Home). *Fax:* (1382) 226745.

WILSON, Robert M.; American theatre and opera director and artist; b. 4 Oct. 1941, Waco, Tex.; s. of D. M. Wilson and Velma Loree Wilson (née Hamilton); ed Univ. of Tex., Pratt Inst.; began creating innovative theatre in New York in the 1960s; worked mainly in Europe in the 1980s and 1990s, directing original works as well as traditional opera and theatre; Guggenheim Fellow 1971, 1980; Trustee Nat. Inst. of Music Theatre; mem. Dramatists Guild, Soc. des Auteurs et Compositeurs Dramatiques, Soc. of Stage Dirs. and Choreographers, PEN American Center, American Acad. of Arts and Letters; hon. Dir American Repertory Theatre; has given lectures and workshops at numerous insts.; Dr. hc Calif. Coll. of Arts and Letters, Pratt Inst. New York City; numerous awards and decorations including the Maharam Award for Best Set Design 1975, Lumen Award 1977, First Prize San Sebastian Film and Video Festival 1984, Picasso Award 1986, Inst. Skowhegan Medal for drawing 1987, Grand Prix Biennale, Barcelona Festival of Cinema Art 1989, Germna Theatre Critics Award 1990, Brandeis Univ. Poses Creative Arts Award 1991, Venice Biennale Golden Lion Award for Sculpture 1993, Dorothy and Lillian Gish Prize 1996, Tadeusz Kantor Prize 1997, Harvard Excellence in Design Award 1998, Pushkin Prize 1999; Most Outstanding Theater Designer of the Seventies, U.S. Inst. of Theater Tech. 1977. *One-man exhibitions of drawings and sculpture:* Iolas Gallery, NY, Palazzi Gallery, Milan, Galerie Fred Lanzenberg, Brussels, Musée Galliera, Paris 1972, 1974, Contemporary Art Center, Cincinatti 1980, Galerie der Stadt, Stuttgart, Galerie Herald Behm, Hamburg 1988, Anne Marie Verna Galerie, Zurich 1989, Museum of Fine Arts, Boston 1991, Centre Georges Pompidou, Paris 1991, Galerie Fred Jahn, Munich 1991, IVAM, Valencia 1992, Museum Boymans-Van Beuningen Rotterdam 1993, Galeria Luis Serpa, Lisbon 1995, Thaddeus Ropac Gallery Salzburg and Paris 1996, Clink Street Vaults, London 1996, Art Cologne, Cologne 1996, Villa Stuck Museum, Munich 1997,

Palazzina dei Giardini, Modena 1998–99, Harvard Grad. School of Design Cambridge Mass. 1999 Rotunda della Besana, Milan 2000, Oberammergau Passion Theater 2000, Guggenheim Museum, New York and Bilbao 2000–01, Kunstindustrimuseet, Copenhagen 2001. *Dance created and choreographed:* Snow on the Mesa (for Martha Graham Dance Co.) 1995. *Stage appearances include:* Deafman Glance 1970, The Life and Times of Joseph Stalin (Dir) 1974, A Letter for Queen Victoria 1974, Einstein on the Beach 1976, 1984, Death, Destruction and Detroit 1979, The Golden Windows 1982, 1985, The Civil Wars 1983–85, Hamletmachine 1986, Doktor Faustus 1989, The Black Rider 1990, King Lear 1990, The Magic Flute 1991, Alice 1993, Der Mond in Gras 1994, The Death of Molière 1994, Hamlet: A Monologue 1995, Prometeo 1997, Saints and Singing 1997, Monsters of Grace 1998, Dream Play 1998, Scourge of Hyacinths 1999, The Days Before 1999, Hot Waters 2000, Relative Light 2000. *Plays directed and designed include:* Deafman Glance 1970, Einstein on the Beach 1976, Death, Destruction and Detroit 1979, The Golden Windows 1982, the CIVIL warS 1983–85, Hamletmachine 1986, Doktor Faustus 1989, The Black Rider 1990, The Magic Flute 1991, Doktor Faustus Lights the Lights 1992, Alice 1992, Madame Butterfly 1993, Hanjo 1994, Hamlet: A Monologue 1995, Time Rocker 1996, Lady from the Sea 1998, Das Rheingold 2000, POEtry 2000, Woyzeck 2001. *Films include:* Overture for a Deafman, Monsters of Grace 1998. *Videos include:* The Spaceman 1976, 1984, Video 50 1978, Stations 1982, La Femme à la Cafétière 1989, Mr. Bojangles' Memory 1991, La Mort de Molière 1994. *Publications include:* The King of Spain 1970, Einstein on the Beach: An Opera in Four Acts (with Philip Glass, q.v., 1976, A Letter for Queen Victoria 1977, Death, Destruction and Detroit 1979, the CIVIL warS 1985, Mr. Bojangles' Memory 1991, RW Notebook 1999. *Leisure interest:* collecting fine art and design. *Address:* RW Work Ltd, 155 Wooster Street, Suite 4F, New York, NY 10012, USA. *Telephone:* (212) 253-7484. *Fax:* (212) 253-7485 (Office). *Website:* www.robertwilson.com (Office).

WILSON, Robert McLachlan, BD, PhD, DD, FBA; British professor of biblical criticism; b. 13 Feb. 1916, Gourock, Scotland; s. of Hugh McLachlan Wilson and Janet N. Struthers; m. Enid Mary Bomford 1945; two s.; ed Greenock Acad., Royal High School, Edinburgh, Edinburgh and Cambridge Univs; Minister of Rankin Church, Strathaven 1946–54; Lecturer in New Testament Language and Literature, St Mary's Coll., Univ. of St Andrews 1954–64, Sr Lecturer 1964–69, Prof. (personal chair) 1969–78, Prof. of Biblical Criticism 1978–83; Assoc. Ed. New Testament Studies 1967–77, Ed. 1977–83; Pres. Studiorum Novi Testamenti Societas 1981; Hon. mem. Soc. of Biblical Literature 1972; Hon. DD (Aberdeen) 1982; Burkitt Medal for Biblical Studies (British Acad.) 1990. *Publications:* The Gnostic Problem 1958, Studies in the Gospel of Thomas 1960, The Gospel of Philip 1962, Gnosis and the New Testament 1968, Commentary on Hebrews 1987, Nag Hammadi and Gnosis (Ed.) 1978, The Future of Coptic Studies (ed.) 1978; Trans. Ed. of: Haenchen, Acts 1971, Foerster, Gnosis Vol. 1 1972, Vol. 2 1974, Rudolph, Gnosis 1983, Schneemelcher, New Testament Apocrypha (revised edn) Vol. I 1991, Vol. II 1992. *Leisure interest:* golf. *Address:* 10 Murrayfield Road, St Andrews, Fife, KY16 9NB, Scotland. *Telephone:* (1334) 474331.

WILSON, Sir Robert Peter, KCMG, FRSA, CIMgt; British businessman; b. 2 Sept. 1943, Carshalton; s. of the late Alfred Wilson and Dorothy Wilson (née Mathews); m. Shirley Elisabeth Robson 1975; one s. one d.; ed Epsom Coll., Sussex Univ., Harvard Business School; Asst Economist Dunlop Ltd 1966–67; Economist Mobil Oil Co. Ltd 1967–70; with Rio Tinto PLC (fmrly RTZ Corpn PLC) 1970–, Man. Dir AM & S Europe 1979–82, Project Dir RTZ Devt Enterprise 1982–83, Head of Planning and Devt RTZ Corpn PLC 1984–86, Dir 1987–, Chief Exec. 1991–97, Chair. 1997–; Dir Rio Tinto Ltd (fmrly CRA Ltd) 1990–(2003), Deputy Chair. 1995–98, Chair. 1999–(2003); Dir The Boots Co. PLC 1991–98, Diageo PLC, BP PLC 1998–, The Economist Group 2002–; Trustee Camborne School of Mines 1993–99; Hon. DSc (Exeter) 1993; Hon. LLD (Dundee) 2001. *Leisure interests:* theatre, opera. *Address:* c/o Rio Tinto PLC, 6 St James's Square, London, SW1Y 4LD, England.

WILSON, Robert Woodrow, PhD; American radio astronomer; b. 10 Jan. 1936, Houston; s. of Ralph Woodrow Wilson and Fannie May (née Willis) Wilson; m. Elizabeth Rhoads Sawin 1958; two s. one d.; ed Rice Univ., California Inst. of Tech.; mem. of Technical Staff, AT & T Bell Labs., Holmdel, NJ 1963–76, Head of Radio Physics Research Dept 1976–94; Sr Scientist, Harvard-Smithsonian Center for Astrophysics 1994–; mem. NAS, American Astronomical Soc., American Physical Soc., Int. Astronomical Union; Henry Draper Award 1977, Herschel Award 1977, Nobel Prize For Physics 1978. *Publications:* numerous articles in scientific journals. *Leisure interests:* running, skiing, playing piano. *Address:* Harvard-Smithsonian Center for Astrophysics, 60 Garden Street, # 42, Cambridge, MA 02138 (Office); 9 Valley Point Drive, Holmdel, NJ 07733, USA (Home). *Telephone:* (617) 496-7744 (Office); (201) 671-7807 (Home). *Fax:* (617) 496-7554.

WILSON, Sandy (see Wilson, Alexander Galbraith).

WILSON, Trevor Gordon, MA, DPhil, FRHistS, FAHA; New Zealand professor of history; b. 24 Dec. 1928, Auckland; s. of the late Gordon Wilson and Winifred Wilson; m. Jane Verney 1957; two d.; ed Mount Albert Grammar School, Univs of Auckland and Oxford; Asst Lecturer in History Canterbury Univ. 1952, Auckland Univ. 1953–55; Research Asst in Govt Univ. of Manchester 1957–59; lecturer then Sr Lecturer in History Univ. of Adelaide 1960–67, Prof. 1968–; Commonwealth Fellow St John's Coll., Cambridge 1972; Visiting Fellow Magdalen Coll., Oxford 1987; Drinko Distinguished Visiting Prof., Marshall Univ., W Va Fall 1989; Nuffield Dominion Travelling

Fellowship 1964–65; Univ. of NZ Overseas Travelling Scholarship 1953; Gilbert Campion Prize (jt winner) 1960, Higby Prize 1965, Adelaide Festival of Arts Literature Award 1988. *Publications:* The Downfall of the Liberal Party (1914–35) 1966, The Political Diaries of C. P. Scott 1911–28 1970, The Myriad Faces of War: Britain and the Great War 1914–18 1986, Command on the Western Front: The Military Career of Sir Henry Rawlinson 1914–1918 (with Robin Prior) 1992, Passchendaele: the Untold Story (with Robin Prior) 1996, The First World War (Cassell History of Warfare) (with Robin Prior) 1999. *Leisure interests:* listening to jazz, watching musical movies, table tennis. *Address:* Department of History, University of Adelaide, North Terrace, S. Australia 5005, Australia. *Telephone:* (8) 8303-5633 (Office). *Fax:* (8) 8303-3443 (Office).

WILSON-JOHNSON, David Robert, BA, FRAM; British baritone; b. 16 Nov. 1950, Northampton; s. of Harry K. Johnson and Sylvia C. Wilson; ed Wellingborough School, Northants., British Inst. of Florence, St Catharine's Coll., Cambridge and Royal Acad. of Music; début at Royal Opera House, Covent Garden in We Come to the River 1976; has since appeared in Billy Budd, L'Enfant et les Sortilèges, Le Rossignol, Les Noces, Boris Godunov, Die Zauberflöte, Turandot, Werther, Madame Butterfly; Wigmore Hall recital début 1977; BBC Promenade Concert début 1981; appeared at Edin. Festival 1976, Glyndebourne Festival 1980 and at festivals in Bath, Bergen, Berlin, Geneva, Graz, Netherlands, Hong Kong, Jerusalem, Orange, Paris and Vienna; Paris Opéra début in Die Meistersinger 1989; played St Francis of Assisi (title role) in Olivier Messiaen's 80th birthday celebrations 1988; American début in Paulus (title role) 1990; English Nat. Opera début (in Billy Budd) 1991, Netherlands Opera début in Birtwistle's Punch and Judy 1993; Founder Dir Ferrandou Summer Singing School 1985–; Gulbenkian Fellowship 1978–81; Nat. Fed. of Music Soc. Award 1977, Evening Standard Award for Opera 1989. *Films include:* A Midsummer Marriage 1988. *Recordings include:* Schubert's Winterreise, Mozart Masses from King's College, Cambridge, Haydn's Nelson Mass, Schoenberg's Ode to Napoleon, King Priam, Punch and Judy, La Traviata, Lucrezia Borgia and Michael Berkeley's Or Shall We Die?, Belshazzar's Feast, L'Enfance du Christ, The Kingdom (Elgar), The Ice Break (Tippett), Odes (Purcell), Caractacus (Elgar), Black Pentecost (Maxwell Davies), Mass in B Minor (Bach) Peter Grimes, Damnation of Faust. *Leisure interests:* swimming, slimming, gardening and growing walnuts in the Dordogne. *Address:* Prinsengracht 455, 1016 HN Amsterdam, Netherlands (Home); 28 Englefield Road, London, N1 4ET, England. *Telephone:* (20) 7254-0941 (London); 5-65-10-94-11 (France); (20) 7728104 (Home). *E-mail:* ferrandou@aol.com (Office); jumbowj@aol.com (Home). *Website:* www.gmn.com (Office).

WILSON OF DINTON, Richard Thomas James Wilson, Baron (Life Peer), cr. 2003, of Dinton in the County of Buckinghamshire, GCB, LLM; British civil servant; b. 11 Oct. 1942; s. of the late Richard Ridley Wilson and Frieda Bell Wilson (née Finlay); m. Caroline Margaret Lee 1972; one s. one d.; ed Radley Coll. and Cambridge Univ.; called to the Bar 1965; Asst Prin. Board of Trade 1966, Pvt. Sec. to Minister of State, Board of Trade 1969–71, Prin. Cabinet Office 1971–73, Dept of Energy 1974, Asst Sec. Dept of Energy 1977–82, Under Sec. 1982, Prin. Establishment and Finance Officer 1982–86; on loan to Cabinet Office Man. and Personnel Office 1986–87, Deputy Sec. Cabinet Office 1987–90; Deputy Sec. (Industry) HM Treasury 1990–92; Perm. Sec. Dept of Environment 1992–94; Perm. Under Sec. of State, Home Office 1994–97; Cabinet Sec. and Head of the Home Civil Service 1997–2002; Master Emmanuel Coll. Cambridge 2002–. *Address:* Emmanuel College, St Andrew's Street, Cambridge, CB2 3AP, England (Office). *Telephone:* (1223) 334942 (Office). *Website:* www.emma.cam.ac.uk (Office).

WILSON OF TILLYORN, Baron (Life Peer), cr. 1992, of Finzean in the District of Kincardine and Deeside and of Fanling in Hong Kong; **David Clive Wilson,** KT, GCMG, PhD, FRSE; British diplomatist and public servant; b. 14 Feb. 1935; s. of Rev. William Skinner Wilson and Enid Wilson; m. Natasha Helen Mary Alexander 1967; two s.; ed Glenalmond School and Keble Coll., Oxford; nat. service, The Black Watch 1953–55; entered Foreign Service 1958, Third Sec., Vientiane 1959–60, Second then First Sec., Peking 1963–65, FCO 1965–68, Cabinet Office 1974–77, Political Adviser, Hong Kong 1977–81, Head S. European Dept, FCO 1981–84, Asst Under-Sec. of State 1984–87; Gov. and Commdr-in-Chief of Hong Kong 1987–92; Chancellor, Univ. of Aberdeen 1997–; Vice-Pres. Royal Scottish Geographical Soc. 1996–; Language Student, Hong Kong 1960–62; Ed. China Quarterly 1968–74; Visiting Scholar, Columbia Univ., New York 1972; Chair. Scottish Hydro-Electric PLC 1993–2000 (Scottish and Southern Energy PLC 1998–2000); mem. Bd of Govs. SOAS 1992–97; mem. Bd British Council 1993–2002 (Chair. Scottish Cttee 1993–2002); Chancellor's Assessor, Univ. of Aberdeen 1993–96; Chair. Council, Glenalmond Coll. 2000–, Advisory Cttee on Business Appointments 2000–, Scottish Peers' Assen 2000–02 (Vice-Chair. 1998–2000); Dir Martin Currie Pacific Trust 1993; Pres. Bhutan Soc. of the UK 1993–; Registrar of the Most Distinguished Order of St Michael and St George 2001–; Hon. Fellow, Keble Coll. Oxford; Hon. LLD (Aberdeen) 1990, (Chinese Univ., Hong Kong) 1996; Hon. DLitt (Sydney) 1991, (Abertay Dundee) 1994. *Leisure interests:* mountaineering, reading, theatre. *Address:* The Master's Lodge, Peterhouse, Cambridge, CB2 1QY; House of Lords, London, SW1A 0PW, England.

WIN AUNG, BSc, PhD; Myanmar politician and diplomatist; b. 28 Feb. 1944, Dawei; m. Daw San Yone; two s. one d.; ed Univ. of Yangon; served as Commdr, Staff Officer in Armed Forces and Ministry of Defence 1965–83, Officer in Prime Minister's Office 1983–84; with Myanmar Embassy, Vientiane, Lao People's Democratic Repub. 1986–88, Singapore 1988–90; Amb. to FRG 1990–96, to Belgium, Netherlands and Austria and to UK 1996–98, to Sweden 1997, to Norway 1998; Perm. Rep. to UN, Vienna, IAEA, UNIDO; Chief of Mission to European Comm.; Minister of Foreign Affairs 1998–; Naing Ngan Daw Sit Smu Htan Tazeik, Pyi Thu Wun Htan Gaung Tazeik. *Publications include:* Nation of Gold; numerous articles in magazines. *Address:* Ministry of Foreign Affairs, Pyay Road, Dagon Township, Yangon, Myanmar (Office). *Telephone:* (1) 222-844 (Office). *Fax:* (1) 222-950 (Office). *E-mail:* mofa.aung@mptmail.net.mm. *Website:* www.e-application.com.mm/mofa.

WINBERG, (Sven) Håkan, LLB; Swedish politician and lawyer; b. 30 July 1931, Ånge; s. of Sven Winberg and Sally Angman; m. Ulla Greta Petersson; Justice, Court of Appeal; MP 1971–82; mem. Exec. Swedish Moderate Party 1972–, mem. Steering Cttee 1975–; mem. Press Assistance Bd 1971–79, Bd of Council for Prevention of Crime 1974–79, Co. Boundaries Cttee 1970–74, Cttee of Inquiry into the Press 1972–75, New Labour Laws Cttee 1976–78, Nat. Police Bd 1977–79, Nordic Council 1977–82; County Councillor 1974–79; Minister of Justice 1979–81; Pres. Court of Appeal, Sundsvall 1982–; mem. Election Review Cttee of the Riksdag 1983–; mem. Parl. Comm. for Investigation into the murder of Prime Minister Olof Palme 1987–88, new Comm. for same investigation 1994; mem. Security Police Cttee 1989–, Court of Law Cttee 1990–. *Leisure interest:* skiing.

WINBLAD, Ann, MA; American finance executive; ed St Thomas Coll.; co-f. Open Systems Inc. 1976–83; fmrly strategic planning consultant; partner Hummer Winblad Venture Partners 1989–. *Publication:* (as co-author) Object-Oriented Software 1990. *Address:* Hummer Winblad Venture Partners, 2nd Floor, 2 South Park, San Francisco, CA 94107, USA.

WINCH, Donald Norman, PhD, FBA, FRHistS; British professor of economic history; b. 15 April 1935, London; s. of Sidney Winch and Iris Winch; m. Doreen Lidster 1983; ed Sutton Grammar School, London School of Econs, Princeton Univ.; Visiting Lecturer Univ. of Calif. 1959–60; Lecturer in Econs Univ. of Edin. 1960–63; Univ. of Sussex 1963–66, Reader 1966–69, Prof. History of Econs 1969–, Dean School of Social Sciences 1968–74, Pro-Vice-Chancellor (Arts and Social Studies) 1986–89; Vice-Pres. British Acad. 1993–94; Visiting Fellow, School of Social Science, Inst. of Advanced Study, Princeton 1974–75, King's Coll., Cambridge 1983, History of Ideas Unit, Australian Nat. Univ. 1983, St Catharine's Coll., Cambridge 1989, All Souls Coll., Oxford 1994; Visiting Prof. Tulane Univ. 1984; Carlyle Lecturer, Oxford Univ. 1995; Prof. Emer. Grad. Research Centre in the Humanities; Publr Sec., Royal Econ. Soc. 1971–; Review Ed. The Economic Journal 1976–83. *Publications:* Classical Political Economy & Colonies 1965, James Mill, Selected Economic Writings 1966, Economics and Policy 1969, The Economic Advisory Council 1930–39 (with S. K. Howson) 1976, Adam Smith's Politics 1978, That Noble Science of Politics (with S. Collini and J. W. Burrow) 1983, Malthus 1987, Riches and Poverty 1996. *Leisure interest:* gardening. *Address:* Arts B, The University of Sussex, Brighton, BN1 9QN, England. *Telephone:* (01273) 678634. *E-mail:* d.winch@sussex.ac.uk (Office).

WINCKLER, Georg; Austrian university rector and professor of economics; b. 27 Sept. 1943, Ostrava, Czechoslovakia; m.; two d.; ed Princeton Univ., USA, Univ. of Vienna; Prof. of Econs, Univ. of Vienna 1978–, Univ. Rector 1999–; with Research Dept IMF 1990–91; Visiting Prof. of Econs, Georgetown Univ., USA 1995; Pres. Austrian Rectors' Conf. 2000–; Vice-Pres. European Univ. Assen 2001–. *Publications:* Central and Eastern Europe: Roads to Growth 1992, Central Banks and Seigniorage: A Study of Three Economies in Transition (European Econ. Review) 1996, Grundzüge der Wirtschaftspolitik Österreichs (co-author) 2001. *Leisure interests:* mountaineering, skiing, reading. *Address:* Office of the Rector, University of Vienna, Dr Karl Lueger-Ring, 1010 Vienna, Austria (Office). *Telephone:* (1) 4277-10010 (Office); (1) 328-12-72 (Home). *Fax:* (1) 4277-9100 (Office). *E-mail:* georg.winckler@univie.ac.at (Office). *Website:* www.univie.ac.at (Office).

WINDLE, Alan Hardwick, PhD, A.R.S.M., FIM, FInstP, FRS; British academic; b. 20 June 1942, Croydon, Surrey; s. of Stuart George Windle and Myrtle Lillian Windle (née Povey); m. Janet Susan Carr 1968; one s. three d.; ed Whitgift School, Imperial Coll. London, Trinity Coll. Cambridge; ICI Research Fellow, Imperial Coll. London 1966–67, lecturer in Metallurgy 1967–75; lecturer in Metallurgy and Materials Science, Cambridge Univ. 1975–92, Fellow Trinity Coll. 1978–, lecturer and Dir of Studies in Natural Sciences, Trinity Coll. 1978–92, tutor 1983–91, Prof. of Materials Science 1992–, Head of Dept of Materials Science, Cambridge Univ. 1996–2001; Visiting Prof. NC State Univ., USA 1980; Exec. Dir Cambridge—MIT Inst. 2000–; Vice-Pres. Inst. of Materials 2001–; Bessemer Medal, Imperial Coll. 1963, Silver Medal, RSA 1963, Rosenhain Medal & Prize, Isle of Man 1987, Swinburne Medal & Prize, Plastics and Rubber Inst. 1992. *Publications:* A First Course in Crystallography 1978, Liquid Crystalline Polymers (with A. M. Donald) 1992. *Leisure interest:* flying light aircraft. *Address:* Department of Materials Science and Metallurgy, Pembroke Street, Cambridge, CB2 3Q2, England. *Telephone:* (01223) 334321. *Fax:* (01223) 335637.

WINDLESHAM, 3rd Baron and Baronet; Baron Hennessy (Life Peer), cr. 1999; **David James George Hennessy,** PC, CVO, MA, DLitt; British politician and fmr college principal; b. 28 Jan. 1932; s. of 2nd Baron Windlesham and Angela Mary Duggan; m. Prudence Glynn 1965 (died 1986); one s. one d.; ed Ampleforth, Trinity Coll., Oxford; Chair. of Bow Group 1959–60, 1962–63; mem. Westminster City Council 1958–62; Dir Rediffusion Television

1965–67; Man. Dir Grampian Television 1967–70; Minister of State Home Office 1970–72; Minister of State Northern Ireland 1972–73; Lord Privy Seal, Leader House of Lords 1973–74; Opposition Leader, House of Lords March–Oct. 1974; Jt Man. Dir ATV Network 1974–75, Man. Dir 1975–81, Chair. 1981; Chair. Independent Television Cos. Asscn 1976–78; Deputy Chair. Queen's Silver Jubilee Appeal 1976–77 and Trust 1977–80; Prin. Brasenose Coll., Oxford 1989–2002, Hon. Fellow 2002; Pres. Victim Support 1992–2001; Chair. Oxford Preservation Trust 1979–89, Parole Bd for England and Wales 1982–88, Oxford Soc. 1985–88; Vice-Chair. Ditchley Foundation 1987–; sits in House of Lords as Lord Hennessy 1999–; Dir W. H. Smith 1986–95, The Observer 1981–89; Trustee, Charities Aid Foundation 1977–81, Community Service Volunteers 1981–2000, Royal Collection Trust 1993–2000; Trustee British Museum 1981–96, Chair. 1986–96; mem. Museums and Galleries Comm. 1984–86; Hon. Bencher, Inner Temple 1999; Visiting Fellow All Souls Coll., Oxford 1986; Visiting Prof. of Public and Int. Affairs, Princeton Univ. 1997, 2002–; Hon. Fellow Trinity Coll., Oxford 1982, Brasenose Coll., Oxford 2002; Hon. LLD (London) 2002. *Publications:* Communication and Political Power 1966, Politics in Practice 1975, Broadcasting in a Free Society 1980, Responses to Crime (Vol. 1) 1987, (Vol. 2) 1993, (Vol. 3) 1996, (Vol. 4) 2001, Windlesham/Rampton Report on Death on the Rock 1989, Politics, Punishment and Populism 1998. *Address:* House of Lords, Westminster, London, SW1A 0PW, England. *E-mail:* windleshamd@ parliament.uk (Office).

WINDSOR, Colin, DPhil, FRS, FInstP; British physicist; b. 28 June 1938, Beckenham, Kent; s. of George Thomas and Mabel Rayment; m. Margaret Lee 1963; one s. two d.; ed Magdalen Coll., Oxford, Clarendon Lab., Oxford; Research Assoc. Yale Univ. 1963–64; scientist UKAEA 1964–96, Programme Area Man. UKAEA Fusion 1996–98; Visiting Fellow Japanese Asscn for Advancement of Science, Sendai 1980; Consultant UKAEA 1998–; Sr Consultant PenOp UK 1998–2000; Hon. Prof. of Physics Univ. of Birmingham 1990–; Duddell Medal, Inst. of Physics 1986. *Publications include:* Pulsed Neutron Scattering 1981, Four Computer Models 1983, Solid State Science, Past, Present and Predicted (ed.) 1987. *Leisure interests:* singing, playing piano and recorder, composing, cycling to work. *Address:* D3, Culham Science Centre, Oxford, OX14 3DB (Office); 116 New Road, East Hagbourne, Oxon., OX11 9LD, England (Home). *Telephone:* (1235) 466652 (Office); (1235) 812083 (Home). *Fax:* (01235) 463414 (Office). *E-mail:* colin.windsor@ukaea.org.uk (Office); colin.windsor@virgin.net (Home). *Website:* www.ukaea.org.uk (Office); freespace.virgin.net/colin.windsor (Home).

WINFREY, Oprah, BA; American broadcaster, actress and producer; b. 29 Jan. 1954, Kosciusko, Miss.; d. of Vernon Winfrey and Vernita Lee; ed Tennessee State Univ.; worked for WVOL radio, Nashville, Tenn. while still at school, subsequently as reporter/anchor, WTVF-TV, Nashville; joined WJZ-TV news, Baltimore, as co-anchor 1976, became co-host, People Are Talking 1978; joined WLS-TV, Chicago as host, AM Chicago, subsequently renamed The Oprah Winfrey Show 1985–99; acting roles: Sofia in The Color Purple 1985, Mrs. Thomas in Native Son 1986, Mattie Michael in The Women of Brewster Place (TV) 1989, Throw Momma From The Train 1988, Listen Up: The Lives of Quincy Jones 1990, Beloved 1998; f. Harpo Productions Inc. 1986, owner and producer 1986–; f., Ed. Dir O The Oprah Magazines 2000–; partner Oxygen Media 2000–; producer of several TV films; numerous awards, including Int. Radio and Television Soc.'s Broadcaster of the Year Award 1988, Lifetime Achievement Award, Nat. Acad. of TV Arts and Sciences 1998. *Publications:* Oprah (autobiog.) 1993, In the Kitchen with Rosie 1996, Make the Connection (with Bob Greene) 1996. *Address:* Harpo Productions, 110 N Carpenter Street, Chicago, IL 60607, USA.

WINGER, Debra; American actress; b. 16 May 1955, Cleveland; d. of Robert Winger and Ruth Winger; m. Timothy Hutton (q.v.) 1986 (divorced); one s.; ed Calif. State Univ., Northridge; served with Israeli army 1972; first professional appearance in Wonder Woman TV series 1976–77. *Films include:* Thank God It's Friday 1978, French Postcards 1979, Urban Cowboy 1980, Cannery Row 1982, An Officer and a Gentleman 1982, Terms of Endearment 1983, Mike's Murder 1984, Legal Eagles 1986, Black Widow 1987, Made in Heaven 1987, Betrayed 1988, The Sheltering Sky, Everybody Wins 1990, Leap of Faith 1992, Shadowlands 1993, A Dangerous Woman 1993, Forget Paris 1995, Big Bad Love 2002. *Address:* c/o CAA, 9830 Wilshire Boulevard, Beverly Hills, CA 90212, USA.

WINGTI, Rt Hon Paias, CMG, PC; Papua New Guinea politician; b. 2 Feb. 1951, Moika Village; five s.; ed Univ. of Papua New Guinea; MP 1977–97; apptd. Asst Speaker and mem. Public Accounts Cttee; elected Govt Whip; Minister for Transport and Civil Aviation 1978–80; Deputy Prime Minister and Minister for Nat. Planning and Devt 1982–84, for Educ. 1984–85; resgnd from Govt, co-f. People's Democratic Movt 1985; Leader of Opposition March–Nov. 1985, 1988–92, 1994; Prime Minister 1985–88, 1992–94. *Leisure interests:* playing golf and watching Rugby League. *Address:* People's Democratic Movement, P.O. Box 972, Boroko, Papua New Guinea. *Telephone:* 277631. *Fax:* 277611.

WINKLER, Hans Günter; German show jumper and company executive; b. 24 July 1926, Barmen; s. of Paul Winkler; m. 4th Debby Malloy 1994; mem. Exec., German Olympic Riding Cttee 1981–; winner of about 1,000 events, incl. over 500 int. events, up to 1964; world's most successful Olympic show jumping rider, took part in six Olympiads 1956–76, winning a still (2002) record haul of five gold medals, one bronze medal (Mexico City) 1968, one

silver medal (Montreal) 1976; World Riding Champion 1954, 1955 (record of 2 wins he shares with Raimondo d'Inzeo); European Champion 1957; Winner, King George V Cup 1965, 1968; Hon. mem. Riding Clubs of Warendorf, Ludwigsburg, Herborn, Darmstadt, Bayreuth, Salzburg, Frankfurt am Main, Mitterfels, Kassel, Hünfeld; Hon. Citizen of Warendorf; Needle of Honour, Senate of West Berlin 1954; Sportsman of the Year 1955, 1956; Gold Band, German Sports Press Asscn 1956; Best Sportsman of the Decade 1960; Needle of Honour, Int. Riding Asscn 1964; Grand Cross of Honour of FRG 1974, FN Award in Gold with Olympic Rings, Laurel Wreath and Diamonds 1976. *Publications:* Meine Pferde und ich (My Horses and I), Pferde und Reiter in aller Welt (Horses and Riders of the World) 1956, Halla D., Geschichte ihrer Laufbahn (Halla D., A History of her Career) 1961, Springreiten (Jumping) 1979, Halla die Olympiadiva: Olympiareiter in Warendorf 1981. *Leisure interests:* skiing, hunting, tennis. *Address:* Dr. Rau Allee 48, 48231 Warendorf, Germany. *Telephone:* (2581) 2361. *Fax:* (2581) 62772. *E-mail:* hgwmt@ warf-online.de (Office).

WINNER, Michael Robert, MA; British film producer and director; b. 30 Oct. 1935, London; s. of the late George Joseph Winner and Helen Winner; ed Downing Coll. Cambridge; Ed. and film critic of Cambridge Univ. paper; entered film industry as film critic and columnist for nat. newspapers and magazines 1951; wrote, produced and directed many documentary, TV and feature films for the Film Producers Guild, Anglo Amalgamated, United Artists 1955–61; Chair. Scimitar Films Ltd, Michael Winner Ltd, Motion Picture and Theatrical Investments Ltd 1957–; Columnist Sunday Times and News of the World; Chief Censorship Officer, Dirs. Guild of GB 1983, mem. Council and Trustee 1983–, Sr mem. 1991–; Founder and Chair. Police Memorial Trust 1984–. *Films:* Play It Cool (dir) 1962, The Cool Mikado (dir, writer) 1962, West 11 (dir) 1963, The System (co-producer and dir) 1963–64, You Must Be Joking (producer, dir, writer) 1964–65, The Jokers (producer, dir, writer) 1966, I'll Never Forget What's 'is Name (producer, dir) 1967, Hannibal Brooks (producer, dir, writer) 1968, The Games (producer, dir) 1969, Lawman (producer, dir) 1970, The Nightcomers (producer, dir) 1971, Chato's Land (producer, dir) 1971, The Mechanic (dir) 1972, Scorpio (producer, dir) 1972, The Stone Killer (producer, dir) 1973, Death Wish (producer, dir) 1974, Won Ton Ton – The Dog Who Saved Hollywood (producer, dir) 1975, The Sentinel (producer, dir, writer) 1976, The Big Sleep (producer, dir, Writer) 1977, Firepower (producer, dir, writer) 1978, Death Wish II (producer, dir, writer) 1981, The Wicked Lady (producer, dir, writer) 1982, Scream For Help (producer, dir) 1983, Death Wish III (producer, dir) 1985, Appointment with Death (producer, dir, writer) 1988, A Chorus of Disapproval (producer, dir, co-writer) 1989, Bullseye! (producer, dir, co-writer) 1990, For the Greater Good (BBC film, actor, dir Danny Boyle) 1990, Decadence (actor, dir Steven Berkoff) 1993, Dirty Weekend (producer, jt screenplay writer) 1993, Parting Shots (producer, dir, writer) 1997. *Theatre:* The Silence of St Just (producer) 1971, The Tempest (producer) 1974, A Day in Hollywood, A Night in the Ukraine (producer) (Evening Standard Award for Best Comedy of the Year 1979). *Radio:* panellist, Any Questions (BBC Radio 4), The Flump (play) 2000. *Television appearances include:* Michael Winner's True Crimes (LWT), panellist, Question Time (BBC One), many variety show sketches. *Publication:* Winner's Dinners 1999, Winner Guide 2002. *Leisure interests:* walking around art galleries, museums and antique shops, eating, being difficult, making table mats, laundry work. *Address:* 219 Kensington High Street, London, W8 6BD, England. *Telephone:* (020) 7734-8385. *Fax:* (020) 7602-9217.

WINOCK, Michel, DLitt; French historian and publisher; b. 19 March 1937, Paris; s. of Gaston Winock and Jeanne Winock (née Dussaule); m. Françoise Werner 1961; two s.; ed Sorbonne; teacher Lycée Joffre, Montpellier 1961–63, Lycée Hoche, Versailles 1963–66, Lycée Lakanal, Sceaux 1966–68; lecturer, Sr lecturer Univ. of Paris VIII-Vincennes à St-Denis 1968–78; Sr lecturer Institut d'Etudes politiques, Paris 1978–, Prof. 1990–; Publr Editions du Seuil, Paris 1969–; radio producer France-Inter 1983–85; Ed.-in-Chief L'Histoire magazine 1978–81, Editorial Adviser 1981–. *Publications:* La république se meurt 1978, La Fière hexagonale 1986, Nationalisme, antisemitisme et fascisme en France 1995, Le siècle des intellectuels (essays on the Medicis) 1997, La guerre de 1914–1918 racontée aux enfants 1998, La France politique XIXe–XXe siecle 2000, Les Voix de la liberté 2001, Les écrivains engagés au XIXe siècle 2001. *Leisure interest:* tennis. *Address:* Institut d'Etudes politiques, 27 rue Saint-Guillaume, 75337 Paris Cedex 07, France. *Telephone:* 1-40-46-51-08. *Fax:* 1-40-46-51-75. *E-mail:* wimi@cybercable.fr, wimi@noos.fr (Office).

WINSLET, Kate Elizabeth; British actress; b. 5 Oct. 1975, Reading; d. of Roger Winslet and Sally Winslet; m. Jim Threapleton 1998 (divorced 2001); one d.; ed Theatre School, Maidenhead; Best Actress Award, Evening Standard British Film Awards 2002, Best Supporting Actress Award, Film Critics' Annual Achievements Awards 2002, European Film Award for Best European Actress 2002. *Television includes:* Get Back, Casualty, Anglo-Saxon Attitudes. *Films:* A Kid in King Arthur's Court, Heavenly Creatures 1994, Sense and Sensibility (BAFTA Award for Best Supporting Actress) 1996, Jude 1996, Hamlet 1996, Titanic (Best European Actress, European Film Acad. 1998, Film Actress of the Year, Variety Club of GB 1998) 1997, Hideous Kinky 1997, Holy Smoke 1998, Quills 1999, Enigma 2000, Iris 2001, Neverland 2002, The Life of David Gale 2002. *Address:* c/o Dallas Smith, Peters Fraser & Dunlop Ltd, 503 The Chambers, Chelsea Harbour, Lots Road,

London, SW10 0XF, England; c/o Hilda Queally, William Morris Agency, 151 South El Camino Drive, Beverly Hills, CA 90212, USA. *Telephone:* (020) 7344-1010.

WINSTON, Baron (Life Peer) cr. 1995, of Hammersmith in the London Borough of Hammersmith and Fulham; **Robert Maurice Lipson Winston,** MB, BS, FRSA, FRCOG, F.SCI.MED.; British obstetrician and gynaecologist; b. 15 July 1940; s. of the late Laurence Winston and of Ruth Winston-Fox; m. Lira Feigenbaum 1973; two s. one d.; ed St Paul's School, London and London Hosp. Medical Coll. Univ. of London; Registrar and Sr Registrar, Hammersmith Hosp. 1970–74; Wellcome Research Sr lecturer, Inst. of Obstetrics and Gynaecology 1974–78; Sr lecturer, Hammersmith Hosp. 1978–81, Consultant Obstetrician and Gynaecologist 1978–; Reader in Fertility Studies, Royal Postgrad. Medical School (RPMS) 1982–86; Prof. of Fertility Studies, Imperial Coll. London 1997–; Chair. Select Cttee of Science and Tech., House of Lords 1999–; Visiting Prof. Univ. of Leuven 1976–77, Mt. Sinai Hosp. New York 1985; Prof. of Gynaecology, Univ. of Texas at San Antonio 1980–81; founder mem. British Fertility Soc.; many other professional appts.; presenter, Your Life In Their Hands, BBC TV 1979–87, Making Babies 1996, The Human Body 1998, The Secret Life of Twins 1999, Child of our Time 2000, Superhuman 2000, Human Instinct 2002; Chancellor Sheffield Hallam Univ. 2001–; Hon. Fellow Queen Mary and Westfield Coll. 1996; Hon. DSc (Cranfield) 2001, (UMIST) 2001, (Oxford Brookes) 2001; Victor Bonney Prize, Royal Coll. of Surgeons 1991–93; Chief Rabbinate Award for Contribution to Soc. 1992–93; Cedric Carter Medal, Clinical Genetics Soc. 1993; Gold Medal, Royal Soc. of Health 1998, Michael Faraday Award, Royal Soc. 1999, Wellcome Award for Science in the Media 2001. *Dir:* Each in his Own Way (Pirandello) Edin. Festival 1969. *Publications:* Reversibility of Sterilization 1978, Tubal Infertility (jtly.) 1981, Infertility: A Sympathetic Approach 1987, Human Instinct 2002; about 300 scientific articles on reproduction. *Leisure interests:* theatre, broadcasting, music, wine, festering. *Address:* The Hammersmith Hospital, Du Cane Road, London, W12 0HS (Office); 11 Denman Drive, London, NW11 6RE, England. *Telephone:* (020) 8383-4152 (Office); (020) 8455-7475. *Fax:* (020) 8458-4980. *E-mail:* r.winston@ic.ac.uk (Office).

WINTER, Frederick Thomas, CBE; British racehorse trainer (retd); b. 20 Sept. 1926, Andover, Hants.; s. of the late Frederick N. Winter and Nancy Flanagan; m. Diana Ruth Pearson 1956; three d.; ed Ewell Castle School; served with 6 Bn Parachute Regt 1944–47; Nat. Hunt jockey (four times champion) 1947–64, trainer (eight times champion) 1964–89. *Leisure interests:* golf, gardening. *Address:* Montague House, Eastbury, Newbury, Berks., RG17 7JN, England. *Telephone:* (01488) 71438.

WINTER, William Forrest, BA, LLB; American lawyer; b. 21 Feb. 1923, Grenada, Miss.; s. of William A. Winter and Inez P. Winter; m. Elise Varner 1950; three d.; ed Univ. of Mississippi; Miss. House of Reps. 1948–56; Miss. state tax collector 1956–64; State Treas. 1964–68; Lt-Gov. of Miss. 1972–76, Gov. 1980–84; Sr Partner, Watkins, Ludlam & Stennis, Jackson, Miss. 1985–; Eudora Welty Prof. of Southern Studies, Millsaps Coll. 1989; Jamie Whitten Prof. of Law, Univ. of Miss. 1989; Chair. Advisory Comm. on Intergovernmental Relations 1993–97; mem. Pres.'s Advisory Bd on Race 1997–. *Address:* 633 North State Street, PO Box 427, Jackson, MS 39202, USA. *Telephone:* (601) 949-4800. *Fax:* (601) 949-4804.

WINTERBOTTOM, Michael; British film director; b. 29 March 1961, Blackburn, Lancashire; ed Oxford Univ.; fmr ed., Thames TV. *Films include:* Butterfly Kisses 1995, Go Now, Jude 1996, Welcome to Sarajevo 1997, I Want you 1998, Resurrection Man (exec. producer) 1998, Wonderland 1999, With or Without You 1999, The Claim 2000, 24 Hour Party People 2002, In This World (Golden Bear, Berlin Film Festival 2003) 2002. *TV series include:* Cracker Mysteries–The Mad Woman in the Attic 1993, Family 1994.

WINTERBOTTOM, Michael, DPhil, FBA; British classicist; b. 22 Sept. 1934, Sale, Cheshire; s. of Allan Winterbottom and Kathleen Mary Winterbottom (née Wallis); m. 1st Helen Spencer 1963 (divorced 1983); two s.; m. 2nd Nicolette Janet Streatfeild Bergel 1986; ed Dulwich Coll., London and Pembroke Coll. Oxford; Domus Sr Scholar, Merton Coll. Oxford 1958–59; Research Lecturer, Christ Church Oxford 1959–62; Lecturer in Latin and Greek, Univ. Coll. London 1962–67; Fellow and Tutor in Classics, Worcester Coll. Oxford 1967–92, Reader in Classical Languages 1990–92; Corpus Christi Prof. of Latin, Fellow of Corpus Christi Coll., Oxford 1993–2001, Fellow Emer. 2001–; Craven Scholar 1954; Derby Scholar 1956; Dr hc (Besançon) 1985. *Publications:* Quintilian (Ed.) 1970, Ancient Literary Criticism (with D. A. Russell) 1972, Three Lives of English Saints 1972, The Elder Seneca (Ed. and Trans.) 1974, Tacitus, Opera Minora (with R. M. Ogilvie) 1975, Gildas (Ed. and Trans.) 1978, Roman Declamation 1980, The Minor Declamations Ascribed to Quintilian (Ed., with commentary) 1984, Sopatros the Rhetor (with D. C. Innes) 1988, Cicero, De Officiis (Ed.) 1994, William of Malmesbury, Gesta Regum Anglorum Vol. I (with R. A. B. Mynors and R. M. Thomson) 1998, William of Malmesbury, Saints' Lives (with R. M. Thomson) 2002. *Leisure interests:* travel, geology, hill walking. *Address:* 53 Thorncliffe Road, Oxford, England. *Telephone:* (1865) 513066.

WINTERFELDT, Ekkehard, Dr rer. nat; German professor of organic chemistry; b. 13 May 1932, Danzig; s. of Herbert Winterfeldt and Herta Winterfeldt; m. Marianne Heinemann 1958; one s. one d.; ed Tech. Hochschule Braunschweig, Tech. Univ. of Berlin; Asst Prof., Tech. Univ. of Berlin 1959, Assoc. Prof. 1967; Prof. and Head of Dept of Organic Chem., Hannover Univ. 1970–; mem. Braunschweigische Wissenschaftliche Gesellschaft, Akad. der

Wissenschaften zu Göttingen; Dr. hc (Liège) 1991; Dozentenstipendium des Fonds der Chemischen Industrie 1969, Emil Fischer Medal (German Chem. Soc.) 1990, Adolf Windaus-Medaille, Univ. of Göttingen 1993, Richard Kuhn-Medaille (Gesellschaft Deutscher Chem.) 1995, Hans Herloft-Inhoffen-Medaille 1998. *Publications:* 175 publs in scientific journals. *Address:* Sieversdamm 34, 30916 Isernhagen, Germany. *Telephone:* (511) 778499.

WINTERS, L. Alan, MA, PhD; British professor of economics; b. 8 April 1950, London; s. of Geoffrey Walter Horace Winters and Christine Agnes Ive; m. 1st Margaret Elizabeth Griffin 1971; m. 2nd Zhen Kun Wang 1997; one s. two d.; ed Chingford Co. High School, Univs. of Bristol and Cambridge; Jr, Research Office, Dept of Applied Econs., Univ. of Cambridge 1971–80; economist, World Bank 1983–85, Div. Chief/Research Man. 1994–99; Prof. of Econs, Univ. of Wales at Bangor 1986–90, Univ. of Birmingham 1990–94, Univ. of Sussex 1999–. *Publications:* Econometric Model of the British Export Sector 1981, International Economics 1984, Europe's Domestic Market 1987, Eastern Europe's International Trade 1994, Sustainable Development 1995, The Uruguay Round and the Developing Countries 1996, Trade Liberalisation and Poverty 2001. *Leisure interests:* walking, music, cricket. *Address:* School of Social Sciences, University of Sussex, Falmer, Brighton, BN1 9QN, England. *Telephone:* (1273) 877273. *Fax:* (1273) 673563.

WINTERS, Robert Cushing, BA, MBA; American insurance company executive; b. 8 Dec. 1931, Hartford, Conn.; s. of George Warren and Hazel Keith (Cushing) Winters; m. Patricia Ann Martini 1962; two d.; ed Yale and Boston Univs.; with Prudential Insurance Co. of America 1953–, Vice-Pres., Actuary 1969–75, Sr Vice-Pres. Cen. Atlantic Home Office 1975–78, Exec. Vice-Pres., Newark 1978–84, Vice-Chair. 1984–86, Chair. and CEO 1987–94, Chair. Emer. 1995–; Fellow Soc. of Actuaries; mem. and fmr Pres. American Acad. of Actuaries; mem. Business Council, Business Roundtable. *Address:* c/o Prudential Insurance Company, 751 Broad Street, Newark, NJ 07102, USA.

WINTERS, Shelley; American actress; b. 18 Aug. 1922, St Louis, Mo.; m. 1st Vittorio Gassmann (divorced); one d.; m. 2nd Anthony Franciosa 1957 (divorced 1960); ed Wayne Univ; Acad. Awards for best supporting actress in The Diary of Anne Frank 1959, A Patch of Blue 1964, Emmy Award for Best Actress 1964, Monte Carlo Golden Nymph Award 1964, Int. Television Award, Cannes Festival 1965. *Films include:* A Thousand and One Nights, A Place in the Sun, Playgirl, Executive Suite, The Diary of Anne Frank 1958, Odds Against Tomorrow, Let No Man Write My Epitaph, Lolita 1962, Wives and Lovers 1963, The Balcony 1964, A House is not a Home 1964, A Patch of Blue, Time of Indifference 1965, Alfie 1965, The Moving Target 1965, The Poseidon Adventure 1972, Cleopatra Jones 1973, Blume in Love 1974, Whoever Slew Auntie Roo 1974, Heaven Save Us from Our Friends 1975, Diamonds 1975, That Lucky Touch 1975, Next Stop Greenwich Village 1976, The Tenant 1976, Pete's Dragon 1977, The Magician 1979, The Visitor 1980, Over the Brooklyn Bridge 1983, The Delta Force 1985, Awakenings 1990, Stepping Out 1991, The Pickle, Portrait of a Lady 1996, Gideon's Webb 1998, La Bamba 1999. *Stage appearances include:* A Hatful of Rain 1955, Girls of Summer 1957, The Night of the Iguana, Cages, Who's Afraid of Virginia Woolf?, Minnie's Boys, Marlon Brando: The Wild One 1996. *Television appearances include:* The Vamp 1972–73, Roseanne (TV series). *Publications:* Shelley also Known as Shirley (autobiog.), One Night Stands of a Noisy Passenger (play) 1971, Shelley II: The Middle of My Century 1989. *Address:* c/o Jack Gilliardi, ICM, 8942 Wilshire Boulevard, Beverly Hills, CA 90211, USA.

WINTERSON, Jeanette, BA; British author; b. 27 Aug. 1959; ed Univ. of Oxford; Whitbread Prize 1985, Llewellyn Rhys Prize 1987, E. M. Forster Award, Golden Gate Award, San Francisco Int. Film Festival 1990, BAFTA Award for Best Drama 1990, FIPA d'Argent Award, Cannes Film Festival 1991, Int. Fiction Award, Festival Letteratura Mantua 1999. *Screenplay:* Great Moments in Aviation 1992. *Television:* Oranges are Not The Only Fruit (BBC) 1990, Orlando – Art That Shook the World (BBC) 2002. *Publications:* fiction: Oranges Are Not The Only Fruit 1985, The Passion 1987, Sexing the Cherry 1989, Written on the Body 1992, Art and Lies 1994, Gut Symmetries 1997, The World and Other Places 1998, The PowerBook 2000, The King of Capri (children's) 2001; essays: Art Objects 1995. *Leisure interests:* opera, ballet, champagne, horses, hens. *Address:* c/o Great Moments Ltd, 40 Brushfield Street, London, E1 6AG, England (Office); c/o ICM, 40 West 57 Street, New York, NY 10019, USA. *E-mail:* info@jeanettewinterson.con. *Website:* www.jeanettewinterson.com.

WINTERTON, George Graham, LLM, JSD; Australian professor of law; b. 15 Dec. 1946, Hong Kong; s. of Walter Winterton and Rita Winterton; m. Rosalind Julian 1979; two s. two d.; ed Hale School, Perth, Univ. of W Australia and Columbia Univ.; Assoc. in Law, Col Univ. 1973–75; staff mem. Univ. of NSW 1975–, Prof. of Law 1992–; mem. Exec. Govt Advisory Cttee, Australian Constitutional Comm. 1985–87, Repub. Advisory Cttee 1993; del. Australian Constitutional Convention 1998; barrister, NSW; barrister and solicitor, Vic. and W Australia; Fulbright Scholarship 1973. *Publications:* Parliament, The Executive and the Governor-General 1983, Australian Constitutional Perspectives (co-ed.) 1992, Monarchy to Republic: Australian Republican Government 1994, We, the People: Australian Republican Government (ed.) 1994, Judicial Remuneration in Australia 1995, Australian Federal Constitutional Law: Commentary and Materials (co-author) 1999. *Leisure interests:* music, reading. *Address:* 5 Park Parade, Bondi, NSW 2026,

Australia (Home); Faculty of Law, University of New South Wales, Sydney, NSW 2052, Australia (Office). *Telephone:* (2) 9385-2245; (2) 9385-2245 (Office); (2) 9389-8290 (Home). *Fax:* (2) 9385-1175; (2) 9385-1175 (Office). *E-mail:* g.winterton@unsw.edu.au (Office).

WINTOUR, Anna; British journalist; b. 3 Nov. 1949; d. of the late Charles Wintour; m. David Shaffer 1984; one s. one d.; ed Queen's Coll. School, London and N London Collegiate School; deputy fashion Harpers & Queen 1970–76, Harpers Bazaar, New York 1976–77; fashion and beauty ed. Viva 1977–78; contributing ed. for fashion and style, Savvy Magazine 1980–81; Sr New York Magazine 1981–83; Creative Dir U.S. Vogue 1983–86; Ed.-in-Chief, Vogue 1986–87; Ed. House & Garden, New York 1987–88; Ed. U.S. Vogue 1988–.

WINWOOD, Stephen Lawrence; British musician and composer; b. Birmingham; s. of Lawrence Samuel Winwood and Lillian Mary Winwood (née Saunders); m. Eugenia Crafton 1987; one s. three d.; singer and musician Spencer Davis Group 1964–67, Traffic 1967–74, Blind Faith 1970; solo artist 1974–; Dir F.S. Ltd; 14 Gold Record Awards, 4 Platinum Record Awards, 2 Grammy Awards. *Albums include:* Arc of a Diver 1980, Talking Back to the Night 1982, Back in the Highlife 1986, Roll With It 1988 (Grammy Award 1989), Chronicles, Refugees of the Heart 1991, Traffic, Far from Home 1994, Junction 7 1997. *Address:* c/o Trinley Cottage, Tirley, Gloucs., GL19 4EU, England. *Telephone:* (1452) 780706. *Fax:* (1452) 780196.

WIRAJUDA, Nur Hassan, MA, LLM, SJD; Indonesian politician; b. 9 July 1948, Tangerang; m.; four c.; ed Univ. of Indonesia, Oxford Univ., UK, Tufts Univ., Harvard Univ. and Univ. of Virginia, USA; practising lawyer (legal aid) and univ. lecturer, Jakarta 1972–75; Legal Council Corp. Sec., Dockyard State Enterprise, Jakarta 1972–73; Head of Section, Secr. of the Foreign Affairs Cttee of the Nat. Council for Political and Security Stabilization, Secr. Gen., Dept of Foreign Affairs 1974–75; Third Sec., then Second Sec. for Political Affairs, Indonesian Embassy, Cairo 1977–81; Head of Section, Politics-Legal Affairs, Directorate of Int. Orgs., Dept of Foreign Affairs 1981, Dir for Int. Orgs. 1993–97; Deputy Dir for Territorial Treaties, Directorate of Legal and Treaty Affairs 1998, Dir Gen. for Political Affairs 2000–01; Counsellor, later Minister Counsellor for Political Affairs, Perm. Mission in Geneva 1989–93; Amb. to Egypt (also Accred to Djibouti) 1997–98; Amb. and Perm. Rep. to the UN, Geneva, World Trade Org. and the Conf. on Disarmament 1998–2000; Personal Rep. of the Pres. to the Group of Fifteen Developing Countries (G-15) 1998–2000; represented the Govt in the sovereignty case concerning Pulau Ligitan and Pulau Sipadan before Int. Court of Justice, The Hague 2000–; Leading Govt Negotiator in the Dialogue on Aceh with Free Aceh Movement reps., Switzerland 2000–. *Address:* c/o Ministry of Foreign Affairs, Jalan Taman Pejambon 6, Jakarta Puscat, Indonesia (Office).

WIRANTO, Gen.; Indonesian army officer; Minister of Defence and Security and C-in-C of Armed Forces –1999; Co-ordinating Minister for Politics and Security 1999–2000; indicted by UN for crimes against humanity in E Timor in 1999 Feb. 2003. *Address:* c/o Office of the Co-ordinating Minister for Politics and Security, Jalan Madan Merdeka Barat 15, Jakarta 10110, Indonesia (Office).

WIRTH, Timothy Endicott, PhD; American politician; b. 22 Sept. 1939, Santa Fe; s. of Cecil Wirth and Virginia Maude Davis; m. Wren Winslow 1965; one s. one d.; ed Harvard and Stanford Univs.; Special Asst to Sec. Dept of Health, Educ. and Welfare 1967, Deputy Asst Sec. for Educ. 1969; Asst to Chair., Nat. Urban Coalition 1968; Vice-Pres. Great Western United Corpn, Denver 1970; Man. Arthur D. Little Inc. 1971–73; mem. 94th–99th Congresses from 2nd Dist Colo; Senator from Colorado 1987–92; Counsellor Dept of State 1993–97; Pres. UN Foundation Jan. 1997–; Ford Foundation Fellow 1964–66; Pres. White House Fellows Asscn 1968–69; mem. Exec. Cttee Denver Council Foreign Relations 1974–75; mem. Bd of Visitors, USAF Acad. 1978–; Adviser, Pres. Comm. on the 80s 1979–80; Democrat. *Address:* United Nations Foundation, 1301 Connecticut Avenue, NW, Washington, DC 20036, USA. *Telephone:* (202) 887-9040 (Office). *Fax:* (202) 887-9021 (Office). *Website:* www.unfoundation.org (Office).

WISDOM, Sir Norman, Kt, OBE; British actor and comedian; b. 4 Feb. 1915; m. 1947 (divorced 1969). *Films include:* Trouble in Store 1953, One Good Turn 1954, There was a Crooked Man 1960, The Girl on the Boat 1962, On the Beat 1962, A Stitch in Time 1963, Double X 1991, Cosmic Brainsuckers 2000. *Plays:* Stage musical Walking Happy, The Legendary Norman Wisdom (touring for Johnny Mans Productions) 1982–96, Norman Wisdom and Friends 2002–03; numerous Royal Variety Performances and pantomimes. *Radio:* Robin Hood (six-part series). *Television:* numerous TV series include Wit and Wisdom 1948–50, Norman 1970, Nobody is Norman Wisdom 1973, A Little Bit of Wisdom 1974; TV Plays include Going Gently 1978; appeared in Bergerac 1982, Casualty 1986, Last of the Summer Wine 1995, Dalziel and Pascoe 2002, The Last Detective 2003. *Achievements:* Best Newcomer Acad. Award 1953, two Broadway Awards, Lifetime Achievement Award British Comedy Awards 1991, Freeman Tirana, Albania 1995, City of London 1995, Douglas (Isle of Man). *Publications:* Trouble in Store (with Richard Dacre) 1991, Don't Laugh at Me (autobiog. with William Hall) 1992, Cos I'm a Fool (with Bernard Bale) 1996, My Turn (with William Hall) 2002. *Leisure interests:* all sports, especially golf and soccer. *Address:* c/o Johnny Mans, Johnny Mans Productions Ltd, PO Box 196, Hoddesdon, Herts., EN10 7WG, England (Office). *Fax:* (1992) 470516 (Office).

WISE, Michael John, CBE, MC, PhD, FRGS, FRSA; British geographer; b. 17 Aug. 1918, Stafford; s. of Harry Cuthbert Wise and Sarah Evelyn Wise; m. Barbara Mary Hodgetts 1942; one s. one d.; ed Saltley Grammar School, Birmingham and Birmingham Univ.; served with RA and Northamptonshire Regt in Middle East and Italy 1941–46; Lecturer in Geography, Univ. of Birmingham 1946–51, LSE 1951–54; Cassel Reader in Econ. Geography, LSE 1954–58, Prof. of Geography 1958–83, Prof. Emer.; Pro-Dir LSE 1983–85, (Hon. Fellow 1988); Erskine Fellow, Univ. of Canterbury, NZ 1970; Chair. Ministry of Agric. Cttee of Inquiry into Statutory Smallholdings 1963–67; Chair. Dept of Transport Landscape Advisory Cttee 1981–90; Chair. Court of Govs, Birkbeck Coll. 1983–89, Fellow 1990–; Pres. Inst. of British Geographers 1974, Int. Geographical Union 1976–80, Geographical Asscn 1976–77; Pres. Royal Geographical Soc. 1980–82; Chair. Dudley Stamp Memorial Trust 1986–; mem. Univ. Grants Cttee, Hong Kong 1966–73, Social Science Research Council 1976–82; Hon. mem. Geographical Soc., USSR 1975, Paris 1984, Mexico 1984, Poland 1986, Asscn Japanese Geographers 1980, Inst. of British Geographers 1989, Geographical Asscn 1990; Hon. Fellow Landscape Inst. 1991; Hon. DUniv (Open Univ.) 1978; Hon. DSc (Birmingham) 1982; Gill Memorial Award of Royal Geographical Soc. 1958, Founder's Medal 1977, Alexander Csoma Körös Medal of Hungarian Geographical Soc. 1980, Tokyo Geographical Soc.'s Medal 1981, Lauréat d'honneur, Int. Geographical Union 1984. *Publications:* Hon. Ed., Birmingham and its Regional Setting 1950, A Pictorial Geography of the West Midlands 1958, Ed. (with E. M. Rawstron), R. O. Buchanan and Economic Geography 1973, General Consultant, An Atlas of Earth Resources 1979, The Ordnance Survey Atlas of Great Britain 1982; numerous papers on economic and urban geography. *Leisure interests:* music, gardening. *Address:* 45 Oakleigh Avenue, Whetstone, London, N20 9JE, England. *Telephone:* (20) 8445-6057.

WISE, Robert E. (Bob); American state official and lawyer; m. Sandy Wise; one s. one d.; ed Duke Univ., Tulane Univ.; pvt. law practice, Charleston, W. Va. 1975–80; attorney legis. council for judiciary comm., W. Va. House of Dels. 1977–78; elected to W. Va. State Senate 1980–82, Congress (W. Va. Second Dist.) 1983–2001, whip-at-large 1986–2001, mem. House Transportation and Infrastructure Cttee; Gov. of W. Va. 2001–; mem. ABA, W. Va. State Bar Asscn. *Leisure interests:* funding PROMISE Scholarships, keeping fit, bluegrass music. *Address:* Office of the Governor, State Capitol Complex, Charleston, WV 25305-0370, USA (Office).

WISE, Robert Earl; American film producer and director; b. 10 Sept. 1914, Winchester, Ind.; s. of Earl W. Wise and Olive Longenecker; m. 1st Patricia Doyle 1942; one s.; m. 2nd Millicent Franklin 1977; ed Franklin Coll., Ind.; joined RKO 1933, apprentice sound effects cutter, then Asst Ed. and later Film Ed.; films edited include Citizen Kane and The Magnificent Ambersons; Film Dir 1943–, partner in independent film co. 1970–2000; Vice-Pres. The Filmakers Group; mem. Bd of Govs, Acad. of Motion Picture Arts and Sciences, Pres. 1985–87; mem. Dirs Guild of America; mem. Nat. Council on the Arts; Irving Thalberg Award, Acad. of Motion Picture Arts and Sciences, D. W. Griffith Award 1988, Life Achievement Award, American Film Inst. 1998. *Films include:* Curse of the Cat People 1944, The Body Snatcher 1945, The Set Up 1949, The Day the Earth Stood Still 1951, The Desert Rats 1953, Executive Suite 1954, Helen of Troy 1955, Tribute to a Bad Man 1956, Somebody Up There Likes Me 1956, Until They Sail 1957, Run Silent, Run Deep 1958, I Want to Live 1958, Odds Against Tomorrow 1959, West Side Story (Acad. Awards for Best Film and Best Dir) 1961, Two for the Seesaw 1962, The Haunting 1963, The Sound of Music (Acad. Awards for Best Film and Best Dir) 1965, The Sand Pebbles 1966, Star! 1968, The Andromeda Strain 1971, Two People 1973, The Hindenburg 1975, Audrey Rose 1977, Star Trek 1979, Rooftops 1989, A Storm in Summer 2000. *Address:* Robert Wise Productions, 2222 Avenue of the Stars, Suite 2303E, Los Angeles, CA 90067, USA.

WISNER, Frank George, BA; American diplomatist; b. 2 July 1938, New York; s. of Frank G. Wisner and Mary E. Knowles; m. 1st Genevieve de Virel 1969 (deceased 1974); one d.; m. 2nd Christine de Ganay 1976; one s. one d. and one step-s. one step-d.; ed Woodberry Forest School, Rugby School and Princeton Univ.; joined US Foreign Service 1961; various posts 1961–75; Special Asst to Under-Sec. for Political Affairs 1975–76; Dir Office of Southern African Affairs 1976–77; Deputy Exec. Sec. 1977–79; Amb. to Zambia 1979–82; Deputy Asst Sec. for African Affairs 1982–86; Amb. to Egypt 1986–91, to Philippines 1991–92, to India 1994–97; Under-Sec. of Defense 1993–94; Bd Dirs Exxon Oil and Gas; Presidential Meritorious Service Awards, Dept of State Meritorious Honor Awards, Vietnam Service Medal, Repub. of Vietnam Mil. Medal of Honour, Dept of Defense Service Medal. *Leisure interests:* hunting, horseback riding, golf. *Address:* American International Group Inc., 18th Floor, 70 Pine Street, New York, NY 10270 (Office); 480 Park Avenue, #18H, New York, NY 10022, USA (Home). *Telephone:* (212) 770-5262 (Office); (212) 355-1765 (Home). *Fax:* (212) 480-5400 (Office); (212) 355-1873 (Home). *E-mail:* frank.wisner@aig.com (Office).

WISSMANN, Matthias; German politician and lawyer; b. 15 April 1949, Ludwigsburg; s. of Paul Wissmann and Margarete Kalcker; ed Univs. of Tübingen and Bonn; lawyer; mem. Fed. Exec. of CDU 1975–; mem. Bundestag 1976–; Pres. European Union of Young Christian Democrats 1976–82; Minister of Research and Technology Jan.–May 1993, of Transport 1993–98; Chair. Parl. Cttee of Econ. and Tech. 1998–2001, Speaker Parl. Group for Econ. and Tech.; CDU. *Publications include:* Zukunftschancen der Jugend 1979, Einsteigen statt Aussteigen 1983, Marktwirtschaft 2000 1993, Soziale

Marktwirtschaft 1998. *Leisure interests:* piano, literature, hockey, tennis, skiing, golf. *Address:* Deutsche Bundestag, Platz der Republik, 11011 Berlin (Office); Am Zuckerberg 79, 71640 Ludwigsburg, Germany (Home). *Telephone:* (30) 22779496 (Office). *Fax:* (30) 22776452 (Office). *E-mail:* matthias .wissmann@bundestag.de.

WISZNIEWSKI, Andrzej, DSc, PhD; Polish university teacher, electrical engineer and politician; b. 15 Feb. 1935, Warsaw; s. of Tadeusz Wiszniewski and Ewa Wiszniewski (née Ciechomska); m. Ewa Lutosławska; one d.; ed Tech. Univ. of Wrocław; researcher Wrocław Univ. of Tech. 1957–, Extraordinary Prof. 1972, Ordinary Prof. 1990–, Rector 1990–96; Univ. of Garyounis Benghazi, Libya 1976–79; Head of Scientific Research Cttee and mem. Council of Ministers 1997–99; Minister of Science 1999–2001; mem. Speech Communication Asscn (USA); mem. Solidarity Trade Union 1980–; mem. Social Movt of Solidarity Election Action 1998–; Hon. mem. Inst. of Electrical Engineers 1999; Kt's Cross Order of Polonia Restituta 1997; Grand Cross Order of Saint Stanisław with Star 1998; Commander Order of Saint Sylvester 1998; Grand Cross Order of Merit (Peru) 2001; Dr hc (Cen. Conn. State Univ.) 1993, (Tech. Univ. of Lvov) 1999, (Tech. Univ. of Wrocław) 2001; City of Wrocław Award 1996, Council of Rectors Award 1998. *Publications:* Measuring Transformers 1983, Algorithms of Numeral Measurements in Electroenergetic Automatics 1990, Schutztechnik in Elektroenergiesystemen (co-author) 1994, Protective Automatics in Electroenergetics Systems 1998, How to Speak and Make Speeches Convincingly 1994, Aphorisms and Quotations: for Orators, Disputants and Banqueters 1997, Measuring and Decision Making Algorithms (jtly), Art of Writing 2003; over 130 articles on electrotechnics and electroenergetics. *Leisure interests:* contemporary literature, dog-walking, skiing, mountaineering, rhetoric. *Address:* Technical University of Wrocław Institute of Power Engineering, Grunwaldski Square 13, 50-370 Wrocław (Office); Krasickiego 18, 51-144 Wrocław, Poland (Home). *Telephone:* (71) 3203487 (Office); (71) 3726477 (Home); (601) 381944. *Fax:* (71) 3203487 (Office). *E-mail:* andyw@elektryk.ie.pwr.wroc.pl (Office); awiszniewski@wr.home.pl (Home). *Website:* www.pwr.wroc.pl/~i-8zas (Office).

WIT, Antoni; Polish conductor and professor of music; b. 7 Feb. 1944, Cracow; m. Zofia Ćwikiewicz; ed State Higher School of Music, Cracow; Asst Conductor Warsaw Philharmonic 1967–70, Gen. and Artistic Dir 2002–; conductor Poznań Nat. Philharmonic 1970–72; Artistic Dir Pomeranian Philharmonic, Bydgoszcz 1974–77; Dir and Artistic Chief Polish Radio Symphony Orchestra and Choir 1977–83; Dir Polish Nat. Radio Symphony Orchestra, Katowice 1983–2000; Artistic Dir Orquesta Filarmonica de Gran Canaria, Las Palmas 1987–91; Prof. Acad. of Music, Warsaw 1997–; has conducted The London Philharmonic, BBC Symphony Orchestra, Berliner Philharmoniker, Royal Philharmonic Orchestra, Orchestre National de Belgique, Tokyo Symphony Orchestra, Montreal Symphony Orchestra, Orquesta Nacional de España; numerous prizes include Second Prize, Herbert von Karajan Conducting Competition, Berlin 1971, Orfeusz (Critics' Award) 1984, 1996, Diapason d'Or, Grand Prix de Disque de la Nouvelle Académie du Disque 1992, MIDEM Classique 2002, Cannes Classical Award 2002. *Recordings include:* symphonies by Tchaikovsky, Górecki, Schumann, Penderecki, etc.; *Compositions:* soundtracks: Kronika wypadków miłosnych (The Chronicle of Love Affairs) 1986, Korczak 1990, Pan Tadeusz (Last Foray in Lithuania) 1999. *Address:* Warsaw Philharmonic – The National Orchestra of Poland, ul. Jasna 5, 00-950 Warsaw, Poland (Office). *Telephone:* (22) 5517100 (Office). *Fax:* (22) 5517200 (Office). *E-mail:* antwit@medianet.pl (Office). *Website:* www .filharmonia.pl (Office).

WITHEROW, John Moore; journalist; b. 20 Jan. 1952, Johannesburg, S. Africa; s. of Cecil Witherow and Millicent Witherow; m. Sarah Linton 1985; two s. one d.; ed Bedford School, Univ. of York, Univ. of Cardiff; two years' voluntary service in Namibia (then SW Africa) after school; posted to Madrid for Reuters; covered Falklands War for The Times 1982; joined The Sunday Times 1984, successively Defence and Diplomatic Corresp., Focus Ed., Foreign Ed., Man. Ed. (news), Acting Ed., The Sunday Times 1994, Ed. 1995–. *Publications:* The Winter War: The Falklands (with Patrick Bishop) 1982, The Gulf War 1993. *Leisure interests:* sailing, skiing, tennis. *Address:* The Sunday Times, 1 Pennington Street, London, E1 9XW, England. *Telephone:* (20) 7782-5640. *Fax:* (20) 7782-5420.

WITHERSPOON, Reese; American actress; b. 22 March 1976, New Orleans; d. of John Witherspoon; m. Ryan Phillippe 1999; one d.; ed Harpeth Hall, Stanford Univ.; f. production co. Type A Films. *Films:* The Man in The Moon 1991, Wildflower (for TV) 1991, Solomon's Choice (for TV), Return to Lonsome Dove (TV mini-series) 1993, A Far Off Place 1993, Jack the Bear, S.F.W. 1995, Fear, Freeway 1996, (Best Actress, Catalonian Int. Film Festival, Cognac Film Festival) 1996, Twilight, Overnight Delivery, Pleasantville 1998, Cruel Intentions (Best Supporting Actress in a Drama Romance, Blockbuster Entertainment Awards) 1999, Election (Best Actress, Nat Soc. of Film Critics) 1999, Best Laid Plans 1999, American Psycho 2000, The Trumpet of the Swan (voice), Little Nicky, Legally Blonde (Best Actress, Cosmo Movie Awards, Best Comedic Performance, MTV Movie Awards) 2001, Sweet Home Alabama 2002, The Importance of Being Earnest. *Television:* Friends, King of the Hill, Saturday Night Live. *Address:* c/o CAA, 9830 Wiltshire Blvd., Beverly Hills, CA 90212-1825, USA (Office).

WITKIN, Joel-Peter, MA, MFA; American photographer; b. b. 13 Sept. 1939, Brooklyn, New York; ed The Cooper Union, New York, Columbia Univ., New York, Univ. of New Mexico; began photography at age 11; photographer, US Army 1961–64; Commdr des Arts et des Lettres 2000; Int. Center of Photography Award, New York City 1988, The Augustus Saint Gaudens Medal, The Cooper Union 1996. *Exhibitions include:* Brooklyn Museum 1986, Centro de Arte Reina Sofía Museum 1988, Palais de Tokyo, Paris 1989, Museum of Modern Art, Haifa, Israel 1990, Guggenheim Museum, New York 1995, Il Castello di Rivoli Museum, Turin, Italy 1995, Museum of Fine Arts, Santa Fe 1998, Wildenstein Gallery, Tokyo 1998, Sterburg Museum Prague 1999, Hotel de Sully, Paris 2000, The Louvre, Paris 2001, Graz Museum, Germany 2003. *Publications:* Joel-Peter Witkin (monograph) 1984, Gods of Earth and Heaven 1994, Guggenheim Museum monograph 1995, The Bone House 1998, Joel-Peter Witkin, Disciple and Master 2000, Songs of Experience 2002, Songs of Innocence 2003. *Address:* 1707 5 Points Road, SW, Albuquerque, NM 87105, USA (Home). *Telephone:* (505) 843-6682 (Office); (505) 842-6511 (Home). *Fax:* (505) 842-1611 (Home). *E-mail:* ddocstar@aol.com (Home).

WITKOP, Bernhard, PhD, ScD; American chemist; b. 9 May 1917, Freiburg (Baden), Germany; s. of Prof. Philipp W. Witkop and Hedwig M. Hirschhorn; m. Marlene Prinz 1945; one s. two d.; ed Univ. of Munich; Dozent Univ. of Munich 1946; Matthew T. Mellon Fellow Harvard Univ., USA 1947; Instructor and Lecturer 1948–50; Special Fellow U.S. Public Health Service 1950–53; Research Fellow Nat. Heart Inst. 1950; Special Fellow, Nat. Inst. of Arthritis and Metabolic Diseases, NIH 1952, Chief of Section on Metabolites 1956–87, Chief of Lab. of Chem., Nat. Inst. of Arthritis, Metabolic and Digestive Diseases 1957–87; NIH Inst. Scholar 1987–92, Hon. Emer. Scholar 1993–; Visiting Prof., Kyoto Univ. 1961, Univ. of Freiburg 1962; Lecturer, Univ. of Zürich 1972; Ed. (USA) FEBS Letters 1979–; mem. NAS, Acad. Leopoldina-Carolina 1972, NAS Comm. on Int. Relations 1978, American Acad. of Arts and Sciences 1978, Paul Ehrlich Foundation, Frankfurt 1979–96, American Philosophical Soc. 1999, Bd of Dirs, Leo Baeck Inst., New York 1992–; Hon. mem. Pharmaceutical Soc. of Japan 1978, Chemical Soc. 1982–, Japanese Biochemical Soc. 1983–, Academia Scientiarum et Artium Europaea, Salzburg 1993–; Order of the Sacred Treasure, Japan; ACS Hillebrand Award 1959, Paul Karrer Medallist, US Sr A. von Humboldt Award (Univ. of Hamburg) 1979, Golden Doctor Diploma (Univ.. of Munich) 1990. *Publications:* Mushroom Poisons 1940, Curare Arrow Poisons 1942, Yohimbine 1943, Kynurenine 1944, Indole Alkaloids 1947–50, Oxidation Mechanisms, Ozonization, Peroxides 1952, Hydroxyaminoacids, Metabolites, Building Stones and Biosynthesis of Collagen 1955, Mescalin and LSD Metabolism 1958, Pharmacodynamic Amines 1960, Nonenzymatic Cleavage and Modification of Enzymes 1961, Gramicidin A 1964, Rufomycin 1964, Photo-Reductions, -Additions, -Cyclizations 1966, Microsomal Hydroxylations, Arenoxide Metabolites, 'NIH-Shift' 1967, Amphibian Venoms, Batrachotoxin, Pumiliotoxin 1968, Norepinephrine Release, Inactivation, False transmitters 1968, Histrionicotoxin, a selective inhibitor of cholinergic receptors 1970–72, Interaction of Polynucleotides Stimulators of Interferon 1973–74, Gephyrotoxin, a Muscarinic Antagonist 1978, Anatoxin-a: The most potent Agonist at the nicotinic receptor 1980–82, Paul Ehrlich: His Ideas and his Legacy, Nobel Symposium 1981, Amphibian Alkaloids 1983, Forty Years of 'Trypto-Fun' 1984, Mind over Matter (lecture at Israel Acad. of Sciences, Jerusalem) 1987, Paul Ehlich's Magic Bullets Revisited. *Leisure interests:* languages, etymology, literature, piano, chamber music, hiking, skating, mountaineering, history and philosophy of science, Japanese style and culture. *Address:* NIDDK, National Institutes of Health, Bethesda, MD 20892 (Office); National Institute of Health–Department of Health, Education & Welfare, Building 8, Room 2A-27, Bethesda, MD 20892; 3807 Montrose Driveway, Chevy Chase, MD 20815, U.S.A. (Home). *Telephone:* (301) 402-4181 (Office); (301) 656-6418 (Home). *Fax:* (301) 402-0240 (Office).

WITTEN, Edward, PhD; American physicist; b. 26 Aug. 1951, Baltimore, Md; s. of Louis Witten and Lorraine Wollach Witten; m. Chiara R. Nappi 1979; one s. two d.; ed Brandeis and Princeton Univs.; Prof. of Physics, Princeton Univ., NJ 1980–87, Inst. for Advanced Study, Princeton 1987–; Fellow American Acad. of Arts and Sciences, American Physical Soc., NAS; McArthur Fellowship 1982; Einstein Medal, Einstein Soc. of Berne, Switzerland 1985, Award for Physical and Math. Sciences, New York Acad. of Sciences 1985, Dirac Medal, Int. Center for Theoretical Physics 1985, Alan T. Waterman Award, Nat. Science Foundation 1986, Fields Medal, Int. Union of Mathematicians 1990. *Publication:* Superstring Theory, 2 Vols (with M. B. Green and J.H. Schwarz) 1987. *Address:* Institute for Advanced Study, Olden Lane, Princeton, NJ 08540, USA. *Telephone:* (609) 734-8021.

WLOSOWICZ, Zbigniew; Polish diplomatist and United Nations official; fmr UN Rep. from Poland, UN Envoy Feb. 1993; mem. UN Security Council; Special Adviser on Inter-Governmental Affairs UNDP 1998–2000; Acting UN Special Rep. of the Sec.-Gen. in Cyprus and Chief of Mission, UNFICYP June 2000–. *Address:* UN Peace-keeping Force in Cyprus (UNFICYP), Department of Peace-keeping Operations, Room S-3727-B, United Nations, New York, NY 10017, USA (Office). *Telephone:* (212) 963-8079 (Office). *Fax:* (212) 963-9222 (Office). *Website:* www.unficyp.org (Office).

WOESSNER, Mark Matthias, DrIng; German business executive; b. 14 Oct. 1938, Berlin; m.; two c.; ed Tech. Univ. Karlsruhe; Man. Asst Bertelsmann AG 1968–70; Production Man. Mohndruck Printing Co. 1970–72, Tech. Dir 1972–74, Man. Dir 1974–76; mem. Exec. Bd Bertelsmann AG, Pres. Printing and Mfg Div. 1976–83, Pres. and CEO 1983–98, Chair. Supervisory Bd

1998–2000; Dep. Chair. Exec. Bd Bertelsmann Foundation 1996–98, Chair. Exec. Bd 1998–2000. *Leisure interest:* sport. *Address:* c/o Bertelsmann Stiftung, Carl-Bertelsmann-Strasse 256 D-, 33311 Gütersloh, Germany.

WOFFORD, Harris Llewellyn, LLB; American writer, attorney and fmr politician; b. 9 April 1926, New York; s. of Harris L. Wofford and Estelle Gardner; m. Emmy Lou Clare Lindgren 1948 (died 1996); two s. one d.; ed Univ. of Chicago and Yale and Howard Univ. Law Schools; admitted DC Bar 1954, U.S. Supreme Court Bar 1958, Pa Bar 1978; Asst to Chester Bowles 1953–54; law assoc. Covington & Burling, Washington, DC 1954–58; legal Asst to Rev. T. Hesburgh, Comm. on Civil Rights 1958–59; Assoc. Prof. Notre Dame Law School 1959–60, on leave 1961–66; Special Asst to Pres. John F. Kennedy 1961–62; Special Rep. for Africa, Dir Ethiopian Program, U.S. Peace Corps. 1962–64; Assoc. Dir Peace Corps, Washington, DC 1964–66; Pres. Coll. at Old Westbury, State Univ. of NY 1966–70, Bryn Mawr (Pa) Coll. 1970–78; Counsel, Schnader, Harrison, Segal and Lewis, Philadelphia and Washington 1979–86; Sec. Labor and Industry, Commonwealth of Pa 1987–91; Senator from Pennsylvania 1991–95; CEO Corpn for Nat. Service 1995–2001; Chair. America's Promise: the Alliance for Youth 2002–; mem. Council on Foreign Relations; Democrat. *Publications include:* It's Up to Us 1946, India Afire (with Clare Wofford) 1951, Of Kennedys and Kings 1980. *Address:* 955 26th Street, NW, Apartment 501, Washington, DC 20037, USA.

WOGAN, Gerald Norman, PhD; American educator; b. 11 Jan. 1930, Altoona, Pa; s. of Thomas B. Wogan and Florence E. (Corl) Wogan; m. Henrietta E. Hoenicke 1957; one s. one d.; ed Juniata Coll. and Univ. of Illinois; Asst Prof. of Physiology, Rutgers Univ., New Brunswick, NJ 1957–61; Asst Prof. of Toxicology, MIT, Cambridge, Mass. 1962–65, Assoc. Prof. 1965–69, Prof. 1969–, Head of Dept of Applied Biological Sciences 1979–88, Dir Division of Toxicology 1988–99, Prof. of Chem. 1989–; Consultant to nat. and int. govt agencies and industries; Fellow American Acad. of Microbiology; mem. NAS, Inst. of Medicine. *Publications:* articles and reviews in professional journals. *Address:* Division of Toxicology, Massachusetts Institute of Technology, 77 Massachusetts Avenue, Room 26-009, Cambridge, MA 02139, USA. *Telephone:* (617) 253-3188.

WOGAN, Michael Terence (Terry), OBE; Irish broadcaster; b. 3 Aug. 1938; s. of the late Michael Thomas Wogan and Rose Wogan; m. Helen Joyce 1965; two s. one d.; ed Crescent Coll., Limerick, Belvedere Coll., Dublin; announcer Radio Telefís Eireann (RTE) 1963, Sr Announcer 1964–66; various programmes for BBC Radio 1965–67; Pye Radio Award 1980, Radio Industries Award (Radio Personality 3 times; TV Personality 1982, 1984, 1985, 1987); TV Times TV Personality of the Year (10 times); Daily Express Award (twice); Carl Alan Award (3 times); Variety Club of GB: Special Award 1982; Showbusiness Personality 1984; Radio Personality of last 21 Years, Daily Mail Nat. Radio Awards 1988; Sony Radio Award, Barcelona Olympics 1993, Best Breakfast Show 1994, Sony Awards 2001, 2002. *Radio programmes include:* Late Night Extra BBC Radio 1967–69; The Terry Wogan Show, BBC Radio One 1969–72, BBC Radio Two 1972–84, 1993, Wake Up to Wogan, BBC Radio Two 1995–. *Television shows include:* Lunchtime with Wogan, ATV; BBC: Come Dancing, Song for Europe, The Eurovision Song Contest, Children in Need, Wogan's Guide to the BBC, Blankety-Blank, Wogan, Terry Wogan's Friday Night Auntie's Bloomers, Wogan's Web, Points of View 2000–01. *Publications:* Banjaxed 1979, The Day Job 1981, To Horse, To Horse 1982, Wogan on Wogan 1987, Wogan's Ireland 1988, Bumper Book of Togs 1995, Is It Me? (autobiog.) 2000. *Leisure interests:* tennis, golf, swimming, reading, writing. *Address:* c/o Jo Gurnett, 2 New Kings Road, London, SW6 4SA, England.

WOICKE, Peter L.; German banker and international finance official; with J. P. Morgan for over 30 years, in particular in Latin America and the Middle East, Head Banking Div., Beirut, Lebanon, Man. Global Gas and Petroleum Group, fmr mem. Exec. Man. Group, Chair. J. P. Morgan Securities Asia, Singapore; Man. Dir World Bank (IBRD) 1999–, Exec. Vice-Pres. IFC 1999. *Address:* International Bank for Reconstruction and Development, 1818 H Street, NW, Washington, DC 20433, U.S.A. (Office). *Telephone:* (202) 477-1234 (Office). *Fax:* (202) 477-6391 (Office). *E-mail:* pic@worldbank.org (Office). *Website:* www.worldbank.org (Office).

WOJTYŁA, Andrzej Franciszek; Polish politician and paediatrician; b. 1 May 1955, Kalisz; s. of Franciszek Wojtyła and Stanisława Wojtyła; m. Ewa Wojtyła; one s. one d.; ed Medical Acad., Poznań, George Washington, Georgetown and La Salle Univs., USA; paediatrician, Children's Ward Mun. Hospital, Pleszew 1980–89; Head, Village Health Service Centre, Jastrzębniki 1985–92; Visiting Researcher, George Washington Univ. 1995, Visiting Prof., Center for Health Policy and Research 1995–96; mem. Solidarity Trade Union 1980–89, Solidarity of Individual Farmers Trade Union 1989–91; Councillor of Commune of Blizanów 1990; mem. Polish Peasant Party Solidarity (PSL Solidarność) 1990–92, Peasant Christian Party (SLCh) 1992–97; Pres. SLCh Voivodship Bd, Kalisz, mem. SLCh Nat. Political Council; mem. Conservative Peasant Party (SKL) 1997–; Deputy to Sejm (Parl.) 1991–93, 1997–, Vice-Chair. Parl. Health Cttee; mem. Parl. Constitutional Responsibility Cttee 1991–93; Minister of Health and Social Welfare 1992–93. *Publication:* Third International Conference: Health Education for Children, International Conference: Health Care Reform in Poland 1995. *Leisure interests:* fitness, walking, history, health care reforms in the world. *Address:* Biuro Poselski, ul. Targowa 24, 62-800 Kalisz, Poland. *Telephone:* (62) 7672604. *Fax:* (62) 7672604. *E-mail:* awojtyla@polbox.com.pl (Home).

WOJTYŁA, HE Cardinal Karol (see John Paul II, His Holiness Pope).

WOLDE-GIORGIS, Girma; Ethiopian head of state; b. Dec. 1925, Addis Ababa; ed School of Social Science, Netherlands, Air Traffic Man. School, Sweden, Air Traffic Control Man. School, Canada; served in Ethiopian Army, rank of Lt 1941–45; trainee, Ethiopian Air Force 1946–47; Instructor in Air Navigation and Air Traffic Control 1948–54; Head Civil Aviation Authority, Eritrean Fed. State, Asmara 1955–57; Dir-Gen. Ethiopian Civil Aviation, mem. bd Ethiopian Airlines 1958; Dir-Gen. Ministry of Commerce, Industry and Planning 1959–60; elected MP, Pres. 1st Session 1961; Vice-Pres. 52nd Int. Parl. Ass., Belgrade 1961; mem. bd Ethiopian Chamber of Commerce 1967, Civil Advisory Council 1973; Vice-Commr to Peace Comm. 1974; Rep. of Ministry of Transport and Communications to Northern Region of Eritrea and Tigrai 1974; mem. Int. Cttee of the Red Cross (ICRC), Head of Logistics to Demobilize ex-Army Personnel 1990; mem. House of People's Reps. Econ. Cttee 2000–01; Pres. of Ethiopia 2001–; Medal of Genet, Mil. Officers' Acad. 1944, Haile Selassie Star, Cavalry 1956, Minilik Star, Cavalry 1960, Haile Selassie Gold Medal 1960, City Council Gold Medal 1971, Red Cross Silver Medal 1988. *Publication:* Air and Men (in Amharic) 1954. *Leisure interests:* farming, afforestation. *Address:* Office of the President, PO Box 1362, Addis Ababa, Ethiopia (Office). *Telephone:* (1) 518677 (Office); (1) 518890 (Home). *Fax:* (1) 518656 (Office).

WOLF, Christa; German writer; b. 18 March 1929, Landsberg/Warthe, fmr GDR; ed Jena and Leipzig; fmr mem. GDR CP, resgnd 1989; Heinrich-Mann Prize 1963, Nationalpreis für Kunst und Literatur (GDR) 1964, Georg-Büchner Prize, Deutsche Akad. der Sprache und Dichtung 1980. *Publications include:* Der geteilte Himmel, Unter den Linden, Moskauer Novelle 1961, Nachdenken über Christa T. 1968, Kein Ort. Nirgends 1979, Kassandra 1983, Störfall 1987, What Remains (short story) 1990, Medea: Stimmen 1996, Hierzulande, Andernorts 2000; several collections of short stories.

WOLF, Markus Johannes (Mischa); German fmr state security official; b. Hechingen, Nr. Stuttgart; s. of Friedrich Wolf; m. 3rd Andrea Wolf; ed Karl-Liebknecht School, Moscow, Comintern School Kuschnarenkovo; emigrated to Switzerland and France 1933, to USSR 1934–45; adopted Soviet citizenship 1939; joined CP 1942; reporter Berlin Radio; 1st Councillor GDR Mission Moscow 1949–51 (changed citizenship to E German); joined Inst. of Econ. Research (secret service) at Ministry for State Security early 1950s, Deputy Minister for State Security; Chief Main Admin. of Foreign Intelligence 1958–87; Maj.-Gen. 1955, Lt-Gen. 1966, Col-Gen. (State Security Service) 1980; sentenced to six years' imprisonment for treason and bribery Dec. 1993; sentence under appeal; Constitutional Court ruled he should not be held criminally accountable; convicted of three kidnappings and given a two-year suspended sentence May 1997; imprisoned for refusing to identify a Cold War agent Jan. 1998; fmr mem. Young Pioneers (radical Stalinist group) 1935, Socialist Unity Party of Germany; Fatherland's Merit Order (Gold) 1969, Order of the Fatherland's War (USSR, 2nd class) 1970. *Publications:* Troika (autobiographical novel) 1989, Memoirs of a Spymaster 1998. *Leisure interest:* culinary skills.

WOLF, Naomi, BA; American author and feminist; b. 15 Nov. 1962, San Francisco, CA; d. of Leonard Wolf and Deborah Wolf; m. David Shipley 1993; one c.; ed Yale Univ.; Rhodes Scholar 1986; Co-Founder and Pres. The Woodhull Inst. for Ethical Leadership 1997–; fmr columnist, George magazine; consultant, Al Gore Presidential campaign 2000. *Publications:* The Beauty Myth: How Images of Beauty Are Used Against Women 1990, Fire With Fire: The New Female Power and How It Will Change in the 21st Century 1993, Promiscuities: The Secret Struggle for Womanhood 1997, Misconceptions: Truth, Lies and the Unexpected on the Journey to Motherhood 2001. *Address:* c/o Royce Carlton Inc., 866 UN Plaza, New York, NY 10017, U.S.A. (Office).

WOLF, Stephen M., BA; American airline executive; b. 7 Aug. 1941, Oakland, Calif.; ed San Francisco State Univ.; American Airlines 1966–81; Pres. and COO Continental Airlines 1982–83; Pres. and CEO Repub. Airlines 1984–86; Chair., Pres. and CEO Tiger Int. Inc. 1986–88; Chair., CEO UAL Corpn 1987–94, also fmr Pres.; Chair. CEO United Airlines 1992–94; Chair. U.S. Air Group Inc. 1996–98 (Pres. 1987–92), Chair. USAIR Inc. 1998–; Sr Adviser Lazard Frères 1994–; Adviser to Chair. of Air France 1994–96; Dir Air Transport Asscn of America and numerous cos. and orgs. *Address:* USAIR Inc., 2345 Crystal Drive, Arlington, VA 22227, USA.

WOLFBEIN, Seymour Louis, PhD; American government official and educator; b. 8 Nov. 1915, New York; s. of Samuel Wolfbein and Fannie Katz; m. Mae Lachterman 1941; two d.; ed Brooklyn Coll. and Columbia Univ.; Research Assoc. U.S. Senate Comm. on Unemployment and Relief 1938; Economist, Research Div., Works Project Admin. 1939–42; Economist, Bureau of Labor Statistics, Dept of Labor 1942–45, Head, Occupational Outlook Div. 1946–49, Head, Manpower and Productivity Div. 1949–50, Manpower and Employment Div. 1950–59, Deputy Asst Sec. of Labor 1959–62, Dir Office of Manpower, Automation and Training 1962–65, Econ. Adviser to Sec. of Labor 1965–67; Visiting Prof. Univ. of Mich. 1950–; Adjunct Prof. American Univ. 1951–; Dean School of Business Admin., Temple Univ. 1967–78, J.A. Boettner Prof. of Business Admin 1978–85; Dean Temple Univ., Japan 1983–85; Pres. T.W.O. Man. Consultants 1986–; Comm. on Human Resources, NAS 1976–; Vice-Pres. World Trade Council 1980–; Fellow, American Statistical Asscn, AAAS; Distinguished Service Award, Dept of Labor 1955 and 1961; Eminent Man of Guidance Award 1970. *Publications:*

Decline of a Cotton Textile City 1942, The World of Work 1951, Employment and Unemployment in the U.S. 1964, Employment, Unemployment and Public Policy 1965, Education and Training for Full Employment 1967, Occupational Information 1968, Emerging Sectors of Collective Bargaining 1970, Work in the American Society 1971, Manpower Policy: Perspectives and Prospects 1973, Labor Market Information for Youths 1975, The Pre-Retirement Years 1977, Establishment Reporting in the USA 1978, The Demography of the Disabled 1988, The Temporary Help Supply Industry 1989, Working and Not Working in the USA, Working Part Time In the USA 1990, To the Year 2000 1991, Our Industrial Future 1991, Our Occupational Future 1992, The World of Work: To the Year 2000 and Beyond 1993, Occupational Futures in the USA 1994, Guidance and Counseling for the Labor Force: Moving Into the Next Millennium 1995, Schooling in the USA: What a Difference a Year Makes 1996, An Election Lesson in Education 1996, The Philadelphia Story 1996, Employment in the USA 1997, Making a Living in the USA 1997, Moving Across the Millennium 1997, The Emerging Geography of the American Economy 1998. *Leisure interest:* painting. *Address:* 4903 Edgemoor, Bethesda, MD 20814, USA. *Telephone:* (215) 563-6740. *Fax:* (215) 854-1892.

WOLFE, Thomas Kennerly, Jr., AB, PhD; American author and journalist; b. 2 March 1931, Richmond, Va; s. of Thomas Kennerly and Helen Hughes; m. Sheila Berger; one s. one d.; ed Washington and Lee Univ. and Yale; reporter Springfield (Mass.) Union 1956–59; reporter, Latin American Corresp. Washington Post 1959–62; reporter, magazine writer New York Herald Tribune 1962–66; magazine writer New York World Journal Tribune 1966–67; Contributing Ed. New York magazine 1968–76, Esquire Magazine 1977–; Contributing Artist Harper's magazine 1978–81; exhibited one-man show of drawings, Maynard Walker Gallery, New York 1965, Tunnel Gallery, New York 1974; mem. American Acad. of Arts and Letters 1999; Hon. DFA (Minneapolis Coll. of Art) 1971, Hon. Litt. D. (Washington and Lee) 1974, Hon. LHD (Va Commonwealth Univ.) 1983, (Southampton Coll., NY) 1984; Front Page Awards for Humour and Foreign News Reporting, Washington Newspaper Guild 1961, Award of Excellence, Soc. of Magazine Writers 1970, Frank Luther Mott Research Award 1973, Va Laureate for Literature 1977, Harold D. Vursell Memorial Award, American Acad. and Inst. of Arts and Letters 1980, American Book Award for Gen. Non-Fiction 1980, Columbia Journalism Award 1980, Citation for Art History, Nat. Sculpture Soc. 1980, John Dos Passos Award 1984, Gari Melchers Medal 1986, Benjamin Pierce Cheney Medal (E Washington Univ.) 1986, Washington Irving Medal (St Nicholas Soc.) 1986. *Publications:* The Kandy-Kolored Tangerine-Flake Streamline Baby 1965, The Electric Kool-Aid Acid Test 1968, The Pump House Gang 1968, Radical Chic and Mau-mauing the Flak Catchers 1970, The New Journalism 1973, The Painted Word 1975, Mauve Gloves and Madmen, Clutter and Vine 1976, The Right Stuff 1979, In Our Time 1980, From Bauhaus to Our House 1981, Bonfire of the Vanities 1987, Ambush at Fort Bragg 1998, A Man in Full 1998, Hooking Up (short stories) 2000. *Address:* c/o Farrar, Straus and Giroux Inc., 19 Union Square W, Floor 11, New York, NY 10003, USA.

WOLFENDALE, Sir Arnold (Whittaker), Kt, PhD, FRAS, FInstP, FRS; British professor of physics; b. 25 June 1927, Rugby; s. of Arnold Wolfendale and Doris Wolfendale; m. Audrey Darby 1951; twin s.; ed Manchester Univ.; Asst Lecturer, Manchester Univ. 1951–54, Lecturer 1954–56; Lecturer, Univ. of Durham 1956–59, Sr Lecturer 1959–63, Reader in Physics 1965–92, Prof. 1965–92, Emer. Prof. 1992–, Head of Dept 1973–77, 1980–83, 1986–89; Chair., Northern Region Action Cttee, Manpower Services Comm. Job Creation Programme 1975–78; Pres. Royal Astronomical Soc. 1981–83, Durham Univ. Soc. of Fellows 1988–, Inst. of Physics 1994–96, European Physical Soc. 1999–; Prof. of Experimental Physics, Royal Inst. of GB 1996–; mem. Science and Eng Research Council 1988–94; Astronomer Royal 1991–95; Fellow Tata Inst. Fund 1996; mem. Academia Europaea 1998; Foreign Fellow, Nat. Acad. of Sciences of India 1990, Indian Nat. Science Acad.; Foreign Assoc. Royal Soc. of SA 1996; Hon. Fellow, Lancs. Polytechnic 1991; Pres. Antiquarian Horological Soc.; Dr. hc (Potchefstroom, Łódź, Teesside, Newcastle, Open Univ., Paisley, Lancaster, Bucharest, Durham, Neofit Rilski Southwest Univ. (Bulgaria); Silver Jubilee Medal 1977, Univ. of Turku Medal 1987, Armagh Observatory Medal 1992, Marian Smoluchowski Medal (Polish Physics Soc.) 1992, Powell Memorial Medal, European Physical Soc. 1996, Freeman Worshipful Co. of Clockmakers, Worshipful Co. of Scientific Instrument Makers, Lancaster. *Publications:* Cosmic Rays 1963; Ed. Cosmic Rays at Ground Level 1973, Origin of Cosmic Rays 1974, Gamma Ray Astronomy 1981, Progress in Cosmology 1982, Gamma Ray Astronomy (with P. V. Ramana Murthy) 1986, Secular, Solar and Geomagnetic Variations in the last 1,000 years 1988; Origin of Cosmic Rays (Co-Ed.) 1981, Obs. Tests of Cosmological Inflation (Co-Ed.) 1991; numerous papers on cosmic radiation. *Leisure interests:* walking, gardening, foreign travel. *Address:* Physics Department, University of Durham, Durham, DH1 3LE (Office); Ansford, Potters Bank, Durham, England (Home). *Telephone:* (191) 384-5642 (Home); (191) 374-2160 (Office). *Fax:* (191) 374-3749 (Office). *E-mail:* a.w.wolfendale@durham.ac.uk (Office).

WOLFENSOHN, James D. (Jim); American international official, business executive and arts administrator; b. 1 Dec. 1933, Sydney, Australia; s. of Hyman Wolfensohn and Dora Weinbaum; m. Elaine Botwinick 1961; one s. two d.; ed Harvard Business School; Pres. J. Henry Schroder Banking Corpn 1970–76; Chair. Salomon Bros. Int. 1977–81; owner, Pres. James D. Wolfensohn Inc. 1981–95, fmr Chair., also CEO; mem. Bd Carnegie Hall; Chair.

Kennedy Center for the Performing Arts 1990–95; Chair. Emer. 1995–; Pres. IBRD June 1995–, Int. Devt Asscn, Int. Finance Corpn, Multilateral Guarantee Agency; Trustee Rockefeller Univ. 1985–94, Howard Hughes Medical Inst. 1987–96; Montblanc de la Culture Award 1992. *Leisure interest:* playing the cello. *Address:* IBRD, 1818 H Street, NW, Washington, DC 20433, USA. *Telephone:* (202) 477-1234. *Fax:* (202) 477-6391. *E-mail:* pic@worldbank.org. *Website:* www.worldbank.org.

WOLFENSTEIN, Lincoln, PhD; American professor of physics; b. 10 Feb. 1923, Cleveland, Ohio; s. of Leo Wolfenstein and Anna Koppel; m. Wilma C. Miller 1957; one s. two d.; ed Univ. of Chicago; Physicist, Nat. Advisory Comm. for Aeronautics 1944–46; Asst Prof., Carnegie-Mellon Univ. 1948–57, Assoc. Prof. 1957–60, Prof. 1960–78, Univ. Prof. 1978–; Guggenheim Fellow 1973–74, 1983–84; mem. NAS; J.J. Sakurai Prize, American Physical Soc. 1992. *Publications:* over 100 papers on theoretical particle and nuclear physics, weak interactions, c.p. violation, neutrino physics. *Address:* Physics Department, Carnegie-Mellon University, 5000 Forbes Avenue, Pittsburgh, PA 15213, USA. *Telephone:* (412) 578-2740.

WOLFF, Hugh; American conductor; b. 21 Oct. 1953, Paris; m. Judith Kogan; three s.; ed Harvard Univ.; Musical Dir NJ Symphony 1985–92; Prin. Conductor Saint Paul Chamber Orchestra 1988–92, Musical Dir 1992–2000; Prin. Conductor Frankfurt Radio Symphony Orchestra 1997–; regularly guest-conducts the major orchestras in N America and Europe. *Address:* c/o Van Walsum Management, 4 Addison Bridge Place, London, W14 8XP, England (Office). *Telephone:* (20) 7371-4343 (Office). *Fax:* (20) 7371-4344 (Office). *E-mail:* vwm@vanwalsum.co.uk (Office). *Website:* www/vanwalsum .co.uk (Office).

WOLFF, Tobias J. A., MA; American writer; b. 19 June 1945, Birmingham, Ala; s. of Arthur S. Wolff and Rosemary Loftus; m. Catherine Dolores Spohn 1975; two s. one d.; ed The Hill School, Univ. of Oxford and Univ. of Stanford; U.S. Army 1964–68; Reporter, Washington Post 1972; Writing Fellow, Stanford Univ. 1975–78; Writer-in-Residence, Ariz. State Univ. 1978–80, Syracuse Univ. 1980–97, Stanford Univ. 1997–; Guggenheim Fellow 1983; Nat. Endowment Fellow 1978, 1984; Hon. Fellow Hertford Coll., Oxford 2000; PEN/Faulkner Award for Fiction 1985, Rea Award for Short Story 1989, Whiting Foundation Award 1989, LA Times Book Prize 1989, Ambassador Book Award 1990, Lila Wallace/Reader's Digest Award 1993, Esquire-Volvo-Waterstone Award for Non-Fiction 1994, Award of Merit, American Acad. of Arts and Letters 2001. *Publications:* Hunters in the Snow 1981, The Barracks Thief 1984, Back in the World 1985, This Boy's Life 1989, In Pharaoh's Army: Memories of a Lost War 1994, The Vintage Book of Contemporary American Short Stories 1994, The Best American Short Stories 1994, The Night in Question 1996. *Address:* English Department, Stanford University, Stanford, CA 94305, USA.

WOLFF, Torben, DSc; Danish deep-sea biologist; b. 21 July 1919, Copenhagen; s. of Jørgen Frederik de Lichtenberg Wolff and Karen Margrethe Lunn; m. Lisbeth Christensen; two d.; ed Copenhagen Univ.; Curator Zoological Museum, Univ. of Copenhagen 1953–66, Chief Curator 1966–80, 1983–89; External Examiner Aarhus Univ. 1966–75, Copenhagen Univ. 1967–79; Sec. Int. Asscn for Biological Oceanography 1970–76; Vice-Pres. Scientific Cttee on Oceanic Research 1980–84; mem. Panel of NATO Marine Sciences Programme 1981–86; mem. Danish Nat. Council for Oceanology 1964–, Sec. 1968–, Chair. 1985–89; mem. Bd Danish Natural History Soc. 1948–50, 1955–68, 1980–85, 1999– (Chair. 1963–68); mem. Adventurers Club of Denmark 1957– (Pres. 1970–73), Bd WWF/Denmark 1980–90, World Innovation Foundation 2001; mem. Bd Denmark's Aquarium 1971–96, Dir 1980–83, 1990–93; Deputy Leader Danish Galathea Deep-Sea Expedition Round the World 1950–52; mem. Danish Atlantide Expedition to West Africa 1945–46; numerous other expeditions; Hon. mem. RSNZ, 1977, Danish Natural History Soc. 1990; Royal Galathea Medal 1955, GEC Gad's Grant of Honour 1964, Popular Science Prize, Danish Asscn of Authors 1983. *Publications:* A Year in Nature 1944, The Systematics and Biology of Isopoda Asellota 1962, Danish Expeditions on the Seven Seas 1967, The History of Danish Zoology 1979, The History of the Danish Natural History Society 1933–83, 1983; numerous scientific and popular scientific papers on crustaceans, deep-sea ecology, history of science, biogs etc. *Leisure interest:* guiding tours abroad to places off the beaten track. *Address:* Zoological Museum, 2100 Copenhagen Ø (Office); Hesseltoften 12, 2900 Hellerup, Denmark (Home). *Telephone:* 39-62-89-71 (Home); 35-32-10-40 (Office). *Fax:* 35-32-10-10 (Office).

WOLFF VON AMERONGEN, Otto; German industrialist; b. 6 Aug. 1918; s. of Otto Wolff and Else von Amerongen; m. Winnie Greger; three d.; Chair. and CEO Otto Wolff AG 1966–86, Chair. Supervisory Bd 1986–90; Chair. and CEO Otto Wolff Industrieberatung und Beteiligungen GmbH 1990–; Chair. and CEO Otto Wolff-Stiftung 1991–; Pres. German Business Asscn. in Russian Fed., Moscow 1995–; Chair., Deputy Chair. and mem. Supervisory Bds. various nat. and int. corpns.; Chair. Cologne Chamber of Commerce and Industry 1966–90, Hon. Chair. 1990–; Chair. German East-West Trade Cttee 1956–2000; Pres. Deutsche Gesellschaft für Osteuropakunde 1971–99; Hon. Chair. Asscn of German Chambers of Commerce and Industry 1988–; Officier, Légion d'honneur, Grosses Bundesverdienstkreuz mit Stern und Schulterband, Gross Kreuz des Bundesverdienstordens 2001. *Address:* Marienburger Strasse 19, 50968 Cologne, Germany. *Telephone:* (221) 9347700. *Fax:* (221) 93477050.

WOLFOWITZ, Paul Dundes, DR.RER.POL; American politician; b. 22 Dec. 1943, Brooklyn, NY; s. of the late Jacob Wolfowitz and of Lillian Dundes; m. Clare Selgin; three c.; ed Cornell Univ., Univ. of Chicago; Man. Intern Bureau of the Budget 1966–67; mem. staff Arms Control and Disarmament Agency 1973–77; Deputy Asst Sec. of Defense for Regional Programs 1977–80, Under-Sec. of Defense for Policy 1989–93, Deputy Sec. of Defense March 2001–; Head of State Dept Policy Planning Staff 1981–82; fmr Asst Sec. of State for E Asian and Pacific Affairs; Amb. to Indonesia 1986–89; lecturer Yale Univ. 1970–73; George F. Kennan Prof. of Nat. Security Strategy, Nat. War Coll. 1993; Dean and Prof. of Int. Relations Paul H. Nitze School of Advanced Int. Studies (SAIS), Johns Hopkins Univ. 1994–2001; mem. Advisory Bd journals Foreign Affairs, National Interest; numerous awards including Presidential Citizen's Award, Dept of Defense Distinguished Public Service Medal, Distinguished Honor Award, Distinguished Civilian Service Medal. *Address:* Department of Defense, 3E 880, 1000 Pentagon, Washington DC 20310, USA (Office). *Telephone:* (703) 697-5737 (Office). *Fax:* (703) 695-1149 (Office). *Website:* www.defenselink.mil (Office).

WOLFRAM, Herwig, DPhil; Austrian historian; b. 14 Feb. 1934, Vienna; s. of Dr. Fritz Wolfram and Rosa Wolfram; m. Adelheid Schoerghofer 1958; three s. one d.; ed Univ. of Vienna; Lecturer 1959–68; Docent, Univ. of Vienna 1967; Assoc. Prof., Los Angeles 1968; Assoc. Prof. of Medieval History 1969, Prof. of Medieval History and Auxiliary Sciences 1971–, Dean Faculty of Arts 1981–83; Dir Inst. für österr. Geschichtsforschung, Vienna 1983–; Fellow Austrian Acad. of Sciences 1985–; Corresp. Fellow Medieval Acad. of America 1990, Royal Historical Soc. London 1995, British Acad. 1996; Theodor-Koerner Foederungspreis 1962, 1964, Kardinal Innitzer-Foederungspreis 1964, Kardinal Innitzerpreis fuer Geisteswissenschaft 1994. *Television:* adviser to Sturm neber Europa I–IV (ZdF, ORF, Arte) 2002. *Publications include:* Splendor Imperii 1963, Intitulatio I 1967, II 1973, III 1988, History of the Goths 1988, Die Geburt Mitteleuropas 1987, Die Goten (7th edn) 2001, Das Reich und die Germanen 1990–92, Salzburg, Bayern, Oesterreich. Die Conversio Bagoariorum et Carantanorum und die Quellen ihrer Zeit 1995, Grenzen und Räume 1995, The Roman Empire and its Germanic Peoples 1997, Konrad II (990–1039): Kaiser dreier Reiche 2000, Die Goten und ihre Geschicte 2001, Die Germanen (7th edn) 2002. *Leisure interests:* sport, music, theatre. *Address:* Institut fuer Oesterreische Geschichtsforschung, Dr. Karl Lueger-Ring 1, 1010 Vienna (Office); Sommeregg 13, 5307, Eugendorf; Wilhelminenstr. 173, 1160 Vienna, Austria (Home). *Telephone:* (1) 427-22-72-60 (Office); (1) 485-63-28 (Home). *Fax:* (1) 427-79-27-2 (Office); (1) 485-63-28 (Home); (6221) 20277 (Home). *E-mail:* herwig.wolfram@univie.ac.at (Office). *Website:* www.univie.ac.at/Geschichtsforschung (Office).

WOLFSON, Dirk Jacob, PhD; Netherlands economist; b. 22 June 1933, Voorburg; s. of Dirk Wolfson and Gerdina Akkerhuys; m. Anna Maaike Hoekstra 1960; three c.; ed Univ. of Amsterdam; Teaching Asst Univ. of Amsterdam 1961–63; Economist, IMF, Washington, DC 1964–70; Dir (Chief Economist), Econ. Policy Div. Netherlands Treasury Dept 1970–75; Prof. of Public Finance, Erasmus Univ. Rotterdam 1975–86, Prof. of Econs 1992–; Rector, Inst. of Social Studies, The Hague 1986–90; mem. Social and Econ. Council 1982–96, Scientific Council for Govt Policy 1990–98; Royal Supervisor, Netherlands Cen. Bank and Chair. Banking Council 1990–99; mem. Senate (Social Democratic Party) 1999–; mem. Royal Netherlands Acad. of Arts and Sciences 1989–; Kt Order of the Netherlands Lion. *Publications:* Public Finance and Development Strategy 1979; numerous books and articles on econ. theory and policy. *Leisure interests:* theatre, hiking. *Address:* Aelbrechtskolk 41a, 3025 HB Rotterdam, Netherlands (Home). *Telephone:* (10) 4779497 (Home). *Fax:* (10) 4764667 (Home). *E-mail:* dwolfson@xs4all.nl (Home).

WOLFSON, Baron (Life Peer), cr. 1985, of Marylebone in the City of Westminster; **Leonard Gordon Wolfson,** Kt; British retail executive; b. 11 Nov. 1927, London; s. of the late Sir Isaac Wolfson and Lady (Edith) Wolfson; m. 1st Ruth Sterling 1949 (divorced 1991); four d.; m. 2nd Estelle Jackson (née Feldman) 1991; one step-s. one step-d.; ed King's School, Worcester; Chair. Great Universal Stores 1981–96, Hon. Pres. 1996– (Dir 1952, Man. Dir 1962–81); Chair. Burberrys Ltd 1978–96, Hon. Pres. 1996–; Founder Trustee Wolfson Foundation 1955–, Chair. 1972–; Pres. Jewish Welfare Bd 1972–82; Patron Royal Coll. of Surgeons 1976; Trustee Imperial War Museum 1988–94; Hon. Fellow Wolfson Coll., Cambridge, Wolfson Coll., St Catherine's Coll. and Worcester Coll., Oxford, Univ. Coll. London, London School of Hygiene and Tropical Medicine 1985, Queen Mary Coll., London Univ. 1985, Univ. of Westminster 1991, Imperial Coll. 1991, Royal Coll. of Eng 1997, Somerville Coll., Oxford 1999, L.S.E. 1999, Inst. of Educ. London Univ. 2001, Israel Museum 2001; Hon. mem. Emmanuel Coll. Cambridge 1996, Royal Coll. of Surgeons Edin. 1997; Hon. FRCP 1977; Hon. FBA 1986, Hon. FRCS 1988; Hon. DCL (Oxon) 1972; Hon. LLD (Strathclyde) 1972, (Dundee) 1979, (Cantab.) 1982, (London) 1982; Hon. DSc (Hull) 1977, (Wales) 1984, (E Anglia) 1986, Hon. D.Univ. (Surrey) 1990, (Glasgow) 1997, Hon. MD (Birmingham) 1992, Dr. hc (Technion) 1995, (Edin.) 1996, Hon. PhD (Tel Aviv) 1971, (Hebrew Univ.) 1978, (Bar Ilan Univ.) 1983, (Weitzmann Inst.) 1988; Sir Winston Churchill Award (British Technion Soc.) 1989. *Leisure interests:* history, economics. *Address:* 8 Queen Anne Street, London, W1G 9LD, England. *Telephone:* (20) 7323-3124 (Office). *Fax:* (20) 7323-3138 (Office).

WOLLHEIM, Richard Arthur, MA, FBA; British philosopher; b. 5 May 1923, London; s. of Eric Wollheim and Constance Wollheim; m. 1st Anne Toynbee (née Powell) 1950 (divorced 1967); two s.; m. 2nd Mary Day Lanier 1969; one d.; ed Westminster School, Balliol Coll. Oxford; army service 1942–45; taught at Univ. Coll. London 1949–82, Grote Prof. 1963–82; Emer. Grote Prof. 1982–; Prof. of Philosophy, Columbia Univ., USA 1982–84; Prof. of Philosophy, Univ. of Calif., Berkeley 1985–; Prof. of Philosophy and the Humanities, Univ. of Calif., Davis 1989–95; mem. American Acad. of Arts and Sciences; Hon. mem. British Psychoanalytic Soc., San Francisco Psychoanalytic Soc.; Award for Services to Psychoanalysis, Int. Psychoanalytic Soc. 1993. *Publications:* F. H. Bradley 1959, Art and its Objects 1968, A Family Romance 1969, Freud 1971, On Art and the Mind 1973, The Thread of Life (William James Lectures, Harvard) 1984, Painting as an Art (Mellon Lectures, Nat. Gallery of Art) 1987, The Mind and Its Depths (essays and lectures) 1993, On the Motions 1999. *Address:* 20 Ashchurch Park Villas, London, W12 9SP, England; 1814 Marin Avenue, Berkeley, CA 94707, USA. *Telephone:* (20) 8743-7708 (London); (510) 525-2599 (Calif.).

WOLPER, David Lloyd; American film and television producer; b. 11 Jan. 1928, New York; s. of Irving S. Wolper and Anna Wolper (née Fass); m. 1st Margaret Dawn Richard 1958 (divorced); two s. one d.; m. 2nd Gloria Diane Hill 1974; ed Drake Univ. and Univ. of Southern California; Vice-Pres. and Treasurer Flamingo Films TV Sales Co. 1948–50; Vice-Pres. W Coast Operations 1954–58; Chair. Bd and Pres. Wolper Productions 1958–, Wolper Pictures Ltd 1968–, The Wolper Org. Inc. 1971–; Pres. Fountainhead Int. 1960–, Wolper TV Sales Co. 1964–, Wolper Productions Inc. 1970–; Vice-Pres. Metromedia Inc. 1965–68; Consultant and Exec. Producer Warner Brothers Inc. 1976–; Dir, fmr Chair. Amateur Athletic Foundation of Los Angeles; Dir Acad. of TV Arts and Sciences Foundation, S. Calif. Cttee for Olympic Games, Univ. of S. Calif. Cinema/TV Dept; mem. Acad. of Motion Picture Arts and Sciences, Acad. of TV Arts and Sciences, Producers' Guild of America, Caucus for Producers, Writers and Dirs.; mem. Bd of Govs. Cedars Sinai Medical Center; mem. Bd of Trustees, American Film Inst., Museum of Broadcasting, LA Country Museum of Art and numerous other appointments; Chevalier, Légion d'honneur 1990; seven Golden Globe Awards, five George Foster Peabody Awards, Distinguished Service Award, US Jr Chamber of Commerce, 46 Emmy Awards, Acad. of TV Arts and Sciences, Monte Carlo Int. Film Festival Award 1964, Cannes Film Festival Grand Prix for TV Programmes 1964, two Acad. Awards: Best Documentary Film 1972, Jean Hersholt Humanitarian Award 1985. *Television productions include:* The Race for Space, The Making of the President, Hollywood and the Stars, March of Time Specials, The Rise and Fall of the Third Reich, The Undersea World of Jacques Cousteau, China: Roots of Madness, Primal Man, Welcome Back, Kotter, Roots, Victory at Entebbe, Roots: The Next Generations, The Thorn Birds, North and South—Books I and II, The Morning After, Napoleon and Josephine and numerous TV films including Men of the Dragon, Unwed Father; has produced numerous feature films and several live special events, including Opening and Closing Ceremonies of 1984 Olympic Games, LA, 100th Anniversary of Unveiling of the Statue of Liberty 1986, Legends, Icons and Superstars of the 20th Century, Celebrate the Century. *Film productions include:* Willy Wonka and the Chocolate Factory; If It's Tuesday, This Must Be Belgium; The Hellstrom Chronicle, Visions of Eight, One is a Lonely Number, Wattstax; Birds Do It, Bees Do It; This is Elvis, Victory at Entebbe, Surviving Picasso, Imagine: John Lennon, I Love My Wife, The Animal Within, Four Days in November, The Bridge at Remagen, The Devil's Brigade, L.A. Confidential. *Publication:* Producer: A Memoir (with David Fisher). *Address:* The David L. Wolper Company, 617 North Rodeo Drive, Beverly Hills, CA 90210, USA. *Telephone:* (310) 278-0619 (Office). *Fax:* (310) 278-3615 (Home). *E-mail:* davidwolper@msn.com (Office). *Website:* www.davidwolper.com (Office).

WOLPERT, Lewis, CBE, DIC, PhD, FRS; British professor of biology as applied to medicine; b. 19 Oct. 1929, South Africa; s. of William Wolpert and Sarah Wolpert; m. Elizabeth Brownstein; two s. two d.; ed Univ. of Witwatersrand, Imperial Coll. London, King's Coll. London; civil engineer S. African Council for Scientific and Industrial Research and Israel Water Planning Dept 1951–54; Reader in Zoology, King's Coll. London 1964–66; Prof. of Biology as Applied to Medicine, Dept of Anatomy and Developmental Biology Univ. Coll. & Middlesex School of Medicine (fmrly at Middx Medical School) 1966–; presenter Antenna (BBC2) 1988–89, TV documentaries and radio interviews with scientists; Chair. MRC Cell Bd 1984–88; Chair. Comm. on the Public Understanding of Science 1994–; mem. various cttees., scientific panels etc.; Hon. DSc (Westminster) 1997, Hon. DUniv (Open Univ.) 1998; Michael Faraday Medal, Royal Soc. 2000. *Publications:* A Passion for Science 1988, The Triumph of the Embryo 1991, The Unnatural Nature of Science 1992, Principles of Development 1998, Malignant Sadness. The Anatomy of Depression 1999. *Leisure interests:* cycling, tennis. *Address:* Department of Anatomy and Developmental Biology, University College London, Gower Street, London, WC1E 6BT, England.

WOLSZCZAN, Aleksander; Polish astronomer; b. 29 April 1946, Szczecinek; m.; one d.; ed Nicolaus Copernicus Univ., Toruń; Dir Astronomy Centre, Nicolaus Copernicus Univ. 1997–2000; Evan Pugh Prof. of Astronomy and Astrophysics, Pa State Univ.; Kt's Cross, Order of Polonia Restituta 1997; Young Astronomer Prize, Polish Astronomical Society 1977, Annual Award, Foundation of Polish Science 1992, Annual Award, Alfred Jurzykowski Foundation 1993, Faculty Scholar Medal, Pa State Univ. 1994, Beatrice M. Tinsley Prize, American Astronomical Society 1996, Casimir Funk Natural Sciences Award, Polish Inst. of Arts and Sciences of America 1996, M. Smoluchowski Medal, Polish Physical Soc. *Publications include:* Interstellar

Interferometry of the Pulsar PSR 1237+25 1987 (co-author), Experimental Constraints on Strong-Field Relativistic Gravity 1992 (co-author), A Planetary System Around the Millisecond Pulsar PSR 1257+12 1992 (co-author), Confirmation of Earth-Mass Planets Orbiting the Millisecond Pulsar PSR B1257+12 1994, Binary Pulsars and Relativistic Gravitation 1994. *Leisure interests:* climbing, hiking. *Address:* The Pennsylvania State University, Department of Astronomy and Astrophysics, 525 Davey Laboratory, University Park, PA 16802, USA (Office). *Telephone:* (814) 863-1756 (Office). *E-mail:* alex@astro.uni.torun.pl (Office).

WOLTER, Frank; German international civil servant; b. 22 Nov. 1943, Seehausen, Bavaria; s. of Dr Hans Wolter and Ilse Wolter (née Henrici); m. Birgit Rein 1975; one s. one d.; ed Univs. of Freiburg, Saarbrücken and Kiel; Research Fellow Kiel Inst. of World Econs 1969–74, Head Research Groups 1974–83; Dir Research Project, German Research Foundation 1977–79; Sr Economist, Econ. Research and Analysis Unit, GATT Secr., Geneva 1983–89, Dir Trade Policies Review Div. 1989–91, Dir Agric. and Commodities 1991–. *Publications:* numerous studies and articles on structural change in industry, int. trade and econ. growth. *Leisure interests:* tennis, skiing, classical music, historical literature, golf. *Address:* 154 rue de Lausanne, 1211 Geneva 21, Switzerland (Office); 38 La Clé des Champs, 01280 Moens, France (Home). *E-mail:* frank.wolter@wto.org (Office); wolterfrank@aol.com (Home).

WONDER, Stevie; American singer, musician and composer; b. Steveland Judkins Morris, 13 May 1950, Saginaw, Mich.; step-s. of Paul Hardaway; m. 1st Syreeta Wright 1971 (divorced 1972); m. 2nd Yolanda Simmons, three c.; ed Michigan School for the Blind; first appeared as solo singer at Whitestone Baptist Church, Detroit 1959; recording artist with Motown, Detroit 1963–70; f. and Pres. Black Bull Music Inc. 1970–, Wondirection Records 1982–; owner KJLH, LA; named Best Selling Male Soul Artist of Year (Nat. Asscn of Record Merchandisers) 1974; Grammy Awards (You Are the Sunshine of My Life, Innervisions, Superstition) 1974, (Fulfillingness' First Finale, Boogie on Reggae Woman, Living for the City) 1975, (Songs in the Key of Life, I Wish) 1977, Acad. and Golden Globe Awards for song I Just Called to Say I Love You 1985, Polar Music Prize, Swedish Acad. of Music. *Singles include:* Fingertips 1963, Uptight/Purple Raindrops 1965, Someday At Christmas/The Miracles of Christmas, I'm Wondering/Everytime I See You I Go Wild 1966, I Was Made to Love Her/Hold Me 1967, Shoo-Be-Doo-Be-Doo-Da-Day/Why Don't You Lead Me To Love, You Met Your Match/My Girl 1968, For Once in My Life, I Don't Know Why, My Cherie Amour, Yester-Me, Yester-You, Yesterday, Never Had a Dream Come True, Signed, Sealed, Delivered, I'm Yours, Heaven Help Us All, Superstition, You are the Sunshine of My Life, Higher Ground, Living For the City, Boogie on Reggae Women, Don't You Worry About a Thing, I Wish, Sir Duke, Another Star, Lately, Jammin', We Are the World (with others), I Just Called to Say I Love You. *Albums include:* Little Stevie Wonder: The Twelve-Year-Old Genius, Tribute To Uncle Ray, Jazz Soul, With A Song In My Heart, At The Beach, Uptight 1966, Down To Earth 1966, I Was Made to Love Her 1967, Someday At Christmas 1967, Stevie Wonder: Greatest Hits 1968, Music Of My Mind 1972, Innervisions 1973, Fulfillingness' First Finale 1975, Songs in the Key of Life 1976, Journey Through the Secret Life of Plants 1979, Hotter than July 1980, Original Musiquarium 1981, Woman in Red 1984, In Square Circle 1986, Characters 1987, Jungle Fever 1991, Inner Peace 1995, Motown Legends 1995. *Address:* c/o Steveland Morris Music, 4616 W Magnolia Boulevard, Burbank, CA 91505, USA; c/o Motown Records, 1755 Broadway, New York, NY 10019.

WONG KAR WAI, BA; Chinese film director; b. 1959, Shanghai; ed Hong Kong Polytechnic; TV drama production training programme Hong Kong TV Broadcasts Ltd 1980–82; Best Dir Award Cannes Film Festival 1997 (for Happy Together). *Films:* As Tears Go By 1988, Days of Being Wild 1990, Days of Being Wild II, Ashes of Time 1994, Chungking Express 1994, Fallen Angels 1995, Happy Together 1997, In the Mood for Love 2000. *Television:* scriptwriter Don't Look Now 1981. *Address:* c/o Jet Tone Films, Flat E, Third Floor, Kalam Court, 9 Grampian Road, Kowloon, Hong Kong Special Administrative Region, People's Republic of China.

WONG YICK MING, Rosanna; Hong Kong administrator and government official; b. 15 Aug. 1952, Hong Kong; ed St Stephen's Girls' School, Univ. of Hong Kong, Univ. of Toronto, LSE, Chinese Univ. of Hong Kong, Univ. of California, Davis; Exec. Dir Hong Kong Fed. of Youth Groups; Chair. Hong Kong Housing Authority, Complaints Cttee of Hong Kong Ind. Comm. Against Corruption, Children's Thalassaemia Foundation, Social Welfare Advisory Cttee 1988–91, Comm. on Youth 1990–91, Police Complaints Cttee 1993; mem. Legis. Council 1985–91, Exec. Council 1988–91, 1992–97, Exec. Council of Hong Kong Special Admin. Region 1997–2002; Patron Mother's Choice, Children's Kidney Trust Fund; mem. Co-ordinating Cttee for Children and Youth at Risk, Exec. Cttee Hong Kong Council of Social Service, Bd World Vision Hong Kong; Hon. Fellow Hong Kong Inst. of Housing 1994; Hon. mem. Chartered Inst. of Housing 1994. *Address:* c/o Executive Council Secretariat, First Floor, Main Wing, Central Government Offices, Central, Hong Kong Special Administrative Region, People's Republic of China.

WOO, John; Chinese film director; b. Yu Sum Woo, 1948, Guangzhou; ed Matteo Ricci Coll., Hong Kong; family moved to Hong Kong 1951; started making experimental 16mm films in 1967; entered film industry 1969 as Production Asst Cathay Film Co., Asst Dir 1971; later joined Shaw Bros as Asst Dir to Zhang Che; arrived in Hollywood 1992, debut with Hard Target 1993. *Films:* The Young Dragons (debut) 1973, The Dragon Tamers, Count-

down in Kung Fu, Princess Chang Ping, From Riches to Rags, Money Crazy, Follow the Star, Last Hurrah for Chivalry, To Hell with the Devil, Laughing Times, Plain Jane to the Rescue, Sunset Warriors (Heroes Shed No Tears), The Time You Need a Friend, Run Tiger, Run, A Better Tomorrow 1986, A Better Tomorrow II, Just Heroes, The Killer 1989, Bullet in the Head, Once a Thief 1990, Hard Boiled 1992, Hard Target 1993, Broken Arrow 1996, Face/Off 1997, King's Ransom, M: I-2 2000, The Last Word (producer), Windtalkers 2002. *Address:* c/o MGM Studios Inc., 2450 Broadway Street, Santa Monica, CA 90404, USA (Office).

WOO, Peter K. C., JP, MBA, DLitt, DSC; Chinese business executive; b. 1946, Shanghai; ed Univ. of Cincinnati, Columbia Business School, USA; Chair. Wheelock & Co. Ltd 1986–96, Hon. Chair. 1996–; Chair. Wharf (Holdings) Ltd 1986–94, Hon. Chair 1994–; Founding Chair. Wheelock NatWest Ltd 1995–, The Wharf (Holdings) Ltd 1992–; Hong Kong (now Hong Kong Special Admin. Region) Affairs Adviser to People's Repub. of China 1993–; mem. Int. Advisory Bd Chemical Banking Corpn 1981–, Nat. Westminster Bank PLC 1992–, Gen. Electric 1994–, Elf Aquitaine 1994–; Dir Standard Chartered Bank PLC 1986–89; mem. Hong Kong (now Hong Kong Special Admin. Region)/United States Econ. Co-operation Cttee 1989–95, Hong Kong Gov.'s Business Council 1993–97, Chair. Hong Kong (now Hong Kong Special Admin. Region) Environment and Conservation Fund Cttee 1994–, Hosp. Authority 1995–; Deputy Chair. Prince of Wales Business Leaders' Forum 1991–; Leader of the Year (Hong Kong Standard) 1995; Cross of Officer, Order of Leopold (Belgium). *Publication:* The Challenge of Hong Kong Plus 1991. *Leisure interests:* golf, tennis. *Address:* Penthouse, Wheelock House, 20 Pedder Street, Central, Hong Kong Special Administrative Region, People's Republic of China.

WOO, Sir PO-SHING, Kt, FCIA., F.I.MGT., FID; British solicitor; b. 19 April 1929, Hong Kong; s. of the late Seaward Woo and of Ng Chiu Man; m. Helen Woo Fong Shuet Fun (Lady Woo) 1956; four s. one d.; ed La Salle Coll., Hong Kong and King's Coll., London; admitted to practice as solicitor in England and Hong Kong 1960; Notary Public 1966; admitted to practice as barrister and solicitor, Supreme Court of Victoria, Australia 1983; founder and Consultant, Woo Kwan Lee & Lo, Solicitors and Notaries 1973; Chair. Kailey Enterprises Ltd, Kailey Devt Ltd; Dir Sun Hung Kai Properties Ltd, Henderson Devt Co. Ltd and over 40 other cos.; mem. Inst. of Admin. Man., Inst. of Trade Mark Agents; f. Woo Po Shing Medal in Law (Hong Kong Univ.) 1982, Woo Po Shing Overseas Summer School Travelling Scholarship (Hong Kong Univ.) 1983, The Po-Shing Woo Charitable Foundation 1994, Woo Po Shing Chair of Chinese and Comparative Law (City Univ.) 1995; fmr mem. Council Univ. of Hong Kong; hon. voting mem. Hong Kong Jockey Club, Po Leung Kuk Advisory Bd, Tung Wah Group of Hosps.; Legal Adviser Chinese Gold and Silver Exchange Soc.; Hon. Pres. and Legal Adviser S. China Athletic Asscn; Patron Woo Po Shing Gallery of Chinese Bronze, Shanghai Museum, The Auckland Observatory (renamed Sir Po-Shing Woo Auckland Observatory Bldg); Hon. Prof. Nankai Univ. of Tianjin, China; Fellow Inst. of Man., Inst. of Dirs, King's Coll., London Univ.; Hong Kong Man. Asscn; Hon. LLD (City Univ. Hong Kong); Hon. LLB (King's Coll. London); World Fellowship of Duke of Edinburgh's Award. *Leisure interests:* travelling, viewing and collecting antiques including Chinese paintings, bronzes and ceramics, racehorses. *Address:* 2/F Kailey Tower, 16 Stanley Street, Central, Hong Kong Special Administrative Region, People's Republic of China. *Telephone:* 2522 4825. *Fax:* 2537 9747.

WOOD, Adrian John Bickersteth, MA, MPA, PhD; British economist; b. 25 Jan. 1946, Woking; s. of the late John H. F. Wood and of Mary E. B. (née Ottley) Brain; m. Joyce M. Teitz 1971; two d.; ed Bryanston School, King's Coll. Cambridge and Harvard Univ.; Fellow, King's Coll. Cambridge 1969–77; Asst Lecturer, Lecturer, Univ. of Cambridge 1973–77; Economist, Sr Economist, IBRD 1977–85; Professorial Fellow, Inst. of Devt Studies, Univ. of Sussex 1985–2000; Chief Economist Dept for Int. Devt 2000–; Harkness Fellowship 1967–69. *Publications:* A Theory of Profits 1975, A Theory of Pay 1978, Poverty and Human Development (with others) 1981, China: Long-Term Development Issues and Options (with others) 1985, North-South Trade, Employment and Inequality 1994. *Leisure interests:* music, art, walking. *Address:* Department of International Development, 1 Palace Street, London, SW1 5HE, England (Office). *Telephone:* (20) 7023-0000. *E-mail:* a-wood@dfid.gov.uk. *Website:* www.dfid.gov.uk.

WOOD, Sir Andrew Marley, GCMG, MA; British diplomatist (retd); b. 2 Jan. 1940, Gibraltar; s. of Robert George Wood; m. 1st Melanie LeRoy Masset 1972 (died 1977); one s.; m. 2nd Stephanie Lee Masset 1978; one s. one d.; ed Ardingly Coll., King's Coll. Cambridge; Foreign Office 1961, served in Moscow 1964, Washington 1967, FCO 1970, Cabinet Office 1971, First Sec., FCO 1973, First Sec. and Head of Chancery, Belgrade 1976, Counsellor 1978, Head of Chancery, Moscow 1979, Head of Western European Dept, FCO 1982, Head of Personnel Operations Dept, FCO 1983, Amb. to Yugoslavia 1985–89, Minister, Washington 1989–92, (Chief Clerk) FCO 1992, Amb. to Russia (also accred to Moldova) 1995–2000; Chair. Britain–Russia Centre, Advisory Council BCB, Exec. Council Russo–British Chamber of Commerce; Dir Foreign and Colonial Investment Trust, PBN Co.; Sr Adviser Ernst and Young; Adviser to HM Govt, BP, Glaxo Smith Kline, Unilever, Advisory Council, Renaissance Capital. *Address:* 15 Platts Lane, London, NW3 7NP, England (Home).

WOOD, Anne, CBE, FRTS; British television producer and educationist; b. 1937, Spennymoor, Co. Durham; m. Barrie Wood; one s. one d.; teacher of

English Language and Literature 1960s; f. Books For Your Children magazine; co-creator and producer TV programme The Book Tower 1979, Ragdolly Anna; Head Children's Programmes TV AM (ITV) 1982–84; f. Ragdoll Ltd (TV production co.) 1984, Creative Dir 1984–; creator (with Robin Stevens) Pob, Rosie and Jim, Tots TV, Brum, Open a Door, Teletubbies (shown in 120 cos. worldwide); Eleanor Farjeon Award for Services to Children's Books 1969, Ronald Politzer Award 1974; for the Book Tower: BAFTA 1979, 1982, Prix Jeunesse 1980; for Tots TV: Prix Jeunesse 1996, BAFTA 1996, 1997; Baird Medal, Royal TV Soc. 1997; numerous awards for Teletubbies including Grand Prize, Winner Pre-School Educ. Category, Prize Int. Contest (Japan) 1997, Children's BAFTA for Best Pre-School Programme 1998, Indies Nickleodeon UK Children's Award 1999, five awards at Int. Licensing Industry Merchandisers' Assen 1999, BBC Audiocall Children's Award 2000; Veuve Clicquot Award for Business Woman of the Year 1999; BAFTA Special Award for Outstanding Contrib. in Children's TV and Film 2000. *Leisure interests:* gardening, reading. *Address:* Ragdoll Limited, Russell House, Ely Street, Stratford-upon-Avon, CV37 6LW, England (Office). *Telephone:* (1789) 404100 (Office). *Fax:* (1789) 404136 (Office). *Website:* www.ragdoll.co.uk (Office).

WOOD, Charles Gerald, FRSL; British scriptwriter and playwright; b. 6 Aug. 1932, St. Peter Port, Guernsey; s. of John Edward Wood and Catherine Mae Wood (née Harris); m. Valerie Elizabeth Newman 1954; one s. one d.; ed King Charles I School, Kidderminster and Birmingham Coll. of Art; corporal 17/21st Lancers 1950–55; factory worker 1955–57; Stage Man., scenic artist, cartoonist, advertising artist 1957–59; Bristol Evening Post 1959–62; mem. Drama Advisory Panel, South Western Arts 1972–73; consultant to Nat. Film Devt Fund 1980–82; mem. Council BAFTA 1991–93; Evening Standard Drama Award 1963 1972, Screenwriters Guild Award 1965, Royal TV Soc. Award 1988, BAFTA Award 1988, Prix Italia 1988, Humanitas Award 2002. *Plays include:* Prisoner and Escort, Spare, John Thomas 1963, Meals on Wheels 1965, Don't Make Me Laugh 1966, Fill the Stage with Happy Hours 1967, Dingo 1967, H 1969, Welfare 1971, Veterans 1972, Jingo 1975, Has 'Washington' Legs? 1978, Red Star 1984, Across from the Garden of Allah 1986; adapted Pirandello's Man, Beast and Virtue 1989, The Mountain Giants 1993, Alexandre Dumas's The Tower 1995. *TV plays include:* Prisoner and Escort, Drill Pig, A Bit of a Holiday, A Bit of an Adventure, Love Lies Bleeding, Dust to Dust. *Screenplays include:* The Knack 1965, Help! 1965, How I Won the War 1967, The Charge of the Light Brigade 1968, The Long Day's Dying 1969, Cuba 1980, Wagner 1983, Red Monarch 1983, Puccini 1984, Tumbledown 1988, Shooting the Hero 1991, An Awfully Big Adventure 1993, England my England (with John Osborne) 1995, The Ghost Road 1996, Mary Stuart 1996, Iris (with Richard Eyre) 1999, Snow White in New York 2001. *TV series:* Don't Forget to Write 1986, My Family and Other Animals 1987, The Settling of the Sun 1987, Sharpe's Company 1994, Sharpe's Regiment 1996, Mute of Malice (Kavanagh QC) 1997, Sharpe's Waterloo 1997, Monsignor Renard 1999. *Publications:* (plays): Cockade 1965, Fill the Stage with Happy Hours 1967, Dingo 1967, H 1970, Veterans 1972, Has 'Washington' Legs? 1978, Tumbledown 1987, Man, Beast and Virtue 1990, The Giants of the Mountain 1994, The Tower 1995, Iris 2002. *Leisure interests:* military and theatrical studies, gardening. *Address:* c/o Sue Rogers, ICM Ltd., Oxford House, 76 Oxford Street, London W1P 1BS, England. *Telephone:* (20) 7636-6565. *E-mail:* charles@wood4760.fsnet.co.uk (Home).

WOOD, Graham Charles, MA, PhD, ScD, F.R.ENG., FRS; British professor of science and engineering; b. 6 Feb. 1934, Farnborough; s. of Cyril Wood and Doris Hilda Wood (née Strange); m. Freda Nancy Waithman 1959; one s. one d.; ed Bromley Grammar School, Kent, Christ's Coll., Cambridge; lecturer, then Sr lecturer, Reader in Corrosion Science UMIST 1961–72, Prof. of Corrosion Science and Eng 1972–97, now Emer. Prof. UMIST and Univ. of Manchester; Vice-Prin. for Academic Devt UMIST 1982–84, Deputy Prin. 1983, Dean of Faculty of Tech. 1987–89, Pro-Vice-Chancellor 1992–97; Chair. Int. Corrosion Council 1993–96; Pres. Inst. of Corrosion Science and Tech. 1978–80; Hon. DSc (UMIST) 2001; U. R. Evans Award, Inst. of Corrosion, C. Wagner Award of Electrochemical Soc., Beilby Medal, Griffith Medal, Inst. of Materials, Cavallaro Medal, European Fed. of Corrosion, European Corrosion Medal, European Fed. of Corrosion. *Publications:* over 400 papers in various learned journals. *Leisure interests:* travel, cricket, walking, history of art, science and politics. *Address:* University of Manchester Institute of Science and Technology, Corrosion and Protection Centre, P.O. Box 88, Manchester, M60 1QD, England. *Telephone:* (161) 200-4850. *Fax:* (161) 200-4865.

WOOD, John; British actor; ed Bedford School, Jesus Coll. Oxford; with Old Vic Co. 1954–56, RSC 1971–. *Stage appearances include:* Enemies, The Man of Mode, Exiles, The Balcony 1971, The Comedy of Errors 1972, Julius Caesar, Titus Andronicus 1972, 1973, Collaborators, A Lesson in Blood and Roses 1973, Sherlock Holmes, Travesties 1974 (Evening Standard Best Actor Award 1974, Tony Award 1976), The Devil's Disciple, Ivanov 1976, Death Trap 1978, Undiscovered Country, Richard III 1979, Piaf, The Provok'd Wife 1980, The Tempest 1988, The Man Who Came to Dinner, The Master Builder 1989, King Lear (Evening Standard Best Actor Award 1991), Love's Labours Lost 1990, The Invention of Love 1997. *Television:* A Tale of Two Cities, Barnaby Rudge 1964–65, The Victorians 1965, The Duel 1966. *Films:* Nicholas and Alexandra 1971, Slaughterhouse Five 1972, War Games 1983, The Madness of King George 1994, Sabrina 1996, Richard III 1996, Jane Eyre 1996, The Gambler 1997, Chocolat 2001. *Address:* c/o Royal Shakespeare Company, Barbican Centre, Silk Street, London, EC2Y 8DS, England.

WOOD, L. John, MA; New Zealand diplomatist; b. 31 March 1944, Kaikoura; s. of Lionel Wood and Margaret Wood; m. 1st Rosemary Taunt 1969 (died 1995); one s.; m. 2nd Rose Newell; ed Lincoln Country Dist High School, Christchurch Boys' High School, Univ. of Canterbury and Balliol Coll. Oxford; joined Ministry of Foreign Affairs 1969; seconded to Treasury 1971–72; Second Sec., later First Sec. Tokyo 1973–76; seconded to Prime Minister's Dept 1976–78; First Sec., later Counsellor and Consul-Gen. Bonn 1978–82; Ministry of Foreign Affairs 1982–83; Minister, Deputy Chief of Mission, Washington, DC 1984–87; Amb. to Iran (also accred to Pakistan and Turkey) 1987–90; Dir N Asia Div. Ministry of External Relations and Trade 1990–91, Deputy Sec. Econ. and Trade Relations 1991–94; Amb. to USA 1994–98, 2001–; Deputy Sec. External Econ. and Trade Policy, Ministry of Foreign Affairs and Trade 1998–2002. *Leisure interests:* rare books and bindings, New Zealand literature, sport, V8 cars. *Address:* New Zealand Embassy, 37 Observatory Circle, NW, Washington, DC 20008, USA; Ministry of Foreign Affairs and Trade, Private Bag 18 901, Wellington, New Zealand. *Telephone:* (202) 328-4851 (Office); (202) 328-4848. *Fax:* (202) 667-5233 (Office). *E-mail:* john.wood@mfat.govt.nz (Office). *Website:* www.mfat.govt.nz (Office).

WOOD, Sir Martin (Francis), Kt, OBE, MA, FRS, DL; British engineer and business executive; b. 19 April 1927; s. of Arthur Henry Wood and Katharine Mary Altham (née Cumberlege) Wood; m. Audrey Buxton (née Stanfield) Wood 1955; one s. one d. one step-s. one step-d.; ed Gresham's, Trinity Coll. Cambridge, Imperial Coll. London, Christ Church Oxford; with Nat. Coal Bd 1953–55; Sr Research Officer, Clarendon Lab., Oxford Univ. 1956–69; f. Oxford Instruments PLC 1959, Chair. 1959–83, Deputy Chair. 1983–; Chair. Nat. Comm. for Superconductivity 1987–91; mem. Advisory Bd for Research Councils 1983–89, ACOST 1990–93, Central Lab. of Research Councils 1995–98; Dir Orbit Precision Machining Ltd 1965–, Oxford Seedcorn Capital Ltd 1986–, Oxford Ventures Group Ltd 1988–, ISIS Innovation Ltd 1989–, Oxford Innovation Ltd 1989–, Newport Tech. Group Ltd 1989–, FARM Africa Ltd 1985–; Tech. Consultant African Medical and Research Foundation; f. Northmoor Trust (for nature conservation), Oxford Trust (for encouragement of study and application of science and tech.); Trustee Oxon Council for Voluntary Action 1994–; Fellow Wolfson Coll., Oxford 1967–94, Hon. Fellow 1994; Hon. Fellow UMIST 1989; Hon. DSc (Cranfield Inst. of Tech.) 1983; Hon. DTech (Loughborough Univ. of Tech.) 1985, Hon. DEng (Birmingham) 1997; DUniv (Open) 1999; Mullard Medal, Royal Soc. 1982. *Address:* c/o Oxford Instruments Group PLC, Old Station Way, Eynsham, Witney, Oxon., OX8 1TL, England. *Telephone:* (1865) 881437.

WOOD, Maurice, MB, BS, FRCGP, FAAFP; American physician; b. 28 June 1922, Pelton, Co. Durham, England; s. of Joseph Wood and Eugenie (Lumley) Wood; m. Erica J. Noble 1948; two s. one d.; ed Chester-le-Street Grammar School and Univ. of Durham; various hosp. appointments 1945–46, 1949-50; Maj., RAMC 1946–49; Sr Partner, Medical Practice, South Shields 1950–71; Gen. Practice Teaching Group, Univ. of Newcastle-upon-Tyne 1969–71; Clinical Asst Dept of Psychological Medicine, South Shields Gen. Hosp. 1966–71; Assoc. Prof., Dir of Research, Dept of Family Practice, Medical Coll. of Va, Va Commonwealth Univ., Richmond, Va 1971–73, Prof. and Dir of Research 1973–87, Prof. Emer. 1987–; Exec. Dir N American Primary Care Research Group 1983–92; Consultant Adviser, WHO 1979–90; other professional appointments and memberships; mem. Inst. of Medicine, NAS; Maurice Wood Award, N American Primary Care Research Group 1995 and other awards and distinctions. *Publications:* International Class of Primary Care 1987, The International Classification of Primary Care in the European Community – with a multilanguage layer (co-ed.) 1993; numerous articles in professional journals and book chapters. *Leisure interests:* sailing, gliding, skiing. *Address:* Department of Family Practice, Medical College of Virginia, Medical College of Virginia Station, Box 251, Richmond, VA 23298-001; Route 1, Box 672, Roseland, VA 22967, USA. *Telephone:* (804) 786-9625; (804) 325-1383. *Fax:* (804) 325-1383. *E-mail:* wood150w@aol.com (Home); wood150w@earthlink.net (Home).

WOOD, Rt Rev Maurice Arthur Ponsonby, DSC, MA, RNR; British ecclesiastic; b. 26 Aug. 1916, London; s. of the late Arthur S. Wood and of Jane Elspeth (née Piper) Wood; m. 1st Marjorie Pennell 1947 (died 1954); two s. one d.; m. 2nd M. Margaret Sandford 1955; two s. one d.; ed Monkton Combe School, Queens' Coll., Cambridge and Ridley Hall, Cambridge; ordained 1940; Curate, St Paul's Portman Square, London 1940–43; Royal Naval Chaplain 1943–47; Rector, St Ebbe's Oxford 1947–52; Vicar and Rural Dean of Islington 1952–61; Prin., Oak Hill Theological Coll., Southgate, London 1961–71; Bishop of Norwich 1971–85; Hon. Chaplain, RNR 1971–, an Hon. Asst Bishop, Diocese of London 1985–, Diocese of Oxford 1989–94; Resident Priest of Englefield 1987–94; entered House of Lords 1975; Chaplain, Commando Assen, Worshipful Co. of Weavers –1995, Freeman 1995–; Chair. Order of Christian Unity 1986–96, Pres. 1996–; Gov. Monkton Combe School, Bath, St Helen's School, Abingdon 1989–; Visitor Luckley-Oakfield School 1990–. *Publications:* Like a Mighty Army 1956, Your Suffering 1959, Christian Stability 1968, To Everyman's Door 1968, Into the Way of Peace 1982, This is our Faith 1985, Comfort in Sorrow 1992. *Leisure interests:* painting, supporting Dr Billy Graham (q.v.) and Norwich City Football Club. *Address:* Stuart Court, High Street, Kibworth Beauchamp, Leicester, LE8 0LR; Abbot's Cottage, Horning, Norfolk, NR12 8NE, England. *Telephone:* (116) 279-6266.

WOOD, Peter, CBE; British business executive; m.; five d.; Founder, CEO Direct Line Insurance 1985–96, Chair. 1996–97; Chair. Privilege Insurance 1993; Vice-Chair. Direct Response Corpn and Homeowners Direct Corpn,

USA; Chair. Esure 2000–; Dir (non-exec.) The Economist Newspaper Ltd 1998–. *Address:* Esure, The Observatory, Castleford Road, Reigate, Surrey, RH2 0SG, England (Office).

WOOD, Peter (Lawrence); British theatre and television director; b. 8 Oct. 1928; s. of Frank Wood and Lucy E. Meeson; ed Taunton School and Downing Coll. Cambridge; Resident Dir Arts Theatre 1956–57; Assoc. Dir Nat. Theatre 1978–89; numerous other productions at theatres in London, Edin., New York, Stratford (Ont.), Vienna etc.; Dir of plays for TV in USA and UK since 1970. *Theatre productions include:* (for Nat. Theatre) The Master Builder 1964, Love for Love 1965, 1985, Jumpers 1972, The Guardsman, The Double Dealer 1978, Undiscovered Country 1979, The Provok'd Wife 1980, On the Razzle 1981, The Rivals 1983, Rough Crossing 1984, Dalliance 1986, The Threepenny Opera 1986, The American Clock 1986, The Beaux' Stratagem 1989, The School for Scandal 1990, (for RSC) Winter's Tale 1960, The Devils 1961, Hamlet 1961, The Beggar's Opera 1963, Travesties 1974, The Strange Case of Dr. Jekyll and Mr. Hyde 1991, Indian Ink 1995, (for Chichester) The Silver King 1990, She Stoops to Conquer 1992, Arcadia 2000, On the Razzle 2001. *Opera productions include:* The Mother of Us All, Santa Fe 1976, Il Seraglio, Glyndebourne 1980, 1988, Don Giovanni, Covent Garden 1981, Macbeth, Staatsoper, Vienna 1982, Orione, Santa Fe 1983, Otello, Staatsoper, Vienna 1987. *Leisure interests:* swimming, sailing, travelling. *Address:* The Old Barn, Batcombe, Somerset, BA4 6HD, England.

WOOD, Ronald Karslake Starr, FRS; British professor of plant pathology; b. 8 April 1919, Ferndale; s. of Percival T. E. Wood and Florence Dix Starr; m. Marjorie Schofield 1947; one s. one d.; ed Ferndale Grammar School and Imperial Coll., London; Ministry of Aircraft Production 1942; Royal Scholar, Lecturer Imperial Coll. 1947, Reader in Plant Pathology 1955, Prof. of Plant Pathology 1964–86, mem. Governing Body, Head Dept of Pure and Applied Biology 1981–84, Sr Research Fellow 1986–, Prof. Emer. 1986–; Dean Royal Coll. of Science 1975; Dir NATO Advanced Study Insts. 1970, 1975, 1980; Sir C. V. Raman Prof. Univ. of Madras 1980; Regent's Lecturer Univ. of Calif. 1981; Otto-Appel Denkmünster 1978; Sec.-Gen. 1st Int. Congress of Plant Pathology 1968, Hon. Pres. 7th Int. Congress (Edin.) 1998; Founder Pres. Int. Soc. for Plant Pathology 1968, British Soc. for Plant Pathology, now Hon. mem.; Commonwealth Fund Fellow 1950, Research Fellow Conn. Agricultural Experimental Station 1957, Fellow American Phytopathological Soc. 1976, Thurburn Fellow Univ. of Sydney 1979; Vice-Chair. Governing Body E Malling Research Station; Gov. Inst. of Horticultural Research; Corresp. mem. Deutsche Phytomedizinische Gesellschaft 1973. *Publications:* Physiological Plant Pathology 1967, Phytotoxins in Plant Diseases (Ed. with A. Ballio and A. Graniti) 1972, Specificity in Plant Diseases (Ed. with A. Graniti) 1976, Active Defence Mechanisms in Plants (Ed.) 1981, Plant Diseases: infection, damage and loss (Ed.) 1984; numerous papers in scientific journals. *Leisure interest:* gardening. *Address:* Department of Biology, Imperial College, London, SW7 2AZ (Office); Pyrford Woods, Pyrford, Nr. Woking, Surrey, England (Home). *Telephone:* (20) 7589-5111 (Office); (19323) 43827 (Home). *Fax:* (20) 7584-2056. *E-mail:* r.carpenter@ic.ac.uk.

WOOD, Ronnie (Ronald); British musician; b. 1 June 1947; m. 1st; one s.; m. 2nd Jo Howard 1985; one s. one d.; guitarist with Jeff Beck Group 1968–69, The Faces 1969–75, The Rolling Stones 1975–; albums with Jeff Beck Group: Truth 1968, Beck-Ola 1969, with The Faces: First Step 1970, Long Player 1971, A Nod's As Good As A Wink... To A Blind Horse 1971, Ooh La La 1973, Coast To Coast Overtures and Beginners 1974, with The Rolling Stones: Black and Blue 1976, Love You Live 1977, Some Girls 1978, Emotional Rescue 1980, Tattoo You 1981, Still Life 1981, Undercover 1983, Rewind 1971–1984 1984, Dirty Work 1986, Steel Wheels 1989, Flashpoint 1991, Voodoo Lounge 1994, solo albums include: Slide on This 1992; films include: Let's Spend the Night Together 1983, Flashpoint 1991; has also played with Bo Diddley, Rod Stewart, Jerry Lee Lewis. *Address:* c/o Monroe Sounds, 5 Church Row, Wandsworth Plain, London, SW18 1ES, England. *Website:* www.ronniewood.com.

WOOD, William B., III, PhD; American professor of biology; b. 19 Feb. 1938, Baltimore, Md; s. of Dr. W. Barry Wood, Jr and Mary L. Hutchins; m. Renate Marie-Elisabeth Hartisch 1961; two s.; ed Harvard Coll., Stanford Univ. and Univ. of Geneva; Nat. Acad. of Sciences—Nat. Research Council Postdoctoral Fellow, Univ. of Geneva 1964; Asst Prof. of Biology, Calif. Inst. of Tech. 1965–68, Assoc. Prof. 1968–70, Prof. 1970–77; Prof. of Molecular Biology, Univ. of Colo, Boulder 1977–, Chair. of Dept 1978–83; mem. NAS, American Acad. of Arts and Sciences, AAAS, American Soc. of Biological Chemists, Soc. for Developmental Biology; U.S. Steel Award in Molecular Biology, NAS 1969. *Publications:* Biochemistry, A Problems Approach (with J. H. Wilson, R. M. Benbow and L. E. Hood) 1974, 1981, Molecular Design in Living Systems 1974, The Molecular Basis of Metabolism 1974, Molecular Biology of Eucaryotic Cells (with L. E. Hood and J. H. Wilson) 1975, Immunology (with L. E. Hood and I. Weissman) 1978, 1984, The Nematode Caenorhabditis Elegans (Ed.) 1988; articles in professional journals. *Leisure interests:* music, tennis, camping. *Address:* Department of Molecular, Cellular and Developmental Biology, Box 347, University of Colorado, Boulder, CO 80309, USA.

WOODHEAD, Christopher Anthony, MA; British academic; b. 20 Oct. 1946, Middx; s. of Anthony Woodhead and Doris Woodhead; m. 1970 (divorced 1995); one d.; ed Wallington Co. Grammar School, Univs. of Bristol and Keele; English teacher Priory School, Shrewsbury 1969–72; Deputy Head of English Newent School, Gloucester 1972–74; Head of English Gordano School, Avon 1974–76; lecturer in English Oxford Univ. 1976–82; English Adviser Shropshire Local Educ. Authority 1982–84, Chief Adviser 1984–86; Deputy Chief Educ. Officer Devon Local Educ. Authority 1988–90, Cornwall Local Educ. Authority 1990–91; Deputy Chief Exec. Nat. Curriculum Council 1990, Chief Exec. 1991–93; Chief Exec. School Curriculum and Assessment Authority 1993–94; HM Chief Inspector of Schools 1994–2001; Prof., Univ. of Buckingham 2002–; columnist, Sunday Times. *Publication:* Class War 2002. *Leisure interests:* rock climbing, running. *Address:* Hendre Gwenllian, Llanfrothen, Penrhyndeudraeth, Gwynedd, LL48 6DJ, Wales.

WOODHOUSE, Rt. Hon. Sir (Arthur) Owen, Kt, PC, KBE, DSC, LLB; New Zealand judge; b. 18 July 1916, Napier; s. of the late Arthur James Woodhouse and Wilhemina Catherine Woodhouse (née Allen); m. Margaret Leah Thorp 1940; four s. two d.; ed Napier Boys' High School and Auckland Univ.; mil. and naval service 1939–45, Lieut.-Commdr. RNZNVR; liaison officer with Yugoslav partisans 1943; Asst to Naval Attaché, British Embassy 1945; joined Lusk, Willis & Sproule, barristers and solicitors 1946; Crown Solicitor, Napier 1953; Judge of Supreme Court 1961–86; a Judge of Court of Appeal 1974–86; Pres. Court of Appeal 1981–86; Founding Pres. Law Comm. 1986–91; Chair. Royal Comm. on Compensation and Rehabilitation in respect of Personal Injury in New Zealand 1966–67, Chair. inquiry into similar questions in Australia 1973–74; Hon. LLD (Victoria Univ. of Wellington) 1978, (Univ. of York, Toronto, Canada) 1981. *Leisure interests:* music, golf. *Address:* 244 Remuera Road, Auckland 1005, New Zealand.

WOODLAND, Alan Donald, PhD, FASSA; Australian professor of econometrics; b. 4 Oct. 1943, Dorrigo, NSW; s. of C. J. Woodland and E. Shephard; m. Narelle Todd 1966; one s. two d.; ed Univ. of New England; lecturer, Univ. of New England 1967–69; Asst Prof. Univ. of British Col 1969–74, Assoc. Prof. 1974–78, Prof. of Econs 1978–81; Prof. of Econometrics, Univ. of Sydney 1982–; Jt Ed. The Economic Record 1987–92; Fellow, Reserve Bank 1981; Fellow, Econometric Soc. *Publication:* International Trade and Resource Allocation 1982. *Leisure interests:* bridge, tennis. *Address:* 5 Rosebery Road, Killara, NSW 2071, Australia. *Telephone:* (2) 9416-3100; (2) 9351-6825. *Fax:* (2) 9351-6409. *E-mail:* a.woodland@econ.usyd.edu.au (Office).

WOODROW, Bill (William Robert), DFA, RA; British artist and sculptor; b. 1 Nov. 1948, nr Henley-on-Thames, Oxon.; s. of Geoffrey W. Woodrow and Doreen M. Fasken; m. Pauline Rowley 1970; one s. one d.; ed Barton Peveril Grammar School and Winchester, St Martin's and Chelsea Schools of Art; numerous solo exhbns in UK, FRG, France, Australia, Netherlands, Belgium, Italy, USA, Canada, Switzerland, Sweden, Ireland and Yugoslavia since 1979; works in many public collections in UK and abroad; Trustee Tate Gallery 1996–2001; elected to Royal Acad. of Arts 2002; finalist in Turner Prize 1986, winner Anne Gerber Award, Seattle Museum of Art, USA 1988. *Exhibitions include:* Fools' Gold, Duveen Galleries, Tate Gallery, London/Institut Mathildenhöhe, Darmstadt 1996, Regardless of History, Fourth Plinth, Trafalgar Square, London 2000–01, Beekeeper, South London Gallery/Mappin Art Gallery, Sheffield 2001, Glyn Vivian Art Gallery, Swansea 2002; has participated in many group exhbns. around the world including British Sculpture in the 20th Century (Whitechapel Gallery), An Int. Survey of Recent Painting and Sculpture (Museum of Modern Art, NY), Skulptur im 20. Jahrhundert (Basle), Carnegie Int. (Pittsburgh) 1985, British Sculpture since 1965 (toured USA) 1987, Great Britain to USSR (Kiev, Moscow) 1990, Metropolis (Berlin) 1991, Ripples across the Water, (Tsurugi and Tokyo) 1994–95, Un Siècle de sculpture anglaise, (Jeu de Paume, Paris) 1996, Sexta Bienal de la Habana (Cuba) 1997, Forjar el Espacio (CAAM, Gran Canaria) 1998 Field Day, Sculpture from Britain (Taipei Fine Arts Museum, Taiwan) 2001; represented Britain at Biennales of Sydney 1982, Paris 1982, São Paulo 1983, 1991, Paris 1985. *Publications include:* Bill Woodrow, Sculpture 1980–86, A Quiet Revolution – Recent British Sculpture, Bill Woodrow, Eye of the Needle, Sculptures 1987–1989, Bill Woodrow, XXI Bienal de São Paulo 1991, In Awe of the Pawnbroker 1994, Fools' Gold 1996. *Address:* 14 Cormont Road, London, SE5 9RA, England. *Telephone:* (20) 7733-2435. *Fax:* (20) 7733-9585. *E-mail:* bill@billwoodrow.com (Office). *Website:* www.billwoodrow.com (Office).

WOODRUFF, Judy Carline, BA; American broadcast journalist; b. 20 Nov. 1946, Tulsa, Okla; d. of William Henry Woodruff and Anna Lee (Payne) Woodruff; m. Albert R. Hunt, Jr 1980; two s. one d.; ed Meredith Coll., Duke Univ.; News Announcer, Reporter WAGA-TV, Atlanta 1970–75; News Corresp. NBC News, Atlanta 1975–76; White House Corresp., NBC News, Washington 1977–83; Corresp. MacNeil-Lehrer News Hour, PBS, Washington 1983–93; Anchor, Sr Corresp. CNN 1993–; Anchor for Frontline (PBS documentary series) 1983–90; mem. Bd of Advisers Henry Grady School of Journalism, Univ. of Ga 1979–82, Bd of Visitors Wake Forest Univ. 1982–88; mem. Bd of Advisers, Benton Fellowship in Broadcast Journalism, Univ. of Chicago 1984–90, Families and Work Inst. 1989–, Freedom Forum First Amendment Center 1992–, Comm. on Women's Health 1993–, Radio and TV News Dirs.' Foundation 1994–; Trustee Duke Univ. 1985–; Co-Chair. Int. Women's Media Foundation 1991– (Founder, Dir 1989–); Kt Fellowship in Journalism, Stanford Univ. 1985–; mem. Nat. Acad. of TV Arts and Sciences, White House Corresps. Asscn; numerous awards. *Publication:* This is Judy Woodruff at the White House 1982. *Address:* Cable News Network, 820 1st Street, NE, Washington, DC 20002, USA.

WOODS, James; American actor; b. 18 April 1947, Vernal, Utah; s. of Gail Woods and Martha Woods; m. 1st Kathryn Greko 1980 (divorced 1983); m. 2nd

Sarah Owen 1989; ed Univ. of California Los Angeles and Massachusetts Inst. of Tech.; first Broadway appearance in Brendan Behan's Borstal Boy; Obie Award for appearance in Brooklyn Acad. of Music Production of Edward Bond's Saved, New York 1971; other stage appearances in 1970s include Moonchildren 1972, The Trial of the Catonsville Nine, Finishing Touches, Conduct Unbecoming; many appearances in films and TV films; two Emmy awards. *Films include:* The Visitors 1971, The Way We Were 1972, The Gambler 1974, Distance 1975, Alex and the Gypsy 1976, The Choirboys 1977, The Onion Field 1979, Black Marble 1980, Fast Walking 1982, Split Image 1982, Videodrome 1983, Once Upon a Time in America 1984, Against All Odds 1984, Joshua Then and Now 1985, Best Seller 1987, Cop 1987, The Boost 1989, True Believer 1989, Immediate Family 1989, Straight Talk 1992, Diggstown, Chaplin 1992, The Getaway 1994, Curse of the Starving Class 1994, Casino 1995, Nixon 1996, Killer: A Journal of Murder, Ghosts of Mississippi 1996, Hercules (voice) 1997, Contact 1997, Vampires 1998, True Crime 1999, Virgin Suicides 2000, Race to Space 2001, John Q 2001, Recess, School's Out (voice) 2001, Riding in Cars with Boys 2001, Scary Movie 2 2001. *Television films include:* Holocaust 1978, Badge of the Assassin 1985, Promise 1986, My Name is Bill. W. 1989, Next Door 1994, The Summer of Ben Tyler 1996, Dirty Pictures 2000, Showtime 2000. *Address:* c/o Guttman Assocs., 118 S. Beverly Drive, Suite 201, Beverly Hills, CA 90210, USA.

WOODS, Michael, PhD; Irish politician; b. 8 Dec. 1935, Bray, Co. Wicklow; m. Margaret Maher; three s. two d.; ed Univ. Coll. Dublin and Harvard Business School, USA; Lecturer, Franciscan Coll. of Agric., Multyfarnham, Co. Westmeath 1958; Head of Dept and Prin. Officer, Agric. Research Inst. 1960–70; Man. Dir F11 Produce Ltd 1970–73, Associated Producer Groups Ltd 1974–79; mem Dáil 1977–; Minister of State, Depts. of Taoiseach and Defence 1979; Minister for Health and Social Welfare 1979–81, March–Dec. 1982, for Social Welfare 1987–91, for Agric. 1991–92, for the Marine 1992, for Social Welfare 1993–94, Health 1994, for Marine and Natural Resources 1997–2000, for Educ. and Science 2000–; Spokesperson on Equality and Law Reform 1994–97; Fianna Fáil. *Publications:* Research in Ireland—Key to Economic and Social Development; numerous tech. and scientific papers. *Address:* Department of Education and Science, Marlborough Street, Dublin 1 (Office); 13 Kilbarrack Grove, Raheny, Dublin 5, Ireland. *Telephone:* (1) 8734700 (Office). *Fax:* (1) 8729553 (Office).

WOODS, Philip Wells (Phil), BMus; American jazz musician (alto saxophonist), composer and teacher; b. 2 Nov. 1931, Springfield, Mass.; s. of Stanley J. Woods and Clara Markley; m. 1st Beverly Berg 1957 (divorced 1973); one s. one d.; m. 2nd Jill Goodwin 1985; two step-d.; ed pvtly. with Harvey LaRose in Springfield, Lenny Tristano in New York, Manhattan School of Music and Juilliard Conservatory; numerous appearances and recordings with bands, as featured performer and with own groups Clark Terry Big Bad Band (co-founder), The European Rhythm Machine (his European group 1968–73), The Phil Woods Quartet 1974–83, The Phil Woods Quintet (leader) 1984–, Phil Woods Little Big Band (leader), Phil Woods Big Band 1998–; featured on soundtrack scores of films The Hustler, Blow-Up, Twelve Angry Men, Boy in a Tree, It's My Turn; Hon. LLD (East Stroudsberg Univ.) 1994; Officier des Arts et des Lettres; recipient of 4 Grammy Awards; Beacon Jazz Award 2001. *Compositions include:* Three Improvisations (saxophone quartet), Sonata for Alto and Piano (Four Moods), Rights of Swing, The Sun Suite, I Remember, The Deer Head Suite, Fill the Woods with Light (for Parsons Dance Co.). *Leisure interests:* computer games, reading, public television, movies. *Address:* P.O. Box 278, Delaware Water Gap, PA 18327, USA. *Telephone:* (570) 421-3145. *Website:* www.philwoods.com (Office).

WOODS, Tiger (Eldrick); American golfer; b. 30 Dec. 1975, Cypress, Calif.; s. of Lt-Col Earl Woods and Kultida Woods; ed Stanford Univ.; winner Int. Jr World Championship 1984–91, Nat. Youth Classic 1990, US Jr Amateur Championship 1991 (youngest winner), 1992, 1993, US Amateur Championships 1994 (youngest winner), 1995, 1996, Las Vegas Invitational competition 1996, Walt Disney Classic 1996, Honda Asian Classic 1997, Mercedes Championships 1997, 2000, US Masters 1997 (youngest winner, broke records for lowest score and greatest margin of victory), 2001, 2002, Bell South Classic 1998, US PGA Championship 1999, 2000, Nat. Car Rental Golf Classic 1999, WGC American Express Championship 1999, AT & T Pebble Beach Nat. Pro-Am. 2000, Bay Hill Invitational 2000, 2001, 2002 US Open 2000, 2002, British Open 2000, winner of numerous other titles; mem. US team World Amateur Team Championship 1994, US Walker Cup team 1995, Ryder Cup 1997, 1999, 2002 (postponed from 2001); contract with Nike 1999 (biggest sponsorship deal in sporting history); f. Tiger Woods Foundation; winner of record prize money (over 33 million dollars at end of 2002); numerous awards including Sports Star of the Year Award 1997, PGA Tour Player of the Year 1997, 1999–2002; Sports Illustrated Sportsman of the Year 1996, 2000. *Leisure interests:* basketball, fishing, sport in general. *Address:* PGA, P.O. Box 109601, 100 Avenue of the Champions, Palm Beach Gardens, FL 33418, USA. *Website:* www.tigerwoods.com.

WOODWARD, Edward, OBE; British actor and singer; b. 1 June 1930, Croydon, Surrey; s. of Edward Oliver Woodward and Violet Edith Woodward; m. 1st Venetia Mary Collett 1952; two s. one d.; m. 2nd Michele Dotrice 1987; one d.; ed Kingston Coll. and Royal Acad. of Dramatic Art; stage debut Castle Theatre, Farnham 1946; in repertory cos. in England and Scotland; London debut, Where There's a Will, Garrick Theatre 1955; 12 LP records as singer and three of poetry and 14 talking book recordings; numerous int. and nat. acting awards, including Golden Globe Award, Emmy Award, Variety Award

(Best Musical Performance). *Other stage appearances include:* Mercutio in Romeo and Juliet, Laertes in Hamlet, Stratford 1958, Rattle of a Simple Man, Garrick 1962, Two Cities (musical) 1968, Cyrano in Cyrano de Bergerac, Flamineo in The White Devil, Nat. Theatre Co. 1971, The Wolf, Apollo 1973, Male of the Species, Piccadilly 1975, On Approval, Theatre Royal Haymarket 1976, The Dark Horse, Comedy 1978, Beggar's Opera (also Dir) 1980, The Assassin 1982, Richard III 1982, The Dead Secret 1992; three productions, New York. *Films include:* Becket 1966, The File on the Golden Goose 1968, Hunted 1973, Sitting Target, Young Winston, The Wicker Man 1974, Stand Up Virgin Soldiers 1977, Breaker Morant 1980, The Appointment 1981, Comeback, Merlin and the Sword 1982, Champions 1983, A Christmas Carol, King David 1984, Uncle Tom's Cabin 1989, Mister Johnson 1990, Deadly Advice 1993, A Christmas Reunion 1994, Gulliver's Travels 1995. *Television include:* over 2000 TV productions; title role in TV serials Callan 1966–71, The Equalizer 1985–89, Over My Dead Body 1990, In Suspicious Circumstances (series) 1991–94, In My Defence 1991, America At Risk (series) 1991–92, Harrison (series, USA) 1993–95, Common as Muck (BBC TV series) 1994, The Woodward File (series) 1995–96, Gulliver's Travels (mini-series) 1995–96, The New Professionals (series) 1998–99, Emma's Boy 2000, Nikita (series) 2000, Night and Day 2001, Messiah 2001. *Leisure interests:* boating, geology. *Address:* c/o Janet Glass, Eric Glass Ltd 28 Berkeley Square, London, W1X 6HD, England. *Telephone:* (20) 7629-7162. *Fax:* (20) 7499-6980.

WOODWARD, Joanne Gignilliat; American actress; b. 27 Feb. 1930, Thomasville, Ga; d. of Wade Woodward and Elinor Trimmier; m. Paul Newman (q.v.) 1958; three d.; ed Louisiana State Univ.; numerous awards including Foreign Press Award for Best Actress 1957, Acad. Award 1957, Nat. Bd Review Award 1957, Best Actress Award, Soc. of Film and TV Arts 1974; Franklin D. Roosevelt Four Freedoms Medal 1991, Kennedy Center Honor 1992. *Films include:* Count Three and Pray 1955, A Kiss Before Dying 1956, The Three Faces of Eve 1957, The Long Hot Summer 1958, Rally Round the Flag Boys 1958, The Sound and the Fury 1959, The Fugitive Kind 1959, From the Terrace 1960, Paris Blues 1961, The Stripper 1963, A New Kind of Love 1963, Signpost to Murder 1964, A Big Hand for the Little Lady 1966, A Fine Madness 1966, Rachel Rachel 1968, Winning 1969, W.U.S.A. 1970, They Might Be Giants 1971, The Effects of Gamma Rays on Man-in-the-Moon Marigolds 1972, The Death of a Snow Queen 1973, Summer Wishes, Winter Dreams 1973, The Drowning Pool 1975, The End 1978, The Shadow Box 1980, Candida (Play) 1981, Harry and Son 1984, The Glass Menagerie 1987, Mr and Mrs Bridge 1990, Philadelphia 1993, My Knees Were Jumping: Remembering the Kindertransports (voice) 1998. *Television includes:* All the Way Home, See How She Runs 1978, Streets of LA 1979, Crisis at Central High 1981, Do You Remember Love? 1985, Blind Spot 1993, Breathing Lessons 1994, James Dean: A Portrait 1996. *Address:* ICM, 40 W 57th Street, New York, NY 10019, USA.

WOODWARD, Adm. Sir John Forster, GBE, KCB; British naval officer (retd); b. 1 May 1932, Marazion, Cornwall; s. of the late Tom Woodward and Mabel B. M. Woodward; m. Charlotte M. McMurtrie 1960; one s. one d.; ed Britannia Royal Naval Coll., Dartmouth; Commanding Officer, HMS Tireless 1961–62, HMS Grampus 1964–65; Exec. Officer, HMS Valiant 1965–67; Commdg Officer, HMS Warspite 1969–71; at Royal Coll. of Defence Studies, then in Directorate of Naval Plans, Ministry of Defence; Commdg Officer, HMS Sheffield 1976–78; Dir of Naval Plans, Ministry of Defence 1978–81; Flag Officer, First Flotilla 1981–83; Sr Task Group Commdr during Falkland Islands campaign 1982; Flag Officer, Submarines and Commdr Submarines, Eastern Atlantic, NATO 1983–84; Deputy Chief of Defence Staff (Commitments) 1985–87; C-in-C Naval Home Command 1987–89, rank of Adm.; Flag Aide-de-Camp to HM the Queen 1987–89; Man. consultant Yachtmaster Ocean (Royal Yachting Asscn); Pres. Falkland Island Memorial Chapel Trust 2001–. *Publications:* Strategy by Matrix 1980, One Hundred Days (autobiog.) 1992. *Leisure interests:* sailing, philately, desktop computers. *Address:* c/o The Naval Secretary, Victory Building, HM Naval Base, Portsmouth, Hants, PO1 3LS, England.

WOODWARD, Kirsten; British couturier; b. 15 Nov. 1959, London; d. of Prof. Woodward and J. B. Woodward; ed London Coll. of Fashion; stall at Hyper Hyper while still a student 1983; Designer Karl Lagerfeld 1984–; f. Kirsten Woodward Hats 1985–; also designed for Lanvin, Victor Edelstein, Betty Jackson, Alistair Blair, The Emanuels, Belleville Sassoon, Katharine Hammnet. *Leisure interests:* boats, horses, geography and ancient history, anthropology, writing.

WOODWARD, Robert Upshur (Bob), BA; American journalist; b. 26 March 1943, Geneva, Ill.; s. of Alfred Woodward and Jane Upshur; m. Elsa Walsh 1989; two c.; ed Yale Univ.; reporter, Montgomery Co. (Md) Sentinel 1970–71; reporter, Washington Post 1971–78, Metropolitan Ed. 1979–81, Asst Man. Ed. 1981–. *Publications:* All the President's Men (with Carl Bernstein) 1974, The Final Days 1976, The Brethren (with Scott Armstrong) 1979, Wired 1984, Veil: The Secret Wars of the CIA 1987, The Commanders 1991, The Man Who Would Be President (with D. S. Broder) 1992, The Agenda: Inside the Clinton White House 1994, The Choice 1996, Shadow: Five Presidents and the Legacy of Watergate 1999, Maestro, Greenspan's Fed and the American Boom 2000, Bush at War... Inside the Bush White House 2002. *Address:* Washington Post Co., 1150 15th Street, NW, Washington, DC 20071, USA.

WOODWARD, Roger Robert, OBE, AC; Australian pianist, conductor and composer; b. 20 Dec. 1942, Sydney; s. of Francis W. Woodward and Gladys A.

Woodward; one s. one d.; ed Conservatorium of Music, Sydney and PWSH, Warsaw; début at Royal Festival Hall, London 1970; subsequently appeared with the five London orchestras; has performed throughout Eastern and Western Europe, Japan and the USA; has appeared at int. festivals and with the maj. orchestras throughout world; extensive repertoire and is noted for interpretation of Chopin, Beethoven, Bach and Twentieth Century Music; Artistic Dir Nat. Chamber Orchestra for Contemporary Music in Australia 'Alpha Centaure' 1989 and festivals in London; performs each season at leading int. festivals works by contemporary composers; Nat. Treas. 1998; Fellow Chopin Inst., Warsaw 1976; Kt (Breffini) 1985. *Leisure interests:* cooking, chess, swimming, gardening, painting, design. *Address:* LH Productions, 2/37 Hendy Avenue, Coogee, NSW 2034, Australia. *E-mail:* woodward@metz.une.edu.au.

WOOLARD, Edgar Smith, Jr., BSc; American business executive; b. 15 April 1934, Washington, NC; s. of Edgar Smith and Mamie (née Boone) Woolard; m. Peggy Harrell 1956; two d.; ed North Carolina State Univ.; fmr Lt, US Army; industrial engineer, Du Pont at Kinston, NC 1957–59, various supervisory and managerial posts 1959–75, Man. Dir textile marketing div. 1975–76, Man. corp. plans dept 1976–77, Gen. Dir products and planning div. 1977–78, Gen. Man. textile fibers, Wilmington, Del. 1978–81, Vice-Pres. textile fibers 1981–83, Exec. Vice-Pres. 1983–85, Vice-Chair. 1985–87, Pres. and COO 1987–89, Chair., CEO 1989–96, Chair. 1996–98, also mem. Bd of Dirs. 1996–; mem. Bd of Dirs. Citicorp, New York, Council for Aid to Educ., New York, IBM, New York, Apple Computer Inc., Cupertino, Calif., Jt Council on Econ. Educ., New York, NC Textile Foundation, Raleigh, Seagram Co., Canada; Int. Palladium Medal Soc. Chimie Industrielle (American Section) 1995. *Address:* c/o Du Pont, 1007 Market Street, Wilmington, DE 19801, USA.

WOOLCOTT, Richard, AC, AO, BA; Australian fmr diplomatist, consultant and company director; b. 11 June 1927, Sydney; s. of Dr and Mrs A. R. Woolcott; m. Birgit Christensen 1952; two s. one d.; ed Frankston High School, Geelong Grammar School, Univ. of Melbourne and London Univ. School of Slavonic and E European Studies; joined Australian Foreign Service 1951; served in Australian missions in London, Moscow (twice), S Africa, Malaya, Singapore and Ghana; attended UN Gen. Ass. 1962; Acting Commr to Singapore 1963–64; High Commr to Ghana 1967–70; accompanied Prime Ministers Menzies 1965, Holt 1966, McMahon 1971, 1972, Whitlam 1973, 1974 and Hawke 1988–91 on visits to Asia, Europe, the Americas and the Pacific; Adviser at Commonwealth Heads of Govt Confs London 1965, Ottawa 1973, Kuala Lumpur 1989; Pacific Forum 1972, 1973, 1988; Australia-Japan Ministerial Cttee 1972, 1973, 1989; Head, S Asia Div., Dept of Foreign Affairs 1973; Deputy Sec. Dept of Foreign Affairs 1974; Amb. to Indonesia 1975–78, to Philippines 1978–82; Perm. Rep. to UN 1982–88; Sec. of Dept of Foreign Affairs and Trade 1988–92; Prime Minister's Special Envoy to develop Asia Pacific Econ. Co-operation 1989; Australian Rep. on UN Security Council 1985–86; rep. of Australia at Non-aligned Summit meeting, Harare 1986; ASEAN Post-Ministerial Conf. 1989, 1990, 1991; Alt. Australian Gov., inaugural EBRD meeting 1991; Chair. Australia Indonesia Inst. 1992–98, Official Establishments Trust 1992–99, Nat. Cttee on Population and Devt 1993–95, Across Asia Multimedia (Hong Kong) 2000–; Dir Auric Pacific (Singapore) 2001–02; mem. int. council of The Asia Soc.; Vice-Pres. Multiple Sclerosis Soc. of Australia 1995–2000; Founding Dir Australasia Centre, Asia Soc. 1997–; Founding Dir or consultant several firms; mem. Bd of Commrs, Lippo Bank, Indonesia 1999–2002; Life Fellow Trinity Coll., Melbourne Univ. 1995; Bintang Mahaputra Utama (Indonesia) 2000. *Publications:* Australian Foreign Policy 1973, The Hot Seat: Reflections on Diplomacy From Stalin's Death to the Bali Bombings 2003; numerous articles, including special features for The Australian, articles for Int. Herald Tribune, Time. *Leisure interests:* writing, cricket, photography. *Address:* PO Box 3926, Manuka, Canberra, ACT 2603 (Office); 19 Talbot Street, Forrest, Canberra, ACT 2603, Australia. *Telephone:* (2) 6295-3206 (Office). *Fax:* (2) 6295-3066 (Office). *E-mail:* rwoolcot@ozemail.com.au (Office and Home) (Home).

WOOLDRIDGE, Hon. Michael Richard Lewis, MB, BSc, MBA; Australian politician; b. 7 Nov. 1956; m. Michele Marion Colman 1988; two s.; ed Scotch Coll., Melbourne, Univ. of Melbourne, Monash Univ.; Resident Medical Staff (Surgical), Alfred Hosp. 1982–85; MP (Liberal Party) for Chisholm, Vic. 1987–88, for Casey, Vic. 1998–; pvt. practice 1985–87; Shadow Minister for Aboriginal Affairs 1990–92; Shadow Minister for Aboriginal and Torres Strait Islander Affairs 1992–93; Deputy Leader of the Opposition, Shadow Minister for Educ., Employment and Training 1993–94, Shadow Minister for Community Services, Sr Citizens and Aged Care 1994–95, for Health and Human Services 1995–96; Minister for Health and Family Services 1996–98, Minister for Health and Aged Care 1998–2002. *Leisure interests:* royal tennis, skiing, reading. *Address:* Parliament House, Canberra, ACT 2600; First Floor, Suite 9, 431 Burke Road, Glen Iris, Vic. 3146, Australia.

WOOLDRIDGE, Richard; British media executive; fmr journalist; fmr Ed. Yorkshire Evening Press; Man. Ed. York and Country Press –1992; Dir Westminster Press (regional newspaper group) 1992–96; joined Int. Herald Tribune 1996, various positions including consultant, Pres. and COO –2003, Chair. and CEO Jan. 2003–. *Address:* International Herald Tribune, 6 bis, rue des Graviers, 92521 Neuilly Cedex, France (Office). *Telephone:* 1-41-43-93-00 (Office). *Fax:* 1-41-43-92-12 (Office). *E-mail:* iht@iht.com (Office). *Website:* www.iht.com (Office).

WOOLF, Baron (Life Peer), cr. 1992, of Barnes in the London Borough of Richmond; **Rt Hon Harry Kenneth Woolf,** PC, LLB; British judge; b. 2 May 1933, Newcastle-upon-Tyne; s. of Alexander Woolf and Leah Woolf; m. Marguerite Sassoon 1961; three s.; ed Glasgow Acad., Fettes Coll., Edin., Univ. Coll. London; Nat. Service, 15/19th Royal Hussars 1954, Capt., Army Legal Services 1955; called to Bar, Inner Temple 1954, began practising 1956; Recorder, Crown Court 1972–79; Jr Counsel, Inland Revenue 1973–74; First Treasury Counsel (Common Law) 1974–79; Judge, High Court, Queen's Bench Div. 1979–86; Presiding Judge, S Eastern Circuit 1981–84; Lord Justice of Appeal 1986–92; Lord of Appeal in Ordinary 1992–96; Master of the Rolls 1996–2000; Lord Chief Justice of England and Wales 2000–; mem. Bd of Man., Inst. of Advanced Legal Studies 1985–94 (Chair. 1986–94); Chair. Lord Chancellor's Advisory Cttee of Legal Educ. 1986–94, Middx Advisory Cttee on Justices of the Peace 1986–90, Magna Carta Trust 1996, Lord Chancellors' Advisory Cttee on Public Records 1996–2000, Council of Civil Justice 1997–2000, Civil Procedure Rules Cttee 1997–2000; Pro-Chancellor London Univ. 1994–2002; Pres. Asscn of Law Teachers 1985–89, Cen. Council of Jewish Social Services 1987–2000, SW London Magistrates' Asscn 1987–93, Asscn of Mems of Bd of Visitors 1994–, Public Records Soc. 1996–2000; Fellow Univ. Coll. London; Visitor Nuffield Coll., Oxford 1996–2000, Downing College, Cambridge 2000–, Univ. Coll., London 1996–2000; Trustee Butler Trust 1991–96, Chair. 1992–96, Pres. 1996–; Special Trustee St Mary's Hosp., Paddington 1993–97; Trustee Jewish Chronicle 1990; Hon. Fellow British Acad. 2002, Acad. of Science; Hon. Fellow Leeds Metropolitan Univ. 1990; Hon. mem. Soc. of Public Teachers of Law 1988; Hon. LLD (Buckingham) 1992, (Bristol) 1992, (London) 1993, (Anglia Poly Univ.) 1994, (Manchester Metropolitan) 1994, (Hull) 2001, (Cranfield) 2001, (Cambridge) 2002, (Exeter) 2002; Hon. DLitt (London) 2002; Hon. DSc (Cranfield) 2002. *Publications:* Protection of the Public – The New Challenge 1990, Declaratory Judgement (Ed. with J. Woolf) 1993, Judicial Review of Administrative Action (Jt Eds De Smith, Woolf & Jowell) (5th edn) 1995; reports: Prisons in England and Wales 1991, Access to Justice (Interim) 1995, (Final) 1996, Principles of Judicial Review (jtly) 1999. *Address:* Royal Courts of Justice, Strand, London, WC2A 2LL, England (Office). *Telephone:* (20) 7936-6766 (Office). *Fax:* (20) 7936-7512 (Office).

WOOLFSON, Michael Mark, MA, PhD DSc, FRAS, CPhys, FInstP, FRS; British professor of physics; b. 9 Jan. 1927, London; s. of Maurice Woolfson and Rose Woolfson (née Solomons); m. Margaret Frohlich 1951; two s. one d.; ed Jesus Coll., Oxford, UMIST; Nat. Service, Royal Engineers 1947–49; Research Asst, Cavendish Lab., Cambridge 1952–54; ICI Fellow Univ. of Cambridge 1954–55; lecturer, Faculty of Tech. Univ. of Manchester 1955–61, Reader 1961–65; Prof. of Theoretical Physics, Univ. of York 1965–94, Prof. Emer. 1994–; Chair. Royal Soc. Planetary Sciences Subcttee. 1979–83, British Crystallographic Asscn 1985–90, British Nat. Cttee for Crystallography 1985–90; Pres. Yorks. Philosophical Soc. 1985–99; Hughes Medal, Royal Soc. 1986, Patterson Award, American Crystallographic Asscn 1990, Gregori Aminoff Medal and Prize, Royal Swedish Acad. of Sciences 1992, Dorothy Hodgkin Prize, British Crystallographic Asscn 1997, Ewald Prize, Int. Union of Crystallography 2002. *Publications:* Direct Methods in Crystallography 1960, The Origin of the Solar System, The Capture Theory 1989, Physical and Non-physical Methods of Solving Crystal Structures 1995, An Introduction to X-ray Crystallography 1997, An Introduction to Computer Simulation 1999, The Origins and Evolution of the Solar System 2000, Planetary Science 2002. *Leisure interest:* winemaking. *Address:* Department of Physics, University of York, York, YO1 5DD (Office); 24 Sandmoor Green, Leeds, LS17 7SB, England (Home). *Telephone:* (1904) 432230 (Office); (113) 266-2166 (Home). *Fax:* (1904) 432214.

WOOLLCOMBE, Rt Rev Kenneth John, MA, STD; British ecclesiastic; b. 2 Jan. 1924, Sutton, Surrey; s. of Rev. Edward P. Woollcombe OBE and Elsie O. Wood; m. 1st Gwendoline R. V. Hodges 1950 (died 1976); m. 2nd Juliet Dearmer 1980; four d.; ed Haileybury Coll., Technical Coll., Wednesbury, St John's Coll., Oxford and Westcott House, Cambridge; Sub-Lt, RDVR 1945–46; Curate, Grimsby Parish Church 1951–53; Fellow, Chaplain and Tutor, St John's Coll., Oxford 1953–60; Prof. of Dogmatic Theology, Gen. Theological Seminary, New York 1960–63; Prin. of Episcopal Theological Coll., Edin. and Canon of St Mary's Cathedral, Edin. 1963–71; Bishop of Oxford 1971–78; Asst Bishop of London 1978–81, Diocese of Worcester 1989–; Canon Residentiary, St Paul's Cathedral 1981–89, Precentor 1982–89; Chair. Soc. for Promotion of Christian Knowledge (SPCK) 1973–79; Chair. Churches' Council for Covenanting 1978–82; Chair. Cttee for Roman Catholic Relations 1985–88; mem. Court of Ecclesiastical Causes Reserved 1984–89; Hon. Fellow St John's Coll., Oxford 1971; Hon. STD (Univ. of the South, Sewanee, Tennessee) 1963; Hon. DD (Hartford, Conn.) 1975. *Publications:* Essays on Typology (co-author) 1957 and contribs to other theological publications. *Leisure interests:* reading, music. *Address:* 19 Ashdale Avenue, Pershore, Worcs., WR10 1PL, England.

WOOLLEY, Kenneth Frank, AM, BArch, LFRAIA; Australian architect; b. 29 May 1933, Sydney; s. of Frank Woolley and Doris May (Mudear) Woolley; m. 1st Cynthia Stuart (divorced 1979); m. 2nd Virginia Braden 1980; two s. one d.; ed Sydney Boys' High School, Univ. of Sydney; Design Architect, Govt Architect's Office, Sydney 1955–56, 1957–63; Asst Architect, Chamberlin, Powell and Bon, London 1956–57; Partner, Ancher, Mortlock, Murray & Woolley, Sydney 1964–69; Dir 1969–75; Dir Ancher, Mortlock & Woolley Pty Ltd, Sydney 1975–; mem. Quality Review Cttee Darling Harbour Redevt.

Authority 1985; Visiting Prof., Univ. of NSW School of Architecture 1983; Visiting Tutor and Critic, Visiting Prof., Univ. of Sydney, Univ. of NSW, NSW Inst. of Tech., Sydney; mem. NSW Bd of Architects 1960–72, NSW Bldg Regulations Advisory Cttee 1960–74, NSW Bd of Architectural Educ. 1969–72, Royal Australian Inst. of Architects Aboriginal Housing Panel 1972–76; Life FRAIA 1976; Sulman Award 1962, Bronze Medal 1962, Wilkinson Award 1962, 1968, 1982, 1987, Blacket Award 1964, 1967, 1969, 1987, Civic Design Award 1983, Gold Medal, Royal Australian Inst. of Architects 1993, numerous other architectural awards. *Major works include:* Australian Embassy, Bangkok, ABC Radio Bldg, Sydney, Hyatt Hotel, Campbell's Cove, Sydney, Control Tower, Sydney Airport, Sydney Town Hall renovations, The Olympics and RAS Exhbn Halls and Hockey Stadium, new offices and city square, three student union bldgs., Univs. in NSW, numerous urban housing devts., radio stations, Vanuatu, Solomon Islands, over 4,000 production houses, State Govt offices, Sydney, Fisher Library, Sydney Univ. *Publications:* numerous papers and articles in architectural journals. *Leisure interests:* golf, sailing, music, drawing. *Address:* LV. 5, 790 George Street, Sydney, NSW 2000, Australia. *Telephone:* 9211-4466 (Office).

WOOLSEY, R. James, MA, LLB; American; b. 1941, Tulsa, Okla; m. Suzanne Haley; three s.; ed Tulsa Cen. High School, Stanford Univ., Oxford Univ., UK and Yale Law School; staff mem. Nat. Security Council 1968–70; Adviser U.S. Del. to Strategic Arms Limitation Talks 1969–70; Gen. Counsel to Senate Cttee on Armed Services 1970–73; Under-Sec. of the Navy 1977–79; del.-at-large to U.S.-Soviet Strategic Arms Reduction Talks and space talks 1983–86; Amb. and U.S. Rep. to negotiations on Conventional Armed Forces in Europe Treaty 1989–91; Chair. CIA task force on future of satellite spying 1991; Dir of CIA 1993–95; Partner Shea & Gardner 1991–93, 1995–; Chair. Advisory Cttee., Clean Fuels Foundation; Dir USF&G 1995, Sun HealthCare Group Inc. 1995, Yurie Systems Inc. 1996; mem. Bd of Govs. Philadelphia Stock Exchange; mem. Pres.'s Comm. on Strategic Forces 1983, Pres.'s Blue Ribbon Comm. on Defense Man. 1985–86, Pres.'s Comm. on Fed. Ethics law Reform 1989, Comm. to Assess the Ballistic Missile Threat to the U.S. 1998, Nat. Comm. on Terrorism 1999–2000; Trustee Center for Strategic and Int. Studies; Rhodes Scholar 1963–65. *Address:* Shea & Gardner, 1800 Massachusetts Avenue, NW, Washington, DC 20036, USA. *Telephone:* (202) 828-2000. *Fax:* (202) 828-2195. *E-mail:* jwoolsey@sheagardner.com. *Website:* www.sheagardner.com.

WOONTON, Robert Philip, PhD; Cook Islands politician; b. 1949; m. Sue Woonton; Minister of Foreign Affairs and Immigration 1999–; Prime Minister Feb. 2002–, portfolio also includes Police, Parl., House of Ariki, Tourism, Agric., Marine Resources, Transport, Airport and Ports Authorities, Nat. Disaster Man. *Address:* Office of the Prime Minister, Government of the Cook Islands, Private Bag, Avarua, Rarotonga, Cook Islands (Office). *Telephone:* 29301 (Office). *Fax:* 20856 (Office). *E-mail:* pmoffice@cookislands.gov.ck (Office); rwoonton@oyster.net.ck (Home). *Website:* www.cook-islands.gov.ck (Office).

WOOSNAM, Ian Harold, MBE; British golfer; b. 2 March 1958, Oswestry, Wales; s. of Harold Woosnam and Joan Woosnam; m. Glendryth Pugh 1983; one s. two d.; ed St Martin's Modern School; professional golfer 1976–; tournament victories: News of the World under-23 Matchplay 1979, Cacharel under-25 Championship 1982, Swiss Open 1982, Silk Cut Masters 1983, Scandinavian Enterprise Open 1984, Zambian Open 1985, Lawrence Batley TPC 1986, 555 Kenya Open 1986, Hong Kong Open 1987, Jersey Open 1987, Cepsa Madrid Open 1987, Bell's Scottish Open 1987, 1990, Lancome Trophy 1987, Suntory World Match-Play Championship 1987, 1990, 2001, Volvo PGA Championship 1988, 1997, Carrolls Irish Open 1988, 1989, Panasonic Euro Open 1988, Am Express Mediterranean Open 1990, Torras Monte Carlo Open 1990, Epson Grand Prix 1990, U.S. Masters 1991, USF+G Classic 1991, Fujitsu Mediterranean Open, Torras Monte Carlo Open 1991, European Monte Carlo Open 1992, Lancôme Trophy 1993, Murphy's English Open 1993, British Masters 1994, Cannes Open 1994, Heineken Classic 1996, Scottish Open 1996, Volvo German Open 1996, Johnnie Walker Classic 1996; team events: Ryder Cup 1983–97, Dunhill Cup 1985, 1986, 1988, 1989, 1990, 1991, 1993, 1995, World Cup 1980, 1982, 1983, 1984, 1985, 1987, 1990, 1991, 1992, 1993, 1994, 1996, 1997; finished top Order of Merit 1987, 1990; ranked No. 1, Sony world rankings 1991; World Cup Individual, PGA Grand Slam 1991; Pres. World Snooker Asscn 1999–; fifth on all-time European earnings list as at 16 Sept. 2002; 29 European PGA Tour titles at end of 2002; now lives in Jersey, Channel Islands. *Publication:* Ian Woosnam's Golf Masterpieces (with Peter Grosvenor) 1991, Golf Made Simple: The Woosie Way 1997. *Leisure interests:* snooker, water skiing, sports, fishing. *Address:* c/o IMG, Pier House, Strand on the Green, London, W4 3NN, England. *Website:* www.woosie.com (Office).

WORCESTER, Robert Milton, BSc; American opinion researcher; b. 21 Dec. 1933, Kansas City; s. of the late C. M. Worcester and Violet Ruth Worcester; m. 1st Joann Ransdell 1958 (deceased); m. 2nd Margaret Noel Smallbone 1982; two s.; ed Univ. of Kansas; Consultant, McKinsey & Co. 1962–65; Controller and Asst to Chair. Opinion Research Corpn 1965–68; Man. Dir Market & Opinion Research Int. Ltd (MORI) 1969–94, Chair. 1973–; fmr Pres. World Asscn for Public Opinion Research; Visiting Prof., City Univ. 1990–2002, LSE 1992– (of Govt 1995–), Strathclyde Univ. 1996–2001; Pres. Environmental Campaigns 2002–; Vice-Pres. Int. Soc. Science Council, UNESCO 1989–94, European Atlantic Group, UNA 1999–, Royal Soc. for Nature Conservation 1995–; Dir (non-exec) Medway Maritime Hospital NHS

Trust; mem. Pilgrims Soc. of GB (Chair. Exec. Cttee 1993–); mem. Court of Govs, LSE, Advisory Bd South East Econ. Devt Agency, European Business Journal, Fulbright Comm. 1995–, Court Middx Univ. 2001–, Council Univ. of Kent 2002–, Advisory Bd Nat. Consumer Council 2002–; Adviser, Prince of Wales's Business Leaders Forum; Specialist Advisor, Treasury Select Cttee 2002–; Gov. Ditchley Foundation; Trustee WorldWide Fund for Nature (WWF-UK) 1988–94, Natural History Museum Devt Trust 1989–94, Magna Carta Kent Foundation 1995–, Wildfowl and Wetlands Trust 2002–; Co-Ed. Int. Journal of Public Opinion Research; consultant to The Times, The Economist; writes monthly columns for Profile (magazine of Inst. of Public Relations) and Parliamentary Monitor; Fellow Market Research Soc. 1997–; Freeman City of London 2001; Hon. DSc (Buckingham) 1999; Hon. DLitt (Bradford) 2001; Hon. DUniv (Middx) 2001; Hon. LLD (Greenwich) 2002; Helen Dinerman Award, World Asscn for Public Opinion Research 1996. *Publications:* Political Communications (with Martin Harrop) 1982, Political Opinion Polling: An International Review (Ed.) 1983, Consumer Market Research Handbook (3rd edn, Ed. with John Downham) 1986, Private Opinions, Public Polls (with Lesley Watkins) 1986, We British (with Eric Jacobs) 1990, British Public Opinion: History and Methodology of Political Opinion Polling in Great Britain 1991, Dynamics of Societal Learning about Global Environmental Change (with Samuel H. Barnes) 1992, Typically British (with Eric Jacobs) 1992, The Millennial Generation (with Madsen Pirie) 1998, The Next Leaders (with Madsen Pirie) 1999, Explaining Labour's Landslide (with Roger Mortimore) 1999, The Big Turn Off (with Madsen Pirie) 2000, How to Win the Euro Referendum: Lessons from 1975 2000, Facing the Future (with Madsen Pirie) 2000, The Wrong Package (with Madsen Pirie) 2001, Explaining Labour's Second Landslide (with Roger Mortimore) 2001. *Leisure interest:* castles, choral music, gardening. *Address:* MORI House, 79–81 Borough Road, London, SE1 1FY (Office); 32 Old Queen Street, London, SW1H 9HP, England. *Telephone:* (20) 7347-3000 (Office); (20) 7222-0232. *Fax:* (20) 7227-0404 (Office). *E-mail:* worc@mori.com (Office). *Website:* www.mori.com (Office).

WORMS, Gérard Etienne; French company director; b. 1 Aug. 1936, Paris; s. of André Worms and Thérèse Dreyfus; m. Michèle Rousseau 1960; one s. one d.; ed Lycées Carnot and Saint-Louis, Ecole Polytechnique and Ecole Nat. Supérieure des Mines, Paris; Engineer, Org. commune des régions sahariennes 1960–62; Head of Dept, Délégation à l'Aménagement du Territoire et à l'Action Régionale 1963–67; Tech. Adviser, Office of Olivier Guichard (Minister of Industry, later of Planning) 1967–69, Office of Jacques Chaban-Delmas (Prime Minister) 1969–71; Asst Man. Dir, Librairie Hachette 1972–75, Man. Dir 1975–81, Dir 1978–81; Prof., Ecole des Hautes Etudes Commerciales 1962–69, Supervisor of complementary courses, Faculty of Letters and Human Sciences, Paris 1963–69; Prof. Ecole Polytechnique 1974–85; Vice-Pres. Syndicat nat. de l'édition 1974–81; Exec. Vice-Pres. Rhône-Poulenc SA 1981–83; Chair. and CEO Compagnie de Suez 1990–95; Pres. Banque Indosuez 1994–95; Pres. Supervisory Bd Rothschild, Compagnie Banque Paris 1995–99, Man. Partner Rothschild et Cie and Rothschild et Cie Banque 1999–, Pres. Centre for research into econ. expansion and business Devt 1996–, Supervisory Council for health information systems 1997–2000, History channel 1997–; mem. bd Telecom Italia 1998–2001, Publicis; Chevalier, Ordre nat. du Mérite; Chevalier, Ordre du Mérite maritime; Officier Légion d'honneur. *Publications:* Les méthodes modernes de l'économie appliquée 1965; various articles on econ. methods in specialized journals. *Address:* Rothschild et Cie, 17 avenue Matignon, 75008 Paris (Office); 61 bis avenue de la Motte Picquet, 75015 Paris, France (Home). *Telephone:* 1-47-83-99-43 (Home).

WORNER, Howard Knox, CBE, DSc, FAA, FTS, FRACI, FIM, FIMM, FAIE, MAIME; Australian metallurgist and scientific consultant; b. 3 Aug. 1913, Swan Hill, Victoria; s. of the late John Worner and Ida Worner; m. Rilda B. Muller 1937 (died 2001); two s. (one deceased) one d.; ed Bendigo School of Mines and Univ. of Melbourne; Lecturer in Metallography, Univ. of Melbourne 1935–38; Research Fellow, Nat. Health and Medical Research Council of Australia 1939–46; Consultant, Defence Forces, on Dental and Surgical Materials 1940–46; tropical scientific service, Australian army 1944–45; Prof. of Metallurgy, Univ. of Melbourne 1947–55, Dean, Faculty of Eng 1953–55; Dir of Research, The Broken Hill Pty Co. Ltd 1956–62; int. consultant 1963; Dir of New Process Devt, CRA Ltd 1964–75; Chair. Nat. Energy Advisory Cttee 1976–77; Chair. Victoria Brown Coal Cttee (later Council) and mem. Nat. Energy Research and Devt Cttee 1976–81; scientific consultant 1981–; Hon. Sec. Australian Acad. of Tech. Sciences 1975–86; Hon. Prof., Univ. of Wollongong 1987–, Dir Microwave Applications Research Centre 1987–88, Dir Microwave and Materials Inst. 1989–, Research Dir Resources Div., ITC Ltd (within Univ.) 1991–; Hon. Fellow Inst. Engineers Australia 1988, Australasian Inst. of Mining and Metallurgy 1989, Australian Acad. of Tech. Sciences and Eng 1993, Australian Inst. of Eng 1993, Australian Inst. of Energy 1994; Hon. DSc (Newcastle, Wollongong, La Trobe); Hon. DEng (Melbourne); ten medals from professional socs and univs and numerous other awards. *Publications:* 210 scientific papers and monographs. *Leisure interests:* mineral collecting, oil painting. *Address:* 28 Parrish Avenue, Mt. Pleasant, NSW 2519, Australia. *Telephone:* (2) 4226-8805 (Office); (2) 4284-4881 (Home). *Fax:* (2) 422-6815 (Office).

WORRALL, Denis John, PhD; South African business executive, politician and lawyer; b. 29 May 1935, Benoni; s. of Cecil John Worrall and Hazel Worrall; m. Anita Denise Ianco 1965; three s.; ed Univ. of Cape Town, Univ.

of SA and Cornell Univ., USA; taught political science, Cornell Univ., Univ. of Calif. at LA, Univ. of Natal, Univ. of SA and Univ. of Witwatersrand; Cornell Research Fellow, Univ. of Ibadan, Nigeria 1962–63; Founder and Ed. New Nation 1967–74; Research Prof. and Dir Inst. for Social and Econ. Research, Rhodes Univ. –1974; Senator for Cape 1974–77; Amb. to Australia 1983–84, to UK 1984–87; Advocate, Supreme Court of SA; MP for Cape Town-Gardens 1977–83; independent cand. for Helderberg in 1987 Election; mem. Pres's. Council 1980–83; f. Ind. Movt 1988; Leader Ind. Party 1988–89; co-founder Democratic Party 1989; MP for Berea, Durban 1989–94; Chair. Omega Investment Research Ltd. *Publications:* South Africa: Government and Politics; numerous articles. *Leisure interests:* reading, tennis. *Address:* Omega Investment Research (Pty) Ltd, P.O. Box 5455, Cape Town 8000; 4 Montrose Terrace, 5 Montrose Street, (Newlands) 7700, Cape Town. *Telephone:* (21) 6897881 (Office); (21) 6857502 (Home).

WORSTHORNE, Sir Peregrine Gerard, Kt, MA; British journalist; b. 22 Dec. 1923, London; s. of Col A. Koch de Gooreynd and the late Baroness Norman; m. 1st Claudia Bertrand de Colasse 1950 (died 1990); one d. one step-s.; m. 2nd Lady Lucinda Lambton 1991; ed Stowe School, Peterhouse, Cambridge and Magdalen Coll., Oxford; editorial staff, Glasgow Herald 1946–48; editorial staff, The Times 1948–50, Washington corresp. 1950–52, Leader writer 1952–55; Leader writer, Daily Telegraph 1955–61; Assoc. Ed. Sunday Telegraph 1961–86, Ed. 1986–89, Ed. Comment Section 1989–91; columnist The Spectator 1997–; Granada TV Journalist of the Year 1981. *Publications:* The Socialist Myth 1972, Peregrinations 1980, By The Right 1987, Tricks of Memory (memoirs) 1993. *Leisure interests:* walking, tennis. *Address:* The Old Rectory, Hedgerley, Bucks., SL2 3UY, England. *Telephone:* (1753) 646167. *Fax:* (1753) 646914.

WOUK, Herman, AB; American writer; b. 27 May 1915, New York; s. of Abraham Isaac Wouk and Esther Levine; m. Betty Sarah Brown 1945; three s. (one deceased); ed Columbia Univ.; radio script-writer for leading comedians, New York 1935–41; presidential consultant to U.S. Treasury 1941; served USNR 1942–46; Visiting Prof. of English, Yeshiva Univ., NY 1952–57; Trustee, Coll. of the Virgin Islands 1961–69; mem. Authors' Guild, USA, Authors' League, Center for Book Nat. Advisory Bd, Library of Congress, Advisory Council, Center for U.S.–China Arts Exchange; Hon. LHD (Yeshiva Univ.); Hon. DLitt (Clark Univ.), (George Washington Univ.) 2001; Hon. DLitt (American Int. Coll.) 1979; Hon. PhD (Bar Ilan) 1990, (Hebrew Univ.) 1997; Hon. DST (Trinity Coll.) 1998; Pulitzer Prize for Fiction 1952, Columbia Univ. Medal for Excellence, Alexander Hamilton Medal, Columbia Univ. 1980, Ralph Waldo Emerson Award, Int. Platform Asscn 1981, Univ. of Calif., Berkeley Medal 1984, Yad Vashem Kazetnik Award 1990, U.S. Navy Memorial Foundation Lone Sailor Award 1987, Washingtonian Book Award (for Inside, Outside) 1986, American Acad. of Achievement Golden Plate Award 1986, Bar Ilan Univ. Guardian of Zion Award 1998, Univ. of Calif. at San Diego UCSD Medal 1998. *Publications:* Aurora Dawn 1947, The City Boy 1948, Slattery's Hurricane 1949, The Traitor (play) 1949, The Caine Mutiny (novel) 1951, The Caine Mutiny Court-Martial (play) 1953, Marjorie Morning-star 1955, Nature's Way (play) 1957, This Is My God 1959, Youngblood Hawke (novel) 1962, Don't Stop the Carnival (novel) 1965, The Winds of War (novel) 1971, War and Remembrance 1978 (screenplay for TV serial 1986), The Winds of War (TV screenplay) 1983, Inside, Outside 1985, The Hope (novel) 1993, The Glory 1994, The Will to Live On 2000. *Leisure interests:* Hebraic studies, travel. *Address:* c/o BSW Literary Agency, 3255 N Street, NW, Washington, DC 20007, USA.

WOUTS, Bernard François Emile; French business executive; b. 22 March 1940, Roubaix; s. of Emile Wouts and Marie Vanderbauwede; m. Annick Memet 1965; two s. one d.; ed Lycée St Louis, Paris; engineer, then Deputy Dir-Gen. and Man. Bayard Presse and Pres. subsidiaries of Bayard Presse group 1966–81; Dir-Gen. Soc. de Publications et d'Editions Réunies 1980–85; Gen. Man. Le Monde 1985–90; Pres. Coopérative des quotidiens de Paris 1988–90; Pres.-Dir-Gen. Le Point 1990–; Pres. SPMI (Syndicat de la Presse Magazine et d'Information) 1995–99, Vice-Pres. 1999–; Pres.-Dir-Gen. Financière Tellendier 2001–. *Publication:* La presse entre les lignes 1990. *Leisure interest:* sailing. *Address:* Le Point, 74 avenue du Maine, 75014 Paris (Office); 1 rue de l'Eglise, 17290 Thairé, France (Home).

WOWEREIT, Klaus, LLB; German politician; b. 1 Oct. 1953, Berlin; Adviser to Senator for Internal Affairs, Berlin 1981–84; mem. Regional Cttee and Del. to Social Democratic Party (SPD), Tempelhof Regional Council 1984–95; Chair. SPD Group, Tempelhof Dist 1981–84, 1999–, Vice-Chair. 1995–99; Mayor of Berlin 2001–; Partner Tempelhof Haus-, Wohnungs- und Grund-stückseigentümerverein Berlin-Lichtenrade eV, Förderverein Bruno eV, European Acad.; mem. Tempelhof Art and Cultural Union (TKK). *Address:* Office of the Bürgermeister, Bezirksstadtrat a.D., 12305 Berlin, Germany (Office). *E-mail:* der-regierende-buergermeister@SKZL.Verwalt-Berlin.de (Office). *Website:* www.berlin.de (Office).

WOYTOWICZ-RUDNICKA, Stefania; Polish soprano concert singer; b. 8 Oct. 1922, Orynin; d. of Michał and Domicela Zwolakowska Woytowicz; m. 1952; ed State Higher School of Music, Cracow; concerts in Europe, USA, Canada, China, Japan; tour of Singapore, Hong Kong, New Zealand, India with Australian Broadcasting Comm.; concert for Pope John Paul II 1995; contract with Deutsche Grammophon; also recorded with RCA Victor, Supraphon, Polskie Nagrania and others; participates in Vienna Festival, Edin. Festival, Warsaw Autumn and others; Pres. Gen. Bd, Warsaw Music Asscn

1977–92; Officer's Cross, Order of Polonia Restituta 1968; First Prize in Prague Spring Int. Singing Competition 1954, State Prize (2nd Class) 1964, Orpheus Prize, Polish Musicians' Asscn 1967, Prize of Minister of Culture and Arts (1st Class) 1975, Prize of Union of Polish Composers 1978, Solidarity Award 1983, Polskie Nagrania Gold Record for recording of Górecki's Symphony No. 3 1997 (Platinum Record 1999), Karol Szymanowski Foundation Award 1998. *Address:* al. Przyjaciół 3 m. 13, 00-565 Warsaw, Poland (Home). *Telephone:* (22) 6281133 (Home).

WRAGG, John, ARCA, RA; British sculptor; b. 20 Oct. 1937, York; s. of Arthur Wragg and Ethel Wragg; ed York School of Art and Royal Coll. of Art; work represented in several public collections including Tate Gallery, London, Contemporary Art Society, Nat. Gallery of Modern Art, Edin., Israel Museum, Wellington Art Gallery, NZ, Sainsbury Centre for Visual Arts, Univ. of East Anglia; Sainsbury Award 1960; winner, Sainsbury Sculpture Competition, Chelsea 1966; Arts Council of GB Major Award 1977; Chantrey Bequest 1981. *One-man exhibitions:* Hanover Gallery 1963, 1966, 1970, Galerie Alexandre Iolas, Paris 1968, York Festival 1969, Bridge St Gallery, Bath 1982, Katherine House Gallery, Marlborough 1984, Quinton Green Fine Art, London 1985, Devizes Museum Gallery 1994, 1996, England & Co. London 1994, L'Art Abstrait, London 1995, 1996, Monumental '96, Belgium 1996, Devizes Museum Gallery 1996, Handel House Gallery, Devizes 2000, Bruton Gallery, Leeds 2000; participant in numerous group exhbns. in UK, Europe and USA 1959–. *Leisure interests:* walking, listening to music, reading. *Address:* 6 Castle Lane, Devizes, Wilts., SN10 1HJ, England. *Telephone:* (1380) 727087. *E-mail:* johnwragg.ra@virgin.net (Office).

WRAN, Hon. Neville Kenneth, AC, QC, FRSA; Australian business executive and fmr politician; b. Sydney; m. 2nd Jill Hickson 1976; one s. one d. and one s. one d. by previous marriage; ed Fort Street Boys' High School, Sydney Univ.; solicitor, then admitted to Bar 1957; apptd. QC 1968; mem. NSW Legis. Council 1970–73; Deputy Leader of Opposition 1971–72; Leader of Opposition in Legis. Council 1972–73; mem. NSW Legis. Ass. for Bass Hill 1973–86; Leader of Opposition 1973–76; Premier of NSW and Minister for Arts (and various other ministerial portfolios) 1976–86; Nat. Pres. Australian Labor Party 1980–86; Chair. CSIRO 1986–91, Lionel Murphy Foundation 1986–2000, Wran Partners Pty Ltd, Victor Chang Cardiac Research Inst.; Dir Cabcharge Australia Ltd; Australian rep. Eminent Persons Group, APEC 1993–95; Gov. Australia-Israel Chamber of Commerce; Foundation mem. Australian Republican Movt; Fellow Powerhouse Museum; Life Gov. Art Gallery of NSW; Hon. LLD (Sydney). *Leisure interests:* reading, tennis, walking. *Address:* GPO Box 4545, Sydney, NSW 2001, Australia. *Telephone:* (2) 9223-4315 (Office). *Fax:* (2) 9223-5267 (Office). *E-mail:* wran@primus.com.au (Office).

WRAY, Gordon Richard, EUR.ING., PhD, DSc, FRS, F.R.ENG., FIMechE, FTI, FRSA; British professor of engineering design; b. 30 Jan. 1928, Farnworth, Lancs.; s. of Joseph Wray and Letitia Wray (née Jones); m. Kathleen Senior 1954; one s. one d.; ed Bolton Tech. Coll. and Univ. of Manchester; Eng Apprentice, Bennis Combustion, Bolton 1943; Design Draughtsman, Dobson and Barlow, Bolton 1946; Sir Walter Preston Scholar, Univ. of Manchester 1949; Devt Eng, Platts (Barton) 1952; Lecturer in Mechanical Eng, Bolton Tech. Coll. 1953; Lecturer in Textile Eng, UMIST 1955; Reader in Mechanical Eng, Loughborough Univ. 1966–70, Prof. and Head of Dept 1970–88; Springer Visiting Prof., Univ. of Calif., Berkeley, USA 1977; Royal Acad. of Eng Prof. in the Principles of Eng Design, Loughborough Univ. of Tech. 1988–93, Dir of Eng Design Inst. 1988–91, Prof. Emer. 1993–; mem. Council, Inst. of Mechanical Engineers 1964–67, Dept of Industry Chief Scientist's Requirements Bd 1974–75, European Soc. for Eng Educ. (SEFI) Cttee on Innovation, Brussels 1980–82, Royal Soc. Working Group on Agricultural Eng 1981–82, Royal Soc. Sectional Cttee 4(1) 1985–89, Cttee of the Eng Profs Conf. 1985–86, Royal Soc./SERC Industrial Fellowships Panel 1986–89, Royal Soc. Mullard Award Cttee 1987–92, Royal Soc. Tech. Activities Cttee 1989–93; mem. Editorial Advisory Bd, Int. Journal of Clothing Science and Tech. 1994–2000; Chair. Judging Panel for William Lee Quater Centenary Tech. Prize 1989, Eng Council/Design Council Working Party on Attaining Competence in Eng Design (The ACED Report) 1989–91; Royal Soc./Royal Acad. of Eng Visiting Lecturer, Australia and NZ 1992; Brunel Lecturer to British Asscn Annual Meeting 1980; Thomas Hawksley Lecturer, Inst. of Mechanical Eng 1989; Bill Aldridge Memorial Lecturer, Textile Inst. (NZ) 1994; Hon. mem. Inst. of Eng Designers 1990; Viscount Weir Prize, Inst. of Mechanical Engineers 1959, Water Arbitration Prize, Inst. of Mechanical Engineers 1972, James Clayton Prize, Inst. of Mechanical Engineers 1975; Warner Medal, Textile Inst. 1976, S. G. Brown Award and Medal, Royal Soc. 1978; First recipient of title 'European Engineer' (Eur.Ing.), Paris 1987. *Publications:* Textile Engineering Processes (contrib.) 1959, Modern Yarn Production from Man-made Fibres 1960, Modern Developments in Weaving Machinery 1961, An Introduction to the Study of Spinning 1962, Contemporary Textile Engineering (contrib.) 1982, Design or Decline: A National Emergency? 1991, State/Industry Linkages 1993, Mechatronic Design in Textile Engineering (contrib.) 1993; numerous papers in learned journals. *Leisure interests:* fell-walking, photography, steam traction engines, theatre, music, gardening, DIY, East Leake Summer Wine Club. *Address:* Stonestack, Rempstone, Loughborough, Leics., LE12 6RH, England.

WRIGHT, Alexander (Alastair) Finlay, MBE, MD; British medical practitioner; b. 19 March 1933, Blantyre, Scotland; s. of Alexander Finlay Wright and Mary Paterson; m. Barbara Lattimer 1957; three s. one d.; ed Hamilton

Acad., Univ. of Glasgow; Gen. Medical Practitioner, medical researcher, teacher 1961–92; Council of Europe Fellowship, France 1976; Chair. Clinical and Research Div. Royal Coll. of Gen. Practitioners 1990–91; mem. Scientific Cttee, Jt Royal Coll. 'Defeat Depression' Campaign 1991–98; Ed. British Journal of Gen. Practice 1991–99; Fellow Royal Coll. of Gen. Practitioners; Hon. Fellow Royal Coll. of Psychiatrists 1998; Sima/Jansson Prize for Research in Gen. Practice 1981, George Abercrombie Award, Royal Coll. of Gen. Practioners 2000. *Publications include:* Medicine and the New Towns of France 1976, Female Sterilisation: The View From General Practice 1981, Depression: Recognition and Management in General Practice 1993, Psychiatry and General Practice (jtly) 1994. *Leisure interests:* walking, spoken French, grandchildren. *Address:* 5 Alburne Crescent, Glenrothes, Fife, KY7 5RE, Scotland. *Telephone:* (1592) 753139. *E-mail:* drafw@blueyonder.co.uk (Home).

WRIGHT, Barbara, MA, LLB, PhD, LittD, SFTCD, MRIA; Irish professor of French literature; b. 8 March 1935, Dublin; d. of W. Edward Robinson and Rosaleen H. Robinson; m. William Wright 1961 (died 1985); one s.; ed Alexandra Coll. Dublin, Trinity Coll. Dublin and Newnham Coll. Cambridge; teaching posts at Univs. of Manchester 1960–61, Exeter 1963–65; mem. staff Trinity Coll. Dublin 1965–, Prof. of French Literature 1978–, Dean, Faculty of Arts (Letters) 1983–86, 1990–96; mem. Academia Europaea; Chevalier, Ordre Nat. du Mérite. *Publications:* Eugène Fromentin's Dominique (critical edn) 1966; studies on Gustave Drouineau 1969, Edgar Quinet 1982, Charles Baudelaire (with D. Scott) 1987; Correspondence of Eugène Fromentin and Gustave Moreau (with P. Moisy) 1972; La Vie et l'œuvre d'Eugène Fromentin (with J. Thompson) 1987; Correspondance d'Eugène Fromentin (2 vols) 1995; Eugène Fromentin: A Life in Art and Letters 2000. *Leisure interest:* music. *Address:* Department of French, Arts Building, Trinity College, Dublin 2 (Office); 1 Lynton Court, Merrion Road, Dublin 4, Ireland (Home). *Telephone:* (1) 6081575 (Office); (1) 6601276 (Home). *Fax:* (1) 6717118. *E-mail:* bwright@tcd.ie (Office).

WRIGHT, Sir David John, GCMG, LVO, MA; British diplomatist and banker; b. 16 June 1944; s. of J. F. Wright; m. Sally Ann Dodkin 1968; one s. one d.; ed Wolverhampton Grammar School, Peterhouse, Cambridge; Third Sec., Foreign Office 1966, Third Sec., later Second Sec., Tokyo 1966–72, FCO 1972–75, Ecole Nat. d'Admin., Paris 1975–76, First Sec., Paris 1976–80, Pvt. Sec. to Sec. of Cabinet 1980–82, Counsellor (Econ.), Tokyo 1982–85, Head Personnel Services Dept FCO 1985–88; Deputy Pvt. Sec. to HRH the Prince of Wales 1988–90 (on secondment); Amb. to Repub. of Korea 1990–94, to Japan 1996–99; Deputy Under-Sec. of State, FCO 1994–96; Group Chief Exec. (Perm. Sec.) British Trade Int. 1999–2002; Vice-Chair. Barclays Capital 2002–; Hon. Fellow Peterhouse, Cambridge 2002; Hon. LLD (Wolverhampton) 1997, (Birmingham) 2000; Grand Cordon, Order of the Rising Sun (Japan) 1998. *Leisure interests:* golf, cooking, military history. *Address:* Barclays Capital, 5 North Colonnade, Canary Wharf, London, E14 4BB, England (Office). *Telephone:* (20) 7773-5599 (Office). *Fax:* (20) 7773-1911 (Office). *E-mail:* david.wright@barcap.com (Office).

WRIGHT, Georg Henrik von, MA, DPhil; Finnish philosopher; b. 14 June 1916, Helsinki; s. of Tor von Wright and Ragni Elisabeth Alfthan; m. Baroness Maria Elisabeth von Troil 1941; one s. one d.; ed Helsinki and Cambridge Univs.; Lecturer in Philosophy, Univ. of Helsinki 1943–46; Prof. of Philosophy, Univ. of Helsinki 1946–61; Prof. of Philosophy, Univ. of Cambridge 1948–51; Visiting Prof., Cornell Univ. 1954, 1958, Univ. of Calif. 1963, Univ. of Pittsburgh 1966, Univ. of Karlsruhe 1975; Research Fellow, Acad. of Finland 1961–86; Andrew D. White Prof.-at-Large, Cornell Univ. 1965–77; Leibniz Prof., Univ. of Leipzig 1994–95; Chancellor of Åbo Acad. 1968–77; Gifford Lecturer Univ. of St Andrew's 1959–60; Tarner Lecturer, Trinity Coll., Cambridge 1969; Woodbridge Lecturer, Columbia Univ. 1972; Nellie Wallace Lecturer, Univ. of Oxford 1978; Tanner Lecturer, Univ. of Helsinki 1984; Pres. Philosophical Soc. of Finland 1962–73, Int. Union of History and Philosophy of Science 1963–65, Inst. Int. de Philosophie, Paris 1975–78; sometime Fellow, Trinity Coll., Cambridge, Hon. Fellow 1983; Fellow, Finnish Soc. of Sciences, Royal Swedish Acad. of Sciences, British Acad., Royal Danish Acad. of Sciences, Norwegian Acad. of Sciences and Letters, European Acad. of Arts, Sciences and Humanities, World Acad. of Arts and Sciences, Academia Europaea; Hon. Foreign mem. American Acad. of Arts and Sciences; Dr. hc (Helsinki, Liverpool, Lund, Turku, Tampere, St Olaf Coll., USA, Buenos Aires, Salta, Bologna, Abo Acad., Tromsø, Stockholm, Leipzig, Innsbruck); Wihuri Foundation Int. Prize 1976, Alexander von Humboldt Foundation Research Award 1986, Tage Danielsson Humanist Award 1998. *Publications:* The Logical Problem of Induction 1941, A Treatise on Induction and Probability 1951, An Essay in Modal Logic 1951, Logical Studies 1957, The Varieties of Goodness 1963, Norm and Action 1963, The Logic of Preference 1963, An Essay in Deontic Logic 1968, Explanation and Understanding 1971, Causality and Determinism 1974, Freedom and Determination 1980, Wittgenstein 1982, Philosophical Papers I–III 1983–84, Intellectual Autobiography 1989, Minervan Pöllö (The Owl of Minerva) 1992, Myten om framsteget (The Myth of Progress) 1993, The Tree of Knowledge 1993, Normen, Werte und Handlungen 1994, Six Essays in Philosophical Logic 1996, In the Shadow of Descartes 1998, Mitt Liv (autobiog.) 2001.

WRIGHT, James Claude, Jr.; American politician; b. 22 Dec. 1922, Fort Worth, Tex.; s. of James C. Wright and Marie (née Lyster) Wright; m. Betty Hay 1972; one s. three d. (by previous m.); ed Weatherford Coll. and Univ. of Texas; army service 1942–45, DFC, Legion of Merit; Partner, advertising and trade extension firm; mem. Texas Legislature 1947–49; Mayor of Weatherford, Tex. 1950–54; mem. League of Texas Municipalities, Pres. 1953; fmr Lay Minister in Presbyterian Church; mem. for Fort Worth (12th District of Tex.), U.S. House of Reps. 1954–89, Deputy Democratic Whip until 1976, Majority Leader in House of Reps. 1976–87; Chair. Democratic Steering and Policy Cttee in House, Vice-Chair. 1976–87, Speaker, House of Reps. 1987–89; mem. Budget Cttee 1974–87; Sr Political Consultant, American Income Life Insurance Co. 1989–; Political Consultant, Arch Petroleum 1989–; fmr ranking mem. Public Works and Transportation Cttee; fmr mem. Govt Operations Cttee; fmr Chair. Comm. on Highway Beautification; Cand. for U.S. Senate 1961. *Publications:* You and Your Congressman 1965, The Coming Water Famine 1966, Of Swords and Plowshares 1968, Worth It All 1993, Balance of Power 1996; co-author: Congress and Conscience 1970, Reflections of a Public Man 1984.

WRIGHT, Sir (John) Oliver, GCMG, GCVO, DSC; British diplomatist; b. 6 March 1921, London; s. of Arthur Wright and Ethel Wright; m. Marjory Osborne 1942; three s.; ed Solihull School and Christ's Coll. Cambridge; Royal Navy 1941–45; joined Foreign Office Nov. 1945; served New York 1946–47, Bucharest 1948–50, Singapore 1950–54, Berlin 1954–56, Pretoria 1957–58; Imperial Defence Coll. 1959; Asst Pvt. Sec. to Foreign Sec. 1960–63, Pvt. Sec. Jan.-Nov. 1963; Pvt. Sec. to Prime Minister 1963–66; Amb. to Denmark 1966–69; UK Rep. to Northern Ireland Govt 1969–70; Deputy Under-Sec. of State and Chief Clerk, FCO 1970–72; Deputy Under-Sec. for EEC and Econ. Affairs 1972–75; Amb. to Fed. Repub. of Germany 1975–81, to USA 1982–86; King of Arms, Most Distinguished Order of St Michael and St George 1987–97; Dir Gen. Tech. Systems Inc. 1990–95, Enviromed PLC 1993–97, Berkeley Hotel 1994–96; Clark Fellow, Cornell Univ. 1987; Lewin Prof., Wash. Univ., St Louis, Mo. 1988; Trustee British Museum, 1986–91, Bd, British Council, Int. Shakespeare Globe Centre; Co-Chair. Anglo-Irish Encounter 1986–91; Chair. British Königswinter Steering Cttee 1987–97; Pres. German Chamber of Commerce and Industry in London 1988–92; Chair. of Govs Reigate Grammar School 1990–97; Hon. Fellow Christ's Coll. Cambridge 1981. *Leisure interests:* theatre, opera. *Address:* Burstow Hall, Horley, Surrey, RH6 9SR, England. *Telephone:* (1293) 783494. *Fax:* (1293) 774044 (Home).

WRIGHT, Karen Jocelyn, MA, MBA, FRSA; American editor and journalist; b. 15 Nov. 1950, New York; d. of Louis David Wile and Grace Carlin Wile; m. 1981; two d.; ed Brandeis and Cambridge Univs., London Grad. School of Business Studies; founder, owner Hobson Gallery, Cambridge 1981–87; co-f. (with Peter Fuller) Modern Painters magazine 1987–, Ed. 1990–; co-f. (with David Bowie, Sir Timothy Sainsbury and Bernard Jacobson) 21 Publishing 1997–; mem. Asscn Int. des Critiques d'Art. *Publications:* (as co-ed.) The Penguin Book of Art Writing 1998, Colour for Kosovo (ed.) 1999, The Grove Book of Art Writing 2000. *Leisure interests:* looking at art, children, reading, theatre, listening to music, skiing. *Address:* 78 Castellain Mansions, Castellain Road, London, W9 1HA, England. *Telephone:* (20) 7407-9247 (Office). *Fax:* (20) 7407-9242 (Office). *E-mail:* info@modernpainters.co.uk (Office); all .wright@virgin.net (Home). *Website:* www.modernpainters.co.uk (Office).

WRIGHT, Rev. Canon (Nicholas) Thomas, MA, DPhil, DD; British theologian and anglican bishop; b. 1 Dec. 1948, Northumberland; s. of Nicholas Irwin Wright and Rosemary Wright (née Forman); m. Margaret Elizabeth Anne Fiske 1971; two s. two d.; ed Sedbergh School, Exeter Coll. Oxford, Wycliffe Hall, Oxford; ordained Beacon 1975, Priest 1976; Jr Resident Fellow Merton Coll. Oxford 1975–78, Jr Chaplain 1976–78; Fellow and Chaplain Downing Coll. Cambridge 1978–81; Asst Prof. of New Testament Studies McGill Univ., Montréal and Hon. Prof. Montréal Diocesan Theological Coll., Canada 1981–86; Lecturer in Theology Univ. of Oxford and Fellow, Tutor and Chaplain, Worcester Coll. Oxford 1986–93; Dean of Lichfield 1994–99; Canon Theologian Coventry Cathedral 1992–99; Canon Theologian of Westminster 2000–03; Bishop of Durham Feb. 2003–; Fellow Inst. for Christian Studies, Toronto 1992–; mem. Doctrine Comm., Church of England 1979–81, 1989–95; regular broadcasts on TV and radio. *Publications include:* Small Faith, Great God 1978, The Work of John Frith 1983, The Epistles of Paul to the Colossians and to Philemon 1987, The Glory of Christ in the New Testament (co-ed.) 1987, The Interpretation of the New Testament 1861–1986 (co-author) 1988, The Climax of the Covenant 1991, New Tasks for a Renewed Church 1992, The Crown and the Fire 1992, The New Testament and the People of God 1992, Who Was Jesus? 1992, Following Jesus 1994, Jesus and the Victory of God 1996, The Lord and His Prayer 1996, What Saint Paul Really Said 1997, For All God's Worth 1997, Reflecting the Glory 1998, The Meaning of Jesus (co-author) 1999, The Myth of the Millennium 1999, Romans and the People of God (co-ed.) 1999, Holy Communion for Amateurs 1999, The Challenge of Jesus 2000, Twelve Months of Sundays, Year C 2000, Easter Oratorio (co-author) 2000, Twelve Months of Sundays, Year A 2001, Luke for Everyone 2001, Mark for Everyone 2001, Paul for Everyone: Galatians and Thessalonians 2002, John for Everyone 2002, Twelve Months of Sundays, Year B 2002, New Interpreter's Bible, Vol. X (contrib.) 2002. *Leisure interests:* music, hillwalking, poetry, cricket, golf. *Address:* Bishop of Durham, Auckland Castle, Bishop Auckland, Co. Durham, DL14 7NR, England (Office). *Telephone:* (1388) 602576 (Office). *Fax:* (1388) 605264 (Office). *E-mail:* bishop.of .durham@durham.anglican.org (Office). *Website:* www.durham.anglican.org (Office).

WRIGHT, Sir Oliver (see Wright, Sir (John) Oliver).

WRIGHT, Paddy; Irish business executive; joined Jefferson Smurfit 1976, fmrly Chief Exec. UK and Ireland, Pres. and COO 1996–2000; fmr Pres. Confed. of Irish Industry.

WRIGHT, Sir Peter Robert, Kt, CBE; British ballet director and choreographer; b. 25 Nov. 1926, London; s. of Bernard Wright and Hilda Foster; m. Sonya Hana 1954; one s. one d.; ed Bedales School and Leighton Park School, Reading; 1944 debut as professional dancer with Ballets Jooss; during 1950s worked with several dance cos. including Sadler's Wells Theatre Ballet; created first ballet, A Blue Rose, for Sadler's Wells 1957; Ballet Master, Sadler's Wells Opera and teacher, Royal Ballet School 1959; teacher and ballet master to ballet co. formed by John Cranko in Stuttgart 1961; choreographed several ballets in Stuttgart including The Mirror Walkers, Namouna, Designs for Dancers, Quintet and mounted his first production of Giselle; producer of TV ballets and choreographer of various London West End musicals and revues during 1960s; Asst Dir The Royal Ballet 1969, later Assoc. Dir; Dir Sadler's Wells Royal Ballet (now The Birmingham Royal Ballet) 1977–95; Dir Laureate, Birmingham Royal Ballet 1995–; Gov. Royal Ballet School 1976–2002, Sadler's Wells Theatre 1987–2000; Special Prof. of Performance Studies, Univ. of Birmingham 1990–; Fellow, Birmingham Conservatoire of Music 1991; Pres. Council of Dance Educ. and Training 1994–99, Friends of Sadler's Wells Theatre 1995–, Benesh Inst. of Choreology 1994–; Vice-Pres. Royal Acad. of Dancing 1993–, Myasthenia Gravis Asscn 1994–; Hon. DMus (London) 1990; Hon. DLitt (Birmingham) 1994; Evening Standard Award for Ballet 1981; Elizabeth II Coronation Award, Royal Acad. of Dancing 1990; Digital Premier Award 1991; Critics Award for Services to the Arts 1995. *Ballets directed include:* many productions in various countries of the full-length classics Giselle, Coppelia, Swan Lake, The Sleeping Beauty, The Nutcracker, but particularly for The Royal Ballet and the Birmingham Royal Ballet. *Leisure interests:* ceramics, gardens, travel, music. *Address:* 10 Chiswick Wharf, London, W4 2SR, England. *Telephone:* (20) 8747-1658. *Fax:* (20) 8400-9939.

WRIGHT, Robert C., LLB; American broadcasting executive; b. 23 April 1943, Hempstead, NY; m. Suzanne Wright 1967; one s. two d.; ed Chaminade High School, Holy Cross Coll. and Univ. of Virginia Law School; career in gen. man. marketing, broadcasting, strategic planning and law; fmr Pres. Cox Cable Communications; later Pres. Gen. Electric Financial Services, Vice-Chair. 2001; Pres. and CEO Nat. Broadcasting Co. (NBC) 1986–2001, Chair. and CEO 2001–. *Address:* General Electric Company, 3135 Easton Turnpike, Fairfield, CT 06431 (Office); National Broadcasting Company Inc., 30 Rockefeller Plaza, 52nd Floor, New York, NY 10112, USA. *Telephone:* (212) 664-4444.

WRIGHT OF RICHMOND, Baron (Life Peer), cr. 1994, of Richmond-upon-Thames in the London Borough of Richmond-upon-Thames; **Patrick Richard Henry Wright,** GCMG, FRCM; British diplomatist (retd); b. 28 June 1931, Reading; s. of the late Herbert H. S. Wright and Rachel Wright (née Green); m. Virginia Anne Gaffney 1958; two s. one d.; ed Marlborough Coll., Merton Coll., Univ. of Oxford; served RA 1950–51; joined Diplomatic Service 1955, Middle East Centre for Arabic Studies 1956–57, Third Sec., British Embassy, Beirut 1958–60, Pvt. Sec. to Amb., later First Sec., British Embassy, Washington 1960–65, Pvt. Sec. to Perm. Under-Sec., FCO 1965–67, First Sec. and Head of Chancery, Cairo 1967–70, Deputy Political Resident, Bahrain 1971–72, Head of Middle East Dept, FCO 1972–74; Pvt. Sec. (Overseas Affairs) to Prime Minister 1974–77; Amb. to Luxembourg 1977–79, to Syria 1979–81, to Saudi Arabia 1984–86; Deputy Under-Sec., FCO 1982–84; Perm. Under-Sec. of State, FCO and Head Diplomatic Service 1986–91; Dir Barclays Bank PLC 1991–96, British Petroleum (now BP Amoco) 1991–2000, De La Rue 1991–2000, Unilever 1991–99, British Airports Authority 1992–98; mem. Council, Royal Coll. of Music 1991–2001; Chair. Royal Inst. for Int. Affairs 1995–99; Gov. Wellington Coll. 1991–2001; Hon. Fellow Merton Coll. Oxford. *Leisure interests:* music, philately, travel. *Address:* c/o House of Lords, London, SW1A 0PW, England.

WRIGLEY, Sir Edward Anthony, Kt, MA, PhD, FBA; British academic; b. 17 Aug. 1931, Manchester; s. of Edward Wrigley and Jessie Wrigley; m. Maria Laura Spelberg 1960; one s. three d.; ed King's School, Macclesfield and Peterhouse, Cambridge; William Volker Research Fellow, Univ. of Chicago 1953–54; Fellow, Peterhouse 1958–79, Sr Bursar 1964–74, Hon. Fellow 1996–; Lecturer in Geography, Univ. of Cambridge 1958–74; Assoc. Dir Cambridge Group for the History of Population and Social Structure 1964–95; mem. Inst. of Advanced Study, Princeton 1970–71; Hinkley Visiting Prof., Johns Hopkins Univ. 1975; Tinbergen Visiting Prof., Erasmus Univ., Rotterdam 1979; Prof. of Population Studies, LSE 1979–88; Pres. Manchester Coll. Oxford 1987–96; Sr Research Fellow All Souls Coll. Oxford 1988–94, Acad. Sec. 1992–94, Fellow 2002–; Prof. of Econ. History, Univ. of Cambridge 1994–97; Master, Corpus Christi Coll. Cambridge 1994–2000; Ed. Econ. History Review 1985–92; Treas. British Acad. 1989–95, Pres. 1997–2001; James Ford Special Lecturer, Oxford 1986; Ellen Macarthur Lecturer, Cambridge 1987; Linacre Lecturer, Oxford 1998; Pres. British Soc. for Population Studies 1977–79; Chair. Population Investigation Cttee 1984–90; Laureate of the Int. Union for the Scientific Study of Population1993; Hon. Fellow LSE 1997; Hon. DLitt (Manchester) 1997, (Sheffield) 1997, (Bristol) 1998, (Oxford) 1999, (Leicester) 1999; Hon. DScS (Edin.) 1998; Founder's Medal, Royal Geographical Soc. 1997. *Publications:* Continuity, Chance and Change 1989,

several works on econ. and demographic history. *Leisure interest:* gardening. *Address:* 13 Sedley Taylor Road, Cambridge, CB2 2PW, England. *Telephone:* (1223) 247614. *E-mail:* tony.wrigley@ntlworld.com (Home).

WU, Sir Gordon, KCMG, BSc; Chinese businessman; b. 3 Dec. 1935, Hong Kong; s. of Chung Wu and Sum (née Kang) Wu; m. Kwok San-Ping Wu 1970; two s. two d.; ed Princeton Univ., USA; Man. Dir Hopewell Holdings, Hong Kong; responsible for construction of colony's tallest bldg, Hopewell Holdings HQ; built China Hotel, Canton, China; built new coal-fired power station for Prov. of Guangdong, China; new motorway linking Hong Kong to Shenzen and Canton now under construction; is responsible for design of many of his own bldgs; Vice-Pres. Hong Kong Real Estate Developer's Asscn 1970–; mem. Chinese People's Political Consultative Conf. 1984–. *Leisure interest:* classical music. *Address:* 641st Floor, Hopewell Centre, 183 Queen's Road East, Hong Kong Special Administrative Region, People's Republic of China. *Telephone:* 25284975. *Fax:* 28612068.

WU, Liang-Yong; Chinese architect; b. 7 May 1922, Nanjing, Jiangsu Prov.; m. Yao Tong-zhen; two s.; ed Nat. Cen. Univ. China, Cranbrook Acad. of Art, Bloomfield Hills, Mich.; Assoc. Prof. of Architecture and Urban Planning, Tsinghua Univ. 1951–61, Prof. 1961–; Dir Inst. of Architectural and Urban Studies 1983–, Centre for Human Settlements 1995–; Visiting Prof. Centre of Urban Studies and Urban Planning, Univ. of Hong Kong 1983, Ecole de Hautes Etudes Sociales, Paris 1987, Univ. of Calif. at Berkeley 1988, Sydney Univ. of Tech. 1993, Univ. of Cambridge 1995; Vice-Pres. Chinese Soc. for Urban Studies 1984–, Int. Union of Architects 1987–90; Pres. Urban Planning Soc. of China 1993–; mem. Academia Sinica 1980; Fellow Chinese Acad. of Science 1980–, Int. Acad. of Architecture 1989, Chinese Acad. of Eng 1995–; Hon. Mem. Architectural Inst. of Japan 1994; Hon. Fellow American Inst. of Architects 1990, Royal Inst. of British Architects 1998; numerous honours and awards including Gold Medal in Architecture for the Ju'er Project 1992, Jean Tschumi Prize, Int. Union of Architects 1996, Chevalier des Arts et des Lettres (France) 1999. *Publications:* A Brief History of Ancient Chinese City Planning 1985, Selected Essays on Urban Planning and Design 1987, Rehabilitating the Old City of Beijing 1999, Reflections at the Turn of the Century. The Future of Architecture 1999. *Leisure interests:* fine arts including painting and calligraphy. *Address:* School of Architecture, Tsinghua University, Beijing 100084 (Office); No. 12, Apt. 10, Tsinghua University, Beijing 100084, People's Republic of China (Home). *Telephone:* (10) 62784567 (Office); (10) 62784507 (Home). *Fax:* (10) 6562768 (Office); (10) 62781048 (Home). *E-mail:* engach@mail.cae.ac.cn (Office); wuly@public.bta.net.cn (Home).

WU BAI; Chinese actor and musician; b. 1968, Chaiyi Prov., Taiwan. *Films:* A Beautiful New World 1998, The Personals, Time and Tide 2000. *Music:* singer, songwriter with China Blue 1993–.

WU BANGGUO; Chinese party official and engineer; b. July 1941, Feidong, Anhui Prov.; ed Radio Electronics Dept, Qinghua Univ., Beijing; joined CCP 1964; worked at Shanghai No. 3 Electronic Tube Factory, progressing from freight worker to Factory Dir –1978; Deputy Man. Shanghai Municipal Electronics Components Industry Co., Shanghai Municipal Electrical Vacuum Device Co. 1979–81; Deputy Sec. Parl. Cttee Shanghai Municipal Instruments Bureau 1981–83; mem. Standing Cttee Shanghai Municipal CCP Cttee 1983–85, Deputy Sec. 1986–89, Sec. 1991–94; alt. mem. CCP Cen. Cttee 1985–92; mem. 14th Cen. Cttee 1992–97; mem. Politburo CCP 1992–; a Shanghai del. to 8th NPC 1993; mem. CCP Secr. 1994–; Vice-Premier of State Council 1995–; mem. 15th CCP Cen. Cttee 1997–2002, 16th CCP Cen. Cttee 2002–; mem. Standing Cttee CCP Politburo 2002–; Chair. Standing Cttee 10th NPC 2003–. *Address:* Quangguo Renmin Daibiao Dahui (National People's Congress), Beijing, People's Republic of China.

WU BOSHAN; Chinese banker; b. 1940; ed Cen. Coll. of Finance and Econs; joined CCP 1965; Pres. Investment Bank of China 1993. *Address:* c/o Investment Bank of China, Beijing, People's Republic of China.

WU DECHANG; Chinese academic; b. 22 Oct. 1927, Beijing; m. Lin Rhi-zhu 1951; one s. two d.; ed Peking Univ. and in USSR; Prof. of Toxicology, Inst. of Radiation Medicine Beijing 1981–; Commdt Mil. Medical Science Acad. of PLA 1990–94; del. to 14th Nat. Conf. CCP 1991–; mem. 8th Nat. Cttee CPPCC 1993–97; Pres. Chinese Soc. of Toxicology; Academician, Chinese Acad. of Eng; Nat. Science and Tech. Awards 1985, 1993, 1995. *Publications:* Radiation Risk and Assessment 1999, Radiation Medicine 2000. *Leisure interest:* classical music. *Address:* Military Medical Science Academy of People's Liberation Army, 27 Tai-Ping Road, Beijing 100850, People's Republic of China. *Telephone:* (10) 68186211. *Fax:* (10) 68214653. *E-mail:* wudc@nic.bmi .ac.cn (Office); wudc@public.bta.net.cn (Office).

WU GUANGYU, Lt-Gen.; Chinese air force officer; b. Dec. 1940, Hongze Co., Jiangsu Prov.; ed middle school and Air Force Aviation School; joined PLA 1958; mem. CCP 1964–; air force pilot and squadron leader 1962–70; various posts in Air Force Aviation 1970–85; Commdr Air Force units, PLA Shanghai Base 1985; Commdr PLA Air Force Command Post 1985–90; Deputy Commdr Nanjing Mil. Regional Air Force 1990–93; Deputy Commdr and Air Force Commdr Jinan Mil. Region 1993; Deputy Commdr PLA Air Force 1995–; Deputy to 6th NPC 1983; alt. mem. 14th CCP Cen. Cttee 1992–97. *Address:* c/o Ministry of National Defence, Jingshanqian Jie, Beijing, People's Republic of China. *Telephone:* (10) 6370000.

WU GUANZHENG; Chinese government official; b. 25 Aug. 1938, Yugan Co., Jiangxi Prov.; s. of Wu Enshui and Dong Gelao; m. Zhang Jinshang 1959;

three s.; ed Power Dept, Qinghua Univ., Beijing; joined CCP 1962; mem. CCP Cttee of Wuhan Gedian Chemical Plant, Deputy Dir Revolutionary Cttee of Wuhan Gedian Chemical Plant 1968–75; Deputy Dir Wuhan Science and Tech. Cttee, Vice-Chair. Wuhan City Asscn of Science and Tech., Deputy Commdr and Dir of Gen. Office, Wuhan City Technical Innovation Headquarters; Dir, Sec. CCP Cttee of Wuhan City Eng Science and Tech. Research Centre 1975–82; standing mem. CCP Cttee of Wuhan City 1982–83; Sec. CCP Cttee and Mayor of Wuhan City 1983–86; Deputy Sec. Jiangxi Prov. CCP Cttee, Acting Gov., Gov. Jiangxi Prov. 1986–95; Sec. CCP Cttee Jiangxi Prov., First Sec. CCP Cttee Jiangxi Prov. Mil. Command 1995–97, Sec. CCP Cttee Shandong Prov. and Prin. of School for CCP Shandong Cttee 1997–; alt. mem. 12th CCP Cen. Cttee 1982–87; mem. 13th CCP Cen. Cttee 1987–92; mem. 14th CCP Cen. Cttee 1992–97; mem. Politburo 15th CCP Cen. Cttee, mem. 15th CCP Cen. Cttee 1997–2002; mem. 16th CCP Cen. Cttee 2002–, mem. Standing Cttee CCP Politburo 2002–. *Leisure interests:* reading, sports. *Address:* 482 Weiyi Road, Jinan City, Shandong, People's Republic of China. *Telephone:* (531) 2033333.

WU GUANZHONG; Chinese painter and university professor; b. Yixing Co., Jiangsu Prov.; ed Nat. Inst. of Fine Arts, Hangzhou; Ecole Nat. Supérieure des Beaux Arts, Paris; Prof. Cen. Inst. of Applied Arts 1980–; exhbns. in Japan, France, Singapore and Hong Kong; mem. 6th CPPCC 1983–87, 7th 1988–92, mem. 8th Nat. Cttee 1993–98; Hon. mem. China Fed. of Literary and Art Circles 1996. *Address:* Central Institute of Applied Arts, 34 Dong Sanhuan North Road, Beijing 100020, People's Republic of China.

WU GUOXIONG, PhD; Chinese meteorologist; b. 20 March 1943, Chaoyang, Guangdong; ed Nanjing Meteorological Inst., Beijing Univ., Imperial Coll. London, UK; Research Fellow, Inst. of Atmospheric Physics Chinese Acad. of Sciences; Chair. Academic Cttee, Nat. Key Lab. of Atmospheric Sciences and Geophysical Fluid Dynamics; Chair. Chinese Cttee for Int. Asscn of Meteorology and Atmospheric Sciences (IAMAS); Academician, Chinese Academy of Sciences 1997–. *Publications:* Time-Mean Statistics of Global General Circulation 1987, Dynamics of Subtropical Anticyclones 2002. *Address:* Institute of Atmospheric Physics, Chinese Academy of Sciences, Qijiahuozi, Beijing 100029 (Office); Room 602, Building 917, Zhong-Guan-Chun, Beijing 100081, People's Republic of China (Home). *Telephone:* (10) 62043356 (Office); (10) 62560155 (Home). *Fax:* (10) 62043526 (Office). *E-mail:* gxwu@lasg.iap.ac.cn (Office). *Website:* www.lasg.ac.cn (Office).

WU HUALUN; Chinese artist; b. June 1942, Tianjin; s. of Wu Bing-Zheng and Wang Yaxin; m. Zeng Wan 1985; ed Cen. Acad. of Arts and Crafts; mem. China Artists' Asscn 1982–, China Calligraphists' Asscn 1986–; Sr Art Ed., China People's Fine Art Publishing House; Prof. 1999–; works have been exhibited many times in Japan, Hong Kong and USA; First Prize, Chinese Paintings Competition 1988; Gold Medal, Japan-China Art Exchange Centre 1988. *Art Exhibitions:* one-man exhbn of paintings 1988, Gallery Triform, Taiwan; TV show featuring figure paintings, Beijing 1998. *Publication:* Chinese Paintings by Wu Hualun 1989. *Leisure interests:* travelling, playing badminton. *Address:* People's Fine Arts Publishing House, 32 Bei Zong Bu Hutong, Beijing 100735, People's Republic of China (Office). *Telephone:* (10) 65244901 (Office).

WU JIANCHANG; Chinese business executive; son-in-law of Deng Xiaoping; fmr Deputy Gen. Man. China Nat. Nonferrous Metals Import and Export Corpn; Vice-Pres. China Nat. Nonferrous Metals Industry Corpn 1984–94, Chair. 1994–. *Address:* China National Nonferrous Metals Industry Corporation, 12B Fuxing Lu, Beijing 100814, People's Republic of China. *Telephone:* (10) 63975588. *Fax:* (10) 63964424.

WU JICHUAN; Chinese party and government official; b. 1937, Changning Co., Hunan Prov.; joined CCP 1960; Vice-Minister of Posts and Telecommunications 1984–90, Minister 1993–98; Minister of Information Industry 1998–2003; Deputy Sec. Henan Prov. CCP Cttee 1990–93; alt. mem., 14th Cen. Cttee 1992–97; Vice-Chair. State Radio Regulatory Cttee; mem. 15th CCP Cen. Cttee 1997–2002, 16th CCP Cen. Cttee 2002–. *Address:* c/o Ministry of Information Industry, 13 Xichangan Jie, Beijing 100804, People's Republic of China.

WU JIEPING; Chinese urologist; b. 22 Jan. 1917, Jiangsu; s. of Wu Jingyi and Cheng Xia; m. 1st Zhao Junkai 1933; m. 2nd Gao Rui 1984; one s. two d.; Prof. Beijing Medical Coll. 1957–; mem. 2nd Medical Coll. Beijing 1960–70; Vice-Pres. Chinese Medical Asscn 1978–84, Pres. 1984–89, Hon. Pres. 1989–; Vice-Pres. Acad. of Medical Sciences 1970–83, Pres. 1983–85, Hon. Pres. 1985–; Vice-Chair. Cen. Council Int. Planned Parenthood Fed. (IPPF) 1986–, Chair. Regional Council 1991–; Vice-Chair. Standing Cttee 8th NPC 1993–98, 9th NPC 1998–; Chair. Jiusan (Sept. 3) Soc. 1997–; Fellow, Chinese Acad. of Science 1981–98, Sr Fellow 1998–; Fellow Chinese Acad. of Eng 1995–98, Sr Fellow 1998–; Hon. Fellow American Coll. of Physicians 1989, American Urological Asscn 1995–, Royal Coll. of Surgeons, Edin., U.K. 1996–. *Leisure interest:* reading. *Address:* National People's Congress, Tiananmen, Beijing 100730, People's Republic of China. *Telephone:* (10) 65135844. *Fax:* (10) 65124876. *E-mail:* egach@mail.cae.ac.cn (Office).

WU JINGHUA; Chinese state official; b. 1931, Mianning Co., Sichuan Prov.; Deputy to 4th NPC 1975; Vice-Minister, State Nationalities' Affairs Comm. 1979; Vice-Chair. Sichuan Prov. People's Congress 1979–83; Pres. Sichuan Prov. Soc. for Agricultural Modernization in Areas Inhabited by Minorities 1981–83; mem. 12th CCP Cen. Cttee 1982–87, 13th Cen. Cttee 1987–93; Sec.

CCP Cttee, Tibet 1985–88; Political Commissar, PLA Tibet Mil. Dist 1985–88; Vice-Minister State Nationalities Affairs Comm. 1985–88, Deputy Sec. Party Group, State Nationalities Affairs Comm. 1988; Vice-Chair. Agric. and Rural Affairs Cttee 9th NPC 1998–. *Address:* c/o Standing Committee of National People's Congress, Beijing, People's Republic of China.

WU JINGLIAN; Chinese economist; b. Jan. 1930, Nanjing, Jiangsu Prov.; ed Fudan Univ.; Asst Research Fellow, Econs Research Inst. of Chinese Acad. of Sciences 1954–79; Assoc. Research Fellow, Econs Inst. of Chinese Acad. of Social Sciences 1979–83, Research Fellow and Prof. 1983–; Vice-Dir Office for Econ. Reform Programmes of State Council, Vice-Chair. Econ. Cttee of CPPCC 1984–; elected one of China's Top Ten Econ. Figures 2000. *Publications:* Explorations into Problems of Economic Reform, Planned Economy or Market Economy. *Address:* c/o Chinese Academy of Social Sciences, Beijing, People's Republic of China.

WU LENGXI; Chinese party official and journalist; b. 1919, Xinhui, Guangdong; ed Wuhan Univ., Lu Xun Acad. of Arts; worked for Mass Daily, Henan 1937; Man. Ed. 7 July Daily, Cen. Plain Mil. Region 1937; Deputy Dir Propaganda Dept, Cen. Plain Mil. Region 1948; Prin. Cadre New China News Agency (NCNA), trained in Pingshanxian, Hebei 1949; Man. Ed. NCNA 1949–50, Deputy Dir 1950–52, Dir 1952–Cultural Revolution; Deputy for Tianjin, 1st NPC 1954–59; mem. Comm. for Cultural Relations with Foreign Countries 1954; Man. Ed. Renmin Ribao (People's Daily) 1958–Cultural Revolution; Deputy for Guangdong, 2nd NPC 1958, 3rd NPC 1964; Deputy Dir Propaganda Dept, CCP Cen. Cttee 1964–Cultural Revolution; mem. Standing Cttee, 3rd NPC 1965–Cultural Revolution; disappeared 1966–72; leading mem. People's Daily 1972; mem. Standing Cttee, 4th NPC 1975; Alt. mem. 11th Cen. Cttee, CCP 1977, 12th Cen. Cttee 1982; Deputy for Shanghai, 5th NPC 1978; mem. Standing Cttee, 5th NPC 1978; Deputy Dir Propaganda Dept, Cen. Cttee 1978; mem. Standing Cttee, Nat. Cttee, 5th CPPCC 1978, 7th 1988–93; fmr Sec. CCP Cttee, Guangdong; Adviser Beijing Journalism Studies Soc. 1980; Alt. mem. 12th Cen. Cttee CCP 1982–87; Minister of Radio and TV 1982–86; Chair. All Journalists' Asscn 1983–; Vice-Pres. China Int. Cultural Exchange Centre 1984–; Pres. Soc. of Radio and TV Oct. 1986–, Soc. for Studies of Radio and TV Oct. 1986–, Chinese Friends Research Foundation 1989–; mem. Standing Cttee 7th CPPCC 1988–93; Vice-Pres. China Int. Cultural Exchange Centre; mem. Educ. and Cultural Cttee 1988–. *Address:* State Council, Beijing, People's Republic of China.

WU MIN, DMed; Chinese geneticist; b. 1925, Changzhou, Jiangsu Prov.; ed Tongji Univ. Medical Coll., USSR Acad. of Medical Science; Research Fellow and then Dir Cytobiology Section of Tumour Research Inst., Chinese Acad. of Medical Science 1961–; Vice-Pres. Council of Chinese Genetics Soc.; mem. Standing Cttee Biology Dept Chinese Acad. of Sciences; mem. 4th Presidium, Chinese Acad. of Sciences 2000–. *Publication:* The Mitotic Caryotype of the Chinese. *Address:* Chinese Academy of Sciences, 52 Sanlihe Road, Beijing 100864, People's Republic of China (Office). *Telephone:* (10) 68597219 (Office). *Fax:* (10) 68511095 (Office).

WU POH-HSIUNG, BSc; Taiwanese politician; b. 19 June 1939, Taoyuan County; m. Dai Mei-yu; two s. one d.; ed Nat. Cheng Kung Univ., Sun Yat-sen Inst. of Policy and Research and Devt; school-teacher 1963–65; mem. Taiwan Prov. Ass. 1968–72; Assoc. Prof. Nan Ya Jr Coll. of Tech. 1972–73; Magistrate, Taoyuan County 1973–76; Dir Inst. of Industry for Workmen and Friends of Labour Asscn, Dir-Gen. Taiwan Tobacco and Wine Monopoly Bureau 1976–80; Dir Inst. of Industrial and Vocational Training for Workmen 1976–80; Chair. Repub. of China Amateur Boxing Asscn 1981–82; Dir Secr., Cen. Cttee, Kuomintang 1982–84, Chair. Cen. Exec. Cttee; Minister of Interior 1984–88, 1991–94; Mayor of Taipei 1988–90; Minister of State 1990–91; apptd. Sec.-Gen. Office of the Pres. 1994; Chair. Cen. Election Comm. 1991–94, Political Party Review Cttee 1991–94. *Address:* c/o Office of the President, 122 Chungking South Road, Sec. 1, Taipei, Taiwan.

WU RENBAO; Chinese farmer and business executive; b. Nov. 1928, Jiangyin, Jiangsu Prov.; joined CCP 1952; Sec. CCP Huaxi Village br., Huazi, Jiangyin Co. 1961–; Gen. Man. Huaxi Agribusiness Co.; Vice-Chair. Chinese Township Enterprises Asscn 1991; named Nat. Model Worker 1989. *Address:* Huaxi Village, Jiangyin, Jiangsu Province, People's Republic of China (Office).

WU SHAOZU, Maj.-Gen.; Chinese politician; b. 1939, Laiyang Co., Hunan Prov.; two s.; ed Qinghua Univ., Beijing; Chair. Student Fed. 1965–82; Deputy, 3rd NPC 1964–66; Vice-Minister State Comm. of Science, Tech. and Industry for Nat. Defence 1982–88; promoted to Maj.-Gen. PLA 1988; Minister State Physical Culture and Sports Comm. 1988–98; Dir State Gen. Bureau for Physical Culture and Sports 1998–2000; mem. 14th and 15th Cen. Cttee CCP 1992–2002; Pres. Chinese Olympic Cttee. *Address:* c/o State General Bureau for Physical Culture and Sports, 9 Tiyuguan Road, Chongwen District, Beijing 100763, People's Republic of China.

WU SHUANGZHAN, Maj.-Gen.; Chinese police officer; b. Feb. 1945, Qingfeng, Henan Prov.; ed PLA Nat. Defence Univ.; joined PLA 1963; joined CCP 1965; Vice-Chief of Staff of Beijing Mil. Area Command and Chief of Staff of the People's Armed Police 1990–92; Deputy Commdr-in-Chief of the People's Armed Police 1992–99, C.-in-C. 1999–. *Address:* People's Armed Police Headquarters, Suzhou Jie, Beijing 100089, People's Republic of China (Office).

WU SHUOING; Chinese economist; b. Jiangyin, Jiangyin Prov.; ed Shanghai East-China People's Revolution Univ.; research student of political econ., Renmin Univ.; fmrly Prof., Pres. of Grad. School, Vice-Pres. Renmin Univ.; Prof., Pres. Peking Univ. 1989–96; mem. Standing Cttee 8th and 9th NPC 1993–. *Publications:* Shenme Shi Zhengzhi Jingyixue (What Is Political Economy?), Zhongguo Shehuizhuyi Jianshe (China's Socialist Construction), Moshi, Yunxing and Kongzhi (Model, Operation and Control). *Address:* Peking University, 1 Loudouqiao, Beijing 100871, People's Republic of China (Office).

WU TIANMING; Chinese film director; b. Oct. 1939, Shaanxi Prov.; m. Mu Shulan; ed Xian Drama School; Head of Xian Film Studio 1983–89; Visiting Scholar Univ. of Calif., USA 1990–91. *Films:* Kith and Kin 1981, River Without Buoys 1983, Life 1984, The Old Well 1987.

WU WEIRAN; Chinese surgeon; b. 14 Oct. 1920, Changzhou, Jiangsu Prov.; s. of Wu Jingyi and Zheng Zhixia; m. Huang Wuchiung 1951; three d.; Deputy Dir Surgery Soc., attached to the Medical Soc. 1972; Deputy Dir Surgery Dept, Beijing Union Medical Coll. Hosp., Chinese Acad. of Medical Sciences 1972; now Prof. of Surgery, Surgical Dept, Beijing Union Medical Coll. Hosp., Chinese Acad. of Medical Sciences; Hon. Dir Beijing Hosp.; alt. mem. 12th CCP Cen. Cttee 1982, mem. 1985, mem. 13th Cen. Cttee 1987–92; mem. Presidium of 14th CCP Nat. Congress 1992. *Leisure interest:* gardening. *Address:* Surgery Department, Beijing Hospital, 1 Dahalu, Dondan, Beijing 100730, People's Republic of China. *Telephone:* 65132266. *Fax:* 65132969.

WU WENJUN; Chinese mathematician; b. 12 May 1919, Jiansu Prov.; ed in USA; returned to China in 1950; Deputy Dir, Math. Inst. Acad. Sinica 1964; mem. Standing Cttee of 5th CPPCC 1978; Deputy Dir, Inst. of Systems Science, Acad. Sinica 1980; mem., Standing Cttee of 6th CPPCC 1983; Pres., Math. Soc. of China 1984; Dir Mathematics and Physics Div. 1992–; mem., Dept of Math. and Physics, Chinese Acad. of Sciences 1985, now Dir; mem. Standing Cttee of 7th CPPCC 1988; mem. 8th CPPCC Nat. Cttee 1993–98.

WU XICHAO; Chinese surgeon; b. Aug. 1922, Malayasia; ed Shanghai Tongji Univ. Medical Coll.; doctor in charge, lecturer, Assoc. Prof., Prof., Vice-Pres. PLA Second Medical Univ. 1949–; Vice-Chair. Medical Soc. of China; Fellow, Chinese Acad. of Sciences; named Model Medical Expert by CCP Cen. Mil. Comm. 1996. *Address:* Chinese People's Liberation Army Second Medical University, Shanghai, People's Republic of China (Office).

WU XU, Maj.-Gen.; Chinese army officer; b. March 1939, Changsu City, Jiangsu Prov.; ed 5th Artillery School and PLA Mil. Acad.; joined PLA 1954; mem. CCP 1959–; various posts in artillery, reconnaissance and training 1956–85; army corps political commissar and army corps Commdr 1985–92; Asst Chief of Gen. Staff 1992; Deputy Chief, PLA Gen. Staff 1995–; mem. 15th CCP Cen. Cttee 1997–2002. *Address:* Ministry of National Defence, Jingshanqian Jie, Beijing, People's Republic of China. *Telephone:* (1) 6370000.

WU XUEQIAN; Chinese politician; b. 1921, Shanghai; joined CCP 1939; Council mem. Asscn for Cultural Relations with Foreign Countries 1954–67; disappeared during Cultural Revolution 1967–77; mem. 5th CPPCC 1978–82; Vice-Minister of Foreign Affairs May–Nov. 1982; Minister of Foreign Affairs 1982–88; State Councillor 1983–88, Vice-Premier State Council 1988–93; mem. 12th Cen. Cttee CCP 1982, 13th Cen. Cttee 1987; mem. Political Bureau of Cen. Cttee 1985–92; Dir Comm. for Commemorating 40th Anniversary of UN 1985; Chair. State Tourism Cttee 1988; mem. Presidium of 14th CCP Nat. Congress 1992; Vice-Chair. 8th Nat. Cttee CPPCC 1993–98; mem. and head numerous dels. abroad; other public appointments. *Address:* State Council, Beijing, People's Republic of China.

WU YI; Chinese politician, engineer and administrator; b. Nov. 1938, Wuhan City, Hubei Prov.; ed Dept of Petroleum Refining, Beijing Petroleum Inst.; joined CCP 1962; Vice-Mayor of Beijing 1988–91; Vice-Minister of Foreign Trade 1991–93; alt. mem. 13th CCP Cen. Cttee 1987–92; mem. 14th CCP Cen. Cttee 1992–97; Minister of Foreign Trade and Econ. Co-operation 1993–98; Chair. Bd of Dirs Foreign Trade Univ. 1995–98; alt. mem. CCP Politburo 1997–2002; mem. 15th CCP Cen. Cttee 1997–2002, 16th CCP Cen. Cttee 2002–; State Councillor 1998–2003, Vice-Premier State Council 2003–; Minister of Public Health 2003–. *Address:* Ministry of Public Health, 1 Xizhinenwai Bei Lu, Xicheng Qu, Beijing 100044 (Office); State Council, Beijing, People's Republic of China. *Telephone:* (10) 68792114 (Office). *Fax:* (10) 64012369 (Office). *Website:* www.moh.gov.cn (Office).

WU YIGONG; Chinese film director; b. 1 Dec. 1938, Chongqing, Sichuan Prov.; s. of Wu Tiesan and Yu Minhua; m. Zhang Wen Rong 1967; one s.; Dir Shanghai Film Bureau, Gen. Man. Shanghai Film Corpn, Vice-Pres. China Film Artists' Asscn 1985–; alt. mem. 14th CCP Cen. Cttee 1992–97, mem. 15th CCP Cen. Cttee 1997–; Vice-Chair. China Fed. of Literary and Art Circles 1996–. *Films include:* University in Exile, The Tribulations of a Chinese Gentleman, Bitter Sea, Evening Rain 1980, A Confucius Family 1992; Golden Rooster Award 1984 for Best Dir of film My Memories of Old Beijing, Magnolia Prize for A Man Aged 18 1988. *Leisure interests:* music, sports. *Address:* 52 Yong Fu Road, Shanghai, People's Republic of China. *Telephone:* 4332558. *Fax:* 4370528.

WU ZUGUANG; Chinese author and dramatist; b. 21 April 1917, Beijing; s. of Wu Ying and Zhou Qin Qi; m. Xin Fengxia 1950; two s. one d; ed China-France Univ.; mem. 6th CPPCC 1983–87, 7th 1988–92, 8th 1993–98; Adviser Chinese Writers' Asscn 1996. *Plays:* Wind Snow Night, Itinerant Entertainer, Xin Fengxia I–XII (TV plays) and others. *Address:* 9-5-7 Gongren Tiyuchang Donglu, Beijing 100020, People's Republic of China. *Telephone:* 65524404.

WU ZUQIANG; Chinese musician and composer; b. 24 July 1927, Beijing; s. of Jing-zhou Wu and Qin-qi (née Zhou) Wu; m. Li-qin Zheng 1953; one s. one d.; Vice-Pres. Cen. Conservatory of Music 1978–82, Pres. 1982–88, now Prof., Hon. Pres.; Vice-Pres. Chinese Musicians' Asscn 1985–; Vice-Exec. Chair. China Fed. of Literary and Art Circles 1988–95, Vice-Chair. 1995; Adviser to China Nat. Symphony Orchestra 1996; alt. mem. 12th CCP Cen. Cttee 1982; Perm. mem. Nat. Cttee 7th, 8th and 9th CPPCC 1988–. *Leisure interests:* literature, fine arts, tourism. *Address:* Central Conservatory of Music, 43 Baojiajie West District, Beijing 100031, People's Republic of China. *Telephone:* (10) 66414887. *Fax:* (10) 66417211.

WUFFLI, Peter A.; Swiss banking executive; b. 26 Oct. 1957; s. of Heinz Wuffli; began career as journalist, Neue Zurcher Zeitung; Man. Consultant, McKinsey & Co. 1984–90, Partner, McKinsey Switzerland 1990–94; joined Swiss Banking Corpn (SBC) 1994, Chief Financial Officer, mem. Exec. Cttee 1994–98; Chief Financial Officer UBS Group (following merger with UBS) 1998–, Chair. and CEO UBS Asset Man. –2001, Pres. UBS Group Dec. 2001–. *Address:* UBS AG, Bahnhofstrasse 45, P.O. Box 8098, Zürich, Switzerland (Office). *Telephone:* (1) 2344100 (Office). *Fax:* (1) 2343415 (Office). *Website:* www.ubs.com (Office).

WULF-MATHIES, Monika, DPhil; German international organization official; b. 17 March 1942, Wernigerode; d. of Carl-Hermann Baier and Margott Baier (née Meisser); m. Carsten Wulf-Mathies 1968; ed Univs. of Hamburg and Freiburg; Br. Asst Fed. Ministry of Econs 1968–71; Head of Dept for Social Policy, Fed. Chancellery 1971–76; mem. ÖTV (Public Services and Transport Workers' Union) 1971–, mem. Man. Exec. Cttee 1976–95, Chair. of ÖTV (representing around 2.3 million workers) 1982–95; Commr for Regional Policies of EU 1995–99; Pres. Public Services Int. 1989–94; mem. Exec. Bd Deutsche Lufthansa AG 1978–95 (Deputy Chair. 1988–95), VEBA 1989–95; mem. SPD 1965–. *Leisure interests:* gardening, cross-country skiing. *Address:* c/o European Commission, 200 rue de la Loi, 1049 Brussels, Belgium.

WUNDERLICH, Paul; German painter, sculptor and lithographer; b. 10 March 1927, Eberswalde; s. of Horst Wunderlich and Gertud Wunderlich (née Arendt); m. 1st Isabella von Bethmann-Hollweg 1957 (divorced 1959); m. 2nd Karin Székessy 1971; two d.; ed Academie Hamburg; Prof. of Drawing and Painting, Acad. Hamburg 1963–68; freelance artist 1969–; Premio Marzotto 1967, Kama Kura Prize, Tokyo 1968, Kunstpreis, Schleswig-Holstein 1986. *Publications:* Monographie Paul Wunderlich Vol. I 1978, Vol. II 1980, Werkverzeichnis der Grafik 1982, Skulpturen und Objekte 1988, Skulpturen und Objekte II 2000, Drypoint I 2000, Drypoint II 2001, Grafik II 2002, Schmuck 2002. *Address:* Haynstrasse 2, 20249 Hamburg, Germany. *Telephone:* (40) 487387. *Fax:* (40) 476312. *E-mail:* www.paul@wunderlich.org (Home).

WUNSCH, Carl Isaac, PhD; American physical oceanographer and university professor; b. 5 May 1941, Brooklyn, New York; s. of Harry Wunsch and Helen (née Gellis) Wunsch; m. Marjory Markel 1980; one s. one d.; ed Mass. Inst. of Tech.; Lecturer in Oceanography, MIT 1966–67, Asst Prof. 1967–70, Assoc. Prof. 1970–75, Prof. of Physical Oceanography 1975–76, Cecil and Ida Green Prof. 1976–, Sec. of Navy Research Prof. 1985–89; Sr Visiting Fellow, Dept of Applied Math. and Theoretical Physics, Cambridge Univ., England 1969, 1974–75, 1981–82; Fulbright Scholar 1981–82; John Simon Guggenheim Foundation Fellow 1981–82; Visiting Sr Scientist, GFDL, Princeton Univ. 1993–94; Visiting Scientist, CNES/CNRS, Toulouse, France 1994; Distinguished Visiting Scientist, Jet Propulsion Lab. 1994–; Chair. Ocean Studies Bd, NRC; Consultant to NAS, NSF; Fellow American Acad. of Arts and Sciences, American Geophysical Union, American Meteorological Soc.; mem. NAS, Royal Astronomical Soc., Soc. for Industrial and Applied Mathematics; James R. Macelwane Award 1971, Maurice Ewing Medal 1990, American Geophysical Union, Founders Prize, Texas Instrument Foundation 1975, A.G. Huntsman Prize 1988, Public Service Medal, NASA 1993, Henry Stommel Prize, American Meteorological Soc. 2000, Moore Distinguished Scholar, Calif. Inst. of Tech. 2000. *Publications:* Evolution of Physical Oceanography (co-ed.), Ocean Acoustic Tomography (co-author), The Ocean Circulation Inverse Problem; many tech. papers. *Leisure interest:* sailing. *Address:* Room 54-1524, Department of Earth, Atmospheric and Planetary Science, Massachusetts Institute of Technology, Cambridge, MA 02139 (Office); 78 Washington Avenue, Cambridge, MA 02140, USA (Home). *Telephone:* (617) 253-5937 (Office). *Fax:* (617) 253-4464.

WURTH, Hubert, LLB; Luxembourg diplomatist; b. 15 April 1952; m. Lydie Polfer (q.v.); two c.; ed Univ. de Paris II, Inst. d'Etudes Politiques, Paris; called to the Luxembourg Bar 1977; Attaché Dept of Int. Econ. Relations, Ministry of Foreign Affairs 1978; Deputy Perm. Rep. to Council of Europe 1979; Chief Sec. to Vice-Pres. of the Govt and Minister for Foreign Affairs, Econ. Affairs and Justice 1981; Deputy Dir of Political Affairs 1986; Amb. to USSR (also accred to Poland, Finland and Mongolia) 1988–92, to the Netherlands 1992–98 (also served as rep. for the Pact on Stability in Europe 1993–95 and on special mission in Fmr Yugoslavia 1996); Perm. Rep. to the UN 1998–. *Exhibitions:* exhbns in Luxembourg, Moscow, Helsinki, Amsterdam, The Hague, New York (Abstract Painting). *Publication:* Monography on Hubert Wurth as a Painter 1998. *Address:* Permanent Mission of Luxembourg to the

United Nations, 17 Beekman Place, New York, NY 10022, USA (Office). *Telephone:* (212) 935-3589 (Office). *Fax:* (212) 935-5896 (Office). *E-mail:* luxembourg@un.int (Office).

WÜTHRICH, Kurt, PhD; Swiss scientist and academic; b. 4 Oct. 1938, Aarberg; m. Marianne Briner 1963; one s. one d.; ed ed. Univs of Bern, Basel and California at Berkeley, USA; mem. tech. staff Bell Telephone Labs 1967–69; Privatdozent, Swiss Fed. Inst. of Tech. (Eidgenössische Technische Hochschule—ETH), Zürich 1970–72, Asst Prof. 1972–76, Assoc. Prof. 1976–80, Prof. of Biophysics 1980– (Chair. Biology Dept 1995–2000); Visiting Miller Research Prof., Univ. of Calif. at Berkeley, USA 1988; Scholar-in-Residence, Johns Hopkins Univ., Baltimore, USA 1992; Sherman Fairchild Distinguished Scholar, Caltech, Pasadena, USA 1994, Visiting Assoc. in Biology and Chemistry 1995; Guest Scientist, The Scripps Research Inst., Calif., USA 1994, Cecil H. and Ida M. Green Visiting Prof. of Structural Biology 2001–; Visiting Prof. Inst. of Physical and Chemical Research (RIKEN), Tokyo, Japan 1997–98, Univ. of Edin., UK 1997–2000; consultant Hoechst AG, Frankfurt, Germany 1985–92, Sandoz Pharma AG, Basel 1987–96, Hoffman-La Roche AG, Basel 1987–, Ciba-Geigy AG, Basel 1989–96, Tripos Inc., St Louis, USA 1992–94, Novartis AG, Basel 1997–; mem. European Molecular Biology Org. (EMBO) 1984, Deutsche Akademie der Naturforscher Leopoldina 1987, Academia Europaea 1989, Schweizerische Akademie der Technischen Wissenschaft (SATW) 2001, Schweizerische Akademie der Medizinischen Wissenschaft (SAMW) 2002; Foreign Fellow, Indian Nat. Science Acad. 1989; Foreign Assoc., US Nat. Acad. of Sciences, India 1992, Académie des Sciences, Inst. de France 2000; Fellow, American Asscn for the Advancement of Science 1998; mem. Schweiz Kommission für Molekularbiologie (SKMB) 1973–76, Pres. 1977–82; mem. council Int. Union of Pure and Applied Biophysics (IUPAB) 1975–78, 1987–90, Sec.-Gen. 1978–84, Vice-Pres. 1984–87; mem. Gen. Cttee Int. Council of Scientific Unions (ICSU) 1980–86, mem. Standing Cttee on the Free Circulation of Scientists 1982–90; mem. Kommission für die Wolfgang Pauli-Vorlesungen, ETH Zürich 1984–92, Pres. 1993–2001; Pres. Züricher Chemiker Gesellschaft 1990–91; mem. Exec. Cttee Schweiz Gesellschaft für Biochemie 1986–92, Pres. Biophysics Section 1985–88; mem. Int. Union of Pure and Applied Chemistry (IUPAC), Comm. on Biophysical Chemistry 1969–99, Chair. 2000–01; mem. Prix Marcel Benoist, Conseil de Fondation, Berne 2001–; mem. bd Centro Stefano Franscini, Monte Verità and ETH Zürich 1989–98, European Molecular Biology Lab., Heidelberg, Germany 1989–95, Nat. Lab. of Biomacromolecules, Academia Sinica, Beijing, China 1989–, Deutsche Forschungsgemeinschaft, Bonn, Germany: Schwerpunktsprogramm "Protein Design" 1989–95, Comm. of the European Communities: Human Capital and Mobility Programme 1992–94, Inst. für Molekulare Biotechnologie, Jena, Germany 1993–96, Ciba Foundation, London, UK 1994–96, Inst. de Biologie Structurale Jean-Pierre Ebel, Grenoble, France 1994–97, Inst. of Biotechnology, Univ. of Helsinki, Finland 1997–, Novartis Foundation, London, UK 1997–, Triad Therapeutics Inc., San Diego, CA, USA 1998–, Genomics Sciences Centre, RIKEN, Tokyo, Japan 2000–, Syrrx Inc., San Diego, CA, USA 2000–, Groupement d'Intérêt Scientifique "Infections à Prions", France 2001–, Nat. Inst. of Chemical Physics and Biophysics (NICPB), Tallinn, Estonia 2001–, Nat. High Field NMR Center (NANUC), Univ. of Alberta, Edmonton, AB, Canada 2001–, Binomix Inc., Pasadena, CA, USA 2002–; Hon. Fellow, Nat. Acad. of Sciences, India 1992; Foreign Hon. mem., American Acad. of Arts and Sciences 1993; Hon mem. Japanese Biochemical Society 1993, Nat. Magnetic Resonance Society of India 1998; Dr hc (Univ. of Siena, Italy) 1997; Hon. DPhil (Univ. of Zürich) 1997; Dr hc (Ecole Polytech. Féd. de Lausanne) 2001; Friedrich-Miescher-Preis, Schweizerische Gesellschaft für Biochemie 1974; Shield of the Faculty of Medicine, Tokyo Univ. 1983; Médaille P. Bruylants, Univ. Catholique de Louvain, Belgium 1986; Stein and Moore Award of the Protein Society, USA 1990; Louisa Gross Horwitz Prize, Columbia Univ., NY 1991; Gilbert Newton Lewis Medal, Univ. of Calif. at Berkeley 1991; Marcel Benoist-Preis, Swiss Confed. 1992; Distinguished Service Award, The Miami Bio/Technology Winter Symposia, USA 1993; Prix Louis Jeantet de Médecine, Fondation Louis Jeantet, Geneva 1993; Kaj Linderstrom-Lang Prize, Carlsberg Foundation, Copenhagen, Denmark 1996; Eminent Scientist of RIKEN, Tokyo, Japan 1997; Kyoto Prize in Advanced Technology, Inamori Foundation, Kyoto 1998; Günther Laukien Prize, Experimental NMR Conf. (ENC), USA 1999; Otto-Warburg-Medaille, Gesellschaft für Biochemie und Molekularbiologie, Germany 1999; Médaille d'Honneur en Argent, Société d'Encouragement au Progrès, Paris, France 2001; Nobel Prize in Chemistry 2002; World Future Award, The World Awards, Vienna, Austria 2002. *Publications:* NMR in Biological Research: Peptitudes and Proteins 1976, NMR of Proteins and Nucleic Acids 1986, NMR in Structural Biology—A Collection of Papers by Kurt Wüthrich 1995; also published 630 papers and reviews. *Address:* Institut für Molekularbiologie & Biophysik, ETH Hönggerberg, HPK, CH-8093 Zürich, Switzerland (Office); The Scripps Reseach Institute, 10550 North Torrey Pines Road, MB-44, La Jolla, CA 92037, USA (Office); Fliederstrasse 7, CH-8304 Wallisellen, Switzerland (Home). *Telephone:* (1) 6332473 (Office); (858) 784-8011 (Office); (1) 8301059 (Home). *Fax:* (1) 6331151 (Office); (858) 784-8014 (Office). *E-mail:* wuthrich@mol.biol.ethz.ch (Office); wuthrich@scripps.edu (Office). *Website:* www.mol.biol.ethz.ch (Office).

WYATT, (Alan) Will, CBE, FRTS; British television executive; b. 7 Jan. 1942, Oxford; s. of Basil Wyatt and Hettie Evelyn Wyatt (née Hooper); m. Jane Bridgit Bagenal 1966; two d.; ed Magdalen Coll. School, Oxford, Emmanuel Coll. Cambridge; trainee reporter, Sheffield Telegraph 1964; Sub-Ed. BBC Radio News 1965; joined BBC TV 1968, Producer Late Night Line-Up, In Vision, The Book Programme, B. Traven – a mystery solved, etc. 1970–77, Asst Head of Presentation (Programmes) 1977, Head Documentary Features 1981, Features and Documentaries Group 1987, Asst Man. Dir BBC Network Television 1988–91; Man. Dir BBC Network TV 1991–96; Chief Exec. BBC Broadcast 1996–99; Chair. Human Capital Ltd 2001–; Chair. BBC Guidelines on Violence 1983, 1987; Dir Broadcasters' Audience Research Bd 1989–91, BBC Subscription TV 1990–93, BBC Enterprises 1991–93, UKTV 1997–99; Vice-Pres. Royal TV Soc. 1997, Euro Broadcasting Union 1998–99; Gov. London Inst. 1990–, Chair. 1999–; Huw Wheldon Memorial Lecture 1996; Royal Inst. Discourse 1996; Pres. Royal TV Soc. 2000–; Dir Coral Eurobet 2000–, Vitec Group 2002–; Gov. Magdalen Coll. School 2000. *Publications:* The Man Who Was B. Traven 1980, Masters of the Wired World (contrib.) 1999; articles on broadcasting in Evening Standard, The Times, Daily Telegraph. *Leisure interests:* fell walking, horse racing, opera, theatre. *Address:* Abbey Willows, The Turnpike, Middle Barton, Oxon., OX7 7DD, England. *Telephone:* (20) 7514-8855 (Office); (1869) 340234 (Home). *Fax:* (1869) 340145 (Home). *E-mail:* will.wyatt@dial.pipex.com (Home).

WYATT, Christopher Terrel, BSc, F.R.ENG., FICE, FRSA, DIC, CBIM; British business executive and engineer; b. 17 July 1927, Ewell, Surrey; s. of Lional H. Wyatt and Audrey Vere Wyatt; m. 1st Doreen Mary Emmerson; three s.; m. 2nd Geertruida Willer 1970; one s.; m. 3rd Patricia Perkins 1990; ed Kingston Grammar School, Battersea Polytechnic and Imperial Coll. London; Charles Brand & Son, Ltd, 1948–54; joined Richard Costain Ltd, 1955, Dir 1970–87, Group Chief Exec. 1975–80, Deputy Chair. 1979–80, Chair. Costain Group PLC 1980–87; Chair. W. S. Atkins Ltd 1987–97; Fellow Royal Acad. of Eng, Inst. of Structural Engineers. *Leisure interest:* sailing. *Address:* Ryderwells Farm, Uckfield Road, Lewes, E. Sussex, BN8 5RN, England. *Telephone:* (1273) 812219.

WYDEN, Ronald Lee, JD; American politician; b. 3 May 1949, Wichita, Kan.; s. of Peter Wyden and Edith Wyden; m. Laurie Oseran 1978; one s.; ed Univ. of Santa Barbara, Stanford Univ. and Univ. of Oregon; campaign aide, Senator Wayne Morse 1972, 1974; Co-founder, Co-Dir Oregon Gray Panthers 1974–80; Dir Oregon Legal Services for Elderly 1977–79; Instructor in Gerontology, Univ. of Oregon 1976, Portland State Univ. 1979, Univ. of Portland 1980; mem. 97th–103rd Congresses from 3rd Oregon Dist 1981–95; Senator from Oregon 1996–; mem. American Bar Asscn; Democrat. *Address:* United States Senate, 516 Hart Senate Office Building, Washington, DC 20510, USA.

WYETH, Andrew N.; American artist; b. 12 July 1917, Chadds Ford, Pa; s. of Newell Converse Wyeth and Carolyn (née Bockius) Wyeth; m. Betsy Merle James 1940; two s.; ed privately; artist, landscape painter 1936–; first one-man exhbn William Macbeth Gallery, New York 1937; one-man gallery exhbns. at Doll and Richard, Boston 1938, 1940, 1942, 1944, 1946, 1950; Macbeth Gallery 1937, 1939, 1941, 1943, 1945, 1948, 1950, 1952; M. Knoedler and Co., New York 1953, 1958, Lefevre Gallery, London 1974, Art Emporium, Vancouver 1977, Mitsukoshi Galleries, Japan 1984; group and other one-man exhbns in USA, Japan, France, Italy, UK and USSR 1980–1993; mem. Nat. Inst. of Arts and Letters, American Acad. of Arts and Sciences, Acad. des Beaux Arts, France; Hon. mem. Soviet Acad. of the Arts 1978; Hon. DFA (Maine, Harvard, Dickinson, Swarthmore, Temple Univ., Delaware, Northeastern Univ., Md); Hon. LHD (Tufts Univ.) 1963; U.S. Presidential Medal of Freedom 1963, Einstein Award 1967, Congressional Gold Medal (first to living American Artist) 1988. *Publication:* Andrew Wyeth: Autobiography (with Thomas Hoving). *Address:* c/o Frank E. Fowler, P.O. Box 247, Lookout Mountain, TN 37350, USA. *Telephone:* (615) 821-3081.

WYLLER, Egil A., DPhil; Norwegian professor emeritus of philosophy; b. 24 April 1925, Stavanger; s. of Trygve Wyller and Anne-Kathrine Wyller; m. Eva Middelthon 1949; three s.; ed Univs of Oslo, Tübingen and Freiburg i. Br.; fmr Prof. of History of the Ideas of Antiquity, Dept of Philosophy, Univ. of Oslo 1969–95 (now Prof. Emer.); Commdr Order of Phoenix (Greece); Kt 1st Class, Order of St Olav (Norway) 2000; Gold Medal of HM King of Norway 1958; Cultural Prize of City of Oslo 1986. *Publications include:* Platons 'Parmenides' 1960, Der späte Platon 1965–1970, Enhet og Annethet I–III 1981, Johannes' Aapenbaring 1985, Prinsesse Europa 1989, Platonismus/ Henologie in der Antike und im Mittelalter I–II (textbook) 1993, Henologisk Skriftserie I–XX 1994–2002, Henologische Perspektiven I–II 1995, Platon und Platonismus 1996, Henrik Ibsen I–II: 1999–2002, Ilenologisk Senftserie I–XX 1993–2002. *Leisure interests:* music, poetry, natural life. *Address:* Institute of Philosophy, University of Oslo, Blindern, Oslo 3 (Office); Kaptein Oppegaards v. 15, 1164 Oslo, Norway (Home).

WYLLIE, Peter John, PhD, FRS; American geologist; b. 8 Feb. 1930, London; s. of George W. Wyllie and Beatrice G. Weaver; m. F. Rosemary Blair 1956; two s. one d. (and one d. deceased); glaciologist, British West Greenland Expedition 1950; geologist, British North Greenland Expedition 1952–54; Asst Lecturer in Geology, Univ. of St Andrews 1955–56; Research Asst to O. F. Tuttle, Pa State Univ. 1956–58, Asst Prof. of Geochem. 1959–60; Research Fellow in Chem., Univ. Leeds 1959–60, Lecturer in Experimental Petrology 1960–61; Assoc. Prof. of Petrology, Pa State Univ. 1961–65; Prof. of Petrology and Geochem., Univ. of Chicago 1965–83, Homer J. Livingston Prof. 1978–83; Chair. Dept of Geophysical Sciences 1979–82; Chair. Div. of Geological and Planetary Sciences, Calif. Inst. of Tech. 1983–87, Prof. of Geology 1983–99, Academic Officer 1994–99, Prof. Emer. 1999–; Vice-Pres. Mineralogical Soc.

of America 1976–77, Pres. 1977–78; Foreign Assoc. NAS 1981; Fellow, American Acad. of Arts and Sciences 1982; Corresp. Fellow, Edin. Geological Soc. 1985–; Foreign Fellow (Corresp. mem.) Indian Geophysical Union 1987; Foreign mem. USSR (now Russian) Acad. of Sciences 1988, Academia Europaea 1996; Foreign Fellow Indian Nat. Science Acad. 1991, Nat. Acad. of Science of India 1992, Chinese Acad. of Science 1996; Louis Murray Visiting Fellow, Univ. of Cape Town March 1987; Vice-Pres. Int. Mineralogical Asscn 1978–86, Pres. 1995–99; Vice-Pres. Int. Union of Geodesy and Geophysics 1991–95, Pres. 1995–99; Hon. Prof. China Univ. of Geosciences, Beijing 1996–; Hon. mem. Mineralogical Soc. of GB and Ireland 1986, German Geological Soc. 2001, Mineralogical Soc. of Russia 1987; Hon. DSc (St Andrews) 1974; Polar Medal 1954, Mineralogical Soc. of America Award 1965, Quantrell Award 1979, Wollaston Medal (Geological Soc., London) 1982, Abraham-Gottlob-Werner-Medaille, German Mineralogical Soc. 1987, Roebling Medal (Mineralogical Soc. of America) 2001, Leopold von Buch Medal (German Geological Soc.) 2001. *Sport:* Heavyweight Boxing Champion, RAF Scotland 1949. *Publications:* Ultramafic and Related Rocks (ed.) 1967, The Dynamic Earth 1971, The Way the Earth Works 1976, Solid-Earth Sciences and Society (Chair. NAS Cttee) 1993; numerous articles in scientific journals. *Leisure interests:* concerts, theatre. *Address:* Division of Geological and Planetary Sciences, California Institute of Technology, Pasadena, CA 91125, USA (Office). *Telephone:* (626) 395-6461 (Office). *E-mail:* wyllie@caltech.edu (Office). *Website:* www.gps.caltech.edu/~wyllie (Office).

WYMAN, Bill (William George); British musician; b. 24 Oct. 1936, Lewisham, London; m. 1st Diane Cory 1959 (divorced 1968); one s.; m. 2nd Mandy Smith 1989 (divorced 1991); m. 3rd Suzanne Accosta 1993; three d.; bassplayer with The Rolling Stones 1962–93; numerous Rolling Stones tours and concerts 1963–90; ARMS Tour UK and USA 1983; Willie and the Poor Boys 1985; Bill Wyman's Rhythm Kings 1998–2002; owner WGW Holdings, WGW Enterprises, Wytel Music, Ripple Records, Ripple Music, Ripple Publications, Ripple Productions, KJM Nominees, Sticky Fingers Restaurant; Lord of the Manor of Gedding and Thornwoods 1968–; Silver Clef Award, Nordoff - Robbins Music Therapy 1982, Grammy Lifetime Achievement Award 1986, inducted into Rock and Roll Hall of Fame 1989, Q Award for Best Live Act 1990, Prince's Trust Award 1991, Ivor Novello Award for Outstanding Contribution to British Music 1991, Blues Foundation, Memphis Literary Award 2002. *Albums include:* The Rolling Stones 1964, The Rolling Stones, No 2 1965, Out of Our Heads 1965, Aftermath 1966, Between the Buttons 1967, Their Satanic Majesties Request 1967, Beggar's Banquet 1968, Let it Bleed 1969, Get Yer Ya-Ya's Out 1969, Sticky Fingers 1971, Exile on Main Street 1972, Goat's Head Group 1973, It's Only Rock 'n' Roll 1974, Black and Blue 1976, Some Girls 1978, Emotional Rescue 1980, Still Life 1982, Primitive Cool 1987, Steel Wheels 1989, Flashpoint 1991, Voodoo Lounge 1994; solo recordings include: Monkey Grip 1974, Stone Alone 1976, Green Ice film soundtrack 1981, Bill Wyman 1981, Digital Dreams 1983, Stuff 1991, Struttin' Our Stuff 1998, Anywhere the Wind Blows 1999, Groovin' 2000, Double Bill 2001, Blues Odyssey 2001. *Singles include:* Come On, I Wanna Be Your Man, Get Off Of My Cloud, 19th Nervous Breakdown, Let's Spend The Night Together, It's All Over Now, Little Red Rooster, (I Can't Get No) Satisfaction, Jumping Jack Flash, Honky Tonk Women, Brown Sugar, Miss You, Ruby Tuesday, Paint It Black, Going To A Go-Go, Emotional Rescue, It's Only Rock 'n' Roll, Harlem Shuffle, Start Me Up, Angie, Undercover Of The Night,; solo singles include: (Si Si) Je Suis Un Rock Star 1981, Come Back Suzanne 1981, A New Fashion 1981. *Films:* Sympathy for the Devil 1970, Gimme Shelter 1970, Ladies and Gentlemen the Rolling Stones 1974, Let's Spend the Night Together 1982, Digital Dreams 1983. *Publications:* Stone Alone – The Story of a Rock and Roll Band 1990 (with Ray Coleman) 1990, Wyman Shoots Chagall 2000, Bill Wyman's Blues Odyssey (with Richard Havers) 2001, Rolling With The Stones (with Richard Havers) 2002. *Address:* c/o Ripple Productions Ltd, 344 Kings Road, London, SW3 5UR, England (Office). *Website:* www.billwyman.com (Office).

WYMAN, Jane (Sarah Jane Fulks); American actress; b. 4 Jan. 1914, St Joseph, Mo.; d. of R. D. Fulks and Emme Reise; m. 1st Myron Futterman 1937; m. 2nd Ronald Reagan (q.v.) 1940 (divorced 1948); one s. one d. (deceased); m. 3rd Fred Karger (divorced); ed Univ. of Missouri; fmr radio singer and chorus girl; TV appearances. *Films include:* My Man Godfrey 1936, Brother Rat 1938, The Lost Weekend 1945, The Yearling 1946, Johnny Belinda 1948 (Acad. Award), State Fright 1950, The Glass Menagerie 1950, The Blue Veil 1951, Magnificent Obsession 1954, All That Heaven Allows 1956, Miracle in the Rain 1956, Holiday for Lovers 1959, Pollyanna 1960, Bon Voyage 1962, How to Commit Marriage 1969. *TV appearances include:* Jane Wyman Theatre 1956–60, Amanda Falcon, Falcon Crest, The Failing of Raymond (film), The Incredible Journey of Dr. Meg Laurel (film). *Address:* c/o Lorimar Productions, 3970 Overland Avenue, Culver City, CA 90230, U.S.A. (Office).

WYN JONES, Ieuan, LLB; British politician and lawyer; b. 22 May 1949, Denbigh, Wales; s. of the late John Jones and of Mair Jones; m. Einan Llywd; three c.; ed Liverpool Polytech.; practised as solicitor 1974–87; MP for Ynys

Môn 1987–2001, mem. Nat. Ass. for Wales (AM) for Ynys Môn 1999–; Chair. Plaid Cymru—The Party of Wales 1980–82, 1990–92, Pres. and Leader 2000–03. *Publication:* Thomas Gee (biog.) 1998. *Leisure interests:* history, sport. *Address:* C2.13, National Assembly for Wales, Pierhead Street, Cardiff Bay, CF99 1NA, Wales (Office). *Telephone:* (29) 2089-8414 (Office). *Fax:* (29) 2089-8269 (Office). *E-mail:* ieuan.wynjones@wales.gov.uk (Office).

WYNDHAM, Henry Mark; British art expert and company director; b. 19 Aug. 1953, London; s. of Hon. Mark Wyndham and Anne Wyndham; m. Rachel Pritchard 1978; three s.; ed Wellesley House, Broadstairs, Eton Coll., Sorbonne, Paris and Sotheby's Fine Art Course; joined Christie's 1974; Head, 19th Century European Picture Dept., Christie's, New York 1978–82, Vice-Pres. 1979; Dir Christie's, London 1983–87; set up Henry Wyndham Fine Art of St James's Art Group 1987–93; set up Portrait Commissions 1992; Chair. Sotheby's UK 1994–, Sotheby's Europe 1997–. *Film:* Tomb Raider 2001. *Television:* Antiques Roadshow 1980s, 1990s. *Leisure interests:* cricket, golf, fishing, shooting, travelling, soccer (Brighton & Hove Albion supporter), visiting museums and art, galleries. *Address:* Sotheby's, 34 New Bond Street, London, W1 (Office); The Old Rectory, Southease, Nr. Lewes, Sussex, BN7 3HX, England (Home). *Telephone:* (20) 7293-5000 (Office).

WYNNE-MORGAN, David; British public relations executive; b. 22 Feb. 1931; s. of John Wynne-Morgan and of the late Marjorie Wynne-Morgan; m. 1st Romaine Ferguson; two s.; m. 2nd Sandra Douglas-Home (divorced); m. 3rd Karin E. Stines; two s.; ed Bryanston School; reporter, Daily Mail 1952–55; foreign corresp., later William Hickey, Daily Express 1955–58; contracted to Sunday Times to write biographical features including ghosting autobiog. of the late Pres. Nasser of Egypt; Founder, Chair. and Man. Dir Partnerplan 1964–80; Man. Dir Extel Public Relations 1980–83, Chair. 1983–84; Chair. and Chief Exec. Hill & Knowlton (UK) Ltd 1984–90, Pres. Hill & Knowlton Europe, Middle East and Africa 1990–94; Chair. Worldwide Exec. Cttee 1994, WMC Communications 1995–, Marketing Group of GB 1989–90; Dir Horsham Corpn 1995–97; Council mem. Lord's Taverners 1992–96; mem. Inst. of Public Relations. *Publications:* biogs of Pietro Annigoni, Margot Fonteyn, Sir Malcolm Sargent. *Leisure interests:* squash (fmr Welsh int.), cricket, tennis, riding, golf. *Address:* WMC Communications, 7 Cheval Place, Knightsbridge, London, SW7 1EW; Lowndes Flat, 136 Brompton Road, London, SW3 1HY, England. *Telephone:* (20) 7591-3999 (WMC Communications). *Fax:* (20) 7591-3910 (WMC Communications).

WYPLOSZ, Charles, PhD, DipEng; French professor of economics; b. 5 Sept. 1947, Vichy; s. of Jacob Wyplosz and Félicia Zanger; m. Claire-Lise Monod 1967; one s. three d.; ed Univ. of Paris, Harvard Univ.; Asst. Assoc., then Full Prof. of Econs, Institut Européen d'Admin des Affaires (INSEAD), Fontainebleau 1978–, Assoc. Dean (Research and Devt) 1986–89; Directeur d'études, EHESS, Paris 1988–95; Prof. of Econs, Grad. Inst. of Int. Studies, Geneva 1995–; Man. Ed. Econ. Policy 1984–2001; mem. Council of Econ. Advisers to Prime Minister of France 1999–, Comm. Economique, Ministry of Finance, France 1999–; mem. Panel of Econ. and Monetary Experts, Cttee for Econ. and Monetary Affairs, European Parl. 2000–; mem. Group of Econ. Analysis, EC 2001–. *Publications:* numerous publs in professional journals; occasional contribs to press. *Leisure interests:* skiing, music, family. *Address:* Graduate Institute of International Studies, 11 avenue de la Paix, 1202 Geneva (Office); 3 rue du Valais, 1202 Geneva, Switzerland (Home). *Telephone:* (22) 9085946 (Office). *Fax:* (22) 7333049 (Office). *E-mail:* wyplosz@hei.unige.ch (Office). *Website:* heiwww.unige.ch/~wyplosz (Office).

WYZNER, Eugeniusz, LLM; Polish diplomatist; b. 31 Oct. 1931, Chełmno; s. of Henryk Wyzner and Janina (née Czaplicka) Wyzner; m. Elżbieta Laudańska 1961; one s.; ed Jagiellonian Univ., Kraków, Warsaw Univ. and Acad. of Int. Law, The Hague; Deputy Perm. Rep. to UN 1961–68; Deputy Dir of Dept at Ministry of Foreign Affairs 1968–71, Dir of Dept 1971–73; Amb., Perm. Rep. to UN, Geneva 1973–78; Dir of Dept, Ministry of Foreign Affairs 1978–81; UN Under-Sec.-Gen. 1982–94; Deputy Minister for Foreign Affairs and Parl. Sec., Ministry of Foreign Affairs 1994–95, Acting Minister for Foreign Affairs Dec. 1995, Sec. Amb. and Rep. to UN 1998–99; Vice-Chair. Int. Civil Service Comm. 1999–; mem. Bd of Dirs Int. Inst. of Space Law, Paris, Int. Peace Acad., New York, Int. Congress Inst. 1987–; Chair. UN Steering Cttee on Status of Women 1989–91, UN Appointments and Promotion Bd 1991–94, UN Exhibits Cttee 1992–94; mem. UN Sr Bd on Services to the Public 1989–94; Amb. ad personam; Gold Cross of Merit; Grand Commdr's Cross, Order of Polonia Restituta; Grand Commdr Order of the Phoenix (Greece); Commdr Légion d'honneur and other decorations. *Publications:* Wybrane zagadnienia z działalności ONZ w dziedzinie kodyfikacji i postępowego rozwoju prawa międzynarodowego, Niektóre aspekty prawne finansowania operacji ONZ w Kongo i na Bliskim Wschodzie, Poland and 50 Years of the United Nations Existence 1995. *Leisure interests:* cross-country skiing, mountain walking, theatre. *Address:* International Civil Service Commission, 2 United Nations Plaza, New York, NY 10017, USA. *Telephone:* (212) 963-8465 (Office). *Fax:* (212) 963-1717 (Office).

X

XI JINPING; Chinese politician; b. June 1953, Fuping, Shaanxi Prov.; s. of Xi Zhongxun; ed Tsinghua Univ.; joined CCP 1974; Vice-Sec., Sec. CCP Zhengding Co. Cttee 1982–85; Vice-Mayor of Xiamen 1985–88; Sec. CCP Ningde Pref. Cttee 1988–90; Sec. CCP Fuzhou Municipal Cttee, Chair. Standing Cttee Fuzhou Municipal People's Congress 1990–96; Vice-Sec. CCP Fujian Prov. Cttee 1995–2000; Deputy Gov. of Fujian 1999–2000, Gov. 2000–. *Publications include:* Research on Developing Chinese Rural Market-orientated Economy, Science and Patriotism (chief ed.). *Leisure interests:* reading, sports. *Address:* Office of the Governor, Fujian Provincial People's Government, Fuzhou, Fujian Province, People's Republic of China (Office). *Telephone:* (591) 7021333 (Office). *Website:* www.fjgov.com.cn (Office).

XI ZEZONG; Chinese scientist; b. 9 June 1927, Shaanxi Prov.; s. of Xi Renyin and Li Mudan; m. Shi Liuyun 1956; one s. one d.; ed Zhongshan Univ.; mem. Chinese Acad. of Sciences 1991; mem. Int. Acad. of History of Science 1993–, Int. Eurasian Acad. of Sciences 1995–; Pres. Chinese Soc. of History of Science and Tech. 1994–. *Address:* Institute for History of Science and Technology, 137 Chao-Nei Street, Beijing 100010, People's Republic of China. *Telephone:* (10) 64043989. *Fax:* (10) 64017637.

XIA PEISU; Chinese computer engineer; b. July 1923; Ed.-in-Chief Journal of Computer Science and Tech.; mem. Chinese Acad. of Sciences 1992–; research fellow Computer Tech. Inst. *Address:* Computer Technology Institute, Zhong Guan Cun, Beijing 100080, People's Republic of China.

XIAN DINGCHANG; Chinese nuclear physicist; b. 15 Aug. 1935, Guangzhou; s. of Xian Jiaqi and Li Zuoming; m.1st Ren Mengmei 1966 (died 1994); two s.; m. 2nd Chu Shiuling 2001; two s.; ed Beijing Univ.; Research Prof. Inst. of High Energy Physics, Academia Sinica; Chair. Chinese Synchrotron Radiation Soc. 1996–; mem. Chinese Acad. of Sciences 1992. *Publication:* Synchrotron Radiation Applications 1997, Contemporary Scientific and Technological Techniques in Ancient Ceramics Research 1999. *Leisure interests:* literature, music. *Address:* Institute of High Energy Physics, 19 Yuquan Road, Beijing 100039, People's Republic of China. *Telephone:* (10) 68235988 (Office); (10) 62568932 (Home). *Fax:* (10) 88215647. *E-mail:* xian@ihep.ac.cn.

XIANG HUAICHENG; Chinese politician; b. 1939, Wujiang Co., Jiangsu Prov.; ed Shandong Univ.; joined CCP 1983; Vice-Minister of Finance 1994–98, Minister of Finance 1998–2003; Vice-Minister State Admin. of Taxation 1994–; mem. 15th CCP Cen. Cttee 1997–2002, 16th CCP Cen. Cttee 2002–. *Address:* Zhongguo Gongchan Dang (Chinese Communist Party), Beijing, People's Republic of China.

XIAO YANG; Chinese party and government official; b. Aug. 1938, Heyuan Co., Guangdong Prov.; ed People's Univ. of China; joined CCP 1966; imprisoned during "Cultural Revolution" 1968–71; Deputy Dir Qujiang Co. CCP Cttee Office, then various party posts 1971–81; Sec. CCP Cttee of Wujiang Region, Shaoguan City, Guangdong Prov. 1981–83; Deputy Sec. Qingyuang Prefectural CCP Cttee, Guangdong 1983; Deputy Chief Guangdong Prov. Procurator's Office, Deputy Sec. CCP Leadership Group 1983–86; Procurator-Gen. Guangdong Prov. Procurator's Office 1986–90; Deputy Procurator-Gen. Supreme Procurator's Office, Deputy Sec. CCP Leadership Group 1990–92; Minister of Justice 1993–98; alt. mem. 14th CCP Cen. Cttee 1992–97; mem. 15th CCP Cen. Cttee 1997–2002, 16th CCP Cen. Cttee 2002–; Pres. Supreme People's Court 1998–. *Address:* Supreme People's Court, 27 Dongjiaominxiang, Beijing 100745, People's Republic of China. *Telephone:* (10) 65136195.

XIE JIN; Chinese film director; b. 1923, Shangyu Co., Zhejiang Prov.; ed Sichuan Nat. Drama School; Film Dir, Datong Film Studio, Shanghai 1948–50; Film Dir, Shanghai Film Studio 1953–88; Exec. Vice-Chair. 5th Nat. Cttee Chinese Fed. of Literary and Art Circles 1988–96, Vice-Chair. 1996–; mem. 8th Nat. Standing Cttee CPPCC 1994–98; a Vice-Pres. Chinese Fed. for the Disabled 1988–; May 1 Labour Medal 1987. *Films include:* Red Girl's Army (Hundred Flavers Award) 1960, Legend of Tian Yun (1st Golden Rooster Best Film Award) 1981, Lotus Town (Golden Rooster Best Film Dir Award) 1987.

XIE JUN; Chinese chess player; b. 30 Oct. 1970, Beijing; Nat. Jr Champion 1984, 1985; Nat. Women's Champion 1989, World Women's Champion 1991, 1993, 1999; now Grandmaster; f. Xie Jun Chess Skill Centre to promote chess in China 2001. *Address:* c/o State General Bureau of Physical Culture and Sports, 9 Tiyuguan Lu, Beijing 100061, People's Republic of China (Office).

XIE QIHUA; Chinese business executive; b. 22 June 1943, Yinxian, Zhejiang; ed Tsinghua Univ.; section chief, Dept Dir, Asst Commdr, Vice-Commdr of Baoshan Iron and Steel Works project; Vice-Chair. and Gen. Man. Baogan Group 1968–; Vice-Chair. and Pres. Shanghai Baosteel Group Corpn; named Nat. Excellent Woman Entrepreneur. *Address:* Baosteel Tower, 370 Pudian Road, Pudong New District, Shanghai, 200122, People's Republic of China (Office). *Telephone:* (21) 68404567 (Office). *Fax:* (21) 68403280 (Office); (21) 68403438 (Office). *Website:* www.baosteel.com (Office).

XIE SHIJIE; Chinese administrator; b. 1934, Liangping Co., Sichuan Prov.; ed South-West Agricultural Coll.; joined CCP 1954; Vice-Gov. of Sichuan Prov. 1986–1993; Sec. CCP Sichuan Prov. Cttee 1993–2000; Chair. Standing Cttee of Sichuan People's Congress 2001–; mem. 14th CCP Cen. Cttee 1992–1997, 15th CCP Cen. Cttee 1997–2002. *Address:* Standing Committee of Sichuan People's Congress, Chengdu, Sichuan Province, People's Republic of China.

XIE TIELI; Chinese film director; b. 1925, Huaiyin Co., Jiangsu Prov.; joined CCP 1942; Film Dir Beijing Film Studio; mem. 5th Nat. Cttee Chinese Fed. of Literary and Art Circles 1988–93, CPCC 8th NPC 1993–98; mem. Educ., Science, Culture and Health Cttee; Vice-Chair. Chinese Film Artists Asscn 1985. *Films include:* February, Violent Storm. *Address:* Beijing Film Studio, 19 Beihuan Xilu Road, Beijing 100088, People's Republic of China.

XIE ZHENHUA; Chinese civil servant; b. Oct. 1949, Tianjin; ed Tsinghua Univ., Wuhan Univ.; joined CCP 1977; teaching Asst Tsinghua Univ.; clerk State Construction Comm.; Dir Radiation Office then Personnel Office of State Environment Protection Bureau (SEPB), Dir Personnel Dept, Vice-Dir 1977–93, Dir 1993–; mem. CCP 15th Cen. Cttee for Discipline Inspection 1997–2002; Global Environment Facility (GEF) Leadership Award (jt winner) 2002. *Address:* State Environment Protection Bureau, Beijing, People's Republic of China.

XIMENES BELO, Mgr Carlos Filipe, SDB; Timor-Leste ecclesiastic; b. 3 Feb. 1948, Baucau, Dili; ordained priest 1980; consecrated Titular Bishop of Lorium 1988; Papal Admin. Dili; active in campaign for human rights in Timor-Leste; fmr Apostolic Admin. to Bishopric of Dili (resgnd 2002); Jt winner Nobel Peace Prize (with José Ramos-Horta, q.v.) 1996. *Address:* Bishop's Residence, Av. Direitos Humanos, Bidan Lecidere, CP 4, Dili 88010, Timor-Leste. *Telephone:* (390) 321177.

XING BENSI; Chinese philosopher and university professor; b. 7 Oct. 1929, Sheng Co., Zhejiang Prov.; s. of Xing Tinxu and Guei Yuyin; m. Zhou Bangyuan 1953; two d.; ed Special School of Russian Language of CCP Cen. Cttee; joined CCP 1950; teacher, Beijing Inst. of Russian Language 1952–56; Asst Researcher and Academic Sec. Inst. of Philosophy under Chinese Acad. of Sciences 1957–66, Deputy Dir, Dir, Vice-Chair. Academic Cttee, under Chinese Acad. of Social Sciences 1978–82, Academician 1983–85; Guest Prof. Qinghua Univ. 1984–; mem. Council for Int. Cultural Exchange 1984; Deputy Gen. Ed. Philosophy Vol. of Chinese Encyclopaedia 1983–; Vice-Pres. CCP Cen. Cttee Party School 1988–; Ed.-in-Chief Party journal Qiushi 1994–; NPC Deputy, Zhejiang Prov.; mem. NPC Law Cttee; Visiting Scholar Columbia Univ. 1981. *Publications:* The Dualism of Ludwig Feurbach's Anthropology 1963, The Social Theory and Historical Viewpoint of Saint-Simon 1964, Humanism in the History of European Philosophy 1978, Philosophy and Enlightenment 1979, The Anthropology of Ludwig Feurbach 1981, Philosophy and Time 1984, Philosophy (Introduction to Philosophy Vol. of Chinese Encyclopaedia) 1987, The Past, Present and Future of Philosophy (Introduction, Little Encyclopaedia of Philosophy) 1987 and many other essays. *Leisure interests:* music, literature, Peking Opera, Chinese calligraphy. *Address:* Institute of Philosophy, Chinese Academy of Social Sciences, Beijing, People's Republic of China.

XING SHIZHONG, Gen.; Chinese army officer; b. Sept. 1938, Licheng Co., Shandong Prov.; ed Nanjing Eng Army School; joined CCP 1957; staff officer in a div. engineer section 1959, a div. operational training section 1965, commdr of corps-affiliated eng bn 1969, regt commdr 1975, chief of corps operational training div. 1978, div. chief of staff 1978, div. commdr 1979, corps commdr 1983, Chief of Staff Lanzhou Mil. Region 1985; rank of Maj.-Gen. 1988, Lt-Gen. 1993; Deputy Commdr Jinan Mil. Region 1995–96; Commandant Nat. Defence Univ. 1995–; rank of Gen. 1998; mem. 15th CCP Cen. Cttee 1997–2002. *Address:* National Defence University, Beijing, People's Republic of China.

XIONG GUANGKAI, Gen.; Chinese diplomatist and army officer; b. March 1939, Nanchang City, Jiangxi Prov.; ed August 1st Middle School, Beijing, PLA Training School for Foreign Languages; joined PLA 1956; joined CCP 1959; translator, secretarial Asst Office of Mil. Attaché, Chinese Embassy, GDR 1960–72; Asst Mil. Attaché, Chinese Embassy, FRG 1972–80; student PLA Military Acad. 1981–83; Asst Div. Chief, Intelligence Dept, Gen. Staff HQ 1983–85, Deputy Dir 1985–87, Dir 1987–88, Asst to Chief of Gen. Staff 1988, Deputy Chief of Gen. Staff 1996–; rank of Maj.-Gen. 1988; alt. mem. 14th CCP Cen. Cttee 1992–97, mem. 15th CCP Cen. Cttee 1997–2002; mem. Cen. Cttee Leading Group on Taiwan 1993–; rank of Lt-Gen. 1993, Gen. 2000; Head of mil. del.to USA 1995. *Address:* c/o Ministry of National Defence, 20 Jingshanqian Jie, Beijing 100009, People's Republic of China.

XIONG SHEN; Chinese mechanical engineer and academic; b. 13 Sept. 1935, Jiangsu Prov.; s. of Shen Baozhang and Xu Shifeng; m. Xia Xuejian 1965; one d.; Tsinghua Univ. teacher, Dept of Eng Mechanics, Tsinghua Univ. 1959–, now Prof. and Dir Fluid Mechanics Lab. 1988–; mem. Evaluation Cttee of Academic Degree of Mechanics 1989–; mem. Advisory Cttee of Int. Symposium on Applications of Laser Techniques to Fluid Mechanics 1988–; Nat. Rep., Int. Congress on Laser Anemometry, Advances and Applications 1989–; Ed. Journal of Experimental Mechanics (China) 1991–, Journal of Aerodynamic Experiments and Measurement and Control (China) 1988–; several prizes including State Prize of Science Congress 1978, Prize of Science and Tech. of State Bureau of Instrumentation Industry 1981, State Prize of Invention 1992, Prize of Zhou Peiyuan Foundation 1992. *Publications* include: *Modern Techniques and Measurements in Fluid Flows* 1989, *Turbulent Correlation Measurement with 2-point LDV System* 1996. *Leisure interests:* music, playing piano and accordion. *Address:* Department of Engineering Mechanics, Tsinghua University, Beijing 100084, People's Republic of China. *Telephone:* (10) 62784476, 62788649. *Fax:* (10) 62785569.

XONGERIN BADAI; Chinese Inner Mongolia administrator, writer and poet; b. 5 June 1930, Bayinguoltng Prefecture, Hejin Co., Xinjiang; s. of Honger Xongerin and Bayinchahan Xongerin; m. 1952; two s. two d.; Pres. Xinjiang Broadcasting and TV Univ. 1982–; Chair. Cttee of Xinjiang Uygur Autonomous Region of CPPCC 1989; mem. Standing Cttee CPPCC 1991. *Publications:* several books of prose, poetry and history in Mongol language and Chinese. *Leisure interests:* history of poetry, writing plays, Mongol history. *Address:* 15 South Beijing Road, Urumqi, Xinjiang, People's Republic of China. *Telephone:* (991) 2825701 (Office); (991) 3839303 (Home). *Fax:* (991) 2823443.

XU ANBI; Chinese potter; b. March 1953, Yixing, Jiangxi Prov.; began practising pottery decoration 1976; exhibited in the U.S., Japan, France, Canada, Australia; named one of the ten best handicraftsmen in China 1997. *Address:* Yixing Jingtao Group, Yixing, Jiangxi Province, People's Republic of China (Office).

XU BING, MFA; Taiwanese artist; b. 8 Feb. 1955, Chongqing; s. of Hua-min Xu and Shi-ying Yang; ed Cen. Acad. of Fine Arts, Beijing; Asst Prof. Printmaking Dept, Cen. Acad. of Fine Arts 1987–, Assoc. Dir 1988–; Hon. Adviser, Dept of Art, Beijing Univ. 1989–; exhbns in China, France, USA, Switzerland, UK, Italy, Japan, Germany, Turkey 1979–; one man exhbns Beijing Art Gallery 1988, Taipei 1988, Taiwan 1990; mem. Chinese Engraving Artists' Asscn 1981–, Chinese Artists' Asscn 1982–, Dir 1985–; Dir Chinese Engraving Artists' Asscn 1986–; mem. Acad. Affairs Cttee, Cen. Acad. of Fine Arts 1988–; mem. Printmaking Artists' Cttee, Chinese Fine Arts Asscn 1989–; mem. Appraisal Cttee, 7th Chinese Nat. Exhbn of Fine Arts 1989; Hon. Fellow, Art Dept, Univ. of Wisconsin at Madison 1990; prizes from Art Exhbns. of Chinese Young Artists' Works 1980, 1985, 8th Exhbn of China's Wooden Paintings 1983, Medal, 9th Chinese Engraving Exhbn 1986, Award for Excellent Prints, Taiwan 1988, Henry E. T. Kok Educ. Foundation Prize for Young Instructors at Insts. of Higher Learning 1989. *Publications:* *Wooden Painting Sketches of Xu Bing* 1986, *Engravings of Xu Bing;* numerous articles in magazines and newspapers. *Leisure interest:* hiking.

XU CAIDONG; Chinese administrator and engineer; b. 1919, Fengxin Co., Jiangxi Prov.; ed Tangshan Inst., Jiaotong Univ., Hebei and Grenoble Inst., France; returned to China 1955; Prof., Guizhou Eng Inst. 1958–; Pres., Science Acad. of Guizhou Prov. 1978; Vice-Gov. Guizhou Prov. 1983; mem. Dept of Tech. Sciences, Academia Sinica 1985–; Vice-Chair. Jiu San Soc. 1983–; mem. 7th Nat. People's Congress, 8th NPC 1993–98, mem. Educ., Science, Culture and Public Health Cttee; NPC Deputy, Guizhou Prov. *Publication:* *The Physical Chemistry of Zinc.* *Address:* Guizhou Provincial People's Government, Guiyang, Guizhou Province, People's Republic of China.

XU CAIHOU, Gen.; Chinese army officer; b. 1943, Wafangdian City, Liaoning Prov.; ed PLA Mil. Eng Acad.; joined CCP 1971; Dir Army Group Political Dept 1985 then Army Group Political Commissar; rank of Maj.-Gen. 1990; Asst Dir PLA Gen. Political Dept 1992, Dir PLA Gen. Political Dept 2003–; Dir Jiefangjun Bao (Liberation Army Daily) 1992, Vice-Dir 1993–99, Exec. Vice-Dir 1999–; Lt-Gen. 1993, Gen. 1999; mem. 15th CCP Cen. Cttee 1997–2002, mem. CCP Cen. Mil. Cttee 1999. *Address:* People's Liberation Army General Political Department, Beijing, People's Republic of China.

XU HOUZE; Chinese geodesist and geophysicist; b. 4 May 1934, Anhui; s. of Xu Zuoren and Jiang Xinghua; m. Yang Huiji 1967; one s. one d.; ed Tongji Univ., Shanghai, Dept of Geodesy; Asst Researcher Inst. of Geodesy and Geophysics, Chinese Acad. of Sciences 1963, Assoc. Prof. 1978, Prof. 1982–; Dir 1983–; Dir Survey and Geophysics Inst. 1992–; mem. Chinese Geophysics Soc. 1978–; Vice-Pres. Int. Gravimetry Cttee and Pres. Perm. Cttee of Earth Tides, Int. Asscn of Geodesy (IAG) 1983–; Vice-Pres. Science-Tech. Soc. of Hubei Prov. 1984–, Chinese Survey and Mapping Soc. 1985–; Prof. Tongji Univ. 1985–, Wuhan Tech. Univ. of Survey and Mapping 1986–; NPC Deputy, Hubei Prov. *Publications:* *The Approximation of Stokes' Function and the Estimation of Truncation Error* 1981, *The Effect of Oceanic Tides on Gravity Tide Observations* 1982, *The Tidal Correction in Astrometry* 1982, *Accuracy Estimation of Loading Correction in Gravity Observation* 1984, *The Effect of Different Earth Models on Load Tide Correction* 1985, *Representation of Gravity Field outside the Earth using Fictitious Single Layer Density* 1984, *Collected Papers on Earth Tides* 1988, *Model of Oceanic Load Tide Correction in Chinese Continent* 1988. *Address:* 54 Xu Dong Road, Wuchang, Hubei 430077, People's Republic of China. *Telephone:* 813405.

XU HUAIZHONG, Maj.-Gen.; Chinese writer; b. 1929, Hebei Prov.; s. of Xu Hongchang and Xin Zhuoliang; m. Yu Zengxiang; one s. two d.; mem. Presidium and Bd of Dirs., Chinese Writers' Asscn 1983–; Deputy Cultural Dir, Gen. Political Dept of PLA 1985–88, Dir 1988–; rank of Maj.-Gen. 1988; mem. Nat. Cttee CPPCC 1993–98; Vice-Chair. Chinese Writers' Asscn 1996–; a Deputy Head Propaganda Dept, CPC 5th Fujian Prov. Cttee 1989–96. *Publications:* *Rainbow over the Earth, On the Tibetan Highlands, Anecdotes from the Western Front, The Wingless Angel* (collection of medium-length novels and short stories), *The Selected Works of Xu Huaizhong* 1989. *Leisure*

interests: playing table tennis and traditional Chinese shadow boxing. *Address:* 21 North Street Andeli, East District, Beijing, People's Republic of China.

XU HUIZI, Gen.; Chinese army officer and party official; b. 9 Dec. 1932, Penglai Co., Shandong Prov.; joined PLA 1948, CCP 1950; Deputy Chief of Gen. Staff 1985–95, rank of Lt-Gen. 1988, rank of Gen. 1994; Pres. Acad. of Mil. Sciences 1995–97; mem. 14th CCP Cen. Cttee 1992–97; mem. Preliminary Working Cttee of the Preparatory Cttee of the Hong Kong Special Admin. Region 1993–97; Vice-Chair. People's Air Defence Cttee 1988–; Deputy Sec. for Discipline Inspection 1994–; apptd Vice-Chair. Cttee of Overseas Chinese Affairs, 9th NPC 1998. *Address:* c/o Standing Committee of National People's Congress, Beijing, People's Republic of China.

XU JIALU; Chinese linguist; b. June 1937, Huai'an Co., Jiangsu Prov.; ed Beijing Normal Univ.; Prof., fmr Vice-Pres. Beijing Normal Univ.; joined China Asscn for Promoting Democracy 1987; Dir State Language Work Cttee 1994–; Vice-Chair. 9th Cen. Cttee of China Asscn for Promoting Democracy, Chair. 10th Cen. Cttee 1997–; mem. Standing Cttee of 7th and 8th NPC; Vice-Chair. Standing Cttee of 9th NPC 1998. *Address:* Beijing Normal University, Xinjiekouwai Street 19, Beijing 100875, People's Republic of China.

XU KUANGDI; Chinese politician and educationist; b. 1937, Tongxiang Co., Zhejiang Prov.; ed Beijing Metallurgy Inst.; joined CCP 1983; Prof., Vice-Pres. Shanghai Industrial Univ.; Dir Shanghai Higher Educ. Bureau; Dir Shanghai Planning Comm.; Vice-Mayor Shanghai Municipality 1992; Vice-Sec. CCP Shanghai Municipal Cttee 1994; Mayor Shanghai Municipality 1995–2001; Sec. CCP Group of Chinese Acad. of Eng 2001–; alt. mem. 14th CCP Cen. Cttee 1992; mem. 15th CCP Cen. Cttee 1997–2002. *Address:* c/o Shanghai Municipal Government, Shanghai, People's Republic of China.

XU QIN; Chinese politician; b. 1928, Suizhong Co., Fengtian (now Liaoning); Prov., joined CCP 1949; Deputy for Jiangxi to 5th NPC 1978; Vice-Gov. Jiangxi 1979–83; Deputy Sec. CCP Cttee, Jiangxi 1981; Vice-Chair. Jiangxi People's Congress 1981, Chair. Feb. 1988; alt. mem. 12th CCP Cen. Cttee 1982–87; mem. 8th NPC 1993–98; NPC Deputy, Jiangxi Prov. *Address:* Jiangxi Provincial Chinese Communist Party, Nanchang, Jiangxi, People's Republic of China.

XU YINSHENG; Chinese government official; b. 12 June 1938; m. Chen Liwen; one s.; World table tennis champion three times; Vice-Minister State Physical Culture and Sport Comm. 1977–98; Vice-Dir State Gen. Admin. of Physical Culture; Pres. Chinese Table Tennis Asscn 1979–, Chinese Boxing Asscn 1987–; Exec. Vice-Chair. Preparatory Cttee for 6th Nat. games 1985; Vice-Pres. Chinese Olympic Cttee 1986–89, 1994–, All-China Sports Fed. 1989–; Exec. Vice-Pres. XIth Asian Games Organizing Cttee 1990–; Pres. Int. Table Tennis Fed. 1997. *Publication:* *How to Play Table Tennis by Dialectics.* *Leisure interests:* tennis, fishing. *Address:* 9 Tiyuguan Road, Beijing, People's Republic of China. *Telephone:* 7012233.

XU YONGQING, Gen.; Chinese army officer; b. 1938, Jiande Co., Zhejiang Prov.; joined PLA 1956; joined CCP 1960; Deputy Army Political Commissar; Army Group Political Commissar; Political Commissar Zhejiang Mil. Provincial Command; Deputy Political Commissar Lanzhou Mil. Area Command 1994; Political Commissar Armed Police; mem. 15th CCP Cen. Cttee 1997–2002; rank of Gen. 2000. *Address:* Armed Police Headquarters, Beijing, People's Republic of China.

XU YONGYUE; Chinese politician; b. July 1942, Zhenping Co., Henan Prov.; ed Beijing Municipal People's Public Security School; joined CCP 1972; served consecutively as Sec. Beijing Municipal People's Public Security School, Gen. Office of Chinese Acad. of Sciences, Gen. Office of Ministry of Educ., Gen. Office of Ministry of Culture 1960–83; Political Sec. to Chen Yun 1983–93; Vice-Sec. Hebei Prov. Cttee 1994–98; Minister of State Security 1998–; alt. mem. 15th CCP Cen. Cttee 1997–2002. *Address:* Ministry of State Security, 14 Dongchangan Jie, Dongcheng Qu, Beijing 100741, People's Republic of China. *Telephone:* (10) 65244702 (Office).

XU YOUFANG; Chinese politician; b. 1939, Guangde Co., Anhui Prov.; ed Anhui Agricultural Coll.; joined CCP 1973; Dir Forestry Industry Bureau, Ministry of Forestry 1985; Vice-Minister for Forestry 1986–93, Minister 1993–97; Deputy Dir State Council Environment Protection Comm.; Dir China Forestry Science and Tech. Comm.; Vice-Chair. Nat. Afforestation Comm. 1993–1996; Pres. China Wildlife Conservation Asscn 1993–96; Sec. CCP Heilongjiang Prov. Cttee 1997–; Chair. Heilongjiang Prov. Congress Standing Cttee 1999–; mem. 15th CCP Cen. Cttee 1997–2002. *Address:* Office of the Governor, Heilongjiang Provincial Government, Harbin City, People's Republic of China.

XU YUANHE; Chinese philosopher; b. 1942, Rugao, Jiangsu Prov.; ed Peking Univ.; Asst Research Fellow, Assoc. Research Fellow then Research Fellow Inst. of Philosophy, Chinese Acad. of Social Sciences 1980–; Dir Oriental Philosophy Research Centre, Chinese Acad. of Social Sciences; State Council Prize 1993. *Publications:* *Origin and Development of Luo Studies, The School of Reason and the Yuan Society, Confucianism and Oriental Culture, Survey of Chinese Civilization.* *Address:* 5 Jian guo men wai Street, Beijing (Office); 502 F2, 2T Bei tai pin zhuang Road, Haichian District, Beijing (Home); Institute of Philosophy, Chinese Academy of Social Sciences, Beijing, People's Republic of China. *Telephone:* (10) 65137744 (Office); (10) 63240875 (Home). *Fax:* (10) 63240815 (Home).

XU ZHENSHI; Chinese photographer, artist and publisher; b. 18 Aug. 1937, Songjiang Co., Shanghai; s. of Xu Weiqing and Jiang Wanying, step-s. of Cheng Shi-fa; m. Zhang Fuhe 1967; one d.; ed No. 1 High School, Songjiang Co., Zhejiang Acad. of Fine Arts; moved to Beijing 1965; Ed. People's Fine Arts Publishing House 1965–86, Dir Picture Editorial Dept 1986–, Ed.-in-Chief 1992–; mem. China Artists' Asscn; Deputy Sec.-Gen. Spring Festival Pictures Research Centre, Publrs' Asscn of China; Deputy Sec.-Gen. and Assoc. Dir Photography Research Centre; mem. Selection Cttee 3rd, 4th and 5th Nat. Exhbns. of Spring Festival Pictures and other exhbns; Assoc. Dir Standing Cttee Spring Festival Pictures; Sr Adviser, Office of East China–UN TIPS Nat. Exploit Bureau 1994–; exhbns in China, Japan, Korea, Hong Kong, Thailand; Vice-Ed.-in-Chief Gouache Vol. of Anthology of Contemporary Chinese Fine Arts 1996; Vice-Pres. Chinese Fan Art Soc. 1997; organized 1st Nat. Exhbn of Calligraphy and Paintings to Help the Poor 1998; Dir Foundation for Underdeveloped Regions in China 1998–; prepared 6th Nat. Exhbn of Spring Festival Pictures 1998; numerous awards including Bronze Medal for albums of photographs, Leipzig Int. Book Exhbn 1987, Nat. Award 1993, Model Ed. Nat. Press and Pubs System 1997, 1998; State Prize for Spring Festival Pictures 2001, two 6th Nat. Exhbn of Spring Festival Pictures Prizes (China) 1998, Chinese Contemporary Art Achievement Prize, Hong Kong. *Publications:* China's Cultural Relics Unearthed during the Great Cultural Revolution 1973, Travel in China (4 vols) 1979–80, Tibet 1981, Travel in Tibet 1981, Costumes of China's Minority Nationalities 1981, Travel in Guilin 1981, Travel Leisurely in China 1981, Travel in Yunnan 1982, China's Flowers in Four Seasons 1982, Poet Li Bai 1983, Native Places of Tang Dynasty Poems 1984, Travel along the Yangtse River 1985, Through the Moongate: A Guide to China's Famous Historical Sites 1986, Waters and Mountains in China 1986, Travel in Guangzhou 1986, China 1987, The Chinese Nation 1989, Poet Du Fu 1989, Selected Works of Xu Zhenshi 1990, 1993, Selected Paintings of Xu Zhenshi 1993, 1994, Boat on the Plateau 1998, Album of Xu Zhenshi's Sketches 1999. *Leisure interest:* sports. *Address:* People's Fine Arts Publishing House, No. 32 Beizongbu Hutong, Beijing, People's Republic of China. *Telephone:* (10) 65244901 (Office); (10) 65246353 (Home).

XU ZHIHONG; Chinese plant physiologist and university president; b. 14 Oct. 1942, Wuxi, Jiangsu Prov.; ed Peking Univ.; research student, Chinese Acad. of Sciences Shanghai Plant Physiology Research Inst.; researcher, Assoc. Research Fellow, Research Fellow, Vice-Dir Chinese Acad. of Sciences Shanghai Plant Physiology Research Inst. 1969–91, Dir 1991–99; Vice-Pres. Chinese Acad. of Sciences and Dir Shanghai Life Science Research Centre 1992–99, mem. 4th Presidium of Depts., Chinese Acad. of Sciences 2000–; Fellow, Chinese Acad. of Sciences 1997–; Pres. Peking Univ. 1999–. *Address:* Peking University, 1 Loudouqiao, Beijing 100871, People's Republic of China (Office). *Telephone:* (10) 62752114 (Office). *Fax:* (10) 62751207 (Office). *Website:* www.pku.edu.cn (Office).

XU ZHIZHAN; Chinese optical scientist; b. Dec. 1938, Changzhou, Jiangsu Prov.; ed Fudan Univ.; research student of physics, Peking Univ.; Dir Chinese Acad. of Sciences Shanghai Optical Precision Machinery Research Inst.; Chief Ed. of Journal of Optics, Vice-Chair. Optical Soc. of China 1992–; Nat. Award

for Natural Sciences numerous times. *Publications:* over 300 essays on laser and related studies. *Address:* Chinese Academy of Sciences Shanghai Optical Precision Machinery Research Institute, Shanghai, People's Republic of China.

XU ZHONGLIN; Chinese politician; b. Dec. 1943, Wujin, Jiangsu Prov.; ed PLA Survey and Cartography Inst., Zhengzhou, CCP Cen. Acad., Beijing; joined CCP 1964; Teaching Asst PLA Survey and Cartography Inst. 1962; Mayor of Xuzhou –1989; Vice-Dir, then Dir Org. Dept, Jiangsu Prov. Cttee 1989–94; Vice-Sec. Jiangsu Prov. Cttee 1994–99, Anhui Prov. Cttee 1999–; Gov. Anhui Prov. 2000–02. *Address:* c/o Anhui People's Government, 221 Changjiang Road, Hefei, Anhui Province, People's Republic of China (Office).

XUE MUQIAO; Chinese politician and economist; b. 25 Oct. 1904, Wuxi Co., Jiangsu Prov.; m. Luo Qiong 1935; three d.; worked in Inst. of Social Sciences attached to Cen. Research Acad. conducting surveys of rural economy 1920s; Prof. of Rural Econs, normal school, Guangxi Prov. 1933; organized Soc. for Research in China's Rural Economy; Ed. Rural China monthly, Shanghai; First Dir of Dept of Training, Anti-Japanese Mil. and Political Acad. of Cen. China, Sec.-Gen. Anti-Japanese Democratic Govt of Shandong Prov., war with Japan 1937–45; successively Sec.-Gen. of Financial and Econ. Comm. of Govt Admin. Council, Vice-Minister in Charge of State Planning Comm., Dir of State Statistical Bureau, Dir Nat. Price Comm.; mem. Council of Social Sciences, Academia Sinica; del. to First, Second and Third Nat. People's Congresses; mem. Nat. Cttee Fifth CPPCC; adviser to State Planning Comm. 1979–, Dir of its Econ. Inst.; Prof., Peking Univ.; Pres. Statistical Soc. 1979, Nat. Statistical Soc.; Hon. Pres. Soc. of Systems Eng 1980; Pres. Planning Soc. 1984–; Adviser, Fed. of Econs Socs. 1981, Office of Restructuring of Econ. System 1984–85; Hon. Dir-Gen. Devt Research Centre 1985–; Hon. Chair. Industrial Co-operative Asscn 1983–; Sr Adviser All-China Fed. of Industry and Commerce 1988–; mem. Academic Cttees. of the Econ. Inst. and Inst. of the World Economy, Chinese Acad. of Social Sciences. *Publications:* The Elementary Knowledge of China's Rural Economy, The ABC of Rural Economy, The Socialist Transformation of China's National Economy, Some Theoretical Problems Concerning the Socialist Economy, Research on Problems Concerning China's Socialist Economy, Research on Price and Currency Problems, Management of the Economy on the Basis of Objective Economic Law, Selected Works of Xue Muqiao, Reforms and the Theoretical Breakthrough, Selected Papers on the Economy. *Address:* Development Research Centre of the State Council, Beijing, People's Republic of China.

XUE WEI; Chinese violinist; b. 21 Dec. 1963, Henan; s. of Xue-Ming and Shang Yi-qing; ed Shanghai Conservatory, Beijing Conservatory of Music and Guildhall School of Music, London; now resides in London appearing regularly with the maj. London orchestras; performs in solo recitals and as concert soloist at int. music festivals; guest soloist with Shanghai Symphony on tour in Japan; Prof. Royal Acad. of Music, London 1989–; numerous prizes including Silver Medal, Tchaikovsky Int. Competition (violin), Moscow 1986; Gold Medal, Carl Flesch Int. Competition 1986; London Philharmonic Soloist of the Year 1986. *Leisure interests:* reading, chess, poker. *Address:* 134 Sheaveshill Avenue, London, NW9, England.

Y

YAACOB, Nik Mohamed; Malaysian businessman; ed Monash Univ., Asian Inst. of Man.; with Sime Darby, fmrly Regional Dir, Dir of Operations, Malaysia, mem. Bd 1990–, mem. Exec. Cttee, CEO 1993–; Dir, DMIB, Sime UEP Properties, Tractors Malaysia holdings, Consolidated Plantations, Port Dickson Power, SD Holdings, Sime Malaysia Region, SIRIM. *Address:* Sime Darby Group, 21st Floor, Wisma Sime Darby, Jalan Raja Laut, 50350 Kuala Lumpur, Malaysia (Office). *Telephone:* (3) 26914122 (Office). *Fax:* (3) 26987398 (Office). *E-mail:* enquiries@simenet.com (Office). *Website:* www .simenet.com (Office).

YAACOBI, Gad, MA; Israeli politician, diplomatist, author and economist; b. 18 Jan. 1935, Moshav Kfar Vitkin; s. of Alexander and Sara Yaacobi; two s. one d.; ed Tel-Aviv Univ. and Harvard Univ., USA; mem. Moshavim Movt 1960–67; Asst to Minister of Agric., Head of Agric. and Settlement Planning and Devt Centre 1960–66; mem. Cen. Cttee Histadrut, Labour Union, Rafi Faction 1966–69; Deputy to Sec. Labour Party 1966–70; MP (Knesset) 1969–92, Parl. Finance Cttee 1969–70, Parl. Defence and Foreign Affairs Cttee 1974; Deputy Minister of Transport 1971–74, Minister 1974–77, of Econs and Planning 1984–88, of Communications 1987–90; mem. Inner Cabinet 1990; Chair. Parl. Econ. Cttee 1977–89; Amb. to UN 1992–96; Chair. Labour Party Econ. Council; Chair. Israel Electric Corpn 1996–99; Chair. and CEO Ports and Railways of Israel 2000; numerous awards. *Publications:* The Power of Quality 1971, The Freedom to Choose 1975, The Government 1980, A Call for Change 1983, On the Razor's Edge 1990; children's books 1988, 1990; Grace of Time (poems) 1991, A Breakthrough: Israel and the UN 1996, New York Diaries: A Place Nearby (poetry) 1997, Heat Lord (novel) 2000, An Aubiography 2002; many articles on Econs and politics. *Leisure interests:* theatre, reading, writing, travelling. *Address:* Ports and Railways Authority, P.O. Box 20121, 61 201 Tel-Aviv (Office); 9 Gordon Street, Tel-Aviv, Israel (Home). *Telephone:* 3-5270662 (Home). *Fax:* 3-5622289 (Office); 3-5273510. *E-mail:* gady@israports.org.il (Office).

YA'ALON, Lt-Gen. Moshe, BA; Israeli army officer; b. 1950, Kiryat Haim; m.; three c.; ed Command and Staff Coll., Kimberly, UK, Univ. of Haifa; drafted into Israeli Defence Force (IDF) 1968, served in Nahal Paratroop Regt; reserve parachuter during Yom Kippur War 1973, participated in liberation of Suez Canal; held several command positions in IDF Paratroop Brigade, Commdr reconnaisance unit during Litani Operation 1978, later Deputy Commdr, apptd Commdr 1990; served in elite unit 1979–82, later Deputy Commdr; fought in Operation Peace for Galilee; retrained in IDF Armoured Corps 1989–90; apptd OC Judea and Samaria, promoted Brig.-Gen. 1992; Commdr of Ground Forces, Tze'elim 1993; apptd OC Intelligence, rank Maj.-Gen. 1995; apptd OC Cen. Command 1998, IDF Deputy Chief-of-Staff 2000, Chief-of-Staff 2002–. *Address:* Office of the Chief-of-Staff, Israeli Defence Force, Ministry of Defence, Kaplan Street, Hakirya, Tel Aviv 67659, Israel (Office). *Telephone:* 3-5692010 (Office). *Fax:* 3-6080343 (Office). *E-mail:* info@mail.idf.il (Office). *Website:* www.idf.il (Office).

YABLOKOV, Alexey Vladimirovich, DSc, D.BIOL.SC.; Russian ecologist; b. 3 Oct. 1933, Moscow; s. of Vladimir Yablokov and Tatiana Sarycheva; m. 1st Eleonora Bakulina 1955 (died 1987); one s.; m. 2nd Dil'bar Klado 1989; ed Moscow Univ.; researcher, Head of Lab., Prof. N. Koltsov Inst. of Developmental Biology 1959–; political activities since late 1980s; Chair. Ichthyological Comm. of USSR Ministry of Fishery 1989–92; USSR People's Deputy 1989–91; Deputy Chair. Comm. on Ecology of USSR Supreme Soviet 1989–91; State Counsellor on Ecology and Public Health to Pres. of Russia 1991–93; Chair. Interagency Comm. on Environmental Security, Russian Security Council 1993–97, Pres. Centre of Russian Environmental Policy 1993–; Corresp. mem. USSR (now Russian) Acad. of Sciences 1984; Chief Scientist Russian Acad. of Sciences 1996–; Pres. Moscow Soc. for Protection of Animals 1988–2001; mem. Exec. Cttee Stockholm Environmental Inst. 1994–98; Environmental Adviser to Pres. EBRD 1997–99; Vice-Pres. World Conservation Union 2001–; Pew Fellowship 1994–97; Severtsev Prize 1976, WASA Prize 1995, Busk Medal 1996, Karpinsky Prize 1997, WWF Gold Medal 2002, Nuclear-free Future World Award 2002. *Publications:* 21 books and numerous articles on population, evolution and conservation biology, zoology, ecology, including Population Biology 1987, Nuclear Mythology 1997, Pesticides as a Toxic Problem 1999. *Leisure interests:* writing, fishing, carpentry. *Address:* World Conservation Union, 28 rue Mauverney, 1196 Gland, Switzerland (Office); Centre for Russian Environmental Policy, 26 Vavilov str., Moscow 119991 (Office); 36-1-56 Vavilova str., Moscow 117296, Russia (Home). *Telephone:* (22) 9990001 (Switzerland) (Office); (095) 9528019 (Moscow) (Office); (095) 1344421 (Home). *Fax:* (22) 9990002 (Switzerland) (Office); (095) 9523007 (Moscow) (Office); (095) 1344421 (Home). *E-mail:* yablokov@voxnet.ru (Home); mail@iucn.org (Office). *Website:* www.iucn.org.

YACOUB, Sir Magdi Habib, Kt, FRCS, FRS; Egyptian cardiac surgeon; b. 16 Nov. 1935, Cairo; m.; one s. two d.; ed Univ. of Cairo; British Heart Foundation Prof. of Cardiothoracic Surgery, Royal Brompton and Nat. Heart Lung Inst. 1986–; Consultant Cardiothoracic Surgeon, Harefield Hosp., Middx 1969–2001; pioneered techniques of repair of complex congenital heart disease, homograft valve surgery and heart, heart-lung and lung transplantation; Hon. MCh (Wales) 1986; Hon. DSc (Loughborough Univ. of Tech.), (Keele) 1995. *Publications:* numerous medical papers. *Leisure interest:* orchid

growing. *Address:* National Heart and Lung Institute, Dovehouse Street, London, SW3 6LY, England. *Telephone:* (20) 7351-8534/3. *Fax:* (20) 7351-8229.

YADLIN, Aharon, BA; Israeli politician and educationalist; b. 17 April 1926, Tel Aviv; s. of Haim Yadlin and Zipora Yadlin; m. Ada Hacohen 1950; three s.; ed Hebrew Univ.; Co-founder Kibbutz Hatzerim; fmr mem. Presidium, Israel Scouts Movement; mem. Exec. Council Histadrut (Israel Fed. of Labour) 1950–52; Prin. Beit Berl (Labour Party's Centre for Educ.) 1956–58; mem. Knesset (Parl.) 1959–79; Deputy Minister of Educ. and Culture 1964–72; Gen. Sec. Israel Labour Party 1972–74; Minister of Educ. and Culture 1974–77; Chair. Educational and Cultural Cttee, Knesset 1977–79; Chair. Beit Berl Coll. of Educ. 1977–85; Chair. Bialik Inst., Books Publishing House and Acad. for Philosophy, Jewish Studies and World Literature 1990–; Sec.-Gen. United Kibbutz Movt (TAKAM) 1985–89; Chair. Beer-Sheva Theatre, Janush Korczak Asscn in Israel, Scientific Cttee Ben Gurion Research Inst. and Archives 1979–85, Yad Tabenkin (Research Centre of Kibbutz Movt), Beith Yatziv Educational Centre, Beer-Sheva, World Labour Zionist Movt 1992–; Chair. Exec. Cttee, Ben Gurion Univ. of the Negev; lecturer and researcher in EFAL (educ. centre of TAKAM); Dr. hc (Ben Gurion Univ. of the Negev) 1988. *Publications:* Introduction to Sociology 1957, The Aim and The Movement 1969; and articles on sociology, education and youth. *Leisure interests:* stamps, gardening. *Address:* World Labour Zionist Movement, Alcharizi 9, Jerusalem (Office); Kibbutz Hatzerim, Mobile Post Hanegev 85420, Israel (Home). *Telephone:* 2-5671184 (Office); 8-6473436 (Home). *Fax:* 2-5671182 (Office); 8-6473199 (Home). *E-mail:* wlzm@jazo.org.il (Office).

YADOV, Vladimir Aleksandrovich, D.PHIL.SC.; Russian sociologist; b. 25 April 1929, Leningrad; m.; one s.; ed Leningrad State Univ., Univ. of Manchester, London School of Econs; with Inst. of Sociological Studies USSR (now Russian) Acad. of Sciences, Inst. of Social and Econ. Problems USSR (now Russian) Acad. of Sciences, Leningrad br. of Inst. of History of Nat. Sciences and Tech.; Dir, Prof. Inst. of Sociology Russian Acad. of Sciences 1986–99, now Dir. Research Centre of Social Transformation; Chief Scientific Researcher 1999–; Dean, Inst. of Sociological Educ. at Repub. Centre of Humanitarian Educ. in St Petersburg 1995–; Pres. Russian Sociological Soc. 1991–; mem. Int. Sociological Asscn 1990– (Vice-Pres. 1990–94); mem. European Asscn of Experimental Social Psychology 1989–, Int. Inst. of Sociology 1990–, Centre for Social Sciences and Documentation, Vienna 1991–; Dr hc (Univs of Tartu and Helsinki). *Publications:* numerous papers on theory and methods of sociology, sociology of labour, social psychology of personality and of science. *Address:* Institute of Sociology, Centre of Social Transformations, Krzhizhanovskogo str. 24/35, korp 5, 117218 Moscow, Russia. *Telephone:* (095) 719-09-40 (Office).

YAGI, Yasuhiro; Japanese engineer; b. 15 Feb. 1920; m.; one s. two d.; ed Imperial Univ., Tokyo; joined Kawasaki Heavy Industries Ltd 1943; Dir and Asst Gen. Supt Mizushima Works 1971–74, Man. Dir 1974–77, Sr Man. Dir Corporate Tech., Engineering and Tubarao Project 1977–79, Exec. Vice-Pres. Corporate Tech. and Tubarao Project 1979–82; Pres. Kawasaki Steel Corpn June 1982–99. *Leisure interests:* golf, Go. *Address:* c/o Kawasaki Steel Corporation, Hibiya Kokusai Building, 2-3, Uchisaiwaicho 2-chome, Chiyoda-ku, Tokyo 100, Japan.

YAGODIN, Gennadiy Alekseyevich; Russian physical chemist; b. 3 June 1927, Vyass, Penza region; s. of Alexei Yagodin and Alexandra Yagodina; m. 1949; one s. one d.; ed Mendeleyev Chemical Tech. Inst., Moscow; mem. CPSU 1948–91; Deputy Dean, Mendeleyev Chemical Tech. Inst., Moscow 1956–59, Dean, Dept of Physical Chemistry 1959–63, Prof. of Chemical Tech. 1959–63, 1966–73, Rector 1973–85; Deputy Dir-Gen. (Head of Dept of Training and Technical Information 1963–64, Head of Dept of Technical Operations 1964–66), IAEA, Vienna 1963–66; USSR Minister of Higher and Secondary Specialized Educ. 1985–89; Chair. State Cttee for Nat. Educ. 1988–91; Rector Int. Univ. in Moscow 1992–2001, First Vice-Pres. 2001–; Deputy, USSR Supreme Soviet 1986–89; mem. Cen. Cttee CPSU 1986–89; Corresp. mem. USSR (now Russian) Acad. of Sciences 1976–; mem. Russian Acad. of Educ.; Order of Lenin; D. Y. Mendeleyev Prize 1981, USSR State Prize 1985. *Leisure interest:* collecting butterflies. *Address:* International University, Leningradsky prosp. 17, 125040 Moscow, Russia. *Telephone:* (095) 250-03-42. *Fax:* (502) 221-10-60; (095) 250-40-49 (Office); (095) 332-13-15 (Home).

YAKER, Layashi; Algerian civil servant; b. 1930, Algiers; m.; three c.; ed Ecole de Commerce, Algiers, Ecole des Hautes Etudes at Sorbonne, Inst. d'Etude du Développement Economique et Social, Univ. of Paris and Conservatoire Nat. des Arts et Métiers, Paris; fmr Prof. Nat. School of Admin., Algiers and Inst. of Political, Diplomatic and Int. Studies, Paris; fmr Assoc. Dir Inst. of Strategic Studies, Algiers; Political Sec. Ministry of Foreign Affairs of Provisional Govt of Algeria in Cairo 1960–61; Head of Mission, Provisional Govt of Algeria to India for S. Asia 1961–62; Minister Plenipotentiary, Ministry of Foreign Affairs and Dir-Gen. for Econ. Social and Cultural Affairs and Int. Cooperation 1962–69; mem. Algerian/French Exec. Bd Org. for Exploitation of Saharan Resources 1963–65; mem. Org. for Industrial Cooperation 1965–70; Gov. African Devt Bank and Alt. Gov. IBRD 1966–68; Minister of Commerce 1969–77; Pres. Council of Ministers, Econ. Comm. for Africa (UNECA) 1973–76; Pres. Council of African Ministers of Commerce

1974–77; mem. Council IPU 1977–79; head of del. to numerous int. confs. 1961–87; MP 1977–79; Amb. to USSR 1979–82, to USA 1982–84; Amb.-at-Large 1985–87; int. consultant 1988–92; UN Under-Sec.-Gen. and Exec. Sec. Econ. Comm. for Africa (UNECA) 1992–95. *Address:* c/o Executive Secretary of the Economic Commission for Africa, P.O. Box 3001, Addis Ababa, Ethiopia.

YAKIŞ, Yaşar; Turkish politician; b. 1938, Akçakoca; m.; one c.; ed Ankara Univ.; joined Ministry of Foreign Affairs 1962; councillor, Turkish Embassy, Damascus, Syria 1980; est. OIC's Standing Cttee for Econ. and Commercial Co-operation 1985; Amb. to Saudi Arabia 1988, to Egypt; Deputy Under-Sec. Ministry of Foreign Affairs, responsible for OIC 1992; Perm. Rep. to UN, Vienna 1998; Minister of Foreign Affairs 2002–; Decoration of King Abdul Aziz, Saudi Arabia 1992. *Address:* Ministry of Foreign Affairs, Disisleri Bakanligi, Yeni Hizmet Binasi, 06520 Balgat, Ankara, Turkey (Office). *Telephone:* (312) 2873556 (Office). *Fax:* (312) 2873869 (Office). *Website:* www .mfa.gov.tr (Office).

YAKOVENKO, Alexander Vladimirovich, CAND.JUR.SC; Russian diplomatist; b. 1954; m.; one d.; ed Moscow State Inst. of Int. Relations; with USSR Mission to UN, New York 1981–86; Head of Div., Dept on Security and Co-operation in Europe, Ministry of Foreign Affairs, Russian Fed. 1986–92; Deputy Dir Dept on Problems of Security and Disarmament, Ministry of Foreign Affairs 1992–97; Perm. Rep. to int. orgs. in Vienna 1997–2000; Dir Information and Press Dept Ministry of Foreign Affairs 2000–. *Address:* Ministry of Foreign Affairs, Smolenskaya-Sennaya pl. 32/34, 121200 Moscow, Russia (Office). *Telephone:* (095) 244-41-19 (Office). *Fax:* (095) 244-41-12 (Office). *Website:* www.mid.ru (Office).

YAKOVLEV, Aleksandr Maksimovich, DJur; Russian lawyer; b. 30 Aug. 1927, Leningrad; s. of Maxim Yakovlev and Maria Yakovleva; m. Eugenia Yakovleva 1950; ed Moscow Inst. of Law; sr research fellow Inst. of Law, USSR Ministry of Internal Affairs, then USSR Ministry of Justice 1957–75; Head Dept of Criminal Law and Criminology USSR (now Russian) Inst. of State and Law, Prof. 1975–94, Chief Researcher 1996–; in democratic movt since late 1980s; USSR People's Deputy 1989–91; mem. Perm. Cttee on Legis. USSR Supreme Soviet 1989–91; Plenipotentiary Rep. of Pres. of Russia at Federal Ass. 1994–96, Expert to Council of Fed. 1997–; Rector New Moscow Law Inst. 1998–; Visiting Prof. Univ. of Manitoba 1990, Rutgers Univ. 1991, Alberta Univ., New York and Toronto Univ. 1992, Emory Univ. Atlanta 1993, 1997; mem. Bd of Dirs Int. Soc. of Social Defence, Paris, UN Cttee Against Torture 1994, Inst. of Sociology of Law for Europe; Hon. LLD (Alberta Univ., Canada) 1991; Merited Lawyer of Russia. *Publications:* The Bear That Wouldn't Dance; Failed Attempts to Reform the Former Constitution of the Soviet Union (with Dale Gibson) 1992, Striving for Law in a Lawless Land 1995, Sociology of Crime 2000, The Social Structure of Society 2003; several other books and more than 100 articles on various aspects of constitutional law, publs in journals. *Leisure interest:* travelling. *Address:* Dolgorukovskaya str. 40, Apt. 153, 127030 Moscow, Russia (Home). *Telephone:* (095) 978-84-97. *Fax:* (095) 978-84-97 (Home); (095) 291-85-74.

YAKOVLEV, Aleksandr Nikolayevich, DHist; Russian politician; b. 2 Dec. 1923, Korolevo, Yaroslavl Region; m.; one s. one d.; ed Yaroslavl Pedagogical Inst.; served in Soviet Army 1941–43; mem. CPSU 1944–91 (expelled); party work, Yaroslavl Dist Cttee CPSU 1946–48; chief lecturer at Yaroslavl Party School and corresp. of Dist newspaper 1948–50; Deputy Head of Dept of Science and Culture, Cen. Cttee of CPSU 1953–56; Instructor with Dept of Propaganda and Agitation of Cen. Cttee CPSU 1962–64; Head of Radio and TV Broadcasting Propaganda Dept of Cen. Cttee CPSU 1964–65; mem. of editorial staff of journal Kommunist; First Deputy Head, Acting Head of Cen. Cttee, Propaganda Dept 1965–73; mem. of Cen. Auditing Comm. of Cen. Cttee CPSU 1971–76; Amb. to Canada 1973–83; Dir Inst. of World Econs and Int. Relations, USSR Acad. Sciences 1983–85; mem. of Council of Nationalities, USSR Supreme Soviet, mem. of USSR Parl. Group Cttee 1984–89; Head of Cen. Cttee CPSU Propaganda Dept 1985–86; mem. Cen. Cttee CPSU 1986–90; Sec. responsible for Propaganda of Cen. Cttee CPSU 1986–90; mem. Political Bureau 1987–90; Head. Int. Policy Comm. 1988–90; People's Deputy 1989–91; mem. Presidential Council 1990–91; Sr Presidential Adviser 1991; Chair. Moscow Public Ass. 1991–; mem. Political Consultative Council Sept.–Dec. 1991; Chair. Presidential Comm. on Rehabilitation of Political Prisoners 1992–; Pres. Democracy Foundation 1993–; Founder and Chair. Russian Party of Social Democracy 1995–; Head, State Radio-TV Co. Ostankino 1993–95; Chair. Bd of Dirs, Russian Public TV 1995–96; Corresp. mem. Acad. of Sciences (Econs Dept) 1984, mem. 1990; Dr hc (Exeter) 1991, (Soka, Japan) 1996. *Publications:* books and articles on Russian 20th century history, critical analyses of Marxist theory and Communist practice; The Slough of Memory (memoirs) 2000. *Leisure interest:* playing chess. *Address:* Presidential Commission on Rehabilitation of Political Prisoners, Ilyinka str. 8/4, Entr. 20, 103132 Moscow, Russia (Office). *Telephone:* (095) 206-24-94 (Office). *Fax:* (095) 206-35-15 (Office).

YAKOVLEV, Veniamin Fedorovich, DJur; Russian politician and lawyer; b. 12 Feb. 1932, Petukhovo, Kurgan Region; s. of Fedor Kuzmich Yakovlev and Domna Pavlovna Yakovleva; m. Galina Ivanovna Yakovleva 1956; two d.; ed Sverdlovsk Inst. of Law; mem. CPSU 1956–91; teacher, then Dir Yakut School of Law 1953–56; Asst Procurator/Attorney-Gen. of Yakut Autonomous Repub. 1956–60; aspirant, teacher, docent, Dean, Pro-Rector Sverdlovsk Inst. of Law 1960–87; Dir All-Union Research Inst. of Soviet Legis. 1987–89; Deputy Chair. Public Comm. of Int. Co-operation on Humanitarian Problems and

Human Rights 1988; USSR Minister of Justice 1989–90; Chair. USSR Supreme Arbitration Court 1991, Supreme Arbitration Court of Russian Fed. 1992–. *Publications:* Civil Law Method of Regulation for Social Relations and more than 150 other Publs. *Leisure interests:* skiing and other sports. *Address:* Supreme Arbitration Court, Maly Kharitonyevski 12, 101000 Moscow, Russia. *Telephone:* (095) 208-11-19. *Fax:* (095) 208-44-00.

YAKOVLEV, Vladimir Anatolyevich, CAND.ECON.SC; Russian politician; b. 25 Nov. 1944, Olekminsk, Yakutia; m. Irina Ivanovna Yakovleva; one s.; ed NW Polytech. Inst.; master on construction sites, Head Repair-Construction Trust 1965–80, Deputy Man. Housing Dept, Leningrad (St Petersburg) 1980–93; First Deputy Mayor of St Petersburg, Russia. Head Cttee on Man. of Municipal Econ. 1993–96; elected Mayor of St Petersburg 1996; mem. Council of Fed. of Russia 1996–2001; Pres. Ass. of Heads of Regions and Repubs. of NW Russia 1997; Pres. Basketball Club Spartacus; Founder and Leader of Vsya Rossiya Movt 1999; Pres. Fed. of Bicycle Sports of St Petersburg; Order of Honour 2000; Merited Constructor of Russia. *Address:* Office of the Governor of St Petersburg, Smolny, 193060 St Petersburg, Russia. *Telephone:* (812) 276-60-94 (Office). *Fax:* (812) 315-98-83 (Office).

YAKOVLEV, Gen. Vladimir Nikolayevich, CAND.MIL.SC.; Russian army officer; b. 17 Aug. 1954, Tver; s. of Nikolai Vassilyevich Yakovlev and Erika Alexeyevna Yakovleva; m. Raisa Anatolyevna Yakovleva; two d.; ed Dzerzhinsky Mil. Acad., Mil. Acad. of Gen. Staff; served with strategic rocket forces incl. Commdr rocket regt 1985–89; Deputy Commdr rocket div. 1989–91, Commdr 1991–93; Head of Staff Rocket Army 1993–94, Commdr 1994–97; Head of Gen. Staff Rocket Troops Jan. 1999–; C-in-C Rocket Strategic Forces of Russian Fed. 1997–2001; Head of Staff for Co-ordination of Mil. Co-operation within CIS 2001–; Prof. Acad. of Mil. Sciences; mem. Russian Acad. of Eng; corresp. mem. Russian Acad. of Rocket and Artillery Sciences; Order of Red Star, Order for Mil. Service, Prize of Russian Pres. for Achievement in Educ. 1998. *Publications include:* Military Work: Science, Art, Vocation 1998, Organizational Activities of General Staff in Rocket Strategic Forces 1999, Rocket Shield of the Motherland 1999, co-author Mil. Encyclopaedic Dictionary of Rocket Strategic Forces. *Leisure interests:* music, reading, tennis, swimming. *Address:* Ministry of Defence, Bolshaya Pirogovskaya str. 23, K-160 Moscow, Russia (Office). *Telephone:* (095) 244-62-14 (Office).

YAKOVLEV, Yegor Vladimirovich; Russian journalist and newspaper editor; b. 14 March 1930; ed Moscow State Historical Archival Inst.; mem. CPSU 1953–91; worked on a number of newspapers: Pravda, Izvestiya, Sovetskaya Rossiya, Moscow Pravda; Founding Ed. Zhurnalist monthly; worked in Prague on staff of World Marxist Review 1972–75; worked on Izvestiya, Moscow 1975–85; Ed. Moscow News weekly 1985–91; Pres. All-Russia Radio and TV Co. Ostankino 1991–92; Founder and Ed. Obshchaya Gazeta weekly 1992–2001; mem. Presidential Political Consultative Council 1991; winner of two int. awards for journalism. *Publications:* more than 20 books; numerous articles on historical and political problems. *Address:* Goncharnaya 1, 109240 Moscow, Russia. *Telephone:* (095) 915-22-88. *Fax:* (095) 615-51-71 (Office). *E-mail:* secretar@og.ru (Office). *Website:* www.og.ru (Office).

YAKOVLEV, Yuri Vassilievich; Russian actor; b. 25 April 1928, Moscow; s. of Vassily Vassilievich Yakovlev and Olga Mikhailovna Ivanova; m. Irina Leonidovna Sergeyeva; two s. one d.; ed Shchukin Higher School of Theatre Art; actor Vakhtangov Acad. Theatre 1952–; Order of Lenin 1988, Order of Red Banner of Labour 1978, Order For Service to Motherland 1996; RSFSR State Prize 1970, USSR State Prize 1979, State Prize of Russia, Crystal Turandot Prize 1998, USSR Peoples' Artist. *Films include:* Idiot 1958, Wind 1959, A Man from Nowhere 1961, Unusual Summer, Hussar Ballad 1962, Anna Karenina 1968, A Theme for a Short Story 1970, Irony of the Fate 1975, Love Earthly 1975, Fate 1978, Ideal Husband 1981, Carnival 1982, Idiot 1983. *Plays include:* Ladies and Hussars, A Play Without Title, My Mocking Happiness, Princess Turandot, Anna Karenina, Great Magic, Casanova, Three Ages of Casanova, Bolingbrook, A Glass of Water, Lessons of the Master, Guilty Without Guilt. *Publications:* Book Album of My Destiny 1997. *Leisure interests:* Russian classical literature, classical music, sports. *Address:* Y. Vakhtangov Academic Theatre, Arbat str. 26, 121002 Moscow (Office); Plotnikov per. 10/28, Apt. 28, 121002 Moscow, Russia (Home). *Telephone:* (095) 241-09-28 (Office); (095) 241-82-71 (Home).

YAKOVLEVA, Olga Mikhailovna; Russian actress; b. 1 March 1941, Alma-Ata, Kazakhstan; ed Moscow Shchepkin Theatre School; actress with Moscow Lenkom Theatre 1962–, Moscow Theatre on Malaya Bronnaya 1967–84, Taganka Theatre 1984–, Moscow Mayakovsky Theatre 1991– and others; Golden Mask Prize 1996. *Plays include:* Moscow Lenkom Theatre: Seagull, My Poor Marat, 104 Pages About Love; Moscow Theatre on Malaya Bronnaya: Three Sisters, Othello, Romeo and Juliet, Marriage, Don Juan; Moscow Taganka Theatre: On the Bottom, Misanthrope; Moscow Mayakovsky Theatre: Napoleon 1; Oleg Tabakov Studio-Theatre: The Last Ones. *Address:* V. Mayakovsky Moscow Academic Theatre, B. Nikitskaya str. 19, 103009 Moscow, Russia (Office). *Telephone:* (095) 290-46-58 (Office).

YAKUNIN, Gleb Pavlovich; Russian politician and ecclesiastic; b. 4 March 1934; m.; one s. two d.; ed Irkutsk Inst. of Agriculture, Moscow Theological Seminary; sexton, Minister in Zaraisk, Dmitrov; expelled from Moscow Theological Seminary and deprived of the right to be a minister for public protest against collaboration of church admin. with CP; Founder and Leader Christian Cttee for Protection of Believers; sentenced to five years' imprisonment and five-year term of exile for anti-Soviet propaganda 1979; then Minister in St Nicholas Church, Shchelykovo Village, Moscow Region; exonerated 1991; active participant of Movt for Democratic Russia, Co-Chair. Coordination Council; People's Deputy of Russia 1990–93; fmr mem. Supreme Soviet of Russia; Chair. Cttee for Protection of Freedom of Conscience 1996; excommunicated by Holy Synod for political activities Dec. 1993; mem. State Duma (Parl.) 1993–95; Chair. L. Tolstoy Cttee for Defence of Freedom of Conscience. *Address:* Bolshoy Golovin per. 22, 103045 Moscow, Russia. *Telephone:* (095) 207-60-69. *Fax:* (095) 207-60-69.

YALÁ, Kumba; Guinea-Bissau politician; b. 1954; mem. Social Renewal Party (PRS); Pres. of Guinea-Bissau and C-in-C of the Armed Forces Feb. 2000–. *Address:* Avenida Unidade Africana, CP 137, Bissau, Republic of Guinea-Bissau (Office). *Telephone:* 211308 (Office). *Fax:* 201671 (Office).

YALOW, Rosalyn Sussman, PhD; American medical physicist; b. 19 July 1921, New York; d. of Simon and Clara (née Zipper) Sussman; m. Aaron Yalow 1943; one s. one d.; ed Hunter Coll., New York, Univ. of Illinois; Asst in Physics, Univ. of Ill. 1941–43, Instructor 1944–45; Lecturer and temp. Asst Prof. in Physics, Hunter Coll., New York 1946–50; Physicist and Asst Chief, Radioisotope Service, Veterans Admin. Hosp., Bronx 1950–70, Acting Chief 1968–70, Chief Radioimmunoassay Reference Lab. 1969, Chief Nuclear Medicine Service 1970–80, Sr Medical Investigator 1972–92, Sr Medical Investigator Emer. 1992–, Dir Solomon A. Berson Research Lab. Veterans Admin. Medical Center 1973–92; Research Prof., Dept of Medicine, Mount Sinai School of Medicine, New York 1968–74, Distinguished Service Prof. 1974–79; Distinguished Prof.-at-Large, Albert Einstein Coll. of Medicine, Yeshiva Univ. 1979–85, Prof. Emer. 1985–; Chair. Dept of Clinical Sciences, Montefiore Hosp., Bronx, NY 1980–85; Solomon A. Berson Distinguished Prof.-at-Large, Mt. Sinai School of Medicine, New York 1986–; Harvey Lecturer 1966, American Gastroenterology Asscn Memorial Lecturer 1972, Joslyn Lecturer, New England Diabetes Asscn 1972, Franklin I. Harris Memorial Lecturer 1973, 1st Hagedorn Memorial Lecturer, Acta Endocrinologica Congress 1973; Pres. Endocrine Soc. 1978–79; mem. NAS 1975–, American Physics Soc., Radiation Research Soc., American Asscn Physicists in Medicine, Biophysics Soc., American Acad. of Arts and Sciences, American Physiology Soc.; Foreign Assoc. French Acad. of Medicine 1981; Fellow New York Acad. of Science, Radiation Research Soc., American Asscn of Physicists in Medicine; Assoc. Fellow in Physics, American Coll. of Radiology, American Diabetes Asscn, Endocrine Soc., Soc. of Nuclear Medicine; more than 60 Hon. doctorates; Jt winner of Nobel Prize for Physiology or Medicine for discoveries concerning peptide hormones 1977 and more than 30 other awards. *Address:* Veterans Administration Medical Center, 130 West Kingsbridge Road, Bronx, New York, NY 10468 (Office); 3242 Tibbett Avenue, Bronx, New York, NY 10463, USA (Home). *Telephone:* (718) 584-9000 (Office). *Fax:* (718) 562-9120 (Office).

YAM, Joseph C. K., CBE, BSc; Hong Kong banker; b. 9 Sept. 1948, Canton, China; s. of Shun Yam and Hok-chun Shum; m. Grace Fong 1972; one s. one d.; ed Univ. of Hong Kong, Inst. of Social Studies, The Hague, Netherlands; demonstrator in Econs, Econs Dept, Univ. of Hong Kong 1970–71; statistician, Census and Statistics Dept, Hong Kong Govt 1971–76, economist, Econ. Services Br. 1976–77, Sr Economist 1977–79, Prin. Asst Sec. (Econ. Services) 1979–82, (Monetary Affairs) 1982–85, Deputy Sec. for Monetary Affairs 1985–91; Dir Office of the Exchange Fund 1991–93; Chief Exec. Hong Kong Monetary Authority 1993–; Banker of the Year in Hong Kong 1995. *Leisure interests:* golf, horse racing, swimming, hiking. *Address:* Hong Kong Monetary Authority, 30/F, 3 Garden Road, Central, Hong Kong Special Administrative Region, People's Republic of China. *Telephone:* 28788196. *Fax:* 28788197. *E-mail:* hkma@hkma.gov.hk (Office). *Website:* www.info.gov.hk/hkma (Office).

YAMAGUCHI, Kenji, MA (ECON.); Japanese government official; b. 19 July 1933, Yamagata; s. of Futao Yamaguchi and Yoshi Yamaguchi; m. Momoe Matsumoto 1962; one s. one d.; ed Univ. of Tokyo; entered Budget Bureau, Ministry of Finance 1956; Nat. Tax Admin. Agency 1963; Ministry of Interior 1966; Econ. Planning Agency 1968; First Sec. Okinawa Reversion Preparatory Cttee, Foreign Minister's Office and Counsellor, Okinawa Bureau, Prime Minister's Office 1969; Int. Finance Bureau, Ministry of Finance 1971; Consul for Japan, Sydney 1972; Counsellor, Personnel Bureau, Prime Minister's Office 1975; Finance Bureau, Ministry of Finance 1977; Dir-Gen. North East Japan Finance Bureau, Ministry of Finance 1981; Special Asst to Minister of Foreign Affairs 1982–87; Exec. Dir for Japan, IBRD and affiliates 1982–87, Dean IBRD Bd 1985–87; Sr Exec. Dir Water Resources Devt Public Corpn 1988–; Co-ordination Leader, Org. for Industry, Science and Cultural Advancement (OISCA) 1987–99; Exec. Adviser Mitsui Trust Bank, Tokyo 1993–99; Chair. Mitsui Trust Int. Ltd, London 1993–99, Mitsui Trust Bank Ltd, Switzerland 1993–97; Exec. Adviser Chiyoda Mutual Life Insurance Co., Tokyo 1997–99; f. WELL (World Economy and Land Lab.) a think-tank seeking a balanced relationship between the nat. econ. and land ownership 1998; Human Life Rescue Award 1954. *Publications:* The World Bank and its Role in the World Economy 1988, The World Bank – How Can Japan Contribute to the World? 1995, Land Policy for Prosperity – Land as Public Property 1997, Land is to be Owned by the Public 2000, A Cool Observation on the Japanese Economy (Okame Hachimoku) 2003; and several books on financial matters, foreign affairs, etc. *Leisure interests:* reading, swimming,

golf. *Address:* 3-16-43 Utsukushiga-Oka, Aoba-ku, Yokohama City 225-0002, Japan. *Telephone:* (45) 901-7309. *Fax:* (45) 901-7309. *E-mail:* well@mx7.ttcn .ne.jp (Office). *Website:* www2.ttcn.ne.jp/~well (Office).

YAMAGUCHI, Shigeru; Japanese judge; b. 4 Nov. 1932, Chiba; ed Kyoto Univ.; Asst Judge, Okayama Dist Court and Okayama Family Court 1957; Judge, Hakodate Dist, Court and Hakodate Family Court 1967; Dir Secr. of Research and Training Inst. for Court Clerks 1969; Judge, Tokyo Dist Court (Presiding Judge of Div.) 1976; Dir Secr. of Tokyo High Court 1980, Judge and Presiding Judge of Div. 1989; Dir Gen. Affairs Bureau, Gen. Secr. of Supreme Court 1983, Justice 1997, Chief Justice of the Supreme Court 1997–; Pres. Kofu Dist Court and Kofu Family Court 1988; Pres. Legal Training and Research Inst. 1991; Pres. Fukuoka High Court 1994. *Address:* Office of the Chief Justice, 4-2, Hayabusa-cho, Chiyoda-ku, Tokyo 102-8651, Japan (Office). *Telephone:* (3) 3264-8111 (Office). *Fax:* (3) 3221-8975 (Office). *Website:* www.courts.go.jp (Office).

YAMAMOTO, Takuma, BEng; Japanese businessman; b. 11 Sept. 1925, Kumamoto; ed Univ. of Tokyo; joined Fujitsu Ltd 1949, Bd Dir 1975–, Man. Dir 1976–79, Exec. Dir 1979–81, Pres. and Rep. Dir 1981–90, Chair. and Rep. Dir 1990–98; Vice-Chair. Communication Industries Asscn of Japan 1986; Chair. Japan Electronic Industry Devt Asscn 1987–89, Vice-Chair. 1989–; Chair. Cttee on Int. Coordination of Econ. Policies (KEIDANREN) 1988–; Hon. Dr. Hum.Litt. (Chaminade Univ. of Honolulu); Blue Ribbon with Medal of Honour 1984. *Leisure interests:* river-fishing, golf, gardening. *Address:* c/o Fujitsu Ltd, 1-6-1 Marunouchi, Chiyoda-ku, Tokyo 100, Japan.

YAMAMOTO, Yohji; Japanese fashion designer; b. 1943, Tokyo; ed Keio Univ. and Bunkafukuso Gakuin school of fashion, Tokyo; launched first collection Tokyo 1977, Paris 1981, New York 1982, first menswear collection, Paris 1984; costume designer for Opéra de Lyon's production of Madame Butterfly 1990, Wagner Opera's production of Tristan und Isolde, Bayreuth 1993, Kanagawa Art Festival Opera Susanoo 1994; launched first perfume Yohji 1996, second perfume Yohji Essential 1998; participant in 25th Anniversary of Pina Bausch Co., Wuppertal 1998; launched first perfume Yohji Homme 1999; designed costumes for the Ryuichi Sakamoto Opera 'Life' 1999; subject of Wim Wenders' film Notebook on Cities and Clothes 1989; So-en Award, Endo Award 1969, Fashion Eds. Club Award, Tokyo 1982, 1991, 1997, Mainichi Fashion Award, Tokyo 1986, 1994, Chevalier, Ordre des Arts et des Lettres 1994, Night of Stars Award Fashion Group, New York 1997, Arte e Moda Award, Pitti Imagine, Florence 1998, Int. Award Council of Fashion Designers of America 1999. *Address:* Yohji Europe, 155 rue Saint Martin, 75003 Paris, France (Office). *Telephone:* 1-42-78-94-11. *Fax:* 1-40-29-94-04.

YAMANI, Sheikh Ahmed Zaki; Saudi Arabian politician; b. 1930, Mecca; ed Cairo Univ., New York and Harvard Univs, USA; Saudi Arabian Govt Service; pvt. law practice; Legal Adviser to Council of Ministers 1958–60; mem. Council of Ministers 1960–86; Minister of State 1960–62; Minister of Petroleum and Mineral Resources 1962–86; Dir Arabian American Oil Company 1962–86; Chair. of Bd of Dirs General Petroleum and Mineral Org. (PETROMIN) 1963–86, Coll. of Petroleum and Minerals, Dhahran 1963–86, Saudi Arabian Fertilizer Co. (SAFCO) 1966–86; f. Centre for Global Energy Studies; Sec.-Gen. Org. of Arab Petroleum Exporting Countries (OAPEC) 1968–69, Chair. 1974–75; mem. several Int. Law Asscns. *Publication:* Islamic Law and Contemporary Issues. *Address:* PO Box 14850, Jeddah 21434, Saudi Arabia.

YAMANI, Hashim ibn Abdullah ibn Hashim al, PhD; Saudi Arabian politician; ed Harvard Univ.; Prof. and later Chair. of Physics Dept, King Fahd Univ. of Petroleum and Minerals; Vice-Pres. King Abdul Aziz City for Science; Minister of Industry and Electricity 1995–; Chair. Sabic. *Address:* Ministry of Industry and Electricity, P. O Box 5729, Omar bin al-Khatab Street, Riyadh 11432, Saudi Arabia. *Telephone:* (1) 477-6666. *Fax:* (1) 477-5441.

YAMASHITA, Yasuhiro, MA; Japanese judo player and coach; b. 1 June 1957, Kumamoto; m. Midori Ono 1986; two s. one d.; ed Kyushu Gakuin High School, Tokai Univ. Sagami High School and Tokai Univ.; nine consecutive times, All Japan Judo Tournament; four-time World Judo Champion; achieved unbroken record of 203 consecutive wins from 1977 till he retd in 1985; gold medallist Olympic Games, Los Angeles 1984; Prof. Dept of Sports, Tokai Univ. 1986–; fmr Team Man. Univ. Judo Team; Man. Japanese Nat. Judo Team 1992–; Nat. Honour Prize (Japan, first amateur sportsman to achieve award); mem. Laurens World Sports Acad. *Publications include:* Young Days with Black Belt, Enjoyable Judo, The Moment of Fight, Osoto-Gari, Judo with Fighting Spirits. *Leisure interests:* reading, playing with my kids, karaoke (with family), dining out. *Address:* 1117 Kitakaname, Hitatsuka Kanagawa, 259–1207 (Office); 661-104 Higashi Koiso, Oiso-machi, Naka-gun, Kanagawa-ken, Japan (Home). *Telephone:* (463) 58-1211 (ext. 3532) (Office); (463) 61-1100. *Fax:* (463) 50-2405 (Office); (463) 61-2120. *E-mail:* judo1117@keyaki.cc.u-tokai.ac.jp (Office).

YAMASSOUM, Nagoum; Chadian politician; Prime Minister of Chad Aug. 2000–. *Address:* Office of the Prime Minister, N'Djamena, Chad (Office).

YAMEY, Basil Selig, CBE, BComm, FBA; British economist; b. 4 May 1919, Cape Town, South Africa; s. of Solomon Yamey and Leah Yamey; m. 1st Helen Bloch 1948 (died 1980); one s. one d.; m. 2nd Demetra Georgakopoulou 1991; ed Tulbagh High School and Univ. of Cape Town; Prof. of Econs LSE 1960–84, Prof. Emer. 1984–; mem. Monopolies and Mergers Comm. 1966–78; Trustee

Nat. Gallery, London 1974–81, Tate Gallery, London 1977–81, Inst. of Econ. Affairs 1987–91; Hon. Fellow LSE 1988. *Publications:* Economics of Resale Price Maintenance 1951, Economics of Underdeveloped Countries (with P. T. Bauer) 1956, Economics of Futures Trading (with B. A. Goss) 1976, Essays on the History of Accounting 1978, Art and Accounting 1989. *Address:* 27B Elsworthy Road, London, NW3 3BT, England. *Telephone:* (20) 7586-9344. *Fax:* (20) 7586-9344.

YAN DONGSHENG, PhD; Chinese academic; b. 10 Feb. 1918, Shanghai; s. of Chi Yan and Yuhan (née Chu) Yan; m. Bi-Rou Sun 1943; one s. one d.; ed Yanjing and Tsinghua Univs., Beijing, Univ. of Illinois, USA; Deputy Dir Inst. of Chem. Eng, Kailan Mining Admin. 1950–54; Research Prof., Inst. of Metallurgy and Ceramics, Acad. of Sciences 1954–60; Deputy Dir Shanghai Ceramic Inst., Acad. of Sciences 1960, Dir 1977; mem. editorial Bd, Chinese Science Bulletin 1961; Vice-Pres. Shanghai Univ. of Science and Tech. 1980, Hon. Pres. 1985–, mem. Acad. Degrees Cttee 1981, Vice-Chair. Fund Cttee 1981; mem. 12th CCP Cen. Cttee 1982; mem. Standing Cttee CPPCC 1987–93, Vice-Chair. Shanghai Municipal CPPCC 1987–93; Pres. Chinese Chemical Soc. 1982–86; Ed.-in-Chief Science in China, Science Bulletin 1987–96, Ceramics Int.; Ed. Material Letters (Int.), Int. Solid State Chem., European Solid State and Inorganic Chem., High Tech Ceramics (Intel); mem. Leading Group for Scientific Work, State Council 1983–88; mem. Chinese Acad. of Sciences (Vice-Pres. 1980–87), Dir Dept of Chem. 1981–93; Party Sec. Chinese Acad. of Sciences 1984–87, Special Adviser 1987–, Sr Fellow 1998–; Sr Fellow Chinese Acad. of Eng 1998–; Pres. Chinese Ceramic Soc. 1983–93, Hon. Pres. 1993–; Pres. Chinese Chemical Soc. 1995–98; Vice-Pres. China–US People's Friendship Asscn 1986–; Titular mem. IUPAC 1987–95; Pres. Fed. of Asian Scientific Acads and Socs 1990–95; Principal Investigator Climb Project, Nanomaterials Research 1992–97, Advisor Climb Project, Nanomaterials and Devices 1997–2002; Hon. mem. Materials Research Socs, India, Japan, USA, Europe; Hon. DSc (Ill., Bordeaux) 1986, (Hong Kong Polytechnic) 1993. *Leisure interests:* tennis, classical music, bridge. *Address:* Chinese Academy of Sciences, 52 San Li He Road, Beijing, People's Republic of China. *Telephone:* (10) 68597289 (Office); (10) 62554019 (Home). *Fax:* (10) 68512458.

YAN HAIWANG; Chinese politician; b. Sept. 1939, Zhengzhou City, Henan Prov.; ed Harbin Architectural Eng Inst.; joined CCP 1966; Vice-Gov. Gansu Prov. 1987, Gov. 1993–97; Vice-Sec. CCP Gansu Provincial Cttee 1988; alt. mem. 14th CCP Cen. Cttee 1992; Sec. CCP Gansu Provincial Cttee 1993–98; mem. 15th CCP Cen. Cttee 1997–2002; currently Deputy Gov. People's Bank of China. *Address:* People's Bank of China, 32 Chengfang Jie, Xicheng Qu, Beijing 100800, People's Republic of China. *Telephone:* (10) 66194114. *Fax:* (10) 66015346. *E-mail:* master@pbc.gov.cn. *Website:* www.pbc.gov.cn.

YAN LIANGKUN; Chinese orchestral conductor; b. Oct. 1923, Wuchang City, Hubei Prov.; Artistic Dir and Conductor, Symphony Orchestra of China Cen. Philharmonic Soc.; Vice-Pres. China Musicians' Asscn 1992–; mem. 6th Nat. Cttee CPPCC 1983–87, 7th 1988–92, 8th 1993. *Address:* Central Philharmonic Society, 11-1 Hepingjie (Peace Street), Beijing 100013, People's Republic of China.

YAN WENJING; Chinese writer; b. 15 Oct. 1915, Wuchang, Hubei; m. 1st Li Shuhua 1939 (died 1976); m. 2nd Kang Zhichiang 1976; one s. five d.; joined CCP 1938; worked in literature Dept of Lu Xun Art Acad., Yan'an; Asst Ed.-in-Chief North East Daily 1945; worked in Propaganda Dept, Cen. Cttee, CCP after 1949; Chief Ed. People's Literature; Dir People's Literature Publishing House, Head 1973–83; mem. Presidium Chinese Writers' Asscn 1985–96, Adviser 1996–; Vice-Pres. China Pen Centre 1982–; writes children's stories. *Publications include:* A Man's Troubles (novel), Nannan and Uncle Whiskers, The Echo, The Little Stream Sings, Next Time Port, Fables of Yan Wenjing, Selected Prose Poems of Yan Wenjing. *Address:* People's Literature Publishing House, Beijing, People's Republic of China. *Telephone:* 5003312.

YANAGISAWA, Hakuo; Japanese politician; mem. LDP; mem. for Shizuoka, House of Reps.; fmr official in Ministry of Finance; Sec. to Chief Cabinet Sec. 1978–80; mem. House of Reps. 1980–; fmr Parl. Vice-Minister; Dir-Gen. Nat. Land Agency 1998–99; Minister of State (Financial Services Agency) and Chair. Financial Reconstruction Comm. March–Oct. 1999, 2000–02. *Leisure interest:* karaoke. *Address:* c/o Financial Services Agency, 3-1-1, Kasumigaseki, Chiyoda-ku, Tokyo 100-8967, Japan (Office).

YANAYEV, Gennadiy Ivanovich, CAND.HIST.SC.; Russian politician; b. 26 Aug. 1937, Perevoz, Perevozovsky region, Gorky Dist; m.; two d.; ed Gorky Agric. Inst. and All-Union Law Inst.; mem. CPSU 1962–91; began work as foreman of mechanisation unit 1959–63; Komsomol work; Second Sec. Gorky village Komsomol Dist Cttee (Obkom), Second, First Sec. Obkom `1963–68; Chair. Cttee of USSR Youth Orgs, then Vice-Chair. of Presidium of Union of Soviet Asscns for Friendship and Cultural Relations with Foreign Countries 1968–86; trade-union work, Sec., Vice-Chair. All-Union Trades Union Fed. 1986–90; mem. Cen. Cttee CPSU, Sec. 1990–91; fmr People's Deputy; mem. CPSU Politburo 1990–91; Vice-Pres. USSR 1990–91; arrested for participation in attempted coup d'état, charged with conspiracy 1992; on trial 1993–94, released after amnesty 1994.

YANDARBIYEV, Zelimkhan; Chechen politician and writer; b. 12 Sept. 1952, Vydrika, Kazakhstan; ed Chechen-Ingush State Univ.; worked as bricklayer, gas well driller 1969–76; proof-reader, engineer-technician, Head Production Div. Chechen-Ingush Publ House 1976–85; mem. USSR Union of

Writers 1985; published a few collections of verses and short stories under pen name Abdul Muslim; Chair. Cttee of Literature Promotion 1985–86; Ed.-in-Chief Raduga (magazine) 1986–89; participant opposition movt for ind. of Chechnya since 1980s; mem. Parl. of Chechnya 1991, Vice-Pres. Chechen Repub. of Ichkeriya (Chechnya) 1993, Acting Pres. (after death of D. Dudayev) 1996; cand. in pres. elections 1997; Personal Rep. of Pres. Maskhadov to Middle East 1999–.

YAÑEZ-BARNUEVO, Juan Antonio, LLB, DIP. I.L.; Spanish diplomatist; b. 15 Feb. 1942, Coria del Río, Seville; s. of the late Luis Yáñez-Barnuevo and Angeles Yañez-Barnuevo; m. Isabel Sampedro 1969; one s.; ed Univs. of Seville, Madrid and Cambridge, School for Int. Civil Servants, Madrid, Hague Acad. of Int. Law and Diplomatic School, Madrid; Sec. of Embassy, Perm. Mission of Spain to UN, New York 1970–73; Deputy Head, Office of Int. Legal Affairs, Ministry of Foreign Affairs 1975–78; Deputy Perm. Rep. to Council of Europe, Strasbourg 1978–82; Dir of Int. Dept of Presidency of Govt (Foreign Policy Adviser to Prime Minister) 1982–91; Amb. and Perm. Rep. of Spain at UN, New York 1991–96; Deputy Dir Diplomatic School 1996–98; Amb.-at-Large 1998–; Head Spanish Del. to UN negotiations on the Int. Criminal Court 1998–; mem. Int. Humanitarian Fact-finding Comm. 2002–; Francisco Tomás y Valiente Prize (Seville) 1998, Jurist of the Year (Madrid Law School) 1999. *Publications:* La Justicia Penal Internacional—Una perspectiva iberoamericana 2001. *Leisure interests:* reading, music, nature. *Address:* Paseo de Juan XXIII 5, 28040 Madrid (Office); c/o Ministry of Foreign Affairs, Plaza de la Provincia 1, 28071 Madrid; Carretera de Húmera, 1 (Aravaca), 28023 Madrid, Spain (Home). *Telephone:* (91) 5339639 (Office). *Fax:* (91) 535 1433 (Office). *E-mail:* hispaunesco@mad.servicom.es (Office).

YANG, Jerry, MS; American computer executive; b. Taiwan; ed Stanford Univ.; co-creator Yahoo! (on-line guide 1994), co-founder, Yahoo! Inc. 1995; Chair. Bd Dirs. 1996–. *Address:* Yahoo! Incorporated, 3420 Central Expressway, 2nd Floor, Santa Clara, CA 95051, USA.

YANG, Hon. Sir Ti Liang, Hon. Mr Justice Yang, Kt, LLB, FCIA; British judge; b. 30 June 1929, Shanghai, China; s. of Shao-nan Yang and Elsie Chun; m. Eileen Barbara Tam 1954; two s.; ed The Comparative Law School of China, Soochow Univ., Shanghai, Univ. Coll. London, UK; called to Bar (with Hons), Gray's Inn 1954; Magistrate, Hong Kong 1956, Sr Magistrate 1963, Dist Judge, Dist Court 1968, Judge of High Court 1975, Justice of Appeal 1980, Vice-Pres. Court of Appeal 1987, Chief Justice of Hong Kong 1988–96; mem. Exec. Council, Hong Kong Special Admin. Region 1997–; Pres. of Ct. of Appeal of Negara Brunei Darussalam 1988–92; Rockefeller Fellow, London Univ. 1963–64; Chair. Kowloon Disturbances Claims Assessment Bd 1966, Compensation Bd 1967, Comm. of Inquiry into the Rainstorm Disasters 1972, into Lelung Wing-sang Case 1976, into McLennan Case 1980; mem. Law Reform Comm. (Chair. Sub-Cttee on law relating to homosexuality 1980) 1980–96; Chair. Chief Justice Working Party on Voir Dire Procs. and Judges' Rules 1979, Univ. and Polytechnic Grants Cttee 1981–84, Hong Kong Univ. Council 1987–; Pro-Chancellor Hong Kong Univ. 1994–; Patron The Soc. for the Rehabilitation of Offenders, Hong Kong; Hon. Pres. Hong Kong Scouts Asscn, Against Child Abuse; Hon. LLD (Chinese Univ. of Hong Kong) 1984, (Hong Kong Polytechnic) 1992; Hon. DLitt (Hong Kong Univ.) 1991; Order of Chivalry (First Class), SPMB, Negara Brunei Darus-salam 1990; Grand Bauhinia Medal 1999. *Publications:* (trans.) General Yue Fei (by Qian Cai) 1995, (trans.) Peach Blossom Fan (novel by Gu Shifàn 1948) 1998. *Leisure interests:* philately, reading, walking, oriental ceramics, travelling, music. *Address:* Executive Council, Central Government Offices, Lower Albert Road, Hong Kong Special Administrative Region, People's Republic of China (Office); Flat 8, Duchess of Bedford House, Duchess of Bedford's Walk, London, W8 7QL, England. *Telephone:* 28498099 (Office).

YANG, Yuyu; Taiwanese artist; ed China, Japan, Italy; Founder Lifescape Museum, Taipei; Int. FRBS 1996. *Works include:* Mountain Grandeur, Solar Permanence, Lunar Brilliance, Dragon's Song, Universe and Life.

YANG BAIBING, Gen.; Chinese army officer; b. Sept. 1920, Tongnan Co., Sichuan Prov.; Deputy Political Commissar, Beijing Mil. Region, PLA 1983–85, Political Commissar 1985; Deputy Dir, Bureau under Int. Liaison Dept, State Council 1985–87; Dir Gen. Political Dept 1987; mem. Cen. Mil. Comm., PRC April 1988, Sec.-Gen. 1989; rank of Gen. 1988; mem. 13th CCP Cen. Cttee 1987–92; mem. 14th CCP Cen. Cttee 1992–97; PLA Deputy to 8th NPC; mem. Politburo 1992–97. *Address:* c/o Politburo, Chinese Communist Party, Beijing, People's Republic of China.

YANG BO; Chinese politician; b. 1920, Shandong; concurrently Dir Research Office and Comprehensive Dept, State Statistics Bureau, State Council; Deputy Dir then Dir Shandong Prov. Statistics Comm.; Vice-Chair. Prov. Revolutionary Cttee, Shandong 1977; Vice-Minister State Planning Comm., State Council 1979; Deputy Man. 7th Dept, China Nat. Tech. Import Corpn (TECHIMPORT) 1980; Vice-Minister State Energy Comm., State Council 1981; Minister of Light Industry 1982–87; Sec. Party Group 1983; mem. 12th Cen. Cttee, CCP 1982–87; Adviser, China-Japan Personnel Exchange Cttee 1985–, NPC Finance and Econ. Cttee; fmr Adviser Internal and Judicial Affairs Cttee; Deputy 7th NPC, mem. Standing Cttee 1988; Chair. Int. Cttee for Promotion of Chinese Industrial Co-operatives (ICCIC) 1992–.

YANG CHENG-ZHI, BSc; Chinese petroleum engineer; b. 8 Aug. 1938, Henan; s. of Yang Xian-zun and Hou Yang; m. Li Yan-qin 1969; one s. one d.; ed Beijing Univ. of Petroleum; Asst Prof. Beijing Univ. of Petroleum 1961–75;

Asst Prof., Vice-Dir Dept of Petroleum Eng Sheng-li Coll. of Petroleum 1976–78; Prof., Sr Research Engineer and Dir of Research for interface chem., Research Inst. of Petroleum Exploration and Devt of Beijing 1979–; Dir Jr Lab. for colloid and interface science, Acad. Sinica and China Nat. Petroleum Co. 1990–; Hon. Prof. Da-qing Univ. of Petroleum 1988–; Visiting Sr Research Engineer Inst. Français du Pétrole 1979–80, 1985–87, 1989–90; mem. China Petroleum Soc., Soc. of Petroleum Engineers of USA; research into enhanced oil recovery, the physical chem. of oil reservoirs, surfactant solution properties, absorption of surfactants and polymers, colloid and interface chem. etc.; Science-Tech. Award in Petroleum Eng 1991, 1996, World Lifetime Achievement Award, ABI, USA 1992 and other awards. *Publications:* Petroleum Reservoir Physics 1975, World Fine Chemical Engineering Handbook (jtly.), Enhanced Oil Recovery Theory and Practice 1995, Improved Oil Recovery 1997, Enhanced Oil Recovery by Chemical Flooding 1999; more than 60 articles in professional journals. *Leisure interests:* collecting stamps and badges. *Address:* Research Institute of Petroleum Exploration and Development, P.O. Box 910, 100083 Beijing (Office); No. 1107, West-Beido Lodging House, Zhixing Road, 100083 Beijing, People's Republic of China (Home). *Telephone:* (10) 62098371 (Office); (10) 62397956 (Home). *Fax:* (10) 62097181 (Office); (10) 62397956 (Home). *E-mail:* ylang@public.fhnet.cn.net (Office).

YANG DEQING; Chinese army officer and politician; b. Sept. 1942, Yingcheng, Hubei Prov.; fmr Divisional Political Commissar and Army Political Dir of PLA Armoured Force, Political Commissar of Acad. of Mil. Economy; Deputy Political Commissar PLA Gen. Logistics Dept 1995–; now Political Commissar, PLA Chengdu Mil. Area Command; mem. Cen. Comm. for Discipline Inspection; Mayor Zhangjiakou City, Hebei Prov. *Address:* Headquarters PLA, Chengdu Military Area Command, Chengdu, Sichuan Province, People's Republic of China (Office).

YANG DEZHONG, Gen.; Chinese army officer and politician; b. 1923, Weinan Co., Shanxi Prov.; joined CCP 1938, First Deputy Dir of Gen. Office 1983–, CCP Cen. Cttee, Dir of Garrison Bureau 1982–; mem. 12th CCP Cen. Cttee 1982–87, 13th 1987–92, 14th 1992–96. *Address:* General Office, Chinese Communist Party Central Committee, Zhong Nan Hai, Beijing, People's Republic of China.

YANG FU-QING; Chinese professor of computer science; b. 6 Nov. 1932, Wuxi, Jiangsu Prov.; ed Tsinghua Univ., Peking Univ.; Prof., Dept of Computer Science and Tech. Peking Univ. 1983–, Dean 1983–99, Dean of Faculty of Information and Eng Science 1999–, Dir Inst. of Software Eng Research 1999–; Dir Nat. Eng Research Centre for Software Eng 1997–; mem. Chinese Acad. of Sciences, Academic Degree Cttee of the State Council; numerous awards and prizes including Special Prize for Advancement of Science and Tech., Electronics Industry Admin. 1996, First Class Prize of the Guang Hua Tech. Fund from the Nat. Defence Tech. Ministry 1996, Science and Tech. Progress Awards of He Liang and He Li Fund 1997. *Publications:* Operating System, Compiler, The Fundamental Theory of Software Engineering, Software Engineering Environment, Software Production Industrialization Technology. *Address:* Department of Computer Science and Technology, Peking University, Beijing 100871, People's Republic of China (Office). *Telephone:* (10) 62751782 (Office). *Fax:* (10) 62751792 (Office). *E-mail:* yang@cs.pku.edu .cn (Office). *Website:* www.cs.pku.edu.cn.

YANG GUOLIANG, Gen.; Chinese army officer; b. March 1938, Zunhua City, Hebei Prov.; ed Beijing Aeronautics Inst.; joined CCP 1961; Vice-Commdr PLA Second Artillery Force 1985; alt. mem. 12th CCP Cen. Cttee 1985, 13th CCP Cen. Cttee 1987; rank of Maj. Gen. 1988, Lt-Gen. 1990; Commdr PLA Second Artillery Force 1992–; rank of Gen. 1998; mem. 14th CCP Cen. Cttee 1992, 15th CCP Cen. Cttee 1997–2002. *Address:* People's Liberation Army Second Artillery Force Headquarters, Beijing, People's Republic of China.

YANG GUOPING, Gen.; Chinese army officer; b. Oct. 1934, Zhongxiang Co., Hubei Prov.; ed PLA Mil. Acad.; joined PLA 1950, fought in Korean War 1951; joined CCP 1956; Staff Officer of Combat Troops, Deputy Section Chief, Section Chief, Deputy Dept Chief, Dept Chief of Combat Troops for Shenyang Mil. Region, Deputy Chief of Staff 1987; Chief of Staff, 14th Army 1983–87; rank of Maj.-Gen. 1988; Chief of Staff, Jinan Mil. Region 1990–94, Deputy Commdr 1994–96; mil. rep. to 14th Cen Cttee CCP 1992; rank of Lt-Gen. 1993; Commdr of People's Armed Police Feb. 1996–; rank of Gen. 1998; mem. 15th CCP Cen. Cttee 1997–2002. *Address:* People's Liberation Army Headquarters of Armed Police, Beijing, People's Republic of China.

YANG GUOQING, MD; Chinese politician and surgeon; b. 1936, Taibei City, Taiwan Prov.; ed Beijing Medical Univ., Kobe Medical Univ., Japan; Dir Beijing Overseas Chinese Office 1990; Vice-Chair. China Asscn of Taiwan Compatriots 1993, Chair. 1997–; Vice-Chair. Cttee of Overseas Chinese Affairs, 9th NPC 1998–. *Address:* China Association of Taiwan Compatriots, Beijing, People's Republic of China.

YANG HUAIQING; Chinese naval officer; b. Feb. 1939, Shouguang Co., Shandong Prov.; joined PLA 1958, CCP 1960; served as Asst of Org. Section under political Dept of frigate detachment; Asst, section chief, deputy Dir and Dir of Cadre Dept of Navy Fleet; Dir political Dept of a naval base; political commissar of a naval base; Deputy Dir Political Dept of PLA Navy, Dir 1992–95; Political Commissar PLA Navy 1995–; rank of Rear-Adm. 1990, Vice-

Adm. 1994, Adm. 2000; Deputy to 8th NPC 1993; mem. 15th CCP Cen. Cttee 1997–. *Address:* Ministry of National Defence, Beijing, People's Republic of China.

YANG JIECHI; Chinese diplomatist; b. May 1950, Shanghai; m.; ed London School of Econs; Counsellor at Embassy to USA 1983–87, Minister 1993–95, Amb. Feb. 2001–; Vice-Minister, Ministry of Foreign Affairs 1998–2001. *Address:* Embassy of the People's Republic of China, 2300 Connecticut Avenue, NW, Washington, DC 20008, USA (Office). *Telephone:* (202) 328-2500 (Office). *Fax:* (202) 588-0032 (Office). *E-mail:* webmaster@china-embassy.org (Office). *Website:* www.china-embassy.org (Office).

YANG JIKE; Chinese scientist and administrator; b. 6 Nov. 1921, Shanghai; m. Wang Anqi; one s. two d.; Prof. Chinese Univ. of Science and Tech. 1966–; Vice-Gov. of Anhui Prov. 1979–88; Vice-Pres. Energy Research Asscn 1982–90, Pres. 1990–; Vice-Chair. China Zhi Gong Dang (Party for Public Interests) 1988–; Pres. Cen. Coll. of Socialism of China (now Cen. Socialist Acad.) 1991–; Vice-Chair. Environmental and Resources Protection Cttee, 8th NPC 1993–98; Vice-Chair. Population Resources and Environment Cttee, 9th NPC of CPPCC 1998–. *Address:* c/o Zhi Gong Dang, Taiping Qiao Street, Xi Cheng District, Beijing, People's Republic of China.

YANG JINGYU; Chinese politician; b. Sept. 1936, Xingyang, He'nan Prov.; ed Beijing Foreign Trade Inst.; joined CCP 1954, Deputy Head Econ. Research Group, Deputy Dir Econ. Law Office, Dir Research Office, Deputy Sec.-Gen. and Deputy Dir Comm. of Legislative Affairs; Sec. to Chair. Standing Cttee of 6th Nat. People's Congress; Dir Legal Affairs Bureau, State Council 1991–95, 1998–, Deputy Sec.-Gen. 1995–98; Del. to 14th and 15th CCP Nat. Congress. *Address:* c/o State Council, Zhongnanhai, Beijing, People's Republic of China.

YANG-KANG LIN (alias Chih-Hung), BA; Taiwanese politician; b. 10 June 1927, Nantou Co.; s. of Chih-Chang Lin and Chen Ruan; m. Chen Ho 1945; one s. three d.; ed Dept of Political Science, Nat. Taiwan Univ.; Chief Admin. Civil Affairs Section, Nantou Co. Govt 1952–61, Sec. 1962–64; Sec. Taiwan Prov. Govt 1964; Chair. Yunlin Co. HQ, Kuomintang 1964–67; Magistrate, Nantou Co. 1967–72; Commr, Dept of Reconstruction 1972–76; Mayor, Taipei Special Municipality 1976–78; Gov. of Taiwan Prov. 1978–81; Minister of Interior 1981–84; Vice-Premier of Exec. Yuan 1984–87; Premier of Judicial Yuan 1987–94; Vice-Chair. Kuomintang 1993–; Sr Adviser to Pres. 1994–; Order of Diplomatic Service Merit, Korea 1977. *Leisure interests:* hiking, reading and studying, music. *Address:* 5 Chao-Chou Street, Taipei, Taiwan. *Telephone:* (2) 3415668. *Fax:* (2) 3923311.

YANG LAN; Chinese broadcaster; b. 1969, Beijing; ed Beijing Foreign Studies Univ.; presenter, Chinese Cen. TV Station 1990–94; producer and presenter, Chinese Channel Phoenix Satellite TV, Hong Kong 1997–99; Co-founder and Chair. Sunshine-Culture Network TV 2000–.

YANG LE (Lo Yang); Chinese mathematician; b. Nov. 1939, Nantong, Jiangsu Prov.; m. Qieyuan Huang; two d.; ed Peking Univ. and Inst. of Mathematics, Chinese Acad. of Sciences; Pres. Acad. of Math. and System Sciences, Chinese Acad. of Sciences 1998–; mem. 4th Presidium of Depts., Chinese Acad. of Sciences 2000–; Research Fellow and Dir Inst. of Math., Chinese Acad. of Sciences; Academician Chinese Acad. of Sciences; Nat. Natural Science Prize, Loo-Keng Hua Math. Prize, Tan Kah Kee Prize, HLHL Prize. *Publication:* Value Distribution Theory 1993. *Address:* Institute of Mathematics, Chinese Academy of Sciences, Zhongguancun, Haidian District, Beijing, People's Republic of China. *Telephone:* (10) 62541848 (Office). *Fax:* (10) 62568356 (Home).

YANG RUDAI; Chinese party official; b. 1926, Renshou, Sichuan Province; joined CCP 1952; cadre in Sichuan 1977–79; Vice-Gov. of Sichuan 1978–82; mem. 12th Cen. Cttee CCP 1982–87; mem. 13th Cen. Cttee CCP 1987–92; mem. Politburo 1987–92; Political Commissar Sichuan Mil. Dist 1983–86; First Sec. Party Cttee 1985; Sec. CCP Sichuan 1983–93; mem. Presidium 14th CCP Nat. Congress 1992; Vice-Chair. 8th Nat. Cttee CPPCC 1993–98, 9th Nat. Cttee 1998–; Hon. Pres. Special Rural Tech. Asscn of China 1995. *Address:* National Committee of Chinese People's Political Consultative Conference, 23 Taipingqiao Street, Beijing, People's Republic of China.

YANG TAIFANG; Chinese politician and expert in telecommunications technology; b. 30 April 1927, Mei Co., Guangdong Prov.; s. of Yang Shukum and Wen Xinyun; m. Wu Youhong 1957; one s. two d.; ed Zhongshan Univ.; Vice-Minister of Posts and Telecommunications 1982–84, Minister 1984–92; mem. 12th Cen. Cttee CCP 1982–87, 13th Cen. Cttee 1987–92; Chair. Overseas Chinese Cttee 8th NPC 1993–98; mem. Presidium 14th CCP Nat. Congress 1992; NPC Deputy, Guangdong Prov.; mem. Standing Cttee 8th NPC 1993–98. Chair. All-China Fed. of Returned Overseas Chinese 1994–. *Leisure interests:* music, bridge, Taiji boxing. *Address:* Overseas Chinese Committee of the National People's Congress, 23 Xijiao Minxiang Road, West District, Beijing 100805, People's Republic of China.

YANG XIZONG; Chinese government official; b. 27 Sept. 1928, Dayi Co., Sichuan Prov.; s. of Yang Qunling and Yang Chunbing; m. Zhou Feng; one s. two d.; alt. mem. CPC Cen. Cttee 1983; Deputy to 6th NPC 1983, NPC Deputy, Sichuan Prov.; Deputy Sec. CPC 4th Cen. Cttee, Sichuan 1983–85; Gov. of Sichuan 1983–85; Chair. Sichuan Prov. 8th People's Congress, Standing Cttee 1993–98; Sec. CCP Prov. Cttee Henan 1985–89; mem. 12th CCP Cen.

Cttee 1985–87, 13th CCP Cen. Cttee 1987–92. *Leisure interest:* reading. *Address:* c/o Sichuan Provincial 8th People's Congress, Chengdu, Sichuan Province, People's Republic of China.

YANG ZHENGWU; Chinese politician; b. Jan. 1941, Longshan Co., Hunan; joined CCP 1969; Deputy Sec. CCP Hunan Prov. Cttee 1990–98, Sec. 1998, currently Chair. Standing Cttee of People's Congress; Chair. Comm. for Comprehensive Man. of Social Security 1993–; Gov. of Hunan Prov. 1995–98; mem. 13th CCP Cen. Cttee 1987–92, 14th CCP Cen. Cttee, 15th CCP Cen. Cttee 1997–2002. *Address:* c/o Office of the Governor, Changsha, Hunan Province, People's Republic of China.

YANG ZHENHUAI; Chinese government official; b. Jan. 1928, Anhui; s. of Yang Licuo and Wu Dingshu; m. Yang Duanyi 1960; one s. one d.; Vice-Minister for Water Resources and Electric Power 1983–88, Minister for Water Resources 1988–93; Sec.-Gen. State Flood Control H.Q. 1986–88, Deputy Head 1988; Deputy Head State Leading Group for Comprehensive Agric. Devt 1990–; Vice-Chair. Environmental and Resources Protection Cttee; alt. mem. 14th CCP Cen. Cttee 1992; Vice-Chair. Agric. and Rural Affairs Cttee, 9th NPC 1998–. *Leisure interests:* reading history, geology, humane studies. *Address:* c/o Standing Committee of National People's Congress, Beijing, People's Republic of China.

YANG ZHENYU; Chinese air force officer; b. 1931, Chifeng City, Rehe (Jehol) (now Liaoning Prov.); ed Air Force Aviation School, Red Flag Air Force Acad., USSR; joined PLA 1947, CCP 1948; Regt literacy teacher of N China Mil. Command 1948–49; joined Chinese People's Volunteers (CPV) in Korea 1951; served in PLA Air Force as Regt Commdr 1962–64, deputy Commdr of div. and chief of staff, PLA Air Force Shanghai Base 1980–81, chief of staff of corps 1983–85, deputy Commdr of command post of PLA Air Force 1985–86; Vice-Pres. Air Force Command Acad. 1986–90, Pres. 1990–; Deputy Commdr PLA Air Force 1994–96; Vice-Pres. China Soc. of Mil. Future Studies 1988–; rank of Maj.-Gen. 1988; a PLA del. to 8th NPC. *Address:* c/o Ministry of National Defence, Beijing, People's Republic of China.

YANG ZHIGUANG; Chinese artist; b. 11 Oct. 1930, Shanghai; s. of Yang Miaocheng and Shi Qinxian; m. Ou Yang 1958; two d.; ed Cen. Acad. of Fine Art; Vice-Pres. and Prof., Guangzhou Acad. of Fine Arts; mem. Council, Chinese Artists' Asscn; mem. Acad. of Traditional Chinese Painting; does traditional Chinese figure painting, calligraphy and seal-making; Artist-in-Residence, Griffis Art Center, Conn., USA Sept. 1990–; one-man show, Center for Int. Art and Culture, New York (Special Award for Outstanding Contribs. to Chinese painting); Gold Medal winner, 7th Vienna World Youth Festival, for picture Sending Food in Heavy Snow 1959. *Publications:* Skill of Chinese Traditional Figure Painting, Selections of Portraits, Chinese Water Colours, Yang Zhiguang's Sketches in China's North-west, Portraits of Modern Chinese Artists, Painting Selections of Mr. and Mrs. Yang Zhiguang. *Leisure interests:* calligraphy, seal-making, poetry. *Address:* Guangzhou Institute of Fine Art, No. 257, Chang Gang Dong Lu Street, Haizhu District, Guangzhou, People's Republic of China. *Telephone:* (20) 84017598 (Home). *Fax:* (20) 84017417 (Home).

YANG ZHUANGSHENG; Chinese business executive; b. Dec. 1942; ed Univ. of Int. Business and Econs.; Gen. Man., Chair. and CEO Science-Tech. Group 1991–. *Address:* Saite Dasha, 19 Jianguomenwai Da Jie, Beijing 100004, People's Republic of China (Office).

YANGLING DUOJI; Chinese politician and academic; b. 24 April 1931, Batang Co., Sichuan Prov.; s. of Yang Yong-an and Basang-wengmo; m. Qumu-a Ying 1954; two s. one d.; Vice-Gov. Sichuan Prov. 1979–81; Perm. Sec. CCP Cttee, Tibet Autonomous Region 1981–86; Vice-Chair. Tibetan People's Govt 1982–83; alt. mem. 12th CCP Cen. Cttee 1982–87; Chair. Tibet Br., CPPCC 1983–86; Vice-Chair. and Vice-Sec. of Party, Sichuan CPPCC 1986–; del. to 7th People's Congress of China 1988–92; del. to 11th Congress of CCP 1980–82, 12th 1982–86, 13th 1987–91; Chair. Tibetan Studies Asscn, Sichuan Prov.; Dean Acad. of Tibetan Studies, Sichuan Prov. 1990–; Ed. Tibetology Research, History of Kong Tibetan 1996–. *Leisure interest:* reading. *Address:* Office of the Vice-Chairman of the Chinese People's Consultative Council, No. 25 Hong Zhao Bi Street, Chengdu, Sichuan, People's Republic of China. *Telephone:* (28) 6753780 (Home). *Fax:* (28) 663393.

YANIN, Valentin Lavrentyevich, DHist; Russian archaeologist; b. 6 Feb. 1929; m.; ed Moscow State Univ.; jr then sr researcher Moscow Univ. 1954–, Prof. 1963, Head Chair. of Archaeology Moscow Univ.; researcher of history and archaeology of Middle Age Russia and of old manuscripts; Chair. of Bd Russian Humanitarian Scientific Fund (RGNF) 1996–; Corresp. mem. USSR (now Russian) Acad. of Sciences 1966, mem. 1990, mem. Presidium 1991–2002; Hon. Citizen of Novgorod; Lenin Prize, USSR State Prize. *Publications include:* Money and Weight Systems of Medieval Russia 1956, Novgorod Posadniki 1962, I Have Sent You a Birch Bark 1965, Act Stamps of Old Russia X–XV Centuries 1970, Novgorod Feudal Ancestral Lands 1982, Novgorod Acts XII–XV Centuries 1991. *Leisure interest:* collecting old vocal recordings. *Address:* RGNF, Yaroslavskaya str. 13, 129366 Moscow, Russia. *Telephone:* (095) 283-55-40 (Office); (095) 335-54-28 (Home).

YANKILEVSKY, Vladimir Borissovich; Russian artist; b. 15 Feb. 1938, Moscow; s. of Boris Yankilevsky and Rosa Yankilevskaya; m. Rimma Solod 1959; one d.; ed Moscow Secondary Art School and Moscow Polygraphic Inst.; took part in Manège exhbn of 1962; participated in first officially permitted Exhbn of avant-garde artists 1975; first retrospective in Moscow 1978; first

retrospectives in the West (New York and Bochum Museum, Germany) 1988; first participation in Sotheby's Auction in Moscow 1988; retrospectives in Paris 1991, Tretyakov Gallery, Moscow 1995–96, Neuhoff Gallery, New York 1996, Mané-Katz Museum, Haifa 2001. *Personal exhibitions:* in Moscow, Prague, New York, San Francisco, Cologne, Chicago, Paris, Bochum, Düsseldorf, Brussels, Leverkusen, Berlin, Uttersberg (Sweden), Haifa. *Group exhibitions:* in Moscow, Italy, Germany, Switzerland, USA, UK, Belgium, France, Japan, Hungary, Korea, Czechoslovakia, Sweden, Poland, Austria, Russia, Israel, Hong Kong. *Animation work includes:* The World of Tales 1973, I Fly to You 1977, I am with You Again 1977. *Television:* Good Evening, Moscow (Moscow, TV Gallery) 1996, Portraits of Artists-Nonconformists (Moscow, TV Gallery, Culture Channel) 2001. *Publications:* Retrospective 1958–1988 1988, Autoportraits 1992, Retrospective 1995–96, Retrospective 1996, Radierungen 1999; Variations on the Other – A Digital-Analog Monograph on the Work of Vladimir Yankilevsky (ed by David Riff) 2002. *Leisure interest:* photography. *Address:* 3 square de Port Royal, 75013 Paris, France. *Telephone:* 1-45-35-91-74. *Fax:* 1-45-35-91-74. *E-mail:* yankilevsky@noos.fr (Home). *Website:* www.yankilevsky.net (Home).

YANKOVSKY, Oleg Ivanovich; Russian actor; b. 23 Feb. 1944, Jezkazgan; m. Lyudmila Zorina; one s.; ed Saratov Drama School; actor Saratov Drama Theatre 1967–73, Moscow Theatre of Lenin Komsomol (now Lenkom) 1973–; leading roles in many theatre productions; debut in film I am Francisc Skorina 1968; Pres. Russian Nat. Festival Cinotaurus 1992; People's Artist of Russia 1984, State Prize of Russia 1989; winner of many int. and Russian prizes at maj. film festivals. *Films include:* Ordinary Wonder, Flights in Dreams and Reality, We, the Undersigned..., Two Hussars, That Munchhausen, Keep Me, My Talisman and others. *Address:* Komsomolsky prospekt 41, Apt. 10, 119270 Moscow, Russia. *Telephone:* (095) 242-32-85 (Home).

YANNARAS, Christos, DPhil, DTheol; Greek professor of philosophy; b. 10 April 1935, Athens; Univ. of Athens 1953–57; Univ. of Bonn 1964–67; Univ. of Paris (Sorbonne) 1968–72; Visiting Prof. Univ. of Geneva 1977–79, Univ. of Crete (Rethymnon) 1979–82; Prof. of Philosophy, Panteios Univ. of Political and Social Studies, Athens 1982–; mem. Acad. Int. des Sciences Humaines, Brussels. *Publications:* The Freedom of Morality 1981, Philosophie sans Rupture 1982, Person and Eros 1984, Critical Ontology 1985, Heidegger and Areopagita 1988, Europe against Hellenism 1990, Meta-modern Metaphysics 1993, The Inhuman Nature of Human Rights 1997, Culture: The Central Problem of Politics 1997, etc. *Address:* 84 Plastira Street, 171 21 Nea Smyrni, Athens, Greece (Home). *Telephone:* (1) 9201843 (Office). *Fax:* (1) 9353697.

YANOFSKY, Charles, PhD; American professor of biology; b. 17 April 1925, New York, NY; s. of Frank Yanofsky and Jennie Kopatz Yanofsky; m. 1st Carol Cohen 1949 (died 1990); three s.; m. 2nd Edna Crawford 1992; ed City Coll. of New York and Yale Univ.; Research Asst in Microbiology, Yale Univ. 1951–53; Asst Prof. of Microbiology, Western Reserve Univ. 1954–58; Assoc. Prof., Dept of Biological Sciences, Stanford Univ., Prof., Dept of Biological Sciences 1961–, Prof. Emer.; Herzstein Prof. of Biology 1967; Pres. Genetics Soc. of America 1969, American Soc. of Biological Chemists 1984; Career Investigator American Heart Asscn 1969–95; mem. NAS, American Acad. of Arts and Sciences; Foreign mem. Royal Soc. 1985–; Hon. mem. Japanese Biochemical Soc. 1985–; Hon. DSc (Univ. of Chicago) 1980, (Yale Univ.) 1981; Eli Lilly Award in Bacteriology 1959, U.S. Steel Award in Molecular Biology 1964, Howard Taylor Ricketts Award 1966, Albert Lasker Award for Basic Medical Research 1971, Selman A. Waksman Award 1972, Louisa Gross Horwitz Prize 1976, Townsend Harris Medal, City Coll. of New York, Mattia Award, Roche Inst. 1982, Genetics Soc. of America Medal 1983, Gairdner Foundation Award 1985, Thomas Hunt Morgan Medal, Genetics Soc. of America 1990, Passano Award 1992, William C. Rose Award of the ASBMB 1997, Abbott-ASM Lifetime Achievement Award 1998. *Publications:* scientific articles in proceedings of Nat. Acad. of Sciences, etc. *Leisure interests:* tennis, growing orchids. *Address:* Department of Biological Sciences, Stanford University, Stanford, CA 94305 (Office); 725 Mayfield Avenue, Stanford, CA 94305, USA. *Telephone:* (650) 725-1835 (Office); (650) 857-9057. *Fax:* (650) 725-8221 (Office).

YAO WENYUAN; Chinese politician and journalist; b. 1924; journalist and youth activist before Cultural Revolution; leading pro-Maoist journalist during Cultural Revolution 1965–68; Ed. Wen Hui Bao 1966, Liberation Daily 1966; mem. Cen. Cultural Revolution Group, CCP 1966; Vice-Chair. Shanghai Revolutionary Cttee 1967–76; Ed. People's Daily 1967–76; mem. Politburo, CCP Cen. Cttee 1969–76; Second Sec. CCP Shanghai 1971; arrested as mem. of Gang of Four Oct. 1976; expelled from CCP July 1977; in detention; on trial Nov. 1980–Jan. 1981; sentenced to 20 years' imprisonment; freed Oct. 1996.

YAO ZHEN, PhD; Chinese scientist; b. 1955; ed Univ. of Edinburgh, UK; Deputy Dir of Shanghai Inst. of Cell Biology, Chinese Acad. of Sciences 1965–; Pres. Chinese Soc. for Cell Biology 1983–86, 1996–99; mem. Div. of Biology, Chinese Acad. of Sciences 1980. *Address:* Shanghai Institute of Cell Biology, Chinese Academy of Sciences, 320 Yueyang Road, Shanghai 200031, People's Republic of China.

YAO ZHENYAN; Chinese banker; Vice-Minister of Water Conservancy and Electric Power 1985–88; Gen. Man. State Energy Investment Corpn 1988–94; Pres. State Devt Bank 1994–98; Vice-Minister State Planning Comm.;

currently Vice-Chair. Financial and Econ. Cttee, Nat. People's Congress. *Address:* c/o State Development Bank, 40 Fucheng Lu, Haidian Qu, Beijing, People's Republic of China.

YAO ZHONGHUA; Chinese artist; b. 17 July 1939, Kunming, Yunnan; s. of the late Yao Penxien and the late Wang Huiyuan; m. Ma Huixian 1969; two s.; ed Cen. Acad. of Fine Arts; one-man show, Beijing 1980, Cité Int. Arts, Paris 1985 and exhbns. in Paris and E Europe; numerous group exhbns. in China, also China Oil Paintings of Present Age Exhbn, New York, USA 1987, Melbourne, Sydney, Australia 1987, Wan Yu Tang Art Gallery, Hong Kong 1989; group Exhbn Beijing Art Gallery 1992; one-man Exhbn Taiwan 1992, Calif., USA 1995; mural for Parl. Hall, Yunnan People's Congress; mem. Council China Artists' Assen; Vice-Pres. Yunnan Painting Inst. *Works include:* Oh, the Land!, Sani Minority's Festival, The Yellow River, Zhenghe's Voyage, The Jinsha River Flowing beside the Jade Dragon Mountain, Chinese Ink and Water. *Publication:* paper on painter Dong Xi Wen, in Chinese Oil Painting and Art Research 1990, Selected Works of Yao Zhonghua 1993. *Leisure interests:* music, literature.

YAQUB, Muhammad, PhD; Pakistani banker and economist; b. 1937, Jalandar, India; s. of Haji Muhammad Shah and Bibi Karim; m. Nasreen Yaqub; two s. one d.; ed Punjab Univ., Yale Univ., Princeton Univ., USA; Asst Dir, Research Dept State Bank of Pakistan 1966–68, Deputy Dir 1968–69, Sr Deputy Dir 1969–72, Sr Prin. Officer, Dir Research Dept 1975, Gov. 1993–99; Sr Economist and Resident Rep., IMF, Saudi Arabia 1975, Fund Resident Adviser to Saudi Arabian Govt, IMF 1977, Divisional Chief, Middle Eastern Dept IMF 1977–80, Asst Div. 1981–82, IMF Rep. to Paris Club, London Club, OECD and co. aid consortia; Consultant IMF, Washington; Prin. Econ. Adviser, Special Section, Ministry of Finance 1992–93; has headed IMF missions to numerous Middle Eastern countries. *Publications:* Major-Macro Economic Policy Issues in Pakistan. *Address:* IMF, 700 19th Street, NW, Washington, DC 20431, USA (Office). *Website:* www.imf.org (Office).

YAR'ADUA, Maj.-Gen. Shehu; Nigerian army officer; b. 5 March 1943, Katsina, Kaduna State; m.; three d.; ed Govt Secondary School, Katsina, Nigerian Mil. Training Coll., Zaria, Royal Mil. Coll., Sandhurst, UK, Command and Staff Coll., UK; Platoon Commdr 1964–65, Battalion Adjutant 1965–67, Co. Commdr 1967, Asst Adjutant Gen., 2nd Div. 1967; commanded 6th Infantry Brigade in Second Infantry Div. with service in Onitsha Sector 1968; commanded 9th Infantry Brigade (based at Warri during civil war) 1969–72; Commr for Transport 1975–76; Chief of Staff, Supreme HQ (Chief of Army Staff) 1976–79; Vice-Pres. Supreme Mil. Council 1976–79; arrested March 1995; farmer; mem. Social Democratic Party; Chair. Nation House Press, Hamada Carpets, Kaduna; fmr Chair. Habib Nigeria Bank Ltd. *Address:* Office of the Chairman, Habib Nigeria Bank Ltd, 1 Keffi Street, P.O. Box 54648, Falomo, Ikoyi, Lagos, Nigeria. *Telephone:* (1) 2663121.

YARMOSHYN, Uladzimir Vasilyevich; Belarus politician and engineer; b. 26 Oct. 1942, Pronsk, Ryazan Region, Russia; m.; two c.; ed Novocherkassk Polytech. Inst., Leningrad Civil Aviation Acad.; turner Electric Locomotive plant, Novocherkassk; Sr engineer, chief mechanical engineer, Deputy Dir Minsk Civil Aviation plant 1965–90; Chair. Exec. Cttee Dist Soviet of People's Deputies, Minsk 1990; Deputy Chair. Minsk City Exec. Cttee, also Head Cttee on Housing and Power Eng 1990–92; First Deputy Chair. then Chair. Minsk City Exec. Cttee 1995–2000; mem. Council in Nat. Ass.; Chair. Council of Ministers 2000–01; Head Belorussian Reps, Mobil Telesystems 2002–. *Address:* Mobil Telesystems, Minsk, Belarus (Office).

YAROV, Yuri Fedorovich; Russian politician; b. 2 April 1942, Mariinsk, Kemerovo Region; m.; one s. one d.; ed Leningrad Tech. Inst., Leningrad Eng Econ. Inst.; worked in factories in Latvia 1964–68, Leningrad Region 1968–76; Dir factory Burevestnik 1978–85; First Sec. Gatchina City CPSU Cttee 1985–87; Deputy Chair. Exec. Cttee Leningrad Regional Soviet of Deputies 1987–89, Chair. 1989–90; Chair. Leningrad Regional Soviet of People's Deputies 1990–91; People's Deputy of Russian Fed. 1990–92; Deputy Chair. Supreme Soviet of Russia 1991–92; Deputy Prime Minister 1992–96; Deputy Head of Pres. Yeltsin's Admin. 1996–, First Deputy 1997–98; Plenipotentiary Rep. of Pres. of the Russian Fed. in Council of Fed. 1998–99; Chair. Exec. Cttee of CIS April 1999–. *Address:* Executive Committee of Commonwealth of Independent States, Varvarka str. 7, 103012 Moscow, Russia. *Telephone:* (095) 206-62-69.

YARROW, Sir Eric Grant, 3rd Bt (cr. 1916), MBE, DL, FRSE; British business executive (retd); b. 23 April 1920, Glasgow; s. of the late Sir Harold Yarrow, 2nd Bt and Eleanor Etheldreda Yarrow; m. 1st Rosemary Ann Young 1951 (died 1957); one s. (deceased); m. 2nd Annette Elizabeth Françoise Steven 1959 (divorced 1975); three s.; m. 3rd Joan Botting 1982; ed Marlborough Coll., Glasgow Univ.; served apprenticeship with G. and J. Weir Ltd; army service in Burma 1939–45, Major Royal Engineers 1945; trained with English Electric Co. 1945–46; Asst Man., Yarrow and Co. Ltd 1946, Dir 1948, Man. Dir 1958–67, Chair. 1962–85, Pres. 1985–86; Chair. Yarrow (Shipbuilders) Ltd 1962–79; Dir Clydesdale Bank 1962–91, Deputy Chair. 1975–85, Chair. 1985–91; Dir Standard Life Assurance 1958–90, Nat. Australia Bank Ltd 1987–91; mem. Council, Royal Inst. Naval Architects 1957–, Vice-Pres. 1965, Hon. Vice-Pres. 1972; mem. Gen. Cttee Lloyd's Register of Shipping 1960–87; Prime Warden, Worshipful Co. of Shipwrights 1970–71; Deacon, Incorpn. of Hammermen of Glasgow 1961–62; fmr mem. Council of Inst. Engineers and Shipbuilders in Scotland; Chair. Exec. Cttee Princess Louise Scottish Hosp., Erskine 1980–86, Hon. Pres. 1986–93; Pres. Scottish Convalescent Home for

Children 1958–70, Burma Star Asscn in Scotland 1989–; Officer, Most Venerable Order of the Hosp. of St John of Jerusalem. *Leisure interests:* golf, family life. *Address:* Cloak, Kilmacolm, Renfrewshire, PA13 4SD, Scotland. *Telephone:* (1505) 872067.

YASHIRO, Eita; Japanese politician; mem. House of Councillors; fmr mem. House of Reps.; Chair. House of Reps. Cttee on Judicial Affairs; fmr Parl. Vice-Minister for Science and Tech.; Minister of Posts and Telecommunications 1999–2000. *Address:* c/o Ministry of Posts and Telecommunications, 1-3-2, Kasumigaseki, Chiyoda-ku, Tokyo 100-0013, Japan (Office).

YASIN, Yevgeny Grigoryevich, D.ECON.SC.; Russian politician and economist; b. 7 May 1934, Odessa; s. of Grigory Yasin and Yevgenia Yasina; m. Lydia Yasina (née Fedoulova); one d.; ed Odessa Inst. of Construction Eng, Moscow State Univ.; worked USSR Cen. Dept of Statistics 1963–73, researcher Cen. Inst. of Econs and Math., USSR (now Russian) Acad. of Sciences 1973–89; Head of Div. State Comm. on Econ. Reform, USSR Council of Ministers (Abalkin Comm.) 1990–91; one of authors of econ. programme 500 Days; Dir-Gen. Direction on Econ. Policy of Russian Union of Industrialists and Entrepreneurs 1991; f. and Dir Expert Inst. of Russian Union of Industrialists and Entrepreneurs 1992–93; mem. Council of Enterprise of Pres. of Russia 1992; Plenipotentiary Rep. of Govt in Parl. 1992–93; Head Analytical Centre of Pres. 1994–; Minister of Econs of Russia 1994–97, Minister Without Portfolio 1997–98; Prof. Higher School of Econs 1992–, Scientific Head 1998–; Head of Govt legislation drafting teams 1992–97. *Address:* Higher School of Economics, Malaya Yakimanka str. 2/1, Moscow, Russia. *Telephone:* (095) 921-79-83; (095) 928-92-90.

YASSIN, Ahmed; Palestinian religious leader; b. 1938, Palestine under British Mandate; ed Al-Azhar Univ., Cairo, Egypt; fled Israel to Gaza Strip 1948; fmrly teacher; fmrly involved in Muslim Brotherhood, jailed for 45 days because of involvement with Muslim Brotherhood; f. Islamic Centre 1973; arrested and sentenced to 13 years' imprisonment for sedition 1984, released 1985; f. Hamas (Islamic resistance movt) 1987; arrested and sentenced to life imprisonment for ordering killing of Palestinians who had allegedly collaborated with Israeli Army 1989, released in trade-off with Jordan for two Israeli agents 1997; placed under house arrest Dec. 2001.

YASSIN, Salim, PhD; Syrian politician and professor of economics; b. 10 Oct. 1937, Lattakia; m. Najwa Ismail 1962; five c.; Dean of Faculty, Aleppo Univ. 1966–68, Vice-Pres. of Univ. 1969–71; Pres. Lattakia Univ. 1971–78; Govt minister 1978–85, Deputy Prime Minister in charge of Econ. Affairs 1985–2000; sentence to ten years' imprisonment for corruption 2001. *Publications:* Theory of Correlation, International Trade, Aggregate Economic Analyses. *Leisure interests:* reading, football, swimming.

YASSUKOVICH, Stanislas Michael, CBE; British/American banker; b. 5 Feb. 1935, Paris, France; s. of Dimitri Yassukovich and Denise Yassukovich; m. Diana Townsend 1961; two s. one d.; ed Deerfield Acad., Mass. and Harvard Univ., USA; U.S. Marine Corps. 1957–61; joined White, Weld and Co. 1961, London Office 1962, Branch Man. 1967–69, Gen. Partner, New York 1969–73, Man. Dir, London 1969–73; Man. Dir European Banking Co. SA Brussels 1983–85, Chief Exec. European Banking Group 1983–85; Chair. Merrill Lynch Europe Ltd 1985–89, Hemingway Properties 1993–; Vice-Chair. Jt Deputy Chair. London Stock Exchange 1986–89, Bristol and West Bldg Soc. (now Bristol & West PLC) 1991–2000, ABC Int. Bank 1993–; Chair. Securities Asscn 1988–91; Chair. Cragnotti & Partners Capital Investment (UK) 1991–96, Park Place Capital 1994–, Henderson EuroTrust PLC 1995–, Easdaq SA 1997–99, Manek Investment Man. Ltd 1997–; Deputy Chair. Flextech PLC 1989–97, South West Water (now Pennon Group PLC) 1993–2000; Dir Royal Nat. Theatre 1991–96, Chair. City Disputes Panel 1993–99; Dir (non-exec.) Henderson Group PLC 1990–98, Telewest PLC 1998–, Atlas Capital Ltd 1999–. *Leisure interests:* hunting, shooting and polo. *Address:* S.M. Yassukovich & Co. Ltd., 42 Berkeley Square, London, W1J 5AW, England (Office). *Telephone:* (20) 7318-0825 (Office). *E-mail:* smycoltd@aol.com (Office).

YASTRZHEMBSKY, Sergey Vladimirovich, CAND.HIST.SC.; Russian politician, journalist and diplomatist; b. 4 Dec. 1953, Moscow; m. Tatyana Victorovna; two c.; ed Moscow State Inst. of Int. Relations, Inst. of Int. Workers' Movt; jr researcher Acad. of Social Sciences Cen. Cttee CPSU 1979–81; on staff journal Problems of the World and Socialism (Prague) 1981–89; Sr staff-mem. Int. Div. Cen. Cttee CPSU 1989–90; Deputy Ed.-in-Chief Megapolis (journal) 1990–91, Ed.-in-Chief VIP journal 1991–92; Dir Dept of Information and Press, Russian Ministry of Foreign Affairs 1992–93; Amb. to Slovakia 1993–96; Press Sec. to Pres. Boris Yeltsin (q.v.) 1996; Deputy Head Pres. Yeltsin's Admin. 1997–98; Vice-Chair. Moscow Govt 1998–99; Asst to Pres. Vladimir Putin (q.v.) Jan. 2000–; Rank II Order of the White Cross (Slovakia); Russian Orthodox Church Order of St Daniil; 850th Anniversary of Moscow Commemorative Medal. *Publications:* Social Democracy in the Contemporary World 1991; essays and articles on current events, contemporary devt of Portugal and European social democracy. *Leisure interests:* tennis, stamp collecting, reading, hunting, downhill skiing. *Address:* Administration of the President, Staraya pl. 4, 103132 Moscow, Russia. *Telephone:* (095) 206-08-31 (Office). *Fax:* (095) 206-91-93 (Office).

YASUI, Kaoru, LLD; Japanese jurist and poet; b. 25 April 1907, Osaka; s. of Harumoto Yasui and Harue Yasui; m. Tazuko Kuki 1936; one s. one d.; ed Tokyo Univ.; Asst Prof. Tokyo Univ. 1932–42, Prof. 1942–48; Prof. Hosei Univ.

1952, Dean Faculty of Jurisprudence 1957–63, Dir 1963–66, Prof. Emer. 1978–; Leader (Chair. etc.) Japan Council Against Atomic and Hydrogen Bombs 1954–65; Pres. Japanese Inst. for World Peace 1965–; Dir Maruki Gallery for Hiroshima Panels 1968–; Chair. Japan-Korea (Democratic People's Repub.) Solidarity Cttee of Social Scientists 1972–; Dir-Gen. Int. Inst. of the Juche Idea 1978–; mem. Lenin Peace Prize Cttee; Hon. mem. Japanese Asscn of Int. Law 1976–; Hon. DJur (San Gabriel Coll., USA); Lenin Peace Prize 1958; Gold Medal (Czechoslovakia) 1965. *Publications:* Outline of International Law 1939, Banning Weapons of Mass Destruction 1955, People and Peace 1955, Collection of Treaties 1960, My Way 1967, The Dialectical Method and the Science of International Law 1970, A Piece of Eternity (Poems) 1977. *Address:* Minami-Ogikubo 3-13-11, Suginami-ku, Tokyo, Japan.

YATES, Peter; British film and theatre producer and director; b. 24 July 1929; s. of Col Robert Yates and Constance Yates; m. Virginia Pope 1960; two s. two d. (one deceased); ed Charterhouse, RADA; entered film industry as studio man. and dubbing Asst with De Lane Lea; Asst Dir The Entertainer, The Guns of Navarone, A Taste of Honey, etc; Golden Globe Best Film Award 1979, Evening Standard Film Award Special Achievement 2001. *Films directed include:* Summer Holiday 1962, Danger Man, Saint (TV series) 1963–65, Robbery 1966, Bullitt 1968, John and Mary 1969, Murphy's War, Mother, Jugs and Speed 1975, The Deep 1976, Breaking Away (also produced) (Golden Globe Best Film) 1979, The Janitor (Eyewitness in USA; also produced) 1980, Krull 1982, The Dresser (also produced) 1983, Eleni 1984, The House on Carroll Street (also produced) 1986, Suspect 1987, An Innocent Man 1989, The Year of the Comet 1992 (also produced), Roommates 1995, The Run of the Country 1996 (also produced), It all Came True 1997, Don Quixote 1999, A Separate Peace 2002. *Plays directed:* The American Dream 1961, The Death of Bessie Smith 1961, Passing Game 1977, Interpreters 1985. *Leisure interests:* tennis, sailing, skiing. *Address:* Judy Daish Associates, 2 St. Charles Place, London, W10 6RG, England.

YATIM, Dato' Rais bin, MA, LLB, PhD; Malaysian politician; b. 15 April 1942, Jelebu, Negeri Sembilan; m. Datin Masnah Mohamat; three s. one d.; ed Univs. of Northern Illinois, Singapore and London; lecturer at ITM, School of Law and also managed own law firm in Kuala Lumpur 1973; mem. Bar Council 1973; mem. Parl. 1974; Parl. Sec. Ministry of Youth, Sport and Culture 1974; Deputy Minister of Law 1976, of Home Affairs 1978; elected to State Ass., Negeri Sembilan 1978; Menteri Besar, Negeri Sembilan 1978; Minister of Land and Regional Devt 1982, of Information 1984–86, of Foreign Affairs 1986–87; Advocate and Solicitor, High Court of Malaysia 1988–; returned to law practice, Kuala Lumpur 1988–; mem. United Malays' Nat. Org. (UMNO) Supreme Council of Malaysia 1982–; Deputy Pres. Semangat 1989–; Minister in Prime Minister's Dept 1999–; mem. Civil Liberty Cttee Bar Council, Kuala Lumpur 1996–98. *Publications:* Faces in the Corridors of Power 1987, Freedom under Executive Power in Malaysia 1995, Zaman Beredar Pesaka Bergilir 1999. *Leisure interests:* photography, writing, travel. *Address:* Putrajaya Prime Minister's Department, 62502 Putrajaya (Office); 41 Road 12, Taman Grandview, Ampang Jaya, 68000 Ampang, Selangor, Malaysia (Home). *Telephone:* (3) 88881434 (Office); (3) 4569621 (Home). *Fax:* (3) 88883539 (Office). *E-mail:* drrais@pc.jaring.my (Home).

YATSKEVICH, Boris Alexandrovich, CAND.GEOL.; Russian geologist; b. 7 Jan. 1948, Lignice, Poland; ed Voronezh State Univ.; Sr technician, Sr geologist, chief geologist Ukhta geological expedition, Komi Autonomous Repub. 1972–86; chief geologist Polar–Urals production geological co. Vorkuta 1986–90; Head of Div. State Cttee on Geology RSFSR 1990–92; Deputy Chair. State Cttee on Geology and use of Mineral Wealth 1992–96; First Deputy Minister of Natural Resources Russian Fed. 1996–99, Minister 1999–2001; mem. Observation Council ALROSA (Diamonds of Russia and Sakha). *Address:* c/o Ministry of Natural Resources of Russian Federation, Bolshaya Gruzinskaya str. 4/6, 123812 Moscow, Russia (Office).

YAU, Carrie, B.SOC.SC.; Hong Kong civil servant; b. Tsang Ka Lai, 4 June 1955; d. of Tsang Hin Yeung and Tsang Choon Kwa; m. Francis Yau; one s.; ed Maryknoll Sisters' School, Diocesan Girls' School, Univ. of Hong Kong; joined Hong Kong Govt as an Admin. Officer 1977, various posts in maj. policy areas, Govt Spokeswoman, Chief Sec.'s Office 1994–95, Dir of Admin. 1997–2000, Sec. for Information Tech. and Broadcasting 2000–; Chair. Bd of Review (Film Censorship), Steering Cttee on Cyberport; Vice-Chair. Broadcasting Authority; mem. Business Advisory Cttee, Services Promotion Strategy Group, Steering Cttee for Third Generation Mobile Service. *Leisure interests:* singing, hiking, family activities. *Address:* Bureau of Information Technology and Broadcasting, 2/F Murray Building, Garden Road, Central, Hong Kong Special Administrative Region, People's Republic of China (Office). *Telephone:* 2189-2283 (Office). *Fax:* 2588-1421 (Office). *E-mail:* tklyau@itbb.gov.hk (Office). *Website:* www.info.gov.hk/itbb/ (Office).

YAVLINSKII, Grigorii Alekseevich, PhD, C.ECON.SC.; Russian politician and economist; b. 10 April 1952, Lvov (now in Ukraine); m.; two s.; ed Plekhanov Inst. of Nat. Econ.; electrician Lvov Co., Raduga 1968–69; Sr researcher, Research Inst. of Man., Ministry of Coal Industry, Moscow 1976–80; Head of Div. Research Inst. of Labour 1980–84; Deputy Chief, Chief of Div., Chief of Dept of Man. USSR State Labour Cttee 1984–89; Chief of Div. State Cttee on Econ. Reform USSR Council of Ministers 1988–90; mem. Pres.'s Political Advisory Council 1990–; Deputy Chair. Council of Ministers of Russian Fed., Chair. State Cttee on Econ. Reform 1990, author of econ.

programme 500 days July–Nov. 1990; Econ. Counsellor of Prime Minister of Russia 1991; Chair. of Council of Scientific Soc. EPI-CENTRE (Cen. for Political and Econ. Studies) 1991–; mem. Econ. Council of Pres. of Kazakhstan 1991–; Deputy Chair. USSR Cttee on Operational Man. of Nat. Econ. Aug.–Dec. 1991; mem. Political Advisory Council of Pres. Gorbachev Oct.–Dec. 1991; co-leader (with Y. Boldyrev and V. Lukin) of pre-election bloc (later political movt then political party) Yabloko 1993, Leader 1995–; mem. State Duma (Parl.) 1993–. *Publications:* Russia – The Search for Landmarks 1993, Incentives and Institutions: The Transition to a Market Economy in Russia 2000; several books on economy of USSR, numerous articles. *Address:* State Duma, Okhotny Ryad 1, 103265 Moscow, Russia. *Telephone:* (095) 292-8944. *Fax:* (095) 292-89-42; (095) 292-93-79.

YAZDI, Ibrahim, PhD; Iranian politician; b. c. 1933; m.; two s. four d.; studied and worked as physician in USA for sixteen years; close assoc. of Ayatollah Khomeini during exile in Neauphlé-le-Château, France Oct. 1978–Feb. 1979; mem. Revolutionary Council during Feb. 1979 revolution; Deputy Prime Minister with responsibility for Revolutionary Affairs Feb.–April 1979; Minister of Foreign Affairs April–Nov. 1979; Special Emissary of Ayatollah Khomeini on Provincial Problems 1979; Supervisor Keyhan Org. 1980–81; Deputy in Parl. for Tehran 1980–84; mem. Foreign Affairs, Health and Welfare Parl. Comms.; WHO Adviser 1991; Sec.-Gen. Liberation Movt of Iran 1995–; arrested Dec. 1997. *Publications:* Final Efforts in Terminal Days: Some Untold Stories of the Islamic Revolution of Iran 1984, Principles of Molecular Genetics 1985, Mutational Changes in Genetic Materials and Repair Systems 1989, The Ills of the Human Heart 1994; papers on herbal and traditional medicine, carcinogenics, the nucleic acid of cancer cells and Islamic and social topics. *Address:* 21 Touraj Lane, Valiasr Avenue, Tehran, 19666 Iran. *Telephone:* (21) 2042558. *Fax:* (21) 2042558.

YAZGHI, Muhammad el-, LenD; Moroccan politician, lawyer and newspaper executive; b. 28 Sept. 1935, Fez; m. Balafrej Souada 1972; two s.; ed Moulay Youssef Coll., Lycée Gouraud, Univ. of Rabat and Ecole Nat. d'Admin., Paris; Dir of Budget, Ministry of Finance 1957–60; Dir Al-Moharir (daily paper) 1975–81, Liberation (daily paper) 1989–; First Sec. Moroccan Press Union 1977–93; Deputy to Parl. 1977–; mem. Political Bureau, Union Socialiste des Forces Populaires (USFP) 1975–91, Joint Vice-Sec. 1992–; currently Minister of Territorial Admin., the Environment, Urban Planning and Housing. *Publications:* articles in magazines and journals. *Leisure interests:* reading, travel. *Address:* Ministry of Territorial Administration, the Environment, Urban Planning and Housing, 36 avenue El Abtal Agdal, Rabat (Office); 5 rue Ibn Tofai, Les Orangers, Rabat, Morocco (Home). *Telephone:* (3) 7763539 (Office). *Fax:* (3) 7763510 (Office). *E-mail:* info@minenv.gov.ma (Office). *Website:* www.minenv.gov.ma (Office).

YAZOV, Marshal Dmitri Timofeevich; Russian military official (retd); b. 1923; ed Frunze Mil. Acad. and Mil. Acad. of Gen. Staff; entered Soviet army 1941–; active service 1941–45; command posts 1945–76; Deputy Commdr of Far Eastern Mil. Dist 1976–79; Commdr of Cen. Group Forces in Czechoslovakia 1979–80; Deputy to USSR Supreme Soviet 1979–89; Commdr of Cen. Asian Mil. Dist 1980; Deputy Minister of Defence Feb.–June 1987, Minister of Defence and Head of Armed Forces 1987–91; mem. of Cen. Cttee of Kazakh CP 1981–87; mem. Presidential Council 1990–91; Cand. mem. of Cen. Cttee of CPSU 1981–91; fmr mem. Politburo; rank of Marshal 1990; arrested 1991, for participation in attempted coup d'état, charged with conspiracy 1992; on trial 1993; released 1994; Chief Mil. Adviser, Ministry of Defence 1998–; Chair. Marshal G. Zhukov Memorial Cttee. *Leisure interests:* theatre, poetry. *Address:* Ministry of Defence, Znamenka str. 19, 103160 Moscow, Russia. *Telephone:* (095) 296-39-66.

YBARRA Y CHURRUCA, Emilio de; Spanish banker; b. 1936, San Sebastián; m.; four c.; ed Jesuit Deusto Univ., Bilbao; joined Banco de Bilbao 1964, mem. Bd of Dirs. 1971, Chief Exec. 1976, Vice-Pres. and Chief Exec. 1986; Sole Vice-Pres. Banco Bilbao-Vizcaya (BBV) (following merger of Banco de Bilbao with Banco de Vizcaya) 1988, Pres. 1990–99, Co-Pres. (following merger with Argentaria SA) Banco Bilbao Vizcaya Argentaria SA (BBVA) 1999–2002. *Address:* c/o Banco Bilbao-Vizcaya Argentaria SA, Paseo de la Castellana 81, 28046 Madrid, Spain.

YE GONGQI; Chinese administrator; b. 1930; joined CCP 1948; Deputy Dir of Shanghai Light Industry Bureau 1976–; Vice-Mayor Shanghai 1985; Chair. Shanghai Municipal 10th People's Congress 1986–. *Address:* Shanghai People's Government, Shanghai, People's Republic of China.

YE LIANSONG; Chinese politician and engineer; b. 1935, Shanghai; ed Jiaotong Univ., Shanghai; engineer, Shijiazhuang Municipal Diesel Plant 1960–80; Vice-Mayor Shijiazhuang 1982–85; mem. Standing Cttee Hebei Prov. CCP Cttee 1983–2000, Deputy Sec. 1998–2000; Vice-Gov. Hebei Prov. 1985–93, Gov. 1993–98; alt. mem. 13th Cen. Cttee CCP 1987–92, mem. 14th Cen. Cttee 1992–97, 15th CCP Cen. Cttee 1997–2002; Deputy to 8th NPC. *Address:* c/o Office of the Governor, Hebei Provincial Government, 1 Weiming Jie Street, Shijiazhuang City, People's Republic of China.

YE RUTANG; Chinese politician; b. 20 March 1940, Zhejiang; s. of Ye Mei and Chen Jiaoru; m. Liu Wenbin 1968; one s. two d.; Minister of Urban and Rural Construction and Environmental Protection 1985–88; Vice-Chair. Environmental Protection Cttee of State Council 1985–88; Vice-Minister of Construction 1988–; Vice-Chair. Chinese Soc. of Science and Tech. for Social Devt 1991–2001; Vice-Chair. Environment and Resources Protection Cttee

2001–; apptd. Pres. Architectural Soc. of China 1992. *Leisure interests:* calligraphy, swimming. *Address:* c/o Ministry of Construction, 9 Sanlihe Road, Beijing 100835, People's Republic of China.

YE SHAOLAN (Ye Qiang); Chinese opera singer, actor and playwright; b. Sept. 1943, Beijing; s. of Ye Shenglan; ed China Acad. of Traditional Operas, Cen. Acad. of Drama; actor, Dir, playwright, Art Dir Zhanyou Peking Opera Troupe, PLA Beijing Mil. Command; mem. Exec. Council of Chinese Dramatists Asscn; won 1st Nat. Theatre Plum Blossom Award 1984; Fulbright Int. Scholar. *Peking operas include:* Lu Bu and Diao Chan, Luo Cheng, Story of the Willow Tree. *Address:* c/o Zhanyou Peking Opera Troupe, People's Liberation Army, Beijing Command, Beijing, People's Republic of China (Office).

YE WEILIN; Chinese writer; b. 1935, Huiyang Co., Guangdong Prov.; s. of Ye Wei; m. Chen Jieni; two c.; joined PLA 1950; Chair. Hainan Writer's Asscn 1990–. *Publications:* The Blue Mulan Rivulet, On the River without Navigation Marks, The First Farewell. *Address:* Hunan Branch of the Writers' Association, Changsha City, Hunan Province, People's Republic of China.

YE WENLING; Chinese writer; b. 1942, Yuhuan, Zhejiang Prov.; ed Literature Inst., Chinese Writers Asscn; worked as kindergarten nurse, school teacher, farm worker, factory worker, Govt office worker, factory clerk before becoming professional writer; fmrly Vice-Chair. He'nan Prov. Fed. of Literary and Art Circles; Chair. Zhejiang Prov. Writers Asscn, Vice-Chair. Fed. of Literary and Art Circles, Zhejiang Prov. *Publications:* Father-Mother Official, The Proud Son of the Sun, Dreamless Valley, Qiu Jin, The Twisting Golden Bamboo Pond, The Brook with Nine Twists, Silent Valley, Selected Short Stories by Ye Wenling, Selected Prose of Ye Wenling, Collected Works of Ye Wenling (8 Vols). *Address:* Zhejiang Writers Association, Hangzhou, Zhejiang Province, People's Republic of China (Office).

YE XIAOGANG; Chinese musical composer; b. 23 Sept. 1955, Shanghai; s. of Ye Chunzi and Ho Ying; m. Xu Jing 1987; ed Eastman School of Music, USA (post-graduate); lecturer Cen. Conservatory of Music, Beijing. *Compositions:* Xi Jiang Yue Symphony 1984, Horizon Symphony 1985, Piano Ballade 1987, Dance Drama: The Love Story of Da Lai VI 1988. *Address:* Central Conservatory of Music, 43 Baojiajie, Beijing, People's Republic of China (Office).

YE XUANPING; Chinese state official; b. Nov. 1924, Meixian Co., Guangdong Prov.; s. of the late Marshal Ye Jianying and Zeng Xianzhi; ed Yan'an Coll. of Natural Sciences, Harbin Polytechnic Univ., Qinghua Univ., studies in USSR 1950–53; joined CCP 1945; Deputy Dir and Chief Engineer Beijing No. 1 Machine-tool Factory 1962–73; Vice-Gov. Guangdong Prov. 1980–85; Chair. Guangdong Prov. Scientific and Tech. Cttee 1980–85; alt. mem. 12th CCP Cen. Cttee 1982, mem. 1985; mem. 13th CCP Cen. Cttee 1987–92, 14th Cen. Cttee 1992–97; Deputy Sec. CCP Cttee, Guangzhou Municipality 1983–85; Acting Mayor Guangzhou 1983, Mayor 1983–85; Deputy for Guangdong Prov. to 6th NPC 1983; Exec. Chair. Preparatory Cttee for 6th NPC Games 1985–89; Gov. of Guangdong 1985–91; Chair. Zhongkai Inst. of Agricultural Tech. 1987–; Vice-Chair. 7th CPPCC Nat. Cttee 1991–93, 8th Nat. Cttee 1993–98, 9th Nat. Cttee 1998–; attended Macao Handover Ceremony as mem. of Chinese Govt. Del. 1999; Hon. Chair. Beijing Science and Eng Univ. 1995–. *Address:* National Committee of Chinese People's Political Consultative Conference, 23 Taipingqiao Street, Beijing, People's Republic of China.

YE YONGLIE; Chinese writer; b. 1940, Wenzhou, Zhejiang Prov.; ed Peking Univ. *Publications:* The Biography of Jiang Qing, The Biography of Zhang Chunqiao, The Biography of Yao Wenyuan, The Biography of Wang Hongwen. *Address:* Shanghai Science Education Film Studio, Shanghai, People's Republic of China.

YEANG, Ken, A.A.DIPL., PhD, RIBA; Malaysian architect and university professor; b. 6 Oct. 1948, Penang; ed Architectural Asscn, London, Univ. of Pennsylvania, Wolfson Coll. Cambridge; Prin. T. R. Hamzah & Yeang Sdn. Bhd. 1976–; external examiner Univ. of Moratuwa 1986–87, Universiti Sains Malaysia 1988–89, 2000–01; Adjunct Prof. Royal Melbourne Inst. of Tech. 1993–, Univ. of Hawaii at Manoa 1999–, Univ. of NSW 2000–; Prof. (Graham Willis Chair) Univ. of Sheffield 1994–; Provost's Distinguished Visitor, Univ. of Southern Calif. 1999; Hon. Fellow Singapore Inst. of Architects 1998; Hon. FAIA 1999; Hon. Academician Int. Acad. of Architecture (Sofia) 2000; Norway Award 1992, Far Eastern Econ. Review Innovation Award 1998, Auguste Perret Prize 1999, Asia Pacific Distinguished Scholar Award 1999, Enterprise 50 Award 1999, Prinz Claus Fonds Award 1999, Sir Robert Mathew Award 2000. *Exhibitions:* participant in exhbns. in New York City 1997, East Berlin 1998 and at Netherlands Inst. of Architecture, Rotterdam 1998, Hayward Gallery 1999, Design Museum 2000. *Publications:* Bioclimatic Skyscrapers 1994, Designing with Nature 1995, The Skyscraper Bioclimatically Considered: A Design Primer 1997, The Green Skyscraper: The Basis for Designing Sustainable Intensive Buildings 1999. *Address:* T. R. Hamzah & Yeang Sdn. Bhd., 8 Jalan 1, Taman Sri Ukay, 6800 Ampang, Selangor, Malaysia (Office). *Telephone:* (3) 42571966 (Office); (3) 42571948. *Fax:* (3) 42561005 (Office); (3) 42569330. *E-mail:* trhy@tm.net.my (Office). *Website:* www.trhamzah-yeang .com/main.htm (Office).

YEFIMOV, Air Marshal Aleksandr Nikolayevich, MSc; Russian air force officer (retd); b. 6 Feb. 1923, Kantemirovka, Voronezh Oblast; ed Voroshilovograd Mil. Air Acad., Mil. Acad. of Gen. Staff; joined CPSU 1943; served in Soviet army 1941; fought on the Western and on 2nd Byelorussian Fronts at

Vyazma, Smolensk, in Byelorussia, Poland and Germany 1942–45; by July 1944 had flown about 100 missions and was made Hero of the Soviet Union; completed his 222nd mission on 8 May 1945; awarded second Gold Star; held various command posts 1945–69; First Deputy C-in-C, Soviet Air Defence Forces 1969–91; Deputy to Supreme Soviet 1946–50, 1974–89; rank of Air Marshal 1975; Commdr of Soviet Air Force and Deputy Minister of Defence 1984–91, Mil. Insp.-Adviser, Ministry of Defence 1991; Chair. CIS Interstate Comm. on use of space and control of air services 1992–96, Council for co-operation with war veterans' unions 1995–; mem. CPSU Cen. Cttee 1986–90; USSR People's Deputy 1989; Hero of the Soviet Union 1944, 1945, Order of Lenin (twice), Order of the Red Banner (five times), Aleksandr Nevsky Order, Merited Mil. Pilot of USSR 1970 and other decorations. *Publication:* Over the Field of Battle 1976. *Address:* c/o Ministry of Defence, Myasnitskaya str. 37, 101000 Moscow, Russia. *Telephone:* (095) 293-31-76.

YEFUNI, Sergey Naumovich; Russian anaesthesiologist and physiologist; b. 24 Jan. 1930; m.; two s.; ed Second Moscow Inst. of Medicine; head of surgery div. municipal hosp. 1954–56; researcher First Moscow Inst. of Medicine 1959–63; Sr researcher, Head of Lab. All-Union Research Cen. of Surgery, USSR Acad. of Medical Sciences 1963–78, Head of Dept 1978–93; Dir-Gen. Inst. of Hyperbaric Medicine 1993–; Corresp. mem. USSR (now Russian) Acad. of Sciences 1979, mem. 1992; research in physiology of breathing, practical problems of anaesthesia, effect of anaesthesia on cardiovascular system; mem. United Scientific Council on complex problem Physiology of Man and Animals; Chair. Comm. Acad. (now Inst.) of Sciences Problems of Hyperbaric Oxygenation; lives in USA; USSR State Prize. *Address:* Institute of Hyperbaric Medicine, 119435 Moscow, Russia. *Telephone:* (095) 246-49-87 (Office); (095) 201-43-68 (Home).

YEGEROV, Adm. Vladimir Grigoryevich; Russian politician; b. 26 Nov. 1938, Moscow; m.; one s., one d.; ed M. Frunze Mil. Naval Higher School, Mil. Naval Acad., Mil. Acad. of Gen. Staff; officer service, Baltic Navy 1964–74, Head of staff, Deputy Commdr, Torpedo-boat Brigade 1974–76, Head, Rocket-boat Brigade 1976–83, Commdr, Motor Rocket-boat Brigade 1983–85, Commdr, Baltic Mil. Navy Base, Mediterranean Fleet of Black Sea Navy 1985–86, First Deputy Commdr, Baltic Navy 1986–91, Commdr 1991–2000; Head of Admin, Gov. of Kaliningrad region 2000–; Hon. mem. Swedish Royal Mil. Navy Soc., Hon. mem. St Petersburg Navy Assembly; Service to the Motherland Order, Mil. Service Order, Arms of Hon. *Address:* Administration of Kaliningrad Region, Office of the Governor, Dmitry Donskogo str. 1, 236007 Kaliningrad, Russia (Office). *Telephone:* (112) 46-75-45 (Office). *Fax:* (112) 46-35-54 (Office). *E-mail:* ako@ako.baltnet.ru (Office). *Website:* www.gov .kaliningrad.ru (Office).

YEGOROV, Sergey Yefimovich; Russian banker; b. 4 Oct. 1927, Orenburg Region; m.; one s. one d.; ed Saratov Inst. of Econ., Acad. of Finance; economist Altai territory branch USSR Gosbank 1950–60; instructor, Head of Sector Dept of Planning and Finance Bodies Cen. CPSU Cttee 1960–74; Chair. of Bd Russian Repub. Bank 1973–; Deputy to RSFSR Supreme Soviet 1973–88; consultant Exec. Bd USSR Gosbank 1988–91; Pres. Asscn of Russian Banks 1991–; mem. Int. Acad. of Information Processes and Tech.; Corresp. mem. Acad. of Man. and Market. *Leisure interests:* theatre, painting. *Address:* Association of Russian Banks, Skatertny per. 20, St 1, Moscow, Russia. *Telephone:* (095) 291-66-30 (Office). *Fax:* (095) 291-66-66 (Office). *E-mail:* arb@arb.ru (Office).

YEGOROV, Vladimir Konstantinovich; Russian politician, philosopher and journalist; b. 30 Oct. 1947, Kanash, Chuvash ASSR; m.; one s.; ed Kazan State Univ.; Deputy Ed. Molodoi Komsomolets, also Head, Dept of Propaganda, Cen. Comsomol Cttee 1974–85; Rector, Gorky. Inst. of Literature in Moscow 1985–87; Deputy Head, Div. of Culture, Ideological Dept, CPSU Cen. Cttee 1987–90; Asst to Pres. Mikhail Gorbachev (q.v.) on Problems of Culture and Religion 1990–91; Chief Scientific Researcher, Analytical Centre at Ministry of Science 1992–96; Prof. Russian Acad. of State Service 1993–; mem. Co-ordination Council, My Motherland; Dir Russian State Library 1996–98; Minister of Culture Russian Fed. 1998–2000; Rector Russian Acad. of State Service 2000–. *Publications:* books including History in our Lives, Intelligentsia and Power, The Star Turns Pale: Reflections on Russian History, From Deadlock to Uncertainty, Many Faces of Russia, numerous articles. *Address:* Academy of State Service, Vernadskogo prosp. 84, 117606 Moscow, Russia. *Telephone:* (095) 436-90-12 (Office).

YEHOSHUA, Abraham B., MA; Israeli writer and university professor; b. 9 Dec. 1936, Jerusalem; s. of Yakov Yehoshua and Malka Rosilio; m. Rivka Kirsninski 1960; two s. one d.; served in paratroopers unit 1954–57; Dir Israeli School in Paris 1964; Gen. Sec. World Union of Jewish Studies, Paris 1964–67; Dean of Students, Haifa Univ. 1967–72, Prof. of Comparative Literature 1972–; Visiting Prof., Harvard Univ., USA 1977, Univ. of Chicago 1988, 1991, Princeton Univ. 1992–; Co-Ed. Keshet 1965–72, Siman Kria 1973–, Tel Aviv Review 1987–; Dr hc (Hebrew Union Coll., Tel-Aviv Univ., Univ. of Turin, Bar Ilan Univ.); Brener Prize, Alterman Prize, Bialik Prize, European B'nai B'rith Award 1993, Israel Prize 1995. *Film adaptations of novels and stories include:* The Lover, Facing the Forests, Continuing Silence, Mr Mani, Open Heart, A Voyage to the End of the Millennium, Early in the Summer of 1970. *Plays:* A Night in May, Last Treatments, Possessions 1986, The Lover, The Night's Babies 1991. *Publications:* Death of the Old Man (short stories) 1963, Three Days and a Child (short stories) 1970, Early in the Summer of 1970 (novella) 1973, Two Plays 1975, The Lover (novel) 1978, Between Right and Right (essays) 1980, A Late Divorce (novel) (Fliano Prize, Italy 1996) 1982, Five Seasons (novel) (Nat. Jewish Book Award 1990, Cavour Prize, Italy 1994) 1988, The Wall and the Mountain (essays) 1988, Mister Mani (novel) (Israeli Booker Prize 1992, Nat. Jewish Book Award 1993, Wingate Prize, UK 1994) 1990, Open Heart (novel) 1994, A Voyage to the End of the Millennium (novel) 1997, The Terrible Power of a Minor Guilt (essays) 1998, The Liberating Bride (novel) 2001. *Address:* 33 Shoshanat Ha-Carme, Haifa, 34322, Israel. *Telephone:* 4-8370001. *Fax:* 4-8375569. *E-mail:* bulli@research.haifa.ac.il (Home).

YEKHANUROV, Yury Ivanovich; Ukrainian politician; b. 23 Aug. 1948, Belkachi, Yakusk; s. of Ivan Mikhailovich Yekhanurov and Galina Mikhailovna Yekhanurova; m. Olga Lvivna Yekhanurova; one s.; ed Kiev Inst. of Nat. Econs, Research Inst. of Econ. State Planning Comm. of Ukraine; master, then head of workshop, chief engineer, Dir Kievmiskbur Co. 1967–77, Head Kievmiskburkomplekt Co. 1978–85; Deputy Head, then Head Burdetal Co. 1988–91; Deputy Head State Econ. Council, Cabinet of Ministers 1991–92; Deputy Head Bd of Verkhovna Rada 1992; Deputy Head, then Head Dept of Econ. Reform and Market Progress, Kiev City Admin. 1992–93; Deputy Minister of the Economy 1993–94; Pres. Union of Small Businesses 1993–94, Dir Council 1996–; Head Supreme Econ. Council 1997–; First Vice-Prime Minister 2000–01; mem. Parl. 2002–. *Address:* House of Government, M. Hrushevskogo str. 12/2, Kiev, Ukraine (Office). *Telephone:* (44) 226-24-72 (Office).

YELLAND, David Ian, BA; British journalist; b. 14 May 1963, Harrogate; s. of John Michael Yelland and Patricia Ann McIntosh; m. Tania Farrell 1996; one s.; ed Brigg Grammar School, Lincs., Coventry Univ.; grad. trainee Westminster Press 1985; trainee reporter Buckinghamshire Advertiser 1985–87; industrial reporter Northern Echo 1987–88; gen. news and business reporter North West Times and Sunday Times 1988–89; city reporter Thomson Regional Newspapers 1989–90; joined News Corpn 1990; city reporter, then City Ed., The Sun 1990–92, New York Corresp. 1992–93, Ed. 1998–2003; Deputy Business Ed., Business Ed., then Deputy Ed. New York Post 1993–98; Sr Vice-Pres. News Corpn, NY 2003–. *Address:* News Corporation, 1211 Avenue of Americas, 8th Floor, New York, NY 10036, USA (Office). *Telephone:* (212) 852-7000 (Office). *E-mail:* dyelland@newscorp.com. *Website:* www.newscorp.com (Office).

YELLEN, Janet Louise, PhD; American economist and government official; b. 13 Aug. 1946, Brooklyn, NY; d. of Julius Yellen and Anna Ruth Yellen (née Blumenthal); m. George Arthur Akerlof 1978; one s.; ed Brown Univ., Yale Univ.; Asst Prof. of Econs Harvard Univ. 1971–76; lecturer LSE 1978–80; Asst Prof. of Econs School of Business Admin. Univ. of Calif. at Berkeley 1980–82, Assoc. Prof. 1982–85, Prof. Haas School of Business 1985–; Bernard T. Rocca Jr Prof. of Int. Business and Trade 1992–; consultant Div. of Int. Finance, Bd Govs. of Fed. Reserve System 1974–75, economist Trade and Financial Studies section 1977–78, mem. 1994–97; Research Fellow MIT 1974; consultant Congressional Budget Office 1975–76, mem. Panel of Econ. Advisers 1993–; Chair. Council of Econ. Advisers 1997–99; research affiliate, Yale Univ. 1976; mem. Advisory Panel on Econs Nat. Science Foundation 1977–78, 1991–92; mem. Brookings Panel on Econ. Activity 1987–88, 1990–91, Sr Adviser 1989–; Lecturer on Macroeconomic Theory, Yrjö Jahnsson Found., Helsinki 1977–78; mem. Council on Foreign Relations 1976–81, American Econ. Asscn; grad. fellow Nat. Science Foundation 1967–71; Guggenheim Fellow 1986–87; Hon. Woodrow Wilson Fellow 1967. *Publications:* The Limits of the Market in Resource Allocation (jtly.) 1977, assoc. Journal of Econ. Perspectives 1987–91, contrib. articles to professional journals. *Address:* Haas School of Business, University of California, Berkeley, CA 94720, USA (Office).

YELTSIN, Boris Nikolayevich; Russian politician (retd); b. 1 Feb. 1931, Sverdlovsk; s. of Nikolai Yeltsin and Klavdia Yeltsina; m. Naina Yeltsina (née Girina) 1956; two d.; ed Urals Polytech. Inst.; construction-worker with various orgs. in Sverdlovsk Dist 1955–68; mem. CPSU 1961–90 (resgnd); First Sec. Sverdlovsk Dist Cen. Cttee CPSU 1976–85; fmr Deputy to Supreme Soviet of USSR; Sec. of Cen. Cttee CPSU 1985–86; First Sec. of Moscow City Party Cttee 1985–87; First Deputy Chair. State Cttee for Construction 1987–89; Head Cttee on Construction Architecture 1989–90; Chair. Inter-Regional Group July 1989; elected to Congress of People's Deputies of the USSR 1989; mem. USSR Supreme Soviet 1989–91; mem. and Chair. RSFSR Supreme Soviet 1990–91; President of RSFSR 1991, of Russia 1991–99; Acting Head Russian Fed. Defence Ministry 1992; Supreme Commdr of Russian Army 1992–99; Olympic Gold Order 1992; German Press Award 1996. *Publications:* Against the Grain (autobiog.) 1990, Three Days 1992, Memoirs: The View From the Kremlin 1990, 1994, 2000. *Leisure interests:* tennis, hunting, film. *Address:* c/o Office of the President, 103073 The Kremlin, korp. 1, Moscow, Russia.

YEMELYANOV, Aleksei Mikhailovich, DEcon; Russian politician and economist; b. 15 Feb. 1935; ed Moscow Univ.; mem. CPSU 1959–90; Lecturer, Prof., Head of Chair Moscow Univ.; mem. Russian Agric. Acad.; USSR People's Deputy 1989–91; Deputy Chair. Cttee on Agric. Problems, USSR Supreme Soviet 1989–91; mem. Pres. Council 1992–; Pres.-Rector Russian State Acad. of State Service 1994–2000, Prof. Dept of Econs 2000–; active participant of democratic movt; mem. of State Duma (Parl.) 1993–95. *Publications:* scientific works and articles on agricultural reforms in Russia. *Address:* Russian Agricultural Academy, Bolshoi Kharitonyevsky per. 21,

107814 Moscow; Academy of State Service, Vernadskogo prosp. 84, 117606 Moscow, Russia. *Telephone:* (095) 923-40-90 (Agricultural Acad.); (095) 436-94-24 (Acad. of State Service).

YEMELYANOV, Stanislav Vasilevich, D.TECH.SC.; Russian management specialist; b. 18 May 1929, Voronezh; s. of Vasilii Yemelyanov and Ludmila (née Chepkova) Yemelyanova; m. Olga Yemelyanova 1952; one s. one d.; ed Moscow Univ.; with Inst. of Control Problems, USSR (now Russian) Acad. of Sciences 1952–76, with Inst. for Systems Analysis 1976– (Dir 1991–), mem. Acad. 1984, mem. Presidium 1988, Acad.-Sec., Dept of Informatics, Computer Science and Automation 1990–; Gen. Dir Int. Inst. for Man. Science 1976–; Head of Chair of Nonlinear Dynamics and Control Processes, Moscow State Univ.; Chair of Engineering Cybernetics, Moscow Steel and Alloys Inst.; mem. editorial Bd Differential Equations, Automatic and Remote Control, Problems of Theory and Practice of Management, Dynamics and Control; research into variable structure control theory; holder of about 100 patents; Lenin Prize 1972, USSR State Prize 1980, Council of USSR Ministers Prize 1981, Russian Fed. State Prize 1994. *Publications:* 7 books; 250 journal articles. *Address:* International Institute for Management Science, Shchepkina Street 8, 129090 Moscow (Office); Academic Zelinskii str. 38/8, Apt. 69, Moscow, Russia (Home). *Telephone:* (095) 208-91-06 (Office); (095) 135-54-69 (Home). *Fax:* (095) 938-16-74.

YEMEN, former King of (see Saif al-Islam, Mohammed al-Badr).

YEMENIDJIAN, Alex, MA; American business executive; ed California State Univ., Northridge, Univ. of Southern California; Man. Partner Parks, Palmer & Yemenidjian; joined Metro-Goldwyn-Mayer (MGM) Grand Inc., Las Vegas 1989, Chief Financial Officer 1994–98, Pres. and COO 1995–99, mem. Bd Dirs. 1999–; Dir MGM Inc., Santa Monica 1997–, Chair. and CEO 1999–; Exec. Tracinda 1990–97, 1999; Chair. United Armenian Fund; mem. Bd Dirs. Kirk Kerkorian's Lincy Foundation. *Address:* Metro-Goldwyn-Mayer Inc., 2500 Broadway Street, Santa Monica, CA 90404, USA (Office). *Telephone:* (310) 449-3000 (Office). *Fax:* (310) 449-3100 (Office). *Website:* www.mgm.com (Office).

YEN CHING-CHANG, MA, LLB; Taiwanese politician; b. 7 April 1948, Tainan; ed Nat. Taiwan Univ., Univ. of Michigan, USA; joined Ministry of Finance 1972, Sr Customs Officer, Taipei Customs Bureau 1972–73, Specialist, Dept of Customs Admin. 1973–77, Sr Specialist in Secr. 1977–78, 1980–84, Exec. Sec. Legal Comm. 1984–85, Taxation and Tariff Comm. 1985–92, Deputy Minister of Finance 1996–2000, Minister of Finance 2000–02; Deputy Dir-Gen. First Bureau, Office of the Pres. 1992–93, Dir-Gen. 1993–96; Prof., Nat. Taiwan Univ., Nat. Chengchi Univ. and Soochoe Univ. 1981–86; Eisenhower Fellowship, USA 1995; Chevalier Ordre nat. du Mérite 1998; Class One Merit Medal, Exec. Yuan 2000. *Publications:* Anti-dumping Act and Customs Policy 1981, Legal Problems of Sino-American Trade Negotiations 1987, Unveiling GATT: Order and Trend of Global Trade 1989, International Economic Law 1991, Laws and Regulations of International Economic Relations 1995, Taxation Law 1998, Understanding and Appreciating French Wines 1997; (in English) Taiwan Trade and Investment Law 1994. *Address:* c/o Ministry of Finance, 2 Aikuo West Road, Taipei, Taiwan (Office).

YENTOB, Alan, LLB; British television administrator; b. 11 March 1947, London; s. of Isaac Yentob and Flora Yentob (née Khazam); one s. one d. by Philippa Walker; ed King's School, Ely, Univ. of Grenoble, France, Univ. of Leeds; BBC gen. trainee 1968, Producer/Dir. 1970–, Head of Music and Arts, BBC-TV 1985–88, Controller, BBC 2 1988–93, BBC 1 1993–96, BBC Dir of Programmes 1996–97; BBC Dir of TV 1997–2000, of Drama, Entertainment and Children's Programmes 2000–; mem. British Film Inst. Production Bd 1985–93, British Screen Advisory Council, Advisory Cttee, Inst. of Contemporary Arts, Council Royal Court Theatre; Gov. Nat. Film School 1998–, S. Bank Bd 1999–; Trustee Architecture Foundation 1992–, Timebank 2001–; Hon. Fellow, RCA, RIBA, Royal TV Soc. *Leisure interests:* swimming, books. *Address:* BBC Television, Television Centre, Wood Lane, London, W12 7RJ, England (Office). *Telephone:* (20) 8743-8000 (Office).

YEO CHEOW TONG, BEng; Singaporean politician; b. 1947; m.; two d.; ed Anglo-Chinese School, Univ. of Western Australia; worked in Econ. Devt Bd 1972–75; joined LeBlond Makino Asia Pte. Ltd (LMA) as Staff Engineer 1975, subsequently promoted to Eng Man., then Operations Dir; Man. Dir LMA and subsidiary co., Pacific Precision Castings Pte. Ltd (PPC) 1981–85; elected MP for Hong Kah 1984; Minister of State for Health and for Foreign Affairs 1985–87; Acting Minister for Health, Sr Minister of State for Foreign Affairs 1987–90, of Health 1990–94, for Community Devt 1991–94, for Trade and Industry 1994–97, of Health and for the Environment 1997–99; Minister for Communications and Information Tech. 1999–2001; Minister of Transport 2001–. *Address:* Ministry of Transport, 460 Alexandra Road, 39–00 PSA Bldg, Singapore 169854. *Telephone:* 62707988. *Fax:* 63757734. *E-mail:* mot@mot .gov.sg. *Website:* www.mot.gov.sg.

YEOH, Michelle, BA; Malaysian actress; b. Nee Yeoh Choo-Keng (sometimes credited as Michelle Khan, Ziqiong Yang or Chi-King Yeung), 6 Aug. 1962, Ipoh, Perak; m. Dickson Poon 1988 (divorced 1992); ed Royal Acad. of Dance, London. *Films:* Owls vs. Dumbo 1984, In the Line of Duty 2 1985, The Target 1985, Magnificent Warriors 1987, Easy Money 1987, The Heroic Trio 1993, Police Story 3 1992 (Part 2 1993), Butterfly Sword 1993, Heroic Trio 2: Executioners 1993, Seven Maidens 1993, Tai-Chi 1993, Wonder Seven 1994,

The Stunt Woman 1996, The Soong Sisters 1997, Tomorrow Never Dies 1997, Moonlight Express 1999, Crouching Tiger, Hidden Dragon 2000. *Address:* c/o Ang Lee, CAA, 9830 Wilshire Boulevard, Beverly Hills, CA 90212, USA.

YEREMIN, Yuri Ivanovich; Russian theatre director; b. 9 March 1944, Kolomna, Moscow Region; s. of Evdokiya Fillippovna Yeremina; m. Nina Petrovna Yeremina 1974; one s. one d.; with Youth Theatre, Rostov-on-Don 1973–77; Gorky Drama Theatre, Rostov-on-Don 1978–80; Cen. Army Theatre, Moscow 1981–87; Dir Pushkin Theatre, Moscow 1987–2000; Prof. Inst. for Advanced Theatre Training, Harvard Univ., USA 1997–; U.S. debut with production of The Paper Gramophone, Hartford Stage Co. 1989; Ward No. 6, dramatic adaptation of Chekhov story, performed at int. drama festivals in USA, France, Italy, Switzerland, Belgium, UK and Canada 1989–91; Vice-Pres. Int. Asscn of Theatre Producers 1991–; People's Artist of Russia 1986, Order for Literature and Art (France) 1989. *Recent productions include:* The Possessed (Dostoevsky adaptation) 1989, Black Monk (Chekhov adaptation) 1990, At Kingdom Gate (Hamsun) 1991, Erick XIV (Strindberg) 1992, The Ghosts (De Filippo) 1992, The History of one Staircase (Buero Valejo) 1993, To Moscow! To Moscow! (adaptation of Chekhov's Three Sisters) 1994, Madame Bovary (Flaubert adaptation) 1994, The Inspector (Gogol) 1994, King Oedipus (Sophocles) 1995. *Productions at American Repertory Theater (Cambridge, Mass.):* The Idiot (Dostoevsky) 1998, Ivanov (Chekhov) 1999, Three Farces and a Funeral (based on Chekhov's comedies) 2000, Othello (Shakespeare) 2001, Silver Age (Roshchin) 2001. *Leisure interests:* painting, writing. *Address:* 7 Soviet Army Street, Apt. 213, 107802 Moscow, Russia. *Telephone:* (095) 281-83-20 (Home); (095) 299-41-36. *E-mail:* yuryer@mail.ru (Home).

YERIN, Army Gen. Victor Fedorovich; Russian politician; b. 17 Jan. 1944, Kazan; m.; two c.; ed Higher School, USSR Ministry of Internal Affairs; regional militiaman; mem. Criminal Investigation Dept Ministry of Internal Affairs, Tatar Autonomous Repub., Chief of Dept 1980–83; Chief of Div. Admin. of struggle against embezzlement of social property 1983–88; First Deputy Minister of Internal Affairs of Armenian SSR 1988–90; Deputy Minister of Internal Affairs of RSFSR, Chief Service of Criminal Militia 1990–91; First Deputy Minister of Internal Affairs of USSR Sept.–Dec. 1991; First Deputy Minister of Security and Internal Affairs of Russian Fed. 1991–92; Minister of Internal Affairs of Russian Fed. 1992–95; Deputy Dir of Foreign Intelligence (SVR) 1995–. Kolpachni per. 11, 101000 Moscow, Russia (Office). *Telephone:* (095) 429-38-50 (Office).

YEROFEYEV, Victor Vladimirovich; Russian writer and critic; b. 19 Sept. 1947, Moscow; m. Veslava (née Skura) Yerofeyeva; one s.; ed Moscow Univ.; expelled from USSR Writers' Union for participation in almanac Metropol, membership restored in 1986; lecturer Maxim Gorky Literature Inst.; seminars on Modern Russian Literature at Univ. of South Calif.; contribs. to Moscow News, Moscow Magazine, New York Review of Books; mem. Bd Russian PEN Centre; named Man of the Year by Moscow Magazine 1990. *Publications:* Anna's Body and End of the Russian Avant-garde (collection of short stories) 1980, Life with an Idiot (novel) 1980, Russian Beauty (novel) 1981, In the Maze of Cursed Questions (collection of essays) 1990, The Pocket Apocalypse 1993, Collected Works (3 vols) 1994–95, The Doomsday 1996, Men 1997, Five Rivers of Life 1998, Encyclopedia of the Russian Soul 2000. *Leisure interest:* travelling. *Address:* 1st Smolensky per. 9, Apt. 1, Moscow, Russia. *Telephone:* (095) 241-02-08.

YERSHOV, Yuri Leonidovich, D.MATH.SCI.; Russian scientist and mathematician; b. 1 May 1940, Novosibirsk; m.; three c.; ed Novosibirsk State Univ.; jr, sr researcher, then Head of Div. Inst. of Math., Siberian br., USSR (now Russian) Acad. of Sciences 1963–85, corresp. mem. Russian Acad. of Sciences 1970, mem. 1991; Rector Novosibirsk Univ. *Publications:* numerous scientific publications including monographs. *Address:* Novosibirsk State University, Pirogova str. 2, 630090 Novosibirsk, Russia (Office). *Telephone:* (3832) 35-78-08 (Office); (3832) 35-51-75 (Home).

YESENBAYEV, Mazhit Tulenbekovich; Kazakhstan politician, engineer and economist; b. 28 April 1949, Pavlodar; ed Kazakh Polytech. Inst., Almaty; fmr Gov. Cen. Karaganda Region; apptd. Minister of Finance 1999–2001, of Economy and Trade 2002–; Order of Parasat 1999. *Publications:* 34 publns on problems of territorial org. of production and optimization of teaching and educational process. *Address:* Ministry of Economy and Trade, Beibitshilik 2, 473000 Astana, Kazakhstan (Office). *Telephone:* (3172) 33-30-03 (Office).

YESIN, Sergey Nikolayevich; Russian writer; b. 18 Dec. 1935, Moscow; s. of Nikolai Yesin and Zinaida (née Afonina) Saprykina; m. Valentina Ivanova; ed Moscow State Univ.; debut as journalist, corresp. Moskovsky Komsomolets, Ed.-in-Chief Krugozor 1972–74; ed. Drama Broadcasting Div. State TV and Broadcasting Cttee 1974–81; Rector Maxim Gorky Literary Inst. 1992–, Prof. 1993; a Founder Club of Ind. Writers 1992; Founder and Vice-Pres. Acad. of Russian Literature 1996; Chair. Int. Union of Social Asscns of Bibliophiles 1997–; State Order of Friendship 1996, Sholohov Literary Award 2000, Moscow Literary Award. *Publications include:* Recollections of August, Memoirs of a Forty-Year-Old, The Imitator, The Spy, Standing in the Doorway, Gladiator 1987, Characters 1990, Selected Stories 1994, In the Season of Salting Pickles 1994, The Current Day 1994, The Mars Eclipse 1994, Tutor 1996, The Power of Culture 1997, Selected Stories 1998, Literary Diaries 1999, 2000, 2001, 2002, Death of Titan 2002, Companion Thoughts 2002. *Leisure interests:* building dachas, home maintenance. *Address:* Tverskoy Boulevard 25, Maxim Gorky Literary Institute, 103104 Moscow; Stroiteley

str. 4, korp. 6, Apt. 43, 117311 Moscow, Russia (Home). *Telephone:* (095) 202-84-22 (Office); (095) 930-35-45 (Home); (095) 203-01-01. *Fax:* (095) 202-76-88 (Office); (095) 203-60-91. *E-mail:* liternity@litinstitut.ru (Office); rectorat@litinstitut.ru (Home). *Website:* www.litinstitut.ru (Office).

YESSENIN-VOLPIN, Alexander Sergeyevich; Russian mathematician, philosopher, poet and mentor of Human Rights Movt; b. 5 Dec. 1924, Leningrad (now St Petersburg); s. of poet Sergey Esenin and Nadiezhda Volpina; m. 1st V. B. Volpina; m. 2nd I. G. Kristi; m. 3rd 1994; one c.; studied at Faculty of Math., Moscow Univ. 1941–46; arrested for his poetry and committed to mental asylum 1949; in exile Karaganda, Kazakh SSR 1950; amnestied 1953; wrote numerous articles on logic and math. and translated extensively; at USSR Acad. of Sciences Inst. of Scientific and Tech. Information 1961–72; dissident activity 1959–; emigrated 1972. *Publications include:* A Free Philosophical Treatise 1959, A Leaf of Spring 1959, 1961, Open Letter to Solzhenitsyn 1970, Report on Committee on Rights of Man 1971, On the Logic of Moral Sciences (in English) 1988; numerous articles in Western and Russian scientific journals (after 1990s). *Leisure interests:* logic, philosophy. *Address:* 1513 North Shore Road, 2nd Floor, Revere, MA 02151, USA. *Telephone:* (781) 289-1072.

YEUTTER, Clayton K.; American government official; b. 10 Dec. 1930, Eustis, Neb.; m. Lillian Jeanne Vierk; two s. two d.; ed Univ. of Nebraska; served USAF 1952–57; ran family farm from 1957; Prof., Dir Agricultural and Tech. Assistance Programme in Bogotá, Colombia 1968–70; Asst Sec. of Agric. in charge of Int. Affairs and Commodity Programs, U.S. Govt 1970–75; Deputy Special Trade Rep. 1975–77, U.S. Trade Rep. 1985–88; Sec. of State for Agric. 1989–91; Chair. Republican Nat. Cttee 1991–92; Counsellor to the Pres. for domestic policy 1992; Pres. Chicago Mercantile Exchange 1978–85; Dir (non-exec.) BAT Industries. *Address:* c/o Republican National Committee, 310 First Street, SE, Washington, DC 20003, USA.

YEVTUSHENKO, Yevgeniy Aleksandrovich; Russian poet; b. 18 July 1933, Zima, Irkutsk Region; m. 1st Bella Akhmadulina 1954; m. 2nd Galina Sokol 1962; one s.; m. 3rd Jan Butler 1978; two s.; m. 4th Maria Novikova 1986; two s.; ed Moscow Literary Inst.; geological expeditions with father to Kazakhstan 1948, the Altai 1949–50; literary work 1949–; mem. Editorial Bd of Yunost magazine 1962–69; People's Deputy of the USSR 1989–91; Sec. USSR Writers' Union 1986–91; Vice-Pres. Soviet PEN Cttee; Prof. Pittsburgh Univ. USA, Univ., Autónoma de Santo Domingo, Dominican Rep.; USSR Cttee for Defence of Peace Award 1965, Order of Red Banner of Labour, Badge of Honour, USSR State Prize 1984. *Films directed include:* Kindergarten 1983, Stalin's Funeral 1987; acted in Ascent (film on Tsiolkovsky). *Publications include:* verse: Scouts of the Future (collected verse) 1952, The Third Snow (lyric verse) 1955, The Highway of Enthusiasts 1956, Zima Junction 1956, The Promise (collected verse) 1960, Moscow Goods Station, The Nihilist, The Apple 1960–61, Do the Russians Want War?, Babi Yar 1961, The Heirs of Stalin, Fears 1962, A Sweep of the Arm 1962, Tenderness 1962, A Precocious Autobiography 1963, The City of Yes and the City of No, Bratskaya Hydro-Electric Power Station 1964, Letter to Yesenin 1965, Italian Tears, A Boat of Communication, Poems Chosen by the Author 1966, Collection of Verses Yelabuga Nail, Cemetery of Whales 1967, That's What Is Happening to Me 1968, It's Snowing White 1969, Kazan University 1971, I am of Siberian Stock 1971, The Singing Domba 1972, Stolen Apples 1972, Under the Skin of the Statue of Liberty (play) 1972, Intimate Lyrics 1973, A Father's Hearing 1975, 1978, From Desire to Desire 1976, Love Poems 1977, People of the Morning 1978, Winter Station 1978, A Dove in Santiago: A Novella in Verse 1978, Heavy Soils 1979, The Face Behind the Face 1979, Ivan the Terrible and Ivan the Fool 1979, Berries (novel) 1981, Ardabiola (short story) 1981, Almost at the End (prose and verse) 1985, A Wind of Tomorrow (essays) 1987, Fatal Half Measures 1989, The Collected Poems 1952–90 1991, Farewell to Red Banner 1992, compiler Twentieth Century Russian Poetry 1994, Don't Die Before You're Dead (novel) 1996, My Very, Very... (poetry) 1996; photography: Divided Twins: Alaska and Siberia, Invisible Threads, Shadows and Faces. *Address:* Kutuzovski Prospekt 2/1, Apt. 101, 121248 Moscow, Russia. *Telephone:* (095) 243-37-69.

YEVTUSHENKOV, Vladimir Petrovich, CAND.ECONS.; Russian economist and business executive; b. 25 Sept. 1948, Kaminshchina, Smolensk region; m.; one s. one d.; ed Moscow Inst. of Chem. Tech., Moscow State Univ.; master Dzerzhinsk plant 1973–75; Deputy Dir, Chief Engineer Karacharovo factory of plastic masses, Moscow 1975–82; Chief Engineer, First Deputy Dir-Gen. Polymerbyt (scientific-production co.), USSR Ministry of Chem. Industry 1982–87; Head Tech. Dept, then Chief Dept of Science and Tech., Moscow City Exec. Cttee 1987–90, Head Cttee on Science and Tech. 1990–; Founder and Pres. Sistema (financial holding Corpn) 1993–; Head Moscow Foundation of Presidential Programmes; counsellor to Mayor of Moscow 1996–; Chair. Bd of Dirs TV-Cen. (TV channel) 1997–99; Lenin's Komsomol Prize. *Address:* Financial Corporation Sistema, Leontyevaky per. 10, 103009 Moscow, Russia (Office). *Telephone:* (095) 229-06-00 (Office).

YEZHOV, Valentin Ivanovich; Russian screenplay writer; b. 21 Jan. 1921, Samara; s. of Ivan Yezhov and Anna Yezhov; m. 1st Olga Sherbova 1951; m. 2nd Natalya Gotovtseva 1976; one s.; ed All-Union State Inst. of Cinematography; Prof. of Cinematography 1989–; mem. CPSU 1951–91; co-author scripts for Our Champions 1954, World Champion 1955, Liana 1956, A Man from the Planet Earth 1958, The House of Gold 1959, The Volga Flows 1962, Wings 1966, Thirty Three 1967, White Sun of the Desert 1969, A Nest of

Gentry 1969, The Legend 1971, This Sweet Word Liberty 1973, Eleven Hopefuls 1974, Siberiade 1977, Meadow Flowers 1981, The Girl and the Grand 1982, Alexander the Small 1982, Moon Rainbow 1983, The First Cavalry 1984, The Rivals 1985, Bow to the Ground 1985, Strawberry Wine 1985, Last Will and Testament 1986, Your Special Correspondent 1986, Igor Savovich 1987, Fellow Townsmen 1988, The Watchmaker and the Hen 1989, Happiness Never Strikes Twice 1990, Esperanza (Mexican co-production) 1990, Maria and Mirabella II 1990, Adjouba (Indian co-production) 1990, Under Aurora (Japanese co-production) 1990, Lord Silver 1991, Sin 1992, My Best Friend General Vasiliy, Son of Joseph 1992, Doctor Andersen 2000; Lenin Prize 1961 for script of film Ballad of a Soldier 1959, State Award of Russia 1997 for script of film White Sun of the Desert. Plays: Nightingale Night 1969, Gunfire Beyond the Dunes 1982, Alyosha 1985. Publications: Siberiada (collected works) 1993, The White Sun of the Desert (collected works) 1994. Leisure interests: fishing, chess. Address: Kutuzovski Prospekt 41, Apt. 20, 121170 Moscow, Russia. Telephone: (095) 249-38-74.

YHAP, Laetitia, DFA; British artist; b. 1 May 1941, St Albans; d. of Leslie Neville Yhap and Elizabeth (née Kogler) Yhap; one s.; ed Camberwell School of Arts and Crafts, Slade School of Fine Art, Univ. Coll. London; Artist-in-Residence Chatham House Grammar School, Ramsgate 1981; works in public collections in UK; mem. of London Group 1971–; exhibited in many nat. and museum-curated shows, British Council, Arts Council, Contemporary Art Soc. etc.; Leverhume Research Award 1962–63; John Moores Prize 1973. Solo exhibitions: numerous one-woman exhbns since 1965, including three solo shows at Piccadilly Gallery 1968, 1970, 1973; most recent maj. solo shows: The Business of the Beach, on tour 1988–89, Life at the Edge, Charleston Farmhouse 1993, Bound By the Sea (retrospective), Berwick Gymnasium 1994, Maritime Counterpoint, Boundary Gallery 1996; most recent In Mono-chrome, Lydd Library Gallery 1998, The Story So Far, Hastings Trust 1999, Being in the Picture, Piers Feetham Gallery, London 2002. Leisure interests: music, attending concerts, playing badminton. Address: 12 The Croft, Hastings, East Sussex, TN34 3HH, England. Telephone: (1424) 426222.

YHOMBI-OPANGO, Brig.-Gen. Jacques-Joachim; Republic of the Congo army officer and fmr Head of State; b. 1939; trained in French army; fmr military attaché at Congolese Embassy, Moscow; Chief of Staff, People's National Army 1968–73, Insp.-Gen. 1973–74; Sec.-Gen. of Council of State with rank of Minister 1974–75, Council of State Delegate responsible for Defence and Security 1974–75; Pres. of Republic, Pres. Council of Ministers, Pres. Mil. Council of Congolese Labour Party 1977–79; arrested 1979, detained 1979–84, released from detention Nov. 1984, rearrested Sept. 1987; Prime Minister of Congo 1993–96; fmr Leader Rassemblement pour la défense et le developpement (RDP); fmr Leader Rassemblement pour la Démocratie et le Développement (RDD); Order of Nat. Flag (N Korea) 1978. Address: c/o Office of the Prime Minister, Brazzaville, Republic of the Congo.

YIANNOPOULOS, Evangelos; Greek politician; b. 1918, Gortynia, Pelo-ponnese; m. Konstantina Yiannopoulou 1954; one s. one d.; ed Athens Univ.; served as officer in Albanian war (wounded) and later in Greek resistance movement in World War II as Bn Commdr in Greek Popular Liberation Army; mem. Nat. Progressive Centre Union; joined Centre Union youth org., Centre Union Party 1960; arrested and deported to remote area 1969, rearrested and imprisoned for political activities 1970; founding mem. Panhellenic Socialist Movement (PASOK); also mem. Cen. Cttee; Pres. Athens Lawyer's Asscn 1976–81; mem. Gov. Council, Inst. of Int. and Alien Law; MP 1981–; Minister of Labour 1981–85, 1985–86, of Merchant Marine 1987–89, of the Aegean March–July 1989, of Labour 1993–94, of Justice 1996–2000. Address: c/o Ministry of Justice, Odos Mesogeion 96, 115 27 Athens, Greece.

YILMAZ, A. Mesut; Turkish politician; b. 6 Nov. 1947, Istanbul; s. of Hasan Yilmaz and Güzide Yilmaz; m. Berna Müren; two s.; ed Istanbul High School for Boys, Faculty of Political Studies, Ankara and in London and Cologne; fmr company Dir in pvt. business sector; Deputy for Rize 1983–; Minister of Culture and Tourism 1986–87, of Foreign Affairs 1987–90, Prime Minister of Turkey June–Nov. 1991, 1996, 1997–98; Deputy Prime Minister and Minister of State –2002; currently Chair. Anavatan Partisi—ANAP (Motherland Party); Vice-Chair. EDU. Address: Anavatan Partisi—ANAP, 13 Cad. 3, Balgat, Ankara (Office); c/o Başbakanlık, Bakanlıklar, Ankara, Turkey. Telephone: (312) 2865000 (Office); (312) 4189056. Fax: (312) 2865019 (Office); (312) 4180476. E-mail: anavatan@anap.org.tr (Office). Website: www.anap.org.tr (Office).

YIN CHANGMIN; Chinese scientist and party and state official; b. 4 Oct. 1923, Nanchang, Jiangxi Prov.; d. of Yin Renqing and Wu Yahui; m. Bei Xiaoliang 1948; two s.; alt. mem. 12th CCP Cen. Cttee 1982, mem. 1986; alt. mem. 13th CCP Cen. Cttee 1987–92; Prof. Hunan Normal Univ. 1979–, Vice-Pres. 1973–81, Pres. 1981–83, Consultant 1985–; Vice-Chair. CPPCC Prov. Cttee, Hunan 1985–92; mem. CCP Cttee, Hunan 1983–85; Vice-Chair. Hunan Branch Asscn for Science and Tech. 1980–85, Hon. Chair. 1985–; mem. Bd of Dirs., Chinese Zoological Soc. 1984; Chair. Bd of Dirs. Hunan Biology Soc. and Zoological Soc. 1981–92, Hunan Zoological Soc. 1992–; Deputy, Nat. Cultural and Educational Conf. 1960; Nat. Red Banner Women's Pacesetter 1959, Model Worker of Hunan Prov. 1960, First Prize for Improvement of Science and Tech., Dept of Agric. and Forestry 1980, First Prize, Nat. Cttee of Educ. and other prizes. Publications: Field Spiders 1980, Textbook of Zoology 1983, Spiders in China: One Hundred New and Newly Recorded Species of the Araneidae and Agelenidae Family 1990, Fauna Sinica; 70 research papers.

Leisure interests: literature, collecting postage stamps. Address: Department of Biology, Hunan Normal University, Changsha, Hunan Province, People's Republic of China. Telephone: (731) 8883310. Fax: (731) 8851226.

YIN JUN; Chinese politician; b. Sept. 1932; alt. mem. 12th CCP Cen. Cttee 1982; Chair. and Gov., Dali Bai Autonomous Pref., Yunnan Prov. 1982–84; Sec. Discipline Inspection Cttee, Yunnan CCP Prov. Cttee 1985; alt. mem. 13th CCP Cen. Cttee 1987; Deputy Sec. Yunnan Prov. Cttee 1989; Chair. Yunnan Prov. 8th People's Congress 1993–98, 9th People's Congress 1998–. Address: Dali Bai Autonomous Prefectural People's Government, Yunnan, People's Republic of China.

YIN KESHENG; Chinese politician; b. 1932; ed Beijing Petroleum Inst.; Vice-Gov., Qinghai 1983; Sec. CCP Cttee, Qinghai 1985–97; mem. 12th CCP Cen. Cttee 1985–87; mem. 13th CCP Cen. Cttee 1987–92, 14th Cen. Cttee 1992–97; Vice-Chair. Nationalities Cttee of 9th NPC 1998–. Address: c/o Standing Committee of National People's Congress, Beijing, People's Republic of China.

YIN WENYING; Chinese entomologist; b. Oct. 1923, Pingxiang Co., Hebei Prov.; ed Zhongyang Univ.; mem. Chinese Acad. of Sciences 1992–; Science and Tech. Progress Award. Address: Shanghai Institute of Entomology, 225 Chongqing Nan Road, Shanghai Municipality, People's Republic of China.

YING, Diane; Taiwanese journalist and publisher; b. Xian, People's Republic of China; ed Univ. of Iowa, USA; emigrated with family from mainland China to Taiwan 1949; fmr reporter, The Philadelphia Inquirer, USA, Taiwan corresp. at various times for Asian Wall Street Journal, New York Times and United Press Int.; Co-founder, Chief Ed. and Publr Commonwealth financial monthly 1981–; teaches journalism at Nat. Chengchi Univ.; Commr Nat. Unification Council. Address: 4th Floor, 87 Sungkiang Road, Taipei, Taiwan.

YISHAI, Eliyahu; Israeli politician; b. 1962, Jerusalem; m.; five c.; fmr Head of Interior Minister's bureau; acting Sec.-Gen., then Leader Shas (Sephardic Torah Guardians) 1991–; Dir-Gen. Shas-affiliated El ha-Ma'ayan Movt; elected to 14th Knesset (Parl.) 1996; Minister of Labour and Social Affairs 1996–2001, of Internal Affairs March 2001–02, also Deputy Prime Minister 2001–02. Address: c/o Shas, Beit Abodi, Rehov Hahida, Bene Beraq, Israel (Office).

YODER, Hatten Schuyler, Jr, PhD; American petrologist; b. 20 March 1921, Cleveland, Ohio; s. of Hatten Schuyler Yoder and Elizabeth Katherine Yoder (née Knieling); m. Elizabeth Marie Bruffey 1959 (deceased); one s. (deceased) one d.; ed Univs. of Chicago and Minnesota and Mass. Inst. of Tech.; active duty, US Naval Reserve 1942–46, MOKO expedition to Siberia 1945–46, Lt-Commdr, retd; Petrologist, Geophysical Lab., Carnegie Inst. of Washington 1948–71, Dir 1971–86, Dir Emer. 1986–; public mem. Foreign Service Selection Bds., Dept of State 1990; mem. Editorial Bd Geochimica et Cosmochimica Acta 1958–68; N American Ed., Journal of Petrology 1959–68, Hon. mem. Advisory Bd 1968–79; Assoc. Ed. American Journal of Science 1972–90; Editorial Bd Earth Sciences History 1993–2000; Consultant Los Alamos Nat. Lab. 1971–; Visiting Prof. of Geochemistry, Calif. Inst. of Tech. 1958; Visiting Prof. of Petrology, Univ. of Tex. 1964, Univ. of Colo 1966, Univ. of Cape Town 1967; new mineral, Yoderite, named in his honour; Participant, Nobel Symposium, Royal Swedish Acad. of Sciences 1979; mem. NAS 1958– (Geology Section Chair. 1973–76); mem. US Nat. Cttee for Geology 1973–76, for Geochemistry 1973–76, on the History of Geology 1982–90; mem. American Philosophical Soc. 1979, (Council 1983–85), Exec. Cttee 1994–, Geochemical Soc. (Organizing and Founding mem., Council 1956–58); Fellow, Mineralogical Soc. of America (mem. Council 1962–64, Vice-Pres. 1970–71, Pres. 1971–72), Geological Soc. of America (mem. Council 1966–68), American Geophysical Union (Pres. Volcanology, Geochemistry and Petrology Section 1961–64, mem. Council 1965–68), American Acad. of Arts and Sciences 1979, Geological Soc. of SA 1988–, Public Mems. Asscn of the Foreign Service (Vice-Pres. 1994–95, 1998–99, Treas. 2000–02); Pres. History of Earth Sciences Soc. 1995–96; Ind. Trustee The Cutler Trust 1992–; Sec.-Treas. Bd of Advisers, The Coll. of Democracy 1985–; Corresp. Fellow, Edin. Geological Soc.; mem. Nat. School Band Asscn; Hon. mem. All-Union Mineralogical Soc. of USSR (now Russia) 1977–, Mineralogical Soc. of GB 1983–, Soc. Française de Minéralogie et de Cristallographie 1986–; Hon. Fellow Geological Soc. of London 1988, Geological Soc. of Finland, Mineralogical Asscn of Canada, World Innovation Foundation 2001; Hon. DEng (Colorado School of Mines) 1995; Dr hc (Univ. of Paris VI) 1981; Nat. High School Band Solo Trombone Championship 1937, Mineralogical Soc. of America Award 1954, Columbia Univ. Bicentennial Medal 1954, Arthur L. Day Medal of Geological Soc. of America 1962, A. L. Day Prize and Lectureship of Nat. Acad. of Sciences 1972, A. G. Werner Medal of German Mineralogical Soc. 1972, Golden Plate Award, American Acad. of Achievement 1976, Wollaston Medal, Geological Soc. of London 1979, Roebling Medal, Mineralogical Soc. of America 1992, Compatriot, Sons of the American Revolution, History of Geology Award, Geological Soc. of America 1998, Professional Achievement Award, Univ. of Chicago Club of Washington Alumni 2000. Publications: Generation of Basaltic Magma 1976, The Evolution of the Igneous Rocks: Fiftieth Anniversary Perspectives (editor) 1979, Planned Invasion of Japan 1945: The Siberian Weather Advantage 1997 and numerous papers. Leisure interests: camping, trombone, rifle and pistol marksmanship, gardening, philately, genealogy. Address: Geophysical Laboratory, 5251 Broad Branch Road, NW, Washington, DC 20015-1305, USA. Telephone: (202) 478-8966 (Office); (301) 365-8758 (Home). Fax: (202) 478-8901 (Office). E-mail: yoder@gl.ciw.edu (Office).

YOH-HAMURA, Shoei, BA; Japanese architect and interior designer; b. 7 March 1940, Kumamoto City; ed Univ. of Keio; interior designer at Int. Design Associates, Tokyo 1964–67; project designer with Nic, Fukuoka 1967–70; Design and Architectural Prin. Yoh and Architects 1970–; Visiting Prof., Grad. School of Architecture, Urban Design and Preservation, Columbia Univ. 1992; Prof., Grad. School of Architecture and Urban Design, Keio Univ. 1996–; Mainichi Design Award 1983, Japan Inst. of Architects Award 1983, 1989, IAKS Award 1993, City of Fukuoka Award 1994, Fukuoka Pref. Award 1998. *Art Exhibitions:* WXYZ Chair. of Glass 1978, Transformation 1980, Light Architecture 1982, Light Architecture II 1984, Forms in Wood 1985, Interface Design 1987, Acquarchitecture 1991. *Leisure interest:* travel. *Address:* Shoei Yoh and Architects, 1-12-30 Heiwa, Minami-ku, Fukuoka-shi, 815-007 (Office); c/o Keio University, 2-15-45 Mita, Minato-Ku, Tokyo 108-8345, Japan. *Telephone:* (92) 521-4782 (Office); (92) 521-4110 (Home); (3) 3453-4511. *Fax:* (92) 521-6718 (Office); (3) 3769-1564. *Website:* www.keio.ac.jp (Office).

YON HYONG MUK; North Korean politician; b. 3 Nov. 1931, N Hamgyong Prov.; worked as farm labourer then technician; Deputy to Supreme People's Ass. 1967–; Vice-Dir then Dir of Dept, Cen. Cttee Workers Party of Korea (KWP); mem. KWP Cen. Cttee Nov. 1970–; Political Bureau 1973–; Vice-Premier, then First Vice-Premier Admin. Council; Sec. to Party Centre; Premier, Admin. Council 1988–92; Party Sec. for Jagang Prov. 1992–; mem. Nat. Defence Comm. 1998–; Order of the Nat. Flag (First Class), Order of Freedom and Independence (First Class); Kim Il-Sung Medal. *Address:* c/o Office of the Premier, Pyongyang, Democratic People's Republic of Korea.

YONLI, Paramanga Ernest, PhD; Burkinabè politician and agricultural economist; b. 1956, Tansarga, Tapoa Prov.; ed Univ. of Benin, Univ. of Paris I (Panthéon-Sorbonne), Nat. Inst. of Agriculture, Paris-Grignon, Ouagadougou Univ.; conducted research into food security and marketing; fmr Minister of the Civil Service and Institutional Devt; Prime Minister of Burkina Faso, Minister of the Econ. and Finance Dec. 2000–. *Address:* Office of the Prime Minister, 03 B.P. 7030, Ouagadougou 03, Burkina Faso (Office).

YOO CHANG-SOON; South Korean politician and businessman; b. 6 Aug. 1918, Anju, Pyongan Nam-do; m.; five s. one d.; ed Hastings Coll., USA; Branch Dir Bank of Korea, Tokyo; Head of US Operations, Bank of Korea, New York 1953; Gov. Bank of Korea 1961–62; Minister of Commerce and Industry 1962–63; Chair. Econ. Planning Bd Feb.–Dec. 1963; Chair. Lotte Confectionery Co. 1967, Counsellor 1985; Chair. Korean Traders' Asscn 1981–82; Prime Minister, Republic of Korea Jan.–June 1982; Pres. Repub. of Korea Nat. Red Cross 1982–; Chair. UN Korean Asscn 1981–; mem. Advisory Council on State Affairs; mem. Seoul Olympics Organizing Cttee 1981. *Leisure interests:* golf, gardening. *Address:* Na-106, Lotte Village, 1494 Seocho-dong, Seocho-gu, Seoul; Alfheim Haus #401, Shinsa-dong, Kangnam-gu, Seoul, Republic of Korea.

YOO CHONG-HA; South Korean politician and diplomatist; b. 28 July 1936; m.; three s.; ed Seoul Nat. Univ., Bonn Univ.; joined Ministry of Foreign Affairs 1959; Third Sec., Bonn Embassy 1963–68; Consul, Chicago May–Oct. 1968, Islamabad 1968–71; Dir SE Asia Div. Ministry of Foreign Affairs 1971–74; Counsellor, Washington Embassy 1974–77; Deputy Dir-Gen. American Affairs Bureau, Ministry of Foreign Affairs 1977–78, Dir-Gen. 1978–80; Minister, Embassy, London 1980–83; Amb. to Sudan 1983–85, to Belgium 1987–89, to EC Feb.–Dec. 1989; Asst Minister for Econ. Affairs, Ministry of Foreign Affairs 1985–87; Vice-Minister of Foreign Affairs 1989–92; Perm. Rep. to UN 1992–94; Sr Adviser to Pres. for Foreign Policy and Nat. Security 1994–96; Minister of Foreign Affairs 1996–98; Order of Service Merit (Red Stripes). *Address:* c/o Ministry of Foreign Affairs, 77, Sejong-no, Jongno-gu, Seoul, Republic of Korea.

YOON SUNG-MIN, Gen.; South Korean army officer and politician; b. 15 Oct. 1926, Muan-kun, Jeolla Nam-do Prov.; m. Chung Hae Woo; two d.; ed Korea Mil. Acad., Korea Army Coll., Nat. Defence Coll., Grad. School of Public Admin., Seoul Nat. Univ.; Regimental Commdr 20th Infantry Div. 1964, Asst Div. Commdr 8th Infantry Div. 1966, apptd. Brig.-Gen. and Asst Chief of Staff for Personnel, Korea Army 1967; Chief of Staff in Viet Nam 1968; Commdg Gen. First Field Army 1979; Chair. Jt Chiefs of Staff 1981; Minister of Nat. Defence 1982–86; Standing Adviser Hyundai Precision & Inc. Co. 1991–; Order of Nat. Security Merit, Tongil Medal, Order of Mil. Service Merit, Ulchi Medal, Chung-Mu Medal, etc. *Leisure interests:* reading, golf and tennis.

YORK, Herbert Frank, PhD; American physicist; b. 24 Nov. 1921, Rochester, NY; s. of Herbert York and Nellie York; m. Sybil Dunford 1947; one s. two d.; ed Rochester and California Univs.; joined staff of Calif. Univ. Radiation Lab. 1943; attached to Y-12 Plant, Oak Ridge, Tenn. 1944–45; Univ. of Calif. Grad. School 1945–49; undertook, with Dr. Hugh Bradner, design and execution of maj. experiment in 'Operation Greenhouse' (Eniwetok) 1950; Asst Prof. of Physics, Univ. of Calif. 1951; headed programme, Livermore weapon Devt lab. 1952–54, Dir 1954–58; Assoc. Dir Univ. of Calif. Radiation Lab. 1954–58; Dir of Research, Advanced Research Projects Div., Inst. for Defense Analyses, Chief Scientist, Dept of Defense Advanced Research and Devt Agency 1958; Dir of Defence Research and Eng 1958–61; Chancellor, Univ. of Calif. at San Diego 1961–64, 1970–72, Dean of Graduate Studies 1969–70, Dir Program in Science, Tech. and Public Affairs 1973–88, Prof. of Physics, Univ. of Calif. 1964–; Consultant in Office of Secretary of Defense 1977–81, 1987, in Exec. Office of Pres. 1977–81; mem. Defense Science Bd 1978–82; Dir Inst. on Global Conflict and Co-operation 1982–88, Dir Emer. 1988–; Amb. to Comprehensive Test Ban Negotiations 1979–81; fmr mem. Army and Air Force Scientific Advisory Bd; Vice-Chair. President's Science Advisory Cttee 1965–67, mem. 1957–58, 1964–68; mem. Gen. Advisory Cttee for Arms Control and Disarmament 1962–69; mem. President's Comm. on Mil. Compensation 1977–78; mem. Bd of Trustees, Aerospace Corpn 1961–87, Bd of Trustees, Inst. for Defense Analyses 1963–95; mem. Bd of Dirs., Educ. Foundation for Nuclear Science; mem. Exec. Cttee Fed. of American Scientists 1970–75, Int. Council, Pugwash Movt 1972–76; Personal Rep. of Sec. of Defense at Anti-Satellite Arms Negotiations, Helsinki 1977, Berne 1978; mem. American Acad. of Arts and Sciences; Lawrence Award 1963, Vannevar Bush Award 2000, Fermi Award 2000. *Publications:* Race to Oblivion 1970, Arms Control Readings 1973, The Advisors 1976, Making Weapons, Talking Peace 1987, A Shield in the Sky (with Sanford Lakoff) 1989, Arms and the Physicist 1995 and various articles on physics and arms control problems. *Address:* University of California, San Diego, IGCC 0518, La Jolla, CA 92093 (Office); 6110 Camino de la Costa, La Jolla, CA 92037, USA (Home). *Telephone:* (858) 459-1776 (Office); (858) 459-1776 (Home). *Fax:* (858) 459-9418.

YORK, Michael (Michael York-Johnson), OBE, BA; British actor; b. 27 March 1942, Fulmer; s. of Joseph Gwynne and Florence Edith (neé Chown) Johnson; m. Patricia McCallum 1968; ed Univ. Coll. Oxford; with Dundee Repertory Co. 1964, Nat. Theatre Co. 1965, guest lecturer; Chair. Calif. Youth Theatre; Chevalier Ordre nat. des. Arts et Lettres. *Stage appearances include:* Any Just Cause 1967, Hamlet 1970, Outcry (Broadway) 1973, Ring Round the Moon 1975, Bent, Cyrano de Bergerac, Whisper in the Mind 1990, The Crucible 1991, Someone to Watch Over Me 1993. *Radio:* Jane Eyre 2002, Alice in Wonderland 2002. *TV appearances include:* The Forsyte Saga, Rebel in the Grave, True Patriot, Much Ado About Nothing, Jesus of Nazareth, A Man Called Intrepid, For Those I Loved, The Weather in The Streets, The Master of Ballantrae, Space, The Far Country, Are You My Mother 1986, Ponce de León 1987, Knot's Landing 1987, The Four Minute Mile 1988, The Lady and the Highwayman 1988, The Heat of the Day 1988, A Duel of Love 1990, The Road to Avonlea 1990, Teklab 1994, September 1995, A Young Connecticut Yankee in King Arthur's Court 1995, Not of This Earth 1995, The Ring 1996, True Women 1996, The Ripper 1997, A Knight in Camelot 1998, Perfect Little Angels 1998, The Haunting of Hell House 2000, The Lot 2001, Founding Fathers, Founding Brothers. *Films include:* The Taming of the Shrew 1966, Accident 1966, Red and Blue 1967, Smashing Time 1967, Romeo and Juliet 1967, The Strange Affair 1967, The Guru 1968, Alfred the Great 1968, Justine 1969, Something for Everyone 1969, Zeppelin 1970, La Poudre d'Escampette 1971, Cabaret 1971, England Made Me 1971, Lost Horizon 1972, The Three Musketeers 1973, Murder on the Orient Express 1974, Great Expectations 1974, Conduct Unbecoming 1974, The Four Musketeers 1975, Logan's Run 1976, Seven Nights in Japan, The Last Remake of Beau Geste 1977, The Island of Dr Moreau 1977, Fedora 1977, The Riddle of the Sands 1978, Final Assignment 1979, Success is The Best Revenge 1984, Dawn 1985, Vengeance 1986, The Secret of the Sahara 1987, Imbalances 1987, Lethal Obsession 1987, The Return of the Musketeers 1988, Till We Meet Again 1989, The Heat of the Day 1989, The Night of the Fox 1990, Eline Vere 1990, Duel of Hearts 1990, The Wanderer 1991, The Long Shadow 1991, Wide Sargasso Sea 1991, Rochade 1991, Discretion Assured 1993, The Shadow of a Kiss 1994, Fall from Grace 1994, Gospa 1995, Goodbye America 1996, Austin Powers 1996, Dark Planet 1996, Wrongfully Accused 1998, One Hell of a Guy 1998, The Omega Code 1999, Borstal Boy 2000, Megiddo 2001, Austin Powers in Goldmember 2002. *Music:* Christopher Columbus: A Musical Journey 2002, Enoch Arden (Tennyson/Strauss) 2003. *Publications:* The Courage of Conviction (contrib.) 1986, Voices of Survival (contrib.) 1987, Travelling Player (autobiog.) 1991, Accidentally on Purpose (autobiog.) 1992, A Shakespearian Actor Prepares 2000, Dispatches From Armageddon 2002. *Address:* c/o Andrew Manson, 288 Munster Road, London, SW6 6BQ, England. *Telephone:* (20) 7386-9158. *Fax:* (20) 7381-8874. *Website:* www.michaelyork.net (Office).

YORK, Susannah; British actress; b. 9 Jan. 1942, London; d. of William Fletcher and Joan Bowring; m. Michael Wells 1960 (divorced 1976); one s. one d.; ed Royal Acad. of Dramatic Art. *Films include:* Tunes of Glory 1960, The Greengage Summer 1961, Freud 1962, Tom Jones 1963, The Seventh Dawn 1964, Act One Scene Nun 1964, Sands of the Kalahari 1965, Scruggs 1966, Kaleidoscope 1966, A Man for All Seasons 1966, Sebastian 1967, The Killing of Sister George 1968, Duffy 1968, Lock up Your Daughters 1969, They Shoot Horses, Don't They? 1969, Country Dance 1970, Jane Eyre 1970, Zee and Co. 1971, Happy Birthday Wanda June 1971, Images 1972 (Best Actress Award, Cannes Film Festival), The Maids, Gold 1974, Conduct Unbecoming 1974, That Lucky Touch 1975, Skyriders 1976, Eliza Fraser 1976, The Shout 1977, The Silent Partner, Superman II 1980, Yellowbeard, Fatal Attraction 1985, A Summer Story 1987, Melancholia 1988, Just Ask for Diamond 1988, Princess 1993. *Plays include:* Wings of a Dove, A Singular Man, Man and Superman, Private Lives, Hedda Gabler (London and New York), Appearances (London and Paris), Peter Pan, Cinderella, The Singular Life of Albert Nobbs, Penthesilea, Fatal Attraction, The Women, The Apple Cart, Agnes of God, The Human Voice, Multiple Choice, A Private Treason, Lyric for a Tango, The Glass Menagerie, A Streetcar Named Desire, Noonbreak, September Tide 1993–94; Dir Salome (Traverse Theatre, Edin.) 1992, Eagle Has Two Heads (Lilian Bayliss Theatre, London) 1994, The First Years/Beginnings 1995, Camino Real 1997; (with RSC) The Merry Wives of Windsor, Camino Real, Hamlet 1997/98, The Ideal Husband 1998/99, The Loves of Shakespeare's Women (also writer) 2001–03. *Television appearances:* The Crucible, Fallen Angels, Second Chance, We'll Meet Again, The Other Side of Me, Macho,

Trainer, Devices and Desires; producer: The Big One 1983. *Publications:* children's books: In Search of Unicorns, Lark's Castle. *Leisure interests:* reading, writing, gardening, travelling, riding, theatre and cinema going. *Address:* c/o Peters, Fraser & Dunlop, 34–43 Russell Street, Drury House, London, WC2B 5HA, England.

YORK, HRH The Duke of; Prince Andrew Albert Christian Edward, Earl of Inverness and Baron Killyleagh, CVO; b. 19 Feb. 1960, London; s. of HM Queen Elizabeth II (q.v.) and Prince Philip, Duke of Edinburgh (q.v.); m. Sarah Ferguson 1986 (divorced 1996); two d., Beatrice Elizabeth Mary, b. 8 Aug. 1988, Eugenie Victoria Helena, b. 23 March 1990; ed Heatherdown Preparatory School, Ascot, Gordonstoun School, Scotland, Lakefield Coll. School, Ont., Canada, Britannia Royal Naval Coll., Dartmouth; joined Royal Navy as Seaman Officer, specializing as a pilot 1979, before entering Royal Naval Coll.; flying training with RAF Leeming, Yorks. and helicopter training at Royal Naval Air Station (RNAS) Culdrose, Cornwall; received Wings 1981; joined front-line unit 820 Naval Air Squadron and embarked in Anti-Submarine Warfare Carrier HMS Invincible; participated in Falklands conflict 1982; served as Flight Pilot in NAS, Type 22 Frigate HMS Brazen 1984–86; returned to 702 NAS as Helicopter Warfare Instructor 1987; joined Type 42 Destroyer HMS Edinburgh as Officer of the Watch 1988–89; returned to RNAS Portland to form HMS Campbeltown Flight; served as Flight Commdr, 829 NAS 1989–91; Army Command and Staff Course, Staff Coll., Camberley 1992; rank of Lt Commdr 1992; commanded Hunt Class Minehunter HMS Cottesmore 1993–94; Sr Pilot, 815 NAS, RNAS Portland 1995–96; joined Ministry of Defence, London as a staff officer, Directorate of Naval Operations 1997–99; rank of Commdr, with Diplomacy Section of Naval Staff, London 1999–2001; Special Rep. for Int. Investment and Trade 2001–; Adm. of the Sea Cadet Corps 1992–; Col-in-Chief Staffordshire Regt 1998–, Royal Irish Regt 1992–, Royal NZ Army Logistic Regt; Hon. Air Commodore RAF Lossiemouth, Morayshire; Patron of over 90 orgs., including Greenwich Hosp., Fight for Sight, Defeating Deafness, Jubilee Sailing Trust, Royal Aero Club; Trustee Nat. Maritime Museum, Greenwich; Chair. Trustees Outward Bound Trust; mem. Advisory Bd of Govs., Lakefield Coll. School; Commodore Royal Thames Yacht Club; Elder Brother Trinity House. *Address:* Buckingham Palace, London, SW1A 1AA, England.

YORKE, Thom; British musician; b. Oct. 1968, Wellingborough, Northamptonshire; ed Exeter Univ.; mem. and lead singer, On A Friday 1987, renamed Radiohead 1991–; also designer of record sleeves; numerous tours, festivals and television appearances; guest vocalist with Drugstore on White Magic for Lovers and El President 1998; guest vocalist with Velvet Goldmine 1998, MTV's 120 Minutes Live 1998; other collabs include: UNKLE 1998, P. J. Harvey 2000; Grammy Award, Best Alternative Rock Performance 1998, Best Alternative Music Album, 2000; Q Award, Best Act in the World Today 2002. *Recordings include:* albums: Pablo Honey 1993, The Bends 1995, OK Computer (No. 1, UK and USA) 1997, Kid A (No. 1, UK and USA) 2000, Amnesiac 2001, I Might Be Wrong 2001; singles: Drill (EP) 1992, Creep 1993, Anyone Can Play Guitar 1993, Pop Is Dead 1993, Stop Whispering 1993, Itch (EP) 1994, My Iron Lung (EP) 1994, My Iron Lung 1994, Live Au Forum (EP) 1995, High and Dry 1995, Fake Plastic Trees 1995, Just 1995, Street Spirit (Fade Out) 1996, The Bends 1996, Paranoid Android 1997, Karma Police 1997, No Surprises 1997, Climbing Up The Walls 1997, Airbag/How Am I Driving? (EP) 1998, Pyramid Song 2001, Knives Out 2001, I Might Be Wrong 2001; Contrib. Help (Bosnia Relief Album) 1995. *Address:* Courtyard Management, 21 The Nursery, Sutton Courtenay, Abingdon, Oxfordshire, OX14 4UA, England (Office). *Website:* www.radiohead.com.

YORONGAR, Ngarledjy; Chadian politician and editorial director; m.; five c.; ed schools and univs in Chad, Canada and France; civil servant and govt official; also worked for int. orgs including OECD, Science and Educ. Admin. and Financial Office in Zaire, Int. Insurance Inst. (IIA) in Cameroon; Cand. in Presidential Elections 1996, 2001; campaigner against human rights violations and corruption, arrested numerous occasions including 1996 and on winning 2001 elections, imprisoned 1998–99; currently Leader, Fédération Action pour le République (FAR); Fed. Exec. Co-ordinator of Federalist Party; Pres. of Foundation for the Respect of Law and Liberties (FORELLI); Editorial Dir of newspapers La Roue and Le Phare Républicain. *Address:* Fédération Action pour la République, BP 4197, N'Djamena, Chad (Office). *Telephone:* 51-45-59. *Fax:* 51-45-59. *E-mail:* yorongar@intnet.td.

YOSELIANI, Otar Davidovich; Georgian film director; b. 2 Feb. 1934, Tbilisi; s. of David Yoseliani and Maria (née Mikaberidze) Yoseliani; m. Rita Semenova 1956; one d.; ed Moscow Univ., Moscow Cinema Inst.; worked as sailor and miner; Tbilisi film studio 1959–76; teacher of cinema, Tbilisi Acad. of Fine Arts; working in France 1982–. *Films include:* Avril 1962, La Chute des Feuilles 1966 (Fipresci Prize, Cannes), Il était un fois un merle chanteur 1970 (Best Foreign Film of the Year, Italy), Pastorale 1976 (Fipresci Prize, Berlin), Sept pièces pour le cinéma noir et blanc 1982, Euskadi 1983, Les favoris de la lune 1984 (Grand Prix, Venice Festival), Le petit monastère en Toscane 1988, Et la lumière fut 1989 (Grand Prix, Venice Festival), Hunting Butterflies 1992 (Tarkovsky Prize 1993), Georgia Alone (TV documentary) 1994, Les Brigandeurs 1996, In Vino Veritas 1999. *Leisure interest:* speleology. *Address:* Mitskewitch 1 korp., 1 Apt. 33, 380060 Tbilisi, Georgia; 14 rue de Rivoli, 75004 Paris, France. *Telephone:* (32) 38-50-58 (Tbilisi); 1-40-26-07-18 (Paris).

YOSHIMURA, Yukio, B.A.(Econs); Japanese business executive and international organization official; b. 9 June 1947, Nishinomiya; s. of Kazuo Yoshimura and Itoko Iijima; m. Tomoko Shibazaki 1977; three s.; ed Tokyo Univ.; Dir Int. Orgs. Div., Ministry of Finance 1991–92, Int. Banking Div. 1992–95; Counsellor, Minister's Secr., in charge of Int. Public Relations 1995–96, Deputy Dir-Gen. Int. Finance Bureau 1996–97; Exec. Dir for Japan, IMF 1997–2001; Sr Adviser to Pres. World Bank Group 2001–; mem. Basle Cttee on Banking Supervision 1984–85; Alt. Exec. Dir World Bank 1988–91; Exec. Dir Inter-American Investment Corpn 1990–91; mem. Group of Ten Working Party on Electronic Money 1996–97. *Address:* World Bank Group, 1818 H Street, NW, Washington, DC 20433, USA (Office). *Telephone:* (202) 473-2862 (Office). *Fax:* (202) 522-3433 (Office).

YOSHINAGA, Sayuri; Japanese film actress; b. 1945; m. Tado Okada; ed Waseda Univ.; film debut in Town with a Cupola 1962; has since appeared in nearly 100 films including The Sound of Waves, The Makioka Sisters, The Diary of Yumechiyo, Ohan, Heaven Station, Killing Time by the Shores of a Mysterious Sea, Joyu; Japan Acad. Award for Best Actress 1985.

YOU XIGUI, Lt-Gen.; Chinese army officer; personal bodyguard to Pres. Jiang Zemin 1994–; fmr acting Dir Bodyguards Bureau PLA, Dir 1996–; alt. mem. 15th CCP Cen. Cttee 1997–. *Address:* People's Liberation Army, c/o Ministry of National Defence, Jingshanqian Jie, Beijing, People's Republic of China.

YOUN, Kong-Hi (Victorinus), STD, DD; North Korean ecclesiastic; b. 8 Nov. 1924, Jinnampo City; s. of (Peter) Sang Youn and (Victoria) Sang Sook Choi; ed St Willibrord's Maj. Seminary, Dok-Won, N. Korea, Urban Coll., Rome, Gregorian Univ., Rome; ordained priest 1950; Asst Priest, Cathedral of Seoul (Myong-Dong) 1950; Chaplain, Pusan UN POW Camp 1951, Vice-Pres. Catholic Library, Pusan 1953; teacher, Song-Shin (Holy Ghost) Middle and High School 1954; Sec. Catholic Conf. of Korea 1960; ordained Bishop 1963–; Ordinary of Su-Won Diocese 1963; Admin. Seoul Archdiocese 1967; Archbishop and Ordinary of Kwangju Archdiocese 1973, Archbishop Emer. 2000; Rep. Kwangju Catholic Coll. Foundation 1974; Chair. Episcopal Conf. of Korea 1975; Rep. of Episcopal Cttee of Bicentennial of Catholic Church in Korea 1980; Episcopal Moderator, Justice and Peace Cttee 1979. *Publication:* Radio Message 1963. *Leisure interest:* mountain climbing. *Address:* Kwangju Catholic University, Nampeong, PO Box 101, Naju-si, Jeonnam 520-710, Republic of Korea. *Telephone:* (61) 337-2181. *Fax:* (61) 337-2185. *E-mail:* vkyoun@mail.kjc.ac.kr (Office).

YOUNG, Bob; Canadian computer executive; b. 19 Jan. 1954; three c.; ed Univ. of Toronto; began career as sales and marketing exec. in computer industry 1976; co-founded Red Hat to develop Linux open-source operating software 1995, now CEO. *Leisure interests:* family holidays, fly-fishing.

YOUNG, Sir Colville (Norbert), GCMG, MBE, JP, DPhil; Belizean Governor-General and academic; b. 20 Nov. 1932, Belize City; s. of Henry Oswald Young and Adney Wilhelmina Young (née Waite); m. Norma Eleanor Trapp 1956; three s. one d.; ed Univ. of West Indies, Univ. of York; Prin. St Michael's Coll., Belize 1974–76; Lecturer in English and Gen. Studies Belize Tech. Coll. 1976–86; Pres. Univ. Coll. of Belize 1986–90, lecturer 1990–93; Gov.-Gen. of Belize 1993–; Arts Faculty Prize, Univ. Coll. of the West Indies 1959, Outstanding Teacher's Award 1987. *Compositions include:* Misa Caribeña, Tiger Dead (folk opera). *Publications:* Creole Proverbs of Belize 1980, Caribbean Corner Calling 1988, Language and Education in Belize 1989, Pataki Full 1990, From One Caribbean Corner (poetry) 1983, contrib. drama and poetry in various anthologies, articles in various publs. *Leisure interests:* creative writing, playing and arranging steelband music, musical composition. *Address:* Belize House, Belmopan, Belize. *Telephone:* (8) 22521; (2) 30881. *Fax:* (8) 22050.

YOUNG, Frances Margaret, OBE, PhD; British professor of theology; b. Frances Margaret Worrall, 25 Nov. 1939, Frome, Somerset; d. of A. Stanley Worrall and Mary Frances (née Marshall) Worrall; m. Robert Charles Young 1964; three s.; ed Bedford Coll., Univ. of London, Girton Coll. Cambridge and Chicago Divinity School; Research Fellow, Clare Hall, Cambridge 1967–68; temporary lecturer Univ. of Birmingham 1971–73, lecturer 1973–84, Sr lecturer 1984–86, Edward Cadbury Prof. 1986–; Head Dept. of Theology 1986–95; Head of School of Philosophy and Theology 1989–93; Dean Faculty of Arts 1995–97; Pro-Vice-Chancellor 1997–2002; ordained Methodist Minister 1984; Hon. DD (Univ. of Aberdeen) 1994. *Publications:* Sacrifice and the Death of Christ 1975, Can These Dry Bones Live? 1982, From Nicaea to Chalcedon 1983, Face to Face: A Narrative Essay in the Theology of Suffering 1985, The Art of Performance 1990, The Theology of the Pastoral Letters 1994, Biblical Exegesis and the Formation of Christian Culture 1997. *Leisure interests:* walking, cycling, camping, travel, music, poetry, literature. *Address:* Department of Theology, University of Birmingham, Birmingham, B15 2TT (Office); 142 Selly Park Road, Birmingham, B29 7LH, England (Home). *Telephone:* (121) 414-5936 (Office); (121) 472-4841 (Home). *E-mail:* f.m.young@bham.ac.uk (Office); fmyoung@lineone.net (Home).

YOUNG, Rt. Hon. Sir George (Samuel Knatchbull), 6th Bt, PC, MA, M.PHIL.; British politician; b. 16 July 1941; s. of Sir George Young, 5th Bt and Elisabeth Knatchbull-Hugessen; m. Aurelia Nemon-Stuart 1964; two s. two d.; ed Eton Coll. and Christ Church Oxford; Economist, Nat. Econ. Devt Office 1966–67; Kobler Research Fellow, Univ. of Surrey 1967–69; Econ. Adviser, Post Office Corpn 1969–74; Councillor, London Borough of Lambeth 1968–71;

mem. Greater London Council for London Borough of Ealing 1970–73; MP for Ealing, Acton 1974–97, for Hampshire NW 1997–; Opposition Whip 1976–79; Parl. Under-Sec. of State, Dept of Health and Social Security 1979–81, Dept of Environment 1981–86; Dir Lovell Partnerships 1987–90; Comptroller of HM Household 1990; Minister of State, Dept of Environment 1990–94; Financial Sec. HM Treasury 1994–95; Sec. of State for Transport 1995–97; Opposition Front Bench Spokesman for Defence 1997–98; Shadow Leader of the House 1998–2000; mem. Conservative Party. *Publications:* Accommodation Services in the UK 1970–80, Tourism, Blessing or Blight? 1973. *Leisure interest:* bicycling. *Address:* House of Commons, London, SW1A 0AA, England. *E-mail:* sirgyoung@aol.com (Office). *Website:* sirgeorgeyoung.org.uk (Office).

YOUNG, Hugo John Smelter, MA; British journalist; b. 13 Oct. 1938, Sheffield; s. of Gerard Young and Diana Young; m. 1st Helen Mason 1966 (died 1989); one s. three d.; m. 2nd Lucy Waring 1990; ed Ampleforth Coll., Balliol Coll., Oxford; with Yorkshire Post 1961; Harkness Fellow 1963; Congressional Fellow, U.S. Congress 1964; Chief Leader Writer, The Sunday Times 1966–77, Political Ed. 1973–84, Jt Deputy Ed. 1981–84; political columnist, The Guardian 1984–; Dir The Tablet 1985–; Chair. The Scott Trust 1989–; mem. UK Advisory Cttee Harkness Fellowships 1990–95 (Chair. 1993–95); Hon. DLitt (Sheffield Univ.) 1993; British Press Awards, Columnist of the Year 1980, 1983, 1985; Granada TV What the Papers Say Awards Columnist of the Year 1985. *Publications:* (co-author): The Zinoviev Letter 1966, Journey to Tranquillity 1969, The Crossman Affair 1974, No, Minister 1982, But, Chancellor 1984, The Thatcher Phenomenon 1986, One of Us 1989 (revised Edn 1991), This Blessed Plot 1998. *Address:* c/o The Guardian, 119 Farringdon Road, London, EC1 3ER, England. *E-mail:* hugoyoung@ compuserve.com (Home). *Website:* www.guardian.co.uk (Office).

YOUNG, John Atherton, AO, DSc, MD, FAA, FRACP; Australian professor of physiology; b. 18 April 1936, Brisbane, Queensland; s. of William Young and Betty Young (née Atherton); ed Brisbane Church of England Grammar School, Univ. of Queensland; Jr Resident Medical Officer, Royal Brisbane Hosp. 1961; Sr Research Officer, Kanematsu Inst., Sydney Hosp. 1962–64; C. J. Martin Travelling Fellow of NH and MRC, Physiology Inst., Free Univ. of Berlin 1965–66; Sr Lecturer, then Assoc. Prof., Univ. of Sydney 1967–76, Prof. of Physiology 1976–, Head of Dept 1976–89, Dean Faculty of Medicine 1989–96, Pro Vice-Chancellor (Health Sciences) 1994–; mem., Deputy Chair., Chair. Cen. Sydney Area Health Service 1989–; Dir Royal Alexandra Hosp. for Children 1989–; Chair. Bd of Govs. Menzies School of Health Research, Darwin 1991–96, Deputy Chair. 1997–2000; Fellow Senate Univ., Sydney 1978–93; Vice-Pres. and Sec. (Biological) Australian Acad. of Science 1998–2002; Pres. Fed. of Asian and Oceanian Physiological Socs 1999–2002, Australian Physiological and Pharmacological Soc. 1996–99; mem. NSW Medical Bd 1999–, Nat. Health and Medical Research Council of Australia 2000–; Alexander von Humboldt Stiftung Research Prize 1999, Prime Minister's Centenary Medal 2003. *Publications:* Morphology of Salivary Glands 1978, Centenary Book of the University of Sydney Medical School 1983, Across the Years 1987; 8 other scientific books, 200 articles in scientific journals and 4 articles in historical journals. *Leisure interests:* history, music. *Address:* College of Health Sciences, Edward Ford Building (A27), University of Sydney, Sydney, NSW 2006, Australia. *Telephone:* (2) 9351-4600. *Fax:* (2) 9351-9926.

YOUNG, Hon. Sir John (McIntosh), AC, KCMG, MA, LLB; Australian judge (retd); b. 17 Dec. 1919, Melbourne; s. of George D. Young and Kathleen M. Young; m. Elisabeth M. Twining 1951; one s. two d.; ed Geelong Grammar School, Brasenose Coll. Oxford, Inner Temple and Univ. of Melbourne; served Scots Guards 1940–46; admitted Victoria Bar 1948; Assoc. to Mr. Justice Dixon, High Court of Australia 1948; practising barrister 1949–74 (QC 1961); Lecturer in Co. Law, Univ. of Melbourne 1957–61; admitted Tasmanian Bar 1964, NSW Bar 1968; consultant, Faculty of Law, Monash Univ. 1968–74; Lt-Gov. of Victoria 1974–95; Chief Justice, Supreme Court of Victoria 1974–91; Chair. Police Bd of Vic. 1992–98; Chancellor, Order of St John in Australia 1982–91; Chief Scout of Australia 1989–96; holder of many other public and charitable offices; Hon. Fellow Brasenose Coll. Oxford 1991; Bailiff, Most Venerable Order of the Hosp. of St John of Jerusalem (GCStJ) 1991; Hon. LLD (Monash) 1986, (Melbourne) 1989. *Publications:* Australian Company Law and Practice (co-author); articles in legal journals. *Leisure interest:* golf. *Address:* 2/18 Huntingtower Road, Armadale, Vic. 3143, Australia.

YOUNG, John Robert Chester, CBE, MA, FRSA; British business executive; b. 6 Sept. 1937; s. of Robert Nisbet Young and Edith Mary Roberts; m. Pauline Joyce Young 1963 (divorced 1997); one s. (one s. deceased) one d.; ed Bishop Vesey's Grammar School, St Edmund Hall, Oxford Univ., Gray's Inn, London; joined Simon & Coates stockbrokers 1961, partner 1965, Deputy Sr Partner 1976; mem. Council London Stock Exchange 1978–82, Dir Policy and Planning 1982–87, Vice-Chair. (non-exec.) Man. Bd 1987–90; CEO and Dir Securities and Futures Authority (fmrly Securities Assocn) 1987–93; Dir Securities and Investment Bd 1993–97, CEO 1993–95; nominated mem. Council of Lloyd's 1996, Deputy Chair. 1997–; mem. Lloyd's Regulatory Bd 1996–, Chair. 1997–; Dir (non-exec.) of E Surrey Healthcare Nat. Health Service Trust 1992–96, of Darby Group PLC 1996–97, of Gartmore Venture Capital Trust 1996–; Public Interest Dir Financial Services Compensation Scheme Ltd 2000–; mem. Ethics Cttee, Securities Inst. 1995–; Adviser to Royal School for the Blind 1997–; fmrly int. athlete, England rugby player and selector. *Leisure interests:* cooking, grandsons, rugby football. *Address:* Office

of the Regulatory Chairman, Lloyds of London, 1 Lime Street, London, EC3M 7HA (Office); Richmond House, Falkland Grove, Dorking, Surrey, RH4 3DL, England (Home). *Telephone:* (20) 7327-1000 (Office). *Fax:* (20) 7327-5599 (Office). *Website:* www.lloydsoflondon.co.uk (Office).

YOUNG, Johnny, BA; American diplomatist; m. Angelena Clark; one s. one d.; ed Temple Univ., Pa; began Foreign Service career as budget and fiscal officer, Antananarivo 1967; Supervisory Gen. Services Officer, Conakry 1970, Nairobi 1972; Admin. Officer and Chargé d'Affaires, Doha 1974; Admin. Counsellor, Bridgetown; Career Devt Officer, Bureau of Personnel 1979; Exec. Dir, Office of the Insp.-Gen. 1981; Admin. Counsellor, Amman 1984; served at The Hague 1985; Amb. (with rank of Minister Counsellor) to Togo, Amb. to Bahrain 1997–2001, to Slovenia 2001–; Meritorious Honor Award, two Group Honor Awards. *Address:* American Embassy, Presernova cesta 31, 1000 Ljubljana, Slovenia (Office). *Telephone:* (1) 2005500 (Office). *Fax:* (1) 2005555 (Office). *E-mail:* email@usembassy.si (Office). *Website:* www .usembassy.si (Office).

YOUNG, Neil; American singer and songwriter; b. 12 Nov. 1945, Toronto, Canada; m. Pegi Young; one s. one d.; began career as lead singer, The Squires; co-f. Buffalo Springfield 1966–69; support to Rolling Stones, Hollywood Bowl 1966; solo artist, with own backing group, Crazy Horse 1969–; with Crosby, Stills, Nash and Young 1969–74; major concerts include Royal Festival Hall, London 1973, The Last Waltz 1976, Miami Music Festival 1977, Live Aid, Philadelphia 1985, Farm Aid II 1987, Nelson Mandela Tribute, Wembley 1990, Bob Dylan's 30th anniversary concert, Madison Square Garden, NY 1992, Reading Festival 1995; Grammy Award, Best New Artist 1970, Melody Maker Poll Winner for Best Int. Group 1971, MTV Video Award 1989, Rolling Stone Critics' Award for Best Album 1989, Bay Area Music Award, Outstanding Album 1993, Q Award for Best Live Act 1993. *Films include:* Rust Never Sleeps (writer and Dir) 1979, Human Highway (writer and Dir) 1982. *Music:* numerous recordings including three albums with Buffalo Springfield, three albums with Crosby, Stills, Nash and Young, numerous solo recordings including Neil Young 1969, After the Goldrush 1970, Crazy Horse 1971, Harvest 1972, Time Fades Away 1973, Tonight's the Night 1975, Comes a Time 1978, Live Rust 1980, Life 1987, American Dream 1988, Freedom 1989, Harvest Moon 1992, Broken Arrow 1996, Year of the Horse 1997. *Address:* c/o Elliot Roberts, Lookout Management, 1460 4th Street, Suite 210, Santa Monica, CA 90404, USA (Office).

YOUNG, Peter Lance, MICE; British business executive; b. 26 June 1938, UK; s. of Harry Aubrey Young and Ethel Freda Young; m. Susan M. Wilkes 1962; three s. one d.; ed Chippenham Grammar School; joined RMC Group PLC 1961, mem. Bd 1977, Deputy Man. Dir 1992, Man. Dir 1993, Group CEO 1996–2000. *Leisure interests:* tennis, gardening. *Address:* c/o RMC Group PLC, RMC House, Coldharbour Lane, Thorpe, Egham, Surrey, TW20 8TD, England.

YOUNG, Richard Stuart; British photographer; b. 17 Sept. 1947, Brocket Hall, Herts.; s. of the late David Young and Hilda Ellison; m. 1st Riita Sinikka Harju 1975 (died 1983); two s.; m. 2nd Susan Manije Walker 1985; one d.; photographer 1974–. *Solo exhbns.:* All Hours 1986, Four Stages of Innocence, RCA 1993, Positive View, Saatchi Gallery 1994, The Night is Young, Grosvenor House 1995, Bad Behaviour, Well Hung Gallery, London 1998. *Publications:* By Invitation Only 1981, Paparazzo 1989. *Leisure interests:* films, travel, books, music, good food. *Telephone:* (20) 8960-4727.

YOUNG, Rosie Margaret, CBE, MD, FRCP, FRCPE, F.R.C.P.(GLAS.), FRACP; British professor of medicine; b. 23 Oct. 1930, Hong Kong; d. of Yeung Shun Hang and Shiu Shui Ying; ed Univ. of Hong Kong; Prof. of Medicine, Univ. of Hong Kong, Hon. Prof. of Medicine 2000; Dean, Faculty of Medicine, Univ. of Hong Kong 1983–85, Pro-Vice-Chancellor 1985–93; Chair. Medical Council of Hong Kong 1988–96; Chair. Hong Kong Educ. Comm. 1993–98; Overseas Adviser, Royal Coll. of Physicians of Edin. 1987–93; mem. Council Royal Australasian Coll. of Physicians 1993–96; JP in Hong Kong 1971; Hon. Fellow Newnham Coll., Cambridge 1988; Gold Bauhinia Star (Hong Kong); Hon. DSc (Hong Kong, Open Learning Inst. of Hong Kong) 1995. *Publications:* over 100 articles in int. medical journals, mostly on diabetes, CHO metabolism and endocrinology. *Address:* Room 413, Professorial Block, Queen Mary Hospital, Pokfulam, Hong Kong Special Administrative Region, People's Republic of China. *Telephone:* 28554253. *Fax:* 28551143.

YOUNG, Simone; Australian conductor and music director; b. 2 March 1961; m. Greg Condon; two d.; ed Sydney Conservatorium of Music; Conductor Vienna Staatsoper, Bastille (Paris), Berlin Staatsoper, Cologne Opera, Royal Opera House (London), Metropolitan Opera (New York), Houston Grand Opera, Los Angeles Opera, New York Philharmonic Orchestra, Oslo Philharmonic Orchestra, Munich Philharmonic Orchestra, Maggio Musicale (Florence), ORF Radio Orchestra Vienna, NDR Hanover, NHK Symphony Orchestra (Japan), Hamburg Philharmonic Orchestra Sydney, Melbourne and West Australian Symphony Orchestras; Chief Conductor Bergen Philharmonic Orchestra 1999–2002; Music Dir Opera Australia 2001–03, Staatsoper Hamburg 2005–; Chevalier Ordre des Arts et des Lettres; Hon. DMus (Monash Univ.) 1998, (Univ. of New South Wales) 2001; Young Australian of the Year 1987. *Repertoire includes:* Rigoletto, Tosca, La Traviata, Oberto, Der fliegende Holländer, Der Rosenkavalier, Macbeth, Elektra, La Bohème, Cavalleria Rusticana, Pagliacci, Tales of Hoffmann, Il Trovatore, Lohengrin, Eugène Onegin, Salomé, Fidelio, Peter Grimes, Wozzeck, La Juive, Der Ring des Nibelungen, Die Meistersinger von Nürnberg, Die Fledermaus, Die Frau ohne Schatten, Faust, Ariadne auf Naxos, Simon Boccanegra, Tannhäuser, Falstaff, Don Carlos, Andrea Chenier, Tristan und Isolde, The Marriage of Figaro, Don Giovanni. *Address:* c/o Arts Management, Level 2, 420 Elizabeth Street, Surry Hills, Sydney, NSW 2010, Australia (Office). *Telephone:* (2) 93102466 (Office). *Fax:* (2) 93105334 (Office). *E-mail:* enquiries@ artsmanagement.com.au (Office).

YOUNG, Wayland (see Kennet, 2nd Baron).

YOUNG OF GRAFFHAM, Baron (Life Peer), cr. 1984, of Graffham in the County of West Sussex; **David Ivor Young,** PC, LLB, DL; British politician and business executive; b. 27 Feb. 1932, London; s. of the late Joseph Young and of Rebecca Young; m. Lita Marianne Shaw 1956; two d.; ed Christ Coll., Finchley and Univ. Coll. London; admitted solicitor 1955; solicitor, Malcolm Slowe, London 1955–56; Exec. Great Universal Stores 1956–61; Chair. Eldonwall Ltd 1961–74, Mfrs Hanover Property Services Ltd 1974–80; Chair. Greenwood Homes Ltd 1976–82; Dir Centre for Policy Studies 1979–82; Special Adviser Dept of Industry 1979–82, of Educ. and Science 1981–82; Chair. Manpower Services Comm. 1982–84; mem., Chair. NEDC 1982–89; Minister without Portfolio 1984–85, Sec. of State for Employment 1985–87, for Trade and Industry and Pres. of Bd of Trade 1987–89; Deputy Chair. Conservative Party 1989–90; Head of Research Project on Tax Simplification, Centre for Policy Studies 2001; Dir Salomon Inc. 1990–94; Head Supervisory Task Force Salomon Bros 1991; Chair. Cable and Wireless 1990–95; Chair. Young Associates Ltd 1996–; Chair. British Org. for Rehabilitation by Training 1975–80 (Pres. 1980–82), Int. Council of Jewish Social and Welfare Services 1981–84, EU–Japan Asscn 1991–97, UCL Council 1995–, London Philharmonic Trust 1995–98, Chichester Festival Theatre Co. Ltd 1997–, Business for Sterling; Pres. Jewish Care 1990–97, Inst. of Dirs 1993–, Nat. Fed. of Enterprise Agencies 1994–98, W Sussex Econ. Forum 1996–; Dir of numerous cos and orgs including Young Assocs Ltd, Acacia City Ltd, Autohit PLC, Elfin Systems Ltd, Pixology Ltd, Pere UK, London Active Man.; Digital Camera Co. Ltd; Industrial Adviser, English Industrial Estates Corpn 1979–80, Special Adviser, mem. 1980–82; DL (W Sussex) 1999; Hon. FRPS 1981; Hon. Fellow Univ. Coll., London 1988. *Publication:* The Enterprise Years: A Businessman in the Cabinet 1990. *Leisure interests:* music, book collecting, photography. *Address:* Young Associates Ltd, Harcourt House, 19 Cavendish Square, London, W1G 0PL, England. *Telephone:* (20) 7447-8800 (Office). *Fax:* (20) 7447-8849 (Office). *E-mail:* young@youngassoc.com (Office).

YOUNG OF OLD SCONE, Baroness (Life Peer), cr. 1997, of Old Scone in the County of Perthshire; **Barbara Scott Young,** MA; British administrator and environmentalist; b. 8 April 1948, Scone; d. of George Young and Mary Young (née Scott); ed Perth Acad., Univ. of Edinburgh, Univ. of Strathclyde; Sector Admin. Greater Glasgow Health Bd 1973–78; Dir of Planning and Devt, St Thomas's Health Dist 1978–79; Dist Gen. Admin. NW Dist Kensington, Chelsea and Westminster Area Health Authority 1979–82; Dist Admin. Haringey Health Authority 1982–85; Dist Gen. Man. Paddington and N Kensington Health Authority 1985–88, Parkside Health Authority 1988–91; Chief Exec. Royal Soc. for the Protection of Birds 1991–98, Vice-Pres. 2000–; Chair. English Nature 1998–2000; Vice-Chair. of BBC 1998–2000; Chief Exec. Environment Agency 2000–; Pres. Inst. of Health Services Man. 1987–88; Vice-Pres. Flora and Fauna Int. 1998–; Patron Inst. of Ecology and Environmental Man. 1993–; mem. BBC Gen. Advisory Council 1985–88, UK Round Table on Sustainable Devt 1995–, World Council Birdlife Int. 1994–98 (Vice-Pres.) 1999–; Trustee Inst. of Public Policy Research 1999–; Hon. DUniv (Stirling) 1995, (Herts.) 1997, (Open Univ., Aberdeen, St Andrews, York) 2000; Hon. DSc (Cranfield) 1998; Green Ribbon Award 2000. *Publications:* What Women Want (contrib.) 1990, Medical Negligence (contrib.) 1990. *Leisure interests:* cinema, gardening. *Address:* Environment Agency, 25th Floor, Millbank Tower, 21–24 Millbank, London, SW1P 4XL, England (Office). *Telephone:* (1454) 624085 (Office). *Fax:* (1454) 624404 (Office). *E-mail:* enquiries@environment-agency.gov.uk. *Website:* www .environment-agency.gov.uk.

YOUNG SEEK CHOUE, LLD; South Korean university chancellor; b. 22 Nov. 1921, Woon San; m. Chung-Myung Oh 1943; two s. two d.; ed Seoul Nat. Univ. and Univ. of Miami; Founder-Pres. Kyung Hee Univ.; Chancellor, Kyung Hee Univ. System; Perpetual Pres. Emer. Int. Asscn of Univ. Pres. (IAUP), fmr Chair.; Chair. High Comm. for Peace; Pres. Inst. of Brighter Soc., Inst. of Int. Peace Studies, Inst. of Asia-Pacific Studies, Centre for Reconstruction of Human Soc., Global Co-operation Soc. Club Int.; Chair. Korean Ass. for Reunion of Ten Million Separated Families, Oughtopian Peace Foundation; initiated UN Int. Day and Year of Peace; recipient of 30 hon. degrees and numerous awards and decorations including UN Special Award for Meritorious Services for Peace 1996. *Publications include:* Democratic Freedom 1948, World Peace through Education 1971, Reconstruction of the Human Society 1975, Oughtopia 1979, World Peace Through Pax UN 1984, World Encyclopedia of Peace 1986, White Paper on World Peace 1991, World Citizenship 1995. *Leisure interests:* golf, tennis, table tennis, travel. *Address:* Office of the Chancellor, Kyung Hee University, 1, Hoegi-Dong, Dongdaemun-gu, Seoul 130-701 (Office); 7-36, 1-Ka, Myungryun-Dong, Jongo-gu, Seoul, Republic of Korea (Home). *Telephone:* (2) 961-0031 (Office); (2) 762-3278 (Home). *Fax:* (2) 962-4343 (Office); (2) 741-3195 (Home). *E-mail:* cie@nms .kyunghee.ac.kr (Office). *Website:* www.kyunghee.ac.kr (Office).

YOUSSOUFI, Abd ar-Rahman el-; Moroccan politician and lawyer; b. 8 March 1924, Tangiers; m. Hélène Youssoufi; ed Univs. of Paris, Poitiers and Nice, Int. Inst. for Human Rights, Strasbourg; activist in union and independence movts.; mem. Istiqlal –1959; left to help set up Union nat. des forces populaires (UNFP), later Union Socialiste des forces populaires (USFP); Asst to Medhi Ben Barka; imprisoned 1959 for anti-state activities; given 2-year prison sentence in political trial in 1963; went into exile in France after release in 1964; spokesman for African and Arab nationalist campaigns and human rights; returned to Morocco early 1980s; Sec. Gen. USFP 1992–93 (left party leadership and went into exile again in protest at outcome of 1993 gen. elections); returned to Morocco 1995 to resume Sec. Gen. post; Prime Minister of Morocco 1998–2002; Grand Collier Ordre de Boyacq, Grande Croix Extra-ordinaire avec Plaque d'Or Ordre du Congrès (Colombia). *Leisure interests:* reading, walking, theatre, music. *Address:* c/o Office of the Prime Minister, Palais Royal, Le Méchouar, Rabat, Morocco.

YSTAD, Vigdis, DPhil; Norwegian professor of Scandinavian literature; b. 13 Jan. 1942, Verdal; d. of Ottar Ystad and Guri Todal; m. 1st Asbjørn Liland 1962; m. 2nd Daniel Haakonsen 1971; one s. one d.; ed Univs. of Trondheim and Oslo; lecturer, Univ. of Oslo 1974, Prof. of Scandinavian Literature 1979–, mem. Univ. Bd 1990–92; Chair. Council for Research in the Humanities 1985; Chair. Bd Centre for Advanced Study, Norwegian Acad. of Science and Letters 1992–93; Vice-Chair. Nat. Acad. of Dramatic Art 1993–96; mem. Norwegian Research Council 1979–85, Norwegian Govt Research Cttee 1982–84; mem. Norwegian Acad. of Science and Letters, Norwegian Acad. for Language and Literature; mem. Bd Nat. Acad. of Art 2000–02, Oslo Acad. of Art 2000–02, Nansenskolen, Lillehammer 2001–; Gen. Ed. Henrik Ibsens skrifter 1998–. *Publications:* Kristofer Uppdals Lyrikk 1978, Henrik Ibsens Dikt 1991, Sigrid Undsel: Et kvinneliv-'livets endeløse gåde' 1993, Ibsens dikt og drama 1996, Contemporary Approaches to Ibsen (Ed.). *Address:* Centre for Ibsen Studies, Box 1116, Blindern, 0316 Oslo (Office); Nils Tollers vei 3, 0851 Oslo, Norway (Home). *Telephone:* 22-85-91-65 (Office); 22-69-10-95 (Home). *Fax:* 22-85-91-69 (Office). *E-mail:* a.v.ystad@ibsen.uio.no (Office).

YU, Nick; Chinese playwright; b. 1971, Anhui Prov.; theatrical Marketing Man.; also part-time playwright; versions of his plays have been performed in Singapore, Japan and USA. *Plays:* The Mental Asylum is Next Door to Heaven, Last Winter 2000, www.com 2001. *Address:* c/o Shanghai People's Art Theatre, 284 Anfu Lu, Shanghai, People's Republic of China (Office).

YU GUANGYUAN; Chinese academic; b. 5 July 1915, Shanghai; ed Qinghua Univ., Beijing; taught in Physics Dept, Lingnan Univ., Guangzhou 1936–37; engaged in youth Movt, land reform, propaganda, culture, journalism, higher educ. and social research 1940s; in CCP Cen. Dept of Propaganda, in charge of social and natural sciences research 1949–75; mem. Academic Cttee, Acad. of Sciences of China 1955–; Deputy Dir State Comm. of Science and Tech. 1964–66, 1977–82; Vice-Pres. Acad. of Social Sciences of China 1978–82, Adviser 1982–87; Pres. Soc. for Study of Marxism, Leninism and Mao Zedong Thought 1980, Soc. of Production Power Economics 1980, Soc. of Research in Dialectics of Nature 1980, Soc. of Territorial Econs 1981; Adviser Environmental Protection Cttee, State Council 1985; Pres. China Environmental Strategy Research Centre 1985; Vice-Pres. China Int. Cultural Centre 1984–; mem. Cen. Advisory Comm. CCP 1982, Pres. Pacific Soc. 1995–. *Publications:* Study of Land Problems in Sui Mi County in China, Exploration of Political Economy of the Socialist Period, Vols I–V, On the Objective Nature of Law, Thesis, Lectures and Notes on Philosophy, Economy of the Primary Period of Socialist China, On the Reform of the Economic Model of China, Economy-Social Development Strategy, Selected Works on Education, My Educational Ideology 1991, On the Central Place of Socialist Market Economy 1992 and numerous other books on Econs and philosophy. *Address:* Chinese Academy of Social Sciences, 5 Jianguomen Nei Da Jie, Beijing 100732, People's Republic of China. *Telephone:* 5137689.

YU GUANGZHONG; Taiwanese university professor, poet, critic, translator and essayist; b. 9 Sept. 1928, Nanjing City, Jiangsu Prov.; m. Wo Chun Fan 1956; four d.; ed Iowa Univ., USA; Chief Ed. of Blue Stars and Modern Literature; Prof. Taiwan Normal Univ., Chinese Univ. of Hong Kong; Kuang Hua Chair. Prof. of English, Nat. Sun Yat-sen Univ. 1998–; Pres. Taipei Chinese Centre, PEN Int. 1990–99; Hon. Fellow Hong Kong Trans. Soc. 1991; Australian Cultural Award 1972; Best Books of the Year 1994, 1996, 1998, 2000 (Taiwan), 1998 (Hong Kong); Nat. Poetry Prize, Wu San-Lian Prose Prize and six others. *Publications:* Elegy of Boatman, Stalactite, Blue Plume, Sirius, White Jade Bitter Gourd, A Tug of War with Eternity, Dream and Geography, Selected Poetry of Yu Guangzhong Vols I and II, The Child of Dogwood–A Life of Yu Guangzhong 1999, The Old Man and the Sea (trans.), The Importance of being Earnest (trans.), Lust for Life (trans.) Bartleby the Scrivener (trans.), Modern English and American Poetry (trans.). *Leisure interests:* travel, hiking, music, museums, maps. *Address:* Foreign Literature Institute, Sun Yat-sen University, 135 Xingang Road, Guanzhou 510275, Guangdong Province, People's Republic of China. *Telephone:* (7) 5564908 (Home); (20) 84112828. *Fax:* (20) 84039173. *E-mail:* adpo@zsu.edu.cn (Office). *Website:* www.zsu.edu.cn (Office).

YU HUA, MA; Chinese writer; b. 1960, Gaotang, Shandong Prov.; ed Beijing Normal Univ.; worked as a dentist for five years. *Publications:* To Live, The Story of Xu Sanguan Selling His Blood, Shouting in the Drizzle, Events of the World Are Like Smoke, One Kind of Reality, Leaving Home for a Long Journey at Eighteen, An Incident, Mistake at Riverside. *Address:* c/o National Human Resources Exchange Centre, Beijing, People's Republic of China (Office).

YU KUO-HWA, BA; Taiwanese politician and banker; b. 10 Jan. 1914, Chekiang; s. of Choping Yu and Eirying Hu; m. Yu Toong Metsung 1946; two s.; ed Tsinghua Univ., Harvard Univ. Graduate School, USA, LSE, UK; Sec. to Pres. of Nat. Mil. Council 1936–44; Alt. Exec. Dir IBRD 1947–50, IMF 1951–55; Pres. Cen. Trust of China 1955–61; Chair. Bd of Dirs. Bank of China 1961–67; Alt. Gov. IBRD 1964–67; Gov. for Repub. of China 1967–69; Minister of Finance 1967–69; Gov. Cen. Bank of China 1969–84; Minister of State 1969–84; Gov. IMF 1969–80, Asian Devt Bank 1969–84; Prime Minister of Taiwan 1984–89; Sr Adviser to Pres. of Taiwan 1989–; Vice-Chair. Kuomintang 1997–; mem. Cen. Standing Cttee, Kuomintang 1979–; Chair. Council for Econ. Planning and Devt 1977–84; Dr. h.c (St John's Univ., Jamaica, New York); Order of Propitious Clouds. *Address:* c/o Office of the President, Taipei, Taiwan.

YU MIN; Chinese physicist; b. Aug. 1926, Ninghe Co., Hebei Prov.; ed Beijing Univ.; mem. Dept of Math. and Physics, Academia Sinica 1985–; Hon. Special Nat. Prizes of Sciences and Tech. 1987, 1989.

YU QIUYU; Chinese writer and critic; b. 1946, Yuyao, Zhenjiang Prov.; ed Shanghai Acad. of Drama; fmrly Prof. and Pres. Shanghai Drama Acad.; Vice-Pres. Shanghai Dramatists Asscn. *Publications:* A Bitter Journey of Culture, Notes Taken while Living in the Mountains, Frost-Cold Long River, Draft History of Dramatic Theories, Dramatic Aesthetic-Psychology, A Narration of the History of Dramatic Culture in China. *Address:* Shanghai Academy of Drama, Shanghai, People's Republic of China (Office).

YU SHYI-KUN; Taiwanese politician; b. 1948, Ilan Co.; ed Chi-li Commercial School, Tung-hai Univ. Dept of Political Science; mem. Seventh Taiwan Prov. Ass. 1981, Eighth 1985; co-f. Democratic Progressive Party (DPP) 1986, elected to First Cen. Standing Cttee 1986, Second 1987, Third 1988, Fourth 1989, Sec. Gen. DPP HQ 1999; Ilan Co. Gov. 1989–97; Exec. Campaign Man. and Spokesperson for DPP cand. Chen Shui-bian's Presidential Campaign 2000; Vice-Premier of Taiwan 2000, also Sec. Gen. Office of the Pres. 2000–02; Premier of Taiwan Jan. 2002–; Deputy Gov. Cen. Bank –2002; f. Lan-yang Cultural and Educ. Foundation 1990, Chair. Taipei Rapid Mass Transit System 1998. *Address:* c/o Office of the President, Chiehshou Hall, 122 Chungking South Road, Sec. 1, Taipei 100, Taiwan (Office). *Telephone:* (2) 23718889 (Office). *Fax:* (2) 23611604 (Office). *E-mail:* public@mail.oop.gov.tw (Office). *Website:* www.oop.gov.tw (Office).

YU WEN; Chinese party official; b. 1918, Shaanxi Prov.; m. Liao Bing; two s. two d.; Deputy Sec.-Gen. Chinese Academy of Sciences 1959; in political disgrace 1967–73; Sec.-Gen. Chinese Acad. of Sciences 1978–83; Perm. Deputy Head, Propaganda Dept CCP 1983–85; Deputy Sec.-Gen. Presidium 6th NPC 1986–; Deputy to 6th NPC for Qinghai Prov. 1986; mem. Standing Cttee NPC 1986–; Vice-Chair. Nationalities Cttee 1986; Head Nat. Examination Cttee for Higher Posts of Journalists 1983; a Vice-Pres. Chinese Acad. of Social Sciences 1990–; Exec. Vice-Pres. Municipal Party School 1990–; a Vice Pres. Asscn for Int. Understanding of China 1993–. *Address:* Central Committee of Chinese Communist Party, Beijing, People's Republic of China.

YU YONGBO, Gen.; Chinese army officer and party official; b. 1931, Fuxian Co., Liaoning Prov.; joined CCP 1948; Dir Political Dept of PLA Nanjing Mil. Area Command 1985–89; Vice-Dir PLA Gen. Political Dept 1989–92, Dir 1992–; rank of Lt-Gen. PLA 1988; mem. Cen. Mil. Comm. 1992–; mem. 14th CCP Cen. Cttee 1992–97; Deputy Head Work Group for Placement of Demobilized Army Officers 1993–; Deputy Head Leading Group for Cracking Down on Smuggling 1993–; rank of Gen.; mem. 15th CCP Cen. Cttee 1997–2002. *Address:* People's Liberation Army Headquarters, c/o Ministry of National Defence, Jingshanqian Jie, Beijing, People's Republic of China.

YU YOUXIAN; Chinese politician; b. 1937, Fenglai Co., Shandong; fmr Vice-Gov. of Henan; Dir Bureau of Press and Publs, State Council 1993–2000; Chair. Asscn of Chinese Publrs. 2000–; mem. CCP Cen. Cttee for Discipline Inspection 1997. *Address:* c/o Press and Publications Administration, State Council, Beijing, People's Republic of China.

YU ZHEN; Chinese politician; b. 1936, Haiyang, Shandong; Vice-Minister of Light Industry 1985–93, Chair. China Nat. Council of Light Industry 1993–98; Pres. China Nat. Light Industrial Machinery Corpn 1983–85; Vice-Minister State Econ. and Trade Comm. 1998–. *Address:* State Economics and Trade Commission, Beijing, People's Republic of China. *Telephone:* 8396250.

YU ZHENGSHENG; Chinese politician; b. April 1945, Shaoxin City, Zhejiang Prov.; ed Harbin Mil. Eng Inst.; joined CCP 1964; Vice-Chair. Exec. Council of Welfare Fund for the Handicapped 1984; Vice-Sec. CCP Yantai City Cttee and Vice-Mayor Yantai City 1985, Mayor 1987; Sec. CCP Qingdao City Cttee and Mayor Qingdao City 1992; alt. mem. 14th CCP Cen. Cttee 1992, mem. 15th CCP Cen. Cttee 1997–2002; Vice-Minister of Construction 1997–98, Minister 1998–2001; Sec. CCP Hubei Prov. Cttee 2001–. *Address:* c/o Ministry of Construction, Baiwanzhuang, Western Suburb, Beijing 100835, People's Republic of China.

YU ZHENWU, Lt-Gen.; Chinese air force officer; b. 1931, Kuangdian Co., Liaoning Prov.; ed PLA Air Force Aviation School; mem. CCP 1947–; Regt Chief Navigating Officer, PLA Air Force 1951; served in Korean War 1953; Group Commdr PLA Air Force 1954–55; Corps Chief Officer in charge of firing training 1957; Regt Commdr 1964; Deputy Div. Commdr 1969–73; Deputy Dir Mil. Training Dept PLA Air Force 1973–77; Dir 1977–79; Corps Commdr 1979–83; Commdr Air Force of Guangdong Mil. Dist 1983–85; Deputy

Commdr PLA Air Force 1985–95, Commdr 1995–97, now Deputy Sec.; alt. mem. 12th and 13th CCP Cen. Cttee. *Address:* c/o Ministry of National Defence, Jingshanqian Jie, Beijing, People's Republic of China.

YUAN ENFENG; Chinese folk singer; b. 22 Jan. 1940, Shaanxi Prov.; d. of Yuan Zaiming and Li Dexian; m. Sun Shao, composer; one s. two d.; ed Dong Yangshi Elementary School, Xian; joined Cultural Troupe of Provincial Broadcasting Station 1951; participated in over 3,000 performances, including numerous solo concerts and 1,000 radio and TV programmes; appearances abroad include Romania, Bulgaria, fmr Czechoslovakia, fmr USSR, Japan, Thailand, Philippines and USA; Hon. Dir and Chair. Folk Music Section, Shaanxi Broadcasting Station 1986–; Vice-Chair. Shaanxi TV Station; mem. Chinese Musicians' Asscn; mem. of Bd, Shaanxi Br., Chinese Cultural Exchange Centre; mem. of many other official orgs; State Actress Award 1987, May Day Labour Medal Award 1993. *TV film:* Silver Bell. *Compositions (with Sun Shao) include:* Millet is Delicious and Caves are Warm, Nowhere is Better than Our North Shaanxi; many recordings and song books; 300 songs on record, cassette and CD. *Leisure interests:* table tennis, fabric weaving. *Address:* Folk Music Section, Provincial Broadcasting and Television Station, Xian, Shaanxi, People's Republic of China. *Telephone:* (29) 7852689.

YUAN GUIREN; Chinese academic; b. Nov. 1950, Guzhen, Anhui Prov.; fmrly Prof. of Philosophy, Vice-Pres., Sec. CCP Cttee, Beijing Normal Univ.; Asst. Mayor of Beijing and Dir Beijing Educational Comm.; Pres. Beijing Normal Univ. 1999–. *Publications:* Zhexue (Philosophy), Ren de Zhexue (The Philosophy of Man), Guanli Zhexue (The Philosophy of Management), Deng Xiaoping Lilun Gailun (Introduction to Deng Xiaoping's Theory). *Address:* Beijing Normal University, 19 Xinjiekouwai Da Jie, Beijing 1000875, People's Republic of China (Office). *Telephone:* (10) 62207960 (Office). *Fax:* (10) 62299974 (Office). *E-mail:* ipo@bnu.edu.cn (Office). *Website:* www.bnu.edu.cn (Office).

YUAN LONGPING; Chinese agronomist; b. 7 Sept. 1930, Beijing; s. of Yuan Xin-Lie and Hua Jing; m. Deng Ze 1964; three s.; teacher Hunan Prov. 1964–; Deputy, 5th NPC 1978–83; Sr Rice Breeder Agric. Acad. of Hunan Prov. 1981–; mem. Standing Cttee 6th CPPCC 1982–88; Vice-Chair. CCP 7th Hunan Prov. Cttee; Dir Hybrid Rice Research Centre under the Hunan Acad. of Agricultural Sciences 1985–; Gold Medal, UN World Property Org. 1985, Laureate of Science Prize, UNESCO 1987, Rank Prize for Food 1988. *Leisure interests:* violin, swimming. *Address:* Hunan Academy of Agricultural Sciences, Mapoling, Furong District, Changsha 410125, Hunan Province, People's Republic of China. *Telephone:* (731) 4080755. *Fax:* (731) 4691877. *E-mail:* lpyuan@public.cs.hn.cn (Office).

YUAN SHOUFANG, Gen.; Chinese army officer; b. Jan. 1939, Jilin City, Jilin Prov.; ed PLA Political Acad.; joined PLA 1958; joined CCP 1962; Dir Army Political Dept 1983; Vice-Dir Political Dept of Ji'nan Mil. Area Command 1985 then Dir; rank of Maj.-Gen. 1988; Asst Dir then Vice-Dir PLA Gen. Political Dept; mem. 14th CCP Cen. Comm. for Discipline Inspection 1992; alt. mem. 15th CCP Cen. Cttee 1997–2002; rank of Gen. 2000. *Address:* People's Liberation Army General Political Department, Beijing, People's Republic of China.

YUAN TSEH LEE, MS, PhD; American professor of chemistry; b. 19 Nov. 1936, Hsinchu, Taiwan; s. of Tsefan Lee and Pei Tsai; m. Bernice Wu 1963; two s. one d.; ed Nat. Taiwan Univ., Nat. Tsinghua Univ. and Univ. of Calif. at Berkeley; postgraduate work in Prof. Bruce Mahan's group, Univ. of Calif. at Berkeley 1962–67; Post-doctoral Fellow, Harvard Univ. 1967–68; Asst Prof. Dept of Chemistry and James Franck Inst. Univ. of Chicago 1968, Assoc. Prof. 1971, Prof. 1973–74; Prof. of Chem. and Prin. Investigator, Lawrence Berkeley Lab. Univ. of Calif. at Berkeley 1974; mem. NAS, Academia Sinica, Taiwan; Fellow, American Acad. of Arts and Science, American Physical Soc.; Nat. Medal of Science 1986; shared Nobel Prize for Chemistry 1986; Dr. hc (Waterloo) 1986; other awards and distinctions. *Address:* Academy Sinica, Nankang, Taipei 11529, Taiwan.

YUAN WEIMIN; Chinese sports administrator and civil servant; b. July 1939, Suzhou, Jiangsu Prov.; joined CCP 1962; joined Chinese Men's Volleyball Team 1962; Chief Coach of Chinese Women's Volleyball Team; Vice-Chair. All-China Sports Fed.; Vice-Chair. Chinese Olympics Cttee; Chair. Chinese Volleyball Asscn, Chinese Football Asscn; Exec. Vice-Chair. Asian Volleyball Fed. 1976–84; Vice-Chair. State Comm. for Physical Culture and Sports 1984–98; Minister in charge of State Gen. Admin. for Sports 2000–; alt. mem. CCP 12th Cen. Cttee 1982–87; mem. CCP 13th and 14th Cen. Cttee 1987–97; alt. mem. CCP 15th Cen. Cttee 1997–2002. *Publication:* My Way of Coaching. *Address:* 9 Tiyuguan Road, Chongwen District, Beijing 100763, People's Republic of China.

YUAN ZHONGYI, MA; Chinese archaeologist; b. 1932, Jiangsu Prov.; m. Liu Yu; one d.; ed East China Teachers' Univ.; Vice-Dir Shaanxi Prov. Archaeological Research Inst. and Curator Qin Shi Huang's Terracotta Army Museum; Del. Fifth People's Congress, Council of China; Outstanding Prof. of Shaanxi Prov., First Class of Nat. Excellence for book on Qin Dynasty Pottery Inscriptions and other book awards. *Publications:* Studies of the Terracotta Army at Qin Shi Huang's Mausoleum, Pottery Inscriptions of the Qin Dynasty, The Pits of Terracotta Warriors and Horses of Qin Shihuang Mausoleum – An Excavation of No. 1 Pit, An Excavation Report on the Bronze Chariots and Horses of Qin Shihuang Mausoleum. *Leisure interest:* handwriting. *Address:* Qin Shi Huang's Terracotta Army Museum, Lintong, Xian, People's Republic of China. *Telephone:* (29) 3911975. *Fax:* (29) 3912829. *E-mail:* zzl@pub.xaonline.sn.cn.

YUASA, Joji; Japanese composer and professor of music; b. 12 Aug. 1929, Koriyama City; s. of Daitaro Yuasa and Otoe Yuasa; m. Reiko Suzuki 1958; one s. one d.; ed Asaka High School, Keio Univ.; orchestral works commissioned by Kousevitzky Music Foundation 1974, Inst. for Research and Co-ordination in Acoustics and Music 1988, Suntory Music Foundation and by orchestras in Japan, Germany and Finland; Prof. of Music, Univ. of Calif. at San Diego 1981–94, Prof. Emer. 1994–; Prof. of Music, Nihon Univ. 1994–; Visiting Prof., Tokyo Coll. of Music; mem. Experimental Workshop, Tokyo 1952; featured composer, Festival of the Arts of this Century, Hawaii 1970, Pacific Music Festival, Sapporo 1990, Music Today Festival, Tokyo 1992; mem. Int. Jury for World Music Days, Int. Soc. for Contemporary Music (ISCM) 1971, 1983, 1992, 2001; Composer-in-Residence, Centre for Music Experiment, Univ. of Calif. at San Diego 1976, NSW Conservatorium of Music, Australia 1980, Univ. of Toronto, Canada 1981; a leader for Int. Composers' Workshops, Amsterdam 1984, 1992; Medal with Purple Ribbon 1997; 8 awards from ISCM 1971–91, Odaka Prizes for Orchestra 1972, 1988, 1997, 2003, Kyoto Music Prize Grand Prix 1995, Suntory Music Prize 1996, Japan Acad. Prize 1999, Imperial Prize 1999. *Film scores:* Osōshiki (The Funeral) (dir Jyuzo Itami), Fukuro no Shiro (The Castle of Owls) (dir Mazathiro Shinoda). *Compositions include:* Time of Orchestral Time 1976, Scenes from Basho (suite) 1980–89, Revealed Time for viola and orchestra 1986, Cosmos Haptic II for piano 1986, Nine Levels by Ze-Ami for chamber ensemble and quadraphonic tape 1988, Eye on Genesis II for orchestra 1992, Piano Concertino 1994, Symphonic Suite; The Narrow Road into the Deep North: Basho 1995, Libera me, in Requiem of Reconciliation 1995. *Radio:* Comet Ikeya (Prix Italia for stereophonic section) 1966, Ai to Shura (Prix Italia for stereophonic section) 1967 and others. *Television:* Yoshinobu Tokugawa (NHK) 1999 and others. *Publications:* To the Cosmology of Music 1981, A Half of the Life – Towards the Open Horizon of Music 1999. *Leisure interests:* skiing, reading. *Address:* 1517 Shields Avenue, Encinitas, CA 92024, USA; 7-16-21-101 Ikegami, Ohta-ku, Tokyo 146-0082, Japan (Home). *Telephone:* (760) 436-3775 (USA); (3) 3754-8710 (Japan). *Fax:* (760) 436-0271 (USA); (3) 3754-8710 (Japan).

YUDASHKIN, Valentin Abramovich; Russian fashion designer; b. 14 Oct. 1963, Bakovka, Moscow Region; m. Marina Vladimirovna Yudashkina; one d.; ed Moscow Industrial Pedagogical Inst.; fashion designer; Founder and Artistic Dir Vali-Moda 1987, Founder and Dir Velentin Yudashkin Presents Co. 1989; participated in maj. fashion shows, including Paris 1990–92, Los Angeles (Beverly Hills Hilton), Israel, Egypt, Italy, etc.; costume designer to several Moscow Theatre New Opera productions; opened Valentin Yudashkin House of Fashion 1993; mem. Paris Haute Couture Syndicate 1996. *Address:* Valentin Yudashkin Fashion House, Kutuzovsky pr. 19, 121151 Moscow, Russia. *Telephone:* (095) 240-11-89 (Office).

YUE QIFENG; Chinese government official; b. 1931, Daming Co., Hebei Prov.; joined CCP 1945; Deputy Sec. Hebei Prov. CCP Cttee 1986–90; Gov. of Liaoning Prov. 1991; Sec. CPC 7th Heilongjiang Prov. Cttee 1994–; mem. 14th CCP Cen. Cttee 1992–97. *Address:* Heilongjiang Provincial Committee of the CPC, 294 Huayuan Street, Harbin 15011, People's Republic of China. *Telephone:* (451) 3630618. *Fax:* (451) 3635140.

YUEN WOO-PING; Chinese film director, actor and choreographer; b. Yuan He-Ping, 1945, Guangzhou, Canton; s. of Yuen Hsiao-Tien; born into a family of Peking Opera artists, learned martial arts; worked with Jackie Chan, Donnie Yen, Ng See Yuen. *Films directed include:* Snake in the Eagle's Shadow 1978, Magnificent Butcher 1979, Drunken Master 1979, Dreadnaught 1981, Drunken Tai-Chi 1984, Mismatched Couples 1985, Tiger Cage 1988, In the Line of Duty 4 1989, Tiger Cage 2 1990, Tiger Cage 3 1991, The Wicked City 1992, Last Hero in China 1993, The Tai Chi Master 1993, The Iron Monkey 1993, Heroes Among Heroes 1993, Wing Chun 1994, Fist of Legend 1994, Fiery Dragon Kid 1995, Tai Chi 2 1996. *Films acted in include:* Miracle Fighters 1982, Mismatched Couples 1985, Eastern Condors 1986, Wicked City 1992, Cinema of Vengeance 1994. *Films choreographed include:* Fist of Legend 1994, Black Mask 1996, The Matrix 1999. *Television:* produced TV Series The Practice 1976.

YULDASHEV, Bekhzad, PhD; Uzbekistan nuclear physicist, administrator and politician; b. 9 May 1945, Tashkent; m.; two s.; ed Tashkent Univ., Moscow Univ.; research in particle and nuclear physics, Jt Inst. of Nuclear Research, Dubna, USSR 1968–71; Sr Researcher, Physical Tech. Inst., Tashkent 1972–83, Head of Lab. 1984–90; Dir-Gen. Inst. of Nuclear Physics, Uzbekistan Acad. of Sciences 1990–, Pres. Acad. of Sciences 2000–; mem. Parl. 2000–; Visiting Prof. Univ. of Washington, Seattle 1977–78, 1980–81, 1989–90; mem. Uzbekistan Acad. of Sciences, American Physical Soc., Scientific Council, Jt Inst. of Nuclear Research, Dubna; Fellow Islamic Acad. of Sciences; Hon. Fellow Indiana Univ. 1997; State Prize in Science and Tech. 1983. *Publications:* more than 250 papers in int. physics journals. *Address:* Uzbekistan Academy of Sciences, Gulyamov St. 70, 700000 Tashkent, Uzbekistan (Office). *Telephone:* (712) 133-68-47 (Office). *Fax:* (712) 133-49-01 (Office). *E-mail:* yuldashev@iae.tashkent.su.

YUMASHEV, Valentin Borisovich; Russian politician and journalist; b. 15 Dec. 1957, Perm; m. 1st; one d.; m. 2nd Tatiana Dyachenko (d. of fmr Pres. Yeltsin, q.v.,); ed Moscow State Univ.; errand boy newspaper Komsomolskaya

Pravda 1976; corresp., Sr corresp. newspaper Komsomolskaya Pravda 1978–87; Moskovsky Komsomolets 1987–89; took part in election campaign of Boris Yeltsin to Supreme Soviet 1988, 1992, 1996; Head of Div., Ed., Deputy Ed.-in-Chief Ogonyok 1987–96; Adviser to Russian Press on mass media 1996–; Head of Admin. Pres. Yeltsin 1997–98; Adviser to Boris Yeltsin 1998–; helped Pres. Yeltsin in writing memoirs. *Leisure interest:* tennis. *Address:* c/o Office of the President, Kremlin, korps 1, Moscow, Russia (Office). *Telephone:* (095) 910-10-89, (095) 206-60-88 (Office).

YUN JONG-YONG, BA; South Korean business executive; b. 21 Jan. 1944, Youngchun, Kyoung-buk; m.; one s. one d.; ed Seoul Nat. Univ., MIT Sloan School, USA; joined Samsung Group 1966, with Samsung Electronics Co. Ltd 1969–, Head Tokyo office 1977–80, Head TV Business Div. 1980–81, Head Video Business Div. 1981–85, Head of Research and Devt Div. 1985–88, Vice-Pres. Electronics Group 1988–90, Vice-Pres. and Rep. Dir Consumer Electronics Business Group 1990–92 (Pres. and Rep. Dir 1992–96), Pres. and CEO Samsung Electronics Co. Ltd 1996–99, Vice-Chair. and CEO Dec. 1999–; Pres. and CEO Samsung Electro-Mechanics Co. Ltd 1992, Samsung Display Devices Co. Ltd 1993, Samsung Japan HQ 1995; Chair. Nat. Acad. of Eng of Korea, Fed. of Korean Information Industries; Prize for Most Successful CEO in Korea (Korea Man. Asscn) 1999; Gold Medal for Contrib. to Industry 1992, Outstanding Achievement in Man. (Inst. of Inc. Engineers) 1998, Asia's Businessman of the Year (Fortune) 2000, CEOs' Choice Award, Asia Business Leader Awards 2002. *Leisure interest:* golf. *Address:* Samsung Electronics Co. Ltd., Samsung Main Building, 250 Taepyeong-ro 2-ga Jung-gu, Seoul 100-742, Republic of Korea (Office). *Telephone:* (2) 727-3355 (Office). *Website:* www .samsungelectronics.com/kr (Office).

YUNIUPINGU, (James) Galarrwuy, AM; Australian community leader and business executive; b. 30 June 1948, Melville Bay, nr Yirrkala, Gove; ed Mission School, Yirrkala, Methodist Bible Coll., Brisbane; active in Gumatj Clan's land struggle in 1960s; joined Interim Northern Land Council 1975, Chair. 1977–80, 1983–; Chair. Gumatj Asscn Inc. 1983–; Public Officer/Dir Yunupingu Industries 1983–; Chair. YBE Pty Ltd 1988–92; Co-Chair. Aboriginal Devt Consultative Forum 2000; Dir Garrangali Crocodile Farm 1991–, Gawpu Marine 1991–; mem. Australian Crocodile Farmers Asscn 1990–, Council for Aboriginal Reconciliation 1991–96; Exec. Dir Yothu Yindi 1992–, Yothu Yindu Foundation 1998–; Gumatj Clan Leader 1979–; also singer and songwriter; Australian of the Year 1978, honoured as one of Australia's Nat. Living Treasures 1998. *Publication:* Our Land Is Our Life. *Leisure interests:* fishing, hunting, songwriting, Australian Rules Football. *Address:* Northern Land Council, P.O. Box 42921, Casuarina, NT 0811, Australia (Office). *Telephone:* (8) 8920-5100 (Office). *Fax:* (8) 8945-2633 (Office).

YUNUS, Muhammad; Bangladeshi banker and professor; m. Afrizi Yunus; one d.; ed Vanderbilt Univ.; Prof. of Econs Chittagong Univ. 1976; f. Grameen Bank Project, pioneering microcredit loans to those in extreme poverty Dec. 1976, changed to ind. bank, Grameen Bank Sept. 1983, now Man. Dir, CEO; Dir UN Foundation; mem. Int. Advisory Group, Fourth World Conference on Women, Beijing 1993–95, Advisory Council for Sustainable Econ. Devt 1993, UN Expert Group on Women and Finance; Founding Man. Dir German Telephones 1998–; Hon. LLD (Warwick) 1996; Independence Day Award, President's Award and Central Bank Award (all Bangladesh), Ramon Magsaysay Award (Philippines), Aga Khan Award for Architecture, Mohamed Shabdeen Award for Science (Sri Lanka), World Food Prize (USA). *Address:* Grameen Bank, Mirpur 2, P.O. Box 1216, Dhaka 1216, Bangladesh. *Telephone:* (2) 801138. *Fax:* (2) 803559. *E-mail:* grameen.bank@grameen.net (Office).

YURKO, Allen; Canadian business executive; b. 1951; COO Siebe 1992–94, CEO 1994–98; CEO Invensys PLC (following merger of Siebe and BTR) 1998–2001. *Address:* c/o Invensys PLC, Carlisle Place, London, SW1P 1BX, England (Office).

YURSKY, Sergei Yurievich; Russian actor, stage manager, film director and writer; b. 16 March 1935, Leningrad (now St Petersburg); s. of the late Yury Yursky and Eugenia Romanova; m. 1st Natalia Tenyakova 1970 (deceased); m. 2nd Daria Jouzskaia 1973; one d.; ed Leningrad Univ., Leningrad Theatrical Inst.; worked for Gorky Theatre, Leningrad 1957–79, Mossoviet Theatre 1978–87 and other theatres in Moscow, Paris and Brussels; acted in films 1960–; one-man performances in 70 cities in USSR 1965–, in Czechoslovakia 1985, Japan 1986, France 1987, 1991, Italy 1987, Switzerland 1989, Israel 1992, Belgium 1993, USA 1994, Germany 1994; world tour with programme 'Pushkin and Others' 1999, including USA, Japan, Germany, France, England and Scotland; with programme 'From the First Person' to USA, Canada, Israel, Lithuania 2002; Order of Honour 1995; People's Artist of the RSFSR 1987, Gold Mask (Moscow) 1998. *Stage roles:* over 60, including Chatsky (Woe from Wit) 1963, Tousenbach (Three Sisters) 1965, Victor Frank (Price) 1968, Henry IV (Henry IV) 1969, Molière (Molière; also dir) 1973, Groznov (Truth is Good, but Happiness is Better; also dir) 1980, Ornifle (Ornifle or Draught; also dir) 1986, King Beranger (The King is Dying, Ionesco) 1992, Azriel (Dibouk!) 1992, Glov (after Gamblers XXI, Gogol; also dir) 1992, Le Baron Cazou (Les Amants Puérils) 1993, Old Man (after Ionescu, also dir) 1994, Foma Opiskin (after Dostoevsky) 1995, Vogler (After The Rehearsal, Bergman) 1996, Malkovic (The Provocation, after Vatsetis; also dir), Libero Bocca (Ferrous Class) 1999, Jazda (The Nobody) 2002. *Radio appearances include roles in:* The Master Builder (also dir) 1996, The Chairs (also dir) 2000. *Television work includes:* Eugene Onegin (eight episodes)

1998. *Films:* A Man from Nowhere 1969, The Golden Calf 1968, The Little Tragedies 1980, The Fall of Condor 1984, Love and Pigeons 1985, The Abyss 1987, The Picture 1989, Chernov/Chernov (also screenplay and dir) 1990 (Prizewinner, Karlovy Vary/Carlsbad Film Festival 1990), The Silencer 1993, Le Bonheur 1993, The Queen Margot 1997, Oligarkh 2003. *Publications:* Who Keeps the Pause 1977, enlarged edn 1989, During the Timeless Times (short stories) 1989, Recognizing (poetry), The Jest (poetry) 1997, The Contents of the Box (short stories) 1999, Play the Life 2002, Spotikatch (35 stories) 2001–03. *Leisure interest:* cat Souss. *Address:* Gagarinsky per. 35, Apt 4, 119002 Moscow, Russia. *Telephone:* (095) 241-52-71. *Fax:* (095) 241-52-71.

YUSHCHENKO, Viktor Andriyovich, CAND.ECON.SC.; Ukrainian economist, banker and politician; b. 23 Feb. 1954, Khoruzhivka, Sumy Region; m.; one s. two d.; ed Ternopil Inst. of Finance and Econ.; economist, Br. Dir USSR State Bank, Ulianivskyi Dist, Sumy Region 1976–85, Deputy Dir of Agric. Credits, Ukrainian Br. of USSR State Bank 1985–87; Dept Dir Ukrainian Bank (fmrly Ukrainian Agro-Industrial Bank) 1987–91, First Deputy Chair. 1991–93; Gov. Nat. Bank of Ukraine 1993–99; Chair. Nasha Ukraina (Our Ukraine) party; Prime Minister of Ukraine 1999–2001; mem. Parl. 2002–; mem. Ukrainian Acad. of Econ. Sciences, Acad. of Econ. and Cybernetics; Dr hc (Kiivo-Mogilanskaya Acad.), (Ostroh Acad.); Global Finance Award 1997. *Publications:* over 250 articles and research papers in Ukrainian and int. journals. *Leisure interests:* painting, pottery, wood-carving. *Address:* c/o Cabinet of Ministers, M. Hrushevskoho str. 12/2, 252008 Kiev, Ukraine.

YUSHKIAVITSHUS, Henrikas Alguirdas; Russian/Lithuanian international civil servant; b. Henrikes Alguirdas Yushkiavitshus, 30 March 1935, Šiauliai, Lithuania; s. of Zigmas Yushkiavitshus and Stefa Biknevitchiutė; m. Elena Samuilytė 1961; one d.; ed Leningrad Electrotechnical Communication Inst.; Dir Technological Dept Lithuanian Radio and TV 1960–66; Dir Tech. Centre, Int. Radio and TV Org. 1966–71; Vice-Chair USSR State Cttee for TV and Radio 1971–90; Chair. Interministerial Cttee for Radio and TV Devt and mem. Interministerial Cttee for Satellite Communications 1971–90; Asst Dir-Gen. for Communication, Information and Informatics, UNESCO 1990–2001, Chargé de mission UNESCO 2001–; Corresp. mem. Russian Eng Acad., mem. Int. Acad. of Electrotechnical Sciences; Fellow Soc. of Motion Picture and TV Engineers (SMPTE), USA; Hon. Academician, Russian Acad. of Information; recipient of several Soviet and Russian decorations etc.; Order of Gediminas, Lithuania 1996; Dr hc (Int. Inst. for Advanced Studies in Systems Research and Cybernetics, Canada);Emmy Directorate Award, US Nat. Acad. of TV Arts and Sciences. *Publications:* contribs to professional journals. *Leisure interests:* tennis, reading, music. *Address:* c/o UNESCO, 1 rue Miollis, 75732 Paris, Cedex 15 (Office); 23 rue Ginoux, 75015 Paris, France (Home). *Telephone:* 1-45-68-13-08 (Office); 1-45-77-20-84 (Home). *Fax:* 1-45-68-57-89 (Office); 1-45-75-21-82 (Home). *E-mail:* henrikas@noos.fr (Home).

YUSUF, Hamza; American theologian; b. (as Mark Hanson), 1959; converted to Islam at age 17; Founder and Dir Zaytuna Islamic Inst., Calif.; Islamic scholar; adviser to Pres. George W. Bush on religious issues. *Address:* Zaytuna Institute, 631 Jackson Street, Hayward, CA 94544-1533, USA (Office). *Telephone:* (510) 582-1979 (Office). *E-mail:* info@zaytuna.org (Office).

YUVENALIY, Metropolitan (Vladimir Kyrillovich Poyarkov); Russian Orthodox ecclesiastic; b. 22 Sept. 1935, Yaroslavl; ed Leningrad Seminary, Moscow Theological Acad.; celibate priest 1960; Sec. Dept of Foreign Relations Moscow Patriarchy 1960; teacher Moscow Seminary 1961–62; Ed. magazine Golos Pravoslavia 1962–63; Dean Russian Orthodox church in West Berlin 1962–63; ordained as archimandrite 1963; Chief Russian Holy Mission in Jerusalem 1963–64; Deputy Chair. Dept of Foreign Relations of Moscow Patriarchy 1964–72, Chair. 1972–81; ordained as bishop 1965; Bishop of Zaraisk, Vicar of Moscow Diocese 1965–69; Bishop of Tula and Belev, Archbishop, Metropolitan 1969–77; perm. mem. Holy Synod 1972–; Metropolitan of Krutitsy and Kolomna 1977–; Chair. Synodal Comm. on Canonization of Saints; Order of Peoples' Friendship 1985, Order of Honour 2000 and other decorations. *Address:* Moscow Diocese, Novodevichy Proezd 1/1, 119435 Moscow, Russia. *Telephone:* (095) 246-08-81.

YUZHANOV, Ilya Arturovich, CAND.ECON.; Russian politician and economist; b. 7 Feb. 1960, Leningrad (now St Petersburg); m.; three c.; ed Leningrad State Univ.; teacher, lecturer in Leningrad insts 1982–90; chief specialist Leningrad Cttee on Econ. Reforms 1990–91; Head of Dept, First Deputy Chair. Cttee on Econ. Devt St Petersburg 1991–94; Chair. Cttee on Land Resources of St Petersburg 1994–97; Chair. State Cttee on Land Resources of Russian Fed. 1997–98; Minister on Land Policy, Construction and Communal Econs May–Sept. 1998; Minister of Antimonopoly Policy and Support for Entrepreneurship 1999–; Medal in Commemoration of 850th Anniversary of Founding of Moscow 1997, Merited Economist of Russian Fed. 2000. *Publications:* monographs and numerous articles in journals and newspapers on antimonopoly and other problems in Econs. *Leisure interest:* sport. *Address:* Ministry of Antimonopoly Policy and Support for Entrepreneurship, Sadovaya-Kudrinskaya str. 11, 123995 Moscow, Russia (Office). *Telephone:* (095) 254-96-97 (Office). *Fax:* (095) 252-66-40 (Office). *E-mail:* gak1@infpres.com (Office). *Website:* www.maprus.ru (Office).

ZACHARIUS, Walter, BA; American publisher; b. 16 Oct. 1923, New York; s. of Abraham Zacharius and Sara Cohen; m. Alice Riesenberg 1948; one s. one d.; ed Coll. of City of New York School of Business, New York Univ., New School of Social Research, Empire State Univ.; served US Army 1942–45; circulation depts McFadden Publishing Inc. 1947–, Popular Library Inc. 1948–49, American Mercury Inc. 1949–51; Circulation Dir Ace News Co., New York 1951–61; Pres. Magnum Royal Publs Inc., New York 1961–; Pres., Chair. of Bd Magnum Communications, New York 1961–; Pres. Lancer Books Inc., New York 1961–75, Walter Zacharius Assoc. 1964–, United Cerebral Palsy of Queens 1986–89; Chair. Bd Kensington Publishing Corpn Inc. 1976–; World War II Medal, American Service Medal; European-African-Middle Eastern Service Medal; Public Relations Award-United Cerebral Palsy of Queens 1970, Award of Honor, UJA Fed. Campaign 1987, UJA Fed.'s Distinguished Service Award 1992, Gallatin Div. of New York City Certificate of Distinction 1993. *Leisure interests:* tennis, horseback riding, art collecting, reading, charity work, piano. *Address:* Kensington Publishing Corporation, 850 3rd Avenue, New York, NY 10022 (Office); 400 East 56th Street, New York, NY 10022, USA (Home). *Telephone:* (212) 407-1500 (Office); (212) 752-0384 (Home). *Fax:* (212) 407-1591 (Office). *E-mail:* wzacharius@kensingtonbooks .com (Office).

ZACHAU, Hans G., Dr rer. nat; German molecular biologist; b. 16 May 1930, Berlin; s. of Dr Erich Zachau and Dr Gertrud Zachau; m. Elisabeth Vorster 1960; three s.; ed Univs. of Frankfurt am Main and Tübingen; Postdoctoral Fellow, MIT and Rockefeller Univ. 1956–58; Max-Planck-Inst. für Biochemie, Munich 1958–61; Inst. für Genetik, Cologne 1961–66; Prof. of Physiological Chemistry and Head of Inst., Univ. of Munich 1967–98, Prof. Emer. 1998–; Chancellor Orden pour le mérite 1992–; mem. Deutsche Akad. der Naturforscher Leopoldina, Austrian, Russian and Bavarian Acads, Academia Europaea; Hon. mem. American Soc. of Biological Chemists; Grosses Bundesverdienstkreuz mit Stern; Bayerischer Verdienstorden; Richard Kuhn Medaille, Otto Warburg Medaille, Maximiliansorden. *Publications:* numerous publs in professional journals. *Address:* Adolf-Butenandt-Institut der Ludwig-Maximilians-Universität, Molekularbiologie, Schillerstrasse 44, 80336 Munich (Office); Pfingstrosenstr. 5a, 81377 Munich, Germany. *Telephone:* (89) 5996429 (Office); (89) 7147575 (Home). *Fax:* (89) 5996425 (Office); (89) 74141733 (Home). *E-mail:* zachau@bio.med.uni-muenchen .de (Office and Home). *Website:* www.med.uni-muenchen.de/biochemie/ zachau (Office).

ZACKHEOS, Sotirios, MA; Cypriot diplomatist; b. 24 Jan. 1950, Nicosia; m.; two c.; ed Univ. of Athens and Stanford Univ., USA; Counsellor Embassy, Moscow 1979–85; Amb. to China (also accred to Japan, Pakistan, The Philippines and Mongolia) 1989–93; Dir of Econ. Affairs, Foreign Ministry 1993, of Political Affairs 1995; Perm. Rep. to UN, Geneva 1996–97, Amb., Perm. Rep. to UN, New York 1997–, Chair. Fourth Cttee (Special Political and Decolonization) 1999; High Commr (non-resident) to St Lucia, Grenada and Trinidad & Tobago 1997–; Amb. (non-resident) to Suriname 1997–; Pancyprian Asscn of Florida Man of the Year Award 2003. *Publications:* contribs to Anthology of Young Cypriot Poets, Justice Pending: Indigenous Peoples and Other Good Causes (contrib.); numerous articles in Cypriot newspapers. *Address:* Permanent Mission of Cyprus to the United Nations, 13 East 40th Street, New York, NY 10016, USA (Office). *Telephone:* (212) 481-6023 (Office). *Fax:* (212) 685-7316 (Office). *E-mail:* cyprus@un.int (Office). *Website:* www.un .int/cyprus.

ZACKIOS, Gerald M.; Marshall Islands government minister and lawyer; ed Int. Maritime Law Inst.; Attorney-Gen. 1995–2001; Minister of Foreign Affairs and Minister in Assistance to the Pres., then Minister of Foreign Affairs and Trade 2001–. *Address:* Ministry of Foreign Affairs and Trade, P.O. Box 1349, Majuro, MH 96960, Marshall Islands.

ZADEK, Peter; British theatre director; b. 19 May 1926, Berlin, Germany; s. of Paul Zadek and Susi Behr; m. (divorced); one s. one d.; emigrated to UK 1933; studied directing at Old Vic, London; Dir Salome (Oscar Wilde), Sweeney Agonistes (T. S. Eliot) 1945–52; Dir with BBC-TV, Wales, Dir The Balcony (Jean Genet), London 1952–57; returned to Fed. Repub. of Germany, Dir in Cologne, Ulm, Hanover 1958–62, Bremen 1962–67, Wuppertal, Stuttgart, Berlin, Munich and TV and cinema films 1967–72; worked on Shakespeare cycle 1972–77; directed film Die wilden Fünfziger (The Wild Fifties) 1982; directed Mozart's Marriage of Figaro, Stuttgart 1983; directed plays Berlin, Munich, Hamburg, Vienna, Paris 1983–, including The Merchant of Venice, Vienna 1989, Measure for Measure, Paris; Dir Berliner Ensemble 1992–95; Dir Antony and Cleopatra, Vienna and Berlin 1994; subject of books by Volker Canaris 1979, M. Lange 1989 and many articles; Fritz Kortner Prize for Best Dir 1988, Erwin Piscator Prize, New York 1989, Kainz Medal, Austria 1990; Commdr des Arts et des Lettres, France 1991. *Publication:* Das wilde Ufer 1990. *Leisure interest:* music. *Address:* 55060 Vecoli, San Martino in Freddana, Italy. *Telephone:* (0583) 349017.

ZADERNYUK, Andrei Fedorovich; Russian engineer; b. 26 July 1943, Orsk, Orenburg region; ed Krasnoyarsk Polytech. Inst., Gorky (Nizhnii-Novgorod) Lobachevsky State Univ.; metal worker, Sr technician Krasnoyarsk-26 1962–66; Sr Technician, Master, Sr Engineer Krasnoyarsk Ore Chem. plant 1966–77; Chief Energy Specialist Production Union of Volga oil

pipeline Nizhnii-Novgorod 1977–92; Dir Dept of Power Energy Complex Admin. of Nizhnii-Novgorod region; Vice-Gov. Nizhnii-Novgorod Region 1992–97; Chair. Fed. Energy Comm. of Russian Fed. 1997–2001; Sign of Hon., Order of the Friendship of Peoples; Labour Veteran Medal. *Address:* Federal Energy Commission, Kitaigorodsky pr. 7, 103074 Moscow, Russia (Office). *Telephone:* (095) 206-80-05 (Office).

ZADORNOV, Mikhail Mikhailovich, CAND.ECON.; Russian politician; b. 4 May 1963, Moscow; s. of Mikhail Zadornov and Raisa Zadornova; m. Natalya Zadornova 1982; one d.; ed G. Plekhanov Inst. of Nat. Econ.; one of authors Programme of Econ. Reforms 500 Days; mem. State Comm. on Econ. Reform, Russian Council of Ministers 1990–91; mem. State Duma (Parl.) (Yabloko faction) 1993–97, (Yabloko Fraction) 1999–; Chair., Cttee on Budget, Taxation, Banks and Finances 1994–97; Minister of Finance 1997–99; Special Rep. of Pres. Boris Yeltsin (q.v.), rank of First Deputy Prime Minister, in negotiations with int. financial orgs 1998–99; Deputy Chair. Cttee on Budget and Taxes, Chair. Sub-Cttee on Monetary Policy, Exchange and Capital Control and the Activities of the Cen. Bank of the Russian Fed. 1999–2003. *Publications:* more than 20 books; numerous articles on Russia's financial problems. *Leisure interest:* playing football. *Address:* State Duma, Okhotny Ryad 1, 103265 Moscow, Russia. *Telephone:* (095) 292-71-98 (Office). *Fax:* (095) 292-90-00 (Office). *E-mail:* zadornov@duma.gov.ru (Office). *Website:* www.zadornov.com (Office).

ZAENTZ, Saul; American film producer; b. Passaic, NJ; served in US army during World War II; settled in San Francisco 1948; worked for Norman Grantz's jazz music label, NY 1954; joined Fantasy Records jazz label, San Francisco 1955, co-owner 1967–; moved into feature film production 1972; f. Saul Zaentz Production Co. and Film Center; Irving G. Thalberg Memorial Award 1997, BAFTA Fellowship 2003. *Films include:* One Flew Over the Cuckoo's Nest 1975 (Acad. Award for Best Picture), Three Warriors 1977, Lord of the Rings 1978, Amadeus 1984, The Unbearable Lightness of Being 1988, At Play in the Fields of the Lord 1991, The English Patient (Acad. Award for Best Picture) 1996; Exec. Producer The Mosquito Coast 1986. *Leisure interests:* reading, music, sports, theatre, film. *Address:* Saul Zaentz & Co., Film Center, 2600 10th Street, Berkeley, CA 94710, USA. *Telephone:* (510) 486-2100. *Fax:* (510) 486-2115. *E-mail:* info@zaentz.com. *Website:* www .zaentz.com.

ZAERA-POLO, Alejandro; Spanish architect; b. b. Madrid; m. Farshid Moussavi; ed Yale Univ., USA; moved to work in London, UK 1993; has worked for Rem Koolhaas, Rotterdam, Netherlands, Zaha Hadid, London, Renzo Piano, Genoa Italy; fmr lecturer, Architectural Asscn, London; co-f. Foreign Office Architects (FOA) with Farshid Moussavi (q.v.), rep. Britain, Architecture Biennale, Venice 2002. *Works include:* medical practice, Groningen, Netherlands, Belgo, Notting Hill, London, Police HQ, Joiosa, Spain, Port Terminal, Yokohama, Japan. *Address:* Foreign Office Architects, 58 Belgrave Road, London SW1V 2BP, England (Office). *Website:* www.f-o-a.net/ (Office).

ZAFIROPOULOS, Vassilis S.; Greek diplomatist (retd); b. 24 Jan. 1934; one s.; ed Univ. of Athens; with Ministry of Finance 1962–67; in charge of press matters UN Information Centre for Greece, Israel, Turkey and Cyprus, Athens 1967–71; joined Diplomatic Service 1971, Third Sec., Ministry of Foreign Affairs 1971–73, Second Sec., Consul, Liège, Belgium 1973–76, First Sec. and Counsellor, Embassy, Nicosia 1976–78, Counsellor for Political Affairs, Embassy, London 1980–84; Head of Cyprus Affairs, Ministry of Foreign Affairs 1984–86; Minister Counsellor, Deputy Perm. Rep. to NATO, Brussels 1986–90, Minister Plenipotentiary 1990, Perm. Rep. to NATO 1993–96; Amb. to Australia and NZ 1991–93, to UK 1996–99; Higher Commdr Order of Phoenix (Greece); Dr hc (Univ. of N London). *Address:* 20B Sirinon Street, Athens 17561, Greece. *Telephone:* (210) 9818946. *Fax:* (210) 9818946.

ZAGAJEWSKI, Adam; Polish writer; b. 21 June 1945, Lvov; s. of Tadeusz Zagajewski and Ludwika Zagajewska; m. Maria Zagajewska; ed Jagiellonian Univ., Cracow; first published poetry and essays in literary reviews in 1960s; first collection of poems 1972; lived in France 1982–2002; lecturer, Univ. of Houston, USA 1988; mem. Polish Writers' Asscn, PEN Club; Koscielscy Foundation Award 1975, Andrzej Kijowski Award 1987, Alfred Jurzykowski Foundation Award 1989, Guggenheim Fellowship 1992, Int. Vilenica Prize (Slovenia) 1996, Tomas Transtromer Prize (Sweden) 2000. *Publications include:* collections of poetry: Jechac do Lwowa (To Go to Lvov) 1985, Pragnienie (Desire) 1999, Without End 2002; essays: Swiat nie przedstawiony (The Non-Represented World—co-author) 1974, Solidarnosc i samotnosc (Solidarity, Solitude) 1986, W cudzym pieknie (Another Beauty) 2000. *Leisure interests:* walking, reading. *Address:* University of Houston, English Department, Houston, TX 77204-3013, USA (Office). *Telephone:* (713) 743-3014 (Office). *Fax:* (713) 743-3215 (Office). *Website:* www.uh.edu.

ZAGALLO, Mario Jorge Lobo; Brazilian footballer and football coach; b. 9 Aug. 1931, Rio de Janeiro; fmrly footballer with Brazilian team Botafogo, Fluminese and Flamengo; played in World Cup Final for Brazil 1958, 1962; football coach 1965–2001; first footballer to attain World Championship as player and then man.; coached Brazilian football team for 1970, 1974 and 1998 World Cups, adviser to nat. coach Brazil 1994–99; fmrly nat. coach Kuwait, Saudi Arabia, UAE; brief return to manage Brazil nat. team for Nov. 2002 friendly against S Korea in Seoul while successor to outgoing manager was sought. *Address:* c/o Confederacão Brasil Futebol, Rua de Alfandega 70 20, 070-001 Rio de Janeiro, Brazil (Office).

ZAGHEN, Paolo, PhD; Brazilian economist and banker; b. Crema, Italy; ed Univ. of São Paulo, Univ. of California at Berkeley; Partner-Dir Lucro DTVM Ltd 1988–91; Open Market Dir Banespa Securities and Exchange Brokers; Financial, Admin. and P.R. Dir Paranapanema Mining, Industry and Construction 1994–96; Dir Cen. Bank 1996–2000; Pres. Bank of Brazil SA 2000–02. *Address:* c/o Banco do Brasil SA, Setor Bancário Sul, SBS, Quadro 4, Bloco C, Lote 32, 70089-900 Brasília DF, Brazil (Office).

ZAGLADIN, Vadim Valentinovich; Russian politician; b. 23 June 1927, Moscow; m. Janetta Rogacheva; one s. three d.; ed Moscow Inst. of Int. Relations; taught at Moscow Inst. of Int. Relations 1949–54; editorial work on various journals 1954–64; editorial post in Prague 1960–64; mem. CPSU 1955–91; mem. Int. Dept, Cen. Cttee of CPSU 1964–67, Deputy Head 1967–82, First Deputy Head 1982–88; mem. Cen. Auditing Cttee 1971–76; cand. mem. Cen. Cttee of CPSU 1976–81, mem. 1981–90; Deputy, Supreme Soviet of USSR and Sec. Foreign Affairs Cttee 1981–89; Chair. Section of Global Problems of Scientific Council of Pres., USSR (now Russian) Acad. of Sciences 1981–; Deputy Chair. Parl. Group of USSR 1981–88; Adviser to fmr Pres. Gorbachev (q.v.) 1988–91; Adviser to Pres. of Int. Foundation for Socio-Econ. and Political Studies (Gorbachev Foundation) 1992–; mem. Russian Acad. of Natural Sciences 1992–; Vice-Pres. Asscn for Euro-Atlantic Co-operation 1991–. *Publications:* over 30 books and numerous articles on political problems. *Address:* Starokonuchenny 26, Apt. 43, 121002 Moscow, Russia. *Telephone:* (095) 241-87-33.

ZAHEDI, Ardeshir, LLB; Iranian diplomatist; b. 16 Oct. 1928, Tehran; s. of Gen. Fazlollah and Khadijeh Zahedi; m. Princess Shahnaz Pahlavi 1957 (dissolved 1964); one d.; ed in Tehran, American Univ. of Beirut and Utah State Univ., USA; Civil Adjutant to His Imperial Majesty the Shah of Iran 1954–79; Amb. to USA 1959–61, to UK 1962–67; Minister of Foreign Affairs 1967–71; Amb. to USA 1973–79 to Mexico 1973–76; sentenced to death (in absentia) by Islamic Revolutionary Court; Hon. LLD (Utah State Univ. 1960, (Chungang Univ. of Seoul) 1969, (E Texas State) 1973, (Kent State) 1974, (St Louis) 1975; numerous decorations including Crown with Grand Cordon, Order of Taj (First Class) 1975.

ZAHIR, Abdul; Afghanistan politician; b. 3 May 1910, Lagham; ed Habibia High School, Kabul and Columbia and Johns Hopkins Univs., USA; practised medicine in USA before returning to Kabul 1943; Chief Doctor, Municipal Hosp., Kabul 1943–50; Deputy Minister of Health 1950–55, Minister 1955–58; Amb. to Pakistan 1958–61, to Italy 1969–71; Chair. House of the People 1961–64, 1965–69; Deputy Prime Minister and Minister of Health 1964–65; Prime Minister of Afghanistan 1971–72.

ZAHIR SHAH (see Mohammed Zahir Shah).

ZAHRADNÍK, Rudolf, DSc, DipEng; Czech physical chemist and university professor; b. 20 Oct. 1928, Bratislava; s. of Rudolf Zahradník and Jindřiška Zahradníková; m. Milena Zahradníková; one d.; ed Czech Tech. Univ., Prague; scientific worker Inst. of Hygiene and Occupational Diseases, Prague 1952–61, Inst. of Physical Chem. and Electrochem., Acad. of Sciences, Prague 1961–83; Prof., Charles Univ., Prague 1967–; Guest Prof. Univs of Würzburg 1965, Darmstadt 1966, Groningen 1967, Osaka 1977, Basel 1981, Vanderbilt Univ. 1990; Dir Jaroslav Heyrovský Inst. of Physical and Electrochem. Prague 1990–93; Pres. Czech Acad. of Sciences 1993–2001, Hon. Pres. 2001–; Pres. Czech Learned Soc. 1994–97; mem. many academic and scientific socs including Int. Acad. of Quantum Molecular Sciences 1982–, World Asscn of Theoretical Organic Chemists, European Acad. of Arts, Science and Literature, Ed. Council Special Journals; Hon. mem. Swiss and German Chemical Socs; Cross of Honour (First Class) for Science and Arts (Austria) 1999; several hon. degrees including Dr hc (Georgetown Univ. Washington, DC) 1996, (Charles Univ. Prague) 1998, (New York) 1998; Jaroslav Heyrovský Golden Plaque Czech Acad. of Sciences 1990, Medal for Merit, Prague 1998. *Publications:* Organic Quantum Chemistry Problems (with P. Cársky) 1973, Elements of Quantum Chemistry (with R. Polák) 1976, Intermolecular Complexes (with P. Hobza) 1988, Thinking as Passion (with Lenka Jaklová) 1998, Rule of Sense 2002. *Leisure interests:* serious music and literature. *Address:* J. Heyrovský Institute of Physical Chemistry, Academy of Sciences of the Czech Republic, Dolejškova 3, 182 23 Prague 8 (Office); Heřmanova 37, 170 00 Prague 7, Czech Republic (Home). *Telephone:* (2) 86583014 (Office); (2) 86583029 (Office); (2) 33382004 (Home). *Fax:* (2) 86582307 (Office); (2) 33382004 (Home). *E-mail:* zahrad@jh-inst.cas.cz (Office). *Website:* www .jh-inst.cas.cz (Office).

ZAINUDDIN, Tun Daim, LLB; Malaysian politician, lawyer and business executive; b. 1938, Alor Star, Kedah State; ed London, Univ. of Calif.; called to the Bar, Lincoln's Inn; magistrate, then Deputy Public Prosecutor; later set up own law firm; Head Peremba 1979–; mem. Dewan Negara (Senate) 1980–82; mem. Dewan Rakat (House of Reps) 1982–; Minister of Finance 1984–91; Chair. Fleet Group; Treas. UMNO; Exec. Dir Nat. Econ. Action Council 1998–; Econ. Adviser to Prime Minister Mahathir bin Mohammad; Minister of Finance and Special Functions 1999–2001; Chair. and Dir numerous cos. *Address:* c/o Ministry of Finance, Block 9, Kompleks Pejabat Kerajaan, Jalan Duta, 50592 Kuala Lumpur, Malaysia (Office).

ZAITSEV, Vyacheslav Mikhailovich (Slava); Russian fashion designer; b. 2 March 1938, Ivanovo; one s.; ed Moscow Textile Inst.; chief designer, All-Union Fashion House 1965–78; chief designer, Moscow Fashion House 'Slava Zaitsev' 1982–, Pres. 1991–; participates in Paris fashion shows 1988–; shows collections worldwide; Prof. Moscow Textile Inst.; has exhibited paintings in the USA and Belgium; Hon. Citizen of Paris 1988; Best Designer Award (Japan) 1989. *Publications:* The Changing Fashion 1980, This Many-Faced World of Fashion 1980. *Leisure interest:* painting. *Address:* Moscow Fashion House, Prospekt Mira 21, 129110 Moscow, Russia. *Telephone:* (095) 971-11-22. *Fax:* (095) 281-55-75.

ZAITSEV, Yury Vladimirovich, DTechSc; Russian engineer and diplomatist; b. 2 Aug. 1933, Moscow; m.; two d.; ed Kuibyshev Moscow Inst. of Construction Eng., Diplomatic Acad. Ministry of Foreign Affairs; Sr researcher Centre for Inst. of Scientific Information on Construction and Architecture, USSR Acad. of Construction and Architecture 1958–59, Research Inst. of Concrete and Reinforced Concrete 1959–64; Prof., Head of Chair., Pro-Rector All-Union Polytechnic Inst. by correspondence 1964–90; Chair. Comm. on Problems of Citizenship at Supreme Soviet, then with Russian Presidency 1990–92; mem. Supreme Soviet of Russian Fed. 1990–93; Perm. Rep. of Russia at int. orgs in Vienna 1992–97; First Deputy Head, Internal Policy Dept of Pres. Yeltsin's Admin 1997–98; mem. Acad. of Tech. Sciences, Acad. of Natural Sciences, Acad. of Eng. *Publications include:* 18 monographs, textbooks, over 200 articles in scientific journals. *Address:* c/o President's Administration, Kremlin 1, Moscow, Russia.

ZAJĄC, Stanisław, ML; Polish politician and lawyer; b. 1 May 1949, Święcany, Krosno Prov.; m.; two c.; ed Jagiellonian Univ., Kraków; employee Regional Court, Jasło; advocate in Krosno and Jasło 1980; advocate for the defence during martial law; adviser NSZZ Solidarity, Carpathian Region; Vice-Chair. Christian Nat. Union (ZChN) 1994–2000, Chair. 2000–; Deputy to Sejm (Parl.) 1991–93, 1997–2001, Vice-Leader Justice Cttee, mem. Parl. Comm. for Spatial, Bldg and Housing Policy; mem. Christian Nat. Union Parl. Caucus 1991–93; Vice-Marshal (Speaker) of Sejm 1997–2001; mem. Solidarity Election Action (AWS) Parl. Caucus 1997–2001. *Address:* Kancelaria Sejmu RP, ul. Sniadeckich 8B, 38-200 Jasło, Poland. *Telephone:* (13) 446 5058.

ZAKARIA, Fareed, PhD; American editor and academic; b. India; m.; one s.; ed Yale and Harvard Univs; Lecturer on Int. Politics and Econs, Harvard Univ., also Head of Project on the Changing Security Environment; Adjunct Prof., Columbia Univ., Cape Western Reserve Univ.; Man. Ed. Foreign Affairs journal 1992–2000; Foreign Policy Adviser to US Admin.; Ed. Newsweek Int. 2000–; Columnist Newsweek (USA), Newsweek Int. and The Washington Post 2001–; speaker at World Econ. Forum, Davos, Switzerland and various univs.; broadcast appearances on Charlie Rose, Firing Line, The NewsHour with Jim Lehrer, The McLaughlin Group, BBC World News and Meet the Press; contrib. to publs including The New York Times, The New Yorker and The Wall Street Journal; wine columnist for Slate (webzine); Overseas Press Club Award. *Publications include:* From Wealth to Power: The Unusual Origins of America's World Role, The American Encounter: The United States and the Making of the Modern World (co-ed.), The Future of Freedom 2003. *Address:* Newsweek International, Newsweek Building, 251 West 57th Street, New York, NY 10019-1894, USA (Office). *E-mail:* editors@newsweek .com (Office). *Website:* www.newsweek-int.com (Office).

ZAKHARCHENYA, Boris Petrovich, DrPhysMathSc; Russian scientist; b. 1 May 1928, Orsha, Vitebsk Region, Belarus; ed Leningrad State Univ.; Jr, then Sr Researcher., Head of Lab., then Head of Div. Leningrad A. Ioffe Inst. of Physics and Tech., USSR (now Russian) Acad. of Sciences 1953–1989, Dir Dept of Physics of Solids 1989–, mem. Russian Acad. of Sciences 1992; Prof. St Petersburg Electromechanical Univ.; Ed.-in-Chief Physics of Solids journal; mem. IUPAP, American Soc. of Physics; Lenin's Prize 1966, USSR State Prize 1977, P. N. Lebedev Great Gold Medal 1996, R. Abramovitz Prize 2001. *Publications:* numerous scientific publs, including monographs. *Address:* A. Ioffe Institute of Physics and Technology, Russian Acad. of Sciences, Politechnicheskaya str. 26, 194021 St Petersburg, Russia (Office). *Telephone:* (812) 247-91-40 (Office); (812) 552-36-72 (Home).

ZAKHAROV, Aleksander Vladimirovich; Russian business executive; b. 3 Oct. 1955, Moscow; m.; three c.; ed G. Plekhanov Moscow Inst. of Nat. Econs, All-Union Acad. of Foreign Trade; expert, sr consultant USSR Chamber of Industry and Commerce 1976–89; Deputy Rep. USSR Chamber of Industry and Commerce in Bulgaria 1989–91; Deputy Dir Centre on Interbank Currency Accounts USSR State Bank (Gosbank) Sept.–Dec. 1991; Dir Moscow Interbank Currency Exchange 1992–. *Leisure interests:* poetry, football. *Address:* Moscow Interbank Currency Exchange, B. Kislovskiy per. 13, 103009 Moscow, Russia. *Telephone:* (095) 234-48-11 (Office). *Fax:* (095) 234-48-46. *Website:* www.micex.com.

ZAKHAROV, Mark Anatolievich; Russian stage and film director; b. 13 Oct. 1933, Moscow; m. Nina Lapshinova; one d.; ed Lunacharsky Theatre Inst. (now Russian Acad. of Theatre Arts); actor since 1955, Stage Dir Theatre of Satire Mayakovsky Theatre 1965–73; Chief Stage Dir Moscow Theatre of Leninsky Komsomol (now 'Lenkom' Theatre) 1973–; teacher, Prof., Russian

Acad. of Theatre Arts 1979–; mem. Pres.'s Council 1996–98; People's Artist of the RSFSR 1988 and numerous govt awards of USSR and Russia. *Television films:* Habitual Miracle 1976, That Very Munchhausen 1979, Formula for Love 1984, To Kill a Dragon 1989. *Plays directed include:* Profitable Place by A. Ostrovsky 1967, Yunona and Avos by A. Voznesensky and A. Rybnikov 1981, Three Girls in Blue by L. Petrushevskaya 1985, Dictatorship of Conscience by M. Shatrov 1986, Wise Man by A. Ostrovsky 1989, Pray for the Dead by Sholom-Aleichem 1989, The Marriage of Figaro by Beaumarchais 1993, The Seagull by Chekhov 1994, King's Games by G. Gorin and M. Anderson 1995, Gambler (Vavvay and Eretic) by Dostoyevsky 1997, Mystification (Dead Souls) by Gogol 1998, City of Millionaires by Eduardo de Filippo 2000. *Publications:* Contacts on Diverse Levels 1988, Super Profession 2000 and numerous Publs on theatre. *Address:* 1st Tverskaya-Yamskaya 7, Apt. 9, Moscow, Russia. *Telephone:* (095) 299-12-61. *Fax:* (095) 234-99-64.

ZAKIS, Juris, DrSc; Latvian solid-state physicist; b. 4 Nov. 1936, Ogre; s. of Roderickh Zakis and Eugenia Zake; m. Anita Zake 1976; three s. two d.; ed Univ. of Latvia, Riga; Prof., Univ. of Latvia 1978, Pro-Rector 1984–87, Rector 1987–2000; Pres. Rectors' Council of Latvia 1995–98; USSR People's Deputy 1989–91; mem. Parl. 1995–; mem. Latvian Acad. of Sciences; Pres. Latvian Acad. of Innovation and Intellectual Property 2000–; Merited Scientist of Latvia 1986, State Emer. Scientist 2002. *Publications:* numerous articles on physics of disordered solids and on higher educ. policy. *Leisure interests:* skiing, linguistics. *Address:* University of Latvia, 19 Rainis Boulevard, Riga, 1586, Latvia. *Telephone:* (2) 929-9918. *Fax:* (2) 728-0807. *E-mail:* jzakis@lanet .lv.

ZAMACHOWSKI, Zbigniew; Polish actor; b. 17 July 1961, Brzeziny; m.; two s. two d.; ed State Higher Film, TV and Theatre School, Łódź; Aleksander Zelwerowicz Award 1993, Gdańsk Film Festival Prize for Best Actor, in Zawrócony 1994, Felix European Film Award, Wiktor Prize 1992, 1993, 1997. *Film roles include:* Zad wielkiego wieloryba 1987, Dotknięci 1988, Bal na dworcu w..., Dekalog X 1989, Ucieczka z kina 'Wolność' 1990, Ferdydurke 1991, Na czarno 1993, Trzy kolory: Biały 1993, Le clandestin (France) 1993, Zawrócony 1994, Pułkownik Kwiatkowski 1995, Sława i chwała 1996, Szczęśliwego Nowego Jorku 1997, "23" 1997, Nie płacz Agnieszko 1997, Ogniem i mieczem (With Fire and sword) 1998, Prymas (Primate) 1999, Weiser Dawidek 1999, Proof of Life 2000, Når nattene blir lange 2000, Cześć Tereska 2000, Wiedźmin 2000, Stacja 2001. *Theatrical roles include:* Płatonow 1992, Amadeus 1993, Wujaszek Wania 1993, Don Juan 1996, Ildefonsjada 1996, Za i przeciw (Taking Sides) 1997, Ślub 1998, Kartoteka (The Card Index) 1999, Wesele (The Wedding) 2000, A Midsummer Night's Dream 2000. *Address:* c/o Agata Domagata, ul. F. Schillera 6m.12, 00-248 Warsaw, Poland. *Telephone:* (48) 501094390. *E-mail:* agat8@idea.net.pl.

ZAMAGNI, Stefano; Italian professor of economics; b. 4 Jan. 1943, Rimini; m. Vera Negri 1968; two d.; ed Univ. of Milan, Univ. of Oxford, UK; Assoc. Dir and Adjunct Prof., Bologna Center, Johns Hopkins Univ. 1977–; Prof. of Econs, Univ. of Bologna 1985–, Chair. Dept of Econs 1985–88, 1991–94, Dean Faculty of Econs 1994–96, Co-ordinator PhD Programme in Econs 1989–93; Pres. ICMC, Geneva 1999–; Vice-Pres. Italian Econ. Assen 1989–92, State Vic. Bank Visiting Prof., Deakin Univ., Geelong, Australia; McDonnell Visiting Scholar, Wider, Helsinki, Finland; Co-Ed. Economia Politica (quarterly) 1983–, Italian Economic Papers 1990–, Journal of International and Comparative Economics, Ricerche Economiche; mem. Exec. Cttee Int. Econ. Assen 1989–, Pontifical Council on Justice and Peace 1992–, Scientific Cttee, J. Maritain Int. Inst. 1995–, Bd of Dirs. UNIBANCA 1999–; mem. Acad. of Sciences; Paul Harris Fellow, Rotary Int. 1995; Accademia Lincei Award; St Vincent Prize in Econs, Capri Prize in Econs 1995, Golden Sigismondo Prize 1997, Gold Medal, Pio Manzu Int. Centre 1998. *Publications:* Microeconomic Theory 1987, The Economic Theories of Production 1989, History of Economic Thought 1991, Value and Capital—Fifty Years Later (with L. McKenzie) 1991, Firms and Markets 1991, Man—Environment and Development: Toward a Global Approach 1991, Market, State and the Theory of Public Intervention 1992, The Economics of Crime and Illegal Markets 1993, Towards a One World Development Path 1993, The Economics of Altruism 1995, An Evolutionary Dynamic Approach to Altruism 1996, Technological Change: Time-Use Policies and Employment 1996, Globalization as Specificity of Post-Industrial Economy 1997, Civil Economy and Paradoxes of Growth in Post-Fordist Societies 1997, Living in the Global Society 1997, Civil Economy, Cultural Evolution and Participatory Development 1999, The Economics of Corruption and Illegal Markets (co-author) 1999, Financial Globalization and the Emerging Economies (co-author) 2000. *Leisure interests:* sports, theatre, classical music. *Address:* Department of Economics, University of Bologna, Piazza Scaravilli 2, 40126 Bologna, Italy. *Telephone:* (051) 2098132. *Fax:* (051) 2098040. *E-mail:* bordoni@economia.unibo.it (Office); veste@economia.unibo.it (Home).

ZAMBELLO, Francesca, BA; American opera and musical director; b. 24 Aug. 1956, New York; ed American School of Paris, Colgate Univ.; Asst Dir Lyric Opera of Chicago 1981–82, San Francisco Opera 1983–84; Artistic Dir Skylight Music Theatre 1984–; Guest Producer San Francisco Opera, Teatro La Fenice, Savonlinna, Festival, Houston Grand Opera, Nat. Opera of Iceland, Seattle Opera, San Diego Opera, Theatre of St Louis, Rome Opera, Théâtre Municipal de Lausanne, Teatro Regio, Parma and Wexford Festival 1988–89; several Olivier awards. *Works directed include:* San Francisco Opera: La Traviata 1983, La Voix Humaine 1986, Faust 1986, La Bohème

1988, Prince Igor; New York Metropolitan Opera: Lucia di Lammermoor 1992; Royal Opera House, Covent Garden: Billy Budd (Bastille Opera, Paris) 1995–96, Arianna 1995–96, The Bartered Bride 2001–; Don Giovanni 2002; English Nat. Opera: Khovanshchina 1995–96; Copenhagen: Tannhäuser 1995–96; Santa Fe Opera: Modern Painters 1995–96; Nat. Theatre: Lady in the Dark 1997; Shaftesbury Theatre, London: Napoleon 2000. *Address:* c/o Columbia Artists, 165 West 57th Street, New York, NY 10019, USA.

ZAMECNIK, Paul Charles, MD; American physician; b. 22 Nov. 1912, Cleveland, Ohio; s. of John Zamecnik and Mary McCarthy; m. Mary Connor 1936; one s. two d.; ed Dartmouth Coll. and Harvard Medical School; Resident, Huntington Memorial Hosp., Boston, Mass. 1936–37; Intern, Univ. Hosps., Cleveland, Ohio 1938–39; Moseley Travelling Fellow of Harvard Univ. at Carlsberg Labs., Copenhagen 1939–40; Fellow Rockefeller Inst., New York 1941–42; Physician, Harvard Univ. and Dir John Collins Warren Labs. at Mass. Gen. Hosp. 1956–79, Hon. Physician 1983–, Exec. Sec. of Cttee on Research 1948–50, Chair. Cttee on Research 1954–56; Chair. Exec. Cttee of Depts. of Medicine, Harvard Medical School 1956–61, 1968–71; Collis P. Huntington Prof. of Oncological Medicine, Harvard Medical School 1956–79, Emer. Prof. 1979–; Prin. Scientist Worcester Foundation for Experimental Biology, Shrewsbury, Mass. 1979–97; Sr Scientist Mass. Gen. Hosp. 1998–; Chair. SAB Hybridon Inc., Cambridge, Mass. 1991–; Jubilee Lecturer, Biochemical Soc., London 1962; Fogarty Scholar 1975, 1978; Foreign mem. Royal Danish Acad. of Sciences; mem. NAS, American Acad. of Arts and Sciences, Asscn American Physicians, American Asscn of Biological Chemists, American Asscn of Cancer Research (Pres. 1964–65); Hon. DSc (Utrecht) 1966, (Columbia) 1971, (Harvard) 1982, (Roger Williams) 1983, (Dartmouth) 1988, (Mass.) 1994; John Collins Warren Triennial Prize 1946, 1950, 1999, James Ewing Award 1963, Borden Award in Medical Sciences 1965, American Cancer Soc. Nat. Award 1967, Passano Award 1970, Presidential Medal of Science 1991, Hudson Hoagland Award 1993, City of Medicine Award, Durham, NC 1995, City of Worcester Science Award 1996, Lasker Lifetime Science Award 1996, Merck Award, ASBC and MB 1997, Annual Orator, Mass. Medical Soc. 1998, Warren Triennial Prize 1999. *Publications include:* Historical and Current Aspects of the Problem of Protein Synthesis (Harvey Lectures Series 54) 1960, Unsettled Questions in the Field of Protein Synthesis (Bio-chemical Journal 85) 1962, The Mechanics of Protein Synthesis and its Possible Alterations in the Presence of Oncogenic RNA Viruses (Cancer Research 26) 1966, Antisense Oligonucleotides as Modulators of Genetic Expression 1992, Antisense Therapy of Drug Resistant Malaria and Bacterial Diseases 1995–98. *Leisure interests:* African art, snorkelling. *Address:* Massachusetts General Hospital, 149 13th Street, Room 1494005, Charlestown, MA 02139 (Office); 101 Chestnut Street, Boston, MA 02108, USA (Home).

ZAMFIR, Gheorghe; Romanian musician; b. 6 April 1941, Găeşti, nr Bucharest; ed self-taught and Bucharest Acad. of Music (studied under Fănică Luca); graduated in conducting at Ciprian Porumbescu Conservatory, Bucharest 1968; toured numerous countries in Europe as student and won first prize in many int. competitions; conductor of 'Ciocirlia' Folk Ensemble in Bucharest 1969; Prof. of Pan-Pipes 1970; formed own orchestra 1970; numerous trips to Europe, Australia, S. America, Canada and USA; numerous recordings. *Address:* Dr. Teohari str. 10, Bucharest, Romania.

ZAMMIT, Ninu, BArch, A.&C.E.; Maltese politician; b. 1952, Zurrieq; m. Margaret Zahra; one s. two d.; ed Univ. of Malta; architect and civil engineer 1975; MP Nationalist Party 1981–; Party Spokesman for Water and Energy 1985–87; Parl. Sec. for Water and Energy 1987–96; Shadow Minister and Opposition Spokesman for Agric. and Fisheries 1996–98; Minister of Agric. and Fisheries 1998–. *Address:* Ministry of Agriculture and Fisheries, Barriera Wharf, Valletta, CMR 02, Malta. *Telephone:* 225236; 225238. *Fax:* 231294.

ZAMMIT DIMECH, Francis, LLD; Maltese politician and lawyer; b. 23 Oct. 1954; s. of George Zammit Dimech; ed St Aloysius Coll. and Univ. of Malta; Pres. Students' Rep. Council of Univ. 1978–79; Vice-Pres. Democratic Youth Community of Europe 1981–83; Nationalist Party MP 1987–; mem. Maltese Parl. Del. to Parl. Ass. of Council of Europe 1987–92; Parl. Sec. later Minister for Transport and Communications 1990–92, 1992–94; Minister for the Environment 1994–96, 1998–2001; Shadow Minister and Opposition Spokesman on Public Works and Environment 1996–98; Pres. Exec. Council Nationalist Party 1997–99; Minister for Resources and Infrastructure 2002–. *Publications:* Poll of 76 1980, The Untruth Game 1986. *Address:* Ministry for Resources and Infrastructure, Floriana CMR 02, Malta. *Telephone:* 21222378. *Fax:* 21243306.

ZAMORA RIVAS, Rubén Ignacio; Salvadorean politician; b. 9 Nov. 1942; s. of Ruben Zamora and Lidia Rivas; m. María Ester Chamorro 1979; five c.; ed Univ. of El Salvador, Univ. of Essex, UK; abandoned studies for priesthood aged 19 and turned to social activism; joined Christian Democratic Party (f. by José Napoléon Duarte 1960); sometime lecturer, Catholic Univ. San Salvador; arrested for political activities 1977; in exile in UK 1977–79; Minister of the Presidency 1979–80; fled to Nicaragua following murder of his brother Mario 1980; Founder and Leader Social Christian Popular Movt (MPSC), Sec.-Gen. Centro Democrática Unido 2001–; returned from exile to San Salvador 1987; Vice-Pres. Nat. Ass. 1991–; Presidential Cand. for 1994 elections; Thinker Prof., Stanford Univ., USA, Notre Dame Univ., IN, USA. *Publications:* El Salvador – heridas que no cierran 1997, La Izquierda

Partidaria Salvadoreña 2003. *Leisure interests:* reading, playing Nintendo. *Address:* Centro Democrática Unido, Boulevard Tutunichapa y Calle Roberto Masserrer 1313, Urb. Médica, San Salvador (Office); 204 Ave. Maquilishuat, Col Vista Hermosa, San Salvador, El Salvador. *Telephone:* 226-1928 (Office); 242-2758 (Home). *Fax:* 225-5883 (Office); 242-2759 (Home).

ZAMYATIN, Leonid Mitrofanovich; Russian diplomatist and journalist (retd); b. 9 March 1922, Nizhni Devitsk, Voronezh Region; m. 1946; one d.; ed Moscow Aviation Inst. and Higher Diplomatic School; mem. CPSU 1944–91; at Ministry of Foreign Affairs 1946–50; First Sec., Secr. of Minister of Foreign Affairs 1950–52; Asst Head, Third European Dept, Ministry of Foreign Affairs 1952–53; First Sec., Counsellor on Political Questions of USSR Mission to UN 1953–57; Soviet Deputy Rep. on Preparatory Cttee and later on Bd of Govs, Int. Atomic Energy Agency (IAEA) 1957–59, Soviet Rep. at IAEA 1959–60; Deputy Head, American Countries Dept, Ministry of Foreign Affairs 1960–62, Head of Press Dept 1962–70, mem. of Collegium of Ministry 1962–70; Dir-Gen. TASS News Agency 1970–78; Deputy to USSR Supreme Soviet 1970–89; Chief, Dept of Int. Information, Cen. Cttee CPSU 1978–85, mem. Cen. Cttee 1981; Amb. to UK 1986–91; Adviser to Chair. Russian Industrialists' and Entrepreneurs' Union 1992–94, to Pres. Bank of St Petersburg 1994–; Lenin Prize 1978; orders and medals of USSR including Order of Lenin (twice). *Publication:* Gorby and Maggie 1995. *Address:* Leont'yevsky per. 10, 103009 Moscow, Russia. *Telephone:* (095) 229-83-75.

ZANDER, Michael, QC; British professor of law; b. 16 Nov. 1932, Berlin, Germany; s. of Walter Zander and Margaret Zander; m. Elizabeth Treeger 1965; one s. one d.; ed Royal Grammar School, High Wycombe, Jesus Coll. Cambridge and Harvard Law School; Sullivan & Cromwell, New York 1958–59; admitted solicitor of Supreme Court 1962; Asst Lecturer, LSE 1963, Lecturer 1965, Sr Lecturer 1970, Reader 1970, Prof. of Law 1977–98, Prof. Emer. 1998–, Convenor (head) 1984–88, 1997–98; legal corresp. The (Manchester) Guardian 1963–88; mem. Royal Comm. on Criminal Justice 1991–93. *Publications:* Lawyers and the Public Interest 1968, Cases and Materials on the English Legal System 1972, 1999, A Bill of Rights 1975, 1997, Legal Services for the Community 1978, The Law-Making Process 1980, 1999, The Police and Criminal Evidence Act 1984, 1995, 2003, A Matter of Justice 1989, The State of Justice 2000. *Leisure interests:* swimming (daily), the cello (not daily). *Address:* 12 Woodside Avenue, London, N6 4SS, England. *Telephone:* (20) 8883-6257. *Fax:* (20) 8444-3348. *E-mail:* zander@legalmusic.u-net.com (Home).

ZANE, Billy; American actor; b. 24 Feb. 1966, Chicago, Ill.; s. of William Zane Sr; m. Lisa Collins 1988 (divorced 1995); ed American School, Switzerland; moved to Hollywood 1984; stage appearances in American Music, New York, The Boys in the Backroom (Actors' Gang, Chicago). *Films:* Back to the Future 1985, Critters 1986, Dead Calm 1989, Back to the Future Part II 1989, Megaville 1990, Memphis Belle 1990, Blood and Concrete: A Love Story 1991, Millions, Femme Fatale 1991, Posse 1993, Orlando 1993, Sniper 1993, Flashfire, Tombstone 1993, The Silence of the Hams 1994, Cyborg Agent, Only You 1994, Tales from the Crypt Presents: Demon Knight 1995, Reflections in the Dark, Danger Zone 1995, The Phantom 1996, This World – Then the Fireworks 1996, Head Above Water 1996, Titanic 1998, Taxman 1999, Morgan's Ferry 1999, Cleopatra 1999, Hendrix 2000, Invincible 2001, The Diamond of Jeru 2001, The Believer 2001, Sea Devils 2002. *Television:* (series) Twin Peaks, Cleopatra; (films) Brotherhood of Justice, The Case of the Hillside Stranglers 1989, Lake Consequence, Running Delilah, The Set Up. *Address:* Creative Artists Agency, 9830 Wilshire Boulevard, Beverly Hills, CA 90212, USA (Office).

ZANKER, Paul, DPhil; German professor of archaeology; b. 7 Feb. 1937, Konstanz; ed Univs. of Munich, Freiburg and Rome; Deutsches Archäologisches Inst. Rome 1963, Dir 1996–; Asst Bonn 1964; lecturer, Freiburg 1967; Prof. Göttingen 1972–; Prof. of Classical Archaeology, Univ. of Munich 1976; mem. Inst. of Advanced Study, Princeton, NJ; mem. Bayerische Akad. der Wissenschaften, British Acad., Accademia Europaea (London), Deutsches Archäologisches Inst. *Publications:* Wandel der Hermesgestalt 1965, Forum Augustum 1968, Forum Romanum 1972, Porträts 1973, Klassizistiche Statuen 1974, Provinzielle Kaiserbildnisse 1983, Augustus und die Macht der Bilder 1987, The Mask of Socrates: The Image of the Intellectual in Antiquity 1995. *Address:* Meiserstrasse 10, 80333 Munich, Germany.

ŽANTOVSKÝ, Michael; Czech politician, scientist and translator; b. 3 Jan. 1945, Prague; s. of Jiří Žantovský and Hana Žantovský; m. 1st. Kristina Žantovská (divorced 1999); one s. one d.; m. 2nd. Jana Žantovský; one s.; ed Charles Univ., Prague, McGill Univ., Montreal; scientific worker in a research inst., Prague 1973–; freelance translator and interpreter 1980–89; activist for ind. creative org. Open Dialogue 1988; founder mem. restored PEN 1989; Press Spokesman for Centre of Civic Forum 1989–90; mem. Advisory Bd to Pres. Václav Havel (q.v.) 1990–91; Press Spokesman to Pres. 1991–92; with Ministry of Foreign Affairs Aug. 1992; Amb. of Czech Repub. to USA 1993–97; mem. Senate 1996–2002; Chair. Senate Comm. for Foreign Affairs, Defence and Security 1996–2002; mem. Civic Democratic Alliance (ODA) March 1997–, Chair. March–Nov. 1997, 2001; Vice-Chair. 1998–2001; mem. Bd of Supervisors OPS Prague – 'European City of Culture 2000' 1999–2001. *Publications:* papers in scientific journals on psychological motivation and

sexual behaviour, author of plays and translator of numerous papers. *Leisure interest:* tennis. *Address:* Senate, Prague, Czech Republic. *Telephone:* (2) 57071111. *Website:* www.senat.cz (Office); www.mzv.cz (Office).

ZANUCK, Richard Darryl, BA; American film company executive; b. 13 Dec. 1934, Beverly Hills, Calif.; s. of Darryl F. Zanuck and Virginia (Fox) Zanuck; m. 1st Lili Gentle; two d.; m. 2nd Linda Harrison 1969; two step-s.; m. 3rd Lili Fini 1978; ed Harvard Mil. Acad. and Stanford Univ.; Story, Production Asst Darryl F. Zanuck Productions 1956, Vice-Pres. 1956–62; President's Production Rep. 20th Century-Fox Studios, Beverly Hills 1962–63, Vice-Pres. in charge of Production 1963–69, Pres. 1969–71, Dir 1966–; Chair. 20th Century-Fox TV Inc.; Sr Vice-Pres. Warner Bros. Inc. 1971–72; Co-founder, Pres. Zanuck/Brown Co. 1972–88; Founder, Propr The Zanuck Co. 1989–; mem. Bd of Govs. Acad. of Motion Picture Arts and Sciences, Screen Producers Guild; Nat. Chair. Fibrosis Asscn 1966–68; mem. Organizing Cttee 1984 Olympics; Trustee, Harvard School; shared Irving J. Thalberg Award 1991; Lifetime Achievement Award, Producer's Guild, America 1993. *Films produced include:* The Sting 1973 (Acad. Award), Jaws 1975, Jaws II 1978, The Island 1980, Neighbors 1982, The Verdict 1983, Cocoon 1985, Target 1985, Cocoon—The Return 1987, Driving Miss Daisy 1989 (Acad. Award), Rush 1991, Rich in Love 1992, Clean State 1993, Wild Bill 1995, Mulholland Falls 1996, Deep Impact 1998, True Crime 1999, Rules of Engagement 2000, Planet of the Apes 2001, Road to Perdition 2001, Reign of Fire 2002. *Address:* Zanuck Co., 9465 Wilshire Boulevard, Suite 930 Beverly Hills, CA 90212, USA.

ZANUSSI, Krzysztof; Polish film director and scriptwriter; b. 17 June 1939, Warsaw; s. of Jerzy Zanussi and Jadwiga Zanussi; m. Elżbieta Grocholska; ed Warsaw and Cracow Univs. and Łódź Higher Film School; Dir TOR State Film Studio 1967–; lecturer, Stage Dept of Higher State School of Film, TV and Drama, Łódź 1970–72; Prof. Univ. of Silesia; has directed numerous short feature films; Vice-Chair., Polish Film Asscn 1971–81; Pres. European Fed. of Film Dirs (FERA) 1990–; mem. Polish Acad. of Arts and Sciences, PEN Club, European Film Acad., Pontificia Accademia delle Arti e Lettere; Dr hc (Moscow WGIC) 1998, (Minsk European Univ. Acad. of Arts, Bucharest); Best Director Cannes Film Festival 1980; Special Jury Prize, Venice Film Festival 1982; Grand Prix Venice 1984; State Prize 1st Class 1984; Kt.'s Cross of Order of Polonia Restituta; Gold Cross of Merit 1981; Chevalier de l'Ordre des Sciences et Lettres 1986; Grand Prix Moscow 2000. *Films include:* Death of Provincial 1966 (awards in Venice, Mannheim, Valladolid and Moscow), Structure of Crystals 1969 (award in Mar del Plata), Family Life 1971 (awards in Chicago, Valladolid and Colombo), Illumination 1973 (Grand Prize in Locarno 1973), The Catamount Killing (USA) 1974, Quarterly Balance 1975 (OCIC Prize, West Berlin Int. Film Festival 1975), Camouflage 1977 (special prize, Tehran Int. Film Festival 1977, Grand Prix, Polish Film Festival 1977), Spiral 1978 (Prize of Journalists, V Polish Film Festival 1978, Cannes 1978, OCIC Prize), Wege in der Nacht 1979 (FRG), Constant Factor 1980 (Best Dir Cannes, OCIC Prize) Contract 1980 (Distribution Prize, Venice Film Festival), From a Far Country 1980 (Donatello Prize, Florence), Versuchung 1981, Imperative (Special Prize and Passinetti Award, Venice), The Unapproachable 1982, Year of the Quiet Sun 1984 (Grand Prix Golden Lion, Venice), The Power of Evil 1985 (OCIC Prize, Montreal), Stan Osiadania 1989, Wherever You Are (Germany, Poland, UK) 1989 (Oecumenical Prize, Moscow, Best Script and Act. European Award, Viareggio 1989), Life for Life (Germany, Poland) 1990, At Full Gallop 1995 (Special Jury Prize, Tokyo), Our God's Brother (Italy, Germany, Poland) 1997, Life as a Fatal, Sexually Transmitted Disease 2000 (Grand Prix, Moscow Int. Film Festival), Supplement 2000. *TV films:* Portrait of the Composer (prizes in Cracow, Leipzig), Face to Face 1967, Credit 1968, Pass Mark 1969, Mountains at Dark 1970, Role (FRG) 1971, Behind the Wall 1971, (Grand Prix, San Remo Int. Film Festival 1972), Hipotese (FRG) 1972, Nachtdienst (FRG) 1975, Penderecki Lutosławski Baird (documentary) 1976, Anatomiestunde (FRG) 1977, Haus der Frauen (FRG) 1978, Mein Krakau (documentary) 1979, Blaubart (FRG, Switzerland) 1984 (Prize, Venice Film Festival), Mia Varsavia 1987, Erloeschene Zeiten 1987, The Silent Touch 1993, Wrong Address (BBC) 1995, Don't Be Afraid (RAI) 1996, Weekend Stories 1995–2000. *Stage plays:* One Flew Over the Cuckoo's Nest 1977, Der König stirbt 1980, Mattatoiò 1982, Day and Night, Duo for One 1983, Hiòb, Les Jeux des Femmes (Paris) 1985, Alle Meine Sonne 1986, Giulio Cesare 1986, Alte Zeiten 1988, Koenig Roger 1988, Geburtstag der Infantin 1989, Regina dei Insort 1989, Death and the Maiden (Poznań and Berlin) 1994, Pl. Presidente (Rome, Florence) 1995, Re Cesare (San Miniatò) 1996, L'uomo che vide (San Miniatò, Borgione) 1998, Herodias et Salomé (Rome) 1998, Amys Way (Essen) 1998, Parenti Terribili (Rome) 2002, Der Beweis (Cologne) 2002. *Television:* Old Times (Harold Pinter) ARD 1988, L'Alouette (Jean Anouilh) TVP 2000, Castine Session 2003. *Publications:* Nowele Filmowe (short feature films) 1976, Scenariusze Filmowe (film scripts) 1978, Un rigorista nella fortezza assediata 1982, Scenariusze Filmowe (film scripts) II, III 1986, IV 1998, The Time to Die (autobiog.) 1997, Weekend Stories 1997, Between Kermess and Salon 1999, Six Scripts (USA) 2001. *Leisure interests:* travel, skiing, horse-riding. *Address:* Studio TOR, ul. Puławska 61, 02-595 Warsaw (Office); ul. Kaniowska 114, 01-529 Warsaw, Poland (Home). *Telephone:* (22) 8455303 (Office); (22) 8392556 (Home). *Fax:* (22) 8455303 (Office). *E-mail:* tor@tor.com.pl (Office).

ZAOURAR, Hocine; Algerian photographer; b. 18 Dec. 1952, Birmandreiss; s. of Mohamed Zaourar and Khedidja Bourahla; teacher of photography, Ecole des Beaux-Arts, Algiers 1983–93; fmrly photojournalist Reuters; photojournalist Agence France-Presse, Algiers 1993–; World Press Photo People in the News, 1st Prize 1997, Prix Munn, Paris 1997, Prix Bayeux des correspondants de guerre 1998, Festival Int. du scoop et du journalisme, 1st Prize 1998. *Exhibitions:* "Algeria: A Country in Mourning", Newseum, Arlington, Va 1998, Stern Magazine, Hamburg 1999, Univ. of Beirut 1999, Maison de la Photographie, Paris 1999. *Address:* c/o Agence France-Presse, 6 rue Abd al-Karim-el-Khettabi, Algiers; 5 Lotissement Tardithe, Birmandreiss, Algiers, Algeria (Home). *Telephone:* 21-72-16-54 (Office); 21-54-16-28 (Home). *Fax:* 21-72-14-89 (Office).

ZAPASIEWICZ, Zbigniew; Polish actor and theatre director; b. 13 Sept. 1934; m.; ed State Higher Theatre School, Warsaw; with Dramatyczny Theatre 1966–83, Man. and Artistic Dir 1987–90; with Powszechny Theatre 1983–87; with Polski Theatre 1990–93; with Współczesny Theatre 1993–; lecturer State Higher Theatre School, Warsaw 1959–94, Dean Faculty of Directing 1980–83; more than 500 film, radio and theatre roles; Gold Cross of Merit 1974, Kt's Cross, Order of Polonia Restituta 1979, Meritorius Activist of Culture Award 1997. *Theatre roles include:* Three Sisters 1963, On All Fours 1972, Macbeth 1972, King Lear 1977, Noc Lintopadowa (November Night) 1987, Ambassador 1995, Tango 1997, Nasze miastro (Our Town) 1998, Kwartet (Quartet) 2001. *Plays directed include:* Dismissal of the Greek Envoys 1980, Horsztynski 1996, Adwokat i róże (Barristers and Roses) 1997, Kwartet 2001. *Film roles include:* Ocalenie 1972, Ziemia obiecana (The Promised Land) 1974, Barwy ochronne (Camouflage) 1976, Bez znieczulenia (Without Anaesthetic) 1978, Matka Królów 1982, Mistrz i Małgorzata (The Master and Margarita) 1988, Życie jako smiertelna choroba przenoszona droga píciowa (Life as a Fatal, Sexually Transmitted Disease) 2000. *Address:* Teatr Współczesny, ul. Mokotowska 13, Warsaw, Poland.

ZAPATERO, José Luis Rodríguez; Spanish politician and lawyer; b. 4 Aug. 1960, Valladolid; m. 1990; two d.; worked as a teacher of law; joined Partido Socialista Obrero Español (PSOE) 1978, Leader, Socialist Youth Org., León 1982, MP 1986–, Leader PSOE Regional Chapter for León 1988, mem. PSOE Fed. Exec. Cttee 1997, Sec.-Gen. July 2000–. *Leisure interests:* jogging, trout fishing. *Address:* Partido Socialista Obrero Español, Ferraz 68 y 70, 28008, Madrid, Spain (Office). *Telephone:* (91) 5820444 (Office). *Fax:* (91) 5820422 (Office). *Website:* www.psoe.es (Office).

ZARB, Frank Gustav, MBA; American government official; b. 17 Feb. 1935, New York; s. of Gustave Zarb and Rosemary (née Antinora) Zarb; m. Patricia Koster 1957; one s. one d.; ed Hofstra Univ.; Graduate trainee, Cities Service Oil Co. 1957–62; Gen. Partner, Goodbody & Co. 1962–69; Exec. Vice-Pres., CBWL-Hayden Stone 1969–71, Exec. Vice-Pres. Hayden Stone 1972–73, 1977; Asst Sec., US Dept of Labor 1971–72; Assoc. Dir Exec. Office of the Pres., Office of Man. and Budget 1973–74; Admin., Fed. Energy Admin. 1974–77; Asst to the Pres. for Energy Affairs 1976; Gen. Partner Lazard Frères 1977–88; Chair. and CEO Smith Barney, Harris Upham 1988–93, Smith Barney Shearson 1993; Chair., CEO Nat. Asscn of Securities Dealers 1997–; Dir Securities Investor Protection Corpn 1988; Vice-Chair. Group Chief Exec. Travelers Inc. 1993–94; Chair., Pres., CEO Alexander & Alexander Services Inc., New York 1994–97; Bd Dirs CS First Boston Inc., Council on Foreign Relations; Chair. Bd of Trustees, Hofstra Univ.; mem. US Presidential Advisory Cttee on Fed. Pay, US Investment Policy Advisory Cttee; mem. Bd of Trustees; Gerald R. Ford Foundation Distinguished Scholar Award, Hofstra Univ. *Publications:* The Stockmarket Handbook 1969, Handbook of Financial Markets 1981, The Municipal Bond Handbook. *Address:* Office of General Counsel, The NASDAQ Stock Market, 1801 K Street, NW, Washington, DC 20006, USA. *Telephone:* (202) 728-8088. *Fax:* (202) 728-8321. *Website:* www.nasdaq.com.

ZARE, Richard Neil, BA, PhD, FRSC, FAAS; American professor of chemistry; b. 19 Nov. 1939, Cleveland, Ohio; s. of Milton Zare and Dorothy Sylvia (Amdur) Zare; m. Susan Leigh Shively 1963; three d.; ed Harvard Univ., Univ. of California, Berkeley; Postdoctoral Research Assoc., Jt Inst. for Lab. Astrophysics, Univ. of Colo 1964–65, Asst Prof., Dept of Physics and Astrophysics 1966–68, Assoc. Prof. 1968–69; Asst Prof., Dept of Chem. MIT 1965–66; Prof. of Chem., Columbia Univ. 1969–77, Higgins Prof. of Natural Science 1975–77; Prof. of Chem., Stanford Univ. 1977– (Marguerite Blake Wilbur Prof. of Natural Science 1987–), Shell Distinguished Prof. of Chem. 1980–85, Fellow 1984–86, Prof. of Physics 1992–; Christensen Fellow, St Catherine's Coll., Oxford 1982; Chair. Nat. Science Foundation Advisory Panel (Chem. Div.) 1980–82, Div. of Chemical Physics, American Physical Soc. 1985–86, NAS Panel on Science and Tech. Centers 1987; Chair. Nat. Research Council's Comm. on Physical Sciences, Math. and Applications 1992–95, Nat. Science Bd 1996–2000; mem. Nat. Research Council's Cttee on Atomic and Molecular Science 1983–85, Directed Energy Weapons Study Panel of American Physical Soc. 1985–87, Govt-Univ.-Ind. Roundtable of NAS 1989–, Nat. Science Bd 1992–2000; Chair. Bd of Dirs Annual Reviews Inc. 1995–; Ed. Chemical Physics Letters 1982–85; mem. Editorial Advisory Bd Chemical Physics, Journal of Molecular Spectroscopy, Annual Reviews, Molecular Physics, Cambridge Univ. Press; mem. NAS 1976– (mem. Council 1995–), ACS, American Acad. of Arts and Sciences, American Philosophical Soc.; Fellow American Physical Soc., Int. Advisory Bd, Optical Soc. of America 1994–, Inst. of Physics 1999–; Foreign mem. Royal Soc. 1999; more than 100 distinguished lecturerships; Hon. DSc (Ariz.) 1990, (Columbia) 1999, (State Univ. of W Georgia) 2001; Dr hc (Uppsala) 2000, (Univ. of York) 2001, (Hunnan Univ.) 2002; numerous honours and awards, including Nat. Medal of Science 1983, Irving Langmuir Prize of the American Physical Soc. 1985,

Kirkwood Award Medal (Yale Univ.) 1986, ACS Willard Gibbs Medal 1990, ACS Peter Debye Award 1991, NAS Award in Chemical Sciences 1991, Harvey Prize 1993, Dannie-Heineman Preis 1993, California Scientist of the Year 1997, Eastern Analytical Symposium Award 1997, NASA Exceptional Scientific Achievement Award 1997, ACS Award in Analytical Chem. 1998, Welch Award in Chem. 1999, ACS E. Bright Wilson Award in Spectroscopy 1999, Nobel Laureate Signature Award for Grad. Educ. in Chem. (ACS) 2000, Arthur L. Schawlow Prize in Laser Science, American Physical Soc. 2000, CaSSS Scientific Achievement Award 2000–01, ACS Charles Lathrop Parsons Award 2001, Madison Marshall Award 2001, Distinguished Chemist Award (ACS Sierra Nevada Section) 2002. *Publications:* Angular Momentum 1988, Laser Experiments for Beginners 1995, Companion to Angular Momentum 1998; over 645 research articles. *Leisure interests:* chess, cooking, music, theatre. *Address:* Department of Chemistry, Stanford University, Stanford, CA 94305-5080; 724 Santa Ynez Street, Stanford, CA 94305, USA (Home). *Telephone:* (650) 723-3062. *Fax:* (650) 723-9262. *E-mail:* zare@stanford.edu (Office). *Website:* zarelab.stanford.edu (Office).

ZASADA, Sobiesław; Polish business executive and racing driver; b. 27 Jan. 1930, Dąbrowa Górnicza; m.; one d.; ed Acad. of Commerce, Cracow; winner of 148 car races including Gran Premio of Argentina 1967, Alps Cup 1968, Press on Regardless 1975; European Champion 1966, 1967, 1971, runner-up 1968, 1969, 1972; gen. agent Mercedes-Benz AG, Poland 1990–; Commdr's Cross, Order of Polonia Restituta 1974, Officer's Cross 1981; Kisiel Award 1996. *Publications:* Car. Race. Adventure 1969, Safe Speed 1971, Remarks and Advice 1978, My Races 1996. *Leisure interests:* skiing, water-skiing, sailing, table-tennis, history, economics, geography. *Address:* Zasada SA, ul. Omulewska 27, 04-128 Warsaw, Poland (Office). *Telephone:* (22) 6116700 (Office).

ZASLAVSKAYA, Tatiana Ivanovna, D.ECON.SC.; Russian economist; b. 9 Sept. 1927, Kiev; ed Moscow Univ.; research at Inst. of Econs of Acad. of Sciences; mem. CPSU 1954–90; mem. Inst. of Econs and Org. of Industrial Eng in Siberian Div. of USSR (now Russian) Acad. of Sciences 1963–87; Corresp. mem. USSR (now Russian) Acad. of Sciences 1968–, mem. 1981–; Dir Public Opinion Research Centre, Moscow 1988–91, Head of Dept 1992–; Pres. of Interdisciplinary Academic Center for Social Sciences (Intercenter), Moscow 1993–; mem. All-Union (now Russian) Agricultural Acad. 1988, Council Int. Fund for Survival and Devt of Humanity 1988; Pres. Sociological Asscn of USSR (now Russia) 1989–91; USSR People's Deputy 1989–91; mem. Pres.'s Consulting Council 1991–; mem. Comm. for Labour, Prices and Social Policy; Hon. mem. Polish Acad. of Sciences; several hon. degrees. *Publications include:* The Principle of Material Interest and Wage-Earning on Soviet Kolkhozes 1958, Contemporary Economics of Kolkhozes 1960, Labour Division on the Kolkhoz 1966, The Migration of the Rural Population in the USSR 1970, A Voice of Reform 1989, The Second Socialist Revolution 1991. *Address:* InterCenter, Vernadskogo prospekt 282, Moscow, Russia. *Telephone:* (095) 938-21-12.

ZATULIN, Konstantin Fedorovich; Russian businessman and economist; b. 7 Sept. 1958, Batumi; m.; one d.; ed Moscow State Univ.; functionary Cen. Komsomol Cttee 1988–89; Dir-Gen. Int. Asscn of Heads of Enterprises 1989–; one of founders Moscow Stock Exchange; Chair. Bd of Co.-Rostok; Pres. Moscow Exchange Union 1992–; mem. Bd Russian Party of Unity and Consent 1993–94; Chair. Businessman for New Russia Union 1993–; Chair. Cttee on CIS affairs and connections with compatriots 1994–; mem. State Duma (Parl.) 1993–95; mem. Govt Comm. on Compatriots Abroad 1994–; Dir Inst. for Problems of Diaspora and Integration (now Inst. of CIS Countries) 1996–; Chair. Fund for Devt of Econ. Reforms; Adviser to Mayor of Moscow 1997; Chair. Bd Moscow Fund of Presidential Programmes 2000–; Chair. Derzhava Movt 1998–, Sochi Friends Club 1998–; mem. Bd Otechestvo political org. 1998; Awards of Russian Govt. *Address:* Institute of CIS Countries, B. Polyanka Street 7, 109180 Moscow (Office); 1st Truzhenikov per. 17, Apt. 79, Moscow, Russia (Home). *Telephone:* (095) 959-34-51 (Office); (095) 248-05-79 (Home). *Fax:* (095) 959-34-49 (Office). *E-mail:* institute@zatulin.ru (Office). *Website:* www.zatulin.ru (Office).

ZAVALA, Silvio, DenD; Mexican historian; b. 7 Feb. 1909, Mérida, Yucatán; s. of Arturo Zavala and Mercedes Vallado; m. Huguette Joris 1951; one s. three d.; ed Univ. del Sureste, Univ. Nacional Autónoma de México and Univ. Central de Madrid, Spain; Centre of Historical Studies, Madrid 1933–36; Sec. Nat. Museum of Mexico 1937–38; founder and Dir Revista de Historia de América (review of Pan-American Inst. of Geography and History) 1938–65; Pres. Historical Comm. of Pan-American Inst. of Geography and History 1946–65; mem. Colegio de México 1940, Pres. 1963–66, Emer. Prof. 1981–; Dir Nat. Museum of History, Chapultepec 1946–54; life mem. El Colegio Nacional 1947; Visiting Prof. Univ. de Puerto Rico 1945, Univ. de la Habana 1946; Prof. of History of Social Insts. of America, Univ. Nacional Autónoma de México; Visiting Prof. Mexico City Coll.; Prof. Smith Coll., Mexico; Chief, Section of Educ., Science and Culture of UN 1947; Visiting Lecturer Harvard 1953, Visiting Prof. Washington (Seattle) and Ghent 1956; Perm. del. to UNESCO 1956–62, mem. Exec. Council 1960–66, Vice-Pres. 1962–64; Vice-Pres. Int. Council of Human Sciences and Philosophy 1959–65, Pres. 1965–71; Amb. to France 1966–75; Hon. Pres. Cttee for 450th Anniversary of Foundation of Mérida de Yucatán; Hon. Pres. 48th Int. Congress of Americanists 1994; mem. Exec. Council, Int. Cttee for Historical Sciences; mem. Nat. Acad. of History and Geography, Mexican Acad. of History 1946, Mexican Acad. of Language

1976; corresp. mem. numerous Acads. of History, etc.; Hon. mem. Historical Assen England 1956, Royal Historical Soc., London 1957, American Historical Assen, Washington, DC 1959, Academia Portuguesa da História 1987; Prof. hc Colegio de San Nicolás, Morelia, Inst. of Latin American Studies Univ. of Texas; Hon. DLitt (Columbia) 1954, (Ghent) 1956, (Toulouse) 1965, (Montpellier) 1967, (Seville) 1990, (Mexico) 1996, (Colima) 1996; Nat. Literary Prize, History Div., Mexico 1969, History Prize, Acad. do Monde Latin, Paris 1974, Arch. C. Gerlach Prize, Panamerican Inst. of Geography and History 1986, Aristotle Medal, UNESCO 1989, Citizen's Merit Medal, Mexico 1991, medals from Universidad Complutense and Panamerican Inst. of Geography and History, El Escorial, Spain 1992, Príncipe de Asturias Prize in Social Sciences 1993, Aguirre Beltrán Medal, Veracruz 1996, Benito Juárez Medal, Sociedad Mexicana de Geografía y Estadística 1997; Grand Officier, Légion d'honneur 1973, Grand-Croix, Ordre nat. du Mérite 1975, Gran Cruz Orden Civil Alfonso X el Sabio 1983, Gran Cruz Orden Isabel la Católica 1997, Iberoamerican History Prize, VII Congress of Iberoamerican Assen of History Academics, Rio de Janeiro 2000. *Publications:* Columbus' Discovery in Art, XIX and XX Centuries 1991, Bio-Bibliografía de S.Z. 1999 and many works on the Spanish colonization of America, Latin American history, New World history. *Address:* Montes Urales 310, Lomas de Chapultepec, Deleg. M. Hidalgo, México, DF, 11000 Mexico. *Telephone:* 5520-4418; 5520-9317. *Fax:* 5645-0464.

ZAVALA BAQUERIZO, Jorge Enrique; Ecuadorean lawyer and politician; b. 13 May 1922, Guayaquil; s. of Oswaldo Zavala Arbaiza and Ana C. Baquerizo Germán de Zavala; m. Carolina Egas Núñez de Zavala; four s.; ed Univ. de Guayaquil; Public Prosecutor, 2nd Criminal Tribunal of Guayas 1947; Prof. of Law, Univ. de Guayaquil; Provincial Counsellor Guayas 1956–58; Vice-Deputy of Guayas 1958–60; Pres. Guayaquil Coll. of Lawyers (twice); Constitutional Vice-Pres. of Republic of Ecuador 1968–72; Congressman Guayas Prov., First Nat. Congressman 1984–88; Pres. Congress 1987–88; Minister of Finance and Public Credit 1988–90; Pres. Acad. de Abogados de Guayaquil 1973–74, 1st Nat. Congress of Lawyers 1960, Nat. Comm. of Human Rights, XXV Curso Int. de Criminología; Vice-Pres. various legal confs.; Prof. Univ. of Guayaquil and Catholic Univ. of Guayaquil; Del. of Sociedad Int. de Criminología; mem. Int. Lawyers' Comm., Int. Lawyers' Assen, American Bar Assen, American Judicature Soc., Int. Assen of Penal Law, Exec. Cttee of World Habeas Corpus; Premio Código Civil 1940; Premio Código Penal 1944; Cotenta Prize for univ. work, Premio al Mérito Científico of Municipality of Guayaquil 1966, 1976; Orden al Mérito en el Grado de Gran Cruz. *Publications:* El Proceso Penal Ecuatoriano, Los Delitos contra la Propiedad, La Pena, Delitos contra la Fe Pública, La Victimología, El Delito de Cheque sin Provisión de Fondos and other books on legal topics. *Address:* Zavala, Carmigniani & Illingworth Abogados, Edificio Amazonas, 8th Floor, General Cordova 401 y V.M. Rendon Guayaquil, Ecuador. *Telephone:* (4) 301007 (Office). *Fax:* (9) 775527 (Office). *E-mail:* zbzci@gye.satnet.net (Office).

ZAVARZIN, Col-Gen. Victor Mikhailovich; Russian army officer; b. 28 Nov. 1948, Zaoleshenka, Kursk Region; m.; two d.; ed Ordzhonikidze Higher Gen. Army School, Frunze Mil. Acad., Acad. of Gen. Staff; Commdg posts in Middle Asia Command 1970–78; Head of Staff of Div. Far E Command 1981–85; Head of Staff, Deputy Commdr, Commdr of Div., Commdr Training Cen. Carpathian Command 1985–90; Commdr United Russian-Turkmen Armed Force in Turkmenistan 1993–94; Commdr United Peacekeeping Forces in Tajikistan 1996–97; Deputy, First Deputy Head of Staff Russian Army, responsible for co-operation with CIS countries April–Oct. 1997; Mil. Rep. of Russia to NATO Headquarters, Brussels Nov. 1997–99; led Russian mil. unit from Bosnia and Herzegovina to Kosovo, Yugoslavia, 1999. *Address:* Avenue de Fré 66, 1180 Brussels (Office); NATO, 1110 Brussels, Belgium. *Telephone:* (2) 374-19-74 (Office). *Fax:* (2) 374-74-56 (Office).

ZAVGAYEV, Doku Gapurovich, CandEcon; Russian (Chechen) politician; b. 22 Dec. 1940; mem. CPSU 1966–91; teacher at elementary school, mechanic, engineer of sovkhoz, man. Regional Union Selkhoztechnika, Dir sovkhoz Znamensky, Chair. Nadterechny Regional Exec. Cttee 1971–72; Chief Repub. Union of Sovkhozes 1972–75; Minister of Agric. of Checheno-Ingush SSR 1975–77; head of div., Second Sec. Checheno-Ingush Regional CP Cttee 1977–89; First Sec. Repub. CP Cttee 1989–91; Chair. Supreme Soviet of Checheno-Ingush Autonomous SSR 1990–91, mem. Cen. CPSU Cttee 1990–91; People's Deputy of RSFSR 1990–93; in Admin. of Pres. of Russia 1994–95; elected Pres. of Chechen Repub. 1995–96; Deputy, Council of Russian Fed. 1995–97; Amb. to Tanzania 1997–; Order of Red Banner of Labour, Badge of Honour; awarded four medals. *Publication:* System of Agric. in Checheno-Ingush Republic. *Leisure interests:* walking, travelling. *Address:* Embassy of Russia, Plot No. 73, Ali Hassan Mwinyi Road, Dar es Salaam, P.O. Box 1905, Tanzania. *Telephone:* (51) 666006 (Office). *Fax:* (51) 666818 (Office). *E-mail:* embruss@intafrica.com (Office).

ZAVOS, Panos Michael, BS, PH.D; American biologist; b. Cyprus; ed Emporia State Univ., Kan., Univ. of Minnesota; long career as reproductive specialist; Founder, Dir and Chief Andrologist Andrology Inst. of America; Co-Founder, Scientific Dir and Chief Embryologist Kentucky Center for Reproductive Medicine; Pres. and Chief Exec. ZDL, Inc.; mem. American Soc. for Reproductive Medicine (ASRM), American Soc. of Andrology (ASA), European Soc. for Human Reproduction and Embryology (ESHRE), M. E. Fertility Soc. (MEFS), Japanese Fertility Soc. and numerous other professional socs.; Hon.

Prof. Chinese Acad. of Science. *Publications:* more than 400 specialist articles on reproduction and infertility. *Address:* 2134 Nicholasville Road, Suite #3, Lexington, KY 40503, USA (Office). *Telephone:* (859) 278-6806 (Office). *Fax:* (859) 278-6906 (Office). *E-mail:* drz@aia-zavos.com (Office). *Website:* www .aia-zavos.com (Office).

ZAWADZKI, Włodzimierz, PhD; Polish scientist; b. 4 Jan. 1939, Warsaw; ed Warsaw Univ.; Prof. 1985; scientific worker and Prof. Inst. of Physics Polish Acad. of Sciences (PAN) 1961–; with Massachusetts Inst. of Tech., Cambridge, USA 1965–67, Ecole Normale Supérieure, Paris 1974; Visiting Prof. Linz Univ. 1978, North Texas State Univ. 1980, Tech. Univ., Munich 1981, Innsbruck Univ. 1983, Univ. Sc. et Tech. du Languedoc Montpellier 1984; mem. Polish Physical Soc.; Annual Prize of Polish Science 1973, Maria Sklodowska-Curie Award 1977, State Prize (1st degree, collective) 1978, Mich. Univ. Award 1995, Marian Smoluchowski Medal 1997. *Publications:* over 170 works on theory of semiconductors; also novels and poetry. *Leisure interests:* literature, music, sports, skiing, tennis, basketball. *Address:* al. J. Ch. Szucha 11 m. 26, 00-580 Warsaw, Poland. *Telephone:* (22) 8410285.

ZAWAHIRI, Ayman, MS, DMed; Egyptian guerrilla leader; b. 9 June 1951; grandson of Rabi'a Zawahiri; ed Cairo Univ.; paediatrician; mem. The Muslim Brotherhood (arrested for membership 1966); imprisoned on firearms charge following Egyptian Pres. Sadat's assassination 1981–84; joined mujahideen troops fighting USSR occupation forces in Afghanistan 1984; co-f. Int. Front for Fighting Jews and Crusaders (with Osama bin Laden, 1998; co-f. al Qa'ida; accused of planning bombings of US embassies in E Africa 1998; mem. Shura (al-Qa'ida body containing reps. from other terrorist groups); personal physician and political adviser to Osama bin Laden; fmr. Leader Vanguards of Conquest Movt, Egyptian Islamic Jihad.

ZAWINUL, Josef Erich; Austrian jazz musician; b. 7 July 1932, Vienna; s. of Josef Zawinul and Maria Zawinul; m. Maxine Byars 1964; three s.; ed Grammar School, Real Gymnasium, Vienna Conservatoire, studied piano under Prof. Valerie Zschörner in Vienna, under Raymond Lewental in New York; studied and played classical, folk and jazz music since early childhood; started as professional musician playing with leading Austrian bands and orchestras throughout Europe 1947–59; moved to USA 1959; pianist for Dinah Washington (jazz singer) and Joe Williams 1959–61; joined Julian Cannonball Adderley's band, writing songs including Mercy, Mercy, Mercy and playing in numerous recordings 1961–69; wrote and played on 5 albums of Miles Davis including album in electric jazz In a Silent Way and Bitches Brew; teamed with Wayne Shorter to form own band Weather Report, working as producer, main composer and keyboard instrumentalist 1970–85; own group Zawinul Syndicate 1985–; Grammy Awards for composition of Mercy, Mercy Mercy 1967, In a Silent Way 1967, Birdland (Best Instrumental Composition) 1977; Weather Report named No. 1 Jazz Band 1972–78, 5 of the 8 Weather Report albums named Jazz Albums of the Year (Downbeat Magazine), No. 1. Synthesizer Player 4 consecutive years, No. 1 Composer, Weather Report No. 1 Group (Jazz Forum). *Recordings include:* The Rise and Fall of the Third Stream, Zawinul 1969, Weather Report 1971, I Sing the Body Electric 1972, Sweetnighter 1973, Mysterious Traveller 1974, Tale Spinning 1975, Black Market 1976, Heavy Weather 1977, Mr. Gone 1978, Night Passage 1980, Lost Tribes 1992, Amen 1992, Symphony: Stories of the Danube. *Leisure interests:* boxing, soccer, swimming, philosophy. *Address:* International Music Network, 278 Main Street, Gloucester, MA 01930, USA.

ZBRUYEV, Alexander Victorovich; Russian actor; b. 31 March 1938, Moscow; m. Ludmila Savelyeva; one d.; ed Shchukin Higher School of Theatre Art; actor Moscow Theatre of Lininsky Comsomol 1961–; f. club and restaurant for actors 1998–; People's Artist of Russian Fed. 1989. *Films include:* My Junior Brother, Two Tickets for a Daytime Seance, Great Change, Romance for Those in Love, I Have You Alone, Circle, Wish for Love, Poor Sasha. *Plays include:* Optimistic Tragedy, Hamlet, Goodbye, Boys, The Day of the Wedding, My Poor Marat, 104 Pages About Love, Wizard, Gambler, The Last Night of the Last Tsar, The Barbarian and Heretic. *Leisure interests:* sports, cars. *Address:* Tverskaya str. 19, Apt. 76, 103050 Moscow, Russia (Home). *Telephone:* (095) 299-99-34 (Home).

ZEA AGUILAR, Leopoldo, PhD; Mexican writer and university professor; b. 30 June 1912, Mexico; s. of Leopoldo Zea and Luz Aguilar; m. 1st Elena Prado Vertiz 1943 (divorced); two s. four d.; m. 2nd María Elena Rodríguez Ozan 1982; Ed. review Tierra Nueva 1940; Prof. Escuela Nacional Preparatoria 1942–47; Prof. Escuela Normal de Maestros 1944–45; Prof. Faculty of Philosophy and Letters, Univ. Nacional Autónoma de México 1944; mem. El Colegio de México 1940; Pres., Cttee for the History of Ideas, Panamerican Inst. of Geography and History; Chief of Dept of Univ. Studies, Sec. of Public Educ. 1953–54; research work, 1954–; mem. Soc. Européenne de Culture 1953–; Dir-Gen. of Cultural Relations Foreign Office; Vice-Pres. Historical Comm. of Pan American Inst. of Geography and History 1961–, Dir of Faculty of Philosophy and Letters 1966–70, Prof. Emer. 1971; Dir-Gen. of Cultural Broadcasting 1970–; Co-ordinator, Co-ordination and Diffusion Cen. for Latin American Studies –1994, Univ. Program 1995–; Dr. hc (Univ. of Paris X) 1984, (Moscow) 1984, (Univ. de la Repub., Uruguay) 1985, (Univ. Nacional Autónoma, Mexico) 1988, (Univ. Fernando Villareal del Perú) 1990; Nat. Prize for Sciences and Arts 1980, decorations from Italy, France, Peru, Yugoslavia, Venezuela, Argentina, Dominican Republic, Brazil, The Philippines and Spain. *Publications:* El Positivismo en México 1943, Apogeo y

Decadencia del Positivismo en México 1944, Ensayos sobre Filosofía en la Historia 1948, Dos Etapas del Pensamiento en Hispanoamérica 1949, La Filosofía como Compromiso 1952, América como Conciencia 1952, Conciencia y posibilidad del Mexicano 1952, El Occidente y la Conciencia de México 1953, La Conciencia del Hombre en la Filosofía 1952, América en la conciencia de Europa 1955, La Filosofía en México 1955, Esquema para una Historia de las ideas en América 1956, Del Liberalismo a la Revolución en la Educación Mexicana 1956, América en la Historia 1957, La Cultura y el Hombre de nuestros Días 1959, Latinoamérica y el Mundo 1960, Ensayos sobre México y Latinoamérica 1960, Democracias y Dictaduras en Latinoamérica 1960, L'Amerique Latine et la Culture Occidentale 1961, El Pensamiento Latino-americano 1963, Latinoamérica en la Formación de nuestro tiempo 1965, Antología de la Filosofía Americana Contemporánea 1968, Latin America and the World 1969, Dependencia y Liberación en la Cultura Latinoamericana 1974, Cultura y Filosofía en Latinoamérica 1976, Dialéctica de la Conciencia Americana 1976, Latinoamérica Tercer Mundo 1977, Filosofía de la Historia Americana 1978, Simón Bolívar 1980, Latinoamérica en la Encrucijada de la Historia 1980, Sentido de la Difusión Cultural Latinoamérica 1981, Filosofía de lo Americano 1983, Discurso desde la Marginación y la Barbarie 1988, 500 Años Después. Descubrimiento e Identidad Latinoamericana 1990, L'Amér-ique Latine face à l'histoire 1991, Regreso de las Carabelas 1993, Filosofar a la altura del Hombre, Discrepar para comprender 1993, Fin de siglo XX. Centuria perdida? 1996, Filosofar a lo universal por lo profundo 1998, Fin de Milenio, Emergencia de los marginados 2000. *Leisure interests:* music, art. *Address:* Torre I de Humanidades, 2° piso, Ciudad Universitaria, Mexico, DF 03410 (Office); Cerrada de las Margaritas 25, Col Florida, 01030 México DF, Mexico (Home). *Telephone:* 622-19-02 (Office); 662-03-77 (Home). *Fax:* 616-25-15.

ZEAYEN, Yusuf; Syrian politician and physician; b. 1931; ed Univ. of Damascus; Minister of Agrarian Reform 1963; mem. Presidential Council 1964–65; Prime Minister of Syria Sept.–Dec. 1965, 1966–68; mem. Baath Party. *Address:* c/o Baath Party, Damascus, Syria.

ZECCHINI, Salvatore, MBA; Italian economist, government official and university professor; b. 17 Nov. 1943, Palermo; m. Eliana de Leva 1971; one s. one d.; ed Columbia Univ. and Univ. of Pennsylvania, USA; economist, Research Dept Banca d'Italia, Dir Research Dept 1972–81, Dir 1981–84; Adviser to Govt of Italy 1978–84; Exec. Dir IMF 1984–89; Special Counsellor, OECD 1989–90, Asst Sec.-Gen. 1990–96, then Deputy Sec.-Gen.; Dir Centre for Co-operation of Economies in Transition 1990–96; Prof. of Int. Econ. Policy, Univ. of Rome 1997–; Econ. Adviser to Minister of Finance 1997–2000, to Minster of Industry and Trade 2001–; Dir Public Investment Evaluation Centre 1997–98. *Publications:* The Transition to a Market Economy (co-ed.) 1991, Lessons from The Economic Transition (ed.) 1996; articles in professional journals and books on Econs and int. finance. *Leisure interests:* history, travel, hiking. *Address:* Ministry of Industry and Trade, Via Molise 2, 00187 Rome, Italy (Office). *Telephone:* (06) 47887952 (Office). *Fax:* (06) 47887952 (Office). *E-mail:* zecchini@flashnet.it (Home).

ZEDILLO PONCE de LEÓN, Ernesto, DEcon; Mexican politician and economist; b. 27 April 1951, Mexico City; m. Nilda Núñez; five c.; ed Instituto Nacional Politécnico, Bradford, Colorado and Yale Univs, USA; joined Partido Revolucionario Institucional (PRI) 1971, with Instituto de Estudios Políticos, Económicos y Sociales (Iepes) (affil. to PRI); econ. researcher Dirección Gen. de Programación Económica y Social; Deputy Man. of Finance and Econ. Research, Banco de Mexico (BANXICO), a Dir in charge of the bank's Ficorca scheme, adviser to Bd of Dirs; teacher Colegio de México; Deputy Sec. for Planning and the Budget 1987–88 (f. Programa Nacional de Solidaridad), Sec. 1988–92, Sec. of Public Educ. 1992–93; campaign man. for the late Luis Donaldo Colosio (fmr presidential cand.) 1993–94; Pres. of Mexico 1994–2000; Head UN High Level Panel on Financing for Devt 2000–01; Prof. of Int. Econs and Politics,Yale Univ., USA; Dir Yale Center for the Study of Globalization 2002–; Hon. LLD (Yale Univ.) 2001; Wilbur Cross Medal 2001. *Address:* Yale Center for the Study of Globalization, Betts House, 393 Prospect Street, New Haven, CT 06511, USA (Office). *Telephone:* (203) 432-1900 (Office). *Fax:* (203) 432-1200 (Office). *Website:* www.ycsg.yale.edu (Office).

ZEFFIRELLI, G. Franco (Corsi); Italian theatrical, opera and film producer and designer; b. 12 Feb. 1923, Florence; ed Liceo Artistico, Florence and School of Agriculture, Florence; designer Univ. Productions, Florence; actor Morelli Stoppa Co.; collaborated with Salvador Dali on sets for As You Like It 1948; designed sets for A Streetcar Named Desire, Troilus and Cressida, Three Sisters; producer and designer of numerous operas at La Scala, Milan 1952– and worldwide; cand. Forza Italia 1994–; Prix des Nations 1976. *Exhibition:* Zeffirelli - The Art of Spectacle (Tokyo, Athens, Florence, Milan). *Operas include:* Lucia di Lammermoor, Cavalleria Rusticana, Pagliacci (Covent Garden) 1959, 1973, Falstaff (Covent Garden) 1961, L'elisir d'amore (Glyndebourne) 1961, Don Giovanni, Alcina (Covent Garden) 1962, Tosca, Rigoletto (Covent Garden) 1964, 1966, 1973, (Metropolitan, New York) 1985, Don Giovanni (Staatsoper-Wien) 1972, (Metropolitan, New York) 1990, Otello (Metropolitan, New York) 1972, Antony and Cleopatra (Metropolitan, New York) 1973, Otello (La Scala) 1976, La Bohème (Metropolitan, New York) 1981, Turandot (La Scala) 1983, 1985, (Metropolitan, New York) 1987, Don Carlos 1992, Carmen 1996, Aida (New Theatre, Tokyo) 1997, (Busetto) 2000, La Traviata (Metropolitan, New York) 1998, Tosca (Rome) 2000, Il Travatore (arena di Verona) 2001. *Theatre:* Romeo and Juliet (Old Vic, London) 1960,

Othello (Stratford) 1961, Amleto (Nat. Theatre, London) 1964, After the Fall (Rome) 1964, Who's Afraid of Virginia Woolf (Paris) 1964, (Milan) 1965, La Lupa (Rome) 1965, Much Ado About Nothing (Nat. Theatre, London) 1966, Black Comedy (Rome) 1967, A Delicate Balance (Rome) 1967, Saturday, Sunday, Monday (Nat. Theatre, London) 1973, Filumena (Lyric, London) 1977, Six Characters in Search of an Author (London) 1992. *Films:* The Taming of the Shrew 1966, Florence, Days of Destruction 1966, Romeo and Juliet 1967, Brother Sun and Sister Moon 1973, Jesus of Nazareth 1977, The Champ 1979, Endless Love 1981, La Traviata 1983, Cavalleria Rusticana 1983, Otello 1986, The Young Toscanini 1987, Hamlet 1990, Sparrow 1994, Jane Eyre 1995, Tea With Mussolini 1998, Callas Forever 2002. *Ballet:* Swan Lake 1985; produced Beethoven's Missa Solemnis, San Pietro, Rome 1971. *Publication:* Zeffirelli by Zeffirelli (autobiog.) 1986. *Address:* Via Lucio Volumnio 37, 00178 Rome, Italy. *Fax:* (06) 7184213.

ZEGLIS, John D., LLB; American telecommunications executive and lawyer; ed Univ. of Illinois, Harvard Law School; began legal career as Assoc., Sidley & Austin 1973, later becoming partner –1984; joined AT&T Wireless Services, Inc. 1984, Corp. Vice-Pres. of Law 1984–86, Gen. Counsel 1986–, Vice-Chair. 1997, Pres. 1997, mem. Bd of Dirs 1997–, later becoming Chair. and CEO; Dir Helmerich and Payne Corpn, Dynergy Corpn, Sara Lee Corpn; fmr Sr Ed. Harvard Law Review; Chair. Bd of Trustees, George Washington Univ.; Trustee, Culver Educ. Foundation, Ind., United Way of Tri-State, NY, United Negro Coll. Fund, NY; mem. Bd Rural School and Community Trust, Washington; mem. Kellogg Advisory Bd, J.L. Kellogg Grad. School of Man.; mem. NW Univ., Univ. of Ill. Business Advisory Council. *Address:* Corporate Customer Services Department, AT&T Wireless Group, 7277 164th Avenue, NE, Redmond, WA 98052, USA (Office). *Website:* www.attws.com (Office).

ZEH BLAH, Moses; Liberian politician; b. 18 April 1947; Amb. to Tunisia and Libya –2000; Vice-Pres. of Liberia July 2000–. *Address:* Office of the Vice-President, Executive Mansion, P.O. Box 10-9001, Capitol Hill, 1000 Monrovia 10, Liberia (Office). *E-mail:* emansion@liberia.net (Office).

ZEIDLER, Eberhard Heinrich, OC, OOnt, LLD, DEng, DArch, FRAIC, RCA, OAA, MAIBC, OAQ; Canadian architect; b. 11 Jan. 1926, Braunsdorf, Germany; s. of Paul Zeidler and Dorothea Dabbert; m. Phyllis Jane Abbott 1957; one s. three d.; ed Bauhaus Weimar and Univ. Fridericiana, Karlsruhe Technische Hochschule; designer, Prof. Egon Eiermann, Karlsruhe 1949–50; Assoc. with Prof. Emanuel Lindner, Osnabrück 1950–51; Assoc.-in-Charge of Design, W & W R. L. Blackwell & Craig, Peterborough 1951–54; partner, Blackwell, Craig & Zeidler Architects, Peterborough and Toronto 1954–57, Craig & Zeidler Architects, Peterborough and Toronto 1957–61, Craig, Zeidler & Strong, Peterborough and Toronto 1961–75, Zeidler Partnership/Architects, Toronto 1975–80, Zeidler Roberts Partnership/Architects, Toronto 1980–2001, Zeidler Grinnell Partnership 2001–; Adjunct Prof. Univ. of Toronto 1983–; Hon. Fellow, American Inst. of Architects 1981; Gold Medal, Royal Architectural Inst. of Canada 1986; more than 100 nat. and int. awards. *Projects include:* Ritz-Carlton, Toronto; Torre Mayor, Mexico City; Casino Niagara, Niagara Falls. *Publications:* Healing the Hospital 1974, Multi-use Architecture in the Urban Context 1983, Zeidler Roberts Partnership – Ethics and Architecture 1999. *Leisure interests:* skiing, tennis. *Address:* Zeidler Grinnell Partnership/Architects, 315 Queen Street West, Toronto, Ont., M5V 2X2, Canada. *Telephone:* (416) 596-8300. *Fax:* (416) 596-1408. *E-mail:* mail@zgpa.net (Office). *Website:* www.zgpa.com (Office).

ZEIGERMAN, HE Dror, PhD; Israeli diplomatist and politician; b. 14 May 1948, Israel; s. of Itzchak Zeigerman; m. Asi Sherf; two s. one d.; ed Hebrew Univ., Jerusalem, George Washington Univ., USA; mil. service 1966–69; Chair. Students' Union, Hebrew Univ., Jerusalem 1969–70; Sec. Israeli Liberal Party, Jerusalem Br. 1970–73; Gen. Sec. Zionist Council in Israel; Head Students' Dept, Jewish Agency and World Zionist Org. 1977–81; Likud Party mem. Knesset (Parl.), mem. Cttees. on Foreign Relations and Security, Immigration and Absorption, Educ. 1981–84; Head Students' Dept, Zionist Org. in Israel, Special Adviser on Student and Youth Matters to Head of Exec. Cttee and Zionist Org. 1987–88; Gen. Man. Israel School of Tourism; Consul-Gen. of Israel, Toronto, Canada 1992–95; Amb. to UK 1998–2000. *Leisure interest:* golf. *Address:* c/o Ministry of Foreign Affairs, Hakirya, Romema, Jerusalem 91950, Israel (Office).

ZELENSKAYA, Yelena Emilyevna; Russian opera singer (soprano); b. 1 June 1961, Baku, Azerbaijan; ed Baku State Conservatory; soloist Moscow Municipal Theatre New Opera 1991–96, Bolshoi Theatre 1996–; tours abroad 1992–; guest singer Wiener Kammeroper 1992–; debut as Lady Macbeth in Lucerne, as Donna Elvira in Savonlinna Opera Festival (Finland), as Aida in Deutsche Oper Dusseldorf 1997, as Lisa in Queen of Spades in Berlin Oper, as Tosca in Norway; participated in Wexford Festival 1999. *Opera:* leading parts include Tatyana in Eugene Onegin, Yaroslavna in Prince Igor, Lady Macbeth in Macbeth, Amelia in Ballo in Maschera, Leonora in La Forza del Destino, Countess in Le Nozze di Figaro, Donna Elvira in Don Giovanni. *Address:* State Academic Bolshoi Theatre, Teatralnaya pl. 1, 103009 Moscow, Russia (Office). *Telephone:* (095) 291-43-45 (Office); (095) 229-75-37 (Home).

ZELENSKY, Igor Anatolyevich; Russian ballet dancer; b. 13 July 1969, Labinsk, Krasnodar Dist.; ed Tbilisi School of Choreography, Leningrad Vaganova School of Choreography; with Mariinsky Opera and Ballet Theatre 1989–; dancer with New York City Ballet 1992–97, guest appearances with Royal Ballet, London, 1996–; Grand Prix and Gold Medal Int. Competition of

Ballet Artists, Paris 1990, Prix de Lumières of Italian Cinema. *Ballets include:* Basil in Don Quixote, Siegfried in Swan Lake, Aki in Corsair, Solor in La Bayadère, Albert in Gisèle, leading roles in Romeo and Julliet, Apollo, Manon, Sleeping Beauty and numerous performances in Europe and the USA. *Address:* Mariinsky Theatre, Teatralnaya pl. 1, St Petersburg, Russia (Office). *Telephone:* (812) 114-12-11 (Office). *Website:* www.kirovballet.com.

ZELEZNY, Jan; Czech athlete; b. 16 June 1966, Mlada Boleslav; s. of Jaroslav Zelezny and Jana Zelezny; fmr mechanic and army col; set five world javelin records; won 91 out of 109 competitions 1991–97; personal best javelin throw (of 98.48m) at Jena, 1996 (still the world record at end of 2002); World Champion 1993, 1995, 2001; silver medal Olympic Games 1988, gold medal 1992, 1996, 2000; mem. IOC 2000–01; Sportsman of the Year, Czech Repub. 2001, Medal of Merit, Czech Repub. 2001. *Leisure interests:* fishing, golf, fine wine. *Address:* Czech Olympic Committee, Benešovská 6, 101 00 Prague 10, Czech Republic. *Telephone:* (2) 71734734 (Office). *Fax:* (2) 71731318 (Office). *E-mail:* info@olympic.cz.

ŽELEZNÝ, Vladimír, DPhil; Czech media executive and politician; b. 3 March 1945, Samara, Russia; m. (divorced); two s.; ed Charles Univ., Prague; worked in radio, TV and newspapers 1970–89; spokesman of Civic Forum during Velvet Revolution 1989–91; Adviser to Prime Minister 1991–92; Dir-Gen. TV Nova 1993–; has written and co-written over a hundred popular science programmes for radio and TV; Senator 2002–. *Publications include:* several popular science studies, including Windows of the Universe Wide Open. *Leisure interests:* plastic arts, astronomy. *Address:* TV Nova, CET 21 Association, Kříženeckého nám. 322, 15252 Prague 5–Barrandov, Czech Republic (Office). *Telephone:* (2) 33100120 (Office). *Fax:* (2) 33100121 (Office). *E-mail:* zeleznyv@senat.cz (Office). *Website:* www.senat.cz (Office); www .tv-nova.cz (Office).

ŻELICHOWSKI, Stanisław; Polish politician; b. 9 April 1944, Księżostany, Zamość Prov.; m.; one s. one d.; ed Dept of Forestry, Agriculture Univ., Warsaw; began career in Presidium of Dist People's Council, Ostrołęka; lecturer, Ciechanów Forest Inspectorate 1969; Forest Insp. Dwukoły Forest Inspectorate 1974; mem. Nat. Forestry Council; mem. United Peasants' Party (ZSL) 1970–89; mem. Tribunal of State 1989–91; mem. Main Exec. Cttee Polish Peasants' Party (PSL) and Pres. Prov. Bd of PSL, Ciechanów 1990–, mem. Comm. for Foreign Affairs; Deputy to Sejm (Parl.) 1985–89, 1991–; Minister of Environmental Protection, Natural Resources and Forestry 1993–97, of the Environment 2001–; Vice-Chair. Parl. Cttee for Environmental Protection, Natural Resources and Forestry 1997–2001. *Leisure interests:* tourism, sports. *Address:* Ministry of Environment, ul. Wawelska 52/54, 00-922, Warsaw, Poland (Office). *Telephone:* (22) 5792400 (Office); (22) 5792222 (Office). *Fax:* (22) 5792224 (Office). *E-mail:* marianna.kuklewska@ mos.gov.pl (Office); info@mos.gov.pl (Office). *Website:* www.mos.gov.pl (Office).

ZELLICK, Graham John, PhD, FRSA, FID, FRSM, CCMI; British university vice-chancellor and professor of law; b. 12 Aug. 1948; m. Jennifer Temkin 1975; one s. one d.; ed Christ's Coll., Finchley, London, Gonville & Caius Coll. Cambridge, Stanford Univ., USA; Lecturer in Laws, Queen Mary and Westfield Coll., Univ. of London 1971–78, Reader in Law 1978–82, Prof. of Public Law 1982–88, Dean Faculty of Laws 1984–88, Head Dept of Law 1984–90, Drapers' Prof. of Law 1988–91, Sr Vice-Prin. and Acting Prin. 1990–91, Prin. 1991–98, Prof. of Law 1991–98, Prof. Emer. of Law 1998–; Dean Faculty of Laws, Univ. of London 1986–88, Deputy Vice-Chancellor 1994–97, Vice-Chancellor and Pres. 1997–2003, mem. Council; Visiting Prof. of Law, Univ. of Toronto 1975, 1978–79; Visiting Scholar, St John's Coll. Oxford 1989; Barrister, Middle Temple 1992, Master of Bench 2001; mem. Competition Comm. Appeal Tribunals 2000–, Competition Appeal Tribunal 2003–, Criminal Injuries Compensation Appeals Panel 2000–; Electoral Commr 2001–; Ed. Public Law 1981–86; Founding Ed. European Human Rights Reports 1978–82; Gov. Tel-Aviv Univ., London Goodenough Trust for Overseas Grads; Trustee Samuel Courtauld Trust; Patron The Redress Trust, London Jewish Cultural Centre; Pres. W London (Reform) Synagogue; Academician Acad. of Learned Socs for the Social Sciences 2000–; Ford Foundation Fellow in Criminal Law and Policy 1970–71; Fellow Inst. of Continuing Professional Devt 1998; mem. of the Court, Drapers' Co. 2000–; Freeman, City of London 1992; Hon. Fellow Soc. of Advanced Legal Studies 1997–, Burgon Soc.; Hon. Fellow Gonville and Caius Coll. Cambridge 2001; Hon. LHD (New York) 2001. *Address:* University of London, Senate House, London, WC1E 7HU (until Sept. 2003) (Office); Burton House, Burton Park, Duncton, Petworth, West Sussex, GU28 0QU, England (Home). *Telephone:* (20) 7862-8004 (Office); (1798) 344746 (Sussex) (Home). *Fax:* (20) 7862-8008 (Office); (20) 7862-8025 (London) (Home); (1798) 344746 (Sussex) (Home). *E-mail:* vice-chancellor@ lon.ac.uk (Office).

ZELLWEGER, Renée, BA; American actress; b. 25 April 1969, Katy, Texas; d. of Emil Zellweger and Kjellfrid Zellweger; ed Katy High School, Univ. of Texas at Austin; Best Comedy Film Actress Award for Nurse Betty, Golden Globes 2001. *Films include:* Dazed and Confused 1993, Reality Bites 1994, Love and a .45 1994, 8 Seconds 1994, The Low Life 1995, Empire Records 1995, The Whole Wide World 1996, Jerry Maguire 1996, Texas Chainsaw Massacre: The Next Generation 1997, Deceiver 1997, One True Thing 1998, A Price Above Rubies 1998, The Bachelor 1999, Me, Myself and Irene 2000, Nurse Betty 2000, Bridget Jones' Diary 2001, Chicago (Golden Globe for Best Actress in a Musical 2003, Screen Actors Guild Award for Best Actress 2003) 2002, Down With Love 2003. *Television includes:* Shake, Rattle and Rock Movie 1993, Murder in the Heartland 1994. *Address:* c/o United Talent Agency, 9560 Wilshire Boulevard, Suite 500, Beverly Hills, CA 90212, USA (Office).

ZELNICK, Strauss, JD, MBA; American business executive; b. 26 June 1957, Boston; s. of Allan Zelnick and Elsa Lee Strauss; m. Wendy Belzberg 1990; two s.; ed Wesleyan and Harvard Univs; called to Bar NY 1984; Dir Int. TV Columbia Pictures Int. Corpn 1983–85, Vice-Pres. Int. TV 1985–86; Sr Vice-Pres. Corp. Devt Vestron Inc. 1986–87, Exec. Vice-Pres. 1987, Pres., COO 1988–89; Pres., COO Twentieth Century Fox 1989–93; Pres., CEO Crystal Dynamics 1993–95; Pres., CEO BMG Entertainment N America 1995–98, BMG Entertainment, New York 1998–; Trustee Wesleyan Univ. 1992–; mem. Bd of Dirs Covenant House 1995–2000. *Leisure interests:* squash, sailing, skiing. *Address:* BMG Entertainment North America, 1540 Broadway, Suite 9W, New York, NY 10036, USA.

ZEMAN, Miloš; Czech politician; b. 29 Sept. 1944, Kolín; m. 2nd Ivana Bednarčíková; one s. (from previous marriage) one d.; ed School of Econs, Prague; teacher, School of Econs, Prague 1969–70; joined CP of Czechoslovakia 1968; expelled 1970; researcher Prognostic Inst., Prague 1971–89; Chair. Czech Social Democratic Party 1993–2001; Chair. of Parl. of Czech Repub. 1996–98; mem. Cttee of Socialist Int. 1997–2002; Prime Minister of Czech Repub. 1998–2002; Chair. Cttee for Protection of Econ. Interests of Czech Repub., Cttee for Handicapped People 1998–; presidential cand. 2003. *Publications:* Confession of a Former Prognosis Maker (with J. Bauer) 1995, Our Post-Totalitarian Crisis and Its Potential Cure 1992; many articles on Econs in papers and magazines. *Leisure interests:* biking, cross-country skiing, science fiction, chess. *Address:* Česká strana sociálně demokratická, Hyberská 7, Prague 1, 11000 Czech Republic (Office). *Telephone:* (2) 96522111 (Office).

ZEMAN, Zbyněk Anthony Bohuslav, MA, DPhil, FRHistS; British historian and writer; b. 18 Oct. 1928, Prague, Czechoslovakia; s. of Jaroslav Zeman and Růžena Zeman; m. 1st Sarah Anthea Collins 1956 (died 1998); two s. one d.; m. 2nd Dagmara Hájková; ed London and Oxford Univs; Asst Ed. Foreign Office (Documents on German Foreign Policy) 1957–58; Research Fellow St Antony's Coll., Oxford 1958–61; mem. ed. staff The Economist 1959–62; Lecturer in Modern History Univ. of St Andrews 1963–70; Head of Research Amnesty Int. 1970–73; Dir European Co-operation Research Group and East-West SPRL 1974–76; Prof. of Cen. and SE European Studies Lancaster Univ. 1976–82, Dir Comenius Centre 1976–82, School of European Studies 1976–82; Research Prof. in European History, Oxford Univ. 1982–96, Prof. Emer. 1996–; Professorial Fellow St Edmund Hall, Oxford 1983–96; Visiting Prof., Univ. of Prague 1990–91. *Publications:* Germany and the Revolution in Russia 1915–1918 (Ed.) 1958, The Break-up of the Habsburg Empire 1914–1918 1961, Nazi Propaganda 1964, (co-author) The Merchant of Revolution, A Life of Alexander Helphand (Parvus) 1965, Prague Spring 1969, A Diplomatic History of the First World War 1971, (Jt) International Yearbook of East–West Trade 1975, The Masaryks 1976, (co-author) Comecon Oil and Gas 1977, Selling the War: Art and Propaganda in the Second World War 1978, Heckling Hitler: Caricatures of the Third Reich 1984, Pursued by a Bear, The Making of Eastern Europe 1989 (revised and enlarged as The Making and Breaking of Communist Europe 1991), The Life of Edvard Beneš 1884–1948 1996, Czechoslovakia in Peace and War 1996, Edvard Beneš, Politicky Životopis 2000, Urangeheimnisse, Der Erzgebirge im Brennpunkt der Weltpolitik (co-author) 2002. *Address:* Čínská 18, Prague 6, Czech Republic. *Telephone:* (2) 24318315 (Home). *Fax:* (327) 324042 (Home). *E-mail:* zbynek.zeman@tiscali.cz (Home).

ZEMECKIS, Robert; American film director and writer; b. May 1952, Chicago; m. Mary Ellen Trainor; ed Univ. of Southern California. *Films include:* I Wanna Hold Your Hand (co-screenplay writer) 1978, Romancing the Stone, Back to the Future (co-screenplay writer), II, III, Death Becomes Her (also co-producer), Trespass (co-screenplay writer), Forrest Gump, Who Framed Roger Rabbit?, Contact, The House on Haunted Hill, Cast Away, What Lies Beneath, Ghost Ship; several TV films. *Address:* c/o Gelfand, Rennert & Feldman, 1880 Century Park East, Suite 900, Los Angeles CA 90067 (Office); c/o Karen Sage, CAA, 9830 Wilshire Boulevard, Beverly Hills, CA 90212; South Side Amusement Bungalow 127, 100 Universal City Plaza, CA 91608, USA.

ZEN, E-An, PhD; American geologist (retd); b. 31 May 1928, Beijing; s. of Hung-chun Zen and Sophia Heng-chih Chen Zen; ed Cornell Univ., Harvard Univ.; went to USA 1946, naturalized US citizen 1963; Research Assoc. Fellow Woods Hole Oceanographic Inst. 1955–56, Research Assoc. 1956–58; Asst Prof. Univ. of NC 1958–59; Geologist US Geological Survey 1959–80, Research Geologist 1980–89; Adjunct Prof., Univ. of Md 1990–; Visiting Assoc. Prof. Calif. Inst. of Technology 1962; Crosby Visiting Prof. MIT 1973; Harry H. Hess Sr Visiting Fellow Princeton Univ. 1981; Fellow Geological Soc. of America (mem. Council 1985–88, Vice-Pres. 1991, Pres. 1992), American Acad. of Arts and Sciences, AAAS, Mineral Soc. of America, Council 1975–77, Pres. 1975–76; mem. Geological Soc. Washington (Pres. 1973); mem. NAS; Arthur L. Day Medal, Geological Soc. of America 1986, Roebling Medal, Mineralogical Soc. of America 1991, Maj. John Coke Medal, Geological Soc. London 1992, and numerous others. *Publications:* about 190 scientific articles and monographs in professional journals. *Address:* Department of Geology, University of Maryland, College Park, MD 20742, USA. *Telephone:* (301) 405-4081.

ZENAWI, Meles; Ethiopian politician and fmr guerrilla fighter; b. 1956; leader of Ethiopian People's Revolutionary Democratic Front (EPRDF) which overthrew regime of Mengistu Haile Mariam (q.v.) 1991; Acting Head of State of Ethiopia May–June, Pres. 1991–95; Prime Minister of Ethiopia 1995–. *Address:* Office of the Prime Minister, P.O. Box 1013, Addis Ababa, Ethiopia. *Telephone:* (1) 552044.

ZENDER, J.W. Hans; German composer and conductor; b. 22 Nov. 1936, Wiesbaden; s. of Dr. Franz Zender and Marianne (née Fromm) Zender; m. Gertrud-Maria Achenbach 1962; ed Acad. Music, Freiburg; studied composition and piano; conductor, Freiburg im Breisgau 1959–63; Chief Conductor, Bonn City Theatre 1964–68; Gen. Dir of Music, Kiel 1969–72; Chief Conductor, Radio Symphony and Chamber Orchestras, Saarbrücken 1972–82; Gen. Dir of Music (Philharmonia and City Opera), Hamburg 1984–87; Chief Conductor Radio Chamber Orchestra, Netherlands Broadcasting Corpn; Prin. Guest Conductor Opéra Nat., Brussels 1987–90; Guest Conductor SWF Symphony Orchestra –1999; Prof. of Composition, Frankfurt Musikhochschule 1988; mem. Freie Akademie der Künste, Hamburg, Akademie der Künste, Berlin, Bayerische Akademie der Künste; numerous recordings. *Major works include:* Canto I–VIII 1965–96, Zeitströme 1974, Mujinokyo 1975, Litanei 1976, Lo-Shu I–VI 1977–89, Hölderlin Lesen (string quartet) 1979, Dialog mit Haydn 1982, Stephen Climax (opera) 1979–84, Don Quixote (opera) 1989–91, Schubert's Winterreise (for soloists, choir, large orchestra and live electronics) 1993–97. *Publication:* Happy New Ears (essays) 1991, Wir steigen niemals in den selben Fluss (essays) 1996. *Leisure interests:* literature, art. *Address:* c/o Astrid Schoeke, Moernckebergallee 41, 30453 Hannover ; Am Rosenheck, 65812 Bad Soden, Germany. *Fax:* (6174) 930054.

ZENG PEIYAN; Chinese politician and electronics engineer; b. Dec. 1938, Shanghai; ed Tsinghua Univ.; joined CCP 1978; Second then First Sec. Science and Tech. Counsellor's Office, Embassy, USA; Dir-Gen. Gen. Office then Dir-Gen. Planning Dept of Ministry of Electronics Industry 1984; Vice-Minister, Ministry of Electronics Industry 1987, Ministry of Machinery-Building and Electronics Industry 1988; alt. mem. 14th CCP Cen. Cttee 1992–97; Deputy Sec.-Gen. and Dir of Office (Minister) Cen. Finance and Econ. Leading Group 1992; Vice-Chair. State Planning Comm. 1993; mem. 15th CCP Cen. Cttee 1997–2002, 16th CCP Cen. Cttee 2002–; Minister of State Devt and Planning Comm. 1998–2003; Chair. Western Region Devt Office, State Council 2000–03, Chair. Information Office, State Council 2001–03, Vice-Premier, State Council 2003–. *Address:* State Council, Beijing, People's Republic of China.

ZENG QINGHONG; Chinese political strategist; s. of Zeng Shan; fmr engineer in rocket and missile design; fmr Deputy Dir-Gen Office, Cen. Cttee of CCP, alt. mem. Cen. Cttee 1992–, Politburo 1997–, mem. Standing Cttee CCP Politburo 2002–; Chief Strategist to Pres. Jiang Zemin –2002, Head CCP Org. Dept 1999–. *Address:* Central Committee of Chinese Communist Party, Beijing, People's Republic of China.

ZENG XIANLIN; Chinese government official; b. 1929, Anyue, Sichuan; Vice-Minister for State Planning Comm. 1986; Vice-Minister for Science and Tech. 1985–87, for State Planning Comm. 1986–87; Minister for Light Industry 1987–93; Vice-Chair. Finance and Econ. Cttee of 9th NPC 1998–; alt. mem. 13th CCP Cen. Cttee 1987–92; alt. mem. 14th CCP Cen. Cttee 1992–97. *Address:* c/o Standing Committee of National People's Congress, Beijing, People's Republic of China.

ZENG YI; Chinese virologist and cancer research specialist; b. 8 March 1929, Guangdong Prov.; s. of Zeng Chin-yao and Chen Chai; m. Li Ze-lin 1953; one s. one d.; ed Shanghai No. 1 Medical Coll.; Vice-Pres. Chinese Acad. of Preventative Medical Science 1989–; Deputy Dir AIDS Prevention Dept 1988–; special interests: tumor viruses, HIV. *Address:* Chinese Academy of Preventative Medicine, 10 Tiantan Xili, Beijing; Institute of Virology, 100 Ying Xin Jie, Beijing, People's Republic of China. *Telephone:* 338621.

ZENTMYER, George Aubrey, Jr, AB, PhD; American professor of plant pathology; b. 9 Aug. 1913, Nebraska; s. of George Aubrey Zentmyer and Mary Strahorn Zentmyer; m. Dorothy Anne Dudley 1941; three d.; ed Univ. of California; Asst Forest Pathologist, US Dept of Agric., San Francisco 1937–40; Asst Plant Pathologist Conn. Agric. Experimental Station, New Haven 1940–44; Asst Plant Pathologist Univ. of Calif. 1944–62, Plant Pathologist and Prof. of Plant Pathology 1962–81, Prof. Emer. 1981–, Chair. Dept of Plant Pathology 1968–73; Pres. American Phytopathological Soc. 1966, Fellow 1968; Pres. Pacific Div. AAAS 1975; Fellow Explorers Club Bd of Dirs, American Phytopathology Soc. Foundation 1986– (Vice-Pres. 1991–), UCR Foundation Bd of Dirs 1993–94; Pres. Bd of Dirs, Riverside Hospice 1984; Pres. Bd of Dirs, UCR Friends of Botanic Gardens 1987–89; Fellow AAAS, mem. Int. Soc. for Plant Pathology, NAS and numerous socs and cttees; Assoc. Ed. Annual Review of Phytopathology 1971–; mem. Bd of Dirs Calif. Museum of Photography 1987–; Vice-Pres. Bd of Dirs, Friends of Mission Inn 1990–91, Pres. 1991–93; Guggenheim Fellow, Australia 1964–65, NATO Sr Science Fellow, England 1971; Award of Honour, Calif. Avocado Soc. 1954, Special Award 1981, Award of Merit, American Phytopathological Soc. 1972, Award of Distinction 1983, Rockefeller Foundation Bellagio Scholar 1985,

Emer. Faculty Award, Univ. of Calif., Riverside 1990, Faculty Public Service Award 1991, Lifetime Achievement Award (Pacific Div., American Phytopathological Soc.) 1991. *Publications:* Recent Advances in Pest Control 1957, Plant Disease Development and Control 1968, Plant Pathology: An Advanced Treatise 1977, Soil-Root Interface 1979, Phytophthora: Its Biology, Taxonomy, Ecology, Pathology 1983, Ecology and Management of Soilborne Plant Pathogens 1985, Compendium of Tropical Fruit Diseases 1994; and numerous papers in scientific journals. *Leisure interests:* fishing, sports, stamp collecting, photography. *Address:* Department of Plant Biology, University of California, Riverside, CA 92521 (Office); 708 Via La Paloma, Riverside, CA 92507, USA (Home). *Fax:* (909) 787-4294.

ZERBO, Col Saye; Burkinabè politician and army officer; b. Aug. 1932, Tougan; joined French army 1950, Upper Voltan army 1961; fmr paratrooper; served Indo-China and Algeria; studied Mil. Coll., Fréjus; courses at Artillery School and Staff Coll. 1966; graduated from Ecole supérieure de guerre 1973; Minister of Foreign Affairs 1974–76; Commdr Combined Regt, Ouagadougou and Dir Bureau of Studies, Armed Forces Staff; led coup to depose Pres. Lamizana Nov. 1980; Pres. of Upper Volta (now Burkina Faso) 1980–82 (overthrown in coup Nov. 1982, arrested Sept. 1983, sentenced to 15 years' imprisonment, May 1984).

ZEROUAL, Gen. Lamine; Algerian head of state and army officer; Minister of Defence July 1993; Supreme Commdr and C-in-C of Armed Forces; Pres. of Algeria 1994–99, also Minister of Defence. *Address:* c/o Office of the President, el-Mouradia, Algiers, Algeria.

ZETSCHE, Dieter; German business executive; b. 5 May 1953, Istanbul; ed Univ. of Karlsruhe, Univ. of Paderborn; joined Research Dept of Daimler-Benz AG 1976–87, Dir of Devt. Dept Mercedes-Benz do Brasil 1987–89, mem. Bd 1988–89, Pres. Mercedes-Benz Argentina 1989–91; Pres. Freightliner Corp., Portland, Ore., USA 1991–92; mem. Bd Mercedes-Benz AG 1992–97, Daimler-Chrysler AG 1997–99, CEO 1999–, Chair. 2000–. *Address:* Daimler-Chrysler AG, 70546 Stuttgart, Germany (Office).

ZEWAIL, Ahmed H., PhD; American (born Egyptian) professor of chemistry and physics; b. 26 Feb. 1946, Damahhour, Egypt; m. Dema Zewail; four c.; ed Alexandria Univ., Univ. of Pennsylvania; IBM Postdoctoral Fellow, Univ. of Calif., Berkeley 1974–76; Asst Prof. of Chemical Physics, Calif. Inst. of Tech. (Caltech) 1976–, Assoc. Prof. 1978–82; Prof. 1982–89, Linus Pauling Prof. of Chemical Physics 1990–94, Linus Pauling Chair. Prof. of Chem. and Prof. of Physics 1995; Dir NSF Lab. for Molecular Sciences 1996–; mem. American Physical Soc., NAS, Académie Européene des Sciences, Arts et Lettres, American Philosophical Soc., Pontifical Acad. of Sciences and others; hon. degrees from Oxford Univ., American Univ., Cairo, Egypt, Katholieke Univ., Leuven, Belgium, Univ. of Pa, USA, Univ. of Lausanne, Switzerland, Swinburne Univ., Australia, Arab Acad. for Science & Tech., Egypt, Alexandria Univ., Egypt, Univ. of New Brunswick, Canada, Univ. of Rome, Univ. of Liège, Belgium; Buck-Whitney Medal, King Faisal Int. Prize, Carl Zeiss Int. Award, Earl K. Plyler Prize, Wolf Prize in Chem., Bonner Chemiepreis, Herbert P. Broida Prize, Order of Merit (First Class), Sciences & Arts, Egypt, Peter Debye Award, Robert A. Welch Award in Chem., Linus Pauling Medal, Benjamin Franklin Medal, E. O. Lawrence Award, Nobel Prize in Chem. 1999, Grand Collar of the Nile, Highest Order of Egypt, Order of Zayed, Highest Presidential Hon., State of UAE, Order of Cedar, Highest Rank of Comm., State of Lebanon, Order of Merit of Tunisia, Vatican Pontifical Acad. Insignia 2000 and numerous other prizes and awards. *Publications:* nearly 400 papers published, 7 books edited, 2 vols published. *Address:* California Institute of Technology, Arthur Amos Noyes Laboratory of Chemical Physics, Mail Code 127-72, Pasadena, CA 91125, USA (Office).

ZHAI TAIFENG; Chinese party official; b. May 1933, Tangshan City, Hebei Prov.; ed Chinese People's Univ. 1955–57; joined CCP 1949; Vice-Chair. Beijing Fed. of Trade Unions 1981; Deputy Sec.-Gen. Propaganda Dept of CCP Cen. Cttee 1986, Sec.-Gen. and Vice-Dir 1991–; Vice-Chair. Chinese Writers' Asscn; mem. 14th CCP Cen. Comm. for Discipline Inspection 1992–97. *Address:* Propaganda Department, Chinese Communist Party Central Committee, Beijing, People's Republic of China.

ZHANG AIPING, Col-Gen.; Chinese politician and army officer; b. 1910, Daxian Co., Sichuan Prov.; joined CCP 1928, Red Army 1929; veteran army and party cadre; mil. cadre in East China 1949–54; Deputy Chief of Gen. Staff PLA 1954–67; rank of Col-Gen. PLA 1955–; alt. mem. 8th Cen. Cttee CCP 1958; criticized and removed from office during Cultural Revolution 1967; Chair. Science and Tech. Comm. for Nat. Defence 1975–77; Deputy Chief of Gen. Staff PLA 1977; mem. 11th Cen. Cttee CCP 1977; a Vice-Premier 1980–82; Minister of Defence 1982–88; mem. 12th Cen. CCP Cttee 1982–85; State Councillor 1982–88; Deputy Sec.-Gen. Mil. Comm. under CCP Cen. Cttee 1982–88; mem. Cen. Mil. Comm. 1983–88; mem. Standing Cttee of Cen. Advisory Comm. 1987–92; mem. Presidium 14th CCP Nat. Congress 1992. *Address:* c/o State Council, Beijing, People's Republic of China.

ZHANG BAIFA; Chinese administrator; b. 1934, Xianghe Co., Hebei Prov.; joined CCP 1954; Vice-Minister of State Capital Construction Comm. 1976–82; Vice-Mayor of Beijing Municipality 1982–97; del. 13th Cen. Cttee CCP 1987–91, del. 14th 1992; Standing Cttee mem. CPC 7th Beijing Municipal Cttee 1992–97; Vice-Chair. Capital Planning and Construction Comm. *Address:* c/o Office of Vice-Mayor, Beijing Municipal Government, Beijing City, People's Republic of China.

ZHANG BAOMING; Chinese administrator; b. Nov. 1940, Qiqihar, Heilongjiang Prov.; ed Fuxin Mining Inst.; joined CCP 1974; Vice-Minister of Coal Industry 1993–98; Dir State Bureau of Coal Industry 1998–. *Address:* State Bureau of Coal Industry, Beijing, People's Republic of China.

ZHANG CHAOYANG; Chinese business executive and inventor; b. 1965, Xi'an, Shaanxi Prov.; ed Tsinghua Univ., Mass. Inst. of Tech.; Chief Rep. in China, Internet Securities 1995–; founder of ITC and the inventor of the Chinese search engine Sohu. *Address:* Guanghua Chang'an Dasha, 7 Jianguomennei Da Jie, Beijing, People's Republic of China. *Telephone:* (10) 65102160.

ZHANG CHENGZHI; Chinese writer; b. 1948, Beijing; ed Beijing Univ.; mem. Inst. of Nationalities, Chinese Acad. of Social Sciences; mem. Chinese Writers' Asscn. *Publications include:* The Black Steed, Rivers of the North, Golden Pastureland.

ZHANG CUNHAO, MSc; Chinese physical chemist; b. Chang Tsun-Hao, Feb. 1928, Tianjin; m. Chi Yunxia; two s.; ed Nanjing Cen. Univ., Univ. of Michigan, USA, Chinese Univ. of Hong Kong; Assoc. Research Fellow, Research Fellow, Vice-Dir, then Dir Dalian Inst. of Chemical Physics, Chinese Acad. of Sciences 1951–, Prof. 1962–; Fellow Chinese Acad. of Sciences 1980–; Hon. Pres. Nat. Natural Science Foundation of China 1999–; Hon. DSc; Nat. Natural Sciences Award (2nd and 3rd Class) 1957, 1982, 1993, 1997, 1999; Chinese Acad. of Sciences Award 1980, 1985, 1989, 1991, 1996, 1997. *Publications:* more than 90 research papers. *Address:* Dalian Institute of Chemical Physics, Chinese Academy of Sciences, Dalian 116023, Liaoning Province (Office); National Natural Science Foundation of China, 83 Shuangqing Road, Beijing 100080; Bldg 817-3, Room 501, Zhong Guan Cun, Beijing 100080, People's Republic of China. *Telephone:* (10) 62327134 (Office); (10) 62554430 (Home). *Fax:* (10) 62327087 (Office). *Website:* zhangch@nsfc .gov.cn (Office).

ZHANG DAINIAN; Chinese philosopher; b. 23 May 1909, Xianxian, Hebei Prov.; ed Peking Teachers' Univ.; Prof. Dept of Philosophy, Qinghua Univ.; Chair. Chinese Soc. of History of Philosophy 1980–; Dir Research Inst. of Ideology and Culture, Qinghua Univ. 1986–. *Publications:* Zhongguo Zhexue Dagang (Outline of Chinese Philosophy), Zhongguo Weiwuzhuyi Sixiang Jian Shi (A Brief History of Chinese Materialism), Zhongguo Zhexue Fawei (An Exploration of Chinese Philosophy). *Address:* Department of Philosophy, Qinghua University, 1 Qinghuayuan, Beijing 100084, People's Republic of China (Office). *Telephone:* 62561144 (Office). *Fax:* 62562768.

ZHANG DEJIANG; Chinese politician; b. Nov. 1946, Taian Co., Liaoning Prov.; ed Yanbian Univ. Kim Il Sung Univ. N Korea; mem. CCP 1971–; Vice-Pres. Yanbian Univ. 1980–83; Deputy Sec. CCP Yanji City Cttee 1983–85; Deputy Sec. CCP Yanbian Korean Autonomous Prefectural Cttee 1985–86; Vice-Minister of Civil Affairs 1986; alt. mem. 14th CCP Cen. Cttee 1992–97; mem. 15th CCP Cen. Cttee 1997–2002; Sec. CCP Jilin Provincial Cttee 1995–98; Sec. CCP Zhejiang Prov. Cttee 1998. *Address:* Zhejiang Provincial Committee of Chinese Communist Party, Hangzhou, People's Republic of China.

ZHANG DELIN; Chinese government and party official; b. Aug. 1939, Beijing; ed Tsinghua Univ., joined CCP 1964; Mayor of Harbin 1990; Vice-Minister of Machine-Bldg and Electronics 1991; Vice-Minister of Machine-Bldg 1993; Vice-Sec. CCP Sichuan Provincial Cttee and Sec. CCP Chongqing City Cttee 1996; Sec. CCP Chongqing Mun. Cttee 1997–99; Mayor of Chongqing 1997–99; mem. 15th CCP Cen. Cttee 1997–2002. *Address:* Chinese Communist Party Chongqing Municipal Committee, Chongqing, Sichuan Province, People's Republic of China.

ZHANG DEQIN; Chinese administrator; b. Dec. 1933, Xiaoxian Co., Anhui Prov.; ed Shanghai Fudan Univ.; Dir State Bureau for Preservation of Cultural Relics 1988–96, Pres. China Cultural Relics Exchange Asscn 1996–; mem. 8th Nat. Cttee CPPCC 1993. *Address:* Administrative Bureau for Museums and Archaeological Data, Beijing, People's Republic of China.

ZHANG DINGHUA; Chinese politician; b. June 1933, Shanxian Co., Henan Prov.; ed Northwest Univ.; joined CCP 1956; Sec. CCP Dagang Petroleum Admin. Bureau Cttee; Dir Propaganda Dept CCP Tianjin Mun. Cttee, Sec. CCP Tianjin Mun. Comm. for Discipline Inspection; mem. 13th CCP Cen. Comm. for Discipline Inspection 1987; Vice-Sec. CCP Inner Mongolia Autonomous Regional Cttee 1988; apptd Vice-Chair. and First Sec. Secr. All-China Fed. of Trade Unions 1991; mem. 14th CCP Cen. Cttee 1992, 15th CCP Cen. Cttee 1997–2002. *Address:* All-China Federation of Trade Unions, 10 Fu Xing Men Wai Jie, Beijing 100865, People's Republic of China. *Telephone:* (10) 68592114. *Fax:* (10) 68552030.

ZHANG FUSEN; Chinese politician; b. March 1940, Shunyi Co., Beijing Municipality; ed Tsinghua Univ.; joined CCP 1958; Vice-Sec. then Sec. CCP Haidian Dist Cttee of Beijing Municipality 1984; mem. Standing Cttee of CCP Beijing Mun. Cttee 1990; Vice-Sec. CCP Xinjiang Uygur Autonomous Regional Cttee 1990; mem. 14th CCP Cen. Cttee 1992; Vice-Minister of Justice; Vice-Sec. CCP Beijing Mun. Cttee 1997–2001; mem. 15th CCP Cen. Cttee 1997–2002, 16th CCP Cen. Cttee 2002–; Minister of Justice 2001–.

Address: Ministry of Justice, 10 Chaoyangmennan Dajie, Chao Yang Qu, Beijing 100020, People's Republic of China (Office). *Telephone:* (10) 65205114 (Office). *Fax:* (10) 65205316.

ZHANG GONG, Gen.; Chinese army officer and party official; b. 1935, Yuanping Co., Shanxi Prov.; joined PLA 1951, CCP 1961; Dir of Political Dept Beijing Mil. Area Command 1985; rank of Maj.-Gen. PLA 1988; Political Commissar Chengdu Mil. Region 1992, Political Commissar Acad. of Mil. Sciences 1994–; rank of Gen. 1998; mem. 14th CCP Cen. Cttee 1992–97, 15th CCP Cen. Cttee 1997–2002. *Address:* Academy of Military Science of People's Liberation Army, Xianghongqi, Haidian District, Beijing, People's Republic of China.

ZHANG GUOGUANG; Chinese politician; b. April 1945, Suizhong Co., Liaoning Prov.; ed Beijing Aeronautics Inst.; joined CCP 1966; Sec. CCP Shenyang City Cttee 1990; Vice-Sec. CCP Liaoning Provincial Cttee 1993–2001; mem. 15th CCP Cen. Cttee 1997–2002; Gov. Liaoning Prov. 1998–2001; Acting Gov., then Gov. Hubei Prov. 2001–. *Address:* Office of the Governor, Hubei People's Government, Wuhan, People's Republic of China (Office).

ZHANG GUOLI; Chinese actor and director; b. 1955, Shaanxi; with Sichuan People's Art Theatre 1983; with China Rail Arts Co. Drama Troupe, Beijing 1993; won 4th Nat. Theatre Plum Blossom Award for Best Actor; MTV Grand Award for Best Dir 1995; Hundred-Flower Award for Best Actor 1996. *Films:* The Trouble-shooters 1988, The Strangers in Beijing 1996, A Long Sigh 2000. *Television:* Hunchback Liu: The Prime Minister 1996, The Legend of Liulichang 1998, Emperor Kangxi Travelling Incognito 1999, Emperor Kangxi Travelling Incognito: A Sequel 2000. *Address:* China Rail Arts Company Drama Troupe, Beijing, People's Republic of China (Office).

ZHANG HAORUO; Chinese politician and engineer; b. 1932, Gongxian Co., Henan Prov.; ed Qinghua Univ. and in USSR; joined CCP 1950; Gov. of Sichuan Prov. 1988–93; Deputy Sec. CCP Sichuan Prov. 1988–93; Minister of Internal Trade 1993–95; Vice-Chair. and Sec. Party Group, State Comm. for Restructuring the Economy 1995–98; Vice-Chair. Environment and Resources Protection Cttee, 9th NPC 1998–. *Address:* c/o Standing Committee of National People's Congress, Beijing, People's Republic of China.

ZHANG HUSHENG; Chinese journalist; fmr Dir Int. Dept, People's Daily, Ed.-in-Chief Overseas Edn 1991–, Deputy Ed.-in-Chief People's Daily 1995–; Head of Information Bureau of 7th NPC Standing Cttee. *Address:* People's Daily, 2 Jin Tai Xi Lu, Chao Yang Men Wai, Beijing 100733, People's Republic of China. *Telephone:* (10) 65092121. *Fax:* (10) 65091982.

ZHANG JIANMIN; Chinese party official; b. 1931, Beijing; Vice-Mayor of Beijing 1984–93; mem. Standing Cttee, Beijing 1987–; alt. mem. 14th CCP Cen. Cttee 1992–97; Chair. Beijing Municipal 10th People's Congress, Standing Cttee 1993–2001; NPC Deputy, Beijing Municipality. *Address:* Beijing Municipal People's Congress, Beijing, People's Republic of China.

ZHANG JIE, BA; Chinese writer; b. 27 April 1937, Beijing; d. of Zhang Shanzhi; ed People's Univ., Beijing; Visiting Prof., Wesleyan Univ., Middletown, Conn., USA 1989–90, 1994–95; Council mem. Chinese Asscn of Writers; mem. Int. PEN (China Br.); mem. Beijing Political Consultative Conf.; Vice-Pres. Beijing Writers' Asscn; has lectured extensively in Europe and USA; Hon. mem. American Acad. and Inst. of Arts and Letters; Nat. Awards for Short Stories, Novella and Novel (only writer to have won all three awards 1949–2000); several other awards. *Publications:* novels: Heavy Wings 1981, Only One Sun 1988, My Unlettered Heart 1998; short stories and novellas: The Ark 1983, Emerald 1985, Collection of Novellas 1986, Inner Fire 1992; short stories: Love Must Not Be Forgotten 1980, Collection of Short Stories and Movie Scripts 1980, On a Green Lawn 1983, A Chinese Woman in Europe 1989, As Long as Nothing Happens, Nothing Will (Malaparte Prize, Italy 1989), You Are My Soul Friend 1990, Gone is the One who Held Me Dearest in the World 1994, Without Words (A Novel in Three Parts) (Laoshe Award 2002, Beijing Govt Literature Award 2002, Selection of Best Fiction Award 2003) 2002; five collections of memoirs. *Leisure interest:* music. *Address:* 501, #97 Qian Men Xi Da Jie, Beijing 100031, People's Republic of China; c/o Tang Di, 20 Hemlock Drive, Sleepy Hollow, NY 10591, USA. *Telephone:* (10) 6603-8673 (Beijing); (914) 631-3761 (USA).

ZHANG JIN; Chinese scientist and university professor; ed Qinghua Univ., Beijing, Beijing Univ. of Aeronautics and Astronautics; specializes in computation of structural dynamics and mechanics of new complex materials for aviation industry; Guest Prof. MIT, USA; Prof., Beijing Univ. of Aeronautics and Astronautics; Guest Research Fellow Univ. of Calif., Berkeley, USA. *Publications include:* The Dynamic Mechanism and Application of New Complex Materials (co-author); scientific papers. *Address:* Beijing University of Aeronautics and Astronautics, 37 Xueyuan Road, Beijing 100083, People's Republic of China.

ZHANG JINGFU; Chinese politician; b. 1914, Feidong Co., Anhui Prov.; fmr Vice-Minister of Local Industry and Vice-Pres. Scientific and Tech. Comm.; alt. mem. 8th Cen. Cttee of CCP 1956; criticized and removed from office during Cultural Revolution 1967; Minister of Finance 1975–79; Gov. and First Sec. Anhui Prov. Cttee 1980–81; First Political Comm. Anhui Mil. Div. 1980–82; State Councillor 1982–88; Minister in Charge of State Econ. Comm. 1982–84; mem. State Finance and Econ. Comm.; mem. 12th Cen. CCP Cttee

1982–87; mem. Standing Comm. of Cen. Advisory Comm. 1987–92; mem. Presidium 14th CCP Nat. Congress 1992; Chair. Guidance Cttee for State Examinations for Econ. Man. Personnel 1983; Hon. Pres. Soc. for Study of Workers' Educ. 1984; Chair. Nat. Industrial Safety Cttee 1985; Pres. Chinese Asscn for Int. Exchange of Personnel 1986–. *Address:* c/o State Economic Commission, Sanlihe, Fuxingmenwai, Beijing, People's Republic of China.

ZHANG JUNJIU; Chinese business executive; Vice-Pres. China North Industries Group 1990–93; Pres. China Ordnance Corpn, China N Industries Group; Gen. Man. China Armament Industry Gen. Corpn 1993–; alt. mem. 14th CCP Cen. Cttee 1992–97; mem. 15th CCP Cen. Cttee 1997–2002; Vice-Pres. and First Sec. Secr. of All-China Fed. of Trade Unions 1998–; Vice-Minister, State Comm. of Science, Tech. and Industry for Nat. Defence 1998–. *Address:* China Ordnance Corporation, Beijing, People's Republic of China.

ZHANG KANGKANG; Chinese writer; b. 1950, Xinhui, Guangdong Prov.; ed Heilongjiang Provincial School of Arts, Coll. Humanities, Luxum Inst. of Literature; farm labourer during Cultural Revolution 1969–77; writer 1972–; Vice-Chair. Heilongjiang Prov. Writers Asscn; won various nat. prizes for novellas and short stories. *Publications:* The Dividing Line 1975, The Red Poppy Flower 1985, The Invisible Companion 1986, The Gallery of Love, Self-selected Works of Zhang Kangkang (5 vols), Cruelty, The Northern Lights, The Fourth World, Sandstorm 1985. *Leisure interests:* music, travel. *Address:* Heilongjiang Provincial Writers Association, Harbin, Heilongjiang Province, People's Republic of China (Office).

ZHANG KEHUI; Chinese politician; b. Zhang Youyi, Feb. 1928, Zhanghua Co., Taiwan; m. Hong Xiaoling; ed Taiwan Teachers' Coll., Xiamen Univ., China; joined CCP 1948; joined Taiwan Democratic Self-Government League 1979; Vice-Dir Taiwan Affairs Office of State Council 1990; Chair. 4th and 5th Councils, All-China Fed. of Taiwan Compatriots 1991–97, Hon. Chair. 6th Council 1997–; Vice-Chair. Taiwan Democratic Self-Government League 5th Cen. Cttee 1992, Chair. 6th Cen. Cttee 1997–; mem. Exec. Council, China Council for Promotion of Peaceful Reunification 1993, Pres. 1994, Pres. 6th Council 1999–; mem. Standing Cttee 8th NPC 1993–98; Vice-Chair. 9th Nat. Cttee of CPPCC 1998–; Adviser Chinese Asscn. of Int. Understanding 1999–. *Address:* National Committee of Chinese People's Political Consultative Conference, 23 Taipingqiao Street, Beijing, People's Republic of China.

ZHANG LICHANG; Chinese administrator; b. 1939, Nanpi Co., Hebei Prov.; joined CCP 1966; Vice-Mayor of Tianjin Municipality 1985, Mayor 1993–98; Deputy Sec. CCP 6th Tianjin Municipal Cttee 1989–92, Sec. CCP 7th Tianjin Municipal Cttee 1992–98; Chair. Tianjin Municipal People's Congress 1998–; currently Chair. Standing Cttee., Tianjin Provincial People's Congress; alt. mem. 13th CCP Cen. Cttee 1987–92, 14th CCP Cen. Cttee 1992–97; mem. 15th CCP Cen. Cttee 1997–2002. *Address:* Tianjin Provincial People's Congress, Tianjin Municipality, People's Republic of China.

ZHANG PING; Chinese writer; b. Nov. 1954, Xi'an, Shanxi Prov.; ed Shanxi Teachers Univ.; teacher Dongjie School, Xinjiang Co.; Shanxi Prov. 1976; Ed. then head, Literature and Arts Div. Linfen Fed. of Literary and Art Circles; Assoc. Chief Ed. Spark Magazine; Vice-Chair. Shanxi Prov. Fed. of Literary and Art Circles; Vice-Chair. Chinese Writers' Asscn 2001–; 7th Nat. Award for Best Short Stories; 5th Mao Dun Award for Literature. *Publications:* The Net of Heaven, Choice, The Murderer, Young Boys and Girls, Sister, Orphans' Tears, The Girl Opposite Me 2001. *Address:* Shanxi Provincial Federation of Literary and Art Circles, Taiyuan, Shanxi Province, People's Republic of China (Office).

ZHANG QUANJING; Chinese politician; b. 1931, Pingyuan Co., Shandong Prov.; mem. CCP 1949–; Deputy Section Chief, CCP Dezhou Pref. Cttee; Deputy Sec. CCP Dezhou Municipal Cttee 1950–66; Div. Chief and Deputy Head, Org. Dept CCP Shandong Provincial Cttee 1971–86; mem. Standing Cttee and Head, Org. Dept CCP Shandong Provincial Cttee 1986–88; Sec. CCP Shandong Provincial Comm. for Inspecting Discipline 1988; Exec. Deputy Dir CCP Cen. Cttee Org. Dept 1991–94, Head 1994–; mem. 8th CCP Nat. Cttee 1993–. *Address:* Organization Department, Central Committee of Communist Party of China, Beijing, People's Republic of China.

ZHANG RENZHI; Chinese landscape artist; b. 7 Dec. 1935, Hebei Prov.; s. of Zhang Pu and Zhang Chen; m. Lang Mei 1966; two s.; ed Cen. Art Inst.; joined Beijing Art Acad. as professional artist; Jt exhbns. Xinxiang, Henan Prov., Macao, Beijing, Japan 1991, Exhbn of Buddhism 1991, Nat. Exhbn 1992, Beseto Arts Festival 1997, etc.; Wintertime Lotus and other works in collection of James Art Museum, Vermont State Univ., USA; Award of Excellence (for 'Quiet Valley'), Nat. Exhbn of Fine Arts 1991; prize for 'Lasting Forever' (burnt pine tree), Bronze Prize (for "Mount Fanjing After Rain"), Nat. Exhbn of Fine Arts 1999. *Solo exhibitions include:* Tianjin, Shen Zhen City 1992, 'Twenty Nocturnal Pieces', Taiwan 1992, Kuang Tong Prov., also Algeria, Germany, Guyana, USA, Hong Kong, Korea, Japan, Thailand, Malaysia, Singapore. *Publications:* Zhang Renzhi's Album of Paintings, (Vol. 2) 1991, Collection of Landscape Paintings 2000. *Leisure interest:* travel. *Address:* Room 501, Building 2, Beijing Arts Institute, Chao Yang District, Beijing, People's Republic of China. *Telephone:* (10) 85973316. *Website:* www .caa.org.cn/beijing/zhangrenzhi (Office).

ZHANG RUIMIN; Chinese business executive; b. Jan. 1949, Laizhou, Shandong Prov.; Dir Qingdao Refrigerator Factory 1984–91; Pres. Haier Group 1991–; voted one of China's Top Ten Econ. Figures 2000. *Address:*

Haier Garden, Haier Industrial Park, Haier Lu, Haier Group, Qingdao 266101, Shandong Province, People's Republic of China. *Telephone:* (532) 8938888. *Fax:* (532) 8938666. *E-mail:* info@haier.com (Office). *Website:* www .haier.com (Office).

ZHANG SHENGMAN; Chinese business executive; b. 1957, Shanghai; ed Fudan Univ., McGill Univ.; Asst to Exec. Dir of World Bank 1983–87; section head and then Vice-Dir Dept of IBRD, Ministry of Finance 1987–92; Deputy Exec. Dir, then Exec. Dir of IBRD 1992–96; Corp. Sec. IBRD 1997–99, Man. Dir 1999–. *Address:* International Bank for Reconstruction and Development, 1818 H Street, NW, Washington, DC 20433, USA. *Telephone:* (202) 477-1234. *Fax:* (202) 477-6391 (Office). *E-mail:* pic@worldbank.org (Office). *Website:* www.worldbank.org.

ZHANG SHOU; Chinese academic and government official; b. 19 July 1930, Changshu Co., Jiangsu Prov.; ed Jiaotong Univ.; joined CCP 1949; taught at Jiaotong Univ. 1953–80, Deputy Dir Dept of Eng and Physics 1958–62, Dept of Naval Architecture 1962–72, Dir 1972–78; Vice-Pres. Jiaotong Univ. 1979, First Vice-Pres. 1980–82; Visiting Scholar at Univ. of Pennsylvania 1981–82; mem. 12th CCP Cen. Cttee 1982; mem. 13th CCP Cen. Cttee 1987–92, 14th CCP Cen. Cttee 1992–, mem. Finance and Econ. Cttee; Vice Minister State Planning Comm. 1983–89; Chair. State Econ. Information Centre 1987–89; Pres. China State Shipbldg. Corpn 1989; Dir State Information Center 1987; Consultant System Eng Asscn of China 1985; Hon. Dir Computer Asscn of China 1987; Deputy Head Leading Group for Introducing Foreign Intellectual Resources 1988; Consultant State Natural Science Foundation of China 1987; mem. 8th NPC 1993–, NPC Deputy, Hubei Prov. *Publications:* Hydrostatics of Naval Architecture 1964, A Concise English-Chinese Naval Architecture Dictionary 1973, Econometrics 1984, Scientific Progress and Economic Development 1988, Reform and Development 1988. *Address:* 5 Yuetan Beijie, Beijing, People's Republic of China.

ZHANG SIQING; Chinese judge; b. 1932, Luoyang City, Henan Prov.; m.; two d.; joined CCP 1952; Deputy Procurator-Gen. Supreme People's Procuratorate of China 1985–93, Procurator-Gen. 1993–98; alt. mem. 13th CCP Cen. Cttee 1987–91; mem. 14th CCP Cen. Cttee 1992–97, 15th CCP Cen. Cttee 1997–2002; Vice-Chair. 9th Nat. Cttee of CPPCC 1998. *Leisure interests:* shadow boxing, swimming, calligraphy. *Address:* National Committee of Chinese People's Political Consultative Conference, 23 Taipingqiao Street, Beijing, People's Republic of China.

ZHANG TAIHENG, Gen.; Chinese army officer; b. 1931, Guangrao Co., Shandong; ed Nanjing Mil. Acad.; joined PLA 1945; platoon leader, 28th Army 1947, Regt leader 1961; Vice-Commdr PLA Chengdu Mil. Area Command 1983, Commdr 1990; Vice-Commdr Nanjing Mil. Area Command 1992; Commdr Jinan Mil. Region 1992–96. *Address:* c/o Ministry of National Defence, Jingshanqian Jie, Beijing, People's Republic of China.

ZHANG TANGMIN; Chinese traditional medical practitioner and chemist; b. 19 March 1939, Kai Jai, Sichuan; s. of Zhang He Ming and Tao Kai Yun; m. Sun Ren Ping 1966; two s. one d.; ed Univ. of Science and Tech. of China; Asst Researcher Inst. of Chem., Academia Sinica 1962–78, Asst Prof. 1978–87, Assoc. Prof. 1987; self-taught in traditional Chinese medicine 1964–; assigned to Beijing Xuanwu Hosp. 1981; opened own epilepsy clinic 1981. *Publications:* New Cure for Epilepsy, Can Epilepsy be Cured?, Fringe Science and Epilepsy, Discussions on the Cure for the Abdomen Type of Epilepsy; and other works on epilepsy. *Address:* Institute of Chemistry, Academia Sinica, Beijing, 100080, People's Republic of China. *Telephone:* (10) 2553979.

ZHANG WANNIAN, Lt-Gen.; Chinese army officer; b. 1 Aug. 1928, Longkou, Shandong; s. of Jin Man Zhang and Li Shi Zhang; m. Pei Zhao Zhong 1954; four d.; alt. mem. 12th CCP Cen. Cttee 1982, 13th CCP Cen. Cttee 1987–92; mem. 14th CCP Cen. Cttee 1992–97, 15th CCP Cen. Cttee 1997–2002; mem. Cen. Mil. Comm. 1992–95, Vice-Chair. 1995–98; Deputy Commdr Wuhan Mil. Region (now Guangzhou Mil. Region) 1982–87, Commdr 1987–90; Commdr Jinan Mil. Region 1990–92; Chief of Gen. Staff PLA 1992–95; mem. CCP Politburo; Sec. Secr. CCP Cen. Cttee. *Address:* c/o Chinese Communist Party Central Committee, Zhong Nan Hai, Beijing, People's Republic of China.

ZHANG WANXIN; Chinese petrochemicals executive; b. 5 May 1930, Harbin; s. of Zhang Xinming and Sun Minying; m. Deng Yinin 1958; one s. one d.; Vice-Pres. China Petrochemical Corpn 1983–88; Chair. and Pres. Int. Multi-Petrochemical Enterprise Ltd (IMPEL), Hong Kong 1989–94; Chair. and CEO Sino-American Corpn (SAAX) 1992–; Pres. Creat Group; Vice-Chair. China Taiwan Study Asscn; Chair. MONTPEL 1992–; Vice-Pres. Devt Research Centre, State Council; part-time Prof., Tsinghua Univ., Beijing; alt. mem. 12th CCP Cen. Cttee 1982; alt. mem. 13th CCP Cen. Cttee 1987; Vice-Chair. China Chemical Eng and Industry Soc.; Prof. Shenzhen Univ. 1983–88, Tsinghua Univ. 1988–93; mem. CCP Cttee, Beijing Municipality 1981–83; Deputy Chief Exec. Econ., Tech. and Social Devt Research Center 1988, Vice-Pres. 1991; alt. mem. 12th and 13th CCP Cen. Cttee; awarded Special Prize of State Cttee for Science and Tech. 1985. *Leisure interest:* listening to music, liberal arts. *Address:* 225 Chaoyangmen, Nei Dajie, Beijing 100010, People's Republic of China. *Telephone:* (10) 65270800; (10) 68578801. *Fax:* (10) 65236060.

ZHANG WEIQING; Chinese politician; b. 1944, Lintong Co., Shaanxi Prov.; ed Peking Univ.; joined CCP 1972; Sec. Communist Youth League Shanxi Provincial Cttee, Vice-Gov. Shanxi Prov.; Vice-Dir Propaganda Dept CCP Shanxi Provincial Cttee; Vice-Minister of State Family Planning Comm. 1994–98, Minister of State 1998–; mem. 15th CCP Cen. Cttee 1997–2002, 16th CCP Cen. Cttee 2002–. *Address:* State Family Planning Commission, 14 Zhichun Lu, Haidan Qu, Beijing 100088, People's Republic of China. *Telephone:* (10) 62046622 (Office). *Fax:* (10) 62051865 (Office). *E-mail:* gjjsw@chinapop.gov.cn (Office). *Website:* www.sfpc.gov.cn (Office).

ZHANG WENKANG; Chinese politician; b. April 1940, Nanhui Co., Shanghai; ed Shanghai No. 1 Medical Coll.; joined PLA 1962, CCP 1996; Vice-Minister Ministry of Public Health 1993–98, Minister 1998–2003; Dir State Admin. of Traditional Chinese Medicine 1993–98, Drugs Licensing Cttee; mem. 15th CCP Cen. Cttee 1997–2002, 16th CCP Cen. Cttee 2002–03. *Address:* c/o Ministry of Public Health, 1 Xizhinenwai Bei Lu, Xicheng Qu, Beijing, People's Republic of China.

ZHANG WENYUE; Chinese politician; b. Oct. 1944, Pucheng Co., Fujian Prov.; ed Beijing Geology Inst.; joined CCP 1965; Dir Geology and Mineral Resources Bureau of Sichuan Prov.; Dir-Gen. Office of Ministry of Geology and Mineral Resources 1986; Dir State Admin. on Mineral Resources 1989; Vice-Minister of Geology and Mineral Resources 1990; mem. CCP Cen. Comm. for Discipline Inspection 1992; Vice-Sec. CCP Xinjiang Uygur Autonomous Regional Cttee 1995–; mem. 15th CCP Cen. Cttee 1997–2002. *Address:* Chinese Communist Party Xinjiang Uygur Autonomous Regional Committee, Urumqi City, Xinjiang Uygur Autonomous Region, People's Republic of China.

ZHANG WULE; Chinese administrator; b. 1937, Anxin Co., Hebei Prov.; ed Beijing Inst. of Iron and Steel Tech. joined CCP 1982; Vice-Gov. Gansu Prov. 1985–93; a Deputy Sec. CPC 8th Gansu Prov. Cttee 1993–; alt. mem. 13th Cen. Cttee CCP 1987–91; mem. 14th 1992; Gov. of Gansu Prov. 1994–96; Vice-Pres. Nat. Cttee of Economy and Trade 1996–. *Address:* c/o Office of the Governor, Gansu Provincial Government, Shengyang City, People's Republic of China.

ZHANG XIANLIANG; Chinese writer; b. 1936, Jiangsu; fmr teacher in Beijing and Ningxia; in political disgrace 1957–79; Vice-Pres. Chinese Writers' Asscn 1985; Best Novel of the Year Awards (China) 1981, 1983, 1984. *Publications include:* Soul and Flesh 1981, Mimosa 1984, Half of Man is Woman 1985, Getting Used to Dying 1989, Grass Soup 1992. *Leisure interest:* Chinese calligraphy. *Address:* Ningxia Writers' Association, Yinchuan City, People's Republic of China.

ZHANG XUANLONG; Chinese business executive; b. 1956, Quanzhou, Fujian Prov.; ed First Jr School of Quanzhou, Fujian; Gen. Man. Hong Kong Kingsun Co. 1980; Gen. Man. and Vice-Chair. Tianjin Stone, a Jt venture with Stone Group; as Vice-Chair. Founder Group, set up Super Chinese Card Dept and brought Founder Golden WPS software into the market 1990; Pres. Founder (Hong Kong) Co. Ltd and Deputy Pres. Founder Group 1992. *Address:* Peking University Founder Group, Beijing, People's Republic of China (Office).

ZHANG XUEZHONG; Chinese politician; b. Feb. 1943, Lanzhou, Gansu Prov.; ed Lanzhou Univ.; joined CCP Dec. 1960; primary school teacher, Sec. of Secr.; People's Air Defence Office, Gansu Prov.; Sec. of Secr., Gen. Office of CCP Gansu Provincial Cttee; Sec. CCP Fafang Commune Cttee, Wuwei Co., Sec. CCP Yuzhong Co. Cttee; Vice-Sec. CCP Lanzhou Mun. Cttee; Sec. CCP Longnan Pref. Cttee 1961–89; Vice-Gov. Gansu Prov. 1989–90; Vice-Sec. CCP Tibet Autonomous Region Cttee 1990–94; Vice-Minister of Personnel 1994–2000, Minister 2000–03; Sec. CCP Sichuan Prov. Cttee 2003–. *Address:* c/o Zhongguo Gongchan Dang (Chinese Communist Party), Beijing, People's Republic of China (Office).

ZHANG YAN; Chinese diplomatist and international organization official; b. 3 Nov. 1950; m. Chen Wangxia; one d.; served with mission to Liberia 1978–83; with Ministry of Foreign Affairs 1983–96, Counsellor, Dept of Int. Organizations and Confs., Ministry of Foreign Affairs March–Aug. 1998; Dir-Gen. Foreign Affairs Office, Yunnan 1996–98; Sr Official, Asia Pacific Econ. Co-operation (APEC) 1998–99, Deputy Exec. Dir 2000, Exec. Dir 2001. *Address:* c/o Ministry of Foreign Affairs, 225 Chaoyangmennei Dajie, Dongsi, Beijing, People's Republic of China.

ZHANG YIMOU; Chinese film actor and director; b. 1951, Xian, Shanxi Prov.; m. Xiao Hua 1982 (divorced 1990); ed Xian Middle School, Beijing Film Acad.; 8th Golden Rooster Best Actor Award for Old Well 1988. *Films include:* The Old Well, Red Sorghum (Hong Gaoliang), Raise the Red Lantern 1991, The Story of Qiu Ju, Keep Cool 1997, Not One Less (Golden Lion, Venice) 1999, The Road Home 1999 (Grand Jury Prize, Berlin 1999), Hero 2002; produced Turandot, Beijing 1998.

ZHANG YOUFU; Chinese ecologist; b. 21 May 1940, Jiangsu Prov.; s. of Zhang Changsheng and Zhong Yinlan; m. Xu Chunlan 1968; two s.; ed Nanking Univ., Chendu Inst. of Geography, Chinese Acad. of Sciences; has been engaged in research work on biological prevention of mudflow damage, soil and water conservation and forest ecology for over 20 years. *Publications:* An Observational Study on Mudflow at Jiangjia Gully, Three Papers 1982, A Brief Introduction of the Programme Against Mudflow By Means of Biology

1983, Mudflow and Forest Vegetation in Jiangjia Gully Basin 1987, Mudflow and its Comprehensive Control 1989, Process of the Erosion, Transportation and Deposition of Debris Flow, Application of Information from Remote Sensing for Preventing Disasters caused by Debris Flow 1990, Application of Information from Remote Sensing for Preventing Disasters caused by Landslides 1990 etc.; papers on measures against debris flow, remote sensing information, etc. *Leisure interest:* photography. *Address:* Chengdu P.O. Box 417, Sichuan 610041, People's Republic of China. *Telephone:* (28) 5581260-375. *Fax:* (28) 5552258.

ZHANG YU; Chinese diplomatist, film actress and diplomatist; b. Oct. 1957, Shanghai City; m. Zhang Jianya; advanced studies, USA 1985–90; mem. 8th NPC 1993–; Amb. to Guyana 1994–99; Hundred Flowers Best Actress Award for Evening Rain 1981; Golden Rooster Best Actress Award for Love at Lushan 1981.

ZHANG YUAN; Chinese film director; b. 1963; ed Beijing Film Acad.; ind. film Dir 1989–; has directed music videos for leading Chinese rock singer Cui Jian; also producer and Dir for MTV; Special Jury Prize, Nantes Film Festival for Mama 1991. *Films:* Mama 1990, Beijing Bastards 1992, The Square 1994, East Palace West Palace 1996, Seventeen Years (Best Dir, Venice Film Festival) 1999.

ZHANG YUNCHUAN; Chinese politician; b. 1946, Dongyang, Zhejiang Prov.; ed Harbin Inst. of Mil. Eng; joined CCP 1973; fmr technician Factory No. 6214, Ministry of Machine Industry No. 6; Vice-Gov. Jiangxi Prov. 1970–95; Exec. Vice-Chair. Xinjiang Uygur Autonomous Region, Vice-Sec. Cttee of Xinjiang Uygur Autonomous Region 1995–99; Sec. Changsha Municipal Cttee 1999–2001; Vice-Sec., then Vice-Gov. Hunan Prov., Gov. 2001–. *Address:* Hunan People's Government, Changsha, Hunan Province, People's Republic of China (Office). *E-mail:* webmaster@hunan.gov.cn (Office). *Website:* www.hunan.gov.cn (Office).

ZHANG ZHIJIAN, Gen.; Chinese army officer; b. 1934, Wenxi Co., Shanxi Prov.; joined PLA 1951; mem. CCP 1956–; teacher, Speeded-Up Educ. School, Chahar Mil. Dist, Hubei (North China) Mil. Region; literacy teacher in div. hosp. of Chinese People's Volunteers, Korea 1953–56; staff officer 1957–69; Chief, Operations and Training Div. PLA Jinan Mil. Region H.Q. 1971–78; Div. Chief of Staff 1978–79; Army Deputy Chief of Staff 1979–80; Div. Commdr 1980–83; Army Commdr 1983–85; Deputy Commdr Jinan Mil. Region 1985; Political Commissar, Chengdu Mil. Region 1994; rank of Gen. 1998; mem. CCP 15th Cen. Cttee 1997–2002. *Address:* Office of the Political Commissar, Chengdu Military Region, People's Republic of China.

ZHANG ZHONGWEI; Chinese politician; b. Feb. 1942, Dujiangyan, Sichuan Prov.; joined CCP 1960; fmrly Dir Agric. and Animal Husbandry, Dept of Sichuan; Vice-Gov. of Sichuan 1993–99, Deputy Gov. 1999–2000, Gov. 2000–. *Address:* Office of the Governor, Sichuan Provincial People's Government, Chengdu, People's Republic of China (Office).

ZHANG ZUOJI; Chinese politician; b. Jan. 1945, Bayan, Heilongjiang Prov.; ed Heilongjiang Univ.; joined CCP 1972; Vice-Minister of Labour 1993–95; Vice-Chief Sec. of State Council 1995–98; Minister of Labour and Social Security 1998–2003. *Address:* c/o Zhongguo Gongchan Dang (Chinese Communist Party), Beijing 100716, People's Republic of China.

ZHAO FULIN; Chinese politician; b. 1932, Daming Co., Hubei Prov.; mem. CCP 1948–; Asst Org. Dept CCP Guanghua Co. Cttee 1949; mem. Secr. CCP Zaoyang Co. Cttee 1956–58; Sec. CCP Jiangling Co. Cttee 1965–66; Deputy Sec. CCP Jingzhou Pref. Cttee 1966–70, 1972–81, Sec. 1981–85; Deputy Sec. CCP Hubei Provincial Cttee and Sec. Comm. for Inspecting Discipline 1985; mem. CCP Comm. for Inspecting Discipline 1985; Chair. Guangxi Zhuang Regional People's Congress Standing Cttee 1995–, Sec. 7th CCP Guangxi Zhuang Autonomous Regional Cttee; mem. 13th and 14th CCP Cen. Cttee. *Address:* Guangxi Zhuang Regional People's Congress, Guangxi, People's Republic of China.

ZHAO GUORONG; Chinese chess player; b. 1961, Heilongjiang Prov.; Chinese Chess Master 1978; Chinese Chess Special Master 1987; Champion, First Chinese Chess Celebrity Championship 1997; AXF Int. Grandmaster. *Address:* c/o State General Bureau of Physical Culture and Sports, 9 Tiyuguan Lu, Beijing 100061, People's Republic of China (Office).

ZHAO LEJI; Chinese politician; b. March 1957, Xi'ning, Qinghai Prov.; ed Peking Univ., Beijing; joined CCP 1975; propaganda clerk Commercial Bureau of Qinghai 1980; Asst to Gov. of Qinghai –1994; Vice-Gov. of Qinghai 1994–98, Acting Gov. 1999, Gov. Jan. 2000–; Vice-Sec. Qinghai Prov. Cttee 1998–. *Address:* Qinghai People's Government, Xi'ning, Qinghai Province, People's Republic of China (Office). *E-mail:* webmaster@qhinfo.com. *Website:* www.qh.gov.cn (Office).

ZHAO QI; Chinese artist; b. Aug. 1954, Jinxian, Liaoning Prov.; ed Lu Xun Acad. of Fine Art; Prof. and Vice-Head Dept of Chinese Painting, Lu Xun Acad. of Fine Art; numerous paintings of historical subjects. *Address:* Lu Xun Academy of Fine Art, Beijing, People's Republic of China.

ZHAO QING, (Ludan); Chinese dancer and choreographer; b. 16 Nov. 1936, Shanghai City; d. of Zhao Dan and Ye Luxi; m. Chen Mingyuan; ed Beijing Dancing Coll.; Prin. actress China Opera and Dance Drama Theatre 1959–, First Grade Dancer 1982–; Prin. Dancer Chinese Art Del. to France, England,

Italy, USA, USSR, Poland, Singapore, Japan, Latin America; mem. 8th Nat. Cttee CPPCC 1993–; mem. China Dancers Asscn; Gold Medal (World Youth Festival); Excellent Performance Award 1980; First Prize Ministry of Culture for "The Sword" (ballet) 1982. *Performances include:* The Lotus Lantern (ballet), Xiaodao Hui (ballet) 1961, Liang Zhu (ballet) 1962, The Red Silk Dance 1978, The Sword 1980, The Poetry of the Sea 1982, Children of the Dragon (TV) 1983–84, Golden Dream (film) 1984–85, Luotuo Xiangzi (ballet) 1986, Luoshen (ballet) 1987, Dance of Calligraphy 1990, The Father and the Daughter (ballet) 1993. *Address:* 2 Nanhuadong Street, Hufang Road, Beijing 100050, People's Republic of China.

ZHAO QIZHENG; Chinese politician; b. Jan. 1940, Beijing; ed China Science and Tech. Univ. 1963; Senior Engineer 1963–84; Dir. of Personnel Resources, Standing Cttee of CCP of Shanghai 1984–91; joined CCP 1979; Vice-Mayor of Shanghai 1991–98; Vice-Dir then Dir Information Office of State Council 1998–. *Address:* 225 Chaoyangmen Neidajie, Beijing, People's Republic of China. *Telephone:* (10) 8652-1199. *Fax:* (10) 6559-2364.

ZHAO RUICHUN; Chinese artist; b. Nov. 1935, Wenzhou, Zhejiang; s. of Zhao Loshu and Huang Shenghong; m. 1st 1956; one d.; m. 2nd Yun Xiuying; one d.; ed Chinese Cen. Fine Arts Inst.; lecturer Guangzhou Inst. of Fine Arts 1959–71; teacher Chinese Cen. Fine Arts Inst. 1980–82; painter Guangzhou Art Acad. 1984–, now Sr Painter; first one-man Exhbn 1962; mem. Chinese Artists' Asscn, Chinese Engraving Asscn; Sec.-Gen. Chinese Asscn of Copper-Plate, Lithographic and Silkscreen Engraving; Ed.-in-Chief Modern Engraving; works exhibited in USA, Japan, England, Australia, New Zealand, Ireland, Singapore, Denmark, Switzerland, Korea, Sweden, Thailand, Canada, USSR, Algeria, Italy and Taiwan. *Publications:* On Engraving Education 1981, Woodcut Techniques 1983, The Practice and Theory of Sketching 1986, Silk-screen Plate Techniques 1987. *Leisure interest:* Chinese cooking. *Address:* Guangzhou Academy of Painting, 130 Shuiyin Road, Guangzhou 510075, Guangdong Province (Office); 609 Dongnan Mansion, Gongyuan Road, Wenzhou 325000, Zhejiang, People's Republic of China (Home). *Telephone:* (20) 87724636 (Office); (577) 88203025 (Home). *Fax:* (577) 88203025 (Home); (577) 88203026. *E-mail:* zrcit@sohu.com (Office).

ZHAO YANXIA; Chinese opera singer; b. 29 April 1928, Beijing; d. of late Zhao Xiaolou; m. Liu Xinyuan; one d.; ed Beijing Performance School; Head First Troupe, Beijing Opera Theatre of Beijing. *Plays include:* Story of Susan, The Pavilion of Red Palm, The Fairy in the Blue Wave, The Story of the White Snake. *Leisure interests:* appreciating music, films, reading, cookery. *Address:* 24 Xisibai 2nd Lane, Beijing 100034, People's Republic of China. *Telephone:* (10) 66161121.

ZHAO ZHONGXIAN, DrSc; Chinese physicist; b. 30 Jan. 1941, Liaoning Prov.; s. of Zhao Desheng and Zhang Naibin; m. Zhou Yaqin 1967; two s.; ed Univ. of Science and Tech. of China; Researcher, Inst. of Physics, Acad. Sinica 1964–; Dir Nat. Lab. for Superconductivity 1991–2000; Chair. Scientific Council, Inst. of Physics 1999–; mem. CPPCC 1993–98; Vice-Pres. China Asscn for Science and Tech. 2001–; Dir Working Cttee on Consultation and Evaluation of Chinese Academia Sinica 2000–04; mem. Presidium Chinese Acad. of Sciences 1998–2004; Vice-Pres. Chinese Physical Soc. 1994–, China Innovation Asscn 1996–; Fellow, Third World Acad. of Sciences 1987, Acad. of Ceramics (Int.) 1989, Chinese Acad. of Sciences 1991; mem. Council of Asscn of Asia Pacific Physical Soc. 1990–97; Special mem. China Center of Advanced Sciences and Tech. 1987; Hon. Fellow India Materials Research Soc. 1991, China Materials Research Soc. 1996; Hon. DSc (Chinese Univ. of Hong Kong) 1988; Hon. Physics Award, Third World Acad. of Sciences 1986, Tan Kah-Kee Material Science Prize 1988, Natural Sciences Prize of China (1st Class) 1990, Wang Dan-ping Science Prize 1992, Science and Tech. Progress Award, Ho Leung Ho Lee Foundation 1997. *Leisure interests:* music, photography, calligraphy. *Address:* Institute of Physics, Chinese Academy of Sciences, Zhong Guan Cun, P.O. Box 603, Beijing 100080 (Office); Building 17-103, Yan-Gui-Yuan, Zhong Guan Cun, Bei Er Tiao, Beijing 100080, People's Republic of China (Home). *Telephone:* (10) 82649190 (Office); (10) 62564951 (Home). *Fax:* (10) 82649486. *E-mail:* zhxzhao@aphy.iphy.ac.cn (Office). *Website:* aphy.iphy.ac.cn (Office).

ZHARIKOV, Alexander Nikolayevich; Russian trade union official and engineer; b. 2 Jan. 1945, Arsenyevo; s. of Nicolai Philippovich Zharikov and Claudia Egorovna Gorodnicheva; m. 1st Olga Borisovna Suhova 1975 (deceased); one s.; m. 2nd Eva Shvachova; one s. one d.; ed Leningrad Shipbuilding Inst.; mil. service 1962–66; Sec. of Youth and Student Org. of Leningrad 1971–74; Chair. Student Council of USSR 1974–78; Vice-Pres. Int. Union of Students 1978–84; official, Int. Dept Cen. Cttee of CPSU 1984–88; Dir Int. Dept USSR All-Union Council 1988–90; Gen. Sec. World Fed. of Trade Unions (WFTU) 1990–; Hon. Prof. (Russian State Univ. of Humanitarian Science); Order of Honour (Russia) 1974. *Publications:* book on world student movt 1979; numerous articles on social issues, labour and trade union relations in newspapers and magazines. *Leisure interests:* swimming, collecting mushrooms, reading, skiing. *Address:* Branicka 112, 14701 Prague 4, Czech Republic (Office). *Telephone:* (2) 44462140 (Office). *Fax:* (2) 44461378 (Office). *E-mail:* wftu@login.cz (Office). *Website:* www.wftu.cz.

ZHARIKOV, Vilen Andreyevich; Russian mineralogist; b. 20 Sept. 1926; m.; two d.; ed Moscow Inst. of Geological Survey; worked as geologist, jr then sr researcher Inst. of Geology of Ore Deposits, Mineralogy and Geochem. 1950–69, Deputy Dir 1969–79; Dir Inst. of Experimental Mineralogy 1979–;

Corresp. mem. USSR (now Russian) Acad. of Sciences 1972, mem. 1987, Academican-Sec. Dept of Geology, Geophysics, Geochem. and Mining Sciences 1991–96; Counsellor to Pres. 1996–; main research in geophysics and experimental mineralogy, petrology; mem. Petrographic Comm. Russian Acad. of Sciences; Chair. Comm. on Int. Programme of Geological Correlation; USSR State Prize. *Publications:* 6 monographs, dozens of articles and communications in scientific journals. *Address:* Department of Geology, Russian Academy of Sciences, Leninsky prospect 32A, 117334 Moscow, Russia (Office). *Telephone:* (095) 938-09-40 (Office, Acad.); (095) 524-50-37 (Inst.).

ZHARIKOV, Yevgeny Ilyich; Russian actor; b. 26 Feb. 1941, Moscow; s. of Ilya Melakhiyevich Zharikov and Anna Grigoryevna Zharikova; m. Natalia Gvozdikova; one s.; ed All-Union Inst. of Cinematography; mem. Union of Cinematographers 1968, Sec. 1999–; mem. Cinema Acad. Nica; Vice-Pres. Guild of Cinema Actors of Russia; f. Moscow Charity Foundation for Actors (Mercy); organized annual Int. Film Actors' Festival ('Sozvezdiye') 1989–99; Pres. Yeugeny Zharikov Social Fund 1999–; Chair. Radio Kitt (Kino, Teatr, TV); mem. Exec. Bd Int. Fed. of Actors; mem. Int. Detective Club; Peoples' Artist of Russian Fed. 1979, USSR State Prize 1987, Order of Honour 1996, Order of Merit for Services to Country 2001. *Film roles include:* What If This Is Love 1960, Ivan's Childhood 1962, Three Plus Two 1963, Russian for You 1966, Snowgirl, Day of Angel, Born by Revolution, Trotsky, Yuri the Long-Handed 1997, Salvation Army 2000. *Leisure interests:* diving, hunting, fishing, sports, Russian and foreign classical literature, serious music. *Address:* Leninsky prospect 123, korp. 1, Apt. 589, 117513 Moscow, Russia (Home). *Telephone:* (095) 438-12-97 (Home). *Fax:* (095) 438-19-58 (Home).

ZHELEV, Zhelyu, PhD; Bulgarian politician; b. 3 March 1935, Veselinovo/ Shumen, Varna Region; s. of Mityu Zhelev and Yordanka Nedelcheva; m. Maria Ivanova Marinova 1966; two d.; ed Univ. of Sofia; fmr librarian in Veselinovo; joined Bulgarian CP but expelled for criticism of Lenin 1964; unemployed 1966–72; initiator for establishment of Cttee for Ecological Protection of City of Ruse 1988; Co-Pres. Club for Protection of Glasnost and Restructuring (now Glasnost and Democracy Club) until Nov. 1989; Chair. UDF (opposition party) 1989–90; Pres. of Bulgaria 1990–96. *Publication:* Fascism 1981. *Leisure interests:* hiking, fishing. *Address:* c/o Office of the President, 2 Dondukov Boulevard, Sofia, Bulgaria. *Telephone:* 871767.

ZHENG HAIXIA; Chinese basketball player; b. 1967, Shandong; started playing basketball aged 12; joined nat. team aged 15, now Capt.; also mem. PLA team; Capt. of Chinese basketball team which won silver medal at Barcelona Olympic Games 1992, gold medal at World Univ. Games 1993, silver medal, Women's World Basketball Championships, Sydney 1994; signed up for two years with WNBA side Los Angeles Sparks 1996–98. *Leisure interests:* music, poetry, knitting. *Address:* c/o State Bureau of Physical Culture and Sports, 9 Tiyuguan Lu, Beijing 100061, People's Republic of China (Office).

ZHENG SILIN; Chinese politician; b. May 1940, Wu Co., Jiangsu Prov.; joined CCP 1965; worked at Dandong Automobile Repair Plant, Liaoning Prov. 1965–81; Dir Dandong TV Parts Factory 1982–83; Vice-Mayor Dandong City 1983–84; Dir Comm. for Foreign Econ. Relations and Trade and Asst Gov., Liaoning Prov. 1984–85; Vice-Gov. Shaanxi Prov. People's Govt 1989–93; Vice-Minister of Foreign Trade and Econ. Co-operation 1993–94; alt. mem. 13th Cen. Cttee CCP 1987–92, 14th Cen. Cttee 1992–97; Deputy Sec. 9th CCP Jiangsu Prov. Cttee; Acting Gov. of Jiangsu Prov. 1994–95, Gov. 1995–98; Vice-Minister State Econ. and Trade Comm. 1998–2000; mem. 15th CCP Cen. Cttee 1997–2002, 16th CCP Cen. Cttee 2002–; Minister of Labour and Social Security 2003–. *Address:* Ministry of Labour and Social Security, 12 Hepinglizhong Jie, Dongcheng Qu, Beijing 100716, People's Republic of China (Office). *Telephone:* (10) 84201235 (Office). *Fax:* (10) 64218350 (Office).

ZHENG WANTONG; Chinese politician; b. May 1941, Tianjin; ed Tianjin Teachers' Coll.; joined CCP 1960; high school teacher, cadre Communist Youth League Hebei Dist Cttee, Tianjin 1961–68; cadre CCP Hebei Dist Cttee, Tianjin 1974–78; cadre then Dir Gen. Office of CCP Tianjin Municipal Cttee 1978–83; Chief Sec. CCP Tianjin Municipal Cttee 1983–88; Vice-Chair. and mem. Secr. All-China Fed. of Trade Unions 1988; Vice-Dir United Front Work Dept of CCP Cen. Cttee 1993–; Vice-Chief Sec. 8th Nat. Cttee of CPPCC 1993–98; mem. CCP Cen. Comm. for Discipline Inspection 1997–; Vice-Chair. 8th Exec. Cttee All-China Fed. of Industry and Commerce 1997–; Vice-Pres. China Overseas Friendship Asscn 1997–; Gen.-Sec. 9th Nat. Cttee of CPPCC 1998–. *Address:* National Committee of Chinese People's Political Consultative Conference, 23 Taipingqiao Street, Beijing, People's Republic of China.

ZHENG XIAOYING; Chinese conductor and professor of music; b. 27 Sept. 1929, Shanghai; d. of Zheng Wei and Wen Siying; m. Liu Enyü 1947; one d.; ed Moscow P.I. Tchaikovsky State Conservatoire, USSR (now Russian Fed.); mem. song and dance troupe 1949; teacher and conductor, Cen. Conservatoire 1950–60, 1963–; conducted Cen. Conservatoire Chorus and Symphony Orchestra, Radio Orchestra of USSR 1961–63, Cen. Philharmonic, China Broadcasting Orchestra, Canberra Orchestra, Hong Kong Philharmonic; Chief Conductor Cen. Opera Theatre 1978–88; Founder, Musical Dir and Conductor Women's Chamber Orchestra, Capital Opera Inst. 1988; Artistic Dir Xiamen Philharmonic Orchestra 1998; appeared at Hong Kong Performing Arts Festival, Savonlinna Opera Festival, Finland, Singapore Inaugural, Macao Int. Music Festival, Chinese Arts Festival; mem. Exec. Council

Chinese Musicians' Asscn; numerous recordings; Special Honour for Outstanding Women 1979, 1983, Nat. First Prize for Conductors 1981, La Donna nel Mondo (Italy) 1983, Médaille d'honneur des arts et des lettres (France). *Leisure interests:* travel, sports. *Address:* Central Conservatory, 43 Baojia Street, 100031 Beijing (Office); (361002) Hai Tan Lu, Gulangyu, Xiamen, People's Republic of China (Home). *Telephone:* (592) 2061549 (Xiamen) (Home); (610) 65520019 (Beijing) (Home). *Fax:* (592) 2061549 (Xiamen) (Home); (610) 65523164 (Beijing) (Home).

ZHENOVACH, Sergey Vassilyevich; Russian theatre director; b. 15 May 1957, Potsdam, Germany; ed Krasnodar Inst. of Culture, Moscow Inst. of Theatre Arts; Dir Youth Theatre Studio Stroitel, Krasnodar 1979, 1982–83; army service 1979–82; teacher Moscow Inst. of Theatre Arts (now Russian Acad. of Theatre Arts) 1990–; Dir Moscow Theatre on Malaya Bronnaya 1992–96, Chief Artistic Dir 1996–; Mayor of Moscow Prize 1992, Golden Mask Prize 1996. *Stage productions include:* The Idiot, King Lear, The Abyss, Miller – Witch, Cheat and Matchmaker, Pannochka, Viy, Illusion. *Address:* Moscow Theatre on Malaya Bronnaya, M. Bronnaya str. 4, 103104 Moscow, Russia (Office). *Telephone:* (095) 290-67-31 (Office).

ZHILINSKY, Dmitry Dmitriyevich; Russian painter; b. 25 May 1927, Sochi; ed Moscow Inst. of Applied and Decorative Arts, Moscow State Surikov Inst. of Fine Arts; teacher Moscow State Surikov Inst. of Fine Arts 1951–74, Prof. 1968; Head of Chair Moscow State Inst. of Polygraphy 1974–81; mem. Exec. Bd USSR Artists' Union 1977; mem. USSR Acad. of Fine Arts 1988; Order, Friendship of Peoples 1994; Silver Medal, Acad. of Fine Arts 1966, Merited Worker of Arts of RSFSR 1983, RSFSR State Repin Prize 1985, Peoples' Artist of RSFSR 1987. *Works include:* Gymnasts 1965, Under the Old Apple Tree 1969, Sunday 1974, Svyatoslav Richter 1985. *Exhibitions:* numerous solo exhbns. in Russia and abroad (Germany, Italy, Holland, Finland, France, etc.). *Address:* Russian Academy of Fine Arts, Prechistenka str. 21, 119034 Moscow, Russia (Office). *Telephone:* (095) 210-36-65 (Office).

ZHIRINOVSKY, Vladimir Volfovich, DPhil; Russian politician; b. 25 April 1946, Alma-Ata, Kazakhstan; m. Galina Zhirinovsky; two s.; ed Inst. of Asian and African Countries and Faculty of Law, Moscow State Univ.; officer, USSR Ministry of Defence, with Gen. Staff of Transcaucasian command 1970–72; with Soviet Soc. of Friendship and Cultural Relations, Cttee for Peace 1973–83; legal consultant, Mir Publs 1983–90; f. 1989 and Chair. Liberal-Democratic Party of Soviet Union (now of Russia; LDPR) 1990–; cand. in Russian Presidential Election 1991; mem. State Duma (Parl.) 1993–, Deputy Chair. 2000–; rank of Col in Army Reserve 1995. *Publications:* The Last Leap South 1993, Political Landscape of Russia 1995, Economic Ideas of a Politician 1996, Geopolitics and the Russian Question 1997, The Zhirinovsky Phenomenon in Russia 1998 and more than 100 other books and publs. *Leisure interests:* volleyball, swimming. *Address:* State Duma, Okhotny Ryad 1, 103009 Moscow; Liberal-Democratic Party of Russia, 1st Basmanny per. 3, 103045 Moscow, Russia. *Telephone:* (095) 292-11-95. *Fax:* (095) 292-92-72.

ZHISLIN, Grigory Yefimovich; Russian violinist; b. 14 May 1945, Leningrad (now St Petersburg); s. of Sarra and Yefim Zhislin; m. Valentina Murashova 1980; one s.; ed Moscow State Conservatory (pupil of Yuny Yankelevich); winner Int. Competitions of Paganini in Genoa 1967 and Queen Elizabeth in Brussels 1976; concerts in USSR and abroad 1966–; participated in maj. music festivals including Maggio Musicale Fiorentino, Warsaw Autumn, Prague Spring, Kuhmi Chamber Music, Berliner Biennale, Pablo Casals in Puerto Rico, Paganini in Genoa and others; teacher Kharkov Inst. of Arts 1971–73, Moscow Gnessin Pedagogical Inst. 1973–, Prof. 1978–90; Royal Coll. of Music London 1990–; Hochschule für Musik Würzburg 1993–; Visiting Prof. Oslo, Krakow, Warsaw Conservatories; master classes USA, Italy, France, Finland, Sweden. *Address:* 25 Whitehall Gardens, London, W3 9RD, England (Home). *Telephone:* (20) 8993-8223. *Fax:* (20) 8993-8295.

ZHITINKIN, Andrei Albertovich; Russian theatre director; b. 18 Nov. 1960; ed Shchukin Theatre High School; Dir Mossoviet Theatre 1991–2001; Head Artistic Dir Drama Theatre, Malaya Bronnaya 2001–; Merited Artist of Russia. *Plays include:* Dog's Waltz 1992, Yellow Angel 1993, All of a Sudden Last Summer 1994, My Poor Marat 1995, He Has Come 1996, Mon Ami 1997, Merchant of Venice 1999. *Address:* Malaya Bronnaya Theatre, Malaya Bronnaya str. 4, 103104 Moscow, Russia (Office). *Telephone:* (095) 290-69-81 (Office).

ZHONG MING, FRSA; Chinese artist; b. 1949, Beijing; elected to Chinese Artists' Asscn 1980; founder mem. Beijing Oil Painting Research Asscn; moved to London 1984; exhibited at Open Exhbn of Royal Soc. of Painters in Watercolour, Bankside Gallery 1984; has also exhibited in Japan and Sweden; speaker at int. symposium The Authentic Garden, Leiden, Netherlands 1990. *Solo exhibitions include:* Camden Arts Centre 1985, Smith's Gallery, Covent Garden 1986, Hong Kong 1988, Taipei 1989. *Publications:* The Craft of Gardens (photographer) 1988; articles on art and cultural subjects in various periodicals. *Address:* 23A Block 2, Ronsdale Garden, 25 Tai Hang Drive, Hong Kong; 51 Sunningwell Road, Oxford, OX1 4SZ, England.

ZHOU DAOJIONG; Chinese banker; b. Dec. 1933, Anhui Prov.; m. Jiang Pei; two s. one d.; ed Cen. Coll. of Finance; joined CCP 1956; Vice-Pres. of People's Construction Bank of China (now China Construction Bank) –1984, Pres. 1985–94; Vice-Pres. State Devt Bank 1994–95; Chair. Chinese Securities Regulatory Comm. 1995–97; Insp. State Council 1998–2000; mem. National

People's Congress 1998–. *Publications:* Latest Financial Practice Handbook (chief ed.), Guide to C.C.B.'s New Investment Vehicles (chief ed.). *Leisure interests:* reading, fishing, playing golf. *Address:* c/o China Construction Bank, 25 Finance Street, Beijing, People's Republic of China (Office). *Telephone:* 67597114 (Office).

ZHOU GANZHI; Chinese architect; b. 1930, Suzhou, Jiangsu Prov.; ed Tsinghua Univ.; joined CCP 1952; Deputy Office Dir State Construction Comm.; Vice-Dir City Planning Research Inst. of State Gen. Admin. of City Construction; Acting Dir Tianjin City Planning Bureau; Sr Architect and Pres. China City Planning and Design Research Acad.; Vice-Minister of Urban and Rural Construction and Environment Protection; Vice-Minister of Construction 1952–98; Chair. Standing Cttee of Civil Eng and Water Conservancy Eng, Dept of Chinese Acad. of Eng 1998–. *Address:* c/o Chinese Academy of Engineering, Beijing, People's Republic of China.

ZHOU GUANGZHAO, MS; Chinese physicist; b. 15 May 1929, Changsha City, Hunan Prov.; s. of Fengjiu Zhou and Zhen-zhao Tao; m. Zheng Aiqin 1955; one d.; ed Tsinghua Univ., Peking Univ.; joined CCP 1952; Dir 9th Research Inst. of Second Ministry of Machine-Bldg Industry; Research Fellow and Dir Physics Research Inst. of Chinese Acad. of Sciences; Vice-Pres. Chinese Acad. of Sciences 1960–87, Pres. 1987–98; alt. mem. 12th CCP Cen. Cttee 1982, mem. 1985; mem. 13th CCP Cen. Cttee 1987–92, 14th CCP Cen. Cttee 1992–97, 15th CCP Cen. Cttee 1997–2002; Vice-Chair. Standing Cttee of 9th NPC 1998; took part in making of China's first atomic bomb and hydrogen bomb; Meritorious Service Medal, CCP Cen. Cttee, State Council and Cen. Mil. Comm. 1999. *Publications:* Language Reform of China 1961, A Free Talk on Chinese Language 1992, Alphabets of the World 1993. *Leisure interests:* swimming, table tennis. *Address:* Chinese Academy of Sciences, 52 San Li He Road, 100864 Beijing, People's Republic of China. *Telephone:* 8597203.

ZHOU HOUJIAN; Chinese business executive; b. Aug. 1957, Qingdao, Shandong Prov.; ed Shandong Univ.; technician, deputy div. head, Man.'s Asst, Vice-Man. then Man. Qingdao TV Plant 1982–94; Pres. and CEO HiSense Group Corp. 1994; awarded the Global Young Entrepreneurs Man. Talent Special Prize 1996; Nat. Wuyi Labour Medal 1998; named one of Top Ten Economic Figures in China 2000. *Address:* HiSense Group Corporation, Qingdao, Shandong Province, People's Republic of China (Office). *Telephone:* (532) 3861992 (Office). *Fax:* (532) 3872882 (Office). *E-mail:* master@hisense .com.cn (Office).

ZHOU KEYU, Gen.; Chinese army officer and party official; b. 1929, Funing Co., Jiangsu Prov.; joined CCP 1945, PLA 1947, Deputy Dir of PLA Gen. Political Dept 1985, Political Commissar Gen. Logistics Dept 1990–95; rank of Lt-Gen. 1988; mem. 14th CCP Cen. Cttee 1992–97; Vice-Chair. Legal Affairs Cttee of 9th NPC 1998–. *Address:* c/o Standing Committee of National People's Congress, Beijing, People's Republic of China.

ZHOU KUNREN, Gen.; Chinese naval officer; b. Sept. 1937, Danyang Co., Jiangsu Prov.; ed PLA Political Acad. and PLA Univ. of Nat. Defence; joined PLA 1956; mem. CCP 1960–; Vice-Dir Political Dept of Navy; rank of Maj.-Gen. 1988; Political Commissar South Sea Fleet; Vice-Political Commissar, PLA Navy 1992, Political Commissar 1992; rank of Lt-Gen. 1993, Gen. 2000; Political Commissar, PLA Gen. Logistics Dept 1995–; mem. 15th CCP Cen. Cttee 1997–2002. *Address:* People's Liberation Army General Logistics Department, Beijing, People's Republic of China.

ZHOU SHENGXIAN; Chinese politician; b. Dec. 1949, Wuzhong, Ningxia Hui Autonomous Region; ed Wuzhong Teachers' Coll.; joined CCP 1972; fmrly teacher Weizhou Middle School, Tongxin Co.; Deputy Magistrate Tongxin Co.; Sec. CCP Tongxin Co. Cttee; Sec. CCP Xiji Co. Cttee; Vice-Sec. Gen. and then Sec. Gen. People's Govt of Ningxia Hui Autonomous Region; Vice-Pres. Govt 1993–2000; Dir State Admin. for Forestry 2000–. *Address:* c/o Minister of Land and Natural Resources, 3 Guanyingyuanxiqu, Xicheng Qu, Beijing 100035, People's Republic of China (Office).

ZHOU TIENONG; Chinese politician; b. Nov. 1938, Shenyang, Liaoning Prov.; ed Peking Univ.; teaching Asst, Harbin Technological Univ. 1960–61; Assoc. Prof. Northeast Heavy Machinery Coll. 1961–83; Vice-Mayor of Qiqihar, Heilongjiang Prov. 1983–91; Vice-Gov. Heilongjiang Prov. 1991–98; Vice-Chair. Cen. Cttee of Kuomintang Revolutionary Cttee 1992–; Vice-Chair. 9th Nat. Cttee of CPPCC 1998–; Pres. Sixth Council of China Council for Promotion of Peaceful Reunification 1999–; Adviser Chinese Asscn of Int. Understanding 1999–. *Address:* National Committee of Chinese People's Political Consultative Conference, 23 Taipingqiao Street, Beijing, People's Republic of China.

ZHOU WEIZHI; Chinese politician and musician; b. 1916, Dongtai Co., Jiangsu Prov.; joined CCP 1938; Dir Central Songs and Dance Troupe; Pres. Cen. Experimental Drama Theatre; Dir Arts Dept of Ministry of Culture; Vice-Minister, then Acting Minister of Culture; Vice-Chair. Chinese Musicians Asscn; Chair. China Fed. of Literary and Art Circles 1996–. *Address:* c/o Ministry of Culture, Jia 83, Donganmen Bei Jie, Dongcheng Qu, Beijing 100701, People's Republic of China.

ZHOU WENYUAN, Maj.-Gen.; Chinese army officer and party official; b. 1940, Tianjin City; ed Hebei Political Teachers Coll.; joined PLA 1961, Deputy Dir PLA Gen. Political Dept 1985; Deputy Political Commissar Shenyang Mil.

Region 1993–; joined CCP 1963; alt. mem. 13th CCP Cen. Cttee 1987–92, 14th 1992–97. *Address:* c/o Ministry of National Defence, Jingshanqian Jie, Beijing, People's Republic of China.

ZHOU XIAOCHUAN, PhD; Chinese central banker; b. Jan. 1948; s. of the late Zhou Jiannan; ed Beijing Chemical Eng Inst., Tsinghua Univ.; Deputy Dir Inst. of Chinese Econ. Reform Research 1986–87; mem. State Council Econ. Policy Group 1986–87; Asst Minister of Foreign Trade and Econ. Co-operation 1986–89; mem. Nat. Cttee on Econ. Reform 1986–91; Deputy Gov. People's Bank of China (PBOC) 1991–95, 1996–98, Gov. Dec. 2002–; Dir State Admin. of Foreign Exchange (SAFE) 1995–98; Pres. China Construction Bank (CCB) 1998–2000; Chair. China Securities Regulatory Comm. (CSRC) 2000–02; Prof. Tsinghua Univ. School of Man., Grad. School PBOC, Univ. of Science and Tech. of China Business School; PBOC Communist Party Sec.; Hon. Pres., Univ. of Science and Tech. of China Business School. *Publications include:* over ten books and over one hundred journal articles on econ. reform including Rebuilding the Relationship Between the Enterprise and the Bank (Sun Zhifang Economics Thesis Prize 1994), Marching Toward an Open Economic System (An Zijie Int. Trade Publication Award 1994), Social Security: Reform and Policy Recommendations (Sun Zhifang Economics Thesis Prize 1997). *Leisure interest:* tennis. *Address:* People's Bank of China, 32 Chenfang Jie, Xicheng Qu, Beijing 100800, China (Office). *Telephone:* (10) 66194114 (Office). *Fax:* (10) 66015346 (Office). *E-mail:* master@pbc.gov.cn (Office). *Website:* www.pbc.gov.cn (Office).

ZHOU XIAOYAN; Chinese musician; b. Wuhan City, Hubei Prov.; ed Shanghai Music School and in France; performed in London, Paris, Geneva, Berlin, Prague and Warsaw; a Vice-Chair. Chinese Musicians' Asscn 1979–; Dir of Vocal Dept Shanghai Conservatory of Music 1987. *Address:* Shanghai Conservatory of Music, Shanghai City, People's Republic of China.

ZHOU XIUJI; Chinese physicist; b. 1936, Zhejiang Prov.; ed Beijing Univ.; c/o mem. Chinese Acad. of Sciences 1992, Environmental and Resources Protection Cttee. *Address:* c/o State Commission of Science, Technology and Industry for National Defence, Za Guaganmennan Jie, Xuawu Qu, Beijing 100053, People's Republic of China.

ZHOU YAOHE, DR.SCI.TECH.; Chinese metallurgist; b. 30 May 1927, Beijing; Pres. Casting Soc. of China Machinery Eng Soc. and Chair. Int. Soc. of Casting; Prof. Northwest Polytechnic Univ.; Fellow Chinese Acad. of Sciences 1991–; Nat. Science and Tech. Advancement Award, Nat. Invention Award and five ministerial awards. *Address:* Northwest Polytechnic University, Xi'an, Shaanxi Province, People's Republic of China (Office).

ZHOU YONGKANG; Chinese politician; b. Dec. 1942, Wuxi City, Jiangsu Prov.; ed Beijing Petroleum Inst.; joined CCP 1964; Dir and Vice-Sec. CCP Cttee of Liaohe Petroleum Exploration Bureau; Mayor Panjin City 1983, Vice-Sec. CCP Panjin City Cttee 1983–85; Vice-Minister of Petroleum Industry 1985; Vice-Gen. Man. Head Office of China Petroleum and Natural Gas Company 1988; alt. mem. 14th CCP Cen. Cttee 1992; Gen. Man. Head Office of China Petroleum and Natural Gas Company 1996–98; Minister of Land Resources 1998–2000; mem. 15th CCP Cen. Cttee 1997–2002, 16th CCP Cen. Cttee 2002–; Sec. CCP Sichuan Prov. Cttee 2000–03; Minister of Public Security 2003–. *Address:* Ministry of Public Security, 14 Dongchangan Jie, Dongcheng Qu, Beijing 100741, People's Republic of China (Office). *Telephone:* (10) 65122831 (Office). *Fax:* (10) 65136577 (Office).

ZHOU YOUGUANG; Chinese economist and linguist; b. 13 Jan. 1906, Changzhou City, Jiangsu Prov.; s. of Zhou Qixian and Xu Wen; m. Zhang Yunhe 1933; one s.; ed Changzhou High School, St John's Univ. and Guanghua Univ. 1927; teaching in Guanghua Univ., Shanghai and other univs. 1927–37; Sinhua Bank, Shanghai and Hong Kong 1937–45; Rep. of Sinhua Bank, to New York and London 1946–48; Prof., Fudan Univ. and Shanghai Coll. of Finance and Econs 1949–55; Research Prof., Cttee for Written Languages Reform of China 1956–87, Research Prof. State Language Comm. and Chinese Social Sciences Acad., Beijing 1987–; visited USA 1990. *Publications:* more than 20 books including Language Reform of China 1961, A Free Talk on Chinese Languages 1992, Alphabets of the World (A Chinese View) 1993. *Address:* Chaonei Nanxiaojie 51, 1-301, Beijing, People's Republic of China. *Telephone:* (10) 65254765.

ZHOU ZHENGQING; Chinese business executive and politician; fmr Deputy Gov. Cen. Bank of China; Deputy Sec. Gen. State Council Sept. 1995–98; mem. Cen. Financial and Econ. Leading Group 1994–; Chair. China Securities Supervisory Comm. 1996–2000. *Address:* c/o State Council, Beijing, People's Republic of China.

ZHOU ZIYU, Gen.; Chinese army officer; Deputy Dir PLA Gen. Political Dept; rank of Gen. 1996; Deputy Sec. Cen. Comm. for Discipline Inspection 1997; mem. 15th CCP Cen. Cttee 1997–2002. *Address:* c/o Central Committee of the Chinese Communist Party, Zhongnanhai, Beijing, People's Republic of China.

ZHU DUNFA, Lt-Gen.; Chinese army officer; b. 1927, Peixian Co., Jiangsu Prov.; joined CCP 1945; Deputy Commdr of PLA Shengyang Mil. Area Command 1985; Commandant PLA Nat. Defence Univ. 1992–95; rank of Lt-Gen. 1988; mem. 14th CCP Cen. Cttee 1992–97. *Address:* Shengyang Military Area Command, People's Liberation Army, Shenyang City, Liaoning Province, People's Republic of China.

ZHU GAOFENG; Chinese politician and engineer; b. May 1935, Ningbo, Zhejiang Prov.; ed Tsinghua Univ., Leningrad Telecommunication Eng Inst.; joined CCP 1964; technician, engineer, Sr Engineer and Chief Engineer Ministry of Posts and Telecommunications 1958–82; Vice-Minister of Posts and Telecommunications 1982–95; Vice-Pres. Chinese Acad. of Eng 1994–. *Address:* Chinese Academy of Engineering, 3 Fuxing Road, Beijing 100038, People's Republic of China. *Telephone:* (10) 68522661 (Office). *Fax:* (10) 68522662 (Office). *E-mail:* engach@mail.cae.ac.cn (Office).

ZHU GUANGYA, PhD; Chinese physicist and state official; b. 1924, Yichang, Hubei Prov.; ed Chongqing and Southwest Assoc. Univs., Univ. of Mich., Atomic Energy Research Inst.; Assoc. Prof. Beijing Univ. 1950–52; Prof., Dir of Teaching and Research, People's Univ., Beijing; joined CCP 1956; with Second Ministry of Machine Bldg Industry 1957–70; alt. mem. 9th CCP Cen. Cttee 1969, 10th Cen. Cttee.; joined PLA 1970; Vice-Minister Comm. of Science, Tech. and Industry for Nat. Defence 1970–82, Dir. of Science and Tech. Cttee 1994–; mem. 11th CCP Cen. Cttee 1977–82, 12th Cen. Cttee 1982–87, 13th Cen. Cttee 1987–92, 14th Cen. Cttee 1992–97; involved in 863 Programme to promote Chinese Devt of high tech. 1981–89; Vice-Pres. China Asscn for Science and Tech. 1982–91, Chair. 1991–95, Hon. Chair. 1996–; Research Fellow, Prof., mem. Chinese Acad. of Sciences and Chinese Acad. of Eng (CAE), Pres. CAE 1994–98, Pres. CCP Leading Group of CAE 1996–; Vice-Chair. 8th Nat. Cttee of CPPCC 1995–98, 9th Nat. Cttee 1998–; Meritorious Service Medal 1999. *Leisure interests:* cycling, classical music, classical literature, playing ping-pong and basketball. *Address:* Commission of Science, Technology and Industry for National Defence, 1 Aimin Street, Xicheng District, Beijing 100034, People's Republic of China (Office). *Telephone:* (10) 66738014 (Office). *Fax:* (10) 66032121 (Office). *E-mail:* engach@mail.cae.ac.cn (Office).

ZHU HOUZE; Chinese party official; b. 16 Jan. 1931, Guiyang Municipality, Guizhou Prov.; s. of Zhu Mei-lu and Xiong Lan-Xian; m. Qiong Zhen-qun 1954; one s. two d.; mem. 12th CCP Cen. Cttee 1982; Sec. CCP Cttee Guiyang Municipality 1982; Sec. CCP Cttee, Guizhou Prov. 1983–85; Head, Propaganda Dept CCP Cen. Cttee 1985–86; Vice-Pres., Sr Research Fellow Research Centre for Rural Devt of the State Council 1987–88; Vice-Chair., First Sec. All-China Fed. of Trade Unions 1989. *Leisure interests:* swimming, music, tennis, photography. *Address:* Jia No. 15, Wan-shou Road, District 6, Beijing 100036, People's Republic of China. *Telephone:* (10) 68211225. *Fax:* (10) 68211225. *E-mail:* z_hz@yahoo.com (Home).

ZHU KAIXUAN; Chinese engineer and administrator; b. 1932, Shanghai City; ed Beijing Aeronautical Inst.; joined CCP 1953; Vice-Minister in charge of State Educ. Comm. 1985–92, Minister 1992–98; Vice-Chair. Acad. Degrees Cttee under State Council 1988; Head Nat. Co-ordination group for Anti-Illiteracy Work 1994–; alt. mem. 14th CCP Cen. Cttee 1992–97; Party Group Sec. State Educ. Comm. 1993–98; Chair. Cttee of Educ., Science, Culture and Public Health, 9th NPC 1998–. *Address:* c/o Standing Committee of National People's Congress, Beijing, People's Republic of China.

ZHU LILAN; Chinese scientist and administrator; b. 18 Aug. 1935, Huzhou Co., Zhejiang Prov.; ed Odessa Univ.; joined CCP 1956; Vice-Minister in charge of State Science and Tech. Comm. 1986–98, Party Group Sec. 1994–; alt. mem. 14th CCP Cen. Cttee 1992; mem. Nat. Leading Group for Science and Tech. 1996–98; Minister of Science and Tech. 1998–2000; mem. 15th CCP Cen. Cttee 1997–2002. *Address:* c/o Ministry of Science and Technology, 15B Fuxing Road, Beijing 100862, People's Republic of China.

ZHU LIN; Chinese actress; b. 22 May 1923, Lianyungang City, Jiangsu Prov.; d. of Zhu Xiaofang and Zhao Shouxuan; m. Diao Guangtan 1943; three s. one d.; ed Huayin Teachers' Coll. and Wuchang Art Training School; actress, Anti-Japanese Performing Group 1938–45, Datong Film Studio 1948–50, China Youth Art Theatre 1950–52, Beijing People's Art Theatre 1953–; Award for Promoting China's Drama 1988, Golden Eagle Prize for Best Supporting Actress, for role of Dowager Empress in film The Last Emperor 1989. *Films:* Weakling, Your Name is Woman 1948, Trials and Hardships 1949, Waiting 1950, The Last Emperor 1989, Su Wu Graze Sheep 1996. *Theatre includes:* Put Down Your Whip 1937, Beautiful Women 1947, Thunderstorm 1953, Three Sisters 1959, Cai Wenji 1959, 1962, 1978, Wu Zetian 1962–64, Death of a Salesman 1983, Win Game 1987, Candied Haws on a Stick 1996, Thunderstorm 1997, Sunrise 2001. *Address:* Room 601, Unit 2, Building 38, Dongzhi Menwai Street, Beijing 100027, People's Republic of China. *Telephone:* (10) 64168165.

ZHU MINGSHAN; Chinese jurist; b. May 1937, Jiutai Co., Jilin Prov.; two s.; ed People's Univ., Beijing; joined CCP 1961; Judge Criminal Court, Supreme People's Court 1978–82, Vice-Pres. 1982–83, Vice-Pres. Supreme People's Court 1983–. *Address:* Supreme People's Court, 27 Dongjiaomin Xiang, Beijing 100745, People's Republic of China.

ZHU QIZHEN; Chinese government official; b. 19 Dec. 1927, Jiangsu; m. Wang Yude 1955; one d.; Gen. Office, Ministry of Foreign Affairs 1949–62; Second Sec., First Sec. Chinese Embassy, UAR 1963–68; Div. Chief African Affairs Dept, Ministry of Foreign Affairs 1969–71, Deputy Dir West Asian and North African Affairs Dept 1972–73; Counsellor, Chinese Embassy, Australia 1973–76; Deputy Dir American and Oceanic Dept, Ministry of Foreign Affairs 1977–81, Dir 1982; Asst Minister, Ministry of Foreign Affairs 1982–84, Vice-Minister 1984–89; Amb. to USA 1989–93; mem. Standing Cttee, Vice-Chair.

Foreign Affairs Cttee, 8th NPC 1993–98, NPC Deputy, Henan Prov.; Chair. China Foundation for Int. Studies and Academic Exchanges 1999–. *Address:* 3 Toutiao, Taijichang, Beijing 100005, People's Republic of China. *Telephone:* (10) 65598131. *Fax:* (10) 65598128.

ZHU RONGJI; Chinese engineer and government official; b. 20 Oct. 1928, Changshan City, Hunan Prov.; m. Lao An; one s. one d.; ed Qinghua Univ.; fmr Deputy Head Production Planning Office, joined CCP 1949; NE China Dept of Industries; Group Head and Deputy Chief of Div., State Planning Comm. 1952–58; teacher, engineer 1958–69; sent for re-educ. during Cultural Revolution 1970–75; Deputy Chief Engineer petroleum pipeline co. 1975–79; Dir Industrial Econs Inst., Chinese Acad. of Social Sciences 1975–79; Div. Chief and Deputy Head of Bureau, State Econ. Comm. 1982, Vice-Minister in charge of State Econ. Comm. 1983–87; Mayor of Shanghai 1987–90; a Vice-Premier, State Council 1991–98, Premier 1998–2003, Dir State Council Production Office 1991; mem. Standing Cttee Political Bureau of CCP Cttee 1993–2003; Gov. People's Bank of China 1993–95; Head State Steering Group of Science, Tech. and Educ. 1998; Chair. Cttee for Construction of Three Gorges Project 1998. *Address:* c/o State Council, Xi Changan Jie, Beijing, People's Republic of China.

ZHU SENLIN; Chinese governor; b. 1930, Chuansha Co., Shanghai; ed Qinghua Univ.; Deputy Sec.-Gen. and Dir-Gen. Gen. Office Guangzhou City Cttee of CCP1981–; later Deputy Sec. Guangzhou City Cttee of CCP and Mayor of Guangzhou City; mem. Guangdong Provincial Cttee of CCP and Sec. Guangzhou City Party Cttee; Deputy Sec. Guangzhou Provincial Party Cttee, Acting Gov. 1991–93, Gov. of Guangdong Prov. 1992–96; Chair. Guangdong Provincial People's Congress; alternate mem. 13th CCP Cen. Cttee, 14th CCP Cen. Cttee 1992–97; Deputy to 7th, 8th and 9th Nat. People's Congress of China. *Address:* 305 Central Dongpeng Road, Guangzhou, People's Republic of China.

ZHU XIAOHUA; Chinese government official; b. 23 Jan. 1940, Xian Municipality, Shanxi Prov.; m. Li Yazhi 1962; three s.; ed Shanghai Univ. of Finance and Econs; with People's Bank of China 1979–90, positions include Deputy Dir, Financial Research Division, Deputy Pres. Shanghai Office, Deputy Gov. People's Bank of China 1993–96; Special Appointee IMF1991–92; apptd Deputy Dir Science and Tech. Dept, State Family Planning Comm. 1992; Deputy Dir Econs Dept, Xinhua News Agency, Hong Kong 1992–93; Dir-Gen. State Admin of Foreign Exchange Control 1993–96; Chair. and CEO China Everbright Holdings Co. Ltd., Hong Kong 1996–99; charged with corruption; expelled frrom Communist Party Aug. 2002; convicted of bribery and sentenced to fifteen years' imprisonment Oct. 2002. *Leisure interests:* literature, sports.

ZHU XU; Chinese actor; b. Feb. 1930, Shenyang, Liaoning Prov.; actor Beijing People's Arts Theatre 1952–. *Films include:* Drum Singers 1987, Xin Xiang 1993, The King of Masks (Best Actor, Tokyo Film Festival) 1996, Shower 1999, Gua Shua 2001. *Address:* Beijing People's Arts Theatre, Beijing, People's Republic of China.

ZHU XUN; Chinese state official; b. 1930, Funing Co., Jiangsu Prov.; ed China People's Univ. and in USSR; Vice-Minister of Geology and Minerals 1982–85, Minister 1985–94; alt. mem. 12th CCP Cen. Cttee 1982, mem. 1985–87, mem. 13th CCP Cen. Cttee 1987–92; mem. 14th CCP Cen. Cttee 1992–97; Sec.-Gen. 8th Nat. Cttee CPPCC 1994–98; Chair. Cttee for Liaison with Hong Kong, Macao, Taiwan and Overseas Chinese Affairs, 9th Nat. Cttee of CPPCC 1998–; Hon. mem. Int. Hydrogeologists' Asscn 1989; Hon. Academician, Russian Acad. of Natural Sciences 1996, of Int. Euro-Asian Acad. of Sciences 1999; Boris Yeltsin Friendship Medal 1999. *Publications:* Introduction to Ore-Seeking Philosophy, Mineral Resources in China, Geoscience and Sustainable Development. *Leisure interests:* swimming, walking, music, film. *Address:* c/o National Committee of Chinese People's Political Consultative Conference, 23 Taipingqiao Street, Beijing, People's Republic of China. *Telephone:* (10) 66191803 (Office); (10) 68321977 (Home). *Fax:* (10) 66191616 (Office).

ZHU YINGHUANG; Chinese journalist; b. 28 Dec. 1943, Shanghai; m. Yao Xiang 1972; one d.; Ed.-in-Chief China Daily; Chair. China Daily Newspaper Group. *Address:* China Daily, 15 Huixin Dongjie, Chao Yang Qu, Beijing 100029, People's Republic of China. *Telephone:* (10) 64918633. *Fax:* (10) 64918377. *Website:* www.chinadaily.com.cn (Office).

ZHU YULI; Chinese aviation industry official; Dir State Bureau of Tech. Supervision 1990–93; Deputy Dir Econ. and Trade Office State Council 1991, Dir of Gen. Office of State Council's Leading Group for "Year of Quality, Variety and Economic Results" 1992; Pres. Aviation Industries of China 1993–; mem. 15th CCP Cen. Cttee 1997–2002. *Address:* Aviation Industries of China, 67 Nan Dajit, Jiaodaokou, Dongcheng Qu, Beijing, People's Republic of China. *Telephone:* (10) 64013322 (Office). *Fax:* (10) 64013648 (Office).

ZHU ZHENDA; Chinese scientist; b. 20 June 1930, Zhejiang Prov.; ed Nanjing Univ.; Head, Dept Desert Research, Geography Inst. 1959–65; Dir Lanzhou Desert Research Inst. 1981, Chinese Acad. of Sciences 1982; awarded China Science Congress Prize 1977. *Address:* Institute of Desert Research, 14 Dong Guan Xilu, Lanzhou, Gansu, People's Republic of China.

ZHUKOV, Alexander Dmitreyevich; Russian politician and economist; b. 1 June 1956; m.; one s.; ed Moscow State Univ., Harvard State Univ.; mem.

All-Union Research Inst. of Systems Studies and State Cttee on Science and Tech. –1980; mem. Chief Currency Econ. Dept, USSR Ministry of Finance 1980–91; Vice-Pres. Avtotractorexport Co., Ministry of Foreign Trade 1991–93; mem. State Duma 1993–; Deputy Chair. Liberal Democratic Union of 12th Dec. 1994–96; Chair. Cttee on Budget, Taxes, Banks and Finance 1998–99, on Budget and Taxes 2000–; mem. Russian Regions Faction 1996–. *Address:* State Duma, 103265 Moscow, Okhotny Ryad 1, Russia (Office). *Telephone:* (095) 292-36-18 (Office). *Fax:* (095) 292-53-05 (Office).

ZHUMALIYEV, Kubanychbek Myrzabekovich; Kyrgyzstan politician and scientist; b. 26 April 1956, Kichik-Ak-Zhol, Osh Region; ed Ryazan' Radio Tech. Inst.; worked as scientific researcher in Frunze Polytechnical Inst. 1978–86, Inst. of Physics Nat. Acad. of Sciences 1986–88; Exec. Dir Scientific Cen. Zhalyn Acad. of Sciences 1988–92; Chair. State Cttee of Science and New Tech. 1992–94; First Vice-Minister of Educ. and Science 1994–95; First Deputy to Sec. of State 1995–96; Head, Admin. of Pres. Akayev 1996–98; Prime Minister of Kyrgyzstan 1998–2001; Gov. of Djelal-Abad Region 1998–2001; Minister of Transport and Communications 2001–02; Deputy Prime Minister 2002–; mem. Nat. Acad. of Sciences. *Address:* Ministry of Transport and Communications, Isanova str. 42, 720017 Bishkek, Kyrgyzstan. *Telephone:* (312) 21-66-72 (Office). *Fax:* (312) 21-36-67 (Office). *E-mail:* di@mtk.bishkek.gov.kg (Office). *Website:* www.mtk.bishkek.gov.kg (Office).

ZHURKIN, Vitaliy Vladimirovich, DPhil; Russian political scientist; b. 14 Jan. 1928, Moscow; m. Dina Zhurkina 1961 (died 1997); one s.; ed Moscow Inst. of Int. Relations; Ed. journal USA: Economics, Politics, Ideology; Deputy Dir USA and Canada Inst. 1971–87; Founder and Dir Inst. of Europe, USSR (now Russian) Acad. of Sciences 1987–99, Hon. Dir 1999–; Sec. Dept of Int. Relations, Acad. of Sciences 1991–97; Corresp. mem. USSR (now Russian) Acad. of Sciences 1984, mem. 1990; mem. Academia Europaea 1990, World Acad. of Art and Science 1994; USSR State Prize 1980. *Publications:* works on the political and mil. aspects of contemporary int. relations. *Address:* Institute of Europe, 18, Korp. 3, Mokhovaya Str., 103873 Moscow, Russia. *Telephone:* (095) 203-73-43 (Office); (095) 230-00-70 (Home). *Fax:* (095) 200-42-98.

ZHVANETSKY, Mikhail Mikhailovich; Russian writer; b. 6 March 1934, Odessa; s. of Emmanuil Moiseevich Zhvanetsky and Raisa Yakovlevna Zhvanetskaya; m.; two s. one d.; ed Odessa Inst. of Naval Eng; worked as technician and engineer, Prodmash factory, Odessa shipbuilding yard 1956–64; literary work 1964–; wrote short stories for Comedy Theatre of A. Raikin; f. Odessa Miniature Theatre (with R. Kartsev and V. Ilchenko) 1970; performed readings of short stories 1970–; stories banned because of criticism of state; Founder and Artistic Dir Moscow Miniature Theatre 1988–; Founder and Ed. Magazin journal 1991; Hon. Citizen of Odessa; Triumph Prize 1994. *Publications include:* Meetings in the Streets 1977, A Year For Two (short stories) 1989, My Life, Stay with Me (novel) 1989, Wir brauchen Helden! (short stories) 1992, My Odessa 1993 (short stories), Complete Works 2001; also stories in newspapers and periodicals. *Address:* Moscow Miniature Theatre, 1st Tverskaya-Yamskaya 16, 125047 Moscow (Office); Lesnaya Str. 4, Apt. 63, 125047 Moscow, Russia (Home). *Telephone:* (095) 250-37-21 (Office); (095) 187-06-48 (Home).

ZHVANIA, Zurab Vissarionovich; Georgian politician; b. 9 Dec. 1963, Tbilisi; m.; two c.; ed Tbilisi State Univ.; Sr Lab. Asst, Jr Researcher Chair of Physiology of Man and Animals, Tbilisi State Univ. 1985–92; Chair. Cen. Exec. Bd of Green Party of Georgia 1988–93; Speaker Green Party of Georgia 1990–93; Chair. European Union of Green Parties 1992–93; one of initiators Union of Citizens of Georgia; one of founders, then Sec.-Gen. Union of Citizens of Georgia 1993–2001; mem. Parl. (Green Faction) 1992–, Chair. 1995–2001. *Address:* House of Government, Tbilisi, Georgia.

ZI HUAYUN; Chinese dancer and scholar; b. 10 March 1936, Tianjin City; d. of Zi Yaohua and Tong Yijun; m. Wang Shouyin 1960; one s. one d.; ed Tianjin Nankai High School, Beijing Normal Univ., Beijing Cen. Drama Coll.; dancer, China Cen. Dance Ensemble 1950–; Dir and Sr Fellow Dance Research Inst. of Chinese Arts Acad. 1987–; Chief Ed. The Art of Dance; prizes include Gold Medal (for Tibetan Dance), 3rd World Youth Festival, Berlin 1950, Bronze Medal (for Flying Apsara), 5th World Youth Festival, Warsaw 1955, Prize for Excellent Performance, 1st Nat. Dancing Competition 1984. *Publications:* Dance and I 1987, Chinese and Foreign Artists 1989, Introduction to Choreography (Co-author) 1991, Treatises on Choreology (Co-author), The Rise and Development of Chinese Folk Dance during the Past 50 Years 1992, Collection of Essays of Hua Yun 1994, Fantasy of Dance 1995, Graceful Life 1997, The Art of Dance and Theory of Dance 1998, The Chinese Dance 1999, Studying Keeps You Young for Ever 2000; Chief Ed. of The Art of Dance. *Address:* Dance Research Institute, Chinese Academy of Arts, 17 Qianhai Xijie, Beijing 100009, People's Republic of China.

ZIA, Begum Khaleda; Bangladeshi politician; b. 15 Aug. 1945; d. of late Iskander Majumder and of Begum Taiyaba Majumder; m. Capt. Ziaur Rahman (later Pres. of Bangladesh) 1960 (deceased); two s.; ed Surendranath Coll., Dinajpur; held captive during Bangladesh's war of independence; Vice-Chair. Nat. Party (BNP) 1982–84, fmr Chair.; helped to form seven-party alliance leading to ousting Pres. Ershad from power 1990; Prime Minister of Bangladesh 1991–96, 2001–, also Minister of the Armed Div., of Defence, of the Cabinet Div., of Power, Energy and Mineral Resources, of Chittagong Hill Tracts Affairs, of the Primary and Mass Educ. Div. and of the Establishment

2001–; Chair. SAARC 1993–94. *Leisure interests:* reading, listening to music, gardening. *Address:* Prime Minister's Office, Old Sangsad Bhaban, Tejgaon, Dhaka (Office); c/o BNP, 29 Minto Road, Dhaka, Bangladesh. *Telephone:* (2) 815100 (Office); (2) 328292. *Fax:* (2) 813244 (Office). *E-mail:* pm@pmo .bdonline.com.

ZICO, (Arthur Antunes Coimbra); Brazilian footballer, football coach and politician; b. 3 March 1953, Rio de Janeiro; m.; one d.; player Flamengo 1972–83, 1986–90, Udinese 1983–86, Kashima Antlers (Japan) 1991–94; player Brazilian nat. team in World Cup 1978, 1982, 1986; 88 caps, 66 goals; became a politician on retirement and apptd. Minister of Sport; retd from politics and launched new J League, Japan; Asst coach to Mario Zagallo (q.v.), World Cup 1998; Man. Japan nat. team July 2002–; South American Footballer of the Year 1977, 1981, 1982, World Footballer of the Year 1993.

ZIDANE, Zinedine ("Zizou"); French footballer; b. 23 June 1972, Marseille; m. Veronique Zidane; two s.; ed Centre de Formation de l'Asscn Sportive, Cannes; Mid-field player with AS Cannes 1988–92 (60 games, 6 goals), with Bordeaux 1992–96 (137 games, 28 goals), with Juventus, Turin 1996–2001, transferred for a record £45million to Real Madrid 2001 (scored winning goal in the Champions League final 2002); winner European Super Cup 1996, European/S. American Cup 1996, League Super Cup 1997, Champion Italy 1997, 1998; mem. French Nat. Team 1994 – in winning team World Cup 1998, Euro 2000; co-owner of brasserie Nulle part ailleurs, Bordeaux; Chevalier, Légion d'honneur; France Football Golden Ball, Best European Footballer 1998, FIFA World Player of the Year, 1998, 2000. *Leisure interests:* music, tennis, boating, cooking, Formula 1 racing. *Address:* c/o Real Madrid Club de Fútbol, Conctia Espina, 28036 Madrid, Spain. *Telephone:* (91) 3984300 (Office). *Fax:* (91) 3440695 (Office). *Website:* www.realmadrid.es (Office); www.zidane.net (Office).

ZIEGLER, Jean, DenD, DenScPol; Swiss university professor, writer and politician; b. 19 April 1934, Berne; s. of Hans Ziegler and Léa Ziegler; m.; one s.; ed Univs. of Geneva, Berne, Paris-Sorbonne and Columbia Univ. New York; with Swiss American Corpn New York 1959; Jr lawyer in training with Theodor Haffner, New York; Asst to Sec.-Gen. of Int. Comm. of Jurists; UN expert, Léopoldville and Elisabethville, Congo 1961–62; Research Assoc. Faculté de Droit, Inst. Africain de Geneva 1963; Prof. Inst. d'Etudes Politiques, Univ. of Grenoble 1967; Faculty of Law and Social and Econ. Sciences, Univ. of Berne 1969; Prof. Faculty of Econ. and Social Sciences, Univ. of Geneva and Univ. Inst. of Devt Studies 1975; Prof. Univ. of Paris I—Sorbonne 1983; numerous research tours in Africa, Latin America and Asia since 1963; City Councillor, Geneva 1963; mem. Swiss Nat. Council 1967–83, 1987–; mem. Fed. Parl. from Geneva; mem. Cen. Cttee Swiss Socialist Party; mem. Exec. Council, Socialist Int.; UN Special Rapporteur for the Right to Food; Adlai Stevenson Peace Award 1964; Chevalier, Ordre des Arts et des Lettres; Bruno Kreisky Peace Prize 2000. *Publications include:* La contre-révolution en Afrique 1963, Vive le pouvoir! ou les délices de la raison d'Etat 1985, Sankara. Un nouveau pouvoir africain (with J. P. Rapp) 1986, Dialogue Est-Ouest (with Y. Popov) 1987, La Suisse lave plus blanc 1990, La victoire des vaincus, oppression et résistance culturelle 1991, Le bonheur d'être Suisse 1993, Il s'agit de ne pas se rendre (with Régis Debray) 1994, L'or du Maniéma (novel) 1996, La Suisse, l'or et les morts 1997, Les seigneurs du crime, les nouvelles mafia contre la démocratie 1999, La faim dans le monde racontée à mon fils 2001; numerous book chapters, articles in reviews, journals, newspapers etc. *Leisure interests:* skiing, tennis, mountaineering. *Address:* University of Geneva, 1211 Geneva 4, Switzerland. *Telephone:* (22) 7058326. *Fax:* (22) 7814100.

ZIEGLER, Peter Alfred, PhD; Swiss professor of global tectonics; b. 2 Nov. 1928, Winterthur; s. of Eugen Ziegler and Adelheid Riggenbach; m. Yvonne M. Bohrer 1960; two s.; ed Univ. of Zürich; joined petroleum industry 1955; field geologist in Israel, Madagascar, Algeria; joined Shell Canada 1958; transferred to Shell Int. Petroleum Maatschappij BV, The Hague 1970; tech. adviser, North Sea exploration 1970–77, exploration consultant Europe, South America, Deputy Head, new ventures and exploration advice with worldwide responsibility 1982, Sr exploration consultant 1984–88, ind. petroleum exploration consultant 1988–; Hon. Lecturer Univ. of Basel 1990–96, Prof. of Global Geology 1996–; Co-ordinator EUCOR-URGENT Project 1999–; mem. Royal Netherlands Acad., Academia Europaea, Polish Acad. of Arts and Sciences, Polish Acad. of Sciences, Russian Acad. of Natural Sciences, New York Acad. of Science; Life mem. Bureau Int. Lithosphere Programme; Hon. mem., Geological Soc. London, Polish Geological Soc., European Union of Geosciences; Dr hc (Moscow State Univ.) 1998, (Tech. Univ. Delft) 2001; Fourmarier Medal (Geological Soc. Belgium), Van Waterschot van der Gracht Medal (Royal Geological and Mining Soc. of the Netherlands), William Smith Medal (Geological Soc. London), J. Neville George Medal (Geological Soc. Glasgow), Leopold von Buch Medal (Deutsche Geologische Gesellschaft), Robert H. Dott Sr Memorial Award (American Asscn of Petroleum Geologists), Special Commendation Award (American Asscn of Petroleum Geologists), Piotr Leonidovich Kapitsa Medal (Russian Acad. of Natural Sciences), S. Müller Medal, European Geophysical Soc. 1998. *Publications include:* Geological Atlas of Western and Central Europe 1982, Evolution of Arctic-North Atlantic and Western Tethys 1988, Evolution of Laurussia, a study in late Palaeozoic plate tectonics 1989, Geodynamics of Rifting (Ed. and Contrib.) 1992, Structure and Prospects of Alpine Basins and Forelands (Ed. and Contrib.) 1996, Peritethyan Rift and Wrench Basins and Passive Margins

(Ed. and Contrib.) 2001. *Leisure interests:* gardening, hiking. *Address:* Kirchweg 41, 4102 Binningen, Switzerland. *Telephone:* (61) 4215535. *Fax:* (61) 4215535.

ZIEGLER, Philip Sandeman, CVO, MA, FRHistS, FRSL; British writer; b. 24 Dec. 1929, Ringwood, Hants.; s. of Colin Louis Ziegler and Dora Ziegler (née Barnwell); m. 1st Sarah Collins 1960 (deceased). m. 2nd Mary Clare Charrington 1971; two s. one d.; ed Eton Coll., New Coll. Oxford; joined Foreign Office 1952, served Vientiane, Paris, Pretoria, Bogotá; Editorial Dir Collins Publishers 1972, Ed.-in-Chief 1979–80, resgnd when apptd. to write official biog. of the late Earl Mountbatten; Chair. London Library 1979–85, Soc. of Authors 1988–90, Public Lending Right Advisory Cttee 1993–96; Hon. DLitt (Westminster Coll., Mo., USA) 1987, (Univ. of Buckingham) 2000; Chancellor's Essay Prize 1950, Heineman Award 1976. *Publications include:* Duchess of Dino 1962, Addington 1965, The Black Death 1969, William IV 1971, Omdurman 1973, Melbourne 1976, Crown and People 1978, Diana Cooper 1981, Mountbatten 1985, Elizabeth's Britain 1926 to 1986 1986, The Sixth Great Power: Barings 1762–1929 1988, King Edward VIII, The Official Biography 1990; ed.: The Diaries of Lord Louis Mountbatten 1920–1922 1987, Personal Diary of Admiral the Lord Louis Mountbatten 1943–1946 1988, From Shore to Shore: The Diaries of Earl Mountbatten of Burma 1953–1979 1989, Brooks's: A Social History (ed. with Desmond Seward) 1991, Wilson: The Authorized Life of Lord Wilson of Rievaulx 1993, London at War: 1939–45 1994, Osbert Sitwell 1998, Britain Then and Now 1999, Soldiers. Fighting Men's Lives 1901–2001 2001. *Address:* 22 Cottesmore Gardens, London, W8 5PR, England. *Telephone:* (20) 7937-1903. *Fax:* (20) 7937-5458.

ZIEJKA, Franciszek; Polish philologist, university rector and writer; b. 10 March 1940, Radłów; m. Maria Gluszek (deceased); two c.; ed Jagiellonian Univ.; academic Jagiellonian Univ. 1963–, Inst. of Polish Studies 1963–, Prof. 1998–, Dean Philological Faculty 1990–93, Vice-Rector 1993–99, Rector 1999–; lector Provençal Univ., Aix-en-Provence 1970–73, Univ. of Lisbon 1979–80; lecturer Inst. des Langues et Civilisations Orientales, Paris 1984–88; mem. United Peasant Party (ZSL) 1962–89, Solidarity Trade Union 1989–93; mem. Polish Acad. of Arts and Sciences 2002–; Hon. Citizen of Tarnòw and Sanok; Officer, Palmes Académiques; Kt's Cross of Order of Polonia Restituta; Order of Cross of the South; Gold Rays with Neck Ribbon of the Order of the Rising Sun; Grand Golden Cross for Services Rendered to the Repub. of Austria; Zygmunt Gloger Prize and Medal, Adamczewski Prize. *TV screenplays include:* Origin of the Legend: The Panorama of Racławice 1981, Polish November 1983, Traugutt 1991. *Radio plays include:* It Happened During Carnival 1996, A Book of Stone About the Past 1996, You Will Be a Pearl for Poland... 1997. *Publications:* Polish and Provençal Studies 1977, The Panorama of Racławice 1984, The Golden Legend of Polish Peasants 1985, Paris and Young Poland 1993, Our Family in Europe 1995, Wyspiański's 'Wedding' in Polish Myths 1997, Poets—Missionaries—Scientists 1998, Mythes polonais. Autour de "La Noce" de Stanisław Wyspiański 2001. *Address:* Uniwersytet Jagielloński, ul. Gołębia 24, 31-007 Cracow (Office); ul. Łepkowskiego 8 m. 48, 31-422 Cracow, Poland (Home). *Telephone:* (12) 4221033 (Office); (12) 4226689 (Office); (12) 4110190 (Home). *Fax:* (12) 4223229 (Office). *E-mail:* rektor@adm.uj.edu.pl (Office). *Website:* www.uj.edu .pl (Office).

ZIELENKIEWICZ, Wojciech Władysław, DSC, PhD; Polish physical chemist; b. 6 June 1933, Warsaw; s. of Edward Zielenkiewicz and Barbara Zielenkiewicz (née Szot); m. Anna Kastrzyńska; one s.; ed Chemistry Faculty of Warsaw Univ.; researcher, Physical Chemistry Inst. of Polish Acad. of Sciences, Warsaw 1955–, Asst, Lecturer 1955–65, Head, Microcalorimetry Lab. 1965–68, Calorimetry Dept 1968–, Asst Prof. 1966–71, Extraordinary Prof. 1971–87, Ordinary Prof. 1987–, Dir of Inst. 1973–90; Gen.-Dir, Polish Acad. of Sciences (PAN) 1968–69, Deputy Gen. Sec. PAN 1969–72, Deputy Sec. PAN Mathematical, Physical and Chemical Sciences Dept 1972–80, Sec. of Dept 1984–89, mem. Presidium 1984–89; Corresp. mem. Real Academia de Ciencias y Artes de Barcelona 1975–, Polish Acad. of Sciences 1977–; titular mem. Thermodynamics Comm. of IUPAC 1976–85; Chair. Comm. of Metrology and Scientific Apparatus of Polish Acad. of Sciences; Ed.-in-Chief Bulletin of the Polish Acad. of Sciences, Chemical Sciences Section 1985–94, Int. Journal Scientific Instrumentation 1972–85, Scientific Instrumentation (Warsaw) 1986–; Pres. Polish Asscn on Calorimetry and Thermal Analysis 1985–91, Hon. mem. 1991–; Commdr's Cross Order of Polonia Restituta; Banner of Works; Gold Cross of Merit and other decorations; awards of Science and Tech. Cttee of PAN, Calvet Medal 1991, W Świętosławski Medal 1994. *Publications:* more than 200 original scientific works in Polish and foreign journals. *Leisure interests:* hiking, reading. *Address:* Instytut Chemii Fizycznej PAN, ul. Kasprzaka 44/52, 01-224 Warsaw (Office); ul. L. Schillera 8 m. 30, 00-248 Warsaw, Poland (Home). *Telephone:* (22) 6324389 (Office). *Fax:* (22) 6325276 (Office). *E-mail:* zivf@ichf.edu.pl (Office). *Website:* www .ichf.edu.pl (Office).

ŽIEMELIS, Vidmantas; Lithuanian lawyer and politician; b. 4 Dec. 1950, Gailiskiai, Moletai Region; ed Vilnius State Univ.; mem. CPSU –1989, voluntarily withdrew from CP; workman, later legal adviser Amalgamation of Chem. Consumer Products 1977–81; Asst to Prosecutor at Vilnius Prosecutor's Office 1981–84; Prosecutor-Gen. Supervision Dept Prosecutor's Office Repub. of Lithuania 1984–90; involved in Sajudis Movt from late 1980s; mem. Council of Sajudis, Vilnius City 1989–90; elected Deputy of Supreme Soviet Repub. of Lithuania Feb. 1990; signatory March 11th Act on Re-establishment of Independence; mem. Seimas (Parl.) Repub. of Lithuania 1992–; mem. Cttee on State Issues and Legal Affairs 1989–96; Minister of Interior 1996–98. *Address:* c/o Conservative Party, Gedimino 1, Suite 302, Vilnius, Lithuania (Office). *Telephone:* (2) 224-747 (Office).

ZIENKIEWICZ, Olgierd Cecil, CBE, PhD, DSc, DipEng, FICE, FRS, FREng; British professor of engineering; b. 18 May 1921, Caterham; s. of the late Casimir Zienkiewicz and Edith V. Penny; m. Helen J. Fleming 1952; two s. one d.; ed Katowice, Poland and Imperial Coll., London; consulting Eng 1945–49; Lecturer, Univ. of Edinburgh 1949–57; Prof. of Structural Mechanics, Northwestern Univ. 1957–61; Prof. and Head Civil Eng Dept and Dir Inst. for Numerical Methods in Eng, Univ. of Wales, Swansea 1961–88, Prof. Emer. 1988–; Naval Sea Systems Command Research Prof. Monterey, Calif. 1979–80; UNESCO Chair. of Numeric Methods in Eng, Univ. of Barcelona 1989–; J. Walter Chair. of Eng, Univ. of Tex., Austin, USA 1989–97; Hon. founder mem. GAMNI, France; Founder Int. Journal of Numerical Methods in Eng 1968–; Pres. Int. Asscn of Computational Mechanics 1986–90; Foreign Assoc. US Nat. Acad. of Eng; Foreign mem. Polish Acad. of Science 1985, Nat. Acad. of Science, People's Repub. of China 1998, Nat. Acad. of Science, Italy 2000; Fellow City and Guilds 1979; Fellow Imperial Coll. 1993; Fellow American Soc. of Civil Engineers; Chevalier des Palmes Académiques 1996; 26 hon. doctorates; J. A. Ewing Research Medal (Inst. of Civil Engineers) 1980, Newmark Medal (American Soc. of Civil Engineers) 1980, Worcester W. Reid Medal (ASME) 1980, Gauss Medal, Acad. of Science, Braunschweig 1987, The Royal Medal 1990, Gold Medal, Inst. of Structural Eng 1992, Gold Medal of Inst. of Math. and its Applications 1992, Leonardo da Vinci Medal of European Soc. for Eng Educ. (SEFI); Timoshenko Medal, ASME 1998, and other awards and prizes. *Publications:* 15 books and 550 articles in professional journals. *Leisure interests:* sailing, skin-diving. *Address:* 29 Somerset Road, Langland, Swansea, SA3 4PG, Wales. *Telephone:* (1792) 368776 (Home).

ZIGUÉLÉ, Martin; Central African Republic politician and insurance company executive; b. 12 Feb. 1957, Paoua; m.; six c.; ed State Coll. of Bangui Rapids, Univ. of Bangui, Int. Inst. of Insurance, Yaoundé, Cameroon; mem. staff Insurance Dept, Ministry of Finance 1978; Asst Gen. Man., then Head various depts. state-owned insurance co. SIRIRI 1988–95; Prin. Insp. of Taxes, seconded to regional insurance co. CICARE; Dir for the Central African Republic, Banque des Etats de l'Afrique Centrale (BEAC); Prime Minister of the Central African Republic 2001–03. *Address:* c/o Office of the Prime Minister, Palais de la Renaissance, Bangui, Central African Republic (Office).

ŽIKEŠ, Ivan; Czech business executive; b. 27 April 1945, Šternov; s. of the late Josef Žikeš and of Vera Žikeš; m. Vera Žikeš; two s.; ed Tech. Univ., Prague; mem. staff Vodní stavby Prague 1969–90; Acting Sec. and owner Recom Reality 1990–; Pres. ARKCMS. *Leisure interest:* golf. *Address:* Recom Reality s.r.o., Varšavská 13, 36001 Karlovy Vary (Office); ARKCMS, Na Chodovci 2880/3, 14100, Prague 4–Sporilov, Czech Republic (Office). *Telephone:* (3) 53228545 (Office). *Fax:* (3) 53228546 (Office). *E-mail:* zikes@recomreality.cz (Office); arkcms@arkcms.cz. *Website:* www.recomreality.cz (Office); www.arkcms.cz.

ZIKMUND, Miroslav; Czech writer; b. 14 Feb. 1919, Plzeň; s. of the late Antonín Zikmund and Magdalena Zikmund; m. Eva Mašková (divorced 1972); one s.; ed Univ. of Econs; Hon. Citizen Zlín 1994, Plzeň 1999, Koprivnice 2000; Order of the Repub. 1953; Golden Plaque Czech Acad. of Sciences 1965, Medal of Merit of Czech Repub. 1999, Gold Medal Silesian Univ. 1999. *Permanent exhibition:* Through Five Continents with Hanzelka and Zikmund, Castle of Zlín 1996–. *Films:* From Morocco to Kilimanjaro 1953, From the Equator to Table Mountain 1953, From Argentina to Mexico 1954, If There be Paradise on Earth 1962. *Television:* numerous documentaries. *Publications:* Over the Cordilleras 1957, Great Waters Iguazu 1957, Amazon Head Hunters 1958 Africa, Dreams and Reality 1952, With the Czech Flag to Kilimanjaro, Conquer the Desert 1954, Over There Behind the River is Argentina 1956, (co-author with Jiří Hanzelka) Between Two Oceans 1959, Crescent Upside Down 1961, Kashmir 1962, Syria 1963, Kurdistan 1963, Thousand and Two Nights 1967, Turkey 1962, Continent under the Himalayas 1969, Political Analysis of the USSR 1989, Ceylon 1991, Life of Dreams and Reality 1997, Blue Mauritius 1999. *Leisure interests:* genealogy, travelling. *Address:* Pod Nivami 2894, 760 01 Zlín, Czech Republic.

ZIMAN, John Michael, DSc, FRS; British physicist; b. 16 May 1925; s. of the late Solomon Netheim Ziman and of Nellie Francis (née Gaster) Ziman; m. Rosemary Milnes Dixon 1951 (died 2001); two adopted s. two adopted d.; ed Hamilton High School, New Zealand, Victoria Coll., Wellington, Balliol Coll., Oxford; Junior Lecturer in Mathematics, Oxford Univ. 1951–53, Pressed Steel Ltd Research Fellow 1953–54; Lecturer in Physics, Cambridge Univ. 1954–64, Fellow of King's Coll. 1957–64, Ed. Cambridge Review 1958–59, Tutor for Advanced Students, King's Coll. 1959–63; Prof. of Theoretical Physics, Univ. of Bristol 1964–69, Melville Wills Prof. 1969–76, Henry Overton Wills Prof. and Dir H. H. Wills Physics Lab. 1976–81, Prof. Emer. 1989–; Visiting Prof. in Depts. of Social and Econ. Studies and Humanities, Imperial Coll. of Science and Tech. 1982–; Chair. Science Policy Support Group 1986–91; Jt Ed., Science Progress 1965–; Hon. Ed. Reports on Progress in Physics 1968–76; Gen. Ed. Cambridge Monographs on Physics; Chair. Council for Science and Society; Rutherford Memorial Lecturer in India and Pakistan 1968; Airey Neave Memorial Award 1981. *Publications:* Electrons

and Phonons 1960, Electrons in Metals 1963, Camford Observed (with Jasper Rose) 1964, Principles of the Theory of Solids 1965, Public Knowledge 1968, Elements of Advanced Quantum Theory 1969, The Force of Knowledge 1976, Reliable Knowledge 1979, Models of Disorder 1979, Teaching and Learning about Science and Society 1980, Puzzles, Problems and Enigmas 1981, An Introduction to Science Studies 1984, The World of Science and the Rule of Law (with Paul Sieghart and John Humphrey) 1986, Knowing Everything about Nothing 1987, Prometheus Bound 1994, Of One Mind 1995, Real Science 2000; numerous articles in scientific journals. *Address:* 27 Little London Green, Oakley, Aylesbury, Bucks., HP18 9QL, England. *Telephone:* (1844) 237464. *Fax:* (1844) 237464.

ZIMBA, Lyonpo Yeshey, MA (ECONS); Bhutanese politician; b. 10 Oct. 1952, Ha; m. Thuji Zangmo; one s. three d.; ed Univ. of Wisconsin; joined civil service in the Royal Secr. 1974, planning officer, Ministry of Planning 1977, Jt Sec. 1991; Chair. Royal Monetary Authority (Cen. Bank) 1986; Minister of Finance July 1998–; Chair. Council of Ministers 2000–01; Silver Medal for Scholastic Achievement, Gold Medal for Best All-Round Coll. Student. *Leisure interests:* nature, walking. *Address:* Ministry of Finance, Tashichhodzong, P.O. Box 103, Thimphu (Office); Royal Monetary Authority, P.O. Box 154, Thimphu, Bhutan. *Telephone:* (2) 322271 (Office); (2) 323111. *Fax:* (2) 323154 (Office). *E-mail:* rma@druknet.net/bt (Office).

ZIMERMAN, Krystian; Polish pianist and conductor; b. 5 Dec. 1956, Zabrze; m. Maria Drygajło; one s. one d.; ed State Higher Inst. of Music, Katowice, student of Prof. Andrzej Jasiński; lecturer Acad. of Music, Basel 1996–; founder and conductor Polish Festival Orchestra 1998; collaboration with conductors Bernstein, von Karajan, Ozawa, Muti, Maazel, Previn, Boulez, Mehta, Haitink, Skrowaczewski, Rattle and others; has performed in numerous European countries and the USA; numerous prizes in prin. pianist competitions in Poland and abroad including First Prize, Beethoven Competition, Hradec Kralové 1973, Grand Prix IX Chopin Int. Pianist Competition, Warsaw 1975, Chigiana's Acad. Award for Best Young Pianist of the Year, Siena 1985, Orfeusz (Critics' Award), Polish Artists of Music Asscn 1988, Grand Prix de Disque, French Acad. 1989, Int. Critics' Award 1989. *Music:* CD recordings include: works for piano and chamber music by Schumann, Grieg (with H. von Karajan), Mozart (with K. Danczowska), Schubert, Brahms, Chopin (with Polish Festival Orchestra – Chopin Piano Concertos), Liszt, Debussy and others. *Address:* Kernmatterstrasse 8B, 4102 Binningen, Switzerland.

ZIMMER, Hans; film score composer; b. 1958, Frankfurt am Main; m. Vicki Carolyn (separated); one d.; ed in England; mem. The Buggles (produced hit song Video Killed the Radio Star); pioneered use of digital synthesizers with computer tech. and traditional orchestras. *Film scores include:* Driving Miss Daisy, Green Card, Pacific Heights, Backdraft, Rain Man, Regarding Henry, Thelma and Louise, The House of the Spirits, The Lion King (Acad. Award 1994), Crimson Tide, Nine Months, Something to Talk About, Beyond Rangoon, Muppet Treasure Island, Broken Arrow, The Preacher's Wife, As Good As It Gets, The Thin Red Line, The Prince of Egypt, Gladiator, Chill Factor, The Road to El Dorado, Mission Impossible II, The Pledge, Hannibal, Pearl Harbor, Black Hawk Down, Spirit; in collaboration with Stanley Myers: Eureka, A World Apart, My Beautiful Laundrette.

ZIMMERMAN, Howard Elliot, PhD; American professor of chemistry; b. 5 July 1926, New York; s. of Charles Zimmerman and May Zimmerman; m. 1st Jane Kirschenheiter 1950 (deceased); three s.; m. 2nd Martha L. Bailey Kaufman 1975 (divorced 1990); one step-s.; m. 3rd Margaret Jane Vick 1991; ed Yale and Harvard Univs; Nat. Research Council Postdoctoral Fellow, Harvard Univ. 1953–54; Instructor Northwestern Univ. 1954–55, Asst Prof. 1955–60; Assoc. Prof. Univ. of Wisconsin 1960–61, Prof. 1961–, Arthur C. Cope Prof. of Chem. 1975–, also Hilldale Prof. of Chem. 1990–; mem. several editorial bds etc.; mem. NAS 1980; Alfred P. Sloan Fellow 1956–60; NRC Postdoctoral Fellowship 1953–54; Sr Humboldt Fellowship 1988; JSPS Fellowship 1988; Yale Chittenden Award 1950, James Flack Norris Award (American Chem. Soc.) 1976, Halpern Award (New York Acad. of Sciences) 1979, Pioneer Award, Nat. Inst. of Chemists 1986, Univ. of Wis. Hilldale Award in Physical Sciences 1990, Arthur C. Cope Scholar Award 1991. *Publications:* Quantum Mechanics for Organic Chemists 1975; 6 book chapters and more than 260 scientific articles. *Leisure interest:* violin. *Address:* Department of Chemistry, University of Wisconsin, 1101 University Avenue, Madison, WI 53706 (Office); 7813 Westchester Drive, Middleton, WI 53562, USA (Home). *Telephone:* (608) 262-1502 (Office); (608) 831-7483 (Home). *Fax:* (608) 262-0381 (Office); (608) 265-4534. *E-mail:* zimmerman@chem.wisc.edu (Office). *Website:* www.chem.wisc.edu/~zimmerman/index.html (Office).

ZIMMERMANN, Frank Peter; German violinist; b. 27 Feb. 1965, Duisburg; m. Young Joo Zimmermann; one s.; ed Folkwang Musikhochschule, Essen, Staatliche Hochschule der Künste, Berlin and with Herman Krebbers in Amsterdam; made debut aged 10 playing Mozart's violin concerto in G major, K 216 in Duisburg; now performs with all maj. orchestras in world and has undertaken extensive tours in Europe, the USA, Japan and Australia; also gives worldwide recitals, with pianists Alexander Lonquich –1994 and Enrico Pace 1998– and with Heinrich Schiff (q.v.) and Christian Zacharias; appeared with English Chamber Orchestra conducted by Sir Colin Davis at Buckingham Palace by special invitation of HRH The Prince of Wales 1991; soloist at Europa Concert given by Berlin Philharmonic under Bernard Haitink at

Royal Albert Hall, London and televised live all over world 1993; recordings include concertos of Tchaikovsky, Brahms, Beethoven, Mozart, Prokofiev, Sibelius, Mendelssohn, Dvořák, Glazunov, Berg, Saint-Saëns, Weill and Stravinsky; in recital with Alexander Lonquich recorded all Mozart and Prokofiev sonatas and works by Ravel, Debussy, Janáček etc.; Brahms Double Concerto with Heinrich Schiff and London Philharmonic Orchestra 1997; Ligeti Violin Concerto with ASKO Ensemble and Reinbert de Leeuw 2001; many other recordings; Premio dell'Accademia Musicale Chigiana, Siena 1990, Rheinischer Kulturpreis 1994; numerous awards and prizes for recordings. *Leisure interests:* gastronomy, sports, wine, arts, literature. *Address:* c/o Riaskoff Concert Management, Concertgebouwplein 15, 1071 LL Amsterdam, Netherlands. *Telephone:* (20) 6645353. *Fax:* (20) 6715106. *E-mail:* mail@riaskoff.nl (Office).

ZIMMERMANN, Friedrich, DJur; German politician; b. 18 July 1925, Munich; s. of Josef Zimmermann and Luise (née Wenger) Zimmermann; m. 1st Erika Mangge 1950 (deceased); one d.; m. 2nd Christel Pratzat 1970 (divorced); one d.; m. 3rd Birgit Kemmler 1988; ed Univ. of Munich; Asst legal officer, Bavarian State Ministry of Justice 1951–54, legal adviser, Bavarian State Chancellery 1954; called to the Bar, Munich 1963; mem. Supervisory Bd, Adler Feuerversicherung AG, Berlin 1955–82, Versicherung für den öffentlichen Dienst AG im Adler-Iduna-Verbund, Berlin 1978–82, Fernsehstudios Munich Atelierbetriebsgesellschaft mbH 1974–82, Chair. July–Sept. 1982; Deputy Chair. Advisory Council, Zweites Deutsches Fernsehen 1964–91; mem. CSU 1948–, now mem. Presidium; mem. Bundestag 1957–90; Fed. Minister of the Interior 1982–89, of Transport 1989–91; Bd Dirs ZDF 1991–; mem. Supervisory Bd Deutsche Lufthansa, Iduna-Nova-Group, ZDF Enterprises GmbH, Fernsehstudio Munich GmbH; Grosses Bundesverdienstkreuz mit stern und Schulterband. *Publications:* Anspruch und Leistung: Widmungen für Franz Josef Strauss 1980, Ausgewählte Bundestagsreden. *Leisure interests:* tennis, skiing, hunting. *Address:* Briennerstrasse 28, 80333 Munich, Germany.

ZIMMERMANN, Reinhard, DrIur; German professor of law; b. 10 Oct. 1952, Hamburg; s. of Fritz Zimmermann and Inge Hansen; ed Univ. of Hamburg and Hamburg Court of Appeal; W P. Schreiner Chair of Roman and Comparative Law and Head of Dept Univ. of Cape Town 1981–88, Deputy Dean and Dean, Faculty of Law 1983–88; Vice-Pres. and Pres. Soc. of South African Teachers of Law 1984–86; Prof. of Roman Law, German Pvt. Law and Comparative Legal History, Univ. of Regensburg 1988–, Dean Faculty of Law 1994–96; Visiting Prof. Univ. of Edin., Tulane Univ., Univ. of Stellenbosch, 1990, 1991, 1992, Max Rheinstein Visiting Prof., Univ. of Chicago Law School 1993, Yale Law School 1998; A. L. Goodhart Prof. of Legal Science, Univ. of Cambridge, UK 1998–99; Dir Max Planck Inst. for Foreign Pvt. and Pvt. Int. Law 2002–; Co-Ed. Zeitschrift für Europäisches Privatrecht, Schriftenreihe zur Europäischen Rechtsgeschichte; mem. Bavarian Acad. of Arts and Sciences; Foreign mem. Royal Netherlands Acad. of Arts and Sciences, Royal Soc. of Edin., Accad. delle Scienze Torino, British Acad.; Hon. LLD (Cape Town) 1991, (Chicago) 1996, (Aberdeen) 2002; Leibniz Prize 1996. *Publications include:* Richterliches Moderationsrecht oder Totalnichtigkeit? 1979, Das römisch-holländische Recht in Südafrika 1983, The Law of Obligations, Roman Foundations of the Civilian Tradition 1993, Southern Cross 1996, Roman Law, Contemporary Law, European Law 2001, Zivilrechtswissenschaft und Schuldrechtsreform 2001, Comparative Foundations of a European Law of Set-Off and Prescription 2002. *Leisure interests:* field hockey, tennis, running, classical music. *Address:* Max-Planck-Institut für ausländisches und internationales Privatrecht, Mittelweg 187, 20146 Hamburg, Germany. *Telephone:* (40) 41900401. *Fax:* (40) 41900402. *E-mail:* r.zimmermann@mpipriv-hh.mpg.de (Office). *Website:* www.mpipriv-hh.mpg.de (Office).

ZINDER, Norton David, PhD; American geneticist and university professor; b. 7 Nov. 1928, New York, NY; s. of Harry Zinder and Jean Gottesman Zinder; m. Marilyn Esteicher 1949; two s.; ed Columbia Univ. and Univ. of Wisconsin; Wisconsin Alumni Fund Fellow, Univ. of Wis. 1948–50, Research Asst 1950–56; Asst, Rockefeller Univ. (then Rockefeller Inst.) 1952–56, Assoc. 1956–58, Assoc. Prof. 1958–64, Prof. 1964–2000, John D. Rockefeller Jr Prof. 1977–2000, Prof. Emer. 2000–, Dean Grad. and Postgrad. Studies 1993–95; mem. of following cttees: Int. Inst. of Cellular and Molecular Pathology (ICP), Brussels 1985, Science and Law Sub-Cttee New York City Bar Asscn 1985, Council on Foreign Relations 1986, NAS/NRC (BAST) Panel on Chemical Weapons Research and Devt Defense 1986, NAS/NRC Chair. to Review the Army Chemical Weapons Stockpile Disposal Program 1987, Alliance Int. Health Care Trust 1984–; mem. Advisory Cttee Celera Genomics 1998–; mem. NAS, American Acad. of Arts and Sciences, American Soc. of Microbiology, American Soc. of Biological Chemists, Genetics Soc. of America, American Asscn for the Advancement of Science, American Soc. of Virology; Scholar of American Cancer Soc. 1955–58; Hon. DSc (Univ. of Wisconsin) 1991; Eli Lilly Award in Microbiology 1962, United State Steel Foundation Award of NAS in Molecular Biology 1966, Medal of Excellence from Columbia Univ. 1969, AAAS Award in Scientific Freedom and Responsibility 1982. *Publications:* Infective Heredity in Bacteria, Cold Spring Harbor Symposium on Quantitative Biology XVIII 1953; and scientific articles in learned journals. *Address:* Rockefeller University, 1230 York Avenue, New York, NY 10021 (Office); 450 East 63rd Street, New York City, NY 10021, USA (Home). *Telephone:* (212) 421-3777.

ZINKERNAGEL, Rolf Martin, PhD; Swiss professor of immunology; b. 6 Jan. 1944, Basel; m.; three c.; ed Mathematisch-Naturwissenschaftliches Gymnasium, Basel, Univ. of Basel, Univ. of Zurich, ANU, Canberra; intern Surgical Dept, Clara-Spital Hosp., affiliated to Faculty of Medicine, Univ. of Basel 1969; Postdoctoral Fellow Lab. for Electron Microscopy, Inst. of Anatomy, Univ. of Basel 1969–70; Postdoctoral Fellow Inst. of Biochem., Univ. of Lausanne 1971–73; Visiting Fellow Dept of Microbiology, John Curtin School of Medical Research, ANU, Canberra 1973–75; Assoc. mem. (Asst Prof.) Dept of Immunopathology, Research Inst. of Scripps Clinic, La Jolla, Calif. 1976–79, Adjunct Assoc. Prof., Dept of Pathology 1977–79, Full Prof. Dept of Immunopathology, Scripps Clinic and Research Foundation 1979; Assoc. Prof. Dept of Pathology, Univ. Hosp., Univ. of Zurich 1979–88, Full Prof. 1988–92, Head Inst. of Experimental Immunology 1992–; mem. numerous scientific advisory bodies including WHO Group of Experts in Vaccine Devt 1985–89, advisory council of Cancer Research Inst. 1988–; mem. Ed. Bds. of immunology, pathology, microbiology and virology journals; mem. numerous professional orgs. including Swiss Soc. of Allergy and Immunology 1971–76 (Pres. 1993–94, Hon. mem. 1996–), Acad. Europaea 1989–, European Network of Immunological Insts. 1990–, Int. Soc. for Antiviral Research 1990–; Fellow American Acad. of Microbiology 1996, Foreign Fellow Nat. Acad. of Science, USA 1996, Australian Acad. of Sciences 1996, American Acad. of Arts and Sciences 1998, Royal Soc. 1998, Acad. Royale de Médicine, Belgium 1998, Berlin-Brandenburgische Akad. der Wissenschaften 1998; Dr. hc (Liège, ANU) 1996, (Oslo, Québec, Genoa) 1997, (Latvian Univ., Riga, Agric. Univ. of Warsaw) 1998; numerous decorations including Inst. for Cancer Research Award 1987; Nobel Prize for Medicine or Physiology 1996. *Publications:* numerous articles in learned journals. *Address:* Department of Pathology, University Hospital, Institute of Experimental Immunology, Schmelzbergstrasse 12, 8091 Zurich (Office); Rebhusstrasse 47, 8126 Zumikon, Switzerland (Home). *Telephone:* (1) 2552989 (Office). *Fax:* (1) 2554420 (Office); (1) 9181940 (Home). *E-mail:* rolf.zinkernagel@pty.usz.ch (Office).

ZINKEVICIUS, Zigmas, DR.HUM.LIT.; Lithuanian philologist; b. 4 Jan. 1925, Juodausiiai, Ukmerge Region; m. Regina Zinkevicienė; two c.; ed Vilnius State Univ.; lab. Asst Vilnius State Univ. 1946–50, Prof., Chair of Lithuanian Language 1950–56, Deputy Dean, Chair of Philology and History 1956–68, Prof., Head, Dept of Lithuanian Language 1967–88; Minister of Educ. and Science, Lithuanian Repub. 1996–98; Chair. Christian-Democratic Party (LKDP); consultant for educ. and science to Lithuanian Pres. 1998–; main research in history of Lithuanian language, dialects and Baltic philology; mem. Swedish Royal Acad. of Letters, History and Antiques, Lithuanian Acad. of Sciences, Norwegian Acad. of Sciences, Lithuanian Catholic Acad. of Sciences 1991, Latvian Acad. of Science 1990; mem. Editorial Bd Baltistica Periodical; J. G. Herder Award. *Publications:* over 20 books, over 500 articles in Lithuanian and foreign languages. *Leisure interests:* yachting, skiing, motor sports, canoeing and boating. *Address:* L R Vyriasybes kanceliarija, Gedimino pr. 11, 2039 Vilnius (Office); Justiniskiu 41-24, 2056 Vilnius, Lithuania (Home). *Telephone:* (3702) 41-08-77.

ZINMAN, David Joel; American conductor; b. 9 July 1936, New York; s. of Samuel Zinman and Rachel Ilo (Samuels) Zinman; m. 1st Leslie Heyman (deceased); one s. one d.; m. 2nd Mary Ingham 1974; one s.; ed Oberlin Conservatory, Ohio and Univ. of Minnesota; studied conducting Berks. Music Center, Tanglewood and with Pierre Monteux; Asst to Monteux 1961–64; Music Dir Nederlands Kamerorkest 1964–77; Music Dir Rochester Philharmonic Orchestra, New York 1974–85, Baltimore Symphony Orchestra 1985–98; Prin. Guest Conductor Rotterdam Philharmonic Orchestra 1977–79, Chief Conductor 1979–82; Music Dir Tonhalle Orchestra, Zurich 1995; Music Dir (desig.) Aspen Music Festival and School 1997, Music Dir 1998–; numerous recordings; Grand Prix du Disque; Edison Award, Gramophone Best Selling Record (Górecki) 1993, Gramophone Award (Jungle Book) 1994, three Grammy awards, Deutschen Schallplatten Prize, Peabody Medal 1996. *Address:* Aspen Music Festival and School, 2 Music School Road, Aspen, CO 81611, USA (Office).

ZINNI, Gen. Anthony; American diplomatist and former military commander; b. 1947, Philadelphia; ed Vilanova Univ.; joined marines 1961, infantry officer 1965, rising to rank of Gen.; active service in Viet Nam (injured 1970), Philippines, Mediterranean, Caribbean, Korea, Turkey, Iraq, Soviet Union, Kenya; Head Unified Task Force Somalia in Operation Restored Hope 1992–93, supervised withdrawal of US forces 1995, also Asst to Special Envoy to Somalia; Deputy Commanding Gen. US Marine Corps. Combat Devt Command, Quantico, Va 1992–94, Commanding Gen. 1st Marine Expeditionary Force 1994–96; Commdr US Cen. Command 1997–2000, in charge of mil. forces in 25 countries in Middle East, Africa and fmr USSR; Head of Persian Gulf forces 1997–2000, Commdr in charge of Operation Desert Fox, Iraq 1998; retd from mil. Aug. 2000; Adviser, Center for Strategic and Int. Studies, Washington 2000–01; US Envoy to the Middle East Nov. 2001–; has participated in diplomatic missions to Somalia, Pakistan, Ethiopia and Eritrea; Defense Distinguished Service Medal, Defense Superior Service Medal (with two oak leaf clusters), Bronze Star Medal with Combat "V", Purple Heart. *Address:* Department of State, 2201 C Street, NW, Washington, DC 20520, USA (Office). *Telephone:* (202) 647-6575 (Office). *Fax:* (202) 647-6575 (Office).

ZINOVIEV, Aleksandr Aleksandrovich, DPhil; Russian philosopher and writer; b. 29 Sept. 1922, Chukhloma, Kostrana Region; m.; two d.; ed Moscow Univ.; mil. service 1944–45; Prof. of Logic & Methodology of Science, Moscow Univ. 1970–78; actively campaigned against party line and discredited in 1970s, expelled 1978, USSR Citizenship restored 1990; returned to Russia 1999; Research post at Univ. of Munich 1978–; mem. Finnish Acad. of Sciences; Prix Tocqueville 1982. *Publications include:* Philosophical Problems of Polyvalent Logic (Russian 1960, English 1963), Principles of the Logical Theory of Scientific Knowledge 1967 (trans. English 1973), An Essay on Polyvalent Logic 1968 (trans. German 1968), Complex Logic 1970 (trans. German Komplexe Logik 1970), Logical Physics 1972, Logische Sprachregeln (with A. N. Wessel) 1975; non-philosophic works: Ziyayushchiye vysoty (Yawning Heights) 1976 (fiction), The Radiant Future 1978, The Yellow House (2 vols) 1980, The Reality of Communism 1983, Homo Sovieticus 1985, The Way to Calvary 1985, The Madhouse 1986, Para Bellum 1987, Gorbachevism 1988, Perestroika in Partygrad 1992, Russian Experiment 1995, On the Way to Supersociety 2000. *Leisure interest:* painting.

ZINSOU, Emile Derlin; Benin politician and physician; b. 23 March 1918; ed Ecole Primaire Supérieure, Ecole Africaine de Médecine, Dakar and Faculté de Médecine, Paris; Represented Dahomey in French Nat. Assembly; fmr Vice-Pres. Assemblée de l'Union française, Senator, Territorial Council; fmr Minister of Economy and of The Plan; fmr Amb. to France; Pres. Supreme Court of Dahomey; Minister of Foreign Affairs 1961–63, 1965–67; Pres. of Dahomey (now Benin) 1968–69; sentenced to death in absentia 1975; pardoned Aug. 1989; Leader Union Nationale pour la Démocratie et le Progrès (UNDP); numerous decorations include Grand Croix Ordre Nat., Dahomey, Grand Officier Légion d'honneur.

ŽIVKOVIĆ, Zoran; Serbia and Montenegro (Serbian) politician; b. 1960; Mayor of Nis 1996–2003; Founding mem., Deputy Chair., First Vice-Pres. and currently Acting Leader Democratic Party (DP); Minister of the Interior, Fed. Govt of Yugoslavia –2003; Prime Minister of Serbia and Montenegro March 2003–. *Address:* Office of the Prime Minister, 11000 Belgrade, Andrićev venac 1, Serbia and Montenegro (Office). *Telephone:* (11) 685872 (Office). *Fax:* (11) 659682 (Office).

ZIZIĆ, Zoran; Serbia and Montenegro (Montenegrin) politician; mem. Socialist People's Party of Montenegro; Prime Minister of the Fed. Govt of Yugoslavia 2000–01; mem. Fed. Parl. of Serbia and Montenegro (fmr Fed. Govt of Yugoslavia). *Address:* c/o Office of the Federal Government, Belgrade, Serbia and Montenegro (Office).

ZLENKO, Anatoliy Maksimovich; Ukrainian diplomatist; b. 2 June 1938, Stavistichl, Kiev Region; s. of Maksim Adamovich Zlenko and Anastasia Efimovna Zlenko; m. Ludmila Ivanovna Zlenko; two d.; ed Kiev Taras Shevchenko Univ.; mem. CPSU 1959–91; diplomatic service since 1967, attaché, Third, Second Sec., Ministry of Foreign Affairs of Ukraine 1967–73; mem. UNESCO Secr., Paris 1973–79; Exec. Sec. Ukrainian Comm. on UNESCO Problems 1979–83; Perm. Rep. of Ukraine in UNESCO 1983–87; Deputy Minister of Foreign Affairs of Ukraine 1987–89, First Deputy Minister 1989–90, Minister 1990–94, 2000–; Rep. to UN 1994–97; Amb. to France 1997–2000 (concurrently to UNESCO and to Portugal 1998–2000); Chevalier de la Légion d'honneur 2000; Order of Merit (Portugal) 2000; Grand Cross, Order of Bernardo O'Higgins (Chile) 2001. *Publications:* Foreign Policy of Ukraine: From Romanticism to Pragmatism 2001, From Nation's Needs to Foreign Policy Priorities 2002; articles in Ukrainian and foreign press on int. relations. *Leisure interests:* history, painting, tennis, volleyball. *Address:* Ministry of Foreign Affairs, No. 1 Mykhailivska Square, 01018 Kiev, Mykhaylivska pl. 1, Ukraine (Office). *Telephone:* (44) 238-15-01 (Office). *Fax:* (44) 226-31-69 (Office). *E-mail:* smin@mfa.gov.ua (Office). *Website:* www.mfa.gov.ua (Office).

ZOBEL DE AYALA, Jaime; Philippine business executive; b. 18 July 1934; s. of Alfonson Zobel de Ayala and Carmen Pfitz y Henero; m. Beatriz Miranda 1985; two s. five d.; ed La Salle Univ., Madrid, Harvard Univ.; with House of Ayala 1958–, Pres. 1984–, then CEO –1995, now Chair.; Amb. to UK 1970–75; fmr Adviser to Pres. Aquino; Hon. LLD (Univ of Philippines) 1991; Chevalier des Arts et des Lettres. *Leisure interests:* photography, scuba diving. *Address:* Ayala Corporation, 7/F Makati Stock Exchange Building, Ayala Avenue, 1254 Makati, Metro Manila 1200, Philippines (Home).

ZOELLICK, Robert Bruce, BA, JD; American politician, lawyer and government official; b. 25 July 1953, Evergreen Park, Ill.; s. of William T. Zoellick and Gladys Zoellick; m. Sherry Lynn Ferguson 1980; ed Swarthmore Coll., Harvard Univ.; Special Asst to Asst Attorney-Gen., Criminal Div., Dept of Justice 1978–79; pvt. law practice 1981–82; Vice-Pres., Asst to Chair. and CEO Bd Fannie Mae 1983–85, Exec. Vice-Pres. Housing and Law 1993–97; Special Asst to Deputy Sec., Deputy Asst Sec. for Financial Instn. Policy, Counsellor to Sec. and Exec. Sec. Treasury Dept 1985–88; Counsellor with rank of Under-Sec. Dept of State 1989–92, Under-Sec. for Econ. and Agricultural Affairs 1991–92; Deputy Chief of Staff, Asst to Pres. 1992–93; Olin Prof. of Nat. Security Affairs, US Naval Acad. 1997–98; Pres., CEO Center for Strategic and Int. Studies 1998–99; US Trade Rep. 2001–; mem. Bd Dirs Alliance Capital, Said Capital, German Marshall Fund US; Dir Aspen Inst. Strategy Group; Sr Int. Adviser Goldman Sachs; Research Scholar Harvard Univ.; Distinguished Service Award (Treasury Dept), Alexander Hamilton Award (State Dept), Kt Commdr's Cross (Germany). *Address:* Office of the United States Trade Representative, Winder Building, 600 17th Street, NW, Washington, DC 20508, USA (Office). *Telephone:* (202) 395-3230 (Office). *Fax:* (202) 395-3911 (Office). *Website:* www.ustr.gov (Office).

ZOHAR, Israel; Israeli artist; b. 7 Feb. 1945, Oktubinsk, USSR; m. 1st Ruth Bregman 1966 (divorced 1974); m. 2nd Arna Meyuhas 1974 (divorced 1982); m. 3rd Wendy Caron 1984; m. 4th Layil Barr; five s. one d.; ed Bezalel Acad. of Art, Jerusalem and with artists A. Yaskil and Ernst Fuchs; lectured at Hebrew Univ. Jerusalem 1979; maj. works include portraits of HRH The Princess of Wales 1990, Henry Catto (fmr US Amb. to UK) 1990, 24ft x 8ft painting of Jacob's Ladder for Music Festival, Exeter Cathedral, UK 1992, portrait of Anne Frank, Music Festival, Bad Kissingen 1992, portrait of Edith Sitwell for Hampstead Festival, London 1995; also writes, adapts and directs plays for theatre including Thomas Mann's Death in Venice (Duke of Cambridge, London), Brecht's The Jewish Wife (Cockpit, London), works by Strindberg, Chekhov, Sartre, Dostoevsky for Café Theatre, London, etc. *Exhibitions:* one-man shows: Ahuva Doron Gallery, Tel Aviv 1970, Bergman Gallery, Tel Aviv, Sara Kishon Gallery, Tel Aviv 1977, 1980, 1997, Artist's House, Jerusalem (retrospective) 1982, 13½ Gallery, Tel Aviv 1986, Musée de l'Athenée, Geneva (retrospective) 1987, Roy Miles Gallery, London 1989, 1993, Museum Panorama Mesdag, The Hague (Homage to Vermeer) 1996, Adler Gallery, Gstaad, Switzerland 1996, Catto Gallery, London 1999, 2001; group exhbns. Salon des Beaux-Arts, Grand Palais, Paris 1985, Prince Albert Museum, Exeter 1992, Roy Miles Gallery, London 1993. *Address:* 10 The Avenue, London, N10 2QL, England. *Telephone:* (20) 8341-1754.

ZOLL, Andrzej; Polish professor of law; b. 27 May 1942, Sieniawa; m.; one s.; ed Jagiellonian Univ., Kraków; Asst Canon Law Dept Jagiellonian Univ., Kraków 1964–75, Asst Prof. 1975–88, Prof. 1988–; Judge Constitutional Tribunal 1989–97, Pres. 1993–97; Vice-Chair. State Election Comm. 1989, Chair. 1990–93; Chair. Legislation Bd attached to the Prime Minister 1998–2000; Commr for Citizens' Rights 2000–; Commdr's Cross, Order of Polonia Restituta 1997, Great Cross of Merit with Star (Germany) 1997, Golden Star on Ribbon of Order of Merit (Austria) 1997, Great Duke Gedymin Order (Lithuania) 1997; Dr hc (Mainz Univ.) 1996. *Publications:* has written 170 works on penal law, philosophy of law and constitutional law including Materialnoprawna problematyka warunkowego umorzenia postępowania karnego 1973, Okoliczności wyłączające bezprawność czynu 1982, O normie prawnej w prawie karnym 1990, Komentarz do kodeksu karnego (co-author) 1998. *Leisure interests:* mountaineering, classical music, books. *Address:* Commissioner for Citizens' Rights Office, al. Solidarności 77, 00-090 Warsaw, Poland (Office). *Telephone:* (22) 5517700 (Office). *E-mail:* brpoinf@brpo.gov.pl (Office). *Website:* www.brpo.gov.pl (Office).

ZOLLINGER, Heinrich Fritz, PhD, DSc; Swiss professor of chemistry and university administrator; b. 29 Nov. 1919, Aarau; s. of Dr Fritz Zollinger and Helene Prior; m. Heidi Frick 1948; three s.; ed Fed. Inst. of Tech. (ETH), Univ. of Basel, MIT; Chemist, Dyestuff Research Dept, CIBA Ltd 1945–60; Lecturer in Dyestuff Chem., Univ. of Basel 1952–60; Prof. of Textile Chem., Fed. Inst. of Tech. 1960–87, Prof. Emer. 1987–, Rector 1973–77; Pres. Organic Chem. Div. of IUPAC 1975–77, Pres. IUPAC 1979–81, Fellow 1999–; Pres. Council Swiss Science Foundation 1979–82; Fellow Swiss Acad. of Eng 1990; Foreign Fellow, Royal Swedish Acad. of Eng 1979, Acad. of Sciences, Göttingen 1984; Hon. Fellow Soc. of Dyers and Colourists (UK) 1981, Chem. Soc. of Japan 1985, Swiss Soc. of Dyers and Colourists (SVCC) 1987, Japanese Soc. of Textile Tech. 1989, Textile Inst. (Manchester) 1989, Shenkar Coll., Ramat Gan, Israel 1991, Romanian Soc. of Dyers and Colourists 1992, Swiss Soc. of Friends of the Weizmann Inst. 1993; Order of the Rising Sun (Japan) 1989; Hon. PhD (Stuttgart) 1976, (Tokyo Inst. Tech.) 1983; Werner Prize 1959, Ruzicka Award 1960, Lewinstein Award 1964, Conrad Prize 1970, O. N. Witt Gold Medal 1980, M. Kehren Gold Medal 1984, Creative Sr Award, Vontobel Foundation, Zürich 2002. *Publications:* Chemie der Azofarbstoffe 1958 (Russian 1960), Diazo and Azo Chemistry 1961, Leitfaden der Farbstoffchemie 1970, Chemie und Hochschule 1978, Color Chemistry 1987, Diazo Chemistry, Part I 1994, Part II 1995, Color: a multidisciplinary approach 1999; volumes on aromatic chemistry in Int. Review of Science 1973, 1976; 320 scientific papers. *Leisure interests:* clarinet, climbing, skiing, sailing, colour studies. *Address:* HUT D14, Eidgenössische Technische Hochschule, 8092, Zürich (Office); Bergstrasse 8, 8700 Küsnacht, Switzerland (Home). *Telephone:* (1) 6324168 (Laboratory); (1) 9105308 (Home). *Fax:* (1) 6321072.

ZOLOTAS, Xenophon, DEcon; Greek university professor; b. 26 March 1904, Athens; s. of the late Efthymios Zolotas; m. Kallirhoe Ritsos 1958; ed Univs. of Athens, Leipzig and Paris; Prof. of Econs Univ. of Thessaloniki 1928, of Athens 1931–68; mem. of Supreme Council of Greece 1932, of Greek del. to the Econ. Council of the Entente Balkanique 1934–39; Chair. Bd of Dirs, Agricultural Bank of Greece 1936–40; Joint Gov. Bank of Greece (after Liberation) Oct. 1944–45; mem. UNRRA Council 1946; Gov. of IMF for Greece 1946–67, 1974–81; mem. Greek Del. to UN Gen. Ass. 1948–53; Del. to Econ. Comm. for Europe 1949–53; mem. Currency Cttee 1950, 1974–81; Vice-Chair. ECE 1952; Minister of Co-ordination Oct. 1952; Gov. Bank of Greece 1955–67, 1974–81, Hon. Gov. 1981–; Minister of Econ. Co-ordination July-Nov. 1974; Prime Minister of Greece 1989–90; mem. "Group of Four" for remodelling of OEEC 1960; mem. Acad. of Athens 1952–; Hon. Pres. Int. Econ. Asscn 1980; Grand Cross of Royal Order of the Phoenix, of the Ordre nat. du Mérite (France), Grand Officier, Légion d'honneur (France) and others. *Publications:* Griechenland auf dem Wege zur Industrialisierung 1926, Wirtschaftsstruktur und Wirtschaftsbeziehungen Griechenlands 1931, L'étalon-or en théorie et en pratique 1933, La question de l'or et le problème monétaire 1938, La théorie économique traverse-t-elle une crise? 1938, La transformation du capitalisme 1953, Monetary Stability and Economic Development 1958, Economic Development and Technical Education 1960, The Problem of the International Monetary Liquidity 1961, Towards a Reinforced Gold Exchange Standard 1961, Economic Development and Private Enterprise 1962, International Monetary Order, Problems and Policies 1962, The Role of the Banks in a Developing Country 1963, The Multicurrency Standard and the International Monetary Fund 1963, Monetary Equilibrium and Economic Development 1965, Remodelling the International Monetary System 1965, Alternative Systems for International Monetary Reform, A Comparative Appraisal 1965, Current Monetary and Economic Developments in Greece 1966, International Labor Migration and Economic Development 1966, Monetary Planning 1967, The Gold Trap and the Dollar 1968, Speculocracy and the International Monetary System 1969, The International Money Mess 1973, From Anarchy to International Monetary Order 1973, The Energy Problem in Greece 1975, Recession and Reflation in the Greek Economy 1975, Developments and Prospects of the Greek Economy 1975, Guidelines for Industrial Development in Greece 1976, Greece in the European Community 1976, International Monetary Vacillations 1976, International Monetary Issues and Development Policies 1977, Inflation and the Monetary Target in Greece 1978, An International Loan Insurance Scheme 1978, The Positive Contribution of Greece to the European Community 1978, The Dollar Crisis and Other Papers 1979, On the Issue of a Stable Monetary Standard 1981, Economic Growth and Declining Social Welfare 1981, The Unruly International Monetary System 1985, The Dollar and the New Form of International Co-operation 1986, The Enigma of the U.S. Trade Deficit 1986, The European Monetary System, The Dollar and the Need for Reform 1987, Co-operation and Disco-ordination in International Monetary Policies, the Need for Rules of Conduct 1988, The European Monetary System and the Challenge of 1992 1988; in Greek: Monetary Stabilization 1929, Economics 1942, Creative Socialism 1944, The Monetary Problem and the Greek Economy 1950, Inflationary Pressures in the Greek Economy 1951, Regional Planning and Economic Development 1961, Human Capital and Economic Development 1968, The Contribution of Exports to Economic Development 1976, Social Welfare and Economic Organization 1976, Consumption, Investment and Monetary Equilibrium 1977, Economic and Monetary Problems in Greece 1979, Progress Towards European Union 1991. *Address:* c/o Bank of Greece, 21 Panepistimou Street, Athens 102 50 (Office); 25 Dionissiou Areopagitou Street, Athens 117 42, Greece (Home). *Telephone:* 3230317 (Office); 9241100 (Home).

ZOLOTOV, Yuri Aleksandrovich, DR.CHEM.; Russian chemist; b. 4 Oct. 1932, Vysokovskoye, Moscow Region; m.; one s.; ed Moscow State Univ.; researcher, Deputy Dir, Head of lab., Inst. of Geochem. and Analytical Chem. 1958–89; Dir N Kurnakov Inst. of Gen. and Inorganic Chem. 1989–99; Distinguished Prof. Moscow Univ.; Corresp. mem., USSR (now Russian) Acad. of Sciences 1970, mem. 1987–; main research in analytical chem., extraction of inorganic compounds, ion chromatography; Hon. mem. Japan Soc. of Analytical Chem. 1991, Göteborg Royal Soc. of Arts and Sciences, Sweden 1999; Dr. hc (Kiev) 1994, (Krasnodar) 1994; Prize of USSR Council of Ministers 1985, USSR State Prize 1972, State Prize of Russia 1991, 2000. *Publications:* 29 books; 680 scientific papers. *Leisure interest:* fishing, writing. *Address:* N Kurnakov Institute of General and Inorganic Chemistry, Leninsky prosp. 31, 119991 Moscow, Russia. *Telephone:* (095) 236-53-27 (Office); (095) 132-20-10 (Home). *Fax:* (095) 952-34-20 (Office). *E-mail:* zolotov@igic.ras.ru (Office).

ZOLOTUKHIN, Valery Sergeyevich; Russian actor, writer and singer; b. 21 June 1941, Bystry Istok, Altai Territory; m.; two c.; ed Moscow Inst. of Theatre Art; with Mossoviet Theatre 1963–64; leading actor Taganka Theatre 1964–; numerous film roles; People's Artist of Russia. *Films:* Bumbarush, The Man with Accordion, The Little Tragedies, The Master of Taiga, Intervention. *Theatre includes:* Zhivago, Alive, Marat and Markise De Sad, Shavashka, Theatre Novel, Medea, The Price. *Publications:* To Istok – River to My Childhood (short stories) 1978, Offering to your Memory (V. Vysotsky memoir) 1992, On the Block of Tagauka 1999, Russian Bath in a Black Style 2000. *Address:* Profsoyuznaya str. 8, korp. 2, Apt. 131, 117292 Moscow, Russia. *Telephone:* (095) 124-21-51.

ZOLTÁN, Imre, MD; Hungarian obstetrician and gynaecologist; b. 12 Dec. 1909, Budapest; s. of E Zoltan; m. Edith Rokay 1953; one d.; ed Pazmany Peter Univ. (now Semmelweis Univ. Budapest); Asst in Dept of Obstetrics and Gynaecology, Univ. Clinic, Pazmany Peter Univ. 1933–46, Assoc. Prof. 1946–50, Prof. and Dir of Dept 1950–79; Sec. Gen. Fed. of Hungarian Medical Socs. 1966–70, Pres. 1974–85; Vice-Pres. Int. Fed. of Gynaecology and Obstetrics 1970–73; Dir Nat. Inst. of Obstetrics and Gynaecology 1973–79, Consulting Prof. 1979–; mem. Presidency of Fed. Hungarian Medical Socs. 1985–; Hon. Life Pres. Hungarian Soc. of Obstetrics and Gynaecology 1979–; Silver Medal, Int. Fed. of Gynaecology and Obstetrics; Officers' Cross Order (Hungary), Order of the Banner (Hungary). *Publications:* Textbooks of Obstetrics and Gynaecology 1951–70, Caesarian Section in Today's Obstetrics 1961; Co-author: Semmelweis. His Life and Work. *Leisure interests:* sport, tennis, gastronomy. *Address:* Bartók Béla ut. 31, 1114 Budapest, Hungary. *Telephone:* 466-7140.

ZONG PU; Chinese writer; b. (as Feng Zhong Pu), 26 July 1928, Beijing; d. of Feng Youlan and Ren Zaikun; m. Cai Zhongde; one d.; ed Qinghua Univ.; mem. editorial bds. Literary Gazette and World Literature. *Publications:* The Red Beans 1957, Melody in Dreams (Nat. Prize for Short Stories) 1978, Who Am I? 1979, Lu Lu 1980, The Everlasting Rock (Nat. Prize for novelette) 1980, Fairy Tales from a Windy Cottage 1984, Bear Palm (short stories) 1985, Lilac Knot (essays) (Nat. Prize for essay) 1986, Retreat to the South (Vol. I of Ordeal) 1988, The Story of a Fish (Nat. Prize for Children's Literature), Discourse on an Iron Flute (essays) 1994, Stories of a Windy Cottage (short stories) 1995, Collected Works (4 Vols) 1996, Hiding in the East (Vol. II of Ordeal) 2000, Who is She? (short story) 2001; numerous essays. *Leisure interests:* music, travel, calligraphy. *Address:* Beijing University, 57 Yan Nan Yuan, Beijing 100871, People's Republic of China.

ZÖPEL, Christoph, DEcon; German politician and economist; b. 4 July 1943, Gleiwitz; s. of Kurt Zöpel and Martha Zöpel (née Grohla); m. Barbara Rössler 1969; two d. one s.; ed Minden, Westphalia, Free Univ. Berlin, Ruhr Univ., Bochum; mem. SDP 1964–, Deputy Chair. SDP in Landtag 1975–78, mem. Exec. Cttee 1986–95, mem. Presidium 1992–95; City Councillor, Bochum 1969–72; mem. Landtag of Land N-Rhine/Westphalia 1972–1990, Minister for Fed. Affairs 1978–80, for Rural and Urban Devt 1980–85, for Urban Devt, Housing and Transport 1985–90; mem. Bundestag 1990–, mem. Cttee on Foreign Affairs 1990–99, Deputy Chair. Cttee on the Affairs of the EU 1991–92, Minister of State, Fed. Foreign Office 1999–; mem. Parl. Ass. OSCE 1994–99; Deputy Mem. N Atlantic Ass. 1998–99; Chair. Cttee on the Economy, Social Cohesion and the Environment, Socialist Int. 2000–. *Address:* Federal Foreign Office, 11013 Berlin, Germany (Office). *Telephone:* 1888172926 (Office). *Fax:* 1888173903 (Office). *Website:* www.auswaertiges-amt.de (Office).

ZORIN, Leonid Genrikhovich; Russian playwright; b. 3 Nov. 1924, Baku, Azerbaijan; s. of Genrikh Zorin and Polina Zorin; m. 1st 1951 (wife deceased); m. 2nd Tatjana Pospelova 1985; one s.; ed Azerbaijan State Univ., M. Gorky Inst. of Literature in Moscow; literary Baku Russian Drama Theatre; later freelance, mem. USSR Union of Writers 1941–, Int. PEN Club, Russian PEN Centre; Grand Prix for the best film script Grandmaster (Festival in Kranje, Yugoslavia), Golden Medal for filmscript Peace to the Newcomer, Venice Film Festival 1961, Prize of All-Union Contest of Playwrights Revival of Russia (for Moscow Nest) 1995, (for Lusgan) 1997. *Plays:* over 40 produced in 15 countries, including Decembrists, Kind Men, The Coronation, The Deck, Warsaw Melody, The Copper Grandmother, The Quotation, The Perished Plot, The Infidelity, The Carnival, The Moscow Nest, Lusgan, The Warsaw Melody 1997, Tsar's Hunt, Roman Comedy, The Invisibles 1999, The Maniac 2000, The Misprint 2001, The Outcome. *Film scripts:* 15 including A Man from Nowhere, The Law, Peace to the Newcomer, Grandmaster, Transit, The Friends and the Years, Pokrovskye Gates, Tsar's Hunt, Hard Sand 2002. *Publications:* (novels and short stories) Old Manuscript 1983, Wanderer 1987, The Topic of the Day 1992, Proscenium 1997, The Plots 1998, The Teetotaller (Banner Prize, Apollon Grigorjev Prize) 2001, The Auction (collection of novels and stories) 2001, Whip (Banner Prize) 2002; numerous essays; Theatre Fantasy (collection of plays) 1974, Selected Plays (2 vols) 1986, The Green Notebooks (collection of essays etc.), The Curtain of the Millennium (collection of later plays) 2002. *Leisure interests:* reading, chess. *Address:* Krasnoarmeyskaya str. 21, Apt. 73, 125319 Moscow, Russia. *Telephone:* (095) 151-43-33 (Home).

ZORIN, Vladimir Yuryevich; Russian politician; b. 9 April 1948, Moscow; m.; three s. one d.; ed Tashkent Inst. of Nat. Econs, Acad. of Public Sciences at Cen. CP Cttee; fmr teacher; People's Deputy of Uzbekistan 1990, Deputy Perm. Rep., Cabinet of Ministers, Repub. of Uzbekistan to Govts. of USSR and Russian Fed. 1991–93; fmr consultant on finance, regional policy and investments in various commercial cos; Deputy, then First Deputy Head Territorial Dept of Fed. Organs of Exec. Power, Chechen Repub.; Co-ordinator Exec. Cttee Int. Movt of Democratic Reforms on Relationship with CIS States 1991–93; mem. State Duma 1995–99; Deputy Head of Govt Del. on Peace Talks in Chechnya 1996; Chair. Perm. Cttee on Problems of Fed. and Regional Policy; Pres. Russian Asscn of Theory and Modelling of Int. Relations; mem. Political Council of Our Home is Russia Movt 1994–99; Deputy Rep. Plenipotentiary of Russian Pres. to Volga Fed. Dist 2000–01, Minister of Fed. Problems, Nat. and Migration Policy, then Minister without Portfolio, in charge of Nationalities Policy 2002–. *Publications:* Chechen Conflict (1991–96): Estimate, Analysis and Ways of Solution, and numerous other publs on politics, history and sociology. *Leisure interests:* chess, painting, Russian folk and classical music, table tennis. *Address:* Office of the Government, Krasnopresnenskaya nab. 2, 103274 Moscow, Russia (Office). *Telephone:* (095) 205-57-35 (Office). *Fax:* (095) 205-42-19. *Website:* www.pravitelstvo.gov.ru.

ZORRILLA, Concepción (China Zorrilla); Uruguayan actress, director and producer; b. 1922; d. of José Luis Zorrilla de San Martin; ed Royal Acad. of Dramatic Art, London; worked with Ars Pulchra group, Uruguayan Independent Theatre; later worked as journalist and as actress and Dir Nat. Theatre of Uruguay; f. with Antonio Larreta and Enrique Guarnero, Theatre of City of Montevideo 1961; directed show Canciones para mirar, New York 1965 and later in Buenos Aires; staged Jacobo Langsner's El Tobogán and Neil Simon's Plaza Suite, Montevideo 1969; has made several films in Argentina; Dir, Como en casa (TV show); newscaster, Radio Belgrano; noted theatrical appearances including one-woman show Hola, hola, un, dos, tres (toured Argentina, Venezuela and USA) and as Emily in Spanish-language version of William Luce's The Belle of Amherst throughout Latin America and in USA 1981.

ZOU'BI, Moneef Rafe' Abdel-Hamid, BEng, MSc; Jordanian engineer; b. 30 Dec. 1963, Amman; s. of Rafe' Abdul Hamid Zou'bi and Wadha Sharif Zou'bi; m.; one s. one d.; ed Bishop's School, Amman, Beeston Coll., Nottingham and Univs of Brighton and Loughborough; Resident Engineer Jordan Royal Corps of Engineers 1988–90; Tech. Affairs Officer Islamic Acad. of Sciences (IAS) 1990–91, Tech. Affairs Dir 1991–95, Deputy Exec. Dir 1995–98, Dir-Gen. May 1998–; Chief Ed. IAS Newsletter; Grad. Mem. Inst. of Civil Engineers (UK), Inst. of Structural Engineers (UK); mem. Asscn of Engineers (Jordan), Licensing Execs Soc. (LES), Jordan Computer Soc., Jordanian Friends of Archaeology Asscn, Arab Youth Forum, Royal Automobile Club of Jordan. *Publications:* Health, Nutrition and Development in the Islamic World (co-author) 1995, Water in the Islamic World (co-author) 1995, An Overview of the Islamic Academy of Sciences 1999, Science Education and Technology Management in the Islamic World (co-author) 2000, Personalities Noble (ed.) 2000, Information Technology for Development in the Islamic World (co-author) 2001; numerous specialist articles. *Leisure interests:* walking, photography, calligraphy, travel, cinema, reading. *Address:* Islamic Academy of Sciences, P.O. Box 830036, Amman (Office); 54 Oqba Bin Nafe' Street, Jabal Amman, Fourth Circle, Jordan (Home). *Telephone:* (6) 5522104 (Office); (6) 5932043 (Home). *Fax:* (6) 5511803 (Office). *E-mail:* mrzoubi@yahoo.com (Office). *Website:* ias-worldwide.org (Office).

ZOU CHENGLU, (Tsou, C.L.), PhD; Chinese biochemist and biophysicist; b. 17 May 1923, Jiangsu; s. of Tsou Dong-hu and Hu Kuei; m. Li Lin (q.v.) 1949; one d.; ed Cambridge Univ., UK; Deputy Dir Inst. of Biophysics, Academia Sinica 1979–83; Visiting Prof., Harvard Univ., USA 1981–82; Dir Nat. Lab. Biomacromolecules 1988–93; Pres. Biochemical Soc. 1993–; mem. Academic Degrees Cttee under State Council 1986–95; mem. Academia Sinica (Dir Div. of Biology 1992–); mem. Nat. Cttee CPPCC 1978, 8th Nat. Cttee 1993–; Hon. mem. American Soc. of Biochem.; China Nat. Natural Science Prize, 1st Class (twice). *Publications:* Current Biochemical Research in China (Ed.) 1989; over 180 research papers. *Leisure interest:* music. *Address:* Institute of Biophysics, Academia Sinica, 15 Datum Road, Beijing 100101, People's Republic of China. *Telephone:* (10) 64889870 (Office); (10) 68422342 (Home). *Fax:* (10) 64872026.

ZOU JIAHUA; Chinese engineer and state official; b. Oct. 1926, Shanghai; s. of late Zou Taofen, elder brother of Zou Jingmeng; ed Moscow; joined CCP 1945; fmr Dir Shenyang No. 2 Machine Tool Plant; Dir Machine Tool Inst., First Ministry of Machine Bldg; Deputy Dir Communication of Science, Tech. and Industry for Nat. Defence; alt. mem. 12th CCP Cen. Cttee 1982–87, mem. 1985; Minister of Ordnance Industry 1985–86, of State Machine-Bldg Industry Comm. 1986–88, of Machine Bldg and Electronics Industry 1988–93, in charge of State Planning Comm. 1991–93; Vice-Premier 1991–98; State Councillor 1988–91; Chair. State Radio Regulatory Cttee 1994–; mem. 13th CCP Cen. Cttee 1987–92, mem. 14th Cen. Cttee 1992–98; mem. CCP Politburo 1992–97; Vice-Chair. Standing Cttee of 9th NPC 1998. *Address:* c/o Standing Committee of National People's Congress, Beijing, People's Republic of China.

ZOU RENJUN, CChem, FRSC; Chinese scientist; b. 16 Jan. 1927, Suzhou City; s. of late Zou Zhangqin and Deng Aiyun; m. Zhao Yaqin 1951; two d.; ed Fudan Univ., Shanghai, Tianjin Univ.; Head Teaching Group, Tianjin Inst. of Chemical Tech. 1958; lecturer, Tianjin Inst. of Tech. 1963; Prof., Hebei Inst. of Tech., Tianjin 1979–; Pres. Hebei Acad. of Sciences, Shijiazhuang 1984–88, Hon. Pres. 1988–; Chair. Hebei Asscn for Science and Tech. 1991–; Fellow Royal Soc. of Chem., London 1982–; numerous awards and prizes, including Gold Medal, State Council of People's Repub. of China 1979, Gay-Lussac Medal, France 1984, Gold Medal, All-China Fed. of Trade Unions 1987, Advanced Worker Award and Gold Medal, State Council 1989. *Publications:* Chemical Reaction Engineering in Basic Organic Chemical Industry 1981, Principles and Techniques of Separation in Petrochemical Industry 1988; more than 50 papers in journals in China, USA, France, Netherlands, Japan etc. *Leisure interest:* music. *Address:* Hebei Academy of Sciences, Friendship Street, Shijiazhuang City 050081, People's Republic of China. *Telephone:* (311) 336002. *Fax:* (311) 332060.

ZOU YU; Chinese government official; b. 3 Oct. 1922, Guangdong Prov.; m. Xue Xialiang 1953; three s. two d.; ed Inst. of Shaanbei; Deputy Dir Public Security Dept Jilin City 1938–49; Deputy Garrison Commdr Shanton Dist 1949–53; Political Commissar Shanton Mil. Sub-Command 1957–75; First Deputy Dir Guangdong Prov. Public Security Dept, Commr Shanton Dist, Leader Guangdong Prov. Govt 1950–77; Dir State Seismological Bureau, State Council 1978–80; Head China Acad. of Sciences 1978–80; Vice-Minister of Justice 1982–83, Minister 1983–88; Pres. Nat. Lawyers Asscn 1986–91; Pres. China Univ. of Political Science and Law 1985–88; mem. Standing Cttee, NPC 1983–88; Deputy Dir Internal and Judicial Affairs Cttee NPC 1988–93; Pres. China Law Soc. 1991; mem. Exec. Cttee LAWASIA 1991, Vice-Pres. 1993; Adviser Internal and Judicial Affairs Cttee. *Publications:* The Strategic Meaning of Spreading Basic Legal Knowledge among the People 1986, The Social Position and Meaning of Civil Conciliation 1987, Dictionary

of Jurisprudence 1991. *Leisure interests:* music, painting, calligraphy. *Address:* No. 6 Nam Dajie, Xizhimen, Beijing 100035, People's Republic of China. *Telephone:* (10) 6033363. *Fax:* (10) 6032251.

ZOUIOUECHE, Nazim Charif Eddine; Algerian engineer and oil company executive; b. 19 Feb. 1940, Algiers; m. Fariel Essid 1971; two s.; ed Ecole Nat Supérieure des Télécommunications, Ecole Nat. Supérieure du Pétrole, Paris; telecommunications engineer, Ministry of Telecommunications 1965–68; production engineer, Elf/Aquitaine 1968–71; Man. Hassi-Messaoud Dist 1971–76; Dir Production Div. Sonatrach 1976–79, Exec. Vice-Pres. and Man. Dir Sonatrach, in charge of Hydrocarbons Div. 1979–85, CEO Transmediterranean Pipeline Co. 1985–93, Chief of Staff Sonatrach 1994–95, Dir-Gen. 1995–; Chair. Observatoire Méditerranéen pour l'Energie (OME) 1995–97; mem. Bd Alfor Drilling Co. (SEDCO/Sonatrach Jt co.) 1977–82. *Leisure interests:* bridge, tennis, horse riding, jogging. *Address:* Sonatrach—Branche Hydrocarbures 8, Chemin du réservoir Hydra, Algiers, Algeria. *Telephone:* (21) 60-03-05; (21) 54-92-00. *Fax:* (21) 48-25-57. *E-mail:* nc_zouioueche@yahoo.fr (Office).

ZOUMBOULAKIS, Petros I.; Greek artist, stage designer and professor of plastic arts; b. 19 April 1937, Athens; ed Polytechnic School of Athens; participant in numerous group exhbns. in Greece especially at Nat. Gallery; work also shown in group exhbns abroad including São Paulo Bienal 1969, Int. Exhbn of Visual Arts, Moscow 1988, 5th Int. Biennale, Cairo 1994, 1st Int. Biennale of Art (CIAC), Rome 1995, Plein Air, Varna 1999; designer of scenery and costumes for both theatre and cinema; illustrator of textbooks used in Greek schools; teacher in applied arts, drawing, colour and stage design, Doxiadis School of Interior Design 1964–86; works in Nat. Gallery, Ministry of Educ. Collection and many public and pvt. collections at home and abroad. *Solo exhibitions include:* Astor Gallery 1970, Zoumboulakis Gallery, Iola 1975, 1977, Rethymnon, Crete 1977, Argo Gallery 1978, Armos Gallery, Thessaloniki 1979, Zalocosta 7 Gallery 1985, New Forms Gallery 1986, 1990, Art Forum Gallery, Thessaloniki 1990, 1992, Agathi Gallery 1991, Citibank, New York 1994, Chrissothemis Gallery 1995, Dimito Gallery, Rethymnou, Crete 1995, Art Forum Gallery, Thessaloniki 1995, Art Deco, Serres 1997, Art Gallery Zante 1997, 2000, Amymoni Gallery, Ioannina 2000, Mun. Gallery-G.I. Katsigna Museum, Larisa 2000, Ektrasi Gianna Grammatopoulou 2001. *Address:* Tsimiski 2, 11471 Athens (Studio); Evrou 18-20, 15234 Athens, Greece (Home). *Telephone:* (1) 3630028 (Studio); (1) 6842088 (Home).

ZOUNI, Opy; Greek artist; b. 4 Feb. 1941, Cairo; d. of John Sarpakis and Helen Sarpakis; m. Alexander Zounis 1965; two s.; ed Athens School of Fine Arts. *Exhibitions:* one-woman exhbns include: Desmos 1973, Athens Gallery 1975, 1978, 1990, 1992, Lausanne Museum of Fine Art 1980, Galerie Jeanneret, Geneva 1982, Contemporary Graphics with Medusa in collaboration with Alexander Iolas 1982, Gallery 3 1984, Peter Noser Gallery, Zurich 1985, Trito Mati 1986, Int. Cultural Centre, Antwerp 1986, Galerie Kara, Geneva 1989, 1991, Vellidio Cultural Centre 1989, Athens French Inst. 1992, Mylos 1993, Galerie Donguy, Paris 1994, Kreonidis Gallery 1996, Art Forum Gallery 1996, Art Athina 4/Amymoni Gallery 1996, Municipal Gallery of Patras 1998, Stiftung für griechische Kultur, Berlin 1999, Museum of Cycladic Art, Athens 1999, Art Forum Gallery 2000, Anemos Gallery, Art Athina 8 2000, Anemos Gallery, Miart Milan 2001, Asscn Mouvement Art Contemporain, Chamalières, France 2001, Art Gallery of the Cyclades, Syros 2002, State Gallery of Contemporary Cypriot Art, Nicosia 2002; group exhbns include: Biennials of São Paolo 1979, Alexandria 1970, Ljubljana 1979, 1983, 1985, 1987, Bradford 1984 and numerous int. exhbns. *Film:* Light – Shadow – Co-incidences? (video-art installation) 1999. *Publications include:* Symmetry 2 1989, Arte e Tecnologia 1993, Symmetry 2000 2002; bilingual monograph 1997; numerous articles in books and reviews. *Address:* 22 Vrilission Street, 152 36 P. Penteli, Greece. *Telephone:* (210) 8042950. *Fax:* (210) 8044264. *E-mail:* zounis@hol.gr (Office).

ZSÁMBÉKI, Gábor; Hungarian theatrical manager and director; b. 30 Dec. 1943, Pécs; s. of János Zsámbéki and Judit Almásy; two d.; ed Faculty of Directing, Budapest Acad. of Dramatic Art and Film Art; Gen. Man. Csiky Gergely Theatre, Kaposvár 1974–78; Prof., Faculty of Acting and Directing, Budapest Acad. of Dramatic Art and Film Art 1978–; Head Dir, Budapest Nat. Theatre 1978–82; Art Dir Katona József Theatre, Budapest 1982–89, Gen. Man. and Stage Dir 1989; Stage Dir Theater tri-bühne, Stuttgart 1988–; Pres. Union des Théâtres de l'Europe, Paris 1998– (mem. Founding Cttee 1989–); Prizes include: BITEF Prize (for The Government Inspector) 1989, French Critics' Prize for Best Foreign Production (for Ubu Roi, Théâtre de l'Odéon, Paris) 1990, Best Foreign Production (for The Government Inspector), Caracas Int. Festival 1990, Merited Artist of the Hungarian Repub., Kossuth Prize. *Productions:* about 150, including classics (Goldoni, Shakespeare, Gogol, Chekhov etc.), modern works (Jarry, Wesker, Gombrowicz) and world premières of contemporary Hungarian plays (Halleluyah by Kornis, Chickenhead by Spiró); productions abroad in Cuba, Czechoslovakia, Finland, Germany, Israel, Norway. *Address:* 1052 Petőfi, Sándor u. 6 (Office); 2011 Budakalász, Duna sétány, Pf. 85, Hungary. *Telephone:* (1) 266-3959 (Office).

ZUBAK, Krešemir; Bosnia and Herzegovina (Croat) politician; b. 29 Nov. 1947, Doboj; m.; two c.; ed Sarajevo Univ.; worked in judicial bodies of Bosnia and Herzegovina; Pres. of Higher Court in Doboj; mem. del. of Croatian population to sign the Washington Agreement and Vienna Agreement; First Pres. of Fed. of Bosnia and Croatia May 1994–97; fmr Croatian Co-Chair. of

Bosnia and Herzegovina; Chair. New Croatian Initiative party. *Address:* Nova Hrvatska Inicijativa, Sime Milutinovića 2/II, Sarajevo, Bosnia and Herzegovina. *Telephone:* (33) 214602. *Fax:* (33) 214603. *E-mail:* nhi@nhi.ba.

ZUBAKIN, Semen Ivanovich; Russian politician; b. 4 May 1952, Verkh-Uimon; m.; two s. one d.; ed All-Union Inst. of Finance and Econs; Asst forestry warden Altai Territory 1972–74; inspector, then Sr Economist, Deputy Head Dept of State Insurance, Gorno-Altai Autonomous Territory 1976–86; inspector, then head of div., Deputy Chair. Cttee on Finance Altai Repub. 1986–91; Deputy Supreme Soviet, Altai Repub.; Chair. Perm. Comm. on Problems of Econ. Reform and Property 1992, Deputy State Ass. 1993; Chief Controller Control Dept, Ministry of Finance of Russian Fed. for Altai Repub. 1994; Chair. of Govt Altai Repub. 1997–2001; mem. State Duma 1995–97; mem. Council of Fed., Russian Fed. 1997–2001; Chair. Russia's Democratic Choice Party, Altai Repub. Div. 1997–. *Address:* c/o Government of Altai Republic, E. Palkina str. 1, 659700 Gozno-Altaisk, Russia (Office).

ZUBAKOV, Vice-Adm. Yurii Antonovich; Russian politician and diplomatist; b. 27 Nov. 1944, Chita; ed KGB Higher School; on staff USSR KGB 1966–89; Deputy Head of sector Cen. CPSU Cttee 1989–90; on staff USSR Security Council 1990–91; Deputy Dir Foreign Intelligence Service USSR (later Russia) 1991–96; Deputy Minister of Foreign Affairs 1996–98; Head of Personnel, Pres. Yeltsin's Admin. 1998–99; Amb. to Lithuania 2000–. *Address:* Embassy of the Russian Federation, Latviju gre 53/54, Vilnius, 2600 Lithuania (Office). *Telephone:* (527) 21763 (Office). *Fax:* (527) 23877 (Office). *E-mail:* rusemb@rusemb.lt.

ZUBEIDI, Mohammed Hamzah al-; Iraqi politician; Deputy Prime Minister March–Sept. 1991, 1995; Prime Minister of Iraq 1991–93.

ZUBERBÜHLER, Daniel; Swiss banking regulator; Dir Fed. Banking Comm. 1997–. *Address:* Eidgenössische Bankenkommission, Sekretariat, Marktgasse 37, Postfach, 3001 Bern, Switzerland. *Telephone:* (31) 3226911.

ZUCKERMAN, Mortimer Benjamin, BA, LLB, LLM, MBA; American (b. Canadian) real-estate developer, publisher and editor; b. 4 June 1937, Montreal, Québec; s. of Abraham Zuckerman and Esther Zuckerman; ed McGill Univ., Pennsylvania Univ., Harvard Univ.; Sr Vice-Pres. Cabot, Cabot and Forbes 1965–69; lecturer, then Assoc. Prof. Harvard Univ. Grad. School of Design 1966–74; visiting lecturer Yale Univ. 1967–69; Chair. Boston Properties Co. 1970–; Dir RET Income Foundation 1976–79, Property Capital Trust Co. 1979–80; Pres., Chair. Atlantic Monthly Co., Boston 1980–; Chair., Ed.-in-Chief US News and World Report 1980–; Propr New York Daily News. *Address:* Boston Properties, 599 Lexington Avenue, Room 1800, New York, NY 10022; US News and World Report, 2400 N Street, NW, Washington, DC 20037, USA.

ZUGAZA MIRANDA, Miguel; Spanish museum director; b. 1964, Durango, Vizcaya; ed Universidad Complutense de Madrid; Dir Reina Sofía Museum of Contemporary Art, Madrid 1994–96; Dir Museum of Fine Arts, Bilbao 1996–2002; Dir Prado Museum, Madrid Jan. 2002–. *Address:* Museo del Prado, Sede Administrativa, c/ Ruiz de Alarcón 23, 28014 Madrid, Spain (Office). *Telephone:* (91) 3302800 (Office). *Fax:* (91) 3302856 (Office). *E-mail:* museo.nacional@prado.mcu.es (Office). *Website:* museoprado.mcu.es/ (Office).

ZUKERMAN, Pinchas; Israeli violinist; b. 16 July 1948, Tel-Aviv; s. of Yehuda Zukerman and Miriam Zukerman; m. 1st Eugenia Rich 1968; two d.; m. 2nd Tuesday Weld (q.v.) 1985 (divorced); ed Israel Conservatory, Acad. of Music, Tel-Aviv, Juilliard School of Music, New York; studied with Ivan Galamian; début in New York with New York Philharmonic 1969, in UK at Brighton Festival 1969; concert and recital performances throughout USA and Europe; appearances as conductor with orchestras worldwide; has performed at Spoleto, Pablo Casals and Edinburgh Festivals; Dir S. Bank Summer Music 1978–80; Musical Dir St Paul Chamber Orchestra 1980–87; Prin. Conductor Dallas Symphony Orch. 1993–95 (Prin. Conductor Int. Summer Music Festival 1990–95); Music Dir Nat. Arts Centre Orchestra, Canada 1998–; Hon. DMus (Brown Univ.) 1989; Leventritt Award 1967. *Address:* c/o Kirshbaum Demler and Associates, 711 West End Avenue, New York, NY 10025, USA. *Telephone:* (212) 222-4843.

ZULEEG, (Friedrich), DJur; German professor and fmr international judge; b. 21 March 1935, Creglingen; s. of Ludwig Zuleeg and Thea Zuleeg (née Ohr); m. Sigrid Feuerhahn 1965; three s. one d.; ed Univs of Erlangen and Hamburg and Bologna Center, Johns Hopkins Univ.; Research Asst, Inst. for Law of the European Communities, Univ. of Cologne 1962–68, Sr Lecturer 1968–71; Prof. of Public Law and Law of the European Communities, Univ. of Bonn 1971–78; Prof. of Public Law, including European and Public Int. Law, Univ. of Frankfurt 1978–88, Jean Monnet Chair of European Law 1998–; Judge, Court of Justice, European Communities 1988–94; Research Fellow Univ. of Calif., Berkeley 1969–70, Visiting Prof. 1996. *Publications:* Die Rechtsform der Subventionen 1965, Das Recht der Europäischen Gemeinschaften im innerstaatlichen Bereich 1969, Subventionskontrolle durch Konkurrentenklage 1974; contrib. to other works. *Leisure interests:* jogging, mountaineering, literature. *Address:* J. W. Goethe-Universität, Senckenberganlage 31, 60054 Frankfurt am Main, Germany. *Telephone:* (69) 79822382. *Fax:* (69) 79828934. *E-mail:* m.zuleeg@jur.uni-frankfurt.de (Office).

ZULFUGAROV, Tofik Nadir oglu; Azerbaijani diplomatist; b. 1 Nov. 1959, Rostov-on-Don; m.; ed Baku State Univ.; researcher, Inst. of Oriental Studies Azerbaijan Acad. of Sciences 1985–91; researcher, Inst. of History Azerbaijan Acad. of Sciences 1991–92; diplomatic service 1992–; took part in negotiations on regulating Nagorny Karabakh conflict, Head of Azerbaijan del. 1992–; Head, Dept of Conflict Problems, Azerbaijan Ministry of Foreign Affairs 1993–94, Minister of Foreign Affairs 1998–2000. *Address:* c/o Ministry of Foreign Affairs, Gendjler Maydani 3, Baku, Azerbaijan.

ZUMA, Jacob; South African politician; b. 12 April 1942, Inkandla, Kwa-Zulu-Natal; joined African Nat. Congress (ANC) 1959; mem. Umkhonto WeSizwe 1962 after ANC banned 1960, arrested 1963, sentenced to ten years' imprisonment; helped re-establish ANC underground structures Natal Prov. 1973–75; left S. Africa 1975; mem. ANC Nat. Exec. Cttee 1977, Deputy Chief Rep., Mozambique –1984, Chief Rep. 1984–87; Head of Underground Structures ANC Head Office, Lusaka, Zambia, 1987, Chief Intelligence Dept, mem. political and mil. council mid-1980s; returned to SA after unbanning of ANC 1990, Chair. S. Natal Region 1990, Deputy Sec.-Gen. ANC 1991, Nat. Chair. 1994–97, Deputy Pres. 1997–; mem. Exec. Cttee Econ. Affairs and Tourism for KwaZulu Natal (KZN) Gov. 1994–99, Chair. ANC in KZN 1994–, est. and patron KZN Reconstruction and Devt Project Bursary Fund; Deputy Pres. of SA 1999–; Nelson Mandela Award for Outstanding Leadership (USA) 1998. *Address:* Office of the Deputy President, Union Buildings, West Wing, Government Avenue, Pretoria 0001, South Africa (Office).

ZUMTHOR, Peter; Swiss architect; b. 1943, Basel; ed Schule für Gestalung, Basel, Pratt Inst., USA; apprenticeship in cabinet-making; architect, Dept. for the Care and Presentation of Monument, Canton Graubünden 1968; tutor, Univ. of Zurich 1978; pvt. practice, Haldenstein, Graubünden 1979–; Visiting Prof. Southern Calif. Inst. of Architecture, USA 1988; workshop leader, Granz Summer Scholl, Austria 1989; Davis Critic, Tulane Univ., USA 1992; Prof., Acad. of Architecture, Mendriso 1996; Hon. mem. Bund Deutcher Artitekten, Germany; Auszeichnung guter Bauten im Kanton Graubünden 1987, 1994, Heinrich Tessenow Medal, Hanover Tech. Univ., Germany 1989, Gulam 1991, Int. Architecture Prize, Neues Bauen in den Alpen 1992, 1995, Best Building, 10 vor 10 1993, Int. Prize, Stone Architecture, Italy 1995, Erich-Schelling Architecture Prize, Germany 1996, Carlsberg Architecture Prize 1998. *Works include:* Churwalden Elementary School, Graubünden 1983, House Räth, Graubünden 1983, Atelier Zumthor, Graubünden 1986, St Benedict Chapel, Graubünden 1989, Chur Art Museum, Graubünden 1990, Gugalun House, Graubünden 1994, Thermal Baths Vals, Graubünden 1996, Bregenz Art Museum, Austria 1997, Topography of Terror, Int. Exhibition and Documentation Centre, Germany 1997, Laban Centre for Music and Dance, UK 1997, Lichtforum Zumtobel Staff, Zurich 1997, Swiss Pavilion, Expo 2000, Germany 1997–2000, Kolumba, Erzbischöfliches Diözesanmuseum, Germany 1997–2000, Cloud Rock Widerness Lodge Moab 1999. *Publications include:* Three Concepts 1997, Peter Zumthor Works: Buildings and Projects 1979–1997 (with Helene Binet) 1998, Thinking Architecture 1998, Swiss Sound Box, Kunsthaus Bregenz 1999. *Address:* Süesswingel 20, 7023 Haldenstein, Switzerland (Office). *Telephone:* (81) 3549292 (Office). *Fax:* (81) 3539293 (Office). *E-mail:* arch@zumthor.ch (Office).

ZUNZI (pseudonym of Wong Kee-kwan); Chinese political cartoonist; m. Chan Ya; ed Chinese Univ. of Hong Kong; worked briefly as print journalist before concentrating on political cartoons; works appear in mass-circulation Chinese-language publs including Ming Pao (daily) and Next (weekly magazine).

ZURABOV, Aleksander Yuryevich, C.ECON.SC.; Russian banker; b. 1956, Leningrad (now St Petersburg); m.; two c.; ed Moscow Inst. of Man., Acad. of Int. Trade; worked with Research Inst. of Marine Transport 1977–89; lecturer Acad. of Int. Trade 1989–91; Head of Div., Head of Dept, mem. Bd Dirs Konversbank 1991–94; Chair. Bd Dirs, Trust and Investments Bank, also Deputy Chair. Bd Dirs, MENATEP Bank 1994–95, Pres. and Chair. Bd MENATEP 1996–; Chair. Bd Dirs Russian Standard Bank 1999–2000; First Deputy Dir-Gen. Aeroflot 1999–. *Address:* MENATEP, Dubininskaya str. 17A, 113054 Moscow, Russia. *Telephone:* (095) 235-90-03 (Office).

ZURABOV, Mikail Yuryevich; Russian civil servant and engineer; b. 3 Oct. 1953, Leningrad; m.; one s. one d.; ed Moscow State Inst. of Man.; lecturer Moscow Inst. of Man. 1975–78; teacher Moscow Higher School of Montage 1981–82; engineer Moscow Research Inst. Orgtechstroi 1982–83; Sr researcher, Head of lab., All-Union Research Inst. of Montage Tech. 1983–88; Deputy Head Montage Co. Mospromtechmontage 1988–92; Dir-Gen. Jt Stock Insurance Co. Max 1992–, also Dir-Gen. Medical Insurance Co. Max-M 1994–98; First Deputy Minister of Public Health May–Sept. 1998; adviser on social problems to Pres. 1998–99; Chair. Bd of Dirs Konversbank; Chair. Pension Fund of Russian Fed. 1999–. *Address:* Pensions Fund of the Russian Federation, Shabolovka str. 4, 117934 Moscow, Russia (Office). *Telephone:* (095) 237-36-37 (Office). *Fax:* (095) 959-83-53 (Office).

ZVEREVA, Natalia (Natasha); Belarus tennis player; b. 16 April 1971, Minsk; d. of Marat Zverev and Nina Zvereva; winner doubles French Open (with Larisa Neiland) 1989, (with Gigi Fernandez, 1992–95, 1997, Wimbledon (with Larisa Neiland) 1991, (with Gigi Fernandez) 1992–94, 1997, US Open (with Pam Shriver) 1991, (with Gigi Fernandez) 1992, 1995, 1996; winner mixed doubles Australian Open 1990, 1995, doubles (with Gigi Fernandez) 1993–94, 1997; four-time Olympian 1988–2000; bronze medallist in doubles (mem. Unified Team), Olympic Games, Barcelona, Spain 1992; winner doubles Pan Pacific (with Gigi Fernandez) 1996; 80 WTA Tour doubles titles by end of 2002; five-time winner of WTA Tour Doubles Team of the Year Award. *Leisure interests:* listening to music, watching water polo, table tennis, nightclubs, reading, cooking, farming.

ZVINAVASHE, Gen. Vitalis; Zimbabwean army officer; b. 1943; Commdr Defence Forces –2002; Chief of Staff, Armed Forces 2003–; est. task force to deal with econ. crisis 2003. *Address:* Office of the Head of the Armed Forces, Defence House, Union Avenue/Third Street, Private Bag 7713, Causeway, Harare, Zimbabwe (Office).

ZWANZIG, Robert Walter, MS, PhD; American professor of chemical physics; b. 9 April 1928, Brooklyn, NY; s. of Walter Zwanzig and Bertha Weil Zwanzig; m. Francis Ryder Zwanzig 1953; one s. one d.; ed Polytechnic Inst. of Brooklyn, Univ. of Southern California and California Inst. of Tech.; Research Fellow, Yale Univ. 1951–54; Asst Prof. of Chem., Johns Hopkins Univ. 1954–58; Physical Chemist Nat. Bureau of Standards, Washington, DC 1958–66; Research Prof., Inst. for Physical Science and Tech., Univ. of Md 1966–80, Distinguished Prof. of Physical Science 1980–88, Prof. Emer. 1988–; Research Chemist NIH 1988–; NAS; Silver Medal, US Dept of Commerce; ACS Peter Debye Award in Physical Chem. 1976, Irving Langmuir Award in Chemical Physics 1984, ACS Joel Hildebrand Award 1994. *Publications:* Non-Equilibrium Statistical Mechanics 2001; more than 140 articles in scientific periodicals. *Address:* Laboratory of Chemical Physics, National Institutes of Health, Bethesda, MD 20892-0520 (Office); 5314 Sangamore Road, Bethesda, MD 20816, USA (Home). *Telephone:* (301) 496-8048 (Office). *Fax:* (301) 496-0825.

ZWAVELING, Albert, MD, PhD; Netherlands professor of surgery (retd); b. 21 July 1927, Schoonebeek; s. of Jan H. Zwaveling and Engeline F. (née Hinnen) Zwaveling; m. 1st Susanna M. van Soest 1952 (died 1966); one s.; m. 2nd Anna M. F. Bloem 1969; two s.; ed State Univ. of Utrecht, University Hosp., Leiden; mil. doctor (rank of maj.) 1954–57; Gen. Practitioner in Indonesia 1957–58; surgical trainee, Leiden 1958–63; Fellow in Oncology, Univ. of Wis., USA 1963–64; Jr Consultant 1964–68; Assoc. Prof. of Surgical Oncology, Leiden Univ. 1968–72; Prof. of Surgery 1972; Head, Dept of Surgery, Univ. Hosp., Leiden 1981–; Chair. Concilium Chirurgicum Utrecht 1985, Medical Staff Univ. Hosp., Leiden 1986; mem. Royal Netherlands Acad. of Sciences 1979; Hon. mem. Dutch Soc. of Oncology, Dutch Asscn of Surgery 1987, Dutch Asscn of Surgical Oncology 1991; awarded Rotgans Medal of Nat. Cancer Inst. 1963, Zwanenberg Award 1969. *Publications:* Dutch Textbook of Oncology, Dutch Textbook of Surgery; 6 monographs on oncology, mainly cancer; more than 120 scientific papers. *Leisure interests:* collecting modern plastic art, gardening. *Address:* University Hospital, Leiden (Office); Vlietpark 4, 2355 CT Hoogmade, Netherlands (Home). *Telephone:* (71) 264005 (Office); (71) 28622 (Home).

ZWERENZ, Gerhard; German writer; b. 3 June 1925, Gablenz; s. of Rudolf Zwerenz and Liesbeth Zwerenz; m. Ingrid Hoffman 1957; one d.; ed Univ. of Leipzig; worked as coppersmith 1939–42; army service 1942–44, deserted to join Red Army 1944; POW in Minsk, USSR 1944–48; obliged to serve with GDR police 1948–50; studied at Leipzig Univ. 1952–56; first Publ 1956; expelled from CP, fled to W Berlin 1957; mem. Bundestag 1994–; Ernst Reuter Prize 1975, Carl-von-Ossietzky-preis 1986, Alternativer Büchnerpreis 1991. *Publications:* 65 books including Aufs Rad geflochten 1959, Die Liebe der toten Männer 1959, Heldengedenktag 1964, Rasputin 1970, Der Widerspruch 1974, Die Westdeutschen 1977, Die Ehe der Maria Braun 1979, Der lange Tod des Rainer-Werner Fassbinder 1982, Rechts und dumm? 1993, Links und lahm 1994, Krieg im Glashaus 2000. *Address:* Brunhildensteg 18, 61389 Schmitten, Germany. *Telephone:* (6082) 1078.

ZWICK, Charles John, BS, PhD; American banker and economist; b. 17 July 1926, Plantsville; s. of Louis C. Zwick and Mabel (née Rich) Zwick; m. Joan Cameron 1952; one s. one d.; ed Univ. of Connecticut and Harvard Univ.; Instructor, Univ. of Conn. 1951; Harvard Univ. 1954–56; Head, Logistics Dept the RAND Corpn 1956–63, mem. Research Council 1963–65; Asst Dir US Bureau of the Budget 1965–68, Dir 1968–69; Pres. Southeast Banking Corpn, Miami 1969, apptd Chair. and CEO 1982; Chair. Bd and CEO Southeast Bank 1982–; Dir Manville Corpn and numerous other cos; Chair. Pres.'s Comm. on Mil. Compensation; Trustee, Carnegie Endowment for Int. Peace, Chair.; mem. Reserve City Bankers Asscn, The Conference Bd, Council of the Int. Exec. Service Corps, Econ. Soc. of S. Fla, Council of 100. *Address:* 4210 Santa Maria Street, Coral Gables, FL 33146, USA. *Telephone:* (305) 666-9208.

ZWICKEL, Klaus; German trade unionist; b. 31 May 1939, Heilbronn; apprentice toolmaker, Nordheim; regional admin. IG Metall-Gewerkschaft für Produktion und Dieustleistung im D6B; mem. Nat. Cttee 1986, Deputy Leader 1989–93, Leader Oct. 1993–; Pres. Int. Metalworkers' Fed.; Deputy Chair. Supervisory Bd Volkswagen AG 1996–; mem. Supervisory Bd (Deputy Chair. 1996–) Vodafone. *Address:* IG Metall, Lyoner Str. 32, 60519 Frankfurt am Main, Germany. *Telephone:* (69) 66930. *Fax:* (69) 66932843. *E-mail:* vorstand@igmetall.de (Office). *Website:* www.igmetall.de (Office).

ŻYCIŃSKI, Archbishop Józef, PhD, DTheol; Polish ecclesiastic and professor of philosophy of science; b. 1 Sept. 1948, Stara Wieś; ed Higher Theological Seminary of the Częstochowa Diocese, Kraków, Pontifical Theology Acad., Kraków, Acad. of Catholic Theology, Warsaw, Catholic Univ. of America, Catholic Univ. of Louvain; Ordained Priest, Częstochowa 1972; Parish Curate, Częstochowa Diocese 1972–74; Higher Theological Seminary of the Częstochowa Diocese, Kraków, Prefect 1974–78, Prefect of Studies 1979–83; Pontifical Acad. of Theology, Kraków, Deputy Dean Philosophy Dept 1982–85, Prof. 1988, Dean Philosophy Dept 1988–91; Ordinary Bishop of Tarnów Diocese, 1990–97; Metropolitan Archbishop of Lublin 1997–; Grand Chancellor Catholic Univ. of Lublin 1997–, Prof. and Head of Dept of Relations between Science and Religion 1998–; mem. Catholic Educ. Congregation, Pontifical Council of Culture; Chair. Polish Episcopate Council for Lay Apostolate; Chair. Programme Council of Catholic Information Agency; mem. European Acad. of Science and Art, Vienna, Russian Acad. of Natural Sciences, Evolutionary and Theoretical Biology Cttee of the Polish Acad. of Sciences. *Publications:* The Universe and Philosophy (jtly) 1980, The Human Person and Philosophy in the Contemporary World (Ed.) 1981, Language and Method 1982, Roads of Those who Think (jtly) 1981, The Galileo Affair: A Meeting of Faith and Science 1985, The Structure of the Metascientific Revolution 1987, To Philosophize in the Context of Science 1987, The Idea of Unification in Galileo's Epistemology 1987, Three Cultures: Science, the Humanities and Religious Values 1987, Theism and Analytical Philosophy (Vol. 1) 1983, (Vol. 2) 1988, The Universe: Machine or Thought (jtly) 1988, The Depth of Being 1988, In the Circle of Science and Belief 1989, Documents from UB Country 1989, Three Cultures 1990, Dilemmas of Evolution (jtly) 1990, Mathematics of Nature, Socratic Meditations (jtly) 1991, The Debate about Universals and Contemporary Science (jtly) 1991, The Galileo Affair 1991, The God of Abraham and Whitehead 1991, Reprieving Nature 1992, Unavoidable Questions (jtly) 1992, Limits of Rationality 1993, Person and Love 1993, Stones and Flowers 1994, Sacrum and Culture 1995, The Seeds of Loneliness 1996, The Elements of Philosophy of Science 1996, Die Zeichen der Hoffnung entdecken 1997, The Invisible Light 1998, The European Community in Spirit 1998, Christian Inspirations in the Rise of Modern Science 2000, Farewell to Nazareth 2000, God of Postmodernists 2001, God and Evolution 2002. *Leisure interests:* literary dailies, poetry, classical music. *Address:* ul. Prymasa St Wyszyńskiego 2, skr. poczt. 198, 20-950 Lublin, Poland. *Telephone:* (81) 5323468. *Fax:* (81) 5346135.

ŻYGULSKI, Kazimierz, HHD; Polish professor and politician; b. 8 Dec. 1919, Wolanka; s. of Zdzisław Żygulski and Maria Żygulska; m. Helena Gutkowa 1955; one s.; ed Univ. of Lwów (now Lvov, Ukraine); in resistance movt in Lwów Voivodship during Nazi occupation; imprisoned in USSR 1944–56; researcher, Sociology and History of Culture Research Centre of Polish Acad. of Sciences, Łódź 1956–59; scientific worker, Philosophy and Sociology Inst. of Polish Acad. of Sciences, Warsaw 1959–90, Head Culture Research Centre 1961–90, Chair. Scientific Council 1987–90, Extraordinary Prof. 1973–83, Ordinary Prof. 1983–; Pro-Rector, State Film, TV and Theatrical Higher School, Łódź 1970–71; Counsellor to Deputy Chair. of Council of Ministers 1971–72; Minister of Culture and Art 1982–86; Pro-Rector, Dir Scientific Research Centre, Warsaw School of Socioeconomic Science 1997–2002; Pres. Warsaw School of Socioeconomic Science 2002–; mem. Polish Cttee ICOM 1972–90, Presidium State Prizes Cttee 1975–83, Presidium Nat. Council for Culture 1983–86; Amb. ad personam 1987; Chair. Polish Nat. Comm. for UNESCO 1987–90; mem. UNESCO Exec. Bd 1987–90, Chair. Int. Cttee of Extra Govt Org., UNESCO 1989–90; mem. European Acad. of Arts, Sciences and Humanities 1989–; Hon. Academician Int. Personnel Acad. (Ukraine) 1999; Officer's Cross Order of Polonia Restituta. *Publications:* Drogi rozwoju kultury masowej (Mass Cultural Ways of Development) 1962, Wstęp do zagadnień kultury (Introduction to the Problems of Culture) 1972, Wartości i wzory kultury (Values and Models of Culture) 1975, Wspólnota śmiechu: Socjologiczne studium komizmu (Community of Laughter: A Sociological Study of the Comical) 1976, Święto i kultura (Holiday and Culture) 1981, Jestem z lwowskiego etapu (I am from Lwów) 1994, Widmo Przyszłości: nowa fala okrucieństwa (Ghost of the Future: New Wave of Atrocities) 1996, Globalne problemy współczesnego świata (The Global Problems of the Contemporary World) 1996, Uwagi o ekstremalnych zjawiskach w kulturze współczesnej (Notes on Extreme Phenomena in Contemporary Culture) 1998, Socialne i ekonomiczne aspekty globalizaçji (The Socio-economic Aspects of Globalization) 1999, Crytając tajne polskie teczki J. Stalina (Reading Secret Materials Concerning Poles from Stalin Times) 1999, Etos edukacji w XXI wieku. Uwagi socjologa (Ethos of Education in the 21st Century. Sociologist Remarks) 2000; numerous research works and monographs on sociology of culture. *Leisure interests:* history of art, photography. *Address:* Wyższa Szkoła Społeczno-Ekonomiczna, ul. M. Kasprzaka 29/31, 01-234 Warsaw (Office); ul. Madalińskiego 50/52 m. 23, 02-581 Warsaw, Poland (Home). *Telephone:* (22) 8770720 (Office); (22) 8498179 (Home). *Fax:* (22) 8770720 (Office).

ZYKINA, Ludmila Georgiyevna; Russian folk singer; b. 10 June 1929, Cheremushki, Moscow Region; ed Ippolitov-Ivanovo School of Music; soloist Pyatnitsky Folk Choir 1947–51; soloist Choir of Russian Song, All-Union Radio 1951–60; soloist Mosconcert 1960–77; Artistic Dir Ensemble Rossia 1977–; Pres. Moscow Regional Charity Public Foundation of Peace 1998–; Pres. Russian Acad. of Folk Art; mem. of Council Our Home is Russia Movt 1995–99; Hero of Socialist Labour; Lenin's Prize 1970, Glinka Prize 1983, Kyrill and Methodius Prize 1998, Ovation Prize 1998, People's Artist of Russia, Ukraine, Azerbaijan. *Address:* Kotelnicheskaya nab. 15, korp. B, Apt. 64, Moscow, Russia (Office). *Telephone:* (095) 245-18-13 (Office).

ŻYLIS-GARA, Teresa; Polish soprano; b. 23 Jan. 1935, Wilno (now Vilnius, Lithuania); m.; one c.; ed State Higher School of Music, Łódź; soloist, Cracow

INTERNATIONAL WHO'S WHO

Philharmonic 1954–58 and Cracow Opera 1958–59; foreign contracts in operas: Oberhausen 1961–63, Städtische Bühnen, Dortmund 1963–65, Deutsche Oper am Rhein, Düsseldorf 1965–70; performances in many countries; regular performances at Metropolitan Opera, New York 1968–; also song recitals; renowned for interpretation of works by Szymanowski; Prof. of Music Art and Pedagogue of Vocal Art, State Higher School of Music, Łódź 1999; Commdr's Cross Order of Polonia Restituta 2000; Prime Minister's Prize (1st Class) 1979. *Debuts abroad:* Paris Opera 1966, San Francisco Opera 1968, Metropolitan Opera, New York 1968, Royal Opera House, Covent Garden 1968, Vienna Opera 1970, Nat. Theatre, Prague 1974, Nat. Theatre, Budapest 1976, Great Theatre, Warsaw 1976, La Scala, Milan 1977, Bolshoi Theatre, Moscow 1978, Teatro Colón, Buenos Aires 1981. *Participation in festivals including:* Glyndebourne 1965, Salzburg 1968, Aix-en-Provence 1972, Orange 1975. *Address:* 16A Boulevard de Belgique, Principality of Monaco. *Telephone:* (93) 305339. *E-mail:* teresa_zylis-gara@monaco377.com (Office).

ZYPRIES, Brigette; German politician; b. 16 Dec. 1953, Kassel; in-service training, Giessen Land Court 1978–80; mem. Academic Staff, Univ. of Giessen 1980–1985; Deputy Head of Div., State Chancellery, Hessen 1985–88; mem. Academic Staff, Fed. Constitutional Court 1988–90; Head of Div., Lower Saxon State Chancellery 1991–95, Head of Dept 1995–97, State Sec. for Women, Labour and Social Affairs 1997–98; with Fed. Ministry of the Interior 1998–2002; State Sec. 1997–2002, Chair. of State Sec. Cttee for Man. of Modern State–Modern Admin. Fed. Govt Programme 1999–; Fed. Minister of Justice Oct. 2002–. *Address:* Federal Ministry of Justice (BMJ), Mohrenstrasse 37, 101117 Berlin, Germany (Office). *Telephone:* (30) 202570 (Office). *Fax:* (30) 20259525 (Office). *E-mail:* poststelle@bmj.bund.de (Office). *Website:* www.bmj.bund.de (Office).

ZYUGANOV, Gennady Andreyevich, DPhil; Russian politician; b. 26 June 1944, Mymrino Village, Orel Region; ed Orel Pedagogical Inst., Acad. of Social Sciences of Cen. CPSU Cttee; worked as teacher in a secondary school 1961–65; CP and trade union functionary 1967; First Sec. Dist, City, Regional Comsomol cttees of Orel, Sec., Second Sec., Head of Propaganda Div. Orel Regional CPSU Cttee 1974–83; Instructor, Head of Propaganda Div. Cen. CPSU Cttee 1983–89; Deputy Head of Ideology Div. Cen. CPSU Cttee 1989–90; mem. Politburo, Sec. Cen. Cttee of CP of Russian Fed.; Chair. Coordination Cttee of Patriotic Forces of Russia 1992–, Co-Chair. Duma of Russian Nat. Sobor 1992–; Co-Chair. Political Council of the Front of Nat. Salvation 1992–; Chair. Cen. Exec. Cttee CP of Russian Fed. at the restorative congress of the CP 1993–; mem. State Duma (Parl.) of Russia 1993–, Head of CP faction; CP Presidential Cand. for 1996 and 1999 elections. *Publications:* Russia and the Contemporary World 1995, Russia, My Homeland (The Ideology of State Patriotism) 1997. *Address:* Communist Party, Zlatoustinsky per, 8/7, 101000 Moscow; State Duma, Okhotny Ryad 1, 103009 Moscow, Russia. *Telephone:* (095) 206-87-89 (Party); (095) 292-87-44 (Duma). *Fax:* (095) 292-56-85.

 1888 www.worldwhoswho.com